AMERICAN MEN & WOMEN OF SCIENCE

AMERICAN MEN & WOMEN OF SCIENCE

PHYSICAL AND BIOLOGICAL SCIENCES

15TH EDITION
VOLUME II
C-F

EDITED BY
JAQUES CATTELL PRESS

R. R. BOWKER COMPANY
NEW YORK & LONDON 1982

International Standard Book Number
      Set: 0-8352-1413-3
    Volume I: 0-8352-1414-1
   Volume II: 0-8352-1416-8
  Volume III: 0-8352-1417-6
  Volume IV: 0-8352-1418-4
   Volume V: 0-8352-1419-2
  Volume VI: 0-8352-1420-6
 Volume VII: 0-8352-1421-4
International Standard Serial Number: 0192-8570
Library of Congress Catalog Card Number: 6-7326

CONTENTS

ADVISORY COMMITTEE

Dr. Dael L. Wolfle, Committee Chairman
Professor Emeritus,
Graduate School of Public Affairs
University of Washington

Dr. Carl D. Douglass
Director,
Division of Research Grants
National Institutes of Health

Mr. Alan Fechter
Head,
Scientific and Technical
Personnel Studies
National Science Foundation

Dr. Harold S. Ginsberg
Professor & Chairman,
Department of Microbiology
College of Physicians and Surgeons
Columbia University

Dr. Allen L. Hammond
Editor, *Science '81,*
American Association for the
Advancement of Science

Dr. Anna J. Harrison
Professor,
Department of Chemistry
Mt. Holyoke College

Dr. William C. Kelly
Executive Director,
Office of Scientific and
Engineering Personnel
National Research Council

Dr. H. William Koch
Director,
American Institute of Physics

Dr. Robert Krauss
Executive Director,
Federation of American Societies
for Experimental Biology

Dr. William J. LeVeque
Executive Director,
American Mathematical Society

Dr. Raymond P. Mariella
Executive Director,
American Chemical Society

Dr. James H. Mulligan, Jr.
Professor,
Department of Electrical Engineering
University of California, Irvine

Dr. Kenneth Prewitt
President,
Social Science Research Council

Dr. Helen M. Ranney
Professor & Chairman,
Department of Medicine
University of California, San Diego

Dr. Matthias Stelly
Executive Vice President,
American Society of Agronomy

Mr. William E. Zimmie
President,
Zimmite Corporation

PREFACE

American Men and Women of Science is without peer as a chronicle of North American scientific endeavor and achievement. It has recorded the careers of over 280,000 scientists and engineers since the first edition appeared in 1906, and continues to provide current information on the leaders in America's research and academic communities.

The Fifteenth Edition contains the biographies of 130,000 women and men; 7,500 appear for the first time. The names of new entrants were submitted for consideration at the editors' request by current entrants and by persons in charge of academic, government and private research programs. All of those included meet the following criteria:

1. Achievement, by reason of experience and training of a stature in scientific work equivalent to that associated with the doctoral degree, coupled with presently continued activity in such work;

   or

2. Research activity of high quality in science as evidenced by publication in reputable scientific journals; or, for those whose work cannot be published because of governmental or industrial security, research activity of high quality in science as evidenced by the judgment of the individual's peers;

   or

3. Attainment of a position of substantial responsibility requiring scientific training and experience to the extent described for (1) and (2).

This edition profiles living scientists in the physical and biological fields as well as public health scientists, engineers, mathematicians, statisticians, and computer scientists. The information is collected by means of direct communication whenever possible. Forms are sent to all entrants for corroboration and updating, and those whose biographies are appearing for the first time receive verification proofs before publication. The information submitted by entrants is included as completely as possible within the boundaries of editorial and space restrictions. Full entries are repeated for former listees who do not return forms but whose current location can be verified in secondary sources. References to the previous edition are given for those who do not return forms and cannot be located, but who are presumed to be still active in science or engineering. A notation is made when an entrant from the previous edition is known to be deceased. Non-citizens of the Americas are included if working in the United States or Canada for a reasonable duration. Information on former entrants who have entered fields other than science and engineering, or who have been retired for ten years and are no longer professionally active has been omitted.

American Men and Women of Science has experienced many changes in its long history, and this edition is no exception. Following the suggestion of the advisory committee, and based on the recommendation of a user survey, the geographic and discipline indexes have been discontinued in printed form. The Fifteenth Edition will be available for on-line searching, however, through BRS, DIALOG and the Jaques Cattell Press. All elements of an entry, including field of interest, experience and location, can be accessed by the use of key words. Although *American Men and Women of Science* is on a three year publication cycle, the on-line database will be updated at more frequent intervals. Previous users of the directory will be pleased to find that the type size has been enlarged in response to many requests.

The Social and Behavioral Sciences section of *American Men and Women of Science* was last published in 1978. The limited acceptance of this section caused the postponement of subsequent editions. Realizing the importance of maintaining current data on the disciplines, the publishers are considering several possibilities for the future. One is the inclusion of selected, appropriate fields in the *Directory of American Scholars,* also a Bowker/Cattell publication. Another plan under consideration is the systematic addition of social and behavioral scientists to the on-line database for eventual publication in an all-inclusive *American Men and Women of Science.*

The editors take this opportunity to thank the Fifteenth Edition advisory committee for their guidance, encouragement and support. Appreciation is expressed to the many scientific societies who provided their membership lists for the purpose of locating former entrants whose addresses had changed.

Comments and suggestions on any aspect of the Fifteenth Edition are encouraged and should be directed to The Editors, *American Men and Women of Science,* P.O. Box 25001, Tempe, Arizona 85282.

Martha Cargill, *Editor*
Renee Lautenbach, *Managing Editor*
Terence Basom, *General Manager*
JAQUES CATTELL PRESS

August, 1982

ABBREVIATIONS

AAAS—American Association for the Advancement of Science
abnorm—abnormal
abstr—abstract(s)
acad—academic, academy
acct—account, accountant, accounting
acoust—acoustic(s), acoustical
ACTH—adrenocorticotrophic hormone
actg—acting
activ—activities, activity
addn—addition(s), additional
Add—Address
adj—adjunct, adjutant
adjust—adjustment
Adm—Admiral
admin—administration, administrative
adminr—administrator(s)
admis—admission(s)
adv—adviser(s), advisory
advan—advance(d), advancement
advert—advertisement, advertising
AEC—Atomic Energy Commission
aerodyn—aerodynamic(s)
aeronaut—aeronautic(s), aeronautical
aerophys—aerophysical, aerophysics
aesthet—aesthetic(s)
AFB—Air Force Base
affil—affiliate(s), affiliation
agr—agricultural, agriculture
agron—agronomic, agronomical, agronomy
agrost—agrostologic, agrostological, agrostology
agt—agent
AID—Agency for International Development
Ala-Alabama
allergol—allergological, allergology
alt—alternate
Alta—Alberta
Am—America, American
AMA—American Medical Association
anal—analysis, analytic, analytical
analog—analogue
anat—anatomic, anatomical, anatomy
anesthesiol—anesthesiology
angiol—angiology
Ann—Annal(s)
ann—annual
anthrop—anthropological, anthropology
anthropom—anthropometric, anthropometrical, anthropometry
antiq—antiquary, antiquities, antiquity

antiqn—antiquarian
apicult—apicultural, apiculture
APO—Army Post Office
app—appoint, appointed
appl—applied
appln—application
approx—approximate(ly)
Apr—April
apt—apartment(s)
aquacult—aquaculture
arbit—arbitration
arch—archives
archaeol—archaeological, archaeology
archit—architectural, architecture
Arg—Argentina, Argentine
Ariz—Arizona
Ark—Arkansas
artil—artillery
asn—association
assoc(s)—associate(s), associated
asst(s)—assistant(s), assistantship(s)
Assyriol—Assyriology
astrodyn—astrodynamics
astron—astronomical, astronomy
astronaut—astronautical, astronautics
astronr—astronomer
astrophys—astrophysical, astrophysics
attend—attendant, attending
atty—attorney
audiol—audiology
Aug—August
auth—author
AV—audiovisual
Ave—Avenue
avicult—avicultural, aviculture

b—born
bact—bacterial, bacteriologic, bacteriological, bacteriology
BC—British Columbia
bd—board
behav—behavior(al)
Belg—Belgian, Belgium
bibl—biblical
bibliog—bibliographic, bibliographical, bibliography
bibliogr—bibliographer
biochem—biochemical, biochemistry
biog—biographical, biography
biol—biological, biology
biomed—biomedical, biomedicine

biomet—biometric(s), biometrical, biometry
biophys—biophysical, biophysics
bk(s)—book(s)
bldg—building
Blvd—Boulevard
Bor—Borough
bot—botanical, botany
br—branch(es)
Brig—Brigadier
Brit—Britain, British
Bro(s)—Brother(s)
byrol—byrology
Bull—Bulletin
bur—bureau
bus—business
BWI—British West Indies

c—children
Calif—California
Can—Canada, Canadian
cand—candidate
Capt—Captain
cardiol—cardiology
cardiovasc—cardiovascular
cartog—cartographic, cartographical, cartography
cartogr—cartographer
Cath—Catholic
CEngr—Corps of Engineers
cent—central
Cent Am—Central America
cert—certificate(s), certification, certified
chap—chapter
chem—chemical(s), chemistry
chemother—chemotherapy
chmn—chairman
citricult—citriculture
class—classical
climat—climatological, climatology
clin(s)—clinic(s), clinical
cmndg—commanding
Co—Companies, Company
coauth— coauthor
co-dir—co-director
co-ed—co-editor
coeduc—coeducation, coeducational
col(s)—college(s), collegiate, colonel
collab—collaboration, coloborative
collabr—collaborator
Colo—Colorado
com—commerce, commercial

ABBREVIATIONS

Comdr—Commander
commun—communicable, communication(s)
comn(s)—commission(s), commissioned
comnr—commissioner
comp—comparative
compos—composition
comput—computation, computer(s),
  computing
comt(s)—committee(s)
conchol—conchology
conf—conference
cong—congress, congressional
Conn—Connecticut
conserv—conservation, conservatory
consol—consolidated, consolidation
const—constitution, constitutional
construct—construction, constructive
consult(s)—consult, consultant(s)
  consultantship(s), consultation, consulting
contemp—contemporary
contrib—contribute, contributing,
  contribution(s)
contribr—contributor
conv—convention
coop—cooperating, cooperation, cooperative
coord—coordinate(d), coordinating,
  coordination
coordr—coordinator
corp—corporate, corporation(s)
corresp—correspondence, correspondent,
  corresponding
coun—council, counsel, counseling
counr—councilor, counselor
criminol—criminological, criminology
cryog—cryogenic(s)
crystallog—crystallographic, crystallograpi-
  ical, crystallography
crystallogr—crystallographer
Ct—Court
Ctr—Center
cult—cultural, culture
cur—curator
curric—curriculum
cybernet—cybernetic(s)
cytol—cytological, cytology
Czech—Czechoslovakia

DC—District of Columbia
Dec—December
Del—Delaware
deleg—delegate, delegation
delinq—delinquency, delinquent
dem—democrat(s), democratic
demog—demographic, demography
demogr—demographer
demonstr—demonstrator
dendrol—dendrologic, dendrological,
  dendrology
dent—dental, dentistry
dep—deputy
dept—department(al)
dermat—dermatologic, dermatological,
  dermatology
develop—developed, developing, development, developmental
diag—diagnosis, diagnostic
dialectol—dialectological, dialectology
dict—dictionaries, dictionary
Dig—Digest
dipl—diploma, diplomate
dir(s)—director(s), directories, directory
dis—disease(s), disorders

Diss Abstr—Dissertation Abstracts
dist—district
distrib—distributed, distribution, distributive
distribr—distributor(s)
div—division, divisional, divorced
DNA—deoxyribonucleic acid
doc—document(s), documentary,
  documentation
Dom—Dominion
Dr—Drive

e—east
ecol—ecological, ecology
econ(s)—economic(s), economical, economy
economet—econometric(s)
ECT—electroconvulsive or electroshock
  therapy
ed—edition(s), editor(s), editorial
ed bd—editorial board
educ—education, educational
educr—educator(s)
EEG—electroencephalogram, electroencephalographic, electroencephalography
Egyptol—Egyptology
EKG—electrocardiogram
elec—electric, electrical, electricity
electrochem—electrochemical, electrochemistry
electrophys—electrophysical, electrophysics
elem—elementary
embryol—embryologic, embryological,
  embryology
emer—emeriti, emiritus
employ—employment
encour—encouragement
encycl—encyclopedia
endocrinol—endocrinologic, endocrinology
eng—engineering
Eng—England, English
engr(s)—engineer(s)
enol—enology
Ens—Ensign
entom—entomological, entomology
environ—environment(s), environmental
enzym—enzymology
epidemiol—epidemiologic, epidemiological,
  epidemiology
equip—equipment
ESEA—Elementary & Secondary Education
  Act
espec—especially
estab—established, establishment(s)
ethnog—ethnographic, ethnographical,
  ethnography
ethnogr—ethnographer
ethnol—ethnologic, ethnological, ethnology
Europ—European
eval—evaluation
evangel—evangelical
eve—evening
exam—examination(s), examining
examr—examiner
except—exceptional
exec(s)—executive(s)
exeg—exegeses, exegesis, exegetic, exegetical
exhib(s)—exhibition(s), exhibit(s)
exp—experiment, experimental
exped(s)—expedition(s)
explor—exploration(s), exploratory
expos—exposition
exten—extension

fac—faculty

facil—facilities, facility
Feb—February
fed—federal
fedn—federation
fel(s)—fellow(s), fellowship(s)
fermentol—fermentology
fertil—fertility, fertilitization
Fla—Florida
floricult—floricultural, floriculture
found—foundation
FPO—Fleet Post Office
Fr—French
Ft—Fort

Ga—Georgia
gastroenterol—gastroenterological, gastroenterology
gen—general
geneal—genealogical, genealogy
geod—geodesy, geodetic
geog—geographic, geographical, geography
geogr—geographer
geol—geologic, geological, geology
geom—geometric, geometrical, geometry
geomorphol—geomorphologic,
  geomorphology
geophys—geophysical, geophysics
Ger—German, Germanic, Germany
geriat—geriatric(s)
geront—gerontological, gerontology
glaciol—glaciology
gov—governing, governor(s)
govt—government, governmental
grad—graduate(d)
Gt Brit—Great Britain
guid—guidance
gym—gymnasium
gynec—gynecologic, gynecological,
  gynecology

handbk(s)—handbook(s)
helminth—helminthology
hemat—hematologic, hematological,
  hematology
herpet—herpetologic, herpetological,
  herpetology
Hisp—Hispanic, Hispania
hist—historic, historical, history
histol—histological, histology
HM—Her Majesty
hochsch—hochschule
homeop—homeopathic, homeopathy
hon(s)—honor(s), honorable, honorary
hort—horticultural, horticulture
hosp(s)—hospital(s), hospitalization
hq—headquarters
HumRRO—Human Resources Research
  Office
husb—husbandry
Hwy—Highway
hydraul—hydraulic(s)
hydrodyn—hydrodynamic(s)
hydrol—hydrologic, hydrological, hydrology
hyg—hygiene, hygienic(s)
hypn—hypnosis

ichthyol—ichthyological, ichthyology
Ill—Illinois
illum—illuminating, illumination
illus—illustrate, illustrated, illustration
illusr—illustrator
immunol—immunologic, immunological,
  immunology

Imp—Imperial
improv—improvement
Inc—Incorporated
in-chg—in charge
incl—include(s), including
Ind—Indiana
indust(s)—industrial, industries, industry
inf—infantry
info—information
inorg—inorganic
ins—insurance
inst(s)—institute(s), institution(s)
instnl—institutional(ized)
instr(s)—instruct, instruction, instructor(s)
instrnl—instructional
int—international
intel—intelligence
introd—introduction
invert—invertebrate
invest(s)—investigation(s)
investr—investigator
irrig—irrigation
Ital—Italian

J—Journal
Jan—January
Jct—Junction
jour—journal, journalism
jr—junior
jurisp—jurisprudence
juv—juvenile

Kans—Kansas
Ky—Kentucky

La—Louisiana
lab(s)—laboratories, laboratory
lang—language(s)
laryngol—laryngological, laryngology
lect—lecture(s)
lectr—lecturer(s)
legis—legislation, legislative, legislature
lett—letter(s)
lib—liberal
libr—libraries, library
librn—librarian
lic—license(d)
limnol—limnological, limnology
ling—linguistic(s), linguistical
lit—literary, literature
lithol—lithologic, lithological, lithology
Lt—Lieutenant
Ltd—Limited

m—married
mach—machine(s), machinery
mag—magazine(s)
maj—major
malacol—malacology
mammal—mammalogy
Man—Manitoba
Mar—March
Mariol—Mariology
Mass—Massachusetts
mat—material(s)
mat med—materia medica
math—mathematic(s), mathematical
Md—Maryland
mech—mechanic(s), mechanical
med—medical, medicinal, medicine
Mediter—Mediterranean
Mem—Memorial
mem—member(s), membership(s)

ment—mental(ly)
metab—metabolic, metabolism
metall—metallurgic, metallurgical,
    metallurgy
metallog—metallographic, metallography
metallogr—metallographer
metaphys—metaphysical, metaphysics
meteorol—meteorological, meteorology
metrol—metrological, metrology
metrop—metropolitan
Mex—Mexican, Mexico
mfg—manufacturing
mfr(s)—manufacture(s), manufacturer(s)
mgr—manager
mgt—management
Mich—Michigan
microbiol—microbiological, microbiology
micros—microscopic, microscopical,
    microscopy
mid—middle
mil—military
mineral—mineralogical, mineralogy
Minn—Minnesota
Miss—Mississippi
mkt—market, marketing
Mo—Missouri
mod—modern
monogr—monograph
Mont—Montana
morphol—morphological, morphology
Mt—Mount
mult—multiple
munic—municipal, municipalities
mus—museum(s)
musicol—musicological, musicology
mycol—mycologic, mycology

n—north
NASA—National Aeronautics & Space
    Administration
nat—national, naturalized
NATO—North Atlantic Treaty Organization
navig—navigation(al)
NB—New Brunswick
NC—North Carolina
NDak—North Dakota
NDEA—National Defense Education Act
Nebr—Nebraska
nematol—nematological, nematology
nerv—nervous
Neth—Netherlands
neurol—neurological, neurology
neuropath—neuropathological, neuro-
    pathology
neuropsychiat—neuropsychiatric, neuro-
    psychiatry
neurosurg—neurosurgical, neurosurgery
Nev—Nevada
New Eng—New England
New York—New York City
Nfld—Newfoundland
NH—New Hampshire
NIH—National Institutes of Health
NIMH—National Institute of Mental Health
NJ—New Jersey
NMex—New Mexico
nonres—nonresident
norm—normal
Norweg—Norwegian
Nov—November
NS—Nova Scotia
NSF—National Science Foundation
NSW—New South Wales

numis—numismatic(s)
nutrit—nutrition, nutritional
NY—New York State
NZ—New Zealand

observ—observatories, observatory
obstet—obstetric(s), obstetrical
occas—occasional(ly)
occup—occupation, occupational
oceanog—oceanographic, oceanographical,
    oceanography
oceanogr—oceanographer
Oct—October
odontol—odontology
OEEC—Organization for European
    Economic Cooperation
off—office, official
Okla—Oklahoma
olericult—olericulture
oncol—oncologic, oncology
Ont—Ontario
oper(s)—operation(s), operational,
    operative
ophthal—ophthalmologic, ophthalmological,
    ophthalmology
optom—optometric, optometrical, optometry
ord—ordnance
Ore—Oregon
org—organic
orgn—organization(s), organizational
orient—oriental
ornith—ornithological, ornithology
orthod—orthodontia, orthodontic(s)
orthop—orthopedic(s)
osteop—osteopathic, osteopathy
otol—otological, otology
otolaryngol—otolaryngological, otolaryn-
    gology
otorhinol—otorhinologic, otorhinology

Pa—Pennsylvania
Pac—Pacific
paleobot—paleobotanical, paleobotany
paleont—paleontological, paleontology
Pan-Am—Pan-American
parasitol—parasitology
partic—participant, participating
path—pathologic, pathological, pathology
pedag—pedagogic(s), pedagogical, pedagogy
pediat—pediatric(s)
PEI—Prince Edward Islands
penol—penological, penology
periodont—periodontal, periodontic(s),
    periodontology
petrog—petrographic, petrographical,
    petrography
petrogr—petrographer
petrol—petroleum, petrologic, petrological,
    petrology
pharm—pharmacy
pharmaceut—pharmaceutic(s), pharmaceu-
    tical(s)
pharmacog—pharmacognosy
pharamacol—pharmacologic, pharmaco-
    logical, pharmacology
phenomenol—phenomenologic(al),
    phenomenology
philol—philological, philology
philos—philosophic, philosophical,
    philosophy
photog—photographic, photography
photogeog—photogeographic, photo-
    geography

photogr—photographer(s)
photogram—photogrammetric, photogrammetry
photom—photometric, photometrical, photometry
phycol—phycology
phys—physical
physiog—physiographic, physiographical, physiography
physiol—physiological, physiology
Pkwy—Parkway
Pl—Place
polit—political, politics
polytech—polytechnic(al)
pomol—pomological, pomology
pontif—pontifical
pop—population
Port—Portugal, Portuguese
postgrad—postgraduate
PQ—Province of Quebec
PR—Puerto Rico
pract—practice
practr—practitioner
prehist—prehistoric, prehistory
prep—preparation, preparative, preparatory
pres—president
Presby—Presbyterian
preserv—preservation
prev—prevention, preventive
prin—principal
prob(s)—problem(s)
proc—proceedings
proctol—proctologic, proctological, proctology
prod—product(s), production, productive
prof—professional, professor, professorial
Prof Exp—Professional Experience
prog(s)—program(s), programmed, programming
proj—project(s), projection(al), projective
prom—promotion
protozool—protozoology
prov—province, provincial
psychiat—psychiatric, psychiatry
psychoanal—psychoanalysis, psychoanalytic, psychoanalytical
psychol—psychological, psychology
psychomet—psychometric(s)
psychopath—psychopathologic, psychopathology
psychophys—psychophysical, psychophysics
psychophysiol—psychophysiological, psychophysiology
psychosom—psychosomatic(s)
psychother—psychotherapeutic(s), psychotherapy
Pt—Point
pub—public
publ—publication(s), publish(ed), publisher, publishing
pvt—private

Qm—Quartermaster
Qm Gen—Quartermaster General
qual—qualitative, quality
quant—quantitative
quart—quarterly

radiol—radiological, radiology
RAF—Royal Air Force
RAFVR—Royal Air Force Volunteer Reserve

RAMC—Royal Army Medical Corps
RAMCR—Royal Army Medical Corps Reserve
RAOC—Royal Army Ordnance Corps
RASC—Royal Army Service Corps
RASCR—Royal Army Service Corps Reserve
RCAF—Royal Canadian Air Force
RCAFR—Royal Canadian Air Force Reserve
RCAFVR—Royal Canadian Air Force Volunteer Reserve
RCAMC—Royal Canadian Army Medical Corps
RCAMCR—Royal Canadian Army Medical Corps Reserve
RCASC—Royal Canadian Army Service Corps
RCASCR—Royal Canadian Army Service Corps Reserve
RCEME—Royal Canadian Electrical & Mechanical Engineers
RCN—Royal Canadian Navy
RCNR—Royal Canadian Naval Reserve
RCNVR—Royal Canadian Naval Volunteer Reserve
Rd—Road
RD—Rural Delivery
rec—record(s), recording
redevelop—redevelopment
ref—reference(s)
refrig—refrigeration
regist—register(ed), registration
registr—registrar
regt—regiment(al)
rehab—rehabilitation
rel(s)—relation(s), relative
relig—religion, religious
REME—Royal Electrical & Mechanical Engineers
rep—represent, representative
repub—republic
req—requirements
res—research, reserve
rev—review, revised, revision
RFD—Rural Free Delivery
rhet—rhetoric, rhetorical
RI—Rhode Island
Rm—Room
RM—Royal Marines
RN—Royal Navy
RNA—ribonucleic acid
RNR—Royal Naval Reserve
RNVR—Royal Naval Volunteer Reserve
roentgenol—roentgenologic, roentgenological, roentgenology
RR—Railroad, Rural Route
rte—route
Russ—Russian
rwy—railway

s—south
SAfrica—South Africa
SAm—South America, South American
sanit—sanitary, sanitation
Sask—Saskatchewan
SC—South Carolina
Scand—Scandinavia(n)
sch(s)—school(s)
scholar—scholarship
sci—science(s), scientific
SDak—South Dakota
SEATO—Southeast Asia Treaty Organization
sec—secondary
sect—section

secy—secretary
seismog—seismograph, seismographic, seismography
seismogr—seismographer
seismol—seismological, seismology
sem—seminar, seminary
sen—senator, senatorial
Sept—September
ser—serial, series
serol—serologic, serological, serology
serv—service(s), serving
silvicult—silvicultural, silviculture
soc(s)—societies, society
soc sci—social science
sociol—sociologic, sociological, sociology
Span—Spanish
spec—special
specif—specification(s)
spectrog—spectrograph, spectrographic, spectography
spectrogr—spectrographer
spectrophotom—spectrophotometer, spectrophotometric, spectrophotometry
spectros—spectroscopic, spectroscopy
speleol—speleological, speleology
Sq—Square
sr—senior
St—Saint, Street(s)
sta(s)—station(s)
stand—standard(s), standardization
statist—statistical, statistics
Ste—Sainte
steril—sterility
stomatol—stomatology
stratig—stratigraphic, stratigraphy
stratigr—stratigrapher
struct—structural, structure(s)
stud—student(ship)
subcomt—subcommittee
subj—subject
subsid—subsidiary
substa—substation
super—superior
suppl—supplement(s), supplemental, supplementary
supt—superintendent
supv—supervising, supervision
supvr—supervisor
supvry—supervisory
surg—surgery, surgical
surv—survey, surveying
survr—surveyor
Swed—Swedish
Switz—Switzerland
symp—symposia, symposium(s)
syphil—syphilology
syst(s)—system(s), systematic(s), systematical

taxon—taxonomic, taxonomy
tech—technical, technique(s)
technol—technologic(al), technology
tel—telegraph(y), telephone
temp—temporary
Tenn—Tennessee
Terr—Terrace
Tex—Texas
textbk(s)—textbook(s)
text ed—text edition
theol—theological, theology
theoret—theoretic(al)
ther—therapy
therapeut—therapeutic(s)

thermodyn—thermodynamic(s)
topog—topographic, topographical,
  topography
topogr—topographer
toxicol—toxicologic, toxicological, toxicology
trans—transactions
transl—translated, translation(s)
translr—translator(s)
transp—transport, transportation
treas—treasurer, treasury
treat—treatment
trop—tropical
tuberc—tuberculosis
TV—television
Twp—Township

UAR—United Arab Republic
UK—United Kingdom
UN—United Nations
undergrad—undergraduate
unemploy—unemployment
UNESCO—United Nations Educational
  Scientific & Cultural Organization
UNICEF—United Nations International
  Childrens Fund
univ(s)—universities, university
UNRRA—United Nations Relief &
  Rehabilitation Administration
UNRWA—United Nations Relief & Works
  Agency
urol—urologic, urological, urology
US—United States

USA—US Army
USAAF—US Army Air Force
USAAFR—US Army Air Force Reserve
USAF—US Air Force
USAFR—US Air Force Reserve
USAR—US Army Reserve
USCG—US Coast Guard
USCGR—US Coast Guard Reserve
USDA—US Department of Agriculture
USMC—US Marine Corps
USMCR—US Marine Corps Reserve
USN—US Navy
USNAF—US Naval Air Force
USNAFR—US Naval Air Force Reserve
USNR—US Naval Reserve
USPHS—US Public Health Service
USPHSR—US Public Health Service Reserve
USSR—Union of Soviet Socialist Republics
USWMC—US Women's Marine Corps
USWMCR—US Women's Marine Corps
  Reserve

Va—Virginia
var—various
veg—vegetable(s), vegetation
vent—ventilating, ventilation
vert—vertebrate
vet—veteran(s), veterinarian, veterinary
VI—Virgin Islands
vinicult—viniculture
virol—virological, virology
vis—visiting

voc—vocational
vocab—vocabulary
vol(s)—voluntary, volunteer(s), volume(s)
vpres—vice president
vs—versus
Vt—Vermont

w—west
WAC—Women's Army Corps
Wash—Washington
WAVES—Women Accepted for Voluntary
  Emergency Service
WHO—World Health Organization
WI—West Indies
wid—widow, widowed, widower
Wis—Wisconsin
WRCNS—Women's Royal Canadian Naval
  Service
WRNS—Women's Royal Naval Service
WVa—West Virginia
Wyo—Wyoming

yearbk(s)—yearbook(s)
YMCA—Young Men's Christian Association
YMHA—Young Men's Hebrew Association
yr(s)—year(s)
YWCA—Young Women's Christian Asso-
  ciation
YWHA—Young Women's Hebrew Asso-
  ciation

zool—zoological, zoology

AMERICAN MEN & WOMEN OF SCIENCE

C

CABANA, ALDEE, b Beloeil, Que, July 20, 35; m 58; c 4. PHYSICAL CHEMISTRY, MOLECULAR SPECTROSCOPY. *Educ:* Univ Montreal, BSc, 58, MSc, 59, PhD(chem), 62. *Prof Exp:* Fel chem, Princeton Univ, 61-63; from asst prof to assoc prof, 63-71, syndicate prof, 75-76, PROF CHEM, UNIV SHERBROOKE, 71-, DEAN, FAC SCI, 78- *Concurrent Pos:* Pres, Syndicate Prof Univ Sherbrooke, 75- *Honors & Awards:* Gerhard Herzberg Award, Spectros Soc Can, 76. *Mem:* Chem Inst Can; Spectros Soc Can; Can Asn Physicists; assoc mem Can Soc Chem Eng. *Res:* Infrared and Raman spectra of molecular crystals; high resolution infrared spectroscopy. *Mailing Add:* Dept Chem Univ Sherbrooke Sherbrooke PQ J1K 2R1 Can

CABANES, WILLIAM RALPH, JR, b Memphis, Tex, Nov 13, 32; m 62; c 1. ORGANIC CHEMISTRY, POLYMER CHEMISTRY. *Educ:* Univ Tex, Austin, BA, 53, MA, 55, PhD(org chem), 57. *Prof Exp:* Res fel chem, Univ Ariz, 62-64; lectr org chem, Univ Minn, Duluth, 64-65; ASSOC PROF ORG CHEM, UNIV TEX, EL PASO, 65- *Concurrent Pos:* R A Welch grant, 67-70. *Mem:* Fel AAAS; NY Acad Sci. *Res:* Organic polymers; polyampholytes. *Mailing Add:* Dept of Chem Univ of Tex El Paso TX 79968

CABANISS, GERRY HENDERSON, b Winter Haven, Fla, Apr 22, 35; m 62; c 3. GEOPHYSICS, TECTONICS. *Educ:* Dartmouth Col, AB, 57; Boston Col, MS, 68; Boston Univ, PhD(geol), 75. *Prof Exp:* GEOPHYSICIST, AIR FORCE GEOPHYSICS LAB, 58- *Mem:* Am Geophys Union. *Res:* The temporal and spatial characteristics of earth crustal deformations at periods longer than one hour. *Mailing Add:* AF Geophysics Lab L G Hanscom AFB MA 01731

CABASSO, ISRAEL, b Jerusalem, Israel, Nov 17, 42. POLYMER CHEMISTRY. *Educ:* Hebrew Univ Jerusalem, BS, 66, MS, 68; Weizmann Inst Sci, PhD(polymer chem), 73. *Prof Exp:* Asst res assoc & teacher chem, Hebrew Univ Jerusalem, 66-68; res asst, Dept Plastic, Weizmann Inst Sci, 68-73; fel, Gulf South Res Inst, 73-74; sr investr polymer chem, 74-75, group leader polymer chem & head & mgr, Polymer Dept, 76-80; PROF & DIR, POLYMER RES INST, STATE UNIV NY SYRACUSE, 80- *Concurrent Pos:* Prof sci, Technicon High Sch, 68-72; sr res assoc, Weizmann Inst Sci, 73-; adj prof polymer dept, Univ Southern Miss, 77-; clin assoc prof biomat dept, La State Univ Med Ctr, New Orleans, 78- *Mem:* Am Chem Soc; Israel Chem Soc. *Res:* Polymer alloys; hollow fiber and synthetic polymeric membrane; synthesis and transport phenomena, for hemodialysis, reverse osmosis, pervaporation, and polymer materials for artificial organs, self extinguish material, and development of ligand polymers. *Mailing Add:* Polymer Res Inst ESF State Univ NY Syracuse NY 13210

CABASSO, VICTOR JACK, b Port Said, Egypt, June 21, 15; US citizen; m 48; c 2. VIROLOGY. *Educ:* Lycee Francais, Egypt, BA, 33; Hebrew Univ, Israel, MS, 38; Sorbonne & Univ Algiers, ScD(bact), 41. *Prof Exp:* Spec investr pub health & hyg, Off Foreign Relief & Rehab Opers, US Dept State, Tunis, 43; chief bacteriologist, Greece & Mid East, UNRRA, 44-46; res virologist, Lederle Labs, 46-58; head virus immunol res dept, Lederle Labs, Am Cyanamid Co, 58-67; dir microbiol res dept, Cutter Labs, 67-69, assoc dir res microbiol, 69-74, dir, 74-76, vpres res & develop, 76-80; CONSULT & LECTR, 80- *Concurrent Pos:* Assoc mem, Pasteur Inst, Tunis; mem comt on stand methods for vet microbiol, Nat Acad Sci; mem working comt microbiol, Nat Comt Clin Lab Stand; mem subcomt rabies, Agr Bd, Nat Res Coun. *Mem:* AAAS; fel NY Acad Sci; fel Am Acad Microbiol; Am Pub Health Asn; Am Soc Microbiol. *Res:* Virology; viral immunology; vaccine development; plasma fractions. *Mailing Add:* 490 Tharp Drive Moraga CA 94556

CABBINESS, DALE KEITH, b Binger, Okla, May 22, 37; m 58; c 2. ANALYTICAL CHEMISTRY. *Educ:* Southwestern State Col, BS, 60; Univ Ark, MS, 65; Purdue Univ, PhD(chem), 70. *Prof Exp:* Chemist, Dow Chem Co, 60-61; res scientist, 69-75; res group leader, Continental Oil Co, 75-81, ASSOC DIR, CONOCO, INC, 81- *Mem:* Am Chem Soc; Sigma Xi. *Res:* Chemical methods of analysis using kinetic techniques, continuous flow procedures, automation of same, and thermo analytical techniques. *Mailing Add:* Conoco Inc PO Box 1267 Ponca City OK 74603

CABBLE, G(EORGE) M(ERRIFIELD), JR, b New York, NY, Sept 24, 15; m 42; c 3. MECHANICAL ENGINEERING. *Educ:* Va Polytech Inst, BSME, 49, MS, 52; Univ Ill, PhD, 58. *Prof Exp:* Self employed, 35-41; rep, Nat Silk Co, Inc, 41-42 & 46-48; asst mech eng, Va Polytech Inst, 48-49, asst prof, 49-51; asst, Univ Ill, 51-54; supvr electromech group, Res Dept, Melpar, Inc, 54; supv engr, Air Brake Div, Westinghouse Air Brake Co, 54-70, sr specialist, 70-75; chief, Wheels & Brake Systs, Amtrak, 77-80; RETIRED. *Concurrent Pos:* Consult engr rwy eng, 52-54 & 80. *Mem:* Fel Am Soc Mech Engrs; Air Brake Asn. *Res:* Friction; braking; adhesion of railway wheels; fatigue of metals; railway engineering. *Mailing Add:* 295-F Lakemoore Dr NE Atlanta GA 30342

CABEEN, SAMUEL KIRKLAND, b Easton, Pa, Jan 22, 31. CHEMISTRY, INFORMATION SCIENCE. *Educ:* Lafayette Col, BA, 52; Syracuse Univ, MS, 55. *Prof Exp:* Asst librn, Am Metal Climax Inc, 56-58; librn, Ford Instrument Co Div, Sperry Rand Corp, 58-64; asst dir, 64-68, DIR, ENG SOCS LIBR, 68- *Mem:* Spec Libr Asn; Am Soc Info Sci; Am Libr Asn. *Mailing Add:* Eng Socs Libr 345 E 47th St New York NY 10017

CABELLI, VICTOR JACK, microbiology, environmental health, see previous edition

CABIB, ENRICO, b Genoa, Italy, Jan 11, 25; m 55; c 3. BIOCHEMISTRY, ENZYMOLOGY. *Educ:* Univ Buenos Aires, PhD(chem), 51. *Prof Exp:* Investr, Inst Biochem Invest, 49-53; vis investr biochem, Col Physicians & Surgeons, Columbia Univ, 53-54; investr, Inst Biochem Invest, 55-58; investr, Sch Sci, Univ Buenos Aires, 58-67; vis scientist, 67-69, RES BIOCHEMIST, NAT INST ARTHRITIS, METAB & DIGESTIVE DIS, 69- *Concurrent Pos:* Instr, Sch Sci, Univ Buenos Aires, 50-53; career investr, Nat Coun Sci & Tech Invests, 60-67; ed, Arch Biochem & Biophys, 70-72 & J Biol Chem, 75-79 & 82- *Mem:* Am Soc Microbiol; Soc Complex Carbohydrates; Fedn Am Sci; Am Soc Biol Chemists. *Res:* Metabolism of carbohydrates, particularly studies on the biosynthesis of di- and poly-saccharides from sugar nucleotides; biosynthesis of yeast cell wall; regulation of glycogen synthesis in yeast and muscle. *Mailing Add:* Nat Inst Arthritis Bldg 10 Rm 9N-115 Bethesda MD 20205

CABLE, CHARLES ALLEN, b Akeley, Pa, Jan 15, 32; m 55; c 2. ALGEBRA, NUMBER THEORY. *Educ:* Edinboro State Col, BS, 54; Univ NC, Chapel Hill, MEd, 59; Pa State Univ, PhD(math), 69. *Prof Exp:* Teacher, high sch, NY, 54-55 & Pa, 57-58; from instr to asst prof math, Juniata Col, 59-67; assoc prof, 69-75, PROF MATH, ALLEGHENY COL, 75-, CHMN DEPT, 70- *Mem:* Am Math Soc; Math Asn Am. *Res:* Group rings where ring is a finite field and group is Abelian; combinatorics and graph theory. *Mailing Add:* Dept of Math Allegheny Col Meadville PA 16335

CABLE, JOE WOOD, b Murray, Ky, Feb 17, 31; m 50; c 3. SOLID STATE PHYSICS. *Educ:* Murray State Univ, AB, 52; Fla State Univ, PhD(chem), 55. *Prof Exp:* PHYSICIST, OAK RIDGE NAT LAB, 55- *Mem:* Am Phys Soc. *Res:* Neutron scattering studies of magnetic materials. *Mailing Add:* Oak Ridge Nat Lab Oak Ridge TN 37830

CABLE, PETER GEORGE, b New York, NY, May 5, 36; m 66. SONAR ENGINEERING. *Educ:* Haverford Col, BA, 58; Columbia Univ, MA, 60; Univ Md, PhD(physics), 66. *Prof Exp:* Physicist, Naval Underwater Systs Ctr, 66-68; res asst prof physics, Univ Md, 69-70; physicist, 71-76, SUPVR PHYSICIST, NAVAL UNDERWATER SYSTS CTR, 76- *Concurrent Pos:* Assoc fac, Mitchell Col, 67-69; adj fac, Hartford Grad Ctr, 77-81. *Mem:* Am Phys Soc; Acoust Soc Am. *Res:* Application of statistical methods to the characterizations of underwater acoustic transmission phenomena, including multipath fluctuations, scattering from rough boundaries and complex objects; acoustical noise and reverberation. *Mailing Add:* 315 Four Mile River Rd Old Lyme CT 06371

CABLE, RAYMOND MILLARD, b Campton, Ky, Apr 22, 09; m 36; c 4. ZOOLOGY. *Educ:* Berea Col, AB, 29; NY Univ, MS, 30, PhD, 33. *Hon Degrees:* ScD, Berea Col, 55. *Prof Exp:* Assoc prof biol, Berea Col, 33-35; from asst prof to prof, 35-75, EMER PROF PARASITOL, PURDUE UNIV, 75- *Concurrent Pos:* Guggenheim fel, Univ PR, 51-52. *Mem:* AAAS; Am Soc Zool; Am Micros Soc; Am Soc Parasitol(vpres, 58, pres, 64); NY Acad Sci. *Res:* Parasitology. *Mailing Add:* Dept of Biol Sci Purdue Univ West Lafayette IN 47907

CABOT, JOHN BOIT, II, b Denver, Colo, Aug 16, 46. NEUROANATOMY, NEUROPHYSIOLOGY. *Educ:* Univ Del, BEA, 69; Univ Va, PhD(physiol), 76. *Prof Exp:* Alfred Sloan Fel physiol & neuroanat, Dept Physiol, Univ Va, 76-79; ASST PROF NEUROBIOL, DEPT NEUROBIOL & BEHAV, STATE UNIV NY AT STONY BROOK, 79- *Concurrent Pos:* Prin investr, Neural Mechamisms Cent Cardiovasc Control, Nat Heart, Lung & Blood Inst, 79-; ad hoc mem, Exp Cardiovasc Study Sect, NIH, 81- *Mem:* Soc Neurosci; AAAS. *Res:* Anatomical, physiological and pharmacological characteristics of central nervous sytem pathways influencing peripheral cardiovascular function; identification of chemically definable inputs of the thoracolumbar sympathetic perganglionic neurons. *Mailing Add:* Dept Neurobiol & Behav Grad Biol Bldg State Univ NY Stony Brook NY 11794

CABOT, MYLES CLAYTON, b Boston, Mass, Oct 23, 48. CELL DIFFERENTIATION, LIPID BIOCHEMISTRY. *Educ:* Western Carolina Univ, BS, 70, MA, 72; Hebrew Univ, PhD(biochem), 76. *Prof Exp:* Damon Runyon-Walter Winchell Cancer Fund fel, 76-78; SCIENTIST BIOCHEM, OAK RIDGE ASSOC UNIVS, 78- *Concurrent Pos:* Consult, USPHS, 78. *Res:* Structure and function of biological membranes; lipid metabolism in cancer cells; membrane modification; tumor promotion; role of lipids in cellular differentiation. *Mailing Add:* Biol Chem Lab Med & Health Sci PO Box 117 Oak Ridge Assoc Univs Oak Ridge TN 37830

CABRAL, GUY ANTONY, b Furnas, Port, Dec 15, 38; US citizen; m 69; c 3. VIROLOGY, ELECTRON MICROSCOPY. *Educ:* Univ Mass, BA, 67; Univ Conn, MS, 70, PhD(parasitol), 74. *Prof Exp:* Fel virol, Baylor Col Med, 74-76, asst prof, 76-78; ASST PROF VIROL, DEPT MICROBIOL, MED COL VA, VA COMMONWEALTH UNIV, 78- *Mem:* Am Soc Microbiol; Am Soc Parasitol; AAAS; Electron Micros Soc Am. *Res:* Viral oncogenesis; analysis of hepatitis type B subunit vaccines; non-A and non-B hepatitis research. *Mailing Add:* Dept Microbiol Va Commonwealth Univ Richmond VA 23298

CABRERA, BLAS, b Paris, France, Sept 21, 46; US citizen; m 72; c 2. LOW TEMPERATURE PHYSICS. *Educ:* Univ Va, BS, 68; Stanford Univ, PhD(physics), 75. *Prof Exp:* RES ASSOC PHYSICS, STANFORD UNIV, 75- *Res:* Testing general relativity with an orbiting precise superconducting gyroscope referenced to a fixed star, using a London moment readout in an ultra-low magnetic field region. *Mailing Add:* Dept of Physics Stanford Univ Stanford CA 94305

CABRERA, EDELBERTO JOSE, b Pinar del Rio, Cuba, Nov 5, 44; US citizen; m 64; c 2. IMMUNOLOGY, IMMUNOPHARMACOLOGY. *Educ:* Univ Ill, Urbana-Champaign, BS, 67, MS, 68, PhD(zool), 72. *Prof Exp:* Res asst malaria, Univ Ill, Urbana-Champaign, 69-72; res scientist immunol, Univ NMex, 72-77; RES SCIENTIST V, NORWICH-EATON PHARMACEUT, 77- *Mem:* AAAS; Fedn Am Soc Exp Biol; Am Asn Immunologists; Sigma Xi. *Res:* Investigation of the immune response of primates and rodents to plasmodial infections; the overall aim of the research is directed toward the preparation of a vaccine against human malaria. *Mailing Add:* Biol Res Div Norwich-Eaton Pharmaceut Norwich NY 13815

CABRI, LOUIS J, b Cairo, Egypt, Feb 23, 34; Can citizen; m 59; c 3. MINERALOGY, GEOCHEMISTRY. *Educ:* Univ Witwatersrand, BSc, 54, Hons, 55; McGill Univ, MSc, 61, PhD(geol, geochem), 65. *Prof Exp:* Geologist, Josan, SA, WAfrica, 56, Sierra Leone Mineral Syndicate, 57-58 & New Amianthus Mines, SAfrica, 59; sci officer mineral, Dept Mines & Tech Surv, Can, 64-65, RES SCIENTIST, DEPT ENERGY, MINES & RES CAN, 66- *Concurrent Pos:* Sci ed, Can Mineralogist, 75-, ed, Platinum-Group Elements & Mineral Geol Recovery, 81. *Honors & Awards:* Waldemar Lindgren Citation, Soc Econ Geol, 66. *Mem:* Mineral Soc Am; Mineral Asn Can; Geol Asn Can; Can Inst Mining & Metall; Prof Inst Pub Serv Can. *Res:* Phase equilibrium research in sulfide and sulfide-type systems and applications to mineralogical problems and to genesis of ore deposits; beneficiation and economic aspects of ore minerals; author of over 85 published papers. *Mailing Add:* Mines Br 555 Booth St Ottawa ON K1A 0G1 Can

CACELLA, ARTHUR FERREIRA, b New Bedford, Mass, Nov 26, 20; m 50; c 5. POLYMER CHEMISTRY. *Educ:* NC State Col, BChE, 47; Inst Textile Technol, MSc, 49; Princeton Univ, MA, 52. *Prof Exp:* Res chemist, Benger Lab, EI du Pont de Nemours & Co, Va, 54-58 & Inst Textile Technol, 59-60; dir res & Deveop, Globe Mfg Co, 60-62; VPRES & LAB DIR, AMELIOTEX, INC, ROCKY HILL, 62- *Mem:* Am Chem Soc; Am Inst Chemists; Am Asn Textile Chemists & Colorists; NY Acad Sci. *Res:* Stress relaxation of nylon; interaction of water vapor with natural and synthetic fibers; solubility of polymers; chemical modification of cotton; polyurethane chemistry of coatings and adhesives; hydrolysis; catalysis; spandex fibers. *Mailing Add:* 16 Hillwood Rd East Brunswick NJ 08816

CACERES, CESAR A, b Puerto Cortes, Honduras, Apr 9, 27. MEDICINE, COMPUTER SCIENCE. *Educ:* Georgetown Univ, BS, 49, MD, 53. *Prof Exp:* Intern med, Boston City Hosp, Mass, 53-54, resident, 54-55; resident, New Eng Med Ctr, 55-56; fel cardiol, George Washington Univ, 56-60, from asst clin prof to assoc prof med, 60-69, prof & chmn dept, 69-71; PRES, CLIN SYSTS ASSOC, 71- *Concurrent Pos:* Chief, Med Systs Develop Lab, USPHS, 60-69; prof elec eng, Univ Md, College Park, 71-76. *Honors & Awards:* Dept Health, Educ & Welfare Super Serv Awards, 63 & 66. *Mem:* Soc Advan Med Systs (past pres); Int Health Eval Asn (past pres); Asn Advan Med Instrumentation (past pres). *Res:* Electrocardiography; cholesterol; cardiology; medical diagnosis; computers in medicine; clinical engineering. *Mailing Add:* 1759 Q St NW Washington DC 20009

CADA, GLENN FRANCIS, b Columbus, Nebr, Nov 2, 49; m 72; c 2. FISHERY BIOLOGY, AQUATIC ECOLOGY. *Educ:* Univ Nebr, BS, 71, PhD(zool), 77; Colo State Univ, MS, 73. *Prof Exp:* Res technician limnol, Univ Nebr, 69-71; res asst aquatic ecol, Colo State Univ, 71-73; res asst ichthyol, 73-76, teaching asst ichthyol & limnol, Univ Nebr, 76-77; RES ASSOC AQUATIC ECOL, OAK RIDGE NAT LAB, 77- *Mem:* Am Fisheries Soc; Sigma Xi; Am Inst Fisheries Res Biol. *Res:* Ichthyoplankton ecology; evironmental impacts of energy technologies, including steam-electric power plants, hydroelectric power, and coal conversion processes. *Mailing Add:* Div of Environ Sci PO Box X Oak Ridge TN 37830

CADA, RONALD LEE, b Columbus, Nebr, June 10, 44; m 66; c 2. PUBLIC HEALTH, MICROBIOLOGY. *Educ:* Colo State Univ, BS, 66, MS, 68; Univ Tex, DrPH, 74. *Prof Exp:* Microbiologist lab, Colo Dept Health, 68-70, consult, 70-72; asst prof dis control, Sch Pub Health, Univ Tex, 74-79; dir med specialties, 81-82, EXT SPECIALIST, ADMIN, UNIV IOWA, 79- *Concurrent Pos:* Lab consult, Community Health Asn, 75-76. *Mem:* Am Pub Health Asn. *Res:* Methods and evaluation of health laboratory quality assurance practice; development of infection control practice and rural health delivery systems; continuing education for rural laboratory personnel. *Mailing Add:* State Hyg Lab Univ Iowa Iowa City IA 52242

CADBURY, WILLIAM EDWARD, JR, b Germantown, Pa, Apr 19, 09; m 33; c 2. PHYSICAL CHEMISTRY. *Educ:* Haverford Col, BS, 31, AM, 32; Univ Pa, PhD(chem), 40. *Hon Degrees:* LLD, Haverford Col, 74. *Prof Exp:* From instr to asst prof chem, Haverford Col, 32-43; actg assoc prof, Univ NC, 43-44; from assoc prof to prof, 44-70, dean col, 51-66, dir post-baccalaureate fel prog, 66-70, EMER PROF CHEM, HAVERFORD COL, 70- *Concurrent Pos:* Assoc ed, J Chem Educ, 50-55; exec dir, Nat Med Fels, Inc, 70-78. *Mem:* Fel AAAS. *Res:* Phase relations in the system sodium sulfate-sodium chromate-water; phase rule studies on aqueous solutions. *Mailing Add:* 10 Railroad Ave Haverford PA 19041

CADE, JAMES ROBERT, b San Antonio, Tex, Sept 26, 27; m 53; c 6. INTERNAL MEDICINE. *Educ:* Univ Tex, MD, 54. *Prof Exp:* Fel, Cornell Univ, 58-61; assoc prof med, 61-72, chief med sch, 72-80, PROF RENAL MED, UNIV FLA, 72- *Mem:* Am Fedn Clin Res; Am Soc Clin Invest; Am Physiol Soc. *Res:* Renal, electrolyte and exercise physiology. *Mailing Add:* Dept of Med Univ of Fla Gainesville FL 32610

CADE, RUTH ANN, b Yazoo City, Miss, Nov 17, 37; m 74; c 2. ENGINEERING, COMPUTER SCIENCE. *Educ:* Miss State Univ, BS, 63; Univ Ala, MA, 68, PhD(eng), 69. *Prof Exp:* Chem engr, Southern Res Inst, 63-64; instr eng mech, Univ Ala, 67-68; asst prof math, 68-75, ASSOC PROF COMPUT SCI, UNIV SOUTHERN MISS, 75- *Mem:* Am Soc Eng Educ; Math Asn Am. *Mailing Add:* Dept Comput Sci & Statist Univ Southern Miss Hattiesburg MS 39401

CADE, STEPHEN C, forestry, see previous edition

CADE, THOMAS JOSEPH, b San Angelo, Tex, Jan 10, 28; m 52; c 5. ORNITHOLOGY. *Educ:* Univ Alaska, AB, 51; Univ Calif, Los Angeles, MA, 55, PhD(zool), 58. *Prof Exp:* Assoc zool, Univ Calif, Los Angeles, 55-58; NSF fel, Mus Vert Zool, Univ Calif, Berkeley, 58-59; from asst prof to prof zool, Syracuse Univ, 59-67; PROF ORNITH, STATE UNIV NY COL AGR, CORNELL UNIV & RES DIR LAB ORNITH, 67-, MEM STAFF INSTR, RES & EXTEN AT ITHACA, 72- *Concurrent Pos:* NSF grants, 60-65 & sr fel, Transvaal Mus, SAfrica, 65-66; USPHS grant, 63-66. *Mem:* Am Soc Mammal; fel Am Ornith Union; Cooper Ornith Soc; Wilson Ornith Soc. *Res:* Population and physiological ecology; behavior of birds and mammals. *Mailing Add:* Cornell Univ Lab Ornith 159 Sapsucker Woods Rd Ithaca NY 14850

CADE, WILLIAM HENRY, b San Antonio, Tex, July 5, 46; m 72; c 1. BEHAVIOR GENETICS, SEXUAL SELECTION. *Educ:* Univ Tex, Austin, BA, 68, MA, 73, PhD(zool), 76. *Prof Exp:* Asst prof, 78-81, ASSOC PROF BIOL, BROCK UNIV, 81- *Concurrent Pos:* Can deleg, Int Ethological Conf, 78 & 81. *Mem:* AAAS; Soc Study Evolution; Animal Behav Soc; Entom Soc Can; Entom Soc Am. *Res:* Insect sexual behavior; selective agents influencing behavior include predators and parasites, female mating preferences and factors affecting male competition; behavior genetics of sexual behavior. *Mailing Add:* Dept Biol Sci Brock Univ St Catharines ON L2S 3A1 Can

CADENHEAD, DAVID ALLAN, b Tillicoultry, Scotland, Aug 5, 30. PHYSICAL CHEMISTRY. *Educ:* Univ St Andrews, BSc, 53; Bristol Univ, PhD(chem), 57. *Prof Exp:* Can Nat Defence fel, Royal Mil Col, Can, 57-59; fel, Alfred Univ, 59-60; asst prof, 60-64, assoc prof, 64-77, res assoc prof biochem, 70-77, PROF CHEM, STATE UNIV NY BUFFALO, 77- *Concurrent Pos:* State Univ NY Buffalo rep, Univs Space Res Asn, 74-; vis prof, San Francisco State Univ, 76. *Mem:* Am Chem Soc; The Chem Soc. *Res:* Adsorption and porosity; monomolecular film studies; surface characterization of phospholipids; molecular interactions in mixed monolayers; cell membrane structure. *Mailing Add:* Dept Chem 112 Acheson Hall State Univ NY Chemistry Rd Buffalo NY 14214

CADIEN, JAMES DAVID, physical anthropology, see previous edition

CADIGAN, FRANCIS C, JR, infectious diseases, tropical medicine, see previous edition

CADIGAN, ROBERT ALLEN, b Glen Falls, NY, June 10, 18; m 44; c 4. GEOLOGY, EXPLORATION GEOCHEMISTRY. *Educ:* Col of Puget Sound, AB, 47; Pa State Univ, MS, 52. *Prof Exp:* Geologist, 48-74, RES GEOLOGIST, US GEOL SURV, 74- *Concurrent Pos:* Adv tech coord comt, Nat Hydrogeochem Surv, US Dept Energy, 75-77; mem, Nat Adv Bd, Am Security Coun; prin investr, Uranium Resource Eval Prog, Delta, Utah Quadrangle, 77- *Mem:* Geol Soc Am; Am Asn Petrol Geologists; Am Soc Econ Paleont & Mineral. *Res:* Textural and geochemical properties of sedimentary rocks; geochemical exploration techniques applied to detecting areas in the United States containing economically important uranium ore deposits; geochemistry of radioactive mineral springs. *Mailing Add:* 9125 W Second Ave Lakewood CO 80226

CADLE, RICHARD DUNBAR, b Cleveland, Ohio, Sept 23, 14; m 40; c 3. PHYSICAL CHEMISTRY. *Educ:* Western Reserve Univ, AB, 36; Univ Wash, PhD(chem), 40. *Prof Exp:* Teaching fel, Univ Wash, 36-38; res chemist, Procter & Gamble Co, 40-47; unit head, Naval Ord Test Sta, Calif, 47-48; sr phys chemist, Stanford Res Inst, 48-54, mgr atmospheric chem physics, 54-63; prog scientist, Nat Ctr Atmospheric Res, 63-66, head, Chem Dept, 66-73, proj scientist, 73-79; CONSULT, 79- *Concurrent Pos:* Asst lectr, Univ Cincinnati, 41-43; consult, Army Chem Corps, 55; vis prof, Ripon Col, 66; mem tech adv comt, Denver Regional Air Pollution Control Agency, 67-72; consult, Gulf South Res Inst, 68-70; mem adv comt air pollution, chem & physics, USPHS, 69-73; panel mem polar meteorol, Nat Acad Sci-Nat Res Coun, 69-73; panel mem atmospheric chem, 70-75; adj prof, Pa State Univ, 72-75. *Mem:* Sigma Xi; Am Chem Soc; Am Geophys Union; Am Meteorol Soc. *Res:* Properties of dilute solutions of colloidal electrolytes; preparation and identification of aerosols; chemical kinetics; atmospheric chemistry. *Mailing Add:* 4415 Chippewa Dr Boulder CO 80303

CADLE, STEVEN HOWARD, b Cincinnati, Ohio, Feb 19, 46; m 68; c 2. ANALYTICAL CHEMISTRY, ENVIRONMENTAL CHEMISTRY. *Educ:* Univ Colo, AB, 67; State Univ NY Buffalo, PhD(chem), 72. *Prof Exp:* Asst prof chem, Vassar Col, 72-73; assoc sr res chemist, 74-77, sr res scientist, 77-81, SR STAFF RES SCIENTIST, GEN MOTORS RES LABS, 81- *Honors & Awards:* Young Author Award, Electrochem Soc, 75. *Mem:* Am Chem Soc. *Res:* Analytical methods of analysis, especially those pertaining to atmospheric pollution problems. *Mailing Add:* Res Labs Gen Motors Tech Ctr Warren MI 48090

CADMAN, EDWIN CLARENCE, b Bandon, Ore, May 14, 45; m 68; c 3. BIOCHEMICAL PHARMACOLOGY, CANCER RESEARCH. *Educ:* Stanford Univ, BA, 67; Univ Ore, MD, 71. *Prof Exp:* Resident, Stanford Med Sch, 71-74; fel oncol, 74-76, asst prof, 76-79, ASSOC PROF MED SCH, YALE UNIV, 79-, CO-CHIEF, SECT MED ONCOL, 81- *Concurrent Pos:* Fac Res Award, Am Cancer Soc, 80. *Mem:* Am Fedn Clin Res; Am Asn Cancer Res; Am Soc Clin Oncol. *Res:* Biochemical modulation and selective killing of cancer cells. *Mailing Add:* Dept Med & Pharmacol Yale Univ New Haven CT 06510

CADMAN, THEODORE W, b Osceola Mills, Pa, Feb 28, 40; m 62; c 2. CHEMICAL ENGINEERING. *Educ:* Carnegie-Mellon Univ, BS, 62, MS, 64, PhD(chem eng), 65. *Prof Exp:* From asst prof to assoc prof, 65-73, PROF CHEM ENG, UNIV MD, COLLEGE PARK, 73-, CHMN DEPT CHEM & NUCLEAR ENG, 78- *Concurrent Pos:* Consult eng, ENSCI, Inc, 72- *Mem:* AAAS; Am Inst Chem Engrs; Am Chem Soc; Instrument Soc Am. *Res:* Computer simulation of chemical, biochemical, and petrochemical processes, process dynamics and process control. *Mailing Add:* Dept of Chem & Nuclear Eng Univ of Md College Park MD 20740

CADMUS, EUGENE L, b Newark, NJ, Aug 28, 22; m 46; c 3. MICROBIOLOGY. *Educ:* Rutgers Univ, BS, 49; Brooklyn Polytech, MS, 51. *Prof Exp:* Res chemist, F W Berk & Co, Inc, 51-56; tech dir chem, Woodridge Chem Co, 56-68; TECH MGR CHEM, VENTRON CORP, 68- *Mem:* Am Soc Testing & Mat; Am Chem Soc; Soc Indust Microbiol. *Res:* Mechanisms of brocide activity in industrial applications, plastics; structure activity relationships for compounds showing microbiological activity. *Mailing Add:* Ventron Corp 154 Andover St Danvers MA 01923

CADMUS, ROBERT R, b Little Falls, NJ, June 16, 14; m 41; c 2. PREVENTIVE MEDICINE, MEDICAL ADMINISTRATION. *Educ:* Col Wooster, AB, 36; Columbia Univ, MD, 40. *Hon Degrees:* DSc, Col Med & Dent NJ, Newark, 71. *Prof Exp:* Dir prof serv patients, Vanderbilt Clin-Columbia-Presby Hosp, NY, 45-48; asst dir, Univ Hosps, Cleveland, Ohio, 48-50; dir, NC Mem Hosp, 50-62; prof hosp admin, Univ NC, 52-66, chmn dept, 62-66; consult dir, NC Mem Hosp & res dir, Educ & Res Found, 62-66; prof prev med & pres, Col Med & Dent, NJ, Newark, 66-71; dir, Med Ctr Southeastern Wis, 71-75; exec dir, 75-79, MED DIR, FOUND FOR MED CARE EVAL SOUTHEASTERN WIS, 79- *Concurrent Pos:* Consult, Nat Inst Arthritis & Metab Dis, 60-64 & Div Hosp & Med Facilities, USPHS, 63; mem comt, Clin Res Ctr, Div Res Facilities & Resources, 64-67; consult, Vet Admin Hosp, East Orange, NJ & USPHS Hosp, Staten Island, NY, 66-71; mem nat adv coun, Gen Med Sci, NIH; mem regional adv group, Health Serv & Ment Health Admin-Regional Med Prog; mem comprehensive health planning coun, Health Serv & Ment Health Admin; clin prof, prev med, Med Col Wis. *Mem:* AMA; Asn Teachers Prev Med; Am Hosp Asn; Am Asn Hosp Consult. *Res:* Administrative medicine. *Mailing Add:* Found Med Care Eval SE Wis 411 E Mason St Milwaukee WI 53202

CADMUS, ROBERT RANDALL, JR, b New York, NY, Oct 30, 46; m 70; c 2. OBSERVATIONAL OPTICAL ASTRONOMY, NUCLEAR PHYSICS. *Educ:* Swarthmore Col, BA, 68; Univ Wis-Madison, MA, 70, PhD(physics), 77. *Prof Exp:* Res asst physics, Univ Wis-Madison, 68-77; res assoc, Dept Physics & Astron, Univ NC, 77-78; ASST PROF PHYSICS, GRINNELL COL, 78- *Concurrent Pos:* Vis asst prof physics, Iowa State Univ, 80-81. *Mem:* Am Phys Soc; Sigma Xi; Aston Soc Pac. *Res:* Determination of stellar angular diameters from lunar occultation observations; study of polarization effects in light ion-induced nuclear reactions; nuclear spectroscopy. *Mailing Add:* Dept of Physics Grinnell Col Grinnell IA 50112

CADOFF, IRVING B(ERNARD), b New York, NY, Aug 7, 27; m; c 2. MATERIALS SCIENCE. *Educ:* City Col New York, BME, 47; NY Univ, MME, 48, DEng Sci, 53. *Prof Exp:* From instr to prof metall eng, NY Univ, 49-73, chmn dept metall & mat sci, 68-73; dir, Westchester Ctr, 75-80, PROF MAT SCI, POLYTECH INST NEW YORK, 73- *Mem:* Am Phys Soc; Am Soc Metals; Am Inst Mining, Metall & Petrol Engrs. *Res:* Theory of the behavior of solids including metals and semiconductors. *Mailing Add:* Westchester Ctr 456 North St White Plains NY 10605

CADOGAN, KEVIN DENIS, b New York, NY, Feb 17, 39; m 61; c 4. PHYSICAL CHEMISTRY. *Educ:* Manhattan Col, BS, 60; Cornell Univ, PhD(phys chem), 66. *Prof Exp:* Res assoc chem, Cornell Univ, 66-67; res assoc chem, Lab Chem Biodynamics, Univ Calif, Berkeley, 67-69; asst prof, 69-74, ASSOC PROF CHEM, CALIF STATE COL, HAYWARD, 74- *Concurrent Pos:* NIH fel, 67-69; Fulbright-Hays lectr, US-UK Educ Comn, 70-71; Fulbright lectr, Inst Educ Technol, Univ Surrey, 70-71. *Mem:* Am Chem Soc. *Res:* Electronic spectroscopy and solid state photochemistry in aqueous and hydrocarbon solutions at cryogenic temperatures; environmental chemistry; induced and natural chemical cycles in the biosphere; scarce chemical research utilization; scientific utopia. *Mailing Add:* Dept Chem Calif State Univ 25800 Hillary St Hayward CA 94542

CADOGAN, W(ILLIAM) P(ATRICK), b Revere, Mass, Nov 2, 19; m 43; c 5. CHEMICAL ENGINEERING. *Educ:* Mass Inst Technol, SB, 41, SM, 46, ScD(chem eng), 48. *Prof Exp:* Chem engr, Standard Oil Co, Ind, 48-51; vpres, Processes Res Inc, 51-56; mgr chem res & develop, Am Mach & Foundry Co, 56-63; vpres res, 63-80, DIR RES, EMHART CORP, 80- *Mem:* AAAS; Sigma Xi; Am Chem Soc; Am Inst Chem Engrs. *Res:* Adsorption of hydrocarbons; glass container forming; packaging machinery; food processing. *Mailing Add:* Emhart Corp PO Box 2730 Hartford CT 06101

CADORET, REMI JERE, b Scranton, Pa, Mar 28, 28; m 50, 69; c 4. PSYCHIATRY. *Educ:* Harvard Univ, AB, 49; Yale Univ, MD, 53. *Prof Exp:* Intern rotating, Robert Packer Hosp, 53-54; res assoc parapsychol, Parapsychol Lab, Duke Univ, 56-58; from asst prof to assoc prof physiol, Med Sch, Univ Man, 58-65; resident psychiat, Sch Med, Wash Univ, 65-68, from asst prof to assoc prof, 68-73; PROF PSYCHIAT, MED SCH, UNIV IOWA, 73- *Mem:* Psychiat Res Soc. *Res:* Genetics of psychiatric illness; nosology of psychiatric conditions; personality; psychiatric epidemiology. *Mailing Add:* Dept of Psychiat 500 Newton Rd Iowa City IA 52240

CADOTTE, JOHN EDWARD, b Minn, Jan 28, 25; m 48; c 5. ORGANIC CHEMISTRY. *Educ:* Univ Minn, MS, 51. *Prof Exp:* Res chemist, Merck & Co, Inc, 51-52, Clinton Foods, Inc, 52-56 & Wood Conversion Co, 56-65; polymer researcher, 65-71, chemist, 66-75, sr chemist, N Star Div, Midwest Res Inst, 75-78; CHIEF CHEMIST, FILMTEC CORP, 78- *Mem:* Am Chem Soc. *Res:* Adhesives; starch; thermosetting resins; Fourdrinier formed board products and coatings; reverse osmosis membranes. *Mailing Add:* 5637 Scenic Dr Minnetonka MN 55343

CADWALLADER, DONALD ELTON, b Buffalo, NY, June 14, 31; m 60; c 3. PHARMACY, MEDICINAL CHEMISTRY. *Educ:* Univ Buffalo, BS, 53; Univ Ga, MS, 55; Univ Fla, PhD(pharm), 57. *Prof Exp:* Interim res prof, mil med supply agency contract, Univ Fla, 57-58; res assoc pharm, Sterling-Winthrop Res Inst, 58-60; group leader, White Labs, Inc, 60-61; from asst prof to assoc prof, 61-68, PROF PHARM, UNIV GA, 68-, HEAD DEPT, 77- *Honors & Awards:* Lunsford-Richardson Pharm Award, 57. *Mem:* Fel AAAS; Am Pharmaceut Asn; fel Acad Pharmaceut Sci. *Res:* Behavior of erythrocytes in various solvent systems; solubility and dissolution of drugs; stability of drugs; drug manufacturing procedures and processes; biopharmaceutics; drug interactions. *Mailing Add:* Dept of Pharm Univ of Ga Athens GA 30602

CADWALLADER, THOMAS E, US citizen. ENGINEERING. *Educ:* Dickinson Col, ScB, 66; Penn State Univ, BS, 66, MS, 67; Vanderbilt Univ, MS, 72. *Prof Exp:* Mem staff, Weston, 67-72 & Weston Europe, Spain, 72-73, PROJ MGR, WESTON, 73- *Mem:* Water Pollution Control Fedn; Am Soc Civil Engrs; dipl Am Acad Environ Engrs. *Res:* Water resources and water quality management; water supply and treatment; stormwater and flood management; in-plant waste control and production; treatment plant operation; process design; air pollution control; solid waste management; environmental assessment. *Mailing Add:* Weston Weston Way West Chester PA 19380

CADY, BLAKE, b Washington, DC, Dec 27, 30; m 60; c 3. SURGERY, ONCOLOGY. *Educ:* Amherst Col, AB, 53; Cornell Univ, MD, 57. *Prof Exp:* Fel surg, Sloan-Kettering Inst & Med Col, Cornell Univ, 65-67; ASSOC CLIN PROF SURG, MED SCH, HARVARD UNIV, 67- *Concurrent Pos:* Staff surgeon, Lahey Clin Found, 67-81. *Mem:* AMA; Am Col Surgeons; Soc Surg Oncol; Soc Head & Neck Surgeons; Soc Surg Alimentary Tract. *Res:* Clinical interest in human tumors and cancers. *Mailing Add:* 110 Francis St Boston MA 02215

CADY, FOSTER BERNARD, b Middletown, NY, Aug 5, 31; m 53; c 3. STATISTICS. *Educ:* Cornell Univ, BS, 53; Univ Ill, MS, 56; NC State Univ, PhD, 60. *Prof Exp:* Soil scientist, Agr Res Serv, USDA, NC State Univ, 57-60; assoc prof statist, Iowa State Univ, 60-68; prof, Univ Ky, 68-71; PROF BIOL STATIST, CORNELL UNIV, 71- *Mem:* Am Statist Asn; Am Soc Agron; Biomet Soc. *Res:* Statistical methods and experimental design in the agricultural and biological sciences. *Mailing Add:* Biomet Unit Cornell Univ Ithaca NY 14850

CADY, GEORGE HAMILTON, b Lawrence, Kans, Jan 10, 06; m 29; c 2. INORGANIC CHEMISTRY, FLUORINE CHEMISTRY. *Educ:* Univ Kans, AB, 27, AM, 28; Univ Calif, PhD(chem), 30. *Prof Exp:* Asst prof chem, Univ S Dak, 30-31; instr inorg chem, Mass Inst Technol, 31-34; res chemist, gen labs, US Rubber Prod, Inc, 34-35 & Columbia Chem Div, Pittsburgh Plate Glass Co, 35-38; from asst prof to prof, 38-72, chmn dept, 61-65, EMER PROF CHEM, UNIV WASH, 72- *Concurrent Pos:* Sect leader, Manhattan Dist Proj, Columbia Univ, 42-43; GN Lewis Mem lectr, 67. *Honors & Awards:* Distinguished Serv Award, Am Chem Soc, 66, Award for Res Fluorine Chem, 72; US Navy Meritorious Pub Serv Citation, 70; Distinguished Serv Citation, Univ Kans, 72. *Mem:* AAAS; Am Chem Soc; Leopoldina Ger Acad Researchers Natural Sci. *Res:* Preparation and properties of fluorides; hypochlorous acid and hypochlorites; determination of rare gases; composition of gas hydrates. *Mailing Add:* Dept Chem BG-10 Univ of Wash Seattle WA 98195

CADY, HOWARD HAMILTON, b Sioux City, Iowa, Jan 15, 31; m 57; c 4. PHYSICAL CHEMISTRY. *Educ:* Univ Wash, BS, 53; Univ Calif, PhD(chem), 57. *Prof Exp:* Asst, Radiation Lab, Univ Calif, 54-57; staff mem, 57-74, SECT LEADER, LOS ALAMOS SCI LAB, UNIV CALIF, 74- *Mem:* AAAS; Am Chem Soc; Am Crystallog Asn; fel Am Inst Chemists. *Res:* General physical chemistry; crystallography. *Mailing Add:* 1373 40th St Los Alamos NM 87544

CADY, JOHN GILBERT, b Seneca Falls, NY, Jan 30, 14; m 40. SOILS. *Educ:* Syracuse Univ, BS, 36; Univ Wis, MS, 38; Cornell Univ, PhD(soils), 41. *Prof Exp:* Asst soils, Univ Wis, 36-38 & Cornell Univ, 38-42; instr agron, Univ Idaho, 42-43; soil scientist, Mil Geol Unit, US Geol Surv, 44-46; soil scientist, Bur Plant Indust, Soils & Agr Eng, USDA, 46-51 & Soil Surv Lab, Soil Conserv Serv, 52-69; LECTR SOIL SCI, JOHNS HOPKINS UNIV, 69- *Concurrent Pos:* Soil mineralogist, Soil Classification Mission, Econ Coop Admin-Belgian Congo Nat Inst Agron Studies, 51-52. *Mem:* AAAS; fel Geol Soc Am; fel Am Soc Agron. *Res:* Soil genesis; weathering; soil mineralogy; relation of soil characteristics to geomorphology, land use and natural vegetation. *Mailing Add:* Dept of Geog & Environ Eng Johns Hopkins Univ Baltimore MD 21218

CADY, K BINGHAM, b Chicago, Ill, Mar 18, 36; c 4. NUCLEAR ENGINEERING. *Educ:* Mass Inst Technol, SB, 56, PhD(nuclear eng), 62. *Prof Exp:* Marine engr, Shipbuilding Div, Bethlehem Steel Co, 56-58, nuclear engr, 58-59; nuclear engr, Jackson & Moreland, Inc, 59-62; asst prof, 62-67, ASSOC PROF NUCLEAR SCI & ENG, CORNELL UNIV, 67- *Concurrent Pos:* Consult, Knolls Atomic Energy Lab, 66-69; nuclear engr, US Atomic Energy Comn, 69-70. *Mem:* Am Nuclear Soc. *Res:* Fast breeder reactor accidents and transients; energy systems analysis; nuclear reactor safety. *Mailing Add:* Ward Lab Cornell Univ Ithaca NY 14853

CADY, LEE (DE), JR, b St Louis, Mo, Nov 22, 27; m 65; c 1. CARDIOLOGY, INDUSTRIAL MEDICINE. *Educ:* Washington Univ, AB, 47, MA, 48, MD, 51; Yale Univ, MPH, 57, DrPH, 59. *Prof Exp:* Intern, Vet Admin Hosp & Baylor Univ, 51-52; epidemic intel officer, USPHS, 52-54; health officer, Int Coop Admin, 54-56; from asst to assoc prof phys med & rehab, NY Univ, 59-64; prof biomath & chmn dept, Univ Tex, Houston, 64-67; staff dir, Comt Emergency Med Care for Los Angeles County, 70-72; CHIEF CARDIOPULMONARY LAB, LOS ANGELES COUNTY OCCUP HEALTH SERV, 72-; ADJ PROF MED, UNIV SOUTHERN CALIF, 67- *Concurrent Pos:* USPHS spec res fel, 58-61. *Mem:* Fel AAAS; fel Am Col Cardiol; fel Am Pub Health Asn; AMA; Asn Comput Mach. *Res:* Cardiovascular disease; epidemiology; preventive medicine; public health; computing machines; statistics. *Mailing Add:* 1718 Warwick Rd San Marino CA 91108

CADY, PHILIP DALE, b Elmira, NY, June 26, 33; m 55; c 5. CIVIL ENGINEERING. *Educ:* Pa State Univ, BS, 56, MS, 64, PhD(civil eng), 67. *Prof Exp:* Engr, Esso Standrad Oil Co, 56-57 & Lago Oil & Transport Co, 57-62; res asst civil eng, 62-67, from asst prof to assoc prof, 67-75, PROF CIVIL ENG, PA STATE UNIV, 75- *Concurrent Pos:* Secy comt, A2-E1, Hwy Res Bd, Nat Acad Sci-Nat Res Coun, 68- *Honors & Awards:* Thompson Award, Am Soc Testing & Mat, 68. *Mem:* Am Soc Civil Engrs; Am Concrete Inst; Am Soc Testing & Mat. *Res:* Durability of portland cement concrete and concrete aggregates. *Mailing Add:* Dept Civil Eng 212 Sackett Bldg Pa State Univ University Park PA 16802

CADY, WALLACE MARTIN, b Middlebury, Vt, Jan 29, 12; m 42; c 3. GEOLOGY. *Educ:* Middlebury Col, BS, 34; Northwestern Univ, MS, 36; Columbia Univ, PhD(geol), 44. *Prof Exp:* Asst geol, Northwestern Univ, 34-36; asst, Columbia Univ, 38-40; substitute tutor, Brooklyn Col, 40-41; from jr geologist to prin geologist, 39-63, RES GEOLOGIST, US GEOL SURV, 63- *Concurrent Pos:* Coun Int Exchange Scholars lectr probs mod tectonics, Voronezh State Univ, USSR, 75. *Mem:* Fel AAAS; Soc Econ Geol; fel Geol Soc Am; Geochem Soc; fel Am Geophys Union. *Res:* Geology of northwestern Washington; regional geology of New England and adjacent Quebec; regional geology of southwestern Alaska; geotectonics; structural geology; metamorphic stratigraphy; archean geology of southwestern Montana. *Mailing Add:* US Geol Surv Box 25046 Fed Ctr Denver CO 80225

CADZOW, JAMES A(RCHIE), b Niagara Falls, NY, Jan 3, 36; m 58; c 4. ELECTRICAL ENGINEERING. *Educ:* Univ Buffalo, BS, 58; State Univ NY, Buffalo, MS, 63; Cornell Univ, PhD(elec eng), 64. *Prof Exp:* Engr, US Army Res & Develop Labs, 58-59; design engr, Bell Aerosysts Corp, 59-61; asst engr, Cornell Aeronaut Labs, 61-62; prof control & commun eng, State Univ NY Buffalo, 64-77; PROF, VA POLYTECH INST & STATE UNIV, 77- *Mem:* Inst Elec & Electronics Engrs. *Res:* Control and signal processing theory; digital filter theory; functional analysis and numerical algorithms; signal and system identification. *Mailing Add:* Dept of Elec Eng Va Polytech Inst & State Univ Blacksburg VA 24060

CAENEPEEL, CHRISTOPHER LEON, b South Bend, Ind, July 1, 42; m 71; c 2. CHEMICAL ENGINEERING. *Educ:* Univ Notre Dame, BS, 64, MS, 64, PhD(chem eng), 70. *Prof Exp:* Chemist, O'Brien Paints, South Bend, Ind, 62-64; teaching asst chem eng, Univ Notre Dame, 64-65 & 66-67; engr, Standard Oil Co, Ohio, 65-66; res asst chem eng, Univ Notre Dame, 67-69; prof chem eng, Calif State Polytech Univ, Pomona, 70-80; WITH AMOCO RES CTR, 80- *Concurrent Pos:* Fac fel, NASA-Am Soc Eng Educ, 71-72; consult, Occidental Res Corp, 73- *Honors & Awards:* Intergovt Personnel Act appt, Environ Protection Agency, Durham, NC, 75-76. *Mem:* Am Soc Eng Educ; Am Inst Chem Engrs; Am Chem Soc; Sigma Xi. *Res:* Reactor design; hydro metallurgy; mass transport; mathematical modelling. *Mailing Add:* PO Box 400 Mail Sta C2 AMOCO Res Ctr Naperville IL 60540

CAESAR, PHILIP D, b New Haven, Conn, Mar 13, 17; m 40; c 2. PETROLEUM CHEMISTRY. *Educ:* Yale Univ, BS, 39; Univ Ill, MS, 48, PhD(chem), 50. *Prof Exp:* Chemist, res dept, Paulsboro Lab, Socony Mobil Oil Co, Mobil Res & Develop Corp, NJ, 39-45, res assoc, 45-56, supvr chem res, 56-60 & catalysis res, 60-64, mgr prod res sect, cent res div, 64-70, mgr explor process res group, Process Res & Tech Serv Div, 70-77; RETIRED. *Mem:* AAAS; Am Chem Soc. *Res:* Thiophene chemistry; composition and properties of petroleum; catalysis research; petroleum processing; fuel cell applications. *Mailing Add:* Box 322 Cruz Bay VI 00830

CAFARELLI, ENZO DONALD, b White Plains, NY, Feb 15, 42; m 67. EXERCISE PHYSIOLOGY. *Educ:* East Stroudsburg State Col, BS, 69, MEd, 70; Univ Pittsburgh, PhD(exercise physiol), 74. *Prof Exp:* Vis asst fel, John B Pierce Found Lab & fel environ physiol, Yale Univ, 74-77; ASST PROF, DEPT PHYS EDUC, YORK UNIV, TORONTO, 77- *Res:* Physiological mechanisms that subserve the sensation of effort during muscular exercise. *Mailing Add:* Dept Off Phys Educ York Univ 302 Tait McKenzie Downsview Can

CAFASSO, FRED A, b New York, NY, Feb 25, 30; m; c 2. MATERIALS CHEMISTRY. *Educ:* New York Univ, PhD(phys chem), 59. *Prof Exp:* Group leader, 66-69, sect head, 69-73, ASSOC DIV DIR, ARGONNE NAT LAB, 73-, SR CHEMIST, 76- *Mem:* Am Chem Soc; AAAS; Res Soc Am. *Res:* Physical and materials chemistry; liquid metals chemistry; high temperature spectroscopy; solution thermodynamics; magnetic properties of solids; electrode processes; alkali metal polyether solutions. *Mailing Add:* 1033 Fair Oaks Oak Park IL 60302

CAFFARELLI, LUIS ANGEL, b Buenos Aires, Argentina, Dec 8, 48. MATHEMATICS. *Educ:* Univ Buenos Aires, MS, 68, PHD(math), 72. *Prof Exp:* Fel math, Univ Minn, 73-75, asst prof, 75-77, assoc prof, 77-79, prof, 79-80; PROF MATH, COURANT INST, NEW YORK UNIV, 80- *Res:* Problems of slump and energy optimization in mathematics and mechanics. *Mailing Add:* 251 Mercer St New York NY 10012

CAFFEY, HORACE ROUSE, b Grenada, Miss, Mar 24, 29; m 54; c 4. AGRONOMY, PLANT BREEDING. *Educ:* Miss State Univ, BS, 51, MS, 55; La State Univ, PhD(agron), 59. *Prof Exp:* Asst, Miss State Univ, 54-55; agronomist, Miss Rice Grower Asn, 55-57; res assoc, Agron Dept, La Exp Sta, 57-58; assoc agronomist, Delta Br Exp Sta, 58-62, prof & supt, Rice Exp Sta, La State Univ, 62-70; assoc dir, La Agr Exp Sta, 70-79, vchancellor admin & dir, Int Progs, 79-80, VCHANCELLOR, INT PROG, CTR AGR SCI & RURAL DEVELOP, LA STATE UNIV, 80- *Concurrent Pos:* Int consult. *Mem:* Am Soc Agron. *Res:* Rice breeding; fertilization and cultural practices; agricultural research administration. *Mailing Add:* Ctr Agr Sci PO Box 19150A Baton Rouge LA 70893

CAFFEY, JAMES E, b Rockdale, Tex, May 5, 34; m 60; c 3. WATER RESOURCES. *Educ:* Tex A&M Univ, BS, 55, MS, 56; Colo State Univ, PhD(civil eng), 65. *Prof Exp:* Instr civil eng, Arlington State Col, 59-61; asst civil engr, Colo State Univ, 61, res asst, 61-65; from asst prof to prof civil eng, Univ Tex, Arlington, 65-74; mgr urban resources dept, Planning Div, Turner, Collie & Braden, Inc, Houston, Tex, 74-76; water resources engr, 76-80, ASSOC, RADY & ASSOCS, INC, 80- *Concurrent Pos:* Engr, Freese, Nichols & Endress, Tex, 65-66, consult, 68-69. *Mem:* Fel Am Soc Civil Engrs; Nat Soc Prof Engrs; Am Geophys Union; fel Am Water Resources Asn; Sigma Xi. *Res:* Classical and stochastic hydrology, including groundwater, surface water and hydrometeorological problems; water resources planning and management from both supply and quality aspects; hydraulic engineering to complement hydrological interests; flood plain management. *Mailing Add:* 1506 Wagonwheel Trail Arlington TX 76013

CAFFREY, JAMES LOUIS, b Camden, NJ, July 2, 46; m 73. PHYSIOLOGY, ENDOCRINOLOGY. *Educ:* Rutgers Univ, BA, 68; Univ Va, PhD(physiol), 73. *Prof Exp:* Fel reproductive endocrinol, Colo State Univ, 73-77; ASST PROF PHYSIOL, N TEX STATE UNIV HEALTH SCI CTR-TEX COL OSTEOP MED, 77- *Mem:* AAAS; Am Physiol Soc; Endocrine Soc; Am Col Sports Med. *Res:* Stress; adrenal cortex/glucocorticoids; adrenal medulla/catecholamines; endogeneous opiates/enkephalines; aging, exercise. *Mailing Add:* NTex State Univ-Tex Col Camp Bowie at Montgomery Ft Worth TX 76107

CAFFREY, ROBERT E, b Scranton, Pa, Mar 9, 20; m 49; c 5. METALLURGY. *Educ:* Pa State Univ, BS, 49, PhD(metall), 55. *Prof Exp:* Res assoc, Pa State Univ, 51-52, instr metall, 52-53; mem tech staff, 54-58, SUPVR, BELL TEL LABS, 58- *Concurrent Pos:* Lectr, Lehigh Univ, 61-63. *Honors & Awards:* Jerome N Behrman Award, 49. *Mem:* Am Soc Metals; Am Inst Mining, Metall & Petrol Engrs; Electrochem Soc; Am Chem Soc; fel Am Inst Chemists. *Res:* High temperature application of metals and alloys in electron devices; insulators and metal deposition by chemical vapor deposition. *Mailing Add:* Bell Tel Labs 555 Union Blvd Allentown PA 18103

CAFLISCH, EDWARD GEORGE, b Union City, Pa, Dec 6, 25; m 52; c 3. ORGANIC CHEMISTRY, ANALYTICAL CHEMISTRY. *Educ:* Allegheny Col, BS, 48; Ohio State Univ, PhD(org chem), 54. *Prof Exp:* Chemist, Plaskon Div, Libbey-Owens-Ford Glass Co, 48-49; asst & instr org chem, Ohio State Univ, 49-52; chemist, 54-80, SR CHEMIST, SOLVENTS & INTERMEDIATES DIV, UNION CARBIDE CORP, 80-; ASST PROF, WVA STATE COL, 80- *Mem:* Am Chem Soc. *Res:* Synthesis of aldehydes; chlorocarbons; fluorocarbons; polymerization of butadiene, pentadienes, and styrene; development of gas and liquid chromatography equipment; petrochemicals; organic analytical research. *Mailing Add:* Union Carbide Corp Tech Ctr 740-4109 South Charleston WV 25303

CAFRUNY, EDWARD JOSEPH, b New Castle, Pa, Dec 17, 24; m 48; c 3. PHARMACOLOGY. *Educ:* Ind Univ, AB, 50; Syracuse Univ, PhD, 55; Univ Mich, MD, 60. *Prof Exp:* From instr to assoc prof pharmacol, Med Sch, Univ Mich, 55-65; prof pharmacol, Sch Med, Univ Minn, 65-68; prof & chmn dept pharmacol & exp therapeut, Med Col Ohio, 68-73; pres, Sterling-Winthrop Res Inst, 73-77; prof pharmacol, Med Col Wis, 77-78; PROF PHARMACOL & DEAN, GRAD SCH BIOMED SCI, COL MED & DENT NJ, 78- *Concurrent Pos:* Consult, Coun on Drugs, Am Med Asn, 63, 64; mem pharmacol & exp therapeut study sect, NIH, 64-68 & anesthesiol training grant comt, 68-71; mem sci adv bd, Pharmaceut Mfg Asn Found, Inc, 68-, pharmacol test comt, Nat Bd Med Examrs, 69-73 & comt on probs of drug safety, Nat Acad Sci-Nat Res Coun, 70-; adj prof pharmacol, Med Col, Cornell Univ. *Mem:* AAAS; Am Soc Pharmacol & Exp Therapeut; NY Acad Sci; Am Soc Nephrol; Am Heart Asn. *Res:* Renal pharmacology; mechanism of action of diuretic agents. *Mailing Add:* Col Med & Dent of NJ Newark NJ 07103

CAGAN, ROBERT H, b Brooklyn, NY, Apr 8, 38; m 68; c 2. BIOCHEMISTRY. *Educ:* Northeastern Univ, BS, 60; Harvard Univ, PhD(biochem), 66. *Prof Exp:* USPHS fel, Nobel Med Inst, Karolinska Inst, Sweden, 66-68; asst prof, 68-75, ASSOC PROF BIOCHEM, MONELL CHEM SENSES CTR, SCH MED, UNIV PA, 75- *Concurrent Pos:* Res chemist, Vet Admin Med Ctr, Philadelphia, 68-; lectr, Gordon Res Conf Taste & Olfaction, NH, 78 & 81, Joint Cong, Europ Chemoreception Res Orgn-Int Symp Olfaction & Taste, Noordwijkerhout, Neth, 80; chmn panel, Winter Conf Brain Res, Idaho, 79 & Colo, 81; gen chmn, Int Symp Biochem Taste & Olfaction, Philadelphia, 80; mem, Commun Sci Study Sect, NIH, 80; contrib ed, Nutrit Rev, 78- *Honors & Awards:* Byron Riegel lectr, Northwestern Univ, 79. *Mem:* AAAS; Am Chem Soc; Swed Biochem Soc; Soc Exp Biol Med; Soc Neurosci. *Res:* Biochemical basis of physiological function; enzymology of phagocytic cells; biochemical mechanisms of taste and olfaction; membrane receptor mechanisms; neurochemistry of gamma-aminobutyric acid; neural development in tissue culture. *Mailing Add:* Monell Chem Senses Ctr Univ of Pa Philadelphia PA 19104

CAGGIANO, JOSEPH ANTHONY, JR, b Brooklyn, NY, July 30, 38; m 64; c 3. NEOTECTONICS. *Educ:* Allegheny Col, BS, 60; Syracuse Univ, MS, 66; Univ Mass, PhD(geol), 77. *Prof Exp:* Instr earth sci & geomorphol, Div Natural Sci, Elmira Col, 64-67; instr phys & hist geol & geomorphol, Dept Geol, Temple Univ, 67-68; asst, Dept Geol, Univ Mass, 68-72; proj geologist, D'Appolonia Consult Engrs, 73-77; STAFF GEOLOGIST & UNIT MGR, ROCKWELL HANFORD OPER, 77- *Concurrent Pos:* Res geologist field mapping, US Geol Surv, Boston, Mass, 70-73. *Mem:* Geol Soc Am; Asn Eng Geologists; Soc Econ Paleontologists & Mineralogists; Seismol Soc Am; Am Quaternary Asn. *Res:* Geologic analyses of late Cenozoic sediments, landforms, structures, contemporary seismicity and deformation to determine the tectonic evolution of an area and its potential impact on engineered facilities. *Mailing Add:* 330 Snyder Rd Richland WA 99352

CAGLE, BEN J, b Ringling, Okla, Sept 28, 21; m 49; c 2. FLUID MECHANICS, ATMOSPHERIC PHYSICS. *Educ:* Univ Okla, BS, 43; Calif Inst Technol, MS, 49. *Prof Exp:* Engr, Calif Inst Technol, 46-60; ENGR, OFF NAVAL RES, 60- *Mem:* Assoc fel Am Inst Aeronaut & Astronaut; Am Geophys Union; Marine Technol Soc. *Res:* Fluid mechanics and geophysics; development of wind tunnel techniques; atmospheric dynamics; ocean engineering; arctic technology. *Mailing Add:* Off of Naval Res 1030 E Green St Pasadena CA 91106

CAGLE, FREDRIC WILLIAM, JR, b Metropolis, Ill, Dec 17, 24. CHEMISTRY. *Educ:* Univ Ill, BS, 44, MS, 45, PhD(chem), 46. *Prof Exp:* Mem sch math, Inst Advan Study, 47-48; fel chem, 48-49, res asst prof, 49-53, from asst prof to assoc prof, 53-60, PROF CHEM, UNIV UTAH, 60- *Concurrent Pos:* Consult, Dow Chem Co, 63- & Pac Northwest Pipeline Corp, 58-61. *Mem:* Am Chem Soc; Am Phys Soc; Am Crystallog Asn. *Res:* Chemical kinetics; theoretical chemistry; x-ray crystallography and crystal structures; applications of computers to chemical problems. *Mailing Add:* Dept of Chem Univ of Utah Salt Lake City UT 84112

CAHILL, CHARLES L, b El Reno, Okla, Feb 23, 33; m 54; c 3. PHYSICAL CHEMISTRY, BIOCHEMISTRY. *Educ:* Okla Baptist Univ, AB, 55; Univ Okla, MS, 57, PhD(biochem), 61. *Prof Exp:* From asst prof to prof chem, Oklahoma City Univ, 61-71; chmn dept, 63-71, assoc dean col arts & sci, 67-71; V CHANCELLOR ACAD AFFAIRS & PROF CHEM, UNIV NC, WILMINGTON, 71- *Concurrent Pos:* NIH res grant, 62-70. *Mem:* AAAS; Am Chem Soc; Endocrine Soc; NY Acad Sci. *Res:* Physicochemical characterization of synthetic polymers and proteins. *Mailing Add:* Univ of NC PO Box 3725 Wilmington NC 28401

CAHILL, GEORGE FRANCIS, JR, b New York, NY, July 7, 27; m 49; c 6. METABOLISM. *Educ:* Yale Univ, BS, 49; Columbia Univ, MD, 53. *Hon Degrees:* MA, Harvard Univ, 66. *Prof Exp:* Intern med, Peter Bent Brigham Hosp, 53-54, from jr resident to sr resident, 54-58; from asst to assoc prof, 58-70, PROF MED, HARVARD MED SCH, 70-; DIR RES, HOWARD HUGHES MED INST, 78- *Concurrent Pos:* Res fel biol chem & Nat Res Coun fel med sci, Harvard Univ, 55-57; sr assoc, Peter Bent Brigham Hosp, 59-64, physician, 68-; dir, Elliott P Joslin Res Lab, 64-78. *Mem:* AAAS; Am Soc Clin Invest; Am Physiol Asn; Am Clin & Climat Asn; Endocrine Soc. *Res:* Metabolism of carbohydrate, lipid and protein. *Mailing Add:* Howard Hughes Med Inst 398 Brookline Ave Boston MA 02215

CAHILL, JERRY EDWARD, b Philadelphia, Pa, Oct 15, 42; m 64; c 4. CHEMICAL PHYSICS, ANALYTICAL INSTRUMENTATION. *Educ:* St Joseph's Col, Pa, BS, 64; Princeton Univ, AM, 67, PhD(chem), 68. *Prof Exp:* Res assoc chem, Univ Southern Calif, 68-70; asst prof chem, Drexel Univ, 70-77; ultraviolet/fluorescence prod specialist, 77-78, appln lab mgr, 78-79, ultraviolet prod mgr, 79-81, DEVELOP ENG MGR, PERKIN-ELMER CORP, 81- *Concurrent Pos:* Merck grant fac develop, Merck Co Found, 70. *Res:* Infrared and Raman spectra of pure and mixed molecular crystals and liquids; intermolecular interactions and motions in condensed matter; vibrational energy transfer and relaxation in condensed matter. *Mailing Add:* Oak Brook Instruments Div Perkin-Elmer Corp 2000 York Rd Oak Brook IL 60521

CAHILL, JONES F(RANCIS), b Middletown, Ohio, Dec 8, 20; m 44; c 3. AERODYNAMICS. *Educ:* Univ Notre Dame, BS, 42. *Prof Exp:* Aeronaut res scientist aerodyn, Langley Res Ctr, Nat Adv Comt Aeronaut, 42-55; aerodyn engr aerodyn design & develop, Flight Sci Div, 55-69, sr staff scientist aerospace res, 69-74, FLIGHT SCI MGR, C-141B PROG, LOCKHEED-GA CO, 74- *Mem:* Assoc fel Am Inst Aeronaut & Astronaut. *Res:* Experimental research on sophisticated high lift systems; scaling problems in transonic aerodynamics associated with shock-boundary layer interactions and shock induced separation. *Mailing Add:* 226 Whitlock Dr SW Marietta GA 30064

CAHILL, KEVIN M, b New York, NY, May 6, 36; m 61; c 5. MEDICINE, TROPICAL MEDICINE. *Educ:* Fordham Univ, AB, 57; Cornell Univ, MD, 61; Univ London & Royal Col Physicians, dipl trop med & hyg, 63; Am Bd Med Microbiol, dipl, 67; Am Bd Prev Med, dipl, 70. *Prof Exp:* CLIN ASSOC PROF MED, NEW YORK MED COL, 65- *Concurrent Pos:* Lectr, Univ Cairo & Univ Alexandria, 63-65; consult, UN Health Serv & USPHS, 65-; mem sci adv bd, Am Found Trop Med, 66-; prof trop med & chmn dept, Royal Col Surgeons, Ireland, 70-; prof pub health & prev med, NJ Col Med, 74-; chmn, Health Planning Comn & Health Res Coun, NY State, 75-, asst to Governor for Health Affairs, 75- *Mem:* Fel Am Col Chest Physicians; Am Pub Health Asn; Am Soc Trop Med & Hyg; Royal Soc Trop Med & Hyg. *Res:* Chest medicine. *Mailing Add:* 850 Fifth Ave New York NY 10021

CAHILL, LAURENCE JAMES, JR, b Frankfort, Maine, Sept 21, 24; m 49; c 3. SPACE PHYSICS. *Educ:* US Mil Acad, BS, 46; Univ Chicago, SB, 50; Univ Iowa, MS, 56, PhD(physics), 59. *Prof Exp:* Asst prof physics, Univ NH, 59-62; chief physics, Hqs NASA, 62-63; from assoc prof to prof physics, Univ NH, 63-68, dir space sci ctr, 67-68; dir Space Sci Ctr, 68-77, PROF PHYSICS, UNIV MINN, MINNEAPOLIS, 77- *Concurrent Pos:* Chmn, US-USSR Comt Co-op Space Res Geomagnetism, 63; mem working group, Int Year Quiet Sun, Int Comt Space Res, 63-64; consult, NASA, 63- *Mem:* Fel Am Geophys Union; Am Phys Soc. *Res:* Investigation of earth's magnetic field by rocket and satellite experiment. *Mailing Add:* Dept of Physics Univ of Minn Minneapolis MN 55455

CAHILL, RICHARD WILLIAM, b Utica, NY, Dec 30, 31; m 68; c 3. PHYSICAL CHEMISTRY, POLYMER CHEMISTRY. *Educ:* Niagara Univ, BS, 58; Purdue Univ, PhD(phys chem), 63. *Prof Exp:* RES SCIENTIST CHEM, LOCKHEED MISSILES & SPACE CO, INC, 63- *Mem:* Am Chem Soc; Sigma Xi. *Res:* The fracture toughness of polymeric materials using the Charpy impact method to obtain the ductile-to-brittle transition temperature and correlation of their chemistry to predict aging trends. *Mailing Add:* 3251 Hanover St Palo Alto CA 94304

CAHILL, THOMAS A, b Paterson, NJ, Mar 4, 37; m 65; c 2. NUCLEAR PHYSICS. *Educ:* Holy Cross Col, BA, 59; Univ Calif, Los Angeles, MA, 61, PhD(physics), 65. *Prof Exp:* Asst prof in residence physics, Univ Calif, Los Angeles, 65-66; NATO fel, Ctr Nuclear Studies, Saclay, France, 66-67; asst prof, 67-71, actg dir, Crocker Nuclear Lab, 72, dir, Inst Ecol, 72-75, assoc prof, 71-76, PROF PHYSICS, UNIV CALIF, DAVIS, 76- *Mem:* Am Chem Soc; Air Pollution Control Asn; Am Phys Soc. *Res:* Investigation of very light nuclei through the techniques of nuclear scattering with emphasis on spin effects; application of nuclear and radiation techniques to ecological problems; air pollution. *Mailing Add:* Dept of Physics Univ of Calif Davis CA 95616

CAHILL, VERN RICHARD, b Tiro, Ohio, May 5, 18; m 46; c 3. MEAT SCIENCE. *Educ:* Ohio State Univ, BSc, 41, MSc, 42, PhD(meat), 55. *Prof Exp:* From instr to PROF ANIMAL SCI, OHIO STATE UNIV, 46- *Concurrent Pos:* Consult meat process, USDA, 79- *Mem:* Am Soc Animal Sci; Am Meat Sci Asn; Inst Food Technologists. *Res:* Carcass yield of edible portion; meat tenderness and preservation; comminuted meat products. *Mailing Add:* 133 Aldrich Rd Columbus OH 43214

CAHIR, JOHN JOSEPH, b Scituate, Mass, Oct 8, 33; m 62; c 4. METEOROLOGY. *Educ:* Pa State Univ, BS, 61, PhD(meteorol), 71. *Prof Exp:* Asst meteorol, Pa State Univ, 61-63; observer, briefer & forecaster, US Weather Bur, 63-64; teacher & researcher, 64-71, PROF METEOROL, PA STATE UNIV, 71-, ASSOC DEAN, COL EARTH AND MINERAL SCI, 80- *Concurrent Pos:* Mem, Nat Acad Sci Comt to Eval Res & Develop of Nat Environ Satellite Serv, Nat Acad Sci-Nat Res Coun Comt Atmospheric Sci, 76; consult, Dept Earth & Gen Sci, Jackson State Univ, 76-77; ed, Monthly Weather Rev, Am Meteorol Soc, 77-; prin investr, Nat Earth Satellite Serv res projs, Off Naval Res, US Nat Weather Serv. *Mem:* Am Meteorol Soc; Am Geophys Union; Royal Meteorol Soc; Sigma Xi; Nat Weather Asn (pres-elect, 80-81, pres, 81-82). *Res:* Synoptic meteorology and local forecasting; jet stream dynamics; cloudiness feedback on climate change; use of real time computer graphics systems in forecasting. *Mailing Add:* Pa State Univ 620 Walker Bldg University Park PA 16802

CAHN, ARNO, b Cologne, Ger, Sept 6, 23; nat; m 50; c 3. ORGANIC CHEMISTRY. *Educ:* Queen's Univ, Ont, BSc, 46; Purdue Univ, PhD(chem), 50. *Prof Exp:* Asst, Purdue Univ, 46-48; sr res chemist, Household Prod Div, Lever Bros Co, 50-53, prin res chemist, 53-56, res assoc, 56-58, chief, Org Sect, 58-63, chief, Detergent Liquids Prod Develop Sect, 63-65, res mgr, Chem & Physics Dept, 65-66, develop mgr household prod, 66-73, dir develop, 73-80, vpres tech develop, 80-81; CONSULT, 81- *Mem:* Am Chem Soc; Am Oil Chemists Soc; fel Am Inst Chemists; Indust Res Inst. *Res:* Kinetics of pyridinium salt formation; synthesis of labelled compounds; structure and physical properties of surface-active agents. *Mailing Add:* Consult Serv Inc 72 E Allison Ave Pearl River NJ 10965

CAHN, DAVID STEPHEN, b Los Angeles, Calif, Jan 12, 40; m 71; c 3. MINERAL ENGINEERING, STATISTICS. *Educ:* Univ Calif, Berkeley, BS, 62, MS, 64, DEng(mineral eng), 66. *Prof Exp:* Engr, Homer Res Labs, Bethlehem Steel Corp, 66-68; group leader, Tech Ctr, Am Cement Corp, 68-71; dir, environ control, 71-77, VPRES, AMCORD INC, 77- *Mem:* Fel

AAAS; Am Inst Mining, Metall & Petrol Engrs; Am Inst Chem Engrs; Air Pollution Control Asn; Am Soc Testing & Mat. *Res:* Comminution; mixing of particulate solids; operations research; mineral dressing; cementitious composite systems; solid waste utilization; stationary source emissions; monitoring of stationary sources, reclamation of surface mined lands. *Mailing Add:* Amcord Inc PO Box 2540 Newport Beach CA 92665

CAHN, JOHN W(ERNER), b Ger, Jan 9, 28; nat US; m 50; c 3. PHYSICAL METALLURGY. *Educ:* Univ Mich, BS, 49; Univ Calif, PhD(chem), 52. *Prof Exp:* Instr, Inst Study Metals, Univ Chicago, 52-54; mem res lab, Gen Elec Co, 54-64; prof metall, Mass Inst Technol, 64-78; CTR SCIENTIST, CTR MAT SCI, NAT BUR STANDARDS, 77- *Concurrent Pos:* Guggenheim fel, 60; chmn, Gordon Conf Phys Metall, 64; vis prof, Israel Inst Technol, 71-72. *Honors & Awards:* Acta Metall Gold Medal, Am Soc Metals, 77. *Mem:* Nat Acad Sci; Am Phys Soc; Am Inst Mining, Metall & Petrol Engrs; Am Soc Metals; Am Acad Arts & Sci. *Res:* Thermodynamics; metallurgical kinetics; phase transformations; surfaces. *Mailing Add:* 223-A153 Nat Bur of Standards Washington DC 20234

CAHN, JULIUS HOFELLER, b Chicago, Ill, Oct 29, 19; m 43, 51; c 2. ASTROPHYSICS. *Educ:* Yale Univ, BA, 42, MS, 47, PhD(physics), 48. *Prof Exp:* Jr engr, Signal Corps Labs, NJ, 42-43; lab asst, Yale Univ, 46-47; asst, gas discharge proj, US Navy, 47-48; asst prof physics, Univ Nebr, 48-50; prin physicist, Battelle Mem Inst, 50-51, asst div consult, 51-59; assoc prof physics & elec eng, 59-70, ASSOC PROF ELEC ENG, PHYSICS & ASTRON, UNIV ILL, URBANA-CHAMPAIGN, 70- *Concurrent Pos:* Consult, Boulder Labs, Nat Bur Standards. *Mem:* Am Phys Soc; Am Astron Soc; Royal Astron Soc; Int Astron Union. *Res:* High current electrical discharges in gases; effects of electrostatic interaction on the electronic velocity distribution function; continuous x-ray absorption; antenna impedance; friction; nondestructive testing; solid state physics; plasma physics; stellar evolution; planetary nebulae; galactic absorption distribution; stellar distances. *Mailing Add:* Dept Aston Univ Ill 1011 W Springfield Ave Urbana IL 61801

CAHN, PHYLLIS HOFSTEIN, fish biology, animal behavior, see previous edition

CAHN, ROBERT NATHAN, theoretical high energy physics, see previous edition

CAHNMANN, HANS JULIUS, b Munich, Ger, Jan 27, 06; nat US; m 45; c 3. ORGANIC CHEMISTRY. *Educ:* Univ Munich, Lic Pharm, 30, PhD(chem), 32. *Prof Exp:* Instr chem, Univ Munich, 31-33 & Univ Paris, 33-36; dir res, Labs, Crinex, 36-39; res assoc org chem, French Pub Health Serv, 39-40; res assoc biochem, Univ Aix Marseille, 40-41; dir res & develop, Biochem Prod Corp, NY, 41-42; res assoc, Mt Sinai Hosp, 42-44; sr chemist, Givaudan-Delawanna, 44-47 & William R Warner, 47-49; sr biochemist, 50-75, EMER SCIENTIST, NIH, 76- *Mem:* Am Chem Soc; Am Thyroid Asn. *Res:* Biochemistry. *Mailing Add:* NIH Bethesda MD 20814

CAHOON, GARTH ARTHUR, b Vernal, Utah, Dec 23, 24; m 48; c 4. HORTICULTURE. *Educ:* Utah State Agr Col, BS, 50; Univ Calif, Los Angeles, PhD(hort sci), 54. *Prof Exp:* Res asst, Dept Floricult & Ornamental Hort, Univ Calif, Los Angeles, 50-54; asst horticulturist, Univ Calif, Riverside, 54-63; assoc prof, 63-67, PROF HORT, OHIO STATE UNIV & OHIO AGR RES & DEVELOP CTR, 67- *Concurrent Pos:* US AID consult, India, 68 & 70; mem, Coun Soil Test & Plant Anal, chmn; hort consult, Food & Agr Orgn, Somalia, Africa, 76-80. *Honors & Awards:* Laurie Award, Am Soc Hort Sci. *Mem:* Fel Am Soc Hort Sci; Int Soc Hort Sci; Weed Sci Soc Am; Am Soc Enol. *Res:* Citrus physiology and nutrition; pomology and viticulture; physiology and nutrition. *Mailing Add:* Dept of Hort Ohio Agr Res & Develop Ctr Wooster OH 44691

CAHOON, JOHN RAYMOND, b Calgary, Alta, Aug 29, 39; m 65; c 3. MATERIALS SCIENCE, ENGINEERING. *Educ:* Univ Man, BSc, 61, MSc, 63, PhD(metall eng), 66. *Prof Exp:* Fel metall, Mellon Inst, Carnegie-Mellon Univ, 66-68; from asst prof to assoc prof mech eng, 68-73, PROF MECH ENG, METALL SCI LAB, UNIV MAN, 73-, HEAD DEPT, 75- *Mem:* Am Soc Metals; Can Inst Mining & Metall. *Res:* Solidification of metals; diffusion in metals; composite materials; corrosion. *Mailing Add:* Dept of Mech Eng Univ of Man Winnipeg Can

CAHOON, MARY ODILE, b Houghton, Mich, July 21, 29. CELL PHYSIOLOGY, RADIATION BIOLOGY. *Educ:* DePaul Univ, BS, 54, MS, 58; Univ Toronto, PhD(cell physiol), 61. *Prof Exp:* From instr to assoc prof, 54-67, chmn dept, 61-73, acad dean, 63-69 & 76-81, PROF BIOL, COL ST SCHOLASTICA, 67-, DEAN, 81- *Concurrent Pos:* Res assoc, McMurdo Sta, Antarctica, 74. *Mem:* Am Soc Zoologists. *Res:* Radiation effects on growth of bacterial cells; calcium variations during crustacean intermolt cycle; ultraviolet resistance of bacterial spores; cold adaptation in metabolism of antarctic fauna. *Mailing Add:* Col of St Scholastica Duluth MN 55811

CAHOY, ROGER PAUL, b Colome, SDak, Feb 19, 27; m 50; c 4. ORGANIC CHEMISTRY. *Educ:* Dakota Wesleyan Univ, BA, 50; Univ SDak, MA, 52; Univ Nebr, PhD(chem), 56. *Prof Exp:* Develop chemist, silicone prod dept, Gen Elec Co, 56-60; res chemist, Spencer Chem Co, 60-63, sr res chemist, 63-77, supvr, 77-80, SR ADV, W GULF OIL CHEM CO, 80- *Mem:* Am Chem Soc; AAAS. *Res:* Organometallic compounds; catalysis; biological active organic compounds; industrial chemicals. *Mailing Add:* 8900 Indian Creek Pkwy 9009 W 67th St Overland Park KS 66210

CAILLE, GILLES, b Montreal, Que, May 5, 35; m 57; c 4. MEDICINAL CHEMISTRY. *Educ:* Univ Montreal, BSc, 59, MSc, 63, PhD(med chem), 69. *Prof Exp:* Monitor instrumental anal & pharmacog, 63-67, prof instrumental anal, 67-69, RES PROF PHARMACOL, UNIV MONTREAL, 69- *Concurrent Pos:* Res fel metab psychotrope, Joliette Res Inst, 69-71, co-dir, 71-74; mem comt pharm, St-Charles Hosp, Joliette, 69-75; consult,

Burroughs Wellcome & Co, 70-76 & Santa Cabrini Hosp, 73-; pres, Biopharm Inc, 71-73. *Mem:* Am Acad Clin Toxicol; Fr Soc Toxicol. *Res:* Metabolism of psychotrope; clinical pharmacology and analytical toxicology. *Mailing Add:* Dept of Pharmacol Fac of Med Univ of Montreal Montreal Can

CAILLEAU, RELDA, b San Francisco, Calif, Feb 1, 09. CELL PHYSIOLOGY. *Educ:* Univ Calif, AB, 30, MA, 31; Univ Paris, DSc, 37. *Prof Exp:* Fr Nat Res fel, Pasteur Inst, Paris, 37-40; asst microbiol vitamin assays, Univ Calif, 41-43; assoc nutritionist & home economist, USDA, 43-46; in charge res, Nat Ctr Sci Res, Ministry Educ, France, 47-49; jr asst res biochemist, Univ Calif, Berkeley, 50-53, asst res biochemist virus cult, 53-55, res assoc oncol & assit res biochemist, cancer res inst, Med Sch, Univ Calif, San Francisco, 55-59; assoc res biochemist, 59-70; RES ASSOC MED, UNIV TEX MD ANDERSON HOSP & TUMOR INST, 70- *Mem:* Tissue Cult Asn; Soc Exp Biol & Med; Soc Cell Biol. *Res:* Effects of various growth media and chemotherapeutic agents upon normal and malignant mouse and human cells in vitro and their chromosomes; establishment of human breast carcinoma cell lines from pleural effusions. *Mailing Add:* Dept Med Univ Tex MD Anderson Hosp & Tumor Inst Houston TX 77025

CAILLIET, GREGOR MICHEL, b Los Angeles, Calif, June 19, 43. ICHTHYOLOGY, MARINE ECOLOGY. *Educ:* Univ Calif, Santa Barbara, BA, 66, PhD(biol), 72. *Prof Exp:* Staff res assoc ichthyol, Univ Calif, Santa Barbara, 71-72; asst prof, 72-77, assoc prof, 77-80, PROF ICHTHYOL, MOSS LANDING MARINE LABS, 80- *Mem:* Am Icthyologists & Herpetologists; Am Fisheries Soc; Ecol Soc Am; Am Soc Limnol & Oceanog. *Res:* Ecology of marine fishes; age, growth and feeding habits of marine fishes, ecology of marine nekton; midwater ecology; fishery biology. *Mailing Add:* Moss Landing Marine Labs PO Box 223 Moss Landing CA 95039

CAILLOUET, CHARLES W, b Baton Rouge, La, Dec 15, 37; m 77; c 4. FISH BIOLOGY. *Educ:* La State Univ, BS, 59, MS, 60; Iowa State Univ, PhD(fishery biol), 64. *Prof Exp:* Asst prof biol, Univ Southwestern La, 64-67; assoc prof, Sch Marine & Atmospheric Sci, Univ Miami, 67-72; supvry fishery biologist, 72-74, fishery biologist, Res Admin, Gulf Coastal Fisheries Ctr, Galveston Facil, 74-77, SUPVRY FISHERY BIOLOGIST & CHIEF, ENVIRON RES & AQUACULT DIV, NAT MARINE FISHERIES SERV, SOUTHEAST FISHERIES CTR, GALVESTON LAB, 77- *Concurrent Pos:* Adj grad fac, Univ Houston, 75-; vis mem grad fac, Tex A&M Univ, 80- *Mem:* AAAS; Am Fisheries Soc; fel Am Inst Fishery Res Biol; Sigma Xi. *Res:* Directs major multi-disciplinary, multi-institutional, and energy-related environmental impact research projects in the Gulf of Mexico; shrimp and sea turtle maniculture research. *Mailing Add:* Nat Marine Fisheries Serv Galveston Lab 4700 Ave U Galveston TX 77550

CAILLOUX, MARCEL LOUIS, b Ottawa, Ont, Dec 8, 14; m 44; c 3. PLANT PHYSIOLOGY. *Educ:* Mt St Louis Col, BA, 35; Univ Montreal, LSc, 40; Univ Paris, DSc, 67. *Prof Exp:* Lab asst & illusr sci publ, Bot Inst, 36, from asst prof to assoc prof, 40-70, PROF PLANT PHYSIOL, UNIV MONTREAL, 70- *Concurrent Pos:* Vchmn res conf plant physiol, Can Nat Res Coun, 54. *Mem:* AAAS; Am Soc Plant Physiologists; Fr-Can Asn Advan Sci; Can Fedn Biol Socs; Can Soc Natural Hist (pres, 47). *Res:* Mechanism of the absorption of water by cells; culture of protoplasts; mechanisms of entry of water in plant protoplasts. *Mailing Add:* Dept of Biol Sci Univ of Montreal Montreal Can

CAIN, BRIAN WILLIAM, b Corpus Christi, Tex, Sept, 10, 41; m 66; c 2. ENVIRONMENTAL CONTAMINANTS. *Educ:* Tex A&I Univ, BS, 65, MS, 68; Univ Ill, PhD(zool), 72. *Prof Exp:* asst prof wildlife ecol, Dept Wildlife, Tex A&M Univ, 72-77; RES BIOLOGIST, US FISH & WILDLIFE SERV, PATUXENT WILDLIFE RES CTR, 78- *Concurrent Pos:* Consult, TerEco Corp, 74-77, LGL Ltd, US Inc, 75-77. *Mem:* Estuarine Res Fedn; Wilson's Ornith Soc; Cooper's Ornith Soc; Wildlife Soc Inc; Southwestern Asn Naturalist. *Res:* Effects of heavy metals on wildlife species; long term release of environmental contaminants by dredge material disposal in estuarine habitats. *Mailing Add:* Patuxent Wildlife Res Ctr US Fish & Wildlife Serv Laurel MD 20708

CAIN, CARL, JR, b Chattanooga, Tenn, Jan 6, 31; m 61; c 2. ANALYTICAL CHEMISTRY, CHEMICAL ENGINEERING. *Educ:* Univ Chattanooga, BS, 52; Univ Tenn, MS, 54, PhD(chem), 56. *Prof Exp:* Proj engr, Cramet, Inc, 56-58; res engr, Develop Lab, Combustion Eng, Inc, 58-61; anal res chemist, Rock Hill Lab, Chemetron Corp, 61-62; staff chem engr, 62-70, supvr, Chem Sect, 70-78, SUPVR, CHEM & METAL ENG GROUP, TENN VALLEY AUTHORITY, 78- *Mem:* Am Chem Soc; Am Soc Mech Eng; Am Soc Testing & Mat. *Res:* Power plant analytical chemistry, especially automatic monitors and controllers; corrosion of metals in aqueous environment; industrial water conditioning. *Mailing Add:* 820 Chestnut St Tower Chattanooga TN 37401

CAIN, CHARLES ALAN, b Tampa, Fla, Mar 3, 43. BIOENGINEERING. *Educ:* Univ Fla, BEE, 65; Mass Inst Technol, MSEE, 67; Univ Mich, PhD(elec eng), 72. *Prof Exp:* Mem tech staff, Bell Labs, Inc, 65-68; asst prof, 72-78, ASSOC PROF ELEC ENG, UNIV ILL, URBANA, 78- *Mem:* sr mem Inst Elec & Electronics Engrs. *Res:* Biological effects and medical applications of microwave energy; mathematical modeling of physiological systems. *Mailing Add:* Dept of Elec Eng Univ of Ill Urbana IL 61801

CAIN, CHARLES COLUMBUS, b Fields, La, Oct 29, 15; m 39; c 2. SOIL SCIENCE. *Educ:* La State Univ, BS, 37; Iowa State Univ, MS, 38, PhD, 56. *Prof Exp:* Jr soil survr, Soil Conserv Serv, USDA, 38-41; asst soil technologist, 41; instr agron & asst agronomist, La State Univ, 41-46; assoc prof, Univ Southwestern La, 46-53, head dept gen agr, 55-65, prof agron, 53-75, dir tech studies, Educ Ctr, New Iberia, 65-75; dir freshman div, Univ, 67-75; AGR CONSULT, 55- *Mem:* Am Soc Agron; Soil Sci Soc Am. *Res:* Soil microscopy; soil morphology and genesis. *Mailing Add:* 720 Girard Park Dr Lafayette LA 70503

CAIN, CHARLES EUGENE, b Ellerbe, NC, June 22, 32; m 58. ORGANIC CHEMISTRY. *Educ:* Univ NC, BS, 54; Duke Univ, MA, 57, PhD(chem), 59. *Prof Exp:* Jr res chemist, Shell Chem Corp, 54; res chemist, E I du Pont de Nemours & Co, 58-60; chmn dept, 60-80, PROF CHEM, MILLSAPS COL, 60- *Mem:* Am Chem Soc; Sigma Xi. *Res:* Reactions of organometallic compounds; reaction mechanisms by relative rates and stereochem effects; electronic versus stereochemical effects in monomers and polymers; analysis of human brain hydrocarbons. *Mailing Add:* Dept of Chem Millsaps Col Jackson MS 39210

CAIN, DENNIS FRANCIS, b Republican City, Nebr, June 4, 30; m 61; c 5. BIOCHEMISTRY, SCIENCE ADMINISTRATION. *Educ:* Creighton Univ, BS, 52; Georgetown Univ, MS, 56; Univ Pa, PhD(biochem), 60. *Prof Exp:* NIH fel, 60-61; assoc biochem, Sch Vet Med, Univ Pa, 61-63, from asst prof to assoc prof, 63-68; biochemist, Surg Neurol Br, 68-74, scientist adminr, Spec Progs, Sci Rev Br, Nat Inst Neurol Dis & Stroke, 74-78; prog dir rev, Div Cancer Res Resources & Ctrs, 78-80, CHIEF, GRANTS REV BD, DIV EXTRAMURAL ACTIV, NAT CANCER INST, NIH, 80- *Concurrent Pos:* Res grant, Nat Inst Neurol Dis & Stroke. *Mem:* AAAS; Am Chem Soc; Sigma Xi. *Res:* Mechanochemistry of muscular contraction; metabolism of phosphorus, nucleic acids and protein in brain tissues. *Mailing Add:* Nat Cancer Inst NIH Westwood Bldg Rm 820 Bethesda MD 20205

CAIN, GEORGE D, b Pittsburgh, Pa, June 1, 40; m 66; c 2. PARASITOLOGY, BIOCHEMISTRY. *Educ:* Sterling Col, BS, 62; Purdue Univ, MS, 64, PhD(biol), 68. *Prof Exp:* Fel, Univ Mass, 68-70; asst prof, 70-75, ASSOC PROF ZOOL, UNIV IOWA, 76-, CHMN DEPT, 80- *Mem:* AAAS; Am Soc Parasitol; Am Soc Zoologists; Nat Speleol Soc; Am Soc Trop Med Hyg. *Res:* Comparative biochemistry of parasite membranes; genetic structure of parasites; lipid metabolism in lower invertebrates. *Mailing Add:* Dept of Zool Univ of Iowa Iowa City IA 52240

CAIN, GEORGE LEE, JR, b Wilmington, NC, Jan 13, 34; m 56; c 1. MATHEMATICS. *Educ:* Mass Inst Technol, BS, 56; Ga Inst Technol, MS, 62, PhD(math), 65. *Prof Exp:* Mathematician, Lockheed-Ga Co, 56-60; from instr to asst prof, 60-68, asst dir, Sch Math, 73-78, assoc prof, 68-80, PROF MATH, GA INST TECHNOL, 80- *Mem:* Soc Indust & Appl Math; Math Asn Am; Am Math Soc. *Res:* Topology; analysis. *Mailing Add:* Sch of Math Ga Inst of Technol Atlanta GA 30332

CAIN, JAMES ALLAN, b Isle of Man, Eng, July 23, 35; div; c 2. GEOLOGY. *Educ:* Univ Durham, BSc, 58; Northwestern Univ, MS, 60, PhD(geol), 62. *Prof Exp:* From instr to asst prof geol, Western Reserve Univ & Case Inst Technol, 61-66; assoc prof, 66-71, PROF GEOL, UNIV RI, 71-, CHMN DEPT, 67- *Concurrent Pos:* Res Corp res grant, 62-65; NSF res grant, 64-66; US Navy Underwater Sound Lab grant, 68; hon res assoc, dept geol sci, Harvard Univ, 73; US Geol Surv res grant, 75; sabbatical leave, Union Oil, Calif & Hanna Mining Co, 80- *Mem:* Geol Soc Am; Brit Geol Soc. *Res:* Quantitative igneous and metamorphic petrology; mineral resources. *Mailing Add:* Dept of Geol Univ of RI Kingston RI 02881

CAIN, JAMES CLARENCE, b Kosse, Tex, Mar 19, 13; c 4. INTERNAL MEDICINE, GASTROENTEROLOGY. *Educ:* Univ Tex, BA, 33, MD, 37; Univ Minn, MMS, 47; Am Bd Internal Med, Am Bd Gastroenterol, dipl. *Prof Exp:* Intern, Protestant Episcopal Hosp, Philadelphia, Pa, 37-39; instr path, Med Sch, Univ Tex, Galveston, 39-40; instr path, 40-41 & 46-48, CONSULT MED, MAYO CLIN, 48-, PROF, MAYO GRAD SCH MED, UNIV MINN, MINNEAPOLIS, 72- *Concurrent Pos:* From asst prof to clin prof med, Mayo Grad Sch Med, Univ Minn, Minneapolis, 54-72; chmn, Combined Comt of Nat Adv Comt to Selective Serv for Selection of Doctors, Dentists, Vet & Allied Med Personnel & Nat Health Resources Adv Comt, 68-69; adv to dir, Selective Serv Syst, 69-70; mem, Nat Adv Heart Coun, Minn State Bd Med Exam & Nat Adv Comt to Health Manpower Comm; chmn, Fed Use of Health Manpower Panel; civilian consult to Surgeon Gen. *Honors & Awards:* Billings Gold Medal Award, AMA, 63. *Mem:* AAAS; AMA; Am Col Physicians; Am Asn Hist Med; Pan-Am Med Asn. *Res:* Lymphatic system; liver and intestinal tract; gastric ulcers. *Mailing Add:* Mayo Clin Dept of Med Rochester MN 55901

CAIN, JAMES THOMAS, b Pittsburgh, Pa, May 2, 42; m 71. ELECTRICAL ENGINEERING. *Educ:* Univ Pittsburgh, BS, 64, MS, 66, PhD(elec eng), 70. *Prof Exp:* Asst instr elec eng, Univ Pittsburgh, 66-70; asst prof, 70-77, ASSOC PROF ELEC ENG, UNIV PITTSBURGH, 77- *Concurrent Pos:* Mem tech staff, Bell Tel Labs, 65; consult, var div of Westinghouse Elec Corp, 72- *Mem:* Inst Elec & Electronics Engrs; Am Soc Eng Educ; Asn Comput Mach. *Res:* Systems analysis and algorithm development for microcomputer based protection, monitoring, and control pf power system; real time computing systems. *Mailing Add:* Dept of Elec Eng Univ of Pittsburgh Pittsburgh PA 15261

CAIN, JEROME RICHARD, b Piqua, Ohio, Apr 26, 47; div; c 2. ALGOLOGY. *Educ:* Miami Univ, BA, 69, MS, 72; Univ Conn, PhD(algol), 75. *Prof Exp:* Scientist, Tech Serv Div, Am Can Co, 69-70; teaching asst bot, Miami Univ, 70-72; res asst, Inst Water Resources, Univ Conn, 72-75; asst prof bot, 75-80, ASSOC PROF BOT, ILL STATE UNIV, 80- *Mem:* Phycol Soc Am; Sigma Xi. *Res:* Algal ecology, nutrition and morphology; environmental regulation of sexual and asexual reproduction in microalgae; algal bioassays for nutrient potential in freshwater ecosystems; effects of toxic substances on growth and reproduction of algae. *Mailing Add:* Dept of Biol Sci Ill State Univ Normal IL 61761

CAIN, JOHN MANFORD, b Morrison, Ill, June 10, 32; m 55; c 2. RESOURCE MANAGEMENT. *Educ:* Univ Wis, BS, 55, MS, 56, PhD(soil sci), 67. *Prof Exp:* Soil scientist, Soil Conserv Serv, USDA, 58-60; teacher, Mich Jr High Sch, 60-61; soil scientist, Soil Conserv Serv, USDA, 61-65; asst prof soil sci, Wis State Univ, River Falls, 66-67; WATER RESOURCE PLANNER, DEPT NATURAL RESOURCES, STATE WIS, 67- *Mem:* Soil Conserv Soc Am; Am Soc Agron; Am Water Resources Asn. *Res:* Use of soil survey materials and techniques for nonagricultural interpretations. *Mailing Add:* Water Qual Planning Sect Box 7921 Madison WI 53707

CAIN, JOSEPH CARTER, III, b Georgetown, Ky, Oct 31, 30; m 68. GEOPHYSICS. *Educ:* Univ Alaska, BS, 52, PhD, 57. *Prof Exp:* Physicist, Geophys Inst, Univ Alaska, 52-57, asst prof geophys res, 57-59; physicist, Goddard Space Flight Ctr, NASA, 59-74; GEOPHYSICIST, ELECTROMAGNETICS & GEOMAGNETISM BR, US GEOL SURV, 74- *Mem:* Am Geophys Union; Int Asn Geomag & Aeronomy; Sigma Xi. *Res:* Magnetic field experiments from spacecraft; geomagnetism; magnetospheric and earth physics; numerical modelling of fields. *Mailing Add:* Stop 964 Box 25046 Lakewood CO 80225

CAIN, LAURENCE SUTHERLAND, b Washington, DC, Feb 4, 46; m 71; c 1. SOLID STATE PHYSICS. *Educ:* Wake Forest Univ, BS, 68; Univ Va, MS, 70, PhD(physics), 73. *Prof Exp:* Res assoc physics, Univ NC, Chapel Hill, 73-76, lectr, 76-78; ASST PROF PHYSICS, DAVIDSON COL, 78- *Mem:* Am Phys Soc; Am Asn Physics Teachers; Sigma Xi. *Res:* Elastic, mechanical, and defect properties of solids through the use of ultrasonic, internal friction, diffusion, and conductivity measurements. *Mailing Add:* Dept of Physics Davidson Col Davidson NC 28036

CAIN, STEPHEN MALCOLM, b Lynn, Mass, Oct 4, 28; m 51; c 2. PHYSIOLOGY. *Educ:* Tufts Col, BS, 49; Univ Fla, PhD(physiol), 59. *Prof Exp:* Physiologist, Chem Corps Med Lab, 53-56; asst physiol, Johns Hopkins Univ, 56; asst, Univ Fla, 56-59, trainee, 59; physiologist, US Air Force Sch Aerospace Med, 59-71, head sect, 60-71, chief respiratory sect, 68-71; PROF PHYSIOL & ASSOC PROF MED, UNIV ALA, BIRMINGHAM, 71- *Mem:* Am Physiol Soc. *Res:* Pulmonary physiology; blood gas transport; tissue hypoxia. *Mailing Add:* Pulmonary Div Dept of Med Univ of Ala Med Ctr Birmingham AL 35294

CAIN, WILLIAM AARON, b Leesville, La, Apr 30, 39; m 59; c 2. IMMUNOLOGY, MICROBIOLOGY. *Educ:* Northwestern State Univ La, BS, 61, MS, 64; La State Univ, PhD(immunol), 66. *Prof Exp:* Res fel, Univ Minn, 66-67; USPHS res fel pediat, 67-69; ASSOC PROF MICROBIOL & IMMUNOL & ADJ ASSOC PROF MED & PEDIAT, HEALTH SCI CTR, UNIV OKLA, 69- *Concurrent Pos:* Immunol consult, Okla Med Res Found, 69-71; allergy immunol consult. *Mem:* Am Soc Microbiol; Am Thoracic Soc. *Res:* Allergy and immediate hypersensitivity; cell mediated immunity and anergy. *Mailing Add:* Dept of Microbiol & Immunol Univ of Okla Health Sci Ctr Oklahoma City OK 73104

CAINE, DRURY SULLIVAN, III, b Selma, Ala, June 9, 32; m 61; c 2. ORGANIC CHEMISTRY. *Educ:* Vanderbilt Univ, BA, 54, MS, 56; Emory Univ, PhD(chem), 61. *Prof Exp:* Fel org chem, Columbia Univ, 61-62; from asst prof to assoc prof, 62-74, PROF CHEM, GA INST TECHNOL, 74- *Mem:* Am Chem Soc; Brit Chem Soc. *Res:* Synthesis of natural products; chemistry of enolate anions. *Mailing Add:* Dept of Chem Ga Inst of Technol Atlanta GA 30332

CAINE, EDSEL ALLEN, invertebrate zoology, ecology, see previous edition

CAINE, T NELSON, b Barrow, Eng, Dec 17, 39; m 66. GEOMORPHOLOGY, HYDROLOGY. *Educ:* Univ Leeds, BA, 61, MA, 62; Australian Nat Univ, PhD(geomorphol), 66. *Prof Exp:* Lectr geog, Univ Canterbury, 66-67; assoc prof geomorphol, 68-80, PROF GEOG, INST ARCTIC & ALPINE RES, UNIV COLO, BOULDER, 80- *Mem:* Glaciol Soc; Am Geophys Union; Am Water Resources Asn; Australian & NZ Asn Advan Sci; Asn Am Geographers. *Res:* Evolution of hillslopes in the alpine environment; snow and glacier hydrology and water resources of the alpine area. *Mailing Add:* Inst of Arctic & Alpine Res Univ of Colo Boulder CO 80302

CAIRD, JOHN ALLYN, b Brooklyn, NY, Dec 24, 47. PHYSICS, LASERS. *Educ:* Rutgers Univ, BSEE, 69; Univ Calif, Los Angeles, MPh, 71; Univ Southern Calif, PhD(physics), 75. *Prof Exp:* Mem tech staff lasers, Hughes Aircraft Co, 69-71, fel, 71-75, staff physicist, 75-76; fel spectros, Chem Div, Argonne Nat Lab, 76-78; sr scientist, Bechtel Nat Inc, 78-81; MEM STAFF APPL PHOTOCHEM, LOS ALAMOS NAT LAB, 81- *Concurrent Pos:* NSF res fel, 76-77. *Mem:* Inst Elec & Electronics Engrs; Am Phys Soc; Optical Soc Am. *Res:* Experimental molecular laser isotope separation; development and spectroscopic analysis of laser devices, atomic structure of lanthanide and actinide elements in crystals and gaseous complexes, electronic transition probabilities and dynamics of energy transfer processes. *Mailing Add:* 337 Cheryl Ct Los Alamos NM 87544

CAIRNCROSS, ALLAN, b Orange, NJ, May 27, 36; m 77; c 3. ORGANIC CHEMISTRY. *Educ:* Cornell Univ, BA, 58; Yale Univ, MS, 59, PhD(org chem), 63. *Prof Exp:* ORG RES CHEMIST, CENT RES DEPT, E I DU PONT DE NEMOURS & CO, INC, 64- *Mem:* Am Chem Soc. *Res:* Stability of tropylium ions; thermal isomerization of tropilidenes; cycloaddition reactions of bycyclobutanes; substituent effects on tropilidene-norcaradiene equilibria, organocopper chemistry and structure, heterocycles, and polymers; photoimaging. *Mailing Add:* 71 W Fourth St New Castle DE 19720

CAIRNIE, ALAN B, b Ayr, Scotland, Nov 18, 32; m 58; c 4. HAZARD EVALUATION, TOXIC CHEMICAL MANAGEMENT. *Educ:* Glasgow Univ, BSc, 54; Aberdeen Univ, PhD(physiol), 58. *Prof Exp:* Sci officer physiol, Rowett Res Inst, Aberdeen, 56-58; lectr, Aberdeen Univ, 58-61; scientist biophys, Inst Cancer Res, London, 61-67; prof biol, Queen's Univ, Ont, 67-76; head radiobiol sect, Defense Res Estab, Ottawa, 76-81; DIR GEN TOXIC CHEMICALS MGT CTR, ENVIRON CAN, 81- *Concurrent Pos:* Vis asst prof, Univ Calif, San Francisco, 65-66; vis assoc prof, Univ Colo, 74. *Mem:* Radiation Res Soc. *Res:* Assessment and control of hazards associated with toxic chemicals; management of multidisciplinary scientific activities; mammalian radiobiology. *Mailing Add:* Defense Res Estab Ottawa Ottawa ON K1A 0Z4 Can

CAIRNS, ELTON JAMES, b Chicago, Ill, Nov 7, 32; m 59, 74; c 1. ELECTROCHEMISTRY, PHYSICAL CHEMISTRY. *Educ:* Mich Col Mining & Technol, BS(chem) & BS(chem eng), 55; Univ Calif, Berkeley, PhD(chem eng), 59. *Prof Exp:* Chemist, US Steel Corp, 53; soils res chemist, Corps Eng, US Army, 54-55; asst thermodyn, Univ Calif, 57-58; phys chemist electrochem, Gen Elec Res Lab, 59-66; phys chemist & group leader, Argonne Nat Lab, 66-70, sect head, 70-73; asst head, electrochem dept, Gen Motors Res Labs, Warren Mich, 73-77; HEAD ENERGY & ENVIRON DIV, LAWRENCE BERKELEY LAB, 78-, ASSOC LAB DIR, 78-; PROF CHEM ENG, UNIV CALIF, BERKELEY, 78- *Concurrent Pos:* Consult, US Dept Interior & US Dept Defense, 69-70, US Dept Defense, 73- & NASA, 71; consult, Mat Res Coun, 73; mem subpanel, US Dept Com Panel on Elec Powered Vehicles, 67; mem org comt, Intersoc Energy Conversion Eng Conf, 69, steering comt, 70-, gen chmn, Conf, 76; mem adv bd, Advances Electrochem & Electrochem Eng, 75-; chmn, Energy Conversion, Am Inst Chem Engrs; mem panel, Nat Acad Sci Comt Motor Vehicle Emissions, 72-73; sci deleg, NATO Conf Air Pollution, Eindhoven, 71; div ed, J Electrochem Soc, 69- *Honors & Awards:* Francis Mills Turner Award, Electrochem Soc, 63; Croft lectr, Univ Mo, 79. *Mem:* AAAS; Electrochem Soc; Am Chem Soc; Am Inst Chem Eng; fel Am Inst Chem. *Res:* Electrochemical energy conversion; thermodynamics; transport phenomena; molten salts; liquid metals; surface chemistry. *Mailing Add:* Energy & Environ Div One Cyclotron Blvd Berkeley CA 94720

CAIRNS, JOHN, JR, b Conshohocken, Pa, May 8, 23; m 44; c 4. LIMNOLOGY. *Educ:* Swarthmore Col, AB, 47; Univ Pa, MS, 49, PhD(protozool), 53. *Prof Exp:* From asst cur to cur limnol, Acad Natural Sci, Philadelphia, 48-66, res assoc, 68; prof zool, Univ Kans, 66-68; res prof, 68-70, Univ prof biol, 70-79, UNIV DISTINGUISHED PROF BIOL, VA POLYTECH INST & STATE UNIV, 79-, DIR CTR FOR ENVIRON STUDIES, 70- *Concurrent Pos:* Lectr dept educ, Temple Univ, 62-63; mem fac, biol sta, Univ Mich, 64-70; trustee, Rocky Mountain Biol Lab, 62-; mem panel fresh-water aquatic life, Nat Acad Sci; mem environ studies bd, Nat Res Coun, 80-83; pres, Sci Adv Bd, US Environ Protection Agency, 79- *Honors & Awards:* Presidential Commendation, 71; Dudley Award, Am Soc Testing & Mat, 78. *Mem:* Fel AAAS; Am Soc Limnol & Oceanog; Soc Protozool; Am Fisheries Soc; Am Micros Soc (pres, 80). *Res:* Ecology of fresh-water Protozoa; response of aquatic organisms to toxic substances; water management; rapid biological information systems; ecology of polluted waters; regional environmental analysis; hazard evaluation, toxic chemicals; restoration of damaged ecosystems. *Mailing Add:* Ctr Environ Studies Va Polytech Inst & State Univ Blacksburg VA 24061

CAIRNS, JOHN MACKAY, b Scranton, Pa, Dec 3, 12; m 48; c 4. EMBRYOLOGY. *Educ:* Hamilton Col, BA, 35; Univ Rochester, MS, 37; Washington Univ, PhD(embryol), 41. *Prof Exp:* Instr, Washington Univ, 41-42; instr, Univ Tex, 46-52, asst prof biol & embryol, 48-52; asst prof histol & embryol, Sch Med, Univ Okla, 52-56; engr, Bell Aircraft Corp, 56-57; sr cancer res scientist, Roswell Park Mem Inst, 57-67, assoc cancer res scientist, 67-80; RETIRED. *Mem:* Am Soc Zoologists; Am Asn Anatomists; Soc Develop Biol; Int Soc Develop Biol. *Res:* Experimental embryology; regional differentiation in mesoderm; application of control system concepts. *Mailing Add:* Mill St RD 1 Springville NY 14141

CAIRNS, ROBERT ROSS, soil chemistry, soil physics, see previous edition

CAIRNS, ROBERT WILLIAM, b Oberlin, Ohio, Dec 23, 09; m 32; c 4. PHYSICAL CHEMISTRY. *Educ:* Oberlin Col, AB, 30; Johns Hopkins Univ, PhD(chem), 32; Harvard Univ, AMP, 51; Univ Del, DSc, 69. *Prof Exp:* Bartol Res Found fel, Johns Hopkins Univ, 33-34; res chemist, Res Ctr, Hercules Inc, 34-40, asst to dir res, 40-41, dir Res Ctr, 41-45, from asst dir res to dir res, 45-65, dir, Co, 60-65, vpres, 65-71; dep asst secy sci & technol, US Dept Com, 71-72; exec dir, Am Chem Soc, 72-77; RETIRED. *Concurrent Pos:* Vchmn res & develop bd & dep asst secy defense, Dept Defense, 53-54; consult, Off Secy Defense, 55-69 & Defense Sci Bd, 56-61, mem exec comt, 65-69; mem nat comt, Int Union Pure & Appl Chem, 58-64; div chem & chem technol, Nat Res Coun, 58-62, pres, 62-64; dir, Indust Res, Indust Res Inst, 55-60, pres, 59-60; mem bd trustees, Gordon Res Conf, 58-61, chmn, 60-61; chmn, Joint Comt Sci & Technol Commun, Nat Acad Sci-Nat Acad Eng, 66-70; mem, Nat Acad Eng, 69-, exec comt, 70-74; sci adv, Gov of Del, 69-71; mem panel on govt labs, President's Sci Adv Comt; chmn bd, Am Chem Soc, 72; consult, 78- *Honors & Awards:* Perkin Medal, Soc Indust Chem, 69; Patent Award, Freedman Found, 72; IRI Medal, Indust Res Inst, 74. *Mem:* Am Chem Soc (pres, 68); Int Union Pure & Appl Chem (pres, 76-77); hon mem Soc Indust Chem; Am Phys Soc; Com Develop Asn. *Res:* Technology of high explosives and propellants; chemical engineering; cellulose, rosin and terpene chemistry; industrial applications of chemicals; polymer chemistry; petrochemicals; research management. *Mailing Add:* 900 Burnt Hill Rd Box 4095 Wilmington DE 19807

CAIRNS, STEPHEN DOUGLAS, b Port Sulphur, La, Nov 26, 49; m 72. SYSTEMATICS, ZOOGEOGRAPHY. *Educ:* La State Univ, BS, 71; Univ Miami, MS, 73, PhD(biol oceanog), 76. *Prof Exp:* RES ASSOC, SMITHSONIAN INST, 79-, FEL ZOOL, 81- *Mem:* Soc Syst Zool. *Res:* Descriptive systematics and zoogeogrphy of deep-water western Atlantic, Antarctic,and Central Pacific scelerctinia and sylasterina (Coelenterata); worldwide revision and phylogenetic analysis of stylasterine genera. *Mailing Add:* Dept Invert Zool NHB-163 W-163 Smithsonian Inst Washington DC 20560

CAIRNS, STEWART SCOTT, b Franklin, NH, May 8, 04; m 28; c 2. MATHEMATICS. *Educ:* Harvard, AB, 26, AM, 27, PhD(math), 31. *Prof Exp:* Instr math, Harvard Univ, 27-28 & Yale Univ, 29-31; from instr to asst prof math, Lehigh Univ, 31-38; asst prof, Queens Col, NY, 38-46; prof math & head dept, Syracuse Univ, 46-48; prof, 48-72, head dept, 48-58, EMER PROF MATH, UNIV ILL, URBANA, 72- *Concurrent Pos:* Mem, Inst Advan Study, 36-37, 59-60, 62-63 & 74-75; consult, Nat Defense Res Comt, 44-46, Rand Corp, 50-70, Res & Develop Bd, 50-52, Dept Defense, 51-70 & NSF, 51-53; mem, Nat Res Coun, 49-54; Fulbright prof, France, 54-55; vis prof, Nat Taiwan Univ, 73; sr US scientist award, Ulm Univ, WGer, 76-77. *Mem:* AAAS; Am Math Soc; Math Asn Am. *Res:* Topology and analysis of manifolds. *Mailing Add:* 607 W Michigan Ave Urbana IL 61801

CAIRNS, THEODORE L, b Edmonton, Alta, July 20, 14; nat US; m 40; c 4. ORGANIC CHEMISTRY. *Educ:* Univ Alta, BSc, 36; Univ Ill, PhD(org chem), 39. *Hon Degrees:* LLD, Univ Alta, 70. *Prof Exp:* Lab asst, Univ Ill, 37-39; instr org chem, Univ Rochester, 39-41; res chemist, E I du Pont de Nemours & Co, 41-45, res supvr, 45-51, lab dir, 51-61, dir basic sci, 62-66, dir res, 66-67, asst dir cent res dept, 67-71, dir cent res & develop dept, 71-79; RETIRED. *Concurrent Pos:* Regents prof, Univ Calif, Los Angeles, 65-66; Fuson lectr, Univ Nev, 68; mem, President Nixon's Sci Policy Task Force, 69, Gov Coun Sci & Technol, 69-72, President's Sci Adv Comt, 70-73 & President's Comt on Nat Medal Sci, 74-75; chmn, Off Chem & Chem Technol, Nat Res Coun, 79-82, mem, Bd Toxicol & Environ Health Hazards, 80-83. *Honors & Awards:* Am Chem Soc Award, 68; Synthetic Org Chem Mfrs Asn US Medal, 68; Perkin Medal, Am Sect, Soc Chem Indust, 73; Cresson Medal, Franklin Inst, 74. *Mem:* Nat Acad Sci. *Res:* Stereochemistry of biphenyls; chemistry of polyamides; reactions of acetylene and carbon monoxide; cyanocarbon chemistry. *Mailing Add:* Box 3941 Greenville DE 19807

CAIRNS, THOMAS W, b Hutchinson, Kans, Nov 13, 31; m 59; c 2. MATHEMATICS. *Educ:* Okla State Univ, BS, 53, MS, 55, PhD(math), 60. *Prof Exp:* Head dept, 69-76, chmn div math sci, 72-80, PROF MATH, UNIV TULSA, 69- *Mem:* Math Asn Am; Am Math Soc; Soc Indust & Appl Math. *Res:* Computing; biomathematics; time series analysis. *Mailing Add:* Dept of Math Sci Univ of Tulsa Tulsa OK 74104

CAIRNS, WILLIAM LOUIS, b St Catharines, Ont, Oct 18, 42. BIOCHEMICAL ENGINEERING, PETROLEUM MICROBIOLOGY. *Educ:* Univ Guelph, BSA, 65; Iowa State Univ, PhD(biochem), 70. *Prof Exp:* Asst prof chem, Univ Ark, Fayetteville, 70-76; res assoc, Max Planck Inst Cell Biol, Heidelberg, 76-78; lectr plant sci, 78-79, ASST PROF BIOCHEM ENG, UNIV WESTERN ONT, 79-, RES ASSOC, 78- *Mem:* Am Chem Soc; AAAS; Am Soc Photobiol; Sigma Xi. *Res:* Microbiol production of surface active agents; biochemical basis of circadian rhythms. *Mailing Add:* Biochem Eng Univ Western Ont London ON N6A 5B8 Can

CAIS, RUDOLF EDMUND, b Prague, Czech, Nov 12, 47; Australian citizen; m 71; c 2. POLYMER CHEMISTRY. *Educ:* Univ Queensland, Australia, BSc Hons, 70, PhD(polymer chem), 75. *Prof Exp:* Consult, 76, MEM TECH STAFF POLYMER CHEM, BELL LABS, 77- *Mem:* Am Chem Soc. *Res:* Nuclear magnetic resonance studies of the structure and dynamics of synthetic macromolecules; polymerization and copolymerization mechanisms. *Mailing Add:* Polymer Chem Res Dept 600 Mountain Ave Murray Hill NJ 07974

CAKMAK, AHMET SEFIK, b Izmir, Turkey, Aug 14, 34; m 60. DYNAMICS. *Educ:* Robert Col Istanbul, BSE, 57; Princeton Univ, MSE, 58, MA, 60, PhD(eng mech), 62. *Prof Exp:* Asst solid mech, Columbia Univ, 60-62; res assoc, 62-63, from asst prof to assoc prof civil eng, 69-71, chmn dept, 71-80, PROF CIVIL ENG, PRINCETON UNIV, 71- *Mem:* Assoc mem Am Soc Civil Engrs; Soc Eng Sci; Am Soc Mech Eng; Soc Rheol. *Res:* Continuum mechanics; statics and dynamics of inelastic media; elastic and viscoelastic systems. *Mailing Add:* Sch of Eng & Appl Sci Princeton Univ Princeton NJ 08544

CALABI, EUGENIO, b Milano, Italy, May 11, 23; nat US; m 52; c 1. MATHEMATICS. *Educ:* Mass Inst Technol, BS, 46; Univ Ill, AM, 47; Princeton Univ, PhD(math), 50. *Prof Exp:* Asst & instr, Princeton Univ, 47-51; asst prof math, La State Univ, 51-55; from asst prof to prof, Univ Minn, 55-64; prof, 64-69, chmn dept, 73-76, THOMAS A SCOTT PROF MATH, UNIV PA, 69- *Concurrent Pos:* Mem, Inst Advan Study, 58-59; Guggenheim fel, 62-63. *Mem:* Am Math Soc. *Res:* Differential geometry of complex manifolds. *Mailing Add:* Dept of Math Grad Sch Univ of Pa Philadelphia PA 19104

CALABI, LORENZO, b Milan, Italy, Apr 11, 22; nat US; m 49; c 4. APPLIED MATHEMATICS. *Educ:* Swiss Fed Inst Technol, dipl, 46; Univ Milan, PhD(math), 47; Univ Strasbourg, PhD(math), 51. *Prof Exp:* Res fel, Inst Advan Math, Italy, 51-52; asst prof, Boston Col, 52-56; res assoc, Parke Math Labs, Inc, 55-56, assoc dir res, 56-74; tech dir, Solo Corp, 74-78; PRES, PARKE MATH LABS, 78- *Concurrent Pos:* Fulbright travel award, 52; lectr, Holy Cross Col, 53-54; assoc prof, Boston Col, 56-59, lectr, 59-62. *Mem:* Asn Comput Mach; Am Math Soc; Soc Indust & Appl Math; Ital Math Union. *Res:* Computer sciences applications. *Mailing Add:* Parke Math Labs One River Rd Carlisle MA 01741

CALABI, ORNELLA, US citizen. IMMUNOLOGY, CHEMOTHERAPY. *Educ:* Hebrew Univ, Jerusalem, MSc, 45; Univ Chicago, MSc, 51; Harvard Univ, DSc(microbiol), 57. *Prof Exp:* Res asst trop med, Hebrew Univ, Jerusalem, 40-45; res asst med, Univ Chicago, 48-49, res asst bact & parasitol, 49-51; instr bact, Brandeis Univ, 53-54; instr microbiol & in-chg trop med, Sch Med, Yale Univ, 56-57; res assoc microbiol, Dept Metall, Mass Inst Technol, 57-58; res assoc path, Children's Hosp, Harvard Med Ctr, Boston, 59-60; instr microbiol, Seton Hall Col Med, NJ, 60-61; res assoc path, New York Med Col, 61-63; microbiologist, Walter Reed Army Inst Res, Washington, DC, 64-70, US CIVIL SERV CAREER SCIENTIST, 67-, *Concurrent Pos:* Vis scientist, Queen Elizabeth Col, Univ London, 71-72; adj dir, Cantonal Inst Bact & Serol, Lugano, Switz, 73-74; consult toxicol, Nat Cancer Inst, NIH, Bethesda, Md, 76- *Mem:* Am Soc Microbiol; AAAS; fel Am Acad Microbiol; NY Acad Sci. *Res:* Pathogenesis of disease; blood and enteric bacterial infections; relapsing fever, shigellosis, melioidosis; humoral and cellular immunity, phagocytosis; chemotherapy, synergism and antagonism of drugs and of oncolytic agents; toxicity tests; mathematical models of drug interaction and their application in biological systems. *Mailing Add:* 5100 Dorset Ave Chevy Chase MD 20815

CALABRESE, ANTHONY, b Providence, RI, Feb 25, 37; m 63; c 2. MARINE ECOLOGY. *Educ:* Univ RI, BS, 59; Auburn Univ, MS, 62; Univ Conn, PhD(zool, ecol), 69. *Prof Exp:* FISHERY BIOLOGIST, NAT OCEANIC & ATMOSPHERIC ADMIN, NAT MARINE FISHERIES SERV, 62- *Mem:* Am Fisheries Soc; Nat Shellfisheries Asn (secy-treas, 74-76, vpres, 76-77, pres elect, 77-78, pres, 78-79); Estuarine Res Fedn; Atlantic Estuarine Res Soc. *Res:* Development of biological information concerning the effect of pollutants on marine organisms, including shellfish, fin fish and crustaceans, to provide a basis for environmental management. *Mailing Add:* Nat Marine Fisheries Serv Northeast Fisheries Ctr Milford CT 06460

CALABRESE, CARMELO, b Kansas City, Mo, Apr 21, 29; m 54; c 2. ELECTRICAL ENGINEERING. *Educ:* Univ Mo-Columbia, BS, 55, MS, 56, PhD, 65. *Prof Exp:* From instr to prof elec eng, Univ Mo-Columbia, 55-75; DIR ELEC SYST RES, CONSOL EDISON CO NEW YORK, INC, 75- *Concurrent Pos:* Res & develop fel, Elec Boat/Gen Dynamics, 66-67; Ford Found grant eng, 66; NSF travel grant, 66. *Mem:* Inst Elec & Electronics Engrs. *Res:* Electric power systems; energy conversion. *Mailing Add:* Consol Edison Co New York Inc 4 Irving Pl New York NY 10003

CALABRESE, DIANE M, b Erie, Pa, Apr 1, 49. ENTOMOLOGY. *Educ:* Gannon Col, BS, 71; Univ Conn, MS, 74, PhD(entomol), 77. *Prof Exp:* Instr biol, Kans State Univ, 77-78; lectr, Univ Tex, El Paso, 78-80; asst prof, Trinity Col, 80-81; ASST PROF BIOL ECOL & GEN BIOL, DICKINSON COL & DIR, FLORENCE JONES REINEMAN WILDLIFE SANCTUARY, 81- *Concurrent Pos:* Ed, newsletter, Women in Entomol, 81- *Mem:* Soc Syst Zool; Entomol Soc Am; Am Soc Zoologists. *Res:* Problems of an evolutionary-ecological nature in systematics; character congruence among ontogenetic, cytogenetic and adult morphological characters in the Gerridae. *Mailing Add:* Dept Biol Dickinson Col Carlisle PA 17013

CALABRESE, JOSEPH C, b Cleveland, Ohio; m 77; c 1. CRYSTALLOGRAPHY, COMPUTING. *Educ:* Univ Wis, PhD(chem), 72. *Prof Exp:* Fel, Univ Milan, 72-73 & Univ Wis, 73-79; CHEMIST, E I DU PONT DE NEMOURS, CO, INC, 80- *Mem:* Am Chem Soc; Am Crystallog Asn. *Res:* Crystallography; crystallographic computing and methodology; organometallic chemistry. *Mailing Add:* Exp Sta E I du Pont de Nemours & Co Inc Wilmington DE 19898

CALABRESE, LUCIO, electrical engineering, see previous edition

CALABRESE, PHILIP G, b Chicago, Ill, Feb 21, 41; div. MATHEMATICS, PHYSICS. *Educ:* Ill Inst Technol, BS, 63, MS, 66, PhD(math), 68. *Prof Exp:* Instr math, Ill Inst Technol, 67-68; asst prof, Naval Postgrad Sch, 68-70; asst prof math, Calif State Col, Bakersfield, 70-75; lectr, Humboldt State Univ, 75-79; SR STAFF ENGR, DECISION SCI, INC, 79- *Concurrent Pos:* Instr, Rosary Col, 66-67; adj prof math, San Diego State Univ, 80- *Mem:* AAAS; Am Math Soc; Math Asn Am. *Res:* Mathematical philosophy, logic and probability; physics, especially quantum theory; probabilistic metric spaces; philosophy. *Mailing Add:* 2911 Luna Ave San Diego CA 92117

CALABRESE, RONALD LEWIS, b Peekskill, NY, Sept 24, 47; m 79; c 1. NEUROBIOLOGY. *Educ:* Cornell Univ, BS, 69; Stanford Univ, AM, 70, PhD(neurobiol), 75. *Prof Exp:* ASST PROF NEUROBIOL, DEPT CELLULAR & DEVELOP BIOL, HARVARD UNIV, 78- *Mem:* Soc Neurosci; AAAS. *Res:* Identification and analysis of neural circuits which generate and coordinate rhythmic behaviors at the cellular level. *Mailing Add:* Biol Labs Harvard Univ 16 Divinity Ave Cambridge MA 02138

CALABRESI, MASSIMO, b Ferrara, Italy, June 2, 03; nat US; m 29; c 2. CARDIOLOGY, GERONTOLOGY. *Educ:* Univ Florence, MD, 26; Yale Univ, DrPH, 44. *Prof Exp:* Instr anat, Univ Florence, 26-27; from instr to assoc prof internal med, Univ Milan, 27-38, fac prof ther, 35-38; from asst clin prof to prof, 59-80, EMER PROF INTERNAL MED, YALE UNIV, 80- *Mem:* Am Heart Asn; AMA; Am Pub Health Asn; NY Acad Sci; Am Col Physicians. *Res:* Physiopathology of cardiac failure; physiology of circulation; cardiac hypertrophy. *Mailing Add:* 300 Ogden St New Haven CT 06511

CALABRESI, PAUL, b Milan, Italy, Apr 5, 30; US citizen; m 54; c 3. PHARMACOLOGY, CHEMOTHERAPY. *Educ:* Yale Univ, BA, 51, MD, 55; Am Bd Internal Med, dipl, 64. *Prof Exp:* Intern, Harvard Med Serv, Boston City Hosp, Mass, 55-56, asst resident, 58-59; proj assoc, Univ Wis, 56-58;from instr to assoc prof med & pharmacol,Yale Univ, 60-68; chmn dept, 68-76, PROF MED, BROWN UNIV, 68- *Concurrent Pos:* Clin fel, Sch Med, Yale Univ, 59-60; field investr, Nat Cancer Inst, 56-60; attend physician, Vet Admin Hosp, West Haven & asst dir, Clin Res Ctr, Yale-New Haven Med Ctr, 60-; assoc physician, Univ Serv, Grace-New Haven Hosp, 60-64, asst attend physician, 64-, assoc coordr cancer teaching, 61- *Mem:* Am Soc Clin Invest; Am Soc Hemat; Am Soc Pharmacol & Exp Therapeut; Am Soc Oncol; Am Fedn Clin Res. *Res:* Medical oncology; hematology; virology; immunology; metabolism of nucleic acids; autoimmune disease; bone marrow function and physiology; antimetabolites in viral and cancer chemotherapy. *Mailing Add:* Dept of Med Sci Brown Univ Providence RI 02912

CALABRETTA, PETER JOSEPH, b Brooklyn, NY, Feb 10, 34; m 57; c 5. ORGANOMETALLIC CHEMISTRY. *Educ:* St John's Univ, NY, BS, 55, MS, 58, PhD(org-organometallic chem), 65. *Prof Exp:* Group leader polymers, Stauffer Chem Co, 65-67; asst dir res, Universal Oil Prod Fragrances, 67-69; dir, Res Fragrances & Flavor Chem, 69-80, VPRES RES & TECH, FELTON INT INC, 80- *Concurrent Pos:* Lectr, City Univ New York, 58-; fel chem, Columbia Univ, 65; consult, NRA, Inc, 64-65. *Mem:* AAAS; Am Chem Soc; fel Am Inst Chem; NY Acad Sci. *Res:* Synthesis of chemicals used in fragrances and flavor formulas. *Mailing Add:* 42 Old Field Lane Great Neck NY 11020

CALABRISI, PAUL, b Naples, Italy, Jan 27, 07; nat; m 40. ANATOMY. *Educ:* Cath Univ Am, BA, 31; George Washington Univ, MA, 40; Cambridge Univ, PhD(anat), 55. *Prof Exp:* From instr to prof anat, Sch Med, George Washington Univ, 39-74; vis prof anat, Univ PR Med Ctr, 74-76; PROF MED SCI, BROWN UNIV, 76- *Concurrent Pos:* Vis lectr, Nat Naval Med Ctr, 47-48, Am Univ, 47-48, Washinton Hosp Ctr, 58, Armed Forces Inst Path, 58, Casualty Hosp, 59 & Nat Univ Athens, 69; consult, Naval Med Res Inst, 47-51; examr, Am Bd Orthop Surg, 48-; lectr, Columbian Hosp for Women & George Washington Hosp, 48-49; lectr & supvr, Trinity Col, Cambridge Univ, 53-55; vis prof, Queen's Univ, Belfast, 69; guest lectr, Prince Georges Hosp, Md. *Honors & Awards:* Cross of Eloy Alfaro, Panama. *Mem:* AAAS; Soc Exp Biol & Med; Am Asn Anatomists; Asn Am Med Cols; Anat Soc Gt Brit & Ireland. *Res:* Embryology; pathology. *Mailing Add:* Dept of Med Sci Brown Univ Providence RI 02912

CALAHAN, DONALD A, b Cincinnati, Ohio, Feb 23, 35; m 59; c 4. ELECTRICAL ENGINEERING. *Educ:* Univ Notre Dame, BS, 57; Univ Ill, MS, 58, PhD(elec eng), 60. *Prof Exp:* From instr to assoc prof elec eng, Univ Ill, 59-65; prof, Univ Ky, 65-66; PROF ELEC ENG, UNIV MICH, 66- *Res:* Investigation of theoretical limitations in the design of electrical networks and of the use of computers in network design. *Mailing Add:* Dept of Elec & Comput Eng 2500 E Eng Bldg Univ Mich Ann Arbor MI 48109

CALAMARI, TIMOTHY A, JR, b New Orleans, La, Nov 12, 36; m 64; c 3. TEXTILE CHEMISTRY. *Educ:* Loyola Univ, La, BS, 58; La State Univ, MS, 61, PhD(chem), 63. *Prof Exp:* RES CHEMIST, SOUTHERN UTILIZATION RES & DEVELOP LAB, USDA, NEW ORLEANS, 63- *Mem:* Am Asn Textile Chemists & Colorists; Sigma Xi; Am Chem Soc; Am Asn Clin Chemists. *Res:* Additive finishing techniques for the development of dimensionally stable cotton fabric; liquid ammonia based treatments for cotton textiles; new fire retardant finishes for cotton and cotton blends; expert on the proper disposal procedures for toxic and dangerous waste chemicals. *Mailing Add:* 1016 Rosa Ave Metairie LA 70005

CALAME, GERALD PAUL, b Lelocle, Switz, Nov 27, 30; US citizen; m 59; c 1. ASTROPHYSICS, PHYSICS. *Educ:* Col of Wooster, BA, 53; Harvard Univ, AM, 55, PhD(physics), 60. *Prof Exp:* Theoret physicist, Knolls Atomic Power Lab, Gen Elec Co, 59-61; from asst prof to assoc prof nuclear eng, Rensselaer Polytech Inst, 61-66; assoc prof, 66-69, PROF PHYSICS, US NAVAL ACAD, 69-, CHMN DEPT, 78- *Concurrent Pos:* Consult, Knolls Atomic Power Lab, 61-66. *Mem:* AAAS; Am Phys Soc; Am Asn Physics Teachers. *Res:* Celestial mechanics; relativity. *Mailing Add:* Dept of Physics US Naval Acad Annapolis MD 21402

CALANDRA, JOSEPH CARL, b Chicago, Ill, Mar 17, 17; m 44; c 4. TOXICOLOGY, BIOCHEMISTRY. *Educ:* Ill Inst Technol, BS, 38; Northwestern Univ, PhD(chem), 42, MD, 50; Am Bd Clin Chem, dipl, 55; Am Bd Indust Hyg, dipl, 62. *Prof Exp:* Instr chem, Ill Inst Technol, 38; from instr chem to assoc prof path, 38-53, chmn dept path, 49-53, PROF PATH, MED SCH, NORTHWESTERN UNIV, 53- *Concurrent Pos:* NIH grant, 58-63; dir toxicol, Indust Bio-Test Labs, Inc, 53-59; pres, Indust Biotest Labs, Inc, 69-76. *Mem:* Fel AAAS; fel Am Soc Clin Pharmacol & Chemother; AMA; Am Indust Hyg Asn; Soc Toxicol. *Res:* Occupational medicine; experimental pathology. *Mailing Add:* Dept of Path Sch Med Northwestern Univ Chicago IL 60611

CALANOG, BLANCA GADDI, b Philippines, July 14, 45; m 72; c 1. NUTRITION, FOOD SCIENCE. *Educ:* Univ Philippines, BS, 65; Univ Wis-Madison, MS, 68, PhD(food sci & microbiol), 73. *Prof Exp:* Metab res dietitian, Univ Chicago Hosp & Clin, 73; instr food & nutrit, Rosary Col, 74; lit scientist, Nat Dairy Coun, 74-79. *Concurrent Pos:* Ed, Dairy Coun Dig, 74-79. *Mem:* Am Inst Nutrit; Am Dietetic Asn; Inst Food Technologists. *Res:* Mycotoxins in foods. *Mailing Add:* 162 Borden Rd Middletown NJ 07748

CALARCO, JOHN RICHARD, nuclear physics, see previous edition

CALARESU, FRANCO ROMANO, b Divaccia, Italy, Apr 12, 31; Can citizen; m 58; c 2. PHYSIOLOGY. *Educ:* Univ Milan, MD, 53; Univ Alta, PhD, 64. *Prof Exp:* Intern, Columbus Hosp, Chicago, 54-55, resident med, 55-56; resident radiother, Jefferson Med Col, 56-58; demonstr physiol, Univ Sask, 58-60; demonstr, Univ Alta, 60-64; scientist, Gatty Marine Lab, Scotland, 64-65; asst prof physiol, Univ Alta, 65-67; assoc prof, 67-72, PROF PHYSIOL, UNIV WESTERN ONT, 72- *Concurrent Pos:* Nat Res Coun Can fel, 58-60; Nat Heart Found Can fel, 60-65; Med Res Coun Can scholar, 65-67; Med Res Coun Can vis prof, Inst Cardiovasc Res, Univ Milan, 74-75. *Mem:* AAAS; Am Physiol Soc; Can Physiol Soc; Soc Neurosci. *Res:* Neural autonomic control. *Mailing Add:* Dept of Physiol Univ of Western Ont London ON N6A 5B8 Can

CALAVAN, EDMOND, b Scio, Ore, Jan 13, 13; m 38; c 4. PLANT PATHOLOGY. *Educ:* Ore State Col, BS, 39, MS, 41; Univ Wis, PhD(plant path), 45. *Prof Exp:* Jr plant pathologist, 45-47, from asst plant pathologist to assoc plant pathologist, 47-59, plant pathologist, Citrus Exp Sta, 59-80, prof, 62-80, EMER PROF PLANT PATH & PLANT PATHOLOGIST, UNIV CALIF, 80- *Mem:* Int Soc Citriculture; Int Orgn Mycoplasmologists; fel Am Phytopath Soc; Int Orgn Citrus Virologist. *Res:* Diseases of citrus; fungal diseases; viral diseases; regulatory plant pathology; mycoplasma diseases of plants. *Mailing Add:* Dept of Plant Path Univ of Calif Riverside CA 92521

CALBERT, HAROLD EDWARD, b Edinburg, Ind, Mar 20, 18; m 42; c 3. BIOCHEMISTRY. *Educ:* Allegheny Col, BA, 39; Univ Wis, MS, 47, PhD(dairy & food technol, biochem), 48. *Prof Exp:* From instr to assoc prof dairy & food indusit, 48-60, PROF FOOD SCI & CHMN DEPT, UNIV WIS-MADISON, 61- *Concurrent Pos:* Chmn environ sci training comt, USPHS. *Mem:* AAAS; Am Dairy Sci Asn; Inst Food Technologists; Am Fisheries Soc. *Res:* Dairy and food chemistry; food plant sanitation; product development; aquaculture. *Mailing Add:* Dept of Food Sci 105 Babcock Hall Univ of Wis Madison WI 53706

CALBO, LEONARD JOSEPH, b New York, NY, Feb 17, 41; m 64; c 2. INDUSTRIAL ORGANIC CHEMISTRY. *Educ:* Manhattan Col, BS, 62; Seton Hall Univ, MS, 64, PhD(org chem), 66; Univ Conn, MBA, 73. *Prof Exp:* Res chemist, Am Cyanamid Co, 66-76; MKT MGR, CATALYSTS & ION EXCHANGE REAGENTS, KING INDUST INC, NORWALK, CT, 76- *Mem:* Am Chem Soc; Am Mgt Asn. *Res:* Surface coatings; cross-linking agents; thermoset amino and polyester resins; development of new resins and cross-linking agents for electrocoating application; catalysts for curing amino resins. *Mailing Add:* King Indust Inc PO Box 588 Norwalk CT 06852

CALCAGNO, PHILIP LOUIS, b New York, NY, Feb 27, 18; m 51. PEDIATRICS. *Educ:* Univ Ga, BS, 40; Georgetown Univ, MD, 43. *Prof Exp:* Rotating intern, Morrisannia City Hosp, New York, 44, resident pediat & internal med, 44-45; chief resident contagious dis, Willard Packer Hosp, 45-46; pediatrician, Floating Hosp, 48; res asst, Children's Hosp, Buffalo, 48-52, assoc pediat, Sch Med, Univ Buffalo, 52-54, from asst prof to assoc prof, 54-62; PROF PEDIAT & CHMN DEPT, GEORGETOWN UNIV, 62- *Mem:* Soc Pediat Res; Am Acad Pediat; NY Acad Sci; Am Pediat Soc; Soc Exp Biol & Med. *Res:* Renal function in infants; physiological studies of the postsurgical state; neurosensory disorders in mental retardation. *Mailing Add:* Georgetown Univ Med Ctr 3800 Reservoir Rd NW Washington DC 20007

CALCATERRA, ROBERT JOHN, b Lincoln, Nebr, Oct 17, 42; m 72; c 3. CHEMICAL ENGINEERING. *Educ:* Univ Nebr, BS, 64, MS, 66; Wash Univ, DSc, 72. *Prof Exp:* Res engr process develop, Monsanto Co, 65-69 & Alcoa, 71-73; res engr, Amoco Chem, Standard Oil Co, Ind, 73-76, sr res engr res planning, 76-80; DIR RES & DEVELOP, ADOLPH COORS CO, 80- *Concurrent Pos:* Affil prof, Dept Chem Eng, Wash Univ, 73-76. *Mem:* Sigma Xi; Am Inst Chem Engrs; Am Soc Eng Educ; Nat Soc Prof Engrs; Technol Transfer Soc. *Res:* Managing brewing, packaging, new products, business planning; technology evaluation and forecasting as it applies to business and research diversification and planning; engineering economics; transport; reaction engineering; mass transfer. *Mailing Add:* 10388 Crestone Mt Littleton CO 80123

CALCOTE, HARTWELL FORREST, b Meadville, Pa, May 20, 20; m 43; c 4. COMBUSTION, PLASMA CHEMISTRY. *Educ:* Cath Univ Am, BACh, 43; Princeton Univ, PhD(phys chem), 48. *Prof Exp:* Instr electronics, Princeton Univ, 43-45, res asst combustion, 45-48; phys chemist, Exp Inc, 48-51, head thermokinetics dept, 52-54, dir res, 55-56; PRES & DIR RES, AEROCHEM RES LABS, INC, 56- *Concurrent Pos:* Mem papers comt, 8th-19th Int Symp on Combustion; mem adv panel, phys chem div, Nat Bur Standards, 66-69; mem, Joint Army-Navy-Air Force Tables Thermochem Working Group, 66-71. *Mem:* AAAS; Am Chem Soc; Am Phys Soc; Am Inst Aeronaut & Astronaut; Combustion Inst. *Res:* Physical chemistry of combustion processes and electrical discharges; electrical properties of flames; radar interference effects in rocket exhausts; instrumentation; soot formation in flames. *Mailing Add:* AeroChem Res Labs Inc PO Box 12 Princeton NJ 08540

CALDECOTT, RICHARD S, b Vancouver, BC, Apr 15, 24; nat; m 47; c 3. GENETICS. *Educ:* Univ BC, BSA, 46; State Col Wash, MS, 48, PhD(radiation genetics), 51. *Prof Exp:* Asst, State Col Wash, 46-49, res assoc, 51; asst prof, Univ Nebr, 51-53; assoc radiobiologist, Brookhaven Nat Lab, 53-54; geneticist, res br, Agr Res Serv, USDA, 54-60 & US Atomic Energy Comn, Washington, DC, 60-63; assoc prof, grad sch, 55-63, prof, 63-65, PROF GENETICS & DEAN COL BIOL SCI, UNIV MINN, ST PAUL, 65-; GENETICIST, CROPS RES DIV, AGR RES SERV, USDA, 63- *Concurrent Pos:* Mem, Nat Acad Sci-Nat Res Coun subcomt on radiation biol; vpres & mem bd dirs, Fresh Water Biol Res Found; mem bd trustees, Argonne Univs Asn, 70-80 & St Paul Sci Mus. *Mem:* AAAS; Genetics Soc Am; Radiation Res Soc; Am Inst Biol Sci. *Res:* Radiobiology; biophysics; cytogenetics. *Mailing Add:* Col of Biol Sci Snyder Hall Univ of Minn St Paul MN 55101

CALDER, DALE RALPH, b St Stephen, NB, Apr 16, 41; m 65; c 2. INVERTEBRATE ZOOLOGY. *Educ:* Acadia Univ, BSc, 64; Col William & Mary, MA, 66, PhD(marine Sci), 68. *Prof Exp:* Assoc marine scientist, Va Inst Marine Sci, 69-73; assoc marine scientist, Marine Resources Res Inst, 73-81; ASSOC CUR & HEAD INVERTEBRATE ZOOL DEPT, ROYAL ONT MUS, 81- *Concurrent Pos:* Nat Res Coun Can fel, 68-69; asst prof marine sci, Univ Va, 69-73; asst prof marine sci, Col William & Mary, 70-73; asst prof marine biol, Col Charleston, 74- *Mem:* Am Soc Zoologists; Soc Syst Zool. *Res:* Ecology of marine fouling organisms; taxonomy and ecology of marine invertebrates, particularly the Hydrozoa and Scyphozoa; ecology of marine benthos. *Mailing Add:* Dept Invert Zool Royal Ont Mus 100 Queens Park Toronto ON M5S 2C6 Can

CALDER, JOHN ARCHER, b Baltimore, Md, Oct 18, 42; m 64. CHEMICAL OCEANOGRAPHY, ORGANIC GEOCHEMISTRY. *Educ:* Southern Methodist Univ, BS, 64; Univ Ill, Urbana, MS, 65; Univ Tex, Austin, PhD(chem), 69. *Prof Exp:* Asst prof oceanog, Fla State Univ, 69-73, assoc prof oceanog, 73-77; MEM STAFF, OFF MARINE POLLUTION ASSESSMENT, NAT OCEANIC & ATMOSPHERIC ADMIN, 77- *Mem:* Geochem Soc; Am Soc Limnol & Oceanog; Am Chem Soc. *Res:* Chemistry of the organic compounds in water and sediment; chemistry of the stable isotopes of carbon and oxygen; biological isotope effects; impacts and management of ocean disposal of wastes. *Mailing Add:* Nat Oceanic & Atmospheric Admin Rockville MD 20852

CALDER, PETER N, b Springhill, NS, April 9, 38; m 64; c 3. ROCK MECHANICS. *Educ:* NS Tech Col, BEng, 63; Queens Univ, MSc, 67, PhD(mining eng), 70. *Prof Exp:* Drilling & Blasting Supvr, Iron Ore Co, Can, 63-65; PROF ROCK MECH & OPEN PIT MINING, QUEENS UNIV, 70-, HEAD, DEPT MINING ENG, 80- *Concurrent Pos:* Consult mining, 70-; chmn rock mech, Underground Blasting Sub-Comt, 77- *Honors & Awards:* Leonard Gold Medal, Eng Inst Can, 70. *Mem:* Can Inst Mining & Metall Engrs; Soc Mining Engrs. *Res:* Computer applications in open pit design; geotechnical aspects of mine design; rock slope reinforcement; drilling and blasting studies. *Mailing Add:* Mining Eng Dept Goodwin Hall Queens Univ Kingston ON K7L 3N6 Can

CALDER, WILLIAM ALEXANDER, III, b Cambridge, Mass, Sept 2, 34; m 55; c 2. PHYSIOLOGICAL ECOLOGY. *Educ:* Univ Ga, BS, 55; Wash State Univ, MS, 63; Duke Univ, PhD(zool), 66. *Prof Exp:* Instr zool, Duke Univ, 66-67, res assoc, 67; asst prof, Va Polytech Inst, 67-69; assoc prof, 69-74, PROF, DEPT ECOL & EVOLUTIONARY BIOL, UNIV ARIZ, 74- *Concurrent Pos:* Mem instrnl staff, Rocky Mountain Biol Labs, 71, 72, 75, 76 & 78; vis prof, Univ New South Wales, 77. *Mem:* AAAS; Am Ornith Union; Cooper Ornith Soc; Fed Am Scientists. *Res:* Physiology of temperature regulation and respiration; environmental physiology; microclimate, heat and water budgets of birds; allometry; mandolin acoustics; biology of ratites. *Mailing Add:* Dept of Ecol & Evolutionary Biol Univ of Ariz Tucson AZ 85721

CALDERON, ALBERTO PEDRO, b Mendoza, Arg, Sept 14, 20; m 50; c 2. MATHEMATICS, CIVIL ENGINEERING. *Educ:* Univ Buenos Aires, dipl civil eng, 47; Univ Chicago, PhD(math), 50. *Prof Exp:* Vis assoc prof, Ohio State Univ, 50-53; mem, Inst Advan Study, Princeton, 55; assoc prof math, Mass Inst Technol, 55-59, prof, 72-75; prof, 59-68, Louis Block prof, 68-72, chmn dept, 70-72, UNIV PROF MATH, UNIV CHICAGO, 75- *Concurrent Pos:* Hon prof, Univ Buenos Aires, 75-; assoc ed, J Functional Anal, J Differential Equations & Advan in Math. *Honors & Awards:* Latin Am Prize Math, IPCLAR, Santa Fe, Arg, 69; Bocher Prize, 78. *Mem:* Nat Acad Sci; Am Acad Arts & Sci; Acad Nacional Ciencias Exactas; Real Acad Ciencias. *Mailing Add:* Univ Chicago Dept Math 5734 University Chicago IL 60637

CALDERON, CALIXTO PEDRO, b Mendoza, Arg, Dec 29, 39. REAL ANALYSIS, HARMONIC ANALYSIS. *Educ:* Univ Buenos Aires, MA, 65, PhD(math), 69. *Prof Exp:* Asst prof math, Univ Buenos Aires, 69-70, assoc prof, 70-72; asst prof, Univ Minn, Minneapolis, 72-74; assoc prof, 76-81, PROF MATH, UNIV ILL, CIRCLE CAMPUS, 81- *Concurrent Pos:* Specialist, Dept Sci Affairs, Pan Am Union, 65-66; vis asst prof, Univ Minn, 69-70; vis assoc prof, Rice Univ, 79. *Mem:* Am Math Soc; Arg Inst Math. *Res:* Real analysis; harmonic analysis; differentiation theory. *Mailing Add:* Math Dept Univ Ill Chicago Circle Chicago IL 60680

CALDERON, NISSIM, b Jerusalem, Israel, Apr 1, 33; US citizen; m 61; c 2. POLYMER CHEMISTRY, ORGANOMETALLIC CHEMISTRY. *Educ:* Hebrew Univ, Jerusalem, MSc, 58; Univ Akron, PhD(polymer chem), 62. *Prof Exp:* Sr res chemist, 62-67, sect head, 67-75, MGR RES & ADMIN, GOODYEAR TIRE & RUBBER CO, 75- *Mem:* Am Chem Soc. *Res:* Developer of the olefin metathesis reaction of homogeneous catalysts; discoverer of the feasibility of cleavage of carbon-to-carbon double bonds by transition metal catalysts. *Mailing Add:* Goodyear Tire & Rubber Co Res Div 142 Goodyear Blvd Akron OH 44316

CALDERONE, JULIUS G, b Detroit, Mich, Aug 2, 28. MEDICAL BACTERIOLOGY, MEDICAL MYCOLOGY. *Educ:* San Jose State Univ, BA, 50; Univ Calif, Los Angeles, PhD(microbiol), 64. *Prof Exp:* Med microbiologist, Tulare County Health Dept, Calif, 51-53; clin lab technologist, US Navy, 53-55; med microbiologist, Orange County Health Dept, Calif, 55-58; asst med microbiol, Univ Calif, Los Angeles, 59-63, fel, 64-65; from asst prof to assoc prof, 65-73, PROF MED MICROBIOL, CALIF STATE UNIV, SACRAMENTO, 73- *Mem:* Am Soc Microbiol; Sigma Xi; Wildlife Dis Asn. *Res:* Bacterial and fungal diseases of animals which may be transmitted to humans. *Mailing Add:* Dept of Biol Sci Calif State Univ Sacramento CA 95819

CALDERONE, RICHARD ARTHUR, b Niles, Ohio, Sept 3, 42; m 70; c 4. MICROBIOLOGY. *Educ:* Ohio Univ, Athens, BS, 65; WVa Univ, PhD(microbiol), 70. *Prof Exp:* Fel mycol, WVa Univ, 70-71; asst prof biol, Washington & Jefferson Col, 71-73; fel med mycol, Skin & Cancer Hosp, Temple Univ, 73-74; asst prof, 74-79, ASSOC PROF MICROBIOL, GEORGETOWN UNIV, 79- *Mem:* Am Soc Microbiol; Med Mycol Soc Am. *Res:* Pathogenesis of endocarditis caused by the yeast Candida albicans, using a rabbit model to study the immune response and how Candida attaches to damaged heart valve endothelium. *Mailing Add:* Microbiol Dept Med Dent Bldg 3900 Reservoir Rd NW Washington DC 20007

CALDERWOOD, KEITH WRIGHT, b Henefer, Utah, July 28, 24; m 50; c 5. GEOLOGY. *Educ:* Brigham Young Univ, BS, 50, MS, 51. *Prof Exp:* Geologist, Phillips Petrol Co, 51-56, staff geologist, 57-59, dist geologist, 59-69; consult geologist, 69-76, PRES, CALDERWOOD & MANGUS, INC, 71- *Mem:* Asn Prof Geol Scientists; Am Asn Petrol Geologists. *Res:* Petroleum and mineral exploration and development. *Mailing Add:* Calderwood & Mangus Inc 7900 Honeysuckle Anchorage AK 99502

CALDWELL, A(RCHIE) LEE, JR, physiology, biochemistry, see previous edition

CALDWELL, AUGUSTUS GEORGE, b Belleville, Can, Apr 7, 23; US citizen; m 48; c 4. SOIL CHEMISTRY. *Educ:* Univ Toronto, BSA, 46, MSA, 48; Iowa State Univ, PhD(soil fertil), 55. *Prof Exp:* Soil surv scientist, Ont Agr Col, 46-52, lectr soil fertil res, 52-54; from asst prof to assoc prof soil chem, Tex A&M Univ, 54-62; PROF AGRON, LA STATE UNIV, BATON ROUGE, 62- *Mem:* Am Soc Agron; Soil Sci Soc Am; Am Chem Soc. *Res:* Soil fertility; soil organic phosphorus; soil tests for phosphorus; plant response to fertilizers; soil characterization; economics of fertilizer use; soil mineralogy. *Mailing Add:* Dept Agron La State Univ Baton Rouge LA 70803

CALDWELL, CARLYLE GORDON, b Little Rock, Ark, Mar 13, 14; m 40; c 1. PLANT CHEMISTRY. *Educ:* Iowa State Col, BS, 36, PhD, 40. *Prof Exp:* Mem staff, 40-47, res dir, 47-55, vpres res, 55-62, dir, 62-66, exec vpres, 66-68, PRES, NAT STARCH & CHEM CORP, 69-, CHIEF EXEC OFFICER, 75-; DIR, RES CORP, 73- *Concurrent Pos:* Chmn, Nat Starch & Chem Corp, 78- *Honors & Awards:* Claude S Hudson Award, Am Chem Soc, 65; Alsberg-Schoch Award, Am Asn Cereal Chemists, 72. *Mem:* Am Chem Soc; Indust Res Inst; Am Inst Chemists; Asn Res Dirs. *Res:* Fractionation of starch; starch derivatives; polymers. *Mailing Add:* Nat Starch & Chem Corp 10 Finderne Ave Bridgewater NJ 08807

CALDWELL, CHRISTOPHER STERLING, b Washington, DC, June 22, 42; m 66; c 1. COMPUTATIONAL FLUID DYNAMICS, NUMERICAL ANALYSIS. *Educ:* Johns Hopkins Univ, BA, 65; Univ Md, MA, 68, PhD(math), 71. *Prof Exp:* Mathematician, Naval Oceanog Off, 70-72; sr mathematician, 72-80, FEL MATHEMATICIAN, BETTIS ATOMIC POWER LAB, 80- *Mem:* Am Math Soc; Soc Indust & Appl Math; Am Nuclear Soc; Sigma Xi. *Res:* Computer simulation of fluid flow. *Mailing Add:* 340 McCombs Rd Venetia PA 15367

CALDWELL, DABNEY WITHERS, b Charlottesville, Va, Mar 26, 27; div; c 4. GEOLOGY. *Educ:* Bowdoin Col, AB, 49; Brown Univ, MA, 53; Harvard Univ, PhD(geol), 59. *Prof Exp:* Geologist, US Geol Surv, 52-54; from instr to asst prof geol, Wellesley Col, 55-67; ASSOC PROF GEOL, BOSTON UNIV, 67-, CHMN GEOL, 81- *Mem:* AAAS; Am Geophys Union; Sigma Xi. *Res:* Glacial geology and fluvial processes in geomorphology; environmental geology; surficial geologic mapping, glacial geology, in the wildlands of northern Maine; groundwater and surface water studies in the northeastern states, in the southern United States and Europe. *Mailing Add:* 725 Commonwealth Ave Boston MA 02215

CALDWELL, DANIEL R, b Oakland, Calif, Feb 29, 36; m 61; c 2. MICROBIOLOGY, BIOCHEMISTRY. *Educ:* Reed Col, BA, 58; Univ Md, MS, 65, PhD(dairy sci), 69. *Prof Exp:* Microbiologist, Agr Res Serv, USDA, Md, 60-69; asst prof microbiol, 69-75, ASSOC PROF MICROBIAL PHYSIOL, UNIV WYO, 75- *Mem:* AAAS; Am Soc Microbiol; Sigma Xi. *Res:* Anaerobic bacterial nutrition and metabolism; rumen microbiology; porphyrin biosynthesis; bacterial carbohydrate fermentation; carbon dioxide fixation; mineral nutrition; anaerobic electron transport; cytochromes in ruminal bacteria. *Mailing Add:* Div of Microbiol & Vet Med Univ of Wyo Laramie WY 82071

CALDWELL, DAVID H(UME), b Lansing, Mich, Aug 9, 14; m 34; c 4. CIVIL ENGINEERING. *Educ:* Univ Calif, BS, 38; Univ Ill, MS, 40, PhD(civil eng), 42. *Prof Exp:* Asst civil eng, Univ Ill, 38-41; city sanit engr, Springfield, Ill, 41; instr sanit eng, Univ Ill, 41-42; asst sanit engr, Calif State Bd Health, 42-43; sanit engr, US War Dept, 43-44; sr sanit engr, US Dept Navy, 44-47; DIR & CHMN, BROWN & CALDWELL CONSULT ENGRS, 76- *Mem:* Fel Am Soc Civil Engrs; Am Water Works Asn; Am Soc Testing & Mat. *Res:* Water supply and treatment; sewage collection and disposal; design; construction; operation; planning. *Mailing Add:* Brown & Caldwell 1501 N Broadway Walnut Creek CA 94596

CALDWELL, DAVID KELLER, b Louisville, Ky, Aug 6, 28. VERTEBRATE BIOLOGY. *Educ:* Washington & Lee Univ, AB, 49; Univ Mich, MS, 50; Univ Fla, PhD(biol), 57. *Prof Exp:* Asst zool, Univ Fla, 52-55, res asst, 55; curatorial asst fishes, State Mus, Fla, 55-57; fishery res biologist, US Fish & Wildlife Serv, 57-60; cur ichthol & marine mammals, Los Angeles County Mus Natural Hist, 60-67; cur & dir res, Marineland of Fla, 67-70; assoc prof, 70-76; RES SCIENTIST, INST ADVAN STUDY COMMUN PROCESSES, UNIV FLA, 76- *Concurrent Pos:* Res assoc, State Mus, Fla, 57-70, field assoc, 75-; res assoc, Ichthol Inst Jamaica, 58-70 & Los Angeles County Mus Natural Hist, 68-80. *Mem:* Am Soc Mammalogists; fel Am Inst Fishery Res Biologists; fel AAAS. *Res:* Marine ichthyology, herpetology, mammalogy, and ecology; zoogeography of fishes; cetology; animal communication. *Mailing Add:* Rte 1 Box 121 St Augustine FL 32084

CALDWELL, DAVID ORVILLE, b Los Angeles, Calif, Jan 5, 25; div; c 2. EXPERIMENTAL HIGH ENERGY PHYSICS. *Educ:* Calif Inst Technol, BS, 47; Univ Calif, Los Angeles, MA, 49, PhD(physics), 53. *Prof Exp:* From instr to assoc prof physics, Mass Inst Technol, 54-63; vis assoc prof, Princeton Univ, 63-64; lectr, Univ Calif, Berkeley, 64-65, PROF PHYSICS, UNIV CALIF, SANTA BARBARA, 65- *Concurrent Pos:* Consult, Radiation Lab, Univ Calif, 50-51, 65-70, Am Sci & Eng, 59-60, Inst Defense Anal, 60-67 & Defense Commun Planning Group, 66-70; NSF fel, Univ Calif, Los Angeles & Edigenossiche Tech Univ, 53-54; physicist, Radiation Lab, Univ Calif, 57, 58 & 64-67; NSF sr fel, 60-61 & Ford Found fel, 61-62; Guggenheim fel, Europ Orgn Nuclear Res, 71-72; mem high energy physics adv panel, Energy Res & Develop Agency & Dept of Energy, 74-78. *Mem:* Fel Am Phys Soc. *Mailing Add:* Dept of Physics Univ of Calif Santa Barbara CA 93106

CALDWELL, DOUGLAS RAY, b Lansing, Mich, Feb 16, 36; m 61; c 2. OCEANOGRAPHY. *Educ:* Univ Chicago, AB, 55, BS, 57, MS, 58, PhD(physics), 64. *Prof Exp:* NSF fel, Cambridge Univ, 63-64; res geophysicist, Inst Geophys & Planetary Physics, Univ Calif, San Diego, 64-68; from asst prof to assoc prof, 68-77, PROF, DEPT OCEANOG, ORE STATE UNIV, 77- *Res:* Physics of fluids; hydrodynamics and magnetohydrodynamics; stability theory; measurements in the oceans. *Mailing Add:* Dept of Oceanog Ore State Univ Corvallis OR 97331

CALDWELL, ELWOOD F, b Gladstone, Man, Apr 3, 23; nat US; m 78; c 2. FOOD SCIENCE. *Educ:* Univ Man, BSc, 43; Univ Toronto, MA, 49, PhD(nutrit), 53; Univ Chicago, MBA, 56. *Prof Exp:* Chemist, Lake of Woods Milling Co, 43-48; res chemist, Can Breweries Ltd, 48-49; chief chemist, Christie, Brown & Co, 49-51; res assoc nutrit, Univ Toronto, 51-53; group leader processing & packaging res, Quaker Oats Co, 53-62, asst dir foods res, 62-69, dir res & develop, 70-72; PROF FOOD SCI & NUTRIT & HEAD DEPT, UNIV MINN, 72- *Concurrent Pos:* Chmn bd dirs, Dairy Qual Control Inst, Inc, St Paul, Minn, 73- *Honors & Awards:* Cert Appreciation Patriotic Civilian Serv, Dept Defense, Army Mat Command, 70. *Mem:* Am Home Econ Asn; Can Inst Food Sci & Technol; fel Inst Food Technol; Am Asn Cereal Chem; Chem Inst Can. *Res:* Food chemistry and technology; experimental, clinical and community nutrition; food service management; educational and research administration. *Mailing Add:* Dept of Food Sci & Nutrit 1334 Eckles Ave St Paul MN 55108

CALDWELL, FRED T, JR, b Hot Springs, Ark, May 12, 25; m 47; c 2. SURGERY. *Educ:* Baylor Univ, BS, 46; Washington Univ, MD, 50. *Prof Exp:* Assoc prof surg, Univ Hosp, State Univ NY Upstate Med Ctr, 58-67; PROF SURG, MED CTR, UNIV ARK, LITTLE ROCK, 67- *Concurrent Pos:* Res fel, Washington Univ, 57-58; Cancer Soc clin fel, 57-58; surg consult, Little Rock Vet Admin Hosp, 67- *Mem:* Am Col Surg; Am Physiol Soc; Soc Univ Surg; Am Surg Asn. *Res:* Energy balance following trauma, particularly after thermal burns; pathogenesis of cholesterol gall stones. *Mailing Add:* Univ of Ark Med Ctr 4301 W Markham St Little Rock AR 72204

CALDWELL, GLYN GORDON, b St Louis, Mo, Jan 14, 34; m 60; c 3. EPIDEMIOLOGY, PUBLIC HEALTH. *Educ:* St Louis Univ, BS, 60; Univ Mo, MS, 62, MD, 66. *Prof Exp:* Intern med, USPHS Hosp, Brighton, Mass, 66-67; resident internal med, Cleveland Metrop Hosp, 69-71; res biologist virol, Ecol Invest Prog, 67-68, actg chief viral dis sect, 68-69, chief oncol & teratology activ, 71-73, asst chief cancer br, Cancer & Birth Defects Div, 73-74, chief field invest sect, 74-77, dep chief cancer br, Bur Epidemiol, 74-77, chief cancer br, Cancer Res Chronic Dis Div, Bur Epidemiol, 77-80, CHIEF CANCER BR, CHRONIC DIS DIV, CTR ENVIRON HEALTH, CTR DIS CONTROL, USPHS, 80- *Concurrent Pos:* Asst prof microbiol, Univ Kans Med Ctr, 67-73; lectr, Univ Mo Med Ctr, Kans City, 71-73; asst prof prev med epidemiol, Emory Univ, 74- *Mem:* Am Soc Microbiol; NY Acad Sci; Am Soc Prev Oncol; Int Asn Comp Res Leukemia & Related Dis. *Res:* Cancer epidemiology; tumor virology; hematology; oncology. *Mailing Add:* Ctr for Dis Control Cancer Br Bur of Epidemiol Atlanta GA 30333

CALDWELL, HENRY CECIL, JR, b Walnut Grove, Miss, Jan 21, 30; m 54; c 3. PHARMACEUTICAL CHEMISTRY, ORGANIC CHEMISTRY. *Educ:* Univ Miss, BS, 52, MS, 54; Univ Kans, PhD(pharmaceut org chem), 57. *Prof Exp:* Sr pharmaceut chemist, 57-62, group leader pharmaceut chem sect, 62-75, ASST DIR, SMITH KLINE & FRENCH LABS, 75- *Mem:* Am Chem Soc; Am Pharmaceut Asn. *Res:* Pharmaceutical product development; Mannich reaction; air suspension coating; drug latentiation; spasmolytics. *Mailing Add:* Smith Kline & French Labs 1500 Spring Garden St Philadelphia PA 19101

CALDWELL, J(OSEPH) J(EFFERSON), JR, b Weatherford, Tex, Oct 22, 15; m 40; c 3. MICROWAVE ELECTRONICS. *Educ:* Tex Tech Col, BS, 37; Mass Inst Technol, ScM, 38. *Prof Exp:* Mem staff, Sperry Gyroscope Co, 38-46; Int Tel & Tel Res Lab, 46-50 & Hughes Aircraft Co, 50-59; researcher strategic systs, Boeing Airplane Co, 59-60; researcher electrooptics, TRW Inc, 60-80; SR STAFF ENGR, SPACE & COMPUT GROUP, HUGHES AIRCRAFT CO, INC, 80- *Concurrent Pos:* Res assoc, Stanford Univ, 38, 41 & 43. *Mem:* Sr mem Inst Elec & Electronics Engrs; Am Phys Soc; Sigma Xi. *Res:* Microwave klystrons, magnetrons and high-powered traveling wave tubes; instrument landing, precision microwave bombing systems and microwave communication systems; atomic frequency standards; laser pumps; electric propulsion; laser target designator; electro-optical systems. *Mailing Add:* Hughes Aircraft Co Inc PO Box 92919 Los Angeles CA 90009

CALDWELL, JERRY, b Tallassee, Ala, May 1, 38; m 62; c 3. IMMUNOGENETICS, MOLECULAR GENETICS. *Educ:* Auburn Univ, BS, 60, MS, 62; Tex A&M Univ, PhD(animal breeding), 69. *Prof Exp:* Asst prof animal sci, Tex A&M Univ, 68-69; fel immunogenetics, Univ Calif, Davis, 69-70; asst prof, 70-79, ASSOC PROF ANIMAL SCI, TEX A&M UNIV, 79- *Mem:* Am Soc Animal Sci; Am Dairy Sci Asn; Int Soc Animal Blood Group Res. *Res:* Immunogenetics, especially antigenic components of red and white blood cells and spermatozoa molecular genetics, especially genetic variation of enzymes and other proteins of mammalian tissues. *Mailing Add:* Immunogenetics Lab Tex A&M Univ Dept Animal Sci College Station TX 77843

CALDWELL, JOHN JAMES, b Winnipeg, Man, Aug 4, 44; m 66; c 3. PLANETARY ATMOSPHERES, ASTRONOMY. *Educ:* Univ Man, BSc Hons, 65; Univ Western Ont, MSc, 66; Univ Wis-Madison, PhD(astron), 71. *Prof Exp:* Res assoc, Univ Wis-Madison, 71-72; res assoc astrophys, Princeton Univ, 72-77; ADJ ASST PROF ATMOSPHERIC SCI, STATE UNIV NY, STONY BROOK, 77- *Concurrent Pos:* Vis prof, Rutgers Univ, 73-77; interdisciplinary scientist space telescope, Marshall Space Flight Ctr, NASA, 78-; vis prof, Univ Hawaii, 81. *Mem:* Am Astron Soc; AAAS. *Res:* Theoretical planetary physics; infrared and radio observation of planets; space astronomy; ultraviolet spectrophotometry of plants. *Mailing Add:* Dept Earth & Space Sci State Univ NY Stony Brook NY 11794

CALDWELL, JOHN R, b Middletown, Conn, Oct 11, 18; m 47; c 5. INTERNAL MEDICINE. *Educ:* Lafayette Col, BA, 40; Temple Univ, MD, 43; Am Bd Internal Med, dipl, 55. *Prof Exp:* Med practitioner, Del, 47-50; staff physician, Med Clins, 52-54, physician-in-charge, Div Hypertension, 54-67, chief, Hypertension Sect, 67-80, STAFF PHYSICIAN, NEPHROL & HYPERTENSION DIV, HENRY FORD HOSP, DETROIT, 80- *Concurrent Pos:* Mem coun arteriosclerosis & mem med adv bd coun high blood pressure res, Am Heart Asn; clin assoc prof internal med, Med Sch, Univ Mich. *Mem:* AAAS; fel Am Col Physicians; AMA; Am Soc Internal Med. *Res:* Causes, effects and treatment of high arterial pressure; renal artery stenosis; pheochromocytoma; primary aldosteronism; pyelonephritis; social and psychologic factors favoring development of hypertension; compliance to treatment. *Mailing Add:* Nephrol & Hypertension Div Henry Ford Hosp Detroit MI 48202

CALDWELL, JOHN THOMAS, experimental nuclear physics, see previous edition

CALDWELL, LARRY D, b Manton, Mich, July 13, 32; m 59; c 4. ECOLOGY. *Educ:* Mich State Univ, BSc, 54, MS, 55; Univ Ga, PhD(zool), 60. *Prof Exp:* Asst prof biol, Southeastern La Col, 59-61; from asst prof to assoc prof, 61-69, PROF BIOL, CENT MICH UNIV, 69- *Mem:* AAAS; Am Soc Mammalogists; Am Ornith Union; Wildlife Soc. *Res:* Population and physiological ecology; mammalian population phenomena; competition in rodent populations; lipid levels and bird migration. *Mailing Add:* Dept of Biol Cent Mich Univ Mt Pleasant MI 48858

CALDWELL, MARTYN MATHEWS, b Denver, Colo, June 28, 41; m 67. PLANT ECOLOGY, PLANT PHYSIOLOGY. *Educ:* Colo State Univ, BS, 63; Duke Univ, PhD(bot), 67. *Prof Exp:* From asst prof to assoc prof, 67-75, PROF ECOL, UTAH STATE UNIV, 75- *Concurrent Pos:* NSF fel, Innsbruck, Austria, 68-69; chmn biol prog, Climatic Impact Assessment Prog, Dept Transp, 73-75; mem nat comt photobiol, Nat Acad Sci, 74-78 & Comt Impacts Stratospheric Change, 75-; Alexander von Humboldt sr US scientist res grant, Fed Repub Ger, 81. *Mem:* Ecol Soc Am; Am Soc Plant Physiologists; Brit Ecol Soc; Australian Soc Plant Physiologists; Soc Range Mgt. *Res:* Physiological ecology of plants under stress in arid and tundra environments; plant photosynthesis, transpiration, water relations, root growth and carbon balance; effects of solar ultraviolet radiation on plants. *Mailing Add:* Ecol Ctr Utah State Univ Logan UT 84322

CALDWELL, MARY ESTILL, b Columbus, Ohio, Feb 12, 96; m 25. BACTERIOLOGY. *Educ:* Univ Ariz, BS, 18, MS, 19; Univ Chicago, PhD(bact), 32. *Prof Exp:* From instr to asst prof biol, 19-32, from assoc prof to prof bact, 32-56, head dept bact, 35-56, PROF PHARMACOL & RES PHARMACOLOGIST, UNIV ARIZ, 57- *Mem:* Am Soc Microbiol; Am Pub Health Asn. *Res:* Viability mycobacterium tuberculosis; variation of certain Salmonellas; antibiotics; cancer chemotherapy; carcinogenesis; anti-inflammatory research. *Mailing Add:* Col of Pharm Univ of Ariz Tucson AZ 85721

CALDWELL, MELBA CARSTARPHEN, b Augusta, Ga, May 4, 21; m 60; c 2. VERTEBRATE ZOOLOGY, COMMUNICATIONS SCIENCE. *Educ:* Univ Ga, BS, 41; Univ Calif, Los Angeles, MA, 63. *Prof Exp:* Fishery aide marine zool, US Fish & Wildlife Serv, Ga, 56-59, fishery res biologist, 59-60; staff res assoc, Allan Hancock Found, Univ Southern Calif, 63-67; asst cur & assoc dir res, Marineland of Fla, 67-69; res instr, 70-76, ASST RES SCI, INST ADVAN STUDY COMMUN PROCESSES, UNIV FLA, 76- *Concurrent Pos:* Res assoc, Los Angeles County Mus Natural Hist, 61-80; field assoc, Fla State Mus, 75- *Mem:* fel AAAS. *Res:* Odontocete cetaceans, especially communication, life history and other aspects of general biology; systematics and distribution of marine fishes and odontocete cetaceans. *Mailing Add:* Rte 1 Box 121 St Augustine FL 32084

CALDWELL, RALPH RUSSELL, b Nanking, China, Sept 23, 22; US citizen; m 45; c 3. ELECTRICAL ENGINEERING. *Educ:* Iowa State Univ, BSEE, 43; Washington Univ, MSEE, 48; Univ Wis, PhD, 52. *Prof Exp:* Instr elec eng, Univ Wis, 48-51, asst prof, 52-54; res engr elec anal, 54-62, SR GROUP ENGR SYSTS ANAL, BOEING CO, 62- *Mem:* Inst Elec & Electronics Engrs; Opers Res Soc Am. *Res:* Systems analysis and applications of new methods of generating electric power for space applications; heat conversion; radiant energy; magneto hydrodynamics using solar and nuclear energy sources; command and control systems design; operations analysis for Inter-Continental Ballistic Missile weapons systems. *Mailing Add:* 8210 SE 67th Mercer Island WA 98040

CALDWELL, RICHARD STANLEY, physiological ecology, aquatic toxicology, see previous edition

CALDWELL, ROBERT WILLIAM, b Brunswick, Ga, Dec 27, 42; m 65; c 2. PHARMACOLOGY, PHYSIOLOGY. *Educ:* Ga Inst Technol, BS, 65; Emory Univ, PhD(basic health sci), 69. *Prof Exp:* Pharmacologist, Div Med Chem, Walter Reed Army Inst Res, 70-72; from asst prof to assoc prof, 72-79, PROF PHARMACOL, CTR HEALTH SCI, UNIV TENN, MEMPHIS, 79- *Mem:* Am Soc Pharmacol & Exp Therapeut; Soc Exp Biol & Med; Soc Neurosci. *Res:* Central nervous system control of hypertension; study of novel cardiac glycosides. *Mailing Add:* Dept Pharmacol Univ Tenn Ctr Health Sci Memphis TN 38163

CALDWELL, ROGER LEE, b Los Angeles, Calif, May 12, 38; m 66; c 2. BIOCHEMISTRY, PLANT PATHOLOGY. *Educ:* Univ Calif, Los Angeles, BS, 61; Univ Ariz, PhD(chem), 66. *Prof Exp:* Nat Acad Sci res assoc, US Food & Drug Admin, Washington, DC, 66-67; from asst prof to assoc prof plant path, 62-80, PROF SOILS, WATER & ENG, UNIV ARIZ, 80-, DIR COUN ENVIRON STUDIES, 74- *Mem:* Am Chem Soc; Am Phytopath Soc; Am Inst Biol Sci; Coun Agr Sci & Technol; Soil Conserv Soc Am. *Res:* Energy alternatives; environmental interactions of agriculture and society; effects of air pollution on plants; pesticide alternatives. *Mailing Add:* Dept Soil Water & Eng Univ Ariz Tucson AZ 85721

CALDWELL, SAMUEL CRAIG, b Kansas City, Mo, Sept 12, 19; m 52; c 1. ELECTRICAL ENGINEERING. *Educ:* Ill Inst Technol, MS, 51. *Prof Exp:* Eng analyst, Gen Elec Co, 51-57, sr syst engr, 57-59, advan develop specialist, 59-60; chief proj engr, Lear-Siegler Inc, Ohio, 60-65; tech staff asst to pres, Joslyn Mfg & Supply Co, Ill, 65-66; consult engr, 66-71; PRES, ELEC TECHNOL, INC, 71- *Mem:* Am Inst Aeronaut & Astronaut; AAAS; Inst Elec & Electronics Engrs. *Res:* Corona discharges phenomena; military system analysis, design and management; advanced control and generation system projects; electronic power conditioning and industrial distribution systems. *Mailing Add:* Elec Technol Inc 2317 Coley Forest Pl Raleigh NC 27612

CALDWELL, SLOAN DANIEL, b Lincolnton, NC, May 26, 43; m 69; c 2. AQUATIC ENTOMOLOGY, INVERTEBRATE ZOOLOGY. *Educ:* Western Carolina Univ, BS, 64; Univ Tenn, MS, 66; Univ Ga, PhD(entom), 73. *Prof Exp:* From instr to asst prof, 69-71, ASSOC PROF BIOL, GA COL, 76- *Concurrent Pos:* Consult, Ga Power Co, 72-73. *Res:* Population, trophic structure and taxonomy of benthic aquatic insects. *Mailing Add:* Dept Biol Ga Col Milledgeville GA 31061

CALDWELL, STEPHEN E, b Columbus, Ohio, Sept 17, 46; m 78. PHYSICS. *Educ:* Ohio State Univ, BSc, 69, MSc, 73, PhD(physics), 74. *Prof Exp:* Mem staff physics, US Army Ballistics Res Lab, 74-76; STAFF MEM PHYSICS, LOS ALAMOS SCI LAB, 76- *Mem:* Am Phys Soc. *Res:* Laser fusion; gas centrifuges. *Mailing Add:* Los Alamos Sci Lab Mail Stop 410 Los Alamos NM 87545

CALDWELL, WILLIAM GLEN ELLIOT, b Millport, Scotland, July 25, 32; m 61; c 3. GEOLOGY. *Educ:* Glasgow Univ, BSc, 54, PhD, 57. *Prof Exp:* Asst lectr geol, Glasgow Univ, 56-57; spec lectr, 57-58, from asst prof to assoc prof, 58-70, PROF GEOL, UNIV SASK, 70-, HEAD, DEPT GEOL SCI, 72- *Mem:* Paleont Soc; Brit Geol Asn; fel Geol Soc Am; Brit Paleont Asn; fel Geol Asn Can (pres, 80-81). *Res:* Stratigraphy and paleontology of Cretaceous System. *Mailing Add:* Dept of Geol Sci Univ of Sask Saskatoon SK S7H 0W0 Can

CALDWELL, WILLIAM L, radiology, deceased

CALDWELL, WILLIAM V, b Boyd, Tex, Sept 3, 17; m 53; c 2. MATHEMATICS. *Educ:* Tex Christian Univ, BA, 51; Univ Mich, MA, 56, PhD(math), 60. *Prof Exp:* Anal engr, transonic lab, Mass Inst Technol, 51-54; asst prof math, Univ Del, 59-61; from asst prof to assoc prof, 61-68, chmn dept, 66-78, PROF MATH, UNIV MICH, FLINT, 68- *Mem:* AAAS; Am Math Soc; Math Asn Am. *Res:* Vector spaces and algebras of light interior functions; theory of quasiconformal functions. *Mailing Add:* Dept of Math Univ of Mich 1321 E Court St Flint MI 48503

CALE, ALBERT DUNCAN, JR, b Windsor, NC, Sept 18, 28; m 54; c 4. MEDICINAL CHEMISTRY. *Educ:* Elon Col, BS, 56; Univ SC, MS, 58. *Prof Exp:* Res chemist, 58-63, sr res chemist, 63-75, res assoc med, 75-81, GROUP LEADER & MGR, A H ROBINS, INC, 81- *Mem:* Am Chem Soc. *Res:* Small ring heterocycles. *Mailing Add:* A H Robins Inc 1211 Sherwood Ave Richmond VA 23220

CALE, WILLIAM GRAHAM, JR, b Philadelphia, Pa, Dec 10, 47; m 74. ECOLOGY. *Educ:* Pa State Univ, BS, 69; Univ Ga, PhD(ecol), 75. *Prof Exp:* Consult ecosyst modeling, Colo State Univ, 74-75; asst prof, 75-80, ASSOC PROF ENVIRON SCI, UNIV TEX, DALLAS, 80- *Mem:* Am Inst Biol Sci; Soc Comput Simulation; AAAS; Ecol Soc Am. *Res:* Ecosystem modeling and systems analysis; theoretical ecology; terrestrial ecology, error analysis. *Mailing Add:* Environ Sci Fac Box 688 Univ of Tex at Dallas Richardson TX 75080

CALE, WILLIAM ROBERT, b Paris, Ont, May 4, 13; m 46; c 2. INORGANIC CHEMISTRY, CHEMICAL ENGINEERING. *Educ:* Univ Toronto, BASc, 35, MASc, 36. *Prof Exp:* Asst to works chemist, Elec Reduction Co Can, Ltd, Erco Industs Ltd, 36-38, works chemist, 38-53, tech serv mgr, 53, mgr res technol serv, 54-55, mgr planning & mkt res div, 56-58, mgr eng serv div, 58-62, mgr chlorate develop dept, 63-64, mgr patents & inventions dept, 64-68, mgr patents & info, 68-78, consult, 78-80. *Concurrent Pos:* Mem exec bd, Can Comt Int Water Pollution Res, 75-77. *Mem:* Fel Chem Inst Can; Can Pulp & Paper Asn. *Res:* Production processes and applications of phosphorus compounds; chlorates and chlorine dioxide; long-range planning market research and patents; environmental affairs. *Mailing Add:* 53 Greenbrook Dr Toronto ON M6M 2J8 Can

CALEDONIA, GEORGE ERNEST, b Boston, Mass, Nov 9, 41; m 65; c 3. PHYSICAL CHEMISTRY, CHEMICAL PHYSICS. *Educ:* Northeastern Univ, AB, 65, MS, 67. *Prof Exp:* Prin scientist gas phase chem, Avco Everett Res Lab, Avco Corp, 67-73; mgr environ sci, 73-80, VPRES RES, PHYS SCI INC, 80- *Mem:* Am Phys Soc; Am Chem Soc; Am Geophy Union. *Res:* Gas phase kinetics; electron excitation phenomena; absorption and transfer of radiative emission; laser physics; discharge physics; pollutant detection and monitoring; reentry physics; aeronomy. *Mailing Add:* Phys Sci Inc 30A Commerce Way Woburn MA 01801

CALEHUFF, GIRARD LESTER, b Williamsport, Pa, Oct 13, 25; m 48; c 5. FLUID MECHANICS, MATHEMATICS. *Educ:* Pa State Univ, BS, 49, MS, 52. *Prof Exp:* Res asst, Pa State Univ, 49-54, asst prof eng res, 54-56; group leader, 56-61, res dir, 61-63, paper mill supt, 63-68, tech dir, 68, res dir, 69-70, asst mgr, 70-75, mill mgr, 75-79, MGR FACIL & PLANNING, WESTVACO CORP, 79- *Mem:* Am Tech Asn Pulp & Paper Indust; Am Soc Mech Engrs; Am Inst Aeronaut & Astronaut; Can Pulp & Paper Asn. *Res:* Turbulent boundary layers in adverse pressure gradients; turbulence measurements in liquids and gases with application to underwater ordnance; dilute fluid suspensions of papermaking fibers; computer control of paper machines. *Mailing Add:* Westvaco Corp 299 Park Ave New York NY 10171

CALENDAR, RICHARD, b Hackensack, NJ, Aug 2, 40; m 69; c 2. MOLECULAR BIOLOGY. *Educ:* Duke Univ, BS, 62; Stanford Univ, PhD(biochem), 67. *Prof Exp:* Fel microbial genetics, Karolinska Inst, Sweden, 67-68; asst prof, 69-72, assoc prof, 72-76, PROF MOLECULAR BIOL, UNIV CALIF, BERKELEY, 76- *Concurrent Pos:* Alexander von Humboldt fel, Max Planck Inst Biochem, Munich, Ger, 73; Guggenheim fel, Karolinska Inst, Sweden, 79-80. *Res:* Gene control, and particle morphogenesis of bacterial viruses. *Mailing Add:* Dept of Molecular Biol Univ of Calif Berkeley CA 94720

CALESNICK, BENJAMIN, b Philadelphia, Pa, Dec 27, 15; m 45; c 1. PHARMACOLOGY. *Educ:* St Joseph's Col, Pa, BS, 38; Temple Univ, AM, 41; Hahnemann Med Col, MD, 44. *Prof Exp:* Lab asst pharmacol, 40-41, assoc, 46-57, asst prof, 57-62, dir human pharmacol, 57-70, PROF PHARMACOL MED, HAHNEMANN MED COL, 62-, DIR DIV HUMAN PHARMACOL, 70- *Concurrent Pos:* Vis instr, Univ Pa, 50; lectr, Women's Med Col Pa, 51-52; chief hypertension clin, St Joseph Hosp, 58- *Mem:* Am Soc Pharmacol & Exp Therapeut; Am Col Clin Pharmacol (pres, 76-78); NY Acad Sci; Soc Exp Biol & Med; Soc Toxicol. *Res:* Human and clinical pharmacology. *Mailing Add:* Div Human Pharmacol Hahnemann Med Col & Hosp Philadelphia PA 19102

CALEY, EARLE RADCLIFFE, b Cleveland, Ohio, May 14, 00; m 25; c 3. ANALYTICAL CHEMISTRY. *Educ:* Baldwin-Wallace Col, BS, 23; Ohio State Univ, MS, 25, PhD(anal chem), 28. *Hon Degrees:* DSc, Baldwin-Wallace Col, 67. *Prof Exp:* Asst chem, Baldwin-Wallace Col, 21-23; teacher, high sch, Ohio, 23-24, prin, 25-27; from instr to asst prof chem, Princeton

Univ, 28-42; chief chemist, Wallace Labs, 42-46; from assoc prof to prof, 46-70, EMER PROF CHEM, OHIO STATE UNIV, 70- *Concurrent Pos:* Chemist Agora Excavation Staff, Athens, Greece, 37; lectr & instr sci & mgt defense & war training, Princeton Univ, 42-45. *Honors & Awards:* Lewis Prize, Am Philos Soc, 40; Ohio J Sci Res Prize, 52; Dexter Award, Am Chem Soc, 66. *Mem:* AAAS; Am Chem Soc; Hist Sci Soc; fel Am Numis Soc. *Res:* Early history of chemistry; direct determination of sodium; analytical chemistry of the alkali and alkaline earth metals; new laboratory apparatus for analytical operations; reactions of hydriodic acid with detection and separation of difficultly soluble compounds; precipitations in nonaqueous solutions; application of chemistry to archaeology. *Mailing Add:* Dept Chem Ohio State Univ Columbus OH 43210

CALEY, WENDELL J, JR, b Philadelphia, Pa, Jan 16, 28; m 52; c 5. PHYSICS. *Educ:* Houghton Col, BS, 50; Univ Rochester, MS, 59; Temple Univ, PhD(physics), 63. *Prof Exp:* Develop engr, Eastman Kodak Co, 53-59; from instr to asst prof physics & head dept, Gordon Col, 61-66; assoc prof, 66-72, head dept, 67-74, PROF PHYSICS, EASTERN NAZARENE COL, 72- *Mem:* Am Asn Physics Teachers. *Res:* Hypervelocity projectiles; optics; laser light scattering in liquids. *Mailing Add:* Dept of Physics Eastern Nazarene Col Quincy MA 02170

CALHOON, DONALD ALAN, b Toledo, Ohio, July 20, 50. MICROBIOLOGY. *Educ:* Va Polytech Inst & State Univ, BS, 72, PhD(microbiol), 79; Univ NH, MS, 75. *Prof Exp:* Physical sci aide, Serol Lab, Fed Bur Invest, 72-73; FEL, ORAL BIOL DEPT, SCH DENT, STATE UNIV NY, BUFFALO, 79- *Mem:* Am Soc Microbiol; AAAS; Int Asn Dent Res; Am Asn Dent Res; Sigma Xi. *Res:* Characterization of periodontopathic bacteria including isolation, biochemical characterization, plasmid isolation, cellular fatty acid and soluble protein analyses of these organisms. *Mailing Add:* Oral Biol Dept State Univ NY 4510 Main St Buffalo NY 14226

CALHOON, ROBERT ELLSWORTH, b Los Angeles, Calif, Dec 29, 38; m 69. QUANTITATIVE GENETICS. *Educ:* San Diego State Univ, AB, 61, MS, 67; Purdue Univ, PhD(genetics), 72. *Prof Exp:* Fel, Purdue Univ, 72-73; asst prof, 73-80, ASSOC PROF BIOL, QUEENS COL, NY, 80- *Mem:* Genetics Soc Am; Am Inst Biol Sci; Sigma Xi. *Res:* Genetic selection and correlated response of quantitative characters in Tribolium and Drosophila. *Mailing Add:* Dept of Biol Queens Col Flushing NY 11367

CALHOON, STEPHEN WALLACE, JR, b Morrow Co, Ohio, Oct 21, 30; m 52; c 3. ANALYTICAL CHEMISTRY. *Educ:* Houghton Col, BS, 53; Ohio State Univ, MSc, 58, PhD(chem), 63. *Prof Exp:* From instr to assoc prof chem, Houghton Col, 56-64, prof, 64-78, head dept, 71-78; DEAN, CENT WESLEYAN COL, 78- *Concurrent Pos:* Asst instr, Ohio State Univ, 60-63. *Mem:* Am Chem Soc; Am Sci Affiliation; Am Asn Higher Educ. *Res:* Simultaneous analysis of carbon, hydrogen and nitrogen in organic compounds; effects of impurities on properties of ultrapure metals; cardiac-pacemaker electrode decomposition product analysis. *Mailing Add:* Dept of Chem Houghton Col Houghton NY 14744

CALHOON, THOMAS BRUCE, physiology, deceased

CALHOUN, BERTRAM ALLEN, b Petoskey, Mich, May 30, 25; m 48; c 5. MAGNETISM. *Educ:* Univ Man, BSc, 47; Wesleyan Univ, MA, 48; Mass Inst Technol, PhD(physics), 53. *Prof Exp:* Asst grad div appl math, Brown Univ, 48-49; asst, Lab Insulation Res, Mass Inst Technol, 49-53; res engr, Westinghouse Res Labs, 53-56; res staff mem, Res Ctr, 56-66, SR PHYSICIST, DEVELOP LAB, IBM CORP, 66- *Mem:* AAAS; fel Am Phys Soc. *Res:* Magnetic properties of ferrites and garnets. *Mailing Add:* IBM Corp 5600 Cottle Rd San Jose CA 95193

CALHOUN, CALVIN L, b Atlanta, Ga, Jan 7, 27; m 48; c 1. CLINICAL NEUROLOGY, ANATOMY. *Educ:* Morehouse Col, BS, 48; Atlanta Univ, MS, 50; Meharry Med Col, MD, 60. *Prof Exp:* Instr biol, Morehouse Col, 50-51; from instr to assoc prof anat & actg chmn dept, 51-72, PROF ANAT & CHMN DEPT, MEHARRY MED COL, 72-, ASSOC PROF MED & DIR DIV NEUROL, 66- *Concurrent Pos:* Resident fel neurol, Univ Minn, 62-65, Nat Inst Neurol Dis & Blindness res fel, 65-66; resource consult, Elem Curric, Minneapolis City Schs, 65-66. *Mem:* AAAS; Am Acad Neurol; Am Asn Anatomists; Nat Med Asn. *Res:* Microscopic anatomy; electron microscopic evaluation of the ultra structure of the evolution of experimental cerebral infarction. *Mailing Add:* 4217 King's Court Nashville TN 37218

CALHOUN, DAVID H, b Chattanooga, Tenn, Nov 9, 42. MICROBIOLOGY, BIOCHEMISTRY. *Educ:* Birmingham Southern Col, BA, 65; Univ Ala, Birmingham, PhD(microbiol), 69. *Prof Exp:* NIH fels, Baylor Col Med, 69-71 & Univ Calif, Irvine, 71-72, instr microbiol, 72-73; asst prof, 73-80, ASSOC PROF MICROBIOL, MT SINAI SCH MED, 80- *Concurrent Pos:* NSF res grant, Mt Sinai Sch Med, 74-76. *Honors & Awards:* Irma T Hirschl Career Scientist Award, 80. *Mem:* Am Soc Microbiol; Sigma Xi; Am Soc Biol Chem; NY Acad Sci. *Res:* Control of gene expression. *Mailing Add:* Dept Microbiol Mt Sinai Sch of Med New York NY 10029

CALHOUN, FRANK GILBERT, b Charleston, WVa, Mar 13, 39; m 66; c 3. TROPICAL AGRICULTURE & AGRONOMY. *Educ:* Ohio State Univ, BS, 61, MS, 68; Univ Fla, PhD(soil sci), 71. *Prof Exp:* Asst prof soil sci & dir, Soil Characterization Lab, Univ Fla, 71-75, assoc prof & chief of party, El Salvador Proj, 75-79; PROF TROPICAL SOILS, TEX A&M UNIV, 79- *Concurrent Pos:* proj develop officer, Int Progs, Tex A&M Univ, 79-; prin investr soil mgt res, WAfrica, 81- *Mem:* Am Soc Agron; Soil Sci Soc Am; Sigma Xi; Int Soc Soil Sci. *Res:* Properties and management of soils in the semi-arid tropics of Africa and meso-America. *Mailing Add:* Soil & Crop Sci Dept Tex A&M Univ College Station TX 77843

CALHOUN, JOHN BUMPASS, b Elkton, Tenn, May 11, 17; m 42; c 2. ECOLOGY. *Educ:* Univ Va, BS, 39; Northwestern Univ, MS, 42, PhD(zool), 43. *Prof Exp:* Instr biol, Emory Univ, 43-44; instr zool & ornith, Ohio State Univ, 44-46; res assoc parasitol, Johns Hopkins Univ, 46-49; NIH spec fel, Jackson Mem Lab, 49-51; psychologist, US Army Med Serv Grad Sch, 51-54; psychologist, Ment Health Intramural Res Prog, 54-71, CHIEF SECT, RES BEHAVIORAL SYSTS, LAB BRAIN EVOLUTION & BEHAV, DIV BIOL & BIOCHEM RES, NIMH, 71- *Mem:* Ecol Soc Am; Wildlife Soc; Am Soc Mammal; Am Soc Naturalists; Soc Gen Systs Res. *Res:* Twenty-four hour activity rhythms; vertebrate ecology and social behavior; natural selection; ecology of the Norway rat; zoogeography; population and mental health; dialogue among scientists; theory of emotion and motivation; environmental design; information and conceptual evolution. *Mailing Add:* NIMH Bldg 110 9000 Rockville Pike Bethesda MD 20205

CALHOUN, JOHN C, JR, b Betula, Pa, Mar 21, 17; m; c 4. PETROLEUM ENGINEERING. *Educ:* Pa State Univ, BS, 37, MS, 41, PhD(petrol & natural gas eng), 46; Ripon Col, Wis, DSc, 75. *Prof Exp:* Eng trainee, Shell Oil Co, Okla, 37; asst petrol eng, Pa State Univ, 37-45; prof petrol & natural gas eng & head dept, Pa State Univ, 50-55; dean eng & dir eng exp sta & eng & exten serv, Tex A&M Univ, 55-57, vpres eng, Col Syst, 57-60, v chancellor for develop, univ syst, 60-63; sci adv, US Dept Interior, DC, 63-65; acting dir, Water Resources Res, 64; vpres progs, 65-71, dean geosci, 69-71, sea grant prog dir, 69-72; vpres acad affairs, 71-77, DISTINGUISHED PROF PETROL ENG, UNIV SYST TEX A&M UNIV, 65-, EXEC V CHANCELLOR PROGS, 77- *Concurrent Pos:* Exec dir & pres, Gulf Univs Res Corp, 66-69; chmn spec study group sonic boom in rel to man, US Dept Interior, 67-68, chmn marine affairs action group, 70; mem comt mineral sci & technol, Nat Acad Sci-Nat Res Coun, 67-69; chmn comt oceanog, Nat Acad Sci, 67-70, chmn ocean sci affairs bd, 70-, chmn naval studies bd, 74-; chmn bd, Univ Corp Atmos Res, 68-71; mem, Presidential Task Force Oceanog, 69; chmn, President's Santa Barbara Oil Spill Panel & Panel on Union Oil Lease, 69; chmn marine affairs action group, 70; coun mem, Tex Coastal & Marine Coun, 72-; mem res coord panel, Gas Res Inst, 77-; dir, Tex Petrol Res Comt, 78- *Mem:* Hon mem Am Inst Mining, Metall & Petrol Engrs; hon mem Am Soc Eng Educ (vpres, 68-71); Am Soc Petrol Engrs (pres, 64); Inst Nautical Archaeol; Marine Technol Soc (pres, 76-77). *Res:* Petroleum and natural gas production; reservoir engineering; core analysis; behavior of porous materials. *Mailing Add:* Tex A&M Univ Syst College Station TX 77843

CALHOUN, MARY LOIS, b Lake City, Iowa, Mar 7, 04. HISTOLOGY, HEMATOLOGY. *Educ:* Iowa State Col, BS, 24, MS, 31, DVM, 39, PhD(histol, hemat), 46. *Prof Exp:* Technician vet anat, Iowa State Col, 28-33, from asst to instr, 33-43, 43; from instr to prof anat, Mich State Univ, 43-72, chmn dept, 48-67, emer prof, 72-79; RETIRED. *Mem:* Am Vet Med Asn; Women's Vet Med Asn; Am Asn Vet Anat; Am Asn Anatomists. *Res:* Microscopic anatomy of the dog and rat and of digestive tract of the chicken; bone marrow of the horse and cow; blood of mouse and swine; comparative histology of the integuments of domestic animals. *Mailing Add:* Dept Anatomy Mich State Univ East Lansing MI 48823

CALHOUN, MILLARD CLAYTON, b Philadelphia, Pa, Aug 25, 35; m 54; c 7. ANIMAL NUTRITION. *Educ:* Univ Del, BS, 58, MS, 60; Univ Conn, PhD(animal nutrit), 67. *Prof Exp:* Res asst animal sci, Univ Del, 58-60; res asst, Univ Conn, 61-66; asst prof animal nutrit, Univ Del, 67-68; asst prof, 68-71, ASSOC PROF ANIMAL SCI, TEX A&M UNIV, 71- *Concurrent Pos:* consult ruminant nutrit & physiology, US AID, Argentina, 72. *Mem:* Am Soc Animal Sci; Am Inst Nutrit; Sigma Xi. *Res:* Endocrine factors in bovine ketosis; fat soluble vitamins and their interrelationships in the bovine; vitamin A and cerebrospinal fluid dynamics; primary acute hypovitaminosis A; feeder lamb nutrition and management; toxic range plants. *Mailing Add:* Agr Res Exten Ctr Tex A&M Univ San Angelo TX 76902

CALHOUN, NOAH ROBERT, b Clarendon, Ark, Mar 23, 21; m 50; c 2. ORAL SURGERY, DENTAL RESEARCH. *Educ:* Howard Univ, DDS, 48; Tufts Univ, MSD(oral surg), 55. *Prof Exp:* Oral surgeon, Vet Admin Hosp, Tuskegee, Ala, 50-52 & Keesler AFB, Miss, 52-53; oral surgeon, Vet Admin Hosp, Tuskegee, Ala, 53-55, chief dent serv, 55-57, oral surgeon, 57-65; oral surgeon, 65-74, CHIEF DENTAL RES, VET ADMIN HOSP, WASHINGTON, DC, 69-, CHIEF DENT RES SERV, 74- *Concurrent Pos:* Mem, Adv Comt, Am Bd Oral Surgeons, 67-71; prof oral surg, Howard Univ, 68; prof lectr, Dent Col, Georgetown Univ; consult, DC Dent Examr Oral Surgeons, 70; mem, Nat Cancer Control Comt, 74 & Cancer Training Control Grant Comt, NIH, 72; consult, Am Bd Oral & Maxillofacial Surg, 81. *Mem:* Inst Med, Nat Acad Sci; Am Dent Asn; Am Soc Oral & Maxillofacial Surg; fel Am Col Dent; fel Int Col Dent. *Res:* The effects of zinc on bone metabolism. *Mailing Add:* Dent Serv Vet Admin Hosp 50 Irving St Washington DC 20422

CALHOUN, RALPH VERNON, JR, b Quincy, Fla, Feb 8, 49; m 71; c 2. GUIDANCE & CONTROL, APPLIED PHYSICS. *Educ:* Univ WFla, BS, 71; Fla State Univ, MS, 74, PhD(physics), 75. *Prof Exp:* Instr physics, Drake Univ, 75-77; PHYSICIST GUID, AIR FORCE ARMAMENT LAB, 77- *Mem:* Am Phys Soc. *Res:* Guidance and control for tactical weapons; radar; millimeterwave phenomonology; electromagnetic scattering. *Mailing Add:* Air Force Armament Lab DLMM Eglin AFB FL 32542

CALHOUN, WHEELER, JR, b Columbus, NMex, Nov 19, 16; m 42; c 3. AGRONOMY. *Educ:* Ore State Univ, BS, 46, MS, 53. *Prof Exp:* Res asst seed prod, 48-51, asst prof res farm oper, 55-65, assoc prof new crop res, 65-77, ASSOC PROF AGRON, ORE STATE UNIV, 77- FARM SUPT, 51- *Concurrent Pos:* Mem sci adv comt, Nat Flax Seed Inst, 63-; oilseed crop specialist, Khuzestan Water & Power Authority, Iran, 72-74. *Mem:* Crop Sci Soc Am; Am Soc Agron; Am Soc Oil Chemists; Int Asn Mechanization Field Exp. *Res:* New crop adaptation; agronomic production; variety testing of grass and legumes for seed production potentials. *Mailing Add:* Dept of Crop Sci Ore State Univ Corvallis OR 97331

CALI, J PAUL, b Providence, RI, Sept 8, 19; m 45; c 4. ANALYTICAL CHEMISTRY, METROLOGY. *Educ:* Brown Univ, BA, 49. *Prof Exp:* Chemist anal chem, US AEC, 49-50; chemist radio chem, Tracer Lab Inc, 50-51; supvry chemist, Cambridge Res Labs, US Air Force, 51-61, supvry chemist anal chem, 63-66; asst to vpres tech admin, Microwave Assoc, 61-62; CHIEF REF MAT, NAT BUREAU STANDARDS, 66- *Concurrent Pos:* Consult, WHO, 76-; mem coun, Nat Comt Clin Lab Standards, 78- *Honors & Awards:* Edward B Rosa Award, Nat Bur Standards, 76; Gold Medal Award, US Dept Com, 76. *Mem:* Int Union Pure & Appl Chem; Am Chem Soc; Am Asn Clin Chem; Int Standards Orgn; Int Orgn Legal Metrol. *Res:* Problems associated with production and certification of reference materials used for improving measurements in industry, environmental protection, health and science. *Mailing Add:* 16405 Kipling Rd Rockville MD 20855

CALIENDO, MARY ALICE, b Warren, Ohio, May 15, 49; m 71; c 2. NUTRITION. *Educ:* Univ Mass, BS, 71; Univ Maine, MS, 72; Cornell Univ, PhD(nutrit), 75. *Prof Exp:* Clin instr nutrit, Syracuse Univ, 74-76, asst prof, 76-78; asst prof, 78-81, ASSOC PROF NUTRIT, UNIV MD, 81- *Concurrent Pos:* Nutrit res consult, Loretto Geriatric Ctr, 76-78, USDA, 78. *Mem:* Am Dietetic Asn; Nutrit Today Soc; Am Pub Health Asn; Soc Nutrit Educ. *Res:* Socio-cultural correlates of nutritional status. *Mailing Add:* 13412 Parkland Rockville MD 20853

CALIGIURI, JOSEPH FRANK, b Columbus, Ohio, Feb 13, 28; m 48; c 4. CONTROL SYSTEMS. *Educ:* Ohio State Univ, BS, 49, MS, 51. *Prof Exp:* Asst proj engr, Sperry Gyroscope Div, Sperry Rand Corp, 51-52, proj engr, 52-56, sr engr, 56-58, eng sect head, 58-60, eng dept head, 60-63, asst chief engr, 63-66, chief engr, 66-69; vpres eng, guid & control systs div, 69-71, pres, 71-77, company vpres, 74-77, sr vpres, 77-81, GROUP EXEC, LITTON INDUSTS, 77-, EXEC PRES, 81- *Mem:* Am Inst Aeronaut & Astronaut; Inst Elec & Electronics Engrs; Am Inst Navig. *Res:* Inertial navigation and guidance systems for marine, aircraft, missile and space; gyroscopes, accelerometers; gimbal and strapdown platforms, electronics and computers; augmented navigation systems through use of optium filters. *Mailing Add:* Litton Indust 360 N Cresent Dr Beverly Hills CA 90210

CALIGIURI, ROBERT DOMENIC, b San Francisco, Calif, July 29, 51; m 74; c 1. ENVIRONMENTALLY ASSISTED CRACKING. *Educ:* Univ Calif, Davis, BS, 73; Stanford Univ, MS, 74, PhD(mat sci), 77. *Prof Exp:* Engr, Failure Anal Assocs, 74-77; metallurgist, Lawrence Livermore Nat Lab, 77-78; MAT SCIENTIST, SRI INT, 78- *Mem:* Am Soc Metals; Am Inst Mining, Metall & Petrol Engrs; Sigma Xi. *Res:* The relationship between microstructure, thermomechanical processing variables and the mechanical physical properties of metals; mechanisms of environmentally assisted cracking in metals; thermomechanical processing. *Mailing Add:* SRI Int AA 289 333 Ravenswood Ave Menlo Park CA 94025

CALIGUIRI, LAWRENCE ANTHONY, b McKees Rocks, Pa, Aug 10, 33; m 66; c 2. IMMUNOLOGY, VIROLOGY. *Educ:* Bethany Col, WVa, BS, 55; Loyola Univ, Ill, MD, 58; Am Bd Pediat, dipl, 64. *Prof Exp:* Intern, Med Ctr, Univ Pittsburgh, 58-59; from resident to chief resident pediat, Children's Hosp, Pittsburgh, 59-62; guest investr animal virol, 64-66, res assoc, 66-68, from asst prof to assoc prof, 68-73, ADJ PROF ANIMAL VIROL, ROCKEFELLER UNIV, 73- *Concurrent Pos:* Prof microbiol & immunol & chmn dept, Albany Med Col, 73-81; consult microbiologist, Albany Med Ctr Hosp, 73-81; vis prof virol, Rockefeller Univ, 80-81; res scholar, Am Cancer Soc, 80-81; adj prof microbiol & vis clin prof pediat, Univ Pittburgh, 81- *Mem:* Soc Gen Microbiol; Am Soc Cell Biologists; Am Soc Microbiol; Am Acad Pediat; Am Asn Immunol. *Res:* Virus-cell interactions and immune defense mechanisms. *Mailing Add:* Allergy & Clin Immunol Assocs 3520 Fifth Ave Pittsburgh PA 15213

CALINGAERT, PETER, b New York, NY, Aug 12, 31; m 63; c 2. COMPUTER SCIENCE. *Educ:* Swarthmore Col, BA, 52; Harvard Univ, AM, 54, PhD(appl math), 55. *Prof Exp:* Res assoc bus data processing, Comput Lab, Harvard Univ, 55-56, res fel & instr appl math, 56-57, asst prof, 57-62; systs planner, Int Bus Mach Corp, 62-63, systs eval mgr, 63-66; comput-related instr systs planning mgr, Sci Res Assocs, 66-68, PROF COMPUT SCI, UNIV NC, CHAPEL HILL, 68- *Concurrent Pos:* Nat lectr, Asn Comput Mach, 69-70 & 73-75. *Mem:* AAAS; Asn Comput Mach; Fedn Am Sci; Inst Elec & Electronics Engrs; AAUP. *Res:* Computer aided design of microelectric systems; program translation; man-machine interaction. *Mailing Add:* New West 035-A Chapel Hill NC 27514

CALIO, ANTHONY JOHN, b Philadelphia, Pa, Oct 27, 29; m 71; c 4. SPACE SCIENCES. *Educ:* Univ Pa, BA, 53. *Hon Degrees:* DSc, Wash Univ, St Louis, 74. *Prof Exp:* Scientist, Bettis Atomic Power Div, Westinghouse Elec Corp, 56-59; mgr nuclear physics sect, Am Mach & Foundry Co, Va, 59-61; exec vpres & mgr opers, Mt Vernon Res Co, 61-63; mem electronic res task group, NASA, Washington, DC, 63-64, chief res eng, Electronics Res Ctr, Boston, 64-65 & Manned Space Sci Prog Off, 65-67, asst dir planetary progs, Off Space Sci & Applns, 67-68, dep dir projs, Sci & Applns Div, Johnson Space Ctr, 68-69, dir sci & applns, 69-75, dep assoc adminr space sci, 75-77, assoc adminr space & terrestrial appln, NASA Hq, Washington, DC, 77-81; DEP ADMINR, NAT OCEANIC & ATMOSPHERIC ADMIN, 81- *Concurrent Pos:* Sloan fel, Stanford Univ Grad Sch Bus, 74-75; mem bd dirs, Ctr Community Design & Res, Rice Univ, 75- *Honors & Awards:* Except Serv Medal, NASA, 69, Except Sci Achievement Medal, 71 & Distinguished Serv Medal, 73. *Mem:* NY Acad Sci; Am Astronaut Soc; Am Geophys Union; Am Inst Aeronaut & Astronaut. *Mailing Add:* 7701 Hamilton Spring Rd Bethesda MD 20034

CALISH, S(YDNEY) R(ALPH), b Boston, Mass, May 15, 20; m 43; c 2. ORGANIC CHEMISTRY, MECHANICAL ENGINEERING. *Educ:* Univ Calif, AB, 41. *Prof Exp:* Tech asst, tech serv dept, W P Fuller & Co, 41; res engr, greases & indust lubes, Calif Res Corp, 45-47, group supvr, 57-62, supv res engr, 62-64, sr eng assoc, Chevron Res Co, 64-67; staff prod engr, Standard Oil Co Calif, 67-70, sr staff prod engr, 70-76; sr staff prod engr, 77-81, CONSULT LUBRICATION ENG, SALES & TECH SERV, CHEVRON USA, INC, 81- *Mem:* Am Soc Lubrication Engrs (pres, 64-65); Soc Automotive Engrs; Am Soc Testing & Mat. *Res:* Lubricant performance testing; evaluation of lubricants; jet engine oils; automatic transmission fluids; gear oils. *Mailing Add:* Chevron USA Inc 555 Market St San Francisco CA 94105

CALISHER, CHARLES HENRY, b New York, NY, July 14, 36; m 79; c 4. MICROBIOLOGY. *Educ:* Philadelphia Col Pharm & Sci, BSc, 58; Univ Notre Dame, MS, 61; Georgetown Univ, PhD(microbiol), 64. *Prof Exp:* Chief cell develop unit, Microbiol Assoc, Inc, Md, 61-65; chief isolation & serol lab, Ctr Dis Control, 65-69, res microbiologist, 69-74; RES MICROBIOLOGIST, USPHS, 74-, CHIEF, ARBOVIRUS REFERENCE BR, VBDD, 73- *Concurrent Pos:* Mem subcomt interrelationships among catalogued arboviruses, Am Comt Arthropod-borne Viruses, 69-; mem arboviruses comt, Res Reference Reagents Bd, Nat Inst Allergy & Infectious Dis, 70-; adj assoc prof, Univ NC, 71-73 & Ga State Univ, 71-75; mem comn viral infections, Armed Forces Epidemiol Bd, Dengue Task Force, 70-73; proj officer, PL 480, Arboviruses in Yugoslavia, 71-; consult lab virol, WHO, 71-; mem reagents comt, Pan Am Health Orgn, 72-75 & expert comt dengue in Caribbean, 72-76; fac affil, Dept Microbiol, Colo State Univ, 75- *Mem:* Am Asn Immunologists; AAAS; Am Soc Microbiol; Am Soc Trop Med & Hyg; Sigma Xi. *Res:* Murine viruses; in vitro growth of tumor cells; cancer viruses; arbovirus ecology and epidemiology. *Mailing Add:* US Pub Health Serv PO Box 2087 Ft Collins CO 80522

CALKIN, MELVIN GILBERT, b New Glasgow, NS, May 20, 36; m 61; c 4. PHYSICS. *Educ:* Dalhousie Univ, BSc, 57, MSc, 58; Univ BC, PhD(physics), 61. *Prof Exp:* With Naval Res Estab, Defence Res Bd Can, 61-62; from asst prof to assoc prof, 62-72, PROF PHYSICS, DALHOUSIE UNIV, 72- *Res:* Classical and quantum electromagnetic theory. *Mailing Add:* Dept of Physics Dalhousie Univ Halifax Can

CALKIN, PARKER E, b Syracuse, NY, Apr 27, 33; m 55; c 2. GLACIAL GEOLOGY. *Educ:* Tufts Univ, BS, 55; Univ BC, MSc, 59; Ohio State Univ, PhD(geol), 63. *Prof Exp:* Res geologist, Tufts Univ, 60-61 & Inst Polar Studies, Ohio State Univ, 61-62; from instr to assoc prof, 63-75, PROF GEOL, STATE UNIV NY BUFFALO, 75- *Concurrent Pos:* Vis res scholar, Scott Polar Res Inst, Cambridge Univ, 70 & Inst Arctic & Alpine Res, Univ Colo, 79. *Mem:* Geol Soc Am; Glaciol Soc; Am Quaternary Asn. *Res:* Geomorphology and glacial geology, particularly in northeastern United States and in polar areas. *Mailing Add:* Dept Geol Sci State Univ of NY 4240 Ridge Lea Rd Buffalo NY 14226

CALKINS, CARROL OTTO, b Sioux Falls, SDak, June 4, 37; m 59; c 2. ECOLOGY, ENTOMOLOGY. *Educ:* SDak State Univ, BS, 59, PhD(entom), 74; Univ Nebr, MS, 64. *Prof Exp:* Res entomologist, Forage Insect Lab, USDA, Lincoln, Nebr, 60-64 & Northern Grain Insects Res Lab, Brookings, SDak, 64-72, res entomologist, insect attractants, Behav & Basic Biol Res Lab, Agr Res Serv, USDA, 72-77; head entom sect, Seibersdorf Lab, Int Atomic Energy Agency, Vienna, 77-80; RES ENTOMOLOGIST INSECT ATTRACTANTS, BEHAV & BASIC BIOL RES LAB, AGR RES SERV, USDA, 80-; ASSOC PROF, UNIV FLA, 80- *Concurrent Pos:* Instr, Univ Nebr, 61-64 & SDak State Univ, 64-72. *Mem:* Ecol Soc Am; Entom Soc Am; Sigma Xi. *Res:* Ecological basis of insect behavior, population dynamics, distribution and abundance; mating behavior, ethology, quality control of mass-reared insects, Tephritidae and Coleoptera. *Mailing Add:* Biol Res Lab-USDA PO Box 14565 Gainesville FL 32604

CALKINS, CHARLES RICHARD, b Racine, Wis, May 30, 21; m 44; c 3. CHEMISTRY. *Educ:* Lawrence Col, BA, 42, MS, 47, PhD, 49. *Prof Exp:* Corp dir res & develop sect, Riegel Paper Corp, 51-65, vpres res & develop, 65-72, pres, Riegel Prod Corp, 72-74; exec vpres, Kerr Glass Mfg Corp, 74-77; vpres environ affairs, Am Paper Inst, 77-79; vpres, Kiray Forest Indust, 79-80; VPRES, SANTA FE ENERGY CO, 81- *Mem:* AAAS; Am Chem Soc; fel Tech Asn Pulp & Paper Indust; Am Inst Chemists. *Res:* Development of specialty and packaging papers. *Mailing Add:* 713 Creekside Lane Houston TX 20007

CALKINS, GEORGE DONALD, b Orrville, Ohio, May 2, 21; m 44; c 7. CHEMICAL ENGINEERING. *Educ:* Wayne State Univ, BS, 42; Univ Pittsburgh, MS, 46. *Prof Exp:* Assoc chemist nuclear fuel reprocessing, Oak Ridge Nat Lab, 47-48, prin scientist, 48-51, asst div chief, 51-54; div chief radioisotopes & radiation, Battelle Mem Inst, 54-58, asst group leader, 58-60, group leader, 60-62, sect chief, 62-64; asst div dir, Atomics Int Div, NAm Aviation, Inc, 64-65, dept dir, 65-69; task force leader, Nat Hwy Safety Bur, 69-70; DIR ENG OPERS, DYNAMIC SCI, 70- *Mem:* Am Chem Soc; Am Soc Testing & Mat; Am Nuclear Soc. *Res:* Safety engineering for aircraft and automobiles. *Mailing Add:* 5831 N Granite Reef Rd Scottsdale AZ 85253

CALKINS, HARMON ELDRED, b Ann Arbor, Mich, July 11, 12; m 38; c 3. BACTERIOLOGY. *Educ:* Transylvania Col, AB, 33; Univ Ky, MS, 37; Univ Pa, PhD(bact), 41. *Prof Exp:* Asst chem & biol, Transylvania Col, 30-33; asst bact, Univ Pa, 38-41 & Johnson Found, 39-41; res bacteriologist, Upjohn Co, 41-48; asst prof bact, Univ Ga, 48-54; assoc prof, SDak State Col, 54-64; assoc prof & assoc bacteriologist, Agr Exp Sta, Univ Idaho, 64-68; assoc prof biol, 68-74, PROF BIOL & CHMN DIV NATURAL SCI & MATH, PAUL QUINN COL, 74- *Concurrent Pos:* Technician, Bur Animal Indust, USDA, 34-35. *Res:* Serological reactivity of protein monolayers; virucidal activity of germicides; development of influenza virus vaccine; bovine liver abscess. *Mailing Add:* Div Natural Sci & Math Paul Quinn Col Waco TX 76704

CALKINS, JAMES A, b Joliet, Ill, Jan 5, 23; m 52; c 1. GEOLOGY. *Educ:* Univ Calif, Berkeley, BA, 50; Univ Ore, MS, 54; Pa State Univ, PhD(geol), 66. *Prof Exp:* GEOLOGIST, US GEOL SURV, 52- *Mem:* Geol Soc Am. *Res:* Geology of the Northwest Himalaya; data storage and retrieval. *Mailing Add:* US Geol Surv Mail Stop 920 Nat Ctr Reston VA 22092

CALKINS, JOHN, b Deming, NMex, Oct 21, 26; m 46; c 3. RADIATION BIOLOGY, PHOTOBIOLOGY. *Educ:* Tex Western Col, BS, 51; Univ Houston, MS, 59; Univ Tex, PhD(biol, physics), 63. *Prof Exp:* From instr to asst prof, 63-69, ASSOC PROF RADIATION MED, UNIV KY, 69- *Mem:* Am Soc Photobiol; Radiation Res Soc; Am Soc Protozoologists. *Res:* Mechanisms and systems for DNA repair; effects of solar ultraviolet radiation; solar ultraviolet photoecology. *Mailing Add:* Dept of Radiation Med 800 Rose St Lexington KY 40536

CALKINS, RUSSEL CROSBY, b Cedar Falls, Iowa, Dec 31, 21; m 76; c 3. ANALYTICAL CHEMISTRY. *Educ:* Univ Northern Iowa, BA, 48; Univ Wis, MS, 51, PhD(chem), 53. *Prof Exp:* Instr chem, Univ Northern Iowa, 48-49; from asst to res asst, Univ Wis, 49-53; chemist, Dow Chem Co, 53-59; sr res chemist, 59-69, STAFF RES CHEMIST, KAISER ALUMINUM & CHEM CORP, 69- *Mem:* AAAS; Soc Appl Spectros; Am Chem Soc; Sigma Xi. *Res:* Exchange properties of nickel complexes; polymer chemistry; analytical research. *Mailing Add:* PO Box 877 Pleasanton CA 94566

CALKINS, WILLIAM GRAHAM, b Chicago, Ill, May 29, 26; m 48; c 4. INTERNAL MEDICINE, GASTROENTEROLOGY. *Educ:* Univ Mich, BS, 46, MD, 50. *Prof Exp:* Intern med, US Naval Hosp, St Albans, NY, 50-51; resident, Gen Hosp, Kansas City, Mo, 51-52; resident, Med Ctr, 54-56, from instr to asst prof, Sch Med, 56-64, ASSOC PROF MED, SCH MED, UNIV KANS, 64- *Concurrent Pos:* Staff physician, Vet Admin Hosp, Kansas City, 61-64, chief med serv, 64-70, staff physician, 70- *Mem:* Fel Am Col Physicians; Am Gastroenterol Asn; Am Pancreatic Asn. *Mailing Add:* Vet Admin Hosp 4801 Linwood Blvd Kansas City MO 64128

CALKINS, WILLIAM HAROLD, b Toronto, Ont, May 28, 18; US citizen; m 43; c 2. INDUSTRIAL CHEMISTRY, POLYMER CHEMISTRY. *Educ:* Univ Calif, BS, 40, PhD(chem), 47. *Prof Exp:* Res chemist, 47-53, sr res supvr, 53-58, res mgr, 58-68, assoc lab dir, plastics dept, 68-75, mgr feedstocks res, Energy & Mat Dept, 75-77, PRIN CONSULT, CENT RES DEPT, E I DU PONT DE NEMOURS & CO, 77- *Mem:* Fel Am Chem Soc; Soc Plastics Engrs; fel AAAS; fel Sigma Xi. *Res:* Petrochemicals; coal liquefaction and gasification; heterogeneous catalysis. *Mailing Add:* Cent Res Dept E I du Pont de Nemours & Co Wilmington DE 19898

CALL, EDWARD PRIOR, b Kent, Ohio, Dec 24, 26; m 54; c 3. REPRODUCTIVE PHYSIOLOGY, AGRICULTURE. *Educ:* Ohio State Univ, BSc, 51; Kans State Univ, PhD(animal breeding), 67. *Prof Exp:* Asst herdsman artificial insemination, Cent Ohio Breeding Asn, 50-51, technician, 51-52; asst prof, 52-58, res asst, 58-63, assoc prof, 63-79, PROF DAIRY SCI & EXTEN SPECIALIST, KANS STATE UNIV, 79- *Mem:* AAAS; Am Dairy Sci Asn; Am Soc Animal Sci. *Res:* Morphology and histology of bovine genitalia; etiology of ovarian dysfunction and reproductive failure; cyclic changes of peripheral hypophyseal and gonadal hormones in the female bovine; management of dairy cattle. *Mailing Add:* Dept Dairy Sci Col Agr Kans State Univ Manhattan KS 66506

CALL, JUSTIN DAVID, b Salt Lake City, Utah, Aug 7, 23; m 51; c 3. CHILD PSYCHIATRY, PEDIATRICS. *Educ:* Univ Utah, BA, 44, MD, 46. *Prof Exp:* Pvt practr, 46-47; intern pediat, Albany Hosp, NY, 47-48; pediat path res, Children's Hosp, Boston, Mass, 48-49; resident pediat, NY Hosp, 49-51; child neuropsychiatrist, Emma Pendleton Bradley Home, 51; resident psychiat, Strong Mem Hosp, 52; from instr to assoc prof, Univ Calif, Los Angeles, 54-68, PROF CHILD & ADOLESCENT PSYCHIAT & PROF, DEPT PEDIAT, UNIV CALIF, IRVINE, 68- *Concurrent Pos:* Mem, Adv Bd, Little Village Nursery Sch, Los Angeles, Exceptional Children's Found; mem, Clin Res Proj Rev Comt, NIMH, 68-72; chmn, Ment Health Adv Bd, Los Angeles County Head 24 Proj, 69-70; training & supervising psychoanalyst, Los Angeles Psychoanal Soc & Inst. *Mem:* Am Psychiat Asn; Am Acad Child Psychiat; Am Acad Pediat; Am Psychoanal Asn. *Res:* Preventive psychiatry; personality development; language acquisition; infant psychopathology. *Mailing Add:* Dept of Psychiat Univ of Calif Irvine CA 92650

CALL, PATRICK JOSEPH, b Portland, Ore, Sept 28, 49; m 74. PHYSICS. *Educ:* Reed Col, BA, 71; Oxford Univ, DPhil(physics), 74. *Prof Exp:* Mem tech staff mat processing, David Sarnoff Res Ctr, RCA Labs, 75-77; SR SCIENTIST THIN FILMS DEVELOP, SOLAR ENERGY RES INST, 77- *Concurrent Pos:* Mem tech staff, Domestic Policy Rev Solar Energy, 78. *Mem:* Am Vacuum Soc; Am Phys Soc. *Res:* Development of thin films and coatings for solar energy applications; analysis of surface and interface properties of thin films. *Mailing Add:* Solar Energy Res Inst 1617 Cole Blvd Golden CO 80401

CALL, REGINALD LESSEY, b Rigby, Idaho, Apr 23, 26; m 50; c 3. PHYSICS. *Educ:* Brigham Young Univ, BS, 51; Univ Utah, PhD(physics), 58. *Prof Exp:* Mem tech staff, Bell Labs, 58-68; ASSOC PROF ELEC ENG, UNIV ARIZ, 68- *Res:* Solid state physics; photovoltaics; solar energy. *Mailing Add:* Dept Elec Eng Univ Ariz Tucson AZ 85721

CALL, RICHARD A, b Gooding, Idaho, July 16, 20; m 44; c 3. PATHOLOGY. *Educ:* Univ Utah, BA, 42, MD, 44; Am Bd Path, dipl. *Prof Exp:* From instr to asst prof, 49-53, ASSOC CLIN PROF PATH, COL MED, UNIV UTAH, 53- *Concurrent Pos:* Asst dir labs, Salt Lake Gen Hosp, 51-52; chief lab serv, Vet Hosp, Salt Lake City, 52-54; fel, Medici Publici, Col Med, Univ Utah, 65; med dir, Utah Valley Hosp, 69-; mem adv bd, Health, Educ & Welfare, Health Ins Benefits Adv Coun Comt, 74-78. *Mem:* AMA; Col Am Pathologists; Am Soc Clin Pathologists; Am Acad Forensic Sci; Int Acad Path. *Res:* Penicillin blood levels; virulence studies in mice of M tuberculosis; causes of death as determined by autopsy in Utah; fluoridosis in man; forensic pathology. *Mailing Add:* Utah Valley Hosp 1034 N 5th West Provo UT 84601

CALLAGHAN, EUGENE, b Snohomish, Wash, Jan 10, 04; m 35; c 2. ECONOMIC GEOLOGY. *Educ:* Univ Ore, AB, 26, AM, 27; Columbia Univ, PhD(geol), 31. *Prof Exp:* Asst, Univ Ore, 26-27; geologist, Metrop Dist, Water Supply Comn, Boston, 29; from asst geologist to sr geologist, US Geol Surv, 30-45; prof econ geol, Ind Univ, 46-49; dir, NMex Bur Mines & Mineral Resources, 49-57; chief geol, Gold Prog, Mineracao Hannaco Ltd, Brazil, 58-60; sr resident geologist, Cyprus Mines Corp, Skouriotissa, 60-65; res prof mineral, 65-68, chmn dept geol & geophys, 68-70, prof geol, 70-72, EMER PROF GEOL & GEOPHYS SCI, UNIV UTAH, 72- *Concurrent Pos:* Geologist, Barton Exped, Persia, 28; econ geologist, Ind State Dept Conserv, 46-49; sr geologist, Utah Geol Surv, 65-67, asst dir, 67-68, assoc dir, 68-; consult geologist, 72- *Mem:* Soc Econ Geol; fel Geol Soc Am; Am Inst Mining, Metall & Petrol Engrs; Brit Inst Mining & Metall. *Res:* Economic geology of magnesite, brucite, gold, tungsten, tin, antimony, copper and clay; Cascade Mountains, Oregon; Eastern Cordillera of Bolivia, Great Basin, Nevada, high plateaus, Utah, Indiana, New Mexico, countries of the Mediterranean region, and the Mideast. *Mailing Add:* 2500 Kensington Ave Salt Lake City UT 84108

CALLAGHAN, OWEN HUGH, b Johannesburg, SAfrica, Oct 2, 27; m 59; c 3. IMMUNOCHEMISTRY. *Educ:* Univ Witwatersrand, MSc, 56; Univ Sheffield, PhD(biochem), 58. *Prof Exp:* Vis scientist, Oxford Univ, 58; res assoc immunol, 59-60, from fac assoc to assoc prof, 61-70, PROF BIOCHEM, CHICAGO MED SCH, 70- *Concurrent Pos:* NIH res career develop award, 63. *Mem:* Brit Biochem Soc; Am Asn Immunologists. *Res:* Enzymology; immunology; histamine release; neurochemistry. *Mailing Add:* Dept of Biochem Chicago Med Sch 2020 W Ogden Ave Chicago IL 60612

CALLAHAM, MAC A, b Ft Payne, Ala, Aug 30, 36; m 60; c 3. WILDLIFE BIOLOGY, FISHERIES. *Educ:* Univ Ga, BS, 58, PhD(wildlife fisheries), 68; George Peabody Col, MA, 61, EdS, 63. *Prof Exp:* Assoc prof biol, Belmont Col, 61-63; assoc prof, 63-72, PROF BIOL, N GA COL, 72- *Mem:* AAAS; Am Fisheries Soc. *Res:* Fishery management; fish blood proteins. *Mailing Add:* Dept of Biol NGa Col Dahlonega GA 30533

CALLAHAM, ROBERT ZINA, b San Francisco, Calif, May 24, 27; m 49; c 2. FOREST ECOLOGY, GENETICS. *Educ:* Univ Calif, BS, 49, PhD(bot), 55. *Prof Exp:* Res forester ecol, Bur Entom & Plant Quarantine, Berkeley Forest Insect Lab, USDA, 49-54; geneticist, Calif Forest & Range Exp Sta, 54-58, leader, Inland Empire Res Ctr, Intermountain Forest & Range Exp Sta, 58-60 & Inst Forest Genetics, 60-63, asst dir, Pac Southwest Forest & Range Exp Sta, 63-64, chief, Br Forest Genetics Res, 64-66, asst to dep chief res, 66-70, dir, Div Forest Insects & Dis Res, 70-73, dir, forest environ res staff, 73-76, DIR, PAC SOUTHWEST FOREST & RANGE EXP STA, US FOREST SERV, BERKELEY, CALIF, 76- *Concurrent Pos:* Mem exec bd, Int Union Forestry Res Orgns, 67-81; ed, Silvae Genetica, 62-66; asst exec dir, Int Union Socs Foresters, 70-74, mem exec bd, 75-79; Cong fel, 72-73. *Mem:* Soc Am Foresters. *Res:* Resistance of pine species and species hybrids to bark beetles and other forest insects; pine hybridization and improvement; geographic variation in forest trees; forestry research administration; renewable resources technical information systems. *Mailing Add:* US Forest Serv Box 245 Berkeley CA 94701

CALLAHAN, ARTHUR BERNARD, b Boston, Mass, Apr 4, 28; m; c 5. BIOPHYSICS, BIOCHEMISTRY. *Educ:* Northeastern Univ, BS, 54; Boston Univ, AM, 55, PhD, 60. *Prof Exp:* Res asst, Boston Univ, 55-56, res assoc, 57-60; instr, Univ RI, 60; fel, Mass Gen Hosp, 61-63; BIOPHYSICIST, OFF NAVAL RES, 64- *Concurrent Pos:* Instr, Boston Univ, 61. *Mem:* Biophys Soc; Cryobiol Soc. *Res:* Membrane biophysics; water and electrolyte regulation. *Mailing Add:* Off Naval Res 495 Summer St Boston MA 02210

CALLAHAN, CLARENCE ARTHUR, b Bay City, Tex, Sept 29, 43; m 66; c 2. ECOLOGY, ENTOMOLOGY. *Educ:* Univ Southwestern La, BS, 66; Auburn Univ, MS, 68; Purdue Univ, PhD(entom), 76. *Prof Exp:* AQUATIC BIOLOGIST LIMNOL, US ENVIRON PROTECTION AGENCY, 72- *Mem:* Am Fisheries Soc; Soc Nematologists. *Res:* Stream Ecology; hazardous waste assessment; neurophysiology. *Mailing Add:* Corvallis Environ Res Lab 200 SW 35th St Corvallis OR 97333

CALLAHAN, DANIEL, b Washington, DC, July 19, 30; m 54; c 6. BIOMEDICAL ETHICS. *Educ:* Yale Univ, BA, 52; Georgetown Univ, MA, 57; Harvard Univ, PhD(phiols), 65. *Hon Degrees:* DSci, Col Med & Dent NJ, 81. *Prof Exp:* Exec ed, Commonwealth Mag, 61-68; assoc staff, The Pop Coun, 69-70; DIR, THE HASTINGS CTR, 69- *Concurrent Pos:* Consult, Pres Comn Pop Growth & the Am Future, 70-71, Comt S-Hemoglobinopathies, Nat Acad Sci, 72, Comn Recombinant DNA Res, NIH, 76 & Med Ethics Comn, Am Col Physicians, 79-; adv bd, Technol in Soc, 81- *Honors & Awards:* Thomas More Medal, Thomas More Asn, 70. *Mem:* Inst Med-Nat Acad Sci; AAAS; Am Philos Asn. *Res:* Biomedical ethics; science and society; social and ethical problems of sicence. *Mailing Add:* The Hastings Ctr 360 Broadway Hastings On Hudson NY 10706

CALLAHAN, HUGH JAMES, b Philadelphia, Pa, July 9, 40; m 61; c 5. IMMUNOCHEMISTRY, GLYCOPROTEIN CHHEMISTRY. *Educ:* St Joseph Univ, BS, 62; Ill Inst Technol, MS, 67; Thomas Jefferson Univ, PhD(biochem), 70. *Prof Exp:* Res assoc, Evanston Hosp, Ill, 62-67; asst prof, 72-76, ASSOC PROF BIOCHEM, THOMAS JEFFERSON UNIV, 76- *Mem:* Am Asn Immnol; Sigma Xi. *Res:* Immunochemical characterization of lymphocyte membrane receptors; physical-chemical studies of antigen-antibody interactions. *Mailing Add:* Dept Biochem Thomas Jefferson Univ 1020 Locust St Philadelphia PA 19107

CALLAHAN, JAMES LOUIS, b Cleveland, Ohio, Sept 25, 26; m 49; c 2. INORGANIC CHEMISTRY. *Educ:* Baldwin-Wallace Col, BS, 50; Western Reserve Univ, MS, 54, PhD, 57. *Prof Exp:* From tech res specialist to supvr catalysis res, 50-70, mgr chem & catalysis res, 70-75, SR CONSULT, STANDARD OIL CO OHIO, 75- *Mem:* Am Chem Soc. *Res:* Catalysis; catalytic conversion of hydrocarbons; solid state chemistry; petrochemicals. *Mailing Add:* Standard Oil Co 4440 Warrensville Center Rd Cleveland OH 44128

CALLAHAN, JAMES THOMAS, b Appalachia, Va, Dec 29, 45; m 68; c 3. RESEARCH ADMINISTRATION, ECOLOGY. *Educ:* Univ SC, BS, 68; Univ Ga, PhD(zool), 72. *Prof Exp:* Asst prog dir, 72-76, ASSOC PROG DIR, ECOSYST STUDIES, NSF, 76- *Concurrent Pos:* Lectr, George Mason Univ, 78; comnr, Int Conv Adv Comn, 79-81. *Mem:* Ecol Soc Am; Am Soc Zoologists; AAAS; Nat Asn Environ Prof. *Res:* Analysis of ecological systems; ecological modeling; nutrient cycles; primary consumer insect populations; science policy; endangered biota; environmental assessment. *Mailing Add:* Div Environ Biol 1800 G St NW Washington DC 20550

CALLAHAN, JEFFREY EDWIN, b Boston, Mass, Sept 24, 43; m 67; c 2. PHYSICAL OCEANOGRAPHY. *Educ:* US Naval Acad, BS, 65; Johns Hopkins Univ, MA, 69, PhD(phys oceanog), 71. *Prof Exp:* Weapons officer, 71-74, mil asst to dir sci & eng, US Naval Oceanog Off, 74-76, cmndg officer, USS AFFRAY, 77-78; PRIN ANALYST, ANAL & TECHNOL, INC, 78- *Mem:* Marine Technol Soc; Am Geophys Union; Sigma Xi; Am Geophys Union. *Res:* Large-scale oceanic circulation and its effect on the distributions of properties in the ocean, particularly polar oceans and their influence on abyssal circulation world-wide. *Mailing Add:* 32 Main St Old Mystic CT 06372

CALLAHAN, JOAN REA, b San Francisco, Calif, Oct 17, 48; m 80; c 1. EVOLUTIONARY BIOLOGY. *Educ:* Univ Calif, Berkeley, AB, 72; Univ Ariz, MS, 75, PhD(zool), 76. *Prof Exp:* Res assoc gen biol, Univ Ariz, 77-80. *Concurrent Pos:* Theodore Roosevelt Mem grant, Am Mus Natural Hist, 76; consult, NSF grant, Dept Psychol, Univ Ga, 78-79; adj res assoc psychol, Univ Ga, 80- *Res:* Behavior and speciation in Eutamias and other sciurids. *Mailing Add:* PO Box 40003 Tucson AZ 85717

CALLAHAN, JOHN EDWARD, b Buffalo, NY, Feb 26, 41; m 65; c 2. GEOLOGY, ECONOMIC GEOLOGY. *Educ:* State Univ NY, Buffalo, BA, 63, MED, 65; Univ NC, Chapel Hill, MS, 68; Queen's Univ, Ont, PhD(geol), 73. *Prof Exp:* assoc prof geol, 70-80, PROF GEOL, APPALACHIAN STATE UNIV, 80- *Concurrent Pos:* Geologist, US Geol Surv, 78-81. *Mem:* Am Inst Engrs; Can Inst Mining & Metall; Asn Explor Geochemists. *Res:* Economic geology and exploration geochemistry. *Mailing Add:* Dept of Geol Appalachian State Univ Boone NC 28608

CALLAHAN, JOHN JOSEPH, b Taylor, Pa, Apr 1, 25; m 53. PHYSICAL CHEMISTRY. *Educ:* Johns Hopkins Univ, BS, 54. *Prof Exp:* Phys chemist, Physicochem Res Div, Chem Res & Develop Lab, 54-60, asst chief chem, Phys Methods Br, 60-62, chief, Agents Reactions Br, 62-66, suprvy chemist, Phys Chem Dept, 66-74, actg chief, Phys Chem Br, Chem Res Div, Chem Lab, 74-77, CHIEF, PHYS ORG SECT, CHEM BR, RES DIV, CHEM SYSTS LAB, EDGEWOOD ARSENAL, US DEPT ARMY, 77- *Res:* Measurement of physical properties; instrumental analysis; purification; reaction rates and mechanisms. *Mailing Add:* Phys Org Sect Chem Br Res Div CSL Aberdeen Proving Ground MD 21010

CALLAHAN, JOHN WILLIAM, b Welland, Ont, July 9, 42; m 69; c 2. BIOCHEMISTRY, NEUROCHEMISTRY. *Educ:* Univ Windsor, BSc, 65, MSc, 66; McGill Univ, PhD(biochem), 70. *Prof Exp:* Med Res Coun Can fel, Univ Calif, Los Angeles, 70-72; INVESTR NEUROSCI, RES INST, HOSP SICK CHILDREN, 72-; ASSOC PROF PEDIAT, FAC MED, UNIV TORONTO, 81-, ASSOC PROF BIOCHEM, 81- *Concurrent Pos:* Med Res Coun Can scholar, 73-78; asst prof pediat, Univ Toronto, 73-81, asst prof biochem, 75-81. *Mem:* Am Soc Neurochem; Can Soc Clin Invest. *Res:* Isolation and characterization of lysosomal hydrolases, especially those enzymes involved in the lysosomal storage diseases; the study of the altered gene products in these diseases. *Mailing Add:* Neurosci Div Hosp Sick Children 555 University Ave Toronto ON M5G 1X8 Can

CALLAHAN, JOSEPH THOMAS, b Concord, NH, Mar 31, 22; m 43; c 3. GEOLOGY. *Educ:* Univ NH, BS, 49; Univ Ariz, MS, 51. *Prof Exp:* Geologist, Ground Water Br, US Geol Surv, 51-55, dist geologist, Ga, 55-61, from assoc chief to chief, Ground Water Br, 61-66; geologist-ground water tech adv, US AID, 66-71; chief underground waste disposal invests, Water Resources Div, 71, chief ground water br, 71-72, REGIONAL HYDROLOGIST, US GEOL SURV, 72- *Honors & Awards:* Meritorious Serv Award, US Dept Interior, 74. *Mem:* Geol Soc Am; Am Water Works Asn; Am Geophys Union. *Res:* Geologic and hydrologic investigations of humid and arid zones, especially in the lower and middle latitudes, and in Korea and Japan. *Mailing Add:* US Geol Surv Water Resources Div Reston VA 22092

CALLAHAN, KEMPER LEROY, b Mt Morris, Pa, July 14, 29; m 59; c 2. PLANT PATHOLOGY. *Educ:* Waynesburg Col, BS, 51; WVa Univ, MS, 53; Univ Wis, PhD(plant path), 57. *Prof Exp:* Cur mus, Waynesburg Col, 47-51; asst, WVa Univ, 51-53; asst, Univ Wis, 53-57; plant pathologist, Forest Serv, USDA, 57-58; plant pathologist, Entom & Path Div, Can Dept Forestry, 58-65; mem fac biol, 65-81, PROF BIOL, GREENSBORO COL, 81- *Mem:* Am Phytopath Soc; Can Phytopath Soc; Am Inst Biol Sci; Am Forestry Asn; Soc Am Foresters. *Res:* Virus diseases of forest trees; natural sciences. *Mailing Add:* Dept of Biol Greensboro Col Greensboro NC 27420

CALLAHAN, KENNETH PAUL, b Pasadena, Calif, Dec 15, 43. INORGANIC CHEMISTRY. *Educ:* Univ Santa Clara, BS, 65; Univ Calif, Riverside, PhD(inorg chem), 69. *Prof Exp:* Scholar inorg chem, Dept Chem, Univ Calif, Los Angeles, 70-74; asst prof chem, Brown Univ, 74-79; SR RES CHEMIST, OCCIDENTAL RES CORP, 79- *Mem:* Am Chem Soc; The Chem Soc; Sigma Xi; NY Acad Sci. *Res:* Metalloborane synthesis; synthesis, spectroscopy and optical activity of coordination compounds; design and synthesis of new ligands; organic chemistry of carboranes; metal-sulfur chemistry; early transition metal chemistry. *Mailing Add:* Occidental Res Corp PO Box 19601 Irvine CA 92713

CALLAHAN, LESLIE G, JR, b Pocomoke City, Md, July 27, 23; m 44; c 2. ELECTRICAL ENGINEERING. *Educ:* US Mil Acad, BS, 44; Univ Pa, MS, 51, PhD(elec eng), 61. *Prof Exp:* Res & develop coordr electronic systs, Continental Army Command, US Army, Ft Monroe, Va, 52-55, tech opers officer, Univ Mich, 58-61, exec officer, Army Res Off, NC, 61-63, dir aviation electronics, Avionics Lab, Ft Monmouth, 65-67; commanding officer, Harry Diamond Labs, Washington, DC, 67-69; PROF INDUST ENG, GA INST TECHNOL, 69- *Concurrent Pos:* Fac fel, US Gen Accounting Off, 75-76. *Mem:* Opers Res Soc Am; Am Soc Eng Educ; AAAS. *Res:* Systems engineering applied to the analysis and design of man-machine systems in the areas of command and control, air defense, surrveillance and avionics. *Mailing Add:* 7105 Duncourtney Dr Atlanta GA 30328

CALLAHAN, LLOYD MILTON, b Hobart, Okla, Mar 28, 34; c 4. AGRONOMY. *Educ:* Okla State Univ, BS, 59, MS, 61; Rutgers Univ, PhD(agron), 64. *Prof Exp:* From asst prof to assoc prof agron, 64-71, assoc prof ornamental hort, 71-78, PROF ORNAMENTAL HORT, UNIV TENN, KNOXVILLE, 78- *Mem:* Am Soc Agron; Weed Sci Soc Am; Crop Sci Soc Am; Sigma Xi. *Res:* Turfgrass management; cellular morphology and anatomy; plant physiology; herbicide phytotoxicity to turfgrasses; disease and sod webworm control. *Mailing Add:* Univ of Tenn Dept of Ornamental Hort & Landscape Design Knoxville TN 37919

CALLAHAN, MARY VINCENT, b Bridgeport, Conn, July 2, 22. CHEMISTRY, INSTRUMENTATION. *Educ:* Col Notre Dame, Md, AB, 43; Cath Univ Am, MS, 45, PhD(chem), 66. *Prof Exp:* Teacher, Inst Notre Dame High Sch, 44-45; teacher, Prep Sch, Col Notre Dame, Md, 46-48, instr chem, Col, 48-50; teacher, NY High Sch, 50-54; from instr to assoc prof, 54-66, PROF CHEM, COL NOTRE DAME, MD, 66-, CHMN DEPT CHEM, 64- *Concurrent Pos:* Vis prof, Summer Sch, Cath Univ Am, 65- *Mem:* AAAS; Am Chem Soc; Soc Appl Spectros. *Res:* Free radicals; pyrolysis of hexachloropropylene; instrumental analysis; infrared spectroscopy; analytical chemistry; molecular structure; amino acids; peptides; complexes. *Mailing Add:* Col of Notre Dame 4701 N Charles St Baltimore MD 21210

CALLAHAN, PHILIP SERNA, b Ft Benning, Ga, Aug 29, 23; m 49; c 4. ENTOMOLOGY. *Educ:* Univ Ark, BA & MS, 53; Kans State Col, PhD(entom), 56. *Prof Exp:* From asst prof to assoc prof entom, La State Univ, 56-63; prof entom, Univ Ga, 63-69; entomologist, Southern Grain Insects Res Lab, Agr Res Serv, 62-69, ENTOMOLOGIST, INSECT ATTRACTANTS, BEHAV & BASIC BIOL RES LAB, USDA, UNIV FLA, 69- *Mem:* Optical Soc Am; Am Ornith Union; Entom Soc Am; NY Acad Sci; fel Explorers Club. *Res:* Ecology and behavior of Lepidoptera; insect biophysics with special reference to theories of infrared and microwave electromagnetic attraction between insects and host plants; methods of insect biotelemetry; nonlinear radiation. *Mailing Add:* Insect Attractants USDA Univ Fla Gainesville FL 32604

CALLAHAN, THOMAS WILLIAM, b Akron, Ohio, Apr 24, 25; m 46; c 2. ELECTRICAL ENGINEERING. *Educ:* Purdue Univ, BS, 47. *Prof Exp:* Staff elec engr, Aluminum Co Am, 47-55, works chief elec eng, 56-64, div mgr, 64-73; from asst dir to assoc dir, 73-81, OPERS DIR, ALCOA LABS, ALUMINUM CO AM, 81- *Mem:* Indust Res Inst; Sigma Xi. *Res:* Research and development for customer and corporate products and processes in the aluminum and related industries; research and development related to all aspects of corporate processes, equipment and control systems. *Mailing Add:* Alcoa Labs Alcoa Center PA 15069

CALLAHAN, WILLIAM PAXTON, III, anatomy, see previous edition

CALLAN, CURTIS, b North Adams, Mass, Oct 11, 42; m 65; c 2. THEORETICAL PHYSICS. *Educ:* Haverford Col, BA, 61; Princeton Univ, PhD(physics), 64. *Prof Exp:* Asst prof physics, Harvard Univ, 67-69; mem, Inst Advan Study, 69-72; PROF PHYSICS, PRINCETON UNIV, 72- *Res:* Quantum field theory with emphasis on applications to elementary particle physics. *Mailing Add:* Joseph Henry Labs Princeton Univ Princeton NJ 08540

CALLAN, EDWIN JOSEPH, b Floral Park, NY, Nov 29, 22; m 46; c 2. ATOMIC PHYSICS, TECHNICAL MANAGEMENT. *Educ:* Manhattan Col, BS, 43; Ohio State Univ, MS, 60. *Prof Exp:* Physicist & chief thermal res sect, Concrete Res Div, Corps Engrs, Miss, 46-53; res & develop adminstr, Directorate Res, Wright Air Develop Ctr, 53-56, chief plans & anal, US Air Force Aerospace Res Labs, 56-68, sci adv, Aerospace Res Labs, 68-75; CONSULT, 75- *Concurrent Pos:* Scholar, Dublin Inst Advan Studies, 64-65; mem conf comt, Nat Conf Admin Res, 72-75; chmn, LOM Ltd. *Mem:* Am Phys Soc; Am Chem Soc. *Res:* Atomic transition rates; thermal and elastic properties of concreting materials; radiation shielding; research management; atomic and ionic energy level calculations and methods; materials science engineering; software systems. *Mailing Add:* 4139 Windcross Lane Orlando FL 32809

CALLANAN, MARGARET JOAN, b Washington, DC, July 31, 26. SCIENCE EDUCATION. *Educ:* Trinity Col, Washington, DC, AB, 48; Cath Univ Am, MS, 50. *Prof Exp:* Chemist, NIH, 50-58; res asst, Nat Res Coun, 58-61; prog officer, 61-74, spec asst, 74-76, PROG MGR, NSF, 76- *Concurrent Pos:* Fel educ for pub mgt, Stanford Univ, 72-73. *Mem:* Fel AAAS; Am Chem Soc. *Res:* Physico-chemical properties of proteins, nucleic acids and protamines; science education; public understanding of science; finding ways to increase the number of women with science careers. *Mailing Add:* NSF 1800 G St NW Washington DC 20550

CALLANTINE, MERRITT REECE, b Hammond, Ind, Jan 6, 36; m 56; c 2. PHYSIOLOGY, ENDOCRINOLOGY. *Educ:* Purdue Univ, BS, 56, MS, 58, PhD(endocrinol), 61. *Prof Exp:* Teaching asst biol sci, Purdue Univ, 58-60; head sect endocrinol, Parke-Davis Res Labs, Mich, 61-70; dir sci & regulatory affairs, 70-72, sr clin investr, Mead Johnson Res Ctr, 72-76; MED-LEGAL LIAISON, LILLY RES LABS, 76- *Concurrent Pos:* Vis assoc prof,

Hahnemann Med Col, 73-78. *Mem:* Endocrine Soc; Am Physiol Soc; Soc Exp Biol & Med; Soc Study Reproduction; AAAS. *Res:* Endocrinology of reproduction, especially control of gonadotrophin secretion, ovarian function and uterine contractility; mechanism of hormone action; nonsteroidal antifertility agents; hormone antagonists; clinical investigation, antineoplastic agents, antibiotics, estrogen replacement therapy and agents to control uterine contractility. *Mailing Add:* 55 Horseshoe Lane Carmel IN 46032

CALLARD, GLORIA VINCZ, b Perth Amboy, NJ, July 20, 38; m 62. COMPARATIVE ENDOCRINOLOGY. *Educ:* Tufts Univ, BS, 59; Rutgers Univ, MS, 63, PhD(zool), 64. *Prof Exp:* Endocrine biochemist, Personal Prod Co Div, Johnson & Johnson, 64-67; lectr, Col William & Mary, 67-72; asst prof, Tufts Univ, 72-73; res assoc & lectr, Boston Univ, 74-75; res assoc obstet & gynec, Harvard Med Sch, 75-79, asst prof, 79-81; ASSOC PROF BIOL SCI, BOSTON UNIV, 81- *Mem:* Endocrine Soc; AAAS; Soc Study Reproduction; Am Soc Zoologists. *Res:* Reproductive physiology; steroid synthesis. *Mailing Add:* Boston Univ 121 Bay St Boston MA 02115

CALLAS, GERALD, b Beaumont, Tex, Oct 14, 32; m 67; c 2. ANATOMY, ELECTRON MICROSCOPY. *Educ:* Lamar State Col, BS, 59; Univ Tex, Galveston, MA, 62, PhD(anat), 66, MD, 67. *Prof Exp:* Intern, John Sealy Hosp, 67-68; asst prof anat, 68-75, ASSOC PROF ANAT, MED BR, UNIV TEX, 75- *Mem:* Am Asn Anatomists. *Res:* Electron microscopy of the lung secondary to altered thyroid function; fine structural changes occurring in the adrenal gland in relation to varying functions of the thyroid gland. *Mailing Add:* Dept Anat Univ Tex Med Br Galveston TX 77550

CALLAWAY, ENOCH, III, b La Grange, Ga, July 12, 24; m 48; c 2. PSYCHIATRY. *Educ:* Columbia Univ, AB, 44, MD, 47. *Prof Exp:* Intern med, Grady Mem Hosp, Emory Univ, 47-48; resident psychiat, Worcester State Hosp, Mass, 48-49; from instr to assoc prof, Psychiat Inst, Univ Md, 52-58; PROF PSYCHIATRY, UNIV CALIF, SAN FRANCISCO, 59- *Concurrent Pos:* USPHS res career investr, 54-58; mem psychopharmacol study sect, NIMH, 63-67, mem alcohol & alcohol probs study sect, 68-72. *Mem:* Am Col Neuropsychopharmacol; Soc Biol Psychiat (vpres, 81); Soc Psychophysiol Res (pres, 81). *Res:* Behavioral neurophysiology as related to psychiatric problems; psychopharmacology. *Mailing Add:* Dept of Psychiat Univ of Calif Med Ctr San Francisco CA 94143

CALLAWAY, JASPER LAMAR, b Cooper, Ala, Apr 5, 11; m 41; c 3. DERMATOLOGY. *Educ:* Univ Ala, BS, 31; Duke Univ, MD, 32. *Prof Exp:* Fel & instr dermat, Univ Pa, 35-37; PROF DERMAT, SCH MED, DUKE UNIV, 37- *Concurrent Pos:* Consult, Vet Admin Hosp, USPHS & Surgeon Gen, US Air Force; mem, Nat Adv Serol Coun; pres, Am Bd Dermat & Syphilol, 58-59; mem, Spec Adv Group, Vet Admin; mem, Cutaneous Dis Sect, Nat Res Coun. *Mem:* Am Dermat Asn (secy, pres, 58-59); Soc Invest Dermat (pres, 55-56); fel Am Col Physicians; Am Asn Prof Dermatologists (pres, 65); Am Acad Dermat. *Res:* Syphilology; manual clinical mycology. *Mailing Add:* Dept of Dermat Duke Hosp Durham NC 27710

CALLAWAY, JOSEPH, b Hackensack, NJ, July 1, 31; m 49; c 3. THEORETICAL PHYSICS. *Educ:* Col William & Mary, BS, 51; Princeton Univ, MA, 53, PhD(physics), 56. *Prof Exp:* Asst prof physics, Univ Miami, 54-60; from assoc prof to prof physics, Univ Calif, Riverside, 60-67; chmn dept physics & astron, 70-73, BOYD PROF PHYSICS, LA STATE UNIV, BATON ROUGE, 67- *Concurrent Pos:* Consult, res labs, Philco Corp, 61-67; sr vis fel, Imp Col, Univ London, 74-75; mem exec comt, APS Div Condensed Matter Physics, 77-79. *Mem:* Fel Am Phys Soc. *Res:* Electron-atom and atom-atom scattering; energy band theory; theory of ferromagnetism; imperfections in crystalline solids. *Mailing Add:* Dept of Physics & Astron La State Univ Baton Rouge LA 70803

CALLAWAY, RICHARD JOSEPH, b Washington, DC, Oct 31, 28; m 56; c 2. PHYSICAL OCEANOGRAPHY. *Educ:* Univ Wash, BS, 56; Ore State Univ, MS, 59. *Prof Exp:* Oceangr, US Fish & Wildlife Serv, Hawaii, 56-58; asst oceanog, Ore State Univ, 58-59; oceangr, US Fish & Wildlife Serv, Wash, 59-60 & US Pub Health Serv, 60-66; OCEANGR, CORVALLIS ENVIRON RES LAB, ENVIRON PROTECTION AGENCY, 66- *Mem:* AAAS; Am Soc Limnol & Oceanog; Am Geophys Union. *Res:* Marine pollution; field and laboratory investigations of municipally and/or industrially caused pollution of marine waters. *Mailing Add:* Corvallis Environ Res Lab 200 SW 35th St Corvallis OR 97330

CALLCOTT, THOMAS ANDERSON, b Columbia, SC, Jan 13, 37; m 61; c 3. SOLID STATE PHYSICS, SURFACE PHYSICS. *Educ:* Duke Univ, BS, 58; Purdue Univ, MS, 62, PhD(physics), 65. *Prof Exp:* Res assoc physics, Purdue Univ, 65; mem tech staff, res div, Bell Tel Labs, 65-68; asst prof, 68-72, assoc prof, 72-78, PROF PHYSICS, UNIV TENN, KNOXVILLE, 78- *Concurrent Pos:* Consult, Oak Ridge Nat Lab, 68-; NSF res grants, 69-77. *Mem:* AAAS; Am Phys Soc. *Res:* Radiation damage effects in crystalline solids; optical x-ray and photoemission measurements on solids; physics of solid surfaces. *Mailing Add:* Dept of Physics Univ of Tenn Knoxville TN 37916

CALLEN, EARL ROBERT, b Philadelphia, Pa, Aug 28, 25; m 50; c 4. SOLID STATE PHYSICS. *Educ:* Univ Pa, AB, 48, MA, 51; Mass Inst Technol, PhD(physics), 54. *Prof Exp:* Physicist, Nat Security Agency, 55-59; with US Naval Ord Lab, 59-68; PROF PHYSICS, AM UNIV, 68- *Mem:* Fel Am Phys Soc. *Res:* Magnetostriction; amorphous magnetism; statistical mechanics of social systems; science and civil liberties; human rights; technology transfer and international development. *Mailing Add:* Dept of Physics Am Univ Washington DC 20016

CALLEN, HERBERT BERNARD, b Philadelphia, Pa, July 1, 19; m 45; c 2. STATISTICAL MECHANICS. *Educ:* Temple Univ, BS, 41, AM, 42; Mass Inst Technol, PhD(physics), 47. *Prof Exp:* Physicist, Kellex Corp, New York, NY, 44-45; electronic res, Princeton Univ, 45; res assoc, Mass Inst Technol, 45-48; from asst prof to assoc prof, 48-56, PROF PHYSICS, UNIV PA, 56- *Concurrent Pos:* Consult, Sperry Rand Corp, 51-; mem adv panel physics, NSF, 66-69, chmn, 69; chmn fac sen, Univ Pa, 70-71; Guggenheim fel, 72; mem, Comn Statist Mech, Int Union Pure & Appl Physics, 72-, chmn 75-78. *Mem:* Fel Am Phys Soc. *Res:* Theoretical physics; theory of solid state; thermodynamics; irreversible statistical mechanics. *Mailing Add:* Dept of Physics Univ of Pa Philadelphia PA 19104

CALLEN, JAMES DONALD, b Wichita, Kans, Jan 31, 41; m 61; c 2. PLASMA PHYSICS. *Educ:* Kans State Univ, BS, 62, MS, 64; Mass Inst Technol, PhD(appl plasma physics), 68. *Prof Exp:* NSF postdoctoral fel, Inst Advan Study, Princeton Univ, 68-69; asst prof aeronaut & astronaut, Mass Inst Technol, 69-72; staff mem, Oak Ridge Nat Lab, 72-75, head, Theory Sect, Fusion Energy Div, 75-79; PROF NUCLEAR ENG & PHYSICS, UNIV WIS-MADISON, 79- *Concurrent Pos:* Consult, Oak Ridge Nat Lab, 69-72. *Mem:* Am Nuclear Soc; Am Phys Soc. *Res:* Plasma physics, mainly magnetic fusion; nuclear reactor engineering. *Mailing Add:* Univ Wis Madison WI 53706

CALLEN, JOSEPH EDWARD, b Moulton, Iowa, Mar 24, 20; m 44; c 2. ORGANIC CHEMISTRY, RESEARCH ADMINISTRATION. *Educ:* Univ Iowa, BS, 42, MS, 43, PhD(org chem), 46. *Prof Exp:* Asst chem, Univ Iowa, 42-43; res chemist, Nat Defense Res Comt, 43-45; res chemist, 46-60, assoc dir res, Proctor & Gamble Co, 60-77; RETIRED. *Concurrent Pos:* Instr, Univ Iowa, 44. *Mem:* Am Chem Soc. *Res:* Synthetic detergents; fats and oils; fluorescent dyes; infrared and ultraviolet spectroscopy; amines; gas chromatography. *Mailing Add:* Star Rte 2 Box 615 Hollister MO 65672

CALLENBACH, JOHN ANTON, b Merchantville, NJ, Apr 9, 08; m 33; c 3. ENTOMOLOGY. *Educ:* Univ Wis, BS, 30, MS, 31, PhD(econ entom), 39. *Prof Exp:* Asst econ entom, Univ Wis, 30-33; Va Smelting Co fel, Va Truck Exp Sta, 33-36; instr econ entom, Univ Wis & agent, Bur Entom & Plant Quarantine, USDA, 36-42; asst prof entom, Univ Idaho, 42-44; asst state entomologist, Mont, 44-46; asst prof zool & entom, Mont State Col, 46-48, assoc prof, 48-53; state entoglist, NDak, & prof agr entom & chmn dept, 53-57, assoc dean agr & assoc dir agr exp sta, 57-69, prof entom, 69-74, chmn dept, 69-73, EMER PROF ENTOM, N DAK STATE UNIV, 74- *Mem:* Entom Soc Am. *Res:* Truck crop and cereal crop insects; mosquitoes. *Mailing Add:* 606 Ninth St S Fargo ND 58103

CALLENDER, JONATHAN FERRIS, b Los Angeles, Calif, Nov 7, 44; m 67; c 3. GEOLOGY, TECTONICS. *Educ:* Calif Inst Technol, BS, 66; Harvard Univ, AM, 68, PhD(geol), 75. *Prof Exp:* Teaching fel geol, Harvard Univ, 67-70, res asst mineral, 70; asst prof, 72-77, ASSOC PROF GEOL, UNIV NMEX, 77- *Concurrent Pos:* Consult, Pub Serv Co, NMex, 73-74 & Sandia Labs, 74-; vis staff scientist, Los Alamos Sci Lab, 74-; proj corresp, US Geodynamics Comt, 75-; pres, NMex Geol Soc, 77; panel mem, Gorleben nuclear disposal site, Fed Repub Ger, 78- *Mem:* Geol Soc Am; Sigma Xi; Am Geophys Union; Mineral Soc Am; Am Asn Petrol Geologists. *Res:* Structural geology and petrology of the Precambrian of New Mexico; tectonics of the Rio Grande rift; nuclear waste disposal in geologic materials; fabric studies of halite; geothermal exploration; geotectonics. *Mailing Add:* Dept of Geol Univ of NMex Albuquerque NM 87131

CALLENDER, WADE LEE, b Kingsville, Ohio, May 27, 26; m 50; c 5. PHYSICAL CHEMISTRY. *Educ:* Col of Wooster, AB, 48; Univ Rochester, PhD(chem), 51. *Prof Exp:* Res chemist, Shell Oil Co, 51-66; sr staff res chemist, Koninklijke-Shell Lab, Amsterdam, 66-68 & Shell Oil Co, 68-73, RES ASSOC, SHELL DEVELOP CO, 73- *Mem:* Catalysis Soc; Am Chem Soc; Am Soc Testing & Mat. *Res:* Mechanism and kinetics of catalytic reactions; analog and digital computing; catalytic reforming; Ziegler-Natta catalysis. *Mailing Add:* Shell Develop Co PO Box 1380 Houston TX 77001

CALLENS, EARL EUGENE, JR, b Memphis, Tenn, Mar 8, 40; m 60; c 10. AEROSPACE ENGINEERING, FLUID DYNAMICS. *Educ:* Ga Inst Technol, BSAE, 62, MSAE, 64; Von Karman Inst Fluid Dynamics, Belg, dipl, 67; Univ Tenn, PhD(aerospace eng), 76. *Prof Exp:* Res engr, 68-77, eng supvr res & testing, Sverdrup Corp, 77-78, asst br mgr, ARO Inc, 78-80; ASST BR MGR, CALSPAN FIELD SERVICES, 81- *Honors & Awards:* Von Karman Prize, Von Karman Inst Fluid Dynamics; 67; HH Arnold Award, Am Inst Aeronaut & Astronaut, 74. *Mem:* Assoc fel Am Inst Aeronaut & Astronaut; Sigma Xi; Nat Mgt Asn; Am Soc Testing Mats. *Res:* Aerothermodynamics; hypersonic flow; wake phenomenology; hypervelocity erosion; technical management. *Mailing Add:* 110 Redbud Lane Tullahoma TN 37388

CALLERAME, JOSEPH, b New York, NY, Feb 9, 50; m 72; c 2. PHYSICS, ACOUSTICS. *Educ:* Columbia Col, BA, 70; Harvard Univ, MA, 71, PhD(physics), 75. *Prof Exp:* Res assoc, Mass Inst Technol, 75-77; sr res scientist physics, 77-80, MGR, MICROWAVE ULTRASONICS LAB, RAYTHEON CO, 80- *Mem:* Inst Elec & Electronics Engrs. *Res:* Surface acoustic wave devices; transducer design; interaction of x-rays with matter; neutron scattering; medical ultrasonics. *Mailing Add:* Raytheon Co Res Div 28 Seyon St Waltham MA 02154

CALLERY, PATRICK STEPHEN, b San Jose, Calif, Nov 30, 44; m 65; c 2. MEDICINAL CHEMISTRY. *Educ:* Univ Utah, BS, 68; Univ Calif, PhD(pharmaceut chem), 74. *Prof Exp:* Fel chem, 73-74, asst prof, 74-78, ASSOC PROF CHEM, UNIV MD, 78- *Concurrent Pos:* Epilepsy Found Am grant & Merck Found develop grant, 78-79; NIH grant, 79-81. *Mem:* Am Chem Soc; Am Soc Mass Spectrometry; Am Asn Col Pharm. *Res:* Biomedical applications of mass sepctrometry; radiopharmaceutical development. *Mailing Add:* Sch Pharm Univ Md 636 W Lombard St Baltimore MD 21201

CALLIHAN, ALFRED DIXON, b Scarbro, WVa, July 20, 08; wid. PHYSICS. *Educ:* Marshall Col, AB, 28; Duke Univ, AM, 31; NY Univ, PhD(physics), 33. *Hon Degrees:* DSc, Marshall Col, 64. *Prof Exp:* From asst to instr physics, Marshall Col, 26-29; asst, Duke Univ, 29-30 & NY Univ, 30-34; tutor, City Col New York, 34-37, from instr to asst prof, 37-48; res physicist, Manhattan Dist Proj, Div War Res, Columbia Univ, 41-45; res physicist, 45-73,

CONSULT, NUCLEAR DIV, UNION CARBIDE CORP, 73-; CONSULT, US ARMY BALLISTICS RES LAB, 73- *Concurrent Pos:* Ed, Nuclear Sci & Eng, 65-; mem, Nuclear Standards Mgt Bd, Am Nat Standards Inst; admin judge, Atomic Safety & Licensing Bd panel, US Nuclear Regulatory Comn. *Mem:* Fel Am Phys Soc; fel Am Nuclear Soc; Sigma Xi. *Res:* Reactor physics. *Mailing Add:* 102 Oak Lane Oak Ridge TN 37830

CALLIHAN, CLAYTON D, b Midland, Mich, June 13, 19; m 57; c 2. CHEMICAL ENGINEERING. *Educ:* Mich State Univ, BS, 54, PhD, 57. *Prof Exp:* Lab technician, Dow Chem Co, Mich, 37-44, sr lab technician, 46-50, res engr, 57-60, sr res engr, La, 60-63; assoc prof, 63-71, PROF CHEM ENG, LA STATE UNIV, BATON ROUGE, 71- *Concurrent Pos:* Consult, 63- *Res:* High polymers and their preparation from cellulose; conversion of cellulosic wastes and microbial proteins. *Mailing Add:* Dept of Chem Eng La State Univ Baton Rouge LA 70803

CALLIHAN, ROBERT HAROLD, b Spokane, Wash, Oct 19, 33; m 54; c 2. AGRONOMY, WEED SCIENCE. *Educ:* Univ Idaho, BS, 57; Ore State Univ, MS, 61, PhD(crop sci), 73. *Prof Exp:* Supt agron, Ore State Univ, 57-60, instr, 60-67; exten specialist potato prod, 67-70, asst exten prof, 69-70, asst res prof agron, 70-75, ASSOC RES PROF AGRON, UNIV IDAHO, 75- *Honors & Awards:* Meritorious Honors Award in Agr, Polish Govt, 77. *Mem:* Weed Sci Soc Am; Am Soc Agron; Crop Sci Soc Am; Potato Asn Am; Europ Asn Potato Res. *Res:* Weed control in potatoes, pulses, forages, and sugar beets; herbigation; crop loss. *Mailing Add:* Plant Sci Dept Univ Idaho Moscow ID 83843

CALLIS, CLAYTON FOWLER, b Sedalia, Mo, Sept 25, 23; m 49; c 2. INORGANIC CHEMISTRY. *Educ:* Cent Col, Mo, AB, 44; Univ Ill, MS, 46, PhD(inorg chem), 48. *Prof Exp:* Instr physics & chem, Cent Col, Mo, 44-45; asst, Univ Ill, 45-47; res chemist, Gen Elec Co, 48-50; res chemist, Monsanto Co, Ala, 51-52 & Ohio, 52-54, res group leader, 54-57 & Mo, 57-59, sr res group leader, 59-60, asst dir res, 60-62, mgr res, 62-69, dir res & devel, Inorg Chem Div, 69-71, Detergents & Fine Chem Div, 71-73 & Detergent & Phosphate Div, 73-75, dir technol planning & eval, 75-77, DIR ENVIRON OPERS & TECHNOL PLANNING, MONSANTO INDUST CHEM CO, 77- *Concurrent Pos:* Civilian with Atomic Energy Comn, 48-50; alt, Indust Res Inst, 75- *Honors & Awards:* St Louis Award, Am Chem Soc, 71. *Mem:* Sigma Xi; Am Inst Chemists; Am Chem Soc; AAAS. *Res:* Chemistry of phosphorus and its compounds; surfactants; detergents; antimicrobials; dentifrices. *Mailing Add:* 2 Holiday Lane St Louis MO 63131

CALLIS, JAMES BERTRAM, b Riverside, Calif, Sept 4, 43; m 68; c 1. SPECTROSCOPY, CANCER DIAGNOSIS. *Educ:* Univ Calif, Davis, BS, 65; Univ Wash, PhD(phys chem), 70. *Prof Exp:* Fel, Dept Chem, Univ Wash, 70-72 & Dept Biophys, Univ Pa, 72-73; res asst prof, 75-78, DIR ANAL SERV, DEPT CHEM, UNIV WASH, 78-, RES ASSOC PROF, 80- *Mem:* Am Chem Soc; AAAS; Soc Appl Spectros. *Res:* Analytical chemistry; development of new types of instrumentation, especially for molecular luminescence and mass spectroscopy; biophysical chemistry; development of new instrumentaton for spectroscopic measurements on living entities. *Mailing Add:* BG-10 Dept Chem Univ Wash Seattle WA 98115

CALLIS, JERRY JACKSON, b Parrott, Ga, July 28, 26. VETERINARY MEDICINE. *Educ:* Ala Polytech Inst, DVM, 47; Purdue Univ, MS, 49. *Hon Degrees:* DSc, Purdue Univ, 79, Long Island Univ, Southampton Col, 80. *Prof Exp:* Vet, Brucellosis Test Lab, Purdue Univ, 48-49, State Vet Res Inst, Holland, 49-51 & Animal Dis Sta, Md, 52-53; in charge res opers, 53-56, asst dir, 56-62, DIR, PLUM ISLAND ANIMAL DIS CTR, 63- *Honors & Awards:* USDA Award, 57; XII Int Vet Cong Prize, Am Vet Med Asn, 74; Am Meat Inst Award, 80. *Mem:* AAAS; Am Vet Med Asn; Tissue Cult Asn; US Animal Health Asn. *Res:* Tissue culture; virology and immunology; foot-and-mouth disease. *Mailing Add:* Plum Island Animal Dis Ctr Box 848 Greenport NY 11944

CALLISON, GEORGE, b Blue Rapids, Kans, June 1, 40; m 62; c 2. EVOLUTIONARY BIOLOGY, VERTEBRATE MORPHOLOGY. *Educ:* Kans State Univ, BS, 62; Univ Kans, MA, 65, PhD(zool), 69. *Prof Exp:* Asst prof zool & asst cur vert paleont, SDak Sch Mines & Technol, 67; asst prof, 69-72, assoc prof, 73-77, PROF BIOL, CALIF STATE UNIV, LONG BEACH, 78- *Concurrent Pos:* Res assoc vert paleont & herpet, Los Angeles County Mus Natural Hist, 69-; consult, Badlands Nat Monument Master Plan, Nat Park Serv, 69 & Fruita Paleont Area, Bur Land Mgt, 77; Long Beach Calif State Col Found res grant, 70; NSF res grants, 77-78 & 79-81. *Mem:* Sigma Xi; Soc Vert Paleont; Soc Study Amphibians & Reptiles. *Res:* Evolutionary interrelationships of primitive snakes; fossil tetrapods from Mesozoic and Cenozoic rocks; comparative anatomical and functional morphological concepts. *Mailing Add:* Dept of Biol Calif State Univ Long Beach CA 90840

CALLOW, ALLAN DANA, b Somerville, Mass, Apr 9, 16; m 43; c 3. SURGERY. *Educ:* Tufts Col, BS, 38, MS, 48, PhD, 52; Harvard Univ, MD, 42; Am Bd Surg, dipl, 52. *Prof Exp:* From instr to prof surg, Med Sch, Tufts Univ, 48-69, vchmn dept surg & chief gen & vascular surg, 71-77; SURG, NEW ENG MED CTR HOSP, 54- *Concurrent Pos:* Trustee, Tufts Univ, 71-77, chmn bd trustees, 77-; trustee, Civic Educ Found; dir, Med Eng Assocs; consult, Surg Gen, Med Dept, US Navy. *Mem:* Asn Am Med Cols; fel Am Col Surg; Am Heart Asn; Soc Vascular Surg; Int Cardiovasc Soc (secy-gen, 68-77, pres, 77-79, pres NAm chap, 74-75). *Res:* Clinical surgery; cardiovascular disease; general and peripheral vascular surgery. *Mailing Add:* New England Med Ctr Hosp 171 Harrison Ave Boston MA 02111

CALLOWAY, DORIS HOWES, b Canton, Ohio, Feb 14, 23; m 81; c 2. NUTRITION. *Educ:* Ohio State Univ, BS, 43; Univ Chicago, PhD(nutrit), 47; Am Bd Nutrit, dipl, 51. *Prof Exp:* Intern dietetics, hosp, Johns Hopkins Univ, 44; res dietician, dept med, Univ Ill, 45; consult nutrit, Med Assocs Chicago, 48-51; nutritionist, QM Food & Container Inst, 51-58, head metab lab, 58-59, chief nutrit br, 59-61; chmn dept food sci & nutrit, Stanford Res Inst, 61-64; PROF NUTRIT, UNIV CALIF, BERKELEY, 63-, PROVOST, PROF SCHS & COLS, 81- *Concurrent Pos:* Assoc ed, Nutrit Rev, 62-68; mem ed bd, J Nutrit, 67-72, Environ Biol & Med, 69-, J Am Dietetic Asn, 74-77 & Interdisciplinary Sci Rev, 75- Mem bd dirs, Am Bd Nutrit, 68-71; mem panel, White House Conf Food, Nutrit & Health, 69; mem bd trustees, Nat Coun Hunger & Malnutrit in US, 69-71; mem Nat Acad Sci-Nat Res Coun Food & Nutrit Bd, 72-75; mem vis comt, Mass Inst Technol, 72-74; mem expert adv panel on nutrit, WHO, 72-; mem adv coun, Nat Inst Arthritis, Metab & Digestive Dis, NIH, 74-77; consult Nutrit Div, Food & Agr Orgn, UN, 74-75; mem adv coun, Nat Inst Aging, NIH, 78-81. *Mem:* Am Inst Nutrit (pres, 82-83); Am Dietetic Asn. *Res:* Human nutrition; protein and energy; gastrointestinal functions. *Mailing Add:* Univ Calif Berkeley CA 94720

CALLOWAY, E DEAN, physical chemistry, see previous edition

CALLOWAY, JEAN MITCHENER, b Indianola, Miss, Dec 18, 23; m 52; c 2. NUMBER THEORY. *Educ:* Millsaps Col, BA, 44; Univ Pa, MA, 49, PhD(math), 52. *Prof Exp:* Asst instr math, Millsaps Col, 44; instr, McCallie Sch, 44-47; asst instr, Univ Pa, 47-52; from asst prof to assoc prof, Carleton Col, 52-60, actg chmn dept, 53-54 & 58-59; chmn dept, 60-73, PROF MATH, KALAMAZOO COL, 60- *Concurrent Pos:* Mem, Inst Advan Study, 59; res assoc, Stanford Univ, 68-69. *Mem:* Am Math Soc; Math Asn Am. *Mailing Add:* Dept of Math Kalamazoo Col Kalamazoo MI 49007

CALMA, VICTOR CHARLES, b Houston, Tex, July 13, 17; m 62. MEDICAL EDUCATION, PEDIATRICS. *Educ:* Rice Univ, BA, 39; Univ Tex, MD, 42. *Prof Exp:* Assoc prof physiol, Univ Houston, 50-51; asst prof, Univ Tex Med Br, Galveston, 51-59, instr pediat, 57-59, asst prof, 59-66, dir adolescent med, 60-66; VPRES MED EDUC, MEM MED CTR, 66- *Concurrent Pos:* Adj prof health sci, Corpus Christi State Univ, 75- *Mem:* AMA; fel Am Acad Pediat; Asn Hosp Med Educ; Am Acad Family Physicians; Alliance Continuing Med Educ. *Res:* Pediatrics; adolescent medicine. *Mailing Add:* Mem Med Ctr 2606 Hosp Blvd Corpus Christi TX 78405

CALMAN, JACK, fluid dynamics, oceanography, see previous edition

CALNE, DONALD BRIAN, b London, Eng, May 4, 36; m 65; c 3. NEUROLOGY, PHARMACOLOGY. *Educ:* Oxford Univ, BSc, 58, MS & BCh, 61, DM, 68. *Prof Exp:* Resident physician med, St Thomas Hosp, London, 63-64; resident physician neurol, Nat Hosps Nervous Dis, London, 65-66 & Univ Col Hosp, London, 67-69; tenured staff physician, Royal Postgrad Med Sch, London, 70-74; CLIN DIR NEUROL, NAT INST NEUROL & COMMUN DIS & STROKE, NIH, 74-, CHIEF EXP THERAPEUT BR, 76- *Concurrent Pos:* Mem adv bd, Advan Neurol, 73- & United Parkinson Found, 75-77; consult neurologist, Nat Naval Med Ctr, Bethesda & Walter Reed Army Med Ctr, Washington, DC, 75- *Mem:* Asn Brit Neurologists; Am Acad Neurol. *Res:* Pharmacological study of mechanisms of synaptic function in the central nervous system in health and disease; use of drugs for the manipulation of synaptic transmission in order to benefit neurological disorders. *Mailing Add:* Rm 6D20 Bldg 10 NIH Bethesda MD 20014

CALNEK, BRUCE WIXSON, b Manchester, NY, Jan 29, 32; m 54; c 2. VETERINARY VIROLOGY. *Educ:* Cornell Univ, DVM, 55, MS, 56. *Prof Exp:* Actg asst prof poultry dis, Cornell Univ, 56-57; assoc prof vet sci, Univ Mass, 57-61; PROF AVIAN DIS, CORNELL UNIV, 61-, CHMN DEPT AVIAN & AQUATIC ANIMAL MED, 77- *Concurrent Pos:* Nat Cancer Inst fel virol, Univ Calif, Berkeley, 67-68; vis scientist oncol, Houghton Poultry Res Sta, Eng, 74-75; cancer res fel, Int Union Against Cancer, 74-75; consult, Virol Study Sect, NIH, 75- *Mem:* Am Vet Med Asn; Am Asn Avian Pathologists; World Vet Poultry Asn. *Res:* Viral oncology, with particular emphasis on the pathogenesis of avian neoplastic diseases of chickens induced by DNA-containing viruses, known as Marek's disease, and RNA-containing viruses causing lymphoid leukosis. *Mailing Add:* Dept of Avian & Aquatic Animal Med Col of Vet Med Cornell Univ Ithaca NY 14853

CALO, JOSEPH MANUEL, b Newark, NJ, Nov 9, 44; m 68; c 2. CHEMICAL ENGINEERING, PHYSICAL CHEMISTRY. *Educ:* Newark Col Eng, BS, 66; Princeton Univ, AM, 68, PhD(chem eng), 70. *Prof Exp:* Atmospheric physicist, Air Force Cambridge Res Labs, Hanscom AFB, 74; res engr, Exxon Res & Eng Co, Florham Park, 74-76; asst prof, Dept Chem Eng, Princeton Univ, 76-81; ASSOC PROF, DIV ENG, BROWN UNIV, 81- *Mem:* Am Inst Chem Engrs; Am Chem Soc; Sigma Xi; AAAS. *Res:* Chemical reactor/reaction engineering; atmospheric physics and chemistry. *Mailing Add:* Div Eng Brown Univ Providence RI 02912

CALOZA, DIONISIO LOPEZ, b Tayug, Pangasinan, Phillipines, May 26, 29; US citizen; m 59; c 1. INFECTIOUS DISEASES, CARDIOVASCULAR MEDICINE. *Educ:* Univ Santo Tomas, Phillipines, MD, 54. *Prof Exp:* Intern, St Clare's Hosp, New York, 55-56, path residency, 56-57, intern med residency, 57-60, res fel, 60-62, personnel & out patient physician, 62-69; asst clin res dir, 70-74, ASSOC CLIN RES DIR, SQUIBB INST MED RES, 74- *Mem:* AMA; Am Soc Microbiol; Am Asn Med Writers. *Res:* Antibiotics; infectious diseases; cardiovascular medicine. *Mailing Add:* 2626 Skytop Dr Scotch Plains NJ 07076

CALPOUZOS, LUCAS, b Detroit, Mich, Oct 20, 27; m 50; c 2. PLANT PATHOLOGY. *Educ:* Cornell Univ, BS, 50; Harvard Univ, AM, 52, PhD(biol), 55. *Prof Exp:* Plant pathologist, R T Vanderbilt Co, 50-51; instr bot, Harvard Univ, 52-53; plant pathologist, Fed Exp Sta, PR, USDA, 55-62; NSF sr fel, Bristol Univ, 62-63; res plant pathologist, Crops Res Div, Agr Res Serv, USDA, 63-67; from assoc prof to prof plant path, Univ Minn, St Paul, 67-71; prof plant sci & head, Dept Plant & Soil Sci, Univ Idaho, 71-80; PROF PLANT SCI & DEAN, SCH AGR & HOME ECON, CALIF STATE UNIV, CHICO, 80- *Mem:* Am Phytopath Soc; Am Soc Agron; Am Soc Hort Sci. *Res:* Crop loss estimates; chemical control of plant diseases; fungus physiology. *Mailing Add:* Sch Agr & Home Econ Calif State Univ Chico CA 95929

CALTAGIRONE, LEOPOLDO ENRIQUE, b Valparaiso, Chile, Mar 1, 27; nat; m 53; c 3. ENTOMOLOGY. *Educ:* Univ Chile, ErAgron, 51; Univ Calif, PhD(entom), 60. *Prof Exp:* Entomologist, Chilean Ministry Agr, 49-62; from jr entomologist to assoc entomologist, 62-75, PROF & ENTOMOLOGIST, UNIV CALIF, BERKELEY, 75- *Concurrent Pos:* John Simon Guggenheim fel, 57-59; lectr, Sch Agr, Cath Univ Chile, 60-62. *Mem:* AAAS; Entom Soc Am; Am Inst Biol Sci. *Res:* Biological control of agricultural insect pests; biology of parasitic Hymenoptera. *Mailing Add:* 1050 San Pablo Ave Albany CA 94706

CALTRIDER, PAUL GENE, b Mineral Wells, WVa, Jan 14, 35; m 56; c 2. MICROBIAL PHYSIOLOGY. *Educ:* Glenville State Col, BS, 56; WVa Univ, MS, 58; Univ Ill, PhD(plant path, microbiol), 62. *Prof Exp:* Sr microbiologist, 62-66, mgr antibiotic qual control & tech serv, 66-76, mgr antibiotic fermentation technol, 76-80, DIR ANTIBIOTIC TECH SERV, ELI LILLY & CO, 80- *Mem:* Am Soc Microbiol; Soc Indust Microbiol; Am Chem Soc. *Res:* Physiology and biochemistry of microorganisms, especially carbohydrate metabolism, antibiotic fermentations and biosynthesis of antibiotics. *Mailing Add:* 307 E McCarty St Indianapolis IN 46285

CALUB, ALFONSO DEGUZMAN, b Aringay, La Union, Philippines, Aug 1, 38; m; c 2. PLANT BREEDING. *Educ:* Univ NH, PhD(plant sci), 72. *Prof Exp:* Res asst, Univ Philippines, 60-64, instr, 64-68; res asst, Univ Ky, 68-69 & Univ NH, 69-72; fel, Univ Nebr, 72-74; dir res & sr plant breeder, Alexandria Seed Co, La, 74-81; SR SCIENTIST, RING AROUND PROD, TEX, 81- *Mem:* Am Soc Agron; Crop Sci Soc Am; AAAS; Sigma Xi. *Res:* Research and development of male strile lines, restorer lines, and hybrids of rice. *Mailing Add:* Ring Around Prod PO Box 778 East Bernard TX 77135

CALUSDIAN, RICHARD FRANK, b Watertown, Mass, Feb 6, 35; m 62; c 3. THEORETICAL PHYSICS. *Educ:* Harvard Univ, BA, 57; Univ NH, MS, 59; Boston Univ, PhD(physics), 65. *Prof Exp:* Physicist, Mat Res Agency, US Dept Army, 65, fel, Natick Labs, 65-66; assoc prof, 66-69, PROF PHYSICS, BRIDGEWATER STATE COL, 69-, CHMN DEPT, 66- *Mem:* Am Asn Physics Teachers. *Res:* Electron-phonon interaction; theory of electrical and thermal conductivity. *Mailing Add:* Dept Physics Bridgewater State Col Bridgewater MA 02324

CALVANICO, NICKOLAS JOSEPH, b New York, NY, Aug 18, 36; m 59; c 2. IMMUNOLOGY, PROTEIN CHEMISTRY. *Educ:* City Col New York, BS, 58; DePaul Univ, MS, 60; Univ Vt, PhD(biochem), 64. *Prof Exp:* Trainee immunol, Div Exp Med, Col Med, Univ Vt, 64-65; res instr med, Sch Med, State Univ NY Buffalo, 68-73; asst prof immunol, Mayo Found Sch Med, Univ Minn, 73-77; asst prof, 77-79, ASSOC PROF, DEPT MED, MED COL WIS, 79-; RES HEALTH SCIENTIST, RES SERV, VET ADMIN CTR, 78- *Concurrent Pos:* Arthritis Found fel, Sch Med, State Univ NY Buffalo, 65-68; consult, Erie County Labs, 68-73; indust consult, 73-77. *Mem:* NY Acad Sci; Am Asn Immunol. *Res:* Hypersensitivity lung disease; immunological mechanisms causing allergic inflammatory lung disease; purification of environmental allergens of annual and microbiol origin; structure and function of Immunoglobulin A. *Mailing Add:* Res Serv/151 Vet Admin Hosp 5000 West National Ave Wood WI 53193

CALVER, JAMES LEWIS, b Pontiac, Mich, June 15, 13; m 45, 70; c 2. MINERALOGY, PHYSICAL GEOLOGY. *Educ:* Univ Mich, AB, 36, MS, 38, PhD(geol), 42. *Prof Exp:* Asst geol, Univ Mich, 35-39; instr geol, Univ Wichita, 40-42; asst prof, Univ Mo, 42-43; assoc geologist, Tenn Valley Authority, 43-47; geologist, Fla Geol Surv, 47-57; comnr mineral resources & state geologist, Va Div, 57-78; RETIRED. *Mem:* Mineral Soc Am; Geol Soc Am; Am Inst Mining, Metall & Petrol Engrs; Am Asn Petrol Geologists; Am Geophys Union. *Res:* Economic geology. *Mailing Add:* 1614 Oxford Rd Charlottesville VA 22903

CALVERLEY, JOHN ROBERT, b Hot Springs, Ark, Jan 14, 32; m 53; c 2. NEUROLOGY. *Educ:* Univ Ore, BS, 53, MD, 55. *Prof Exp:* Resident neurol, State Univ Iowa Hosps, 56; fel med, Mayo Found, 57, resident neurol, 57-59; neurologist, Wilford Hall US Air Force Hosp, San Antonio, Tex, 60-62; chief neurol serv, 62-64; from asst prof to assoc prof, 64-70, chief div, 66-73, PROF NEUROL, MED BR, UNIV TEX, GALVESTON, 70-, CHMN DEPT, 73- *Concurrent Pos:* Asst examr, Am Bd Neurol & Psychiat, 65-77, dir, 77-; nat consult neurol, Surgeon Gen, US Air Force, 73- *Mem:* Am Neurol Asn; Asn Res Nerv & Ment Dis; Am Acad Neurol; Am Epilepsy Soc; Asn Univ Prof Neurol. *Res:* Medical education. *Mailing Add:* Dept of Neurol Univ of Tex Med Br Galveston TX 77550

CALVERT, ALLEN FISHER, b San Diego, Calif, Aug 1, 27; m 55; c 4. BIOCHEMICAL GENETICS. *Educ:* Univ San Francisco, BS, 52; Univ Calif, PhD(biochem), 62; Am Bd Clin Chem, dipl, 72. *Prof Exp:* Fel biochem, Univ Hawaii, 62-64; biochemist, Clin Invest Ctr, US Naval Hosp, Oakland, Calif, 64-65; biochemist, Med Genetics Div, 65-81, ASSOC PROF PEDIAT & CHILD HEALTH, DEPT PEDIAT, COL MED, HOWARD UNIV, 74- *Mem:* Am Soc Human Genetics; Am Asn Clin Chem. *Res:* Inborn errors of metabolism; screening for children's diseases of genetic origin; ultra micro methods; cyclic nucleotide metabolism in health and in disease. *Mailing Add:* Dept of Pediat Col of Med Howard Univ Washington DC 20059

CALVERT, CRAIG STEVEN, b Hartford, Conn, Apr 17, 54; m 78; c 1. CLAY MINEROLOGY. *Educ:* Univ RI, BS, 76; NC State Univ, MS, 78; Tex A&M Univ, PhD(soil sci), 81. *Prof Exp:* Res & teaching asst soil mineral, NC State Univ, 76-78; res & teaching asst soil mineral & basic soils, Tex A&M Univ, 78-81; RES CHEMIST, EXXON PROD RES CO, 81- *Mem:* Soil Sci Soc Am; Am Soc Agron; Clay Minerals Soc; Mineral Soc Gt Brit. *Res:* Studies of clay minerals and clay diagenesis; clay minerals in soils and in petroleum reservoirs. *Mailing Add:* 10122 Limewood Ln Sugarland TX 77478

CALVERT, DAVID VICTOR, b Chaplin, Ky, Feb 26, 34; m 57; c 2. SOIL FERTILITY. *Educ:* Univ Ky, BS, 56, MS, 58; Iowa State Univ, PhD(soil fertil), 62. *Prof Exp:* Asst soils chemist, Citrus Exp Sta, 62-67, from assoc prof to prof soil chem, 67-78, DIR, AGR RES CTR, UNIV FLA, 78- *Concurrent Pos:* Off collabr, Soil & Water Conserv Div, Agr Res Serv, USDA, 69-; consult, Jamaican Sch Agr, 70. *Mem:* AAAS; Am Soc Agron; Sigma Xi; Soc Citricult. *Res:* Chemistry of soil phosphorus; soil-plant tracer studies with Nitrogen-fifteen isotope; soil chemistry-fertility, drainage and irrigation with citrus. *Mailing Add:* Agr Res Ctr Box 248 Univ Fla Ft Pierce FL 33450

CALVERT, JACK GEORGE, b Inglewood, Calif, May 9, 23; m 46; c 2. PHOTOCHEMISTRY, PHYSICAL CHEMISTRY. *Educ:* Univ Calif, Los Angeles, BS, 44, PhD(chem), 49. *Prof Exp:* Nat Res Coun Can fel, 49-50; from asst prof to prof, 50-74, chmn dept, 64-68, Kimberly prof, 74-81, EMER PROF CHEM, OHIO STATE UNIV, 81-; SR SCIENTIST, NAT CTR ATMOSPHERIC RES, 82- *Concurrent Pos:* Chmn, Nat Air Pollution Manpower Develop Adv Comt, 68-69, Nat Adv Comt Conserv Found, 69-72, Comt on Aldehydes, Nat Acad Sci, 79-81 & Environ Chem & Physics Rev Panel, Environ Protection Agency, 80-; Air Pollution Res Grants Adv Comt, Environ Protection Agency, 70-72; mem, Chem & Physics Adv Comt on Air Pollution, 73-76, Comt on Health Effects of Air Pollutants, Nat Acad Sci, 73-74, USA-USSR Joint Comt on Atmospheric Modelling & Aerosols, 75- & vis comt of Brookhaven Nat Lab, Dept Energy & Environ, 76-; Simon Guggenheim Mem Fel, 77-78. *Honors & Awards:* Inovative Res in Environ Sci & Technol Award, Am Chem Soc, 81. *Mem:* Fel AAAS; Am Chem Soc; fel Am Inst Chemists. *Res:* Atmospheric chemistry; photochemistry; reaction kinetics. *Mailing Add:* Div Atmospheric Chem & Aeronomy Nat Ctr Atmospheric Res Boulder CO 80303

CALVERT, JAMES BOWLES, b Columbus, Ohio, May 28, 35. OPTICAL PHYSICS. *Educ:* Mont State Col, BS, 56, MS, 59; Univ Colo, PhD(physics), 63. *Prof Exp:* Res physicist, 59-63, from lectr to asst prof physics, 62-66, assoc prof astron, 76-80, ASSOC PROF PHYSICS, UNIV DENVER, 66- *Mem:* Am Inst Physics; Am Phys Soc; Am Asn Physics Teachers; Nat Soc Prof Engrs. *Res:* Energy transfer in molecular collisions; fluctuations in light beams; coherence theory; atomic structure. *Mailing Add:* Dept of Physics & Astron Univ of Denver Denver CO 80208

CALVERT, LAURISTON DERWENT, b Tasmania, Dec 10, 24; m 54; c 2. CHEMISTRY, CRYSTALLOGRAPHY. *Educ:* Univ NZ, BS, 46, BA, 48, MS, 49, PhD(crystal struct anal), 52. *Prof Exp:* Nat Res Coun fel, 52-54; from asst res officer to sr res officer, 54-73, PRIN RES OFFICER, NAT RES COUN CAN, 73- *Concurrent Pos:* Co-ed, Struct Reports. secy, Can Nat Comt Crystallog, 69- *Res:* Low and high temperature and high pressure x-ray diffraction; powder diffraction; single-crystal structure analysis; inter-metallic compounds. *Mailing Add:* Nat Res Coun Can Ottawa Can

CALVERT, OSCAR HUGH, b Dallas, Tex, Oct 28, 18; m 44; c 4. PLANT PATHOLOGY. *Educ:* Okla State Univ, BS, 43; Univ Wis, MS, 45, PhD(plant path), 48. *Prof Exp:* Asst bot & plant path, Okla State Univ, 42-44; asst, Penicillin Proj, US Army & Dept Bot, Univ Wis, 44-45, asst, Dept Plant Path, 45-48; asst plant pathologist, Dept Plant Physiol & Path, Agr & Mech Col Tex, 48-52; plant pathologist, USDA, 52-54; consult plant path & nursery retail sales mgr, Lambert Landscape, 54-58; asst prof field crops, 58-67, from asst prof to assoc prof plant path, 67-75, PROF PLANT PATH, UNIV MO-COLUMBIA, 75- *Concurrent Pos:* Vis prof, Res Inst Plant Protection, Budapest, Hungary, 69-70. *Mem:* AAAS; Am Soc Agron; Mycol Soc Am; Am Phytopath Soc. *Res:* Diseases of field crops. *Mailing Add:* 405 S William Columbia MO 65201

CALVERT, RALPH LOWELL, b Howard, Kans, Jan 10, 10; wid; c 2. MATHEMATICS. *Educ:* Southwestern Col, Kans, AB, 37; Univ Ill, AM, 38, PhD(math, astron), 50. *Prof Exp:* From instr to assoc prof math & astron, Utah State Univ, 40-49; asst prof, Univ Wyo, 49-51; res mathematician, Sandia Corp, 51-73; RETIRED. *Res:* Systems analysis. *Mailing Add:* 415 Adams St NE Albuquerque NM 87108

CALVERT, THOMAS W(ILLIAM), b Dunaskin, Scotland, Apr 12, 36; m 59; c 2. BIOMEDICAL ENGINEERING, COMPUTER SCIENCE. *Educ:* Univ London, BSc, 57; Wayne State Univ, MSEE, 64; Carnegie Inst Technol, PhD(elec eng), 67. *Prof Exp:* Elec design engr, Imp Chem Indust, Ltd Eng, 57-60; electronic engr, Canadair Ltd, Can, 60-61; lectr elec eng, Western Ont Inst Technol, 61-64; instr, Wayne State Univ, 64-65; instr, Carnegie-Mellon Univ, 66-67, asst prof elec eng & bioeng, 67-69, assoc prof elec eng & bioeng & chmn biotech prog, 69-72; PROF KINESIOL & COMPUT SCI, SIMON FRASER UNIV, 77-, DEAN, FAC INTERDISCIPLINARY STUDIES, 77- *Mem:* Inst Elec & Electronics Engrs; Soc Neurosci; Can Med & Biol Eng Soc; Comput Sci Asn; Asn Prof Engrs BC. *Res:* Pattern recognition; in particular feature extraction with application to vector cardiograms; modelling the nervous system; reading aids for the blind; systems theory in physiology; languages for human movement; computer graphics. *Mailing Add:* Fac of Interdisciplinary Studies Simon Fraser Univ Burnaby BC V5A 1S6 Can

CALVERT, WYNNE, b Columbus, Ohio, Mar 4, 37; m 58; c 3. ATMOSPHERIC PHYSICS. *Educ:* Mont State Col, BS, 58; Univ Wis, MS, 59; Univ Colo, PhD(astrogeophys), 62. *Prof Exp:* Physicist, Nat Bur Stand, 60-62; asst prof physics, Mont State Col, 62-63; proj leader cent radio propagation lab, Nat Bur Stand, 63-65; chief rocket & satellite exp sect, Aeronomy Lab, 65-67, CONSULT TO AERONOMY LAB, ENVIRON RES LABS, NAT OCEANIC & ATMOSPHERIC ADMIN, 67- *Mem:* Int Sci Radio Union; Am Geophys Union; Sigma Xi. *Res:* Ionospheric physics and plasma physics. *Mailing Add:* 900 35th St Boulder CO 80303

CALVIN, CLYDE LACEY, b Winlock, Wash, June 22, 34; m 60; c 2. PLANT ANATOMY. *Educ:* Wash State Univ, BS, 60; Purdue Univ, MS, 62; Univ Calif, Davis, PhD(bot), 66. *Prof Exp:* NIH fel, Univ Calif, Santa Barbara, 65-66; asst prof bot, Calif State Col, Long Beach, 66-67; assoc prof biol, Ore Col Educ, 67-68; ASSOC PROF BIOL, PORTLAND STATE UNIV, 68- *Mem:* Bot Soc Am; Int Soc Plant Morphol. *Res:* Plant anatomy and ultrastructure; tissue relations between dicotyledonous parasites and their hosts. *Mailing Add:* Dept of Biol Portland State Univ Portland OR 97207

CALVIN, LYLE D, b Nebr, Apr 12, 23; m 52; c 3. STATISTICS. *Educ:* Parsons Jr Col, AB, 43; NC State Univ, BS, 47, PhD, 53; Univ Chicago, BS, 48. *Prof Exp:* Asst, NC State Univ, 47-50, asst statistician, 52-53; biometrician, G D Searle & Co, 50-52; assoc prof, 53-57, chmn dept, 62-81, PROF STATIST, ORE STATE UNIV, 57-, STATISTICIAN, EXP STA, 53-, DIR, SURV RES CTR, 73-, DEAN, GRAD SCH, 81- *Concurrent Pos:* Vis prof, Univ Edinburgh, 67 & Univ Cairo, 71-72; mem epidemiol & biomet training comt, Nat Inst Gen Med Sci, 68-72; mem Am Statist Asn comt, Bur of Census, 71-77. *Mem:* Fel AAAS; Biomet Soc (pres, NAm Region, 64-65, secy, 80-); fel Am Statist Asn; Royal Statist Soc; Int Statist Inst. *Res:* Experimental design and analysis; sampling methods. *Mailing Add:* Dept Statist Ore State Univ Corvallis OR 97331

CALVIN, MELVIN, b St Paul, Minn, Apr 8, 11; m 42; c 3. ORGANIC CHEMISTRY. *Educ:* Mich Col Mines, BS, 31; Univ Minn, PhD(chem), 35. *Hon Degrees:* Numerous from US & foreign univs & cols, 55-79. *Prof Exp:* Rockefeller grant, Univ Manchester, 35-37; instr chem, 37-40, from asst prof to prof, 41-71, dir, Bio-Org Div, Lawrence Radiation Lab, 46-80, dir, Lab Chem Biodynamics, 60-80, PROF MOLECULAR BIOL, UNIV CALIF, BERKELEY, 63-, UNIV PROF CHEM, 71- . *Concurrent Pos:* Off investr, Nat Defense Res Comt, Univ Calif, 41-44, Manhattan Dist Proj, 44-45; mem US deleg, Int Conf Peaceful Uses Atomic Energy, Geneva, Switz, 55; mem joint comt, Int Union Pure & Appl Chem, 56; chem adv comt, US Air Force Off Sci Res, 51-55; vchmn exec coun, Armed Forces-Nat Res Coun Comt Bio-Astronaut, 58-62; mem, President's Sci Adv Comt, 63-65; bd sci counr, NIMH, 68-71; vchmn comt sci & pub policy, Nat Acad Sci, 71, chmn, 72-75; mem energy res adv bd, Dept Energy, 81. *Honors & Awards:* Nobel Prize in Chem, 61; Sugar Res Found Prize, 50; Flintoff Medal & Prize, The Chem Soc, 55; Hales Award, Am Soc Plant Physiol, 56; Richards Medal, Am Chem Soc, 56, Award Nuclear Appln in Chem, 57, Nichols Medal, 58; Davy Medal, Royal Soc, 64; Priestly Medal, 78; Gold Medal, Am Inst Chemists, 79; Oesper Prize, Am Chem Soc, 81. *Mem:* Nat Acad Sci; AAAS; Am Chem Soc (pres-elect, 70, pres, 71); fel Am Phys Soc; Am Soc Biol Chem. *Res:* Physical chemistry; photosynthesis and chemical biodynamics; plant physiology; chemical evolution; molecular biology; chemical and viral carcinogenesis; solar energy conversion (biomass and artificial photosynthesis). *Mailing Add:* Lab of Chem Biodynamics Univ of Calif Berkeley CA 94720

CALVIN, WILLIAM HOWARD, b Kansas City, Mo, Apr 30, 39. NEUROPHYSIOLOGY, BIOPHYSICS. *Educ:* Univ Wash, PhD(physiol & biophys), 66. *Prof Exp:* Asst physics, Northwestern Univ, 61; from instr neurol surg & physiol-biophys to asst prof neurol surg, 67-73, ASSOC PROF NEUROL SURG, UNIV WASH, 74- *Concurrent Pos:* Nat Acad Sci travel grants to int cong, 66 & 71; NIH grant, 71-; NIH sr int fel, 78-79; vis prof neurobiol, Hebrew Univ Jerusalem, 78-79. *Mem:* Int Brain Res Orgn; Int Asn Study Pain; Biophys Soc; Am Physiol Soc; Soc Neurosci. *Res:* Neuronal processes involved in repetitive discharge, coding of information, integration at single cell level; neuronal mechanisms of epilepsy and central pain. *Mailing Add:* Dept Neurol Univ Wash Seattle WA 98195

CAMACHO, ALVRO MANUEL, b Trinidad, WI, Mar 1, 27; US citizen; m 56; c 4. PEDIATRIC ENDOCRINOLOGY. *Educ:* Creighton Univ, 46-49, MD, 53. *Prof Exp:* Intern, Charity Hosp, New Orleans, La, 53-54; resident pediat, Med Br Hosps, Univ Tex, 55-58; fel pediat endocrinol, Children's Hosp, Ohio State Univ, 58-60; fel, Johns Hopkins Hosp, Baltimore, 60-61, instr pediat, 61-63; asst prof, Sch Med, Wayne State Univ, 63-64; from asst prof to assoc prof, 64-72, PROF PEDIAT, COL MED, UNIV TENN, MEMPHIS, 72-, CHIEF SECT PEDIAT ENDOCRINOL, 64- *Honors & Awards:* Lederle Med Fac Award, 66. *Mem:* Am Fedn Clin Res; Endocrine Soc; Soc Pediat Res; Am Pediat Soc. *Mailing Add:* Dept of Pediat Univ of Tenn Memphis TN 38103

CAMARDA, HARRY SALVATORE, b New York, NY, Sept 23, 38. PHYSICS. *Educ:* New York Univ, BS, 63; Columbia Univ, MA, 65, PhD(physics), 70. *Prof Exp:* Res assoc physics, Nevis Labs, Columbia Univ, 70-71; res assoc, Nat Bur Standards, 71-73; sr physicist, Lawrence Livermore Lab, 74-79; ASSOC PROF PHYSICS, PA STATE UNIV, DELAWARE CO CAMPUS, 79- *Concurrent Pos:* Nat Bur Standards res award, Nat Res Coun, 71; consult, Lawrence Livermore Lab, 79-82. *Mem:* Am Phys Soc; Sigma Xi; NY Acad Sci. *Res:* Statistical properties of excited nuclei; neutron resonance interactions; low energy nuclear optical model. *Mailing Add:* Pa State Univ Delaware Co Campus 25 Yearsley Mill Rd Media PA 19063

CAMBEL, ALI B(ULENT), b Merano, Italy, Apr 9, 23; nat US; m 46; c 4. ENERGY TECHNOLOGY & POLICY. *Educ:* Robert Col, Istanbul, BS, 42; Calif Inst Technol, MS, 46; Univ Iowa, PhD(mech eng), 50. *Prof Exp:* From instr to asst prof mech eng, Univ Iowa, 47-53; from assoc prof to prof, Northwestern Univ, 53-61, Walter P Murphy distinguished prof, 61-68, dir gas dynamics lab, 53-66, chmn dept, 57-66; dean col eng, Wayne State Univ, 68-70, exec vpres acad affairs, 70-72; corp vpres, Gen Res Corp, Washington, DC, 72-74; dep asst dir, NSF, 74-75; chmn dept civil, mech & environ eng, 75-80, PROF ENG & APPL SCI, GEORGE WASHINGTON UNIV, 75-, DIR OFF ENERGY PROG, 75- *Concurrent Pos:* Lectr & chmn symp, Nat Acad Sci, 64; dir res & eng support div, Inst Defense Anal, 66-67, vpres res, 67-68; staff dir, President's Interdept Energy Study; adv & consult to advan res proj agency, Dept Defense & Aeronaut Systs Div, Off Sci & Technol; indust consult; mem eng sci adv comt, Air Force Off Sci Res. *Honors & Awards:* Pendray Award, Am Inst Aeronaut & Astronaut, 59; McGraw Res Award, Am Soc Eng Educ, 60; NSF Excellence Award, 75. *Mem:* Am Soc Mech Engrs; Am Inst Aeronaut & Astronaut; Am Soc Eng Educ. *Res:* Magnetogasdynamics; energetics; social change. *Mailing Add:* Tompkins Hall George Washington Univ Washington DC 20652

CAMBEY, LESLIE ALAN, b Sydney Australia, May 15, 34; m 56; c 4. PHYSICS. *Educ:* Univ New SWales, BS, 55, PhD(physics), 60. *Prof Exp:* Fel physics, McMaster Univ, 60-62; sr res scientist, Nuclide Corp, Pa, 62-65, dir res, 65-67; mgr custom prod, CEC|Anal Instruments Div, Bell & Howell Co, Calif, 67-70; vpres, 70-80, EXEC VPRES, MAT RES CORP, 80- *Mem:* Inst Elec & Electronic Engrs. *Res:* Atomic mass determinations; ion sputtering; ion optics; mass spectroscopy. *Mailing Add:* 100 Gotleib Dr Pearl River NY 10965

CAMBRAY, JOSEPH, physical organic chemistry, bioorganic chemistry, see previous edition

CAMDEN, JAMES BERGER, chemical engineering, numerical analysis, see previous edition

CAME, PAUL E, b Dover, NH, Feb 25, 37; m 60; c 2. MICROBIOLOGY, VIROLOGY. *Educ:* St Anselm's Col, AB, 58; Univ NH, MS, 60; Hahnemann Med Col, PhD(microbiol), 64. *Prof Exp:* Instr microbiol, Med Units, Univ Tenn & res virologist, St Jude Hosp, 63-65; res assoc biophys cytol, Rockefeller Univ, 65-67; sr virologist, 67-70, mgr dept virol, 70-74, assoc dir microbiol sci & virol, Schering-Plough Corp, 74-75; HEAD DEPT MICROBIOL, STERLING-WINTHROP RES INST, 75- *Mem:* AAAS; NY Acad Sci; Am Asn Immunologists; Am Asn Cancer Res; Am Soc Microbiol. *Res:* Mechanisms of cellular resistance to viruses; mechanisms of virus oncogenicity; chemotherapy of virus and microbial diseases. *Mailing Add:* Dept of Microbiol Sterling-Winthrop Res Inst Rensselaer NY 12211

CAMERINI-OTERO, RAFAEL DANIEL, b Buenos Aires, Arg, Jan 15, 47; US citizen; m 69. MOLECULAR BIOLOGY, HUMAN GENETICS. *Educ:* Mass Inst Technol, BS, 66; NY Univ, MD, 73, PhD(microbiol), 73. *Prof Exp:* Intern pediat, Bellevue Hosp Med Ctr, NY Univ, 73-74; res assoc molecular biol, 74-77, SR INVESTR, MOLECULAR BIOL LAB, HUMAN BIOCHEM GENETICS SECT, NAT INST ARTHRITIS, METAB & DIGESTIVE DIS, NIH, 77- *Mem:* Am Chem Soc; Biophys Soc; Am Soc Biol Chem. *Res:* Molecular biology of morphogenesis and differentiation; developmental genetics; chromatin and chromosome structure; physical biochemistry of macromolecules; pediatrics; human and medical genetics. *Mailing Add:* Nat Inst Arthritis Metab Bldg 10 Rm 9N-238 Bethesda MD 20205

CAMERMAN, ARTHUR, b Vancouver, BC, Apr 12, 39. PHARMACEUTICAL CHEMISTRY, PHARMACOLOGY. *Educ:* Univ BC, BSc Hons, 61, PhD(chem), 64. *Prof Exp:* Fel molecular biol, Royal Inst Great Brit, 64-66; sr fel & res assoc biol struct & pharm, 67-71, res asst prof med neurol & pharmacol, 71-75, res assoc prof, 75-81, RES PROF, UNIV WASH, 81- *Concurrent Pos:* vis investr, Howard Hughes Med Inst, 71-72; affil, Child Develop & Mental Retardation Ctr, 76-, alcohol & drug abuse Inst, Univ Wash, 77- *Mem:* AAAS; Am Crystallog Asn; Am Chem Soc; Am Soc Neurochem; Am Soc Pharmacol & Exp Therapeut. *Res:* Stereochemical basis of drug and biological molecule action; use of crystallography to determine three-dimensional molecular conformations of anti-epileptic and anti-cancer drugs. *Mailing Add:* Div Neurol RG-20 Univ Wash Seattle WA 98195

CAMERMAN, NORMAN, b Vancouver, BC, Apr 12, 39. MOLECULAR BIOLOGY, X-RAY CRYSTALLOGRAPHY. *Educ:* Univ BC, BSc, 61, PhD(chem), 64. *Prof Exp:* Nat Res Coun Can overseas fel, Royal Inst Gt Brit, 64-66; Med Res Coun Can prof asst, 67-69, asst prof, 69-75, assoc prof, 75-79, PROF BIOCHEM, UNIV TORONTO, 79- *Concurrent Pos:* Med Res Coun Can scholar, 69-73. *Mem:* AAAS; Am Crystallog Asn. *Res:* Molecular basis of biological activity; molecular structure determinations of drugs, hormones and other biologically-active substances; correlation of structure and actions. *Mailing Add:* Dept Biochem Univ Toronto Toronto ON M5S 1A1 Can

CAMERO, ARTHUR ANTHONY, b Tampa, Fla, June 29, 47. CHEMICAL ENGINEERING. *Educ:* Univ Fla, BS, 69; Princeton Univ, MA, 72, PhD(chem eng), 75. *Prof Exp:* Engr process design, Monsanto Co, 70; engr, Exxon Res & Eng Co, 75-76, res engr, 76-78, sr engr res & develop, 78-80; MEM STAFF, FLUOR ENGRS & CONSTRUCTORS, 80- *Mem:* Am Inst Chem Engrs; Am Chem Soc. *Res:* Coal gasification; coal liquefaction; kinetics; catalysis. *Mailing Add:* Fluor Engrs & Constructors PO Box 35000 Houston TX 77035

CAMERON, ALASTAIR GRAHAM WALTER, b Winnipeg, Can, June 21, 25; US citizen; m 55. THEORY. *Educ:* Univ Man, BSc, 47; Univ Sask, PhD(physics), 52. *Hon Degrees:* AM, Harvard Univ, 73; DSc, Univ Sask, 77. *Prof Exp:* Asst prof phys, Iowa State Col, 52-54; from asst to sr res officer, Atomic Energy Can, Ltd, 54-61; sr scientist, Goddard Inst Space Studies, 61-66; prof space phys, Belfer Grad Sch Sci, Yeshiva Univ, 66-73; PROF ASTRON, HARVARD UNIV, 73- *Concurrent Pos:* Vis lectr phys, Yale Univ, 62-68; adj prof phys, NY Univ, 63-65; consult, Nat Aeronaut & Space Admin, 66-; mem vis comt, Bartol Res Found, Franklin Inst, 74-; chmn, Nat Acad Sci-NRC Space Sci Bd, 76-82. *Honors & Awards:* Bronze Medal, Univ Liege, 59. *Mem:* Nat Acad Sci; Am Acad Arts & Sci; Royal Soc Can; Am Astron Soc; Am Geophys Union. *Res:* Theoretical research in nuclear physics, astrophysics, and planetary sciences, including nuclear astrophysics, stellar formation and evolution of the solar system and of planets. *Mailing Add:* Harvard Col Observ 60 Garden St Cambridge MA 02138

CAMERON, ALEXANDER MENZIES, b Yonkers, NY, Sept 5, 30; m 52; c 3. VETERINARY PATHOLOGY. *Educ:* Colo State Univ, BS, 61, DVM, 62; Univ Calif, Davis, PhD(comp path), 70. *Prof Exp:* Vet clinician small animals, pvt pract, NMex, 62-63 & Calif, 64-66; field vet dis eradication, USDA, Calif, 63-64; asst prof vet path, Col Vet Med, Univ Ill, 70-76; mem staff path serv proj, 76-79, DIR, DIV PATH, NAT CTR TOXICOL RES, 80- *Concurrent Pos:* Assoc prof path, Med Sch, Univ Ark, 76-79. *Mem:* Am Col Vet Pathologists; Am Vet Med Asn; Int Acad Path; Soc Toxicol Path; Am Asn Lab Animal Sci. *Res:* Development of mammary neoplasms in animals; toxicologic pathology. *Mailing Add:* Div Path Nat Ctr Toxicol Res Jefferson AR 72079

CAMERON, BARRY WINSTON, b NS, Feb 7, 40; US citizen; m 68. PALEOECOLOGY. *Educ:* Rutgers Univ, AB, 62; Columbia Univ, AM, 65, PhD(geol), 68. *Prof Exp:* Teaching asst geol, Columbia Univ, 62-64; from instr to asst prof geol, 67-72, ASSOC PROF GEOL, BOSTON UNIV, 72- *Concurrent Pos:* NSF grant, 70-72, 77-79. *Mem:* Sigma Xi; Paleont Soc; Geol Soc Am; Soc Econ Paleont & Mineral; Int Sed Asn. *Res:* Trace fossils, especially algal, sponge and worm borings; calcareous algae; paleoecology, sedimentation and stratigraphy of medial Ordovician limestones of New York and Ontario; cyclic sedimentation, especially punctuated aggradational cycles; evolution of benthonic marine invertebrate fossil communities; geologic computer applications. *Mailing Add:* Boston Univ Dept of Geol 725 Commonwealth Ave Boston MA 02215

CAMERON, BRUCE FRANCIS, b Damariscotta, Maine, Sept 10, 34; m 57; c 2. PHYSICAL BIOCHEMISTRY, HEMATOLOGY. *Educ:* Harvard Univ, BS, 56; Univ Pa, MD, 60, PhD(biochem), 62. *Prof Exp:* Vis res assoc chem, Am Univ Beirut, 62-63; res assoc, Univ Ibadan, 63-65; sr staff scientist, New Eng Inst Med Res, 66-69; assoc prof med, Sch Med, Univ Miami, 69-78; sr scientist, Papanicolaou Cancer Res Inst, 71-78; ASSOC PROF PEDIAT MED, SCH MED, UNIV CINCINNATI, 78-; DIR, CINCINNATI COMPREHENSIVE SICKLE CELL CTR, CHILDREN'S HOSP RES FOUND, 78- *Concurrent Pos:* NIH fel, 60-63; Am Heart Asn advan res fel, 67-69; vis scientist, Am Univ Beirut, 65; investr, Howard Hughes Med Inst, 69-71; adj prof life sci, New Eng Inst Grad Sch, 71-74; estab investr, Am Heart Asn, 72-77, mem, Coun on Basic Sci. *Mem:* AAAS; Am Heart Asn; Am Soc Hemat; Soc Anal Cytol; NY Acad Sci; Am Soc Biol Chemists. *Res:* Physical chemistry of hemoglobin; erythrocyte physiology; membrane physiology; membrane transport; studies in sickle cell anemia; biophysical instrumentation with minicomputer systems. *Mailing Add:* Comprehensive Sickle Cell Ctr Elland & Bethesda Ave CH-B-22 Cincinnati OH 45229

CAMERON, DAVID GEORGE, b Streaky Bay, South Australia, March 13, 47; Can citizen; m 69; c 3. VIBRATIONAL SPECTROSCOPY. *Educ:* Monash Univ, Australia, BSc, 67; LaTrobe Univ, BSc, Hons, 68, PhD, 72. *Prof Exp:* Fel, 72-74, STAFF, NAT RES COUN, CAN, 74- *Concurrent Pos:* Assoc ed, Appl Spectros, 82- *Mem:* Soc Appl Spectros. *Res:* Infrared and Raman spectroscopy of biological systems; data reduction in infrared and Raman spectroscopy. *Mailing Add:* Div Chem Nat Res Coun Can 100 Sussex Dr Ottawa ON K1A 0R6 Can

CAMERON, DAVID GLEN, b Great Falls, Mont, Dec 6, 34; m 61; c 2. POPULATION GENETICS, EVOLUTIONARY BIOLOGY. *Educ:* Princeton Univ, AB, 57; Stanford Univ, PhD(biol), 66. *Prof Exp:* Res assoc environ med, US Army Med Res Labs, Ft Knox, Ky, 57-59; asst prof genetics, Univ Alta, 64-69; assoc prof zool & head dept zool & entom, 70-74, ASSOC PROF BIOL & GENETICS, MONT STATE UNIV, 74- *Concurrent Pos:* Secy & trustee, Rocky Mountain Biol Labs, Crested Butte, Colo, 68-74. *Mem:* AAAS; Am Inst Biol Sci; Genetics Soc Am; Soc Study Evolution; Am Soc Human Genetics. *Res:* Ecological, populational, genetic and evolutionary aspects of genetic polymorphisms in natural populations of small rodents, European rabbits, elk and trout; blood groups serum proteins isoenzymes; human genetics. *Mailing Add:* Dept of Biol Mont State Univ Bozeman MT 59717

CAMERON, DON FRANK, b El Paso, Tex, Aug 13, 47; m 69; c 2. TESTICULAR PATHOLOGY. *Educ:* Univ STenn, BA, 69; Med Univ SC, MS, 72, PhD(anat), 77. *Prof Exp:* Instr anat path, Greenville Tech Educ Ctr, Allied Health Sch, 71-72; instr, 76-80, ASST PROF ANAT, COL MED, UNIV FLA, 80- *Concurrent Pos:* Prin investr, Col Med, Univ Fla, NIH, 82- *Mem:* SEastern Electron Micros Soc; AAAS; Am Asn Anatomists; Sigma Xi. *Res:* Male infertility with specific involvement in subfertility associated with varicocele, pituitary adenoma and diabetes; elucidation of mechanisms of spermatogenesis with special emphasis on steroli cell structure and function. *Mailing Add:* JHMHC PO Box J-235 Gainesville FL 32601

CAMERON, DONALD EUGENE, b Sayre, Pa, Oct 1, 22; m 44; c 5. FOOD MICROBIOLOGY. *Educ:* Cornell Univ, BS, 43. *Prof Exp:* Proj leader microbiol, Cent Labs, Gen Foods Corp, 43-53, prod & process develop, 53-59, qual control mgr, Birds Eye Baby Foods, 59-62, technologist, Jell-O Plant, 62-64, bacteriologist, Tech Serv, 64-66, asst qual control supvr, 66-67, QUAL CONTROL SUPT, FOOD PROD DIV, GEN FOODS CORP, 68- *Mem:* Inst Food Technol; Am Soc Microbiol. *Res:* Processing of raw cacao and green coffee; microbiology of food plant processes; new product development. *Mailing Add:* Dover Oper Gen Foods Corp PO Box 600 Dover DE 19901

CAMERON, DONALD FORBES, b Edmonton, Alta, Aug 19, 20; m 44; c 4. ANESTHESIOLOGY. *Educ:* Univ Alta, BA, 47, MD, 49; FRCPS(C) cert. *Prof Exp:* Lectr pharmacol, 50-62, asst prof pharmacol & anesthesia & asst dean fac med, 62-65, assoc dean, 65-74, assoc prof, 65-73, PROF ANESTHESIA, UNIV ALTA, 73-, DEAN FAC MED, 74- *Concurrent Pos:* Mem, Med Coun Can, 62-, pres, 74-75; mem bd gov, Univ Hosp, 74-; mem gen coun, Can Med Asn, 75- *Honors & Awards:* Order of Brit Empire. *Mem:* Fel Am Col Anesthesiol. *Mailing Add:* Fac of Med Univ of Alta Edmonton Can

CAMERON, DOUGLAS EWAN, b New Brunswick, NJ, Apr 5, 41; c 5. TOPOLOGY. *Educ:* Miami Univ, BA, 63; Univ Akron, MS, 65; Va Polytech Inst & State Univ, PhD(topol), 70. *Prof Exp:* Instr math, Community & Tech Col, Univ Akron, 65-66 & Va Polytech Inst & State Univ, 66-69; from instr to asst prof, 69-74, assoc prof, 74-80, PROF MATH, UNIV AKRON, 80- *Mem:* Am Math Soc; Math Asn Am. *Res:* Properties of maximal and minimal topologies, specifically covering axioms; filters and their use in the study of point set topology. *Mailing Add:* Dept of Math & Statist Univ of Akron Akron OH 44325

CAMERON, DOUGLAS GEORGE, b Eng, Mar 11, 17; m 46; c 6. MEDICINE. *Educ:* Univ Sask, BSc, 37; McGill Univ, MD & CM, 40; Oxford Univ. *Prof Exp:* Res asst, Nuffield Dept Clin Med, Oxford Univ, 48; sr med res fel, Nat Res Coun Can, 49-52; assoc physician, 51-57, asst dir, 52-57, DIR & PHYSICIAN-IN-CHIEF, UNIV CLIN, MONTREAL GEN HOSP, 57-; PROF MED, FAC MED, McGILL UNIV, 57-, CHMN DEPT, 74- *Concurrent Pos:* Asst prof med, McGill Univ, 49-57, chmn dept, 64-69. *Honors & Awards:* Officer, Order Can, 78. *Mem:* Fel Am Col Physicians; Am Soc Clin Invest; Royal Col Physicians & Surgeons Can (pres, 78); Asn Am Physicians; Am Clin & Climat Asn. *Mailing Add:* 3655 Drummond St McGill Univ Montreal Can

CAMERON, DUNCAN MACLEAN, JR, b St Albans, Vt, May 15, 31; m 55; c 3. ZOOLOGY, ECOLOGY. *Educ:* Univ Maine, BS, 54, MEd, 60; Univ Calif, Davis, PhD, 69. *Prof Exp:* Teacher, Pub Schs, Maine & Ohio, 56-61; instr bot, Univ Maine, 61-62; res zoologist, Univ Calif, Davis, 62-64, teaching asst zool, 64-66, assoc, 66-67, lectr, 67-68; fel, Univ BC, 68-69; asst prof biol, 69-73, ASSOC PROF BIOL, YORK UNIV, 73-, DIR, DIV NATURAL SCI, 80- *Concurrent Pos:* Vis prof entom, Univ Maine, 78-79. *Mem:* AAAS; Am Inst Biol Sci; Ecol Soc Am; Am Soc Mammal; Can Soc Zool. *Res:* Population ecology of small mammals; ecological processes, especially competition; ecology of pitcher-plants and their insect associates. *Mailing Add:* Dept of Biol York Univ Toronto ON M3S 1P3 Can

CAMERON, EDWARD ALAN, b Brockville, Ont, July 4, 38; m 64; c 2. FOREST ENTOMOLOGY, FOREST PEST MANAGEMENT. *Educ:* Ont Agr Col, BSA, 60; Univ Calif, Berkeley, MS, 67, PhD(entom), 74. *Prof Exp:* Entomologist, Commonwealth Inst Biol Control, 60-65; asst prof, 70-75, ASSOC PROF ENTOM, PA STATE UNIV, UNIVERSITY PARK, 75- *Concurrent Pos:* Collabr, USDA, 71-; gastdozent, Entomologisches Inst, Zurich, Switzerland, 79-80. *Mem:* Entom Soc Can; Entom Soc Am; Int Orgn Biol Control. *Res:* Bionomics, ecology and control of forest insects; gypsy moth management. *Mailing Add:* Dept Entom Pa State Univ University Park PA 16802

CAMERON, EDWARD ALEXANDER, b Manly, NC, Nov 10, 07; m 37; c 1. MATHEMATICS. *Educ:* Univ NC, AB, 28, AM, 29, PhD(math), 36. *Prof Exp:* From instr to prof, 29-72, EMER PROF MATH, UNIV NC, CHAPEL HILL, 72- *Concurrent Pos:* Ford Found fel, 51-52; NSF sci fac fel, 65-66; consult, NSF. *Mem:* Am Math Soc; Math Asn Am (treas, 68-72). *Res:* Algebra. *Mailing Add:* 404 Laurel Hill Rd Chapel Hill NC 27514

CAMERON, EUGENE NATHAN, b Atlanta, Ga, Aug 10, 10; m; c 3. ECONOMIC GEOLOGY. *Educ:* NY Univ, BS, 32; Columbia Univ, AM, 34, PhD(geol), 39. *Prof Exp:* Asst geol, NY Univ, 30-35; asst, Columbia Univ, 36-37, lectr, 37-39, instr, 39; assoc geologist, US Geol Surv, 42-44, geologist, 46, sr geologist, 46-50; from assoc prof to prof econ geol, 47-70, chmn dept geol, 55-60, Van Hise distinguished prof econ geol, 70-80, EMER PROF GEOL, UNIV WIS-MADISON, 80- *Concurrent Pos:* Geologist, US Geol Surv, 37-39; asst, State Geol & Natural Hist Surv, Conn, 41-42; consult, NASA, 62-63 & 64-67; deleg, Int Comn Ore Micros, 62-64; mem, Comt Mineral Resources & Environ, 73-75; mem, US Nat Comt Geol, 74-77. *Mem:* Fel Geol Soc Am; fel Mineral Soc Am; Soc Econ Geologists (secy, 61-69, vpres, 69, pres, 74). *Res:* Mineralogy; economic geology of pegmatite mineral deposits; internal structure of granitic pegmatites; optical properties of ore minerals; chromite deposits; lunar samples; investigation of origin of chromite deposits in the Bushveld Complex; analysis of mineral resource problems. *Mailing Add:* Dept of Geol & Geophys Univ of Wis Madison WI 53706

CAMERON, GUY NEIL, b San Francisco, Calif, May 1, 42. ECOLOGY, POPULATION BIOLOGY. *Educ:* Univ Calif, Berkeley, BA, 63; Calif State Col, Long Beach, MA, 65; Univ Calif, Davis, PhD(zool), 69. *Prof Exp:* Asst res zoologist, Univ Calif, Berkeley, 69-71; asst prof, 71-76, ASSOC PROF BIOL, UNIV HOUSTON, 77- *Concurrent Pos:* Consult, Gulf Univs Res Consortium, 73, Dames & Moore Environ Engrs, 74 & 75; assoc ed, J Mammal, 80- *Mem:* Ecol Soc Am; Am Soc Naturalists; Am Soc Mammalogists; Brit Ecol Soc; Soc Study Evolution. *Res:* Investigation of role of interspecific interactions in demographic and genetic aspects of natural populations by experimental perturbation; contribution of decomposer organisms to community dynamics; stability of arthropod food chains. *Mailing Add:* Dept Biol Univ Houston Houston TX 77004

CAMERON, H RONALD, b Oakland, Calif, June 30, 29; m 57; c 2. PLANT PATHOLOGY. *Educ:* Univ Calif, BS, 51; Univ Wis, PhD(plant path), 55. *Prof Exp:* Agt, USDA, Univ Wis, 53-55; from asst plant pathologist to assoc prof pathologist, 55-70, PLANT PATHOLOGIST, ORE STATE UNIV, 70- *Concurrent Pos:* NSF fel, Stanford Univ, 62-63; NATO sr fel, East Malling Res Sta, Eng, 72. *Res:* Virus and bacterial diseases of fruit and nut trees; genetics of pathogenicity. *Mailing Add:* Dept of Bot & Plant Path Ore State Univ Corvallis OR 97331

CAMERON, IRVINE R, b Fredericton, NB, June 24, 19; m 45; c 2. POLYMER CHEMISTRY. *Educ:* Univ NB, BS, 41; Univ Toronto, MS, 42. *Prof Exp:* From sci officer to dir eng planning & coord, Chief Tech Serv Br, Can Forces Hq, 70-72; dir gen mat develop planning, 72-76; dir, Gen Res & Develop Serv, Dept Nat Defence, Can, 76-80; RETIRED. *Mem:* Fel Chem Inst Can; assoc fel Can Aeronaut & Space Inst; Am Inst Aeronaut & Astronaut; Prof Inst Pub Serv Can; Can Soc Chem Eng. *Res:* High explosives; propellants for guns and rockets; development of composite rocket propellants of polyurethane type resulting in the Black Brant series of sounding rockets; equipment development; military applications. *Mailing Add:* 4 Riopelle Ct Kanata ON K2K 1J1 Can

CAMERON, IVAN LEE, b Los Angeles, Calif, Jan 4, 34; m 55; c 3. ZOOLOGY, ANATOMY. *Educ:* Univ Redlands, BS, 56; Univ Southern Calif, MS, 59; Univ Calif, Los Angeles, PhD(anat), 63. *Prof Exp:* Biologist, Oak Ridge Nat Lab, 63-65; from asst prof to assoc prof, 65-74, PROF ANAT, UNIV TEX HEALTH SCI CTR, SAN ANTONIO, 74-; assoc prof, 68-74, PROF ANAT, UNIV TEX HEALTH SCI CTR, SAN ANTONIO, 74- *Mem:* Am Asn Anatomists; Am Soc Cell Biol; Am Asn Cancer Res. *Res:* Nuclear-cytoplasmic environmental interactions; chemical changes during the cell-growth-duplication cycle; feedback control of cellular proliferation. *Mailing Add:* Dept of Anat Univ of Tex Health Sci Ctr San Antonio TX 78284

CAMERON, J A, b Pittsburg, Okla, Oct 7, 29; m 53; c 2. MEDICAL MICROBIOLOGY. *Educ:* Maryville Col, BS, 51; Univ Tenn, MS, 55, PhD, 58. *Prof Exp:* Asst, Univ Tenn, 56-58; from instr to assoc prof bact, 58-73, PROF, BIOL SCI GROUP, UNIV CONN, 73- *Concurrent Pos:* Res assoc, Calif Inst Technol, 68-69. *Mem:* AAAS; Am Soc Microbiol; Soc Gen Microbiol. *Res:* Host parasite relationships in bacterial diseases. *Mailing Add:* Microbiol Sect Biol Sci Group Univ of Conn Storrs CT 06268

CAMERON, JAMES N, b Hanover, NH, May 28, 44; m 63; c 2. PHYSIOLOGY. *Educ:* Univ Wis, Madison, BS, 66; Univ Tex, Austin, PhD(zool), 69. *Prof Exp:* NIH fel, Univ BC, 69-73; assoc prof zoophysiol, Univ Alaska & Inst Arctic Biol, 73-75; ASSOC PROF ZOOLOGY, MARINE SCI INST, UNIV TEX, 75- *Concurrent Pos:* Secy, Div Comp Physiol & Biochem, Am Soc Zool, 78-79. *Res:* Physiology of respiration, circulation and ion regulation; acid-base regulation; comparative physiology. *Mailing Add:* Port Aransas Marine Lab Univ of Tex Port Aransas TX 78373

CAMERON, JAMES WAGNER, b Falls City, Nebr, Apr 23, 13; m 38; c 2. PLANT GENETICS, PLANT BREEDING. *Educ:* Univ Mo, AB, 38; Harvard Univ, AM, 43, PhD(genetics), 47. *Prof Exp:* Asst genetics, Harvard Univ, 41-42; res assoc, Off Sci Res & Develop Contract, 43-45; asst genetics, Harvard Univ, 45-46; from jr geneticist to assoc geneticist, Citrus Res Ctr, 47-60, lectr hort sci, Univ, 60-64, geneticist, 60-80, prof hort sci, 64-80, EMER PROF, CITRUS RES CTR, UNIV CALIF, RIVERSIDE, 80- *Concurrent Pos:* Sr scholar, East-West Ctr, Univ Hawaii, 62-63; Fulbright lectr, Aegean Univ, Turkey, 70-71; Fulbright travel grant, Palermo Univ, Italy, 76. *Mem:* Am Soc Agron; Am Soc Hort Sci; Sigma Xi; Am Genetic Asn. *Res:* Breeding and genetics of citrus and maize. *Mailing Add:* Dept Botany & Plant Sci Univ of Calif Riverside CA 92521

CAMERON, JOHN, b Glasgow, Scotland, Aug 12, 39. METALLURGICAL ENGINEERING, PYROMETALLURGY. *Educ:* Royal Col Sci & Technol, Scotland, ARCST, 62, DRC, 64; Univ Strathclyde, PhD(metall), 66. *Prof Exp:* Fel, Nat Res Coun Can, NS, 66-68; res assoc, Univ BC, 68-70; asst prof, 70-77, ASSOC PROF, QUEEN'S UNIV, ONT, 77- *Mem:* Am Soc Metals; Am Inst Mining, Metall & Petrol Engrs; assoc Brit Iron & Steel Inst; assoc Brit Inst Metals; Can Inst Mining & Metall. *Res:* Electroslag remelting; vacuum arc remelting; electroslag welding; physical properties of slags, oxides of refractory metals; pyrometallurgy; extractive processes; radioactive waste management; pyrometallurgical processes. *Mailing Add:* Dept Metall Eng Queen's Univ Kingston ON K7L 3N6 Can

CAMERON, JOHN ALEXANDER, b Toronto, Ont, May 19, 36; m 58; c 3. NUCLEAR PHYSICS. *Educ:* Univ Toronto, BA, 58; McMaster Univ, PhD(physics), 62. *Prof Exp:* NATO fel nuclear orientation, Clarendon Lab, Oxford Univ, 62-64; from asst prof to assoc prof, 64-74, PROF PHYSICS & ASSOC DEAN SCH GRAD STUDIES, McMASTER UNIV, 74- *Concurrent Pos:* Sloan Found fel, 67-68; vis scientist, Cent Res Inst Physics, Hungary, 70; mem fac sci, Univ Paris, 71. *Mem:* Can Asn Physicists. *Res:* Atomic beams; nuclear orientation; angular correlation studies; hyperfine structure in atoms and solids; nuclear moments; nuclear reactions and spectroscopy. *Mailing Add:* Dept of Physics McMaster Univ Hamilton ON L8S 4L8 Can

CAMERON, JOHN RODERICK, b Wis, Apr 21, 22; m 47; c 2. MEDICAL PHYSICS. *Educ:* Univ Chicago, BS, 47; Univ Wis, MS, 49, PhD(nuclear physics), 52. *Prof Exp:* Asst prof, Univ Sao Paulo, 52-54; proj assoc, Univ Wis, 54-55; asst prof nuclear physics, Univ Pittsburgh, 55-58; from asst prof to assoc prof, 58-65, dir, Biomed Eng Ctr, 69-76, dir, Med Physics Div, 74-81, PROF RADIOL & BIOMED ENG, UNIV WIS-MADISON, 65-, FARRINGTON DANIELS PROF MED PHYSICS, 79-, CHMN, DEPT MED PHYSICS, 81- *Concurrent Pos:* Secy-gen, Int Orgn Med Physics, 69-76; consult, Vet Admin Hosp, Madison, Atomic Energy Comn, Washington, Int Atomic Energy Asn, Vienna, Austria, Bur Radiation Health, Fed Drug Admin, 71- *Honors & Awards:* Coolidge Award, Am Asn Physicists Med, 80. *Mem:* Am Phys Soc; Am Asn Physicist in Med (pres, 68); Soc Nuclear Med; Health Physics Soc; Radiation Res Soc. *Res:* Radiation dosimetry using thermoluminescence; physics of diagnostic radiology; physics of bones; general applications of physics to medicine. *Mailing Add:* 118 N Breese Terr Madison WI 53705

CAMERON, JOSEPH MARION, b Edinboro, Pa, Apr 6, 22; m 46; c 4. MATHEMATICAL STATISTICS. *Educ:* Univ Akron, BS, 42; NC State Col, MS, 47. *Prof Exp:* Math statistician, 47-63, chief statist eng lab, 63-68, chief off measurement serv, Inst Basic Standards, Nat Bur Standards, 68-77; CONSULT STATIST, 77- *Mem:* Inst Math Statist; fel Am Statist Asn; Biomet Soc. *Res:* Application of statistics in physical sciences. *Mailing Add:* 12502 Gould Rd Wheaton MD 20906

CAMERON, LOUIS MCDUFFY, b Richmond, Va, Dec 16, 35; m 59. APPLIED PHYSICS. *Educ:* Univ Richmond, BS, 57; George Washington Univ, MS, 62; Georgetown Univ, PhD(physics), 66. *Prof Exp:* Physicist, NIH, 58-61 & Naval Res Lab, Washington, DC, 61-66; physicist, 66-70, supvry physicist, 70-75, assoc dir, 75-80, DIR, NIGHT VISION & ELECTRO OPTICS LAB, FT BELVOIR, VA, 80- *Concurrent Pos:* Edison Mem training scholar, Naval Res Lab, Washington, DC, 64-65. *Honors & Awards:* Ann Award, Night Vision Lab, 75; Res & Develop Achievement Award, US Army, 75. *Mem:* Am Phys Soc. *Res:* Liquid crystal physics; basic research including thermodynamics, light scattering, x-ray, microscope; development of a set of common modules utilized in infrared thermal imaging systems for all of the Department of Defense; electro-optics. *Mailing Add:* Night Vision Lab Ft Belvoir VA 22060

CAMERON, MALCOLM LAURENCE, b NS, Oct 23, 18; m 52; c 3. PHYSIOLOGY. *Educ:* Dalhousie Univ, BSc, 50, MSc, 51; Cambridge Univ, PhD(insect physiol), 53. *Prof Exp:* Nat Res Coun Can fel biol, Univ NB, 53-55; from asst prof to assoc prof, Univ Sask, 55-65; assoc prof, 65-67, asst dean arts & sci, 69-77, PROF BIOL, DALHOUSIE UNIV, 67- *Res:* Insect hormones, enzymes and virology; excretory processes; invertebrate fine structure. *Mailing Add:* Dept of Biol Dalhousie Univ Halifax NS B3H 3J5 Can

CAMERON, MARGARET DAVIS, b Montgomery, Tex, Apr 25, 20. ORGANIC CHEMISTRY. *Educ:* Tex Women's Univ, BA, 42; Univ Houston, MS, 48; Tulane Univ, PhD(chem), 51. *Prof Exp:* Fulbright scholar & Ramsay mem fel, Univ Leeds, 51-52; USPHS fel, Ohio State Univ, 52-53; res chemist, Monsanto Co, 53-56; from assoc prof to prof chem, 56-72, REGENTS PROF CHEM, LAMAR UNIV, 72- *Mem:* Am Chem Soc; The Chem Soc. *Res:* Chemistry of acetylenic and heterocyclic compounds. *Mailing Add:* 4060 Howard St Beaumont TX 77705

CAMERON, ROBERT ALAN, b Edmonton, Alta, Oct 19, 26; m 52; c 3. EXPLORATION GEOLOGY. *Educ:* Dalhousie Univ, BSc, 48; Univ Toronto, MASc, 53; McGill Univ, PhD(geol), 56. *Prof Exp:* Lectr geol, Univ NB, 52; geologist, Imperial Oil Ltd, Alta, 52-53 & Malartic Gold Fields Ltd, Que, 56-57; chief geologist, E Malartic Mines Ltd, 57-62; area supvr, McIntyre Porcupine Mines Ltd, 62; asst prof mining, NS Tech Col, 62-68; prin, Sudbury Campus, Cambrian Col, 68-69; ASSOC PROF GEOL, LAURENTIAN UNIV, 69- *Mem:* Fel Geol Asn Can; Can Inst Mining & Metall; Can Geophys Union. *Res:* Geological and geophysical exploration methods. *Mailing Add:* 1818 Hawthorne Dr E Sudbury ON P3A 1M6 Can

CAMERON, ROBERT HORTON, b Brooklyn, NY, May 17, 08; m 31; c 2. MATHEMATICS. *Educ:* Cornell Univ, AB, 29, AM, 30, PhD(math), 32. *Prof Exp:* Instr math, Cornell Univ, 29-33; Nat Res fel, Brown Univ, Princeton Univ & Inst Advan Study, 33-35; from instr to assoc prof, Mass Inst Technol, 35-45; prof, 45-74, chmn dept, 57-63, EMER PROF MATH, UNIV MINN, MINNEAPOLIS, 74- *Concurrent Pos:* Mem panel, Off Sci Res & Develop Proj, Appl Math Group, NY Univ, 44-45. *Honors & Awards:* Chauvenet Prize, Math Asn Am, 44. *Mem:* AAAS; Am Math Soc; Math Asn Am. *Res:* Mathematical analysis; almost periodic functions and transformations; partial differential equations; integration in function space; non-linear integral equations. *Mailing Add:* 3519 Stinson Blvd NE Minneapolis MN 55418

CAMERON, ROY (EUGENE), b Denver, Colo, July 16, 29; m 56, 78; c 2. SCIENCE ADMINISTRATION, ECOLOGY. *Educ:* Wash State Univ, BS, 53 & 54; Univ Ariz, MS, 58, PhD(plant sci), 61. *Prof Exp:* Res chemist, Hughes Aircraft Co, 55-56; sr scientist, Jet Propulsion Lab, Calif Inst Technol, 61-68, mem tech staff, 68-73; pres, Darwin Res Inst, Calif, 73-74; dep dir land reclamation lab, Environ Impact Studies Div, 75-77, DIR, ENERGY RESOURCES TRAINING & DEVELOP, RECLAMATION LAB, ENVIRON IMPACT STUDIES DIV, ARGONNE NAT LAB, 77- *Concurrent Pos:* Consult, Med Sch, Baylor Univ, 66-68; Jet Propulsion Lab team leader, Antarctic Exped, 66-74; vis scientist, Am Soc Agron, 67-69; prin investr, NSF res grant Antarctic microbial ecol, 69-74; Smithsonian Inst study grant Moroccan desert, 69-70; consult, Ecol Ctr, Utah State Univ, 70-72; Dept Com grants, Native Am energy/environ, 78-80. *Mem:* AAAS; World Future Soc; Soil Sci Soc Am; Am Inst Biol Sci; Ecol Soc Am. *Res:* Desert soil microbiology; blue-green algae; microbial ecology; soil science; polar ecology; environmental monitoring; coal mine reclamation; Native American energy and environmental training; general environmental sciences; numerous publications. *Mailing Add:* Argonne Nat Lab 9700 S Cass Ave Argonne IL 60439

CAMERON, WINIFRED SAWTELL, b Oak Park, Ill, Dec 3, 18; m 53; c 2. ASTRONOMY. *Educ:* Northern Ill Univ, BE, 40; Ind Univ, MA, 52. *Prof Exp:* Asst astron, Weather Forecasts, Inc, 42-46 & 49-50; instr, Mt Holyoke Col, 50-51; astron res asst, US Naval Observ, 51-58; aerospace technologist, Lab Space Physics, 59-71, AEROSPACE TECHNOLOGIST & ACQUISITION SCIENTIST, NAT SPACE SCI DATA CTR, GODDARD SPACE FLIGHT CTR, NASA, 71- *Honors & Awards:* Asteroid 1575 named Winifred, Minor Planets Ctr, 52; Spec Act Award, NASA, 66, Apollo Achievement Award, 70, Exceptional Contrib to Educ Award, 71, Qual Increase Award, 73, & Spec Achievement Award, 77. *Mem:* Int Astron Union; Am Astron Soc; Am Geophys Union; Int Asn Planetology; Int Platform Asn. *Res:* Measurements of sunspots; lunar surface and scientific aspects research; scientific results of Mercury program of manned spaceflight; science data acquisition and analyses for Data Center of lunar and planetary surface features and lunar transient phenomena. *Mailing Add:* Nat Space Sci Data Ctr Code 601 Goddard Space Flight Ctr Greenbelt MD 20771

CAMHI, JEFFREY MARTIN, b New York, NY, May 16, 41; m 65; c 1. NEUROPHYSIOLOGY, ANIMAL BEHAVIOR. *Educ:* Tufts Univ, BS, 63; Harvard Univ, PhD(biol), 67. *Prof Exp:* Asst prof biol, 67-77, MEM FAC CORNELL UNIV, 77- *Mem:* AAAS; Soc Neurosci. *Res:* Single-unit neurophysiology and behavior in arthopods; development of behavior and of the nervous system. *Mailing Add:* Sect of Neurobiol & Behav Cornell Univ Langmuir Lab Ithaca NY 14850

CAMIEN, MERRILL NELSON, b Redlands, Calif, Dec 10, 20; m 44; c 2. BIOLOGICAL CHEMISTRY. *Educ:* Univ Calif, Los Angeles, AB, 43, MA, 45, PhD(microbiol), 48. *Prof Exp:* Res assoc biochem, Univ Calif, Los Angeles, 48-50; Fulbright res scholar, Univ Liege, 50-51; jr res chemist, Univ Calif, Los Angeles, 51-53, from asst res chemist to assoc res chemist, 53-62; res chemist, Vet Admin Ctr, Los Angeles, 62-63; res assoc, Mt Sinai Hosp, 64-65, sr scientist, 65-68; res physiologist, Dept Med, Ctr Health Sci, Univ Calif, Los Angeles, 68-70; res biochemist & head biochem & microbiol, Nucleic Acid Res Inst, Int Chem & Nuclear Corp, 69-70, head biol, microbiol & parasitol, 70-71, head neuropharmacol, 71-73; res assoc, 73-76, ASST RES BIOCHEMIST, UNIV CALIF, IRVINE, 76- *Mem:* Fel AAAS; Am Soc Microbiol; Am Soc Biol Chem; Soc Exp Biol & Med. *Res:* Studies relating to physical biochemistry of bacteriophage DNAs. *Mailing Add:* 1606 Warwick Ln Newport Beach CA 92660

CAMIENER, GERALD WALTER, b Detroit, Mich, Aug 15, 32; m 53; c 3. BIOCHEMISTRY, MICROBIOLOGY. *Educ:* Wayne State Univ, AB, 54; Mass Inst Technol, PhD(biochem), 59. *Prof Exp:* Teaching asst microbiol, Wayne State Univ, 53-54; res biochemist, Upjohn Co, 59-72; pres, ICN Life Sci Group, ICN Pharmaceut, 72-76; PRES, AM RES PROD CO, 76- *Mem:* Am Soc Biol Chemists; Am Asn Clin Chemists; AAAS; Am Chem Soc. *Res:* Biosynthesis of thiamine; isolation and purification of enzymes; tissue culture and antitumor antibiotics; enzyme inhibitors; immunology; immunosuppression; delayed hypersensitivity. *Mailing Add:* Am Res Prod Co PO Box 21009 South Euclid OH 44121

CAMILLO, VICTOR PETER, b Bridgeport, Conn, Jan 23, 45; m 66; c 1. PURE MATHEMATICS. *Educ:* Univ Bridgeport, BA, 66; Rutgers Univ, PhD(math), 69. *Prof Exp:* Asst prof math, Univ Calif, Los Angeles, 69-70; asst prof, 70-74, ASSOC PROF MATH, UNIV IOWA, 74- *Mem:* Am Math Soc. *Res:* Theory of rings. *Mailing Add:* Dept of Math Univ of Iowa Iowa City IA 52242

CAMIN, JOSEPH HARVEY, zoology, see previous edition

CAMINITA, BARBARA HOBSON, b Cranston, RI, Aug 18, 11; div; c 2. MICROBIOLOGY. *Educ:* Univ Md, BS, 38, MS, 48. *Prof Exp:* From jr bacteriologist to assoc bacteriologist, Div Indust Hyg, NIH, Md, 40-51; microbiologist, Off Naval Res, 51-62 & US Naval Weapons Lab, Va, 62-68; asst prof, 70-78, ASSOC PROF BIOL, MERCER UNIV, 78- *Concurrent Pos:* NIH fel, Univ Md, 48-50. *Mem:* AAAS; Am Soc Microbiol; Biophys Soc; Am Inst Biol Sci. *Res:* Air-borne infection; Entamoeba histolytica; Neisseria gonorrhoeae. *Mailing Add:* 240 Merritt Ave Macon GA 31204

CAMMARATA, ARTHUR, b Montclair, NJ, Jan 6, 40; m 62; c 1. PHYSICAL ORGANIC CHEMISTRY. *Educ:* Upsala Col, BS, 60; Rutgers Univ, PhD(phys org chem), 65. *Prof Exp:* Asst prof chem, Med Col Va, 65-68; assoc prof, 68-71, chmn, Pharmaceut Sect, 69-72, PROF CHEM, SCH PHARM, TEMPLE UNIV, 71- *Mem:* AAAS; Am Chem Soc; Acad Pharmaceut Sci; Am Asn Cols Pharm. *Res:* Molecular pharmacology; stereochemistry of medicinals; computers in pharmaceutical sciences. *Mailing Add:* Dept of Med Chem Temple Univ Sch of Pharm Philadelphia PA 19140

CAMMARATA, J BARRY, b Baltimore, Md, Mar 12, 48. PHYSICS. *Educ:* Col William & Mary, BS, 69; Univ Calif, Berkeley, MA, 71; Univ Md, PhD(physics), 74. *Prof Exp:* Res physicist, Lawrence Livermore Lab, 69-70; scholar, Stanford Univ, 74-76; ASST PROF PHYSICS, VA POLYTECH INST & STATE UNIV, 76- *Mem:* Am Phys Soc; Sigma Xi. *Res:* Theoretical studies of pion interactions, chiral symmetry and applications of current algebra and field theory in intermediate energy nuclear and particle physics. *Mailing Add:* Dept of Physics Va Polytech Inst & State Univ Blacksburg VA 24060

CAMMARATA, JOHN, b Brooklyn, NY, Oct 6, 22; m 54; c 2. ELECTRICAL ENGINEERING. *Educ:* Brooklyn Polytech Inst, BEE, 43; Hofstra Univ, MBA, 61. *Prof Exp:* Res asst, Brooklyn Polytech Inst, 42; engr, Gen Elec Co, NY, 43-46; develop engr, Arma Div, Am Bosch Arma, Garden City, 46-50, asst chief engr, 50-61, mgr prod reliability, 61-64, works mgr mfg opers, 64-65, dir, 65-66; gen mgr, Barden Leemath Div, Barden Corp, 66-68; mgr indust eng, Int Tel & Tel Corp, 68-77; CONSULT ENGR, 77- *Mem:* Fel Inst Environ Sci; Inst Elec & Electronics Engrs; Nat Soc Prof Engrs; Am Mgt Asn. *Res:* Servomechanisms; gun fire control systems; analogue computers; missile guidance systems; electromagnetic compatibility. *Mailing Add:* 30 Lilac Dr Syosset NY 11791

CAMMARATA, PETER S, b Chicago, Ill, Dec 26, 20; m 52; c 3. BIOCHEMISTRY, PHYSICAL ORGANIC CHEMISTRY. *Educ:* Univ Chicago, BS, 43, MS, 47; Univ Wis, PhD(physiol chem), 51. *Prof Exp:* Res assoc cancer res, Univ Chicago, 47-49; asst prof biochem, Yale Univ, 52-54; sr chemist, 54-55, biochem supvr, 56-62, nat prod supvr, 62-64, asst dir biochem, 64-70, dir biochem res div, 70-74, RES ADV, G D SEARLE & CO LABS, 75- *Honors & Awards:* Am Inst Chemists Award, 39. *Mem:* Am Chem Soc. *Res:* Enzymology; sulfated polysaccharides; proteases; prostaglandins; biochemical pharmacology and endocrinology; medicinal chemistry. *Mailing Add:* G D Searle & Co Box 5110 Chicago IL 60680

CAMOUGIS, GEORGE, b Concord, Mass, May 10, 30; m 61; c 3. ENVIRONMENTAL RESEARCH, ENVIRONMENTAL TOXICOLOGY. *Educ:* Tufts Univ, BS, 52; Harvard Univ, MA, 57, PhD(biol), 58. *Prof Exp:* Asst comp anat, Tufts Univ, 50-52; lab asst parasitol, Harvard Univ, 55; from asst prof to assoc prof physiol, Clark Univ, 58-64; sr neurophysiologist, Astra Pharmaceut Prod, Inc, 64-66, head neuropharmacol sect, 66-68; PRES & RES DIR, NEW ENG RES, INC, 68- *Concurrent Pos:* Res scientist, NY State Dept Health, 60; panel mem undergrad sci equip prog, NSF, 64 & 65; affil assoc prof, Clark Univ, 64-68, affil prof, 68-; mem corp, Bermuda Biol Sta Res, Inc, 68-; adj prof, Worcester Polytech Inst, 70- *Mem:* Soc Environ Toxicol Chem; Am Soc Zoologists; Biophys Soc; Am Physiol Soc; NY Acad Sci. *Res:* Environmental assessments; toxic materials; natural resources; public health. *Mailing Add:* 7 Wheeler Ave Worcester MA 01609

CAMP, ALBERT T(ALCOTT), b Jamestown, NY, Jan 6, 20; m 42; c 3. CHEMICAL ENGINEERING. *Educ:* Yale Univ, BEng, 41; Mass Inst Technol, MS, 56. *Prof Exp:* Res chemist, Hercules Powder Co, 41-50; chem engr & head propellant develop br, US Naval Ord Test Sta, 50-55 & Propellants Div, 55-59; dir, Propellants Div, Lockheed Propulsion Co, 59-64; dir develop, US Navy Propellant Plant, 64-65, dir res & develop, 65-67; assoc tech dir develop & technol, 67-69, dir sci & eng dept, 69-71, head fleet support dept, 71-72, actg tech dir, 72-73; spec asst to tech dir, Naval Ord Sta, 74-75, chief technologist, 75-80, CONTRACTOR CONSULT PROPELLANTS, PROPULSION & EXPLOSIVES TECHNOL, NAVAL SURFACE WEAPONS CTR, 81-; PRES, BRENTLAND DAIRY CORP, 77- *Concurrent Pos:* Consult, Thiokol Corp, 80-81. *Mem:* Am Chem Soc; Am Defense Prep Asn; Sigma Xi; Am Inst Aeronaut & Astronaut; AAAS. *Res:* Mechanism of solid propellant burning; catalysis of solid propellant burning; paint and varnish chemistry; synthesis of new nitrate esters; polymer chemistry; chemistry of propellants and explosives. *Mailing Add:* R-11 Bldg 600 Naval Surface Weapons Ctr Indian Head MD 20640

CAMP, BENNIE JOE, b Greenville, Tex, Mar 19, 27; m 52; c 2. BIOCHEMISTRY. *Educ:* ETex State Univ, BS, 49; Tex A&M Univ, MS, 53, PhD(biochem), 56. *Prof Exp:* From asst prof to assoc prof biochem, 56-66, PROF BIOCHEM & BIOPHYS & VET PHYSIOL & PHARMACOL, TEX A&M UNIV, 66- *Mem:* Am Chem Soc; hon fel Am Col Vet Toxicol; Am Inst Chemists; Sigma Xi. *Res:* Chemistry of poisonous plants and toxicology of environmental pollutants. *Mailing Add:* Col of Vet Med Tex A&M Univ College Station TX 77843

CAMP, DAVID CONRAD, b Atlanta, Ga, Aug 20, 34; m 61; c 2. EXPERIMENTAL NUCLEAR PHYSICS. *Educ:* Emory Univ, BA, 55; Ind Univ, MA, 58, MS, 59, PhD(physics), 63. *Prof Exp:* SR STAFF PHYSICIST, NUCLEAR CHEM DIV, LAWRENCE LIVERMORE LAB, UNIV CALIF, 63-, MGR, SAFEGUARDS TECHNOL PROG, 79- *Concurrent Pos:* Mem staff, Inter-Univ Reactor Inst, Delft Technol Univ, 71-72; consult, Mobil Res & Develop Corp, 74 & Environ Protection Agency, 80-83; adj asst prof radiol, Sch Med Univ Calif, 74-; instr appl sci, Univ Calif, Davis at Livermore, 77- *Mem:* AAAS; Am Phys Soc; Inst Nuclear Mat Mgt. *Res:* Nuclear instrumentation development program manager; multi-element multi-technique intercomparison studies; design of Si(Li) and Ge(Li) detector systems, x-ray fluorescence and gamma-ray spectrometry systems; x-ray, gamma-ray spectroscopy; nuclear safeguards instrumentation. *Mailing Add:* Lawrence Livermore Lab L-233 Univ of Calif Livermore CA 94550

CAMP, DAVID THOMAS, b Toledo, Ohio, Nov 26, 37; m 60; c 2. CHEMICAL ENGINEERING, METALLURGICAL ENGINEERING. *Educ:* Carnegie Inst Technol, BS, 58, MS, 60, PhD(chem eng), 63. *Prof Exp:* Develop engr photog processing equip, Eastman Kodak Co, 59-60; instr metall eng, Carnegie Inst Technol, 62-63, asst prof, 63-65; from asst prof to assoc prof chem eng, Univ Detroit, 65-74, prof & chmn dept, 74-76; SR PROCESS SPECIALIST, DOW CHEM CO, 76- *Mem:* Am Inst Mining, Metall & Petrol Engrs; Am Inst Chem Engrs; Am Soc Eng Educ. *Res:* Process engineering and design; absorption and catalysis. *Mailing Add:* Dow Chem Co Bldg 826 Midland MI 48640

CAMP, EARL D, b Magazine, Ark, June 12, 18; m 48; c 1. PLANT PATHOLOGY. *Educ:* Tex Tech Univ, BS, 41; Univ NMex, MS, 43; Univ Iowa, PhD(bot), 52. *Prof Exp:* War res staff & investr med mycol, Columbia Univ, 43-44; from instr to assoc prof biol, 45-59, dept chmn, 59-71, PROF BIOL, TEX TECH UNIV, 59- *Mem:* Fel AAAS. *Res:* Plant morphology and pathology; developmental anatomy of woody monocots. *Mailing Add:* Dept Biol Sci Tex Tech Univ Lubbock TX 79409

CAMP, ELDRIDGE KIMBEL, b Tamaqua, Pa, Sept 6, 15; m 47; c 2. ELECTROCHEMISTRY. *Educ:* Pa State Univ, BS, 38. *Prof Exp:* Apprentice exec, Collins & Aikman Corp, 39-40, foreman dyer, 40-42; res chemist metallic corrosion, Westinghouse Res Labs, 46-56; staff engr elec contacts, Prod Develop Lab, Int Bus Machine Corp, 56-57, mgr finishes & corrosion lab, 57-59, mem tech staff, Mat & Processes Labs, 59-60; DIR RES & MEM TECH STAFF, AM CHEM & REFINING CO, INC, 60- *Mem:* Am Electroplaters Soc; Am Chem Soc; Electrochem Soc; Am Soc Test & Mat. *Res:* Electrode processes applied to electrodeposition; anodizing; electropolishing; galvanic corrosion; surface studies; the study of mechanical and physical properties of precious metal film deposits and processes. *Mailing Add:* Am Chem & Refining Co PO Box 4067 10 Sheffield Waterbury CT 06714

CAMP, FRANK A, III, b Dallas, Tex, Feb 25, 47; m 70; c 2. AQUATIC ECOLOGY. *Educ:* NTex State Univ, BA, 69, MS, 71; Va Polytech Inst & State Univ, PhD(zool), 75. *Prof Exp:* Sr aquatic biologist, WAPORA Inc, 74-75, dir, Ill Div, 75-76; vpres, Jack McCormick & Assocs, 76-78; SR PROJ MGR, TERA CORP, 78- *Concurrent Pos:* Environ eng consult. *Mem:* AAAS; Sigma Xi. *Res:* Benthic diversity studies; continuous flow and static algal bioassays; bioassays at all trophic levels. *Mailing Add:* TERA Corp Suite 300 3131 Turtle Creek Blvd Dallas TX 75219

CAMP, FRANK RUDOLPH, JR, b North Adams, Mass, Oct 6, 19; m 44. IMMUNOLOGY. *Educ:* Emory Univ, AB, 48, MS, 54. *Prof Exp:* Chief lab serv, US Army Hosp, Bad Kreuznach, Ger, 52-54, instr immunohemat, Med Field Serv Sch, Ft Sam Houston, Tex, 54-57, asst dir, Europe Blood Bank, US Army, Landstuhl, Ger, 57-60, fel immunohemat, Walter Reed Army Inst Res, Washington, DC, 60-61, immunohematologist, 61-65, dir blood transfusion div, US Army Med Res Lab, Ky, 65-72, cmndg officer, Lab, 72-74; SCI DIR-DIR, LOUISVILLE REGION, AM RED CROSS BLOOD SERV, 74- *Concurrent Pos:* Asst clin prof path, Univ Louisville Sch Med; consult, Chief Mil Hist & Ctr of Mil Hist, US Army Med Hist Div, Washington. *Mem:* AAAS; Am Acad Forensic Sci; Genetics Soc Am; Am Soc Human Genetics; Int Soc Hemat. *Res:* Immunohematology; quantitative hemagglutination; erythrocyte metabolism and preservation; blood group genetics; tissue compatibility. *Mailing Add:* Am Red Cross Blood Serv 510 E Chestnut St Louisville KY 40201

CAMP, FREDERICK WILLIAM, b Washington, DC, July 1, 34; m 57; c 3. CHEMICAL ENGINEERING. *Educ:* Columbia Univ, AB, 56, BS, 57; Princeton Univ, MSE, 61, PhD(chem eng), 62. *Prof Exp:* Res engr, Process Develop, Sun Oil Co, 62-75, MGR SYNFUELS TECHNOL, SUNOCO ENERGY DEVELOP CO, 75- *Mem:* Am Chem Soc. *Res:* Athabasca tar sands; development and mathematical modeling of petroleum and petrochemical processes; conversion of coal and oil shale to synthetic fuels. *Mailing Add:* Sunoco Energy Develop Co 12700 Park Central Pl Dallas TX 75251

CAMP, HANEY BOLON, b Rome, Ga, May 29, 38; m 59; c 3. ENTOMOLOGY, TOXICOLOGY. *Educ:* Auburn Univ, BS, 60, MS, 63; Univ Calif, Riverside, PhD(entom), 68. *Prof Exp:* Regist coordr, Agr Div, 69-71, toxicologist, 71-72, dir regist & toxicol, 72-75, dir biochem, 75-78, spec asst to vpres res & develop, 78-79, VPRES RES & DEVELOP, CIBA-GEIGY CORP, 79- *Mem:* Soc Toxicol; Am Chem Soc; Entom Soc Am; Sigma Xi. *Res:* Insecticide chemistry; toxicology; mode of action of pesticides; environmental impact; metabolism in plants and animals; governmental regulation of pesticides. *Mailing Add:* 5 Anson Circle Greensboro NC 27407

CAMP, LESLIE WILFORD, b San Luis Obispo, Calif, Apr 16, 26; m 46; c 7. GEOLOGY. *Educ:* Brigham Young Univ, BA, 50; Johns Hopkins Univ, AM, 51. *Prof Exp:* Geologist, Fuels Br, US Geol Surv, 51-54; sr explor geologist, Columbia Geneva Div, US Steel Corp, 54-63; opers supvr, Crest Explor, Ltd, Stand Oil Co Calif, 63-66; sr geologist, Bear Creek Mining Co, 66-68; proj mgr indust minerals div, Kennecott Explor Inc, 68-70, proj mgr financial eval, 70-71, prof mgr, Kennecott Explor Servs, 72-74, mgr admin, Kennecott Corp Explor Group, 75-80; CHIEF GEOLOGIST, TETON EXPLOR DRILLING, INC, 80- *Mem:* Geol Soc Am; Am Inst Mining, Metall & Petrol Eng; Can Inst Mining & Metall; Soc Econ Geol. *Res:* Economic geology. *Mailing Add:* Teton Explor Drilling, Inc PO Drawer A-1 Casper WY 82602

CAMP, MARK JEFFREY, b Toledo, Ohio, Dec 19, 47. PALEOECOLOGY, MALACOLOGY. *Educ:* Univ Toledo, BSc, 70, MSc, 72; Ohio State Univ, PhD(geol), 74. *Prof Exp:* Asst prof geol, Earlham Col, 74-76; ASST PROF GEOL, UNIV TOLEDO, 76- *Mem:* Paleont Soc. *Res:* Comprehensive study of Pleistocene lacustrine deposits in Ohio, Michigan and Indiana, with emphasis on ecologic relationships of fauna and flora, distribution of species, glacial history, stratigraphy and origin of sediments. *Mailing Add:* 856 McKinley Ave Toledo OH 43605

CAMP, PAUL R, b Middletown, Conn, Dec 29, 19; m 58; c 3. SOLID STATE PHYSICS. *Educ:* Wesleyan Univ, BA, 41; Harvard Univ, MA, 47; Pa State Col, PhD(physics), 51. *Prof Exp:* Physicist, US Naval Res Lab, 41-44; instr, Wesleyan Univ, 47-48; physicist, Res Lab, Radio Corp Am, 51-53; Ford intern physics, Reed Col, 53-54; from asst prof to assoc prof, Polytech Inst Brooklyn, 54-61; chief, Mat Res Br, Cold Regions Res & Eng Lab, 61-63, physicist at large, 63-65; visiting physicist, Comn Col Physics, Univ Mich, 65-67; head dept physics, 67-73, PROF PHYSICS, UNIV MAINE, ORONO, 73- *Concurrent Pos:* Consult, Rand Corp, 56-61. *Mem:* Int Glaciol Soc; Am Phys Soc; Am Asn Physics Teachers. *Res:* Physics of ice. *Mailing Add:* Dept of Physics Bennett Hall Univ of Maine Orono ME 04473

CAMP, RONALD LEE, b Indianapolis, Ind, Apr 16, 44; m 72. PHYSICAL ORGANIC CHEMISTRY. *Educ:* Univ Mich, BS, 66; Mass Inst Technol, PhD(org chem), 71. *Prof Exp:* Res chemist polymer chem, Union Carbide Corp, 70-73; RES SUPVR ORG CHEM RES & DEVELOP, BASF WYANDOTTE CORP, 73- *Mem:* Am Chem Soc. *Res:* Synthesis of organic pesticides; process research and development for agricultural chemicals; polymer synthesis; surfactant synthesis. *Mailing Add:* BASF Wyandotte Corp 1609 Biddle Ave Wyandotte MI 48192

CAMP, RUSSELL R, b Corning, NY, Mar 26, 41; m 65. PLANT PATHOLOGY, ELECTRON MICROSCOPY. *Educ:* Baldwin-Wallace Col, BS, 64; Miami Univ, MA, 66; Univ Wis, PhD(bot), 70. *Prof Exp:* Asst prof, 70-75, ASSOC PROF BIOL, GORDON COL, 75- *Mem:* AAAS; Am Inst Biol Sci; Mycol Soc Am; Bot Soc Am; Am Phytopath Soc. *Res:* Electron microscopy of host parasite relations of fungal pathogens and their respective plant host. *Mailing Add:* Gordon Col Dept of Biol 255 Grapevine Rd Wenham MA 01984

CAMPAGNUOLO, CARL JOSEPH, mechanical engineering, physics, see previous edition

CAMPAIGNE, ERNEST EDWIN, b Chicago, Ill, Feb 13, 14; m 41; c 3. MEDICINAL CHEMISTRY. *Educ:* Northwestern Univ, BS, 36, MS, 38, PhD(biochem), 40. *Prof Exp:* Lab asst, Northwestern Univ, 36-40, res fel chem, 41-42; instr, Bowdoin Col, 40-41; instr prev med & pub health, Sch Med, Univ Tex, 42-43; from instr to prof, 43-79, EMER PROF CHEM, IND UNIV, BLOOMINGTON, 79- *Concurrent Pos:* Assoc biochemist, M D Anderson Hosp Cancer Res, Univ Tex, 42-43; with Comt Med Res, 44; res partic, Oak Ridge Inst Nuclear Studies, 55; consult, Off Surgeon Gen, Walter Reed Army Inst Res, 59-62; vis lectr, Univ Calif, San Francisco, 62; consult, NIH, 60-64, mem Coun Pub Comt, 60-62 & Policy Comt, 62-64, chmn, Med Div, 68; chmn med comn, Int Union Pure & Appl Chem, 69-73; consult, Drug Dvelop Comt, Div Cancer Treatment, Dept Health Educ & Welfare, 75-79. *Mem:* AAAS; Am Chem Soc; Soc Exp Biol & Med; fel NY Acad Sci; The Chem Soc. *Res:* Heterocyclic chemistry; central nervous system agents; antimetabolites; physiologically active and organic sulfur compounds. *Mailing Add:* Dept of Chem Ind Univ Bloomington IN 47401

CAMPANA, RICHARD JOHN, b Everett, Mass, Dec 5, 18; m 45; c 2. FOREST PATHOLOGY. *Educ:* Univ Idaho, BSF, 43; Yale Univ, MF, 47, PhD(forest path), 52. *Prof Exp:* Instr forestry, Pa State Univ, 47; asst prof bot, NC State Univ, 47-49; asst plant pathologist, USDA, 49-52; from asst plant pathologist to assoc plant pathologist, Ill Nat Hist Surv, 52-58; chmn plant sci PhD prog, 68-72, head dept bot & plant path, 58-68, PROF BOT & FOREST PATH, UNIV MAINE, 58- *Concurrent Pos:* Consult, Salt Prod Assocs, Ill, 55-57, State Chamber Com, Ill, 55-58, Morton Arboretum, 55-58, Tower Grove Park, Mo, 56-57 & Ill Munic League, 56-58; vis prof, NY State Col Forestry, Syracuse Univ, 67; guest botanist, Brookhaven Nat Lab, 67-71; ed, Phytopath News, 70-76; chmn, Orono Conserv Comn, 70-; pres, Maine Asn Conserv Comn, 72-73. *Honors & Awards:* Award of Merit, Orono Conserv Comn, 75; Award, Int Soc Arborists, 75. *Mem:* AAAS; Bot Soc Am; Am Phytopath Soc; Can Phytopath Soc; Int Soc Arborists (pres, 66-67). *Res:* Diseases of forest shade and ornamental trees and woody shrubs. *Mailing Add:* Dept Bot Univ Maine Orono ME 04469

CAMPANELLA, PAUL JOSEPH, II, ECOLOGY, ENVIRONMENTAL MANAGEMENT. *Educ:* Brown Univ, BA, 67; Syracuse Univ, PhD(ecol), 72. *Prof Exp:* Fel behav ecol, Smithsonian Trop Res Inst, 72-74; res scientist pop ecol, Gorgas Mem Lab Trop Med, 74-76; INSTR ANIMAL BEHAV, POP BIOL & HUMAN ECOL, CANAL ZONE COL, 73-; ENVIRON & ENERGY CONTROL OFFICER ENVIRON MGT, PANAMA CANAL CO, 73- *Mem:* AAAS; Ecol Soc Am. *Res:* Territoriality and spacing systems; evolution of mating systems; community stability. *Mailing Add:* Box 298 Balboa Panama

CAMPANELLA, SAMUEL JOSEPH, b Washington, DC, Dec 26, 26; m 58; c 1. ELECTRONICS, COMMUNICATIONS. *Educ:* Cath Univ Am, BS, 50, DSc(elec eng), 65; Univ Md, College Park, MS, 57. *Prof Exp:* Electronics scientist sonar, Naval Res Lab, Washington, DC, 50-53; electronics engr commun, MELPAR Inc, Falls Church, 53-57, mgr electronics res lab, 57-64,

mgr electronics res & develop ctr, 64-67; mgr signal processing lab, 67-73, DIR COMMUN PROCESSING LABS, COMSAT LABS, WASHINGTON, DC & CLARKSBURG, MD, 73- *Mem:* Fel Inst Elec & Electronics Engrs; fel AAAS; Am Inst Aeronaut & Astronaut; Sigma Xi. *Res:* Advanced communication satellite technology in time division multiple access; frequency division multiple access; digital speech interpolation; source encoding of speech and video; modulation techniques and on-board communications processing. *Mailing Add:* COMSAT Labs Clarksburg MD 20734

CAMPARO, JAMES CHARLES, b Newark, NJ, Mar 15, 56; m 79; c 1. ATOMIC & MOLECULAR PHYSICS. *Educ:* Columbia Univ, BA, 77, MA, 78, MPhil & PhD(chem), 81. *Prof Exp:* MEM TECH STAFF, AEROSPACE CORP, 81- *Mem:* Am Phys Soc. *Res:* Atomic physics; optical pumping in atomic clocks. *Mailing Add:* MS Ab/1667 Aerospace Corp PO Box 92957 Los Angeles CA 90009

CAMPAU, EDWARD JUNIOR, b Alto, Mich, July 5, 16; m 51; c 2. ENTOMOLOGY. *Educ:* Mich State Col, BS, 38; Stanford Univ, MA, 40; Univ Wis, PhD(econ entom), 42. *Prof Exp:* Asst entom, Mich State Col, 38-39; tech asst, Stanford Univ, 39-40; field inspector, State Dept Agr, Mich, 40; Cent Wis Canneries, 41; asst, Wis Alumni Res Found, 41-42; insecticides & fungicides group leader, Stand Oil Co (Ind), 46-58; entomologist, Lilly Res Labs, 58-70, staff asst plant sci res, 70-81; RETIRED. *Mem:* AAAS; Entom Soc Am. *Res:* Field control of codling moth, grapeberry moth and pea aphid; morphology of beetles; fungicides; weed killers; aerosols; household and agricultural insecticides; influence of clay diluents on toxicity of rotenone in ground cube when used for pea aphid control. *Mailing Add:* 114 Willow Rd Greenfield IN 46140

CAMPBELL, ADA MARIE, b Jewell, Iowa, Apr 1, 20. FOOD CHEMISTRY. *Educ:* Iowa State Univ, BS, 42, MA, 45; Cornell Univ, PhD(food sci, nutrit), 56. *Prof Exp:* Instr food & nutrit, NDak State Univ, 45-50; asst home economist exp sta, NMex State Univ, 50-52; actg asst prof food & nutrit, Univ Calif, Los Angeles, 52-53; asst foods, Cornell Univ, 53-56; asst prof food & nutrit, Univ Calif, Los Angeles, 56-61; assoc prof food sci, 61-67, PROF FOOD SCI, UNIV TENN, 67- *Mem:* AAAS; Am Asn Cereal Chem; Inst Food Technol; Am Oil Chem Soc. *Res:* Food lipids. *Mailing Add:* Col of Home Econ Univ of Tenn Knoxville TN 37916

CAMPBELL, ALAN, b Alexandria, Egypt, Aug 28, 44; Can & Brit citizen; m 71. ECOLOGY, ZOOLOGY. *Educ:* McGill Univ, BSc, 67; Univ Man, MSc, 69; Simon Fraser Univ, PhD(biol), 74. *Prof Exp:* Fel stored prod insects, Agr Can, 73-75; res proj dir tick res, Dept Biol, Acadia Univ, 75-78; RES SCIENTIST LOBSTER BIOL, DEPT FISHERIES & OCEANS, CAN, 78- *Mem:* Can Soc Zoologists; Entom Soc Am; Entom Soc Can; Sigma Xi; Crustaceans Soc. *Mailing Add:* Fisheries & Oceans Can Biol Sta St Andrews NB E0G 2X0 Can

CAMPBELL, ALAN NEWTON, b Halifax, Eng, Oct 29, 99; m 31; c 1. PHYSICAL CHEMISTRY. *Educ:* Univ London, PhD(phys chem), 24; Aberdeen Univ, DSc, 29. *Hon Degrees:* DSc, Univ Manitoba, 82. *Prof Exp:* Asst chem, Aberdeen Univ, 25-30; from asst prof to prof phys chem, 30-69, head dept, 45-68, EMER PROF PHYS CHEM, UNIV MANITOBA, 69- *Concurrent Pos:* Mem, Nat Res Coun Can, 51-57. *Honors & Awards:* Chem Inst Can Medal, 71. *Mem:* Fel Royal Soc Can; fel Royal Inst Chem. *Res:* Electrochemistry; phase rule. *Mailing Add:* Dept Chem Univ Manitoba Winnipeg MB R3B 2E9 Can

CAMPBELL, ALFRED, organic chemistry, see previous edition

CAMPBELL, ALFRED DUNCAN, b Zion, Ill, Dec 25, 19; m 43; c 2. BIOCHEMISTY. *Educ:* Univ Ill, BS, 43; Purdue Univ, MS, 48, PhD(agr biochem), 50. *Prof Exp:* Asst, State Exp Sta, Ind, 46-50; asst div head, Fleischmann Labs, Stand Brands Inc, 50-57; asst res dir, Clinton Corn Processing Co, 57-62; chief, Food Contaminants Br, 62-71, DEP DIR, DIV CHEM & PHYSICS, FOOD & DRUG ADMIN, 71-, RES COORDR OFF SCI, 73- *Concurrent Pos:* Mem food contaminants comn, Int Union Pure & Appl Chemists, 69- *Mem:* AAAS; Am Chem Soc; Inst Food Tech; fel Am Inst Chem. *Res:* Enzymology; intermediary metabolism; lipid metabolism; carboxylation reactions; bacterial and physiological genetics. *Mailing Add:* Dept of Biol Sci Stanford Univ Stanford CA 94305

CAMPBELL, ALICE DEL CAMPILLO, b Santurce, PR, May 30, 28; m 58; c 2. BIOCHEMISTRY. *Educ:* Columbia Univ, AB, 47; NY Univ, MS, 53; Univ Mich, PhD(biochem), 60. *Prof Exp:* Asst biochem, Pub Health Res Inst, NY, 47-48; dept pharmacol, NY Univ, 48-54; instr, Sch Med, Univ PR, 54-56; res assoc biol, Univ Rochester, 60-68; res assoc, 68-77, SR RES ASSOC BIOL SCI, STANFORD UNIV, 77- *Mem:* Am Chem Soc; Sigma Xi; fel Am Inst Chem. *Res:* Enzymology; intermediary metabolism; lipid metabolism; carboxylation reactions; bacterial and physiological genetics. *Mailing Add:* Dept of Biol Sci Stanford Univ Stanford CA 94305

CAMPBELL, ALLAN BARRIE, b Winnipeg, Man, Mar 28, 23; m 50; c 1. PLANT BREEDING. *Educ:* Univ Man, BSA, 44, MSc, 48; Univ Minn, PhD(genetics, plant breeding), 54. *Prof Exp:* RES SCIENTIST WHEAT BREEDING, CAN DEPT AGR, 49- *Mem:* Agr Inst Can; Can Soc Agron; Royal Soc Can. *Res:* Breeding improved varieties of common wheat with special emphasis on resistance to stem rust and leaf rust. *Mailing Add:* Res Sta Agr Can 195 Dafoe Rd Winnipeg MB R3T 2M9 Can

CAMPBELL, ALLAN McCULLOCH, b Berkeley, Calif, Apr 27, 29; m 58; c 2. MICROBIAL GENETICS. *Educ:* Univ Calif, BS, 50; Univ Ill, MS, 51, PhD(bact), 53. *Prof Exp:* Instr bact, Sch Med, Univ Mich, 53-57; res assoc genetics, Carnegie Inst, 57-58; from asst prof to prof biol, Univ Rochester, 58-68; PROF BIOL, STANFORD UNIV, 68- *Concurrent Pos:* Fel, Nat Found Inst Pasteur, 58-59; USPHS res career award, 62-68; Found Microbiol lectr, 70-71; mem genetics study sect, NIH, 64-69, mem recombinant, DNA Adv Comt, 77-81. *Mem:* Nat Acad Sci; AAAS; Am Soc Microbiol; Am Soc Nat. *Res:* Genetics of bacteriophage; lysogeny; biochemical genetics. *Mailing Add:* Dept of Biol Sci Stanford Univ Stanford CA 94305

CAMPBELL, ARTHUR B, b Ann Arbor, Mich, Sept 3, 43; m 71; c 1. RADIATION EFFECTS, SINGLE EVENT UPSETS. *Educ:* Union Col NY, BS, 65; Univ Del, MS, 67, PhD(physics), 71. *Prof Exp:* Fel, Univ Salford, Eng, 71-72 & McMaster Univ, Can, 72-75; res physicist, Bur Mines, US Govt, 75-79; RES PHYSICIST, NAVAL RES LAB, 79- *Mem:* Inst Elec & Electronic Engrs. *Res:* Radiation effects in materials including semiconductor devices and metals; including ion implantation and single event upsets in semiconductor memories. *Mailing Add:* Code 6611 Naval Res Lab Washington DC 20375

CAMPBELL, ASHLEY SAWYER, b Montclair, NJ, Dec 24, 18; m 42; c 6. THERMODYNAMICS. *Educ:* Harvard Univ, BS, 40, SM, 47, ScD(mech eng), 49. *Prof Exp:* Engr, Wright Aero Corp, 40-45; asst dean, Harvard Univ, 48-49, asst prof, 49-50; dean eng, Univ Maine, 50-57 & Tufts Univ, 57-68; prof mech eng, Univ Maine, 68-79. *Res:* Thermodynamics of combustion engines. *Mailing Add:* Dept of Mech Eng Univ of Maine Orono ME 04473

CAMPBELL, BARBARA KNAPP, b Denver, Colo, June 14, 08; m 33. MEDICINAL CHEMISTRY. *Educ:* Univ Chicago, BS, 29, MS, 31; Pa State Col, PhD(org chem), 37. *Prof Exp:* Teacher, Maret Sch, Washington, DC, 33; res assoc chem, Univ Notre Dame, 37-44; lectr, Univ Ind, 45-53; consult, Mead Johnson Res Labs, 53-73; CONSULT & SCI TRANSLATOR, CAMPBELL & ASSOCS, 73- *Concurrent Pos:* Instr, St Mary's Col (Ind), 39-40; with Off Sci Res & Develop; Nat Defense Res Comt, 42-45. *Mem:* Fel AAAS; Am Chem Soc; Sigma Xi. *Res:* Synthetic drugs, especially for malaria and cancer; amino alcohols and ethylenimines; aliphatic hydrocarbons; reduction of organic compounds; preparation and reactions of aliphatic tertiary aminoalcohols; infrared spectroscopy. *Mailing Add:* 8216 Petersburg Rd Evansville IN 47711

CAMPBELL, BENEDICT JAMES, b Philadelphia, Pa, Oct 17, 27; m 52; c 2. BIOCHEMISTRY. *Educ:* Franklin & Marshall Col, BS, 51; Northwestern Univ, PhD(biochem), 56. *Prof Exp:* Res biochemist, Glidden Co, 55-58 & Armour Co, 58-60; assoc prof, 60-67, chmn dept, 73-77, PROF BIOCHEM, SCH MED, UNIV MO-COLUMBIA, 67- *Mem:* AAAS; Am Chem Soc; NY Acad Sci; Am Soc Biol Chemists; Biophys Soc. *Res:* Biochemical research; graduate education. *Mailing Add:* Dept of Biochem Univ of Mo Med Ctr Columbia MO 65201

CAMPBELL, BERNERD EUGENE, b Wooster, Ohio, Nov 1, 38; m 66; c 3. HIGH ENERGY LASERS. *Educ:* Otterbein Col, BS, 61. *Prof Exp:* Researcher physics, US Army Missile Command, Redstone Arsenal, 61-63; RES SCIENTIST HIGH ENERGY LASER STUDIES, BATTELLE COLUMBUS LABS, BATTELLE MEM INST, 64- *Mem:* Sigma Xi. *Res:* High energy laser device technology. *Mailing Add:* Battelle Columbus Labs 505 King Ave Columbus OH 43201

CAMPBELL, BERRY, b St Paul, Minn, Mar 21, 12; m 33; c 4. NEUROLOGY. *Educ:* Univ Calif, Los Angeles, AB, 32; Johns Hopkins Univ, PhD(anat), 35. *Prof Exp:* Asst zool, Univ Calif, 32; asst prof anat, Sch Med, Univ Okla, 37-42; from asst prof to prof anat, Med Sch, Univ Minn, 43-58; res prof neurosurg, Loma Linda Univ, 58-66; prof, 66-77, actg chmn dept, 66-72, EMER PROF PHYSIOL, MED SCH, UNIV CALIF, IRVINE, 77- *Concurrent Pos:* Nat Res Coun fel med sci, Western Reserve Univ, 35-37; Guggenheim fel, Rockefeller Inst, 40-42; fel neurol, Col Physicians & Surgeons, Columbia Univ, 42-43; hon res fel, Univ Col, Univ London, 53-54; field naturalist, Roosevelt Wildlife Forest Exp Sta, Syracuse Univ, 32; vis asst prof, Sch Med, Univ Tenn, 42; vis prof, Columbia Univ, 53; res prof, Calif Col Med, 64-66; mem attend staff, Los Angeles County Hosp & Rancho Los Amigos, 64-68; consult physiol, Ctr Marital & Sexual Studies, 71- *Mem:* AAAS; Am Acad Neurol; Harvey Soc; Am Soc Ichthyologists & Herpetologists; Am Neurol Asn. *Res:* Distribution of vertebrates; evolution of mammals; anatomy and physiology of the nervous systems; encephalitis and multiple sclerosis; immunology; milk antibodies. *Mailing Add:* 444 N Alta Vista Ave Monrovia CA 91016

CAMPBELL, BONITA JEAN, b Annapolis, Md, Sept 15, 43; div; c 1. INDUSTRIAL ENGINEERING, MANAGEMENT SCIENCE. *Educ:* Colo State Univ, BS, 67; Univ Redlands, MS, 73; Pepperdine Univ, MBA, 73; Univ Calif, Los Angeles, PhD(opers res), 79. *Prof Exp:* Assoc engr, Robinson Eng, 65-68; indust engr, Kaiser Steel Corp, 68-72; acct mgr, Info Systs Div, Gen Elec, 72-73; asst prof quant methods, Pepperdine Univ, 73-75; asst prof, 75-81, ASSOC PROF, CALIF STATE UNIV, NORTHRIDGE, 81-, DIR, WOMENS ENG PROG, 75- *Concurrent Pos:* Consult statistician, Thomas J Dudley & Assoc, 73-75 & L E Chuba Res Assoc, 75-76; adj prof, Pepperdine Univ, 75-77; proj dir, NSF grants, 77-; mem tech staff, Aerospace Corp, 77- *Honors & Awards:* Aerospace Woman of the Year, 79. *Mem:* Am Inst Indust Engrs; Soc Women Engrs; Asn Women Sci. *Res:* Time series analysis, particularly parameter estimation; statistical quality control, particularly sampling designs and plans. *Mailing Add:* Sch Eng & Comput Sci Calif State Univ Northridge CA 91330

CAMPBELL, BONNALIE OETTING, b Springfield, Mo, Aug 21, 33; m 60; c 2. PHYSIOLOGY, ENDOCRINOLOGY. *Educ:* Southwest Mo State Univ, AB, 55; Northwestern Univ, MS, 58, PhD(physiol), 64. *Prof Exp:* Instr biochem, Univ Houston, 66-71, instr physiol, 71-73, ASST PROF PHYSIOL, BAYLOR COL MED, 73- *Concurrent Pos:* NASA grants, 70-; consult endocrinol, Vet Admin Hosp, Houston, 73- *Mem:* AAAS; Am Soc Zoologists; assoc Am Physiol Soc. *Res:* Adrenocorticotropic hormone; circadian rhythms. *Mailing Add:* Dept of Physiol Baylor Col of Med Houston TX 77030

CAMPBELL, BRUCE (NELSON), JR, b Northampton, Mass, Apr 21, 31; m 56; c 4. BIOCHEMISTRY, ORGANIC CHEMISTRY. *Educ:* Williams Col, AB, 52; Univ Conn, PhD(chem), 58. *Prof Exp:* Asst instr chem, Univ Conn, 55-56; from asst prof to prof chem, MacMurray Col, 57-73, chmn dept chem, 72-73; chmn dept, 73-78, PROF CHEM STATE UNIV NY POTSDAM, 73- *Concurrent Pos:* NSF sci fac fel, Mich State Univ, 65-66; vis prof, Dept

Biochem, Univ Ill, Urbana, 73, vis res prof, 80-81. *Mem:* Sigma Xi; AAAS; Am Chem Soc. *Res:* Enzyme isolation and reactions; micelle catalysis; theoretical and synthetic organic chemistry; innovation in chemical education. *Mailing Add:* Dept of Chem State Univ of NY Potsdam NY 13676

CAMPBELL, BRUCE CARLETON, b Trenton, NJ, May 15, 49. HOST-PLANT RESISTANCE, INSECT-PLANT INTERACTIONS. *Educ:* Rutgers Univ, BA, 71, MS, 76; Univ Calif, Davis, PhD(entomol), 80. *Prof Exp:* Res assoc entomol, Univ Calif, Davis, 78-80; RES ENTOMOLOGIST, USDA- *Mem:* Entomol Soc Am; Phytochem Soc NAm; AAAS. *Res:* Host-plant resistance with respect to the effects of plant natural products on insect development, metabolism and feeding behavior. *Mailing Add:* USDA-WRRC 800 Buchanan St Berkeley CA 94710

CAMPBELL, BRUCE HENRY, b Madison, SDak, Oct 27, 40; m 63; c 3. ANALYTICAL CHEMISTRY. *Educ:* Univ Kans, BS, 62; Univ SDak, MA, 65; Univ Tex, PhD(chem), 68. *Prof Exp:* From asst prof to assoc prof chem, Univ Southern Miss, 67-72; fel, Clarkson Col Technol, 72-74; mgr res anal serv, J T Baker Chem Co, 74-75, sr chemist, 75-81; SR RES CHEMIST, AM CYANAMID CO, STAMFORD, CONN, 81- *Concurrent Pos:* Ed, Critical Rev Anal Chem, 75- *Mem:* Am Chem Soc; Electrochem Soc; Chem Notation Asn. *Res:* Applied and theoretical electrochemistry; general analytical chemistry. *Mailing Add:* Am Cyanamid Co 1937 W Main Stamford CT 06904

CAMPBELL, C(OLIN) K(YDD), b St Andrews, Scotland, May 3, 27; Can citizen; m 54; c 3. ELECTRICAL ENGINEERING, MATERIALS SCIENCE. *Educ:* Univ St Andrews, BSc Hons, 52, PhD(physics), 60; Mass Inst Technol, SM, 53. *Prof Exp:* Commun engr, Diplomatic Wireless Serv, Eng, 46-47 & Foreign Off, 47; commun engr, Brit Embassy, Washington, DC, & Brit deleg to UN, NY, 47-48; design engr, Atomic Instrument Co, Mass, 54-57; proj engr, A Kusko Inc, 57; from asst prof to assoc prof, 60-67, chmn dept, 65-69, prof elec eng, 67-80, PROF ELEC & COMPUT ENG, MCMASTER UNIV, 80- *Concurrent Pos:* Mem, Brit deleg, Meeting of Nobel Physics Prizewinners, Bavaria, 59; vis res prof, Univ BC, 70; Nat Res Coun Can sr res fel, 70. *Mem:* Inst Elec & Electronics Engrs; Sigma Xi; Can Soc Elec Eng; fel Eng Inst Can; fel Royal Soc Arts. *Res:* Thin film physics; synthesis of thin film electronic filter devices; low temperature physics and superconductivity; masers and lasers; surface acoustic wave devices. *Mailing Add:* Dept Elec & Comput Eng 1280 Main St W Hamilton ON L8S 4L7 Can

CAMPBELL, CARL WALTER, b Decatur, Ill, Jan 10, 29; m 51; c 5. PLANT PHYSIOLOGY, HORTICULTURE. *Educ:* Ill State Norm Univ, BSEd, 51; Kans State Col, MS, 52; Purdue Univ, PhD(plant physiol), 57. *Prof Exp:* Plant physiologist, Agr Mkt Serv, USDA, 57-60; asst horticulturist, 60-66, assoc horticulturist, 66-70, PROF HORT & HORTICULTURIST, AGR RES & EDUC CTR, UNIV FLA, 70- *Mem:* AAAS; Am Inst Biol Sci; Am Pomol Soc; Am Soc Hort Sci; Soc Econ Bot. *Res:* Plant growth regulators; post-harvest physiology of fruits; horticultural and physiological aspects of selection, propagation and production of tropical and subtropical fruit crops. *Mailing Add:* Agr Res & Educ Ctr Univ of Fla 18905 SW 280th St Homestead FL 33031

CAMPBELL, CARLOS BOYD GODFREY, b Chicago, Ill, July 27, 34; m 79; c 4. NEUROANATOMY, ZOOLOGY. *Educ:* Univ Ill, BS, 55, MS, 57, MD, 63, PhD(anat), 65. *Prof Exp:* Surgical intern, Presby-St Lukes Hosp, Chicago, Ill, 63-64; neuroanatomist, Walter Reed Army Inst Res, Washington, DC, 64-67; from asst prof to assoc prof anat & physiol, Ctr Neural Sci, Ind Univ, Bloomington, 67-74; resident physician, Dept Neurol, Los Angeles County-Univ Southern Calif Med Ctr, 73-74; assoc clin prof anat, Calif Col Med, Univ Calif, Irvine, 75-77, resident physician, dept radiol sci, 75-77; vis assoc biol, Calif Inst Technol, 76-77; prof anat & head dept, Sch Med, Univ PR, 77-79; RES NEUROLOGIST, WALTER REED ARMY INST RES, 79- *Concurrent Pos:* Adj prof anat, Georgetown Univ, 80- *Mem:* Am Asn Anat; Am Soc Zoologists; Am Primatol Soc; Soc Neurosci; Int Primatol Soc. *Res:* Comparative neuroanatomy; systematic zoology; comparative neurology of motor and sensory systems; primate nervous systems; primate evolution. *Mailing Add:* Div Neuropsychiat Walter Reed Army Inst Res Washington DC 20012

CAMPBELL, CATHERINE CHASE, b New York, NY, July 1, 05; m 30; c 1. PALEONTOLOGY, GEOMORPHOLOGY. *Educ:* Oberlin Col, BA & MA, 27; Radcliffe Col, MA, 30, PhD(micropaleont), 32. *Prof Exp:* Instr geol, Mt Holyoke Col, 27-29; tech writer meteorol, Long Range Weather Forecasting Unit, US Army Air Force, 43-45; tech ed rocket proj, Calif Inst Technol, 45-46; underwater ord, US Naval Ord Test Sta, 47-51, supvr pub ed, 51-61; GEOLOGIST, US GEOL SURV, 61- *Mem:* Fel Geol Soc Am; Geosci Info Soc; Asn Earth Sci Ed; Soc Tech Commun. *Res:* Environmental geology. *Mailing Add:* US Geol Surv 345 Middlefield Rd Menlo Park CA 94025

CAMPBELL, CATHY, b Lamar, Mo, Jan 8, 49. STATISTICS. *Educ:* Univ Mo-Columbia, BS, 70, MA, 71; Southern Methodist Univ, PhD(statist), 77. *Prof Exp:* Res asst biostatist, Univ NC, 73-74; ASST PROF STATIST, UNIV MINN, 77- *Mem:* Am Statist Asn; AAAS; Int Biomet Soc. *Res:* Analysis of data from complex sample surveys; replication methods of variance estimation. *Mailing Add:* Dept of Appl Statist Rm 352 1994 Buford Ave St Paul MN 55108

CAMPBELL, CHARLES EDWIN, b Columbus, Ohio, Dec 11, 42; m 65; c 2. PHYSICS. *Educ:* Ohio State Univ, BS, 64; Washington Univ, St Louis, PhD(physics), 69. *Prof Exp:* Res assoc physics, Univ Wash, 69-71 & Stanford Univ, 71-73; asst prof, 73-76, assoc prof, 76-81, PROF PHYSICS, UNIV MINN, MINNEAPOLIS, 81- *Concurrent Pos:* Vis prof, Inst Theoret Physics, Univ Cologne, 81-82. *Mem:* Am Phys Soc. *Res:* Many-body theory; theory of quantum fluids; physical absorption. *Mailing Add:* Sch of Physics & Astron Univ of Minn Minneapolis MN 55455

CAMPBELL, CHARLES HAYWOOD, b Sanford, NC, Dec 8, 24; m 47; c 4. VETERINARY MICROBIOLOGY. *Educ:* Univ NC, BA, 49, MSPH, 51, PhD(parasitol), 54. *Prof Exp:* Instr parasitol, Univ NC, 50-54; instr microbiol & immunol, State Univ NY Downstate Med Ctr, 54-56; immunologist, Plum Island Animal Dis Lab, USDA, 56-58; sr cancer res scientist virol, Roswell Park Mem Inst, 58-60; RES MICROBIOLOGIST, PLUM ISLAND ANIMAL DIS CTR, USDA, 60- *Mem:* Am Soc Microbiol; Am Acad Microbiol. *Res:* Antigenic studies of Trichinella spiralis; natural resistance to foot-and-mouth disease; virus selection and recombination. *Mailing Add:* USDA Plum Island Animal Dis Ctr Box 848 Greenport NY 11944

CAMPBELL, CHARLES J, b Nanton, Alta, Can, Nov 25, 15; US citizen; m. FISH BIOLOGY, FISHERIES MANAGEMENT. *Educ:* Wash State Univ, BS, 38. *Prof Exp:* Jr fishery biologist, US Forest Serv, 39-40; from field biologist to chief basin invests, Fishery Div, Ore Wildlife Comn, 41-59, chief fisheries, US Bur Land Mgt, 59-75, asst chief fisheries, Ore Dept Fish & Wildlife, 75-78, environ specialist, 78-79; ENVIRON SCIENTIST, VTN OREGON, INC, 79- *Mem:* Am Fisheries Soc (pres, 73); Am Inst Fisheries Res Biol; Wildlife Soc. *Res:* Fishery biology, management and adminstration; ecology of fish. *Mailing Add:* 921 SW Cheltenham St Portland OR 97201

CAMPBELL, CHARLOTTE CATHERINE, b Winchester, Va, Dec 4, 14. MEDICAL MYCOLOGY. *Educ:* George Washington Univ, BS, 51; Am Bd Med Microbiol, dipl. *Hon Degrees:* DSc, Lowell Tech Inst, 72. *Prof Exp:* Technician, Dept Bact, Walter Reed Army Inst Res, 41-43, bacteriologist, 43-46, med mycologist, 46-49, chief mycol sect, 49-62; from assoc prof to prof med mycol, Sch Pub Health, Harvard Univ, 62-73; prof med mycol & chmn dept med sci, Sch Med, Southern Ill Univ, 73-77; co-prin investr, US/USSR Prog Microbiol, Am Soc Microbiol, 77-80; RETIRED. *Concurrent Pos:* Consult, Vet Admin-US Armed Forces Comn Histoplasmosis & Coccidioidomycosis, 54-62 & Mid Am Res Unit, CZ, 57-62; assoc ed, Sabouraudia; assoc in med, Peter Bent Brigham Hosp, 63-73; mem sci adv bd, Gorgas Mem Inst; mem panel rev skin test antigens, Food & Drug Admin. *Honors & Awards:* Medals, US War Dept, 48 & US Dept Army, 61; Rhoda Benham Medallion for Meritorious Contrib Med Mycol, 78; Isham Award, 79. *Mem:* Fel AAAS; Am Pub Health Asn; Am Thoracic Soc; Am Acad Microbiol; Med Mycol Soc of the Americas (pres, 70). *Res:* Antigenic analysis of systemic mycotic agents; epidemiology and ecology of histoplasmosis; serologic diagnosis and chemotherapy of systemic mycoses. *Mailing Add:* 120 Pembroke St Boston MA 02118

CAMPBELL, CLARENCE L, JR, b Indianapolis, Ind, Sept 24, 21; m. VETERINARY MEDICINE. *Educ:* Ohio State Univ, DVM, 45. *Prof Exp:* Vet pvt pract, Ill, 45; field vet, Fla Livestock Sanit Bd, Fla Dept Agr, 45-48, asst state vet, 48-52, state vet & secy, 53-61, STATE VET & DIR DIV ANIMAL INDUST, FLA DEPT AGR & CONSUMER SERV, 61- *Concurrent Pos:* Pres, Nat Assembly State Vet, 56-57. *Honors & Awards:* Meritorious Serv Award, USDA, 62; Cert Serv Award, Am Vet Med Asn, 68. *Mem:* US Animal Health Asn (pres, 65-66); Am Vet Med Asn; Am Asn Equine Practitioners. *Res:* Regulatory veterinary medicine. *Mailing Add:* Fla Dept of Agr & Consumer Serv Rm 328 Mayo Bldg Tallahassee FL 32301

CAMPBELL, CLEMENT, JR, b Milton, Pa, Oct 22, 30; m 66; c 1. CHEMISTRY. *Educ:* Bucknell Univ, BS, 51. *Prof Exp:* Res chemist, Pyrotechnics Lab, 51-74 & Explosives Div, 74-77, RES CHEMIST, ENERGETIC MAT DIV, US ARMY RES & DEVELOP COMMAND, PICATINNY, 77- *Mem:* AAAS; Am Chem Soc; Sigma Xi; NAm Thermal Anal Soc. *Res:* Pre-ignition and ignition reactions of explosive, propellant and pyrotechnic materials; reactions of powdered metals; decomposition of inorganic oxidants; thermoanalysis; gas chromatography/mass spectrometry applied to energetic materials; characterization of environmental pollutants from ammunition plants. *Mailing Add:* 29 Cory Rd Flanders NJ 07836

CAMPBELL, CLYDE DEL, b Wheeling, WVa, Apr 1, 30; m 56; c 1. ORGANIC CHEMISTRY, BIOCHEMISTRY. *Educ:* WLiberty State Col, AB & BS, 53; NC State Col, MS, 55; WVa Univ, PhD(biochem, org chem), 58. *Prof Exp:* Asst biol chem, NC State Col, 53-55 & WVa Univ, 55-58; instr chem, WLiberty State Col, 58-61; sr res chemist, Mobay Chem Co, WVa, 61-68; chmn div sci & math, 68-70, assoc acad dean, 70-73, DEAN ADMIN, WLIBERTY STATE COL, 73- *Mem:* AAAS; Am Chem Soc. *Res:* Isolation and identification of chlorophyll and carotenoid pigments; nitrogen metabolism in ruminants; function of vitamin B12 in nitrogen metabolism; carbohydrate analysis of foodstuffs; polyurethanes; isocyanates; plastics and synthetic resins; intermediary metabolism. *Mailing Add:* WLiberty State Col West Liberty WV 26074

CAMPBELL, COLIN, b Washington, DC, June 24, 27; m 52; c 3. OBSTETRICS & GYNECOLOGY, MEDICAL ADMINISTRATION. *Educ:* Stanford Univ, AB, 49; Temple Univ, EdM, 67; McGill Univ, MD, CM, 53. *Prof Exp:* Instr obstet & gynec, Temple Univ, 61-64; from asst prof to prof obstet & gynec, Univ Mich, Ann Arbor, 64-78, from asst dean to assoc dean student affairs, 72-78; DEAN & PROF OBSTET & GYNEC, SCH PRIMARY MED CARE, UNIV ALA, HUNTSVILLE, 78- *Concurrent Pos:* Consult, Wayne County Gen Hosp, 65-; examr, Am Bd Obstet & Gynec, 69-76. *Mem:* Fel Am Col Obstet & Gynec. *Res:* Erythroblastosis fetalis; medical education. *Mailing Add:* Sch of Primary Med Care 109 Governors Dr Huntsville AL 35801

CAMPBELL, CONSTANCE SUE, reproductive biology, behavioral endocrinology, deceased

CAMPBELL, CONSTANTINE ALBERGA, b Montego Bay, W Indies, Jan 18, 34; m 60. SOIL CHEMISTRY. *Educ:* Univ Toronto, BSA, 60, MSA, 61; Univ Sask, PhD(soil chem), 65. *Prof Exp:* Lectr soil chem & physics, Univ Sask, 63-64; Res scientist soil chem, 65-77, HEAD SOIL CHEM, 77- *Concurrent Pos:* Can rep nitrogen prog, Food & Agr Orgn UN/Int Atomic Energy Agency; Assoc ed, Can J Soil Sci, 81- *Mem:* Can Soc Soil Sci; Am Soc Agron. *Res:* Influence of environmental conditions on changes in soil nitrogen status and soil nitrogen availability to plants. *Mailing Add:* 75 MacDonald Crescent Swift Current SK S9H 1P5 Can

CAMPBELL, DAN NORVELL, b Mt Enterprise, Tex, Sept 10, 28; m 51; c 2. ANALYTICAL CHEMISTRY, HEALTH SCIENCE. *Educ:* Southern Methodist Univ, BS, 52, MS, 53; Am Acad Indust Hyg, cert, 81. *Prof Exp:* From res chemist to sr res chemist, 55-75, PROCESS SPECIALIST, MONSANTO CO, 70-, INDUST HYG ANAL SPECIALIST, 76- *Mem:* Am Chem Soc; Am Ind Hyg Asn. *Res:* Chromatographic separations in analytical chemistry involving both gas and liquid chromatography. *Mailing Add:* 1223 Sunset Lane Monsanto Co Texas City TX 77590

CAMPBELL, DAVID KELLY, b Long Beach, Calif, July 23, 44; m 67; c 2. THEORETICAL HIGH ENERGY PHYSICS, FIELD THEORY. *Educ:* Harvard Col, AB, 66; Cambridge Univ, PhD(theoret physics), 70. *Prof Exp:* Res assoc theoret high energy physics, Univ Ill, 70-72; mem, Inst Advan Study, Princeton, 72-74; STAFF MEM, THEORET DIV, LOS ALAMOS SCI LAB, 74- *Concurrent Pos:* Fel, Ctr Advan Study, Univ Ill, 70-72; Oppenheimer fel, Los Alamos Sci Lab, 74-77. *Mem:* Am Phys Soc; AAAS. *Res:* Relativistic quantum field theory models of elementary particle physics; pion condensation in nuclear matter at high density; nonlinear phenomena in field theory and condensed matter systems. *Mailing Add:* Theory Div T-8 Los Alamos Sci Lab Los Alamos NM 87545

CAMPBELL, DAVID OWEN, b Merriam, Kans, Nov 11, 27; m 54; c 3. RADIOCHEMISTRY, INORGANIC CHEMISTRY. *Educ:* Univ Kansas City, BA, 47; Ill Inst Technol, PhD(chem), 53. *Prof Exp:* CHEMIST, OAK RIDGE NAT LAB, 53- *Honors & Awards:* Special Award, Am Nuclear Soc, 81. *Mem:* Am Chem Soc; Am Nuclear Soc. *Res:* Decontamination of nuclear equipment; molten salt and fluoride volatility fuel processing; transuranium element chemistry and chemistry of protactinium; nuclear reactor fuel reprocessing; radioactive waste treatment, nuclear reactor safety. *Mailing Add:* 102 Windham Rd Oak Ridge TN 37830

CAMPBELL, DAVID PAUL, b Seattle, Wash, May 12, 44; m 69; c 1. GENETICS. *Educ:* Western Wash State Col, BA, 67; Wash State Univ, PhD(genetics), 76. *Prof Exp:* ASST PROF GENETICS, CALIF STATE POLYTECH UNIV, POMONA, 75- *Mem:* AAAS; Am Soc Plant Physiologists; Int Plant Tissue Cult Asn. *Res:* Ultrastructural changes in germinating seed tissues of the Solanaceae. *Mailing Add:* Dept of Biol Sci Calif State Polytech Univ Pomona CA 91768

CAMPBELL, DEWAYNE E, b Ligonier, Pa, Aug 2, 23; m 46; c 4. FISHERIES. *Educ:* Univ Mich, BSF, 50. *Prof Exp:* Fisheries res technician, Inst Fisheries Res, Fisheries Div, Mich Dept Conserv, 47-49; fishery biologist, Benner Spring Fish Res Sta, Pa Fish Comn, 50-60, southwest regional fisheries mgr, 60-62; chief biol sect, Environ Planning Div, Neilan Engrs, Inc, Pa, 62-65; ZONE FISHERIES BIOLOGIST, NAT FORESTS MICH, US FOREST SERV, 65- *Concurrent Pos:* Consult mem, Environ Res Inst Inc, DC, 62-65. *Mem:* Am Fisheries Soc; Wildlife Soc. *Res:* Evaluation of aquatic resources. *Mailing Add:* Hiawatha Nat Forest US Forest Serv Escanaba MI 49829

CAMPBELL, DONALD A, electrical engineering, microbiology, see previous edition

CAMPBELL, DONALD BRUCE, b New South Wales, Australia. PLANETARY SCIENCES. *Educ:* Univ Sydney, BS, 63, MS, 65; Cornell Univ, PhD(astron), 71. *Prof Exp:* Res assoc astron, Cornell Univ, 71-73; mem staff, Haystack Observ, Northeast Radio Observ Corp, 73-74; res assoc, 74-76, sr res assoc, 76-79, ASSOC DIR, ARECIBO OBSERV, CORNELL UNIV, 79- *Mem:* Am Astron Soc; Am Geophys Union; Int Astron Union. *Res:* Investigation of planetary surfaces and atmospheres by means of ground based radar. *Mailing Add:* Arecibo Observ Box 995 Arecibo PR 00612

CAMPBELL, DONALD EDWARD, b Brooklyn, NY, Sept 3, 28; m 52; c 4. CHARACTERIZATION OF GLASSES & CERAMICS. *Educ:* Union Col, BS, 49; Rensselaer Polytech Inst, PhD(chem), 52. *Prof Exp:* Asst AEC contract, Rensselaer Polytech Inst, 50-52; from instr to asst prof chem, SDak State Col, 52-55; res chemist glass res & develop lab, 55-63, leader anal chem group tech serv res dept, 63-65, mgr chem anal res dept, 65-73, SR RES ASSOC, CORNING GLASS WORKS, 73-, MGR PHYS ANAL CHEM RES SERV, CORNING-EUROPE, CENTRE EUROP RECHERCHE, 75- *Concurrent Pos:* Mem, Nat Res Coun, eval panel anal chem progs & activ, Nat Bur Standards, 75-81; mem subcomt A2 durability & anal of glass, Int Comn Glass, 80- *Mem:* Am Chem Soc; Am Phys Soc; Brit Soc Glass Technol; Am Ceramics Soc; Sigma Xi. *Res:* Chlorosilanes; aluminum soaps; solvent extraction of inorganic ions; chemical analysis of ceramic materials; materials characterization; physical and chemical properties of glass and related materials. *Mailing Add:* Corning Europe Inc BP No 3 77211 Avon Cedex Avon France

CAMPBELL, DONALD GRAY, b Valley Stream, NY, Aug 14, 43; m 64; c 3. REPRODUCTIVE PHYSIOLOGY. *Educ:* Cornell Univ, BS, 65; Univ Guelph, MS, 67; Rutgers Univ, PhD(reproductive physiol), 75. *Prof Exp:* Lab mgr semen processing, Select Sires, Inc, 67-70; sect head physiol, 70-80, MGR RES SERV, ANIMAL HEALTH PROD DIV, SCHERING CORP, 81- *Mem:* Am Soc Animal Sci; Soc Study Reproduction. *Res:* Estrous synchronization in cattle, horses, dogs and cats. *Mailing Add:* Animal Health Prod Div Schering Corp Galloping Hill Rd Kenilworth NJ 07033

CAMPBELL, DONALD L, b Waverly, Iowa, July 16, 40. INORGANIC CHEMISTRY. *Educ:* Iowa State Univ, BS, 62; Univ Ill, Urbana, PhD(inorg chem), 69. *Prof Exp:* Chemist, Liquid Carbonic Div, Gen Dynamics Corp, 62-65; asst prof, 69-78, ASSOC PROF CHEM, UNIV WIS-EAU CLAIRE, 78- *Mem:* Am Chem Soc; AAAS. *Res:* Coordination chemistry of the lanthanide ions; thermodynamic parameters for complex formation and factors effecting complex stability; heavy metals in the environment. *Mailing Add:* Dept Chem Univ Wis Eau Claire WI 54701

CAMPBELL, DONALD R, b Youngstown, Ohio, Oct 12, 30; m 56; c 2. ANALYTICAL CHEMISTRY, RADIOCHEMISTRY. *Educ:* Univ Akron, BS, 53. *Prof Exp:* Jr res chemist, 53-59; sr res chemist, 60-68, res scientist, 69-71, GROUP LEADER, GEN TIRE & RUBBER CO, 71- *Mem:* Am Chem Soc; Am Inst Chemists. *Res:* Analytical chemistry of high polymers; application of radiochemical techniques to elucidation of the structure and composition of polymers and to the determination of functional groups in polymers; synthesis of isotopically-substituted compounds. *Mailing Add:* Gen Tire & Rubber Co Akron OH 44329

CAMPBELL, DOUGLAS ARTHUR, b Duluth, Minn, Feb 17, 42. MOLECULAR GENETICS. *Educ:* Ind Univ, Bloomington, BA, 64; Univ Wash, PhD(genetics), 69. *Prof Exp:* Lectr microbiol, Dept Life Sci, Univ Calif, Riverside, 69-70; NIH fel biol, Univ Chicago, 70-72 & postdoctoral fel, Dept Genetics, Univ Calif, Berkeley, 73-75; asst prof biol, Col Holy Cross, Worcester, Mass, 75-81; PRES & RES DIR, MICROGENE ASSOCS, INC, 81- *Mem:* Sigma Xi; Genetics Soc Am; AAAS; NY Acad Sci. *Res:* Genetics and radiation genetics of bacteriophage T4; effects of radiation on genetic recombination in yeast; chromosome behavior in yeast aneuploids; mechanism of genetic recombination in yeast; applied microbiology. *Mailing Add:* MicroGene Assocs Inc PO Box 134 W Millbury MA 01586

CAMPBELL, DOUGLAS MICHAEL, b San Pedro, Calif, May 4, 43; m 66; c 4. MATHEMATICAL ANALYSIS. *Educ:* Harvard Univ, BS, 67; Univ NC, Chapel Hill, PhD(math), 71. *Prof Exp:* from asst prof to assoc prof, 71-79, PROF MATH, BRIGHAM YOUNG UNIV, 79- *Concurrent Pos:* Russian translr, Am Math Soc, 71-; reviewer, Math Rev, 74- *Honors & Awards:* Maeser Award, 81. *Mem:* Am Math Soc; Sigma Xi; Math Asn Am. *Res:* Geometric function theory. *Mailing Add:* Dept Math Brigham Young Univ Provo UT 84602

CAMPBELL, EARL WILLIAM, b Bowling Green, Ohio. HEMATOLOGY. *Educ:* Harvard Col, BA, 58; Univ Rochester, MD, 62. *Prof Exp:* USPHS fel, Sch Med, Univ Utah, 67-68; instr med, WVa Univ, 68-69, asst prof, Med Ctr, 69-70; pvt pract, Md, 70-73; asst prof, Mich State Univ, 73-74, assoc prof med, 74-78; PROF MED, MED COL OHIO, 78- *Concurrent Pos:* Investr, Acute Leukemia Group B, 68-72, Nat Polycythemia Rubra Vera Group, 73- & Mich Hemophilia Home Care Proj, 74-; consult hemat, Baltimore Cancer Res Inst, Nat Cancer Inst, 71-72; dir, Hemophilia Clin, Lansing Area, 74- *Mem:* AMA; fel Am Col Physicians; Am Soc Hemat. *Res:* Clinical investigation of polycythemia and related myeloproliferative diseases with the Polycythemia Rubra Vera Group; projects on antithrombin III, platelet factor IV. *Mailing Add:* Med Col Ohio Toledo OH 43614

CAMPBELL, EDWARD CHARLES, b Brooklyn, NY, Dec 25, 13; m 36; c 3. PHYSICS. *Educ:* Univ Mich, BS, 34; Ohio State Univ, PhD(physics), 38. *Prof Exp:* Instr physics, Minn State Teachers Col, 38-42; vis asst prof, Princeton Univ, 42-46; sr physicist, Oak Ridge Nat Lab, 46-69; chmn dept physics, 69-71, PROF PHYSICS, NDAK STATE UNIV, 69- *Concurrent Pos:* Res physicist, Ctr Study Nuclear Energy, Belg, 57-58. *Mem:* Fel Am Phys Soc; Sigma Xi; Am Nuclear Soc. *Res:* Nuclear isomers; reactor physics; pulsed neutron techniques. *Mailing Add:* Dept of Physics NDak State Univ Fargo ND 58102

CAMPBELL, EDWIN STEWART, b Ada, Ohio, Aug 18, 26; m 49. CHEMICAL PHYSICS. *Educ:* Johns Hopkins Univ, AB, 45; Univ Mich, MSc, 48; Univ Calif, PhD, 51. *Prof Exp:* Instr quant & qual anal, St Martin's Col, 48; asst, Univ Calif, 48-51; lectr & fel, Univ Southern Calif, 51-52; proj assoc, Naval Res Lab, Univ Wis, 52-55; asst prof chem, 55-61, ASSOC PROF CHEM, NY UNIV, 62- *Mem:* AAAS; Am Phys Soc; Fedn Am Scientists; NY Acad Sci. *Res:* Energetics of hydrogen bonding, its implications for structure and properties; structure of liquid and solid water; theory of flame propagation; statistical mechanics. *Mailing Add:* Dept of Chem NY Univ New York NY 10003

CAMPBELL, EVAN EDGAR, b Texarkana, Tex, Spet 13, 22; m 47; c 3. INDUSTRIAL HYGIENE. *Educ:* Univ Denver, BS, 47, MS, 53. *Prof Exp:* Indust hyg chemist, Med Sch, Univ Colo, 48-51; chemitoxicologist, Denver Gen Hosp, 51-53; indust hyg chemist, Los Alamos Nat Lab, Univ Calif, 53-62, sect leader indust hyg & radiobioassay, 62-73, asst group leader indust hyg group, 73-74, alt group leader, indust hyg group, 74-80; MGR, INDUST HYG, DIAMOND SHAMROCK CORP, DALLAS, 80- *Mem:* Am Indust Hyg Asn (pres, 76-77). *Res:* Air sampling and analysis of work room air; distribution of nuclides in tissue of workers exposed to nuclides; radio bioassay to evaluate worker exposure. *Mailing Add:* 423 Estante Way Los Alamos NM 87544

CAMPBELL, FERRELL RULON, b Afton, Wyo, Nov 14, 37; m 70; c 1. ANATOMY. *Educ:* Utah State Univ, BS, 60, MS, 63; Univ Chicago, PhD(anat), 66. *Prof Exp:* From instr to asst prof anat, Stanford Univ, 66-73; ASSOC PROF ANAT, UNIV LOUISVILLE, 73- *Mem:* Am Asn Anat. *Res:* Hematology. *Mailing Add:* Dept Anat Sch Med Univ of Louisville Louisville KY 40208

CAMPBELL, FINLEY ALEXANDER, b Kenora, Ont, Jan 5, 27; m 53; c 3. GEOLOGY. *Educ:* Univ Man, BSc, 50; Queen's Univ, Ont, MA, 56; Princeton Univ, PhD(geol), 58. *Prof Exp:* Geologist, Prospectors Airways Co, Ltd, 50-56; explor geologist, Mining Corp Can, 56-58; asst prof geol, Univ Alta, 58-62, assoc prof, 62-65; head dept, 65-70, acad vpres, 71-76, PROF GEOL, UNIV CALGARY, 65- *Concurrent Pos:* Vpres, Capital Resources, Univ Calgary, 70- *Mem:* Royal Soc Can; Geol Asn Can; Mineral Asn Can; Mineral Soc Am; Can Soc Petrol Geol. *Res:* Economic geology; mineralogy; petrology; geochemistry. *Mailing Add:* 3408 Benton Dr NW Calgary AB T2L 1W8 Can

CAMPBELL, FRANCIS JAMES, b Toledo, Ohio, July 29, 24; m 48; c 7. RADIATION CURING, RADIATION DAMAGE. *Educ:* Univ Toledo, BS, 48. *Prof Exp:* HEAD MAT SECT, RADIATION SCI DIV, US NAVAL RES LAB, 58- *Concurrent Pos:* US del, Int Electrotechnol Comn, 64- *Concurrent Mem:* Sigma Xi; Am Chem Soc; sr mem Inst Elec & Electronics Engrs; Am Soc Testing & Mat; fel Am Inst Chemists. *Res:* Radiation curing adhesives and composites; radiation and thermal effects on spacecraft materials, thermal control coatings, solar arrays and electrical insulation for nuclear power and aerospace equipment. *Mailing Add:* Div 6654 Naval Res Lab Washington DC 20375

CAMPBELL, FRANK LESLIE, entomology, deceased

CAMPBELL, GARY THOMAS, b Granite City, Ill, Nov 11, 46; m 68; c 2. NEUROENDOCRINOLOGY. *Educ:* Wash Univ, BS, 68; Northwestern Univ, PhD(biol sci), 72. *Prof Exp:* Res biologist, Monsanto Chem Co, 68; res assoc biol sci, Northwestern Univ, 69, teaching asst, 70-72; instr physiol, Med Col Va, 72-73, asst prof, 73-75; asst prof physiol, Univ Nebr Med Ctr, Omaha, 75-76; MEM FAC, DEPT PHYSIOL, MED COL VA HEALTH SCI CTR, 76- *Mem:* AAAS; Sigma Xi; Am Soc Zoologists. *Res:* Description of the cytoarchitecture in brain-pituitary control systems using immunohistochemical methods. *Mailing Add:* Dept of Physiol Med Col Va Health Sci Ctr Richmond VA 23298

CAMPBELL, GAYLON SANFORD, b Blackfoot, Idaho, Aug 20, 40; m 64; c 8. AGRICULTURAL METEOROLOGY, SOIL PHYSICS. *Educ:* Utah State Univ, BS, 65, MS, 66; Wash State Univ, PhD(soils), 68. *Prof Exp:* Captain, US Army Atmospheric Sci Lab, 68-70; from asst prof to assoc prof biophys & soils, 70-80, PROF SOILS, WASH STATE UNIV, 80- *Concurrent Pos:* Consult, Pac Northwest Labs, Battelle Mem Inst, 73-; vis fel, Sci Res Coun, Eng, 77-78. *Mem:* Am Meteorol Soc; Soil Sci Soc Am; Am Soc Agron. *Res:* Evapotranspiration, plant and soil water measurement; computer models of evaporation, transpiration and water uptake by plants; energy budgets of plants and animals. *Mailing Add:* Dept of Agron & Soils Wash State Univ Pullman WA 99163

CAMPBELL, GEORGE MELVIN, b Prospect, Pa, May 14, 29; m 59; c 2. PHYSICAL CHEMISTRY, ANALYTICAL CHEMISTRY. *Educ:* Hiram Col, BA, 54; Vanderbilt Univ, MS, 56, PhD(chem), 63. *Prof Exp:* Mem health physics staff, Argonne Nat Lab, 56-58; instr pub health, Univ Minn, 58-60; MEM CHEM STAFF, LOS ALAMOS SCI LAB, UNIV CALIF, 63- *Mem:* Am Chem Soc; fel Am Inst Chemists; Sigma Xi; AAAS. *Res:* Electrochemical investigations in fused salts and other nonaqueous media; thermodynamic properties of plutonium compounds; photochemistry of plutonium compounds. *Mailing Add:* CMB-11 Los Alamos Sci Lab Los Alamos NM 87544

CAMPBELL, GEORGE S(TUART), b Sauquoit, NY, Nov 29, 26; m 51; c 2. AERONAUTICS. *Educ:* Rensselaer Polytech Inst, BS, 47, BAE, 49; Calif Inst Technol, MS, 51, PhD(aeronaut), 56. *Prof Exp:* Aeronaut res scientist, Nat Adv Comt Aeronaut, 47-53; sr scientist, Hughes Aircraft Co, 54-63; head dept aerospace eng, 63-71, PROF AEROSPACE ENG, UNIV CONN, 63- *Mem:* Am Inst Aeronaut & Astronaut; Am Phys Soc; Am Soc Eng Educ; Inst Asn Math & Comput Simulation; Soc Naval Architects & Marine Engrs. *Res:* Aerodynamics; flight mechanics. *Mailing Add:* Dept of Mech Eng U-139 Univ of Conn Storrs CT 06268

CAMPBELL, GEORGE WASHINGTON, JR, b Loma Linda, Calif, Sept 22, 19; m 42; c 4. INDUSTRIAL CHEMISTRY. *Educ:* Univ Calif, Los Angeles, AB, 42; Univ Southern Calif, MS, 47, PhD, 51. *Prof Exp:* Asst, Manhattan Proj, Univ Chicago, 42-43; rubber compounder, Goodyear Tire & Rubber Co, Calif, 43-45; lab assoc chem, Univ Southern Calif, 45-47, asst, 47-51, res assoc, Off Naval Research Proj, 51-52; assoc prof chem, Univ Houston, 53-57, chief investr, Off Ord Res Proj, 52-57; sr res chemist, US Borax Res Corp, 57-63, res supvr, 63-71, mgr, Pilot Plant Res Dept, 71-77, MGR PROCESS RES, US BORAX RES CORP, 77- *Concurrent Pos:* From instr to prof, George Pepperdine Col, 45-53, head dept, 45-53. *Honors & Awards:* Honor Scroll Award, Am Inst Chemists, 76. *Mem:* Am Chem Soc; fel Am Inst Chemists; Am Soc Testing & Mat; Nat Asn Corrosion Eng. *Res:* Boron chemistry; corrosion; process development. *Mailing Add:* US Borax Res Corp Pilot Plant Res Dept Boron CA 93516

CAMPBELL, GERALD ALLAN, b Cincinnati, Ohio, May 30, 46; m 67. ORGANIC POLYMER CHEMISTRY. *Educ:* Univ Cincinnati, BS, 67; Ohio State Univ, PhD(org chem), 71. *Prof Exp:* sr res chemist, 71-77, LAB HEAD POLYMER CHEM, EASTMAN KODAK CO, 77- *Mem:* Am Chem Soc. *Res:* Synthesis of monomers and their subsequent polymerizations to materials of interest in photographic science. *Mailing Add:* Eastman Kodak Co Res Labs 1669 Lake Ave Rochester NY 14650

CAMPBELL, GILBERT SADLER, b Toronto, Ont, Jan 4, 24; US citizen; m 47; c 6. SURGERY. *Educ:* Univ Va, BA, 43, MD, 46; Univ Minn, MS, 49, PhD(surg), 54. *Prof Exp:* Intern, Univ Minn Hosp, 46, asst physiol, Med Sch, 47-48, instr, 48-49, chief resident surg, Hosp, 53-54; from instr to asst prof, 54-58; prof & chief thoracic surg, Med Ctr Okla & chief surgeon, Vet Admin Hosp, 58-65; PROF SURG & HEAD DEPT MED CTR, UNIV ARK, LITTLE ROCK, 65- *Concurrent Pos:* Markle scholar, Univ Minn, 54-58. *Honors & Awards:* Horsley Prize, 54. *Mem:* Soc Exp Biol & Med; Soc Univ Surg; Am Asn Thoracic Surg; Am Col Surg; Am Physiol Soc. *Res:* Cardiovascular surgery; pulmonary physiology. *Mailing Add:* Dept of Surg Univ of Ark Med Ctr Little Rock AR 72205

CAMPBELL, GRAHAM HAYS, b Houston, Tex, Aug 17, 36; m 60; c 2. COMPUTER SCIENCES. *Educ:* Rice Univ, BA, 57; Yale Univ, MS, 58; Univ Calif, Berkeley, PhD(physics), 65. *Prof Exp:* From asst physicist to assoc physicist appl math, 66-69, COMPUTER SCIENTIST, BROOKHAVEN NAT LAB, 69- *Mem:* Asn Comput Mach. *Res:* Computer networks; symbolic algebraic manipulation by computers; operating systems theory. *Mailing Add:* Dept of Appl Math Brookhaven Nat Lab Upton NY 11973

CAMPBELL, GRAHAM LE MESURIER, b London, Eng, Nov 25, 41; US citizen; m 68; c 1. DEVELOPMENTAL CYTOLOGY, NEUROIMMUNOLOGY. *Educ:* Cambridge Univ, BA, 64; Univ Pa, PhD(biol), 70. *Prof Exp:* Res asst mammalian cytogenetics, Med Res Coun, Harwell, UK, 64-66; res assoc develop cytol, Wistar Inst, 71-76; DIR VIROL IMMUNOL & BIOL, CANCER INFO DISSEMINATION & ANAL CTR, FRANKLIN INST, 76- *Res:* Functional analysis of purified populations isolated from central nervous systems and neuro systems. *Mailing Add:* Franklin Inst 20th St & Race St Philadelphia PA 19103

CAMPBELL, HALLOCK COWLES, b Cortland, NY, June 4, 10; m 36, 63; c 2. CHEMISTRY. *Educ:* Hamilton Col, BS, 32; Harvard Univ, AM, 34, PhD(chem), 36. *Prof Exp:* Master in chg chem, Browne & Nichols Sch, Mass, 35-38; instr, Queens Col (NY), 38-43; res chemist, Arcos Corp, 43-45, assoc dir res & eng, 45-56, dir res, 56-68, dir res & technol, 68-73; mgr educ, Am Welding Soc, 73-76; CONSULT WELDING EDUC, 76- *Concurrent Pos:* Asst lectr, Eve Tech Sch, Temple Univ, 45-55, co-dir metall, 55-61, dir, 61-73. *Honors & Awards:* Nat Meritorious Cert, Am Welding Soc, 73. *Mem:* AAAS; Am Chem Soc; Am Welding Soc; fel Am Soc Metals; fel Am Inst Chemists. *Res:* Kinetics of thermal explosions; arc welding electrodes; properties of low alloy and high alloy weld metal; thermal explosion of ethylazide gas. *Mailing Add:* 746 Fiddlewood Rd Vero Beach FL 32960

CAMPBELL, HAROLD ALEXANDER, b Zion, Ill, June 27, 09; m 38; c 3. BIOCHEMISTRY. *Educ:* Univ Ill, BS, 35; Univ Wis, PhD(agr chem), 39. *Prof Exp:* Asst, Exp Sta, Univ Wis, 35-39; res chemist & mgr, Cent Labs, Gen Foods Corp, 39-61; vis investr, Walker Lab, Sloan-Kettering Inst Cancer Res, 62-69; RES ASSOC ONCOL, McARDLE LAB CANCER RES, UNIV WISMADISON, 69- *Mem:* Am Chem Soc. *Res:* Isolation of dicumarol hemorrhagic agent in sweet clover disease and its use for the treatment of humans as an anticoagulant; the relationship of L-asparaginase enzyme activity to the antileukemia activity of certain preparations including guinea pig serum; isolation and assay of biological materials of medical significance. *Mailing Add:* 5113 St Cyr Middleton WI 53562

CAMPBELL, HOWARD ERNEST, b Detroit, Mich, Sept 20, 25; m 72; c 4. MATHEMATICS. *Educ:* Univ Wis, BS, 46, MS, 47, PhD(math), 49. *Prof Exp:* Asst, Univ Wis, 46-49; instr math, Univ Pa, 49-51; asst prof, Emory Univ, 51-56; from asst prof to assoc prof, Mich State Univ, 56-63; chmn dept, 63-78, PROF MATH, UNIV IDAHO, 63- *Concurrent Pos:* Chmn comt exam math test, Gen Exam, Col Level Exam Prog, Col Entrance Exam Bd & Educ Testing Serv, 65-75. *Mem:* Am Math Soc; Math Asn Am; Sigma Xi. *Res:* Nonassociative algebras. *Mailing Add:* Box 423 Washington ID 84780

CAMPBELL, HOWARD WALLACE, b Baltimore, Md, Oct 23, 35; m 65; c 3. ENVIRONMENTAL SCIENCES, POPULATION BIOLOGY. *Educ:* Univ Fla, BA, 58; Univ Calif, Los Angeles, MA, 63, PhD(sensory physiol), 67. *Prof Exp:* Fel ctr biol natural systs, Wash Univ, 67-68 & ctr neurobiol sci, Med Sch, Univ Fla, 68-69; asst cur, Fla State Mus, 69-70; asst prof zool, Univ Fla, 70-72; consult ecologist, Jack McCormick & Assoc, 72-73; staff scientist, Off Endangered Species, Washington, DC, 73-74, CHIEF FIELD STA, NAT FISH & WILDLIFE LAB, FISH & WILDLIFE SERV, 74- *Concurrent Pos:* Mem, Crocodile Spec Group, Int Union Conserv Nature & Natural Resources Survival Serv Comn, 71- *Mem:* Am Soc Zool; Sigma Xi; Ecol Soc; Soc Study Amphibians & Reptiles. *Res:* Impact of land-use practices on ecosystem dynamics; population biology, ecology, behavior and physiology of crocodilians and sirenians; behavior and ecology of amphibians and reptiles. *Mailing Add:* Nat Fish & Wildlife Lab 412 NE 16th Ave Rm 250 Gainesville FL 32601

CAMPBELL, HUGH JOHN, organic chemistry, physical organic chemistry, see previous edition

CAMPBELL, IAIN MALCOLM, b Glasgow, Scotland, June 15, 40; Brit citizen; m 73; c 1. BIOCHEMISTRY, ANALYTICAL CHEMISTRY. *Educ:* Glasgow Univ, BS, 62, PhD(chem), 65. *Prof Exp:* Vis asst prof, 67-69, asst prof, 69-74, ASSOC PROF BIOCHEM, UNIV PITTSBURGH, 74- *Concurrent Pos:* Merck Found fac develop award, 70-71. *Mem:* The Chem Soc; Am Chem Soc; Am Soc Mass Spectrometry; Am Oil Chemist's Soc; AAAS. *Res:* Control and biological function of plant and fungal secondary metabolism; natural product biosynthesis; biomass conversion; mode of drug action; radio gas chromatography; gas chromatography/mass spectrometry; liquid chromatography/mass spectrometry. *Mailing Add:* Dept Biol Sci Rm 605 GSPH Univ Pittsburgh Pittsburgh PA 15261

CAMPBELL, IAN HENRY, b Melbourne, Australia, Jan 31, 42; m 71; c 4. GEOLOGY. *Educ:* Univ Western Australia, BSc, 66; Univ London, DIC & PhD(geol), 73. *Prof Exp:* Field geologist, Western Mining Corp Ltd, 66-69; proj geologist, Australian Selection Party Ltd, 73-74; res fel geol, Univ Melbourne, 74-76 & Queen's Univ, Kingston, 76-77; res fel geol, 77-79, ASST PROF, UNIV TORONTO, 79- *Mem:* Am Geophys Union. *Res:* Igneous and experimental petrology; layered intrusions; magmatic ore deposits; rare earth element geochemistry. *Mailing Add:* Earth & Planetary Sci Erindale Col Univ Toronto Mississauga ON L5L 1C6 Can

CAMPBELL, JACK JAMES RAMSAY, b Vancouver, BC, Mar 29, 18; m 42; c 4. BACTERIOLOGY. *Educ:* Univ BC, BSA, 39; Cornell Univ, PhD(bact), 44. *Prof Exp:* Asst bact, Cent Exp Farm, Ottawa, 39-40; asst, Queen's Univ (Ont), 44-46; assoc prof dairying, 46, prof, 47-65, PROF MICROBIOL & HEAD DEPT, UNIV BC, 65- *Concurrent Pos:* Vis lectr, Johns Hopkins Univ, 52; res assoc, Univ Ill, 54. *Mem:* AAAS; Am Soc Microbiol; Brit Soc Gen Microbiol; Can Soc Microbiol; Royal Soc Can. *Res:* Bacterial physiology. *Mailing Add:* Dept of Microbiol Univ of BC Vancouver BC V6T 1W5 Can

CAMPBELL, JAMES, b Glasgow, Scotland, July 18, 07; m 54; c 4. PHYSIOLOGY, BIOCHEMISTRY. *Educ:* Univ Toronto, BA, 30, MA, 32, PhD, 38. *Prof Exp:* Res assoc physiol, McGill Univ, 32-33; res assoc, Sch Hyg, 33-40, from asst prof to assoc prof, 40-58, prof physiol, 58-72, spec lectr, 72-77, EMER PROF, UNIV TORONTO, 77- *Mem:* Am Physiol Soc; Am Chem Soc; Am Diabetes Asn; Can Biochem Soc; Brit Biochem Soc. *Res:* Proteolytic enzymes; digestion; nutrition; hormonal control of metabolism; growth hormone; insulin. *Mailing Add:* Dept of Physiol Univ of Toronto Toronto ON M5S 1A8 Can

CAMPBELL, JAMES A, b Mowequa, Ill, Nov 29, 17; m 44; c 3. MEDICINE, CARDIOLOGY. *Educ:* Knox Col, Ill, AB, 39; Harvard Med Sch, MD, 43. *Prof Exp:* Resident path, Univ Chicago, 41-42; from intern to resident med, Boston City Hosp, 43-44; Harvey Cushing fel surg, Johns Hopkins Univ, 47-48; asst prof med, Presby Hosp, Univ Ill, 48-51; dean, Albany Med Col, 51-53; prof med & chmn dept, St Luke's Hosp, 53-57; prof med & chmn dept, Presby-St Luke's Hosp, 57-64, pres, 64-69; PRES & CHIEF EXEC OFFICER, RUSH-PRESBY-ST LUKE'S MED CTR, 69-; PROF MED, RUSH MED COL, 71- *Res:* Cardiac physiology. *Mailing Add:* 1753 W Congress Pkwy Chicago IL 60612

CAMPBELL, JAMES A, b Chipley, Fla, Apr 12, 28; m 55; c 5. BIOLOGY, ECOLOGY. *Educ:* Fla Agr & Mech Univ, BS, 51, MEd, 56; Pa State Univ, DEd(biol sci), 62. *Prof Exp:* Sci teacher, Roulhac High Sch, 51-56; div chmn biol, Rosenwald Jr Col, 58-64; assoc prof, Tenn State Univ, 64-74; ADJ PROF NATURAL SCI & DIR, NATURAL SCI & MATH DEPT, AM BAPTIST COL, 74- *Mem:* AAAS; Nat Asn Biol Teachers. *Res:* Fresh water ecology; influence of selected abiotic factors on population density. *Mailing Add:* 2707 Bronte Ave Nashville TN 37207

CAMPBELL, JAMES ALEXANDER, b Guelph, Ont, Oct 10, 13; m 39; c 2. FOOD SCIENCE, NUTRITION. *Educ:* Univ Toronto, BSA, 36; McGill Univ, MSc, 38, PhD(agr chem), 47. *Prof Exp:* Agr asst animal nutrit, Chem Div, Sci Serv, Can Dept Agr, Ottawa, 38-41, chemist, Vitamin & Physiol Res Lab, 41-48; chief, Vitamins & Nutrit Lab, Dept Nat Health & Welfare, 48-62, dir res labs, 63-67, sr sci adv foods, 67-71, actg dir, Nutrit Bur, Food & Drug Directorate, 71-73, dep dir, Caribbean Food & Nutrit Inst, 73-76; NUTRIT CONSULT, 76- *Concurrent Pos:* Past vpres & dir, Prof Inst Pub Serv Can, 52-56; consult, Protein Adv Group, WHO-Food & Agr Orgn-UNICEF, 61-; vis prof food technol & nutrit, Am Univ Beirut, 62-63; treas, Int Union Nutrit Sci, 75. *Mem:* Am Inst Nutrit; Animal Nutrit Res Coun; fel Chem Inst Can; Can Inst Food Technol; Nutrit Soc Can (past pres). *Res:* Chemical, microbiological and biological assays for vitamins; studies with rats; protein evaluation; physiological availability of drugs and vitamins; evaluation of drugs in oral prolonged action dosage forms; food chemistry; nutrition surveys; food and nutrition policy. *Mailing Add:* 1785 Riverside Dr Suite 2204 Ottawa ON K1G 3T7 Can

CAMPBELL, JAMES ARTHUR, b Elyria, Ohio, Oct 1, 16; m 38; c 2. PHYSICAL CHEMISTRY. *Educ:* Oberlin Col, AB, 38; Purdue Univ, MS, 39; Univ Calif, PhD(chem), 42. *Hon Degrees:* DSc, Beaver Col, 73. *Prof Exp:* Instr chem, Manhattan Proj, Univ Calif, 42-45, instr plutonium res, 44-45; from asst prof to prof chem, Oberlin Col, 45-57; dir chem educ mat study, 60-63; PROF CHEM & CHMN DEPT, HARVEY MUDD COL, 57- *Concurrent Pos:* Advan educ fel, Cambridge Univ, 52-53; Guggenheim fel, Kyoto Univ & Cambridge Univ, 63-64; UNESCO sci teaching adv, Asia, 69-70; NSF fac fel, Ctr Pop Studies, Harvard, 70; resident scholar, Villa Serbelloni, 72; AAAS exchange lectr, 73; vis prof, Chinese Univ Hong Kong, 75-76 & Univ Nairobi, 81. *Honors & Awards:* Mfg Chem Teaching Award, 62; James Flack Norris Award, Am Chem Soc, 64, Sci Apparatus Makers' Award, 72. *Mem:* AAAS; Am Chem Soc; The Chem Soc; Int Union Pure & Appl Chem. *Res:* X-ray diffraction; vapor pressure measurement; absorption spectrometry; films for education in chemistry. *Mailing Add:* Dept of Chem Harvey Mudd Col Claremont CA 91711

CAMPBELL, JAMES B, b Fraserburgh, Scotland, Sept 16, 39; m 66. MEDICAL MICROBIOLOGY. *Educ:* Aberdeen Univ, BSc, 62; Univ Alta, PhD(biochem), 65. *Prof Exp:* Asst biochem, Univ Alta, 62-65, fel, 65-66; trainee virol, Wistar Inst, 66-67, res asst, 67-68; asst prof, 68-70, ASSOC PROF VIROL, UNIV TORONTO, 70- *Concurrent Pos:* Spec lectr, Sch Hyg, Univ Toronto, 67-68; consult virol & biochem, Extendicare Diag Serv, Div Extendicare, Can Ltd, Willowdale, Ont, 71- *Mem:* Am Soc Microbiol; Can Soc Microbiol. *Res:* Pathogenesis and biochemistry of animal viruses; serodiagnosis of virus infections. *Mailing Add:* Dept of Microbiol & Parasitol Fac of Med Univ of Toronto Toronto ON M5S 1A1 Can

CAMPBELL, JAMES FRANKLIN, b Meridian, Miss, Oct 25, 41. AERONAUTICAL ENGINEERING. *Educ:* Miss State Univ, BS, 63; Va Polytech Inst & State Univ, MS, 68, PhD(aerospace eng), 73. *Prof Exp:* Aerospace engr, 63-72, aeronaut res engr, 72-75, head, appl aerodyn group, 75-81, ASST HEAD, NAT TRANSONIC FACIL, AERODYN BR, LANGLEY RES CTR, NASA, 81- *Honors & Awards:* NASA Lifting Body Res Award, 70 & Viking Team Award, 77. *Mem:* Assoc fel Am Inst Aeronaut & Astronaut. *Res:* Fluid and flight mechanics; aerodynamics. *Mailing Add:* Mail Stop 287 NASA Langley Res Ctr Hampton VA 23665

CAMPBELL, JAMES FULTON, b Philadelphia, Pa, Nov 24, 32; m 55, 69; c 3. HEALTH SCIENCES, SCIENCE WRITING. *Educ:* Rutgers Univ, BSc, 55; Univ Va, MA, 60, PhD(psychol), 64. *Prof Exp:* Res assoc autonomic psychophysiol, Fels Res Inst, 62-64, USPHS fel psychophysiol, 64-65; asst prof, Antioch Col, 63-65; res assoc psychol, McGill Univ, 65-68, asst prof, 68-73; ASSOC PROF PSYCHOL, CARLETON UNIV, 73- *Concurrent Pos:* Proj officer, Ont Educ Commun Authorities, 75-79. *Mem:* Can Psychol Asn. *Res:* Behavioral management of obesity and health; psychological factors in rehabilitation. *Mailing Add:* Dept of Psychol Carleton Univ Ottawa ON K1S 5B6 Can

CAMPBELL, JAMES L, b Los Angeles, Calif, Sept 28, 24; m 60; c 3. INVERTEBRATE ZOOLOGY. *Educ:* Univ Calif, Berkeley, AB, 49, MA, 51; Univ Calif, Los Angeles, PhD(zool), 67. *Prof Exp:* Assoc prof, 55-77, PROF BIOL, LOS ANGELES VALLEY COL, 77- *Mem:* AAAS. *Res:* Malacology, study of digestive system of Haliotis cracherodii; echinoderm biology, study of echinoid hoemol system; freshwater primary productivity; marine invertebrates. *Mailing Add:* Dept of Biol Los Angeles Valley Col Van Nuys CA 91401

CAMPBELL, JAMES NICOLL, b St Thomas, Ont, June 15, 30; m 54; c 4. MICROBIOLOGY, BIOCHEMISTRY. *Educ:* Univ Western Ont, BA, 51; Univ BC, BA, 55, MSc, 57; Univ Chicago, PhD(microbiol), 60. *Prof Exp:* From asst prof to assoc prof, 60-69, PROF MICROBIOL, UNIV ALTA, 69- *Mem:* Am Soc Microbiol; Can Biochem Soc. *Res:* Interaction of bacteria with plant and animal host species; isolation and characterization of bacterial enzymes. *Mailing Add:* Dept of Microbiol Univ of Alta Edmonton AB T6G 2E9 Can

CAMPBELL, JAMES STEWART, b Bear River, NS, June 10, 23; m 47; c 5. PATHOLOGY. *Educ:* Dalhousie Univ, BSc, 43, MD, 47; Am Bd Path, dipl, 52; Royal Col Path, fel, 71; FRCPS(C). *Prof Exp:* Asst path, Med Sch, Tufts Univ, 49-52, instr, 52-53; from asst prof to prof path, Univ Ottawa, 53-74, prof & head dept, 79-81; prof path & chmn dept, Mem Univ Nfld, 74-79. *Concurrent Pos:* From jr asst pathologist to asst pathologist, New Eng Med Ctr, 49-53; registr, Registry for Tissue Reactions to Drugs, Ottawa, 70-; consult pathologist, Can Tumor Ref Ctr, 58- & Nat Defence Med Ctr, Ottawa, 61-; pathologist, Ottowa Gen Hosp, 53-74, head, Dept Lab Med, 79-81; chmn dept lab med, Gen Hosp St John's, 76-; head path sect, Toxicol Res Div, Health & Wealthfare Can, 81. *Mem:* Int Acad Path; Can Med Asn; Can Asn Path; fel Am Col Path. *Res:* Endocrine and gynecologic pathology

CAMPBELL, JAMES WAYNE, b Highlandville, Mo, Mar 2, 32; m 60; c 2. COMPARATIVE BIOCHEMISTRY, COMPARATIVE PHYSIOLOGY. *Educ:* Southwest Mo State Col, BS, 53; Univ Ill, MS, 55; Univ Okla, PhD(zool), 58. *Prof Exp:* Asst zool, Univ Ill, 53-55 & Univ Okla, 55-56; Nat Acad Sci-Nat Res Coun fel, Johns Hopkins Univ, 58-59; from instr to assoc prof biol, 59-70, chmn dept, 74-78, PROF BIOL, RICE UNIV, 70- *Concurrent Pos:* NIH spec fel, Univ Wis, 64-65; USPHS career develop award, 66-70; consult prev med, NASA Manned Spacecraft Ctr, Houston, 69-71; consult, BMS, NSF, 72-73 & 74-75, DAR, NSF, 78-79, prog dir, Regulatory Biol, 73-74, div dir, Physiol, Cellular & Molecular Biol, NSF, 79-81. *Mem:* Fel AAAS; Biochem Soc, Eng; Am Physiol Soc; Am Soc Zool; Am Soc Biol Chemists. *Res:* Comparative biochemistry of invertebrates and vertebrates. *Mailing Add:* Dept of Biol Rice Univ Houston TX 77001

CAMPBELL, JEPTHA EDWARD, JR, b Atlanta, Ga, Sept 16, 23; m 49; c 3. FOOD SCIENCE. *Educ:* Rollins Col, BS, 47; Univ Wis, MS, 49, PhD(biochem, physiol), 51. *Prof Exp:* Proj assoc biochem, Univ Wis, 51-52; group leader radiobiol, Mound Lab, Monsanto Chem Co, 52-55; chief food chem, USPHS, 55-70; chief microbiol, Biochem Br, Div Microbiol, 70-71, ASST DIR, CINCINNATI FOOD RES LABS, FOOD & DRUG ADMIN, 71- *Honors & Awards:* Serv Award, US Dept Health, Educ & Welfare, 62. *Mem:* Am Chem Soc; Am Inst Nutrit; Am Pub Health Asn; Asn Off Agr Chem. *Res:* Nutrition; radiobiology; food technology; analytical food chemistry. *Mailing Add:* Cincinnati Food Rec Labs FDA 1090 Tusculum Ave Cincinnati OH 45226

CAMPBELL, JOHN ALEXANDER, b Detroit, Mich, July 7, 40; m 69. PULMONARY MEDICINE, BIOMEDICAL ENGINEERING. *Educ:* Univ Mich, BSE, 62, MSE, 64, PhD(bioeng), 67; Rush Med Col, MD, 74. *Prof Exp:* Chem engr, process develop dept, Parke, Davis & Co, Mich, 64-65; asst attend biomed engr, Presby-St Luke's Hosp, 67-74; resident internal med, Univ Ill Med Ctr, 74-77; FEL, PULMONARY MED, NORTHWESTERN UNIV MED SCH, 77-, INSTR, 78- *Mem:* Am Inst Chem Engrs; Am Thoracic Soc; fel Am Col Chest Physicians; Sigma Xi. *Res:* Mathematical models of physiological systems; patient monitoring, using computers; artificial organs; exercise physiology; computer applications in clinical medicine and research. *Mailing Add:* Marshfield Clinic 1000 N Oak Marshfield IL 54449

CAMPBELL, JOHN ARTHUR, b Muskogee, Okla, Nov 2, 30; m 53; c 3. PETROLOGY, SEDIMENTARY ROCKS. *Educ:* Univ Tulsa, BGeol, 55; Univ Colo, MS, 57, PhD(geol), 66. *Prof Exp:* From instr to assoc prof geol, Colo State Univ, 57-74; res geologist, US Geol Surv, 74-81; PROF GEOL, FT LEWIS COL, 81- *Mem:* Fel AAAS; fel Geol Soc Am; Am Asn Petrol Geol; Soc Econ Paleont & Mineral. *Res:* Petrology, stratigraphy and depositional environment of paleozoic rocks of the southern Rocky Mountains; uranium in paleozoic rocks of the southwestern United States. *Mailing Add:* Dept Geol Ft Lewis Col Durango CO 81301

CAMPBELL, JOHN BRYAN, b Fairmont, Nebr, Mar 30, 33; m 56; c 4. ENTOMOLOGY. *Educ:* Univ Wyo, BS, 61, MS, 63; Kans State Univ, PhD(entom), 66. *Prof Exp:* Entomologist, Agr Res Serv, USDA, Univ Nebr-Lincoln, 66-70; assoc prof, 70-78, PROF ENTOM, UNIV NEBR, NORTH PLATTE STA, 78- *Mem:* Entom Soc Am. *Res:* Biology and ecology of rangeland grasshoppers and livestock insects; biology and control of livestock insects in Central Plains. *Mailing Add:* Dept of Entom Univ of Nebr North Platte NE 69101

CAMPBELL, JOHN C(ARL), b Wilsey, Kans, Apr 20, 20; m 41; c 4. OCCUPATIONAL SAFETY, AGRICULTURAL ENGINEERING. *Educ:* Kans State Univ, BS, 47; Ore State Univ, MS, 49. *Prof Exp:* Exten agr engr, Ore State Univ, 48-54; exten agr engr, Univ Ill, 54-55; assoc prof gen eng, 56-65, head dept, 66-72, assoc prof indust eng, 73-77, ASSOC PROF INDUST & GEN ENG & DIR SAFETY, ORE STATE UNIV, 78- *Mem:* Am Soc Safety Engrs; Am Soc Agr Engrs; Am Soc Eng Educ. *Mailing Add:* Dept Indust & Gen Eng Ore State Univ Corvallis OR 97331

CAMPBELL, JOHN DUNCAN, b Hamilton, Ont, Apr 22, 23; m 54; c 2. PALEOBOTANY. *Educ:* McMaster Univ, BA, 44; Univ BC, MA, 49; McGill Univ, PhD, 52. RES OFFICER, ALTA RES COUN, 53- *Mem:* Can Inst Mining & Metall; Am Soc Testing Mat; Int Asn Plant Taxonomists. *Res:* Paleoclimatic extremes and dendroclimatology of Alberta Foothills coal-mining zone; coal systematics, distribution and occurrence, palaeoecology and wood of Cretaceous and Tertiary continental deposits of Central Canada. *Mailing Add:* Alta Res Coun 11315 87th Ave Edmonton Can

CAMPBELL, JOHN HOWLAND, b Oklahoma City, Okla, Mar 9, 38; m 62; c 2. ANATOMY. *Educ:* Calif Inst Technol, BA, 60; Harvard Univ, PhD(biol), 64. *Prof Exp:* ASSOC PROF ANAT, SCH MED, UNIV CALIF, LOS ANGELES, 64- *Concurrent Pos:* NSF grants, Pasteur Inst, Paris, France, 64-65 & Commonwealth Sci & Indust Res Orgn, Canberra, Australia, 65-66. *Mem:* AAAS; Am Asn Anat. *Res:* Genetics; molecular evolution; biological pattern formation; immunology. *Mailing Add:* Dept of Anat Sch Med Univ of Calif Sch of Med Los Angeles CA 90024

CAMPBELL, JOHN HYDE, b Ithaca, NY, Dec 2, 47; m 68; c 2. PHYSICAL CHEMISTRY. *Educ:* Rochester Inst Technol, BS, 70; Univ Ill, MS, 72, PhD(phys chem), 75. *Prof Exp:* Chemist, Eastman Kodak Co, 67-70; res chemist energy systs, 75-80, PROJ LEADER, NUCLEAR WASTE FORM DEVELOP, LAWRENCE LIVERMORE LAB, UNIV CALIF, 80- *Mem:* Am Phys Soc; Am Chem Soc; Am Inst Chem Engrs. *Res:* Development of waste form for disposal of high-level radioactive waste; operation and analysis of pilot-scale oil shale retorts; investigation of fundamental reaction chemistry of oil shale retorting. *Mailing Add:* Lawrence Livermore Lab Univ of Calif Livermore CA 94550

CAMPBELL, JOHN MORGAN, b Virden, Ill, Mar 24, 22. PETROLEUM ENGINEERING. *Educ:* Iowa State Univ, BS, 43; Univ Okla, MS, 48, PhD, 51. *Prof Exp:* Develop engr & supvr, E I du Pont de Nemours & Co, 43-46; spec instr, Univ Okla, 46-50; mgr Process Equip Div, Black Sivalls & Bryson, Inc, 51-54; prof petrol eng & chmn dept, 54-64, Erle P Halliburton prof, 64, distinguished prof, 64-70; pres, Int Petrol Inst, 70-78; PRES, JOHN M CAMPBELL & CO, 78- *Concurrent Pos:* Pres, John M Campbell & Co, 68-70; consult, over twenty companies & Secy Navy. *Mem:* Am Inst Mining, Metall & Petrol Engrs; Am Inst Chem Eng. *Res:* PVT behavior of hydrocarbon systems; adsorption; flow of fluids in porous media; engineering economics. *Mailing Add:* John M Campbell & Co 121 Collier Norman OK 73069

CAMPBELL, JOHN OWEN, b Louisville, Ky, July 19, 19; m 59; c 5. ELECTRONIC ENGINEERING. *Educ:* Ga Inst Technol, BS, 41. *Prof Exp:* Engr, Gen Elec Co, 41-42, BuShips, US Dept Navy, 42-43, B-29 prog, Bell Aircraft Co, 43-44 & atomic bomb proj, Tenn Eastman Corp, 44-45; res radar engr, Hughes Aircraft Co, 49-52; proj sonar engr, Bendix Pac Div, 52-54; res scientist, Lockheed Missiles & Space Co, 54-56; exec vpres, electronic develop, Aerosystronics Corp, 56-59; sr proj engr, satellite systs, Space Technol Labs, Thompson Ramo Wooldridge, Inc, 59-63; CONSULT MGR ENGR, 63- *Mem:* NY Acad Sci. *Res:* Systems analysis; conceptual design and long range planning for military weapons systems; communication satellite systems; integrated urban communications systems; air and water traffic control systems; engineering planning for nuclear power plants. *Mailing Add:* 15955 Community St Sepulveda CA 91343

CAMPBELL, JOHN RAYMOND, b San Diego, Calif, Feb 6, 44; m 76; c 1. OCEAN ENGINEERING, FLUID MECHANICS. *Educ:* San Diego State Univ, BS, 69; Colo State Univ, PhD(fluid mech), 74. *Prof Exp:* Res assoc, fluid mech & ocean eng, Univ Del, Newark, 74-76; asst prof hydraulic ocean eng, Purdue Univ, 77-78; staff scientist, Los Alamos Sci Lab, 78-81; consult, 80-81, STAFF MEM, FLOW SCI, INC, LOS ALAMOS, NMEX, 81- *Concurrent Pos:* Consult, Midocean Motion Pictures, 79-80, Ft Sill Okla, 80-81, Newark Del Water Comn, 76-77. *Mem:* Inst Elec & Electronics Engrs; Am Meteorol Soc. *Res:* Computer graphics and computer generated movies to visualize physical processes in atmospheric dispersion, superconductors, underground stress field engineering and in oceanographic dispersion modelling. *Mailing Add:* 320 Rim Rd Los Alamos NM 87544

CAMPBELL, JOHN RICHARD, b Pratt, Kans, Jan 16, 32; m 62; c 3. PEDIATRIC SURGERY. *Educ:* Univ Kans, BA, 54, MD, 58; Am Bd Surg, dipl, 64, cert pediat surg, 75. *Prof Exp:* Intern, Univ Pa Hosp, 58-59; surg resident, Med Ctr, Univ Kans, 59-63; asst instr pediat surg, Sch Med, Univ Pa, 65-67; from asst prof to assoc prof, 67-72, PROF SURG & PEDIAT, MED SCH, UNIV ORE, 72-, CHIEF PEDIAT SURG, 67- *Concurrent Pos:* Surg resident, Children's Hosp Philadelphia, 65-67. *Mem:* Am Pediat Surg Asn; Am Col Surg; Am Acad Pediat; AMA. *Res:* Pediatric surgery and oncology; shock in the newborn infant. *Mailing Add:* Dept of Surg Univ of Ore Med Sch Portland OR 97201

CAMPBELL, JOHN ROY, b Goodman, Mo, June 14, 33; m 54; c 3. DAIRY SCIENCE. *Educ:* Univ Mo, BS, 55, MS, 56, PhD(nutrit), 60. *Prof Exp:* From asst prof to prof dairy husb, Univ Mo-Columbia, 70-77; PROF DAIRY SCI, UNIV ILL, URBANA, 77- *Concurrent Pos:* Southern Ice Cream Mfrs fel, 55-56; Danforth assoc, 70. *Honors & Awards:* Distinguished Teaching Award, Ralston-Purina Co, 74. *Mem:* AAAS; Am Dairy Sci Asn (pres, 80-81); Am Soc Animal Sci; NY Acad Sci. *Res:* Dairy cattle physiology, especially health, nutrition, production and management; recycling corrugated paper through ruminants in the production of meat and milk. *Mailing Add:* Univ Ill Col Agr Urbana IL 61801

CAMPBELL, JUDITH LYNN, b New Haven, Conn, Mar 24, 43. DNA REPLICATION. *Educ:* Wellesley Col, BA, 65; Harvard Univ, PhD, 74. *Prof Exp:* Res assoc molecular biol, Harvard Med Sch, 74-77; ASST PROF CHEM BIOL & MOLECULAR BIOL, CALIF INST TECHNOL, 77- *Concurrent Pos:* NIH res career develop award, 79-83. *Mem:* Fedn Am Soc Exp Biol. *Res:* Genetic and biochemical studies on the regulation of DNA replication in prokaryotes and eukaryotes; regulation of plasmid replication. *Mailing Add:* Dept Chem 164-30 Calif Inst Technol Pasadena CA 91125

CAMPBELL, KATHERINE SMITH, b Boston, Mass, Apr 10, 43; m 71; c 1. TIME SERIES. *Educ:* Radcliffe Col, BA, 64; Univ Md, MA, 69; Univ NMex, PhD(math), 79. *Prof Exp:* Asst mem tech staff, Bellcomm, Inc, Wash, DC, 64-66; asst math, Univ Md, 66-68; scientist, EG&G, Los Alamos, NMex, 72-75; STATISTICIAN, LOS ALAMOS NAT LAB, 75- *Concurrent Pos:* Lectr math, Univ NMex, 72. *Mem:* Am Statist Asn; Inst Math Statist. *Res:* Application of statistics in geological exploration; nuclear safeguards and reliability. *Mailing Add:* S-1/MS-600 Los Alamos Nat Lab Los Alamos NM 87545

CAMPBELL, KENNETH, b San Francisco, Calif, June 1, 99; m 30; c 4. MECHANICAL ENGINEERING. *Educ:* Harvard Univ, AB, 21, SB, 23. *Hon Degrees:* DSc, Bard Col, 56. *Prof Exp:* Mem staff, Bethlehem Steel Co, 23-28; asst chief engr, Trent Anthracite Corp, 28-29; mem staff, Sanderson & Porter, 29-33; from test engr to sr proj engr, Wright Aero Div, Curtiss-Wright Corp, 34-45, dir res, 45-51, tech dir, 51-55, gen mgr, Res Div, 55-58, sci & eng adv & pres staff, 58-64; consult, Thiokol Chem Corp, 64-76; CONSULT, INST DEFENSE ANAL, DC, 64- *Concurrent Pos:* Mem tech mission propulsion eng, US Navy, Ger, 45; mem consult bd, Nuclear Engine Propulsion Aircraft, 49-51. *Honors & Awards:* Wright Bros Medal, Soc Automotive Engrs, 44 & Manley Medal, 45. *Mem:* Soc Automotive Engrs; fel Am Inst Aeronaut & Astronaut. *Res:* Air breathing propulsion; compression; fluid dynamics; thermoionic conversion to electricity; ionic propulsion; radioisotopes and radiation; heat transfer; combustion; components of jet, turbofan and turboshaft power plants. *Mailing Add:* 245 E Ridgewood Ave Ridgewood NJ 07450

CAMPBELL, KENNETH EUGENE, JR, b Jackson, Mich, Nov 4, 43. AVIAN PALEONTOLOGY, HISTORICAL BIOGEOGRAPHY. *Educ:* Univ Mich, BS, 66, MS, 67; Univ Fla, Phd(zool), 73. *Prof Exp:* Asst prof geol & zool, Univ Fla, 75-77; CUR VERT PALEONT, NATURAL HIST MUS, LOS ANGELES, 77- *Mem:* Am Ornith Soc; Wilson Ornith Soc; Cooper Ornith Soc; Soc Vert Paleont; Sigma Xi. *Res:* Avian paleontology and osteology; cenozoic geology and paleontology of South America. *Mailing Add:* Natural Hist Mus 900 Exposition Blvd Los Angeles CA 90007

CAMPBELL, KENNETH LYLE, b St Paul, Minn, May 3, 48. REPRODUCTIVE ENDOCRINOLOGY, BIOCHEMISTRY. *Educ:* Augsburg Col, BA, 70; Univ Mich, MS, 71, PhD(biochem), 76. *Prof Exp:* Anal chemist, Fed Water Qual Lab, Duluth, 70; NIH fel ovarian function, Reprod Endocrinol Prog, Dept Path, 76-79, RES INVESTR, REPROD ENDOCRINOL PROG, CTR HUMAN GROWTH & DEVELOP, UNIV MICH, 79- *Concurrent Pos:* Inst for Environ Qual fel, Dept Biochem, Univ Mich, 72-75. *Mem:* Soc Study Reprod. *Res:* Granulosa cell function and structure of the membrana granulosum; biochemical characterization of hormone action and hormone metabolism; toxicological actions of environmental contaminants on reproductive organs. *Mailing Add:* Reprod Endocrinol Prog Univ of Mich Ann Arbor MI 48109

CAMPBELL, KENNETH NIELSEN, b Hillsdale, Mich, May 31, 05; m 33. MEDICINAL CHEMISTRY. *Educ:* Univ Chicago, BS, 28, PhD(org chem), 32. *Prof Exp:* Asst, Univ Chicago, 29-32; fel, Pa State Col, 33-34, asst chem, 34-35; Univ Ill, 35-36; instr org chem, Univ Notre Dame, 36-38, asst prof, 38-40, assoc prof, 40-45, prof, 45-54; dir med chem, Mead Johnson Res Ctr, 53-70, consult, 70-73; PHARMACEUT CONSULT, CAMPBELL & ASSOCS, 73- *Concurrent Pos:* Pharmaceut indust consult, 44-53; researcher cancer chemother, NIH, 45-54; consult, USPHS, 49-52; lectr, Univ Tex, 58. *Honors & Awards:* Ind Technol Col Citation of Merit, 58; Univ Notre Dame Alumni Sci Award, 65; Tri-State Coun Sci & Eng Tech Achievement Award, 73. *Mem:* Fel AAAS; fel Am Inst Chem; Am Chem Soc; Sigma Xi; NY Acad Sci. *Res:* Aliphatic hydrocarbons; reduction; synthetic drugs; antimalarials and growth inhibitors; amines; quinolines; ethyleneimines; acetylenes. *Mailing Add:* 8216 Petersburg Rd Evansville IN 47711

CAMPBELL, KENNETH WILFORD, b Ingersoll, Ont, Aug 21, 42; m 65; c 3. PLANT BREEDING, PLANT CYTOGENETICS. *Educ:* Univ Guelph, BSc, 71, PhD(plant breeding & genetics), 75. *Prof Exp:* res scientist, Agr Can Res Br, 74-81; RES SCIENTIST, CIBA GEIGY SEEDS, LTD, 81- *Concurrent Pos:* Mem, Barley Subcomt, Can Comt Grain Breeding, 75- *Mem:* Genetics Soc Can; Crop Sci Soc Am. *Res:* Breeding superior six-row, and recently two-row barley for the Canadian prairies, with emphasis on malting quality; intercrosses of two-row and six-row types and haploidy; breeding superior barley varieties for Ontario; barley doubled hapolid technique. *Mailing Add:* Ciba Geigy Seeds Ltd Alto Craig ON N0M 1A0 Can

CAMPBELL, KEVIN PETER, b Brooklyn, NY, Jan 19, 52; m 74; c 2. CALCIUM TRANSPORT, MUSCLE PHYSIOLOGY. *Educ:* Manhattan Col, BS, 73; Univ Rochester, MS, 76, PhD(biophysics), 79. *Prof Exp:* Fel, Med Res Coun Can, Univ Toronto, 78-81; ASST PROF PHYSIOL, UNIV IOWA, 81- *Concurrent Pos:* Prin investr, Am Heart Asn grant in aid, 82-85. *Mem:* Biophys Soc; NY Acad Sci; AAAS; Sigma Xi. *Res:* Structure and function of the sarcoplasmic reticuum membrane in skeletal and cardiac muscle; molecular mechanisms of calcium movements across excitable membranes. *Mailing Add:* Dept Physiol & Biophys Univ Iowa Iowa City IA 52242

CAMPBELL, KIRBY I, b San Jose, Calif, Jan 12, 33; m 54; c 1. ENVIRONMENTAL HEALTH, TOXICOLOGY. *Educ:* Univ Calif, Davis, BS, 55, DVM, 57; Harvard Univ, MPH, 64. *Prof Exp:* Vet, Butte Vet Hosp, Oroville, Calif, 59-61; proj vet officer, Air Pollution Res Ctr, Univ Calif, Riverside, USPHS, 61-63, actg chief chronic & explor toxicol unit, Health Effects Res Prog, Nat Air Pollution Control Admin, 64-68, dep chief, 68-70, chief vet med, 68-70; chief comp & reprod toxicity sect, Toxicol Div, US Environ Protection Agency, Cincinnati, 72-76, chief, Functional Pathol Br, Lab Studies Div, 76-79, sr toxcologist, Toxicol Div, Health Effects Res Lab, 79-81. *Concurrent Pos:* Mem proj group, Air Pollution Res Adv Comt, Coord Res Coun, 68-72. *Mem:* Am Vet Med Asn; Am Col Vet Toxicologists. *Res:* Experimental biology, environmental toxicology, including inhalation; experimental laboratory animal science; mammalian, submammalian, in vivo, in vitro bioassay systems; immune response and defense systems; reproductive function and developmental biology. *Mailing Add:* Health Effects Res Lab US Environ Protection Agency Cincinnati OH 45268

CAMPBELL, LARRY EDWIN, b Gas City, Ind, Feb 21, 41; c 4. PHYSICAL INORGANIC CHEMISTRY. *Educ:* Purdue Univ, BSChE, 63, PhD(chem), 67. *Prof Exp:* Sr res chem, Corning Glass Works, 66-68, mgr silicate chem res, 68-71, mgr surface chem res, 71-75; mgr chem res & develop, Englehard Indust Div, 75-77, gen mgr chem catalyst dept, 77-81, VPRES ELECTRONIC MAT SYSTS, ENGLEHARD MINERALS & CHEM CO, 81- *Mem:* Am Chem Soc; Am Inst Chem Engrs; Am Soc Testing & Mat. *Res:* Catalyst preparation, characterization, evaluation; preparation of precious metal salts, compounds; refining electrochemistry; fuel cells; biological use of precious metals; electronic materials. *Mailing Add:* Englehard Minerals & Chem 1221 Ave Americas New York NY 10020

CAMPBELL, LARRY ENOCH, b Brookville, Pa, July 21, 38; m 65; c 3. SOLID STATE PHYSICS. *Educ:* Carnegie Inst Technol, BS, 60, MS, 62, PhD(physics), 66. *Prof Exp:* Appointee physics, Argonne Nat Lab, asst prof, 68-73, ASSOC PROF PHYSICS, HOBART & WILLIAM SMITH COLS, 73- *Concurrent Pos:* Sci asst, Tech Univ Munich, 72-73. *Mem:* Am Phys Soc. *Res:* Application of the Mössbauer effect to solid state and nuclear physics problems. *Mailing Add:* Dept of Physics Hobart & William Smith Cols Geneva NY 14456

CAMPBELL, LAURENCE JOSEPH, b Belmont, WVa, Feb 26, 37; m 71; c 1. LOW TEMPERATURE PHYSICS. *Educ:* Mass Inst Technol, SB & SM, 61; Univ Calif, San Diego, La Jolla, PhD(physics), 65. *Prof Exp:* Res assoc physics, Univ Ill, Urbana, 65-67; STAFF MEM PHYSICS, LOS ALAMOS SCI LAB, 67- *Concurrent Pos:* Vis res scientist, Univ Calif, Berkeley, 79; vis scientist, Acad Sci, USSR, 80-81. *Mem:* Am Phys Soc; AAAS. *Res:* Superfluid hydrodynamics; quantized vortices. *Mailing Add:* MS-764 Los Alamos Nat Lab Los Alamos NM 87545

CAMPBELL, LINZY LEON, b Panhandle, Tex, Feb 10, 27; m 53. MICROBIOLOGY, BIOCHEMISTRY. *Educ:* Univ Tex, BA, 49, MS, 50, PhD(bact, biochem), 52. *Prof Exp:* Res scientist I marine microbiol, Dept Bact, Univ Tex, 47-50, res scientist II food bact, 50-51; Nat Microbiol Inst res fel plant biochem, Univ Calif, 52-54; from asst prof & asst bacteriologist to assoc prof hort & assoc bacteriologist, State Col Wash, 54-59; assoc prof microbiol, Western Reserve Univ, 59-62; prof microbiol, Univ Ill, Urbana-Champaign, 62-72, dir sch life sci, 71-72, head dept, 63-71; PROF MICROBIOL & PROVOST & VPRES ACAD AFFAIRS, UNIV DEL, 72- *Concurrent Pos:* Ed, J Bact, Am Soc Microbiol, 64-65, ed-in-chief, 65-78. *Mem:* Fel AAAS; Am Chem Soc; Am Soc Biol Chem; Am Soc Microbiol (pres, 73-74); Brit Soc Gen Microbiol. *Res:* Microbial metabolism; enzymes; fermentations; food microbiology; thermophilic microorganisms. *Mailing Add:* 104 Hullihen Hall Univ of Del Newark DE 19711

CAMPBELL, LOIS JEANNETTE, b Toledo, Ohio, Nov 16, 23. GEOLOGY. *Educ:* Univ Mich, BS, 44; Ohio State Univ, PhD(glacial geol), 55. *Prof Exp:* Jr geologist statist & eval, Humble Oil & Refining Co, 45-47; from instr to asst prof, 54-75, ASSOC PROF GEOL, UNIV KY, 75- *Mem:* Am Asn Petrol Geologists; Geol Soc Am; Nat Asn Geol Teachers. *Res:* Pleistocene geology; late paleozoic invertebrates; geomorphology. *Mailing Add:* Dept of Geol Univ of Ky Lexington KY 40506

CAMPBELL, LORNE ARTHUR, b Saskatoon, Sask, Nov 10, 23; m 47. PHARMACOLOGY. *Educ:* Univ BC, BScAg, 53, MSc, 54; Univ Calif, Davis, PhD(comp pharmacol & toxicol), 62. *Prof Exp:* Fel, Univ Calif Med Sch, 62-63; dir path & toxicol, Smith Kline & French Lab, 63-67; asst prof pharmacol, Tex A&M Univ, 67-69; head toxicol, Abbott Lab, 69-71; staff officer, Comt Food Protection, Nat Res Coun, Nat Acad Sci, 71-73; food regulations adminr, Sunkist Growers, Inc, 73-76; mgr biomed group, Stanford Res Inst, 76-77; vpres, 78-81, DIR, NAT CANCER INST CARCINOGENESIS BIOASSY PROG, TRACTOR JITOC INT, 77-, PRES, 81- *Concurrent Pos:* Chmn, Nutrit Labeling Comt, United Fresh Fruit & Veg Asn, 74-76; mem, Bd Dirs, Indust Comt Citrus Additives & Pesticides, 74-76. *Mem:* Inst Food Technologists; Asn Food & Drug Offs; Sigma Xi. *Res:* The role of dietary fiber in nutrition; role of pectin as a dietary fiber; the safety of low methoxyl pectin. *Mailing Add:* Tracor Jitco Inc 1776 E Jefferson St Rockville MD 20852

CAMPBELL, LOUIS LORNE, b Winnipeg, Man, Oct 20, 28; m 54; c 3. MATHEMATICS, INFORMATION THEORY. *Educ:* Univ Man, BSc, 50; Iowa State Univ, MS, 51; Univ Toronto, PhD(math), 55. *Prof Exp:* Defence sci serv officer, Defence Res Telecommunications Estab, Can, 54-58; from asst prof to assoc prof math, Univ Windsor, 58-63; assoc prof, 63-67, PROF MATH, QUEEN'S UNIV, ONT, 67-, HEAD, DEPT MATH & STATIST, 80- *Mem:* Am Math Soc; Soc Indust & Appl Math; Can Math Soc; Inst Elec & Electronics Engrs; Statist Soc Can. *Res:* Information measures; source coding; sampling theorem; signal processing. *Mailing Add:* Dept of Math & Statist Queen's Univ Kingston Can

CAMPBELL, MALCOLM JOHN, b Wollongong, Australia, Aug 16, 37. SPACE PHYSICS. *Educ:* Univ Sydney, BSc, 58, PhD(physics), 63. *Prof Exp:* Fel space res, Goddard Space Flight Ctr, NASA, Md, 63-65; assoc, Ctr Radiophysics & Space Res, Cornell Univ, 65-72; res assoc, State Univ NY at Syracuse Univ, 72-73; asst prof, 73-80, ASSOC PROF SPACE PHYSICS, WASH STATE UNIV, 80- *Mem:* Am Geophys Union; Am Phys Soc. *Res:* Atmospheric physics and chemistry. *Mailing Add:* Air Res Dana 306 Wash State Univ Pullman WA 99164

CAMPBELL, MARY KATHRYN, b Philadelphia, Pa, Jan 20, 39. BIOPHYSICAL CHEMISTRY. *Educ:* Rosemont Col, BA, 60; Ind Univ, PhD(phys chem), 65. *Prof Exp:* Instr radiol sci, Johns Hopkins Univ, 65-68; from asst to assoc prof, 68-81, PROF CHEM, MOUNT HOLYOKE COL, 81- *Concurrent Pos:* Vis scientist, Inst Molecular Biol, Univ Paris, 74-75; vis prof chem, Univ Ariz, 81-82. *Mem:* Am Chem Soc. *Res:* Specific interactions between proteins and nucleic acids; physical chemistry of nucleic acids and proteins. *Mailing Add:* Dept of Chem Mt Holyoke Col South Hadley MA 01075

CAMPBELL, MICHAEL DAVID, b Lancaster, Ohio, Aug 8, 41; m 65; c 5. GROUNDWATER GEOLOGY, EXPLORATION GEOLOGY. *Educ:* Ohio State Univ, BA, 66; Rice Univ, MA, 76. *Prof Exp:* Staff mineral geologist, Continental Oil Co of Australia, Ltd, 66-69; dist geologist, United

Nuclear Corp, Wyo, 69-70; consult econ geologist, Rice Univ, 70-76; DIR, ALT ENERGY, MINERAL & ENVIRON PROGS, KEPLINGER & ASSOCS, INC, HOUSTON, 76- Concurrent Pos: Abstr ed, Ground Water, 66-70; tech consult, Water Well J, 71-73; UN tech expert, 76-; mem proj on ground water igneous & metamorphic rocks, UNESCO, 76-; spec lectr, Petroleos Mexicanos, Mexico City, 79. Mem: Am Inst Prof Geol Scientists; Soc Econ Geologists; Geol Soc Am; Am Inst Mining Engrs. Res: Ground water and mineral development; exploration mining; groundwater pollution; geochemistry; geothermal energy; uranium, coal, precious metals, base metals and strategic minerals; resource assessment; geotechnical investigations. Mailing Add: Keplinger & Assocs Inc 1200 Milam St Houston TX 77002

CAMPBELL, MICHAEL FLOYD, b Sparta, Ill, Nov 5, 42; m 64; c 2. FOOD SCIENCE, SOY PROTEINS. Educ: Univ Ill, BS, 64, MS, 66, PhD(food sci), 68. Prof Exp: Microbiologist, R J Reynolds Indust, 68-70; sr food scientist, Libby McNeill & Libby, 70-71; sr food scientist, 71-73; group leader veg proteins, 73-80, GROUP MGR PROTEIN PRODUCT DEVELOP, A E STALEY MFG CO, 80- Concurrent Pos: vchmn, Ill State Coun on Nutrit, 77-; chmn, Sci & Nutrit Comt, Food Protein Coun, 80- Mem: Inst Food Technologists; Am Asn Cereal Chemists. Res: Vegetable protein products and process development; corn sweeteners; food starches; food microbiology. Mailing Add: A E Staley Mfg Co 2200 E Eldorado Decatur IL 62525

CAMPBELL, MILTON HUGH, b Billings, Mont, Sept 2, 28; m 52; c 4. NUCLEAR ENGINEERING, ANALYTICAL CHEMISTRY. Educ: Mont State Col, BS, 51; Univ Wash, MS, 61. Prof Exp: Head analyst chem, Ideal Cement Co, 51-53 & 55; jr chemist, Hanford Atomic Prod Oper, Gen Elec Co, 55-57, anal chemist, 57-59, process chemist, 59-61, sr engr, 61-65; sr engr, Chem Processing Div, Isochem Inc, 65-67, staff engr, 67, mgr separations chem lab, Res & Develop, Atlantic Richfield Hanford Co, 67-73, mgr waste mgt & storage technol, 73-74; STAFF ENGR, EXXON NUCLEAR CO, INC, 74-; Am Soc Testing & Mat; Am Nuclear Soc; Inst Nuclear Mat Mgt. Mem: Am Chem Soc. Res: Inorganic ion exchange and liquid-liquid separations; nucleonics; gas chromatography; spectrophotometric analysis; thermochemistry; radioactive material measurements; waste management; safety analysis and environmental analysis; project management. Mailing Add: 2119 Beech Richland WA 99352

CAMPBELL, NEIL ALLISON, b Los Angeles, Calif, Apr 17, 46; m 66; c 1. CELL BIOLOGY, PLANT PHYSIOLOGY. Educ: Calif State Univ, Long Beach, BS, 67; Univ Calif, Los Angeles, MA, 68; Univ Calif, Riverside, PhD(biol), 75. Prof Exp: Instr biol, San Bernadino Valley Col, 69-77; asst prof biol, Cornell Univ, 77-80; ASSOC PROF BIOL, SAN BERNARDINO VALLEY COL, 80-; ASSOC RES BOTANIST, UNIV CALIF, RIVERSIDE, 80- Mem: Am Soc Plant Physiologists; Sigma Xi. Res: Structure and function of plant cells; physiology of salt tolerance; physiology of plant movements. Mailing Add: Dept Biol San Bernardino Valley Col San Bernardino CA 92405

CAMPBELL, NEIL JOHN, b Los Angeles, Calif, Aug 26, 25; Can citizen; m 54; c 2. PHYSICAL OCEANOGRAPHY. Educ: McMaster Univ, BSc, 50, MSc, 51; Univ BC, PhD(physics), 55. Prof Exp: Phys oceanogr Pac oceanog group, Fisheries Res Bd Can, 55, Atlantic oceanog group, 55-59, oceanogr in chg, 59-63; CHIEF OCEANOGR, MARINE SCI BR, DEPT ENERGY, MINES & RESOURCES, 63-; DIR-GEN, MARINE SCI & INFO DIRECTORATE, DEPT FISHERIES & OCEANS, ONT, CAN, 70- Concurrent Pos: Lectr, Dalhousie Univ, 60-63; first vchmn, Intergovt Oceanog Comn, UNESCO, 78-80, 80- Res: Arctic and environmental oceanography. Mailing Add: Marine Sci Br Dept of Energy, Mines & Res Ottawa ON K1A 0G1 Can

CAMPBELL, NORMAN E ROSS, b Ft William, Ont, Oct 11, 20; m 47; c 2. MICROBIOLOGY. Educ: Ont Agr Col, BSA, 44; Univ Man, MSc, 49, PhD(microbiol), 60. Prof Exp: From asst prof to assoc prof, 49-68, chmn div biol sci, 74-80, PROF MICROBIOL, UNIV MAN, 69- Mem: Can Soc Microbiol; Arctic Inst NAm. Res: Soil microbiology; nitrogen fixation in subarctic and arctic soils. Mailing Add: 861 Lynn St Ft Garry Winnipeg Can

CAMPBELL, PAUL GILBERT, b Minneapolis, Minn, Sept 25, 25; m 51. ORGANIC CHEMISTRY. Educ: Univ Md, BS, 50; Univ SC, MS, 53; Pa State Univ, PhD(org chem), 57. Prof Exp: Chemist, NIH, 50-51; sr chemist, J T Baker Chem Co, 57-59 & Allied Chem Corp, 59-60; CHEMIST, NAT BUR STAND, 60- Honors & Awards: Silver Medal, Dept Com, 67. Mem: AAAS; Am Chem Soc; Am Soc Test & Mat. Res: Organic synthesis; bituminous building materials; organic coatings. Mailing Add: Nat Bur of Stand Bldg Res Div B-348 Washington DC 20234

CAMPBELL, PETER HALLOCK, b Flushing, NY, Mar 16, 40. TAXONOMY & ECOLOGY OF PHYTOPLANKTON. Educ: Swarthmore Col, BA, 62; Univ NC, PhD(bot), 73. Prof Exp: Teaching asst bot, 69-70, RES ASSOC, UNIV NC, CHAPEL HILL, 72- Res: Taxonomy and ecology of the phytoplankton of North Carolina lakes, preparation of a guide to these algae. Mailing Add: 1005 1/2 S Columbia Chapel Hill NC 27514

CAMPBELL, PRISCILLA ANN, b Mineola, NY, Aug 19, 40; m; c 2. IMMUNOLOGY. Educ: Colo Col, BA, 62; Univ Colo, MS, 65, PhD(cell biol), 68. Prof Exp: Fel immunol, Univ Calif, San Diego, 68-70 & Nat Jewish Hosp, Denver, 70-72; MEM STAFF, DIV BASIC IMMUNOL, DEPT MED, NAT JEWISH HOSP, DENVER, 72- Concurrent Pos: Asst prof path, Univ Colo Med Ctr, Denver, 72-78, assoc prof, 78-; NIH grant, 74-; mem study sect, NIH, 79-83. Mem: AAAS; Am Asn Immunologists; Am Soc Exp Path; Am Soc Microbiol; Reticuloendothelial Soc. Res: Cell biology of immune response; resistance to bacterial infection. Mailing Add: Div Basic Immunol Nat Jewish Hosp Denver CO 80206

CAMPBELL, RALPH EDMUND, b Providence, Utah, Sept 22, 27; m 52; c 5. FOREST SOILS. Educ: Utah State Univ, BS, 50, MS, 54. Prof Exp: Soil scientist, Exp Sta, SDak State Univ & USDA, 50-54 & NMex Agr Ext Sta, Tucumcari, 54-55, soil scientist, Southern Montana Res Ctr, Agr Res Serv, Mont, 55-64, res soil scientist, 64; RES SOIL SCIENTIST, ROCKY MOUNTAIN FOREST & RANGE EXP STA, US FOREST SERV, 64- Mem: Soil Sci Soc Am; Am Soc Agron. Res: Soil fertility, moisture and management; forest soils problems related to nutrient cycling, sediment movement, water quality and forest climate. Mailing Add: Rocky Mountain Forest & Range Exp Sta US Forest Serv Flagstaff AZ 86001

CAMPBELL, RAYMOND EARL, b Ranger, Tex, Jan 4, 41; m 65; c 2. HORTICULTURE. Educ: Okla State Univ, BS, 63, MS, 66; Kans State Univ, PhD(hort), 72. Prof Exp: County exten agent, Coop Exten Serv, Okla State Univ, Coal County, 63-64 & Delaware County, 66-67; instr agr, Friends Univ, 67-68; county exten agent hort, Coop Exten Serv, Kans State Univ, 68-70; exten specialist voc hort, Va Polytech Inst & State Univ, 72-74; exten specialist veg crops, 74-77, ASSOC PROF HORT, OKLA STATE UNIV, 77- Mem: Am Soc Hort Sci. Res: Investigation of environmental influence on vegetable crop production and yield with particular emphasis on temperature and humidity; investigation of applications of artificial soil mixes to greenhouse vegetable growing and vegetable crop alternatives. Mailing Add: Dept Hort Okla State Univ Stillwater OK 74074

CAMPBELL, RICHARD DANA, b Oklahoma City, Okla, June 12, 39; m 63; c 2. DEVELOPMENTAL BIOLOGY. Educ: Harvard Univ, BA, 61; Rockefeller Inst, PhD(biol), 65. Prof Exp: Asst prof organismic biol, 65-70, assoc prof develop & cell biol, 70-74, PROF DEVELOP & CELL BIOL, UNIV CALIF, IRVINE, 74- Mem: Am Soc Zool; Am Soc Cell Biol; Soc Develop Biol. Mailing Add: Dept of Develop & Cell Biol Univ of Calif Irvine CA 92717

CAMPBELL, RICHARD M, b Logan, Ohio, July 29, 30; m 54; c 2. ELECTRICAL ENGINEERING. Educ: Ohio State Univ, BEE, 54, MSc, 56, PhD(electron devices), 66. Prof Exp: Res asst, Electron Device Lab, Ohio State Univ, 55-56, res assoc, Lab & instr elec eng, Univ, 56-62; staff mem, RCA Labs, 62-63; from instr to asst prof, 63-77, ASSOC PROF ELEC ENG, OHIO STATE UNIV, 77- Concurrent Pos: Consult, Electronics Co, 62 & Edmund C Frost & Co, 67. Mem: Inst Elec & Electronics Engrs. Res: Electron optics problems in television type pickup tubes and microwave tubes. Mailing Add: Dept of Elec Eng Electronics Lab Ohio State Univ 2015 Neil Ave Columbus OH 43210

CAMPBELL, ROBERT A, b Toledo, Ohio, Dec 21, 24; m 49; c 3. PEDIATRICS. Educ: Univ Calif, Berkeley, AB, 54; Univ San Francisco, MD, 58; Am Bd Pediat, dipl, 63, cert pediat nephrol, 74. Prof Exp: Res asst, Cancer Res Genetics Lab, Univ Calif, Berkeley, 54-58; USPHS fel pediat biochem, 61-63, assoc prof, 63-71, dir, Pediat Renal-Metab Lab, 63-80, PROF PEDIAT, MED SCH, UNIV ORE, 71- Mem: AAAS; Am Acad Pediat. Res: Metabolic disorders of infancy and childhood; cancer. Mailing Add: Dept of Pediat Univ of Ore Health Sci Ctr Portland OR 97201

CAMPBELL, ROBERT BENONI, b Providence, Utah, Feb 14, 21; m 42; c 5. AGRONOMY. Educ: Utah State Agr Col, BS, 43, MS, 51. Prof Exp: Asst soil scientist, USDA, 46-51; sr agronomist, Exp Sta, Hawaiian Sugar Planters Asn, 53-56; SOIL SCIENTIST, SCI EDUC ADMIN-FED RES, USDA, 66- Mem: Am Soc Agron. Res: Agricultural physics related to the physical environment of plants. Mailing Add: USDA Sci Educ Admin-Fed Res PO Box 3039 Florence SC 29501

CAMPBELL, ROBERT HENRY, analytical chemistry, organic chemistry, see previous edition

CAMPBELL, ROBERT LOUIS, b Westerville, Ohio, Nov 16, 25; m 49; c 3. NEUROSURGERY. Educ: Baldwin-Wallace Col, BS, 45; Ohio State Univ, MD, 49; Am Bd Neurol Surg, dipl, 60. Prof Exp: From instr to asst prof, 57-64, PROF NEUROL SURG & DIR MED CTR, IND UNIV, INDIANAPOLIS, 65- Concurrent Pos: Consult, Vet Admin Hosp, Indianapolis, 59- & Naval Hosp, Great Lakes, Ill, 63-; mem, Subarachnoid Hemorrhage Study Sect, NIH, 62-; mem consult staff, Wishard Mem Hosp, 65- Mem: Cong Neurol Surg; Am Asn Neurol Surg; fel Am Col Surgeons; Soc Neurol Surgeons; AMA. Res: Spinal cord neurotransmitters; cerebral vasospasm. Mailing Add: Dept of Neurol Surg Ind Univ Med Ctr Indianapolis IN 46202

CAMPBELL, ROBERT NOE, b Fairmont, Minn, Nov 16, 29; m 54; c 3. PLANT PATHOLOGY. Educ: Univ Minn, BS, 52, MS, 54, PhD(plant path), 57. Prof Exp: Asst plant path, Univ Minn, 52-54, instr, 54-56; plant pathologist, Forest Prod Lab, 57-59; from asst prof to assoc prof plant path, 59-69, PROF PLANT PATH & PLANT PATHOLOGIST EXP STA, UNIV CALIF, DAVIS, 69- Mem: Am Phytopath Soc; Bot Soc Am; AAAS. Res: Cause and control of diseases of vegetable crops; fungal transmission of plant viruses. Mailing Add: Dept of Plant Path Univ of Calif Davis CA 95616

CAMPBELL, ROBERT SAMUEL, b La Harpe, Ill, Aug 15, 04; m 32, 54; c 4. BOTANY. Educ: Univ Chicago, BS, 25, MS, 29, PhD(plant ecol), 32. Prof Exp: Range examr, Jornada Exp Range, US Forest Serv, NMex, 25-34, asst chief div range res, Washington, DC, 34-43, in chg range utilization studies, 37-43, chief div range & watershed mgr res, Southern Forest Exp Sta, 43-63; CONSULT ECOLOGIST, 69- Concurrent Pos: Ed, J Range Mgt, 50-52 & 63-69. Honors & Awards: Superior Serv Award, USDA, 61. Mem: Ecol Soc Am; Am Inst Biol Sci; Soc Am Foresters; Soc Range Mgt (vpres, 57, pres, 58). Res: Range ecology; forest range management; research methods. Mailing Add: RR 7 S 36th St Quincy IL 62301

CAMPBELL, ROBERT SEYMOUR, b Saskatoon, Sask, Sept 9, 13; nat US; m; c 4. ZOOLOGY, LIMNOLOGY. *Educ:* Univ Sask, BA, 34, MA, 35; Univ Mich, PhD(zool), 39. *Prof Exp:* Teaching asst biol, Univ Sask, 32-35; teaching asst zool & asst limnol, Univ Mich, 35-39; asst prof biol, Cent Mich Univ, 39-44; from assoc prof to prof zool, Coop Fishery Unit Sch Forestry, Fisheries & Wildlife, Univ Mo-Columbia, 44-78; RETIRED. *Mem:* Assoc Am Soc Limnol & Oceanog; assoc Ecol Soc Am; assoc Am Fisheries Soc; Wildlife Soc; fel Am Inst Fishery Res Biol. *Res:* Limnology and fisheries biology; acid pollution in strip-mine lakes; thermal pollution. *Mailing Add:* Sch Forestry Fisheries & Wildlife Univ Mo Columbia MO 65201

CAMPBELL, ROBERT TERRY, b Greenwood, Miss, July 27, 32; m 54; c 2. PAPER TECHNOLOGY, TECHNICAL MANAGEMENT. *Educ:* Miss Col, BS, 54; Univ NC, Chapel Hill, MA, 59. *Prof Exp:* From res chemist to chief pulp res, 59-75, mgr pulp res, Erling Riis Res Lab, 75-80, MGR TECH PLANNING, INT PAPER CO, 81- *Mem:* Tech Asn Pulp & Paper Indust. *Res:* Development and improvement of processes to convert wood and other fiber sources into bleached pulp for papermaking and regenerated cellulose manufacture. *Mailing Add:* Technol Planning Int Paper Co 122 Berndale Dr Westport CT 06880

CAMPBELL, ROBERT WAYNE, b Concordia, Kans, Dec 19, 40; m 60; c 3. POLYMER CHEMISTRY. *Educ:* Kans State Univ, BS, 62; Purdue Univ, PhD(org chem), 66. *Prof Exp:* Res chemist, 66-68, group leader polymer res, 68-73, proj leader explor plastics & fibers, 73-78, sect supvr chem synthesis, 78-80, PROD DEVELOP MGR, PHILLIPS PETROL CO, 80- *Mem:* Am Chem Soc; Soc Plastics Engrs (secy, 75, treas, 76, pres, 78). *Res:* Synthetic and reaction mechanism aspects of organo-sulfur chemistry; mass spectral fragmentation of sulfonate esters and related materials; polymer synthesis and characterization, including structure-property correlation; sulfur chemical synthesis and applications; specialty chemical commercial development. *Mailing Add:* 1330 Cherokee Hills Ct Bartlesville OK 74003

CAMPBELL, RONALD WAYNE, b Cherryvale, Kans, July 26, 19; m 43; c 3. HORTICULTURE. *Educ:* Kans State Univ, BS, 43, MS, 46; Mich State Univ, PhD(hort), 57. *Prof Exp:* From asst prof to assoc prof, 46-61, head dept hort & forestry, 66-80, PROF HORT, KANS STATE UNIV, 61- *Mem:* AAAS; Am Soc Hort Sci; Am Soc Plant Physiol; Weed Sci Soc Am; Am Pomol Soc. *Res:* Physiological studies of influences of agricultural chemicals on plants; winter hardiness and water relations studies; stock and scion relationships. *Mailing Add:* Dept of Hort & Forestry Kans State Univ Manhattan KS 66506

CAMPBELL, RUSSELL HARPER, b Bakersfield, Calif, Apr 20, 28; m 53; c 2. EARTH SCIENCE, ENGINEERING GEOLOGY. *Educ:* Univ Calif, BA, 51. *Prof Exp:* GEOLOGIST, US GEOL SURV, 51- *Mem:* Fel Geol Soc Am; Am Geophys Union; Soc Econ Paleontologists & Mineralogists. *Res:* Engineering geology, economic geology, structure and stratigraphy of the western Transverse Ranges, California; earthquake hazards; earthquake tectonics; landslides and mudflows; stratigraphy and structure of northwestern Alaska; uranium deposits of southeastern Utah. *Mailing Add:* Off of Earthquake Studies Nat Ctr MS 905 Reston VA 22092

CAMPBELL, SAMUEL GORDON, b Oban, Scotland, Dec 10, 33; m 61; c 3. IMMUNOLOGY. *Educ:* Glasgow Univ, BVMS, 56; Toronto Univ, MVSc, 59; Cornell Univ, PhD(vet microbiol), 64. *Prof Exp:* House physician vet med, Vet Sch, Univ Glasgow, 56-57; asst vet microbiol, Ont Vet Col, 57-59; NY State Col Vet Med, Cornell Univ, 61-64; sr lectr, Sch Vet Sci, Melbourne Univ, 64-66; asst prof, NY State Col Vet Med, 67-70, dir int educ, 68-74, ASSOC PROF VET MICROBIOL, NY STATE COL VET MED, CORNELL UNIV, 70-, ACTG HEAD DEPT MICROBIOL, 74- *Concurrent Pos:* Consult, Vet Educ, Rockefeller Found, Brazil & Peru, 68 & Dept Microbiol, Tuskegee Inst, 73; external examr, Univ Guelph, 73, Melbourne Univ, 74; vis prof crib death res, Prof Coombs, Cambridge Univ, 74-75; consult hemoprotozoan dis, USAID, Colombia & Kenya, 75. *Mem:* Royal Col Vet Surg. *Res:* Immunological responses of cattle, sheep, and goats. *Mailing Add:* Dept of Vet Microbiol Cornell Univ NY State Col of Vet Med Ithaca NY 14853

CAMPBELL, STEPHEN LA VERN, b Bell Plaine, Iowa, Dec 8, 45. MATHEMATICS, APPLIED MATHEMATICS. *Educ:* Dartmouth Col, AB, 67; Northwestern Univ, MS, 68, PhD(math), 72. *Prof Exp:* Instr, Marquette Univ, 69-72; from asst prof to assoc prof, 72-81, PROF MATH, NC STATE UNIV, 81- *Mem:* Soc Indust & Appl Math. *Res:* Singular systems of differential equations and their applications in engineering and biology; bounded linear operators in Banach spaces. *Mailing Add:* Dept of Math NC State Univ Raleigh NC 27650

CAMPBELL, STEWART JOHN, b Calgary, Alta, July 22, 47; m 70; c 4. OILSEED CHEMISTRY, OILSEED PROCESSING. *Educ:* Univ Alta, BSc, 69, PhD(chem), 73. *Prof Exp:* Res scientist & plant breeder, Res Br, Agr Can, 73-79; STAFF MEM PLANNING & DEVELOP, UNITED OILSEED PROD LTD, 79- *Concurrent Pos:* Plant breeder, Can Expert Comt Grain Crops, 73- *Mem:* Chem Inst Can; Agr Inst Can; Am Asn Cereal Chemists; Can Seed Growers Asn; Am Oil Chem Soc. *Res:* Improvement of oilseed and grain crops adapted to western Canada through research in plant breeding, crop production, and oilseed quality. *Mailing Add:* United Oilseed Prod LTD Box 1620 Lloydminster AB Can

CAMPBELL, SUZANN KAY, b New London, Wis, Apr 19, 43. PHYSICAL THERAPY. *Educ:* Univ Wis-Madison, BS, 65, MS, 68, PhD(neurophysiol), 73. *Prof Exp:* Phys therapist, Cent Wis Colony & Training Sch, 65-68; instr phys ther, Sch Med, Univ Wis-Madison, 68-70, consult, Univ Family Health Serv, 71-72; asst prof, 72-77, ASSOC PROF PHYS THER, SCH MED, UNIV NC, CHAPEL HILL, 77- *Concurrent Pos:* Consult, Div Dis of Develop & Learning, Biol Sci Res Ctr, Univ NC, Chapel Hill, 72-; vis lectr phys ther & res fel, Psychophysiol Sect, Dept Pediat & Psychol, Univ Wis-Madison, 81; ed, Phys & Occup Ther in Pediat. *Honors & Awards:* Golden Pen Award, Am Phys Ther Asn, 78. *Mem:* AAAS; Am Phys Ther Asn; Soc Res Child Develop. *Res:* Infants with central nervous system dysfunction; identification, psychoaffective and sensorimotor development, interaction with mother, and effectiveness of physical therapy in promoting development. *Mailing Add:* Div of Phys Ther 221 H Univ of NC Sch of Med Chapel Hill NC 27514

CAMPBELL, THOMAS COLIN, b Annandale, NJ, Mar 14, 34; m 62; c 5. BIOCHEMISTRY, NUTRITION. *Educ:* Pa State Univ, BS, 56; Cornell Univ, MS, 57, PhD(animal nutrit), 62. *Prof Exp:* Res biologist, Woodard Res Corp, 61-63; res assoc toxicol, Mass Inst Technol, 63-65; from asst prof to prof biochem, Va Polytech Inst & State Univ, 65-75; PROF NUTRIT BIOCHEM, DIV NUTRIT SCI, CORNELL UNIV, 75- *Concurrent Pos:* Campus coordr, Philippine Nat Nutrit Prog; NIH res career develop award, 74. *Mem:* Am Inst Nutrit; Am Soc Pharmacol & Exp Therapeut; Soc Toxicol; Sigma Xi. *Res:* Study of metabolism; mechanism of action and human consumption patterns of aflatoxin; nutrition-toxin interactions; environmental health; international nutrition. *Mailing Add:* Div of Nutrit Sci Cornell Univ Ithaca NY 14853

CAMPBELL, THOMAS COOPER, b Decatur, Ill, Feb 29, 32; m 57; c 2. PHYSICAL ORGANIC CHEMISTRY, PETROLEUM ENGINEERING. *Educ:* Millikin Univ, BS, 57; Emory Univ, MS, 63; Ga Inst Technol, PhD(chem), 68. *Prof Exp:* Res chemist, Monsanto Co, 67-69, sr res chemist, 69-74; res & develop assoc, PQ Corp, 74-80; MGR, ENHANCED OIL RECOVERY ENG, AMINOIL USA, 80- *Mem:* Soc Petrol Engrs; Am Chem Soc; Sigma Xi. *Res:* enhanced oil recovery; alkaline waterflooding; sodium silicate applications and technology, surface chemistry; surfactant applications and formulations. *Mailing Add:* Aminoil USA Inc PO Box 191 Huntington Beach CA 92648

CAMPBELL, THOMAS HODGEN, b Toronto, Ohio, Dec 9, 24. MYCOLOGY. *Educ:* Ohio State Univ, BSc, 46, MSc, 49; Univ Wis, PhD(bot), 52. *Prof Exp:* Instr bot, Univ Tenn, 52-53; biologist, Am Cyanamid Co, NY, 53-54; from asst prof to assoc prof bot, Univ Tenn, 54-61; assoc prof biol, 61-65, head dept, 65-69, prof biol, 65-80, EMER PROF BIOL, COL STEUBENVILLE, 80- *Mem:* AAAS; Mycol Soc Am; Bot Soc Am; Am Phytopath Soc; Mycol Soc France. *Res:* Morphology, cytology and variation of Penicillium chrysogenum; taxonomy and history of mycology. *Mailing Add:* 2601 S Berry Rd Norman OK 73069

CAMPBELL, TRAVIS AUSTIN, b Washington, DC, Aug 20, 43; m 75. PLANT BREEDING. *Educ:* Univ Md, BS, 66, MS, 72, PhD, 80. *Prof Exp:* Agronomist plant breeding & weed sci, 67-76, RES AGRONOMIST PLANT BREEDING, USDA, 76- *Mem:* Am Soc Agron; Am Soc Hort Sci. *Res:* New crops breeding. *Mailing Add:* Sci & Educ Admin-Agr Res USDA Rm 339 BG001 Beltsville MD 20705

CAMPBELL, VIRGINIA WILEY, b Denver, Colo, Sept 5, 37; m 57; c 2. MOLECULAR BIOLOGY, IMMUNOLOGY. *Educ:* Univ Colo, BA, 59, BS, 61; Univ Mich, PhD(microbiol), 79. *Prof Exp:* RES ASSOC, DEPT MICROBIOL, UNIV MICH, 79- *Mem:* AAAS. *Res:* Gene organization in eucaryotic cells, expression, and regulation in immunoglobulin-producing cells. *Mailing Add:* Dept Microbiol & Immunol Med Sci Bldg II Ann Arbor MI 48109

CAMPBELL, W(ILLIAM) M(UNRO), b Alvinston, Ont, Jan 21, 15; m 41; c 2. CHEMICAL ENGINEERING. *Educ:* Univ Toronto, BASc, 38; Case Western Reserve Univ, MS, 40; Univ Ill, PhD(chem eng), 50. *Prof Exp:* Asst, Case Western Reserve Univ, 38-40; plant res engr & group leader, Shawinigan Chems, Ltd, 41-46; asst prof chem eng, Queen's Univ, Can, 46-47; instr, Univ Ill, 47-50; group leader, Chem Eng Br, Atomic Energy Can, Ltd, 50-51, head br, 51-56, dir, Chem & Metall Div, 56-65; dir res, Ont Res Found, 65-70; mgr indust appln, Atomic Energy Can, Ltd, 70-71, spec adv to vpres, 71-76; proj dir, W L Wardrop & Assoc Ltd, 76-78; RETIRED. *Mem:* Chem Inst Can. *Res:* Process development based on acetylene; Fischer-Tropsch process; radiochemical processing; solvent extraction; nuclear fuel development; metallurgy. *Mailing Add:* 6 Radcliffe Crescent London ON N6H 3X4 Can

CAMPBELL, W P, b Lloydminster, Sask, Aug 1, 22; m 50; c 3. PLANT PATHOLOGY. *Educ:* Univ Alta, BSc, 49; Univ Toronto, PhD(bot), 53. *Prof Exp:* Res officer plant path, 49-73, chief plant inspection & quarantines, 73-77, CHIEF PLANT PROTECTION DIV, CAN DEPT AGR, 77- *Mem:* Am Phytopath Soc; Can Phytopath Soc; Agr Inst Can. *Res:* Ergot of cereals and grasses; pesticides. *Mailing Add:* Plant Protection Div Can Agr Cent Exp Farm Ottawa ON K1A 0C5 Can

CAMPBELL, WALLACE G, JR, b Lockport, NY, July 25, 30; m 57; c 4. PATHOLOGY. *Educ:* Harvard Univ, AB, 53; Cornell Univ, MD, 57. *Prof Exp:* Asst path, Cornell Univ, 58-61, instr, 61-62; from asst prof to assoc prof, 64-71, PROF PATH, EMORY UNIV, 71- *Concurrent Pos:* USPHS trainee path, 59-62. *Mem:* Am Asn Path; Int Acad Path; Am Soc Nephrology; AAAS; Soc Exp Biol Med. *Res:* Experimental hypertension; cardiovascular and renal pathology; coagulation of blood; cellular pathology; arthritis; pneumocystis; vaccinia virus toxicity; endocrine tumors of the pancreas. *Mailing Add:* Dept of Path Emory Univ Atlanta GA 30322

CAMPBELL, WALLACE HALL, b New York, NY, Feb 6, 26; m 56; c 2. ATMOSPHERIC PHYSICS, GEOMAGNETISM. *Educ:* La State Univ, BS, 50; Vanderbilt Univ, MA, 53; Univ Calif, Los Angeles, PhD(physics), 59. *Prof Exp:* Grad res geophysicist, Inst Geophys, Univ Calif, Los Angeles, 55-57, jr res geophysicist, 57-59; asst prof geophys res, Geophys Inst, Univ Alaska, 59-60; group leader ultra low frequency res, Cent Radio Propagation Lab, Nat Bur Stand, 60-65, chief geomagnetism res, Aeronomy Lab, Inst Telecommun Sci & Aeronomy, Environ Sci Serv Admin, 65-67; dir geomagnetism lab, Environ Res Labs, Nat Oceanic & Atmospheric Agency, 67-71, head space magnetism res, 71-73; RESEARCHER EXTERNAL GEOMAGNETIC FIELD, US GEOL SURV, 73- *Concurrent Pos:* Mem various working groups, Int Asn Geomagnetism & Aeronomy, 64- *Honors & Awards:* Boulder Scientist Award, Sigma Xi, 63. *Mem:* Sigma Xi; Am Geophys Union; Soc

Explor Geophysicists; AAAS; Soc Terrestrial Magnetism & Elec Japan. *Res:* Upper atmospheric physics; geomagnetic phenomena; natural ultra low frequency field variations; auroral luminosity fluctuations. *Mailing Add:* US Geol Surv Mailstop 964 Fed Ctr Box 25046 Denver CO 80225

CAMPBELL, WARREN ADAMS, b Berkeley, Calif, June 14, 36; m 58. ASTRONOMY. *Educ:* Willamette Univ, BA, 58; Univ Wis, MS, 60, PhD(astron), 65. *Prof Exp:* Asst prof math, Wash State Univ, 65-70; ASST PROF PHYSICS, UNIV WIS, RIVER FALLS, 70- *Mem:* Am Astron Soc. *Res:* Forbidden oxygen and nitrogen lines in the spectra of planetary nebulae. *Mailing Add:* Dept of Physics Univ of Wis River Falls WI 54022

CAMPBELL, WILBUR HAROLD, b Santa Ana, Calif, Apr 23, 45; m 81. ENZYMOLOGY, BIOINORGANIC CHEMISTRY. *Educ:* Pomona Col, BA, 67; Univ Wis-Madison, PhD(biochem), 72. *Prof Exp:* Res assoc, Univ Ga, 72-73, Mayo Clin, 73-74 & Mich State Univ, 74-75; asst prof chem, 75-80, ASSOC PROF CHEM, COL SCI & FORESTRY, STATE UNIV NY, 80- *Mem:* Am Chem Soc; Am Soc Plant Physiologists; Japanese Soc Plant Physiologists. *Res:* Plant biochemistry; focusing on photosynthetic carbon metabolism and nitrogen metabolism; enzymed nitrate reductase; microcomputing for biochemical research. *Mailing Add:* Dept Chem State Univ NY Col Environ Sci & Forestry Syracuse NY 13210

CAMPBELL, WILLIAM (ALOYSIUS), b Newcastle, NB, Apr 18, 06; US citizen; m 32; c 5. DEVELOPMENTAL ANATOMY, ELECTRON MICROSCOPY. *Educ:* St Francis Xavier Univ, BA, 27; St Francis Col (Pa), MS, 29. *Prof Exp:* Asst prof biol & physics, St Francis Col (Pa), 27-29, biol & head dept, 29-38; asst prof, Canisius Col, 38; from asst prof to assoc prof, 38-73, EMER ASSOC PROF BIOL, COL HOLY CROSS, 73- *Mem:* Nat Asn Biol Teachers. *Res:* Comparative anatomy, histology and cytology; developmental anatomy; electron microscopy; experimental embryology. *Mailing Add:* 73 Willow Hill Rd Cherry Valley MA 01611

CAMPBELL, WILLIAM ANDREW, b Paterson, NJ, Jan 29, 06; m 36; c 3. FOREST PATHOLOGY. *Educ:* Pa State Teachers Col, BS, 29; Univ Colo, AM, 31; Pa State Col, PhD(mycol, plant path), 35. *Prof Exp:* Asst forest pathologist, Div Forest Path, Bur Plant Indust, USDA, 36-42, forest pathologist, Guayule Res Proj, Salinas, Calif, 42-46, pathologist, Div Forest Path, Georgia, 46-53, sr pathologist, 53-54, plant pathologist, Southeastern Forest Exp Sta, US Forest Serv, 54-71; prof plant path, Univ Ga, 71-73; CONSULT FORESTRY, 73- *Mem:* Am Phytopath Soc; Mycol Soc Am. *Res:* Diseases of native tree species, particularly root diseases and wood decay; fungi affecting roots of plants. *Mailing Add:* 260 Milledge Heights Athens GA 30601

CAMPBELL, WILLIAM B(UFORD), b Clarksdale, Miss, Nov 23, 35; m 63; c 2. CERAMIC ENGINEERING, MINERALOGY. *Educ:* Ga Inst Technol, BCerE, 58, MSCerE, 60; Harvard Univ, AM, 62; Ohio State Univ, PhD, 67; NY Univ Med Sch, PGMed, 80. *Prof Exp:* Asst prof ceramic eng, Ga Inst Technol, 58-59, res asst, Eng Exp Sta, 58-60; res assoc crystal res, Harvard Univ, 60-62; sr scientist, Lexington Labs, Inc, Cambridge, 62, progs dir & vpres, 63-67; from asst prof to assoc prof ceramic eng, Ohio State Univ, 67-73; assoc prof, Dept Eng, Univ Tenn, 73-77; SR PARTNER, CAMPBELL, CHURCHILL, ZIMMERMAN & ASSOCS, 77-; PRES & CHMN, SOUTHEASTERN MOBILITY CO, INC, 77-; PARTNER, BRAE ARDEN FARMS & BRAE ARDEN RANCH, 79- *Concurrent Pos:* Res analyst, US Air Force, 65-69; res scientist, Arctic Inst NAm, 60; mem, Int Conf Crystal Growth, 66 & task group biomat, Nat Acad Eng. *Mem:* Am Ceramic Soc; Mineral Soc Am; Nat Inst Ceramic Engrs; Am Inst Chem Engrs; Can Ceramic Soc. *Res:* Experimental mineralogy; crystal synthesis; bioceramic materials; pigment degradation mechanisms; thermal effects on reaction kinetics; forensic sciences. *Mailing Add:* 717 Kempton Rd Knoxville TN 37919

CAMPBELL, WILLIAM BRYSON, b Sulphur Springs, Tex, Mar 25, 47; m 75. PHARMACOLOGY. *Educ:* Univ Tex, Austin, BS, 70; Univ Tex Southwestern Med Sch, PhD(pharmacol), 74. *Prof Exp:* Fel pharmacol, Med Col Wis, 74-75, instr, 75-76; asst prof, 76-81, ASSOC PROF PHARMACOL, UNIV TEX SOUTHWESTERN MED SCH, 81- *Concurrent Pos:* Coun, high blood pressure res. *Mem:* Am Fedn Clin Res; Am Soc Pharmacol & Exp Therapeut; Am Heart Asn. *Res:* Pharmacology of vasoactive substances and their relationship to the kidney, the adrenal gland and the peripheral vasculature in hypertension. *Mailing Add:* Dept Pharmacol Univ Tex Health Sci Ctr Dallas TX 75235

CAMPBELL, WILLIAM CECIL, b Londonderry, Ireland, June 28, 30; nat US; m 62; c 3. ZOOLOGY. *Educ:* Univ Dublin, BA, 52; Univ Wis, MS, 54, PhD(zool, vet sci), 57. *Prof Exp:* Asst parasitol, Univ Wis, 53-57; res assoc, Merck Inst Therapeut Res, 57-66, dir parasitol, 66-72, dir, Merck, Sharp & Dohme Vet Res & Develop Lab, Australia, 72-73, sr investr, 73-76, dir basic parasitol, 77-78, SR DIR BASIC PARASITOL, MERCK INST THERAPEUT RES, 78- *Concurrent Pos:* Adj prof parasitol, Univ Pa, 77-; mem exec comt, Int Comn Trichinellosis, 72-76, vpres, 76-80, pres, 80- *Mem:* Am Soc Parasitol (vpres, 79); Am Soc Trop Med & Hyg. *Res:* Parasitology; helminthology; chemotherapy. *Mailing Add:* Merck Inst for Therapeut Res Rahway NJ 07065

CAMPBELL, WILLIAM FRANK, b Mt Vernon, Ill, Sept 23, 28; m 54; c 4. RADIATION BOTANY, PLANT PHYSIOLOGY. *Educ:* Univ Ill, BS, 56, MS, 57; Mich State Univ, PhD(radiation bot), 64. *Prof Exp:* Collabr hort, Agr Res Serv, USDA, 64-68, assoc prof plant physiol, 68-77, PROF PLANT SCI, UTAH STATE UNIV, 77- *Mem:* AAAS; Am Soc Hort Sci; Am Inst Biol Sci; Am Soc Agron; Bot Soc Am. *Res:* Effects of ionizing radiation in successive generations on developing and dormant plant embryos; plant growth, physiological responses histo and cyto-chemical and ultrastructural changes as influenced by environmental stresses; ultrastructural plant cytology. *Mailing Add:* Dept of Plant Sci Utah State Univ Logan UT 84322

CAMPBELL, WILLIAM H, b Fayette, Ala, July 20, 40. MATHEMATICS. *Educ:* Univ Ala, Tuscaloosa, BA, 62, MA, 63, PhD, 69. *Prof Exp:* Mathematician, Gen Dynamics Corp, Conn, 63-64; instr math, Univ Ala, Huntsville, 64-66, ASST PROF MATH, UNIV ALA, BIRMINGHAM, 69- *Mem:* Am Math Soc; Math Asn Am. *Mailing Add:* Dept of Math Univ of Ala Birmingham AL 35233

CAMPBELL, WILLIAM HOWARD, b Lakeview, Ore, Aug 13, 42; m 67; c 2. PHARMACOLOGY. *Educ:* Ore State Univ, BS, 65, MS, 68; Purdue Univ, PhD(pharm), 71. *Prof Exp:* Asst prof pharm, Ore State Univ, 71-75; CHMN DEPT PHARM PRACT, SCH PHARM, UNIV WASH, 75- *Concurrent Pos:* Sr investr, Health Serv Res Ctr, Ore Region, Kaiser Found, Portland, 71-; sr consult, Vet Admin Hosp, 75- *Mem:* Am Pub Health Asn; Am Pharmaceut Asn. *Res:* Assessment of drug systems operation within general medical care, specifically adverse drug reactions, drug use review and control, and technological applications. *Mailing Add:* Sch of Pharm Univ of Wash Seattle WA 98195

CAMPBELL, WILLIAM JACKSON, b Wichita Falls, Tex, Oct 23, 29; m 51; c 3. CLINICAL BIOCHEMISTRY. *Educ:* NTex State Univ, BA, 49; Univ Tex, MS, 52, MS, 53; Ohio State Univ, PhD(phys chem), 60. *Prof Exp:* Chief dept biochem, Walter Reed Army Inst Res, 60-64; prog adminr, clin chem, Nat Inst Gen Med Sci, 64-74; EXEC DIR CLIN CHEM, AM ASN CLIN CHEM, 74- *Concurrent Pos:* Lectr, Am Univ, 61-73; prof lectr, 63-65, adj prof, 65-73. *Mem:* Sigma Xi; Am Chem Soc; Am Asn Clin Chemists. *Mailing Add:* Am Asn Clin Chem 1725 K St NW Washington DC 20006

CAMPBELL, WILLIAM JOSEPH, b Washington, DC, July 31, 26; m 48; c 2. PHYSICAL CHEMISTRY. *Educ:* Univ Md, BS, 50, PhD(chem), 56. *Prof Exp:* Asst phys chem, Univ Md, 51; phys chemist, 51-56, supvry phys chemist, 56-62, supvry res chemist, 62-80, RES DIR, US BUR MINES, 80- *Honors & Awards:* Dept Interior Meritorious Serv Award, 62. *Mem:* NY Acad Sci; Am Chem Soc; Soc Appl Spectros; Am Inst Min, Metall & Petrol Eng; fel Am Inst Chem. *Res:* Fluorescent x-ray spectroscopy; x-ray diffraction; high temperature physical chemistry; auger spectroscopy; environmental chemistry; mineral particulates; electron optics; chemical-instrumental methods of analysis. *Mailing Add:* 2720 Hambleton Rd Riva MD 21844

CAMPBELL, WILLIAM JOSEPH, meteorology, oceanography, see previous edition

CAMPBELL, WILLIAM ROBERT, toxicology, see previous edition

CAMPBELL, WILLIAM VERNON, b Chester, SC, May 4, 24; m 47; c 2. ENTOMOLOGY. *Educ:* Miss State Univ, BS, 51, MS, 52; NC State Univ, PhD(entom), 58. *Prof Exp:* Entomologist, Insect Control, Entom Res Br, Agr Res Serv, USDA, Tidewater Field Sta, Va, 52-53 & wheat stem sawfly proj, Cereal & Forage Insects Sect, Entom Res Br, NDak, 53-55; asst entom, 55-58, from asst prof to assoc prof, 59-69, PROF ENTOM, NC STATE UNIV, 70- *Concurrent Pos:* Assoc ed, Peanut Sci, Int Workshop, 80 & 81; consult, Int Crops Res Inst for Semi-Arid Tropics, India, 81. *Mem:* Entom Soc Am; Am Peanut Res Educ Soc. *Res:* Biology and control of insects; plant resistance to insects attacking field and forage crops; plant and insect histology. *Mailing Add:* Dept Entom NC State Univ PO Box 5215 Raleigh NC 27650

CAMPENOT, ROBERT BARRY, b East Orange, NJ, Mar 30, 46. NEUROBIOLOGY. *Educ:* Rutgers Univ, BA, 68; Univ Calif, Los Angeles, MS, 71; Mass Inst Technol-Woods Hole Oceanog Inst, PhD(biol oceanog), 76. *Prof Exp:* res fel neurobiol, Harvard Med Sch, 75-78; ASST PROF NEUROBIOL, CORNELL UNIV, 78- *Res:* Developmental neurobiology. *Mailing Add:* Sect Neurobiol & Behav Cornell Univ Ithaca NY 14850

CAMPER, NYAL DWIGHT, b Lynchburg, Va, May 12, 39. PLANT PHYSIOLOGY, PLANT BIOCHEMISTRY. *Educ:* NC State Univ, 62, PhD(crop sci), 67. *Prof Exp:* Res asst herbicide physiol, NC State Univ, 62-66; asst prof plant physiol, 66-71, assoc prof, 74-77, PROF PLANT PHYSIOL, CLEMSON UNIV, 77- *Concurrent Pos:* Dir student sci training prog, NSF, 68-70. *Mem:* Sigma Xi; Tissue Cult Asn; Am Chem Soc; Am Soc Plant Physiol; Weed Sci Soc. *Res:* Physiology and biochemistry of herbicide action, mechanisms of action and the biological systems involved. *Mailing Add:* Dept of Plant Path & Physiol Clemson Univ Clemson SC 29631

CAMPILLO, ANTHONY JOSEPH, lasers, biophysics, see previous edition

CAMPION, JAMES J, b Philadelphia, Pa, July 14, 39; m 69. ANALYTICAL CHEMISTRY, PHYSICAL CHEMISTRY. *Educ:* La Salle Col, BA, 61; Univ Pittsburgh, PhD(nonaqueous solutions), 66. *Prof Exp:* Off Saline Water res assoc, Univ Pittsburgh & Mellon Inst, 67-68; asst prof, 68-73, ASSOC PROF ANAL CHEM, STATE UNIV NY COL NEW PALTZ, 73- 68-73. *Mem:* Am Chem Soc; Sigma Xi. *Res:* Solution chemistry of electrolytes and nonelectrolytes in aqueous and nonaqueous solvents. *Mailing Add:* Dept of Chem State Univ of NY Col of Paltz New Paltz NY 12561

CAMPISI, LOUIS SEBASTIAN, b New York, NY, Aug 9, 35; m 63; c 1. INORGANIC CHEMISTRY. *Educ:* City Col New York, BS, 56; Fordham Univ, MS, 60, PhD(inorg chem), 64. *Prof Exp:* Asst prof chem, 62-69, assoc prof, 69-77, PROF CHEM, IONA COL, 78- *Mem:* Am Chem Soc; Sigma Xi. *Res:* Chemistry of uranium and thorium; coordination chemistry. *Mailing Add:* Dept of Chem Iona Col New Rochelle NY 10801

CAMPLING, C(HARLES) H(UGH) R(AMSAY), b Melville, Sask, Nov 30, 22; m 46; c 3. ELECTRICAL ENGINEERING. *Educ:* Queen's Univ, Can, BSc, 44; Mass Inst Technol, SM, 48. *Prof Exp:* Instr math, Queen's Univ, Can, 45-46; asst elec eng, Mass Inst Technol, 46-48, res engr, 48-49; jr res officer, Nat Res Coun Can, 49-50; assoc prof elec eng, Royal Mil Col, 50-55; assoc prof, 55-63, head dept, 67-77, PROF ELEC ENG, QUEEN'S UNIV, ONT, 63- *Honors & Awards:* Ross Medal, Eng Inst Can, 62. *Mem:* Inst Elec & Electronics Engrs; fel Eng Inst Can; Can Soc Elec Eng (pres, 78-80). *Res:* Digital systems. *Mailing Add:* Dept of Elec Eng Queen's Univ Kingston ON K7L 3N6 Can

CAMPO, ROBERT D, b New York, NY, Feb 18, 30; m 57; c 5. BIOCHEMISTRY, BIOLOGY. *Educ:* St John's Univ, NY, BS, 52, MS, 57; Rockefeller Inst, PhD(biochem), 63. *Prof Exp:* From instr to asst prof biochem, 63-70, assoc prof, 70-75, PROF ORTHOP SURG, SCH MED, HEALTH SCI CTR, TEMPLE UNIV, 75- *Mem:* Soc Exp Biol & Med; Am Rheumatism Asn; Orthop Res Soc. *Res:* Radiation biology; acid mucopolysaccharides; protein polysaccharides of cartilage; bone formation; calcification and degradation enzymes of cartilage; organic matrices of cartilage and bone. *Mailing Add:* Dept of Orthop Surg Temple Univ Health Sci Ctr Philadelphia PA 19140

CAMPOLATTARO, ALFONSO, b Naples, Italy, Jan 4, 33; US citizen; m 60; c 3. THEORETICAL PHYSICS. *Educ:* Univ Naples, PhD(theoret physics), 59. *Prof Exp:* Res physicist, Univ Naples, 60-65, assoc prof theoret physics, 63-65; NATO fel, Palmer Physics Lab, Princeton Univ, 65-66; vis asst prof, Univ Calif, Irvine, 66-67, actg assoc prof, 67-68; vis assoc prof, 68-70, assoc prof, 70-71, PROF PHYSICS, UNIV MD, BALTIMORE COUNTY, 71- *Concurrent Pos:* Res physicist, Naval Surface Weapon Ctr, White Oak, Silver Spring, Md, 68- *Honors & Awards:* Young Physicist Prize, Ital Physics Soc, 62; US Navy Achievement Awards, 70 & 78. *Mem:* Am Asn Univ Prof; French Soc Phys Chem; AAAS; Am Phys Soc. *Res:* Mathematical aspects of quantum field theory; relativistic astrophysics; combustion theory; detonation theory; solid state physics; particle accelerators. *Mailing Add:* Dept of Physics Univ of Md Baltimore County Baltimore MD 21228

CAMRAS, MARVIN, b Chicago, Ill, Jan 1, 16; m 51; c 5. MAGNETISM, ELECTRONICS. *Educ:* Armour Inst Technol, BS, 40; Ill Inst Technol, MS, 42. *Hon Degrees:* LLD, Ill Inst Technol, 68. *Prof Exp:* Physicist, 40-45, sr physicist, 45-59, sr engr, 59-65, sci adv, 65-69, SR SCI ADV, IIT RES INST, 69- *Concurrent Pos:* Engr & draftsman, Delta Star Elec Co, Ill, 39; ed, Trans on Audio, Inst Elec & Electronics Eng, 58-64; chmn, Nat Comt II, Int Electrotech Comn; mem S4 comt, Am Nat Stand Inst; dir, Midwest Acoust Conf, 69-72; mem, Nat Inventors Coun, 72; instr elec eng, Ill Inst Technol, 78. *Honors & Awards:* Distinguished Serv Award, Ill Inst Technol, 48; Scott Medal, 55; Citation, Ind Tech Col, 58; Achievement Award, Inst Elec & Electronics Eng, 58, Consumer Electronics Award, 64 & Broadcasting Papers Award, 64; US Camera Award, 59; Idust Res Prod Award, 66; John Potts Gold Medal Award, Audio Eng Soc, 69; Washington Award, Western Soc Engrs, 79. *Mem:* Nat Acad Eng; hon mem Audio Eng Soc; fel AAAS; fel Inst Elec & Electronics Eng; fel Acoust Soc Am. *Res:* Magnetic recording; stereophonic sound; electronics; magnetism; video recording. *Mailing Add:* Technol Ctr IIT Res Inst 10 W 35th St Chicago IL 60616

CANADY, WILLIAM JAMES, b New York, NY, Dec 8, 24; m 55; c 1. BIOCHEMISTRY. *Educ:* Fordham Univ, BS, 46; George Washington Univ, MS, 50, PhD(biochem), 55. *Prof Exp:* From instr to assoc prof, 58-69, PROF BIOCHEM, MED CTR, WVA UNIV, 69- *Concurrent Pos:* Fel chem, Univ Ottawa, 55-57. *Mem:* Am Chem Soc; Soc Exp Biol & Med. *Res:* Vitamin K; methodology; mechanism of enzyme action; thermodynamics of ionization and solution processes. *Mailing Add:* Med Ctr WVa Univ Morgantown WV 26506

CANALE, RAYMOND PATRICK, b Cortland, NY, Nov 20, 41; m 68; c 2. SANITARY & BIOCHEMICAL ENGINEERING. *Educ:* Syracuse Univ, BS, 64, MS, 66, PhD(sanit eng), 68. *Prof Exp:* From asst prof to assoc prof, 68-77, PROF CIVIL ENG, UNIV MICH, 77- *Mem:* Am Soc Civil Engrs; Water Pollution Control Fedn; Am Chem Soc. *Res:* Biological treatment of domestic and industrial wastes; stream and estuarine pollution; mass transfer in open channel flow; predator-prey relationships in microbial cultures; mathematical ecology. *Mailing Add:* Dept of Civil Eng 304 W Eng Bldg Univ of Mich Ann Arbor MI 48104

CANALE-PAROLA, ERCOLE, b Frosinone, Italy, Sept 13, 29; US citizen; m 54; c 2. MICROBIOLOGY. *Educ:* Univ Ill, BS, 56, MS, 57, PhD(microbiol), 61. *Prof Exp:* NIH fel, Hopkins Marine Sta, Stanford Univ, 61-63; from asst prof to assoc prof microbiol, 63-67, PROF MICROBIOL, UNIV MASS, 73- *Concurrent Pos:* Vis scientist, Woods Hole Oceanographic Inst, 69, Dept Biol, Amherst Col, 78. *Mem:* Am Soc Microbiol; Am Acad Microbiol; Soc Gen Microbiol. *Res:* Bacterial physiology; microbial ecology; spirochetes; sarcinae; bacterial pigments; evolution of microorganisms; cellulose degradation by anaerobic bacteria. *Mailing Add:* Dept of Microbiol Univ of Mass Amherst MA 01003

CANAL-FREDERICK, GHISLAINE R, b Metz, France, Mar 31, 33; div; c 4. PSYCHOPHYSIOLOGY, HUMAN NEUROPSYCHOLOGY. *Educ:* Univ Md, BS, 71; Howard Univ, MS, 74, PhD(neuropsychol), 78. *Prof Exp:* Psychologist clinic & res, Surg Neurol Br, 73-76, RES PSYCHOLOGIST CLINIC & RES, FUNCTIONAL NEUROSURG, CLINICAL NEUROSCI, NAT INST NEUROL & COMMUNICATIVE DISORDERS & STROKE, 76- *Mem:* Am Psychol Asn; Soc Neurosci; Grad Women Sci; AAAS. *Res:* Human neuropsychology; cerebral organization; cognition; hemispheric asymmetry; age, sex, and hand related factors in cerebral organization. *Mailing Add:* 5003 Elsmere Pl Bethesda MD 20014

CANARY, JOHN JOSEPH, b Mineola, NY, Jan 9, 25; m 51; c 7. METABOLISM, ENDOCRINOLOGY. *Educ:* St John's Col, NY, BS, 47; Georgetown Univ, MD, 51. *Prof Exp:* NIH trainee metab dis, Georgetown Univ, 54-55; from instr to assoc prof, 56-68, actg dir radioisotope lab, Univ Hosp, 58, dir gen clin res ctr, 73-78, PROF MED, SCH MED, GEORGETOWN UNIV, 68-, DIR DIV & CLINICS ENDOCRINOL & METAB, UNIV HOSP, 59- *Concurrent Pos:* Res fel, NIH, 55-57; clin instr biochem, Sch Med, Georgetown Univ, 57-60, spec lectr, 70-; consult & lectr endocrinol, Nat Naval Med Ctr, 58-; consult metab, Walter Reed Army Inst Res, 61-; consult metab & endocrinol, NIH, 76-; mem, Comt Diabetes in Caribbean, WHO/Pan Am Health Orgn; consult traditional med, diabetes & cardiovasc dis, WHO, 79- *Mem:* AAAS; Am Fedn Clin Res; Endocrine Soc; Am Soc Bone & Mineral Res; Am Soc Clin Invest. *Res:* Study of the density and chemical composition of human bone in various disease states, particularly osteoporosis and the effects of therapy thereon; body composition and density. *Mailing Add:* Sch Med Georgetown Univ Washington DC 20007

CANAVAN, ROBERT I, b Ridgefield Park, NJ, July 31, 27. MATHEMATICS. *Educ:* Woodstock Col, Md, AB, 50; NY Univ, PhD(math), 57; Univ Innsbruck, lic theol, 61. *Prof Exp:* Instr math, LeMoyne Col, NY, 51-52; from asst prof to assoc prof, St Peter's Col, NJ, 62-69; assoc prof, 69-74, PROF MATH, MONMOUTH COL, NJ, 74- *Mem:* Am Math Soc; Math Asn Am; Soc Indust & Appl Math. *Res:* Ordinary and partial differential equations. *Mailing Add:* Dept of Math Monmouth Col West Long Branch NJ 07764

CANAVERA, DAVID STEPHEN, forest genetics, see previous edition

CANAWATI, HANNA N, b Bethlehem, Palestine, Nov 18, 38; m 68; c 3. CLINICAL MICROBIOLOGY, MEDICAL TECHNOLOGY. *Educ:* Damascus Univ, BS, 64; Roosevelt Univ, MS, 71; Chicago Med Sch, PhD(med microbiol), 74. *Prof Exp:* CHIEF MICROBIOL, RANCHO LOS AMIGOS HOSP & JOHN WESLEY COUNTY HOSP, 75-; asst prof path, Sch Med, Univ Southern Calif, 75-81. *Concurrent Pos:* Lectr med technol, Masters Prog, Calif State Univ, Dominguez Hills, 76-; microbiol consult, 81- *Mem:* Am Soc Microbiol; Am Acad Microbiol; NY Acad Sci. *Res:* Clinical significance of anaerobes in diabetic patients; bacteriologic study of liver patients spontaneous bacterial pertitonitis; methicillin resistan staph aureus characteristics and drug resistance; in vitro evaluation of cephalosporins against clinically isolated bacteria. *Mailing Add:* Rancho Los Amigos Hosp 7601 E Imperial Hwy Downey CA 90242

CANCIO, MARTA, b San Sebastian, PR, Dec 8, 28; m 52, 64; c 3. BIOCHEMISTRY. *Educ:* Univ PR, BS, 49; Univ Mo, MS, 52, PhD(biol chem), 54. *Prof Exp:* Assoc biochem, Sch Med, Univ PR, 54-67, asst prof biochem & nutrit, 67-71; chief biochemist, 54-66, SUPVRY RES CHEMIST, VET ADMIN HOSP, 66-; ASSOC PROF BIOCHEM & NUTRIT, SCH MED, UNIV PR, RIO PIEDRAS, 71- *Mem:* NY Acad Sci; Am Fedn Clin Res; Am Inst Nutrit; Am Soc Clin Nutrit; Latin Am Nutrit Soc. *Res:* Lipid and protein chemistry; malabsorption; tropical sprue; immunochemistry; hyperlipidemias. *Mailing Add:* 39 Jazmin St San Francisco Rio Piedras PR 00927

CANCRO, ROBERT, b New York, NY, Feb 23, 32; m 56; c 2. PSYCHIATRY. *Educ:* Fordham Univ, 48-51; State Univ NY, MD, 55, DrMedSci, 62; Am Bd Psychiat & Neurol, cert psychiat, 62. *Prof Exp:* Dir alcohol res ward & instr psychiat, State Univ NY Downstate Med Ctr, 62-66; psychiatrist, Menninger Found, 66-69, mem fac, Menninger Sch Psychiat, 67-69; vis assoc, Ctr Advan Study & vis prof, Dept Comput Sci, Univ Ill, Urbana, 69-70; prof psychiat, Univ Conn, Farmington, 70-76; PROF & CHMN DEPT PSYCHIAT, NY UNIV, 76- *Concurrent Pos:* Consult, Dept Comput Sci, Univ Ill, 67 & Topeka State & Vet Admin Hosps, Topeka, Kans, 67-69. *Mem:* AAAS; Am Psychiat Asn; Asn Am Med Cols; AMA; NY Acad Sci. *Res:* Prediction of outcome in schizophrenia; nature of pathology in schizophrenia and in addictions. *Mailing Add:* Dept Psychiat NY Univ Med Ctr New York NY 10016

CANDELAS, GRACIELA C, b PR, 22; US citizen. MOLECULAR BIOLOGY. *Educ:* Univ PR, BS, 44; Duke Univ, MS, 59; Univ Miami, PhD(molecular biol), 66. *Prof Exp:* Instr biol, 51-57, from asst prof to assoc prof, 61-71, PROF BIOL, UNIV PR, RIO PIEDRAS, 71- *Concurrent Pos:* Vis prof biol, Syracuse Univ, 69-71, City Col New York, 74-75 & Rockefeller Univ, 79-80; prof cell & molecular biol, Med Col Ga, 72-74; princ investgr, NSF proj, 81-83. *Mem:* Int Soc Develop Biol; Am Soc Cell Biol; Sigma Xi; Int Cell Res Orgn. *Res:* Using a pair of fibroin producing glands, which is a one protein system, from the spider Nephila Clavipes as a model system in the study of the synthesis of a large protein and its processing and regulation; molecular biology of differentiating systems. *Mailing Add:* Dept Biol Univ PR Rio Piedras PR 00931

CANDER, LEON, b Philadelphia, Pa, Oct 7, 26; m 54; c 2. INTERNAL MEDICINE, CLINICAL PHYSIOLOGY. *Educ:* Temple Univ, MD, 51. *Prof Exp:* Intern, Southern Div, Einstein Med Ctr, 51-52; fel physiol, Dept Physiol & Pharmacol, Grad Sch Med, Univ Pa, 52-54, instr, 54-55, assoc, 55-56; from asst resident to resident med, Beth Israel Hosp, Boston, 56-58; sr instr, Med Sch, Tufts Univ, 58-60; from asst prof to assoc prof, Hahnemann Med Col & Hosp, 60-66, head, Sect Chest Dis, 60-66; prof physiol & internal med & chmn dept, Med Sch, Univ Tex, San Antonio, 66-72; chmn, Dept Med, 72-80, HEAD, SECT CHEST DIS, DAROFF DIV, ALBERT EINSTEIN MED CTR, PHILADELPHIA, 80-; PROF MED, JEFFERSON MED COL, 72- *Concurrent Pos:* Asst lab instr, Sch Auxiliary Med Sci, Univ Pa, 53-55, Am Col Physicians res fel, 54-55; asst, Harvard Med Sch, 57-58; fel, Nat Acad Sci-Nat Res Coun; Markle scholar acad med, Hahnemann Med Col & Hosp, 61-66. *Mem:* Am Fedn Clin Res; Am Physiol Soc; Am Col Physicians. *Res:* Clinical pulmonary physiology. *Mailing Add:* 317 Cherry Lane Wynnewood PA 19096

CANDIA, OSCAR A, b Buenos Aires, Arg, Apr 30, 35; m 60; c 3. PHYSIOLOGY, BIOPHYSICS. *Educ:* Univ Buenos Aires, MD, 59. *Prof Exp:* Instr basic physics, Univ Buenos Aires, 60-61, head lab & res assoc biophysics, 62-63; res assoc, Univ Louisville, 64-65, asst prof, 65-68; assoc prof ophthal, 68-77, ASSOC PROF PHYSIOL & PROF OPHTHAL, MT SINAI SCH MED, 78- *Concurrent Pos:* Res fel electrophysiol, Univ Buenos Aires, 60-62; NIH career develop award, 66-71; res assoc, Arg Nat Res Coun, 60-63; mem, Vision Res Prog Comt, Nat Eye Inst, 79-83. *Mem:* Biophys Soc; Asn Res Ophthal; Am Physiol Soc. *Res:* Ion transport in biological membranes, models; instrumentation. *Mailing Add:* Dept of Ophthal Mt Sinai Sch of Med New York NY 10029

CANDIDO, EDWARD PETER MARIO, b Noranda, Que, Mar 28, 46; m 69; c 2. BIOCHEMISTRY, MOLECULAR BIOLOGY. *Educ:* McGill Univ, BSc, 68; Univ BC, PhD(biochem), 72. *Prof Exp:* Fel, Med Res Coun Lab Molecular Biol, Cambridge, Eng, 72-73; asst prof, 73-78, ASSOC PROF BIOCHEM, UNIV BC, 78- *Concurrent Pos:* Res grants, BC Health Care Res Found, 79-81, Med Res Coun Can, 73-83 & NIH, 76-82. *Mem:* Can Biochem Soc; Am Soc Biol Chemists. *Res:* Regulation of gene activity in eukaryotic cells; structure and function of chromosomal proteins. *Mailing Add:* Dept Biochem Univ BC Vancouver BC V6T 1W5 Can

CANDLAND, CALVIN TAYLOR, physics, ballistics, see previous edition

CANDY, J(AMES) C(HARLES), b Crickhowell, Wales, Sept 27, 29; US citizen; m 54; c 1. ELECTRONIC ENGINEERING. *Educ:* Univ Wales, BSc, 51, PhD(electronics), 54. *Prof Exp:* Res engr, S Smith & Sons, Eng, 54-56; sr sci officer, Atomic Energy Res Estab, 56-59; res assoc, Dept Physics, Univ Minn, 59-60; MEM TECH STAFF, BELL TEL LABS, 60- *Mem:* Inst Elec & Electronics Engrs. *Res:* High-speed electronic circuits; television transmission. *Mailing Add:* Commun Systs Div Bell Tel Labs Inc Holmdel NJ 07733

CANE, DAVID EARL, b Sept 22, 44. BIO-ORGANIC CHEMISTRY, NATURAL PRODUCTS CHEMISTRY. *Educ:* Harvard Col, AB, 66; Harvard Univ, MA, 67, PhD(chem), 71. *Prof Exp:* NIH fel, 71; res assoc org chem, Swiss Fed Inst Technol, 71-73; from asst prof to assoc prof, 73-80, PROF CHEM, BROWN UNIV, 80- *Concurrent Pos:* vis assoc prof, Univ Chicago, 80; mem, Bio Organic Natural Prod Study Sect, NIH, 80-84; chmn, Gordon Res Conf Natural Prod, 82; res fel, Alfred P Sloan, 78-82; nat res career develop award, NIH, 78-83. *Mem:* Am Chem Soc; The Chem Soc. *Res:* Biosynthesis of natural products; stereochemistry and synthetic methods. *Mailing Add:* Dept Chem Brown Univ Providence RI 02912

CANE, LESLIE SHELDON, b Passaic, NJ, June 15, 47. ANATOMY. *Educ:* Marietta Col, BS, 69; Univ Louisville, PhD(anat), 78. *Prof Exp:* ASST PROF ANAT, MED CTR, LOYOLA UNIV, 78- *Mem:* Sigma Xi; Electron Micros Soc Am. *Res:* Biochemical and physiological changes occuring with behaviorly induced hypoxic states. *Mailing Add:* Dept Anat Loyola Univ 2160 S First Ave Maywood IL 60153

CANE, MARK A, b Brooklyn, NY, Oct 20, 44; m 68; c 2. OCEANOGRAPHY, METEOROLOGY. *Educ:* Harvard Univ, BA, 65, MS, 68; Mass Inst Technol, PhD(meteorol), 76. *Prof Exp:* Math analyst, Comput Appln Inc, 66-70; asst prof math, New Eng Col, 70-72; fel oceanog, Nat Res Coun, 75-76; analyst, Sigma Data Serv Inc, 76-78; earth scientist oceanog, Goddard Space Flight Ctr, NASA, 78-79; ASST PROF OCEANOG, MASS INST TECHNOL, 79- *Concurrent Pos:* Adj asst prof, Dept Geol Sci, Columbia Univ, 77-78. *Mem:* Am Meteorol Soc. *Res:* Dynamics of equatorial ocean circulation; air-sea interaction; use of satellite data in numerical weather prediction. *Mailing Add:* Rm 54-1724 Mass Inst of Technol Cambridge MA 02139

CANELLAKIS, EVANGELO S, b Tientsin, China, June 20, 22; nat US; m 48, 75; c 2. BIOCHEMISTRY. *Educ:* Nat Univ Athens, BS, 47; Univ Calif, PhD(biochem), 51. *Prof Exp:* Res asst, Univ Calif, 48-50, asst, 50-51; Nat Found Infantile Paralysis fel, Dept Physiol Chem, Univ Wis, 51-54; Squibb fel pharmacol, Yale Univ, 54-55, from instr to assoc prof, 55-64, PROF PHARMACOL, YALE UNIV, 64- *Concurrent Pos:* Res career develop award, USPHS, 58-63, res career prof, 63-; ed, Biochimica Biophysica Acta, 69. *Mem:* Am Soc Biol Chem; Am Asn Cancer Res; Brit Biochem Soc; Hellenic Chem Soc. *Res:* Amino acid metabolism; pyrimidine metabolism; mechanisms in nucleic acid synthesis; diacridines; relationship of biochemical sites of action of antitumor drugs to their antineoplastic properties; control and regulation of enzymatic activities. *Mailing Add:* Dept Pharmacol 123 York St New Haven CT 06511

CANELLAKIS, ZOE NAKOS, b Lowell, Mass, Sept 7, 27; m 48; c 2. BIOCHEMISTRY. *Educ:* Vassar Col, BA, 47; Univ Calif, MS, 51; Univ Wis, PhD(physiol chem), 54. *Prof Exp:* Asst biochem, 54-55, instr, 55-59, res assoc, 59-67, asst dean, Grad Sch, 72-77, SR RES ASSOC, DEPT PHARMACOL, MED SCH, YALE UNIV, 67- *Res:* Amino acid metabolism; protein and nucleic acid synthesis; polyamines. *Mailing Add:* Dept of Pharmacol Yale Univ Med Sch New Haven CT 06520

CANELLOS, GEORGE P, b Boston, Mass, Nov 1, 34; m 58; c 3. INTERNAL MEDICINE, ONCOLOGY. *Educ:* Harvard Univ, AB, 56; Columbia Univ, MD, 60; Am Bd Internal Med, dipl, 68. *Prof Exp:* Intern, Mass Gen Hosp, Boston, 60-61; clin fel, Harvard Med Sch, 61-62; asst resident, Mass Gen Hosp, Boston, 62-63; clin assoc, Nat Cancer Inst, 63-65; sr resident, Mass Gen Hosp, Boston, 65-66; res asst hemat, Royal Postgrad Med Sch London, 66-67; sr investr, Nat Cancer Inst, 67-75, asst chief med br, 73-75, clin dir, 74-75; CHIEF DIV MED, SIDNEY FARBER CANCER CTR, 75-; ASSOC PROF MED, HARVARD MED SCH, 75-; SR ASSOC MED, PETER BENT BRIGHAM HOSP, 75- *Concurrent Pos:* Asst clin prof, Dept Med, Georgetown Univ, 68-74, assoc clin prof, 74- *Mem:* Am Soc Hemat; Am Fedn Clin Res; Am Asn Cancer Res; Am Soc Clin Oncol; fel Am Col Physicians. *Res:* Cell biology as related to disorders of hemopoiesis. *Mailing Add:* Sidney Farber Cancer Ctr 44 Binney St Boston MA 02115

CANERDAY, THOMAS DONALD, invertebrate pathology, economic entomology, see previous edition

CANFIELD, CARL REX, JR, b Oregon, Ill, May 15, 23; m 52; c 3. ENGINEERING RESEARCH. *Educ:* Ill Inst Technol, BS. *Prof Exp:* Tool designer, Delta Star Elec Co, 42-43; engr, Armour Res Found, 46-51; res engr, Cent Res, Borg-Warner Corp, 51-59, chief engr prod develop, Carne Co, 58-59, dir eng, Marvel-Schebler Prod Div, 59-65, gen mgr, Simms Marvel-Schebler Ltd, London, Eng, 65-68, mgr eng, Warner Elec Brake & Clutch Co, 68-72; vpres res & develop, Schwitzer, Wallace Murray Corp, 72-77, vpres & gen mgr, 77-79, PRES, ENG COMPONENTS GROUP, WALLACE MURRAY CORP, 79- *Mem:* Instrument Soc Am; Soc Automotive Engrs. *Res:* Special instrumentation for road testing of automatic transmissions of cars, trucks and special vehicles; development of wet friction materials for automatic transmissions and fuel injection equipment for cars and trucks. *Mailing Add:* Wallace Murray Corp 9333 N Meridian St Suite 360 Indianapolis IN 46260

CANFIELD, CRAIG JENNINGS, b Pasadena, Calif, May 11, 32; m 54; c 7. CLINICAL PHARMACOLOGY, MALARIOLOGY. *Educ:* Univ Ore, BS, 55, MD, 57. *Prof Exp:* Resident med, Walter Reed Gen Hosp, 60-63; chief dept med clin res, SEATO Med Res Lab, 64-66; fel hemat, Walter Reed Gen Hosp, 68-69, asst dir malaria & chief clin pharm, Walter Reed Army Inst Res, 70-75, dir div med chem, 75-78, DIR DIV EXP THERAPEUT, WALTER REED ARMY INST RES, 78- *Concurrent Pos:* Prin investr antiparasitic notices of claimed investigational exemption for a new drugs, US Army Med Res & Develop Command, 70-; mem malarial chemother task force, WHO, 75-; prof pharmacol, Uniformed Serv Univ, 77- *Honors & Awards:* Gorgas Medal, 79. *Mem:* Fel Am Col Clin Pharmacol; fel Am Col Physicians; Am Soc Trop Med & Hyg; Am Fedn Clin Res; Am Soc Pharmacol & Exp Therapeut. *Res:* Antiparasitic drug development, especially malaria; hematology; clinical research and pharmacology; diagnosis and treatment of malaria. *Mailing Add:* Div of Exp Therapeut Walter Reed Army Inst of Res Washington DC 20012

CANFIELD, EARL RODNEY, b Atlanta, Ga, July 27, 49; m 73; c 1. COMBINATORICS. *Educ:* Brown Univ, ScB, 71; Univ Calif, San Diego, PhD(math), 75. *Prof Exp:* asst prof comput sci, 75-80, ASSOC PROF STATIST & COMPUT SCI, UNIV GA, 80- *Concurrent Pos:* Prin investr, NSF grant, 78-79; vis asst prof comput sci, Univ Calif, San Diego, 78-79. *Res:* Asymptotic and probabilistic methods in combinatorics and analysis of algorithms. *Mailing Add:* Dept of Statist & Comput Sci Univ of Ga Athens GA 30602

CANFIELD, EARLE LLOYD, b Des Moines, Iowa, Oct 24, 18; m 47; c 3. MATHEMATICS, STATISTICS. *Educ:* Drake Univ, BA, 40; Northwestern Univ, MA, 44; Iowa State Univ, PhD, 50. *Prof Exp:* Teacher high schs, Iowa, 40-46, prin, 43-46; from instr to assoc prof math, 46-58, PROF MATH, DRAKE UNIV, 58-, DEAN GRAD STUDIES, 57- *Concurrent Pos:* Consult, Des Moines Secondary Sch Math Teachers, 51-52; Des Moines consult sch math study group, Yale Univ, 60-61 & Stanford Univ, 61-62; consult, Coun Grad Schs; mem exec comt, Midwestern Asn Grad Schs, 71-75, chmn, 73-74; mem exec comt, Coun Grad Schs in US, 75-76 & 77-80. *Mem:* Math Asn Am. *Res:* Statistical analysis, experimental educational data; mathematical statistics; teaching mathematics, experimental materials. *Mailing Add:* Dept of Math Drake Univ 25th & University Ave Des Moines IA 50311

CANFIELD, JAMES HOWARD, b Elmhurst, Ill, Dec 25, 30; m 50; c 2. ORGANIC CHEMISTRY, INFORMATION SCIENCE. *Educ:* Purdue Univ, BSc, 51; Univ Calif, PhD(chem), 54. *Prof Exp:* Res chemist, Elastomers Chem Dept, Jackson Lab, E I du Pont de Nemours & Co, Inc, 56-58; res proj chemist, Whittier Res Lab, Am Potash & Chem Corp, 58-59; res mgr, Magna Prods, Inc, 59-64; propellant specialist, Foreign Tech Div, 65-67, chem specialist, 67-69, tech adv, Info Systs Div, Air Force Syst Command, 70-78, TECH ADV, INFO SERV DIV, FOREIGN TECH DIV, WRIGHT-PATTERSON AFB, 78- *Mem:* Am Chem Soc; The Chem Soc; Am Soc Info Sci. *Res:* Organic synthesis; general polymer chemistry; organoboron derivatives. *Mailing Add:* 2298 Jacavanda Dr Dayton OH 45431

CANFIELD, RICHARD CHARLES, b Detroit, Mich, Dec 9, 37; m 78; c 3. SOLAR PHYSICS, RADIATIVE TRANSFER. *Educ:* Univ Mich, BS, 59, MS, 61; Univ Colo, PhD(astrogeophysics), 68. *Prof Exp:* Vis scientist, High Altitude Observ, Nat Ctr Atmospheric Res, 68-69; fel, Neth Orgn Sci Res, 69-70; astrophysicist, Sacramento Peak Observ, 70-76; assoc res physicist, 76-80, RES PHYSICIST, UNIV CALIF, SAN DIEGO, 80- *Concurrent Pos:* Mem adv comn, High Altitude Observ Nat Ctr Atmospheric Res, 74-78; mem optical & infrared subcomt, Astron Adv Comt, NSF, 79-; mem comt solar and space physics, Nat Acad Sci, 77-80; mem, Space Sci Bd, Nat Acad Sci, 80- *Mem:* Am Astron Soc; Int Astron Union. *Res:* Radiative transfer; application and development of theory of radiative transfer line formation to solar and astrophysical problems, including chromospheric heating, solar flares and solar velocity field, and quasar emission line regions. *Mailing Add:* Ctr for Astrophysics & Space Sci Univ Calif San Diego La Jolla CA 92093

CANFIELD, ROBERT CHARLES, b Forsyth, Mont, Mar, 17, 22; m 56; c 7. CLINICAL RESTORATIVE DENTISTRY, ORAL ANATOMY. *Educ:* Univ Wash, DDS, 51, cert biomed instrumentation, 68. *Prof Exp:* Clin asst, 51-56, clin assoc, 56-67, from asst to assoc prof, 67-74, PROF DENT, UNIV WASH, 74-, ASST DEAN REGIONAL EDUC, 79- *Concurrent Pos:* Vis prof, Zahnartz Inst, Univ Vienna, Austria, 66; Danforth Assoc, 71; dir student affairs, Univ Wash, 76-79; adj prof neurosurg, Univ Wash, 81; affil, Ctr Res Oral Biol. *Mem:* Int Asn Study Pain; Pierre Fauchard Academie. *Res:* Cerebral responses to tooth pulp stimulation in laboratory animals and man; axonal degeneration patterns in cat brainstem trigeminal nucleus after tooth pulp removal; estimation of sensation magnitude elicited by tooth pulp stimulation in man. *Mailing Add:* Sch Dent SC-62 Univ Wash Seattle WA 98195

CANFIELD, ROBERT E, b New York, NY, June 4, 31; m 54; c 3. MEDICINE, ENDOCRINOLOGY. *Educ:* Lehigh Univ, BS, 52; Univ Rochester, MD, 57. *Prof Exp:* From intern to asst resident med, Presby Hosp, 57-59; res assoc, NIH, 59-62; NIH spec res fel, Enzymol Lab, Nat Ctr Sci Res France, 62-63; from asst prof to assoc prof, 63-72, PROF MED, COL PHYSICIANS & SURGEONS, COLUMBIA UNIV, 72-, DIR, CLIN RES CTR, 80- *Mem:* Am Soc Biol Chemists; Am Soc Clin Invest; Endocrine Soc; fel Royal Soc Med; Asn Am Physicians. *Res:* Protein chemistry, especially related to endocrine and metabolism disorders in man; studies of lysozyme, human chorionic gonadotropin, fibrinogen and Pagets disease of bone. *Mailing Add:* 601 W 113 St Apt 11E New York NY 10025

CANFIELD, WILLIAM H, b Oklahoma City, Okla, May 24, 20. SPEECH PATHOLOGY, AUDIOLOGY. *Educ:* Northwestern Univ, BS, 42; Columbia Univ, MA, 50, EdD(speech), 59. *Prof Exp:* Instr speech, Hofstra Col, 50-57; instr speech path, Teachers Col, Columbia Univ, 57-58, res assoc, 58-60, asst prof, 60-63; assoc prof, 63-68, PROF SPEECH PATH & AUDIOL, ADELPHI UNIV, 68- *Concurrent Pos:* Consult speech ther, St Barnabas Hosp, Bronx, NY, 59- & St Luke's Hosp, New York, 59- *Mem:* Am Speech & Hearing Asn; Speech Commun Asn; Am Cleft Palate Asn. *Res:* Laryngectomy, cleft palate, Parkinson's disease. *Mailing Add:* Dept of Speech Path & Audiol Adelphi Univ Garden City NY 11530

CANHAM, JOHN EDWARD, b Buffalo, NY, Sept 10, 24; m 47; c 7. MEDICINE, NUTRITION. *Educ:* Columbia Univ, MD, 49. *Prof Exp:* Intern, Letterman Gen Hosp, US Army, San Francisco, Calif, 49-50, resident internal med, 51-53, physician, 8th Sta Hosp, Kobe, Japan, 50-51, mem staff internal med, Us Army Hosp, Ft Belvoir, Va, 54-56, chief med serv, US Army Hosp, Wurzburg, Ger, 57-60, chief metab div, US Army Med Res & Nutrit Lab, 61-64, dir res lab, 64-66, comdr, 121st Evacuation Hosp, Ascom, Korea, 66-67, dir res lab, US Army Med Res & Nutrit Lab, 67-73, dir res lab, Letterman Army Inst Res, 73-79; DIR CLIN RES, MED PROD, CUTTER LABS, INC, 79- *Concurrent Pos:* Chief prev med, Wurzburg Med Serv Area, Ger, 57-60; clinician, Interdept Comt Nutrit for Nat Defense, Uruguay Nutrit Surv, 62; affil prof, Colo State Univ, 64-66 & 68-; US Army liaison rep, Nutrit Study Sect, NIH & Food & Nutrit Bd, Nat Acad Sci-Nat Res Coun, 64-78; US deleg, Far East Conf Nutrit, Manila, Philippines, 67; consult nutrit to Surgeon Gen, US Army, 69-79; mem food formulation res panel, US Dept Defense, 70-78. *Honors & Awards:* Joseph Goldberger Award Clin Nutrit, AMA, 71. *Mem:* Am Inst Nutrit; Am Soc Clin Nutrit; Am Col Clin Nutrit; Asn Mil Surg US; Am Bd Nutrit. *Res:* Nutrition research including applied, clinical and parenteral nutrition, nutrient requirements and nutritional biochemistry; acclimatization, metabolic and nutritional aspects of environment stress. *Mailing Add:* Med Prod Div Cutter Labs Inc 4th & Parker Sts Berkeley CA 94710

CANHAM, PETER BENNET, b Toronto, Ont, Apr 26, 41; m 64; c 2. BIOPHYSICS. *Educ:* Univ Toronto, BASc, 62; Univ Waterloo, MSc, 64; Univ Western Ont, PhD(biophys), 67. *Prof Exp:* Proj engr, Can Govt, 62-63; lectr biophys, 67-68, asst prof, 68-74, assoc prof, 74-79, PROF BIOPHYS, UNIV WESTERN ONT, 79- *Mem:* Biophys Soc; Can Physiol Soc. *Res:* Physics of the blood vessel wall, in particular at bifurcations. *Mailing Add:* Dept of Biophys Univ of Western Ont London ON N6A 5C1 Can

CANHAM, RICHARD GORDON, b Arlington, Va, Aug 30, 28; m 52; c 3. PHYSICAL CHEMISTRY. *Educ:* Col William & Mary, BS, 50; Johns Hopkins Univ, MA, 54, PhD, 59. *Prof Exp:* Chemist, Nat Bur Stand, 50-55; from asst prof to assoc prof chem, Col William & Mary, 56-62; assoc prof, Col Charleston, 62-64; assoc prof chem, 64-69, chmn dept phys sci, 71-73, PROF CHEM, OKLA BAPTIST UNIV, 69-, CHMN, DEPT PHYS SCI, 80- *Mem:* Am Chem Soc. *Res:* Electromotive force of cells; pH in aqueous and nonaqueous media. *Mailing Add:* 4002 N Aydelotte Shawnee OK 74801

CANIS, WAYNE F, b Elmira, NY, Aug 30, 39; m 68. GEOLOGY. *Educ:* Colgate Univ, AB, 61; Univ Mo-Columbia, MA, 63, PhD(geol), 67. *Prof Exp:* Explor geologist, Shell Oil Co, 67-70; assoc prof phys sci, Livingston Univ, 70-80; ASSOC PROF GEN SCI, UNIV NALA, 80- *Mem:* Soc Econ Paleontologists & Minerologists; Am Asn Petrol Geol; Brit Palaeont Asn; Paleont Soc; Geol Soc Am. *Res:* Biostratigraphy; conodonts; holothurian sclerites. *Mailing Add:* Dept Physics & Gen Sci Univ NAla Florence AL 35632

CANIZARES, CLAUDE ROGER, b Tucson, Ariz, June 14, 45. X-RAY ASTRONOMY. *Educ:* Harvard Univ, AB, 67, MS, 68, PhD(physics), 72. *Prof Exp:* Mem res staff, Ctr Space Res, 71-74, asst prof physics, 74-78, ASSOC PROF PHYSICS, MASS INST TECHNOL, 78- *Concurrent Pos:* Fel Alfred P Sloan Found. *Mem:* Int Astron Union; Am Phys Soc; Am Astron Soc. *Res:* Optical and X-ray studies of X-ray sources; design and construction of X-ray satellite experiments. *Mailing Add:* Rm 37-501 Mass Inst of Technol Cambridge MA 02139

CANIZARES, ORLANDO, b Havana, Cuba, May 27, 10; nat US; m 38; c 3. DERMATOLOGY. *Educ:* Univ Paris, MD, 35. *Prof Exp:* PROF CLIN DERMAT & SYPHILOL, GRAD MED SCH, NY UNIV, 53-; VIS DERMATOLOGIST & SYPHILOLOGIST, BELLEVUE HOSP, 54- *Concurrent Pos:* Consult, Vet Admin, NY & USPHS Hosp, Staten Island; chief dermat serv, St Vincent's Hosp. *Mem:* AAAS; Am Dermat Asn; fel Am Col Physicians. *Mailing Add:* 3 E 69th St New York NY 10021

CANN, CARMAN DENNIS, materials science, see previous edition

CANN, HOWARD M, b Chicago, Ill. HUMAN GENETICS, PEDIATRICS. *Educ:* Univ Colo, BA, 50, MD, 54. *Prof Exp:* From asst prof to assoc prof pediat, 64-77, assoc prof genetics, 74-77, PROF PEDIAT & GENETICS, SCH MED, STANFORD UNIV, 77- *Concurrent Pos:* NIH res career develop award, 63-68; John & Mary R Markle Found scholar acad med, 66; NIH spec res fel, Genetics Lab, Dept Biochem, Oxford Univ, 71-72; adv sci group on inherited blood clotting dis, WHO, 71. *Mem:* Am Soc Human Genetics; Soc Pediat Res; Am Acad Pediat; Am Fedn Clin Res. *Res:* Human gene mapping with particular emphasis on HLA region linkage relationships; prenatal diagnosis of genetic disorders. *Mailing Add:* Dept of Pediat Stanford Univ Sch of Med Stanford CA 94305

CANN, JOHN RUSWEILER, b Bethlehem, Pa, Dec 11, 20; m 46; c 3. BIOPHYSICAL CHEMISTRY, MOLECULAR BIOPHYSICS. *Educ:* Moravian Col, BS, 42; Lehigh Univ, MS, 43; Princeton Univ, MA, 45, PhD(phys chem), 46. *Prof Exp:* Res asst, Manhattan Proj, Princeton Univ, 43-46; res asst, SAM Lab, Carbon & Carbide Chem Corp, 46; res assoc & instr, Cornell Univ, 47; from asst prof to assoc prof, 51-63, PROF BIOPHYS, UNIV COLO HEALTH SCI CTR, DENVER, 63- *Concurrent Pos:* Res fel, Calif Inst Technol, 47-48, sr res fel, 48-50; NIH res grants biophys, Univ Colo Med Ctr, Denver, 51-; USPH spec res fel, Carlsberg Found Biol Inst, Denmark, 61-62; abstractor, Excerpta Medica, 52-; mem planning group biophys mat, Nat Inst Gen Med Students, 65, ad hoc mem biophys & biophys chem B study sect, 67, mem sect A, 76. mem adv panel molecular biol, Div Biol & Med Sci, NSF, 67-70; mem, Molecular & Cellular Biophysics Study Sect, NIH, 81. *Mem:* Fel AAAS; Am Chem Soc; Am Asn Immunol; Am Asn Biol Chemists; Biophys Soc. *Res:* Separation, purification and characterization of proteins; electrophoresis; ultracentrifugation; interaction of proteins with each other and with small molecules; theory of electrophoresis and ultracentrifugation of reacting macromolecules; CD of proteins and peptides. *Mailing Add:* Dept Biophys & Genetics Univ Colo Health Sci Ctr Denver CO 80262

CANN, MALCOLM CALVIN, b Yarmouth, NS, Feb 9, 24; m 49. ORGANIC CHEMISTRY, BIOCHEMISTRY. *Educ:* Sir George Williams Col, BSc, 53; McGill Univ, MSc, 55, PhD(biochem), 58. *Prof Exp:* Chemist, Food & Drug Directorate, Can Dept Nat Health & Welfare, 57-66; instr biochem sci, Eastern Ont Inst Technol, 66-67; MASTER SCH TECHNOL, ALGONQUIN COL, 67- *Mem:* Can Biochem Soc; Can Inst Chem. *Res:* Bioassay of corticotropin by means of isolated adrenal tissue, adrenal ascorbic acid and plasma corticosteroids; absorption and toxicity of pesticides in rats of various age groups. *Mailing Add:* 2150 Berwick Ave Ottawa ON K2C 0Y3 Can

CANN, MICHAEL CHARLES, b Schenectady, NY, May 6, 47. ORGANIC CHEMISTRY. *Educ:* Marist Col, BA, 69; State Univ NY Stony Brook, MA, 72, PhD(org chem), 73. *Prof Exp:* NSF fel & assoc instr org chem, Univ Utah, 73-74; lectr org chem, UNiv Colo, Denver, 74-75; asst prof, 75-78, ASSOC PROF ORG CHEM, UNIV SCRANTON, 78- *Mem:* Am Chem Soc. *Res:* The synthesis of aromatic, heterocyclic cations; mechanism of the decomposition 3, 6-Dihydro-1,2-Oxazenes; mechanism of the formation of the Grignard reagent. *Mailing Add:* Dept of Chem Univ of Scranton Scranton PA 18510

CANNELL, DAVID SKIPWITH, b Washington, DC, Jan 29, 43; m 67; c 1. THERMAL PHYSICS. *Educ:* Mass Inst Technol, BS, 65, PhD(physics), 70. *Prof Exp:* Asst prof, 70-76, assoc prof, 76-79, PROF PHYSICS, UNIV CALIF, SANTA BARBARA, 79- *Concurrent Pos:* Hertz fel, Hertz Found, 67-70; Sloan fel, Alfred P Sloan Found,73-75; Guggenheim fel, Guggenheim Found, 78; consult, Dow Chem, 82- *Res:* Condensed matter physics, including critical phenomena, laser light scattering and the behavior of systems far from equilibrium. *Mailing Add:* Dept Physics Univ Calif Santa Barbara CA 93106

CANNELL, GLEN H, b Abraham, Utah, Aug 5, 19; m 42, 66; c 6. SOIL PHYSICS. *Educ:* Utah State Univ, BS, 48, MS, 50; Wash State Univ, PhD(agron, soil physics), 55. *Prof Exp:* Soil scientist, Agr Res Serv, USDA, NDak, 54-56; soil physicist, 56-74, PROF SOIL PHYSICS, UNIV CALIF, RIVERSIDE, 74- *Concurrent Pos:* Assoc prog dir, Div Pre-Col Educ Sci, NSF, Washington, DC, 69-71. *Mem:* Am Soc Agron; Soil Sci Soc Am; Am Soc Hort Sci. *Res:* Soil physics, with emphasis on soil-water-plant relations, soil water movement, soil physical properties and instrumentation for measurement of soil water. *Mailing Add:* Dept Soil Physics Univ Calif PO Box 112 Riverside CA 92502

CANNEY, FRANK COGSWELL, b Ipswich, Mass, Oct 8, 20; m 44; c 1. GEOLOGY. *Educ:* Mass Inst Technol, SB, 42, PhD(geol), 52. *Prof Exp:* Asst geol, Mass Inst Technol, 49-51; geologist, 51-70, CHIEF EXPLOR RES BR, US GEOL SURV, 70- *Mem:* Soc Econ Geol; Am Inst Mining, Metall & Petrol Engrs; Geol Soc Am; Am Geochem Soc; Am Chem Soc. *Res:* Geochemical prospecting for mineral deposits; geochemistry of minor elements in the weathering cycle; remote sensing applied to exploration for mineral deposits. *Mailing Add:* US Geol Surv Fed Ctr Mail Stop 955 Box 25046 Denver CO 80225

CANNING, T(HOMAS) F, b Boston, Mass, May 26, 27; m 51, 79; c 2. CHEMICAL ENGINEERING. *Educ:* Yale Univ, BE, 50. *Prof Exp:* Prod engr, Merck & Co, Inc, 51-56; develop engr, Nat Res Corp, 56-58; sr res engr, Am Potash & Chem Corp, 58-62, proj engr, 62-65, head crystallization sect, 65-67, head chem eng sect, 67-70, proj mgr, 70-73, mgr plant tech servs, 73-77, mgr eng servs, 78-79, MGR PROCESS DEVELOP, KERR-MCGEE CHEM CORP, 80- *Mem:* Am Inst Chem Engrs; Am Chem Soc. *Res:* Process improvement and development, design leading to boric acid, salt cake and soda ash processes; process development in liquid-liquid extraction, crystallization, evaporation, heat transfer and solar evaporation. *Mailing Add:* 548 E Dana Ave Ridgecrest CA 93555

CANNON, ALBERT, b Charleston, SC, Jan 15, 21; m 43; c 4. CLINICAL PATHOLOGY. *Educ:* Col Charleston, BS, 41; Med Col SC, MD, 49. *Prof Exp:* Intern surg, George Washington Univ Hosp, 49-50; mem surg staff, Charleston Naval Hosp, 50; resident path, US Naval Med Sch, 51-55, instr, 55-57, chief anat path, 57-58; asst prof path, Med Sch, Georgetown Univ, 58-59; asst prof, 59-70, PROF CLIN PATH, MED UNIV SC, 70- *Concurrent Pos:* Lectr lab med, US Naval Hosp, Charleston, SC; med dir, ARC Blood Ctr. *Mem:* AMA; Asn Clin Scientists. *Res:* Anatomic pathology of central nervous system; hematology; histochemistry; clinical chemistry; blood banking. *Mailing Add:* Dept of Clin Path Med Univ of SC Charleston SC 29403

CANNON, DONALD CHARLES, b Independence, Mo, Nov 14, 34; m 58; c 4. CLINICAL PATHOLOGY, IMMUNOLOGY. *Educ:* Harvard Univ, BA, 56; Univ Chicago, MD, 60, PhD(path), 64. *Prof Exp:* Intern path, Med Ctr, Univ Calif, Los Angeles, 60-61; instr, Univ Chicago, 63-64; instr, Univ NC, 64-65; asst prof, State Univ NY Upstate Med Ctr & asst attend pathologist, State Univ Hosp, 65-68, chief diag reagents sect, Div Biol Stand, NIH, 68-69, asst sect chief clin chem serv, Clin Path Dept, 69-70; asst dir, Bio-Sci Labs, Van Nuys, Calif, 70-71, dir, 71-74; chmn dept, 74-80, PROF PATH & LAB MED, MED SCH, UNIV TEX, HOUSTON, 74- *Mem:* AAAS; Acad Clin Lab Physicians & Scientists; AMA; Col Am Pathologists; Am Soc Clin Pathologists. *Res:* Clinical chemistry; blood banking; health care management systems. *Mailing Add:* Dept of Path & Lab Med PO Box 20708 Houston TX 77025

CANNON, DONALD JOSEPH, b Boston, Mass, Sept 28, 40; m 68; c 3. BIOCHEMISTRY. *Educ:* Harvard Univ, AB, 62; Boston Univ, MA, 65, PhD(med sci, biochem), 68. *Prof Exp:* Staff scientist, Boston Biomed Res Inst, 72-77; ASST PROF BIOCHEM, UNIV ARK MED SCI, 78-; RES CHEMIST, VET ADMIN HOSP, LITTLE ROCK, 78- *Concurrent Pos:* Res fel biochem, Univ Hawaii, 68-69; fel in aging, Boston Biomed Res Inst, 70-72. *Mem:* Am Chem Soc; Geront Soc; Sigma Xi. *Res:* Biochemistry and metabolism of connective tissue proteins; enzymology; gerontology. *Mailing Add:* Vet Admin Med Ctr 300 E Roosevelt Rd Little Rock AR 72206

CANNON, GLENN ALBERT, b Easton, Md, Apr 11, 40; m 62; c 2. PHYSICAL OCEANOGRAPHY. *Educ:* Drexel Inst, BS, 63; Johns Hopkins Univ, MA, 65, PhD(oceanog), 69. *Prof Exp:* Res asst prof oceanog, Univ Wash, 69-70, res oceangr, Pac Marine Environ Lab, Nat Oceanic & Atmospheric Agency, 70-73; prog dir, NSF, 73-75; RES OCEANOGR, PAC MARINE ENVIRON LAB, NAT OCEANIC & ATMOSPHERIC ADMIN, UNIV WASH, 75-, AFFIL ASSOC PROF OCEANOG, 79- *Concurrent Pos:* Mem adv panel oceanog, NSF, 72-73, 75-76. *Mem:* Am Geophys Union. *Res:* Physical oceanography; estuarine and coastal circulation. *Mailing Add:* Pac Marine Environ Lab NOAA Dept of Oceanog Univ of Wash Seattle WA 98105

CANNON, HELEN LEIGHTON, b Wilkinsburg, Pa, Apr 30, 11; m 35; c 1. GEOCHEMISTRY. *Educ:* Cornell Univ, AB, 32; Univ Pittsburgh, MS, 34. *Prof Exp:* Asst geol, Northwestern Univ, 32-33 & Univ Okla, 34-35; geologist, Oil Geol, Gulf Oil Co, 35-36; geologist minor metal commodity admin, 42-46, geologist geochem prospecting methods, 46-62, GEOLOGIST EXPLOR RES, US GEOL SURV, 62- *Concurrent Pos:* Chmn subcomt geochem environ in health & dis, Nat Res Coun, 69-73. *Mem:* Fel AAAS; fel Geol Soc Am; Asn Explor Geochemists; Int Asn Geochem & Cosmochem. *Res:* Botanical methods of prospecting; trace element distribution in soils and plants as related to geology, health and disease. *Mailing Add:* US Geol Surv Rte 3 Box 77B Santa Fe NM 87501

CANNON, HOWARD S(UCKLING), b Chicago, Ill, Sept 23, 26; m 47; c 5. METALLURGICAL ENGINEERING, PHYSICAL METALLURGY. *Educ:* Carnegie Inst Technol, BS, 50; Rensselaer Polytech Inst, MS, 51, PhD(phys metall), 54. *Prof Exp:* Res engr, Linde Air Prod, 53-55; supvr phys metall, Amco Res, Inc, 55-58; dir phys metall lab, Cent Res & Eng, Continental Can Co, 58-63, dir res inorg mat, Corp Res & Develop, 63-69 & new technol, Metall Div, 70-73, asst to vpres res & eng, 73-76, gen mgr technol & econ, 76-78; DIR RES, RASSELSTEIN (STEEL), W GER, 78- *Mem:* Am Soc Metals; Am Inst Mining, Metall & Petrol Engrs. *Res:* Liquid phase sintering; cooper alloy development; metallic and ceramic coating development; casting research; aluminum and tinplate container technology; steel and aluminum production economics; tinplate and automotive steel research. *Mailing Add:* 5470 Andernach Kolner Strasse 4 West Germany

CANNON, JERRY WAYNE, b Lambert, Miss, June 24, 42; m 63. BIOCHEMISTRY. *Educ:* Univ Miss, BSc, 64; Drexel Univ, PhD(chem), 69. *Prof Exp:* Instr biochem, Sch Med, Univ Miss, 68-70; asst res prof, 70-78, ASSOC PROF CHEM, MISS COL, 78- *Mem:* Am Chem Soc. *Res:* Pathway of steroid biosynthesis; synthesis and biological testing of chemical analogs of digitalis. *Mailing Add:* Dept of Chem Miss Col Clinton MS 39056

CANNON, JOHN BURNS, b Spartanburg, SC, Mar 5, 48. BIOCHEMISTRY, BIOINORGANIC CHEMISTRY. *Educ:* Duke Univ, BS, 70; Princeton Univ, PhD(chem), 74. *Prof Exp:* Res chemist, Dept Chem, Univ Calif, San Diego, 74-76; instr chem, Northern Ill Univ, 77-79; ASST PROF CHEM, CLEVELAND STATE UNIV, 79- *Mem:* Am Chem Soc; Sigma Xi; Am Asn Clin Chem. *Res:* Kinetics and model studies of heme proteins; interaction of hemes and hemeproteins with liposomes; animal model studies of porphyrias. *Mailing Add:* Asst prof chem Northern Ill Univ Cleveland OH 44115

CANNON, JOHN FRANCIS, b Monroe, Utah, Dec 14, 40; m 62; c 8. PHYSICAL CHEMISTRY, INORGANIC CHEMISTRY. *Educ:* Brigham Young Univ, BS, 65, PhD(phys chem), 69. *Prof Exp:* Fel, Georgetown Univ, 69-70; assoc dir high pressure data ctr, 70-72, assoc dir ctr high pressure res, 72-78, ASST PROF CHEM, BRIGHAM YOUNG UNIV, 78- *Mem:* Am Chem Soc; Sigma Xi. *Res:* High pressure, high temperature synthesis of inorganic compounds, especially intermetallics and compounds containing lanthanide elements; x-ray crystallography. *Mailing Add:* Dept of Chem Brigham Young Univ Provo UT 84601

CANNON, JOHN N(ELSON), b Salt Lake City, Utah, July 27, 27; m 51; c 6. MECHANICAL ENGINEERING. *Educ:* Univ Utah, BSME, 52, MS, 55; Stanford Univ, PhD, 65. *Prof Exp:* Aeronaut engr, N Am Aviation, 55-57; from asst prof to assoc prof, 57-68, chmn dept, 62-80, PROF MECH ENG, BRIGHAM YOUNG UNIV, 68- *Concurrent Pos:* Lectr, Univ Southern Calif, 56. *Mem:* Am Inst Aeronaut & Astronaut; Am Soc Mech Engrs; Am Soc Eng Educ. *Res:* Fluid mechanics; thermodynamics; heat transfer and combustion. *Mailing Add:* Dept of Mech Eng Sci Brigham Young Univ Provo UT 84602

CANNON, JOHN ROZIER, b McAlester, Okla, Feb 3, 38; m 57; c 3. MATHEMATICS. *Educ:* Lamar State Col, BA, 58; Rice Univ, MA, 60, PhD(math), 62. *Prof Exp:* Assoc mathematician, Brookhaven Nat Lab, 62-64; NATO fel, 64-65; mem fac math, Purdue Univ, 65-66, prof, 68-69; assoc prof, Univ Minn, Minneapolis, 66-68; prof math, Univ Tex, Austin, 69-81; PROF MATH, WASH STATE UNIV, 81- *Concurrent Pos:* Consult, Mobil Oil Corp, 67-69 & Gen Motors Res Labs, 77-; vis prof, Tex Tech Univ, 73-74, Colo State Univ, 79, Univ Firenze, 79 & Han-Meitner Inst, Berlin, 79. *Mem:* Am Math Soc; Soc Indust & Appl Math; Sigma Xi; Math Asn Am. *Res:* Ordinary and partial differential equations; numerical analysis. *Mailing Add:* Dept Math Wash State Univ Pullman WA 99163

CANNON, JOSEPH G, b Decatur, Ill, Sept 30, 26; m 60; c 4. MEDICINAL CHEMISTRY. *Educ:* Univ Ill, BS, 51, MS, 53, PhD(pharmaceut chem), 57. *Prof Exp:* Asst prof pharmaceut, Univ Wis, 56-60, assoc prof pharmaceut chem, 60-62; assoc prof, 62-65, PROF MED CHEM, UNIV IOWA, 65-, ASST DEAN GRAD AFFAIRS, COL PHARM, 76- *Mem:* Am Chem Soc; fel Am Inst Chemists; fel Acad Pharmaceut Sci. *Res:* Organic synthesis; structure-activity relationships; nitrogen heterocycles. *Mailing Add:* Col of Pharmacy Univ of Iowa Iowa City IA 52242

CANNON, LAWRENCE ORSON, b Logan, Utah, June 11, 35; m 59; c 3. MATHEMATICS. *Educ:* Utah State Univ, BS, 58; Univ Wis, MS, 59; Univ Utah, PhD(math), 65. *Prof Exp:* From instr to asst prof math, Utah State Univ, 61-63; instr, Univ Utah, 63-64; from asst prof to assoc prof, 65-77, PROF MATH, UTAH STATE UNIV, 78- HEAD DEPT, 69- *Concurrent Pos:* Vis prof, Rutgers Univ, 68-69. *Mem:* Am Math Soc. *Res:* Upper semicontinuous decompositions of 3-manifolds; wild and tame surfaces. *Mailing Add:* Dept of Math Utah State Univ Logan UT 84322

CANNON, M(OODY) DALE, b Wheeler, Tex, Dec 11, 21; m 47; c 4. AGRICULTURAL ENGINEERING. *Educ:* Okla State Univ, BS, 50; Univ Mo, MS, 53. *Prof Exp:* Exten agr engr, Kans State Col, 53-56; asst prof agr eng & asst agr eng, univ agr exp sta, 56-73, ASSOC PROF AGR ENG & ASSOC AGR ENGR, COTTON RES CTR, UNIV ARIZ, 73- *Mem:* Am Soc Agr Engrs; Coun Agr Sci & Technol. *Res:* Mechanization of cotton production research. *Mailing Add:* Univ of Ariz Cotton Res Ctr 4201 E Broadway Phoenix AZ 85040

CANNON, MARVIN SAMUEL, b Toledo, Ohio, Feb 10, 40; m 73. HUMAN ANATOMY, CELL BIOLOGY. *Educ:* Univ Toledo, BS, 60, MS, 65; Ohio State Univ, PhD(human anat), 69. *Prof Exp:* Asst prof biol sci, Capital Univ, 71-73; asst prof anat, Univ Tex Med Br Galveston, 73-76; ASSOC PROF ANAT, TEX A&M UNIV, 76- *Concurrent Pos:* Bremer Found Fund fel, Ohio State Univ, 71-73; Am Heart Asn grant, 80-81. *Mem:* AAAS; Am Asn Anat; Pan Am Asn Anat; Am Inst Biol Sci. *Res:* Microvasculature metabolism. *Mailing Add:* Dept of Human Anat Olin E League Res Ctr College Station TX 77843

CANNON, ORSON SILVER, b Salt Lake City, Utah, Nov 21, 08; m 34; c 5. PHYTOPATHOLOGY. *Educ:* Utah State Col, BS, 35, MS, 37; Cornell Univ, PhD(plant path), 42. *Prof Exp:* Asst plant path, Utah State Agr Col, 33-37; asst exten plant pathologist, Pa State Col, 42-43; head dept, Crop Res Lab, H J Heinz Co, Ohio, 43-48; plant pathologist, Bur Plant Indust, Soils & Agr Eng, USDA, 48-57, head dept bot & plant path, 57-74, EMER PROF BOT & PLANT PATH, UTAH STATE UNIV, 74- *Mem:* AAAS; Am Phytopath Soc; Am Soc Hort Sci; Am Soc Plant Physiol. *Res:* Bacterial wilt of alfalfa; vegetable diseases; mosaic resistance in cucumbers; anthracnose resistance in tomatoes; curly top and wilt resistance in tomatoes. *Mailing Add:* 1407 E 17th N Logan UT 84321

CANNON, PETER, b Chatham, Eng, Apr 20, 32; m 55; c 4. PHYSICAL CHEMISTRY. *Educ:* Univ London, BSc, 52, PhD(chem), 55. *Prof Exp:* Mem staff, Overseas Chem Dept, Procter & Gamble Co, 55-56; phys chemist, Gen Elec Res Lab, 56-65, mgr opers anal, Gen Elec Info Systs, 65-67; mgr sensors & mat, Gen Elec Mfg & Process Automation Bus Div, 67-69, mgr sensors & microelectronics, 69-72, strategy develop automation & machine tools bus, 72-73; dir new prod develop, 73-75, vpres, Bus Develop, Util & Indust Opers Div, 75-76; STAFF VPRES RES & VPRES, SCI CTR, ROCKWELL INT CORP, 76- *Concurrent Pos:* Adj prof, Polytech Inst Brooklyn, 64-69; lectr, Grad Sch Bus Admin, Univ Va, 65-67. *Mem:* Am Chem Soc; Am Phys Soc; Royal Soc Chem. *Res:* Administrative product development programs and business strategy planning; physics and chemistry of surfaces and the solid state; catalysis; super-pressure reactions, especially diamonds; operations analysis and research, especially mathematical programming. *Mailing Add:* Rockwell Int Sci Ctr 1049 Camino Dos Rios Thousand Oaks CA 91360

CANNON, PHILIP JAN, b Washington, DC, Nov 15, 40; m 61; c 2. GEOMORPHOLOGY. *Educ:* Univ Okla, BS, 65, MS, 67; Univ Ariz, PhD(geol), 73. *Prof Exp:* Geologist, US Geol Surv, 67-72; res scientist geol, Tex Bur Econ Geol, 72-74; asst prof geol, Univ Alaska, 74-81; CHIEF GEOLOGIST, PLANETARY DATA, FAIRBANKS, ALASKA, 81- *Concurrent Pos:* Mem Sithylemenkat meteorite impact crater discovery group, Alaska, 77. *Mem:* Am Soc Photogram; Sigma Xi; Nat Stereoscopic Asn; Am Soc Petrol Geologists. *Res:* Geomorphic investigations of Alaska and geologic mapping of coastal areas using side-looking airborne radar imagery; regional geologic explorations using radar and landsat imageries of North America; author of sixteen publications in various journals. *Mailing Add:* Planetary Data PO Box 60675 Fairbanks AK 99706

CANNON, RAYMOND JOSEPH, JR, b Hartford, Conn. MATHEMATICS, AIR POLLUTION. *Educ:* Col Holy Cross, AB, 62; Tulane Univ, PhD(math), 67. *Prof Exp:* Asst prof math, Vanderbilt Univ, 67-69; asst prof, Univ NC, Chapel Hill, 69-74; assoc prof math, Stetson Univ, 74-80; ASSOC PROF MATH, BAYLOR UNIV, 80- *Concurrent Pos:* Off Naval Res fel, Univ Mich, 68-69; vis assoc prof, Baylor Univ, 78-79. *Mem:* Am Math Soc; Math Asn Am. *Res:* Quasiconformal mappings; functions of a complex variable; topological analysis. *Mailing Add:* Dept Math Baylor Univ Waco TX 76798

CANNON, ROBERT H, JR, b Cleveland, Ohio, Oct 6, 23; m 45; c 7. ENGINEERING, DYNAMICS. *Educ:* Univ Rochester, BS, 44; Mass Inst Technol, ScD(mech eng), 50. *Prof Exp:* Chief scientist, US Air Force, 66-68; prof aeronaut & astronaut & chmn dept, Stanford Univ, 59-70, dir, Guid & Control Lab, 59-70; US asst secy transp, US Dept Transp, 70-74; prof eng & chmn div eng & appl sci, Calif Inst Technol, 74-80; PROF ENG, STANFORD UNIV, 80- *Concurrent Pos:* Chmn, Electronics Res Ctr Adv Group, NASA, 68-70 & Res Adv Subcomt Guid, Control & Navig, 68-70; chmn, Assembly Eng, Nat Res Coun, 74-75 & Energy Eng Bd, 75- & mem gov bd, 78- *Honors & Awards:* Secy Award Outstanding Achievement, Dept Transp, 74. *Mem:* Nat Acad Eng; fel Am Inst Aeronaut & Astronaut. *Res:* Dynamics and automatic control; inertial guidance and automatic flight control of air, water and spacecraft; hydrofoil boats; wave actuated pumps. *Mailing Add:* Eng Dept Stanford Univ Stanford CA 94305

CANNON, ROBERT LAURENCE, b Kinston, NC, Sept 16, 39; m 69. IMAGE PROCESSING. *Educ:* Univ NC, BS, 61, PhD(comput sci), 73; Univ Wis, Madison, MS, 63. *Prof Exp:* Instr, Philander Smith Col, Ark, 65-66; instr, Wilmington Col, 67-68, asst prof math, 68-69; asst prof, 73-77, ASSOC

PROF COMPUT SCI, UNIV SC, 77-, CHMN, DEPT, 80- *Mem:* Asn Comput Mach; Inst Elec & Electronics Engrs. *Res:* Image processing techniques are applied in petrography; thin sections of oil field rocks are analyzed for shape, density and other properties of pores and surrounding minerals. *Mailing Add:* Dept Comput Sci Univ SC Columbia SC 29208

CANNON, ROBERT YOUNG, b Boise, Idaho, Sept 11, 17; m 48; c 3. DAIRY SCIENCE. *Educ:* Iowa State Univ, BS, 39; Ohio State Univ, MS, 40; Univ Wis, PhD(dairy indust), 49. *Prof Exp:* PROF FOOD SCI, AUBURN UNIV, 48- *Mem:* Am Dairy Sci Asn; Inst Food Technol; Int Asn Milk, Food & Environ Sanit. *Res:* Dairy foods processing; quality control of foods; food plant sanitation. *Mailing Add:* Dept of Animal & Dairy Sci Auburn Univ Auburn AL 36830

CANNON, THEODORE WILES, cloud physics, see previous edition

CANNON, WALTON WAYNE, b Ark, Jan 8, 18; m 48; c 3. ELECTRICAL ENGINEERING. *Educ:* Univ Ill, BSEE, 48, MSEE, 49, PhD(elec eng), 55. *Prof Exp:* Asst microwave magnetrons, Univ Ill, 46-49, res assoc microwave devices, 49-51; from assoc prof to prof elec eng, Univ Ark, 51-61; electronics scientist, Deco Electronics, Va, 61-64; prof elec eng, Va Polytech Inst, 64-69; chmn dept, 69-80, PROF ELEC ENG, WVA UNIV, 69- *Concurrent Pos:* NSF fel, 59-60; consult, Ark Educ TV Asn & Transvideo Corp. *Mem:* Am Soc Eng Educ; Inst Elec & Electronics Engrs; Nat Soc Prof Engrs. *Res:* Radio-frequency mass spectrometry; satellite communication; semiconductor electronics; electronic circuits and systems; communication systems; general electrical engineering. *Mailing Add:* Dept of Elec Eng Eng Scis Bldg WVa Univ Evansdale Campus Morgantown WV 26506

CANNON, WILLIAM CHARLES, b San Diego, Calif, Oct 5, 26; m 60; c 1. PHYSICS, AEROSOL SCIENCE. *Educ:* Wash State Univ, BS, 50; Univ Calif, Los Angeles, MA, 63, PhD(physics), 71. *Prof Exp:* Res engr flight test instrumentation guided missile, NAm Aviation, Downey, 53-55; design engr preliminary anal nuclear reactor res, Atomic Int Div, NAm Aviation Co, Canoga Park, 55-57, sr res eng mat sci, Douglas Aircraft Co, 57-60; res autonetics, Anaheim, 60-62; res asst low temperature physics res, Univ Calif, Los Angeles, 61-71; SR RES SCIENTIST AEROSOL PHYSICS, BIOL DEPT, BATTELLE PAC NORTHWEST LABS, RICHLAND, 72- *Concurrent Pos:* Physicist & consult thermionics res, Jet Propulsion Lab, Pasadena, 69-71. *Mem:* AAAS; Sigma Xi. *Res:* Aerosol science research in instrumentation and measurement methods and in relation of aerosol properties to respiratory deposition and biological effects of aerosol inhalation. *Mailing Add:* 2177 Crestview Ave Richland WA 99352

CANNON, WILLIAM FRANCIS, III, b Troy, NY, Aug 11, 40; m 69. GEOLOGY. *Educ:* Syracuse Univ, AB, 62, PhD(geol), 68; Miami Univ, MS, 64. *Prof Exp:* GEOLOGIST, US GEOL SURV, 67- *Mem:* Geol Asn Can; Soc Mining Engrs; AAAS; Geol Soc Am. *Res:* Mineral resources and geology of Precambrian rocks in the Lake Superior area. *Mailing Add:* US Geol Surv Nat Ctr Stop 954 Reston VA 22092

CANNON, WILLIAM NATHANIEL, b Atlanta, Ga, Oct 15, 27; m 51; c 4. ORGANIC CHEMISTRY. *Educ:* NGa Col, BS, 48; Univ Ga, MS, 50. *Prof Exp:* Chemist, Rohm & Haas Co, Redstone Arsenal, Ala, 50-52; org chemist, 52-57, appln res chemist, 57-66, process chemist, 66-67; sr org chemist, 67-74, RES SCIENTIST, ELI LILLY & CO, 74- *Mem:* Am Chem Soc; Soc Indust Microbiol (secy, 66-67). *Res:* Synthesis of organic compounds for testing and evaluation as agricultural chemicals. *Mailing Add:* 814 Spy Run Dr Cumberland IN 46229

CANNON, WILLIAM NELSON, JR, b Wilmington, Del, Jan 7, 32; m 62; c 3. ENTOMOLOGY. *Educ:* Univ Del, BS, 53, MS, 60; Ohio State Univ, PhD(entom), 63. *Prof Exp:* Sanitarian, Del State Bd Health, 56-58; res assoc entom, Ore State Univ, 63-65; RES ENTOMOLOGIST, FORESTRY SCI LAB, NORTHEASTERN FOREST EXP STA, US FOREST SERV, 65- *Mem:* Entom Soc Am. *Res:* Insect-host plant relationships; insect biology; cost-effective integrated pest management strategies. *Mailing Add:* Forestry Sci Lab USDA NE Forest Exp Sta Delaware OH 43015

CANNONITO, FRANK BENJAMIN, b New York, NY, Oct 19, 26; m 53, 77; c 2. ALGEBRA, MATHEMATICAL LOGIC. *Educ:* Columbia Univ, BS, 59, MA, 61; Adelphi Univ, PhD(math), 65. *Prof Exp:* Res mathematician, Res Dept, Grumman Aircraft Eng Corp, 60-62; staff mathematician, Tech Anal Off, Hughes Aircraft Co, 62-64, mgr info sci progs, 64-66; from asst prof to assoc prof math, 66-77, vchmn dept, 69-72, PROF MATH, UNIV CALIF, IRVINE, 77- *Concurrent Pos:* Sr staff mathematician, Hughes Aircraft Co, 66-69; prin investr, Air Force Off Sci Res grant, 66-73; Army Res Off Conf & NSF Conf grants, 69; assoc ed, Info Sci, 68- *Mem:* Am Math Soc; Asn Symbolic Logic. *Res:* Fine degrees of solvability of the word problem and related decision problems in group theory; subgroups of finitely presented groups. *Mailing Add:* Dept of Math Univ of Calif Irvine CA 92717

CANO, FRANCIS ROBERT, b New York, NY, Apr 25, 44; m 69; c 3. MICROBIOLOGY, BIOCHEMISTRY. *Educ:* St John's Univ, NY, BS, 65, MS, 67; Pa State Univ, PhD(microbiol), 70. *Prof Exp:* Res assoc, Inst Microbiol, Rutgers Univ, 71-72; res bacteriologist vaccine res, 72-75, group leader vaccine res, 75-76, mgr biol prod & process improv vaccine develop, 76-79, mgr biol prod & develop, 79-80, MGR BIOL, LEDERLE LABS DIV, AM CYANAMID CO, 80- *Concurrent Pos:* Instr, Rockland Community Col, 74-76; consult, Fisher Diagnostics, 77. *Mem:* Am Soc Microbiol; AAAS. *Mailing Add:* Lederle Labs Pearl River NY 10965

CANO, GILBERT LUCERO, b Mesilla, NMex, Jan 7, 32; m 52; c 4. EXPERIMENTAL ATOMIC PHYSICS. *Educ:* NMex State Univ, BS, 54, MS, 60, PhD(physics), 64. *Prof Exp:* MEM RES STAFF, SANDIA CORP, 64- *Mem:* Am Phys Soc. *Res:* Charge spectroscopy of laser-induced blow-off; laser-induced fusion; atomic stopping power of thin metallic films; ion-atom interactions; fast reactor safety. *Mailing Add:* Sandia Labs Div 4426 Albuquerque NM 87115

CANOLTY, NANCY LEMMON, b Washington, Ind, Mar 1, 42; m 68; c 2. NUTRITION. *Educ:* Purdue Univ, BS, 63, MS, 68; Univ Calif, Berkeley, PhD(nutrit), 74. *Prof Exp:* asst prof nutrit, Univ Calif, Davis, 73-80; ASSOC PROF FOODS & NUTRIT, UNIV GA, 80- *Mem:* Inst Food Technologists; Sigma Xi; Am Inst Nutrit; AAAS; Am Oil Chemists. *Res:* Influence of nutrition upon human lactation, infant nutrition; protein and energy utilization. *Mailing Add:* Dept Foods & Nutrit Univ Ga Athens GA 30602

CANON, ROY FRANK, b Eagle Pass, Tex, Sept 10, 42; div. MATERIALS SCIENCE. *Educ:* Univ Tex, BES, 64; Univ Tex, Austin, PhD(mech eng), 68. *Prof Exp:* Engr & scientist, Tracor, Inc, Tex, 65-67; asst metallurgist, Argonne Nat Lab, 68-69; engr/scientist, Tracor, Inc, 69-72; tech dir, Turbine Support Div, 72-76, VPRES CHROMALLOY COMPRESSOR TECHNOL, CHROMALLOY AM CORP, 76- *Mem:* Am Soc Metals; Metall Soc. *Res:* Mechanical properties of ceramic nuclear fuel materials; composite materials; development of new repair procedures and protective coatings for gas turbine components; new abradable seals for gas turbine applications. *Mailing Add:* Turbine Support 4430 Director Dr San Antonio TX 78220

CANONICO, DOMENIC ANDREW, b Chicago, Ill, Jan 18, 30; m 55; c 5. METALLURGY, MATERIAL SCIENCE. *Educ:* Mich Technol Univ, BS, 51; Lehigh Univ, MS, 61, PhD(metall eng), 63. *Prof Exp:* Metallurgist metal joining, Ill Inst Technol Res, 53-58; instr metall, Lehigh Univ, 58-62; engr metal joining, Homer Res Lab, Bethlehem Steel Corp, 62-64; supvr process control, Aerospace Components Div, Atlas Chem, 64-65; metallurgist metal joining, Nuclear Div, Oak Ridge Nat Lab, Union Carbide Corp, 65-74, group leader pressure vessel technol, 74-81; DIR, METALL & MAT LAB, COMBUSTION ENG, INC, 81- *Concurrent Pos:* Consult, Nuclear Regulatory Comn, 73- & Adv Comt on Reactor Safeguards, 75-; mem, Pressure Vessel Res Comt. *Honors & Awards:* Rene D Wasserman Award, Am Welding Soc, 78; Lincoln Gold Medal. *Mem:* Am Soc Mech Engrs; Am Welding Soc; fel Am Soc Metals; Sigma Xi; Am Soc Testing & Mat. *Res:* Fracture toughness and weldability of materials for application in energy-producing systems; impact properties; fracture mechanics; creep; fatigue; solidification mechanics; weldment discontinuities; brazing; materials design; ferrous metallurgy. *Mailing Add:* Combustion Eng Inc 911 W Main St Chattanooga TN 37402

CANONICO, PETER GUY, b Tunis, Tunisia, June 12, 42; US citizen; m 69; c 2. CELL BIOLOGY, TOXICOLOGY. *Educ:* Bucknell Univ, BS, 64; Univ SC, MS, 66; Rutgers Univ, PhD(physiol), 69. *Prof Exp:* res scientist cell physiol, 69-80, CHIEF, DEPT ANTIVIRAL STUDIES, US ARMY MED RES INST INFECTIOUS DIS, 80- *Concurrent Pos:* Assoc prof, Hood Col, 76- *Honors & Awards:* Res & Develop Medal, Dept Army, 75. *Mem:* Am Soc Cell Biol; Am Physiol Soc; AAAS; Am Soc Microbiol; Soc Exp Biol & Med. *Res:* Effects of infections and inflammation on cellular functions and physiology and morphology of subcellular organelles; studies of host cellular defense mechanisms to microbial infection; antiviral drug development; toxicology and mechanisms of action of antiviral compounds. *Mailing Add:* Chief Dept Antiviral Studies USAMRIID, Virology Div Frederick MD 21701

CANRIGHT, JAMES EDWARD, b Delaware, Ohio, Mar 1, 20; m 43; c 4. PALYNOLOGY, PALEOBOTANY. *Educ:* Miami Univ, AB, 42; Harvard Univ, AM, 47, PhD(biol), 49. *Prof Exp:* Teaching fel biol, Harvard Univ, 46-49; from instr to prof bot, Ind Univ, 49-63; chmn dept, 64-72, PROF BOT, ARIZ STATE UNIV, 64- *Concurrent Pos:* Am Philos Soc res grant, 53-54; NSF travel grant, Int Bot Cong, Paris, 54, Edinburgh, 64 & Leningrad, 75; res grants, 54-; consult, Mene Grande Oil Co, Venezuela, 58; Guggenheim fel, Indonesia & Malaya, 60-61; vis scientist US-China coop sci prog, Nat Taiwan Univ, 71. *Mem:* Fel AAAS; Int Orgn Paleobot; Bot Soc Am; Am Inst Biol Sci; Int Comn Palynol. *Res:* Tertiary and Cretaceous palynology; paleobotany of the Paleozoic. *Mailing Add:* Dept of Bot & Microbiol Ariz State Univ Tempe AZ 85281

CANTAROW, WALTER DANIEL, b Hartford, Conn, Apr 1, 47. IMMUNOCHEMISTRY, CANCER IMMUNOLOGY. *Educ:* Yale Univ, BS, 69; Tufts Univ, PhD(biochem), 75. *Prof Exp:* Fel, Univ Wis, 75-78; Res assoc, Tufts Univ, 78-80, consult, Tufts Cancer Res Ctr, 80-81; SR RES ASSOC, MALLORY INST PATH, 80- *Concurrent Pos:* Lectr, Tufts Univ, 78-81. *Mem:* AAAS; Reticuloendothelial Soc; Int Soc Oncodevelop Biol & Med. *Res:* Development and evaluation of assays for tumor markers; immunologic means to aid in its destruction. *Mailing Add:* Mallory Inst Path 784 Mass Ave Boston MA 02118

CANTE, CHARLES JOHN, b Brooklyn, NY, Oct 31, 41; m 73. PHYSICAL CHEMISTRY, SURFACE CHEMISTRY. *Educ:* City Col New York, BS, 63, MA, 65, PhD(phys chem), 67; Iona Col, MBA, 72. *Prof Exp:* Lectr chem, City Col New York, 64-67; phys chemist, Phys Res Lab, Edgewood Arsenal, Dept Army, 67-68, res & develop coordr, 68-69; sr chemist, Tech Ctr, 69-71, group leader,, 71-73, personnel assoc, 73-75, mgr new technol res, NY, 75, field res mgr, Res Dept, Pet Foods Div, 76-80, MGR, DIV TECH RES, GEN FOODS CORP, 80- *Concurrent Pos:* E I du Pont de Nemours teaching award, 66-67. *Mem:* AAAS; Am Chem Soc; NY Acad Sci. *Res:* Colloid chemistry; food chemistry. *Mailing Add:* Res Dept Gen Foods Corp 250 N St White Plains NY 10625

CANTELMO, ANGELA, b Oct 2, 48; US citizen. BIOLOGY, MARINE ECOLOGY. *Educ:* Northeastern Univ, BA, 71; City Univ New York, PhD(biol), 77. *Prof Exp:* Fel biol, Univ WFal, 76-77; ASST PROF BIOL, RAMAPO COL NJ, 77- *Concurrent Pos:* Theodore Roosevelt Mem fel, Am Mus Natural Hist, 75. *Mem:* AAAS; Am Soc Zoologists; Estuarine Res Fedn; Sigma Xi. *Res:* Physiological ecology of invertebrates; hydromineral balance in decapod crustaceans; molt physiology of crustaceans; effects of toxic substances on crustacean physiology. *Mailing Add:* Sch of Theoret & Appl Sci Ramapo Col of NJ Mahwah NJ 07430

CANTELMO, FRANK RONALD, b Newark, NJ, Jan 10, 45; m 70. ECOLOGY. *Educ:* Fairleigh Dickinson Univ, BS, 70; City Univ New York, PhD(biol), 78. *Prof Exp:* Aquatic biologist, US Dept Interior, Environ Protection Agency, 66-69; environ scientist, Barnstead Inc, 70-71; lectr biol, City Univ New York, 71-76; ECOLOGIST, HUDSON RIVER SURV SERV GROUP, TEX INSTRUMENTS INC, 78- *Concurrent Pos:* Res assoc, Univ Univ WFla, 76-77. *Mem:* Am Soc Limnol & Oceanog; Int Asn Meiobenthologists; Am Soc Zoologists; Sigma Xi. *Res:* Ecology of estuarine and marine meiofauna; vertical and horizontal zonation patterns of estuarine nematodes; effects of biocides on the structure and function of meiofauna communities established in experimental systems. *Mailing Add:* Hudson River Ecol Surv Serv Group Tex Instruments Inc Buchanan NY 10511

CANTELO, WILLIAM WESLEY, b Medford, Mass, Sept 11, 26; m 58; c 3. ENTOMOLOGY. *Educ:* Boston Univ, AB, 48; Univ Mass, MS, 50, PhD(entom), 52. *Prof Exp:* Asst entomologist, Bartlett Tree Res Labs, 52-54, assoc entomologist, 54-55; staff entomologist, US Naval Forces, Marianas, 56-61; entom adv, US Opers Mission, Ministry Agr, Thailand, 61-66; RES ENTOMOLOGIST, USDA, 66- *Mem:* AAAS; Entom Soc Am. *Res:* Flies infesting commercial mushroom crops; economic entomology; insect population dynamics and ecology. *Mailing Add:* USDA BARC-E Bldg 470 Beltsville MD 20705

CANTER, LARRY WAYNE, b Nashville, Tenn, May 25, 39; m 62; c 2. SANITARY ENGINEERING, PUBLIC HEALTH. *Educ:* Vanderbilt Univ, BE, 61; Univ Ill, MS, 62; Univ Tex, PhD(civil eng), 67. *Prof Exp:* Sanit engr, USPHS, 62-65; asst prof civil eng, Tulane Univ, 67-69; from asst prof to assoc prof, 69-76, PROF CIVIL ENG & DIR, UNIV OKLA, 76- *Res:* Water and wastewater treatment. *Mailing Add:* Dept of Civil Eng Univ of Okla Norman OK 73069

CANTER, NATHAN H, b Philadelphia, Pa, Nov 17, 42; m 64; c 1. POLYMER PHYSICS. *Educ:* Temple Univ, AB, 63; Princeton Univ, MS, 65, PhD(chem), 66. *Prof Exp:* RES ASSOC, CORP RES LABS, EXXON RES & ENG CO, 66- *Mem:* AAAS; Am Chem Soc; Am Phys Soc. *Res:* Statistical and solid state physics; physical chemistry; polymer physics and chemistry. *Mailing Add:* Exxon Res & Eng Corp Res Lab PO Box 45 Linden NJ 07036

CANTERBURY, S(AMUEL) L(UTHER), JR, b Bristow, Okla, Sept 14, 10; m 31; c 3. ELECTRICAL ENGINEERING. *Educ:* Marquette Univ, BEE, 34; Agr & Mech Col Tex, MS, 37, PhD(elec eng), 45. *Prof Exp:* Instr eng, Kilgore Col, 35-37, head eng dept, 37-45, dean eng, 45-76; RETIRED. *Concurrent Pos:* Coordr civil aeronaut authority war training sch, Navy V-5, 39-44; prof, Marquette Univ, 48; Piper Found prof, 64; vis prof, Tex A&M Univ & Grad Fac, 66. *Mem:* Am Soc Eng Educ; Inst Elec & Electronics Engrs. *Res:* Prediction of cold front storms by means of electronics. *Mailing Add:* 1219 E North St Kilgore TX 75662

CANTERNA, RONALD WILLIAM, b Freeport, Pa, May 3, 46. GLOBULAR CLUSTERS, PHOTOMETRY. *Educ:* Colgate Univ, BA, 68; Univ Wash, Seattle, PhD(astron), 76; Univ Wyo, BEd, 82. *Prof Exp:* Instr astron, Univ Wash, 76-77; asst prof, La State Univ, 77-79; ASST PROF ASTRON & PHYSICS, UNIV WYO, 79- *Concurrent Pos:* Spec asst to pres res & develop, Univ Wash, Seattle, 76-77; res fel, Italian Nat Coun Res, 80. *Mem:* Sigma Xi; Asn Astron Educrs; Astron Soc Pac. *Res:* Properties of globular clusters of the Milky Way galaxy and their role in the chemical evolution and history of galaxy formation; design, development and use of the Washington photometric system for stellar photometry. *Mailing Add:* Dept Physics & Astron Univ Wyo Laramie WY 82071

CANTILLI, EDMUND JOSEPH, b Yonkers, NY, Feb 12, 27; m 48; c 3. TRANSPORTATION ENGINEERING. *Educ:* Columbia Univ, BA, 54, BS, 55; Yale Univ, MS, 57; Polytech Inst Brooklyn, PhD(transp), 72. *Prof Exp:* Sr traffic engr, New York Port Authority, 55-61, terminals engr, 61-63, proj planner & engr safety res & studies, 63-65, supvry engr traffic control, 65-67, supvry engr traffic safety, 67-69; res assoc transp eng, 69-72, assoc prof, 72-77, PROF TRANSP PLANNING & ENG, POLYTECH INST NEW YORK, 77- *Concurrent Pos:* VPres transp eng, Urbitran Assoc Inc, 73-81; pres & chmn bd transp safety, Inst Safety Transp, 77-; vpres forensic eng, Tech & Med Forensic Consults, Inc, 81-; pres & chmn bd consult eng, Adeboh Assocs, Inc, 81-; pres transp & environ safety, Edmund J Cantilli, 81- *Mem:* Fel Inst Transp Engrs; fel Am Soc Civil Engrs; Am Inst Cert Planners; Am Planning Asn; Am Soc Safety Engrs. *Res:* Transportation safety; traffic safety; transportation system safety; environmental impact assessment, including air, water, noise, social and planning; pedestrian safety. *Mailing Add:* Polytechnic Inst NY 333 Jay Brooklyn NY 11201

CANTIN, GILLES, b Montreal, Que, Apr 29, 27; US citizen; m 52; c 1. ENGINEERING SCIENCE, MATHEMATICS. *Educ:* Polytech Sch, Montreal, BSc, 50; Stanford Univ, MSc, 60; Univ Calif, Berkeley, PhD(eng sci), 68. *Prof Exp:* Prof math & physics, Tech Sch, Rimouski, 50-52; prof physics, Royal Mil Col, 52-54; eprof eng, Univ Col, Ethiopia, 54-59; from asst prof to assoc prof mech eng, 60-71, PROF MECH ENG, NAVAL POSTGRAD SCH, 71- *Concurrent Pos:* Consult, Nat Comt for Ethiopia, Int Geophys Year, 57-58; vis prof, Univ Technol Compiegne, France, 76- *Mem:* Soc Naval Architects & Marine Engrs; Am Soc Mech Engrs; Am Soc Eng Educ. *Res:* Stress analysis; structural mechanics; computer methods; development of finite element methods. *Mailing Add:* 17 via Ladera Monterey CA 93940

CANTIN, MARC, b Que, Aug 7, 33; m 59; c 1. MEDICINE. *Educ:* Laval Univ, MD, 58; Univ Montreal, PhD, 62. *Prof Exp:* Asst, Inst Exp Med & Surg, Univ Montreal, 58-62; instr path, Sch Med, Univ Chicago, 64-65; from asst prof to prof path, Univ Montreal, 65-80; DIR, LAB PATHOBIOL, CLIN RES INST MONTREAL, 80- *Concurrent Pos:* USPHS fel, 62-63 & grant, 64-66; fel path, Sch Med, Univ Chicago, 62-64; Chicago Heart Asn fel, 63-65 & grant, 64-66; Ill Heart Asn fel, 63-65. *Mem:* Am Heart Asn; Can Med Asn. *Res:* Relationships between juxtaglomerular apparatus and adrenal cortex in experimental situations; atrial specific granules structure and function; ultrastructural cytochemistry; ultrastructural immunocytochemistry; ultrastructural radioautography. *Mailing Add:* Clin Res Inst Montreal 110 Pine Ave W Montreal PQ H2W 1R7 Can

CANTINO, EDWARD CHARLES, b Berkeley, Calif, Oct 31, 21; m 45; c 2. MYCOLOGY. *Educ:* Univ Calif, AB, 43, PhD(plant physiol), 48. *Prof Exp:* Sr lab technician, Div Plant Nutrit, Univ Calif, 43-44; chemist, Am Cyanamid Co, Calif, 44-45; res chemist, Aerojet Eng Corp, 45; from asst prof to assoc prof bot, Univ Pa, 48-56; PROF BOT, MICH STATE UNIV, 56- *Concurrent Pos:* Guggenheim fel, 50-51; res collabr, Brookhaven Nat Lab, 55; vis prof, Univ Geneva, 60; consult, NIH, 63-66 & NSF, 63-; ed-in-chief, Experimental Mycol, 75- *Honors & Awards:* Distinguished Fac Award, Mich State Univ, 64. *Mem:* Am Soc Microbiol; Am Acad Microbiol; Bot Soc Am; Am Soc Cell Biol; Mycol Soc Am. *Res:* Physiological mycology; physiology of fungi; biology of aquatic phycomycetes; cell differentiation. *Mailing Add:* Dept of Bot & Plant Path Mich State Univ East Lansing MI 48824

CANTLEY, LEWIS CLAYTON, b Charleston, WVa, Feb 20, 49. MEMBRANE TRANSPORT, CELL DIFFERENTIATION. *Educ:* WVa Wesleyan Col, BS, 71; Cornell Univ, PhD(phys chem), 75. *Prof Exp:* Fel, 75-78, asst prof, 78-81, ASSOC PROF BIOCHEM, FAC ARTS & SCI, HARVARD UNIV, 81- *Concurrent Pos:* Instr & scholar, Dreyfus Found, 81; estab investr, Am Heart Asn, 81. *Mem:* Am Heart Asn; Am Soc Biol Chemists; Biophys Soc; Med Found. *Res:* Structures, mechanisms and regulation of proteins which transport ions across eucaryotic cell membranes; investigation of affects of cation fluxes on cell differentiation. *Mailing Add:* Biol Lab Harvard Univ 16 Divinity Ave Cambridge MA 02138

CANTLIFFE, DANIEL JAMES, b New York, NY, Oct 31, 43; m 65; c 4. PLANT PHYSIOLOGY, VEGETABLE CROPS. *Educ:* Delaware Valley Col, BS, 65; Purdue Univ, MS, 67, PhD(plant physiol), 71. *Prof Exp:* Res asst, Purdue Univ, 65-69; res assoc, Cornell Univ, 69-70; res scientist, Hort Res Inst Ont, 70-74; from asst prof to assoc prof, 74-81, PROF SEED PHYSIOL, UNIV FLA, 81- *Concurrent Pos:* Vis prof, Univ Hawaii, 79-80. *Mem:* Am Soc Hort Sci; Am Soc Plant Physiologists; Am Soc Agron; Crop Sci Soc Am; Sigma Xi. *Res:* Basic studies and applications with seeds as plant growth units, including the physiology of fruit development, seed formation, seed germination, seed dormancy, and seed vigor. *Mailing Add:* Dept of Veg Crops Univ of Fla Gainesville FL 32611

CANTLON, JOHN EDWARD, b Sparks, Nev, Oct 6, 21; m 44; c 4. ECOLOGY. *Educ:* Univ Nev, BS, 47; Rutgers Univ, PhD(bot), 50. *Prof Exp:* Asst prof bot, George Washington Univ, 50-52, assoc prof, 52-53; sr ecologist, Phys Res Lab, Boston Univ, 53-54; assoc prof bot, 54-58, prof, 58-69, provost, 69-75, VPRES RES & GRAD STUD, MICH STATE UNIV, 75- *Concurrent Pos:* Mem adv panel environ biol, NSF, 61-64, prog dir environ biol, 65-66, mem adv comt, div environ sci, 66-69, adv comt instnl relations, 70-74; gov bd, Am Inst Biol Sci, 63-66; adv comt health physics, Oak Ridge Nat Lab, 66-69, adv coun, 71-75; exec comt, Div Biol & Agr, Nat Res Coun, 67-71, coun natural resources, 73-81, chmn environ studies bd, 78-81; chmn sci adv bd, Environ Protection Agency, 78-81. *Mem:* AAAS; Ecol Soc Am (secy, 58-63, vpres, 67-68, pres, 68-69); Am Inst Sci; Bot Soc Am; Am Soc Naturalists. *Res:* Pattern in communities; physiological ecology; Alaskan tundra vegetation; research and academic administration. *Mailing Add:* Admin Bldg Mich State Univ East Lansing MI 48824

CANTOR, CHARLES ROBERT, b Brooklyn, NY, Aug 26. BIOPHYSICAL CHEMISTRY. *Educ:* Columbia Col, AB, 63; Univ Calif, Berkeley, PhD(chem), 66. *Prof Exp:* From asst prof to prof chem, 66-81, PROF & CHMN HUMAN GENETICS & DEVELOP, COL PHYSICIANS & SURGEONS, COLUMBIA UNIV, 81- *Concurrent Pos:* Alfred P Sloan fel, 69-71; NIH study sect, 71-75; Guggenheim fel, 73-74; Sherman Fairchild Distinguished vis scholar, Calif Inst Technol, 75-76; mem cellular & molecular basis dis rev comt, Nat Inst Gen Med Sci, 77-81; bd trustees, Cold Spring Harbor Labs, 78- *Honors & Awards:* Eastman Kodak Award, 65; Fresenius Award Chem, 72; Eli Lilly Award, 78. *Mem:* Harvey Soc; Am Soc Biol Chem; Biophys Soc; fel Acad Arts & Sci. *Res:* Optical properties and conformation of nucleic acids and proteins; structure of the ribosome; mechanism of protein synthesis; affinity labelling; structure of chromatin; photochemical crosslinking; macromolecular assembly. *Mailing Add:* Dept Human Genetics & Develop Med Sch Columbia Univ New York NY 10032

CANTOR, DAVID GEOFFREY, b London, Eng, Apr 12, 35; US citizen; m 58; c 2. MATHEMATICS, COMPUTER SCIENCES. *Educ:* Calif Inst Technol, BS, 56; Univ Calif, Los Angeles, PhD(math), 60. *Prof Exp:* Asst prof math, Univ Wash, 62-64; PROF MATH & COMPUT SCI, UNIV CALIF, LOS ANGELES, 64- *Concurrent Pos:* Sloan Found fel, 67; prin investr, NSF, 68- *Mem:* Am Math Soc; Math Asn Am; Soc Indust & Appl Math; Asn Comput Mach; Inst Elec & Electronics Engrs. *Res:* Number theory; combinatorics; algorithms. *Mailing Add:* Dept of Math Univ of Calif Los Angeles CA 90024

CANTOR, DAVID MILTON, b Grand Rapids, Mich, June 30, 52. ANALYTICAL CHEMISTRY. *Educ:* Mich State Univ, BS, 73; Univ Ill, MS, 75, PhD(chem), 77. *Prof Exp:* CHEMIST ANAL, PHILLIPS PETROL CO, 77- *Mem:* Am Chem Soc; Soc Appl Spectros. *Res:* Spectroscopy, in particular nuclear magnetic resonance; application to analysis of polymers, hydrocarbon mixtures including petroleum fractions and alternate fuels; chemical structures; computer control and optimization of analytical instrumentation. *Mailing Add:* Phillips Petrol Co Res & Develop Bartlesville OK 74004

CANTOR, ENA D, b Montreal, Que, Mar 1, 20; m. MICROBIOLOGY, IMMUNOLOGY. *Educ:* McGill Univ, BA, 40, BSc, 42, PhD(microbiol, immunol), 68; Harvard Univ, MA, 46. *Prof Exp:* Technician, Royal Victoria Hosp, Can, 42-44; res technician, RI Hosp, Providence, 55-57; res technician, Mass Mem Hosp, 58-59; chief technician, Jewish Gen Hosp, Can, 60-62; techician, McGill Univ, 62-63; mem staff clin virol, Royal Victoria Hosp &

McGill Univ, 68-69; chief sanit virol sect, 69-71, chief gen bact sect, 71-79, SPEC BACT ANAEROBES, MINISTRY SOCIAL AFFAIRS, MONTREAL, 79- Mem: Am Soc Microbiol; Can Pub Health Asn; Can Fedn Biol Sci; Can Soc Microbiol; Can Soc Immunol. Res: Enteroviruses; serum proteins; population studies of norms; enterococci, especially chemical and immunological studies; lysogeny of Lancefield group B streptococci. Mailing Add: Div Spec Bacteriol Ministry Social Affairs Labs Ste-Anne-De-Bellevue PQ H7B 1B7 Can

CANTOR, KENNETH P, b Mt Vernon, NY, 1941. EPIDEMIOLOGY. Educ: Oberlin Col, BA, 62; Univ Calif, Berkeley, PhD(biophys), 69; Harvard Sch Pub Health, MPH, 73. Prof Exp: Res adminr health effects, US Environ Protection Agency, 73-75; EPIDEMIOLOGIST CANCER EPIDEMIOL, NAT CANCER INST, 75- Mem: Soc Epidemiol Res; NY Acad Sci; AAAS; Soc Risk Analysis. Res: Environmental cancer epidemiology. Mailing Add: Nat Cancer Inst 3C07 Landow Bldg Bethesda MD 20205

CANTOR, MARVIN H, b Brooklyn, NY, Nov 17, 35. CELL PHYSIOLOGY. Educ: Boston Univ, AB, 57; Mass Inst Technol, SM, 59; Univ Calif, Los Angeles, PhD(zool), 64. Prof Exp: Fel zool, Syst-Ecol Prog, Marine Biol Lab, Woods Hole, 64-65; from asst prof to assoc prof biol, 65-71, PROF BIOL, CALIF STATE UNIV, NORTHRIDGE, 71- Mem: AAAS; Soc Protozool; Am Soc Zool; NY Acad Sci. Res: Cell growth and metabolism; cell synchrony; regulation of metabolism. Mailing Add: Dept of Biol Calif State Univ Northridge CA 91330

CANTOR, STANLEY, b Brooklyn, NY, Sept 23, 29; m 50; c 3. PHYSICAL CHEMISTRY. Educ: Tulane Univ, BS, 51, MS, 53, PhD(chem), 55. Prof Exp: MEM RES STAFF, OAK RIDGE NAT LAB, 55- Concurrent Pos: Exchange fel, Atomic Energy Res Estab, Eng, 63-64. Mem: AAAS; Am Chem Soc; Sigma Xi. Res: Properties of energy storage materials; thermal analysis; nuclear reactor chemistry; chemistry of energy systems; energy information analysis. Mailing Add: PO Box X Oak Ridge Nat Lab Oak Ridge TN 37830

CANTOW, MANFRED JOSEF RICHARD, b Oberhausen, Ger, Mar 21, 26; m 61. PHYSICAL CHEMISTRY, POLYMER PHYSICS. Educ: Univ Mainz, BS, 52, MS, 55, PhD(phys chem), 59. Prof Exp: Sr res chemist, Calif Res Corp, 60-66; Chevron Res Co, 66-67; asst dir, Airco Cent Res Labs, 67-71; ADV CHEMIST, IBM CORP, 71- Concurrent Pos: Lectr exten, Univ Calif, Berkeley, 62- Mem: Am Chem Soc. Res: Characterization of polymers; polymer fractionation; physical properties of polymers; polymerization and modification of vinyl polymers. Mailing Add: IBM Corp Monterey & Cottle Rds San Jose CA 95193

CANTRALL, IRVING JAMES, b Springfield, Ill, Oct 6, 09; m 32; c 2. ENTOMOLOGY. Educ: Univ Mich, AB, 35, PhD(entom), 40. Prof Exp: Asst Orthoptera, mus zool, Univ Mich, 34-37; tech asst, 37-42; jr aquatic biologist, Tenn Valley Authority, 42, asst aquatic biologist, 42-43; asst prof biol, Univ Fla, 46-49; from asst prof to prof zool, 49-77, EMER PROF ZOOL, UNIV MICH, ANN ARBOR, 78-, EMER CUR INSECTS, MUS ZOOL, 78- Concurrent Pos: Mem Univ Mich exped, South & Southwest US, 35, Mex, 41, 53, 59, Guatemala, 56, Cent Am, 61; cur, Edwin S George Reserve, Mus Zool, 49-59, cur insects, 59-77. Mem: AAAS; Soc Syst Zool; Ecol Soc Am; Soc Study Evolution; Entom Soc Am. Res: Taxonomy of new world Acridoidea. Mailing Add: Mus of Zool Univ of Mich Ann Arbor MI 48109

CANTRALL, CYRUS D, III, b Bartlesville, Okla, Oct 4, 40; m 72. PHYSICS, THEORETICAL CHEMISTRY. Educ: Harvard Univ, AB, 62; Princeton Univ, MA, 64, PhD(physics), 68. Prof Exp: From asst prof to assoc prof physics, Swarthmore Col, 67-74; staff mem, Laser Res & Technol Div, Los Alamos Sci Lab, 73-76, assoc group leader, Theoret Chem & Molecular Physics, 76-78, staff mem, Theoret Div Off, 78-79; PROF PHYSICS & DIR, CTR QUANTUM ELECTRONICS & APPL, UNIV TEX,, DALLAS, 80- Concurrent Pos: Vis res fel, Princeton Univ, 70-71; adj prof physics, Univ NMex, 76-; assoc prof, Univ Paris, 80; consult, Los Alamos Nat Lab, 79- Mem: Fel Am Phys Soc; Am Asn Physics Teachers; Am Chem Soc; fel Optical Soc Am; Inst Elec & Electronics Engrs. Res: Lasers and their applications in physics, chemistry and industrial processing; laser isotope separation; multiphoton excitation of polyatomic molecules; nonlinear optics and pulse propagation; molecular spectroscopy; quantum optics; quantum theory of measurement. Mailing Add: Univ Tex-Dallas Dept Physics PO Box 688 Richardson TX 75080

CANTRELL, ELROY TAYLOR, b Mobile, Ala, May 10, 43; m 67; c 2. PHARMACOLOGY, CANCER. Educ: Ark State Univ, BS, 65; Univ Tenn, MS, 68; Baylor Col Med, PhD(pharmacol), 71. Prof Exp: Fel pharmacol, Baylor Col Med, 71-72; res assoc med genetics, M D Anderson Hosp, 72-73; asst prof, 73-76, chmn dept, 73-80, ASSOC PROF PHARMACOL, TEX COL OSTEOP MED, 76- Concurrent Pos: Consult, NIH, Environ Protection Agency & Becton Dickinson Res Ctr, 75-79. Mem: Am Soc Pharmacol & Therapeut; NY Acad Sci; Am Thoracic Soc. Res: The metabolism of chemical carcinogens by human tissues. Mailing Add: Dept of Pharmacol Tex Col Osteop Ft Worth TX 76107

CANTRELL, GRADY LEON, b Louisville, Ky, Feb 18, 36; m 54; c 1. MATHEMATICS. Educ: Univ Louisville, BA, 64; Univ Ky, MS, 66, PhD(math), 68. Prof Exp: Asst prof, 68-71, ASSOC PROF MATH, MURRAY STATE UNIV, 71- Mem: Math Asn Am. Res: Analytic function theory; continuous functions. Mailing Add: Dept of Math Murray State Univ Murray KY 42071

CANTRELL, JAMES CECIL, b Palmersville, Tenn, Sept 14, 31; m 54; c 3. TOPOLOGY. Educ: Bethel Col, BS, 53; Univ Miss, MS, 55; Univ Tenn, PhD(math), 61. Prof Exp: Instr, Dresden High Sch, 53-54; instr math, Univ Tenn, 61-62; from asst prof to assoc prof, 62-70, PROF MATH, UNIV GA, 70-, HEAD DEPT, 74- Concurrent Pos: Mem, Inst Advan Study, 66-67; Alfred P Sloan res fel, 66-68. Mem: Am Math Soc. Res: Topological embeddings of manifolds. Mailing Add: Dept Math Univ Ga Athens GA 30601

CANTRELL, JAMES R, b Norman, Okla, Aug 8, 22; m 53; c 5. SURGERY. Educ: Johns Hopkins Univ, AB, 44, MD, 46. Prof Exp: Intern, Johns Hopkins Univ Hosp, 46-47, asst resident surgeon, 47-48 & 50-52, from resident surgeon to surgeon, 52-60, dir tumor clin, 58-60, asst surg, Sch Med, Johns Hopkins Univ, 47-48 & 50-52, from instr to assoc prof, 52-60; prof surg, Univ Wash, 60-75; DIR SURG EDUC, SWED HOSP MED CTR, SEATTLE, 75- Concurrent Pos: Consult, Vet Admin Hosp, 60- Mem: Asn Thoracic Surg; Am Col Surgeons; AMA; Soc Univ Surgeons; Am Surg Asn. Res: Neoplastic and cardiopulmonary disease. Mailing Add: 1221 Madison Seattle WA 98104

CANTRELL, JOHN LEONARD, b Billings, Mont, Feb 7, 39; m 62; c 4. IMMUNOLOGY, IMMUNOGENETICS. Educ: Mont State Univ, BS, 67, MS, 69; Univ Calif, Los Angeles, PhD(immunol), 72. Prof Exp: Fel, Jackson Lab, Maine, 72-74; asst mem, Okla Med Res Found, 74-76; sr staff elect cancer, Nat Inst Allergy & Infectious Dis, NIH, 76-81; CHIEF IMMUNOL, RIBI IMMUNOCHEM RES, MONT, 81- Concurrent Pos: Asst prof, Med Sch, Univ Okla, 74-76; mem clin staff, Univ Hosp & Clin, Univ Okla & Children's Mem Hosp, Oklahoma City, 74-76. Mem: Transplantation Soc; Am Asn Cancer Res; Am Asn Immunologists; Sigma Xi; Am Col Radiol. Res: Cancer immunology; immunotherapy; immunogenetics of transplantation immunology. Mailing Add: Ribi Immunochem Res Inc PO Box 1409 Hamilton MT 59840

CANTRELL, JOSEPH SIRES, b Parker, Kans, July 31, 32; m 58; c 3. PHYSICAL CHEMISTRY, SOLAR PHYSICS. Educ: Kans State Teachers Col, AB, 54; Kans State Univ, MS, 57, PhD(phys chem), 61. Prof Exp: Res chemist, Procter & Gamble Co, 61-66; mem fac chem, 65-69, ASSOC PROF CHEM, MIAMI UNIV, 69- Mem: Electrochem Soc; Am Chem Soc; Am Crystallog Asn; Int Solar Energy Soc. Res: Chemical kinetics; x-ray crystal structure; mesomorphic structure; thin film and interfacial structure; electron diffraction; chemical applications of solar energy; photoelectrochemical processes; electrochemistry. Mailing Add: Dept of Chem Miami Univ Oxford OH 45056

CANTRELL, RONALD P, b Shamrock, Tex, May 1, 43; m 68; c 2. GENETICS. Educ: Tex Tech Univ, BS, 66; Purdue Univ, MS, 69, PhD(genetics), 70. Prof Exp: Plant breeder maize, Cargill Inc, 71-75; PROF GENETICS, PURDUE UNIV, 75- Mem: Am Soc Agr; Am Genetic Soc; Can Genetics Asn. Res: Sorghum genetics. Mailing Add: Dept of Agron Purdue Univ West Lafayette IN 47907

CANTRELL, THOMAS SAMUEL, b Spartanburg, SC, Aug 29, 38. ORGANIC CHEMISTRY. Educ: Univ SC, BS, 58, MS, 59; Ohio State Univ, PhD(chem), 64. Prof Exp: NSF fel org chem, Columbia Univ, 64-65; asst prof chem, Rice Univ, 65-70; res chemist, NIH, 70-71; asst prof chem, 71-72, ASSOC PROF CHEM, AM UNIV, 72- Mem: Am Chem Soc; The Chem Soc. Res: Organic photochemistry; nonbenzenoid aromatic compounds. Mailing Add: Dept of Chem Am Univ Washington DC 20016

CANTRELL, WILLIAM ALLEN, b Everton, Ark, Nov 6, 20; m 45; c 2. PSYCHIATRY. Educ: McMurry Col, BS, 40; Univ Tex Med Br Galveston, MD, 43; Am Bd Psychiat & Neurol, cert psychiat, 51. Prof Exp: Intern, US Naval Hosp, Corona, Calif, 43-44; resident neuropsychiat, Univ Tex Med Br Hosps, 49-50, asst prof, 50-51; pvt pract, Houston, 51-63; clin prof, 63-68, PROF PSYCHIAT, BAYLOR COL MED, 68- Concurrent Pos: Asst prof neuropsychiat, Univ Tex Med Br, 51-54; clin asst prof psychiat, Baylor Col Med, 51-63; from asst chief to sr attend, Psychiat Serv, Methodist Hosp, 52-; clin assoc prof psychiat, Univ Tex Grad Sch Biomed Sci Houston, 59-; attend staff, Psychiat Serv, Ben Taub Gen Hosp, 63-; asst examr, Am Bd Psychiat & Neurol, 64-; consult psychiat, Social Security Admin, Bur Hearings & Appeals, 64- & Vet Admin Hosp, Houston, 67-; adj prof, Inst Relig, Houston, 68- Mem: AAAS; Cent Neuropsychiat Asn (pres, 76-77); fel Am Psychiat Asn; Am Col Psychiat. Res: Undergraduate medical education, especially methodology and evaluation; doctor-patient relationship as a factor in the quality of health care delivery. Mailing Add: Dept of Psychiat Baylor Col of Med Houston TX 77030

CANTRELL, WILLIAM FLETCHER, b Young Harris, Ga, Oct 29, 16; m 47; c 2. CHEMOTHERAPY. Educ: Univ Ga, BS, 38, MS, 39; Univ Chicago, PhD, 49. Prof Exp: Instr zool, Univ Ga, 39-40; asst parasitol & pharmacol, Univ Chicago, 41-46; from asst prof to prof pharmacol, Univ Louisville, 49-59; mem staff, Lab Parasite Chemother, NIH, 59-62; assoc prof, 63-78, PROF PHARMACOL, UNIV TENN, MEMPHIS, 78- Mem: Am Soc Pharmacol; Am Soc Parasitol; Am Soc Trop Med & Hyg; Soc Exp Biol & Med. Res: Transmission of malaria by mosquitoes; chemotherapy of malaria; mode of action of chemotherapeutic drugs; antigenic variation in trypanosomes; drug resistance. Mailing Add: 1682 Estate Dr Memphis TN 38117

CANTRILL, JAMES EGBERT, b Frankfort, Ky, Sept 2, 33; m 56; c 6. ORGANIC CHEMISTRY. Educ: Univ Notre Dame, BS, 55; Mass Inst Technol, PhD(org chem), 59. Prof Exp: Res chemist, Eastman Kodak Co, NY, 59-60; instr chem, St Thomas Moore Col, 60-61, asst prof & chmn dept, 61-63; develop chemist, Plastics Dept, Gen Elec Co, 63-67; mgr res & advan develop, 67-69; mgr res lab, Foster Grant Co, Inc, 69-74, bus develop mgr, 74-77; BUS DEVELOP MGR PETROCHEM, AM HOECHST CO, 77- Mem: Am Chem Soc. Res: Polymer synthesis; reaction kinetics and mechanisms. Mailing Add: Am Hoechst Co Rte 202-206 N Somerville NJ 08876

CANTU, ANTONIO ARNOLDO, b Laredo, Tex, Jan 5, 41. FORENSIC SCIENCE, QUANTUM CHEMISTRY. Educ: Univ Tex, Austin, BS, 63, PhD(chem physics), 67. Prof Exp: Fel, Univ Alta, 68-71; Orgn Am States fel & vis prof, Inst Physics, Univ Mex, 70; res assoc, Res Coun Alta, 71-72; chemist, Law Enforcement Assistance Admin, US Dept Justice, 72-73; FORENSIC CHEMIST, BUR ALCOHOL, TOBACCO & FIREARMS, US DEPT TREAS, 73- Mem: Soc Appl Spectros; Am Chem Soc; Sigma Xi. Res: Development of techniques to improve conventional methods of ink and paper analysis in the examination of questioned documents; application of statistical pattern recognition techniques to the individualization of physical evidence. *Mailing Add:* Bur of ATF Lab US Treas Dept 1401 Research Blvd Rockville MD 20850

CANTWELL, EDWARD N(ORTON), JR, b Chicago, Ill, Jan 13, 27; m 48; c 2. FUELS, LUBRICANTS. *Educ:* Northwestern Univ, BSME, 49, MS, PhD(mech eng), 53. *Prof Exp:* Engr, 52-62, div head, 62-79, RES MGR, E I DU PONT DE NEMOURS & CO, INC, 79- *Mem:* Soc Automotive Engrs; Combustion Inst. *Res:* Combustion of fuels in internal combustion engines; effect of fuels, lubricants and additives on all aspects of engine performance; future engines; measurement and control of vehicle emissions; effect of emissions on the environment. *Mailing Add:* 2400 Heather Rd W Wilmington DE 19803

CANTWELL, FREDERICK FRANCIS, b Brooklyn, NY, May 22, 41; m 64; c 3. ANALYTICAL CHEMISTRY. *Educ:* Allegheny Col, BA, 63; Univ Iowa, PhD(chem), 72. *Prof Exp:* Sr scientist anal chem, Endo Labs Inc, E I du Pont de Nemours & Co, Inc, 64-70, asst dir anal res, 72-74; asst prof, 75-80, PROF CHEM, UNIV ALTA, 80- *Concurrent Pos:* Nat Res Coun Can res grants, 75- *Mem:* Am Chem Soc; Chem Inst Can; Sigma Xi. *Res:* Liquid chromatographic research on novel stationary phases including preparation, studies of retention mechanisms and application to drug analysis; solvent extraction applied to flow injection analysis and metal speciation. *Mailing Add:* Dept Chem Univ Alta Edmonton AB T6G 2E8 Can

CANTWELL, GEORGE E, b Darlington, Pa, May 5, 29; m 50; c 10. INSECT PATHOLOGY. *Educ:* Kent State Univ, BS, 51, MA, 55; Univ Md, PhD(systematics), 60. *Prof Exp:* Histologist, 57-58, INSECT PATHOLOGIST, USDA, 58- *Concurrent Pos:* Lectr, Prince Georges Community Col, 60- *Mem:* Soc Invert Path. *Mailing Add:* One Greentree Pl Greenbelt MD 20770

CANTWELL, JOHN CHRISTOPHER, b St Louis, Mo, Aug 12, 36; m 64. MATHEMATICS, DIFFERENTIAL TOPOLOGY. *Educ:* St Louis Univ, BS, 57; Univ Notre Dame, PhD(math), 62. *Prof Exp:* Asst, Inst Advan Study, 62-64; asst prof, Univ Iowa, 64-67; from asst prof to assoc prof, 67-73, PROF MATH, ST LOUIS UNIV, 73- *Mem:* Asn Mem Inst Advan Study; Am Math Soc; Math Asn Am; Nat Speleol Soc. *Res:* Convex geometry; foliations; morse theory; differential and combinatorial manifolds. *Mailing Add:* 2351 Parkridge St Louis MO 63144

CANTWELL, THOMAS, b Buffalo, NY, June 25, 27; m 51; c 3. GEOLOGY, GEOPHYSICS. *Educ:* Mass Inst Technol, SB, 48, PhD(geophys), 60; Harvard Univ, MBA, 51. *Prof Exp:* Chem engr, Ionics Inc, 51-52; liaison officer, Mass Inst Technol, 52-54, res assoc nuclear eng, 54-58, asst prof geophys, 60-63; pres, Geosci, Inc, 63-70; pres, Petrol Holdings, Inc, 70-77; PRES, INDEPENDENT EXPLOR CO, 78- *Concurrent Pos:* Lectr, Mass Inst Technol, 63-65; vpres data processing, Mandrel Industs, 66-69, pres, 69-70; adj prof, Stanford Univ, 78- *Mem:* Am Phys Soc; Am Asn Petrol Geol; Soc Explor Geophys; Soc Petrol Engrs; fel Royal Geog Soc. *Res:* Oil and gas exploration techniques; sedimentary basin studies; mineral exploration. *Mailing Add:* 3960 Braxton Dr Houston TX 77063

CANTY, EUGENE THOMAS, b New York, NY, June 8, 25; m 46; c 3. ELECTRONIC ENGINEERING. *Educ:* Columbia Univ, BS, 46, MS, 47. *Prof Exp:* Electronics engr missile guid, Fairchild Engine & Airplane Corp, 47-50; sect head electronic design, Avion Instrument Corp, 50-52, res consult, Avion Div, ACF Industs, Inc, 53-56; exec engr intel systs, Int Tel & Tel Corp, 56-60; prog mgr, Lunar Vehicle Systs, Defense Res Labs, 60-67, PROG MGR, TRANSP SYSTS STUDIES, TRANSP RES DEPT, GEN MOTORS CORP, 67- *Concurrent Pos:* Mem, Hwy Res Bd, Nat Acad Sci-Nat Res Coun. *Mem:* Inst Elec & Electronics Engrs. *Res:* Application of electronic, microwave, physical and applied mathematics technologies to unique control and information handling problems of complex systems. *Mailing Add:* Gen Motors Corp Res Labs Tech Ctr Warren MI 48090

CANVIN, DAVID T, b Winnipeg, Man, Nov 8, 31; m 57; c 4. PLANT PHYSIOLOGY, PLANT BIOCHEMISTRY. *Educ:* Univ Man, BSA, 56, MSc, 57; Purdue Univ, PhD(plant physiol), 60. *Prof Exp:* Res assoc plant sci, Univ Man, 60-63, assoc prof, 63-65; PROF BIOL, QUEEN'S UNIV, ONT, 65-, HEAD DEPT, 80- *Concurrent Pos:* Secy-treas, Biol Coun Can. *Honors & Awards:* Gold Medal, Can Soc Plant Physiologists. *Mem:* AAAS; Am Soc Plant Physiol; Can Soc Cell Biol; Can Soc Plant Physiol; fel Royal Soc Can. *Res:* Intermediary metabolism in plants; environmental physiology. *Mailing Add:* Dept Biol Queen's Univ Kingston ON K7L 3N6 Can

CAPALDI, EUGENE CARMEN, b Philadelphia, Pa, Apr 10, 37; m 63; c 2. ORGANIC CHEMISTRY. *Educ:* Univ Pa, BS, 59; Univ Del, MS, 61, PhD(org chem), 64. *Prof Exp:* Res chemist, 63-66, sr res chemist, 66-76, coordr toxicol, 76-78, chem prod supvr, 78-80, admin mgr, 80-81, MGR TOXICOL & PROD SAFETY, ARCO CHEM CO, DIV ATLANTIC RICHFIELD CORP, 81- *Mem:* Am Chem Soc. *Res:* Synthesis of new monomers and chemical intermediates; polyester and polyurethane chemistry; toxicology and product safety. *Mailing Add:* Arco Chem Co 3801 W Chester Pike Newtown Square PA 19073

CAPDEVILA, JORGE H, biochemistry, pharmacology, see previous edition

CAPE, JOHN ANTHONY, b Helena, Mont, Nov 2, 29; m 62; c 3. SOLID STATE PHYSICS. *Educ:* Carroll Col (Mont), AB, 51; Mont State Univ, MS, 53; Univ Notre Dame, PhD(physics), 58. *Prof Exp:* Prof math & physics, Carroll Col (Mont), 55-56; asst physics, Univ Notre Dame, 57, instr, 57-58; res assoc, Univ Ill, 58-60; res specialist, Atomics Int, 60-64; mem tech staff, 64-72, group leader solid state sci, 72-77, prog mgr energy conversion, 74-78, PROJ MGR CONCENTRATOR SOLAR CELLS, SCI CTR, ROCKWELL INT CORP, 81- *Concurrent Pos:* Vis res assoc, Stanford Univ, 69. *Mem:* Fel Am Phys Soc. *Res:* Magnetic properties of materials; optical properties of magnetic materials; semiconductors; physical properties of surfaces and interfaces; superconductivity; solar photovoltaic energy conversion. *Mailing Add:* Sci Ctr Rockwell Int Corp Thousand Oaks CA 91360

CAPE, RONALD ELLIOT, b Montreal, Can, Oct 11, 32; m 56; c 2. BIOCHEMISTRY. *Educ:* Princeton Univ, AB, 53; Harvard Univ, MBA, 55; McGill Univ, PhD(biochem), 67. *Prof Exp:* Pres, Prof Pharmaceut Corp, 57-67, chmn, 67-73; managing partner, Cetus Sci Lab, 71-72, pres, 72-78, CHMN & CHIEF EXEC OFFICER, CETUS CORP, 78- *Concurrent Pos:* Med Res Coun Can Centennial fel, Univ Calif, Berkeley, 67-70; pres, Cape Farley Inc, 71-75. *Mem:* Am Soc Microbiol; Can Biochem Soc; Royal Soc Health; Sigma Xi; Soc Cosmetic Chemists. *Res:* Mutation and gene manipulation of industrial microorganisms. *Mailing Add:* Cetus Corp 600 Bancroft Way Berkeley CA 94710

CAPECCHI, MARIO RENATO, b Verona, Italy, Oct 6, 37; US citizen; m 63. CELL BIOLOGY. *Educ:* Antioch Col, BS, 61; Harvard Univ, PhD(biophys), 67. *Prof Exp:* Soc Fels jr fel biophys, Harvard Univ, 66-68, from asst prof to assoc prof biochem, Med Sch, 68-73; PROF BIOL, UNIV UTAH, 73- *Concurrent Pos:* Estab investr, Am Heart Asn, 69-72; NIH Career Develop Award, 72-74; Am Cancer Soc Fac Res Award, 74-79. *Honors & Awards:* Am Chem Soc Biochem Award, 69. *Mem:* Am Soc Biol Chem; Am Biochem Soc. *Res:* Gaining an understanding of how the information encoded in the gene is translated by the cell; expression in Eucaryotic and Procaryotic cells; somatic cell genetics. *Mailing Add:* Dept of Biol Univ of Utah Salt Lake City UT 84112

CAPEHART, BARNEY LEE, b Galena, Kans, Aug 20, 40; m 61; c 3. SYSTEM ENGINEERING. *Educ:* Univ Okla, BSEE, 61, MEE, 62, PhD(syst eng), 67. *Prof Exp:* Lectr eng, Northeastern Univ, 64-65; mem tech staff, Aerospace Corp, Calif, 67-68; asst prof indust & syst eng, Grad Eng Educ Syst, Univ Fla, 68-72; assoc prof indust eng, Univ Tenn, Knoxville, 72-73; assoc prof, 73-79, PROF INDUST & SYSTS ENG, UNIV FLA, 79- *Concurrent Pos:* Consult, Martin-Marietta Corp, Fla, 69. *Mem:* Fel AAAS; Inst Elec & Electronics Engrs; Am Inst Indust Engrs; Sigma Xi. *Res:* Digital simulation techniques; environmental applications of systems analysis and operations research and energy conservation. *Mailing Add:* Dept Indust & Systs Eng Univ Fla Gainesville FL 32611

CAPEL, CHARLES EDWARD, b Troy, NY, Dec 26, 22; m 45; c 2. MATHEMATICS. *Educ:* NY State Teachers Col, Albany, BA, 47; Univ Rochester, MA, 50; Tulane Univ, PhD(math), 53. *Prof Exp:* Instr math, Geneseo State Teachers Col, 47-49 & Tulane Univ, 50-51; asst prof, Miami Univ, 53-58; res mathematician, Westinghouse Res Lab, Pa, 58-60; PROF MATH, MIAMI UNIV, 60- *Mem:* Am Math Asn; Math Soc Am. *Res:* Inverse limit spaces; functions; fixed points. *Mailing Add:* Dept of Math Miami Univ Oxford OH 45056

CAPELETTI, TAMI LEE, metallurgy, see previous edition

CAPEN, CHARLES CHABERT, b Tacoma, Wash, Sept 3, 36; m 68. VETERINARY PATHOLOGY. *Educ:* Wash State Univ, DVM, 60; Ohio State Univ, MSc, 61, PhD(vet path), 65; Am Col Vet Pathologists, dipl. *Prof Exp:* Res assoc, 60-62, from instr to prof vet pathobiol, 62-72, PROF ENDOCRINOL, COL MED, OHIO STATE UNIV, 72-, ACTG CHMN, 81- *Concurrent Pos:* Consult path, Food & Drug Admin, 73-; mem coun, Am Col Vet Pathologists, 75-81. *Honors & Awards:* Borden Res Award, Am Vet Med Asn, 75. *Mem:* AAAS; Am Vet Med Asn; Endocrine Soc; Int Acad Path; Am Soc Exp Path. *Res:* Comparative and veterinary pathology; endocrine and metabolic diseases; calcium metabolism; ultrastructure of thyroid and parathyroid glands; metabolic bone disease. *Mailing Add:* Dept Vet Pathobiol Ohio State Univ 1925 Coffey Rd Columbus OH 43210

CAPEN, CHARLES FRANKLIN, JR, b Gilman, Ill, Jan 1, 26; m 56; c 3. PLANETARY SCIENCES, EDUCATION LECTURING. *Educ:* Spartan Col Aeronaut Eng, dipl, 46 & 49. *Prof Exp:* Dir astrophys, Smithsonian Astrophys Observ, Shiraz, Iran Sta, Int Geophys Year, 57-61; sr scientist & resident astronr, Table Mountain Observ, Jet Propulsion Lab, Calif Inst Technol, 62-70; ASTRONR PLANETS, PLANETARY RES CTR, LOWELL OBSERV, 70-; SR RES ASTRON, BRAESIDE OBSERV, 76- *Honors & Awards:* Inst Environ Sci Award, 69; Bruce Blair Gold Medal, 70; Apollo Achievement Award, NASA, 71. *Mem:* Int Astron Union; Am Astron Soc. *Res:* Observation and research on planets, comets, meteors; color photography and colorimetry of planets and comets; martian meteorology and surface variations; history of planetary science and its modern applications. *Mailing Add:* Lowell Observ Box 1269 Flagstaff AZ 86001

CAPERON, JOHN, b Milford, Utah, Apr 14, 29; m 64; c 3. ECOLOGY, OCEANOGRAPHY. *Educ:* Univ Utah, BS, 52; Scripps Inst Oceanog, Univ Calif, PhD(oceanog), 65. *Prof Exp:* Scientist, Int Bus Mach Corp, 53-59; oceanogr, Supreme Allied Comdr Atlantic Antisubmarine Warfare Res Ctr, Off Naval Res, London, 65-69; assoc prof, 69-74, PROF OCEANOG, UNIV HAWAII AT MANOA, 74- *Mem:* Ecol Asn Am. *Res:* Population dynamics; marine ecology. *Mailing Add:* Dept of Oceanog Univ of Hawaii Honolulu HI 96822

CAPERS, EVELYN LORRAINE, b Los Angeles, Calif, Dec 20, 25; m 58; c 1. CLINICAL MICROBIOLOGY. *Educ:* Univ Calif, Berkeley, BA, 46; Univ Southern Calif, PhD(bact), 71. *Prof Exp:* Med technologist, Childrens Hosp Los Angeles, 47-66; med microbiologist, Martin Luther King Jr Gen Hosp, Los Angeles County Dept Health Serv, 71-74; ASST DIR MICROBIOL, BIO-SCI LABS, 74- *Concurrent Pos:* Asst clin prof path, Sch Med, Univ Southern Calif, 73- *Mem:* Am Soc Microbiol; Sigma Xi. *Res:* Diagnostic microbiology and serology. *Mailing Add:* Bio-Sci Lab 7600 Tyrone Ave Van Nuys CA 91405

CAPETOLA, ROBERT JOSEPH, b Norristown, Pa, Oct 25, 49; m 76; c 2. PHARMACOLOGY. *Educ:* Philadelphia Col Pharm & Sci, BS, 71; Hahnemann Med Col, MS, 74, PhD(pharmacol), 75. *Prof Exp:* Res assoc pharmacol, Hahnemann Med Col, 75-76; sr pharmacologist, Wyeth Lab, Inc, 76-78; scientist, 78-79, sr scientist, 79-81, GROUP LEADER, HYPERSENSITIVITY DIS, ORTHO PHARMACEUT CORP, 81- *Mem:*

Am Soc Pharmacol & Exp Therapeut; Am Rheumatism Asn; Soc Exp Biol & Med; Soc Invest Dermat; Am Chem Soc. *Res:* Therapeutic control of inflammatory and allergic disorders; immunopharmacology; rheumatoid arthritis and asthma; analgesics and dermatopharmacology. *Mailing Add:* 1776 Turk Rd Doylestown PA 18901

CAPIAUX, RAYMOND, b Lille, France; US citizen; m; c 5. GAS DYNAMICS, PLASMA PHYSICS. *Educ:* Swiss Fed Inst Technol, BS, 49, MS, 50. *Prof Exp:* Res engr, Sulzer Bros, Switz, 50-53; sr propulsion aeronaut engr, Convair Div, Gen Dynamics, Tex, 53-56; supvr aerodyn design, Curtiss-Wright Corp, 56-57; staff engr, Fairchild Engine & Airplane Corp, 57-58; res specialist dynamics & performance, Palo Alto Res Lab, 58-61, staff scientist, Mech & Math Sci Lab, 61-63, sr staff scientist, Aerospace Sci Lab, 63-66, mgr, 67-70, dir eng sci, 70, dir res, Palo Alto Res Lab, 70-75, VPRES RES & DEVELOP, PALO ALTO RES LAB, LOCKHEED MISSILES & SPACE CO, INC, 75- *Concurrent Pos:* Mem, Defense Atomic Support Agency, 66- *Mem:* Am Inst Aeronaut & Astronaut. *Res:* Gas dynamics phenomena associated with ballistic and molecular physics. *Mailing Add:* Palo Alto Res Lab 3251 Hanover St Palo Alto CA 94304

CAPIZZI, ROBERT L, b Philadelphia, Pa, Nov 20, 38; m 65; c 4. ONCOLOGY, CLINICAL PHARMACOLOGY. *Educ:* Temple Univ, BS, 60; Hahnemann Med Col, MD, 64. *Prof Exp:* Fel clin pharmacol, Hahnemann Med Col, 65-66; fel med & pharmacol, 67-69, from asst prof to assoc prof med & pharmacol, Sch Med, Yale Univ, 72-77; PROF MED & PHARMACOL & CHIEF, DIV MED ONCOL, UNIV NC, 77- *Concurrent Pos:* Fac develop award clin pharmacol, Pharmaceut Mfrs Asn, 73; investr, Howard Hughes Med Inst, 76. *Mem:* Am Asn Cancer Res; Am Soc Clin Oncol; Am Soc Clin Pharmacol & Therapeut. *Res:* Cancer chemotherapy; chemical mutagenesis. *Mailing Add:* Div of Med Oncol Sch of Med Univ NC Chapel Hill NC 27514

CAPLAN, ARNOLD I, b Chicago, Ill, Jan 5, 42; m 65; c 2. DEVELOPMENTAL BIOLOGY, BIOCHEMISTRY. *Educ:* Ill Inst Technol, BS, 63; Johns Hopkins Univ, PhD(biochem), 66. *Prof Exp:* Fel anat, Johns Hopkins Univ Med Sch, 66-67; fel biochem, Brandeis Univ, 67-68, fel biol, 68-69; ass prof biol, 69-74, assoc prof biol & anat, 74-81, PROF BIOL, CASE WESTERN RESERVE UNIV, 81- *Mem:* AAAS; Soc Develop Biol; Soc Cell Biol. *Res:* Biochemical control of phenotypic expression, especially in chick embryo limb mesodermal cells; biochemical development of muscle, cartilage and bone. *Mailing Add:* Dept of Biol Case Western Reserve Univ Cleveland OH 44106

CAPLAN, DONALD, b Ottawa, Ont, Sept 24, 17; m 41; c 2. SURFACE CHEMISTRY, PHYSICAL METALLURGY. *Educ:* Queen's Univ, Ont, BSc, 40, MSc, 41; Rensselaer Polytech Inst, PhD(metall), 55. *Prof Exp:* Plant chemist & metallurgist, Hull Iron & Steel Foundries Ltd, 41-46; res chemist corrosion chem, Nat Res Coun Can, 46-53; res fel phys chem, Rensselaer Polytech Inst, 53-56; SR RES OFFICER CORROSION CHEM, NAT RES COUN CAN, 56- *Res:* Mechanism and kinetics of high temperature oxidation of metals; corrosion of metals and alloys; materials selection for resistance to corrosion. *Mailing Add:* Chem Div Nat Res Coun of Can Ottawa Can

CAPLAN, GERALD, b Eng, Mar 6, 17; nat US; m 42; c 1. PSYCHIATRY, PSYCHOANALYSIS. *Educ:* Univ Manchester, BSc, 37, MB & ChB, 40, MD, 45; Royal Col Physicians & Surgeons, DPM, 42; Royal Col Psychiatrists, FRCPsych, 71. *Hon Degrees:* MA, Harvard Univ, 70. *Prof Exp:* Asst med officer, Birmingham City Ment Hosp, Eng, 40-43; dep med supt, Swansea Ment Hosp, Eng, 43-45; psychiatrist, Tavistock Clin, London, 45-48; adv psychiat, Ministry Health, Israel, 48-49; psychiat dir, Lasker Ment Hyg & Child Guid Ctr, Jerusalem, 49-52; lectr ment health, Sch Pub Health, 52-54, assoc prof, Sch Pub Health, dir community ment health prog & psychiat dir, Harvard Family Guid Ctr, 54-64, clin prof psychiat, Harvard Med Sch, 64-70, prof psychiat, 70-78, dir lab community psychiat, 64-78, MER PROF PSYCHIAT, HARVARD MED SCH, HARVARD UNIV, 78-; EMER PROF PSYCHIAT & PROF CHILD PSYCHIAT, HEBREW UNIV, JERUSALEM, 78-; DIR, DEPT CHILD PSYCHIAT, HADASSAH HOSP, JERUSALEM, 78- *Concurrent Pos:* Chmn, Mass Adv Coun Ment Health & Retardation, 68; sr psychiat consult, Peace Corps, 61-71 & Off Econ Opportunity, 67-70. *Mem:* Law & Soc Asn; fel Am Pub Health Asn; Am Psychiat Asn; Am Orthopsychiat Asn; Int Asn Child & Adolescent Psychiat & Allied Professions (hon pres). *Mailing Add:* 30 King David St Jerusalem Israel

CAPLAN, JOHN D(AVID), b Weiser, Idaho, Mar 5, 26; m 52; c 3. CHEMICAL ENGINEERING. *Educ:* Ore State Univ, BS, 49; Wayne State Univ, MS, 55. *Prof Exp:* Head fuels & lubricants dept, 63-67, tech dir basic & appl sci, 67-69, EXEC DIR, GEN MOTORS RES LABS, 69- *Honors & Awards:* Crompton-Lanchester Medal, Brit Inst Mech Engrs, 64. *Mem:* Nat Acad Eng; Am Chem Soc; Am Inst Chem Engrs; Soc Automotive Engrs. *Res:* Engine fuels and combustion; automotive air pollution. *Mailing Add:* Exec Dept Gen Motors Res Labs Warren MI 48090

CAPLAN, PAUL E, b Far Rockaway, NY, Feb 29, 24; m 49; c 5. CHEMICAL ENGINEERING, INDUSTRIAL HYGIENE. *Educ:* Middlebury Col, AB, 44; Univ Colo, BSChE, 48; Univ Calif, Berkeley, MPH, 49; Am Acad Indust Hyg, dipl, 62; Bd Cert Safety Prof, cert, 71. *Prof Exp:* From asst indust hyg engr to sr indust hyg engr, Bur Occup Health, Calif State Dept Pub Health, 49-60 & adv, Bur Radiol Health, 60-71; DEP DIR DIV TECH SERVS, NAT INST OCCUP SAFETY & HEALTH, 71- *Concurrent Pos:* Mem threshold limits value comt, air sampling instruments comt, agr health comt & hyg guides comt, Am Conf Govt Indust Hyg. *Mem:* Am Conf Govt Indust Hyg; Am Indust Hyg Asn; Health Physics Soc; Am Pub Health Asn; Am Soc Testing & Mat. *Res:* Evaluation and control of hazards involved in use of agricultural chemicals and compressed air; development of techniques of air sampling for general environmental hazards evaluation. *Mailing Add:* Nat Inst Occup Safety & Health 4676 Columbia Pkwy Cincinnati OH 45226

CAPLAN, PAULA JOAN, b Springfield, Mo, July 7, 47; c 4. SEX DIFFERENCES. *Educ:* Harvard Univ, AB, 69; Duke Univ, MA, 71, PhD(psychol), 73. *Prof Exp:* Postdoctoral fel, Neuropsychol Res Unit, Hosp Sick Children, 74-77; clin & res psychologist, Family Court Clin, Clarke Inst Psychiat, 77-80; asst prof, 80-81, ASSOC PROF APPL PSYCHOL, ONT INST STUDIES EDUC, 81-; ASST PROF PSYCHIAT, UNIV TORONTO, 79- *Mem:* Am Orthopsychiat Asn; Can Psychol Asn. *Res:* Research methodology; sex differences in intelligence, play, aggression, achievement behavior and spatial abilities; children's learning; hand preference development in infants; child abuse. *Mailing Add:* Dept Appl Psychol Ont Inst Studies Educ Toronto ON M5S 2R8 Can

CAPLAN, PHILIP JUDAH, b Detroit, Mich, May 25, 27; m 52; c 4. SOLID STATE PHYSICS. *Educ:* Yeshiva Univ, BA, 48; Wayne State Univ, MS, 52. *Prof Exp:* PHYSICIST, ELECTRONICS TECHNOL & DEVICES LAB, US ARMY, 52- *Res:* Semiconductor interface defects; electron spin resonance of solids; nuclear magnetic resonance in ferromagnetic materials; dynamic nuclear polarization; optical spectra of laser materials. *Mailing Add:* US Army Electronics Technol & Devices Lab Ft Monmouth NJ 07703

CAPLAN, RICHARD MELVIN, b Des Moines, Iowa, July 16, 29; m 52; c 4. DERMATOLOGY. *Educ:* Iowa State Univ, BS, 49; Univ Iowa, MA, 51, MD, 55. *Prof Exp:* From asst prof to assoc prof, 61-69, PROF DERMAT, COL MED, UNIV IOWA, 69-, ASSOC DEAN CONTINUING MED EDUC, 70- *Mem:* Soc Med Sch Dirs Continuing Med Educ; Am Acad Dermat; Am Dermat Asn; Soc Med Col Dirs. *Mailing Add:* Dept of Dermat Univ of Iowa Col of Med Iowa City IA 52240

CAPLAN, YALE HOWARD, b Baltimore, Md, Dec 27, 41; m 65; c 3. TOXICOLOGY. *Educ:* Univ Md, BS, PhD(med chem), 68. *Prof Exp:* Asst pharmaceut chem, Sch Pharm, Univ Md, 64-65; res assoc toxicol & cancer chemother, Sinai Hosp, Baltimore, Md, 68-69, supvr surg res div, 69; asst toxicologist, 69-74, CHIEF TOXICOLOGIST, OFF CHIEF MED EXAMR, STATE OF MD, BALTIMORE, 74- *Concurrent Pos:* Res consult, Sinai Hosp, Baltimore, Md, 70-74; consult toxicologist, Cent Labs Assoc Md Pathologists, 71-72; instr toxicol, Sch Med, Univ Md, 72-73, clin asst prof path, 73-77, clin assoc prof, 77-, dir grad prog legal med (toxicol), 74-, assoc mem grad fac, 74-77, mem grad fac,77-, asst prof med chem, Sch Pharm & dir toxicol, Md Med Lab, 77-; lectr, Sch Hyg & Pub Health, Johns Hopkins Univ, 73-, consult appl physics lab, 73-; consult, Allied Chem Co, 75-78 & Ctr Human Toxicol, Univ Utah, 79-; prof lectr, Dept Forensic Sci, George Washington Univ, 74-76. *Mem:* AAAS; fel Soc Forensic Toxicologists (secy, 76-78, vpres, 79); fel Am Acad Forensic Sci; Int Asn Forensic Toxicol; fel Am Inst Chemists. *Res:* Analytical forensic and clinical toxicology, particularly development of procedures for analysis and chemical diagnosis in drug related death; experimental toxicology, particularly relationship of toxic concentrations and effects of drugs. *Mailing Add:* 8100 Tapscott Ct Pikesville MD 21208

CAPLE, GERALD, b International Falls, Minn, Apr 3, 35; m 64. ORGANIC CHEMISTRY. *Educ:* St Olaf Col, BA, 57; Fla State Univ, PhD(org chem), 63. *Prof Exp:* Res assoc chem, Ore State Univ, 63-65, asst prof, 65-66; asst prof, 66-70, ASSOC PROF CHEM, NORTHERN ARIZ UNIV, 70- *Mem:* Am Chem Soc. *Res:* Organic synthesis and mechanisms. *Mailing Add:* Dept of Chem Northern Ariz Univ Flagstaff AZ 86001

CAPLE, RONALD, b International Falls, Minn, Dec 7, 37; m 59; c 4. ORGANIC CHEMISTRY. *Educ:* St Olaf Col, BA, 60; Univ Mich, MS, 62, PhD(org mechanisms), 64. *Prof Exp:* NSF fel, Univ Colo, 64-65; from asst prof to assoc prof, 65-74, PROF ORG CHEM, UNIV MINN, DULUTH, 74- *Mem:* Am Chem Soc. *Res:* Intermediates in bridged polycyclic compounds. *Mailing Add:* Dept of Chem Univ of Minn Duluth MN 55812

CAPLIN, SAMUEL MILTON, b Cleveland, Ohio, Oct 28, 17; m 42, 53; c 3. BOTANY. *Educ:* Univ Akron, BS, 39, MS, 41; Univ Chicago, PhD(plant physiol), 46. *Prof Exp:* NIH fel growth & metabolism plant tissue cult, 47-49; res assoc bot, Univ Rochester, 49-50, asst prof, 50-56; asst prof, ELos Angeles Col, 56-60; from asst prof to assoc prof bot, 60-67, chmn dept bot & coordr biol, 67-69, PROF BOT, CALIF STATE UNIV, LOS ANGELES, 67- *Mem:* AAAS; Am Soc Plant Physiol; Bot Soc Am; Tissue Cult Asn; Int Asn Plant Tissue Cult. *Res:* Environmental parameters and radiation on growth of excised carrot root tissues. *Mailing Add:* Dept of Botany Calif State Univ Los Angeles CA 90032

CAPLIS, MICHAEL E, b Ypsilanti, Mich, July 25, 38; m 56; c 7. BIOCHEMISTRY, TOXICOLOGY. *Educ:* Eastern Mich Univ, BS, 62; Purdue Univ, MS, 64, PhD(biochem), 70. *Prof Exp:* Teacher physics, math & chem, St John High Sch, 58-62; asst biochem, Purdue Univ, 62-67, res asst, 67-69; instr med, 69-80, ASST PROF BIOCHEM, DIV ALLIED HEALTH, SCH MED, IND UNIV, 80- *Concurrent Pos:* Anal biochemist, State of Ind, 62-67; toxicologist, Ind Criminal Justice Comn, Region I, 70; dir, Northwest Ind Criminal & Toxicol Lab, 70- *Mem:* AAAS; Am Asn Clin Chem; Am Chem Soc; Am Acad Clin Toxicol; Am Asn Crim Lab Dirs. *Res:* Analytical biochemistry-toxicology; mechanism of action of toxic chemicals and drugs; resistance to toxic action of chemicals and drugs; development of instrumental analytical procedures for study of chemicals, drugs and their metabolites in biological systems; applications of spectrochemical and electrochemical methods. *Mailing Add:* Div Allied Health Sch Med Ind Univ Indianapolis IN 46202

CAPLOW, MICHAEL, b New York, NY, May 20, 35; m 59; c 2. BIOCHEMISTRY, ENZYMOLOGY. *Educ:* NY Univ, DDS, 59; Brandeis Univ, PhD(biochem), 63. *Prof Exp:* Asst biochem, Yale Univ, 63-70; assoc prof, 70-73, PROF BIOCHEM, 73- & PROF ORAL BIOL, SCH DENT, UNIV NC, CHAPEL HILL, 78- *Mem:* AAAS; Am Chem Soc. *Res:* Enzyme kinetics and mechanisma mechanisms; chemistry of microtubules, biosynthesis of dextrans by cariogenic microorganisms. *Mailing Add:* Dept of Biochem Univ of NC Chapel Hill NC 27514

CAPO, BERNARDO GUILLERMO, b Guayama, Dec 28, 08; m 30; c 2. AGRICULTURE. *Educ:* Univ PR, BS, 29; Cornell Univ, MS, 41, PhD(agr), 42. *Prof Exp:* Anal chemist, Fertil & Feed Control, PR Dept Agr, 29-36; soils chemist, 36-42, head soils div, 42-43, biometrician, 43-48, head dept agron & hort, 44-52, asst dir res, 48-49, actg dir, 49-50, assoc dir, 52-65, TECH CONSULT, AGR EXP STA, UNIV PR, RIO PIEDRAS, 67- *Concurrent Pos:* Tech dir, Ancram Paper Mills, NY, 46-48; prof col soc sci, Univ PR, 48-49; proj mgr, UN Spec Fund Proj 101, Damascus Agr Res Sta, 64-65; statist consult, Urban Renewal & Housing Admin, 68-69; consult, Agr Coun PR, 69-71. *Mem:* Am Statist Asn; Inst Math Statist. *Res:* New fertilizer equation; leaf composition as index of availability of nutrients in the soil; optimum economic quantity of fertilizer based on leaf analysis; statistical analysis of research data. *Mailing Add:* 1749 Santa Praxedes St Rio Piedras PR 00926

CAPOBIANCO, MICHAEL F, b Brooklyn, NY, Oct 4, 31; m 65. MATHEMATICS, STATISTICS. *Educ:* Polytech Inst Brooklyn, BChE, 52, MChE, 54, PhD(math), 64; Columbia Univ, MA, 57. *Prof Exp:* Statistician, Am Cyanamid Co, 54-55; from instr to asst prof math, St John's Univ, 55-63; mathematician, Repub Aviation Corp, 63; lectr math, Polytech Inst Brooklyn, 63-64, asst prof, 64-66; assoc prof, 66-71, PROF MATH, ST JOHN'S UNIV, NY, 71- *Concurrent Pos:* Consult, Maimonides Hosp Brooklyn, 66- *Mem:* Am Math Soc; Math Asn Am; Biomet Soc; Soc Indust & Appl Math. *Res:* Statistical decision theory; statistical inference in digraphs; traffic analysis; combinatorics; statistics in the life sciences, especially psychology, economics, sociology, biophysics and cybernetics; tensor analysis and differential geometry. *Mailing Add:* Dept of Math St John's Univ Staten Island NY 10301

CAPON, BRIAN, b Wallasey, Eng, Dec 27, 31. BOTANY. *Educ:* La Sierra Col, BA, 58; Univ Chicago, MS, 60, PhD(bot), 61. *Prof Exp:* From asst prof to assoc prof, 61-71, chmn dept, 69-71, PROF BOT, CALIF STATE UNIV, LOS ANGELES, 71- *Res:* Physiology of desert plants. *Mailing Add:* Dept of Biol Calif State Univ Los Angeles CA 90032

CAPONE, DOUGLAS GEORGE, b Newark, NJ, April 30, 50; c 79; c 1. MARINE MICROBIOLOGY, MICROBIAL ECOLOGY. *Educ:* Univ Miami, BS, 73, PhD(marine sci), 78. *Prof Exp:* Grad res asst marine sci, Rosenstiel Sch Marine & Atmospheric Sci, Univ Miami, 74-78, fel, 79; RES ASST PROF, MARINE SCI RES CTR, STATE UNIV NY STONY BROOK, 79- *Mem:* Am Soc Microbiol; Am Soc Limnol & Oceanog; AAAS; Phycol Soc Am; Sigma Xi. *Res:* Role and importance of microorganisms in marine ecosystems, particularly in elemental cycles; interactions of the microbiota and environmental pollutants. *Mailing Add:* Marine Sci Res Ctr State Univ NY Stony Brook NY 11794

CAPONE, JAMES JOSEPH, immunochemistry, bacteriology, see previous edition

CAPONETTI, JAMES DANTE, b Boston, Mass, Mar 15, 32; m 66. BOTANY. *Educ:* Mass Col Pharm, BS, 54, MS, 56; Harvard Univ, AM, 59, PhD(biol), 62. *Prof Exp:* Asst prof, 61-71, ASSOC PROF BOT, UNIV TENN, KNOXVILLE, 71- *Mem:* Fel AAAS; Bot Soc Am; Int Soc Plant Morphol; Am Fern Soc; Int Plant Propagators' Soc. *Res:* Morpho-genesis and propagation of vascular plants, mostly Pteridophytes, by tissue culture. *Mailing Add:* Dept of Bot Univ of Tenn Knoxville TN 37996

CAPONIO, JOSEPH FRANCIS, b Canton, Mass, Mar 25, 26; m 57; c 2. BIOCHEMISTRY. *Educ:* St Anselm's Col, AB, 51; Georgetown Univ, PhD(biochem), 59. *Prof Exp:* Sr analyst, Libr Cong, 55-58; chief bibliog div, Off Tech Serv, US Dept Com, 58-61; dir tech info, Defense Document Ctr, Div Sci Area, US Dept Defense, 61-64; sci info officer, NIH, 64-70; assoc dir, Nat Agr Libr, 70-74; dir, Environ Sci Info Ctr, 74-79, DEP DIR, NAT TECH INFO SERV, NAT OCEANIC & ATMOSPHERIC ADMIN, DEPT COM, 79- *Concurrent Pos:* Mem off critical tables, Nat Acad Sci-Nat Res Coun, 64- *Honors & Awards:* Silver Medal, Dept Com. *Mem:* Am Chem Soc; Am Soc Info Sci; AAAS. *Res:* Protein and enzyme chemistry; information science. *Mailing Add:* 8417 Ft Hunt Rd Alexandria VA 22308

CAPORALE, LYNN HELENA, b New York, NY, Sept 3, 47. BIOCHEMISTRY, IMMUNOLOGY. *Educ:* Brooklyn Col, BS, 67; Univ Calif, Berkeley, PhD(molecular biol), 73. *Prof Exp:* Nat Inst Allergy & Infectious Dis fel path, Med Sch, NY Univ, 73-74; assoc researcher leukemia, Sloan Kettering Inst Cancer Res, 75-76; res assoc biochem, Rockefeller Univ, 76-77; ASST PROF BIOCHEM, SCH MED & DENT, GEORGETOWN UNIV, 78- *Concurrent Pos:* Adj asst prof, Rockefeller Univ, 78- Am Lung Asn res grant, 78-79; NIH res grant, 78-81. *Mem:* AAAS; NY Acad Sci; Fedn Am Scientist; Sigma Xi. *Res:* Biochemistry of the immune response; the complement cascade; inflammation; immune RNA; interaction of cells and serum macromolecules; proteases; peptide synthesis. *Mailing Add:* Sch Med & Dent 3900 Reservoir Rd NW Washington DC 20007

CAPORALI, RONALD VAN, b Arnold, Pa, June 22, 36; m 56; c 4. MECHANICAL ENGINEERING, CERAMIC SCIENCE. *Educ:* Pa State Univ, BS, 58, MS, 64, PhD(ceramic sci), 69. *Prof Exp:* Ceramic technologist, Am Glass Res, 58-62; res asst glass struct, Pa State Univ, 62-69; sr glass scientist, Am Glass Res, 69-76; OWNER-CONSULT, GLASS TECHNOL, 76- *Mem:* Am Ceramic Soc; Brit Soc Glass Tech; Soc Soft Drink Technologists; Am Soc Testing & Mat; AAAS. *Res:* Structure and strength of glasses; fracture analysis. *Mailing Add:* RD 1 Box 19 West Sunbury PA 16061

CAPOSSELA, HARRY JAMES, b Bridgeport, Conn, Feb, 24, 44. NUCLEAR ENGINEERING, NUCLEAR PHYSICS. *Educ:* Rensselaer Polytech Inst, BS, 66; Mass Inst Technol, MS, 68. *Prof Exp:* NUCLEAR ENGR NUCLEAR REACTOR CORE DESIGN & ANAL METHODS DEVELOP, KNOLLS ATOMIC POWER LAB, GEN ELEC CO, 68- *Mem:* Am Nuclear Soc; AAAS. *Res:* Nuclear reactor physics; nuclear reactor core design. *Mailing Add:* Knolls Atomic Power Lab PO Box 1072 River Rd Schenectady NY 12301

CAPOTOSTO, AUGUSTINE, JR, analytical chemistry, see previous edition

CAPP, GRAYSON L, b Seattle, Wash, Aug 11, 36; m 59; c 3. BIOCHEMISTRY. *Educ:* Seattle Pac Col, BS, 58; Univ Ore, MS, 62, PhD(biochem), 67. *Prof Exp:* Instr chem, Los Angeles Pac Col, 59-60; res assoc biochem, Ore Primate Ctr, 61-63; NIH fel protein struct, Duke Univ, 66-68; asst prof biochem, 68-70, asst prof chem, 70-73, ASSOC PROF CHEM & PRE-PROF HEALTH SCI ADV, SEATTLE PAC COL, 73- *Concurrent Pos:* NIH sr fel, Univ Wash, 69-70. *Mem:* AAAS; Am Chem Soc. *Res:* Protein subunit structure and function with studies of glutamic dehydrogenase and human hemoglobin. *Mailing Add:* 903 W Fulton Seattle WA 98119

CAPP, JOHN PAUL, b Latrobe, Pa, June 17, 21; m 53; c 3. CHEMICAL ENGINEERING, INORGANIC CHEMISTRY. *Educ:* St Vincent Col, BS, 43. *Prof Exp:* Chemist, Synthetic Liquid Lab, US Bur Mines, 46-49, chemist, Underground Gasification Coal Field Sta, 49-53, chemist,, Metall Lab, 53-54, chem engr, 55-59, engr, Div Mineral Tech, 54-55, chem engr, Morgantown Coal Res Ctr, 59-74, supvry chem engr, Off Surface Mining & Reclamation Res, 74-80; CONSULT, 80- *Mem:* Am Chem Soc. *Res:* Reclamation of surface mine spoils; underground gasification of coal-synthesis of rare or depleted minerals; utilization, processing and disposal of solid wastes from coal. *Mailing Add:* 40 Citadel Rd Morgantown WV 26505

CAPP, MICHAEL PAUL, b Yonkers, NY, July 1, 30; m 57; c 4. RADIOLOGY, PEDIATRICS. *Educ:* Roanoke Col, BS, 52; Univ NC, MD, 58. *Prof Exp:* Intern pediat, Med Ctr, Duke Univ, 58-59, resident radiol, 59-62, assoc, 6263, from asst prof to assoc prof radiol, 63-70, dir diag radiol, 66-70, asst prof pediat, 68-70; PROF RADIOL & CHMN DEPT, COL MED, UNIV ARIZ, 70- & CHIEF STAFF AZ MED CTR, UNIV HOSP, 77- *Mem:* Soc Pediat Radiol; AMA; Radiol Soc NAm; Am Roentgen Ray Asn; Am Col Radiol; Asn Univ Radiologists. *Res:* Congenital heart disease, particularly left ventricular function. *Mailing Add:* Dept of Radiol Univ of Ariz Col of Med Tucson AZ 85724

CAPP, WALTER B(ERNARD), b Munhall, Pa, Apr 18, 33; m 65. OPERATIONS RESEARCH. *Educ:* Carnegie Inst Technol, BS, 55, MS, 57. *Prof Exp:* Engr econ eval, Gulf Res & Develop Co, 57-60, proj engr opers res, 60-63, sr proj engr, 63-66, sect supvr, Opers Res Sect, 66-71, tech adv, Computation & Commun Serv Dept, 71-75, MGR MGT SCI, GULF OIL CORP, 76- *Mem:* Inst Mgt Sci. *Res:* Management science; economic analysis; statistical analysis; linear programming; computer programming. *Mailing Add:* 5 Worthington Rd Pittsburgh PA 15238

CAPPALLO, ROGER JAMES, b Cleveland, Ohio, Sept 30, 49; m 71; c 1. VERY LONG BASELINE INTERFEROMETRY. *Educ:* Mass Inst Technol, SB, 71, PhD(planetary sci), 80. *Prof Exp:* Res assoc, Mass Inst Technol, 80; RES SCIENTIST, HAYSTACK OBSERV, 80- *Mem:* Am Geophys Union. *Res:* Techniques and applications of very long baseline interferometry for geodesy and astronomy; modelling of the moon's rotation. *Mailing Add:* Haystack Observ Rte 40 Westford MA 01886

CAPPAS, C, b Cairo, Egypt, Mar 14, 26; US citizen; m 56. PHYSICAL CHEMISTRY, MATHEMATICS. *Educ:* Berea Col, BA, 56; Univ Fla, PhD(phys chem), 62. *Prof Exp:* Res assoc phys chem, Princeton Univ, 62, group leader dielectrics, 62-64; assoc prof chem, Oglethorpe Univ, 65-67; ASSOC PROF CHEM, UNIV S ALA, 67- *Mem:* AAAS; Am Chem Soc; Sigma Xi. *Res:* Chemical kinetics; determination of physical constants; polymer chemistry; solid state chemistry. *Mailing Add:* Dept of Chem Univ of S Ala Mobile AL 36688

CAPPEL, CARL ROBERT, b Connersville, Ind, Nov 17, 42. ORGANIC CHEMISTRY, PHOTOGRAPHIC CHEMISTRY. *Educ:* Ball State Univ, BS, 69; Univ Ill, MS, 72, PhD(chem), 73. *Prof Exp:* Asst chem, Univ Ill, 69-73; SR RES CHEMIST, EASTMAN KODAK CO, 73- *Mem:* Sigma Xi; Soc Photog Scientists & Engrs. *Res:* Investigation and application of organic chemistry to photographic science. *Mailing Add:* 69 Hermitage Rd Rochester NY 14617

CAPPELL, SYLVAIN EDWARD, b Brussels, Belg, Sept 10, 46; US citizen; m 66; c 3. TOPOLOGY. *Educ:* Columbia Univ, 66; Princeton Univ, PhD(math), 69. *Prof Exp:* Princeton nat fel, Princeton Univ, 66-69, from instr to asst prof math, 69-74; assoc prof, 74-78, PROF MATH, COURANT INST, NY UNIV, 78- *Concurrent Pos:* Woodrow Wilson Found fel, 66-67; NSF fel, 66-68; Danforth Found fel, 66-69; vis lectr, Harvard Univ, 70-71; Sloan Found fel, 71-73; vis prof, Weizmann Inst, Israel, 72, Inst Hautes Etudes Sci, 73 & Harvard Univ, 81. *Res:* Manifolds and submanifolds. *Mailing Add:* Courant Inst of Math Sci 251 Mercer St New York NY 10012

CAPPELLETTI, RONALD LOUIS, experimental solid state physics, metal physics, see previous edition

CAPPELLINI, RAYMOND ADOLPH, b Pittsburgh, Pa, Jan 30, 26; m 50; c 4. PLANT PATHOLOGY. *Educ:* Duquesne Univ, BEd, 50; Pa State Univ, MS, 52; Cornell Univ, PhD, 55. *Prof Exp:* Asst res specialist plant path, 55-61, assoc prof, 61-67, PROF PLANT PATH, RUTGERS UNIV, 67-, CHMN DEPT PLANT PATH, 71- *Mem:* Am Phytopath Soc; Mycol Soc Am. *Res:* Market diseases; fungus physiology. *Mailing Add:* Dept of Plant Path Cook Col Rutgers Univ New Brunswick NJ 08903

CAPPS, DAVID BRIDGMAN, b Jacksonville, Ill, Jan 25, 25; m 48; c 3. MEDICINAL CHEMISTRY. *Educ:* Ill Col, AB, 48; Univ Nebr, MS, 50, PhD(org chem), 52. *Hon Degrees:* DSc, Ill Col, 79. *Prof Exp:* Res chemist, Chemstrand Corp, 52-56; from assoc res chemist to res scientist, 56-77, SR SCIENTIST ORG CHEM, RES LABS, PARKE, DAVIS & CO, 77- *Mem:* Am Chem Soc; AAAS. *Res:* Synthesis of experimental drugs for the control of cancer and of infectious diseases, and the study of relationships between molecular structure and biological activities. *Mailing Add:* 1406 Brooklyn Ann Arbor MI 48104

CAPPS, MARY JAYNE, physiological psychology, sensory physiology, see previous edition

CAPPS, RICHARD H, b Wichita, Kans, July 1, 28; m 55, 75. THEORETICAL PHYSICS. *Educ:* Univ Kans, AB, 50; Univ Wis, MS, 52, PhD(physics), 55. *Prof Exp:* Fel, Univ Calif, Berkeley, 55-57; actg asst prof physics, Univ Wash, 57-59; fel, Cornell Univ, 58-60; from asst prof to prof, Northwestern Univ, 60-67; PROF PHYSICS, PURDUE UNIV, 67- *Concurrent Pos:* Fulbright & Guggenheim fel, Univ Rome, 62-63; consult, Argonne Nat Lab, Ill, 60-70. *Mem:* Am Phys Soc. *Res:* Theory of the interactions of fundamental particles. *Mailing Add:* Dept of Physics Purdue Univ West Lafayette IN 47907

CAPPUCCI, DARIO TED, JR, b Plains, Pa, Aug 19, 41. VETERINARY MEDICINE. *Educ:* Univ Calif, Davis, BS, 63, DVM, 65, MS, 66; Am Bd Vet Pub Health, dipl, 73; Am Registry Cert Animal Scientists, dipl, 75; Univ Calif, San Francisco, PhD(comp path), 76. *Prof Exp:* Head carnivore unit, NIH Animal Ctr, Md, 66-67; vet epidemiologist, Zoonoses Surveillance Unit, Nat Communicable Dis Ctr, Ga, 68; researcher vet med & sci, Independent Invest Studies, 69; vet, Vet Lab Serv, Calif Dept Agr, 69-70; pub health vet, Calif Dept Health, 70-76; pvt pract, 76-78; VET EPIDEMIOLOGIST, FOOD & DRUG ADMIN, MD, 78- *Concurrent Pos:* Mem subcomt pub health, Nat Brucellosis Comt, 68-69; pub health serv med epidemiol preceptor, 80- *Mem:* Am Vet Med Asn; Am Soc Animal Sci; AAAS; Wildlife Dis Asn; NY Acad Sci. *Res:* Reproductive pathophysiology; veterinary public health; comparative medicine; supervision of laboratory animal breeding colony; animal science. *Mailing Add:* 1077 Sanchez St San Francisco CA 94114

CAPRA, J DONALD, b Burlington, Vt, July 20, 37; m 58; c 2. MEDICINE, IMMUNOLOGY. *Educ:* Univ Vt, BS, 59, MD, 63. *Prof Exp:* Intern, St Luke's Hosp, New York, 64, resident, 65; sr surgeon, NIH, 6567; guest investr, Rockefeller Univ, 6769; assoc prof microbiol, Mt Sinai Sch Med, 69-74; PROF MICROBIOL, UNIV TEX HEALTH SCI CTR, DALLAS, 74- *Concurrent Pos:* USPHS fel, 65-67. *Mem:* Am Asn Immunologists; Am Rheumatism Asn. *Res:* Immunogenetics; protein sequences; antibody combining site. *Mailing Add:* Dept of Microbiol Univ of Tex Health Sci Ctr Dallas TX 75235

CAPRANICA, ROBERT R, b Los Angeles, Calif, May 29, 31; m 58. NEUROBIOLOGY, ELECTRICAL ENGINEERING. *Educ:* Univ Calif, Berkeley, BS, 58; NY Univ, MEE, 60; Mass Inst Technol, ScD(elec eng), 64. *Prof Exp:* Mem tech staff commun res, Bell Tel Labs, NJ, 58-69; assoc prof neurobiol & elec eng, 69-75, PROF NEUROBIOL & BEHAVIOR & ELEC ENG, CORNELL UNIV, 75- *Concurrent Pos:* Ed, J Comp Physiol. *Mem:* AAAS; Am Soc Zool; fel Acoust Soc Am; Am Physiol Soc; Soc Neurosci. *Res:* Animal sound communication; auditory neurophysiology. *Mailing Add:* Langmuir Lab Sect of Neurobiol Cornell Univ Ithaca NY 14850

CAPRETTA, UMBERTO, b Nereto, Italy, Mar 5, 22; US citizen; m 50; c 2. ANALYTICAL CHEMISTRY. *Educ:* Univ Naples, Dr indust chem, 52. *Prof Exp:* Teacher high sch, Italy, 52-55; lab technician, 55-60, anal chemist, 60-68, SR ENGR, EASTMAN KODAK CO, 68- *Mem:* AAAS; fel Am Inst Chemists; Am Chem Soc; NY Acad Sci. *Res:* Instrumental analysis; x-ray emission; polarography; atomic absorption; development of new methods and techniques. *Mailing Add:* 187 River St Rochester NY 14612

CAPRI, ANTON ZIZI, b Czernowitz, Romania, Apr 20, 38; Can citizen; m 60; c 3. PARTICLE PHYSICS, MATHEMATICAL PHYSICS. *Educ:* Univ Toronto, BASc, 61; Princeton Univ, MA, 65, PhD(physics), 67. *Prof Exp:* Res physicist, Kimberly-Clark Corp, 61-63; fel, 67-68, vis asst prof theoret physics, 68-69, asst prof, 69-73, assoc prof, 73-79, PROF THEORET PHYSICS, UNIV ALTA, 79- *Concurrent Pos:* Sr res fel, Alexander von Humboldt Found, 75-76. *Mem:* Am Phys Soc. *Res:* Higher spin field theories; existence of solutions in quantum field theory. *Mailing Add:* Theoret Physics Inst Univ of Alta Edmonton AB T6G 2E1 Can

CAPRIO, JAMES R, b Niagara Falls, NY, Apr 8, 39; m 58; c 2. ELECTRICAL ENGINEERING, APPLIED MATHEMATICS. *Educ:* State Univ NY, Buffalo, BS, 61, MS, 63; Cornell Univ, PhD(elec eng), 66. *Prof Exp:* Asst electronics engr, Cornell Aeronaut Lab, Cornell Univ, 61-62, assoc electronics engr, 62-66, res electronics engr, 66-67, prin electronics engr, 67-74; ASST MGR, SYSTS ENG DIV, COMPTEK RES, INC, 74- *Concurrent Pos:* Asst prof elec eng, State Univ NY, Buffalo, 67-74; consult prin engr, Cornell Aeronaut Lab, 67- *Mem:* Inst Elec & Electronics Engrs; Soc Indust & Appl Math; Math Asn Am. *Res:* Radar systems and signal processing; statistical communications theory; detection and estimation of signal wave forms and parameters; digital filtering. *Mailing Add:* Systs Eng Dept 455 Cayuga Rd Buffalo NY 14225

CAPRIO, JOHN THEODORE, b Norfolk, Va, June 22, 45; m 68. SENSORY PHYSIOLOGY. *Educ:* Old Dominion Univ, BS, 67; Fla State Univ, PhD(physiol), 76. *Prof Exp:* Asst prof, 76-80, ASSOC PROF PHYSIOL, LA STATE UNIV, 80- *Concurrent Pos:* Prin investr, Nat Inst Neurol & Commun Disorders & Stroke grant, 79-81 & 81-84. *Mem:* Soc Neurosci; Sigma Xi; AAAS; Europ Chemoreception Res Orgn. *Res:* Chemical senses; olfaction and taste in aquatic organisms. *Mailing Add:* Dept of Zool & Physiol La State Univ Baton Rouge LA 70803

CAPRIO, JOSEPH MICHAEL, b New Brunswick, NJ, Nov 7, 23; m 51; c 3. AGRICULTURAL METEOROLOGY, MICROCLIMATOLOGY. *Educ:* Rutgers Univ, BS, 47, MS, 50; Calif Inst Technol, BS, 48; Utah State Univ, PhD(biometeorol), 70. *Prof Exp:* Agrometeorologist, Am Inst Aerological Res, 50-53; statistician & agronometeorologist, Citrus Exp Sta, Univ Calif, 53-55; from asst prof to assoc prof agr climat, 55-63, PROF AGR CLIMAT, MONT STATE UNIV, 63- *Concurrent Pos:* Mem, past chmn & secy, Tech Comt Western Regional Proj W-48, 57-75 & W-148, 76-81; mem, Tech Comt Great Plains Regional Proj GP-1, 59-61; climat expert, UN World Meteorol Orgn, Iran, 62-63; mem phenology panel, US Int Biol Prog, 67-70; co-invest, Earth Resources Technol Satellite-1, Phenology Satellite Exp, NASA, 72-74; vis scientist, Div Land Use Res, Commonwealth Indust & Sci Orgn, Canberra, Australia, 73-74; mem, UN World Meteorol Orgn Working Group on Methods of Forecasting Agr Crop Develop & Ripening, 75-79; ecologist-meterologist workshop chmn, Panel Biol Indicators Climatic Change, 76; Agristars NASA Prog, 80- *Mem:* Am Meteorol Soc; Int Soc Bioclimat & Biometeorol; Am Soc Agron; Soil Sci Soc Am. *Res:* Biometeorology; agrometeorology, including statistical climatic analysis; mapping of climatic elements in mountainous areas; study of weather effects on crop production; plant phenology; soil physics; hydrology. *Mailing Add:* Dept of Plant & Soil Sci Mont State Univ Bozeman MT 59715

CAPRIO, MARIO J(OSEPH), b Newark, NJ, Sept 7, 20; m 50; c 2. CHEMICAL ENGINEERING. *Educ:* NY Univ, BS, 42; Carnegie Inst Technol, BChE, 47. *Prof Exp:* Sr res engr, 48-68, PURCHASING AGT, ALUMINUM CO AM, 68- *Mem:* Am Ceramic Soc. *Mailing Add:* 505 Clyde St New Kensington PA 15068

CAPRIOGLIO, GIOVANNI, b Rome, Italy, Aug 9, 32; m 58; c 1. ELECTROCHEMISTRY. *Educ:* Univ Milan, DSc(indust chem), 56. *Prof Exp:* Asst prof electrochem, Univ Modena, 57-59 & Univ Milan, 59-62; consult, Gen Atomic Div, Gen Dynamics Corp, 61-62, staff mem, 62-67; proj mgr, Gulf Gen Atomic, Inc, 67-70; assoc dir lab, 70-73, MGR MAT & CHEM DEPT, GEN ATOMIC CO, 73- *Mem:* Int Soc Electrochem; Electrochem Soc; Am Nuclear Soc. *Res:* High temperature materials; corrosion; batteries; thermochemical hydrogen production. *Mailing Add:* Gen Atomic Co PO Box 81608 San Diego CA 92138

CAPRIOLI, RICHARD MICHAEL, b New York, NY, Apr 12, 43; m 71. BIOCHEMISTRY, MASS SPECTROMETRY. *Educ:* Columbia Univ, BS, 65, PhD(biochem), 69. *Prof Exp:* Res assoc chem, Purdue Univ, 69-70, from asst prof to assoc prof, 70-75; assoc prof, 75-80, PROF BIOCHEM, MED SCH, UNIV TEX, HOUSTON, 80- *Mem:* Am Soc Biol Chemists; Am Soc Mass Spectrometry. *Res:* Peptide sequencing by mass spectrometry; intermediary metabolism using stable isotopes; mechanisms of enzyme action. *Mailing Add:* Dept Biochem Univ Tex Med Sch Houston TX 77025

CAPRIOTTI, EUGENE RAYMOND, b Brackenridge, Pa, June 20, 37; m 60; c 1. ASTRONOMY, PHYSICS. *Educ:* Pa State Univ, BS, 59; Univ Wis, PhD(astron), 62. *Prof Exp:* Res fel astron, Calif Inst Technol, 62-63; asst prof, Univ Calif, Berkeley, 63-64; sr engr, Westinghouse Elec Corp, 64; from asst prof to assoc prof astron, 64-73, PROF ASTRON, OHIO STATE UNIV, 73-, CHMN DEPT, 78-; DIR, PERKINS OBSERV, 78- *Concurrent Pos:* Vis assoc prof, Steward Observ, Univ Ariz, 69-70. *Mem:* Am Astron Soc. *Res:* Active galactic nuclei, quasars, gaseous nebulae and interstellar medium. *Mailing Add:* Dept of Astron Ohio State Univ Columbus OH 43210

CAPRON, ALEXANDER MORGAN, b Hartford, Conn, Aug 16, 44; m 69; c 1. SCIENCE POLICY. *Educ:* Swarthmore Col, BA, 66; Yale Univ, LLB, 69; Univ Pa, MA, 76. *Prof Exp:* lectr & res assoc, Yale Univ, 70-72, vis lectr law, 76-77; PROF LAW, UNIV PA, 72-, PROF HUMAN GENETICS, 76- *Concurrent Pos:* Prin investr, NIH grant, 74-77 & mem, Consensus Develop Conf Caesarean Childbirth, 80; mem, Biomed Res & Develop Adv Panel, Off Technol Assessment, US Cong, 76; assoc ed, Am J Human Genetics, 77-80; mem, Adv Comt Experimentation, Fed Judicial Ctr, Wash, DC, 78-81; exec dir, Presidents Comn Study Ethical Prob Med, Biomed & Behav Res, 80- *Mem:* Inst Med-Nat Acad Sci; fel Inst Soc Ethics & Life Sci; AAAS; NY Acad Sci. *Res:* Ethical, social and legal implications of developments in the life sciences and the impact of governmental policies and legal rules on medicine and the biomedical and behavorial sciences. *Mailing Add:* Suite 555 2000 K St Northwest Washington DC 20006

CAPSHEW, CHARLES EDWARD, b Fletcher, Okla, Nov 1, 46; m 70; c 3. ORGANIC CHEMISTRY. *Educ:* Southwestern Okla State Univ, BS, 68; Univ Tex, Austin, PhD(org chem), 77. *Prof Exp:* res chemist catalysis, 77-79, res & develop staff planner, 80-81, SR RES CHEMIST, PHILLIPS PETROL CO, 81- *Mem:* Am Chem Soc; Soc Plastics Engrs. *Res:* Development of catalysts for olefin polymerization and other industrial reactions; development of commercial manufacturing procedures for industrial catalysts. *Mailing Add:* 247 RB-6 PRC Bartlesville OK 74004

CAPSTACK, ERNEST, b Fall River, Mass, June 9, 30; m 58; c 2. ORGANIC CHEMISTRY, BIOCHEMISTRY. *Educ:* Mass Inst Technol, BS, 52; Univ RI, MS, 54; Brown Univ, PhD(chem), 59. *Prof Exp:* Res chemist, E I du Pont de Nemours & Co, 58-60; res fel, Steroid Training Prog, Worcester Found Exp Biol, 60-61; res assoc, Clark Univ, 61-62; scientist, Worcester Found Exp Biol, 62-64; vis asst prof, Clark Univ, 62-64; assoc prof chem, 64-66, PROF CHEM, W VA WESLEYAN COL, 66-, CHMN DEPT, 67- *Mem:* Am Chem Soc; Sigma Xi. *Res:* Organic and steroid synthesis; steroid and terpene biosynthesis and metabolism; science and religion; death and dying. *Mailing Add:* Dept of Chem WVa Wesleyan Col Buckhannon WV 26201

CAPURRO, LUIS R A, physical oceanography, marine meteorology, see previous edition

CAPUTI, ROGER WILLIAM, b Newark, NJ, Jan 9, 35; m 59; c 3. PHYSICAL CHEMISTRY. *Educ:* Calif Inst Technol, BS, 57, PhD(phys chem), 60. *Prof Exp:* Radiol chemist, US Naval Radiol Defense Lab, 57-60; teaching asst, Phys Chem Lab, Calif Inst Technol, 60-64; chemist, US Naval Radiol Defense Lab, 64-68; chemist, Vallecitos Nuclear Ctr, 68-70, mgr prod qual & applns lab, 70-72; sr scientist, Track Etch Develop Lab, 72-76, SR SCIENTIST, CORE CHEM LAB, VALLECITOS NUCLEAR CTR, GEN ELEC CO, 76- *Mem:* NY Acad Sci. *Res:* Experimental and theoretical studies of breeder reactor fuel-cladding-coolant interactions; etching of ion damage tracks in plastics; development of microbiological culturing techniques on membrane filters; modeling of membrane filter theory; instrumentation; analysis of nuclear weapons effects; oceanography. *Mailing Add:* Gen Elec Vallecitos Nuclear Ctr Vallecitos Rd Pleasanton CA 94566

CAPUTO, JOSEPH ANTHONY, b Jersey City, NJ, May 10, 40; m 65; c 2. PHYSICAL ORGANIC CHEMISTRY. *Educ:* Seton Hall Univ, BS, 62, MS, 64; Univ Houston, PhD(phys org chem), 67. *Prof Exp:* Fel org chem, Duke Univ, 67-68; from instr to assoc prof org chem, State Univ NY Col Buffalo, 68-77, chmn dept chem, 74-77; PROF CHEM & DEAN SCH SCI, SOUTHWEST TEX STATE UNIV, 77-, VPRES ACAD AFFAIRS, 80- *Mem:* The Chem Soc; Am Chem Soc. *Res:* Linear free energy relationships; electronic transmission; reaction mechanisms; diazoalkanes; phosphorus heterocycles; antimalarial compounds. *Mailing Add:* Sch of Sci Southwest Tex State Univ San Marcos TX 78666

CAPUZZO, JUDITH M, b Manchester, NH, Dec 29, 47; m 72. PHYSIOLOGICAL ECOLOGY, POLLUTION ECOLOGY. *Educ:* Stonehill Col, BS, 69; Univ NH, MS, 71, PhD(zool), 74. *Prof Exp:* Instr biol, Framingham State Col, 74-75; fel, 75-76, investr, 75-76, asst scientist, 76-79, ASSOC SCIENTIST BIOL OCEANOG, WOODS HOLE OCEANOG INST, 80- *Concurrent Pos:* Lectr, Cornell Univ & Univ Pa, 77-; vis prof, Bridgewater State Col, 78-; participant, Nat Acad Sci Workshop Petrol Marine Environ, 81 & Planning Comt Workshop Land vs Sea Disposal Indust & Domestic Wastes, 82- *Mem:* AAAS; Am Soc Zoologists; Sigma Xi; World Mariculture Soc; Estuarine Res Fedn. *Res:* Comparative physiology of marine larval and postlarval crustaceans including studies of energetics and nutrition; assimilative capacity of the oceans for waste disposal with a consideration of the effects of pollutants on the physiology of marine animals. *Mailing Add:* Woods Hole Oceanog Inst Woods Hole MA 02543

CAPWELL, ROBERT J, b Binghamton, NY, July 6, 40; m 62; c 2. PHYSICAL CHEMISTRY. *Educ:* Ohio State Univ, BS, 63; Pa State Univ, MS, 65; Univ Pittsburgh, PhD(phys chem), 70; Rider Col, MBA, 80. *Prof Exp:* Chemist, Gulf Res & Develop Co, 65-68; res scientist phys chem, N L Industs, Inc, 70-72, sect leader phys & anal chem 72-73, dept head anal & tech specialist, Cent Res Lab, 73-76, res & develop mgr, Indust Chem Div, 76-81; MFG ENG MGR, YIELD MGT, GTD IBM CORP, 81- *Mem:* Am Chem Soc; Soc Appl Spectros. *Res:* Infrared and Raman spectroscopy; structure of matter; chemical instrumentation; molten salt chemistry; flame retardants; plastics additives; reaction mechanisms; electroless plating; process control; statistical quality control; printed circuit boards. *Mailing Add:* 139 Dorchester Dr East Windsor NJ 08520

CARABATEAS, PHILIP M, b New York, NY, Jan 20, 30; m 60; c 2. ORGANIC CHEMISTRY, MEDICINAL CHEMISTRY. *Educ:* Polytech Inst, Brooklyn, BS, 55; Rensselaer Polytech Inst, PhD(chem), 62. *Prof Exp:* From asst res chemist to res chemist, 55-70, SR RES CHEMIST, ORG CHEM, STERLING-WINTHROP RES INST, 70- *Mem:* Am Chem Soc. *Res:* Synthesis of nitrogen heterocycles, analgesics, antitussives and antifertility agents. *Mailing Add:* Sterling-Winthrop Res Inst Rensselaer NY 12144

CARACENA, FERNANDO, b El Paso, Tex, Mar 13, 36; m 69; c 2. ATMOSPHERIC PHYSICS, PHYSICS. *Educ:* Univ Tex, El Paso, BS, 58; Case Western Reserve Univ, MA, 66, PhD(physics), 68. *Prof Exp:* Atmosphere physicist, White Sands Missile Range, Dept Defense, 58-61, sci programmer, Ballistic Res Labs, Aberdeen Proving Grounds, Md, 59-61; asst prof physics, Metrop State Col, 69-76; ATMOSPHERE PHYSICIST, ATMOSPHERIC PHYSICS & CHEM LABS, ENVIRON RES LABS, NAT OCEANIC & ATMOSPHERIC ADMIN, 76- *Concurrent Pos:* Fel, Workshop on Relativistic Wave Equations, Cleveland State Univ, Off Naval Res, 69. *Mem:* AAAS; Am Phys Soc; Sigma Xi. *Res:* Severe local storms, flash floods, and infrared remote sensing; air safety, especially clear air turbulence, low altitude wind shear, and meteorology of wind-shear-related aircraft accidents. *Mailing Add:* Nat Oceanic & Atmospheric Admin Chem Lab RX8 Boulder CO 80303

CARACO, THOMAS BENJAMIN, b West Palm Beach, Fla, Nov 7, 46; m 79; c 1. ECOLOGY, ANIMAL BEHAVIOR. *Educ:* Univ Rochester, AB, 68; Syracuse Univ, PhD(biol), 77. *Prof Exp:* Fel ecol, Univ Ariz, 77-79; ASST PROF BIOL, UNIV ROCHESTER, 79- *Mem:* Ecol Soc Am; Animal Behav Soc; AAAS. *Mailing Add:* Dept Biol Univ Rochester Rochester NY 14627

CARADUS, SELWYN ROSS, b Auckland, NZ, Nov 10, 35; m 59; c 2. MATHEMATICAL ANALYSIS. *Educ:* Univ Auckland, BSc, 57, MSc, 58; Univ Southern Calif, MA, 62; Univ Calif, Los Angeles, PhD(math), 65. *Prof Exp:* Jr lectr math, Univ Auckland, 58-60; from asst prof to assoc prof, 64-76, PROF MATH, QUEEN'S UNIV, ONT, 77- *Mem:* Am Math Soc; Can Math Cong. *Res:* Theory of linear operators in Banach space. *Mailing Add:* Dept of Math Queen's Univ Kingston ON K7L 3N6 Can

CARAM, HUGO SIMON, b Buenos Aires, Arg, Mar 14, 45; m 70; c 2. CHEMICAL ENGINEERING. *Educ:* Univ Buenos Aires, BS, 67; Univ Minn, PhD(chem eng), 77. *Prof Exp:* Process engr petrol refining, Shell Compania Argentino de Petroleo Sociedad Anonimo, 70-72; res asst chem eng, Univ Minn, 72-77; asst prof, 77-81, ASSOC PROF CHEM ENG, LEHIGH UNIV, 81- *Mem:* AAAS; Am Inst Chem Engrs. *Res:* Coal gasification in fluid and fixed beds; multiphase flows; reactor analysis; mathematical modeling. *Mailing Add:* Dept Chem Eng Lehigh Univ Bethlehem PA 18015

CARAPELLA, S(AM) C(HARLES), JR, b Tuckahoe, NY, Jan 27, 23. PHYSICAL METALLURGY. *Educ:* Mich State Col, BS, 44; Univ Notre Dame, MS, 48, PhD(phys metall), 50. *Prof Exp:* Metallurgist, Allison Div, Gen Motors Corp, 44; res metallurgist, 50-57, sect head, 57-59, supt high purity metals develop, 59-74, SUPT BYPROD METALS, ASARCO, INC, 74- *Mem:* Am Soc Metals; Sigma Xi. *Res:* nonferrous physical metallurgy; properties of less common metals. *Mailing Add:* 114 Walter St South Plainfield NJ 07080

CARAS, GUS J(OHN), b Karitsa, Greece, Jan 20, 29; US citizen; m 59; c 3. CHEMICAL ENGINEERING, INFORMATION SCIENCE. *Educ:* Ga Inst Technol, BS, 58, MS, 67. *Prof Exp:* Process engr, Redstone Div, Thiokol Chem Corp, Ala, 58-61, chem engr, 61-62; chem engr struct & mech lab, Res & Develop Dept, US Army Missile Command, 62-63, info scientist, Redstone Sci Info Ctr, Res & Develop Directorate, 63-67; info scientist pesticides prog, Food & Drug Admin, 67-69, chief tech data unit, Div Community Studies, 69-73, CHIEF STATIST SERV ACTIV, CTR DISEASE CONTROL, HEALTH & HUMAN SERV, 73- *Concurrent Pos:* Instr math, statist & comput sci, Ga State Univ & De Kalb Community Col, 76- *Mem:* Am Soc Info Sci; Am Inst Aeronaut & Astronaut; Am Inst Chem Engrs; Am Statist Asn. *Res:* Research and development in field of solid propellant rockets; analysis and interpretation of scientific and technical literature; design and administration of information storage and retrieval systems; mathematical statistics; computer science. *Mailing Add:* 1659 Clairmont Pl NE Atlanta GA 30329

CARASSO, ALFRED SAMUEL, b Alexandria, Egypt, Apr 9, 39; m 64; c 1. MATHEMATICS. *Educ:* Univ Adelaide, BS, 60; Univ Wis-Madison, MS, 64, MA, 65, PhD(math), 68. *Prof Exp:* Meteorologist, Bur Meteorol, Australia, 60-62; asst prof math, Mich State Univ, 68-69; from asst prof to assoc prof, 69-74, PROF MATH & STATIST, UNIV NMEX, 75- *Concurrent Pos:* Consult, Los Alamos Nat Lab, 72; prin invest, Res Partial Differential Equations, US Army Res Off Grant, 76. *Mem:* Am Math Soc; Soc Indust & Appl Math. *Res:* Partial differential equations; numerical analysis. *Mailing Add:* Dept of Math Univ of NMex Albuquerque NM 87131

CARAWAY, JAMES SPENCE, b Jacksonville, Fla, July 30, 43; m 66; c 2. MEDICINE, RADIOLOGY. *Educ:* Duke Univ, BA, 65; Univ Tenn, MD, 69; Am Bd Radiol, dipl, 74. *Prof Exp:* ASST PROF RADIOL, COL MED, UNIV S FLA, 77- *Mem:* Am Col Radiol; Radiol Soc NAm. *Mailing Add:* Dept of Radiol Univ of SFla Tampa FL 33620

CARAWAY, WENDELL THOMAS, b Xenia, Ohio, Nov 4, 20; m 44. BIOCHEMISTRY. *Educ:* Wilmington Col, BS, 42; Miami Univ, MA, 43; Johns Hopkins Univ, PhD(biochem), 50; Am Bd Clin Chem, dipl. *Prof Exp:* Asst chemist, Ohio River Div Labs, US Corps Engr, 43-45, mat engr & head chem lab, 45-46; biochemist, RI Hosp, 50-57; BIOCHEMIST, FLINT CLIN PATHOLOGISTS, 57- *Concurrent Pos:* Mem bd dirs, Nat Registry Clin Chem, 67-73. *Honors & Awards:* Ames Award in Clin Chem, Garulet Award, 78. *Mem:* AAAS; Am Chem Soc; Am Asn Clin Chem (pres, 65). *Res:* Kinetics and mechanisms of reactions; serum enzyme assays; ultramicrochemical methods of blood analysis; drug effects on lab tests. *Mailing Add:* 1102 Woodside Dr Flint MI 48503

CARBAJAL, BERNARD GONZALES, III, b New Orleans, La, Feb 15, 33; m 54; c 2. SOLID STATE CHEMISTRY, SEMICONDUCTORS. *Educ:* Univ Minn, PhD(chem), 58. *Prof Exp:* Asst chem, Univ Minn, 54-56; asst prof, Col St Thomas, 57-60; mem tech staff, 60-69, mgr multilevel tech prog, Components Group, 69-73, mgr advan circuit technol, 72-74, mgr design support, 74-76, prog mgr, Automated Array Assembly, 76-80, PROG MGR COMPLEMENTARY METAL-OXIDE SEMICONDUCTOR TECHNOL PROD ENG, TEX INSTRUMENTS, INC, 80- *Mem:* Am Chem Soc. *Res:* Organic semiconductors; thin film polymers; electrical conduction in organic materials; semiconductor processing; metal-oxide-semiconductor devices; thin films; interconnection technology; solar photovoltaic technology; complimentary metal-oxide semiconductor technology. *Mailing Add:* Tex Instruments Inc PO Box 225012 Dallas TX 75265

CARBALLO-QUIROS, ALFREDO, b San Jose, Costa Rica, Nov 28, 19; m 45; c 3. PLANT BREEDING, QUANTITATIVE GENETICS. *Educ:* Iowa State Col, MS, 57; NC State Col, PhD(plant breeding), 62. *Prof Exp:* Head maize sect, Ministry Agr, Costa Rica, 48-51, head lowland crops, 51-54; coordr, Cent Am Coop Maize Proj, Rockefeller Found, 55-56 & 58-59; geneticist, Inter-Am Inst Agr Sci, Orgn Am States, Costa Rica, 62-63; dir maize prog, Nat Inst Agr Invest & Mendoza Found, Venezuela, 63-66; consult maize prog, Food & Agr Orgn, UAR, 66-67; geneticist maize prog, 69-70, GENETICIST, INT MAIZE TESTING PROG, INT MAIZE & WHEAT IMPROV CTR, MEX, 70- *Concurrent Pos:* Del, Inter-Am Conf Crop Sci, Peru, 63 & Colombia, 70; del annual meeting, Cent Am Coop Maize Improv Proj, 67. *Mem:* NY Acad Sci; Crop Sci Soc Am; Latin Am Soc Crop Sci; Sigma Xi; Agron Eng Soc Costa Rica. *Res:* Intra-population improvement of maize populations through a quantitative genetics approach. *Mailing Add:* Apartado 2591 San Jose Costa Rica

CARBARY, JAMES F, b June 5, 51. MAGNETOSPHERIC PHYSICS. *Educ:* Univ Ill, BS, 73; Rice Univ, MS, 76, PhD(space physics), 78. *Prof Exp:* Res assoc, Rice Univ, 77-78; RES ASSOC, APPL PHYSICS LAB, JOHN HOPKINS UNIV, 78- *Mem:* Am Geophys Union. *Res:* Research involving magnetospheres of Earth, Jupiter and Saturn. *Mailing Add:* Appl Physics Lab Johns Hopkins Univ Laurel MD 20707

CARBERRY, EDWARD ANDREW, b Milwaukee, Wis, Nov 20, 41; m 67; c 2. INORGANIC CHEMISTRY, ORGANOMETALLIC CHEMISTRY. *Educ:* Marquette Univ, BS, 62; Univ Wis, PhD(inorg chem), 68. *Prof Exp:* PROF CHEM, SOUTHWEST MINN STATE UNIV, 68- *Mem:* Am Chem Soc; Am Sci Glassblowers Soc. *Res:* Preparation, spectroscopic and bonding studies of inorganic and organometallic compounds, especially organosilicon compounds; catenated group IV chemistry emphasizing polysilanes and polygermanes linear and cyclic. *Mailing Add:* Dept of Chem Southwest Minn State Univ Marshall MN 56258

CARBERRY, JAMES JOHN, b Brooklyn, NY, Sept 13, 25; m 59; c 2. CHEMICAL ENGINEERING. *Educ:* Univ Notre Dame, BS, 50, MS, 51; Yale Univ, PhD, 57. *Prof Exp:* Chem process engr, Explosives Dept, E I du Pont de Nemours & Co, NJ, 51-53; consult, Olin-Mathieson Chem Corp, Conn, 54-57; sr res engr, Eng Dept, E I du Pont de Nemours & Co, 57-61; from asst prof to assoc prof chem eng, 61-66, PROF CHEM ENG, UNIV

NOTRE DAME, 66- *Concurrent Pos:* Consult, Am Oil Co, 62- & Catalytica & Assocs, Inc, 74-; NSF sr fel, Cambridge Univ, 65-66; Hays-Fulbright sr scholar, Univ Rome, 74; Sir Winston Churchill fel, Cambridge Univ, 79. *Honors & Awards:* Yale Eng Asn Award; R H Wilhelm Award, Am Inst Chem Engrs, 76. *Mem:* AAAS; fel NY Acad Sci; fel Am Inst Chem; Am Inst Chem Engrs; Am Chem Soc. *Res:* Kinetics; heterogeneous catalysis; heat and mass transfer; nitric acid manufacture; catalytic reactor technology. *Mailing Add:* Dept of Chem Eng Univ of Notre Dame Notre Dame IN 46556

CARBERRY, JUDITH B, b Oil City, Pa, Mar 10, 36; m 81; c 2. POLLUTION CONTROL. *Educ:* Cornell Univ, BS, 58; Univ Notre Dame, MS, 69, PhD(environ eng), 72. *Prof Exp:* Fel environ eng, Univ Col, London, 72-73; asst prof, Univ Del, 73-78, assoc prof, 78-79; sr fel, The Technion, Israel, 79-80; ASSOC PROF ENVIRON ENG, UNIV DEL, 80- *Concurrent Pos:* Asst dir filtration, NATO Advan Study Inst, 73, partic wastewater, 76, dir & lectr sludge, 79; consult, Planners & Assocs, 73-74, Howard L Robertson, Inc, 75-76, US Naval Ship Res & Develop Ctr, 77-78, Ecolsci, Inc, US Environ Protection Agency, 80-81; guest lectr, Univ Del, 73, Duke Univ, Tulane Univ, Va Polytech, & The Technion, Israel; prin investr grants, US Off Water Res & Technol & US Environ Protection Agency, 73-; tech reviewer, US Environ Protection Agency & NSF, 78- *Mem:* Water Pollution Control Fedn; Asn Environ Eng Profs; Soc Women Engrs. *Res:* Interfacial phenomena of liquid/particulate reactions and resulting fundamental effects on liquid/solid separation processes; biological particulate transport and adsorption reactions in engineered systems and sediment particle reactions with pollutants in natural systems. *Mailing Add:* Dept Civil Eng Univ Del Newark DE 19711

CARBIENER, WAYNE ALAN, b St Joseph Co, Ind, Feb 21, 36; m 58; c 4. NUCLEAR ENGINEERING. *Educ:* Purdue Univ, BS, 58, MS, 62; Ohio State Univ, PhD(nuclear eng), 75. *Prof Exp:* Res engr nuclear sci, Battelle Columbus Labs, 62-71, sect mgr nuclear eng & sci, 71-75, prog mgr nuclear eng, 76-78; dept mgr technol develop, Battelle/ONWI, 78-81, MGR, OFF NAT WEAPONS TEST INTEGRATION, BATTELLE/BPMD, 81-. *Mem:* Am Soc Mech Eng. *Res:* Development and application of technology to isolation of nuclear waste; earth science, nuclear science, geology, engineering and materials science. *Mailing Add:* Off Nat Weapons Sta Integration 505 King Ave Columbus OH 43201

CARBNO, WILLIAM CLIFFORD, b Tessier, Sask, July 30, 30; m 53; c 1. MATHEMATICS EDUCATION. *Educ:* Univ Sask, BEd, 61, BA, 63, MEd, 64; Univ Toronto, PhD, 76. *Prof Exp:* Asst prof, 67-80, ASSOC PROF MATH EDUC & EDUC PSYCHOL, BRANDON UNIV, 80- *Concurrent Pos:* Chmn sub-comt on math prog, Coun Develop Math Curric, Man, 70-73; mem, Elem Math Curric Comt, 71-72; vis prof math educ, Univ Sask, 78-79. *Mem:* Can Soc Studies Educ; Can Asn Res Educ. *Res:* Child development; models for memory and cognition. *Mailing Add:* Fac of Educ Brandon Univ Brandon Can

CARBON, JOHN ANTHONY, b Sharon, Pa, Jan 1, 31; m 50; c 2. BIOCHEMISTRY. *Educ:* Univ Ill, BS, 52; Northwestern Univ, PhD(biochem), 55. *Prof Exp:* Res assoc biochem, Med Sch, Northwestern Univ, 55-56; sr res chemist, Org Chem Dept, Abbott Labs, 56-63, res assoc, Biochem Dept, 63-68; assoc prof biochem, 68-70, PROF BIOCHEM, UNIV CALIF, SANTA BARBARA, 70- *Concurrent Pos:* Consult, Abbott Labs, 74- & Appl Molecular Genetics, 80- *Mem:* Am Soc Biol Chemists; AAAS; Genetics Soc Am. *Res:* Nucleic acids; transfer RNA; viral DNA; bacterial plasmids; molecular cloning; yeast molecular genetics; chromosome structure. *Mailing Add:* Dept of Biol Sci Univ of Calif Santa Barbara CA 93106

CARBON, MAX W(ILLIAM), b Monon, Ind, Jan 19, 22; m 44; c 5. NUCLEAR ENGINEERING. *Educ:* Purdue Univ, BS, 43, MS, 47, PhD(heat transfer & thermodyn), 49. *Prof Exp:* Thermodynamacist, Hanford Works, Gen Elec Co, 49-50, pile engr, 50-51, head heat transfer unit, 52-55, head contract eng unit, 55; chief thermodyn sect, Res & Advan Develop Div, Avco Mfg Corp, 55-58; prof mech eng & chmn nuclear eng comt, 59-63, PROF NUCLEAR ENG & CHMN DEPT, UNIV WIS, MADISON, 63- *Concurrent Pos:* Mem, Adv Comt Reactor Safeguards, US Nuclear Regulatory Comn, 75-, vchmn, 78, chmn, 79. *Mem:* AAAS; Am Soc Mech Engrs; Am Soc Eng Educ; Am Nuclear Soc; Am Asn Univ Professors. *Res:* Nuclear power; heat transfer. *Mailing Add:* Dept of Nuclear Eng Univ of Wis Madison WI 53706

CARBONE, GABRIEL, b New York, NY, Sept 4, 27; m 53; c 1. ENVIRONMENTAL CHEMISTRY. *Educ:* Brooklyn Col, BS, 49. *Prof Exp:* Chemist, Food & Water Chem Lab, 55-67, sr chemist, 67-70, PRIN CHEMIST & DIR FOOD & WATER CHEM LAB, BUR LABS, NEW YORK CITY HEALTH DEPT, 70- *Concurrent Pos:* Mem fumigant bd, New York City Health Dept, 70- *Res:* Alternate standards for sharer rapid pasteurization test for dairy products and differentiation of residual and reactivated phosphatase in dairy products; nitrites and nitrates in meat products. *Mailing Add:* Food & Water Chem Lab Bur Labs 455 1st Ave New York NY 10016

CARBONE, JOHN VITO, b Sacramento, Calif, Dec 13, 22; m 46; c 3. MEDICINE. *Educ:* Univ Calif, BA, 45, MD, 48. *Prof Exp:* From instr to assoc prof, 51-66, PROF MED, SCH MED, UNIV CALIF, SAN FRANCISCO, 66- *Concurrent Pos:* Giannini fel med, 54-55; consult to Surgeon Gen, US Army, 58 & Letterman Hosp, Travis AFB, San Francisco. *Res:* Gastroenterology; metabolic aspects of liver disease. *Mailing Add:* Sch of Med Univ of Calif San Francisco CA 94143

CARBONE, PAUL P, b White Plains, NY, May 2, 31; m 54; c 7. ONCOLOGY. *Educ:* Albany Med Col, MD, 56. *Prof Exp:* Intern med, USPHS Hosp, Baltimore, Md, 56-57, mem med staff, Savannah, Ga, 57-58; resident internal med, San Francisco, Calif, 58-60; sr investr, Nat Cancer Inst, 60-65, head solid tumor serv, 65-68, chief med br, 68-72, assoc dir med oncol, Div Cancer Treatment, 72-76; PROF HUMAN ONCOL & MED & CHIEF CLIN ONCOL, UNIV WIS, 76-, CHMN DEPT HUMAN ONCOL, 77-;

DIR, WIS CLIN CANCER CTR, 78- *Mem:* Am Soc Hemat; Am Fedn Clin Res; Am Asn Cancer Res; Am Soc Clin Oncol; Am Soc Clin Invest. *Res:* Research in cancer chemotherapy, immunology and hematology. *Mailing Add:* Wis Clin Ctr K4/614 600 Highland Ave Madison WI 53792

CARBONE, RICHARD EDWARD, b Bronx, NY, Sept 26, 44; m 70; c 2. METEOROLOGY, ATMOSPHERIC PHYSICS. *Educ:* NY Univ, BS, 66; Univ Chicago, MS, 69. *Prof Exp:* Analyst opers res, Grumman Aerospace, 68-70; res scientist meteorol, Univ Chicago, 72-74 & Meteorol Res Inc, 74-75, mgr atmospheric physics, 75-76; staff scientist III meteorol, 76-81, MGR FIELD OBSERV FACIL, NAT CTR ATMOSPHERIC RES, 81- *Mem:* Am Meteorol Soc; Sigma Xi. *Res:* Storm kinematics; microphysics; precipitation physics; remote sensing of atmosphere; Doppler radar. *Mailing Add:* Nat Ctr Atmospheric Res PO Box 3000 Boulder CO 80307

CARBONE, ROBERT JAMES, b Hartford, Conn, Aug 17, 30; m 53; c 3. FAMILY PRACTICE MEDICINE, PHYSICS. *Educ:* Univ Conn, BA, 52, MA, 53, PhD, 56; MD, 79. *Prof Exp:* Asst, Univ Conn, 54-56; physicist, Lincoln Lab, Mass Inst Technol, 56-60 & 62-68 & Bomac Labs, Inc, 61-62; physicist, Philips Res Labs, Technol Univ Eindhoven, 68-69 & Lincoln Lab, Mass Inst Technol, 70-72; alternate group leader, Los Alamos Sci Lab, Univ Calif, 72-76. *Concurrent Pos:* Family pract resident physician, East Tenn State Univ, Bristol, Tenn, 79-80, Johnson City, 81-82. *Mem:* Am Phys Soc; AMA; Am Acad Family Pract. *Res:* Radiofrequency gas discharges; heavy ion-atom interactions; chemical and gaseous lasers; direct current discharges; laser applications in fusion and isotope separation. *Mailing Add:* 2704 Oakland Ave Johnson City TN 37601

CARBONELL, JAIME GUILLERMO, b Montevideo, Uruguay, July 29, 53; US citizen; m 75; c 2. COGNITIVE SCIENCE, NATURAL LANGUAGE PROCESSING. *Educ:* Mass Inst Technol, SB, 75; Yale Univ, BS, 76, PhD(comput sci), 79. *Prof Exp:* Res programmer comput sci, Bolt Beranek & Newman, 71-75; res fel, Yale Univ, 76-79; ASST PROF COMPUT SCI, CARNEGIE-MELLON UNIV, 79- *Concurrent Pos:* Consult various orgn, 78- *Mem:* Asn Comput Ling; Asn Comput Mach; Cognitive Sci Soc; NY Acad Sci; Am Asn Artificial Intel. *Res:* Artificial intelligence focusing on computer models of analogical reasoning, planning and counterplanning, natural language processing, man-machine interfaces, modeling human memory and inference processes; knowledge engineering focusing on rule-based expert systems and real time decision-making. *Mailing Add:* Comput Sci Dept Carnegie-Mellon Univ Pittsburgh PA 15213

CARBONELL, ROBERT JOSEPH, b El Salvador, Mar 20, 27; m 50; c 5. FOOD SCIENCE. *Educ:* Nat Univ El Salvador, BS, 48; Purdue Univ, MS, 50. *Prof Exp:* Res chemist, Sanit Eng Div, Inst Inter Am Affairs, El Salvador, 45-46, asst head dept chem, Ctr Nat Agron, 46-52, head green coffee processing div, 52-53; assoc prof biochem, Sch Agron, Nat Univ El Salvador, 51-52, assoc prof org anal, Sch Pharmaceut Chem, 51-53; res chemist res & develop food prod, Fleischmann Labs, Standards Brands Inc, 53-54, group leader, 54-57, div head, 57-59, dir, Consumer Prod Res Dept, 59-63, dir, Div Res & Develop, 63-65, mgr, 65-69, dir res, 69-73, corp dir prod & develop planning, 73-74, mgr, Fleischmann Indust Mfg, 74-75, mgr grocery prod mfg, 75, vpres res & develop, 75-81; EXEC VPRES TECHNOL, NABISCO BRANDS INC, 81- *Concurrent Pos:* Mem, Coffee Processing Surv Comn, El Salvador Govt, 52; abstr, Chem Abstr, 53-54. *Mem:* Am Chem Soc; Inst Food Tecnol. *Res:* Composition of fats and oils from tropical species of Salvadorean Flora; nutritional value of coffee pulp; treatment of waste waters from coffee processing plants; effect of crossing upon chemical composition of sunflower oil; coffee bean mucilage. *Mailing Add:* Nabisco Brands Inc 15 River Rd Wilton CT 06897

CARBONI, RUDOLPH A, b Yonkers, NY, Nov 10, 22; m 49; c 4. ORGANIC CHEMISTRY. *Educ:* Columbia Univ, AB, 47, AM, 48; Mass Inst Technol, PhD(org chem), 53. *Prof Exp:* Res chemist, Charles Pfizer & Co, 48-50; res chemist, Cent Res Dept, 53-61, res supvr, Org Chem Dept, 62-67, div head explor intermediates, 67-68, lab mgr, 68-70, res & develop mgr permasep prod, 70-73, TECH MGR ELECTRONIC PROD DIV, PHOTOPROD DEPT, E I DU PONT DE NEMOURS & CO, 73- *Mem:* Am Chem Soc; Am Asn Textile Chem & Colorists. *Res:* Cyanocarbon chemistry; new polynitrogen systems; organofluorine chemistry; antibiotic research; inductive and field effects; dye studies and oxidation catalysts; reverse osmosis; photopolymer systems for printed circuit and microelectronic device fabrication. *Mailing Add:* Photoprod Dept E I du Pont de Nemours & Co Wilmington DE 19803

CARBONNEAU, ROCH, physiology, endocrinology, see previous edition

CARD, HOWARD CLARENCE, solid state electronics, semiconductors, see previous edition

CARD, KENNETH D, b Ont, Jan 23, 37; m 59; c 2. GEOLOGY. *Educ:* Queen's Univ (Ont), BSc, 59; Princeton Univ, MA, 62, PhD(geol), 63. *Prof Exp:* Resident geologist, 63-66; field geologist, 66-74, sr geologist, Ont Div Mines, 74-77; GEOLOGIST, PRECAMBRIAN SUBDIV, GEOL SURV CAN, 77- *Mem:* Fel Geol Soc Am; fel Geol Asn Can. *Res:* Regional geology; precambrian stratigraphy, structure and metamorphism. *Mailing Add:* Geol Surv of Can 588 Booth St Ottawa Can

CARD, PETER J, b Manchester, NH, Sept 17, 49; m 77. CARBOHYDRATE CHEMISTRY. *Educ:* Univ NH, BS, 72; Ohio State Univ, PhD(chem), 76. *Prof Exp:* Fel, Harvard Univ, 76-77; RES CHEMIST, CENT RES DEPT, E I DU PONT DE NEMOURS & CO, INC, 77- *Mem:* Am Chem Soc. *Res:* Studies in the areas of organosulfur chemistry; strained ring systems; work towards a synthesis of erythromycin; chival synthesis from carbohydrates; synthesis of modified sugars; glycosylation reactions. *Mailing Add:* Cent Res & Develop Dept Exp Sta E I du Pont de Nemours & Co Inc Wilmington DE 19898

CARD, ROGER JOHN, b Grand Rapids, Mich, Oct 31, 47. HETEROGENEOUS CATALYSIS. *Educ:* Hope Col, BS, 69; Iowa State Univ, MS, 71, PhD(org chem), 75. *Prof Exp:* Asst prof org chem, Univ Kebangsaan Malaysia, 75-77; fel, Bowling Green State Univ, 77-78; res scientist chem, 78-80, SR RES CHEMIST, AM CYANAMID CO, 80- *Mem:* Am Chem Soc; The Chem Soc. *Res:* Study of mechanisms of catalytic processes; design of improved catalysts; design and application of polymer supported catalysts. *Mailing Add:* Am Cyanamid Co 1937 W Main St Stamford CT 06904

CARDE, RING RICHARD TOMLINSON, b Hartford, Conn, Sept 18, 43; m 74; c 2. INSECT PHEROMONES. *Educ:* Tufts Univ, BS, 66; Cornell Univ, MS, 68, PhD(entom), 71. *Prof Exp:* Fel, NY State Agr Exp Sta, Cornell Univ, 71-75; from asst prof to assoc prof entom, Mich State Univ, 75-80; PROF AND HEAD ENTOM, UNIV MASS, 80- *Honors & Awards:* Ciba-Geigy Award, Entom Soc Am, 81. *Mem:* Entom Soc Am; Entom Soc Can; AAAS; Sigma Xi; Soc Study Evolution. *Res:* Insect pheromones and behavior; pheromone identification; use of pheromones in pest management; biosystematics of the Lepidoptera. *Mailing Add:* Dept Entom Univ Mass Amherst MA 01003

CARDELL, ROBERT RIDLEY, JR, b Atlanta, Ga, Nov 11, 31; m 59; c 3. CELL BIOLOGY. *Educ:* Ga Southern Col, BS, 56; Univ Va, MS, 59, PhD(biol), 62. *Prof Exp:* Asst biol, Univ Va, 56-59, instr, 59-60; asst biophys, Edsel B Ford Inst Med Res, 60-62, res assoc, 62-64; res assoc biol & instr, Harvard Univ, 64-67; assoc prof anat, Sch Med, Univ Va, 67-70, prof, 70-79; PROF & CHAIR ANAT & CELL BIOL, COL MED, UNIV CINCINNATI, 79- *Mem:* Am Soc Cell Biol; Am Asn Anat; Endocrine Soc. *Res:* Ultrastructure of cells; morphological action of hormones; cell biology; cellular endocrinology. *Mailing Add:* Dept Anat & Cell Biol Col Med Univ Cincinnati Charlottesville VA 22901

CARDEN, ARNOLD EUGENE, b Birmingham, Ala, Apr 27, 30; m 52; c 6. ENGINEERING. *Educ:* Ala Polytech Inst, BSME, 52; Univ Ala, MS, 56; Univ Conn, PhD(metall), 72. *Prof Exp:* Res engr, Alcoa Res Labs, 56-58; from asst prof to assoc prof eng mech, 58-71, PROF ENG MECH, UNIV ALA, TUSCALOOSA, 71- *Concurrent Pos:* Res partic, Oak Ridge Nat Lab, 59-; NSF fel, Dept Metall, Univ Conn, 69-70; fel, Inst Mat Sci, 71-72. *Mem:* Am Soc Mech Engrs; Am Soc Metals; Am Soc Eng Educ; Nat Asn Corrosion Engrs. *Res:* Mechanics; mechanics of materials; methods of mechanical testing; material properties. *Mailing Add:* Dept of Aerospace Eng Mech Eng & Univ of Ala University AL 35486

CARDENAS, CARLOS GUILLERMO, b Laredo, Tex, June 25, 41; m 65; c 2. ORGANIC CHEMISTRY. *Educ:* Univ Tex, BS, 62, PhD(org chem), 65. *Prof Exp:* Asst prof chem, US Naval Postgrad Sch, 65-67; res chemist, Phillips Petrol Co, 67-69, group leader, 69; sr chemist, 69-71, sect mgr, 71-74, MGR RES, GLIDDEN-DURKEE DIV, SCM CORP, 75- *Concurrent Pos:* Off Naval Res grant, 65-67. *Mem:* Am Chem Soc; The Chem Soc. *Res:* Olefin synthesis and reaction mechanisms; nuclear magnetic resonance; Diels-Alder reactions; base catalysis; organometallics; terpenes. *Mailing Add:* Glidden-Durkee Div SCM Corp PO Box 389 Jacksonville FL 32201

CARDENAS, MANUEL, b San Diego, Tex, Sept 18, 42; m 68; c 2. EXPERIMENTAL STATISTICS. *Educ:* Tex A&I Univ, BS, 68, MA, 70; Tex A&M Univ, PhD(statist), 74. *Prof Exp:* Comput programmer, Tex Real Estate Res Ctr, 72-73; asst prof, 74-80, ASSOC PROF STATIST, NMEX STATE UNIV, 80- *Mem:* Am Statist Soc; Biometric Soc. *Res:* Survey sampling and compartmental modeling; the derivation of the distribution of models with time-dependent transition probabilities, particularly as applied to bio-medical sciences. *Mailing Add:* Dept of Exp Statist Box 3130 NMex State Univ Las Cruces NM 88003

CARDENAS, MARY JANET M, b Miami, Okla, Jan 31, 42; m 60, 79; c 4. OCULOMOTOR DISORDERS, PROTEIN CHEMISTRY. *Educ:* Okla State Univ, BA, 63; Univ Ill, MS, 65, PhD(biochem), 67. *Prof Exp:* Res assoc protein synthesis, Ore State Univ, 67; instr chem, Col Nueva Granada, 69-71; fel, Ore State Univ, 71-73, asst prof biochem & biophysics, 73-78; assoc prof chem, Univ NC, Chapel Hill, 78-81; HEALTH SCI ADMINR, NAT EYE INST, NIH, 81- *Concurrent Pos:* Grants Assoc, NIH, 80-81. *Mem:* AAAS; Am Chem Soc; Am Asn Biol Chemists; NY Acad Sci; Sigma Xi. *Res:* Sensorimotor aspects of vision; studies on pyruvate kinase isozymes and isozyme hybrids; enzymes which phosphorylate or dephosphorylate proteins. *Mailing Add:* Nat Eye Inst Nat Inst Health Bethesda MD 20205

CARDER, DAVID ROSS, b Wayne, Nebr, Aug 14, 40; m 63; c 2. MANAGEMENT SYSTEMS, CIVIL ENGINEERING. *Educ:* Univ Calif, Los Angeles, BS, 63; Stanford Univ, PhD(civil eng), 74. *Prof Exp:* Staff engr consulting, Allied Technol & Capital Inc, 64-65; gen engr construct, Angeles Nat Forest, 65-66; indust engr fire mgt systs res, Riverside Fire Lab, 66-68, indust engr equip develop, San Dimas Equip Develop Ctr, 68-69; indust engr trans systs anal, Transp Systs Planning Proj, 69-71; gen engr mgt systs anal, Prog & Legis, 71-74, PROJ LEADER MULTIRESOURCE MGT RES, ROCKY MOUNTAIN EXP STA, FOREST SERV, USDA, 74- *Concurrent Pos:* Adj fac, Northern Ariz Univ, 75- & Tex Tech Univ, 77- *Mem:* Sigma Xi; Soc Am Foresters. *Res:* Forest management systems engineering; mathematical modeling of the effects of man on forest biophysical processes; communication and display techniques for use in evaluating tradeoffs among management alternatives and in negotiating decisions. *Mailing Add:* Forestry Sci Lab Northern Ariz Univ Flagstaff AZ 86001

CARDER, KENDALL L, b Norfolk, Nebr, Sept 11, 42. PHYSICAL OCEANOGRAPHY. *Educ:* Ore State Univ, MS, 67, PhD(oceanog), 70. *Prof Exp:* From asst prof to assoc prof, 69-74, PROF OCEANOG, UNIV S FLA, ST PETERSBURG, 74- *Concurrent Pos:* Deleg, Int Oceanog Cong, Tokyo, 70; NSF grant, 70-71; Off Naval Res grant, 72-; Off Water Resources res grant, 74-; del, Int Union Geod Geophys, Grenoble, 75; oceanoptics & polar prog mgr, Hq & prog scientist for NIMBUS-7 coast zone color scanner satellite & scanning multichannel microwave radiometer sensors, NASA, 80-82, mem satellite ocean color sci working group, 81- *Mem:* Am Geophys Union; Optical Soc Am. *Res:* Distribution and dynamics of marine particulates and their effects on the submarine light field; satellite sensing of ocean variables. *Mailing Add:* Marine Sci Dept Univ of SFla 830 First St S St Petersburg FL 33701

CARDIASMENOS, APOSTLE GEORGE, b Oakland, Calif. MICROWAVE ENGINEERING, SOLID STATE PHYSICS. *Educ:* Univ Calif, Berkeley, BSEE, 70; Univ Mass, MSEE, 76, PhD(physics & astron), 78. *Prof Exp:* Sr engr microwaves, Five Col Radio Observ, 75-77; sr scientist millimeter waves, 77-80, DIV MGR, MILLIMETER SUBSYSTS DIV, ALPHA INDUSTS, 80- *Concurrent Pos:* Consult microwaves, TRG Div, Alpha Industs, 75-77. *Mem:* Inst Elec & Electronics Engrs. *Res:* Low noise microwave millimeter wave and infrared receivers and devices; masers, lasers and related devices. *Mailing Add:* Millimeter Subsysts Div Alpha Industs 20 Sylvan Rd Woburn MA 01801

CARDIFF, ROBERT DARRELL, b San Francisco, Calif, Dec 5, 35; m 62; c 3. PATHOLOGY, VIROLOGY. *Educ:* Univ Calif, Berkeley, BS, 58, PhD(zool), 68; Univ Calif, San Francisco, MD, 62; Am Bd Path, dipl, 69. *Prof Exp:* Rotating intern, Kings County Gen Hosp, Brooklyn, 62-64; instr path & resident anat path, Sch Med, Univ Ore, 64-66; staff pathologist, Dept Neuropsychiat, Walter Reed Army Inst Res, Washington, DC, 68-71; assoc prof, 71-77, PROF PATH, SCH MED, UNIV CALIF, DAVIS, 77- *Mem:* AAAS; Am Soc Microbiol; Am Asn Cancer Res; Int Acad Path; Am Asn Path & Bact. *Res:* Mammary tumor systems; control of viral expression; molecular biology of RNA tumor viruses; host-virus relationships; virus structure and function. *Mailing Add:* Dept Path Univ Calif Sch Med Davis CA 95616

CARDILLO, FRANCES M, b Rome, NY, Apr 19, 32. BIOLOGY. *Educ:* Col St Rose, BS, 53, MA, 61; St Bonaventure Univ, PhD(biol), 67. *Prof Exp:* Instr bot, Immaculate Conception Jr Col, 66-67; asst prof, Ladycliff Col, 67-69; assoc prof, Quincy Col, 69-71; assoc prof, Ladycliff Col, 71-75; ASSOC PROF BIOL, MANHATTAN COL, 75- *Concurrent Pos:* NSF Acad Year exten grant, 69-71. *Mem:* AAAS; Am Inst Biol Sci; Bot Soc Am; Am Fern Soc; Tissue Culture Asn. *Res:* Anatomy of Lycopodium species; biochemical studies of Crossosoma. *Mailing Add:* Dept of Biol Manhattan Col Riverdale NY 10471

CARDILLO, MARK J, b Passaic, NJ, Aug 20, 43. CHEMICAL PHYSICS. *Educ:* Stevens Inst Technol, BS, 64; Cornell Univ, PhD(chem), 70. *Prof Exp:* Res assoc chem, Brown Univ, 69-71; Nat Res Coun Italy fel, Inst Physics, Univ Genoa, 71-72; res assoc, Mass Inst Technol, 72-75; MEM STAFF, BELL LABS, 75- *Mem:* Am Chem Soc; Am Phys Soc. *Res:* Gas-surface interactions; molecular beams; scattering; reaction kinetics; chemical dynamics on surfaces; high temperature mass spectrometry. *Mailing Add:* Bell Labs Murray Hill NJ 07974

CARDINAL, ANDRE, b Valleyfield, Que, May 12, 35; m 59; c 2. PHYCOLOGY. *Educ:* Univ Montreal, MSc, 61; Univ Paris, DSc(phycol), 64. *Prof Exp:* Biologist, Marine Biol Sta Grande-Riviere, 64-68; MEM FAC UNIV LAVAL, 68- *Mem:* Phycol Soc Am; Brit Phycol Soc; Phycol Soc France; Int Phycol Soc. *Res:* Ecology, taxonomy and morphology of marine algae; marine phycology. *Mailing Add:* Dept of Biol Univ of Laval Quebec PQ G1K 7P4 Can

CARDINAL, JOHN ROBERT, b Flint, Mich, Dec 24, 43; m 70; c 2. MICELLAR SYSTEMS, CONTROLLED RELEASE DRUG DELIVERY SYSTEMS. *Educ:* Univ Mich, BS, 67; Univ Wis, MS 69, PhD(pharm), 73. *Prof Exp:* Res asst, Univ Mich, 66-67; res asst, Univ Wis, 67-71, teaching asst pharmaceut, 70-71; asst prof pharmaceut, Univ Utah, 71-79, assoc prof, 79-82; PROJ LEADER, NOVEL DRUG DELIVERY SYSTS, PFIZER CO, 82- *Concurrent Pos:* Vis prof, Upjohn Co, 80. *Mem:* Acad Pharmaceut Sci; Am Chem Soc; AAAS; Controlled Release Soc; NY Acad Sci. *Res:* Solubilization in micellar systems; mechanisms of cholesterol gallstone formation and of solute permeation through skin; novel drug delivery systems; author or co-author of approximately 30 articles. *Mailing Add:* Cent Res Pfizer Pharmaceut Co Groton CT 06340

CARDINALE, GEORGE JOSEPH, b New York, NY, Mar 30, 36; m 64; c 2. BIOCHEMISTRY. *Educ:* Fordham Univ, BS, 57; Ohio State Univ, PhD(org chem), 65. *Prof Exp:* Fel biochem, Brandeis Univ, 65-67, res assoc, 67-70; asst mem physiol chem, 70-78, ASST TO DIR SCI AFFAIRS, ROCHE INST MOLECULAR BIOL, 78- *Concurrent Pos:* Adj assoc prof, Dept Pharmacol & Toxicol, Univ RI, 74- *Mem:* Int Inflammation Club. *Res:* Prolyl hydroxylase and its role in collagen biosynthesis; factors affecting collagen synthesis; role of collagen in atherosclerosis. *Mailing Add:* Roche Inst of Molecular Biol Nutley NJ 07110

CARDINET, GEORGE HUGH, III, b Oakland, Calif, Oct 28, 34; m 57; c 4. COMPARATIVE PATHOLOGY. *Educ:* Univ Calif, BS, 60, DVM, 63, PhD(comp path), 66. *Prof Exp:* From asst prof to assoc prof anat, Neuromuscular Res Lab, Kans State Univ, 66-74; assoc prof, 74-76, PROF ANAT, UNIV CALIF, DAVIS, 76-, PROF PHYS MED & REHAB, 78-, ASSOC DEAN SCH VET MED, 76- *Concurrent Pos:* NIH fel, 63-66 & 73-74. *Mem:* AAAS; Am Asn Anat; Am Soc Zool; Electron Micros Soc Am; Am Asn Vet Anat. *Res:* Investigations of myopathies in domestic animals including clinical enzymology; enzyme histochemistry and electromicroscopy. *Mailing Add:* Dept of Anat Univ of Calif Sch of Vet Med Davis CA 95616

CARDIS, ANGELINE BAIRD, b Trenton, NJ, Mar 28, 43; m 62; c 3. ORGANIC CHEMISTRY, AGRICULTURAL CHEMISTRY. *Educ:* Temple Univ, BA, 72, PhD(org chem), 77. *Prof Exp:* Res chemist, Agr Chem Group, FMC Corp, 76-80; SR RES CHEMIST POLYMERS RES & DEVELOP, MOBIL CHEM CO, 80- *Mem:* Am Chem Soc; AAAS. *Res:* Synthesis of biologically active compounds; structure- activity relationships; alkaloid synthesis and biosynthesis; polyethylene product development; blown and cast film extrusion. *Mailing Add:* FMC Corp PO Box 8 Princeton NJ 08540

CARDMAN, LAWRENCE SANTO, b Mt Vernon, NY, Oct 7, 44; m 68; c 2. NUCLEAR PHYSICS. *Educ:* Yale Univ, BA, 66, PhD(physics), 72. *Prof Exp:* Actg instr physics, Electron Accelerator Lab, Yale Univ, 71-72; Nat Acad Sci-Nat Res Coun res fel, Ctr Radiation Res, Nat Bur Standards, 72-73; asst prof, 73-78, ASSOC PROF PHYSICS, PHYSICS RES LAB, UNIV ILL, 78- *Mem:* Sigma Xi; Am Phys Soc. *Res:* Photonuclear physics; elastic and inelastic electron scattering studies of nuclear structure. *Mailing Add:* Dept of Physics Univ of Ill Urbana IL 61801

CARDNER, DAVID V, b Wilmington, Del, June 15, 35; m 61; c 3. CHEMICAL ENGINEERING. *Educ:* Rice Univ, BS, 57, PhD(chem eng), 63. *Prof Exp:* Res engr, Plastics Dept, 63-67, asst div supt process res, 67-68, asst div supt nylon tech, 68-72, asst div supt eng liaison, 72-74, SR ENG PROCESS COMPUT CONTROL, E I DU PONT DE NEMOURS & CO, 74- *Concurrent Pos:* Mem, Tex State Republican Exec Comt, 76-80; comnr, Sabine River Compact Admin, 81- *Mem:* Am Inst Chem Engrs; fel Am Inst Chem. *Res:* Computer control of processes; non-linear programming; model studies; process simulations. *Mailing Add:* E I Du Pont de Nemours & Co PO Box 1089 Orange TX 77630

CARDON, BARTLEY LOWELL, b Berkeley, Calif, Sept 3, 40. PHYSICS. *Educ:* Univ Calif, Berkeley, AB, 63; Purdue Univ, MS, 66; Univ Ariz, PhD(physics), 77. *Prof Exp:* Res assoc physics, Univ Ariz, 72-77; res fel astrophys, 77-79, RES ASSOC ASTROPHYS, HARVARD COL OBSERV, 79- *Mem:* Sigma Xi; Optical Soc Am; Am Asn Physics Teachers. *Res:* Beam-foil spectroscopy; spectroscopy of atoms and molecules; experimental determinations of oscillator strengths of atoms and molecules. *Mailing Add:* Ctr for Astrophys 60 Garden St Cambridge MA 02138

CARDON, SAMUEL ZELIG, b Chicago, Ill, Nov 24, 18; m 58; c 2. CHEMISTRY. *Educ:* Univ Chicago, BS, 39, MS, 41; Western Reserve Univ, PhD(org chem), 50. *Prof Exp:* Chemist, Harshaw Chem Co, 44-48; org chemist, Lubrizol Corp, 49-51; chemist, Horizons, Inc, 51-53 & Rand Develop Corp, 53-64; secy-treas, 64-80, CHEMIST, GEN TECH SERV, INC, 64, PRES, 80- *Mem:* Am Chem Soc; Am Asn Small Res Co (pres). *Res:* Organic and inorganic synthesis; biological regulation and dynamics; chemical carcinogenesis and inhibition; water purification; research management. *Mailing Add:* Gen Tech Serv Inc 8794 West Chester Pike Upper Darby PA 19082

CARDONE, VINCENT J, meteorology, see previous edition

CARDOSO, SERGIO STEINER, b Belem-Para, Brazil, June 26, 27; m 54; c 4. PHARMACOLOGY, BIOLOGICAL RHYTHMS. *Educ:* Univ Brazil, MD, 52; Univ Sao Paulo, PhD(pharmacol), 64. *Prof Exp:* From asst prof to assoc prof pharmacol, Univ Sao Paulo, 61-68, from asst prof to assoc prof, 67-76, PROF PHARMACOL, SCH MED, UNIV TENN, MEMPHIS, 77- *Mem:* Am Soc Pharmacol & Exp Therapeut. *Res:* Possible role of circadian mitotic rhythms as related to cancer chemotherapy. *Mailing Add:* Dept of Pharmacol Univ of Tenn Med Sch Memphis TN 38163

CARDUS, DAVID, b Barcelona, Spain, Aug 6, 22; m 51; c 4. CARDIOLOGY, BIOMATHEMATICS. *Educ:* Univ Montpellier, BA, 42; Univ Barcelona, MD, 49. *Prof Exp:* Intern, Hosp Clin, Univ Barcelona, 49-50; resident, Sanitarium of Puig de Olena, Barcelona, 50-53; res assoc physiol, Postgrad Sch Cardiol, Med Sch, Univ Barcelona, 54-55; from instr to asst prof physiol & rehab, 60-65, assoc prof rehab, 65-69, assoc prof physiol, 65-73, PROF PHYSIOL, COL MED, BAYLOR UNIV, 73-, PROF REHAB & HEAD CARDIOPULMONARY LAB, 69-, DIR DIV BIOMATH, 70- *Concurrent Pos:* French Govt res fel, 53-54; Brit Coun res fel, 57; Inst Int Educ fel, Lovelace Found, 57-60; head work tolerance eval unit, Tex Inst Rehab & Res, 60; adj prof math sci, Rice Univ, 70- *Mem:* AAAS; Am Col Cardiol; Am Col Chest Physicians; AMA; NY Acad Sci. *Res:* Experimental exercise and respiratory physiology; mathematical and computer applications to the study of physiological systems; body comcomposition of humans with extensive muscular paralysis; physiology of urinary bladder; benefit continued studies of rehabilitation medicine. *Mailing Add:* Tex Inst for Rehab & Res PO Box 20095 Houston TX 77025

CARDWELL, ALVIN BOYD, b Lenoir City, Tenn, Oct 16, 02; m 30; c 2. SOLID STATE PHYSICS. *Educ:* Univ Chattanooga, BS, 25; Univ Wis, MS, 27, PhD(physics), 30. *Hon Degrees:* DSc, Univ Chattanooga, 61. *Prof Exp:* Asst physics, Univ Wis, 26-29; from asst prof to assoc prof, Tulane Univ, 30-36; prof, 36-73, head dept physics & physicist in charge, Eng Exp Sta, 37-53, physicist in charge, Agr Exp Sta, 47-53, assoc dean sch arts & sci, 53-55, dir bur gen res, 54-67, head dept physics & physicist in charge, Eng Exp Sta, 57-67, Agr Exp Sta, 57-73, EMER PROF PHYSICS, KANS STATE UNIV, 73- *Concurrent Pos:* Res physicist, Clinton Eng Works, Tenn Eastman Corp, Oak Ridge, Tenn, 43-46. *Mem:* AAAS; fel Am Phys Soc; Am Asn Physics Teachers. *Mailing Add:* Rt 3 Box 310E Kingston TN 37763

CARDWELL, DUDLEY H, b Lawyers, Va, Oct 21, 01; m 35; c 1. PETROLEUM GEOLOGY, STRUCTURAL GEOLOGY. *Educ:* Univ Va, BS, 23, MS, 25. *Prof Exp:* Field geologist, Sun Oil Co, 29-44, dist geologist, 44-59, sr geologist, 59-66; PETROL GEOLOGIST, WVA GEOL SURVEY, 67- *Concurrent Pos:* Mem, Comt Statist on Drilling & Nat Petrol Coun, 68-; mem, Oil Reserves Subcomt for WVa, Am Petrol Inst, 69-, chmn, 74-78. *Mem:* Am Asn Petrol Geologists. *Res:* Petroleum and structural geology. *Mailing Add:* WVa Geol Surv PO Box 879 Morgantown WV 26505

CARDWELL, JOE THOMAS, b Vernon, Tex, Feb 19, 22; m 42; c 2. DAIRY CHEMISTRY. *Educ:* Tex Technol Col, BS, 47, MS, 49; NC State Col, PhD, 56. *Prof Exp:* Vet voc teacher, Knox County Voc Sch, Tex, 47; instr dairy mfg, Tex Technol Col, 47-50; res asst dairy chem, NC State Col, 50-52; from asst prof to assoc prof dairy mfg, 52-64, ASSOC PROF DAIRY SCI, MISS STATE UNIV & DAIRY CHEMIST, AGR EXP STA, 64- *Mem:* Inst Food Technol; AAAS; Am Dairy Sci Asn. *Res:* Milk plant sanitation; oxidized flavor development in milk; influence of calcium chloride on yield of cheddar cheese; frozen cultures; chocolate milk; flavor components of foods; products made from delactosed milk; method of detecting NFOM in fluid milk; new products developed from sweet whey. *Mailing Add:* Miss State Univ Col of Agr Drawer DD Mississippi State MS 39762

CARDWELL, PAUL H, b Metamora, Mich, Aug 24, 12; m 39; c 4. COLLOID CHEMISTRY. *Educ:* Cent Mich Teacher's Col, AB, 35; Univ Mich, PhD(chem), 41. *Prof Exp:* Chief chemist, Dowell Inc, 41-52, dir lab, 52-54; tech specialist, Dow Chem Co, Mich, 54-65, asst mgr apparatus & instruments, 65-67, mgr apparatus & instruments bus, 67-69; dir res, Deepsea Ventures Inc, 69-75; CONSULT OCEAN NODULE PROCESSING, 75- *Mem:* AAAS; Am Chem Soc; Am Inst Aeronaut & Astronaut; Am Inst Mining, Metall & Petrol Eng; Electrochem Soc. *Res:* Contact angles; colloid chemistry; resins; corrosion inhibitors; chemical removal of aluminum from oil wells; reproducible contact angles on reproducible metal surfaces; extractive metallurgy. *Mailing Add:* Zanoni VA 23191

CARDWELL, VERNON BRUCE, b Ft Morgan, Colo, Oct 8, 36; m 54; c 4. AGRONOMY, CROP PHYSIOLOGY. *Educ:* Colo State Univ, BS, 58, MS, 61; Iowa State Univ, PhD(crop prod), 67. *Prof Exp:* Res asst agron, Colo State Univ, 58-60, asst agronomist, 60-64; instr agron, Iowa State Univ, 64-67; from asst prof to assoc prof, 67-78, PROF AGRON, UNIV MINN, ST PAUL, 78- *Mem:* Am Soc Agron; Crop Sci Soc Am; Coun Agr Sci & Technol. *Res:* Seed physiology; seed quality wheat; low temperature germination corn & soybeans. *Mailing Add:* Dept of Agron Univ of Minn St Paul MN 55108

CARDWELL, WILLIAM THOMAS, JR, b Boulder, Colo, May 27, 17; m 47. ENGINEERING. *Educ:* Calif Inst Technol, BS, 38, MS, 39. *Prof Exp:* Chemist, Standard Oil Co, Calif, 39-41, petrol engr, 41-47, res engr, Chevron Res Co, 47-48, sr res engr, 48-56, res assoc, 56-66, sr res assoc, Chevron Res Co, 66-80; RETIRED. *Mem:* Am Chem Soc; Am Inst Mining, Metall & Petrol Engrs; Acoust Soc Am. *Res:* Physical chemistry of drilling fluids; physics and mathematics of oil reservoirs; patents; physics of musical wind instruments. *Mailing Add:* Chevron Res Co Box 446 La Habra CA 90631

CAREN, LINDA DAVIS, b Corsicana, Tex, Apr 17, 41; m 63; c 2. MEDICAL MICROBIOLOGY, BIOLOGY. *Educ:* Ohio State Univ, BSc, 62; Stanford Univ, AM, 65, PhD(med microbiol), 67. *Prof Exp:* Tech ed, Tech Info Div, NASA Ames Res Ctr, 72-76; ASST PROF BIOL, UNIV SANTA CLARA, 78- *Concurrent Pos:* Nat Acad Sci fel, 67; consult, Encycl Britannica, 68; instr, DeAnza Col, 77-78; vis lectr, Dept Biol Univ Santa Clara, 74-78, NASA grant, 78-82. *Mem:* Int Soc Study Origins Life; Am Soc Microbiol; AAAS; Sigma Xi. *Res:* Role of complement in resistance to disease and in the rejection of skin grafts; use of the enzyme-linked immunosorbent blocking assay to detect anti-influenza antibody; effects of environmental pollutants on immune response and resistance to disease; use of enzyme-linked immunosorbent blocking assay to detect gene dosage effects on anitgens in the Duffy, Rhesus and Serum Serologic systems. *Mailing Add:* Dept of Biol Univ of Santa Clara Santa Clara CA 95053

CAREN, ROBERT POSTON, b Columbus, Ohio, Dec 25, 32; m 63. PHYSICS. *Educ:* Ohio State Univ, BS, 53, MS, 54, PhD(physics), 61. *Prof Exp:* Sr physicist, NAm Aviation Inc, Ohio, 59-60; instr physics, Ohio State Univ, 60-61; res scientist & sr mem res lab, 62-68, mgr infrared progs lab, 68-70, dir eng sci lab, 70-75, DIR PALO ALTO RES LABS, LOCKHEED MISSILES & SPACE CO, 75- *Concurrent Pos:* Lectr, Univ Santa Clara. *Honors & Awards:* IR-100 Award, 67. *Mem:* Am Phys Soc; Am Asn Physics Teachers; assoc fel Am Inst Aeronaut & Astronaut; Am Defense Preparedness Asn. *Res:* Development of advanced infrared sensor systems and subsystems; radiation heat transfer theory; nuclear effects on materials; experimental low temperature research. *Mailing Add:* Lockheed 5201 3251 Hanover Bldg 201 Palo Alto CA 94304

CARES, WILLIAM RONALD, b Dearborn, Mich, 41; m; c 1. SURFACE CHEMISTRY, CHEMICAL KINETICS. *Educ:* Case Inst Technol, BSChE, 63; Univ Ill, MS, 65, PhD(chem), 69. *Prof Exp:* Res fel, Rice Univ, 69-71; res chemist, US Naval Res Lab, 71-73; res chemist catalysis, Petro-Tex Chem Corp, 73-76; SR RES CHEMIST, M W KELLOGG CO, 76- *Mem:* Am Chem Soc; Am Inst Chem Engrs; Royal Soc Chem; Catalysis Soc; Sigma Xi. *Res:* Kinetics and mechanics of heterogeneous catalytic reactions; flue gas desulfurization chemistry; kinetics of surface reactions; environmental chemistry; chemical engineering. *Mailing Add:* M W Kellogg Res & Develop Ctr 16200 Park Row-Indust Park Ten Houston TX 77084

CARESS, EDWARD ALAN, b Columbus, Nebr, Feb 6, 36; m 61; c 3. ORGANIC CHEMISTRY. *Educ:* Dartmouth Col, AB, 58; Univ Rochester, PhD(org chem), 63. *Prof Exp:* Fel, Univ Rochester, 63; res assoc org chem, Mass Inst Technol, 63-65; from asst prof to assoc prof, 65-78, PROF CHEM, GEORGE WASHINGTON UNIV, 78-, ASST DEAN GRAD SCH ARTS & SCI, 71- *Mem:* Am Chem Soc; The Chem Soc. *Res:* Organic reaction mechanisms; photochemistry of organic compounds; resolution of organic compounds through use of platinum complexes; structure determination. *Mailing Add:* Dept Chem George Washington Univ Washington DC 20052

CARET, ROBERT LAURENT, b Biddeford, Maine, Oct 7, 47; m 69. ORGANIC & ENVIRONMENTAL CHEMISTRY. *Educ:* Suffolk Univ, BA, 69; Univ NH, PhD(org chem), 74. *Prof Exp:* Res assoc, Bio-Res Inst, 67-69; teacher chem, Rumford High Sch, 69-70; teaching asst, Univ NH & Suffolk Univ, 66-72; vis asst prof, 74-75, instr, 75-76, ASST PROF CHEM, TOWSON STATE UNIV, 76-, DEAN SCI, 81- *Concurrent Pos:* Lectr, Suffolk Univ, 72-73. *Honors & Awards:* Outstanding Young Chemist Award, DC Instit Chemists, 81. *Mem:* Sigma Xi; Am Chem Soc; Am Asn Univ Prof. *Res:* Stereochemistry, conformational analysis; nuclear magnetic resonance including Carbon-13 nmr and their use in the study of organosulfur compounds; flavor and fragance compounds. *Mailing Add:* Dept of Chem Towson State Univ Towson MD 21204

CARETTO, ALBERT A, JR, b Baldwin, NY, May 16; 28; m 60; c 2. NUCLEAR CHEMISTRY, PHYSICAL CHEMISTRY. *Educ:* Rensselaer Polytech Inst, BS, 50; Univ Rochester, PhD(chem), 54. *Prof Exp:* Nuclear chemist, Brookhaven Nat Lab, 54-56; nuclear chemist, Univ Calif, Berkeley, 56-57, res chemist, Livermore, 58-59; asst prof chem, 57-58, from asst prof to assoc prof, 59-67, chmn dept, 70-74, PROF CHEM, CARNEGIE-MELLON UNIV, 67- *Concurrent Pos:* Sabbatical Award, Europ Ctr Nuclear Res, 64-65 & Europ Ctr Nuclear Res, Geneva, Switz, 74-75. *Mem:* AAAS; Am Chem Soc; Am Phys Soc. *Res:* Nuclear reactions induced with high energy particles; nuclear spectroscopy; radiochemical effects of recoil atoms. *Mailing Add:* Dept Chem Carnegie-Mellon Univ Pittsburgh PA 15213

CAREW, DAVID P, b Monson, Mass, Oct 21, 28; m 51; c 3. PHARMACY. *Educ:* Mass Col Pharm, BS, 52, MS, 54; Univ Conn, PhD(pharm), 58. *Prof Exp:* Asst instr pharmacog, Univ Conn, 54-57; from asst prof to assoc prof, 57-65, PROF PHARMACOG, UNIV IOWA, 65-, ASST DEAN, COL PHARM, 75- *Concurrent Pos:* Collab scientist, UN Cannabis Res Prog; mem adv panel, US Pharmacopaeia, 71- *Honors & Awards:* M L Huit Award, 80. *Mem:* Fel AAAS; Am Soc Pharmacog (vpres, 64-65, pres, 65-66); Am Pharmaceut Asn; fel Acad Pharmaceut Sci; Int Plant Tissue Cult Asn. *Res:* Natural product research; products with therapeutic activity; plant tissue culture and biosynthesis; antibiotics. *Mailing Add:* Col of Pharm Univ of Iowa Iowa City IA 52242

CAREW, JOHN FRANCIS, b Brooklyn, NY, June 26, 37; m 63; c 3. NUCLEAR ENGINEERING, NUCLEAR PHYSICS. *Educ:* St John's Univ, BS, 60, MS, 63; NY Univ, PhD(physics), 68. *Prof Exp:* Physicist, Sperry Gyroscope Co, 64-65; prof physics, St John's Univ, 65-68; physicist, Knolls Atomic Power Lab, Gen Elec, 68-72, mgr monitoring syst, Nuclear Energy Div, 72-76; PHYSICIST, BROOKHAVEN NAT LAB, 76- *Concurrent Pos:* Res assoc, NY Univ, 66-68. *Mem:* Am Nuclear Soc; Am Phys Soc. *Res:* Nuclear energy systems; atomic and nuclear physics. *Mailing Add:* Dept Nuclear Energy Brookhaven Nat Lab Upton LI NY 11973

CAREW, LYNDON BELMONT, JR, b Lynn, Mass, Nov 27, 32; m 60; c 2. ANIMAL NUTRITION, HUMAN NUTRITION. *Educ:* Univ Mass, BS, 55; Cornell Univ, PhD(animal nutrit), 61. *Prof Exp:* Res asst poultry nutrit, Cornell Univ, 55-58, res assoc, 58-59, res asst, 59-61; tech dir, Colombian Nat Poultry Prog & Animal Nutrit Lab, Colombian Agr Prog, Rockefeller Found, Bogota, 61-65; sr res assoc poultry sci, Cornell Univ, 65-66; head poultry res sect, Hess & Clark Div, Richardson Merrill Corp, Ohio, 66-69; assoc prof animal sci & nutrit, 69-75, PROF ANIMAL SCI & HUMAN NUTRIT, UNIV VT, 75- *Concurrent Pos:* Mem tech comt, Animal Nutrit Res Coun, 72-; sci prog mgr, Int Nutrit Proj, Univ Vt, 80-; USDA regional steering comt, poultry nutrit, 81- *Mem:* AAAS; Am Inst Nutrit; Poultry Sci Asn; Soc Exp Biol & Med. *Res:* Nutrition-endocrine interactions; essential fatty acid metabolism; thyroid function; metabolizable energy; energy metabolism; general poultry nutrition; nutritive properties of fats; Lat Am poultry science; dietary fat, amino acids and hormone function; biochemistry. *Mailing Add:* Univ Vt Dept Animal Sci Biores Lab 655 Spear St Burlington VT 05401

CAREW, THOMAS EDWARD, b Columbus, Ga, Dec 18, 43; m 65. METABOLISM, CARDIOVASCULAR PHYSIOLOGY. *Educ:* Johns Hopkins Univ, BA, 65; Cath Univ Am, MSE, 67, PhD(bioeng), 71. *Prof Exp:* Res engr, Nat Heart & Lung Inst, 69-72; ASST RES PHYSIOLOGIST, UNIV CALIF, SAN DIEGO, 72- *Concurrent Pos:* Consult, NSF, 72-; vis prof, Tromso Univ, 77. *Mem:* Fel Am Heart Asn; Am Physiol Soc; AAAS; NY Acad Sci. *Res:* Studies of lipoprotein metabolism relating to atherosclerosis: tissue sites of degradation of lipoproteins; studies of in vivo and in vitro studies of lipoprotein receptors and their importance in determining cellular cholesterol balance. *Mailing Add:* Dept Med (M-013-D) Univ Calif San Diego La Jolla CA 92093

CAREY, ALFRED W(ILLIAM), JR, b New York, NY, May 5, 24; m 46; c 3. REFRIGERATION. *Educ:* Polytech Inst Brooklyn, BMechE, 49. *Prof Exp:* Res engr, Super Engine Div, White Motors Co, 49-53; prin mech engr, Battelle Mem Inst, 53-55, proj leader mech res, 55-59, asst div chief, 59-61, assoc staff engr prime movers, 61-62; proj mgr combustion res, 62-66, mgr, 66-70, mgr advan develop, 70-71, dir advan prod planning, 71-75, dir combustion res, 75-77, SR TECH ADV RES, CUMMINS ENGINE CO, INC, 77-, DIR ADVAN CONTROLS, 80- *Mem:* Am Soc Automotive Engrs. *Res:* Heat power; combustion phenomena in compression and spark ignition reciprocating engines; refrigeration, particularly unconventional systems; fuel injection systems. *Mailing Add:* Cummins Engine Co Inc-50165 Columbus IN 47201

CAREY, ANDREW GALBRAITH, JR, b Baltimore, Md, Apr 11, 32; m 57; c 2. BIOLOGICAL OCEANOGRAPHY. *Educ:* Princeton Univ, AB, 55; Yale Univ, PhD(zool), 62. *Prof Exp:* Asst prof oceanog, 61-71, ASSOC PROF OCEANOG, ORE STATE UNIV, 71- *Concurrent Pos:* Marshal fel, Denmark, 70; Japan Soc Prom Sci vis prof, Univ Tokyo, 77. *Mem:* AAAS; Am Soc Limnol & Oceanog; Am Soc Zoologists; Ecol Soc Am; Marine Biol Asn UK. *Res:* Marine benthic ecology; community, energetics, deep sea; invertebrate zoology; polar ecology. *Mailing Add:* Sch of Oceanog Ore State Univ Corvallis OR 97331

CAREY, BERNARD JOSEPH, b Pittsburgh, Pa, Feb 28, 41; m 66; c 2. COMPUTER SCIENCE. *Educ:* Univ Pittsburgh, BS, 62; Univ Calif, Santa Barbara, MS, 69, PhD(elec eng comput sci), 71. *Prof Exp:* Design engr, Guid & Control, Litton Industs, 63-68; res asst speech processing, Univ Calif, Santa Barbara, 69-71; asst prof, 71-77, ASSOC PROF COMPUT SCI, UNIV CONN, 77- *Concurrent Pos:* Consult microprocessing syst, Rogers Corp, 75- *Mem:* Inst Elec & Electronics Engrs. *Res:* Multiprocessor systems design; applications of microprocessors. *Mailing Add:* U-157 Univ of Conn Storrs CT 06268

CAREY, CYNTHIA, b Denver, Colo, July 17, 47. PHYSIOLOGICAL ECOLOGY, COMPARATIVE PHYSIOLOGY. *Educ:* Occidental Col, Los Angeles, AB, 69, MA, 70; Univ Mich, PhD(zool), 76. *Prof Exp:* Asst physiol, Univ Mich, 70-74, res asst, 74-76; ASST PROF PHYSIOL, UNIV COLO, 76- *Honors & Awards:* Marcia Brady Tucker Award, Am Ornithologist's Union, 73; A Brazier Howell Award, Cooper Ornith Soc, 75. *Mem:* Am Ornithologist's Union; Am Soc Zoologists; Am Soc Ichthyologists & Herpetologists; Cooper Ornith Soc; AAAS. *Res:* Physiological adaptation of animals to stressful environments. *Mailing Add:* Dept of EPO Biol Univ of Colo Boulder CO 80309

CAREY, DAVID CROCKETT, b Montclair, NJ, Oct 2, 39. HIGH ENERGY PHYSICS, PARTICLE PHYSICS. *Educ:* Mass Inst Technol, BS, 62; Univ Mich, MS, 64, PhD(physics), 67. *Prof Exp:* Technician, Forrestal Res Ctr, Princeton-Penn Accelerator, 59-60; instr physics & math, Upsala Col, 62; res assoc physics, City Col New York, 67-69; PHYSICIST, NAT ACCELERATOR LAB, 69- *Mem:* AAAS; Am Phys Soc. *Res:* Theoretical and experimental investigations into strong interaction dynamics; design of particle accelerators and external beams. *Mailing Add:* Nat Accelerator Lab Batavia IL 60510

CAREY, FRANCIS ARTHUR, b Philadelphia, Pa, May 28, 37; m 63; c 3. ORGANIC CHEMISTRY. *Educ:* Drexel Univ, BS, 59; Pa State Univ, PhD(org chem), 63. *Prof Exp:* NIH fel, Harvard Univ, 63-64; asst prof, 66-71, ASSOC PROF CHEM, UNIV VA, 71- *Mem:* Am Chem Soc. *Res:* Structural and synthetic organic chemistry. *Mailing Add:* Dept of Chem Univ of Va Charlottesville VA 22903

CAREY, JOHN HUGH, b Windsor, Ont, Jan 28, 47; m 70; c 3. PHOTOCHEMISTRY. *Educ:* Univ Windsor, BSc, 70, MSc, 72; Carleton Univ, PhD(chem), 74. *Prof Exp:* Nat Res Coun Can fel, 74-76, res consult, 76-78, RES SCIENTIST, NAT WATER RES INST, 78- *Mem:* InterAm Photochem Soc. *Res:* Photochemistry of natural waters and of solution-sediment interface; photochemical aspects of pollution and water treatment processes; fate and effects of synthetic organic compounds in natural waters. *Mailing Add:* Nat Water Res Inst 867 Lakeshore Rd Burlington ON L7R 4A6 Can

CAREY, JOHN JOSEPH, b Boston, Mass, Dec 10, 11; m 37; c 3. ELECTRICAL ENGINEERING, SAFETY ENGINEERING. *Educ:* Mass Inst Technol, BSEE, 34, MSEE, 53. *Prof Exp:* Elec-mech engr, Panama Canal, 34-41; elec designer, Jackson & Moreland Engrs, 41-42; instr elec eng, Univ NMex, 45; instr, Univ Kans, 45-46; prof, 46-72, EMER PROF ELEC ENG, UNIV MICH, ANN ARBOR, 72-; CONSULT ELEC ENGR, 72- *Concurrent Pos:* Test engr, Gen Elec Co, 39; consult, Commonwealth Assocs, Mich, 52, Gen Elec Co, Ind, 55, Fargo Eng Co, Mich, 55-, Consumers Power Co, 60, Climax Molybdenum Co, Mich, 62- & Mich Consol Gas Co, 63-; eng guid coordr, Engrs Coun Prof Develop, 67-70; Univ Mich rep, Am Power Conf & mem gen & elec prog comts, 67-72. *Mem:* Nat Soc Prof Engrs; Inst Elec & Electronics Engrs; Am Soc Eng Educ. *Res:* Energy conversion; systems engineering; engineering economics. *Mailing Add:* 3486 Woodland Rd Ann Arbor MI 48104

CAREY, KRISTEN ERLING, b Adelaide, S Australia, Dec 4, 49. MICROBIOLOGY, GENETICS. *Educ:* Flinders Univ, S Australia, BSci, 71; Monash Univ, Australia, PhD(microbial genetics), 74; State Col Educ, Australia, dipl educ, 74. *Prof Exp:* Lectr, Med Sch, Univ Mich, 74-76, res assoc microbiol, 76-77; ASST PROF BOT, BUTLER UNIV, 77- *Mem:* Am Soc Microbiol; Am Asn Univ Prof. *Res:* Gene expression in bacteria and the role of plasmids in evolution of microbial populations; implications for eucaryote systems; aims and function of education practices. *Mailing Add:* Dept of Bot 4600 Sunset Ave Indianapolis IN 46208

CAREY, LARRY CAMPBELL, b Coal Grove, Ohio, Nov 5, 33; m 56; c 4. SURGERY. *Educ:* Ohio State Univ, BSc, 55, MD, 59. *Prof Exp:* Intern surg, New York Hosp, Cornell Univ, 59-60; resident, Marquette Integrated Residency Prog, 60-64, chief admin resident, Marquette Univ, 64-65, from asst prof to prof surg, Sch Med, Univ Pittsburgh, 68-74; PROF SURG & CHMN DEPT, COL MED, OHIO STATE UNIV, 75- *Concurrent Pos:* Markle Scholar acad med, 65-70; William S Middleton lectr, Wis State Med Soc, 65; consult, Milwaukee County Gen Hosp, Wis, 65-, Milwaukee Lutheran Hosp, 65-, Columbia Hosp, 65- & St Luke's Hosp, 68-; asst clin prof, Boston Univ, 66-67. *Mem:* AAAS; fel Am Col Surg; AMA; Soc Univ Surg; Soc Surg Alimentary Tract. *Res:* Pancreatic physiology; bioelectric phenomena; shock. *Mailing Add:* Dept Surg Col Med Ohio State Univ Columbus OH 43210

CAREY, MARTIN CONRAD, b Clonmel, Ireland, June 18, 39; US citizen; m 72; c 2. GASTROENTEROLOGY, MOLECULAR BIOPHYSICS. *Educ:* Nat Univ Ireland, MB, BCh, BAO, 62, MD, 81. *Prof Exp:* Clin fel gastroenterol, Boston Univ Hosp, 69-70; res fel & assoc biophys, Sch Med, Boston Univ, 70-73, asst prof med, 73-75; asst prof, 75-79, ASSOC PROF MED, SCH MED, HARVARD UNIV, 79-, LAWRENCE J HENDERSON ASSOC PROF HEALTH SCI & TECHNOL, 79-; ASSOC MED GASTROENTEROL, BRIGHAM & WOMENS HOSP, 79- *Concurrent Pos:* Int Fogarty fel, NIH, 68; fel, Med Res Found, Boston, 72; mem, Nat Inst Arthritis, Metab & Digestive Dis res subcomt, 72-73; fel, J S Guggenheim Found, 74; Acad Career Develop Award, NIH, 75; ad hoc mem, NIH Gen Med A Spec Study Sect, 75-78; assoc ed, J Lipid Res, 78- *Honors & Awards:* Gold Medal, Nat Univ Ireland; McArdle Prize; McArdle, Kennedy, Macennis, Bellingham & Smith Gold Medals. *Mem:* Am Gastroenterol Asn; Am Soc Study Liver Dis; Am Oil Chem Soc; Am Soc Clin Invest. *Res:* Physical chemistry and pathophysiology of alimentary tract lipids in health and disease. *Mailing Add:* Harvard Med Sch Brigham & Womens Hosp Boston MA 02115

CAREY, MICHAEL DEAN, b South Bend, Ind, Apr 18, 46; m 67; c 3. ECOLOGY, ANIMAL BEHAVIOR. *Educ:* Wittenberg Univ, BA, 68; Ind Univ, MA, 76, PhD(ecol), 77. *Prof Exp:* Instr zool & ecol, Clark Col, Vancouver, Wash, 76-77; asst prof biol & ecol, Cent Mich Univ, 77-78; ASST PROF BIOL, ECOL & ANIMAL BEHAV, UNIV SCRANTON, 78- *Concurrent Pos:* Vis lectr, Univ Minn, ITASCA Sta, 81. *Mem:* Am Ornithologists Union; Cooper Ornith Soc; Ecol Soc Am; Sigma Xi; Wilson Ornith Soc. *Res:* Avian breeding sociobiology; evolution of mating systems and territoriality in passerines; empirical field tests of current evolutionary models. *Mailing Add:* Dept of Biol Univ of Scranton Scranton PA 18510

CAREY, PAUL L, b Arrowsmith, Ill, Nov 4, 23; m 48; c 5. BIOCHEMISTRY. *Educ:* Ill Wesleyan Univ, BS, 48; Kansas State Col, MS, 50; Purdue Univ, PhD(biochem), 58. *Prof Exp:* Jr biochemist, Smith, Kline & French Labs, 50-53; asst, Purdue Univ, 53-54, Walter G Karr fel, 54-57; mgr spec chows lab, Ralston Purina, 58-62; chemist, Penick & Ford, Ltd, 62-65; biochemist, R J Reynolds Co, 65-68; group leader, 68-70; assoc scientist, 70-78, SCIENTIST, RALSTON PURINA CO. 78- *Concurrent Pos:* Instr, Winston Salem State Teachers Col, 67. *Mem:* AAAS; Am Chem Soc. *Res:* Nutrition; chemistry of biological materials; process research and development. *Mailing Add:* Cent Res Dept Ralston Purina Co 900 Checkerboard Sq Plaza St Louis MO 63188

CAREY, SUSAN THERESA, b New York, NY. BOTANY, MYCOLOGY. *Educ:* Columbia Univ, AB, 52, MA, 53, PhD(bot), 66. *Prof Exp:* Res asst mycol, Charles Pfizer & Co, Inc, 53-57; res asst, Columbia Univ, 59-60; res asst, 64-65, res fel, 65-67, RES ASSOC MYCOL, NY BOT GARDEN, 67- *Concurrent Pos:* Adj prof bot, Fordham Univ, 73; NIH grants, 73-74, 76-78 & 78-80. *Mem:* Am Inst Biol Sci; Bot Soc Am; Brit Mycol Soc; Mycol Soc Am; Torrey Bot Club. *Res:* Antibiotics from fungi; biologically active metabolites from pyrenomycetes; morphology; taxonomy; chemotaxonomy of pyrenomycetes. *Mailing Add:* NY Bot Garden Bronx NY 10458

CAREY, WILLIAM DANIEL, b New York, NY, Jan 29, 16; m 44; c 5. SCIENCE POLICY. *Educ:* Columbia Univ, BA, 40, MA, 41; Harvard Univ, MPA, 42. *Prof Exp:* Asst dir, Exec Off US Pres, Bur Budget, 66-69; vpres, Arthur D Little, Inc, 69-74; EXEC OFFICER & PUBL, AAAS, 75- *Concurrent Pos:* Chmn, US aide, US-USSR Bilateral Group Sci Policy, 73-; trustee, Russell Sage Found & Mitre Corp, 78-; gov, Ctr Creative Leadership, 79-81; chmn vis comt, US Nat Bur Standards, 80-81. *Honors & Awards:* Ralph Coates Roe Medal, Am Soc Mech Engrs, 79. *Mem:* Nat Acad Sci-Inst Med; Nat Acad Pub Admin; Am Soc Pub Admin. *Mailing Add:* AAAS 1776 Massachusetts Ave NW Washington DC 20036

CARFAGNO, DANIEL GAETANO, b Syracuse, NY, Aug 17, 35; m 58; c 2. PHYSICAL CHEMISTRY, ENVIRONMENTAL MONITORING. *Educ:* Le Moyne Col, NY, BS, 57; Syracuse Univ, PhD(phys chem), 65. *Prof Exp:* Sr res chemist, 67-67, res group leader, 67-69, res specialist, 69-73, GROUP LEADER, ENVIRON LAB, MONSANTO RES CORP, 73- *Mem:* Am Chem Soc. *Res:* Phase equilibria; x-ray diffraction; differential thermal analysis; purification of alkaline earth metals; physical properties of plutonium and its compounds; isotopic fuels; environmental monitoring for radioactive materials. *Mailing Add:* Monsanto Res Corp Mound Facility PO Box 32 Miamisburg OH 45342

CARGILL, B(URTON) F(LOYD), b Mich, Apr 12, 22; m 46; c 2. AGRICULTURAL ENGINEERING. *Educ:* Mich State Univ, BSAE, 47, MSAE, 52; Univ Mo, PhD, 60. *Prof Exp:* Proj engr & instr res, 47-50, proj leader, 50-55, from asst prof to assoc prof, 55-69, PROF AGR ENG, MICH STATE UNIV, 69- *Concurrent Pos:* Prof farm struct, Exten, Mich State Univ, 55, fruit & veg harvesting, handling & storage coordr, 67. *Mem:* AAAS; Am Soc Agr Engrs. *Res:* Fruit and vegetable storages; methods engineering; effect of environment on storage; building design; materials handling. *Mailing Add:* Dept of Agr Eng Mich State Univ East Lansing MI 48824

CARGILL, ROBERT LEE, JR, b Marshall, Tex, Sept 11, 34; m 65; c 3. ORGANIC CHEMISTRY. *Educ:* Rice Univ, BA, 55; Mass Inst Technol, PhD(org chem), 60. *Prof Exp:* NIH fel org chem, Univ Calif, Berkeley, 60-62; from asst prof to assoc prof chem, 67-73, PROF CHEM, UNIV SC, 73- *Mem:* Am Chem Soc; The Chem Soc. *Res:* Photochemistry; isomerization reactions, especially in small ring compounds; structure and synthesis of natural products; synthesis and properties of highly strained molecules. *Mailing Add:* Dept of Chem Univ of SC Columbia SC 29208

CARGO, DAVID GARRETT, b Pittsburgh, Pa, Dec 28, 24; m 49; c 6. ZOOLOGY. *Educ:* Univ Pittsburgh, BS, 49, MS, 50. *Prof Exp:* Biologist, State of Md, 50-60; RES ASSOC MARINE BIOL, CHESAPEAKE BIOL LAB, UNIV MD, SOLOMONS, 60- *Res:* Biology and ecology of marine invertebrates, especially Crustacea and coelenterates. *Mailing Add:* St Leonard Prince Frederick MD 20678

CARGO, GERALD THOMAS, b Dowagiac, Mich, Mar 2, 30; m 56; c 2. MATHEMATICAL ANALYSIS. *Educ:* Univ Mich, BBA, 52, MS, 53, PhD(math), 59. *Prof Exp:* Asst math, Willow Run Res Ctr, Univ Mich, 55-56; asst prof, 59-63, assoc prof, 63-77, PROF MATH, SYRACUSE UNIV, 77- *Concurrent Pos:* Resident res assoc, Coun, Nat Bur Standards, 61-62; NSF res grant, 63-66; res analyst, Aerospace Res Labs, 67- *Mem:* Am Math Soc; Math Asn Am; Sigma Xi. *Res:* Boundary behavior of analytic functions; inequalities and convex functions; Hardy classes and Nevanlinna theory; Tauberian theorems; mathematical microbiology; zeros of polynomials. *Mailing Add:* Dept of Math Syracuse Univ Syracuse NY 13210

CARHART, RICHARD ALAN, b Evanston, Ill, Aug 30, 39; m 60; c 3. THEORETICAL HIGH ENERGY PHYSICS, MATHEMATICAL PHYSICS. *Educ:* Northwestern Univ, BA, 60; Univ Wis, MA, 62, PhD(physics), 64. *Prof Exp:* Res assoc physics, Univ Wis, 64 & Brookhaven Nat Lab, 64-66; asst prof, 66-70, ASSOC PROF PHYSICS, UNIV ILL, CHICAGO CIRCLE, 70- *Mem:* Am Phys Soc. *Res:* Parity violations in quantum electro-dynamics; nucleon electromagnetic form factors and other topics in theoretical elementary particle physics; nonlinear ordinary and partial differential equations of physics. *Mailing Add:* Dept of Physics Box 4348 Univ of Ill at Chicago Circle Chicago IL 60680

CARICO, JAMES EDWIN, b Galax, Va, Mar 20, 37; m 59; c 2. INVERTEBRATE ZOOLOGY, ARACHNOLOGY. *Educ:* ETenn State Univ, BS, 59; Va Polytech Inst & State Univ, MS, 64, PhD(zool), 70. *Prof Exp:* From asst prof to assoc prof, 64-72, PROF BIOL, LYNCHBURG COL, 72- *Concurrent Pos:* Res grant, Va Acad Sci, 71; res fel arachnology, Harvard Univ, 72. *Mem:* Am Arachnological Soc; Brit Arachnological Soc. *Res:* Taxonomy; ecology; evolution in the spider family Pisauridae; evolution and construction behavior of spider webs. *Mailing Add:* 511 Brevard St Lynchburg VA 24501

CARIM, HATIM MOHAMED, b Hyderabad, India, July 17, 46. BIOMEDICAL ENGINEERING, ELECTROCHEMISTRY. *Educ:* Osmania Univ, India, BS, 67, 71; Drexel Univ, MS, 73, PhD(biomed eng), 76. *Prof Exp:* Teaching asst, Drexel Univ, 75-76; PROD DEVELOP SPECIALIST BIOMED ENG, MED PROD DIV, 3M CO, 77- *Mem:* Electrochem Soc; Soc Biomat; Inst Elec & Electronics Engrs; Sigma Xi. *Res:* Biomedical diagnostic techniques; biomaterials; bioelectrodes. *Mailing Add:* 270-2A Med Prod Div 3M Ctr 3M Co St Paul MN 55144

CARITHERS, JEANINE RUTHERFORD, b Boone, Iowa, Sept 26, 33; m 53; c 3. ANATOMY, NEUROENDOCRINOLOGY. *Educ:* Iowa State Univ, BS, 56, MS, 65; Univ Mo, PhD(anat), 68. *Prof Exp:* Asst prof, 68-72, assoc prof vet anat, 72-76, PROF & CHAIR VET ANAT, IOWA STATE UNIV, 79- *Concurrent Pos:* Assoc prof, Univ Louis Pasteur, 76-77. *Mem:* Am Asn Anatomists; Am Asn Vet Anatomists; Soc Neurosci; Sigma Xi; AAAS. *Res:* Neuroendocrinology, neurosecretion; role of the central neverous system in regulation of blood pressure and body fluid homeostasis. *Mailing Add:* Dept of Vet Anat Iowa State Univ Ames IA 50011

CARITHERS, WILLIAM CORNELIUS, JR, experimental high energy physics, see previous edition

CARL, JAMES DUDLEY, b Centralia, Ill, June 4, 35; m 61. GEOCHEMISTRY. *Educ:* Mo Sch Mines, BS, 57; Univ Ill, MS, 60, PhD(geol), 61. *Prof Exp:* Asst prof geol, Cent Mo State Col, 61-63 & Ill State Univ, 63-68; ASSOC PROF GEOL, STATE UNIV NY COL POTSDAM, 68- *Mem:* Geol Soc Am; Geochem Soc; Mineral Soc Am. *Res:* Petrology; mineralogy; geochemical and structural studies of igneous and metamorphic rocks from coastal Maine and the Northwest Adirondacks, New York; major and trace element variation. *Mailing Add:* Dept of Geol State Univ of NY Potsdam NY 13676

CARL, PHILIP LOUIS, b Cleveland, Ohio, Dec 6, 39; m 64. MOLECULAR GENETICS, BIOCHEMISTRY. *Educ:* Harvard Univ, BA, 61; Univ Calif, Berkeley, MS, 63, PhD(biophys), 68. *Prof Exp:* Jane Coffin Childs Mem Fund fel med res, 68-70; asst prof microbiol, Univ Ill, Urbana, 70-77, vis asst prof chem, 77-80; RES ASSOC PROF PHARMACOL, UNIV NC, CHAPEL HILL, 80- *Mem:* AAAS; Am Soc Microbiol. *Res:* Molecular biology of DNA replication carcinogenesis and cancer chemotherapy. *Mailing Add:* Dept Pharmacol FLOB Bldg 231H Univ NC Chapel Hill NC 27514

CARLAN, ALAN J, b New York, NY, Feb 15, 30; m 51; c 3. SOLID STATE PHYSICS, PHYSICAL ELECTRONICS. *Educ:* Brooklyn Col, BA, 51; Worcester Polytech Inst, MS, 57. *Prof Exp:* Physicist, Am Optical Co, Mass, 53-57 & Hoffman Elec, Ill, 57-58; fel, Mellon Inst, 58-61; supv engr, Syntron Co, Pa, 61-62; pres, Power Components, Inc, 62-66; chief engr, Zener Diodes, Int Rectifier Corp, 66-67; sr tech specialist & group scientist, NAm Rockwell Corp, 67-70; oper mgr, Int Rectifier Corp, 70-73; mgr advan develop, Rockwell Int, 73-76; mem tech staff, 76-80, SR ENGR SPECIALIST, LARGE SCALE & VERY LARGE SCALE TECHNOL, AEROSPACE CORP, 80- *Concurrent Pos:* Adv fel, Mellon Inst, 61, vis fac fel, 66. *Mem:* Am Phys Soc; Inst Elec & Electronics Engrs; Electrochem Soc. *Res:* Investigation and development of improved metal-oxide semiconductors, MNOS integrated circuits and power devices; developed improved manufacturing technologies and processes. *Mailing Add:* 4951 Rock Valley Rd Rancho Palos Verdes CA 90274

CARLANDER, KENNETH DIXON, b Gary, Ind, May 25, 15; m 39, 75. FISHERIES. *Educ:* Univ Minn, BS, 36, MS, 38, PhD(zool), 43. *Prof Exp:* Lab technician, Work Proj Admin, Univ Minn, 36-38; fishery biologist, Minn State Dept Conserv, 38-46; from asst prof to prof zool, 46-74, DISTINGUISHED PROF, IOWA STATE UNIV, 74- *Concurrent Pos:* Leader, Iowa Coop Fishery Res Unit, 46-65; consult, Ford Found, Egypt, 65-66; vis prof, Satya Wacana Christian Univ, Java Indonesia, 78 & Texas A&M Univ, 80. *Mem:* AAAS; Am Fisheries Soc (pres, 60); Am Soc Limnol & Oceanog; Am Soc Ichthyol & Herpet; Biomet Soc. *Res:* Fishery biology; fish population estimation; limnology; age and growth of fishes. *Mailing Add:* Dept of Animal Ecol Iowa State Univ Ames IA 50011

CARLBERG, DAVID MARVIN, b Los Angeles, Calif, Feb 9, 34; m 62; c 2. MICROBIOLOGY, VIROLOGY. *Educ:* Univ Calif, Los Angeles, BA, 56, PhD(microbiol), 63. *Prof Exp:* Chemist, Riker Labs, Inc, 56-58; head formula off, Rexall Drug & Chem Co, 58; res engr, McDonnell Douglas Corp, 63-65; mem staff, Hughes Aircraft Co, 65-66; from asst prof to assoc prof, 66-75, PROF MICROBIOL, CALIF STATE UNIV LONG BEACH, 75- *Mem:* Am Soc Microbiol; Am Inst Aeronaut & Astronaut; AAAS. *Res:* Microbial genetics; halobacteria; collection, detection and analysis of microorganisms in air and on surfaces; bio-instrumentation; exobiology. *Mailing Add:* Dept Microbiol Calif State Univ Long Beach CA 90840

CARLBORG, FRANK WILLIAM, b Chicago, Ill, Nov 23, 28; m 56; c 3. STATISTICS. *Educ:* Ripon Col, BA, 50; Univ Ill, MS, 54; Univ Chicago, PhD(statist), 64. *Prof Exp:* Mathematician, Aerial Measurements Lab, Northwestern Univ, 54-55; consult opers res, Booz-Allen & Hamilton, Inc, 55-57; asst prof math, Rockford Col, 57-61; instr statist, Grad Sch Bus, Univ Chicago, 63-64; assoc prof math, Northern Ill Univ, 64-67; INDEPENDENT STATIST CONSULT, 67- *Mem:* Am Statist Asn. *Res:* Experimental design and analysis of experimental results. *Mailing Add:* 400 S Ninth St St Charles IL 60174

CARLE, GLENN CLIFFORD, b San Bernardino, Calif, Aug 17, 36; m 64; c 1. EXOBIOLOGY, PLANETARY ATMOSPHERES. *Educ:* Calif State Polytech Univ, BS, 63. *Prof Exp:* Chemist, 63-80, CHIEF, SOLAR SYST EXPLOR OFF, AMES RES CTR, NASA, 81- *Concurrent Pos:* Co-investr, Viking Biol Gas Exchange Exp, 71-76 & Pioneer Venus Gas Chromatograph, 75-78. *Honors & Awards:* Newcomb Cleveland Award, AAAS, 76. *Mem:* Am Chem Soc. *Res:* Advanced instrument concepts, primarily gas chromatography, for future spacecraft flights which will be used to explore the solar system; major emphasis is on greater sensitivity to volatile molecules. *Mailing Add:* Ames Res Ctr NASA MS 239-12 Moffett Field CA 94035

CARLE, KENNETH ROBERTS, b Keene, NH, Sept 16, 29; m 57; c 4. PHYSICAL ORGANIC CHEMISTRY. *Educ:* Middlebury Col, AB, 51; Univ NH, MS, 53; Del Univ, PhD(chem), 55. *Prof Exp:* Asst, Gen Chem Lab, Univ NH, 51-52 & Qual Chem Lab, Del Univ, 52-53; res chemist org chem, Am Cyanamid Co, 55-59; assoc prof chem, 59-62, head dept, 62-69, PROF CHEM, HOBART & WILLIAM SMITH COL, 62-, HEAD DEPT, 78- *Concurrent Pos:* Instr, Bridgeport Eng Inst, 57-; Fulbright-Hays lectr, Univ Manila, 66-67; vis res prof, Silliman Univ, Philippines, 74-75. *Mem:* AAAS; Am Chem Soc. *Res:* Organic synthesis; polymers; kinetics; rubber chemistry; structure determination of myeloma proteins. *Mailing Add:* Dept of Chem Hobart & William Smith Col Geneva NY 14456

CARLEN, PETER LOUIS, b Edmonton, Alta, July 22, 43; m 70; c 2. NEUROLOGY, NEUROPHYSIOLOGY. *Educ:* Univ Toronto, MD, 67; FRCP(C), 72. *Prof Exp:* Intern, Montreal Gen Hosp, 67-68, resident internal med, 68-69; instr neurophysiol, Dept Zool, Hebrew Univ, Jerusalem, 69-70; resident neurol, Univ Toronto, 70-72; fel neurophysiol neurobiol unit, Hebrew Univ, 72-74; SR PHYSICIAN & HEAD NEUROL PROG, ADDICTION RES FOUND CLIN INST, 74-; STAFF NEUROLOGIST, TORONTO WESTERN HOSP, UNIV TORONTO, 74-, RES ASSOC, PLAYFAIR NEUROSCI UNIT, 79-, ASSOC PROF, DEPT MED & PHYSIOL, UNIV TORONTO, 81- *Mem:* Fel Can Neurol Soc; fel Am Acad Neurol; Soc Neurosci; AAAS; Can Physiol Soc. *Res:* Neurobiology; acute and chronic effects of psychoactive drugs on neuronal function in man and animal; cellular neurophysiology; neural modelling. *Mailing Add:* 33 Russell St Toronto ON M5S 2S1 Can

CARLEONE, JOSEPH, b Philadelphia, Pa, Jan 30, 46; m 68; c 2. ENGINEERING MECHANICS. *Educ:* Drexel Univ, BS, 68, MS, 70, PhD(appl mech), 72. *Prof Exp:* Eng trainee mech eng, Philadelphia Naval Shipyard, 63-68, mech engr power plants, 68; res assoc composite mat, Drexel Univ, 72-73; CHIEF ENGR MECH, DYNA EAST CORP, 73- *Concurrent Pos:* NDEA fel, Drexel Univ, 68-71, adj prof, 74-75 & 77- *Mem:* Sigma Xi; Am Soc Mech Engrs; Am Defense Preparedness Asn. *Res:* Response of metals to high explosives; shaped charges; ballistics; the mechanics of fiber-reinforced composites; impact of plates and membranes. *Mailing Add:* 7709 Brous Ave Philadelphia PA 19152

CARLETON, BLONDEL HENRY, b Portland, Ore, Dec 8, 04; m 35; c 5. PHYSIOLOGY. *Educ:* Univ Ore, BA, 26; Univ Rochester, PhD(physiol), 36. *Prof Exp:* Asst zool, Univ Ore, 26-27; asst physiol, Sch Med, Univ Rochester, 33-36; instr biol & physics, Ga Teachers Col, 36-38; from asst prof to prof zool, 38-75, chmn fac biol, 67-70, EMER PROF ZOOL, UNIV PORTLAND, 75- *Mem:* Sigma Xi; Am Asn Biol Teachers. *Res:* Excitability of amphibian muscle; narcosis and excitability in nerve; oxygen metabolism of muscle and nerve. *Mailing Add:* 6705 N Wilbur Ave Portland OR 97217

CARLETON, HERBERT RUCK, b Rockville Centre, NY, Dec 5, 28; m 51; c 3. ULTRASONICS, OPTICAL PHYSICS. *Educ:* Univ Southern Calif, BA, 58; Cornell Univ, PhD(theoret physics), 64. *Prof Exp:* Test methods engr, Sperry Gyroscope Corp, 49-54; design engr, Gilfillan Bros, Inc, 54-55; sr engr, Canoga Corp, 55-56; prin engr, Bendix Pac Corp, Calif, 56-58; staff mem, Res Ctr, Sperry Rand Corp, 62-67; assoc prof mat sci, 67-73, joint assoc prof mat sci & elec sci, 73-75, JOINT PROF MAT SCI & ELEC SCI, STATE UNIV NY, STONY BROOK, 75- *Concurrent Pos:* Consult, Bendix Pac Corp, 59-60 & Defense Systs Dept, Gen Elec Corp, 60-62; vis scientist, IBM San Jose Res Lab, 74, consult, 74-75. *Mem:* Optical Soc Am; Am Phys Soc; sr mem, Inst Elec & Electronics Eng. *Res:* Ultrasonic spectroscopy; optical properties of materials; strain-optic properties; non-crystalline solids; elastic properties of crystals; brillouin scattering; hypersonics; ultrasonic amplification in peizoelectric semiconductors. *Mailing Add:* Dept Mat Sci State Univ NY Stony Brook NY 11794

CARLETON, NATHANIEL PHILLIPS, astrophysics, see previous edition

CARLETON, RICHARD ALLYN, b Providence, RI, Mar 15, 31; m 54; c 4. CARDIOLOGY. *Educ:* Dartmouth Col, AB, 52; Dartmouth Med Sch, cert, 53; Harvard Med Sch, MD, 55. *Prof Exp:* Intern med, Boston City Hosp, 55-56, asst resident, 56-57, sr resident, 57-58, sr med resident, Metab Sect, 59-60; from asst prof to assoc prof, Med Sch, Univ Ill, 62-68; assoc dir cardiol, Sect Cardiorespiratory Dis, Rush-Presby-St Luke's Med Ctr, 62-68, dir cardiol, 68-72; prof med, Rush Med Col, 68-72; prof, Univ Calif, San Diego, 72-74; prof med & chmn dept, Dartmouth Med Sch, 74-76; PROF MED, BROWN UNIV MED PROG, 76- *Concurrent Pos:* Res fel, Harvard Med Sch, 58-59; Burton E Hamilton res fel, Cardiol Div, Thorndike Mem Labs, Boston City Hosp, Mass, 58-59; teaching fel, Sch Med, Tufts Univ, 59-60; asst med, Harvard Med Sch, 56-58; from asst attend physician to assoc attend physician, Rush-Presby-St Luke's Med Ctr, 62-67, attend physician, 67-72; chief cardiol, San Diego Vet Admin Hosp, 72-74 & Mem Hosp, Pawtucket, RI, 76-; fel coun cardiol, Am Heart Asn. *Mem:* Fel Am Col Cardiol; Am Soc Clin Invest; fel Am Col Physicians; Asn Univ Cardiologists. *Res:* Heart disease prevention; cardiac rehabilitation; exercise physiology. *Mailing Add:* Mem Hosp Pawtucket RI 02860

CARLEY, CHARLES TEAM, JR, b Greenville, Miss, Dec 27, 32; m 55; c 4. MECHANICAL ENGINEERING. *Educ:* Miss State Univ, BS, 55; Va Polytech Inst, MS, 61; NC State Univ, PhD(mech eng), 65. *Prof Exp:* Instr mech eng, Va Polytech Inst, 58-60; asst prof, Miss State Univ, 60-61; asst, NC State Univ, 61-64; assoc prof, 64-68, PROF MECH ENG, MISS STATE UNIV, 68-, HEAD DEPT, 69- *Mem:* Am Soc Mech Engrs; Am Soc Eng Educ. *Res:* Heat transmission; thermodynamics; bioengineering. *Mailing Add:* Dept Mech Eng Miss State Univ State College MS 39762

CARLEY, DAVID DON, b Battle Creek, Mich, July 2, 35. THEORETICAL PHYSICS. *Educ:* Western Mich Univ, BS, 57; Univ Mich, MS, 58; Univ Fla, PhD(physics), 63. *Prof Exp:* Proj engr, Noise & Vibration Lab, Gen Motors Corp, 58-60; res assoc, Univ Fla, 64; from asst prof to assoc prof, 64-75, PROF PHYSICS, WESTERN MICH UNIV, 75- *Mem:* Am Phys Soc. *Res:* Statistical mechanics; theory of fluids. *Mailing Add:* Dept of Physics Western Mich Univ Kalamazoo MI 49008

CARLEY, HAROLD EDWIN, b Syracuse, NY, July 8, 42; m 65; c 3. PLANT PATHOLOGY, SOIL SCIENCE. *Educ:* Cornell Univ, BS, 64; Univ Idaho, MS, 66; Univ Minn, St Paul, PhD(plant path), 69. *Prof Exp:* Proj leader agr bactericide-viricide develop, 69-71, GROUP LEADER FUNGICIDES, ROHM AND HAAS CO, 71- *Mem:* Am Hort Soc; Am Forestry Soc; AAAS; Am Phytopath Soc. *Res:* Discovery, optomization, and early development of chemical and biological plant disease control agents. *Mailing Add:* Rohm and Haas Co Spring House PA 19477

CARLEY, JAMES F(RENCH), b New York, NY, July 16, 23; m 81; c 3. POLYMER & OIL SHALE ENGINEERING. *Educ:* Cornell Univ, BS, 44, BChE, 47, PhD(chem eng), 51. *Prof Exp:* Instr statist & acct, Cornell Univ, 49-50; res chem engr, Plastics Processing, E I du Pont de Nemours & Co, 50-55; eng ed, Mod Plastics, 56-59; assoc prof chem eng, Univ Ariz, 59-61; tech dir, Prodex Corp, 61-64; develop assoc, Celanese Plastics Co, 64; from assoc prof to prof chem eng, eng design & econ eval, Univ Colo, Boulder, 64-76; STAFF SCIENTIST, OIL SHALE PROJ, LAWRENCE LIVERMORE NAT LAB, 76- *Mem:* Am Inst Chem Engrs; Soc Plastics Engrs. *Res:* Rheology, processing and engineering design of plastics; applied statistics; fluid flow and heat transfer; oil shale technology. *Mailing Add:* Lawrence Livermore Nat Lab PO Box 808 Livermore CA 94550

CARLEY, THOMAS GERALD, b Greenville, Miss, July 3, 35. STRUCTURAL MECHANICS. *Educ:* La State Univ, BS, 58, MS, 61; Univ Ill, PhD(theoret & appl mech), 65. *Prof Exp:* Res engr, Boeing Co, 65-66; asst prof mech eng, Southern Methodist Univ, 66-68; from asst prof to assoc prof, 68-77, PROF ENG SCI & MECH, UNIV TENN, 77- *Concurrent Pos:* Consult, Union Carbide Corp, 68- *Mem:* Sigma Xi; Am Soc Eng Educ. *Res:* Structural dynamics; seismic engineering; noise and vibration. *Mailing Add:* 7113 Merrick Dr Knoxville TN 37916

CARLILE, CLAYTON GEORGE, organic chemistry, see previous edition

CARLILE, ROBERT NICHOLS, b National City, Calif, Apr 24, 29; m 52; c 3. ELECTRICAL ENGINEERING. *Educ:* Pomona Col, BA, 51; Stanford Univ, MS, 53, EE, 56; Univ Calif, Berkeley, PhD(elec eng), 63. *Prof Exp:* Mem tech staff, Hughes Aircraft Co, 54-57, proj engr, 58-59; assoc prof elec eng, 63-69, PROF ELEC ENG, UNIV ARIZ, 69- *Concurrent Pos:* Vis res prof, Plasma Physics Lab, Princeton Univ, 69-70. *Mem:* Inst Elec & Electronics Engrs; Am Phys Soc. *Res:* Electromagnetic pulse (EMP), phenomenology; fusion plasmas; electric power generation, transmission, and distribution. *Mailing Add:* Dept of Elec Eng Univ of Ariz Tucson AZ 85721

CARLIN, CHARLES HERRICK, b Rockford, Ill, Jan 25, 39; m 65; c 2. ORGANIC CHEMISTRY. *Educ:* Carthage Col, AB, 61; Johns Hopkins Univ, MA, 63, PhD(org chem), 66. *Prof Exp:* From asst prof to assoc prof, 66-75, assoc dean col, 77-79, PROF CHEM, CARLETON COL, 75- *Concurrent Pos:* Sci adv, Food & Drug Admin, 69- *Mem:* AAAS; Sigma Xi. *Res:* Synthetic and mechanistic organic electrochemisty. *Mailing Add:* Dean's Off Carleton Col Northfield MN 55057

CARLIN, HERBERT J, b New York, NY, May 1, 17; m 40; c 2. ELECTROPHYSICS, ELECTRONICS. *Educ:* Columbia Univ, BS, 38, MS, 40; Polytech Inst Brooklyn, DEE, 47. *Prof Exp:* Design engr, Meter Div, Westinghouse Elec Co, NJ, 40-45; instr elec eng, Microwave Res Inst, Polytech Inst Brooklyn, 45-53, res prof, 53-66; dir, Sch Elec Eng, 66-75, J PRESTON LEVIS PROF ENG, CORNELL UNIV, 66- *Concurrent Pos:* Assoc dir, Microwave Res Inst, Polytech Inst Brooklyn, 56-61, head electrophys dept, 61-66; NSF sr res fel, 64-65; mem eval panel, Electromagnetics Dept, Nat Bur Standards; mem vis comt, Lehigh Univ & Univ Pa, 79-; vis prof elec eng, Mass Inst Technol, 72-73 & Univ Genoa, 74; vis res scientist, Ctr Nat d'Etudes des Telecommun, Paris, 79-80. *Mem:* Fel Inst Elec & Electronics Engrs. *Res:* Network theory; microwave components, techniques and measurements. *Mailing Add:* Sch Elec Eng Phillips Hall Cornell Univ Ithaca NY 14853

CARLIN, RICHARD LEWIS, b Boston, Mass, July 28, 35; m 59; c 2. INORGANIC CHEMISTRY. *Educ:* Brown Univ, BS, 57; Univ Ill, MS, 59, PhD, 60. *Prof Exp:* From instr to asst prof chem, Brown Univ, 60-67; assoc prof, 67-70, PROF CHEM, UNIV ILL, CHICAGO CIRCLE, 70- *Concurrent Pos:* Vis prof, Kamerlingh Onnes Lab-Oratorium, Leiden. *Mem:* Am Chem Soc; Am Phys Soc. *Res:* Electronic structure of transition metal compounds; synthetic inorganic chemistry; magnetism and spectroscopy; magnetism at low temperatures. *Mailing Add:* Dept Chem Univ Ill Chicago Circle Chicago IL 60680

CARLIN, ROBERT BURNELL, b St Paul, Minn, Nov 13, 16; m 52; c 5. ORGANIC CHEMISTRY. *Educ:* Univ Minn, BCh, 37, PhD(org chem), 41. *Prof Exp:* Asst, Univ Minn, 37-40; Lalor Found fel, Univ Ill, 41-42, instr org chem, 42-43; instr, Univ Rochester, 43-46; assoc prof, 46-52, head dept chem, 60-67 & assoc dean, Col Eng & Sci, 67-70, BECKER PROF ORG CHEM, CARNEGIE-MELLON UNIV, 52- *Concurrent Pos:* Consult, Koppers Co, Inc, 52-; Reilly lectr, Univ Notre Dame, 56; chmn, Gordon Res Conf Org Reactions & Processes, 56; mem comt, Off Ord Res, 56-59; eval postdoctoral fel applns, Nat Acad Sci-Nat Res Coun, 55-58, NSF, 55-59 & Air Force Off Sci Res, 66-68. *Mem:* Fel AAAS; Am Chem Soc. *Res:* Molecular rearrangements, such as, benzidine and alkyl group migrations; Fischer indole synthesis; polymer synthesis and structure; synthesis of bicyclic N heterocycles. *Mailing Add:* Dept Chem Mellon Inst Carnegie-Mellon Univ Pittsburgh PA 15213

CARLISLE, DAVID BREZ, b Salford, Eng, Mar 12, 26. MARINE BIOLOGY, FRESH WATER BIOLOGY. *Educ:* Oxford Univ, BA, 47, MS, 51, DPhil(zool), 54, DSc(zool), 63. *Prof Exp:* Zoologist, Marine Biol Asn UK, 51-62; head lab res div, Anti Locust Res Ctr, 62-69; prof biol & chmn dept, Trent Univ, 69-72; adv, Water Qual Res, 72-78, RES SCIENTIST, DEPT ENVIRON, INLAND WATERS DIRECTORATE, GOVT CAN, 78- *Mem:* Fel Brit Inst Biol; fel Zool Soc London; fel Linaean Soc London; fel Am Anthrop Asn; fel AAAS. *Res:* Comparative endocrinology of arthropods; tunicate biology; physiological ecology; environment induced changes in the endocrine systems of arthropods; environmental biology; fluid mechanics. *Mailing Add:* Inland Waters Directorate Place Vincent Massey Hull PQ J8I 1V0 Can

CARLISLE, DONALD, b Vancouver, BC, June 21, 19; m 44; c 4. ECONOMIC GEOLOGY. *Educ:* Univ BC, BASc, 42, MASc, 44; Univ Wis, PhD(geol), 50. *Prof Exp:* Geologist, Consol Mining & Smelting Co, Can, 44-46; lectr geol, 49-50, from instr to assoc prof, 51-64, assoc dean grad div, 67-74, PROF GEOL & MINERAL RESOURCES, UNIV CALIF, LOS ANGELES, 64- *Mem:* Fel Geol Soc Am; Soc Econ Geol; Am Inst Mining, Metall & Petrol Engrs; Geol Asn Can; Int Asn Sedimentologists. *Res:* Mineral economics and economic theory; mineral deposits and geochemistry; areal studies. *Mailing Add:* Dept of Earth & Space Sci Univ of Calif Los Angeles CA 90024

CARLISLE, FRANK JEFFERSON, JR, b Fargo, NDak, Feb 8, 20; m 44; c 5. SOIL SCIENCE. *Educ:* NDak State Col, BS, 42; Univ Wis, MS, 47; Cornell Univ, PhD, 54. *Prof Exp:* Soil scientist, Soil Conserv Serv, USDA, 47-54, soil correlator, 54-60; head Soil Surv Lab, Soil Conserv Serv, USDA, Nebr, 60-61, asst dir soil classification & correlation, 61-73, asst dir soil surv invest, 73-77; RETIRED. *Mem:* Soil Sci Soc Am; Am Soc Agron. *Res:* Soil classification, morphology and genesis. *Mailing Add:* PO Box 65 St Inigoes MD 20684

CARLISLE, GENE OZELLE, b Bivins, Tex, Feb 11, 39; m 61; c 1. INORGANIC CHEMISTRY. *Educ:* E Tex State Univ, BSc, 61, MSc, 65; N Tex State Univ, PhD(chem), 69. *Prof Exp:* Teacher high sch, Tex, 61-62; instr chem, Texarkana Col, 62-65; asst prof physics, 65-66; instr chem, N Tex State Univ, 66-67; res assoc, Univ NC, 69-70; asst prof chem, 70-74, ASSOC PROF CHEM, W TEX STATE UNIV, 74- *Mem:* Am Chem Soc; Am Phys Soc; Am Inst Physics. *Res:* Synthesis of transition metal complexes and applications of information gained from spectral and magnetic studies of these complexes to structural and bonding problems in coordination chemistry. *Mailing Add:* Dept of Chem W Tex State Univ Canyon TX 97016

CARLISLE, JOHN GRIFFIN, JR, b Port Washington, NY, May 25, 11; m 43; c 3. MARINE BIOLOGY. *Educ:* Loyola Univ (Calif), BS, 36. *Prof Exp:* Jr biologist, Marine Fisheries, 45-51, MARINE BIOLOGIST, MARINE FISHERIES, CALIF DEPT FISH & GAME, 51- *Mem:* Am Fisheries Soc; fel Am Inst Fishery Res Biologists. *Res:* Marine ecology; life histories of fishes and molluscs; marine habitat development. *Mailing Add:* 350 Golden Shore Long Beach CA 90802

CARLISLE, VICTOR WALTER, b Bunnell, Fla, Oct 3, 22; m 50; c 3. SOIL MORPHOLOGY. *Educ:* Univ Fla, BSA, 47, MS, 53, PhD(soils), 62. *Prof Exp:* Asst soil surveyor, Fla Agr Exp Sta, 47-54; asst soils, Inst Food & Agr Sci, 54-60, from instr to asst prof, 60-67, asst chemist, Agr Exp Sta, 62-67, assoc prof & assoc chemist, 67-74, PROF SOIL SCI, INST FOOD & AGR SCI, UNIV FLA, 74- *Concurrent Pos:* Consult, US AID, Univ Costa Rica, 66, Battelle Mem Inst subcontract, 67 & Jamaica Sch Agr, 70; course coordr, Orgn Trop Studies, Inc, Costa Rica, 68. *Mem:* Soil Sci Soc Am; Int Soc Soil Sci; Clay Minerals Soc; Am Asn Quaternary Environ. *Res:* Soil genesis, classification and mapping; source of parent materials of soils; weathering; soil mineralogy. *Mailing Add:* Inst of Food & Agr Sci Univ of Fla Gainesville FL 32611

CARLITZ, LEONARD, b Philadelphia, Pa, Dec 26, 07; m 31; c 2. MATHEMATICS. *Educ:* Univ Pa, AB, 27, AM, 28, PhD(math), 30. *Prof Exp:* Nat Res fel math, Calif Inst Technol, Univ Pa & Cambridge Univ, 30-32; from asst prof to prof, 32-64, JAMES B DUKE PROF MATH, DUKE UNIV, 64- *Concurrent Pos:* Mem, Inst Adv Study, 35-36. *Mem:* Am Math Soc; Math Asn Am; Soc Indust & Appl Math. *Res:* Theory of numbers; arithmetic of polynomials and power series; combinatorial analysis; special functions. *Mailing Add:* Dept Math Duke Univ Durham NC 27706

CARLITZ, ROBERT D, b Durham, NC, June 10, 45. ELEMENTARY PARTICLE PHYSICS. *Educ:* Duke Univ, BS, 65; Calif Inst Technol, PhD(physics), 70. *Prof Exp:* Asst prof physics, Univ Chicago, 72-77; ASSOC PROF PHYSICS, UNIV PITTSBURGH, 77- *Concurrent Pos:* Vis prof, Univ Wash, 76-77, Univ Mich, 79. *Res:* Field theory. *Mailing Add:* Dept Physics & Astron Univ Pittsburgh 3941 O'Hara St Pittsburgh PA 15260

CARLOCK, JOHN TIMOTHY, b Paterson, NJ, Nov 7, 51; m 77; c 2. ORGANIC CHEMISTRY. *Educ:* Col St Rose, BA, 73; Brigham Young Univ, PhD(org chem), 77; Med Sch, Univ Okla, MD, 81. *Prof Exp:* Res scientist chem, Continental Oil Co, 77-78; ASSOC PROF MED, HEALTH SCI CTR, UNIV OKLA, 82- *Concurrent Pos:* Fel, Chem Dept, Univ Jubljana. *Honors & Awards:* Coston Award Outstanding Biomed Res, 80. *Mem:* Am Chem Soc; Am Acad Family Practrs; AMA. *Res:* Heterogeneous catalysis synthesis and implementation; heterocyclic photochemistry; organic synthesis; medicine and medicinal chemistry; clinical research. *Mailing Add:* Suite 2 5527 S Sunnylane Dr Oklahoma City OK 73135

CARLONE, ROBERT LEO, b Morristown, NJ, Sept 1, 48. DEVELOPMENTAL BIOLOGY, NEUROBIOLOGY. *Educ:* Amherst Col, BA, 70; Univ NH, MSc, 75, PhD(zool), 78. *Prof Exp:* fel, Muscular Dystrophy Asn Can, 78-80; MULTIPLE SCLEROSIS SOC CAN FEL, MCMASTER UNIV, 81- *Concurrent Pos:* Chmn, Third Biennial Forum on Regeneration, McMaster Univ, 81. *Mem:* Soc Develop Biol Inc; Tissue Cult Asn; Am Soc Cell Biol. *Res:* Cellular biology of regeneration; neurotrophic interactions involved in amphibian limb regeneration; cell biology and biochemistry of cellular proliferation in regenerating systems. *Mailing Add:* Dept of Neurosci McMaster Univ Med Ctr Hamilton ON L8S 4L8 Can

CARLOTTI, RONALD JOHN, b Martins Ferry, Ohio, Sept 20, 42; m 69; c 3. NUTRITIONAL BIOCHEMISTRY. *Educ:* Ohio State Univ, BS, 64; WVa Univ, MS, 66, PhD(nutrit biochem), 70. *Prof Exp:* Res asst biochem, Col Agr, WVa Univ, 66-70; res assoc enzymol, Univ Iowa, 71-72, asst res scientist infant nutrit, 72-73, res assoc enzymol, 73-74; nutritionist human nutrit, Res Dept, Kellogg Co, 74-77; mgr, 77-80, GROUP MGR, NUTRIT & BASIC RES, FRITO-LAY, INC, 80- *Mem:* Am Chem Soc; AAAS; Inst Food Technologists; Am Meat Sci Asn. *Res:* Development of nutrit labeling, review of nutrit advert; investigation on sodium, potassium and other nutrient ineractions with essential hyprtension in rats; relationship of salt, fat, kind of fat, level of fat and salt on growth and development of rats and non-human primates; isolation, purification and immunochemical characterization of lactate dehydrogenase from Morris hepatomas. *Mailing Add:* Frito-Lay Inc Res Dept 900 North Loop 12 Irving TX 75061

CARLQUIST, PHILIP RICH, b Salt Lake City, Utah, Mar 25, 10; m 33; c 3. MICROBIOLOGY. *Educ:* Univ Utah, BA, 35; Univ Calif, MPH, 38; Yale Univ, PhD(bact), 51. *Prof Exp:* Bacteriologist, Utah State Health Dept, 35-37, 38-39; dir state health lab, Dept Health, Wyo, 39-41; chief div bact, Army Med Sch, US Army, 46-48; bacteriologist, Europe, 50-54, Fourth Army Med Lab, 54-59 & Madigan Army Hosp, Wash, 59-65; MICROBIOLOGIST, DEKALB GEN HOSP, 65- *Concurrent Pos:* Mem comt Enterobacteriacaea, Int Asn Microbiol Socs, 47- *Mem:* assoc mem Am Soc Clin Path; Brit Soc Gen Microbiol; Am Soc Microbiol. *Res:* Diagnostic medical bacteriology, particularly enterices and anaerobes. *Mailing Add:* DeKalb Gen Hosp 2701 N Decatur Rd Decatur GA 30033

CARLQUIST, SHERWIN, b Los Angeles, Calif, July 7, 30. BOTANY. *Educ:* Univ Calif, BA, 52, PhD(bot), 56. *Prof Exp:* Asst prof bot, Grad Sch, Claremont Cols, 56-61, assoc prof, 61-66; prof, 66-77, VIOLETTA L HORTON PROF BOT, CLAREMONT GRAD SCH & POMONA COL, 76- *Honors & Awards:* Gleason Prize, NY Bot Garden, 67. *Mem:* Bot Soc Am; Am Soc Plant Taxon. *Res:* Comparative anatomy of flowering plants; Compositae, Rapateaceae; problems of insular floras and faunas; wood anatomy; ecological plant anatomy. *Mailing Add:* Rancho Santa Ana Bot Garden Claremont CA 91711

CARLS, RALPH A, b Ringtown, Pa, Aug 9, 38; m 59; c 2. BACTERIOLOGY. *Educ:* Mansfield State Col, BS, 60; Okla State Univ, MS, 64; Univ Wis, PhD(bact), 71. *Prof Exp:* Teacher pub schs, 60-66; prof microbiol, 70-81, PROF BIOL, EDINBORO STATE COL, 81- *Mem:* Am Soc Microbiol. *Res:* Microbial ecology; contamination control and biological indicators. *Mailing Add:* Dept of Biol Edinboro State Col Edinboro PA 16444

CARLSEN, RICHARD CHESTER, b San Francisco, Calif, Feb 5, 40; m 69; c 2. NEUROPHYSIOLOGY. *Educ:* Univ Calif, Berkeley, AB, 63; Univ Ore, PhD(physiol), 73. *Prof Exp:* Res assoc neurophysiol, Duke Univ Med Ctr, 73-76. ASST PROF HUMAN PHYSIOL, SCH MED, UNIV CALIF, DAVIS, 76- *Concurrent Pos:* Muscular Dystrophy Asn fel physiol & pharmacol, Duke Univ, 74-76; NIH fel, 75. *Mem:* Am Physiol Soc; Soc Neurosci; Sigma Xi. *Res:* Development and plasticity of synaptic connections in the spinal cord; trophic relationship between nerve and muscle. *Mailing Add:* Dept of Human Physiol Univ of Calif Sch of Med Davis CA 95616

CARLSON, A BRUCE, b Cleveland, Ohio, Jan 31, 37; m 59; c 3. ELECTRICAL & SYSTEMS ENGINEERING. *Educ:* Dartmouth Col, AB, 58; Stanford Univ, MS, 60, PhD(elec eng), 64. *Prof Exp:* ASSOC PROF ELEC ENG, RENSSELAER POLYTECH INST, 63- *Concurrent Pos:* Commun consult, NY State Dept Health, 66-68. *Mem:* Inst Elec & Electronics Engrs; Am Soc Eng Educ. *Res:* Communication systems; engineering education; systems analysis; social context of engineering; electronics. *Mailing Add:* Dept Elec & Systs Eng Rensselaer Polytech Inst Troy NY 12181

CARLSON, ALBERT DEWAYNE, JR, b Colfax, Iowa, Dec 8, 30; m 56; c 2. INVERTEBRATE PHYSIOLOGY. *Educ:* Univ Iowa, BA, 52, MS, 59, PhD(zool), 60. *Prof Exp:* assoc prof, 60-76, PROF NEUROBIOL, STATE UNIV NY STONY BROOK, 76- *Mem:* Soc Exp Biol. *Res:* Neural and cellular control of luminescent responses of larval and adult fireflies; neurobiology and behavior of fireflies and aquatic invertebrates. *Mailing Add:* Dept Neurobiol & Behav State Univ NY Stony Brook NY 11794

CARLSON, ALLAN DAVID, b Fargo, ND, June 19, 39; m 60; c 4. NUCLEAR PHYSICS. *Educ:* Concordia Col, Moorhead, Minn, 61; Univ Wis-Madison, MS, 63, PhD(physics), 66. *Prof Exp:* Staff assoc physics, Gen Atomic Div Gen Dynamics Corp, 66-67; staff mem, Gulf Gen Atomic, 67-70;

staff scientist, Gulf Energy & Environ Systs, 70-72; NUCLEAR PHYSICIST, NAT BUR STANDARDS, 72- Concurrent Pos: Mem, US Nuclear Cross Sect Adv Comt, 70-72 & Cross Sect Eval Working Group, 72-, chmn, 80. Mem: Am Phys Soc. Res: Experimental nuclear physics; neutron cross sections; fluctuations in total neutron cross sections; capture cross sections; resonance parameters; light element, capture and fission cross section standards; neutron reaction mechanisms. Mailing Add: B119 Nat Bur of Standards Ctr for Radiation Res Washington DC 20234

CARLSON, ARTHUR, JR, b Buffalo, Kans, June 5, 22; m 53; c 3. VETERINARY PHARMACOLOGY. Educ: Kans State Univ, DVM, 50; Univ Mo, MS, 67. Prof Exp: Pvt pract, Humboldt, Kans, 50-62; res assoc pharmacol res, Haver-Lockhart Labs, Kansas City, 62-64, assoc dir pharmacol res, 64-65, dir pharmacol res, 65-68, vpres pharmacol res, 68-74; DIR QUAL ASSURANCE, BAYVET CORP, SHAWNEE, KANS, 74- Mem: Am Vet Med Asn; Am Pharmaceut Asn; Animal Health Inst; Am Soc Vet Physiol & Pharmacol. Res: Calcium and amino acid metabolism; Escherichia coli endotoxin, vaccine adjuvants, prolonged-release oral medications, and antiviral agents. Mailing Add: 9205 W 89th Shawnee KS 66204

CARLSON, ARTHUR STEPHEN, b Brooklyn, NY, Oct 24, 19; m 41; c 2. PATHOLOGY. Educ: Brooklyn Col, AB, 41; Cornell Univ, MD, 52; Am Bd Path, Am Bd Nuclear Med, Nat Bd Med Exam, dipl. Prof Exp: Asst bacteriologist, Brooklyn Col, 41-42; instr path, Med Col, Cornell Univ, 53-56, lectr, 56-69; assoc pathologist, 56-74, CHIEF PATHOLOGIST, COMMUNITY HOSP AT GLEN COVE, 74-, ATTEND-IN-CHARGE, NUCLEAR MED SECT, 81- Concurrent Pos: From intern to resident, NY Hosp, 52-55, provisional asst, 55-57; res fel, NY Heart Asn, 55-56; pres, NY State Bd Med Examr; inspector, Inspection & Accreditation Prog, Am Asn Blood Banks; clin asst prof path, Med Col, Cornell Univ, 69-77, clin assoc prof, 77- Mem: AAAS; Col Am Path; Am Asn Path & Bact; Int Acad Path. Res: Pathological and bacteriological biochemistry; morphological pathology. Mailing Add: Community Hosp Glen Cove NY 11542

CARLSON, BILLE CHANDLER, b Jamaica Plain, Mass, June 27, 24; wid; c 2. APPLIED MATHEMATICS. Educ: Harvard Univ, BA & MA, 47; Oxford Univ, PhD(physics), 50. Prof Exp: Staff mem radiation lab, Mass Inst Technol, 43-44; instr physics, Princeton Univ, 50-52, res assoc, 52-54; from asst prof to prof physics, 54-65, PROF PHYSICS & MATH, AMES LAB, IOWA STATE UNIV, 65- Concurrent Pos: Sr res fel math, Calif Inst Technol, 62-63; visitor, Poincare Inst, Univ Paris, 71-72; vis prof, Inst Phys Sci & Technol, Univ Md, 80-81. Mem: Fel Am Phys Soc; Am Math Soc; Soc Indust & Appl Math; Math Asn Am. Res: Special functions, particularly elliptic integrals and R-functions. Mailing Add: Depts of Physics & Math Iowa State Univ Ames IA 50011

CARLSON, BRUCE ARNE, b St Paul, Minn, Apr 8, 46; m 68. ORGANIC CHEMISTRY, ORGANOMETALLIC CHEMISTRY. Educ: Cornell Univ, AB, 68; Purdue Univ, PhD(org chem), 73. Prof Exp: res chemist org chem, Cent Res & Develop Dept, 73-76, res chemist, Chem Dyes & Pigments Dept, 77-78, PROD MGR, METHANOL PROD DIV, E I DU PONT DE NEMOURS & CO, INC, 78-82. Mem: Am Chem Soc; Fedn Am Scientists; Sigma Xi. Res: Exploratory chemistry of organoboranes and boron hydrides; heterocyclic chemistry based on HCN and unusual diazo and diazonium ion chemistry; chemistry of chromophores. Mailing Add: Chem & Pigments Dept B16379 E I du Pont de Nemours & Co Inc Wilmington DE 19898

CARLSON, BRUCE MARTIN, b Gary, Ind, July 11, 38; m 68; c 2. ANATOMY, DEVELOPMENTAL BIOLOGY. Educ: Gustavus Adolphus Col, BA, 59; Cornell Univ, MS, 61; Univ Minn, MD & PhD(anat), 65. Prof Exp: From asst prof to assoc prof, 66-75, prof anat, 75-79, PROF BIOL SCI, UNIV MICH, ANN ARBOR, 79- Concurrent Pos: US Acad Sci exchange fel, Inst Develop Biol, Moscow, USSR, 65-66 & Inst Physiol, Prague, Czech, 71, 72, 74, 75, 77, 78 & 79; Fulbright fel, Hubrecht Lab, Utrecht, Neth, 73-74; Josiah Macy Jr fel, Univ Helsinki, 81-82. Honors & Awards: Newcomb-Cleveland Award, AAAS, 74. Mem: Int Soc Develop Biol; Am Asn Anat; Am Soc Zool; Am Soc Ichthyologists & Herpetologists; Soc Develop Biol. Res: Regeneration; muscle transplantation; bone induction and morphogenesis. Mailing Add: Dept Anat Univ Mich Ann Arbor MI 48104

CARLSON, CHARLES MERTON, b Duluth, Minn, Apr 3, 34; wid. THEORETICAL CHEMISTRY. Educ: Univ Calif, Riverside, AB, 56; Univ Utah, PhD(chem), 60. Prof Exp: Staff scientist, Metall Dept, Brookhaven Nat Lab, NY, 60-62; res specialist, Solid State Physics Group, Boeing Sci Res Labs, 62-70; VIS SCHOLAR, COMPUT SCI GROUP, UNIV WASH, 71- Mem: Am Phys Soc; Am Chem Soc; Soc Indust & Appl Math. Res: Basic theoretical research in quantum chemistry and statistical mechanics as applied to molecules and solids. Mailing Add: 6507 1/2 Parker Ct NW Seattle WA 98117

CARLSON, CHARLES WENDELL, b Eaton, Colo, May 15, 21; m 43; c 5. ANIMAL NUTRITION. Educ: Colo State Univ, BS, 42; Cornell Univ, MSA, 48, PhD(animal nutrit), 49. Prof Exp: Asst poultry husb, Cornell Univ, 46-49; from asst prof to assoc prof, 49-56, PROF POULTRY HUSB, S DAK STATE UNIV, 56-, LEADER POULTRY RES, 67- Concurrent Pos: Res assoc, Wash State Univ, 62-63; prin non-ruminant nutritionist, Coop States Res Serv, USDA, Washington, DC, 75-76. Honors & Awards: Nat Turkey Fedn res award, 61. Mem: Fel AAAS; Am Chem Soc; fel Poultry Sci Asn (pres, 70-71); Am Inst Nutrit. Res: Poultry; biochemistry; amino acid and energy metabolism; growth factors; calcification. Mailing Add: Dept of Animal Sci SDak State Univ Brookings SD 57007

CARLSON, CLARENCE ALBERT, JR, b Moline, Ill, Apr 3, 37; m 58; c 2. FISH BIOLOGY, AQUATIC ECOLOGY. Educ: Augustana Col, Ill, AB, 58; Iowa State Univ, MS, 60, PhD(zool), 63. Prof Exp: Asst prof biol, Augustana Col, Ill, 62-66; asst prof fishery biol & asst leader NY Coop Fishery Unit,

Cornell Univ, 66-72; assoc prof, 72-78, PROF FISHERY BIOL, COLO STATE UNIV, 78- Mem: Am Fisheries Soc; Ecol Soc Am; Am Inst Biol Sci. Res: Ecology of fishes; river ecology; environmental effects of energy development; aquatic radioecology. Mailing Add: Dept Fishery & Wildlife Biol Colo State Univ Ft Collins CO 80523

CARLSON, CURTIS RAYMOND, b Providence, RI, May 22, 45; m 73. VISION, IMAGE PROCESSING. Educ: Worcester Polytech, BS, 67; Rutgers Univ, PhD(mech eng), 73. Prof Exp: Mem tech staff, 73-81, HEAD IMAGE QUALITY & HUMAN PERCEPTION RES, SARNOFF RES LABS, RCA, 81- Mem: Sigma Xi; Optical Soc Am; Soc Info Display; Asn Res Vision & Ophthalmology. Res: Human visual perception; display image quality; image processing. Mailing Add: Sarnoff Res Labs Rte 1 Princeton NJ

CARLSON, DALE ARVID, b Aberdeen, Wash, Jan 10, 25; m 48; c 4. SANITARY ENGINEERING, CIVIL ENGINEERING. Educ: Univ Wash, BSCE, 50, MSCE, 51; Univ Wis, PhD(civil eng), 60. Prof Exp: Engr, City Water Dept, Aberdeen, 51-55; from instr to assoc prof civil eng, 55-67, chmn dept, 71-76, PROF CIVIL ENG, UNIV WASH, 67-, DIR SOLID WASTES MGT PROG, 69-, DEAN COL ENG, 76- Concurrent Pos: Asst, Wis Alumni Res Found, 60; co-prin investr, US Corps Engrs, states of Ore & Wash, Northwest Pulp & Paper Asn, 60-61 & City of Anacortes, 63-64; prin investr, USPHS, 61-65, Metrop Engrs, Wash, 63-64, Munic of Metrop Seattle, 64-65 & Northwest Pulp & Paper Asn, 64-; mem, Wash State Bd Health, 64-72, chmn, 71-72; vis prof, Tech Univ Denmark, Copenhagen, 70-; vis scientist, Royal Col Agr, Uppsala, Sweden, 76 & 78. Mem: Am Soc Civil Engrs; Water Pollution Control Fedn; Am Water Works Asn; Am Asn Prof Sanit Engrs; Int Asn Water Pollution Res. Res: Biological treatment of domestic and industrial wastes; water quality; solid wastes management; odor removal by soil columns. Mailing Add: Col of Eng Univ of Wash Seattle WA 98195

CARLSON, DANA PETER, b Red Wing, Minn, Oct 31, 31; m 56; c 4. ORGANIC CHEMISTRY. Educ: Univ Minn, BS, 53; Carnegie Inst Technol, MS, 56, PhD(chem), 57. Prof Exp: From res chemist to sr res chemist, Plastics Dept, 57-71, res assoc, 71-81, RES FEL, E I DU PONT DE NEMOURS & CO, INC, 81- Mem: Am Chem Soc. Res: Fluorocarbon chemistry; synthesis of monomers and polymers. Mailing Add: E I du Pont de Nemours & Co Inc PO Box 1217 Parkersburg WV 26101

CARLSON, DAVID ARTHUR, b Muskegon, Mich, Nov 28, 40; m 63; c 2. ORGANIC CHEMISTRY, ANALYTICAL CHEMISTRY. Educ: Kalamazoo Col, BA, 62; Univ Hawaii, MS, 66, PhD(phys org chem), 70. Prof Exp: Res chemist, Anaconda Wire & Cable Res Lab, 62-63; RES CHEMIST, USDA, 69- Mem: Am Chem Soc; AAAS; Entom Soc Am. Res: Biologically active natural products; identification of insect sex attractant hormones and stimulant pheromones in mosquitoes, houseflies and tsetse flies; pesticide analysis; gas chromatography; mass spectrometry. Mailing Add: Insects Affecting Man Res Lab USDA Gainesville FL 32604

CARLSON, DAVID EMIL, b Weymouth, Mass, Mar 5, 42; m 66; c 2. SOLID STATE PHYSICS. Educ: Rensselaer Polytech Inst, 63; Rutgers Univ, PhD(physics), 68. Prof Exp: Res scientist physics, US Army Nuclear Effects Lab, mem tech staff physics, 70-76, HEAD PHOTOVOLTAIC DEVICE DEVELOP, RCA LABS, NJ, 77- Honors & Awards: Ross Coffin Purdy Award, Am Ceramic Soc, 76. Mem: Am Phys Soc; Inst Elec & Electronics Engrs; Electrochem Soc; Sigma Xi. Res: Ion motion in glasses and insulators; thin film photovoltaic devices. Mailing Add: RCA Labs Princeton NJ 08540

CARLSON, DAVID HILDING, b Chicago, Ill, Nov 10, 36; m 59; c 4. MATHEMATICS. Educ: San Diego State Col, AB, 57; Univ Wis, MS, 59, PhD(math), 63. Prof Exp: Instr math, Univ Wis, Milwaukee, 62-63; from asst prof to assoc prof, 63-73, PROF MATH, ORE STATE UNIV, 73- Concurrent Pos: Fulbright-Hays lectr, Univ of Repub Uruguay, 65-66; vis prof, Kent State Univ & Univ Coimbra, Port, 70-71. Mem: Am Math Soc; Math Asn Am. Res: Matrix theory, especially inertia theory and location of eigenvalues. Mailing Add: Dept of Math Ore State Univ Corvallis OR 97331

CARLSON, DAVID L, b Minneapolis, Minn, Sept 3, 36. ELECTRICAL & BIOMEDICAL ENGINEERING. Educ: Univ Minn, BSEE, 59; Iowa State Univ, MS, 61, PhD(elec eng), 64. Prof Exp: Asst prof, 64-67, ASSOC PROF BIOMED ENG, IOWA STATE UNIV, 67- Mem: Inst Elec & Electronics Engrs. Res: Electronic instrumentation; respiratory assistance for newborn infants; medical ultrasound. Mailing Add: Dept of Biomed Eng Iowa State Univ Ames IA 50011

CARLSON, DAVID STEN, b New Bedford, Mass, Aug 30, 48; m 70; c 2. ANATOMY, DENTAL RESEARCH. Educ: Univ Mass, Amherst, BA, 70, MA, 72, PhD(anthrop), 74. Prof Exp: Teaching fel anthrop, Univ Mass, Amherst, 70-74, lectr, 73-74; asst prof anthrop, Wayne State Univ, 74-76; ASST PROF ANAT, UNIV MICH, 78-, ASST RES SCIENTIST, CTR HUMAN GROWTH & DEVELOP, 78- Concurrent Pos: Marshall fel, Am Scandanavian Found, 73; assoc, Sch Med, Wayne State Univ, 74-76; scholar, Univ Mich, 75-77; co-ed, Human Biol. Mem: AAAS; Am Asn Phys Anthropologists; Human Biol Coun. Res: Analysis of the phylogenetic and ontogenetic factors influencing the form and function of the craniofacial complex. Mailing Add: Ctr for Human Growth & Dev Univ of Mich Ann Arbor MI 48103

CARLSON, DON MARVIN, b Walhalla, NDak, Mar 11, 31; m 51; c 4. GLYCOPROTEINS, GENE EXPRESSION. Educ: NDak State Univ, BS, 56; Univ Ill, MS, 58; Mich State Univ, PhD(biochem), 61. Prof Exp: Instr, Univ Mich, 63-64; from asst prof to assoc prof biochem, Case Western Reserve Univ, 64-75; dept head, 75-81, PROF BIOCHEM, PURDUE UNIV, 81- Concurrent Pos: NIH Physiol Chem Study Sect, 76-80. Mem: Am Soc Biol Chemists; Soc Complex Carbohydrates (secy, 74-80); Am Chem Soc. Res: Chemistry and biosynthesis of glycoproteins; regulation of gene expression. Mailing Add: Dept Biochem Purdue Univ West Lafayette IN 47907

CARLSON, DONALD EUGENE, radiobiology, immunobiology, see previous edition

CARLSON, DOUGLAS W, b Jamestown, NDak, Jan 7, 30; m 54; c 2. PHYSICAL CHEMISTRY. *Educ:* Univ NDak, BS, 55; Univ Del, MS, 57, PhD(phys chem), 59. *Prof Exp:* Fel, Princeton Univ, 59-61; res chemist, Minn Mining & Mfg Co, Minn, 61-64; res chemist, E I du Pont de Nemours & Co, Del, 64-67, tech rep, 67-70; dir res, Springfield Res Ctr, Dayco Corp, 70-79; SR VPRES, BANDAG INC, 80- *Mem:* Am Chem Soc. *Res:* Polymer chemistry; photochemistry. *Mailing Add:* RR 3 Box 525 Q Muscantine IA 52761

CARLSON, EDWARD H, b Lansing, Mich, Apr 29, 32; m 60; c 3. SOLID STATE PHYSICS. *Educ:* Mich State Univ, BS, 54, MS, 56; Johns Hopkins Univ, PhD(physics), 59. *Prof Exp:* Instr physics, Johns Hopkins Univ, 59-60; NSF fel, State Univ Leiden, 60-61; asst prof, Univ Ala, 61-65; from asst prof to assoc prof, 65-74, PROF PHYSICS, MICH STATE UNIV, 74- *Mem:* Am Phys Soc. *Res:* Rare earth spectra; electron and nuclear magnetic spin resonance; ordered magnetic states; atomic and molecular structure. *Mailing Add:* Dept of Physics Mich State Univ East Lansing MI 48824

CARLSON, ELOF AXEL, b Brooklyn, NY, July 15, 31; m 59; c 5. GENETICS. *Educ:* NY Univ, BA, 53; Ind Univ, PhD, 58. *Prof Exp:* Lectr genetics, Ind Univ, 57-58 & Queen's Univ, 58-60; asst prof zool, Univ Calif, Los Angeles, 60-65, assoc prof, 65-68; prof biol, 68-75, DISTINGUISHED TEACHING PROF BIOL, STATE UNIV NY, STONY BROOK, 75- *Mem:* Fel AAAS; Genetics Soc Am. *Res:* Gene structure and function; chemical and radiation induced mutagenesis; mosaicism in Drosophila and man; history of genetics. *Mailing Add:* Dept of Biol State Univ of NY Stony Brook NY 11794

CARLSON, EMIL HERBERT, b Portland, Ore, Oct 25, 29; m 51; c 4. ORGANIC CHEMISTRY. *Educ:* Willamette Univ, BS, 51; Carnegie Inst Technol, MS, 54, PhD(chem), 56. *Prof Exp:* Asst chem lab, Carnegie Inst Technol, 51-52, asst org qual lab, 52-53, sr asst, 53-54; res chemist, 5S-64, prod specialist org div, Mo, 64-65, mkt analyst, 65-70, RES SPECIALIST, AGR DIV, MONSANTO CO, 70- *Mem:* Am Chem Soc; NY Acad Sci; Sigma Xi. *Res:* Agricultural chemicals; functional fluids; intermediate chemicals. *Mailing Add:* Monsanto Co PO Box 473 Muscatine IA 52761

CARLSON, ERIC DUNGAN, b Kansas City, Mo, Jan 19, 29; m 70; c 2. ASTRONOMY. *Educ:* Wash Univ (St Louis), AB, 50; Northwestern Univ, MS, 65, PhD(astron), 68. *Prof Exp:* Mgt trainee printing, R R Donnelley & Sons Co, 56-58; asst to ed-in-chief encycl writing, Consol Bk Publs, 58-61; SR ASTRONR, ADLER PLANETARIUM, 68- *Mem:* Am Astron Soc. *Res:* Peculiar emissionline stars. *Mailing Add:* Adler Planetarium 1300 S Lake Shore Dr Chicago IL 60605

CARLSON, ERIC THEODORE, b Westbrook, Conn, Aug 22, 22; m 50; c 1. PSYCHIATRY. *Educ:* Wesleyan Univ, BA, 44; Cornell Univ, MD, 50. *Prof Exp:* Intern int med, New York Hosp, 50-51, asst res psychiat, 51-55, psychiatrist out-patients, 55-56, asst attend psychiatrist, 52-60, assoc attend psychiatri st, 60-70, ATTEND PSYCHIATRIST, NEW YORK HOSP, 70-; CLIN PROF PSYCHIAT, MED COL, CORNELL UNIV, 70- *Concurrent Pos:* Asst psychiat, Med Col, Cornell Univ, 52-53, instr, 53-58, from clin asst prof to clin assoc prof, 58-70; consult psychiatrist, Hosp Spec Surg, New York. *Mem:* AAAS; Am Psychiat Asn; Am Col Psychiatrists; Int Soc Hist Med; Am Asn Hist Med. *Res:* Medical education; development of psychiatric thought. *Mailing Add:* 60 Sutton Pl S New York NY 10022

CARLSON, ERNEST HOWARD, b Seattle, Wash, Dec 23, 33. GEOLOGY, MINERALOGY. *Educ:* Univ Wash, BSc, 56; Univ Colo, MSc, 60; McGill Univ, PhD(crystal growth), 66. *Prof Exp:* Geologist, US Geol Surv, 58-60; instr geol, Villanova Univ, 65-66; asst prof, 66-75, ASSOC PROF GEOL, KENT STATE UNIV, 75- *Concurrent Pos:* Vis prof, Pahlavi Univ, Shiraz, Iran, 70-71. *Mem:* Am Crystallog Asn; Geol Soc Am; Mineral Soc Am; Sigma Xi. *Res:* Experimental mineralogy; exploration geochemistry. *Mailing Add:* Dept of Geol Kent State Univ Kent OH 44242

CARLSON, F ROY, JR, b Boston, Mass, Aug 1, 44; m 67. COMPUTER SCIENCE. *Educ:* Univ Rochester, BS, 67; Univ Southern Calif, PhD, 70. *Prof Exp:* Asst prof elec eng & comput sci, 70-76, ASST DEAN, SCH ENG & DIR ENG COMPUT LAB, UNIV SOUTHERN CALIF, 76- *Mem:* Inst Elec & Electronics Engrs; Asn Comput Mach. *Res:* Design of computer based instructional systems, utilizing natural language processing and artificial intelligence techniques for the presentation of instructional material. *Mailing Add:* Eng Comput Lab Univ of Southern Calif Univ Park Los Angeles CA 90007

CARLSON, FRANCIS DEWEY, b Syracuse, NY, June 29, 21; m 50; c 3. BIOPHYSICS. *Educ:* Johns Hopkins Univ, AB, 42; Univ Pa, PhD(biophys), 49. *Prof Exp:* Asst, Electroacoust Lab, Harvard Univ, 42-43, res assoc, 43-46; asst, Univ Pa, 46-49; from instr to assoc prof biophys, 49-60, chmn dept, 56-74, PROF BIOPHYS, JOHNS HOPKINS UNIV, 60- *Concurrent Pos:* NSF sr fel, 61-62. *Mem:* AAAS; Am Phys Soc; Biophys Soc. *Res:* Mechano-chemistry of muscular contraction; molecular biology; neurophysiology. *Mailing Add:* Dept of Biophys Johns Hopkins Univ Baltimore MD 21218

CARLSON, FREDERICK PAUL, b Aberdeen, Wash, May 26, 38; m 70; c 4. OPTICS, ELECTROMAGNETICS. *Educ:* Univ Wash, BSEE, 60, PhD(elec eng), 67; Univ Md, MS, 64. *Prof Exp:* Instr & control engr elec eng, US Navy, US Atomic Energy Comn, 60-64; res engr, Boeing Aerospace Co, 65-66; from asst prof to prof, Univ Wash, 67-79; vpres, 77-79, actg pres, 79-80, PROF APPL PHYSICS, 77-, PRES, ORE GRAD CTR, 80- *Concurrent Pos:* Vis scholar, Pac Lutheran Theol Sem, Berkeley, 75-76; vis prof, Stanford Univ, 75-76; consult, Naval Res Adv Comt, 76-79. *Mem:* Optical Soc Am; sr mem Inst Elec & Electronics Engrs; Am Geophys Union. *Res:* Optical data processing; optical computing; biomedical applications of optical data processing and pattern recognition. *Mailing Add:* Oregon Grad Ctr 19600 NW Walker Rd Beaverton OR 97006

CARLSON, GARY, b Los Angeles, Calif, Mar 6, 28; m 54; c 5. COMPUTER SCIENCES, INTELLIGENT SYSTEMS. *Educ:* Univ Calif, Los Angeles, BS, 56, MA, 58, PhD(indust psychol), 62. *Prof Exp:* Res asst, Western Data Processing Ctr, Univ Calif, Los Angeles, 58-59; sr opers res specialist, Indust Dynamics Dept, Hughes Aircraft Co, Calif, 59-61; with, Info Systs, Inc, 61-63; dir, Comput Res Ctr, Brigham Young Univ, 63-70, dir comput serv, 70-79; PRES, COMPUT TRANSLATION, INC, 79- *Concurrent Pos:* Mem, Utah State Citizens Comt Rev State Comput Orgn, 68-69. *Mem:* Asn Comput Mach; AAAS. *Res:* Computer administration; computer performance measurement and monitoring. *Mailing Add:* Comput Translation Inc 1455 S State St 3 Orem UT 84057

CARLSON, GARY ALDEN, b Hastings, Nebr, Apr 18, 41; m 62, 81; c 2. PHYSICAL CHEMISTRY. *Educ:* Univ Idaho, BS, 63; Univ Calif, Berkeley, PhD(phys chem), 66. *Prof Exp:* MEM TECH STAFF PHYS CHEM, SANDIA LABS, 66- *Mem:* Am Chem Soc. *Res:* Free radical studies; rapid scan infrared spectroscopy; high temperature chemisty; detonation chemistry; exploding wires; pulsed electron beam energy deposition; plasma spectroscopy; nonequilibrium phase changes; liquid metal fast breeder reactor safety research; medical devices development. *Mailing Add:* Div 2151 Sandia Labs Albuquerque NM 87185

CARLSON, GARY P, b Buffalo, NY, Feb 21, 43; m 68; c 4. TOXICOLOGY, PHARMACOLOGY. *Educ:* St Bonaventure Univ, BS, 65; Univ Chicago, PhD(pharmacol), 69. *Prof Exp:* From asst prof to assoc prof pharmacol, Univ RI, 69-75; assoc prof, 75-80, PROF TOXICOL, PURDUE UNIV, 80- *Mem:* Soc Toxicol; Am Soc Pharmacol & Exp Therapeut; Am Indust Hyg Asn; NY Acad Sci. *Res:* Toxicity of pesticides, drugs, chemicals; drug metabolism. *Mailing Add:* Dept Pharmacol & Toxicol Purdue Univ West Lafayette IN 47907

CARLSON, GARY WAYNE, b Idaho Falls, Idaho, Oct 10, 44; m 72; c 3. NUCLEAR PHYSICS. *Educ:* Univ Utah, BA, 68, PhD(physics), 73. *Prof Exp:* PHYSICIST NUCLEAR PHYSICS, LAWRENCE LIVERMORE LAB, 72- *Res:* Fission cross section measurements; nuclear explosives. *Mailing Add:* Lawrence Livermore Lab PO Box 808 Livermore CA 94550

CARLSON, GERALD EUGENE, b Wausa, Nebr, Oct 28, 32; m 54; c 3. ENVIRONMENTAL PHYSIOLOGY, AGRONOMY. *Educ:* Iowa State Univ, BS, 58, MS, 59; Pa State Univ, PhD(forage physiol), 63. *Prof Exp:* Res agronomist, Crop Res Div, 63-66, res leader, Humid Pasture & Range, 66-72, lab chief, Light & Plant Growth Lab, 72-79, NAT RES PROG LEADER, BELTSVILLE AGR RES CTR, AGR RES SERV, USDA, 79- *Concurrent Pos:* Vis foreign scientist, Japanese Inst Sci & Technol, 70. *Mem:* Fel Am Soc Agron; Crop Sci Soc Am; Soc Range Mgt. *Res:* Identification of factors limiting light utilization by plants including the effect of temperature and light on photosynthesis, respiration and translocation. *Mailing Add:* Rm 314 Bldg 005 Beltsville Agr Res Ctr Beltsville MD 20705

CARLSON, GERALD LEROY, b Kane, Pa, July 13, 32; m 59; c 6. ANALYTICAL CHEMISTRY. *Educ:* Grove City Col, BS, 54; Univ Pittsburgh, MS, 57, PhD(chem), 60. *Prof Exp:* Res assoc, Mellon Inst, 54-60, res fel, 60-61; res chemist, Alcoa Res Labs, Alcoa Aluminum Co Am, 61-62; res fel, Mellon Inst, 62-67 & Mellon Inst Sci, Carnegie-Mellon Univ, 67-74; sr scientist, 74-78, MGR ANAL CHEM, WESTINGHOUSE RES LABS, 78- *Mem:* Soc Appl Spectros; Am Chem Soc; Coblentz Soc. *Res:* Molecular spectroscopy; mass spectrometry; water chemistry. *Mailing Add:* Westinghouse Res Labs Beulah Rd Pittsburgh PA 15235

CARLSON, GERALD LOWELL, b Jackson, Minn, Dec 2, 29; m 56; c 2. BIOLOGICAL CHEMISTRY. *Educ:* Luther Col, Iowa, AB, 51; Univ Ga, MS, 56; Mass Inst Technol, PhD(biochem), 61. *Prof Exp:* Donner Found res fel med, 61-62; Given Found res fel, 62-63; asst prof biochem, 63-69, ASSOC PROF BIOCHEM, MED CTR, UNIV ALA, 69- *Concurrent Pos:* Lalor Found res grant, 63-64. *Mem:* AAAS; Am Soc Zool; Soc Gen Physiol. *Res:* Mechanisms of enzyme action; germ cell differentiation; autoimmunity; biochemistry of regeneration and metamorphosis. *Mailing Add:* Dept of Biochem Univ of Ala Med Ctr Birmingham AL 35294

CARLSON, GERALD MICHAEL, b Clayton, Wash, Sept 26, 46; m 67; c 2. BIOCHEMISTRY. *Educ:* Wash State Univ, BS, 69; Iowa State Univ, PhD(biochem), 75. *Prof Exp:* Res assoc, Inst Enzyme Res, Univ Wis, 75-78; ASST PROF BIOCHEM, DEPT CHEM, UNIV SOUTH FLA, 78- *Concurrent Pos:* NIH fel, 76-78. *Res:* Regulation at molecular level of glycogenolysis and gluconeogenesis. *Mailing Add:* Dept Chem Univ South Fla Tampa FL 33620

CARLSON, GLENN RICHARD, b New Haven, Conn, Oct 22, 45; m 67; c 2. SYNTHETIC ORGANIC CHEMISTRY. *Educ:* Bates Col, BS, 67; Mich State Univ, PhD(org chem), 71. *Prof Exp:* Res assoc org chem, Univ Chicago, 71-73; res chemist, 73-81, SECT MGR, ROHM & HAAS CO, 81- *Mem:* Am Chem Soc. *Res:* Synthesis of biologically active molecules; development of new synthetic methods in organic chemistry. *Mailing Add:* Rohn & Haas Co Res Div Labs 727 Norristown Rd Spring House PA 19477

CARLSON, GORDON ANDREW, b Jamestown, NY, Jan 11, 17; m 41; c 3. INORGANIC CHEMISTRY. *Educ:* Wittenberg Col, AB, 40; Ohio State Univ, PhD(chem), 44. *Prof Exp:* Res chemist, Columbia Chem Div, Pittsburgh Plate Glass Co, Ohio, 44-50, asst chief chemist, WVa, 50-51 & Columbia-Southern Chem Co, 51-55, asst dir res, 55-62; dept head inorg res, 62-65, SR RES ASSOC, CHEM DIV, BARBERTON CHEM TECH CTR, PITTSBURGH PLATE GLASS CO, 65- *Mem:* Am Chem Soc; Electrochem Soc. *Res:* Chlor-alkali cells; coordination compounds; rare earths; alkalies and chlorine; industrial electrochemistry; metal halides and inorganic chlorinations; chemical metallurgy. *Mailing Add:* 254 Tanglewood Trail Wadsworth OH 44281

CARLSON, H(ENNING) MAURICE, b Moline, Ill, Feb 13, 16; m 43; c 4. MECHANICAL ENGINEERING. *Educ:* Univ Minn, BS, 39, BME, 43; Univ Louisville, MME, 55; Rutgers Univ, MEngSc, 75. *Prof Exp:* Teacher, High Sch, Minn, 39-41; asst, Univ Minn, 41-42, instr math, 43-44; res engr, Fuels Div, Battelle Mem Inst, 44-49; from asst prof to assoc prof mech eng, Univ Louisville, 49-57; prof, 57-59, dir eng, 59-62, head, Dept Mech Eng, 57-78, prof, 78-81, EMER PROF, LAFAYETTE COL, 81- *Concurrent Pos:* Mem, Student Develop Comt, Engrs Coun Prof Develop, 60-62, chmn, 63-66, mem ethics comt, 66- *Honors & Awards:* Lincoln Arc Welding Award, 47. *Mem:* Am Soc Mech Engrs; Am Soc Eng Educ; Nat Soc Prof Engrs. *Res:* Engineering education and administration; thermodynamics; fluid mechanics; machine design; consult energy conservation and alternatives; air pollution and control; educational administration. *Mailing Add:* Dept of Mech Eng Lafayette Col Easton PA 18042

CARLSON, HAROLD C(ARL) R(AYMOND), b Easthampton, Mass, July 18, 08; m 55. MECHANICAL ENGINEERING & METALLURGY. *Prof Exp:* Design engr, Otis Elevator Co, NY, 29-40; chief engr, Lee Spring Co, Brooklyn, NY, 40-46 & Fischer Mfg Co, 46-48; pres & chief consult engr, Carlson Co, 48-70; CONSULT ENGR, 70- *Honors & Awards:* Mach Design Award, 51. *Mem:* Fel Am Soc Mech Engrs; Am Soc Testing & Mat. *Res:* Mechanical spring engineering; design of mechanical products; metallurgy of springs; design of machinery for automation; consultant on management and manufacturing problems; physical testing of fatigue of metals and spring specifications. *Mailing Add:* 611B Lake Point Dr Lakewood NJ 08701

CARLSON, HARRY WILLIAM, b Philadelphia, Pa, Oct 11, 24; m 45; c 2. AERODYNAMICS, FLUID MECHANICS. *Educ:* Va Polytech Inst, BS, 52. *Prof Exp:* Engr, Langley Res Ctr, NASA, 52-71, sect head aeronaut, Langley Res Ctr, 68-80; RETIRED. *Concurrent Pos:* Mem sonic boom res panel, Interagency Noise Abatement Prog, 68. *Honors & Awards:* Awards, NASA, 66 & 68. *Mem:* Am Inst Aeronaut & Astronaut. *Res:* Design and evaluation of supersonic aircraft aerodynamic configurations, sonic boom generation phenomena and development of prediction and minimization techniques. *Mailing Add:* 122 Dogwood Dr Newport News VA 23606

CARLSON, HARVE J, b Jerome, Idaho, June 10, 11; m 37; c 3. BACTERIOLOGY, VIROLOGY. *Educ:* Univ Wash, BS, 34; Univ Mich, MSPH, 40, DPH, 43. *Prof Exp:* Lab technician, Idaho State Dept Health, 36-39, asst bacteriologist, 39-40; asst bacteriologist, Univ Mich, 40-41, res assoc, 41-42, instr bact, 42-43; asst prof pediat res, Western Reserve Univ, 46-51; biologist, Off Naval Res, Calif, 51-56, sci liaison off, Eng, 56-58, head microbiol br, 58-59; prog dir facil & spec prog, Div Biol & Med Sci, NSF, 59-60, from dep asst dir to dir div, 60-72; SCI & EDUC CONSULT, 72- *Mem:* Am Soc Microbiol; Am Soc Exp Biol & Med. *Res:* Antibiotics; ultraviolet irradiation; airborne organisms; oligiodynamics of metals; effects on bacteria and viruses; effect of chemical agents of poliomyelitis virus; research administration. *Mailing Add:* 406 Dorset Dr Cocoa Beach FL 32931

CARLSON, HERBERT CHRISTIAN, JR, b Brooklyn, NY, May 10, 37; div; c 2. ATMOSPHERIC PHYSICS, SPACE SCIENCE. *Educ:* Cooper Union, BEE, 59; Cornell Univ, MSc, 62, PhD(radio propagation), 65. *Prof Exp:* Res assoc/sr res assoc, Arecibo Observ, Nat Astronomy & Ionosphere Ctr, Cornell Univ, 65-69; res assoc, Dept Space Physics, Rice Univ, 69-70, Dept Geol & Geophys, Yale Univ, 70; head ionosphere dept, Arecibo Observ, Nat Astronomy & Ionosphere Ctr, Cornell Univ, 70-73; sr res scientist atmospheric physics, Inst Phys Sci, Univ Tex, Dallas, 73-77; prog dir aeronomy, NSF, 77-81; CHIEF, IONOSPHERIC PHYSICS BR, AIR FORCE GEOPHYS LAB, 81- *Concurrent Pos:* Mem, Comt Solar-Terrestrial Res Panel, Nat Acad Sci, 72-75; mem, Sci Adv Comt, Stanford Res Inst Int, 72-77, consult, 72-77; coordr, Incoherant Scattering Working Group, Int Union Radio Union, 73-77; mem, Sci Adv Comt, Nat Astronomy & Ionosphere Ctr, 74-77; mem, Stratosphere Working Group Subcomt, Intergovt Comt Atmosphere Sci, 77-79. *Mem:* Am Geophys Union; AAAS; Int Union Radio Sci. *Res:* Upper atmospheric, radio, and space physics; application of radio and optical techniques, and in situ measurements, to studies of the ionosphere/thermosphere especially thermal balance, chemistry and transport; areas of plasma physics. *Mailing Add:* Air Force Geophys Lab PHY Hanscom AFB MA 01731

CARLSON, HUGH DOUGLAS, b Haileybury, Ont, Aug 29, 22; m 50; c 2. ECONOMIC GEOLOGY. *Educ:* Queen's Univ (Ont), BSc, 49, PhD(geol), 53; Univ Toronto, MASc, 50. *Prof Exp:* Resident geologist, Ont Dept Mines, 53-56; consult geologist, 56-57; asst prof geol, Univ SDak, 57-60, assoc prof, 60-63; res geologist, Ont Dept Mines, 63-67; CONSULT GEOLOGIST, 67- *Mem:* AAAS; Geol Asn Can; Can Inst Mining & Metall; Mineral Asn Can. *Mailing Add:* 110 Martin St Porcupine Can

CARLSON, IRVING THEODORE, b Colbert, Wash, July 14, 26; m 52; c 2. PLANT BREEDING. *Educ:* Wash State Univ, BS, 50, MS, 52; Univ Wis, PhD(agron), 55. *Prof Exp:* Asst wheat breeding, Wash State Univ, 50-52; asst forage grass breeding, Univ Wis, 52-55; asst wheat breeding, Wash State Univ, 55-56; asst prof field crops, NC State Col, 56-60; assoc prof agron, 60-73, PROF AGRON, IOWA STATE UNIV, 73- *Mem:* Am Soc Agron; Am Forage & Grassland Coun. *Res:* Breeding and evaluation of forage crops, including orchard grass, reed canary grass, smooth bromegrass, tall fescue, alfalfa and birdsfoot trefoil. *Mailing Add:* Dept of Agron Iowa State Univ Ames IA 50011

CARLSON, JAMES ANDREW, b Lewiston, Idaho, Nov 14, 46; m 73. PURE MATHEMATICS. *Educ:* Univ Idaho, BS, 67; Princeton Univ, PhD(math), 71. *Prof Exp:* Asst prof math, Stanford Univ, 71-73 & Brandeis Univ, 73-75; asst prof, 75-79, ASSOC PROF MATH, UNIV UTAH, 79- *Concurrent Pos:* Sloan fel, 78-79. *Res:* Algerbraic geometry particularly Hodge theory and moduli problems. *Mailing Add:* Dept Math Univ Utah Salt Lake City UT 84112

CARLSON, JAMES C, b Mankato, Minn, Jan 4, 28; div; c 3. RADIOLOGICAL PHYSICS, COMPUTER SYSTEMS DESIGN. *Educ:* Univ Minn, AB, 51, MS, 56. *Prof Exp:* Cancer res scientist, Roswell Park Mem Inst, 54-57; RADIOL PHYSICIST, HACKLEY HOSP, MUSKEGON, MICH, 57- *Concurrent Pos:* Consult, Vet Admin Hosp, Wood, Wis, 60- *Mem:* Radiol Soc NAm; Soc Nuclear Med; Health Physics Soc; Am Asn Physicists Med; Soc Comput Med. *Res:* computer programming for nuclear medicine; hospital computer systems; radiology data management. *Mailing Add:* Nuclear Med Dept Hackley Hosp Muskegon MI 49443

CARLSON, JAMES GORDON, b Port Allegany, Pa, Jan 24, 08; m 36; c 3. CYTOLOGY, RADIOBIOLOGY. *Educ:* Univ Pa, AB, 30, PhD(cytol), 35. *Prof Exp:* Demonstr biol, Bryn Mawr Col, 30-31, instr, 31-35; instr zool, Univ Ala, 35-39, from asst prof to assoc prof, 39-46; sr biologist, NIH, USPHS, Md, 46-47; prof zool, Univ Tenn, Knoxville, 47-62, head dept zool & entom, 47-67, dir, Inst Radiation Biol, 55-75, Alumni Distinguished Serv Prof, 62-78, EMER PROF, UNIV TENN, KNOXVILLE, 78- *Concurrent Pos:* Rockefeller fel, Carnegie Inst, Cold Spring Harbor Biol Lab & Univ Mo, 40-41; USPHS spec fel, Univ Heidelberg, 64-65; spec consult, USPHS, 43-46, 47-48; consult, Oak Ridge Nat Lab, Tenn, 47-78; mem comt biol & agr fels, Nat Res Coun, 49-52. *Mem:* AAAS (vpres, 55); Radiation Res Soc; Am Soc Cell Biol; Am Inst Biol Sci. *Res:* Effects of fixatives on staining reactions; orthopteran cytology; effects of ultraviolet and ionizing radiations on chromosomes and cell division; effect of chemical agents on chromosomes and cell division. *Mailing Add:* Dept of Zool Univ of Tenn Knoxville TN 37916

CARLSON, JAMES H, b Cleveland, Ohio, June 10, 35; m 62; c 2. GENETICS. *Educ:* Fenn Col, BS, 58; Ohio State Univ, MS, 60, PhD(genetics), 63. *Prof Exp:* Asst instr zool, Ohio State Univ, 61-63; asst prof biol, Fairleigh Dickinson Univ, 63-66; assoc prof, 66-70, chmn dept, 70-74, PROF BIOL, RIDER COL, 70- *Mem:* AAAS; Genetics Soc Am; Am Genetic Asn. *Res:* Penetrance, expressivity and chromosomal control of a wing venation mutant system in Drosophila melanogaster. *Mailing Add:* Dept of Biol Rider Col Trenton NJ 08602

CARLSON, JAMES ROY, b Windsor, Colo, Mar 9, 39; m 61; c 2. BIOCHEMISTRY. *Educ:* Colo State Univ, BS, 61; Univ Wis-Madison, MS, 64, PhD(biochem), 66. *Prof Exp:* Asst prof, 66-71, assoc prof, 71-76, PROF ANIMAL SCI, WASH STATE UNIV, 76- CHMN GRAD PROG NUTRIT, 73- *Mem:* Am Inst Nutrit; Am Soc Animal Sci; Am Thoracic Soc; Soc Exp Biol Med. *Res:* Nutritional biochemistry, involving amino acid and protein metabolism and enzyme adaptation in response to nutritional factors. *Mailing Add:* Dept of Animal Sci Wash State Univ Pullman WA 99164

CARLSON, JANET LYNN, b Minneapolis, Minn, Aug 31, 52; m 76. SYNTHETIC ORGANIC CHEMISTRY. *Educ:* Hamline Univ, St Paul, Minn, BA, 74; Stanford Univ, PhD(org chem), 78. *Prof Exp:* ASST PROF ORG CHEM, MACALESTER COL, ST PAUL, MINN, 78- *Mem:* Am Chem Soc. *Res:* Synthesis of natural products (including pheromones) and of sweeteners. *Mailing Add:* Chem Dept Macalester Col St Paul MN 55105

CARLSON, JOHN BERNARD, b Virginia, Minn, Jan 23, 26; m 49. PLANT ANATOMY. *Educ:* St Olaf Col, BA, 50; Iowa State Col, PhD(plant anat), 53. *Prof Exp:* Instr bot, Iowa State Col, 54; from asst prof to assoc prof, 54-67, PROF BOT, UNIV MINN, DULUTH, 67- *Mem:* Bot Soc Am. *Res:* Developmental morphology of soybeans and other plants; floral anatomy of wild rice. *Mailing Add:* Dept of Biol Univ of Minn Duluth MN 55812

CARLSON, JOHN GREGORY, b Minneapolis, Minn, Mar 25, 41; c 2. HUMAN LEARNING & EMOTION, BEHAVIORAL MEDICINE. *Educ:* Univ Minn, BA, 63, PhD(psychol), 67. *Prof Exp:* From asst prof to assoc prof, PROF PSYCHOL, UNIV HAWAII, 67- *Concurrent Pos:* Vis prof, Univ Minn, 75, Univ NMex, 76 & Univ Colo, 80; Nat Inst Mental Health fel, Inst Behav Sci, 75-76. *Mem:* Am Psychol Asn; Biofeedback Soc Am. *Res:* Behavioral medicine; biofeedback applications; emotion and human learning. *Mailing Add:* Dept Psychol Univ Hawaii Honolulu HI 96822

CARLSON, JOHN W, b Topeka, Kans, Nov 10, 40; m 61; c 2. MATHEMATICS. *Educ:* Kans State Univ, BS, 63, MS, 64; Univ Mo-Rolla, PhD(math), 70. *Prof Exp:* Instr math, Washburn Univ, 64-67; instr, Univ Mo-Rolla, 67-70; asst prof, 70-74, ASSOC PROF, EMPORIA STATE UNIV, 74- *Mem:* Am Math Soc; Math Asn Am. *Res:* Topology; quasi-uniform spaces. *Mailing Add:* Dept of Math Emporia State Univ Emporia KS 66802

CARLSON, JON FREDERICK, b Newport News, Va, July 3, 40; m 66; c 2. ALGEBRA. *Educ:* Old Dom Col, BA, 62; Univ Va, MA, 65, PhD(math), 67. *Prof Exp:* Instr math, Univ Va, 67-68; asst prof, 68-76, ASSOC PROF MATH, UNIV GA, 76- *Mem:* AAAS; Am Math Soc; Math Asn Am. *Res:* Representations of group algebra of finite groups. *Mailing Add:* Dept of Math Univ of Ga Athens GA 30602

CARLSON, KEITH DOUGLAS, b Los Angeles, Calif, Feb 28, 33. PHYSICAL CHEMISTRY. *Educ:* Univ Redlands, BS, 54; Univ Kans, PhD(chem), 60. *Prof Exp:* Fulbright scholar theoret chem, Oxford Univ, 60-62, hon Am Ramsey fel, 61-62; from asst prof to prof chem, Case Western Reserve Univ, 62-79; SR CHEMIST, ARGONNE NAT LAB, 79- *Concurrent Pos:* Consult, Gen Elec Co, 74-79; mem, High Temperature Sci & Technol Comt, Nat Res Coun, 71-73; chmn, Gordon Res Conf High Temperature Chem, 72. *Mem:* Am Phys Soc; Am Chem Soc; Sigma Xi. *Res:* High temperature chemistry; thermodynamics and materials properties; solid state chemistry. *Mailing Add:* Chem Div Argonne Nat Lab Argonne IL 60439

CARLSON, KEITH J, b White Bear Lake, Minn, June 3, 38; m 65. GEOLOGY. *Educ:* Gustavus Adolphus Col, BS, 60; Iowa State Univ, MS, 62; Univ Chicago, PhD(paleozool), 66. *Prof Exp:* Asst prof, 67-74, ASSOC PROF GEOL, GUSTAVUS ADOLPHUS COL, 74- *Mem:* Soc Vert Paleont; Soc Study Evolution. *Res:* Vertebrate paleontology. *Mailing Add:* Dept of Geol Gustavus Adolphus Col St Peter MN 56082

CARLSON, KENNETH THEODORE, b Douglas, NDak, June 18, 21; m 49; c 3. CHEMISTRY. *Educ:* Minot State Col, BS, 47; Colo State Col, MA, 53. *Prof Exp:* Instr high schs, NDak, 47-48, 49-51, prin, 51-54; asst prof physics & chem, 54-55, from asst prof to assoc prof chem, 55-69, PROF SCI, MAYVILLE STATE COL, 69-, CHMN DEPT SCI, 75- *Mem:* Am Chem Soc; Nat Sci Teachers Asn. *Res:* History of chemistry, especially as it pertains to chemical education in the United States. *Mailing Add:* Dept of Sci Mayville State Col Mayville ND 58257

CARLSON, KERMIT HOWARD, b Jamestown, NY, Dec 31, 13; m 46; c 2. MATHEMATICS. *Educ:* Upsala Col, BA, 39; Univ Iowa, MS, 41; Univ Wis, PhD, 54. *Prof Exp:* Instr math, Mich State Univ, 51-54; PROF MATH, VALPARAISO UNIV, 54- *Mem:* Am Math Soc; Math Asn Am. *Res:* Area theory; harmonic functions; calculus of variations; topology. *Mailing Add:* Dept of Math Valparaiso Univ Valparaiso IN 46383

CARLSON, KRISTIN ROWE, b Minneapolis, Minn, July 31, 40. PSYCHOPHARMACOLOGY. *Educ:* Univ Mich, BA, 62; McGill Univ, MA, 63, PhD(psychol), 66. *Prof Exp:* NIMH fel, Univ Waterloo, 66-68; asst prof pharmacol & psychol, 68-75; res asst prof pharmacol, Sch Med, Univ Pittsburgh, 75-77; ASSOC PROF PHARMACOL, SCH MED, UNIV MASS, 77- *Concurrent Pos:* Mem, Pharmacol Sci Rev Comt, Nat Inst Gen Med Sci, 80-84. *Mem:* Sigma Xi; Am Soc Pharmacol & Exp Therapeut; Soc Neurosci. *Res:* Effects of psychoactive drugs on behavior and neurochemistry. *Mailing Add:* Dept of Pharmacol Sch of Med Univ of Mass 55 Lake Ave N Worcester MA 01605

CARLSON, LAWRENCE EVAN, b Milwaukee, Wis, Dec 22, 44; c 1. MECHANICAL ENGINEERING, BIOENGINEERING. *Educ:* Univ Wis, BS, 67; Univ Calif, Berkeley, MS, 68, DEng, 71. *Prof Exp:* Asst prof mat eng, Univ Ill, Chicago Circle, 71-74; asst prof eng design, 74-78, ASSOC PROF MECH ENG, UNIV COLO, BOULDER, 78- *Concurrent Pos:* Consult, Prosthetics Res Lab, Northwestern Univ, 71-75; NSF travel grants, Yugoslavia, 72, 75 & res initiation grant, 73-74; NIH res career develop award, 76-81; prin investr, Vet Admin grants, 76- *Honors & Awards:* Ralph R Teetor Award, Soc Automotive Engrs, 76. *Mem:* Am Soc Mech Engrs; Sigma Xi. *Res:* Rehabilitation engineering; upper-limb prosthetics; orthotics. *Mailing Add:* Dept Mech Eng Campus Box 427 Univ Colo Boulder CO 80309

CARLSON, LESTER WILLIAM, b Warren, Wis, Sept 12, 33; m 54; c 5. PLANT PATHOLOGY, SILVICULTURE. *Educ:* Carroll Col, Wis, BS, 55; Okla State Univ, MS, 59; Univ Wis, PhD(plant path), 63. *Prof Exp:* Asst prof plant path, SDak State Univ, 63-66; forest pathologist, 66-74, proj leader, 74-77, prog specialist, Tree Biol, 77-80, FORESTRY ADV, CAN FORESTRY SERV, 80- *Mem:* Can Phytopath Soc; Can Inst Forestry. *Res:* Plant disease control; nursery cultural practices; tree seedling physiology; forest regeneration and reclamation; forest management and conservation; general environmental sciences. *Mailing Add:* Can Forestry Serv Place Vincent Massey Ottawa ON K1A 1G5 Can

CARLSON, LEWIS JOHN, b Valley City, NDak, Oct 4, 24; m 50; c 2. PAPER CHEMISTRY. *Educ:* Jamestown Col, BS, 47; Univ Iowa, MS, 50. *Prof Exp:* Teacher high sch, NDak, 47-48; res chemist, Rayonier, Inc, 50-60; sr chemist, Minn Mining & Mfg Co, 60-62; res chemist, 62-70, supvr coating appln res, 70-76, mgr coating & process develop, 76-80, MGR, PAPER PROD DEVELOP, CROWN ZELLERBACH CORP, 80- *Tech Asn Pulp & Paper Indust.* *Res:* Wood chemistry; carbohydrate; organic synthesis; polymers; paper coatings and treatments. *Mailing Add:* 232 NW 19th Camas WA 98607

CARLSON, MARVIN PAUL, b Creston, Iowa, Sept 27, 35; div; c 3. GEOLOGY. *Educ:* Univ Nebr, BS, 57, MS, 63, PhD(geol), 69. *Prof Exp:* Stratigrapher, 58-63, PRIN GEOLOGIST, CONSERV & SURV DIV, UNIV NEBR, 63-, ASST DIR, 70-, PROF, 76- *Concurrent Pos:* Grad Fac fel, Univ Nebr & assoc state geologist, 70-; Res chmn, Interstate Oil Compact Comn, 71; adv comt mem, Nat Gas Surv, Fed Power Comn, 75. *Mem:* Fel Geol Soc Am; AAAS; Sigma Xi. *Res:* Remote sensing of natural resources; land use planning; long range effect of man on natural resource systems. *Mailing Add:* 113 NH Univ of Nebr Lincoln NE 68588

CARLSON, MERLE WINSLOW, b Minneapolis, Minn, June 5, 42. ORGANIC CHEMISTRY, ENVIRONMENTAL CHEMISTRY. *Educ:* Univ Minn, BA, 64; Northwestern Univ, PhD(chem), 69. *Prof Exp:* Res assoc org chem, Univ Wis, 69-70; instr, Northwestern Univ, 70-71; asst prof, State Univ NY, Stony Brook, 71-72; asst prof, 72-77, ASSOC PROF ORG CHEM, BUTLER UNIV, 77- *Concurrent Pos:* Chmn phosphate task force, Ind Senate Environ & Ecol Comt, 73-74; co-chmn environ studies prog, Butler Univ, 75-; pres, Environ Monitoring Serv, Inc, 75-; bd mem, founder & consult, Wolf Tech Serv, Inc, 76- *Mem:* Am Chem Soc; Am Asn Arson Investrs; AAAS. *Res:* Synthesis of small-ring organic compounds and cycloaddition reactions; absorption of chlorinated hydrocarbons by plants. *Mailing Add:* Dept of Chem Butler Univ Indianapolis IN 46208

CARLSON, NORMAN ARTHUR, b Geneseo, Ill, Aug 5, 39; m 67; c 1. ORGANIC CHEMISTRY. *Educ:* Augustana Col, Ill, BA, 61; Univ Wis-Madison, MS, 63; Univ Mich, PhD(org chem), 67. *Prof Exp:* CHEMIST, ORG CHEM DEPT, E I DU PONT DE NEMOURS & CO, INC, WILMINGTON, 67- *Mem:* Am Chem Soc. *Mailing Add:* Sharpless Rd Hockessin DE 19707

CARLSON, OSCAR NORMAN, b Mitchell, SDak, Dec 21, 20; m 46; c 3. METALLURGY. *Educ:* Yankton Col, BA, 43; Iowa State Univ, PhD(chem), 50. *Prof Exp:* Prof chem, 50-62, chmn, Dept Metall & chief div, Inst Atomic Res, 62-66, PROF MAT, SCI, & ENG, IOWA STATE UNIV, 62- *Concurrent Pos:* Vis scientist, Max Planck Inst Metallfürschung, Stuttgart, 74-75. *Mem:* Am Chem Soc; Am Soc Metals; Am Inst Mining, Metall & Petrol Engrs; AAAS. *Res:* Phase equilibria; preparation of high purity metals; metallurgy of uranium, thorium, vanadium and yttrium; mass transport of solutes in metals at high temperatures. *Mailing Add:* Dept of Metall Iowa State Univ Ames IA 50011

CARLSON, OSCAR VERDELL, entomology, invertebrate zoology, see previous edition

CARLSON, PAUL ROLAND, b St Paul, Minn, Nov 23, 33; m 57; c 2. MARINE GEOLOGY. *Educ:* Gustavus Adolphus Col, BA, 55; Iowa State Univ, MS, 57; Ore State Univ, PhD(oceanog), 67. *Prof Exp:* Res asst eng geol, Soil Eng Lab, Iowa State Univ, 55-57; geologist, US Army Corps Engrs, 57-58; instr geol, Gustavus Adolphus Col, 58-59; teacher gen sci, Cleveland Consol Schs, 59-61; instr geol, Pac Lutheran Univ, 61-63; res assoc geol oceanog, Ore State Univ, 63-67; GEOLOGIST, US GEOL SURV, 67- *Mem:* Geol Soc Am; Am Geophys Union; Soc Econ Paleont & Mineral. *Res:* Sedimentology; submarine canyons; processes of sedimentation; estuaries, especially San Francisco Bay; acoustical subbottom profiling; oceanographic factors affecting estuaries. *Mailing Add:* US Geol Surv 345 Middlefield Rd Menlo Park CA 94025

CARLSON, PHILIP R, b Evanston, Ill, June 2, 31; m 54; c 3. MATHEMATICS. *Educ:* Bethel Col (Minn), BS, 53; Univ Minn, BS, 57, MS, 65, PhD, 71. *Prof Exp:* Teacher high sch, Minn, 57-59; instr math, 60-67, from asst prof to assoc prof, 67-71, PROF MATH, BETHEL COL (MINN), 71- *Concurrent Pos:* Programmed Course in Algebra for High Sch Teachers, 60-66; dir, Job Corps Math Proj Minn Nat Lab, 67-68; vis scholar math, Cambridge Univ (Eng), 73-74. *Mem:* Math Asn Am; Nat Coun Teachers of Math. *Res:* Mathematics, algebraic theory. *Mailing Add:* Dept of Math Bethel Col St Paul MN 55101

CARLSON, RICHARD EUGENE, b Wausa, Nebr, Oct 19, 40; m 60; c 2. AGRONOMY. *Educ:* Univ Nebr, BS, 67; Iowa State Univ, MS, 69, PhD(agr climat), 71. *Prof Exp:* Researcher & teaching asst, Iowa State Univ, 67-68; NDEA fel, 68-71; photointerpreter, Purdue Univ, 71; from asst prof to assoc prof, 71-79, PROF AGR CLIMAT, IOWA STATE UNIV, 79- *Mem:* Am Soc Agron; Crop Sci Soc Am; Soil Sci Soc Am; Am Meteorol Soc. *Res:* Microclimate studies on corn and soybeans with emphasis on moisture stress and photosynthesis. *Mailing Add:* Dept of Agron Iowa State Univ Ames IA 50010

CARLSON, RICHARD FREDERICK, b St Paul, Minn, June 19, 36; m 57; c 3. PHYSICS. *Educ:* Univ Redlands, BS, 57; Univ Minn, MS, 62, PhD, 64. *Prof Exp:* Asst res physicist, Univ Calif, Los Angeles, 64, asst prof physics, 64-67; asst prof, 67-71, coordr dept, 70-72, assoc prof, 71-77, PROF PHYSICS, UNIV REDLANDS, 77-, CHMN PHYSICS & CHMN SCI FAC, 81- *Mem:* Am Phys Soc; Am Sci Affil. *Res:* Experimental nuclear physics; nuclear structure; few nucleon problem. *Mailing Add:* Dept Physics Univ Redlands Redlands CA 92373

CARLSON, RICHARD OSCAR, b Flushing, NY, June 2, 26; m 52; c 3. SEMICONDUCTOR DEVICES, SENSORS. *Educ:* Columbia Univ, AB, 47, AM, 49, PhD(physics), 52. *Prof Exp:* Asst, Columbia Univ, 47-50, physicist, Hudson Labs, 52-54; PHYSICIST, GEN ELEC CORP RES & DEVELOP CTR, 54- *Mem:* Fel Am Phys Soc; Electrochem Soc; sr mem Inst Elec & Electronics Eng. *Res:* Processing of silicon devices and integrated circuits; experimental transport measurements on pure and doped semiconductor crystals; temperature and humidity sensors; silicon device packaging; electron and gamma irradiation. *Mailing Add:* Gen Elec Corp R&D Ctr PO Box 43 Schenectady NY 12305

CARLSON, RICHARD PATRICK, b Great Bend, Kans, June 8, 39; m 64; c 2. IMMUNOINFLAMMATORY PHARMACOLOGY. *Educ:* Emporia State Univ, Kans, BA, 62; Hahnemann Med Col, Pa, MS, 74; Thomas Jefferson Univ, PhD, 76. *Prof Exp:* Sci instr biol, physics, chem & geol, Larned High Sch, Kans, 62-66; res biologist, Merck Sharp & Dohme Res Lab, 66-76; sr res pharmacologist, USV Pharm Corp, 76-78; SUPVR IMMUNOINFLAMMATORY PHARM, WYETH LABS, RADNOR, PA, 78- *Mem:* Sigma Xi; Res Soc. *Res:* Testing of experimental drugs (potential novel antiarthritic and antiallergic) using in vitro and in vivo animal and cellular models which detect antiinflammatory and immunologic activities, for example, effects on cell and humoral immunity and immediate hypersensitivity. *Mailing Add:* 112 Rosewood Dr Lansdale PA 19446

CARLSON, RICHARD RAYMOND, b Chicago, Ill, Sept 15, 23; m 51; c 3. NUCLEAR PHYSICS. *Educ:* Univ Chicago, PhD(physics), 51. *Prof Exp:* Res assoc physics, Univ Chicago, 51; from asst prof to assoc prof, 51-63, PROF PHYSICS, UNIV IOWA, 63- *Concurrent Pos:* Guggenheim fel, Oxford Univ, 59; mem staff, Los Alamos Sci Lab, Univ Calif, 56; physicist, Oak Ridge Nat Lab, 52. *Mem:* Am Phys Soc. *Mailing Add:* Dept Physics Univ Iowa Iowa City IA 52241

CARLSON, RICHARD WALTER, b Los Angeles, Calif, May 22, 54; m 76. ISOTOPE GEOCHEMISTRY, GEOCHRONOLOGY. *Educ:* Univ Calif, San Diego, BA, 76; Scripps Inst Oceanog, PhD(earth sci), 80. *Prof Exp:* Res asst, Scripps Inst Oceanog, 76-80; res fel, 80-81, MEM STAFF, DEPT TERRESTRIAL MAGNETISM, CARNEGIE INST, 81- *Mem:* Am Geophys Soc. *Res:* Isotope geochemistry; structure of chemical heterogeneity in the earth's mantle; chronology of planetary differentiation; formation of planetary crusts; techniques for high precision isotopic analysis. *Mailing Add:* Dept Terrestrial Magnetism 5241 Broad Branch Rd NW Washington DC 20015

CARLSON, ROBERT BRUCE, b Virginia, Minn, Sept 15, 38; m 60. ENTOMOLOGY. *Educ:* Univ Minn, Duluth, BS, 60; Mich State Univ, MS, 62, PhD(entom), 65. *Prof Exp:* Assoc insect ecologist, NCent Forest Exp Sta, US Forest Serv, 65-67; asst prof entom, 68-71, assoc prof, 71-80, PROF ENTOM, NDAK STATE UNIV, 80- *Mem:* AAAS; Ecol Soc Am; Entom Soc Am; Entom Soc Can. *Res:* Ecology. *Mailing Add:* Dept of Entom NDak State Univ Fargo ND 58102

CARLSON, ROBERT FRITZ, b Sweden, June 27, 09; nat US; m 49; c 3. HORTICULTURE. *Educ:* Univ Minn, BS, 44; Mich State Univ, MS, 49, PhD, 52. *Prof Exp:* Res assoc pomol, NY Exp Sta, Cornell Univ, Geneva, NY, 44-46; from asst prof to assoc prof, 46-66, PROF HORT, MICH STATE UNIV, 66- *Concurrent Pos:* Vis prof, Univ Uppsala, Lund & Agr Exp Stas, Sweden, 53; agr res adv to Univ Ryukyus, Okinawa, Japan, 56-58; speaker, Apricot Symp, Yugoslavia, 68 & Int Hort Congs, Israel, 70 & Poland, 74; consult, US AID to Uruguay, 75. *Honors & Awards:* Stark Award, Am Soc Hort Sci, 66; Paul Shepard Award, Am Pomol Soc, 73; Gold Medal, Mass Hort Soc & Wilder Award, Am Pomol Soc, 74; Norman Jay Colman Award, Am Asn Nurserymen, 78. *Mem:* Fel Am Soc Hort Sci; Am Pomol Soc; Int Hort Soc. *Res:* Rootstock physiology; dormancy problems in tree fruits; rootstocks for various tree fruits. *Mailing Add:* Dept of Hort Mich State Univ East Lansing MI 48824

CARLSON, ROBERT G(USTAV), b Brooklyn, NY, June 6, 28; m; c 3. METALLURGY, CERAMIC ENGINEERING. *Educ:* Polytech Inst Brooklyn, BME, 51; Rensselaer Polytech Inst, MME, 55; Univ Cincinnati, PhD(metall), 62. *Prof Exp:* Mem staff, CheMet Prog, 51-52, metall engr, Aeronaut & Ord Div, 52-53, asst refractory metals, Res Lab, 53-55, assoc, Lamp Metals & Components Dept, 55-58, mgr advan mat, Advan Engine & Technol Dept, 58-66, mgr composite mat, 66-70, sr composites engr, Mat & Process Technol Lab, 70-77, mgr, Boron Aluminum Fabrication, 77-81, MGR, TURBINE SHROUDS, AIRCRAFT MACH GROUP, MAT & PROCESS TECHNOL LAB, GEN ELEC CO, 81- *Honors & Awards:* Turner Award, 60. *Mem:* Am Inst Mining, Metall & Petrol Engrs; Am Soc Metals; Electrochem Soc. *Res:* Development of composite structural materials; refractory alloys; alkali metal corrosion behavior. *Mailing Add:* Aircraft Engine Group Gen Elec Co M85 Cincinnati OH 45215

CARLSON, ROBERT GEORGE, b Grand Rapids, Mich, Apr 1, 22; m 42; c 2. VETERINARY PATHOLOGY. *Educ:* Mich State Univ, DVM, 52; Purdue Univ, MS, 54, PhD(vet path), 56; Am Col Lab Animal Med, dipl; Am Col Vet Path, dipl. *Prof Exp:* Instr vet sci, Purdue Univ, 52-56, asst prof, 56; res assoc, Upjohn Co, 56-61, sect head path, 61-74, int adv, Japan Upjohn, Ltd, 74-78, dir res, Japan Upjohn Ltd & mgr path & toxicol res unit, 78-80, DIR PRODUCT DEVELOP JAPAN UPJOHN LTD & GROUP MGR, PROD RES & DEVELOP, UPJOHN CO, 80- *Mem:* Am Vet Med Asn; Am Col Vet Path; Am Col Lab Animal Med; Soc Toxicol; Europ Soc Toxicol. *Res:* Veterinary pathology; toxicology and pathology research. *Mailing Add:* Kalamazoo MI

CARLSON, ROBERT GIDEON, b Chicago, Ill, Feb 4, 38; m 62; c 2. ORGANIC CHEMISTRY. *Educ:* Univ Ill, BS, 59; Mass Inst Technol, PhD(org chem), 63. *Prof Exp:* From asst prof to assoc prof chem, 63-72, PROF CHEM, UNIV KANS, 72- *Concurrent Pos:* Alfred P Sloan Found fels fel, 70-72. *Mem:* Am Chem Soc; The Chem Soc. *Res:* Synthetic organic chemistry; structure and synthesis of natural products; highly strained ring systems; photochemical reactions of organic compounds. *Mailing Add:* Dept of Chem Univ of Kans Lawrence KS 66044

CARLSON, ROBERT KENNETH, b Chicago, Ill, July 7, 28; m 54; c 2. INORGANIC CHEMISTRY. *Educ:* Northwestern Univ, PhB, 54. *Prof Exp:* Asst chemist, Great Lakes Carbon Corp, 49-50, chemist, 53-57; res chemist, Borg-Warner Corp, 57-59; mat engr, Chance Vought Corp, 59-60, res scientist, 60-62; sr scientist, Res Ctr, Ling-Temco-Vought Corp, 62-63, head mat sci, 63-64, prog mgr, Carbon & Graphite Div, 64-67; vpres & gen mgr, 67-77, PRES & CHIEF EXEC OFFICER, POCO GRAPHITE INC, UNION OIL CO, CALIF, 77- *Concurrent Pos:* Prin investr, US Air Force Indust res grant, 61-62. *Mem:* Sigma Xi; Am Chem Soc; fel Am Inst Chemists; Am Carbon Soc (chmn, 79-). *Res:* Synthesis of new carbon and graphite products; high temperature refractory oxides for rocket and missile application; synthesis of salts of organo phosphoric acids. *Mailing Add:* Poco Graphite Union Oil Co Calif PO Box 2121 Decatur TX 76234

CARLSON, ROBERT L, b Gary, Ind, May 22, 24; m 50; c 5. STRUCTURAL MECHANICS. *Educ:* Purdue Univ, BS, 48, MS, 50; Ohio State Univ, PhD(eng), 62. *Prof Exp:* Res engr, Battelle Mem Inst, 50-60, res assoc, 60-62; res engr, US Steel Res Lab, 62-63; res assoc, Dept Aeronaut, Stanford Univ, 63-65, assoc prof, 65-66; PROF AEROSPACE ENG, GA INST TECHNOL, 66- *Concurrent Pos:* Lectr, Int Union Theoret & Appl Mech Colloquium, 60; consult, EIMAC Div, Varian Assocs, 65-66 & US Air Force Flight Dynamics Lab, 68. *Honors & Awards:* Charles Dudley Medal, Am Soc Testing & Mat, 59. *Mem:* Am Inst Aeronaut & Astronaut Engrs; Soc Exp Stress Anal. *Res:* Phase of structural mechanics which deals with the conditions of external loading and/or temperature environment which lead to failure due to instability and fracture. *Mailing Add:* 4738 Cambridge Dr Dunwoody GA 30338

CARLSON, ROBERT LEONARD, b Duluth, Minn, Feb 26, 32; m 58; c 2. PHOTOGRAPHIC CHEMISTRY. *Educ:* Univ Minn, BA, 58; Univ Ill, PhD(inorg chem), 62. *Prof Exp:* PROD DEVELOP MGR, 3M CO, 62- *Res:* Metal ion complexes and molecular complexes in non-aqueous solvents; electrochemistry; photoconductors; photographic chemistry; color photographic imaging systems. *Mailing Add:* 2243 Berland Pl St Paul MN 55119

CARLSON, ROBERT M, b Cokato, Minn, Oct 30, 40; m 62; c 2. ORGANIC CHEMISTRY. *Educ:* Univ Minn, BChem, 62; Princeton Univ, PhD(chem), 66. *Prof Exp:* Fel, Harvard Univ, 65-66; from asst prof to assoc prof org chem, 66-74, PROF CHEM, UNIV MINN, DULUTH, 74- *Mem:* Sigma Xi; Am Chem Soc. *Res:* Total synthesis of natural products; new synthetic methods; environmental organic chemistry. *Mailing Add:* Dept of Chem Univ of Minn Duluth MN 55812

CARLSON, ROBERT MARVIN, b Denver, Colo, Mar 18, 32; m 62; c 1. SOIL CHEMISTRY, PLANT NUTRITION. *Educ:* Colo State Univ, BS, 54; Univ Calif, Berkeley, PhD(soil sci), 62. *Prof Exp:* Soil scientist, USDA, 52-54; sr lab technician, Univ Calif, Berkeley, 55-62; prog specialist, Ford Found, Arg, 62-65; asst pomologist, 65-71, ASSOC POMOLOGIST, UNIV CALIF, DAVIS, 71- *Concurrent Pos:* Vis res prof, Nat Univ South, Arg, 62-65. *Mem:* Am Soc Agron; Soil Sci Soc Am; Am Chem Soc. *Res:* Analytical chemistry. *Mailing Add:* Dept of Pomol Univ of Calif Davis CA 95616

CARLSON, ROBERT WARNER, b Waseca, Minn, Oct 26, 41; m 63; c 2. AERONOMY, ATOMIC PHYSICS. *Educ:* Calif State Polytech Col, San Luis Obispo, BS, 63; Univ Southern Calif, PhD(physics), 70. *Prof Exp:* Res scientist, Jet Propulsion Lab, Calif Inst Technol, 63-66; res engr, 66-70, RES PHYSICIST, UNIV SOUTHERN CALIF, 70- *Concurrent Pos:* Consult, Jet Propulsion Lab, Calif Inst Technol, Gen Dynamics Corp & var indust orgn, 67- *Mem:* AAAS; Optical Soc Am; Am Geophys Union. *Res:* Atomic and molecular physics and their application to atmospheric and astrophysical problems. *Mailing Add:* Dept of Physics Univ of Southern Calif Los Angeles CA 90007

CARLSON, ROGER, b St Joseph, Mo, Aug 15, 37; m 60; c 1. MATHEMATICAL STATISTICS. *Educ:* Univ Kansas City, BS, 59, MA, 60; Harvard Univ, PhD(statist), 64. *Prof Exp:* Asst prof, 63-69, ASSOC PROF MATH, UNIV MO-KANSAS CITY, 69- *Mem:* Am Statist Asn. *Res:* Foundations of statistical inference; applications of mathematics to social sciences. *Mailing Add:* Dept of Math Univ of Mo Kansas City MO 64110

CARLSON, ROGER HAROLD, b Winnebago, Ill, May 31, 41; m 66; c 4. MICROBIOLOGY, ENVIRONMENTAL HEALTH. *Educ:* Univ Ill, BS, 64; Univ Mich, MS, 66, PhD(environ health sci), 76. *Prof Exp:* Res scientist, Conductron Corp, McDonnell-Douglas, 66-67; res asst, Univ Mich, 71-73; DIR PUB HEALTH LABS, KANS DEPT HEALTH & ENVIRON, 76- *Concurrent Pos:* Consult, Environ Control Technol Corp, 73-74 & Coca-Cola Export Co, Atlanta, Ga, 74-75; adj asst prof, Dept Microbiol, Kans Univ, 77- *Mem:* Am Soc Microbiol; Am Pub Health Asn; Water Pollution Control Fedn. *Res:* Active carbon absorption of viruses from waters and waste waters; microwave and chemical disinfection processes; biological indicators of water pollution, environmental cancers research. *Mailing Add:* Dept of Health & Environ 740 Forbes Bldg Topeka KS 66620

CARLSON, RONALD H, industrial chemistry, see previous edition

CARLSON, ROY DOUGLAS, b San Bernardino, Calif, Dec 29, 44; m 66; c 3. BIOPHYSICS. *Educ:* Pomona Col, BA, 66; Univ Wis-Madison, MA, 68, PhD(biophys), 73. *Prof Exp:* NIH fel, Univ Tenn-Oak Ridge Grad Sch Biomed Sci & Biol Div, Oak Ridge Nat Lab, 73-76, res assoc, 76-77; sr res assoc, 77-78, asst biophysicist, 78-80, ASSOC BIOPHYSICIST, BROOKHAVEN NAT LAB, 80- *Mem:* Am Crystallog Asn; Biophys Soc. Biophys Soc. *Res:* Res: Neutron scattering studies and physical biochemistry of chromatin and of histone complexes; macromolecular structure and assembly. *Mailing Add:* Biol Dept Brookhaven Nat Lab Upton NY 11973

CARLSON, ROY W(ASHINGTON), b Bigstone, Minn, Sept 23, 00; m 27; c 2. CIVIL ENGINEERING. *Educ:* Univ Redlands, AB, 22; Univ Calif, MS, 33; Mass Inst Tech, ScD(mat), 39. *Hon Degrees:* ScD, Univ Redlands, 51. *Prof Exp:* Assoc prof physics, Univ Redlands, 24-25; res engr, Southern Calif Edison Co, 25-27; testing engr, Los Angeles County, 27-31; res engr, Univ Calif, 31-34, assoc prof, 35-36; asst prof civil eng, Mass Inst Tech, 34-35, assoc prof, 36-43, consult engr, 36-65; RES ASSOC, UNIV CALIF, BERKELEY, 65- *Concurrent Pos:* Engr, Radiation Lab, Univ Calif, 43-44 & Los Alamos Sci Lab, Los Alamos, NMex, 44-45. *Honors & Awards:* Dudley Medal, Am Soc Testing & Mat; Wason Medal & Turner Medal, Am Concrete Inst, 67. *Mem:* Fel Am Soc Civil Engrs; hon mem Am Concrete Inst; hon mem Brazil Concrete Inst; Nat Acad Eng. *Res:* Inventor of electrical instruments for measuring stress, strain, temperature and pressure. *Mailing Add:* 55 Maryland Ave Berkeley CA 94707

CARLSON, STANLEY DAVID, b St Paul, Minn, Sept 4, 34; m 58, 69; c 5. ENTOMOLOGY, PHYSIOLOGY. *Educ:* Univ Minn, BS, 56; Univ Nebr, MS, 61; Kans State Univ, PhD(entom, physiol), 65. *Prof Exp:* Res entomologist, Stored Prod Insects Res Br, Agr Res Serv, USDA, Kans, 59-64; asst prof entom, Va Polytech Inst, 65-67; NIH spec fel physiol, Karolinska Inst, Sweden, 67-69 & biol, Yale Univ, 69-70; NSF fel, Univ Ill, Urbana, 70-71; from asst prof to assoc prof, 71-76, PROF ENTOM, UNIV WIS-MADISON, 80- *Concurrent Pos:* Entomologist, Colo Dept Agr, 59; USDA res grant, 65-; consult, Panogen Div, Morton Chem Co, 61-62; mem, Neurosci Training Comt, Univ Wis, 73-; NIH & NSF grants. *Mem:* AAAS; Entom Soc Am; Am Inst Biol Sci; Scand Physiol Soc; Sigma Xi. *Res:* Sensory physiology of insects; physiology of insect vision and visual pigments; neuroanatomy: ultrastructure of compound eye, optic tract, and blood-brain barrier. *Mailing Add:* Dept of Entom Univ of Wis Madison WI 53706

CARLSON, THOMAS ARTHUR, b Waterbury, Conn, Apr 1, 28; m 50. MOLECULAR PHYSICS. *Educ:* Trinity Col, Conn, BS, 50; Johns Hopkins Univ, MA, 51, PhD(chem), 54. *Prof Exp:* SR RES STAFF MEM, OAK RIDGE NAT LAB, 54- *Concurrent Pos:* Guggenheim fel, 67; ed, J Electron Spectroscopy, 72-77. *Mem:* Am Chem Soc; fel Am Phys Soc; AAAS. *Res:* Electron spectroscopy; Auger and electron shake-off phenomena; hot atom chemistry; atomic physics; synchrotron radiation. *Mailing Add:* Physics Div Oak Ridge Nat Lab PO Box X Oak Ridge TN 37830

CARLSON, TOBY NAHUM, b Brooklyn, NY, Nov 4, 36; m 69; c 2. METEOROLOGY. *Educ:* Mass Inst Technol, BS, 58, MS, 60; Univ London, PhD(meteorol), 65. *Prof Exp:* Res meteorologist, Weather Serv, Inc, on contract to Air Force Cambridge Res Lab, 61-62, Nat Hurricane Res Lab, Nat Oceanic & Atmospheric Admin, Environ Res Lab, 65-74; ASSOC PROF METEOROL, PA STATE UNIV, 74- *Honors & Awards:* Distinguished Authorship, Nat Oceanic & Atmospheric Admin, 74. *Mem:* Am Meteorol

Soc. *Res:* Modelling urban heat fluxes, heatbudget surface temperature; investigation of aerosol transport and effects of aerosol layer on solar radiation balance over equatorial Atlantic. *Mailing Add:* Dept of Meteorol Pa State Univ University Park PA 16802

CARLSON, WAYNE R, b Moline, Ill, Dec 31, 40; m. CYTOGENETICS. *Educ:* Rockford Col, BA, 62; Ind Univ, Bloomington, MA, 67, PhD(zool), 68. *Prof Exp:* Assoc prof genetics, 68-77, ASSOC PROF BOT, UNIV IOWA, 77- *Concurrent Pos:* NSF res grant, 75-77. *Res:* Cytogenetics of maize, especially the B chromosome. *Mailing Add:* Dept of Bot Univ of Iowa Iowa City IA 52242

CARLSON, WILLARD EMMETT, b Ft Dodge, Iowa, May 11, 23; m 50; c 4. PAPER CHEMISTRY, PROCESS ENGINEERING. *Educ:* Iowa State Univ, BS, 47; Lawrence Col, MS, 49. *Prof Exp:* Dir res, Whiting-Plover Paper Co, 52-57; from supvr res & develop, Cent Tech Dept to mgr cent res, St Regis Paper Co, 57-64, mgr develop, 64-66, tech dir, Kraft Div, 66-81; PRES & CONSULT PULP & PAPER, WILLARD CARLSON ASSOC PAPER CO, 81- *Mem:* Tech Asn Pulp & Paper Indust. *Res:* Pulp and paper research; coatings; natural and synthetic fibrous web formation; fiber bonding; water removal; elastic and resilient properties of fibrous webs; Kraft odor abatement. *Mailing Add:* St Regis Paper Co 150 E 42nd St New York NY 10017

CARLSON, WILLIAM DWIGHT, b Denver, Colo, Nov 5, 28; m 50; c 2. VETERINARY RADIOLOGY, RADIATION BIOLOGY. *Educ:* Colo State Univ, DVM, 52, MS, 56; Univ Colo, PhD(radiol), 58; Am Bd Vet Radiol, dipl, 62. *Prof Exp:* Vet, 52-53; asst prof dept med, Colo State Univ, 53-55, Am Vet Med Asn fel, 55-57, assoc prof & radiologist, Col Vet Med, 57-62, prof radiol, 64-68, chmn dept radiol & radiation biol, 64-68, dir radiol health animal res lab, Univ-USPHS, 62-68, pres bd trustees, Colo State Univ Res Found, 66-68; PRES, UNIV WYO, 68- *Concurrent Pos:* Civilian adv, US Army Gen Command & Staff Sch, Ft Leavenworth, Kans, 69-72; consult, USPHS, 62-, Vet Admin Med Facil, 68-, Am Inst Biol Sci, 69-70, NASA, 69- & Surg Gen, US Air Force, 70-; mem bd comnr, Nat Comn on Accrediting, 69-72; mem nat adv coun health res facil, NIH, 69-73; secy adv comt coal mine safety res, Dept Interior, 71; mem bd visitors, Air Univ, 73- *Mem:* AAAS; Am Soc Nuclear Med; Am Vet Radiol Soc; Am Vet Med Asn; Radiol Soc NAm. *Res:* Diagnostic, therapeutic, radioactive isotopes; lower animals. *Mailing Add:* Box 3434 Univ Sta Laramie WY 82070

CARLSON, WILLIAM H, horticulture, see previous edition

CARLSON, WILLIAM THEODORE, b Lyons, Nebr, Mar 27, 33; m 60; c 2. INFORMATION SCIENCE. *Educ:* Univ Nebr, BS, 57, MS, 59. *Prof Exp:* Asst & instr agron, Univ WVa, 59-62; asst analyst, 62-63, chief plant sci, 63-66, CHIEF AGR & APPL BIOL SCI, SCI INFO EXCHANGE, SMITHSONIAN INST, 66- *Concurrent Pos:* Adv, Agr Res Inst-Nat Acad Sci, 66- *Mem:* Am Soc Agron; Am Soc Info Sci. *Res:* Forage management; weed control; information storage and retrieval system design; agricultural and plant sciences; environmental biology; water resources; pesticides and agronomy. *Mailing Add:* 1915 Plyers Mill Rd Wheaton MD 20902

CARLSSON, DAVID JAMES, b Hartlepool, Eng, Oct 2, 40; Can citizen; m 65; c 2. FIBER SCIENCE, POLYMER CHEMISTRY. *Educ:* Univ Birmingham, Eng, BSc, 62, PhD(chem), 65. *Prof Exp:* Fel phys chem, 65-67, assoc res officer, 67-77, SR RES OFFICER TEXTILE SCI, NAT RES COUN CAN, 77- *Mem:* Fel Chem Inst Can; Chem Soc. *Res:* Light induced degradation of fiber forming polymers; mechanisms and stabilization; fiber microstructure, characterization and correlation with physical properties. *Mailing Add:* Div of Chem Nat Res Coun of Can Ottawa Can

CARLSSON, ERIK, b Vingaker, Sweden, Mar 31, 24; m 51; c 2. RADIOLOGY. *Educ:* Karolinska Inst, Sweden, MD, 52, PhD, 70. *Prof Exp:* Mem staff, Radiol Dept, Karolinska Sjukhuset, Stockholm, Sweden, 54-57, pediat roentgenol, 55-57 & thorax roentgenol, 60-62; from asst prof to assoc prof radiol, Sch Med, Wash Univ, 58-64; assoc prof radiol, head cardiovasc radiol & staff mem, Cardiovasc Res Inst, Med Ctr, 64-68, PROF RADIOL, UNIV CALIF, SAN FRANCISCO, 68- *Concurrent Pos:* NIH training grant & consult. *Mem:* Asn Univ Radiol; NY Acad Sci; Sigma Xi; AAAS; Am Heart Asn. *Res:* Diagnostic and cardiovascular radiology. *Mailing Add:* Univ of Calif Med Ctr San Francisco CA 94143

CARLSTEAD, EDWARD MEREDITH, b Chillicothe, Mo, Aug 1, 25; m 50; c 3. METEOROLOGY, COMPUTER SCIENCE. *Educ:* Univ Calif, Los Angeles, BS, 46; US Naval Postgrad Sch, MS, 53. *Prof Exp:* Analyst, Joint Weather Bur-Air Force-Navy Anal Ctr, Washington, DC, 49-51; chief analyst, Joint Numerical Weather Prediction Unit, Md, 56-59; res meteorologist, Fleet Numerical Weather Facility, 59-62; officer in chg opers anal, Pac Command Detachment, Naval Command Systs Support Activity, 62-65; chief sci serv div, Pac Regional Hq, Nat Weather Serv, Environ Sci Serv Admin, 65-71, meteorologist in chg, Nat Weather Serv Forecast Off, Nat Oceanic & Atmospheric Admin, Honolulu, 71-78; CHIEF, FORECAST DIV, NAT METEOROL CTR, NAT OCEANIC & ATMOSPHERIC ADMIN, WASHINGTON, 78- *Mem:* Am Meteorol Soc; Sigma Xi. *Res:* Programming of digital computers to analyze and predict wind and temperature fields in the tropics; improvement of forecasting techniques; physical oceanography; operations analysis. *Mailing Add:* Nat Meteorol Ctr Washington DC 20233

CARLSTEN, JOHN LENNART, b Minneapolis, Minn, Feb 4, 47. LASER SPECTROSCOPY, QUANTUM ELECTRONICS. *Educ:* Univ Minn, BS, 69; Harvard Univ, MA, 71, PhD(physics), 74. *Prof Exp:* Res assoc, Joint Inst Lab Astrophysics, 74-76; sr res assoc, 76-79; asst prof physics, Univ Colo, 76-79; staff mem, 79-81, ASSOC GROUP LEADER, LOS ALAMOS NAT LAB, 81- *Mem:* Am Phys Soc. *Res:* Study of spontaneous and stimulated scattering processes, such as stimulated Raman scattering, laser excitation of atomic and molecular systems and excited-state spectroscopy. *Mailing Add:* MS 564 Los Alamos Nat Lab Los Alamos NM 87545

CARLSTONE, DARRY SCOTT, b Vinita, Okla, May 15, 39; m 62; c 2. PARTICLE PHYSICS. *Educ:* Univ Okla, BS, 61; Purdue Univ, MA, 64, PhD(physics), 68. *Prof Exp:* Asst prof, 67-72, assoc prof, 72-76, PROF PHYSICS, CENT STATE UNIV, OKLA, 76-, CHMN DEPT, 78- *Mem:* Am Phys Soc; Am Asn Physics Teachers. *Res:* Theoretical particle physics with special interest in symmetry principles. *Mailing Add:* Dept of Physics Cent State Univ Edmond OK 73034

CARLTON, BRUCE CHARLES, b Burrillville, RI, Aug 3, 35; m 56; c 2. GENETICS. *Educ:* Univ NH, BS, 57; Mich State Univ, MS, 58, PhD(genetics), 60. *Prof Exp:* Asst hort, Mich State Univ, 57-59; USPHS trainee, Stanford Univ, 60-62; from asst prof to assoc prof biol, Yale Univ, 62-71; prof biochem & microbiol, 71-79, PROF MOLECULAR & POP GENETICS, UNIV GA, 80- *Concurrent Pos:* USPHS res grant, 63-1 NSF res grant, 65-; fel, Silliman Col, 69-71. *Mem:* Am Soc Microbiol. *Res:* Mechanisms of genetic control through studies of mutationally-altered proteins and structure and function of circular DNA elements; correlation between specific plasmias and S-endotoxin production in bacillus thuringiensis. *Mailing Add:* 523 Biol Sci Bldg Univ of Ga Athens GA 30602

CARLTON, DONALD MORRILL, b Houston, Tex, July 20, 37; m 61; c 3. ENVIRONMENTAL SCIENCE, ORGANIC CHEMISTRY. *Educ:* Univ St Thomas, Tex, BA, 58; Univ Tex, Austin, PhD(org chem), 62. *Prof Exp:* Staff mem & group leader polymer sci, Sandia Corp, 62-65; asst dir res, Tracor Inc, 65-69; PRES & 'BD CHMN, RADIAN CORP SUBSID HARTFORD STEAM BOILER INSPECTION & INS CO, 69- *Concurrent Pos:* Dir, Nat Coun Prof Serv Firms & Centex Chap, Am Red Cross. *Mem:* Am Chem Soc. *Res:* Energy and environmental science and engineering. *Mailing Add:* Radian Corp PO Box 9948 Austin TX 78766

CARLTON, JAMES THEODORE, b Ft Worth, Tex, Feb 15, 48. MARINE BIOLOGY, INVERTEBRATE ZOOLOGY. *Educ:* Univ Calif, Berkeley, BA, 71; Univ Calif, Davis, PhD(ecol), 79. *Prof Exp:* Sr sci asst invertebrate zool, 71-73, RES ASSOC, CALIF ACAD SCI, 75- *Concurrent Pos:* Lectr geol & paleobiol, Univ Calif, Davis, 75-76; staff res assoc zool, Bodega Marine Lab-Naval Arctic Res Lab, 76; vis asst prof biol, Univ Ore-Ore Inst Marine Biol, 78; scholar, NSF Nat Needs, Woods Hole Oceanog Inst, 78-79, guest investr, 79-80, investr, 80-81. *Mem:* AAAS; Am Malacol Union; Ecol Soc Am; Soc Syst Zool; Am Soc Zool. *Res:* History, biogeography, and ecology of temperate estuarine invertebrates; biogeography of man-dispersed marine and estuarine invertebrates; systematics and biology of marine mollusks; biology of hermit crabs and their symbionts. *Mailing Add:* Dept of Invert Zool Golden Gate Park San Francisco CA 94118

CARLTON, PAUL F(LEMING), b Rolla, Mo, Oct 17, 23; m 42; c 4. CIVIL ENGINEERING. *Educ:* Mo Sch Mines, BS, 47. *Hon Degrees:* CE, Mo Sch Mines, 59. *Prof Exp:* Eng inspector, State Hwy Dept, Mo, 47-48; soils engr, St Louis Dist Off, US Corps Engrs, 48-51; proj engr, Tech Develop Ctr, Civil Aeronautics Admin, 51-53; chief res br, Ohio River Div Labs, US Corp Engrs, 53-63; proj officer, Hq US Army Nat Command, 63-67, chief, Spec Proj Div, US Corps Engrs Strategic Studies Group, 67-68, chief, Environ Sci Br, 68-71, chief, Mil Engr & Topography Res, Off Chief Engrs, 71-74, chief, Res Br, Combat Support Syst, Off Dep Chief Staff for Res & Develop, 74-80; RETIRED. *Mem:* Am Soc Civil Engrs. *Res:* Rigid pavement for roads and airfields; soil stabilization; ground mobility research. *Mailing Add:* 4800 Prestwick Dr Fairfax VA 22030

CARLTON, RICHARD WALTER, b Nov 23, 42; US citizen; m 66; c 2. SEDIMENTARY PETROLOGY. *Educ:* Wash State Univ, BS, 65; Ore State Univ, MS, 68, PhD(geol), 72. *Prof Exp:* GEOLOGIST, OHIO GEOL SURV, 70- *Mem:* Soc Econ Paleontologists & Mineralogists. *Res:* Chlorite-illite ratios used in conjunction with stratigraphic and petrographic studies to reconstruct the paleogeography of Lower Silurian clastic rocks in Ohio; mineralogic and petrographic characterization of Middle and Upper Devonian shales in Ohio; petrographic and mineralogic studies of Ohio's Devonian age black shales; prediction of the degree of washability of coal using automated image analysis. *Mailing Add:* Dept Natural Resources Div Geol Surv Fountain Sq Columbus OH 43224

CARLTON, ROBERT AUSTIN, b Brownsville, Tenn, Apr 30, 27; m 50; c 2. ZOOLOGY. *Educ:* Lambuth Col, BS, 50; George Peabody Col, MA, 51; Ala Polytech Inst, PhD(zool), 58. *Prof Exp:* Instr biol, Northeast Miss Jr Col, 51-54; zool, Ala Polytech Inst, 54-56; assoc prof biol, Delta State Col, 56-64; PROF BIOL, LAMBUTH COL, 64- *Mem:* Nat Wildlife Fed. *Res:* Vertebrate ecology; natural history of vertebrates. *Mailing Add:* Lambuth Col Jackson TN 38302

CARLTON, TERRY SCOTT, b Peoria, Ill, Jan 29, 39; m 60; c 2. THEORETICAL CHEMISTRY. *Educ:* Duke Univ, BS, 60; Univ Calif, Berkeley, 63. *Prof Exp:* Asst prof chem, 63-69, assoc prof, 69-76, PROF CHEM, OBERLIN COL, 76- *Concurrent Pos:* Vis prof chem, Univ NC, 76. *Mem:* Am Phys Soc. *Res:* Quantum theory; electron density and electron correlation in atoms. *Mailing Add:* Dept Chem Oberlin Col Oberlin OH 44074

CARLTON, THOMAS A, JR, b Vivian, La, May 3, 27; m 50; c 4. CIVIL ENGINEERING. *Educ:* Tex A&M Univ, BS, 50, MS, 55; Univ Tex, PhD(civil eng), 62. *Prof Exp:* Asst prof civil eng, Lamar State Col, 53-56, asst prof mech eng mech, Univ Tex, 56-59; assoc prof civil eng, Miss State Univ, 59-61; assoc prof eng mech, 61-64, PROF CIVIL ENG, UNIV ALA, TUSCALOOSA, 64- *Concurrent Pos:* Res assoc, George C Marshall Space Flight Ctr, Nat Aeronaut & Space Admin, 62-64. *Mem:* Am Soc Eng Educ; Soc Exp Stress Anal. *Res:* Theoretical soil mechanics; orthotropic thin shell stability; experimental stress analysis. *Mailing Add:* Col of Eng Univ of Ala University AL 35486

CARLTON, VIRGINIA, b Rosebud, Tex, Mar 20, 18. MATHEMATICS. *Educ:* Centenary Col, BS, 39; Tulane Univ, MA, 40; Northwestern Univ, PhD, 59. *Prof Exp:* Teacher high sch, La, 40-41; instr math, Wesleyan Col, 41-46, prof & head dept, 50-55; asst prof, Centenary Col, 46-48; assoc prof, Northwestern State Col, 48-50; lectr, Northwestern Univ, 55-57; PROF MATH, CENTENARY COL, 57-, HEAD DEPT, 57- *Concurrent Pos:* Ford fel, Fund Advan Educ, 53-54; Fulbright lectr, Ghana, 63-64 & Liberia, 70-72. *Mem:* Am Math Soc; Nat Coun Teachers Math; Math Asn Am; Sigma Xi. *Res:* Teaching of mathematics. *Mailing Add:* Dept of Math Centenary Col Shreveport LA 71104

CARLTON, WILLIAM HERBERT, b Statesboro, Ga, Oct 6, 40; m 62; c 3. MEDICAL PHYSICS. *Educ:* Emory Univ, BS, 62, MS, 64; Rutgers Univ, PhD(radiation biophys), 69; Am Bd Health Physics, dipl, 70; Am Bd Radiol, dipl & cert radiol physics, 73. *Prof Exp:* Lectr radiation sci, Rutgers Univ, 64-69; asst prof, 69-74, ASSOC PROF RADIOL, MED COL GA, 74- *Concurrent Pos:* Consult Colgate-Palmolive Res Lab, 68-69 & Vet Admin Hosp, Augusta, Ga, 70- *Mem:* Am Asn Physicists in Med; Soc Nuclear Med; Health Physics Soc. *Res:* Low energy x-ray absorption; x-ray dose measurements; lacrimal scanning. *Mailing Add:* Dept of Radiol Med Col of Ga Augusta GA 30902

CARLTON, WILLIAM WALTER, b Owensboro, Ky, June 17, 29; m 55; c 2. VETERINARY PATHOLOGY, VETERINARY TOXICOLOGY. *Educ:* Univ Ky, BS, 53, MS, 56; Fla Southern Col, BS, 54; Auburn Univ, DVM, 60; Purdue Univ, PhD(vet path), 63; Am Col Vet Path, dipl. *Prof Exp:* Instr path, Purdue Univ, 60-62; asst prof, Mass Inst Technol, 62-65; assoc prof, 65-68, PROF PATH, SCH VET MED, PURDUE UNIV, WEST LAFAYETTE, 68- *Mem:* Am Inst Nutrit; Am Asn Avian Path; Am Soc Exp Path; Int Acad Path; Soc Toxicol. *Res:* Nutritional and toxicological diseases, especially of cardiovascular and nervous systems. *Mailing Add:* Dept of Vet Microbiol Purdue Univ Sch of Vet Med West Lafayette IN 47906

CARLUCCI, ANGELO FRANCIS, b Plainfield, NJ, Feb 17, 31. MICROBIAL ECOLOGY, MARINE MICROBIOLOGY. *Educ:* Rutgers Univ, BS, 53, MS, 56, PhD(microbiol), 59. *Prof Exp:* Asst microbiol, Tela RR Co, United Fruit Co, Honduras, 59-61; jr res biologist, Scripps Inst Oceanog, Univ Calif, San Diego, 61-62, postgrad res biologist, 62-64, asst res biologist, Inst Marine Resources, assoc res microbiologist, 71-77, RES MICROBIOLOGIST, INST MARINE RESOURCES, UNIV CALIF, SAN DIEGO, 77-, LECTR, 70- *Mem:* AAAS; Am Soc Microbiol; Am Soc Limnol & Oceanog; Sigma Xi; Western Soc Naturalists. *Res:* General marine microbiology; nitrogen cycle in the sea; vitamins and metabolites in marine ecology; survival of bacteria in seawater; phytoplankton-bacterial interactions; microbiology of sea surface. *Mailing Add:* Inst Marine Resources A-018 Univ Calif San Diego La Jolla CA 92093

CARLUCCI, FRANK VITO, b New York, NY, Apr 23, 48. LIQUID CHROMATOGRAPHY, AUTOMATED CHEMISTRY. *Educ:* Richmond Col, City Univ New York, BS, 71; Stevens Inst Technol, MS, 76; Rutgers Univ, PhD(food chem), 82. *Prof Exp:* Asst scientist, Schering-Plough Corp, 71-76; SR RES SCIENTIST, E R SQUIBB & SONS, INC, 77- *Concurrent Pos:* Assoc scientist, Hoeschst-Roussel, 77. *Mem:* Am Soc Testing & Mat; Am Inst Chemists. *Res:* Application of high performance liquid chromatography in developing a quantitative assay for specific amines and amino acids found in protein foods and an equation which will index the degree of decomposition. *Mailing Add:* 4B Boxwood Mall Old Bridge NJ 08857

CARLUCCIO, FRANK, b Newark, NJ, Aug 31, 19; m 59; c 1. CHEMICAL ENGINEERING. *Educ:* Newark Tech Sch, AE, 41; Newark Col Eng, BS, 43; Columbia Univ, MS, 47. *Prof Exp:* Jr scientist, Univ Calif, Los Alamos, 44-46; chem engr, Food Mach & Chem Corp, 47-56; chem engr, 56-60, prog mgr, 60-67, SUPVR, GAF CORP, 67- *Mem:* Am Inst Chem Engrs. *Res:* Liquid extraction; high pressure research; process development. *Mailing Add:* 8 Gloria Dr Towaco NJ 07082

CARLUCCIO, LEEDS MARIO, b Leominster, Mass, Sept 12, 36; m 61; c 3. BOTANY, MORPHOLOGY. *Educ:* Mass Col Pharm, BS, 58, MS, 60; Cornell Univ, PhD(paleobot), 66. *Prof Exp:* Instr gen bot, Cornell Univ, 64-66; from asst prof to assoc prof, 66-72, PROF GEN BOT, CENT CONN STATE COL, 72- *Concurrent Pos:* Mem Int Orgn Paleobot. *Mem:* Bot Soc Am; Sigma Xi; Am Asn Univ Prof. *Res:* Anatomy and morphology of the progymnosperms of Devonian floras. *Mailing Add:* Dept of Biol Cent Conn State Col New Britain CT 06050

CARLYLE, JACK WEBSTER, b Cordova, Alaska, Feb 23, 33; m 70; c 1. ANALYSIS OF ALGORITHMS. *Educ:* Univ Wash, BA, 54, MS, 57; Univ Calif, Berkeley, MA & PhD(elec eng), 61. *Prof Exp:* Asst prof elec eng, Princeton Univ, 61-63; asst prof eng, 63-68, assoc prof, 68-74, prof & chmn dept, 75-80, PROF COMPUT SCI, UNIV CALIF, LOS ANGELES, 80- *Concurrent Pos:* Vis scientist, Thomas J Watson Res Ctr, IBM, 73. *Mem:* Asn Comput Mach; Inst Elec & Electronics Engrs; Inst Math Statist; Am Math Soc; Soc Indust & Appl Math. *Res:* Computer science theory; stochastic sequential machines; nonparametric methods in signal detection; communication systems. *Mailing Add:* Comput Sci Dept 3731 Boelter Hall Univ Calif Los Angeles CA 90024

CARMACK, MARVIN, b Dana, Ind, Sept 1, 13; m 60. ORGANIC CHEMISTRY. *Educ:* Univ Ill, AB, 37; Univ Mich, MS, 39, PhD(org chem), 40. *Prof Exp:* Asst org chem, Univ Ill, 40-41; Towne instr, Univ Pa, 41-44, from asst prof to prof, 44-53; PROF ORG CHEM, IND UNIV, BLOOMINGTON, 53- *Concurrent Pos:* Guggenheim fel, Swiss Fed Inst Technol, 49-50; Fulbright res scholar, Commonwealth Sci & Indust Res Orgn, Melbourne, 60-61. *Mem:* AAAS; Am Chem Soc; NY Acad Sci; The Chem Soc; Swiss Chem Soc. *Res:* Natural products; organic sulfur chemistry; heterocyclic compounds. *Mailing Add:* Dept of Chem Ind Univ Bloomington IN 47405

CARMAN, CHARLES JERRY, b Tucumcari, NMex, Nov 14, 38; m 61; c 4. RESEARCH MANAGEMENT, PHYSICAL POLYMER CHEMISTRY. *Educ:* Eastern NMex Univ, BS, 61; Univ Calif, MS, 63. *Prof Exp:* Res chemist, 63-65, sr res chemist, 65-71, res assoc, 71-77, sr res & develop assoc, 77-79, mgr, Tech Resources Engineered Prod Group, 79-81, MGR CORPORATE RES, RES & DEVELOP CTR, B F GOODRICH CO, 81- *Mem:* Am Chem Soc; Sigma Xi. *Res:* Manage broadbase basic technologies in polymer physics, composites, synthesis; materials research and develop and product development; nuclear magnetic resonance of polymers; relationships of polymer molecular structure and physical properties; nuclear relaxation and polymer molecular motion; electron spin resonance; structure and function of homogeneous and heterogeneous catalysts. *Mailing Add:* B F Goodrich 9921 Brecksville Rd Brecksville OH 44141

CARMAN, GEORGE MARTIN, b Jersey City, NJ, June 2, 50. BIOCHEMISTRY, MICROBIOLOGY. *Educ:* William Paterson Col, BA, 72; Seton Hall Univ, MS, 74; Univ Mass, PhD(biochem), 76. *Prof Exp:* Fel biochem, Med Sch Univ Tex, 77-78; ASST PROF FOOD ENZYM, RUTGERS UNIV, 78- *Concurrent Pos:* Robert A Welch Found, Tex, fel, 77-78. *Mem:* Am Soc Microbiol; Sigma Xi; Inst Food Technol. *Res:* Membrane structure and function and phospholipid metabolism. *Mailing Add:* Dept of Food Sci Rutgers Univ New Brunswick NJ 08903

CARMAN, GLENN ELWIN, b Waterloo, Iowa, June 8, 14; m 41; c 2. ENTOMOLOGY. *Educ:* State Univ Iowa, BS, 36; Cornell Univ, PhD(entom), 42. *Prof Exp:* Res entomologist, Rohm & Haas Co, 42-43; from jr entomologist to assoc entomologist, Agr Exp Sta, 43-53, chmn dept, Univ Calif, 63-69, entomologist, Citrus Res Ctr & Agr Exp Sta, 53-81, prof, 60-81, EMER PROF ENTOM, UNIV CALIF, RIVERSIDE, 81- *Mem:* Fel AAAS; Entom Soc Am. *Res:* Insect toxicology; economic entomology; biology and control of citrus scale insects; evaluation of application equipment; reentry studies; ant and snail control on citrus crops. *Mailing Add:* 5368 Pinehurst Dr Riverside CA 92504

CARMAN, MAX FLEMING, JR, b Lansing, Mich, Oct 2, 24; m 47; c 2. GEOLOGY. *Educ:* Univ Calif, Los Angeles, AB, 48, PhD(geol), 54. *Prof Exp:* Asst, Univ Calif, Los Angeles, 51-54; asst prof, Univ Houston, 54-57; prof geol, Petrobras Petrol Co, Brazil, 57-59; assoc prof geol, 59-64, assoc dean col arts & sci, 61-65, PROF GEOL, UNIV HOUSTON, 64- *Concurrent Pos:* NSF & Fulbright sr res fel, Victoria, NZ, 63. *Mem:* Geol Soc Am; Mineral Soc Am; Geochem Soc; Brazilian Geol Soc. *Res:* Petrology; petrography; areal and structural geology. *Mailing Add:* Dept of Geol Univ of Houston Houston TX 77004

CARMAN, PHILIP DOUGLAS, b Ottawa, Can, Oct 28, 16; m 51; c 3. OPTICS. *Educ:* Univ Toronto, BA, 40; Univ Rochester, MSc, 51. *Prof Exp:* Optical instruments, Res Enterprises Ltd, 40; from jr physicist to sr res officer, Nat Res Coun Can, 41-81; RETIRED. *Concurrent Pos:* Consult optics, 81- *Mem:* Fel Optical Soc Am; Can Asn Physicists; Can Inst Surv; Am Soc Photogrammetry & Remote Sensing. *Res:* Performance of photographic and photogrammetric systems; optical instrument design and testing. *Mailing Add:* 1332 Snowdon St Ottawa Can

CARMEAN, WILLARD HANDY, b Philadelphia, Pa, Jan 4, 22; m 49; c 3. FOREST SOILS. *Educ:* Pa State Univ, BS, 43; Duke Univ, MF, 47, PhD(forest soils), 53. *Prof Exp:* Res forester soil res & forest surv, Pacific Northwest Forest Exp Sta, 46-51; soil scientist forest soils, Cent States Forest Exp Sta, 53-67, proj leader, NCent Forest Exp Sta, 67-79; ASSOC PROF FOREST SOILS, LAKEHEAD UNIV, ONT, 79- *Concurrent Pos:* Forest soils consult, Malaysia, UN Food & Agr Orgn, 74. *Mem:* AAAS; Soc Am Foresters; Soil Sci Soc Am; Ecol Soc Am; Am Soil Conserv Soc. *Res:* Relations between tree growth and factors of soil and topography. *Mailing Add:* Sch Forestry Lakehead Univ Thunder Bay ON P7B 5E1 Can

CARMEL, RALPH, b Riga, Latvia, Aug 8, 40; US citizen; m 67; c 2. HEMATOLOGY. *Educ:* Yeshiva Univ, BA, 59, BHL, 59; NY Univ, MD, 63. *Prof Exp:* USPHS res fel hemat, Mt Sinai Sch Med, 66-68; res assoc, Aerospace Med Lab, Lackland AFB, 68-70; Wellcome fel, St Mary's Hosp Med Sch, London, 71; from asst prof to assoc prof med, Wayne State Univ, 72-75; chief hemat, Grace Hosp, Detroit, 75; assoc prof, 75-81, PROF MED, SCH MED, UNIV SOUTHERN CALIF, 81- *Mem:* Am Soc Hemat; Am Soc Clin Nutrit; Am Inst Nutrit; Am Fedn Clin Res; Am Soc Clin Invest. *Res:* Megaloblastic anemia and folic acid and vitamin B-12 metabolism, with special interest in the transport of vitamin B-12 and in the proteins binding vitamin B-12. *Mailing Add:* Univ Southern Calif Sch of Med 2025 Zonal Ave Los Angeles CA 90033

CARMELI, MOSHE, b June 15, 33; US citizen; m 61; c 3. THEORETICAL PHYSICS. *Educ:* Hebrew Univ, Jerusalem, MSc, 60; Israel Inst Technol, PhD(physics), 64. *Prof Exp:* Lectr physics, Israel Inst Technol, 64; res assoc physics, Lehigh Univ, 64-65; res assoc physics, Univ Md, 65-67, asst prof, 67-68; res physicist, US Air Force, Wright-Patterson AFB, 67-69, sr scientist, 69-72; assoc prof, 72-74, head dept, 73-77, PROF PHYSICS, BEN GURION UNIV, 74- *Mem:* Fel Am Phys Soc; AAAS; Am Asn Univ Profs; Sigma Xi; Int Soc Gen Relativity & Gravitation. *Res:* General relativity and gauge theory. *Mailing Add:* Dept of Physics Ben Gurion Univ Beer Sheva Israel

CARMEN, ELAINE (HILBERMAN), b New York, NY, Mar 26, 39. PSYCHIATRY. *Educ:* City Col NY, BS, 59; Sch Med, NY Univ, MD, 64; Am Bd Psychiat & Neurol, dipl, 77. *Prof Exp:* Intern, NC Mem Hosp, 64-65, resident, 65-66; staff physician, John Umstead Hosp, 67-69, resident psychiat, 69-72; instr, 72-74, asst prof, 74-79, ASSOC PROF PSYCHIAT, SCH MED, UNIV NC, 79-, ASST DIR PSYCHIAT RESIDENCY TRAINING, 77- *Concurrent Pos:* Mem, Panel of Spec Populations, President's Comn Mental Health, 77-78. *Mem:* Fel Am Psychiat Asn; Am Med Women's Asn; Asn Acad Psychiat; Nat Women's Health Network. *Res:* Sex roles; psychological consequences of sexual inequality; violence against women. *Mailing Add:* Dept of Psychiat Sch of Med Univ of NC Chapel Hill NC 27514

CARMER, SAMUEL GRANT, b Buffalo, NY, Dec 19, 32; m 60; c 3. BIOMETRICS. *Educ:* Cornell Univ, BS, 54; Univ Ill, Urbana, MS, 58, PhD(agron), 61. *Prof Exp:* Res fel biomath, NC State Col, 61-62; from asst prof to assoc prof, 62-71, PROF BIOMET, UNIV ILL, URBANA-CHAMPAIGN, 71- *Mem:* Am Soc Agron; Am Statist Asn; Biomet Soc; Crop Sci Soc Am. *Res:* Biomathematics; teaching graduate level courses and providing individual advice on problems of experimental design; statistical analysis and data processing by computer. *Mailing Add:* Dept Agron Turner Hall 1102 S Goodwin Ave Urbana IL 61801

CARMI, SHLOMO, b Cernauti, Romania, July 18, 37; US citizen; m 63; c 3. FLUID MECHANICS, HEAT TRANSFER. *Educ:* Univ Witwatersrand, BSc, 62; Univ Minn, MS, 66, PhD(aeronaut eng), 68. *Prof Exp:* From asst prof to assoc prof, 68-78, PROF MECH ENG, COL ENG, WAYNE STATE UNIV, 78- *Concurrent Pos:* Fac res award, Wayne State Univ, 70; sr lectr, Technion, Israel Inst Technol, Haifa, 70-72, vis prof, I Taylor Chair, Mech Eng Dept Technion, 77-78; US Army Res Off award & US Dept Energy grant, 77-79; Dow Chem Co/DOE grant, 78-79; assoc ed, J Fluids Eng, 81- *Mem:* Am Phys Soc; Soc Natural Philos; Am Soc Mech Engrs. *Res:* Hydrodynamic stability and turbulence by linear and nonlinear theories; eigenvalue bounds; variational and numerical solutions; computer codes for differential equations in fluid mechanics and heat and mass transfer; applied mathematics and modeling; stability studies in fluid, thermal, chemical and biological systems. *Mailing Add:* Dept of Mech Eng Wayne State Univ Detroit MI 48202

CARMICHAEL, DAVID JAMES, b Casterton, Australia, June 2, 36; m 68; c 1. PROTEIN CHEMISTRY. *Educ:* Univ Melbourne, BAgrSci, 60; Univ Nottingham, PhD(food sci), 66. *Prof Exp:* Technologist, Kraft Foods Ltd, 60-63; demonstr food sci, Univ Nottingham, 63-66; Am Dent Asn fel, Northwestern Univ, 66-67; Helen Hay Whitney Found fel, 67-68; assoc prof, 68-73, PROF DENT, UNIV ALTA, 73-, DIR, RES & GRAD STUDIES, FAC DENT, 76- *Concurrent Pos:* Med Res Coun Can grant, 73-76; vis scientist, Med Res Coun Can, 75; vis prof Monash Univ, Clayton, Australia, 75-76. *Mem:* Brit Biochem Soc; Int Asn Dent Res. *Res:* Collagen research; biochemical characterization of normal and lathyritic dentin matrix collagen; immunohistochemical study of collagen fibrillogenesis. *Mailing Add:* Fac of Dent Univ of Alta Edmonton AB T6G 2E8 Can

CARMICHAEL, DONALD C(HARLES), b Cincinnati, Ohio, May 22, 33; m 56. SOLAR ENERGY, MATERIALS SCIENCE. *Educ:* Purdue Univ, BS, 55, MS, 57. *Prof Exp:* Metall engr, Allison Div, Gen Motors Corp, 55; prin metall engr, 56-63, asst div chief advan mat develop, 63-65, chief mat appln div, 66-71, MGR SOLAR PHOTOVOLTAICS, BATTELLE MEM INST, 71- *Mem:* Am Soc Metals; Am Vacuum Soc; Int Solar Energy Soc. *Res:* Development of metallic, ceramic and composite materials; materials compatibility; diffusion; nuclear materials; powder metallurgy; coating technology; vacuum coating; thin films; sputtering; hot-isostatic-pressing process; solar photovoltaic conversion; solar energy systems and applications. *Mailing Add:* Battelle Mem Inst 505 King Ave Columbus OH 43201

CARMICHAEL, GREGORY RICHARD, b Marengo, Ill, June, 16, 52; m 75. CHEMICAL ENGINEERING. *Educ:* Iowa State Univ, BS, 74; Univ Ky, MS, 75, PhD(chem eng), 79. *Prof Exp:* Asst prof, 78-82, ASSOC PROF CHEM ENG, UNIV IOWA, 82- *Mem:* Am Inst Chem Engrs; Am Chem Soc; Air Pollution Control Asn; Am Meteorol Soc; Sigma Xi. *Res:* Mathematical modeling of the transport, chemical reaction and removal processes affecting the distribution of trace species in the lower troposphere. *Mailing Add:* 129 Chem Bldg Univ Iowa Iowa City IA 52242

CARMICHAEL, HALBERT HART, b St Louis, Mo, Aug 29, 37; m 58; c 2. CHEMICAL KINETICS. *Educ:* Univ Tenn, BS, 59; Univ Calif, PhD(chem), 63. *Prof Exp:* Nat Bur Stand fel, 63-64; asst prof, 64-69, assoc prof, 69-78, PROF CHEM, NC STATE UNIV, 78- *Mem:* Am Chem Soc. *Res:* Photochemistry and radiation chemistry of gases. *Mailing Add:* Dept of Chem NC State Univ Raleigh NC 27607

CARMICHAEL, IAN STUART, b London, Eng, Mar 29, 30; m 70; c 4. PETROLOGY, GEOCHEMISTRY. *Educ:* Cambridge Univ, BA, 54; Univ London, PhD(geol), 59. *Prof Exp:* Lectr geol, Imp Col, Univ London, 58-63; assoc prof, 65-67, chmn dept geol & geophysics, 72-76, assoc dean grad div, 76-78, PROF GEOL, UNIV CALIF, BERKELEY, 67- *Concurrent Pos:* Sr foreign scientist, NSF, Univ Chicago, 63; Miller res prof, Miller Inst Sci Res, 67-68; ed-in-chief, Contrib to Mineral & Petrol, 74- *Mem:* Am Geophys Union; Mineral Soc Am; Mineral Soc Gt Brit & Ireland. *Res:* Origin and cooling history of igneous rocks. *Mailing Add:* Dept of Geol Univ of Calif Berkeley CA 94720

CARMICHAEL, J W, JR, b Lamesa, Tex, Feb 9, 40. PHYSICAL CHEMISTRY, INORGANIC CHEMISTRY. *Educ:* Eastern NMex Univ, BS, 61; Univ Ill, MS, 63, PhD(phys chem), 65. *Prof Exp:* Asst chem, Univ Ill, 62-65; asst prof, Univ Ark, 65-70; asst prof, 70-73, assoc prof, 73-77, PROF CHEM, XAVIER UNIV LA, 77- *Concurrent Pos:* Pre-Health Professions adv, 74- *Mem:* Am Chem Soc; Nat Asn Minority Med Educ; The Chem Soc; Nat Sci Teachers Asn. *Res:* Teaching approaches which make chemistry more accessible to the underprepared. *Mailing Add:* Dept of Chem Xavier Univ of La New Orleans LA 70125

CARMICHAEL, LELAND E, b Huntington Park, Calif, June 15, 30; m 57; c 3. VETERINARY MICROBIOLOGY. *Educ:* Univ Calif, AB, 52, DVM, 56; Cornell Univ, PhD(virol), 59. *Prof Exp:* Asst bact, State Univ NY Vet Col, Cornell Univ, 56-59, res assoc virol, 59-63, asst prof infectious dis & John M Olin Chair, 63-69, PROF VET VIROL & JOHN M OLIN PROF VIROL & VET MICROBIOL, STATE UNIV NY VET COL, CORNELL UNIV, 69- *Concurrent Pos:* NIH grant, 61-81; Scientific dir, James A Baker Inst for Animal Health, 75- *Honors & Awards:* Gaines Award, Am Vet Med Asn, 75. *Mem:* Am Vet Med Asn; NY Acad Sci; US Livestock Sanit Asn; Am Soc Microbiol; Infectious Dis Soc Am. *Res:* Infectious diseases of domestic animals, principally viral and mycoplasmal diseases; infectious hepatitis; immunology; pathogenesis. *Mailing Add:* Vet Virus Res Inst Snyder Hall SUNY Vet Col Cornell Univ Ithaca NY 14850

CARMICHAEL, RALPH HARRY, b Freetown, Ind, Jan 20, 23; m 42; c 1. PHARMACOLOGY. *Educ:* Ind Univ, BS, 49; Butler Univ, MS, 56. *Prof Exp:* Assoc chemist, 50-56, supvr clin chem, 56-62, dept head clin chem & hemat, 62-70, DEPT HEAD DRUG METAB, LILLY LAB CLIN RES, ELI LILLY & CO, 70- *Mem:* Am Chem Soc; Am Asn Clin Chemists; NY Acad Sci. *Res:* Drug metabolism. *Mailing Add:* 2732 Parkwood Dr Indianapolis IN 46224

CARMICHAEL, RICHARD DUDLEY, b High Point, NC, Mar 13, 42; m 67. MATHEMATICAL ANALYSIS. *Educ:* Wake Forest Col, BS, 64; Duke Univ, AM, 66, PhD(math), 68. *Prof Exp:* Asst prof math, Va Polytech Inst & State Univ, 68-71; assoc prof, 71-80, PROF MATH, WAKE FOREST UNIV, 80- *Mem:* Am Math Soc; Math Asn Am; Soc Indust & Appl Math; Calcutta Math Soc. *Res:* Theory of distributions; complex variables. *Mailing Add:* Dept of Math Wake Forest Univ Winston-Salem NC 27109

CARMICHAEL, ROBERT STEWART, b Toronto, Ont, Jan 11, 42; m 67. GEOPHYSICS, GEOLOGY. *Educ:* Univ Toronto, BASc, 63; Univ Pittsburgh, MS, 64, PhD(earth & planetary sci), 67. *Prof Exp:* Teaching asst geol, Univ Pittsburgh, 63-64 & 66-67; fel geophys, Osaka Univ, 67-68; geophysicist, Explor & Prod Res Ctr, Shell Develop Co, 69-72; asst prof, Mich State Univ, 73-77; ASSOC PROF GEOL, UNIV IOWA, 77- *Concurrent Pos:* Prin investr, NSF & NASA grants. *Mem:* Am Geophys Union; Sigma Xi; Soc Explor Geophys; Soc Terrestrial Magnetism & Elec. *Res:* Rock magnetism; computer analysis; properties of earth materials; high-pressure geophysics; exploration geophysics; engineering geophysics. *Mailing Add:* Dept of Geol Univ of Iowa Iowa City IA 52242

CARMICHAEL, RONALD L(AD), b Independence, Mo, Sept 29, 21; m 43; c 2. MINING ENGINEERING. *Educ:* Mo Sch Mines, BS, 44, MS, 47; Colo Sch Mines, ScD(mining eng), 52. *Prof Exp:* Jr mining engr, US Bur Mines, 44-45; mine engr, Rock Island Coal Co, 45-46; instr mining, Mo Sch Mines, 47-48; teaching fel chem mining & metall eng, Ore State Col, 48-49, instr, 49-50; prin mining engr, Battelle Mem Inst, 52-57, proj leader, 57-62, sr metals economist & engr, 62-68; from assoc prof to prof eng mgt, 68-78, PROF MINING ENG, UNIV MO-ROLLA, 78- *Concurrent Pos:* Lectr, Ohio State Univ, 57, 66; consult, Oak Ridge Nat Lab, 80- *Mem:* Am Inst Mining, Metall & Petrol Engrs; Sigma Xi. *Res:* Metals and minerals economics; management theory; engineering-economics of the production, transportation refining, processing, fabrication and utilization of metals and minerals. *Mailing Add:* Dept of Mining Eng Univ of Mo Rolla MO 65401

CARMICHAEL, STEPHEN WEBB, b Detroit, Mich, July 17, 45; m 70. HUMAN ANATOMY. *Educ:* Kenyon Col, AB, 67; Tulane Univ, PhD(anat), 71. *Prof Exp:* Asst prof biol, Delgado Col, 69-71; from instr to asst prof anat, 71-75, ASSOC PROF ANAT, SCH MED, WVA UNIV, 75- *Concurrent Pos:* Fel, Giorgio Cini Found, Milan, 73. *Mem:* Am Asn Anat; Electron Micros Soc Am; Am Soc Cell Biol. *Res:* Morphological aspects of secretion; adrenal medullary cytology. *Mailing Add:* Dept of Anat WVa Univ Med Ctr Morgantown WV 26506

CARMODY, GEORGE R, b Brooklyn, NY, Mar 29, 38; m 62; c 3. POPULATION GENETICS. *Educ:* Columbia Univ, AB, 60, PhD(zool), 67. *Prof Exp:* Teaching asst zool, Columbia Univ, 61-62; USPHS fel, Univ Chicago, 67-68; asst prof, 69-74, assoc chmn, Dept Biol, 73-76, ASSOC PROF BIOL, CARLETON UNIV, 74- *Concurrent Pos:* Ford Found genetics training grant fel, Univ Chicago, 68-69; vis sr fel, Genetics Dept, Univ Nottingham, Eng, 76-77. *Mem:* AAAS; Genetics Soc Am; Soc Study Evolution; Genetics Soc Can. *Res:* Speciation in Drosophila; protein polymorphisms; maintenance of genetic variability in natural populations; genetic variability in cave-dwelling organisms; DNA sequence variation. *Mailing Add:* Dept Biol Carleton Univ Ottawa ON K1S 5B6 Can

CARMON, JAMES LAVERN, b Ga, May 7, 26; m 46; c 1. STATISTICS, GENETICS. *Educ:* Univ Ga, BSA, 48; Univ Md, MS, 50; NC State Col, PhD(statist), 55. *Prof Exp:* Instr, animal husb, Univ Ga, 50-55, from asst prof to assoc prof, 55-58, statistician, Col Exp Sta, 56-59, assoc dir, Inst Statist, 59, DIR COMPUT CTR, UNIV GA, 59-, ASST VCHANCELLOR COMPUT SYSTS, 68- *Concurrent Pos:* NIH res fel statist, Va Polytech Inst, 63-64. *Mem:* Asn Comput Mach. *Res:* Statistics, genetics, and computer and information science. *Mailing Add:* Off of Comput Activ Univ of Ga Athens GA 30602

CARMONY, DONALD DUANE, b Indianapolis, Ind, Sept 16, 35; m 61; c 2. HIGH ENERGY PHYSICS. *Educ:* Ind Univ, BS, 56; Univ Calif, Berkeley, PhD(physics), 62. *Prof Exp:* Res physicist, Lawrence Radiation Lab, Univ Calif, Berkeley, 61-62, res physicist & lectr, Univ Calif, Los Angeles, 62-63, res physicist, Univ Calif, San Diego, 63-66; assoc prof, 66-75, PROF PHYSICS, PURDUE UNIV, 75- *Concurrent Pos:* Alexander von Humboldt sr scientist award, 72-73; Sr Fulbright scholar, 79-80. *Mem:* Fel Am Phys Soc. *Res:* Experimental high energy physics; high energy hadron collisions; neutrino interactions; study of pion-pion interactions and strange meson resonances. *Mailing Add:* Dept of Physics Purdue Univ Lafayette IN 47907

CARMOUCHE, L(OUIS) N(ORMAN), b Newton, Kans, Aug 7, 16; m 39; c 3. CHEMICAL ENGINEERING. *Educ:* Univ Kans, BS, 38. *Prof Exp:* Chem engr, Midland Div, Dow Chem Co, 39-40, plant supt, 40-42, tech expert, 44-46, gen mgr, Ludington Div, 46-60, gen mgr, Saginaw Bay Div, 60-63, mgr basic opers, Midland Div, 63-67, gen mgr, Packaging Div, 67-68, mgr, Functional Chem & Serv Dept, 68-69, mgr, Functional Prod & Systs Dept, 69-79, corp prod dir, Exec Dept, 79-81; PRES, TRANSTEL SERV CO, 81- *Concurrent Pos:* Prod supt, Ludington Plant, Dow Magnesium Corp, 42-45. *Mem:* Am Inst Chem Engrs. *Res:* Heat transfer; crystallization; pyrometric processes; drying; management science. *Mailing Add:* 4412 Orchard Midland MI 48640

CARNAHAN, BRICE, b New Philadelphia, Ohio, Oct 13, 33. CHEMICAL ENGINEERING, APPLIED MATHEMATICS. *Educ:* Case Inst Technol, BS, 55, MS, 57; Univ Mich, PhD(chem eng), 65. *Prof Exp:* Lectr chem eng, 60-61, asst dir, Ford Found Proj, 61-63, instr chem eng & biostatist, 63-65, from asst prof to assoc prof, 65-70, asst dir, NSF Proj, 65, PROF CHEM ENG & BIOSTATIST, UNIV MICH, 70- *Concurrent Pos:* Vis prof, Univ Pa, 70; mem, Comt Comput Aids Chem Eng Educ, Nat Acad Eng. *Mem:* AAAS; Am Asn Comput Mach; Am Inst Chem Engrs. *Res:* Numerical mathematics; digital computer applications; radiation chemistry. *Mailing Add:* Dept of Chem Eng Univ of Mich Ann Arbor MI 48409

CARNAHAN, CHALON LUCIUS, b Beverly, Mass, Sept 17, 33; m 60; c 2. GROUNDWATER HYDROLOGY. *Educ:* Calif Inst Technol, BS, 55; Univ Calif, Berkeley, MS, 58; Univ Nev, Reno, PhD(hydrol), 75. *Prof Exp:* Radiol chemist, US Naval Radiol Defense Lab, 57-62; sr radiochemist, Hazleton-Nuclear Sci Corp, 62-65; mgr phys chem dept, 65-67; sr assoc scientist, Isotopes, a Teledyne Co, 67-69, scientist & group leader, 69-70, Teledyne Isotopes, 70-71; res assoc, Desert Res Inst, Univ Nev, 71-76; supvry assoc, Environ Sci Assocs, 76-78; STAFF SCIENTIST, LAWRENCE BERKELEY LAB, UNIV CALIF, 78- *Mem:* AAAS; Am Geophys Union. *Res:* Physical and chemical effects of underground nuclear explosions; nuclear reactions; thermodynamics of irreversible processes in flow through porous media; contamination transport in ground water. *Mailing Add:* Bldg 90-1140 Lawrence Berkeley Lab Univ Calif Berkeley CA 94720

CARNAHAN, HOWARD LEON, b Erie, Kans, Mar 25, 20; m 45, 73; c 2. GENETICS, PLANT BREEDING. *Educ:* Kans State Col, BS, 42; Univ Minn, MS, 47, PhD(plant genetics), 49. *Prof Exp:* Asst, Univ Minn, 42, res assoc, 46-48; asst prof agron, Pa State Univ, 49-52; res agronomist, US Regional Pasture Res Lab, 53-57, agronomist in chg, 57-60; res agronomist, Agr Res Serv, USDA, 60-65; dir res, Arnold-Thomas Seed Serv, 65-69; DIR PLANT BREEDING, CALIF COOP RICE RES FOUND, 69- *Honors & Awards:* Serv to Agr Award, Prof Agr Technicians Asn, 79. *Mem:* Am Soc Agron; Crop Sci Soc Am; Am Genetic Asn. *Res:* Forage plant breeding; cytogenetics; agronomy; rice breeding. *Mailing Add:* Calif Coop Rice Res Found PO Box 306 Biggs CA 95917

CARNAHAN, JAMES CLAUDE, b Yonkers, NY, Nov 25, 43; m 71; c 2. POLYMER CHEMISTRY, PHYSICAL ORGANIC CHEMISTRY. *Educ:* Columbia Univ, BS, 69; State Univ NY, Albany, PhD(chem), 74. *Prof Exp:* Res fel org chem, Univ Saarlandes, WGer, 74-75; STAFF CHEMIST ORG CHEM, RES & DEVELOP CTR, GEN ELEC CO, 75- *Mem:* Am Chem Soc. *Res:* Liquid and gas chromatography; polymer characterization and molecular weights. *Mailing Add:* Res & Develop Ctr PO Box 8 Schenectady NY 12301

CARNAHAN, JAMES ELLIOT, b Kaukauna, Wis, Jan 26, 20; m 44; c 4. ENTOMOLOGY, ENVIRONMENTAL BIOLOGY. *Educ:* Univ Wis, BS, 42, MS, 44, PhD(org chem), 46. *Prof Exp:* Asst chem warfare agents, Univ Wis, 42-46; res chemist, 46-56, RES SUPVR, E I DU PONT DE NEMOURS & CO, 56- *Honors & Awards:* Hoblitzelle Nat Award Res Agr Sci, Tex Res Found, 65. *Mem:* Am Chem Soc; Am Soc Plant Physiol; Am Soc Biol Chem; Entom Soc Am. *Res:* Organic synthesis; catalytic chemistry; polymer chemistry; biological nitrogen fixation; plant biochemistry; agricultural chemicals, drugs and air pollution effects on plants. *Mailing Add:* E I du Pont de Nemours & Co Wilmington DE 19898

CARNAHAN, ROBERT D, b Pontiac, Mich, June 14, 31; m 53; c 4. METALLURGY, MATERIALS SCIENCE. *Educ:* Mich Tech Univ, BS, 53; Northwestern Univ, PhD(mat sci), 63. *Prof Exp:* Res scientist, Honeywell Res Ctr, Minn, 56-59, res metallurgist, Ord Div, Minneapolis-Honeywell Regulator Co, 59; asst fracture of ceramics, Northwestern Univ, 60-62, resident damping ceramics, 62; mem tech staff, Aerospace Corp, 62-66, staff scientist, 66-68; dir mat sci lab, Universal Oil Prod, 68-73; DIR RES, ELEC & ELECTRONICS LAB, GOULD INC, 73- *Mem:* Am Inst Mining, Metall & Petrol Engrs; Electrochem Soc; Inst Elec & Electronics Engrs. *Res:* The relation of structure of metals and nonmetals to mechanical and physical behavior, especially the role of dislocations in the microstrain region and relation to macroplastic flow; dimensional stability and microplastic behavior of solids; gas phase catalysis; solid state sensors; ink jet writing devices; thin film deposition of precision resistors; surface physics and chemistry of solids. *Mailing Add:* 40 Gould Ctr Rolling Meadows IL 60008

CARNAHAN, ROBERT EDWARD, b Kaukauna, Wis, Jan 5, 25; m 50; c 2. ORGANIC CHEMISTRY. *Educ:* Univ Wis, BS, 47; Univ Ill, MS, 48, PhD(org chem), 50. *Prof Exp:* Res chemist, Pfizer, Inc, 50-55, patent agent, 55-60; patent agent, Mead Johnson & Co, 60-69, dir patents, 69-81; DIR PATENTS, BRISTOL-MYERS CO, 81- *Mem:* Am Chem Soc; AAAS. *Res:* Medicinal chemistry. *Mailing Add:* Bristol Lab Box 657 Syracuse NY 13201

CARNALL, WILLIAM THOMAS, b Denver, Colo, May 23, 27; m 50; c 3. PHYSICAL CHEMISTRY. *Educ:* Colo State Univ, BS, 50; Univ Wis, PhD(chem), 54. *Prof Exp:* Asst, Univ Wis, 52-54; SR CHEMIST, ARGONNE NAT LAB, 54- *Concurrent Pos:* Sigma Xi fel, Munich, 61-62. *Mem:* Am Chem Soc. *Res:* Chemistry of the actinide elements; theory of lanthanide and actinide element spectra. *Mailing Add:* 5333 Seventh Ave La Grange IL 60525

CARNELL, DAVID W(ASHBURN), b Hartford, Conn, June 14, 21; m 43; c 3. CHEMICAL ENGINEERING. *Educ:* Tufts Col, BS, 41; Mass Inst Technol, MS, 42. *Prof Exp:* Chem engr, 42-52, res supvr, 52-61, sr supvr, 61-67, res assoc, 67-73, sr supvr, 73-75, res mgr, Res & Develop Div, 75-80, TECH FEL, DU PONT CAPE FEAR PLANT, E I DU PONT DE NEMOURS & CO, INC, 80- *Mem:* Am Inst Chem Engrs. *Res:* Process and product development; chemicals and polymers; plastics. *Mailing Add:* Cape Fear Plant PD E I du Pont de Nemours & Co Inc Wilmington NC 28401

CARNELL, PAUL HERBERT, b Oakfield, Wis, May 27, 17; m 42; c 5. PETROLEUM CHEMISTRY. *Educ:* Albion Col, AB, 39; Western Reserve Univ, PhD(chem), 43. *Hon Degrees:* DrLaws, Alderson Broaddus Col, 73. *Prof Exp:* Res chemist, Phillips Petrol Co, 43-47; dir res, Leonard Refining, Inc, 47-48; asst prof, Marietta Col, 48-49; asst prof, Albion Col, 48-52, head chem dept, 52-66; mem staff, 66-68, asst dir, Div Instl Develop, Bur Higher & Continuing Educ, US Off Educ, Dept Health, Educ & Welfare, 68-81, ASST DIR, OFF POSTSEC EDUC, DEPT EDUC, 81- *Concurrent Pos:* Res Corp grant, 52; res assoc, Yale Univ, 59-60; NIH res grants, 59-; Am Chem Soc vis scientist, 59-; assoc prof dir acad years insts, NSF, 64-65. *Mem:* Am Chem Soc; NY Acad Sci. *Res:* Petroleum chemistry; Treating with hydrofluoric acid, lubricating oils, fuel oils, fuel oil stability, and viscosity; synthetic membranes. *Mailing Add:* Off Postsec Educ Dept Educ Washington DC 20202

CARNES, DAVID LEE, JR, b Youngstown, Ohio, Mar 16, 46; m 71. COMPARATIVE PHYSIOLOGY. *Educ:* Allegheny Col, BS, 68; Rice Univ, MA, 74, PhD(biol), 75. *Prof Exp:* Res assoc biol, Rice Univ, 74-75; res assoc pharmacol, Univ Mo-Columbia & Harry S Truman Vet Admin Hosp, 75-79; RES ASSOC, MED & ENDOCRINE DIV, CHILDREN'S HOSP MED CTR & INSTR ORAL BIOL, HARVARD SCH DENT MED, 79- *Mem:* NY Acad Sci; AAAS; Am Soc Bone & Mineral Res. *Res:* Interrelationship of Parathyroid hormone, calcitonin and vitamin D, as they relate to the control of calcium metabolism. *Mailing Add:* Children's Hosp Med Ctr Endocrine Div G-1221 300 Longwood Ave Boston MA 02115

CARNES, JAMES EDGAR, human anatomy, see previous edition

CARNES, JAMES EDWARD, b Cumberland, Md, Sept 27, 39. CONSUMER ELECTRONICS, SOLID STATE ELECTRONICS. *Educ:* Pa State Univ, BS, 61; Princeton Univ, MA, 67, PhD(electron device physics), 70. *Prof Exp:* mem tech staff solid state electronics, 69-77, mgr integrated circuit develop, Consumer Electronics Div, 77-78, mgr technol applns, 78-81, DIR, NEW PROD LAB, CONSUMER ELECTRONICS DIV, RCA LABS, 81- *Concurrent Pos:* Lectr, Short Course Prog, Univ Calif, Los Angeles, 73- *Mem:* Inst Elec & Electronics Engrs. *Res:* Experimental and analytical studies of metal-oxide-silicon integrated circuits, specifically charge-coupled devices including understanding of physics of operation and optimum design for imaging, memory and signal processing applications; application of integrated circuit technology to consumer products; advanced development of consumer electronics video products. *Mailing Add:* RCA New Prod Lab 600 N Sherman Dr Indianapolis IN 46201

CARNES, JOSEPH JOHN, b Rock Island, Ill, Aug 3, 17; m 42; c 5. ORGANIC CHEMISTRY. *Educ:* St Ambrose Col, BS, 39; Univ Iowa, MS, 41, PhD(org chem), 43. *Prof Exp:* Chemist, Nat Defense Res Comt contract, Univ Iowa, 42-43; sr chemist, Am Cyanamid Co, 43-51, group leader, 51-54, sect mgr, 54-59, dir appl res, 59-63, dir contract res, 63-68; dir advan planning, New Eng Inst, 68-69, vpres, 69-75; RETIRED. *Mem:* Fel AAAS; Am Chem Soc; fel Am Inst Chemists. *Res:* Synthetic organic chemistry; process development; ring closure of N-chloroamines; nitrogen mustards; chemical warfare agents; surface active agents; organic phosphorus insecticides; new product development; paper and industrial chemicals; rocket propellant chemistry; energy conversion. *Mailing Add:* c/o A Lacurci 2 Haviland Rd Ridgefield CT 06877

CARNES, WALTER ROSAMOND, b Winona, Miss, Oct 7, 22; m 46; c 2. ENGINEERING MECHANICS, AEROSPACE ENGINEERING. *Educ:* Ga Inst Tech, BS, 49, MS, 54; Univ Ill, PhD(mech), 64. *Prof Exp:* Instr math, Ga Inst Tech, 50-51, 53-55, from instr to asst prof aeronaut eng, 55-59; assoc prof, 59-63, PROF AEROSPACE ENG & ENG MECH, 63-, ASSOC DEAN ENG & DIR INSTR, COL ENG, 70- *Mem:* Nat Soc Prof Engrs; Am Soc Eng Educ. *Res:* Structural dynamics. *Mailing Add:* Col of Eng Miss State Univ Drawer DE Mississippi State MS 39762

CARNES, WILLIAM HENRY, b Ft Worth, Tex, Nov 2, 09; m 50. PATHOLOGY. *Educ:* Columbia Univ, AB, 32; Johns Hopkins Univ, MD, 36. *Prof Exp:* Asst res & path, City Hosps, Baltimore, Md, 36-38; assoc path, Sch Med, Johns Hopkins Univ, 38-39; instr, Columbia Univ, 39-41; from asst prof to assoc prof, Stanford Univ, 41-47; from asst prof to assoc prof, Johns Hopkins Univ, 47-51; from assoc prof to prof, Stanford Univ, 51-56; prof path & head dept, Univ Utah, 56-68; prof, 68-77, EMER PROF PATH, UNIV CALIF, LOS ANGELES, 77- *Mem:* AAAS; Am Asn Path; Am Soc Cell Biol; Am Soc Exp Path; Soc Exp Biol & Med. *Res:* Experimental pathology. *Mailing Add:* Dept of Path Univ of Calif Sch of Med Los Angeles CA 90024

CARNESALE, ALBERT, b Bronx, NY, July 2, 36; m 62; c 2. NUCLEAR ENGINEERING, PUBLIC POLICY. *Educ:* Cooper Union, BME, 57; Drexel Inst Technol, MS, 61; NC State Univ, PhD(nuclear eng), 65. *Prof Exp:* Sr engr, Martin Co, Md, 57-62; assoc prof nuclear eng, NC State Univ, 62-69; scientist, US Arms Control & Disarmament Agency, 69-72; prof univ studies, NC State Univ, 72-74; assoc dir prog sci & int affairs, 74-78, PROF PUB POLICY, J F KENNEDY SCH GOVT, HARVARD UNIV, 78- *Concurrent Pos:* Consult, Southern Interstate Nuclear Bd, Ga, 63-69; USAEC & Res Triangle Inst, NC, 65-69 & US Nuclear Regulatory Comn, 75-77; adv, US Deleg to Strategic Arms Limitation Talks with Soviet Union, 70-72; expert/consult, US Arms Control & Disarmament Agency, 72- & US Dept State, 77-; head US deleg, Int Nuclear Fuel Cycle Eval, 78-80. *Mem:* AAAS; Am Soc Eng Educ; Am Nuclear Soc. *Res:* Nuclear energy policy, nuclear weapons policy and other national and international policy issues having substantial scientific and technological dimensions. *Mailing Add:* J F Kennedy Sch Govt Harvard Univ Cambridge MA 02138

CARNEY, BRUCE WILLIAM, b Guam, Nov 30, 46; US citizen; m 71. ASTRONOMY. *Educ:* Univ Calif, Berkeley, BA, 69; Harvard Univ, AM, 71, PhD(astron), 78. *Prof Exp:* Sci & eng asst, US Army Ballistics Res Lab, 71-74; fel astron, Dept Terrestrial Magnetism, Carnegie Inst Washington, 78-80; ASST PROF ASTRON, UNIV NC, CHAPEL HILL, 80- *Mem:* Am Astron Soc; Astron Soc Pac; Sigma Xi. *Res:* Observational aspect of stellar and galactic evolution; particularly Population II systems. *Mailing Add:* Dept Physics & Astron Phillips Hall 039A Univ NC Chapel Hill NC 27514

CARNEY, D(ENNIS) J(OSEPH), b Charleroi, Pa, Mar 19, 21; m 43; c 5. METALLURGY. *Educ:* Pa State Col, BS, 42; Mass Inst Technol, DSc, 49. *Prof Exp:* Metallurgist, US Steel Corp, Clairton, 42-43, physicist, South Works, 49-50, gen supvr metals res, 50-51, chief develop metallurgist, 51-54, supt elec furnaces, 54-56, open hearth, 56, div supt steel prod, Duquesne Works, 56-59, asst gen supt, Homestead Dist Works, 59-63, gen supt, Duquesne Works, 63-65, vpres long range facil planning, 65-68, vpres appl res, 68-72, vpres res, 72-74; vpres opers, 74-75, exec vpres & dir, 75-76, chief operating officer, 76-77, pres, 76-79, CHIEF EXEC OFFICER, WHEELING-PITTSBURGH STEEL CORP, 77-, CHMN BD, 78- *Concurrent Pos:* Metallurgist, Naval Res Lab, 43-45; asst, Carnegie Inst Technol, 46-47 & Mass Inst Technol, 47-49. *Honors & Awards:* Fairless Award, Am Inst Mining Engrs, 78. *Mem:* Am Inst Mining, Metall & Petrol Engrs; Int & Am Iron & Steel Inst; distinguished life mem Am Soc Metals. *Res:* Gases in steel; hardenability; quenching of steel; sinter; machinability; blast furnace and open hearth studies. *Mailing Add:* Wheeling-Pittsburgh Steel Corp 4 Gateway Ctr Pittsburgh PA 15230

CARNEY, DARRELL HOWARD, b Boise, Idaho, April 15, 48; m 71; c 2. CELL SURFACES, GROWTH CONTROL. *Educ:* Col Idaho, BS, 70; Univ Conn, PhD(develop biol), 75. *Prof Exp:* Res fel, Univ Calif, Irvine, 75-78; ASST PROF BIOCHEM, UNIV TEX MED BR, 78- *Concurrent Pos:* prin invest grant, 79-82, Res Career Develop Award, Nat Cancer Inst, 82-87. *Mem:* Am Soc Cell Biol; Sigma Xi. *Res:* Molecular events that lead to initiation of cell proliferation including characterization of the thrombin receptor, visualization of thrombin-receptor interactions, and determining the role of microtubules in these initiation events. *Mailing Add:* Div Biochem Univ Tex Med Br Galveston TX 77550

CARNEY, EDWARD J, b Rochester, NY, May 15, 29; m 51; c 5. STATISTICS, COMPUTER SCIENCES. *Educ:* Univ Rochester, AB, 51, MS, 58; Iowa State Univ, PhD(statist), 67. *Prof Exp:* Asst factory eng dept, Bausch & Lomb Optical Co, 54-58; staff asst area commun proj, Gen Dynamics Electronics, 58-59; instr indust eng, Iowa State Univ, 59-63, asst prof indust eng & statist, 63-67, assoc prof statist, 67-74, PROF COMPUT SCI & STATIST, UNIV RI, 74- *Mem:* Inst Math Statist; Am Statist Asn; Asn Comput Mach. *Res:* Design of experiments; variances of variance component estimates; statistical computations. *Mailing Add:* Comput Sci & Exp Statist Univ of RI Kingston RI 02881

CARNEY, GORDON C, b Glasgow, Scotland, Sept 15, 34; m 60; c 2. INVERTEBRATE PHYSIOLOGY. *Educ:* Univ Durham, BSc, 57, MSc, 60; Univ Minn, PhD(entom), 64. *Prof Exp:* Jr res officer, Atomic Energy Can, Ltd, 63-64, asst res officer, 64-66; asst prof biol, Bowling Green State Univ, 66-69; lectr biol, 69-74, SR LECTR CELL PHYSIOL, BRISTOL POLYTECH, 74- *Mem:* Marine Biological Asn UK. *Res:* Metabolism of invertebrate mitochondria; physiological effects of pollutants on aquatic invertebrates; binding of heavy metals by marine algae and its effect on primary production; dietary and environmental uptake of cadmium by daphnia. *Mailing Add:* Dept of Sci Bristol Polytechnic Bristol BS16 1QY England

CARNEY, JOHN FRANCIS, III, civil engineering, see previous edition

CARNEY, JOHN MICHAEL, b Chicago, Ill, Jan 27, 47; m 73; c 1. BEHAVIORAL PHARMACOLOGY. *Educ:* St Mary's Col, BS, 68; San Diego State Univ, MS, 70; Univ Mich, PhD(pharmacol), 76. *Prof Exp:* Teaching asst human anat, San Diego State Univ, 68-70 & neurophysiol, Univ Mich, 70-71; fel, Med Col Va, 76-78; ASST PROF PHARMACOL & ADJ ASST PROF PSYCHIAT, UNIV OKLA, 78- *Concurrent Pos:* Nat Inst Drug Abuse fel, 76-78; prin investr, Hoechst- Roussel Pharmaceut Inc, 78-80, consult, Frankfurt, 78-; prin investr, Nat Inst Drug Abuse grant, 78-81; mem, Int Study Group Invest Drugs as Reinforcers. *Mem:* Sigma Xi; Behav Pharmacol Soc. *Res:* Drug abuse; alcoholism; neurobiology of epilepsy; behavioral teratology; mental retardation and drugs. *Mailing Add:* Dept of Pharmacol Col of Med PO Box 26901 Oklahoma City OK 73190

CARNEY, RICHARD WILLIAM JAMES, b Novelty, Mo, June 19, 34; m 57; c 3. ORGANIC CHEMISTRY. *Educ:* McPherson Col, BS, 57; Iowa State Univ, MS, 61, PhD(org chem), 62. *Prof Exp:* Sr chemist, sr res chemist & sr staff chemist, 62-72, sr staff scientist process res, 72-75, MGR, CHEM DEVELOP RES, CIBA PHARMACEUT CO, 75- *Concurrent Pos:* Vis scientist, Basel, 68. *Mem:* Am Chem Soc; Am Inst Chem; NY Acad Sci. *Res:* Diterpenes; chemistry of heterocyclics. *Mailing Add:* Pharmaceut Div Ciba-Geigy Corp Summit NJ 07901

CARNEY, ROBERT GIBSON, b Ann Arbor, Mich, Apr 25, 14; m 39; c 4. DERMATOLOGY. *Educ:* Univ Mich, AB, 35, MD, 39. *Prof Exp:* Intern med, 39-40, resident dermat, 40-43, assoc, 46-47, from asst prof to assoc prof, 47-54, PROF DERMAT, UNIV IOWA HOSPS, 61- *Concurrent Pos:* Consult, Comt Rev, US Pharmacopeia, 50-; consult, Am Acad Dermat Adv Comt, Food & Drug Admin, 61- *Mem:* Am Acad Dermat; Soc Invest Dermat. *Res:* Topical therapy and pharmaceuticals; incontinentia pigmenti. *Mailing Add:* Dept of Dermat Univ of Iowa Hosp Iowa City IA 52240

CARNEY, ROBERT SPENCER, b Memphis, Tenn, Aug 9, 45. BIOLOGICAL OCEANOGRAPHY, MARINE BIOLOGY. *Educ:* Duke Univ, BS, 67; Tex A&M Univ, MS, 71; Ore State Univ, PhD(oceanog), 77. *Prof Exp:* Res asst biol oceanog, Ore State Univ, 71-76; res collabr, Smithsonian Inst, 76-77, res collabr, 77-81; asst prog dir biol, 78-80, PROG DIR BIOL OCEANOG, NSF, 80-81. *Mem:* Sigma Xi; AAAS. *Res:* Marine benthic ecology; quantitative analysis of ecological data; deep-sea community ecology; functional morphology of deep-sea animals; evolution and systematics of deep-sea holothurians and other echinoderms; radioactive waste disposal. *Mailing Add:* Biol Oceanog Prog 1800 G St NW Washington DC 20550

CARNEY, ROSE AGNES, b Chicago, Ill. PHYSICS. *Educ:* DePaul Univ, BS, 42, MS, 46; Ill Inst Technol, PhD, 61. *Prof Exp:* Asst metal labs, Univ Chicago, 42-43; instr, Army Spec Training Prog, De Paul, 43-44, instr physics, 44-46; chmn physics & math, St Xavier Col, Ill, 46-48; assoc prof physics, 48-59, PROF MATH & CHMN DEPT, ILL BENEDICTINE COL, 59-, CHMN DIV NATURAL SCI, 69- *Concurrent Pos:* Consult, Argonne Nat Lab, 62, 63, 64. *Mem:* Am Asn Physics Teachers; Math Asn Am. *Res:* Molecular spectroscopy; mathematical physics. *Mailing Add:* Dept of Math Ill Benedictine Col Lisle IL 60532

CARNEY, WILLIAM J, b Wheeling, WVa, Apr 12, 23; m 46; c 3. CHEMICAL ENGINEERING. *Educ:* WVa Univ, BSChE, 44, MSChE, 51, PhD(chem eng), 54. *Prof Exp:* Chemist, Paper Makers Chem Div, Exp Sta, Hercules Powder Co, Del, 46-47, tech serv engr, Paper Makers Chem Div, Mich, 47-49; res proj engr, Res Div, 53-60, sect head, 60-65, DEPT MGR, POLYESTER RES & DEVELOP DIV, GOODYEAR TIRE & RUBBER CO, 65- *Res:* Research engineering, process design and development and applied polymer chemistry in field of linear polyesters for textile and industrial fibers, plastic films, plastic containers, coatings and adhesives. *Mailing Add:* 1034 N Portage Path Akron OH 44313

CARNEY, WILLIAM PATRICK, b Dillon, Mont, July 1, 38; m 65; c 2. HELMINTHOLOGY, ZOONOTIC DISEASES. *Educ:* St Edwards Seminary, Kenmore, Wash, BA, 60; Western Mont Col, Dillon, BS, 62; Univ Mont, Missoula, PhD(zool), 67; Johns Hopkins Univ, MPH, 76. *Prof Exp:* Res assoc parasitol, Minot State Col, NDak, 67-69, Naval Med Res Inst, 69-70; res scientist parasitol, Naval Med Res Unit, Jakarta, 70-74 & Naval Med Res Inst, 74-75, Naval Med Res Unit, Taipei, 76-79; Officer-in-charge infectious dis, Naval Med Res Unit-Jakarta, 79-81; PROG MGR INFECTIOUS DIS, NAVAL MED RES & DEVELOP COMMAND, 81- *Concurrent Pos:* Ed assoc, Chinese J Microbiol, 76-79; vis assoc prof, Nat Taiwan Univ, 77-79; Nat Yang-Ming Med Col, 78-79; consult, Western Pac Region, WHO, 79. *Mem:* Am Soc Parasitologists; Am Micros Soc; Wildlife Dis Asn; Am Malocol Union. *Res:* Epidemiological investigations of tropical infectious diseases of man with emphasis of snail-transmitted diseases in Southeast Asia. *Mailing Add:* Naval Med Res & Develop Command Nat Naval Med Ctr Bethesda MD 20814

CARNIGLIA, STEPHEN C(HARLES), b San Francisco, Calif, Jan 15, 22; m 47; c 2. RESEARCH MANAGEMENT, RESEARCH ADMINISTRATION. *Educ:* Univ Calif, Berkeley, BS, 43, MS, 45, PhD(chem), 54. *Prof Exp:* Instr chem, Marin Col, 46-51; chemist, Radiation Lab, Univ Calif, 51-53 & Calif Res & Develop Co, 53; res dir inorg chem, Westvaco Mineral Prod Div, FMC Corp, 53-56; mgr mat & process res, Atomics Int Div, NAm Rockwell Corp, 56-68 & Rocketdyne Div, 68-70; MGR APPL CHEM RES & DEVELOP, KAISER ALUMINUM & CHEM CORP, 70- *Concurrent Pos:* Mem, Nat Acad Sci-Mat Adv Bd Comts Ceramics, 60-67. *Mem:* Am Catalysis Soc; fel Am Ceramic Soc; Am Ceramic Soc (vpres, 80-81). *Res:* Chemistry, physics and mechanics of materials, especially at high temperatures; inorganic chemical processes and reactions; catalysis. *Mailing Add:* 115 Wilshire Ct Danville CA 94526

CARNOW, BERTRAM WARREN, b Philadelphia, Pa, June 19, 22; m 75; c 6. ENVIRONMENTAL HEALTH, THORACIC DISEASES. *Educ:* NY Univ, BA, 47; Chicago Med Sch, MB & MD, 51. *Prof Exp:* Intern, Cook County Hosp, Chicago, 51-52; resident cardiol, Michael Reese Hosp, Chicago, 52-53, resident clin internal med, 53-55; physician pvt pract, 55-69; clin assoc, 64-65, asst clin prof, 65-67, from asst prof to assoc prof, 67-70, dir, Div Occupational Med, Cook County Hosp, 77-79, PROF PREV MED & COMMUNITY HEALTH, SCH MED, UNIV ILL, CHICAGO, 70-, PROF OCCUP & ENVIRON MED, SCH PUB HEALTH, 72-, DIR, OCCUPATIONAL SAFETY & HEALTH, EDUC RES CTR, 77- *Concurrent Pos:* Consult & attend physician, Michael Reese Hosp, 55-72 & Univ Ill Hosp, 70-; chest consult, Union Health Serv, 57-76; med dir, Chicago Lung Asn, 69-77; dir, Environ Health Resource Ctr, Ill Inst Environ Qual, 70-78; mem bd cert preventive med and occupational med; dir, Great Lakes Ctr Occupational Safety & Health, Univ Ill, 76- *Mem:* AAAS; Am Thoracic Soc; fel Am Pub Health Asn; fel Am Col Chest Physicians; fel Royal Soc Health. *Res:* Effects of environmental hazards on health, including air pollution morbidity and mortality; health and energy; occupational diseases including pneumoconiosis, metals, and noise. *Mailing Add:* Dept Prev Med Abraham Lincoln Sch Med Univ Ill Chicago IL 60680

CARNS, HARRY ROBERT, b Cedar Rapids, Iowa, Nov 17, 17; m 37; c 3. PLANT PHYSIOLOGY. *Educ:* Univ Iowa, BS, 39, MS, 41; Univ Calif, Los Angeles, PhD(bot), 51. *Prof Exp:* Plant physiologist, Cotton Field Sta, USDA & Delta Br Exp Sta, Miss, 50-57; plant physiologist, Dept Bot, Univ Calif, Los Angeles, 57-61; leader cotton physiol invests, Plant Indust Sta, USDA, 61-72, CHMN, PLANT PHYSIOL INST, BELTSVILLE AGR RES CTR, USDA, MD, 72- *Mem:* AAAS; Am Soc Plant Physiol; Am Inst Biol Sci; NY Acad Sci; Am Soc Photobiol. *Res:* Physiology of the cotton plant; plant growth regulators; foliar and fruit abscission; phytotoxicity of agricultural chemicals; defoliation; bioconversion to fuels. *Mailing Add:* Plant Physiol Inst USDA Beltsville Agr Res Ctr West Beltsville MD 20705

CARO, LUCIEN G, b Toulon, France, July 5, 28; US citizen; m 54; c 2. MOLECULAR BIOLOGY. *Educ:* Univ Tulane, BS, 57; Yale Univ, PhD(biophys), 59. *Prof Exp:* NSF fel & guest investr cell biol, Rockefeller Inst, 59-61; Helen Hay Whitney fel & res assoc, 61-64; biophysicist, Oak Ridge Nat Lab, 64-70; PROF MOLECULAR BIOL, UNIV GENEVA, 70- *Concurrent Pos:* NSF res grant, 64; vis investr, Inst Molecular Biol, Univ Geneva, Switz, 62-64. *Mem:* AAAS; Swiss Soc Cellular & Molecular Biol; Am Soc Microbiol; Swiss Soc Microbiol. *Res:* Control of DNA replication; plasmids; electron microscopy; autoradiography. *Mailing Add:* Dept Molecular Biol Univ Geneva 30 quai E Ansermet Geneva Switzerland

CAROFF, LAWRENCE JOHN, b Beaverdale, Pa, Aug 26, 41; c 3. ASTROPHYSICS. *Educ:* Swarthmore Col, BS, 62; Cornell Univ, PhD(appl physics), 67. *Prof Exp:* Res scientist astrophys, 67-81, ACTG DEP DIV CHIEF, SPACE SCI DIV, AMES RES CTR, NASA, 81- *Mem:* Int Astron Union; Am Astron Soc. *Res:* Theoretical research into nature of quasars and active galaxies; cosmology; galactic infrared sources; infrared observations from aircraft and ground observations of galactic H II regions, stars and planets. *Mailing Add:* Ames Res Ctr MS 245-1 NASA Moffett Field CA 94035

CAROL, BERNARD, b New York, NY; c 4. MATHEMATICAL STATISTICS, COMPUTERS. *Educ:* Columbia Univ, MA, 49. *Prof Exp:* Statistician, Metrop Life Ins Co, 49-61; biostatistician & dir comput ctr, NY Med Col, 61-68; biomathematician, Dept Biostatist, Montefiore Hosp & Med Ctr, 68-71; DIR BIOSTATIST, AYERST LABS, AM HOME PROD, 71- *Mem:* Inst Math Statist; Biomet Soc; Am Statist Asn; Asn Comput Mach; Opers Res Soc Am. *Res:* Mathematical statistics applied to medicine marketing, insurance, design of computer files, validation of aptitude tests, sampling company files, teaching with heavy use of computers. *Mailing Add:* Ayerst Labs 685 Third Ave New York NY 10017

CAROLIN, VALENTINE MOTT, JR, b Sayville, NY, Aug 23, 18; m 52; c 2. INSECT ECOLOGY. *Educ:* Syracuse Univ, BS, 39, MS, 42. *Prof Exp:* Scout, Bur Entom & Plant Quarantine, USDA, NJ, 39; survr, Radio Corp Am Commun, Inc, NY, 39-40; asst, State Univ NY Col Forestry, Syracuse Univ, 40-42; entomologist, Bur Entom & Plant Quarantine, USDA, 46-54, Pac Northwest Forest & Range Exp Sta, US Forest Serv, 54-74, supvry res entomologist, Pac Northwest Forest & Range Exp Sta, 74-76; CONSULT ENTOMOLOGIST, 77- *Mem:* Entom Soc Am; Soc Am Foresters; Entom Soc Can. *Res:* Biological control factors, especially parasites of forest insects; ecology of spruce budworm; western hemlock looper; techniques for field fumigation of European pine shoot moth; associated insects on western conifers. *Mailing Add:* 9030 SE Mill St Portland OR 97216

CAROME, EDWARD F, b Cleveland, Ohio, May 22, 27; m 51, 77; c 6. PHYSICS. *Educ:* John Carroll Univ, BS & MS, 51; Case Inst Technol, PhD(physics), 54. *Prof Exp:* From asst prof to prof physics, John Carroll Univ, 54-68; liaison scientist, London Br, Off Naval Res, 68-69; PROF PHYSICS, JOHN CARROLL UNIV, 69- *Concurrent Pos:* Sr res assoc, Hansen Labs Physics, Stanford Univ, 78-79. *Mem:* Fel Am Phys Soc; fel Acoust Soc Am; fel Brit Phys Soc; European Phys Soc. *Res:* Theoretical nuclear structure; theoretical and experimental studies of ultrasonic waveguides; absorption and dispersion of ultrasound in liquids; propagation of acoustic transients; laser induced effects in liquids and solids; acoustically induced effects in optical fibers. *Mailing Add:* Dept of Physics John Carroll Univ Cleveland OH 44118

CARON, AIMERY PIERRE, b Paris, France, Apr 20, 30; US citizen; m 56; c 1. PHYSICAL CHEMISTRY. *Educ:* Univ Calif, Los Angeles, BS, 55; Univ Southern Calif, MS, 58, PhD(crystallog chem), 62. *Prof Exp:* Lab asst, Univ Southern Calif, 55, US Air Force & Army fel, 62-63; mem res staff phys chem, Space Mat Lab, Northrop Corp, 63-66; asst prof chem, Univ Mass, 66-68; mgr, C & M Caron, Inc, VI, 68-69; admin officer, 69-73, asst to pres, 72-77, ASSOC PROF CHEM, COL VI, 73-, DIR COMMUNITY SERVS, 77- *Mem:* Am Crystallog Asn. *Res:* Determination of molecular structures by x-ray diffraction; inorganic syntheses; infrared spectroscopy; general physical chemistry; scientific computer programming. *Mailing Add:* Col of VI St Thomas VI 00801

CARON, DEWEY MAURICE, b North Adams, Mass, Dec 25, 42; m 65. ENTOMOLOGY, APICULTURE. *Educ:* Univ Vt, BS, 64; Univ Tenn, Knoxville, MS, 66; Cornell Univ, PhD(entom), 70. *Prof Exp:* Instr entom, Cornell Univ, 68, admin asst, Dept Entom, 69-70; asst prof apicult, Univ Md, 70-81, actg chmn entom, 80-81; CHMN ENTOM & APPL ECOL, UNIV DEL, 81- *Mem:* Entom Soc Am; Am Inst Biol Sci; Bee Res Asn. *Res:* Pollination ecology; biology and behavior of bees and wasps. *Mailing Add:* Dept Entom & Appl Ecol Univ Del Newark DE 19711

CARON, E(DGAR) LOUIS, b Chicago, Ill, July 31, 22; m 48; c 5. ORGANIC CHEMISTRY, INFORMATION SCIENCE. *Educ:* Tex A&M Univ, BSEE, 44; Bradley Univ, BS, 47; Univ Ill, MS, 48. *Prof Exp:* Res chemist, 48-66, SCI SYSTS ANALYST, UPJOHN CO, 66- *Mem:* Am Chem Soc; Drug Info Asn; Asn Comput Mach; Asn Syst Mgt; Am Inst Chem. *Res:* Large data base scientific and managerial information storage and retrieval computer systems. *Mailing Add:* Res & Develop Div Upjohn Co 301 Henrietta St Kalamazoo MI 49001

CARON, PAUL R(ONALD), b Fall River, Mass, July 14, 34; m 60; c 1. ELECTRICAL ENGINEERING, COMPUTER ENGINEERING. *Educ:* Bradford Durfee Col Tech, BSEE, 57; Brown Univ, MSc, 60, PhD(eng), 63. *Prof Exp:* Asst elec eng, Brown Univ, 57-63; mem tech staff, Plasma Res Lab, Aerospace Corp, 63-65; assoc prof elec eng, Southeastern Mass Tech Inst, 65-66; staff mem, Electronics Res Ctr, NASA, 66-70; assoc prof, 70-74, PROF ELEC ENG, SOUTHEASTERN MASS UNIV, 74- *Mem:* Inst Elec & Electronics Engrs. *Res:* Electromagnetic theory; antennas; micro processors. *Mailing Add:* Dept of Elec Eng Southeastern Mass Univ North Dartmouth MA 02747

CARON, RICHARD EDWARD, b Pawtucket, RI, April 7, 50. INTEGRATED PEST MANAGEMENT. *Educ:* Univ Maine, Orono, BS, 72, NC State Univ, Raleigh, MS, 76, PhD(entom), 81. *Prof Exp:* Res asst, NC State Unv, 76-78; ASST PROF ENTOM, AGR EXT SERV, UNIV TENN, 81- *Mem:* Sigma Xi; Entom Soc Am. *Res:* Corn earworm production on corn relative to survival factors; bollweevil diapause and longevity; effects of soil-applied pesticides; cultivar; planting date on soybean arthropods. *Mailing Add:* 605 Airways Blvd Jackson TN 38301

CARONE, FRANK, b New Kensington, Pa, Nov 28, 27; m 52; c 5. PATHOLOGY. *Educ:* WVa Univ, AB, 48; Yale Univ, MD, 52. *Prof Exp:* Instr, Sch Med, Yale Univ, 59-60; from asst prof to prof, 60-69, MORRISON PROF PATH & DEP CHMN DEPT, SCH MED, NORTHWESTERN UNIV, CHICAGO, 69- *Concurrent Pos:* Life Inst Med Res Fund res fel, 57-59; Markle scholar, 64-69; dir labs, Northwestern Mem Hosp, Chicago, 61- *Mem:* Am Fedn Clin Res; Int Acad Path; Am Soc Exp Path. *Res:* Renal pathophysiology employing micropuncture techniques; light and electron microscopic study of human renal disease. *Mailing Add:* Dept of Path Northwestern Univ Med Sch Chicago IL 60611

CAROSELLI, REMUS FRANCIS, b Providence, RI, Oct 4, 16; m 48; c 3. TEXTILE CHEMISTRY. *Educ:* Univ RI, BS, 37. *Prof Exp:* Process control technologist, Ashton Plant, Owens-Corning Fiberglas Corp, 41-46, chief chemist, 46-48, proj mgr textile res, 48-50, asst res mgr, 50-57, lab mgr textile process & prod develop, 57-60, mgr textile prod develop lab, 60-73; PRES, R F CAROSELLI PROD DEVELOP SERV, 74- *Concurrent Pos:* Mem res adv bd, Textile Inst, Princeton Univ. *Mem:* Am Chem Soc; Asn Textile Chemists & Colorists. *Res:* Textiles, plastics, coatings and research and development organization. *Mailing Add:* 230 Colonel John Gardner Rd Narragansett RI 02882

CAROTHERS, STEVEN WARREN, b Prescott, Ariz, Dec 19, 43; m; c 3. ECOLOGY. *Educ:* Northern Ariz Univ, BS, 66, MS, 69; Univ Ill, Urbana, PhD(ecol), 74. *Prof Exp:* Asst ornithologist, Mus Northern Ariz, 66-67; teaching asst biol, Northern Ariz Univ, 67-68; asst cur zool, Mus Northern Ariz, 69-70; instr ornith, Northern Ariz Univ, 70; teaching asst biol, Univ Ill, 70-71; cur zool, 71-74, RES ECOLOGIST, MUS NORTHERN ARIZ, 74- *Concurrent Pos:* Artist in Residence, Univ Ill, 79; instr, Dept Environ Sci, Univ Va; pvt consult fed burro problems, Dept Navy. *Mem:* Am Ornithologists Union; Am Soc Mammalogists; Cooper Ornith Soc; Wilson Ornith Soc. *Res:* Work with federal agencies and private institutions at designing proper land-use management plans particularly those affecting non-game wildlife. *Mailing Add:* Mus of Northern Ariz Colton Res Ctr Flagstaff AZ 86001

CAROTHERS, ZANE BLAND, b Philadelphia, Pa, Nov 7, 24; m 52; c 2. BOTANY. *Educ:* Temple Univ, BS, 50, MEd, 52; Univ Michigan, PhD(bot), 58. *Prof Exp:* Instr bot, Univ Ky, 57-59; from asst prof to assoc prof, 59-76, assoc head dept, 70-72, PROF BOT, UNIV ILL, URBANA-CHAMPAIGN, 76- *Mem:* Brit Bryol Soc; Bot Soc Am; Am Bryol & Lichenol Soc; Electron Microscope Soc Am; Int Soc Plant Morphologists. *Res:* Ultrastructure of gametogenesis in bryophytes and nonvascular plants; anatomy of vascular plants. *Mailing Add:* Dept of Bot Univ of Ill Urbana-Champaign Urbana IL 61801

CAROVILLANO, ROBERT L, b Newark, NJ, Aug 2, 32; m 52; c 3. SPACE PHYSICS, ASTROPHYSICS. *Educ:* Rutgers Univ, AB, 54; Ind Univ, PhD(physics), 59. *Prof Exp:* From asst prof to assoc prof, 59-67, PROF PHYSICS, BOSTON COL, 67-, CHMN DEPT, 69- *Concurrent Pos:* Vis fac, Mass Inst Technol, 67-68; assoc ed, Cosmic Electrodynamics, 69-72 & Rev Geophys-Space Physics, 75-78. *Mem:* AAAS; Am Phys Soc; Am Geophys Union (secy magnetospheric sect, 70-76); Am Asn Physics Teachers; NY Acad Sci. *Res:* Theoretical studies on the solar wind, the magnetosphere, the ionosphere and auroras; plasma physics. *Mailing Add:* Dept of Physics Boston Col Chestnut Hill MA 02167

CAROW, JOHN, b Ladysmith, Wis, Aug 26, 13; m 42; c 2. FORESTRY. *Educ:* Univ Mich, BSF, 37, MF, 38. *Prof Exp:* Field asst forest surv, Appalachian Forestry Exp Sta, 37-38, jr forester, 39-42; forest statistician, Am Paper & Pulp Asn, 38-39; shelterbelt asst, US Forest Serv, 39; res forester, Southeastern Forestry Exp Sta, 42-46; from instr to prof, 47-78, EMER PROF FOREST MGT, UNIV MICH, 78- *Mem:* Fel Am Foresters. *Res:* Forest mensuration, inventory techniques, logging cost analysis; forest management. *Mailing Add:* Sch Natural Resources Univ of Mich Ann Arbor MI 48109

CAROZZI, ALBERT VICTOR, b Geneva, Switz, Apr 26, 25; nat US; m 49; c 2. GEOLOGY. *Educ:* Univ Geneva, MS, 47, DSc(geol mineral), 48. *Prof Exp:* Lectr spec geol, Univ Geneva, 48-53, asst prof geol, Univ Ill, Urbana-Champaign, 57-59, assoc mem, Ctr Advan Study, 69-70, prof geol, 59-80; RETIRED. *Concurrent Pos:* Asst vis prof, Univ Ill, 55-56; Am Asn Petrol Geol distinguished lectr, 59; adv, Govt Ivory Coast, Africa, 60-; corresp mem, Int Comt Hist of Geol Sci, 68-; consult adv, Petroleo Brasileiro SAm, Brazil, 69- & Philippine Oil Develop Co, Manila, 70- *Honors & Awards:* Davy Award, Univ Geneva, 49, 54; Plantamour-Prevost Award, 55. *Mem:* Fel Geol Soc Am; Am Asn Petrol Geol; Soc Econ Paleont & Mineral; Hist Sci Soc. *Res:* Sedimentary petrology, such as models of deposition of carbonate rocks and sandstones, experimental studies on porosity in carbonate rocks; history of geology; oil exploration. *Mailing Add:* Dept of Geol 254 Nat Hist Bldg Univ of Ill Urbana-Champaign Urbana IL 61801

CARP, GERALD, b New York, NY, Aug 20, 24; m 48; c 2. ELECTRONIC ENGINEERING, PHYSICS. *Educ:* City Col New York, BEE, 48; Polytech Inst Brooklyn, MSEE, 60. *Prof Exp:* Instr elec eng, City Col New York, 48-50; chief weapons effects nuclear weapons, US Army Res & Develop Lab, 50-60; mgr radiation effects opers, Gen Elec Co, 60-66; dir adv develop educ tech, Gen Learning Corp, 66-67; consult info syst, Gen Elec Co, 67-68; group leader sensor-tech, Mitre Corp, 68-74; chief appl technol, Drug Enforcement Admin, 74-76; chief aviation sect res & develop, Fed Aviation Admin, 76-81; MEM DIV STAFF, MITRE CORP, 81- *Honors & Awards:* Inventors Award, Gen Elec Co, 65. *Mem:* Sigma Xi; Inst Elec & Electronics Engrs. *Res:* Application of nuclear techniques; gamma and neutron interactions; image analysis, pattern recognition to detection of bulk explosives; sensor technology. *Mailing Add:* 8613 Fox Run Potomac MD 20854

CARP, RICHARD IRVIN, b Philadelphia, Pa, May 10, 34; m 60; c 1. MICROBIOLOGY, VIROLOGY. *Educ:* Univ Pa, BA, 55, VMD, 58, PhD(microbiol), 62. *Prof Exp:* Asst virol, Wistar Inst, 58-62, fel, 62-63; virol res dir, Alembic Chem Co, India, 63-64; assoc, Wistar Inst, 64-68; MEM STAFF, INST BASIC RES MENT RETARDATION, 68-; PROF MICROBIOL, STATE UNIV NY DOWNSTATE MED CTR, 77- *Concurrent Pos:* Vis prof, Div Biochem Virol, Col Med, Baylor Univ, 66-; adj prof, City Univ New York, 69- *Mem:* Am Soc Microbiol. *Res:* Slow infections of the central nervous system with particular interest in scrapie and the search for the causes of multiple sclerosis and amyotrophic lateral sclerosis; viruses that cause birth defects and mental retardation, such as the cytomegaloviruses. *Mailing Add:* Inst Basic Res Ment Retardation 1050 Forest Hill Rd Staten Island NY 10314

CARPELAN, LARS HJALMAR, b Calif, June 9, 13; m 54; c 3. ECOLOGY. *Educ:* San Jose State Univ, AB, 34; Stanford Univ, PhD, 53. *Prof Exp:* Res assoc algal physiol, Hopkins Marine Sta, Stanford Univ, 53-54; res assoc zoo-fisheries, Univ Calif, Los Angeles, 54-56; from asst prof to assoc prof, 56-71, PROF BIOL, UNIV CALIF, RIVERSIDE, 71- *Mem:* Ecol Soc Am; Am Soc Limnol & Oceanog. *Res:* Aquatic biology; brackish waters. *Mailing Add:* Dept of Biol Univ of Calif Riverside CA 92507

CARPENTER, ADELAIDE TROWBRIDGE CLARK, b Athens, Ga, June 24, 44. GENETICS. *Educ:* NC State Univ, BS, 66; Univ Wash, MS, 69, PhD(genetics), 72. *Prof Exp:* NIH fel cytogenetics, Univ Wis-Madison, 72-74; res assoc, Dept Anat, Duke Univ, 74-75, asst adj prof, 75-76, asst med res prof, 76; asst prof cytogenetics, 76-79, ASSOC PROF BIOL, UNIV CALIF, SAN DIEGO, 79- *Concurrent Pos:* assoc ed, Genetics, 80- *Mem:* Genetics Soc Am; Am Soc Naturalists; Am Soc Cell Biol; AAAS. *Res:* Analysis of meiotic mutants in Drosophila melanogaster females, particularly recombination-defectives, by electron microscopy and effects on somatic crossing-over and chromosome maintenance. *Mailing Add:* Dept Biol B-022 Univ Calif San Diego La Jolla CA 92093

CARPENTER, ALDEN B, b Newton, Mass, Feb 24, 36; m 61; c 2. GEOCHEMISTRY. *Educ:* Harvard Univ, AB, 57, PhD(geol), 63. *Prof Exp:* From asst prof to assoc prof geol, 63-73, prof geol, Univ Mo-Columbia, 73-81; SR RES ASSOC, CHEVRON OIL FIELD RES CO, LA HABRA, CALIF, 81- *Mem:* Mineral Soc Am; Mineral Asn Can; Geochem Soc; Soc Econ Paleontologists & Mineralogists; Am Asn Petrol Geologists. *Res:* Geochemistry of subsurface waters; diagenesis of sandstones and carbonate rocks. *Mailing Add:* Chevron Oil Field Res Co Box 446 La Habra CA 90631

CARPENTER, ANNA-MARY, b Ambridge, Pa, Jan 14, 16. ANATOMY. *Educ:* Geneva Col, AB, 36; Univ Pittsburgh, MS, 37, PhD(microtech), 40; Univ Minn, MD, 58. *Hon Degrees:* DSc, Geneva Col, 68. *Prof Exp:* Asst, Univ Pittsburgh, 38-40; instr lab tech, Moravian Col Women, 41-42; chmn biol curricula, Scranton-Keystone Jr Col, 42-44; res assoc path dept, Children's Hosp, Pittsburgh, 44-53; lectr mycol, Sch Med, Univ Pittsburgh, 46-53 & Western Reserve Univ, 53-54; from instr to assoc prof, 54-65, PROF ANAT, SCH MED, UNIV MINN, MINNEAPOLIS, 65- *Mem:* AAAS; Histochem Soc (secy, 74-75, treas, 75-79, pres, 80-81); Am Asn Anat; Int Soc Human & Animal Mycol; Int Soc Stereology (secy-treas, 72-). *Res:* Mycology; histochemistry; quantitation; diabetes. *Mailing Add:* 153 Orlin Ave SE Minneapolis MN 55414

CARPENTER, BARRY KEITH, b Hastings, Eng, Feb 13, 49; m 74. ORGANIC CHEMISTRY, ORGANOMETALLIC CHEMISTRY. *Educ:* Warwick Univ, BSc, 70; Univ Col, Univ London, PhD(chem), 73. *Prof Exp:* NATO fel, Yale Univ, 73-75; asst prof, 75-81, ASSOC PROF CHEM, CORNELL UNIV, 81- *Concurrent Pos:* Mem, A P Sloan Found, 80-82. *Mem:* Royal Soc Chem; Am Chem Soc. *Res:* Mechanistic organic and mechanistic organometallic chemistry. *Mailing Add:* Dept of Chem Cornell Univ Ithaca NY 14853

CARPENTER, BENJAMIN H(ARRISON), b Buckhannon, WVa, Apr 5, 21; m 41; c 3. CHEMICAL ENGINEERING, POLLUTION CONTROL. *Educ:* WVa Wesleyan Col, BS, 41; WVa Univ, MS, 61. *Prof Exp:* Res chemist, Union Carbide Corp, 48, mgr qual control systs, 49-53, group leader eng statist, 54-63, eng consult chem div, 64-69; SR ENGR STATIST RES DIV, RES TRIANGLE INST, 69-, HEAD INDUST PROCESS STUDIES SECT, 77- *Mem:* Am Chem Soc; Am Statist Asn; Am Soc Qual Control; Air Pollution Control Asn; Am Iron & Steel Inst. *Res:* Quality of life research; new industrial processes; energy efficient processes; industrial pollution control; environmental assessment of industrial processes. *Mailing Add:* 1220 Huntsman Dr Durham NC 27713

CARPENTER, BRUCE H, b Rapid City, SDak, Feb 5, 32; m 52, 75; c 2. PLANT PHYSIOLOGY. *Educ:* Calif State Col, Long Beach, AB, 57, MA, 58; Univ Calif, Los Angeles, PhD(bot), 62. *Prof Exp:* Instr biol, 57-59, from asst prof to prof, Calif State Univ, Long Beach, 62-75, chmn dept, 67-72, assoc vpres acad affairs-acad personnel, 72-75; PROVOST & ACAD V PRES, WESTERN ILL UNIV, 75- *Concurrent Pos:* Nat Sci Found res grant, 63- *Mem:* AAAS; NY Acad Sci; Am Soc Plant Physiol. *Res:* Plant photoperiodism and Circadian rhythms. *Mailing Add:* Western Ill Univ Macomb IL 61455

CARPENTER, C(LIFFORD) LEROY, b New York, NY, Apr 25, 15; m 56; c 2. CHEMICAL ENGINEERING, ENVIRONMENTAL PROTECTION. *Educ:* Columbia Univ, AB, 37, AM, 40, BS, 41; Polytech Inst Brooklyn, DChE, 51. *Prof Exp:* Chemist, Columbia Univ, 41-42; chemist & chem engr, Esso Labs, Standard Oil Co, 42-45; asst, Dept Chem, Columbia Univ, 46-47; sr proj engr res & develop, Colgate-Palmolive- Peet Co, 48-49, group leader process develop synthetic detergents, 49-52; head process & eng, Develop Sect, Chem Develop Dept, W R Grace & Co, 52-53, head process eng, Grace Chem Co, 53-54; vpres & tech dir, Summers Fertilizer Co Inc & Northern Chem Industs Inc 54-57; head process design & econ new prods, Res Dept, Cabot Corp, 57-62, assoc dir titania, 62-64; consult, 64-65; head process eng & econ eval, Abcor, Inc, 65-67; mgr advan study & proj anal, Ledgemont Lab, Kennecott Copper Corp, 67-69, prog mgr, 69-70, consult & admin asst, 70-71; dir develop, Koch Eng Co, Inc, 71-73; MANAGING DIR, ASSOC PROF, INC, 73- *Mem:* Am Chem Soc; Am Inst Chem Engrs. *Res:* Hydrogenation; hydroforming; Fischer-Tropsch type synthesis; entrainment separation; extraction; synthetic detergents; ammonia and urea; synthesis gas; polyofins; chloride route silica and titania pigments; coal conversion; multicomponent separations. *Mailing Add:* 4921 Elmwood Pkwy Metairie LA 70003

CARPENTER, CAROLYN VIRUS, b Chicago, Ill, Jan 1, 40; m 64; c 3. BIOCHEMISTRY, MICROBIOLOGY. *Educ:* Univ Ill, Urbana, BS, 63; Univ Ill, Chicago Med Ctr, PhD(biochem), 68. *Prof Exp:* Fel biochem, 68-75, res assoc biochem & molecular biol, Northwestern Univ, 75-76; RES SCIENTIST, WEYERHAEUSER CO, 76- *Mem:* Am Chem Soc. *Res:* Mechanism of action of anti-metabolites; specificity profiles of the enzymes involved in cell wall biosynthesis in bacteria; symbiotic nitrogen fixation in non-legumes. *Mailing Add:* 16463 6th Ave SW Seattle WA 98166

CARPENTER, CHARLES, b Newark, NJ, July 17, 08; m 36; c 3. CHEMISTRY. *Educ:* Syracuse Univ, BS, 29, MS, 31; Darmstadt Tech Univ, Dr Ing, 33. *Prof Exp:* Asst chem, Carnegie Inst Technol, 34-36; chief chemist, asst dir & tech dir, Herty Found Lab, 36-39; tech dir & gen supt, Southland Paper Mills, 39-47; asst to vpres, NY & Pa County, 47-50; vpres, White Star Paper Co, 51; CONSULT, 52- *Mem:* Soc Am Foresters; Tech Asn Pulp & Paper Indust. *Res:* Cellulose, wood and pulp chemistry. *Mailing Add:* 2345 Wildwood Dr Montgomery AL 36111

CARPENTER, CHARLES C J, b Savannah, Ga, Jan 5, 31; m 58; c 3. INFECTIOUS DISEASE. *Educ:* Princeton Univ, AB, 52; Johns Hopkins Univ, MD, 56. *Prof Exp:* From asst prof to prof med, Johns Hopkins Univ, 62-73; CHMN, DEPT MED, CASE WESTERN RESERVE UNIV, 73-; PHYSICIAN-IN-CHIEF, UNIV HOSPS CLEVELAND, 73- *Concurrent Pos:* Res career develop award, Johns Hopkins Univ, 64-69; mem US deleg, US-Japan Coop Med Sci Prog, 65-, chmn cholera panel, 66-73; mem cholera adv comt, NIH, 66-73; mem expert adv panel bact dis, WHO, 67-; trustee, Int Ctr Infectious Dis Res, Bangladesh, 79-; mem exec comt, Bd Sci & Technol Int Develop, Inst Med-Nat Acad Sci, 81-83; chmn elect, Am Bd Internal Med, 82-83. *Mem:* Am Soc Clin Invest; Infectious Dis Soc Am; Asn Profs Med; Asn Am Physicians (secy, 76-80). *Res:* Defining the pathophysiology, immunology and optimal means of treating cholera and other dehydrating diarrheal diseases. *Mailing Add:* Dept Med Univ Hosps Adelbert Rd Cleveland OH 44106

CARPENTER, CHARLES CONGDEN, b Denison, Iowa, June 2, 21; m 47; c 3. ZOOLOGY, BEHAVIOR ETHOLOGY. *Educ:* Univ Northern Mich, BA, 43; Univ Mich, MS, 47, PhD(zool), 51. *Prof Exp:* Instr zool, Univ Mich, 51-52 & Wayne State Univ, 52; from instr to assoc prof, 53-66, PROF ZOOL, UNIV OKLA, 66-, CUR REPTILES, MUS ZOOL, 54- *Concurrent Pos:* NY Zool Soc grant-in-aid, Jackson Hole Res Sta, 51; NSF grant, 56-75; treas, Grassland Res Found, 58-62; mem, Galapagos Int Sci Proj, 64; mem, Sci Adv Comt, Charles Darwin Found for Galapagos Islands. *Mem:* Am Soc Zoologists; Ecol Soc Am; Am Soc Ichthyologists & Herpetologists; Am Soc Mammal; fel Animal Behav Soc (secy, 65-68). *Res:* Ecology and behavior of vertebrates; herpetology; dynamics of populations and space relationships of reptiles and amphibians; comparative ecology and behavior. *Mailing Add:* Dept of Zool Univ of Okla Norman OK 73019

CARPENTER, CHARLES PATTEN, b Sellersville, Pa, July 5, 10; m 34; c 2. TOXICOLOGY, BACTERIOLOGY. *Educ:* Franklin & Marshall Col, BS, 31; Univ Pa, AM, 34, PhD(med sci), 37. *Prof Exp:* Instr bact, Hyg Dept, Med Sch, Univ Pa, 36-39, asst prof pub health & prev med, Lab, 39-40; Union Carbide indust fel, Mellon Inst, 40-46, sr fel, 46-56, from asst admin fel to admin fel, 56-75, ADV FEL, CARNEGIE-MELLON UNIV, MELLON INST RES, 75- *Mem:* AAAS; Am Chem Soc; Am Soc Toxicol; Am Indust Hyg Asn. *Res:* Toxicity of synthetic organic chemicals; industrial hygiene. *Mailing Add:* Carnegie-Mellon Univ 4400 5th Ave Pittsburgh PA 15213

CARPENTER, DAVID FRANCIS, b Springfield, Mass, Dec 24, 45; m 68; c 2. MICROBIAL PHYSIOLOGY. *Educ:* Univ Vt, BA, 67; Univ NH, PhD(microbiol), 71. *Prof Exp:* Nat Acad Sci-Nat Res Coun assoc, Washington, DC, 71-73; res microbiologist, Food Sci Lab, US Army Natick Develop Ctr, 73-77; MGR MICROBIOL RES & DEVELOP, TRAVENOL LABS, INC, 77- *Mem:* Am Soc Microbiol; Soc Indust Microbiol; Sigma Xi; Am Chem Soc. *Res:* Microbiology research and development on medical devices and health care specialties. *Mailing Add:* Travenol Labs 6301 Lincoln Ave Morton Grove IL 60053

CARPENTER, DAVID O, b Fairmont, Minn, Jan 27, 37; m 61; c 2. NEUROPHYSIOLOGY, BIOPHYSICS. *Educ:* Harvard Univ, BA, 59, MD, 64. *Prof Exp:* Med officer neurophysiol, Lab Neurophysiol, NIMH, 65-72; chmn, Neurol Dept, Armed Fores Radiobiol Res Inst, 73-80; DIR, CTR LABS & RES, NY STATE DEPT HEALTH, 80- *Concurrent Pos:* Fel neurophysiol, Sch Med, Harvard Univ, 64-65. *Mem:* Am Physiol Soc; Soc Gen Physiol; Soc Neurosci; Int Brain Res Orgn; Am Pub Health Asn. *Res:* Electrogenic sodium pumps in Aplysia neurons; neurotransmitter substances in Aplysia and mammalian nervous systems; ionic basis of action potentials in invertebrate neurons; significance of cell size in spinal motor neurons; supraspinal control mechanisms. *Mailing Add:* Ctr Labs & Res NY State Dept Health Albany NY 12201

CARPENTER, DELMA RAE, JR, b Salem, Va, Apr 15, 28; m 52; c 3. PHYSICS ENGINEERING. *Educ:* Roanoke Col, BS, 49; Cornell Univ, MS, 51; Univ Va, PhD(physics), 57. *Prof Exp:* Instr physics, 51-53, from asst prof to assoc prof, 56-62, proj dir res labs, 60-68, dep dir, 63-65, head dept physics, 69-74, PROF PHYSICS, VA MIL INST, 63-, DIR RES LABS, 65- *Concurrent Pos:* Res assoc, US Army Ord Contract, 53, 54, 56 & 60; consult, US Army Res Off, 71-75; chmn, Sci Mus Va, 73-78, chmn bd trustees, 73- *Mem:* Fel AAAS; Am Asn Physics Teachers; Soc Res Adminr. *Res:* Ordnance development and design; heat transfer in satellite instruments; physics teaching demonstrations. *Mailing Add:* Dept of Physics Va Mil Inst Lexington VA 24450

CARPENTER, DEWEY KENNETH, b Omaha, Nebr, June 30, 28; m 55; c 3. PHYSICAL CHEMISTRY, POLYMER CHEMISTRY. *Educ:* Syracuse Univ, BS, 50; Duke Univ, AM, 52, PhD(chem), 55. *Prof Exp:* Res assoc chem, Cornell Univ, 55-56; res assoc & instr, Duke Univ, 56-58; from asst prof to assoc prof chem, Ga Inst Technol, 58-69; assoc prof, 69-74, PROF CHEM, LA STATE UNIV, BATON ROUGE, 74- *Concurrent Pos:* Vis fel, Dartmouth Col, 67-68 & Stanford Univ, 76. *Mem:* Am Chem Soc; Am Sci Affil; Sigma Xi; Biophys Soc; Am Crystallog Asn. *Res:* Physical chemistry of high polymers; physical chemistry of macromolecules in solution. *Mailing Add:* Dept Chem La State Univ Baton Rouge LA 70803

CARPENTER, DOROTHY IRENE, b South Bend, Ind, Aug 12, 15. MATHEMATICS. *Educ:* Ashland Col, AB, 37; Univ Mich, MA, 44. *Prof Exp:* Instr math, Denison Univ, 46-53; assoc prof math, 53-80, chmn dept, 70-80, EMER PROF MATH, ASHLAND COL, 80- *Mem:* Nat Coun Teachers Math; Math Asn Am. *Res:* History of mathematics. *Mailing Add:* 407 Claremont Ave Ashland OH 44805

CARPENTER, DWIGHT WILLIAM, b Paducah, Ky, July 25, 36; m 58; c 3. PHYSICS. *Educ:* Univ Ky, BS, 58; Univ Ill, Urbana-Champaign, MS, 59, PhD(physics), 65. *Prof Exp:* Res assoc physics, Univ Ill, Urbana-Champaign, 64-66; asst prof, Duke Univ, 66-72; PROF MATH & PHYSICS & CHMN DIV SCI & MATH, LIMESTONE COL, 72- *Mem:* Asn Comput Mach; Am Phys Soc; Am Asn Physics Teachers; Math Asn Am. *Res:* Elementary particle physics. *Mailing Add:* Div of Sci & Math Limestone College Gaffney SC 29340

CARPENTER, EDWARD J, b Buffalo, NY, Mar 28, 42; m 67; c 2. BIOLOGICAL OCEANOGRAPHY. *Educ:* State Univ NY Col Fredonia, BS, 64; NC State Univ, MS, 67, PhD(zool), 70. *Prof Exp:* NSF fel biol oceanog, Woods Hole Oceanog Inst, 70-71, from asst scientist to assoc scientist, 71-75; ASSOC PROF BIOL, STATE UNIV NY STONY BROOK, 75- *Concurrent Pos:* Mem, US-USSR Comt Ocean Pollution, 73-; US-Japanese joint res prog, 79- *Mem:* Am Soc Limnol & Oceanog; Estuarine Res Fedn; Sigma Xi; Phycol Soc Am. *Res:* Nitrogen cycling in marine environment; physiology of nitrogen incorporation by algae; denitrification and nitrogen fixation; entrainment of plankton through coastal power plants; effects of pollutants on microorganisms. *Mailing Add:* Marine Sci Res Ctr State Univ of NY Stony Brook NY 11794

CARPENTER, EDWIN DAVID, b Great Falls, Mont, Aug 3, 32. ORNAMENTAL HORTICULTURE. *Educ:* Wash State Univ, BS, 57; Mich State Univ, MS, 62, PhD(hort), 64. *Prof Exp:* Sr exp aide, Coastal Wash Res & Exten Unit, Wash State Univ, 57-60; from asst prof to assoc prof, 64-67, PROF ORNAMENTAL HORT, UNIV CONN, 77-, CHMN HORT SECT, DEPT PLANT SCI, 71- *Concurrent Pos:* Mem, Northeast Regional Tech Comn, Plant Hort Introd, USDA, 65-, chmn, 72-79. *Mem:* Am Soc Hort Sci; Am Hort Soc; Int Plant Propagators Soc; Am Soc Bot Gardens & Arboretums; Int Soc Hort Sci. *Res:* Plant anatomy, taxonomy and ecology. *Mailing Add:* Dept of Plant Sci Univ of Conn Storrs CT 06268

CARPENTER, ESTHER, b Meriden, Conn, June 4, 03. ZOOLOGY. *Educ:* Ohio Wesleyan Univ, AB, 25, Univ Wis, MS, 27; Yale Univ, PhD(zool), 32. *Hon Degrees:* DSc, Ohio Wesleyan Univ, 56. *Prof Exp:* Asst zool, Univ Wis, 25-27; lab technician, Yale Univ, 28-29; lab technician biol, Albertus Magnus Col, 30-32; lab technician, Dept Embryol, Carnegie Inst, 32-33; lab technician, 33-34, from instr to prof, 34-63, Myra MSampson prof, 63-68, EMER PROF ZOOL, SMITH COL, 68- *Concurrent Pos:* Instr, Albertus Magnus Col, 33-34; Howald Scholar, Ohio State Univ, 42-43; res, Strangeways Res Lab, Eng, 53-54, 61; Sophia Smith fel, 73-80. *Mem:* AAAS; Am Soc Cell Biol; Am Soc Zool; Soc Develop Biol; Am Asn Anat. *Res:* Experimental embryology; vital staining and transplantation in amphibia; regeneration in Eisenia foetida; tissue culture-differentiation of avian thyroid and femora; differentiation and physiological activities of embryonic thyroid glands in vitro; age changes in rat pituitary. *Mailing Add:* 55 Prospect St Northampton MA 01060

CARPENTER, FRANCES LYNN, b Oklahoma City, Okla, Feb 14, 44. ECOLOGY, EVOLUTION. *Educ:* Univ Calif, Riverside, BA, 66; Univ Calif, Berkeley, PhD(zool), 72. *Prof Exp:* ASSOC PROF ECOL, UNIV CALIF, IRVINE, 72- *Concurrent Pos:* NSF res grants, 78-80 & 81-83. *Mem:* Ecol Soc Am; Am Soc Naturalists; Soc Study Evolution; Cooper Ornith Soc; Am Ornithologists Union. *Res:* Energetics of plant-pollinator coevolved relationships; pollination strategies; behavior and resource partitioning in avian nectar-eaters; territoriality; comparison of generalist and specialist adaptive strategies in plants, birds, insects. *Mailing Add:* Dept of Ecol & Evolutionary Biol Univ of Calif Irvine CA 92717

CARPENTER, FRANK G(ILBERT), b Washington, DC, Mar 26, 20; m 45; c 6. CHEMICAL ENGINEERING. *Educ:* Univ Md, BS, 42; Univ Del, MChE, 46, PhD(chem eng), 49. *Prof Exp:* Res assoc, Nat Bur Stand, 49-63; dir cane sugar ref res proj, 63-81, RES LEADER SUGAR PROCESSING, SOUTHERN REGIONAL LAB, USDA, 81- *Honors & Awards:* Award, Sugar Indust Technologists, 75. *Mem:* Am Chem Soc; Sugar Indust Technologists; AAAS; Inst Food Tech; Asn Off Anal Chemists. *Res:* Sugar refining research; fluid flow; colorimetry; turbidimetry; adsorption; chromatography; surfaces. *Mailing Add:* 29 Crane St New Orleans LA 70124

CARPENTER, FRANK GRANT, b Toledo, Ohio, Oct 8, 23; m 51; c 2. PHYSIOLOGY. *Educ:* Ohio State Univ, BSc, 48; Columbia Univ, PhD, 51. *Prof Exp:* Asst physiol, Ohio State Univ, 48 & Columbia Univ, 49-51; instr, Univ Rochester, 52-54; asst prof, Med Col, Cornell Univ, 54-57; from asst prof to assoc prof, Dartmouth Med Sch, 57-67; assoc prof, 67-71, PROF PHARMACOL, UNIV ALA, BIRMINGHAM, 71-, PROF ANESTHESIOL, 73- *Concurrent Pos:* Fel, Univ Rochester, 51-54. *Mem:* Am Physiol Soc; Harvey Soc; Am Soc Pharmacol & Exp Therapeut. *Res:* Anesthesia; nerve metabolism; autonomic neuroeffectors. *Mailing Add:* Dept of Pharmacol Univ of Ala Birmingham AL 35294

CARPENTER, FRANK MORTON, b Boston, Mass, Sept 6, 02. ENTOMOLOGY. *Educ:* Harvard Univ, AB, 26, MS, 27, ScD, 29. *Prof Exp:* Nat Res Coun fel zool, 28-31, assoc entom, 31-32, from asst prof to prof, 36-39, chmn dept, 53-59, prof entom & Agassiz prof zool, 36-69, Fisher Prof natural hist, 69-72, asst cur invert paleont, Mus Comp Zool, 32-36, cur fossil insects, 36-72, EMER FISHER PROF NATURAL HIST, EMER AGASSIZ PROF ZOOL, HARVARD UNIV & HON CUR FOSSIL INSECTS, MUS COMP ZOOL, 72- *Concurrent Pos:* Assoc, Carnegie Inst, 31-32; ed, Psyche, 46- *Honors & Awards:* Paleont Soc Medal, 75. *Mem:* Fel Am Acad Arts & Sci. *Res:* Paleoentomology and insect evolution; North American Neuroptera; Permian insects of Kansas and Oklahoma; Carboniferous insects of North America and Europe. *Mailing Add:* Biol Labs Harvard Univ Cambridge MA 02138

CARPENTER, FREDERICK DONALD, b San Diego, Calif, Aug 11, 27; m 51; c 3. NUCLEAR ENGINEERING, QUALITY ASSURANCE. *Educ:* San Diego State Col, BS, 51. *Prof Exp:* Chemist, Scripps Inst, Univ Calif, 51; chemist mat lab, US Naval Air Sta, San Diego, 51-52, chemist eval br, Navy Electronics Lab, 52-57; staff mem metall, 57-71, mgr, Hot Cells Opers, 65-71, mgr Qual Control Fuel Dept, 71-73, dir, Quality Assurance, 73-75, MGR, QUALITY SYSTS DEPT, GEN ATOMIC CO, 73- *Concurrent Pos:* Consult, Dent Div, Bur Med, US Navy, 55-57. *Mem:* Am Nuclear Soc; Int Metallog Soc; sr mem Am Soc Qual Control. *Res:* Irradiation effects on surface reaction of metals; carbide fuel conversion studies; development of thermoelectric and thermionic materials; high temperatures material compatibility studies between fueled carbides and refractory metals; materials irradiation, capsule design, construction, operation; nuclear systems. *Mailing Add:* Gen Atomic Co PO Box 81608 San Diego CA 92138

CARPENTER, FREDERICK HILTMAN, b Cortez, Colo, June 8, 18; m 43; c 4. BIOCHEMISTRY. *Educ:* Stanford Univ, AB, 40, AM, 41, PhD(biochem), 44. *Prof Exp:* Lab asst biochem, Stanford Univ, 40-43, actg instr, 42; res asst, Med Col, Cornell Univ, 43-45, res assoc, 45-48; from asst prof to assoc prof, 49-62, dean div biol sci, 72-78, PROF BIOCHEM, UNIV CALIF, BERKELEY, 62- *Concurrent Pos:* Spec consult, NIH, 46-47, mem biochem study sect, 65-69; Royal Victor fel, 43; Rockefeller fel, 48; Guggenheim fel, 64; vis sci, Technische Hochschule, Aachen, WGer, 71-72 & Birkbeck Col, London, 78-79. *Mem:* AAAS; Am Chem Soc; Am Soc Biol Chem. *Res:* Chemistry and synthesis of penicillin; chemistry of nucleic acid; action of mustard gas; synthesis, degradation and isolation of peptides; theory and practice of chromatography; biological activity in insulin and leucine amino peptidase. *Mailing Add:* Dept Biochem Univ Calif Berkeley CA 94720

CARPENTER, GAIL ALEXANDRA, b New York, NY, Dec 23, 48. BIOMATHEMATICS. *Educ:* Univ Colo, Boulder, BA, 70; Univ Wis-Madison, MA, 72, PhD(math), 74. *Prof Exp:* Instr appl math, Mass Inst Technol, 74-76; asst prof, 76-80, ASSOC PROF MATH, NORTHEASTERN UNIV, 80- *Mem:* Am Math Soc. *Res:* Mathematical biology, using methods of topological dynamics; study of excitable membrane and network phenomena. *Mailing Add:* Dept of Math Northeastern Univ Boston MA 02115

CARPENTER, GARY GRANT, b San Francisco, Calif, Aug 25, 29. PEDIATRICS. *Educ:* Rutgers Univ, AB, 56; Jefferson Med Col, MD, 60. *Prof Exp:* From instr to asst prof, Sch Med, Temple Univ, 65-68; ASSOC PROF PEDIAT, JEFFERSON MED COL, 68- *Concurrent Pos:* Training fel metab & amino acids, St Christopher's Hosp Children, Pa, 62-63; asst prog dir, clin res ctr, St Christopher's Hosp Children, 65-68. *Mem:* AAAS; Ny Acad Sci. *Res:* Amino acid metabolism; cytogenetics. *Mailing Add:* Dept of Pediat Jefferson Med Col Philadelphia PA 19107

CARPENTER, GENE BLAKELY, b Evansville, Ind, Dec 15, 22; m 49; c 2. PHYSICAL CHEMISTRY, CRYSTALLOGRAPHY. *Educ:* Univ Louisville, BA, 44; Harvard Univ, MA, 45, PhD(phys chem), 47. *Prof Exp:* Nat Res fel, Calif Inst Technol, 47-48, res fel, 48-49; from instr to assoc prof chem, 49-63, PROF CHEM, BROWN UNIV, 63- *Concurrent Pos:* Guggenheim fel, Univ Leeds, 56-57; vis prof, State Univ Groningen, 63-64; Fulbright-Hays lectr, Univ Zagreb, 71-72. *Mem:* Am Chem Soc; Am Crystallog Asn. *Res:* Crystal structure by x-ray diffraction; potential-energy modelling of crystals. *Mailing Add:* Dept of Chem Brown Univ Providence RI 02912

CARPENTER, GENE PAUL, economic entomology, see previous edition

CARPENTER, GRAHAM JOHN CHARLES, b Cardiff, Wales, UK, Jan 3, 39. METAL PHYSICS. *Educ:* Univ Wales, BSc Hons, 61, PhD(metall), 64. *Prof Exp:* Res demonstr metall, Univ Wales, 63-64; res fel, Cambridge Univ, 64-67; res officer mat sci, Chalk River Nuclear Labs, 67-81; RES SCIENTIST, CAN METALL RES LABS, OTTAWA, 81- *Concurrent Pos:* Vis res assoc, Atomic Energy Res Estab, Harwell, 75-76. *Mem:* Micros Soc Can. *Res:* Electron microscopy, precipitation phenomena, radiation damage, radiation growth, zirconium and titanium alloys. *Mailing Add:* Phys Metall Res Lab Can Metall 568 Booth St Ottawa ON K1A OG1 Can

CARPENTER, HARRY C(LIFFORD), b Richey, Mont, Oct 25, 21; m 52; c 2. CHEMICAL ENGINEERING. *Educ:* Mont State Col, BS, 48, MS, 49. *Prof Exp:* RES CHEM ENGR, PETROL RES CTR, US BUR MINES, 49- *Mem:* AAAS; Am Chem Soc; Am Inst Chem Engrs. *Res:* Refining of shale oil by hydrogenation, hydro cracking and other catalytic processes; retorting of oil shale by in situ methods. *Mailing Add:* 1322 Canby Laramie WY 82070

CARPENTER, HARRY WELLINGTON, b Chicago, Ill, Mar 6, 31; m 59; c 4. CERAMICS. *Educ:* Univ Ill, BS, 55. *Prof Exp:* Engr, Chicago Vitreous Corp, 55; sr res engr, Atomics Int Div, 58-65, mem tech staff, Rockedyne Div, 65-69, MEM TECH STAFF, POWER DIV, N AM ROCKWELL CORP, 69- *Mem:* Am Soc Metals; Sigma Xi. *Res:* Materials research and development, particularly relating to ceramic and ceramic-metal systems for high-temperature applications. *Mailing Add:* 19945 Acre St Northridge CA 91324

CARPENTER, IRVIN WATSON, JR, b Washington, DC, Nov 29, 23; m 48; c 3. PLANT TAXONOMY. *Educ:* Purdue Univ, BSF, 48, MS, 50, PhD(bot), 52. *Prof Exp:* Instr forestry, Purdue Univ, 52-53; from asst prof to prof biol, 53-72, CHMN BIOL, APPALACHIAN STATE UNIV, 72- *Mem:* Bot Soc Am; AAAS. *Res:* Flora of southern Appalachians. *Mailing Add:* Dept Biol Appalachian State Univ Boone NC 28606

CARPENTER, JACK WILLIAM, b Worthington, Ohio, July 17, 25; m 50; c 2. THEORETICAL PHYSICS. *Educ:* Mass Inst Technol, BS, 51, MS, 52, PhD(physics), 57. *Prof Exp:* Proj scientist & sr physicist, Allied Res Assoc, Inc, 57-58, chief proj scientist, 58; vpres geophys div & sr physicist, Am Sci & Eng, Inc, Cambridge, 58-69; PRES & DIR, VISIDYNE, INC, MASS, 69- *Res:* Plasma physics; nuclear weapons effects; magnetohydrodynamics; nuclear physics; infrared spectroscopy. *Mailing Add:* Visidyne Inc S Bedford Burlington MA 01803

CARPENTER, JAMES E(DWIN), b Woodsville, NH, Mar 21, 32; m 64; c 3. STRUCTURAL ENGINEERING. *Educ:* Univ Cincinnati, CE, 54; Purdue Univ, MSCE, 60, PhD(struct eng), 65. *Prof Exp:* Engr & inspector, Fay, Spofford & Thorndike, Inc, 57-59; assoc develop engr, Res & Develop Div, Portland Cement Asn, 61-65, develop engr, 65-68, sr res engr, 68-75; mem staff, Concrete Technol Corp, 75-79; PROJ MGR, ANDERSEN-BJORNSTAD-KANE-JACOBS, INC, SEATTLE, WASH, 80- *Mem:* Am Soc Civil Engrs; Am Concrete Inst. *Res:* Structural research in reinforced and prestressed concrete. *Mailing Add:* 16463 Sixth Ave SW Seattle WA 98166

CARPENTER, JAMES E(UGENE), b Syracuse, NY, Jan 19, 21; m 43; c 3. MECHANICAL ENGINEERING, SCIENCE POLICY. *Educ:* Univ Syracuse, BS, 43; Univ Buffalo, MS, 51. *Prof Exp:* Test engr, Res Lab, Curtiss-Wright Corp, 43-44; res engr, Cornell Aeronaut Lab, Inc, 46-50, head struct lab, 50-58, prof mgr, 58-62, br head, 62-64, from asst dept head to dept head, 64-69, sr staff scientist, 69-70; mem comn govt procurement, 70-73; POLICY ANALYST, NSF, 73- *Res:* Strain gauge and structural research; hypersonic materials. *Mailing Add:* 3412 Mansfield Rd Falls Church VA 22041

CARPENTER, JAMES FRANKLIN, b Brookfield, Mo, Apr 10, 23; m 47; c 1. MATERIALS SCIENCE, PHYSICAL CHEMISTRY. *Educ:* Cent Methodist Col, AB, 48; Northwestern Univ, MS, 50; St Louis Univ, PhD(phys chem), 58. *Prof Exp:* Chemist, Mallinckrodt Chem Works, 50-58; asst mgr res chem, Mallinckrodt Nuclear Corp, 58-60; group leader, United Nuclear Corp, 60-62; SR STAFF ENGR CHEM, McDONNELL DOUGLAS CORP, 62- *Concurrent Pos:* Comt mem nat mat adv bd, Comt Characterization Org Matrix Composites, 78-80. *Mem:* Soc Advan Mat & Proc Eng; Am Inst Aeronaut & Astronaut. *Res:* Physical-organic chemistry; characterization of advanced resin composites and structural adhesives; quality assurance criteria of structural resins based on the physiochemical properties. *Mailing Add:* 11701 Tescord Dr St Louis MO 63128

CARPENTER, JAMES H(EISKELL), b Baltimore, Md, Mar 10, 28; m 50; c 2. OCEANOGRAPHY. *Educ:* Univ Va, BA, 49; Johns Hopkins Univ, MA, 52, PhD(oceanog), 57. *Prof Exp:* Res assoc, Johns Hopkins Univ, 56-58, from asst prof to assoc prof oceanog, 58-71, NSF grant, 72-73; PROF OCEANOG, ROSENSTIEL SCH MARINE & ATMOSPHERIC SCI, UNIV MIAMI, 73- *Concurrent Pos:* Mem subcomt environ effects, Adv Comt to Fed Radiation Coun, Nat Res Coun-Nat Acad Sci. *Mem:* AAAS; Am Geophys Union; Am Soc Limnol & Oceanog. *Res:* Factors influencing the distribution and abundance of materials in shallow water environments. *Mailing Add:* Rosenstiel Sch of Marine & Univ of Miami Miami FL 33149

CARPENTER, JAMES L(INWOOD), JR, b Fredericksburg, Va, Jan 6, 25; m 47; c 2. INDUSTRIAL ENGINEERING. *Educ:* Col William & Mary, BA, 49, MA, 50. *Prof Exp:* Elec engr, Navy Bur Ships, 50-53 & Newport News Shipbldg & Drydock Co, 53-56; elec engr, Missile Div, Chrysler Corp, 56-57, dept mgr, 57-59, dir plans & prog, Adv Proj Off, Defense Group, 50-61; dir logistics support, 61-72, DIR SYSTS ENG, MARTIN MARIETTA CORP, 72- *Concurrent Pos:* Recipient, Greer Award for Contrib to Logistics Mgt, 70. *Mem:* Fel Soc Logistics Engrs (past pres); Syst Safety Soc. *Res:* Engineering analysis of man-machine interface, especially information processing and management. *Mailing Add:* 5214 Alleman Dr Orlando FL 32809

CARPENTER, JAMES WILLIAM, b Shamokin, Pa, Sept 7, 35; m 58; c 4. ORGANIC CHEMISTRY. *Educ:* Lebanon Valley Col, BS, 60; Univ Nebr, MS, 63, PhD(org chem), 65. *Prof Exp:* Instr chem, Univ Nebr, 64-65; CHEMIST, EASTMAN KODAK CO, 65- *Mem:* Soc Photog Sci & Eng. *Res:* Photographic chemistry. *Mailing Add:* 120 Campfire Rd N Henrietta NY 14467

CARPENTER, JAMES WOODFORD, b Union, Ky, Jan 6, 22; m 49; c 2. ANIMAL SCIENCE. *Educ:* Univ Ky, BS, 52, MS, 53; Univ Fla, PhD(meat technol), 59. *Prof Exp:* Plant mgr, 54-59, asst meat scientist, 59-66, assoc meat scientist, 66-71, PROF & MEAT SCIENTIST, MEAT LAB, UNIV FLA, 71- *Honors & Awards:* Educ & Cult Medal, Govt S Vietnam, 70. *Mem:* Am Soc Animal Sci; Am Meat Sci Asn. *Res:* Meat animal carcass evaluation, especially quality and palatability factors. *Mailing Add:* Dept of Animal Sci Univ of Fla Gainesville FL 32611

CARPENTER, JOHN HAROLD, b Owatonna, Minn, May 1, 29; m 53; c 2. HIGH TEMPERATURE CHEMISTRY. *Educ:* Macalester Col, BA, 51; Purdue Univ, MS, 53, PhD(chem), 55. *Prof Exp:* Chemist, Univ Calif, 54-55, res chemist, Lawrence Radiation Lab, 55-68; assoc prof chem, 68-71, PROF CHEM, ST CLOUD STATE UNIV, 71-, CHMN CHEM DEPT, 73- *Mem:* Am Chem Soc; Am Ceramic Soc. *Res:* Structures, vapor pressures and thermodynamics of high melting inorganic compounds. *Mailing Add:* Dept of Chem St Cloud State Univ St Cloud MN 56301

CARPENTER, JOHN MARLAND, b Williamsport, Pa, June 20, 35; m 59; c 4. SOLID STATE PHYSICS, NUCLEAR ENGINEERING. *Educ:* Pa State Univ, BS, 57; Univ Mich, MSE, 58, PhD(nuclear eng), 63. *Prof Exp:* Res assoc nuclear eng, Univ Mich, Ann Arbor, 60-63, fel, Inst Sci & Technol, 63-64, from asst prof to prof, 64-76; vis scientist, 71-72 & 73, SR PHYSICIST & TECH DIR, ARGONNE NAT LAB, 75- *Concurrent Pos:* Consult, Solid State Sci Div, Argonne Nat Labs, 69-71, mem comt intense neutron sources. *Mem:* Am Nuclear Soc; Am Phys Soc; AAAS; Sigma Xi. *Res:* Neutron inelastic scattering; neutron diffraction; amorphous solids; molecular spectroscopy; nuclear reactor instrumentation and control, Cerenkov counters; proton recoil counters; neutron thermalization; pulsed moderators; pulsed spallation neutron sources; neutron scattering instrumentation. *Mailing Add:* Argonne Nat Lab Intense Pulsed Neutron Source Argonne IL 60439

CARPENTER, JOHN RICHARD, b Galveston, Tex, May 20, 38; m 58; c 3. GEOCHEMISTRY. *Educ:* Rice Univ, BA, 59; Fla State Univ, MS, 62, PhD(geochem geol), 64. *Prof Exp:* Asst geol, Fla State Univ, 63-64; geologist, Fla Geol Surv, 64; US Naval Oceanog Off, 64-66; from asst prof to assoc prof geol, 66-77, actg head dept, 69-70, PROF GEOL, UNIV SC, 77-, DIR GRAD STUDIES & ASST CHMN DEPT GEOL, 74- *Concurrent Pos:* Sr col consult, 72-74, sr staff mem, Earth Sci Teacher Prep Proj, 73- *Mem:* Mineral Soc Am; Geochem Soc; Int Asn Geochem & Cosmochem; Nat Asn Geol Teachers. *Res:* Element distribution in coexisting phases of metamorphic and igneous rocks; geochemistry and petrogenesis of ultramafic rocks; structural control of metamorphic mineral assemblages; geochemistry of opaque minerals; alternative structure modes for earth science education. *Mailing Add:* Dept of Geol Univ of SC Columbia SC 29208

CARPENTER, KENNETH HALSEY, b El Dorado Kans, June 22, 39; m 71; c 3. ELECTROMAGNETICS. *Educ:* Kans State Univ, BSEE, 61, MS, 62; Tex Christian Univ, PhD(physics), 66. *Prof Exp:* Columbia Res Corp, 66-68; assoc prof physics, ETenn State Univ, 68-75; Union Carbide Corp, Nuclear Div & Comput Sci Div, Oak Ridge Nat Lab, 75-79; ASSOC PROF ELEC ENG, UNIV MO-ROLLA, 79- *Mem:* Am Phys Soc; Inst Elec & Electronics Engrs. *Res:* Plasma diagnostics for magnetic confinement fusion and computing applications to this area. *Mailing Add:* Elec Eng Dept Univ Mo Rolla MO 65401

CARPENTER, KENNETH JOHN, b London, Eng, May 17, 23. NUTRITION. *Educ:* Cambridge Univ, BA, 44, PhD(nutrit), 48, ScD, 75. *Prof Exp:* Sci officer nutrit, Rowett Inst, Aberdeen, Scotland, 48-56; reader, Cambridge Univ, 56-77; PROF EXP NUTRIT, UNIV CALIF, BERKELEY, 77-, CHMN DEPT, 81- *Concurrent Pos:* Kellogg fel, Harvard Univ, 55-56; bursar, Food Res Inst, Mycone, 62. *Mem:* Brit Nutrit Soc; Am Nutrit Soc; Am Asn Cereal Chemists. *Res:* Availability of vitamins and amino acids in processed foods. *Mailing Add:* Dept of Nutrit Sci Univ of Calif Berkeley CA 94720

CARPENTER, KENT HEISLEY, b Williamsport, Pa, Apr 30, 38; m 72; c 2. HYDROMETALLURGY, CHEMICAL PROCESSING. *Educ:* Pa State Univ, BS, 61. *Prof Exp:* Asst res engr, Dept Nuclear Eng, Univ Mich, 61-65; assoc res engr, Conductron Div, McDonnel Douglass, 65-69; owner/mgr, Sports Car Serv, Inc, 69-72; sr proj engr, Thetford Corp, 72-75; SR RES ASSOC, CLIMAX MOLYBDENUM CO, AMAX, 75- *Res:* Hydro-and pyro-metallurgical processing of nickel and cobalt ores; reduction of metal oxide powders; crystallization of molybdenum and tungsten salts; elevated temperature and fluid bed processing. *Mailing Add:* 1438 Crawford Lane Ann Arbor MI 48105

CARPENTER, LEE GRAYDON, b Milestone, Sask, Aug 15, 25; US citizen; m; c 2. INDUSTRIAL CHEMISTRY. *Educ:* Univ Sask, BSc, 49, MSc, 51; Columbia Univ, PhD(phys chem), 56. *Prof Exp:* Reduction engr, Aluminum Co Can, 56-57; sect head alkali metal salts, Am Potash & Chem Corp, 57-60; dept mgr radiation & radiochem, Aerojet-Gen Corp, 60-70; sr engr, 73-78, staff engr, 78-79, group leader, 79-80, SR TECH SUPVR, ALUMINUM CO AM, 80- *Mem:* Am Chem Soc; Chem Inst Can; AAAS. *Res:* Recovery of aluminum from domestic ores and treatment of waste gases and residues resulting from recovery methods. *Mailing Add:* Alcoa Labs Box 772 New Kensington PA 15068

CARPENTER, LYNN ALLEN, b Cushing, Okla, Apr 25, 43. MICROWAVE ENGINEERING, SAFETY ENGINEERING. *Educ:* Okla State Univ, BS, 64; Univ Ill, Urbana-Champaign, 66, PhD(physics), 71. *Prof Exp:* Res asst elec eng, Univ Ill, 68-71, res assoc, 71-72; asst prof, 72-79, ASSOC PROF ELEC ENG, PA STATE UNIV, 79- *Concurrent Pos:* Res trainee simulation, NASA Manned Spacecraft Ctr, 65; mem staff radar systems, Mass Inst Technol, 68. *Mem:* Am Geophys Soc; Int Sci Radio Union; Inst Elec & Electronics Engrs. *Res:* development of measurements of the Doppler shift for incoherent-scatter radar systems. *Mailing Add:* 314 Elec Eng Pa State Univ University Park PA 16802

CARPENTER, MALCOLM BRECKENRIDGE, b Montrose, Colo, July 7, 21; m 49; c 3. ANATOMY, PHYSIOLOGY. *Educ:* Columbia Univ, BA, 43; Long Island Col Med, MD, 47; Am Bd Psychiat & Neurol, dipl, 55. *Prof Exp:* Asst neurol, 47 & 48-50, from instr to assoc prof anat, 53-62, prof anat, Columbia Univ, 62-76; prof anat & neurol, Pa State Univ, 76-78; PROF & CHMN DEPT ANAT, UNIFORMED SERV UNIV HEALTH SCI, BETHESDA, MD, 78- *Concurrent Pos:* Fel neurol, Columbia Univ, 48-50; Markle scholar med sci, 53-58; surg intern, Bellevue Hosp, NY, 47-48; asst res neurologist, Neurol Inst, NY, 50 & 52-53; consult, Nat Inst Neurol Dis & Blindness, 62-66 & 68-72; mem, Inst Brain Res Orgn; ed, Neurology, 63-72, Am J Anat, 68-74, J Comp Neurol, 71-80 & Neurobiology, 71; mem, Anat Test Comt, Nat Bd Med Examr, 77- *Mem:* Am Asn Anat; Asn Res Nerv & Ment Dis; Am Neurol Asn; Am Acad Neurol; NY Acad Med. *Res:* Neuroanatomic, neurophysiologic and neuropathologic study of motor disturbances, particularly those due to disease of basal ganglia. *Mailing Add:* 4301 Jones Bridge Rd Bethesda MD 20014

CARPENTER, MARTHA STAHR, b Bethlehem, Pa, May 29, 20; m 51; c 1. ASTRONOMY. *Educ:* Wellesley Col, BA, 41; Univ Calif, MA, 43, PhD, 45. *Prof Exp:* Asst astron, Univ Calif, 41-44; instr, Wellesley Col, 45-47; from asst prof to assoc prof, Cornell Univ, 47-54; res grant radio astron, Australian Commonwealth Sci & Indust Res Org, 54-55; res assoc, Ctr Radiophysics & Space Res, Cornell Univ, 55-69; lectr, 69-77, ASSOC PROF ASTRON, UNIV VA, 73- *Mem:* AAAS; Am Astron Soc; Am Asn Variable Star Observers (2nd vpres, 48-49, lst vpres, 49-51, pres, 51-54). *Res:* Galactic structure; radio astronomy. *Mailing Add:* Dept of Astron Univ of Va 416 Cabell Hall Charlottesville VA 22903

CARPENTER, MARY PITYNSKI, b Detroit, Mich, Feb 20, 26; m 47; c 3. BIOCHEMISTRY. *Educ:* Wayne Univ, BS, 46; Univ Mich, MA, 48, PhD(zool), 52. *Prof Exp:* Res assoc zool, Univ Mich, 51-53; res assoc biochem, Okla Med Res Found, 54-58, biochemist, 58-66; from asst prof to assoc prof biochem, 65-69, PROF BIOCHEM & MOLECULAR BIOL, SCH MED, UNIV OKLA, 69- *Concurrent Pos:* Assoc mem, Okla Med Res Found, 69-76, mem, 76- *Mem:* AAAS; Am Soc Biol Chem; Am Chem Soc; Am Inst Nutrit; Brit Biochem Soc. *Res:* Biochemistry of mammalian testis; metabolism of unsaturated fatty acids and prostaglandins; mixed function oxidases; function of vitamin E. *Mailing Add:* 1218 Cruce Norman OK 73069

CARPENTER, NANCY JANE, b Detroit, Mich, Nov 15, 46. GENETICS. *Educ:* Albion Col, BA, 68; Univ Mich, MS, 69, PhD(zool), 72. *Prof Exp:* asst prof, 73-79, ASSOC PROF ZOOL, UNIV TULSA, 79- *Concurrent Pos:* Scholar, Univ Mich, 73; assoc clin genetics, Children's Med Ctr, 75-81, assoc dir clin genetics, 81-; clin asst prof pediat, Univ Okla Med Col, Tulsa, 78- *Mem:* Am Soc Human Genetics; Genetics Soc Am; AAAS; Sigma Xi. *Res:* Cytogenetics and clinical genetics. *Mailing Add:* Dept Clin Genetics Children's Med Ctr 5300 E Skelly Dr Tulsa OK 74135

CARPENTER, PAUL GERSHOM, b Salem, Ore, Jan 16, 14; m 37; c 2. ORGANIC CHEMISTRY. *Educ:* Willamette Univ, AB, 35; Ore State Col, MS, 37; Univ Wis, PhD(org chem), 41. *Prof Exp:* Asst, Ore State Col, 35-37 & Univ Wis, 37-38; asst prof chem, Willamette Univ, 38-39; asst, Wis Alumni Res Found, 39-40 & Univ Wis, 40-41; res chemist, Hercules Powder Co, 41-42, asst group leader, 42-45; sales res investr, Phillips Petrol Co, 45-47, chief prod res sect, 47-51; mgr synthetic rubber res br, Copolymer Rubber & Chem Corp, 51-56, vpres res & develop, 56-60, pres & chief exec off, 60-69; pres & chief exec off, Polyform, Inc, 70-73; develop mgr, Draco Inc, 73-78; VPRES, HOUSTON-SIMPLEX CORP, 78- *Concurrent Pos:* Chem & petrol consult, 69- *Mem:* Am Chem Soc; Sigma Xi. *Res:* Hydrogenation; organic synthesis; polymerization; petroleum production; synthetic rubber. *Mailing Add:* 1325 Marilyn Dr Baton Rouge LA 70815

CARPENTER, RAY WARREN, b Berkeley, Calif, Sept 29, 34; m 55; c 3. MATERIALS SCIENCE, SOLID STATE PHYSICS. *Educ:* Univ Calif, Berkeley, BS, 58, MS, 59, PhD(metall), 66. *Prof Exp:* Res asst alloy thermodyn, Inst Eng Res, Univ Calif, 56-59; sr metallurgist, Aerojet-Gen Nucleonics, 59-65 & Stanford Res Inst, 65-66; sr mem staff res, Oak Ridge Nat Lab, 66-80; PROF SOLID STATE SCI & ENG & DIR, REGIONAL FACIL HIGH RESOLUTION ELECTRON MICROS, ARIZ STATE UNIV, TEMPE, 80- *Concurrent Pos:* Prof metall eng, Univ Tenn, 76-77 & Vanderbilt Univ, Nashville, 79-80. *Honors & Awards:* Analytical Electron Micros Award, Int Metallog Soc, 76 & 77. *Mem:* Am Inst Mining, Metall & Petrol Engrs, Metall Soc; Electron Micros Soc Am. *Res:* Techniques and instrumentation for high resolution analytical electron microscopy and applications to material science and solid state physics; phase transformations and interfaces in metals, ceramics and semiconductors; structural analysis of solids; electron microscopy. *Mailing Add:* Ctr Solid State Sci PSB-255 Ariz State Univ Tempe AZ 85287

CARPENTER, RAYMON T, b Topeka, Kans, Jan 14, 29; m 53; c 1. NUCLEAR PHYSICS. *Educ:* Univ Kans, BS, 54, MS, 56; Northwestern Univ, PhD(nuclear physics), 62. *Prof Exp:* Asst instr physics, Univ Kans, 54-56; asst instr physics, Northwestern Univ, 56-58; physicist, Argonne Nat Lab, 58-62; asst prof physics, 62-65, ASSOC PROF PHYSICS, UNIV IOWA, 65- *Mem:* AAAS. *Res:* Experimental nuclear structure physics of light nuclei, using accelerated lithium and helium ions as projectiles; gamma ray spectroscopy. *Mailing Add:* Dept of Physics Univ of Iowa Iowa City IA 52240

CARPENTER, RAYMOND ALLISON, molecular spectroscopy, see previous edition

CARPENTER, RICHARD A, b Kansas City, Mo, Aug 22, 26; m 48; c 3. POLICY ANALYSIS. *Educ:* Univ Mo, BS, 48, MA, 49. *Prof Exp:* Chemist, Shell Oil Co, 49-51; asst mgr, Midwest Res Inst, 51-58; mgr, Callery Chem Co, 58-64; sr specialist sci & tech, Libr Cong, 64-69, chief, Environ Policy Div, Cong Res Serv, 69-72; exec dir comn nat resources, Nat Res Coun, Nat Acad Sci, 72-77; RES ASSOC, ENVIRON & POLICY INST, EAST-WEST CTR, 77- *Mem:* Fel AAAS; Am Chem Soc; Sci Res Soc Am; Ecol Soc Am. *Res:* Air pollution; environmental chemistry; technology assessment; boron chemistry; rocket propellants. *Mailing Add:* Environ & Policy Inst 1777 East-West Rd Honolulu HI 96848

CARPENTER, RICHARD M, b Cambridge, Mass, Apr 3, 43; m 69. ELECTRICAL ENGINEERING, APPLIED MATHEMATICS. *Educ:* Tufts Univ, BSEE, 64; Harvard Univ, MS, 66. *Prof Exp:* Aerospace technologist, Electronics Res Ctr, NASA, Mass, 66-70; sr mem tech staff & head comput-aided design, New Prod Line Eng Div, RCA Comput Systs Div, Marlboro, 70-72; chief elec engr, Massa Div, Dynamics Corp Am, 72-75; vpres eng, Massa Corp, Hingham, Mass, 75-76; VPRES, MASSA PROD CORP, HINGHAM, MASS, 77- *Mem:* Inst Elec & Electronics Engrs. *Res:* Effective design procedures for engineers in a computer-aided circuit design environment; computer-aided circuit design; high speed logic circuit design; development of microprocessor based electo-acoustic control systems. *Mailing Add:* Massa Prod Corp 280 Lincoln St Hingham MA 02043

CARPENTER, ROBERT DEAN, b Paris, Mo, Dec 12, 24; m 51; c 4. ANALYTICAL CHEMISTRY. *Educ:* Iowa State Univ, BS, 52. *Prof Exp:* Chemist, Com Solvents Corp, 52-54; chemist, 54-59, res chemist, 59-65, sr scientist, 65-72, ASSOC PRIN SCIENTIST CHEM, PHILIP MORRIS USA, 72- *Res:* Chemistry of tobacco and cigarette smoke; analysis of components and elucidation of mechanisms. *Mailing Add:* Philip Morris Res Ctr Box 26603 Richmond VA 23261

CARPENTER, ROBERT FRANCIS, molecular physics, see previous edition

CARPENTER, ROBERT HALSTEAD, b Pasadena, Calif, June 24, 14; m 41; c 2. GEOLOGY. *Educ:* Stanford Univ, AB, 40, MA, 43, PhD(geol), 48. *Prof Exp:* Geologist, Anaconda Copper Mining Co, Mont, 42-44 & Int Smelting & Ref Co, Utah, 44-46; from asst prof to prof geol, Colo Sch Mines, 47-74; PROF GEOL, UNIV GA, 74- *Concurrent Pos:* Consult geologist, NY & Honduras Rosario Mining Co, Honduras, 49-52, Molybdenum Corp Am, 53-, Thomp Creek Coal & Coke, 53-, Utah Construct Co, 54 & UN Spec Fund Proj, Baldwin Mines, Burma, 63; Fulbright res scholar, italy, 57-58; pres, Int Mineral Eng, 63- *Mem:* Geol Soc Am; Soc Econ Geologists; Am Inst Mining, Metall & Petrol Eng. *Res:* Economic and structural geology; geochemistry of ore deposits. *Mailing Add:* Dept of Geol Univ of Ga Athens CA 30602

CARPENTER, ROBERT LELAND, b St Louis, Mo, June 27, 42; m 65; c 4. AEROSOL PHYSICS. *Educ:* Univ Mo-Rolla, BS, 65; Univ Tenn, PhD(molecular biol), 75. *Prof Exp:* Res asst plasma physics, Los Alamos Sci Lab, 65-66; engr, McDonnell Douglas Corp, 66-70; SR STAFF INHALATION TOXICOL, LOVELACE BIOMED & ENVIRON RES INST, 75- *Mem:* AAAS; Am Chem Soc. *Res:* Inhalation toxicology of airborne effluents source characterization and aerosol generation; aerosol physics. *Mailing Add:* Inhalation Toxicol Res Inst Box 5890 Albuquerque NM 87185

CARPENTER, ROBERT RAYMOND, b Connellsville, Pa, Mar 6, 33; m 54; c 2. INTERNAL MEDICINE. *Educ:* Univ Pittsburgh, BS, 54; Univ Rochester, MD, 57. *Prof Exp:* Intern, King County Hosp, 57-58; resident, Sch Med, Univ Wash, 58-60; clin investr & attend physician, Lab Clin Invest, Nat Inst Allergy & Infectious Dis, 62-63, actg chief clin immunol, 63-64; asst prof med, Baylor Col Med, 64-68; from asst prof to assoc prof med & community med, Univ Pittsburgh, 68-72; PROF INTERNAL MED & DIR PRIMARY CARE-COMMUNITY MED, UNIV MICH, ANN ARBOR, 72- *Concurrent Pos:* Markle scholar, 64; consult infectious dis, Georgetown Univ Serv, DC Gen Hosp, 62-63 & Montefiore Hosp, Pittsburgh, 68-71; consult immunol, Vet Admin Hosp, Houston, 64-68, dir immunol & infectious dis, 68; attend physician, Ben Taub Gen Hosp, Houston, 64-68; dir health care, Western Pa Regional Med Prog, Pittsburgh, 68-72. *Mem:* Am Asn Immunol; Am Col Physicians; Am Fedn Clin Res; Am Hosp Asn; Am Col Prev Med. *Res:* Immunology; infectious disease; health care. *Mailing Add:* Primary Care-Community Med Univ of Mich Med Ctr Ann Arbor MI 48104

CARPENTER, ROGER EDWIN, b Tucson, Ariz, Oct 13, 35; m 62, 73; c 2. ZOOLOGY. *Educ:* Univ Ariz, BA, 57; Univ Calif, Los Angeles, PhD(zool), 63. *Prof Exp:* Assoc biol, Univ Calif, Riverside, 61-63; from asst prof to assoc prof zool, 63-70, chmn dept, 71-75, PROF ZOOL, SAN DIEGO STATE UNIV, 70- *Mem:* AAAS; Am Soc Mammal; Am Soc Zoologists. *Res:* Environmental physiology of vertebrates. *Mailing Add:* Dept of Zool San Diego State Univ San Diego CA 92182

CARPENTER, ROLAND LEROY, b Los Angeles, Calif, Apr 26, 26; m 51; c 1. ASTRONOMY, ASTROPHYSICS. *Educ:* Los Angeles State Col, BA, 51; Univ Calif, Los Angeles, MA, 64, PhD, 66. *Prof Exp:* Electronics technician, Collins Radio Co, 52-55, engr digital commun, 55-57, group supvr, 57-59; res engr, Calif Inst Technol, 59-62, scientist, 62-68; assoc prof physics, Calif State Col, 68-77; MEM STAFF LUNAR & PLANETARY SCI SECT, JET PROPULSION LAB, CALIF INST TECHNOL, 68-; PROF PHYSICS, CALIF STATE UNIV, LOS ANGELES, 77- *Mem:* AAAS; Am Astron Soc; Royal Astron Soc. *Res:* Radar astronomy, especially studies of nearer planets by earth-based radar; galaxies; planetary astronomy. *Mailing Add:* Dept of Physics 5151 State University Dr Los Angeles CA 90032

CARPENTER, ROY, US citizen. MARINE CHEMISTRY, GEOCHEMISTRY. *Educ:* Wash & Lee Univ, BS, 61; Univ Calif, San Diego, PhD(chem), 68. *Prof Exp:* Asst prof marine chem & geochem, 68-73, ASSOC PROF OCEANOG, UNIV WASH, 73- *Mem:* Am Chem Soc. *Res:* Chemical reactions in the oceans and marine sediments. *Mailing Add:* Dept Oceanog WB-10 Univ of Wash Seattle WA 98195

CARPENTER, RUSSELL LE GRAND, b Meriden, Conn, Nov 7, 01; m 29; c 2. RADIOBIOLOGY, HISTOLOGY. *Educ:* Tufts Col, BS, 24; Harvard Univ, PhD(zool), 28. *Hon Degrees:* ScD, Tufts Univ, 77. *Prof Exp:* Instr anat, Col Physicians & Surgeons, Columbia Univ, 28-31, assoc, 31-35, asst prof, 35-38; lectr ophthal, Harvard Med Sch, 53-80; prof, 38-68, EMER PROF ZOOL, TUFTS UNIV, 68-; RES BIOLOGIST, BUR RADIOL HEALTH, USPHS, 70- *Concurrent Pos:* Mem corp, Marine Biol Lab, Woods Hole, 33-; instr, Harvard Univ, 46-53; mem teaching staff, Lancaster Course Ophthal, 52-; consult microwave radio-biol, USPHS, 69-70; consult, Retina Found, 64-75. *Mem:* Am Asn Anat; Am Soc Zoologists; Asn Res Vision & Ophthal; fel Am Acad Arts & Sci; Int Microwave Power Inst. *Res:* Anatomy and histology of the vertebrate eye; biological effects of microwave radiation with particular reference to the eye. *Mailing Add:* Bur of Radiol Health 109 Holton St Winchester MA 01890

CARPENTER, SAMMY, b Bolckow, Mo, July 20, 28; m 50; c 2. ORGANIC CHEMISTRY. *Educ:* Northwest Mo State Col, AB & BS, 50; Univ Mo, PhD(chem), 58. *Prof Exp:* Asst chem, Univ Mo, 54-57, asst instr, 58; res chemist, Celanese Corp Am, 58-64; from asst prof to assoc prof, 64-77, PROF CHEM, NORTHWEST MO STATE UNIV, 77- CHMN DEPT, 68- *Concurrent Pos:* Guest chemist, Nat Bur Stand, 52-54. *Mem:* Am Chem Soc; Sigma Xi; AAAS. *Res:* Substituted styrenes; organometallics and epoxides. *Mailing Add:* Dept of Chem Northwest Mo State Univ Maryville MO 64468

CARPENTER, STANLEY JOHN, b Mansfield, Ohio, Feb 12, 36; m 63; c 3. CYTOLOGY. *Educ:* Oberlin Col, AB, 58; Univ Iowa, PhD(zool), 64. *Prof Exp:* Trainee path, 64-66, instr anat & cytol, 66-67, asst prof, 67-73, chmn dept, 78-80, ASSOC PROF ANAT, DARTMOUTH MED SCH, 73- *Res:* Cell fine structure; choroid plexus, placenta, embryo. *Mailing Add:* Dept of Anat Dartmouth Med Sch Hanover NH 03755

CARPENTER, STEPHEN RUSSELL, b Kansas City, Mo, July 5, 52; m 79. LIMNOLOGY, AQUATIC BOTANY. *Educ:* Amherst Col, BA, 74; Univ Wis, Madison, MS, 76, PhD(bot), 79. *Prof Exp:* ASST PROF BIOL, UNIV NOTRE DAME, 79- *Mem:* AAAS; Am Soc Limnol & Oceanog; Brit Ecol Soc; Ecol Soc Am; Sigma Xi. *Res:* Aquatic plant ecology; detital processing and dynamics in lakes and streams; lake succession; modeling ecological systems; statistical analysis of ecological data. *Mailing Add:* Dept Biol Univ Notre Dame Notre Dame IN 46556

CARPENTER, STEVE HAYCOCK, b Cedar City, Utah, May 15, 38; m 60; c 2. SOLID STATE PHYSICS. *Educ:* Univ Utah, BS, 59, PhD(physics), 64. *Prof Exp:* Asst elec & magnetic lab, Univ Utah, 60-62; res physicist, Aerojet-Gen Corp Div, Gen Tire & Rubber Co, 64-65; From lectr to assoc prof & res physicist, 65-74, sr res physicist, Dept of Physics & Metall, 74-76, chmn, Dept Physics, 76-80, PROF, DEPT PHYSICS & METALL, UNIV DENVER, 74- *Concurrent Pos:* Astron head, Physics Div, Denver Res Inst, Univ Denver, 76-77; Invited Fulbright-Hays lectr, Byelo Russian Polytech Inst, Minsk, USSR, 76; panel mem, NSF Reviewer Panel for res invitation grants in mat sci; chmn, NSF Site Visit Team, Mich Tech Univ; reviewer, J Applied Physics; key reader, Metallurgical Transactions; consult, Lawrence Livermore Nat Labs, Rocky Flats, Dunegan-Enduco. *Mem:* Am Phys Soc. *Res:* Defects, including impurities, and their interactions in crystals by means of internal friction measurements; non destructive testing particularily using acoustic emission methods and techniques; explosion welding and powder compaction. *Mailing Add:* Dept of Physics Univ of Denver Denver CO 80208

CARPENTER, T J, b Middlebourne, WVa, Jan 9, 27; m 49; c 3. ORGANIC CHEMISTRY, ANALYTICAL CHEMISTRY. *Educ:* WVa Univ, BS, 49, MS, 51. *Prof Exp:* Plant chemist, Corning Glass Works, Pa, 54-56, supv chem eng, NY, 56-57, mfg eng consult, 57-61, mgr chem & metall eng dept, Tech Staff Div, 61-64; sr mem tech staff, Signetics Corp, 64-65, sect head, Process Improv, 65-66; mgr process technol dept, 66-71, DIR PROCESS TECHNOL, CORNING GLASS WORKS, 71- *Mem:* Am Chem Soc; Am Ceramic Soc; Am Inst Chem Eng. *Res:* Chemical process engineering. *Mailing Add:* HP-ME-3-D6 Corning Glass Works Corning NY 14830

CARPENTER, WILL DOCKERY, b Moorhead, Miss, July 13, 30; m; c 2. PLANT PHYSIOLOGY. *Educ:* Miss State Univ, BS, 52; Purdue Univ, MS, 56, PhD(plant physiol), 58. *Prof Exp:* Plant biochemist, Inorg Chem Div, Monsanto Chem Co, 58-60, market develop dept, Agr Div, Monsanto Co, 60-75, mgr dept, 68-70, dir dept, 71-75, dir prod develop, 75-76, dir environ oper, 77-80, DIR, ENVIRON MGT, CORP ENVIRON POLICY STAFF, MONSANTO AGR PROD CO, 80- *Concurrent Pos:* Mem, NCent Weed Control Conf, pres, 77. *Mem:* Weed Sci Soc Am (treas, 75, pres, 80). *Res:* Respiration and carbohydrate metabolism; soil fertility; herbicides; agriculture. *Mailing Add:* Monsanto Agr Prod Co 800 N Lindbergh Blvd St Louis MO 63166

CARPENTER, WILLIAM GRAHAM, b West Liberty, WVa, May 7, 31; m 65; c 3. POLYMER CHEMISTRY. *Educ:* WVa Wesleyan Col, BS, 53; Univ Md, MS, 56, PhD(org chem), 60. *Prof Exp:* Res chemist, Stamford Res Labs, Am Cyanamid Co, 59-63; sr chemist, Plastics Div, Moorehead-Patterson Res Ctr, Am Mach & Foundry Co, 63-64 & Org Div, Cent Res Labs, Interchem Corp, Bloomfield, 64-67; sr chemist, NL Industries Inc, 67-79; TECH MGR, CORROSION ENG DIV, PENNWALT CORP, 79- *Mem:* Am Chem Soc; Soc Plastics Engrs. *Res:* Fiber process development; polyamides containing phosphorus; addition polymerization; synthesis and evaluation of high temperature polymers; compounding epoxy resins; block copolymers; epoxide polymerization; water soluble polymers, thickeners and retention aids. *Mailing Add:* 216 O'Hara Manor Dr Pittsburgh PA 15238

CARPENTER, WILLIAM JOHN, b Pittsburgh, Pa, Sept 15, 27; m 52; c 3. FLORICULTURE. *Educ:* Univ Md, BS, 49; Mich State Univ, PhD(hort), 53. *Prof Exp:* From asst prof to prof hort, Kans State Univ, 53-66; prof hort, Mich State Univ, 68-75; PROF & CHMN DEPT ORG HORT, UNIV FLA, 75- *Mem:* Am Soc Hort Sci. *Res:* Measuring and programming of the greenhouse environment; supplemental lighting of greenhouse crops; floriculture crop physiology; administrative responsibility for Florida's teaching, extension and research programs in organic horticulture. *Mailing Add:* Dept Ornamental Hort Univ of Fla Gainesville FL 32611

CARPENTER, ZERLE LEON, b Thomas, Okla, July 21, 35; m 58; c 2. ANIMAL SCIENCE, FOOD SCIENCE. *Educ:* Okla State Univ, BS, 57; Univ Wis, MS, 60, PhD(animal sci), 62. *Prof Exp:* Res assoc, Univ Wis, 58-62; from asst prof to assoc prof, 62-70, PROF ANIMAL SCI, TEX A&M UNIV, 70-, HEAD DEPT, 80- *Mem:* Am Meat Sci Asn; Am Soc Animal Sci; Inst Food Tech. *Res:* Determination of histological, biochemical and physical characteristics of beef, pork and lamb muscle as related to quantitative and qualitative components of meat animal species. *Mailing Add:* Dept of Animal Sci Tex A&M Univ College Station TX 77843

CARPENTIER, ROBERT GEORGE, b Paris, France, Oct 3, 29. PHYSIOLOGY, CARDIOLOGY. *Educ:* Univ Chile, BS, 49, MD, 57. *Prof Exp:* Instr path & physiol, Col Med, Univ Chile, 57-59, asst prof cardiol, 60-64, from asst prof to prof path & physiol, 65-76; ASSOC PROF PHYSIOL, COL MED, HOWARD UNIV, 76- *Concurrent Pos:* NIH fel cardiac electrophysiol, J E Fogarty Int Ctr Advan Study Health Sci, State Univ NY, Brooklyn, 70-72. *Mem:* Am Physiol Soc; Am Heart Asn; AAAS; NY Acad Sci. *Res:* Cardiovascular physiology, in particular cardiac electrophysiology and pharmacology. *Mailing Add:* Dept of Physiol & Biophys 520 West St NW Washington DC 20059

CARPER, WILLIAM ROBERT, b Syracuse, NY, Feb 8, 35; m 66; c 3. ENZYMOLOGY. *Educ:* State Univ NY Albany, BS, 60; Univ Miss, PhD(chem), 63. *Prof Exp:* Welch Fund fel chem, Texas A&M Univ, 63-65; asst prof, Calif State Col Los Angeles, 65-67; assoc prof, 67-70, PROF BIOCHEM, WICHITA STATE UNIV, 70- *Concurrent Pos:* NIMH spec fel, Univ SFla, 72-73, URRP fel, 80-81. *Mem:* Am Chem Soc; The Chem Soc; Asn Biol Chemists; Sigma Xi. *Res:* Structure and function of proteins. *Mailing Add:* Dept of Chem Wichita State Univ Wichita KS 67208

CARPINO, LOUIS ALBERT, b Des Moines, Iowa, Dec 13, 27; m 58; c 6. CHEMISTRY. *Educ:* Iowa State Col, BS, 50; Univ Ill, MS, 51, PhD(org chem), 53. *Prof Exp:* Assoc prof org chem, 54-67, PROF CHEM, UNIV MASS, AMHERST, 67- *Concurrent Pos:* Alexander von Humboldt Award, 74. *Mem:* Am Chem Soc; The Chem Soc; Soc Ger Chem; Swiss Chem Soc; Chem Soc Japan. *Res:* Small-ring heterocycles; non-benzenoid aromatic systems; new amino-protecting groups; organo-nitrogen and organo-sulfur chemistry; polymeric organic reagents; peptide synthesis. *Mailing Add:* Dept of Chem Univ of Mass Amherst MA 01003

CARR, ALBERT A, b Covington, Ky, Dec 20, 30; m 56; c 4. ORGANIC CHEMISTRY, MEDICINAL CHEMISTRY. *Educ:* Xavier Univ, BS, 53, MS, 55; Univ Fla, PhD(org chem), 58. *Prof Exp:* SECT HEAD ORG CHEM, MERRELL-DOW PHARMACEUT, INC, 58- *Mem:* Am Chem Soc. *Res:* Pharmaceuticals; psychotherapeutics; design preparation and characterization of psychotherapeutic, cardiovascular and antiallergy agents. *Mailing Add:* Merrell-Dow Pharmaceut Inc 2110 E Galbraith Rd Cincinnati OH 45215

CARR, ARCHIE FAIRLY, JR, b Mobile, Ala, June 16, 09; m 37; c 5. ZOOLOGY. *Educ:* Univ Fla, BS, 33, MS, 34, PhD(herpet), 37. *Prof Exp:* Asst biol, 33-37, instr biol sci, 38-40, asst prof, 40-44, from assoc prof to prof, 45-59, GRAD RES PROF ZOOL, UNIV FLA, 59- *Concurrent Pos:* Mem, Univ Fla exped, Mex, 39-40, 41, Shire Valley Surv, Nyasaland, Africa, 52, Am Philos Soc exped, Trinidad & Costa Rica, 53, Univ Fla-Fla State Mus exped, Panama & Costa Rica, 54, Nat Sci Found, Cent Am, 55-, Brazil, West Africa, Portugal, Azores, 56, Mex, Spain, SAfrica, Argentina, Chile & Costa Rica, 57, 58, Off Naval Res, Nat Sci Found, Leeward Islands of Hawaiian Archipelago, 62, EAfrica & Madagascar, 63; prof, Escuela Agricola Panamericana, 45-49; biologist, United Fruit Co, 49; res assoc, Am Mus Natural Hist, 49-; assoc, Fla State Mus, 53-; tech adv to faculty sci & letters, Univ Costa Rica, 56-57; tech dir, Caribbean Conserv Corp, 59-; head marine turtle group, Survival Serv Comn, Int Union Conserv Nature, 63- *Honors & Awards:* Elliot Medal, Nat Acad Sci, 55; Burroughs Award, 56; Gold Medal, World Wildlife Fund, 73; Edward W Browning Award, 75. *Mem:* Am Soc Ichthyol & Herpet (vpres, 41); Am Soc Nat; fel Am Soc Fishery Res Biologists. *Res:* Zoogeography of turtles; ecology of reptiles and amphibians of Florida; tropical natural history; ecology and migration of sea turtles. *Mailing Add:* Dept of Zool Univ of Fla Gainesville FL 32611

CARR, BRUCE R, b Ann Arbor, Mich. OBSTETRICS & GYNECOLOGY, ENDOCRINOLOGY. *Educ:* Univ Mich, BS, 67, MD, 71. *Prof Exp:* Resident obstet & gynec, 71-75, fel reproductive endocrinol, 78-80, ASST PROF OBSTET & GYNEC, HEALTH SCI CTR, UNIV TEX, 80- *Mem:* Am Col Obstet & Gynec; Endocrine Soc; Am Fertil Soc. *Res:* Endocrinology of pregnancy; lipoprotein metabolism and cholesterol synthesis in human fetal adrenal and human corpus luteum; regulation of cholesterol synthesis in liver tissue. *Mailing Add:* Univ Tex Health Sci Ctr 5323 Harry Hines Blvd Dallas TX 75235

CARR, BURCH, b Indianapolis, Ind, Apr 17, 35; m 59; c 2. SPEECH PATHOLOGY. *Educ:* Denison Univ, BA, 57; Ohio Univ, MA, 62, PhD(speech path), 64. *Prof Exp:* Asst prof speech path, Univ Vt, 64-66; asst prof & dir speech path, Okla State Univ, 66-67; asst prof, Univ of Wis-Milwaukee, 67-69; chmn dept, 69-81, PROF SPEECH PATH, OKLA STATE UNIV, 81- *Mem:* Acoustical Soc Am; Am Speech & Hearing Asn; Speech Commun Asn. *Res:* Phonetics; stuttering. *Mailing Add:* 120 Hanner Hall Okla State Univ Stillwater OK 74074

CARR, CHARLES JELLEFF, b Baltimore, Md, Mar 27, 10; m 32; c 3. PHARMACOLOGY, CHEMISTRY. *Educ:* Univ Md, BS, 33, MS, 34, PhD(pharmacol), 37. *Hon Degrees:* DSc, Purdue Univ, 64. *Prof Exp:* From asst prof to prof pharmacol, Univ Md, 37-55; prof, Purdue Univ, 55-57; head pharmacol unit, Psychopharmacol Serv Ctr, NIMH, 57-63; chief sci anal br, Life Sci Div, Army Res Off, chief res & develop hqs, US Dept Army, Va, 63-67; dir life sci res off, Fedn Am Socs Exp Biol, 67-77; exec dir, 77-79, SCI COUNR, FOOD SAFETY COUN, 80- *Concurrent Pos:* Adj prof, Univ Md, 57-; managing ed, Regulatory Toxicol & Pharmacol, 81- *Mem:* Soc Pharmacol & Exp Therapeut; Am Chem Soc; Am Pharmaceut Asn; NY Acad Sci; Am Col Neuropsychopharmacol. *Res:* Carbohydrate metabolism; general anesthetic agents; hypotensive alkylnitrites; psychopharmacology; genetic basis for drug metabolic effects. *Mailing Add:* 6546 Belleview Dr Columbia MD 21046

CARR, CHARLES WILLIAM, b Minneapolis, Minn, July 20, 17; m 45; c 2. BIOCHEMISTRY. *Educ:* Univ Minn, BChem, 38, MS, 39, PhD(phys chem), 43. *Prof Exp:* Jr chemist, 39-43, res fel, 43-46, from instr to assoc prof, 46-64, actg head dept, 74-76, PROF BIOCHEM, UNIV MINN, MINNEAPOLIS, 64-, ASSOC HEAD DEPT, 76- *Mem:* Am Chem Soc; Am Soc Biol Chem; Soc Exp Biol & Med; NY Acad Sci; Am Soc Cell Biol. *Res:* Membrane structure and permeability; ion binding with proteins and other biopolymers; ionic effects on enzymes. *Mailing Add:* Dept Biochem Univ Minn Minneapolis MN 55455

CARR, CLIDE ISOM, b Creston, Mont, June 9, 20; m 45; c 3. RESEARCH ADMINISTRATION, TECHNICAL MANAGEMENT. *Educ:* Univ Mont, BA, 42; Univ Calif, PhD(chem), 49. *Prof Exp:* Asst, Univ Calif, 46-49; res chemist, Gen Labs, US Rubber Co, 49-55, Naugatuck Chem, 55-56 & Calif Res Corp, 56-57; res chemist & group leader, Res Ctr, US Rubber Co, 57-60, dept mgr, Fiber Res, 60-61 & Elastomer Res, 61-66, mgr tire eng, 66-69, mgr elastomer res, Uniroyal Res Ctr, Uniroyal Inc, 69-79, dir tire res, 79-81; RETIRED. *Mem:* AAAS; Am Chem Soc; Sigma Xi. *Res:* Management of tire technology and elastomer applications; plastics; fibers; rubber; tires; polymers. *Mailing Add:* 10802 Meade Dr Sun City AZ 85351

CARR, DANIEL OSCAR, b Kansas City, Kans, May 1, 34. BIOCHEMISTRY. *Educ:* Univ Mo-Kansas City, BS, 56; Iowa State Univ, PhD(biochem), 60. *Prof Exp:* From instr to asst prof, 63-69, ASSOC PROF BIOCHEM, UNIV KANS MED CTR, KANSAS CITY, 69- *Concurrent Pos:* USPHS fel, Univ Kans Med Ctr, Kansas City, 60-63. *Mem:* AAAS; Am Chem Soc; Am Soc Biol Chemists. *Res:* Mechanisms of enzymic catalysis, roles of vitamins and coenzymes with emphasis upon drug metabolism and clinical biochemistry. *Mailing Add:* Dept of Biochem Univ Kans Med Ctr Kansas City KS 66103

CARR, DAVID HARVEY, b Southport, Eng, Jan 10, 28; Can citizen; m 51; c 1. ANATOMY, CYTOGENETICS. *Educ:* Univ Liverpool, MB, ChB, 50, DSc, 70. *Prof Exp:* Lectr, Univ Western Ont, 58-61, from asst prof to assoc prof, 61-67; assoc prof, 67-70, PROF ANAT, COL HEALTH SCI, MCMASTER UNIV, 70- *Concurrent Pos:* Can Soc Study Fertil res award, 61. *Mem:* Am Asn Anat; Can Fedn Biol Soc; Genetics Soc Am. *Res:* Chromosome studies in clinical syndromes and spontaneous abortions. *Mailing Add:* Dept of Anat Col Health Sci McMaster Univ Hamilton ON L8S 4L8 Can

CARR, DAVID TURNER, b Richmond, Va, Mar 12, 14; m 79; c 1. INTERNAL MEDICINE, ONCOLOGY. *Educ:* Med Col Va, MD, 37; Univ Minn, MS, 47. *Prof Exp:* Intern, Grady Hosp, Ga, 37-38, asst resident, 38-39; chest serv, Bellevue Hosp, New York, 40-41, chief resident, 41-42; physician, Mt Morris Tuberc Hosp, 42-43; from asst prof to assoc prof med, Mayo Med Sch, 53-64, prof med, 64-79, chmn dept oncol & dir, Mayo Comprhensive Cancer Ctr, 74-75, consult, Mayo Clin, 47-79; PROF MED, M D ANDERSON HOSP & TUMOR INST, 79- *Mem:* Am Lung Asn (vpres, 71-72); Am Cancer Soc; fel Am Col Physicians; Am Thoracic Soc (vpres, 63-64); Int Asn Study Lung Cancer (vpres, 74-75, pres, 76, treas, 76-). *Mailing Add:* M D Anderson Hosp & Tumor Inst Tex Med Ctr Houston TX 77030

CARR, DENISE BENCIVENGA, b Brooklyn, NY, Feb 8, 52; m 72. ORGANOMETALLIC CHEMISTRY. *Educ:* Mt Holyoke Col, BA, 73; Princeton Univ, MA, 76, PhD(chem), 78. *Prof Exp:* SR RES CHEMIST ORGANOMETALLIC CHEM, MERCK SHARP & DOHME, 78- *Mem:* Am Chem Soc. *Res:* Applications of organometallic chemistry to organic synthesis. *Mailing Add:* R-203-801 Merck Sharp & Dohme Rahway NJ 07065

CARR, DODD S(TEWART), b Chicago, Ill, Dec 19, 25; m 53; c 2. ELECTRODEPOSITION OF METALS. *Educ:* Loyola Col, BS, 45; Johns Hopkins Univ, MSE, 48, DrEng(chem eng), 50; Rutgers Univ, MBA, 61. *Prof Exp:* Res chemist nickel plating, Int Nickel Co, 49-52; asst dir electrochem res, Bart Mfg Co, 52-56, dir res, Bart Labs & Design, Inc, 56-59; tech asst to vpres, Freeport Nickel Co, 59-60; vpres & tech dir, Bart Mfg Corp, 60-65; vpres & secy, Hill Cross Co, Inc, 65-66; proj mgr chem res, 66-67, mgr, 67-69, MGR CHEM RES & PATENTS, INT LEAD ZINC RES ORGN, INC, 69- *Concurrent Pos:* Consult, WHO, 74, 76 & 79. *Honors & Awards:* Silver Medal, Am Electroplaters Soc, 52. *Mem:* Fel Am Inst Chem; NY Acad Sci; sr mem Am Chem Soc; Electrochem Soc; Am Ceramics Soc. *Res:* Organolead chemical applications; zinc oxide stabilization of plastics against ultraviolet light degradation; zinc paint pigments; lead-acid batteries; antifouling coatings for shipbottoms; ceramic foodware safety; electroforming; nickel plating; wood preservatives; patenting and licensing. *Mailing Add:* 649 Lake St Newark NJ 07104

CARR, DONALD DEAN, b Fredonia, Kans, Mar 28, 31; m 55; c 4. GEOLOGY. *Educ:* Kans State Univ, BS, 53, MS, 58; Ind Univ, Bloomington, PhD(geol), 69. *Prof Exp:* Teacher pub sch, 59-60; geologist, Humble Oil & Ref Co, 60-62 & Geosci Div, Tex Instruments Co, 62-63; GEOLOGIST, COAL & INDUST MINERALS SECT, IND GEOL SURV, 63- *Concurrent Pos:* Subj ed, Indust Minerals, Encycl Mat Sci & Eng; prof, Ind Univ. *Mem:* Geol Soc Am; Am Asn Petrol Geologists; Am Inst Mining, Metall & Petrol Engrs; Am Inst Prof Geol. *Res:* Sedimentology; stratigraphy; geomorphology; economic geology of coal and industrial minerals. *Mailing Add:* Ind Geol Surv 611 N Walnut Grove Bloomington IN 47405

CARR, DUANE TUCKER, b Gunnison, Colo, July 6, 32; m 54; c 2. CHEMISTRY. *Educ:* Western State Col Colo, BA, 54; Purdue Univ, PhD(phys chem), 62. *Prof Exp:* Instr chem, Wabash Col, 60-61; asst prof 61-67, ASSOC PROF CHEM, COE COL, 67- *Concurrent Pos:* Asst prof chem, Agr Col, Haile Selassie Univ, 68-70. *Mem:* AAAS; Am Chem Soc. *Res:* Molecular structure, carbon-13 splittings in fluorine magnetic resonance spectra. *Mailing Add:* 1829 D Ave NE Cedar Rapids IA 52402

CARR, EDWARD ALBERT, JR, b Cranston, RI, Mar 3, 22; m 52; c 2. PHARMACOLOGY, INTERNAL MEDICINE. *Educ:* Brown Univ, AB, 42; Harvard Univ, MD, 45. *Prof Exp:* Intern, RI Hosp, 45-46; asst resident internal med, Cushing Hosp, 48; instr, Harvard Med Sch, 49-51; resident internal med, Pa Hosp, 51-52; from asst prof to prof internal med & pharmacol, Univ Mich, Ann Arbor, 53-74, dir, Upjohn Ctr Clin Pharmacol, 66-74; prof med & Pharmacol & chmn dept Pharmacol, Univ Louisville, 74-76; PROF MED & PHARMACOL & CHMN DEPT PHARMACOL & THERAPEUT, STATE UNIV NY BUFFALO, 76- *Concurrent Pos:* Res fel pharmacol, Harvard Med Sch, 48-49; exchange fel, St Bartholomew's Hosp, London, 52-53; mem pharmacol training comt, 64-66 & pharmacol-toxicol comt, Nat Inst Gen Med Sci, 70-74; mem revision comt, US Pharmacopeia, 65-75; mem, US Joint Comn Prescription Drug Use, 76- *Mem:* AAAS; Am Col Physicians; Am Soc Pharmacol & Exp Therapeut; Am Soc Clin Pharmacol & Therapeut (pres, 74-75); Am Thyroid Asn. *Res:* Clinical pharmacology; drug allergy; thyroid; radioisotopes; translation of animal data to human pharmacology. *Mailing Add:* Dept of Pharmacol & Therapeut State Univ NY Med Sch Buffalo NY 14214

CARR, EDWARD FRANK, b St Johnsbury, Vt, Aug 18, 20; m 54; c 3. PHYSICS. *Educ:* Mich State Univ, BS, 43, PhD(physics), 54. *Prof Exp:* Asst physics, Mich State Univ, 48-53, instr, 53-54; asst prof, St Lawrence Univ, 54-57; from asst prof to assoc prof, 57-69, PROF PHYSICS, UNIV MAINE, ORONO, 69- *Mem:* Am Phys Soc; Am Asn Physics Teachers. *Res:* physics of liquid crystal, particularly electrical properties. *Mailing Add:* Dept of Physics Univ of Maine Orono ME 04473

CARR, EDWARD MARK, b Warsaw, Poland, Sept 16, 18; nat US; m 44; c 2. ANALYTICAL CHEMISTRY. *Educ:* Univ Minn, BCh, 49, MS, 52. *Prof Exp:* Res chemist process develop, E I du Pont de Nemours & Co, 52-53; res chemist, Toni Div, Gillette Co, 53-56, res supvr anal chem sect, 56-61, res assoc, 61-64; mgr anal chem group, Noxzema Chem Co, 64-69, mgr anal chem, 69-78, SR RES SCIENTIST, NOXELL CORP, 78- *Mem:* Am Chem Soc; Soc Cosmetic Chemists. *Res:* Analytical chemistry of cosmetic materials and products; physical chemistry of surface active agents; emulsion polymerization. *Mailing Add:* 9605 Labrador Lane Cockeysville MD 21030

CARR, FREDDIE KAY, b Clinton, NC; m 65; c 2. PHARMACOLOGY, PHARMACEUTICAL CHEMISTRY. *Educ:* NC State Univ, BS, 67; Univ NC, PhD(pharmaceut chem), 75. *Prof Exp:* Nat Res Serv res fel & instr physiol, Albany Med Col, 75-78; ASST PROF PHARMACOL, PHILADELPHIA COL OSTEOP MED, 78- *Mem:* Am Chem Soc; Am Physiol Soc; Sigma Xi. *Res:* Cardiovascular and biochemical sequelae of circulatory shock. *Mailing Add:* Dept of Pharmacol Philadelphia Col of Osteop Med Philadelphia PA 19131

CARR, GEORGE LEROY, b Upperco, Md, Dec 11, 27; m 52; c 3. PHYSICS, SCIENCE EDUCATION. *Educ:* Western Md Col, BS, 48, MEd, 59; Cornell Univ, PhD(sci educ, physics), 69. *Prof Exp:* Teacher high sch, Md, 48-51; chmn dept sci, Milford Mill High Sch, 53-61; instr physics, Cornell Univ, 63-64; chmn dept sci, Pikesville High Sch, Md, 64-65; asst prof educ & physics, Western Md Col, 65-66; from asst prof to assoc prof, 66-70, PROF PHYSICS, UNIV LOWELL, 70- *Concurrent Pos:* Consult, Phys Sci Study Comt, 57-61; adv, Univ Lowell Prof Improv Prog, 69-71. *Mem:* AAAS; Am Asn Physics Teachers; Am Geophys Union. *Res:* Problem-solving in physics; environmental applications of physics; teaching of physics. *Mailing Add:* 2 Gifford Lane Chelmsford MA 01824

CARR, GERALD DWAYNE, b Pasco, Wash, Apr 1, 45; m 68. SYNTHETIC BOTANY, EVOLUTION. *Educ:* Eastern Wash State Col, BA, 68; Univ Wis-Milwaukee, MS, 70; Univ Calif, Davis, PhD(bot), 75. *Prof Exp:* Assoc bot, Univ Calif, Davis, 74-75; ASST PROF BOT, UNIV HAWAII, 75- *Concurrent Pos:* Consult bot, Kuakini Hosp & Home, 76. *Mem:* Soc Study Evolution; Am Soc Plant Taxonomists; Bot Soc Am; Int Asn Plant Taxon. *Res:* Biosynthetic and evolutionary studies of the Pacific states and Hawaiian tarweeds; biosystematics and cytogenetics of the Hawaiian flora. *Mailing Add:* Dept of Bot Univ of Hawaii Honolulu HI 96822

CARR, HERMAN YAGGI, b Alliance, Ohio, Nov 28, 24; m 59; c 2. CONDENSED STATE PHYSICS. *Educ:* Harvard Univ, BS, 48, MA, 49, PhD(physics), 53. *Prof Exp:* From asst prof to assoc prof, 52-64, PROF PHYSICS, RUTGERS COL, 64- *Concurrent Pos:* Guggenheim fel, 67. *Mem:* Fel Am Phys Soc; Am Asn Physics Teachers. *Res:* Nuclear magnetic resonance; physics of fluids; phase transitions. *Mailing Add:* Dept of Physics Rutgers Univ Box 849 New Brunswick NJ 08903

CARR, HOWARD EARL, b Headland, Ala, Sept 16, 15; m 39; c 2. PHYSICS. *Educ:* Auburn Univ, BS, 36; Univ Va, AM, 39, PhD(physics), 41. *Prof Exp:* Asst, Univ Va, 39-40; from asst to assoc prof physics, Univ SC, 41-44; physicist, Ford, Bacon, Davis Corp, Manhattan Dist, Oak Ridge, Tenn, 44; asst prof physics, US Naval Acad, 46-48; assoc prof, head dept, 53-78, PROF PHYSICS, AUBURN UNIV, 53- *Mem:* AAAS; fel Am Phys Soc; Am Asn Physics Teachers. *Res:* Isotope separation; thermal diffusion in liquids; mass spectrography; negative ions. *Mailing Add:* Dept of Physics Auburn Univ Auburn AL 36830

CARR, JACK A(LBERT), b Burlington, Ont, Apr 18, 20; m 42; c 2. CHEMICAL ENGINEERING. *Educ:* Univ Toronto, BASc, 41. *Prof Exp:* Mem staff, Dunlop Can Ltd, 40-41, compounder indust rubber goods, 45-49, head natural latex process control, 49-53; asst mgr, Dunlop Res Ctr, 53-65, asst gen mgr, 65-70, gen mgr, 71-80; RETIRED. *Mem:* Am Chem Soc; Chem Mkt Res Asn; emer mem Indust Res Inst; hon mem Can Res Mgt Asn; fel Chem Inst Can. *Res:* Polymer and polymerization chemistry; polymer physics. *Mailing Add:* 12 Plateau Circle Don Mills ON M3C 1M8 Can

CARR, JAMES DAVID, b Ames, Iowa, Apr 3, 38; m 68; c 2. ANALYTICAL CHEMISTRY. *Educ:* Iowa State Univ, BS, 60; Purdue Univ, PhD(anal chem), 66. *Prof Exp:* Technician gas chromatog, Ivorydale Labs, Procter & Gamble Co, 60; res fel chem, Univ NC, 65-66; asst prof, 66-70, ASSOC PROF CHEM, UNIV NEBR-LINCOLN, 71-, VCHMN DEPT, 81- *Concurrent Pos:* Vis assoc prof chem, Purdue Univ, 74-75. *Mem:* Am Chem Soc. *Res:* Kinetics and mechanism of ligand exchange reactions; optically active multidentate ligands; oxidation kinetics by ferrate VI; water quality analysis and treatment. *Mailing Add:* Dept Chem Univ Nebr Lincoln NE 68588

CARR, JAMES W(OODFORD), JR, b Columbus, Miss, Mar 13, 21; m 46. CHEMICAL ENGINEERING. *Educ:* Miss State Univ, BS, 43; Mass Inst Tech, MS, 47. *Prof Exp:* HEAD BUS & OPER SERV, EXXON RES & DEVELOP LABS, 47- *Mem:* Am Inst Chem Engrs; Instrument Soc Am. *Res:* Fluid solids; pilot plant engineering; process control instrumentation and techniques. *Mailing Add:* Exxon Res & Develop Lab 4045 Scenic Hwy Baton Rouge LA 70805

CARR, JAN, b London, Eng, Jan 22, 43; Can citizen; m 66; c 2. ELECTRICAL POWER SYSTEMS. *Educ:* Ryerson Polytech Inst, dipl, 63; Univ Toronto, BASc, 68; Univ Waterloo, MASc, 70, PhD(elec eng), 72. *Prof Exp:* Asst proj eng, Motorola Electronics Inc, 67-68; res engr, Saskatchewan Power Corp, 72-77; consult, 77-80; pres, Amicus Eng Corp, 80-81; CONSULT, 81- *Concurrent Pos:* Adj prof, Univ Waterloo, 73; assoc ed, Can J Elec Eng, 82- *Mem:* Inst Elec & Electronics Engrs; Inst Elec Engrs; Can Soc Elec Engrs; Eng Inst Can. *Res:* Instrumentation and simulation of electric power systems particularly with respect to protective relaying; high-voltage direct current transmission and distribution systems. *Mailing Add:* 85 McDougall Rd Waterloo ON N2L 2W4 Can

CARR, JEROME BRIAN, b Syracuse, NY, Dec 17, 38; m 61; c 3. OCEANOGRAPHY, LIMNOLOGY. *Educ:* St Louis Univ, BS, 61; Boston Col, MS, 65; Rensselaer Polytech Inst, PhD(oceanog), 71. *Prof Exp:* Phys oceanogr, US Naval Oceanog Off, Md, 61-62; oceanogr-geophysicist, Sperry Rand Res Ctr, Mass, 63-66; oceanogr, Gen Dynamics/Electronics, NY, 66; vis asst prof oceanog & geol, Purdue Univ, 66-67; oceanogr, Raytheon Corp, RI, 67-68 & Hazeltine Corp, Braintree, 69-70; environ consult, 70-71; environ scientist, Lowell Technol Inst Res Found, 71-72 & Anal Systs Eng Corp, 72-74; PRES & TECH DIR, CARR RES LAB, INC, 74- *Mem:* AAAS; Am Geophys Union; Am Inst Mining, Metall & Petrol Engrs; Aquatic Plant Mgt Soc; US Naval Inst. *Res:* Study of space-time variations of the ocean's thermal structure and relations to underwater acoustics; global tectonics; urban hydrology; developed new lake management techniques using iron and nitrogen control and using biological substitutions; hazardous waste site restoration. *Mailing Add:* 17 Waban St Wellesley MA 02181

CARR, JOHN B, b Olympia, Wash, Aug 29, 37; m 60; c 4. AGRICULTURAL CHEMISTRY MANAGEMENT. *Educ:* St Martin's Col, BSc, 59; Univ Wash, PhD(med chem), 63. *Prof Exp:* NIH fel med chem, Univ Kans, 63-64; org res chemist, 64-77, supvr detergent applications, 77-80, bus researcher, 80-81, MGR ORG CHEM, SHELL DEVELOP CO, 81- *Res:* Lipio metabolism; animal physiology and growth; parasitology; insecticides; herbicides; surfactants. *Mailing Add:* Shell Develop Co PO Box 4248 Modesto CA 95352

CARR, JOHN WEBER, III, b Durham, NC, May 16, 23; m 49; c 3. MATHEMATICS. *Educ:* Duke Univ, BS, 43; Mass Inst Technol, MS, 49, PhD(math), 51. *Prof Exp:* Res assoc, Mass Inst Technol, 51-52; res mathematician, Univ Mich, 52-55, asst & assoc prof, 55-59; assoc prof & dir res comput ctr, Univ NC, 59-62, prof, 62-63; assoc prof, 63-66, chmn grad group comput & info sci, 66-73, PROF COMPUT & INFO SCI, MOORE SCH ENG, UNIV PA, 66- *Concurrent Pos:* Lectr math, Univ Mich, 53-55; ed, Comput Reviews, 59-63; vis prof, Jiao Tong Univ, Shanghai, China, 78, 79 & 81; vis prof, NW Telecommun Eng Inst, Xian, China, 78-79; tech consult, UN Develop Prog, Hong Kong Productivity Ctr, Govt Hong Kong, 81. *Mem:* Am Math Soc; Asn Comput Mach (pres, 57-58). *Res:* Solution of Schrodinger equation; computing machinery logic and programming theory; numerical analysis; artificial intelligence; problem solving and programming theory. *Mailing Add:* Moore Sch Elec Eng Univ Pa Philadelphia PA 19104

CARR, JULIUS JAY, biochemistry, deceased

CARR, LAURENCE A, b Ann Arbor, Mich, Mar 21, 42; m 64; c 2. PHARMACOLOGY. *Educ:* Univ Mich, BS, 65; Mich State Univ, MS, 67, PhD(pharmacol), 69. *Prof Exp:* Asst, Mich State Univ, 66; from asst prof to assoc prof, 69-81, PROF PHARMACOL, UNIV LOUISVILLE, 81- *Concurrent Pos:* Fulbright res scholar, 80-81. *Honors & Awards:* Bristol Lab Award, 65. *Mem:* Am Soc Pharmacol & Exp Therapeut; AAAS; Soc Neurosci; Int Soc Neuroendocrinol. *Res:* Brain catecholamines and reproductive hormones; effects of drugs on the synthesis, release and metabolism of brain catecholamine. *Mailing Add:* Dept of Pharmacol & Toxicol Univ Louisville Louisville KY 40292

CARR, LAWRENCE JOHN, b De Kalb, Ill, July 4, 39; m 66; c 1. ORGANIC CHEMISTRY, POLYMER CHEMISTRY. *Educ:* St Mary's Col, Minn, BA, 62; Univ Ariz, PhD(org chem), 66. *Prof Exp:* Res chemist, Arco Chem, Atlantic Richfield, 66-71 & A-M Corp, 72-73; group leader chem, 73-79, STAFF SCIENTIST, BORG-WARNER CORP, 79- *Mem:* Am Chem Soc; Sigma Xi. *Res:* Process research on organic and polymeric products; applications research on new chemical products. *Mailing Add:* Borg-Warner Corp Wolf & Algonquin Rds Des Plaines IL 60018

CARR, MALCOLM WALLACE, b New York, NY, Oct 8, 99; m 42. ANATOMY, SURGICAL PATHOLOGY. *Educ:* Univ Pa, DDS, 22; Am Bd Oral & Maxillofacial Surg, dipl. *Prof Exp:* Instr oral surg, Col Physicians & Surgeons, Columbia Univ & clin asst vis oral surgeon, Vanderbilt Clin, 23-25; from asst attend to assoc attend, Fifth Ave Hosp, 23-36; assoc prof oral surg, NY Med Col & assoc oral surgeon, Flower & Fifth Ave Hosps, 36-65; CONSULT, 65- *Concurrent Pos:* Assoc, St Mary's Hosp, Children, 33-35; dir & vis oral surgeon, Metrop Hosp, 34-55, consult, 55-; dir & vis oral surgeon, Knickerbocker Hosp, 35-41, consult, 41-65; lectr, Grad Sch Med, Univ Pa, 36-41, 46-55, lectr, Sch Dent, 38-41; attend oral surgeon & dir outpatinet clin, St Luke's Hosp, 40-62, consult, 62-; consult-instr, Bur Med & Surg, US Dept Navy, St Albans, NY, 48-55; attend oral surgeon, NY Polyclin Med Sch & Hosp, 49-55, prof oral surg, 49-55; dir dent & vis oral surgeon, Bird S Coler Mem Hosp, 51-55, consult, 55-65; consult, Metrop Med Ctr, NY Col Med, 56- *Honors & Awards:* Hon fel, Royal Col Surg, Eng; comdr, Order Knights Hosp St John Jerusalem, 75. *Mem:* AAAS; fel Am Col Dent (pres, 45); AMA; Am Soc Anesthesiol; NY Acad Med. *Res:* Acute infections of face and neck; fractures of the Maxillae; oral surgery; neoplastic diseases. *Mailing Add:* 530 Park Ave New York NY 10021

CARR, MEG BRADY, b Belvidere, Ill, May 13, 49; m 72. REGRESSION ANALYSIS, NUMERICAL METHODS. *Educ:* Fla State Univ, BA, 71, PhD(appl math), 80; NC State Univ, MA, 72. *Prof Exp:* Grad asst, Nat Ctr Atmospheric Res, 75-80; ASST PROF COMPUT SCI, UNIV OKLA, 80- *Mem:* Am Statist Asn. *Res:* Applied mathematics, numerical methods, statistics, regression analysis and time series analysis; applications of mathematics and statistics to meteorology. *Mailing Add:* Sch Elec Eng & Comput Sci Univ Okla 202 W Boyd St Rm 219 Norman OK 73019

CARR, MICHAEL H, b Leeds, Eng, May 26, 35; US citizen; m 61; c 5. ASTROGEOLOGY, GEOCHEMISTRY. *Educ:* Univ London, BSc, 56; Yale Univ, MS, 57, PhD(geol), 60. *Prof Exp:* Res assoc geophys, Univ Western Ont, 60-62; geologist, US Geol Surv, 62-74, chief, Br Astrogeol Studies, 74-78. *Mem:* AAAS; Geol Soc Am; Am Geophys Union. *Res:* Geology of the moon and the planets; lunar stratigraphy; chemistry of the lunar regolith; geologic history of Mars; Martian volcanism; planetary exploration; trace element geochemistry; electron microprobe analysis. *Mailing Add:* US Geol Surv 345 Middlefield Rd Menlo Park CA 94025

CARR, MICHAEL JOHN, b Portland, Maine, Nov 12, 46; m 72. GEOLOGY. *Educ:* Dartmouth Col, AB, 69, MS, 71, PhD(geol), 74. *Prof Exp:* ASST PROG GEOL, RUTGERS UNIV, 74- *Mem:* Geol Soc Am; Am Geophys Union. *Res:* The relation of volcanos and active faults to underthrusting at convergent plate margins, with special emphasis on the Central American convergent plate margin. *Mailing Add:* Dept of Geol Rutgers Univ New Brunswick NJ 08903

CARR, NORMAN L(OREN), b Ill, Dec 7, 24; m 48; c 4. CHEMICAL ENGINEERING. *Educ:* Univ Ill, BS, 46; Univ Minn, MS, 50; Ill Inst Tech, PhD(chem eng), 53. *Prof Exp:* Process chem engr, Mallinckrodt Chem Works, 46-48; asst, Univ Minn, 48-49 & Ill Inst Tech, 49-50; res engr, Pure Oil Co, 52-59; SR STAFF ENGR, CHEM & MINERALS DIV, GULF RES & DEVELOP CO, 59- *Mem:* Am Chem Soc; Am Inst Chem Engrs. *Res:* Process simulation using analog and digital computers; reactor dynamics and control; fluidization heat transfer; viscosity of natural gases at high pressures; isomerization; kinetics; separations; chemical reaction engineering; coal liquefaction; uranium extraction. *Mailing Add:* 4215 El Rancho Dr Allison Park PA 15101

CARR, PAUL HENRY, b Boston, Mass, May 12, 35; m 60; c 3. SOLID STATE PHYSICS. *Educ:* Mass Inst Technol, BS, 57, MS, 61; Brandeis Univ, PhD(solid state physics), 66. *Prof Exp:* Res physicist, Calibration Ctr, Redstone Arsenal, Ala, 61-62; res physicist, 62-68, supvry res physicist, Air Force Cambridge Res Lab, 68-76, MEM STAFF, ELECTROMAGNETIC SCI DIV, ROME AIR DEVELOP CTR, 76- *Mem:* Am Phys Soc; Sigma Xi; fel Inst Elec & Electronics Engrs. *Res:* Electron paramagnetic resonance; vacuum standards and measurements; nonlinear phenomena in microwave ultrasonics; microwave phonons; kilomegacycle ultrasonics; microwave frequency elastic surface waves; surface acoustic wave signal processing. *Mailing Add:* Rome Air Develop Ctr Hanscom AFB Bedford MA 01731

CARR, PETER WILLIAM, b Brooklyn, NY, Aug 16, 44; m 66; c 3. ANALYTICAL CHEMISTRY. *Educ:* Polytech Inst Brooklyn, BS, 65; Pa State Univ, PhD(anal chem), 69. *Prof Exp:* Res assoc path, Med Sch, Stanford Univ, 68-69; from asst prof to assoc prof, Univ Ga, 69-77; assoc prof, 77-81, PROF CHEM, UNIV MINN, MINNEAPOLIS, 81- *Concurrent Pos:* Consult, Leeds & Northrup Co, 70-78; pres, Symp Anal Chem Pollutants Inc, 74- & Minn Chromatography Forum, 78-; consult, 3M Co, 79- *Mem:* Am Chem Soc; Am Asn Clin Chemists; NAm Thermal Anal Soc. *Res:* Bioanalytical chemistry; immobilized enzymes; high performance liquid chromatography; affinity chromatography; thermoanalytical chemistry; clinical chemistry; ion selective electrodes; electroanalytical chemistry. *Mailing Add:* Dept of Chem 207 Pleasant St Minneapolis MN 55455

CARR, RICHARD DEAN, b Columbus, Ohio, June 29, 29; m 53; c 4. DERMATOLOGY. *Educ:* Ohio State Univ, BA, 51, MD, 54. *Prof Exp:* Asst prof dermat, 63-65, dir div, 67-69, ASSOC PROF DERMAT, COL MED, OHIO STATE UNIV, 65- *Mem:* AMA; Am Acad Dermat; Soc Invest Dermat; Am Col Physicians; Am Asn Prof Dermat. *Res:* Clinical dermatology. *Mailing Add:* 1840 Zollinger Rd Columbus OH 43221

CARR, ROBERT CHARLES, b Oakland, Calif, Nov 13, 46. PARTICULATE EMISSIONS CONTROL. *Educ:* Univ Calif, Berkeley, BS, 68, MS, 70. *Prof Exp:* Res asst combustion res, Univ Calif, Berkeley, 68-72; sr engr power plant emissions testing, KVB Eng, 72-74; tech mgr particulate emissions control, 74-82, PROG MGR AIR QUAL CONTROL, ELEC POWER RES INST, 82- *Res:* Particulate emission control devices for pulverizer coal power plants; fabric filtration; electrostatic precipitation; development of particulate measurement instrumentation; nitro-oxygen emsission control; dry sulfonyl emission control; integrated environmental control systems. *Mailing Add:* 3412 Hillview Ave Elec Power Res Inst PO Box 10412 Palo Alto CA 94303

CARR, ROBERT H, b Ames, Iowa, June 3, 35; m 62. PHYSICS. *Educ:* Cornell Univ, BA, 57; Iowa State Univ, PhD(solid state physics), 63. *Prof Exp:* Res officer physics, Commonwealth Sci & Indust Res Orgn, Australia, 63-64; from asst prof to assoc prof, 64-72, PROF PHYSICS, CALIF STATE UNIV, LOS ANGELES, 72- *Mem:* Am Asn Physics Teachers; Cryogenic Soc Am (past pres). *Res:* Measurement of low temperature characteristics of materials. *Mailing Add:* Dept of Physics Calif State Univ Los Angeles CA 90032

CARR, ROBERT JOSEPH, b Milwaukee, Wis, Mar 27, 31. NUCLEAR CHEMISTRY, ANALYTICAL CHEMISTRY. *Educ:* Univ Calif, Los Angeles, BS, 51; Univ Calif, Berkeley, PhD(chem), 56. *Prof Exp:* From instr to asst prof chem, Wash State Univ, 55-61; chemist, Shell Develop Co, 61-67; prof chem, Merritt Col, Oakland, 67-70; PROF CHEM, COL ALAMEDA, 70- *Mem:* Am Chem Soc. *Res:* Nuclear reactions and spectroscopy; activation analysis; Mossbauer effect spectroscopy; application of radio-isotopes to problems in physical and analytical chemistry. *Mailing Add:* Dept of Chem Col of Alameda Alameda CA 94501

CARR, ROBERT WILSON, JR, b Montpelier, Vt, Sept 7, 34; m 58; c 3. CHEMICAL KINETICS, LASER PHOTOCHEMISTRY. *Educ:* Norwich Univ, BS, 56; Univ Vt, MS, 58; Univ Rochester, PhD(phys chem), 62. *Prof Exp:* Asst prof, 65-69, assoc prof, 69-76, PROF CHEM ENG, UNIV MINN, MINNEAPOLIS, 76- *Concurrent Pos:* Res fel, Harvard Univ, 63-65, lectr chem, 64-; asst ed, J Phys Chem, 70-80; NSF fel, Cambridge Univ, 71-72; Hon Ramsay Mem fel, 71-72; Fullbright scholar, 82. *Mem:* AAAS; Am Chem Soc; Sigma Xi. *Res:* Gas kinetics; photochemistry; energy transfer; unimolecular reactions; laser induced reactions. *Mailing Add:* Dept of Chem Eng & Mat Sci Univ of Minn Minneapolis MN 55455

CARR, ROGER BYINGTON, b Haverhill, Mass, Mar 25, 36; m 60; c 2. ASTRONOMY, PHYSICS. *Educ:* Bucknell Univ, BS, 63; Univ Fla, MS, 65, PhD(physics, astron), 67. *Prof Exp:* From instr to asst prof astron, Carleton Col, 67-72; asst prof physics, Alfred Univ, 72-76, res geophysicist, 76-77; vis asst prof, St John Fisher Col, 78; DIR EXTENDED EDUC, STATE UNIV NY AGR & TECH COL, ALFRED, 78- *Mem:* Am Astron Soc; Am Meteorol Soc; Sigma Xi. *Res:* Atmospheric extinction; eclipsing binary stars. *Mailing Add:* Sch of Allied Health Technol State Univ NY Agr & Technol Col Alfred NY 14802

CARR, RONALD E, b Newark, NJ, Sept 17, 32; m 57; c 2. OPHTHALMOLOGY, VISUAL PHYSIOLOGY. *Educ:* Princeton Univ, AB, 54; Johns Hopkins Univ, MD, 58; NY Univ, MS, 63. *Prof Exp:* Intern, Cornell-Bellevue Med Serv, 58-59; resident ophthal, Med Ctr, NY Univ, 59-62; clin assoc ophthal, NIH, Md, 63-64, actg assoc ophthalmologist, 64-65; asst prof, 65-69, assoc prof, 69-71, PROF OPHTHAL, MED CTR, NY UNIV, 71- *Concurrent Pos:* Fel ophthal, Med Ctr, NY Univ, 62-63; attend physician, Univ Hosp, NY, 65-; chief ophthal serv, Goldwater Mem Hosp, 67-77; dir retinal clin, Bellevue Hosp, 70- *Mem:* Am Acad Ophthal & Otolaryngol; Am Col Surg; Asn Res Ophthal; Am Ophthal Soc. *Res:* Clinical applications of visual electrophysiology; hereditary diseases of the retina; drug induced retinal degenerations. *Mailing Add:* Dept of Ophthal NY Univ Med Ctr New York NY 10016

CARR, RONALD IRVING, b Toronto, Ont, May 17, 35; m 68; c 2. IMMUNOLOGY, ALLERGY. *Educ:* Univ Toronto, BA, 58, MD, 62; Rockefeller Univ, PhD(immunol), 69. *Prof Exp:* Sr fel immunol, Nat Jewish Hosp, 69-70; asst prof, 70-77, ASSOC PROF MED, UNIV COLO MED CTR, DENVER, 78-; MEM STAFF, DEPT MED, NAT JEWISH HOSP RES CTR, 70- *Concurrent Pos:* Mem, Pulmonary, Allergy & Clin Immunol Adv Comt, Food & Drug Admin, 73-76 & chmn, 76-77; mem bd of dirs, Lupus Found Am Inc, 77- *Mem:* Am Asn Immunologists; Am Acad Allergy; Am Rheumatism Asn. *Res:* Mechanisms of food hypersensitivity and possible food related immune disease; factors regulating mucosal immunity; regulatory mechanisms and defects in systemic lupus erythematosus; immune complexes in disease. *Mailing Add:* Nat Jewish Hosp 3800 E Colfax Ave Denver CO 80206

CARR, RUSSELL L K, b Wakefield, Mich, Apr 26, 26; wid; c 2. ORGANIC CHEMISTRY. *Educ:* Ohio State Univ, BSc, 51, PhD(chem), 55. *Prof Exp:* From chemist to sr chemist, 55-64, res supvr, 64-66, sect mgr res, 66-70, MGR RES, HOOKER CHEM CORP, 70- *Mem:* Am Chem Soc. *Res:* Organic fluorine chemistry; fluorinations; hydrogenations, catalysis; organic phosphorus chemistry; reactions of elemental phosphorus and of esters of phosphorus acids; synthesis of phosphines; polymer chemistry. *Mailing Add:* 3405 Baseline Rd Grand Island NY 14072

CARR, SCOTT BLIGH, b Linton, Ky, Oct 11, 34; m 56; c 2. ANIMAL NUTRITION. *Educ:* Western Ky State Col, BS, 56; Univ Ky, MS, 63, PhD(dairy nutrit), 67. *Prof Exp:* Exten specialist forages, 67-71, ASST PROF RUMINANT NUTRIT & SCIENTIST-IN-CHARGE FORAGE TESTING LAB, VA POLYTECH INST & STATE UNIV, 71-, EXTEN SPECIALIST FORAGE EVAL, 77- *Mem:* Am Dairy Sci Asn; Am Soc Animal Sci. *Res:* Forages; dairy and beef nutrition. *Mailing Add:* Dept of Animal Nutrit Va Polytech Inst & State Univ Blacksburg VA 24060

CARR, STEPHEN HOWARD, b Dayton, Ohio, Sept 29, 42; m 67. POLYMER SCIENCE & TECHNOLOGY. *Educ:* Univ Cincinnati, BS, 65; Case Western Reserve Univ, MS, 67, PhD(polymer sci), 70. *Prof Exp:* From asst prof to assoc prof, 70-78, PROF MAT SCI & CHEM ENG, NORTHWESTERN UNIV, 78- *Concurrent Pos:* Assoc surg res, Evanston Hosp, 73- *Honors & Awards:* Ralph R Teeter Award, Soc Automotive Engrs, 80. *Mem:* AAAS; Am Chem Soc; Am Phys Soc; Am Soc Metals; Soc Plastic Engrs. *Res:* Molecular organization in the polymer solid state; electrical polarization and electrical conductivity in polymeric solids; biopolymers; mechanical behavior of polymers. *Mailing Add:* Dept of Mat Sci & Eng Northwestern Univ Evanston IL 60201

CARR, THOMAS DEADERICK, b Ft Worth, Tex, Jan 2, 17; m 61; c 1. PHYSICS, ASTRONOMY. *Educ:* Univ Fla, BS, 37, MS, 39, PhD(physics), 58. *Prof Exp:* Physicist & head blast measurement sect, Ballistic Res Lab, Aberdeen Proving Ground, Md, 40-45; civilian scientist with US Navy Bur Ord, 46; physicist & head antenna & propagation sect & staff mem directorate range develop, Air Force Missile Test Ctr, Patrick Air Force Base, Fla, 50-56; from asst prof to assoc prof, 58-69, PROF PHYSICS & ASTRON, UNIV FLA, 69-, ASSOC CHMN ASTRON, 77- *Mem:* Am Phys Soc; Am Astron Soc; Am Geophys Union. *Res:* Radio astronomy; geophysics; radio propagation; cosmic radiation; x-ray diffraction; blast measurements; ballistics; guided missile instrumentation. *Mailing Add:* Dept of Physics & Astron Univ of Fla Gainesville FL 32603

CARR, TOMMY RUSSELL, b Hardtner, Kans, July 30, 46; m 71; c 2. ANIMAL SCIENCE, FOOD SCIENCE. *Educ:* Kans State Univ, BS, 69, MS, 70; Okla State Univ, PhD(food sci), 75. *Prof Exp:* Res asst animal sci, Kans State Univ, 69-70; instr animal & food sci, Okla State Univ, 70-74; asst prof, 74-80, ASSOC PROF ANIMAL SCI, UNIV ILL, 80- *Mem:* Am Meat Sci Asn; Am Soc Animal Sci; Inst Food Technologists. *Res:* Growth and composition of meat animals and in methods used to evaluate compositional differences in both live animals and carcasses. *Mailing Add:* 205 Meat Sci Lab Univ Ill 1503 S Maryland Urbana IL 61801

CARR, WALTER JAMES, JR, b Knob Noster, Mo, May 6, 18; m 53; c 2. PHYSICS. *Educ:* Mo Sch Mines, BS, 40; Stanford Univ, EE, 42; Carnegie Inst Technol, DrSc(physics), 50. *Prof Exp:* From physicist to adv physicist, 42-65, mgr theoret physics dept, 65-70, CONSULT MAGNETISM, WESTINGHOUSE RES LABS, 70- *Mem:* Am Phys Soc; Inst Elec & Electronics Engrs. *Res:* Solid state physics; ferromagnetism; superconductivity. *Mailing Add:* Westinghouse Res Lab Beulah Rd Pittsburgh PA 15235

CARR, WILLIAM EDWARD STATTER, marine ecology, see previous edition

CARR, WILLIAM N, b Thayer, Mo, June 5, 36; m 63; c 1. BIOENGINEERING, BIOMEDICAL ENGINEERING. *Educ:* Carnegie Mellon Univ, BS & MS, 59, PhD(elec eng), 62; Southern Methodist Univ, MBA, 67. *Prof Exp:* Mem tech staff, Tex Instruments, Inc, 62-66; prof electronic sci & dir electronic sci ctr, Southern Methodist Univ, 67-69; pres, Zentron Int, Inc, 69-78; DIR ENG, DATAPOINT CORP, 79- *Concurrent Pos:* Assoc prof, Col Med, Baylor Univ, 67-78. *Mem:* AAAS; Am Phys Soc; Electrochem Soc; Inst Elec & Electronics Engrs; Soc Nuclear Med. *Mailing Add:* PO Box 40269 San Antonio TX 78229

CARRABINE, JOHN ANTHONY, b Cleveland, Ohio, Nov 8, 28; m 51; c 6. X-RAY CRYSTALLOGRAPHY, INORGANIC CHEMISTRY. *Educ:* John Carroll Univ, BS, 51, MS, 53; Case Western Reserve Univ, PhD, 70. *Prof Exp:* Chemist, Thompson Prods, Inc, 51-56; supvr phys res, Brush Beryllium Co, 56-66; asst prof, 66-72, assoc prof, 72-77, PROF CHEM, JOHN CARROLL UNIV, 77-, CHMN, CHEM DEPT, 81- *Concurrent Pos:* Lectr, Eve Col, John Carroll Univ, 56-66. *Mem:* Am Chem Soc. *Res:* Crystal and molecular structures of metal complexes of biochemically important substances; physical metallurgy of beryllium. *Mailing Add:* Dept of Chem John Carroll Univ North Park & Miramar Blvd Cleveland OH 44118

CARRADINE, WILLIAM RADELL, JR, b Austin, Tex, Jan 30, 41; m 63; c 2. CHEMICAL ENGINEERING. *Educ:* Tex Technol Col, BS, 64, MS, 65; Univ Tex, Austin, PhD(chem eng), 70. *Prof Exp:* RES ENGR, CONTINENTAL CHEM, CONTINENTAL OIL INC, 69- *Mem:* Am Inst Chem Engrs; Sigma Xi. *Res:* Economic analysis; process simulation; process development. *Mailing Add:* 2323 Turner Ponca City OK 74601

CARRAHER, CHARLES EUGENE, JR, b Des Moines, Iowa, May 8, 41; m 63; c 7. POLYMER CHEMISTRY, PHYSICAL CHEMISTRY. *Educ:* Sterling Col, BA, 63; Univ Mo-Kansas City, PhD(chem), 67. *Prof Exp:* Teaching asst chem, Univ Mo, 63-67; from asst prof to prof chem, Univ SDak, 67-76, dir, Gen Chem Prog, 67-76, chmn, Sci Div, 72-74; PROF CHEM & CHMN DEPT, WRIGHT STATE UNIV, 76- *Concurrent Pos:* Petrol Res Fund grant, 68-; Nat Sci Found grant, 70-73; adv, Sen McGovern, 72-75; Res Fund grant, 73-75; Nat tour speaker, 75-76; Am Chem Soc-Petrol Res Fund grants, 74-82; ed, Polymer Educ Newsletter, Advan Organometall & Inorganic Polymers, Advan Interfacial Synthesis; Plenary speaker, Royal Chem Soc Australia, 79. *Mem:* AAAS; Am Inst Chemists; Sigma Xi (pres-elect, 71-72, pres, 72-73); Am Chem Soc. *Res:* Preparation and characterization of phosphorus containing extended polar polymers and organometallic polymers; practical and theoretical molecular weight distribution determinations; published 15 books and 250 papers. *Mailing Add:* Wright State Univ Dayton OH 45431

CARRANO, ANTHONY VITO, b New York, NY, Mar 22, 42; m 64; c 2. CYTOGENETICS, BIOPHYSICS. *Educ:* Rensselaer Polytech Inst, BS, 64; Univ Calif, Berkeley, MB, 70, PhD(biophys), 72. *Prof Exp:* Fel, Div Biol & Med Res, Argonne Nat Lab, Ill, 72-73; biophysicist, Biomed Div, 73-80, LEADER CELL BIOL & MUTAGENESIS, LAWRENCE LIVERMORE LAB, UNIV CALIF, 80- *Concurrent Pos:* Adj asst prof, Sch Med, Univ Calif, Davis, 74; assoc ed, Radiation Res, 76-79. *Mem:* Am Soc Cell Biol; Am Soc Human Genetics; Radiation Res Soc; Genetics Soc Am; Environ Mutagen Soc. *Res:* Flow of chromosomes; mechanisms of sister chromatid exchange and chromosomal aberration production and persistence; human population monitoring for environmental exposure; chromosome structure; medical genetics. *Mailing Add:* Biomed Div L-452 Lawrence Livermore Lab Livermore CA 94550

CARRANO, RICHARD ALFRED, b Bridgeport, Conn, Oct 1, 40; div; c 2. PHARMACOLOGY, TOXICOLOGY. *Educ:* Univ Conn, BS, 63, MS, 65, PhD(pharmacol & biochem), 67. *Prof Exp:* Res pharmacologist, ICI US, Inc, 66-67, supvr gen pharmacol, 68-74; mgr pharmacol & toxicol, 74-77, DIR PRECLIN RES, ADRIA LABS, INC, 77- *Mem:* Am Chem Soc; Am Soc Pharmacol & Exp Therapeut; Am Pharmaceut Asn; NY Acad Sci. *Res:* Development of new drugs by guiding the studies to demonstrate efficacy and to prove safety in animals for extrapolation to man, administration of the relationships between regulatory and clinical research groups which are necessary to obtain this goal. *Mailing Add:* Adria Labs Inc Box 16529 Columbus OH 43216

CARRANO, SALVATORE ANDREW, b New Haven, Conn, Feb 2, 15. INORGANIC CHEMISTRY. *Educ:* Yale Univ, BS, 35; Boston Col, MS, 55, PhD(chem), 63. *Prof Exp:* Anal chemist, New Haven Clock Co, 35-38; res chemist, Seymour Mfg Co, 38-53; asst instr chem, Boston Col, 53-55, from asst prof to prof, 56-80, EMER PROF CHEM, FAIRFIELD UNIV, 80-; SR SCIENTIST, RES & DEVELOP DIV, AVCO, 55- *Concurrent Pos:* Teaching fel, Boston Col, 60-63; vis prof, Univ Tenn, 71. *Mem:* Am Chem Soc; Sigma Xi. *Res:* Structure and bonding studies of transition metal complexes utilizing chemical symmetry and group theory. *Mailing Add:* Dept of Chem Fairfield Univ Fairfield CT 06430

CARRARA, PAUL EDWARD, b San Francisco, Calif, Sept 16, 47. HOLOCENE CLIMATIC CHANGES. *Educ:* San Francisco State Col, BA, 69; Univ Colo, MSc, 72. *Prof Exp:* Res assoc, Inst Arctic & Alpine Res, Univ Colo, 72-74; GEOLOGIST, US GEOL SURV, 74- *Mem:* Int Glaciol Soc; Geol Soc Am; Am Quaternary Asn. *Res:* Holocene climatic changes and tree-ring analysis to date geomorphologic events. *Mailing Add:* US Geol Survey Fed Ctr MS 913 Box 25046 Denver CO 80225

CARRASQUER, GASPAR, b Valenica, Spain, Dec 21, 25; nat US; m 79; c 4. MEDICINE. *Educ:* Univ Valenica, MD, 51. *Prof Exp:* Intern, North Hudson Hosp, NJ, 53; resident internal med, City Hosp New York, 54-55 & Louisville Gen Hosp, Ky, 55-56; from instr to assoc prof med, 59-70, PROF EXP MED, SCH MED, UNIV LOUISVILLE, 71-, ASSOC PHYSIOL, 61- *Concurrent Pos:* Fel, Sch Med, Univ Louisville, 56-59; res fel, Am Heart Asn, 58-60, adv res fel, 60-62; USPHS career develop award, 67-72; estab investr, Am Heart Asn, 62-67. *Mem:* Am Physiol Soc; Am Biophys Soc; Soc Exp Biol & Med. *Res:* Renal physiology; ion transport; concentration mechanism of the urine. *Mailing Add:* Dept of Med Univ Loouisville PO Box 35260 Louisville KY 40292

CARRASQUILLO, ARNALDO, b Santa Isabel, PR, July 12, 37; m 63; c 2. MEDICINAL CHEMISTRY, SCIENCE EDUCATION. *Educ:* Univ PR, Rio Piedras, BS, 59, MS, 66; Ohio State Univ, PhD(org chem), 71. *Prof Exp:* Instr chem, Univ PR, Rio Piedras, 59-62, res asst, 62-63; res asst, PR Nuclear Ctr, 63-65 & Ohio State Univ, 70-71; from asst prof to assoc prof, 71-78, PROF CHEM, CATH UNIV PR, 78- *Concurrent Pos:* Biomed res dir, Cath Univ PR, 74-76. *Mem:* Am Chem Soc. *Res:* The synthesis of biologically important molecules, isolation and characterization of biologically active natural products; exploratory organic chemistry; the study and analysis of organic compounds in the biosphere. *Mailing Add:* PO Box 105 Sta 6 Ponce PR #00732

CARRAWAY, CORALIE ANNE CAROTHERS, b Montgomery, Ala; c 2. BIOCHEMISTRY, CELL BIOLOGY. *Educ:* Miss State Univ, BS, 61; Okla State Univ, PhD(biochem), 74. *Prof Exp:* Res asst biochem, Dept of Chem, Univ Ill, 63-66; lab technician, Univ Calif, Berkeley, 67-68; res assoc, Okla State Univ, 74-75; actg asst prof bact, Univ Calif, Los Angeles, 75-76; res assoc, Okla State Univ, 76-78, asst res biochemist, 78-81; ASST PROF, DEPT ONCOL, SCH MED, UNIV MIAMI, 81- *Concurrent Pos:* Fel Okla Heart Asn, Dept Biochem, Okla State Univ, 77-78. *Mem:* AAAS; Am Soc Cell Biol. *Res:* Regulation of plasma membrane functions; involvement of plasma membrane and cytoskeleton in differentiation and neoplastic transformation. *Mailing Add:* Dept Oncol Sch Med Univ Miami Coral Gables FL 33124

CARRAWAY, KERMIT LEE, b Utica, Miss, Mar 1, 40; m 62; c 1. BIOCHEMISTRY. *Educ:* Miss State Univ, BS, 62; Univ Ill, PhD(org chem), 66. *Prof Exp:* NIH res fel biochem, Univ Calif, 66-68; from asst prof to assoc prof biochem, Okla State Univ, 68-75, prof biochem, 75-81; PROF & CHMN ANAT, SCH MED, UNIV MIAMI, 81- *Concurrent Pos:* Mem, Molecular Cytol Study Sect, NIH, 75-78. *Mem:* Am Soc Cell Biol; Am Soc Biol Chemists. *Res:* Membrane biochemistry; protein chemistry. *Mailing Add:* Dept Anat Sch Med Univ Miami Miami FL 33101

CARREAU, PIERRE, b Montreal, Que, Nov 14, 39; m 63; c 3. CHEMICAL ENGINEERING, RHEOLOGY. *Educ:* Univ Montreal, BSc, 63, MSc, 65; Univ Wis, PhD(chem eng), 68. *Prof Exp:* Asst chem eng, 64-65, asst prof, 68-77, assoc prof chem eng, 77-80, chmn dept, 77-80, PROF, POLYTECH SCH, UNIV MONTREAL, 80- *Concurrent Pos:* Nat Res Coun Can res grant, 69-72; prof consult, Nat Res Coun-Bobtex Corp, Can, 69- *Mem:* Sr mem Chem Inst Can; Can Soc Chem Engrs; Soc Rheol. *Res:* Constitutive equations for viscoelastic fluids; transport phenomena applied to polymeric systems. *Mailing Add:* Dept of Chem Eng Univ of Montreal Polytech Sch Montreal PQ H3C 3A7 Can

CARREGAL, ENRIQUE JOSE ALVAREZ, b Padron, Spain, July 2, 32; US citizen; m 60; c 2. MEDICINE, PHYSIOLOGY. *Educ:* Univ Santiago, MD, 54, PhD(med), 60. *Prof Exp:* House doctor, Hosp Clin, Santiago, 54-55; instr physiol, Univ Santiago Med Dch, 55; fel physiol, Span Pharmacol Inst Madrid, 56-59; fel radiol, Univ Madrid, 57-59; fel neurophysiol, Coun Sci Invest, 60; res fel, Inst Med Res, Huntington Mem Hosp, Pasadena, Calif, 60-63; neurophysiologist, Stanford Res Inst, 63-65; assoc prof physiol, 66-69, ASSOC PROF NEUROSURG, SCH MED, UNIV SOUTHERN CALIF, 70- *Concurrent Pos:* Consult, Huntington Mem Hosp, Pasadena, Calif & City of Hope Nat Med Ctr, Duarte. *Mem:* AAAS; Am Physiol Soc; Soc Neurosci; Span Soc Physiol Sci. *Res:* Neurophysiology of pain and sensory mechanism, neural control of respiration; synaptology. *Mailing Add:* 1870 Alpha Ave S Pasadena CA 91030

CARREIRA, LIONEL ANDRADE, b Worcester, Mass, Nov 1, 44; m 70; c 1. PHYSICAL CHEMISTRY, MOLECULAR SPECTROSCOPY. *Educ:* Worcester Polytech Inst, BS, 66; Mass Inst Technol, PhD(phys chem), 69. *Prof Exp:* Fel chem, Univ Fla, 69-71; res assoc, Univ SC, 71-73; instr, 73-75, ASST PROF CHEM, UNIV GA, 75- *Mem:* Am Chem Soc; Sigma Xi. *Res:* Studies of far infrared and Raman spectra of simple polyatomic molecules having large amplitude oscillations, quasi-linear molecules with anomalously low frequency bending modes and other molecules with unusual vibrational potential functions. *Mailing Add:* Dept of Chem Univ of Ga Athens GA 30601

CARREKER, R(OLAND) P(OLK), JR, b Birmingham, Ala, Aug 6, 25; m 48; c 3. METALLURGICAL ENGINEERING, MATERIALS ECONOMICS. *Educ:* Univ Ill, BS, 45, MS, 47; Rensselaer Polytech Inst, PhD(metall eng), 55. *Prof Exp:* Asst, Gen Elec Res Lab, 47-52, res assoc, 52-57, metall engr, 57-70, consult mat resources, Mat Resources Oper, 70-73, MGR MAT TECH & ECON ANAL, MAT RESOURCES OPER, GEN ELEC CO, 73- *Mem:* Am Soc Metals; Am Inst Mining, Metall & Petrol Engrs. *Res:* Deformation of metals; continuous casting; process development; economic analysis; mineral ventures evaluation; business systems for strategic planning and forecasting. *Mailing Add:* 12 Elmwood Lane Westport CT 06880

CARRERA, GUILLERMO MANUEL, b Vieques, PR, Jan 3, 13; m 45; c 2. PATHOLOGY. *Educ:* Univ PR, BS, 34; Tulane Univ, MD, 37. *Prof Exp:* Instr, 45-53, assoc prof path, 53-75, head dept, Ochsner Med Ctr, 54-72, CLIN PROF PATH, TULANE UNIV, 75- *Mem:* AAAS; Am Asn Exp Path; Soc Exp Biol & Med; Am Asn Pathologists; AMA. *Mailing Add:* Dept of Path Ochsner Med Ctr New Orleans LA 70121

CARRICK, LEE, b Detroit, Mich, Oct 31, 43; m 67. EXPERIMENTAL INFECTIOUS DISEASES. *Educ:* Wayne State Univ, BS, 66; PhD(biol), 73. *Prof Exp:* Technologist, 69-70, res asst, 70-74, instr, 74-76, ASST PROF MICROBIOL, MED SCH, WAYNE STATE UNIV, 76- *Mem:* Soc Exp Biol & Med; Sigma Xi; Am Soc Microbiol; Am Inst Biol Sci; AAAS. *Res:* Murine models of opportunistic infections and granulomatous diseases with emphasis on the fractionation and characterization of lympholines and studies of their role in the activation of macrophages for cell-mediated immunity and fibroblasts in chronic inflammation. *Mailing Add:* Dept Immunol & Microbiol Sch Med Wayne State Univ 540 E Canfield Detroit MI 48201

CARRICK, WAYNE LEE, b Benton, Ark, Feb 23, 27; m 49; c 5. ORGANIC CHEMISTRY, POLYMER CHEMISTRY. *Educ:* Univ Ark, BS, 52, MS, 53, PhD(phys org chem), 55. *Prof Exp:* Res chemist, 54-56, group leader, 56-65, assoc dir res & develop, Union Carbide Corp, 65-77; VPRES RES & DEVELOP, CHEMPLEX CO, 77- *Mem:* Am Chem Soc. *Res:* Reactions mechanisms; kinetics; catalysis; organic compounds of transition metals; high polymers. *Mailing Add:* RR 2 Box 106-C Long Grove IL 60047

CARRICO, CHRISTINE KATHRYN, b Charlottesville, Va, April 25, 50. SCIENCE ADMINISTRATION. *Educ:* Hollins Col, BA, 71; Yale Univ, PhD(pharmacol), 76. *Prof Exp:* Fel assoc pharmacol, Yale Univ, 76-77; res assoc, Nat Cancer Inst, 77-79, HEALTH SCIENTIST ADMINR, PHARMACOL SCI, NAT GEN MED SCI, NIH, 79- *Mem:* Am Soc Pharmacol & Exp Therapeut. *Res:* Molecular pharmacology; clinical pharmacology; drug metabolism and drug disposition. *Mailing Add:* 4521 Maple Ave Bethesda MD 20814

CARRICO, ROBERT JOSEPH, b Mishawaka, Ind, Dec 27, 38; m 76. BIOCHEMISTRY. *Educ:* Purdue Univ, BS, 64; Univ Wis, PhD(biochem), 68. *Prof Exp:* Res asst biochem, Univ Wis, 68-69; fel, Univ Gothenburg, 69-71; RES SCIENTIST BIOCHEM, MILES LABS, INC, 71- *Concurrent Pos:* Fel biochem, Albert Einstein Col Med, 71-72. *Res:* Applications of immobilized enzymes in clinical chemistry; activities of modified substrates and cofactors with enzymes; monitoring of therapeutic drugs in blood. *Mailing Add:* Miles Labs Inc 1127 Myrtle St Elkhart IN 46514

CARRIER, GEORGE FRANCIS, b Millinocket, Maine, May 4, 18; m 46; c 3. ENGINEERING & APPLIED MATHEMATICS. *Educ:* Cornell Univ, ME, 39, PhD(appl mech), 44. *Prof Exp:* From asst prof to prof eng, Brown Univ, 46-52; Gordon McKay prof mech eng, 52-72, T JEFFERSON COOLIDGE PROF APPL MATH, HARVARD UNIV, 72- *Concurrent Pos:* Mem bd trustees, Rensselaer Polytech Inst; mem coun eng col, Cornell Univ; Assoc ed, J Fluid Mech. *Honors & Awards:* Richards Mem Award, 63 & Timoshenko Medal, 78, Am Soc Mech Engrs; Von Karman Medal, Am Soc Civil Engrs, 77; Von Karman Prize, Soc Indust & Appl Math, 79; Appl Math & Numerical Analysis Award, Nat Acad Sci, 80; Silver Centennial Medal, Am Soc Mech Engrs, 80. *Mem:* Nat Acad Sci; Am Acad Arts & Sci; Am Soc Mech Engrs; Nat Acad Eng; fel Am Acad Arts & Sci. *Res:* Applied mathematics; hydrodynamics. *Mailing Add:* Pierce Hall Harvard Univ Cambridge MA 02138

CARRIER, GERALD BURTON, b Punxsutawney, Pa, Aug 24, 27; m 49; c 3. MATERIALS SCIENCE, PHYSICS. *Educ:* Bowling Green State Univ, BA & BS, 50; Ohio State Univ, MS, 56. *Prof Exp:* RES PHYSICIST GLASS & CERAMICS, CORNING GLASS WORKS, 52- *Concurrent Pos:* Math instr, Elmira Col. *Mem:* Electron Micros Soc Am. *Res:* Electron microscopy of glasses; glass ceramics; ceramics. *Mailing Add:* Corning Glass Works Sullivan Park Corning NY 14830

CARRIER, STEVEN THEODORE, b Havre, Mont, Nov 8, 38; m 63; c 2. MEDICAL STATISTICS, BIOSTATISTICS. *Educ:* Calif Polytech State Univ, BS, 67; Tex A&M Univ, PhD(statist), 75. *Prof Exp:* Analyst math, Naval Weapons Ctr, Calif, 67-68; statistician, Am Cyanamid Co, 71-75, group leader statist anal, Lederle Labs, 75-77; mgr statist sect, Med Oper Dept, Cutter Labs, Berkeley, 77-79; SECT HEAD, BIOSTATIST DEPT, PHARMACEUT PROD DIV RES & DEVELOP, ABBOTT LABS, 79- *Mem:* Drug Info Asn; Am Statist Asn; Biometrics Soc; Soc Clin Trials. *Res:* New statistical methods for the design and analysis of clinical trial data. *Mailing Add:* 3804 11th St Winthrop Harbor IL 60096

CARRIER, W(ILLIAM) DAVID, III, b Allentown, Pa, Dec 21, 43; m 65; c 2. GEOTECHNICAL ENGINEERING. *Educ:* Mass Inst Technol, SB, 65, SM, 66, ScD(civil eng), 68. *Prof Exp:* Lunar soil mech specialist, Johnson Space Ctr, NASA, 68-73; asst chief soils engr, Bechtel, Inc, San Francisco, 73-77; mgr solid waste systs, Woodward-Clyde Consults, 77-78; mgr, Geotech Group, 78-80, DIR ENG, BROMWELL ENG, 80- *Concurrent Pos:* Consult geotech engr, Lunar & Planetary Inst, Houston, 77-78; mem, US Comt Large Dams. *Honors & Awards:* Norman Medal, Am Soc Civil Engrs & Cert Commendation, Johnson Space Ctr, NASA, 72. *Mem:* Am Soc Civil Engrs; Int Soc Soil Mech & Found Engrs; Nat Soc Prof Engrs; Am Inst Mining Engrs. *Res:* Geotechnical properties of industrial and mining solid wastes; development of new methods of disposal. *Mailing Add:* Bromwell Eng PO Box 5467 Lakeland FL 33803

CARRIERE, RITA MARGARET, b Toronto, Ont, Can, Apr 25, 30. HISTOLOGY. *Educ:* McGill Univ, BSc, 50, MSc, 54, PhD, 60. *Prof Exp:* Lectr histol, Univ Montreal, 55-57, asst prof histol, embryol & endocrinol, 57-60; ASST PROF ANAT, STATE UNIV NY DOWNSTATE MED CTR, 60- *Mem:* Sigma Xi; Am Soc Cell Biol. *Res:* Liver growth and differentiation; age changes in rat orbital glands; intestinal epithelium; dynamics of cell populations. *Mailing Add:* 495 Lenox Rd Brooklyn NY 11203

CARRIG, COLIN BRUCE, veterinary radiology, see previous edition

CARRIGAN, CHARLES ROGER, b Pasadena, Calif, Sept 7, 49; m 76; c 1. FLUID MECHANICS, HEAT TRANSFER. *Educ:* Univ Calif, Los Angeles, BA, 71, MS, 73, PhD(geophys), 77. *Prof Exp:* Res fel, Dept Geod & Geophys, Cambridge Univ, 77-78 & 79, NATO fel, 78-79; res geophysicist, Inst Geophys & Planetary Physics, Univ Calif, Los Angeles, 79-80; MEM TECH STAFF, GEOPHYS RES DIV, SANDIA NAT LABS, 80- *Mem:* Am Geophys Union; Sigma Xi. *Res:* Natural convection and heat transfer in geophysical and astrophysical systems; laboratory studies of the stability of convecting fluids; fluid mechanics of volcanism. *Mailing Add:* Geophys Res Div 5541 Sandia Nat Labs Albuquerque NM 87115

CARRIGAN, P H, JR, b Gloucester, Mass, Apr 19, 28; m 51, 75. HYDRAULIC ENGINEERING, HYDROLOGY. *Educ:* Univ Calif, Los Angeles, BS, 49; Ga Inst Technol, MS, 63; Colo State Univ, PhD, 75. *Prof Exp:* Hydraul engr, 49-66, res hydrologist, 66-72, sr staff hydrologist, 72-79, RES MGR, US GEOL SURV, 79- *Mem:* Am Soc Civil Engrs; Am Geophys Union; Inst Asn Hydraul Res; Sigma Xi. *Res:* Fluid mechanics; turbulent diffusion; transport of radionuclides in streams; statistical hydrology. *Mailing Add:* US Geol Surv Nat Ctr Stop 432 Reston VA 22092

CARRIGAN, RICHARD ALFRED, b Somerville, Mass, May 11, 06; m 31; c 1. ENVIRONMENTAL CHEMISTRY, SCIENCE ADMINISTRATION. *Educ:* Univ Fla, BS, 32; Cornell Univ, PhD(soil chem), 48. *Prof Exp:* High sch teacher, Fla, 32-33; lab supvr, Magnolia Petrol Co, Tex, 33-38; from asst chemist to assoc chemist exp sta, Univ Fla, 38-45, from assoc biochemist to biochemist, 45-51, prof soils, Col Agr, 48-51; supvr anal chem, Armour Res Found, Ill, 51-60; prog dir sci facil eval group, Div Inst Prog, 60-64, staff assoc, 64-70, prog mgr, Div Inst Develop, 70-71, prog mgr, Div Advan Environ Res & Technol, 71-78, prog mgr, Div Prob-focused Res Applns, 78-79, PROG DIR, DIV ATMOSPHERIC SCI, NSF, 80- *Concurrent Pos:* Specialist anal chem, Union of Burma Appl Res Inst, 54-55. *Mem:* Fel AAAS; Am Chem Soc; fel Am Inst Chem; Soil Sci Soc Am; Am Geophys Union. *Res:* Chemistry of minor elements in soils; spectrographic analysis; pasture fertility; chemistry of cobalt in soils; spectroscopy of plasmas; federal grant administration. *Mailing Add:* 2475 Virginia Ave NW Apt 304 Washington DC 20037

CARRIGAN, RICHARD ALFRED, JR, b Miami, Fla, Feb 17, 32; m 54; c 2. ELEMENTARY PARTICLE PHYSICS. *Educ:* Univ Ill, BS, 53, MS, 56, PhD(physics), 62. *Prof Exp:* Jr physicist, Firestone Tire & Rubber Co, 53; res physicist, Carnegie Inst Technol, 61-64, asst prof physics, 64-68; dir personnel serv, 72-76, asst dir, 76, PHYSICIST, FERMI NAT ACCELERATOR LAB, 68-, ASST HEAD, RES DIV, 77- *Concurrent Pos:* Guest res assoc, Brookhaven Nat Lab, 62-63, guest asst physicist, 63-67; consult, Am Inst Res, 63-64; sr Fulbright fel, Deutsches Elektron-Synchrotron, 67-68. *Mem:* AAAS; Am Phys Soc; Sigma Xi. *Res:* Experimental elementary particle physics; particle scattering; magnetic monopole hypothesis. *Mailing Add:* Fermi Nat Accelerator Lab Box 500 Batavia IL 60510

CARRIKER, MELBOURNE ROMAINE, b Santa Marta, Colombia, Feb 25, 15; US citizen; m 43; c 4. MALACOLOGY, MARINE INVERTEBRATE BIOLOGY. *Educ:* Rutgers Univ, BS, 39; Univ Wis, PhM, 40, PhD(invert zool), 43. *Hon Degrees:* DSc, Beloit Col, 68. *Prof Exp:* Asst zool, Univ Wis, 39-43; instr, Rutgers Univ, 46-47, asst prof, 47-54; assoc prof, Univ NC, 54-61; fisheries res biologist & chief shellfish mortality prog, Biol Lab, US Bur Com Fisheries, Md, 61-62; dir systs-ecol prog, Marine Biol Lab, 62-72, investr, 72-73; PROF, COL MARINE STUDIES, UNIV DEL, 73- *Concurrent Pos:* Mem ornith exped, 34; trustee, Int Oceanog Found, 64-; mem corp, Marine Biol Lab, 62-78; adv comt biol study of plant site, Conn Yankee Atomic Power Plant, 65-75; adv comt oceanic biol to Off Naval Res, Am Inst Biol Sci, 66-69; adj prof, Univ RI, 65-73 & Boston Univ, 68-73; bioinstrumentation coun, 69-72; mem, President's Fed Water Pollution Control Adv Bd, 69-75; assoc mus comp zool, Harvard Univ, 67-73; res fel, Acad Natural Sci, Philadelphia, 68-; mem adv bd, Quarterly Rev Biol, 68-; mem ecol adv comt, Environ Protection Agency Sci Adv Bd, 75-78; assoc, Del Mus Natural Hist, 75-77. *Mem:* AAAS; Am Soc Zool; Ecol Soc Am; Atlantic Estuarine Res Soc (pres, 61); Nat Shellfisheries Asn (pres, 57-59). *Res:* Anatomy, histology, behavior, ecology and physiology of gastropods; ecology and ultrastructure of bivalve larvae; estuarine and marine ecology; mechanisms of penetration of calcareous substrata by invertebrates, especially of boring gastropods; ultrastructure and chemistry of bivalve shell. *Mailing Add:* Col of Marine Studies Univ of Del Lewes DE 19958

CARRIKER, ROY C, b Spokane, Wash, July 21, 37; m 65. PHYSICS. *Educ:* Wash State Univ, BS, 60; Trinity Col, Conn, MS, 63; Univ Conn, PhD(physics), 68; Harvard Univ, MBA, 76. *Prof Exp:* Sr engr, Pratt & Whitney Aircraft Div, United Aircraft Corp, 60-65, res engr, United Aircraft Res Labs, 65-66, sr res engr, 66-68, supvr optical technol, 68-69, chief electronic instrumentation, 69-70; tech dir, Precision Metals Div, Hamilton Watch Co, 70-72; dir eng & develop, Hamilton Technol, Inc, 72-74; pres, R C Carriker & Assoc, 74-76; GEN MGR, SERMETEL INC, 76-; V PRES, TELEFLEX INC, 78- *Res:* Solid state physics, especially rare earth-transition metal alloys, transport properties and superconductivity; optics, especially spectroscopy of flames and plasmas, coherent optics and holography; instrumentation techniques. *Mailing Add:* Sermetel Int Hq Limerick Rd Limerick PA 19468

CARRINGTON, ELSIE REID, b Philadelphia, Pa, Sept 19, 11; m 43. OBSTETRICS & GYNECOLOGY. *Educ:* Wheaton Col, Ill, AB, 33; Temple Univ, MD, 41, MS, 49; Am Bd Obstet & Gynec, dipl. *Prof Exp:* Assoc prof, Sch Med, Temple Univ, 58-61; res prof, Med Col Pa, 61-67, prof obstet & gynec & chmn dept, 67-77; prof obstet & gynec, Univ NMex, 77-80. *Concurrent Pos:* Adj prof obstet & gynec, Univ NMex, 80- *Mem:* AMA; Am Asn Obstet & Gynec; Asn Prof Gynec & Obstet; Am Col Obstet & Gynec. *Res:* Carbohydrate metabolism in pregnancy; fetal and neonatal welfare; placental function; monitor study of fetal and neonatal instantaneous heart rate patterns. *Mailing Add:* Dept of Gynec & Obstet Univ of NMex Albuquerque NM 87131

CARRINGTON, THOMAS JACK, b Amarillo, Tex, June 1, 29; m 56; c 2. GEOLOGY. *Educ:* Univ Ky, BS, 58, MS, 60; Va Polytech Inst, PhD(geol), 65. *Prof Exp:* Petrol consult, Ky, 59; asst prof geol, Birmingham-Southern Col, 61-65, actg chmn dept, 61-62 & 63-65, chmn, 65-67, assoc prof, 65-67; PROF GEOL & HEAD DEPT, AUBURN UNIV, 67- *Concurrent Pos:* Dir, Nat Sci Found undergrad res participation prog & equip grant, Birmingham-Southern Col, 63-64. *Mem:* Geol Soc Am; Nat Asn Geol Teachers. *Res:* Stratigraphy, origin and areal distribution of geologic rock formations in the Talladega Group, Alabama; geologic structural development in the Piedmont area of Alabama. *Mailing Add:* Dept of Geol Auburn Univ 8080 Haley Center Auburn AL 36830

CARRINGTON, TUCKER, b Cincinnati, Ohio, Oct 19, 27; m 57; c 3. PHYSICAL CHEMISTRY. *Educ:* Univ Va, BS, 48; Calif Inst Technol, PhD(chem), 52. *Prof Exp:* Instr chem, Yale Univ, 52-54; phys chemist, Nat Bur Standards, 56-68, Nat Acad Sci-Nat Res Coun resident res assoc, 56-57; PROF CHEM, YORK UNIV, 68- *Honors & Awards:* Silver Medal, Combustion Inst, 62. *Mem:* Am Phys Soc; Chem Inst Can. *Res:* Energy transfer between resolved quantum states of small molecules in gases. *Mailing Add:* Dept of Chem York Univ Toronto ON M3J 1P3 Canada

CARROCK, FREDERICK E, b Utica, NY, Oct 9, 31; m 59; c 1. PHYSICAL CHEMISTRY, ORGANIC CHEMISTRY. *Educ:* Syracuse Univ, BA, 54, MS, 56; State Univ NY, Syracuse, PhD(chem), 59. *Prof Exp:* Asst, State Univ NY, Syracuse, 54-56; res chemist, US Rubber Co, 59-61; supvr lab develop res, Rexall Chem Co, 61-65, asst mgr process develop res, Dart Industs Inc, 65-70, dir prod develop, 70-78; MGR TECH DEVELOP, MOBIL CHEM CO, 78- *Mem:* Am Chem Soc; fel Am Inst Chemists. *Res:* Free radical and polymer chemistry. *Mailing Add:* 151 Albright Lane Paramus NJ 07652

CARROLL, ARTHUR PAUL, b New Orleans, La, Aug 1, 42. PLANT PHYSIOLOGY, PLANT BIOCHEMISTRY. *Educ:* Col Santa Fe, BS, 65; Purdue Univ, PhD(biol), 75. *Prof Exp:* Teacher biol & chmn dept, Archbishop Rummel High Sch, 65-70; instr, Purdue Univ, 75-76; asst prof biol, 76-77, CHMN DEPT SCI, COL SANTA FE, 77- *Concurrent Pos:* Consult, Controls for Environ Pollution, 78- *Mem:* AAAS; Am Soc Plant Physiol. *Res:* Development and reproductive behavior of the green alga, chlorella pyrenoidosa, grown in synchronous cultures. *Mailing Add:* Dept of Sci Col of Santa Fe Santa Fe NM 87501

CARROLL, BENJAMIN L, physical chemistry, applied mathematics, see previous edition

CARROLL, BERNARD JAMES, b Sydney, Australia, Nov 21, 40; m 66; c 2. EXPERIMENTAL PSYCHIATRY, PSYCHOPHARMACOLOGY. *Educ:* Univ Melbourne, BSc, 61, MB, BS, 64, DPM, 69, PhD(endocrinol), 72. *Prof Exp:* Resident med officer, Royal Melbourne Hosp, 65-66, sr house physician, 66-67; clin supvr psychiat, Univ Melbourne, 67-68, med res fel, 68-69; sr res officer, Nat Health & Med Res Coun, 69-70, res fel, 70-71; asst prof psychiat, Univ Pa, 71-73; assoc prof, 73-76, PROF PSYCHIAT, UNIV MICH, ANN ARBOR, 76-, ACTG CHMN, 81-, RES SCIENTIST, MENT HEALTH RES INST, 73-, ASSOC DIR CLIN RES, 77- *Concurrent Pos:* Royal Australian Col Physicians traveling fel endocrinol, 70; Nat Health & Med Res Coun Australia Charles J Martin overseas fel, 71; mem extramural grants comt, Ill Dept Ment Health, 73-, chmn, 76-; consult, Intramural Prog Rev, 75; assoc ed, Psychoneuroendocrinology, 75- *Mem:* Int Soc Psychoneuroendocrinol; Int Col Neuropsychopharmacol; AAAS; Soc Biol Psychiat. *Res:* Clinical psychobiology of depression and mania; clinical and experimental psychopharmacology; behavioral pharmacology; psychoendocrinology; neuroendocrinology. *Mailing Add:* Ment Health Res Inst Univ of Mich Ann Arbor MI 48109

CARROLL, BURT HARING, b Tenafly, NJ, Mar 20, 96; m 24; c 3. CHEMISTRY. *Educ:* Cornell Univ, ChB, 17; Univ Wis, PhD(chem), 22. *Prof Exp:* Mem staff, Arthur D Little, Inc, 17; assoc chemist, Nat Bur Standards, 22-29, chemist, 29-33; chemist, Eastman Kodak Co, 33-45, supvry scientist, 45-51, sr res assoc, 52-61; prof, 62-81, EMER PROF PHOTOG SCI, ROCHESTER INST TECHNOL, 81- *Concurrent Pos:* Vis lectr, Soc Photo Sci & Eng, 76. *Honors & Awards:* Jansen Medal, French Photog Soc; Henderson Medal, Royal Photog Soc, 51; Centennial Medal, Sch Eng, Columbia Univ, 64; Lieven Gevaert Medal, Soc Photog Sci, 77. *Mem:* Am Chem Soc; fel Optical Soc Am; hon mem Soc Photog Sci & Eng; Royal Photog Soc; Ger Photog Soc. *Res:* Optical sensitization; photographic emulsion making; photographic theory. *Mailing Add:* Sch of Photog Arts & Sci One Lomb Memorial Dr Rochester NY 14623

CARROLL, CATHERINE, b Salmon Arm, BC, Oct 27, 18. NUTRITION. *Educ:* McGill Univ, BHS, 39; Univ Chicago, SM, 54; Mich State Univ, PhD(nutrit), 60. *Prof Exp:* Dietitian, Royal Inland Hosp, Kamloops, Can, 41-50; dietitian, Vancouver Gen Hosp, 50-53, asst dir dietetics, 54-57; assoc prof, 60-66, PROF NUTRIT, UNIV ARK, FAYETTEVILLE, 66- *Mem:* AAAS; Am Dietetic Asn; Am Inst Nutrit; Can Dietetic Asn. *Res:* Interrelationships in carbohydrate and lipid metabolism; amino acid imbalance; ethanol metabolism and liver lipids. *Mailing Add:* Dept of Home Econ Univ of Ark Fayetteville AR 72701

CARROLL, DANA, b Palm Springs, Calif, Sept 2, 43; m 66; c 2. MOLECULAR BIOLOGY. *Educ:* Swarthmore Col, BA, 65; Univ Calif, Berkeley, PhD(chem), 70. *Prof Exp:* Fel cell biol, Beatson Inst Cancer Res, 70-72; fel develop biol, Carnegie Inst Washington Dept Embryol, 72-75; asst prof microbiol, 75-81, ASSOC PROF CELL, VIRAL, MOLECULAR BIOL, MED CTR, UNIV UTAH, 81- *Mem:* Am Soc Microbiol; Sigma Xi. *Res:* Sequence organization in specific, isolated genes of Xenopus, and its relation to their evolution and developmental regulation; genetic recombination. *Mailing Add:* Dept Cell Viral Molecular Biol Univ of Utah Med Ctr Salt Lake City UT 84132

CARROLL, DENNIS PATRICK, b Minneapolis, Minn, Feb 6, 41; m 67; c 3. ELECTRIC POWER SYSTEMS, COMPUTER SIMULATION. *Educ:* Univ Md, BS, 64; Univ Wis, MS, 65, PhD(elec eng), 69. *Prof Exp:* Electronics eng, US Naval Air Test Ctr, 64-65; asst prof, Univ Wis-Milwaukee, 69-70, Clarkson Col Tech, 70-73; assoc prof, 73-79, PROF ELEC ENG, PURDUE UNIV, 79- *Concurrent Pos:* Exec vpres, Simulation Technologies, Inc, 77- *Mem:* Sr mem, Inst Elec & Electronics Engrs. *Res:* Analysis of electric power systems; applications of computer simulation; control system theory. *Mailing Add:* Sch of Elec Eng Purdue Univ West Lafayette IN 47907

CARROLL, DEVINE PATRICK, b Los Angeles, Calif, April 30, 53; m 74; c 2. ARACHNOLOGY, ECOLOGY. *Educ:* Univ Calif, Riverside, BS, 75, PhD(entom), 79. *Prof Exp:* FEL RESEARCHER, WASH STATE UNIV, 80- *Mem:* Entom Soc Am; Am Arachnological Soc. *Res:* Apple aphid ecology, including natural enemies and modeling of growth and development. *Mailing Add:* Tree Fruit Res Ctr Wash State Univ Wenatchee WA 98801

CARROLL, EDWARD ELMER, b North Bergen, NJ, Feb 13, 30; m 58; c 3. NUCLEAR ENGINEERING. *Educ:* Harvard Univ, AB, 50; Univ Pa, MS, 52, PhD(physics), 60. *Prof Exp:* Fel scientist, Bettis Atomic Power Lab, Westinghouse Elec Corp, 59-66; assoc prof nuclear eng, 66-76, actg chmn dept, 76-80, PROF NUCLER ENG, UNIV FLA, 76- *Concurrent Pos:* Vis staff mem, Los Alamos Sci Lab. *Mem:* Am Phys Soc; Am Nuclear Soc. *Res:* Fast neutron cross-section measurements; pulse neutron measurements; nuclear spectroscopy. *Mailing Add:* Dept of Nuclear Eng Univ of Fla Gainesville FL 32601

CARROLL, EDWARD JAMES, JR, b San Diego, Calif, Dec 25, 45; m 68; c 2. DEVELOPMENTAL BIOLOGY, BIOCHEMISTRY. *Educ:* Sacramento State Col, BA, 68; Univ Calif, Davis, PhD(biochem), 72. *Prof Exp:* Fel develop biol, Scripps Inst Oceanog, 72-75; asst prof zool, Univ Md, College Park, 75-76; asst prof, 76-80, ASSOC PROF BIOL, UNIV CALIF, RIVERSIDE, 80- *Mem:* AAAS; Am Soc Cell Biol; Am Soc Zoologists; Soc Develop Biol. *Res:* Biochemistry of fertilization and activation of embryonic metabolism. *Mailing Add:* Dept of Biol Univ of Calif Riverside CA 92521

CARROLL, EDWARD MAJOR, b Corsicana, Tex, Dec 30, 16; m 41; c 2. MATHEMATICS EDUCATION. *Educ:* Bishop Col, BS, 39; Columbia Univ, MA, 52, EdD(math educ), 64. *Prof Exp:* Asst to pres, Bishop Col, 39-52, asst prof math & physics, 52-57; teacher math, Dwight Morrow High Sch, Englewood, NJ, 58-65; PROF MATH & MATH EDUC, NY UNIV, 65- *Concurrent Pos:* Vis prof, Univ Wis-Madison, 64; consult-writer, Educ Serv Inc, Mass, 65; mem comt examr, Nat Teacher Exam, Educ Testing Serv, NJ, 69-73; vis prof, Univ Monsoura, Repub Egypt, 81. *Mem:* Am Math Soc; Am Educ Res Asn; Math Asn Am; Nat Coun Teachers Math; AAAS. *Res:* Learning and teaching of mathematics in early childhood. *Mailing Add:* 933 Shimkin Hall NY Univ New York NY 10003

CARROLL, F IVY, b Norcross, Ga, Mar 28, 35; m 57; c 2. ORGANIC CHEMISTRY. *Educ:* Auburn Univ, BS, 57; Univ NC, PhD(chem), 61. *Prof Exp:* Sr chemist, 60-67, group leader, 67-71, asst dir, 71-75, DIR ORG & MED CHEM, RES TRIANGLE INST, 75- *Mem:* Am Chem Soc; The Chem Soc. *Res:* Synthesis of compounds of potential chemotherapeutic value; analgesics, depressants, stimulants, hallucinogens, antiradiation agents, antiparasitic agents, antifertility agents, anticancer agents and cancer prevention (retinoids); application of organic physical methods to biological problems, circular dichroism, and hydrogen and carbon 13 nuclear magnetic resonance. *Mailing Add:* Res Triangle Inst PO Box 12194 Research Triangle Park NC 27709

CARROLL, FELIX ALVIN, JR, b High Point, NC, Aug 17, 47; m 72; c 1. ORGANIC CHEMISTRY, PHOTOCHEMISTRY. *Educ:* Univ NC, Chapel Hill, BS, 69; Calif Inst Technol, PhD(org chem), 73. *Prof Exp:* Chemist polymer chem, Burlington Indust Res Ctr, 68-69; asst prof chem, 72-80, ASSOC PROF CHEM, DAVIDSON COL, 80- *Concurrent Pos:* Res grant, Res Corp, 73- & NC Sci & Technol Comt, 75-79; chem exhibit design consult, Discovery Pl Sci Mus, Charlotte, NC, 77- *Mem:* Am Chem Soc; AAAS; Inter-Am Photochem Soc; Sigma Xi. *Res:* Photochemical and photophysical processes; intersystem crossing; heavy atom effects; singlet quenching; exciplexes; kinetics and mechanisms of photochemical reactions; pheromones; history of chemistry. *Mailing Add:* Dept Chem Davidson Col Davidson NC 28036

CARROLL, FLOYD DALE, b Mt Clare, Nebr, Jan 8, 14; m 44; c 1. ANIMAL HUSBANDRY. *Educ:* Univ Nebr, BS, 37; Univ Md, MS, 39; Univ Calif, PhD(animal nutrit), 48. *Prof Exp:* Prin technician, 48-49, from instr to assoc prof, 49-64, prof, 64-70, EMER PROF ANIMAL HUSB, UNIV CALIF, DAVIS, 70- *Concurrent Pos:* Fulbright fel, Univ Ceylon, 55-56. *Res:* Vitamin B synthesis in the horse; nutrition in range beef production; beef production under hot climatic conditions; dwarfism in beef cattle; factors affecting beef carcass grades; composition and palatability. *Mailing Add:* Dept of Animal Sci Univ of Calif Davis CA 95616

CARROLL, FRANCIS W, b Philadelphia, Pa, Aug 22, 32; m 59; c 4. MATHEMATICAL ANALYSIS. *Educ:* St Joseph's Col, Pa, BS, 54; Purdue Univ, MS, 56, PhD(math), 59. *Prof Exp:* Asst prof math, Purdue Univ, 59-60, Mich State Univ, 60 & Univ Wisconsin-Milwaukee, 60-61; from asst prof to assoc prof, 61-75, PROF MATH, OHIO STATE UNIV, 75- *Mem:* Am Math Soc; Math Asn Am; AAAS. *Res:* Complex analysis; functional equations. *Mailing Add:* Dept Math Ohio State Univ Columbus OH 43210

CARROLL, GEORGE C, b Alton, Ill, Feb 11, 40; m 68; c 2. MYCOLOGY. *Educ:* Swarthmore Col, BA, 62; Univ Tex, PhD(bot), 66. *Prof Exp:* Asst prof, 67-72, ASSOC PROF BIOL, UNIV ORE, 72- *Concurrent Pos:* Vis prof, Swiss Fed Inst Technol, Inst Gen Bot, 73-74. *Mem:* Mycol Soc Am; Bot Soc Am; Am Soc Microbiol; Soc Gen Microbiol; Brit Mycol Soc. *Res:* Ultrastructure of spore formation in fungi; evolution of the fungi; ecology of fungi in terrestrial ecosystems; microbiology of the coniferous forest canopy. *Mailing Add:* Dept of Biol Univ of Ore Eugene OR 97403

CARROLL, GERALD V, b Meriden, Conn, Apr 9, 21. GEOLOGY. *Educ:* Lehigh Univ, BA, 43; Yale Univ, PhD(geol), 52. *Prof Exp:* Instr, Lehigh Univ, 50-51; instr, Trinity Col, Conn, 51-53; asst prof geol, Dartmouth Col, 53-54; assoc prof, Agr & Mech Col, Univ Tex, 54-59; vis assoc prof, Pa State Univ, 59-61; assoc prof, 61-65, PROF GEOL, GEORGE WASHINGTON UNIV, 65- *Res:* Petrology. *Mailing Add:* Dept of Geol George Washington Univ Washington DC 20052

CARROLL, HARVEY FRANKLIN, b New Haven, Conn, Aug 25, 39. PHYSICAL CHEMISTRY. *Educ:* Hunter Col, AB, 61; Cornell Univ, PhD(phys chem), 69. *Prof Exp:* Sr chemist, Chem Div, Uniroyal Inc, Conn, 68-69; asst prof, 70-75, chairperson, 76-79, ASSOC PROF, DEPT PHYS SCI, KINGSBOROUGH COMMUNITY COL, CITY UNIV NY, 75- *Concurrent Pos:* Vis prof, Dept Physical Chem, Hebrew Univ, Jersalem, Israel, 79-80. *Mem:* Am Chem Soc; Sigma Xi. *Res:* High temperature gas phase chemical kinetics; shock tubes; homogeneous isotope exchange reactions in ultra clean systems; unimolecular reactions; chemical and nutrition education. *Mailing Add:* Dept of Phys Sci Kingsborough Community Col Brooklyn NY 11235

CARROLL, JAMES BARR, b Chicago, Ill, Mar 25, 29; m 52; c 6. SCIENCE ADMINISTRATION, SCIENCE POLICY. *Educ:* Brown Univ, ScB, 52, MS, 57; Univ Conn, PhD(physics), 67. *Prof Exp:* Res engr, United Aircraft Res Labs, 55-68; staff scientist, Royal Prod Co, Litton Industs, 68-72; consult, Off Planning & Mgt, US Environ Protection Agency, 72-74; dir, Off Energy Supply Progs, Fed Energy Admin, 74; CONSULT, 74- *Concurrent Pos:* Lectr, Trinity Col, Conn, 65-66 & Univ Conn, 68. *Mem:* Am Phys Soc. *Res:* Technology assessment; computer modeling techniques; energy research. *Mailing Add:* 63 Pippin Dr Glastonbury CT 06033

CARROLL, JAMES H(ENRY), b Knoxville, Tenn, Mar 14, 23. CHEMICAL ENGINEERING. *Educ:* Univ Tenn, BS, 47. *Prof Exp:* Engr polymerization, Res Div, Borger, Tex, 47-50, asst sect mgr, 50-54, tech asst to br mgr, 55, sect mgr, 56-72, mgr, Carbon Black Develop Ctr, Toledo, Ohio, 72-79, SECT MGR, CARBON BLACK DEVELOP, PHILLIPS PETROL CO, BARTLESVILLE, OKLA, 72- *Mem:* Am Chem Soc. *Res:* Synthetic rubber; carbon black. *Mailing Add:* Carbon Black Develop Ctr 275 Millard Ave Toledo OH 43605

CARROLL, JAMES JOSEPH, b Scranton, Pa, Dec 12, 35; m 60; c 1. BIOCHEMISTRY, CLINICAL CHEMISTRY. *Educ:* Univ Scranton, BS, 57; Pa State Univ, MS, 60, PhD(biochem), 62; NAT Registry Clin Chem, cert; Fairleigh Dickinson Univ, MBA, 77. *Prof Exp:* Scientist, Sandoz Pharmaceut, 62-65; scientist, Warner-Lambert Res Inst, 65-71, sr scientist, 71-73, sr res assoc, Warner-Lambert Co, Inc, 73-76, mgr planning & coord, Warner-Lambert Res Inst, 76-77, PROD MGR, GEN DIAGNOSTICS INT, WARNER-LAMBERT INT, 77- *Concurrent Pos:* Mem adj fac, Dept Mkt, Econ & Finance, Col Bus Admin, Fairleigh Dickinson Univ, Madison, NJ, 77- *Mem:* Am Chem Soc; Am Asn Clin Chemists; Asn Clin Scientists; Biomed Mkt Asn. *Res:* Cholesterol metabolism; drug metabolism; creation and development of enzyme assays for use in diagnostics reagents; immuno-enzyme assays for isoenzymes. *Mailing Add:* Warner-Lambert Co Inc Morris Plains NJ 07950

CARROLL, JOHN MILLAR, b Philadelphia, Pa, Dec 6, 25; m 44; c 7. INDUSTRIAL ENGINEERING, ELECTRONICS. *Educ:* Lehigh Univ, BS, 50; Hofstra Univ, MA, 55; NY Univ, DEngSc, 68. *Prof Exp:* Asst ed, Electronics Mag, 52-54, assoc ed, 54-57, managing ed, 57-64; assoc prof indust eng, Lehigh Univ, 64-68; PROF COMPUT SCI, UNIV WESTERN ONT, 68- *Concurrent Pos:* Secy field-test panel, Nat Stereophonic Radio Comt, 59-60; mem comt info handling, Eng Serv Libr, 64-68; trustee, Eng Index, 68-71; consult, Can Privacy & Comput Task Force, 71 & Comput Security, Royal Can Mounted Police, 75-76. *Mem:* Sr mem Inst Elec & Electronics Engrs. *Mailing Add:* Dept of Comput Sci Univ of Western Ont London Can

CARROLL, JOHN TERRANCE, b Hibbing, Minn, Oct 31, 42; m 67; c 1. PARTICLE PHYSICS, COMPUTER SCIENCE. *Educ:* St Mary's Col, Winona, Minn, 64; Univ Wis, Madison, MA, 66, PhD(physics), 71. *Prof Exp:* Res assoc physics, 71-75, MATHEMATICIAN PHYSICS, STANFORD LINEAR ACCELERATOR CTR, 75- *Concurrent Pos:* Sci assoc, Europ Orgn Nuclear Res, 81-82. *Mem:* Am Phys Soc. *Res:* Elementary particle physics; bubble chamber studies of hadronic interactions; development and application of new computer hardware and software techniques for data acquisition and analysis. *Mailing Add:* Stanford Linear Accelerator Ctr PO Box 4349 Stanford CA 94305

CARROLL, KENNETH GIRARD, b Pittsburgh, Pa, Feb 18, 14; m 45; c 1. PHYSICS. *Educ:* Carnegie Inst Technol, BS, 34, MS, 35; Yale Univ, PhD(physics), 39. *Prof Exp:* Instr physics, NC State Col, 39-40; physicist, Nat Adv Comt Aeronaut, Va & Ohio, 40-44, Elastic Stop Nut Corp Am, NJ, 44-46 & res lab, US Steel Corp, 46-54; head physics sect, Int Nickel Co Res Lab, 54-61; sr scientist, Sperry Rand Res Ctr, 61-67 & NASA Electronics Res Ctr, 67-70; vis scientist, Forsyth Dent Ctr, Boston, 70-71; physicist, Argonne Nat Lab, 74-77; CONSULT, 77- *Concurrent Pos:* Nat Acad Sci-Nat Res Coun vis scientist, US Army Natick Labs, 65-66. *Mem:* Am Phys Soc; Electron Micros Soc; Sigma Xi. *Res:* X-ray diffraction and spectroscopy; electron microscopy; physical metallurgy; application of electron beam instruments to biological systems; detection and localization of trace metals in single biological cells. *Mailing Add:* 2424 Pennsylvania Ave NW Washington DC 20037

CARROLL, KENNETH KITCHENER, b Carrolls, NB, Mar 9, 23; m 50; c 3. BIOCHEMISTRY, NUTRITION. *Educ:* Univ NB, BSc, 43, MSc, 46; Univ Toronto, MA, 46; Univ Western Ont, PhD(med), 49. *Prof Exp:* From asst prof to prof med res & actg head dept, 54-68, PROF, BIOCHEM DEPT, UNIV WESTERN ONT, 68- *Concurrent Pos:* Can Life Ins Off Asn fel, Dept Med Res, Univ Western Ont, 49-52; Merck & Co fel, Dept Chem, Cambridge Univ, 52-53, Agr Res Coun Can fel, 53-54; hon secy, Can Fedn Biol Socs, 67-71;

mem coun on atherosclerosis, Am Heart Asn. *Mem:* AAAS; Am Oil Chem Soc; Am Soc Biol Chem; Chem Inst Can; Can Physiol Soc. *Res:* Lipid metabolism, cholesterol; atherosclerosis; mammary cancer; polyprenols. *Mailing Add:* Dept of Biochem Univ of Western Ont London ON N6A 5C1 Can

CARROLL, MARCUS NEWMAN, JR, physiology, pharmacology, see previous edition

CARROLL, MICHAEL M, b Thurles, Ireland, Dec 8, 36; US citizen; m 64; c 2. ROCK MECHANICS, BIOMECHANICS. *Educ:* Nat Univ Ireland, BA, 58, MA, 59; Brown Univ, PhD(appl math), 65. *Hon Degrees:* DSc, Nat Univ Ireland, 79. *Prof Exp:* Res assoc, Div Appl Math, Brown Univ, 64-65; asst prof, 65-69, assoc prof, 69-75, PROF APPL MECH, DEPT MECH ENG, UNIV CALIF, BERKELEY, 75- *Concurrent Pos:* Visitor, Sch Theoret Physics, Dublin Inst Advan Studies, 71-72; vis prof, Univ Col Cork, Ireland, 77; consult, Thoratec Labs, Berkeley, Calif, 76- & Terra Tek Inc, Salt Lake City, Utah, 77-; affil mem, Dept Cardiovasc Surg, Pac Med Ctr, 77- *Mem:* Am Soc Mech Engrs; Acoust Soc Am; Soc Rheology; Sigma Xi. *Res:* Continuum mechanics, with emphasis on nonlinear phenomena; mechanics of porous materials; mechanics of oil and gas reservoirs; acoustics; nonlinear optics; biomechanics. *Mailing Add:* Dept Mech Eng Univ Calif Berkeley CA 94720

CARROLL, MURRAY NORMAN, b Calgary, Alta, June 14, 23; m 52. PHYSICAL CHEMISTRY. *Educ:* Univ BC, BA, 47; McGill Univ, PhD(chem), 52. *Prof Exp:* Res chemist, Celanese Corp Am, 51-55 & Borden Chem Co, 55-61; assoc chemist, Div Indust Res, Wash State Univ, 61-66; sect head, Forest Prod Lab, Can Dept Forestry & Rural Develop, 66-70; RES MGR, WOOD PROD DIV, CAN DEPT ENVIRON, 70- *Mem:* Forest Prod Res Soc. *Res:* Synthetic textiles; pulp and paper; adhesive chemistry; wood products. *Mailing Add:* Western Forest Prod Lab 6620 NW Marine Dr Vancouver BC V6T 1X2 Can

CARROLL, PAUL JOSEPH, low temperature physics, see previous edition

CARROLL, PAUL TREAT, b San Francisco, Calif, Oct 22, 43; m 68; c 2. PHARMACOLOGY, TOXICOLOGY. *Educ:* Univ Calif, Berkeley, AB, 66; San Jose State Univ, MA, 69; Univ Md, PhD(pharmacol), 73. *Prof Exp:* Scientist urol, Alcon Labs, 69-70; fel neurochem, Johns Hopkins Univ, 73-76; asst prof pharmacol, Univ RI, 76-81; ASSOC PROF PHARMACOL, MED SCH, TEX TECH UNIV, 81- *Concurrent Pos:* SmithKline Corp fel, Johns Hopkins Univ, 74-76; NSF neurobiol grant, 78-81. *Mem:* Soc Neurosci; Am Soc Pharmacol & Exp Therapeut. *Res:* Central cholinergic metabolism. *Mailing Add:* Dept Pharmacol & Exp Therapeut Tex Tech Univ Health Sci Ctr Lubbock TX 79430

CARROLL, RAYMOND JAMES, b Yokohama, Japan, Apr 21, 49, US citizen; m 72. STATISTICS, BIOSTATISTICS. *Educ:* Univ Tex, Austin, BA, 71; Purdue Univ, MS, 72, PhD(statist), 74. *Prof Exp:* Asst prof statist, 74-78, ASSOC PROF STATIST, UNIV NC, CHAPEL HILL, 78- *Concurrent Pos:* Co-prin investr, Air Force Off Sci Res, 76-; statist consult, NC State Fisheries Off, 76-78 & Ctr Dis Control, 78-79; vis consult, Nat Heart, Lung & Blood Inst, 80- *Mem:* Inst Math Statist; Am Statist Asn; Biomet Soc; Sigma Xi. *Res:* Robustness of statistical inference, statistics of accounting, transformations. *Mailing Add:* Dept of Statist Univ of NC Chapel Hill NC 27514

CARROLL, ROBERT BAKER, b Tuscaloosa, Ala, Apr 8, 21; div; c 4. ORGANIC CHEMISTRY, PLANT PATHOLOGY. *Educ:* Univ Ala, BS, 42; La State Univ, BS, 47, MS, 49, PhD(plant path), 51. *Prof Exp:* Asst jr pyrometrist, Ensley-Fairfield Works, US Steel Corp, Ala, 41; asst res chemist, Swann Chem Co, 41-42; asst res chemist, Exp Sta, Hercules Powder Co, Del, 42-43, explosives chemist, Radford Ord Works, Va, 42-43; asst plant physiologist, Boyce Thompson Inst Plant Res, NY, 50-52; microbiologist, Biochem Res Lab, Borden Co, 52-53; independent consult microanal, 53-68; PRES, O D V, INC, 68- *Mem:* AAAS; Am Ord Asn; Sigma Xi; Weed Sci Soc Am; Am Inst Chemists. *Res:* Food and flavors; pharmaceuticals; pesticides; instrumentation; plant physiology; agronomy; alcoholic beverages; plastics; oils and fats; microanalytical methods using all forms of chromatography; forensic chemistry, especially analysis of drugs and narcotics; field identification of narcotics and dangerous drugs. *Mailing Add:* ODV Inc PO Box 305 South Paris ME 04281

CARROLL, ROBERT BUCK, b Wellsburg, WVa, June 27, 40; m 63; c 3. SOYBEAN PATHOLOGY, SOIL-BORNE DISEASES. *Educ:* WVa Univ, BS, 62, MS, 64; Pa State Univ, PhD(plant pathol), 71. *Prof Exp:* Res asst plant pathol, WVa Univ, 62-64; res asst plant pathol, Pa State Univ, 64-70, instr, 70-71; exten specialist, 71-77, ASSOC PROF PLANT PATHOL, UNIV DEL, 77- *Concurrent Pos:* Asst dept chmn, Plant Sci Dept, Univ Del, 77-; assoc ed, Plant Dis J, Am Phytopathol Soc, 81- *Mem:* Am Phytopathological Soc; NY Acad Sci. *Res:* Soybean pathology with emphasis on the effect of changing cultural practices (tillage, herbicides, varieties) on the incidence of root and stem diseases. *Mailing Add:* Plant Sci Dept 146 Agr Hall Newark DE 19711

CARROLL, ROBERT J, b Conshohocken, Pa, Aug 24, 28; m 59; c 4. PHYSICAL CHEMISTRY. *Educ:* Drexel Univ, BS, 58. *Prof Exp:* RES CHEMIST, EASTERN REGIONAL RES CTR, USDA, 55- *Mem:* Electron Micros Soc Am; AAAS. *Res:* Electron microscopy; ultrastructural investigations of meat, milk proteins, lactation and leathers. *Mailing Add:* Eastern Regional Res Ctr 600 E Mermaid Lane Philadelphia PA 19118

CARROLL, ROBERT LYNN, b Kalamazoo, Mich, May 5, 38; wid; c 1. VERTEBRATE PALEONTOLOGY. *Educ:* Mich State Univ, BS, 59; Harvard Univ, MA, 61, PhD(biol), 63. *Prof Exp:* Nat Res Coun Can fel, 62-63; NSF fel, 63-64; assoc cur geol, Redpath Mus, 64-69, assoc prof vert paleont, 69-74, dir Redpath Mus, 79-80, PROF VERT PALEONT, MCGILL UNIV, 74-, CUR, REDPATH MUS, 69- *Honors & Awards:* Schuchert Award, Paleont Soc, 78. *Mem:* Soc Vert Paleont (vpres, 81-82 & pres, 82-83);

Soc Study Evolution; Am Soc Zool; Paleont Soc; Linnean Soc London. *Res:* Anatomy and phylogeny of Carboniferous, Permian and Triassic amphibians and reptiles--labyrinthodonts, microsaurs, captorhinomorphs and eosuchians; origin of lizards and Lissamphibia. *Mailing Add:* Redpath Mus McGill Univ 859 Sherbrooke St W Montreal PQ H3A 2K6 Can

CARROLL, ROBERT WAYNE, b Chicago, Ill, May 10, 30; m 57, 74, 79; c 2. MATHEMATICS. *Educ:* Univ Wis, BS, 52; Univ Md, PhD(math), 59. *Prof Exp:* Res aeronaut scientist, Nat Adv Comt Aeronaut, Ohio, 52-54; Nat Sci Found fel, 59-60; asst prof math, Rutgers Univ, 60-63, assoc prof, 63-64; assoc prof, 64-67, PROF MATH, UNIV ILL, URBANA-CHAMPAIGN, 67- *Concurrent Pos:* Nat Sci Found res grant, 63-70. *Mem:* Math Soc Am. *Res:* Partial differential equations; functional analysis; differential geometry; mathematical physics; Lie groups; author or co-author of 3 books on focertto in preparation and over 80 research articles. *Mailing Add:* Dept of Math Univ of Ill Urbana IL 61801

CARROLL, ROBERT WILLIAM, b Geneva, NY, Jan 16, 38. PHYSICAL CHEMISTRY. *Educ:* Hobart Col, BS, 59; Fordham Univ, PhD(phys chem), 65. *Prof Exp:* Res chemist, Inmont Corp, 65-68; sr scientist photoconductor res & develop, Optonetics, Inc, 69-70; asst prof chem, Herbert H Lehman Col, 71-78; asst prof chem, Manhattan Col, Mt St Vincent Univ, 79-80; ASST PROF CHEM, FORDHAM UNIV, 81- *Mem:* Am Chem Soc; Sigma Xi; AAAS; NY Acad Sci; fel Am Inst Chemists. *Res:* Kinetics of hydrocarbon pyrolysis; field emission and field ionization microscopy; heterogeneous catalysis. *Mailing Add:* Dept Chem Fordham Univ Bronx NY 10468

CARROLL, SAMMY RAY, research management, physical chemistry, see previous edition

CARROLL, SAMUEL EDWIN, b Thamesville, Ont, Dec 20, 28; m; c 2. CARDIOVASCULAR SURGERY, THORACIC SURGERY. *Educ:* Univ Western Ont, BA, 56, MD, 53. *Prof Exp:* Trainee surg, Victoria Hosp, 53-58; registr, Edgware Gen Hosp, London, Eng, 59-60; CARDIOVASC SURGEON, DEPT VET AFFAIRS, WESTMINSTER HOSP, 63-; CHIEF SURGEON, ST JOSEPH'S HOSP, 66-; PROF SURG, UNIV WESTERN ONT, 66- *Concurrent Pos:* Res fel hypothermia, Surg Lab, Children's Hosp Med Ctr, Boston, Mass, 61; Ont Heart Found res fel, 61-, grant in aid, 64-; res asst, St Mark's Hosp, London, Eng, 59-60; examr, Royal Col Physicians & Surgeons Can, 68-74. *Mem:* Fel Am Col Cardiol; fel Am Col Chest Physicians; fel Am Col Surg; NY Acad Sci; Can Cardiovasc Soc. *Res:* Hypothermia; small vessel anastomosis; surgical shock. *Mailing Add:* St Joseph's Hosp London ON N6A 4V2 Can

CARROLL, THOMAS JOSEPH, b Pittsburgh, Pa, April 26, 12. PHYSICS. *Educ:* Univ Pittsburgh, AB, 32; Yale Univ, PhD(physics), 36. *Prof Exp:* Lab asst physics, Yale Univ, 32-36; prof math & physics, Col New Rochelle, 36-41; radio engr, Signal Corps Labs, Ft Monmouth, NJ, 41-43, physicist, Off Chief Signal Officer, Washington, DC, 43-46; Bur Standards, 46-51, Lincoln Lab, Mass Inst Technol, 51-58 & Bendix Radio Co, 58-68; res prof, Dept Elec Eng, George Washington Univ, 68-70; CONSULT, 70- *Concurrent Pos:* Mem, Int Sci Radio Union. *Mem:* Am Phys Soc; Inst Elec & Electronics Engrs; Optical Soc Am; Acoust Soc Am; Am Asn Physics Teachers. *Res:* Microwave radio propagation; twilight scatter propagation; molecular spectra; Faraday effect in molecular spectra. *Mailing Add:* 162 Lake Shore Rd Brighton MA 02135

CARROLL, THOMAS WILLIAM, b Los Angeles, Calif, Aug 22, 32; m 52; c 4. PLANT PATHOLOGY, PLANT VIROLOGY. *Educ:* Calif State Polytech Col, BS, 54; Univ Calif, Davis, MS, 62, PhD(plant path), 65. *Prof Exp:* NIH res plant pathologist, 65-66; from asst prof to assoc prof bot, 66-74, PROF PLANT PATH, MONT STATE UNIV, 74- *Mem:* Am Phytopath Soc. *Res:* Plant virology; electron microscopy. *Mailing Add:* Dept of Plant Path Mont State Univ Bozeman MT 59717

CARROLL, WALTER WILLIAM, b Chicago, Ill, June 25, 15; m; c 2. CANCER, SURGERY. *Educ:* Northwestern Univ, MD, 41, MS, 44. *Prof Exp:* From instr to prof surg, Med Sch, Northwestern Univ, 42-74; MED DIR, ST VINCENT MED CTR, LOS ANGELES, 74-; CLIN PROF SURG, UNIV SOUTHERN CALIF MED SCH, 74- *Concurrent Pos:* Surg attend staff, Passavant Mem Hosp Exp Study, Nat Res Coun, 42-45; assoc div surg, Cook County Hosp & staff physician, Commonwealth Edison Co, 44-46; courtesy surg staff, St Joseph Hosp; assoc dir, Joint Comn Accreditation of Hosps, 70-74; mem bd dirs, Cent Area Teaching Hosp, Inc, 74-77, pres, 76-77. *Mem:* Am Col Surg; Am Geriat Soc; Am Radium Soc; Am Pub Health Asn; Int Soc Surg. *Res:* Nerve repair; wound healing; soft tissue tumor surgery; venous surgery. *Mailing Add:* 67 Agape Village Hwy 79 Warner Springs CA 92086

CARROLL, WILLIAM ROBERT, b Logan, Utah, June 9, 16; m 41; c 4. BIOCHEMISTRY. *Educ:* Swarthmore Col, AB, 38; Harvard Univ, AM, 40, PhD(physiol), 42. *Prof Exp:* Scientist dir, Nat Inst Arthritis, Metab & Digestive Dis, 48-71; TEACHER SCI, BALLOU HIGH SCH, WASHINGTON, DC, 71- *Concurrent Pos:* Res fel, Med Col, Cornell Univ, 46-48. *Mem:* AAAS; Am Soc Biol Chem; Nat Sci Teachers Asn. *Res:* Influence of estrogen on the metabolism of the uterus; enzyme reactions; metabolism of amino acids; effect of x-rays on proteins; physical chemistry of proteins and nucleic acids. *Mailing Add:* 4802 Broad Brook Dr Bethesda MD 20814

CARRON, NEAL JAY, b Jersey City, NJ, May 27, 41. PHYSICS. *Educ:* Mass Inst Technol, BS, 63; Univ Ill, MS, 65, PhD(physics), 69. *Prof Exp:* Res assoc physics, Rice Univ, Houston, Tex, 69-71; RES STAFF MEM PHYSICS, MISSION RES CORP, SANTA BARBARA, 71- *Mem:* Am Phys Soc. *Res:* Plasma physics; charged particle beams; inertial confinement fusion. *Mailing Add:* 662 Burtis Santa Barbara CA 93111

CARROTHERS, P(ERCIVAL) J(OHN) G(ODBER), b Edinburgh, Scotland, July 3, 21; Can citizen; m 60; c 3. FISHING GEAR TECHNOLOGY, TEXTILE TECHNOLOGY. *Educ:* Univ BC, BASc, 44; Mass Inst Technol, SM, 52; Univ Toronto, MEng, 71. *Prof Exp:* Asst chemist pulp & paper, Pac Mills, Ltd, 44; chem engr in chg res, Com Fishing Gear & Related Prod, Edward Lipsett, Ltd, 45-54; RES ENGR, CAN DEPT FISHERIES & OCEANS, 54- *Mem:* Textile Res Inst; Can Inst Textile Sci; Eng Inst Can; Can Soc Mech Eng. *Res:* Engineering research on commercial and exploratory fishing gear; mechanics; techniques for fishery resource inventory. *Mailing Add:* Biol Sta Dept of Fisheries & Oceans St Andrews NB E0G 2X0 Can

CARROZZA, JOHN HENRY, b Bridgeport, Conn, Dec 14, 44; m 77; c 2. MICROBIOLOGY, IMMUNOLOGY. *Educ:* Fairfield Univ, BS, 66; Univ Conn, PhD(virol), 72. *Prof Exp:* Lab dir vet vaccine, Amerlab Inc, 71-78; dir res & develop vet vaccine, 78-80, GEN MGR, KEEVET LABS, 80- *Mem:* Am Soc Microbiol; AAAS. *Res:* Veterinary vaccines, including those for Marek's Disease, rabies, pseudorabies, viral arthritis, fowl cholera. *Mailing Add:* Keevet Labs PO Box 1706 Anniston AL 36202

CARRUTH, BETTY RUTH, b Comanche, Tex. NUTRITION. *Educ:* Tex Tech Univ, BS, 65, MS, 68; Univ Mo, PhD(human nutrit, sociol), 74. *Prof Exp:* Instr nutrit, Tex Tech Univ, 68-71; res dietitian, Med Ctr & instr med dietetics, Dept Human Nutrit, Foods & Food Systs Mgt, Univ Mo, 74; asst prof nutrit, Univ Minn, St Paul, 74-78; dir nutrit, adolescent health training proj, Dept Pediat, Univ Tex Health Sci Ctr, Dallas, 78-81; HEAD DEPT NUTRIT & FOOD SCI, UNIV TENN, KNOXVILLE, 81- *Mem:* Am Dietetic Asn; Soc Adolescent Med; Sigma Xi. *Res:* determination of significant nutritional and socio-health needs of youth; attitude measurement. *Mailing Add:* Dept Nutrit & Food Sci Univ Tenn Knoxville TN 37916

CARRUTH, JAMES HARVEY, b Baton Rouge, La, Aug 17, 38; m 65; c 2. PURE MATHEMATICS. *Educ:* La State Univ, BS, 61, MS, 63, PhD(math), 66. *Prof Exp:* Asst prof, 66-69, assoc prof, 70-76, PROF MATH, UNIV TENN, KNOXVILLE, 76- *Mem:* Am Math Soc; Math Asn Am. *Res:* Topological semigroups. *Mailing Add:* Dept of Math Univ of Tenn Knoxville TN 37916

CARRUTH, WILLIS LEE, b Summit, Mass, Feb 21, 09; m 37; c 2. PHYSICAL CHEMISTRY. *Educ:* Asbury Col, BA, 35; Univ Ky, MS, 38. *Prof Exp:* Instr chem, Asbury Col, 35-36 & Univ SDak, 36-38; instr chem & physics, Lewis & Clark Col, 38-39, from asst prof to prof chem, 39-44; prof, Nebr Wesleyan Univ, 44-46; assoc prof math, Col Puget Sound, 46-47, from asst prof to prof chem, 47-58; mem staff, Res & Develop, Appl Physics Corp, 58-74; TECH DIR, TINSLEY REPLICATION GROUP, TINSLEY LABS, INC, 74- *Concurrent Pos:* Registr & admin secy fac, Lewis & Clark Col, 42-44; consult scientist, Varian Assocs, 74- *Mem:* Fel AAAS; Am Chem Soc; Optical Soc Am. *Res:* Spectroscopy; instrumental methods of analysis; optics. *Mailing Add:* 2120 Maginn Dr Glendale CA 91202

CARRUTHERS, CHRISTOPHER, b Motherwell, Scotland, Mar 17, 09; nat US; m 40, 59; c 4. CANCER. *Educ:* Syracuse Univ, BS, 33, MS, 35; Univ Iowa, PhD(biochem), 38. *Prof Exp:* Asst chem, Syracuse Univ, 33-35; asst chem, Univ Iowa, 35-38; res assoc, Barnard Free Skin & Cancer Hosp, 42-48; mem div cancer res, Med Sch, Wash Univ, 48-53; assoc cancer res scientist, Rosewell Park Mem Inst, 53-66; prin cancer res scientist, 66-79; RETIRED. *Concurrent Pos:* Res fel, Barnard Free Skin & Cancer Hosp, 38-42; instr, Sch Med, Wash Univ, 41-44; assoc res prof, Med Sch, State Univ, NY Buffalo, 56-79. *Mem:* Fel AAAS; fel NY Acad Sci; Am Soc Biol Chem; Am Asn Cancer Res; Soc Exp Biol & Med. *Res:* Polarography in biochemistry and cancer research; biochemistry of epidermis, cell particulates and carcinogenesis; immunology and biochemistry of epidermal proteins and of membranes of various types of rat mammary carcinomas and in rat liver carcinogenesis; metabolism of azocarcinogens by rat liver and distribution of ligandin in azocarcinogen-treated rat liver and azocarcinogen-induced liver tumors; necotine as a cocarcinogen in mouse skin. *Mailing Add:* Roswell Park Mem Inst Orchard Park Labs Orchard Park NY 14127

CARRUTHERS, JOHN ROBERT, b Toronto, Ont, Sept 12, 35; m 57; c 2. MATERIALS SCIENCE. *Educ:* Univ Toronto, BASc, 59, PhD(metall), 66; Lehigh Univ, MS, 61. *Prof Exp:* Mem tech staff semiconductor mat, Bell Tel Labs, 59-63; lectr mat sci, Univ Toronto, 64-65; asst prof, 65-67; mem tech staff crystal chem, Bell Tel Labs, 67-75, head crystal growth & glass res & develop dept, Bell Labs, Murray Hill, NJ, 75-77; dir mat processing, Space Div, NASA, 77-81; PROJ MGR MAT CHARACTERIZATION, SOLID STATE LAB, HEWLETT-PACKARD, PALO ALTO, CALIF, 81- *Concurrent Pos:* Consult, Off Applns, NASA, 74-77. *Mem:* AAAS; Am Phys Soc. *Res:* Crystal growth and evaluation, especially influences of fluid convection and phase equilibria on crystal growth, space processing, optical fibers for communications. *Mailing Add:* Hewlett-Packard Labs Page Mill Rd Palo Alto CA 94304

CARRUTHERS, LUCY MARSTON, b Kansas City, Mo, Jan 20, 37; m 58, 69; c 3. PHYSICAL CHEMISTRY, SCIENTIFIC COMPUTING. *Educ:* Swarthmore Col, BA, 58; Rutgers Univ, MS, 61, PhD(theoret chem), 64. *Prof Exp:* Programmer physics & eng, Mat Sci Ctr, Cornell Univ, 67-69; programmer astronomy, Hale Observ, Pasadena, Calif, 69-70; sr programmer chem, Cornell Univ, 70-73; staff mem weapons physics, TD-Div, 73-75, STAFF MEM REACTOR PHYSICS, Q-DIV, LOS ALAMOS NAT LAB, 75- *Mem:* Am Nuclear Soc; Asn Comput Mach; Asn Women Sci; Grad Women Sci. *Res:* Computer calculations and analysis of gas-cooled reactors, fuels, and structural analysis. *Mailing Add:* Group Q-13 Mail Stop 576 Los Alamos Nat Lab Los Alamos NM 87545

CARRUTHERS, PETER A, b Lafayette, Ind, Oct 7, 35; m 55, 69, 81; c 3. THEORETICAL PHYSICS. *Educ:* Carnegie Inst Technol, BS & MS, 57; Cornell Univ, PhD(theoret physics), 61. *Prof Exp:* From asst prof to prof physics, Cornell Univ, 61-73; LEADER THEORET DIV, LOS ALAMOS SCI LAB, UNIV CALIF, 73- *Concurrent Pos:* NSF fel, 60-61; Sloan res fel, 63-65; vis assoc prof, Calif Inst Technol, 65, vis prof, 69-70 & 77-78; NSF sr fel, Univ Rome, 67-68; mem bd dirs & trustee, Aspen Ctr Physics, 75-, bd trustees, 79-; mem, Physics Adv Panel, NSF, 75-80, chmn, 78-80, mem, High Energy Physics Adv Panel, 78-; mem NAS comn, US-USSR Physics Coop, 78- *Mem:* Fel Am Phys Soc; AAAS. *Res:* Theory of strong interactions of elementary particles; symmetries of elementary particles. *Mailing Add:* Los Alamos Sci Lab UC PO Box 1663 Los Alamos NM 87544

CARRUTHERS, RAYMOND INGALLS, b Pomona, Calif, Jan 4, 51; m 71; c 3. EPIZOOTIOLOGY. *Educ:* Calif Polytech State Univ, BS, 75; Mich State Univ, MS, 79, PhD(entom), 81. *Prof Exp:* Res asst, Mich State Univ, 76-81; ASST PROF ENTOM, CORNELL UNIV, 81- *Mem:* Entom Soc Am; Entom Soc Can. *Res:* Principles of population ecology and system science are used in the development and implementation of integrated pest management for agriculture; biological control using insect parasites and pathogens. *Mailing Add:* Dept Entom Cornell Univ Ithaca NY 14853

CARRYER, HADDON MCCUTCHEN, b Unionville, Mo, Aug 25, 14; m 41; c 3. INTERNAL MEDICINE, ALLERGY. *Educ:* Drake Univ, BA, 35; Northwestern Univ, BM, 38, MS & MD, 39; Univ Minn, PhD(med), 48. *Prof Exp:* Asst med, Mayo Grad Sch, Univ Minn, 42-43, consult, 43-, from instr to assoc prof, Mayo Med Sch, 46-73, PROF MED, MAYO MED SCH, 73- *Concurrent Pos:* Consult, Div Med, Mayo Clin, 43- *Mem:* Fel Am Acad Allergy; fel Am Col Physicians; AMA. *Res:* Executive health periodic examinations. *Mailing Add:* Mayo Med Sch Rochester MN 55901

CARSKI, THEODORE ROBERT, b Baltimore, Md, June 22, 30; m 54; c 4. IMMUNOLOGY, MICROBIOLOGY. *Educ:* Johns Hopkins Univ, AB, 52; Univ Md, MD, 56; Am Bd Microbiol, dipl, 65. *Prof Exp:* Med intern, Univ Md, 56-57; sr asst surgeon, Commun Dis Ctr, Ala, 57-60; dir med res, Baltimore Biol Lab Div, B-D Labs, Inc, 60-68; dir microbiol, 68-70, from asst dir to dir, Huntingdon Res Ctr, 70-74, assoc med dir, 74-75, CORP MED DIR, BECTON, DICKINSON & CO, 75- *Mem:* Am Soc Microbiol. *Res:* Fluorescent antibody techniques; mycoplasma; medical immunology; bacteriology and virology; clinical research drugs and diagnostic reagents. *Mailing Add:* Becton Dickinson & Co Box 243 Cockeysville MD 21030

CARSOLA, ALFRED JAMES, b Los Angeles, Calif, June 6, 19; m 47; c 7. OCEANOGRAPHY, MARINE GEOLOGY. *Educ:* Univ Calif, Los Angeles, AB, 42; Univ Southern Calif, MS, 47; Scripps Inst, Univ Calif, PhD(oceanog), 53. *Prof Exp:* Asst, Univ Southern Calif, 46-47; geophysicist & oceanographer, Electronics Lab, US Navy, 47-60; staff scientist, Lockheed-Calif Co, 60-67, head oceanics div, 67-71; environ res scientist, Southern Calif Coastal Res Proj, 71-72; chief staff scientist, Lockheed Ocean Lab, Lockheed Missiles & Space Co, 72-75; INSTR, SAN DIEGO & GROSSMONT COMMUNITY COL, UNIV SAN DIEGO & SAN DIEGO STATE UNIV, 75- *Concurrent Pos:* Instr, San Diego State Col, 56-59, Loyola Univ, 63, Univ San Diego, 59 & Univ Calif, Los Angeles, 60-61, 62. *Mem:* AAAS; Soc Econ Paleont & Mineral; Am Geophys Union; fel Geol Soc Am; Am Soc Limnol & Oceanog. *Res:* Marine sediments; arctic marine seafloor, bathymetry and geomorphology; Seamount sediments; nearshore physical marine processes; micropaleontology; physical oceanography and acoustical oceanography. *Mailing Add:* 3569 Addison St San Diego CA 92106

CARSON, BOBB, b Minneapolis, Minn, July 16, 43. SEDIMENTOLOGY. *Educ:* Carleton Col, BA, 65; Univ Wash, MS, 67, PhD(geol oceanog), 71. *Prof Exp:* Asst prof, 71-76, assoc prof, 76-82, PROF GEOL, LEHIGH UNIV, 82- *Concurrent Pos:* Consult, Off Marine Geol, US Geol Surv, Woods Hole, Mass, 75-76; sci staff, Deep-sea drilling proj, Leg 57, 77. *Mem:* AAAS; Am Geophys Union; Geol Soc Am; Soc Econ Paleontologists & Mineralogists; Int Asn Sedimentologists. *Res:* Quaternary continental margin sedimentation, northwest pacific ocean; tectonic modification of deep-sea sediments related to subduction; agglomeration of fine-grained sediments. *Mailing Add:* Bldg 31 Dept Geol Sci Lehigh Univ Bethlehem PA 18015

CARSON, BONNIE L BACHERT, b Kansas City, Kans, Aug 11, 40; div; c 1. INFORMATION SCIENCE. *Educ:* Univ NH, BA, 63; Ore State Univ, MS, 66. *Prof Exp:* Teaching asst chem, Ore State Bd Higher Educ, 63-66; lab instr, Univ Waterloo, 68-69; asst abstractor, Chem Abstracts Serv, 69-71; Russian translator, 71-73; asst chemist, 73-75, assoc chemist, 75-80, SR CHEMIST, MIDWEST RES INST, 80- *Mem:* Am Chem Soc; Am Inst Chemists; NY Acad Sci; Soc Environ Geochem & Health; AAAS. *Res:* Assessment and compilation of information on the magnitude of human exposure to, the health effects of, and the environmental fate of toxic chemicals. *Mailing Add:* Midwest Res Inst 425 Volker Blvd Kansas City MO 64110

CARSON, CHESTER CARROL, b Passaic, NJ, Nov 21, 18; m 47; c 2. ANALYTICAL CHEMISTRY. *Educ:* Newark Col Eng, BS, 41; Rensselaer Polytech Inst, MS, 59. *Prof Exp:* Control chemist, Rayon Prod, Celanese Corp Am, Md, 41-42; CHEMIST, LARGE STEAM TURBINE-GENERATOR DEPT, GEN ELEC CO, 46- *Mem:* Am Soc Testing & Mat; Am Chem Soc; fel Am Inst Chemists; Sigma Xi. *Res:* Sampling and analysis of atmospheric particulates at gas turbine sites; sampling and analysis of pyrolysates detected in large gas-cooled generators; measurement of hydrogen in steel, of hydrogen, oxygen and nitrogen in steel and metals; problems in gas systems; immediate detection of local overheating in gas-cooled electrical machines; problems in water-cooled systems of generator stators. *Mailing Add:* Mat & Processes Lab Gen Elec Co Schenectady NY 12345

CARSON, EUGENE WATSON, JR, b Cumberland, Va, Mar 27, 39; m 60; c 3. AGRONOMY, PLANT BIOCHEMISTRY. *Educ:* Va Polytech Inst & State Univ, BS, 61, MS, 63; NC State Univ, PhD(soil sci), 66. *Prof Exp:* Va Coun Hwy Invest & Res asst turf & hwy, Va Polytech Inst & State Univ, 60-63; res asst plant physiol, NC State Univ, 63-66; assoc prof, 66-72, PROF AGRON, VA POLYTECH INST & STATE UNIV, 72- *Mem:* Am Soc Agron; Crop Sci Soc Am. *Res:* Plant ecology. *Mailing Add:* Dept of Agron Va Polytech Inst & State Univ Blacksburg VA 24060

CARSON, FREDERICK WALLACE, b Quincy, Mass, Mar 18, 40; m 69. ORGANIC CHEMISTRY, BIOCHEMISTRY. *Educ:* Mass Inst Technol, BS, 61; Washington Univ, MA, 63; Univ Chicago, PhD(chem), 65. *Prof Exp:* NIH fel org chem, Princeton Univ, 65-66; asst prof org chem & biochem, Ind Univ, Bloomington, 66-70; asst prof, 70-71, ASSOC PROF ORG CHEM & BIOCHEM, AM UNIV, 72- *Concurrent Pos:* Grants, Washington Heart Asn, 72, NIMH, 73, US Dept Interior, 75, Petrol Res Fund, Biomed Sci & Res Corp. *Mem:* AAAS; Am Chem Soc; The Chem Soc; NY Acad Sci. *Res:* Biochemical mechanisms; model enzyme systems; enzyme kinetics; stereochemistry; organosulfur chemistry. *Mailing Add:* Dept of Chem American Univ Washington DC 20016

CARSON, GEORGE STEPHEN, b Lakewood, Ohio, Dec 7, 48; m 69; c 2. MATHEMATICS. *Educ:* Univ Tenn, Knoxville, BS, 70; Univ Calif, Riverside, PhD(math), 75. *Prof Exp:* Lectr math, Calif State Col, San Bernardino, 75-76; mem tech staff, B-1 Div Rockwell, 76-77 & GTE Automatic Elec Labs, Northlake, Ill, 77-78; assoc prin engr, Elec Systs Div, Harris Corp, Melbourne, Fla, 78-81; CONSULT, HERMOSA BR, WPL INC, 81- *Mem:* Am Math Soc; Math Asn Am; AAAS; Sigma Xi; Inst Elec & Electronics Engrs. *Res:* Approximation theory; computer graphics; computer software engineering, digital signal processing. *Mailing Add:* 13254 Jefferson Ave Hawthorne CA 90250

CARSON, GEORGE WALTER, b Salem, Ind, May 26, 04; m 27; c 3. MATHEMATICS. *Educ:* Hanover Col, AB, 27; Univ Ill, AM, 35. *Prof Exp:* Head dept math, Pikeville Col, 35-41; prof, Grove City Col, 42-58; assoc prof, Univ Redlands, 58-61; prof, 61-71, EMER PROF MATH, CALIF STATE POLYTECH UNIV, 71- *Res:* Mathematics education. *Mailing Add:* 234D Paseo Quinta Green Valley AZ 85614

CARSON, GORDON B(LOOM), b High Bridge, NJ, Aug 1, 11; m 37; c 4. INDUSTRIAL & MECHANICAL ENGINEERING. *Educ:* Case Inst Technol, BS, 31; Yale Univ, MS, 32, ME, 38. *Hon Degrees:* DEng, Case Inst Technol, 57; LLD, Rio Grande Col, 73. *Prof Exp:* Instr mech eng, Case Inst Technol, 32-36; engr, Am Ship Bldg Co, 36; from asst prof to assoc prof indust eng, Case Inst Technol, 37-44; dir res, Cleveland Automatic Mach Co, 39-44; mgr eng, Selby, Selby Shoe Co, 44-49, secy of corp, 49-53; dean eng, Ohio State Univ, 53-58; prof indust eng & vpres, 58-71; prof mgt & exec vpres, Albion Col, 71-77; ASST TO THE CHANCELLOR, NORTHWOOD INST, 77- *Concurrent Pos:* Chmn tool & die comt, Fifth Regional War Labor Bd, 44-45; chmn, Ohio Selective Serv Adv Bd Sci & Tech Personnel, 55-70; vpres, Ohio State Univ Res Found & dir, Knowledge Commun Fund, 67-; vpres, Ga Ctr Automation & Soc, Univ Ga, 69-71; dir, Accuray Corp, Cardinal Fund, 65. *Mem:* Fel AAAS; fel Am Soc Mech Engrs; Nat Soc Prof Engrs; Am Soc Eng Educ; fel Am Inst Indust Engrs (pres, 56-57). *Res:* Automation, especially as it relates to manufacturing process and to the control of atmospheric and water pollution; energy use reduction. *Mailing Add:* 5413 Gardenbrook Dr Midland MI 48640

CARSON, HAMPTON LAWRENCE, b Philadelphia, Pa, Nov 5, 14; m 37; c 2. EVOLUTIONARY BIOLOGY. *Educ:* Univ Pa, AB, 36, PhD(zool), 43. *Prof Exp:* Instr zool, Univ Pa, 38-42; from instr to prof, Wash Univ, 43-70; PROF GENETICS, UNIV HAWAII, 71- *Concurrent Pos:* Mem Wheelock Exped, Labrador, 34; prof biol, Univ Sao Paulo, 51 & 77; Fulbright res scholar, Univ Melbourne, 61. *Mem:* Nat Acad Sci; Soc Study Evolution (pres, 71); Am Soc Naturalists (pres, 73); AAAS; Am Acad Arts & Sci. *Res:* Population genetics; genetic systems and their relation to evolution; cytogenetics and evolution of drosophila and other insects. *Mailing Add:* Dept of Genetics Univ of Hawaii Honolulu HI 96822

CARSON, J DAVID, b Lehi, Utah, Dec 19, 17; m 42; c 6. GENETICS. *Educ:* Colo State Univ, BS, 47; Univ Calif, PhD(genetics), 53. *Prof Exp:* Asst & assoc poultry sci & animal genetics, Utah State Univ, 52-64; chmn dept, 64-76, PROF BIOL SCI, UNIV OF THE PACIFIC, 64- *Concurrent Pos:* Consult, West-Line Breeders, Wash, 56-58; NIH res grant, 61. *Mem:* Genetics Soc Am; Poultry Sci Asn. *Res:* Genetics of reproduction in domestic turkeys as influenced through hybridization and natural selection; genetic forces regulating serum cholesterol levels in white mice; dietary interactions. *Mailing Add:* Dept of Biol Sci Univ of the Pacific Stockton CA 95211

CARSON, JAMES ESTLE, b Canton, Ohio, Dec 21, 21; m 48; c 2. METEOROLOGY. *Educ:* Kent State Univ, BS, 43; Univ Chicago, SM, 48, PhD(meteorol), 60. *Prof Exp:* Res asst meteorol, Univ Chicago, 47-51; asst prof, Rutgers Univ, 51-53; meteorologist, US Army Natick Res & Develop Command, 53-55; asst prof physics, Iowa State Univ, 55-61; METEOROLOGIST, ARGONNE NAT LAB, 61- *Mem:* Am Meteorol Soc; Sigma Xi; Air Pollution Control Asn. *Res:* Meteorology; micrometeorology; turbulent transfer and diffusion; thermal pollution; cooling tower effluents. *Mailing Add:* Environ Statements Proj Bldg 11 Argonne Nat Lab Argonne IL 60439

CARSON, JAMES ROLLAND, b Omaha, Nebr, Feb 21, 14; m 47; c 4. POULTRY SCIENCE. *Educ:* Ore State Col, BS, 37; Cornell Univ, MS, 42, PhD(animal breeding), 49. *Prof Exp:* Asst, Cornell Univ, 40-42 & 46-48; asst prof poultry sci, Univ Conn, 48-55; assoc prof, 55-59; regional coordr, NCent Regional Poultry Breeding Proj, USDA, 59-62; prof, 62-80, EMER PROF POULTRY SCI, PURDUE UNIV, 80- *Mem:* AAAS; Poultry Sci Asn; Am Genetic Asn. *Res:* Poultry management and physiology. *Mailing Add:* 350 Sylvia West Lafayette IN 47906

CARSON, JOHN WILLIAM, b Tallahassee, Fla, Aug 22, 44; m 66; c 2. MECHANICAL ENGINEERING. *Educ:* Northeastern Univ, BS, 67; Mass Inst Technol, SM, 68, PhD(mech eng), 71. *Prof Exp:* Res engr, 70-76, V PRES, JENIKE & JOHANSON INC, 76- *Res:* Storage and flow of bulk solids; two phase flow; pressures on bin walls; controlled feeding of fine materials. *Mailing Add:* Jenike & Johanson Inc 2 Executive Park Dr North Billerica MA 01862

CARSON, JOHNNY LEE, b Asheville, NC, Feb 6, 49; m 73. ENVIRONMENTAL BIOLOGY, CYTOPATHOLOGY. *Educ:* Western Carolina Univ, BS, 71; Univ NC, PhD(bot), 75. *Prof Exp:* RES ASSOC PATH, SCH MED, UNIV NC, CHAPEL HILL, 75- *Mem:* Sigma Xi. *Res:* Cytopathological studies of effects of environmental pollutants in mammals; cytology-ecology of algae and fungi. *Mailing Add:* Dept of Path Sch of Med Univ NC Chapel Hill NC 27514

CARSON, PAUL LANGFORD, US citizen. MEDICAL PHYSICS, ULTRASONIC RESEARCH. *Educ:* Colo Col, BS, 65; Univ Ariz, PhD(physics), 72. *Prof Exp:* From instr to assoc prof radiol, Med Ctr, Univ Colo, Denver, 71-81; ASSOC PROF RADIOL SCI, MED SCH, UNIV MICH, 81- *Mailing Add:* Dept Radiol Mich Hosp Ann Arbor MI 48109

CARSON, PAUL LLEWELLYN, b Ames, Iowa, Mar 27, 19; m 53; c 4. SOIL FERTILITY. *Educ:* Northwest Mo State Teachers Col, BS, 41; Iowa State Col, MS, 47. *Prof Exp:* Teacher pub schs, Mo, 41; agronomist, 48-78, PROF AGRON, S DAK STATE UNIV, 69- *Concurrent Pos:* Adv, Rockefeller Found, Colombia, SA, 67-68; consult, USAID, Pakistan, 76, Brazil, 78 & Botzwana, 81-82. *Mem:* Am Soc Agron; Soil Sci Soc Am. *Res:* Soil management; soil testing to determine fertilizers needed for farmers soils. *Mailing Add:* Dept of Plant Sci S Dak State Univ Brookings SD 57006

CARSON, RALPH S(T CLAIR), b Durham, NC, Dec 22, 22; m 49; c 2. ELECTRICAL ENGINEERING. *Educ:* Ind Inst Tech, BS, 45; Univ Mich, MS, 52; Univ Ill, PhD(elec eng), 64. *Prof Exp:* Eng asst, Farnsworth Radio & TV Corp, 45-46; instr electronics, Ind Inst Tech, 46-51, chmn, Dept Electronic Eng, 52-60; from res asst to res assoc elec eng, Univ Ill, 61-64; assoc prof, 64-65, PROF ELEC ENG, UNIV MO-ROLLA, 65- *Mem:* Sr mem Inst Elec & Electronics Engrs; Am Soc Eng Educ. *Res:* Electronic devices and circuits. *Mailing Add:* Dept of Elec Eng Univ of Mo Rolla MO 65401

CARSON, ROBERT CLELAND, b Akron, Ohio, Mar 11, 24; m 51; c 4. MATHEMATICS. *Educ:* Purdue Univ, BS, 48, MS, 50; Univ Wis, PhD(math), 53. *Prof Exp:* Asst prof math & statist, Lehigh Univ, 53-57; asst prof math, Western Reserve Univ, 57-58; mathematician, Goodyear Aircraft Corp, Ohio, 58-63; coordr res, 63-71, asst dean grad studies, 68-71, ASSOC PROF MATH, UNIV AKRON, 63- *Mem:* Am Math Soc; Am Statist Asn; Soc Indust & Appl Math. *Res:* Variational methods and stochastic processes. *Mailing Add:* 1537 Maple St W Barberton OH 44203

CARSON, ROBERT JAMES, III, b Lexington, Va. GEOLOGY, GEOMORPHOLOGY. *Educ:* Cornell Univ, AB, 63; Tulane Univ, MS, 67; Univ Wash, PhD(geol), 70. *Prof Exp:* Geologist, Texaco Inc, La, 63-67; from asst to assoc prof geol, NC State Univ, 70-74; asst prof, 75-80, ASSOC PROF GEOL & CHMN DEPT, WHITMAN COL, 80- *Concurrent Pos:* Consult, Wash State Dept Ecol & Div Geol & Earth Resources, 69- *Mem:* AAAS; Geol Soc Am; Int Glaciol Soc; Am Quaternary Asn. *Res:* Quaternary and environmental geology of the Olympic Peninsula, Washington. *Mailing Add:* Dept Geol Whitman Col Walla Walla WA 99362

CARSON, STANLEY FREDERICK, b San Francisco, Calif, Oct 4, 12; m 44; c 3. MICROBIOLOGY. *Educ:* Stanford Univ, AB, 34, PhD(microbiol), 41. *Prof Exp:* Sr microbiologist, Merck & Co, 42-45 & Wyeth Inst Appl Biochem, Pa, 45-46; sr microbiologist, 47-48, prin biologist, 48-67, from asst dir to dep dir, 48-77, CONSULT, BIOL DIV, OAK RIDGE NAT LAB, 77- *Concurrent Pos:* E R Squibb lectr, Rutgers Univ, 58; Haskin Labs fel, Stanford Univ, 41-42; mem, NSF Adv Panel Molecular Biol, 55-57, Adv Panel Spec Facilities & Progs, 61-70; vpres, Microbial Metab Div, Int Cong Microbiol, Italy, 53; assoc ed, J Bact, 51-56 & Bact Rev, 58-64, Grants Mag, 77-81; hon res prof, Univ Ga, 60-77; prof biomed sci, Univ Tenn, 67-77, emer prof, 77- *Mem:* Fel AAAS; Am Chem Soc; Am Soc Biol Chemists; Am Soc Microbiol. *Res:* Biochemistry and physiology of microorganisms; intermediary metabolism; enzyme mechanisms; isotopic tracers. *Mailing Add:* 109 Pleasant Rd Oak Ridge TN 37830

CARSON, STEVEN, b Brooklyn, NY, Oct 17, 25; m 48; c 2. PHARMACOLOGY. *Educ:* Wash Univ, BS, 48; NY Univ, MS, 50, PhD(biol pharmacol), 58. *Prof Exp:* Asst, Pub Health Res Inst, NY, 48-49; chief chemist, NY Med Col, 49-51; pharmacologist, Endo Labs, Inc, 51-58, vpres & sci dir, Food & Drug Res Labs, Inc, 59-72; vpres & dir sci affairs, Biomet Testing, Inc, 72-75; adj assoc prof, ASSOC PROF, ST JOHN'S UNIV, NY, 80- *Concurrent Pos:* Mem bd forum advan toxicol, Univ Tenn. *Mem:* NY Acad Sci; fel Soc Cosmetic Chemists; Am Soc Pharmacol & Exp Therapeut; fel Royal Soc Health; fel Soc Cosmetic Chemists. *Res:* Pharmacology of central nervous depressants and stimulants; pharmacological properties of marine products and marine inhabitants; toxicological evaluations of food additives; drug supplements; respiratory physiology and pharmacology in laboratory animals exposed to environmental irritant; clinical pharmacology. *Mailing Add:* Toxicon Assoc Inc PO Box 373 Ryder Station Brooklyn NY 11234

CARSON, STEVEN DOUGLAS, b Bartlesville, Okla, Apr 9, 51. BIOCHEMICAL GENETICS. *Educ:* Rice Univ, BA, 73; Univ Tex Med Br, Galveston, PhD(human genetics), 78. *Prof Exp:* Welch undergrad fel, Rice Univ, 70-72; student asst chem, US Environ Protection Agency, 72-73; res technician, Univ Tex Med Br Galveston, 73-78; FEL, DEPT MOLECULAR BIOPHYSICS & BIOCHEM, SCH MED, YALE UNIV, 78- *Concurrent Pos:* Fel, NSF, 78-79; fel, NIH, 79- *Mem:* AAAS; Am Soc Human Genetics; NY Acad Sci. *Res:* Protein function in biological regulation such as human biochemical genetics and membrane biochemistry; plasma proteins including clotting factors and lipoproteins, cystic fibrosis, lipid vesicles, tissue factor and monoclonal antibodies. *Mailing Add:* Dept Molecular Biophysics & Biochem Yale Univ PO Box 3333 New Haven CT 06510

CARSON, VICTOR S(TUART), b Pocatello, Idaho, June 29, 08; m 29. ELECTRICAL ENGINEERING. *Educ:* Ore State Col, BS, 38; Stanford Univ, Engr, 40, PhD(elec eng), 46. *Prof Exp:* Instr radio commun, Ore Inst Tech, 28-30; chief engr, KOIN Broadcasting Sta, 30-35; design engr, Hewlett-Packard Co, 40-41; asst prof elec eng, Univ Conn, 41-42; asst prof, Stanford Univ, 42-45, res assoc microwaves, 45-46, assoc prof elec eng & dir, Loran Res Lab, 46-47; physicist, Watson Labs, US Air Force, 47-48; prof elec eng, NC State Col, 48-57 & San Jose State Col, 57-59; mem tech staff, Space Tech Labs, TRW Systs, 59-65, consult space systs, 65-67; prof eng, 67-72, EMER PROF ENG, SAN FRANCISCO STATE COL, 72- *Concurrent Pos:* Tech consult, US Air Force, 48-50. *Mem:* Fel Inst Elec & Electronics Engrs. *Res:* Micro-wave electronics; long range electronic navigation; electromagnetic radiation and propagation; electronic computers. *Mailing Add:* 141 Sir Francis Ct Capitola CA 95010

CARSTEA, DUMITRU, b Comuna - Paduroiu, Romania, Mar 22, 30; US citizen; m 56; c 4. ENVIRONMENTAL ENGINEERING, SOIL CHEMISTRY. *Educ:* MS & BS, Agr Inst, Bucharest, 54; Ore State Univ, MS, 65, PhD(soil chem, clay mineral), 67. *Prof Exp:* Res scientist, Romanian Acad Sci, 54-60; res asst clay mineral & soil chem, Ore State Univ, 61-66; res scientist, proj leader, Can Dept Agr, 66-67; soil scientist, chemist, & hydrologist, US Geol Surv, 67-68, res hydrologist & proj leader, 68-70; environ tech staff & task leader, 74-76, group leader, Mitre Corp, Washington Opers, 76-78; prog mgr & dept head, Environ Sci & Eng, Hittman Corp, 78-80; MGR, ENVIRON ENG DEPT, SYST DEVELOP CORP, 80- *Concurrent Pos:* Consult environ & natural resource areas, 76- *Mem:* Am Chem Soc; Int Soc Soil Sci; AAAS; Nat Geophys Soc; Soil Sci Soc Am. *Res:* Environmental/energy analysis of coal gasification and coal liquefaction technologies; environmental analysis, regulation, planning and engineering; erosion and sedimentation; water quality and wastewater treatment; soil and hydrological studies; waste management; clay mineralogy. *Mailing Add:* 13563 Point Pleasure Dr Chantilly VA 22021

CARSTEN, ARLAND L, b Hastings, Minn, Apr 17, 30; m 69; c 1. RADIOBIOLOGY, HEALTH PHYSICS. *Educ:* Mankato State Col, BSc, 53, MS, 56; Univ Rochester, PhD(biol), 57. *Prof Exp:* From asst to sr assoc radiation biol, Univ Rochester, 55-64; assoc health physicist, 57-62, vis assoc biologist, 62-64, assoc scientist, 66-70, SCIENTIST, MED RES CTR, BROOKHAVEN NAT LAB, 70-; ASSOC PROF PATH, STATE UNIV NY STONY BROOK, 73- *Concurrent Pos:* Res fel, Royal Dent Col, Copenhagen, Denmark, 65-66; health physics fel adv, AEC, 60-62; lectr, Am Inst Biol Sci Prog, Med Educ Nat Defense, 61-63; res assoc neurol, Columbia Univ, 64-72; res assoc, Lerner Marine Lab, Bimini, Bahamas. *Mem:* AAAS; Radiation Res Soc; Health Physics Soc; Am Soc Hemat; Int Soc Exp Hemat. *Res:* Acute and late effects of ionizing radiation on mammals, particularly genetic and effects on hematopoietic and nervous tissues; protection against and recovery from radiation injury to man. *Mailing Add:* Med Res Ctr Brookhaven Nat Lab Upton NY 11973

CARSTEN, MARY E, b Berlin, Ger, Mar 2, 22; nat US; m 64. BIOCHEMISTRY. *Educ:* NY Univ, AB, 46, MS, 48, PhD(biochem), 51. *Prof Exp:* Instr, NY Univ, 52-53; res assoc dept microbiol, Col Physicians & Surg, Columbia Univ, 53-55; asst res physiol chemist, Dept Physiol Chem, 56-61, assoc res biochemist, Depts Biol Chem & Med, 61-63, assoc prof, Depts Physiol, Obstet & Gynec, 63-70, PROF OBSTET & GYNEC, SCH MED, UNIV CALIF, LOS ANGELES, 70- *Concurrent Pos:* Nat Found Infantile Paralysis fel, 54-55; Am Cancer Soc fel, Univ Calif, Los Angeles, 55-57; estab investr, Los Angeles County Heart Asn, 61-64; USPHS res career develop award, 64-69 & 69-74. *Honors & Awards:* Res Award, Los Angeles County Heart Asn, 62, 63, 64. *Mem:* Hon mem Soc Gynecol Invest; Am Soc Biol Chem; Am Chem Soc; NY Acad Sci; Am Physiol Soc. *Res:* Ion exchange chromatography; amino acids; protein chemistry; immunochemistry; skeletal, heart and smooth muscle proteins and calcium transport; prostaglandins; myometrial and uterine physiology. *Mailing Add:* Dept Obstet & Gynec Univ Calif Sch Med Los Angeles CA 90024

CARSTENS, ALLAN MATLOCK, b Aurora, Ill, Jan 14, 39; m 60; c 3. OPERATIONS RESEARCH. *Educ:* Univ NMex, BS, 61, MS, 63, PhD, 67. *Prof Exp:* Instr math, Wash State Univ, 66-67, asst prof, 67-70; from asst prof to assoc prof, Mankato State Col, 70-73; sr programmer, 73-76, SUPV PUB REL PROGRAMMER, SPERRY RAND CORP, UNIVAC, 76- *Mem:* Asn Comput Mach; AAAS; Am Math Soc; Math Asn Am. *Res:* Generalized topological spaces; convergence algebras; products of pretopologies; structures of the lattices of pretopologies, pseudotopologies, limitierungen. *Mailing Add:* UNIVAC Sperry Rand Corp 2276 Highcrest Dr Roseville MN 55113

CARSTENS, EARL E, b Rochester, NY, March 26, 50; m 75; c 1. NEUROPHYSIOLOGY, NEUROSCIENCE. *Educ:* Cornell Univ, BS, 72; Univ NC, PhD(neurobiol), 77. *Prof Exp:* Fel, Univ Heidelberg, Ger, 77-80; ASST PROF PHYSIOL, UNIV CALIF, DAVIS, 80- *Mem:* Soc Neurosci. *Res:* Neurophysiological investigations of neural systems in brain which modulate spinal neurons transmitting information on pain. *Mailing Add:* Dept Animal Physiol Univ Calif Davis CA 95616

CARSTENS, ERIC BRUCE, b Lethbridge, Alta; m 79. ANIMAL VIROLOGY, INSECT VIROLOGY. *Educ:* Univ Alta, BSc, 68, MSc, 74; Univ Sherbrooke, PhD(virol), 77. *Prof Exp:* Fel virol, Inst Genetics, Univ Cologne, Ger, 77-79; ASST PROF VIROL, DEPT MICROBIOL & IMMUNOL, QUEENS UNIV, ONT, 80- *Mem:* Can Soc Microbiol; Micros Soc Can; Am Soc Microbiol; Am Soc Virol. *Res:* Gene structure and function of insect viruses particularly baculoviruses; mode of replication of these viruses so that their genes may be favorably altered leading to better pest control agents. *Mailing Add:* Dept Microbiol & Immunol Queens Univ Kingston ON K7L 3N6 Can

CARSTENS, JOHN C, b Chicago, Ill, Oct 8, 37; m 67. PHYSICS. *Educ:* Monmouth Col, Ill, AB, 59; Univ Mo-Rolla, PhD(physics), 66. *Prof Exp:* Fel, Univ Mo-Rolla, 66-67; asst prof physics, Western Ill Univ, 67-68; ASSOC PROF PHYSICS & SR INVESTR, CLOUD PHYSICS CTR, UNIV MO-ROLLA, 68- *Concurrent Pos:* Resident res assoc, Argonne Lab, 66-67. *Res:* Mass and heat transport problems in cloud physics; droplet growth. *Mailing Add:* Dept of Physics Norwood Hall Univ of Mo Rolla MO 65401

CARSTENS, MARION ROBERT, b Reardan, Wash, Oct 1, 19; m 41; c 3. HYDRAULIC ENGINEERING. *Educ:* Wash State Univ, BS, 41; Univ Iowa, MS, 47, PhD(hydraul eng), 50. *Prof Exp:* Res assoc, Iowa Inst Hydraul Res, 46-47; instr civil eng, Wash State Univ, 47-49, assoc prof, 50-51; from assoc prof to prof, Ga Inst Technol, 51-78; RETIRED. *Concurrent Pos:* Dir res & prof, Southeast Asia Treaty Orgn Grad Sch Eng, Bangkok, Thailand, 59-61; consult, Ga Iron Works & Tubexpress Systs, Inc, 78- *Mem:* Fel Am Soc Civil Engrs; Am Soc Mech Engrs. *Res:* Sediment transportation; open-channel flow; slurry pipelines; pneumatic capsules pipelines. *Mailing Add:* PO Box 803 Dablenega GA 30345

CARSTENS, ROBERT L(OWELL), b Sisseton, SDak, July 31, 22; m 48; c 1. TRANSPORTATION ENGINEERING. *Educ:* Iowa State Univ, BS, 43, MS, 64, PhD(transp eng). 66. *Prof Exp:* Construct engr, Kramme & Jensen Construct Co, 48 & Jensen Construct Co, 48-50; maintenance engr, Arabian Am Oil Co, 54-61; hwy engr, US Agency Int Develop, 62-63; assoc prof civil eng, 64-70, PROF CIVIL ENG, IOWA STATE UNIV, 70- *Concurrent Pos:* Mem transp res bd, Nat Res Coun. *Mem:* Am Soc Civil Engrs; Am Soc Eng Educ; Nat Soc Prof Engrs; Inst Transp Engrs. *Res:* Traffic safety; traffic engineering; transportation planning; transportation economics. *Mailing Add:* Dept of Civil Eng Iowa State Univ Ames IA 50011

CARSTENSEN, EDWIN L(ORENZ), b Oakdale, Nebr, Dec 8, 19; m 47; c 5. BIOMEDICAL ULTRASOUND, BIOELECTRIC PHENOMENA. *Educ:* Case Western Reserve Univ, MS, 47; Univ Pa, PhD(physics), 55. *Prof Exp:* Asst, Case Western Reserve Univ, 41-42; mem sci staff, Div War Res, Columbia Univ, 42-45, head lab sect, Navy Under-Water Sound Ref Lab, 45-48; res assoc & asst prof, Moore Sch Elec Eng, Univ Pa, 48-55; biophysicist, Ft Detrick, Md, 56-61; assoc prof elec eng, 61-72, PROF ELEC ENG, UNIV ROCHESTER, 72- *Mem:* Fel Acoustical Soc Am; Inst Elec & Electronics Engrs; Biophys Soc; Biomed Eng Soc; Am Inst Ultrasound Med. *Res:* Acoustical and dielectric properties of biological materials; biological effects of ultrasonic and electric fields. *Mailing Add:* Dept of Elec Eng Univ of Rochester Rochester NY 14627

CARSTENSEN, JENS T(HUROE), b Brooklyn, NY, Jan 9, 26; m 46; c 3. CHEMICAL ENGINEERING. *Educ:* Tech Univ Denmark, MS, 50; Stevens Inst Technol, MS, 64, PhD(phys chem), 67. *Prof Exp:* Develop chemist pharmaceut chem, Lederle Labs, Am Cyanamid Co, 50-53, formulation chemist, 53-55, dept head, Process Improv Lab, 55-57, tech asst to pharmaceut prod mgr, 57-59, dept head encapsulation, 59-60; group leader, Pharmaceut Res Dept, Hoffmann-La Roche, Inc, 60-67; assoc prof pharm, 67-72, PROF PHARM, UNIV WIS-MADISON, 72- *Concurrent Pos:* Assoc prof, Fac Pharm, Univ Paris-Sud, 77-78. *Honors & Awards:* Ebert Award, Acad Pharmaceut Sci, 76, Res Achievement Award, 77; Gent Res Award, Belgium, 78; IPT Award, Acad Pharm Sci, 79. *Mem:* AAAS; NY Acad Sci; Am Pharmaceut Asn; Am Chem Soc. *Res:* Physical pharmacy; kinetics; diffusion controlled processes; tableting and encapsulation operations. *Mailing Add:* 573 Pharm Bldg Univ of Wis N Charter St Madison WI 53706

CARSWELL, ALLAN IAN, b Toronto, Ont, Oct 4, 33; m 56; c 3. OPTICAL PHYSICS. *Educ:* Univ Toronto, BApplSci, 56, MA, 57, PhD(physics), 60. *Prof Exp:* Nat Res Coun Can fel, Inst Theoret Physics, Amsterdam, 60-61; sr mem sci staff plasma physics, RCA Victor Co, 61-65, dir optical & microwave physics lab, 65-68; dir grad prog physics, 71-80, PROF PHYSICS, YORK UNIV, 68-; pres, Optech Inc, 74- *Mem:* Am Phys Soc; Can Asn Physicists; Can Aeronaut & Space Inst; Optical Soc Am; Asn Prof Engrs. *Res:* Laser systems and applications; atmospheric optics; lidar; light scattering. *Mailing Add:* Dept of Physics York Univ Toronto ON R7A 5Z7 Can

CART, ELDRED NOLEN, JR, b Irvington, Ky, Jan 6, 34; m 56; c 3. CHEMICAL ENGINEERING. *Educ:* Univ Louisville, BChE, 57; Ohio State Univ, MS, 60. *Prof Exp:* Sect head, Esso Res Labs, Humble Oil & Refining, 60-69; sr staff anal, Corp Planning Dept, Exxon USA, 69-71; sr staff adv, Logistics Dept, Esso 71-76; planning mgr, Govt Res Lab, 76-79, planning mgr, Contract Res Office, 79-81, SR STAFF ADVR, NEW FACIL PROJ, EXXON RES & ENG CO, 81- *Mem:* Am Inst Chem Eng. *Res:* Systems study on future fuels and prime movers for aircraft, marine, railroad, and pipelines; use of coal on residential and commercial sectors. *Mailing Add:* Exxon Res & Eng Co PO Box 101 Florham Park NJ 07932

CARTE, IRA F, b Winona, WVa, Jan 21, 38; m 62; c 1. GENETICS. *Educ:* Va Polytech Inst, BS, 63, MS, 66, PhD(genetics), 68. *Prof Exp:* GENETICIST, PERDUE FARMS, INC, 68- *Mem:* Poultry Sci Asn; Am Genetic Asn. *Res:* Population genetics of chickens. *Mailing Add:* Buckingham Ct Salisbury MD 21801

CARTEN, ANDREW SYLVESTER, JR, b Boston, Mass, Jan 3, 22; m 49; c 8. ATMOSPHERIC PHYSICS, INSTRUMENTATION. *Educ:* Col of Holy Cross, AB, 43; Tufts Univ, MS, 47. *Prof Exp:* Indust engr, Friez Div, Bendix Corp, Md, 47-54; design engr, Air Force Cambridge Res Ctr, 54-58; systs engr, Air Force Electronics Systs Div, 58-60; sr engr, Air Force Cambridge Res Labs, 60-71; BALLOON SYSTS ENGR, AIR FORCE GEOPHYSICS LAB, 71- *Concurrent Pos:* Prog chmn, Sec Symp on Meteorol Observ & Instruments, 72 & 8th Air Force Cambridge Res Labs Sci Balloon Symp, 74. *Mem:* Am Meteorol Soc; Am Inst Aeronaut & Astronaut. *Res:* Scientific and military high altitude balloon systems; aerospace instrumentation; parachute technology. *Mailing Add:* Air Force Geophys Lab LCB Hanscom AFB MA 01731

CARTER, ANNE COHEN, b New York, NY, Nov 27, 19; m 47; c 2. ENDOCRINOLOGY, BREAST ONCOLOGY. *Educ:* Wellesley Col, BA, 41; Cornell Univ, MD, 44; Am Bd Internal Med, dipl. *Prof Exp:* From instr to asst prof med, Med Col, Cornell Univ, 46-55; from asst prof to assoc prof, State Univ NY Downstate Med Ctr, 55-68, prof med, 67-82; PROF MED, NY MED COL, 82- *Concurrent Pos:* Fel, Russell Sage Inst Path, 51-55; mem, Cancer Clin Training Comt, Nat Cancer Inst, 71-74, mem, Cancer Control Treatment & Rehab Rev Comt, 74-76 & Clin Cancer Prog, Proj Rev Comt, 76-80. *Mem:* Fel AAAS; Soc Exp Biol & Med; Endocrine Soc; Am Soc Clin Oncol; Am Diabetes Asn. *Res:* Endocrinology and metabolism. *Mailing Add:* NY Med Col Westchester County Med Ctr Valhalla NY 10595

CARTER, ASHLEY HALE, b Glen Ridge, NJ, June 27, 24; m 72; c 3. ELECTROPHYSICS. *Educ:* Harvard Univ, AB, 45; Brown Univ, ScM, 50, PhD(physics), 63. *Prof Exp:* Res assoc underwater explosions, Woods Hole Oceanog Inst, 46-47; underwater acoustics, res anal group, Brown Univ, 51-53; mem tech staff, 53-65, head eng mech & physics dept, 65-71, HEAD ELEC PROTECTION & INTERFERENCE DEPT, BELL TEL LABS, 71- *Concurrent Pos:* Lectr, Fairleigh Dickinson Univ, 72-75; lectr, Drew Univ, 75-76, adj assoc prof, 76-81, adj prof, 81- *Mem:* Am Phys Soc; NY Acad Sci; Inst Elec & Electronics Engrs. *Res:* Electromagnetic interference; electrical protection techniques; physics of gas discharge; optical waveguides; propagation of waves in inhomogeneous media; underwater acoustics. *Mailing Add:* 420 River Rd Chatham NJ 07928

CARTER, BETTINA BUSH, b Woburn, Mass, Sept 4, 10; m 29, 51; c 3. IMMUNOBIOLOGY, ENVIRONMENTAL BIOLOGY. *Educ:* Univ Mich, AB, 29, MS, 45; Univ Pittsburgh, PhD(bact, biochem), 51. *Prof Exp:* Jr lab technician div labs, NY State Dept Health, 37-40; chief serologist, La State Health Labs, 40-41; chief serologist, Ky State Health Dept, 41-43; chief serologist, Ill Br Lab, Chicago, 43-44; res immunologist, Inst Path, WPa Hosp, Pittsburgh, 44-53; asst prof microbiol, Col Med, State Univ NY Syracuse, 53-55; from asst prof biol to assoc prof biol, Univ Western Mich, 55-59; res assoc, Sch Med, Univ Louisville, 59-63, assoc prof natural sci, Univ Louisville, 60-63; from adj assoc prof bact to prof bact, Syracuse Univ, 65-70; prof biol & chmn dept sci & math, Cazenovia Col, 70-73; adj prof, Div Environ Technol, Fla Int Univ, 74-78; EDUC CONSULT, WARD'S NATURAL SCI ESTAB, 69- *Concurrent Pos:* Lectr, Duquesne Univ, 46-49. *Honors & Awards:* Gerber Award, 56; Zonta Int Woman's Year, 75. *Mem:* AAAS; Am Chem Soc. *Res:* RH factor; effect of nutrition on antibody formation; serology of syphilis; complement fixation; algal immune patterns; environment; effect of plant auxins on animal cells. *Mailing Add:* 5220 SW 60 Pl Miami FL 33155

CARTER, BRIAN GEOFFREY, b Manchester, Eng, May 3, 35; Can citizen; m 58; c 2. IMMUNOBIOLOGY. *Educ:* Univ London, BSc, 56, MSc, 57, PhD(immunol), 61. *Prof Exp:* Instr pediat, Univ Pa, 64-65; asst prof microbiol & immunol, McGill Univ, 68-69; asst prof, 69-76, ASSOC PROF IMMUNOL, UNIV MAN, 76- *Concurrent Pos:* USPHS trainee, 62-64; Nat Multiple Sclerosis Soc fel, 66-68. *Mem:* Can Soc Immunol; Brit Soc Immunol; Am Asn Immunol. *Res:* Cellular aspects of antibody heterogeneity; differentiation of immunocompetent cells; cellular mechanisms underlying the synthesis of different immunoglobulin classes. *Mailing Add:* Dept of Immunol Univ of Man Winnipeg MB R3E 0W3 Can

CARTER, CAROL SUE, b San Francisco, Calif, Dec 25, 44; m 70; c 1. ETHOLOGY. *Educ:* Drury Col, BA, 66; Univ Ark, Fayetteville, PhD(zool), 69. *Prof Exp:* Instr biol, Drury Col, BA, 66; NIH trainee, Mich State Univ, 69-70; NIH fel, WVa Univ, 70-71; adj asst prof biol, 70-72; res fel psychopharmacol, Ill Dept Ment Health, 72-74; asst prof, 74-77, ASSOC PROF, DEPT PHYSIOL, ECOL, ETHOL & EVOLUTION, UNIV ILL, CHAMPAIGN, 77- *Concurrent Pos:* NSF & NIH res grants. *Mem:* AAAS; Soc Neurosci; Animal Behav Soc. *Res:* Mechanisms regulating mammalian reproductive behavior; utilization of endocrine, neuroendocrine and pharmacological techniques to study the physiological basis of behavior. *Mailing Add:* 829 Psychol Bldg Univ of Ill Champaign IL 61820

CARTER, CHARLES CONRAD, b Seattle, Wash, July 20, 24; m 48; c 4. NEUROLOGY. *Educ:* Reed Col, BA, 46; Univ Ore, MD, 48. *Prof Exp:* Intern, Good Samaritan Hosp, 48-49; resident neurol, Med Sch, Wash Univ, 54-56; from asst prof to prof neurol, Health Sci Ctr, Univ Ore, 62-79, actg head div, 74-75. *Concurrent Pos:* Nat Inst Neurol Dis & Stroke grant, Sch Med, Wash Univ, 69-70; vis assoc prof neurol, Sch Med, Wash Univ, 69-70. *Mem:* AMA; Am Acad Neurol. *Res:* Cerebral blood flow. *Mailing Add:* 525 W 26th St Eugene OR 97405

CARTER, CHARLES EDWARD, b Boise, Idaho, Aug 25, 19; m 46; c 2. BIOCHEMISTRY. *Educ:* Reed Col, BA, 41; Cornell Univ, MD, 44. *Prof Exp:* Prin biochemist, Oak Ridge Nat Lab; asst prof med, Sch Med, Western Reserve Univ, 50-53; assoc prof pharmacol, Sch Med, Yale Univ, 53-57, prof, 57-64; dir dept pharmacol, Sch Med, Case Western Reserve Univ, 64-72, prof, 64-76; mgr biomed progs, Div Biomed & Environ Res, Dept Energy, Washington, 76-80; WITH NAT INST ENVIRON HEALTH, NIH, 80- *Mem:* Am Soc Biol Chemists. *Res:* Biochemistry of nucleic acids. *Mailing Add:* Nat Inst Environ Health NIH Research Triangle Park NC 27709

CARTER, CHARLES WILLIAMS, JR, b Montpelier, Vt, Nov 25, 45; m 68; c 2. PROTEIN CRYSTALLOGRAPHY. *Educ:* Yale Univ, BA, 67; Univ Calif, San Diego, MS, 68, PhD(biol), 72. *Prof Exp:* Fel chem, Univ Calif, San Diego, 72-73; vis scientist, Med Res Coun Lab Molecular Biol, Cambridge, Eng, 73-74; asst prof, 74-80, ASSOC PROF BIOCHEM & ANAT, UNIV NC, 80- *Concurrent Pos:* Prin investr, NIH, 75-, Nat Sci Found, 76-78. *Mem:* Biophys Soc; Am Soc Biol Chemists; Am Crystallographic Soc. *Res:* structure determination by x-ray crystallography of electron transport proteins and macromolecules responsible for incorporating tryptophan into proteins, including the alpha subunit of tryptophan synthetase; tryptophan tRNA synthetase and tRNA tryptophan. *Mailing Add:* Dept Biochem 231 H Univ NC Chapel Hill NC 27514

CARTER, CLINT EARL, b Durant, Okla, Apr 28, 41; m 62; c 2. ANIMAL PHYSIOLOGY, PARASITOLOGY. *Educ:* La Sierra Col, BA, 65; Loma Linda Univ, MA, 67; Univ Calif, Los Angeles, PhD(zool), 71. *Prof Exp:* Teaching assoc microbiol, San Bernardino Valley Jr Col, 66-67; teaching asst gen biol & cell & comp physiol, Univ Calif, Los Angeles, 67-68; teaching assoc fel gen zool & cell physiol, Univ Mass, 71-72; asst prof, 72-80, ASSOC PROF BIOL, VANDERBILT UNIV, 80-, DIR GRAD STUDIES, 77- *Mem:* Am Soc Parasitologists; AAAS; Sigma Xi. *Res:* Immunoparasitology and parasite physiology. *Mailing Add:* 1523 Sam Houston Dr Brentwood TN 37027

CARTER, DAVID, b Brooklyn, NY, April 1, 20; m 43; c 2. PHYSICS. *Educ:* City Col, BEE, 45; Stanford Univ, PhD(physics), 51. *Prof Exp:* Tutor, City Col, 43-44; radio engr, Hallicrafters, Inc, Ill, 45-46; elec engr, Aladdin Radio Industs, 46; instr elec eng, Ill Inst Technol, 46-47; asst physics, Stanford Univ, 47-49; asst prof elec eng, NY Univ, 51-52; sr res engr, Gen Dynamics Div, Convair, 52-55; PROF PHYSICS, SAN JOSE STATE UNIV, 55- *Concurrent Pos:* Instr, Radio-TV Inst, NY, 45 & Am TV Inst Technol, Chicago, 46; electronics engr, Argonne Nat Lab, 46-47; lectr, San Diego State Col, 53 & Univ Calif, Los Angeles, 53-55; consult, Varian Assocs, 56- *Mem:* Inst Elec & Electronics Engrs. *Res:* Microwave tubes and antennas. *Mailing Add:* Dept of Physics San Jose State Univ San Jose CA 95192

CARTER, DAVID L, b Cleveland, Ohio, June 27, 33; m 57; c 2. SOLID STATE SCIENCE. *Educ:* Ohio State Univ, BSc & MSc, 56; Columbia Univ, PhD(physics), 62. *Prof Exp:* Res asst microwave physics, Radiation Lab, Columbia Univ, 58-62; res assoc solid state physics, Univ Pa, 62-64; vis prof, Physics Lab, Ecole Normale Superieure, Paris, 64-66; mem tech staff solid state microwave physics, Physics Res Lab, Tex Instruments, Inc, 66-68, mgr electron transport physics br, 68-71; staff scientist, Chief Tech Off, Singer Co, 71-74; mgr photoreceptor res, Xerox Corp, 74-77; dir res & develop progs, Singer Co, Fairfield, NJ, 77-80; SUPVR TECHNOL ASSESSMENT GROUP, BELL LABS, MURRAY HILL, NJ, 80- *Concurrent Pos:* Consult, Nuclear Res Assocs, 61-62, TRG Inc, 61-64 & Philco Res Labs, 62-64; chmn, Conf Physics Semimetals & Narrow Gap Semiconductors, Dallas, 70; assoc ed, Inst Elec & Electronics Engrs Trans on Electron Devices, 81- *Mem:* Am Phys Soc; Inst Elec & Electronics Engrs. *Res:* Microwave interactions with solids; microwave solid state masers; narrow gap semiconductors; electro-optics technology; technical management; solid state physics. *Mailing Add:* 136 Bellevue Ave Upper Montclair NJ 07043

CARTER, DAVID LAVERE, b Tremonton, Utah, June 10, 33; m 53; c 3. WATER QUALITY. *Educ:* Utah State Univ, BS, 55, MS, 57; Ore State Univ, PhD(soil sci), 61. *Prof Exp:* Lab technician soil sci, Utah State Univ, 52-54; phys sci aid, Soil Conserv Serv, USDA, 54-55; instr, Ore State Univ, 56; soil scientist, Soil & Water Conserv Res Div, 56-60, res soil scientist & line proj leader, 60-65, res soil scientist, 65-75, SUPVRY SOIL SCIENTIST, AGR RES SERV, USDA, 75- *Honors & Awards:* Emmett J Culligan Award, World Water Soc, 75. *Mem:* AAAS; fel Am Soc Agron; fel Soil Sci Soc Am; Int Soc Soil Sci; Soil Conserv Soc Am. *Res:* Salt and ion movement through soils; erosion and sediment control on irrigated land; irrigation and drainage water quality. *Mailing Add:* Snake River Conserv Res Ctr Agr Res Serv USDA Rte 1 Box 186 Kimberly ID 83341

CARTER, DAVID MARTIN, b Doniphan, Mo, June 10, 36; m 61; c 3. DERMATOLOGY. *Educ:* Dartmouth Col, AB, 58; Harvard Med Sch, MD, 61; Yale Univ, PhD(biol), 71. *Prof Exp:* Intern med & surg, Med Ctr, Univ Rochester, 61-62, asst resident med, 62-63; surgeon, Venereal Dis Br, Commun Dis Ctr, USPHS, 63-65; resident dermat, Hosp Univ Pa, 65-67; asst prof, 70-73, assoc prof, 73-77, PROF DERMAT, SCH MED, YALE UNIV, 77- *Concurrent Pos:* Med investr, Howard Hughes Med Inst, 70-77. *Mem:* Am Acad Dermat; Soc Invest Dermat; Am Dermat Asn. *Res:* Defenses of cutaneous cells against ultraviolet irradiation. *Mailing Add:* Dept of Dermat Yale Univ Sch of Med New Haven CT 06510

CARTER, DAVID SOUTHARD, b Victoria, BC, Mar 25, 26; US citizen; m 49; c 4. MATHEMATICS. *Educ:* Univ BC, BA, 46, MA, 48; Princeton Univ, PhD(math physics), 52. *Prof Exp:* Asst math physics, Princeton Univ, 49-52; mem staff, Los Alamos Sci Lab, Calif, 52-58; NSF res grant math & instr math sci, NY Univ, 57-58; vis assoc prof, Univ Wash, 58 & Univ Calif, Berkeley, 59-61; actg chmn dept, 69-80, PROF MATH, ORE STATE UNIV, 61- *Concurrent Pos:* Consult, Lockheed Missiles & Space Co, 59- *Mem:* Am Math Soc. *Res:* Applied analysis; hydrodynamics; statistical mechanics; control and stability theory; numerical analysis and computation. *Mailing Add:* Dept of Math Ore State Univ Corvallis OR 97331

CARTER, DON, b Norborne, Mo, Jan 6, 26. CHEMICAL ENGINEERING. *Educ:* Univ Mo, BS, 49; NC State Col, MS, 51; Wash Univ, DSc(chem eng), 64. *Prof Exp:* Res engr, 51-59, proj leader, 60-63, sr group leader, 63-69, prin engr, Corp Eng Dept, 69-74, MONSANTO FEL, MONSANTO CO, 74- *Concurrent Pos:* Lectr, Wash Univ, 66-70. *Mem:* Am Inst Chem Engrs. *Res:* Polymer process development; separations operations; gas chromatography; automatic control. *Mailing Add:* Corp Eng Dept Monsanto Co 800 N Lindbergh Blvd St Louis MO 63166

CARTER, EARL THOMAS, b Baltimore, Md, July 7, 22; m 47; c 3. PHYSIOLOGY. *Educ:* Northwestern Univ, BS, 34, MD, 48, MS, 50; Univ Tex, PhD(physiol), 55. *Prof Exp:* Staff physician, Chicago Munic Tuberc Sanitarium, 50-51; third yr resident med, Chicago Wesley Mem Hosp, 55-56; asst prof physiol & prev med, Ohio State Univ, 56-60; asst prof med, 60-73, PROF PREV MED, MAYO CLIN & MAYO GRAD SCH MED & CHMN DIV, CLIN, 73- *Concurrent Pos:* Staff physician, Univ Hosp & Ohio Tuberc Hosp, 56-60; consult, Mayo Clin, 60- *Res:* Environmental medicine and environmental physiology. *Mailing Add:* 200 First St SW Rochester MN 55901

CARTER, ELMER BUZBY, b Brooklyn, NY, Mar 28, 30; m 57; c 2. COMPUTER SCIENCE. *Educ:* Haverford Col, SB, 53; Fla State Univ, MS, 60, PhD(physics), 62. *Prof Exp:* Res assoc physics, Rice Univ, 62-63, asst prof, 63-65; asst prof, Strasbourg Univ, 65-66; assoc prof physics, 66-71, ASSOC PROF, COMPUT & INFO SCI & URBAN STUDIES, TRINITY UNIV, 71- *Concurrent Pos:* NSF comput sci resident, Syst Develop Corp, Santa Monica, Calif & Sch Archit & Urban Planning, Univ Calif, Los Angeles, 70-71. *Mem:* AAAS; Am Phys Soc; Asn Comput Mach. *Res:* Urban studies; data base organization; information systems; systems ethics. *Mailing Add:* Dept of Comput & Info Sci Trinity Univ San Antonio TX 78284

CARTER, ELOISE, b Waterproof, La, June 9, 45. NUTRITION. *Educ:* Southern Univ, Baton Rouge, BS, 67; Tuskegee Inst, MS, 69; Kans State Univ, PhD(foods & nutrit), 76. *Prof Exp:* Instr nutrit, NC Cent Univ, 69-73, Kans State Univ, 73-76; HEAD DEPT HOME ECON, TUSKEGEE INST, 76- *Mem:* Am Dietetic Asn; AAAS; Am Home Econ Asn; Sigma Xi. *Res:* Human nutrition; food eating habits and patterns. *Mailing Add:* Dept Home Econ Tuskegee Institute AL 36088

CARTER, FAIRIE LYN, b Biloxi, Miss, Oct 1, 26. ANALYTICAL CHEMISTRY. *Educ:* Miss State Col for Women, BS, 48; Univ NC, MA, 50. *Prof Exp:* Asst anal chem, Univ NC, 48-50; asst cur limnol, Acad Nat Sci Philadelphia, 50-54; assoc chemist, E Reg Res Ctr, 55-57, res chemist, S Reg Res Ctr, 57-65, RES CHEMIST, FORESTRY SCI LAB, US FOREST SERV, USDA, 65- *Mem:* Am Chem Soc; Am Oil Chem Soc; Sigma Xi; Entom Soc Am. *Res:* Termite biochemistry; termiticides; wood extractives; composition of natural products; amino acids; lipids; chromatography. *Mailing Add:* Forestry Sci Lab US Forest Serv PO Box 2008 GMF Gulfport MS 39503

CARTER, FREDERICK J, b Vernon, NY, Dec 16, 29; m 61; c 5. MATHEMATICS. *Educ:* Le Moyne Col, NY, BS, 56; Univ Detroit, MA, 58. *Prof Exp:* Instr math, Le Moyne Col, NY, 58-63; from instr to asst prof, 63-70, chmn dept, 70-74, ASSOC PROF MATH, ST MARY'S UNIV, TEX, 70-, UNDERGRAD ADV, 74- *Mem:* Am Math Soc; Math Asn Am. *Res:* Integral transforms and distribution theory. *Mailing Add:* Dept of Math St Mary's Univ San Antonio TX 78284

CARTER, G CLIFFORD, b Oak Park, Ill, Nov 12, 45; m 66; c 2. SONAR SIGNAL PROCESSING, ACOUSTICAL SIGNAL PROCESSING. *Educ:* US Coast Guard Acad, BS, 67; Univ Conn, MS, 72, PhD(elec eng), 76. *Prof Exp:* ENGR, US NAVAL UNDERWATER SYSTS CTR, 69- *Concurrent Pos:* Adj fac mem, Univ Conn; adj prof, Kans State Univ. *Mem:* Inst Elec & Electronics Engrs; Am Statistical Asn. *Res:* Sonar signal processing; passive localization and estimation of spectral densities; coherence and time delay. *Mailing Add:* Code 3331 Bldg 80 Naval Underwater Systs Ctr New London CT 06320

CARTER, GEORGE EMMITT, JR, b Fayetteville, NC, Jan 18, 46; m 70; c 2. PLANT PHYSIOLOGY. *Educ:* Wake Forest Univ, BS, 68, MA, 70; Clemson Univ, PhD(plant physiol), 73. *Prof Exp:* Asst prof, 73-78, ASSOC PROF PLANT PHYSIOL, CLEMSON UNIV, 78- *Mem:* Am Soc Plant Physiologists; Sigma Xi; AAAS. *Res:* Mechanism of dormancy in plants; quantitative analysis of plant growth regulators; peach tree physiology; pesticide residue analysis; protein electrophoresis. *Mailing Add:* Dept of Plant Path & Physiol Clemson Univ Clemson SC 29631

CARTER, GEORGE H, b Dobbs Ferry, NY, June 16, 16; m 46; c 3. PSYCHIATRY. *Educ:* Williams Col, BA, 38; Harvard Univ, MD, 43. *Prof Exp:* From instr to asst prof prev med, 50-53, from instr to asst prof psychiat, 53-59, ASSOC PROF PSYCHIAT, SCH MED, BOSTON UNIV, 59- *Concurrent Pos:* Resident fel psychiat, Harvard Med Sch, 48, teaching fel, 48-49; Commonwealth Fund fel, 66-67; asst, Univ Hosp, 50-55, asst vis physician, 55-59, vis physician, 59-; chmn residency training psychiat, Med Ctr, Boston Univ, 71-74 & curriculum coordr, 74-75, clin dir family ther, 74-75; asst chief inpatient serv psychiat, Bedford Vet Admin Hosp, 75-78, dir family ther, 78-; neurolinguistic prog practr, 81. *Mem:* Am Med Soc; Am Psychiat Asn; Am Psychoanal Asn. *Res:* Psychotherapy; family therapy. *Mailing Add:* 16 Ash St Cambridge MA 02138

CARTER, GERALD BATE, b Belle Fourche, SDak, Aug 26, 21; m 44; c 3. ANALYTICAL CHEMISTRY. *Educ:* Univ Kansas, BS, 43, MS, 48. *Prof Exp:* Army ord civilian chemist, Sunflower Ord Works, 43-46; chemist, US Potash Co, 46-47; from proj leader to sect leader anal res, Houston Res & Develop Lab, Indust Chem Div, Shell Chem Co, 48-68, dept head anal, biol sci res ctr, Shell Develop Co, Modesto, Calif, 68-76, MEM STAFF, SHELL OIL CO, HOUSTON, 76- *Mem:* Am Chem Soc; Sigma Xi. *Res:* Separation techniques and instruments; spectroscopy; chromatography; physical measurement; radiochemistry. *Mailing Add:* Shell Oil Co PO Box 2463 Houston TX 77001

CARTER, GESINA C, b Nootdorp, Netherlands, Dec 15, 39; US citizen; m 62; c 3. SOLID STATE PHYSICS, MAGNETICS. *Educ:* Univ Mich, BS, 60; Carnegie Inst Technol, MS, 62, PhD(physics), 65. *Prof Exp:* Res assoc acoust, Cath Univ, 65-66; physicist, Nat Bur Standards, 66-78; EXEC SECY, NUMERICAL DATA ADV BD, NAT ACAD SCI, 78- *Concurrent Pos:* Vis researcher, Phys Spectrometry Lab, Fac Sci, Univ Grenoble, 75-76. *Honors & Awards:* Silver Medal, Dept Com, 77. *Mem:* Am Phys Soc; Am Inst Physics; Am Soc Info Sci; NY Acad Sci; Am Soc Testing & Mat. *Res:* Magnetism in metals; band structure and electronic behavior in metals; transport properties in metals; nuclear magnetic resonance in metals and alloys; thermodynamics and phase diagrams; critical data evaluation; metal-hydrogen systems. *Mailing Add:* Nat Acad of Sci Washington DC 20418

CARTER, GILES FREDERICK, b Lubbock, Tex, Mar 22, 30; m 54; c 3. METALLURGICAL CHEMISTRY, ARCHAEOLOGICAL CHEMISTRY. *Educ:* Tex Tech Univ, BS, 49; Univ Calif, Berkeley, PhD(chem), 53. *Prof Exp:* Asst chem, Univ Calif, 49-50, chemist radiation lab, 50-52; res chemist, E I du Pont de Nemours & Co, 52-63, staff scientist, 63-67; dir state tech serv, 67-70, assoc prof, 70-75, PROF CHEM, EASTERN MICH UNIV, 75- *Mem:* Am Chem Soc; Am Numis Soc; Am Soc Metals; Sigma Xi; Royal Numis Soc. *Res:* X-ray fluorescence analyses of ancient coins; diffusivity measurements in metals. *Mailing Add:* 1303 Grant St Ypsilanti MI 48197

CARTER, H KENNON, experimental nuclear physics, see previous edition

CARTER, HARRY HART, b Ponca, Nebr, Mar 14, 21; m 46; c 7. PHYSICAL OCEANOGRAPHY. *Educ:* US Coast Guard Acad, BS, 43; Scripps Inst Oceanog, MS, 48. *Prof Exp:* Res assoc, Johns Hopkins Univ, 63-68, res scientist, Chesapeake Bay Inst, 68-77; PROF MARINE SCI, STATE UNIV NY, STONY BROOK, 77- *Concurrent Pos:* Pres, Hydrocon, Inc, 70-78; prof part-time, Marine Sci, State Univ NY, Stony Brook, 75-77. *Mem:* AAAS; Sigma Xi. *Res:* Estuarine circulation and mixing; coastal oceanography. *Mailing Add:* MSRC State Univ of NY Stony Brook NY 11794

CARTER, HARVEY PATE, b Friendship, Tenn, Dec 15, 27; m 51; c 1. COMPUTER SCIENCE. *Educ:* David Lipscomb Col, BA, 49; Vanderbilt Univ, MA, 50, PhD(math), 59. *Prof Exp:* Instr math, David Lipscomb Col, 50-51, assoc prof, 53-57; sr mathematician, Oak Ridge Nat Lab, 57-68, asst dir math div, 64-68; assoc prof math, Univ Tenn, Knoxville, 68-70; dir math div, Oak Ridge Nat Lab, 69-73; DIR COMPUT SCI DIV, UNION CARBIDE NUCLEAR DIV, UNION CARBIDE CORP, 73- *Mem:* Asn Comput Mach. *Res:* Applications of computer techniques to scientific and engineering problems; management of computer facilities. *Mailing Add:* Union Carbide Nuclear Div PO Box X Oak Ridge TN 37830

CARTER, HERBERT EDMUND, b Morresville, Ind, Sept 25, 10; m 33; c 2. CHEMISTRY, BIOCHEMISTRY. *Educ:* DePauw Univ, AB, 30; Univ Ill, AM, 31, PhD(chem), 34. *Hon Degrees:* ScD, DePauw Univ, 51, Univ Ill, 74, Univ Ind, 74; DHL, Thomas Jefferson Univ, 75. *Prof Exp:* From instr to prof chem, Univ Ill, Urbana-Champaign, 32-67, head dept, 54-67, acting dean grad col, 63-65, vchancellor acad affairs, 67-71; coordr interdisciplinary progs, 71-77, head, Dept Biochem, 77-81, RES FEL, OFF ARID LANDS STUDIES, UNIV ARIZ, 81- *Concurrent Pos:* Mem div chem & chem technol, Nat Res Coun, 50-55, mem-at-large & mem exec comt, 57-59; mem mgt comt, Gordon Res Conf, 53-56, mem coun, 59-; chmn biochem study sect, NIH, 54-56, chmn biochem training grant comt, 58-61; mem nat comt, Int Union Pure & Appl Chem, 55-62, chmn, 60-62; mem bd sci counr, Nat Heart Inst, 57-59; mem nat comt, Int Union Biochem, 62-65; mem, President's Comt Nat Medal Sci, 63-66; chmn sect biochem, Nat Acad Sci, 63-66, mem coun, 66-69; mem Nat Sci Bd, 64-, chmn, 70-74; mem bd trustees, Nutrit Found, 70-; mem bd trustees, Argonne Univ Assoc, 80- *Honors & Awards:* Lilly Award, 43; Nichols Medal, 65; Award Lipid Chemistry, Am Oil Chem Soc, 66; Kenneth A Spencer Award, 68; Alton E Bailey Award, 70. *Mem:* Nat Acad Sci; AAAS; Am Chem Soc; Am Soc Biol Chemists (pres, 56-57); Am Oil Chem Soc. *Res:* Fatty acid metabolism; biochemistry of amino acids; chemistry of streptomycin and other antibiotic substances; biochemistry of complex lipids of plants and animals; structure of bacterial lipopolysaccharides. *Mailing Add:* 6205 Ariz Health Sci Ctr Univ of Ariz Tucson AZ 85721

CARTER, HOWARD PAYNE, b Houston, Tex, Sept 9, 21; m 52; c 2. ZOOLOGY. *Educ:* Tuskegee Inst, BS, 41; Columbia Univ, MA, 48; Univ Calif, MA, 57; Univ Wis, PhD(protozool), 64. *Prof Exp:* Instr, 50-54, from asst prof to assoc prof, 54-70, dean, Col Arts & Sci, 68-78, PROF BIOL, TUSKEGEE INST, 70-, . *Concurrent Pos:* Res assoc, Carver Res Found, 58- *Mem:* AAAS; Sigma Xi; Soc Protozool; Am Soc Parasitol; Am Micros Soc. *Res:* Infraciliature of ciliated protozoa; morphology of parasitic and freeliving protozoa; ciliate ultrastructure. *Mailing Add:* PO Box 773 Tuskegee Institute AL 36088

CARTER, HUBERT KENNON, b Athens, Ga, Apr 23, 41; m 62; c 3. EXPERIMENTAL NUCLEAR PHYSICS. *Educ:* Univ Ga, BS, 63; La State Univ, MS, 65; Vanderbilt Univ, PhD(physics), 69. *Prof Exp:* Asst prof physics, Furman Univ, 68-74; MEM FAC RES, UNIV ISOTOPE SEPARATOR, OAK RIDGE ASSOC UNIVS, 72-, SCIENTIST PHYSICS, 73- *Mem:* Am Phys Soc; AAAS. *Res:* The study of nuclei far from stability with an isotope separator on-line to a heavy-ion cyclotron and with fast atom-laser spectroscopy. *Mailing Add:* Bldg 6000 Oak Ridge Nat Lab Oak Ridge TN 37830

CARTER, IRVING DOYLE, b Brewer, Maine, July 4, 18; m 39; c 2. CHEMISTRY, CHEMICAL ENGINEERING. *Educ:* Northeastern Univ, BS, 42. *Prof Exp:* Anal chemist, 42-45, res chemist, 45-53, APPL STATISTICIAN, AM CYANAMID CO, 53- *Mem:* Am Soc Qual Control; Am Statist Asn. *Res:* Statistical consultation in the planning, design, execution, analysis and evaluation of research and development programs in the fields of chemistry and engineering. *Mailing Add:* Chem Res Div Am Cyanamid Co 1937 W Main St Stamford CT 06904

CARTER, JACK FRANKLIN, b Lodgepole, Nebr, Oct 1, 19; m 41; c 5. AGRONOMY. *Educ:* Univ Nebr, BS, 41; State Col Wash, MS, 47; Univ Wis, PhD(agron, plant path), 50. *Prof Exp:* Res & teaching fel agron, State Col Wash, 41 & 46-47; res asst agron & plant path, Univ Wis, 47-50; assoc prof & assoc agronomist, 50-59, PROF AGRON & AGRONOMIST, NDAK STATE UNIV, 59-, CHMN DEPT, 60- *Mem:* Coun Agr Sci & Technol, (pres, 78-79); Am Soc Agron; Crop Sci Soc Am (pres, 72-73). *Res:* Forage crop production and management; pasture research; forage crop diseases. *Mailing Add:* 1345 11th St N Fargo ND 58102

CARTER, JACK LEE, b Kansas City, Kans, Jan 23, 29; m 51; c 3. BOTANY. *Educ:* Kans State Teachers Col, BS, 50, MS, 54; Univ Iowa, PhD(bot), 60. *Prof Exp:* Assoc prof biol & head dept, Northwestern Col, Iowa, 55-58 & Simpson Col, 60-62; assoc prof & coordr res & inst grants, Kans State Teachers Col, 62-66; assoc dir biol sci curric study, Univ Colo, 66-68; PROF BIOL, COLO COL, 68- *Concurrent Pos:* Ed, Am Biol Teacher, 70-74. *Mem:* AAAS; Nat Asn Biol Teachers; Bot Soc Am; Am Soc Plant Taxonomists; Am Inst Biol Sci. *Res:* Developmental and systematic botany. *Mailing Add:* Dept of Biol Colo Col Colorado Springs CO 80903

CARTER, JAMES CLARENCE, b New York, NY, Aug 1, 27. THEORETICAL PHYSICS. *Educ:* Spring Hill Col, BS, 52; Fordham Univ, MS, 53; Catholic Univ, PhD(physics), 56; Woodstock Col, STL, 59. *Prof Exp:* From instr to asst prof, 60-67, acad vpres, 70-74, ASSOC PROF PHYSICS, LOYOLA UNIV, LA, 67-, PRES, 74- *Concurrent Pos:* NSF exten grant, 63-64; NSF res grant, Loyola Univ, La, 66-70; Nat Acad Sci-Nat Res Coun resident res assoc, Nat Bur Standards, 64-65. *Mem:* Am Phys Soc; Am Asn Physics Teachers. *Res:* Nuclear structure; symmetries of elementary particles. *Mailing Add:* President Loyola Univ New Orleans LA 70118

CARTER, JAMES EDWARD, b Great Neck, NY, Nov 3, 29; m 51; c 3. OBSTETRICS & GYNECOLOGY, PATHOLOGY. *Educ:* Univ Vt, BA, 51; NY Med Col, MD, 55. *Prof Exp:* Assoc prof, 70-73, PROF OBSTET & GYNEC & PATH, SCH MED, IND UNIV, INDIANAPOLIS, 73-, ASSOC DEAN STUDENT & CURRICULAR AFFAIRS, 73- *Mem:* AAAS; Am Col Obstet & Gynec; Electron Micros Soc Am. *Mailing Add:* Ind Univ Sch Med 1100 W Michigan St Indianapolis IN 46202

CARTER, JAMES EVAN, b Calgary, Alta, Can, Oct 26, 41; m 65; c 4. PHARMACEUTICAL ANALYSIS, PHARMACEUTICAL QUALITY CONTROL. *Educ:* Brigham Young Univ, BS, 66, MS, 69; Univ Utah, PhD(mech chem), 75. *Prof Exp:* Biochemist & prin investr, Utah State Div Health & Utah Community Pesticide Study, 69-73; GROUP LEADER ANAL DEVELOP, AM CRITICAL CARE, DIV AM HOSP SUPPLY CORP, 75- *Mem:* Am Pharmaceut Asn; Am Chem Soc; Asn Off Anal Chemists. *Res:* Pharmaceutical analysis and control in-vitro; methods development; compatibility studies of drugs in solution; analysis of drugs in feed. *Mailing Add:* Am Critical Care 1600 Waukegan McGaw Park IL 60085

CARTER, JAMES HARRISON, II, b Biloxi, Miss, July 4, 45; m 65; c 2. HEMATOLOGY SYSTEMS, TECHNICAL MANAGEMENT. *Educ:* Ga Inst Technol, BS, 66, PhD(chem), 70. *Prof Exp:* Asst clin chemist, Med Lab Assoc, 70-71; gen mgr, Diag Lab, Biomed Prod Corp, 71-75; LAB DIR, VET DIAG, VET CLIN LAB, 75-; SR SCIENTIST, RES & DEVELOP, COULTER ELECTRONICS INC, 78- *Concurrent Pos:* Lab consult, James H Carter, PhD, Lab Consult, 75-; prin investr, Broward County Bd Comn, 81- *Mem:* Am Asn Clin Chem; Confr Public Health Lab Dir. *Res:* Automated instrument applications to non-human clinical specimens; design and development of hematology reagent and control systems for use with Coulter electronic cell counting; blood cellular components, stabilization and handling. *Mailing Add:* 700 W 83rd St Hialeah FL 33014

CARTER, JAMES M, b Cass Co, Mich, Dec 7, 21; m 51; c 4. VETERINARY PHYSIOLOGY. *Educ:* Mich State Univ, DVM, 51; Purdue Univ, MS, 63, PhD(physiol), 65. *Prof Exp:* Pvt vet practr, Ind, 51-61; Am Vet Med Asn fel, 61-63, asst, 63-65, asst prof, 65-68, ASSOC PROF VET PHYSIOL, PURDUE UNIV, WEST LAFAYETTE, 68- *Mem:* Am Vet Med Asn; Am Soc Vet Physiol & Pharmacol. *Res:* Renal and respiratory physiology, especially fluid and electrolyte and acid-base balance studies. *Mailing Add:* Sch Vet Med Purdue Univ West Lafayette IN 47906

CARTER, JOHN C H, b Toronto, Ont, Sept 16, 25; m 49. MARINE BIOLOGY, FRESH WATER BIOLOGY. *Educ:* Univ Toronto, BA, 48; McGill Univ, MSc, 61, PhD(zool), 63. *Prof Exp:* Res fel, Systs & Ecol Prog, Marine Biol Lab, 63-65; ASSOC PROF BIOL, UNIV WATERLOO, 65- *Mem:* Am Soc Limnol & Oceanog. *Res:* Hydrography and plankton of landlocked fiords of Canadian Arctic; Arctic plankton; ecology of estuarine and freshwater copepods. *Mailing Add:* Dept of Biol Univ of Waterloo Waterloo ON N2L 3G1 Can

CARTER, JOHN HAAS, b Trevorton, Pa, Oct 25, 30; m 54; c 3. OPTOMETRY. *Educ:* Pa State Col Optom, OD, 53; Univ Ind, MS, 59, PhD, 62. *Prof Exp:* Asst div optom, Univ Ind, 57-59, res asst, 59-62; res assoc prof physiol optics, Pa Col Optom, 62-66, res prof, 66-70; dir visual sci div, 71-73, acad dean, 73-77, PROF PHYSIOL OPTICS, NEW ENG COL OPTOM, 70- *Mem:* Fel AAAS; fel Am Acad Optom. *Res:* Physiological optics; infrared self-recording refractionometer; nature of stimulus to accomodative mechanism of the eye. *Mailing Add:* New Eng Col Optom 424 Beacon St Boston MA 02115

CARTER, JOHN LEMUEL, JR, b Clarksville, Tex, Mar 17, 20; m 47; c 3. NUCLEAR REACTOR COMPUTER CODES, PHYSICS. *Educ:* Baylor Univ, BA, 41; Brown Univ, MSc, 43; Cornell Univ, PhD(physics), 53. *Prof Exp:* Engr sound div, US Naval Res Lab, 43-45; engr, US Naval Underwater Sound Reference Lab, 45-47; asst physics, Cornell Univ, 47-52; engr measurements lab, Gen Elec Co, Mass, 52-55, physicist, Hanford Atomic Prod Oper, 55-58, supvr theoret physics res unit, Hanford Labs, 58-63, tech specialist, 63-64; res assoc, Reactor Physics Dept, Pac Northwest Lab, Battelle Mem Inst, 65-77; SR ENGR, EXXON NUCLEAR CO, 77- *Mem:* Am Phys Soc; Am Nuclear Soc. *Res:* Nuclear reactor physics; solid state theory; digital computer codes. *Mailing Add:* 78 McMurray Rd Richland WA 99352

CARTER, JOHN LYMAN, b Sisseton, SDak, Mar 14, 34; m 63. INVERTEBRATE PALEONTOLOGY. *Educ:* Univ NDak, BS, 59; Univ Cincinnati, PhD(geol), 66. *Prof Exp:* Res assoc paleont & cur, Univ Ill, Urbana-Champaign, 66-72; ASSOC CUR, CARNEGIE MUS NATURAL HIST, 72- *Mem:* Paleont Soc; Soc Syst Zool; Brit Palaeont Asn; Int Palaeont Asn; Soc Econ Paleont & Mineral. *Res:* Late Paleozoic Brachiopoda and biostratigraphy. *Mailing Add:* Carnegie Mus Nat Hist 4400 Forbes Ave Pittsburgh PA 15213

CARTER, JOHN NEWTON, b Columbia, Mo, Jan 24, 21; m 48; c 3. AGRONOMY. *Educ:* Univ Mo, BS, 43; Univ Ill, MS, 48, PhD(soil fertil), 50. *Prof Exp:* Spec res asst agron, Univ Ill, 47-50; prin soil scientist, Battelle Mem Inst, 51-55; SOIL SCIENTIST SOIL & WATER CONSERV, AGR RES SERV, USDA, 55- *Mem:* Am Soc Agron; Soil Sci Soc Am; Am Soc Sugar Beet Technologists. *Res:* Sugarbeet nitrogen nutrition; soil fertility; soil nitrogen transformations; soil organic matter; plant nutrition. *Mailing Add:* Snake River Conserv Res Sta USDA-ARS Rt 1 Box 186 Kimberly ID 83341

CARTER, JOHN PAUL, JR, b Charlottesville, Va, July 23, 51. PHARMACEUTICAL CHEMISTRY. *Educ:* Univ Tenn, AB, 73, PhD(chem), 78. *Prof Exp:* Res assoc, Ore State Univ, 78-80; SR SCIENTIST, ADRIA LAB INC, 81- *Mem:* Am Chem Soc; Royal Inst Chem. *Res:* Cancer chemotheraphy; synthesis of natural products; new synthetic reactions. *Mailing Add:* Adria Lab Res Park PO Box 16529 Columbus OH 43216

CARTER, JOHN ROBERT, b Buffalo, NY, Apr 21, 17; m 43; c 2. PATHOLOGY. *Educ:* Hamilton Col, BS, 39; Univ Rochester, MD, 43. *Prof Exp:* Asst path, Univ Iowa, 44, from instr to prof, 44-59; prof path & oncol & chmn dept, Med Ctr, Univ Kans, 59-66; prof path, chmn dept & dir, Inst Path, 66-81, PROF PATH & PROF PATH, DEPT ORTHOP, CASE WESTERN RESERVE UNIV, 81- *Concurrent Pos:* Dir path, Univ Hosps, Cleveland, 66-81, dir, Musculoskeletal Path Lab, 81- *Mem:* Am Soc Clin Path; Am Soc Exp Path; Col Am Path; Am Asn Path & Bact (treas, 61-62, secy-treas, 62-65, vpres, 66-67, pres, 67-68); Int Acad Path. *Res:* Blood coagulation; musculoskeletal neoplasms. *Mailing Add:* Inst of Path Case Western Reserve Univ Cleveland OH 44106

CARTER, JOHN VERNON, b Boise, Idaho, Dec 21, 40; m 64; c 3. BIOPHYSICAL CHEMISTRY. *Educ:* Whittier Col, BA, 62; Purdue Univ, PhD(org chem), 67. *Prof Exp:* Res scientist org chem, Koppers Co, Inc, Pa, 67-68; res fel, Univ Pittsburgh, 68-70; from asst prof to assoc prof chem, Adams State Col, 70-74; res assoc chem, Univ Minn, Minneapolis, 74-76; asst prof, 76-81, ASSOC PROF HORT SCI, UNIV MINN, ST PAUL, 81- *Mem:* Am Soc Plant Physiol; Sigma Xi; Am Chem Soc. *Res:* Plant stress physiology. *Mailing Add:* Dept of Hort Sci Univ of Minn St Paul MN 55108

CARTER, JOSEPH GAYLORD, b Honolulu, Hawaii, Dec 14, 47; m 69; c 2. PALEOBIOLOGY, PALEONTOLOGY. *Educ:* UniV Kans, BS, 70; Yale Univ, PhD(paleobiol), 76. *Prof Exp:* Asst prof geol, Colgate Univ, 74-76; asst prof, 76-81, ASSOC PROF GEOL, UNIV NC, 81- *Concurrent Pos:* Explor geologist, Union Oil Co, 70. *Honors & Awards:* W A Tarr Award. *Mem:* Sigma Xi; Paleont Soc; Paleont Res Inst. *Res:* Ecology and evolution of the Mollusca, especially shell microstructure and evolution of Middle Paleozoic benthic and post-Paleozoic endolithic communities. *Mailing Add:* Dept Geol Univ NC Chapel Hill NC 27514

CARTER, KENNETH, b Morecambe, Eng, Feb 6, 14; m 40, 70; c 3. MEDICINE, PHARMACEUTICAL CHEMISTRY. *Educ:* Univ London, MRCS & LRCP, 47. *Prof Exp:* Res chemist, Glaxo Labs, Eng, 38-42, med dir, Buenos Aires, 48-50, dir, Qual Control & Prod, 49-57; res liaison officer & secy, Therapeut Res Corp Gt Brit, 46-48; dir develop, Smith Kline & French, Pa, 52-54, med dir & dir develop, Eng, 54-57; sci dir, Ames Co, Ind, 57-58, vpres res & med affairs, 58-62, Miles Labs, Inc, 62-65; vpres & dir med affairs, Syntex Int, 65-71, corp vpres regulatory affairs, Syntex Corp, 71-79; consult, Drug Surveillance Res Unit, Southampton Univ, Eng, 80-81; CONSULT, 81- *Concurrent Pos:* House physician, Postgrad Med Sch, Univ London, 47-48; mem, Royal Col Surgeons; mem, Bd Dirs, Royal Soc Med Found, Inc, 68- *Mem:* Fel Pharmaceut Soc Gt Brit; fel Royal Soc Med; Brit Med Asn; Brit Harvein Soc. *Res:* Administration of research, development and medical operations; disciplines necessary for developing new diagnostic and therapeutic agents, such as chemistry, biochemistry, immunology, toxicology, pharmacology, clinical pharmacology and clinical research; government regulatory affairs. *Mailing Add:* 24612 Olive Tree Lane Los Altos Hills CA 94022

CARTER, KENNETH NOLON, b Columbia, SC, Oct 2, 25; m 54; c 1. ORGANIC CHEMISTRY. *Educ:* Erskine Col, AB, 47; Vanderbilt Univ, MS, 49, PhD(chem), 51. *Prof Exp:* HEAD DEPT CHEM, PRESBY COL, 51-, CHARLES A DANA PROF, 70- *Mem:* Am Chem Soc. *Res:* Organic synthesis; molecular rearrangements. *Mailing Add:* Dept of Chem Presby Col Clinton SC 29325

CARTER, LARK POLAND, b Lytton, Iowa, June 26, 30; m 54; c 2. AGRONOMY. *Educ:* Iowa State Univ, BS, 53, MS, 56, PhD(agron), 60. *Prof Exp:* Asst prof agron, Mont State Univ, 60-62, asst dean, Col Agr, 62-65, assoc dean, Col Agr & asst dir, Agr Exp Sta, 65-80; asst dir higher educ, USDA, Washington, DC, 80-81; DEAN, SCH AGR & NATURAL RESOURCES, CALIF POLYTECH STATE UNIV, SAN LUIS OBISPO, 81- *Mem:* Am Soc Agron. *Res:* Field crop production; forage management; seed certification; grass and legume seed production. *Mailing Add:* Sch Agr & Natural Resources Calif Polytech State Univ San Luis Obispo CA 93407

CARTER, LEE, b Rock Island, Ill, Sept 8, 17; m 45; c 3. CHEMICAL ENGINEERING, ENGINEERING ECONOMICS. *Educ:* Purdue Univ, BS, 40; Cornell Univ, MS, 45. *Prof Exp:* Lab asst, Universal Oil Prod Co, 37-38, pilot plant operator, 40-42; mgr tech serv, Va-Carolina Chem Corp, 47; from res engr to mgr, Calgary Off, E B Badger & Sons Co & Stone & Webster, 47-63; mgr eng reports, R W Booker & Assocs, Inc, 63-69, sr vpres & dir proj studies div, 69-72; CONSULT ENGR, 72- *Concurrent Pos:* Mem investment mission, US Dept Com, Colombia, 65. *Mem:* AAAS; Am Inst Chem Engrs; Chem Inst Can; fel Brit Inst Petrol. *Res:* Technical-economic investigations of project feasibility; industrial development studies; coal conversion; production of olefins; port development studies. *Mailing Add:* 622 Belson Ct Kirkwood MO 63122

CARTER, LELAND LAVELLE, b Oberlin, Kans, Nov 27, 37; m 58; c 4. REACTOR PHYSICS, NUCLEAR ENGINEERING. *Educ:* Northwest Nazarene Col, BA, 61; Univ Wash, MS, 64, PhD(nuclear eng), 69. *Prof Exp:* Physicist, Gen Elec Co, 62-63; physicist, Pac Northwest Labs, Battelle Mem Inst, 64-65; nuclear engr, Los Alamos Sci Lab, Univ Calif, 69-73, alt group leader neutron transport, 74-77; prin engr, 77-81, FEL ENGR, WESTINGHOUSE HAMFORD CO, 81- *Mem:* Am Nuclear Soc. *Res:* Application of the Monte Carlo method to solve three-dimensional particle transport problems on the digital computer; adjoint simulation, neutron cross-sections, nonlinear radiative transport, criticality, unbiased sampling schemes and shielding for neutron energies 0-50 million electron volts. *Mailing Add:* W/F121B Box 1970 Richland WA 99352

CARTER, LEO F, b Warwick, NY, Dec 20, 39; m 61; c 2. CHEMICAL ENGINEERING. *Educ:* Syracuse Univ, BChE, 61, MChE, 63; Univ Mich, PhD(chem engr), 67. *Prof Exp:* sr specialist, 67-80, GROUP LEADER, EXPLOR & FUNDAMENTAL POLYMER RES, MONSANTO CO, SPRINGFIELD, MASS, 80- *Mem:* Am Chem Soc; Am Inst Chem Engrs. *Res:* Multiphase polymer structure-properties relationships; polymerization kinetics and process modeling; rheology of fiber suspensions; laminar flow in porous ducts. *Mailing Add:* 489 Main St Wilbraham MA 01095

CARTER, LINDA G, b Mansfield, Ohio, Sept 23, 49. SYNTHETIC ORGANIC CHEMISTRY. *Educ:* Case Western Reserve Univ, BA, 71; Purdue Univ, MS, 73; Univ Ill, PhD(org chem), 80. *Prof Exp:* Res chemist, Monsanto Agr Prod Co, 73-76; RES CHEMIST, BIOCHEM DEPT, E I DU PONT DE NEMOURS & CO, 80- *Mem:* Am Chem Soc. *Res:* Agrichemical research; metalation chemistry. *Mailing Add:* Exp Sta E324/313 Dept Biochem E I du Pont de Nemours Wilmington DE

CARTER, LOREN SHELDON, b Nampa, Idaho, Jan 10, 39; m 68. PHYSICAL CHEMISTRY, INORGANIC CHEMISTRY. *Educ:* Ore State Univ, BS, 61, MS, 66; Wash State Univ, PhD(phys chem), 70. *Prof Exp:* Reactor engr, Phillips Petrol Co, 61-63; from asst prof to assoc prof, 70-79, PROF CHEM, BOISE STATE UNIV, 79- *Mem:* Am Chem Soc. *Res:* Surface adsorption on clays; transference number measurements using a centrifuge in organic solvents; hydrocarbons in the environment; chemotaxonomy of cacti. *Mailing Add:* Dept of Chem Boise State Univ Boise ID 83725

CARTER, MARY EDDIE, b Americus, Ga, March 14, 25. ORGANIC CHEMISTRY. *Educ:* La Grange Col, BA, 46; Univ Fla, MS, 49; Univ Edinburgh, PhD, 56. *Prof Exp:* Instr chem, La Grange Col, 46-47; microscopist, Calloway Mills, 47-48; textile chemist, Southern Res Inst, 49-51; chemist, West Point Mfg Co, 51-53; res chemist, Am Viscose Corp, 56-62, res assoc, FMC Corp, Am Viscose Div, Res & Develop, 62-71; chief textiles & clothing lab, SMNRD, Agr Res Serv, 71-73, dir, Southern Regional Res Ctr, 73-80, ASSOC ADMIN, SCI & EDUC-AGR RES SERV, USDA, 80- *Honors & Awards:* Herty Award, Am Chem Soc, 79. *Mem:* Am Chem Soc; Am Asn Textile Chemists & Colorists; Inter-Soc Color Coun; Fiber Soc; Sigma Xi. *Res:* Naturally occurring polymers for fiber, food and feed, including safety, nutrition and processing aspects. *Mailing Add:* Rm 302-A Admin Bldg Agr Res Serv USDA Washington DC 20250

CARTER, MARY KATHLEEN, b Franklinton, La, July 11, 22. PHARMACOLOGY. *Educ:* Tulane Univ, BA, 49, MS, 53; Vanderbilt Univ, PhD(pharmacol), 55. *Prof Exp:* Asst pharmacol, Tulane Univ, 49-52; asst, Vanderbilt Univ, 52-53; res assoc, Med Ctr, Univ Kans, 55-57; from instr to assoc prof, 57-73, PROF PHARMACOL, MED SCH, TULANE UNIV, 73- *Concurrent Pos:* USPHS fel, Med Ctr, Univ Kans, 55-57, sr res fel, Med Sch, Tulane Univ, 57-61. *Mem:* AAAS; Soc Exp Biol & Med; Am Soc Pharmacol & Exp Therapeut; Am Soc Nephrology. *Res:* Renal pharmacology; transport of electrolytes and sugars; cholinesterases. *Mailing Add:* Dept of Pharmacol Tulane Univ Sch of Med New Orleans LA 70112

CARTER, MASON CARLTON, b Wash, DC, Jan 14, 33; m 53. PLANT PHYSIOLOGY, FORESTRY. *Educ:* Va Polytech Inst, BS, 55, MS, 57; Duke Univ, PhD(forestry), 59. *Prof Exp:* Asst plant physiol, Va Polytech Inst, 55-56; res forester, Southeastern Forest Exp Sta, USDA, 59-60; asst prof forestry, Auburn Univ, 60-66, assoc prof forestry & bot, 66-70, alumni assoc prof, 70-72, alumni prof, 72-73; PROF FORESTRY & NATURAL RESOURCES & CHMN DEPT, PURDUE UNIV, WEST LAFAYETTE, 73- *Mem:* Am Forestry Asn; Soc Am Foresters. *Res:* Mechanisms of herbicidal action; physiology of woody plants. *Mailing Add:* Dept of Forestry & Natural Resources Purdue Univ West Lafayette IN 47907

CARTER, MELVIN K, physical chemistry, environmental chemistry, see previous edition

CARTER, MELVIN WHITEHEAD, sanitary engineering, see previous edition

CARTER, MELVIN WINSOR, b Phoenix, Ariz, Jan 22, 28; m 50; c 5. APPLIED STATISTICS, BIOMETRICS. *Educ:* Ariz State Univ, BS, 53; NC State Col, MS, 54, PhD, 56. *Prof Exp:* Asst nutrit, NC State Col, 52-56; asst prof statist, Purdue Univ, 56-58; exp statist, NC State Col, 58-61; assoc prof, 61-66, PROF STATIST, BRIGHAM YOUNG UNIV, 66- *Concurrent Pos:* Vis prof, NC State Univ, 67-68 & Texas A&M Univ, 71; biostatistician, Upjohn Co, 75. *Mem:* Am Statist Asn; Biomet Soc. *Res:* Biometrics; nutrition; endocrinology; biochemistry; methodology for the analysis of unbalanced designs. *Mailing Add:* Dept of Statist Brigham Young Univ Provo UT 84601

CARTER, NEVILLE LOUIS, b Los Angeles, Calif, Aug 21, 34; m 56; c 3. GEOLOGY, GEOPHYSICS. *Educ:* Pomona Col, AB, 56; Univ Calif, Los Angeles, MA, 58, PhD(geol), 63. *Prof Exp:* Res geophysicist, Univ Calif, Los Angeles, 61-63, asst, 63; res geologist, Shell Develop Co, 63-66; assoc prof geol & geophys, Yale Univ, 66-71; prof geophys, earth & space sci, State Univ NY Stony Brook, 71-78; HEAD AND PROF GEOPHYSICS, FAC ASSOC, CTR TECTONOPHYSICS, TEXAS A&M UNIV, 78- *Mem:* Am Geophys Union; Geol Soc Am. *Res:* Tectonophysics; experimental and natural deformation of rocks and minerals. *Mailing Add:* Dept of Earth & Space Sci State Univ of NY Stony Brook NY 11794

CARTER, ORWIN LEE, b Geneseo, Ill, Aug 22, 42; m 66; c 2. PHYSICAL CHEMISTRY, IMMUNOLOGY. *Educ:* Univ Iowa, BS, 64; Univ Ill, MS, 65, PhD(x-ray crystallog), 67; Rider Col, MBA, 75. *Prof Exp:* Asst prof phys chem, US Mil Acad, 67-70; from scientist to sr scientist, Rohm & Haas Co, 70-74; dir, Prod Develop, Micromedic Systs, Inc, 74-77; assoc dir, Immunodiagnostics, 77-78, act dir, Res Ctr, 78-79, vpres, Admin & Planning, 79-80, VPRES & GEN MGR, MANUAL IMMUNOASSAY, IMMUNODIAGNOSTICS, BECTON DICKINSON & CO, 80- *Mem:* Am Chem Soc; Am Asn Clin Chemists; Sigma Xi. *Res:* Immunoassay by radioisotope techniques; enzymatic assays in clinical chemistry. *Mailing Add:* 1090 High Mountain Rd Franklin Lakes NJ 07417

CARTER, PAUL BEARNSON, b Spanish Fork, Utah, Feb 17, 18; m 42; c 1. BACTERIOLOGY. *Educ:* Univ Utah, BS, 48, MS, 50, PhD(bact), 55. *Prof Exp:* Instr bact, Univ Utah, 50-55, res instr anat, 55-56; asst prof biol, 56-62, assoc prof, 62-77, PROF BIOL, UTAH STATE UNIV, 77- *Mem:* Am Soc Microbiol; NY Acad Sci; Sigma Xi. *Res:* Pathogenic microbiology; medical mycology; immunology; inflammation. *Mailing Add:* Dept Biol Utah State Univ Logan UT 84322

CARTER, PAUL RICHARD, b St Louis, Mo, Apr 14, 22; m 44; c 2. MEDICINE, SURGERY. *Educ:* Union Col, Nebr, BA, 44; Loma Linda Univ, MD, 48; Am Bd Surg, dipl; Am Bd Thoracic Surg, dipl. *Prof Exp:* Surg resident, Los Angeles County Gen Hosp, 50-52, 54-56; thoracic surg resident, Olive View Sanitarium, Calif, 56-57; head physician surg, Los Angeles County Gen Hosp, 57-66; assoc prof surg, Univ Calif-Calif Col Med, 67-68; assoc prof in residence, 68-70, prof surg, Col Med, Univ Calif, Irvine, 70-76; CHIEF THORACIC SURG, PETTIS VET ADMIN HOSP, LOMA LINDA, CA, 76-; PROF SURG, LOMA LINDA UNIV, 76- *Concurrent Pos:* Fulbright scholar, Oxford Univ, 59; assoc prof surg, Sch Med, Loma Linda Univ, 62-66; chief surg, Rancho Los Amigos Hosp, 66-68; sr attend surgeon, Los Angeles County Gen Hosp & White Mem Hosp, Los Angeles; chief surg, Orange County Med Ctr, 70-76; mem sr staff, Intercommunity Hosp, Covina; mem active staff, Queen of the Valley Hosp, West Covina. *Mem:* Fel Am Col Surg; Am Col Chest Physicians; Am Asn Thoracic Surg; Soc Thoracic Surg. *Res:* Mesenteric vascular occlusion; subphrenic abscess; volvulus of the colon and gall-bladder; pseudotumors of the lung; traumatic thoracic injuries; gallstone obstruction; surgical significance of sternal fracture; rupture of the bronchus; segmental reversal of small intestine; use of the Celestin tube for inoperable carcinoma of the esophagus and cardia; bronchotomy; diaphragmatic hernia. *Mailing Add:* 227 W Badillo Covina CA 91723

CARTER, PAUL RICHARD, surface chemistry, see previous edition

CARTER, PHILIP BRIAN, microbiology, immunology, see previous edition

CARTER, R OWEN, JR, b Sligo, La, Aug 18, 15; m 44; c 3. TOXICOLOGY & SAFETY EVALUATION, PHYSICAL CHEMISTRY. *Educ:* Centenary Col, BS, 35; Univ Wis, PhD(phys chem), 39. *Prof Exp:* Sr chemist, Procter & Gamble Co, 39-41; res assoc, Nat Defense Res Comt Proj, Univ Wis, 41-44; SR CHEMIST, PROCTER & GAMBLE CO, 44- *Mem:* Am Chem Soc; Am Acad Dermat; Sigma Xi. *Res:* Molecular-kinetic study of proteins; gelatinization of high polymers; fats and oils; soaps and detergents; toxicology and safety evaluation. *Mailing Add:* 6309 Lisbon Cincinnati OH 45213

CARTER, RALPH E(DGAR), b Vancouver, BC, Nov 25, 23; nat US; m 51; c 1. METALLURGY. *Educ:* Univ BC, BASc, 48, MASc, 49; Univ London, PhD(metall), 53. *Prof Exp:* Res metallurgist, Atomic Energy Can, Ltd, 49-51 & Can Bur Mines, 53-55; res ceramist, 55-75, mgr silicon iron prog, Corp Res & Develop, 75-77, MGR STRUCT MAT & CORROSION BR, CORP RES & DEVELOP, GEN ELEC CO, 77- *Mem:* Am Ceramic Soc. *Res:* High temperature physical chemistry and kinetics. *Mailing Add:* Gen Elec Res & Develop Ctr PO Box 8 Schenectady NY 12301

CARTER, RICHARD P(ENCE), b Alderson, WVa, Jan 3, 15; m 39; c 3. CHEMICAL ENGINEERING. *Educ:* Va Polytech Inst, BS, 36; Purdue Univ, PhD(chem eng), 40. *Prof Exp:* Asst, Purdue Univ, 36-40; chem engr, Pilot Plant Develop, Exp Sta, Hercules Inc, Wilmington, Del, 40-42, head pilot plant dept, 42-43, chem engr, 43-45, chief chemist, 45-51, asst plant mgr, 51-59, tech asst to plant mgr, 59-61, tech mgr, NJ, 61-65, sr scientist, Allegany Ballistics Lab, 65-66, div mgr, Polymers Tech Ctr, Hercules Inc, 69-70, oper mgr, 71-80; ENGR CONSULT PLASTICS PROCESSING, 80- *Mem:* Am Chem Soc; Am Inst Chem Engrs; Am Inst Aeronaut & Astronaut. *Res:* Organic chemical development; synthetic resins development; esterification; distillation; thermal cracking; hydrogenation; general engineering; explosives and solid rocket development; plastics processes. *Mailing Add:* 510 Ruxton Dr Wilmington DE 19809

CARTER, RICHARD THOMAS, b Portland, Ore, Apr 4, 36; m 57; c 3. PARASITOLOGY, INVERTEBRATE ZOOLOGY. *Educ:* Portland State Univ, BS, 63; Ore State Univ, MA, 67, PhD(parasitol), 73. *Prof Exp:* Instr biol, Portland State Col, 62-63; asst prof, 68-73, ASSOC PROF BIOL, PAC UNIV, 73-, CHMN DEPT, 74- *Mem:* Sigma Xi. *Res:* Investigations into life stage development in Nanophyetus salmincola as related to life history. *Mailing Add:* Dept of Biol Pac Univ Forest Grove OR 97116

CARTER, ROBERT DUNCAN, b Twin Falls, Idaho, Mar 2, 29; m 50; c 3. ENTOMOLOGY. *Educ:* Univ Calif, BS, 50, PhD(entom), 54; Am Registry Prof Entomologists, cert. *Prof Exp:* Entomologist, Bur Entom, Calif State Dept Agr, 50; entomologist, 55-70, mgr entom res, Agr Res Ctr, 70-81, MGR ENTOM & PESTICIDE CONTROL, DEL MONTE CORP, 81- *Concurrent Pos:* Consult, Ariz Auditor Gen, 79, USDA New Pest Detection & Survey Comt, 80. *Mem:* Entom Soc Am; Am Phytopath Soc. *Res:* Arthropods in relation to plant disease; agricultural entomology; pest management. *Mailing Add:* 7644 Surrey Lane Oakland CA 94605

CARTER, ROBERT ELDRED, b Minneapolis, Minn, July 14, 23; m 46; c 3. PEDIATRICS, HEMATOLOGY. *Educ:* Univ Minn, BS, 45, MB, 46, MD, 48. *Prof Exp:* From instr to asst prof pediat, Univ Chicago, 56-59; from asst prof to prof, Univ Iowa, 59-67, from asst dean to assoc dean, 61-67; prof pediat, assoc dean & dir, Sch Med, Univ Miss, 67-70; dean med educ prog, 70-74, prof microbiol & pediat, 74-78, EMER PROF, UNIV MINN, DULUTH, 78- *Concurrent Pos:* John & Mary R Markle scholar med sci, 57-62. *Mem:* Soc Pediat Res. *Res:* Biological effects of ionizing radiations; general hematology and bone marrow function. *Mailing Add:* PO Box 504 Corrales MN 87048

CARTER, ROBERT EMERSON, b Philadelphia, Pa, Feb 3, 20; m 47; c 11. PHYSICS. *Educ:* Washington Col, BS, 42; Univ Ill, MS, 47. *Prof Exp:* Jr physicist, Off Sci Res & Develop, Purdue Univ, 42-43, instr eng sci & war mgt training, 42-43; jr physicist, Los Alamos Sci Lab, Univ Calif, 43-45; asst nuclear res, Univ Ill, 46-48; mem staff, Los Alamos Sci Lab, 48-63; chmn phys sci dept, Armed Forces Radiobiol Res Inst, 63-75; head, Reactor Sci Div, Inst Resource Mgt, Bethesda, 76-80, PROJ MGR, US NUCLEAR REGULATORY COMN, 80- *Concurrent Pos:* Consult, AEC, 47-48, Dept Army, 59-63; instr, Los Alamos Grad Ctr, Univ NMex, 56-63; mem, Subcomt Res Reactors Comt Phys Sci, Nat Acad Sci-Nat Res Coun, 64-69. *Mem:* Am Nuclear Soc; Am Phys Soc; AAAS; Sigma Xi. *Res:* Nuclear physics; nuclear engineering; molecular and atomic physics; mathematical physics; radiation physics; medical physics; radiation biology. *Mailing Add:* 9512 Edgeley Rd Bethesda MD 20814

CARTER, ROBERT EVERETT, b Jamaica, NY, Dec 3, 37; m 62, 75; c 3. PHYSICAL ORGANIC CHEMISTRY. *Educ:* Columbia Col, BA, 58; Calif Inst Technol, PhD(org chem), 62; Gothenburg Univ, Fil Dr, 70. *Prof Exp:* NIH fel gen med sci, Inst Org Chem, Gothenburg Univ, 62-65, lectr org chem, 64-65; consult, A B Hassle Co, 65-67; res assoc, 68-70, docent, Div Org Chem, 70-76, LECTR ORG CHEM, LUND INST TECHNOL, 77- *Res:* Applications of computers and computer graphics to organic chemistry. *Mailing Add:* Div of Org Chem Chem Ctr Lund Inst of Technol Lund Sweden

CARTER, ROBERT L(EROY), b Leavenworth, Kans, Aug 22, 18; m 41; c 5. ENERGY CONVERSION, RADIOACTIVE WASTE MANAGEMENT. *Educ:* Univ Okla, BS, 41; Duke Univ, PhD(physics), 49. *Prof Exp:* Technician, Eastman Kodak Co, 41-42, physicist, Tenn Eastman Corp, 45-46; res asst physics, Duke Univ, 46-49; res engr, Atomics Int Div, NAm Aviation, Inc, 49-53, group leader mat tech, 53-56, nuclear reactor proj engr, 56-59, sr res specialist direct energy conversion, 59-62; assoc prof elec eng, 62-63, PROF ELEC & NUCLEAR ENG, UNIV MO-COLUMBIA, 63- *Concurrent Pos:* Vis staff mem, Los Alamos Sci Lab, 68-69. *Mem:* Am Phys Soc; Am Nuclear Soc; Am Soc Eng Educ; Nat Soc Prof Engrs. *Res:* Mass spectrography; microwave spectroscopy; radiation effects; nuclear reactor materials; energy conversion; low level radioactive waste management. *Mailing Add:* Dept of Elec Eng Univ of Mo Columbia MO 65201

CARTER, ROBERT LEONIDAS, b Atlanta, Ga, Aug 31, 09; m 34; c 2. SOIL FERTILITY. *Educ:* Univ Ga, BS, 31, MS, 33. *Prof Exp:* Ed adv, Civilian Conservation Corps, 34-35 & Soil Scientist, USDA, 35-46; soil scientist, Ga Coastal Plain Exp Sta, 46-74; prof agron, 46-74, EMER PROF AGRON, UNIV GA, 74- *Mem:* Am Soc Agron; Am Chem Soc; Soil Conserv Soc Am. *Res:* Soil classification and survey; soil conservation and soil fertility research; soil and plant micronutrient research. *Mailing Add:* 1207 N Central Ave Tifton GA 31794

CARTER, ROBERT SAGUE, b Poughkeepsie, NY, Nov 15, 25; m 49; c 4. NUCLEAR PHYSICS. *Educ:* Princeton Univ, AB, 48; Harvard Univ, MA, 49, PhD(physics), 52. *Prof Exp:* Assoc physicist, Brookhaven Nat Lab, 52-56; physicist, Westinghouse Res Labs, 56-58; physicist, 58-69, CHIEF REACTOR RADIATION DIV, NAT BUR STANDARDS, 69- *Mem:* Am Nuclear Soc; fel NY Acad Sci; Am Phys Soc. *Res:* Elementary particle physics; neutron physics; reactor engineering. *Mailing Add:* 14710 Pettit Way Potomac MD 20854

CARTER, ROY MERWIN, b Mauston, Wis, Jan 5, 13; m 40; c 2. WOOD TECHNOLOGY. *Educ:* Univ Minn, BSF, 35; Mich State Univ, MS, 39. *Prof Exp:* Asst, Mich State Univ, 36-38; dist forester, Wis State Dept Conserv, 38-39; instr & exten forester, Univ Wis, 39-42; chief procurement inspector woodcraft, Army Air Force, 42-43; wood process engr, Fairchild Aircraft Corp, 43-44; forest utilization specialist, US Forest Serv, 44-48; PROF WOOD TECHNOL, SCH FOREST RESOURCES, NC STATE UNIV, 48- *Mem:* Soc Am Foresters; Forest Prod Res Soc (2nd vpres, 49, 1st vpres, 50, pres, 51). *Res:* Wood moisture relations; wood preservation and finishing; gluing; plant operations and processes for wood industries. *Mailing Add:* Dept Wood & Paper Sci NC State Univ Sch Forest Res Raleigh NC 27650

CARTER, SIDNEY, b Boston, Mass, Dec 8, 12; m 45; c 3. NEUROLOGY. *Educ:* Dartmouth Col, AB, 34; Boston Univ, MD, 38. *Prof Exp:* Intern, St Mary's Hosp, Waterbury, Conn, 38-39; resident psychiat, Westboro State Hosp, Mass, 39-40; resident neurol, Boston City Hosp, 40-42; asst, Harvard Med Sch, 41-42; chief, Div Child Neurol, Columbia-Presby Med Ctr, 54-78; from instr to prof neurol, 47-78, EMER PROF NEUROL & PEDIAT, COL PHYSICIANS & SURGEONS, COLUMBIA UNIV, 78-; CHIEF DEPT NEUROL, BLYTHEDALE CHILDREN'S HOSP, 78- *Concurrent Pos:* Asst, Div Neuropsychiat, Montefiore Hosp, 46-47, adj attend neurologist, 48-52; from asst attend neurologist to attend neurologist, Columbia-Presby Hosp, 48-; attend neurologist, Lawrence Hosp, Bronxville, 52-, consult, 78-; consult, Morristown Mem Hosp, NJ, 53- *Mem:* Am Psychiat Asn; Am Acad Neurol; AMA; Am Acad Cerebral Palsy; Int League Against Epilepsy. *Res:* Epilepsy; pediatric neurology. *Mailing Add:* Blythedale Children's Hosp Valhalla NY 10959

CARTER, STEFAN A, b Warsaw, Poland, Mar 25, 28; Can citizen; m 58; c 2. PHYSIOLOGY. *Educ:* Univ Man, MD & BSc, 54, MSc, 56. *Prof Exp:* Lectr, 58-59, from asst prof to assoc prof, 59-77, prof physiol, Fac Med, 77-81, PROF MED, UNIV MAN, 81- *Concurrent Pos:* Clin res fel, NY Hosp-Cornell Med Ctr, 56-67; Nat Res Coun Can fel physiol, Mayo Found, Univ Minn, 57-58; Man Heart Found grant-in-aid, 59-76; dir cardiovasc sect, Clin Invest Unit, St Boniface Gen Hosp, 58-; dir long term anticoagulant & peripheral vascular dis clin, St Boniface Hosp, 67-; mem coun circulation, Am Heart Asn, 69; St Boniface Gen Hosp Res Found grant-in-aid, 77- *Mem:* Can Physiol Soc; Can Soc Clin Invest; Can Cardiovasc Soc. *Res:* Vasomotor regulation in diabetes; function and elasticity of medium-sized arteries and arterial pressure pulses in health and arterial diseases; arterial occlusive disease in the limbs; biofeedback and vasodilators in Raynaud's diseases. *Mailing Add:* 234 Elm St Winnipeg MB 43M 3N5 Can

CARTER, STEPHEN KEITH, b New York, NY, Oct 30, 37; m 66; c 2. INTERNAL MEDICINE, ONCOLOGY. *Educ:* Columbia Col, AB, 59; New York Med Col, MD, 63. *Prof Exp:* Intern med, Lenox Hill Hosp, 63-64, resident, 64-66, chief resident, 66-67; spec asst to sci dir chemother, Nat Cancer Inst, 67-68, chief cancer ther eval br, 68-73, assoc dir cancer ther eval, 73-74, dep dir div cancer treatment, 74-76; DIR, NORTHERN CALIF CANCER PROG, PALO ALTO, 76- *Concurrent Pos:* Consult prof med, Stanford Univ, 76-; clin prof med, Univ Calif, San Francisco, 76- *Mailing Add:* Northern Calif Cancer Prog Suite 200 1801 Page Mill Rd Bldg B Palo Alto CA 94304

CARTER, THOMAS EDWARD, JR, b Athens, Ga, Jan 23, 53; m 75. QUANTITATIVE GENETICS, STATISTICS. *Educ:* Univ Ga, BS, 75; NC State Univ, Raleigh, MS, 77, PhD(plant breeding), 80. *Prof Exp:* RES GENETICIST SOYBEAN, AGR RES SERV, NC STATE UNIV, USDA, 81- *Concurrent Pos:* Prin investr & res grant, Drought Tolerance in Soybeans, 81- *Mem:* Crop Sci Soc Am; Am Soc Agron; Biomet Soc. *Res:* Genetics of drought tolerance in soybean; development of stategies for plant breeding using quantitative genetics; application of plant physiology to plant breeding; efficiency of breeding methods. *Mailing Add:* 1239 Williams Hall NC State Univ Raleigh NC 27607

CARTER, W(ILLIS) MERLE, b Paris, Ky, Nov 28, 16; m 40; c 2. MECHANICAL ENGINEERING. *Educ:* Univ Ky, BS, 38, MS, 46; Univ Mich, PhD(mech eng), 53. *Prof Exp:* Designer, Mawen Motor Corp, 38-42, chief designer, 42-44; engr, Aeronaut Res Lab, 44-46, prof mach design, 46-65, chmn dept mech eng, 60-65, PROF MECH ENG, UNIV KY, 65- *Mem:* Am Soc Mech Engrs; Am Soc Eng Educ. *Res:* Refrigeration and internal combustion engines. *Mailing Add:* Dept of Mech Eng Univ of Ky Lexington KY 40506

CARTER, WALTER HANSBROUGH, JR, b Winchester, Va, Mar 20, 41; m 63; c 3. BIOSTATISTICS. *Educ:* Univ Richmond, BS, 63; Va Polytech Inst, MS, 66, PhD(statist), 68. *Prof Exp:* Asst prof biomet, 72-79, PROF BIOSTATIST, MED COL VA, VA COMMONWEALTH UNIV, 79- *Mem:* Sigma Xi; Am Statist Asn; Biomet Soc. *Res:* Treatment optimization in combination chemotherapy of cancer; clinical trials; design and analysis of response surface experiments. *Mailing Add:* Dept Biostatist Box 32 Med Col Va Sta Richmond VA 23298

CARTER, WILLIAM ALFRED, b Ada, Okla, Sept 16, 35. ZOOLOGY, ORNITHOLOGY. *Educ:* ECent State Col, BS, 57; Okla State Univ, MS, 60, PhD(zool), 65. *Prof Exp:* Instr biol, Northwestern State Col, Okla, 63-64; from asst prof to assoc prof, 64-71, PROF BIOL, E CENT OKLA STATE UNIV, 71-, CHMN DEPT, 72- *Concurrent Pos:* Res assoc ornith, Stovall Mus, Univ Okla, 71-; Okla coordr, US Fish & Wildlife Breeding Bird Surv, 74-; consult, Environ Impact Assessment, Williams Bros Eng Co, 75-78. *Mem:* Am Ornithologists Union; Am Soc Ichthyologists & Herpetologists; Cooper Ornith Soc; Wilson Ornith Soc; Sigma Xi. *Res:* Ecology and distribution of birds and herps. *Mailing Add:* Dept of Biol ECent Okla State Univ Ada OK 74820

CARTER, WILLIAM CASWELL, b Waterville, Maine, Jan 16, 17; m 42; 57; c 3. MATHEMATICS. *Educ:* Colby Col, AB, 38; Harvard Univ, PhD(math), 47. *Prof Exp:* Mathematician, Ballistic Res Lab, Aberdeen, 47-52; instr math, Univ Md, 47-51, Johns Hopkins Univ, 51-52; mathematician, Computer Dept, Raytheon Mfg Co, 52-55; dept mgr systs anal, Datamatic, Minn-Honeywell, 55-59; sr engr, Res Div, Int Bus Mach Corp, 59-61, data systs div, 61-66, STAFF MEM, IBM MACH RES CTR, 66- *Concurrent Pos:* Instr, Boston Univ, 52-58. *Mem:* Am Math Soc; Asn Comput Mach; Soc Indust & Appl Math; fel Inst Elec & Electronics Eng. *Res:* Fault tolerant computer system design and design methods; combinatorial math; computer systems design and analysis; logic design and methods of logic design; computer systems programming. *Mailing Add:* 3 Shagbark Lane Woodbury CT 06798

CARTER, WILLIAM DOUGLAS, b Keene, NH, Apr 24, 26; m 50; c 4. GEOLOGY. *Educ:* Dartmouth Col, AB, 49. *Prof Exp:* Geol field asst, Permafrost, US Geol Surv, 48-49, petrol res, 50, geologist uranium explor prog, 51-57, mining geologist & tech adv to Govt Chile, AID, 57-62, commodity geologist, Light Metals & Indust Minerals Br, Resources Res Group, 62-65, geol coordr remote sensing eval & coord staff, 65-67, chmn mineral & land resources working group, Earth Resources Observ Systs Prog, 67-70; asst mgr, Applications Res, Earth Resources Observational Systs Prog, US Geol Surv, 70-74, res scientist, 75-81; CONSULT GEOLOGIST, 82- *Concurrent Pos:* Lectr remote sensing, Am Asn Petrol Geologists Continuing Educ Prog, 75- *Honors & Awards:* Alan Gordon Award, Am Soc Photogram, 78. *Mem:* Fel Geol Soc Am; Soc Econ Geologists; Am Asn Petrol Geologists; Am Soc Photogrammetry; Yugoslav Acad Sci. *Res:* Use of satellite data in studies of the tectonics and location of ore deposits in the United States and Andes Mountain region, South America; mineral and energy deposits, chiefly uranium, copper, silica, phosphate and potash; photogeology; remote sensing; space applications. *Mailing Add:* 1925 Newton Square Bldg E2 Reston VA 22091

CARTER, WILLIAM EUGENE, b Steubenville, Ohio, Oct 16, 39; m 61; c 3. GEODESY. *Educ:* Univ Pittsburgh, BS, 61; Ohio State Univ, MS, 65; Univ Ariz, PhD(civil eng), 73. *Prof Exp:* Chief astron surv team, 1381st Geodetic Surv Squad, US Air Force, 61-63, chief, Astron Surv Br, 1st Geodetic Surv Squad, 66-69, res geodesist lunar laser ranging, Air Force Cambridge Res Lab, 69-72; Lure proj mgr, Inst Astron, Univ Hawaii, 72-76; asst chief, Gravity, Astron & Satellite Br, 77-79, CHIEF, GRAVITY, ASTRON & SPACE GEOD DIV, NAT GEODETIC SURV, 79- *Concurrent Pos:* Mem, Lunar Ranging Exp Team, 75-76. *Mem:* Am Geophys Union; Am Cong Surv & Mapping; Am Astron Soc. *Res:* Application of radio interferometric surveying to the studies of polar motion, earth rotation, crustal deformations, plate motion; research and development of advanced geodetic instrumentation and observational methods. *Mailing Add:* Nat Geodetic Survey C-15 Rockville MD 20852

CARTER, WILLIAM HAROLD, b Houston, Tex, Nov 17, 38; div; c 2. OPTICAL PHYSICS. *Educ:* Univ Tex, BS, 62, MS, 63, PhD(elec eng), 66. *Prof Exp:* Res assoc elec eng, Univ Tex, 63-66, instr, 66; contract monitor optics, US Army Mil Intel Corps, 67-69; res assoc physics, Univ Rochester, 69-70; RES PHYSICIST OPTICS, OPTICAL SCI DIV, NAVAL RES LAB, 71-; PROF ELEC ENG, UNIV NEBR-LINCOLN, 81- *Concurrent Pos:* Asst prof lectr, George Washington Univ, 68-69, assoc prof lectr, 71-75; vis res fel, Univ Reading, Eng, 76-77; assoc ed, J Optical Soc Am, 79-85. *Mem:* Int Soc Optical Eng; Am Phys Soc; Optical Soc Am; Sigma Xi; Cosmos Club. *Res:* Electromagnetic wave propagation; holography; digital image processing; coherence theory; angular spectrum representation; radio astronomy; laser resonater theory; scattering theory; microscopy; electromagnetic beam theory. *Mailing Add:* Code 7740 Naval Res Lab Washington DC 20375

CARTER, WILLIAM WALTON, b Pensacola, Fla, Nov 7, 21; m 45; c 4. PHYSICS. *Educ:* Carnegie Inst Technol, BS, 43; Calif Inst Technol, PhD(physics), 49. *Prof Exp:* Researcher radar, Naval Res Labs, 44-46; staff mem, sect chmn & group leader physics & eng, Los Alamos Sci Labs, 49-59; chief scientist, Missile Command, US Army, 59-67; asst dir defense res & eng, Off Secy Defense, 67-71; TECH DIR, US ARMY ELECTRONIC RES & DEVELOP COMT, HARRY DIAMOND LABS, 71- *Mem:* Am Phys Soc; AAAS; assoc Am Inst Aeronaut & Astronaut. *Res:* Nuclear physics; weapons and their effects; electronics and electronic components; spectroscopy. *Mailing Add:* 2800 Powder Mill Rd Adelphi MD 20783

CARTERETTE, EDWARD CALVIN HAYES, b Mt Tabor, NC, July 10, 21; m 55; c 1. PSYCHOACOUSTICS, NEUROPSYCHOLOGY. *Educ:* Univ Chicago, AB, 49; Harvard Univ, AB, 52; Ind Univ, MA, 54, PhD(psychol), 57. *Prof Exp:* Res staff mem acoustics lab, Mass Inst Technol, 51-52; from instr to asst prof psychol, Univ Calif, Los Angeles, 56-63, assoc prof exp psychol, 63-68; vis assoc prof psychol, Univ Calif, Berkeley, 65-66; PROF EXP PSYCHOL, UNIV CALIF, LOS ANGELES, 68- *Concurrent Pos:* NSF fel, Royal Inst Technol, Stockholm, Sweden & Cambridge Univ, Eng, 60-61; NSF sr fel, Inst Math Studies in Soc Sci, Stanford Univ, 64-65; rev ed, J Auditory Res, 60-69; assoc ed, Perception & Psychophysics, 71- & Music Perception, 81-; mem, Brain Res Inst, Univ Calif, Los Angeles, 74-; distinguished vis, Am Psychol Asn, 79- *Mem:* Fel Acoust Soc Am; fel AAAS; fel Am Psychol Asn; fel Soc Exp Psychologists (secy-treas, 82-); Psychonomic Soc. *Res:* Psychoacoustics, hearing and speech perception; neuropsychology; mathematical models of cognitive processes. *Mailing Add:* Dept Psychol Univ Calif Los Angeles CA 90024

CARTIER, GEORGE THOMAS, b Scranton, Pa, Jan 26, 24; m 46; c 2. APPLIED CHEMISTRY. *Educ:* Haverford Col, AB, 49. *Prof Exp:* Asst org chem, Smith Kline & French, 49-51; tech liaison & mkt develop, Quaker Chem Prods, 51-55; lab dir, Res & Develop Qual Control, A M Collins Div, Int Paper Co, 55-61; consult chemist, Web Processing, 61-65; pres, Keystone Filter Media Co, 65-74; CONSULT, 74- *Mem:* Am Chem Soc; Tech Asn Pulp & Paper Indust; Asn Consult Chemists & Chem Engrs; Filtration Soc. *Res:* High polymer applications research; decorative and functional paper and paper board coatings research and development; market development; fibrous filter media; high efficiency filter construction. *Mailing Add:* 311 Middle Rd Falmouth ME 04105

CARTIER, JEAN JACQUES, b Beauharnois, Que, Apr 1, 27; m 54. ENTOMOLOGY. *Educ:* Univ Montreal, BA, 48, BS, 52, MS, 53; Kans State Univ, PhD(entom), 56. *Prof Exp:* Res officer, Res Sta, 53-69, res coordr entom, Res Br, Cent Exp Farm, 69-75, asst dir gen, 75-78, dir gen, Res Br, Eastern Region, 78-80, DIR GEN, RES BR, ONT REGION, CAN DEPT AGR, 80- *Mem:* Entom Soc Am; Entom Soc Can. *Res:* Crop plants resistance to insects; biology of aphids, particularly aphid biotypes. *Mailing Add:* Res Br Ont Region Off Cent Exp Farm K W Neatby Bldg Ottowa ON K1A 0C5 Can

CARTIER, PETER G, b Green Bay, Wis. PHYSICAL CHEMISTRY, POLYMER CHEMISTRY. *Educ:* Lawrence Univ, BA, 68; Cornell Univ, PhD(phys chem), 73. *Prof Exp:* SR CHEMIST, ROHM AND HAAS CO, 73- *Mem:* Am Chem Soc. *Res:* Surface chemistry; the development and characterization of adsorbents and ion exchange resins; reverse osmosis membranes. *Mailing Add:* 13 Chelfield Rd Glenside PA 19038

CARTIER, RAYMOND MARTIN, b New York, NY, Sept 1, 31; m 61; c 2. CHEMICAL ENGINEERING. *Educ:* Polytech Inst Brooklyn, BChE, 53, MChE, 54, PhD(chem eng), 57; Xavier Univ, Ohio, MBA, 62. *Prof Exp:* Chem engr, Exp Develop Div, 59-61, group leader, 61-63, head consult, Winton Hill Tech Ctr, 63-69, sect head, 69-76, MGR RES & DEVELOP MATH, TECH INFO SERV & SYSTS CONTROL RESOURCES, MIAMI VALLEY LABS & WINTON HILL TECH CTR, PROCTER & GAMBLE CO, 76- *Res:* High pressure alkylations; liquid extraction; freeze and spray drying; size reduction; chemical engineering mathematics; statistical design and analysis of experiments; computer applications. *Mailing Add:* Winton Hill Tech Ctr Procter & Gamble Co 6000 Center Hill Cincinnati OH 45224

CARTLEDGE, FRANK, b Emory, Ga, Aug 26, 38; m 61. ORGANIC CHEMISTRY. *Educ:* King Col, BA, 60; Iowa State Univ, PhD(org chem), 64. *Prof Exp:* Nat Sci Found res fel organosilicon chem, Univ Sussex, 64-65; fel, Univ Gottingen, 65-66; asst prof, 66-71, ASSOC PROF CHEM, LA STATE UNIV, BATON ROUGE, 71- *Mem:* Am Chem Soc. *Res:* Synthesis and kinetics of reactions of group four organic compounds. *Mailing Add:* Dept of Chem La State Univ Baton Rouge LA 70803

CARTMILL, MATT, b Los Angeles, Calif; m 71; c 1. PHYSICAL ANTHROPOLOGY. *Educ:* Pomona Col, BA, 64; Univ Chicago, MA, 66, PhD(primate evolution), 70. *Prof Exp:* Assoc anat, Med Ctr, 69-70, asst prof, 70-74, sociol & anthrop, Duke Univ, 70-74, ASSOC PROF ANTHROP, DUKE UNIV, 74-, PROF ANAT, 81- *Concurrent Pos:* NIH career develop award, 75; co-managing ed, Int J Primatol, 78. *Mem:* Am Anthrop Asn; Am Asn Phys Anthrop; Am Soc Mammal; Primate Soc Gt Brit; Int Primate Soc. *Res:* Primate evolution. *Mailing Add:* Dept Anat Duke Univ Med Ctr Durham NC 27710

CARTON, CHARLES ALLAN, b New York, NY, Feb 28, 20; m 57; c 2. NEUROSURGERY. *Educ:* Yale Univ, BA, 41; Columbia Univ, MD, 44; Am Bd Neurol Surg, dipl, 55. *Prof Exp:* Intern med & surg, Bellevue Hosp, New York, 44-45; asst resident neurol & neuropath, Neurol Inst, NY, 47-48, fel neurosurg, 49, asst resident, 50-51, chief resident, 52; asst prof, Baylor Col Med, 53-56; asst clin prof, Albert Einstein Col Med, 56-58, assoc clin prof, 58-61; assoc clin prof & mem attend staff, 61-74, CLIN PROF NEUROSURG, MED CTR, UNIV CALIF, LOS ANGELES, 74- *Concurrent Pos:* Asst resident, Presby Hosp, New York, 49; chief neurosurg, Vet Admin Hosp, Houston, 53; asst attend neurosurgeon, Jefferson Davis Hosp, 54; asst neurosurgeon, Methodist Hosp & Clin; asst neurosurgeon, M D Anderson Hosp, 55; exec officer, Div Neurosurg, Montefiore Hosp, New York, 56, chief, 58; vis neurosurgeon, Bronx Munic Hosp Ctr, 58; vis neurosurgeon, Morrisania Hosp, 59; adj, Cedars Lebanon Hosp, Los Angeles, 61, asst, 63; asst, Mt Sinai Hosp, 64; attend & co-chief neurosurg, Cedars-Sinai Med Ctr, 71-75. *Mem:* AAAS; Am Asn Neuropath; Am Acad Neurol; fel Am Col Surg; AMA. *Res:* Cerebrovascular disease aneurysm and small vessel anastomosis; hydrocephalus. *Mailing Add:* Dept Surg Univ Ca Los Angeles Sch Med Los Angeles CA 90024

CARTON, ROBERT WELLS, b Chicago, Ill, Nov 22, 20; m 47; c 4. INTERNAL MEDICINE. *Educ:* Princeton Univ, AB, 42; Northwestern Univ, MD, 46. *Prof Exp:* From clin asst to prof med, Col Med, Univ Ill, 51-70; assoc dean, 70-76, RUSH MED COL, 70-, DIR PULMONARY MED, 76- *Mem:* Fel Am Col Physicians. *Res:* Correlation of pulmonary structure and function; chronic bronchopulmonary infections; pulmonary function testing. *Mailing Add:* 1725 W Harrison Chicago IL 60612

CARTWRIGHT, BRIAN GRANT, astrophysics, see previous edition

CARTWRIGHT, DAVID CHAPMAN, b Minneapolis, Minn, Dec 2, 37; m 65; c 2. CHEMICAL PHYSICS, MOLECULAR PHYSICS. *Educ:* Hamline Univ, BS, 62; Calif Inst Technol, MS, 63, PhD(chem physics, physics), 68. *Prof Exp:* NATOfel atmospheric physics, Max Planck Inst Extraterrestrial Physics, 67-68; fel physics, Univ Colo, Boulder, 68-69; mem tech staff, Space Physics Lab, Aerospace Corp, 69-74; staff mem, Theoret Div, 74-75, alt group leader, Laser Theory Group, Theoret Div, 75-76, group leader, 75-80, div leader, 80, ACTG DIV LEADER, THEORET CHEM & MOLECULAR PHYSICS GROUP, LOS ALAMOS NAT LAB, 80- *Mem:* Am Phys Soc; Am Geophys Union. *Res:* Electron impact processes in atoms and molecules; structure of simple molecules; auroral and ionospheric processes; gas laser processes; theory of low energy electron scattering by atoms and molecules; physics of auroras and airglow. *Mailing Add:* AP Div MS 563 Los Alamos Nat Lab PO Box 1663 Los Alamos NM 87545

CARTWRIGHT, GEORGE EASTMAN, internal medicine, deceased

CARTWRIGHT, HUGH MANNING, b Hitchin, UK. PHYSICAL CHEMISTRY, SPECTROSCOPY. *Educ:* Univ EAnglia, BSc, 69, PhD(chem), 72. *Prof Exp:* Asst prof, 73-76, SR LAB INSTR CHEM, UNIV VICTORIA, BC, 77- *Concurrent Pos:* Fel, Univ Victoria, BC, 73-74; instr & consult, BC Govt, 78- *Res:* Spectroscopic investigation of thin films and adsorbed molecules; chemical education; technical and scientific writing. *Mailing Add:* Dept of Chem Univ of Victoria Victoria BC V8W 2Y2 Can

CARTWRIGHT, KEROS, b Los Angeles, Calif, July 25, 34; m 62; c 4. HYDROGEOLOGY. *Educ:* Univ Calif, Berkeley, AB, 59; Univ Nev, MS, 61; Univ Ill, PhD(geol), 73. *Prof Exp:* Asst hydrol, US Geol Surv, 60-61; res asst, 61-63, from asst geologist to assoc geologist, 63-74, GEOLOGIST & HEAD, HYDROGEOLOGY & GEOPHYSICS SECT, ILL GEOL SURV, 74- *Mem:* Am Geophys Union; Geol Soc Am; Am Inst Mining, Metall & Petrol Engrs. *Mailing Add:* Ill State Geol Surv Urbana IL 61801

CARTWRIGHT, THOMAS CAMPBELL, b York, SC, Mar 8, 24; m 46; c 4. ANIMAL BREEDING. *Educ:* Clemson Col, BS, 48; Tex A&M Univ, MS, 49, PhD, 54. *Prof Exp:* Animal husbandman & geneticist, Agr Exp Sta, 52-58, PROF ANIMAL BREEDING, TEX A&M UNIV, 58- *Mem:* AAAS; Am Genetic Asn; Am Soc Animal Sci. *Res:* Population genetics; genetics of cattle. *Mailing Add:* Dept of Animal Sci Tex A&M Univ College Station TX 77843

CARTWRIGHT, THOMAS EDWARD, b Monessen, Pa, April 27, 16; m 41; c 4. BIOPHYSICS. *Educ:* Univ Pittsburgh, BS, 39, MS, 49, PhD(biophys), 54. *Prof Exp:* Research asst virol, 47-49, res assoc biophys, 51-59, asst prof, 59-61, ASSOC PROF BIOPHYS, UNIV PITTSBURGH, 61- *Mem:* AAAS; Biophys Soc; Nat Sci Teachers Asn. *Res:* Biophysical properties of viruses and toxins. *Mailing Add:* Dept of Biophys Univ of Pittsburgh Pittsburgh PA 15213

CARTY, ARTHUR JOHN, b Hookergate, Eng, Sept 12, 40; m 67; c 3. INORGANIC CHEMISTRY, ORGANOMETALLIC CHEMISTRY. *Educ:* Univ Nottingham, BSc, 62, PhD(chem), 65. *Prof Exp:* Asst prof chem, Mem Univ Nfld, 65-67; asst prof, 67-69, assoc prof chem, 79-75, PROF CHEM, UNIV WATERLOO, 75- *Concurrent Pos:* Royal Soc Nuffield Found fel, 74; actg dir, Guelph-Waterloo Ctr Grad Studies in Chem, 75-76; dir, Guelph-Waterloo Ctr Grad Studies Chem, 76-79; chmn, Chem Grants Selection Comt, Nat Sci & Eng Res Coun, 79-80, group chmn chem, 80- *Mem:* Am Chem Soc; Chem Inst Can. *Res:* Synthetic and structural inorganic and organometallic chemistry; metal clusters and reactivity patterns for unsaturated molecules in clusters; chemistry of metal acetylides and metal carbonyls; phosphinoacetylenes as ligands and synthons; phosphido bridged bi-and polynuclear complexes; bioinorganic chemistry of heavy metals including mercury, lead and cadmium. *Mailing Add:* Dept of Chem Univ of Waterloo Waterloo ON N2L 3G1 Can

CARTY, DANIEL T, b Greenville, Tex, Aug 19, 35; m 59; c 2. ORGANIC CHEMISTRY, POLYMER CHEMISTRY. *Educ:* Univ Calif, Riverside, BA, 61; Univ Hawaii, MS, 63; Stanford Univ, PhD(chem), 68. *Prof Exp:* Chemist, Stanford Res Inst, 63-65; res assoc, Inst Org Chem, Karlsruhe Tech Univ,

Ger, 67-68; chemist, Rohm and Haas Co, Bristol, Pa, 68-72; sr res assoc, Fibers Pioneering Res, 72-76; sr res assoc, Plastics Pioneering Res, Pa, 76-77, proj leader textile chem res, 77-79, MKT DEVELOP MGR CHEM SPECIALTIES, PACIFIC REGION, PLASTICS PIONEERING RES, CA, 79- *Res:* Homopolymers and copolymers of acrylates and their alloys with other polymeric systems; chemistry of novel small ring hydrocarbons and valence bond isomers of benzene; chemical modification of nylon and polyester fibers. *Mailing Add:* 50 Tyrrel Danville CA 94526

CARUBELLI, RAOUL, b Cordoba, Arg, June 17, 29; US citizen; m 59; c 2. BIOCHEMISTRY. *Educ:* Cordoba Nat Univ, PhD(biochem), 60. *Prof Exp:* Lab instr anal chem pharmaceut drugs & quant anal & biol chem, Cordoba Nat Univ, 53-56; res assoc biochem, Okla Med Res Found, 57-59, biochemist, 60-64, sr investr, 64-65, assoc, 65-67, assoc mem, 67-73; from asst prof to assoc prof biochem, 63-70, prof, 70-81, DISTINGUISHED MED RES FOUND PROF BIOCHEM & MOLECULAR BIOL, SCH MED, UNIV OKLA, 70-; MEM STAFF, OKLA MED RES FOUND, 73- *Concurrent Pos:* USPHS res grants, 62-; NIH res career develop award, 68-72; vis investr, Max Planck Inst Virus Res, Ger, 63-64; vis investr, Ger Cancer Res Ctr, Heidelberg, 76-77. *Mem:* AAAS; Sigma Xi; Am Chem Soc; Am Soc Biol Chem. *Res:* Biological and carbohydrate chemistry; chemistry and metabolism of carbohydrates and glycoproteins; chemical carcinogenesis. *Mailing Add:* Biomembrane Res Lab Okla Med Res Found 825 NE 13 St Oklahoma City OK 73104

CARUCCIO, FRANK THOMAS, b New York, NY, Sept 7, 35; m 63; c 1. GROUNDWATER GEOLOGY, ENVIRONMENTAL GEOLOGY. *Educ:* City Col NY, BS, 58; Pa State Univ, MS, 63, PhD(geol), 67. *Prof Exp:* Res assoc geol, Pa State Univ, 67-68; asst prof, State Univ NY Col New Paltz, 68-70, assoc prof, 70-71; ASSOC PROF GEOL, UNIV SC, 71- *Concurrent Pos:* State Univ NY Res Found grant, 69; consult geologist, Res Ctr, Uniroyal, Inc, NY, 69-71; Environ Protection Agency res grants, 73-75, 75-76, 76-77, 77-78 & 78-81, demonstration grant, 75-78 & NSF grant, 80-83; mem, G W Resource & Coal Mining Comt, Nat Res Coun, Nat Acad Sci. *Mem:* Am Geophys Union; Am Water Works Asn; Water Resources Asn; Water Pollution Control Fedn; Soc Environ Geochem & Health. *Res:* Groundwater, its occurrence, movement and quality in relation to the hydrogeologic environment; interactions of pollutants within the hydrogeologic regime and their affects on the ground water potability; surface coal mining; environmental impacts (acid mine drainage). *Mailing Add:* Dept of Geol Univ of SC Columbia SC 29208

CARUOLO, EDWARD VITANGELO, b Providence, RI, Nov 1, 31; m 53; c 4. ANIMAL PHYSIOLOGY, MEDICAL PHYSIOLOGY. *Educ:* Univ RI, BS, 53; Univ Conn, MS, 55; Univ Minn, PhD(physiol), 63. *Prof Exp:* Instr physiol, Univ Minn, 60-63; asst prof, 63-68, ASSOC PROF EXP PHYSIOL, NC STATE UNIV, 68-, CHMN FAC PHYSIOL, 74- *Mem:* Am Dairy Sci Asn; Am Physiol Soc; Nat Mastitis Coun. *Res:* Physiology of milk secretion and ejection in health and disease; general experimental animal physiology; animal models in byssinosis. *Mailing Add:* Grinnells Animal Health Lab NC State Univ Raleigh NC 27607

CARUSO, FRANK LAWRENCE, b Hackensack, NJ, Nov 18, 49; m 75. PLANT PATHOLOGY, PLANT PHYSIOLOGY. *Educ:* Gettysburg Col, AB, 71; Univ Mass, MS, 75; Univ Ky, PhD(plant path), 78. *Prof Exp:* Res asst plant path, Univ Mass, 72-74, Univ Ky, 74-78; MEM STAFF, DEPT BOT & PLANT PATH, UNIV MAINE, ORONO, 78- *Mem:* Am Phytopathological Soc; Sigma Xi. *Res:* Physiology of diseased plants; bacterial and fungal diseases of fruits. *Mailing Add:* Dept Bot & Plant Path Univ Maine Orono ME 04469

CARUSO, FRANK SAN CARLO, b Hartford, Conn, Aug 29, 36; m 55, 73; c 3. PHARMACOLOGY. *Educ:* Trinity Col, Conn, BS, 58; Univ Rochester, MS, 61, PhD(pharmacol), 63. *Prof Exp:* Sr pharmacologist, Bristol Labs, 63-65, asst dir pharmacol-cardiovasc res, 65-66, coordr biol screening, 67-72, asst dir clin pharmacol, 72-74, dir clin analgesic res, 74-80; DIR CLIN PHARMACOL, REVLON HEALTH CARE GROUP, 80- *Mem:* AAAS; NY Acad Sci; Am Soc Clin Pharmacol & Therapeut; Int Asn Study Pain; fel Col Clin Pharmacol. *Res:* Sodium fluoride effects on renal function in dogs; pharmacological and toxicological effects on blood pressure, heart rate and respiration; narcotics and analgesics, narcotics and antagonists. *Mailing Add:* 243 Marling Ave Tarrytown NY 10591

CARUSO, SEBASTIAN CHARLES, b Jamestown, NY, March 7, 26. ENVIRONMENTAL CHEMISTRY. *Educ:* Alfred Univ, BA, 49; Univ Pittsburgh, PhD, 54. *Prof Exp:* Asst, Univ Pittsburgh, 49-50, res asst, 50-54; fel, 54-66, SR FEL, CARNEGIE-MELLON UNIV, 66- *Mem:* AAAS; Am Chem Soc; Am Soc Testing & Mat. *Res:* Lipid chemistry; micro-isolation and identification of organic substances obtained from natural sources; biochemistry of water pollution; gas chromatography; chemical analysis of surface waters and air. *Mailing Add:* Carnegie-Mellon Univ 4400 Fifth Ave Pittsburgh PA 15213

CARUTHERS, JOHN QUINCY, b Columbia, Tenn, Feb 28, 13; m 49; c 3. BACTERIOLOGY. *Educ:* Hampton Inst, BS, 33; Iowa State Univ, MS, 41. *Prof Exp:* Instr bact, Atlanta Col Mortuary Sci, 38-62, pres, 53-62; ASST PROF BIOL, SPELLMAN COL, 62- *Concurrent Pos:* Instr pub schs, Ga, 33-59. *Mem:* Am Soc Microbiol; Nat Sci Teachers Asn. *Res:* Physiological bacteriology; antibiotic resistance in staphylococci. *Mailing Add:* 668 Fielding Ln SW Atlanta GA 30311

CARUTHERS, LEO THOMAS, JR, b Sheffield, Ala, July 12, 25; m 52; c 4. HEALTH PHYSICS. *Educ:* Univ Richmond, BS, 53. *Prof Exp:* Field rep, USAEC, Oak Ridge, Tenn, 54-57, health physicist, Savannah River Opers Off, SC, 57-58; RADIATION PROTECTION OFFICER, NC STATE UNIV, 58- *Concurrent Pos:* US AEC fel, Agr Econ Div, Vanderbilt Univ, 53-54. *Mem:* Health Physics Soc. *Mailing Add:* 214 David Clark Labs NC State Univ Raleigh NC 27607

CARUTHERS, MARVIN HARRY, b Des Moines, Iowa, Feb 11, 40; c 2. NUCLEIC ACID CHEMISTRY. *Educ:* Iowa State Univ, BS, 62; Northwestern Univ, PhD(biochem), 68. *Prof Exp:* Fel biochem, Univ Wis, 68-70, Mass Inst Technol, 70-72; asst prof, 73-77, assoc prof, 77-79, PROF BIOCHEM, UNIV COLO, 80- *Concurrent Pos:* Prin investr, various NIH & NSF grants, 73-; career develop award, NIH, 75-80; Guggenheim fel, John Simon Guggenheim Mem Found, 80-81. *Mem:* Am Chem Soc; AAAS; Fedn Am Soc Exp Biologists; Sigma Xi. *Res:* Nucleic acid chemistry; biochemistry. *Mailing Add:* Dept Chem Campus Box 215 Univ Colo Boulder CO 80309

CARVAJAL, FERNANDO, b San Jose, Costa Rica, June 4, 13; nat US; m 41; c 4. MICROBIOLOGY. *Educ:* Univ Costa Rica, BS, 38; Cornell Univ, MS, 42; La State Univ, PhD(mycol), 43. *Prof Exp:* Res mycologist & dir field studies, Inst del Cafe, San Jose, Costa Rica, 39; res mycologist, Exp Sta, La State Univ, 43-44; sr res mycologist, Schenley Res Labs, 44-49, head div microbiol, 49-54; co-head div microbiol, Schering Corp, 54-57, head div microbiol & vpres, Formet Labs, 57-61; dir res & labs, Arroyo Pharmaceut Corp, 61-72; mgr, fermentation prod, Upjohn Mfg Corp, 72-76, res & develop, 76-78; CONSULT, 79- *Concurrent Pos:* Fel, US Off Educ. *Honors & Awards:* Cert Merit, La State Univ, 42. *Mem:* Sigma Xi; Am Soc Microbiol; Mycol Soc Am; Am Chem Soc. *Res:* Bacteriology; studies on genetics, mutations, physiology and fermentation of fungi and bacteria; plant pathology; antibiotics; discovery of the sexual state of Colletotrichum falcatum; synthesis of steroids; bacteriophages; production of vitamins by microbial fermentation. *Mailing Add:* 4681 Armadillo St Boca Raton FL 33433

CARVALHO, SERGIO EDUARDO RODRIGUES DE, b Rio de Janeiro, Brazil, Nov 1, 36; m 61; c 4. COMPUTER SCIENCE. *Educ:* Cath Univ Rio de Janeiro, Brazil, BEE, 61, MSc, 69; Univ Waterloo, PhD(comput sci), 74. *Prof Exp:* Engr instrumentation org & methods data processing, Petroleo Brasileiro SA, 62-68; assoc prof comput sci, Cath Univ Rio de Janeiro, Brazil, 74-76; fel, IBM Res Lab, Calif, 76-77; assoc prof comput sci, Univ Colo, 77-79; assoc prof comput sci, Cath Univ Rio de Janeiro, 79-81; ASSOC PROF COMPUT SCI, UNIV COLO, 81- *Concurrent Pos:* Adj prof, Cath Univ Rio de Janeiro, 68-69; consult, Digital Systs Lab, 74-76, Pikes Peak Reg Libr Dist, 78- *Res:* Design and implementation of programming languages and of small, on line, data base systems and languages. *Mailing Add:* Dept Elec Eng & Comput Sci Univ Colo Colorado Springs CO 80907

CARVELL, KENNETH LLEWELLYN, b N Andover, Mass, May 1, 25. FOREST ECOLOGY. *Educ:* Harvard Univ, BA, 49; Yale Univ, MF, 50; Duke Univ, DF, 53. *Prof Exp:* Assoc forester, Agr Exp Sta & assoc prof silvicult, 53-64, PROF FOREST ECOL & FOREST ECOLOGIST, WVA UNIV, 64- *Res:* Forest regeneration methods and improvement cuttings for hardwood forests; use of chemical herbicides in forest improvement work; ecological effects of herbicides on electric transmission line rights-of-way. *Mailing Add:* Div Forest WVa Univ Morgantown WV 26505

CARVER, CHARLES E(LLSWORTH), JR, b Burlington, Vt, May 27, 22; m 50; c 3. CIVIL ENGINEERING. *Educ:* Univ Vt, BS, 47; Mass Inst Technol, MS, 49, ScD(civil eng), 55. *Prof Exp:* Instr civil eng, Univ Vt, 47; res asst hydrodyn, Mass Inst Technol, 47-49 & 51-55; instr civil eng, Univ Mass, 49-51; sr engr, Glenn L Martin Co, 55-56; res assoc phys oceanog, Woods Hole Oceanog Inst, 56-58; assoc prof civil eng, 58-62, PROF CIVIL ENG, UNIV MASS, 62- *Concurrent Pos:* Lectr, Johns Hopkins Univ, 55-56; consult, Gen Elec Co, 58-60; res & adv develop, Avco Corp, 63. *Mem:* Am Soc Civil Engrs; Am Soc Eng Educ; Sigma Xi. *Res:* Boundary layer control; non-Newtonian flow; oxygen transfer in bubble and spray aeration processes; undersea weapons systems; aircraft weapons systems; wave energy conversion devices. *Mailing Add:* Dept Civil Eng Univ Mass Amherst MA 01003

CARVER, DAVID HAROLD, b Boston, Mass, Apr 18, 30; m 63; c 3. PEDIATRICS, INFECTIOUS DISEASES. *Educ:* Harvard Col, AB, 51; Duke Univ, MD, 55. *Prof Exp:* Asst prof pediat, microbiol & immunol, Albert Einstein Col Med, 63-66; from assoc prof to prof pediat, Sch Med, Johns Hopkins Univ, 73-76, assoc prof microbiol, 67-76; PROF & CHMN DEPT PEDIAT, UNIV TORONTO, 76-; PHYSICIAN-IN-CHIEF, HOSP FOR SICK CHILDREN, TORONTO, 76- *Concurrent Pos:* Res fel pediat, Med Sch, Western Reserve Univ, 56-58; USPHS res fel, Children's Hosp Med Ctr & Harvard Med Sch, 61-63; mem comt infectious dis, Am Acad Pediat, 73-79. *Honors & Awards:* Schaffer Award, Johns Hopkins Univ Hosp, 73; Bain Award, Hosp for Sick Children, 78. *Mem:* Soc Pediat Res; Infectious Dis Soc Am; Am Pediat Soc; Am Acad Pediat; Am Soc Microbiol. *Res:* Virology. *Mailing Add:* Hosp for Sick Children 555 University Ave Toronto ON M5G 1X8 Can

CARVER, EUGENE ARTHUR, b Randolph, Vt, Dec 28, 44; m 70; c 2. GENETICS, METEORITICS. *Educ:* Univ Md, BS, 67; Univ Chicago, MS, 70, PhD(chem), 74. *Prof Exp:* Res assoc meteoritics, Goddard Space Flight Ctr, NASA, 72-74; ED CHEM, CHEM ABSTR SERV, INC, 74- *Mem:* Meteoritic Soc. *Res:* Solar system history as inferred from meteorites and lunar samples with emphasis on fission-track dating and geochronology; genetics of dogs with special emphasis on coat colors. *Mailing Add:* 3725 Rome Corners Rd Galena OH 43021

CARVER, GARY PAUL, b Brooklyn, NY, 42; m 75. EXPERIMENTAL SOLID STATE PHYSICS. *Educ:* Clarkson Col Technol, BS, 63; Cornell Univ, PhD(physics), 70. *Prof Exp:* Res asst, Lab Atomic & Solid State Physics, Cornell Univ, 66-69; res physicist solid state, Naval Surface Weapons Ctr, White Oak Lab, 69-77; physicist, 77-80, SUPVRY PHYSICIST, SEMICONDUCTOR MAT & PROCESSES DIV, NAT BUR STANDARDS, GAITHERSBURG, MD, 80- *Concurrent Pos:* Vis scientist, Clarendon Lab, Oxford Univ, 76. *Mem:* Am Phys Soc; AAAS; Inst Elec & Electronics Engrs. *Res:* Development of measurement methods for detection and characterization of bulk and interface traps in oxides and oxide/semiconductor interfaces and of defect centers in semiconductors; correlation of results with properties of microelectronic semiconductor devices; design and analysis of test structures for materials and process characterization and for radiation effects. *Mailing Add:* Bldg 225 Rm A331 Nat Bur of Standards Washington DC 20234

CARVER, JAMES CLARK, b Lake Charles, La, Dec 16, 45; m 69; c 2. SURFACE CHEMISTRY, ANALYTICAL CHEMISTRY. *Educ:* Centenary Col La, BS, 67; Univ Tenn, PhD(inorg chem), 72. *Prof Exp:* Res assoc anal chem, Univ Ga, 71-73, elec spectros lab supvr surface characterization, 73-74, lectr anal chem, 74-75; asst prof, Tex A&M Univ, 75-78; SR CHEMIST SURFACE CHARACTERIZATION, EXXON RES & DEVELOP LABS, EXXON CORP, 78- *Concurrent Pos:* Prin investr, Petrol Res Fund grant, 76-78, Robert A Welch Found grant, 77-78. *Mem:* Am Chem Soc; Am Vacuum Soc; Am Phys Soc. *Res:* Surface characterization of catalysts using x-ray photoelectron spectroscopy; scanning auger electron spectroscopy; secondary ion mass spectroscopy and low energy ion scattering spectrometry. *Mailing Add:* Exxon Res & Develop Labs PO Box 2226 Baton Rouge LA 70821

CARVER, JOHN GUILL, b Mt Juliet, Tenn, Feb 10, 24; m 56; c 4. PHYSICS ENGINEERING. *Educ:* Ga Inst Technol, BS, 50; Yale Univ, MS, 51, PhD(physics), 55. *Prof Exp:* Res asst physics, Yale Univ, 51-55; sr engr, Aircraft Nuclear Propulsion Dept, Gen Elec Co, 55-56, task leader, 56-60, specialist advan reactor physics develop, Atomic Power Equip Dept, 60-62, mgr fuels & irradiations physics, 62-67; mgr advan res & technol, Space Div, NAm Rockwell Corp, 67-70, supvr advan res, 70-77, supvr electro-optics technol, 77-79, MGR, SHUTTLE SYSTS STUDY, SPACE DIV, ROCKWELL INTERNAT CORP, 79- *Concurrent Pos:* Chmn, Tech Comt Sensor Systs, Am Inst Aeronaut & Astronaut, 74-75. *Mem:* Fel AAAS; assoc fel Am Inst Aeronaut & Astronaut; Am Phys Soc; Sigma Xi. *Res:* Particle accelerators; neutron cross sections; nuclear shielding; neutron spectrometry; physics of plutonium fuel cycle; infrared sensor systems; research reactor operation. *Mailing Add:* 3079 Pinewood St Orange CA 92665

CARVER, JUNE HARRIS, cell & molecular biology, see previous edition

CARVER, KEITH ROSS, b Beech Creek, Ky, May 18, 40; m 65; c 1. ELECTRICAL ENGINEERING, ELECTROMAGNETICS. *Educ:* Univ Ky, BS, 62; Ohio State Univ, MS, 63, PhD(elec eng), 67. *Prof Exp:* Res asst elec eng, radio observ, Ohio State Univ, 62-66, res assoc, 66-67; asst prof, Univ Ky, 67-69; assoc prof, 66-77, group supvr, E M Res & Develop Group, Phys Sci Lab, 78-81, PROF ELEC ENG, NMEX STATE UNIV, 77-; PROG MGR, RADAR REMOTE SENSING SYSTS, NASA HQ, WASHINGTON, DC, 81- *Concurrent Pos:* Mem, URSI Comn F, 77- *Honors & Awards:* C Holmes MacDonald Award, 76. *Mem:* Am Soc Photogram; Inst Elec & Electronics Engrs. *Res:* Antenna design and measurement microwave remote sensing; radio wave propagation; Remote sensing instrumentation and antenna design and measurement. *Mailing Add:* Code ER-2 NASA HQ Washington DC 20546

CARVER, MICHAEL BRUCE, b Wales, Mar 3, 41; Can citizen; m; c 2. NUMERICAL ANALYSIS. *Educ:* McMaster Univ, Can, BEng, 63; Birmingham Univ, MSc, 65. *Prof Exp:* Res engr aerodynamics, English Elec Co, 63-65; res engr hydrodynamics, 65-69, simulation analyst numerical math, 69-80, res engr computational thermalhydraulics, 80-81, HEAD, FLUID DYNAMICS SECT, ATOMIC ENERGY CAN LTD, 81- *Concurrent Pos:* Lectr, Algonquin Col Tech, 71- & Univ Ottawa, 79- *Mem:* Asn Prof Engrs Ont; Int Asn Math & Comput Simulation. *Res:* Simulation, numerical analysis, solution of differential equation systems, computational thermal hydraulic analysis of single and two phase flows. *Mailing Add:* Atomic Energy of Can Ltd Chalk River Nuclear Labs Chalk River ON K0J 1J0 Can

CARVER, MICHAEL JOSEPH, b Omaha, Nebr, Apr 4, 23; m 48; c 3. BIOCHEMISTRY. *Educ:* Creighton Univ, BS, 47, MS, 48; Univ Mo, PhD(biochem), 52. *Prof Exp:* Instr chem, Creighton Univ, 48-49; supvr anal dept, Cudahy Labs, 52-56; assoc res prof, 56-66, PROF BIOCHEM, UNIV NEBR MED CTR, OMAHA, 66-, ASST DEAN COL MED, 70- *Mem:* AAAS; Am Chem Soc; Am Inst Chem; Soc Exp Biol & Med; Am Soc Neurochem. *Res:* Cytochemistry; electrophoresis; protein chemistry; neurochemistry; psycotropic drugs; mental retardation. *Mailing Add:* 553 S 90th Omaha NE 68114

CARVER, O(LIVER) T(HOMAS), b Charleston, WVa, July 14, 24; m 50; c 3. ELECTRICAL ENGINEERING. *Educ:* WVa Univ, BSEE, 49. *Prof Exp:* Engr, 49-55, leader syst design, 55-59, leader, Aerospace Systs Div, 59-61, mgr test systs anal, 61-76, MGR, ATE SYSTS, RCA CORP, 76- *Concurrent Pos:* Spec lectr, George Washington Univ, 65-66. *Mem:* Am Inst Aeronaut & Astronaut; Inst Elec & Electronics Engrs. *Res:* Automatic test systems analysis; advanced test technique and development. *Mailing Add:* Ate Systs RCA Corp Bedford St Box 588 Burlington MA 01803

CARVER, ROBERT E, b Kansas City, Mo, Jan 6, 31; div; c 2. SEDIMENTARY PETROLOGY, HYDROGEOLOGY. *Educ:* Mo Sch Mines, BSMinE, 53; Univ Mo, AM, 59, PhD(geol), 61. *Prof Exp:* Geologist, Bellaire Res Labs, Texaco, Inc, 61-64; from asst prof to assoc prof, 64-80, asst head dept, 71-80, PROF GEOL, UNIV GA, 80- *Concurrent Pos:* Vis prof, Univ Rio Grande do Sul, Brazil, 72; assoc ed, J Sedimentary Petrol, 80-; consult. *Mem:* Fel Geol Soc Am; Am Asn Petrol Geologists; Soc Econ Paleontologists & Mineralogists; Int Asn Sedimentol; AAAS. *Res:* Sedimentary petrology; industrial mineralogy; hydrogeology; geology and natural resources of the southeast Atlantic coastal plain. *Mailing Add:* Dept Geol Univ Ga Athens GA 30602

CARVER, THOMAS RIPLEY, physics, deceased

CARY, ARTHUR SIMMONS, b Sacramento, Calif, Nov 30, 25; m 57; c 3. HIGH ENERGY PHYSICS. *Educ:* Fisk Univ, BA, 49, MA, 51; Univ Calif, Riverside, MA & PhD(physics), 69. *Prof Exp:* Instr phys sci, Dillard Univ, 54-56; assoc prof physics, Tenn State Univ, 56-63; from asst prof to assoc prof, Harvey Mudd Col, 69-74; asst prof, 74-80, ASSOC PROF PHYSICS, CALIF POLYTECH STATE UNIV, 80- *Honors & Awards:* Fulbright lectr, Univ Liberia, WAfrica, 80-81. *Mem:* Am Phys Soc; Am Asn Physics Teachers; Nat Sci Teachers Asn. *Res:* High energy experimental physics; nuclear emulsion; bubble chamber. *Mailing Add:* Dept of Physics Calif Polytech State Univ San Luis Obispo CA 93407

CARY, BOYD BALFORD, JR, acoustics, fluid physics, see previous edition

CARY, HOWARD BRADFORD, b Columbus, Ohio, May 24, 20; m 42; c 2. WELDING ENGINEERING. *Educ:* Ohio State Univ, BIE, 42. *Prof Exp:* Welding engr, Fisher Tank Div, Gen Motors Corp, Mich, 42-44, process engr, 46; welding res engr, Battelle Mem Inst, 46-48, welding engr, 48-51, welding supt, 51-55, asst gen works mgr, 56-58; asst gen works mgr, Marion Power Shovel Co, 58-59; dir, 59-76, VPRES WELDING SYSTS, HOBART BROS CO, 76-, PRES, HOBART SCH WELDING TECHNOL, 80- *Concurrent Pos:* US deleg, Comn XIV Int Inst Welding. *Mem:* Am Soc Metals; Am Welding Soc (pres, 80-81); Nat Soc Prof Engrs; Am Soc Mech Engrs. *Res:* Development of automatic metal-arc welding process for steel and aluminum utilizing atomsphere generated outside of the arc; welding education; welding process development. *Mailing Add:* 1492 Surrey Rd Troy OH 45373

CASABELLA, PHILIP A, b Albany, NY, Feb 18, 33; m 60; c 2. PHYSICS. *Educ:* Rensselaer Polytech Inst, BS, 54, MS, 57; Brown Univ, PhD(physics), 59. *Prof Exp:* Res assoc physics, Brown Univ, 59-60; from asst prof to assoc prof, 61-69, chmn dept physics & astron, 68-77, PROF PHYSICS, RENSSELAER POLYTECH INST, 69- *Mem:* AAAS; Sigma Xi; Fel Am Phys Soc. *Res:* Nuclear magnetic resonance and pure quadruple resonance in solids. *Mailing Add:* 209 Colonial Ave Albany NY 12208

CASAD, BURTON M, b Mooreland, Okla, Nov 19, 33; m 54; c 4. CHEMICAL ENGINEERING. *Educ:* Okla State Univ, BS, 55, MS, 57, PhD(chem eng), 60. *Prof Exp:* Process engr, Phillips Petrol Co, 55-56; asst chem eng, Okla State Univ, 56-59; res engr corrosion, 59-63, res group leader, 63-67, sect supvr mat & eng, gas processing, 67-76, SECT DIR RECOVERY SECT, CONTINENTAL OIL CO, 76- *Mem:* Nat Asn Corrosion Engrs; Am Inst Chem Engrs. *Res:* Corrosion of oil and gas well equipment; corrosion; water treating; enhanced oil recovery processes. *Mailing Add:* 1504 Pecan Rd Ponca City OK 74601

CASADABAN, MALCOLM JOHN, b New Orleand, La, Aug 12, 49; m 77; c 1. MOLECULAR GENETICS, GENE EXPRESSION. *Educ:* Mass Inst Technol, SB, 71; Harvard Univ, PhD(microbiol & molecular genetics), 76. *Prof Exp:* Res fel, Stanford Univ, 76-79; ASST PROF MOLECULAR BIOL, DEPT BIOPHYSICS & THEORET BIOL, UNIV CHICAGO, 80- *Concurrent Pos:* Asst prof, Dept Biochem, Univ Chicago & Comt Genetics, 80- *Mem:* Am Soc Microbiol; AAAS. *Res:* Gene expression, structures, and function; analysis of genetic control elements by DNA fusion and cloning in prokaryotic and eukaryotic cells; mechanisms of DNA transposition. *Mailing Add:* Dept Biophysics & Theoret Univ Chicago 920 E 58th St Chicago IL 60637

CASADY, ALFRED JACKSON, b Milton, Iowa, Feb 16, 16; m 41; c 2. AGRONOMY, PLANT BREEDING. *Educ:* Kans State Univ, BS, 48, MS, 50, PhD(agron), 62. *Prof Exp:* Agronomist plant breeding, Agr Res Serv, USDA, Kans State Univ, 49-70; PROF AGRON, KANS STATE UNIV, 70- *Concurrent Pos:* Res agronomist, USDA, 76- *Mem:* Am Soc Agron. *Res:* Breeding and selection of cereal crops for improved yield; insect and disease resistance. *Mailing Add:* Dept of Agron Kans State Univ Manhattan KS 66506

CASADY, ROBERT BARNES, b Los Angeles, Calif, Nov 29, 17; m 43; c 3. PHYSIOLOGY, RESEARCH ADMINISTRATION. *Educ:* Univ Calif, BS, 41, PhD(comp physiol), 48. *Prof Exp:* Instr zool & jr zoologist, Exp Sta, Univ Calif, 48-50; asst prof animal indust, NC State Univ, 50-57; supt, US Rabbit Exp Sta, Animal Res Div, Calif, 57-65, res animal husbandman, Animal Husb Div, Agr Res Ctr, 65-67, ASST DIR INT PROGS DIV, AGR RES CTR, USDA, 67- *Concurrent Pos:* Res assoc, Inst Co-op Res, Johns Hopkins Univ, 53-54. *Mem:* AAAS. *Res:* Rabbit physiology; nutrition; genetics and management. *Mailing Add:* 1320 Chilton Dr Silver Springs MD 20904

CASAGRANDE, ARTHUR, b Haidenschaft, Austria, Aug 28, 02; nat US; m 40; c 2. CIVIL ENGINEERING. *Educ:* Vienna Tech Univ, Ing, 24, Dr tech, 33. *Hon Degrees:* Dr tech, Vienna Tech Univ, 65; SM, Harvard Univ, 42; Dr, Nat Univ, Mex, 51; Dr hc, Univ Leige, Belg, 75. *Prof Exp:* Asst hydraul, Vienna Tech Univ, 24-26; res asst, US Bur Pub Roads, 26-32; lectr soil mech, 32-35, from asst prof to assoc prof civil eng, 34-46, prof soil mech & found eng, 46-73, EMER PROF SOIL MECH & FOUND ENG, HARVARD UNIV, 73- *Concurrent Pos:* Asst to Prof Terzaghi, 26-30; consult, 32- *Mem:* Nat Acad Eng; AAAS; Am Soc Civil Engrs; Am Soc Eng Educ; Int Soc Soil Mech & Found Eng (pres, 61-65). *Res:* Soil mechanics new testing apparatus; frost action in soils; seepage; stress-deformation and strength characteristics of soils and soft rocks; liquefaction of sands; earth and rockfill dams. *Mailing Add:* Pierce Hall Harvard Univ Cambridge MA 02138

CASAGRANDE, DANIEL JOSEPH, b Bridgeport, Conn, Jan 25, 45; m 64; c 2. ORGANIC GEOCHEMISTRY. *Educ:* Univ Scranton, BSc, 66; Pa State Univ, PhD(fuel sci), 70. *Prof Exp:* Fel org geochem, Univ Calgary, 71; prof org geochem, Governors State Univ, 71-79; SR RES SPECIALIST, EXXON PROD RES CO, 79- *Concurrent Pos:* Consult, Village Park Forest South, Ill, 72-, Armour Dial, Inc, 72, Izaak Walton League, 73, Kerr-McGee Corp, 75-78, Shell Oil Co, 76 & Cities Serv Oil Co, 78. *Honors & Awards:* Colin Roscoe Award, Am Chem Soc. *Mem:* Am Chem Soc; Geol Soc Am; The Chem Soc; Geochem Soc; AAAS. *Res:* Organic geochemistry of sulfur, metals, amino acids, porphyrins in sediments, petroleum, peat, lignite and coal. *Mailing Add:* Exxon Prod Res Co PO Box 2189 Houston IL 77001

CASAGRANDE, LEO, b Austria, 1903. CIVIL ENGINEERING. *Educ:* Tech Univ Vienna, Civil Engr, 28, Dr Tech, 33. *Prof Exp:* Design engr, Ger, 28-30; res asst, Mass Inst Technol, 30-32 & Inst Soil Mech, Tech Univ Vienna & Berlin, 32-34; mem staff, Soils & Found Div, Ger Hwys, Berlin, 34-45; res engr, Bldg Res Sta, Watford, Eng, 46-50; prof found eng, Harvard Univ, 56-72; CONSULT ENGR, 50- *Concurrent Pos:* Hon prof soil mech, Tech Univ Braunschweig, 40-45. *Mem:* Nat Acad Eng; Am Soc Civil Eng; NY Acad Sci. *Mailing Add:* Casagrande Consults 40 Massachusetts Ave Arlington MA 02174

CASALE, GEORGE PASCO, b New Britain, Conn, June 28, 43; m 68; c 3. CELL BIOLOGY, IMMUNOLOGY. *Educ:* Providence Col, AB, 65; Univ Notre Dame, PhD(microbiol), 72. *Prof Exp:* Asst cancer res scientist immunol, Roswell Park Mem Inst, 71-73; res assoc immunol, 74-75, RES ASSOC CELL BIOL, UNIV CONN HEALTH CTR, 75- *Mem:* AAAS; Am Soc Cell Biol. *Res:* Biochemical aspects of erythroid differentiation and development; immunogenetic and biochemical aspects of macrophage recognition and destruction of neoplastic cells. *Mailing Add:* Dept of Anatomy Univ of Conn Health Ctr Farmington CT 06032

CASALI, LIBERTY, b Vivian, WVa, Oct 15, 11. CHEMISTRY. *Educ:* Duke Univ, BS, 33; Univ Colo, PhD(phys chem), 52. *Prof Exp:* Teacher pub schs, WVa, 33-42; asst chemist, Gen Elec Co Labs, Mass, 42-45; asst gen qual phys chem lab, Wheaton Col, Mass, 45-47; instr math, Univ Colo, 48-50, asst chem, 47-51; from instr to asst prof chem, Russell Sage Col, 52-61; assoc prof chem & physics, Winthrop Col, 61-65 & Bridgewater Col, 65-66; from assoc to prof, 67-77, EMER PROF CHEM, JAMES MADISON UNIV, 77- *Concurrent Pos:* Abstractor, Chem Abstr. *Mem:* Am Chem Soc. *Res:* Heats of reaction of some fluroolefins; molecular spectra; history of science. *Mailing Add:* 722 S Main St Apt B3 Harrisonburg VA 22801

CASALS, JORDI, b Viladrau, Spain, May 15, 11; nat US; m 41; c 1. VIROLOGY. *Educ:* Instituto Nacional, BS, 28; Univ Barcelona, MD, 34. *Prof Exp:* Asst resident physician, Med Sch Hosp, Univ Barcelona, 34-36; asst path, Sch Med, Cornell Univ, 37-38; asst, Dept Path & Bact, Rockefeller Inst, 38-52, virus res prog, Rockefeller Found, 52-69; prof, 69-80, PROF EMER & SR RES SCIENTIST EPIDEMIOL, YALE UNIV, 80- *Concurrent Pos:* Consult, Walter Reed Army Med Ctr; mem, Surgeon Gen's Virus Comn, Japan, 47. *Mem:* AAAS; fel Soc Exp Biol & Med; fel NY Acad Sci. *Res:* Arthropod-borne virus infections. *Mailing Add:* Dept of Epidemiol Yale Univ New Haven CT 06520

CASANOVA, JOSEPH, b Stafford Springs, Conn, May 31, 31; m 56; c 4. ORGANIC CHEMISTRY. *Educ:* Mass Inst Technol, SB, 53; Carnegie Inst Technol, MS, 56, PhD(org chem), 57. *Prof Exp:* Res chemist, E I du Pont de Nemours & Co, Del, 57; res chemist & dir res, Chem Warfare Lab, Army Chem Ctr, 58-59; NIH res fel, Harvard Univ, 59-61; from asst prof to assoc prof, 61-74, dean undergrad studies, 78-80, assoc vpres planning & resources, 80-81, PROF CHEM, CALIF STATE UNIV, LOS ANGELES, 74- *Concurrent Pos:* Vis prof, Ind Univ, 65-66; Fulbright scholar, Dept Org Chem, Univ Lund, Sweden, 70-71. *Mem:* Am Chem Soc; The Chem Soc. *Res:* Sulfonium salts; organic boron compounds; isocyanides; electroorganic chemistry. *Mailing Add:* Dept of Chem Calif State Univ Los Angeles CA 90032

CASARETT, ALISON PROVOOST, b New York, NY, Apr 17, 30; c 2. RADIOBIOLOGY. *Educ:* St Lawrence Univ, BS, 51; Univ Rochester, MS, 53, PhD(radiation biol), 57. *Prof Exp:* Res assoc radiation biol, Univ Rochester, 53-58, instr, 58-63; asst prof, 63-69, ASSOC PROF PHYSICAL BIOL, CORNELL UNIV, 69-, ASSOC DEAN GRAD SCH, 73-, VPROVOST, 78- *Mem:* Radiation Res Soc. *Res:* Physiological, endocrinological and pathological effects of radiation on mammals. *Mailing Add:* Sage Grad Ctr Cornell Univ Ithaca NY 14853

CASARETT, GEORGE WILLIAM, b Rochester, NY, Aug 17, 20; m 44; c 2. PATHOLOGY. *Educ:* Univ Rochester, PhD(anat), 52. *Prof Exp:* Jr res assoc, 41-43, asst path, Manhattan Proj, 43-47, chief path unit, Atomic Energy Proj, 47-49, asst chief radiation tolerance sect, 49-52, scientist, 52-62, res assoc radiation ther, 59-68, from instr to assoc prof, 53-59, prof radiation biol, 63-66, chief, Radiation Path Sect, 62-80, PROF RADIATION BIOL & BIOPHYS, SCH MED, UNIV ROCHESTER, 63-, PROF RADIOL, 68-, CHIEF, RADIATION PATH SECT, 62- *Concurrent Pos:* Consult, Surgeon Gen, US Army, 61-70, sci comt effects atomic radiation, UN, 63-, US Armed Forces Radiobiol Res Inst, 64-70 & coun, Am Asn Advan Aging Res; mem, US deleg, UN Conf Peaceful Uses Atomic Energy, Switz, 55, subcomt effects radiation, Nat Acad Sci, 56-64, subcomt nat comt radiation protection, 56-, adv comt to Fed Radiation Coun, 66-70, nat coun radiation protection, 62-, comt on radiation effects, 73- & Int Comn Radiol Protection, 67-70, chmn comt on biol effects of radiation, Nat Acad Sci; mem cancer res training comt, Nat Cancer Inst, 69- *Honors & Awards:* Award & Silver Medal, Am Roentgen Ray Soc, 59; Award, Radiol Soc NAm, 59. *Mem:* AAAS; Am Asn Anat; Am Soc Exp Path; fel Am Geront Soc; fel NY Acad Sci. *Res:* Oncology; pathology and hematology of radiations; radioactive substances; radiation biology; gerontology; sterility. *Mailing Add:* Dept Radiation Biol & Biophys Univ Rochester Sch Med Rochester NY 14642

CASASENT, DAVID P(AUL), b Washington, DC, Dec 8, 42; m 64; c 4. INFORMATION PROCESSING, RADAR. *Educ:* Univ Ill, Urbana-Champaign, BS, 64, MS, 65, PhD(elec eng), 69. *Prof Exp:* Asst prof, 69-76, PROF ELEC ENG, CARNEGIE-MELLON UNIV, 76- *Concurrent Pos:* Consult, Digital Equip Corp, 70-, Off Naval Res, 75-, Dept Defense, 77-, NSF & Rome Air Develop Ctr, 78-, NASA & Gen Dynamics, 80-; res contract, Off Naval Res, 71-, Air Force Off Sci Res, 75- *Honors & Awards:* B Carlton Award, Inst Elec & Electronics Engrs, 76. *Mem:* Fel Inst Elec & Electronics Engrs; fel Optical Soc Am; Soc Photo-Optical Instrumentation Engrs. *Res:* On-line real-time optical image and signal processing; pattern recognition radar and C3 I signal processing; missile guidance, optimal control, real-time light modulators; hybrid optical-digital data processing. *Mailing Add:* Dept of Elec Eng Carnegie-Mellon Univ Pittsburgh PA 15213

CASASSA, EDWARD FRANCIS, b Portland, Maine, Nov 10, 24; m 54; c 3. PHYSICAL CHEMISTRY OF MACROMOLECULES. *Educ:* Univ Maine, BS, 45; Mass Inst Technol, PhD(phys chem), 53. *Prof Exp:* Chemist, E I du Pont de Nemours & Co, 45-48; asst, Mass Inst Technol, 49-52; proj assoc chem, Univ Wis, 52-56; fel, 56-59, SR FEL, MELLON INST, 59-, PROF CHEM, CARNEGIE-MELLON UNIV, 67- *Concurrent Pos:* Lectr, Univ Pittsburgh, 56-59; asst ed, J Polymer Sci, 65-69, assoc ed, 69- *Mem:* AAAS; Am Phys Soc; Am Chem Soc. *Res:* Physical chemistry of polymers and proteins; statistical mechanics; light scattering. *Mailing Add:* Dept Chem 4400 Fifth Ave Pittsburgh PA 15213

CASCARANO, JOSEPH, b Brooklyn, NY, Oct 26, 28; m 54; c 2. CELL PHYSIOLOGY. *Educ:* NY Univ, BA, 50, MS, 53, PhD(biol), 56. *Prof Exp:* US Pub Health Serv fels, Univ Minn, 56-57, NY Univ, 57-58, instr path, Sch Med, 58-59, asst prof, 59-65; assoc prof zool, 65-70, PROF CELL BIOL, UNIV CALIF, LOS ANGELES, 70- *Honors & Awards:* Distinguished Teaching Award, Univ Calif, Los Angeles, 70. *Mem:* AAAS; Am Physiol Soc; Am Soc Cell Biol; Soc Exp Biol & Med. *Res:* Cation transport; cell permeability; anaerobic energy metabolism; relation of cell function to energy metabolism; mitochondrial biogenesis; metabolic regulation, heart metabolism; acclimation and adaptation of animals to altitude. *Mailing Add:* Dept of Biol Univ of Calif Los Angeles CA 90024

CASCIANO, DANIEL ANTHONY, b Buffalo, NY, Mar 1, 41; m 64; c 2. CELL BIOLOGY. *Educ:* Canisius Col, BS, 62; Purdue Univ, PhD(cell biol), 71. *Prof Exp:* Res asst tissue cult, Roswell Park Mem Inst, 63-64; res asst cell biol, Purdue Univ, 65-66, asst microbiol, 69; investr biochem, Univ Tenn, 71-73; res biologist, 73-79, DIR, DIV MUTAGENESIS RES, NAT CTR TOXICOL RES, 79- *Res:* Development of mammalian somatic cell systems capable of in vitro metabolism of promutagens and procarcinogens. *Mailing Add:* Div of Mutagenic Res Nat Ctr of Toxicol Res Jefferson AR 72079

CASE, ARTHUR ADAM, b Manhattan, Kans, Dec 3, 10; m 40; c 4. VETERINARY MEDICINE. *Educ:* Kans State Col, BS, 37, MS, 39, DVM, 42; Am Bd Vet Toxicol, dipl, 72. *Prof Exp:* Asst parasitol, Kans State Col, 35-41; from instr to asst prof path, Ohio State Univ, 42-47; assoc prof, 47-51, prof vet med & surg & exten vet, 51-81, chief toxicol vet clin staff, 67-81, EMER PROF VET MED & SURG, COL VET MED, UNIV MO, 81- *Concurrent Pos:* Exten vet, Vet Continuing Educ, 73-81. *Mem:* Fel AAAS; Am Vet Med Asn; Am Asn Vet Clinicians; Am Asn Path & Bact; Am Soc Parasitol. *Res:* Parasitology; pathology; infectious diseases of swine; toxicology, especially poisonous plants; white snake-root poisoning, green acorn-oak leaf poisoning, bullnettle nighshade poisoning and mold toxicities. *Mailing Add:* 1508 Ross Columbia MO 65201

CASE, CARL TYLER, plasma physics, see previous edition

CASE, CLINTON MEREDITH, b Oregon City, Ore, Nov 20, 40; m 65; c 2. SURFACE PHYSICS, HYDROLOGY. *Educ:* Linfield Col, BA, 63; Univ Nev, Reno, MS, 67, PhD(physics), 70. *Prof Exp:* Res assoc hydrol, 70-72, asst res prof, 73-75, assoc res prof, 75-80, RES PROF HYDROL, CTR WATER RESOURCES RES, DESERT RES INST, UNIV NEV, RENO, 80- *Concurrent Pos:* Fulbright scholar, 63. *Mem:* Am Geophys Union; Am Phys Soc; Am Vacuum Soc; Am Asn Physics Teachers. *Res:* Statistical mechanics of cooperative phenomena, including surface effects; theoretical groundwater hydrology; experimental solid state physics. *Mailing Add:* 985 Akard Dr Reno NV 89503

CASE, DAVID ANDREW, b Akron, Ohio, Oct 12, 48. PHYSICAL CHEMISTRY. *Educ:* Mich State Univ, BS, 70; Harvard Univ, AM, 72, PhD(chem physics), 77. *Prof Exp:* ASST PROF CHEM, UNIV CALIF, DAVIS, 77- *Mem:* Am Chem Soc. *Res:* Theoretical chemistry; electronic structures of inorganic compounds and metalloenzymes; dynamics of proteins; relativistic effects in molecular electronic structures. *Mailing Add:* Dept of Chem Univ of Calif Davis CA 95616

CASE, JAMES B(OYCE), b Lincoln, Ill, Oct 26, 28; m 58; c 1. PHOTOGRAMMETRY, GEODESY. *Educ:* Stanford Univ, BS, 50; Ohio State Univ, MS, 57, PhD(geod sci), 59. *Prof Exp:* Res fel glacier mapping, Ohio State Univ & Am Geog Soc, 56-59; prin investr, Ohio State Univ Res Found, 59-60; sr photogrammetrist, Broadview Res Corp, 60-61; prin scientist, Autometric Oper, Raytheon Co, 61-71; supvry geodesist, US Army Topog Command, 71-72; phys scientist, Topog Ctr, 72-79, STAFF PHOTOGRAMMETRIST, HQ, DEFENSE MAPPING AGENCY, 79- *Concurrent Pos:* Ed-in-chief, Photogram Eng & Remote Sensing, 75- *Mem:* AAAS; Brit Cartog Soc; Can Cartog Asn; Can Inst Surv; Sigma Xi. *Mailing Add:* 1210 Colonial Rd McLean VA 22101

CASE, JAMES EDWARD, b Mountain View, Ark, Feb 15, 33; m 55, 72; c 5. GEOLOGY, GEOPHYSICS. *Educ:* Univ Ark, BS, 53, MS, 54; Univ Calif, Berkeley, PhD(geol), 63. *Prof Exp:* Instr geol & math, Lamar State Col, 54-55; geologist, US Geol Surv, 55, geologist & geophysicist, 56-58, geophysicist, 58-65, chief Denver area pub unit & geologist, 66; assoc prof geol & geophys, Tex A&M Univ, 66-69 & Univ Mo, 69-71; GEOPHYSICIST, US GEOL SURV, CALIF, 71- *Mem:* Fel Geol Soc Am; Am Geophys Union; Seismol Soc Am; Soc Explor Geophys; Am Asn Petrol Geol. *Res:* Gravity; magnetic data; correlation of geophysical data with geologic structure; tectonics of northern South America and Caribbean region; geophysical expression of mafic and ultramafic belts; tectonostratigraphic terranes. *Mailing Add:* US Geol Surv 345 Middlefield Rd Menlo Park CA 94025

CASE, JAMES FREDERICK, b Bristow, Okla, Oct 27, 26; m 50; c 3. COMPARATATIVE PHYSIOLOGY. *Educ:* Johns Hopkins Univ, PhD(biol), 51. *Prof Exp:* Physiologist avian physiol, USDA, 51-52; insect physiologist, Med Labs, Army Chem Ctr, Md, 55-57, from asst prof to assoc prof zool, Univ Iowa, 57-63; assoc prof, 63-69, PROF NEUROBIOL, UNIV CALIF, SANTA BARBARA, 69- *Mem:* AAAS. *Res:* Invertebrate physiology. *Mailing Add:* Dept of Biol Univ of Calif Santa Barbara CA 93018

CASE, JAMES HUGHSON, b Franklinville, NY, May 25, 28; m 51; c 3. AUTOMATA THEORY. *Educ:* Ala Polytech Inst, BS, 50; Tulane Univ, PhD(math), 54. *Prof Exp:* Asst prof math, Univ Utah, 54-59; asst prof, Univ Rochester, 59-61; assoc prof, 61-68, PROF MATH, UNIV UTAH, 68- *Concurrent Pos:* Consult, Gen Dynamics/Electronics, 60-61. *Mem:* Am Math Soc. *Res:* Automata theory; general topology. *Mailing Add:* Dept of Math Univ of Utah Salt Lake City UT 84112

CASE, JOHN WILLIAM, b Clinton, Iowa, Oct 28, 42; m 68; c 3. RECURSIVE FUNCTION THEORY. *Educ:* Iowa State Univ, Ames, BS, 64; Univ Ill, Urbana, MS, 66, PhD(math), 69. *Prof Exp:* Asst prof comput sci, Univ Kans, Lawrence, 69-73; asst prof, 73-75, ASSOC PROF COMPUT SCI, STATE UNIV NY BUFFALO, 75- *Concurrent Pos:* Vis fel comput sci, Yale Univ, New Haven, Conn, 80-81; vis assoc prof comput sci, NY Univ, New York, 80-81. *Mem:* Asn Comput Mach; AAAS; Am Math Soc; Asn Symbolic Logic; Europ Asn Theoret Comput Sci. *Res:* Recursive function theory in computer science including the theory of inductive inference machines; theoretical applications of self-referential machines or programs; abstract structure of programs; relative succinctness of programs in language hierarchies; biologically motivated automata theory. *Mailing Add:* Comput Sci Dept State Univ NY 4226 Ridge Lea Rd Amherst NY 14226

CASE, KENNETH E(UGENE), b Oak Ridge, Tenn, Aug 12, 44; m 66; c 2. INDUSTRIAL ENGINEERING, QUALITY ASSURANCE. *Educ:* Okla State Univ, BS, 66, MS, 67, PhD(indust eng), 69. *Prof Exp:* Technician, Aerotron Radio Co, Okla, 59-63; prod engr, Humble Oil Co, Okla, 65; elec engr, Collins Radio Co, Iowa, 66; instr indust eng, Okla State Univ, 67-68; from asst prof to assoc prof indust eng & opers res, Va Polytech Inst & State Univ, 69-74; mgt scientist, GTE Data Serv, Tampa, Fla, 74-75; assoc prof indust eng, 75-80, PROF & HEAD INDUST ENG, SCH INDUST ENG & MGT, OKLA STATE UNIV, 80- *Concurrent Pos:* Mgt consult, Cities Serv Oil Co, Milwaukee & Tulsa, 68-69; invited lectr, US Army Logistics Ctr, 70; fac fel, NASA-Am Soc Eng Educ Systs Design Prog, 70; consult, Tenn Valley Authority, 70-71, Gen Motors, Va & Brunswick Corp, 73, TRW Reda Pump, 76, Walker, Jackman, Livingston, Attys, Okla, 77, Stang Hydronics, Inc, Okla & Boeing Com Airplane Co, Wash, 78, Detroit Diesel Allison Div, Gen Motors, Ind, 79, Mercury Marine, Okla, 80 & Remington Arms, Inc, Conn, 80-81; ed, Appl Probability & Statist Dept, Am Inst Indust Engrs Trans, 77-80; dir conf prog coord, Inst Indust Engrs, 79-82; Dir prof regist, Inst Indust Engrs, 81. *Honors & Awards:* Ralph R Teetor Award, Soc Automotive Engrs, 77. *Mem:* Sr mem Am Inst Indust Engrs; sr mem Am Soc Qual Control; Nat Soc Prof Engrs. *Res:* Quality program management and computation of complex system reliability; economically-based quality control planning; inspection error and its adverse effects on quality; resource allocation under constraints. *Mailing Add:* Sch of Indust Eng & Mgt Okla State Univ Stillwater OK 74074

CASE, KENNETH MYRON, b New York, NY, Sept 23, 23. PHYSICS. *Educ:* Harvard Univ, SB, 45, MA, 46, PhD(physics), 48. *Prof Exp:* Mem staff physics, Los Alamos Sci Lab, 44-45; Nat Res fel, 45-48; fel, Inst Adv Study, 48-50, asst prof physics, Univ Mich, 50-52, from assoc prof to prof chem, 53-67; PROF PHYSICS, ROCKEFELLER UNIV, 67- *Concurrent Pos:* Consult, Los Alamos Sci Lab, 48-; res assoc, Radiation Lab, Univ Calif, 49 & Univ Rochester, 50. *Mem:* Nat Acad Sci. *Res:* Neutron diffusion; field theory; relativistic wave equations. *Mailing Add:* Dept of Physics Rockefeller Univ New York NY 10021

CASE, LLOYD ALLEN, b Ontario, Ore, Jan 1, 43; m 62; c 7. PHYSICS, COMPUTER SCIENCE. *Educ:* Brigham Young Univ, BS, 64, PhD(physics), 68. *Prof Exp:* Teaching asst physics, Brigham Young Univ, 62-68, res asst, 64-68; asst prof, Ind Univ Southeast, 68-71, chmn dept natural sci, 70-72, assoc prof physics, 72-76; res fel, NASA-Ames Lab & Stanford Univ, 71-72; prof & dir comput serv, Ind Univ Southeast, 76-79; mgr, Syst Comput Technol Corp, Malvern, Pa, 79-81; PRES, UNIV NEV SYST & DIR COMPUT SERV, 81- *Concurrent Pos:* NSF fel, Univ Colo, 68; Ind Univ res grant, 71. *Mem:* Am Phys Soc; Am Asn Physics Teachers; Sigma Xi. *Res:* Hardware; software; consulting; audits; astrophysics; general relativity. *Mailing Add:* 660 Winchester Dr Reno NV 89506

CASE, MARVIN THEODORE, b Anna, Ill, Dec 20, 34; m 58; c 2. VETERINARY PATHOLOGY, TOXICOLOGY. *Educ:* Univ Ill, BS, 57, DVM, 59, MS, 64, PhD(vet path), 68; Am Bd Toxicol, dipl, 80. *Prof Exp:* Vet, Ill State Dept Agr, 61-62; from instr to asst prof vet path, Col Vet Med, Univ Ill, 62-69; head path-toxicol sect, 69-71, mgr path, 71-75, MGR PATH-TOXICOL, RIKER LABS, 75- *Concurrent Pos:* Dep vet Los Angeles County, Calif & assoc prof comp med, Univ Southern Calif, 69-71. *Mem:* AAAS; Am Asn Advan Lab Animal Sci; Am Vet Med Asn; NY Acad Sci; Int Acad Path. *Res:* Neoplasia; toxicology; animal diseases; teratology. *Mailing Add:* Riker Labs Bldg 218-3 3-M Ctr St Paul MN 55101

CASE, MARY ELIZABETH, b Crawfordsville, Ind, Dec 10, 25. MICROBIAL GENETICS. *Educ:* Maryville Col, Tenn, BA, 50; Univ Tenn, MS, 50; Yale Univ, PhD(bot), 57. *Prof Exp:* Res assoc genetics, Yale Univ, 57-72; assoc prof zool, 72-79, ASSOC PROF MOLECULAR & POP GENETICS, UNIV GA, 80- *Mem:* Am Soc Microbiol; Am Genetics Soc. *Res:* Genetics of microorganisms; neurospora crassa. *Mailing Add:* Molecular & Pop Genetics Univ of Ga Athens GA 30602

CASE, NORMAN MONDELL, b Milton, Ore, Oct 12, 17. HUMAN ANATOMY. *Educ:* Col Med Evangelists, BS, 49; Univ Southern Calif, MS, 54; Loma Linda Univ, PhD(anat), 58. *Prof Exp:* Tech asst anat, 50-54, from asst instr to asst prof, 54-75, ASSOC PROF ANAT, LOMA LINDA UNIV, 75- *Mem:* Am Asn Anat; Electron Micros Soc Am; assoc AMA; Royal Micros Soc. *Res:* Electron microscopy of the optic lobe in Octopus. *Mailing Add:* Dept Anat Loma Linda Univ Loma Linda CA 92354

CASE, ROBERT B, b Columbus, Ohio, July 19, 20; m 61; c 1. CARDIOLOGY, PHYSIOLOGY. *Educ:* Ohio Wesleyan Univ, BA, 43; Mass Inst Technol, BS, 43; Columbia Univ, MD, 48. *Prof Exp:* Res assoc cardiac physiol, Sch Pub Health, Harvard Univ, 52-54; DIR LAB EXP CARDIOL, ST LUKE'S HOSP, 56-, ASSOC PROF MED, COL PHYSICIANS & SURGEONS, COLUMBIA UNIV, 72- *Concurrent Pos:* Nat Heart Inst res fel, 52-54; NY Heart Asn sr res fel, 56-61; USPHS res career develop award, 62-67; chief cardiac consult clin, City Health Dept, New York, 62-70; asst clin prof med, Col Physicians & Surgeons, Columbia Univ, 80- *Mem:* Am Physiol Soc; Am Fedn Clin Res. *Res:* Cardiac physiology; coronary artery disease. *Mailing Add:* St Luke's Hosp 421 W 113th St New York NY 10025

CASE, ROBERT OLIVER, b Ft Thomas, Ky, Nov 17, 35. APPLIED MECHANICS, MACHINE DESIGN. *Educ:* US Mil Acad, BS, 58; Univ Ala, Tuscaloosa, MS, 62, PhD(eng mech), 68. *Prof Exp:* Res assoc, Univ Ala, 66-68; asst prof, 68-77, assoc prof, 77-80, PROF MECH ENG, FLA ATLANTIC UNIV, 80-, CHMN DEPT, 77- *Mem:* Soc Exp Stress Anal. *Res:* Photoelastic investigations of thin-walled structures and non-isotropic structures. *Mailing Add:* Dept of Mech Eng Fla Atlantic Univ Boca Raton FL 33431

CASE, RONALD MARK, b Wausau, Wis, Oct 7, 40; m 63; c 2. WILDLIFE ECOLOGY. *Educ:* Ripon Col, AB, 62; Univ Ill, Urbana, MS, 64; Kans State Univ, PhD(biol), 71. *Prof Exp:* Instr ecol, Univ Mo, 71-72; from asst prof to assoc prof, 72-80, PROF WILDLIFE, UNIV NEBR, 80- *Concurrent Pos:* Consult ecol, Midwest Res Inst, 71-72, Mits Kawamoto & Assocs, 72-73. *Mem:* Wildlife Soc; Ecol Soc Am; Am Inst Biol Sci; Am Soc Naturalists; Am Ornithologists Union. *Res:* Pocket gophers and grasslands; population dynamics and damages to forage; bioenergetics of Bobwhites; study of population status of wild canids, especially swift fox and red fox in Nebraska. *Mailing Add:* Dept Forestry Fisheries & Wildlife Univ Nebr Lincoln NE 68583

CASE, TED JOSEPH, b Sioux City, Iowa, July 19, 47. EVOLUTIONARY ECOLOGY. *Educ:* Univ Redlands, BS, 69; Univ Calif, Irvine, PhD(biol), 74. *Prof Exp:* Res assoc & lectr entomol, Univ Calif, Davis, 73-75; asst prof biol, Purdue Univ, 75-78; ASST PROF BIOL, UNIV CALIF, SAN DIEGO, 78- *Concurrent Pos:* Assoc ed, Univ Calif Publ Entomol, 80-81. *Res:* Evolutionary ecology; island biogeography; lizard ecology. *Mailing Add:* Biol Dept C016 Univ Calif San Diego La Jolla CA 92093

CASE, VERNA MILLER, b Lebanon, Pa, Aug 17, 48; m 76; c 2. ETHOLOGY, ANIMAL BEHAVIOR. *Educ:* Pa State Univ, BS, 70, MS, 72, PhD(zool), 74. *Prof Exp:* ASST PROF BIOL, DAVIDSON COL, 74- *Mem:* Animal Behav Soc; AAAS. *Res:* Development and regulation of vertebrate social systems; relationship between social systems, the ecological setting in which they occur and the evolutionary history of the species. *Mailing Add:* Dept of Biol Davidson Col Davidson NC 28036

CASE, VERNON WESLEY, b Kitchener, Ont, May 7, 35; m 58; c 3. SOIL FERTILITY. *Educ:* Univ BC, BSA, 58; Cornell Univ, MSc, 61. *Prof Exp:* Res officer res br, Can Dept Agr, 61-68; agr specialist, Res & Develop, Int Minerals & Chem Corp, 68-73; instr soils & plant nutrit, Triton Col, 73-74; MGR AGRON SERV LAB, INT MINERALS & CHEM CORP, 74- *Mem:* Am Soc Agron; Int Soc Soil Sci; Coun Agr Sci & Technol. *Res:* Fertilizer evaluation and plant nutrition research; land reclamation and environmental concerns in agriculture; manager analysis soil, plant and miscellaneous agricultural samples. *Mailing Add:* 1331 S First St Int Minerals & Chem Corp Terre Haute IN 47808

CASE, WILLIAM BLEICHER, b Elmira, NY, Oct 16, 41; m 80; c 1. PLASMA PHYSICS. *Educ:* Syracuse Univ, BS, 63, MS, 66, PhD(physics), 71. *Prof Exp:* Instr physics, Syracuse Univ, 70-72; vis asst prof, State Univ NY, Binghamton, 74-75; asst prof physics, Hobart & William Smith Cols, 75-80; ASST PROF PHYSICS, GRINNELL COL, 80- *Mem:* Am Phys Soc. *Res:* Electron beam instabilities; microwave generation using electron beams. *Mailing Add:* Dept Physics Grinnell Col Grinnell IA 50112

CASELLA, ALEXANDER JOSEPH, b Taylor, Pa, Aug 10, 39; m 66; c 2. BIOPHYSICS, ENERGY STUDIES. *Educ:* Villanova Univ, BS, 61; Drexel Inst Technol, MS, 64; Pa State Univ, PhD(physics), 69. *Prof Exp:* Physicist, Frankford Arsenal, Philadelphia, 61-65; asst prof physics, Jacksonville Univ, 69-74; ASSOC PROF ENVIRON STUDIES, SANGAMON STATE UNIV, 74- *Mem:* AAAS; Am Asn Physics Teachers. *Res:* Lasers; biophysics of visual systems; solar energy; energy technology. *Mailing Add:* Dept Environ Studies Sangamon State Univ Springfield IL 62708

CASELLA, CLARENCE J, b New York, NY, Nov 9, 29; m 59; c 5. GEOLOGY. *Educ:* Hunter Col, BA, 56; Columbia Univ, PhD(geol), 62. *Prof Exp:* Lectr geol, Hunter Col, 58-60 & Brooklyn Col, 60-61; asst prof, Villanova Univ, 61-65; asst prof, Dept Earth Sci, 65-68, ASSOC PROF, DIV GEOL, NORTHERN ILL UNIV, 68- *Mem:* AAAS; Geol Soc Am. *Res:* Structure and petrology of metamorphic rocks; lunar geology. *Mailing Add:* Dept of Geol Northern Ill Univ De Kalb IL 60115

CASELLA, JOHN FRANCIS, b Oneida, NY, June 9, 44; m 68; c 2. POLYMER CHEMISTRY. *Educ:* Clarkson Col Technol, BS, 66, MS, 71, PhD(phys chem), 73. *Prof Exp:* Res assoc phys chem of proteins, Grad Dept Biochem, Brandeis Univ, 72-74; Res scientist polymer characterization, Ethicon, Inc, 74-80; MEM STAFF, I O LAB CORP, 80- *Concurrent Pos:* Am Cancer Soc fel, 74. *Mem:* Am Chem Soc; AAAS; NY Acad Sci. *Res:* Physical chemistry of macromolecules; solution properties of synthetic polymers and how they correlate with processability and final properties of the polymer. *Mailing Add:* I O Lab Corp 695 W Terrace Dr San Dimas CA 91773

CASELLA, RUSSELL CARL, b Framingham, Mass, Nov, 6, 29; m 52; c 2. PHYSICS. *Educ:* Mass Inst Technol, BS, 51; Univ Ill, MS, 53, PhD(physics), 56. *Prof Exp:* Physicist, Air Force Cambridge Res Ctr, 51-52; asst, Univ Ill, 53-54, from res asst to assoc, 54-58; physicist, Int Bus Machines Res Lab, 58-65; physicist, 65-69, ELEM PARTICLE & SOLID STATE THEORIST, REACTOR RADIATION THEORY DIV, NAT BUR STANDARDS, 69- *Honors & Awards:* Silver Medal Award, US Dept Com, 73. *Mem:* Am Phys Soc. *Res:* Theoretical high energy physics; theoretical solid state physics. *Mailing Add:* 1485 Dunster Lane Potomac MD 20854

CASEMAN, A(USTIN) BERT, b Phoenix, Ariz, Feb 13, 22; m 46; c 1. CIVIL ENGINEERING, STRUCTURAL ENGINEERING. *Educ:* Utah State Univ, BS, 47, MS, 48; Mass Inst Technol, DSc (civil eng), 61. *Prof Exp:* From instr to asst prof civil eng, Wash State Univ, 48-56; assoc prof, 56-62, PROF CIVIL ENG, GA INST TECHNOL, 62- *Concurrent Pos:* NSF fac fel, 57. *Mem:* Am Soc Civil Engrs; Am Concrete Inst; Sigma Xi. *Res:* Structural theory; design of thin shell structures. *Mailing Add:* Sch of Civil Eng Ga Inst of Technol Atlanta GA 30332

CASERIO, MARJORIE C, b London, Eng, Feb 26, 29; nat US; m 57; c 2. ORGANIC CHEMISTRY. *Educ:* Univ London, BSc, 50; Bryn Mawr Col, MA, 51, PhD(chem), 56. *Prof Exp:* Assoc chemist, Fulma Res Inst, Eng, 52-53; from asst to instr chem, Bryn Mawr Col, 53-56; fel, Calif Inst Tech, 56-64; from asst prof to assoc prof, 65-71, PROF CHEM, UNIV CALIF, IRVINE, 71- *Concurrent Pos:* John S Guggenheim Found fel, 75-76. *Honors & Awards:* Garvan Medal, Am Chem Soc, 75. *Mem:* Am Chem Soc; The Chem Soc; Sigma Xi. *Res:* Reaction mechanisms in organic chemistry. *Mailing Add:* Dept of Chem Univ of Calif Irvine CA 92717

CASEY, ADRIA CATALA, b Havana, Cuba, Apr 24, 34; m 66; c 2. CHEMICAL HAZARD ASSESSMENT, MEDICINAL CHEMISTRY. *Educ:* Univ Havana, BS, 56; Univ Miami, MS, 62; Clarkson Col Technol, PhD(org chem), 64. *Prof Exp:* Asst prof chem, Univ Villanueva, Cuba, 56-60; instr, Clarkson Col Technol, 64-65; res chemist, Textile Fibers, E I du Pont de Nemours & Co, Inc Exp Sta, Del, 65-66; mem staff chem, NEng Inst, 66-73; asst prof chem, Univ Bridgeport, Conn, 73-75; sr res chemist, 75-77, sr label adminr environ health & safety, 77-81, MGR, CHEM HAZARD ASSESSMENT & COMMUN, STAUFFER CHEM CO, 81- *Mem:* Sigma Xi; Am Chem Soc; Sci Res Soc Am; Int Soc Heterocyclic Chem. *Res:* Synthesis; organic synthesis of specialty chemicals; regulatory classification of chemicals. *Mailing Add:* Stauffer Chem Co Legal Dept/Labeling Westport CT 06880

CASEY, CAROL A, b Chamberlain, SDak, Dec 10, 53. NITROGEN METABOLISM IN FISH. *Educ:* Augustana Col, Sioux Falls, SDak, BA, 76; Rice Univ, MS, 80, PhD(biol), 81. *Prof Exp:* Res asst, Rice Univ, 76-80; FEL BIOCHEM, UNIV MINN, 80- *Concurrent Pos:* Lab asst biol, Rice Univ, 76-78. *Res:* Obtaining information concerning nitrogen metabolism in fishes specifically on aspects of ammoniagenesis in teleosts as well as osmoregulation in elasmobranchs. *Mailing Add:* RR #1 Mitchell SD 57301

CASEY, CHARLES P, b St Louis, Mo, Jan 11, 42; m 68. ORGANIC CHEMISTRY. *Educ:* St Louis Univ, BS, 63; Mass Inst Technol, PhD(org chem), 68. *Prof Exp:* Fel org chem, Harvard Univ, 67-68; from asst prof to assoc prof, 68-77, PROF ORG CHEM, UNIV WIS, MADISON, 77- *Honors & Awards:* Eastman Kodak Award, Mass Inst Technol, 67. *Mem:* Am Chem Soc; The Chem Soc. *Res:* Mechanism of organometallic reactions; metal carbene complexes; CO reduction; homogeneous catalysis. *Mailing Add:* Dept Chem Univ Wis Madison WI 53706

CASEY, DANIEL EDWARD, b West Springfield, Mass, Jan 1, 47. PSYCHOPHARMACOLOGY, MOVEMENT DISORDERS. *Educ:* Univ Va, BA, 69, MD, 72. *Prof Exp:* Resident, Dept Psychiat, Brown Univ, 74-76; instr, 76-77, asst prof psychiat, 77-80, ASST PROF, DEPT NEUROL, ORE HEALTH SCI UNIV, 79-, ASSOC PROF, DEPT PSYCHIAT, 80- *Concurrent Pos:* Vis res scientist, Sct Hans Hosp, Denmark, 78; assoc investr, Vet Admin Res Career Develop Prog, 76-78, res assoc, 78-81, clin investr, 81-84; dir, Tardive Dyskinesia Clin, Ore Health Sci Univ, 76-; affil scientist, Ore Regional Primate Res Ctr, 80- *Mem:* Am Psychiat Asn; Col Int Neuropsychopharmacol; Soc Biol Psychiat; AAAS. *Res:* Biological psychiatry with emphasis on clinical drug trials and nonhuman primate models of tardive dyskinesia and schizophrenia; neurotransmitter mechanisms of dopamine, acetylcholine, gaba and endorphins. *Mailing Add:* 3250 Southwest Doschdale Dr Portland OR 97201

CASEY, HAROLD W, b Reuter, Mo, Sept 24, 32; m 55; c 2. VETERINARY PATHOLOGY. *Educ:* Univ Mo-Columbia, BS, 54, DVM, 57; Tulane Univ, MPH, 58; Univ Calif, Davis, PhD(comp path), 65; Am Col Vet Pathologists, dipl, 66. *Prof Exp:* US Air Force, 58-80, vet, Nouasseur AFB, 58-59, asst chief vet serv, Morocco, 59-61, res scientist biol div, Hanford Atomic Works, 61-63, chief anat path sect, 65-67, chief cytolpath br, 67-70, chief vet path br, Air Force Sch Aerospace Med, 70-71, chmn gen vet path br, 71-74, chmn dept vet path, Armed Forces Inst Path, 74-80; DIR PATH, TOXIGENICS, INC, 80- *Concurrent Pos:* mem, Fac Discussants, Charles Louis Davis, DVM Found, 72-, prog dir, Gross Path Div, 74-80, Adv Bd, 76-; head, WHO Int Ref Ctr Comp Path, 75-80; mem, Comt Histol Classification of Lab Animal Tumors, Inst Lab Animal Resources, Nat Res Coun, 75-79, Carnivores Subcomt, Comt on Animal Models for Res on Aging, 78-80. *Mem:* Int Acad Path; AAAS; Am Vet Med Asn; Am Col Vet Path. *Res:* Comparative pathology, including ultrastructure and the biological effects of ionizing radiation with special interest in non-human primate pathology. *Mailing Add:* Toxigenics Inc 1800 E Pershing Rd Decatur IL 62526

CASEY, HELEN LILES, b Greer, SC, Oct 5, 22; m 43; c 2. BACTERIOLOGY, IMMUNOLOGY. *Educ:* Univ SC, BS, 43; Fla State Univ, MS, 53; Purdue Univ, PhD(immunol), 58. *Prof Exp:* Lab technician bact, Shannon WTex Mem Hosp, San Angelo, Tex, 43-45; lab technician, Doctor's Lab, San Angelo, 45; med technician, Alvin Mem Hosp, Alvin, Tex, 46-47; head technician, Clin Lab, McLeod Infirmary, Florence, SC, 47-48; asst chief & med technician serol, Venereal Dis Res Lab, USPHS, Durham, NC, 48-50; med bacteriologist in chg venereal dis serol lab, Chamblee, Ga, 50-54, chief virus serol lab & supvry med bacteriologist, Viral & Rickettsial Dis Sect, Lab Br, Commun Dis Ctr, Atlanta, 57-61, chief immuno-serol unit, Virol Sect, 61-72, chief autoimmune dis lab, Viral Immunol Br, 72-77, CHIEF IMMUNOL, PERINATAL VIROL BR, LAB BUR, CTR DIS CONTROL, 78-; ASSOC CLIN PROF, DEPT MED, RHEUMATOL & IMMUNOL DIV, MED SCH, EMORY UNIV, 73- *Concurrent Pos:* Fel rheumatic dis, Southwestern Med Sch, Dallas, 71-72. *Mem:* Am Rheumatism Asn; AAAS; Sigma Xi; Am Soc Microbiol; Am Pub Health Asn. *Res:* Viral antigen-antibody reactions in relation to diagnostic work; possible viral etiology of rheumatoid arthritis; detection of various types immune-complexes in serum or body fluids of patients with rheumatic diseases; production of antigens for newer viruses; crude versus purified antigens for diagnosis of viral diseases. *Mailing Add:* Virol Div Ctr for Dis Control Atlanta GA 30333

CASEY, HORACE CRAIG, JR, b Houston, Tex, Dec 4, 34; m 60; c 2. ELECTRICAL ENGINEERING. *Educ:* Okla State Univ, BS, 57; Stanford Univ, MS, 59, PhD(elec eng), 64. *Prof Exp:* Res & develop engr electronics, Hewlett-Packard Co, 57-62; MEM TECH STAFF, BELL LABS, 64- *Mem:* Am Phys Soc. *Res:* Semiconductor materials and devices; electronic instrumentation. *Mailing Add:* Bell Labs Rm 1C 350 Murray Hill NJ 07974

CASEY, JAMES, b Tipperrary, Ireland, Sept 15, 49; div; c 1. MECHANICS OF CONTINUOUS MEDIA. *Educ:* Nat Univ Ireland, BE, 71; Univ Calif, Berkeley, PhD(eng sci), 80. *Prof Exp:* ASST PROF MECH ENG, UNIV HOUSTON, 80- *Concurrent Pos:* Lectr, Univ Calif, Berkeley, 80. *Mem:* Am Soc Mech Engrs. *Res:* Continuum mechanics; large strain elasticity and plasticity; directed media; continuum thermodynamics; history of mechanics. *Mailing Add:* Dept Mech Eng Univ Houston 4800 Calhoun Houston TX 77004

CASEY, JAMES PATRICK, b Syracuse, NY, Aug 5, 15; m 41; c 2. CHEMISTRY. *Educ:* Syracuse Univ, BS, 37; State Univ NY, MS, 47. *Prof Exp:* Head paper serv lab, A E Staley Mfg Co, 37-46; assoc prof pulp & paper mfg, State Univ NY, 46-51; dir tech serv, A E Staley Mfg Co, 51-56, dir res, 56-59; vpres res & develop, Union Starch & Ref Co, 59-67, vpres mkt & develop, Union Div, 67-70, vpres res, Marschall Div, 70-76, CONSULT, MILES LABS, 76- *Mem:* Am Chem Soc; fel Tech Asn Pulp & Paper Indust; Am Asn Cereal Chem; Indust Res Inst. *Res:* Paper; starch; textiles; adhesives; consumer products; foods; synthetic resin emulsions; vegetable oils; chemical technology; enzymes; food cultures; microbiology; fermentation; cereal processing. *Mailing Add:* PO Box 1598 Tyron NC 28782

CASEY, JOHN EDWARD, JR, b Cranston, RI, Dec 2, 30; m 56; c 2. ORGANIC CHEMISTRY. *Educ:* Providence Col, BS, 52, MS, 57. *Prof Exp:* Control chemist, Allied Chem Corp, 52; asst chem, Providence Col, 55-57; org chemist, Smith Kline & French Labs, 57-64; process chemist, Geigy Chem Corp, RI, 64-66; develop chemist, Rohm and Haas Co, 66-71; mgr process develop, Yardney Elec Corp, 71-76; mgr electrochem progs, GTE LABS, 76-77, mgr prod, Power Sources Ctr, 77-78; dir qual assurance, Altus Corp, 78-80, mgr eng admin, 80-81; OWNER & DIR, BRYANT BUR, MOUNTAIN VIEW, CALIF, 81- *Mem:* Am Chem Soc. *Res:* Correlation of chemical structure and biological activity; natural products; waste treatment; environmental chemistry; battery technology; electronic engineering. *Mailing Add:* 297 Barbara Ave Mountain View CA 94040

CASEY, KENNETH L, b Ogden, Utah, Apr 16, 35; m 58; c 3. NEUROPHYSIOLOGY, NEUROLOGY. *Educ:* Whitman Col, BA, 57; Univ Wash, MD, 61. *Prof Exp:* Intern, NY Hosp-Cornell Med Ctr, 61-62; res assoc psychol, McGill Univ, 64-66; from asst prof to assoc prof physiol, 66-74, resident neurol, 71-74, assoc prof physiol & neurophysiol, 74-75, assoc prof neurol, 75-78, PROF NEUROL, UNIV MICH, ANN ARBOR, 78-, PROF PHYSIOL, 75-; CHIEF, NEUROL SERV, VET ADMIN MED CTR, ANN ARBOR, 80- *Mem:* Am Neurol Asn; Int Asn Study Pain; Am Pain Soc; Soc Neurosci; Am Acad Neurol. *Res:* Neurophysiological correlates of behavior; neurophysiology of limbic system; somatosensory neurophysiology and neural mechanism of pain sensation. *Mailing Add:* Neurol Serv Vet Admin Med Ctr 2215 Fuller Rd Ann Arbor MI 48105

CASEY, RICHARD GEORGE, information science, see previous edition

CASH, DEWEY BYRON, b Wadley, Ala, Dec 22, 30; m 54; c 2. MATHEMATICAL ANALYSIS. *Educ:* Auburn Univ, BS, 55, MEd, 57, MS, 64. *Prof Exp:* Teacher high schs, Fla & Ga, 55-58; assoc prof, 58-76, PROF MATH, COLUMBUS COL, 76- *Mem:* Math Asn Am. *Res* Differential equations. *Mailing Add:* Dept Math Columbus Col Columbus GA 31907

CASH, FLOYD LEE, b Wichita Falls, Tex, July 14, 26; m 49; c 2. ELECTRICAL ENGINEERING. *Educ:* Univ Okla, BS, 46; Univ Tex, MS, 51, PhD(elec eng), 55. *Prof Exp:* Instr eng, Midwestern Univ, 47-50; instr elec eng, Univ Tex, 53-54; engr, Elgen Corp, 54-56, res engr, 56-58; dir tech training, Opers Dept, Lane-Wells, 58-59; actg chmn dept, 69-77, PROF ELEC ENG, UNIV TEX, ARLINGTON, 59-, CHMN DEPT, 77- *Concurrent Pos:* Consult, Saturn Electronics Corp, Tex, 61-; consult, Astronaut Div, Ling-Temco-Vought, Inc, 61-63, Aeronaut Div, 62-63 & Electronics Div, 62; consult, Signatrol Corp, Ill, 63- & Hunt Electronics Corp, Tex, 63-; ed, J Soc Prof Well Log Analysts, 62. *Mem:* Sr mem Inst Elec & Electronics Engrs; Soc Petrol Engrs; Am Inst Mining, Metall & Petrol Engrs; Soc Prof Well Log Analysts. *Res:* Electromagnetic wave propagation; antennas; radar cross section measurements; oil well log analysis; application of computers to geophysical measurements and interpretations of these measurements. *Mailing Add:* Dept of Elec Eng Univ of Tex Arlington TX 76010

CASH, ROWLEY VINCENT, b Waterville, NY, June 7, 17; m 51; c 3. HISTORY OF CHEMISTRY. *Educ:* Colgate Univ, AB, 39; Ind Univ, PhD(chem), 52. *Prof Exp:* Asst chem, Ind Univ, 39-42; head dept, Olivet Col, 42-51; from asst prof to prof, 57-81, res prof, 69-75, PROF EMER CHEM, CENT CONN STATE COL, 81- *Concurrent Pos:* Vis prof, North Adams State Col, 81. *Mem:* Fel AAAS; Hist Sci Soc; Am Chem Soc; fel Am Inst Chemists; Soc Hist Technol. *Res:* History of chemistry; contributions by Scandinavian chemists. *Mailing Add:* 119 Elizabeth Lane Mount Dora FL 32757

CASH, WILLIAM DAVIS, b Chesnee, SC, Feb 23, 30; m 61; c 3. BIOLOGICAL CHEMISTRY. *Educ:* Univ NC, BS, 51, PhD(pharmaceut chem), 54. *Prof Exp:* Res assoc biochem, Med Col, Cornell Univ, 54, from instr to assoc prof, 56-68; DIR BIOCHEM, CIBA-GEIGY CORP, 68- *Mem:* AAAS; Am Chem Soc; Am Soc Biol Chemists; NY Acad Sci. *Res:* Diabetes; prostaglandin biochemistry; platelet biochemistry; neurochemistry. *Mailing Add:* Ciba-Geigy Corp Ardsley NY 10502

CASHEL, MICHAEL, b Worthington, Minn, Feb 18, 37; m 62; c 3. BIOCHEMISTRY, GENETICS. *Educ:* Amherst Col, AB, 59; Western Reserve Univ, MD, 63; Univ Wash, PhD(genetics), 68. *Prof Exp:* HEAD, SECT MOLECULAR REGULATION, LAB MOLECULAR GENETICS, NAT INST CHILD HEALTH & HUMAN DEVELOP, 67- *Mem:* Am Soc Biol Chem. *Res:* Regulation of RNA synthesis; transcription specificity of RNA polymerase and nucleotide synthesis; protein synthesis; metabolic dormancy and cell physiology. *Mailing Add:* Molecular Genetics Bldg 6 Rm 335 Nat Inst Child Health Bethesda MD 20205

CASHIN, KENNETH D(ELBERT), b Lowell, Mass, May 10, 21; m 44; c 3. CHEMICAL ENGINEERING. *Educ:* Worcester Polytech Inst, BS, 47, MS, 48; Rensselaer Polytech Inst, PhD, 55. *Prof Exp:* From asst prof to assoc prof, 48-63, assoc dean, Eng Sch, 78-81, PROF CHEM ENG, UNIV MASS, 81- *Concurrent Pos:* Consult, Army Chem Corps, 56-57; NSF grants, 57-58, 75-77 & 79-81; adv to establish dept chem eng, Col Petrol & Minerals, Dhahran, Saudi Arabia, 68-70. *Mem:* Am Chem Soc; Am Inst Chem Engrs; Am Soc Eng Educ; Sigma Xi. *Res:* Fluidization of solid particles in gas streams; heat transfer by radiation; spectroscopic studies in fluorine supported flames and other combustion phenomena. *Mailing Add:* Dept of Chem Eng Univ of Mass Amherst MA 01003

CASHION, PETER JOSEPH, b Boston, Mass, June 26, 40; m 67; c 4. BIOCHEMISTRY. *Educ:* Boston Col, BSc, 64; Tufts Univ, PhD(biochem), 69. *Prof Exp:* Fel biochem, Univ Wis, 69-70; fel, Mass Inst Technol, 70-72; asst prof, 72-75, ASSOC PROF BIOCHEM, UNIV NB, 75- *Mem:* Am Chem Soc; Can Biochem Soc. *Res:* Nucleic acid chemistry. *Mailing Add:* 821 Hansom St Fredericton Can

CASHWELL, EDMOND DARRELL, b Groveland, Fla, Feb 14, 20; m 45; c 1. APPLIED MATHEMATICS. *Educ:* Univ Wis, PhD(math), 49. *Prof Exp:* Jr physicist, AEC, Metal Lab, Univ Chicago, 44-45 & Clinton Labs, 45-46; instr math, Univ Wis, 49 & Ohio State Univ, 49-51; MEM STAFF MATH, LOS ALAMOS SCI LAB, 51- *Mem:* Am Math Soc; Am Nuclear Soc. *Res:* The Monte Carlo method, especially as applied to transport problems in physics; differential equations; number theory; probability theory and random processes. *Mailing Add:* 1426 43rd St Los Alamos NM 87544

CASIDA, JOHN EDWARD, b Phoenix, Ariz, Dec 22, 29; m 56; c 2. TOXICOLOGY. *Educ:* Univ Wis, BS, 51, MS, 52, PhD(entom, biochem), 54. *Prof Exp:* Res asst, Univ Wis, 46-53; med entomologist, Camp Detrick, Md, 53; from asst prof to prof entom, Univ Wis, 54-63; PROF ENTOM & INSECT TOXICOLOGIST, UNIV CALIF, BERKELEY, 64- *Concurrent Pos:* Haight travel fel, 58-59; Guggenheim fel, 70-71; int res award pesticide chem, Am Chem Soc, 70. *Honors & Awards:* Medal, Seventh Int Cong Plant Protection, Paris, 70. *Mem:* AAAS; Am Chem Soc; Entom Soc Am. *Res:* Pesticide chemistry; comparative biochemistry. *Mailing Add:* Div of Entom Univ of Calif Berkeley CA 94720

CASIDA, LESTER EARL, JR, b Columbia, Mo, Aug 25, 28; m 53; c 2. MICROBIOLOGY, ECOLOGY. *Educ:* Univ Wis, BS, 50, MS, 51, PhD(bact), 53. *Prof Exp:* Bacteriologist, Abbott Labs, 51 & Pabst Labs, 53-54; res biochemist, Charles Pfizer & Co, Inc, 54-57; asst prof bact, 57-62, assoc prof microbiol, 62-66, PROF MICROBIOL, PA STATE UNIV, 66- *Mem:* Am Soc Microbiol; Am Chem Soc; Brit Soc Gen Microbiol. *Res:* Microbial physiology and ecology; industrial microbiology. *Mailing Add:* Dept of Microbiol S-101 Frear Bldg Pa State Univ University Park PA 16802

CASILLAS, EDMUND RENE, b Westwood, Calif, Nov 24, 38; m 62; c 2. BIOCHEMISTRY. *Educ:* Calif State Univ, BA, 63; Ore State Univ, PhD(biochem), 68. *Prof Exp:* Res assoc biochem, Ore State Univ, 64-68; fel, Ore Regional Primate Res Ctr, 69-71, res scientist reproductive physiol, 71-76; ASSOC PROF CHEM, NMEX STATE UNIV, 76- *Concurrent Pos:* Mem, Pop Res Comt, Nat Inst Child Health & Human Develop, 79-83. *Mem:* Am Soc Biol Chemists; Soc Study Reproduction; Am Chem Soc; Soc Study Fertil; Sigma Xi. *Res:* Reproductive processes in male animal with emphasis on spermatozoan maturation in the epididymis and regulatory mechanisms involved in spermatozoa physiology and metabolism. *Mailing Add:* Dept of Chem NMex State Univ Box 3C Las Cruces NM 88003

CASJENS, SHERWOOD REID, b Kesley, Iowa, July 10, 45; m 72. BIOCHEMISTRY. *Educ:* Mich State Univ, BS & MS, 67; Stanford Univ, PhD(biochem), 72. *Prof Exp:* ASSOC PROF, DEPT CELLULAR, VIRAL & MOLECULAR BIOL, SCH MED, UNIV UTAH, 74- *Concurrent Pos:* NIH res grant, 75-82, NSF res grant, 79-84. *Res:* Structure and assembly of viruses; genetics and biochemistry of bacteriophage P22 morphogenesis. *Mailing Add:* Dept Cellular Viral & Molecular Biol Univ Utah Med Ctr Salt Lake City UT 84132

CASKEY, ALBERT LEROY, b Wichita, Kans, Nov 26, 31; m 57; c 2. ANALYTICAL CHEMISTRY. *Educ:* Southeast Mo State Col, BS, 53; Iowa State Col, MS, 55, PhD(anal chem), 61. *Prof Exp:* Asst prof chem, Southeast Mo State Col, 58-61, assoc prof, 61-64; ASSOC PROF CHEM, SOUTHERN ILL UNIV, CARBONDALE, 64- *Concurrent Pos:* Chem consult & tech witness legal proc, 60-; NSF grants, 63-77; Off Water Resources Res grants, 65-75. *Mem:* AAAS; Am Chem Soc; Soc Appl Spectros. *Res:* Chelation systems; substituent effects in chelation; water pollution; spectrophotometric methods; ion exchange; inorganic reactions; biological effects of trace substances. *Mailing Add:* Dept of Chem Southern Ill Univ Carbondale IL 62901

CASKEY, CHARLES (DIRXON), JR, b Fannin Co, Tex, Oct 26, 07; m 31; c 3. ANIMAL NUTRITION. *Educ:* Okla Agr & Mech Col, BS, 29; Cornell Univ, PhD, 40. *Prof Exp:* Lab asst agr chem, Okla Agr & Mech Col, 29; chief chemist, State Bd Agr, Okla, 29-37; dir southern states labs, 40-43, V PRES IN CHARGE RES, CO-OP MILLS, INC, 43- *Mem:* Am Chem Soc; Poultry Sci Asn; Am Dairy Sci Asn. *Res:* Manganese requirements in poultry. *Mailing Add:* 701 Morningside Dr Towson MD 21204

CASKEY, CHARLES THOMAS, b Lancaster, SC, Sept 22, 38; m 60; c 2. HUMAN GENETICS. *Educ:* Duke Univ, MD, 63; Am Bd Internal Med, dipl, 77. *Prof Exp:* Intern & resident, Sch Med, Duke Univ, 63-65; res assoc, Nat Heart & Lung Inst, 65-67, sr investr, 65-70, head med genetics, 70-71; HEAD MED GENETICS, BAYLOR COL MED, 71- *Concurrent Pos:* Howard Hughes investr, Baylor Col Med, 71. *Mem:* Am Soc Genetics; Am Soc Biol Chem; Fedn Am Socs Exp Biol; Am Soc Clin Invest. *Res:* The mechanism of polypeptide chain determination; somatic cell genetics, inborn error of metabolism and medical genetics. *Mailing Add:* Baylor Col of Med 1200 Moursund Ave Houston TX 77030

CASKEY, GEORGE R, JR, b Chicago, Ill, Feb 15, 28; m 52; c 2. MATERIALS SCIENCE. *Educ:* Univ Ill, BS, 50; Mass Inst Technol, SM, 52, PhD(mat sci), 69. *Prof Exp:* Res scientist, 52-64 & 68-75, STAFF METALLURGIST, SAVANNAH RIVER LAB, E I DU PONT DE NEMOURS & CO, 75- *Concurrent Pos:* Vis prof mats eng, Va Polytech, 81. *Mem:* Metall Soc; Am Inst Mining, Metall & Petrol Engrs. *Res:* Alloy theory and electronic structure; radiation damage in reactor materials; physical metallurgy of uranium; hydrogen solution and transport in metals; hydrogen damage and fracture. *Mailing Add:* Savannah River Lab E I du Pont de Nemours & Co Inc Aiken SC 29801

CASKEY, JAMES EDWARD, JR, b Heath Springs, SC, Mar 13, 18; m 42; c 2. METEOROLOGY, SCIENCE COMMUNICATIONS. *Educ:* Furman Univ, BS, 39; Duke Univ, MA, 40; Univ Chicago, cert prof meteorol, 42. *Prof Exp:* Observer, US Weather Bur, Charleston, SC, 41, meteorologist, Washington, DC, 46; asst prof physics, Furman Univ, 46-48; meteorologist, US Weather Bur, Washington, DC, 48-65; chief sci info & doc, Environ Sci Serv Admin, Nat Oceanog & Atmospheric Admin, Rockville, Md, 66-70, dir, Environ Sci Info Ctr, 71-74; DIR PUBL & TECH ED, AM METEOROL SOC, 74- *Concurrent Pos:* Ed, Monthly Weather Rev, 48-68; US mem comn bibliog & publ, World Meteorol Orgn, 54-59. *Honors & Awards:* Silver Medal, Dept Com, 58. *Mem:* AAAS; Am Meteorol Soc; Am Geophys Union; Counc Eng & Sci Soc Execs. *Res:* Synoptic and dynamic meteorology; climatology and forecasting. *Mailing Add:* 21 Flume Rd Magnolia MA 01930

CASKEY, JERRY ALLAN, b Galion, Ohio, Sept 8, 38; m 63; c 3. CHEMICAL ENGINEERING. *Educ:* Ohio Univ BS, 61; Clemson Univ, MS, 63, PhD(chem eng), 65. *Prof Exp:* Chem engr, Dow Chem Co, 65-67, res engr, 67; asst prof chem eng, Va Polytech Inst & State Univ, 67-72; assoc prof, 73-78, PROF CHEM ENG, ROSE-HULMAN INST TECHNOL, 78- *Concurrent Pos:* vis res prof, Israel Inst Tech, 72. *Mem:* Am Inst Chem Engrs; Am Soc Eng Educ; Int Solar Energy Soc. *Res:* Solar heating technology; water resources engineering. *Mailing Add:* Dept Chem Eng Rose-Hulman Inst 5500 Wabash Ave Terre Haute IN 47803

CASLER, DAVID ROBERT, b Norwich, NY, May 25, 20; m 42; c 2. PHARMACEUTICS. *Educ:* Union Col, NY, BS, 41. *Prof Exp:* Apprentice, Lathrop's Pharm, 41-42, pharmacist, 42, 46-47; from res asst to res assoc, 47-61, assoc mem, 61-63, res pharmacist, 63-74, sr res pharmacist, 74-79, GROUP LEADER, CLIN PACKAGING & PROD DEVELOP PILOT LAB, STERLING-WINTHROP RES INST, 64-, RAW MAT MGR, 79-, CLIN SUPPLIES COORDR, 81- *Concurrent Pos:* Chmn flavor test panel, Sterling-Winthrop Res Inst, 59-67, div narcotics officer, 81- *Mem:* Am Pharmaceut Asn; Acad Pharm Sci. *Res:* Flavors; flavor test panel methodology; perfumery; liquid processing and processing equipment; surfactants and emulsions; packaging equipment. *Mailing Add:* Prod Develop Div Sterling-Winthrop Res Inst Rensselaer NY 12144

CASLER, MICHAEL DARWIN, b Green Bay, Wis, Oct 31, 54; m 77. GRASS BREEDING, QUANTITATIVE GENETICS. *Educ:* Univ Ill, Urbana, BS, 76; Univ Minn, MS, 79, PhD(plant breeding), 80. *Prof Exp:* ASST PROF AGRON, UNIV WIS-MADISON, 80- *Mem:* Am Soc Agron; Crop Sci Soc Am. *Res:* Breeding cool-season grasses for improved nutritive value and production; utilizing maximum heterozygosity in perennial grasses; evaluating selection systems for improving varietal performance; improving adapted cool-season grass varieties. *Mailing Add:* Dept Agron Univ Wis 1575 Linden Dr Madison WI 53706

CASO, LOUIS VICTOR, b Union City, NJ, July 6, 24. HISTOLOGY, IMMUNOLOGY. *Educ:* Manhattan Col, BS, 47; Columbia Univ, AM, 49; Rutgers Univ, BS, 54, PhD(zool), 58. *Prof Exp:* Instr biol sci, Col Pharm, Rutgers Univ, 49-54, asst zool, Univ, 55-58; asst res prof pharmacol, Sch Med, George Washington Univ, 59-60; asst prof anat, Col Med, Ohio State Univ, 61-64; asst prof histol, 64-68, ASSOC PROF ANAT SCI, SCH DENT, TEMPLE UNIV, PA, 68- *Concurrent Pos:* NIH grant, 62-63; Am Cancer Soc grants, 63-64 & 73-74. *Mem:* Am Asn Anat; NY Acad Sci; Tissue Cult Asn. *Res:* Effects of viral hemagglutination on human erythrocyte antigens; effects of homologous antiserum on cell growth and morphology; immunology of cancer; action of phytohemagglutinin and neuraminidase on cell growth; antigenicity; cytochemistry; histochemistry and function of thymus gland. *Mailing Add:* Sch of Dent Temple Univ Philadelphia PA 19140

CASO, MARGUERITE MIRIAM, b Union City, NJ, Mar 2, 19. CHEMISTRY. *Educ:* Col Mt St Vincent, AB, 40; Fordham Univ, MS, 55, PhD(chem), 58. *Prof Exp:* Chemist, Colgate-Palmolive-Peet Co, 41-42; chemist, Nat Starch Prod Co, 42-44; teacher sci, Holy Cross Acad, New York, 46-53; lectr chem, Fordham Univ, 54-55; from instr to assoc prof chem, Col Mt St Vincent, 55-77; vis assoc prof, 77-80, ASSOC PROF CHEM, ST JOSEPH'S COL, 80- *Concurrent Pos:* Dir undergrad res prog, Nat Sci Found, 62- *Mem:* AAAS; Am Chem Soc. *Res:* Analytical and inorganic chemistry; nonaqueous solution; infrared spectroscopy; complexes. *Mailing Add:* Dept of Chem St Joseph's Col Philadelphia PA 19131

CASOLA, ARMAND RALPH, b Newark, NJ, Feb 21, 18; m 54; c 5. PHARMACEUTICAL CHEMISTRY, MEDICINAL CHEMISTRY. *Educ:* City Col NY, BS, 40; Fordham Univ, MS, 50, PhD(org chem), 56. *Prof Exp:* Res chemist, Am Cyanamid Co, 54-59; sr scientist, Strasenburgh Labs, 59-65;

chemist, Div New Drugs, Bur Med, 65-66, supvry chemist, Div Dent & Surg Adjs, Off New Drugs, 66-70, chief chemist, Bur Drugs, 70-72, SUPVRY CHEMIST, DIV ANTI INFECTIVE DRUG PRODS, BUR DRUGS, FOOD & DRUG ADMIN, 72- *Mem:* AAAS; Am Chem Soc; NY Acad Sci; Acad Pharmaceut Sci; Sigma Xi. *Res:* Synthetic organic chemistry; intermediates; chemotherapeutics; analgesics; hypotensives. *Mailing Add:* Food & Drug Admin 5600 Fishers Lane Rockville MD 20857

CASON, JAMES, JR, b Murfreesboro, Tenn, Aug 30, 12; m 35; c 2. ORGANIC CHEMISTRY. *Educ:* Vanderbilt Univ, AB, 34; Univ Calif, MS, 35; Yale Univ, PhD(org chem), 38. *Prof Exp:* Asst & Nat Cancer Inst fel, Harvard Univ, 38-40; instr org chem, DePauw Univ, 40-41; from instr to asst prof, Vanderbilt Univ, 41-45; from asst prof to assoc prof, 45-52, PROF ORG CHEM, UNIV CALIF, BERKELEY, 52- *Mem:* Am Chem Soc; Sigma Xi. *Res:* Structure and synthesis of natural products; branched-chain acids; cyclic reaction intermediates. *Mailing Add:* Dept Chem Univ Calif Berkeley CA 94720

CASON, JAMES LEE, b Shongaloo, La, Feb 22, 22; m 46; c 2. DAIRY HUSBANDRY, NUTRITION. *Educ:* La Polytech Inst, BS, 48; Mich State Univ, MS, 50; NC State Col, PhD(dairy husb, nutrit), 56. *Prof Exp:* Actg asst prof dairy husb, La Polytech Inst, 49; instr, Univ Ark, 50-53, asst prof, 53-54; asst prof, Rutgers Univ, 56-59; assoc prof, Univ Md, 59-68, prof, 68-70; PROF AGR & HEAD DEPT, COL PURE & APPL SCI, NORTHEAST LA UNIV, 69- *Mem:* Am Soc Animal Sci; Biomet Soc; Am Dairy Sci Asn. *Res:* Dairy cattle nutrition, particularly forage utilization. *Mailing Add:* Dept of Agr Northeast La Univ Monroe LA 71209

CASON, NEAL M, b Chicago, Ill, July 26, 38; c 5. HIGH ENERGY PHYSICS. *Educ:* Ripon Col, AB, 59; Univ Wis, MS, 61, PhD(physics), 64. *Prof Exp:* Res assoc high energy physics, Univ Wis, 64-65; from instr to assoc prof, 65-76, PROF PHYSICS, UNIV NOTRE DAME, 76- *Concurrent Pos:* Woodrow Wilson fel. *Mem:* Am Phys Soc. *Res:* Multi-particle production at high energy; associated production of strange particles; meson spectroscopy. *Mailing Add:* Dept of Physics Univ of Notre Dame Notre Dame IN 46556

CASORSO, DONALD ROY, pathology, see previous edition

CASPARI, ERNST WOLFGANG, b Berlin, Ger, Oct 24, 09; nat US; m 38. DEVELOPMENTAL GENETICS, BEHAVIORAL GENETICS. *Educ:* Univ Gottingen, PhD(zool), 33; Wesleyan Univ, MA,50. *Prof Exp:* Asst zool, Univ Gottingen, 33-35; asst microbiol, Univ Istanbul, 35-38; fel biol, Lafayette Col, 38-41, asst prof, 41-44; asst prof zool, Univ Rochester, 44-45, res assoc, 45-46; assoc prof biol, Wesleyan Univ, 46-47; res assoc genetics, Carnegie Inst Washington, NY, 47-49; prof biol, Wesleyan Univ, 49-60; prof, 60-75, chmn dept, 60-65, EMER PROF BIOL, UNIV ROCHESTER, 75- *Concurrent Pos:* Ctr Advan Study Behav Sci fel, Stanford Univ, 56-57 & 65-66; ed, Advan Genetics, 60- & Genetics, 68-72; guest prof, Inst Genetics, Univ Giessen, Ger, 75-76; Alexander von Humboldt Found US sr scientist award, 81-82. *Honors & Awards:* Dobzhavsky Mem Award, Res Behav Genetics. *Mem:* Am Soc Naturalists (vpres, 61); Genetics Soc Am (treas, 51-53, vpres, 65, pres, 66); fel Am Acad Arts & Sci; Behav Genetics Asn; hon mem Am Soc Naturalists. *Res:* Physiological genetics; genetics of behavior; genetic transformation in Ephestia; effect of base analogues on development. *Mailing Add:* Dept Biol Univ Rochester Rochester NY 14627

CASPARI, MAX EDWARD, b Frankfurt-on-Main, Ger, Mar 17, 23; nat US; m 51; c 3. SOLID STATE PHYSICS. *Educ:* Wesleyan Univ, AB, 48; Mass Inst Technol, PhD(physics), 54. *Prof Exp:* Asst insulation res lab, Mass Inst Technol, 48-54; from instr to assoc prof, 54-64, PROF PHYSICS, UNIV PA, 64- *Concurrent Pos:* Chmn dept physics, Univ Pa, 68-73. *Mem:* Am Phys Soc. *Res:* Hyperfine interactions; perturbed angular correlations; magnetism; surfaces. *Mailing Add:* 1520 Spruce St Philadelphia PA 19102

CASPARY, DONALD M, b New York, NY, Sept 1, 43; m 67; c 2. AUDITORY NEUROSCIENCE, SENSORY NEUROBIOLOGY. *Educ:* Univ Wis, BA, 65; Syracuse Univ, MS, 68; New York Univ, PhD(biol), 71. *Prof Exp:* Fel neurobiol, Nat Inst Neurol & Commun Disorders & Stroke, State Univ NY, Albany, 71-72; asst prof neurobiol, 73-76, ASSOC PROF PHARMACOL, SCH MED, SOUTHERN ILL UNIV, 76-, ASSOC PROF OTOLARYNGOL, DEPT SURG, 82- *Concurrent Pos:* Consult, Callier Hearing & Speech Ctr, Dallas, Tex, 73-76; NIH prin investr & co-investr, Nat Inst Neurol & Commun Disorders & Stroke, 79-82. *Mem:* Acoust Soc Am; Soc Neurosci; AAAS; Sigma Xi; Asn Res Otol. *Mailing Add:* Dept Pharmacol Sch Med Southern Ill Univ PO Box 3926 Springfield IL 62708

CASPE, SAUL, b New York, NY, Mar 1, 05; m; c 2. BIOCHEMISTRY. *Educ:* Polytech Inst Brooklyn, BS, 30. *Prof Exp:* Asst nutrit chemist, Col Physicians & Surgeons, Columbia Univ, 21-23; develop chemist, H A Metz Labs, NY, 24-30; res engr & fel, Casa Biochemica, France, 30-31; consult chemist, 32-35; assoc dir res, Philip Morris & Co, 35-55; res biochemist, Jewish Mem Hosp, NY, 58-60; CONSULT RES BIOCHEMIST, 60- *Concurrent Pos:* Field interviewer, Lea-Mendota Res Group, 66-75, field rep, Int Med Serv Am, 75; consult chemist, Lab Indust Hyg, 67-; assoc Hodgkins dis study, St Vincent's Hosp, NY; vol, Neo-Guardian Placement Proj, 75-79. *Mem:* Am Chem Soc; fel Am Inst Chem. *Res:* Enzyme chemistry and physiology; creatine metabolism; organic synthesis of tertiary amines; sulphur drugs; biologicals of value in wound healing. *Mailing Add:* PO Box 608 Grand Cent Sta New York NY 10017

CASPER, BARRY MICHAEL, b Knoxville, Tenn, Jan 21, 39; m 61. THEORETICAL PHYSICS. *Educ:* Swarthmore Col, BA, 60; Cornell Univ, PhD(theoret physics), 66. *Prof Exp:* Consult, Inst Defense Anal, 62-63; instr physics, Cornell Univ, 65-66; from asst prof to assoc prof, 66-77, PROF PHYSICS, CARLETON COL, 77- *Concurrent Pos:* Nat coun mem, Fedn Am Scientist, 71-75; chmn, Forum Physics & Soc, Am Phys Soc, 74; res fel, Prog Sci & Int Affairs, Harvard Univ, 75-76; humanities fel, Rockefellar Found, 75-76; NSF fel, Sci Appl to Societal Probs, 76-77. *Mem:* Am Phys Soc; Am Asn Physics Teachers. *Res:* Elementary particle research; arms control research; scientist and public policy; history of science. *Mailing Add:* Dept of Physics Carleton Col Northfield MN 55057

CASPER, JOHN MATTHEW, b Middletown, Pa, Jan 28, 46; m 71; c 1. PHYSICAL CHEMISTRY. *Educ:* Univ Scranton, BS, 67; Univ SC, PhD(chem), 71. *Prof Exp:* Res assoc chem, Univ Md, 71-73; asst prof chem, Polytech Inst NY, 73-80; MEM STAFF, IBM INSTRUMENTS, INC, 80- *Concurrent Pos:* Consult, Church & Dwight Co, Inc, 75- *Mem:* Am Chem Soc; Coblentz Soc; Soc Appl Spectros. *Res:* Application of vibrational spectroscopy to studies of chemical structure and bonding. *Mailing Add:* IBM Instruments Inc PO Box 332 Danbury CT 06810

CASPERS, HORST J, b Reitsch, Ger, Mar 3, 25; m 61. PHYSICAL CHEMISTRY, ANALYTICAL CHEMISTRY. *Educ:* Univ Munich, dipl, 55, Dr rer nat(phys chem), 58. *Prof Exp:* Res scientist spectros, Siemens & Halske Res Labs, 59-61; supvr anal chem, Res Div, Am Stand Corp, NB, 61-68; mgr anal res sect, 68-71, mgr inorg res sect, 71-74, MGR ANAL TECH SUPPORT SECT, STAUFFER CHEMS, 75- *Mem:* Am Chem Soc; Soc Ger Chem. *Res:* Kinetic studies of donor-acceptor complexes of polymers with Friedel-Crafts catalysts; investigation of polarized molecules by ultraviolet spectroscopy; low temperature infrared spectroscopy of semiconductor materials; research on clay-organic compounds. *Mailing Add:* 12 Wildwood Rd Saddle River NJ 07458

CASPERS, HUBERT HENRI, b Oostkamp, Belg, June 5, 29; US citizen; m 59; c 2. SOLID STATE PHYSICS, SPECTROSCOPY. *Educ:* Univ Calif, Los Angeles, BA, 53, MA, 58, PhD(spectros), 62. *Prof Exp:* RES PHYSICIST & HEAD LUMINESCENT MAT SECT, US NAVAL ELECTRONICS LAB CTR, SAN DIEGO, 62- *Mem:* Am Phys Soc. *Res:* Rare earth solid state spectroscopy; infrared and Raman spectroscopy on solids. *Mailing Add:* 4744 70th St La Mesa CA 92041

CASPERSON, LEE WENDEL, b Portland, Ore; m 74; c 2. QUANTUM ELECTRONICS, LASER PHYSICS. *Educ:* Mass Inst Technol, BS, 66; Calif Inst Technol, MS, 67, PhD(elec eng & physics), 71. *Prof Exp:* Asst prof, 71-76, assoc prof, 76-80, PROF ELEC ENG, UNIV CALIF, LOS ANGELES, 80- *Concurrent Pos:* Consult, Northrop Res & Technol Ctr, 73-78, TRW, 76-; vis prof, Dept Physics, Univ Auckland, NZ, 81. *Mem:* Sigma Xi; Optical Soc Am; Inst Elec & Electronic Engrs. *Res:* Quamtum electronics; laser physics; beam propagation; optical resonators; waveguides; scattering; laser media; laser instabilities. *Mailing Add:* 7731-D Boetler Hall Sch Eng & Appl Sci Univ Calif Los Angeles CA 90024

CASPI, ELIAHU, b Warsaw, Poland, June 10, 13; US citizen; m 48; c 1. ORGANIC CHEMISTRY, BIOCHEMISTRY. *Educ:* Clark Univ, PhD(org chem), 55. *Prof Exp:* Scientist, Anal Chem, Israel Stand Inst, 43-50; from staff res scientist to sr res scientist, 51-70, PRIN RES SCIENTIST, WORCESTER FOUND EXP BIOL, 71- *Concurrent Pos:* US Pub Health Serv res career prog award, 63-72. *Mem:* Fel AAAS; Am Chem Soc; Am Soc Biol Chemists; Royal Soc Chem; Am Heart Asn. *Res:* Bioorganic chemistry of natural products; biosynthesis and metabolism of hormones; biosynthesis of sterols in relation to cancer. *Mailing Add:* Worcester Found for Exp Biol Shrewsbury MA 01545

CASS, CAROL E, b Lexington, Ky, Oct 18, 42; m 66. CELL BIOLOGY, BIOCHEMISTRY. *Educ:* Univ Okla, BS, 63, MS, 65; Univ Calif, Berkeley, PhD(cell biol), 71. *Prof Exp:* Fel cancer chemother, 70-73, asst prof, 74-80, ASSOC PROF BIOCHEM, CANCER RES UNIT, UNIV ALTA, 80- *Mem:* Can Biochem Soc; Can Soc Cell Biol; Am Asn Cancer Res; Tissue Cult Asn; NY Acad Sci. *Res:* Nucleoside transport in mammalian cells, biochemical and biological mechanisms of anti-neoplastic agents; mechanisms of resistance to anti-neoplastic agents. *Mailing Add:* Cancer Res Unit McEachern Lab Univ of Alta Edmonton AB T6G 2E8 Can

CASS, DAVID D, b Indianapolis, Ind, Sept 1, 38; m 66. PLANT EMBRYOLOGY. *Educ:* Butler Univ, BS, 61; Univ Okla, PhD(bot), 67. *Prof Exp:* US Pub Health Serv fel, Univ Calif, Berkeley, 66-68, lectr biol, 68-69; from asst prof to assoc prof, 69-80, PROF BOT, UNIV ALTA, 80-, CHMN DEPT, 79- *Mem:* Can Bot Asn (secy, 78-80); Int Soc Plant Morphologists; Soc Econ Bot; Bot Soc Am. *Res:* Vascular plant embryology, especially fertilization mechanisms and early embryo and pollen tube development; determining roles of embryo sac transfer cells; histochemistry; electron microscopy. *Mailing Add:* Dept of Bot Univ of Alta Edmonton AB T6G 2E9 Can

CASS, GLEN R, b Pasadena, Calif, Apr 18, 47; m 76; c 1. AIR POLLUTION CONTROL, AEROSOL MECHANICS. *Educ:* Univ Southern Calif, BS, 69; Stanford Univ, MS, 70; Calif Inst Technol, PhD(environ eng), 78. *Prof Exp:* Engr, Naval Undersea Ctr, Pasadena, 69; commissioned officer, US Pub Health Serv, 70-73; sr res fel & instr, 78-79, ASST PROF ENVIRON ENG, CALIF INST TECHNOL, 79- *Concurrent Pos:* consult, S Coast Air Quality Mgt Dist, 78; mem res screening comt, Calif Air Resources Bd, 80- *Mem:* Sigma Xi; NY Acad Sci. *Res:* Air pollution control strategy design; aerosol mechanics; air pollution source characteristics and control technology; visibility; fluid mechanics applied to air quality problems; environmental economics. *Mailing Add:* Environ Eng Sci Dept Calif Inst Tech Pasadena CA 91125

CASS, THOMAS ROBERT, b San Francisco, Calif, Nov 25, 36; m 59; c 2. MATERIALS SCIENCE. *Educ:* Univ Calif, Berkeley, BS, 58, MS, 61, PhD(metall), 66. *Prof Exp:* NSF fel metall, Univ Paris, Orsay, 65-66; res scientist, Dept Mat Res, Orlando Div, Martin Aerospace Group, Martin-Marietta Corp, Fla, 66-68, chief adv mat res & develop, 68-70; mem res staff, Fairchild Res & Develop Lab, Fairchild Camera & Instrument Corp, 70-71; mem tech staff, Hewlett-Packard Solid State Lab, 71-78, MEM TECH STAFF, HEWLETT-PACKARD INTEGRATED CIRCUIT LAB, 78- *Concurrent Pos:* vis prof, Univ Estadual de Campinas, Brazil, 77. *Mem:* Am Phys Soc; Electron Micros Soc Am. *Res:* Characterization of electronic materials and devices; transmission and scanning electron microscopy; x-ray double crystal diffractometry; x-ray topography; diffraction contrast theory; ion implantation into semiconductors. *Mailing Add:* Hewlett-Packard Labs 3500 Deer Creek Rd Palo Alto CA 94304

CASSADY, GEORGE, b Los Angeles, Calif, Aug 9, 34; m 57; c 3. MEDICINE, PEDIATRICS. *Educ:* Duke Univ, MD, 58. *Prof Exp:* Intern pediat, Duke Univ Med Ctr, 58-59, resident pediat, 60; clin assoc, Med Invest & Genetic Unit, Nat Inst Dent Res, 60-62; sr resident pediat, Children's Hosp Med Ctr, Boston, Mass, 62-63; from asst prof to assoc prof pediat, 64-70, PROF PEDIAT, MED CTR, UNIV ALA, BIRMINGHAM, 70-, DIR NEWBORN DIV, 65-, ASSOC PROF OBSTET & GYNEC, 77- *Concurrent Pos:* Fel pediat cardiol, Duke Hosp, Durham, NC, 59; teaching fel, Harvard Med Sch, 62-63; res fel newborn physiol, Boston Lying-In Hosp & Harvard Med Sch, 63-64; mem bd cert, Am Acad Pediat; chmn maternal & child health comt, State Ala. *Mem:* Am Soc Human Genetics; fel Am Acad Pediat; Soc Pediat Res; Am Fedn Clin Res; NY Acad Sci. *Mailing Add:* Dept of Pediat Univ of Ala Birmingham AL 35294

CASSADY, JOHN MAC, b Vincennes, Ind, Aug 16, 38; m 59; c 5. ORGANIC CHEMISTRY, MEDICINAL CHEMISTRY. *Educ:* DePauw Univ, BA, 60; Case Western Reserve Univ, MS, 62, PhD(org chem), 64. *Prof Exp:* Res assoc, Case Western Reserve Univ, 64-65; NIH fel, Univ Wis, 65-66; from asst prof to assoc prof, 66-74, assoc dept head, 74-80, PROF MED CHEM & HEAD DEPT, SCH PHARM & PHARMACOL SCI, PRUDUE UNIV, 80- *Mem:* AAAS; Am Chem Soc; Royal Soc Chem; fel Acad Pharmaceut Sci; Am Soc Pharmacog. *Res:* Isolation and structure elucidation of tumor inhibitors from plants; synthesis of potential tumor inhibitors including pyrimidines, xanthones, acridonea and anthracyclinenes; synthesis of dopaminergic agents. *Mailing Add:* Dept of Med Chem Sch of Pharm Purdue Univ West Lafayette IN 47907

CASSADY, PHILIP EARL, fluid dynamics, applied physics, see previous edition

CASSAN, STANLEY MORRIS, b Montreal, Que, Nov 3, 36; US citizen; m 61. PULMONARY DISEASES, INTERNAL MEDICINE. *Educ:* McGill Univ, BSc, 58, MD CM, 62; Univ Minn, PhD(pulmonary med, path), 70. *Prof Exp:* NIH fel pulmonary med, Med Ctr, Stanford Univ, 71-72; adj assoc prof med & chief respiratory intensive care unit, Med Ctr, 72-79, CLIN ASSOC PROF MED, UNIV CALIF, LOS ANGELES, 80- *Honors & Awards:* Mayer Res Award, Am Col Chest Physicians, 70. *Mem:* fel Am Col Chest Physicians; fel Am Col Physicians; Am Lung Asn. *Res:* Morphometry in pulmonary disease; glycolysis and redox ratio in human erythrocytes; pollutants and pulmonary carcinoma. *Mailing Add:* Suite 665W 2001 Santa Monica Blvd Santa Monica CA 90404

CASSANOVA, ROBERT ANTHONY, b Columbia, SC, Apr 12, 42; m 64; c 2. SOLAR ENERGY, BIOMASS CONVERSION TECHNOLOGY. *Educ:* NC State Univ, BS, 64; Univ Tenn Space Inst, 67; Ga Inst Technol, PhD(aerospace eng), 75. *Prof Exp:* Res engr, ARO, Inc, 64-67; res engr, Sch Aerospace Eng, 67-77, sr res engr, Eng Exp Sta, 77, ASSOC LAB DIR, ENG EXP STA, GA INST TECHNOL, 79-, DIR, SOLAR THERMAL ADVAN RES CTR, 81- *Concurrent Pos:* Consult, various energy related private industs, 75- *Mem:* Sigma Xi; AAAS; Solar Thermal Test Facility User's Asn; Int Asn Hydrogen Energy. *Res:* Research and development of advanced energy systems using high temperature solar energy; biomass and integration of advanced high temperature materials into energy systems. *Mailing Add:* Energy & Mat Sci Lab Eng Exp Sta Ga Inst Technol Atlanta GA 30332

CASSEDAY, JOHN HERBERT, b Pasadena, Calif, Aug 11, 34; m 65; c 2. NEUROSCIENCES, PSYCHOLOGY. *Educ:* Univ Calif, Riverside, BA, 60; Ind Univ, MA, 63, PhD(psychol), 70. *Prof Exp:* USPHS trainee, Duke Univ, 70-72, lectr, Dept Psychol, 72-76, asst prof otolaryngol, 72-79, asst prof psychol, 76-80, ASSOC PROF PSYCHOL, DUKE UNIV, 80-, ASSOC MED RES PROF, DEPT SURG, MED CTR, 79- *Concurrent Pos:* NSF grant, 72-75 & 77-; NIH grant, 75- *Mem:* AAAS; Acoust Soc Am; Soc Neurosci. *Res:* Hearing. *Mailing Add:* Lab of Otolaryngol Duke Univ Med Ctr Durham NC 27710

CASSEDY, EDWARD S(PENCER), JR, b Washington, DC, Aug 19, 27; m 52; c 4. ELECTRICAL ENGINEERING, PHYSICS. *Educ:* Union Col, BS, 49; Harvard Univ, SM, 50; Johns Hopkins Univ, DEng, 59. *Prof Exp:* Engr, Potomac Elec Power, 50-51; electronics engr, US Naval Ord Lab, 51-54; res assoc eng, Johns Hopkins Univ, 54-58, res scientist, 58-60; from asst prof to assoc prof electrophys, 60-68, PROF ELEC ENG, POLYTECH INST NEW YORK, 68- *Concurrent Pos:* Vis staff, Los Alamos Nat Lab, 74-76 & Brookhaven Nat Lab, 79-80. *Honors & Awards:* Annual award, Nat Electronics Conf, 65; inst premium award, Brit Inst Elec & Electronics, 66; citation in physics, Am Inst Physics, 70. *Mem:* Fedn Am Sci; Am Phys Soc; Inst Elec & Electronics Engrs; Int Asn Energy Economists. *Res:* Antenna and scattering theory; theory of guided waves; nonlinear interaction of waves; electromagnetic theory; plasmas; power systems; energy policies; economics. *Mailing Add:* Dept of Elec Eng 333 Jay St New York NY 11201

CASSEDY, GEORGE H, b Mechanicville, NY, Sept 11, 22; m 48; c 3. CHEMICAL ENGINEERING. *Educ:* Rensselaer Polytech Inst, BChE, 47. *Prof Exp:* Supvr prod, 47-56, sr engr tech sect, 56-57, sr supvr, 57-60, sr supvr, Res & Develop Div, 60-62, facil supvr, 62-64, supt eng serv, 64-70, div head, 70-72, chief supvr technol, 72-73, chief supvr energy mgt coord, 73-74, supt utilities, 74-75, supt environ, 75-77, supt planning, 77-78, SUPT ENVIRON CONTROL, E I DU PONT DE NEMOURS & CO, INC, 78- *Mem:* Am Inst Chem Engrs. *Res:* Fluorinated hydrocarbon and organolead processes; process development facilities, environmental and energy. *Mailing Add:* E I du Pont de Nemours & Co Inc Chambers Works Deepwater NJ 08023

CASSEL, D KEITH, b Bader, Ill, July 23, 40; m 65; c 2. SOIL PHYSICS. *Educ:* Univ Ill, BS, 63; Univ Calif, Davis, MS, 64, PhD(soil physics), 68. *Prof Exp:* Lab technician, Univ Calif, Davis, 65-68; assoc prof soil physics, NDak State Univ, 68-74; assoc prof, 74-80, PROF SOIL PHYSICS, NC STATE UNIV, 80- *Mem:* Soil Sci Soc Am; Soil Conserv Soc Am; Int Soc Soil Sci; Am Soc Agron. *Res:* Water and solute movement in unsaturated soils; tillage and modification of hardpan soils. *Mailing Add:* Dept of Soil Sci NC State Univ Raleigh NC 27607

CASSEL, DAVID GISKE, b Ainsworth, Nebr, Dec 12, 39; m 66; c 2. PHYSICS, ELEMENTARY PARTICLE PHYSICS. *Educ:* Calif Inst Technol, BS, 60; Princeton Univ, MA, 62, PhD(physics), 65. *Prof Exp:* NSF fel, Europ Orgn Nuclear Res, Geneva, Switz, 65-66; asst prof, 66-71, assoc prof, 71-79, PROF PHYSICS, CORNELL UNIV, 79- *Concurrent Pos:* Humboldt Found sr fel, Physics Inst, Bonn Univ, 73-74. *Mem:* Am Phys Soc. *Res:* Pi meson form factor; theory of neutron storage rings; neutral K meson decays; symmetries of electromagnetic interactions; neutral K meson photoproduction; inelastic electron scattering; electron-positron annihilation. *Mailing Add:* Newman Lab Cornell Univ Ithaca NY 14850

CASSEL, DAVID WAYNE, b Toronto, Can, Sept 21, 36; US citizen; m 60; c 3. ALGEBRA. *Educ:* Greenville Col, BS, 59; Syracuse Univ, MA, 62, PhD(math), 67. *Prof Exp:* Instr math, Messiah Col, 62-64; Danforth teacher, Syracuse Univ, 65-67; from asst prof to assoc prof, 67-73, PROF MATH, CHMN DEPT, REGISTR, MESSIAH COL, 73-, DIR COMPUT SERV, 77- *Mem:* Am Math Soc; Math Asn Am. *Res:* Homological algebra; structure of projective modules as it relates to the base ring. *Mailing Add:* Dept Math Messiah Col Grantham PA 17027

CASSEL, JAMES MARTIN, b New Kensington, Pa, Nov 21, 18; m 44; c 4. DENTAL MATERIALS. *Educ:* Washington & Jefferson Col, BS, 42; Georgetown Univ, MS, 55, PhD(chem), 68. *Prof Exp:* Leather technologist, 46-47, res chemist leather, 47-62, res chemist, polymer characterization, 62-68, CHIEF DENT & MED MAT SECT, NAT BUR STANDARDS, 68- *Concurrent Pos:* Prog mgr, Synthetic Implants, Nat Bur Standards, 75-77. *Honors & Awards:* Alsop Award, Am Leather Chem Asn, 59; Dept Com Silver Award, 59 & Gold Award, 77. *Mem:* Am Chem Soc; AAAS; Int Asn Dent Res. *Res:* Chemical and physical studies of natural polymers; dental materials and synthetic surgical implants. *Mailing Add:* Dent & Med Mat Sect Nat Bur Standards Washington DC 20234

CASSEL, JOSEPH FRANKLIN, b Reading, Pa, July 9, 16; m 43; c 4. ORNITHOLOGY, ECOLOGY. *Educ:* Wheaton Col, BS, 38; Cornell Univ, MS, 41; Univ Colo, PhD(zool), 52. *Prof Exp:* From instr to asst prof zool, Colo State Univ, 46-50; from asst prof to assoc prof, 50-61, chmn dept, 53-63, 69-77, PROF ZOOL, NDAK STATE UNIV, 61- *Concurrent Pos:* NSF sci fac fel, Mus Comp Zool, Harvard Univ, 63-64. *Mem:* Sigma Xi; Am Ornithologists Union; Am Inst Biol Sci; Ecol Soc Am; Soc Study Evolution. *Res:* Population dynamics; speciation; creationism and evolution; birds and mammals of North Dakota. *Mailing Add:* Dept of Zool NDak State Univ Fargo ND 58105

CASSEL, WILLIAM ALWEIN, b Philadelphia, Pa, Mar 25, 24; m 49; c 2. MICROBIOLOGY. *Educ:* Philadelphia Col Pharm, BS, 46, MS, 47; Univ Pa, PhD(microbiol), 52. *Prof Exp:* Jr bacteriologist, Philadelphia Gen Hosp, 47-48, lab tech asst, 48-50; asst instr microbiol, Univ Pa, 50-51; res assoc, Hahnemann Med Col, 53 52-53; from asst prof to assoc prof, 53-69, PROF MICROBIOL, EMORY UNIV, 69- *Concurrent Pos:* Med fac award, Lederle Labs, 55-58; USPHS res career develop award, 60-65. *Mem:* AAAS; Am Soc Microbiol; Soc Exp Biol & Med; Am Asn Immunol; Tissue Culture Asn. *Res:* Variation in viruses; relation of viruses to cancer; microbial cytology; animal virology; oncolytic viruses; genetics. *Mailing Add:* Dept of Microbiol Emory Univ Atlanta GA 30322

CASSELL, EUGENE ALAN, b Quarryville, Pa, June 11, 34; m 61; c 3. SANITARY ENGINEERING. *Educ:* Pa State Univ, BS, 56; Mass Inst Technol, SM, 58; Univ NC, Chapel Hill, PhD(sanit eng & water resources), 64. *Prof Exp:* Sanit engr, Div Radiol Health, USPHS, 59-61; from asst prof to assoc prof civil eng, Clarkson Col Technol, 64-75; PROF NATURAL RESOURCES, SCH NATURAL RESOURCES, UNIV VT, 75- *Concurrent Pos:* Consult to various consult eng firms, 64-69 & various govt agencies, 65-69. *Mem:* Water Pollution Control Fedn; Am Water Works Asn; Am Soc Civil Engrs. *Res:* Chemical and biological treatment of waste sludges and slurries; flotation; refuse collection optimization. *Mailing Add:* Sch of Natural Resources Univ of Vt Burlington VT 05401

CASSELL, GAIL HOUSTON, b Alexander City, Ala, Jan 25, 46; m 67; c 1. MICROBIOLOGY, INFECTIOUS DISEASES. *Educ:* Univ Ala, BS, 69; Univ Ala, Birmingham, MS, 71, PhD(microbiol), 73. *Prof Exp:* Biol technician virol & drug metab, Southern Res Inst, 64-67; res assoc molecular biol, Univ Ala, 67-68; res asst, 68-70, instr, 70-73, asst prof microbiol, 74-78, ASST PROF COMP MED, UNIV ALA, BIRMINGHAM, 73-, ASSOC PROF MICROBIOL, 78- *Concurrent Pos:* NIH grants, 73- & res career develop award, 77-82; Vet Admin grants, 73-; resident microbiol, Vet Admin Hosp, Birmingham, 70-; mem mycoplasmas comt, WHO. *Mem:* Am Soc Microbiol; Recticuloendothel Soc; Am Thoracic Soc. *Res:* Host-parasite relationships in mycoplasmal diseases and the phagocytic cell in host resistance. *Mailing Add:* Dept of Microbiol Univ of Ala Birmingham AL 35294

CASSELMAN, JOHN MALCOLM, b Sydenham, Ont, Apr 25, 40; m 64; c 2. FISHERIES, ZOOLOGY. *Educ:* Ont Agr Col, BSAgr, 64; Univ Guelph, MS, 69; Univ Toronto, PhD(zool), 78. *Prof Exp:* Consult aquatic biol fisheries, 73-74; sr aquatic biologist, James F MacLaren Ltd, 74-76; RES SCIENTIST, FISHERIES BR, RES SECT, ONT MINISTRY NATURAL RESOURCES, 76- *Mem:* Am Fisheries Soc; Am Soc Ichthyologists & Herpetologists; Can Soc Zoologists; Freshwater Biol Asn; Soc Int Limnol. *Res:* Aquatic biology, fisheries, coolwater species, Esocidae; environmental physiology, temperature, photoperiod, nutrition, hormone control, and aquatic acidification; laboratory and natural environment; physiology of growth as related to age and growth determination from calcified tissue. *Mailing Add:* Fisheries Br Res Sect Box 50 Maple ON L0J 1E0 Can

CASSELMAN, WARREN GOTTLIEB BRUCE, b Vancouver, BC, July 26, 21; m 50; c 2. PHARMACOLOGY, PUBLIC HEALTH ADMINISTRATION. *Educ:* Univ BC, BA, 43, MA, 44; Univ Toronto, MD, 49, PhD(physiol), 52. *Prof Exp:* Asst, Banting & Best Dept Med Res, Univ

Toronto, 49-52, res assoc, 52-55, assoc prof, 55-58, assoc prof histol, Dept Anat, 57-58; sr res histochemist, Dept Neuropath, NY State Psychiat Inst, 58-59; assoc mem in chg div cell biol, Inst Muscle Dis, Inc, NY, 59-61; head training sect, Geigy Chem Corp, 61-65; prof pharmacol, Univ Toronto, 65-66; med dir, Pharmaceut Div, Geigy (Can) Ltd, 65-70, head clin pharmacol unit, 70; clin pharmacol adv, Drug Adv Bur, Dept Nat Health & Welfare, Can, 70-72, dir bur, 72-73, dir gen, Drugs Directorate, 73-74, sr adv med, Health Protection Br, 74-80, sr med adv, Int Health Servs, 75-80 ; PROF FAC MED & DIR OUTREACH PROG, HEALTH SCI FACULTIES, UNIV WESTERN ONTARIO, 80- *Concurrent Pos:* Merck fel natural sci, Cytol Lab, Oxford Univ, 53-54; res assoc psychiat, Col Physicians & Surgeons, Columbia Univ, 59-65; Merck lectr, Univs BC, Alta & Sask, 61. *Honors & Awards:* Starr Medal, Univ Toronto, 57. *Mem:* Am Physiol Soc; Can Physiol Soc; Pharmacol Soc Can; Can Med Asn. *Res:* pharmacokinetics; histochemistry; primary health care; health planning. *Mailing Add:* Health Sci Bldg Univ Western Ontario London ON N6A 5C1 Can

CASSEN, PATRICK MICHAEL, b Chicago, Ill, May 13, 40; m 65; c 1. GAS DYNAMICS, MAGNETOHYDRODYNAMICS. *Educ:* Univ Mich, BAeroE, 62, MS, 63, PhD(aeronaut & astronaut eng), 67. *Prof Exp:* RES SCIENTIST, SPACE SCI DIV, AMES RES CTR, NASA, 67- *Honors & Awards:* Newcomb-Cleveland Award, AAAS, 79. *Mem:* Am Geophys Union; Acad Appl Sci. *Res:* Magnetohydrodynamic boundary layers; magnetospheric physics; origin and evolution of the solar system. *Mailing Add:* MS 245-3 Ames Res Ctr NASA Moffett Field CA 94035

CASSEN, THOMAS JOSEPH, b Chicago, Ill. PHYSICAL CHEMISTRY. *Educ:* Polytech Inst Brooklyn, BS, 61, PhD(phys chem), 66. *Prof Exp:* Res assoc chem, Univ Calif, Riverside, 66-68 & Univ Ariz, 68-70; NIH spec fel, 70; coordr, Gen Chem Labs, Univ Ariz, 71; asst prof chem, Univ Ga, 72-80; ASST PROF CHEM, UNIV NC, CHARLOTTE, 80- *Mem:* Am Chem Soc; AAAS. *Res:* Molecular spectroscopy. *Mailing Add:* Dept of Chem Univ of Ga Athens GA 30602

CASSENS, DANIEL LEE, b Dixon, Ill, Dec 15, 46; m 70; c 2. FORESTRY, WOOD TECHNOLOGY. *Educ:* Univ Ill, Urbana, BS, 68; Univ Calif, Berkeley, MS, 69; Univ Wis-Madison, PhD(forestry), 73. *Prof Exp:* Wood prods technologist, US Forest Prods Lab, 70-73; exten specialist, Coop Exten Serv, La State Univ, 73-77; asst prof, 77-80, ASSOC PROF FORESTRY, PURDUE UNIV, 80- *Concurrent Pos:* Co-prin investr proj, NC Regional Off Pesticide Impact Assessment Prog, 78; co-investr, Spec Appropriation State Ind Proj, 78-81; wood prods technologist, TIM Tech Inc, 78-; prin investr, various grants, 79-82. *Mem:* Forest Prods Res Soc; Soc Wood Sci & Technol; Sigma Xi. *Res:* Technology transfer and wood products processing including log and lumber stain; biodeterioration of residential structures; fuel values of wood residues; wood drying, and log and lumber grading. *Mailing Add:* Dept of Forestry & Natural Resources Purdue Univ West Lafayette IN 47907

CASSENS, PATRICK, b Litchfield, Ill, Oct 21, 38; m 62; c 2. MATHEMATICAL ANALYSIS. *Educ:* St Louis Univ, BS, 60, MS, 62, PhD(math), 66. *Prof Exp:* Teaching asst math, St Louis Univ, 62-64; from instr to asst prof, Univ Mo, St Louis, 64-68; from asst prof to assoc prof math, State Univ NY Col, Oswego, 68-76, assoc dean arts & sci, 73-76; vpres acad affairs, Siena Col, 77-79, VPRES ACAD AFFAIRS, CENT STATE UNIV, OKLA, 79- *Mem:* AAAS; Am Math Soc; Math Asn Am. *Res:* Summability theory and natural boundaries of functions; 2-metric geometry. *Mailing Add:* Box 223 Newtonville NY 12128

CASSENS, ROBERT G, b Morrison, Ill, June 10, 37; m 60; c 1. BIOCHEMISTRY. *Educ:* Univ Ill, BS, 59; Univ Wis, MS, 61, PhD(biochem), 63. *Prof Exp:* From asst prof to assoc prof, 64-71, PROF MEAT & ANIMAL SCI, UNIV WIS-MADISON, 71-, CHMN DEPT, 81- *Concurrent Pos:* Fulbright grant, Australia, 63. *Mem:* Inst Food Technol; Am Soc Animal Sci. *Res:* Meat science; examination of muscle ultrastructure as effected by rate of postmortem glycolysis; function of zinc in muscle; effect of temperature on rigor mortis and associated changes; histochemistry of fiber types; myoglobin localization; fate of nitrite in cured meat; phosphorylase fluorescent antibody. *Mailing Add:* Muscle Biol Lab Univ of Wis Madison WI 53706

CASSERBERG, BO R, b Halsingborg, Sweden, Oct 3, 41; m 63; c 3. PHYSICS. *Educ:* Univ Minn, Minneapolis, BPhys, 64; Princeton Univ, PhD(physics), 68. *Prof Exp:* Asst prof, 68-74, ASSOC PROF PHYSICS, UNIV MINN, DULUTH, 74- *Res:* Hyperfine structure; magnetic resonance. *Mailing Add:* Dept of Phys Univ of Minn Duluth MN 55812

CASSIDY, CARL EUGENE, b Salineville, Ohio, Dec 4, 24; m 61; c 2. ENDOCRINOLOGY, INTERNAL MEDICINE. *Educ:* Kenyon Col, AB, 46; Western Reserve Univ, MD, 48. *Prof Exp:* Asst, 54-56, clin instr, 56-58, instr, 58-59, sr instr, 59-62, from asst prof to assoc prof, 62-73, CLIN PROF MED, SCH MED, TUFTS UNIV, 73-, PROG DIR, POSTGRAD MED INST, 78- *Concurrent Pos:* Res fel, New Eng Ctr Hosp, 54-56; trainee, Nat Inst Arthritis & Metab Dis, 54-56; asst physician, New Eng Ctr Hosp, 56-68, physician, 68-71; physician-in-chief, Med Ctr Western Mass, 72-77; pvt pract, 77- *Mem:* Endocrine Soc; AMA; Am Thyroid Asn; Am Col Physicians. *Res:* Diseases of endocrine glands; antithyroid drugs; radioiodine; hormones of reproductive system; pituitary hormones. *Mailing Add:* PO Box 68 Prudential Ctr Sta Boston MA 02199

CASSIDY, ESTHER CHRISTMAS, b Washington, DC, Aug 5, 33; div; c 3. PHYSICS, ELECTRICAL ENGINEERING. *Educ:* Manhattanville Col, Purchase, NY, BA, 55. *Prof Exp:* Physicist/proj mgr aerodyn res, Nat Bur Standards, 55-61, physicist/proj mgr high speed elec & optical measurements, 61-66, physicist/proj mgr high voltage elec measurements, 66-73, gen phys scientist cong affairs, 74-75; gen phys scientist, Energy Res & Develop Admin, Dept Energy, 75-78; SUPVRY GEN PHYS SCIENTIST & DIR CONG AFFAIRS, NAT BUR STANDARDS, 78- *Concurrent Pos:* Sci & technol fel, Dept Com, Nat Bur Standards, 73-74. *Honors & Awards:* Silver Medal, Dept Com, Nat Bur Standards, 70, Distinguished Service Award, 63; Special Achievement Award, Energy Res & Develop Admin, Dept Energy, 77. *Mem:* Am Phys Soc; sr mem Inst Elec & Electronic Engrs. *Res:* High-speed electro-optical; high voltage electrical measurements; time resolved spectroscopic; high-speed photographic studies of ultra high-temperature gases and electrical insulating materials. *Mailing Add:* Asst to the Dir for Cong Affairs Nat Bur Standards Washington DC 20234

CASSIDY, HAROLD GOMES, b Havana, Cuba, Oct 17, 06; nat US; m 34. ORGANIC CHEMISTRY, SCIENCE WRITING. *Educ:* Oberlin Col, AB, 390, AM, 32; Yale Univ, PhD, 39. *Hon Degrees:* DSc, St Thomas Inst, 72. *Prof Exp:* Res instr chem, Oberlin Col, 32-33; res chemist, Wm S Merrell Co, Ohio, 33-36; instr chem, Oberlin Col, 36-37; from instr to prof, 38-72, EMER PROF CHEM, YALE UNIV, 72- *Concurrent Pos:* Chmn, Gordon Conf Separation & Purification, 56 & Comt Grants-in-Aid, Nat Exec Bd, Soc Sigma Xi, 69; Nat Sigma Xi lectr, 60 & 65; Ayd lectr, 62; Korzybski Mem lectr, 62; Res Soc spec lectr, 63; Danforth vis lectr, Asn Am Cols Arts Prog, 68 & 71; Sigma Xi centennial lectr, Ohio State Univ, 70; seminar leader libr arts educ, Danforth Workshop, 62-65; sr fel sci, Ctr Advan Studies, Wesleyan Univ, 65-66; consult, Improv Sci Educ in India, 69 & Nat Humanities Fac, 70; prof-at-large, Hanover Col, 72-; Green Honors Chair prof, Tex Christian Univ, 74; assoc ed, Am J Sci. *Mem:* Fel AAAS; Am Chem Soc. *Res:* Oxidation-reduction; chromatography; cybernetics; science education. *Mailing Add:* 605 W Second St Madison IN 47250

CASSIDY, JAMES EDWARD, b Springfield, Mass, Aug 17, 28; m 59; c 2. METABOLISM, ANALYTICAL CHEMISTRY. *Educ:* Univ Mass, BS, 49; Univ Vt, MS, 54; Rensselaer Polytech Inst, PhD(chem), 58. *Prof Exp:* Asst chemist eng exp sta, Univ NH, 49-50; chemist, Army Chem Ctr, 51-52; asst dept chem, Univ Vt, 53-54; asst, Rensselaer Polytech Inst, 54-57; res chemist, Am Cyanamid Co, 58-64; res assoc, 64-69, group leader, 69-8O, SR GROUP LEADER, CIBA-GEIGY CORP, 80- *Mem:* Am Chem Soc; Sigma Xi; NY Acad Sci; Int Soc Study Xenobitics. *Res:* Metabolism of pesticides and herbicides in soil, plants and animals; separations and instrumentation. *Mailing Add:* 503 Tangle Dr Jamestown NC 27282

CASSIDY, JAMES T, b Oil City, Pa, Sept 10, 30; m 55; c 2. RHEUMATOLOGY. *Educ:* Univ Mich, BS, 53, MD, 55. *Prof Exp:* From instr to assoc prof internal med, 62-73, PROF MED & PEDIAT, MED SCH, UNIV MICH, ANN ARBOR, 73- *Concurrent Pos:* Fel, Rackham Arthritis Res Unit, Med Sch, Univ Mich, Ann Arbor, 61-62; Arthritis Found fel, 63-66. *Mem:* Soc Pediat Res; Am Asn Immunol; Am Rheumatism Asn; Am Fedn Clin Res. *Res:* Immunology. *Mailing Add:* R4633 Kresge Med Res Bldg Univ of Mich Med Sch Ann Arbor MI 48109

CASSIDY, JOHN J(OSEPH), b Gebo, Wyo, June 21, 30; m 53; c 3. HYDROLOGY, HYDRAULIC ENGINEERING. *Educ:* Mont State Col, BS, 52, MS, 60; Univ Iowa, PhD(fluid mech), 64. *Prof Exp:* Hwy engr, US Bur Pub Roads, 52-53; design engr, Mont State Water Conserv Bd, 55-58; instr fluid mech, Mont State Col, 58-60; mech, Univ Iowa, 60-63; from asst prof to prof civil eng, Univ Mo-Columbia, 63-72, chmn dept, 72-74; asst chief hydraul engr, 74-75, chief hydrol engr, 75-79, dir, State Washing Water Res Ctr, 79-81, CHIEF HYDROL ENGR, BECHTEL INC, 81- *Concurrent Pos:* Off, US Coast & Geod Surv, 52; eng resident, US Bur Reclamation, 69-70; chmn Am Soc Civil Engrs, Hydraul Div, 78-79. *Mem:* Am Soc Civil Engrs; Am Water Resources Asn. *Res:* Flood hydrology; reservoir operation studies; water resources; design of hydraulic structures. *Mailing Add:* Bechtel Inc PO Box 3965 San Francisco CA 94119

CASSIDY, PATRICK EDWARD, b East Moline, Ill, Nov 8, 37; m 81; c 1. CHEMISTRY. *Educ:* Univ Ill, BS, 59; Univ Iowa, MS, 62, PhD(chem), 63. *Prof Exp:* Fel, Univ Ariz, 63-64; mem tech staff polymer chem, Sandia Corp, 64-66; sr scientist-group leader, Tracor, Inc, 66-69, asst to dir res lab, 69-71; from asst prof to assoc prof, 71-80, PROF CHEM, SOUTHWEST TEX STATE UNIV, 80- *Concurrent Pos:* Vpres, Tex Res Inst, 75- *Mem:* Am Chem Soc; Soc Plastics Engrs; fel Am Inst Chemists. *Res:* Polyphenylene; polyphenylethers; ferrocenes and other organo-metallics; thermal analyses of polymers; epoxy resin modifications; urethanes; high-temperature polymers; adhesives; coupling agents; phenolics; permeation through polymers; heterocyclic polymers; polyimidines; polymer backbone reactions. *Mailing Add:* Dept Chem Southwest Tex State Univ San Marcos TX 78666

CASSIDY, RICHARD MURRAY, b St John, NB, Oct 28, 44; m 66; c 2. CHROMATOGRAPHY, INDUSTRIAL CHEMISTRY. *Educ:* Univ King Col, BSc, 65; Dalhousie Univ, MSc, 67; McMaster Univ, Phd(anal chem), 70. *Prof Exp:* Fel, Dalhousie Univ, 71-72, res assoc, 72-73; RES SCIENTIST, ATOMIC ENERGY CAN LTD, 73- *Mem:* Chem Inst Can. *Res:* Development of new chromatography techniques for the determination of organic and inorganic materials. *Mailing Add:* Atomic Energy of Canada Ltd Chalk River Nuclear Lab Chalk River ON K0J 1J0 Can

CASSIDY, SAMUEL H, b Escanaba, Mich, Oct 3, 22; m 56. MATHEMATICS. *Educ:* Univ Minn, Minneapolis, BA, 48; Univ Mich, MS, 50. *Prof Exp:* Instr math, Napa Col, 54-57; mathematician, US Naval Radiol Defense Lab, 57-69; mathematician, 69-81, SCIENTIST III, NAVAL UNDERSEA CTR, 81- *Mem:* AAAS. *Res:* Computer systems analysis. *Mailing Add:* Naval Ocean Systs Ctr Code 7232 San Diego CA 92152

CASSIDY, WILLIAM ARTHUR, b New York, NY, Jan 3, 28; m 61; c 3. GEOCHEMISTRY, GEOLOGY. *Educ:* Univ NMex, BS, 52; Pa State Univ, PhD(geochem), 61. *Prof Exp:* Mem staff seismic comput, Superior Oil Co Calif, 52-53; res scientist meteoritics, Lamont Geol Observ, Columbia Univ, 61-67; assoc prof, 68-81, PROF GEOL & PLANETARY SCI, DEPT GEOL & PLANETARY SCI, UNIV PITTSBURGH, 81- *Concurrent Pos:* Prin investr, NSF grants Antarctic Search Meteorites, 76- *Mem:* Am Geophys Union; Meteoritical Soc. *Res:* Origin and evolution of planetary and subplanetary bodies; element abundances and fractionations; meteorites and meteorite craters; lunar & planetary surface phenomena. *Mailing Add:* Dept Geol & Planetary Sci Univ Pittsburgh Pittsburgh PA 15260

CASSIE, ROBERT MACGREGOR, b Lowville, NY, May 22, 35; m 71. GEOLOGY. *Educ:* St Lawrence Univ, BS, 56; Univ Wis, PhD(geol), 65. *Prof Exp:* Sr res mineralogist, Chem Div, Pittsburgh Plate Glass Co, 62-65, res supvr, Minerals Res, 65-66; asst prof geol, Col Wooster, 66-67; asst prof, 67-73, ASSOC PROF GEOL, STATE UNIV NY COL BROCKPORT, 73- *Concurrent Pos:* Sr fel, Geophys Lab, Carnegie Inst, 69-70. *Mem:* Geol Soc Am; Am Geophys Union; Nat Asn Geol Teachers; AAAS. *Res:* Petrology and structure of metamorphic and igneous terrains; silicate phase equilibria. *Mailing Add:* Dept of Earth Sci State Univ NY Col Brockport NY 14420

CASSIM, JOSEPH YUSUF KHAN, b Khoi, Iran, June 12, 24; m 68. BIOMACROMOLECULAR PHYSICAL CHEMISTRY. *Educ:* Univ Ill, BA, 51; Univ Chicago, PhD(biophysics), 65. *Prof Exp:* Res & develop physicist, Indust Condenser Corp, 51-58; res fel, Dept Biophysics, Univ Chicago, 65; res biophysicist, Cardiovasc Res Inst, Univ Calif, San Francisco, 65-68; asst prof, Dept Biophysics, 68-71, assoc prof, 71-78, assoc prof, 78-81, PROF, DEPT MICROBIOL, OHIO STATE UNIV, 81- *Mem:* Biophys Soc; Am Soc Photobiol. *Res:* Structure-function studies of biomacromolecules and membranes by means of spectroscopic and spectropolarimetric analysis; purple membrane of Halobacterium halobuim. *Mailing Add:* Dept Microbiol Ohio State Univ 484 W 12th St Columbus OH 43210

CASSIN, JOSEPH M, b Lowell, Mass, July 21, 28; m 69. MICROBIAL ECOLOGY. *Educ:* Cath Univ Am, AB, 52; St John's Univ, AM, 58; Howard Univ, MS, 64; Fordham Univ, PhD(microbial ecol), 68. *Prof Exp:* Teacher, sec schs, 52-67; asst prof microbial ecol, Inst Marine Sci, 68-78, asst prof, 68-75, ASSOC PROF BIOL, ADELPHI UNIV, 76- *Concurrent Pos:* Instr, Sci Honors Prog, Sch Eng, Columbia Univ, 59-60; inst dir biol sci curric study, NY Archdiocese Sci Coun, 64-65; res asst microbial ecol, Fordham Univ, 66-78; dir, Adelphi Inst Marine Sci, 76-78 & NSF precol, Inst Marine Biol, 78-79; consult var environ co, Water Qual, Ecosyst Anal, Aerial Photog. *Mem:* Phycol Soc Am; Ecol Soc Am; Am Inst Biol Sci. *Res:* Phytoplankton physiology and taxonomy. *Mailing Add:* Dept of Biol Adelphi Univ Garden City NY 11530

CASSIN, SIDNEY, b Mass, June 8, 28; m 50; c 4. PHYSIOLOGY. *Educ:* NY Univ, BA, 50; Univ Tex, MA, 54, PhD(physiol), 57. *Prof Exp:* From instr to assoc prof physiol, 57-68, PROF PHYSIOL, COL MED, UNIV FLA, 68- *Concurrent Pos:* NIH spec fel, Nuffield Inst Med Res, Oxford Univ, 62-63. *Mem:* Sigma Xi; Can Physiol Soc; Perinatal Res Soc; Am Physiol Soc; Soc Exp Biol & Med. *Res:* Respiratory physiology; neonatal anoxia; fetal and newborn pulmonary circulation; renal physiology. *Mailing Add:* Dept of Physiol Col of Med Univ of Fla Gainesville FL 32601

CASSINELLI, JOSEPH PATRICK, b Cincinnati, Ohio, Aug 23, 40; c 3. ASTROPHYSICS. *Educ:* Xavier Univ, Ohio, BS, 62; Univ Ariz, MS, 65; Univ Wash, PhD(astron), 70. *Prof Exp:* Res asst, Kitt Peak Nat Observ, 63-65; res engr aerospace sci, Boeing Co, Wash, 65-66; res assoc, Joint Inst Lab Astrophys, Colo, 70-72; from asst prof to assoc prof, 72-81, PROF ASTRON, UNIV WIS-MADISON, 81- *Concurrent Pos:* Vis scientist, Space Res Lab, Astron Inst Utrecht, 75 & Harvard Smithsonian Ctr Astrophys, 81. *Mem:* Am Astron Soc; Int Astron Union. *Res:* Theoretical studies of the structure of the stellar atmosphere of hot stars; radiative transfer in stellar atmospheres and studies of stellar coronae and stellar winds; satellite observations of ultraviolet and x-ray emission from hot stars; structure of supermassive stars. *Mailing Add:* Washburn Observe Astron Dept 475 N Charter St Univ Wis Madison WI 53706

CASSOLA, CHARLES A(LFRED), b Haverhill, Mass, Aug 6, 13; m 46. MATERIALS ENGINEERING. *Educ:* Northeastern Univ, BS, 37. *Prof Exp:* Inspector eng mat, Naval Air Mat Ctr, 40-42; Bur Aeronaut resident rep, Singer Mfg Co, 42-46; mat engr, Naval Air Eng Ctr, 46-56, head plastics br, 57-58, supt high polymer div, 58-70, supt high polymer div, Naval Air Develop Ctr, 70-74; CONSULT, 74- *Mem:* Am Soc Testing & Mat; Soc Aerospace Mat & Process Eng. *Res:* Applied research and development in high polymer materials, primarily those related to fields of structural plastics, elastomers; sealants and textiles as utilized in military aircraft. *Mailing Add:* 1108 Merrick Ave Collingswood NJ 08108

CASSOLA, ROBERT LOUIS, b Brooklyn, NY, June 9, 41; m 65; c 2. NUCLEAR & THEORETICAL PHYSICS, SYSTEMS ANALYSIS. *Educ:* Polytech Inst Brooklyn, BS, 62; Ohio Univ, PhD(nuclear physics), 66. *Prof Exp:* Sr res physicist, Battelle Mem Inst, 66-68; lectr physics, Ohio State Univ, 67-68; fac res fel nuclear physics, Univ Wash, 68-69; staff specialist, 69-77, sr consult systs anal, 77-80, MGR TECH RESOURCES, CONTROL DATA CORP, MINNEAPOLIS, 80- *Concurrent Pos:* Fac res fel, Univ Wash, 68-69; lectr physics, Univ Minn, 74- *Honors & Awards:* Dr Charles Kidd Award, Fed Coun Sci & Technol, 68. *Mem:* Sigma Xi; Am Phys Soc. *Res:* Theoretical nuclear physics, especially nuclear reaction theories and nuclear structure; systems analysis, with special emphasis on simulation; analysis of data processing systems which utilize distributed architectures. *Mailing Add:* 4810 W Coventry Rd Minnetonka MN 55343

CASTAGNA, MICHAEL, b Janesville, Wis, Oct 21, 27; m 55; c 4. BIOLOGICAL OCEANOGRAPHY, AQUACULTURE. *Educ:* Fla State Univ, BS, 53, MS, 55. *Prof Exp:* Asst cur marine studios, Marineland, Fla, 55-56; res biologist, US Dept Interior Fish & Wildlife Serv, 56-62; asst prof, 62-70, ASSSOC PROF, COL WILLIAM & MARY, 70-; SR MARINE SCIENTIST, VA INST MARINE SCI, 62- *Concurrent Pos:* Adj prof, Univ del Norte, Chile. *Mem:* Estuarine Res Fedn (treas, 73-75, secy, 75-77, pres, 77-79); Nat Shellfisheries Asn (secy-treas, 72-74, vpres, 74-75, pres, 76-77); World Mariculture Soc; Am Malacol Union. *Res:* Larval behavior, mariculture; natural history of mollusks. *Mailing Add:* Locustville VA 23404

CASTAGNOLI, NEAL, JR, b Los Angeles, Calif, Sept 6, 36; m 57; c 5. ORGANIC CHEMISTRY, MEDICINAL CHEMISTRY. *Educ:* Univ Calif, Berkeley, BS, 59, MA, 61, PhD(chem), 64. *Prof Exp:* NIH fel, Higher Inst Health, Italy, 64-65; fel, Imp Col, Univ London, 65-67; from asst prof to assoc prof, 67-77, PROF CHEM & PHARMACEUT CHEM, MED CTR, UNIV CALIF, SAN FRANCISCO, 77-, V CHMN DEPT PHARMACEUT CHEM & MED CHEM, 77- *Mem:* Am Chem Soc; Royal Soc Chem; NY Acad Sci. *Res:* Synthesis, metabolism and pharmacological activity of centrally active compounds. *Mailing Add:* Dept of Chem 926 Med Sci Bldg San Francisco CA 94143

CASTALDI, COSMO RAYMOND, b Sudbury, Ont, Nov 12, 20; m 51; c 4. DENTISTRY. *Educ:* Univ Toronto, DDS, 44; Northwestern Univ, MSD, 51. *Prof Exp:* Demonstr children's dent, Northwestern Univ, 51-52; asst prof, Ind Univ, 52-56; prof, Univ Alta, 56-65; prof, Dept Restorative Dent, Univ Man, 65-69; PROF PEDIAT DENT & HEAD DEPT, SCH DENT MED, UNIV CONN, 69- *Mem:* Int Asn Dent Res; Am Dent Asn; Am Acad Pedodontics; Am Asn Advan Sci; Am Soc Testing Mat. *Res:* Dental epidemiology, dental care for adolescents, handicapped children, dental caries; sports medicine. *Mailing Add:* Dept Pediat Dent Univ Conn Health Ctr Farmington CT 06032

CASTANEDA, ALDO RICARDO, b Genoa, Italy, July 17, 30; US citizen; m 56; c 3. THORACIC SURGERY, CARDIOVASCULAR SURGERY. *Educ:* San Carlos Univ, Guatemala, MD, 56; Univ Minn, PhD(surg), 63, MS, 64. *Prof Exp:* From instr to prof surg, Univ Minn, Minneapolis, 63-72; prof cardiovasc surg & cardiovasc surgeon-in-chief, PROF SURG, HARVARD MED SCH & CHIEF DEPT CARDIAC SURG, CHILDREN'S HOSP MED CTR, 77- *Concurrent Pos:* Mem adv coun, Cardiovasc Surg Coun, Am Heart Asn, 68. *Mem:* AAAS; Am Asn Thoracic Surg; Am Col Cardiol; Am Col Surg; Am Surg Asn. *Res:* Cardiac physiology; extracorporeal circurlation and its biologic effects; combined cardiopulmonary transplantation. *Mailing Add:* Dept of Cardiac Surg Children's Hosp Med Ctr Boston MA 02115

CASTANER, DAVID, b New York, NY, Aug 4, 34; m 62; c 3. SYSTEMATIC BOTANY. *Educ:* City Col New York, BS, 61; Iowa State Univ, MS, 63, PhD(plant path), 65. *Prof Exp:* Asst plant path, Iowa State Univ, 61-65; from asst prof to assoc prof, 66-73, PROF BOT & CUR HERBARIUM, CENT MO STATE UNIV, 73- *Mem:* Mycol Soc Am; Bot Soc Am; Am Soc Plant Taxon. *Res:* Flora of Johnson County, Missouri; genus Carex. *Mailing Add:* Dept Biol Cent Mo State Univ Warrensburg MO 64093

CASTANERA, ESTHER GOOSSEN, b Winnipeg, Man, July 19, 20; nat US. BIOCHEMISTRY, NUTRITION. *Educ:* Univ Man, BSc, 42; Univ Calif, PhD(animal nutrit), 54. *Prof Exp:* Chemist nitrocellulose & small arms ammunition, Defence Industs, Ltd, Can, 42-44; chemist, Can Breweries Ltd & Graham's Dried Foods, Ltd, 44-45; technician hematol & serol, Can Red Cross Blood Transfusion Serv, 46-48; asst pentosuria, Dept Biol Chem, Sch Med, Creighton Univ, 48-49, Univ Calif, 49-54; asst microenzyme methods, Dept Pharmacol, Sch Med, Univ Wash, 54-55; biochemist cellulose metabolism in rats, Chem Div, US Army Med Nutrit Lab, Colo, 56-57; res biochemist pyridoxine & pregnancy, Univ Calif, 57-58; biochemist res assoc pharmacol, Bio-Med Div, US Radio Defense Lab, 58-60; res biochemist, Univ Calif, Berkeley, 61-65; res chemist, Calif State Dept Pub Health, 65-67; RES BIOCHEMIST, MED CTR, UNIV CALIF, SAN FRANCISCO, 67- *Mem:* AAAS; fel Am Inst Chem; Am Chem Soc. *Res:* Radioactive tracers in metabolism; microbiochemical techniques; enzymology. *Mailing Add:* 1417 Grizzly Peak Blvd Berkeley CA 94708

CASTANO, JOHN ROMAN, b New York, NY, June 10, 26; m 51; c 1. GEOLOGY, GEOCHEMISTRY. *Educ:* City Col NY, BS, 48; Northwestern Univ, MS, 50. *Prof Exp:* Asst, Northwestern Univ, 48-50; from geol trainee to sr staff geologist, 50-77, PROJ LEADER GEOCHEM SERV, SHELL DEVELOP CO, 75- *Concurrent Pos:* US Nat Comn Geochem, 77-80. *Mem:* Geol Soc Am; Am Asn Petro Geologists; Soc Econ Paleontologists & Mineralogists; Int Comn Coal Petrol. *Res:* Petrology and genesis of ancient and recent sand bodies; environment of deposition of sedimentary iron ores; coal petrology; organic geochemistry. *Mailing Add:* Shell Develop Co Box 481 Houston TX 77001

CASTATER, ROBERT DEWITT, b Janesville, Wis, Jan 27, 22; m 44; c 2. OPERATIONS ANALYSIS. *Educ:* Milton Col, BS, 47; State Univ Iowa, MS, 52. *Prof Exp:* OPERS ANALYST & DIV CHIEF, STRATEGIC AIR COMMAND, OFFUTT AFB, 57- *Res:* Bomber penetration analysis; war planning; analysis; war games; operational test and evaluation; electronic counter measures. *Mailing Add:* 11421 Hickory Rd Omaha NE 68144

CASTELFRANCO, PAUL ALEXANDER, b Florence, Italy, Oct 16, 21; nat US; m 54; c 2. PLANT PHYSIOLOGY. *Educ:* Univ Calif, AB, 43, MS, 50, PhD(agr chem), 54; Harvard Univ, STB, 57. *Prof Exp:* Asst, Dept Agr Biochem, Univ Calif, 51-54, jr res biochemist, 55-56; USPHS fel biochem, Med Sch, Tufts Col, 57-58; from asst botanist to assoc botanist, 58-65, assoc prof, 65-70, PROF BOT, UNIV CALIF, DAVIS, 70- *Concurrent Pos:* Guggenheim Mem Found fel, 73-74. *Mem:* Am Soc Plant Physiologists; Am Soc Photobiol; Am Soc Biol Chemists. *Res:* Chlorophyll biosynthesis. *Mailing Add:* Dept of Bot Univ of Calif Davis CA 95616

CASTELL, ADRIAN GEORGE, b Formby, Eng, Sept 9, 35; Can citizen; m 61; c 2. ANIMAL SCIENCE, ANIMAL NUTRITION. *Educ:* Univ Reading, BSc, 59; Univ Hawaii, MS, 62; Univ Alta, PhD(animal nutrit), 67. *Prof Exp:* RES SCIENTIST ANIMAL NUTRIT, AGR CAN RES BR, 67- *Mem:* Brit Soc Animal Prod; Can Soc Animal Sci (secy, 78-81, pres 82-83); Agr Inst Can. *Res:* Swine production, management and nutrition; evaluation of new or potential sources of nutrients for livestock. *Mailing Add:* Agr Can Res Sta PO Box 610 Brandon MB R7A 5Z7 Can

CASTELL, JOHN DANIEL, b Guelph, Ont, Apr 19, 43; m 66, 75, 80; c 6. MARINE SCIENCES, NUTRITIONAL BIOCHEMISTRY. *Educ:* Dalhousie Univ, BSc Hons, 65, MSc, 66; Ore State Univ, PhD(food sci), 70. *Prof Exp:* Fel, Hormel Inst, Univ Minn, 70; RES SCIENTIST MARINE NUTRIT, DEPT FISHERIES & OCEANS, FISHERIES & ENVIRON SCI, 71-; ASSOC PROF BIOL, DALHOWSIE UNIV, 81- *Concurrent Pos:* Mem comt, Natural & Renewable Resources, Nat Res Coun, 81- *Mem:* Nat

Shellfish Asn; World Maricult Soc. *Res:* Nutritional requirements of marine species of commercial interest for aquaculture with a main emphasis on lobsters and minor emphasis on oysters and salmonids. *Mailing Add:* 18 Garsham Rd Halifax NS B3H 3J5 Can

CASTELLA, FRANK ROBERT, b Asbury Park, NJ, Nov 9, 36; m 62; c 2. ENGINEERING. *Educ:* City Col New York, BEE, 58; Univ Calif, Los Angeles, MS, 60. *Prof Exp:* Elec eng circuit design, Litton Industs, 60-62; physicist navig systs, Appl Physics Lab, Johns Hopkins Univ, 62-66; elec eng antenna systs, Gen Elec Co, 66-69; elec eng commun systs, Radiation Inc/Harris Corp, 69-72; PHYSICIST RADAR SYSTS, APPL PHYSICS LAB, JOHNS HOPKINS UNIV, 72- *Mem:* Inst Elec & Electronics Engrs. *Res:* Design and analysis of radar systems and communication systems; radar signal processing and tracking systems; detection theory. *Mailing Add:* 5621 Phelps Luck Dr Columbia MD 21045

CASTELLAN, GILBERT WILLIAM, b Denver, Colo, Nov 21, 24; m 56; c 4. PHYSICAL CHEMISTRY. *Educ:* Regis Col, Colo, BS, 45; Cath Univ, PhD(chem), 49. *Hon Degrees:* ScD, Regis Col, Colo, 67. *Prof Exp:* AEC fel theoret physics, Univ Ill, 49-50; from instr to prof chem, Cath Univ Am, 50-69, asst head dept, 63-65; assoc dean phys sci & eng, grad sch, 69-74, assoc chmn dept, 73-77, PROF CHEM, UNIV MD, COLLEGE PARK, 69- *Concurrent Pos:* Consult, Naval Res Lab, 56-63 & Melpar, Inc, 63-67; NSF fel, Max Planck Inst Phys Chem, Gottingen, 62-63. *Mem:* Am Phys Soc; Electrochem Soc; Am Chem Soc. *Res:* Chemical relaxation; electrochemical thermodynamics and kinetics. *Mailing Add:* Dept of Chem Univ of Md College Park MD 20742

CASTELLAN, NORMAN J, b Everett, Wash, Jan 11, 12; wid; c 3. CIVIL ENGINEERING. *Educ:* Univ Colo, BS, 33, MS, 34. *Prof Exp:* Instr civil eng, Univ Colo, 34; sr rodman, US Bur Pub Rd, 34, sr levelman, 35; instrumentman, US Coast & Geod Surv, 34-35; bridge draftsman, Colo State Hwy Dept, 35-36; sr engr, US Bur Reclamation, 36; instr math & civil eng, Colo Sch Mines, 36-39, asst prof, 39-41; asst to dist mgr, War Prod Bd, 41-43, dep regional dir, 47; self employed consult engr, 47-55; assoc prof civil eng, 55-59, head dept civil eng, 60-63, chmn div eng, 62-67, head dept civil eng, 69-76, prof civil eng, 59-80, EMER PROF CIVIL ENG, SACRAMENTO STATE COL, 80- *Honors & Awards:* Western Elec Fund-Am Soc Eng Educ Award, 70-71. *Mem:* Am Soc Civil Engrs; Am Soc Eng Educ. *Res:* Structural analysis. *Mailing Add:* Sch of Eng Sacramento State Col Sacramento CA 95819

CASTELLANA, FRANK SEBASTIAN, b Flushing, NY, Feb 5, 42. BIOMEDICAL ENGINEERING, MEDICINE. *Educ:* Queens Col, NY, BS, 63; Columbia Univ, BS, 63, MS, 64, EngScD(fluid mech), 69; Albert Einstein Col Med, MD, 76. *Prof Exp:* Res engr, heat transfer res facility, 68-69, asst prof chem eng, 69-73, ASSOC PROF CHEM ENG, COLUMBIA UNIV, 77-, RES ASSOC, DEPT ST LUKE'S HOSP, 77- *Concurrent Pos:* Med intern, Hosp Ctr, St Luke's Hosp, 76-77. *Mem:* Am Inst Chem Eng; Am Chem Soc. *Mailing Add:* Dept of Chem Eng Columbia Univ New York NY 10027

CASTELLANO, SALVATORE, MARIO, b Trieste, Italy, Sept 28, 25; US citizen; m 53. NUCLEAR MAGNETIC RESONANCE, INDUSTRIAL CHEMISTRY. *Educ:* Liceo Scientifico, Trieste, Italy, dipl, 43, Polytech Milan, Italy, PhD(chem), 51. *Prof Exp:* Asst prof phys & indust chem, Inst Indust Chem, Polytech Milan, 51-58, dir, Nuclear Magnetic Resonance Lab, 60-62; fel, Mellon Inst, 62-75, PROF BIOPHYS CHEM, DEPT BIOL SCI, CARNEGIE-MELLON UNIV, 75- *Concurrent Pos:* Vis prof, Inst Phys Chem, Univ Padova, 74; fel, Chem Dept, Mass Inst Technol, 58-60; consult, Montecatini Co, 53-58, Assoreni Assocs, 79-81. *Mem:* Int Soc Magnetic Resonance. *Res:* Catalitic studies and industrial developments of oxosyntesis and of other high-pressure syntesis utilizing carbon monoxide and hydrogen gas mixtures; structural studies of chemical and biochemical compounds by means of high resolution nuclear magnetic resonance; mathematical algorithms and computer programs for the analysis of nuclear magnetic resonance spectra. *Mailing Add:* 6346 Burchfield Ave Pittsburgh PA 15217

CASTELLI, VITTORIO, b Rome, Italy, Apr 8, 34; US citizen; m 57; c 1. MECHANICAL ENGINEERING. *Educ:* Columbia Univ, MS, 59, PhD(mech eng), 62. *Prof Exp:* From instr to asst prof mech eng, 59-68, prof, 69-80, ADJ PROF MECH ENG, COLUMBIA UNIV, 80- *Concurrent Pos:* Engr, Franklin Inst, 59-62, sr staff res engr, 62-63, consult, 63-; consult, Conductron Corp, Calif, 64-, AiResearch Corp, Ariz, 64-, Autonetics Div, NAm Aviation, Inc, 64-, Mech Tech Inc, 64-, Rohr Corp, 65-, Xerox Data Systs, 68-, Appl Magnetics Corp, 68-, Comput Peripherals Co, 69-70 & Control Data Corp, 69- *Res:* Fluid mechanics; incompressible and compressible fluid lubrication; applications of computers to engineering problems. *Mailing Add:* Dept of Mech Eng Columbia Univ New York NY 10027

CASTELLI, WALTER ANDREW, b Iquique, Chile, May 5, 29; m 53; c 2. ANATOMY. *Educ:* Univ Chile, DDS, 57; Univ Mich, MS, 64. *Prof Exp:* Instr anat, Concepcion Univ, 57-62, instr anat & res assoc physiopath, 64-66; from asst prof to prof anat, Univ Mich, Ann Arbor, 66-82; PROF ANAT, SCH MED, UNIV CONCEPCION, CHILE, 82- *Concurrent Pos:* W K Kellogg Found fel anat, Univ Mich, 62-64. *Mem:* Int Asn Dent Res. *Res:* Gross anatomy; vascular studies; head and neck area; experimental tooth transplants in monkeys; periodontal studies. *Mailing Add:* Dept of Anat 3725 Med Sci II Univ of Mich Ann Arbor MI 48109

CASTELLI, WILLIAM PETER, b New York, NY, Nov 21, 31; m 61; c 3. EPIDEMIOLOGY, CARDIOLOGY. *Educ:* Yale Col, BS, 53; Cath Univ Louvain, MD, 59. *Prof Exp:* DIR LABS, FRAMINGHAM HEART STUDY, NAT HEART, LUNG & BLOOD INST, NIH, 65- *Concurrent Pos:* Harvard Med Sch fel, 61-65, lectr prev med, 65-; chmn subcomt criteria & methods, Coun Epidemiol, Am Heart Asn, 78- *Res:* To identify those factors associated with subsequent development of cardiovascular disease, such as lipid measures of lipoproteins, hypertension, cigarette smoking, diabetes mellitus overweight and physical activity. *Mailing Add:* Framingham Heart Study 118 Lincoln St Framingham MA 01701

CASTELLINO, FRANCIS JOSEPH, b Pittston, Pa, Mar 7, 43; m 65; c 3. BIOCHEMISTRY. *Educ:* Univ Scranton, BS, 64; Univ Iowa, MS, 66, PhD(biochem), 68. *Prof Exp:* NIH fel biochem, Duke Univ, 68-70; from asst prof to assoc prof, 70-77, PROF BIOCHEM, UNIV NOTRE DAME, 77-, DEAN, COL SCI, 79- *Res:* Structure function relationships in proteins. *Mailing Add:* Dept of Chem Univ of Notre Dame Notre Dame IN 46556

CASTELLION, ALAN WILLIAM, b North Tonawanda, NY, May 1, 34; m 61; c 2. RESEARCH ADMINISTRATION, PHARMACOLOGY. *Educ:* Univ Buffalo, BS, 56; Univ Utah, PhD(pharmacol), 64. *Prof Exp:* Teaching asst pharmacog, Univ Utah, 56-58, pharm, 58-59 & pharmacol, 59-63, res asst, 63-64; sr pharmacologist, Neuropharmacol Sect, Dept Neurol & Cardiol, Res & Develop Div, Smith Kline & French Labs, 66-67, sr scientist, Dept Pharmacol, 67-69; chief, Sect Pharmacol, 70-77, asst mgr sci affairs, 77-80, DIR COMPLIANCE, NORWICH-EATON PHARMACEUT, 80- *Concurrent Pos:* Smith Kline & French res fel, Col Med, Univ Utah, 64-66. *Honors & Awards:* Lunsford Richardson Pharm Award, 64. *Mem:* Sr mem Acad Pharmaceut Sci; Am Soc Pharmacol & Exp Therapeut; Sigma Xi; Regulatory Affairs Prof Soc; Am Pharmaceut Asn. *Res:* Pharmaceutical research and development; pharmaceutical regulatory affairs; compliance and quality assurance; toxicology; pharmacy. *Mailing Add:* Bradley Hill Rd Oxford NY 13830

CASTELLO, JOHN DONALD, b Paterson, NJ, May 1, 52. FOREST VIROLOGY, FOREST PATHOLOGY. *Educ:* Montclair State Col, BA, 73; Wash State Univ, MS, 75; Univ Wis, PhD(plant path), 78. *Prof Exp:* ASST PROF PLANT PATH, MICROBIOL & FOREST PATH, COL ENVIRON SCI & FORESTRY, STATE UNIV NY, 78- *Mem:* Am Phytopath Soc. *Res:* Virus diseases of shade, ornamental and forest tree species in an attempt to relate virus infection with dieback and decline diseases of major tree species in the northeast. *Mailing Add:* State Univ NY Environ Sci & Forestry Syracuse NY 13210

CASTELLUCCI, NICHOLAS THOMAS, b Roseto, Pa, May 1, 38; c 3. ORGANIC POLYMER CHEMISTRY. *Educ:* Moravian Col, BS, 58; Univ Pittsburgh, MS, 60. *Prof Exp:* Res asst, Mellon Inst, 58-65; asst, Pittsburgh Corning, 66-71; Scientist chem, PPG Indust Inc, 72-80; WITH RES LAB, US STEEL CORP, 80- *Honors & Awards:* IR-100 Award, Indust Res Mag, 70. *Mem:* Nat Asn Corrosion Engrs; Am Chem Soc. *Mailing Add:* Res Lab US Steel Corp 125 Jamison Lane MS 19 Monroeville PA 15146

CASTELNUOVO-TEDESCO, PIETRO, b Florence, Italy, Jan 5, 25; US citizen; m 57; c 2. PSYCHOANALYSIS, PSYCHOSOMATIC MEDICINE. *Educ:* Univ Calif, Los Angeles, BA, 45; Univ Calif, Berkeley, MA, 48; Sch Med, Boston Univ, MD, 52. *Prof Exp:* Physician inpatient unit psychiat, Boston City Hosp, 58-59; asst prof to prof psychiat, Sch Med, Univ Los Angeles, 59-75; JAMES G BLAKEMORE PROF PSYCHIAT, SCH MED, VANDERBILT UNIV, 75- *Concurrent Pos:* Asst psychiat, Harvard Med Sch, 58-59; chmn, Dept Psychiat, Harbor Gen Hosp, Calif, 59-75; Training & supv analyst, St Louis Psychoanal Inst, 77- *Mem:* fel Am Psychiat Asn; Am Psychoanal Asn; Am Psychosom Soc; fel Am Col Psychiatrists; fel Am Col Psychoanalysts. *Res:* psychotherapy; psychiatric education; author or coauthor of 85 publications. *Mailing Add:* Dept Psychiat Sch Med Vanderbilt Univ Nashville TN 37232

CASTEN, RICHARD FRANCIS, b New York, NY, Nov 1, 41; m 64. NUCLEAR PHYSICS. *Educ:* Col of the Holy Cross, BS, 63; Yale Univ, MS, 64, PhD(physics), 67. *Prof Exp:* Fel nuclear physics, Niels Bohr Inst, Univ Copenhagen, 67-69 & Los Alamos Sci Lab, 69-71; from asst physicist to physicist, 71-81, GROUP LEADER, NEUTRON NUCLEAR STRUCTURE GROUP, BROOKHAVEN NAT LAB, 81- *Mem:* Sigma Xi; NY Acad Sci; AAAS; Am Phys Soc. *Res:* Nuclear structure, especially collective modes such as pairing, vibrational, rotational excitations, Coulomb excitation, one and two nucleon transfer reactions, gamma ray deexcitations, Nilsson, Coriolis, interacting Boson approximation models. *Mailing Add:* Physics Dept Brookhaven Nat Lab Upton NY 11973

CASTEN, RICHARD G, b Philadelphia, Pa, May 14, 43; m 70. APPLIED MATHEMATICS. *Educ:* Temple Univ, AB, 65; Calif Inst Technol, PhD(appl math), 70. *Prof Exp:* Math technician magnetohydrodyn, Gen Elec Co, 64-65; math technician satellite orbits, Aerospace Corp, 66; res fel appl math, Calif Inst Technol, 70; asst prof math, Purdue Univ, West Lafayette, 70-77; MEM TECH STAFF, AEROSPACE CORP, 77- *Mem:* Soc Indust & Appl Math. *Res:* Biomathematics. *Mailing Add:* Aerospace Corp 2350 El Segundo Blvd El Segundo CA 90245

CASTENHOLZ, RICHARD WILLIAM, b Chicago, Ill, May 9, 31; m 54; c 2. BOTANY, MICROBIOLOGY. *Educ:* Univ Mich, BS, 52; Wash State Univ, PhD(bot), 57. *Prof Exp:* Asst bot, Wash State Univ, 53-57; from instr to assoc prof, 57-69, PROF BIOL, UNIV ORE, 69- *Concurrent Pos:* John Simon Guggenheim fel, 70-71; Fulbright scholar, Norway, 77-78. *Mem:* Ecol Soc Am; Phycol Soc Am; Am Soc Limnol & Oceanog; Am Soc Microbiol; Brit Soc Gen Microbiol. *Res:* Physiology and ecology of marine and freshwater algae; biology of thermophilic microorganisms. *Mailing Add:* Dept of Biol Univ of Ore Eugene OR 97403

CASTENSCHIOLD, RENE, b Mount Kisco, NY, Feb 7, 23; m 47; c 3. ELECTRICAL ENGINEERING. *Educ:* Pratt Inst, BEE, 44. *Prof Exp:* Design engr, Gen Elec Co, 44-47; sr prod engr, Am Transformer Co, 47-50; EXEC ENG MGR, AUTOMATIC SWITCH CO, 51- *Concurrent Pos:* Lectr, NJ Inst Technol, 67-79. *Mem:* Fel Inst Elec & Electronics Engrs; Nat Soc Prof Engrs; Instrument Soc Am. *Res:* Research and development of automatic transfer switches and generator controls; author of over 20 papers and articles on design, ground-fault protection, system coordination and controls for emergency power. *Mailing Add:* Lee's Hill Rd New Vernon NJ 07976

CASTER, KENNETH EDWARD, b New Albany, Pa, Jan 26, 08; m 33. GEOLOGY, PALEONTOLOGY. *Educ:* Cornell Univ, AB, 29, MS, 31, PhD(stratig), 33. *Prof Exp:* Asst entom, Cornell Univ, 28-30, asst geol, 29-30, instr paleont, 30-32, instr geol, 32-35; researcher, Paleont Res Inst, NY, 35-36; cur paleont, Mus, 36-40, fel, Grad Sch, 37-78, from asst prof to prof, 40-78, EMER PROF GEOL, UNIV CINCINNATI, 78- *Concurrent Pos:* Asst head dept sci, NY State Norm Sch, Geneseo, 35-36; Nat Res Coun grant-in-aid, 35-37; trustee, Paleont Res Inst, NY, 39-, vpres, 41-43 & 65, pres, 44, 45, 51-54 & 66; trustee, Cushman Found, 51-56; vis prof awards, US Dept State, 45-47; prof, Sao Paulo, 45-48; mem, Pan Am Cong Mining, Eng & Geol, 47 & US comn geol, 60-64; Guggenheim fel geol studies, SAm, 47-48, SAfrica, 54-55, Australia & NZ, 56; Fulbright vis fel, Univ Tasmania, 55-56 & Univ Cologne, 64; German Res Asn grant, 64; US rep, Int Paleont Union, 60-; US off del, Int Geol Cong, 60 & 64. *Honors & Awards:* Gondwana Medal, India, 55; Paleont Soc Medal, 76. *Mem:* AAAS; Am Asn Petrol Geol; fel Paleont Soc (secy, 47-55, vpres, 57, pres, 59); fel Geol Soc Am; Soc Vert Paleont. *Res:* Invertebrate paleontology; paleozoic stratigraphy; paleogeography; Southern Hemisphere historical geology; early echinoderm history; fossil arachnida; problematica. *Mailing Add:* 425 Riddle Rd Cincinnati OH 45220

CASTER, WILLIAM OVIATT, b Topeka, Kans, Dec 7, 19; m 43; c 4. NUTRITION. *Educ:* Univ Wis, BA, 42, MS, 44; Univ Minn, PhD(physiol chem), 48. *Prof Exp:* Asst inorg chem, Univ Wis, 42-43; chemist, Lab Physiol Hyg, Univ Minn, 44-46, chemist, Physiol Hyg, 46-47, asst prof physiol chem, 51-63; biochemist, Nutrit Unit, USPHS, 48-51; assoc prof, 63-70, PROF NUTRIT, UNIV GA, 70- *Concurrent Pos:* USPHS fel, Nat Heart Inst, 56-61. *Mem:* AAAS; Am Soc Biol Chemists; Am Inst Nutrit; Brit Nutrit Soc. *Res:* Human nutrition; water and electrolyte metabolism; radiobiology; chemistry and function of cardiovascular system. *Mailing Add:* 368 Dawson Hall Sch of Home Econ Univ of Ga Athens GA 30602

CASTILLO, JESSICA MAGUILA, b Zamboanga City, Philippines, Jan 6, 38. INSECT PATHOLOGY, NEMATOLOGY. *Educ:* Univ Philippines, BS, 58; Univ Mass, MS, 65; Univ Md, PhD(plant path), 68. *Prof Exp:* Asst instr zool, Univ Philippines, 58-62; res assoc nematol, Univ Mass, 68-70; assoc prof biol, Mindanao State Univ, 70-72; res assoc nematol, Univ Mass, 72-74; asst dir microbiol, Quipse Labs, Ill, 74; fel, Boyce Thompson Res Inst, 75-77, consult, 78; INSTR, STATE UNIV NY AGR & TECH COL, FARMINGDALE, 78- *Mem:* AAAS; Am Inst Biol Sci; Soc Nematologists; Soc Invert Path. *Mailing Add:* 61-15 98th St Rego Park NY 11374

CASTLE, GEORGE SAMUEL PETER, b Belfast, North Ireland, May 30, 39; Can citizen; m 61; c 3. ELECTRICAL ENGINEERING. *Educ:* Univ Western Ont, BESc, 61, PhD(elec eng), 69; Imp Col, Univ London, DIC, 63; Univ London, MSc, 63. *Prof Exp:* Assoc mem sci staff microwave commun systs, Res & Develop Lab, Northern Elec Co, 63-66; lectr eng sci, 68-69, from asst prof to assoc prof, 69-79, PROF ENG SCI & CHMN, DEPT ELEC ENG, UNIV WESTERN ONT, 79- *Mem:* Inst Elec & Electronics Engrs. *Res:* Application of electrostatic forces to engineering problems. *Mailing Add:* 6 Brentwood Pl London ON N6G 1X6 Can

CASTLE, GORDON BENJAMIN, b Portland, Ind, Aug 10, 06; m 31; c 2. ZOOLOGY. *Educ:* Wabash Col, AB 28; Univ Calif, AM, 30, PhD(zool), 34. *Prof Exp:* Asst biol, Termite Invest Comt, Univ Calif, 28-31; from instr to prof, Univ Mont, 34-62; actg head dept, 37-38, chmn dept, 38-49, dir biol sta, 38-62, sr acad dean & dean col arts & sci, 49-52, dean grad sch, 52-57, acting pres, 58-59, chmn dept, 62-64, vpres univ, 64-67, prof, 62-77, EMER PROF ZOOL, ARIZ STATE UNIV, 77- *Mem:* AAAS; Ecol Soc Am; Am Soc Zoologists. *Res:* Social and aquatic insects. *Mailing Add:* 521 E Loyola Dr Tempe AZ 85282

CASTLE, JOHN EDWARDS, b Minneapolis, Minn, June 10, 19; m 42; c 3. APPLIED CHEMISTRY. *Educ:* Carleton Col, BA, 40; Univ Wis, PhD(org chem), 44. *Prof Exp:* Asst chem, Univ Wis, 40-42, tech asst, Off Sci Res & Develop Contract, 42-43; chemist cent res dept, E I du Pont de Nemours & Co, Inc, 43-50, res supvr, 50-61, asst lab dir, 61-63, assoc dir mat res, 63-65, lab dir, Electrochem Dept, 65-68, asst res dir, 68-72, mgr environ prods sect, Indust Chem Dept, 72-74, res mgr energy & mat dept, 74-77, environ control mgr cent res dept, 78; consult, 78-79. *Concurrent Pos:* Adj prof, Col Marine Studies, Univ Del, 79- *Mem:* Am Chem Soc; Am Inst Chem Engrs. *Res:* Contact catalysis; organic synthesis; polymers; biochemistry; chitin, mucopolysaccharides; bioenergy processes. *Mailing Add:* Col Marine Studies Univ Del Lewes DE 19958

CASTLE, JOHN GRANVILLE, JR, b Buffalo, NY, Sept 9, 24; m 46; c 5. MAGNETIC RESONANCE, PHYSICAL OPTICS. *Educ:* State Univ NY Buffalo, BA, 47; Yale Univ, PhD(physics), 50. *Prof Exp:* Instr physics, State Univ NY Buffalo, 50-51; assoc res physicist, Cornell Aeronaut Lab, 51-52; res assoc, State Univ NY Buffalo, 53-55; res physicist, Westinghouse Res Lab, 55-58, adv physicist, Westinghouse Res & Develop Ctr, 58-67; prof elec eng & res assoc, Learning Res & Develop Ctr, Univ Pittsburgh, 67-69; dir, Div Natural Sci & Math, Univ Ala, Huntsville, 70-71, prof physics 69-80; MEM TECH STAFF, SANDIA NAT LAB, 80- *Concurrent Pos:* Vis scientist, High Energy Physics Lab, Stanford Univ, 70-71; clin prof therapeut radiol, Med Ctr, Univ Ala, Birmingham, 70-80; consult, US Army Missile Command, 72- *Mem:* AAAS; Am Phys Soc. *Res:* Cryogenic engineering; solid state physics; medical instrumentation; educational media; microwave and optical properties of solids; infrared properties of gases; biomedical engineering. *Mailing Add:* Div 2362 Sandia Nat Lab Albuquerque NM 87185

CASTLE, KAREN G, b Elizabeth, NJ, Sept 23, 48; m 71. ASTRONOMY, PHYSICS. *Educ:* Univ Mich, BS, 70, MS, 72, PhD(astron), 75. *Prof Exp:* Fel physics & instr, Univ Calgary, 75-78; assoc sr comput programmer, Lockheed Electronics Co, 78-80, ENGR, SR LOCKHEED ENG & MGT SERV, LOCKHEED AIRCRAFT CORP, 80- *Concurrent Pos:* Lectr, Downtown Campus, Univ Houston, 81. *Mem:* Am Astron Soc; AAAS; Astron Soc Pac; Sigma Xi; Am Inst Aeronaut & Astronaut. *Res:* Dynamics of mass exchange in binary star systems; orbital mechanics. *Mailing Add:* Lockheed Electronics Co 1830 NASA Rd 1 Houston TX 77058

CASTLE, MANFORD C, b Coeburn, Va, Apr 27, 42; m 69; c 3. PHARMACOLOGY. *Educ:* Berea Col, BA, 65; Univ Kans, PhD(pharmacol), 72. *Prof Exp:* Vol chem teacher, Peace Corps, Univ Antioquia, Colombia, 66-68; clin instr pharmacol, Univ Kans, 72-73; staff assoc & NIH fel, Nat Inst Gen Med Sci, 73-75; staff assoc pharmacol, Nat Cancer Inst, 75-76; asst prof, 76-78, ASSOC PROF, DEPT PHARMACOL, E VA MED SCH, NORFOLK, 78- *Concurrent Pos:* Consult, Nat Cancer Inst, 78-80; prin investr, Nat Heart, Lung & Blood Inst, 77-80. *Mem:* AAAS; Am Soc Pharmacol & Exp Therapeut; Drug Metab Soc; Int Union Pharmacol. *Res:* Metabolism and disposition of drugs, particularly cardiac glycosides and cancer chemotherapeutic agents; alteration of these processes by other drugs; methods involve use of radioactive tracers and high-pressure liquid chromatography. *Mailing Add:* Eastern Va Med Sch PO Box 1980 Norfolk VA 23501

CASTLE, PETER MYER, b Detroit, Mich, Apr 19, 40; m 61; c 3. CHEMICAL PHYSICS, HIGH TEMPERATURE CHEMISTRY. *Educ:* Univ Mich, BS, 62; Purdue Univ, PhD(phys chem), 70. *Prof Exp:* Vis asst prof phys chem, Purdue Univ, 70; sr engr, 70-80, FEL SCIENTIST PHYS CHEM, WESTINGHOUSE RES LABS, 80- *Concurrent Pos:* Instr night sch, Community Col Allegheny County, Boyce Campus, 74-; adj prof, Kans State Univ. *Mem:* Am Soc Mass Spectrometry. *Res:* Studies of infrared, visible and near ultraviolet laser photolysis reactions for synthetic applications and understanding of fundamental photophysical processes; high temperature mass spectrometric investigations of liquid vapor and solid-vapor equilibria in fused salt systems. *Mailing Add:* Westinghouse Res Labs Beulah Rd Pittsburgh PA 15235

CASTLE, RAYMOND NIELSON, b Boise, Idaho, June 24, 16; m 37; c 8. CHEMISTRY. *Educ:* Idaho State Univ, BS, 39; Univ Colo, MA, 41, PhD(chem), 44. *Prof Exp:* Asst chem, Univ Colo, 39-42; instr, Univ Idaho, 42-43; instr, Univ Colo, 43-44; res chem, Battelle Mem Inst, 44-46; asst prof chem, Univ NMex, 46-47, pharmaceut chem, 47-50, from assoc prof to prof chem, 50-70, chmn dept, 63-70; prof chem, Brigham Young Univ, 70-81; GRAD RES PROF CHEM, UNIV SOUTH FLA, 81- *Concurrent Pos:* Res fel, Univ Va, 52-53; ed, J Heterocyclic Chem; vis prof, Univ Fla, 79. *Mem:* Am Chem Soc; fel Royal Soc Chem; Pharmaceut Soc Japan; Int Soc Heterocyclic Chem. *Res:* Organic chemistry; optical crystallography; optical crystallographic properties of organic compounds; synthesis of cinnolines; pyridazines; pyridines, polycyclic thiophenes; other related heterocycles of medicinal interest. *Mailing Add:* Dept Chem Univ South Fla Tampa FL 33620

CASTLE, RICHARD THOMAS, physics, see previous edition

CASTLE, ROBERT O, b Berkeley, Calif, Dec 31, 26; m 54; c 2. GEOLOGY, TECTONICS. *Educ:* Stanford Univ, BS, 48; McGill Univ, MSc, 49; Univ Calif, Los Angeles, PhD(geol), 64. *Prof Exp:* Instr geol, Univ Mass, 49-50; geol field asst, 50-51, geologist, 51-52, GEOLOGIST, US GEOL SURV, 54- *Mem:* Geol Soc Am; Asn Eng Geologists. *Res:* Tectonics engineering geology; igneous petrology; contemporary crustal deformation. *Mailing Add:* US Geological Survey 345 Middlefield Rd Menlo Park CA 94025

CASTLE, WILLIAM BOSWORTH, b Cambridge, Mass, Oct 21, 97; m 33; c 2. CLINICAL MEDICINE, HEMATOLOGY. *Educ:* Harvard Univ, MD, 21; FRACP; FRCP, 64. *Hon Degrees:* SM, Yale Univ, 33; MD, Univ Utrecht, 36; SD, Univ Chicago, 52; LLD, Jefferson Med Col, 64; DSc, Harvard Univ, 64, Univ Pa, 66, Marquette Univ, 69, Mt Sinai Sch Med, 72; LHD, Boston Col, 66; hon FRCPS(C), 65; hon FRCP(E), 67. *Prof Exp:* Intern, Mass Gen Hosp, 21-23; asst physiol, Sch Pub Health, 23-25, instr, Med Sch, 24-25, asst med, 25-29, from instr to prof, 29-57, George Richards Minot prof, 57-63, Francis Weld Peabody fac prof, 63-68, EMER FRANCIS WELD PEABODY FAC PROF MED, HARVARD UNIV, 68- *Concurrent Pos:* Dir anemia comn, Rockefeller Found, PR, 31; assoc dir, Thorndike Mem Lab, Boston City Hosp, 32-48, dir lab, 48-63, dir second & fourth med serv, 40-63, hon dir lab, 63-; distinguished physician, Vet Admin, 68-72; sr physician, Vet Admin Hosp, West Roxbury, Mass, 72-73, consult, 73-79. *Honors & Awards:* Phillips Prize, Am Col Physicians, 32; Perpetual Student, Med Col, St Bartholomew's Hosp, London, 70. *Mem:* Nat Acad Sci; AAAS; master Am Col Physicians; fel Am Inst Nutrit, 73; hon mem Am Soc Hemat. *Res:* Clinical medicine; etiology and therapy of pernicious anemia, sprue; anemias in pregnancy; hookworm anemia; relation asmotic fragility to cell shape; hemolytic effects of oxidants; mechanism of hemolytic anemias; splenic filtration; redcell viscosity of sicklemia; vitamin B12 intrinsic factor relations. *Mailing Add:* 22 Irving St Brookline MA 02146

CASTLEBERRY, GEORGE E, b Herring, Okla, Mar 20, 18; m 44. INORGANIC CHEMISTRY. *Educ:* Southwestern State Col, Okla, BS, 39; Univ Okla, MS, 51, PhD(sci educ), 68. *Prof Exp:* Prin & teacher, E Walnut Schs, Okla, 40-41; teacher, Clinton High Sch, 41-42, teacher & asst prin, 45-58; PROF CHEM, SOUTHWESTERN STATE COL, OKLA, 58- *Mem:* Am Chem Soc; Nat Sci Teachers Asn. *Res:* Science education; graduate education of secondary school science teachers of Oklahoma public schools; orthoaminobenzenethiol as a reagent for the gravimetric determination of selenium in compounds. *Mailing Add:* Dept of Chem Southwestern State Col Weatherford OK 73096

CASTLEMAN, ALBERT WELFORD, JR, b Richmond, Va, Jan 7, 36; m 76; c 2. CHEMICAL PHYSICS. *Educ:* Rensselaer Polytech Inst, BChE, 57; Polytech Inst Brooklyn, MSc, 63, PhD, 69. *Prof Exp:* Engr, Olin Mathieson Chem Corp, 57-58; engr, Brookhaven Nat Lab, 58-66, scientist, 66-75; PROF CHEM, UNIV COLO, 75- *Concurrent Pos:* Adj prof atmospheric chem, Dept Earth & Space Sci & Mech, State Univ NY Stony Brook, 73-75; fel, Coop Inst Res Environ Sci, Univ Colo, 75-; consult, Mfg Chemists Sherman Fairchild Distinguished Scholar, Calif Inst Technol, 77; Asn; consult, Adv Comt Reactor Safeguard, AEC, 58-75, Reactor Safety Div, US Nuclear Regulatory Comn, 75-81; adv, Nat Ctr Atmospheric Res, 75-; mem, Subcomn Ions, Aerosols & Radioactivity, Int Comn Atmospheric Electricity, Int Asn

Meteorol & Atmospheric Physics; mem comt & chmn panel fates of pollutants, Nat Acad Sci/Nat Res Coun Environ Res Assessment Comt. *Mem:* Am Chem Soc; Am Phys Soc; Am Geophys Union; Int Asn Meteorol & Atmospheric Physics (secy, 74-75); Sigma Xi. *Res:* Nucleation phenomena, molecular properties of small clusters; kinetics of association reactions, solvation phenomena, statistical mechanics; aerosol and surface chemistry; laser photochemistry; catalysis atmospheric chemistry. *Mailing Add:* Dept Chem Univ Colo Boulder CO 80309

CASTLEMAN, BENJAMIN, b Everett, Mass, May 17, 06; m 35; c 3. PATHOLOGY. *Educ:* Harvard Univ, BA, 27; Yale Univ, MD, 31. *Hon Degrees:* MD, Gothenburg Univ, 66. *Prof Exp:* Instr path, 35-42, assoc, 43-48, asst prof, 48-53, clin prof, 53-61, prof, 61-70, Shattuck prof path anat, 70-72, EMER SHATTUCK PROF PATH ANAT, HARVARD MED SCH, 72-; HON PATHOLOGIST, MASS GEN HOSP, 74- *Concurrent Pos:* Asst pathologist, Mass Gen Hosp, 35-42, pathologist, 42-43, chief dept path, 53-74; consult pathologist, hosps. *Mem:* Am Asn Path & Bact; Am Soc Clin Path; Am Soc Exp Path; Am Acad Arts & Sci; Int Acad Path. *Res:* Hypertension; parathyroid and thymus glands; myasthenia gravis; pulmonary disease. *Mailing Add:* Dept of Path Mass Gen Hosp Boston MA 02114

CASTLEMAN, L(OUIS) S(AMUEL), b St Johnsbury, Vt, Nov 24, 18; m; c 4. PHYSICAL METALLURGY. *Educ:* Mass Inst Technol, BS, 39, ScD, 50. *Prof Exp:* Metallurgist, Sunbeam Elec Mfg Co, 39-41; asst metall, Mass Inst Technol, 47-50; sr scientist, Westinghouse Atomic Power Div, 50-52, supvry scientist, 53-54; metall specialist, Gen Tel & Electronics Labs, Inc, Sylvania Elec Prod, Inc, 54-64; adj prof, 55-64, PROF PHYS METALL, POLYTECH INST NEW YORK, 64- *Concurrent Pos:* Res assoc, sch mines, Columbia Univ, 57-58; chmn fac senate, Polytech Inst New York. *Mem:* Am Inst Mining, Metall & Petrol Engrs; Am Phys Soc; fel AAAS. *Res:* Phase transformations; mechanical properties of metals and alloys; effects of nuclear radiations on properties of metals and alloys; diffusional phenomena; electronic materials. *Mailing Add:* Polytech Inst of New York 333 Jay Brooklyn NY 11201

CASTLES, THOMAS R, b St Louis, Mo, Oct 27, 37; m 59; c 3. PHARMACOLOGY. *Educ:* Grinnell Col, BA, 59; Univ Iowa, MS, 62, PhD(pharmacol), 65. *Prof Exp:* From assoc pharmacologist to prin pharmacologist, 67-70, Midwest Res Inst, 67-77; MGR TOXICOL LAB, STAUFFER CHEM CO, 77- *Mem:* Am Soc Pharmacol & Exp Therapeut; Soc Am Toxicol. *Res:* Thiazide diuretics; aldosterone; carbonic anhydrose inhibitors; pharmacology and toxicology of antimalarial compounds; analgesic tolerance. *Mailing Add:* Stauffer Chem Co 1200 South 47th Richmond CA 94804

CASTLETON, KENNETH BITNER, b Salt Lake City, Utah, July 29, 03; m 31; c 4. SURGERY. *Educ:* Univ Utah, AB, 23, Univ Pa, MD, 27; Univ Minn, PhD(surg), 33; Am Bd Surg, dipl. *Prof Exp:* Instr anat, 33-34, phys diagnosis, 35-36, surg anat, 38-43, assoc clin prof surg, 43-62, prof surg & dean, Col Med, 62-69, vpres med affairs, 69-71, EMER PROF SURG, UNIV UTAH, 71- *Concurrent Pos:* Pvt pract, 33-62. *Mem:* Fel Am Col Surg. *Res:* Clinical surgery; gastroenterology; experimental physiology. *Mailing Add:* 1235 E 2nd South 303 Salt Lake City UT 84102

CASTNER, THEODORE GRANT, JR, b Orange, NJ, June 17, 30; m 67; c 2. SOLID STATE PHYSICS. *Educ:* Cornell Univ, BEng, 53; Univ Ill, MS, 55, PhD(physics), 58. *Prof Exp:* Physicist, Gen Elec Res Labs, 58-63; assoc prof, 63-70, PROF PHYSICS, UNIV ROCHESTER, 70- *Concurrent Pos:* Guggenheim fel, Swiss Fed Inst Technol, 69-70 & Sandia Labs, 76-77. *Mem:* Fel Am Phys Soc; Am Asn Phys Teachers; Am Sect Int Solar Soc. *Res:* Electron spin resonance phenomena in solids; impurities in insulators, semiconductors; cooperative phenomena in magnetic materials; spin-lattice relaxation; dielectric phenomena and Metal-Insulator transition in doped semiconductors; magnetoelectric effect. *Mailing Add:* Dept Physics & Astron Univ Rochester Rochester NY 14627

CASTO, CLYDE CHRISTY, b Edmond, Okla, Oct 8, 12; m 42; c 2. ANALYTICAL CHEMISTRY. *Educ:* Cent State Col, BS, 36; Univ Mich, MS, 48. *Prof Exp:* Anal chemist, George W Gooch Lab, Los Angeles, 36-38, anal chemist, Commercial Lab, 38-40; res chemist, Consol Electrodyn Corp, Calif, 40-41; anal chemist, George W Gooch Lab, Los Angeles, 41-42; anal res chemist, Basic Magnesium, Nev, 42-44; head anal res & develop, Tenn Eastman Corp, Oak Ridge, 44-46; res chemist, Rayon Dept, E I du Pont de Nemours & Co, 48-50, res supvr textile fibers dept, Nylon Res Div, 50-56; sect head anal instrumental, Am Potash & Chem Corp, Nev, 56-57; lab dir, vpres & partner, George W Gooch Labs, Calif, 57-59; staff chemist, Aerojet-Gen Corp, 59-60; mgr phys & anal chem dept, Rocket Power, Inc, Ariz, 60-64; chief chemist, Off State Chemist, State Ariz, 64-77; RETIRED. *Mem:* Am Chem Soc. *Res:* Light metals; uranium chemistry; nylon and polyesters; chemicals and high energy fuels; solid propellants; agricultural chemicals. *Mailing Add:* 2149 Nicklaus Dr Mesa AZ 85205

CASTON, J DOUGLAS, b Ellenboro, NC, June 16, 32; m 58; c 3. BIOCHEMISTRY, EMBRYOLOGY. *Educ:* Lenoir-Rhyne Col, BA, 54; Univ NC, MA, 58; Brown Univ, PhD(biol), 61. *Prof Exp:* From sr instr to assoc prof anat, 63-75, PROF ANAT, SCH MED, CASE WESTERN RESERVE UNIV, 75- *Concurrent Pos:* Fel develop biol, Carnegie Inst of Wash, 61-63; Am Cancer Soc grants. *Mem:* Biophys Soc; Am Soc Gen Physiol; Soc Develop Biol. *Res:* Control of metabolic pathways during development; catecholamine synthesis; protein and ribonucleic acid synthesis; folate binding macromolecules. *Mailing Add:* Dept of Anat Sch of Med Case Western Reserve Univ Cleveland OH 44106

CASTON, RALPH HENRY, b Akron, Ohio, Nov 22, 15; m 46; c 3. PHYSICS. *Educ:* Univ Akron, MS, 39; Univ Notre Dame, PhD(physics), 42. *Prof Exp:* Mem staff, Nat Defense Res Comt Proj, Radiation Lab, Mass Inst Technol, 42-45; MEM TECH STAFF, KIMBERLY-CLARK RES & DEVELOP LAB, 45- *Mem:* Am Phys Soc. *Res:* Physics of rubber; radar; general physics in the paper industry; operations research; computer process control. *Mailing Add:* Kimberly-Clark Res & Develop Lab Neenah WI 54956

CASTONGUAY, RICHARD NORMAN, b Worcester, Mass, Dec 22, 39; m 73; c 2. PHYSICAL CHEMISTRY, MATERIALS ENGINEERING. *Educ:* Col Holy Cross, BS, 62; Cornell Univ, PhD(phys chem), 67. *Prof Exp:* Corp tech dir, MICA Corp, 68-78; MGR ELEC ELECTRONIC MATRIX DEVELOP & APPL LABS, RESINS DEPT, CIBA GEIGY CORP, 78- *Concurrent Pos:* Consult, Gallil Corp, 74-77; consult, AILTECH Div, Cutler Hammer, 77-78. *Mem:* Am Phys Soc; Int Soc Hybrid Microelectronics; Soc Advan Mat & Process Eng. *Res:* Polymer chemistry; polymeric material characteristics including electrical, electronic and structural; resistance materials characteristics. *Mailing Add:* 18 Pondcrest Rd Danbury CT 06810

CASTONGUAY, THOMAS T(ELISPHORE), b Lead, SDak, Nov 20, 09; m 40; c 5. CHEMICAL ENGINEERING, PHYSICAL CHEMISTRY. *Educ:* Univ Detroit, BMetEng, 31; Iowa State Col, PhD(chem eng, phys chem), 41. *Prof Exp:* Instr chem & eng, Univ Detroit, 31-34 & Iowa State Col, 36-40; asst prof chem eng, Univ Kans, 40-41, acting head dept, 41-42, assoc prof, 42-46; prof & head dept, 46-77, EMER PROF CHEM ENG, UNIV N MEX, 77- *Concurrent Pos:* Chem dir, Ames Prods Co, 33-36, consult chem engr, 33-36; engr consult, 77- *Mem:* Am Chem Soc; Am Soc Eng Educ; Am Inst Chem Engrs; Brit Soc Engrs. *Res:* Catalysis and high pressure; dehydration; fertilizers; waterproofing of paper; production of dichloro-diphenyl-trichloroethane. *Mailing Add:* 923 Vassar Dr NE Albuquerque NM 87106

CASTOR, CECIL WILLIAM, b Detroit, Mich, Oct 9, 25; m 48; c 3. INTERNAL MEDICINE, RHEUMATOLOGY. *Educ:* Univ Mich, MD, 51; Am Bd Internal Med, dipl, 58. *Prof Exp:* Intern & resident internal med, 51-55; from instr to assoc prof internal med, 55-67, PROF INTERNAL MED, MED SCH, UNIV MICH, ANN ARBOR, 67- *Concurrent Pos:* Arthritis & Rheumatism Found fel, 55-57, sr investr, 57-62; USPHS career res develop award, 63-67; mem study sect gen med, NIH, 70-74; fel comt & prof educ comt, Arthritis Found. *Honors & Awards:* Int Geigy Rheumatism Award, 15th Int Cong Rheumatol France, 81. *Mem:* Fel Am Col Physicians; Am Soc Clin Invest; Am Fedn Clin Res; Am Rheumatism Asn; Tissue Cult Asn. *Res:* Regulation of connective tissue cells, in vitro and in vivo, especially on the hormonal control of mucopolysaccharide and collagen synthesis. *Mailing Add:* Dept Internal Med Univ Mich Med Ctr Ann Arbor MI 48104

CASTOR, JERE GEORGE, b Newark, Ohio, Aug 31, 28; div; c 5. MECHANICAL ENGINEERING, MANAGEMENT. *Educ:* Univ Ill, BS, 51. *Prof Exp:* Proj engr constant speed drives, Sundstrand Aviation, 51-54, group engr advan develop & hydromech systs, 54-58, systs mgr B-70 hydromech systs & Hotelect Prog, 58-62; proj engr TSE-36 helicopter engine, Airesearch Mfg Co Ariz, 62-66, prog mgr TPE-331 turboprop engine prod improv, 66-70, prog mgr advan technol & propulsion engines, 70-73, prog mgr space power unit reactor, 73-76, prog dir, Advan Concepts & Advan Power Systs, 76-77, PROJ ENGR, COMPOUND CYCLE TURBINE ENG PROG, DEFENSE ADVAN RES PROJS AGENCY, US AIR FORCE, GARRETT TURBINE ENGINE CO, 77- *Mem:* Am Soc Mech Engrs; Soc Automotive Engrs; Am Inst Aeronaut & Astronaut. *Res:* Prime propulsion engines systems; aerospace gas turbines and transportation; secondary power systems; aerospace hydraulics; turbo compound engines; aerospace and transportation in industry. *Mailing Add:* Garrett Turbine Engine Co 111 S 34th St Phoenix AZ 85034

CASTOR, JOHN I, b Fresno, Calif, Jan 5, 43. ASTROPHYSICS. *Educ:* Fresno State Col, BS, 61; Calif Inst Technol, PhD(astron), 67. *Prof Exp:* Res fel physics, Calif Inst Technol, 66-67; res assoc astrophys, 67-69, asst prof, 69-72, assoc prof, 72-78, PROF PHYSICS & ASTROPHYS, UNIV COLO, BOULDER, 78-, FEL JOINT INST LAB ASTROPHYS, 70- *Mem:* Fel Royal Astron Soc; Am Astron Soc; Int Astron Union. *Res:* Stellar interiors; pulsating stars; radiative transfer; stellar radiation hydrodynamics. *Mailing Add:* Dept of Physics & Astrophysics Univ of Colo Boulder CO 80309

CASTOR, LAROY NORTHROP, b Philadelphia, Pa, Sept 27, 24; m 53; c 4. CELL BIOLOGY, CELL CYCLE. *Educ:* Mass Inst Technol, BS, 48; Univ Pa, PhD(biophys), 54. *Prof Exp:* Am Cancer Soc fel, Univ Toronto, 55; fel, Univ Pa, 56-57; assoc biophysics, Johnson Res Found, 57-63; sr investr cell biol, Biochem Res Found, Del, 63-66; asst mem, 66-78, ASSOC MEM, INST CANCER RES, 78- *Mem:* Am Soc Cell Biol; Tissue Cult Asn; Am Asn Cancer Res. *Res:* Protein synthesis and degradation in relation to control of the cell cycle; cell kinetics; sensitivity of cell cultures to anti-cancer drugs. *Mailing Add:* Inst for Cancer Res 7701 Burholme Ave Fox Chase Philadelphia PA 19111

CASTRACANE, V DANIEL, b Philadelphia, Pa, Aug 16, 40; m 77; c 2. REPRODUCTIVE PHYSIOLOGY, ENDOCRINOLOGY. *Educ:* Temple Univ, BA, 62; Villanova Univ, MS, 66; Rutgers Univ, PhD(zool), 72. *Prof Exp:* Fel steroid biochem, Worcester Found Exp Biol, 72-73; fel reprod physiol, Sch Med, Case Western Reserve Univ, 73-76; ASSOC FOUND SCIENTIST REPROD ENDOCRINOL, SOUTHWEST FOUND FOR RES & EDUC, 76- *Mem:* Endocrine Soc; Soc Study Reprod; Am Soc Primatologists. *Res:* Utero-ovarian relationships; pubertal endocrinology; corpus luteum; endocrinology of pregnancy. *Mailing Add:* Southwest Found for Res & Educ PO Box 28147 San Antonio TX 78284

CASTRANOVA, VINCENT, b Trenton, NJ, March 18, 49; m 70. CELLULAR PHYSIOLOGY, RESPIRATORY PHYSIOLOGY. *Educ:* Mt St Marys Col, BS, 70; WVa Univ, PhD(physiol), 74. *Prof Exp:* Fel physiol, WVa Univ, 70-74; fel, Yale Univ, 74-76, res fac, 76-77; asst prof, 77-81, ASSOC PROF, WVA UNIV, 81- *Concurrent Pos:* Res physiologist, Nat Inst Occup Safety & Health, 77- *Mem:* Am Physiol Soc; Biophys Soc; Soc Toxicol. *Res:* Isolation and characterization of lung cells surfactant release by alveolar type II epithelial cells excitation-secretion coupling in alveolar macrophages, volume regulation by pneumocytes and toxicity of metals on lung cells. *Mailing Add:* Appalachian Lab Occup Safety 944 Chestnut Ridge Rd Morgantown WV 26505

CASTRIC, PETER ALLEN, b Pendleton, Ore, Sept 26, 38; m 65; c 1. MICROBIAL PHYSIOLOGY, MICROBIAL BIOCHEMISTRY. *Educ:* Ore State Univ, BS, 61; Mont State Univ, PhD(microbiol), 69. *Prof Exp:* Fel microbiol, Dept Bot & Microbiol, Mont State Univ, 64-69, biochem, Dept Biochem & biophysics, Univ Calif, Davis, 69-70 & Dept Biochem, Univ Mich, Ann Arbor, 70-71; asst prof, 71-74, assoc prof, 74-80, PROF BIOL & MICROBIOL, DEPT BIOL SCI, DUQUESNE UNIV, PITTSBURGH, 80- *Mem:* Am Soc Biol Chemists; Am Soc Microbiol; AAAS. *Res:* Bacterial secondary metabolism; examination of hydrogen cyanide biosynthesis by pseudomonas aeruginosa; urea metabolism in yeasts and algae; characterization of urea amidolyase in these microbes. *Mailing Add:* 620 N Meadowcraft Ave Pittsburgh PA 15216

CASTRILLON, JOSE P A, b Buenos Aires, Arg, Jan 4, 26; m 64; c 2. ORGANIC CHEMISTRY, RADIOCHEMISTRY. *Educ:* Univ Buenos Aiers, Dr(chem), 51. *Prof Exp:* Scientist chem, Atanor, SAM, Arg, 50-52, Squibb, SA, 53-55, Arg AEC, 56-64 & PR Nuclear Ctr, 64-73; div head phy sci, PR Nuclear Ctr, 73-76; MEM FAC & HEAD DEPT CHEM, PAN AM UNIV, 76- *Concurrent Pos:* Fel Arg Coun, Univ Colo, 60-61; prof org chem, Univ Asuncion, 71-72. *Mem:* Am Chem Soc; Arg Chem Soc. *Res:* New solvents and solutes in liquid scintillation counting; synthesis of sulfur heterocycles as potential schistosomicides, trypanosomicides and antitumor agents; conformational studies of flexible ring systems. *Mailing Add:* Dept Chem Pan Am Univ Edinburg TX 78539

CASTRO, ALBERT JOSEPH, b Santa Clara, Calif, May 13, 16; m 37; c 3. ORGANIC CHEMISTRY. *Educ:* San Jose State Col, AB, 39; Stanford Univ, AM, 42, PhD(org chem), 45. *Prof Exp:* Res chemist, Calif Res Corp, 44-47; asst prof chem, Univ Ariz, 47-49; from asst prof to assoc prof, 49-58, PROF CHEM, SAN JOSE STATE UNIV, 58- *Concurrent Pos:* Asst, Univ Santa Clara, 49; consult, Nassau Chems, Inc, 49-53; vis lectr, Johns Hopkins Univ, 54-55; vis scholar, Stanford Univ, 78; Nat Sci Found reviewer, Chem Div, Chem Synthesis & Anal Sect, 79; ad hoc consult, Minority Biomed Support Prog, NIH, 79. *Mem:* Fel Am Inst Chemists; Am Chem Soc; Brit Chem Soc; Sigma Xi. *Res:* Composition of ether solutions of the Grignard reagent; synthesis and structure of compounds related to chelidonine; reaction of epoxides and ammonia; synthesis of arylethylenes; Friedel-Crafts reaction; natural products; chemistry of pyrroles; compounds of possible pharmacological value. *Mailing Add:* Dept of Chem San Jose State Univ San Jose CA 95192

CASTRO, ALBERTO, b San Salvador, El Salvador, Nov 15, 33; m 56; c 5. BIOCHEMISTRY, ENDOCRINOLOGY. *Educ:* Univ Houston, BS, 58; Univ El Salvador, PhD(biol chem), 62. *Prof Exp:* From asst prof to prof microbiol & biochem, Univ El Salvador, 58-63, dir grad res & coordr-dir gen studies & preprof curric, 65-66; asst prof pediat, Sch Med, Univ Ore, 70-73; assoc prof, 73-77, PROF MED & PATH, SCH MED, UNIV MIAMI, 77-, DIR, HORMONE RES LAB, 73- *Concurrent Pos:* Prof basic sci & head dept, Univ El Salvador, 65-68; NIH sr res fel diabetes & metab, Sch Med, Univ Ore, 66-70; dir endocrinol lab, United Med Lab, 70-73; consult, Union Carbide Corp, NY, 73-; sr scientist, Papanicolaou Cancer Res Inst, 73-75. *Mem:* AAAS; Am Chem Soc; Am Inst Chem; NY Acad Sci. *Res:* Carbohydrate biochemistry, metabolism and modes of action; hormone mechanisms and the interrelationship to hypertension and primary aldosteronism. *Mailing Add:* 6275 SW 123rd Terrace Miami FL 33156

CASTRO, ANTHONY J, b Chicago, Ill, Nov 30, 30; m 81; c 3. ORGANIC POLYMER CHEMISTRY. *Educ:* Univ Chicago, MS, 58, PhD(chem), 62; John Marshall Law Sch, JD, 75. *Prof Exp:* Res supvr polymer chem, Continental Can Co, 62-65; mgr polymer chem, 65-80, ASST DIR RES, ARMAK CO, MCCOOK, 80- *Mem:* AAAS; NY Acad Sci; Am Chem Soc; Soc Plastics Engrs. *Res:* Investigation into areas of unconventional polymer formation; preparation of novel polymeric materials from conventional polymerision techniques; preparation of novel microporous thermoplastics. *Mailing Add:* 710 W Roscoe Chicago IL 60657

CASTRO, CHARLES E, b Santa Clara, Calif, Nov 17, 31; m 53; c 7. ORGANIC CHEMISTRY. *Educ:* San Jose State Col, AB, 53; Univ Calif, Davis, PhD(phys chem), 57. *Prof Exp:* Res chemist, Shell Develop Co, Calif, 57-60; from asst chemist to assoc chemist, 60-70, CHEMIST & PROF BIOL CHEM, UNIV CALIF, RIVERSIDE, 70- *Mem:* Am Chem Soc. *Res:* Reactions of organics with transition metal species; anthelmintics; mode of action; hemes and hemeprotein redox mechanisms. *Mailing Add:* Dept Nematol Univ Calif Riverside CA 92521

CASTRO, GEORGE, b Los Angeles, Calif, Feb 23, 39; m 63; c 4. RESEARCH MANAGEMENT, PHYSICAL CHEMISTRY. *Educ:* Univ Calif, Los Angeles, BS, 60; Univ Calif, Riverside, PhD(chem), 65. *Prof Exp:* Fel chem, Univ Pa, 65-67 & Calif Inst Technol, 67-68; staff mem res, 68-69, proj leader org photoconductors, 69-73, mgr org solids, 73-75, MGR PHYS SCI, IBM SAN JOSE RES LAB, 75- *Mem:* Am Physical Soc. *Res:* Electronic properties of organic solids. *Mailing Add:* IBM Res Lab 5600 Cottle Rd San Jose CA 95193

CASTRO, GILBERT ANTHONY, b Port Arthur, Tex, Apr 24, 39; m 61; c 2. PHYSIOLOGY, MICROBIOLOGY. *Educ:* Lamar State Col, BS, 61; Univ Ark, MS, 63; Univ Tex, PhD(microbiol), 66. *Prof Exp:* NIH fel zool, Univ Mass, 66-68; from asst prof to assoc prof parasitol & lab pract, Med Ctr, Univ Okla, 69-72; assoc prof, 72-77, PROF PHYSIOL, UNIV TEX MED SCH HOUSTON, 77- *Mem:* Am Physiol Soc; Am Soc Trop Med & Hyg; Am Soc Parasitol; Soc Exp Biol & Med. *Res:* Intestinal physiology; host-parasite relationships; physiology and immunology of host-parasite systems; pathogenesis of gastrointestinal parasites. *Mailing Add:* Dept of Physiol Univ of Tex Med Sch Houston TX 77025

CASTRO, PETER, b Mayaguez, PR, July 20, 43; US citizen. MARINE ZOOLOGY, PARASITOLOGY. *Educ:* Univ PR, Mayagüez, BS, 64; Univ Hawaii, MS, 66, PhD(zool), 69. *Prof Exp:* Res assoc, Dept Marine Sci, Univ PR, Mayagüez, 70; instr, Dept Biol Sci, Univ PR, Rio Piedras, 70-71; asst prof, 72-75, ASSOC PROF BIOL SCI, CALIF STATE POLYTECH UNIV, POMONA, 75- *Concurrent Pos:* Vis investr, Hopkins Marine Sta, Stanford Univ, 71-82 & Smithsonian Trop Res Inst, 74; lectr, Moss Landing Marine Labs, 73. *Mem:* AAAS; Am Soc Zoologists. *Res:* Ecological, physiological and behavioral aspects of marine symbioses. *Mailing Add:* Dept of Biol Sci Calif State Polytech Univ Pomona CA 91768

CASTRO, PETER S(ALVATORE), b Chicago, Ill, July 5, 26; m 58; c 1. ELECTRICAL ENGINEERING. *Educ:* Northwestern Univ, BSEE, 51, MSEE, 56, PhD(elec eng), 59. *Prof Exp:* Elec engr, Motorola, Inc, Ill, 51-53; res scientist, Lockheed Res Lab, 59-72; chief engr, Spectrotherm Corp, 72-76; CHIEF ENGR, RAYTEK DIV OF OCLI, 76- *Mem:* AAAS; Inst Elec & Electronics Engrs. *Res:* Circuit theory, mainly of distributed parameter networks; analog applications of thin magnetic films; infrared optics and instrumentation-thermography. *Mailing Add:* 901 Madonna Way Los Altos CA 94022

CASTRO, WALTER ERNEST, b Peekskill, NY, Dec 31, 34; m 58; c 3. FLUID & ENGINEERING MECHANICS. *Educ:* State Univ NY Agr & Tech Inst, Delhi, AAS, 54; Ind Inst Technol, BSME, 59; Clemson Univ, MSME, 62; Univ WVa, PhD (eng mech), 66. *Prof Exp:* Instr mech eng, 59-61, asst prof eng mech, 61-62 & 65-67, assoc prof, 67-73, PROF MECH ENG & MECH, CLEMSON UNIV, 73- *Mem:* Am Soc Eng Educ; Am Soc Mech Engrs. *Res:* Experimental mechanics; turbulence; transition; two phase flow; turbulence suppression using high polymer additives. *Mailing Add:* Dept of Mech Eng Clemson Univ Clemson SC 29631

CASTRONOVO, FRANK PAUL, JR, b Newark, NJ, Jan 2, 40; m 77; c 1. MEDICAL PHYSICS, RADIOPHARMACOLOGY. *Educ:* Rutgers Univ, Newark, BS, 62, New Brunswick, MS, 64; Johns Hopkins Univ, PhD(radiol sci), 70; Am Bd Radiol, dipl, 78; Am Bd Sci Nuclear Med, dipl, 79. *Prof Exp:* Res sci radiopharmacol, Squibb Inst Med Res, 64-65; asst physicist, 70-80, RADIATION SAFETY OFFICER, MASS GEN HOSP, 80-, RADIOPHARMACOLOGIST, 80-; ASST PROF RADIOL, HARVARD MED SCH, 76- *Concurrent Pos:* Consult med physics & radiopharmaceut sci, Boston hosps, 74-; adj clin prof radiopharmacol, Mass Col Pharm, 76-; vis scientist, Mass Inst Technol, 75- *Honors & Awards:* Nat Res Award, Parenteral Drug Asn, 69. *Mem:* Soc Nuclear Med; Radiopharmaceut Sci Coun; Am Asn Physicists in Med; Am Pharmaceut Asn; Am Soc Hosp Pharmacists. *Res:* Research and development of radiopharmaceuticals; clinical radiopharmacology; quantitative skeletal imaging; ultra-short-lived generator-produced radionuclides; medical physics dosimetry; hospital personnel radiation exposure. *Mailing Add:* Dept of Radiol Mass Gen Hosp Boston MA 02114

CASTRUCCIO, PETER ADALBERT, b New York, NY, Jan 11, 25; m 51. ENGINEERING & THEORETICAL PHYSICS. *Educ:* Univ Genoa, DrEng(elec eng), 46. *Prof Exp:* Asst proj engr, Bendix Radio, Md, 46-50; proj engr, Aircraft Armaments, Inc, 50-55; head preliminary design, Westinghouse Elec Corp, Md, 55-58, dir astronaut, 58-59; tech dir, Aeronca Mfg Co, 59-61; dir adv space progs, Fed Systs Div, IBM Corp, Bethesda, 61-68, dir advan progs, Ctr Sci Studies, Gaithersburg, 68-73; PRES, ECOSYSTS INT, INC, 73- *Concurrent Pos:* Lectr, Space Inst, Univ Md, 59 & 60. *Honors & Awards:* Award, Am Inst Aeronaut & Astronaut, 58. *Mem:* Sr mem Inst Elec & Electronics Engrs; Am Astronaut Soc; Am Inst Aeronaut & Astronaut; Am Ord Asn. *Res:* Terminal guidance systems for radar and optical guided missiles; space technology, especially celestial mechanics, guidance and control, systems techniques, optical and inertial sensors, communications techniques and land survey techniques from ultrahigh flying platforms. *Mailing Add:* ECOSysts Int Inc PO Box 225 Gambrills MD 21054

CASWELL, ANTHONY H, b Exeter, Eng, Sept 23, 40. CELL BIOLOGY, MUSCLE. *Educ:* Cambridge Univ, Eng, BA, 62; Univ Col Wales, Britain, PhD, 66. *Prof Exp:* Asst prof med, biochem & pharmacol, 70-73, assoc prof, 73-81, PROF PHARMACOL, MED SCH, UNIV MIAMI, 81- *Res:* Mechanism of excitation-contraction coupling in muscle; transverse tubules from skeletal muscle; preparing transverse-tubule vesicles from skeletal muscle with limited contamination from other sources; investigation of transverse-tubules and their interaction with sarcoplasmic reticulum for an understanding of muscle function and contraction. *Mailing Add:* Univ Miami 1600 NW 10th Ave Box 016189 Miami FL 33101

CASWELL, HAL, b Los Angeles, Calif, Apr 27, 49. ECOLOGY, MATHEMATICAL ECOLOGY. *Educ:* Mich State Univ, BS, 71, PhD(zool), 74. *Prof Exp:* NSF fel zool, Mich State Univ, 71-74, res assoc, 74-75; from asst prof to assoc prof biol sci, Univ Conn, 75-81; ASSOC SCIENTIST, WOODS HOLE OCEANOG INST, 81- *Concurrent Pos:* Res assoc, Univ Calif, Berkeley, 80-81. *Mem:* Ecol Soc Am; AAAS; Int Soc Plant Pop Biol; Brit Ecol Soc. *Res:* Population and community ecology; evolutionary demography and life history theory; plant population biology. *Mailing Add:* Biol Dept Woods Hole Oceanog Inst Woods Hole MA 02543

CASWELL, HERBERT HALL, JR, b Marblehead, Mass, May 21, 23; m 48; c 6. ECOLOGY, ORNITHOLOGY. *Educ:* Harvard Univ, SB, 48; Univ Calif, Los Angeles, MA, 50; Cornell Univ, PhD(zool), 56. *Prof Exp:* PROF BIOL, EASTERN MICH UNIV, 55-, HEAD DEPT, 74- *Mem:* Ecol Soc Am; Wilson Ornith Soc; Am Ornith Union; Am Inst Biol Sci; Sigma Xi. *Res:* Terrestrial ecology. *Mailing Add:* Dept of Biol Eastern Mich Univ Ypsilanti MI 48197

CASWELL, JOHN N(ORMAN), b Brooklyn, NY, June 26, 20; m 46; c 2. ELECTRICAL ENGINEERING. *Educ:* Cooper Union, BEE, 41; Brooklyn Polytech Inst, MEE, 49. *Prof Exp:* From asst proj engr to sr proj engr, Sperry Gyroscope Co, Great Neck, 41-52, head eng sect, 52-57, head eng dept, 57-

62, mgr Polaris systs opers, 62-67, equip eng mgr Polaris/Poseidon prog Systs Mgt Div, 67-70; prog mgr safeguard, 70-73, mgr spec studies, 73-74, poseidon extended operating cycle prog mgr, 74-81, AUTOMATED MAT SYSTS PROG CONTROL MGR, SPERRY CORP, 81- *Mem:* Am Inst Elec & Electronics Engrs. *Res:* Radar systems requiring precise three coordinate automatic tracking for fire control applications and precise navigation systems. *Mailing Add:* Sperry Corp Marcus Ave & Lakeville Rd Great Neck NY 11020

CASWELL, LYMAN RAY, b Omaha, Nebr, Sept 29, 28; m 64; c 3. ORGANIC CHEMISTRY. *Educ:* Ind Univ, BS, 49, MA, 50; Mich State Univ, PhD(org chem), 56. *Prof Exp:* Asst prof chem, Ohio Northern Univ, 55-56; head, Chem Dept, Upper Iowa Univ, 56-61; from asst prof to assoc prof, 61-68, actg chmn dept, 67-70 & 73-79, PROF CHEM, TEX WOMAN'S UNIV, 68-, CHMN DEPT, 79- *Mem:* AAAS; Am Chem Soc; Am Inst Chemists. *Res:* Heterocyclic compounds; cyclic imides and anhydrides; ultraviolet visible and fluorescence spectra. *Mailing Add:* Dept of Chem Tex Woman's Univ Denton TX 76204

CASWELL, RANDALL SMITH, b Eugene, Ore, Feb 7, 24; m 45; c 6. PHYSICS. *Educ:* Mass Inst Technol, SB, 47, PhD(physics), 51. *Prof Exp:* Assoc prof physics, Univ Ky, 50-52; res partic solid state physics, Oak Ridge Nat Lab, 52; physicist neutron physics, 52-69, dep dir, Ctr Radiation Res, 69-78, CHIEF, NUCLEAR RADIATION DIV, NAT BUR STANDARDS, 78- *Concurrent Pos:* Adj prof physics, Am Univ, 57-71; mem, Nat Coun Radiation Protection & Measurement, 67-; chmn neutron measurements sect, Adv Comt, Standards Ionizing Radiation Measurement, 69-; mem, Int Comn Radiation Units & Measurement, 75-, secy, 79-; assoc ed, Radiation Res, 77-80. *Honors & Awards:* Gold Medal, US Dept Com, 79. *Mem:* Fel Am Phys Soc; Radiation Res Soc. *Res:* Neutron cross sections; physics and dosimetry. *Mailing Add:* Ctr for Radiation Res Nat Bur Standards Washington DC 20234

CASWELL, ROBERT LITTLE, b San Francisco, Calif, Jan 27, 18; m 57; c 1. PESTICIDE CHEMISTRY. *Educ:* Univ Calif, Berkeley, BS, 39. *Prof Exp:* Chemist pesticides, Agr Res Serv, USDA, 41-42 & 46-64, asst chief staff, Off Enforcement Chem, Pesticides Regulation Div, 64-70, Off Pesticides, 70-72, chemist, Criteria & Eval Div, Off Pesticides, Environ Protection Agency, 72-76; CONSULT, 76- *Mem:* AAAS; Am Chem Soc. *Res:* Development of chemical methods of analysis for pesticides. *Mailing Add:* 11626 35th Pl Beltsville MD 20705

CATACOSINOS, PAUL ANTHONY, b New York, NY, Sept 29, 33; m 58; c 3. GEOLOGY, STRATIGRAPHY. *Educ:* Univ NMex, BA, 57, MA, 62; Mich State Univ, PhD(geol), 72. *Prof Exp:* Explor geologist, Mountain Fuel Supply Co, 62-66; explor geologist, Consumers Power Co, 67-69; from instr to assoc prof geol, Delta Col, 69-80, prof, 80-82; MEM STAFF, ROM ENERGY CORP, 82- *Honors & Awards:* Bergstein Award, Delta Col, 72. *Mem:* Am Asn Petrol Geologists; fel Geol Soc Am; Soc Explor Paleontologists & Mineralogists; Sigma Xi; Am Astron Soc. *Res:* Origin and evolution of the Michigan Basin; detailed analysis of the Cambrian and Ordovician stratigraphic sections; precambrian sediments of Michigan. *Mailing Add:* Rom Energy Corp 30200 Telegraph Rd Suite 159 Birmingham MI 48010

CATALANO, ANTHONY WILLIAM, b Brooklyn, NY, Feb 8, 47; m 72. SOLID STATE CHEMISTRY, PHYSICAL CHEMISTRY. *Educ:* Rensselaer Polytech Inst, BS, 68; Brown Univ, PhD(chem), 72. *Prof Exp:* Fel, Div Eng, Brown Univ, 72-74; staff scientist, Inst Energy Conversion, Univ Del, 79-81; mgr mat develop & anal, 79-81; MEM TECH STAFF, RCA LABS, PRINCETON, NJ, 81- *Mem:* Am Chem Soc; Am Vacuum Soc. *Res:* Solid state chemistry, particularly electrical and optical properties of new materials with application to photovoltaic devices; crystal growth and defect chemistry of zinc phosphorous and development of photovoltaic devices. *Mailing Add:* David Sarnoff Res Ctr RCA Labs Princeton NJ 08540

CATALANO, RAYMOND ANTHONY, b Westland, Pa, Feb 21, 38. INVERTEBRATE ZOOLOGY, AQUATIC ENTOMOLOGY. *Educ:* Edinboro State Col, BS, 60; Ind Univ, Pa, MS, 67; Brigham Young Univ, PhD(zool), 78. *Prof Exp:* Educr sci, Avella Area High Sch, Pa, 60-65 & biol, Gateway High Sch, Pa, 65-67; PROF BIOL, CALIF STATE COL, PA, 67- *Concurrent Pos:* Col dir, Marine Sci Consortium, 71-80; res assoc, Ctr Health & Environ Studies, Brigham Young Univ, 75; environ consult, Western Pa Conserv, 77-; educ consult, Acad Year Biol Inst, NSF, 78-79. *Mem:* NAm Benthological Soc; Am Soc Limnol & Oceanog; Int Asn Theoret & Appl Limnol; Ecol Soc Am. *Mailing Add:* Dept Biol Calif State Col California PA 15419

CATALANOTTO, FRANK ALFRED, b Brooklyn, NY, Aug 4, 44; m 69; c 1. DENTAL RESEARCH, PEDODONTICS. *Educ:* NJ Col Dent, DMD, 68; Harvard Univ, cert pedodontics, 71. *Prof Exp:* Instr pedodontics, Sch Dent Med, Harvard Univ, 69-71; assoc epidemiologist, Naval Dent Res Inst, Great Lakes, Ill, 72-74; ASSOC PROF PEDODONTICS, HEALTH CTR, UNIV CONN, FARMINGTON, 74- *Concurrent Pos:* Asst pedodontics, Childrens Hosp Med Ctr, Boston, 69-71; Nat Inst Dent Res career develop award, 71. *Mem:* Am Dent Asn; Int Asn Dent Res; Am Acad Pedodontics. *Res:* Oral sensation and perception, including taste, smell, touch; physiology and biochemistry of taste and taste bud function. *Mailing Add:* Dept Pediat Dent Univ Conn Health Ctr Farmington CT 06032

CATALDI, HORACE A(NTHONY), b Brooklyn, NY, Apr 24, 18; m 51; c 5. CHEMICAL ENGINEERING. *Educ:* City Col New York, BChE, 40; Univ Ill, MS, 47, PhD(chem eng), 49. *Prof Exp:* Asst physicist, US Navy Dept, 41-44; phys chemist, Manhattan Proj, Columbia Univ, 44-45; asst dept supvr, Carbide & Carbon Chem Corp, Oak Ridge, 45-46; spec res asst, Univ Ill, 46-49; asst proj engr, Standard Oil Co, Ind, 50-53; res & develop chemist, 53-59, sprvr phys chem, 59-62, SPECIALIST, THERMOPLASTIC RECORDING MAT, GEN ELEC CO, 62- *Mem:* Electrochem Soc; Am Chem Soc; Am Asn Corrosion Engrs. *Res:* Demaagnetization of ships; acoustics; development of counting circuits; mixing of free gas jets; light scattering in critical region; corrosion-erosion reactions at high temperatures; materials for thermoplastic recording. *Mailing Add:* 2516 E Menlo Blvd Milwaukee WI 53211

CATALDO, DOMINIC ANTHONY, b Altoona, Pa, June 17, 42; m 65; c 1. PLANT PHYSIOLOGY, BIOCHEMISTRY. *Educ:* Ohio State Univ, BS, 66; Univ Dayton, MS, 68; Yale Univ, MPh & PhD(plant physiol), 72. *Prof Exp:* Instr biol, Univ Dayton, 66-67; res assoc, Dept Agron, Univ Wis, 72-74; res scientist, 74-80, STAFF SCIENTIST PLANT PHYSIOL, BATTELLE-NORTHWEST LABS, 80- *Mem:* Am Soc Plant Physiol; Am Forestry Soc. *Res:* Trace metal metabolism; source-sink relations, nitrogen metabolism, membrane transport mechanisms in plant physiology; kinetics and specificity of root absorption of nutrient and non-nutrient species. *Mailing Add:* Battelle-Northwest Labs PO Box 999 Richland WA 99352

CATALDO, JOSEPH C, b New York, NY, Apr 1, 37; c 2. WATER RESOURCE ENGINEERING, ENVIRONMENTAL ENGINEERING. *Educ:* City Univ New York, BCE, 60, MSCE, 64, PhD(eng), 69. *Prof Exp:* Naval architech eng, Brooklyn Naval Shipyard, 60-63; lectr, City Univ New York, 63-69, asst prof, 69-71; water resource engr, TAMS, 71-73; environ engr, Dames & Moore, 73-75; asst prof, 75-80, PROF ENG, COOPER UNION, 75- *Mem:* Am Soc Civil Engrs. *Res:* Hydraulic engineering; sanitary engineering; thermal pollution. *Mailing Add:* 173 Greenridge Ave White Plains NY 10605

CATALFOMO, PHILIP, b Providence, RI, Dec 27, 31; m 62; c 2. PHARMACOGNOSY. *Educ:* Providence Col, BS, 53; Univ Conn, BS, 58; Univ Wash, MS, 60, PhD(pharmacog), 63. *Prof Exp:* From asst prof to prof pharmacog, Sch Pharm, Ore State Univ, 63-75; head dept, 66-75; PROF PHARMACOG & DEAN, SCH PHARM, UNIV MONT, 75- *Concurrent Pos:* Am Found Pharmaceut Educ Gustavus A Pfeiffer Mem res fel, 69-70. *Mem:* AAAS; Am Soc Pharmacog; Am Pharmaceut Asn; Acad Pharmaceut Sci. *Res:* Investigation of higher plants and fungi for pharmacologically active components; secondary metabolism of marine fungi and mycorrhizal fungi. *Mailing Add:* Sch Pharm Univ Mont Missoula MT 59812

CATALONA, WILLIAM JOHN, b Cleveland, Ohio, Nov 14, 42; m 66; c 1. UROLOGIC ONCOLOGY, TUMOR IMMUNOLOGY. *Educ:* Otterbein Col, BS, 64; Yale Med Sch, MD, 68. *Prof Exp:* Intern surg, Yale New Haven Hosp, 68-69; resident, Univ Calif, San Francisco, 69-70; clin assoc, Surg Br, Nat Cancer Inst, NIH, 70-72; resident urol, Johns Hopkins Hosp, 72-76; ASSOC PROF SURG, WASHINGTON UNIV, 76- *Concurrent Pos:* Asst ed, J Urol, 78- *Honors & Awards:* James Ewing Prize, James Ewing Soc, 72; Grayson Carroll Prize, Am Urol Soc, 74; C E Alken Res Prize, Alken Soc, Bern, Switz, 79. *Mem:* Am Asn Immunologists; Am Asn Cancer Res; Am Urol Asn; Am Col Surg; Soc Int Urol. *Res:* Cancer research in the general area of tumor immunology; specific areas of investigation include regulation of host immunologic responses; lymphokines; interferon as an antitumor agent. *Mailing Add:* 4989 Barnes Hosp Plaza St Louis MO 63110

CATANACH, WALLACE M, JR, b Philadelphia, Pa, Aug 24, 30; m 53; c 4. MECHANICAL ENGINEERING, MECHANICS. *Educ:* Pa State Univ, BS, 52; Bradley Univ, MSME, 58; Lehigh Univ, PhD(mech eng), 67. *Prof Exp:* Res design engr, Caterpillar Tractor Co, 54-59; asst prof mech eng, Lafayette Col, 59-65; res asst mech, Lehigh Univ, 65-67; asst prof mech eng, 67-70, ASSOC PROF MECH ENG, LAFAYETTE COL, 70- *Mem:* Am Soc Mech Engrs; Am Soc Eng Educ. *Res:* Fracture mechanics; fatigue crack propagation in cylindrical shells. *Mailing Add:* Dept of Mech Eng Lafayette Col Easton PA 18042

CATANESE, CARMEN ANTHONY, b Niagara Falls, NY, Apr 27, 42; m 67; c 2. PHYSICS, ELECTRICAL ENGINEERING. *Educ:* Xavier Univ, BS, 64; Yale Univ, MS, 65, PhD(physics), 70. *Prof Exp:* Mem tech staff, 70-79, group leader, kinescope systs res, 79-81, DIR PICTURE TUBE SYSTS RES, RCA LABS, 81- *Concurrent Pos:* Consult, NSF, Educ Directorate, 75-76. *Mem:* Am Phys Soc; Soc Info Display; Inst Elec & Electronic Engrs. *Res:* Magnetic materials; solid state physics; display engineering; electron optics. *Mailing Add:* David Sarnoff Res Ctr RCA Labs Princeton NJ 08540

CATANZARO, EDWARD JOHN, b Jamaica, NY, Nov 4, 33; m 62; c 2. GEOCHEMISTRY. *Educ:* Brooklyn Col, BS, 55; Univ Wyo, MA, 57; Columbia Univ, PhD(geochem), 62. *Prof Exp:* Geologist, US Geol Surv, Washington, DC, 62-63; res chemist, Nat Bur Standards, 63-69; asst prof geol, Southampton Col, 69-71; assoc prof, 71-76, PROF CHEM, FAIRLEIGH DICKINSON UNIV, 76- *Concurrent Pos:* Vis sr res assoc, Lamont-Doherty Geol Observ, NY, 70- *Mem:* Geol Soc Am; Geochem Soc; Am Geophys Union. *Res:* Atomic weights of chemical elements; natural isotopic variations in strontium and lead; geochemistry and petrology of Precambrian rocks; mass spectrometric techniques and development; trace metal concentrations and movements in natural waters. *Mailing Add:* Dept of Chem Fairleigh Dickinson Univ Teaneck NJ 07666

CATAPANE, EDWARD JOHN, b Brooklyn, NY, Oct 13, 51. NEUROBIOLOGY, NEUROCHEMISTRY. *Educ:* Fordham Univ, BA, 73, MS, 75, PhD(physiol), 77. *Prof Exp:* Asst prof, 77-82, ASSOC PROF BIOL, CITY UNIV NEW YORK, 82- *Mem:* Soc Neurosci; AAAS; NY Acad Sci; Am Soc Zoologists. *Res:* Neurobiological studies of the interactions among monoaminergic neurotransmitters and neuroactive peptidergic substances in the nervous system; peripherally innervated organs of invertebrates. *Mailing Add:* 2105 Gerritsen Ave Brooklyn NY 11229

CATCHINGS, ROBERT MERRITT, III, b Washington, DC, Apr 2, 42; m 70. SOLID STATE PHYSICS. *Educ:* Univ Mich, BS, 64; Wayne State Univ, MS, 66, PhD(physics), 70. *Prof Exp:* ASST PROF PHYSICS, HOWARD UNIV, 70- *Res:* Magnetization, electrical conductivity and nuclear magnetic resonance studies of amorphous solids. *Mailing Add:* 7015 Fitzpatrick Dr Laurel MD 20810

CATCHPOLE, HUBERT RALPH, b London, Eng, May 13, 06; nat US. PHYSIOLOGY. *Educ:* Cambridge Univ, BA, 28, MA, 79; Univ Calif, PhD(physiol), 33. *Prof Exp:* Asst, Univ Calif, 34-35 & Cutter Labs, 35-36; from instr to asst prof physiol, Yale Univ, 36-43, Commonwealth Fund fel, 41-43; assoc path, 46-47, asst prof, 47-51, res assoc prof, 51-61, res prof path, 61-75, PROF HISTOL & EMER PROF PATH, UNIV ILL COL MED, 75- *Concurrent Pos:* Vis prof humanities, Rush Univ, 80- *Mem:* Assoc Am Physiol Soc; assoc Endocrine Soc; assoc Brit Soc Endocrinol; Asn Am Anat Soc. *Res:* Physiology of reproduction, aeroembolism and capillary vessels; lactogenic and gonadotrophic hormones; biophysics of ionic distribution in connective tissue and cells; histochemistry of connective tissue. *Mailing Add:* Dept of Histol Univ of Ill Col of Dent Chicago IL 60612

CATE, JAMES RICHARD, JR, b Winters, Tex; m 64; c 2. ENTOMOLOGY. *Educ:* Tex A&M Univ, BS, 67, MS, 68; Univ Calif, Berkeley, PhD(entom), 75. *Prof Exp:* Res asst entom, Tex A&M Univ, 66-68, res assoc, 68-71; res asst, Univ Calif, Berkeley, 71-72, res assoc, 72-74; ASST PROF ENTOM, TEX A&M UNIV, 74- *Mem:* Entom Soc Am; Entom Soc Can; Int Orgn Biol Control; Sigma Xi. *Res:* Population ecology and biological control of insect pests of cotton. *Mailing Add:* Dept of Entom Tex A&M Univ College Station TX 77843

CATE, ROBERT BANCROFT, b Manchester, NH, July 26, 24; m 51. REMOTE SENSING, SOIL SCIENCE. *Educ:* Dartmouth Col, BA, 45; NC State Univ, MSc, 60, PhD(soil sci), 70. *Prof Exp:* Admin asst & vconsul, US Foreign Serv, Calcutta, India & Rio de Janerio, Brazil, 46-52; govt pub rels specialist, San Francisco, 53-56; off mgr, Kaiser Aluminio, Lida, Belem, Brazil, 56-57; soil chemist, Brit Guiana Soil Surv Proj, Food & Agr Orgn, 61-63; vis assoc prof, NC State Univ & regional dir, Agency Int Develop Int Soil Testing Proj, Brazil 64-73, Guatemala, 74-75 & Colombia, 76; STAFF SCIENTIST, SYSTS & SERV DIV, LOCKHEED ENG & MGT SERV CO, INC, 77- *Mem:* Am Soc Agron; Soil Sci Soc Am; Int Soc Soil Sci. *Res:* New statistical methods for correlation and utilization of soil analyses and plant response data; use of landsat data to estimate world crop production, using new theory of invariant color. *Mailing Add:* Lockheed Eng & Mgt Serv Co C09 1830 NASA Rd 1 Houston TX 77058

CATE, RODNEY LEE, b Coleman, Tex, Dec 8, 50; m 72; c 1. PROTEIN CHEMISTRY, PEPTIDE ENDOCRINOLOGY. *Educ:* Tarleton State Univ, BS, 73; Ariz State Univ, PhD(chem), 77. *Prof Exp:* Res chemist biochem, Univ Calif, Los Angeles, 77-78; ASST PROF CHEM, MIDWESTERN STATE UNIV, 78- *Concurrent Pos:* Scholar, Univ Calif, Los Angeles, 77-78; consult, Nimbus Tech Control Ctr, 78-; sect officer, Am Chem Soc, 81- *Mem:* Am Chem Soc; Sigma Xi; Am Asn Advan Sci. *Res:* Enzymology, protein structure and function, protein purification, and metabolic regulation. *Mailing Add:* Dept of Chem Midwestern State Univ Wichita Falls TX 76308

CATE, THOMAS RANDOLPH, b Nashville, Tenn, Feb 19, 35; m 56; c 5. VIROLOGY, CLINICAL MEDICINE. *Educ:* Vanderbilt Univ, BA, 56, MD, 59. *Prof Exp:* Asst prof med, Sch Med, Washington Univ, 66-68; assoc prof med, Duke Univ, 68-75; ASSOC PROF MICROBIOL & MED, BAYLOR COL MED, 75- *Concurrent Pos:* Consult, Microbiol Labs, Barnes Hosp, 66-68. *Mem:* Infect Dis Soc Am; Am Soc Microbiol; Am Thoracic Soc; Am Fedn Clin Res. *Res:* Pathogenesis of respiratory virus infections with a major focus on mechanisms of resistance. *Mailing Add:* Dept of Microbiol Baylor Col of Med 1200 Moursund Houston TX 77030

CATENHUSEN, JOHN ALFONS, b Tecumseh, Nebr, June 17, 09; m 41; c 2. PLANT ECOLOGY. *Educ:* Univ Wis, PhB, 37, PhM, 39, PhD(bot), 48. *Prof Exp:* Biologist, Arboretum & Wildlife Refuge, Univ Wis, 41-43; asst div mgr, Trop Plantation, Haiti, 43-44; res botanist, Firestone Plantations Co, Liberia, WAfrica, 44-51; assoc prof biol & head dept, Col of Steubenville, 52-55; prof biol & head, Div Sci & Math, Hillsdale Col, 55-81; RETIRED. *Mem:* AAAS. *Res:* Plant taxonomy; animal ecology; plant breeding; Hevea brasiliensis. *Mailing Add:* Baw Beese Heights Rte 3 Hillsdale MI 49242

CATER, CARL MALCOM, biochemistry, deceased

CATER, EARLE DAVID, b San Antonio, Tex, Apr 4, 34; m 63, 71. PHYSICAL CHEMISTRY. *Educ:* Trinity Univ, BS, 54; Univ Kans, PhD(chem), 60. *Prof Exp:* Resident assoc chem, Argonne Nat Lab, 58-60, res assoc, 60-61; from asst prof to assoc prof, 61-77, PROF CHEM, UNIV IOWA, 78- *Concurrent Pos:* Vis chemist, Oxford Univ, 71; mem ad hoc comt, High Temperature Sci & Technol, Nat Res Coun, 75-77; div ed high temperature sci & technol, J Electrochem Soc, 77-; chmn, Gordon Res Conf High Temperature Chem, 78. *Mem:* AAAS; Electrochem Soc; Am Chem Soc. *Res:* High temperature physical chemistry; thermodynamics of vaporization processes; solid phase reactions at high temperatures; variable valence phenomena in rare earth compounds; electron microscopy of inorganic crystals, particularly of nonstoichiometric compounds. temperature mass spectrometry. *Mailing Add:* Dept of Chem Univ of Iowa Iowa City IA 52242

CATER, FRANK SYDNEY, b Chicago, Ill, June 27, 34. MATHEMATICS. *Educ:* Univ Southern Calif, BA, 56, MA, 57, PhD(math), 60. *Prof Exp:* Asst prof math, Univ Ore, 60-65; from asst prof to assoc prof, 65-70, PROF MATH, PORTLAND STATE UNIV, 70- *Concurrent Pos:* Referee, Math Mag, 72- *Mem:* Am Math Soc; Math Asn Am. *Res:* Analysis and real variables. *Mailing Add:* Dept of Math Portland State Univ Portland OR 97207

CATES, DAVID MARSHALL, b Salisbury, NC, Jan 7, 22; m 48; c 2. POLYMER CHEMISTRY, TEXTILE CHEMISTRY. *Educ:* NC State Col, BS, 49, MS, 51; Princeton Univ, PhD(chem), 55. *Prof Exp:* PROF TEXTILE CHEM, NC STATE UNIV, 55- *Mem:* Am Chem Soc; Fiber Soc; Am Asn Textile Chemists & Colorists. *Res:* High polymers and textile fibers; absorption chemistry. *Mailing Add:* 3 David Clark Lab NC State Univ Raleigh NC 27607

CATES, GEOFFREY WILLIAM, b Toronto, Ont, Oct 4, 23; m 48; c 5. CLINICAL PATHOLOGY. *Educ:* Univ Toronto, MD, 47; FRCP(C). *Prof Exp:* Labs dir, Saskatoon City Hosp, 58-63, lectr, 56-63, assoc prof & asst dir labs, Univ Hosp, 63-67, PROF PATH, UNIV SASK, 67-, ASSOC DIR LABS UNIV HOSP, 67- *Mem:* Am Soc Clin Path; Can Asn Path; Can Med Asn; Int Acad Path. *Res:* Practice of clinical pathology in relationship to patient care and undergraduate teaching of morbid anatomy. *Mailing Add:* Univ Hosp Saskatoon SK S7H 0W0 Can

CATES, LINDLEY A, b Chicago, Ill, Nov 20, 32; m 57; c 2. MEDICINAL CHEMISTRY, ORGANIC CHEMISTRY. *Educ:* Univ Minn, BS, 54; Univ Colo, MS, 58, PhD(pharmaceut chem), 61. *Prof Exp:* Instr pharm, Univ Colo, 58-61; from asst prof to assoc prof, 61-68, PROF MED CHEM, COL PHARM, UNIV HOUSTON, 68-, CHMN MED CHEM & PHARMACOG, 73- *Concurrent Pos:* Prin investr, NIH grants, 62-; Robert A Welch Found grant, 69-74. *Mem:* Am Pharmaceut Asn; Am Chem Soc; Am Asn Cancer Res; Acad Pharmaceut Sci. *Res:* Synthesis of organophosphorus compounds as potential chemotherapeutics. *Mailing Add:* Col of Pharm Univ of Houston Houston TX 77004

CATES, VERNON E, b Parsons, Kans, Feb 17, 31; m 66; c 2. ANALYTICAL CHEMISTRY, INORGANIC CHEMISTRY. *Educ:* Kans State Univ, BS, 53, MS, 56, PhD(chem), 62. *Prof Exp:* Teacher high sch, Kans, 56; instr chem, Centenary Col, 56-59; from asst prof to assoc prof, ETex State Univ, 62-67; chmn dept, 67-80, PROF CHEM, DALLAS BAPTIST COL, 67- *Mem:* Am Chem Soc. *Res:* Gas chromatography; analytical oxidizing agents; analytical methods; teaching innovations. *Mailing Add:* Dallas Baptist Col Dept of Chem 7007 W Kiest Dallas TX 75211

CATHCART, JOHN ALMON, b Sparta, Ill, Jan 17, 16; m 41; c 2. ORGANIC CHEMISTRY. *Educ:* Monmouth Col, Ill, BS, 37; Ohio State Univ, PhD(org chem), 41. *Prof Exp:* Asst chem, Ohio State Univ, 37-41; Anna Fuller Fund fel, Ohio State Univ, 41-42; from instr to asst prof chem & math, Monmouth Col, 42-45; res chemist, Eastman Kodak Co, 45-51, develop engr, 51-60, patent search specialist, 60-64, supvr info sect, Patent Dept, 64-74, patent search specialist, 74-81; RETIRED. *Mem:* Am Chem Soc. *Res:* Polynuclear hydrocarbons; polymers; organic synthesis, patents. *Mailing Add:* 65 Kemphurst Rd Rochester NY 14612

CATHCART, JOHN VARN, b St George, SC, Nov 28, 23; m 66. PHYSICAL CHEMISTRY. *Educ:* Clemson Col, BS, 47; Univ Va, PhD(chem), 51. *Prof Exp:* CHEMIST, PHYS CHEM METAL SURFACES, OAK RIDGE NAT LAB, 51- *Mem:* AAAS; Am Soc Metals; Electrochem Soc Inc; Am Inst Mining, Metall & Petrol Engrs; fel Am Soc Metals. *Res:* Oxidation of metal surfaces; stress effects during oxidation; diffusion in oxides. *Mailing Add:* 4609 Clinchview Lane Knoxville TN 37921

CATHER, JAMES NEWTON, b Carthage, Mo, Mar 17, 31; m 51; c 2. ZOOLOGY. *Educ:* Southern Methodist Univ, BS, 54, MS, 55; Emory Univ, PhD, 58. *Prof Exp:* Instr biol, Emory Univ, 58; from instr to assoc prof zool, 58-73, from assoc chmn to actg chmn, Div Biol Sci, 76-79, leader, Dept Exp Biol, 75-76, PROF ZOOL, UNIV MICH, 73-, . *Concurrent Pos:* Upjohn fac fel, 65; instr embryol, Marine Biol Lab, 66-67; vis prof, Ore Inst Marine Biol, 69 & 74, Bermuda Biol Sta, 72, Univ Utreclet, 73 & Friday Harbor Lab, 81. *Mem:* AAAS; Malacol Soc London; Am Soc Zoologists; Soc Develop Biol; Int Soc Develop Biol. *Res:* Cellular differentiation; molluscan development; invertebrate embryology. *Mailing Add:* Div of Biol Sci Dept Zool Univ of Mich Natural Sci Bldg Ann Arbor MI 48109

CATHEY, EVERETT HENRY, b Little Rock, Ark, Jan 9, 31; m 61; c 2. GEOLOGY. *Educ:* Univ Ark, BA, 56, MS, 60; Univ Ariz, PhD(admin & geophysics), 76. *Prof Exp:* Asst prof physics, Fort Hays St Univ, 62-64; NASA fel geophysics, Colo State Univ, 64-67; assoc prof geol & physics, Amarillo Col, 67-69; prof sci, Cent Ariz Col, 69-80; PROJ GEOLOGIST, GULF OIL CORP, 81- *Concurrent Pos:* Dept chmn gen studies, Cent Ariz Col, 75-78, dean continuing educ, 78-79; NSF fel acoustic emissions, Lockheed Ga Co, 76; NASA fel, Geophysics Br, Goddard Space Flight Ctr, Greenbelt, Md, 77. *Mem:* Soc Explor Geophysicists. *Res:* Atmospheric geophysics; paleoclimatology; acoustics; gravity; science administration. *Mailing Add:* 1643 Valley Parkway Claremore OK 74017

CATHEY, LECONTE, b Statesville, NC, Oct 18, 23; m 48; c 5. RADIATION PHYSICS. *Educ:* Davidson Col, BS, 47; Emory Univ, MS, 48; Univ NC, PhD(physics), 52. *Prof Exp:* Sr res physicist, Savannah River Lab, 52-67; PROF PHYSICS, UNIV SC, 68- *Concurrent Pos:* Mem grants rev comt, Dept Health, Educ & Welfare & Environ Protection Agency, 71. *Mem:* AAAS; Am Asn Univ Prof; Sigma Xi; Am Phys Soc; Inst Elec & Electronic Engrs. *Res:* Instrumentation; radiation measurement; Mossbauer spectroscopy. *Mailing Add:* 1225 Belt Line Blvd Columbia SC 29205

CATHEY, WADE THOMAS, JR, b Greer, SC, Nov 26, 37. ELECTRICAL ENGINEERING, OPTICS. *Educ:* Univ SC, BS, 59, MS, 61; Yale Univ, PhD(elec eng), 63. *Prof Exp:* Asst elec eng, Univ SC, 59-60 & Yale Univ, 60-62; sr res engr, Autonetics Div, N Am Aviation, Inc, Calif, 62-63, res specialist, 63-64, group scientist, 64-68; assoc prof elec & comput eng, 68-72, assoc chmn dept, 70-75, PROF ELEC & COMPUT ENG, UNIV COLO, DENVER, 72- *Concurrent Pos:* Vis prof, Univ Reading, Eng, 72-73 & Univ Calif, San Diego, 81. *Mem:* Fel Optical Soc Am; sr mem Inst Elec & Electronics Engrs. *Res:* Holography; imaging theory; tomography; laser sytems; optical communications sytems; coherent optics; optical information processing. *Mailing Add:* 359 Pine Brook Hills Boulder CO 80302

CATHEY, WILLIAM NEWTON, b Pulaski, Tenn, Feb 20, 39; m 63. SOLID STATE PHYSICS. *Educ:* Univ Tenn, BS, 61, MS, 62, PhD(solid state physics), 66. *Prof Exp:* Fel, Nat Res Coun Can, 66-67; asst prof, 67-74, ASSOC PROF PHYSICS, UNIV NEV, RENO, 74-, DEPT CHMN, 79- *Concurrent Pos:* Consult, Reno Metall Ctr, US Bur Mines, Nev. *Mem:* Am Phys Soc; Am Asn Physics Teachers. *Res:* Electronic structure of metals using Mossbauer effect; hydrogen storage alloys. *Mailing Add:* Dept of Physics Univ of Nev Reno NV 89557

CATHLES, LAWRENCE MACLAGAN, III, b Brooklyn, NY, Feb 9, 43; m 74. GEOPHYSICS. *Educ:* Princeton Univ, AB, 65, PhD(geophys), 71. *Prof Exp:* Sr geophysicist, Ledgemont Lab, Kennecott Copper Corp, 71-78; ASSOC PROF GEOL, Pa State Univ, 78- *Concurrent Pos:* Mem adv coun, Dept Geol & Geophys Sci, Princeton Univ, 73- *Mem:* Am Geophys Union; AAAS. *Res:* Earth's viscosity structure inferred from isostatic rebound phenomena; physics and chemistry of copper sulfide leaching from waste dumps; physics and chemistry of igneous intrusive environments. *Mailing Add:* Dept of Geol 116 Deike Bldg University Park PA 16802

CATHOU, RENATA EGONE, b Milan, Italy, June 21, 35; US citizen; div. IMMUNOLOGY. *Educ:* Mass Inst Technol, BS, 57, PhD(biochem), 63. *Prof Exp:* Res assoc phys chem, Mass Inst Technol, 62-65, fel, 64-65; res assoc biochem, Med Sch, Harvard Univ, 65-69, instr med, 69-70; asst prof, 70-73, assoc prof, 73-78, PROF BIOCHEM & PHARMACOL, SCH MED, TUFTS UNIV, 78- *Concurrent Pos:* Am Heart Asn grant, 69-; Nat Inst Allergy & Infect Dis grant, 71-; sr investr, Arthritis Found, 70-75. *Mem:* Biophys Soc; AAAS; Am Asn Immunol; Am Chem Soc; Am Soc Biol Chem. *Res:* Structure, conformation and function of biological macromolecules in the immune response. *Mailing Add:* Dept of Biochem & Pharmacol Tufts Univ Med Sch Boston MA 02111

CATIGNANI, GEORGE LOUIS, b Nashville, Tenn, Apr 9, 43; m 72. NUTRITIONAL BIOCHEMISTRY. *Educ:* Vanderbilt Univ, BA, 67, PhD(biochem), 74. *Prof Exp:* Res assoc toxicol, Ctr Environ Toxicol, Dept Biochem, Vanderbilt Univ, 74-75; staff fel nutrit biochem, Lab Nutrit & Endocrinol, Nat Inst Arthritis, Metab & Digestive Dis, 75-78; ASST PROF FOOD SCI, NC STATE UNIV, 78- *Mem:* Am Inst Nutrit; AAAS; Inst Food Technol; Sigma Xi. *Res:* Mechanism of action of vitamin E; identification, characterization and function of specific cytoplasmic tocopherol binding protein and its role in vitamin E action. *Mailing Add:* Dept of Food Sci 218 Schaub Hall NC State Univ Raleigh NC 27650

CATLETT, DUANE STEWART, b Fremont, Nebr, July 13, 40; m 61; c 1. PHYSICAL CHEMISTRY, CHEMICAL METALLURGY. *Educ:* Nebr Wesleyan Univ, BA, 63; Iowa State Univ, PhD(phys chem), 67. *Prof Exp:* Asst prof chem, Minot State Col, 67-68; asst prof, Pac Lutheran Univ, 68-70; staff mem, 70-74, ALT GROUP LEADER MAT TECHNOL GROUP, LOS ALAMOS SCI LAB, 74- *Mem:* Am Vacuum Soc; Am Soc Metals. *Res:* Gas-solid kinetics and its theory of the rate-determining processes, such as nucleation and diffusion; thermodynamics of solution; thin film deposition processes; hot-atom chemistry and radiolysis of condensed media. *Mailing Add:* Group CMB-6/ms-770 Los Alamos Sci Lab Los Alamos NM 87545

CATLIN, AVERY, b New York, NY, Jan 29, 24; m 46; c 4. MATERIALS SCIENCE. *Educ:* Univ Va, BEE, 47, MA, 49, PhD(physics), 60. *Prof Exp:* From instr to asst prof elec eng, 49-61, assoc prof mat sci, 61-67, acting chmn dept, 61-62, assoc dean eng & appl sci, 67-74, PROF MAT SCI, UNIV VA, 67-, EXEC V PRES, 74- *Mem:* AAAS; Am Phys Soc; Inst Elec & Electronics Engrs; Am Inst Mining, Metall & Petrol Engrs; Am Soc Eng Educ. *Res:* Solid state physics; properties of thin films; electron microscopy; electronic properties of solids; biomaterials. *Mailing Add:* Pavilon VIII Univ Va Charlottesville VA 22903

CATLIN, B WESLEY, b Mt Vernon, NY, June 26, 17. MICROBIOLOGY. *Educ:* Univ Calif, Los Angeles, AB, 42, MA, 44, PhD(microbiol), 47. *Prof Exp:* Med lab technician, Challis Clin Lab, Calif, 39-41; med lab technician, Seaside Mem Hosp, 42; chief lab technologist, Santa Barbara Gen Hosp, 43; teaching asst bact, Univ Calif, Los Angeles, 43-47, res assoc, 47-49; res assoc genetics, Carnegie Inst Wash, 49-50; from asst prof microbiol to prof, Med Col Wis, 50-76; mem fac, Marquette Univ Sch Med, 76-80, PROF MICROBIOL, MED COL WIS, 80- *Mem:* AAAS; Am Soc Microbiol; Soc Study Evolution; Genetics Soc Am; Brit Soc Gen Microbiol. *Res:* Neisseriaceae; genetic transformation. *Mailing Add:* Dept Microbiol Med Col Wis PO Box 26509 Milwaukee WI 53226

CATLIN, DON HARDT, b New Haven, Conn; m 73; c 2. INTERNAL MEDICINE, CLINICAL PHARMACOLOGY. *Educ:* Yale Univ, BA, 60; Univ Rochester, MD, 65. *Prof Exp:* Resident chief, Med Sch, Univ Calif, Los Angeles, 68-69; maj med, Walter Reed Army Inst Res, 69-72; asst prof, 72-78, ASSOC PROF MED & PHARMACOL, SCH MED, UNIV CALIF, LOS ANGELES, 78- *Concurrent Pos:* Dir, Ctr Study Drug Induced Dis, 76- *Res:* Clinical pharmacology of opiates and endorphins; basic mechanisms of drug dependence; pharmacokinetics and pharmacodynamics. *Mailing Add:* Sch of Med Univ of Calif Los Angeles CA 90024

CATLIN, DONALD E, b Erie, Pa, Apr 29, 36; m 61; c 2. MATHEMATICS. *Educ:* Pa State Univ, BS, 58, MA, 61; Univ Fla, PhD(math), 65. *Prof Exp:* Instr math, Univ Fla, 64-65; ASST PROF MATH & STATIST, UNIV MASS, 65-, VCHMN DEPT MATH, 70-71, 77- *Concurrent Pos:* Mem, Inst Fundamental Studies. *Mem:* Am Math Soc; Math Asn Am. *Res:* Systems theory; optimal filtering and estimation; marine navigation. *Mailing Add:* Dept of Math Univ of Mass Amherst MA 01002

CATLIN, FRANCIS I, b Hartford, Conn, Dec 6, 25; m 48; c 3. OTOLARYNGOLOGY. *Educ:* Johns Hopkins Univ, MD, 48, ScD, 59. *Prof Exp:* Intern, Union Mem Hosp, 48-49; intern otolaryngol, Johns Hopkins Hosp, 50 & 52-53, asst resident, 53-54 & 55, otolaryngologist, 56-72; from instr to asst prof otolaryngol, Johns Hopkins Univ, 56-63, asst prof audiol & speech, Sch Hyg & Pub Health, 60-70, assoc prof otolaryngol, Sch Med, 63-72, sci dir, Info Ctr Hearing, Speech & Dis Human Commun, 68-72, assoc prof audiol & speech, Pub Health Admin, 70-72; PROF OTORHINOLARYNGOL & COMMUN SCI, BAYLOR COL MED, 72-; CHIEF-OF-SERV, DEPT OTOLARYNGOL, TEX CHILDREN'S & ST LUKE'S EPISCOPAL HOSPS, HOUSTON, 72- *Concurrent Pos:* Consult, Vet Admin Hosp, Perry Point, 61-72; spec consult, Neurol & Sensory Dis Serv Prog, US Dept Health, Educ & Welfare, 63-64; mem communicative dis res training comt, Nat Inst Neurol Dis & Blindness, 63-65; mem prof adv coun, Nat Easter Seal Soc Crippled Children & Adults, 73- *Honors & Awards:* Cert audiol, Am Speech & Hearing Asn, 65; Award of Merit, Am Acad Ophthal & Otolaryngol, 74. *Mem:* AMA; fel Am Acad Opthal & Otolaryngol; fel Am Laryngol, Rhinol & Otol Soc; Am Broncho-Eophagol Asn; Am Speech & Hearing Asn. *Res:* Hearing problems in audiology including instrumentation; infectious diseases involving the paranasal sinuses. *Mailing Add:* St Luke's-Tex Children's Hosps PO Box 20269 Houston TX 77030

CATLIN, PETER BOSTWICK, b Ross, Calif, Sept 22, 30; m 52; c 3. PLANT PHYSIOLOGY, POMOLOGY. *Educ:* Univ Calif, BS, 52, MS, 55, PhD(plant physiol), 58. *Prof Exp:* Asst pomologist, 58-64, ASSOC POMOLOGIST, UNIV CALIF, DAVIS, 64-, LECTR POMOL, 69- *Mem:* Am Soc Hort Sci. *Res:* Physiology and biochemistry of plant growth and development; respiratory metabolism; chemical taxonomy. *Mailing Add:* Dept of Pomol Univ of Calif Davis CA 95616

CATLIN, SETH, mathematical logic, see previous edition

CATO, BENJAMIN RALPH, JR, b Belmont, NC, Aug 24, 25; m 48; c 3. MATHEMATICS. *Educ:* Duke Univ, AB, 48, AM, 50. *Prof Exp:* Instr math & physics, Univ Ariz, 50-52; instr math, Univ Md, 52-55; from asst prof to assoc prof, 55-74, PROF MATH, COL WILLIAM & MARY, 74- *Concurrent Pos:* Assoc prof, Summer Inst High Sch Teachers, Nat Sci Found, 59-, assoc dir, 60-68, dir, 68-75. *Mem:* Am Math Soc; Math Asn Am. *Res:* Partial differential equation; integral equations; analysis; linear operators. *Mailing Add:* Dept Math Col of William & Mary Williamsburg VA 23185

CATON, RANDALL HUBERT, b Minneapolis, Minn, Aug 19, 42; m 69; c 1. METAL PHYSICS, LOW TEMPERATURE PHYSICS. *Educ:* Univ Minn, BS, 65; Univ Pa, MS, 67; City Univ New York, PhD(physics), 72. *Prof Exp:* Res assoc physics, Univ Ill, 72-74; assoc physicist, Brookhaven Nat Lab, 74-78; ASST PROF PHYSICS, CLARKSON COL TECHNOL, 78- *Mem:* Am Phys Soc; Sigma Xi. *Res:* Low temperature physics; electrical properties and heat capacity of metals; magnetic materials; superconductivity; radiation damage in superconductors. *Mailing Add:* Dept of Physics Clarkson Col Potsdam NY 13676

CATON, ROY DUDLEY, JR, b Fresno, Calif, June 7, 30. ELECTROANALYTICAL CHEMISTRY. *Educ:* Fresno State Col, BS, 52, MA, 53; Ore State Univ, PhD(chem), 63. *Prof Exp:* Chemist, Chem & Radiol Labs, US Army Chem Ctr, Md, from asst prof to assoc prof, 62-75, PROF CHEM, UNIV NMEX, 75- *Concurrent Pos:* Petrol Res Fund grant, 63-64. *Mem:* Am Chem Soc; Electrochem Soc. *Res:* Polarography and coulometry of metals in fused salt media; electrode potentials of metals in fused alkali metaphosphates; ion exchange and liquid chromatography detectors. *Mailing Add:* Dept of Chem Univ of NMex Albuquerque NM 87131

CATRAMBONE, JOSEPH ANTHONY, SR, b Chicage, Ill, Sept 21, 24; m 51; c 12. MATHEMATICS, DATA PROCESSING. *Educ:* St Benedict's Col, BS, 47; Univ Maine, MA, 53. *Prof Exp:* Instr math & chem, Damar Acad, 47-50; mathematician adv bd on simulation secretariat, Univ Chicago, 53-54, syst res, 54-56, group leader, Inst Syst Res, 56-58, sr mathematician & asst dir labs appl sci, 58-61; sr scientist sci comput ctr, Serv Bur Corp, 62-63; opers analyst res inst, Ill Inst Technol, 63-68; dir admin data processing, 68-72, asst vpres data processing, 72-78, ASSOC VPRES ADMIN INFO SYSTS, UNIV ILL, CHICAGO CIRCLE, 78- *Concurrent Pos:* Instr math, Walton Col Com, 52-, Loyola Univ, 56- & Chicago Jr Col, 57-58. *Mem:* Am Math Soc. *Res:* Military weapons systems analyses and evaluations; operations research; applied mathematics. *Mailing Add:* 3023 N 77th Ct Elmwood Park IL 60635

CATRAVAS, GEORGE NICHOLAS, b Argostoli, Greece, June 22, 16; US citizen. ORGANIC CHEMISTRY, BIOCHEMISTRY. *Educ:* Univ Athens, DCh, 37; Univ Leeds, PhD(org chem), 47; Sorbonne, DSc, 53. *Prof Exp:* Instr org chem, Nat Univ Athens, 37-40; res chemist, Lever Bros & Unilever, Eng, 47-49; in charge res, Nat Ctr Sci Res, France, 50-54; Foreign Oper Admin-Nat Acad Sci fel, Univ Chicago, 54-56, asst prof, 56-63; head biochem res, Technicon Corp, 63-66; proj dir, Molecular Biol Exp, 66-72, chief div neurochem, 72-77, CHMN BIOCHEM DEPT, ARMED FORCES RADIOBIOL RES INST, 77- *Concurrent Pos:* Prof lect, Am Univ, 67- & adj prof, 72- *Honors & Awards:* Except Serv Civilian Award, Gold Medal, Defense Nuclear Agency, 73. *Mem:* AAAS; Am Soc Biol Chemists; Radiation Res Soc; NY Acad Sci; Royal Soc Chem. *Res:* Intermediary metabolism of lipids; control mechanisms; membranes; action of ionizing radiations on cell constituents; mammalian central nervous system; opiates; microwaves. *Mailing Add:* Armed Forces Radiobiol Res Inst Defense Nuclear Agency Bethesda MD 20014

CATSIFF, EPHRAIM HERMAN, PHYSICAL CHEMISTRY, POLYMER CHEMISTRY. *Educ:* Pa State Col, BS, 45; Univ Southern Calif, MS, 48; Polytech Inst Brooklyn, PhD(polymer chem), 52. *Prof Exp:* Res asst chem, Princeton Univ, 51-53, res assoc chem, 53-57; chemist, Shell Develop Co, Calif, 57-62; supvr phys properties sect, Res Dept, Thiokol Chem Corp, 62-67, head polymer physics & instrumental res, 67-69, head explor polymer res, 69-74; group leader polymer physics, 74-79, SR SCIENTIST, COMPOSITE PROD RES, CIBA-GEIGY CORP, 79- *Mem:* Am Chem Soc; Soc Rheol; Soc Plastics Engrs; NY Acad Sci; NAm Thermal Anal Soc. *Res:* Creep and stress relaxation of crystalline and amorphous polymers; swelling behavior of filled rubbers; Mullins effect; melt viscometry; epoxy resins characterization; reinforced composites; dynamic mechanical analysis; thermal analysis. *Mailing Add:* 21 Southern Rd Hartsdale NY 10530

CATSIMPOOLAS, NICHOLAS, b Athens, Greece, Feb 9, 31; US citizen; m 59; c 3. BIOPHYSICS. *Educ:* Athens Univ, BS, 55 Univ Tenn, MS, 62, PhD(biochem), 64. *Prof Exp:* Biochemist, King Gustaf V Res Inst, Sweden, 59-60; sr res scientist, Res Ctr, Cent Soya Co , Chicago, 65-73; adj assoc prof, Stritch Sch Med, Loyola Univ, 72-73; assoc prof, Mass Inst Technol, 73-80; PROF, SCH MED, BOSTON UNIV, 80- *Mem:* AAAS; Am Soc Biol Chem; NY Acad Sci; Am Chem Soc; Biophys Soc. *Res:* Protein and cell biophysics; electrophoresis. *Mailing Add:* Biophys Lab Mass Inst Technol Rm 56-307 Cambridge MA 02139

CATT, KEVIN JOHN, b Melbourne, Australia, Sept 24, 32; US citizen; m 69; c 2. ENDOCRINOLOGY, BIOCHEMISTRY. *Educ:* Univ Melbourne, MB, BS, 56, MD, 60; Monash Univ, Australia, PhD(biochem), 67; FRACP, 71. *Prof Exp:* Sr lectr, Dept Med, Monash Univ, 64-68, reader med, 68-69; assoc prof, Endocrine Unit, Dept Med, Med Ctr, Cornell Univ, 69-70; vis scientist, 70-77, CHIEF, SECT HORMONAL REGULATION ENDOCRINOL, NAT INST CHILD HEALTH & HUMAN DEVELOP, NIH, 73-, CHIEF, ENDOCRINOL & REPRODUCTION RES BR, 76- *Concurrent Pos:* Assoc clin prof med, Georgetown Univ, 71-; lectr, Sect Endocrinol, Royal Soc Med, 76; Charles E Culpeper prof, Sch Med, Univ Va, 81. *Honors & Awards:* Eric Sussman Prize Res, Royal Australian Col Physicians, 70. *Mem:* Royal Australian Col Physicians; Coun High Blood Pressure Res; Endocrine Soc; Am Soc Clin Invest; Am Soc Biol Chemists. *Res:* Mechanisms of peptide hormone receptors and regulation of pituitary, gonadal and adrenal functions; regulation of renin-angiotensin system and control of aldosterone secretion. *Mailing Add:* Endocrinol & Reproduction Res Br NIH Bldg 10 Rm 12N204 Bethesda MD 20205

CATTANEO, L(OUIS) E(MILE), b Philadelphia, Pa, June 21, 20; m 49; c 5. STRUCTURAL ENGINEERING. *Educ:* Cath Univ Am, BCE, 42. *Prof Exp:* Asst prof civil eng, Cath Univ Am, 46-56; STRUCT RES ENGR, NAT BUR STANDARDS, 56- *Mem:* Am Soc Testing & Mat; Soc Exp Stress Anal; Am Concrete Inst. *Res:* Structures and materials of construction; live loads in buildings. *Mailing Add:* 5438 MacBeth St Hyattsville MD 20784

CATTANI, RAY AUGUST, b San Bernadino, Calif, Feb 18, 30; m 54; c 5. AGRICULTURAL CHEMISTRY, SOIL CHEMISTRY. *Educ:* Brigham Young Univ, BA, 57; Ore State Univ, 57-60, MS, 60; Univ Ariz, PhD(agr chem), 63. *Prof Exp:* Asst soil chem, Ore State Univ, 57-60; NSF res asst agr chem, Univ Ariz, 60-63; mem chem fac, Phoenix Col, 63-66, Mesa Community Col, 66-67, acad dean, 67-73; exec dean, Scottsdale Community Col, 73-76; pres, Reedley Col, 76-81; CHANCELLOR, STATE CTR COMMUNITY COL DIST, 81- *Concurrent Pos:* Consult & examr, NCent Asn Comn Higher Educ, 69-76, Western Asn, 76- *Mem:* AAAS; Am Soc Plant Physiol; Am Chem Soc; Am Inst Chem. *Res:* Inorganic and organic chemistry; quantitative analysis. *Mailing Add:* 8350 S Frankwood Reedley CA 93654

CATTELL, MCKEEN, b Garrison, NY, Nov 17, 91; m 22; c 4. PHARMACOLOGY. *Educ:* Columbia Univ, BS, 14; Harvard Univ, AM, 17, PhD(physiol), 20, MD, 24. *Hon Degrees:* DSc, Univ Antioquia, Columbia. *Prof Exp:* Teaching fel physiol, Harvard Med Sch, 14-17, teaching fel pharmacol, 20-24; from instr to asst prof physiol, 24-36, assoc prof pharmacol in charge dept, 36-43, prof & head dept, 43-56, prof clin pharmacol, 56-59, EMER PROF CLIN PHARMACOL, MED COL, CORNELL UNIV, 59-; ED, J CLIN PHARMACOL, 61- *Concurrent Pos:* Mem div biol & agr, Nat Res Coun, 37-46, vchmn, 41-43; mem pharmacol study sect, USPHS, 46-47; mem teaching mission, Austria, 47, Columbia, 48 & Japan, 50; chmn adv comt chem-biol coord ctr, Nat Res Coun & physiol-pharmacol sub-comt, 49-50, mem div med sci, 50-53; vis prof, Univ Tokyo, 59. *Mem:* AAAS; Am Soc Pharmacol & Exp Therapeut (treas, 44-47, pres, 51); fel NY Acad Med; fel NY Acad Sci; Am Col Clin Pharmacol & Chemother (pres, 63-64). *Res:* Traumatic shock; physiological effects of hydrostatic pressure; nerve-muscle physiology; mechanism of digitalis action. *Mailing Add:* Dept of Pharmacol Cornell Univ Med Col New York NY 10021

CATTERALL, JAMES F, b Providence, RI, 1949; m 70; c 1. EUKARYOTIC GENE EXPRESSION, HORMONE-GENE INTERACTION. *Educ:* Colgate Univ, AB, 71; Northwestern Univ, Evanston, MS, 72, PhD(molecular biol), 76. *Prof Exp:* Fel, Dept Cell Biol, Baylor Col Med, 76-78 & res instr, 78-79; STAFF SCIENTIST, POP COUN, 79-; ASST PROF, ROCKEFELLER UNIV, 79- *Concurrent Pos:* Vis scientist, Lab Molecular Biol, Cambridge, UK, 78. *Mem:* Am Soc Cell Biol; Am Soc Microbiol; AAAS; NY Acad Sci. *Res:* Studies of eukaryotic gene structure and regulation of gene expression by steroid hormones; application of gene-product specific immuno assay to recombinant DNA methodology for selection of specific low abundance sequences. *Mailing Add:* Rockefeller Univ 1230 York Ave New York NY 10021

CATTERALL, WILLIAM E(DWARD), b Chicago, Ill, May 29, 20; m 44, 70, 76; c 2. CHEMICAL ENGINEERING. *Educ:* Purdue Univ, BS, 40; Mass Inst Technol, ScD, 42. *Prof Exp:* Res asst prof chem eng, Univ Pa, 43-46; chem engr, Esso Res & Eng Co, 46-54, sect head, 54-57, eng assoc, 57-63, sr eng assoc, 63-71; RETIRED. *Concurrent Pos:* Consult chem eng, 42-43. *Mem:* Am Chem Soc; Am Inst Chem Engrs. *Res:* Process design and economic evaluation in field of petrochemicals. *Mailing Add:* 5929 E 32nd St Tucson AZ 85711

CATTERSON, ALLEN DUANE, b Denver, Colo, June 26, 29; m 50; c 3. PREVENTIVE MEDICINE, AEROSPACE MEDICINE. *Educ:* Univ Colo, BA, 51, MD, 55; Ohio State Univ, MS, 61. *Prof Exp:* Gen pract, Colo, 58-59; resident aviation med, Ohio State Univ, 59-61; chief resident, Lovelace Found Med Educ & Res, 61-62; actg asst chief, Ctr Med Opers Off, NASA Manned Spacecraft Ctr, 62-63, assoc chief, 63-64, asst to chief, Ctr Med Prog, 64-65, chief flight med br, Ctr Med Off, 65-66, dep dir med res & opers, 66-71; pres, Aerospace Med Consult, 71-76; PRES, AIRPORT MED ASSOCS, 76- *Concurrent Pos:* Mem air traffic controller career comt, US Dept Transp, 69-70. *Honors & Awards:* Except Serv Award, NASA, 69; Melbourne W Boynton Award, Am Astronaut Soc, 71. *Mem:* Fel Aerospace Med Asn; fel Am Col Prev Med. *Res:* Environmental physiology. *Mailing Add:* Airport Med Assocs PO Box 60385 Houston TX 77205

CATTO, PETER JAMES, b Boston, Mass, Mar 23, 43; m 69; c 2. PLASMA PHYSICS. *Educ:* Mass Inst Technol, BS & MS, 67; Yale Univ, PhD(eng & appl sci), 72. *Prof Exp:* Mem sch natural sci, Inst Advan Study, Princeton, NJ, 71-73; asst prof plasma physics, Univ Rochester, 73-78; STAFF SCIENTIST, SCI APPLN, INC, BOULDER, COLO, 78- *Concurrent Pos:* Consult, Fusion Energy Div, Oak Ridge Nat Lab, 74-79 & Magnetic Fusion Energy Prog, Lawrence Livermore Nat Lab, 79- *Mem:* Am Phys Soc. *Res:* Equilibrium, stability, and transport in conventional and tandem mirrors, bumpy tori, and tokamaks. *Mailing Add:* Sci Appln Inc 934 Pearl St Boulder CO 80302

CATTOLICO, ROSE ANN, b Philadelphia, Pa, July 2, 43. DEVELOPMENTAL BIOLOGY, MOLECULAR BIOLOGY. *Educ:* Temple Univ, BA, 65, MA, 67; State Univ NY Stony Brook, PhD(develop biol), 73. *Prof Exp:* Res assoc biol, Brookhaven Nat Lab, 67-68; fel biol, McGill Univ, 73-75; asst prof, 75-81, ASSOC PROF BOT, UNIV WASH, 81- *Concurrent Pos:* Res grant, Univ Wash, 75 & NSF grant, 76- *Mem:* Soc Develop Biol; Soc Plant Physiologists; Am Soc Cell Biol; Phycological Soc Am; Asn Women Sci. *Res:* Control of organelle biogenesis, nucleic acid and protein metabolism during growth and development of synchronized unicellular algae. *Mailing Add:* Dept Bot Univ Wash Seattle WA 98195

CATTON, IVAN, b Vancouver, BC, June 29, 34; US citizen; m 61; c 3. HEAT TRANSFER, FLUID MECHANICS. *Educ:* Univ Calif, BS, 59, PhD(eng), 66. *Prof Exp:* Engr, Douglas Aircraft Co, 59-62, scientist, 65-67; res engr, 62-65, from asst prof to assoc prof eng, 67-76, PROF ENG, UNIV CALIF, LOS ANGELES, 76- *Concurrent Pos:* Consult, Douglas Aircraft Co, 62-, Rand Corp, 67-, Atomics Int, 70- & Adv Comt Reactor Safeguards, US Nat Res Coun, 74- *Honors & Awards:* Heat Transfer Mem Award, Am Soc Mech Engrs, 81. *Mem:* Am Soc Mech Engrs; Am Phys Soc; Am Inst Aeronaut & Astronaut; foreign fel Royal Meteorol Soc. *Res:* Thermal stability of fluids; electroconvection in dielectrics; natural convection in confined regions; free surface flows under low gravity conditions; heat transfer in nuclear plants; environmental transport processes; numerical methods. *Mailing Add:* Rm 2567 Boelter Hall Univ of Calif Los Angeles CA 90024

CATURA, RICHARD CLARENCE, b Arkansas, Wis, July 31, 35; m 59; c 3. PHYSICS, X-RAY ASTRONOMY. *Educ:* Univ Minn, BS, 57; Univ Calif, Los Angeles, MS, 59, PhD(physics), 62. *Prof Exp:* Res physicist, Univ Calif, Los Angeles, 62-63; res assoc elem particle physics, Princeton Univ, 63-66; res scientist, 66-73, STAFF SCIENTIST, LOCKHEED PALO ALTO RES LAB, 73- *Concurrent Pos:* Math consult, Radioisotope Serv, Vet Admin, Los Angeles, Calif, 59-62. *Mem:* Am Phys Soc; Int Astron Union; Am Astron Soc. *Res:* Nuclear physics; transport of high intensity charged particle beams; properties of wide-gap spark chambers; elementary particle physics; solar and cosmic x-ray astronomy. *Mailing Add:* Lockheed Palo Alto Res Lab 3251 Hanover St Palo Alto CA 94304

CATY, JEAN LOUIS, b Matheson, Ont, Mar 12, 43; m 69. GEOLOGY, SEDIMENTOLOGY. *Educ:* Univ Montreal, BS, 67, MS, 70, PhD(geol), 76. *Prof Exp:* ASST PROF EARTH SCI, UNIV QUE, CHICOUTIMI, 72- *Mem:* Geol Asn Can; Can Inst Mining & Metall. *Res:* Stratigraphy, structural geology, geochemistry and sedimentology of the northern edge of the Archean Greenstone Belt, Chibougamau, Province of Quebec. *Mailing Add:* Dept Earth Sci Univ Que Quebec Can

CATZ, BORIS, b Russia, Feb 15, 23; US citizen; m; c 4. MEDICINE. *Educ:* Nat Univ Mex, BS, 41, MD, 47; Univ Southern Calif, MS, 51. *Prof Exp:* Intern, Gen Hosp, Mexico City, 45-46; adj prof, Sch Med, Nat Univ Mex, 47-48; instr, 52-54, asst clin prof, 54-59, ASSOC CLIN PROF MED, UNIV SOUTHERN CALIF, 59- *Concurrent Pos:* Practicing physician, Los Angeles, 51-; chief thyroid clin, Los Angeles County Hosp, 59-69, sr consult, 70- *Mem:* Am Thyroid Asn; fel Am Col Physicians; Soc Exp Biol & Med; Endocrine Soc; fel Am Col Nuclear Med. *Res:* Thyroid disease. *Mailing Add:* Suite 404 435 N Roxbury Dr Beverly Hills CA 90210

CATZ, CHARLOTTE SCHIFRA, b Paris, France; US citizen. PEDIATRICS, TERATOLOGY. *Educ:* Univ Buenos Aires, MD, 52. *Prof Exp:* Staff physician, Pediat Serv, Hosp Fernandez, Buenos Aires, Arg, 51-56, supvr, Pediat Tuberc Clin, 55-56; teaching asst pediat, Stanford Univ, 59-61; asst dir, Pediat Out-Patient Clin, Palo Alto Med Ctr, Calif, 63-66; from asst prof to assoc prof pediat, State Univ NY Buffalo, 66-75; pediat med officer, 75-80, HEAD, PREGNANCY & PERINATOLOGY SECT, NAT INST CHILD HEALTH & HUMAN DEVELOP, 80- *Concurrent Pos:* Pvt pract pediat, Inst Padua, Buenos Aires, 53-56; actg instr, Sch Med, Stanford Univ, 63-64; assoc attend physician, Children's Hosp, Buffalo, NY, 69-75, clin dir, Birth Defects Ctr, 70-75; Fulbright sr res scholar & guest prof, Univ Rene Descartes, Paris, 73-74; Nat Inst Child Health & Human Develop liaison officer to comt on drugs, Am Acad Pediat, 75- *Mem:* Am Acad Pediat; AAAS; Am Soc Pharmacol & Exp Therapeut; Asn Ambulatory Pediat Serv. *Mailing Add:* Pregnancy & Infancy Br Human Develop Landow C709 Bethesda MD 20014

CATZ, JEROME, b New Brunswick, NJ, Dec 11, 32; m 52; c 3. PRODUCT SAFETY, INSTRUMENTATION. *Educ:* Mass Inst Technol, SB & SM, 56, ME, 58, ScD, 60. *Prof Exp:* Asst prof mech eng, Mass Inst Technol, 60-65; assoc prof mech eng, 65-70, interim dean, Sch Eng, 72, assoc dean, 72-75, interim dean, 75-77, PROF MECH ENG, UNIV MIAMI, 70-, CHMN DEPT, 78- *Concurrent Pos:* Consult engr, 64- *Mem:* Am Soc Mech Eng; Nat Soc Prof Engrs; Am Soc Eng Educ; Am Soc Testing & Mat; Am Soc Safety Engrs. *Res:* Solid ionic arrays as transducers for the measurement of displacement, temperature and heat flux and for use as energy conversion devices. *Mailing Add:* Univ Miami PO Box 248294 Coral Gables FL 33124

CAUDILL, REGGIE JACKSON, b Branson, Mo, Oct 20, 49; m 70; c 2. AUTOMATED VEHICLE SYSTEMS. *Educ:* Univ Ala, BSME, 71, MSMH, 73; Univ Minn, PhD(mech eng), 76. *Prof Exp:* Engr dynamic anal, Teledyne-Brown Eng Co, 71-72; res asst, Univ Ala, 72-73, Univ Minn, 73-76; asst prof, Univ Mo-Columbia, 76-77; ASST PROF, PRINCETON UNIV, 77- *Concurrent Pos:* Consult, US Urban Mass Transp Admin & NJ Dept Environ Protection, 78, US Environ Protection Agency, 79 & Transp Systs Ctr, Econ, Inc, 80-81; prin investr, US Dept Transp, 78-80, Nat Sci Found, 80- *Honors & Awards:* Teeter Award, Soc Automotive Engrs. *Mem:* Soc Automotive Engrs; Advan Transit Asn; Am Soc Mech Engrs. *Res:* Design, analysis, and microprocessor implementation of control laws for automated vehicle systems-urban transit, inter-city freight, and industrial material handling; development and integration of computer-aided design, manufacturing, and robotic systems. *Mailing Add:* E414 Eng Quadrangle Princeton Univ Princeton NJ 08544

CAUDLE, DANNY DEARL, b Maud, Tex, Oct 8, 37; m 64; c 4. PHYSICAL CHEMISTRY, CORROSION. *Educ:* Centenary Col, BS, 61; Univ Okla, PhD(phys chem), 66. *Prof Exp:* Res asst chem res inst, Univ Okla, 62-66; res scientist, 66-72, CORROSION & CHEM SPECIALIST, PROD DEPT, CONTINENTAL OIL CO, 72- *Mem:* Am Chem Soc; Nat Asn Corrosion Eng; Soc Petrol Eng. *Res:* Oil field chemical problems, and environmental engineering. *Mailing Add:* 8835 Sharpview Houston TX 77036

CAUGHEY, DAVID ALAN, b Grand Rapids, Mich, Mar 5, 44; m 69; c 2. AERODYNAMICS, COMPUTATIONAL FLUID DYNAMICS. *Educ:* Univ Mich, BSE, 65; Princeton Univ, MA, 67, PhD(aerospace eng), 69. *Prof Exp:* Scientist aerodynamics, McDonnell Douglas Res Labs, 71-75; asst prof, 75-80, ASSOC PROF AEROSPACE ENG, SIBLEY SCH MECH & AEROSPACE ENG, CORNELL UNIV, 80- *Concurrent Pos:* Vis asst prof, Cornell Univ, 74-75; consult, McDonnell Douglas Corp, 75- *Honors & Awards:* Lawrence Sperry Award, Am Inst Aeronaut & Astronaut, 79. *Mem:* Am Inst Aeronaut & Astronaut; Sigma Xi. *Res:* Numerical techniques for predicting aerodynamic characteristics of flight vehicles, especially in the transonic flow regime. *Mailing Add:* 218 Upson Hall Cornell Univ Ithaca NY 14853

CAUGHEY, JOHN LYON, JR, b Rochester, NY, May 30, 04; m 37; c 1. MEDICAL EDUCATION. *Educ:* Harvard Univ, AB, 25, MD, 30; Columbia Univ, MScD, 35. *Prof Exp:* Intern med, Presby Hosp, New York, 30-32, from asst resident to resident, 32-37; from asst to assoc, Columbia Univ, 35-45; asst dean, 45-48, asst prof med, 45-48, assoc prof clin med, 48-69, prof med & med educ, 69-74, assoc dean, 48-70, dean student affairs, 70-74, EMER PROF MED & MED EDUC, SCH MED, CASE WESTERN RESERVE UNIV, 74-, EMER DEAN STUDENT AFFAIRS, 74-, EMER PROF FAMILY MED, 75- *Concurrent Pos:* Asst physician, Presby Hosp, New York, 37-45; tech aide, Comt Med Res, Off Sci Res & Develop, 43-45. *Honors & Awards:* Abraham Flexner Award, Asn Am Med Col, 74. *Res:* Constitutional medicine; comprehensive health services. *Mailing Add:* Sch Med Case Western Reserve Univ Cleveland OH 44106

CAUGHEY, THOMAS KIRK, b Scotland, Oct 22, 27; m 52; c 4. APPLIED MECHANICS. *Educ:* Glasgow Univ, BSc, 48; Cornell Univ, MME, 52; Calif Inst Technol, PhD(eng sci), 54. *Prof Exp:* Instr appl mech, 52-54, from asst prof to assoc prof, 55-62, PROF APPL MECH, CALIF INST TECHNOL, 62- *Concurrent Pos:* Consult engr, Jas Howden & Co, Scotland, 49-51, 54-55, NAm Electronics, 55-58, Aeronaut Eng Res Inc, 58-62, Inca Inc, 62-68, Jet Propulsion Lab, Calif Inst Technol, 69- & Tetra-Tech Inc, 70- *Mem:* AAAS; Am Math Soc; Soc Indust & Appl Math; Seismol Soc Am. *Res:* Non-linear mechanics; vibrations; acoustics; electronics; applied mathematics; classical physics. *Mailing Add:* Calif Inst of Technol 1201 E California Pasadena CA 91125

CAUGHEY, WINSLOW SPAULDING, biochemistry, deceased

CAUGHLAN, CHARLES NORRIS, b Pullman, Wash, Jan 20, 15; m 36; c 4. PHYSICAL CHEMISTRY. *Educ:* Univ Wash, BS, 36, PhD(chem), 41. *Prof Exp:* Instr chem, Mont State Col, 41-44; chemist, Eastman Kodak Co, 44-46; from asst prof to assoc prof, 46-51, head dept chem, 67-73, PROF CHEM, MONT STATE UNIV, 51- *Mem:* Am Chem Soc; Am Crystallog Asn. *Res:* Hydrogen bonds in acetoxime; Raman spectroscopy; dielectric properties of polymers and titanium compounds; structures; metal alkoxides; x-ray diffraction; structures of organic phosphates, organic titanates, organic vanadates and natural products. *Mailing Add:* Dept of Chem Mont State Univ Bozeman MT 59715

CAUGHLAN, GEORGEANNE ROBERTSON, b Montesano, Wash, Oct 25, 16; div; c 4. PHYSICS, ASTROPHYSICS. *Educ:* Univ Wash, BS, 37, PhD(physics, 64. *Prof Exp:* From instr to assoc prof, 57-74, PROF PHYSICS, MONT STATE UNIV, 74- *Mem:* Fel Am Phys Soc; Am Astron Soc; Am Asn Physics Teachers; Int Astron Union; Sigma Xi. *Res:* Nuclear astrophysics and the analysis of synthesis of elements in the stars. *Mailing Add:* Dept of Physics Mont State Univ Bozeman MT 59717

CAUGHLAN, JOHN ARTHUR, b Pittsfield, Ill, Apr 29, 21; m 42; c 4. ORGANIC CHEMISTRY. *Educ:* Univ Ill, BS, 42; Univ Nebr, MS, 44. *Prof Exp:* Lab foreman, Tenn Eastman Corp, 44-46; res chemist, 46-50, develop chemist, 50-54, head evaluation sect, 54-56; asst asst to dir prod develop, 56-57, asst dir prod develop, 57-60, mgr process chem, 60-62, asst to dir res, 62-67, asst dir res, 67-69, asst dir, Chem Group Res & Develop, 69-72, mgr admin res & develop, Indust Div, 72-76, tech asst, 76-81, TECH ASSOC TO DIR CORP QUAL STAND, MALLINCKRODT INC, 81- *Mem:* Am Chem Soc; Am Pharmaceut Asn. *Res:* Amino ketones; opium alkaloids; organic chemistry; analysis of pharmaceutical chemicals; columbium; tantalum; industrial chemicals. *Mailing Add:* Mallinckrodt Inc 3600 N Second St St Louis MO 63147

CAUL, JEAN FRANCES, b Cleveland, Ohio, Aug 19, 15. FOOD SCIENCE. *Educ:* Lake Erie Col, AB, 37; Ohio State Univ, MA, 38, PhD(physiol chem), 42. *Prof Exp:* Res chemist, Borden Co, NY, 42-44; sr proj leader, Arthur D Little, Inc, 44-67; distinguished prof, 67-70, PROF FOODS & NUTRIT, COL HOME ECON, KANS STATE UNIV, 70- *Concurrent Pos:* Vis instr, Inst Food Sci, Giessen, Ger, 60. *Mem:* Am Chem Soc; Inst Food Technol; NY Acad Sci. *Res:* Food technology; flavor measurement; consumer product testing; catfish flavor and preflavoring. *Mailing Add:* Dept of Foods & Nutrit Kans State Univ Manhattan KS 66506

CAULDER, JERRY DALE, b Gideon, Mo, Nov 7, 42; m 63; c 1. WEED SCIENCE. *Educ:* Southeast Mo State Univ, BS & BA, 64; Univ Mo, MS, 66, PhD(agron), 69. *Prof Exp:* Res asst weed sci, Univ Mo, 66-70; mkt develop specialist, 69-71, mgr, Colombia, SA, 71-73, develop assoc, 73, tech mgr herbicides, 73-74, NEW PROD MGR, MONSANTO CO, 74- *Res:* Coordination of the discovery, development and manufacture of herbicides and plant growth regulators. *Mailing Add:* 7 Devondale Lane St Louis MO 63131

CAULFIELD, DANIEL FRANCIS, b Brooklyn, NY, Aug 4, 35; m 60; c 2. POLYMER CHEMISTRY. *Educ:* Brooklyn Col, BS, 57; Polytech Inst Brooklyn, PhD(chem), 62. *Prof Exp:* Res Assoc chem, Polytech Inst Brooklyn, 62; fel Cornell Univ, 62-65; RES CHEMIST, FOREST PROD LAB, US FOREST SERV, 65- *Mem:* Am Chem Soc; Tech Asn Pulp & Paper Indust. *Res:* Light scattering; scattering and diffraction of x-rays. *Mailing Add:* Forest Prod Lab US Forest Serv Madison WI 53705

CAULFIELD, JAMES BENJAMIN, b Minneapolis, Minn, Jan 1, 27; m 50; c 3. MEDICINE, PATHOLOGY. *Educ:* Miami Univ, BA, 47; Univ Ill, BS, 48, MD, 50. *Prof Exp:* Vis investr, Rockefeller Inst Med Res, 55-56; from instr to asst prof path, Med Ctr, Univ Kans, 56-59; from asst prof to assoc prof path, Harvard Med Sch, 59-75; CHMN DEPT PATH, SCH MED, UNIV SC, 75- PATH, HARVARD MED SCH, 70- *Concurrent Pos:* USPHS fel, 56-58; asst path, Mass Gen Hosp, 59-75, assoc pathologist, 69-75; pathologist, Shrine Burns Inst, Boston, Mass, 70-75. *Mem:* Int Acad Path. *Res:* Electron microscopy; spontaneous and induced alterations in fine structure of cells. *Mailing Add:* Dept Path Sch Med Univ SC Columbia SC 29208

CAULK, DAVID ALLEN, b Minneapolis, Minn, Sept 24, 50; m 72; c 2. APPLIED MECHANICS. *Educ:* Rensselaer Polytech Inst, BS, 72; Univ Calif, Berkeley, MS, 74, PhD(eng sci), 76. *Prof Exp:* Assoc sr res engr, 76-80, STAFF RES ENGR ENG MECH, GEN MOTORS RES LABS, 80- *Mem:* Am Soc Mech Engrs; Sigma Xi. *Res:* Fluid mechanics; metal plasticity; polymer processing; continuum mechanics. *Mailing Add:* Dept Eng Mech Gen Motors Res Labs Warren MI 48090

CAULTON, M(ARTIN), b Bronx, NY, Aug 28, 25; m 49; c 2. PHYSICS, ELECTRONIC ENGINEERING. *Educ:* Rensselaer Polytech Inst, BS, 50, MS, 52, PhD(physics), 54. *Prof Exp:* Fulbright fel cosmic ray physics, Imp Col, Univ London, 54-55; mem tech staff, Bell Tel Labs, 55-58; asst prof physics, Union Col, NY, 58-60; MEM TECH STAFF, RCA LABS, 60- *Concurrent Pos:* Adj prof elec eng, Drexel Univ, Philadelphia, 61-71; vis prof, Israel Inst Technol, 71-72. *Mem:* Am Phys Soc; fel Inst Elec & Electronic Engrs. *Res:* High-energy nuclear physics; low-noise traveling-wave-tubes; microwave propagation in electron beams; microwave solid-state electronics; microwave integrated circuits. *Mailing Add:* David Sarnoff Res Ctr RCA Corp Princeton NJ 08540

CAUNA, NIKOLAJS, b Riga, Latvia, Apr 4, 14; US citizen; m 42. ANATOMY, CELL BIOLOGY. *Educ:* Riga Univ, MD, 42; Univ Durham, MSc, 54, DSc, 61. *Prof Exp:* Student demonstr anat, Univ Riga, 35-42, lectr, 42-44; med practitioner, WGer, 44-46; lectr anat, Baltic Univ, Ger, 46-48; from lectr to reader, Durham, Eng, 48-61; PROF ANAT, SCH MED, UNIV PITTSBURGH, 61-, CHMN DEPT, 75- *Concurrent Pos:* Res grants, Royal Soc Eng, 59-61, Am Cancer Soc, 62-63 & USPHS, 62- *Mem:* Am Asn Anat; Histochem Soc; Am Soc Cell Biol; Anat Soc Gt Brit & Ireland; fel Royal Micros Soc. *Res:* Development and evolution of tetrapod limbs; development, structure and function of the peripheral receptor organs; control mechanism of the autonomic nervous system; fine structure and functions of the human nasal respiratory mucosa; urticaria. *Mailing Add:* Sch Med Univ of Pittsburgh Pittsburgh PA 15261

CAUSA, ALFREDO G, b Montevideo, Uruguay, June 25, 28; US citizen. POLYMER SCIENCE, TEXTILES. *Educ:* Sch Chem & Chem Eng, Montevideo, BSc, 58; Case Inst Technol, MS, 62; Univ Akron, PhD(polymer sci), 68. *Prof Exp:* Chemist textile chem, SAm Subsidiaries, Courtaulds, Ltd, 52-58; res chemist indust fibers, Textile Fibers Div, Can Indust Ltd, 61-64; res chemist polymers, Tarrytown Tech Ctr, Union Carbide Corp, 68-70; PRIN CHEMIST TIRE REINFORCING TECHNOL, GOODYEAR TIRE & RUBBER CO, 70- *Mem:* Am Chem Soc; AAAS. *Res:* Failure modes in tires and other fiber-reinforced composites; fiber fracture; polymer and fiber microstructure; chemistry of fiber finishes and adhesives; chemistry and physics of interfaces. *Mailing Add:* Goodyear Tire & Rubber Co Plant 1 Dept 469B 1144 E Market St Akron OH 44316

CAUSEY, ARDEE, b Baton Rouge, La, July 8, 15; m 38; c 2. CHEMICAL ENGINEERING. *Educ:* Univ La, BS, 36; Univ Mich, MSE, 37. *Prof Exp:* Lab analyst, E I du Pont de Nemours & Co, 37-39, operating supvr camphor plant, 40-46; supvr, 46-56, SYSTS ANALYST, ETHYL CORP, 56- *Mem:* Am Inst Chem Engrs; Am Chem Soc. *Res:* Tetra ethyl lead; oils, fats and wax; organic solvent; fine chemicals; electronic computer. *Mailing Add:* 666 Parlange Dr Baton Rouge LA 70806

CAUSEY, GEORGE DONALD, b Baltimore, Md, July 9, 26; m 61; c 4. AUDIOLOGY, SPEECH PATHOLOGY. *Educ:* Univ Md, BA, 50, MA, 51; Purdue Univ, PhD(audiol, speech path), 54. *Prof Exp:* Asst chief audiol clin, DC Health Dept, 54-55; chief acoust res audiol, Vet Benefits Off, 55-64; CHIEF CENT AUDIOL & SPEECH PATH PROG, VET ADMIN HOSP, 64- *Concurrent Pos:* Res prof, Univ Md, 56-80, dir, Biocommun Lab, 67-80; mem comt hearing, bioacoust & biomech, Nat Acad Sci-Nat Res Coun, 67-; mem comt hearing aids, Am Nat Standards Inst, 67-; clin assoc prof surg, Georgetown Univ Med Ctr, 76-; res prof, Catholic Univ of Am, 80- *Mem:* Fel Am Speech & Hearing Asn; Acoust Soc Am; Sigma Xi; Inst Elec & Electronics Engrs. *Res:* Hearing impairment and measurement techniques; hearing aids. *Mailing Add:* 3504 Dunlop Chevy Chase MD 20015

CAUSEY, MILES KEITH, b Monroe, La, Dec 23, 40; m 63; c 1. WILDLIFE BIOLOGY. *Educ:* La State Univ, BS, 62, MS, 64, PhD(entom), 68. *Prof Exp:* asst prof, 68-75, assoc prof, 75-80, PROF ZOOL & ENTOM, AUBURN UNIV, 80- *Mem:* AAAS; Wildlife Soc; Am Soc Mammal. *Res:* Wildlife biology and conservation, especially pesticide-wildlife relationships and environmental degradation. *Mailing Add:* Dept of Zool & Entom Auburn Univ Auburn AL 36830

CAUSEY, NELL BEVEL, invertebrate zoology, deceased

CAUSEY, WILLIAM MCLAIN, b Cleveland, Miss, Feb 6, 38; m 73; c 1. MATHEMATICAL ANALYSIS. *Educ:* Univ Miss, BS, 60, MA, 62; Univ Kans, PhD(math), 66. *Prof Exp:* Asst prof math, Miss State Univ, 66-67; asst prof, Univ Cincinnati, 67-68; assoc prof, 68-73, PROF MATH, UNIV MISS, 73- *Mem:* Am Math Soc; London Math Soc. *Res:* Complex variables; univalent functions. *Mailing Add:* Dept of Math Univ of Miss University MS 38677

CAUTHEN, SALLY EUGENIA, b Montgomery, Ala, Oct 1, 32. BIOCHEMISTRY. *Educ:* Abilene Christian Col, BS, 53; La State Univ, Baton Rouge, MS, 57; Oxford Univ, PhD(biochem), 65. *Prof Exp:* Asst prof chem, Abilene Christian Col, 56-67; asst prof, Tex Tech Univ, 67-68; PROF CHEM, NORTHEAST LA UNIV, 68- *Mem:* AAAS; Am Chem Soc; Am Soc Microbiol. *Res:* Vitamins and coenzymes, especially biotin, folic acid and vitamin B12; methionine biosynthesis in bacteria; enzymology, especially atropinesterase and methyltransferase; azolesterases related to schizophrenia. *Mailing Add:* Dept of Chem Northeast La Univ Monroe LA 71209

CAUTIS, C VICTOR, b Braila, Romania, June 18, 46; US citizen; m 70; c 1. ELECTROMAGNETIC WAVE PROPAGATION, COMPUTER SCIENCE. *Educ:* Univ Bucharest, Romania, dipl physics, 70; Columbia Univ, New York, MPh, 76, PhD(physics), 77. *Prof Exp:* Res assoc physics, Joint Inst Nuclear Res, Dubna, USSR, 72-73; res asst, Columbia Univ, 74-77; res assoc physics, Stanford Linear Accelerator Ctr, Stanford Univ, 77-81; SR SCIENTIST, TECHNOL COMMUN INT, MOUNTAIN VIEW, CALIF, 81- *Mem:* Am Phys Soc; Inst Elec & Electronics Engrs. *Res:* Electromagnetic wave propagation and radio direction finding. *Mailing Add:* Technol Commun Int 1625 Stierlin Rd Mountain View CA 94043

CAVA, MICHAEL PATRICK, b Brooklyn, NY, Feb 13, 26; m 51; c 1. ORGANIC CHEMISTRY. *Educ:* Harvard Univ, BS, 46; Univ Mich, MS, 48, PhD(chem), 51. *Prof Exp:* Fel, Harvard Univ, 51-53; from asst prof to prof chem, Ohio State Univ, 53-65; prof, Wayne State Univ, 65-69; PROF CHEM, UNIV PA, 69- *Mem:* Am Chem Soc. *Res:* Natural products chemistry; strained ring systems; organosulfur, selenium, and tellurium chemistry. *Mailing Add:* Dept of Chem Univ of Pa Philadelphia PA 19104

CAVAGNA, GIANCARLO ANTONIO, b Milano, Italy, June 3, 38. ORGANIC CHEMISTRY, PAPER CHEMISTRY. *Educ:* Univ Pavia, PhD(org chem), 61. *Prof Exp:* Org res chemist, Inst Carlo Erba Therapeut Res, Italy, 61-63; res chemist, 63-74, SR RES CHEMIST, RES CTR, WESTVACO CORP, 74- *Mem:* Am Chem Soc; Tech Asn Pulp & Paper Indust. *Res:* Organic and colloid chemistry of the papermaking process; chemistry of wood by-products. *Mailing Add:* Westvaco Corp Res Ctr Johns Hopkins Rd Laurel MD 20707

CAVALIERE, ALPHONSE RALPH, b New Haven, Conn, Jan 23, 37; m 61; c 3. BOTANY. *Educ:* Ariz State Univ, BS, 60, MS, 62; Duke Univ, PhD(mycol), 65. *Prof Exp:* Vis asst prof bot, Duke Univ, 65-66; from asst prof to assoc prof, 66-75, PROF BIOL & CHMN DEPT, GETTYSBERG COL, 75- *Concurrent Pos:* Assoc mem, Surtsey Res Soc, Iceland, 65- *Mem:* Mycol Soc Am; Am Inst Biol Sci. *Res:* Fungi of Iceland; mycological research on the new volcanic upthrust, Surtsey; marine fungi of Eastern US; marine algae of Bermuda. *Mailing Add:* Dept Biol Gettysburg Col Gettysburg PA 17325

CAVALIERI, ANTHONY JOSEPH, II, b Ft Bragg, NC, Sept 8, 51; m 70; c 1. ENVIRONMENTAL PLANT PHYSIOLOGY. *Educ:* Univ NC at Wilmington, BS, 75; Univ SC, PhD(biol), 75. *Prof Exp:* Fel, Dept Bot, Univ Ill, 80-81; RES PHYSIOLOGIST, DEPT CORN BREEDING, PIONEER HI-BRED INT INC, 81- *Mem:* Am Asn Plant Physiologists; Am Soc Agron; Crop Sci Soc Am; Sigma Xi. *Res:* Plant physiology; environmental limitations on crop yield; plant water relations. *Mailing Add:* Pioneer Hi-Bred Int Inc Dept Corn Breeding PO Box 85 Johnston IA 50131

CAVALIERI, DONALD JOSEPH, b New York, NY, May 5, 42; m 70; c 1. PHYSICS. *Educ:* City Col New York, BS, 64; Queens Col, New York, MA, 67; NY Univ, PhD(meteorol), 74. *Prof Exp:* Physicist, US Naval Appl Sci Lab, 66-67; from instr to asst prof physics, State Univ NY, 67-70; nat res coun res assoc meteorol, Nat Geophys & Solar-Terrestrial Data Ctr, Nat Oceanog & Atmospheric Admin, 74-76; vis asst prof physics & atmospheric sci, Drexel Univ, 76-77; staff scientist, Systs & Appl Sci Corp, 77-79; PHYS SCIENTIST, GODDARD LAB ATMOSPHERIC SCI, NASA, 79- *Mem:* Am Geophys Union; Am Meteorol Soc. *Res:* Statistical association of stratospheric and ionospheric planetary scale waves; large scale atmosphere-sea ice interactions; passive microwave remote sensing of the cryosphere. *Mailing Add:* Code 912-1 Goddard Lab Atmospheric Sci Goddard Space Flight Ctr NASA Greenbelt MD 20771

CAVALIERI, ERCOLE LUIGI, b Milan, Italy, Feb 10, 37. CHEMICAL CARCINOGENESIS. *Educ:* Univ Milan, DSc, 62. *Prof Exp:* Fel, Polytech Zurich, 63-64; lectr & res assoc, Dept Chem, Univ Montreal, 65-67; asst prof, 67-68; res assoc, Melvin Calvin Lab, Lawrence Berkeley Lab, 68-70; asst prof res, Dept Biochem, 71-74, assoc prof, 74-81, PROF RES, DEPT BIOCHEM & BIOMED CHEM, EPPLEY INST RES CANCER, UNIV NEBR MED CTR, 81- *Concurrent Pos:* Proj leader environ carcinogenesis, Sect Polycyclic Hydrocarbons, Pub Health Servs, Nat Cancer Inst, 72-79; prin investr contracts, 79-81; prin investr grants, Nat Cancer Inst, 73-76, Nat Inst Environ Health Sci, 79-85; mem sci adv comt, Nat Cancer Inst, 77. *Mem:* Am Chem Soc; AAAS; Am Asn Cancer Res; Fedn Am Scientists; Europ Asn Cancer Res. *Res:* Carcinogenesis of polycyclic aromatic hydrocarbons with reference to their reaction mechanisms; enzymology of activation; binding to cellular macromolecules; metabolism and tumorgenicity. *Mailing Add:* Eppley Inst Res Cancer Univ Nebr Med Ctr 62nd & Dewey Omaha NE 68105

CAVALIERI, LIEBE FRANK, b Philadelphia, Pa, Aug 26, 19; c 3. PHYSICAL BIOCHEMISTRY. *Educ:* Univ Pa, BS, 43, MS, 44, PhD(chem), 45. *Prof Exp:* Asst instr, Univ Pa, 43; fel amino compounds & sugars, Ohio State Univ, 45; fel, 46-48, from asst to assoc, 48-60, assoc dir, 61-68, asst prof biochem, 52-54, assoc prof, 54-60, PROF BIOCHEM, SLOAN-KETTERING DIV, CORNELL UNIV, 60-, MEM, 60- *Concurrent Pos:* Fel, Columbia Univ, 50. *Mem:* AAAS; Am Chem Soc; Am Soc Biol Chem; Harvey Soc. *Res:* Macromolecular structure of nucleic acids; DNA replication. *Mailing Add:* Div Molecular Biol Walker Lab 145 Boston Post Rd Rye NY 10580

CAVALIERI, RALPH R, b New York, NY, Jan 15, 32; m 57; c 1. ENDOCRINOLOGY, NUCLEAR MEDICINE. *Educ:* NY Univ, BA, 52, MD, 56; Am Bd Internal Med, dipl, 65; Am Bd Nuclear Med, dipl, 73. *Prof Exp:* Intern med, Third Div, Bellevue Hosp, 56-57, resident, 57-59; mem staff nuclear med, US Naval Hosp, Bethesda, Md, 59-61; NATO fel biochem, Nat Inst Med Res, Eng, 61-62; USPHS spec fel nuclear med, Johns Hopkins Univ Hosp, 62-63; CHIEF NUCLEAR MED SERV, VET ADMIN HOSP, 63-; PROF MED & RADIOL, MED CTR, UNIV CALIF, SAN FRANCISCO, 78- *Concurrent Pos:* From asst clin prof to assoc clin prof med & radiol, Med Ctr, Univ Calif, San Francisco, 63-78. *Mem:* Soc Nuclear Med; Asn Am Physicians; Endocrine Soc; Am Fedn Clin Res; Am Soc Clin Invest. *Res:* Thyroid physiology and biochemistry; endocrine control of metabolism; application of radioisotope techniques to medicine. *Mailing Add:* Vet Admin Med Ctr 42nd Ave & Clement San Francisco CA 94121

CAVALLARO, MARY CAROLINE, b Everett, Mass, Feb 2, 32. PHYSICS, SCIENCE EDUCATION. *Educ:* Simmons Col, BS, 54, MS, 56; Ind Univ, EdD, 72. *Prof Exp:* Instr physics & math, Sweet Briar Col, 55-56; instr physics, Simmons Col, 56-58 & Randolph-Macon Woman's Col, 58-59; asst prof, Framingham State Col, 61-63; asst to dean grad studies, 72-78, PROF PHYSICS, SALEM STATE COL, 63-, VCHMN PHYSICS, DEPT CHEM & PHYSICS, 80- *Concurrent Pos:* Boston Univ teaching fel, 59-61, lectr, 61-62. *Mem:* Am Phys Soc; Am Asn Physics Teachers; Asn Educ Teachers Sci; Nat Sci Teachers Asn. *Res:* Administration in higher education; institutional research graduate education. *Mailing Add:* Dept of Physics Salem State Col Salem MA 01970

CAVALLITO, CHESTER JOHN, b Perth Amboy, NJ, May 7, 15; m 40; c 3. ORGANIC CHEMISTRY, PHYSIOLOGICAL CHEMISTRY. *Educ:* Rutgers Univ, BS, 36; Ohio State Univ, AM, 38, PhD(chem), 40. *Prof Exp:* Asst entom, NJ Exp Sta, 36; res chemist, Goodyear Tire & Rubber Co, 40-41, Winthrop Chem Co, 42-46 & Sterling-Winthrop Res Inst, 46-50; res dir, Irwin, Neisler & Co, 51-63; vpres & dir res, Neisler Labs, Inc, 63-66; prof med chem, Sch Pharm, Univ NC, Chapel Hill, 66-70; exec vpres, Ayerst Labs, 70-78; ADJ PROF MED CHEM, SCH PHARM, UNIV NC, CHAPEL HILL, 78- *Concurrent Pos:* Lectr pharmacol, Univ Ill, 62-66. *Mem:* Fel AAAS; Am Chem Soc; Am Soc Microbiol; fel NY Acad Sci; Acad Pharmaceut Sci. *Res:* Medicinals, synthetic and natural; mechanisms of drug action; research administration. *Mailing Add:* Rte 3 Box 152 Hillsborough NC 27278

CAVANAGH, DENIS, b Paisley, Scotland, Dec 27, 23; US citizen; m 51; c 3. OBSTETRICS & GYNECOLOGY. *Educ:* Univ Glasgow, MB, ChB, 52; FRCOG. *Prof Exp:* Mike Hogg Award, Postgrad Sch Med, Univ Tex, 59; from asst prof to prof obstet & gynec, Univ Miami, 59-66; prof & chmn dept, Sch Med, St Louis Univ, 66-77; PROF OBSTET & GYNEC, UNIV S FLA, 77- *Mem:* AAAS; AMA; fel Am Col Surg; fel Am Col Obstet & Gynec; Am Gynec Soc. *Res:* Diagnosis and treatment of gynecological cancer; clinical and laboratory aspects of septic shock; eclamptogenic toxemia. *Mailing Add:* Dept of Obstet & Gynec Univ of S Fla Col of Med Tampa FL 33620

CAVANAGH, TIMOTHY D, b Berkeley, Calif, Aug 16, 38; m 63; c 2. MATHEMATICS. *Educ:* Calif State Univ, Sacramento, AB, 59, MA, 62; Ohio State Univ, PhD(math educ), 65. *Prof Exp:* From asst prof to assoc prof, 65-73, PROF MATH, UNIV NORTHERN COLO, 73- *Concurrent Pos:* Vis prof, Univ Col, Galway, Ireland, 70-71. *Mem:* Math Asn Am; Nat Coun Teachers Math; Am Educ Res Asn. *Res:* Mathematics education. *Mailing Add:* Dept of Math Univ of Northern Colo Greeley CO 80639

CAVANAH, LLOYD (EARL), b Keytesville, Mo, Sept 18, 19; m 48; c 2. AGRONOMY. *Educ:* Univ Mo, BS, 48, MS, 50. *Prof Exp:* From instr to assoc prof, 48-74, supt dept res farm, 62-77, PROF AGRON, UNIV MO-COLUMBIA, 74- *Concurrent Pos:* Exec secy-treas, Mo Seed Improv Asn, Univ Mo, 55-62; dir, Mo Found Seeds. *Mem:* Am Soc Agron. *Res:* Quality seeds; factors that affect the cleanliness and germination of seeds. *Mailing Add:* Dept Agron 135 Mumford Hall Univ Mo Columbia MO 65211

CAVANAUGH, JAMES RICHARD, b Philadelphia, Pa, Sept 17, 34; m 61; c 5. MAGNETIC RESONANCE SPECTROSCOPY. *Educ:* St Joseph's Col, Philadelphia, BS, 56; Columbia Univ, New York, MS, 57, PhD(chem), 60. *Prof Exp:* Res chemist indust res, Mobil Oil Co, Princeton, 60-65; chemist res spectros, 65-72, leader, 72-81, LAB CHIEF GOVT RES, EASTERN REGIONAL RES CTR, USDA, 81- *Concurrent Pos:* Instr chem, St Joseph's Col, Philadelphia, 67-73. *Mem:* Am Chem Soc; AAAS; Fedn Anal Chem & Spectros Soc. *Res:* Applications of nuclear magnetic resonance and other spectroscopy techniques to systems of biological and biochemical interest. *Mailing Add:* Agr Res Serv Eastern Regional Res Ctr USDA 600 E Mermaid Lane Philadelphia PA 19118

CAVANAUGH, ROBERT J, b Scranton, Pa, Nov 11, 42; m 64; c 3. ORGANIC CHEMISTRY. *Educ:* Carnegie-Mellon Univ, BS, 64; Univ Pittsburgh, PhD(org chem), 67. *Prof Exp:* SR RES CHEMIST, E I DU PONT DE NEMOURS & CO, INC, 69- *Mem:* Am Chem Soc. *Res:* Reactions of enamines; catalytic oxidation; polymer synthesis. *Mailing Add:* E I Du Pont de Nemours & Co Washington WV 26181

CAVAZOS, LAURO FRED, b King Ranch, Tex, Jan 4, 27; m 54; c 10. ANATOMY. *Educ:* Tex Tech Col, BA, 49, MA, 51; Iowa State Univ, PhD(physiol), 54. *Prof Exp:* Teaching asst, Tex Tech Col, 49-51; res asst, Iowa State Col, 51-54; from instr to assoc prof anat, Med Col Va, 54-64; prof anat & chmn dept, Tufts Univ, 64-72, assoc dean, Sch Med, 72-73, actg dean,

73-75, dean, 75-80; PROF BIOL SCI & PRES, TEX TECH UNIV & PROF ANAT & PRES, HEALTH SCI CTR, 80- *Mem:* Am Asn Anat; Asn Am Med Cols; AAAS; Sigma Xi; Histochem Soc. *Res:* Physiology; histochemistry, electron microscopy and biochemistry of male reproductive system; hormonal factors; fine structure of cells of steroid secretion. *Mailing Add:* Off Pres Health Sci Ctr Tex Tech Univ Lubbock TX 79409

CAVE, MAC DONALD, b Philadelphia, Pa, May 14, 39; div; c 2. ANATOMY, CELL BIOLOGY. *Educ:* Susquehanna Univ, BA, 61; Univ Ill, MS, 63, PhD(anat), 65. *Prof Exp:* Am Cancer Soc Swed-Am Exchange fel, Inst Genetics, Univ Lund, 65-66; USPHS fel, Max Planck Inst Biol, 66-67; asst prof anat & cell biol, Sch Med, Univ Pittsburgh, 67-72; assoc prof, 72-79, PROF ANAT, COL MED, UNIV ARK, 79- *Mem:* AAAS; Am Asn Anat; Am Soc Cell Biol. *Res:* The replication and structure of the genetic machinery, synthesis of chromosomal proteins and nucleic acids, organization and localization of genes coding for ribosomal RNA, their amplification during oogenesis and their expression during development. *Mailing Add:* Dept Anat Col Med Univ Ark 4301 W Markham Little Rock AR 72201

CAVE, WILLIAM THOMPSON, b Winnipeg, Man, June 8, 17; US citizen; m 41; c 2. PHYSICAL CHEMISTRY. *Educ:* Univ Man, BSc, 39; Oxford Univ, DPhil(phys chem), 48. *Prof Exp:* Res chemist, Shawinigan Chems Co, 44-46 & 48-51; res mgr, Cent Res Dept, Monsanto Chem Co, 51-68, tech dir, Monsanto Co, 68-70, DIR NUCLEAR OPERS, MOUND LAB, MONSANTO RES CORP, 70- *Concurrent Pos:* Mem inspection bd, UK & Can, 40-44. *Mem:* Fel AAAS; NY Acad Sci; Am Chem Soc; Soc Appl Spectros. *Res:* Spectroscopy; organic chemistry; instrumentation. *Mailing Add:* 539 Elderwood Rd Kettering OH 45429

CAVELL, RONALD GEORGE, b Sault St Marie, Ont, Oct 15, 38; m 60; c 2. INORGANIC CHEMISTRY. *Educ:* McGill Univ, BSc, 58; Univ BC, MSc, 60, PhD(inorg chem), 62; Cambridge Univ, PhD, 64. *Prof Exp:* From asst prof to assoc prof, 64-74, PROF CHEM, UNIV ALTA, 74- *Honors & Awards:* Alcan Lectr Award, Chem Inst Can, 79. *Mem:* Chem Inst Can; The Chem Soc; Am Chem Soc. *Res:* X-ray and ultraviolet photoelectron spectroscopy; chemistry of simple and complex transition metal halides; particularly fluorides; halogen and perfluoroalkyl derivatives of phosphorus. *Mailing Add:* Dept of Chem Univ of Alta Edmonton AB T6G 2E8 Can

CAVENDER, JAMES C, b Tuxedo, NY, July 27, 36; m 64; c 2. MYCOLOGY. *Educ:* Union Col, BS, 58; Univ Wis, MS, 61, PhD(bot), 63. *Prof Exp:* Res assoc bact, Univ Wis, 63-64; asst prof biol, Wabash Col, 64-69; asst prof, 69-70, ASSOC PROF BOT, OHIO UNIV, 71- *Mem:* AAAS; Bot Soc Am; Mycol Soc Am. *Res:* Ecology, taxonomy and morphology of cellular slime molds. *Mailing Add:* Dept of Bot Ohio Univ Athens OH 45701

CAVENDER, JAMES VERE, JR, b San Antonio, TX, Oct 10, 22; m 45; c 2. ORGANIC POLYMER CHEMISTRY. *Educ:* Agr & Mech Col, Tex, BSc, 48. *Prof Exp:* Res chemist, Monsanto Chem Co, Mo, 48-51, res chemist, Tex, 51-54, res group leader, 54-74, SR PROCESS SPECIALIST, MONSANTO CO, 74- *Mem:* Am Chem Soc. *Res:* Linear polyolefin process development; Ziegler chemistry; organic synthesis; organic medicinals. *Mailing Add:* Monsanto Co PO Box 1311 Texas City TX 77590

CAVENDER, PATRICIA LEE, b Warren, Ohio, Sept, 26, 50; m 77; c 1. AGRICULTURAL CHEMISTRY. *Educ:* Allegheny Col, BS, 72; Univ Ill, PhD(org chem), 77. *Prof Exp:* Fel, Schering Plough, Inc, 77-79; RES CHEMIST, AGR CHEM DIV, FMC CORP, INC, 80- *Mem:* Am Chem Soc; AAAS; Sigma Xi. *Mailing Add:* FMC Corp Inc Princeton NJ 08540

CAVENESS, WILLIAM FIELDS, neurophysiology, clinical neurology, deceased

CAVENEY, STANLEY, b Chester, Eng, Mar 26, 45; m 69; c 1. CELL BIOLOGY, DEVELOPMENTAL BIOLOGY. *Educ:* Univ Witwatersrand, S Africa, BSc, 68; Oxford Univ, DPhil(zool), 71. *Prof Exp:* Asst prof, 73-77, ASSOC PROF ZOOL, UNIV WESTERN ONT, 77- *Mem:* Am Soc Cell Biol; Can Soc Cell Biol; Soc Develop Biol. *Res:* Cell biology of insect development; cellular interactions and communication during insect metamorphosis. *Mailing Add:* Dept of Zool Univ of Western Ont London ON N6A 5B8 Can

CAVENY, ELMER LEONARD, b NC, May 26, 07; m 30; c 1. PSYCHIATRY. *Educ:* Emory Univ, MD, 30; Am Bd Psychiat, dipl; Am Bd Prev Med, dipl. *Prof Exp:* Asst clin prof psychiat, Womens Med Col, Philadelphia, 48-51; clin prof, Georgetown Univ, 52-55; prof psychiat & neurol & chmn dept, 55-58, PROF PSYCHIAT, MED COL ALA, 59- *Concurrent Pos:* Chief neuropsychiat treatment & training ctr, US Naval Hosp, Philadelphia, 48-51, chief neuropsychiat serv, Nat Naval Med Ctr, Bethesda, 51-53, head neuropsychiat br, Bur Med & Surg, US Navy Dept, Washington, DC, 53-55; pvt pract, 59-63. *Mem:* Fel Am Col Physicians; Am Psychoanal Asn; fel Am Psychiat Asn; AMA. *Res:* Psychological structure of man through psychiatry and psychoanalysis. *Mailing Add:* 3516 Robin Dr Birmingham AL 35223

CAVENY, LEONARD HUGH, combustion, energy conversion, see previous edition

CAVERS, PAUL BRETHEN, b Toronto, Ont, Jan 18, 38; m 61; c 4. PLANT ECOLOGY, WEED SCIENCE. *Educ:* Ont Agr Col, BSA, 60; Univ Wales, PhD(weed ecol), 63; Univ London, 72. *Prof Exp:* Lectr, 63-64, asst prof, 64-69, assoc prof, 69-78, PROF ECOL, UNIV WESTERN ONT, 78- *Concurrent Pos:* Chmn subcomt life hist studies, Can Weed Comt; grant selection comt pop biol, Nat Res Coun Can, 73-76. *Mem:* Weed Sci Soc Am; Ecol Soc Am; Brit Ecol Soc; Agr Inst Can; Can Bot Asn(pres, 73-74). *Res:* Comparative ecology of closely related species living in the same area including the following genera: Rumex, Polygonum, Setaria and Melilotus; seed dispersal and dormancy; seedling establishment; dynamics of seed and plant populations. *Mailing Add:* Dept of Plant Sci Univ of Western Ont London ON N6A 5B8 Can

CAVERS, S(TUART) D(ONALD), b Vancouver, BC, Sept 23, 20; m 48; c 4. CHEMICAL ENGINEERING. *Educ:* Univ BC, BASc, 42, MASc, 46; Calif Inst Technol, PhD(chem eng), 51. *Prof Exp:* Jr chem engr, Consol Mining & Smelting Co of Can, Ltd, 42-44; asst chem, Univ BC, 45-46, instr, 46-47; asst chem eng, Calif Inst Technol, 47-50; from asst prof to assoc prof, Univ Sask, 50-55; res engr, BC Res Coun, 55-56; assoc prof, 56-64, PROF CHEM ENG, UNIV BC, 64- *Concurrent Pos:* Nat Res Coun sr res fel, 67-68. *Mem:* Fel Chem Inst Can; Can Soc Chem Eng. *Res:* Material transfer; liquid-liquid extraction; backmixing and axial dispersion, drop coalescence, drop-size distributions; internal sampling of columns; design of non-mechanically agitated liquid-liquid contactors. *Mailing Add:* Dept of Chem Eng Univ BC 2216 Main Mall Vancouver BC V6T 1W5 Can

CAVERT, HENRY MEAD, b Minneapolis, Minn, Mar 30, 22; m; c 3. PHYSIOLOGY, MEDICAL SCHOOL ADMINISTRATION. *Educ:* Univ Minn, MD, 51, PhD(physiol), 52. *Prof Exp:* From asst to assoc prof physiol, 51-68, asst dean med sch, 57-64, PROF PHYSIOL, MED SCH, UNIV MINN, MINNEAPOLIS, 68-, ASSOC DEAN, 64- *Concurrent Pos:* Am Heart Asn res fel, 51-54, estab investr, 54-57; Nat Heart Inst spec res fel biochem & vis prof biochem, Sch Med, Univ Edinburgh, 61-62; mem heart prog proj comt, Nat Heart & Lung Inst, 66-69, consult, 69-; mem, Basic Sci Coun, Am Heart Asn. *Mem:* AAAS; Am Physiol Soc; Asn Am Med Cols; Sigma Xi; Am Med Asn. *Res:* Transport of sugars and amino acids across muscle cell membranes; effects of muscle activity on transmembrane transport; metabolism of myocardium; physician manpower needs and supply. *Mailing Add:* 145 Owre Hall Mayo Box 293 Univ of Minn Med Sch Minneapolis MN 55455

CAVES, CARLTON MORRIS, b Muskogee, Okla, Oct 24, 50. THEORETICAL PHYSICS. *Educ:* Rice Univ, BA, 72; Calif Inst Technol, PhD, 79. *Prof Exp:* Res fel, 79-81, SR RES FEL, CALIF INST TECHNOL, 82- *Mem:* Am Phys Soc. *Res:* Theoretical investigations of experimental gravitation; quantum-mechanical limitations on high-precision measurements, especially as related to gravitational-wave detection; nonlinear quantum optics. *Mailing Add:* Calif Inst Tech 130-33 Pasadena CA 91125

CAVES, THOMAS COURTNEY, b Pryor, Okla, Apr 8, 40; m 64; c 1. THEORETICAL CHEMISTRY. *Educ:* Univ Okla, BA, 62; Columbia Univ, PhD(chem physics), 68. *Prof Exp:* NASA res fel atomic physics, Harvard Col Observ, 68-69, res assoc, 69; asst prof, 69-74, ASSOC PROF CHEM, NC STATE UNIV, 74- *Concurrent Pos:* Vis fel, Gen Elec Res & Develop Ctr, 81-82. *Mem:* Am Phys Soc; Am Chem Soc. *Res:* Ab initio calculation of atomic and molecular properties; scattered wave x-alpha calculations on atomic clusters; semiempirical Green's function method for calculating atomic properties. *Mailing Add:* Dept of Chem NC State Univ Raleigh NC 27650

CAVEY, MICHAEL JOHN, b Elkhorn, Wis, Oct 8, 46. MORPHOLOGY, EMBRYOLOGY. *Educ:* Univ Va, BA, 68; Univ Wash, MS, 71, PhD(zool), 73. *Prof Exp:* Res scientist anat, Sch Med, Univ Southern Calif, 74-76; ASST PROF BIOL, UNIV CALGARY, 76- *Concurrent Pos:* NIH fel, 75-76. *Mem:* Sigma Xi; Am Soc Zoologists; Western Soc Naturalists; Can Soc Zoologists; Am Asn Anatomists. *Res:* Fine structure and differentiation of contractile tissues and intercellular junctions; morphogenetic movements in marine invertebrates and their subcellular mechanisms; histology. *Mailing Add:* Dept Biol 2500 University Dr NW Calgary AB T2N 1N4 Can

CAVIN, WILLIAM PINCKNEY, b Spartanburg, SC, June 2, 25; m 50; c 2. ORGANIC CHEMISTRY. *Educ:* Wofford Col, AB, 45; Duke Univ, AM, 46; Univ NC, PhD(chem), 53. *Prof Exp:* Asst, Duke Univ, 45-46; from instr to prof, 46-62, JOHN M REEVES PROF CHEM, WOFFORD COL, 62-, CHMN DEPT, 71- *Concurrent Pos:* NSF fac fel-vis prof chem, Brown Univ, 65-66. *Mem:* Am Chem Soc. *Res:* Isotope effect of carbon-14 in organic reactions; kinetics and mechanisms of organic reactions. *Mailing Add:* Dept of Chem Wofford Col Spartanburg SC 29301

CAVINESS, BOBBY FORRESTER, b Asheboro, NC, Mar 24, 40; m 61; c 1. COMPUTER ALGEBRA, ANALYSIS OF ALGORITHMS. *Educ:* Univ NC, Chapel Hill, BS, 62; Carnegie-Mellon Univ, MS, 64, PhD(math), 68. *Prof Exp:* Asst prof math, Duke Univ, 67-70; asst prof comput sci, Univ Wis-Madison, 70-75; assoc prof comput sci, Ill Inst Technol, 75-76; from assoc prof to prof math sci, Rensselaer Polytech Inst, 76-79; chairperson computer sci, 79-81, PROF COMPUTER SCI & MATH, UNIV DEL, 81- *Concurrent Pos:* NSF grant, 69-70, 71-74 & 76-78; assoc ed, Asn Comput Mach Transactions Math Software, 75-77; nat lectr, Asn Comput Mach, 81-82. *Mem:* Asn Comput Mach; Math Asn Am; Soc Indust & Appl Math; AAAS; Fedn Am Scientists. *Res:* Symbolic and algebraic computation; recursive systems for symbolic mathematics; analysis of algorithms. *Mailing Add:* Dept Math Sci Rensselaer Polytech Inst Troy NY 12181

CAVINESS, VERNE STRUDWICK, JR, b Raleigh, NC, July 25, 34; m 62; c 2. NEUROLOGY, NEUROPATHOLOGY. *Educ:* Duke Univ, BA, 56; Oxford Univ, DPhil(exp path), 60; Harvard Univ, MD, 62. *Prof Exp:* asst prof, 71-76, ASSOC PROF NEUROL, HARVARD MED SCH, 76-; DIR RES NEUROPATH DEVELOP, EUNICE KENNEDY SHRIVER CTR, 76- *Concurrent Pos:* NIH spec res fel, Harvard Med Sch, 69-71; asst neurologist, Mass Gen Hosp, 71-; sr investr, E K Shriver Inst, 71- *Mem:* AAAS; Am Neurol Asn; Am Acad Neurol. *Res:* Developmental neuroanatomy and neuropathology. *Mailing Add:* E K Shriver Inst 200 Trapelo Rd Waltham MA 02154

CAVITT, STANLEY BRUCE, b Red Oak, Tex, Apr 5, 34; m 65; c 1. PETROLEUM CHEMISTRY. *Educ:* NTex State Col, BA, 56, MS, 57; Univ Tex, PhD(chem), 61. *Prof Exp:* Chemist, Am Oil Co, 61-63; res chemist, Jefferson Chem Co, Inc, 63-69, PROJ CHEMIST, TEXACO CHEM CO, INC, 69- *Mem:* Am Chem Soc; The Catalysis Soc. *Res:* Catalyst research; petrochemicals; organic synthesis. *Mailing Add:* Texaco Chem Co Inc PO Box 15730 Austin TX 78761

CAVONIUS, CARL RICHARD, b Santa Barbara, Calif, Dec, 23, 32. NEUROSCIENCE. *Educ:* Wesleyan Univ, BA, 53; Brown Univ, MSc, 61, PhD(psychol), 62. *Prof Exp:* USPHS fel, Brown Univ, 62-63; res scientist, Human Sci Res, Inc, 63-65; dir, Eye Res Found, 65-71; Von Humboldt fel, Univ Munich, 71-73; J McKeen Cattell Fund fel, Cambridge Univ, 73-74; chief sci officer lab med phys, Univ Amsterdam, 74-75; PROF NEUROPHYS, UNIV DORTMUND, W GERMANY, 76- *Concurrent Pos:* From asst prof to assoc prof, Sch Med, Univ Md, 64-70; res dir, Inst Pedestrian Res, 73-74; dir, Inst Arbeitsphysiol, 80-81. *Mem:* Am Psychol Asn; Optical Soc Am; Psychonomic Soc; Exp Psychol Soc. *Res:* Sensory coding and processing; human psychophysics, especially visual; human factors and applied physiology. *Mailing Add:* Inst for Occup Physiol Ardeystrasse 67 D-4600 Dortmund Germany, Federal Republic of

CAWEIN, MADISON JULIUS, b Bloomfield, NJ, Jan 31, 26; m 69; c 4. HEMATOLOGY, CLINICAL PHARMACOLOGY. *Educ:* Harvard Univ, BA, 49; Tulane Univ, MD, 54; Univ Minn, MS, 59. *Prof Exp:* Assoc prof med, Med Sch, Univ Ky, 60-66; dir clin pharmacol, Eaton Labs, 66-68; assoc prof clin pharmacol, Univ Tenn, 68-70; DIR CLIN PHARMACOL, MERRELL DOW PHARM, INC, 70- *Concurrent Pos:* Consult, Vet Admin Hosp, Lexington, Ky, 60-66; USPHS Hosp, Lexington, 60-66; St Mary's Hosp, Lexington, 59-66, Univ Ky Hosp, 60-66, Vet Admin Hosp, Johnson City, Tenn, 68-70 & Univ Tenn Mem Hosp, Knoxville, 68-70; lectr, Roswell Park Mem Inst, 64. *Mem:* Am Soc Hemat; Am Soc Clin PHarmacol & Therapeut; Am Fedn Clin Res; NY Acad Sci. *Res:* Genetics of erythrocyte enzymes; hemoglobinopathy; leukemoid reactions; pharmacogenetics; drug interactions; carcinogenesis; pharmacology of 1-dihydroxyphenylalanine. *Mailing Add:* Merrell Dow Pharm Inc 2110 E Galbraith Rd Cincinnati OH 45215

CAWLEY, EDWARD PHILIP, b Jackson, Mich, Sept 1, 12; m 39; c 2. DERMATOLOGY. *Educ:* Univ Mich, AB, 36, MD, 40; Am Bd Dermat, dipl, 47. *Prof Exp:* Asst prof dermat, Med Sch, Univ Mich, 48-51; PROF DERMAT & CHMN DEPT, SCH MED, UNIV VA, 51- *Concurrent Pos:* Dir, Am Bd Dermat, 58-67, pres. *Mem:* Am Dermat Asn; Soc Invest Dermat; AMA; NY Acad Sci. *Res:* Medical mycology and dermatopathology. *Mailing Add:* Dept of Dermat Univ of Va Sch of Med Charlottesville VA 22901

CAWLEY, EDWARD T, b Chicago, Ill, Mar 13, 31; m 55; c 5. ECOLOGY. *Educ:* Northern Ill State Teachers Col, BS, 53; Univ Wis, MS, 58, PhD(bot), 60. *Prof Exp:* From asst prof to assoc prof, 60-71, PROF BIOL, LORAS COL, 71-, DIR, ENVIRON RES CTR, 73- *Concurrent Pos:* Mem Iowa State Preserves Adv Bd, 63-75, chmn, 63-68; consult ed, Brown Publ Co. *Mem:* Sigma Xi; Ecol Soc Am. *Res:* Fresh water ecology-diversity indices; ecology of upper Mississippi River. *Mailing Add:* Dept of Biol Loras Col Dubuque IA 52001

CAWLEY, JOHN JOSEPH, b Somerville, Mass, Sept 18, 32; m 56; c 6. PHYSICAL ORGANIC CHEMISTRY. *Educ:* Boston Col, BS, 55; Harvard Univ, MA, 57, PhD(chem), 61. *Prof Exp:* Fel, Univ Wash, 60-61; asst prof, 61-69, ASSOC PROF CHEM, VILLANOVA UNIV, 69- *Mem:* Am Chem Soc; The Chem Soc. *Res:* Chromic acid oxidations; hydrolytic processes in concentrated acid media; chemistry of acetals, especially of dioxolans and dioxoles; reductions of B-keto systems; epihalohydrin chemistry. *Mailing Add:* Dept of Chem Villanova Univ Villanova PA 19085

CAWLEY, LEO PATRICK, b Oklahoma City, Okla, Aug 11, 22; m 48; c 3. PATHOLOGY, CLINICAL IMMUNOLOGY. *Educ:* Okla State Univ, BS, 48; Univ Okla, MD, 52; Am Bd Path, dipl, 57, cert clin chem, 65, cert blood banking, 73, cert radioisotopic path, 74, Am Bd Nuclear Med, dipl, 76, Am Bd Med Lab Immunol, dipl, 81. *Prof Exp:* Intern path, Wesley Hosp, Wichita, Kans, 52-53, resident, 53-54; resident, Wayne County Gen Hosp, Eloise, Mich, 54-57; clin pathologist & assoc dir labs, 57-69, dir labs, 69-76, DIR RES & DEVELOP, DEPT LAB MED, WESLEY MED CTR, 76- *Concurrent Pos:* Clin assoc prof path, Sch Med, Univ Kansas, Wichita, 77-80, prof, 80-; sci dir, Wesley Med Res Found. *Mem:* AAAS; Am Soc Clin Pathologists; Am Soc Human Genetics; Am Soc Exp Path; Am Chem Soc. *Res:* Biochemistry; characterization of proteins other than hemoglobin of human erythrocytes, using methods based on column chromatography, electrophoresis, analytic electrophoresis, immunoelectrophoresis and gas chromatography. *Mailing Add:* Wesley Med Res Found 550 N Hillside Wichita KS 67214

CAWLEY, ROBERT, b Scranton, Pa, Jan 29, 36; m 58; c 4. THEORETICAL PHYSICS, THEORETICAL MECHANICS. *Educ:* Mass Inst Technol, BS, 58, MS, 60, PhD(physics), 65. *Prof Exp:* Asst prof physics, Clarkson Col Technol, 65-67; RES PHYSICIST, NUCLEAR PHYSICS DIV, NAVAL SURFACE WEAPONS CTR, 67- *Mem:* Am Phys Soc. *Mailing Add:* Nuclear Physics Br Naval Surface Weapons Ctr Silver Spring MD 20910

CAWLEY, WILLIAM ARTHUR, b New York, NY, Dec 11, 25; m 51; c 6. ENVIRONMENTAL ENGINEERING. *Educ:* Harvard Univ, AB, 46; Tufts Univ, BS, 50; Mass Inst Technol, MS, 55. *Prof Exp:* Jr sanit engr, Mass Dept Pub Health, 50, asst sanit engr, 52-54; sanit engr, Rayonier, Ind, 55-59; tech ed, Scranton Pub Co, 59; staff consult, Res Dept, Mead Corp, 59-63; mgr eng, Sewage & Waste Treatment Dept, Cochrane Div, Crane Co, 63-66; chief pollution control tech br, Fed Water Qual Admin, 66-68, dir, Div Process Res & Develop & Div Water Qual Res, 68-71; dep dir, Off Prog Mgt, Off Res & Develop, 71-75, dir, Tech Support Div, 75-78, DEP DIR, INDUST ENVIRON RES LAB, OFF RES & DEVELOP, US ENVIRON PROTECTION AGENCY, 78- *Mem:* Am Soc Civil Engrs; Water Pollution Control Fedn; Am Inst Chem Engrs; Am Acad Environ Engrs. *Res:* Methods of municipal and industrial waste treatment; water quality control; water reuse. *Mailing Add:* Indust Environ Res Lab US Environ Protection Agency Cincinnati OH 45268

CAWTHON, GEORGE M, JR, US citizen. ELECTRICAL ENGINEERING. *Prof Exp:* Test engr flight controls, General Dynamics/Ft Worth, 64-65; sr electronic engr, Sperry Rand Space Support, 65-68; sr syst engr, 68-76, mgr progs telemetry instrumentation, 76-77, ENG MGR, ELECTRO-PRODS DIV, SCIENTIFIC-ATLANTA INC, 77- *Res:* Servo control systems; antenna pedestals; program management; telemetry antenna systems test and evaluation. *Mailing Add:* Scientific-Atlanta Inc 3845 Pleasantdale Rd Atlanta GA 30340

CAYEN, MITCHELL NESS, b Montreal, Que, Nov 6, 38; m 67; c 2. BIOCHEMISTRY. *Educ:* McGill Univ, BSc, 59, MSc, 61, PhD(agr chem), 65. *Prof Exp:* RES BIOCHEMIST & HEAD METAB SECT, AYERST RES LABS, 65-, SR RES ASSOC, 80- *Concurrent Pos:* Fel coun arteriosclerosis, Am Heart Asn. *Mem:* Am Soc Pharmacol & Exp Therapeut; AAAS; Can Biochem Soc; NY Acad Sci; Sigma Xi. *Res:* Lipid metabolism; pathogenesis of atherosclerosis; drug metabolism; pharmacokinetics. *Mailing Add:* 5625 Hudson Ave Cote St Luc Montreal PQ H4W 2K3 Can

CAYER, DAVID, b Hartford, Conn, Nov 5, 13; m 42; c 2. GASTROENTEROLOGY. *Educ:* Duke Univ, AB, 35, MD, 38; Am Bd Internal Med, dipl, 46; Am Bd Gastroenterol & Am Bd Nutrit, dipl, 51. *Prof Exp:* Res physician, NC Sanitarium Tuberc, 39; from intern to resident, Med Sch, Duke Univ, 39-42, asst physiol & pharm, 41, instr med, 42-44; asst prof med, 45-49, assoc prof, 49-53, prof gastroenterol, 53-56, PROF MED, BOWMAN GRAY SCH MED, WAKE FOREST UNIV, 56- *Concurrent Pos:* Consult, US Vet Admin, NC, 48 & Nat Cancer Inst. *Honors & Awards:* Silver Medal, AMA, 51, Billings Medal, 51 & 71, Gold Medal, 71. *Mem:* AAAS; fel AMA; fel Am Col Physicians; Am Gastroscopic Soc; fel Am Col Clin Pharmacol & Chemother. *Res:* Digestive diseases. *Mailing Add:* 2240 Cloverdale Ave Winston-Salem NC 27103

CAYFORD, AFTON HERBERT, b Hollywood, Calif, Dec 15, 29; m 51; c 4. MATHEMATICAL ANALYSIS, NUMBER THEORY. *Educ:* La Verne Col, BA, 51; Univ Calif, Los Angeles, MA, 58, PhD(math), 61. *Prof Exp:* Mem tech staff, Hughes Aircraft Co, 56-58; instr math, Univ BC, 59-62; res scientist, Jet Propulsion Lab, Calif Inst Technol, 62-63; asst prof, 62-70, ASSOC PROF MATH, UNIV BC, 70- *Mem:* AAAS; Am Math Soc; Math Asn Am; Can Math Cong; Sigma Xi. *Res:* Analytic number theory and properties of certain classes of entire functions of complex variable with special characteristics on finite point sets; growth rate. *Mailing Add:* Dept of Math Univ of BC Vancouver BC V6T 1W5 Can

CAYLE, THEODORE, b New York, NY, Mar 1, 28; m 49; c 4. ENZYMOLOGY, INDUSTRIAL MICROBIOLOGY. *Educ:* Brooklyn Col, BA, 49, MA, 51; Univ Ill, PhD(plant physiol, biochem), 56. *Prof Exp:* Asst, Brooklyn Col, 49-51; asst, Univ Ill, 51-53, 55-56; instr biol, Univ Wash, 56-58; biochemist, Wallerstein Labs, 58-62, mgr biochem res, 62-65, asst dir res, 65-70, dir res, 70-73; pres, CCF Consult Corp, 74-75; vpres tech dir, Dairyland Food Labs, Inc, 75-77; PROJ ASSOC, UNIV WIS-MILWAUKEE, 78-; MGR MICROBIOL & ENZYMOL, KRAFT, INC, 79- *Mem:* Am Dairy Sci Asn; Am Chem Soc; Am Asn Cereal Chem; Sigma Xi; Am Soc Microbiol. *Res:* Dairy, fermentation and enzyme chemistry. *Mailing Add:* 7451 N Beach Ct Fox Point WI 53217

CAYWOOD, STANLEY WILLIAM, JR, b Akron, Ohio, Aug 10, 24; m 59. ORGANIC CHEMISTRY. *Educ:* Harvard Univ, AB, 48, AM, 49; Univ NH, MS, 50; Cornell Univ, PhD(org chem), 53. *Prof Exp:* res chemist, Elastomers Dept, 53-80, RES ASSOC, POLYMER PROD DEPT, E I DU PONT DE NEMOURS & CO, INC, 80- *Concurrent Pos:* Vis prof, Clarkson Col Technol, 64-65. *Res:* Polymer synthesis, elastomer testing, evaluation and processing; polymer colloids, synthesis, and characterization. *Mailing Add:* 115 Watford Rd Westgate Farms Wilmington DE 19808

CAYWOOD, THOMAS E, b Lake Park, Iowa, May 9, 19; m 41; c 3. OPERATIONS RESEARCH. *Educ:* Cornell Col, AB, 39; Northwestern Univ, MA, 40; Harvard Univ, PhD(math), 47. *Prof Exp:* Tutor math, Northwestern Univ, 39-40; tutor, Harvard Univ, 41-42, spec res assoc physics, 42-45, asst, 46; sr mathematician & coordr res, Inst Air Weapons Res, Ill, 47-52; supvr opers res, Armour Res Found, 52-53; partner, Caywood-Schiller Assoc, 53-61, Peat, Marwick, Caywood, Schiller & Co, 62-66 & Caywood-Schiller Assoc, 66-70; vpres, Caywood-Schiller Div, A T Kearney Co, 71-78; PROF LECTR MGT SCI & PROD MGT, UNIV CHICAGO, 78- *Concurrent Pos:* Lectr sch bus, Univ Chicago, 53-57; consult, Off Asst Secy Defense, 53-60 & opers eval group, US Navy, 60-61; pres, Invests Opers Mex, SA, 59-60; mem alumni bd dir, Cornell Col, 62-65, trustee, 64-, pres bd trustees, 70-72; mem statist comt, Nat Acad Sci-Nat Res Coun, 60-63; mem defense sci bd & chmn ord panel, Off Dir Defense Res & Eng, 60-64; chmn task force, Gun Systs Acquisition, Defense Sci Bd, 75; ed, Opers Res, Opers Res Soc Am, 61-68. *Honors & Awards:* George E Kimball Medal, Opers Res Soc Am, 74. *Mem:* Am Math Soc; Am Inst Indust Eng; Opers Res Soc Am (vpres, 68-69, pres, 69-70); Math Asn Am; Inst Mgt Sci. *Res:* Applied mathematics; operational research; theory of games; probability; evaluation engineering. *Mailing Add:* Grad Sch of Bus Univ of Chicago Chicago IL 60637

CAYWOOD, WILLIAM PARKS, b Pittsburgh, Pa, June 30, 21; m 51; c 2. ELECTRICAL ENGINEERING. *Educ:* Carnegie-Mellon Univ, BS, 42, MS, 43, PhD(elec eng), 52. *Prof Exp:* Instr elec eng, Carnegie-Mellon Univ, 43-46, asst prof, 48-54, lectr math, 58; ASSOC PROF ANAL METHODS, DUQUESNE UNIV, 68-; CONUSLT ELEC ENGR & PROPRIETOR, POINT CONSULT, 49- *Concurrent Pos:* Spec consult, Off Secy Defense, 48-52. *Mem:* Sr mem Inst Elec & Electronics Engrs. *Res:* Electrical circuit for cardiac defibrillator; high temperature electrical machines; all electrical taxi meter; high power synchronous demodulator. *Mailing Add:* 5740 Beulah Lane Murrysville PA 15668

CAZEAU, CHARLES J, b Rochester, NY, June 25, 31; m 60; c 2. GEOLOGY. *Educ:* Univ Notre Dame, BS, 54; Fla State Univ, MS, 55; Univ NC, PhD(geol), 62. *Prof Exp:* Explor Geologist, Humble Oil & Refining Co, Tex, 55-56, 57-58; asst prof geol, Clemson Col, 60-63; asst prof, 63-67, ASSOC PROF GEOL, STATE UNIV NY BUFFALO, 67- *Concurrent Pos:* Sigma Xi study grant, 64-65; consult, Union Camp Corp, 74-75. *Mem:* Am Asn Petrol Geologists; Soc Econ Paleontologists & Mineralologists; AAAS; Nat Asn Geol Teachers. *Res:* Detrital mineralogy; recent sediments; Triassic and Pleistocene geology; geoarchaeology of West Mexico; cultural resources. *Mailing Add:* Dept of Geol State Univ of NY Buffalo NY 14214

CAZIER, MONT ADELBERT, b Cardston, Alta, May 27, 11; US citizen; m 55; c 3. SYSTEMATIC ENTOMOLOGY. *Educ:* Univ Calif, BS, 35, PhD(entom), 42. *Prof Exp:* Asst cur entom, Dept Insects & Spiders, Am Mus Natural Hist, 41-43, assoc cur, 46-51, cur, 52-59, chmn dept, 46-59, founder & dir, Southwestern Res Sta, 55-59, resident dir, 50-62; PROF ZOOL, ARIZ STATE UNIV, 68- *Concurrent Pos:* Res entomologist, Univ Calif, 62-64. *Res:* Bionomic entomology; biology; ecology and behavior studies in aculeate Hymenoptera, Coleoptera and Diptera. *Mailing Add:* Dept of Zool Ariz State Univ Tempe AZ 85287

CAZIN, JOHN, JR, b Wheeling, WVa, July 2, 29; m 53; c 3. MICROBIOLOGY, MEDICAL MYCOLOGY. *Educ:* Univ NC, BS, 52, MS, 54, PhD(bact), 57. *Prof Exp:* Instr, 57-58, assoc, 58-59, from asst prof to assoc prof, 59-72, PROF MICROBIOL, UNIV IOWA, 72- *Mem:* Am Soc Microbiol; Mycol Soc Am; Int Soc Human & Animal Mycol; fel Am Acad Microbiol; Med Mycol Soc of the Americas. *Res:* Antibiotics and c-albicans; nutrition and sporulation of allescheria; extracellular nucleases from yeasts; virulence and immunology of cryptococus, allescheria and phycomycetes; morphology and physiology of phycomycetes; antigenic peptides of alternaria. *Mailing Add:* Dept Microbiol Col Med Univ of Iowa Iowa City IA 52240

CEAGLSKE, NORMAN H(UGO), b Merrill, Wis, Feb 16, 07; m 29; c 3. CHEMICAL ENGINEERING. *Educ:* Univ Wis, BS, 28, MS, 29, PhD(chem eng), 36. *Prof Exp:* Asst to indust engr, Wis Gas & Elec Co, 29-30; instr chem eng, Univ Wis, 30-36; instr metall, Univ Iowa, 36-40; asst & assoc prof chem eng, Wash Univ, 40-46; prof, 46-74, EMER PROF CHEM ENG, UNIV MINN, MINNEAPOLIS, 74- *Concurrent Pos:* Res engr, Anheuser-Busch, Inc, 42-46; vis prof, Case Inst Technol, 52; Fulbrigh grant, Norweg Inst Technol, 58-59. *Mem:* Instrument Soc Am; Am Soc Eng Educ; Am Inst Chem Engrs. *Res:* Drying; capillary flow; plastics; distillation; fluid flow; automatic control. *Mailing Add:* Dept of Chem Eng Univ of Minn Minneapolis MN 55455

CEASAR, GERALD P, b New York, NY, Jan 8, 40; m 67. CHEMICAL PHYSICS. *Educ:* Manhattan Col, BS, 62; Columbia Univ, PhD(chem), 67. *Prof Exp:* Air Force Off Sci Res fel chem, Calif Inst Technol, 68-69; NATO & Ramsay Mem fel, Univ Bristol & Oxford Univ, 69; asst prof, Univ Rochester, 69-74; SCIENTIST, WEBSTER RES CTR, XEROX CORP, 74- *Mem:* Am Phys Soc; Am Chem Soc. *Res:* Surface physics and chemistry; photoelectron and auger spectroscopies; electronic structure of molecules and solids; solid state chemistry; thin film technology; optical spectroscopy; magnetic resonance spectroscopy; liquid crystals; amorphous semiconductor physics. *Mailing Add:* Xerox Webster Res Ctr Webster NY 14580

CEBALLOS, RICARDO, b Cadiz, Spain, Jan 12, 30; m 57; c 3. PATHOLOGY, NEUROLOGY. *Educ:* Univ Madrid, MD, 53. *Prof Exp:* Intern, Dept Physiol, Med Sch, Univ Madrid, 47-49, intern, Dept Internal Med, 49-52, rotating intern, 52-53; assoc prof path, Clin Concepcion, Madrid, 55-57; instr, Med Ctr, Univ Ala, 58, asst prof, 58-60; asst pathologist & dir labs, Hotel Dieu Hosp, Kingston, Ont, 60-63; asst dir anat path, 63-64, dir, 64-76, CERT PATHOLOGIST, UNIV HOSP & HILLMAN CLIN, BIRMINGHAM, 76-; PROF PATH & ASSOC PROF NEUROL, MED CTR, UNIV ALA, 69- *Concurrent Pos:* Fel, Menendez & Pelayo Univ, Spain, 53; fel path, Inst Clin & Med Invest, 53-54; Doherty Found fel histochem & path, Med Sch, Univ Ala, 55; Marquesa de Pelayo Found fel, Spain, 56; Med Res Coun Can fel, 62; intern, Dept Path, Gen Hosp, Prov Diputacion of Madrid, Spain, 50-53; secy, Int Cong Internal Med, 56; consult, Vet Admin Hosp, Tuskegee, Ala, 58-60 & 64-67; lectr, Med Sch, Queen's Univ, Ont, 60-63; assoc prof path & instr neurol & med, Med Ctr, Univ Ala, 64-69; consult, WHO. *Mem:* Int Acad Path; AMA; Latin Am Soc Path. *Res:* Pituitary changes in head trauma; neuropathology; hyperparathyroidism; congenital heart disease. *Mailing Add:* Dept Path Univ Hosp Birmingham AL 35233

CEBRA, JOHN JOSEPH, b Philadelphia, Pa, May 7, 34; m 56; c 4. IMMUNOBIOLOGY, IMMUNOCHEMISTRY. *Educ:* Univ Pa, AB, 55; Rockefeller Inst, PhD(immunochem), 60. *Prof Exp:* Nat Found fel immunol, Weizmann Inst Sci, 60-61; from instr to assoc prof microbiol, Col Med, Univ Fla, 61-67; assoc prof biol, Johns Hopkins Univ, 67-69, prof, 69-80; prof biol, 80-81, ANNENBERG PROF NATURAL SCI, UNIV PA, 81-, CHMN DEPT, 80- *Concurrent Pos:* NIH career develop award, 64-67; vis prof immunochem, St Mary's Hosp Med Sch, London, 66-67; mem study sect, Nat Inst Allergy & Infectious Dis, 67-71; instr-in-charge physiol course, Marine Biol Lab, Woods Hole, Mass, 72-76. *Honors & Awards:* Eli Lilly Award Microbiol & Immunol, Am Soc Microbiol, 68. *Mem:* Am Asn Immunologists; Am Soc Microbiol. *Res:* Protein chemistry; structure of immunoglobulins; interaction of antigen, antibody and complement components; cellular synthesis of immunoglobulin polypeptide chains. *Mailing Add:* 212 Biol Bldg G5 Univ Pa Philadelphia PA 11104

CEBULAK, WALTER S(TANLEY), b Saginaw, Mich, Nov 8, 43; m 65; c 2. METALLURGICAL ENGINEERING. *Educ:* Mich Technol Univ, BS, 65, MS, 67. *Prof Exp:* GROUP LEADER POWDER & FORGINGS DIV, ALCOA LABS, ALUMINUM CO AM, 77- *Mem:* Am Soc Metals; Am Inst Mining, Metall & Petrol Engrs; Metall Soc. *Res:* Powder metallurgy; atomization; materials synthesis; rapid solidification; aluminum alloy development; physical metallurgy. *Mailing Add:* Powder & Forgings Div Alcoa Labs Alcoa Center PA 15069

CEBULL, STANLEY EDWARD, b Albany, Calif, June 1, 34; m 56; c 3. STRUCTURAL GEOLOGY. *Educ:* Univ Calif, Berkeley, AB, 57, MA, 58; Univ Wash, PhD(geol), 67. *Prof Exp:* Geologist, Tex Petrol Co, Venezuela, 58-62; from asst prof to assoc prof, 67-81, PROF GEOSCI, TEX TECH UNIV, 81- *Mem:* Am Geophys Union; Am Asn Petrol Geologists; Geol Soc Am. *Res:* Tectonic geology. *Mailing Add:* Dept of Geosci Texas Tech Univ Lubbock TX 79409

CECCHI, JOSEPH LEONARD, b Chicago, Ill, Mar 29, 47; m 70; c 2. PLASMA PHYSICS, ATOMIC PHYSICS. *Educ:* Knox Col, AB, 68; Harvard Univ, AM, 69, PhD(physics), 72. *Prof Exp:* Res assoc atomic physics, Argonne Nat Lab, 67; res staff mem plasma physics, 72-79, RES PHYSICIST & HEAD, MAT PHYSICS GROUP, PLASMA PHYSICS LAB, PRINCETON UNIV, 79- *Concurrent Pos:* Vpres & sr scientist, Princeton Sci Consult, Inc, Plainsboro, NJ, 79- *Mem:* Am Phys Soc; Am Vacuum Soc. *Res:* Controlled thermonuclear fusion by the Tokamak method of magnetic confinement, with specific interests in impurity transport, fundamental atomic processes, plasma-limiter interaction, and materials physics. *Mailing Add:* Plasma Physics Lab Princeton Univ PO Box 451 Princeton NJ 08540

CECH, CAROL MARTINSON, b Albert Lea, Minn, Dec 26, 47; m 70. BIOPHYSICAL CHEMISTRY, BIOCHEMISTRY. *Educ:* Grinnell Col, BA, 70; Univ Calif, Berkeley, PhD(chem), 75. *Prof Exp:* Jane Coffin Childs fel biochem, Harvard Univ, 75-77; ASST PROF CHEM, UNIV COLO, 78- *Mem:* Biophys Soc. *Res:* RNA polymerase-DNA interactions; gene regulation. *Mailing Add:* Dept of Chem Univ of Colo Boulder CO 80309

CECH, FRANKLIN CHARLES, b Cleveland, Ohio, Nov 26, 19; m 42; c 4. FOREST GENETICS. *Educ:* Univ Ohio, AB, 42; Mont State Univ, BSF, 49, MF, 53; Tex A&M Univ, PhD(physiol, genetics), 57. *Prof Exp:* Nurseryman, Mont State Univ, 49-53; silviculturist, Tex Forest Serv, 55-57; res silviculturist, Int Paper Co, 57-64; assoc prof, 64-69, PROF FOREST GENETICS, WVA UNIV, 69- *Mem:* Soc Am Foresters. *Res:* Forest genetics and tree improvement with southern pines and northern hardwoods; silvicultural research in regeneration of species. *Mailing Add:* Div of Forestry WVa Univ Morgantown WV 26506

CECH, JOSEPH JEROME, JR, b Berwyn, Ill, Dec 5, 43; m 67; c 2. PHYSIOLOGICAL ECOLOGY. *Educ:* Univ Wis-Madison, BS, 66; Univ Tex, Austin, MA, 70, PhD(zool), 73. *Prof Exp:* assoc fisheries sci, Portland Maine, 73-75; ASST ASSOC PROF FISHERIES BIOL, UNIV CALIF, DAVIS, 75- *Mem:* Am Inst Biol Sci; Ecol Soc Am; Am Fisheries Soc; Sigma Xi; Estuarine Res Fedn. *Res:* Investigations in the physiological adjustments and adaptations of marine and freshwater fishes to their environments with emphasis on respiratory, circulatory and hematological responses to extreme environments or environmental changes. *Mailing Add:* Dept of Wildlife & Fisheries Biol Univ of Calif Davis CA 95616

CECH, ROBERT E(DWARD), b Minneapolis, Minn, Mar 23, 24; m 50; c 3. METALLURGY. *Educ:* Univ Wis, BS, 48, PhD(metall eng), 67; Rensselaer Polytech Inst, MS, 54. *Prof Exp:* Metallurgist, Gen Elec Res Lab, 48-62 & 65-70; instr metall, Univ Wis, 62-65; consult, 70-77; CONSULT, GEN MOTORS, 77- *Honors & Awards:* Mathewson Award, Am Inst Mining, Metall & Petrol Engrs, 62; Award, Indust Res Mag, 69. *Mem:* Am Inst Mining, Metall & Petrol Engrs; Am Soc Metals; NY Acad Sci. *Res:* Metallurgical reaction kinetics; technology of cobalt-rare earth and ferrite magnets. *Mailing Add:* RD 1 Hetcheltown Rd Scotia NY 12302

CECH, THOMAS ROBERT, b Chicago, Ill, Dec 8, 47; m 70. BIOCHEMISTRY, MOLECULAR BIOLOGY. *Educ:* Grinnell Col, BA, 70; Univ Calif, Berkeley, PhD(chem), 75. *Prof Exp:* Nat Cancer Inst fel molecular biol, Dept Biol, Mass Inst Technol, 75-77; ASST PROF CHEM, DEPT CHEM, UNIV COLO, BOULDER, 78- *Concurrent Pos:* Prin investr NIH res grant, 78-; res career develop award, NIH, 80. *Mem:* Am Soc Biol Chemists. *Res:* Ribonucleic acid splicing; chromatin structure and transcriptional regulation; extrachromosomal genes in Tetrahymena; photochemical cross-linking of DNA and RNA with psoralen derivatives. *Mailing Add:* Dept of Chem Univ of Colo Boulder CO 80309

CECICH, ROBERT ALLEN, plant anatomy, see previous edition

CECIL, DAVID ROLF, b Tulsa, Okla, July 12, 35; m 58; c 1. MATHEMATICS. *Educ:* Univ Tulsa, BA, 58; Okla State Univ, MS, 60, PhD(math), 62. *Prof Exp:* Sales engr fluid dynamics, Black, Sivalls & Bryson, 57-58; sr res mathematician, Atlantic Ref Co, 62; asst prof math, North Tex State Univ, 62-69; prof, Butler Univ, 69-70; assoc prof, 70-73, PROF MATH, TEX A&I UNIV, 73-, CHMN DEPT MATH, 80- *Concurrent Pos:* Consult, Region 2, Educ Serv Ctr. *Mem:* Am Math Soc; Sigma Xi. *Res:* Vector lattices; topological algebra; group generalizations, computer applications. *Mailing Add:* Dept Math Tex A&I Univ Kingsville TX 78363

CECIL, HELENE CARTER, b Tunkhannock, Pa, Jan 25, 33; m 54; c 1. REPRODUCTIVE PHYSIOLOGY. *Educ:* Univ Md, BS, 63, PhD(poultry physiol), 68. *Prof Exp:* RES PHYSIOLOGIST, USDA, 57- *Mem:* Am Physiol Soc; Am Chem Soc; Poultry Sci Asn; AAAS. *Res:* Avian reproductive environmental pollutants on reproduction. *Mailing Add:* Avian Physiol Lab Bldg 262 USDA Beltsville MD 20705

CECIL, SAM REBER, b San Francisco, Calif, Feb 22, 16; m 47; c 2. FOOD SCIENCE. *Educ:* Milligan Col, BS, 37; Univ Ga, MSA, 54. *Prof Exp:* Asst biochem, Sch Med, Vanderbilt Univ, 37-39, asst nutrit, 40-41; asst food technologist, 41-43, assoc food technologist, 43-58, food scientist, 58-67, PROF FOOD SCI RES, AGR EXP STA, UNIV GA, 67- *Concurrent Pos:* Jr food technologist, Ore State Col, 56-58; mem sci adv coun, Refrigeration Res Found, 74-79. *Mem:* AAAS; Inst Food Technologists; Am Chem Soc; Am Oil Chem Soc. *Res:* Canning and freezing of fruits and vegetables; storage of canned foods, military and civil defense rations; effects of newer cultural practices on processing and product quality of peanuts. *Mailing Add:* 1119 Maple Dr Griffin GA 30223

CECIL, THOMAS E, b Louisville, Ky, Dec 13, 45; m 71; c 3. GEOMETRY. *Educ:* Col Holy Cross, AB, 68; Brown Univ, PhD(math), 73. *Prof Exp:* Asst prof math, Vassar Col, 73-78; asst prof, 78-80, ASSOC PROF MATH, COL HOLY CROSS, 80- *Concurrent Pos:* NSF basic res grants, 75 & 76. *Mem:* Am Math Soc; Math Asn Am; Sigma Xi. *Res:* Taut immersions of manifolds; differential geometry. *Mailing Add:* Dept of Math Col of the Holy Cross Worcester MA 01610

CECILE, MICHAEL PETER, b Chapleau, Ont, Oct 15, 46. EARTH SCIENCES, STRATIGRAPHY. *Educ:* Univ Waterloo, BSc, 70; Carleton Univ, MSc, 73, PhD(geol), 76. *Prof Exp:* RES SCIENTIST GEOL, GEOL SURV CAN, 77- *Concurrent Pos:* Fel, Geol Surv Can-Nat Res Coun Can, 76-77. *Mem:* Geol Asn Can; Can Soc Petrol Geologists. *Res:* Proterozoic and archean geology; paleozoic stratigraphy; economic geology. *Mailing Add:* Geol Surv of Can 3303 33rd St NW Calgary Can

CEDAR, FRANK JAMES, b Ottawa, Ont, Aug 28, 45. ENVIRONMENTAL LAW. *Educ:* Carleton Univ, BSc, 67, BA, 81; Univ Alta, PhD(synthetic org chem), 73. *Prof Exp:* CHEM EVAL OFFICER, REGISTRATION OF PESTICIDES, PESTICIDES DIV, AGR CAN, 73- *Concurrent Pos:* exec secy, consult Comt Indust bio-test pesticide, 81- *Mem:* Chem Inst Can; Am Chem Soc; Soc Environ Toxicol; Can Wood Preserv Asn. *Res:* Evaluates data submitted to government by industry for the registration of wood preservatives and industrial biocides. *Mailing Add:* Pesticides Div Agr Can Carling Ave Ottawa ON K1A 0C5 Can

CEDER, JACK G, b Spokane, Wash, Aug 25, 33; m 55; c 2. PURE MATHEMATICS. *Educ:* Univ Wash, BS, 55, MS, 57, PhD(math), 59. *Prof Exp:* From asst prof to assoc prof, 59-74, PROF MATH, UNIV CALIF, SANTA BARBARA, 74- *Mem:* Am Math Soc. *Res:* Abstract topological spaces; real functions. *Mailing Add:* Dept of Math Univ of Calif Santa Barbara CA 93106

CEDERBERG, JAMES W, b Oberlin, Kans, Mar 16, 39; m 67; c 2. MOLECULAR PHYSICS, PHYSICS. *Educ:* Univ Kans, AB, 59; Harvard Univ, AM, 60, PhD(physics), 63. *Prof Exp:* Lectr & res fel physics, Harvard Univ, 63-64; from asst prof to assoc prof, 64-80, PROF PHYSICS, ST OLAF COL, 80- *Concurrent Pos:* NSF sci fac fel, Duke Univ, 69-70; res assoc, Harvard Univ, 76-77. *Mem:* Am Phys Soc; Am Asn Physics Teachers. *Res:* Molecular beams; rotational magnetic moments and magnetic interactions in molecules; molecular hyperfine interactions. *Mailing Add:* Dept of Physics St Olaf Col Northfield MN 55057

CEFOLA, MICHAEL, b Barile, Italy, Oct 22, 08; US citizen; m 48. NUCLEAR CHEMISTRY, INORGANIC CHEMISTRY. *Educ:* City Col BS, 33; New York, BS, 33; NY Univ, PhD(chem), 41. *Prof Exp:* Instr microchem, NY Univ, 41-42; instr chem, City Col New York, 41-42; res assoc, Univ Chicago, 42-44; mem staff, Radiation Lab, Mass Inst Technol, 44-45; microchemist, Socony-Vacuum Oil Co, NY, 45-47; chemist, Gen Elec Co, 47-50; from assoc prof to prof, 50-72, EMER PROF CHEM, FORDHAM UNIV, 72- *Mem:* Am Chem Soc; hon mem Am Microchem Soc; fel NY Acad Sci. *Res:* Ultramicrochemistry in radiochemistry; high vacuum technique; chemistry of chelate compounds. *Mailing Add:* 179 Bell Rd Scarsdale NY 10583

CEGLIO, NATALE MAURO, b New York, NY, Sept 6, 44. X-RAY OPTICS, MICROFABRICATION. *Educ:* Columbia Univ, BA, 66, BS, 67, Mass Inst Technol, MS, 69, PhD(physics), 76. *Prof Exp:* Instr physics, Naval Postgrad Sch, 69-73; physicist, 76-80, DEP GROUP LEADER, LAWRENCE LIVERMORE LAB, 81- *Res:* X-ray and thermonuclear burn imaging; time and space resolved x-ray spectroscopy; microfabrication for x-ray optics applications; physics of high temperature, high density plasmas; carbon dioxide gas lasers and gas discharge phenomena. *Mailing Add:* L-473 PO Box 808 Lawrence Livermore Lab Livermore CA 94550

CEGLOWSKI, WALTER STANLEY, b Newark, NJ, Nov 24, 32; m 64; c 1. MICROBIOLOGY. *Educ:* Univ Vt, BS, 54; Rutgers Univ, MS, 56, PhD(dairy microbiol), 62. *Prof Exp:* Lab asst rickettsial dis, Walter Reed Army Inst Res, DC, 56-58; res asst dairy bact, Rutgers Univ, 58-62; res biochemist, Immunol Lab, Plum Island Animal Dis Lab, USDA, 62-65; fel dept microbiol, Sch Med, Temple Univ, 65-67; asst prof & dir immunoserol lab, 67-70; assoc prof microbiol, Pa State Univ, 70-79; PROF MICROBIOL & DIR, IMMUNOL LAB, SCH MED, TEMPLE UNIV, 79- *Concurrent Pos:* Vis Scientist, Nat Cancer Inst, 77. *Mem:* Am Soc Microbiol; Am Asn Immunol; fel NY Acad Sci. *Res:* Applied microbiology and immunology. *Mailing Add:* Dept Microbiol & Immunol Sch Med Temple Univ Philadelphia PA 19140

CEITHAML, JOSEPH JAMES, b Chicago, Ill, May 23, 16; m 42; c 2. BIOCHEMISTRY. *Educ:* Univ Chicago, BS, 37, PhD(biochem), 41. *Prof Exp:* Res assoc biochem, 41-45, from asst prof to assoc prof, 46-58, PROF BIOCHEM, UNIV CHICAGO, 58-, DEAN STUDENTS, DIV BIOL SCI, 51- *Mem:* AAAS; Asn Am Med Cols; Am Soc Biol Chem. *Res:* Isolation of anterior pituitary hormones; metabolism of the malaria parasite; isolation and study of plant enzymes; biochemical genetics. *Mailing Add:* Pritzker Sch of Med 5724 S Ellis Ave Chicago IL 60637

CELANDER, EVELYN FAUN, b Ottumwa, Iowa, Nov 4, 26; wid; c 3. BIOCHEMISTRY. *Educ:* Drake Univ, BA, 48; Col Osteop Med & Surg, MS, 67. *Hon Degrees:* DSc, Col Osteopth Med & Surg, 78. *Prof Exp:* Reader & res asst, State Univ Iowa & Univ Tex Med Br, 48-55; res technician, Univ Tex Med Br, 55-59, res assoc physiol, 59-61; from instr to asst prof, 61-71, ASSOC PROF BIOCHEM, COL OSTEOP MED & SURG, 71- *Res:* Control and function of fibrinolytic enzyme system in health and disease; biosynthesis of radioactive protein substances; computer technology as applied to information retrieval, data processing and instruction. *Mailing Add:* Dept Biochem Col Osteop Med & Surg Des Moines IA 50312

CELAURO, FRANCIS L, b Jersey City, NJ, Sept 12, ll; m 40; c 3. MATHEMATICS. *Educ:* NY Univ, AB, 37, AM, 39, PhD(math), 52. *Prof Exp:* Instr math, NY Univ, 37-40; asst prof, Loyola Col, 40-43; mathematician, Nat Bur Standards, 43-45; asst prof math, Lehigh Univ, 45-49; prof, East Tenn State Col, 54-57; prof, Cent Mich Univ, 57-62; prof, 62-76, EMER PROF MATH, GEORGE PEABODY COL, 76- *Concurrent Pos:* NSF award, Princeton Univ, 60; consult math, sci & eng. *Mem:* Math Asn Am; Am Asn Univ Professors. *Res:* Applied mathematics; psychology of mathematics learning at college level; factors associated with retention of college mathematics. *Mailing Add:* 1347 Burton Valley 1347 Burton Valley Rd Nashville TN 37215

CELESIA, GASTONE G, b Genoa, Italy, Nov 22, 33. NEUROLOGY, NEUROPHYSIOLOGY. *Educ:* Univ Genoa, MD, 59; McGill Univ, MS, 65. *Prof Exp:* Resident neurol, Montreal Neurol Inst, 62-65; from asst prof to prof neurol, Med Ctr, Univ Wis-Madison, 66-76, dir lab EEG & clin neurophysiol, 70-76; prof neurol & vchmn dept, St Louis Univ, 76-79; PROF NEUROL & VCHMN DEPT, CTR HEALTH SCI, UNIV WIS-MADISON, 79- *Concurrent Pos:* Fel neurophysiol, Med Ctr, Univ Wis-Madison, 60-62 & Montreal Neurol Inst, 64-65; demonstr, McGill Univ, 63-65; clin investr, Vet Admin Hosp, 66-70, consult, 70-76; consult, Cent Wis Colony, 70-76; chief, Neurol Serv, William S Middleton Mem Vet Hosp, 79- *Mem:* Am Acad Neurol; Soc Neurosci; Am Epilepsy Soc; Am EEG Soc; AMA. *Res:* Electroencephalography; auditory cortex; sensory system. *Mailing Add:* Dept Neurol Wm Middleton Va Hosp 2500 Overlook Terrace Madison WI 53705

CELESK, ROGER A, b Chicago, Ill, Sep 13, 49; m 80; c 1. MICROBIAL ADHERENCE, ELECTRON MICROSCOPY. *Educ:* Univ Ill, BS, 71, Univ Notre Dame, PhD(microbiol), 77. *Prof Exp:* Fel, NIH, 76, Inst Cancer Res, 76-77, & Nat Inst Dent Res, 77-79; ASST PROF BIOL, UNIV DAYTON, 79- *Mem:* Am Soc Microbiol; Am Asn Gnotobiotics; N Am Soc Sigma Xi. *Res:* Microbial ecology and pathogenesis; host-miroflora interactions; bacterial adherence on surfaces; gnotobiotics; electron microscopy; ultrastructural analysis. *Mailing Add:* 222 Sherman Hall Univ Dayton Dayton OH 45469

CELIANO, ALFRED, b Orange, NJ, Aug 8, 28. CHEMICAL KINETICS, PHYSICAL INORGANIC CHEMISTRY. *Educ:* Seton Hall Univ, AB, 49; Catholic Univ, STL, 53; Fordham Univ, MS, 56, PhD(chem), 59. *Prof Exp:* Chmn dept, 59-80, PROF CHEM, SETON HALL UNIV, 59- *Mem:* AAAS; Am Chem Soc. *Res:* The stability and kinetics of formation and substitution of inorganic complexes. *Mailing Add:* Dept of Chem Seton Hall Univ South Orange NJ 07079

CELIK, HASAN ALI, b Bozkir, Turkey. ALGEBRA. *Educ:* Middle East Tech Univ, BS, 64, MS, 65; Univ Calif, Santa Barbara, PhD(math), 71. *Prof Exp:* Asst math, Middle East Tech Univ, 64-66; from asst prof to assoc prof, 71-80, PROF MATH, CALIF STATE POLYTECH UNIV, POMONA, 80- *Mem:* Am Math Soc; Math Asn Am. *Res:* Non-associative algebra including flexible-antiflexible algebras; Jordan-Lie-Alternative Rings. *Mailing Add:* Dept of Math Calif State Polytech Univ Pomona CA 91768

CELINSKI, OLGIERD J(ERZY) Z(DZISLAW), b Warsaw, Poland, Nov 22, 22; nat Can; m 51; c 1. ELECTRICAL ENGINEERING. *Educ:* Polish Univ Col, Dipl Ing, 50; Univ Ottawa, MSc, 61. *Prof Exp:* Develop engr electronics, Airmec Labs, 50-51; digital cts, Comput Devices, Can, 52-54; mail sorting, Post Off Lab, 54-57; asst prof elec eng, Univ Ottawa, 57; pres, Northern Energy, 76-81; PRES, INTERACTIVE LEARNING CONTRACTORS INC, 81- *Concurrent Pos:* Univ deleg & consult electronics res, Karachi, Univ Ottawa, 64-66. *Mem:* Brit Inst Elec Engrs. *Res:* Learning processes; computer modeling of human activity; man-machine systems; electrical measurements. *Mailing Add:* 169 Henderson Ave Ottawa ON K1N 7P7 Can

CELIS, ANTONIO JUAN, b Manila, Philippines, Nov 14, 33; nat US; m 59; c 2. CIVIL & STRUCTURAL ENGINEERING. *Educ:* Univ Santo Tomas, Manila, BSCE, 53; Okla State Univ, MSCE, 55, PhD, 57. *Prof Exp:* Res assoc, Okla State Univ, 54-55; struct engr, Roof Struct Inc, Mo, 55-56; instr civil eng, St Louis Univ, 56-58; asst prof, Univ Alta, 58-60 & St Louis Univ, 60-68; ASSOC PROF CIVIL ENG, UNIV MO-ROLLA, 68- *Concurrent Pos:* Assoc mem, Hanlon & Assocs, Mo; prin, Celis, Zeiter & Assocs; advr struct engr, Sverdrup & Parcel Inc, Mo, 56-58; consult struct sect, Dept Pub Works, Edmonton, Can Bank Bldg & Equip Corp Am, Mo, 60-61; NSF sci fac fel, 64; bldg comnr, City of University City, Mo, 68-69; pres, A J Celis & Assocs, Consult Prof Engrs. *Mem:* Fel Am Soc Civil Engrs; Am Asn Eng Educ; Nat Soc Prof Engrs; Inst Asn Bridge & Struct Eng; Int Asn Shell & Spatial Struct. *Res:* Theoretical stress analysis; space frames; shells and plates; rigid frames; zero sideways axis of rigid frames; matrices for curvilinear structures; long span reticulated shell structures and domes. *Mailing Add:* 1572 Hudson Rd Dellwood MO 63136

CELIS, ROBERTO T F, b La Paz, Entre Rios, Arg, Apr 22, 30; m 63; c 2. MOLECULAR BIOLOGY, MICROBIOLOGY. *Educ:* Univ Buenos Aires, MD, 57, PhD(biochem), 64. *Prof Exp:* Res assoc microbiol, Univ Buenos Aires, 60-62, lectr, 62-64, asst prof, 64-66; asst prof microbiol, 72-75, ASSOC PROF MICROBIOL, MED SCH, NY UNIV, 75- *Concurrent Pos:* Trainee genetics, Med Sch, NY Univ, 68-70; NIH res grant, 73- *Mem:* NY Acad Sci; Am Soc Microbiol. *Res:* Transport of basic amino acids on escherichia coli. *Mailing Add:* Dept of Microbiol NY Univ Med Sch New York NY 10016

CELITANS, GERARD JOHN, b Riga, Latvia, Feb 1, 37; US citizen; m 66. BIOPHYSICS, NUCLEAR PHYSICS. *Educ:* Univ New South Wales, BSc, 59, PhD(nuclear & radiation chem), 63. *Prof Exp:* Res officer, Australian Atomic Energy Res Estab, Southerland, NSW, 63-64; res scientist, New Eng Inst Med Res, Conn, 64-66; assoc prof chem & physics, Hiram Scott Col, 66-67; assoc prof chem, Fla Atlantic Univ, 67-68; actg chmn, 77-79, ASSOC PROF BIOENG, UNIV TEX HEALTH SCI CTR, SAN ANTONIO, 68-, PLANNING OFFICER, 79- *Concurrent Pos:* Vis prof & res assoc, New Eng

Inst Med Res, 66- *Mem:* Asn Am Med Cols; Am Phys Soc. *Res:* Low energy positronium; gamma-ray interaction and spectroscopy; sub-nanosecond electronics. *Mailing Add:* Planning Off Univ Tex Health Sci Ctr San Antonio TX 78284

CELLA, RICHARD JOSEPH, JR, b Philadelphia, Pa, Nov 2, 42; m 64; c 1. POLYMER CHEMISTRY, PHYSICAL CHEMISTRY. *Educ:* Univ Del, BS, 64; Cornell Univ, PhD(phys chem), 69. *Prof Exp:* res chemist, 69-76, tech serv rep, Elastomer Chem Dept, 76-80, SR MKT REP, POLYMER PROD DEPT, E I DU PONT DE NEMOURS & CO, INC, 80- *Res:* X-ray diffraction studies of polymer structure; morphology and solid state characterization of polymers; physical and mechanical properties of elastomers; adhesives; technical sales. *Mailing Add:* Polymer Prod Dept E I Du Pont de Nemours & Co Inc Wilmington DE 19898

CELLARIUS, RICHARD ANDREW, b Oakland, Calif, July 28, 37; m 59; c 2. BOTANY, BIOPHYSICS. *Educ:* Reed Col, BA, 58; Rockefeller Univ, PhD(biol), 65. *Prof Exp:* USPHS fel, 65-66; asst prof bot, Univ Mich, 66-72; MEM FAC, EVERGREEN STATE COL, 72- *Mem:* AAAS; Sigma Xi; Am Soc Photobiol; Am Soc Plant Physiol; Am Inst Biol Sci. *Res:* Light reactions of photosynthesis, photochemistry, plant physiology, photobiology; environmental policy. *Mailing Add:* Evergreen State Col Olympia WA 98505

CELLI, VITTORIO, b Parma, Italy, Aug 13, 36; m 62; c 1. SOLID STATE PHYSICS. *Educ:* Univ Pavia, DSc(physics), 58. *Prof Exp:* Res assoc solid state physics, Univ Ill, 59-61, asst prof, 61-62; asst res physicist, Univ Calif, San Diego, 62-64; lectr & asst theoret physics, Univ Bologna, 64-66; assoc prof physics, 66-69, PROF PHYSICS, UNIV VA, 69- *Concurrent Pos:* Fulbright scholar, 59-62; prof extraordinary, Univ Trieste & guest scientist, Int Ctr Theoret Physics, Trieste, 73-74; Humboldt sr US scientist award, 81. *Honors & Awards:* Docent, Ital Ministry Educ, Rome, 65. *Mem:* Fel Am Phys Soc; Ital Phys Soc. *Res:* Theoretical physics; theoretical solid state physics; surface science. *Mailing Add:* 210 Magnolia Dr Charlottesville VA 22903

CELMER, WALTER DANIEL, b Plymouth, Pa, Sept 13, 25; m 46, 79; c 4. BIO-ORGANIC CHEMISTRY. *Educ:* Bucknell Univ, BS, 47; Univ Ill, PhD(biochem), 50. *Prof Exp:* Res chemist, 50-54, res supvr, 54-61, res mgr, 61-72, RES ADV, PFIZER INC, 72- *Concurrent Pos:* Ed, Antimicrobial Agents & Chemother, 72-79. *Mem:* Am Chem Soc; Am Soc Biol Chem; Am Soc Microbiol; Int Platform Asn. *Res:* Discovery from microbial sources of novel chemical entities possessing biological activities, especially antibiotics and to elucidate their structures, stereochemistry, biogenesis, as well as to prepare and study their synthetic modifications. *Mailing Add:* Cent Res Pfizer Inc Groton CT 06340

CELMINS, AIVARS KARLIS RICHARDS, b Riga, Latvia, Apr 10, 27; m 55; c 3. APPLIED MATHEMATICS, NONLINEAR DATA ANALYSIS. *Educ:* Hannover Tech Univ, BS, 50, MS, 53; Clausthal Tech Univ, PhD(geophys), 57. *Prof Exp:* Mathematician, Seismos GmbH, Ger, 53-57; asst sect head explor geophys, Petrobras-DEPEX, Brazil, 57-58, sect head gravity, 59-61; sr mathematician, Inst Instrumental Math, Bonn, Ger, 61-64; RES MATHEMATICIAN, US ARMY BALLISTIC RES LAB, 64- *Concurrent Pos:* Instr, Univ Del, 65-70. *Mem:* Asn Comput Mach; Europ Asn Explor Geophysicists; Ger Soc Appl Math & Mech. *Res:* Numerical mathematics and its applications to technical and physics problems, particularly in the fields associated with fluid dynamics, engineering and exploration geophysics; numerical solution of partial differential equations; nonlinear model fitting to data. *Mailing Add:* Ballistic Res Lab Aberdeen Proving Ground MD 21005

CELOTTA, ROBERT JAMES, b New York, NY, Nov 18, 43; m 66; c 2. ATOMIC & MOLECULAR PHYSICS, SURFACE PHYSICS. *Educ:* City Col New York, BS, 64; NY Univ, PhD(physics), 69. *Prof Exp:* Res asst physics, NY Univ, 64-69; res assoc, Joint Inst Lab Astrophys, Univ Colo, 69-71; PRIN SCIENTIST PHYSICS, RADIATION PHYSICS DIV, NAT BUR STANDARDS, 71- *Concurrent Pos:* Instr physics, NY Univ, 64-69. *Honors & Awards:* Silver Medal, US Dept of Com, 78. *Mem:* fel Am Phys Soc; AAAS. *Res:* Surface physics; atomic and molecular physics; electron polarization phenomena. *Mailing Add:* Radiation Physics Div Nat Bur Standards Washington DC 20234

CELS, ROBERT, b Levuka, Fiji Islands, Jan 3, 23; US citizen; m 64; c 2. PHYSICAL CHEMISTRY, ELECTROCHEMISTRY. *Educ:* Univ NZ, BS, 45; Case Western Reserve Univ, PhD(electrochem), 55. *Prof Exp:* Chemist, Vacuum Oil Co, NZ, 47-50; chemist, Werner G Smith, Ohio, 50-51; chemist, Harshaw Chem Co, 51-52; res chemist, Kemet Dept, Linde Co, Union Carbide Corp, 54-65; res specialist, Res Ctr, Babcock & Wilcox Co, 65-81. *Mem:* Electrochem Soc; Sigma Xi. *Res:* Solid electrolyte tantalum capacitors; tantalum analyses for trace impurities; chemisorption of gases by alkaline earth metal films; silicon and germanium films prepared by high vacuum evaporation; silicon pressure transducers and silicon devices; corrosion research at high temperatures and pressures using electrochemical techniques. *Mailing Add:* 12839 Hoover Ave NW Uniontown OH 44685

CEMBER, HERMAN, b Brooklyn, NY, Jan 14, 24; m 43; c 2. RADIOBIOLOGY, HEALTH PHYSICS. *Educ:* City Col New York, BS, 49; Univ Pittsburgh, MS, 52, PhD(biophys), 60; Environ Engrs Intersoc Bd, dipl; Am Bd Health Physics, dipl. *Prof Exp:* Res assoc health physics, Grad Sch Pub Health, Univ Pittsburgh, 50-54, from asst prof to assoc prof indust hyg, 54-60; asst prof indust health, Col Med, Univ Cincinnati, 60-64; PROF CIVIL ENG, NORTHWESTERN UNIV, EVANSTON, 64- *Concurrent Pos:* Health physics consult, Carnegie Inst Technol, 52-60; radiol safety officer, Univ Pittsburgh, 52-60; lectr, US Naval Training Prog, Westinghouse Atomic Power Div, 52-55; tech expert occup health, Int Labour Off, Switz, 61-62; vis prof indust health, Col Med, Univ Cincinnati, 64-65; Fulbright vis prof environ health, Hadassah Med Sch, Hebrew Univ Jerusalem, 72-73; pres, Radiation Safety Serv, Inc, Evanston, Ill. *Mem:* AAAS; Radiation Res Soc; Health Physics Soc; Am Acad Environ Engrs; fel Am Pub Health Asn. *Res:* Biological effects of radiation; experimental lung cancer. *Mailing Add:* Technol Inst Northwestern Univ Evanston IL 60201

CEMBROLA, ROBERT JOHN, b New York, NY, April 3, 49; m 77. POLYMER PHYSICS. *Educ:* Rochester Inst Technol, BS, 72, MS, 73; Univ Mass, MS, 77, PhD(polymer sci), 78. *Prof Exp:* fel polymer sci, Kyoto Univ, Japan, 78-79; sr res chemist, 79-80, GROUP LEADER POLYMER PHYSICS, GEN TIRE & RUBBER CO, 80- *Mem:* Am Chem Soc. *Res:* Solid state physics of polymers; structure-property relationships; rheo-optical study of deformation mechanisms of semi-crystalline polymers. *Mailing Add:* 196 Willson Ave Tallmadge OH 44278

CENCE, ROBERT J, b Cleveland, Ohio, July 16, 30; m 54; c 2. PHYSICS. *Educ:* Univ Calif, Berkeley, AB, 52, PhD(physics), 59. *Prof Exp:* Res assoc physics, Lawrence Radiation Lab, Univ Calif, 59-63, instr, Univ Calif, Berkeley, 62-63; assoc prof, 63-74, PROF PHYSICS & ASTRON, UNIV HAWAII, 74- *Mem:* Am Phys Soc. *Res:* Elementary particle physics. *Mailing Add:* Dept of Physics Univ of Hawaii Honolulu HI 96822

CENCI, HARRY JOSEPH, b Brooklyn, NY, Oct 2, 30; m 54; c 6. ORGANIC CHEMISTRY, POLYMER CHEMISTRY. *Educ:* Brooklyn Col, BS, 53; Univ Pa, MS, 55, PhD(org chem), 57. *Prof Exp:* Head synthesis lab, 57-74, proj leader indust coatings, 74-77, proj leader, Emulsion Synthesis, 77-79, DEPT MGR, CHEM PROCESS RES, ROHM & HAAS CO, 79- *Mem:* Am Chem Soc. *Res:* Shythesis and application of industrial coatings; polymer synthesis; modifiers for polyvinyl chloride; emulsion and solution polymerization; physical organic chemistry; reactions of cis and trans cyclohexane -1, 3- diols; synthesis and reactions of 1, 2- difluoro-1, 2-dicyanoethylene; photochemistry. *Mailing Add:* Rohm & Haas Co Res Lab Box 219 Bristol PA 19007

CENEDELLA, RICHARD J, b Pittsburgh, Pa, Jan 12, 39; m 64; c 1. BIOCHEMISTRY, PHARMACOLOGY. *Educ:* Pa State Univ, BS, 61; Jefferson Med Col, PhD(biochem), 66. *Prof Exp:* Res assoc, 65-68, from asst prof to prof pharmacol, Sch Med, WVa Univ, 68-76; PROF & CHMN, DEPT BIOCHEM, KIRKSVILLE COL OSTEOP MED, 76- *Res:* Fatty acid metabolism; lipid pharmacology; mechanism of action of hypolipemic drugs; cataracts. *Mailing Add:* Dept of Biochem Kirksville Col Osteop Med Kirksville MO 63501

CENGEL, JOHN ANTHONY, b East Chicago, Ind, July 21, 36; m 62; c 3. PHYSICAL ORGANIC CHEMISTRY. *Educ:* Purdue Iniv, BS, 58, PhD(phys chem), 65; Ore State Univ, MS, 59. *Prof Exp:* From proj chemist to sr proj chemist, 65-70, SR RES SCIENTIST, AMOCO CHEM CORP, STAND OIL CO IND, 70- *Concurrent Pos:* AEC grant, 63-65. *Mem:* Am Chem Soc; Inst Chem Eng; Soc Plastics Indust; Am Soc Test & Mat. *Res:* Infrared spectroscopy; metal carbonyl chemistry; polymer development; cellular plastics; viscous polymers; petroleum and gasoline additives. *Mailing Add:* Dept of Res & Develop PO Box 400 Amoco Chem Corp Naperville IL 60540

CENTER, ELIZABETH M, b Sterling, Ill, Aug 11, 28; m 51; c 1. GENETICS. *Educ:* Augustana Col, AB, 50; Stanford Univ, PhD(genetics), 57. *Prof Exp:* Res asst anat, 51-61, res assoc, 61-69, instr biol sci, 68-71, lectr biol sci, Stanford Univ, 71-78; asst prof, 77-79, PROF BIOL, COL NOTRE DAME, CALIF, 79- *Mem:* NY Acad Sci; Am Soc Zoologists; Genetics Soc Am; Am Soc Anat; Sigma Xi. *Res:* Developmental genetics. *Mailing Add:* Dept Biol Col Notre Dame Belmont CA 94002

CENTER, ROBERT E, b Breslau, Ger, Nov 12, 35; m 59; c 3. LASERS, CHEMICAL PHYSICS. *Educ:* Univ Sydney, BSc, 56, BE, 58, MEngSc, 59, PhD(gas dynamics), 63. *Prof Exp:* Scientist gas dynamics, Jet Propulsion Lab, Calif Inst Technol, 63-67; prin res scientist, Avco Everett Res Lab, 67-75; dir laser res, 75-79, VPRES RES, MATH SCI NORTHWEST, 79- *Mem:* Am Phys Soc. *Res:* Scattering of fast electrons in gases; vibrational relaxation in anharmonic diatomic molecules under conditions of thermal nonequilibrium; high temperature gas phase kinetics; visible and ultraviolet electric discharge laser development. *Mailing Add:* 7633 NE 14th Ave Bellevue WA 98004

CENTIFANTO, YSOLINA M, b Panama, Aug 12, 28; US citizen; m 53; c 3. BACTERIOLOGY. *Educ:* Univ Panama, BS, 51; Western Reserve Univ, MS, 54; Univ Fla, PhD(bact), 64. *Prof Exp:* Asst prof physiol & genetics, Univ Panama, 55-56; res biologist, Kodak Trop Res Lab, Panama, 57; res biologist, Eastman Kodak Res Lab, NY, 58-61; res assoc virol, Ophthal Div, 64-65, from instr to assoc prof ophthal & microbiol, Col Med, Univ Fla, 65-77; PROF OPHTHAL & MICROBIOL, COL MED, La State Univ, 78- *Mem:* AAAS; Am Chem Soc; Am Soc Microbiol; Asn Res Vision & Ophthal. *Res:* Viral and bacterial infections of the eye; pathogenesis of disease and its relation to host defense mechanisms, such as interferon and antibody synthesis; carcinoma of the prostate; studies on recurrent viral infections. *Mailing Add:* Sch Med La State Univ 1542 Tulane Ave New Orleans LA 70112

CENTNER, ROSEMARY LOUISE, b Newport, Ky, Sept 23, 26. ORGANIC CHEMISTRY. *Educ:* Our Lady of Cincinnati Col, BA, 47; Univ Cincinnati, MS, 49. *Prof Exp:* Libr asst tech libr, 49-52, br librn, 52-56, tech librn, 56-66, mgr tech info serv, 66-72, mgr div info consults, 72-73, mgr, NDA Coord, 73-75, mgr biomed commun, 75-80, MGR TECH COMMUN, PROCTER & GAMBLE CO, 80- *Mem:* AAAS; Am Chem Soc; Am Med Writers Asn. *Res:* Scientific information; information retrieval; technical translation. *Mailing Add:* Paper Prod Div Procter & Gamble Winton Hill Tech Ctr 6100 Center Hill Rd Cincinnati OH 45224

CENTOFANTI, LOUIS F, b Youngstown, Ohio, July 25, 43; m 63; c 3. INORGANIC CHEMISTRY. *Educ:* Youngstown State Univ, BS, 65; Univ Mich, MS, 67, PhD(chem), 68. *Prof Exp:* Fel chem, Univ Utah, 68-69; asst prof, Emory Univ, 69-73; sr res chemist, Monsanto Co, 73-; regional adminr, US Dept Energy, 79-81; PRES, PPM, INC, 81- *Mem:* Am Chem Soc. *Res:* Synthetic and physical inorganic chemistry. *Mailing Add:* Atlanta GA 30345

CENTOLA, GRACE MARIE, anatomy, endocrinology, see previous edition

CENTORINO, JAMES JOSEPH, b Salem, Mass, July 18, 23; wid; c 5. MARINE STUDIES. *Educ:* Boston Univ, AB, 50, AM, 51. *Prof Exp:* Teacher jr high sch, Mass, 53-S6; from instr to assoc prof geog & earth sci, 56-81, PROF GEOG, SALEM STATE COL, 81- *Concurrent Pos:* Dir earth sci div, NSF In-Serv Inst, 59-67 & Coop Col-Sch Sci Prog, 71; Consult, Soc Studies Curric Projs, 62, Boston Univ Mapping Serv, 63 & Mass Coastal Environ, Mass Coastal Zone Mgt, 75; Sea Grant proposal reviewer, 77; coordr, Marine Studies Prog, Salem State Col, 77-, asst dir, Inst Marine Sci & Related Studies, NSF, 77-78, staff assoc, 78-79, assoc & dir, 79-80; assoc dir, Marine Sci Summer Inst, NSF, 80-81; mem bd dir, Mass Bay Marine Studies Consortium, 80- & Mass Marine Educrs, 81. *Mem:* Int Oceanog Found; The Oceanic Soc; Nat Marine Educ Asn; Nat Geog Soc. *Res:* Air pollution in the Boston area; locational patterns of the New England shoe industry; local conservation problems; marine education and research. *Mailing Add:* Dept of Geog Salem State Col Salem MA 01970

CENTURY, BERNARD, b Chicago, Ill, June 15, 28; m 58; c 4. PHARMACOLOGY. *Educ:* Univ Chicago, PhB, 46, BS & MS, 51, PhD(pharmacol), 53. *Prof Exp:* Biochemist, Biochem Res Lab, Elgin State Hosp, 54-59, res assoc, 59-74, actg dir, 69-74; asst prof biol chem, Univ Ill Col Med, 62-74; mem staff, dept biochem, Michael Reese Med Ctr, 74-77; CLIN CHEMIST, LAB DEPT, ST MARY'S HOSP, WATERBURY, CONN, 77- *Concurrent Pos:* NSF fel pharmacol, Univ Chicago, 53-54. *Mem:* AAAS; Am Chem Soc; Am Inst Nutrit; Am Soc Pharmacol & Exp Therapeut; Am Asn Clin Chem. *Res:* Biochemistry of mental diseases; relationships of dietary lipids to vitamin E deficiency; effect of diet lipids on metabolism of essential fatty acids and tissue compositions; effect of diet lipids on pharmacological responses. *Mailing Add:* St Mary's Hosp Lab Dept 56 Franklin Cheshire CT 06410

CEPEDA, JOSEPH CHERUBINI, b Del Rio, Tex, Apr 19, 48. PETROLOGY, VOLCANOLOGY. *Educ:* Univ Tex, Austin, BS, 70, PhD(geol), 77; NMex Inst Mining & Technol, MS, 72. *Prof Exp:* Instr, Appalachian State Univ, 76-77; ASST PROF GEOL, DEPT GEOSCI, W TEX STATE UNIV, 77- *Mem:* Geol Soc Am; Mineral Soc Am. *Res:* Field relations and chemistry of igneous and metamorphic rocks; computer applications to geologic problems. *Mailing Add:* Dept of Geosci WTex State Univ Canyon TX 79016

CEPERLEY, DAVID MATTHEW, b Charleston, WVa, Dec 26, 49. STATISTICAL PHYSICS, PHYSICAL CHEMISTRY. *Educ:* Univ Mich, BS, 71; Cornell Univ, PhD(physics), 76. *Prof Exp:* Fel physics, Univ Paris XI, 76-77; fel, Courant Inst, 77-78; staff chemist, Lawrence Berkeley Lab, 78-81, STAFF SCIENTIST, NAT RESOURCE COMPUT CHEM, LAWRENCE LIVERMORE NAT LAB, 81- *Mem:* Am Phys Soc; AAAS. *Res:* Computer simulation of many-body systems; particularly quantum and polymeric systems; Monte Carlo Methods. *Mailing Add:* Lawrence Livermore Lab L71 Livermore CA 94550

CEPONIS, MICHAEL JOHN, b Brooklyn, NY, June 25, 16; m 51; c 6. PLANT PATHOLOGY. *Educ:* Cornell Univ, BS, 50, MS, 53. *Prof Exp:* Plant pathologist, Tischler Res Serv, NJ, 53-55; from asst plant pathologist to plant pathologist, 55-63, RES PLANT PATHOLOGIST, AGR RES SERV, USDA, NEW BRUNSWICK, NJ, 63- *Mem:* Am Phytopath Soc; Am Soc Hort Sci. *Res:* Market diseases of fruits and vegetables. *Mailing Add:* USDA PO Box 231 New Brunswick NJ 08903

CEPRINI, MARIO Q, b Jamaica, NY, Sept 30, 25; m 49; c 3. ORGANIC CHEMISTRY, POLYMER & POLYMER ADDITIVES. *Educ:* Queens Col, NY, BS, 47; St John's Univ, NY, MS, 61, PhD(org chem), 67. *Prof Exp:* Jr chemist, NY State Racing Comn Lab, 47-52, chemist, 52-60; jr chemist, Hoffmann-LaRoche Inc, NJ, 60-64, assoc chemist, 64-65; sr chemist, 67-69, group leader metallo-org, 70-72, group leader process develop, 72-75, group leader polymer additives, 75-77, SR RES SCIENTIST, HEYDEN DIV, TENNECO CHEM, INC, GARFIELD, NJ, 70-, LAB MGR POLYMER & ADDITIVES RES, INTERMEDIATES DIV, PISCATAWAY, 78- *Mem:* Soc Plastics Engrs; Am Chem Soc; Sigma Xi. *Res:* Peptide and amino acid chemistry; antibiotics; organic synthesis; polymer additives; process development; polymer synthesis. *Mailing Add:* 513 Ocean Point Ave Cedarhurst NY 11516

CERAMI, ANTHONY, b Newark, NJ, Oct 3, 40. MEDICAL BIOCHEMISTRY. *Educ:* Rutgers Univ, BS, 62; Rockefeller Univ, PhD(biochem), 67. *Prof Exp:* Asst prof biochem, 69-72, assoc prof & head lab, 72-78, PROF BIOCHEM, ROCKEFELLER UNIV, 78- *Concurrent Pos:* Fel, Harvard Med Sch, 67-68 & Jackson Lab, 68-69; med adv bd, Cooley's Anemia Vol, Inc, 75- & Cooley's Anemia Blood & Res Found, 78-; res coun, Diabetic Retinopathy Found, 77-; res coun, Pub Health Res Inst, NY, 78- *Mem:* Am Soc Hemat; Am Soc Biol Chemists; Am Soc Pharmacol & Exp Therapeut; Am Soc Study Blood. *Res:* Diabetes, beta-thalassemia, sickle cell anemia, parasitology. *Mailing Add:* Lab Med Biochem Rockefeller Univ 1230 York Ave New York NY 10021

CERANKOWSKI, LEON DENNIS, b Philadelphia, Pa, July 31, 40; m 63. PHYSICAL CHEMISTRY. *Educ:* Drexel Univ, BS, 63; Princeton Univ, MA, 65, PhD(chem), 69. *Prof Exp:* Chemist, USDA, 61-64; instr phys chem, Princeton Univ, 67-69; SCIENTIST, POLYMER LAB, POLAROID CORP, 69- *Mem:* AAAS; Am Chem Soc. *Res:* Physical chemistry of electrolyte and macromolecular solutions. *Mailing Add:* Polaroid Corp 549 Technol Sq Cambridge MA 02139

CERBULIS, JANIS, b Smiltene, Latvia, Dec 5, 13; nat US; m 52; c 3. BIOCHEMISTRY, AGRICULTURE. *Educ:* Acad Agr, Jelgava, Latvia, PhD(agr), 44; Univ Pa, MS, 57; Rutgers Univ, PhD(biochem), 67. *Prof Exp:* Adminr & instr hort, Baltic Univ, Ger, 47-49; res chemist, Stephen F Whitman & Sons, Pa, 51-55 & Borden Chem Co, 55-56; RES CHEMIST, FOOD SCI LAB, EASTERN REGIONAL RES CTR, AGR RES SERV, USDA, 56- *Concurrent Pos:* USPHS maintenance grant, 61-63; Am Cancer Soc res grant-in-aid, 63; abstractor, Chem Abstracts, 58-76. *Mem:* Am Chem Soc; Ger Soc Fat Res; Sigma Xi. *Res:* Growing of grass seeds, vegetable seeds and medicinal plants; food value of grass; phenolic resins; earthworm chemical composition; whey composition; lactose chemistry; milk proteins and lipids; milk clotting; milk composition and relationship among milk constituents. *Mailing Add:* RD 2 Box 940 Boyertown PA 19512

CERCING, THURE E, b Elmhurst, Ill, Nov 16, 49; m 74. GEOLOGY, GEOCHEMISTRY. *Educ:* Iowa State Univ, BS, 72, MS, 73; Univ Calif, Berkeley, 77. *Prof Exp:* Res assoc geol, Oak Ridge Nat Lab, 77-79; ASST PROF GEOL & GEOPHYS, COL MINES, UNIV UTAH, 79- *Mem:* Geol Soc Am; Soc Econ Paleontologists & Mineralogists. *Res:* Radioactive waste disposal; geochemistry of lake sediments; volcanic ash correlation and dating. *Mailing Add:* Univ Utah Col Mines 717 William Browning Blvd Salt Lake City UT 84112

CERCONE, NICHOLAS JOSEPH, b Pittsburgh, Pa, Dec 18, 46. COMPUTER SCIENCE. *Educ:* Col Steubenville, BS, 68; Ohio State Univ, MS, 70; Univ Alta, PhD(comput sci), 75. *Prof Exp:* Programmer design automation, Int Bus Mach Corp, 68-69; instr comput sci, Ohio State Univ, 70-71; instr comput, Int Bus Mach Corp, 71-72; asst prof comput sci, Old Dom Univ, 75-76; ASST PROF COMPUT SCI, COMPUT SCI PROG, SIMON FRASER UNIV, 76- *Mem:* Asn Comput Mach; Inst Elec & Electronics Engrs; Royal Photographic Soc. *Res:* Artificial intelligence; natural language processing; representation of knowledge. *Mailing Add:* Comput Sci Dept Simon Fraser Univ Burnaby BC V5A 1S6 Can

CEREFICE, STEVEN A, b Newark, NJ, Aug 10, 43; m 67. ORGANIC CHEMISTRY, ORGANOMETALLIC CHEMISTRY. *Educ:* Rutgers Univ, BA, 65; Columbia Univ, MA, 66, PhD(org chem), 69. *Prof Exp:* RES CHEMIST ORG CHEM, AMOCO CHEM CORP, 70- *Mem:* AAAS; Am Chem Soc. *Res:* Organic synthesis; photochemistry of hydrocarbons; small ring compounds; bicyclic-polycyclic hydrocarbons; transition metal-catalyzed cycloaddition and electrocyclic reaction of polycyclic hydrocarbons; catalysis and mechanisms studies. *Mailing Add:* 1254 Hearthside Ct Naperville IL 60565

CERIMELE, BENITO JOSEPH, b Cincinnati, Ohio, May 11, 36; m 63; c 4. BIOMATHEMATICS, COMPUTER SCIENCES. *Educ:* Xavier Univ, Ohio, BS, 57, MS, 59; Univ Cincinnati, PhD(math), 63; Ind Univ, MBA, 76. *Prof Exp:* Reactor physicist, Gen Elec Co, Ohio, 57-59; from instr to asst prof math, Xavier Univ, Ohio, 62-66; NIH fel biomath, NC State Univ, 66-68, asst prof, 68-70; sr systs analyst, Lilly Res Labs, Eli Lilly & Co, 70-78; MGR, SCI INFO SERV, MERRELL DOW PHARMACEUT, 78- *Concurrent Pos:* Adj asst prof biostatist, Sch Med, Ind Univ, 76-; adj asst prof biomath, Sch Med, Univ NC, Chapel Hill, 68-70. *Mem:* Biometrics Soc; Asn Comput Mach. *Res:* Biometry; pharmacokinetics; scientific applications programming. *Mailing Add:* Merrell Dow Pharmaceut PO Box 68511 Indianapolis IN 46268

CERINI, COSTANTINO PETER, b Philadelphia, Pa, Nov 19, 31; m 60; c 2. VIROLOGY, IMMUNOLOGY. *Educ:* La Salle Col, BS, 53; Lehigh Univ, MS, 60, PhD(virol), 64. *Prof Exp:* Res virologist, 64-70, GROUP LEADER, LEDERLE LABS DIV, AM CYANAMID CO, 70- *Mem:* AAAS; Am Soc Microbiol; Tissue Cult Asn; NY Acad Sci. *Res:* Virus immunology; research and development of human viral vaccines. *Mailing Add:* Lederle Labs Pearl River NY 10965

CERKANOWICZ, ANTHONY EDWARD, b Bayonne, NJ, Feb 19, 41; m 66; c 5. COMBUSTION, MECHANICAL ENGINEERING. *Educ:* Stevens Inst Technol, ME, 62, MS, 64, PhD(thermodyn), 70. *Prof Exp:* Res engr combustion, Vitro Labs, 67-69; vpres, Photochem Industs, 69-74; STAFF ENGR COMBUSTION, EXXON RES & ENG CO, 74- *Concurrent Pos:* Chmn, Stevens Inst Honor Syst Adv Coun, 75-77. *Mem:* Am Soc Mech Engrs; Combustion Inst. *Res:* Pioneering research of techniques for photochemical ignition and enhancement of combustion in unsensitized fuel-air mixtures; utilization of catalytic combustion techniques in advanced power systems. *Mailing Add:* Exxon Res & Eng Co PO Box 45 Linden NJ 07036

CERKLEWSKI, FLORIAN LEE, b Danville, Pa, May 28, 49. NUTRITION. *Educ:* Pa State Univ, BS, 71; Univ Ill, Urbana, PhD(nutrit), 76. *Prof Exp:* Fel trace metals, Kettering Lab, Univ Cincinnati, 76; asst prof nutrit, Marquette Univ, 76-79; ASST PROF FOODS & NUTRIT, OREGON STATE UNIV, 79- *Mem:* Am Inst Nutrit. *Res:* Trace metal nutrition in health and disease; nutritional biochemistry interactions with toxic metals; nutrition and dental caries. *Mailing Add:* Dept Foods & Nutrit Oregon State Univ Corvallis OR 97331

CERMAK, J(ACK) E(DWARD), b Hastings, Colo, Sept 8, 22; m 49; c 2. FLUID MECHANICS, WIND ENGINEERING. *Educ:* Colo State Univ, BS, 48; Cornell Univ, PhD, 59. *Prof Exp:* Assoc prof eng mech, 47-59, vpres res found, 66-69, pres, 69-72, chmn eng sci major prog, 68-71, PROF IN CHARGE FLUID MECH & WIND ENG PROG, COLO STATE UNIV, 59-, DIR, FLUID DYNAMICS & DIFFUSION LAB, 63- *Concurrent Pos:* NATO fel, Cambridge Univ, 61-63; lectr, Univ Tex, Cambridge Univ, Israel Inst Technol, Univs Hokkaido, Moscow, Warsaw, Madrid & Marseille, 63-; res grants numerous govt agencies and industrial organizations; consult numerous labs & indust co; chmn, Comn on Nat Disasters, Nat Res Coun; pres, Wind Eng Res Coun Inc, 71-; US ed, Int J Wind Engineering, 74-; pres, Int Asn Wind Eng, 75-79. *Honors & Awards:* Freeman Scholar, Am Soc Mech Engrs, 74. *Mem:* Nat Acad Eng; Am Soc Civil Engrs; Am Soc Mech Engrs; Am Soc Eng Educ; Am Acad Mech. *Res:* Geophysical fluid mechanics, simulation of atmospheric motions by special wind tunnels, atmospheric diffusion and turbulence; structural aerodynamics; wind engineering; electrokinetics. *Mailing Add:* Col Eng Colo State Univ Ft Collins CO 80523

CERMAK, JAMES OTTO, mechanical & nuclear engineering, see previous edition

CERNANSKY, NICHOLAS P, b Pittsburgh, Pa, Mar 10, 46; m 70. AIR POLLUTION, ALTERNATE & SYNTHETIC FUELS. *Educ:* Univ Pittsburgh, BS, 67; Univ Mich, MS, 68; Univ Calif, Berkeley, MPH, 73, PhD(mech eng), 74. *Prof Exp:* Develop engr modeling, Westinghouse Power Circuit Breaker Div, 67; air pollution engr vehicle emissions, Nat Air Pollution Control Admin, 68-70; res asst mech eng, Univ Calif, Berkeley, 70-74; asst prof, 75-79, ASSOC PROF MECH ENG, DREXEL UNIV, 79- *Concurrent Pos:* Mem technol panel staff, Comt Motor Vehicle Emissions, 74, Diesel Impact Study Comt, Nat Acad Sci, 79-81. *Honors & Awards:* Ralph R Teetor Award, Soc Automotive Engrs, 76. *Mem:* Air Pollution Control Asn; AAAS; Am Soc Mech Eng; Soc Automotive Engrs; Combustion Soc. *Res:* Analytical and experimental research problems in the areas of fundamental combustion studies, practical combustion systems, propulsion, air pollution, vehicular air pollution, energy and fuel conservation, fuels technology and environmental sciences. *Mailing Add:* Dept Mech Eng Drexel Univ Philadelphia PA 19104

CERNI, TODD ANDREW, b Milwaukee, Wis, Apr 28, 47. CLOUD PHYSICS, RADIATIVE TRANSFER. *Educ:* Marquete Univ, BS, 69, Ind Univ, MS, 71, Univ Ariz, PhD(atmospheric sci), 78. *Prof Exp:* Res assoc, Dept Physics, 76-78, res assoc, 78-79, ASST PROF ATMOSPHERIC SCI & ENG, DEPT ATMOSPHERIC SCI, UNIV WYO, 79- *Mem:* Am Phys Soc; Am Meteorol Soc. *Res:* Cloud physics; radiative transfer; atmospheric instrumentation. *Mailing Add:* Dept Atmospheric Sci Univ Wyo PO Box 3038 Univ Sta Laramie WY 82071

CERNICA, JOHN N, b Romania, May 14, 32; US citizen; m 59; c 5. CIVIL ENGINEERING. *Educ:* Youngstown Univ, BS, 54; Carnegie Inst Technol, MS, 55, PhD(civil eng), 57. *Prof Exp:* Asst prof civil eng & actg head dept, 57-58, assoc prof, 58-61, PROF CIVIL ENG, YOUNGSTOWN STATE UNIV, 61- *Concurrent Pos:* Panelist, NSF; examiner, Ohio State Bd Registr Prof Engrs & Surveyors. *Mem:* Am Soc Eng Educ; Am Soc Civil Engrs; Am Concrete Inst; Nat Soc Prof Engrs. *Res:* Structures and soil mechanics. *Mailing Add:* Dept of Civil Eng Youngstown State Univ Youngstown OH 44555

CERNOSEK, STANLEY FRANK, JR, b Shiner, Tex, Dec 19, 40; m 68; c 2. IMMUNOCHEMISTRY. *Educ:* Pan Am Col, BA, 63; Univ Tex, Austin, PhD(chem), 69. *Prof Exp:* Res assoc peptide chem, Sch Med, Univ Pittsburgh, 68-70; fel biochem, Grad Dept Biochem, Brandeis Univ, 70-73; asst prof dept biochem, Col Med, Univ Ark, 73-80; res chemist, Nat Ctr Toxicol Res, 78-80; WITH BECKMAN INSTRUMENT, INC, 80- *Mem:* Am Chem Soc; Royal Soc Chem; Biophys Soc; Sigma Xi. *Res:* Synthetic protein and peptide syntheses; sequential polypeptide syntheses; physical biochemistry; development and applications of radioimmunoassays for chemical carcinogens, hormones and environmental toxicans. *Mailing Add:* Beckman Instrument Inc PO Box C-196000 Irvine CA 92713

CERNUSCHI, FELIX, b Montevideo, Uruguay, May 17, 08; m 47; c 2. PHYSICS, ASTROPHYSICS. *Educ:* Univ Buenos Aires, CE, 32; Cambridge Univ, PhD(physics), 38. *Prof Exp:* Res worker, Cordoba Observ, Argentina, 38-39; prof phys sci, Nat Univ Tucuman, Argentina, 39-43; res assoc astrophys, Harvard Col Observ, 44-46; sci adv phys sci, UNESCO, France, 47-48; invited prof physics, Univ PR, 49-50; prof astron, Univ of the Repub, Uruguay, 50-78, prof physics, 55-78, dir dept astron & physics, 55-78, dir fac humanities & sci, 57-78; PROF PHYSICS, FAC ENG, UNIV BUENOS AIRES, 78- *Concurrent Pos:* Argentine Asn Adv Sci fel, 38-39; Guggenheim fel, 44-46; prof physics & dir fac eng, Univ Buenos Aires, 57-68; mem, Radioastronomy Comn, Univ Buenos Aires, 59-63 & Nat Coun Sci & Tech Invests, Argentina, 59-; invited lectr, Inter-Am Conf Physics, Brazil, 63 & Inter-Am Conf Sci & Technol, DC, 64. *Honors & Awards:* Phys Sci Prize, Buenos Aires City, 65. *Mem:* Fel AAAS; fel Am Phys Soc; Am Astron Soc; Argentine Nat Acad Sci; Argentine Physics Asn. *Res:* Statistical mechanics and its application to liquid state, solid state and astrophysics; interstellar matter; polarization of stellar light; cosmogony; methods for teaching science and organization of universities; transition solid-liquid; solar energy applications. *Mailing Add:* Larrea 1065 (8 B) 1117 Buenos Aires Argentina

CERNY, JOSEPH, III, b Montgomery, Ala, Apr 24, 36; m 59; c 2. NUCLEAR CHEMISTRY. *Educ:* Univ Miss, BS, 57; Univ Calif, Berkeley, PhD(nuclear chem), 61. *Prof Exp:* From asst prof to assoc prof, 61-71, chmn dept, 75-79, PROF CHEM, UNIV CALIF, BERKELEY, 71-; RES CHEMIST, LAWRENCE BERKELEY LAB, 71-, HEAD, NUCLEAR SCI DIV & ASSOC DIR, 79- *Concurrent Pos:* Consult, US Army Res Off, 63-65; Guggenheim fel, Oxford Univ, 69-70; vis fel, Australian Nat Univ, Canberra, 75. *Honors & Awards:* E O Lawrence Award, US AEC, 74. *Mem:* Am Chem Soc; fel Am Phys Soc; Fedn Am Sci; AAAS. *Res:* Low energy nuclear science utilizing stripping or pickup reactions; studies of nuclei far from stability with an on-line mass separator; studies of isobaric analogue states and exotic nuclei. *Mailing Add:* Lawrence Berkeley Lab Bldg 88 Berkeley CA 94720

CERNY, LAURENCE CHARLES, b Cleveland, Ohio, Mar 5, 29; m 55; c 3. BIOPHYSICAL CHEMISTRY. *Educ:* Case Inst Technol, BS, 51, MS, 53; State Univ Ghent, PhD(phys chem), 56. *Prof Exp:* Asst prof chem, John Carroll Univ, 56-60; PROF CHEM, UTICA COL, 60- *Concurrent Pos:* Fel, Med Sch, Univ Minn, 58-59; res assoc hemodynamics, St Vincent Hosp, 59-60; estab investr, Masonic Med Res Lab, 62-67, career develop award, 67-; US-Czech exchange fel, Nat Acad Sci. 67. *Mem:* Fel Am Inst Chem; Biophys Soc; Am Chem Soc; Soc Rheol; Am Heart Asn. *Res:* Hemorheology; hemodynamics; polymers; chemical education; plasma expanders. *Mailing Add:* Masonic Med Res Lab Utica NY 13501

CERRETA, KENNETH VINCENT, b Jersey City, NJ, June 12, 42; m 75; c 1. PHARMACOLOGY. *Educ:* Marist Col, BA, 64; Univ Md, MS, 70; Col Med & Dent NJ, PhD(pharmacol), 76. *Prof Exp:* Asst biochemist, Hoffmann-La Roche Inc, 69-70; assoc biochemist, Roche Inst Molecular Biol, 70-73; fel pharmacol, Univ Calif, San Francisco, 76-77; ASST PROF PHARMACOL, SCH MED, UNIV SDAK, 77- *Concurrent Pos:* Lilly Res Inst grant, Univ SDak, 77-78, Smith-Kline Inc grant, 78-79. *Mem:* AAAS; NY Acad Sci; Sigma Xi. *Res:* Neuropharmacology of drugs producing analgesia and sedation, and biochemical factors associated with their mechanism of action. *Mailing Add:* Sect on Pharmacol-DBPP Univ of SDak Sch of Med Vermillion SD 57069

CERRONI, ROSE E, b Weirton, WVa, Mar 29, 30. BIOLOGY, PHYSIOLOGY. *Educ:* Col of Steubenville, BS, 52; Vanderbilt Univ, MA, 55, PhD(biol), 59. *Prof Exp:* Instr nursing sci, Wheeling Hosp Sch Nursing, 52-53; instr microbiol, Vanderbilt Univ, 55-56; NIH fel, Carlsberg Biol Inst, 60-61; res assoc, Temple Univ, 61-62; asst prof biol, West Liberty State Col, 62-67; PROF BIOL, COL STEUBENVILLE, 67- *Mem:* Am Inst Biol Sci. *Res:* Physiology and ultra structure of the nucleus of acanthamoeba radioautographic studies on tetrahymena pyriformis to determine aspects of the mechanism of heat-induced division sychrony. *Mailing Add:* Dept of Biol Univ Steubenville Steubenville OH 43952

CERVENKA, JAROSLAV, b Prague, Czech, Mar 15, 33; US citizen; m 59; c 2. MEDICAL GENETICS, CANCER. *Educ:* Charles Univ, Czech, MD, 58; Czech Acad Sci, CSc(med genetics), 68. *Prof Exp:* Act chief genetics, Lab Plastic Surg, Prague, 67-68; asst prof, 68-71, assoc prof, 71-78, PROF GENETICS, SCH DENT, UNIV MINN, 78-, PROF MED, MED SCH, 78-, DIR, DIV CYTOGENETICS & CELL GENETICS, 79- *Concurrent Pos:* Staff consult, Sch Dent, Univ Minn, 66-, mem staff, Grad Sch, 69-, Genetic Clin, Health Sci Ctr, 72- *Mem:* Am Soc Human Genetics; Int Dermatoglyphics Asn; Sigma Xi; Int Found Human Health. *Res:* Cytogenetics of cancer; genetics of congenital abnormalities; prenatal diagnosis of genetic disease; clinical cytogenetics. *Mailing Add:* Div of Oral Path & Hum Gen Univ of Minn Sch of Dent Minneapolis MN 55455

CERVONI, PETER, b Jamaica, NY, Mar 4, 31; m 64; c 3. PHARMACOLOGY. *Educ:* St John's Univ, NY, BS, 52; Univ Wash, MS, 55, PhD(pharmacol), 57. *Prof Exp:* Asst pharmacol, Univ Wash, 52-57; pharmacologist, US Army Chem Warfare Labs, 57-59; asst prof pharmacol, Univ Miss, Jackson, 60-61; from instr to asst prof, State Univ NY Brooklyn, 61-66; sr res pharmacologist, Wellcome Res Lab, Burroughs Wellcome & Co, 66-70; sect head cardiovasc/autonomic pharmacol, USV Pharmaceut Corp, 70-71, mgr biol res & develop, 71-73, dir & res scientist, 73-75, dir pharmacol, Pharmaceut Res & Develop, 75-79; HEAD, DEPT CARDIOVASC BIOL RES, MED RES DIV, AM CYANAMID CORP, 79- *Concurrent Pos:* Life Ins Med Res Fund fel, 59-60. *Mem:* Am Heart Asn; Sigma Xi; AAAS; Am Soc Pharmacol & Exp Therapeut; fel NY Acad Sci. *Mailing Add:* Biol Res Lederle Labs Am Cyanamid Corp Pearl River NY 10965

CERWONKA, ROBERT HENRY, b Endicott, NY, Mar 16, 31; m 57; c 2. MARINE ECOLOGY. *Educ:* State Univ NY, Albany AB, 53, MA, 57; Univ Conn, PhD, 68. *Prof Exp:* From instr to assoc prof, 59-69, PROF BIOL, STATE UNIV NY COL POTSDAM, 69-, CHMN, BIOL DEPT, 79- *Mem:* Ecol Soc Am; Am Soc Limnol & Oceanog; Am Ornith Union; Sigma Xi. *Res:* Filtering rates of bivalve mollusks. *Mailing Add:* Dept of Biol State Univ of NY Col Potsdam NY 13676

CESARI, LAMBERTO, b Bologna, Italy, Sept 23, 10; m 39. MATHEMATICAL ANALYSIS. *Educ:* Univ Pisa, PhD(math), 33. *Hon Degrees:* Dr, Univ Perugia, Italy. *Prof Exp:* Asst prof math, Univ Rome, 37-39; assoc prof, Univ Pisa, 39-42; from assoc prof to prof, Univ Bologna, 42-48; vis prof, Inst Adv Study, 48, Univ Calif, 49 & Univ Wis, 50; vis prof, Purdue Univ, 50, prof, 52-60; PROF MATH, UNIV MICH, 60-, R L WILDER PROF, 75- *Mem:* Am Math Soc; Math Asn Am; Soc Indust & Appl Math; Math Union Italy. *Res:* Real functions; calculus of variations; surface area theory; asymptotic behavior of differential equations; numerical analysis; ordinary and partial differential equations; optimal control theory; nonlinear analysis. *Mailing Add:* Dept of Math Univ of Mich Ann Arbor MI 48104

CESCAS, MICHEL PIERRE, b Bordeaux, France, Sept 23, 36; m 68; c 2. SOIL CHEMISTRY, SOIL FERTILITY. *Educ:* Laval Univ, BSc, 60; Univ Ill, Urbana, MSc, 65, PhD(agron), 68. *Prof Exp:* Res asst agron, Univ Ill, Urbana, 60-61, 63-68; from asst prof soil chem to prof, 68-77, PROF SOIL SCI, LAVAL UNIV, 77-, HEAD DEPT, 77- *Honors & Awards:* Scarseth's Award, Am Soc Agron. *Mem:* AAAS; Am Soc Agron; Soil Sci Soc Am; Int Soc Soil Sci; Am Chem Soc. *Res:* Electron probe analysis of soils and related materials; phosphorus evolution in soils; rock phosphate transformation with time; analytical chemistry methodology in soil testing and analysis; adsorption phenomena in soils; optimization of fertilization of important crops; use of manures. *Mailing Add:* Dept Soils Laval Univ Fac Agr & Food Sci Quebec PQ G1K 7P4 Can

CESS, ROBERT D, b Portland, Ore, Mar 3, 33; m 53; c 2. ATMOSPHERIC SCIENCES. *Educ:* Ore State Univ, BS, 55; Purdue Univ, MS, 56; Univ Pittsburgh, PhD(mech eng), 60. *Prof Exp:* Res engr, Westinghouse Res Labs, 56-60, consult, 60-64; assoc prof mech eng, NC State Col, 60-61; assoc prof eng, 61-65, prof, 65-75, prof atmospheric sci, 75-81, LEADING PROF, STATE UNIV NY STONY BROOK, 81- *Concurrent Pos:* NSF res grant, 60-; deleg, US/USSR Bilateral Agreement Environ Protection, 78-79; assoc ed, J Quant Spectros Radiation Transfer; vis prof, Leningrad State Univ, 80; mem, Carbon Dioxide & Climate Rev Panel, Nat Res Coun, 81-82. *Mem:* AAAS; Am Phys Soc. *Res:* Atmospheric radiation; climate modeling. *Mailing Add:* Lab Planetary Atmospheres Res State Univ NY Stony Brook NY 11794

CESSNA, JOHN CURTIS, b Johnstown, Pa, Apr 15, 26; m 47; c 2. ORGANIC CHEMISTRY. *Educ:* Augustana Col, BA, 50; Iowa State Col, MS, 52. *Prof Exp:* Res chemist, Nat Carbon Res Lab, 52-64; sr res chemist, Consumer Prod Div, 64-72, sr res chemist, 72-81, STAFF ELECTROCHEMIST, BATTERY PRODS DIV, UNION CARBIDE CORP, 81- *Mem:* Am Chem Soc; Electrochem Soc; Nat Asn Corrosion Eng. *Res:* Corrosion studies relating to batteries and coolants; basic and applied research on batteries. *Mailing Add:* Battery Prods Div 12900 Snow Rd Parma OH 44130

CESSNA, LAWRENCE C, JR, b Cumberland, Md, Feb 1, 39; m 60; c 2. POLYMER PHYSICS, CHEMICAL ENGINEERING. *Educ:* Johns Hopkins Univ, BES, 61; Rensselaer Polytech Inst, PhD(polymer sci), 65. *Prof Exp:* Res assoc polymer sci, Rensselaer Polytech Inst, 65-66; res engr, 66-70, sr res engr, 70-73, res scientist, 73, mgr mat sci div, Hercules Res Ctr, 73-77, asst dir develop projs, 77-80, dir technol mkt, 80-81, DIR DEVELOP, HERCULES INC, 81- *Mem:* Indust Res Inst; Soc Chem Indust; Soc Plastics Engr; Am Chem Soc. *Res:* Ultimate properties of high polymers; physical and mechanical behavior of polymers and polymer based composite materials; chemical engineering fundamentals. *Mailing Add:* 111 Neptune Dr Newark DE 19711

CETAS, ROBERT CHARLES, plant pathology, deceased

CETERA, MARGARET MARY, b Chicago, Ill, May 31, 53. ANALYTICAL CHEMISTRY. *Educ:* Ill Benedictine Col, BS, 75; ECarolina Univ, MS, 81. *Prof Exp:* Asst res chemist, CPC Int, Argonne, Ill, 75-77, asst plant chemist, 77-78; sci tech res asst, Ill Legis Coun, 78-79; RES ASSOC, EAST CAROLINA UNIV, 82- *Mem:* Am Chem Soc. *Res:* Instrument-computer interfacing; programmed experiments for physically impaired persons. *Mailing Add:* Dept Chem East Carolina Univ Greenville NC 27834

CETRON, MARVIN J, b Brooklyn, NY, July 5, 30; m 55; c 2. RESEARCH MANAGEMENT, INDUSTRIAL ENGINEERING. *Educ:* Pa State Univ, BS, 52; Columbia Univ, MS, 59, cert exec develop, 58; Am Univ, PhD(res & develop mgt), 70. *Prof Exp:* Head performance statist sect, Naval Appl Sci Lab, NY, 52-54, head mgt planning, rev br, 54; eng asst to tech dir opers res, 56-58, independent res coordr, Naval Marine Eng Lab, Md, 58-63, head prog mgt off, 63-64, planning dir, 64-66, head tech forecasting & appraisal, HQ Naval Mat Command, DC, 66-71; FOUNDER & PRES, FORECASTING INT, LTD, 71- *Concurrent Pos:* Ed-in-chief, Technol Assess J, 69-; adj prof, Am Univ & Mass Inst Technol, 70-; mem, Coast Guard Res & Develop Adv Comt. *Honors & Awards:* Armed Forces Mgt Lit Award, 69 & 70; Armed Forces Mgt Award, 70. *Mem:* AAAS; Am Inst Indust Engrs. *Res:* Technological forecasting; operations research in research and development; research and development planning; project selection and resource allocation models; technology assessment. *Mailing Add:* 1001 N Highland St Arlington VA 22210

CETRULO, CURTIS L, obstetrics, see previous edition

CEVALLOS, WILLIAM HERNAN, b Quito, Ecuador, Mar 11, 32; US citizen; m 56; c 4. BIOCHEMISTRY, METABOLISM. *Educ:* Mt St Mary's Col, Md, BS, 54; St John's Univ, NY, MS, 56; Georgetown Univ, PhD(biochem), 60. *Prof Exp:* Asst microbiol, St John's Univ, NY, 54-56, lab instr histol, 55-56; asst biochem, Georgetown Univ, 56-59, lab instr chem, Sch Nursing, 57-59; res assoc biochem, Sinai Hosp, Baltimore, Md, 59-64; res assoc, Smith Kline & French Labs, 64-68; RES ASSOC BIOCHEM, DIV RES, LANKENAU HOSP, 68- *Concurrent Pos:* NIH fel, 60-62, grant, 62-64. *Mem:* NY Acad Sci. *Res:* Lipid metabolism related to atherosclerosis and heart disease; hormonal and chemotherapeutic control of cholesterol metabolism; relationship of circulating and dietary lipids to platelets and thrombosis. *Mailing Add:* 22 Fairfield Rd Devon PA 19333

CEVASCO, ALBERT ANTHONY, b New York, NY, Sept 4, 40; m 63; c 2. ORGANIC CHEMISTRY. *Educ:* Manhattan Col, BS, 62; Fordham Univ, PhD(org chem), 68. *Prof Exp:* Asst chem, Fordham Univ, 62-67; res chemist, Explor Res & Develop Dept, Bound Brook, 67-69, res chemist, Decision Making Systs, 69-70, process res chemist, Dyes Tech Dept, 70-75, SR RES CHEMIST, AGR RES CTR, AM CYANAMID CO, PRINCETON, NJ, 75- *Mem:* Am Chem Soc; Sigma Xi. *Res:* Heterocyclic syntheses; organic luminescers; dye and brightener intermediates process research and development; process research and development of agricultural organic chemicals, animal health products, pesticides and synthetic pyrethroids. *Mailing Add:* 21 Kingswood Dr Belle Mead NJ 08502

CEZAIRLIYAN, ARED, b Istanbul, Turkey, May 9, 34; US citizen; m 70; c 1. THERMAL PHYSICS, MATERIALS SCIENCE. *Educ:* Robert Col, Istanbul, BSME, 57; Purdue Univ, Lafayette, MSME, 60, PhD, 63. *Prof Exp:* PHYSICIST, NAT BUR STANDARDS, 63- *Concurrent Pos:* Consult, Thermophys Properties Res Ctr, Purdue Univ, 68-; mem, Int Orgn Comt, Europ Thermophys Properties Conf, 74-; chmn, Int Thermophysics Cong, 76-; ed-in-chief, Int J Thermophysics, 80- *Honors & Awards:* Spec Act Award, US Dept Com, 70; Silver Medal Award, 75; Spec Achievement Award, Nat Bur Standards, 77; Distinguished Eng Alumnus Award, Purdue Univ, 78; Gold Medal Award, US Dept Com, 80; Heat Transfer Mem Award, Am Soc Mech Engrs, 81. *Mem:* AAAS; Am Phys Soc; Am Soc Mech Engrs; Sigma Xi. *Res:* High temperature thermophysics; material properties; calorimetry; high temperature thermometry; high speed pyrometry; optics; transient measurement techniques. *Mailing Add:* Thermophysics Div Nat Bur of Standards Washington DC 20234

CHA, DAE YANG, b Korea, Sept 25, 36; m 65; c 3. CHEMICAL ENGINEERING. *Educ:* Seoul Nat Univ, BS, 59, MSE, 61; Univ Calif, Berkeley, MS, 63; Univ Mich, PhD(chem eng), 68. *Prof Exp:* CHEM ENGR, UPJOHN CO, 66- *Mem:* Am Inst Chem Engrs; Am Chem Soc. *Res:* Heterogeneous catalysis; separation and purification of antibiotics and steroids from fermentation medium; process development on fine chemicals and specialty polymers. *Mailing Add:* 2030 Aberdeen Dr Kalamazoo MI 49008

CHA, SUNGMAN, b Chungpyong, Korea, Mar 1, 28; m 60; c 3. BIOCHEMISTRY, PHARMACOLOGY. *Educ:* Yonsei Univ, Korea, MD, 54; Univ Wis, PhD(pharmacol), 63. *Prof Exp:* Asst pharmacol, Univ Wis, 59-61, trainee, 61-63; from asst prof to assoc prof, 63-76, PROF MED SCI, BROWN UNIV, 76- *Mem:* Am Soc Biol Chem. *Res:* Metabolism of nucleotides including analogues; enzymology of cancer cells. *Mailing Add:* Div of Biomed Sci Brown Univ Providence RI 02912

CHAAPEL, DONALD WILLIAM, electrical engineering, see previous edition

CHABAI, ALBERT JOHN, b Mont, Feb 1, 29; m 58; c 6. PHYSICS. *Educ:* Mont State Col, BS, 51; Lehigh Univ, MS & PhD(physics), 58. *Prof Exp:* Mem physics res staff, 58-65, div supvr, Adv Systs Develop, 65-71, DIV SUPVR, COMPUTATIONAL PHYSICS & MECH, SANDIA LABS, 71- *Mem:* AAAS. *Res:* Fluid dynamics. *Mailing Add:* 2607 Haines Ave NE Albuquerque NM 87102

CHABRECK, ROBERT HENRY, b Lacombe, La, Mar 18, 33; m 54; c 4. WILDLIFE MANAGEMENT, ECOLOGY. *Educ:* La State Univ, Baton Rouge, MS, 57, PhD(bot), 70. *Prof Exp:* Refuge biologist, La Wildlife & Fisheries Comn, 57-59, res biologist, 59-66, res supvr, 66-67; asst leader, La Coop Wildlife Res Unit, 67-72; assoc prof, 72-77, PROF FORESTRY & WILDLIFE MGR, LA STATE UNIV, BATON ROUGE, 77- *Mem:* Wildlife Soc. *Res:* Wetland ecology, especially wetland management, life history studies of American alligator and waterfowl. *Mailing Add:* Sch of Forestry & Wildlife Mgt La State Univ Baton Rouge LA 70803

CHACE, FENNER ALBERT, JR, b Fall River, Mass, Oct 5, 08; m 34; c 1. ZOOLOGY. *Educ:* Harvard Univ, AB, 30, AM, 31, PhD(biol), 34. *Prof Exp:* Asst cur mar invert, Mus Comp Zool, Harvard Univ, 34-42, cur Crustacea, 42-46, cur marine invert, US Nat Mus, 46-63; sr zoologist, 63-68, res assoc, 68-78, EMER ZOOLOGIST, SMITHSONIAN INST, 78- *Concurrent Pos:* Asst biol, Harvard Univ, 35, Agassiz fel, 35-39, tutor biol, 40-41. *Mem:* AAAS; Soc Syst Zool; Crustacean Soc. *Res:* Taxonomy, morphology and distribution of decapod Crustacea. *Mailing Add:* Dept Invert Zool Smithsonian Inst Washington DC 20560

CHACE, FREDERIC MASON, b Swansea, Mass, Aug 24, 06; m 43. MINING GEOLOGY. *Educ:* Brown Univ, PhB, 29, MA, 32; Harvard Univ, PhD(geol), 47. *Prof Exp:* Geologist, Bendigo Mines Ltd, Australia, 34-36; consult geologist, Mining Co of Oruro, Boliva, 37; geologist, Cerro de Pasco Copper Corp, Peru, 38-40; indust specialist, War Prod Bd, Washington, DC, 42-45; commodity geologist, US Geol Surv, 46-47; staff geologist, 47-51; regional geologist, M A Hanna Co, Minn & Mich, 51-52; mining geologist, Gold Fields Am Develop Co, Ltd, 52-55; asst dir explor, M A Hanna Co, 55-61, chief geologist, Hanna Mining Co, 61-68, vpres geol & explor, 68-74; CONSULT, 74- *Mem:* Am Inst Min, Metall & Petrol Eng; Soc Econ Geol; Geol Soc Am. *Res:* Structural control of ore deposits; paragenesis of ore minerals; mineral exploration and mineral economics; gold, copper and iron ore deposits. *Mailing Add:* 3611 Medford Rd Durham NC 27705

CHACE, MILTON A, b Takoma Park, Md, Mar 19, 34; m 58; c 3. DYNAMICS, MECHANICAL ENGINEERING. *Educ:* Cornell Univ, BEP, 57; Univ Mich, MSME, 62, PhD(mech eng), 64. *Prof Exp:* Engr, US Atomic Energy Comn, 57-59; mech engr, Atomic Power Develop Assocs, 59-61; staff engr, Systs Develop Div, IBM Corp, 64-67; assoc prof mech eng, 67-75, PROF MECH ENG, UNIV MICH, 75- *Concurrent Pos:* Dir, Comput-Aided Design Lab, 71- & Mech Dynamics Inc, 77- *Mem:* Am Soc Mech Engrs. *Res:* Dynamics of mechanical systems; digital computer simulation of systems; computer aided design. *Mailing Add:* 3265 N Maple Rd Ann Arbor MI 48105

CHACE, WILLIAM GEORGE, JR, horticulture, plant physiology, see previous edition

CHACKERIAN, CHARLES, JR, b San Francisco, Calif, Feb 6, 35; c 3. PHYSICAL CHEMISTRY, MOLECULAR SPECTROSCOPY. *Educ:* Univ Calif, Berkeley, BS, 58; Univ Wash, PhD(chem), 64. *Prof Exp:* RES SCIENTIST, AMES RES CTR, NASA, 64- *Mem:* Am Phys Soc. *Res:* Shock waves; high temperature chemical kinetics and molecular relaxation; infrared spectroscopy related to planetary and stellar spectroscopy; gas lasers. *Mailing Add:* Ames Res Ctr NASA Moffett Field CA 94035

CHACKO, GEORGE KUTTICKAL, b Trivandrum, India, July 1, 30; US citizen; m 57; c 2. SYSTEMS MANAGEMENT, STATISTICS. *Educ:* Madras Univ, MA, 50; Indian Statist Inst, advan cert, 51; Univ Calcutta, BC, 52; New Sch Soc Res, PhD(econometrics), 59. *Prof Exp:* Consult opers res, Union Carbide Corp, New York, 62-63; mem tech staff, Res Anal Corp, McLean, Va, 63-65 & MITRE Corp, Washington, DC, 65-67; sr staff scientist, TRW Systs, Washington Opers, 67-70; PROF SYSTS MGT, UNIV SOUTHERN CALIF, 70- *Concurrent Pos:* Fel, Western Mgt Sci Ctr, Univ Calif, Los Angeles, 61; consult space systs anal, Inst Creative Studies, Washington, DC, 68-70; consult comput sci, US Dept of Defense, Indust Col Armed Forces, 70; consult mil opers res, Milcom Systs, Rockville, Md, 71-72; consult info sci, King Res, Rockville, Md, 75-76; consult comput aided mgt controls, On-Line Systems, McLean, Va, 79-, prin investr adaptive forecasting, 81. *Mem:* Fel AAAS; fel Am Astronaut Soc; Opers Res Soc Am; Inst Mgt Sci. *Res:* Major systems acquisition management; management information systems; technological forecasting and control; computer networking in editorial processing and national development; computer aided management controls in public and private sectors. *Mailing Add:* 6809 Barr Rd Bethesda MD 20816

CHACKO, GEORGE KUTTY, b Kottarakkara, India, Feb 15, 33; m 62; c 3. BIOCHEMISTRY. *Educ:* Univ Col, Trivandrum, India, BSc, 56; Maharaja's Col, Ernakulam, MSc, 58; Univ Ill, Urbana, PhD(food chem, biochem), 66. *Prof Exp:* Fel biochem, Univ Wash, 66-67; fel, Univ Ariz, 67-68; res asst prof, 68-74, res assoc prof biochem & physiol, 74-77, ASSOC PROF BIOCHEM, MED COL PA, 77- *Mem:* Am Chem Soc; Am Oil Chemists Soc; AAAS. *Res:* Biochemical characterization of axon plasma membranes; structure and function of platelet complex lipids. *Mailing Add:* Dept of Biochem & Physiol Med Col of Pa Philadelphia PA 19129

CHACKO, SAMUEL K, b Kottarakara, India, Feb 7, 42; US citizen; m 68; c 3. PATHOBIOLOGY, BIOCHEMISTRY. *Educ:* Kerala Vet Col & Res Inst, DVM, 63; Univ Pa, PhD(path), 69. *Prof Exp:* Instr path, Comp Cardiovasc Studies Unit, 65-66, USPHS trainee, 66-69, assoc prof, 74-81, PROF PATH, DEPT PATHOBIOL, SCH VET MED & GRAD SCH ARTS & SCI, UNIV

PA, 81- Concurrent Pos: Prin investr, Cardiovasc Studies Unit, Univ Pa, 69-75 & Pa Muscle Inst, 72-76; exp pathologist, Molecular Cardiol Sect, Cardiol Br, Nat Heart, Lung & Blood Inst, 75-77; consult, NIH Prog Proj grant, 76; prin investr, Nat Heart, Lung & Blood Inst res grant, 78. Mem: Am Soc Exp Path; Am Soc Cell Biol; Int Soc Heart Res; Sigma Xi. Res: Regulation of actomyosin ATPase and contraction in smooth muscle; cytoplasmic filaments in smooth muscle and endothelial cells; contractile protein structure and function in development, growth and aging in cardiac and smooth muscle. Mailing Add: Lab of Path Rm 305 Univ of Pa Sch of Vet Med Philadelphia PA 19104

CHACKO, ROSY J, b Neendoor, Kerala; India citizen; m 70. MYCOLOGY, FOREST PATHOLOGY. Educ: Univ Kerala, BSc, 59; Agra Univ, MSc, 62; Univ Mont, PhD(bot), 72. Prof Exp: Lectr, Univ Kerala, 62-67; teaching asst bot, Univ Mont, 68-72; res technician forest path, Col Forestry, Univ Idaho, 73-74, res scientist, 74-77; RES TECHNICIAN PLANT PATH, WASH STATE UNIV, 77- Concurrent Pos: Mem mus subcomt, Wash State Univ, 78- Mem: Mycol Soc Am. Res: Collect and identify fruiting bodies of Ascomycetes and Basidiomycetes that decay timber; make aseptic isolations from sporophores/decay; study the morphology using light and electron microscopic observations. Mailing Add: Dept Hort Wash State Univ Pullman WA 99164

CHACON, RAFAEL VAN SEVEREN, b El Salvador, Cent Am, June 10, 31; nat US; wid; c 4. MATHEMATICS. Educ: Univ Rochester, BS, 51; Syracuse Univ, PhD(math), 56. Prof Exp: Instr, Ohio State Univ, 56-58; asst prof math, Univ Wis, 58-61; assoc prof, Brown Univ, 61-64 & Ohio State Univ, 64-69; prof, Univ Minn, Minneapolis, 69-74; PROF MATH, UNIV BC, 74- Mem: Am Math Soc; fel Royal Soc Can. Res: Probability theory; ergodic theory; functional analysis. Mailing Add: Dept Math Univ BC Vancouver BC V6T 1W5 Can

CHADDE, FRANK ERNEST, b Chicago, Ill, June 23, 29; m 53; c 4. ANALYTICAL CHEMISTRY. Educ: Univ Ill, BS, 51. Prof Exp: Control chemist, 51-52, anal chemist, 54-63, mgr anal res dept, 63-67, mgr chem control dept, 67-69, MGR ANAL LAB, ABBOTT LABS, 69- Mem: Am Soc Qual Control; Am Chem Soc; Acad Pharmaceut Sci. Res: Ultra violet spectroscopy; colorimetry; titrimetric analysis; polarography. Mailing Add: D-866 Anal Labs Abbott Lab North Chicago IL 60064

CHADDOCK, JACK B, b Cameron, WVa, Dec 6, 24; m 55. MECHANICAL ENGINEERING. Educ: Univ SC, BS, 45; Univ WVa, BS, 48; Mass Inst Technol, MS, 49, MechE, 52, ScD(mech eng), 55. Prof Exp: From instr to asst prof mech eng, Mass Inst Technol, 50-57; assoc prof, Rensselaer Polytech Inst, 57-59; prof, Purdue Univ, 59-66; PROF MECH ENG & CHMN DEPT, DUKE UNIV, 66-, DIR, CTR STUDY ENERGY CONSERV, 75- Concurrent Pos: Fulbright lectr, Inst Technol, Helsinki, 55- 56; vis prof, Univ NSW, Australia, 73; vis prof, Bldg Res Estab, Eng, 80; pres, John B Pierce Found, New York, 81- Mem: Fel Am Soc Heat, Refrig & Air Cond Engrs (pres, 81-82); Int Inst Refrig; Am Soc Mech Engrs; Am Soc Eng Educ; Sigma Xi. Res: Heat and mass transfer; two-phase flow; building energy systems; solar heating and cooling. Mailing Add: Dept Mech Eng & Mat Sci Duke Univ Durham NC 27706

CHADDOCK, RICHARD E(ASTMAN), b Colon, Panama, Dec 10, 16; m 41; c 2. CHEMICAL ENGINEERING. Educ: Univ Mich, PhD(chem eng), 41. Prof Exp: Chem engr, Atlas Powder Co, Del, 40-45; asst to dir res, Hercules Inc, 45-48, mgr, Sales Res Div, 48-55, dir develop, 55-66, dir planning, 66-68, dir, Environ Affairs, 68-79; PRES, ENVIRON MGT INC, 79- Mem: Am Inst Chem Engrs; Am Chem Soc; Chem Mkt Res Asn (pres, 57). Res: Liquid vapor equilibrium in hydrocarbon-water systems; unsteady state heat transfer to liquids in tanks; practical aspects in design of liquid agitators; market research engineering. Mailing Add: Environ Mgt Inc PO Box 1057 Port Orange FL 32019

CHADER, GERALD JOSEPH, b Buffalo, NY, Apr 15, 37; c 3. BIOCHEMISTRY. Educ: Univ Buffalo, BA, 59; Univ Louisville, PhD(biochem), 66. Prof Exp: High sch teacher, NY, 59-60; instr, Med Sch & tutor, Dept Biochem & Molecular Biol, Harvard Univ, 71; biochemist, 71-75, CHIEF, SECT RETINAL METAB, NAT EYE INST, 75- Concurrent Pos: Fel biochem, Sch Med, Univ Louisville, 66-67; fel biol chem, Harvard Med Sch, 67-69. Mem: Am Soc Biol Chemists; Am Soc Neurochem. Res: Mechanism of action of vitamin A, involving vitamin-receptor interactions and study of these interactions in relation to retinal function. Mailing Add: Lab of Vision Res Bldg 6 Rm BIA-07 Nat Eye Inst Bethesda MD 20205

CHADHA, KAILASH CHANDRA, b Churu, India, July 1, 43; US citizen; m 71; c 2. INTERFERONS. Educ: Univ Rajasthan, India, BSc, 62; Indian Agr Res Inst, New Delhi, MSc, 64; Univ Guelph, PhD(virol), 68. Prof Exp: Nat Res Coun fel virol, Can Dept Agr, 68-70; cancer res scientist I, 70-72, cancer res scientist II, 73-76, CANCER RES SCIENTIST IV INTERFERON & MICROBIOL, ROSWELL PARK MEM INST, 76- Concurrent Pos: Res prof, Niagara Univ, 78-; assoc res prof, Dept Microbiol, State Univ NY Buffalo, 79- Mem: NY Acad Sci; Am Soc Microbiol. Res: Mammalian interferons: their purification, physico-chemical characterization and mechanism of action; gene expression in virally transformed mammalian cells. Mailing Add: Dept Cell & Tumor Biol Roswell Park Mem Inst 666 Elm St Buffalo NY 14263

CHADI, D J(AMES), b Teheran, Iran, Oct 10, 47. SOLID STATE PHYSICS. Educ: Cooper Union, BS, 69; Univ Calif, Berkeley, PhD(physics), 74. Prof Exp: MEM RES STAFF, XEROX PALO ALTO RES CTR, 74- Mem: Am Phys Soc; Am Vacuum Soc. Res: Electronic and structural properties of solids; semiconductor surfaces. Mailing Add: 3333 Coyote Hill Rd Palo Alto CA 94304

CHADWICK, DAVID HENRY, b Sutton, NH, Aug 8, 18; m 44; c 3. INDUSTRIAL ORGANIC CHEMISTRY. Educ: Univ NH, BS, 40, MS, 42; Univ Ill, PhD(org chem), 46. Prof Exp: From asst to instr chem, Univ NH, 40-42; asst, Univ Ill, 42-46; res chemist, Monsanto Chem Co, 46-49, res group leader, 49-59; asst dir res, 59-67, dir process res dept, 67-78, DIR ANAL RES & TESTING SERV, MOBAY CHEM CO, 78- Concurrent Pos: Anal lab control supvr, Clinton Eng Works, Tenn Eastman Corp, 44-45; res chemist, Nat Defense Res Comt Contract, Monsanto Chem Co, 43; instr chem, Univ Ill, 46. Mem: Am Chem Soc. Res: Molecular rearrangements; stable vinyl alcohols; addition of Grignard reagents to aronitriles; synthetic detergents; organophosphorus compounds; isocyanates; tall oil; polyurethanes; polyesters; polycarbonates. Mailing Add: Res Dept Mobay Chem Corp New Martinsville WV 26155

CHADWICK, DUANE G(EORGE), b LaGrande, Ore, Jan 24, 25; m 51; c 7. ELECTRICAL ENGINEERING. Educ: Utah State Univ, BSEE, 52; Univ Wash, MSEE, 57. Prof Exp: Res engr, Boeing Airplane Co, 53-57; asst prof, 57-65, ASSOC PROF ELEC ENG, UTAH STATE UNIV, 65- Res: Electronic control mechanisms; hydrologic instrumentation; solar powered water pumps. Mailing Add: Dept of Elec Eng UMC 41 Utah State Univ Logan UT 84322

CHADWICK, GEORGE F, b Buffalo, NY, July 11, 30; m 52; c 4. PLASTICS CHEMISTRY, CHEMICAL ENGINEERING. Educ: Univ Buffalo, BA, 51; Pa State Univ, MA, 56. Prof Exp: Asst petrol, Pa State Univ, 51-54; chemist, Durez Plastics Div, Hooker Chem Corp, 54-57; res scientist, Airco Electronics, 57-64, res supvr, 64-65, develop supvr, 65-67, mgr develop electronics, 67-72, mgr process eng, 73-78; consult eng, Mesch & Assocs, 78-80; SR DEVELOP, AGR-CHEM DIV, FMC CORP, 80- Mem: Am Chem Soc; Soc Plastics Engrs; Am Inst Chem Engrs; fel Brit Plastics Inst. Res: Plastics; rheology; conductivity of fine dispersed conductive materials in plastics composites; environmental chemistry. Mailing Add: FMC Corp Agr-Chem Div 100 Niagara St Middleport NY 14105

CHADWICK, HAROLD KING, b Bay Shore, NY, May 28, 30; m 55; c 5. FISHERIES. Educ: Cornell Univ, BS, 52; Univ Mich, MS, 56. Prof Exp: FISHERY BIOLOGIST, CALIF DEPT FISH & GAME, 56- Mem: Am Fisheries Soc. Res: Investigation of Sacramento River striped bass population including harvest and natural mortality rates and strength of year classes; reservoir ecology; fisheries management. Mailing Add: Calif Dept of Fish & Game 4001 N Wilson Way Stockton CA 95205

CHADWICK, JUNE MARIE, microbiology, see previous edition

CHADWICK, ROBERT AULL, b Milwaukee, Wis, May 4, 29; m 51; c 2. GEOLOGY. Educ: Princeton Univ, AB, 51; Univ Wis, PhD(geol), 56. Prof Exp: Geologist, Eagle-Picher Co, 56-59; asst prof geol, Long Beach State Col, 59-61; from asst prof to assoc prof, 61-73, PROF GEOL, MONT STATE UNIV, 73- Concurrent Pos: NSF grants attend, Conf Struct & Origin Volcanic Rocks, Wayne State Univ, 62 & Geol of Scand, Int Field Inst, 63; consult, Mont Power Co, 73; res grants, Mont Power Co, 74, US Environ Protection Agency & US Geol Surv, 75. Mem: Fel Geol Soc Am; Am Geophys Union. Res: Petrology; economic geology; Tertiary volcanic rocks of southwestern Montana; geology of pegmatites; paleomagnetism of volcanic rocks; geology of Montana coal deposits; geothermal energy potential of Montana. Mailing Add: Dept of Earth Sci Mont State Univ Bozeman MT 59715

CHADWICK, WALLACE LACY, b Loring, Kans, Dec 4, 97; m 21; c 2. CIVIL ENGINEERING. Hon Degrees: Dr Eng Sci, Univ Redlands, 65. Prof Exp: Statistician & plant engr, Calif Alkali Co, 20-21; draftsman, Southern Calif Edison Co, 22-24, div engr, 24-28, transmission engr, Big Creek-San Joaquin Hydroelec Proj, 28-31; dir design & construct many dams & power sta, construct Colo River Aqueduct & from engr to sr engr, Metrop Water Dist Southern Calif, 31-37, spec assignment, 38; from civil engr to chief ciVil engr, Southern Calif Edison Co, 37-44, mgr eng dept, 45-50, vpres, 51-62; CONSULT ENG DAMS, TUNNELS, HYDRO, THERMAL & NUCLEAR POWER PLANTS & ELEC UTILITY PROBS, 62- Concurrent Pos: Chmn, Joint Res Coun Power Plant Air Pollution Control, Los Angeles, 56-62; mem joint bd environ studies, Nat Acad Sci & Nat Acad Eng, 65-69; pres bd trustees, Univ Redlands, 56-69, chmn exec comt, 69-75; mem exec comt, US comt, Int Comn Large Dams, 70-76; mem US comt, World Energy Conf. Honors & Awards: Philip T Sprague Award, Instrument Soc Am, 63; Golden Beaver Award, 69; Rickey Medal, Am Soc Civil Eng, 71. Mem: Nat Acad Eng; hon mem fel Am Soc Mech Eng; fel Inst Elec & Electronics Engrs; Am Soc Civil Eng (pres, 64-65); Am Concrete Inst. Mailing Add: 200 Howe Bldg 180 S Lake Ave Pasadena CA 91101

CHAE, CHI-BOM, b Seoul, Korea, Sept 25, 40; US citizen; m 70; c 2. GENE REGULATION. Educ: Seoul Nat Univ, BS, 63; Univ NC, PhD(biochem), 67. Prof Exp: Asst prof, 70-76, ASSOC PROF, DEPT BIOCHEM, UNIV NC, 76- Mem: Am Asn Biol Chemists; AAAS. Res: Chromatin structure; association of globin RNA with nuclear matrix; genetic engineering; globin gene. Mailing Add: Dept Biochem Univ NC Chapel Hill NC 27514

CHAE, KUN, b Seoul, Korea, Apr 13, 44; m 73; c 2. MEDICINAL CHEMISTRY, ENVIRONMENTAL CHEMISTRY. Educ: Seoul Nat Univ, BS, 66; Univ NC, Chapel Hill, MS, 71, PhD(med chem), 73. Prof Exp: Vis fel, 73-74, staff fel, 74-77, RES CHEMIST, NAT INST ENVIRON HEALTH SCI, RES TRIANGLE PARK, 78- Mem: Am Chem Soc; Sigma Xi. Res: Organic synthesis and metabolic studies of lipids; synthesis and analysis of chlorinated aromatics; toxicological and metabolic studies of polychlorinated biphenyls; synthesis and characterization of antigens for immunochemical studies. Mailing Add: 5112 Lazywood Lane Durham NC 27712

CHAE, SOO BONG, b Musan, Korea, June 22, 39; m 67; c 2. MATHEMATICS. Educ: Seoul Nat Univ, BS, 62; Emory Univ, MA, 63; Univ Rochester, PhD(math), 70. Prof Exp: PROF MATH, NEW COL UNIV S FLA, 70- Mem: Am Math Soc; Math Asn Am. Res: Functional analysis; general topology. Mailing Add: New Col of Univ of SFla Sarasota FL 33580

CHAE, YONG SUK, b Chochiwen, Korea, July 29, 30; m 62; c 2. CIVIL ENGINEERING, ENGINEERING MECHANICS. *Educ:* Dartmouth Col, AB, 56, MS, 57; Univ Mich, PhD(civil eng), 64. *Prof Exp:* Civil engr, Howard, Needles, Tammen & Bergendoff, 60-61; from asst prof to assoc prof, 64-71, PROF CIVIL ENG, RUTGERS UNIV, 71-, ASSOC DEAN, 81- *Concurrent Pos:* Consult, US Army Cold Regions Res & Eng Lab, Mineral Fibre Prod Bur, Continental Oil Co, Singer Co, Dames & Moore, Charles Kupper Int & NL Industries; NATO sr fel sci, Dept State-NSF, 75. *Mem:* Am Soc Civil Engrs. *Res:* Soil mechanics; soil dynamics; foundation engineering; physics of snow, ice and frozen soil; earthquake engineering; environmental effects of construction. *Mailing Add:* Col of Eng Rutgers Univ PO Box 909 Piscataway NJ 08854

CHAE, YOUNG C, b Seoul, Korea, Mar 31, 32; m 59; c 2. CHEMICAL ENGINEERING, POLYMER SCIENCE. *Educ:* SDak Sch Mines & Technol, BS, 59; Case Inst Technol, PhD(chem eng), 62. *Prof Exp:* Sr res chemist, 62-65, res proj leader, 65-66, group leader, 66-70, sr group leader, Org Res Dept, 70-73, com develop mgr, 73-78, MGR COM DEVELOP, MONSANTO NEW ENTERPRISE DIV, MONSANTO CO, 78- *Mem:* Am Chem Soc; Am Inst Chem Engrs; Soc Plastics Indust; Soc Plastics Engrs; Am Mgt Asn. *Res:* Physical characterization of polymers; reinforced plastics; cellular plastics; surface coatings; plasticizers; flame retardant polymers and process development. *Mailing Add:* Monsanto Co 800 N Lindbergh St Louis MO 63166

CHAET, ALFRED BERNARD, b Boston, Mass, June 7, 27; m 50; c 3. PHYSIOLOGY. *Educ:* Univ Mass, BS, 49, MS, 50; Univ Pa, PhD(zool), 53. *Prof Exp:* Asst, Univ Pa, 51-53; instr zool, Univ Maine, 53-56; asst prof physiol, Sch Med, Boston Univ, 56-58; from assoc prof to prof biol, Am Univ, 58-66; provost, 67-76, PROF BIOL, UNIV WFLA, 66-, ASSOC V PRES, 76- *Concurrent Pos:* Res, Marine Biol Lab, Woods Hole, 49, 51-53 & 55-58 & corp mem; res assoc, Boston City Hosp, 56-; NIH spec fel & vis scholar, Scripps Inst, Calif, 64-65; assoc dean sci, Univ WFla, 66-67; chmn, Fla Panhandle Health Systs Agency, Inc. *Mem:* AAAS; Am Soc Zool; Soc Gen Physiol; Am Soc Physiol; Soc Biophys. *Res:* Shedding substance in starfish-invertebrate neurohormone; absorption properties of echinoderm tube feet; adhering mechanisms in invertebrates; toxic factor in heat death; thiaminase. *Mailing Add:* 8877 Scenic Hills Dr Pensacola FL 32504

CHAFETZ, HARRY, b New York, NY, Oct 27, 29; m 55; c 2. ORGANIC CHEMISTRY. *Educ:* City Col New York, BS, 50; Pa State Univ, PhD(chem), 54. *Prof Exp:* From chemist to res chemist, 56-61, group leader, 61-70, RES ASSOC, BEACON RES LABS, TEXACO INC, 70- *Mem:* Am Chem Soc. *Res:* Organic synthesis; petrochemicals; free radical chemistry; halogenetion and oxidation reactions; lubricant additives; hydrocarbon chemistry; syngas chemistry. *Mailing Add:* PO Box 509 Beacon NY 12508

CHAFETZ, MORRIS EDWARD, b Worcester, Mass, Apr 20, 24; m 46; c 3. PSYCHIATRY. *Educ:* Tufts Univ, MD, 48; Am Bd Psychiat & Neurol, dipl, 56. *Prof Exp:* Dir alcohol clin, Mass Gen Hosp, 57-68, dir acute psychiat serv, 61-68, psychiatrist, 64-70, dir clin psychiat serv, 68-70; actg dir, Div Alcohol Abuse & Alcoholism, Nat Inst Alcohol Abuse & Alcoholism, NIMH, 70-71, dir, 71-75; PRES, HEALTH EDUC FOUND, 75- *Concurrent Pos:* Mem ad hoc rev bd res in alcoholism, NIMH, 58-61; mem subcomt alcoholism, Mass Ment Health Planning Proj, 63-; assoc clin prof psychiat, Harvard Med Sch, 68-70. *Mem:* Group Advan Psychiat. *Res:* Treatment, prevention and dynamics of alcoholism and alcohol-related disorders; psychiatric care of urban poor. *Mailing Add:* Health Educ Found 600 New Hampshire Ave NW Suite 452 Washington DC 20037

CHAFFEE, ELEANOR, b Cambridge, Mass, Oct 9, 34. PHYSICAL INORGANIC CHEMISTRY. *Educ:* Mt Holyoke Col, BA, 56; Harvard Univ, MAT, 62; Wellesley Col, MA, 67; Brown Univ, PhD(chem), 71. *Prof Exp:* Res physicist photoconductivity, Stanford Res Inst, 56-57; res physicist phys chem, Arthur D Little, Inc, 59-61; teacher chem, Am High Sch, Lugano, Switz, 62-63 & Lexington High Sch, Mass, 63-65; fel chem, State Univ NY Buffalo, 71-72; RES CHEMIST INORG CHEM, EASTMAN KODAK CO, NY, 72- *Res:* Kinetics and mechanisms of oxidation of substrates, their catalysis by metals, and their complexes; peroxide chemistries. *Mailing Add:* 1786 Lake Rd Webster NY 14580

CHAFFEE, MAURICE AHLBORN, b Wilkes-Barre, Pa, Jan 10, 37; m 59; c 2. ECONOMIC GEOLOGY, GEOCHEMISTRY. *Educ:* Colo Sch Mines, Geol E, 59; Univ Ariz, MS, 64, PhD(econ geol, mineral), 67. *Prof Exp:* Mine geologist, NJ Zinc Co, Va, 60-62; GEOLOGIST, US GEOL SURV, 67- *Mem:* Geol Soc Am; Soc Econ Geol; Asn Explor Geochem; Sigma Xi. *Res:* Geology and hydrothermal alteration of mineral deposits; trace element chemistry related to mineral deposits; development of new methods and concepts for application of trace element chemistry to mineral exploration. *Mailing Add:* US Geol Survey Fed Ctr MS 955 PO Box 25046 Denver CO 80225

CHAFFEE, ROBERT GIBSON, b Rutland, Vt, Mar 6, 14; m 38; c 5. PALEONTOLOGY. *Educ:* Dartmouth Col, AB, 36; Univ Pa, MS, 41; Columbia Univ, PhD, 52. *Prof Exp:* Field asst, Am Mus Natural Hist, NY, 26-28; asst cur geol & paleont, Acad Natural Sci, Pa, 38-42; photogrammetrist, Alaskan Br, US Geol Surv, 42-44; cur geol, Dartmouth Col Mus, 48-68, dir, 68-75, dir, Montshire Mus, 76-80; RETIRED. *Res:* Vertebrate paleontology; stratigraphy. *Mailing Add:* Lyme N Hanover NH 03755

CHAFFEE, ROWAND R J, b El Paso, Tex, Nov 4, 25; m 53; c 6. PHYSIOLOGY, BIOCHEMISTRY. *Educ:* Univ NMex, BS, 46, BA, 51, MS, 52; Harvard Univ, PhD(biol sci), 57. *Prof Exp:* Asst prof zool, Univ Redlands, 58-59; NIH fel cellular physiol, Univ Calif, Berkeley, 59-60; asst prof zool, Univ Calif, Riverside, 60-64; mem staff cellular physiol, Los Alamos Sci Lab, 64-69; PROF ERGONOMICS, UNIV CALIF, SANTA BARBARA, 69- *Mem:* AAAS; Am Soc Mech Engrs; Am Physiol Soc; Soc Exp Biol & Med; Brit Ergonomics Res Soc. *Res:* Biochemistry of hibernating; cold and heat acclimation; cellular physiology; mitosis; enzyme kinetics; primate temperature; altitude acclimation biochemistry. *Mailing Add:* Dept of Ergonomics Univ of Calif Santa Barbara CA 93106

CHAFFEY, CHARLES ELSWOOD, b Montreal, Que, Jan 22, 41; m 71; c 2. CHEMICAL ENGINEERING, RHEOLOGY. *Educ:* McGill Univ, BSc, 61, PhD(chem), 65. *Prof Exp:* assoc prof, 67-80, PROF CHEM ENG, UNIV TORONTO, 80- *Res:* Rheology of suspensions and reinforced polymer melts. *Mailing Add:* Dept of Chem Eng Univ of Toronto Toronto ON M5S 1A4 Can

CHAFFIN, DON B, b Sandusky, Ohio, Apr 17, 39; m 66; c 1. INDUSTRIAL ENGINEERING, BIOENGINEERING. *Educ:* Gen Motors Inst, BIE, 62; Univ Toledo, MSIE, 64; Univ Mich, PhD(eng), 67. *Prof Exp:* Jr draftsman, Mack Iron Steel Co, Ohio, 55-57; quality control engr, New Departure Div, Gen Motors Corp, Ohio, 60-62, inspection foreman, 62-63; proj engr, Micrometrical Div, Bendix Corp, Mich, 63-64; asst prof phys med, Univ Kans, 67-68; asst prof indust eng, 68-70, assoc prof indust eng & bioeng, 70-77, PROF INDUST & OPERS ENG, UNIV MICH, 77- *Concurrent Pos:* Bioeng grant, Western Elec Co, 67-71, NASA, 70-71, Aerospace Med Res Labs, 70-71 & Nat Inst Occupational Safety & Health, 71-72; consult, Bendix Corp, Mich, 64. *Mem:* Human Factors Soc; Nat Soc Prof Engrs; Am Inst Indust Engrs; Biomed Eng Soc; Brit Ergonomics Res Soc. *Res:* Effects and applications of electromyography for bettering human performance; concepts of mechanics to the study of the skeletal-muscle system; expanding the teaching of physiological, neurological, and anatomical concepts as related to the bettering of man-machine systems. *Mailing Add:* Col of Eng Univ of Mich Ann Arbor MI 48105

CHAFFIN, ROGER JAMES, b Ripon, Wis, Apr 29, 41; m 63; c 3. ELECTRICAL ENGINEERING, SOLID STATE PHYSICS. *Educ:* Univ Wis, Madison, BS, 63, MS, 64, PhD(plasma eng), 67. *Prof Exp:* Asst plasma res, Univ Wis, Madison, 63-67; tech staff mem, 67-74, SUPVR, EXPLOR RADAR DEVELOP, SANDIA CORP, 74- *Mem:* Sr mem Inst Elec & Electronics Engrs. *Res:* Radiation effects in microwave semiconductor devices; radar fuzing research; compound semiconductor device physics. *Mailing Add:* Div 5133 Sandia Labs Albuquerque NM 87185

CHAFFIN, TOMMY L, b Dallas, Tex, Apr 11, 43; m 65. ORGANIC CHEMISTRY. *Educ:* Okla State Univ, BS, 65; Univ Ill, PhD(org chem), 69. *Prof Exp:* Sr res chemist, 69-75, tech mgr, 75-80, TECH DIR, 3M CO, ST PAUL, 80- *Mem:* Am Chem Soc. *Res:* Stereospecific alkylations; anionic block copolymers; Friedel-Crafts chemistry. *Mailing Add:* 3M Co 209-1W 3M Ctr St Paul MN 55101

CHAGANTI, RAJU SREERAMA KAMALASANA, b Samalkot, India, Mar 12, 33; m 66; c 2. GENETICS. *Educ:* Andhra Univ, India, BSc, 54, MSc, 55; Harvard Univ, PhD(biol), 64. *Prof Exp:* Demonstr & res asst bot, Andhra Univ, India, 55-61, lectr, 61-67; mem sci staff, Med Res Coun Radiobiol Unit, Harwell, Eng, 67-71; res assoc & assoc investr, Lab Human Genetics, New York Blood Ctr, 71-76; DIR, LAB CANCER GENETICS & CYTOGENETICS & ATTEND GENETICIST & CYTOGENETICIST, MEM, SLOAN-KETTERING CANCER CTR, 76-; ASST PROF GENETICS, GRAD SCH MED SCI, CORNELL UNIV, 74- *Concurrent Pos:* consult, Lab Human Genetics, New York Blood Ctr, 76-; assoc prof, Dept Path, Cornell Univ Med Col, 78- *Mem:* Am Soc Human Genetics; Genetics Soc Am; Tissue Cult Asn; Sigma Xi; Am Soc Cell Biol. *Res:* Human and mammalian genetics; genetic control of chromosome form and behavior at mitosis and meiosis; chromosome change in neoplastic cells. *Mailing Add:* Mem Sloan-Kettering Cancer Ctr 1275 York Ave New York NY 10021

CHAGNON, ANDRE, b Montreal, Que, Aug 16, 32; m 58; c 2. VIROLOGY, TISSUE CULTURE. *Educ:* Univ Montreal, BA, 53, BSc, 57, PhD(bact), 60. *Prof Exp:* Res asst, 78-80, PROF VIROL, INST ARMAND-FRAPPIER, 80- *Concurrent Pos:* Dir sci technol info, Pub Rel. *Mem:* Tissue Cult Asn; Fr-Can Asn Advan Sci; Can Soc Microbiol; Soc Cryobiol. *Mailing Add:* Inst of Armand-Frappier CP100 Ville de Laval Can

CHAGNON, JEAN YVES, b Quebec, Can, May 27, 34; m 66; c 2. SEISMIC MICROZONATION. *Educ:* Laval Univ, BA, 54; Ecole Polytech, BASc, 58; McGill Univ, MSc, 61, PhD(geol), 65. *Prof Exp:* Engr geol geotech, Quebec Ministry Natural Resources, 64-72, head, Dept Geotech, 72-77; prof eng geol, 77-78, head, Dept Geol, 78-79, PROF ENG GEOL, LAVAL UNIV, 79- *Concurrent Pos:* Mem, Asn Comt Geotech Res, Nat Res Coun Can, 75-81, Subcomt, 79-82 & subcomt, Urgan Eng Terrain Problems, 79-82; consult, Eng Geol Hydro-Quebec, 78-82; assoc ed, Can Geotech J, 77-82. *Mem:* Geol Asn Can; Eng Inst Can; Can Geotech Soc. *Res:* Behavior of sensitive clays and landslides in these clays; seismic microzonation; geotechnical mapping. *Mailing Add:* 778 Francois-Artesu Ste-Foy PQ G1V 3G7 Can

CHAGNON, PAUL ROBERT, b Woonsocket, RI, Nov 11, 29. NUCLEAR PHYSICS. *Educ:* Col of the Holy Cross, BS, 50; Johns Hopkins Univ, PhD(physics), 55. *Prof Exp:* Assoc, Univ Mich, 55, instr, 55-57, asst prof physics, 57-63; from asst prof to assoc prof, 63-69, PROF PHYSICS, UNIV NOTRE DAME, 69- *Mem:* Am Phys Soc. *Res:* Nuclear spectroscopy. *Mailing Add:* Dept of Physics Univ of Notre Dame Notre Dame IN 46556

CHAHINE, MOUSTAFA TOUFIC, b Beirut, Lebanon, Jan 1, 35; US citizen; m 60; c 1. FLUID PHYSICS, ATMOSPHERIC PHYSICS. *Educ:* Univ Wash, BS, 56, MS, 57; Univ Calif, Berkeley, PhD(fluid physics), 60. *Prof Exp:* Res assoc fluid dynamics, Univ Calif, Berkeley, 58-60, teaching assoc aeronaut, 59-60; staff scientist, Jet Propulsion Lab, 60-78, MGR, DIV EARTH & SPACE SCI, JET PROPULSION LAB, CALIF INST TECHNOL, 78- *Concurrent Pos:* Vis scientist, Mass Inst Technol, 69-70; mem earth surv panel, NASA, 69-75; assoc prof, Am Univ Beirut, 71-72; sci consult, Naval Postgrad Sch, Monterey, Calif, 74-77. *Honors & Awards:* Exceptional Sci Achievement Medal, NASA, 69. *Mem:* Fel Am Inst Physics; Am Meteorol Soc. *Res:* Thermodynamics and statistical fluid physics; strong shock waves and remote sensing of planetary atmospheres; long range numerical weather prediction. *Mailing Add:* Jet Propulsion Lab Calif Inst of Technol Pasadena CA 91103

CHAI, AN-TI, b Honan, China, 39. MOLECULAR SPECTROSCOPY. *Educ:* Nat Taiwan Univ, BS, 61; Kans State Univ, MS, 66, PhD(physics), 68. *Prof Exp:* Asst prof physics, Mich Technol Univ, 68-73; interim asst prof & asst res scientist, Interdisciplinary Ctr for Aeronomy & Atmospheric Sci, Univ Fla, 74-76; GEN PHYSICIST, LEWIS RES CTR, NASA, 76- *Concurrent Pos:* Adv, Nat Res Coun, NASA Lewis Res Ctr, 80-81; adj assoc prof elec eng & appl physics, Case Western Reserve Univ, 81. *Res:* Spectroscopy; atmospheric optics; solar irradiance measurements; standardization and methodology of solar cell measurements; photovoltaic device fabrication and theory; Fluid physics under low, or near zero, gravity environment. *Mailing Add:* NASA-Lewis Res Ctr 21000 Brook Park Cleveland OH 44135

CHAI, CHEN KANG, b Hopeh, China, Feb 14, 16; m 54; c 2. GENETICS. *Educ:* Army Vet Col, China, DVM, 37; Mich State Col, MS, 49, PhD(animal breeding), 51. *Prof Exp:* Asst, Mich State Col, 49-51; US Dept State fel, 51-52, res fel, 52-55, res assoc, 56, staff scientist, 57-67, SR STAFF SCIENTIST, JACKSON LAB, 67- *Concurrent Pos:* Vis fel, Mass Inst Technol, 52-53; Guggenheim fel, 62-63. *Mem:* Fel AAAS; Am Genetic Asn; Genetics Soc Am; Biomet Soc; Am Asn Phys Anthrop. *Res:* Quantitative genetics; genetic study of endocrine variation; mouse and rabbit genetics; genetic variations in Taiwan aborigines. *Mailing Add:* Jackson Lab Bar Harbor ME 04609

CHAI, HYMAN, b Lithuania, Dec 15, 20; US citizen; m 76; c 2. ALLERGY, IMMUNOLOGY. *Educ:* Univ Witwatersrand, MB, ChB, 43, Clin MD, 51; Royal Col Physicians & Surgeons, DCH, 51, FRCP(E), 74; Am Bd Allergy & Immunol, cert, 75. *Prof Exp:* Intern, Johannesburg Gen Hosp, 44-45; res pediat, Transvaal Mem Hosp, 45-46; fel allergy-immunol, 62-64, head div med, 64-75, assoc clin prof pediat, Sch Med, Univ Colo, 73-80, dir clin serv & res, Nat Asthma Ctr, Denver, 75-80, SR STAFF PHYSICIAN, DEPT PEDIAT & MED, NAT JEWISH HOSP & NAT ASTHMA CTR, 80-; ASSOC PROF PEDIAT, SCH MED, UNIV COLO, 80- *Concurrent Pos:* Assoc clin prof pediat, Sch Med, Univ Colo, 73-80, assoc prof, 80-; mem task force, Nat Inst Allergy & Infectious Dis, 77-78; co-investr, Nat Inst Heart, Lung & Blood grants, 75- & Environ Protection Agency grant, 78- *Mem:* Fel Am Acad Allergy; Am Col Allergy; fel Am Thoracic Soc; fel Am Col Chest Physicians. *Res:* Pulmonary physiology of asthma; immunology associated chest disease; allergic process, including immunology. *Mailing Add:* Nat Asthma Ctr 1999 Julian St Denver CO 80204

CHAI, WINCHUNG A, b Hunan, China, Aug 21, 39; US citizen; m 69; c 1. MATHEMATICAL ANALYSIS, APPLIED MATHEMATICS. *Educ:* Wittenberg Univ, BA, 60; NY Univ, MS, 64; Polytech Inst Brooklyn, PhD(math), 68. *Prof Exp:* Mathematician, Am Tel & Tel Co, 60-63 & Aerospace Res Ctr, Gen Precision Inc, NJ, 63-68; ASSOC PROF MATH, MONTCLAIR STATE COL, 68- *Concurrent Pos:* Sr consult, Comput Sci & Mgt Info Systs. *Mem:* Am Math Soc; Math Asn Am; Soc Indust & Appl Math; Asn Comput Mach. *Res:* Applied mathematics and computer science. *Mailing Add:* Dept of Math Montclair State Col Upper Montclair NJ 07043

CHAIKEN, JAN MICHAEL, b Philadelphia, Pa, Oct 19, 39; m 39; c 2. MATHEMATICS. *Educ:* Carnegie Inst Technol, BS, 60; Mass Inst Technol, PhD(math), 66. *Prof Exp:* From instr to asst prof math, Cornell Univ, 64-68; RESEARCHER, RAND CORP, 68- *Concurrent Pos:* Res assoc, Mass Inst Technol, 67-68; adj assoc prof, Univ Calif, Los Angeles, 72-80; assoc ed, Opers Res, 75-77; fac mem, Rand Grand Inst, 81- *Mem:* AAAS; NY Acad Sci; Opers Res Soc Am. *Res:* Allocation of urban services; models of criminal careers. *Mailing Add:* Rand Corp 1700 Main St Santa Monica CA 90406

CHAIKEN, ROBERT FRANCIS, b Brooklyn, NY, Dec 19, 28; m 53; c 3. CHEMICAL PHYSICS. *Educ:* Univ Ill, BS, 49; Brooklyn Polytech Inst, MS, 58; Univ Calif, Riverside, PhD(chem), 66. *Prof Exp:* Res chemist, Tracerlab Inc, 50-51 & US Testing Co, 51-53; res assoc, George Wash Univ, 53-57; res assoc, Aerojet-Gen Corp, 57-59, tech specialist, 59-61, tech consult, 61-68; sr chem physicist, Stanford Res Inst, 68-70; SUPVRY RES CHEMIST, PITTSBURGH MINING RES CTR, US BUR MINES, 70- *Concurrent Pos:* Lectr, Univ Pittsburgh, 72-76, Pa State Univ, 81-82. *Mem:* AAAS; Am Chem Soc; Combustion Inst (asst treas, 74-78). *Res:* High temperature and pressure reaction kinetics; theory of combustion and detonation processes; fire and explosion safety; in situ combustion of fossil fuels. *Mailing Add:* Pittsburgh Res Ctr US Bur Mines PO Box 18070 Pittsburgh PA 15236

CHAIKIN, LAWRENCE, b New York, NY, Mar 14, 14; m 43; c 2. ORAL SURGERY. *Educ:* NY Univ, BA, 34, DDS, 37. *Prof Exp:* From instr to assoc prof, 38-78, CLIN PROF ORAL SURG, COL DENT, NY UNIV, 78- *Concurrent Pos:* Assoc vis oral surgeon, Bellevue Hosp; lectr & clinician; consult oral surgeon, NShore Hosp, Manhasset, NY. *Mem:* Fel Am Col Dent; fel Am Asn Oral & Maxillofacial Surgeons. *Res:* Local anesthesia in dentistry. *Mailing Add:* 23 Bond St Great Neck NY 11021

CHAIKIN, PAUL MICHAEL, b Brooklyn, NY, Nov 14, 45; m 77; c 1. SOLID STATE PHYSICS. *Educ:* Calif Inst Technol, BS, 66; Univ Pa, PhD(physics), 71. *Prof Exp:* From asst prof to assoc prof, 72-80, PROF PHYSICS, UNIV CALIF, LOS ANGELES, 80- *Concurrent Pos:* Consult, IBM Res Labs, 75-76; A P Sloan Found fel, 77-81; assoc prof physics, D'orsay Centre, Univ Paris South, 78-79. *Mem:* Am Phys Soc. *Res:* Superconductivity; magnetism; thermoelectricity; metal-insulator transitions; organic conductors; quasi-one-dimensional compounds, thin metal films, colloids and colloidal crystals. *Mailing Add:* Dept of Physics Univ of Calif Los Angeles CA 90024

CHAIKIN, PHILIP, b Washington, DC, Dec 23, 48; m 74; c 1. BIOPHARMACEUTICS, PHARMACOKINETICS. *Educ:* Univ Md, BS, 72, PharmD, 77. *Prof Exp:* Scientist, 78-80, SR SCIENTIST, DRUG METAB DIV, ORTHO PHARMACEUT CORP, 80- *Concurrent Pos:* Fel pharmacokinetics, Univ Md, 78. *Mem:* Am Soc Hosp Pharmacists; Am Col Clin Pharmacol. *Res:* Preclinical and clinical pharmacokinetics and biopharmaceutics including mechanisms of absorption, distribution, metabolism and excretion of drug substances. *Mailing Add:* 922 Merritt Dr Somerville NJ 08876

CHAIKIN, SAUL WILLIAM, b New York, NY, Dec 25, 21; div; c 2. CHEMISTRY. *Educ:* Brooklyn Col, BA, 43; Univ Chicago, MS, 48, PhD(chem), 48. *Prof Exp:* Asst chem, Toxicity Lab, Univ Chicago, 43-45; res assoc, Univ Calif, Los Angeles, 48-49; asst prof anal chem, Univ WVa, 49-51; sr chemist, Stanford Res Inst, 51-64, mgr surface chem sect, Electronic Mat Dept, 64-68; mgr chem res dept, Memorex Corp, 68-69; dir res, Xidex Corp, 69-76; INSTR CHEM, DEANZA COL, 77- *Concurrent Pos:* Res Corp grantee, 50; consult chem. *Mem:* Am Chem Soc; Sigma Xi; Soc Photog Sci & Eng. *Res:* Development of analytical methods; organic reductions with complex metal hydrides; chelate formation; organoboron chemistry; vapor pressure determination; chromatography; microscopy; surface contamination; permeability; soldering and fluxes. *Mailing Add:* 10480 Ann Arbor Ave Cupertino CA 95014

CHAISSON, ERIC JOSEPH, b Lowell, Mass, Oct 26, 46; m 76. ASTROPHYSICS, RADIO ASTRONOMY. *Educ:* Univ Lowell, BS, 68; Harvard Univ, AM, 69, PhD(astrophys), 72. *Prof Exp:* Res assoc, Harvard-Smithsonian Observ, 72-74; asst prof, 74-79, ASSOC PROF ASTROPHYS, HARVARD UNIV, 79- *Concurrent Pos:* Nat Acad Sci fel, 72-74; Alfred P Sloan Found res fel, 76-79; chmn pub educ, Harvard-Smithsonian Ctr, 78-; Harlow Sliopley vis prof, Am Astron Soc, 79-; mem sci working group, Extraterrestrial Intel, NASA, 79- *Honors & Awards:* B J Bok Prize, Harvard Univ, 77, A C Smith Prize, 78; C R Mingins Award, Univ Lowell. *Mem:* AAAS; Am Astron Soc; Am Asn Physics Teachers; Fedn Am Scientists; Int Astron Union. *Res:* Gaseous nebulae; interstellar matter; cosmic evolution; extraterrestrial intelligence. *Mailing Add:* Harvard-Smithsonian Ctr for Astrophysicis 60 Garden St Cambridge MA 02138

CHAIT, ARNOLD, b New York, NY, Jan 20, 30; m 65; c 3. MEDICINE. *Educ:* NY Univ, BA, 51; Univ Utrecht, MD, 57; Am Bd Radiol, dipl, 63. *Prof Exp:* Intern, Kings County Hosp, NY, 58-59, resident radiol, 59-62; from instr to assoc prof, State Univ NY Downstate Med Ctr, 62-67; from asst prof to assoc prof, 67-74, PROF RADIOL, UNIV PA, 74- *Concurrent Pos:* Attend physician, Philadelphia Vet Admin Hosp, 69-76; consult, Children's Hosp Philadelphia, 74-76; chmn, Dept Radiol, Grad Hosp, 76-, chmn med staff, 81-83. *Mem:* Inter-Am Col Radiol; Soc Cardiovasc Radiol; Radiol Soc NAm; Am Roentgen Ray Soc; fel Am Col Radiol. *Res:* Cardiovascular radiology. *Mailing Add:* Dept Radiol Grad Hosp 19th & Lombard Sts Philadelphia PA 19104

CHAIT, EDWARD MARTIN, b Brooklyn, NY, May 8, 42; m 66; c 2. ANALYTICAL CHEMISTRY, MASS SPECTROMETRY. *Educ:* Cornell Univ, AB, 64; Purdue Univ, PhD(anal chem), 68. *Prof Exp:* Applns supvr, 67-74; prod mgr instruments, 74-79, RES ASSOC, E I DU PONT NEMOURS & CO, INC, 79- *Concurrent Pos:* Ed, J Chem, Biol & Environ Instrumentation; mem adv panel, Ctr Anal Chem, Nat Bur Standards. *Mem:* Am Soc Mass Spectrometry; Am Chem Soc; Am Soc Testing & Mat. *Res:* Organic mass spectrometry; molecular spectroscopy; field ionization phenomena; biomedical gas chromatography/mass spectrometry; environmental analysis; electrophoresis, immunoassay, clinical chemistry; bioanalytical chemistry; biotechnology; business and venture management. *Mailing Add:* Du Pont Photo Products Dept Exp Sta 352 Wilmington DE 19898

CHAKERIAN, GULBANK DONALD, b Parlier, Calif, Dec 21, 33; m 58; c 2. MATHEMATICS. *Educ:* Univ Calif, Berkeley, AB, 55, PhD(math), 60. *Prof Exp:* Instr math, Calif Inst Technol, 60-63; lectr, 63-64, asst prof, 64-69, PROF MATH, UNIV CALIF, DAVIS, 69- *Mem:* Am Math Soc; Math Asn Am. *Res:* Integral geometry and convex bodies. *Mailing Add:* Dept of Math Univ of Calif Davis CA 95616

CHAKKALAKAL, DENNIS ABRAHAM, b Irinjalakuda, India, Mar 16, 39; m 70. BIOPHYSICS, BIOENGINEERING OF THE MUSCULOSKELETAL SYSTEM. *Educ:* Madras Univ, BSc, 58; Marquette Univ, MS, 62; Washington Univ, PhD(physics), 68. *Prof Exp:* Assoc prof physics, Southern Univ, 69-80; MEM STAFF, VET ADMIN MED CTR, OMAHA, 80- *Concurrent Pos:* NIH/NRSA fel biophysics & bioengineering & asst prof, Rensselaer Polytech Inst, 76-80. *Mem:* Orthop Res Soc; Sigma Xi; Bioelec Repair & Growth Soc. *Res:* Many-body theory (physics); biophysical aspects of bone physiology, pathology and fracture healing; electrical stimulation of osteogenesis; bioengineering aspects of the musculoskeletal system relevant to clinical orthopaedics and rehabilitation. *Mailing Add:* Vet Admin Med Ctr 4101 Woolworth Ave Omaha NE 68105

CHAKKO, MATHEW K(ANJHIRATHINKAL), b Kunnamkulam, India, Mar 29, 34; m 65; c 1. ENGINEERING MECHANICS, COMPOSITES MATERIAL SCIENCE. *Educ:* Univ Kerala, BScEng, 55; Syracuse Univ, MME, 61, PhD(mech eng), 65. *Prof Exp:* Inspector factories, Govt Travancore-Cochin, India, 55-56; asst dist engr, Shell Oil Co India, 56-57; trainee, Hindustan Steel, Ltd, 57-58; res asst mech eng, Syracuse Univ, 58-64; res engr, 65-67, sr res engr, 67-70, res assoc, 70-76, SR RES & DEVELOP ASSOC, RES & DEVELOP CTR, B F GOODRICH CO, 76- *Mem:* Am Chem Soc. *Res:* Stress analysis; viscous heating and heat transfer in rubber products; composite material science; fatigue of composite and polymeric materials; contact problems in elasticity; contact stress fatigue of metals; metal rolling. *Mailing Add:* B F Goodrich Res & Develop Ctr 9921 Brecksville Rd Brecksville OH 44141

CHAKLADER, ASOKE CHANDRA DAS, b Bamrail, India, Sept 1, 30; m 59; c 2. CERAMICS, INORGANIC CHEMISTRY. *Educ:* Univ Calcutta, BSc, 49, Bengal Ceramic Inst, dipl ceramic technol, 51; Univ Leeds, PhD(ceramics), 57. *Prof Exp:* Sr lab asst, Nat Metall Lab, Jamshedpur, India, 51-54; Exhib 1851 sr studentship, Univ Leeds, 57-59; res assoc metall, 59-64, from asst prof to assoc prof, 64-71, PROF METALL, UNIV BC, 71- *Mem:* Inst Ceramics Engrs; Am Soc Metals; Am Ceramic Soc; Can Ceramic Soc; Brit Ceramic Soc. *Res:* Kinetics of solid state transition, especially of silica and silicate system; sintering variables; theory of hot pressing. *Mailing Add:* Dept of Metall Univ of BC Vancouver Can

CHAKO, NICHOLAS, b Hotove, Albania, Nov 11, 10; nat US; m 52; c 1. MATHEMATICS. *Educ:* France, BS, 28; Johns Hopkins Univ, PhD(physics), 34; Sorbonne, DSc, 66. *Prof Exp:* Prof math & physics & head dept, State Gym, Albania, 36-37; staff mem, Crufts Lab & tutor physics, Harvard Univ, 38-40; staff mem, Spectros Lab, Mass Inst Technol, 40-41; assoc prof physics, Kans State Univ, 46-47 & Ala Polytech Inst, 47-49; Fulbright exchange prof, State Univ Utrecht, 50-51; guest prof math & physics, Chalmers Univ Technol, Sweden, 51-52; res assoc, Inst Math Sci, NY Univ, 53-56; ASSOC PROF MATH, QUEENS COL, NY, 56- *Concurrent Pos:* Lectr, Ill Inst Technol, 40-41; consult, Balkan Affairs, Off Strategic Serv, DC, 42-45; consult & math physicist, Russell Elec Co, Ill, 42-46; Fulbright grant to Holland, 50-51; lectr, Univ Lund, 52; prof, French Atomic Energy Ctr, Saclay & Univ Paris, 66-67; vis lectr, Laval Univ, 68. *Honors & Awards:* Annual Prize, Royal Soc Eng & Chalmers Alumni Asn Sweden, 52. *Mem:* Am Phys Soc; Inst Elec & Electronics Engrs; Am Math Soc; NY Acad Sci; Acoust Soc Am. *Res:* Absorption of light by organic compounds; geometrical and electron optics; crystal vibrations and acoustics fields; diffraction; special functions; asymptotic integration. *Mailing Add:* Dept of Math Queens Col Flushing NY 11367

CHAKRABARTI, BIRESWAR, physical chemistry, physical biochemistry, see previous edition

CHAKRABARTI, CHUNI LAL, b Patuakhali, India, Mar 1, 20; m 62; c 1. ANALYTICAL CHEMISTRY, INORGANIC CHEMISTRY. *Educ:* Univ Calcutta, BSc, 41; Univ Birmingham, MSc, 60; Queen's Univ, Belfast, PhD(chem), 62, DSc(chem), 80; FRIC, 63. *Prof Exp:* Supvr chemist, Metal & Steel Factory, Govt India, 41-45; chemist-in-charge, Mines & Indust Dept, Govt Burma, 45-52, chief chemist & mgr, Mineral Resources Develop Corp, 52-59; vis asst prof & fel, La State Univ, 63-65; group leader res ctr, Noranada Mines Ltd, 65; asst prof, 65-67, assoc prof anal & inorg chem, 67-76, PROF CHEM, CARLETON UNIV, CAN, 76- *Honors & Awards:* Gerhard Herzberg Award, Spectros Soc Can, 77; Fisher Sci Award, Chem Inst Can, 81. *Mem:* Fel Chem Inst Can; Am Chem Soc; Brit Soc Anal Chem. *Res:* Atomic-absorption, atomic-fluorescence and emission spectroscopy; determination of ultratrace elements in air and water; speciation and complexation of trace metals in the aquatic environment; the effect of heavy-metals-organics interactions on the fixation and release of heavy metals (of geochemical and biochemical interest) in the aquatic environment; electroanalytical techniques for characterization and quantitation of trace metal species. *Mailing Add:* Dept of Chem Carleton Univ Colonel By Dr Ottawa ON K1S 5B6 Can

CHAKRABARTI, PARITOSH M, b Apr 1, 40; US citizen; m 68; c 2. ORGANIC CHEMISTRY, PHYSICAL CHEMISTRY. *Educ:* Univ Calcutta, India, BS, 57, MS, 59, DSc(org chem), 64. *Prof Exp:* Fel chem, Ohio State Univ, 64-66 & Univ Hull, Eng, 67-68; asst prof, Mich Technol Univ, 68-69; sr res chemist, FMC Corp, NJ, 69-72; group leader surfactants res, 72-74, res mgr surfactants, 74-77, TECH DIR ORG CHEM, GAF CORP, 77- *Mem:* Am Chem Soc; Asn Res Dirs. *Res:* Organic chemicals, particularly agricultural chemicals; acetyene derived chemicals, surfactants, other fine chemicals and specialty chemicals; analytical chemistry. *Mailing Add:* Res & Develop 1361 Alps Rd Wayne NJ 07470

CHAKRABARTI, SIBA GOPAL, b Rangpur, Bengal, July 1, 23; m 59; c 2. BIOCHEMISTRY. *Educ:* Univ Calcutta, BSc, 45; Rutgers Univ, MS, 60, PhD(biochem), 63. *Prof Exp:* Chemist, Bhartia Elec Steel Co, India, 45-47 & Burn & Co, Ltd, 47-53; assoc chemist, Sam Tour & Co, Inc, NY, 53-54; res assoc biochem, Sloan-Kettering Inst Cancer Res, 54-58; res asst, Rutgers Univ, 58-60; clin chemist, Middlesex Gen Hosp, NJ, 60-62 & St Joseph's Hosp, Hamilton, Ont, 63-65; asst prof dermat & indust health, Med Ctr, Univ Mich, Ann Arbor, 68-73; assoc prof dermat, 73-78, PROF DERMAT, COL MED, HOWARD UNIV, 79- *Concurrent Pos:* NIH res trainee dermat, Univ Mich, 65-68. *Mem:* Am Chem Soc; Soc Invest Dermat; Int Pigment Cell Soc; NY Acad Sci; AAAS. *Res:* Epidermal protein synthesis and characterization of epidermal pre-keratins; control mechanisms in epidermal differentiation; Melanogenesis: chemistry and biology of melanin pigment; metabolism of photoactive compounds; experimental photochemotherapy; chemistry and biology of pigmentation of skin and hair and epidermal differentiation and keratinization. *Mailing Add:* Dept of Dermat Howard Univ Col of Med Washington DC 20059

CHAKRABARTY, ANANDA MOHAN, b Sainthia, India, Apr 4, 38; US citizen; m 65; c 2. MICROBIOLOGY, GENETICS. *Educ:* St Xavier's Col, India, BSc, 58; Calcutta Univ, MSc, 60, PhD(biochem), 65. *Prof Exp:* Sr sci officer biochem, Calcutta Univ, 64-65; res assoc, Univ Ill, Urbana, 65-71; staff microbiologist, Gen Elec Co, 71-79; PROF MICROBIOL, UNIV ILL MED CTR, 79- *Concurrent Pos:* Adj prof, Dept Biol, State Univ NY, 76-79. *Honors & Awards:* Scientist of the Year Award, Industrial Res Mag, 75, IR-100, 75. *Mem:* Am Soc Microbiol; AAAS; Am Soc Biol Chemists; Soc Indust Microbiol; NY Acad Sci. *Res:* Evolution and application of hydrocarbon degradative plasmids in Pseudomonas; molecular cloning and genetic engineering with plasmids; genetic basis of hydrocarbon biodegradation; microbial biodegradation of environmental pollutants. *Mailing Add:* Dept of Microbiol Univ of Ill Med Ctr PO Box 6998 Chicago IL 60680

CHAKRABARTY, MANOJ R, b Bajitpur, Bangladesh, Jan 1, 33; div; c 2. PHYSICAL INORGANIC CHEMISTRY. *Educ:* Univ Calcutta, BS, 51, MS, 54; Univ Toronto, PhD(inorg chem), 62. *Prof Exp:* Instr chem, Bengal Eng Col, India, 55-56; lectr, Indian Sch Mines, 56-57; sessional instr, Univ Alta, 57-59; assoc res scientist mat chem, Ont Res Found, 62-63; from asst prof to assoc prof chem, 63-69, PROF CHEM, MARSHALL UNIV, 69- *Mem:* Am Chem Soc. *Res:* Coordination compounds; inorganic reaction kinetics; analytical chemistry. *Mailing Add:* Dept of Chem Marshall Univ Huntington WV 25701

CHAKRABARTY, RAMESWAR PRASAD, b Sylhet, Bangladesh, June 2, 35; US citizen; m 71; c 2. STATISTICS. *Educ:* Univ Gauhati, India, BS, 55, MS, 57; Tex A&M Univ, PhD(statist), 68. *Prof Exp:* Lectr statist, Univ Gauhati, 58-59; statistician, Tea Res Asn of India, 59-64; vis asst prof, Univ Ga, 67-69; statistician, Fertilizer Asn of India, 69-71; asst prof statist, Univ Ga, 71-76; ASSOC PROF COMPUT SCI, JACKSON STATE UNIV, 76- *Concurrent Pos:* Reviewer, Math Rev, 76-; NSF grant, 77. *Mem:* Int Asn Surv Statist; Am Statist Asn; Biomet Soc; Asn Comput Mach; Sigma Xi. *Res:* Ratio methods of estimation, variance estimation in surveys; jack-knife statistics; statistical consulting on designs of surveys, experiments and data analysis. *Mailing Add:* Dept of Comput Sci Jackson State Univ Jackson MS 39217

CHAKRABORTY, JYOTSNA, b Calcutta, India, June 1, 34; m 54; c 1. REPRODUCTIVE PHYSIOLOGY, CELL PHYSIOLOGY. *Educ:* City Col, Univ Calcutta, BS, 54, Sci Col, MS, 56; Inst Nuclear Physics, Calcutta, PhD(zool & biophysics), 62. *Prof Exp:* Res asst cell biol, Inst Nuclear Physics, 60-62; fel, Iowa State Univ, Ames, 62-63; lectr, Inst Nuclear Physics, 65-69; Ford Found fel, Harbor Gen, Med Ctr, Univ Calif, Los Angeles, 69-70; asst prof, 72-75, ASSOC PROF CELL PHYSIOL & REPRODUCTIVE PHYSICS, MED COL OHIO TOLEDO, 75- *Concurrent Pos:* Dir ultra structure res, Biophysics Lab, Inst Nuclear Physics, Calcutta, India, 65-69; dir, Electron Micros Lab, Dept Physiol, Med Col Ohio, 70-; prin investr grant, NIH, 76-80, Stranhan Found, 81-83; vis scholar, Cambridge Univ, Eng, 77. *Mem:* Soc Study Reproduction; AAAS; Am Soc Andrology; Electron Micros Soc India. *Res:* Light and electron microscopic studies of male and female reproductive tracts, mammary glands, spermatozoa, eggs, early embryos and prostate glands; hydridomas and monoclonal antibodies of cell surface antigens. *Mailing Add:* CS #10008 Dept Physiol Med Col Ohio Toledo OH 43699

CHAKRABORTY, RANAJIT, b Calcutta, India, Apr 17, 46; m 74. POPULATION GENETICS, HUMAN GENETICS. *Educ:* Indian Statist Inst, Calcutta, BStatist, 67, MStatist, 68, PhD(biostatist), 71. *Prof Exp:* From lectr to sr lectr statist, Indian Statist Inst, Calcutta, 71-72; vis consult genetics, Pop Genetics Lab, Univ Hawaii, 72-73; res assoc pop genetics, Health Sci Ctr, 73, asst prof, 73-78, ASSOC PROF POP GENETICS, GRAD SCH & HUMAN ECOL, SCH PUB HEALTH, UNIV TEX, HOUSTON, 78- *Concurrent Pos:* Assoc ed, South Asian Anthrop; Am Col Epidemiol fel, 81. *Mem:* Genetics Soc Am; Am Soc Human Genetics; Am Soc Phys Anthropologists; Am Soc Dermatoglyphics. *Res:* Statistical methods for genetic determination of quantitative traits; analysis of pedigree data for detection and estimation of familial aggregation of various disorders; mathematical theories of molecular evolution and population dynamics; medico-legal genetics. *Mailing Add:* Ctr for Demog & Pop Genetics 1100 Holcombe Blvd Rm 1109 Houston TX 77030

CHAKRABURITY, KALPANA X, b India. BIOCHEMISTRY. *Educ:* Univ Calculta, BSc, 61, MSc, 64, PhD(biochem), 68. *Prof Exp:* Asst prof, 73-80, ASSOC PROF BIOCHEM, MED COL WIS, 80- *Mem:* Am Soc Biol Chemists; Sigma Xi. *Res:* Enzymology, chemistry of nucleic acids protein nucleic acid interactions; structure and function of transfer RNA; regulation of ribosomal reactions. *Mailing Add:* Dept of Biochem Med Col of Wis Milwaukee WI 53226

CHAKRAVARTI, DIPTIMAN, b Sylhet, Assam, Sept 19, 28; m 55; c 2. RADIOCHEMISTRY, FOOD CHEMISTRY. *Educ:* Univ Calcutta, BSc, 48; Univ Mass, MS, 51; Wash State Univ, PhD(animal s ci), 55. *Prof Exp:* Food technologist fisheries res, Col Fisheries, Univ Wash, 57-58, from res instr to res assoc prof radiochem, Lab Radiation Biol, 58-66; mgr life sci advan mkt develop, Corning Glass Works, NY, 66-67, head life sci dept & mgr com develop, 67-69; PRES & CHIEF EXEC OFF, INNOVA CORP, 69- *Concurrent Pos:* Consult indust orgns, 56-; head anal radio chem div, Univ Wash, 61-66; dir, Oper Interface, Am Chem Soc Environ Conf, 70, chmn centennial comt, Puget Sound Sect, Am Chem Soc, 75-76; mem bd dirs, Inst Technol Corp; mem bd trustees, Pac Sci Ctr Found, Seattle; mem, Bd Regents, Wash State Univ; mem collegium, Div Natural Sci, Pac Lutheran Univ. *Mem:* Am Chem Soc; Inst Food Technol; NY Acad Sci. *Res:* Food technology; radiochemical analysis of environmental biological samples, methodology and microanalytical techniques; electrochemistry and metal process quality control; industrial ion-exchange processes; oil pollution control in industrial and marine environment; pollution control; environmental science and aquaculture; technology transfer. *Mailing Add:* Innova Corp 550 Mercer St Suite 100 Seattle WA 98109

CHAKRAVARTI, KALIDAS, b Gobindapur, India. PHYSICAL CHEMISTRY, SURFACE CHEMISTRY. *Educ:* Univ Calcutta, BS, 57, MS, 59, PhD(chmem), 64. *Prof Exp:* Res assoc Univ Calcutta, 64-65; res fel, Univ Minn, Minneapolis, 65-66; res assoc, Lehigh Univ, 67-69; SR SCIENTIST, ALLIED CORP, 69- *Mem:* Am Chem Soc; fel Am Inst Chemists. *Res:* Physical chemistry of macromolecules and biopolymers; colloid and surface chemistry; synthetic fibers and synthetic polymers; fiber surface science; adhesion and bonding of elastomers; fiber finishes. *Mailing Add:* Fibers & Plastics Tech Ctr Allied Corp PO Box 31 Petersburg VA 23803

CHAKRAVORTY, S(AILENDRA) K(UMER), b Calcutta, India, Jan 5, 22; m 56; c 3. PETROLEUM ENGINEERING. *Educ:* Univ Calcutta, BSc, 42, MSc, 44; Colo Sch Mines, PE, 47; Univ Kans, PhD(petrol geol & eng), 51. *Prof Exp:* Lectr geol, Univ Calcutta, 44-45; instr petrol eng, Univ Kans, 47-48; supvr petrol eng & geol, Dept Mineral Resources, Sask, 51-52, chief oil & gas conserv officer, 52-53; chief petrol engr, New Superior Oils Can Ltd, 54-56, prod mgr, 56-59; sr staff engr, 59-76, div petrol engr, 77-80, SUPVR FORMATION EVAL, HUDSON'S BAY OIL & GAS CO, LTD, 80- *Mem:* Can Asn Prof Engrs; Am Inst Mining, Metall & Petrol Engrs; Can Inst Mining & Metall; Can Well Logging Soc; Sigma Xi. *Mailing Add:* Hudson's Bay Oil & Gas Co Ltd 700-Second St SW Calgary AB T2P 0X5 Can

CHAKRIN, ALAN LEONARD, b New York, NY, Mar 7, 40; m 64; c 2. LABORATORY COMPUTER SYSTEMS, CLINICAL CHEMISTRY. *Educ:* Brooklyn Col, BA, 61; Univ Chicago, PhD(biochem), 69. *Prof Exp:* Res assoc biochem, Univ Chicago, 69-70; instr, 70-74, assoc path, Med Sch, Northwestern Univ, Chicago, 74-81; actg dir clin chem, Vet Admin Lakeside Hosp, Chicago, 80-81; biochemist, 70-81, CONSULT CLIN CHEM, NORTHWESTERN MEM HOSP, 81-; SUPVR QUOTATION SYSTS, CHICAGO MERCANTILE EXCHANGE, 81- *Mem:* Am Chem Soc; Am Asn Clin Chemists; Asn Comput Mach. *Res:* Applications of digital computers in clinical laboratories; laboratory statistics and quality control. *Mailing Add:* Chicago Mercantile Exchange 444 W Jackson Chicago IL 60606

CHAKRIN, LAWRENCE WILLIAM, b Brooklyn, NY, Oct 21, 38; m 64. PHARMACOLOGY. *Educ:* Long Island Univ, BSc, 62; Univ Minn, PhD(neuropharmacol), 67. *Prof Exp:* USPHS fel, Cambridge, Eng, 67-68; asst dir biol res, Smith Kline & French Labs, 68-77, res pharmacologist, 68-80, assoc dir biol res, 77-80; dir pharmacol, 80, VPRES BIOL, STERLING-WINTHROP RES INST, 80- *Mem:* Am Soc Pharmacol & Exp Therapeut; Am Soc Neurochem; Am Acad Allergy. *Res:* Respiratory pharmacology; pharmacology of immediate hypersensitivity reactions; central nervous system neuropharmacology; cholinergic mechanisms. *Mailing Add:* Sterling-Winthrop Res Inst Columbia Pike Rensselaer NY 12144

CHAKY, REBECCA CAROL, b Lexington, Ky. PLASMA PHYSICS. *Educ:* Univ Cent Fla, BS, 74; Univ Kans, MS, 76, PhD(physics), 81. *Prof Exp:* Res asst & teaching asst, Dept Physics & Astron, Univ Kans, 74-81; MEM TECH STAFF, DEFENSE & SPACE SYSTS GROUP, TRW, 81- *Mem:* Am Phys Soc; Soc Physics Students. *Res:* spacecraft-plasma interactions; computer simulation. *Mailing Add:* TRW M2/1161 One Space Park Redondo Beach CA 90278

CHALABI, A FATTAH, b Mosul, Iraq, Apr 12, 24; m 56. CIVIL ENGINEERING. *Educ:* Univ Baghdad, BSc, 46; Univ Mich, MSc, 52, PhD(civil eng), 56. *Prof Exp:* Supt bldgs, Iraqi Pub Works Dept, 46-49; designer struct eng, Ayres, Lewis, Norris & May, 50-56; asst prof civil eng, Univ Baghdad, 56-59; asst prof mech eng, 59-60, from assoc prof to prof civil eng, 60-78, G I ALDEN PROF ENG, WORCESTER POLYTECH INST, 78- *Concurrent Pos:* Consult, Tippit, Abbott, McCarthy & Straton, Iraq, 56-59; consult engr, 60-81. *Mem:* Am Soc Civil Engrs; Am Concrete Inst; Am Soc Eng Educ. *Res:* Laboratory performance of concrete masonry units made with lightweight aggregate; thermal properties of concrete; construction management and structures information systems. *Mailing Add:* Dept Civil Eng Worcester Polytech Inst Worcester MA 01609

CHALDER, GEOFFREY HAY, b Newcastle-on-Tyne, Eng, Apr 27, 30; m 54, 70; c 5. METALLURGY. *Educ:* Univ Durham, BSc, 51. *Prof Exp:* Sci officer, Culcheth Labs, UK Atomic Energy Authority, Eng, 51-55; res officer, Chalk River Nuclear Labs, Atomic Energy Can Ltd, 55-70; mgr fuels, Nuclear Labs, Combustion Eng, Inc, 70-73; sr sci adv, Halden Reactor Proj, Norway, 73-76; MGR MAT & SERVS PROGS, NUCLEAR POWER SYSTS, COMBUSTION ENG, INC, 76- *Res:* Nuclear materials research and development. *Mailing Add:* Combustion Eng Inc Windsor CT 06095

CHALEFF, DEBORAH TARDY, b Syracuse, NY. DEVELOPMENTAL BIOLOGY, GENETICS. *Educ:* William Smith Col, BS, 74; Cornell Univ, PhD(genetics), 81. *Prof Exp:* FEL, CARNEGIE INST WASHINGTON, 80- *Mem:* Genetics Soc Am. *Res:* Molecular mechanisms by which maize controlling transposable elements alter or regulate gene expression and influence developmental processes. *Mailing Add:* 1625 N Rodney St Wilmington DE 19806

CHALEFF, ROY SCOTT, b New York, NY, Oct 30, 47; m 76. GENETICS, PLANT PHYSIOLOGY. *Educ:* Amherst Col, BA, 68; Yale Univ, MPhil, 70, PhD(biol), 72. *Prof Exp:* Fel biol, Brookhaven Nat Lab, 72-74; sr sci officer appl genetics, John Innes Inst, Norwich, Eng, 74-76; asst prof plant breeding, Cornell Univ, 76-80; RES SCIENTIST, EXP STA, E I DU PONT DE NEMOURS & CO, INC, WILMINGTON, DEL, 80- *Concurrent Pos:* AID grant, 78-80. *Mem:* Genetics Soc Am. *Res:* Selection and characterization of mutants using cultured cells of higher plants especially tobacco and rice. *Mailing Add:* E I du Pont de Nemours & Co Inc Exp Sta Wilmington DE 19899

CHALFANT, FOREST EARLE, b Huntington, Ind, Oct 4, 34; m 55; c 3. INDUSTRIAL ENGINEERING. *Educ:* Gen Motors Inst, BA, 57. *Prof Exp:* Sr design engr, 63-64, sr develop engr, 64-69, asst engr in charge, 69-75, eng group mgr, 75, engr in charge, Comput Systs Eng, 75-80, engr in charge, Prod Test Lab, 80-81, SR CONSULT ENGR, QUALITY CONTROL ACTIVITY, FISHER BODY DIV, GEN MOTORS, 82- *Res:* Computer aided design systems development and management. *Mailing Add:* 6168 Sandshores Dr Troy MI 48098

CHALFANT, RICHARD BRUCE, b Akron, Ohio, Aug 15, 29; m 53; c 3. ENTOMOLOGY. *Educ:* Univ Akron, BS, 54; Univ Wis, MS, 56, PhD(entom), 59. *Prof Exp:* Asst prof entom, Sch Agr, NC State Univ, 59-66; assoc prof, 66-80, PROF ENTOM, GA COASTAL PLAIN EXP STA, UNIV GA, 80- *Concurrent Pos:* Int agr, Africa. *Mem:* Entom Soc Am. *Res:* Biology, control and management of insects affecting vegetable crops; host-plant resistance; integrated pest management. *Mailing Add:* Ga Coastal Plain Exp Sta Univ of Ga Tifton GA 31794

CHALGREN, STEVE DWAYNE, b Ft Dodge, Iowa, Jan 3, 40; m 62; c 2. MICROBIOLOGY, VIROLOGY. *Educ:* Univ Iowa, BA, 61; Univ Mo, MS, 65, PhD(microbiol, virol), 68. *Prof Exp:* ASSOC PROF BIOL, RADFORD COL, 68- *Concurrent Pos:* Microbiol consult, Labs, Radford Community Hosp, Va, 68- *Mem:* Am Soc Microbiol. *Res:* Diagnostic microbiology. *Mailing Add:* Dept of Biol Radford Col Box 597 Radford VA 24142

CHALKLEY, DONALD THOMAS, b Lake Charles, La, Feb 8, 20; m 42, 66; c 6. EMBRYOLOGY, SCIENCE POLICY. *Educ:* Oberlin Col, BA, 42; Amherst Col, MA, 47; Princeton Univ, PhD(zool, embryol), 50. *Prof Exp:* Mem staff, Dept Biol, Princeton Univ, 50; asst prof, Univ Notre Dame, 50-56; prog analyst, Nat Cancer Inst, USPHS, 56-59, exec secy, Path Study Sect, Div Res Grants, 59-66, Reproductive Biol Study Sect, 66-67, spec asst to dir, 67-72, chief, Inst Rels Br, 72-74, dir, Off Protection Res Risks, NIH, 74-79; RETIRED. *Concurrent Pos:* From asst referral officer to assoc referral officer, Div Res Grants, USPHS, 62-67; asst to vchancellor, Univ Miss Med Ctr, 65-66. *Res:* Research and training grant administration; policy development and implementation; legal and ethical aspects of research. *Mailing Add:* 9242 E Parkhill Dr Bethesda MD 20014

CHALKLEY, G ROGER, b Sleaford, Eng, June 28, 39; m 62; c 3. BIOCHEMISTRY. *Educ:* Oxford Univ, BA, 61, MA & DPhil(chem), 64. *Prof Exp:* Res fel biol, Calif Inst Technol, 64-67; from asst prof to assoc prof biochem, 67-73, PROF BIOCHEM, ENDOCRINOL & GENETICS, UNIV IOWA, 73- *Res:* Structure and function of chromosomal nucleoproteins; mode of action of steroid hormones; interaction of carcinogens with nuclear material. *Mailing Add:* Dept of Biochem Univ of Iowa Iowa City IA 52242

CHALKLEY, ROGER, b Cincinnati, Ohio, June 21, 31. MATHEMATICS, ALGEBRA. *Educ:* Univ Cincinnati, ChE, 54; AM, 56, PhD(math), 58. *Prof Exp:* Instr math, Univ Cincinnati, 57-58; mathematician, Oak Ridge Nat Lab, 58-59; asst prof math, Knox Col, Ill, 60-62; from asst prof to assoc prof, 62-79, PROF MATH, UNIV CINCINNATI, 80- *Mem:* Am Math Soc; Math Asn Am. *Res:* Algebraic differential equations. *Mailing Add:* Dept Math Univ Cincinnati Cincinnati OH 45221

CHALLICE, CYRIL EUGENE, b London, Eng, Jan 17, 26; m 51. PHYSICS, BIOPHYSICS. *Educ:* Univ London, BSc, 46, PhD(physics), 49, DSc(biophys), 75; Imp Col, Univ London, ARCS, 46, DIC, 49; Univ Alta, PEng, 74. *Prof Exp:* Biophysicist, Nat Inst Med Res, Eng, 49-52 & Wright-Fleming Inst Microbiol, 52-54; biophysicist & lectr physics, St Mary's Hosp Med Sch, London, 54-57; from asst prof to assoc prof physics, 57-63, head dept, 63-71, vdean, Fac Arts & Sci, 73-76, PROF PHYSICS, UNIV CALGARY, 63- *Concurrent Pos:* NIH fel, 56; NY State Dept Health fel, 58-59; chmn, Nat Comt Biophys, Can, 75-81. *Mem:* Fel AAAS; Biophys Soc; Electron Micros Soc Am; NY Acad Sci; fel Brit Inst Physics. *Res:* Structure of biological systems using light and electron microscopy, and electrophysiological methods; structure and function of the heart. *Mailing Add:* 2916 14th Ave NW Calgary AB T2N 1N3 Can

CHALLIFOUR, JOHN LEE, b Bristol, Eng, June 13, 39; m 67; c 3. MATHEMATICAL PHYSICS. *Educ:* Univ Calif, Berkeley, BA, 60; Cambridge Univ, PhD(theoret physics), 63. *Prof Exp:* Instr math, Princeton Univ, 63-65, lectr, 65-66; asst prof physics, Brandeis Univ, 66-68; assoc prof, 68-78, PROF MATH & PHYSICS, IND UNIV, BLOOMINGTON, 78- *Concurrent Pos:* Vis prof, Univ Gottingen, 70-71, Univ Bielefeld, 75-76 & Univ BC, 80-81. *Mem:* Am Math Soc; Am Phys Soc. *Res:* Axiomatic and constructive quantum field theory; theory of distributions; partial differential operators. *Mailing Add:* Dept of Phys Ind Univ Bloomington IN 47401

CHALLINOR, DAVID, b New York, NY, July 11, 20; m 52; c 4. FOREST ECOLOGY. *Educ:* Harvard Univ, BA, 43; Yale Univ, MF, 59, PhD(forest ecol), 66. *Prof Exp:* Forestry asst, Conn Agr Exp Sta, 59-60; dep dir, Peabody Mus Natural Hist, Yale Univ, 60-66; spec asst trop biol, Mus Nat Hist, Smithsonian Inst, 66-67, dep dir, 67-69, dir off int activ, 69-71, ASST SECY SCI, SMITHSONIAN INST, 71- *Mem:* Soc Am Foresters; Ecol Soc Am; Wildlife Soc; fel AAAS. *Res:* Tree-soil interactions in temperate and tropical forest environments. *Mailing Add:* Asst Secy Sci Smithsonian Inst Washington DC 20560

CHALLONER, DAVID REYNOLDS, b Appleton, Wis, Jan 31, 35; m 58; c 3. INTERNAL MEDICINE, ENDOCRINOLOGY. *Educ:* Lawrence Col, BS, 56; Harvard Univ, MD, 61. *Prof Exp:* Intern, Columbia-Presby Hosp, 61-62, asst resident, 62-63; res assoc, Lab Metab, Nat Heart Inst, 63-65; chief resident, King County Hosp, Univ Wash, 65-66, USPHS spec fel endocrinol, 66-67; from asst prof to prof med & biochem & asst chmn dept med, Sch Med, Ind Univ, Indianapolis, 67-75; PROF INTERNAL MED & DEAN, ST LOUIS UNIV SCH MED, 75- *Mem:* Inst Med-Nat Acad Sci; Endocrine Soc; Am Physiol Soc; Am Diabetes Asn; Am Fedn Clin Res (pres). *Res:* Control mechanisms in intermediary and oxidative metabolism. *Mailing Add:* St Louis Univ Sch of Med 1402 S Grand Blvd St Louis MO 63104

CHALMERS, BRUCE, b London, Eng, Oct 15, 07; nat US; m 38; c 5. APPLIED PHYSICS. *Educ:* Univ London, BSc, 29, PhD, 32, DSc, 63. *Hon Degrees:* AM, Harvard Univ, 53. *Prof Exp:* Lectr physics & math, Sir John Cass Inst, London, 32-38; physicist, Tin Res Inst, 38-41; sr sci officer, Brit Ministry of Supply, 41-44; head metall div, Royal Aircraft Estab, Farnborough, 44-46; Atomic Energy Res Estab, Harwell, 46-48; prof phys metall, Univ Toronto, 48-53; McKay prof metall, 53-78, EMER PROF METALL, HARVARD UNIV, 78- *Concurrent Pos:* Marberg lectr, 60; Australian Inst Metals lectr, 63; master, John Winthrop House, Harvard Univ, 64-74. *Honors & Awards:* Albert Sauveur Award, Am Soc Metals, 61; Clamer Medal, Franklin Inst, 64. *Mem:* Nat Acad Sci; fel Am Acad Arts & Sci; hon mem French Metall Soc, Indian Inst Metals & Japan Inst Metals. *Res:* Processes of solidification; plastic deformation; structure of grain boundaries; fracture of metals and other substances. *Mailing Add:* Div Applied Sci Harvard Univ Cambridge MA 02138

CHALMERS, JOHN HARVEY, JR, b St Paul, Minn, Mar 5, 40. BIOCHEMICAL GENETICS, MUSICAL ACOUSTICS. *Educ:* Stanford Univ, AB, 62; Univ Calif, San Diego, PhD(biol), 68. *Prof Exp:* NIH-USPHS fel genetics, Univ Wash, 68-71; NIH-USPHS trainee, Univ Calif, Berkeley, 71-73; res fel appl microbiol, Merck Sharp & Dohme Res Labs, 73-75; asst prof biochem, 76-80, ASST PROF PATH, BAYLOR COL MED, TEX MED CTR, 80- *Concurrent Pos:* Ed-publ, Xenharmonikon, 73-79; scolar-in-residence, Ossubau Island Proj, 79 & Fonduzione Rockefeller Cult Ctr, Bellugio, Italy, 80. *Mem:* Sigma Xi; AAAS; Genetics Soc Am; Am Soc Microbiol. *Res:* Biochemical genetics; industrial microbiology; fungal genetics; musical acoustics and experimental music; molecular virology. *Mailing Add:* Dept Path Baylor Col Med Tex Med Ctr Houston TX 77030

CHALMERS, JOSEPH STEPHEN, b Detroit, Mich, Feb 26, 38; m 62; c 3. THEORETICAL PHYSICS. *Educ:* Wayne State Univ, BS, 60, MA, 62, PhD(physics), 67. *Prof Exp:* Assoc prof, 67-80, PROF PHYSICS, UNIV LOUISVILLE, 80- *Mem:* Am Phys Soc. *Res:* Theory of scattering of elementa ry particles by optical potentials; paramagnetic resonance of free radicals. *Mailing Add:* Dept of Physics Univ of Louisville Louisville KY 40208

CHALMERS, ROBERT ANTON, b Wildwood, NJ, Nov 4, 30; m 56; c 2. NUCLEAR PHYSICS. *Educ:* Princeton Univ, AB, 52; Northwestern Univ, PhD(physics), 63. *Prof Exp:* STAFF SCIENTIST, LOCKHEED MISSILES & SPACE CO, INC, 63- *Mem:* Am Phys Soc. *Res:* Low energy nuclear physics research with electrostatic accelerator and development of computer-oriented laboratory instrumentation. *Mailing Add:* 450 Adobe Pl Palo Alto CA 94304

CHALMERS, ROBERT KENNY, pharmacy, pharmacology, see previous edition

CHALMERS, THOMAS CLARK, b Forest Hills, NY, Dec 8, 17; m 42; c 4. INTERNAL MEDICINE, GASTROENTEROLOGY. *Educ:* Columbia Col, MD, 43; Am Bd Internal Med, dipl, 50. *Prof Exp:* Intern med, Presby Hosp, New York, 43-44; res fel, Malaria Res Unit, Goldwater Mem Hosp, NY Univ, 44-45; resident, 2nd & 4th Med Serv, Boston City Hosp, 45-47, out-patient physician, 47-48; dir hepatitis study, Comn Liver Dis, Armed Forces Epidemiol Bd, 51-53; chief med serv, Lemuel Shattuck Hosp, Boston, 55-68; asst chief med dir res & educ, Vet Admin, DC, 68-70; prof med, Sch Med, George Washington Univ, 70-73; PRES, MT SINAI MED CTR, PROF MED, PRES & DEAN, MT SINAI SCH MED, 73- *Concurrent Pos:* Asst, Harvard Med Sch, 47-49, from instr to asst clin prof, 49-61, lectr, 61-; pvt pract internal med, Cambridge, Mass, 47-53; asst physician, Thorndike Mem Lab, Boston City Hosp, 47-53, assoc vis physician, 2nd & 4th Med Serv, 55-68; jr physician, Mt Auburn Hosp, Cambridge, 47-53, assoc vis physician, 55-68; lectr, Sch Med, Tufts Univ, 55-61, prof, 61-68; consult, Faulkner Hosp, Jamaica Plain, Mass, 55-68; assoc staff, New Eng Hosp Ctr, Boston, 55-68; mem training comt, Nat Heart Inst, 61-65, mem spec rev panel, Coronary Drug Proj, 66-69, mem diet-heart rev panel, 68, mem policy bd, Urokinase-Streptokinase Pulmonary Embolism Trial, 68-72; mem cancer chemother collab prog rev comt, Nat Cancer Inst, 65-66; mem comt epidemiol & vet follow-up studies, Nat Acad Sci-Nat Res Coun, 65-69, 72-, mem ad hoc comt hepatitis-associated antigen tests, 70-71; mem subcomt on liver, Adv Comt Gen Med, Army Surg Gen Adv Comt, 65-72; mem sci adv comt, Pharmaceut Mfrs Asn Found, 66-68, mem adv comt to fac develop awards in clin pharmacol, 66-70; mem coop studies eval comt, Vet Admin, 70-74; chmn nat coop Crohn's dis study adv bd, Nat Inst Arthritis, Metab & Digestive Dis, 71-78; mem hyper-immune gamma globulin trials policy bd, Nat Heart & Lung Inst, 72-75; chmn rev panel new drug regulation, Food & Drug Admin, 75-76; mem, Bd Regents, Nat Libr Med, 78-79. *Mem:* Inst of Med of Nat Acad Sci; Am Asn Study Liver Dis (pres, 59); Am Clin & Climat Asn; Am Col Physicians; Am Gastroenterol Asn (pres, 69). *Res:* Clinical trials; clinical epidemiology. *Mailing Add:* Mt Sinai Sch of Med 1 Gustave L Levy Pl New York NY 10029

CHALOUD, J(OHN) HOYT, b Omaha, Nebr, Feb 16, 20; m 53; c 2. CHEMICAL ENGINEERING. *Educ:* Iowa State Col, BS(chem eng). *Prof Exp:* Engr process develop, 46-53, sect head tech serv, 53-54, sect head prod develop, 54-58, dept head tech serv, 58-59, assoc dir soap prod develop, 59-69, dir, Explor Develop Div, 69-71, dir, Soap Technol Div, 71-73, dir corp res & develop, prof & regulatory serv, 73-74, dir food prod develop, 74-78, mgr int corp res & develop, 78-81, CONSULT, PROCTER & GAMBLE, 81- *Concurrent Pos:* Mem weights & measures adv comt, Nat Bur Standards, 62-; mem tech comt, Nutrition Found, 74-78; trustee, Food Safety Coun, 76-78. *Mem:* AAAS; Am Chem Soc; Am Inst Chem Engrs; Am Oil Chem Soc. *Res:* Synthetic detergents; glycerine; fatty acids and alcohols. *Mailing Add:* 204 Poage Farm Rd Cincinnati OH 45215

CHALQUEST, RICHARD ROSS, b Denver, Colo, Nov 4, 29; m 54; c 7. VETERINARY MEDICINE, MICROBIOLOGY. *Educ:* Wash State Univ, BS, 51, DVM, 57; Cornell Univ, MS, 59, PhD(path), 60. *Prof Exp:* Asst prof vet microbiol, Wash State Univ, 60-62; res vet, Pfizer Inc, 62-63, mgr agr res & develop, 63-65, dir, 65-72; PROF AGR & DIR DIV AGR, ARIZ STATE UNIV, 72- *Concurrent Pos:* Mem gov bd, Agr Res Inst, Nat Res Coun, Nat Acad Sci, 67-70. *Mem:* Am Asn Avian Path; Am Vet Med Asn; Poultry Sci Asn; Am Asn Vet Parasitol. *Res:* Agricultural research. *Mailing Add:* Div of Agr Ariz State Univ Tempe AZ 85281

CHALUPA, LEO M, b Ger, Mar 28, 45; US citizen; m 66. NEUROSCIENCES, VISION. *Educ:* Queens Col, BA, 66; City Univ New York, PhD(neuropsychol), 70. *Prof Exp:* Res physiologist psychol, Brain Res Inst, Univ Calif, Los Angeles, 70-75; asst prof, 75-78, ASSOC PROF PSYCHOL, UNIV CALIF, DAVIS, 78- *Concurrent Pos:* Fel, Brain Res Inst, Univ Calif, Los Angeles, 70-72; Guggenheim fel, 78. *Honors & Awards:* US-USSR Scientist Exchange Award, Nat Acad Sci, 74. *Mem:* AAAS; Soc Neurosci; Am Psychol Asn. *Res:* Visual neurophysiology and neuropsychology; plasticity of the visual system. *Mailing Add:* Dept of Psychol Univ of Calif Davis CA 95616

CHALUPA, WILLIAM VICTOR, b New York, NY, Dec 11, 37; m 60; c 2. ANIMAL NUTRITION. *Educ:* Rutgers Univ, BS, 58, MS, 59, PhD(nutrit), 62. *Prof Exp:* Asst dairy sci, Rutgers Univ, 58-59, asst instr, 59-62, res fel nutrit, 62-63; from asst prof to assoc prof, Clemson Univ, 63-71; mgr rumen metabolic res, Smith Kline Animal Health Prod Div, 71-76; assoc prof, 76-80, PROF NUTRIT, SCH VET MED, UNIV PA, 80- *Concurrent Pos:* Vis scientist, USDA, Md, 69-70; adj assoc prof, Sch Vet Med, Univ Pa, 75- *Honors & Awards:* Am Feed Mfrs Award, 81. *Mem:* AAAS; Am Soc Animal Sci; Am Dairy Sci Asn; Am Inst Nutrit. *Res:* Energy and protein utilization of foodstuffs by ruminant and monogastric animals; biochemistry of rumen metabolism. *Mailing Add:* Sch Vet Med Univ Pa New Bolton Ctr Kennett Square PA 19348

CHALUPNIK, JAMES DVORAK, b Bay City, Tex, Nov 10, 30; m 57; c 1. MECHANICS. *Educ:* Tex Tech Col, BSME, 53; Univ Tex, MSEM, 60, PhD(eng mech), 64. *Prof Exp:* Instr mech eng, Univ Tex, 57-58, res asst, 61-64; supvr, Lockheed Missile & Space Co, 58-59, scientist, 59-61; from asst prof to assoc prof mech eng, 64-76, PROF MECH ENG, UNIV WASH, 76- *Mem:* AAAS; Am Soc Mech Engrs; Soc Exp Stress Anal; Am Soc Eng Educ; Acoust Soc Am. *Res:* Acoustics and noise studies; dynamic behavior of materials and structures; mechanical vibrations. *Mailing Add:* Dept of Mech Eng NYS FU-10 Univ of Wash Seattle WA 98195

CHAMBERLAIN, A(DRIAN) R(AMOND), b Mich, Nov 11, 29; m 54, 79; c 2. ENGINEERING. *Educ:* Mich State Univ, BS, 51; Wash State Univ, MS, 52; Colo State Univ, PhD, 55. *Hon Degrees:* DEng, Mich State Univ, 71; LHD, Univ Denver, 72. *Prof Exp:* Fulbright grantee, Univ Grenoble, France, 55-56; chief eng sect, Colo State Univ, 57-59, chief eng res & actg dean col eng, 59-61, vpres, 60-66, exec vpres & treas, 66-69, pres, 69-80; PRES, MITCHELL & CO, 81-; EXEC ENGR, SIMONS, LI & ASSOCS, INC, 81- *Concurrent Pos:* Mem bd trustees, Colo State Univ Res Found, 58-63 & 69-73, pres, 59-60; mem bd dirs, Univ Nat Bank, 62-74, chmn bd, 64-69; mem adv comt environ sci, NSF, 67-69, chmn, 67, mem & chmn comn weather modification, 64-66; mem adv comt on air qual criteria, Nat Air Pollution Control Admin, US Pub Health Serv, 67-70; trustee, Univ Corp Atmos Res, 67-81, chmn bd trustees, 77-79; trustee, Nat Cystic Fibrosis Res Fedn, 71-; mem bd dir, Nat Ctr Higher Educ Mgt Systs, 74-77, chmn bd, 78-79; pres, State Bd Agr Univs Systs, 78-80; hon prof, El Inst Politecnico, Nacional de Mexico; chmn, Nat Asn Land-Grant Cols & Univs, 80 & mem exec comn, 76-81; mem, NSF Dirs Adv Coun, 78-80; pres, Black Mountain Ranch, Inc, 68-; mem bd dirs, Mitchell & Co, 68-74 & 79-, Simons, Li & Assocs, Inc, 80- & exec comt, Solaron Corp, 81- *Honors & Awards:* Order of Aztec Eagle, Repub Mexico. *Mem:* AAAS; Am Soc Civil Engrs; Sigma Xi. *Res:* Fluid mechanics, hydrology & water resources; financial systems. *Mailing Add:* 1319 Stonehenge Dr Ft Collins CO 80525

CHAMBERLAIN, CHARLES CALVIN, b Evart, Mich, Jan 23, 20; m 46; c 2. ANIMAL NUTRITION. *Educ:* Mich State Univ, BS, 41, MS, 48; Iowa State Univ, PhD, 59. *Prof Exp:* From instr to assoc prof animal nutrit, 49-71 & from asst animal husbandman to assoc animal husbandman, 52-71, PROF ANIMAL NUTRIT, UNIV TENN, 71- *Mem:* Am Soc Animal Sci. *Res:* Cattle and swine. *Mailing Add:* Dept of Animal Sci Univ of Tenn Knoxville TN 37916

CHAMBERLAIN, CHARLES CRAIG, b Milford, Utah, June 1, 33; m 59; c 4. MEDICAL PHYSICS, RADIOBIOLOGY. *Educ:* Univ Calif, Los Angeles, BA, 59, MA, 61, PhD(med physics), 67. *Prof Exp:* Instr, 67-70, ASST PROF RADIOL, STATE UNIV NY UPSTATE MED CTR, 70-, ASSOC PROF, COL HEALTH RELATED PROFESSIONS, 81- *Mem:* Health Physics Soc; Am Asn Physicists in Med; Am Inst Ultrasound Med. *Res:* Effects of heat and radiation on mammalian cells in culture; physics of diagnostic radiology. *Mailing Add:* Dept Radiol State Univ NY Upstate Med Ctr Syracuse NY 13210

CHAMBERLAIN, CRAIG STANLEY, b Sacramento, Calif, Jan 14, 47; m 74. INORGANIC CHEMISTRY, MATERIALS SCIENCE. *Educ:* Calif State Univ, Sacramento, BS, 69, MS, 73; Univ Ill, Urbana, PhD(chem), 78. *Prof Exp:* Forensic chemist, US Army Criminal Invest Lab, 69-71; SR CHEMIST MAT SCI, 3M CO, 78- *Mem:* Am Chem Soc; Sigma Xi; Audobon Soc. *Mailing Add:* 201-2E 3M Ctr St Paul MN 55144

CHAMBERLAIN, DAVID LEROY, JR, b Kansas City, Kans, Sept 2, 17; m 45; c 3. ORGANIC CHEMISTRY, CHEMICAL ENGINEERING. *Educ:* Univ Kans, BS, 44, MS, 50; Univ Southern Calif, PhD(org chem), 53. *Prof Exp:* Lab asst, Univ Kans, 43-44; chem engr & tech asst to opers, Rayon Mfg, E I du Pont de Nemours & Co, 44-46; lab asst, Univ Kans, 46-47; res org chemist, Callery Chem Co, 53-56; sr org chemist, Stanford Res Inst, 56-72; consult, 72-73; RES ASSOC, NAT FOREST PROD ASN-NAT BUR OF STAND, 73- *Mem:* Am Chem Soc; fel Am Inst Chem; Combustion Inst; Sigma Xi. *Res:* Thermal degradation of organic materials; chemistry of organic-inorganic interfaces; chemistry of fire retardant materials; fire test methods for materials. *Mailing Add:* 12209 Pawnee Dr Gaithersburg MD 20760

CHAMBERLAIN, DILWORTH WOOLEY, b Milford, Utah, June 1, 33; m 58; c 6. ICHTHYOLOGY. *Educ:* Calif State Univ, Los Angeles, BS, 65; Univ Southern Calif, PhD(biol), 80. *Prof Exp:* Res asst, Sch Med, Univ Southern Calif, 59-72, res assoc, 72-74; sci advisor, 74-80, SR SCI ADVISOR ENVIRON PROTECTION, ATLANTIC RICHFIELD CO, 80- *Concurrent Pos:* Chmn, Task Force Oil Effects Salmon, Am Petrol Inst, 80- & Task Force Natural Perturbations, 80- *Mem:* AAAS; Sigma Xi; Soc Petrol Indust Biologists. *Mailing Add:* Atlantic Richfield Co 515 S Flower St Los Angeles CA 90071

CHAMBERLAIN, DONALD F(RANK), b Wayzata, Minn, July 14, 14; m 40; c 5. CHEMICAL ENGINEERING. *Educ:* Univ Minn, BChE, 36, PhD(chem eng), 40. *Prof Exp:* Asst, Univ Minn, 36-40; res engr, Nat Aniline Div Allied Chem & Dye Corp, 40-46; from asst prof to prof chem eng, Wash Univ, 46-56, vchmn dept, 52-55; adminr, US Govt (classified), 55-76, asst dir, Off Sci Intel, Cent Intel Agency, 63-65, dir, 65-73, inspector gen, 73-76; RETIRED. *Concurrent Pos:* Lectr eng sci & mgt war training, Cornell Univ, 43-45. *Mem:* Am Inst Chem Engrs; Am Chem Soc. *Res:* Foreign science and technology. *Mailing Add:* 500 S Ramona Ave Indialantic FL 32903

CHAMBERLAIN, DONALD WILLIAM, b Green Bay, Wis, Nov 28, 05; m 45; c 3. PLANT PATHOLOGY. *Educ:* St Norbert Col, BA, 29; Univ Wis, MA, 32, PhD(plant path), 43. *Prof Exp:* Instr hort, Univ Wis, 43-45; asst agron, Agr Exp Sta, Univ Ky, 45-46; assoc pathologist, 46-56, PATHOLOGIST, CROPS RES DIV, AGR RES SERV, USDA, 56-; PROF PLANT PATH, UNIV ILL, URBANA-CHAMPAIGN, 75- *Concurrent Pos:* From asst prof to assoc prof plant path, Univ Ill, Urbana-Champaign, 56-75. *Mem:* AAAS; Am Phytopath Soc. *Res:* Bacterial and fungus diseases of soybean; disease resistance; occurrance of races of Pseudomonas glycinea in Illinois; resistance to Phytophthora rot in soybean as expressed in roots or stems. *Mailing Add:* 2022 Boudreau Dr Urbana IL 61801

CHAMBERLAIN, ERLING WILLIAM, b Oslo, Norway, Jan 5, 34; US citizen; m 57. MATHEMATICS. *Educ:* Columbia Univ, AB, 55, MA, 56, PhD(math), 61. *Prof Exp:* From asst prof to assoc prof, 62-70, PROF MATH, UNIV VT, 70- *Concurrent Pos:* NSF res grants, 63-70. *Mem:* Am Math Soc. *Res:* Asymptotic theory of ordinary differential equations in the complex domain, especially with regard to factorization of differential operators. *Mailing Add:* Dept of Math Univ of Vt Burlington VT 05401

CHAMBERLAIN, JACK G, b Detroit, Mich, May 15, 33; m 55; c 4. DEVELOPMENTAL ANATOMY. *Educ:* Occidental Col, BA, 55; San Diego State Col, MA, 57; Univ Calif, Berkeley, PhD(anat), 62. *Prof Exp:* Instr anat, Univ Calif, Berkeley, 62-63; instr, Univ Mich Sch Med, 63-64; asst prof, Univ Calif, San Francisco, 64-72; assoc prof anat, 72-80, PROF ANAT, SCH DENT, UNIV OF PAC, 80-, CHMN DEPT, 72- *Concurrent Pos:* Fac grant, Univ Calif, 62-64; Rackham fac & local cancer res grants, Univ Mich, 63-64, fac grant, 64-65, USPHS grant, 65-70. *Mem:* Soc Develop Biol; Am Asn Anat. *Res:* Normal and abnormal developmental biology, especially pathogenesis of central nervous system abnormalities induced by antivitamins; scanning electron microscopy. *Mailing Add:* Dept of Anat Univ of the Pac San Francisco CA 94115

CHAMBERLAIN, JAMES LUTHER, b West Chester, Pa, May 16, 25; m 51; c 3. ZOOLOGY. *Educ:* Cornell Univ, BS, 48; Univ Mass, MS, 51; Univ Tenn, PhD(zool), 57. *Prof Exp:* Asst proj leader, WVa Conserv Comn, 48-49; field agt, US Fish & Wildlife Serv, Mass, 51; instr zool, State Teachers Col, NY, 52-53; res assoc, La State Univ, 55-57; assoc prof biol, Randolph-Macon Woman's Col, 57-69; chmn div sci & math, 69-74, PROF BIOL, UTICA COL, 74- *Concurrent Pos:* Res grant, US Forest Serv. *Mem:* Ecol Soc Am; Am Soc Mammal; Am Soc Ichthyologists & Herpetologists; Am Ornithologists Union; Wildlife Soc. *Res:* Marsh ecology; vertebrate ecology. *Mailing Add:* Div of Sci & Math Utica Col Utica NY 13502

CHAMBERLAIN, JOHN, b Detroit, Mich, Jan 15, 23; m 50; c 3. FLUIDS. *Educ:* Mass Inst Technol, SB, 44. *Prof Exp:* Res engr, Res Lab, 46-52, asst proj engr, 52-55, proj engr, 55-68, DEVELOP ENGR, PRATT & WHITNEY AIRCRAFT DIV, UNITED AIRCRAFT CORP, 68- *Honors & Awards:* George Mead gold medal eng achievement, United Aircraft Corp, 65. *Mem:* Am Inst Aeronaut & Astronaut. *Res:* Combustion and cooling systems for airbreathing engines and rockets. *Mailing Add:* 8141 S Elizabeth Ave Lake Park FL 33410

CHAMBERLAIN, JOHN PAUL, b Chicago, Ill, Nov 4, 43; m 67; c 1. DEVELOPMENTAL BIOLOGY. *Educ:* Princeton Univ, AB, 65; Univ Miami, PhD(biol), 70. *Prof Exp:* Fel biochem & microbiol, Univ Wash, 70-73; ASST PROF BIOL, UNIV MICH, ANN ARBOR, 73- *Mem:* Soc Develop Biol. *Res:* Gene regulation and genetic control of embryonic development. *Mailing Add:* Div of Biol Sci Univ of Mich Ann Arbor MI 48109

CHAMBERLAIN, JOSEPH MILES, b Peoria, Ill, July 26, 23; m 45; c 3. ASTRONOMY. *Educ:* US Merchant Marine Acad, BS, 44; Bradley Univ, BA, 47; Columbia Univ, AM, 50, EdD, 62. *Prof Exp:* Instr nautical sci, US Merchant Marine Acad, 47-50, asst prof astron & meteorol, 50-52; asst astronomer, Am Mus-Hayden Planetarium, NY, 52-53, chmn & astronomer, 53-64; asst dir, Am Mus Natural Hist, 64-68; prof astron, Northwestern Univ, 68-77; DIR, ADLER PLANETARIUM, 68-, PRES, 76- *Concurrent Pos:* Instr, Naval Reserve Officer Sch, NY, 54-55; consult, Norman Porter & Assocs, NY, 54-; lectr, Nat Artists Corp, NY, 55-57; instr, Hunter Col, 64-68; prof lectr, Univ Chicago, 68-71. *Mem:* Int Planetarium Soc; Am Astron Soc; Am Asn Mus (vpres, 71-74, pres, 74-75); Am Polar Soc; Int Planetarium Director's Conf (vchmn, 72-78, chmn, 78-). *Res:* Determination of geodetic coordinates by astronomic methods; planetarium education and administration. *Mailing Add:* Adler Planetarium 1300 S Lake Shore Dr Chicago IL 60605

CHAMBERLAIN, JOSEPH WYAN, b Boonville, Mo, Aug 24, 28; m 49; c 3. AERONOMY, ASTRONOMY. *Educ:* Univ Mo, AB, 48, AM, 49; Univ Mich, MS, 51, PhD(astron), 52. *Prof Exp:* Proj scientist aurora & airglow, US Air Force Cambridge Res Ctr, 51-53; res assoc Yerkes Observ, Univ Chicago, 53-55, from asst prof to prof, 55-62; assoc dir planetary sci div, Kitt Peak Nat Observ, 62-70, astronr, 70-71; dir, Lunar Sci Inst, 71-73; PROF SPACE PHYSICS & ASTRON, RICE UNIV, 73- *Concurrent Pos:* Mem exec comt, Assembly Math Phys Sci, Nat Res Coun-Nat Acad Sci, 74-78; ed, Rev Geophys & Space Physics, 74-80; sect chmn, Nat Acad Sci. *Mem:* Nat Acad Sci; fel AAAS; Am Astron Soc; Am Phys Soc; fel Am Geophys Union. *Res:* Planetary atmospheres; aurora and airglow; aeronomy of the stratosphere; atmospheric pollution ; climate. *Mailing Add:* Dept Space Physics & Astron Rice Univ Houston TX 77001

CHAMBERLAIN, MALCOLM, b Binghamton, NY, June 7, 25; m 50; c 2. ORGANIC CHEMISTRY. *Educ:* Bowdoin Col, BS, 47; Mass Inst Technol, PhD(org chem), 51. *Prof Exp:* Res chemist, 51-54, proj leader, 54, group leader, 55, asst lab dir cellulose & plastics lab, 56-60, staff asst exec res, 61-67, admin asst human health res, 67-69, asst mgr, Corp Res & Develop, Indust Rels, 69-77, employee rels mgr, 71-80, RES ASSOC, ORG CHEM, DOW CHEM CO, 80- *Mem:* AAAS; Am Chem Soc. *Res:* Synthetic organic chemistry; autoxidation of polymers; plastics; carbohydrate derivatives. *Mailing Add:* Dow Chem Co 1414 Crescent Dr Midland MI 48640

CHAMBERLAIN, NUGENT FRANCIS, b Henderson, Tex, Mar 10, 16; m 43; c 3. SPECTROSCOPY, ELECTRON MICROSCOPY. *Educ:* Agr & Mech Col Tex, ChE, 38. *Prof Exp:* Tech trainee, Humble Oil & Ref Co, 38, from jr chemist to chemist, 39-41, from res chemist to sr res chemist, 41-59, sr res chem engr, 59-61, res specialist, 61-63, res assoc, 63-66, res assoc Esso Res & Eng Co, 66-69, sr res assoc, 69-74, SR RES ASSOC, BAYTOWN RES & DEVELOP DIV, EXXON RES & ENG CO, 74- *Honors & Awards:* Southeastern Tex Sect Award & Southwest Regional Award, Am Chem Soc, 69. *Mem:* Am Chem Soc; fel Am Inst Chemists; Microbeam Anal Soc; Electron Micros Soc Am; Am Soc Testing & Mat. *Res:* Nuclear magnetic resonance spectroscopy; electron microscopy. *Mailing Add:* Exxon Res & Eng Co Baytown Res & Dev Div Box 4255 Baytown TX 77520

CHAMBERLAIN, OWEN, b San Francisco, Calif, July 10, 20; m 43, 80; c 4. EXPERIMENTAL HIGH ENERGY PHYSICS. *Educ:* Dartmouth Col, AB, 41, Univ Chicago, PhD(physics), 49. *Prof Exp:* From instr to assoc prof, 48-58, PROF PHYSICS, UNIV CALIF, BERKELEY, 58- *Concurrent Pos:* Civilian physicist, Manhattan Dist, Berkeley & Los Alamos, 42-46; Guggenheim fel, 57-58; Loeb lectr, Harvard Univ, 59. *Honors & Awards:* Nobel Prize, 59. *Mem:* Nat Acad Sci; fel Am Phys Soc; fel AAAS. *Res:* Fission; Alphaparticle decay; neutron diffraction in liquids; high energy nucleon scattering; antinucleons. *Mailing Add:* Dept Physics Univ Calif Berkeley CA 94720

CHAMBERLAIN, PHYLLIS IONE, b Belfast, NY, Oct 22, 38. INORGANIC CHEMISTRY. *Educ:* Houghton Col, BS, 60; State Univ NY Buffalo, PhD(chem kinetics), 68. *Prof Exp:* Teacher pub sch, NY, 60-62; asst prof, 67-75, ASSOC PROF CHEM, ROBERTS WESLEYAN COL, NY, 75- *Concurrent Pos:* Danforth Assoc, 78- *Mem:* Am Chem Soc; Am Sci Affil. *Res:* Kinetics and mechanisms of the reactions of transition metal complexes of organic ligands. *Mailing Add:* Roberts Wesleyan Col 2301 Westside Dr Rochester NY 14624

CHAMBERLAIN, ROBERT ENGLISH, b Utica, NY, Jan 15, 21; m 48; c 2. MICROBIOLOGY. *Educ:* Rensselaer Polytech Inst, BS, 44, MS, 47; Univ Mich, PhD(bact), 52; Am Bd Med Microbiol, dipl. *Prof Exp:* Asst, Behr Manning Corp, NY, 44; lab asst zool, Rensselaer Polytech Inst, 46-47; instr, Univ Mich, 51-52; head microbiol sect, Smith Kline & French Labs, 52-61; group supvr microbiol, Nat Drug Co, 61-65; CHIEF MED MICROBIOL SECT, NORWICH-EATON PHARMACEUT, 65- *Mem:* Am Soc Microbiol; AAAS. *Res:* Antimicrobial agents. *Mailing Add:* Norwich-Eaton Pharmaceut Norwich NY 13815

CHAMBERLAIN, ROBERT GLENN, b Atascadero, Calif, May 8, 39; m 60; c 4. MATHEMATICAL MODELING, SYSTEMS ANALYSIS. *Educ:* Calif Inst Technol, BS, 60, MS, 61. *Prof Exp:* Mech engr spacecraft, US Air Force, 61-64; sr engr, 64-67, MEM TECH STAFF, JET PROPULSION LAB, CALIF INST TECHNOL, 67- *Concurrent Pos:* Mgr SAMICS Develop, Low Cost Solar Array Proj, Jet Propulsion Lab, Calif Inst Technol, 75- *Mem:* Opers Res Soc Am; AAAS; Inst Mgt Sci; Sigma Xi. *Res:* Cost and performance modeling of energy production systems; modeling of the economics of energy system component manufacturing. *Mailing Add:* Jet Propulsion Lab 506-316 4800 Oak Grove Dr Pasadena CA 91109

CHAMBERLAIN, ROY WILLIAM, b Stanton, Calif, July 24, 16; m 44; c 1. MEDICAL ENTOMOLOGY, VIROLOGY. *Educ:* Mont State Col, BS, 42; Johns Hopkins Univ, ScD(parasitol), 49. *Prof Exp:* Chief arbovirus vector lab, 49-67, chief arbovirus infections unit, 67-68, DEP CHIEF VIROL DIV, CTR DIS CONTROL, USPHS, 68- *Mem:* Am Soc Trop Med & Hyg; Sigma Xi; Am Mosquito Control Asn. *Res:* Arthropod transmission of virus diseases of man and animals; behavior of arboviruses in insects and vertebrates. *Mailing Add:* Virol Div Ctr for Dis Control Atlanta GA 30333

CHAMBERLAIN, S(AVVAS) G(EORGIOU), b Nicosia, Cyprus, Mar 21, 41; m 65; c 1. ELECTRONICS, SEMICONDUCTOR PHYSICS. *Educ:* Univ Southampton, MSc, 66, PhD(electronics), 68. *Prof Exp:* Proj leader optoelectronics & device physics, Allen Clark Res Ctr, Plessey Co Ltd, Eng, 68-69; asst prof electronics, 69-77, PROF ELEC ENG, UNIV WATERLOO, 77- *Mem:* Inst Elec & Electronics Engrs; assoc mem Brit Inst Elec Engrs; Brit Inst Physics & Phys Soc. *Res:* Solid state semiconductor devices; integrated circuits; device modeling; accurate numerical solutions of p-n junctions and transistors; optoelectronic devices including charge coupled devices. *Mailing Add:* Dept of Elec Eng Univ of Waterloo Waterloo Can

CHAMBERLAIN, THEODORE KLOCK, b Detroit, Mich, July 18, 30. GEOLOGY, OCEANOGRAPHY. *Educ:* Univ NMex, BS, 52; Scripps Inst Oceanog, Univ Calif, MS, 53, PhD(oceanog), 60. *Prof Exp:* Res marine geologist, Scripps Inst Calif, 56-60; oceanogr, Tokyo Univ Fisheries, Tokyo, 60-62; assoc prof & asst chmn dept oceanog, Univ Hawaii, 62-67; sr oceanogr & mgr sci div, Ocean Sci & Eng Inc, 67-71; dir, Chesapeake Res Consortium, Johns Hopkins Univ, 72-75; head earth resources dept, 75-80, PROF, COLO STATE UNIV, 75- *Concurrent Pos:* Nat Acad Sci-Nat Res Coun fel, 60-62. *Mem:* Am Soc Limnol & Oceanog; AAAS; Royal Siam Soc. *Res:* Littoral processes, physical limnology, marine placers, exploration geology; earth resources development. *Mailing Add:* Dept of Earth Resources Colo State Univ Ft Collins CO 80523

CHAMBERLAIN, WILLIAM MAYNARD, b Montreal, Que, Apr 7, 38; m 61; c 2. AQUATIC BIOLOGY. *Educ:* Univ Toronto, BS, 61, PhD(zool), 68. *Prof Exp:* Res assoc, Limnol Res Ctr, Univ Minn, Minneapolis, 67-69; asst prof, 69-76, ASSOC PROF LIFE SCI, IND STATE UNIV, 76- *Concurrent Pos:* Partic, Gordon Res Conf, 66 & 70 & Int Symp Eutrophication, 67. *Mem:* Am Soc Limnol & Oceanog; Ecol Soc Am. *Res:* Nutrient circulation studies on phosphorus in aquatic ecosystems; assay procedures for available phosphorus; temperature effects on cladoceran populations; nutrient cycles. *Mailing Add:* Dept of Life Sci Ind State Univ Terre Haute IN 47809

CHAMBERLAND, BERTRAND LEO, b Manchester, NH, Mar 17, 34; m 65; c 3. INORGANIC CHEMISTRY. *Educ:* St Anselms Col, AB, 55; Col of the Holy Cross, MS, 56; Univ Pa, PhD(inorg chem), 60. *Prof Exp:* Res chemist, Nat Carbon Co, Ohio, 56-57 & E I du Pont de Nemours & Co, Inc, 60-69; PROF CHEM, UNIV CONN, 69- *Mem:* Am Chem Soc; Royal Soc Chem; Am Ceramic Soc; Am Crystallog Soc. *Res:* Inorganic synthesis of molecular and solid state compounds; preparation, characterization and crystal growth of solid state materials; high pressure synthesis and reactions. *Mailing Add:* Dept of Chem Univ of Conn Storrs CT 06268

CHAMBERLIN, EARL MARTIN, b Cochranville, Pa, Dec 4, 14; m 47; c 7. ORGANIC CHEMISTRY. *Educ:* Philadelphia Col Pharm & Sci, ScB, 36; Boston Univ, AM, 37; Harvard Univ, AM, 44, PhD(org chem), 46. *Prof Exp:* Asst org chem, Merck & Co, 38-40, admin asst to dir res, 40-41, res chemist, 46-47, staff asst to vpres & sci dir, 48-49, res chemist, 49-59, mgr develop res, 59-68, dir, Synthetic Prep Lab, Process Res, Merck & Co, 69-77, sr dir process res, Merck Sharp & Dohme Res Labs, 77-79; RETIRED. *Concurrent Pos:* lectr, Union Col Cranford, NJ, 78-79. *Mem:* Am Chem Soc; fel Am Inst Chemists. *Res:* Synthetic organic chemistry; alkaloids; fatty acids; quinones; organic therapeutic agents; steroidal hormones; organometallic chemistry. *Mailing Add:* 2028 Hilltop Rd Westfield NJ 07090

CHAMBERLIN, HARRIE ROGERS, b Cambridge, Mass, June 13, 20; m; c 4. PEDIATRICS. *Educ:* Harvard Univ, AB, 42, MD, 45. *Prof Exp:* Instr pediat, Sch Med, Yale Univ, 51-52; from instr to assoc prof, 53-70, PROF PEDIAT & DIR DIV FOR DIS OF DEVELOP & LEARNING, CHILD DEVELOP INST, SCH MED, UNIV NC, CHAPEL HILL, 70- *Concurrent Pos:* Mem, White House Ad Hoc Adv Comt Ment Retardation, 63-65; consult, Div Hosp & Med Facil, USPHS, 65-68. *Mem:* AMA; Am Acad Pediat; assoc Am Acad Neurol; Am Pediat Soc; Am Acad Cerebral Palsy & Develop Med. *Res:* Mental retardation; developmental neurology in the infant and child. *Mailing Add:* Dept of Pediat Univ of NC Chapel Hill NC 27514

CHAMBERLIN, HOWARD ALLEN, b Dayton, Ohio, Nov 17, 21; m 46; c 3. POLYMER CHEMISTRY, TEXTILE CHEMISTRY. *Educ:* Ohio State Univ, BSc, 44; NC State Univ, MSc, 68. *Prof Exp:* Chemist, Monsanto Cent Res Labs, Ohio, 44-51; chemist, Res & Develop Labs, Chemstrand Corp, Ala, 52-55, develop group leader, Acrylic Fiber Plant, 55-59, res chemist, Chemstrand Res Ctr, Monsanto Co, 60-67; RES CHEMIST, HOOKER RES CTR, HOOKER CHEM CORP, 67- *Mem:* Am Chem Soc. *Res:* Polymer process development and improvement; synthetic fiber technical assistance and development in acrylic fiber plant; application of polymerization technology to textile fabric finishes and flame retardants to plastics; research approaches. *Mailing Add:* Hooker Chem Corp Res Ctr Box 8 MPO Niagara Falls NY 14302

CHAMBERLIN, JAMES WESLEY, organic chemistry, see previous edition

CHAMBERLIN, JOHN MACMULLEN, b Old Hickory, Tenn, Oct 12, 35; m 65; c 1. INORGANIC CHEMISTRY, PHYSICAL CHEMISTRY. *Educ:* Western Ky Univ, BS, 57; Duke Univ, MA, 61, PhD(inorg chem), 64. Prof Coordr coordr med technol, 65-78, asst to dean, Col Appl Arts & Health, 72-78, ASSOC PROF INORG & PHYS CHEM, WESTERN KY UNIV, 64- *Res:* Potentiometric and polarographic determination of stability constants of complex ions in molten salts; corrosion of metals in molten salts. *Mailing Add:* Dept of Chem Western Ky Univ Bowling Green KY 42101

CHAMBERLIN, RICHARD ELIOT, b Cambridge, Mass, Mar 20, 23; m 53; c 4. MATHEMATICS. *Educ:* Univ Utah, AB, 43; Harvard Univ, AM, 47, PhD(math), 50. *Prof Exp:* Asst prof math, 49-51, from asst prof to assoc prof, 52-70, PROF MATH, UNIV UTAH, 70- *Mem:* Am Math Soc. *Res:* Algebraic topology; critical points of polynomials. *Mailing Add:* Dept of Math Univ of Utah Salt Lake City UT 84112

CHAMBERLIN, THOMAS LELAND, b Hamilton, Ohio, Oct 12, 46. PETROLEUM GEOLOGY, STRATIGRAPHY. *Educ:* Mich State Univ, East Lansing, BS, 68; Univ Ill, Urbana, MS, 71, PhD(geol), 75. *Prof Exp:* Geologist petrol geol, Texaco, Inc, 75-78; DISTRICT GEOLOGIST PETROL GEOL, PETROL, INC, 78- & OFF MGR, 81- *Concurrent Pos:* Res asst, Ill State Geol Surv, 69-74. *Mem:* Am Asn Petrol Geologists; Soc Econ Paleontologists & Mineralogists. *Res:* The regional geologic analysis of selected areas to be evaluated in terms of hydrocarbon accumulation and production. *Mailing Add:* PO Box 22 Franktown CO 80116

CHAMBERLIN, WILLIAM BRICKER, III, b Cleveland, Ohio, Aug 8, 43; m 75. ORGANIC CHEMISTRY. *Educ:* Miami Univ, Oxford, Ohio, BA, 66, MS, 70. *Prof Exp:* Teacher sci, Roosevelt Jr High, Ohio, 68-69; asst instr chem, Miami Univ, Oxford, Ohio, 69-70; chemist, 70-72, PROJ MGR CHEM, LUBRIZOL CORP, 72- *Mem:* Am Chem Soc; Soc Automotive Engrs. *Res:* Development of additives to improve engine lubrication. *Mailing Add:* Lubrizol Corp 29400 Lakeland Blvd Wickliffe OH 44092

CHAMBERS, ALFRED HAYES, b Reading, Pa, Nov 15, 14; m 45. PHYSIOLOGY. *Educ:* Swarthmore Col, AB, 36; Univ Pa, PhD(physiol), 42. *Prof Exp:* Asst instr physiol, Univ Pa, 37-42, instr, 42-45, assoc, 45-47, asst prof, 47-48; from asst prof to assoc prof, 48-70, PROF PHYSIOL & BIOPHYSICS, UNIV VT, 70- *Concurrent Pos:* NIH spec fel, 61, 62. *Mem:* Am Physiol Soc. *Res:* Metabolism; respiration; hearing. *Mailing Add:* Dept of Physiol Univ of Vt Burlington VT 05401

CHAMBERS, BARBARA MAE FROMM, b Syracuse, NY, Nov 23, 40; m 62; c 4. MATHEMATICS. *Educ:* Univ Ala, BS, 62, MA, 64, PhD(math), 69. *Prof Exp:* Asst math, Univ Ala, 62-69; consult, Washington, DC, 69-70; lectr, Univ Va, Fairfax, 70-71; asst prof math, George Mason Univ, 71-79; ASSOC PROF MATH, NORTHERN VA COMMUNITY COL, 79- *Concurrent Pos:* NASA fel, 63; adv, Northern Va Sci Fair, 72-81. *Mem:* Math Asn Am. *Res:* Analytic function theory and applications. *Mailing Add:* 4220 Dandridge Terr Alexandria VA 22309

CHAMBERS, CARL COVALT, b Philadelphia, Pa, May 8, 07; m 30; c 3. ELECTRICAL ENGINEERING, COMMUNICATIONS. *Educ:* Dickinson Col, BS, 29; Univ Pa, ScD(elec eng), 34. *Hon Degrees:* DSc, Dickinson Col, 72. *Prof Exp:* Jr engr, Tech Test Dept, Radio Corp Am Mfg Co, Camden, 29-30, engr, Tube Div, Radio Corp Am Victor Co, 30-32; from instr to prof elec eng, 33-72, actg dean, 49-50, dean 50-53, vpres eng affairs, 53-72, univ prof, 72-75, EMER UNIV PROF ENG, MOORE SCH, UNIV PA, 75- *Concurrent Pos:* Consult engr, 34-; consult, Edward Starn Co, Pa, 36-54; with Off Sci Res & Develop, 44; dir res, Int Resistance Co, 44-47, consult, 47-54; mem-at-large, US comt, Int Electrotech Comn. *Mem:* Nat Acad Engrs; AAAS; Am Phys Soc; Inst Elec & Electronics Engrs; Am Soc Eng Educ. *Res:* Radio systems theory; radio interference; electronic control; electricity and magnetism; physical electronics. *Mailing Add:* Estero Woods Village Apt 322 Estero FL 33928

CHAMBERS, CHARLES MCKAY, JR, b Hampton, Va, June 22, 41; m 62; c 4. ACADEMIC ADMINISTRATION, MATHEMATICAL SCIENCES. *Educ:* Univ Ala, BS, 62, MS, 63, PhD(physics), 64; George Washington Univ, JD, 76. *Prof Exp:* Aerospace engr, Marshall Space Flight Ctr, NASA, 62-63; res assoc physics, Univ Ala, 63-64; NSF res fel, Harvard Univ, 64-65; from asst prof to assoc prof math, Univ Ala, 65-69; charter officer & dir, Univ Assocs, Inc, 69-72; assoc dean, George Washington Univ, 72-77; staff assoc & legal adv, 77-79, acting pres, 80-81, GEN COUN, COUN POSTSEC ACCREDITATION, WASHINGTON, DC, 81- *Concurrent Pos:* Dir, NSF and NASA grants Ala math talent search; consult, US Air Force, Salk Inst, US Cong, US Off Educ, NSF, Am Asn Higher Educ, Coun Grad Schs US, US Dept Agr, Amor Coun Educ, Nat League Nursing, Nat Inst Drug Abuse, Law Enforcement Assistance Admin, Fund Improv Postsecondary Educ & Ctr Mediation Higher Educ. *Mem:* AAAS; Am Math Soc; Am Asn Physics Teachers; Am Asn Univ Adminrs. *Res:* Development and administration of interdisciplinary programs; abstract harmonic analysis; group representation theory; quantative science in policy studies. *Mailing Add:* 4220 Dandridge Terr Alexandria VA 22309

CHAMBERS, DAVID SMITH, b Clarksville, Tex. APPLIED STATISTICS. *Educ:* Univ Tex, AB, 39, MBA, 47. *Prof Exp:* Spec instr math, Univ Tex, 38-41; asst state supvr div wage-hour, US Dept Labor, Miss, 41-42; regional examr, Off Price Admin, Tex, 42-43; instr aeronaut eng, Univ Tex, 43-44, instr appl math & astron, 44-46, instr bus statist, 46-47; from asst prof to prof statist, Univ Tenn, Knoxville, 58-81; CONSULT PRODUCTIVITY & QUAL CONTROL, 81- *Concurrent Pos:* Mem bd dirs, Engr Joint Coun, 72-74. *Honors & Awards:* Eugene Grant Award, Am Soc Qual Control. 70. *Mem:* AAAS; Am Soc Qual Control (pres, 71-72); Am Statist Asn; Am Soc Test & Mat; NY Acad Sci. *Res:* Quality control. *Mailing Add:* Dept Statist Univ Tenn Knoxville TN 37916

CHAMBERS, DERRELL LYNN, b Los Angeles, Calif, Feb 3, 34; m 54; c 3. ENTOMOLOGY. *Educ:* Whittier Col, BA, 55; Ohio State Univ, MS, 57; Ore State Univ, PhD, 65. *Prof Exp:* Biol aide entom res div, Whittier Lab, Agr Res Serv, USDA, 55; forestry aide, US Forest Serv, Ohio, 56-57; asst zool & entom, Ohio State Univ, 56-57; entomologist, Entom Res Div, Mexican Fruit Flies Invest Lab, Agr Res Serv, USDA, Mexico City, 57-59, entomologist, Pioneering Res Lab Insect Physiol, Md, 59-61; asst, Sci Res Inst, Ore State Univ, 61-64; sr entomologist, Entom Res Div, Arid Areas Citrus Insects Invest Lab, Agr Res Serv, Calif, 65-67, invests leader, Mex Fruit Flies Invest Lab, 68, Hawaiian Fruit Flies Invest Lab, Honolulu, 69-72, LAB DIR INSECT ATTRACTANTS & BIOL RES LAB, AGR RES SERV, USDA, 72- *Concurrent Pos:* Consult, various govt agencies and progs. *Mem:* Am Inst Biol Sci; Entom Soc Am. *Res:* Insect physiology and behavior. *Mailing Add:* Insect Attract & Biol Res Lab PO Box 14565 Gainesville FL 32604

CHAMBERS, DOYLE, b Line, Ark, Mar 24, 18; m 43; c 3. ANIMAL GENETICS, ANIMAL BREEDING. *Educ:* La State Univ, BS, 40, MS, 47; Oklahoma State Univ, PhD(animal breeding), 50. *Prof Exp:* Asst animal sci, La State Univ, 40-42, instr, 45-47; from assoc prof to prof, Okla State Univ, 50-62, assoc dir, Agr Exp Sta, 62-64; DIR AGR EXP STA, LA STATE UNIV, BATON ROUGE, 64-, PROF ANIMAL SCI, 77- *Concurrent Pos:* Don M Tyler distinguished prof, Okla State Univ, 61. *Mem:* Fel AAAS; Am Soc Animal Sci. *Res:* Inheritance of quantitative traits of economic importance in beef cattle and swine, including growth and carcass traits, maternal traits and efficiency of feed use; dwarfism and cancer eye studies. *Mailing Add:* Agr Exp Sta PO Drawer E La State Univ Baton Rouge LA 70893

CHAMBERS, EDWARD LUCAS, b Manhattan, NY, Jan 27, 17; m 54; c 2. CELL PHYSIOLOGY. *Educ:* Princeton Univ, BA, 38; NY Univ, MD, 43. *Prof Exp:* Intern, 2nd Div, Bellevue Hosp, 43-44, asst resident, 4th Div, 44; asst prof anat, Sch Med, Johns Hopkins Univ, 50-52; assoc prof, Sch Med, Univ Ore, 53-54; assoc prof physiol, 54-63, chmn grad prog cellular & molecular biol, 60-71, prof physiol & biochem, 63-73, PROF PHYSIOL & BIOPHYS, SCH MED, UNIV MIAMI, 73- *Concurrent Pos:* Mem corp, Marine Biol Lab, Woods Hole, Mass. *Mem:* Soc Gen Physiol; Am Physiol Soc; Am Soc Cell Biol. *Res:* Ion exchanges between cell and environment; cell activation and fertilization; cell metabolism; micromanipulation. *Mailing Add:* Dept of Physiol & Biophys Univ Miami Sch Med PO Box 016430 Miami FL 33101

CHAMBERS, FRANK WARMAN, b Washington, DC, Nov 10, 48; m 75; c 1. PLASMA PHYSICS, COMPUTATIONAL PHYSICS. *Educ:* St Joseph's Col, BS, 70; Mass Inst Technol, PhD(physics), 75. *Prof Exp:* Res assoc plasma physics, Mass Inst Technol, 76; PHYSICIST PLASMA PHYSICS, LAWRENCE LIVERMORE LAB, UNIV CALIF, 76- *Mem:* Am Phys Soc. *Res:* Theoretical research on the interaction of charged particle beams with gases; computer simulation of plasma phenomena; linear stability analysis. *Mailing Add:* L-321 PO Box 808 Livermore CA 94550

CHAMBERS, HOWARD WAYNE, b Buda, Tex, Dec 27, 39. TOXICOLOGY. *Educ:* Tex A&M Univ, BS, 61, MS, 63; Univ Calif, Berkeley, PhD(entom), 66. *Prof Exp:* Res entomologist, Univ Calif, 66-68; from asst prof to assoc prof, 68-79, PROF ENTOM, MISS STATE UNIV, 79- *Mem:* Am Chem Soc; Entom Soc Am. *Res:* Insecticide chemistry; mechanism of action and metabolism of insecticides; insecticide synergists; resistance to insecticides. *Mailing Add:* PO Drawer EM Miss State Univ Mississippi State MS 39762

CHAMBERS, JAMES PATRICK, biochemistry, microbiology, see previous edition

CHAMBERS, JAMES Q, b Kansas City, Mo, Jan 14, 38; m 64. ANALYTICAL CHEMISTRY. *Educ:* Princeton Univ, AB, 59; Univ Kans, PhD(chem), 64. *Prof Exp:* Asst prof chem, Univ Colo, 64-69; asst prof, 69-71, ASSOC PROF CHEM, UNIV TENN, 71- *Res:* Mechanisms and kinetics of electrode reactions; electrosynthetic methods; electron paramagnetic resonance; ultraviolet and visible spectroscopy of radical ions. *Mailing Add:* Dept of Chem Univ of Tenn Knoxville TN 37916

CHAMBERS, JAMES RICHARD, b Birmingham, Ala, Aug 20, 14; m 39; c 1. ORGANIC CHEMISTRY. *Educ:* Columbia Union Col, BA, 39; Western Reserve Univ, MS, 49; Tex A&M Univ, PhD(org chem), 58. *Prof Exp:* Asst chem, Columbia Union Col, 39-41; prin, Nashville Jr Acad, 41-42; chief chemist, Pennzoil Co, 42-46; head chem dept, Atlantic Union Col, 46-54; instr chem, Southwestern Jr Col, 54-56; asst, Agr & Mech Col Tex, 56-58; head sci dept, Southwestern Jr Col, 58-60; assoc prof, 60-61, PROF CHEM, WALLA WALLA COL, 61- *Mem:* Am Chem Soc. *Res:* Organic synthesis; organophosphorus chemistry; biochemistry. *Mailing Add:* Dept of Chem Walla Walla Col College Place WA 99324

CHAMBERS, JAMES VERNON, b Pekin, Ill, Mar 12, 35; m 57; c 1. FOOD SCIENCE. *Educ:* Ohio State Univ, BSc, 61, MSc, 66, PhD(food sci), 72. *Prof Exp:* Head microbiologist div qual control, Ross Labs Div, Abbott Labs, 61-68; lab dir, Div Food, Dairies & Drugs, Ohio Dept Agr, 69-71; asst prof food sci, Univ Wis, River Falls, 72-74; assoc prof & exten specialist dairy mfg, 74-81, ASSOC PROF ANIMAL SCI, PURDUE UNIV, 78- *Concurrent Pos:* Consult microbiol food waste treatment & mgt pract, A & P Tea Co, 77-, Durkee-Glidden, 78-, Holly Milk, Inc, 79-, Dairymen, Inc, 80- & Pollio Dairy Prod, Inc, 81. *Mem:* Inst Food Technologists; Am Soc Microbiol: Water Pollution Control Fedn; Am Dairy Sci Asn; Int Asn Milk Food & Environ Sanitarians Inc. *Res:* Translocation of Xanthine oxidase from milk into the blood and possible effect on cholesterol accumulation; managing subclinical mastitis in the dairy cow. *Mailing Add:* Smith Hall Rm 101-D Purdue Univ West Lafayette IN 47907

CHAMBERS, JOHN EDWARD, phycology, electron microscopy, see previous edition

CHAMBERS, JOHN MCKINLEY, b Toronto, Ont, Apr 28, 41; m 71. STATISTICS, COMPUTER SCIENCE. *Educ:* Univ Toronto, BSc, 63; Harvard Univ, AM, 65, PhD(statist), 66. *Prof Exp:* supvr statist, 66-81, HEAD, ADVAN SOFTWARE, BELL LABS, 81- *Concurrent Pos:* Vis lectr math, Imp Col, Univ London, 66-67; vis lectr statist, Harvard Univ, 69 & Princeton Univ, 71; assoc ed, J Am Statist Asn, 71-74. *Mem:* Fel Am Statist Asn; fel Royal Statist Soc; Asn Comput Mach; Brit Comput Soc; Int Statist Inst. *Res:* Analytical and statistical computing; graphics; software systems; expert software. *Mailing Add:* Bell Tel Labs Murray Hill NJ 07974

CHAMBERS, JOHN WILLIAM, b Richmond, Ky, Nov 7, 29; m 65; c 2. ENDOCRINOLOGY, PHARMACOLOGY. *Educ:* Eastern Ky State Col, BS, 58; Vanderbilt Univ, PhD(pharmacol), 65. *Prof Exp:* From res asst to asst prof pharmacol, Vanderbilt Univ, 64-70; asst prof, Med Col Va, 70-76; assoc prof, 76-78, PROF PHARMACOL & CHMN DEPT, WVA SCH OSTEOPATH MED, 78- *Concurrent Pos:* NIH-USPHS fel, 65-66. *Mem:* AAAS; Am Soc Pharmacol & Exp Therapeut; assoc Am Chem Soc; NY Acad Sci. *Res:* Effects of hormones and drugs on amino acid transport and metabolism, on membrane function and on enzyme activity. *Mailing Add:* Dept Pharmacol WVa Sch of Osteopath Med Lewisburg WV 24901

CHAMBERS, KATHLEEN CAMILLE, b Polson, Mont, July 14, 47. ANIMAL PHYSIOLOGY. *Educ:* Portland State Univ, BS, 71; Univ Wash, PhD(psychol), 75. *Prof Exp:* Asst prof, Portland State Univ, 75-78; assoc prof physiol basis motivation, 78-79; ASST SCIENTIST, ORE REGIONAL PRIMATE RES CTR, 79- *Concurrent Pos:* Collab scientist, Ore Regional Primate Res Ctr, 76-79. *Mem:* Animal Behav Soc; Int Primatological Soc; Am Soc Primatologists. *Res:* Physiological determinants of the sex difference in the acquisition and extinction of a conditioned food oversion primate rodent; primate sexual behavior; physiological correlates of sexual behavior in aging primates. *Mailing Add:* Ore Regional Primate Res Ctr 505 NW 185th Ave Beaverton OR 97006

CHAMBERS, KENTON LEE, b Los Angeles, Calif, Sept 27, 29; m 58; c 2. BOTANY. *Educ:* Whittier Col, AB, 50; Stanford Univ, PhD(biol), 56. *Prof Exp:* Actg instr biol sci, Stanford Univ, 54-55; from instr to asst prof bot, Yale Univ, 56-60; assoc prof, 60-65, PROF BOT, ORE STATE UNIV, 65-, CUR HERBARIUM, 60- *Concurrent Pos:* Prog dir syst biol, NSF, 67-68. *Mem:* AAAS; Am Soc Plant Taxonomists (pres, 79); Soc Study Evolution; Bot Soc Am; Asn Trop Biol. *Res:* Taxonomy and biosystematics of angiosperms, especially Compositae; flora of Oregon. *Mailing Add:* Dept of Bot Ore State Univ Corvallis OR 97331

CHAMBERS, LARRY WILLIAM, b Hamilton, Ont, Oct 6, 46; m 74; c 1. EPIDEMIOLOGY, HEALTH PROGRAMS EVALUATION. *Educ:* McMaster Univ, BA Hons, 70, MSc, 73; Mem Univ Nfld, PhD(community med), 78. *Prof Exp:* Res asst, Dept Clin Epidemiol & Biostatist, McMaster Univ, 70-71; lectr, Div Community Med, Mem Univ Nfld, 73-76; asst prof, 76-78; asst prof, 78-81, ASSOC PROF HEALTH CARE EVAL & EPIDEMIOL, DEPT CLIN EPIDEMIOL & BIOSTATIST, MCMASTER UNIV, 81- *Concurrent Pos:* Prin investr, Family Pract Nurses Nfld, Nat Health Res & Develop Prog, 73-78, Indexes Health-Prof & Lay Perspectives, 79-81; co-investr, Home Centered Videotaped Coun Rural Parents Hearing Impaired Children, 77-79 & Trial Home Care Chronically Ill Elderly, 79-82; consult, Can Health Surv, 75-; Nfld Cancer Treatment & Res Found, 76-78; Metrop Ment Health Planning Bd Halifax, NS, 77-, Sch Pub Health, Univ NC & Div Family Med, Duke Univ, 78- & Expert Group Qual Care Assessment, Can Physiotherapy Asn & Nat Health & Welfare, 78-; prin investr, Health Care Eval Sem, St John's, Nat Health Res & Develop Prog, 77- & Workshops Rev Health Progs, 79-81; vis prof, Univ Sierra Leone, 80. *Mem:* Can Pub Health Asn; Soc Epidemiol Res; Am Pub Health Asn; Int Epidemiol Asn; Can Asn Teachers Social & Prev Med. *Res:* Development of measures of health status; quantification of quality in health care assessment; cancer epidemiology; research methodology in the health sciences. *Mailing Add:* Clin Epidemiol & Biostatist 1200 Main St W Hamilton ON L8N 3Z5 Can

CHAMBERS, LEE MASON, b St Marys, WVa, Mar 17, 36; m 60; c 1. ANALYTICAL CHEMISTRY, ELECTROCHEMISTRY. *Educ:* Marshall Univ, BS, 58; Univ Ill, MS, 60, PhD(anal chem), 63. *Prof Exp:* Staff chemist, Ivorydale Tech Ctr, 62-66, group leader res & develop, 66-70, mem staff, Packaging Develop, 76-79, STAFF ANAL CHEMIST & GROUP LEADER, WINTON HILL TECH CTR, PROCTOR & GAMBLE CO, 79- *Mem:* Am Chem Soc; Sigma Xi. *Res:* Development of chemical and instrumental methods for analysis. *Mailing Add:* Proctor & Gamble Co 6100 Center Hill Rd Cincinnati OH 45224

CHAMBERS, LESLIE ADDISON, b Mystic, Iowa, Oct 11, 05; m 30; c 4. ENVIRONMENTAL HEALTH, ZOOLOGY. *Educ:* Tex Christian Univ, BS, 27, MS, 28; Princeton Univ, PhD(biol), 30. *Prof Exp:* Asst prof biol, Tex Christian Univ, 30-32; Johnson Found fel med physics, Univ Pa, & instr pediat sch med, 32-36, assoc med physics & lectr biophys, 36-42, assoc pediat, 36-46, from asst prof to assoc prof biophys, 42-46; chief phys defense div, Biol Labs, Chem Corps, US Army, 46-51; dir res, R A Taft Sanit Eng Ctr, USPHS, 51-56, dir res, Los Angeles Air Pollution Control Dist, 56-60; prof biol & dir Hancock Found, Univ Southern Calif, 60-68; PROF ENVIRON HEALTH, UNIV TEX SCH PUB HEALTH HOUSTON, 68-, DIR INST ENVIRON HEALTH, 69-71. *Concurrent Pos:* Consult, USPHS, 56-; NSF, 63- & Pan Am Health Orgn, 75-; adj prof, Environ Sci & Eng Dept, Rice Univ, 74- *Mem:* AAAS; Am Soc Microbiol; Am Physiol Soc; Am Chem Soc; fel NY Acad Sci. *Res:* Biological and chemical properties of viruses; physical fractionation of rickettsiae; physical properties of bacterial cells; environmental health; air pollution; aerobiology; marine biology. *Mailing Add:* Univ of Tex Sch of Pub Health PO Box 20168 Houston TX 77025

CHAMBERS, RALPH ARNOLD, b Harlan, Ky, Sept 5, 33; m 53; c 2. POLYMER CHEMISTRY. *Educ:* Presby Col, SC, BS, 59; Vanderbilt Univ, PhD(chem), 63. *Prof Exp:* From chemist to sr chemist, 62-67, sr res chemist, 67-71, res assoc, 71-75, SUPT DEVELOP & CONTROL, TENN EASTMAN CO, 75- *Mem:* Am Chem Soc; Sigma Xi; Tech Asn Pulp & Paper Indust. *Res:* Chemistry of cellulose and its derivatives. *Mailing Add:* Tenite Plastics Div Tenn Eastman Co Kingsport TN 37660

CHAMBERS, RICHARD, b London, Eng, Apr 22, 23; m 56. NEUROLOGY. *Educ:* Oxford Univ, BA, 44, BM & BCh, 47, MA, 48; FRCP(C), 59; FRCP(London), 76. *Prof Exp:* Instr, Univ Toronto, 57-60; assoc prof, NJ Col Med & Dent, 60-61, prof, 61-66; PROF NEUROL, JEFFERSON MED COL, 66- *Concurrent Pos:* Fel neurol, Harvard Med Sch, 51-53 & 56; scholar, Royal Col Physicians, Eng, 55-56. *Mem:* Am Acad Neurol; Am Asn Neuropath. *Res:* Cortical physiology; fructose metabolism; virus encephalitis; peripheral neuropathy. *Mailing Add:* Dept of Neurol Jefferson Med Col Philadelphia PA 19107

CHAMBERS, RICHARD LEE, b Algona, Iowa, Feb 26, 47; m 78; c 3. GEOPHYSICS, SEISMIC STRATIGRAPHY. *Educ:* Univ Mont, BA, 70, MS, 71; Mich State Univ, PhD(geol), 75. *Prof Exp:* Res scientist chem sedimentology, Great Lakes Environ Res Lab, Dept of Com, 73-80; SR RES GEOLOGIST, PHILLIPS PETROL CO, 80- *Mem:* Sigma Xi. *Res:* Program development, data acquisition, processing and interpretation of marine seismic data; sedimentary basin analysis for potential hydrocarbon deposits; development of new marine seismic techniques for data acquisition and interpretation. *Mailing Add:* 179 GB Phillips Petrol Co Bartlesville OK 74004

CHAMBERS, ROBERT J, b Atlanta, Ga, Sept 23, 30; m 74; c 2. ASTRONOMY. *Educ:* Univ Wash, BSc, 52; Univ Calif, Berkeley, PhD(astron), 64. *Prof Exp:* From instr to assoc prof, 67-73, PROF ASTRON, POMONA COL, 73-, DIR, BRACKETT OBSERV, 64- *Concurrent Pos:* NSF sci fac fel, Univ Calif, Berkeley, 69-70. *Mem:* AAAS; Am Astron Soc; assoc Am Soc Mech Engrs. *Res:* Galactic star clusters; astronomical instrumentation. *Mailing Add:* F P Brackett Observ Pomona Col Claremont CA 91711

CHAMBERS, ROBERT ROOD, b Lincoln, Nebr, May 23, 23; m 65; c 3. ORGANIC CHEMISTRY. *Educ:* Univ Nebr, AB, 44; Univ Ill, PhD(org chem), 47; DePaul Univ, JD, 51. *Prof Exp:* Res chemist, Sinclair Res Inc, 47-50, group leader, 50-52, div dir, 52-59, tech mgr, 59-66, vpres, 67-68, pres, 68, vpres res, Sinclair Oil Corp, 68-69, pres, Nuclear Mat & Equip Co, 70-71, Arco Nuclear Co, 71-75 & Arco Med Prod Co, 75-77, pres, Arco Solar Inc, 77-80, pres, Arco Environ & Ardev, 78-80, VPRES, ATLANTIC RICHFIELD CO, 69- *Mem:* Am Chem Soc; Brit Chem Soc. *Res:* Petroleum; petrochemicals. *Mailing Add:* Atlantic Richfield Co 515 South Flower St Los Angeles CA 90071

CHAMBERS, ROBERT WARNER, b Oakland, Calif, Oct 27, 24; m 49; c 3. BIOCHEMISTRY, MOLECULAR BIOLOGY. *Educ:* Univ Calif, AB, 49, PhD(biochem), 54. *Prof Exp:* Asst biochem, Univ Calif, 51-54; Life Ins Med Res Fund, Res Coun fel, 54-56; from instr to prof biochem, Sch Med, NY Univ, 56-81; CARNEGIE & ROCKEFELLER PROF BIOCHEM & HEAD

DEPT, DALHOUSIE UNIV, HALIFAX, NS, CAN, 81- *Concurrent Pos:* NSF grant, 58-62; Nat Inst Gen Med Sci grant, 60-78; New York Health Res Coun grant, 64-70; Am Cancer Soc grant, 70-72; Nat Cancer Inst grant, 74-78; career scientist, Health Res Coun City New York, 62-72; mem subcomt purines & pyrimidines, Comt Biol Chem, Nat Acad Sci-Nat Res Coun, 62, chmn, 64; mem comt res etiology of cancer, Am Cancer Soc, 66-69; mem postdoctoral fel comt, NSF, 67; Nat Acad Sci-Nat Res Coun & Polish Acad Sci exchange scientist, 68. *Mem:* AAAS; Am Chem Soc; Royal Soc Chem; Am Soc Biol Chem; fel NY Acad Sci. *Res:* Photochemistry of nucleic acids; structure-action relationships in transfer RNA; synthesis of oligonucleotides; mutagenesis and carcinogenesis; molecular mechanisms of mutation by carcinogens; precise nature of the carcinogen-induced lesions in DNA that produce mutations and the relationship of these mutations to tumor production. *Mailing Add:* Dept Biochem Sir Charles Tupper Bldg Dalhousie Univ Halifax NS B3H 4H7 Can

CHAMBERS, VAUGHAN CRANDALL, (JR), b Philadelphia, Pa, June 14, 25; m 48; c 4. ORGANIC CHEMISTRY. *Educ:* Swarthmore Col, AB, 47; Mass Inst Technol, PhD(org chem), 50. *Prof Exp:* Chemist, Org Photog Mat, 50-59, sr chemist, 59-60, res assoc, 60-61, res supvr, 61-64, RES MGR PHOTO PROD DEPT, E I DU PONT DE NEMOURS & CO, INC, 64- *Mem:* Am Chem Soc; Soc Photog Sci & Eng. *Res:* Physical organic study of small carbocyclic compounds; photography, sensitizing dyes; polymers for use in photographic products. *Mailing Add:* 602 Duncan Rd Cragmere Wilmington DE 19809

CHAMBERS, WILBERT FRANKLIN, b Cameron, WVa, Feb 26, 23; m 57; c 2. NEUROANATOMY. *Educ:* WVa Univ, BS, 46, MS, 47; Univ Wis, PhD(anat), 52. *Prof Exp:* Instr anat, Univ Pittsburgh, 49-52; fel, Vanderbilt Univ, 52-54, instr, 54-55; from instr to assoc prof, Univ Vt, 55-67; assoc prof, 67-71, PROF ANAT, DARTMOUTH MED SCH, 71- *Mem:* Am Asn Anat; Am Soc Zool. *Res:* Morphology of primate brain; nervous system function in altered endocrine states; the subcommissural organ and water metabolism; effect of amphethamines on the reticular activation response; gonadatrophic centers of the hypothalamus; the thyroid release factors region of the hypothalamus. *Mailing Add:* Dept of Anat-Cytol Dartmouth Med Sch Hanover NH 03755

CHAMBERS, WILLIAM EDWARD, b Ravenswood, WVa, Aug 14, 33; m 55; c 3. ANALYTICAL CHEMISTRY. *Educ:* Marshall Univ, BS, 55; Univ Ill, MS, 57, PhD(anal chem), 60. *Prof Exp:* Anal chemist, Parma Res Center, Union Carbide Corp, 59-63, supvr anal div, 63-68, asst dir advan technol projs, Carbon Prod Div, 68-73, dir carbon fiber develop, 73-75, gen mgr res & develop, Parma Tech Ctr, 75-76, VPRES TECHNOL, CARBON PROD DIV, UNION CARBIDE CORP, 76- *Mem:* Soc Appl Spectros; Am Chem Soc. *Res:* Flame spectroscopy; nuclear magnetic resonance. *Mailing Add:* 17 Heritage Dr Danbury CT 06810

CHAMBERS, WILLIAM HYLAND, b St Louis, Mo, July 30, 22; m 45; c 4. NUCLEAR SCIENCE. *Educ:* Cornell Univ, BA, 43, MS, 48; Ohio State Univ, PhD(physics), 50. *Prof Exp:* Asst, Cornell Univ, 46-48; asst, Ohio State Univ, 48-49; mem staff & group leader, 50-77, from asst div leader to assoc div leader, 77-79, DEPUTY ASSOC DIR, LOS ALAMOS NAT LAB, 79- *Concurrent Pos:* With AEC Combined Opers Planning Group, Oak Ridge, 67. *Mem:* Fel AAAS; Inst Nuclear Mat Mgt; Am Phys Soc; Am Nuclear Soc. *Res:* Nuclear weapon development; detection of nuclear detonations in space; solar flare x-rays; soft x-ray spectrometry; nuclear safeguards and arms control; nuclear material detection and identification. *Mailing Add:* 336 Andanada Los Alamos NM 87544

CHAMBLEE, DOUGLAS SCALES, b Zebulon, NC, Jan 4, 21; m 49; c 3. AGRONOMY. *Educ:* NC State Univ, BS, 44, MS, 47; Iowa State Univ, PhD(agron), 49. *Prof Exp:* Res instr agron, 43-47, from asst prof, to assoc prof, 48-60, PROF AGRON, NC STATE UNIV, 60- *Concurrent Pos:* Mem, NC State Mission, Peru, 61-64; agent div forage crops, USDA. *Mem:* Fel Am Soc Agron. *Res:* Moisture requirements of alfalfa; grass mixtures; fertility and management of permanent pastures; sod-seeding legumes in grass pastures; legume inoculation. *Mailing Add:* Dept Crop Sci NC State Univ Raleigh NC 27650

CHAMBLISS, GLENN HILTON, b Jasper, Tex, Feb 14, 42; m 65; c 1. MICROBIOLOGY. *Educ:* Univ Tex, Austin, BA, 65; Miami Univ, MA, 67; Univ Chicago, PhD(microbiol), 72. *Prof Exp:* Fel, Jane Coffin Childs Mem Fund Med Res, 71-73; fel, Phillipe Found, 73-74; ASST PROF BACT, UNIV WIS-MADISON, 74- *Concurrent Pos:* Fel microbiol, Inst Microbiol, Univ Paris-Sud, 72-74. *Mem:* Am Soc Microbiol; Fedn Europ Biol Socs; NY Acad Sci. *Res:* Examination of the involvement of translational controls in regulating temporal gene expression during bacterial sporulation. *Mailing Add:* Dept of Bact Univ of Wis Madison WI 53706

CHAMBLISS, KEITH WAYNE, b Flora, Ill, Dec 16, 26; m 56; c 3. IMMUNOCHEMISTRY. *Educ:* Univ Ill, AB, 48; Univ Ind, AM, 50, PhD(biochem), 52; Am Bd Clin Chem, dipl, 61. *Prof Exp:* Res immunochemist serol, US Army Med Serv Grad Sch, 52-53; res biochemist agr chem, Univ Wyo, 55-56; clin chemist, Toledo Hosp, Ohio, 56-61; sect head immunol, Ames Res Lab Div, Miles Labs Inc, 62-73; dir immunochem res & develop, 73-77, dir appl res, 78-81, SR RES ASSOC ONCOL RES & DEVELOP, AM DADE DIV, AM HOSP SUPPLY CORP, 81- *Mem:* Am Chem Soc; Am Asn Clin Chem. *Res:* Monoclonal antibodies and antibody-antigen reactions applied to diagnostic tests. *Mailing Add:* DADE Div Am Hosp Supply Corp PO Box 520672 Miami FL 33152

CHAMBLISS, OYETTE LAVAUGHN, b Chapman, Ala, Nov 4, 36; m 61; c 2. VEGETABLE CROPS. *Educ:* Auburn Univ, BS, 58, MS, 62; Purdue Univ, PhD(plant breeding), 66. *Prof Exp:* Res horticulturist, Veg Breeding Lab, Crops Res Div, Agr Res Serv, USDA, 66-70; assoc prof veg crops, 70-78, PROF VEG CROPS, AUBURN UNIV, 78- *Honors & Awards:* Marion Meadows Award, Am Soc Hort Sci, 66, Asgrow Award, 72. *Mem:* Am Soc Hort Sci; Am Hort Soc; AAAS; Am Inst Biol Sci. *Res:* Developing insect resistant varieties and investigating nature of resistance in cucumber and cowpea. *Mailing Add:* Dept Hort Auburn Univ Auburn AL 36849

CHAMBRE, PAUL L, b Kassel, Ger, Aug 7, 18; US citizen; m; c 3. APPLIED MATHEMATICS, ENGINEERING SCIENCE. *Educ:* Univ Calif, Berkeley, BS, 41, PhD(eng), 51; NY Univ, MS, 47. *Prof Exp:* From asst prof to assoc prof math, 53-62, prof math & eng sci, 62-76, PROF MATH NUCLEAR ENG, UNIV CALIF, BERKELEY, 76- *Concurrent Pos:* Consult to US Off Naval Res, 53-; consult, Nat Acad Sci, 81- *Res:* Differential equations; classical analysis; rarified gas dynamics; chemical reactions in flowing systems; neutron transport theory; nuclear waste isolation. *Mailing Add:* Dept of Nuclear Eng Univ of Calif Berkeley CA 94720

CHAMEIDES, WILLIAM LLOYD, b New York, NY. Nov 21, 49; m 69. AERONOMY. *Educ:* State Univ NY Binghamton, BA, 70; Yale Univ, MPh, 73, PhD(atmospheric sci), 74. *Prof Exp:* Res investr, Space Physics Res Lab, Univ Mich, 74-75, asst res scientist, 75-76; asst prof physics & atmospheric sci, Univ Fla, 78-80; ASSOC PROF GEOPHYS SCI, GA INST TECHNOL, 80- *Mem:* Am Geophys Union; AAAS. *Res:* Theoretical studies of the physical and chemical phenomena of planetary atmospheres with specific attention to the processes that control the abundances of trace gases in the earth's lower atmosphere; participation in experiments to measure trace gases from space. *Mailing Add:* Dept Geophys Sci Ga Inst Technol Atlanta GA 30332

CHAMIS, CHRISTOS CONSTANTINOS, b Sotira, Greece, May 16, 30; US citizen; m 66; c 3. ENGINEERING MECHANICS. *Educ:* Cleveland State Univ, BCE, 60; Case Western Reserve Univ, MSEM, 62, PhD(mech of solids), 67. *Prof Exp:* Designer indust struct & draftsman consult eng firms, Undergrad Coop Prog, Cleveland, Ohio, 55-60; asst stress & struct anal, Case Western Reserve Univ, 60-62, composite mech, 64-68; res mathematician, B F Goodrich Res Ctr, 62-64; AEROSPACE ENGR, LEWIS RES CTR, NASA, 68- *Concurrent Pos:* Tech sem lectr, George Washington Univ. *Mem:* Am Soc Civil Engrs; Am Inst Aeronaut & Astronaut; Am Soc Mech Engrs; Soc Advan Mat & Process Eng; Am Soc for Testing & Mat. *Res:* Advanced structural analysis, composite mechanics, integrated computer programs for structural and stress analysis, structural dynamics and impact. *Mailing Add:* 24534 Framingham Dr Westlake OH 44145

CHAMPAGNE, PAUL ERNEST, b Woonsocket, RI, Nov 27, 46; m 68; c 2. COAL PROCESSING TECHNOLOGY, ENERGY PROCESS SYSTEMS DESIGN. *Educ:* Univ RI, BS, 69. *Prof Exp:* Assoc res engr, US Steel Corp Res Ctr, 69-73; res engr tech & econ eval, Ledgemont Lab, Kennecott Copper Corp, 73-74; process res eng, US Steel Corp Res Ctr, 74-75, plant process engr, Coal & Coke Opers, 75-77, plant asst supvr coking, 77-78, div engr coal & coking opers, 78-79; mgr core opers, Semet-Sorway Div, Allied Chem Corp, 79; MGR COAL & ENERGY TECHNOL, SCI TECHNOL CTR, KOPPERS CO, INC, 80- *Mem:* Am Inst Chem Engrs; Am Inst Mech Engrs; Am Foundrymens Soc; Eastern States Blast Furnace & Coke Oven Asn. *Res:* Liquid state direct reduction steelmaking; gas/solid fluidized bed direct reduction; fluidized bed design; coal characterization and carbonization; formcoke; e; coal gasification; alternate solid fuels; carbonization research; coal process technology. *Mailing Add:* 1345 Foxwood Dr Monroeville PA 15146

CHAMPE, PAMELA CHAMBERS, b San Francisco, Calif, Aug 29, 45; m 69; c 2. BIOCHEMISTRY, MEDICAL EDUCATION. *Educ:* Stanford Univ, BA, 67; Purdue Univ, MS, 69; Rutgers Univ, PhD(microbiol), 74. *Prof Exp:* Res asst microbiol, 69-73, teaching specialist microbiol & biochem, 73-74, instr biochem, 74-77, ASST PROF BIOCHEM, COL MED & DENT NJ-RUTGERS MED SCH, 77- *Concurrent Pos:* Lectr comprehensive med rev prog, Kuwait, 81- *Mem:* AAAS; Sigma Xi; Nat Asn Med Minority Educr; Asn Am Med Col; NY Acad Sci. *Res:* Development of improved methods of medical education, especially pertaining to the presentation of basic science courses, with a focus on biochemistry. *Mailing Add:* 17 Beech Lane Edison NJ 08820

CHAMPE, SEWELL PRESTON, b Montgomery, WVa, Nov 24, 32; m 59, 69; c 2. MOLECULAR BIOLOGY, GENETICS. *Educ:* Mass Inst Technol, SB, 54; Purdue Univ, PhD(biophys), 59. *Prof Exp:* Am Cancer Soc fel, Purdue Univ, 59-61, from asst prof to assoc prof biol, 61-69; PROF MICROBIOL, RUTGERS UNIV, 69- *Concurrent Pos:* NIH res career award, 63- *Res:* Bacteriophage structure and genetics; microbial development. *Mailing Add:* 17 Beech Lane Edison NJ 08817

CHAMPION, KENNETH STANLEY WARNER, b Sydney, Australia, Dec 7, 23; m 48; c 4. PHYSICS. *Educ:* Univ Sydney, BSc, 44; Univ Birmingham, PhD, 51. *Prof Exp:* Asst lectr physics, Univ Queensland, 46-49; hon res fel, Univ Birmingham, 51-52; res assoc, Mass Inst Technol, 52-54; asst prof, Tufts Univ, 54-59; sect chief, Space Physics Labs, 59-63, CHIEF, ATMOSPHERIC STRUCT BR, AIR FORCE CAMBRIDGE RES LABS, 63- *Concurrent Pos:* Res assoc, Comput Ctr, Mass Inst Technol, 56-59; consult, Photochem Lab, Geophys Res Directorate, Air Force Cambridge Ctr, 56-59; vis prof, Univ Adelaide, 64; chmn working group 4, Comt Space Res, Int Coun Sci Unions, 74-79; chmn task group on Comt Int Reference Atmosphere, Comt Space Res, 79- *Honors & Awards:* Guenter Loeser lectr, 62. *Mem:* Am Geophys Union; Am Phys Soc; Am Meteorol Soc; fel Brit Phys Soc; Sigma Xi. *Res:* Plasma physics; effects of electromagnetic and magnetic fields; measurement of cross sections for atomic processes; upper atmosphere physics; properties and processes of the atmosphere; model atmospheres. *Mailing Add:* 6 Rolfe Rd Lexington MA 02173

CHAMPION, WILLIAM (CLARE), b Rockford, Ill, Mar 12, 30; m 63. ORGANIC CHEMISTRY. *Educ:* Univ Ill, BS, 52; Cornell Univ, PhD(org chem), 58. *Prof Exp:* Asst org chem, Cornell Univ, 54-57; fel, Iowa State Univ, 58-59; from asst prof to assoc prof, 59-73, PROF ORG CHEM, COLO COL, 73- *Mem:* Am Chem Soc; Am Crystallog Asn. *Res:* Synthetic organic chemistry; x-ray crystallography. *Mailing Add:* Dept of Chem Colo Col Colorado Springs CO 80913

CHAMPLIN, ARTHUR KINGSLEY, b Portland, Maine, Nov 30, 38; m 66; c 2. REPRODUCTIVE BIOLOGY, GENETICS. *Educ:* Williams Col, BA, 61, MA, 63; Univ Rochester, PhD(biol), 69. *Prof Exp:* NIH trainee biol, Univ Rochester, 65-69; fel biol & reproduction physiol, Jackson Lab, 69-71; asst prof, 71-80, ASSOC PROF BIOL & CHMN, DIV NATURAL SCI, COLBY COL, 80- *Mem:* Soc Study Reproduction; Am Soc Zoologists; AAAS. *Res:* Genetic and environmental factors affecting mammalian reproduction and early development. *Mailing Add:* Dept of Biol Colby Col Waterville ME 04901

CHAMPLIN, KEITH S(CHAFFNER), b Minneapolis, Minn, Aug 20, 30; m 54; c 2. ELECTRICAL ENGINEERING. *Educ:* Univ Minn, BS, 54, MS, 55, PhD(elec eng), 58. *Prof Exp:* Asst, 54-55, from asst prof to assoc prof, 58-66, PROF ELEC ENG, UNIV MINN, MINNEAPOLIS, 66- *Concurrent Pos:* Exchange prof, Sorbonne, 63. *Mem:* Inst Elec & Electronics Engrs; Am Phys Soc. *Res:* Semiconductors; microwave electronics; solid state devices; fluctuation phenomena. *Mailing Add:* 5437 Elliot Ave Minneapolis MN 55417

CHAMPLIN, ROBERT L, b Casper, Wyo, Oct 9, 30; m 53; c 3. ENVIRONMENTAL ENGINEERING. *Educ:* Univ Wyo, BS, 59, MS, 61; Harvard Univ, MA, 64, PhD(water chem), 69. *Prof Exp:* From instr to assoc prof, 59-77, PROF CIVIL & ENVIRON ENG, UNIV WYO, 77- *Mem:* Am Chem Soc; Nat Soc Prof Engrs; Am Water Works Asn; Water Pollution Control Fedn; Nat Asn Corrosion Engrs. *Res:* Water quality; pollution; aqueous corrosion. *Mailing Add:* Box 3295 Univ Sta Laramie WY 82071

CHAMPLIN, WILLIAM G, b Rogers, Ark, Sept 10, 23; m 51; c 1. MEDICAL MICROBIOLOGY. *Educ:* Northeastern State Univ, Okla, BS, 48; Univ Ark, MS, 65, PhD(microbiol), 71. *Prof Exp:* SUPV MICROBIOLOGIST, VET ADMIN HOSP, 53- *Concurrent Pos:* Consult, Fayetteville City & Washington Regional Med Ctr, 71-75; guest lectr immunol & vis prof microbiol, Univ Ark, 71-75. *Mem:* Am Soc Microbiol; Am Soc Clin Pathologists; Sigma Xi. *Res:* Rapid diagnosis of viral diseases by cell culture and indirect immunofluorescence of clinical material. *Mailing Add:* Vet Admin Hosp Fayetteville AR 72701

CHAMPNEY, WILLIAM SCOTT, b Cleveland, Ohio, Jan 15, 43; m 66; c 3. MOLECULAR GENETICS, RIBOSOMES. *Educ:* Univ Rochester, AB, 65; State Univ NY Buffalo, PhD(biol), 70. *Prof Exp:* Instr microbiol, Col Med, Univ Calif, Irvine, 70-72; asst prof biochem, Univ Ga, 72-79; ASST PROF GENETICS, UNIV TEXAS, 79- *Mem:* Am Soc Biol Chemists; AAAS; Sigma Xi; Am Soc Microbiol. *Res:* Genetics of bacterial ribosomes; protein-nucleic acid interactions. *Mailing Add:* Div Life Sci Univ Tex San Antonio TX 78285

CHAN, ALBERT (YU-CHUNG), b Canton, China, Mar, 28, 49; US citizen. BIOCHEMICAL PHARMACOLOGY, ELECTROPHYSIOLOGY. *Educ:* Univ Calif, Berkeley, AB, 72; Calif State Univ, Long Beach, MS, 75; Univ Nebr Med Ctr, PhD(pharmacol), 80. *Prof Exp:* Staff res assoc, Naval Biomed Res Lab, Oakland, 72; res asst, Calif State Univ, Long Beach, 72-75, Univ Nebr Med Ctr, 75-80; FEL, SOUTHWESTERN MED SCH, UNIV TEX, 80- *Res:* Regulation of the activity of pineal serotonin N-acetyltransferase, and enzyme controlling the synthesis of melatonin; electrical activity of the nucleus ventromedalis hypothalami in relation to reproduction. *Mailing Add:* Univ Tex Health Sci Ctr 5323 Harry Hines Blvd Dallas TX 75235

CHAN, ALBERT SUN CHI, b Kwong Tung, China, Oct 30, 50; m 77; c 1. HOMOGENEOUS CATALYSIS, ORGANOMETALLIC CHEMISTRY. *Educ:* Int Christian Univ, AB, 75; Univ Chicago, MS, 76, PhD(chem), 79. *Prof Exp:* SR RES CHEMIST, MONSANTO CO, 79- *Mem:* Am Chem Soc. *Res:* Organometallic chemistry and its use in homogeneous catalysis; kinetics and mechanisms of homogeneous catalytic reactions; catalytic activation of carbon monoxide and the use of synthesis gas for selective organic reactions. *Mailing Add:* Monsanto Co 800 N Lindbergh Blvd St Louis MO 63167

CHAN, ALLAN P, b Montreal, Que, Oct 2, 21; m 48. RESEARCH MANAGEMENT, PLANT SCIENCE. *Educ:* McGill Univ, BSc, 44, MSc, 46; Ohio State Univ, PhD(floricult), 49. *Prof Exp:* Res asst, Macdonald Col, McGill Univ, 44-46; officer-in-chg floricult res, Cent Exp Farm, 47-59; head ornamental plant sect, 59-62, from asst dir to dir, Inst, 62-73, res coordr, 73-78, PROG ANALYST, RES BR EXEC, PLANT RES INST, 78- *Mem:* Am Inst Biol Sci; Am Soc Hort Sci; Int Soc Hort Sci; Agr Inst Can; Am Asn Bot Gardens & Arboretums. *Res:* Floriculture research; plant physiology and anatomy; controlled environment facilities. *Mailing Add:* Plant Res Inst Central Exp Farm Ottawa Can

CHAN, AN SOO, histology, embryology, see previous edition

CHAN, ARTHUR WING KAY, b Hong Kong, June 24, 41; m 67; c 1. BIOCHEMISTRY, PHARMACOLOGY. *Educ:* Australian Nat Univ, BSc, 66, PhD(org chem), 69. *Prof Exp:* Res assoc org chem, Wash Univ, 69-71, res assoc pharmacol, Med Sch, 71-73; res scientist III, 73-76, res scientist IV, 76-79, RES SCIENTIST V, RES INST ON ALCOHOLISM, 79- *Concurrent Pos:* Res assoc prof pharmacol, State Univ NY Buffalo, 74-; prin investr of res grant, Nat Inst Alcohol Abuse & Alcoholism, 75-77, NY State Health Res Coun, 76-77 & 78-79 & Nat Inst Drug Abuse, 80-81; sponsor postdoctoral fel, Nat Inst Neurol, Commun Dis & Strokes, 76-78; mem exec comt, NY State Coun Res Scientist. *Mem:* Sigma Xi; Res Soc Alcoholism; Am Soc Pharmacol & Exp Therapeut. *Res:* Organic chemistry; quantitative histochemistry; central nervous system effects of alcohol; alcohol-drug interaction; thiamine deficiency; kidney metabolism. *Mailing Add:* Res Inst on Alcoholism 1021 Main St Buffalo NY 14203

CHAN, BERTRAM KIM CHEONG, b Hong Kong, Nov 28, 37; US citizen; m 69. NUCLEAR HARDENING. *Educ:* Univ New South Wales, Austraila, BSc (hons I), 62, MESc, 68; Univ Sydney, PhD(eng), 66. *Prof Exp:* Res scientist nuclear eng, Australian Atomic Energy Comn Res Estab, 65-67; fel, Univ Waterloo & Atomic Energy Can Ltd, 68-69; res assoc biomed eng, Univ Southern Calif, 69-70; assoc prof math, Loma Linda Univ, 70-71; prof chem & math, Mid East Col, Lebanon, 71-78; prof chem, Atlantic Union Col, 78-80; SR RES ENGR ELECTRONIC SYSTS ENG, DEPT VULNERABILITY ANAL & PARTS DEVELOP, LOCKHEED MISSILES & SPACE CO, LOCKHEED CORP, 80- *Mem:* Royal Australian Chem Inst; UK Inst Chem Engrs. *Res:* Electromagnetic pulse interactions with space vehicles; air mitigation effects on electromagnetic pulses; systems generated electromagnetic pulses; transient analysis of waveforms; computer-aided and experimental analysis of latch-up in integrated circuits. *Mailing Add:* 1534 Orillia Ct Sunnyvale CA 94087

CHAN, BOCK G, b Kwantung, China, June 15, 35; US citizen; m 68. PHYTOCHEMISTRY. *Educ:* Cornell Univ, PhD(plant physiol), 70. *Prof Exp:* Experimentalist mineral nutrit biochem, Dept Pomol, Cornell Univ, 60-61 & 63-67, res assoc photosynthesis, Dept Veg Crops, 70-71; fel biochem, 71-73, res plant physiologist, 73-81, SUPVRY PLANT PHYSIOLOGIST, WESTERN REGIONAL RES CTR, AGR RES SERV, USDA, 81- *Mem:* Sigma Xi; Phytochem Soc NAm; Am Soc Plant Physiol. *Res:* Phytochemical basis and the physiology of plant resistance to insects, other pests and pathogens, with special emphasis on the economical crop plants; investigation into enzymology and biosynthetic pathways of the biologically active compounds. *Mailing Add:* Western Regional Res Ctr 800 Buchanan Albany CA 94710

CHAN, CHEUNG-KING, botany, horticulture, see previous edition

CHAN, CHIA HWA, high energy physics, theoretical physics, see previous edition

CHAN, CHIU YEUNG, b Hong Kong, Feb 28, 41; Brit citizen; m 70; c 1. MATHEMATICAL ANALYSIS, APPLIED MATHEMATICS. *Educ:* Univ Hong Kong, BSc, 65; Univ Ottawa, MSc, 67; Univ Toronto, PhD(math), 69. *Prof Exp:* From asst prof to assoc prof, 69-81, PROF MATH, FLA STATE UNIV, 81- *Mem:* Soc Indust & Appl Math; Am Acad Mechanics; Am Math Soc. *Res:* Partial differential equations, including Stefan problems, Sturmian theory, nuclear reactor kinetics, heat conduction, heat radiation, extremum principles, nonlinear Euler-Poisson-Darboux equations, and mathematical modelling; biomathematics and physical mathematics. *Mailing Add:* Dept of Math Fla State Univ Tallahassee FL 32306

CHAN, DANIEL WAN-YUI, b China, Dec 29, 49; m 76. BIOCHEMISTRY, CLINICAL CHEMISTRY. *Educ:* Univ Ore, BA, 72; State Univ NY, Buffalo, PhD(biochem), 76. *Prof Exp:* Teaching asst biochem, State Univ NY, Buffalo, 72-76, res instr, 76-77; asst prof & assoc dir clin chem, 77-78, co-dir, 79-80, DIR CLIN CHEM, DEPT LAB MED, JOHNS HOPKINS UNIV HOSP, 81- *Concurrent Pos:* Fel, Erie County Lab, Meyer M Hosp, Buffalo, 76-77. *Mem:* Am Asn Clin Chem; Endocrine Soc; Int Soc Clin Enzym; Nat Acad Clin Biochem; Acad Clin Lab Physicians & Scientists. *Res:* Reproductive and thyroid endocrinology; radioimmunoassay development; therapeutic drug monitoring. *Mailing Add:* Dept of Lab Med Johns Hopkins Hosp Baltimore MD 21205

CHAN, DAVID S(IU-POON), b Hong Kong, July 23, 40; US citizen; m 75; c 2. PEPTIDE HORMONES. *Educ:* San Jose State Univ, BA, 64, MS, 70; Univ Southern Miss, PhD(biochem), 73. *Prof Exp:* Teaching asst chem, Univ Southern Miss, 70-73; res fel biol chem, Harvard Univ, 73-75, res assoc, 75-77; PRIN CHEMIST, BECKMAN INSTRUMENTS, INC, 78- *Concurrent Pos:* Vpres, Gemini Sci, Inc, 77- *Mem:* Am Soc Neurochem. *Res:* Instrumentation designed for proteins, peptides and nucleotide synthesis, purification and analysis. *Mailing Add:* Beckman Instruments Inc 1050 Page Mill Rd Palo Alto CA 94304

CHAN, EDDIE CHIN SUN, b Singapore, May 13, 31; Can citizen. MICROBIAL PHYSIOLOGY EDUniv Tex, El Paso, BA, 54; Univ Tex, Austin, MA, 57; Univ Md, PhD(microbiol), 60. *Prof Exp:* Nat Res Coun Can fel, 60-62; asst prof microbiol & biochem, Univ NB, 62-65; asst prof, 65-68, ASSOC PROF MICROBIOL & IMMUNOL, McGILL UNIV, 68- *Concurrent Pos:* Nat Res Coun Can & Med Res Coun Can grants. *Mem:* AAAS; Am Soc Microbiol; Can Soc Microbiol. *Res:* Anaerobes of periodontal disease; textbooks in general microbiology. *Mailing Add:* Dept of Microbiol & Immunol McGill Univ Montreal Can

CHAN, EDWARD YUETCHUN, b Canton, China, Dec 25, 49. FOUNDRY CATALYSIS. *Educ:* State Univ NY, Fredonia, BS, 73; Brown Univ, PhD(org chem), 79. *Prof Exp:* RES CHEMIST, QUAKER OATS CO, 79- *Mem:* Am Chem Soc. *Res:* Syntheses of furan-based resins and polymers; syntheses of foundry binders and catalysts. *Mailing Add:* 3 Villa Verde Dr 318 Buffalo Grove IL 60090

CHAN, HAK-FOON, b Hong Kong, Oct 10, 42; m 68; c 1. AGRICULTURAL CHEMISTRY. *Educ:* Chung Chi Col, Chinese Univ, Hong Kong. dipl sci, 64; Bowling Green State Univ, MA, 68; Univ Mich, PhD(org chem), 71. *Prof Exp:* Fel chem, Univ Rochester, 71-73; sr chemist fungicide & biocide, 73-80, AGR PROD AREA MKT MGR, PACIFIC REGION, ROHM AND HAAS CO, 81- *Mem:* Am Chem Soc; Royal Soc Chem. *Res:* To prepare for evaluation organic compounds which possess fungicidal, bactericidal and biocidal activities. *Mailing Add:* 524 Matterhorn Dr Walnut Creek CA 94598

CHAN, HARVEY THOMAS, JR, b Astoria, Ore, Mar 5, 40; m 66; c 3. FOOD SCIENCE. *Educ:* Ore State Univ, BSc, 63, PhD(food sci), 69; Univ Hawaii, MSc, 66. *Prof Exp:* Res asst food sci, Univ Hawaii, 63-65 & Ore State Univ, 65-68; FOOD TECHNOLOGIST, AGR RES SERV, USDA, 68- *Concurrent Pos:* Affil grad fac, Dept Food Sci, Univ Hawaii, 69-80, Dept

Hort, 80- *Mem:* Inst Food Technologists (secy-treas, 73-74 & 76, chmn-elect, 78-79); Am Chem Soc; Sigma Xi. *Res:* Chemical and biochemical composition of tropical fruits and vegetables; process and product development of tropical fruits and vegetables; changes in nutrients and biochemical constituents during processing. *Mailing Add:* USDA-Agr Res Serv PO Box 917 Hilo HI 96720

CHAN, JAMES C, b Hong Kong, Nov 20, 37; m 64. MICROBIOLOGY. *Educ:* Int Christian Univ Tokyo, BA, 61; Univ Rochester, PhD(microbiol), 66. *Prof Exp:* Sr res scientist, Squibb Inst Med Res, 66-68; asst prof med, Sch Med, Ind Univ, Indianapolis, 68-71; asst prof biochem virol, Baylor Col Med, 71-72; asst virologist, 72-78, asst prof, 72-79, dir, Virol Prog, 80-81, ASSOC PROF VIROL, CANCER CTR, M D ANDERSON HOSP & TUMOR INST, UNIV TEX, 79-, ASSOC VIROLOGIST, 79-, CHMN, HYBRIDOMA STUDY GROUP, 80- *Concurrent Pos:* Ind Univ fac res grant & Little Red Door, Inc cancer res grants, 69 & 70; Am Cancer Soc inst grant, 68-70; St Joseph Co, Inc cancer res grant, 71-72; NIH biomed res grant, 78-79; hybridoma res grant, UCF, 80- *Mem:* AAAS; Am Soc Microbiol; Am Asn Cancer Res; Int Leukemia Asn. *Res:* Biochemical changes in cells following infection by tumor viruses, such as RNA tumor viruses; virus induced tumor; host resistance; studies of viral involvement in neoplastic diseases in animals and man; monoclonal antibodies. *Mailing Add:* Dept of Virol Cancer Ctr Univ Tex M D Anderson Hosp & Tumor Inst Houston TX 77030

CHAN, KAI CHIU, b Canton, China, May 16, 34; US citizen; m 66; c 2. DENTISTRY. *Educ:* Chiba Univ, Japan, BS, 58; Tokyo Med & Dent Univ, DDS, 62; Univ Iowa, MS, 64, DDS, 67. *Prof Exp:* From instr to asst prof, 64-71, assoc prof, 71-76, PROF OPER DENT, COL DENT, UNIV IOWA, 76- *Mem:* Am Asn Dent Schs; Am Dent Asn; Int Asn Dent Res; Acad Oper Dent. *Res:* Burnished amalgam surfaces; retention pins; dental cements. *Mailing Add:* Col of Dent Univ of Iowa Iowa City IA 52242

CHAN, KA-KONG, Hong Kong; m 68; c 3. MEDICINAL CHEMISTRY. *Educ:* Univ NB, PhD(chem), 66. *Prof Exp:* Fel organic chem, Univ NB, 66-67; fel Univ BC, 67-69; res fel biochem, Harvard Univ, 69-70; RES SCIENTIST MED & ORG CHEM, HOFFMAN-LA ROCHE INC, 70- *Mem:* Am Chem Soc. *Res:* Synthesis of natural products; asymmetric synthesis of natural vitamin E; solid phase peptide synthesis; synthesis of fluorinated retinoids; design and synthesis of enzyme inhibitors. *Mailing Add:* Chem Res Dept Hoffman-La Roche Inc 340 Kingsland St Nutley NJ 07110

CHAN, KENNETH KIN-HING, b Hong Kong, Nov 30, 40; US citizen; m 72; c 2. CLINICAL PHARMACOLOGY, PHARMACEUTICAL CHEMISTRY. *Educ:* Calif State Univ, San Jose, BS, 64; Univ Calif, Davis, MS, 68; Univ Calif, San Francisco, PhD(pharmaceut chem), 72. *Prof Exp:* Res biochemist, Stanford Univ/Vet Admin Hosp, Palo Alto, 64-66; res assoc pharmaceut chem, 72-73, asst prof, 73-79, ASSOC PROF PHARM, SCH PHARM, UNIV SOUTHERN CALIF, 79-, DIR, PHARMACOANALYTIC LAB, COMPREHENSIVE CTR, 80- *Concurrent Pos:* Prin investr, NIH grants, Nat Cancer Inst, 74-75 & 76-79, co-prin investr, 75-76; proj investr, NIH grants, Nat Cancer Inst, Western Cancer Study Group pharmacokinetics, 75-76 & Los Angeles County/Univ Southern Calif Cancer Ctr, 74-77 & 80-83. *Mem:* Am Chem Soc; AAAS; Am Asn Cancer Res. *Res:* Drug metabolism; pharmacokinetics; isotope labeling synthesis; cancer chemotherapy; pharmacology of anticancer drugs; drug analysis; chemical structure and biological activities; nuclear magnetic resonance; mass spectrometry. *Mailing Add:* 605 Indiana Place South Pasadena CA 91030

CHAN, KWOKLONG ROLAND, b Shanghai, China, Oct 18, 33. ATMOSPHERIC CHEMISTRY, ATMOSPHERIC PHYSICS. *Educ:* Univ Hong Kong, BSc, 56; Stanford Univ, MS, 58, PhD(elec eng), 63. *Prof Exp:* Res asst, Radiosci Lab, Stanford Univ, 58-62; asst prof elec eng, Univ Hawaii, 62-63; res scientist, Instrument Div, 63-64, res scientist, Space Sci Div, Ames Res Ctr, 64-80, asst mgr, Upper Atmosphere Res Prog, Washington, DC, 80-81, ASST CHIEF, ATMOSPHERIC EXP BR, AMES RES CTR, NASA, 81- *Mem:* Inst Elec & Electronics Engrs; Am Geophys Union. *Res:* Study of the earth's neutral and ionized atmospheres by experimental technique using ground-based, airborne, balloon-borne or spacecraft instruments; electrical engineering. *Mailing Add:* Space Sci Div Ames Res Ctr NASA Moffett Field CA 94035

CHAN, LAI KOW, b Hong Kong, Nov 5, 40; m 67. STATISTICS. *Educ:* Hong Kong Baptist Col, BSc, 62; Univ Western Ont, MA, 64, PhD(statist), 66. *Prof Exp:* Instr, Univ Toronto, 65-66; from asst prof to prof statist, Univ Western Ont, 66-80; PROF STATIST & HEAD DEPT, UNIV MAN, 80- *Concurrent Pos:* Hon res fel, Univ Col, London, 73-74; vis prof, Univ Umea, 80- *Mem:* Fel Am Statist Asn; Inst Statist Inst; Opers Res Soc Am; Inst Math Statist. *Res:* Estimation problems in linear models; optimization methods; rehabilitized risk assessment of large technological systems. *Mailing Add:* Dept Statist Univ Man Winnipeg MB R3T 2N2 Can

CHAN, LEE-NIEN LILLIAN, b Hong Kong, Sept 28, 41; m 69; c 3. DEVELOPMENTAL BIOLOGY, CELL BIOLOGY. *Educ:* Acadia Univ, BSc, 63; Univ Wis, MS, 66; Yale Univ, PhD(biol), 71. *Prof Exp:* Assoc in res, Yale Univ, 67, res assoc molecular biophys & biochem, 71; res assoc biol, Mass Inst Technol, 71-73; asst prof physiol, Univ Conn Health Ctr, 73-78; ASSOC PROF CELL BIOL, UNIV TEX MED BR GALVESTON, 78- *Concurrent Pos:* NIH res grant. *Mem:* Am Soc Cell Biol; Am Soc Hematol; Soc Develop Biol; Am Soc Biol Chem. *Res:* Development of eukaryotes; regulation of specific gene expression; erythropoiesis; differentiation of red cell membrane. *Mailing Add:* Dept of Human Biol Chem & Genetics Univ of Tex Med Br Galveston TX 77550

CHAN, LELAND, environmental health, see previous edition

CHAN, MAUREEN GILLEN, b Brooklyn, NY, June 2, 39; m 63. POLYMER CHEMISTRY. *Educ:* Chestnut Hill Col, BS, 61; Stevens Inst Technol, MS, 65. *Prof Exp:* Sr tech aide chem, 62-64, assoc mem tech staff, 64-74, mem tech staff, 74-78, SUPVR, POLYOLEFIN STABILIZATION GROUP, BELL LABS, 78- *Mem:* Am Chem Soc; Soc Plastics Engrs; NAm Thermal Anal Soc; Am Soc Testing & Mat. *Res:* Stabilization of high polymers. *Mailing Add:* Bell Labs Murray Hill NJ 07974

CHAN, MOSES HUNG-WAI, b Hsi-an, China, Nov 23, 46; m 72; c 1. LOW TEMPERATURE PHYSICS. *Educ:* Bridgewater Col, BA, 67; Cornell Univ, MS, 70, PhD(exp physics), 74. *Prof Exp:* asst lectr, Univ Hong Kong, 69-70; res asst, Cornell Univ, 70-73; res assoc physics, Duke Univ, 73-76 ; asst prof physics, Univ Toledo, 76-79; ASST PROF, PA STATE UNIV, 79- *Mem:* Am Phys Soc; Sigma Xi. *Res:* Low temperature properties of quantum fluids and solids, and critical phenomena of fluids; thermodynamic study of phase transition in two and three dimensional systems. *Mailing Add:* Dept Physics 104 Davey Lab Penn State Univ University Park PA 16802

CHAN, PAUL C, b Hong Kong, Mar 15, 36; m 64; c 1. CIVIL ENGINEERING, APPLIED MECHANICS. *Educ:* Univ Hong Kong, BSc, 58; Worcester Polytech Inst, MSc, 62; Tex A&M Univ, PhD(civil eng), 68. *Prof Exp:* Asst prof, 66-77, ASSOC PROF CIVIL ENG, NJ INST TECHNOL, 77- *Mem:* Geol Soc Am; Seismol Soc Am. *Res:* Soil structure interaction; soil behavior under dynamic loadings; stress waves propagation. *Mailing Add:* Dept of Civil Eng NJ Inst of Technol Newark NJ 07102

CHAN, PETER SINCHUN, b Kwang-tung, China, Dec 1, 38; m 64; c 3. PHARMACOLOGY, BIOCHEMISTRY. *Educ:* Nat Taiwan Univ, BSc, 61; Univ Cincinnati, MSc, 64; Ind Univ, Bloomington, PhD(pharmacol, org chem), 67. *Prof Exp:* Res fel med chem, Univ Mich, 67-68; instr pharmacol, Med Br, Univ Tex, Galveston, 68-69, asst prof, 69-70; res pharmacologist, 70-73, group leader & prin res pharmacologist, 73-75, head dept cardiovasc-renal pharmacol, Lederle Labs Div, 75-76, GROUP LEADER & PRIN RES PHARMACOLOGIST, MED RES DIV, AM CYANAMID CO, 76- *Mem:* Am Soc Pharmacol & Exp Therapeut; Soc Exp Biol & Med; Am Heart Asn; Am Chem Soc. *Res:* Cardiovascular and renal pharmacology; pharmacological and biochemical approaches for the search of new drugs and to study mechanisms of drug actions, drug design and regulation of enzyme systems of pharmacologic importance. *Mailing Add:* Med Res Div American Cyanamid Co Pearl River NY 10965

CHAN, PHILLIP C, b Amoy, China, June 14, 28; US citizen; m 65; c 1. BIOCHEMISTRY. *Educ:* Monmouth Col, Ill, BS, 52; Columbia Univ, MA, 53, PhD(chem), 57. *Prof Exp:* Fel, Sch Med, Johns Hopkins Univ, 57-59; Jane Coffin Childs fel, Max Planck Inst Cell Chem, Ger, 59-60; asst prof, 60-67, assoc prof, 67-76, PROF BIOCHEM, STATE UNIV NY DOWNSTATE MED CTR, 76- *Mem:* Am Chem Soc; Harvey Soc; Am Soc Biol Chem. *Res:* Reactive oxygen species in biological systems. *Mailing Add:* Dept Biochem State Univ of NY Downstate Med Ctr Brooklyn NY 11203

CHAN, PING-KWONG, b Sun Wei, Kwangtung, China, Oct 22, 49; #1977. GENERAL TOXICOLOGY, RISK ASSESSMENT. *Educ:* Northeastern Univ, BSc, 75; Univ Miss Med Sch, PhD(toxicol), 81. *Prof Exp:* Pharmacist, Osco Drug Co, 75-76; TOXICOLOGIST, ROHM & HAAS CO, 80- *Mem:* Sigma Xi. *Res:* Toxicology and risk assessment in product development; mechanism of toxicity; metabolism; pharmacokinetics; mycotoxins. *Mailing Add:* Toxicology Dept Rohm & Haas Co Spring House PA 19477

CHAN, PO CHUEN, cell biology, see previous edition

CHAN, RAYMOND KAI-CHOW, b Hong Kong, Oct 10, 33; m 60; c 2. PHYSICAL CHEMISTRY. *Educ:* Univ Toronto, BA, 58, PhD(phys chem), 61. *Prof Exp:* Nat Res Coun Can fel, 61-62; asst prof, 62-71, ASSOC PROF CHEM, UNIV WESTERN ONT, 71- *Mem:* Chem Inst Can; NAm Thermal Anal Soc. *Res:* Molecular solid phase transitions under pressure, supercooled liquids and glassy plastic crystals by thermally stimulated depolarization, dielectric properties and differential thermal analysis; air pollution, especially sulfur dioxide limestone/dolomite reaction using thermogravimetry. *Mailing Add:* Dept of Chem Univ of Western Ont London N6A 5B7 Can

CHAN, RICHARD K S, b Kwongtung, China, Nov 22, 34; m 65; c 1. PHYSICAL CHEMISTRY, POLYMER PHYSICS. *Educ:* Cheng Kung Univ, Taiwan, BSc, 57; State Univ NY, PhD(phys chem), 63; Syracuse Univ, PhD(phys chem), 63. *Prof Exp:* Instr phys chem, Chung Chi Col, Hong Kong, 57-59; res assoc, Univ Ill, 62-64; res engr, Dow Chem Co, 64-67; sr res chemist, 67-70, RES SCIENTIST, POLYMER RES, AIR PROD & CHEM, INC, 70- *Mem:* Am Chem Soc; Am Inst Chem Engrs. *Res:* Application of solid and fluid mechanics to polymer field; polymer characterization; kinetics of homo- and copolymerization. *Mailing Add:* Polymer Res Dept Air Prod & Chem Inc PO Box 538 Allentown PA 18105

CHAN, SAMUEL H P, b Nanking, China, Aug 1, 41; m 71. BIOCHEMISTRY, MOLECULAR BIOLOGY. *Educ:* Int Christian Univ, Tokyo, BA, 64; Univ Rochester, PhD(biochem), 69. *Prof Exp:* Asst, Univ Rochester, 64-69; res assoc biochem & fel, Cornell Univ, 69-71; asst prof, 71-76, ASSOC PROF BIOCHEM, SYRACUSE UNIV, 76- *Mem:* AAAS; Am Chem Soc; NY Acad Sci; Sigma Xi. *Res:* Physical, chemical and enzymatic properties of cytochromes and cytochrome oxidase; resolution and reconstitution of inner mitochondrial membrane; mechanism of oxidative phosphorylation. *Mailing Add:* Dept of Biol Syracuse Univ Syracuse NY 13210

CHAN, SHAM-YUEN, b Hong Kong; Brit citizen; m 75. BIOCHEMISTRY, MICROBIOLOGY. *Educ:* Hong Kong Baptist Col, BS, 73; Univ Notre Dame, PhD(microbiol), 78. *Prof Exp:* Fel, Lobund Lab, Univ Notre Dame, 78-81, res asst prof prostate cancer, Dept Microbiol, 81-82; RES SCIENTIST, RECOMBINANT DNA GROUP, MILES LAB, INC, 82- *Mem:* Am Soc Microbiol; NY Acad Sci; Sigma Xi; AAAS; Gnotobiotic Asn. *Res:* Characterization and isolation of tissue plasminogen activators using tissue culture and biochemical techniques. *Mailing Add:* Miles Lab Inc PO Box 932 Elkhart IN 46515

CHAN, SHIH HUNG, b Taiwan, Nov 8, 43; US citizen; m 70; c 2. HEAT TRANSFER, FLUID MECHANICS. *Educ:* Taipei Inst Technol, dipl, 63; Univ NH, 66; Univ Calif, Berkeley, PhD(mech eng), 69. *Prof Exp:* From asst prof to assoc prof mech eng, NY Univ, 69-73; assoc prof, Polytech Inst NY, 73-74; res staff nuclear eng, Argonne Nat Lab, 74-75; assoc prof, 75-80, PROF MECH ENG, UNIV WIS, MILWAUKEE, CHMN, 79- *Concurrent Pos:* Prin investr grants, NSF, Dept Energy & NIH, 70-; consult, Gen Elec Co, 81 & Arrgonne Nat Lab, 75- *Mem:* Am Nuclear Soc; Am Soc Mech Eng; Sigma Xi. *Res:* Thermal radiative transfer; radiation properties of gases and nuclear reactor materials; fouling heat transfer; thermal hydraulic analyses of nuclear reactors; two-phase flow; condensation; melting and solidification. *Mailing Add:* Dept Mech Eng Univ Wis PO Box 784 Milwaukee WI 53201

CHAN, SHU FUN, b Canton, China, July 27, 39; m 69; c 2. CHEMISTRY. *Educ:* Sun Yat Sen Univ, BSc, 60; Univ Hong Kong, BSc, 66, PhD(chem), 71. *Prof Exp:* Chemist, Chiap Hwa Mfg Co, Hong Kong, 63-65; teaching asst, Univ Hong Kong, 66-70; lectr inorg chem, Nanyang Univ, 70-78; sr res assoc, 78-80, CHEM ASSOC, BROOKHAVEN NAT LAB, NY, 80- *Concurrent Pos:* Fel, State Univ NY, Buffalo, 77. *Mem:* Am Chem Soc; Chem Soc London. *Res:* Kinetic and mechanistic studies of substitution reactions; electron transfer reactions of coordination compounds. *Mailing Add:* 830 Brookhaven Nat Lab Upton NY 11973

CHAN, SHU-GAR, b Canton, China, Aug 18, 27; US citizen; m 56. ELECTRICAL ENGINEERING. *Educ:* Univ Wash, Seattle, BS, 52; Columbia Univ, MS, 54; Univ Kans, PhD(elec eng), 64. *Prof Exp:* Lectr elec eng, City Col New York, 54-58; instr, Univ Mich, 58-60 & Univ Kans, 61-62; ASSOC PROF, NAVAL POSTGRAD SCH, 64- *Mem:* Inst Elec & Electronics Engrs; Sigma Xi. *Res:* Network theory; computer-aided design; topology. *Mailing Add:* Dept of Elec Eng Naval Postgrad Sch Monterey CA 93940

CHAN, SHUNG KAI, b Hong Kong, Mar 31, 35; m 63. BIOCHEMISTRY. *Educ:* WVa Univ, AB, 56; Univ Wis, PhD(biochem), 62. *Prof Exp:* Asst res chemist, Samuel Robert Noble Found, 58-59; sr res biochemist, Abbott Labs, 62-66; asst prof, 66-70, ASSOC PROF BIOCHEM, MED CTR, UNIV KY, 70- *Mem:* AAAS; Am Chem Soc; Brit Biochem Soc; Am Soc Biol Chem. *Res:* Glycoproteins, structure and function; glycoproteins, biosynthesis and regulation. *Mailing Add:* Dept of Biochem Univ of Ky Med Ctr Lexington KY 40506

CHAN, SHU-PARK, b Canton, China, Oct 10, 29; m 56; c 2. ELECTRICAL ENGINEERING. *Educ:* Va Mil Inst, BS, 55; Univ Ill, MS, 57, PhD(elec eng), 63. *Prof Exp:* Instr math & elec eng, Va Mil Inst, 57-59, asst prof math, 61-63; instr, Univ Ill, 60-62, res assoc, co-ord sci lab, 62-63; assoc prof elec eng, 63-68, PROF ELEC ENG, UNIV SANTA CLARA, 68-, CHMN DEPT, 69- *Concurrent Pos:* NSF res grant, 64-65; conf chmn, Fourth Asilomar Conf Circuits & Systs, 70; ed Int Ser Eng & Scis, Nat Taiwan Univ Press, 73-; spec chair elec eng, Nat Taiwan Univ, 73; overseas consult, Nat Sci Coun, Repub China, 76-; invited lectr, Acad Sinica, Peking, 80; hon prof, Elec Eng Dept, Univ Hong Kong, 80. *Honors & Awards:* Commendation for contrib in elec eng, Calif State Senate, 72. *Mem:* Inst Elec & Electronics Engrs; Am Soc Eng Educ. *Res:* Linear graph theory and its applications to electrical networks; circuit theory; computer-aided analysis and design of linear active networks and systems. *Mailing Add:* Dept of Elec Eng & Comput Sci Univ of Santa Clara Santa Clara CA 95053

CHAN, SIU-KEE, b Canton, China, Sep 11, 36; US citizen; m 66; c 2. FINITE ELEMENT ANALYSIS, PLASTICITY. *Educ:* Cheng Kung Univ, BSME, 59, Univ Va, MMSc, 62, Univ Ill, PhD(mech), 66. *Prof Exp:* Engr, Hayes Int Aircraft Co, 66; FEL ENGR, WESTINGHOUSE RES LABS, 66- *Mailing Add:* Westinghouse Res Labs Beulah Rd Pittsburgh PA 15235

CHAN, STEPHEN, b Wuchow, China, July 28, 42; c 2. ENDOCRINOLOGY. *Educ:* Univ Hong Kong, BSc, 66, MSc, 68; Univ Hull, PhD(zool), 71. *Prof Exp:* Res assoc, Boston Univ, 71-72; asst prof, Rutgers Univ, 72-77; ASSOC PROF BIOL, STATE UNIV NY BROCKPORT, 77- *Mem:* Soc Study Reproduction; Soc Endocrinol; Soc Exp Biol & Med. *Res:* Mammalian reproduction with emphasis on prenatal biology and aging mechanisms. *Mailing Add:* Dept of Biol Sci State Univ of NY Brockport NY 14420

CHAN, SUNNEY IGNATIUS, b San Francisco, Calif, Oct 5, 36; m 64; c 1. BIOPHYSICAL CHEMISTRY, BIOPHYSICS. *Educ:* Univ Calif, Berkeley, BS, 57, PhD(chem), 60. *Prof Exp:* NSF fel physics, Harvard Univ, 60-61; asst prof chem, Univ Calif, Riverside, 61-63; from asst prof to assoc prof chem physics, 63-68, actg exec officer chem, 77-78, exec officer chem, 78-80, PROF CHEM PHYSICS, CALIF INST TECHNOL, 68-, PROF BIOPHYS CHEM, 76-, MASTER STUDENT HOUSES, 80- *Concurrent Pos:* Consult, Unified Sci Assocs, 63-64, Div Gen Med Sci, USPHS, 70-74, Procter & Gamble Co, 74-; Merck Sharp & Dohme Res Labs, 74- & McGaw Labs, 77-79; Sloan fel, 65-67; Guggenheim Mem fel, 68-69; mem ed rev bd, Appl Spectros, 68-70; assoc ed, Ann Rev Magnetic Resonance, 70; Reilly lectr, Univ Notre Dame, 73. *Mem:* AAAS; Am Phys Soc; Am Chem Soc; Am Soc Biol Chemists; fel NY Acad Sci. *Res:* Physical methods for the determination of molecular structure; applications of magnetic resonance spectroscopy to biological problems, particularly membrane structure and function, protein-lipid interactions and mechanisms of ion and electron transport. *Mailing Add:* Dept of Chem Calif Inst of Technol Pasadena CA 91125

CHAN, TAK-HANG, b Hong Kong, June 28, 41. ORGANIC CHEMISTRY. *Educ:* Univ Toronto, BSc, 62; Princeton Univ, MA, 63, PhD(chem), 65. *Prof Exp:* Asst prof, 66-71, assoc prof, 72-77, PROF CHEM, McGILL UNIV, 78- *Concurrent Pos:* Res fel, Harvard Univ, 65-66. *Mem:* Am Chem Soc; The Chem Soc; Chem Inst Can; AAAS. *Res:* Synthesis of complicated natural products; structural determination of natural products; mechanisms of organic reactions; new synthetic methods with silicon, sulfur and phosphorus compounds. *Mailing Add:* Dept of Chem McGill Univ Montreal Can

CHAN, TAT-HUNG, b Hong Kong, Aug 21, 51. AUTOMATA THEORY, COMPUTATIONAL COMPLEXITY. *Educ:* Dartmouth Col, AB, 74; Cornell Univ, MS & PhD(comput sci), 80. *Prof Exp:* Programmer, Asiadata Ltd, Hong Kong, 75-76; ASST PROF COMPUT SCI, UNIV MINN, 80- *Mem:* Asn Comput Mach; Soc Indust & Appl Math. *Res:* Complexity theory; programming logics and program verification. *Mailing Add:* Dept Comput Sci Technol Col Univ Minn 207 Church St SE Minneapolis MN 55455

CHAN, TEH-SHENG, b Taiwan, China. HUMAN GENETICS, MICROBIOLOGY. *Educ:* Nat Taiwan Univ, MD, 63; Yale Univ, PhD(molecular biol), 69. *Prof Exp:* Intern, Nat Taiwan Univ Hosp, 62-63; asst prof physiol, Sch Med, Univ Conn, Farmington, 73-78; ASSOC PROF MICROBIOL, UNIV TEX MED BR GALVESTON, 78- *Concurrent Pos:* Helen Hay Whitney fel, Rockefeller Univ, 69-71 & Mass Inst Technol, 71-73. *Mem:* Am Soc Microbiol; AAAS. *Res:* Somatic cell genetics; inborn errors of purine metabolism; viral gene transfer in mammalian cells. *Mailing Add:* Dept of Microbiol Univ of Tex Med Br Galveston TX 77550

CHAN, VINCENT SIK-HUNG, b Hong Kong, Sept 1, 49. PLASMA PHYSICS, ELECTRICAL ENGINEERING. *Educ:* Univ Wis-Madison, BSEE, 72, MSEE, 73, PhD(plasma physics), 75. *Prof Exp:* SR SCIENTIST FUSION, GEN ATOMIC CO, 75- *Mem:* Am Phys Soc. *Res:* Radio-frequency heating of fusion plasmas, wave propagation and instabilities in plasmas and transport phenomena in plasmas. *Mailing Add:* Fusion Div Gen Atomic Co PO Box 81608 San Diego CA 92138

CHAN, WAH CHUN, b Kwangtung, China, Oct 8, 34; Can citizen; m 67; c 4. CONTROL ENGINEERING, OPERATIONS RESEARCH. *Educ:* Nat Taiwan Univ, BSc, 58; Univ NB, MSc, 61; Univ BC, PhD(control), 65. *Prof Exp:* Asst, Univ NB, 59-61; res asst, Univ BC, 64-65; mem sci staff, Res & Develop Labs, Northern Elec Co, 65-67; from asst prof to assoc prof elec eng, 67-77, PROF ELEC ENG, UNIV CALGARY, 77- *Honors & Awards:* 73 Ambrose Fleming Premium, Brit Inst Elec Engrs, 74. *Mem:* Sr mem Inst Elec & Electronics Engrs. *Res:* Optimal control systems; poWer systems; telecommunication and queueing systems; reliability. *Mailing Add:* Dept of Elec Eng Univ of Calgary Calgary AB T2N 1N4 Can

CHAN, WAH YIP, b Shanghai, China, Dec 1, 32; nat US; m 61; c 2. PHARMACOLOGY. *Educ:* Univ Wis, BA, 56; Columbia Univ, PhD(pharmacol), 61. *Prof Exp:* From res assoc biochem to assoc prof pharmacol, 60-76, PROF PHARMACOL, MED COL, CORNELL UNIV, 76- *Concurrent Pos:* mem basic pharmacol adv comt, Pharmaceut Mfrs Asn Found, 73-; mem, Pharmacol Study Sect, NIH, 77; consult, Prog Proj Rev, Nat Heart Lung & Blood Inst & NIH, 81. *Mem:* Soc Exp Biol & Med; Am Soc Pharmacol & Exp Therapeut; Soc Study Reproduction; Harvey Soc; NY Acad Sci. *Res:* Pharmacology of neurohypophysial hormones and polypeptides; renal pharmacology; uterine pharmacology. *Mailing Add:* Dept of Pharmacol Cornell Univ Med Col New York NY 10021

CHAN, WAI MAY, b China, Oct 7, 34; US citizen. MICROBIOLOGY, BIOCHEMISTRY. *Educ:* Wheaton Col, Ill, BS, 52; Northwestern Univ, MT, 54; Iowa State Univ, MS, 56. *Prof Exp:* Asst res microbiologist taxon of antibiotic producing microorganisms, Parke Davis & Co, 56-61; sr med technologist clin lab, Olin Mem Hosp, Mich State Univ, 62-63; res assoc microbial biochem, Squibb Inst Med Res, 63-71; SR BIOLOGIST MICROBIOL PHARMACEUT ANAL, SYNTEX RES, 71- *Mem:* Soc Indust Microbiol; Am Soc Microbiol; Nat Registry Microbiol; Am Soc Clin Pathologists; Am Chem Soc. *Res:* Taxonomical study of antibiotic producers; modes of action of antimicrobial agents in cell free systems and in cell walls; analysis of antibiotics and preservatives used in pharmaceutical products. *Mailing Add:* Syntex Res 3401 Hillview Ave Palo Alto CA 94304

CHAN, WAI-YEE, b Canton, China, Apr 28, 50; m 76; c 1. BIOCHEMICAL GENETICS, MEDICAL BIOCHEMISTRY. *Educ:* Chinese Univ, Hong Kong, BSc 74; Univ Fla, PhD(biochem), 77. *Prof Exp:* Teaching asst biochem, Univ Fla, 74-77; fel, 77-78, res assoc pediat, 78-79, ASST PROF PEDIAT & BIOCHEM, UNIV OKLA, 79- *Concurrent Pos:* Staff affil, GEM Serv, dir, Trace Element Lab & asst sci dir, Biochem Genetics Lab, Okla Children's Hosp, 79-; consult, Vet Admin Med Ctr, Oklahoma City, Okla, 81-; consult ed, J Am Col Nutrit, 82- *Mem:* Am Inst Nutrit; NY Acad Sci; Am Soc Biol Chem; Soc Ped Res; Biochem Soc. *Res:* Molecular mechanisms of inborn errors of metabolism; trace element genetic metabolic disorders and roles in infant nutrition and development; polyamine metabolism in humans in health and diseases. *Mailing Add:* Dept Pediat Univ Okla Health Sci Ctr PO Box 26901 Oklahoma City OK 73190

CHAN, WING CHENG RAYMOND, b Canton, China, Feb 19, 36; US citizen; m 62; c 3. CHEMICAL ENGINEERING, PROCESS DEVELOPMENT & DESIGN. *Educ:* Univ Calif, BS, 60; Univ Minn, Minneapolis, PhD(chem eng), 64. *Prof Exp:* Res engr, Uniroyal, Inc, 64-65, sr engr, Chem Div, 65-66, sr res engr, 66-69, res scientist, 69-76, ENG ASSOC, UNIROYAL CHEM CO, 76- *Mem:* Am Inst Chem Engrs; Am Chem Soc. *Res:* Computer simulation and optimization of chemical processes; reaction kinetics and reactor engineering; interfacial heat and mass transfer; applied mathematics in chemical engineering; fluid-fluid separation. *Mailing Add:* Uniroyal Chem Co Div Eng Elm St Naugatuck CT 06770

CHAN, YAT YUNG, b Hong Kong, March 12, 36; US citizen; m 66; c 1. AERODYNAMICS, FLUID MECHANICS. *Educ:* Nat Taiwan Univ, BSc, 56; Univ Sydney, Australia, MEngSc, 60; Univ Toronto, PhD(aerodynamic eng), 65. *Prof Exp:* Sci officer, Weapons Res Estab, Australia, 60-61; asst res officer, 65-67, assoc res officer, 67-75, SR RES OFFICER, NAT RES COUN, CAN, 75- *Concurrent Pos:* Sessional lectr, Carleton Univ, Ottawa, Can, 81- *Mem:* Am Inst Aeronaut & Astronaut. *Res:* Boundary layer theory, computational methods for two and three-dimensional, laminar and turbulent flow; organized structure of jet turbulence with application to jet noise; transonic wind tunnel wall interference; transonic three dimensional flows. *Mailing Add:* Nat Aeronaut Estab Nat Res Coun Can Montreal Rd Ottawa ON R1A 0K6 Can

CHAN, YICK-KWONG, b China, Oct 14, 35; m 69. BIOMETRY. *Educ:* Taiwan Prov Col Agr, BS, 55; Univ Minn, MS, 60, PhD(biostatist), 66. *Prof Exp:* Asst prof pub health, Yale Univ, 66-68; assoc prof biomet & head regional statist off, Southeastern Cancer Study Group, Emory Univ, 68-74; asst chief, Coop Stud Prog Coord Ctr, Vet Admin Med Ctr & assoc prof, Univ Md, 74-75; CHIEF, COOP STUDIES PROG COORD CTR, VET ADMIN MED CTR, WEST HAVEN & LECTR PUB HEALTH & BIOMET, YALE UNIV, 75- *Mem:* Fel Am Pub Health Asn; Am Statist Asn; Inst Math Statist; Biomet Soc. *Res:* Application of statistics to clinical trials, epidemiology and bioassays; epidemic simulations. *Mailing Add:* Vet Admin Coop Studies Prog Vet Admin Med Ctr West Haven CT 06516

CHAN, YUN LAI, b Taiwan; US citizen; m 68; c 2. RENAL PHYSIOLOGY, MEMBRANE BIOPHYSICS. *Educ:* Kaohsiung Med Col, BS, 65; Col Med, Nat Taiwan Univ, MS, 67; Sch Med, Univ Louisville, PhD(pharamacol), 71. *Prof Exp:* Instr renal pharmacol, Sch Med, Univ Louisville, 71-74, physiol, Sch Med, Yale Univ, 74-76; asst prof, 76-81, ASSOC PROF PHYSIOL, COL MED, UNIV ILL, 81- *Concurrent Pos:* Res assoc, renal physiol, Max Planck Inst Biophysics, 72-73; prin investr, NIH, 81. *Mem:* Am Physiol Soc; Am Soc Nephrol; Am Fedn Clin Res; Sigma Xi; NY Acad Sci. *Res:* Neural and hormonal control of renal function; cellular mechanisms of renal tubular transport. *Mailing Add:* Dept Physiol Col Med Univ Ill PO Box 6998 Chicago IL 60680

CHANANA, ARJUN DEV, b Lyallpur, Punjab, India, Nov 6, 30; m 63; c 2. EXPERIMENTAL PATHOLOGY, SURGERY. *Educ:* Univ Rajasthan, MB & BS, 55; FRCS(E) & FRCS, 60. *Prof Exp:* Internship, residencies & postdoctoral work surg, 55-60; chief resident surg, Bolton Dist Gen Hosp, Eng, 60-63; asst scientist, 63-66, assoc scientist, 66-69, actg head, Div Hemat, 68-69, scientist, 69-77, SR SCIENTIST, MED DEPT, BROOKHAVEN NAT LAB, 79- *Concurrent Pos:* Asst attend physician, Hosp of Med Res Ctr, Brookhaven Nat Lab, 63-65, assoc attend physician, 65-70, attend physician, 70-, chief of staff, 74-; assoc prof, Health Sci Ctr, State Univ NY Stony Brook, 70-; res consult surg, Nassau County Med Ctr, 70- *Mem:* Am Soc Hemat; Soc Exp Biol & Med; Transplantation Soc; Radiation Res Soc; Am Soc Exp Path. *Res:* Lymphocytopoiesis; transplantation immunology; leukemia; extracorporeal irradiation of blood and lymph; pulmonary biology. *Mailing Add:* Med Dept Brookhaven Nat Lab Upton NY 11973

CHANCE, BRITTON, b Wilkes-Barre, Pa, July 24, 13; m 38, 56; c 12. BIOPHYSICS, BIOCHEMISTRY. *Educ:* Univ Pa, BS, 35, MS, 36, PhD(phys chem), 40; Univ Cambridge, PhD(physiol), 42, DSc, 52. *Hon Degrees:* MD, Karolinska Inst, Sweden, 62; DSc, Med Col Ohio, 74, Semmelweise Univ, Budapest, 76 & Hahnemann Med Col, Philadelphia, 77. *Prof Exp:* Actg dir, Johnson Res Found, 40-41, asst prof biophys, 41-49, prof, 49-64, DIR JOHNSON RES FOUND, UNIV PA, 49-, JOHNSON PROF BIOPHYS & PHYS BIOCHEM, SCH MED, 64- *Concurrent Pos:* Investr, Off Sci Res & Develop, 41; res assoc, Radiation Lab, Mass Inst Technol, 41-42, group leader, 41-45, assoc div head, 42-45, mem vis comt, 54-56; sci consult to attache for res, USN, London, 48; consult, NSF, 51-56, mem physics panel comt on growth, 52-57; mem vis comt, Bartol Res Found, 55-59; Harvey lectr, 54; Phillips lectr, 56 & 65; Pepper lectr, 57; mem, President's Sci Adv Comt, 59; mem comn blood & blood derivatives, Am Red Cross & Nat Res Coun; exchange scholar, USSR, 63; foreign fel, Churchill Col, Univ Cambridge, 66; Keilin lectr, 66; Hackett lectr, 66; Redfearn lectr, 70; mem adv coun, Nat Inst Alcoholism, 71-75; vpres, Int Union Pure & Appl Biophys, 72-75, pres, 75-78, hon vpres, 78-81. *Honors & Awards:* Presidential Cert of Merit, 50; Paul Lewis Award, 50; Morlock Award, 61; Genootschaps Medal, Dutch Biochem Soc, 65; Franklin Medal, 66; Harrison Howe Award, Rochester Chap, Am Chem Soc, 66, Philadelphia Chap Award, 69, Nichols Award, NY Chap, 70; Pa Award for Excellence, 68; Heineken Medal, Royal Neth Acad Sci & Lett, 70; Gairdner Award, 72; Post-Cong Festschrift, 73; Semmelweis Medal, 74; Nat Medal Sci, 74. *Mem:* Nat Acad Sci; fel Am Phys Soc; Am Soc Biol Chem; Am Chem Soc; Am Acad Arts & Sci. *Res:* Automatic ship steering; photoelectric control units; radar timing and computing devices; sensitive spectrophotometers; enzyme-substrate compounds and reaction mechanisms of catalases; peroxidases, dehydrogenases; cytochromes; kinetics of multienzyme systems; oscillating enzyme systems; cation accumulation; cell oxygen requirements; non invasive optical and PWMR studies of organ biochemistry. *Mailing Add:* Johnson Res Found Univ of Pa Sch of Med Philadelphia PA 19104

CHANCE, C(LAYTON) W(ILLIAM), b Peoria, Ill, Feb 27, 22; m 44; c 3. ENGINEERING GRAPHICS. *Educ:* Bradley Univ, BS, 43; Univ Tex, MEd, 55, PhD, 63. *Prof Exp:* Draftsman eng dept, Euclid Div, Gen Motors Corp, 46-47, specification writer, sales promotion dept, 47-49, serv lit writer, serv dept, 49-52; teacher, pub sch, 52-53; from instr to asst prof eng drawing & discriptive geometry, Univ Tex, Austin, 53-66, res engr defense res lab, 55-57; acting dean instr, Mo Western Col, 66-67; ASSOC PROF ENG & TECHNOL, NORTHERN ARIZ UNIV, 67- *Concurrent Pos:* Wagner & Eng Found scholar, Univ Tex, 58; US Off Educ grant, 59. *Mem:* Am Soc Eng Educ. *Res:* Applications relating to Olgyay method of overhang shading evaluation to portable school buildings; overhead projector; colored transparency method of communication; counseling. *Mailing Add:* Fac Box 15600 Northern Ariz Univ Flagstaff AZ 86011

CHANCE, CHARLES JACKSON, b Belen, NMex, Apr 18, 14; m 36; c 2. ZOOLOGY, FISHERIES. *Educ:* Berea Col, AB, 35; Univ Tenn, MS, 42. *Prof Exp:* Aquatic biologist, Fisheries Mgt, Tenn Conserv Dept, 40-48; aquatic biologist, 48-58, chief aquatic biologist, 58-60, CHIEF FISHERIES & WATERFOWL RESOURCES BR, TENN VALLEY AUTHORITY, 60- *Mem:* AAAS; Am Inst Biol Sci; Am Fisheries Soc; Wildlife Soc. *Res:* Fisheries populations and management. *Mailing Add:* 4304 Gaines Rd Knoxville TN 37918

CHANCE, KELLY VAN, b Shamrock, Tex, Jan 19, 47; m 72; c 1. CHEMICAL PHYSICS. *Educ:* Univ Hawaii, BS, 70; Harvard Univ, AM, 72, PhD(chem physics), 77. *Prof Exp:* PHYSICIST, SMITHSONIAN ASTROPHYS OBSERV, HARVARD-SMITHSONIAN CTR ASTROPHYS, 77- *Res:* Molecular spectroscopy; atmospheric chemistry; chemical astrophysics. *Mailing Add:* Smithsonian Astrophys Observ 60 Garden St Cambridge MA 02138

CHANCE, ROBERT L, b Detroit, Mich, Feb 1, 24; m 52; c 4. ANALYTICAL CHEMISTRY, INORGANIC CHEMISTRY. *Educ:* Wayne State Univ, BS, 48. *Prof Exp:* Sr res chemist, 49-54, group leader inorg anal chem, 54-61, sr res chemist, 62-78, sr res scientist, 78-81, STAFF RES SCIENTIST, GEN MOTORS RES LABS, 81- *Mem:* Am Chem Soc; Nat Asn Corrosion Engrs; Am Soc Testing & Mat. *Res:* General and automotive corrosion research; electrochemical polarization techniques; surface analysis; engine coolants; inhibitor systems; coatings; alloy compositions; metallurgical structure; metal deformation; heat treatment; cavitation phenomena; corrosion surveys. *Mailing Add:* Gen Motors Res Labs Phys Chem Dept Gen Motors Tech Ctr Warren MI 48090

CHANCE, RONALD E, b Lapeer, Mich, Jan 17, 34; m 61; c 1. BIOCHEMISTRY, METABOLISM. *Educ:* Purdue Univ, BS, 56, MS, 59, PhD(biochem), 62. *Prof Exp:* Asst prof biochem, Purdue, 62-63; sr biochemist, 63-69, res scientist, 69-77, RES ASSOC, ELI LILLY & CO, 78- *Concurrent Pos:* USDA grant, 62-63. *Mem:* AAAS; Am Chem Soc; Am Soc Animal Sci. *Res:* Animal nutrition, amino acid requirements and interrelationships in Chinook salmon and weanling pigs; chemistry of protein hormones; isolation, purification, characterization and chemistry of protein hormones. *Mailing Add:* Dept Biochem Lilly Res Labs Indianapolis IN 46206

CHANCE, RONALD RICHARD, b Memphis, Tenn, July 24, 47; m 67; c 2. SOLID STATE CHEMISTRY. *Educ:* Delta State Univ, BS, 70; Dartmouth Col, PhD(chem), 74. *Prof Exp:* staff physicist, Allied Chem Corp, 74-77, GROUP LEADER, ALLIED CORP, 77- *Mem:* Am Phys Soc; Am Chem Soc. *Res:* Optical and electrical properties of conjugated polymers; theory of fluorescence and energy transfer in layered systems; photoconduction and exciton dynamics in molecular crystals. *Mailing Add:* Mat Res Ctr Allied Chem Corp Morristown NJ 07960

CHAND, RAM, b Shaharsultan, India, Oct 8, 39; m 69; c 2. ENGINEERING MECHANICS. *Educ:* Panjab Univ, India, BSc, 65, Indian Inst Technol, India, M(tech), 68; Univ Iowa, MS, 73, PhD(mech & hydraul), 74. *Prof Exp:* Res asst, Nat Aeronaut Lab, India, 65-66; sr lectr appl mech, Engr Col, India, 68-70; sr instr dynamics & solid mech, Univ Iowa, 72-73; sr engr, Rockwell Int, 74-77; LECTR ADVAN MATH, UNIV NC, CHARLOTTE, 80- *Concurrent Pos:* Consult, Nuclear Power Serv, NJ, 77- *Mem:* Am Soc Mech Engrs; Soc Exp Stress Anal. *Res:* Applications of optimization techniques; finite element methods; analytical and experimental stress analysis (non-destructive testing) in engineering mechanics and biomedical engineering; computer aided engineering designs; stress analysis in nuclear industry. *Mailing Add:* 8340 Knights Bridge Rd Charlotte NC 28210

CHANDAN, RAMESH CHANDRA, b Lahore, Pakistan, July 5, 34; m 60; c 3. FOOD TECHNOLOGY, BIOCHEMISTRY. *Educ:* Panjab Univ, India, BSc, 53, Hons, 55, MSc, 56; Univ Nebr, Lincoln, PhD(dairy mfg), 63. *Prof Exp:* Lectr chem, Panjab Univ, India, 56-57; lectr dairy chem, Nat Dairy Res Inst, India, 57-59; from asst to assoc dairy sci, Univ Nebr, Lincoln, 59-66; scientist dairy technol, Unilever, Ltd, Eng, 67-69; mgr res & develop, Dairylea Coop, Inc, 70-74; vpres, Whey Prod & Tech Serv, Purity Cheese Co, Anderson Clayton Foods, 74-76; ASSOC PROF, FOOD SCI & HUMAN NUTRIT DEPT, MICH STATE UNIV, 76- *Mem:* Am Dairy Sci Asn; Inst Food Technologists; Am Chem Soc; fel Am Inst Chemists; Am Mgt Asn. *Res:* Physico-chemical properties of milk; lipases; lysozymes; lipids; milk protein; microbial chemistry and enzymes; diary product technology; cultures; cultured products; food product development; whey protein manufacturing technology, quality control, cheese product development; whey fractionation. *Mailing Add:* 139 Food Sci Bldg Mich State Univ East Lansing MI 48824

CHANDER, JAGDISH, b Toba Tek Singh, India, Mar 7, 33; m 65; c 3. EXPERIMENTAL NUCLEAR PHYSICS. *Educ:* DAV Col, Jullundur, India, BSc, 52; Panjab Univ, India, BA, 53 & 54; Univ Rajasthan, MSc, 56; Univ Erlangen, Dr rer nat(physics), 61. *Prof Exp:* Demonstr chem, DAV Col, Jullundur, 52-53; demonstr, DSD Col, Gurgaon, 53-54; lectr physics, DAV Col, Jullundur, 56-68; lectr, Birla Sci Col, Pilani, 62 & Panjab Univ, 62-66; asst prof, 66-67, assoc prof, 67-70, PROF PHYSICS & ASTRON, UNIV WIS-STEVENS POINT, 70- *Concurrent Pos:* Res assoc, Siemens Res Lab, Erlangen, Ger, 61; dir, NSF Undergrad Res Partic, 68-71; acad year exten grant col teachers, NSF, 69-70; vis prof, Birla Inst Technol & Sci, Pilani, India, 79. *Mem:* Am Phys Soc; Am Asn Physics Teachers. *Res:* Low energy nuclear physics; semiconductor radiation detectors; teaching of physics. *Mailing Add:* 806 Crescent Ct Plover WI 54467

CHANDER, SATISH, b Muzaffargarh, Pakistan, Dec 25, 37; Canadian citizen; m 61; c 2. VETERINARY PATHOLOGY, DIAGNOSTIC SEROLOGY. *Educ:* Punjab Univ, India, BVSc, 56, MVSc, 60; Vet Sch, Hannover, Ger, DVM, 68; Ont Vet Col, Guelph, PhD(oncol), 71. *Prof Exp:* Res asst, Regional Animal Nutrit Ctr, 59-60; asst res officer, Punjab Agr Univ, 60-65, asst prof path, Vet Sch, 65-66; hematologist, Vet Sch, Hannover, Ger, 68; lectr, Ont Vet Col, 71-72; RES SCIENTIST, AGR CAN, OTTAWA, 72- *Concurrent Pos:* Volkswagen Works Award, Vet Sch, Hannover, Ger, 67-68. *Mem:* Can Asn Vet Pathologists; Can Vet Med Asn; Int Asn Comp Res Leukemia & Related Dis. *Res:* Etiology, diagnosis and epizootiology of leukemia in cattle (Bovine Leukosis). *Mailing Add:* Agr Can Animal Path Div 801 Fallowfield Rd Ottawa ON K2H 8P9 Can

CHANDLER, A BLEAKLEY, b Augusta, Ga, Sept 11, 26; m; c 2. PATHOLOGY. *Educ:* Med Col Ga, MD, 48. *Prof Exp:* Intern, Baylor Univ Hosp, 48-49; resident path, Univ Hosp, Augusta, Ga, 49-50; from asst prof to assoc prof, 53-62, PROF PATH, MED COL GA, 62-, CHMN DEPT, 75- *Concurrent Pos:* Nat Cancer Inst trainee path, Med Col Ga, 50-51; Commonwealth Fund res fel, Inst Thrombosis Res, Norway, 63-64. *Mem:* Am Asn Hist Med; Int Acad Path; Am Soc Exp Path; Am Path & Bact. *Res:* In vitro thrombosis; experimental and human cardiovascular pathology. *Mailing Add:* Dept of Path Med Col of Ga Augusta GA 30902

CHANDLER, ALBERT MORRELL, b Pontiac, Mich, July 10, 32; m 59; c 3. BIOCHEMISTRY. *Educ:* Wayne State Univ, BS, 55, PhD(biochem), 62. *Prof Exp:* Pharmacist, Mich, 51-56; res assoc anat, Wayne State Univ, 63-66; from asst prof to assoc prof, 66-73, PROF BIOCHEM, SCH MED, UNIV OKLA, 73- *Concurrent Pos:* NIH fels, Ohio State Univ, 61-63. *Mem:* AAAS; Am Chem Soc. *Res:* Plasma protein metabolism; hepatic nucleic acid metabolism; regulation of hexosamine synthesis. *Mailing Add:* Dept of Biochem Univ of Okla Oklahoma City OK 73190

CHANDLER, ALFRED BERTRAM, b Geelong, Australia, Nov 30, 16; nat US; m 41; c 1. INORGANIC CHEMISTRY, ANALYTICAL CHEMISTRY. *Educ:* Univ Tenn, BS, 47. *Prof Exp:* Chemist, Aluminum Co Am, Tenn, 40-43; chemist-spectroscopist, Tenn Eastman Co, 43-47; chief chemist, Foote Mineral Co, 47-65; managing dir, Int Div, Andrew S McCreath & Son, Inc, 65-68; SCIENTIST, ROY F WESTON, INC, 68- *Concurrent Pos:* Dir, Andrew S McCreath & Son, Inc, 61- *Mem:* Am Chem Soc; Am Soc Testing & Mat; Am Inst Mining, Metall & Petrol Eng. *Res:* Instrumentation; emission and x-ray spectroscopy; flame photometry; atomic absorption; environmental science; waste water treatability. *Mailing Add:* Process Develop Lab Roy F Weston Inc Weston Way West Chester PA 19380

CHANDLER, ARTHUR CECIL, JR, b Hinton, WVa, Feb 14, 33; m 57; c 4. MEDICINE, OPHTHALMOLOGY. *Educ:* Fla Southern Col, AB, 53; Univ Tenn, MS, 55; Duke Univ, MD, 59; Am Bd Ophthal, dipl, 65. *Prof Exp:* Instr surg, Sch Med, Stanford Univ, 63-65; assoc, 65-66, asst prof, 66-70, ASSOC PROF OPHTHAL, SCH MED, DUKE UNIV, 70-, ASSOC ANAT, 67- *Concurrent Pos:* Consult, Durham Vet Admin Hosp, 65-, chief ophthal, 66-; consult, Watts Hosp & Sea Level Hosp. *Mem:* AAAS; fel Am Col Surg; AMA; Am Asn Ophthal. *Res:* Prevention and treatment of amblyopia ex anopsia. *Mailing Add:* Box 3802 Duke Univ Med Ctr Durham NC 27710

CHANDLER, CARL DAVIS, JR, b Pulaski, Va, Jan 25, 44; m 66; c 2. ANALYTICAL CHEMISTRY. *Educ:* Emory & Henry Col, BS, 65; ETenn State Univ, MA, 67; Va Polytech Inst & State Univ, PhD(chem), 73. *Prof Exp:* ANAL GROUP AREA SUPVR CHEM, RADFORD ARMY AMMUNITION PLANT, HERCULES INC, 67- *Concurrent Pos:* Lectr short course liquid chromatography, Am Chem Soc, 73-; consult, US Army Res Off, Picatinny Arsenal. *Mem:* Am Chem Soc. *Res:* Investigation of column efficiency improvements in gas and liquid chromatography; analysis of propellants and explosives; development of pollution abatement processes and pollution measuring instrumentation specifically for various explosives and propellants. *Mailing Add:* 50 Aldrin St Dublin VA 24084

CHANDLER, CHARLES H(ORACE), b Weihsien, Shantung, China, July 10, 18; div. PHYSICS, ENGINEERING. *Educ:* Col of Wooster, BA, 40; Ohio State Univ, MSc(physics), 46. *Prof Exp:* Mem tech staff, David Sarnoff Res Ctr, 46-54; eng leader, Radio Corp Am, 54-57; chief electronics engr, Gillette Safety Razor Co, 58-60, mgr electronic process develop, 60-62; prin engr, Booz-Allen Appl Res, Inc, 62-64, assoc dir develop & design div, 64-66; sr tech consult, Eng Div, Am Safety Razor Co, 66-71; in charge new prod develop, Micro Switch, Div Honeywell Inc, 71-74; independent consult, Jarrell-Ash, Div Fischer Sci Corp & Ball Bros Res, Inc, 74-77; instrumentation specialist, Centronics Data Comput Corp, 77-78; PROJ ENGR, STANLEY TOOLS, DIV STANLEY WORKS, INC, 78- *Concurrent Pos:* Cert client instr, Kepner-Tregoe Mgt Course. *Mem:* Sigma Xi; sr mem Instrument Soc Am; fel AAAS; Inst Defense Prep; Soc Photo-Optical Instrumentation Engrs. *Res:* Propagation in dielectric materials; television circuit development; radar systems and special displays; electronic navigation, bombing, military data-handling systems; applications of electronics in production control systems; manufacturing engineering; bring new technology (including lasers) to bear on inspection and printing of steel tape rules. *Mailing Add:* Stanley Tools Div 600 Myrtle St New Britain CT 06050

CHANDLER, CLAY MORRIS, b McKenzie, Tenn, Nov 2, 27; m 56; c 2. ZOOLOGY. *Educ:* Bethel Col, Tenn, BS, 50; George Peabody Col, MA, 54; Ind Univ, PhD(zool), 65. *Prof Exp:* Asst prof biol, WGa Col, 59-61; prof zool, Bethel Col, Tenn, 65-70; PROF BIOL, MID TENN STATE UNIV, 70- *Concurrent Pos:* Consult environ mgt, planning & eng, Nashville, 77- *Mem:* AAAS; NAm Benthological Soc. *Res:* Ecology and systematics of freshwater triclad Turbellaria. *Mailing Add:* Dept Biol Mid Tenn State Univ Murfreesboro TN 37132

CHANDLER, COLSTON, b Boston, Mass, June 7, 39; m 65; c 3. THEORETICAL PHYSICS, SCATTERING THEORY. *Educ:* Brown Univ, ScB, 61; Univ Calif, Berkeley, PhD(physics), 67. *Prof Exp:* Asst prof, 66-68, 70-73, assoc prof, 73-78, PROF PHYSICS, UNIV N MEX, 78- *Concurrent Pos:* Vis prof, Bonn Univ, Ger, 78. *Mem:* AAAS; Am Phys Soc; Sigma Xi; Am Asn Univ Professors; Int Asn Math Physicists. *Res:* Nonrelativistic quantum mechanical scattering theory. *Mailing Add:* Dept Physics & Astron Univ NMex Albuquerque NM 87131

CHANDLER, DAVID, b New York, NY, Oct 15, 44; m 66; c 2. CHEMICAL PHYSICS, STATISTICAL MECHANICS. *Educ:* Mass Inst Technol, SB, 66; Harvard Univ, PhD(chem physics), 69. *Prof Exp:* Res chemist, Univ Calif, San Diego, 69-70; asst prof, 70-75, assoc prof chem, Univ Ill, Urbana, 75-77; vis prof chem, Columbia Univ, 77-78; PROF CHEM, UNIV ILL, URBANA, 78- *Concurrent Pos:* Sloan fel, 72-76; Guggenheim fel, 81-82. *Mem:* Am Inst Physics; Am Phys Soc; Am Chem Soc; fel AAAS. *Res:* Statistical mechanics; structure and dynamics of simple and complex molecular liquids; aqueous solutions; theory of chemical reactions in condensed phases. *Mailing Add:* Dept of Chem Univ Ill Sch of Chem Sci Urbana IL 61801

CHANDLER, DEAN WESLEY, b Chicago, Ill, June 5, 44. PHYSICAL CHEMISTRY, ANALYTICAL CHEMISTRY. *Educ:* Harvard Univ, BA, 67; Northwestern Univ, PhD(chem), 73. *Prof Exp:* Lectr chem, State Univ NY Albany, 73-74, vis asst prof, 74-75; ASST PROF CHEM, WILLIAMS COL, 75-, ASST DEAN, 78- *Mem:* Am Chem Soc; Am Inst Physics. *Res:* Development of new physical techniques which might prove useful as tools for chemical analysis. *Mailing Add:* Dept of Chem Williams Col Williamstown MA 01267

CHANDLER, DONALD ERNEST, b San Bernardino, Calif, Nov 22, 25; m 46; c 3. PHYSICS. *Educ:* US Naval Acad, BS, 46; Univ Calif, Los Angeles, MA, 54, PhD(physics), 58. *Prof Exp:* Tech officer, Electronic Systs, Off Naval Res, US Navy, 55-57, physicist, Armed Forces Spec Weapons Proj, 57-59, proj officer, Adv Res Proj Agency, 59-63, sr prog officer, Electronics Lab, 63-66, proj mgr, Advan Res Proj Agency, 66-68; mem tech staff, 68-71, mgr phys sci, Tempo, 71-81, MGR PHYS SCI, GEN ELEC CO, 81- *Mem:* Acoustical Soc Am; Am Geophys Union. *Res:* Propagation of acoustic waves in media exhibiting relaxation; propagation of electromagnetic waves in ionized gases. *Mailing Add:* Tempo Gen Elec Co 816 State St Santa Barbara CA 93103

CHANDLER, DONALD STEWART, b Red Bluff, Calif, Sept 23, 49; m 76; c 1. SYSTEMATIC ENTOMOLOGY, MEDICAL ENTOMOLOGY. *Educ:* Univ Calif, Davis, BS, 71; Univ Ariz, MS, 73; Ohio State Univ, PhD(entom), 76. *Prof Exp:* Entomolgist, Bur Land Mgt, 76-77; sr operator, Mosquito Abatement Dist, Butte County, Calif, 78-81; ENTOMOLOGIST, UNIV NH, 81- *Honors & Awards:* R E Snodgrass Mem Award, Entom Soc Am, 74. *Mem:* Entom Soc Am; Soc Systematic Zoologists; Sigma Xi. *Res:* Biology, zoogeography and systematics of Anthicidae and Pselaphidae beetle families. *Mailing Add:* Dept Entomology Univ NH Durham NH 03824

CHANDLER, FRANCIS WOODROW, JR, b Milledgeville, Ga, July 25, 43; m 68; c 2. VETERINARY PATHOLOGY. *Educ:* Univ Ga, BS, 66, DVM, 67, PhD(vet path), 73; Am Col Vet Pathologists, dipl. *Prof Exp:* Vet med officer, Venereal Dis Res Lab, Ctr Dis Control, 67-70; resident, Dept Vet Path, Col Vet Med, Univ Ga, 70-73; CHIEF, PATH BR, HOST FACTORS DIV, CTR INFECTIOUS DIS, CENTERS DIS CONTROL, USPHS, 73-; CONSULT PATHOLOGIST, FOOD & DRUG ADMIN, 77- *Mem:* Int Acad Path; NY Acad Sci; Am Asn Lab Animal Sci; Sigma Xi. *Res:* Animal models of human venereal diseases; pneumocystis carinii pneumonia; mycotic diseases; anemia and neoplasia; surface ultrastructure of cells; Legionnaires' disease; algal infections (protothecosis); immunohistologic diagnosis of infectious diseases. *Mailing Add:* Host Factors Div Bldg 1/2301 Ctr Infectious Dis Centers Dis Control Atlanta GA 30333

CHANDLER, FREDERICK WILLIAM, b Epsom, Surrey, Eng, May 17, 38; Can-Brit citizen; m 69; c 2. PALEOCLIMATES, CLASTIC SEDIMENTOLOGY. *Educ:* Reading Univ, Eng, BSc, 62; London Univ, BSc, 64; Univ Western Ont, PhD(geol), 69. *Prof Exp:* Field geologist proterozoic stratig, Ont Geol Surv, 70-72; RES SCIENTIST SEDIMENTOLOGY, REDBEDS, PALEOCLIMATES & MINERALIZATION IN SEDIMENTS, GEOL SURV CAN, OTTAWA, 72- *Mem:* Geol Asn Can (secy-treas, Precambrian Div, 76-78). *Res:* Sedimentology and mineralization; tectonics; red beds of Canada, clastic sedimentology. *Mailing Add:* Geol Surv of Can Rm 483 601 Booth St Ottawa ON K1A 0E8 Can

CHANDLER, H(ENRY) M(ILLIGAN), JR, b Middletown, Conn, June 3, 21. ELECTRICAL ENGINEERING. *Educ:* Princeton Univ, BSE, 42, MSE, 47. *Prof Exp:* Asst mech eng, 42-43, instr, 43, instr elec eng, 43-44, lectr, 46-47, asst prof, 47-59, sr prof tech staff mem, Plasma Physics Lab, 59-67, SR STAFF MEM, PLASMA PHYSICS LAB, PRINCETON UNIV, 67- *Concurrent Pos:* Civilian with US Navy, 44. *Mem:* AAAS; sr mem Inst Elec & Electronics Engrs. *Res:* Electronic voltage regulators; radar detection of floating ice; radar sea return. *Mailing Add:* Plasma Physics Lab Princeton Univ PO Box 451 Princeton NJ 08544

CHANDLER, HORACE W, b Brooklyn, NY, May 23, 27; m 54; c 2. PHYSICAL CHEMISTRY, CHEMICAL ENGINEERING. *Educ:* Cornell Univ, BChE, 50; NY Univ, MChE, 55; Columbia Univ, DrEngSc, 60. *Prof Exp:* Tech trainee, Gen Chem Div, Allied Chem & Dye Corp, 50-51; chem engr, Gen Aniline & Film Corp, 51-53; res engr, Columbia Mineral Beneficiation Labs, 53-58; tech coordr, Radiation Applns, Inc, 58-60; tech adv to pres, Isomet Corp, 60-68; CHMN DEPT PHYS SCI & MATH, BERGEN COMMUNITY COL, 68- *Concurrent Pos:* Lectr, Stevens Inst Technol, 60. *Mem:* Am Inst Chem Eng; Am Chem Soc. *Res:* Radiation, polymer and high temperature chemistry; life support systems. *Mailing Add:* Dept of Physical Sci & Math Bergen Community Col Paramus NJ 07652

CHANDLER, J RYAN, b Charleston, SC, July 30, 23; m 41; c 3. SURGERY, OTOLARYNGOLOGY. *Educ:* Duke Univ, MD, 47; Am Bd Otolaryngol, dipl. *Prof Exp:* PROF OTOLARYNGOL, SCH MED, UNIV MIAMI, 52-, CHMN DEPT, 72- *Concurrent Pos:* Consult, Vet Admin Hosp, Miami, Fla, 57 & NIH Commun Dis Training Grant Comt, 60-64. *Mem:* Am Soc Head & Neck Surg; Soc Head & Neck Surg; Am Laryngol Asn; Am Otol Soc; Am Acad Otolaryngol. *Res:* Otology and head and neck cancer surgery; otolaryngology teaching. *Mailing Add:* Dept Otolaryngol D48 Univ Miami Sch Med PO Box 016960 Miami FL 33101

CHANDLER, JAMES HARRY, III, b New Orleans, La, Apr 26, 50. ORGANIC CHEMISTRY. *Educ:* Univ Tenn, Knoxville, BSc, 73, PhD(org chem), 78. *Prof Exp:* Res assoc chem, Int Paper Co, 78-81; CHEMIST, ANAL QUAL ASSURANCE OFF, US ARMY ENVIRON HYG AGENCY, 81- *Mem:* Am Chem Soc. *Res:* Performing technical audits and inspection of Army environmental labs and data. *Mailing Add:* 6705C Townbrook Dr Baltimore MD 21207

CHANDLER, JAMES MICHAEL, b Wichita, Kans, Sept 30, 43; m 68; c 2. CROP SCIENCE, WEED SCIENCE. *Educ:* WTex State Univ, BS, 65; Okla State Univ, MS, 68, PhD(agron), 71. *Prof Exp:* Res asst, Okla State Univ, 69-71; RES AGRONOMIST WEED RES, SOUTHERN WEED SCI LAB, RES SER, USDA, 71- *Mem:* Weed Sci Soc Am; Coun Agr Sci & Technol; Am Soc Agron; Crop Sci Soc Am; Sigma Xi. *Res:* Agronomy and botany related to weed science and the development of principles and practices for economical control of weeds. *Mailing Add:* Southern Weed Sci Lab PO Box 225 Stoneville MS 38776

CHANDLER, JASPER S(CHELL), b Allen, Nebr, July 21, 11; m 38; c 4. MECHANICAL ENGINEERING. *Educ:* Ga Inst Tech, BS, 34, MS, 36; Pa State Col, PhD(mech eng), 38. *Prof Exp:* Machinist's apprentice, NC & St Louis RR, 29-34; asst, Eng Lab, Ga Inst Technol, 34-36; asst Diesel Lab, Pa State Col, 36-38; res engr, Physics Div, 38-57, sr res assoc, 58-76, CONSULT, EASTMAN KODAK CO, 76- *Honors & Awards:* Jour award, Soc Motion Picture & TV Engrs, 47. *Mem:* Fel Soc Motion Picture & TV Engrs; Soc Photog Sci & Eng. *Res:* Motion picture film handling equipment; cameras; projectors; printers; perforators and special equipment. *Mailing Add:* 185 Dorian Lane Rochester NY 14626

CHANDLER, JERRY LEROY, b Little Falls, Minn, Sept 14, 40; m 69; c 2. BIOMATHEMATICS. *Educ:* Okla State Univ, BS, 63, PhD(biochem), 68. *Prof Exp:* Instr biochem, Okla State Univ, 68-69; chemist & dept leader, Zentrallaor fur Mutigeni Tatsprnfung, 69-72; res assoc biochem, Okla State Univ, 73-74; health standards mgr, 75-77, sect chief, 77-80, SCI ADVISOR, NAT INST OCCUP SAFETY & HEALTH, 80- *Concurrent Pos:* Fac mem, NIH Found Advan Educ Sci, 81-82. *Mem:* Soc Risk Anal; Environ Mutagen Soc. *Res:* Development of mathematical models of dose-response relationships derived from biochemical mechanisms of action. *Mailing Add:* 7412 Churchill Rd McLean VA 22101

CHANDLER, JOHN EDWARD, b Knoxville, Tenn, Feb 26, 41; m 64; c 2. REPRODUCTIVE PHYSIOLOGY. *Educ:* Southern Benedictine Col, BA, 64; Univ Tenn, MS, 69; Va Polytech Inst & State Univ, PhD(animal sci), 77. *Prof Exp:* Asst biologist cancer chemother, Southern Res Inst, 64-66; res assoc reproduction physiol, Comp Animal Res Lab, 67-69; nutrit biochemist amino acid nutrit, Smith Kline Corp, 69-73; asst, Va Polytech Inst, 73-77; asst prof, 77-80, ASSOC PROF REPRODUCTION PHYSIOL, LA STATE UNIV, 80- *Concurrent Pos:* Asst mgr, La Animal Breeders Coop, 77-80, res mgr, 80- *Mem:* Am Soc Animal Sci; Am Dairy Sci Asn. *Res:* Biocolloidal aspects of semen with respect to semen preservation, metabolism and interaction with the female environment. *Mailing Add:* Dept Dairy Sci La State Univ Baton Rouge LA 70893

CHANDLER, KIRBY, physical anthropology, deceased

CHANDLER, LELAND, entomology, see previous edition

CHANDLER, LOUIS, b Rumania, Jan 15, 22; nat US; m 43. BIOPHYSICS, RADIATION PHYSICS. *Educ:* Univ Chicago, BS, 43; Univ Ill, MS, 47, PhD(biophysics), 54. *Prof Exp:* Instr physics, Univ Chicago, 43-44; physicist, Manhattan Dist, Chicago, Oak Ridge, Calif, 44-46; asst physics, Univ Ill, 46-48; physicist, Anderson Phys Lab, 48-49; chief physicist, Swift & Co, 55-57; from asst prof to assoc prof, Univ Ill, 57-67; prof environ sci, 67-76, dir grad prog radiol health, 68-69, chmn, Dept Radiation Sci, 76-77, PROF RADIATION SCI, RUTGERS UNIV, 67- *Concurrent Pos:* Pres, Radiation Control, Inc, 59-67; res prof, Univ Tokyo, 63-64; fel adv, AEC, 68-70; first officer dosimetry, Int Atomic Energy Agency, Vienna, 70-72; vis prof, Kyushu Univ, Japan, 78. *Mem:* Am Phys Soc; Radiation Res Soc; Am Asn Physics Teachers; Health Phys Soc; Am Asn Physicists in Med. *Res:* Effect of small dose radiation on cell growth; radiation protection legislation; applications of Mossbauer effect; dosimetry in high level radiation processing and low level environmentally stimulated irradiators. *Mailing Add:* 36 N Ross Hall Blvd Piscataway NJ 08854

CHANDLER, MICHAEL LYNN, pharmacology, biochemistry, see previous edition

CHANDLER, RAY JAMES, corrosion, see previous edition

CHANDLER, REGINALD FRANK, b Edmonton, Alta, Sept 18, 41; m 62; c 2. NATURAL PRODUCTS CHEMISTRY, ETHNOBOTANY. *Educ:* Univ Alta, BSc, 62, MSc, 65; Univ Sydney, PhD(pharmaceut chem), 69. *Prof Exp:* Lectr phytochem, Univ Sydney, 65-68; asst prof, 68-74, ASSOC PROF PHARM, DALHOUSIE UNIV, 74- *Concurrent Pos:* Secy-treas, Asn Fac of Pharm Can, 72-74. *Mem:* Am Soc Pharmacol; Ethno-Pharmacol Soc; Chem Inst Can; Am Chem Soc; Soc Econ Bot. *Res:* Investigation of the medicinal phytochemical and ethnobotanical aspects of maritime flora with particular emphasis on the traditional Micmac and Malecite Indian medicines. *Mailing Add:* Col of Pharm Dalhousie Univ Halifax NS B3H 3J5 Can

CHANDLER, RICHARD EDWARD, b Ft Pierce, Fla, Sept 9, 37; m 61; c 1. MATHEMATICS. *Educ:* Fla State Univ, BS, 59, MS, 60, PhD(math), 63. *Prof Exp:* Res assoc, Duke Univ, 63-65; asst prof math, 65-67, assoc prof, 67-72, PROF MATH, NC STATE UNIV, 72- *Mem:* Math Soc; Math Asn Am. *Res:* General topology, especially Hausdorff compactifications. *Mailing Add:* Dept of Math NC State Univ Raleigh NC 27650

CHANDLER, ROBERT FLINT, JR, b Columbus, Ohio, June 22, 07; m 31; c 3. AGRONOMY. *Educ:* Univ Maine, BS, 29; Univ Md, PhD(pomol), 34. *Hon Degrees:* LLD, Univ Maine, 51; DH, Cent Luzon State Univ, 71; ScD, Univ Notre Dame, 71, Univ Philippines, 72, Univ NH, 72 & Univ Md, 75; LittD, Univ Singapore, 71. *Prof Exp:* Horticulturist, State Dept Agr, Maine, 29-31; asst, Exp Sta, Univ Md, 31-34; Nat Res Found fel forestry, Univ Calif, 34-35; from asst prof to prof forest soils, Cornell Univ, 35-47; dean col agr & dir exp sta, Univ NH, 47-50, pres, 50-54; asst dir agr, Rockefeller Found, 54-57, assoc dir agr sci, 57-65, spec field staff mem, Asian Veg Res & Develop

Ctr, Taiwan, 65-75; CONSULT INT AGR, 75- *Concurrent Pos:* Vis prof, Agr Mech Col Tex, 40; soil scientist, Rockefeller Found, 46-47; dir, Int Rice Res Inst, Laguna, Philippines; dir, Near East Found. *Honors & Awards:* Gold Medal Award, Govt India, 66; Sitari-I-Imtiaz Award, Govt Pakistan, 68. *Mem:* Fel Am Acad Arts & Sci; Am Soc Agron; Crop Sci Soc Am; Soc Int Develop. *Res:* Chemical composition of forest tree leaves and litter; vegetation as soil-forming factor; potassium nutrition of alfalfa; agricultural education and research in the Far East; administration of scientific research. *Mailing Add:* Petersham Rd Templeton MA 01468

CHANDLER, ROGER EUGENE, b Elmira, NY, Sept 16, 34; m 56; c 2. ORGANIC CHEMISTRY. *Educ:* Colgate Univ, BA, 56; Mass Inst Technol, PhD(org chem), 61. *Prof Exp:* Res chemist, Esso Res & Eng Co, 61-64, proj leader detergent additives, 64-66, res coordr, Paramins Div, Enjay Chem Co, 66-67, sect head detetergent additives, 67-68, sect head res dept, Esso Petrol Co, Eng, 68-70, head engine testing activity, Enjay Additives Lab, 70-73, sr adv environ conserv & health, 73-78, sr adv, African Affairs, Exxon Corp, 78-80, MGR, PUB AFFAIRS DEPT, EXXON ENTERPRISES, 80- *Mem:* Am Chem Soc; Soc Automotive Engrs; Air Pollution Control Asn; Water Pollution Control Fedn. *Res:* Lubricating oil additives; environmental conservation. *Mailing Add:* 809 Village Green Westfield NJ 07090

CHANDLER, WILLIAM DAVID, b Brantford, Ont, Jan 29, 40; m 61; c 4. PHYSICAL ORGANIC CHEMISTRY. *Educ:* Queen's Univ, Ont, BSc, 62, PhD(chem), 65. *Prof Exp:* NATO fel, Pa State Univ, 65-66 & Rutgers Univ, 66-67; from asst prof to assoc prof, 67-74, PROF CHEM & HEAD DEPT, UNIV REGINA, 74- *Mem:* AAAS; fel Chem Inst Can; Am Chem Soc. *Res:* Organic synthesis; diphenyl ether chemistry; natural product chemistry of algae. *Mailing Add:* Dept Chem Univ Regina Regina Can

CHANDLER, WILLIS THOMAS, b Argyle, Minn, Feb 15, 23; m 57. METALLURGY. *Educ:* Univ Minn, BMetE, 44, PhD(metall), 55. *Prof Exp:* Asst metall, Manhattan Proj, Univ Chicago, 44 & Mass Inst Technol, 44-45; asst, Univ Minn, 45-48, res assoc, Nuclear Eng Propulsion Aircraft Proj, 48-50; asst prof, Northwestern Univ, 50-53 & Univ Notre Dame, 53-59; sr res engr, 59-62, prin scientist, 62-77, PROJ ENG ADV METALL & FRACTURE MECH, ROCKETDYNE DIV, ROCKWELL INT, 77- *Mem:* AAAS; Am Inst Mining, Metall & Petrol Engrs; Am Soc Metals. *Res:* Metallurgy of high temperature and refractory alloys; transformations in metals; hydrogen embrittlement of refractory metals; erosion and corrosion of metals; hydrogen-environment embrittlement. *Mailing Add:* 22714 Margarita Dr Woodland Hills CA 91364

CHANDRA, DHANESH, b Hyderabad, India, Oct 10, 44. EXTRACTIVE METALLURGY, COMPOSITE MATERIALS. *Educ:* Osmenia Univ, India, BEng, 67; Univ Ill, MS, 72; Univ Denver, PhD(metall & mat sci), 76. *Prof Exp:* Mgr planning control, Hyderabad Asbestos Cement Prod, India, 68-70; res asst, Col Eng, 72-76, SR RES METALLURGIST & HEAD STRATEGIC MAT CTR, DENVER RES INST, UNIV DENVER, 76- *Concurrent Pos:* Teaching asst mat characterization, Univ Denver, 75; prin investr grants, US Bur Mine Projs, 76-, Magnasep Corp, 78-79, & Cent Naz Cat Unico Bibl Italiana, Bibl, 76-; consult, Colburn Eng, Denver, 77-, Rocky Mountain Energy Co, Wyoming, 80- *Mem:* Am Soc Metals; Am Inst Mining & Metall Engrs. *Res:* Extractive metallurgy of metals: nickel, cobalt, chronium, magnese, aluminum and gold; bench scale process development involving kinetic thermodynamic, electron-optical microscopic evaluation; recycling of metals and alloy; unidirectional solidification of metal oxide eutectics for use in electronic materials; fabricating alumium-graphite composite. *Mailing Add:* 4904 S Flower Way Denver CO 80123

CHANDRA, G RAM, b India, Feb 10, 33; m. BIOCHEMISTRY. *Educ:* Agra Univ, BS, 51, MS, 53; Univ Alta, PhD(biochem), 62. *Prof Exp:* Res asst biochem, Indian Agr Res Inst, 55-59; scientist, Res Inst Advan Studies, 62-65; scientist, Mich State Univ, 65-66; SCIENTIST, AGR RES SERV, USDA, 66- *Res:* Biological volatiles; senescence; plant nutrition; hormones. *Mailing Add:* 14028 Cricket Ln Silver Spring MD 20904

CHANDRA, JAGDISH, b Hyderabad, India, Oct 11, 35; US citizen; m 61; c 3. MATHEMATICS. *Educ:* Osmania Univ, India, BA, 55, MA, 57; Rensselaer Polytech Inst, PhD(math), 65. *Prof Exp:* Instr math, Rensselaer Polytech Inst, 65-66; res mathematician, US Army Arsenal, Watervliet, 66-70; chief appl math br, 70-73, assoc dir math div, 73-74, DIR MATH DIV, US ARMY RES OFF, DURHAM, 74- *Concurrent Pos:* Adj asst prof, Rensselaer Polytech Inst, 66-70, Union Col, 68-69; adj assoc prof, Duke Univ, 74-80, adj prof, 80- *Mem:* Am Math Soc; Soc Indust & Appl Math. *Res:* Mathematical analysis, nonlinear differential and integral equation; operator inequalities; mathematical theories of combustion. *Mailing Add:* US Army Res Off PO Box 12211 Research Triangle Park NC 27709

CHANDRA, KAILASH, b Kanpur, UP, India, Aug 20, 38; m 61; c 3. PHYSICS. *Educ:* Agr Univ, BSc, 56, MSc, 58; Gorakhpur Univ, PhD(physics), 67. *Prof Exp:* Lectr physics, KK Degree Col, India, 58-60; res fel, Coun Sci & Indust Res, 60-62; lectr, Gorakhpur Univ, 62-68; res assoc, Univ Ga, 68-69; assoc prof, 69-73, PROF PHYSICS, SAVANNAH STATE COL, 73- *Concurrent Pos:* Vis res fel, Nat Bur Standards, Washington, 78 & NASA Langley Res Ctr, Hampton, Va, 80. *Mem:* Am Asn Physics Teachers; Am Phys Soc. *Res:* Molecular spectroscopy; laser spectroscopy; competency based education in physics; microcomputers in education. *Mailing Add:* 110 Paradise Dr Savannah GA 31406

CHANDRA, PRADEEP, b Rajasthan, India, July 4, 44. INTERNAL MEDICINE, HEMATOLOGY. *Educ:* Univ Rajasthan, India, MB, BS, 66; Am Bd Internal Med, dipl, 72, cert hemat, 74. *Prof Exp:* House officer & registr, SMS Med Col Hosp, Univ Rajasthan, 67-68; resident internal med, Wyckoff Heights Hosp, Brooklyn, NY, 68-69; from resident to chief resident, Bronx Lebanon Hosp Ctr, 69-71; clin fel hemat, Long Island Jewish Hosp, New Hyde Park, NY, 71-73; asst prof, 76-80, ASSOC PROF MED, STATE UNIV NY STONY BROOK, 80-; DIR EDUC & ASSOC ATTEND

PHYSICIAN, DEPT ONCOL, MONTEFIORE HOSP & MED CTR, BRONX, NY, 80- *Concurrent Pos:* Nat Leukemia Asn grants, 75 & 76; assoc scientist, Brookhaven Nat Lab, 74-77, res collabr, 81-, attend physician & prin investr leukemia study, Hosp Med Res Ctr, 74-81, scientist-in-chg, Clin Hemat Lab & Blood Bank, 77-81. *Honors & Awards:* Physician Recognition Award, AMA, 78. *Mem:* Am Soc Hemat; Am Fedn Clin Res; fel Int Soc Hemat; fel Am Col Physicians; Soc Exp Biol & Med. *Res:* Study of lymphocytes in health and disease; special interest in chronic lymphocytic leukemia, measurement of body burden of leukemic cells; growth of lymphocytes and bone marrow cells in cultures; chrono-oncology and oncology. *Mailing Add:* Dept Oncol Montefiore Hosp 111 E 210th St Bronx NY 10467

CHANDRA, PURNA, b Khatauli, India, June 23, 29; m 64. AGRICULTURAL MICROBIOLOGY. *Educ:* Agra Univ, BSc, 49, MSc, 51; Ore State Univ, PhD(bact), 58. *Prof Exp:* Instr bact, Ore State Univ, 58-59; lectr, Univ Bagdad, 59-60; microbiologist, Can Dept Agr Res Sta, Sask, 60-63; asst prof biol, Mt Allison Univ, 63-67; assoc prof, 67-70, PROF BIOL, LAKE SUPERIOR STATE COL, 70- *Concurrent Pos:* Vis scientist, Appl Biochem Div, Dept Sci & Indust Res, New Zealand, 81. *Mem:* AAAS; Am Soc Microbiol; Soil Sci Soc Am. *Res:* Decomposition of organic matter in soils; nitrogen transformation in soils; biocidal effect on soil microorganisms; soil respiration studies; microbial ecology. *Mailing Add:* Dept of Biol Sci Lake Superior State Col Sault Ste Marie MI 49783

CHANDRA, SURESH, b Etah, India, July 25, 39; m 64; c 2. FLUID MECHANICS, CHEMICAL ENGINEERING. *Educ:* Allahabad Univ, BSc, 57; Banaras Hindu Univ, BSc, 61; Univ Louisville, MChE, 62; Colo State Univ, PhD(fluid mech), 67. *Prof Exp:* Asst prof mech eng, Univ Miami, 66-71; PROF MECH ENG & CHMN DEPT, A&T STATE UNIV, NC, 71-, DEAN, SCH ENG, 77- *Concurrent Pos:* Partic, Am Soc Eng Educ-Ford Found Residency Prog eng pract, 69. *Mem:* Am Soc Mech Engrs; Am Inst Aeronaut & Astronaut; Am Soc Eng Educ. *Res:* Diffusion in turbulent boundary layers; heat transfer in metallic conduits. *Mailing Add:* Sch of Eng A&T State Univ of NC Greensboro NC 27411

CHANDRA, SUSHIL, b Varanasi, India, Dec 31, 31; m 55; c 3. AEROSPACE & ATMOSPHERIC PHYSICS. *Educ:* Benares Hindu Univ, BSc, 52, MSc, 54; Pa State Univ, PhD(physics), 61. *Prof Exp:* Lectr physics, U P Col, Varanasi, 54-58; res asst atmospheric physics, Pa State Univ, 59, instr physics, 60-61; Nat Acad Sci resident res assoc, Goddard Space Flight Ctr, NASA, Md, 61-64; scientist, Nat Phys Lab, India, 64-66; AEROSPACE TECHNOLOGIST, GODDARD SPACE FLIGHT CTR, NASA, 66- *Mem:* Am Geophys Union. *Res:* Physics of the upper atmosphere; aeronomy; ionosphere. *Mailing Add:* Code 624 Goddard Space Flight Ctr NASA Greenbelt MD 20771

CHANDRAN, KRISHNAN BALA, b Madurai City, India, May 16, 44; m 72; c 2. BIOMECHANICS, MECHANICAL ENGINEERING. *Educ:* Madras Univ, BS, 63; Wash Univ, MS, 69, DSc(biomed eng), 72. *Prof Exp:* Tool engr, Hindustan Motors Ltd, Calcutta, India, 66-67; asst prof orthop, Biomech Lab, Med Sch, Tulane Univ, 74-78; ASSOC PROF, DIV MAT ENG, COL ENG, UNIV IOWA, 78- *Mem:* Am Acad Mechanics; Am Soc Mech Engrs; Am Soc Biomech; Am Heart Asn; Sigma Xi. *Res:* Investigations on traumatology of the human head and spine; hemodynamics at arterial curvature sites in relation to the origin of atherosclerosis; left ventricular dynamics with emphasis on the non invasive diagnosis of myocardial infarction; flow dynamics past prosthetic heart valves. *Mailing Add:* Div of Mat Eng Col of Eng Univ of Iowa Iowa City IA 52242

CHANDRAN, SATISH RAMAN, b Oct 6, 38; US citizen; m 66; c 2. ENTOMOLOGY, PARASITOLOGY. *Educ:* Univ Kerala, BS, 55, MS, 58; Univ Ill, Urbana, PhD(entom), 66. *Prof Exp:* Res scientist, Univ Ill, Urbana, 64-66; from instr to asst prof biol, Univ Ill, Chicago Circle, 66-72; assoc prof, 72-77, PROF BIOL, KENNEDY-KING COL, 77- *Mem:* Entom Soc Am; Am Inst Biol Sci; Nat Asn Biol Teachers. *Res:* Developmental morphology due to thermal stress in mosquitoes; microsomal oxidase activity in insects; toxicity of the photoisomere of cyclodiene insecticides of freshwater animals; lepidopteran morphology. *Mailing Add:* 1648 Western Ave Flossmoor IL 60422

CHANDRASEKARAN, BALAKRISHNAN, b Lalgudi, India, June 20, 42. COMPUTER SCIENCE, ELECTRICAL ENGINEERING. *Educ:* Univ Madras, BE, 63; Univ Pa, PhD(elec eng), 67. *Prof Exp:* Eng res specialist, Data Recognition Lab, Philco-Ford Corp, 67-69, eng specialist, Advan Eng & Res, 69, from asst prof to assoc prof, 69-77, PROF COMPUT & INFO SCI, OHIO STATE UNIV, 77- *Concurrent Pos:* Consult, LNK Corp, Md, 69-72 & Lawrence Livermore Nat Labs, 80. *Mem:* Inst Elec & Electronics Engrs; Asn Comput Mach; AAAS; Am Asn Artificial Intel. *Res:* Artificial intelligence, computer graphics, medical diagnosis by computer; intelligent and learning systems; statistical pattern recognition. *Mailing Add:* Dept of Comput & Info Sci Ohio State Univ Columbus OH 43210

CHANDRASEKARAN, SANTOSH KUMAR, b Delhi, India. CHEMICAL ENGINEERING, BIOMEDICAL ENGINEERING. *Educ:* Indian Inst Technol, Bombay, BTech, 64; Univ Calif, Berkeley, MS, 65, PhD(chem eng), 71. *Prof Exp:* Res asst chem eng, Univ Calif, Berkeley, 64-65, res & teaching assoc, 67-71; sr engr, E I du Pont de Nemours Inc, 65-67; develop engr, Alza Corp, 71-76, dir systs develop, 74-81, prin scientist, 76-81; DIR RES & DEVELOP, ABCOR, INC, 81- *Mem:* Am Chem Soc; Am Inst Chem Engrs; Sigma Xi. *Res:* Polymer and pharmaceutical chemistry; design and development of drug delivery systems; ultrafiltration and reverse osmosis. *Mailing Add:* Abcor Inc 850 Main St Wilmington MA 01887

CHANDRASEKHAR, B S, b Bangalore, India, May 24, 28; div; c 2. PHYSICS. *Educ:* Mysore Univ, BSc, 47; Univ Delhi, MSc, 49; Oxford Univ, DPhil(physics), 52. *Prof Exp:* Res assoc physics, Univ Ill, 52-54; res physicist, Westinghouse Res Labs, 54-59, fel physicist, 59-61, sect mgr cryophysics,

61-63; prof physics, 63-67, chmn physics dept, 65-67, chmn biol dept & dean sci, 67-, PERKINS PROF PHYSICS, CASE WESTERN RESERVE UNIV, 67- *Concurrent Pos:* Vis scientist, Oxford, 54-55; sr vis res fel, Imp Col, London, 61; consult, Bell Tel Labs, 65, 66 & 68, Argonne Nat Lab, 65-68, Lewis Res Ctr, 66 & NSF Inst Progs, 71; vis prof, Univ Ill, Urbana-Champaign, 77; Fulbright-Hays fel, Imperial Col, London & Univ Cambridge, 78; vis prof, Eidgenoessische Technische Hochschule, Zurich Switzerland, 80-81. *Mem:* Fel Am Phys Soc. *Res:* Liquid helium; superconductivity; electronic properties of solids. *Mailing Add:* Dept of Physics Case Western Reserve Univ Cleveland OH 44106

CHANDRASEKHAR, SUBRAHMANYAN, b Lahore, India, Oct 19, 10; nat US; m 36. ASTRONOMY, ASTROPHYSICS. *Educ:* Univ Madras, BA, 30; Cambridge Univ, PhD(theoret physics), 33, ScD(astrophys), 42. *Prof Exp:* Fel, Trinity Col, Cambridge Univ, 33-37; res assoc, 36-37, from asst prof to prof, 37-45, DISTINGUISHED SERV PROF, YERKES OBSERV, UNIV CHICAGO, 46- *Concurrent Pos:* Ed, Astrophys J, 52-71. *Honors & Awards:* Bruce Gold Medal, Astron Soc Pac, 52; Gold Medal, Royal Astron Soc, 53; Rumford Medal, Am Acad Arts & Sci, 57; Royal Medal, Royal Soc, 62; Nat Medal of Sci, 66; Henry Draper Medal, 71; Heineman Prize, Am Phys Soc, 74. *Mem:* Nat Acad Sci; Am Acad Arts & Sci; Am Astron Soc; Royal Astron Soc; Royal Soc. *Res:* Internal constitution of stars; white dwarfs; dynamics of stellar systems; theory of stellar atmospheres; radiative transfer; hydrodynamics and hydromagnetics; general relativity. *Mailing Add:* Lab for Astrophys & Space Res 933 E 56th St Chicago IL 60637

CHANDRASHEKAR, MUTHU, b Banares, India, Feb 24, 47; m 69. MECHANICAL ENGINEERING, SYSTEMS ENGINEERING. *Educ:* Indian Inst Technol, Kanpur, India, BTech, 69; Univ Waterloo, Ont, MASc, 70, PhD(syst design), 73. *Prof Exp:* Vis prof syst sci, Univ Paraibe, Brazil, 74; vis prof energy systs, Dept Elec Eng & Syst Sci, Mich State Univ, 76; asst prof, 73-79, ASSOC PROF COMPUT DESIGN, UNIV WATERLOO, ONT, 79- *Concurrent Pos:* Consult, Can Centre Inland Waters, Burlington, 74, Can Elec Asn, Montreal, 78 & Nat Res Coun, 78. *Mem:* Int Solar Energy Soc. *Res:* System theory; thermodynamics; networks; energy systems analysis; solar heating simulation; computer aided design of large scale engineering systems; water distribution. *Mailing Add:* Dept of Syst Design Univ of Waterloo Waterloo ON N2L 3G1 Can

CHANDROSS, EDWIN A, b Brooklyn, NY, Oct 13, 34; m 61; c 2. ORGANIC CHEMISTRY, PHYSICAL CHEMISTRY. *Educ:* Mass Inst Technol, BS, 55; Harvard Univ, MA, 57, PhD(org chem), 60. *Prof Exp:* MEM TECH STAFF CHEM, BELL TEL LABS, 59-, HEAD, ORG CHEM RES & DEVELOP DEPT, 80- *Concurrent Pos:* Instr, Rutgers Univ, 62-63. *Mem:* AAAS; Am Chem Soc; The Chem Soc. *Res:* Photochemistry; fluorescence spectroscopy; chemiluminescence. *Mailing Add:* Bell Tel Labs Murray Hill NJ 07974

CHANDROSS, RONALD JAY, b New York, NY, Mar 21, 35; m 59; c 2. BIOPHYSICS. *Educ:* Polytech Inst Brooklyn, BS, 56; Mass Inst Technol, PhD(phys chem), 61. *Prof Exp:* Sr physicist, Gen Dynamics/Astronaut, 61-63; res chemist, Gen Chem Div, Allied Chem Corp, 63-66; fel biol, Mass Inst Technol, 66-68; res fel, Dept Surg, Mass Gen Hosp, 68-69; res assoc, Lab Reproductive Biol, 69-77, res asst prof, 77-82, RES ASSOC PROF, UNIV NC, CHAPEL HILL, 82- *Mem:* Am Crystallog Asn; Am Phys Soc; AAAS; Biophys Soc. *Res:* X-ray, electron diffraction; electron microscopy; structure of collagen and related substances; membrane structures; steroid structure-activity relationships. *Mailing Add:* 111 Swing Bldg Univ of NC Div of Health Affairs Chapel Hill NC 27514

CHANEY, ALLAN HAROLD, b Kerrville, Tex, Dec 11, 23; m 48; c 2. ZOOLOGY. *Educ:* Tulane Univ, BS, 46, MS, 49, PhD(zool), 58. *Prof Exp:* Instr comp anat, Tulane Univ, 50; from asst prof to assoc prof zool, Ark Polytech Col, 53-59; prof & head dept, Del Mar Col, 59-63; assoc prof, 63-66, PROF BIOL, TEX A&I UNIV, 66- *Mem:* Am Soc Syst Zool; Am Soc Ichthyologists & Herpetologists. *Res:* Herpetology; systematics; marine biology; ornithology. *Mailing Add:* 1208 W Richard Kingsville TX 78363

CHANEY, CHARLES LESTER, b Denver, Colo, Dec 21, 30; m 61; c 1. ANALYTICAL CHEMISTRY. *Educ:* Univ Wash, BS, 58. *Prof Exp:* Chemist, US Bur Mines, Nev, 58-60 & Md, 60-62; res asst anal chem, 62-67, staff assoc, 67-80, SR SCIENTIST, GEN ATOMIC CO, 80-; OWNER & MGR, SPECTRA CO, 71- *Mem:* Am Chem Soc; Soc Appl Spectros; Am Soc Testing & Mat. *Res:* Design, construct spectroscopy equipment and instrumentation; spectrographic analysis. *Mailing Add:* 2987 Governor Dr San Diego CA 92122

CHANEY, DAVID WEBB, b Cleveland, Ohio, Dec 19, 15; m 38; c 1. ORGANIC CHEMISTRY. *Educ:* Swarthmore Col, AB, 38; Univ Pa, MS, 40, PhD(org chem), 42. *Prof Exp:* Asst sect leader, Am Viscose Corp, 42-52; sr res group leader, Chemstrand Corp, 52-53, asst dir res, 53-58, exec dir res, 58-60, vpres & exec dir, Chemstrand Res Ctr, Inc, 60-65, tech dir new prod & basic res, 65-67; dean, Sch Textiles, NC State Univ, 67-81, prof textiles, 77-81; RETIRED. *Mem:* AAAS; Am Soc Eng Educ; Am Chem Soc; Am Asn Textile Chem & Colorists. *Res:* Organic synthetic fluorine compounds, especially fluorovinyls; vinyl copolymers; condensation polymers; synthetic fibers. *Mailing Add:* Sch of Textiles NC State Univ Raleigh NC 27650

CHANEY, GEORGE L, b Coffeyville, Kans, Mar 16, 30; m 52; c 4. MATHEMATICS. *Educ:* Univ Kans, BS, 53, PhD(math educ), 67; Kans State Col Pittsburg, MS, 59. *Prof Exp:* High sch teacher, Kans, 53-56; teacher math, Coffeyville Community Col, 56-61; prof, Kans State Col Pittsburg, 62-64 & 66-68; PROF MATH, OTTAWA UNIV, KANS, 68- *Mem:* Math Asn Am. *Mailing Add:* Dept of Math Ottawa Univ Ottawa KS 66067

CHANEY, ROBERT BRUCE, JR, b Helena, Mont, Aug 22, 32; m 63; c 2. AUDIOLOGY. *Educ:* Univ Mont, BA, 58, MA, 60; Stanford Univ, PhD(audiol), 65. *Prof Exp:* Audiologist, Vet Admin, 60-62; res psychologist, US Navy Electronics Lab, Calif, 63-64; from asst prof to assoc prof audiol, 64-77, PROF COMMUN SCI & DISORDERS, UNIV MONT, 77- *Mem:* Acoust Soc Am; Am Speech & Hearing Asn. *Res:* Speech and hearing science; acoustical theory of speech production; neurological basis of speech perception. *Mailing Add:* Speech & Hearing Clin Univ of Mont Missoula MT 59812

CHANEY, ROBIN W, b Cleveland, Ohio, Dec 13, 38. NUMERICAL ANALYSIS, OPERATIONS RESEARCH. *Educ:* Ohio State Univ, BS, 60, PhD(math), 64. *Prof Exp:* Asst prof math, Western Wash State Col, 64-67 & Univ Calif, Santa Barbara, 67-69; PROF MATH, WESTERN WASH STATE COL, 69- *Concurrent Pos:* NSF fel, 66-67; vis incof, Chalmers Inst Technol, Sweden, 72-73. *Mem:* AAAS; Am Math Soc; Soc Indust & Appl Math; Inst Mgt Sci. *Res:* Convergence analysis of optimization algorithms. *Mailing Add:* Dept of Math Western Wash State Col Bellingham WA 98225

CHANEY, STEPHEN GIFFORD, b Ware Co, Pa, Feb 8, 44; m 68. BIOCHEMISTRY. *Educ:* Duke Univ, BS, 66; Univ Calif, Los Angeles, PhD(biochem), 70. *Prof Exp:* Am Cancer Soc fel microbiol, Sch Med, Washington Univ, 70-72; ASST PROF BIOCHEM, SCH MED, UNIV NC, CHAPEL HILL, 72- *Res:* Nucleic acid research; control mechanisms. *Mailing Add:* Dept of Biochem Univ of NC Chapel Hill NC 27514

CHANEY, WILLIAM R, b McAllen, Tex, Dec 2, 41; m 68; c 2. FORESTRY, PLANT PHYSIOLOGY. *Educ:* Tex A&M Univ, BS, 64; Univ Wis, PhD(tree physiol), 69. *Prof Exp:* Asst prof, 70-73, assoc prof, 73-81, PROF TREE PHYSIOL, PURDUE UNIV, WEST LAFAYETTE, 81- *Concurrent Pos:* Fel, Dept Forestry, Univ Wis, 69-70. *Mem:* Am Soc Plant Physiol; Ecol Soc Am; Soc Am Foresters. *Res:* Water relations of woody species; minoland reclamation, mycorrhizae. *Mailing Add:* Dept of Forestry & Nat Resources Purdue Univ West Lafayette IN 47906

CHANG, ALBERT YEN, b China, Apr 15, 36; m 64. BIOCHEMISTRY. *Educ:* Nat Taiwan Univ, 58; Univ Calif, Berkeley, MA, 62; Univ Ill, Urbana, PhD(biochem), 65. *Prof Exp:* SR SCIENTIST IV DIABETES RES, UPJOHN CO, 67- *Mem:* AAAS; Am Chem Soc; Am Diabetes Asn; Soc Exp Biol Med; Am Soc Biol Chemists. *Res:* Etiology of diabetes; control of diabetic complications; glycoprotein metabolism; regulation of enzymes in mammalian systems. *Mailing Add:* Diabetes & Atherosclerosis Res Upjohn Co Kalamazoo MI 49001

CHANG, BERKEN, atomic physics, see previous edition

CHANG, BETTY, b China; US citizen. GERONTOLOGY. *Educ:* Columbia Univ, BS, 61, MAEd, 61; Univ Calif, San Francisco, DNS, 77. *Prof Exp:* Lectr med-surg nursing, Nursing Sci Prog, Queens Col, 61-68; asst prof family & med-surg nursing, San Francisco State Univ, 68-73; asst prof, 77-81, ASSOC PROF MED-SURG NURSING, UNIV CALIF, LOS ANGELES, 81- *Mem:* Geront Soc; Am Coun Nurse Researchers. *Res:* Care of the elderly, particularly evaluation of care from the patient's perspective. *Mailing Add:* Sch of Nursing Univ of Calif Ctr for Health Sci Los Angeles CA 90024

CHANG, BOMSHIK, b Inchon, Korea, Feb 6, 31; m; c 2. MATHEMATICS. *Educ:* Seoul Nat Univ, BA, 54, MA, 56; Univ BC, PhD, 59. *Prof Exp:* From lectr to asst prof, 58-69, ASSOC PROF MATH, UNIV BC, 69- *Mem:* Am Math Soc; Math Asn Am; Can Math Cong. *Res:* Group theory; Lie algebra. *Mailing Add:* Dept of Math Univ of BC Vancouver BC V6T 1W5 Can

CHANG, BUNWOO BERTRAM, b Kwongtung, China, Oct 9, 47; m 70; c 2. GEOPHYSICS. *Educ:* St John's Univ, Collegeville, Minn, BA, 71; Rice Univ, Houston, MA, 74, PhD(physics), 76. *Prof Exp:* Fel, Div Labs & Res, NY State Dept Health, 76-77; res physicist oil & gas explor, MRD Assoc, Inc, 80-81; VPRES GEOPHYS RES, O'CONNOR RES INC, DENVER, 82- *Concurrent Pos:* co-prin investr, Res Proj, Nat Sci Found, 77-80. *Mem:* Am Phys Soc; Soc Explor Geophysicists; Eur Asn Explor Geophysicists. *Res:* Development of advanced seismic analysis algorithms and interpretation for oil and gas exploration; modeling inversion calculations and the use of pattern recognition techniques. *Mailing Add:* O'Connor Res Inc 730 17th St Denver CO 80202

CHANG, CATHERINE TEH-LIN, b China. PHOTOCHEMISTRY, PHOTOGRAPHIC CHEMISTRY. *Educ:* Nat Taiwan Univ, BS, 58; Washington Univ, PhD(chem), 64. *Prof Exp:* Res chemist, 64-69, sr res chemist, 69-75, RES ASSOC, PHOTO PROD DEPT, E I DU PONT DE NEMOURS & CO, INC, 75- *Mem:* Am Chem Soc; Soc Photog Scientists & Engrs. *Res:* Stereochemical course of the diazomethane-carbonyl reaction; acid-catalyzed cyclization of farnesol; photopolymerization; photoimaging systems. *Mailing Add:* Photo Prod Dept Exp Sta E I du Pont de Nemours & Co Inc Wilmington DE 19898

CHANG, CHAE HAN JOSEPH, b Seoul, Korea, July 7, 29; US citizen; m 56; c 4. RADIOLOGY. *Educ:* Severance Union Med Col, MD, 53; Am Bd Radiol, dipl, 59; Nagoya Univ, PhD(med sci), 66. *Prof Exp:* Resident radiol, Emory Univ Hosp, 55-58, instr, Sch Med, 58-59; chief, Man Mem Hosp, WVa, 59-63; from assoc prof to prof, Sch Med, WVa Univ, 64-70; PROF RADIOL, SCH MED, UNIV KANS, 70- *Mem:* AMA; fel Am Col Radiol; Radiol Soc NAm; Am Roentgen Ray Soc; Asn Univ Radiol. *Res:* Roentgenological measurement of the right descending pulmonary artery in normal state and pulmonary hypertension; computed tomographic evaluation of the breast. *Mailing Add:* Dept of Radiol Univ of Kans Med Ctr Kansas City KS 66103

CHANG, CHARLES C, b Liaoning, China. May 28, 39; m 73. PHYSICAL CHEMISTRY. *Educ:* Taiwan Nat Normal Univ, BS, 66; Univ Wis, Milwaukee, MS, 69; Johns Hopkins Univ, PhD(phys chem), 72. *Prof Exp:* Fel catalysis, Johns Hopkins Univ, 72-73; assoc sr res chemist, Gen Motors Res Lab, 73-79; STAFF RES CHEMIST, AMOCO OIL RES, 79- *Mem:* Am Chem Soc; Catalysis Soc. *Res:* Heterogeneous catalysis on interactions of gases with the surface of metal catalysts. *Mailing Add:* Amoco Oil Res Ctr Box 400 H2 Naperville IL 60566

CHANG, CHARLES HUNG, b Szechwan, China, Apr 4, 25; US citizen; m 56; c 3. SYNTHETIC ORGANIC CHEMISTRY. *Educ:* Nat Cent Polytech Col, China, dipl, 45; Univ Mont, MS, 55; Wayne State Univ, PhD(org chem), 59. *Prof Exp:* Chem engr, Taiwan Fertilizer Co, 47-54; res assoc chem, Wayne State Univ, 58-61; res chemist, GAF Corp, 61-65; res specialist dyestuffs, 65-73; RES ASSOC DYESTUFFS, SCOTT ALTHOUSE RES CTR, CROMPTON & KNOWLES CORP, 73- *Mem:* Am Chem Soc. *Res:* Design and synthesis of organic dyestuffs and intermediates. *Mailing Add:* Crompton & Knowles Corp PO Box 341 Reading PA 19603

CHANG, CHARLES YU-CHUN, b Harbin, China, Sept 18, 41; US citizen; m 69; c 1. PHARMACEUTICAL CHEMISTRY. *Educ:* Tamkang Col, Taiwan, BS, 64; Am Univ, MS, 74. *Prof Exp:* Res chemist, Kingdom Pharmaceut Co, Taiwan, 65-67; instr tech & mil Mandarin Chinese, Berlitz Lang Inst, Washington, DC, 67-69; dir qual control, Mifflin McCambridge Co, Riverdale, 69-76; REV CHEMIST, US FOOD & DRUG ADMIN, 76- *Mem:* Nat Asn Pharmaceut Mfrs. *Res:* Large scale purification and disinfection of water; origination of rapid pharmaceutical tests and analyses; activation parameters for hydrogen-deuterium exchanges. *Mailing Add:* 8715 23rd Court Adelphi MD 20783

CHANG, CHEN CHUNG, b Tientsin, China, Oct 13, 27; nat US; m 51, 77; c 4. MATHEMATICAL LOGIC. *Educ:* Harvard Univ, AB, 49; Univ Calif, PhD(math), 55. *Prof Exp:* Lectr math, Univ Calif, 54-55; instr, Cornell Univ, 55-56; asst prof, Univ Southern Calif, 56-58; from asst prof to assoc prof, 58-64, PROF MATH, UNIV CALIF, LOS ANGELES, 64- *Concurrent Pos:* NSF sr fel, Inst Advan Study, 62-63; Fulbright sr res fel, UK, 66-67; vis fel, All Souls Col, Oxford Univ, 66-67; consult ed, J Symbolic Logic, Asn Symbolic Logic, 68-77; mem US nat comt, Int Union Hist & Philos of Sci, 70-72; ed, Ann Math Logic, 70-76. *Mem:* Asn Symbolic Logic. *Res:* Logic. *Mailing Add:* 26332 C N Oak Highland Dr Newhall CA 91321

CHANG, CHENG ALLEN, b Taiwan, Mar 28, 52; m 77; c 2. SEPARATION SCIENCE, INORGANIC STEREOCHEMISTRY. *Educ:* Nat Taiwan Univ, BS, 74; Univ Pittsburgh, PhD(chem), 78. *Prof Exp:* Asst prof, Wellesley Col, 78-79; vis scientist, Mass Inst Technol, 78-79; res assoc, Univ Maine, 79-80; ASST PROF TEACHING & RES, UNIV TEX, EL PASO, 80- *Mem:* Am Chem Soc; Sigma Xi; AAAS; NY Acad Sci. *Res:* High performance liquid chromatography with substitution-inert metal complexes; synthesis and stereochemical studies of metal complexes of ion-selective multidentate ligands; determination of metal speciation in the environment. *Mailing Add:* Dept Chem Univ Tex El Paso TX 79968

CHANG, CHI, b China, Mar 3, 44; Can citizen; m 73; c 3. SOIL PHYSICS, SOIL PHYSICAL CHEMISTRY. *Educ:* Chung-Hsing Univ, Taiwan, BSc, 67; Univ Man, MSc, 72, PhD(soil physics), 76. *Prof Exp:* Res scientist soil sci, Hydrol Res Div, Environ Can, 76-78; res scientist, Soil Res Inst, 75-76, RES SCIENTIST SOIL SCI, LETHBRIDGE RES STA, AGR CAN, 78- *Mem:* Soil Sci Soc Am; Am Soc Agron; Am Geophys Union. *Res:* Water and nitrate movement in soils under irrigated field conditions; relations of soil physical properties and soil management to salinity of irrigated soils. *Mailing Add:* 4013 Glacier Ave Lethbridge AB T1J 3P2 Can

CHANG, CHI KWONG, b Nanking, China, Dec 25, 47; m 71; c 2. ORGANIC CHEMISTRY, BIOINORGANIC CHEMISTRY. *Educ:* Fu Jen Cath Univ, Taiwan, BS, 69; Univ Calif, San Diego, PhD(chem), 73. *Prof Exp:* Res chemist, Univ Calif, San Diego, 73-75; fel, Univ BC, 75-76; asst prof, 76-79, ASSOC PROF CHEM, MICH STATE UNIV, 79- *Concurrent Pos:* vis scientist, Brookhaven Nat Lab, 79; A P Sloan fel, 80-82; Camille & Henry Dreyfus teacher-scholar, 80-84. *Mem:* Am Chem Soc. *Res:* Synthesis of macrocyclic ligands, porphyrins and metalloporphyrins; models for metalloenzymes; biological oxygen binding and activation. *Mailing Add:* Dept Chem Mich State Univ East Lansing MI 48824

CHANG, CHIA-CHENG, b Tamsui, Taiwan, May 28, 39; m 65; c 3. MECHANISM OF CARCINOGENESIS, SOMATIC CELL GENETICS. *Educ:* Chung-Hsing Univ, BS, 62; Univ Mo, PhD(genetics), 71. *Prof Exp:* Investr somatic cell genetics, Biol Div, Oak Ridge Nat Lab, 71-72; fel, human genetics, Dept Human Genetics, Med Sch, Univ Mich, 72-74; res assoc, DNA repair & mutagenesis, Dept Human Develop, 74-75, asst prof human develop, Dept Pediat & Human Develop, 75-79, ASSOC PROF, MICH STATE UNIV, 79- *Honors & Awards:* Young Environ Scientist Award, Nat Inst Environ Health Sci, NIH, 78-81. *Mem:* Genetic Soc Am; AAAS; Tissue Culture Asn; Environ Mutagen Soc; Sigma Xi. *Res:* Using mutagen sensitive mutants to study mechanisms of mutagenesis in human and mammalian cells; role of cell-cell communication in tumor promotion; development of assay systems for environmental mutagens and promoters. *Mailing Add:* B240 Life Sci Bldg Mich State Univ East Lansing MI 48824

CHANG, CHIEH CHIEN, b Peiping, China, July 21, 13; nat US; m; c 3. ENGINEERING, ATMOSPHERIC SCIENCES. *Educ:* Nat Northeastern Univ, Peiping, BS, 32; Calif Inst Technol, MS, 41, PhD, 50. *Prof Exp:* Instr, Tsing Hua Univ, China, 34-40, supvr wind tunnel proj, 35-37; res asst to Prof T von Karman, Calif Inst Technol, 40-42; design engr, US Plywood Corp, NY, 42-43; design engr, Glenn Martin Co, Md, 43-46, res engr in charge supersonic aerodyn, 46-47; assoc prof aeronaut, Johns Hopkins Univ, 47-52, contract res dir, 51-52; res prof, Inst Fluid Dynamics & Appl Math, Univ Md, 52-54; prof fluid mech, Univ Minn, 54-62; vis prof & dir plasma space sci lab, 62-63, prof space sci & appl physics & head dept, 63-71, prof aerospace &

atmospheric sci, 71-77, PROF MECH ENG, CATH UNIV AM, 77- *Concurrent Pos:* Lectr, Chinese Air Force Acad, 39-40; mem aeroelasticity comt, Appl Physics Lab, Johns Hopkins Univ, 48-50; consult, Off Sci Res, US Air Force, 51-53, Gen Mills Corp, 55-58, Int Continental Ballistic Missile Prog, Gen Elec Co, 56-58, Los Alamos Sci Lab, 58-59 & Lawrence Radiation Lab, Univ Calif, 59-63; Guggenheim fel, 52-53; sr staff scientist, Phys Res Labs, Aerospace Corp, 61-62; US Atomic Energy Comn rep, Int Conf Plasma Physics & Controlled Nuclear Fusion Res, Salzburg, Austria, Sept, 62; rep, Univ Corp Atmospheric Res. *Honors & Awards:* Gold Medal Award, Chinese Govt, 67. *Mem:* AAAS; Am Phys Soc; fel Am Inst Aeronaut & Astronaut; Am Geophys Union; Am Soc Mech Engrs. *Res:* Concept of ring vortex cavity reactor for space nuclear propulsion; superfast thermalization of plasma for controlled thermonuclear fusion reactor; honeycomb sandwich structures used in flying vehicles; tornado and hurricane modeling. *Mailing Add:* Sch of Eng & Archit Cath Univ of Am Washington DC 20064

CHANG, CHIEN-WU, b Keelung, Taiwan, Feb 28, 46; m 76. PHYSICAL CHEMISTRY OF METALS. *Educ:* Tunghai, Univ, Taiwan, BS, 69; State Univ NY at Buffalo, MS, 74, PhD(chem eng), 77. *Prof Exp:* Assoc process engr, China Fluor Eng & Construct Co, 70-71; teaching & res asst, Tunghai Univ, 71-72; res assoc, Mass Inst Technol, 76-79; physicist, Space Div, Gen Elec Co, 79-81; GROUP LEADER, KAWECKI BERYLCO INDUST DIV, CABOT CORP, 82- *Mem:* Am Inst Chem Engrs; Am Phys Soc. *Res:* Momentum heat and mass transfer in materials processing; high temperature chemical reaction; magnetohydrodynamics application in materials processing; process system analysis and control. *Mailing Add:* Kawecki Berylco Indust Inc Cabot Corp PO Box 567 Boyertown PA 19512

CHANG, CHIH-PEI, b Chungking, China, Feb 10, 45; US citizen; m 71. ATMOSPHERIC DYNAMICS, METEOROLOGY. *Educ:* Nat Taiwan Univ, BS, 66; Univ Wash, PhD(atmospheric sci), 72. *Prof Exp:* Asst prof, 72-76, ASSOC PROF METEOROL, NAVAL POSTGRAD SCH, 76- *Concurrent Pos:* Prin investr & proj dir, Nat Environ Satellite Serv grant, 73-78 & NSF grant, 75-79; adv ed, Papers Meterol Res, 78-80; res consult, Chinese Nat Sci Coun, 77-79. *Mem:* Am Meteorol Soc; Sigma Xi. *Res:* Theoretical and observational studies of large-scale meteorology in the tropical and subtropical atmosphere, including planetary scale circulations, monsoons, and synoptic disturbances. *Mailing Add:* Dept of Meteorol Naval Postgrad Sch Monterey CA 93940

CHANG, CHIN HAO, b Haining, Chekiang, China, July 2, 26; m 61; c 1. ENGINEERING MECHANICS. *Educ:* Univ Taiwan, BS, 53; Va Polytech Inst, MS, 57; Univ Mich, PhD(eng mech), 62. *Prof Exp:* Asst prof eng mech, Univ Ala, Tuscaloosa, 60-64; assoc prof, 64-77, PROF ENG MECH, UNIV ALA, 77- *Mem:* Am Soc Mech Engrs; Am Soc Eng Educ; Sigma Xi; Am Acad Mech. *Res:* Structural mechanics. *Mailing Add:* Dept Eng Mech Univ Ala PO Box 2908 University AL 35486

CHANG, CHIN HSIUNG, b Tainan, Taiwan, May 19, 39; US citizen; m 70; c 2. INORGANIC CHEMISTRY, PHYSICAL CHEMISTRY. *Educ:* Nat Taiwan Univ, BS, 62; Rice Univ, PhD(inorg chem), 67. *Prof Exp:* Sr scientist, Avco Everett Res Lab Inc, 71-73; STAFF CHEMIST, EXXON RES & ENG CO, 73- *Mem:* AAAS; Am Chem Soc; Electrochem Soc; NY Acad Sci; Sigma Xi. *Res:* Solid state chemical researches on materials for electrochemical systems adsorption and catalysis. *Mailing Add:* Exxon Res & Eng Co Corp Res Labs Box 45 Linden NJ 07036

CHANG, CHIN-AN, b Sian, China, June 13, 43; m 66; c 4. PHYSICAL CHEMISTRY, MATERIALS SCIENCE. *Educ:* Chung-Hsing Univ, Taiwan, BS, 63; Colo State Univ, MS, 67; Univ Calif, Berkeley, PhD(phys chem), 70. *Prof Exp:* Vis assoc prof chem, Tsing-Hua Univ, Taiwan, 70-71; res assoc, Tex A&M Univ, 71-72; res fel, Calif Inst Technol, 72-73; chemist, Lawrence Berkeley Lab, Calif, 73-75; RES STAFF MEM, T J WATSON RES CTR, IBM CORP, NY, 75- *Mem:* Am Phys Soc; Electrochem Soc. *Res:* Growth and characterization of thin film semiconductors; chemical physics of molecular structure and properties. *Mailing Add:* T J Watson Res Ctr IBM Corp Yorktown Heights NY 10598

CHANG, CHIN-CHUAN, b Laiyang, China, Oct 5, 25; m 45; c 3. ENDOCRINOLOGY, REPRODUCTIVE PHYSIOLOGY. *Educ:* Cath Univ Peiping, BS, 48; NY Univ, MA, 61; Univ Wis-Madison, PhD(endocrinol, reprod physiol), 67. *Prof Exp:* Instr biol, Nat Defense Med Col, Taiwan, 55-58; instr zool, Nat Taiwan Univ, 58-63, assoc prof, 63-65; res assoc endocrinol, 69-70, staff scientist, 71-77, SR INVESTR, BIOMED DIV, POP COUN, ROCKEFELLER UNIV, 77- *Concurrent Pos:* Res fel med, Pop Coun, Rockefeller Univ, 67-69. *Mem:* AAAS; Am Fertil Soc; Endocrine Soc; NY Acad Sci. *Res:* Relationship between blastocyst and endometrium in process of implantation and requirements of ovarian hormones for formation of deciduomata; endocrine activity of steroids released through dimethylpolysiloxane membrane; more effective methods in contraception. *Mailing Add:* Pop Coun Rockefeller Univ York Ave & 66th St New York NY 10021

CHANG, CHING HSONG, b Erh-Shui, Taiwan, Nov 9, 48; m 76; c 1. MOLECULAR ENDOCRINOLOGY, REPRODUCTIVE PHYSIOLOGY. *Educ:* Nat Taiwan Inst Agr, Dipl, 70; Kans State Univ, MS, 74; Clemson Univ, PhD(physiol nutrit), 78. *Prof Exp:* Grad res asst genetics, Kans State Univ, 72-74; grad res asst physiol, Clemson Univ, 74-78; fel biochem, Baylor Col Med, 78-82. *Res:* Mechanism of hormonal actions in mammals; purification and characterization of androgen receptors from various target organs. *Mailing Add:* Dept Cell Biol Baylor Col Med Tex Med Ctr Houston TX 77030

CHANG, CHING MING, b Nanking, China, Oct 13, 35; m 64; c 2. FLUID PHYSICS, ENGINEERING SCIENCE. *Educ:* Aachen Tech Univ, Dipl Ing, 62, DrIng(fluid physics), 67. *Prof Exp:* Res assoc, Shock Tube Lab, Inst Mech, Aachen Tech Univ, 62-64, instr, 64-67, res assoc, 67; vis asst prof eng mech, NC State Univ, 68-70, asst prof, 70-73; sr engr, 73-75, consult, 75, supvr, 75-

78, ENG ASSOC, LINDE DIV, UNION CARBIDE CORP, 78- *Concurrent Pos:* Deleg, Int Coun Sci Unions, Madrid, 65, London, 67; asst ed, Plasma Physics, 71-72; adj assoc prof eng sci, aerospace & nuclear eng, State Univ NY Buffalo, 75-79, adj prof eng, 79- *Mem:* AAAS; Am Phys Soc; Am Soc Mech Engrs; Nat Soc Prof Engrs; Air Pollution Control Asn. *Res:* Heat transfer; energy conversion; electrohydrodynamics; applied mechanics; electrostatic precipitation; thermal sciences and air pollution. *Mailing Add:* Linde Div Union Carbide Corp PO Box 44 Tonawanda NY 14150

CHANG, CHING SHUNG, b China, Dec 19, 47. GEOTECHNICAL ENGINEERING, SOIL MECHANICS. *Educ:* Chen Kung Univ, BS, 69; Univ SC, MS, 71; Univ Calif, Berkeley, PhD(soil mech), 76. *Prof Exp:* Res engr, Univ Calif, Berkeley, 76-77; asst prof civil eng, State Univ NY Buffalo, 77-79; ASST PROF CIVIL ENG, UNIV MASS, 79- *Mem:* Am Soc Civil Engrs; Int Soc Soil Mechs & Found Eng. *Res:* Stress/strain behavior of soil; application of computers in geotechnical engineering. *Mailing Add:* 91 Stony Hill Rd Amherst MA 01002

CHANG, CHING-JEN, b Keelung, Taiwan, Feb 2, 41; m 67; c 1. PHYSICAL ORGANIC CHEMISTRY. *Educ:* Tunghai Univ, Taiwan, BS, 63; Marquette Univ, MS, 67; Univ Calif, Berkeley, PhD(org chem), 71. *Prof Exp:* Res fel chem, Univ Fla, 71-73; SR CHEMIST COATINGS, ROHM & HAAS CO, 73- *Mem:* Am Chem Soc. *Res:* Carbanions; ion-pairs structures; water soluble polymers; hydrophobic association; ionic association; polyurethanes; thickeners; emulsion polymerization; surfactants and dispersants; rheology of polymer solutions and dispersions; acrylic monomers and polymers. *Mailing Add:* Res Labs Rohm & Haas Co Norristown & McKean Rds Spring House PA 19477

CHANG, CHING-JER, b Hsin-chu, Taiwan, Oct 17, 42. NATURAL PRODUCTS CHEMISTRY, MEDICINAL CHEMISTRY. *Educ:* Nat Taiwan Cheng Kung Univ, BS, 65; Ind Univ, PhD(org chem), 72. *Prof Exp:* Res asst chem, Nat Taiwan Univ, 66-67; teaching asst, NMex Highlands Univ, 68; res & teaching asst, Ind Univ, 68-72; res assoc, 72-73, asst prof, 73-78, ASSOC PROF MED CHEM & PHARMACOG, PURDUE UNIV, WEST LAFAYETTE, 78- *Mem:* Am Chem Soc; The Chem Soc; Am Soc Pharmacog; Phytochem Soc NAm; Am Pharmaceut Asn. *Res:* Structure elucidation, stereochemistry, biosynthesis and partial synthesis of natural products; interaction of small molecules and drugs with macromolecules; biomedical application of spectroscopy. *Mailing Add:* Dept of Med Chem & Pharmacog Purdue Univ Sch of Pharm West Lafayette IN 47907

CHANG, CHIN-HAI, b Taiwan, China; US citizen. IMMUNOCHEMISTRY, IMMUNOLOGY. *Educ:* Nat Taiwan Univ, BS, 65; Washington Univ, PhD(develop biochem), 71. *Prof Exp:* Fel physiol chem, Roche Inst Molecular Biol, 71-73; asst prof cancer res, Sch Med, Tufts Univ, 73-76; MGR IMMUNOCHEM RES, SYVA RES INST, PALO ALTO, 76- *Concurrent Pos:* Consult immunochem, Leary Lab, 73-76. *Mem:* AAAS; Int Res Group Carcinoembryonic Proteins; Am Asn Clin Chem; NY Acad Sci; Am Soc Microbiologists. *Res:* Immunodiagnostics; clinical chemistry; biochemistry; tumor immunology; microbiology. *Mailing Add:* Syva Res Inst 3181 Porter Dr Palo Alto CA 94303

CHANG, CHRISTOPHER TEH-MIN, b Nanking, China, Apr 2, 36; m 69; c 1. ELECTRICAL ENGINEERING. *Educ:* Nat Taiwan Univ, BSEng, 57; Univ Southern Calif, MSEE, 62, PhD(elec eng), 68. *Prof Exp:* Teaching asst physics, Taipei Inst Technol, Taiwan, 59-60; test engr, ALWAC Comput Div, El-tronics, Calif, 61-62; design engr, Appl Res Lab, Calif, 62-63; res asst electromagnetic theory & superconductivity, Univ Southern Calif, 63-68; asst elec engr, High Energy Fac Div, Argonne Nat Lab, 68-73; MEM TECH STAFF, CENT RES LAB, TEX INSTRUMENTS, INC, 73- *Mem:* Am Phys Soc; Inst Elec & Electronics Engrs. *Res:* Superconductivity, microwave circuits, magnetic bubble device design and material developments. *Mailing Add:* Cent Res Labs Tex Instruments Inc PO Box 225936 MS 134 Dallas TX 75265

CHANG, CHU HUAI, b Fukien, China, Oct 1, 17; m 59; c 2. RADIOLOGY. *Educ:* St John's Univ, China, BS, 41, MD, 44. *Prof Exp:* From instr to asst prof radiol, Sch Med, Yale Univ, 54-62; assoc prof & assoc attend radiologist, Med Ctr, 62-67, PROF RADIOL, COL PHYSICIANS & SURGEONS, COLUMBIA UNIV, 67-, ATTEND RADIOLOGIST, COLUMBIA-PRESBY MED CTR, 67-, DIR, RADIATION THER DIV, 70- *Concurrent Pos:* Res fel radiol, Sch Med, Univ Calif, 47-49; res fel, Sch Med, Yale Univ, 50-51. *Mem:* AAAS; Sigma Xi; Am Soc Therapeut Radiol; Am Col Radiol; Asn Univ Radiol. *Res:* Radiation therapy and radiobiology. *Mailing Add:* Col Physicians & Surgeons Columbia Univ New York NY 10032

CHANG, CHUAN CHUNG, b Tainan, Formosa, Nov 28, 38; m 63; c 2. PHYSICS. *Educ:* Rensselaer Polytech Inst, BS, 62; Cornell Univ, PhD(physics), 67. *Prof Exp:* Res asst physics, Cornell Univ, 63-67; MEM TECH STAFF, BELL LABS, 67- *Res:* Surface physics; crystallography; electron diffraction; electron spectroscopy; electronics materials. *Mailing Add:* 2C-136 Bell Labs Murray Hill NJ 07974

CHANG, CLIFFORD WAH JUN, b Honolulu, Hawaii, July 25, 38. ORGANIC CHEMISTRY. *Educ:* Univ Southern Calif, BS, 60; Univ Hawaii, PhD(chem), 64. *Prof Exp:* Jr chemist, Cyclo Chem Corp, Calif, 59; asst marine chemist, Hawaii Marine Lab, 61; fel chem, Univ Ga, 64-68; from asst prof to assoc prof, 68-79, PROF CHEM, UNIV WEST FLA, 79- *Concurrent Pos:* Vis prof, Univ Okla, 76-77 & Univ Hawaii, 77 & 81. *Mem:* Am Chem Soc; The Chem Soc; Sigma Xi; Am Soc Pharmacog. *Res:* Structural determinations and synthesis of natural products. *Mailing Add:* Dept Chem Univ West Fla Pensacola FL 32504

CHANG, DANIEL P Y, b Shanghai, China, Mar 25, 47; US citizen; m 69; c 2. AEROSOL SCIENCE, AIR POLLUTION CONTROL. *Educ:* Calif Inst Technol, BS, 68, MS, 69, PhD(mech eng), 73. *Prof Exp:* Res fel environ health eng, Calif Inst Technol, 73; asst prof, 73-80, ASSOC PROF CIVIL ENG,

UNIV CALIF, DAVIS, 80- *Concurrent Pos:* Prin investr, Res Initiation Award, NSF, 75-77; co-investr contracts, Environ Protection Agency, 77-79, proj dir, Air Pollution Area Training Ctr, 78-81. *Mem:* Air Pollution Control Asn; AAAS; Sigma Xi; Am Asn Aerosol Res. *Mailing Add:* Dept Civil Eng Univ Calif Davis CA 95616

CHANG, DAVID BING JUE, b Seattle, Wash, June 27, 35; m 59; c 4. APPLIED PHYSICS. *Educ:* Univ Wash, Seattle, BS, 56; Calif Inst Technol, PhD(physics), 62. *Prof Exp:* Staff physicist, Gen Atomic, 63-66; sr fel, Univ Wash, 66-68; staff physicist, Boeing Co, 68-73; dep asst secy sci & technol, US Dept Commerce, 73-77; mgr res planning, 77-78, HEAD APPL PHYSICS, OCCIDENTAL RES CORP, 78- *Concurrent Pos:* Res & develop comt, US-Israel, US Govt & US-Japan Sci Comt, 75; fel, Univ Calif, San Diego, 61-63; affil investr, Va Mason Res Ctr, 71-82; consult, Firlands Hosp, 72-73; affil assoc prof, Dept Physics & Biophysics, Univ Wash, 68-82; adj prof, Dept Physics, Univ Calif, Irvine, 81-82; prof physics, Inst Basic Res, Harvard Univ. *Mem:* Am Phys Soc; AAAS; Inst Elec & Electronics Engrs. *Res:* Analyses of collective effects in molecules and semiconductors, in fusion and space plasmas, in biophysics and astrophysics; gauge theory of gravitation; development of technology policy; energy technologies. *Mailing Add:* 14212 Livingstone Tustin CA 92680

CHANG, DING, b Kwiechow, China, Sept 2, 40; m 72; c 2. ORGANIC CHEMISTRY, BIOCHEMISTRY. *Educ:* Nat Taiwan Norm Univ, BS, 66; Univ NB, PhD(org chem), 71. *Prof Exp:* Res assoc chem, Univ NB, 71-72; res fel, Inst Biomed Res, Univ Tex, Austin, 72-77; prin res chemist, Bioprods Dept, Beckman Instruments Inc, 77-79; VPRES & MFG DIR, PENINSULA LABS, INC, 79- *Mem:* Am Chem Soc. *Res:* Synthetic chemistry of natural products; alkaloids, peptides and proteins. *Mailing Add:* 611 Taylor Way #2 Belmont CA 94002

CHANG, DONALD CHOY, b Kwangtung, China, Aug 28, 42. BIOPHYSICS, CELL PHYSIOLOGY. *Educ:* Nat Taiwan Univ, BS, 65; Rice Univ, MA, 67, PhD(physics), 70. *Prof Exp:* Res assoc physics, Rice Univ, 70-74; instr, 73-74, ASST PROF BIOPHYS, BAYLOR COL MED, 74- *Concurrent Pos:* Welch Found fel biophys, Baylor Col Med, 70-73; adj asst prof physics, Rice Univ, 74-; vis lectr biophysics, Beijing Univ, 81- *Mem:* AAAS; Am Phys Soc; Biophys Soc. *Res:* Nuclear magnetic resonance studies of cellular water and ions; cellular transport; electrobiophysics and mechanisms of nerve excitation. *Mailing Add:* Dept Physics Rice Univ Houston TX 77001

CHANG, EDDIE LI, b Nanking, China, Oct 4, 48; US citizen. LIGHT-SCATTERING, LIPID MEMBRANES. *Educ:* Antioch Col, BS, 71; Univ Ore, PhD(chem-physics), 77. *Prof Exp:* Res assoc, Dept Chem, Univ Wash, 77-79; Nat Res Coun fel, 79-81, RES PHYSICIST, NAVAL RES LAB, 81- *Mem:* Biophys Soc. *Res:* Physical properties of lipid membranes; interaction of lipids with proteins; use of artificial lipid bilayers as membrane models. *Mailing Add:* Optical Probes Code 510 Naval Res Lab Washington DC 20375

CHANG, ELFREDA TE-HSIN, b Peiping, China, Dec 13, 35; US citizen. THERMODYNAMICS, PHYSICAL CHEMISTRY. *Educ:* Univ Mich, BSE, 57, MS, 59, PhD(phys chem), 63. *Prof Exp:* MEM TECH STAFF CHEM, AEROSPACE CORP, 62- *Mem:* Sigma Xi. *Res:* Low and high temperature calorimetry; thermodynamics of gas-condensed-phase equilibria; solubility of gases in propellants; compaitbility of materials with propellants; physical chemistry of propellants. *Mailing Add:* Aerospace Corp 2350 E El Segundo Blvd El Segundo CA 90245

CHANG, EPPIE SHENG, b Shanghai, China, Aug 20, 46; US citizen; m 68; c 2. BIOCHEMISTRY, NUTRITION. *Educ:* Univ Calif, Berkeley, BA, 67, MA, 71. *Prof Exp:* Res lab asst, Dept Nutrit Sci, Univ Calif, 67-68, res asst, 68-70; asst res scientist, Ames Prod Develop Lab, 71-74, assoc res scientist, 74-77, RES SCIENTIST, AMES BLOOD CHEM LAB, MILES LAB, 77- *Mem:* Am Asn Clin Chem. *Res:* Development of simple clinical, serum tests for diagnostic application. *Mailing Add:* Ames Blood Chem Lab Miles Lab 1127 Myrtle St Elkhart IN 46514

CHANG, ERNEST SUN-MEI, b Berkeley, Calif, Dec 7, 50. ENDOCRINOLOGY, CELL BIOLOGY. *Educ:* Univ Calif, Berkeley, AB, 73; Univ Calif, Los Angeles, PhD(biol), 78. *Prof Exp:* ASST PROF ANIMAL SCI, UNIV CALIF, DAVIS, 78- *Concurrent Pos:* Am Cancer Soc fel, Univ Chicago, 78. *Mem:* AAAS; Tissue Cult Asn; World Maricult Soc; Am Soc Zoologists. *Res:* Molecular action of insect and crustacean hormones; invertebrate zoology; aquaculture of marine invertebrates. *Mailing Add:* Bodega Marine Lab PO Box 247 Bodega Bay CA 94923

CHANG, FA YAN, b Shantung, China, May 5, 32; m 60; c 2. WEED SCIENCE, PLANT PHYSIOLOGY. *Educ:* Nat Taiwan Univ, BSc, 53; Univ Alta, MSc, 66, PhD(plant sci), 69. *Prof Exp:* Asst agronomist, Taiwan Tobacco Res Inst, Repub China, 54-64; instr weed sci, Univ Alta, 69-70; res assoc, Univ Guelph, 70-74; HERBICIDE EVAL OFFICER, AGR CAN, 74- *Concurrent Pos:* Nat executive, Can Weed Comt, 75-; mem, Plant Growth Regulator Working Group. *Mem:* Agr Pesticide Soc Can; Weed Sci Soc Am; Can Soc Plant Physiol. *Res:* Weed control; herbicide physiology and antidotes. *Mailing Add:* Pesticides Div K W Neatby Bldg Carling Ave Ottawa ON K1A 0C6 Can

CHANG, FRANK KENG, b Anhwei, China, Feb 12, 22; US citizen; m 62; c 1. SEISMOLOGY, PETROLEUM EXPLORATION. *Educ:* Nat Hunan Univ, BS, 46; St Louis Univ, MS, 58. *Prof Exp:* Petrol engr drilling & production, Chinese Petrol Corp, 46-52; chief seismologist, US Antarctic Res Proj, Arctic Inst NAm, NSF, 58-60 & res assoc, Geophys & Polar Res Ctr, Univ Wis, 60-61; RES GEOPHYSICIST, ENG WATERWAYS EXP STA, US ARMY, 66- *Concurrent Pos:* Geophys engr seismic data process petrol explor, Tex Instrument, Inc, 66. *Mem:* Seismol Soc Am; Soc Explor Geophysicists; Am Geophys Union; Sigma Xi. *Res:* Earthquake resistant design; site characterization of earthquake ground motions by power spectral densities; strong motion duration, spectral content and predominant period; a quantitative earthquake intensity scale; permanent displacement analysis treating slides an embankment as a rigid block on an inclined plane. *Mailing Add:* US Army Engr Waterways Exp Sta PO Box 631 Vicksburg MS 39180

CHANG, FRANKLIN, b Princeton, NJ, Feb 12, 42; m 67; c 1. PHYSIOLOGY, ENTOMOLOGY. *Educ:* Univ Md, BS, 63; Univ Ill, PhD(entom), 69. *Prof Exp:* Asst prof biol, Alma Col, Mich, 69-70; asst prof entom, 70-74, ASSOC PROF ENTOM, UNIV HAWAII, 74- *Mem:* Sigma Xi; AAAS; Entom Soc Am; Am Inst Biol Sci. *Res:* Carbohydrate and lipid metabolism in insects; endocrinology. *Mailing Add:* Dept of Entom Univ of Hawaii 3050 Maile Way Honolulu HI 96822

CHANG, FRANKLIN SHIH CHUAN, b Nanking, China, Dec 30, 15; US citizen; m 38, 69; c 4. POLYMER CHEMISTRY. *Educ:* Purdue Univ, MS, 49; Univ Md, PhD(chem), 52. *Prof Exp:* Group leader anal & phys chem, Mystik Adhesive Prod, Inc, 52-60; mgr polymer physics, Ingersoll Res Ctr, Borg-Warner Corp, 60-79, staff scientist, 79-80; CONSULT, 80- *Mem:* Am Chem Soc. *Res:* Physical testing of viscoelastic materials; adhesion and adhesives; infrared spectrometry; molecular structure; submicron particle size distribution measurements; polymer physics. *Mailing Add:* 320 S Maple Mt Prospect IL 60018

CHANG, FREDDY WILFRED LENNOX, b Kwang Tung, China, Sept 18, 35; Trinidad & Tobago citizen; m 65; c 3. OPTOMETRY, PHARMACOLOGY. *Educ:* Sir George Williams Univ, BSc, 65; Univ Waterloo, OD, 70; Ind Univ, Bloomington, MS, 73, PhD(physiol optics), 76. *Prof Exp:* Res technician urol, Royal Victoria Hosp, Montreal, 65-67; clinician optom, Drs J D Price & G Grant, Kitchener, Ont, 70; assoc instr optom, Ind Univ, Bloomington, 70-74; asst prof optom, Univ Ala, Birmingham, 74-77; instr pharmacol, 76-77; asst prof optom, 77-80, ASSOC PROF OPTOM & ADJ ASSOC PROF PHARMACOLOGY, MEDICAL SCI PROG, IND UNIV, BLOOMINGTON, 80- *Concurrent Pos:* Am Optom Found fel, 71-74; consult pharmacol, Nat Bd Examr Optom, 74- & Tex State Bd Optom, 78; dir continuing educ, Sch Optom, Univ Ala, Birmingham, 76-77 & Sch Optom, Ind Univ, 77- *Mem:* Am Acad Optom; Asn Res Vision & Ophthal; Am Optom Asn; Sigma Xi. *Res:* Ocular pharmacology, specifically toxicology; physiological disposition of drugs in the eye. *Mailing Add:* Ind Univ Sch of Optom 800 E Atwater Bloomington IN 47401

CHANG, FREDERIC CHEWMING, b San Francisco, Calif, Aug 5, 05; m 32; c 3. ORGANIC CHEMISTRY. *Educ:* Harvard Univ, MA, 40, PhD(org chem), 41. *Prof Exp:* From instr to asst prof chem, Lingnan Univ, 30-38, cur dept, 32-38; res assoc, Stanford Univ, 41-42; spec res assoc, Off Sci Res & Develop, Harvard Univ, 42-46; prof chem & chmn dept, Lingnan Univ, 46-51; lectr chem & res assoc path, Univ Tenn, Memphis, 51-59, prof pharmacog, Col Pharm, 59-72, prof biochem, Col Basic Med Sci, 59-76; DISTINGUISHED RES PROF BIOCHEM, COL MED, UNIV SOUTH ALA, 76- *Mem:* AAAS; Am Chem Soc; Royal Soc Chem; Am Soc Pharmacog; Phytochem Soc NAm. *Res:* Naphthoquinones; antimalarials; steroids; medicinal plants; bile acids. *Mailing Add:* Dept of Biochem Univ SAla Mobile AL 36688

CHANG, GEORGE CHUNYI, b Shangai, China, Aug 23, 35; m 63; c 3. APPLIED MECHANICS, STRUCTURAL ENGINEERING. *Educ:* Taiwan Col Eng, BS, 59; Univ Ill, MS, 62, PhD(struct eng), 66. *Prof Exp:* Struct engr, Severud-Elstad-Krueger & Assocs, 62-63; res asst, Col Eng, Univ Ill, 63-66; res engr, Boeing Airplane Co, Wash, 66-68, res specialist, 68-69; asst prof aerospace eng, US Naval Acad, 69-73; assoc prof, 73-75; br chief energy res, US Dept Energy, 75-79; PROF & ASSOC DEAN ENG, CLEVELAND STATE UNIV, 79- *Concurrent Pos:* Instr, Highline Col, 67-68; lectr, Univ Md, College Park, 69-70; consult, Spacecraft Lab, Commun Satellite Corp, Washington, DC, 69-73, US Dept Energy, 80-82. *Mem:* Am Inst Aeronaut & Astronaut; Am Soc Eng Educ; Am Acad Mech. *Res:* Problems in the areas of applied mechanics, engineering design, computer methods, renewable energy and conservation technology. *Mailing Add:* Col Eng Cleveland State Univ Cleveland OH 44115

CHANG, GEORGE WASHINGTON, b Madison, Wis, Feb 22, 42. MICROBIAL PHYSIOLOGY, PHARMACOLOGY. *Educ:* Princeton Univ, AB, 63; Univ Calif, Berkeley, PhD(biochem), 67. *Prof Exp:* Vis scientist, Lab Molecular Biol, NIH, 67-68; NIH fel biochem, 68-70, asst prof, 70-76, ASSOC PROF FOOD MICROBIOL, NUTRIT SCI DEPT, UNIV CALIF, BERKELEY, 76- *Mem:* Am Soc Microbiol; Inst Food Technologists. physiology; intestinal microflora and microecology. *Res:* Intestinal microflora and its interaction with diet and disease; microbiological and biochemical tools for clinical chemistry and pharmacology. *Mailing Add:* Dept of Nutrit Sci Univ of Calif Berkeley CA 94720

CHANG, H K, b Shenyang, China, July 9, 40; US citizen. BIOMEDICAL ENGINEERING. *Educ:* Nat Taiwan Univ, BS, 62; Stanford Univ, MS, 64; Northwestern Univ, PhD(biomed eng), 69. *Prof Exp:* From asst prof to assoc prof eng sci, State Univ NY Buffalo, 69-76; assoc prof, 76-80, PROF PHYSIOL & BIOMED ENG, MCGILL UNIV, 80- *Mem:* Am Physiol Soc; Am Thoracic Soc; Biomed Eng Soc; Am Inst Chem Engrs; Am Soc Civil Engrs. *Res:* Respiratory physiology and bio-fluid mechanics with special emphasis on gas transport and blood flow in the lung. *Mailing Add:* 3655 Drummond St Fac Med McGill Univ Montreal PQ H3G 1Y6 Can

CHANG, HAI-YAIN (HOWARD), b Chiangsu, China, Nov 12, 39. FLUID DYNAMICS, HYDRAULICS. *Educ:* Cheng Kung Univ, Taiwan, BS, 62; Colo State Univ, MS, 65, PhD(fluid mech, hydraul), 67. *Prof Exp:* Asst prof civil eng, Colo State Univ, 67; from asst prof to assoc prof aerospace eng, 67-77, PROF CIVIL ENG, SAN DIEGO STATE UNIV, 77- *Concurrent Pos:* Consult, Rohr Corp, 68- *Honors & Awards:* Outstanding Contrib Aerospace Eng Award, Am Inst Aeronaut & Astronaut, 70. *Mem:* Am Inst Aeronaut & Astronaut. *Res:* River mechanics; hydraulics; turbulence; hydraulic analogy; potential flows; compressible flows. *Mailing Add:* Dept of Eng San Diego State Univ San Diego CA 92182

CHANG, HAN-CHUAN LIU, b Kwangsi, China; US citizen; m 63; c 2. MOLECULAR SPECTROSCOPY. *Educ:* Tunghai Univ, Taiwan, BS, 60; Univ Southern Calif, MS, 64, PhD(physics), 73. *Prof Exp:* Teaching asst physics, Tunghai Univ, Taiwan, 60-61; res asst neurophysiol, Med Sci Res, Rancho Los Amigos Hosp, Downey, Calif, 64-66; MEM TECH STAFF, LOGICON, SAN PEDRO, 73- *Res:* Optics; energy sources. *Mailing Add:* Logicon Inc 21535 Hawthorne Blvd Torrance CA 90503

CHANG, HAO-JAN, b Shantung, China. POLYMER CHEMISTRY, ORGANIC CHEMISTRY. *Educ:* Chung-Yuan Col, BS, 68; Univ Mass, PhD(chem), 74. *Prof Exp:* Sr res chemist, Eastman Kodak Co, 74-78; SR POLYMER CHEMIST, MEMOREX CO, 78- *Mem:* Am Chem Soc; AAAS. *Res:* Structural and mechanistic study of polymer chemistry. *Mailing Add:* 3637 Slopeview Dr San Jose CA 95122

CHANG, HARRY LO, b China, Sept 4, 35; m 63; c 3. CHEMICAL ENGINEERING. *Educ:* Tunghai Univ, Taiwan, BS, 60; Rice Univ, PhD(chem eng), 67. *Prof Exp:* Res engr, Mobil Res & Develop Corp, 67-70, sr res engr, 70-75; enhanced recovery mgr, 75-80, MGR, ENHANCED RECOVERY RES, CITIES SERV CO, 80- *Mem:* Soc Petrol Engrs; Am Inst Mech Engrs. *Res:* Thermodynamics; vapor liquid equilibrium of hydrocarbons; mass transport phenomenon; improved oil recovery research; enhanced recovery processes. *Mailing Add:* 6616 E 108th Tulsa OK 74133

CHANG, HENRY, b Shanghai, China, Dec 2, 44; US citizen; m 76; c 1. BIOENGINEERING, SCIENCE EDUCATION. *Educ:* Harvard Univ, BS, 65; Med Sch, Harvard Univ, MD, 69; diplomate, Am Bd Int Med, 75 & 78. *Prof Exp:* Fel hemat & oncol, Children's Hosp, Boston, 73-76; asst prof, Dept Pediat, New York Univ, 76-79; ASST PROF HEMAT & ONCOL, DEPT MED, ALBERT EINSTEIN COL MED, 79- *Concurrent Pos:* Vis asst prof, Med Biochem, Rockefeller Univ, 76-78. *Mem:* Am Soc Hematol. *Res:* Blood disorders; red cells; hemoglobin biochemistry; molecular biology; cell growth and differentiation, especially of bone marrow; gene control; pharmacology and drug design. *Mailing Add:* Ullman 925 Albert Einstein Col Med 1300 Morris Park Ave Bronx NY 10461

CHANG, HERBERT YU-PANG, b Shanghai, China, Nov 25, 37. ELECTRICAL ENGINEERING. *Educ:* Univ Ill, BS, 60, MS, 62, PhD(elec eng), 64. *Prof Exp:* MEM TECH STAFF, BELL TEL LABS, 64- *Mem:* Fel Inst Elec & Electronics Engrs. *Res:* Basic and/or applied research in areas of telephone switching systems design, system maintenance techniques, computer software systems and computer aided design systems. *Mailing Add:* 405 Charles Ave Naperville IL 60540

CHANG, HOU-MIN, b Chiayi, Taiwan, Aug 29, 38; m 66; c 2. WOOD CHEMISTRY. *Educ:* Nat Taiwan Univ, BA, 62; Univ Wash, MS, 66, PhD(wood chem), 68. *Prof Exp:* Fel, 68-69, vis asst prof, 69, asst prof, 70-73, assoc prof, 73-77, PROF WOOD & PAPER SCI, NC STATE UNIV, 77- *Mem:* Am Chem Soc; Am Tech Asn Pulp & Paper Indust. *Res:* Species variation in wood lignins; isolation and characterization of cellulase lignin; characterization of residual lignin in kraft pulps of various yield; delignification by oxygen and alkali; lignin biodegradation. *Mailing Add:* Dept of Wood & Paper Sci NC State Univ Raleigh NC 27607

CHANG, HOWARD HOW CHUNG, b Honolulu, Hawaii, Nov 16, 22; m 52; c 1. THEORETICAL PHYSICS. *Educ:* Calif Inst Technol, BS, 44; Univ Calif, MA, 49; Harvard Univ, PhD(physics), 55. *Prof Exp:* Instr physics, Clarkson Tech Inst, 49-50; instr math, Univ Hawaii, 50-52; mem tech staff, Microwave Lab, Gen Elec Co, 55-57; physicist, Rand Corp, Calif, 57-58 & Hughes Aircraft Co, 58-61; sr math physicist, Stanford Res Inst, 61-76; STAFF SCIENTIST, LOCKHEED MISSILES & SPACE CO, 76- *Concurrent Pos:* Liaison physicist, Off Naval Res, London, 69-70. *Mem:* Am Phys Soc; AAAS. *Res:* Electromagnetic theory; plasma physics; controlled fusion; solar energy; macroscopic applications of superconductivity; energy storage; energy economics. *Mailing Add:* 337 Los Altos Ave Los Altos CA 94022

CHANG, HSIEN-HSIN, b Yuan-lin, China, June 16, 42; m 69, 81. ORGANIC CHEMISTRY. *Educ:* Nat Taiwan Univ, BS, 65; Univ Miami, MS, 69; Univ Wash, PhD(org chem), 74. *Prof Exp:* Teaching assoc chem, Univ Wash, 73-74; res assoc biochem, molecular & cell biol, Cornell Univ, 74-76; group leader, The Quaker Oats Co, 76-77; sr scientist, Pillsbury Co, 77-80; STAFF CHEMIST, QUAKER OATS CO, 80- *Mem:* Am Chem Soc; Am Oil Chemists Soc. *Res:* Metabolism of coenzymes; synthesis of biologically significant compounds; enzyme modification of food ingredients; microwave interaction with foods. *Mailing Add:* Quaker Oats Co 617 W Main St Barrington IL 60010

CHANG, HSING-TZE RUAN, protein chemistry, nutritional biochemistry, see previous edition

CHANG, HSU, b China, Feb 3, 32; US citizen; m 61; c 3. MAGNETISM, ELECTRICAL ENGINEERING. *Educ:* Univ Taiwan, BS, 53; Carnegie Inst Technol, MS, 57, PhD(elec eng), 59. *Prof Exp:* Asst elec eng, Univ Taiwan, 54-55; MEM RES STAFF, INT BUS MACH CORP, 59- *Concurrent Pos:* Vis assoc prof, Carnegie Inst Technol, 64-66; rev ed & ed-in-chief, Trans Magnetics, 67-72; tech prog co-chmn, Int Magnetics Conf, 70, 71 & 73. *Mem:* Fel Inst Elec & Electronics Engrs. *Res:* Electromagnetic field theory; magnetization reversal phenomena; magnetic memory devices and systems; magnetic bubbles; data bases. *Mailing Add:* 947 Fox Meadow Rd Yorktown Heights NY 10598

CHANG, I-DEE, b Anhwei, China, Mar 21, 22; m 70. AERONAUTICS, MATHEMATICS. *Educ:* Nat Cent Univ, China, BS, 44; Kans State Univ, MS, 55; Calif Inst Technol, PhD(aeronaut, math), 59. *Prof Exp:* Res fel aeronaut, Calif Inst Technol, 59-61; from asst prof to assoc prof, 62-69, PROF AERONAUT & ASTRONAUT, STANFORD UNIV, 70- *Mem:* Am Inst Aeronaut & Astronaut; Am Phys Soc; Biomed Eng Soc. *Res:* Viscous fluid theory; singular perturbation methods; bio-fluid mechanics. *Mailing Add:* 948 Wing Pl Stanford CA 94305

CHANG, IFAY F, b Chung King, China, Apr 4, 42; m 68; c 1. SOLID STATE PHYSICS, ELECTRICAL ENGINEERING. *Educ:* Cheng Kung Univ, Taiwan, BS, 63; Univ RI, MS, 66, PhD(elec eng), 68. *Prof Exp:* Sr assoc engr, Components Div, 68-69, staff engr, Vt, 69-70, MEM RES STAFF, IBM WATSON CTR, INT BUS MACHINES CORP, NY, 70- *Concurrent Pos:* Lectr, Syracuse Univ, 68-69; vis lectr, Univ Tex, Austin, 76-77; consult, IBM Off Prods Div, Austin, 76-77. *Mem:* Am Phys Soc; Inst Elec & Electronics Engrs; fel Soc Info Display; Electrochem Soc; Soc Info Display (treas). *Res:* Lattice dynamics; optical and electrical properties of solids and solid films; impurities and imperfections in solids; mixed crystals; infrared and raman spectroscopy; solid state devices and microelectronics; display device and technology; electrochromism; electroluminescence; rescence and phosphors. *Mailing Add:* PO Box 218 18-150 IBM Watson Res Ctr Yorktown Heights NY 10598

CHANG, IK-CHIN, b Suncheon, Korea, Jan 5, 16; m 42; c 3. IMMUNOLOGY. *Educ:* Yonsei Univ, Korea, MD, 40, DmSc(microbiol), 60; Johns Hopkins Univ, MPH, 54. *Prof Exp:* Dep dir bioprod, Nat Health Inst, Korea, 40-56; assoc prof microbiol, Yonsei Univ Col, 57-60; prof, Cath Med Col, Korea, 60-66; res assoc, Sch Pub Health, Univ Pittsburgh, 66-69; BACTERIOLOGIST BIO-PROD, BUR DIS CONTROL & LAB SERV, MICH DEPT PUB HEALTH, 69- *Mem:* Am Soc Microbiol. *Res:* Establishment of standard procedure in toxic factors in Pertussis vaccine. *Mailing Add:* 529 Keenway Circle Lansing MI 49001

CHANG, I-LOK, b Amoy, China, July 9, 43; US citizen; m 70; c 1. MATHEMATICAL ANALYSIS. *Educ:* Calif Inst Technol, BS, 65; Cornell Univ, PhD(math), 71. *Prof Exp:* From instr to asst prof, 70-76, ASSOC PROF MATH, AM UNIV, 76- *Mem:* Am Math Soc; AAAS. *Res:* Functions of a complex variable; numerical analysis. *Mailing Add:* Dept of Math Statist Comput Sci Am Univ Washington DC 20016

CHANG, IN-KOOK, b Choonchun, Korea, Aug 24, 43; m 71; c 2. PLANT PHYSIOLOGY. *Educ:* Seoul Nat Univ, BS, 66; Va Polytech Inst & State Univ, MS, 70; Univ Chicago, PhD(biol), 74. *Prof Exp:* Asst prof plant physiol, Va Polytech Inst & State Univ, 75-77; res biologist, 77-78, SR RES BIOLOGIST, DIAMOND SHAMROCK CORP, 78- *Mem:* AAAS; Am Soc Plant Physiologists; NY Acad Sci; Weed Sci Soc Am. *Res:* Plant growth and development; effects of growth regulators on crop productivity; plant hormone metabolism; mode of action of herbicides, degradation of herbicides and growth regulators in plants and soils. *Mailing Add:* T R Evans Res Ctr Diamond Shamrock Corp Painesville OH 44077

CHANG, IRENE CHING LAI, b Peiping, China, July 14, 16; m 41; c 2. NUTRITION. *Educ:* Nanking Univ, BS, 39; MS, 42; State Univ Wash, PhD(foods nutrit), 49. *Prof Exp:* Lab instr gen org & anal chem, Nanking Univ, 39-42, instr chem, 42-45; res asst foods & nutrit, State Univ Wash, 46-48; res assoc, Syracuse Univ, 48-51, from asst prof to assoc prof, 51-56; res scientist, Joseph E Seagram & Sons, 56-64; res assoc biochem, NC State Univ, 65-75; RETIRED. *Mem:* Inst Food Technologists; Am Chem Soc. *Res:* Mineral metabolism and nutrition. *Mailing Add:* 516 Emerson Dr Raleigh NC 27609

CHANG, JACK CHE-MAN, b Shanghai, China, Nov 19, 41; m 65. ANALYTICAL CHEMISTRY. *Educ:* Asbury Col, BA, 61; Univ Ill, Urbana, MS, 63, PhD(chem), 65. *Prof Exp:* Res assoc electrochem luminescence, Mass Inst Technol, 66-67; SR RES CHEMIST, EASTMAN KODAK CO, 67- *Res:* Electrochemistry of organic compounds. *Mailing Add:* Eastman Kodak Co Res Labs 343 State St Rochester NY 14650

CHANG, JAMES C, b Shanghai, China, Aug 8, 30; m 70. PHYSICAL CHEMISTRY, INORGANIC CHEMISTRY. *Educ:* Mt Union Col, BS, 57; Univ Calif, Los Angeles, PhD(chem), 64. *Prof Exp:* Res chemist, E R Squibb & Sons Div, Olin Mathieson Chem Co, 59-62; asst prof chem, State Col Iowa, 64-67; from asst prof to assoc prof, 67-74, actg head dept, 75-77, PROF CHEM, UNIV NORTHERN IOWA, 74- *Concurrent Pos:* Vis scientist, Univ Copenhagen, 69-70. *Mem:* Am Chem Soc. *Res:* Inorganic synthesis and substitution reactions of inorganic complex compounds. *Mailing Add:* Dept of Chem Univ of Northern Iowa Cedar Falls IA 50613

CHANG, JAW-KANG, b Cholon, South Vietnam, Aug 11, 42; US citizen; m 62. BIOCHEMISTRY. *Educ:* Nat Taiwan Univ, BS, 65; Univ NB, Fredericton, PhD(org chem), 69. *Prof Exp:* Res fel paptide chem, Inst Biomed Res, Univ Tex, Austin, 69-73; sr develop chemist, Dept Bio-Prod, Beckman Instruments Inc, 73-77; res dir, 77-80, VPRES, PENINSULA LABS, INC, 80- *Res:* Synthetic chemistry of natural products; alkaloids, peptides and proteins; design and synthesis of analogs of biological active peptides. *Mailing Add:* Peninsula Labs Inc 611 Taylor Way Suite 2 Belmont CA 94002

CHANG, JEFFREY PEH-I, b Changteh, China, Oct 10, 17; US citizen; c 2. CELL BIOLOGY. *Educ:* Nat Cent Univ, Chungking, BS, 41; Univ Ill, MS, 46, PhD(zool), 49. *Prof Exp:* From asst prof to assoc prof, Univ Tex Postgrad Sch Biomed Sci, 55-62; from asst biologist to assoc biologist, Univ Tex M D Anderson Hosp & Tumor Inst Houston, 55-64, actg chief sect exp path, 59-64, biologist & prof biol, 64-72; PROF CELL BIOL, UNIV TEX MED BR GALVESTON, 72- *Concurrent Pos:* Spec consult, Nat Cancer Inst, 58-61 & Sch Aerospace Med, Brooks AFB, 62-64; consult, Univ Tex M D Anderson Hosp & Tumor Inst Houston, 72-76; res consult, Nat Sci Coun, Repub China, 74-; academician, Academia Sinica, Repub China. *Mem:* AAAS; Am Soc Cell Biol; Am Soc Exp Path; Am Asn Cancer Res; Histochem Soc. *Res:* Ultrastructural and histochemical studies of cells and tissues; initiation and mechanism of carcinogenesis; tumor production and biology. *Mailing Add:* Dept of Human Biol Chem & Genet Univ of Tex Med Br Galveston TX 77550

CHANG, JEN-SHIH, b Tokyo, Japan, Sept 6, 47; Canadian citizen; m 74; c 2. PLASMA PHYSICS. *Educ:* Musashi Inst Technol, BEng, 69, MEng, 71; York Univ, PhD(space sci), 76. *Prof Exp:* Lectr elec eng, Yomiuri Inst Physics & Technol, 71-72; researcher environ sci, Nat Ctr Sci Res, France, 73-74; proj scientist, York Univ, 75-78, asst prof plasma physics, 78-79; ASSOC PROF ENG PHYSICS, MCMASTER UNIV, 80- *Mem:* Physics Soc Japan; Inst Elec Engrs Japan; Am Geophys Union; Can Soc Chem Eng; Chem Inst Can. *Res:* Heat, mass, aerosol and charge transport problem in a variable property fluid; electrostatic charging of aerosol particle; plasma diagnostic techniques; glow discharge positive column; lighting to object; two phase flow. *Mailing Add:* McMaster Univ Hamilton ON L8S 4K1 Can

CHANG, JHY-JIUN, b China, May 29, 44; US citizen; m 68; c 2. SOLID STATE PHYSICS. *Educ:* Nat Taiwan Univ, BS, 66; Case Western Reserve Univ, MS, 69; Rutgers Univ, PhD(physics), 73. *Prof Exp:* Res asst prof physics, Univ Calif, Santa Barbara, 73-76; sr res fel, Calif Inst Technol, 77; ASST PROF PHYSICS, WAYNE STATE UNIV, 77- *Res:* X-ray and electron spectroscopy; phase transition and thermal and dynamic properties of organic conductors; nonequilibrium superconductivity; Josephson effects in superconducting tunnel junctions. *Mailing Add:* Dept Physics Wayne State Univ Detroit MI 48202

CHANG, JOHN CHUAN, b Peiping, China, Apr 19, 19; US citizen; m 49; c 6. PHYSICAL METALLURGY, PROCESSING METALLURGY. *Educ:* Chiao Tung Univ, BS, 42; Univ Calif, Berkeley, MS, 48. *Prof Exp:* Res engr temper brittleness steel proj, Res Inst, Univ Calif, Berkeley, 47-50; radiographer, Gen Metals Corp, 51-52; metallographer, US Steel Corp, 52-54; jr engr, Boeing Co, 54-56, assoc res engr, 56-58, res engr, 58-63; SR METALLURGIST, ROHR INDUSTS, 64- *Concurrent Pos:* Instr metall, Southwestern Col, Calif, 70- *Mem:* Am Soc Metals; fel Am Inst Chem; Metall Soc; Am Soc Metals. *Res:* Research and development in titanium, iron, nickel and aluminum alloys. *Mailing Add:* 575-19 Otay Lakes Rd Chula Vista CA 92010

CHANG, JOHN H(SI-TEH), b Hopei, China, Mar 9, 37; m 63; c 2. COMPUTER SCIENCE, SYSTEMS PLANNING & ANALYSIS. *Educ:* Nat Taiwan Univ, BS, 60; Yale Univ, MS, 66, PhD(elec eng), 68. *Prof Exp:* Engr, Int Bus Mach Corp, 63-68, res staff mem, IBM Thomas J Watson Res Ctr, 68-73, sr engr & proj supvr, data processing econ, 73-78, MGR SYSTS EVAL & DATA PROCESSING ECON, IBM CORP, 78- *Concurrent Pos:* Res asst, Yale Univ, 65-68; asst prof, NY Univ, 69-70; lectr, Univ Conn, Stamford, 70-72; adj assoc prof math, Pace Univ, 77-79; adj prof computer sci, Polytech Inst NY, 79- *Mem:* Inst Elec & Electronics Engrs. *Res:* Investigate problems of data processing technologies and economics for systems evaluation, planning, and demand prediction. *Mailing Add:* IBM Corp Armonk NY 10504

CHANG, JOSEPH YUNG, b Nanking, China, Jan 30, 32; nat US; m 63. PHYSICAL CHEMISTRY. *Educ:* Taiwan Col Eng, BS, 53; Univ Notre Dame, MS, 57, PhD(phys chem), 58. *Prof Exp:* Res assoc & fel, Univ Notre Dame, 58-61; proj scientist, Res Div, Philco Corp, 61; assoc res scientist, NY Univ, 61-63; res scientist, 63-76, SR RES SCIENTIST, GRUMMAN AEROSPACE CORP, 76- *Mem:* AAAS; Am Phys Soc; Am Chem Soc; Am Nuclear Soc. *Res:* Radiation chemistry and effects on solid state materials; radiation conversion of wastes; solar energy conversion; fusion radiation effects. *Mailing Add:* Res Ctr Plant 26 Grumman Aerospace Corp Bethpage NY 11714

CHANG, JUANG-CHI (JOSEPH), b Nanking, China, Apr 24, 36. COMMUNICATION SYSTEMS, ELECTRONICS ENGINEERING. *Educ:* Nat Taiwan, BS, 59; Univ BC, MASc, 61; Iowa State Univ, PhD(elec eng), 65. *Prof Exp:* Res assoc elec eng, Res Inst, Univ Ala, Huntsville, 64-65, asst prof, 65-66; specialist, Lockheed-Ga Co, 66-67, staff engr, Lockheed Electronics Co, 67-74; MEM TECH STAFF, THE AEROSPACE CORP, 74- *Mem:* Inst Elec & Electronics Engrs. *Res:* Communication theory; telecommunication systems; satellite communications; microwave devices; multiple beam antennas. *Mailing Add:* The Aerospace Corp 2350 E El Segundo Blvd El Segundo CA 90245

CHANG, JULIUS SHIH-YU, b Chunking, China, Oct 5, 40; US citizen; m 66; c 2. ATMOSPHERIC SCIENCE, COMPUTATIONAL PHYSICS. *Educ:* Univ Ill, BS, 62; Univ Calif, Berkeley, MA, 65 & 67; State Univ NY Stony Brook, PhD(appl math), 72. *Prof Exp:* Mem staff theoret physics, 66-69, consult, 69-72, mem staff, 72-74, group leader geophysics, 74-76, group leader comput physics, 76-79, DEP DIV LEADER THEORETICAL PHYSICS, LAWRENCE LIVERMORE LAB, UNIV CALIF, 79- *Concurrent Pos:* Consult, Energy Res & Develop Agency, 75-78; mem, Panel Atmospheric Chem & Transport, Nat Res Coun, Nat Acad Sci, 75-80; vis scientist climate res, Nat Ctr Atmospheric Res, 78-79; mem sci adv comt, High Altitude Pollution Prog, Fed Aviation Admin, 78-; mem, Int Ozone Comt, 80-; mem, Int Comt Meteorol Upper Atmosphere, 80- *Mem:* AAAS; Am Geophys Union. *Res:* Atmospheric chemistry; stratospheric and tropospheric modeling; computational physics; numerical solution of ordinary and partial differential equations; numerical hydrodynamics. *Mailing Add:* Lawrence Livermore Lab PO Box 808 Livermore CA 94550

CHANG, JUN HSIN, b Yangmei, Taiwan, Rep China; US citizen; m 70; c 3. CHEMISTRY. *Educ:* Nat Taiwan Norm Univ, BS, 67; Univ Detroit, MS, 71; State Univ NY Buffalo, PhD(org chem), 76. *Prof Exp:* Res assoc chem, Rice Univ, 75-76; RES ASSOC ORG SYNTHESIS, AGR CHEM GROUP, FMC CORP, 76- *Mem:* Am Chem Soc. *Res:* Organic synthesis in natural products, pesticides and pharmaceutical drugs. *Mailing Add:* FMC Corp Agr Chem Group 100 Niagara St Middleport NY 14105

CHANG, JUNG-CHING, b Taipei, Taiwan, Jan 13, 39; m 65; c 1. ANALYTICAL CHEMISTRY, PHYSICAL CHEMISTRY. *Educ:* Tamkang Col, BS, 63; Univ PR, MS, 69; Univ Mo-Kansas City, PhD(phys chem), 75. *Prof Exp:* Chem engr adhesives, Taiwan Sugar Corp, 64-67; res assoc org chem, Univ Ore, 76-77; fel polymer sci, Univ Cincinnati, 77-79; anal chemist, ICN Pharmaceut, Inc, 77-81; RES CHEMIST, ASHLAND CHEM CO, 81- *Mem:* Sigma Xi; NY Acad Sci; Am Chem Soc. *Res:* Thermal analysis; microwave and infrared spectroscopy; chemical kinetics; photochemistry;

mass spectrometry; electron spin resonance; photoelectron spectroscopy; x-ray diffraction methods in polymer science; combined gas chromatography and mass spectrometry; liquid chromatography; atomic absorption spectroscopy; mini computers and computer programming. *Mailing Add:* 5245 Portland St # 103 Columbus OH 43220

CHANG, KAI, b Canton City, China, Apr 27, 48; Taiwan Citizen; m 73. MICROWAVE ENGINEERING, SOLID STATE ELECTRONICS. *Educ:* Nat Taiwan Univ, BSEE, 70; State Univ NY Stony Brook, MS, 72; Univ Mich, PhD(elec eng), 76. *Prof Exp:* Res asst microwave solid state circuits, Cooley Electronics Lab, Univ Mich, 72-76; consult engr microwave tubes & circuits, Shared Appl Ind, Harris Corp, 76-78; MEM TECH STAFF MICROWAVE ENG, ELECTRON DYNAMICS DIV, HUGHES AIRCRAFT Co, 78- *Mem:* Inst Elec & Electronics Engrs. *Res:* Research, development and consulting on microwave solid state circuits; millimeter wave devices and techniques; electron optics and microwave tubes; electromagnetic theory; antenna and communication electronics. *Mailing Add:* Electron Dynamics Div 3100 W Lomita Blvd Torrance CA 90509

CHANG, KAUNG-JAIN, b Fu-Jain Province, China, May 14, 45; m 74; c 2. ROCK MECHANICS, MATERIALS SCIENCE. *Educ:* Cheng KKung Univ, Taiwan, BE, 67; Univ Iowa, ME, 72, DPhil(solid mech), 74. *Prof Exp:* Fel viscoplasticity, Div Mat Eng, Univ Iowa, 75; res assoc creep metals, Dept Theoret & Appl Mech, Cornell Univ, 76-77; SR INVESTR & ASST PROF ROCK MECH, ROCK MECH & EXPLOSIVES RES CTR, UNIV MO-ROLLA, 77- *Mem:* Am Soc Mech Engrs; AAAS. *Res:* Investigation of the fracture phenomena and the constitutive properties of rocks and other materials. *Mailing Add:* Rock Mech & Explosives Res Ctr Univ of Mo Rolla MO 65401

CHANG, KENNETH SHUEH-SHEN, b Taipei, Taiwan, Jan 3, 29; c 5. MICROBIOLOGY, ONCOLOGY. *Educ:* Nat Taiwan Univ, MD, 51; Univ Tokyo, DMSc, 60. *Prof Exp:* Asst microbiol, Col Med, Nat Taiwan Univ, 51-55, lectr, 55-59, from assoc prof to prof, 59-67; sr virologist, Flow Labs, 67-69, med officer, Lab Biol, 69-70, HEAD, SECT VIRAL ONCOGENESIS, LAB CELL BIOL, NAT CANCER INST, 70- *Concurrent Pos:* WHO fel, Commonwealth Serum Labs & Dept Microbiol, Univ Melbourne, 56; Nat Acad Sci fel, Dept Med Microbiol & Immunol, Univ Calif, Los Angeles, 62-64; head Bacillus Calmette-Guerin Vaccine Lab, Taiwan Serum & Vaccine Inst, 57-58; head microbiol & serol sect, Dept Clin Path, Nat Taiwan Univ Hosp, 58-67. *Mem:* Am Asn Cancer Res; Am Soc Microbiol; Tissue Cult Asn; Am Asn Immunologists; Int Asn Comp Res Leukemia & Related Dis. *Res:* Cancer virology and immunology; clinical microbiology. *Mailing Add:* Lab of Cell Biol Nat Cancer Inst Bethesda MD 20014

CHANG, KERN KO NAN, b Shanghai, China, Sept 9, 18; m 48; c 3. ELECTRONIC PHYSICS. *Educ:* Nat Cent Univ, China, BS, 40; Univ Mich, MS, 42; Polytech Inst Brooklyn, DEE, 54. *Prof Exp:* Engr, Cent Radio Mfg Co, 40-45, mem staff, Radio Corp Am Labs, 48-62, head microwave solid-state device group, 62-72, FEL, RCA LABS, 72- *Honors & Awards:* RCA Labs Achievement Awards, 56, 60, 64 & 67; CIE Achievement Award, 70. *Res:* Magnetrons; traveling wave tubes; beam-focusing devices; parametric amplifiers; tunnel diode amplifiers and converters; solid-state microwave devices; light emitting and avalanche devices; CR tubes and display systems. *Mailing Add:* RCA Labs Princeton NJ 08540

CHANG, KUANG-CHOU, b Taipei, Taiwan, Jan 2, 49; m. PHYSICAL ORGANIC CHEMISTRY. *Educ:* Tunghai Univ, Taiwan, BS, 70; Univ Minn, PhD(org chem), 75. *Prof Exp:* Res asst hydrogen bonding, Univ Minn, 71-74; res fel solution kinetics, Brandeis Univ, 74-76; mem staff, Bell Labs, 76-77; SCIENTIST, POLAROID CORP, 77- *Res:* Spectroscopic studies of reaction kinetics and structure determination; physics and chemistry of semiconductor photographic science and engineering. *Mailing Add:* Polaroid Corp 750 Main St 4B Cambridge MA 02139

CHANG, KUO WEI, b Shanghai, China, Nov 21, 38; m 63; c 1. BIOMEDICAL ENGINEERING. *Educ:* Nat Taiwan Univ, BS, 60; Univ Cincinnati, MS, 63; Princeton Univ, MA, 67, PhD(aerospace sci), 69. *Prof Exp:* Engr, First Naval Shipyard, Chinese Navy, 60-62; res asst aerospace eng, Univ Cincinnati, 62-64; asst res aerospace sci, Princeton Univ, 64-68; sr scientist physics, 68-71, mgr biosensors dept, 71-75, TECH APPL SCI LABS, GULF & WESTERN CO, 75-; PRES, INDUST & BIOMED SENSORS CORP, 75- *Mem:* Am Phys Soc; Asn Advan Med Instrumentation; Inst Elec & Electronics Engrs. *Res:* Aerospace sciences; plasma physics; magnetohydrodynamics; biophysics; fluid mechanics; kinetic theory of gases; electronics. *Mailing Add:* Indust & Biomed Sensors Corp 1345 Main St Waltham MA 02154

CHANG, KWANG-POO, b Taipei, Taiwan, Nov 12, 42; m 72; c 1. PARASITOLOGY, CELL BIOLOGY. *Educ:* Nat Taiwan Univ, BSc, 65; Univ Guelph, MS, 68, PhD(biol), 72. *Prof Exp:* Fel parasitol, 72-74, from res assoc to asst prof, 74-79, ASSOC PROF, ROCKEFELLER UNIV, 79- *Mem:* Am Soc Microbiol; Am Soc Parasitologists; Am Soc Trop Med Hyg; Am Soc Cell Biol; Soc Protozool. *Res:* Cell biology of invertebrates; intracellular symbiosis, including structural and physiological aspects of cellular interactions between prokaryotic symbiotes and insect or protozoan hosts; intracellular parasitism in mammalian Leishmaniasis. *Mailing Add:* Rockefeller Univ New York NY 10021

CHANG, L(EROY) L(I-GONG), b Honan, China, Jan 20, 36; m 62. SEMICONDUCTORS, SOLID STATE PHYSICS. *Educ:* Nat Taiwan Univ, BS, 57; Univ SC, MS, 61; Stanford Univ, PhD, 63. *Prof Exp:* Mem res staff, Thomas J Watson Res Ctr, Int Bus Mach Corp, 63-68; assoc prof elec eng, Mass Inst Technol, 68-69; MEM RES STAFF, THOMAS J WATSON RES CTR, IBM CORP, 69- *Mem:* Am Phys Soc; Am Vacuum Soc; Inst Elec & Electronics Engrs. *Res:* Semiconductor physics, devices and materials. *Mailing Add:* Thomas J Watson Res Ctr IBM Corp PO Box 218 Yorktown Heights NY 10598

CHANG, LAY NAM, b Singapore, June 1, 43; m 67; c 1. QUANTUM FIELD THEORY. *Educ:* Columbia Univ, AB, 64; Univ Calif, Berkeley, PhD(physics), 67. *Prof Exp:* Res assoc, Mass Inst Technol, 67-69 & The Enrico Fermi Inst, Univ Chicago, 69-71; asst prof physics, Univ Pa, 71-78; ASSOC PROF PHYSICS, VA POLYTECH INST & STATE UNIV, 78- *Concurrent Pos:* Vis scientist, Niels Bohr Inst, 74 & Brookhaven Nat Lab, 76. *Res:* Theoretical physics; field theory; particle physics. *Mailing Add:* Physics Dept Va Polytech Inst & State Univ Blacksburg VA 24061

CHANG, LENA, b Yunan, Mainland China, Dec 23, 38; US citizen; m 61; c 2. ACTUARIAL SCIENCE, STATISTICAL MATHEMATICS. *Educ:* Univ Ill, BS, 58, MS, 60, PhD(math), 64. *Prof Exp:* Lectr math, Mich State Univ, 61-62; instr, Univ Ill, Champaign-Urbana, 64-65; asst prof, Univ Ill, Chicago Circle, 65-74; vis assoc prof actuarial sci, Dept Ins & Risk, Temple Univ, 74-76; actuary-statistician, State Rating Bur, Div Ins, Mass, 76-79; INDEPENDENT MATH, ACTUARIAL STATIST, INS CONSULT, CHANG & CUMMINGS, 79- *Concurrent Pos:* Res sci mathematician, Sci Lab, Ford Res Ctr, Ford Motor Co, Mich, 60-61; assoc investr group representation theory, Off Naval Res, 62-64 & NSF res grant, 65-68; expert & consult, US Gen Acct Off, Washington, DC, 74-75; consult actuary, Gordon Assocs, 75-76 & Off State Auditor Gen, Commonwealth of Pa, 76. *Mem:* Am Math Soc; Am Risk & Ins Asn; Am Statist Asn; Sigma Xi. *Res:* Actuarial and mathematical studies of insurance legislation costs; insurance rate filings including auto, worker's compensation products liability and health; loss reserve and investment income; actuarial analysis; operations research; computer science. *Mailing Add:* 6 Beacon Boston MA 02202

CHANG, LOUIS WAI-WAH, b Hong Kong, July 1, 44; US citizen; m 68; c 2. EXPERIMENTAL PATHOLOGY. *Educ:* Univ Mass, Amherst, BA, 66; Tufts Univ, MS, 69; Univ Wis-Madison, PhD(path), 72. *Prof Exp:* Instr path, 72-73, dir path lab, Univ Wis-Madison, 72-76, asst prof path, 73-76; assoc prof, 77-80, PROF PATH, MED CTR, UNIV ARK, 80-, DIR PATH GRAD PROG, 77- *Concurrent Pos:* NIH & NSF res grants, 73-80; consult, Nat Inst Health, Environ Protection Agency & I J Life Systs, Inc, 79- *Mem:* Am Asn Pathologists; Am Asn Neuropath; Soc Neurosci; Soc Toxicol. *Res:* Environmental toxicology; heavy metal toxicology; experimental pathology on brain, liver, and kidney; histochemistry; electron microscopy; developmental biology and teratology; author of seventy publications. *Mailing Add:* Dept Path Univ Ark Med Ctr Little Rock AR 72201

CHANG, LUCY MING-SHIH, b China, Aug 20, 42; US citizen. BIOCHEMISTRY. *Educ:* Western Reserve Univ, AB, 64, Ind Univ, PhD(biochem), 68. *Prof Exp:* Res assoc biochem, Univ Ky, 68-70, asst prof, 70-72; from asst prof to assoc prof, Univ Conn, 72-77; PROF BIOCHEM, UNIFORMED SERV UNIV HEALTH SCI, 77- *Mem:* AAAS; Am Soc Biol Chem. *Res:* Enzymatic synthesis of DNA in eukaryotic cells. *Mailing Add:* Uniformed Serv Univ Health Sci 4301 Jones Bridge Rd Bethesda MD 20014

CHANG, LUKE LI-YU, b Honan, China, Sept 18, 35; US citizen; m 59; c 2. MINERALOGY. *Educ:* Nat Taiwan Univ, BS, 57; Univ Chicago, PhD(geophys sci), 63. *Prof Exp:* Sr scientist mineral & ceramic sci, Tem-Pres Res, Inc, 63-67; asst prof geol, Cornell Univ, 67-70; assoc prof geol, Miami Univ, 70-75, prof, 75-81; PROF GEOL & CHMN DEPT, UNIV MD, 81- *Concurrent Pos:* Contrib ed, Phase Diagrams Ceramist, Am Ceramic Soc & Nat Bur Standards, 74- *Mem:* Fel Mineral Soc Am; Am Ceramic Soc; Geochem Soc; Mineral Soc Gt Brit; Can Mineral Soc. *Res:* Mineral synthesis and equilibrium relations in the systems of carbonates, sulfides, and oxides; crystal chemistry of tungstates. *Mailing Add:* Dept of Geol Univ Md College Park MD 20742

CHANG, M(ELVIN) C(HEN-SIANG), mineral & metallurgical engineering, see previous edition

CHANG, MEI LING (WU), b Kiangsi, China, Mar 1, 15; US citizen; m 53. NUTRITIONAL BIOCHEMISTRY. *Educ:* Ginling Col, China, BS, 38; Ore State Univ, MS, 49, PhD(nutrit), 51. *Prof Exp:* Res asst histochem of brain, Sch Med, Wash Univ, 51-53; res assoc nutrit, Ore State Univ, 53-54; res assoc nutrit biochem, Univ Ill, 54-62; RES CHEMIST, HUMAN NUTRIT DIV, USDA, 62- *Mem:* Am Inst Nutrit. *Res:* Vitamin metabolism; histochemistry of brain; dietary effect on enzyme system; carbohydrate metabolism. *Mailing Add:* Nutrit Inst Agr Res Serv USDA Beltsville MD 20705

CHANG, MIN CHUEH, b Taiyuan, China, Oct 10, 08; US citizen; m 48; c 3. PHYSIOLOGY. *Educ:* Tsing Hua, China, BSc, 33; Univ Edinburgh, dipl Agr, 39; Univ Cambridge, PhD, 41, ScD, 69. *Prof Exp:* Res fel, Sch Agr, Univ Cambridge, 41-45; res assoc, 45-56, sr scientist, 56-70, PRIN SCIENTIST, WORCESTER FOUND EXP BIOL, 71-; ADJ PROF BIOL, BOSTON UNIV, 74- *Concurrent Pos:* Assoc prof, Boston Univ, 51-61, res prof, 61-74. *Honors & Awards:* Ortho Award, 50; Lasker Award, 54; Ortho Medal, 61; Hartman Award, 70; Marshall Medal, 71; Francis Amory Prize, 75. *Mem:* AAAS; Am Physiol Soc; Am Asn Anatomists; Am Acad Arts & Sci; Soc Study Fertility. *Res:* Physiology of reproduction; mammalian germ cells; animal husbandry. *Mailing Add:* Worcester Found for Exp Biol 222 Maple Ave Shrewsbury MA 01545

CHANG, MINGTEH, b Fukien, China, Jan 18, 39; m 70; c 1. FOREST HYDROLOGY. *Educ:* Nat Chung-Hsing Univ, Taiwan, BS, 60; Pa State Univ, MS, 68; WVa Univ, PhD(forest hydrol), 73. *Prof Exp:* Watershed technologist, Mountainous Agr Resources Develop Bur, Govt of Taiwan, 61-64; teaching asst surv, Chung-Hsing Univ, 64-67; res assoc hydrol, Water Res Inst, WVa Univ, 73-75; asst prof forest hydrol, 75-80, ASSOC PROF FOREST HYDROL, SCH FORESTRY, STEPHEN F AUSTIN STATE UNIV, 80-, GROUP LEADER FOREST RESOURCES RES, 73- *Mem:* Am Geophys Union; Soc Am Foresters; Soil Conserv Soc Am. *Res:* Quantitative analysis and interpretation of hydrologic and climatologic data; physical and physiologic processes of the soil-plant-atmosphere system in forest environment. *Mailing Add:* Sch of Forestry Box 6109 Stephen F Austin State Univ Nacogdoches TX 75961

CHANG, MORRIS, b Chekiang, China, July 10, 31; US citizen; m 53; c 1. ELECTRONICS. *Educ:* Mass Inst Technol, BS, 52, MS, 53; Stanford Univ, PhD(elec eng), 64. *Prof Exp:* Sr engr, Sylvania Elec Prods, Inc, 55-58; mgr germanium develop, 58-61, mgr, Germanium Small Signal Dept, 64-67, vpres, Semiconductor Circuits Div, 67-72, group vpres, Semiconductor Group, 72-75, group vpres, Worldwide Semiconductors Opers, 75-78, group vpres, World Consumer Opers, 78-80, SR VPRES CORP QUALITY & RELIABILITY, TEX INSTRUMENTS, INC, 80- *Mem:* Inst Elec & Electronics Engrs. *Res:* Semiconductor electronics. *Mailing Add:* Tex Instruments Inc PO Box 225474 Dallas TX 75265

CHANG, NGEE PONG, b Singapore, Dec 24, 40; m 65; c 2. THEORETICAL HIGH ENERGY PHYSICS. *Educ:* Ohio Wesleyan Univ, BA, 59; Columbia Univ, PhD(physics), 63. *Prof Exp:* Res assoc physics, Columbia Univ, 62-63; res fel, Inst Advan Study, 63-64; res assoc, Rockefeller Univ, 64-65; vis prof, 65-66, PROF PHYSICS, CITY COL NEW YORK, 66- *Concurrent Pos:* Vis prof, Max Planck Inst Physics & Astrophysics, Munich, WGer, 73 & Univ Tokyo, Res Inst Fundamental Physics & Kyoto Univ, 74; Japan Soc Promotion Sci fel, 74. *Mem:* Am Phys Soc; AAAS; NY Acad Sci; fel Am Phys Soc. *Res:* Field theory of weak interactions; symmetries; kinematics at infinite momentum; impact parameter representation; infinite energy scattering; non-abelian gauge theories; quark dynamics; grand unified field theories; asymptotic freedom; renormalization group analysis. *Mailing Add:* Dept of Physics City Col of New York New York NY 10031

CHANG, PAUL K(EUK), b Inchon, Korea, Apr 8, 13; nat US; m 55; c 2. MECHANICAL & AEROSPACE ENGINEERING. *Educ:* Berlin Tech, Dipl Ing, 40, Dr Ing, 63; NY Univ, MAE, 48; Harvard Univ, MS, 49; Univ Notre Dame, DSc, 51. *Prof Exp:* Aeronaut engr, Siebel Flugzeug-Werke, Ger, 40-41; Betriebs asst, Daimler-Benz Motoren, 42; mech engr, Brown-Boveri Co, 46-47; instr, Univ Notre Dame, 49-52; design engr, AiResearch Mfg Co, 52-54; res specialist, Lockheed Aircraft Corp, 54-58; assoc prof mech eng, 59-63, prof, 63-80, EMER PROF MECH ENG, CATH UNIV AM, 80- *Concurrent Pos:* Consult, David Taylor Model Basin, US Naval Res Lab, US Naval Ord Lab, 58-; Fulbright lectr, Madrid, 64-65; vis prof, Orgn Am States, Lima, Peru, 73 & Nat Acad Sci, Bucharest, Romania & Sofia, Bulgaria, 77-78. *Mem:* Am Soc Mech Engrs; assoc fel Am Inst Aeronaut & Astronaut. *Res:* Flow separation; fluid mechanics; heat transfer. *Mailing Add:* 8005 Falstaff Rd McLean VA 22101

CHANG, PAUL PENG-CHENG, b Kiangsu, China, Aug 19, 31; US citizen; m 67; c 2. STRUCTURAL ENGINEERING, CIVIL ENGINEERING. *Educ:* Cheng-Kung Univ, Taiwan, BS, 56; Univ Okla, ME, 66. *Prof Exp:* Field engr power house construct, Taiwan Power Co, 58-64; engr power house design, Sargent & Lundy Engrs, Inc, 66-68; eng supvr, Bechtel Power Corp, 68-74; prin engr power house design, Kaiser Eng Power Corp, 74-80; SUPV STRUCT ENGR POWER HOUSE DESIGN, GIBBS & HILL, INC, 80- *Concurrent Pos:* Founder & pres, PPC Consult Engrs, 72- *Mailing Add:* 300 Lakeside Dr Oakland CA 94623

CHANG, PAULINE (WUAI) KIMM, b Shanghai, China, Jan 19, 26; nat US; m 52; c 2. ORGANIC CHEMISTRY. *Educ:* Wellesley Col, BA, 49; Univ Mich, MS, 50, PhD(chem), 55. *Prof Exp:* From res asst to res assoc, 55-66, SR RES ASSOC PHARMACOL, SCH MED, YALE UNIV, 66- *Mem:* Am Chem Soc; Royal Soc Chem. *Res:* Synthetic organic chemistry; medicinal chemistry; synthesis of labeled compounds. *Mailing Add:* Dept of Pharmacol Yale Univ Sch of Med New Haven CT 06510

CHANG, PEI KUNG (PHILIP), b Shantung Province, China, Jan 9, 36; US citizen; m 66; c 1. FOOD SCIENCE, BIOCHEMISTRY. *Educ:* Nat Taiwan Univ, BS, 60; Colo State Univ, MS, 64; Univ Wis, PhD(food sci), 69; New York Inst Technol, MBA, 82. *Prof Exp:* Res asst nutrient anal green veg, Colo State Univ, 62-64; res asst egg white & yolk protein, Univ Wis, 64-68; RES ASSOC FOOD INGREDIENTS, EASTERN RES CTR, STAUFFER CHEM CO, 68- *Mem:* Inst Food Technologists; Am Asn Cereal Chemists. *Res:* Egg and milk proteins; developed process cheese emulsifier, whey protein recovery process and egg albumen and whole egg replacers; egg yolk extender for mayonnaise; process for lowering thermogelation temperature of whey protein; process for improving gelation of egg albumen. *Mailing Add:* 232 Coachlight Sq Montrose NY 10548

CHANG, PEI WEN, b China, Apr 26, 23; nat US; m 51; c 3. VETERINARY PATHOLOGY. *Educ:* Mich State Univ, DVM, 51; Univ RI, MS, 60; Yale Univ, PhD, 65. *Prof Exp:* Gen practitioner, Ind, 51-53; area veterinarian, Ind Livestock Sanit Bd, 53-55; asst prof & asst res prof animal path, 55-60, assoc prof, 60-66, PROF ANIMAL PATH, UNIV RI, 66- *Concurrent Pos:* Danforth fel, 61-63. *Mem:* Am Vet Med Asn. *Res:* Animal virology; characterization of animal viruses. *Mailing Add:* Dept of Animal Path Univ of RI Kingston RI 02881

CHANG, PETER HON, b Shanghai, China, Feb 19, 41; US citizen; m 68; c 2. BIOENGINEERING. *Educ:* Univ Calif, Berkeley, BS, 64, MS, 66, PhD(bioeng), 70. *Prof Exp:* Res engr, Sondell Sci Instruments, Calif, 65-70; staff scientist, Hewlett Packard Co, 70-71; prod mgr instrumentation, 71-77, MGR INSTRUMENT QUAL ASSURANCE, AMES CO DIV, MILES LABS, INC, 77- *Concurrent Pos:* Mem bd dirs, VIR Electronics, Ltd, Hong Kong, 73- & Nike Enterprise Ltd, 75- *Mem:* Inst Elec & Electronics Engrs. *Res:* Glucose controlled insulin infusion system--an instrumentation system to simulate pancreatic endocrine function of a normal subject for diabetic research; instrument manufacturing management, especially in quality assurance. *Mailing Add:* Miles Labs Inc 1127 Myrtle St Elkhart IN 46514

CHANG, PO-CHENG, fluid mechanics, see previous edition

CHANG, POTTER CHIEN-TIEN, b Canton, China, Mar 21, 34; US citizen; m 61; c 2. BIOSTATISTICS. *Educ:* Nat Taiwan Univ, BS, 58; Univ Minn, MS, 66, PhD(biometry), 68. *Prof Exp:* From asst prof to assoc prof, 68-81, PROF & HEAD, DIV BIOSTATIST, SCH PUB HEALTH, UNIV CALIF, LOS ANGELES, 81- *Mem:* Am Statist Asn; Biometric Soc. *Res:* Statistical methodology; application of statistics in medical research. *Mailing Add:* Div of Biostatist Univ of Calif Sch of Pub Health Los Angeles CA 90024

CHANG, RAYMOND, b Hong Kong, Mar 6, 39; m 68. PHYSICAL CHEMISTRY. *Educ:* Univ London, BSc, 62; Yale Univ, MS, 63, PhD(phys chem), 66. *Prof Exp:* Res fel, Wash Univ, 66-67; asst prof chem, Hunter Col, 67-68; from asst prof to assoc prof, 68-78, PROF CHEM, WILLIAMS COL, 78- *Mem:* Am Chem Soc. *Res:* Electron spin resonance and nuclear magnetic resonance; chemical kinetics of fast reactions; photosynthesis; conformation of proteins. *Mailing Add:* Dept Chem Williams Col Williamstown MA 01267

CHANG, REN-FANG, b Nanking, China, Jan 14, 38; m 68. THERMODYNAMICS, LASERS. *Educ:* Taiwan Nat Univ, BS, 60; Univ Md, PhD(physics), 68. *Prof Exp:* Res assoc physics, 68-71, asst prof physics & astron, Univ Md, 71-78; RES PHYSICIST, NAT BUR STANDARDS, 78- *Honors & Awards:* NASA Apollo Achievement Award. *Mem:* AAAS; Am Phys Soc; Sigma Xi. *Res:* Measurements of thermophysical properties; measurements on scattered laser light from samples undergoing phase transitions; studies of optical properties of retro reflector. *Mailing Add:* Nat Bur Standards Bldg 221 Rm A311 Washington DC 20234

CHANG, RICHARD C(HI-CHENG), b Nanking, China, Jan 19, 18; US citizen; m 41; c 2. CHEMICAL ENGINEERING, POLYMER CHEMISTRY. *Educ:* Nanking Univ, BS, 40; Syracuse Univ, MChE, 50, PhD(chem eng), 54. *Prof Exp:* Instr chem, Nanking Univ, 40-42; chem engr, Cheng-tu Tannery, China, 42-43; sr chem engr, Chamois Tannery, 43-46; supt Tannery No 2, Taiwan Animal Prod Co, 46-48; res engr, Syracuse Univ, 54-56; sect leader synthetic rubber, Am Synthetic Rubber Corp, 56-64; sr res chem engr, Chemstrand Res Ctr, Inc, Monsanto Co, 64-74; sr res specialist, Monsanto Triangle Park Develop Ctr, 74-81; RETIRED. *Mem:* Am Chem Soc; Am Inst Chem Engr. *Res:* Synthetic fibers; leather tanning and synthetic rubber. *Mailing Add:* 516 Emerson Dr Raleigh NC 27609

CHANG, RICHARD KOUNAI, b Hong Kong, June 22, 40; m 61; c 3. SOLID STATE PHYSICS, QUANTUM ELECTRONICS. *Educ:* Mass Inst Technol, BS, 61; Harvard Univ, MS, 62, PhD(solid state physics), 65. *Prof Exp:* Res fel solid state physics, Harvard Univ, 65-66; asst prof, 66-69, assoc prof, 70-76, PROF ENG & APPL SCI, YALE UNIV, 76- *Concurrent Pos:* Consult, Sanders Inc & Sandia Nat Labs. *Mem:* Fel Am Phys Soc; fel Optical Soc Am. *Res:* Nonlinear optics; Raman spectroscopy; solid state laser emission; surface science. *Mailing Add:* Yale Univ PO Box 2157 Yale Sta New Haven CT 06520

CHANG, ROBERT CHI-HENG, polymer chemistry, see previous edition

CHANG, ROBERT SHIHMAN, b China, July 26, 22; nat US; m 51; c 4. VIROLOGY. *Educ:* St John's Univ, China, MD, 46; Harvard Univ, DSc, 52. *Prof Exp:* Assoc prof microbiol, Harvard Univ, 54-68; PROF MED MICROBIOL, SCH MED, UNIV CALIF, DAVIS, 68- *Concurrent Pos:* Med dir, Davis Free Clinics, 78-; dir, Tissue Typing Lab, Med Ctr, Univ Calif, Davis, 79- *Mem:* AAAS; Soc Exp Biol & Med. *Res:* Virology; immunology; preventive medicine. *Mailing Add:* Sch Med Univ Calif Davis CA 95616

CHANG, SHAO-CHIEN, b Mar 1, 30; Can citizen; m; c 2. MATHEMATICS. *Educ:* Taiwan Norm Univ, BSc, 56; Carleton Univ, Ont, MSc, 63, PhD(math), 68. *Prof Exp:* Teacher, Taipei Chien Kuo High Sch, 55-56; supvr, Chnong Hwa NTS Sch, KL Malaysia, 57-62; sessional lectr math, Carleton Univ, Ont, 63-65; lectr, 65-67, asst prof, 67-73, ASSOC PROF MATH, BROCK UNIV, 73- *Mem:* Am Math Soc; Math Asn Am; Can Math Cong. *Res:* Mathematical logic, especially syntatical transforms; summability, especially classical and functional analytical method; sequences. *Mailing Add:* Dept of Math Brock Univ St Catharines ON L2S 3A1 Can

CHANG, SHAU-JIN, b Kiangsu, China, Jan 7, 37; m 64; c 2. ELEMENTARY PARTICLE PHYSICS, MATHEMATICAL PHYSICS. *Educ:* Taiwan Univ, BS, 59; Tsing Hua Univ, Taiwan, MS, 61; Harvard Univ, PhD(physics), 67. *Prof Exp:* Mem physics, Inst Advan Study, 67-69; from asst prof to assoc prof, 69-74, PROF PHYSICS, UNIV ILL, URBANA, 74- *Concurrent Pos:* Mem, Inst Advan Study, Princeton, 72-73; Alfred P Sloan fel, 72-74; vis physicist, Fermi Nat Accelerator Lab, 75. *Mem:* fel Am Phys Soc; Chinese Astron Soc. *Res:* Various theoretical topics in quantum field theory; elementary particle physics; nonlinear iterative system. *Mailing Add:* Dept Physics Univ Ill Urbana IL 61801

CHANG, SHAW FAI, b Anhwei, China, July 26, 33; US citizen; m 60; c 4. BIOCHEMICAL PHARMACOLOGY. *Educ:* Taiwan Col Eng, BS, 55; Univ Minn, MS, 62. *Prof Exp:* Jr biochemist chem carcinogenesis, Vet Admin Hosp, 62-64; associated res biochemist drug metab, Parke, Davis & Co, 64-69; sr biochem pharmacologist, 69-71, res specialist, 71-72, SR RES SPECIALIST DRUG METAB, RIKER LABS, INC, 3M CO, 78- *Mem:* Am Chem Soc; AAAS; Sigma Xi. *Res:* Study of the physical translocation and biochemical modification of central nervous system and anti-inflammatory agents in laboratory animals and human volunteers; development of extremely sensitive analytical method in quantitating drug residues in biological fluids. *Mailing Add:* Riker Labs Inc 3M Ctr Bldg 270-35 St Paul MN 55144

CHANG, SHELDON S L, b Peking, China, Jan 20, 20; m 45; c 2. ELECTRICAL ENGINEERING. *Educ:* Nat Southwest Assoc Univ, China, BS, 42; Tsinghua Univ, MS, 44; Purdue Univ, PhD(elec eng), 47. *Prof Exp:* Design engr, Cent Radio Works, China, 43-44; design engr, Robbins & Myers, Inc, Ohio, 46-47, res & develop engr, 48-52; instr, Purdue Univ, 47-48; from asst prof to prof elec eng, NY Univ, 52-63; PROF ELEC ENG, STATE UNIV NY STONY BROOK, 63- *Concurrent Pos:* Consult, Robbins & Meyers, Inc, 52- & Marine & Air Armament Div, Sperry Gyroscope Co Div, Remington Rand, 56-68; vis Mackay prof, Univ Calif, Berkeley, 69-70. *Mem:* Fel Inst Elec & Electronics Engrs; Am Phys Soc; Am Math Soc. *Res:* Optimal control systems theory; energy conversion; feedback communication systems; electronics. *Mailing Add:* Dept of Elec Eng Col of Eng State Univ NY Stony Brook NY 11794

CHANG, SHEN CHIN, entomology, biochemistry, deceased

CHANG, SHIH LU, b China, Dec 28, 13; nat US; m 48; c 2. MICROBIOLOGY, PUBLIC HEALTH. *Educ:* Yale-in-China Med Col, MD, 35; Harvard Univ, DPH, 41; Am Bd Microbiol, dipl. *Prof Exp:* Res fel sanit eng, Harvard Univ, 41-44, res fel comp path & trop med, 42-46, fac instr sanit biol & instr comp path & trop med, 44-46, from asst prof to assoc prof sanit biol, 46-54; sr surgeon, Microbiol Sect, Robert A Taft Sanit Eng Ctr, USPHS, 54-59, med dir, 59-70; chief etiology, Div Water Hyg, Water Supply Res Lab, Nat Environ Res Ctr, Environ Protection Agency, 70-75, chief etiology, Health Effects Res Lab, 75-77; RETIRED. *Concurrent Pos:* Responsible envestr projs, Off Sci Res & Develop, Nat Res Coun, Off Qm Gen & Surgeon Gen Off, USPHS, 41-54; instr environ microbiol, Beijing, China, 79-80. *Mem:* AMA; Am Pub Health Asn; Am Acad Microbiol; AAAS; Royal Soc Health. *Res:* Bacteriology and parasitology in relation to public health and sanitary engineering, especially in field of disinfection and on epidemiology of amebic meningoencephalitis and recreational waters. *Mailing Add:* 1035 Juanita Dr Walnut Creek CA 94595

CHANG, SHIH-GER, b Taipei, China, Oct 24, 41. PHYSICAL CHEMISTRY, ENVIRONMENTAL CHEMISTRY. *Educ:* Kung Univ, Taiwan, BS, 64; Univ Detroit, MS, 68; Univ Calif, Berkeley, PhD(phys chem), 71. *Prof Exp:* Res assoc mat res, 71-72, res assoc chem kinetics, 72-73, STAFF CHEMIST ATMOSPHERIC AEROSOL RES, LAWRENCE BERKELEY LAB, 73- *Mem:* Am Chem Soc; Am Phys Soc. *Res:* Chemical characterization of air pollutants, and study of chemical reaction of air pollutants; study of surface chemistry of solids; development of a plant flue gas desulfurization and denitrification process. *Mailing Add:* Energy & Environ Div Univ of Calif Berkeley CA 94720

CHANG, SHIH-YUNG, b Hopei, China, Feb 10, 38; m 64; c 1. QUANTUM CHEMISTRY. *Educ:* Nat Taiwan Univ, BS, 60; Kans State Univ, MS, 65; Univ Wash, PhD(phys chem), 69. *Prof Exp:* Res assoc chem, Univ Calif, Santa Barbara, 69-70; NIH fel, Johns Hopkins Univ, 70-71; mem sci staff, Wolf Res & Develop Corp, 71-73; SR PHYS CHEMIST, ENVIROSPHERE CO, EBASCO SERV INC, 73- *Concurrent Pos:* Adj asst prof, Dept Pharmacol, Mt Sinai Sch Med, City Univ New York, 76-; staff engr, Gibbs & Hill, Inc. *Mem:* Am Phys Soc; Sigma Xi. *Res:* Ab-initio study of molecular wave functions and physical properties; perturbation theory of molecular polarizabilities, force constants and dipole moments; perturbational approach to the determination of molecular electrostatic interaction potential for drug design. *Mailing Add:* 12 Kory Dr Kendall Park NJ 08824

CHANG, SHU-PEI, b Sinwui, China, Oct 11, 22; US citizen; m 69; c 1. POLYMER CHEMISTRY, INDUSTRIAL ORGANIC CHEMISTRY. *Educ:* Nat Checkiang Univ, BS, 45; Univ Louisville, PhD(chem), 63. *Prof Exp:* Chem engr & soil scientist, Taiwan Sugar Co, 46-59; res fel, Univ Louisville, 63-64; RES CHEMIST, HORT & SPEC CROPS, NORTHERN REGIONAL RES CTR, USDA, 64- *Mem:* Am Chem Soc; AAAS; Am Oil Chemist's Soc. *Res:* Plasticizers, lubricants and extenders from new seed oils or their derived fatty acids; addition and condensation polymerizations; application of calorimetric, chromatographic and spectroscopic methods to analysis. *Mailing Add:* 1815 N University St Peoria IL 61604

CHANG, SHU-SING, b Shanghai, China, Feb 18, 35; m 60; c 2. PHYSICAL CHEMISTRY. *Educ:* Univ Taiwan, BS, 56; Univ Mich, MS, 59, PhD(chem), 62. *Prof Exp:* Chemist, Cent Res Lab, Allied Chem Corp, 61-63; chemist, Inorg Solids Div, 63-64, CHEMIST, POLYMER DIV, NAT BUR STANDARDS, 64- *Mem:* Am Phys Soc; Am Chem Soc; Am Soc Testing & Mat. *Res:* Thermodynamic properties of globular molecules, plastic crystals, vitreous state and polymers; calorimetry, diffusion, migration and automation. *Mailing Add:* Polymer Div Nat Bur of Standards Washington DC 20234

CHANG, SHUYA, b Shanghai, China, Dec 20, 47. INDUSTRIAL CHEMISTRY. *Educ:* Fu-Jen Catholic Univ, Taiwan, BS, 69; Univ Miami, MS, 71; Tex A&M Univ, PhD(chem), 74. *Prof Exp:* Fel, Univ Ga, 74-76 & Pulp & Paper Res Inst, Can, 76-77; researcher, 77-80, SR RESEARCHER POLYMER, UNION INDUST RES INST, 80- *Concurrent Pos:* Assoc Prof, Fu-Jen Catholic Univ, 78 & Nat Tsing Hwa Univ, 81- *Mem:* Soc Plastics Engrs. *Res:* Polymer characterizations-thermal properties and molecular weight distributions; process modification, property modification, new fibers, characterization and industrial application. *Mailing Add:* 1021 Kuang Fu Rd Hsinchu Taiwan

CHANG, STEPHEN SZU SHIANG, b Peiking, China, Aug 15, 18; nat US; m 52. FOOD CHEMISTRY. *Educ:* Nat Chi-nan Univ, BS, 41; Kans State Univ, MS, 49; Univ Ill, PhD(food chem), 52. *Prof Exp:* Res chemist, Universal Pharmaceut Corp, China, 41-44; assoc engr, Nat Resources Comn China, 44-46; supt prod, Chinchow Pulp & Paper Mill, 46-47; res assoc food chem, Univ Ill, 52-55; res chemist, Swift & Co, 55-57; sr res chemist, A E Staley Mfg Co, 57-60; assoc prof food sci, 60-62, PROF FOOD SCI, RUTGERS UNIV, 62-, CHMN, FOOD SCI DEPT, 77- *Honors & Awards:* Spec Award, Potato Chip Inst Int; Putnam Food Award, Putnam Publ Co; Bailey Award & lipid chem award, Am Oil Chem Soc; Distinguished Food Scientist Award, NY Inst Food Technol. *Mem:* Inst Food Technologists; Am Chem Soc; Am Oil Chem Soc (pres, 70); NY Acad Sci. *Res:* Flavor stability of fats and oils; chemical reactions involved in the processing of edible fats and oils; mechanisms of the autoxidation of unsaturated fatty acids; chemistry of food emulsifiers; chemistry of food flavors; isolation and identification of flavor compounds in foods. *Mailing Add:* Dept of Food Sci Rutgers Univ New Brunswick NJ 08903

CHANG, SUK CHUL, b Hamhung, Korea, June 19, 23; m 67; c 2. PATHOLOGY, CYTOLOGY. *Educ:* Seoul Nat Univ, MD, 48; Washington Univ, PhD(path anat), 56. *Prof Exp:* Intern, 34th Gen Hosp, US Army, Korea, 48-49; assistantship, Seoul Univ Hosp, 49-52; instr path, Col Med, Univ Utah, 57-59; lectr, Univ Toronto, 59-61; assoc prof, Post-Grad Sch Med, Univ Tex & assoc pathologist, M D Anderson Hosp & Tumor Inst, 62-68, dir cytol, Sch Cytotechnol, 64-68; assoc prof, 69-72, PROF PATH, HAHNEMANN MED

COL, 72-, DIR DIV CYTOPATH & SCH CYTOTECHNOL, 70- *Concurrent Pos:* Vis pathologist, Toronto Gen Hosp, 59-61. *Mem:* Col Am Path; Am Soc Cytol; Am Soc Clin Path. *Res:* Anatomic pathology; exfolitive cytology; cancer research in lung and female reproductive organs; epidemiology; early detection of cancer. *Mailing Add:* Div of Cytopath Hahnemann Med Col Philadelphia PA 19102

CHANG, SUN-YUNG ALICE, b Ci-an, China, Mar 24, 48; m 73. MATHEMATICAL ANALYSIS. *Educ:* Nat Taiwan Univ, BA, 70; Univ Calif, Berkeley, PhD(math), 74. *Prof Exp:* Asst prof math, State Univ NY Buffalo, 74-75; Hedrick Asst Prof Math, Univ Calif, Los Angeles, 75-77; asst prof math, Univ Md, College Park, 77-80; ASSOC PROF, UNIV CALIF, LOS ANGELES, 80- *Concurrent Pos:* Solan fel, 80-81. *Mem:* Am Math Soc. *Res:* Investigation of behavior of analytic functions in the complex plane and in several complex variables, approximation of bounded functions by analytic functions. *Mailing Add:* Dept Math Univ Calif Los Angeles CA 90024

CHANG, TAI MING, b Taiwan, China, Nov 14, 38; m 66; c 2. CHEMICAL ENGINEERING, POLYMER SCIENCE. *Educ:* Nat Taiwan Univ, BS, 61; WVa Univ, MS, 65, PhD(chem eng), 67. *Prof Exp:* Sr res engr, Goodyear Tire & Rubber Co, Akron, 67-70, group leader res & develop, 70-75; eng specialist, 75-81, SR SPECIALIST, MONSANTO CO, 81- *Mem:* Am Chem Soc; Am Inst Chem Engrs. *Res:* Polymerization engineering; solid state polymerization; system simulation and optimization; fluidization; heat and mass transfer; polymer processing; polyvinyl butyral product and process. *Mailing Add:* 50 Canterbury Lane Longmeadow MA 01106

CHANG, TAI YUP, b Korea, Oct 25, 33; m 62; c 2. AIR POLLUTION, QUANTUM CHEMISTRY. *Educ:* Seoul Nat Univ, BS, 58, MS, 60; Univ Wis-Madiosn, PhD(theoret chem), 66. *Prof Exp:* Res fel theoret chem, Univ Wis-Madison, 67 & Harvard Univ, 67-69; res scientist, 69-80, STAFF SCIENTIST, CHEM DEPT, RES STAFF, FORD MOTOR CO, 80- *Mem:* Am Phys Soc; Air Pollution Control Asn; Am Meteorol Soc; Am Chem Soc. *Res:* Atomic and molecular physics; development and application of the perturbation theory; air pollution modeling, urban air quality modeling including atmospheric dispersion and photochemistry; global balance of trace gases. *Mailing Add:* Chem Dept Res Staff Ford Motor Co PO Box 2053 Dearborn MI 48121

CHANG, TA-YUAN, b Kwei-Chow, China, Apr 8, 45; m 72; c 2. LIPID METABOLISM, BIOCHEMICAL REGULATION. *Educ:* Nat Taiwan Univ, BS, 67; Univ NC, Chapel Hill, PhD(biochem), 73. *Prof Exp:* Fel, Washington Univ Med Sch, 73-76; ASST PROF BIOCHEM, DARTMOUTH MED SCH, 76- *Mem:* Am Soc Biol Chemists; Am Chem Soc. *Res:* Regulation of cholesterol biosynthesis in mammalian cells. *Mailing Add:* Dept Biochem Dartmouth Med Sch Hanover NH 03755

CHANG, TE WEN, b Nanchang, China, Oct 12, 20; US citizen; m 52; c 5. INFECTIOUS DISEASES, VIROLOGY. *Educ:* Nat Cent Univ, AB, 41, MD, 45. *Prof Exp:* Resident & asst med, Nat Cent Univ Hosp, 46-49; intern, St Joseph Hosp, Kansas City, 50; res fel virol, Univ Kans, 50-52; fel med, Mass Mem Hosp & Boston Univ, 52-57; instr med, 58-59, asst prof med & microbiol, 60-67, ASSOC PROF MED, NEW ENG MED CTR, TUFTS UNIV, 68- *Concurrent Pos:* Asst physician, New Eng Med Ctr Hosp, 60; assoc prof sch med, Tufts Univ, 68. *Mem:* AAAS; Fedn Clin Invest; Am Soc Microbiol; Infectious Dis Soc Am; Am Pub Health Asn. *Res:* Treatment and prevention of viral diseases in man; clostridium difficile infections. *Mailing Add:* Dept of Med New Eng Med Ctr Hosp Boston MA 02111

CHANG, THOMAS MING SWI, b Swatow, China, Apr 8, 33; Can citizen; m 58; c 4. PHYSIOLOGY, MEDICAL RESEARCH. *Educ:* McGill Univ, BSc, 57, MD, CM, 61, PhD(physiol), 65; FRCP(C), 72. *Prof Exp:* Intern, Montreal Gen Hosp, 61-62; sessional lectr, 64-65, lectr, 65-66, from asst prof to assoc prof, 66-72, dir, Artificial Organ Res Unit, 75-79, PROF PHYSIOL, MCGILL UNIV, 72-, PROF MED, 75-, DIR, ARTIFICIAL CELLS & ORGANS RES CTR, 79-; CAREER INVESTR, MED RES COUN CAN, 68- *Concurrent Pos:* Med Res Coun Can fel, 62-65, scholar, 65-68. *Mem:* Am Physiol Soc; Can Physiol Soc; Am Biophys Soc; Int Soc Artificial Organs; fel Royal Col Physicians Can. *Res:* Artificial and biological membranes; artificial cells and artificial organs; microencapsulation of enzymes, detoxicants and other biologically active materials for biomedical research and clinical applications. *Mailing Add:* McGill Univ 3655 Drummond St Montreal PQ H3G 1Y6 Can

CHANG, TIEN SUN, b Mukden, China, Feb 28, 31; nat US; m 61. PHYSICS, MECHANICS. *Educ:* Univ Ill, BS, 52, MS, 53 & 54, PhD(theoret & appl mech), 55; Univ Mich, PhD(theoret physics), 63. *Prof Exp:* Asst theoret & appl mech, Univ Ill, 52-54, assoc, 54-55, from instr to asst prof, 55-57; from assoc prof to prof eng mech, Va Polytech Inst, 57-67; NSF prof continuum mech, NC State Univ, 67-76, grad prof nuclear eng & chmn mech prog, 68-76; VIS PROF & MEM STAFF RES, MASS INST TECHNOL, 76- *Concurrent Pos:* Develop engr, Reactor Div, Oak Ridge Nat Lab, 62, res engr, 63, consult, 63-; vis prof, Cambridge Univ, 64-65 & 69, vis lectr, Dept Appl Math & Theoret Physics, 68; lectr & topic organizer, Langley Res Ctr, NASA, 64-65; vis prof, Lehigh Univ, 69, Cornell Univ, 70 & Mass Inst Technol, 71; invited lectr, jointly sponsored by Academia Sinica, Nat Taiwan Univ & Nat Tsing Hua Univ, Taiwan, 70; consult-lectr, adv group aerospace res & develop, NATO, 65-66; ed, Plasma Physics, 67-80; hon res fel, Harvard Univ, 78-79; consult, Nat Magnet Lab, 77-79. *Honors & Awards:* Thompson Award, Am Soc Testing & Mat, 58. *Mem:* AAAS; Am Geophys Union; fel Am Phys Soc. *Res:* Theoretical and solid state physics; magnetohydrodynamics; plasma physics; fluid mechanics; rheology; radiation gas dynamics; superfluids; hypervelocity impact; nonlinear waves; biomathematics; continuum mechanics; space physics. *Mailing Add:* Mass Inst Technol PO Box 6 Cambridge MA 02139

CHANG, TIEN-DING, b Chwansha, China, Oct 13, 21; m 51; c 2. GENETICS. *Educ:* Chekiang Univ, BS, 44; Univ Minn, MS, 60; Iowa State Univ, PhD(genetics), 63. *Prof Exp:* Teacher high schs, China, 44-46; agronomist, Taiwan Agr Res Inst, 46-57; cytogeneticist, Dept Med Genetics, Children's Hosp Winnipeg, 64-69; res assoc genetics, Univ Mo-Columbia, 69-74; RES ASSOC CELLULAR & BIOCHEM GENETICS, SLOAN-KETTERING INST CANCER RES, 74- *Concurrent Pos:* Damon Runyon Mem Fund vis investr, Biol Div, Oak Ridge Nat Lab, 63-64; cytogeneticist, Jenkins Found for Res, Salinas, Calif, 73-74. *Mem:* Genetics Soc Am; Genetics Soc Can; Tissue Culture Asn; NY Acad Sci. *Res:* Plant and mammalian cytogenetics. *Mailing Add:* Sloan-Kettering Inst 145 Boston Post Rd Rye NY 10580

CHANG, TIEN-LIN, b Chekiang, China, Nov 22, 43; US citizen; m 71; c 2. ELECTRICAL ENGINEERING, COMPUTER SCIENCE. *Educ:* Nat Taiwan Univ, BS, 65; Rice Univ, MS, 69, PhD(elec eng), 71. *Prof Exp:* Res asst elec eng, Rice Univ, 67-71, fel, 71; MEM TECH STAFF INFO SCI, ROCKWELL INT CORP, 71- *Mem:* Sigma Xi; sr mem Inst Elec & Electronics Engrs. *Res:* Digital signal processing in the areas of filter structure design; applications in image processing and telecommunications; pattern recognition, artificial intelligence, and intelligent machines. *Mailing Add:* Rockwell Int MS/BA61 3370 Miraloma Anaheim CA 92803

CHANG, TIMOTHY SCOTT, b Shaowu, China, May 30, 25; m 55; c 4. POULTRY PATHOLOGY, AVIAN MICROBIOLOGY. *Educ:* Fukien Christian Univ, BA, 46; Duke Univ, MDiv, 51; NC State Univ, BS, 52; Ohio State Univ, MS, 53, PhD(poultry path, avian microbiol), 57. *Prof Exp:* Teacher pub sch, China, 46-48; asst poultry sci, Ohio State Univ, 51-57; dir bact res lab, Whitmoyer Labs, Inc, Rohm and Haas Co, Pa, 57-65; group leader vet microbiol, Vet Res Div, Norwich Pharmacal Co, NY, 65-66, sect chief, 66-69; div mgr diagnostic reagents, Burroughs Wellcome Co, 69-70; dir animal technol dept, S B Penick & Co, CPC Int, Inc, 70-72; assoc prof, 71-77, PROF POULTRY PATH & AVIAN MICROBIOL, MICH STATE UNIV, 77- *Concurrent Pos:* Vis lectr, China, 79, 80 & 81. *Mem:* Am Poultry Sci Asn; Am Soc Microbiol; World Poultry Sci Asn; Am Asn Avian Pathologists; NY Acad Sci. *Res:* Function of Bursa of Fabricius in antibody production; immuno-response; poultry diseases; microbial fermentation; antibiotic properties-effects; radiation effects; sanitation-disinfectant; toxicological effects; avian microbiology. *Mailing Add:* Dept Animal Sci Mich State Univ East Lansing MI 48824

CHANG, TSONG-HOW, b Nanking, China, Oct 11, 29; m; c 3. STATISTICAL MODELING, ENGINEERING ECONOMICS. *Educ:* Nat Taiwan Univ, BS, 53; WVa Univ, MS, 58; Univ Wis, Madison, PhD(mech eng), 72. *Prof Exp:* Sr analyst oper res, Minneapolis Honeywell, 60-61; asst prof indust eng, Miss State Univ, 63-66; asst prof, 69-75, ASSOC PROF INDUST ENG, UNIV WIS, MILWAUKEE, 75-, DEPT CHAIR INDUST & SYST ENG, 79- *Concurrent Pos:* Adv prof, Shanghai Inst Mech Eng, China, 79- *Mem:* Sigma Xi; Oper Res Soc Am; Am Inst Indust Engrs. *Res:* Statistical modeling and engineering; economic analysis of industrial and manufacturing engineering systems; analysis of survival data for life expectancy predictions and engineering reliability. *Mailing Add:* Dept Indust & Syst Eng Univ Wis PO Box 784 Milwaukee WI 53201

CHANG, T(AO)-Y(UAN), b Taiwan, China, Mar 1, 37; m 63; c 2. QUANTUM ELECTRONICS, PLASMA PHYSICS. *Educ:* Nat Taiwan Univ, BS, 59; Stanford Univ, MS, 62; Univ Calif, Berkeley, PhD(elec eng), 66. *Prof Exp:* Engr electronics, Machtronics Inc, Calif, 62; res asst, Univ Calif, Berkeley, 62-66, acting asst prof elec eng, 66-67; MEM TECH STAFF, BELL TEL LABS, 67- *Honors & Awards:* Sr Am Sci Award, Alexander von Humboldt Found, Fed Repub Ger, 79. *Mem:* Inst Elec & Electronics Engrs; Optical Soc Am. *Res:* Instabilities in mirror confined plasmas; infrared mixing in nonlinear crystals; precision spectroscopy of carbon dioxide laser; infrared and far-infrared generation by optical pumping; molecular-beam epitaxy. *Mailing Add:* Bell Tel Labs 4F429 Holmdel NJ 07733

CHANG, WEN-HSUAN (WAYNE), b Tsingtao, China, Mar 28, 26; m 59; c 2. ORGANIC CHEMISTRY. *Educ:* Fu Jen Univ, China, BSc, 48; Wesleyan Univ, MA, 56; Northwestern Univ, PhD, 59. *Prof Exp:* Assoc engr, Taiwan Agr & Chem Works, Formosa, 49-54; sr res chemist, 58-65, from res assoc to sr res assoc, 65-69, scientist, 69-71, sr scientist, 71-73, MGR, PIONEER POLYMER RES DEPT, PPG INDUSTS, 73- *Mem:* Am Chem Soc; NY Acad Sci; Royal Soc Chem. *Res:* Organic chemical synthesis; reaction mechanisms; kinetics; polymer synthesis. *Mailing Add:* PPG Industs PO Box 9 Rosanna Dr Allison Park PA 15101

CHANG, WILLIAM, b Kiangsu, China, Apr 4, 31; m 55; c 3. ELECTRICAL ENGINEERING, APPLIED PHYSICS. *Educ:* Univ Mich, BS, 52, MS, 53; Brown Univ, PhD(elec eng), 57. *Prof Exp:* Res assoc & lectr elec eng, Stanford Univ, 57-59; from asst prof to assoc prof, Ohio State Univ, 59-65; prof elec eng, Washington Univ, 65-79, chmn dept, 65-71, dir, Lab Appl Electronic Sci, 71-79, Samuel Sachs prof, 76-79; PROF ELEC ENG, UNIV CALIF, SAN DIEGO, 79- *Mem:* Am Optom Asn; Am Phys Soc; fel Inst Elec & Electronics Engrs. *Res:* Quantum electronics; lasers; masers; electromagnetic field theory; infra-red systems; integrated optics. *Mailing Add:* Dept Elec Eng & Comput Sci Univ Calif San Diego La Jolla CA 92093

CHANG, WILLIAM WEI-LIEN, b Taipei, Taiwan, Feb 7, 33; m 65; c 3. HISTOLOGY, PATHOLOGY. *Educ:* Nat Taiwan Univ, MD, 58; Ohio State Univ, MSc(path), 66; McGill Univ, PhD(anat), 70; Am Bd Path, dipl, 78. *Prof Exp:* Asst pharmacol, Nat Taiwan Univ, 60-61; rotating intern med, Buffalo Gen Hosp, 61-62; from asst resident to resident path, Ohio State Univ, 62-66; from asst prof to assoc prof anat, Mt Sinai Sch Med, 70-79; mem fac, Grad Sch, City Univ New York, 72-79; ASSOC PROF MATH, MED CTR, WVA UNIV, 79- *Concurrent Pos:* Clin fel, Am Cancer Soc, Dept Path, Ohio State Univ, 64-65; Ont Heart Asn fel, Dept Path, Queen's Univ, Ont, 66-67; Nat Cancer Inst res grant, Dept Anat, Mt Sinai Sch Med, 74-77. *Mem:* Am Asn Anat; Am Soc Cell Biol; Int Acad Path; AAAS. *Res:* Cell population kinetics of colon and salivary glands; chemical carcinogenesis of colon. *Mailing Add:* WVa Univ Med Ctr Morgantown WV 26506

CHANG, WILLIAM Y B, b Amoy, China, June 1, 48; m 77; c 1. PRIMARY PRODUCTIVITY, MODELS ECOSYSTEMS. *Educ:* Univ Pac, MS, 73; Ind Univ, MA, 75, PhD(ecol & math), 79. *Prof Exp:* Assoc instr zool & math, Ind Univ, 76-78; res investr ecol & statist, 79-80, ASST RES SCIENTIST, GREAT LAKES RES DIV, UNIV MICH, 80- *Concurrent Pos:* Eigenmann fel biol, Ind Univ, 78, consult statist & comput, 78. *Mem:* AAAS; Am Soc Limnol Oceanog; Int Asn Great Lakes Res; Am Statist Asn. *Res:* Statistical models to ascertain and understand the dynamic interactions between biotic and abiotic components in an aquatic environment and the reasons for changes in environments. *Mailing Add:* Great Lakes Res Div Univ Mich Ann Arbor MI 48109

CHANG, Y AUSTIN, US citizen; m 56; c 3. CHEMICAL METALLURGY, THERMODYNAMICS. *Educ:* Univ Calif, Berkeley, BS, 54, PhD(metall), 63; Univ Wash, MS, 55. *Prof Exp:* Chem engr, Stauffer Chem Co, Calif, 56-59; res metallurgist, Lawrence Radiation Lab, Univ Calif, Berkeley, 63; sr metall engr, Aerojet-Gen Corp, Calif, 63-67; assoc prof, Univ Wis-Milwaukee, 67-70, chmn dept mat, 71-78, prof mat eng, 70-80, assoc dean res, Grad Sch, 78-80; PROF, DEPT METALL & MINERAL ENG, UNIV WIS-MADISON, 80- *Concurrent Pos:* Prin investr, NSF, 70-; mem int coun, Data Syst for Phase Diagrams, Am Soc Mat-Nat Bur Stand, 78-; mem bd, Goodwill Residential Community, Inc, Milwaukee, 78-80; mem, Wis Gov Asian Am Adv Coun, 80-82. *Mem:* Am Inst Mining, Metall & Petrol Engrs; fel Am Soc Metals; Sigma Xi; Nat Asn Corrosion Engrs. *Mailing Add:* Dept Metall & Mineral Eng 1509 University Ave Madison WI 53706

CHANG, YEW CHUN, b Yinping, China, Oct 10, 41; Can citizen; m 69; c 2. PHYSICAL CHEMISTRY, ORGANIC CHEMISTRY. *Educ:* Univ BC, BSc, 64, MSc, 66; Univ Sussex, DPhil(chem), 68. *Prof Exp:* Sr chemist imaging, Energy Conversion Devices Inc, 70-71, org chem mgr, 71-74; scientist liquid toners, Xerox Res Ctr, Can Ltd, 74-79; sr scientist oil res, Syncrude Can, 79-80; SUPVR ENERGY RES & DEVELOP, ARCO, 80- *Concurrent Pos:* Fel, Yale Univ, 68-69 & Univ Calif, Los Angeles, 69-70; hon consult, Indust Adv Coun, Univ Waterloo, 76-79. *Mem:* Assoc mem, Am Chem Soc; Soc Photog Scientists & Engrs; Chem Inst Can; Inter-Am Photochem Soc; Am Physics Soc. *Res:* Examined particles; clay in oil emulsions; surfactant dependent on colloids; natural gas components separation and processing; oil sands development; non-fossil fuel energy; thermoelectrics; hydrogen generation and storage; photochemistry and solar energy. *Mailing Add:* Arco Solar Indust 911 Wilshire Blvd Los Angeles CA 90017

CHANG, YI-CHI, pharmacology, see previous edition

CHANG, YI-HAN, b Peking, China, May 26, 33; US citizen; m 63. BIOCHEMICAL PHARMACOLOGY, IMMUNOLOGY. *Educ:* Stetson Univ, BS, 56; Pa State Univ, PhD(org chem), 61; Univ Conn, PhD(pharmacol), 65. *Prof Exp:* Res chemist, Pfizer, Inc, 60-63, res biochem pharmacologist, 63-68, res supvr, 68-72, group mgr, 72-75; ASSOC PROF MED & PHARMACOL, SCH MED, UNIV CALIF, LOS ANGELES, 75-, EXEC DIR RES, RHEUMATOL DIV, 78- *Mem:* Am Soc Pharmacol & Exp Therapeut; Am Chem Soc. *Res:* Anti-inflammatory and immunosuppressive agents; etiology and pathology of rheumatoid arthritis and hypersensitivity diseases; in vitro, in vivo models of cell-mediated hypersensitivity; drug metabolism; mechanism of action of colchicine. *Mailing Add:* 1024 Somer Rd Los Angeles CA 90024

CHANG, YOON IL, b Pyungbuk, Korea, Apr 12, 42; US citizen; m 66; c 3. NUCLEAR ENGINEERING. *Educ:* Seoul Nat Univ, BS, 64; Tex A&M Univ, ME, 67; Univ Mich, PhD(nuclear sci), 71. *Prof Exp:* Nuclear engr, Nuclear Assurance Corp, 71-74; nuclear engr, 74-76, group leader, 76-77, sect head, 77-78, ASSOC DIR, APPL PHYSICS DIV, ARGONNE NAT LAB, 78- *Mem:* Am Nuclear Soc. *Res:* Reactor physics; nuclear fuel cycle analysis; reactor core design analysis; advanced reactor concept evaluation. *Mailing Add:* Appl Physics Div 9700 S Cass Ave Argonne IL 60439

CHANG, YUNG-FENG, b Taiwan, China, Nov 15, 35; m 68; c 2. BIOCHEMSITRY, MICROBIOLOGY. *Educ:* Nat Taiwan Univ, BS, 58, MS, 60; Univ Pittsburgh, PhD(biochem), 66. *Prof Exp:* Res asst biochem, Nat Taiwan Univ, 61-62; res asst, Univ Pittsburgh, 62-66; res assoc, Sch Med, 66-70, asst prof histol & embryol, Sch Dent, 70-71, asst prof microbiol, 71-74, assoc prof microbiol, 74-79, PROF BIOCHEM, SCH DENT, UNIV MD, BALTIMORE, 79- *Concurrent Pos:* Prin investr, NIH res grants. *Mem:* Am Chem Soc; Am Soc Microbiol; Am Soc Biol Chem; Int Asn Dent Res. *Res:* Lysine metabolism and regulation of enzyme in Pseudomonas putida; isoenzymes of glutaric semialdehyde dehydrogenase; cariostatic effects of amino acids on dental plaque formation and cell wall biosynthesis of streptococcus mutans; lysine metabolism in the mammalian brain; neurochemical and developmental aspects of the metabolic pathways of lysine in the rat. *Mailing Add:* Dept Biochem Univ of Md Sch of Dent Baltimore MD 21201

CHANG, YUNG-KWANG, physics, materials science, see previous edition

CHANG, YU-WEI, b Chen-Kiang, Kiangsu, China, July 14, 19; m 53; c 4. ORGANIC CHEMISTRY. *Educ:* Nat Cent Univ, China, BS, 40; Univ Wash, PhD, 53. *Prof Exp:* Res fel, Columbia Univ, 52-56; res assoc, Worcester Found Exp Biol, 56-58; res fel org chem, Harvard, 58-60; RES CHEMIST, JACKSON LAB, E I DU PONT DE NEMOURS & CO, INC, 60- *Res:* Synthetic organic chemistry; reaction mechanisms. *Mailing Add:* 3 Lori Ln Cragmoor Woods Wilmington DE 19809

CHANG-FANG, CHUEN-CHUEN, b Taipei, Taiwan, June 21, 30; US citizen; m 61; c 3. PARTICLE PHYSICS. *Educ:* Nat Taiwan Univ, BS, 53; Univ SC, MS, 57; Duke Univ, PhD(physics), 61. *Prof Exp:* Teaching asst physics, Prov Tainan Eng Col, 53-55; instr, Univ Miami, 60-61; sr physicist, Controls for Radiation, 61-62; asst prof physics, Southern Ill Univ, Carbondale, 66-72; vis assoc prof, Nat Taiwan Univ, 72-73; asst prof physics, Southern Ill Univ, Carbondale, 73-78; consult, Argonne Nat Lab, Argonne, Ill, 80-81. *Mem:* Am Phys Soc; Am Asn Physics Teachers. *Res:* Phenomenological analysis of anti-proton-proton interaction at 2.32 GeV/c. *Mailing Add:* 1605 W Freeman Carbondale IL 62901

CHANGNON, STANLEY ALCIDE, JR, b Donovan, Ill, Apr 14, 28; m 50; c 3. CLIMATOLOGY. *Educ:* Univ Ill, BS, 51, MS, 56. *Prof Exp:* Proj supvr cloud physics, Univ Ill, 52-54; assoc scientist, 55-65, prof climat scientist, 65-70, actg head, 70-71, head, Atmospheric Sci Sect, 71-79, CHIEF, ILL STATE WATER SURV & PROF, UNIV ILL, 75- *Concurrent Pos:* NSF res grants, 65-; mem nat comt, Comt Weather Info for Agr, 65; mem, Nat Comt Severe Local Storms & Nat Comt Weather Modification. *Honors & Awards:* Robert Horton Award, Am Geophys Union, 64; Award, Bldg Res Inst, 65; Abby Award, Meteorol Soc, 81. *Mem:* Am Meteorol Soc; Am Geophys Union; AAAS. *Res:* Climatology of Lake Michigan, Illinois and Middle West; severe storms; physical geography; weather modification; agrometeorology; irrigation; urban industrial effects on precipitation. *Mailing Add:* Atmospheric Sci Sect Univ Ill 271A Water Resrcs Urbana IL 61801

CHANIN, LORNE MAXWELL, b Roland, Man, Aug 14, 27; m 50; c 3. PLASMA PHYSICS. *Educ:* Univ Man, BS, 49; Univ NMex, MS, 51; Univ Pittsburgh, PhD(physics), 59. *Prof Exp:* Res engr, Westinghouse Res Labs, 51-59; res scientist & sect head, Honeywell Res Ctr, 59-65; assoc prof, 65-68, PROF ELEC ENG, UNIV MINN, MINNEAPOLIS, 68- *Concurrent Pos:* Consult, US Bur Mines. *Mem:* Am Phys Soc; Inst Elec & Electronics Engrs; Europ Phys Soc. *Res:* Atomic physics; interactions and reactions involving electrons, ions and excited atoms; plasma physics; electrical discharges; gaseous electronics; plasma chemistry. *Mailing Add:* Dept of Elec Eng Univ of Minn Minneapolis MN 55455

CHANLETT, EMIL T(HEODORE), b New York, NY, Dec 30, 15; m 46; c 2. SANITARY ENGINEERING. *Educ:* City Col New York, BS, 37; Columbia Univ, MS, 39; Am Bd Indust Hyg, Dipl, 62. *Prof Exp:* Asst sanit engr, US Pub Health Serv, 41-43; from asst to assoc prof sanit eng, 46-58, PROF SANIT ENG, UNIV NC, 58- *Concurrent Pos:* W K Kellogg Found field fel, 38-39; spec lectr, Sch Pub Health, Johns Hopkins Univ, 46; consult, Brazilian Govt, Inst Inter-Am Affairs & Spec Pub Health Serv, Amazon River Basin, 48; consult occup & radiol health, State Bd Health, NC; mem, NC Atomic Energy Adv Bd; mem, State Bd Refrig Exam, NC; mem, Sanitarians' Joint Coun, 58-64, chmn, 63, secy, 61 & 64; alternate mem, NC State Bd Sanit Exam, 63-; mem, Am Intersoc Bd Cert Sanitarians, 64. *Mem:* Am Water Works Asn; Water Pollution Control Fedn; Am Indust Hyg Asn; Air Pollution Control Asn; Inter-Am Asn Sanit Engrs (vpres, US sect, 62-64). *Res:* Industrial hygiene; radiological health; air pollution control; public health. *Mailing Add:* Dept of Environ Sci & Eng Univ of NC Chapel Hill NC 27514

CHANLEY, JACOB DAVID, b New York, NY, Jan 8, 18; m 42; c 2. BIOCHEMISTRY. *Educ:* City Col New York, BS, 38; Univ Chicago, MS, 40; Harvard Univ, MA, 42, PhD(chem), 44. *Prof Exp:* Asst, Mt Sinai Hosp, 40-41; res worker, War Prod Bd, Columbia Univ, 44-45; res chemist, Mt Sinai Hosp, 45-67; ASSOC PROF BIOCHEM, SCH MED & GRAD SCH, CITY UNIV NEW YORK, 67- *Concurrent Pos:* Fel chem, Harvard Univ, 41-44; Rockefeller traveling fel, Oxford Univ, 49-50; Dazian Found fel, 49-50; sr res assoc, Mt Sinai Hosp, 67-70. *Mem:* AAAS; Am Chem Soc; The Chem Soc; Am Soc Biol Chemists. *Res:* Chemistry; steroid saponins of marine origin; metabolism of adrenergic transmitters; enzyme kinetics. *Mailing Add:* Mt Sinai Sch of Med Fifth Ave & 100th St New York NY 10029

CHANMUGAM, GANESAR, b Colombo, Ceylon, Oct 24, 39; m 66; c 2. THEORETICAL ASTROPHYSICS. *Educ:* Univ Ceylon, BSc, 61; Cambridge Univ, BA, 63; Brandeis Univ, PhD(physics), 70. *Prof Exp:* Instr physics, Univ Mass, Amherst, 63-64; res fel astrophys, Inst Astrophys, Univ Liege, Belg, 69-71; res assoc, 71-72, asst prof, 72-78, ASSOC PROF PHYSICS & ASTRON, LA STATE UNIV, BATON ROUGE, 78- *Concurrent Pos:* Vis fel, Joint Inst Lab Astrophysics, Univ Colo, Boulder, 79-80. *Mem:* Am Phys Soc; Am Astron Soc; Int Astron Union; Royal Astron Soc. *Res:* Physics of dense matter with astrophysical applications to white dwarfs; neutron stars. *Mailing Add:* Dept of Physics & Astron La State Univ Baton Rouge LA 70803

CHANNEL, LAWRENCE EDWIN, b Boise, Idaho, Mar 17, 27; m 47; c 5. PHYSICS. *Educ:* Pasadena Col, AB, 50; Univ Calif, Los Angeles, MA, 55. *Prof Exp:* Physicist, US Naval Ord Test Sta, Pasadena, Calif, 53-57; opers analyst, Mass Inst Technol physics eval group, US Dept Navy, Washington, DC, 57-63; res & develop scientist, 63-67, dept mgr, 67-69, DIV MGR, LOCKHEED-CALIFORNIA CO, 69- *Concurrent Pos:* Asst physics, Univ Calif, Los Angeles, 54; part-time instr, Pasadena Col, 64-65 & 69. *Mem:* Acoust Soc Am; Am Inst Aeronaut & Astronaut; Am Helicopter Soc. *Res:* Underwater acoustics; military operations research. *Mailing Add:* Lockheed Calif Co 2555 N Hollywood Way Burbank CA 91503

CHANNELL, ROBERT BENNIE, b Gallman, Miss, July 4, 24. SYSTEMATIC BOTANY. *Educ:* Miss State Col, BS, 47, MS, 49; Duke Univ, PhD, 55. *Prof Exp:* Pub sch teacher, 47-49; instr bot, Miss State Col, 49-51; asst, Duke Univ, 51-54; asst cur, Herbarium, 54-55; botanist, Gray Herbarium-Arnold Arboretum, Harvard, 55-57; from asst prof to assoc prof biol, 57-69, chmn dept, 63-73, PROF BIOL, VANDERBILT UNIV, 69- *Mem:* Am Soc Plant Taxon; Int Asn Plant Taxon. *Res:* Conventional and experimental taxonomy of vascular plants, particularly Compositae and Cyperaceae; flora of the Southeastern United States. *Mailing Add:* Dept of Biol Substa B Vanderbilt Univ Nashville TN 37240

CHANNIN, DONALD JONES, b Evanston, Ill, Aug 29, 42. PHYSICS, OPTICS. *Educ:* Case Western Reserve Univ, BS, 64; Cornell Univ, PhD(physics), 70. *Prof Exp:* MEM TECH RES STAFF, SARNOFF RES CTR, RCA LABS, 70- *Concurrent Pos:* Vis prof, Inst Physics & Chem, San Carlos, Univ Sao Paulo, Brazil, 77. *Mem:* Am Phys Soc; Optical Soc Am. *Res:* Solid state physics; electro-optical phenomenon; liquid crystals; injection lasers; optical communications systems. *Mailing Add:* Sarnoff Res Ctr RCA Labs Princeton NJ 08540

CHANNING, CORNELIA POST, b Boston, Mass, Apr 23, 38. ENDOCRINOLOGY. *Educ:* Hood Col, BA, 61; Harvard Univ, MA, 63, PhD(biochem), 66. *Prof Exp:* Fel reproductive physiol, Sch Vet Med, Univ Cambridge, 65-67; from instr to asst prof physiol, Sch Med, Univ Pittsburgh, 67-73; assoc prof, 73-76, PROF PHYSIOL, SCH MED, UNIV MD, BALTIMORE, 76- *Concurrent Pos:* Nat Inst Child Health & Human Develop fel, res grant, 68-85, contract grant, 70-78; Am Cancer Soc grant, 68; Pop Coun New York res grant, 72-77; WHO grant, 75 & 77-80; mem bladder-prostate adv comt, Nat Cancer Inst, 72-73; mem study sect on molecular cytol, NIH, 74-77; Southern Med Asn res award, 76; Ford Found grant, 77-80; Soc Study Reprod res award, 78. *Honors & Awards:* Newcomb Cleveland Prize, AAAS, 69; Erntoppenheimer Mem Award, Endocrine Soc, 78. *Mem:* Am Physiol Soc; Soc Study Reproduction; Endocrine Soc; Soc Exp Biol & Med; Tissue Cult Asn. *Res:* Reproductive physiology and biochemistry of the mammalian ovary; use of tissue culture as a method for studying the mechanisms of luteinization in the rhesus monkey, pig and human; control of ovarian steroidogenesis; control of oocyte meiosis. *Mailing Add:* Dept of Physiol Univ of Md Sch of Med Baltimore MD 21201

CHANNON, STEPHEN R, b Washington, DC, Aug 13, 47; m 69; c 1. NONLINEAR DYNAMICS. *Educ:* Ohio State Univ, BS, 70; Rutgers Univ, PhD(physics), 81. *Prof Exp:* Physicist, Fusion Energy Corp, 74-77; consult physicist-programmer, 81-82, DIR THEORY PROG, FUSION ENERGY CORP, 82- *Concurrent Pos:* Dir opers, Consortium Early Testing Advan Feul Fusion, 81-; vis assoc prof, Univ Buenos Aires, 82- *Mem:* Am Physics Soc. *Res:* Nonlinear dynamics; physics of the Mioma concept for controlled fusion (high ion energy plasma confined in a simple magnetic mirror). *Mailing Add:* Fusion Energy Corp PO Box 2005 Princeton NJ 08540

CHANOCK, ROBERT MERRITT, b Chicago, Ill, July 8, 24; m 48; c 2. PEDIATRICS, BACTERIOLOGY. *Educ:* Univ Chicago, BS, MD, 47. *Prof Exp:* Asst prof res pediat, Sch Med, Univ Cincinnati, 54-56; asst prof epidemiol, Sch Pub Health, Johns Hopkins Univ, 56-57; MED DIR, LAB INFECT DIS, NAT INST ALLERGY & INFECT DIS, 57-, VCHMN, BD VACCINE DEVELOP, 64-; PROF CHILD HEALTH & DEVELOP, SCH MED, GEORGE WASHINGTON UNIV, 71- *Concurrent Pos:* Nat Res Coun fel, 50-51; Nat Found Infantile Paralysis fel, 51-52; sr res fel, USPHS, 56-57; virologist, Children's Hosp DC, 57-; mem int nomenclature comt myxoviruses, 7th & 8th Int Microbiol Cong; mem, Armed Forces Epidemiol Bd, Comn Acute Respiratory Dis, assoc mem, Comn Influenza; dir int ref ctr respiratory viruses, WHO, 62-; mem int comt nomenclature bacteria, Int Asn Microbiol Soc, 69-72; clin prof, Georgetown Univ, 70-71. *Honors & Awards:* E Mead Johnson Award Pediat Soc, 64; USPHS Meritorious Serv Medal, 65; Squibb Award, Infect Dis Soc Am, 69; USPHS Distinguished Serv Medal, 71. *Mem:* Nat Acad Sci; Soc Pediat Res; Am Soc Microbiol; Am Epidemiol Soc; Am Soc Clin Invest. *Res:* Respiratory virus diseases; virus microbiology. *Mailing Add:* Lab of Infect Dis Nat Inst Allergy & Infect Dis Bethesda MD 20014

CHANOWITZ, MICHAEL STEPHEN, b Chicago, Ill, May 12, 43. PHYSICS. *Educ:* Cornell Univ, BA, 63, PhD(physics), 71. *Prof Exp:* SR STAFF SCIENTIST, LAWRENCE BERKELEY LAB, 79- *Res:* Theoretical elementary particle physics. *Mailing Add:* 50A 3115 Lawrence Berkeley Lab Berkeley CA 94720

CHAN-PALAY, VICTORIA, b Singapore, Oct 9; 45; US citizen; m c 2. NEUROSCIENCES. *Educ:* Smith Col, AB, 65; Tufts Univ, PhD, 69; Harvard Med Sch, MD, 75. *Hon Degrees:* DSc, Smith Col, 79. *Prof Exp:* Res asst biophys, New Eng Med Ctr, Boston, 65-66; teaching asst histol & gross anat, Sch Med, Tufts Univ, 68-69; instr, 70-72, asst prof, 72-78, ASSOC PROF NEUROBIOL, HARVARD MED SCH, 78-; ASSOC PROF NEUROBIOL, WHITAKER COL HEALTH SCI, MASS INST TECHNOL, 78- *Concurrent Pos:* Asst prof neurobiol, Mass Inst Technol, 72-78; Alfred P Sloan res fel neurosci, 76; vis guest scientist, Brain Res Inst, Kyoto Univ, 78; mem, Neurolog Disorders Proj Rev, 78-; White House fel & staff asst to Secy Defense, The Pentagon, 79-80; Tarbox distinguished lectr, Tarbox Parkinson's Dis Inst, Tex, 79, Louise Harkness Ingalls fel, 79-80; chair comt sci, Bd Counr, Smith Col, 80-; mem bd dirs, Nat Ctr Therapeut Riding, 81-; mem adv coun spec prog, WETA TV, Washington, DC, 81- *Honors & Awards:* William F Milton Fund Award, Harvard Univ, 73; Leon Reznick Mem Prize, Harvard Med Sch, 75. *Mem:* Am Asn Anat; Am Asn Cell Biol; Soc Neurosci; Am Asn Univ Women; Am Med Women's Asn. *Res:* Brain network analyses and the decoding of chemicals that are utilized in cellular communication; author or coauthor of over 50 publications. *Mailing Add:* Dept Neurobiol Harvard Med Sch Boston MA 02115

CHANSON, SAMUEL T, b Can citizen. PERFORMANCE EVALUATION, OPERATING SYSTEMS. *Educ:* Hong Kong Univ, BSc, 69; Univ Calif, Berkeley, MSc, 71, PhD(elec eng & comput sci), 74. *Prof Exp:* Asst prof elec eng, Purdue Univ, 74-75; asst prof, 75-82, ASSOC PROF COMPUT SCI, UNIV BC, 82- *Mem:* Asn Comput Mach; Comput Soc; Inst Elec & Electronics Engrs. *Res:* Computer systems performance evaluation; system load control; bottleneck detection and removal; computer selection methodology; computer design problems. *Mailing Add:* Dept Comput Sci Univ BC Vancouver BC V6T 1W5 Can

CHANT, DONALD A, b Toronto, Ont, Sept 30, 28; m 75; c 1. ENTOMOLOGY. *Educ:* Univ BC, BA, 50, MA, 52; Univ London, PhD(zool), 56. *Hon Degrees:* LLD, Dalhousie Univ, 76. *Prof Exp:* Res officer, Res Inst, Can Dept Agr, 56-60; dir entom & plant path, Res Lab, Vineland, Ont, 60-64; chmn dept biol control, Univ Calif, Riverside, 64-67; chmn dept zool, 67-75; vpres & provost, 75-80, DIR, CTR TOXICOL, UNIV TORONTO, 80- *Concurrent Pos:* Mem, Nat Comt Pesticide Use in Agr, Can, 61-64 & subcomt insect control, Nat Res Coun-Nat Acad Sci. *Mem:* Fel Entom Soc Can; Can Soc Zool (pres, 74-75); fel Royal Entom Soc; fel Royal Soc Can. *Res:* Acarology; taxonomy and ecology of predacious phytoseiid mites; principles of predation; biological control. *Mailing Add:* Can Ctr Toxicol Rm 103 121 St Joseph St Toronto ON M5S 1A1 Can

CHANTELL, CHARLES J, b Chicago, Ill, May 19, 31; m 57; c 2. VERTEBRATE ANATOMY. *Educ:* Univ Ill, BS, 61; Univ Notre Dame, MS, 63, PhD(biol), 65. *Prof Exp:* ASSOC PROF BIOL, UNIV DAYTON, 65- *Mem:* Soc Vert Paleont; Am Soc Ichthyologists & Herpetologists; Soc Study Amphibians & Reptiles. *Res:* Evolution, phylogeny and osteology of the lower vertebrates. *Mailing Add:* Dept of Biol Univ of Dayton Dayton OH 45469

CHANTRY, WILLIAM AMDOR, b Corning, Iowa, Sept 21, 24; m 49; c 3. CHEMICAL ENGINEERING, PHYSICAL CHEMISTRY. *Educ:* Univ Iowa, BS, 49, MS, 51; Cornell Univ, PhD(chem eng), 53. *Prof Exp:* Technologist, Sherwin Williams Co, Ill, 49-50 & Shell Chem Corp, Calif, 53-56; from technologist to sr technologist, Shell Chem Corp, Tex, 56-59; from res engr to sr res engr Dacron res lab, 59-67, res assoc, 67-71, develop assoc, 71-75, DEVELOP FEL TEXTILE FIBERS DEPT, KINSTON PLANT, E I DU PONT DE NEMOURS & CO, 75- *Mem:* Am Inst Chem Engrs; Sigma Xi; Fiber Soc; Textile Inst. *Res:* Liquid-liquid extraction; heat exchanger design; polymerization kinetics; spinning and drawing on synthetic fibers; fabric finishing; textile fibers product development; fiber spinning; polymerization; heat transfer and fluid flow. *Mailing Add:* 1708 St George Pl Kinston NC 28501

CHAO, ALEXANDER WU, accelerator theory, see previous edition

CHAO, B(EI) T(SE), b Kiangsu, China, Dec 18, 18; nat US; m 48; c 2. MECHANICAL ENGINEERING, HEAT TRANSFER. *Educ:* Chiao-Tung Univ, BS, 39; Univ Manchester, PhD(mech eng), 47. *Prof Exp:* Engr-in-chg, Small Tools & Gage Div, Cent Mach Works, Nat Resources Comn, China, 41-44; assoc prof, 53-55, assoc mem, Ctr Advan Study, 63-64, head thermal sci div, Dept Mech Eng, 70-75, PROF MECH ENG, UNIV ILL, URBANA-CHAMPAIGN, 55-, HEAD DEPT MECH & INDUST ENG, 75- *Concurrent Pos:* Spec consult, Scully-Jones & Co, 52-55; mem reviewing staff, Southwest Res Inst, 53-56; spec consult, Chicago Opers Off, AEC, 62; mem reviewing staff, Zentralblatt fur Mathematik, Berlin, 66-; tech ed, J Heat Transfer, Am Soc Mech Engrs, 75-81; mem Westinghouse Awards Comn, Am Soc Eng Educ, 75-81; consult, Argonne Nat Lab, 76-; mem US eng educ deleg to China, Nat Acad Sci, Am Coun Learned Soc & Soc Sci Res Coun, 78; mem, Adv Screening Comn Eng, Fulbright-Hayes Awards Prog, 79-81, chmn, 80; mem, Comn on Recommendation for US Army Basic Sci Res, Nat Res Coun, 80-83. *Honors & Awards:* Blackall Award, Am Soc Mech Engrs, 57, Heat Transfer Award, 71; Western Elec Fund Award, Am Soc Eng Educ, 73, Mech Eng Outstanding Teaching Award, 75. *Mem:* Nat Acad Eng; Am Soc Eng Educ; Soc Eng Sci; fel Am Soc Mech Engrs. *Res:* Heat and mass transfer; fluid mechanics; multiphase flows. *Mailing Add:* 704 Brighton Dr Urbana IL 61801

CHAO, CHONG-YUN, b Kunming, China, July 5, 31; m 56; c 2. MATHEMATICS. *Educ:* Univ Iowa, BA, 53, MS, 54; Univ Mich, PhD(math), 61. *Prof Exp:* Instr math, Coe Col, 54-56; mathematician, Res Ctr, Int Bus Mach Corp, 61-63; assoc prof math, 63-66, PROF MATH & STATIST, UNIV PITTSBURGH, 66- *Mem:* Am Math Soc; Math Asn Am. *Res:* Lie algebras, groups and graphs. *Mailing Add:* Dept of Math Univ of Pittsburgh Pittsburgh PA 15213

CHAO, EDWARD CHING-TE, b Soochow, China, Nov 30, 19; nat US; m 42; c 3. GEOLOGY. *Educ:* Nat Southwest Assoc Univ, BS, 41; Univ Chicago, PhD(geol), 48. *Prof Exp:* Jr geologist, Geol Surv Szechuan, China, 41-45; fel petrol & geochem, Univ Chicago, 48-49; GEOLOGIST, US GEOL SURV, WASHINGTON, DC, 49- *Mem:* Geol Soc Am; Mineral Soc Am; Geochem Soc. *Res:* Petrology; geochemistry; mineralogy; impact metamorphism; lunar petrology; coal petrology; geology. *Mailing Add:* US Geol Surv Nat Ctr 12201 Sunrise Valley Dr Reston VA 22092

CHAO, FU-CHUAN, b Hong Kong, Feb 8, 19; US citizen; m 47; c 3. BIOCHEMISTRY. *Educ:* Lingnan Univ, BA, 41; Univ Calif, Berkeley, PhD(biochem), 51. *Prof Exp:* Res fel biochem, Univ Calif, Berkeley, 51-52, jr res biochemist, 52-53; res instr biochem, Univ Utah, 53-55; res assoc, Stanford Univ, 55-61, biophys chemist, Stanford Res Inst, 61-74; res chemist, Univ San Francisco & VA Hosp, Palo Alto, 74-78; BIOCHEMIST, SMITHKLINE INSTRUMENTS, INC, 78- *Concurrent Pos:* Am Heart Asn fel, 55-61. *Mem:* AAAS; Am Chem Soc; fel Am Inst Chemists; NY Acad Sci; Am Soc Microbiol. *Res:* Stability of ribonucleoproteins in solution; purification of viruses by chemical methods; prognosis of cancer; metabolism of marijuana; quantitative extraction of polychlorinated biphenyls from milk and blood; immunochemistry. *Mailing Add:* 1524 Channing Ave Palo Alto CA 94303

CHAO, JIA-ARNG, b Hunan, China, July 8, 41; m 67; c 1. MATHEMATICS. *Educ:* Nat Taiwan Normal Univ, BS, 64; Nat Tsing Hua Univ, MS, 66; Washington Univ, PhD(math), 72. *Prof Exp:* Teaching & res asst math, Washington Univ, 66-71, instr, 72; ASST PROF MATH, UNIV TEX, AUSTIN, 72- *Mem:* Am Math Soc. *Res:* Harmonic analysis on local fields. *Mailing Add:* Dept of Math Univ of Tex Austin TX 78712

CHAO, JING, b Zhejiang, China, Nov 7, 24; m 52; c 1. PHYSICAL CHEMISTRY. *Educ:* Nat Cent Univ, China, BS, 47; Carnegie-Mellon Univ, MS, 61, PhD(phys chem), 62. *Prof Exp:* Asst chem engr, Hsinchu Res Inst, Chinese Petrol Corp, 47-53; assoc chem engr, Union Indust Res Inst, Ministry Econ Affairs, China, 53-57; phys chemist, Thermal Res Lab, Dow Chem Co, 61-69; sr thermodynamicist, 69-73, asst dir molecular thermodyn, 73-78, RES SCIENTIST, THERMODYN RES CTR, TEX A&M UNIV, 78- *Mem:* Am Chem Soc; Sigma Xi. *Res:* Thermochemistry; chemical thermodynamics; collection, analysis of chemical data and critical evaluation of physical and thermodynamic properties for chemical substances. *Mailing Add:* Thermodyn Res Ctr Tex Eng Exp Sta Tex A&M Univ College Station TX 77843

CHAO, JOWETT, b Chekiang, China, Nov 16, 15; nat US; m 39; c 1. PARASITOLOGY. *Educ:* WChina Union Univ, BS, 39; Nat Cent Univ, China, MS, 42; Cornell Univ, PhD(entom), 49. *Prof Exp:* Instr gen zool, WChina Union Univ, 39-40; entomologist, Ministry Agr & Forestry, China, 42-44; teacher chem, Putney Sch, Vt, 47-48; chemist, Vitaminerals, Inc, Calif, 48-54; from asst res zoologist to assoc res zoologist, Univ Calif, Los Angeles, 54-65, res zoologist, 65-77; RETIRED. *Concurrent Pos:* Nat Found Infantile Paralysis fel, 57; lectr, Immaculate Heart Col, Calif, 58-59; Inter-Am Prog Trop Med fel, La State Univ, 61; mem int panel workshop malaria immunol, Walter Reed Army Inst Res, 63; consult, Ore State Univ, 75; Nat Acad Sci exchange scientist, Czechoslovakia and Poland, 78; lectr, Nat Acad Sci, Peoples Repub China, 79. *Mem:* AAAS; Am Soc Trop Med & Hyg; Soc Protozool; Am Soc Parasitol; Am Mosquito Control Asn. *Res:* In vitro culture of plasmodium; internal microorganisms; in vitro culture of insect cells and the insect phase of blood parasites; reptilian hemogregarine life cycle and transmission; invertebrate tissue culture. *Mailing Add:* 228 S Palm Dr Beverly Hills CA 90212

CHAO, KWANG CHU, b Chungking, China, June 7, 25; m 53; c 3. CHEMICAL ENGINEERING. *Educ:* Chekiang Univ, BS, 48; Univ Wis, MS, 52, PhD(chem eng), 56. *Prof Exp:* Asst eng, Taiwan Alkali Co, 48-51, chem engr, 52-54; res assoc, Univ Wis, 56-57; res engr, Chevron Res Co, 57-63; assoc prof chem eng, Ill Inst Technol, 63-64 & Okla State Univ, 64-68; PROF CHEM ENG, PURDUE UNIV, 68- *Concurrent Pos:* Indust consult, 64-; dir res grants, NSF, Petrol Res Fund, Am Petrol Inst, Gas Processors Asn, Elec Power Res Inst & Gulf Found. *Mem:* Fel Am Inst Chem Engrs; Am Chem Soc; Sigma Xi. *Res:* Thermodynamics; molecular theory; equilibrium properties of fluids; theory of solutions; surface phases. *Mailing Add:* Sch of Chem Eng Purdue Univ West Lafayette IN 47907

CHAO, LI-PEN, b Hunan, Repub of China, Apr 14, 33; m 67; c 2. NEUROCHEMISTRY, BIOCHEMISTRY. *Educ:* Chung Hsing Univ, Taiwan, BS, 57; Univ Minn, MS, 64, PhD(biochem), 67. *Prof Exp:* Teaching asst plant physiol, Chung Hsing Univ, Taiwan, 59-60; res asst biochem, Univ Minn, 61-67; asst res biochemist, Sch Med, Univ Calif, San Francisco, 67-70; from asst res neurologist to assoc res neurologist, 70-79, RES NEUROLOGIST, SCH MED, UNIV CALIF, LOS ANGELES, 79- *Mem:* AAAS; Am Chem Soc; Sigma Xi; Am Soc Neurochem; Int Soc Neurochem. *Res:* Chemistry of enzymes and proteins--isolation, purification and characterization by various chemical and physical methods; chemistry of cholinergic nerve transmission and localization of cholinergic neurons. *Mailing Add:* Dept Neurol Univ Calif Sch Med Los Angeles CA 90024

CHAO, MIN-TE, b Hupei, China, Jan 23, 38; US citizen; m 65; c 2. STATISTICS. *Educ:* Nat Taiwan Univ, BS, 61; Univ Calif, Berkeley, MA, 65, PhD(statist), 67. *Prof Exp:* mem tech staff, Bell Labs, 68-78, DIST MGR, ANAL SUPPORT CTR, AM TEL & TEL CO, 78- *Concurrent Pos:* Assoc ed, Bull Acad Sinica, 75-78. *Mem:* Am Statist Asn. *Res:* Large sample theory; stochastic approximating; models for error process in telecommunication applications; traffic theory; survey sampling; non-linear regression. *Mailing Add:* Rm 7134 M1 Am Tel & Tel Co 295 N Maple Ave Basking Ridge NJ 07920

CHAO, MOU SHU, b Changsha, China, Nov 20, 24; nat US; m 68. ELECTROCHEMISTRY, ANALYTICAL CHEMISTRY. *Educ:* Nat Cent Univ, China, BS, 47; Univ Ill, MS, 57, PhD(anal chem), 61. *Prof Exp:* Asst chem, Nat Cent Univ, China, 47-49; technician, Taiwan Fertilizer Co, 50-53, asst engr, 53-55; chemist, Spec Serv Lab, 60-63, res chemist, Electro & Inorg Res Lab, 63-72, res specialist, 72-79, RES LEADER, INORG LAB, DOW CHEM CO, 80- *Mem:* Am Chem Soc; Electrochem Soc; Am Inst Chemists; Sigma Xi. *Res:* Chemical instrumentation; electrode kinetics. *Mailing Add:* Cent Res-Inorg Lab Dow Chem Co Midland MI 48640

CHAO, RAUL EDWARD, b Havana, Cuba, Dec 21, 39; US citizen; m 64. CHEMICAL ENGINEERING, MANAGEMENT. *Educ:* Univ PR, Mayaguez, BSChE, 61; Johns Hopkins Univ, PhD(chem eng), 65. *Prof Exp:* Instr chem eng, Johns Hopkins Univ, 61-63, res asst, 63-65; proj engr, Exxon Res & Eng Co, NJ, 65-68; chmn, Dept Chem Eng, Univ PR, Mayaguez, 68-77; CHMN, DEPT CHEM ENG, UNIV DETROIT, 77- *Concurrent Pos:* Consult, NASA-Houston, 73-77 & Rockwell Int, Columbus, Ohio, 78- *Mem:* Am Inst Chem Engrs; Am Chem Soc. *Res:* Polymer processing; heat transfer; reaction engineering; process synthesis emphasizing renewable resources, alternate feedstocks and economic analyses of processes, as well as planning and forecasting. *Mailing Add:* Chem Eng Dept Univ Detroit 4001 W McNichols Rd Detroit MI 48221

CHAO, SHERMAN S, b Nanking, China, Aug 16, 47; m 75. CHEMICAL SPECTROSCOPY, TRACE ANALYSIS. *Educ:* Tamkang Univ, BS, 70; Loyola Univ, MS, 74, PhD(anal chem), 77. *Prof Exp:* Res fel, Univ Mo, Columbia, 76-77; sr chemist, Nalco Chem Co, 77-80; SUPVR RES SERV, INST GAS TECHNOL, 80- *Concurrent Pos:* Res assoc, Chem Dept, Loyola Univ, 80- *Mem:* Am Chem Soc; Soc Appl Spectros. *Res:* Method development, analytical trouble shooting and analytical basic reseach in fields of energy research, environmental chemistry, trace element analysis, spectroscopy and separation science. *Mailing Add:* Inst Gas Technol 34224 S State St Chicago IL 60616

CHAO, TAI SIANG, b Yangchow, China, Sept 26, 19; US citizen; m 49; c 3. CHEMICAL ENGINEERING, ORGANIC CHEMISTRY. *Educ:* Nat Cent Univ, Chungking, BS, 41; Purdue Univ, MS, 49, PhD(chem eng), 53. *Prof Exp:* Engr, Chungking Battery Plant, Cent Elec Mfg Works, China, 41-47; res assoc chem, Purdue Univ, 53-55; sr res chemist, Archer Daniels Midland Co, 55-61; res chemist, Sinclair Res, Inc, Div Sinclair Oil Corp, 61-69, sr res chemist, 69-74, res assoc, 74-78, SR RES ASSOC, ATLANTIC RICHFIELD CO, 79- *Concurrent Pos:* Wright Air Develop Ctr fel, Purdue Univ, 53-54; Off Naval Res fel, 54-55. *Mem:* Am Chem Soc; fel Am Inst Chemists. *Res:* Engine oils and synthetic lubricants, gasoline, distillates and heavy fuels; additives for lubricants and fuels, especially antioxidants, flow improvers, friction modifiers, organic phosphorus, nitrogen, fluorine and silicon compounds. *Mailing Add:* 2449 Troy Circle Olympia Fields IL 60461

CHAO, TSUN TIEN, b Anhwei, China, July 23, 18; US citizen; m 47; c 3. GEOCHEMISTRY, ANALYTICAL CHEMISTRY. *Educ:* Nat Cent Univ, China, BS, 42; Ore State Univ, MS, 59, PhD(soil chem), 60. *Prof Exp:* Jr soil chemist, Nat Agr Res Bur, China, 44-45, 46-48; assoc agronomist, Taiwan Sugar Exp Sta, 48-52, soil technologist, 52-56; res fel soil chem, Ore State Univ, 56-59, res assoc, 59-61, asst prof, 61-64; from assoc soil chemist to soil chemist, Pineapple Res Inst, 64-67; RES CHEMIST, US GEOL SURV, 66- *Mem:* Soil Sci Soc Am; Am Soc Agron; Geochem Soc; Am Chem Soc; AAAS. *Res:* Geochemistry of heavy metals in the weathering zone; research in methods of chemical analysis for geochemical exploration. *Mailing Add:* US Geol Surv Federal Ctr Denver CO 80225

CHAO, YU-SHENG, b China, Sept 1, 45; m 73; c 1. BIOCHEMISTRY. *Educ:* Nat Taiwan Univ, BS, 69; Univ Miami, MS, 74, PhD(biochem), 77. *Prof Exp:* Fel, Univ Calif, San Francisco, 77-80; SR RES BIOCHEMIST, MERCK SHARP & DOHME RES LAB, 80- *Concurrent Pos:* Mem, Am Heart Asn. *Res:* Effects of pharmacological agents on lipoprotein metabolism. *Mailing Add:* Merck Sharp & Dohme Res Lab Dept Biochem PO Box 2000 Rahway NJ 07065

CHAPARAS, SOTIROS D, b Lowell, Mass, May 4, 29; m 56; c 2. MICROBIOLOGY, IMMUNOLOGY. *Educ:* Northeastern Univ, BS, 51; Univ Mass, MS, 53; St Louis Univ, PhD(microbiol), 58; Am Bd Med Microbiol, dipl, 74. *Prof Exp:* Instr microbiol, Sch Med, St Louis Univ, 58-59; instr, Sch Med, Univ Southern Calif, 59-60; sr scientist, 60-68, DIR MYOBACT & FUNGAL ANTIGENS BR, BUR BIOLOGICS, FOOD & DRUG ADMIN, 68- *Concurrent Pos:* Assoc prof, Howard Univ, 62-; fac chmn microbiol & immunol, NIH, 62-; chmn sci assembly on microbiol & immunol, Am Thoracic Soc, 74-75; panel mem, US-Japan Tuberc Panel, US-Japan Med Coop Prog, 75-; chmn adv comt, Trudeau Inst, 78-; lectr, Med Sch, Univ Md, 80-; WHO consult tuberculosis, 81- *Honors & Awards:* Commendation Medal, USPHS, 72. *Res:* Pathogenicity, immunity and hypersensitivity in tuberculosis; standardization of skin test reagents; immunity in cancer; immunology of fungi. *Mailing Add:* Bur of Biologics Food & Drug Admin Bethesda MD 20205

CHAPAS, RICHARD BERNARD, b Cleveland, Ohio, Dec 5, 45; m 68; c 3. PHOTOGRAPHIC CHEMISTRY. *Educ:* St Vincent Col, BS, 68; Univ Ill, PhD(chem), 72. *Prof Exp:* sr res chemist, Eastman Kodak Co, 72-78; asst prof chem, Gordon Jr Col, Barnesville, Ga, 78-80; SR DEVELOP CHEMIST, JOHNSON & JOHNSON, 80- *Concurrent Pos:* Mem adj fac, Rochester Inst Technol, 73-78, Mercer County Community Col, 80- *Mem:* Am Chem Soc; Soc Photog Scientists & Engrs. *Res:* Photographic systems development and analysis; light sensitive materials production; medical devices product development. *Mailing Add:* 2 Standfort Ct East Windsor NJ 08520

CHAPATWALA, KIRIT D, b Surat, India; US citizen; m 77; c 1. HEAVY METAL TOXICITY. *Educ:* Gujarat Univ, India, BSc, 70; Miss State Univ, MS, 73, PhD(microbiol & biochem), 78. *Prof Exp:* Tech asst microbiol, Miss State Univ, 71-76, res asst, 72, 73 & 74, res fel, 78; asst prof, 78-80, ASSOC PROF BIOL & MICROBIOL, SELMA UNIV, 80- *Mem:* Am Soc Microbiol; Sigma Xi. *Res:* Effect of cadmium on renal and hepatic gluconeogenic and Adenosine Triphosphate enzymes; study the chemical composition of phage D-11 receptor sites on Mycobacterium phlei. *Mailing Add:* Dept Biol Selma Univ Selma AL 36701

CHAPEL, JAMES L, b Ont, Jan 1, 20; US citizen; m 52; c 3. CHILD PSYCHIATRY. *Educ:* Univ Toronto, MD, 54. *Prof Exp:* Assoc child psychiat, Univ Iowa Psychopath Hosp, 66; PROF PSYCHIAT & CHIEF SECT CHILD PSYCHIAT, COL MED, UNIV MO-COLUMBIA, 66- *Concurrent Pos:* Consult child psychiat, Bd Control, Iowa, 66; consult, Bd Training Schs, Mo, 67- & Boone & Calloway County Juv Courts, 67- *Mem:* Fel Am Col Psychiat; Am Psychiat Asn. *Res:* Diagnosis, evaluation and treatment of attention span deficit with hyperactivity; the biological and biochemical basis of abnormal behaviors of children. *Mailing Add:* Univ of Mo Med Ctr 807 Stadium Rd Columbia MO 65201

CHAPEL, RAYMOND EUGENE, b Marlow, Okla, Jan 31, 21; m 43; c 3. MECHANICAL ENGINEERING. *Educ:* Okla Agr & Mech Col, BS, 42, MS, 51. *Prof Exp:* From asst prof to assoc prof mech eng, 51-68, asst dir eng res, Off Eng Res, 65-67, PROF MECH & AEROSPACE ENG, OKLA STATE UNIV, 68-, ASSOC DIR ENG RES, OFF ENG RES, 67- *Mem:* Assoc fel Am Inst Aeronaut & Astronaut; Am Soc Eng Educ; Nat Soc Prof Engrs. *Res:* Machine analysis and design; aerospace structures. *Mailing Add:* Off of Eng Res Okla State Univ Stillwater OK 74074

CHAPERON, EDWARD ALFRED, b Burlington, Vt, Sept 24, 30; m 62; c 2. IMMUNOLOGY, MICROBIOLOGY. *Educ:* LeMoyne Col, BS, 57; Marquette Univ, MS, 59; Univ Wis-Madison, PhD(zool), 65. *Prof Exp:* NIH fel immunol, Med Ctr, Univ Colo, Denver, 65-68; asst prof, 68-71, ASSOC PROF MICROBIOL, SCH MED, CREIGHTON UNIV, 71- *Mem:* Am Asn Immunol; Am Soc Microbiol; Reticuloendothelial Soc. *Res:* Cellular immunology. *Mailing Add:* Dept of Med Microbiol Creighton Univ Sch of Med Omaha NE 68178

CHAPIN, CHARLES EDWARD, b Porterville, Calif, Oct 25, 32; m 58; c 3. GEOLOGY. *Educ:* Colo Sch Mines, Geol Engr, 54, DSc(geochem), 65. *Prof Exp:* Asst prof geol, Univ Tulsa, 64-65; asst prof, NMex Inst Mining & Technol, 65-68, assoc prof & head geosci dept, 68-70; geologist, 70-76, SR GEOLOGIST, NMEX BUR MINES, 76- *Concurrent Pos:* Adj prof geosci, NMex Inst Mining & Technol, 70- *Honors & Awards:* Van Diest Gold Medal, Colo Sch Mines, 80. *Mem:* Geol Soc Am; Soc Econ Paleontologists & Mineralogists; Am Geophys Union. *Res:* Volcanology; mineral deposits; tectonics. *Mailing Add:* NMex Bur of Mines Socorro NM 87801

CHAPIN, DAVID LAMBERT, b Detroit, Mich, May 24, 48; US citizen. NUCLEAR ENGINEERING. *Educ:* Univ Mich, BSE, 70, MSE, 71, PhD(nuclear eng), 74. *Prof Exp:* Researcher fusion reactors, Princeton Plasma Physics Lab, NJ, 74-76; RESEARCHER FUSION REACTORS, WESTINGHOUSE ELEC CORP, 76- *Mem:* Am Nuclear Soc; Am Phys Soc; Sigma Xi. *Res:* Controlled fusion reactor design, especially related to computational nuclear engineering and systems studies. *Mailing Add:* 49 Roycroft Ave Pittsburgh PA 15228

CHAPIN, DOUGLAS SCOTT, b Muskegon, Mich, July 14, 22; m 44; c 4. PHYSICAL CHEMISTRY. *Educ:* Kans State Col, BS, 44; Ill Inst Technol, MS, 48; Ohio State Univ, PhD(chem), 54. *Prof Exp:* Researcher, Nat Bur Standards, 47; asst, Cryogenic Lab, Ohio State Univ, 48-51; sr cryogenic oper, Herrick L Johnston, Inc, 52; asst, Cryogenic Lab, Ohio State Univ, 53-54; cryogenic engr, Herrick L Johnston, Inc, 54; from asst prof to assoc prof chem, Univ Ariz, 54-66; assoc prog dir grad fels & traineeships, 66-68; prog dir, 68-73; head fels & traineeships sect, 73-77, dir fac oriented progs, 77-78, STAFF ASSOC, SCI PERSONNEL IMPROV DIV, NAT SCI FOUND, 78- *Concurrent Pos:* Staff mem, Lincoln Lab, Mass Inst Technol, 63-64. *Mem:* AAAS; Faraday Soc; Am Chem Soc. *Res:* Low temperature kinetics; ortho-parahydrogen catalysis; separation of ortho-parahydrogen; low temperature thermodynamics of gases absorbed on solids; solid state chemistry of transition metal oxides. *Mailing Add:* Div Sci Personnel Improv Nat Sci Found Washington DC 20550

CHAPIN, EARL CONE, b Farmington, Ill, Feb 5, 19; m 45; c 3. ORGANIC CHEMISTRY. *Educ:* Univ Ill, BS, 41; Pa State Univ, MS, 42, PhD(org chem), 44. *Prof Exp:* Res chemist, Monsanto Chem Co, 44-50, res group leader, 51-62; chmn dept phys sci, 62-68, dean sch arts & sci, 68-74, PROF CHEM, WESTERN NEW ENGLAND COL, 62- *Mem:* Am Chem Soc. *Res:* Synthetic polymers; organic synthesis. *Mailing Add:* Sch of Arts & Sci Western New England Col Springfield MA 01119

CHAPIN, EDWARD WILLIAM, JR, b Baltimore, Md, May 28, 43. MATHEMATICAL LOGIC. *Educ:* Trinity Col, Conn, BS, 65; Princeton Univ, MA, 67, PhD(math), 69. *Prof Exp:* asst prof math, Univ Notre Dame, 69-77; CHMN MATH & COMPUT SCI, UNIV MD, EASTERN SHORE, 77- *Mem:* AAAS; Am Math Soc; Math Asn Am; Asn Symbolic Logic; Soc Indust & Appl Math. *Res:* Algebraic structure of deductive systems; non-standard measure theory; stochastic models of set theory; modal logic. *Mailing Add:* Rte 1 Box 81-B Firetower Rd Hebron MD 21830

CHAPIN, F STUART, III, b Portland, Ore, Feb 2, 44; m 66; c 2. PLANT ECOLOGY. *Educ:* Swarthmore Col, BA, 66; Stanford Univ, PhD(biol), 73. *Prof Exp:* Vis instr biol, Univ Javeriana, Colombia, 66-68; instr biol, Stanford Univ, 69-73; asst prof, 73-78, ASSOC PROF PLANT PHYSIOL ECOL, UNIV ALASKA, 78- *Concurrent Pos:* Guggenheim fel, 79-80. *Mem:* Am Ecol Soc; Brit Ecol Soc; Scand Soc Plant Physiol. *Res:* Plant nutritional ecology; nutrient absorption and allocation; root growth; adaptations of arctic and taiga plants to low temperature and nutrient availability; plant responses to grazing; nutrient cycling. *Mailing Add:* Inst of Arctic Biol Univ of Alaska Fairbanks AK 99701

CHAPIN, HENRY J(ACOB), b Scranton, Pa, May 26, 08; m 42; c 2. METALLURGY. *Educ:* Haverford Col, BS, 29; Mass Inst Technol, BS, 32. *Prof Exp:* Metallurgist, Am Brake Co, 42-58, sr metallurgist, 58-65; sr metallurgist, Abex Inc, 65-73; RETIRED. *Concurrent Pos:* With Off Sci Res & Develop, 44; consult, 73- *Mem:* Am Welding Soc; Am Soc Metals. *Res:* Ferrous metallurgy; manganese steel; abrasion resistant steels and irons. *Mailing Add:* 61 Oweno Rd Mahwah NJ 07430

CHAPIN, JOAN BEGGS, b St Louis, Mo, Feb 8, 29; div; c 3. SYSTEMATICS. *Educ:* Kans State Univ, BS, 50; La State Univ, MS, 59, PhD(entom), 71. *Prof Exp:* From res asst to asst prof, 57-77, ASSOC PROF, DEPT ENTOM, LA STATE UNIV, 77- *Mem:* Entom Soc Am; Sigma Xi; Coleopterists Soc. *Res:* Taxonomy of beneficial and economic pest insects which occur in Louisiana and the surrounding region; coccinellidae systematics. *Mailing Add:* Dept Entom La State Univ Baton Rouge LA 70803

CHAPIN, JOHN LADNER, b New York, NY, Sept 1, 16; m 50; c 3. RESPIRATORY PHYSIOLOGY. *Educ:* Denison Univ, AB, 39; Univ Rochester, PhD(physiol), 50. *Prof Exp:* Instr physiol, Sch Med, La State Univ, 50; from instr to asst prof, Sch Med, Univ Colo, 51-65; PROF PHYSIOL, INST CHILD STUDY, UNIV MD, COLLEGE PARK, 65- *Mem:* AAAS; Am Ornithologists Union; Am Physiol Soc; NY Acad Sci; Am Inst Biol Sci. *Res:* Respiratory and environmental physiology; man and his environment; physical aspects of human development. *Mailing Add:* 2400 Parker Ave Wheaton MD 20902

CHAPLER, CHRISTOPHER KEITH, b Des Moines, Iowa, July 19, 40; m 61; c 3. MEDICAL PHYSIOLOGY. *Educ:* Drake Univ, BA, 62, MA, 64; Univ Fla, PhD(physiol), 67. *Prof Exp:* Can Heart Found fel, 67; from asst prof to assoc prof, 68-79, PROF PHYSIOL, QUEEN'S UNIV, ONT, 79- *Mem:* Am Physiol Soc; Can Physiol Soc; Can Fedn Biol Sci; Fedn Am Soc Exp Biol. *Res:* Muscle metabolism; cardiovascular physiology. *Mailing Add:* Dept Physiol Queen's Univ Kingston ON K7L 3N6 Can

CHAPLIN, FRANK S(PRAGUE), b Nova Scotia, May 14, 10; nat US; m 39; c 4. MECHANICAL ENGINEERING. *Educ:* Mass Inst Technol, BS, 32. *Prof Exp:* Stress analyst rail car eng, E G Budd Mfg Co, Pa, 34-39, chief of stress, 39-42 & aviation div, 42-43; prin engr, Artil Div, Off Chief Ord, 43-45; sect chief friction & ballistics res, Franklin Inst Labs, 45-48, assoc dir mech eng, 49-58; CONSULT MECH DEVELOP, 58- *Mem:* Am Soc Mech Engrs; Soc Exp Stress Anal; Nat Soc Prof Engrs. *Res:* Friction and lubrication; structures; machine development; planetariums; towers. *Mailing Add:* Rte 2 Box 290A Blounts Creek NC 27814

CHAPLIN, HUGH, JR, b New York, NY, Feb 4, 23; m 45; c 4. MEDICINE. *Educ:* Princeton Univ, AB, 43; Columbia Univ, MD, 47. *Prof Exp:* From intern to resident, Mass Gen Hosp, 47-50; physician in chg, Clin Ctr Blood Bank, NIH, 53-55; from instr to asst prof, 55-62, dir student health serv, 56-57, assoc dean, Med Sch, 57-63, assoc prof & dir, Johnson Insts Rehab, 64-65, PROF MED & PREV MED & KOUNTZ PROF PREV MED, MED SCH, WASH UNIV, 65- *Concurrent Pos:* Fel, Brit Postgrad Med Sch, London, 51-53; Nat Inst Arthritis & Metab Dis trainee, Med Sch, Wash Univ, 55-56; Commonwealth Fund res fel, Wright-Fleming Inst, London, 62-63, Josiah Macy Scholar, 75-76; mem, Am Bd Internal Med, 56. *Mem:* Am Soc Hematol; Am Soc Clin Invest; Asn Am Physicians; Royal Soc Med. *Res:* Hematology; secondary hemolytic anemia. *Mailing Add:* 159 Linden Ave St Louis MO 63105

CHAPLIN, JAMES FERRIS, b Lamar, SC, Nov 10, 20; m 45; c 2. GENETICS. *Educ:* Clemson Univ, BS, 48; NC State Col, MS, 52, PhD(plant breeding, genetics), 59. *Prof Exp:* Asst agronomist, Clemson Col, 48-57; res agronomist, Pee Dee Exp Sta, 57-65, sr scientist, Oxford Tobacco Res Lab, 65-67, leader tobacco breeding & dis invests, Plant Sci Res Div, 67-72, DIR, OXFORD TOBACCO RES LAB, USDA, 72-; PROF CROP SCI, NC STATE UNIV, 65- *Honors & Awards:* Award for Distinguished Contrib to Tobacco Sci, Coop Ctr Sci Res Relating to Tobacco. *Mem:* Fel Am Soc Agron; Am Genetics Asn. *Res:* Tobacco breeding and genetics for disease resistance, chemical constituents and agronomic characteristics. *Mailing Add:* USDA Tobacco Res Lab Agr Res Serv Southern Region Oxford NC 27565

CHAPLIN, MICHAEL H, b Olney, Ill, Aug 22, 43; m 65; c 1. PLANT PHYSIOLOGY, NUTRITION. *Educ:* Univ Ky, BS, 65; Rutgers Univ, MS, 66; Mich State Univ, PhD(hort), 68. *Prof Exp:* DIR PLANT ANAL LAB & ASSOC PROF HORT, ORE STATE UNIV, 68- *Mem:* Am Soc Hort Sci. *Res:* Nutritional status of economic crops as it affects quality, yield and maturation processes. *Mailing Add:* Dept of Hort Ore State Univ Corvallis OR 97331

CHAPLIN, NORMAN JOHN, b Hamilton, Ont, Oct 10, 18; US citizen; m 42; c 2. SOLID STATE PHYSICS, ELECTRONICS. *Educ:* Univ Toronto, BASc, 49, MASc, 50. *Prof Exp:* Mem tech staff, Can Radio Mfg Corp, 52-56; mem tech staff, Bell Labs, 56-80; RETIRED. *Mem:* Inst Elec & Electronics Engrs. *Res:* Solidification of alloys; semiconductor devices; reliability physics; integrated circuits; spectrochemical analysis. *Mailing Add:* 3155 South Dr Allentown PA 18103

CHAPLIN, ROBERT LEE, JR, b Savannah, Ga, Mar 22, 23; m 56; c 1. PHYSICS. *Educ:* Clemson Univ, BS, 48; NC State Col, MS, 53, PhD(physics), 62. *Prof Exp:* Instr physics, NC State Col, 56-60; res asst, Univ NC, 60-61, fel, 61-62; from asst prof to assoc prof, 62-74, PROF PHYSICS, CLEMSON UNIV, 74- *Concurrent Pos:* Res partic, Oak Ridge Nat Lab, 63, 74 & 76. *Mem:* Sigma Xi; Am Phys Soc. *Res:* Defect state of metal crystals as produced by electron irradiation damage and removed by thermal annealing. *Mailing Add:* Dept Physics Clemson Univ Clemson SC 29631

CHAPLIN, SUSAN BUDD, b Los Angeles, Calif, Nov 12, 46; m 73; c 1. PHYSIOLOGY. *Educ:* Occidental Col, AB, 68; Cornell Univ, PhD(physiol), 73. *Prof Exp:* Res assoc agr eng, Cornell Univ, 73-74; asst prof biol, Occidental Col, 74-75; ASST PROF BIOL SCI, UNIV MO-COLUMBIA, 75- *Mem:* Cooper Ornith Soc; Am Soc Zoologists; Am Physiol Soc; Sigma Xi. *Res:* Physiological ecology; thermoregulation of vertebrates and insects; energy budgets; overwintering physiology of birds and insects. *Mailing Add:* Div of Biol Sci Tucker Hall Univ of Mo Columbia MO 65201

CHAPLINE, GEORGE FREDERICK, JR, theoretical physics, theoretical astrophysics, see previous edition

CHAPLINE, WILLIAM RIDGELY, (JR), b Lincoln, Nebr, Jan 10, 91; m 21; c 2. RANGE MANAGEMENT, FORESTRY. *Educ:* Univ Nebr, BS. *Prof Exp:* Grazing asst, US Forest Serv, 13-14, examr grazing, 15-20, from inspector to sr inspector in charge grazing res, 20-35, chief div range res, 35-52; chief forest conserv sect, Food & Agr Orgn, UN, Rome, 52-54; prof int course on pastures, Inst Interam Agr Sci, Montevideo, 54-55; consult, Ministry Agr, Arg & Chile, 55, Inst Interam Agr Sci, Peru, 55 & Govt of Spain, 56-57; consult watershed mgt, Charles Lathrop Pack Forestry Found, 57-59; CONSULT, 59- *Concurrent Pos:* Spec investr, USDA, 17-18; consult, Civilian Conserv Corp, 34-36, US Navy, 44, Forest Serv, USDA, 67-69, Am Univ African Drought Proj, 74- & Vols Int Tech Assistance; coordr spec course, Colo State Univ, 67. *Honors & Awards:* Cert Merit, Soc Range Mgt, 67. *Mem:* AAAS; Soc Foresters; Soc Range Mgt; hon mem Grassland Soc Southern Africa. *Res:* Forest, range and watershed management; ecology; range plants; livestock production; erosion control; range re-seeding; worldwide rangeland management and improvement. *Mailing Add:* 4225 43rd St NW Washington DC 20016

CHAPMAN, ALAN J(ESSE), b Los Angeles, Calif, June 22, 25; m 50; c 2. MECHANICAL ENGINEERING. *Educ:* Rice Inst, BS, 45; Univ Colo, MS, 49; Univ Ill, PhD(mech eng), 53. *Prof Exp:* From instr to assoc prof mech eng, 46-58, assoc prof, 55-63 & 64-69, vpres admin, 69-70, dean eng, 75-80, PROF MECH ENG, RICE UNIV, 58- *Concurrent Pos:* Consult, Anderson-Greenwood & Co, 54-, Manned Spacecraft Ctr, NASA, Houston, 63- & Shell Develop Co, 63- *Mem:* Fel Am Soc Mech Engrs; assoc fel Am Inst Aeronaut & Astronaut; Am Soc Eng Educ. *Res:* Heat transfer; fluid dynamics. *Mailing Add:* Dept of Mech Eng Rice Univ PO Box 1892 Houston TX 77001

CHAPMAN, ALAN T, b Columbus, Ohio, Nov 20, 29; m 53; c 3. CERAMIC ENGINEERING. *Educ:* Rutgers Univ, BS, 51; Ohio State Univ, MS, 57, PhD(ceramic eng), 60. *Prof Exp:* Res assoc ceramics, Ohio State Univ, 55-60; ceramic engr, Oak Ridge Nat Lab, Union Carbide Nuclear Co, 60-65; assoc prof ceramic eng, 65-76, HOOD PROF CERAMIC ENG, GA INST TECHNOL, 76- *Concurrent Pos:* Traveling lectr, Oak Ridge Inst Nuclear

Studies, 63-64. *Honors & Awards:* B Mifflin Hood Chair of Ceramics. *Mem:* Am Ceramic Soc. *Res:* Phase relations in ceramic materials for nuclear applications and single crystal growth of nonmetallic materials. *Mailing Add:* Sch of Ceramic Eng Ga Inst of Technol Atlanta GA 30322

CHAPMAN, ALBERT LEE, b Anderson, Mo, Nov 5, 33; m 56; c 4. ANATOMY. *Educ:* Univ Mo, AB, 56, MS, 59; Univ Nebr, PhD(anat), 62. *Prof Exp:* From instr to assoc prof, 62-74, PROF ANAT, UNIV KANS MED CTR, KANSAS CITY, 74- *Concurrent Pos:* Spec fel, Viral Lymphoma & Leukemia Br, Nat Cancer Inst, 69- *Mem:* Am Asn Anat; AAAS; NY Acad Sci; Soc Exp Biol & Med; Electron Micros Soc Am. *Res:* Electron microscopic studies of lymphatic tissues, especially leukemic tissue and virus. *Mailing Add:* Dept of Anat Univ Kans Med Ctr Kansas City KS 66103

CHAPMAN, ARTHUR BARCLAY, b Windermere, Eng, Oct 25, 08; nat US; m 34; c 3. GENETICS, ANIMAL BREEDING. *Educ:* State Col Wash, BS, 30; Iowa State Col, MS, 31; Univ Wis, PhD(genetics), 35. *Prof Exp:* Asst genetics, Univ Wis, 31-36; Nat Res fel agr, Iowa State Col & Chicago, 36-37; from instr to prof genetics, 37-75, EMER PROF GENETICS, UNIV WIS-MADISON, 75- *Concurrent Pos:* Rockefeller Found res & teaching award, Poland, 60; Fulbright & Guggenheim Mem Found fels, NZ, 66-67 & Midwest Univ Consortium Int Activities-AID, Indonesia, 73; vis prof, Cairo Univ, Egypt, 77. *Honors & Awards:* Animal Breeding & Genetics Award, Am Soc Animal Sci, 68, Morrison Award, 74. *Mem:* Fel AAAS; Biomet Soc; Genetics Soc Am; fel Am Soc Animal Sci (vpres, 63-64, pres, 64-65); Am Dairy Sci Asn. *Res:* Animal breeding; genetic effects of irradiation. *Mailing Add:* 1117 Risser Rd Madison WI 53705

CHAPMAN, ARTHUR OWEN, b Heber, Utah, Mar 16, 13; m 41; c 2. HISTOLOGY, PATHOLOGY. *Educ:* Brigham Young Univ, AB, 41; Univ Kans, MA, 49; Univ Nebr, PhD(med sci), 53. *Prof Exp:* Asst instr zool, Univ Kans, 46-47, asst instr anat, 47-49; instr, Col Med, Univ Nebr, 49-53, asst prof, 53-59; assoc prof, 59-67, prof, 67-80, EMER PROF ZOOL, BRIGHAM YOUNG UNIV, 80- *Mem:* Am Asn Anatomists. *Res:* Nervous system; irradiation effects on the brain and on embryos; thiamin deficiency and mercury effects on the brain. *Mailing Add:* Dept of Zool 259 WIDB Brigham Young Univ Provo UT 84601

CHAPMAN, CARL JOSEPH, b New York, NY, July 4, 39; m 65. SYSTEMATIC BOTANY. *Educ:* Univ NH, BS, 61, PhD(bot), 65. *Prof Exp:* Fel, Univ NH, 65; instr bot, Univ RI, 65-66; res assoc, Univ Fla, 66-67; from asst prof to assoc prof biol, 67-77, PROF BIOL, CONCORD COL, 77- *Mem:* Bot Soc Am; Sigma Xi. *Res:* Floristic studies; scanning electron microscopy studies of fern spores. *Mailing Add:* Dept of Biol Concord Col Athens WV 24712

CHAPMAN, CARLETON ABRAMSON, b Groveton, NH, Oct 14, 11; m 40; c 1. GEOLOGY. *Educ:* Univ NH, BS, 33; Harvard Univ, AM, 35, PhD(petrog), 37. *Prof Exp:* Asst petrog, Harvard Univ, 34-35, instr, 35-37; instr geol, 37-39, assoc, 39-42, from asst prof to assoc prof, 45-48, PROF GEOL, UNIV ILL, URBANA-CHAMPAIGN, 48- *Mem:* AAAS; fel Geol Soc Am; fel Mineral Soc Am; Am Geochem Soc; fel Geol Soc London. *Res:* Petrology; igneous and metamorphic geology; mineralogy; structural geology. *Mailing Add:* Dept of Geol Univ of Ill Urbana IL 61801

CHAPMAN, CARLETON BURKE, b Sycamore, Ala, June 11, 15; m 40; c 3. MEDICINE. *Educ:* Davidson Col, AB, 36; Oxford Univ, BS, 38; Harvard Univ, MD, 41, MPH, 44; Am Bd Internal Med, dipl, 48; Am Bd Cardiovasc Dis, 53. *Hon Degrees:* MA, Dartmouth Col, 68; LLD, Davidson Col, 68. *Prof Exp:* From intern to resident med, Boston City Hosp, Mass, 41-44; from instr to asst prof med, Med Sch, Univ Minn, 47-53; prof, Southwestern Med Sch, Univ Tex, 53-66; dean, Dartmouth Med Sch, 66-73, vpres, 72-73; pres, Commonwealth Fund, New York, 73-80; PROF HIST MED, ALBERT EINSTEIN COL MED, BRONX, 80- *Concurrent Pos:* Rockefeller Found fel, Sch Pub Health, Harvard Univ, 44; asst, Harvard Med Sch, 43; consult, Surgeon-Gen, US Army, 44 & US Vet Admin, 47-; fel, Coun Clin Cardiol, Am Heart Asn. *Mem:* AAAS; Am Acad Arts & Sci; Am Soc Clin Invest; fel Am Col Cardiol; Am Heart Asn (pres, 64-65). *Res:* Cardiovascular disease; morals and ethics of bioscience and medicine. *Mailing Add:* Thetford VT 05074

CHAPMAN, CHARLES R, ecology, deceased

CHAPMAN, CLARK RUSSELL, b Palo Alto, Calif, May 13, 45; m 66; c 1. PLANETARY SCIENCES. *Educ:* Harvard Col, AB, 67; Mass Inst Technol, MS, 68, PhD(planetary sci), 72. *Prof Exp:* Res scientist astrosci, Res Inst, Ill Inst Technol, 71-72; RES SCIENTIST, PLANETARY SCI INST, SCI APPLN, INC, 72- *Concurrent Pos:* Consult, Task Group Mercury Nomenclature, Int Astron Union, 74-75 & Lunar Sci Inst Coun, Univ Space Res Asn, 75-78; mem sci adv group inner solar syst, NASA, 75-77; mem, Lunar Sci Rev Panel, 75-77, 80-81; mem organizing comt Comn 15, Int Astron Union, 76-, vpres, 79-82, mem, Comns 16 & 17, 77-; mem comt planetary explor, Nat Acad Sci, 77-80; assoc ed, J Geophys Res, 76-78; mem, Infrared Telescope Opers Working Group, NASA, 81-84. *Mem:* AAAS; Am Astron Soc; Am Geophys Union; Meteoritical Soc. *Res:* Spectrophotometry of planets, satellites, asteroids and compositional interpretation; analysis of telescopic and spacecraft imagery of planetary atmospheres and surfaces; cratering and impact-erosional processes; planetary accretion; Jupiter's atmospheric circulation; comparative planetology. *Mailing Add:* 6160 N Montebella Tucson AZ 85704

CHAPMAN, DAVID J, b Kingston, WI, Dec 12, 39; m 63; c 1. PLANT BIOCHEMISTRY, PHYCOLOGY. *Educ:* Univ Auckland, BSc, 60; Univ Calif, PhD(marine biol), 65. *Hon Degrees:* DSc, Univ Auckland, 79. *Prof Exp:* Res assoc marine biol, Scripps Inst, Calif, 65-66; res assoc biol, Brookhaven Nat Lab, 66-67; asst prof, Univ Chicago, 68-73; assoc prof, 73-78, PROF BIOL, UNIV CALIF, LOS ANGELES, 78- *Concurrent Pos:* Ger Acad Exchange award, Univ Saarlandes, 70; distnguished vis scientist, Nat Res Coun Can, 79-80. *Mem:* Am Chem Soc; Linnean Soc London; Am Soc Plant Physiol; Bot Soc Am; Phycol Soc Am. *Res:* Phycology, algal, chloroplast and natural product biochemistry; chemical taxonomy, phylogeny. *Mailing Add:* Dept of Biol Univ of Calif Los Angeles CA 90024

CHAPMAN, DAVID MACLEAN, b Thunder Bay, Ont, Jan 3, 35. ANATOMY, ZOOLOGY. *Educ:* Univ Man, BSc, 59, MSc, 61; Univ Cambridge, PhD(zool), 64. *Prof Exp:* PROF ANAT, MED COL, DALHOUSIE UNIV, 64- *Mem:* Can Soc Zool; Marine Biol Asn UK. *Res:* Electron microscopy of cnidarians. *Mailing Add:* Dept of Anat Dalhousie Univ Halifax Can

CHAPMAN, DEAN R(ODEN), aeronautical engineering, see previous edition

CHAPMAN, DEREK D, b Lincoln, Eng, Feb 13, 32; m 58; c 2. ORGANIC CHEMISTRY. *Educ:* Univ Nottingham, BSc, 53, PhD(org chem), 56. *Prof Exp:* Lectr chem, SE Essex Tech Col, Eng, 60-61; sr res chemist, 62-66, RES ASSOC, EASTMAN KODAK CO, 66- *Concurrent Pos:* Fel, Univ Rochester, 56-59, Hull Univ, 59-60 & Univ Rochester, 61-62. *Mem:* Am Chem Soc; Soc Chem Indust; Brit Chem Soc. *Res:* Synthesis of alkaloids; structure determination of antibiotics; synthesis of photographically useful compounds. *Mailing Add:* 7 Andony Rochester NY 14624

CHAPMAN, DOUGLAS GEORGE, b Provost, Alta, Mar 20, 20; nat US; m 43; c 3. BIOMETRICS. *Educ:* Univ Sask, BA, 39; Univ Calif, MA, 40, PhD(math), 49; Univ Toronto, MA, 44. *Prof Exp:* Meteorologist, Meteorol Serv Can, 41-46; asst prof math, Univ BC, 46-48; asst math statist, Univ Calif, 48-49; from asst prof to prof math, 49-68, dir ctr quantitative sci, 68-71, DEAN COL FISHERIES, UNIV WASH, 71- *Concurrent Pos:* Guggenheim fel, Oxford Univ, 54-55; vis prof, NC State Univ, 58-59 & Univ Calif, San Diego, 63-64; adv NPac Fur Seal Comn, 59-; chmn spec study group, Int Whaling Comn, 61-64, sci comn, 65-74; mem, Wash State Census Bur, 65-68; mem comn nat statist, Nat Acad Sci, 71-74 & ocean affairs bd, 72-76; chmn comn sci adv, Marine Mammal Comn, 76- *Mem:* Fel Inst Math Statist; Biomet Soc; fel Am Statist Asn; Am Fisheries Soc; AAAS. *Res:* Mathematical statistics theory; population estimation; population dynamics. *Mailing Add:* Col of Fisheries Univ of Wash Seattle WA 98195

CHAPMAN, DOUGLAS WILFRED, b Can, Sept 21, 21; nat US; m 53; c 2. ORGANIC CHEMISTRY. *Educ:* Univ Calif, BS, 48; Mass Inst Technol, PhD(chem), 51. *Prof Exp:* Res chemist, 51-65, RES ASSOC, MALLINCKRODT INC, 65- *Mem:* Am Chem Soc. *Res:* Organic synthesis; cosmetic pigments; x-ray contrast media. *Mailing Add:* 48 Greendale Dr St Louis MO 63121

CHAPMAN, FLOYD BARTON, b Zaleski, Ohio, Apr 1, 11. HORTICULTURE. *Educ:* Ohio State Univ, AB, 32, AM, 33, PhD(zool), 38. *Prof Exp:* Asst bot, Ohio State Univ, 32-35; field ecologist, State Div Conserv, Ohio, 35-38, game mgt technician, 38-40; asst biologist, Fish & Wildlife Serv, US Dept Interior, 40-42; forest game technician, State Div Wildlife, Ohio, 45-47, from asst chief to assoc chief game sect, 47-57; res ecologist, Malabar Farm, Friends of the Land, Ohio, 58-63; horticulturist, Adjunctive Ther Dept, Harding Hosp Ohio, 63-78; HORTICULTURIST, INNISWOOD GARDENS METRO PARK, 78- *Mem:* Am Soc Mammal; Am Rock Garden Soc; Am Hort Soc; fel Royal Hort Soc. *Res:* Ecology of white-tailed deer, tree squirrels and ruffed grouse; ecology of forest game animals; nature interpretation; environmental ecology; seed germination in alpine plants. *Mailing Add:* 392 Walhalla Rd Columbus OH 43202

CHAPMAN, GARY ADAIR, b Corvallis, Ore, Aug 30, 37; m 60; c 2. AQUATIC BIOLOGY, WATER POLLUTION. *Educ:* Ore State Univ, BSc, 59, MSc, 65, PhD(fisheries), 69. *Prof Exp:* Agr res technician, USDA, 60-62; FISHERIES BIOLOGIST, US ENVIRON PROTECTION AGENCY, 68- *Honors & Awards:* Superior Serv Medal, US Environ Protection Agency, 72, Except Serv Medal, 76. *Mem:* Am Fisheries Soc; Sigma Xi; Soc Environ Toxicol & Chem; AAAS; Am Soc Testing & Mat. *Res:* Pollution effects on aquatic organisms; salmonid biology and toxicity bioassays; chemistry and toxicity of heavy metals in water. *Mailing Add:* Western Fish Toxicol Sta 1350 SE Goodnight Ave Corvallis OR 97330

CHAPMAN, GARY ALLEN, b Bryan, Tex, Mar 25, 38; m 62; c 1. SOLAR PHYSICS. *Educ:* Univ Ariz, BS, 60, PhD(astron), 68. *Prof Exp:* Asst astronr, Univ Hawaii, 68-69; mem tech staff solar physics, Aerospace Corp, 69-77; assoc prof, 77-80, PROF ASTROPHYSICS, CALIF STATE UNIV, NORTHRIDGE, 80-, DIR, SAN FERNANDO OBSERV, 79- *Mem:* AAAS; Am Astron Soc; Am Phys Soc; Sigma Xi; Int Astron Union. *Res:* Fine structure of solar magnetic fields and solar faculae, the effect of faculae on solar oblateness measurements, solar spectroscopy and photometry. *Mailing Add:* Dept of Physics & Astron 18111 Nordhoff St Northridge CA 91330

CHAPMAN, GARY THEODORE, b Elmwood, Wis, Apr 28, 34; m 56; c 4. FLUID MECHANICS, AERODYNAMICS. *Educ:* Univ Minn, BA, 57; Stanford Univ, MS, 63, PhD(aeronaut, astronaut), 70. *Prof Exp:* Res scientist fluid mech, 57-71, res scientist aerodyn, 71-73, chief aerodyn res br, 74-78, STAFF SCIENTIST FLUID MECH, AMES RES CTR, NASA, 78- *Concurrent Pos:* Vis prof aerodyn, Iowa State Univ, 73-74, proj scientist, 79-81. *Mem:* AAAS; Am Inst Aeronaut & Astronaut; Am Soc Eng Educ; Sigma Xi. *Res:* Basic fluid mechanics; viscous flows including separation; vortices and turbulence; bodies and winged bodies at high angles of attack and flow modeling. *Mailing Add:* M S 20ZA-1 NASA Ames Res Ctr Moffett Field CA 94035

CHAPMAN, GEORGE BUNKER, b Bayonne, NJ, June 10, 25. CYTOLOGY. *Educ:* Princeton Univ, AB, 50, AM, 52, PhD, 53. *Prof Exp:* Asst instr biol, Princeton Univ, 50-52, asst res, 52-53, res assoc, 54-56; asst prof zool, Harvard, 56-60; assoc prof anat, Med Col, Cornell Univ, 60-63; PROF BIOL & CHMN DEPT, GEORGETOWN UNIV, 63- *Concurrent Pos:* Res biologist, Labs Div, Radio Corp of Am, 53-56. *Mem:* Am Soc Microbiol; Sigma Xi; Am Soc Microbiol. *Res:* Bacteriophagy; bacterial and general cytology; fine structure of human skin, eye, uterus, and gallbladder; electron microscopy of fish coelenterates and protozoa. *Mailing Add:* Dept of Biol Georgetown Univ Washington DC 20057

CHAPMAN, GEORGE DAVID, b Windsor, Ont, June 8, 40; m 72; c 2. OPTICAL PHYSICS, ATOMIC PHYSICS. *Educ:* Assumption Univ, BSc, 61; Univ Windsor, MSc, 64, PhD(physics), 65. *Prof Exp:* Overseas fel, Nat Res Coun, Oxford Univ, 65-67; res officer physics, 68-80, SR RES OFFICER PHYSICS, NAT RES COUN, 80- *Concurrent Pos:* Lectr, Carleton Univ, 70-71. *Mem:* Can Asn Physicists. *Res:* Holography; interferometry; optical data processing; quantum optics; atomic spectroscopy; level crossings; lifetimes. *Mailing Add:* Div of Physics Nat Res Coun Ottawa ON K1A 0R6 Can

CHAPMAN, GLENN WALLACE, JR, b Albany, Ga, Oct 12, 35; m 63; c 2. LIPID CHEMISTRY. *Educ:* Univ Ga, BS, 65, MS, 70. *Prof Exp:* Phys sci technician plant physiol, Agr Res Serv, USDA, Watkinsville, Ga, 65-67, biol lab technician, 67-72, chemist field crops & oil seeds, Athens, Ga, 71-76; RES CHEMIST OIL SEEDS, FED RES SERV, SOUTHERN REGION, RICHARD B RUSSELL RES CTR, 76- *Mem:* Am Oil Chemists' Soc. *Res:* The effect of storage conditions on chemical and microbial deterioration of hybrid sunflower seed; soybean lipase. *Mailing Add:* Richard B Russell Res Ctr PO Box 5677 Athens GA 30613

CHAPMAN, HAROLD CLYDE, b Kalamazoo, Mich, Dec 1, 21; m 44; c 4. ENTOMOLOGY. *Educ:* Mich State Univ, BS, 48, MS, 50; Rutgers Univ, PhD, 59. *Prof Exp:* Asst, Mich State Univ, 49-50; forest entomologist, Div Forest Insects, 50-51, med entomologist, Entom Res Div, Insects Affecting Man & Animals Res Br, Fla, 51-52, Nev, 58-61 & Calif, 61-64, location leader, sci & educ admin-agr res, 64-81, res leader & surv res entomologist, 76-81, COLLABR & CONSULT, GULF COAST MOSQUITO RES LAB, AGR RES SERV, USDA, 81- *Concurrent Pos:* Assoc, Rutgers Univ, 55-58. *Mem:* Soc Invert Path; Am Mosquito Control Asn (pres, 75-76). *Res:* Biological and ecological control research on mosquitoes. *Mailing Add:* USDA Gulf Coast Mosquito Res Lab Chennault Campus Lake Charles LA 70601

CHAPMAN, HERBERT L, JR, b Kansas City, Mo, July 15, 23; m 55; c 4. ANIMAL NUTRITION. *Educ:* Univ Fla, BSA, 48, MSA, 51; Iowa State Univ, PhD(animal nutrit), 55. *Prof Exp:* Asst animal husbandman, 51-53, from asst animal nutritionist to animal nutritionist, 55-65, prof animal sci, 65-80, ANIMAL NUTRITIONIST & DIR, AGR RES CTR, AGR EXP STA, UNIV FLA, 65- *Mem:* Fel AAAS; Am Soc Biol Sci; Am Registry Cert Animal Scientists; Am Soc Animal Sci. *Res:* Mineral requirement and interrelations in beef cattle; vitamin interrelations; nutritional requirements of all classes of beef cattle; pasture crop evaluation; chemical residues in beef cattle. *Mailing Add:* Agr Res Ctr Univ of Fla Ona FL 33865

CHAPMAN, JOE ALEXANDER, b Westpoint, Tenn, Oct 23, 19; m 41; c 3. PLANT ECOLOGY. *Educ:* Carson Newman Col, BS, 40; Peabody Col, MA, 47; Univ Tenn, PhD, 57. *Prof Exp:* High sch teacher, 41-42 & 42-44; from asst prof to assoc prof biol, 47-51, PROF BIOL & HEAD DEPT, CARSON NEWMAN COL, 53- *Concurrent Pos:* Pres, Appalachian Elec Coop, 79- *Mem:* AAAS; Ecol Soc Am; NY Acad Sci. *Res:* Taxonomy. *Mailing Add:* Carson Newman Col Jefferson City TN 37760

CHAPMAN, JOHN E, b Springfield, Mo, July 5, 31. PHARMACOLOGY. *Educ:* Southwest Mo State Col, BS(educ) & BS(biol, chem), 54; Univ Kans, MD, 58; Am Bd Clin Pharmacol, dipl. *Prof Exp:* Instr pharmacol, Med Ctr, Univ Kans, 61-62, asst prof, 62-67, asst acad dean, Med Sch, 63-65, assoc dean, 65-67; assoc dean educ, 67-72, actg dean, 72-73, actg vchancellor med affairs, 73-75, DEAN, VANDERBILT UNIV SCH MED, 75- *Concurrent Pos:* Chmn & bd dirs, Health Educ Media Asn, Coun Deans. *Mem:* Am Soc Pharmacol & Exp Therapeut; Am Col Clin Pharmacol (vpres & regent). *Res:* Role of humoral agents in central nervous system activity; medical school and medical center administration; medical education. *Mailing Add:* Sch of Med Vanderbilt Univ Nashville TN 37203

CHAPMAN, JOHN FRANKLIN, JR, b Oakdale, Calif, Apr 11, 45; m 68. CLINICAL BIOCHEMISTRY, LABORATORY MEDICINE. *Educ:* San Jose State Col, BA, 68; Calif State Univ, Fresno, MS, 72; Univ NC, Chapel Hill, MPH, 76, DrPH(lab practice), 78. *Prof Exp:* Pub health microbiologist, Fresno County Dept Health, 68-72, sr pub health microbiologist, 72-73, dir, Pub Health Labs, 73-75; fel clin chem, 78-79, ASST PROF PATH & ASSOC DIR CLIN CHEM, DEPT PATH, DIV LAB MED, UNIV NC, CHAPEL HILL, 79- *Mem:* Nat Acad Clin Biochem; Asn Clin Lab Physicians & Scientists; Asn Clin Scientists; Am Asn Clin Chem; Sigma Xi. *Res:* High resolution two dimensional electrophoresis in detection of tumor markers and other markers of disease; laboratory determination of amniotic fluid phospholipids in the detection of fetal lung maturity. *Mailing Add:* 31 Polks Landing Chapel Hill NC 27514

CHAPMAN, JOHN HERBERT, physics, deceased

CHAPMAN, JOHN JUDSON, b Valdosta, Ga, May 10, 18; m 47; c 4. GEOLOGY. *Educ:* Univ Ill, PhD(geol), 53. *Prof Exp:* Topog engr, US Geol Surv, 41-44 & 46-47; sr geologist, Creole Petrol Corp, 48-51; asst prof geol & head dept, Southern State Col, 53-57, prof geol & chmn div natural sci, 57-68; prof earth sci & head dept, 68-80, PROF GEOL, WEST CAROLINA UNIV, 80-; CONSULT PETROL GEOLOGIST, MAGNOLIA, ARK, 81- *Mem:* AAAS; Geol Soc Am; Am Asn Petrol Geologists; Nat Asn Geol Teachers; Am Inst Prof Geologists. *Res:* Physical stratigraphy; petroleum geology. *Mailing Add:* Dept of Earth Sci Western Carolina Univ Cullowhee NC 28723

CHAPMAN, JOHN S, b Sweetwater, Tex, Jan 30, 08; m 32; c 1. MEDICINE. *Educ:* Southern Methodist Univ, BA & BS, 27, MA, 28; Univ Tex, MD, 32. *Prof Exp:* Clin asst prof med, Univ Tenn, 43; clin asst, 43-45, from clin instr to clin assoc prof, 45-52, PROF MED, UNIV TEX HEALTH SCI CTR DALLAS, 52- Prof Exp: Tuberc consult, Vet Admin Hosp, Dallas, 46; civilian consult, Brooke Army Hosp, 64; consult, Bur Radiol Health & ETex Tuberc Hosp, Tyler; ed-in-chief, Arch Environ Health, AMA, 71-75. *Mem:* AAAS; Am Col Physicians; Am Thoracic Soc. *Res:* Eosinophilic leucocyte; mycobacteria; juvenile tuberculosis. *Mailing Add:* 5323 Harry Hines Blvd Dallas TX 75235

CHAPMAN, JOSEPH ALAN, b Salem, Ore, Apr 28, 42; m 78. WILDLIFE ECOLOGY. *Educ:* Ore State Univ, BS, 65, MS, 67, PhD(wildlife sci), 70. *Prof Exp:* Wildlife biologist, US Fish & Wildlife Serv, 65-67; res asst, Dept Fisheries & Wildlife, Ore State Univ, 67-69; fac res asst, Natural Resources Inst, Univ Md, 69-70, res asst prof, 70-74, res assoc prof & head, Appalachian Environ Lab, 74-78, PROF & HEAD, APPALACHIAN ENVIRON LAB & COL PARK STA, UNIV MD, 78- *Concurrent Pos:* Adj prof wildlife sci, Garrett Community Col, 73-; adj assoc prof biol, Frostburg State Col, 73-; guest lectr wildlife ecol, WVa Univ, Univ Md & Univ Ohio, 73- *Mem:* Wildlife Soc; Am Soc Mammalogists; Cooper Ornith Soc; Ecol Soc Am; Australian Wildlife Soc. *Mailing Add:* CEES Appalachian Environ Lab Univ of Md Frostburg MD 21532

CHAPMAN, JUDITH-ANNE WILLIAMS, b Timmins, Ont, Aug 17, 49; m; c 1. MEDICAL STATISTICS. *Educ:* Univ Waterloo, BS, 71, PhD(statist), 74. *Prof Exp:* Fel statist, 74-76, STATIST CONSULT CANCER RES, NAT CANCER INST CAN, UNIV WATERLOO, 76- *Mem:* Can Oncol Soc; Am Statist Asn; Can Statist Asn. *Res:* Use of statistics in analysing cancer mortality and incidence data; regional differences in Ontario; different statistics for significance tests; case-control study in bladder cancer. *Mailing Add:* 11 Dayman Ct Kitchener Can

CHAPMAN, KENNETH REGINALD, b Croydon, Eng, Apr 10, 24; m 46; c 5. EXPERIMENTAL NUCLEAR PHYSICS. *Educ:* Univ London, BSc, 50 & 51, MSc, 60, PhD(nuclear physics), 65. *Prof Exp:* Develop engr, Mullard Radio Valve Co, UK, 40-47; res demonstr physics, Univ Col, Univ Leicester, 51-56; res assoc, Univ Birmingham, 56-66; ACCELERATOR PHYSICIST, FLA STATE UNIV, 66- *Mem:* Brit Inst Physics; Brit Inst Elec Eng. *Res:* Accelerator and nuclear physics; ion source research; accelerator development. *Mailing Add:* Dept of Physics Fla State Univ Tallahassee FL 32306

CHAPMAN, KENT M, b Minneapolis, Minn, Oct 28, 28; m 51; c 4. BIOPHYSICS. *Educ:* Univ Minn, BA, 49, MS, 53, PhD(biophys), 62. *Prof Exp:* From asst prof to assoc prof physiol, Univ Alta, 58-65; chmn neurosci sect, Div Biol & Med Sci, 73-76, ASSOC PROF MED SCI, BROWN UNIV, 65- *Mem:* AAAS; Biophys Soc; Am Physiol Soc; Soc Neurosci. *Res:* Neurophysiology; sensory transduction and encoding; electrophysiology; insect mechanoreceptors; vertebrate cardiac mechanoreceptors. *Mailing Add:* Div of Biol & Med Box G Brown Univ Providence RI 02912

CHAPMAN, LLOYD WILLIAM, b Pasadena, Calif, Jan 5, 38; m 68; c 2. PHYSIOLOGY. *Educ:* Univ Calif, Los Angeles, BA, 61; Univ Southern Calif, PhD(physiol), 71. *Prof Exp:* From instr to asst prof physiol, Sch Med, Univ Southern Calif, 72-78; ASST PROF PHYSIOL, COL OSTEOP MED OF PAC, 78- *Concurrent Pos:* Consult, Medi Legal Inst, Los Angeles, 72-; vpres, Med Res Found Heart Dis, Los Angeles, 77-; res assoc, Cedars-Sinai Med Ctr, Los Angeles; res assoc, Univ Calif, Riverside. *Mem:* Assoc mem Am Physiol Soc. *Res:* Fluid and electrolyte balance; reflex regulation of circulation. *Mailing Add:* Col Osteop Med the Pac 309 Pomona Mall East Pomona CA 91766

CHAPMAN, LORING FREDERICK, b Los Angeles, Calif, Oct 4, 29; m 54; c 3. NEUROSCIENCES, BEHAVIORAL BIOLOGY. *Educ:* Univ Nev, BS, 50; Univ Chicago, PhD(biopsychol), 55. *Prof Exp:* Res asst, Dept Med, Univ Chicago, 52-55; from asst prof to assoc prof psychol, Dept Med, Col Med, Cornell Univ, 54-61; assoc prof med psychol, Dept Psychiat, Univ Calif, Los Angeles, 61-65; prof, Univ Ore, 65-66 & Georgetown Univ, 66-67; prof behav biol & chmn dept, prof psychiat & neurol, 67-79, prof neurol, 67-81, PROF PSCHIATRY & HUMAN PHYSIOL, SCH MED, UNIV CALIF, DAVIS, 79- *Concurrent Pos:* Nat Acad Sci award, 57, 59 & 61; Wilson prize, 58; partic, Skin Conf, 59, 76; vis scientist, Univ Sao Paulo, 59; partic, Ciba Found Conf, London, Eng, 60; consult, Nat Inst Neurol Dis, 62-; USPHS career develop award, 64; dir res, Fairview Hosp, 65-66; chief lab & behav biol br, NIH, 66-67; mem & res behav biologist, Calif Primate Res Ctr, 67- mem, Comt, Nat Inst Neurol Dis & Blindness, 67-68 & Res & Training Comt, Nat Inst Child Health & Human Develop, 68-73; Commonwealth Fund award & vis scientist, Univ Col, Univ London, 70; consult, NASA, 73- & Calif Med Facility, Vacaville, 74-; vis prof pharmacol & physiol, Fac Med, Botucatu, Brazil, 77; vis scientist, Univ Florence, Italy, 79-80; Fogarty Serv Int fel, 79-80. *Mem:* Am Physiol Soc; Soc Neurosci; Am Neurol Asn; Royal Soc Med; Aerospace Med Asn. *Res:* Brain function; biology of behavior; primatology; mental retardation; mental illness and deviant behavior; pain; pleasure; addiction; behavioral and reproductive hazards of psychoactive Druss; coding principles in neural systems; memory; psychopharmacology; neuropeptides; aerospace physiology; environmental physiology. *Mailing Add:* Dept Psychiat Sch of Med Univ of Calif Davis CA 95616

CHAPMAN, ORVILLE LAMAR, b New London, Conn, June 26, 32; m 55, 81; c 2. ORGANIC CHEMISTRY. *Educ:* Va Polytech Inst, BS, 54; Cornell Univ, PhD(chem), 57. *Prof Exp:* From instr to prof chem, Iowa State Univ, 57-76; PROF CHEM, UNIV CALIF, LOS ANGELES, 76- *Concurrent Pos:* Alfred P Sloan Found res fel, 61- *Honors & Awards:* Award in Pure Chem, Am Chem Soc, 68; Founders Prize, Tex Instrument Found, 74; Arthur C Cope Award, Am Chem Soc, 78. *Mem:* Nat Acad Sci; Am Chem Soc; The Chem Soc. *Res:* Organic photochemistry; reactive intermediates; natural products; insect, fish and mammalian pheromones. *Mailing Add:* Dept of Chem Univ of Calif 405 Hilgard Ave Los Angeles CA 90024

CHAPMAN, PETER JOHN, b Wolverhampton, Eng, Oct 26, 36; m 69; c 2. BIOCHEMISTRY, MICROBIOLOGY. *Educ:* Univ Leeds, BSc, 58, PhD(biochem), 61. *Prof Exp:* Assoc biochem, Univ Ill, Urbana, 61-64; lectr, Univ Hull, 64-66; from asst prof to assoc prof, 66-77, PROF BIOCHEM, UNIV MINN, ST PAUL, 77- *Mem:* Biochem Soc; Am Soc Biol Chemists; Am Soc Microbiol; Soc Gen Microbiol; Soc Indust Microbiol. *Res:* Microbial metabolism of synthetic and naturally-occurring compounds; regulation and organization of genes specifying catabolic enzymes; evolutionary relationships of degradative enzymes. *Mailing Add:* Dept of Biochem Univ of Minn St Paul MN 55101

CHAPMAN, R KEITH, b Oak Lake, Man, Oct 31, 16; m 42; c 3. ENTOMOLOGY. *Educ:* Ont Agr Col, BSA, 40; Univ Wis, PhD(entom), 49. *Prof Exp:* Lectr entom & zool, Ont Agr Col, 40-45; asst entom, 45-47, from instr to assoc prof, 47-59, PROF ENTOM, UNIV WIS-MADISON, 59- *Mem:* Entom Soc Am; Potato Asn Am; Am Phytopath Soc. *Res:* Insect transmission of plant disease; vegetable insects and their control. *Mailing Add:* Dept of Entom Univ of Wis Col Agr & Life Sci Madison WI 53706

CHAPMAN, RAMONA MARIE, b Columbus, Ky, Sept 17, 45. ONCOLOGY, HEMATOLOGY. *Educ:* Memphis State Univ, BS, 68; Univ Tenn, MD, 70. *Prof Exp:* Intern med, St Pauls Hosp, Dallas, 70-71 & residency, 71-72; residency internal med, Mt Zion Hosp, San Francisco, 72-73; fel hemat & oncol, Scripps Clin & Res Found, 73-76; hon sr registr oncol, St Bartholomews Hosp, London, 76-79; mem staff oncol, US Army, Walter Reed Army Med Ctr, 79-81 & mem hemat, Walter Reed Army Inst Res, 81-82; DIR, ST JOHNS REGIONAL ONCOL CTR, MO, 82- *Concurrent Pos:* Asst prof, Dept Med, Uniformed Serv Univ Health Sci, 79-82. *Mem:* AAAS; Am Women's Med Asn. *Res:* Effects of cancer chemotherapy on sexual function and fertility in humans; possibility of gonadal protection via hormonal gonadal suppression during chemotherapy. *Mailing Add:* St Johns Regional Oncol Ctr 2727 McClelland Blvd Joplin MO 64801

CHAPMAN, RAY LAVAR, b Blackfoot, Idaho. NUCLEAR ENGINEERING, PROPULSION. *Educ:* Brigham Yound Univ, BS, 49, MS, 51. *Prof Exp:* Sr dynamics engr stability & control, Gen Dynamics Corp, 51-58; assoc prof nuclear eng, Univ Ariz, 58-61; staff engr dept propulsion, Martin Marietta Corp, 61-73; PROJ ENGR NUCLEAR ENG, EG&G IDAHO INC, 74- *Concurrent Pos:* Consult, Army Electronic Proving Ground, 58-61. *Res:* Two phase fluid flow; critical heat flux, nuclear propulsion; hybrid propulsion. *Mailing Add:* EG&G Idaho Inc PO Box 1625 Idaho Falls ID 83401

CHAPMAN, RICHARD ALEXANDER, b Teague, Tex, Sept 24, 32; m 54; c 4. SEMICONDUCTORS. *Educ:* Rice Univ, BA, 54, MA, 55, PhD, 57. *Prof Exp:* Asst physics, Rice Univ, 54-56; physicist, Vallecitos Atomic Lab, Gen Elec Corp, 57-59; physicist, 59-64, mgr mat physics br, 64-71, mgr infrared devices br, 71-76, SR MEM TECH STAFF, CENT RES LAB, TEX INSTRUMENTS INC, 76- *Concurrent Pos:* Mem bd gov, Rice Univ, 75-79. *Mem:* Fel Am Phys Soc. *Res:* Semiconductor memories; optoelectronic devices and physics; charge coupled devices and infrared imagers; photovoltaic infrared detectors; light emitting diodes and digital displays; photoluminescence and infrared properties of impurities in semiconductors; semiconductor materials. *Mailing Add:* 7240 Briarcove Dr Dallas TX 75240

CHAPMAN, RICHARD DAVID, b Atlanta, Ga, June 25, 28; m 55; c 4. ORGANIC CHEMISTRY, POLYMER CHEMISTRY. *Educ:* Univ Fla, BS, 49; Northwestern Univ, MS, 51, PhD(org chem), 54. *Prof Exp:* Sr chemist, Chemstrand Corp, 53-58; group leader, 58-60, res chemist, Chemstrand Res Ctr, 60-69, res specialist 69-76, sr res specialist, Monsanto Textiles Co, 76-80, SR TECHNOL SPECIALIST, MONSANTO PLASTICS & RESINS CO, 80- *Res:* Polymer chemistry; condensation polymers; melt spinning. *Mailing Add:* Tech Ctr Monsanto Textiles Co PO Box 12830 Pensacola FL 32575

CHAPMAN, ROBERT DEWITT, b Erie, Pa, July 13, 37; m 64; c 2. ASTROPHYSICS. *Educ:* Pa State Univ, BS, 59; Harvard Univ, PhD(astron), 65. *Prof Exp:* Asst prof astron, Univ Calif, Los Angeles, 64-67; astronomer, 67-77, ASSOC CHIEF, LAB ASTRON & SOLAR PHYSICS, GODDARD SPACE FLIGHT CTR, NASA, 77- *Concurrent Pos:* Vis lectr, Univ Md, 70-75; lectr, Montgomery Col, 81. *Honors & Awards:* Sci Writing Award, Am Inst Physics-US Steel Found, 74. *Mem:* Am Astron Soc; Int Astron Union. *Res:* Structure of the outermost layers of the sun and stars and related physical problems. *Mailing Add:* Lab for Astron & Solar Physics Code 680 NASA Goddard Space Flight Ctr Greenbelt MD 20771

CHAPMAN, ROBERT EARL, JR, b Borger, Tex, Jan 11, 41; m 61; c 2. BIOPHYSICS. *Educ:* Yale Univ, MS, 66, PhD, 68. *Prof Exp:* Fel biophys, Univ Calif, San Diego, 68; CHIEF PHOTOG SCIENTIST, UNICOLOR DIV, PHOTOSCI INC, 68- *Concurrent Pos:* Guest lectr, Lansing Community Col, Mich, 81- *Res:* Photographic science; photo chemistry. *Mailing Add:* Unicolor Div Photosci Inc 7200 Huron River Dr Dexter MI 48130

CHAPMAN, ROBERT MILLS, b Chicago, Ill, Aug 29, 18; m 45, 68; c 1. GEOLOGY. *Educ:* Northwestern Univ, BS, 41. *Prof Exp:* Geologist, Alaskan Br, 42-47, in charge Fairbanks off, 47-55 & geochem explor br, Colo, 55-61, in charge off, College, Alaska, 61-69, GEOLOGIST, ALASKAN GEOL BR, US GEOL SURV, 70- *Mem:* Fel Geol Soc Am; Soc Econ Geol; Am Asn Petrol Geol; fel Arctic Inst NAm. *Res:* Alaskan geology; structure and stratigraphy of interior region; geochemical exploration; mineral deposits; history of the geological surrey in Alaska. *Mailing Add:* US Geol Surv 345 Middlefield Rd Menlo Park CA 94025

CHAPMAN, ROBERT PRINGLE, b Hartland, NB, Sept 12, 26; m 50; c 3. PHYSICS. *Educ:* Mt Allison Univ, BS, 47; McGill Univ, MS, 49; Univ Sask, PhD(physics), 53. *Prof Exp:* Sci officer, Defence Res Estab Atlantic, 53-73, HEAD OCEAN ACOUSTICS SECT, DEFENCE RES ESTAB PAC, 73- *Mem:* Acoustical Soc Am. *Res:* Underwater acoustics; physics of aurora borealis; mass spectroscopy. *Mailing Add:* 1245 Rockcrest Victoria BC V9A 4W4 Can

CHAPMAN, ROGER CHARLES, b New Orleans, La, July 14, 36; m 61; c 3. FORESTRY, STATISTICS. *Educ:* Col William & Mary, BS, 59; Duke Univ, MF, 59; Univ Calif, Berkeley, MA, 65; NC State Univ, PhD(forestry), 79. *Prof Exp:* Res forester, US Forest Serv, 59-66; statistician biomet, 66-69; asst prof biomet, Sch Forestry, Duke Univ, 69-73; asst prof, 73-80, ASSOC PROF BIOMET, DEPT FORESTRY, WASH STATE UNIV, 80- *Mem:* Am Statist Asn; Biomet Soc; Soc Am Foresters. *Res:* Forest growth and yield; estimation theory; forest resources sampling. *Mailing Add:* Dept Forestry & Range Mgt Wash State Univ Pullman WA 99164

CHAPMAN, ROSS ALEXANDER, b Oak Lake, Man, Dec 10, 13; m 42; c 2. FOOD SCIENCE. *Educ:* Univ Toronto, BSA, 40; McGill Univ, MSc, 41, PhD(chem), 44. *Hon Degrees:* DSc, Univ Guelph, 72. *Prof Exp:* Asst prof, MacDonald Col, McGill Univ, 44-48; head food sect, Food & Drug Div, Dept Nat Health & Welfare, Ottawa, 48-55, head food sect, WHO, Geneva, 55-57, asst dir sci serv, 58-63, asst dir gen food, 63-65, asst dep minister food & drugs, 65-71, spec adv, Off Dep Minister Health, 71-72, dir-gen int health serv, 72-73; consult food legis & control, South Pac Comn, New Caledonia, 75-76; consult, Pan Am Health Orgn, Washington, DC, 77-78 & Trinidad, Tobago & Brazil, 80. *Concurrent Pos:* Head Can deleg, UN Comn Narcotic Drugs, 70-73; mem deleg, UN Conf Protocol Psychotropic Substances, 71. *Res:* Methods of determination of thiamine and riboflavin; ferric thiocyanate methods for fat peroxides and its application to milk powders and fats and oils; methods for determination of antioxidants in fat and oils; behavior of antioxidants; methods for arsenic in fruits and vegetables and tocopherol in butter fat; food and drug legislation. *Mailing Add:* 655 Richmond Rd Unit 48 Ottawa ON K2A 3Y3 Can

CHAPMAN, RUSSELL LEONARD, b Brooklyn, NY, May 30, 46; m 69; c 2. PHYCOLOGY. *Educ:* Dartmouth Col, AB, 68; Univ Calif, Davis, MS, 70, PhD(bot), 73. *Prof Exp:* Asst prof, 73-77, ASSOC PROF BOT, LA STATE UNIV, BATON ROUGE, 77-, ASSOC DEAN, COL ARTS & SCI, 79- *Mem:* Phycol Soc Am; Bot Soc Am; Int Phycol Soc; Brit Phycol Soc; Electron Micros Soc Am. *Res:* Cytology, ultrastructure and biochemistry of Cephaleuros and related chroolepidaceous green algae including Phycopeltis and Trentepohlia. *Mailing Add:* Dept of Bot La State Univ Baton Rouge LA 70803

CHAPMAN, SALLY, b Philadelphia, Pa, July 28, 46. CHEMISTRY. *Educ:* Smith Col, AB, 68; Yale Univ, PhD(chem), 73. *Prof Exp:* Fel chem, Univ Calif, Irvine, 73-74 & Univ Calif, Berkeley, 75; asst prof, 75-80, ASSOC PROF CHEM, COLUMBIA UNIV, 80- *Mem:* Am Chem Soc; Am Phys Soc. *Res:* Classical trajectory studies of a variety of bimolecular reactive systems; emphasizing energy use and energy disposal and its relationship to the potential energy surface or surfaces. *Mailing Add:* Dept Chem Barnard Col Columbia Univ New York NY 10027

CHAPMAN, SHARON K, b Hutchinson, Kans, Nov 3, 39. PHARMACOLOGY, MEDICAL SCIENCE. *Educ:* Kans State Col Pittsburg, BS, 61; Univ Fla, PhD(med sci), 70. *Prof Exp:* Asst prof pharmacol, Sch Pharm, Univ Md, 70-72; pharmacologist biochem res, Vet Admin Hosp, Gainesville, Fla, 72-75; asst prof pharmacol, Col Med, Univ Fla, 75- *Concurrent Pos:* Pharmaceut Mfrs Asn Found res grant, 77; grad coordr, Dept Pharmacol, Col Med, Univ Fla, 78-80. *Mem:* Am Soc Pharmacol & Exp Therapeut. *Res:* Biochemical mechanisms of action of drugs and foreign chemicals; chemotherapeutics; polyamine chemistry; cyclic nucleotides. *Mailing Add:* Dept Clin Res Merrell Dow Pharmaceuticals Cincinnati OH 45215

CHAPMAN, STEPHEN R, b San Francisco, Calif, Oct 21, 36; m 58; c 2. POPULATION GENETICS, AGRONOMY. *Educ:* Univ Calif, Davis, BS, 59, MS, 63, PhD(genetics), 66. *Prof Exp:* Lab tech agron, Univ Calif, Davis, 60-66; asst prof agron & genetics, Univ Mont, 66-70; from assoc prof to prof, Mont State Univ, 70-77; ASSOC DEAN & DIR INSTRUC, COL AGR SCI, CLEMSON UNIV, 77- *Mem:* Am Soc Agron. *Res:* Population genetics and ecology of forage grasses. *Mailing Add:* Col Agr Sci Clemson Univ Clemson SC 29631

CHAPMAN, THOMAS EVERETT, b Globe, Ariz, Feb 16, 39; m 65; c 2. VETERINARY PHYSIOLOGY. *Educ:* Univ Calif, Davis, BS, 62, DVM, 64, PhD(physiol), 69. *Prof Exp:* From asst prof to assoc prof physiol, Kans State Univ, 69-78; ASSOC PROF PHYSIOL, ORE STATE UNIV, 78- *Res:* Water metabolism in ruminants and poultry; gluconeogenesis and glucose utilization in ruminants; propionate production and propionate-lactate interrelations in ruminants. *Mailing Add:* Sch of Vet Med Ore State Univ Corvallis OR 97331

CHAPMAN, THOMAS WOODRING, b Wilkinsburg, Pa, Sept 21, 40; m 66. CHEMICAL ENGINEERING. *Educ:* Yale Univ, BE, 62; Univ Calif, Berkeley, PhD(chem eng), 67. *Prof Exp:* Asst prof, 67-77, PROF CHEM ENG, UNIV WIS-MADISON, 78- *Mem:* Am Inst Chem Engrs; Am Chem Soc; Am Inst Mining, Metall & Petrol Engrs. *Res:* Mass transfer and separation operations; transport properties; electrochemical and hydrometallurgical processes. *Mailing Add:* Dept of Chem Eng Univ of Wis Madison WI 53706

CHAPMAN, TOBY MARSHALL, b Chicago, Ill, Nov 16, 38; m 61; c 3. BIO-ORGANIC CHEMISTRY, POLYMER CHEMISTRY. *Educ:* Univ Ill, BS, 60; Polytech Inst Brooklyn, PhD(chem), 65. *Prof Exp:* Res fel biol chem, Harvard Med Sch, 65-67; asst prof, 67-74, ASSOC PROF CHEM, UNIV PITTSBURGH, 74- *Mem:* Am Chem Soc. *Res:* New methods of peptide and oligonucleotide synthesis; determination of biopolymer structure; vinyl copolymerization; synthesis of phosphorus containing polymers; synthesis of sugar phosphates. *Mailing Add:* Dept of Chem Univ of Pittsburgh Pittsburgh PA 15260

CHAPMAN, VERNE M, b Sacramento, Calif, Oct 4, 38; m 68. GENETICS. *Educ:* Calif State Polytech Col, BS, 60; Ore State Univ, MS, 63, PhD(genetics), 65. *Prof Exp:* Asst prof biol, Millersville State Col, 65-66; fel, Jackson Lab, 66-68; res fel, Yale Univ, 68-72; ASSOC CANCER RES SCIENTIST, ROSWELL PARK MEM INST, 72-; ASST PROF GENETICS, STATE UNIV NY BUFFALO, 73- *Mem:* Soc Develop Biol; Genetics Soc Am. *Res:* Biochemical genetics and developmental genetics of the mouse. *Mailing Add:* Dept of Molecular Biol Roswell Park Mem Inst Buffalo NY 14263

CHAPMAN, WARREN HOWE, b Chicago, Ill, Oct 30, 25; c 5. UROLOGY. *Educ:* Mass Inst Technol, BS, 46; Univ Chicago, MD, 52. *Prof Exp:* Intern, St Luke's Hosp, Chicago, 52-53; resident urol, Univ Chicago Clins & instr, Sch Med, 53-57; res assoc, Western Wash State Col, 63-66; clin assoc, Dept Surg, Univ Wash Affil Hosps, 57-62, clin instr, 62-66, from asst prof to assoc prof urol, 66-73, PROF UROL, UNIV WASH, 73-, ADMIN OFF DEPT, 66- *Mem:* AMA; Am Urol Asn; Am Asn Cancer Res; Asn Am Med Cols; Soc Univ Urol. *Res:* Renal and adrenal hypertension; carcinoma of the bladder; microsurgery. *Mailing Add:* Dept of Urol RL10 Univ of Wash Seattle WA 98195

CHAPMAN, WILLIAM EDWARD, b Miami, Fla, Aug 23, 45; m 75. PATHOLOGY. *Educ:* Univ Conn, Storrs, BA, 72; Univ Conn, Farmington, MD, 76. *Prof Exp:* Resident path, 76-78, FEL IMMUNOL, DEPT PATH, SCH MED, UNIV CONN, FARMINGTON, 78- *Res:* Babesiosis; immunopathology of the lung. *Mailing Add:* Dept of Path Univ of Conn Sch of Med Farmington CT 06032

CHAPMAN, WILLIAM FRANK, b Hanover, NH, July 26, 44; m 67. GLACIAL GEOLOGY. *Educ:* Univ NH, BS, 66; Univ Mich, MS, 68, PhD(geol), 72. *Prof Exp:* ASSOC PROF GEOL, SLIPPERY ROCK STATE COL, 71- *Mem:* Geol Soc Am; Am Quaternary Asn; AAAS; Nat Asn Geol Teachers; Sigma Xi. *Res:* Study of the glacial geology of the Oil City Quadrangle, Pennsylvania. *Mailing Add:* Dept of Geol Slippery Rock State Col Slippery Rock PA 16057

CHAPMAN, WILLIE LASCO, JR, b Chattanooga, Tenn, Dec 17, 28; m 58; c 2. COMPARATIVE PATHOLOGY. *Educ:* Univ Tenn, BS, 50; Auburn Univ, DVM, 57; Colo State Univ, MS, 63; Univ Wis, PhD(vet sci), 68. *Prof Exp:* Pvt pract, 57-62; resident radiol, Colo State Univ, 62-63; asst prof vet med & surg, Sch Vet Med, Univ Ga, 63-64; res fel comp path, Univ Wis, 64-67; asst prof path, 67-71, assoc prof med & surg & head dept, 71-75, assoc prof path, 75-77, PROF PATH, COL VET MED, UNIV GA, 77- *Concurrent Pos:* NIH spec fel, Dept Path & Regional Primate Res Ctr, Univ Wis, 65-67. *Mem:* Am Vet Med Asn; Am Animal Hosp Asn; Am Asn Lab Animal Sci; Int Acad Path. *Res:* Neoplasms; mechanisms of immunity to blood parasites; chemotherapy of leishmaniasis. *Mailing Add:* Dept of Path Univ of Ga Col of Vet Med Athens GA 30602

CHAPPEL, CLIFFORD, b Guelph, Ont, Aug 23, 25; m 54, 70; c 4. BIOLOGY. *Educ:* Ont Vet Col, DVM, 50; McGill Univ, MSc, 53, PhD(invest med), 59. *Prof Exp:* Assoc dir biol res, Ayerst Res Labs, 53-65; pres & dir, Bio-Res Labs, Ltd, 65-76; vpres & dir res, Connlab Holdings Ltd, 76-78; PRES, FDC CONSULTS, INC, 78- *Concurrent Pos:* Lectr, Dept Invest Med, McGill Univ. *Mem:* Soc Exp Biol & Med; Am Soc Pharmacol; Pharmacol Soc Can. NY Acad Sci; Am Soc Toxicol; Europ Soc Toxicol; Soc Toxicol Can. *Res:* Pharmacology; toxicology. *Mailing Add:* FDC Consults Inc 364 Robin Ave Beaconsfield PQ H9W 1R8 Can

CHAPPEL, SCOTT CARLTON, b Syracuse, NY, Apr 22, 50; m 76. NEUROENDOCRINOLOGY. *Educ:* Pa State Univ, BS, 72; Univ Md, PhD(physiol), 76. *Prof Exp:* Fel, Ore Regional Primate Res Ctr, 76-78, asst scientist reproduction, 78-79; ASST PROF, DEPT OBSTET-GYNEC, UNIV PA, 79- *Concurrent Pos:* Res grants, Cammack Trust Fund, 78-79 & NIH, 78-80 & 81-83. *Mem:* Soc Study Reproduction; Endocrine Soc; Am Physiol Soc; NY Acad Sci. *Res:* Reproductive endocrinology and neuroendocrinology. *Mailing Add:* Dept Obstet-Gynec Univ Pa 3400 Spruce St Philadelphia PA 19104

CHAPPELEAR, DAVID C(ONRAD), b Dayton, Ohio, Mar 2, 31; div; c 2. CHEMICAL ENGINEERING. *Educ:* Yale Univ, BE, 53; Princeton Univ, MA, 59, PhD(chem eng), 60. *Prof Exp:* Res engr, Plastics Div, Res Dept, Monsanto Co, 53-54 & 56, sr res engr, 60-64, res specialist, 64-65, group supvr, 65, process tech mgr, 65-70, mgr process technol, 70-76, process technol dir, 77, technol dir, 78-80; DIR, CORP RES & DEVELOP, RAYCHEM CORP, MENLO PARK, 80- *Concurrent Pos:* Vis lectr, Univ Mass, 61-68, adj assoc prof, 68- *Mem:* Am Inst Chem Engrs; Am Chem Soc; NY Acad Sci. *Res:* Polymer product and process development; chemical reactor design; colloidal chemistry; radiation chemistry; flow of dispersed systems. *Mailing Add:* 2049 Fallenleaf Lane Los Altos CA 94022

CHAPPELEAR, JOHN EMERSON, b Enid, Okla, Feb 13, 29; m 55; c 4. APPLIED MATHEMATICS, PHYSICS. *Educ:* Univ Okla, BS, 50; Ind Univ, MS, 52, PhD(physics), 54. *Prof Exp:* From physicist to sr physicist, 54-64, res assoc, 64-66, sr res assoc, 66-74, SR STAFF MATHEMATICIAN, SHELL DEVELOP CO, 74- *Concurrent Pos:* Lectr, Univ Houston, 68-70 & Rice Univ, 70-71. *Mem:* Soc Petrol Engrs. *Res:* Computer science; petroleum reservoir engineering; numerical solution of systems of non-linear partial differential equations. *Mailing Add:* Shell Dev Co 1 Shell Plaza PO Box 2463 Houston TX 77001

CHAPPELL, CHARLES FRANKLIN, b St Louis, Mo, Dec 7, 27; m 51; c 3. METEOROLOGY, ATMOSPHERIC PHYSICS. *Educ:* Wash Univ, BS, 49; Colo State Univ, MS, 66, PhD(atmospheric sci), 71. *Prof Exp:* Flight test engr, MacDonnell Aircraft Corp, 50-55; anal & forecasting, Nat Weather Serv, 56-67; res meteorologist, Dept Atmospheric Sci, Colo State Univ, 67-70; assoc prof meteorol, Utah State Univ, 70-72; res meteorologist, Off Weather Modification, 72-73, sr scientist & dep dir, Atmospheric Physics & Chem Lab, 73-79, ACTG DIR, OFF WEATHER RES & MODIFICATION, ENVIRON RES LABS, NAT OCEANIC & ATMOSPHERIC AGENCY, 79- *Concurrent Pos:* Adj prof, Utah State Univ, 72-74; assoc mem grad fac, Colo State Univ, 73-, vis assoc prof, 74. *Mem:* Am Geophys Union; Am Meteorol Soc; Sigma Xi; Weather Modification Asn. *Res:* Parameterization of severe convection in mesoscale numerical models, genesis and organization of mesoscale convective systems, and mesoscale modeling of precipitation over mountainous terrain; severe storm prediction. *Mailing Add:* Rb 3 Rm 567 Environ Res Lab NOAA 30th & Marine Boulder CO 80302

CHAPPELL, CHARLES RICHARD, b Greenville, SC, June 2, 43; m 68; c 1. MAGNETOSPHERIC PHYSICS. *Educ:* Vanderbilt Univ, BA, 65; Rice Univ, PhD(space sci), 69. *Prof Exp:* Consult, Lockheed Palo Alto Res Lab, 68, assoc res scientist, 68-70, res scientist, 70-73, staff scientist, 73-74; chief, Magnetospheric & Plasma Physics Br, 74-80, CHIEF, SOLAR TERRESTRIAL PHYSICS DIV, SPACE SCI LAB, MARSHALL SPACE FLIGHT CTR, NASA, 80- *Concurrent Pos:* Assoc res physicist, Univ Calif, San Diego, 73-74. *Mem:* Am Geophys Union; AAAS; Int Asn Geomagnetism & Aeronomy; Int Union Radio Sci. *Res:* Space science; study of low energy particle population of the magnetosphere; the plasmasphere and ionosphere; magnetospheric convection. *Mailing Add:* 2803 Downing Ct Huntsville AL 35801

CHAPPELL, ELIZABETH, b Chicago, Ill, Jan 26, 27; m 73; c 2. PHARMACOLOGY. *Educ:* St Xavier Col, BS, 45; Univ Ill, MS, 47, PhD(pharmacol), 61. *Prof Exp:* Instr sci, St Xavier Col, 47-48; res asst pharmacol, 48-53, chem, 56-57, sr pharmacologist, 60-74, REGULATORY AFFAIRS MGR, ABBOTT LABS, 74- *Res:* General pharmacology, including blood coagulation, enzyme induction, antidiabetic drugs and general screening procedures; enzymology; biogenic amines and cyclic amp. *Mailing Add:* Abbott Labs North Chicago IL 60064

CHAPPELL, GUY LEE MONTY, b Marysville, Ohio, Aug 23, 40; m 62; c 2. RUMINANT NUTRITION, PHYSIOLOGY. *Educ:* Va Polytech Inst, MS, 65, PhD(ruminant nutrit), 66. *Prof Exp:* Asst prof, 66-70, assoc prof, 70-77, PROF SHEEP EXTEN & RES, UNIV KY, 78- *Mem:* Am Soc Animal Sci; Sigma Xi. *Res:* Factors affecting cellulose digestibility in the ruminant; factors affecting roughage utilization ruminants; high energy rations for early weaned lambs; intensive sheep production; youth progams in animal science. *Mailing Add:* Dept Animal Sci Univ Ky Lexington KY 40506

CHAPPELL, RICHARD LEE, b Buffalo, NY, Mar 9, 38; m 68; c 2. NEUROBIOLOGY. *Educ:* Princeton Univ, BSE, 62; Johns Hopkins Univ, PhD(biophys), 70. *Prof Exp:* Test engr nuclear eng, Naval Reactors, US AEC, 62-66; from asst prof to assoc prof, 70-79, PROF BIOL SCI, HUNTER COL, 80- *Concurrent Pos:* Consult, Gifted Student Develop Prog, Inc, 78- *Mem:* AAAS; Asn Res Vision & Ophthal; Inst Elec & Electronics Engrs; Soc Neurosci; Soc Gen Physiologists. *Res:* Electrophysiology; pharmacology; neuroanatomy and information processing with emphasis on the retina and visual systems. *Mailing Add:* Dept of Biol Sci Hunter Col 695 Park Ave New York NY 10021

CHAPPELL, SAMUEL ESTELLE, b Abingdon, Va, Apr 18, 31; m 78; c 1. PHYSICS. *Educ:* Va State Col, BS, 52; Pa State Univ, MS, 59, PhD(physics), 62. *Prof Exp:* Physicist radiation physics, 62-72, physicist info specialist, 72-78, PHYSICIST STANDARDS SPECIALIST, NAT BUR STANDARDS, 78- *Concurrent Pos:* Sci fel, Off of President's Spec Trade Rep, 76-77. *Mem:* Am Phys Soc; AAAS; Sigma Xi; Am Soc Testing Mat. *Res:* Experimental work in ionizing radiation dosimetry and radiation effects on materials; coordination of National Bureau of Standards staff participation in domestic and international standards organization; facilitates international cooperative projects in science and technology. *Mailing Add:* Phys A353 Nat Bur of Standards Washington DC 20234

CHAPPELL, WILLIAM ADRIAN, b Belvidere, NC, Oct 22, 25; m 52; c 3. VIROLOGY. *Educ:* Univ NC, AB, 47, MSPH, 51, PhD, 64. *Prof Exp:* Microbiologist, Virus & Rickettsia Div, Ft Detrick, 51-66; chief arbovirus ref lab, Nat Commun Dis Ctr, 66-70, chief, Viral & Rickettsial Prod Br, 70-81, CHIEF BIOL PRODUCTS PRODUCTION, BIOL PRODUCTS DIV, CTR DIS CONTROL, USPHS, 81- *Mem:* Sigma Xi; Am Soc Microbiol; Am Soc Trop Med & Hyg; Tissue Cult Asn. *Res:* Medical virology; aerobiology, viruses and bacteria; combined infections; arboviruses; Bedsonia agents; viral, rickettsial, mycoplasmal, bacterial, fungal and parasitic reagent development and production. *Mailing Add:* Biol Prod Div Ctr for Dis Control Atlanta GA 30333

CHAPPELLE, DANIEL EUGENE, b Washington, DC, Mar 15, 33; div; c 3. FOREST ECONOMICS. *Educ:* Colo State Univ, BS, 56; Duke Univ, MF, 59; State Univ NY Col Forestry, Syracuse Univ, PhD(forestry econ), 65. *Prof Exp:* Res forester econ, Southeastern Forest Exp Sta, US Forest Serv, 56-61; res asst forestry econ, State Univ NY Col Forestry, Syracuse Univ, 61-64; economist, Pac Northwest Forest & Range Exp Sta, US Forest Serv, 64-66, prin economist, 66-68; assoc prof resource econ, Mich State Univ, 68-71, PROF RESOURCE ECON, MICH STATE UNIV, 71- *Mem:* Am Econ Asn; Regional Sci Asn; Asn Evolutionary Econ. *Res:* Natural resource economics; regional economics and regional science; land use modeling. *Mailing Add:* Dept Resource Develop Mich State Univ East Lansing MI 48824

CHAPPELLE, EMMETT W, b Phoenix, Ariz, Oct 24, 25; m 47; c 4. BIOCHEMISTRY, PHOTOBIOLOGY. *Educ:* Univ Calif, BA, 50; Univ Wash, MS, 54. *Prof Exp:* Instr biochem, Meharry Med Col, 50-52; res assoc, Stanford Univ, 55-58; scientist biochem, Res Inst Advan Studies, 58-63; biochemist, Hazleton Labs, 63-66; exobiologist, 66-70, astrochemist, 70-73, Photobiologist, 73-77, AGR REMOTE SENSING SCIENTIST, GODDARD SPACE FLIGHT CTR, NASA, 77- *Concurrent Pos:* Consult, Appl Magnetics Corp, 73-74; NASA fel, Johns Hopkins Univ, 75- *Mem:* Am Chem Soc; NY Acad Sci; Am Soc Photobiol. *Res:* Metabolism of iron in mammalian systems; methods for quantitative assay of proteins and amino acids; carbon monoxide utilization by green plants; bioluminescence; methods for microbial determination; interstellar molecules; remote spectral analysis of agricultural crops. *Mailing Add:* 2502 Allendale Rd Baltimore MD 21216

CHAPPELLE, THOMAS W, b Petersburg, Ind, Feb 11, 18; m 52; c 1. MECHANICAL ENGINEERING, OPERATIONS RESEARCH. *Educ:* Univ Cincinnati, ME, 41; George Washington Univ, MEA, 65. *Prof Exp:* Engr, Cincinnati Milling & Grinding Mach, Inc, 41-42 & Atlanta Chem Warfare Procurement Dist, 42-43; asst prof mech eng, chmn com eng dept & coordr co-op plan, Univ Denver, 46-48; personnel dir & asst to contract adminr, Res Labs, Bendix Aviation Corp, 48-51; chief oper capability team & dep chief opers anal, Hqs, Strategic Air Command, 51-55 & 57-58; chief, Off Opers Anal, Hqs, Eighth Air Force, 55-57; br chief, Anal Serv Inc, 58-60, vpres, 60-76; dir prog planning & anal, 76-77, asst to chief scientist, 77-80, DEP DIR MGT SUPPORT OFFICE, HQ, NASA, 80- Mem: AAAS; Opers Res Soc Am; Am Astronaut Soc; Nat Space Club. Res: Long-range planning of aeronautical and space research and development. Mailing Add: Apt A114 6166 Leesburg Pike Falls Church VA 22044

CHAPPELOW, CECIL CLENDIS, JR, b Kansas City, Mo, Apr 12, 28; m 47; c 5. ORGANIC CHEMISTRY. Educ: Univ Southern Calif, BA, 51; Univ Mo-Kansas City, MA, 57, PhD, 68. Prof Exp: Sr chemist, Chem Div, 50-66, prin chemist, 66-68, head org & polymeric mat sect, 68-70, head org & polymer chem, 70-73, mgr indust progs, 73-75, HEAD MAT SCI, MIDWEST RES INST, 75- Mem: Am Chem Soc; Sigma Xi. Res: Synthesis, physicochemical characterization; structure-property correlation; substituted ureas and sulfamides; organometallic monomers and polymers; epoxidation and hydroxylation reactions; hydrogen-fluoride catalyzed condensations; metal chelating agents; biomedical polymer systems; cellulose conversion and utilization; corrosion protective coatings; synthetic polymeric membranes. Mailing Add: Midwest Res Inst Phys Sci Div 425 Volker Blvd Kansas City MO 64110

CHAPPELOW, CECIL CLENDIS, III, b Culver City, Calif, July 5, 48; m 78. CHEMICAL ENGINEERING. Educ: Univ Mo-Columbia, 70; Univ Calif, Berkeley, PhD(chem eng), 74. Prof Exp: Sr res engr, MPM Div, Pfizer, Inc, 73-77; sr process engr, 77-78, SECT MGR RES & DEVELOP, AIR PROD & CHEM, INC, 78- Mem: Am Inst Chem Engrs. Res: Emulsion polymerization; process and product development with application to adhesives and nonwovens; phase equilibria with emphasis on gas-liquid solutions. Mailing Add: Air Prod & Chem Inc PO Box 538 Allentown PA 18105

CHAPPLE, PAUL JAMES, b St Helier, UK, July 19, 33. CELL BIOLOGY, VIROLOGY. Educ: Univ Bristol, BSc, 57, PhD, 60. Prof Exp: Res asst, Univ Bristol, Eng, 59-60; res fel, Ministry Agr, Fisheries & Food, Worplesdon, Eng, 60-63; mem sci staff, Common Cold Unit, Med Res Coun, Nat Inst Med Res, Salisbury, 63-66; managing dir & pres, Flow Labs Ltd, Scotland, 66-72, vpres, Int Opers, Flow Labs, Inc, Rockville, 72-74; Dir, W Alton Jones Cell Sci Ctr, Lake Placid, 74-81; PRES, TKI, INC, 81- Concurrent Pos: Vis scientist, Microbiol Res Estab, Porton, Eng, 62-63; WHO consult, 64-65; co-investr, United Cerebral Palsy Res & Educ Found Inc, 75-78, Nat Heart, Lung & Blood Inst, 77-78 & Nat Inst Allergy & Infectious Dis, 77-79; prin investr, Nat Heart, Lung & Blood Inst, 77-78 & Nat Inst Aging, 77-80; prog dir, NIH, 78-79; dir, Bank Lake Placid. Mem: AAAS; Am Soc Microbiol; Am Soc Cell Biol; Soc Gen Microbiol; Tissue Cult Asn. Res: New cell substrate for virus diagnosis and propagation; culture and study of differentiated cells. Mailing Add: Rds End Placid Heights Lake Placid NY 12946

CHAPPLE, WILLIAM DISMORE, b Boston, Mass, July 24, 36; m 63; c 1. NEUROPHYSIOLOGY, COMPARATIVE PHYSIOLOGY. Educ: Harvard Univ, BA, 58; Syracuse Univ, MA, 60; Stanford Univ, PhD(biol), 65. Prof Exp: Res biologist, Control Systs Lab, Stanford Res Inst, 63-65; NATO fel, Cambridge Univ & Bristol Univ, 65-66; asst prof, 66-70, assoc prof, 70-80, PROF BIOL, UNIV CONN, 80- Mem: Fel AAAS; Soc Neurosci; Brit Soc Exp Biol. Res: Comparative neurophysiology; neural basis of patterned movement. Mailing Add: Biol Sci Group U-42 Univ of Conn Storrs CT 06268

CHAPPLE, WILLIAM MASSEE, structural geology, tectonics, deceased

CHAPUT, RAYMOND LEO, b Manchester, NH, Mar 29, 40; m 62; c 5. RADIATION BIOLOGY, HEALTH PHYSICS. Educ: St Anselm Col, BA, 62; Univ Rochester, MS, 65; Univ Tenn, PhD(zool), 67. Prof Exp: Prin investr, Armed Forces Radiobiol Res Inst, 67-73; head non ionizing radiation sect, Naval Bur Med & Surg, 73-75; chief nuclear submarine med sect, Naval Undersea Med Inst, 75-78; dir radiation health, Pearl Harbor Naval Shipyard, 78-81; CHIEF EXP PATH DIV, ARMED FORCES RADIOBIOL RES INST, 81- Concurrent Pos: Comt mem, Am Nat Standard Inst, 73-75. Mem: Health Physics Soc; Sigma Xi. Res: Amino acid and metabolism in insect larvae and pupae; the effects of ionizing radiation on insect hematocytes; effects of ionizing radiation on animal behavior; neurochemistry and supportive treatment after irradiation using bone marrow and peripheral blood elements. Mailing Add: Armed Forces Radiobiol Inst Nat Naval Med Ctr Bethesda MD 20014

CHAR, DONALD F B, b Honolulu, Hawaii, Mar 25, 25; m 51; c 5. PUBLIC HEALTH, PEDIATRICS. Educ: Temple Univ, MD, 50. Prof Exp: Intern, Atlantic City Hosp, 50-51; resident pediat, St Christopher's Hosp Children, 53-56; dir med educ, Kauikeolani Children's Hosp, 56-59 & 62-65; from instr to asst prof pediat, Med Sch, Univ Wash, 59-63; DIR STUDENT HEALTH & PROF PEDIAT, UNIV HAWAII, 65- Concurrent Pos: Fel pediat cardiol, St Christopher's Hosp Children, 55-56; res instr, Med Sch, Univ Wash, 62-63; lectr, East-West Training Prog Med Practitioners, Apia, WSamoa, 65; hon consult, Health Ctr, Chinese Univ, Hong Kong, 73; vis prof pediat, Med Sch, Hong Kong Univ, 73; fel, East West Ctr, 80-81. Mem: Am Acad Pediat; Am Col Health Asn. Res: Immune status in adrenalectomized animals; health care of foreign students. Mailing Add: Student Health Serv Univ Hawaii 1710 East West Rd Honolulu HI 96822

CHAR, WALTER F, b Honolulu, Hawaii, May 27, 20; m 48; c 3. PSYCHIATRY. Educ: Temple Univ, MD, 45; Am Bd Psychiat & Neurol, cert psychiat, 52, cert psychoanal, 58, cert child psychiat, 60. Prof Exp: Intern, Med Ctr, Temple Univ, 45-46; resident psychiat, Univ Pittsburgh, 48-49; resident, Med Ctr, Temple Univ, 49-52, resident psychiat, Sch Med & dir child psychiat, Med Ctr, 52-62; chmn dept psychiat, 67-69, PROF PSYCHIAT, SCH MED, UNIV HAWAII, 67-, ASSOC CHMN DEPT, 69- Concurrent Pos: Pvt pract psychiat & psychoanal, 52-; consult psychiat, Child & Family Serv, Honolulu, 62-, Cath Social Serv & Army Tripler Gen Hosp,

65- Mem: Am Psychiat Asn; Am Psychoanal Asn; Am Acad Child Psychiat; Am Orthopsychiat Asn; Am Col Psychoanal. Res: Evaluation of admission procedure of medical students; transcultural psychiatry. Mailing Add: Univ of Hawaii Sch of Med 1356 Lusitana St Honolulu HI 96813

CHARACHE, PATRICIA, b Newark, NJ, Dec 26, 29; m 51; c 1. MEDICINE. Educ: Hunter Col, BA, 52; NY Univ, MD, 57. Prof Exp: Intern med, Baltimore City Hosps, 57-58; res assoc immunol, Childrens Hosp & Harvard Univ, 62-64; from instr to asst prof med, 64-73, asst prof microbiol, 70-79, ASSOC PROF MED & LAB MED, JOHNS HOPKINS UNIV, 73- Concurrent Pos: USPHS fel res med, Univ Pa, 58-59, Porter fel, 59-60; USPHS fel infect dis, Johns Hopkins Univ, 60-62; res career develop award, Nat Inst Allergy & Infect Dis, 69- Mem: Am Soc Clin Pharmacol; Reticuloendothelial Soc; Infect Dis Soc Am; Am Soc Microbiol; Fedn Clin Res. Res: Immunology and infectious disease, emphasizing bacterial-host interaction; medical microbiology. Mailing Add: Dept of Lab Med Johns Hopkins Hosp Baltimore MD 21205

CHARACHE, SAMUEL, b New York, NY, Jan 12, 30; m 51; c 1. MEDICINE. Educ: Oberlin Col, BA, 51; NY Univ, MD, 55; Am Bd Internal Med, dipl & cert hemat; Am Bd Clin Path, dipl & cert hemat. Prof Exp: Clin assoc, NIH, 56-58; resident med, Hosp Univ Pa, 58-60; from asst prof to assoc prof, 66-78, PROF MED, SCH MED, JOHNS HOPKINS UNIV, 78-, PROF PATH, 81- Concurrent Pos: USPHS, 56-58; fel hemat, Johns Hopkins Hosp, 60-62 & 64-66; fel biol, Mass Inst Technol, 62-64. Mem: Asn Am Physicians; Am Soc Hemat. Res: Hematology. Mailing Add: Dept Med Johns Hopkins Hosp Baltimore MD 21205

CHARACKLIS, WILLIAM GREGORY, b Annapolis, Md, Aug 21, 41; m 64; c 2. CHEMICAL ENGINEERING, ENVIRONMENTAL ENGINEERING. Educ: Johns Hopkins Univ, BES, 64; PhD(environ eng), 70; Univ Toledo, MSChE, 67. Prof Exp: Res engr, Olin-Matheson Chem Corp, 64-65; res asst chem eng, Univ Toledo, 65-67; res asst environ eng, Johns Hopkins Univ, 67-70; from asst prof to assoc prof, 70-78, PROF ENVIRON ENG & CHMN DEPT, RICE UNIV, 78- Concurrent Pos: Merck Found fac develop grant, 72; NSF fac sci fel, 76; NSF fac sci fel, Swiss Fed Inst Water Resources & Water Pollution Control, 77-78. Mem: Am Inst Chem Engrs; Int Asn Water Pollution Res; Water Pollution Control Fedn. Res: Microbial engineering, biofouling, water and wastewater engineering. Mailing Add: Dept of Environ Sci & Eng PO Box 1892 Houston TX 77001

CHARAP, STANLEY H, b Brooklyn, NY, Apr 21, 32; m 55; c 2. SOLID STATE SCIENCE. Educ: Brooklyn Col, BS, 53; Rutgers Univ, PhD(physics), 59. Prof Exp: Asst physics, Rutgers Univ, 53-55, instr, 57-58; physicist, Res Ctr, Int Bus Mach Corp, 58-64; res scientist, Res Div, Am Stand Corp, 64-65, supvr solid state physics, 65-66, mgr physics & electronics, 66-68; assoc prof, 68-71, PROF ELEC ENG, CARNEGIE-MELLON UNIV, 71-, ASSOC HEAD ELEC ENG, 80- Concurrent Pos: Consult, Westinghouse Res Labs, 69-; ed, Inst Elec & Electronics Engrs Trans on Magnetics, 75-81. Mem: Am Phys Soc; Inst Elec & Electronics Engrs; Magnetics Soc; Sigma Xi. Res: Magnetic domains, magnetic hysteresis models; theory of solid state; magnetism of solids. Mailing Add: Dept Elec Eng Carnegie Mellon Univ Pittsburgh PA 15213

CHARBENEAU, GERALD T, b Mt Clemens, Mich, July 22, 25; m 47; c 3. DENTISTRY. Educ: Univ Mich, DDS, 48, MS, 49. Prof Exp: Teaching fel dent, Sch Dent, Univ Mich, Ann Arbor, 48-49; from instr to assoc prof, 49-65, PROF DENT, SCH DENT, UNIV MICH, ANN ARBOR, 65-, CHMN DEPT OPER DENT, 69- Mem: Am Dent Asn; Int Asn Dent Res; Am Acad Restorative Dent; Acad Oper Dent. Res: Operative and general restorative dentistry with specific relationship of dental materials to these clinical areas. Mailing Add: 2062 Dent Sch of Dent Univ of Mich Ann Arbor MI 48109

CHARBONNEAU, LARRY FRANCIS, b Faribault, Minn, Aug 14, 39; m 66; c 2. ORGANIC POLYMER CHEMISTRY. Educ: Mankato State Col, BS, 64; Univ Ill, Urbana-Champaign, MS, 69, PhD(org chem), 72. Prof Exp: Chem technician polymer chem, 3M Co Cent Res, 60-62, chemist photochem, 64-67; assoc sr res chemist org polymer chem, Gen Motors Res Labs, Warren, Mich, 72-77; SR RES CHEMIST ORG POLYMER CHEM, CELANESE RES CO, 77- Mem: AAAS; Am Chem Soc. Res: Synthesis of high performance polymers for industrial yarns and engineering plastics. Mailing Add: 166 Lafayette Ave Chatham NJ 07928

CHARBONNIER, FRANCIS MARCEL, b Monaco, Apr 28, 27; nat US; m 52; c 6. PHYSICS. Educ: Polytech Sch Paris, Dipl d'Ing, 49; Univ Wash, PhD(physics), 52. Prof Exp: Engr, Militaire de l'Armement, France, 52-55; sr physicist, Linfield Res Inst, 56-57, tech asst to sci, 57-59, asst dir, 59-62; dir res & develop div, Field Emission Corp, 62-64; vpres & res dir, 64-73; ENG MGR, McMINNVILLE DIV, HEWLETT-PACKARD CO, 74- Mem: Am Asn Physicists Med; Am Phys Soc; Inst Elec & Electronics Engrs. Res: Field emission; electron physics, optics and devices; medical x-ray systems; pulsed radiation sources. Mailing Add: Hewlett-Packard Co McMinnville Div 1700 S Baker St McMinnville OR 97128

CHARD, RONALD LESLIE, JR, b Pomeroy, Wash, Sept 23, 30; m 54; c 5. PEDIATRIC ONCOLOGY & HEMATOLOGY. Educ: Wash State Univ, BS, 52; Univ Wash, MD, 63. Prof Exp: Fel, 66-68, ASSOC DIR PEDIAT HEMAT & ONCOL, CHILDREN'S ORTHOP HOSP & MED CTR, 69-; ASSOC CHMN LEUKEMIA STUDIES, CHILDREN'S CANCER STUDY GROUP, 73- Concurrent Pos: Nat Cancer Inst fel, 66; clin prof pediat, Sch Med, Univ Wash, 75-; chmn leukemia task force, Coop Groups Report 1979, Nat Cancer Inst, Children's Cancer Study Group, Southwest Oncol Group, Cancer & Leukemia Group B, 78- Mem: Am Soc Clin Oncol; Int Soc Exp Hemat. Mailing Add: 5070 Harold Pl Seattle WA 98105

CHAREN, GEORGE, b Newark, NJ, June 18, 13; m 43; c 3. PHYSICS, CHEMISTRY. *Educ:* Columbia Univ, AB, 34, MA, 37; Univ Colo, EdD(sci), 62. *Prof Exp:* Pub sch instr, NJ, 38-41; head dept develop & prod fermentations, Apex Chem Co, 41-46 & S B Penick & Co, 46-48; high sch instr, NY, 56-58; instr phys sci, Univ Colo, 59-60; assoc prof sci & coordr physics, Jersey City State Col, 60-67; PROF PHYS SCI & MATH & DEAN INSTR, BERGEN COMMUNITY COL, 67- *Concurrent Pos:* Mem inserv inst, Esso Found & NY Univ, 57-58 & Newark Col Eng, 61-62; mem univ phys sci study comt physics, 62-63; mem acad year inst, NSF, Univ Colo, 58-59. *Mem:* AAAS; Nat Sci Teachers Asn; Am Asn Physics Teachers. *Res:* Nuclear physics. *Mailing Add:* Bergen Community Col 400 Paramus Rd Paramus NJ 07652

CHARETTE, LAURENT A, b Gogama, Ont, Jan 2, 24; m 48; c 4. ANIMAL PRODUCTION, ANIMAL BREEDING. *Educ:* Ont Agr Col, BSA, 48; Univ Minn, St Paul, MS, 51, PhD(animal breeding), 57. *Prof Exp:* Res officer animal sci, Exp Farm, Can Dept Agr, Ont, 48-62; dir dept animal sci, 62-74, prof animal sci, 62-77, PROF ZOO TECH, FAC AGR & FOOD SCI, LAVAL UNIV, 77- *Mem:* Can Soc Animal Prod; Am Soc Animal Sci. *Res:* Effects of sex and age of castration in swine; crossbreeding beef breeds; crossbreeding dairy and beef cattle. *Mailing Add:* Dept of Animal Sci Laval Univ Fac of Agr & Food Sci Quebec Can

CHARGAFF, ERWIN, b Austria, Aug 11, 05; US citizen; m 29; c 1. BIOCHEMISTRY. *Educ:* Univ Vienna, Dr phil(chem), 28. *Hon Degrees:* ScD, Columbia Univ & Dr phil, Univ Basel, 76. *Prof Exp:* Milton Campbell res fel, Yale Univ, 28-30; asst dept bact & pub health, Univ Berlin, 30-33; res assoc, Pasteur Inst, 33-34; res assoc, 35-38, from asst prof to prof, 38-74, chmn dept, 70-74, EMER PROF BIOCHEM, COL PHYSICIANS & SURGEONS, COLUMBIA UNIV, 74- *Concurrent Pos:* Guggenheim fels, 49 & 57-58; vis prof, Wenner Grens Inst, Univ Stockholm, 49, Univs Rio de Janeiro, Sao Paulo & Recife, 59, Cornell Univ & Univs Naples & Palermo, 66 & Biol Sta, Naples, 69; Harvey lectr, Rockefeller Univ, 56; Plenary Cong lectr, Int Biochem Cong Vienna, 58; vis lectr, Univs Tokyo, Kyoto, Sendai & others, 58; Jesup lectr, Columbia Univ, 59; first K A Forster lectr, Mainz, 68 & Miescher Mem lectr, Basel, 69; mem comt growth, Nat Res Coun, 52-54; mem adv coun biol, Oak Ridge Nat Lab, 58-67; Albert Einstein chair, Col France, 65-80. *Honors & Awards:* Pasteur Medal, Paris, 49; Carl Neuberg Medal, 58; Soc Chem Biol Medal, Paris, 61; Charles Leopold Mayer Prize, Acad Sci, Paris, 63; Dr H P Heineken Prize, Royal Neth Acad Sci, 64; Bertner Found Award, 65; Gregor Mendel Medal, Halle, Ger, 73; Nat Medal Sci, 74; New York Acad Med Medal, 80. *Mem:* Nat Acad Sci; fel Am Acad Arts & Sci; for mem Royal Swed Physiol Soc; Ger Acad Sci; Am Philos Soc. *Res:* Lipids; lipoproteins; blood coagulation; metabolism of amino acids and inositol; chemistry and biosynthesis of nucleic acids and nucleoproteins; phosphotransferases and other enzymes. *Mailing Add:* 350 Cent Park W New York NY 10025

CHARI, NALLAN C, b Rajahmundry, India, Nov 2, 31; m 54; c 1. CHEMICAL ENGINEERING. *Educ:* Benares Hindu Univ, BS, 54; Univ Mich, MS, 57, ScD(chem eng), 60. *Prof Exp:* Instr chem eng, Benares Hindu Univ, 54-55; asst eng res inst, Univ Mich, 55-60; staff chem engr, Tech Ctr, Owens-Illinois Glass Co, 60-67, chief programmer, 67-70, mgr process comput control, 70-73, mgr systs develop, 73-77, MGR PROCESS ENG & CONTROL, OWENS-ILLINOIS, INC, 77- *Mem:* Am Chem Soc; Am Inst Chem Engrs; Tech Asn Pulp & Paper Indust; Can Pulp & Paper Asn; Nat Soc Prof Engrs. *Res:* Thermodynamics; process dynamics and control; pulp and paper process design and systems engineering study. *Mailing Add:* Owens-Illinois Inc PO Box 1035 Toledo OH 43666

CHARKES, N DAVID, b New York, NY, Aug 13, 31; m 53; c 3. NUCLEAR MEDICINE. *Educ:* Columbia Univ, AB, 52; Washington Univ, MD, 55. *Prof Exp:* USPHS fel arthritis & metab dis, 60-61; assoc radiol, 62-66, clin asst prof, 66, assoc prof radiol & med, 66-71, dir, Dept Nuclear Med, Hosp, 66-80, PROF RADIOL & ASSOC PROF MED, SCH MED, TEMPLE UNIV, 71-, RES PROF NUCLEAR MED & PROF MED, 80- *Concurrent Pos:* Dir radioisotope unit, North Div, Albert Einstein Med Ctr, 62-66; consult nuclear med, Walson Army Hosp, Ft Dix, NJ, 67- & Vet Admin Hosp, Wilmington, Del; Fogarty Sr Internat fel, 76. *Mem:* Soc Nuclear Med; Am Fedn Clin Res. *Mailing Add:* Temple Univ Sch of Med Broad & Ontario Sts Philadelphia PA 19122

CHARKOUDIAN, JOHN CHARLES, b Springfield, Mass, July 29, 41. INORGANIC CHEMISTRY, PHOTOGRAPHIC CHEMISTRY. *Educ:* Bates Col, BS, 63; Babson Col, MBA, 66; Boston Univ, MS, 67; Va Polytech Inst & State Univ, PhD(phys inorg chem), 70. *Prof Exp:* SCIENTIST PHOTOG CHEM, POLAROID CORP, 70- *Mem:* AAAS; Am Chem Soc; Soc Photog Scientists & Engrs. *Res:* Mechanism of photographic development electron spin resonance applied to photographic science; fast reaction kinetics; stopped flow and temperature jump kinetics. *Mailing Add:* 86 Henry Cambridge MA 02139

CHARLANG, GISELA WOHLRAB, b Berlin, Ger, May 31, 38; US citizen; m 69. MICROBIAL GENETICS, MICROBIAL ECOLOGY. *Educ:* Univ Chicago, BA, 61, MS, 62, PhD(bot), 64. *Prof Exp:* NSF fel, Univ Liverpool, 64-65; instr bot, Univ Chicago, 65-66; asst prof biol, Grand Valley State Col, 66-68; res assoc, Univ Ill, Urbana, 68-69; res fel, 69-73, assoc scientist, 73-79, scientist, 79-80, MEM PROF STAFF, DIV BIOL, CALIF INST TECHNOL, 80- *Mem:* AAAS; Asn Women in Sci; Am Asn Univ Women. *Res:* Siderophores and iron transport in Neurospora crassa and other fungi; effects of low water activity environments on membranes; isolation and characterization of membrane receptors for siderophores. *Mailing Add:* Div Biol Calif Inst Technol Pasadena CA 91125

CHARLAP, LEONARD STANTON, b Wilmington, Del, Aug 1, 38. MATHEMATICS. *Educ:* Mass Inst Technol, BS, 59; Columbia Univ, PhD(math), 62. *Prof Exp:* Mem, Inst Advan Study, 62-64; from asst prof to assoc prof math, Univ Pa, 64-69; assoc prof, 69-70, PROF MATH, STATE UNIV NY STONY BROOK, 70- *Mem:* Am Math Soc. *Res:* Differential geometry; differential topology; homological algebra; flat Riemannian manifolds. *Mailing Add:* Dept of Math State Univ of NY Stony Brook NY 11794

CHARLEBOIS, CLARENCE THOMAS, b Rouyon, Que, Apr 20, 49. NEUROSCIENCE, SCIENCE POLICY. *Educ:* McGill Univ, BSc & dipl ethology, 70. *Prof Exp:* Researcher neurosci, Inst Exp Psychol, Oxford Univ, 70-73; sci adv, Sci Coun Can, 75-77; TOXIC SUBSTANCES POLICY ANALYST US-CAN, ENVIRON CAN, 77- *Mem:* Can Pub Health Asn. *Res:* Neurophysiological control of hunger and thirst; regulation of toxic substances. *Mailing Add:* 2-230 Nelson Ottawa Can

CHARLES, DONALD FOSTER, b Iloilo, Philippines, Oct 16, 22; m 44; c 3. PHYSICAL CHEMISTRY. *Educ:* Univ Calif, AB, 47. *Prof Exp:* RES CHEMIST, CALIF & HAWAIIAN SUGAR REFINING CO, 47- *Mem:* Am Chem Soc. *Res:* Physical properties of sucrose solutions; technology of sugar refining; chemistry of cane sugar colorants; high performance liquid chromaography of refinery products, sugars, organic acids, and sugar polymers. *Mailing Add:* C & H Sugar Refining Co Crockett CA 94525

CHARLES, EDGAR DAVIDSON, JR, b Florence, SC, Apr 26, 43; m 65; c 1. PUBLIC HEALTH. *Educ:* Pembroke State Univ, BS, 66; Univ Ala, Tuscaloosa, MS, 68, PhD(econ), 71. *Prof Exp:* ASST PROF HOSP & HEALTH ADMIN, UNIV ALA, BIRMINGHAM, 71-, ASSOC PROF PUB HEALTH, 76-, ACTG CHMN DIV HEALTH CARE ORGN, 78- *Concurrent Pos:* WHO fel, 74. *Mem:* Am Econ Asn; Am Pub Health Asn. *Res:* Health care organization and health economics. *Mailing Add:* Dept of Pub Health SOM|SPAH Univ of Ala Univ Sta Birmingham AL 35294

CHARLES, GEORGE WILLIAM, b Columbus, Ohio, Dec 24, 15; m 39; c 2. PHYSICS. *Educ:* Ohio State Univ, BA, 37, PhD(physics), 47. *Prof Exp:* Asst physics, Ohio State Univ, 38-42; instr, NC State Col, 42-44; physicist, Naval Ord Lab, 44-46; asst prof physics, Univ Okla, 47-52; sr res physicist, Mound Lab, 52-54; PHYSICIST, OAK RIDGE NAT LAB, 54- *Mem:* Optical Soc Am. *Res:* Atomic spectroscopy; physical optics; heat; spectra of columbium and molybdenum in the extreme ultraviolet; spectra of polonium and of rare earths. *Mailing Add:* Oak Ridge Nat Lab Physics Div 840 W Outer Dr Oak Ridge TN 37830

CHARLES, HARRY KREWSON, JR, b Audubon, NJ, May 29, 44; m 70. ELECTRICAL ENGINEERING, SOLID STATE PHYSICS. *Educ:* Drexel Univ, BS, 67; Johns Hopkins Univ, DPhil(elec eng), 72. *Prof Exp:* Engr aerospace technol elec & commun eng, Goddard Space Flight Ctr, NASA, 68; res assoc solid state physics, 72-73; engr sr staff elec eng & solid state physics, 73-79, sect supvr microelectronics group, 79-81, ASST GROUP SUPVR MICROELECTRONICS, APPL PHYSICS LAB, JOHNS HOPKINS UNIV, 81- *Mem:* Inst Elec & Electronics Engrs; Am Phys Soc; Int Soc Hybrid Microelectronics; Int Solar Energy Soc; Electron Micros Soc Am. *Res:* Electrical engineering, with emphasis on hybrid microelectronics; thin film resistors, integrated circuits and solar cells. *Mailing Add:* Appl Physics Lab Johns Hopkins Rd Laurel MD 20810

CHARLES, MICHAEL EDWARD, b Leicester, Eng, Dec 20, 35; Can citizen; m 59; c 2. CHEMICAL ENGINEERING. *Educ:* Imp Col, Univ London, BASc, 57; Univ Alta, MASc, 59, PhD(chem eng), 63. *Prof Exp:* Res officer, Res Coun Alta, 57-61; res engr, Imp Oil Ltd, Calgary, 63-64; from asst prof to assoc prof chem eng, 64-71, asst chmn dept, 70-75, PROF CHEM ENG, UNIV TORONTO, 71-, CHMN DEPT, 75- *Concurrent Pos:* Dir, Chem Eng Res Consults Ltd, 65-, vpres, 70-75; consult, Imp Oil Ltd, 66 & 74, Milltronics Ltd, 67-71, Wolfe Spiral Pipe Co Ltd, 71-73, Atomic Energy Can Ltd, 72- & Olympia-York Construct, 74; sci adv, Worthington Ltd, Can, 70-74. *Mem:* Can Soc Chem Eng; Can Res Mgt Asn; fel Chem Inst Can. *Res:* Fluid mechanics of complex systems with industrial significance, especially pipeline transport of solids in slurry and capsule form; two-phase gas-liquid flows in tubular reactors, furnaces and boilers; continuous particle size determination and behavior of oil spills. *Mailing Add:* Dept of Chem Eng Univ of Toronto Toronto ON M5S 2R8 Can

CHARLES, R(ICHARD) J(OSEPH), b Elfros, Sask, Sept 8, 25; US citizen; m 50; c 1. METALLURGY. *Educ:* Univ BC, BS, 48, MS, 49; Mass Inst Technol, ScD(metall), 54. *Prof Exp:* Asst prof metall, Mass Inst Technol, 54-56; res assoc, Gen Elec Res Lab, 56-64 & 65-69, actg mgr, Metals & Ceramics Studies Sect, 64-65, mgr, Properties Br, 69-72, MGR, CERAMICS BR, GEN ELEC CO, CORP RES & DEVELOP, 72- *Concurrent Pos:* Chmn, Gordon Conf Glass, 59-60; adj prof ceramics, Mass Inst Technol, 76-, Robert S Williams lectr, 76. *Honors & Awards:* Raymond Award, Am Inst Mining, Metall & Petrol Engrs, 57; George W Morey Award, Am Ceramic Soc, 72; Coolidge Fel, Gen Elec Co, 74. *Mem:* Am Inst Mining, Metall & Petrol Engrs; Am Ceramic Soc. *Res:* Mechanical properties of brittle materials; electrical and physical chemical properties of oxides, silicates, refractory compounds and metals; permanent magnetism and superconductivity. *Mailing Add:* Gen Elec Co Corp Res & Develop PO Box 8 Schenectady NY 12345

CHARLES, ROBERT WILSON, b Altoona, Pa, Sept 1, 45. GEOCHEMISTRY. *Educ:* Bucknell Univ, BS, 67; Mass Inst Technol, PhD(geol), 72. *Prof Exp:* Fel geochem, Univ BC, 73-74; STAFF MEM GEOCHEM, LOS ALAMOS SCI LAB, 74- *Mem:* AAAS; Mineral Soc Am; Am Geophys Union. *Res:* Experimental determination of phase equilibria suitable to describe mineral assemblages found in nature; experimentation involves the routine use of high pressure-temperature hydrothermal equipment to duplicate natural conditions. *Mailing Add:* Los Alamos Sci Lab CNC-11 M/S 514 Univ of Calif Los Alamos NM 87545

CHARLESWORTH, LLOYD JAMES, JR, b Allentown, Pa, Feb 17, 34; m 66; c 1. SEDIMENTOLOGY. *Educ:* Lehigh Univ, BA, 56; Univ Mich, MS, 58, PhD(geol), 68. *Prof Exp:* Sr geologist, NJ Bur Geol & Topog, 61-67; res assoc geol, Univ Mich, 67-68; sr geologist, NJ Bur Navig, 68; vis scholar, Univ

Mich, 68-69; ASSOC PROF GEOL & DIR SUBSURFACE DATA CTR, UNIV TOLEDO, 69- *Mem:* AAAS; Geol Soc Am; Soc Econ Paleontologists & Mineralogists; Sigma Xi; Int Asn Great Lakes Res. *Res:* Sedimentology, sedimentary petrography, geomorphology, and process-response conditions of sedimentation, especially in Holocene paludal, coastal and continental shelf sedimentary environments, particularly New Jersey, Lake Erie and Florida regions. *Mailing Add:* Dept of Geol Univ of Toledo Toledo OH 43606

CHARLESWORTH, ROBERT K(ORIDON), b Idaho Falls, Idaho, July 26, 23; m 52; c 2. CHEMICAL ENGINEERING. *Educ:* Univ Wash, BS, 44; Univ Wis, MS, 47; Purdue Univ, PhD(chem eng), 51. *Prof Exp:* Instr chem, Idaho State Col, 47-48; from res & develop engr to sr res engr, 51-68, RES GROUP LEADER, DOW CHEM CO, 68- *Mem:* Am Chem Soc; Am Inst Chem Engrs. *Res:* High polymers; chemical engineering unit operations. *Mailing Add:* 24 Los Banos Ct Walnut Creek CA 94598

CHARLET, LAURENCE DEAN, b Danville, Ill, Oct 6, 46; m 69; c 2. ENTOMOLOGY. *Educ:* San Diego State Univ, BS, 69; Univ Calif, Riverside, MS, 73, PhD(entom), 75. *Prof Exp:* Res entomologist, Univ Calif, Riverside, 75-78; RES ENTOMOLOGIST, OILSEEDS RES UNIT, USDA, 78- *Mem:* Int Orgn Biological Control; Entom Soc Am; Entom Soc Can; Sigma Xi. *Res:* Bionomics of pine and citrus mites; ecology of domestic mites; pest management and biological control of sunflower insect pests. *Mailing Add:* Dept Entom Agr Res Serv USDA NDak State Univ Fargo ND 58105

CHARLEY, PHILIP J(AMES), b Melbourne, Australia, Aug 18, 21; US citizen; m 48; c 3. MECHANICAL & METALLURGICAL ENGINEERING, CHEMISTRY. *Educ:* Univ Wis, BS, 43; Univ Southern Calif, MS, 47, PhD, 60. *Prof Exp:* Test engr, Gen Elec Co, 43-44; lectr, Univ Southern Calif, 47-49; proj engr, Standard Oil Co, 48-55; vpres, 55-70, PRES, TRUESDAIL LABS, INC, 70- *Mem:* AAAS; Am Soc Test & Mat; Am Soc Mech Engrs; Am Soc Metals; Am Chem Soc. *Res:* Analytical mechanics; organometallic compounds; trace metal metabolism; air pollution problems; forensic engineering and chemistry. *Mailing Add:* Truesdail Labs 4101 N Figueroa St Los Angeles CA 90065

CHARLIER, ROGER HENRI, b Antwerp, Belg, Nov 10, 21; nat US; m 58; c 2. GEOLOGY, GEOGRAPHY. *Educ:* Colonial Univ, Belg, BPol & Admin Sci, 40; Free Univ Brussels, MPolSc, 41, MS, 45; Univ Liege, BS(geol) & BS(geog), 43; Univ Erlangen, PhD(phys geog), 47; Indust Col Armed Forces, dipl, 53; McGill Univ, cert, 53; Univ Paris, LittD(cult geog), 57, ScD(geol, oceanog), 58. *Prof Exp:* Prof geog, Col Baudouin, Belg, 41-42; personal student asst geol, Univ Liege, 43-44; press corresp, 45-51; assoc prof geog & chmn dept, Poly Univ, 51-52; prof phys sci & chmn dept, Finch Col, 52-55; chmn dept geol & geog, Hofstra Univ, 55-58; adj prof geol, Univ Paris, 58-59; vis prof educ, Univ Minn, 59-60; prof geol & geog, Parsons Col, 60-61; dir bur educ travel & study abroad, 61-63, chmn area earth sci, 62-63, coordr earth sci progs, 63-66, vchmn dept geog & environ studies, 67-71, PROF GEOG, GEOL & OCEANOG, NORTHEASTERN ILL UNIV, 61- *Concurrent Pos:* Dept dir, UNRRA, 46-47; res analyst, US Govt, 47, 49 & 50; bursar, Carnegie Corp, 53; vis lectr, NY Univ, 53-58, Hunter Col, 57-58 & Univ Aix-Marseille, 58-60; Fr Govt spec fel, 58-59; resident scholar, Northeastern Ill Univ, 62-65; vis prof, Western NMex Univ, 62-65; NSF grants, 63, 64; vis prof, De Paul Univ, 64-66; vis scientist, Govt SAfrica, 68, Rhodesia, 68, Romania, 68, Israel, 69; exchange sr scientist, NSF, 68, Romanian Acad Sci, 68, Nat Res Coun Romania, 70 & Int Res & Exchange Comn, 69; sr NATO fel & grant, 70; prof oceanog, Fac Sci, Univ Bordeaux, 70-74; extraordinary prof, Flemish Free Univ Brussels, 70-; spec consult, World Tourism Orgn, UNESCO, 73-; exec dir, Inst Develop Riverine & Estuarine Systs, 74-76; sr Fulbright fel, 76; NSF grant, 78; Nat Acad Sci exchange sr scientist, Romania & Bulgaria, 79; Belgian NSF grants, 78, 79, 80 & 81. *Honors & Awards:* Francois Franck Prize, 39; Belg Govt Prize, 39; City of Antwerp Prize, 39; Cross of the Rhine, Belg; Gold Medal for Excellence in Educ, Belg; Medal for Touristic Merit, Belg; Knight, Order of Acad Palms, France; Comdr, Arts-Sci-Lett, France; Knight, Order of Leopold, Belg; Gold Medal Advan of Progress, France; Great Medal, Univ Bordeaux, France, 73; Great Gold Medal Arts-Sci-Lett, France, 79. *Mem:* Asn Am Geogr; Nat Asn Geol Teachers; fel Geol Soc Am; Marine Technol Soc; Am Soc Oceanog. *Res:* Oceanography; coastal erosion; sedimentary processes; applications of statistics to the domain of the earth sciences; regional geography of Europe; ocean energies; ocean economics. *Mailing Add:* 4055 N Keystone Ave Chicago IL 60641

CHARLOCK, THOMAS PETER, b New York, NY, Nov 25, 47. CLIMATE MODELING, ATMOSPHERIC RADIATION. *Educ:* Fordham Col, BS, 69; Univ Ariz, MS, 75, PhD(atmospheric sci), 79. *Prof Exp:* Grad asst, Dept Atmospheric Sci, Univ Ariz, 72-79; res assoc, Rosentiel Sch Marine & Atmospheric Res, Univ Miami, 79-81; STAFF SCIENTIST ATMOSPHERIC SCI, NAT CTR ATMOSPHERIC RES, 81- *Mem:* Am Meteorol Soc; AAAS; Am Geophys Union. *Res:* Mathematical modeling of global climate and atmospheric radiation; analysis of the effects of clouds, gases, aerosol and upper ocean structure on the earths radiation budget. *Mailing Add:* Nat Ctr Atmospheric Res PO Box 3000 Boulder CO 80307

CHARLTON, DAVID BERRY, b Vancouver, BC, Jan 26, 04; nat US; m 30; c 4. CHEMISTRY, BACTERIOLOGY. *Educ:* Univ BC, BA, 25; Cornell Univ, MS, 29; Iowa State Col, PhD(bact), 33. *Prof Exp:* Asst bacteriologist, Portland, Ore, 26-28; instr bact, Ore State Col, 29-31 & Univ Nebr, 31-32; owner & dir, Charlton Labs, 34-71, CONSULT, MEI-CHARLTON INC, 71- *Concurrent Pos:* Instr bact, Ore State Col, 34-36. *Mem:* AAAS; Am Chem Soc; Am Pub Health Asn. *Res:* Food bacteriology; sanitary bacteriology; chlorine compounds as germicides. *Mailing Add:* MEI-Charlton Inc 2233 SW Canyon Rd Portland OR 97201

CHARLTON, GORDON RANDOLPH, b Newport News, Va, Aug 30, 37; m 65; c 2. RESEARCH ADMINISTRATION, HIGH ENERGY PHYSICS. *Educ:* Ohio State Univ, BSc, 57; WVa Univ, MSc, 60; Univ Md, PhD(physics), 66. *Prof Exp:* Res asst high energy physics, Univ Md, 62-66; physicist, Ecole Polytechnique, Paris, 66-69; asst physicist, High Energy Physics Div, Argonne Nat Lab, 69-72; res assoc, Stanford Linear Accelerator Ctr, 72-73; syst mgr Physics Dept, Univ Toronto, 73-75; PHYSICIST HIGH ENERGY PHYSICS, OFF ENERGY RES, DEPT ENERGY, 75- *Mem:* Am Phys Soc. *Res:* Experimental high energy physics; computer controlled film-measuring machines and data processing. *Mailing Add:* Div High Energy Physics Dept Energy Washington DC 20545

CHARLTON, HARVEY JOHNSON, b Dillwyn, Va, Aug 18, 34; m; c 3. MATHEMATICS. *Educ:* Va Polytech Inst, BS, 60, MS, 62, PhD(math), 66. *Prof Exp:* Proj physicist, Atomic Energy Div, Babcock Wilcox Co, Va, 57-59; instr math, Va Polytech Inst, 60-66; ASST PROF MATH, NC STATE UNIV, 66- *Mem:* Am Math Soc; Asn Symbolic Logic. *Res:* Modern topology. *Mailing Add:* Dept of Math NC State Univ Box 5126 Raleigh NC 27601

CHARLTON, JAMES LESLIE, b St Thomas, Ont, Dec 12, 42; m 64; c 2. PHOTOCHEMISTRY, ORGANIC CHEMISTRY. *Educ:* Univ Western Ont, BSc, 65, PhD(chem), 68. *Prof Exp:* Nat Res Coun Can fel, Calif Inst Technol, 68-70; asst prof, 70-74, assoc prof, 74-81, PROF CHEM, UNIV MAN, 81- *Mem:* Am Chem Soc; Can Inst Chem. *Res:* Photochemical kinetics; organic synthesis; photochemical synthesis. *Mailing Add:* Dept of Chem Univ of Man Winnipeg MB R3B 2E9 Can

CHARLTON, THOMAS, b Chicago, Ill, Nov 14, 35; m 59; c 6. ELECTRICAL ENGINEERING, PHYSICS. *Educ:* Univ Notre Dame, BSEE, 57; Ohio State Univ, MSEE, 58, PhD(elec eng), 61. *Prof Exp:* Sr engr, Mil Electronics Div, Motorola Inc, 61-64, sect head antennas & microwave components, 64-65; dir adv develop, 65-66, dir res & develop, 66-70, dir eng, 70-76, MGR ADV PROD RES, ANDREW CORP, 76- *Mem:* Inst Elec & Electronics Engrs. *Res:* Advanced antenna concepts and systems; transmission lines and waveguide; development of tracking systems and advanced communications antennas. *Mailing Add:* Andrew Corp 14445 Rameys Lane Orland Park IL 60462

CHARM, STANLEY E, b Boston, Mass, Oct 18, 26; m 52; c 3. BIOCHEMICAL ENGINEERING. *Educ:* Univ Mass, BS, 50; Wash State Col, MS, 52; Mass Inst Technol, BS, 55, ScD(food tgchnol), 57. *Prof Exp:* Res chemist, Am Home Foods Div, Am Home Prod Corp, NY, 52-53; asst food technol, Mass Inst Technol, 53-55, instr, 55-57, asst prof nutrit & food sci, 57-63; ASSOC PROF PHYSIOL & SCI DIR NEW ENG ENZYME CTR, SCH MED, TUFTS UNIV, 63- *Concurrent Pos:* NIH res grant, 61-; consult, Gen Foods Corp, Del, 61-66 & Bur Commercial Fisheries, US Fish & Wildlife Serv, Mass, 63- *Mem:* Inst Food Technol; Soc Rheol; Soc Cryobiol; Am Inst Chem Engrs. *Res:* Food engineering; rheology; biomedical engineering. *Mailing Add:* Tufts Univ Sch of Med 136 Harrison Ave Boston MA 02111

CHARMAN, HOWARD PRENTIS, medical research, see previous edition

CHARMATZ, RICHARD, micropaleontology, see previous edition

CHARMBURY, H(ERBERT) BEECHER, b Hanover, Pa, Sept 21, 14; m 38; c 2. COAL PREPARATION. *Educ:* Gettysburg Col, AB, 36; Univ Pa, MS, 37; Pa State Univ, PhD(fuel technol), 42. *Prof Exp:* Asst petrol & natural gas, Pa State Univ, 37-39, asst fuel technol, 39-42, from asst prof to assoc prof, 42-50, assoc prof mineral prep eng, 50-53, asst dean planning & develop, Col Earth & Mineral Sci, 71-73, prof, 53-80; RETIRED. *Concurrent Pos:* Secy mines & mineral industs, Commonwealth of Pa, 63-71; consult coal mining, prep & environ probs, 73- *Honors & Awards:* Environ Conserv Award, Am Inst Mining, Metall & Petrol Engrs, 76, Percy Nicholls Award, 77; Environ Conserv Award, Nat Audubon Soc, 77. *Mem:* Am Chem Soc; Am Gas Asn; Am Inst Mining, Metall & Petrol Engrs. *Res:* Mineral preparation engineering; coal preparation. *Mailing Add:* 420 S Corl St Apt 8 State College PA 16801

CHARNES, ABRAHAM, b Hopewell, Va, Sept 4, 17; m 50; c 3. MATHEMATICS, ECONOMICS. *Educ:* Univ Ill, AB, 38, MS, 39, PhD(math), 47. *Prof Exp:* Off Naval Res fel, Univ Ill, 47-48; from asst prof to assoc prof math, Carnegie Inst Technol, 48-52, assoc prof indust admin, 52-55; prof math & dir res dept transportation & indust mgt, Purdue Univ, 55-57; res prof appl math & econ, Northwestern Univ, 65-68; Walter P Murphy prof, 68-78, JESSE H JONES PROF BIOMATH, GEN BUS & MGT SCI, PROF MATH, GEN BUS & COMPUT SCI & DIR, CTR CYBERNETIC STUDIES, UNIV TEX, AUSTIN, 73- *Concurrent Pos:* Ed, J Inst Mgt Sci, 54- *Mem:* Fel AAAS; fel Economet Soc; Opers Res Soc Am; Asn Comput Mach; Inst Mgt Sci (vpres, 58, pres, 60). *Res:* Topological algebra; functional analysis; differential equations; aerodynamics; hydrodynamic theory of lubrication; statistics; extremal methods; game theory; mathematical theory of management science; biomathematics. *Mailing Add:* BEB 203E Univ of Tex Austin TX 78712

CHARNEY, ELLIOT, b New York, NY, June 1, 22; m 47; c 3. CHEMICAL PHYSICS. *Educ:* City Col New York, BS, 42; Columbia Univ, PhD, 56. *Prof Exp:* Res chemist, Manhattan Proj, 42-45, tech adv, 45-48; consult, US AEC, 48-50; consult writer, Kellex Corp, 50-54; res scientist, Lab Phys Biol, 56-72, chief, Sect Spectros & Struct, 72-80, CHIEF, LAB CHEM PHYS, NIH, 80- *Concurrent Pos:* Asst, Columbia Univ, 51-55; vis scientist, Univ Oxford, 62-63; vis fac assoc, Dartmouth Col, 74. *Mem:* Am Phys Soc; NY Acad Sci. *Res:* Infrared and ultraviolet spectroscopy; optical rotatory dispersion; structure and interactions of molecules in condensed phases; electro-optic properties; biopolymers. *Mailing Add:* NIH Bldg 2 Room B1-03 Bethesda MD 20205

CHARNEY, JULE GREGORY, meteorology, deceased

CHARNEY, MICHAEL, b New York, NY, Aug 6, 11; m 41, 66; c 5. PHYSICAL ANTHROPOLOGY, FORENSIC ANTHROPOLOGY. *Educ:* Univ Tex, Austin, BA, 34; Univ Colo, Boulder, PhD(anthrop), 69; Am Bd Forensic Anthrop, dipl. *Prof Exp:* Chief lab serv clin path, Station Hosp, Camp Gordon, Ga, 45-46; chief bacterologist cancer res, Longevity Res

Found, NY, 47-48; dir clin path, Hackensack Bio-Chem Lab, NJ, 46-65; asst prof anthrop, Idaho State Univ, 68-72; from assoc prof to prof, 71-76, EMER PROF ANTHROP & LECTR, COLO STATE UNIV, 77-, DIR, CTR HUMAN IDENTIFICATION, 80- *Concurrent Pos:* Co-dir, Forensic Sci Lab, Colo State Univ, 73, assoc prof zool, 74-, dir, Forensic Sci Lab; dep coroner, Larimer County, Colo, 75- *Mem:* Fel Royal Anthrop Inst Gt Brit; Am Asn Phys Anthropologists; Am Acad Forensic Sci; Soc Study Human Biol; Soc Study Biol. *Res:* Problems in facial restoration as an aid in identification of human remains; problems in sexing, racing, age estimation, stature and weight of human remains. *Mailing Add:* Ctr Human Identification Colo State Univ Ft Collins CO 80523

CHARNEY, WILLIAM, b Russia, Jan 10, 18; nat US; m 47; c 2. MICROBIOLOGY. *Educ:* Johns Hopkins Univ, BA, 40; Rutgers Univ, PhD(microbiol), 53. *Prof Exp:* Bacteriologist, Rare Chems, Inc, 46-50; microbiologist, 53-70, assoc dir microbiol develop, 70-73, DIR MICROBIOL DEVELOP, SCHERING CORP, 73- *Mem:* Am Soc Microbiol; Am Chem Soc; NY Acad Sci. *Res:* Microbial transformation of steroids; vitamin B-12; antibiotics. *Mailing Add:* 110 Christopher St Montclair NJ 07042

CHARNICKI, WALTER FRANCIS, b Haverhill, Mass, Mar 6, 21; m 46; c 2. PHARMACEUTICAL CHEMISTRY. *Educ:* Mass Col Pharm, BS, 43, MS, 48; Purdue Univ, PhD(pharmaceut chem), 51. *Prof Exp:* Control chemist, E L Patch Co, 43, 46; instr, Franklin Tech Inst, 47-48; res assoc, Merck Sharp & Dohme Res Lab, 51-59; dir prod develop, 59-71, VPRES TECH OPERS, DORSEY LABS, SANDOZ INC, 71- *Concurrent Pos:* Retail pharmacist, 43, 46-48. *Mem:* Am Chem Soc; Am Pharmaceut Asn; NY Acad Sci. *Res:* Synthesis of organic medicinal agents; sterile and tablet pharmaceuticals. *Mailing Add:* Dorsey Labs Sandoz Inc PO Box 83288 Lincoln NE 68501

CHARNY, EUGENE JOSEPH, b Philadelphia, Pa, Dec 31, 27; m 53; c 3. PSYCHOANALYSIS. *Educ:* Swarthmore Col, BA, 50; Univ Pa, MD, 54; Pittsburgh Psychoanal Inst, dipl, 67. *Prof Exp:* Intern, Grad Hosp, Univ Pa, 54-55; clin dir, State Hosp, Mayview, Pa, 60-61; instr, Western Psychiat Inst, Med Sch, Univ Pittsburgh, 61-64, asst prof psychiat, 64-76. *Concurrent Pos:* Teaching fel psychiat, Western Psychiat Inst, Univ Pittsburgh, 55-58; teaching analyst, Pittsburgh Psychoanal Inst. *Mem:* AAAS; Am Acad Psychoanal; Am Psychiat Asn; Am Psychosom Soc. *Res:* Human communication; linguistic-kinesic analysis of psychotherapy films; general systems theory; psychoanalytic theory. *Mailing Add:* 405 Med Arts Bldg 3700 Fifth Ave Pittsburgh PA 15213

CHAROLA, ASUNCION ELENA, b Arg, Feb 23, 42. ANALYTICAL CHEMISTRY, PHYSICAL CHEMISTRY. *Educ:* Nat Univ La Plata, lic(anal chem), 67, lic(indust chem), 69, Dr(anal chem), 74. *Prof Exp:* Chief anal chem, Nat Univ La Plata, 72-74; fel, NY Univ, 74-76; asst prof chem, Manhattan Col, 78-81; ASSOC CHEM, METROP MUS ART, 81- *Concurrent Pos:* Warner-Lambert fel, NY Univ, 76- *Mem:* Arg Chem Asn; Am Chem Soc; AAAS; US-Int Coun Monuments & Sites. *Res:* Solid state chemistry; polymorphism; x-ray crystallography; electron microscopy; spectroscopy of solids; electroanalytical chemistry. *Mailing Add:* Objects Conserv Metrop Mus Art Fifth Ave at 82nd St New York NY 10028

CHARON, NYLES WILLIAM, b Minneapolis, Minn, Sept 13, 43; m 69. MICROBIOLOGY. *Educ:* Univ Minn, BA, 65, MS, 69, PhD(microbiol), 72. *Prof Exp:* Teaching res asst microbiol, Univ Minn, 65-72; fel biol sci, Stanford Univ, 72-74; asst prof, 74-80, ASSOC PROF MICROBIOL, WVA UNIV, 80- *Mem:* AAAS; Am Soc Microbiol; Sigma Xi; Am Leptospirosis Res Conf. *Res:* Late gene regulation in bacteriophage lambda; biochemical and genetic studies of the spirochete Leptospira, their relative sensitivity to ultraviolet-light irradiation, membrane fluidity, structure, means for motility and isoleucine biosynthesis. *Mailing Add:* Dept Microbiol WVa Univ Med Ctr Morgantown WV 26506

CHARPIE, ROBERT ALAN, b Cleveland, Ohio, Sept 9, 25; m 47; c 4. THEORETICAL PHYSICS. *Educ:* Carnegie Inst Technol, BS, 48, MS, 49, DSc(theoret physics), 50. *Hon Degrees:* PhD, Denison Univ, 65. *Prof Exp:* Physicist, Westinghouse Elec Corp, 47-50; physicist, Oak Ridge Nat Lab, 50-55, asst dir, 55-61, dir, Reactor Div, 58-61; mgr advan develop, Union Carbide Corp, 61-63, gen mgr develop dept, 63-64, dir technol, 64-66, pres electronics div, 66-68; pres, Bell & Howell Co, 68-69; PRES CABOT CORP, 69- *Concurrent Pos:* Asst, US Mem Seven-Nation Adv Comt, Int Conf Peaceful Uses Atomic Energy, 55, coordr, US Fusion Res Exhib, 58, secy gen adv comt, AEC, 59-63; ed-in-chief, Proc Int Conf, 55; gen ed, Int Monogr Ser on Nuclear Energy, 55-60; ed, J Nuclear Energy, 55-60; mem, Oak Ridge Bd Ed, 57-61; mem adv comn UN sci activities, State Dept, 61-; mem panel, Civilian Technol Pakistan, President's Sci Adv Comn, 61-, mem panel oceanog, President's Sci Adv Comt, 65; trustee, Carnegie Inst Technol, 62- *Honors & Awards:* Award, US Chamber Com, 55. *Mem:* Nat Acad Eng; fel Am Nuclear Soc; fel Am Phys Soc; fel NY Acad Sci; Sigma Xi. *Res:* Theoretical, nuclear and reactor physics. *Mailing Add:* Cabot Corp 125 High St Boston MA 02110

CHART, JEROME JAMES, endocrinology, see previous edition

CHARTERS, ELAINE MARY, b Springfield, Ohio, Aug 15, 32. GENERAL BIOLOGY, MICROBIOLOGY. *Educ:* Our Lady Cincinnati Col, BA, 54; Cath Univ Am, MA, 60, PhD(biol), 63. *Prof Exp:* Med technologist, Mercy Hosp, Springfield, Ohio, 55-56; from instr to prof biol, Edgecliff Col, 62-80, PROF BIOL, XAVIER UNIV, 80- *Mem:* Nat Asn Biol Teachers; Sigma Xi; Am Soc Clin Path. *Res:* Effects of anoxia on liver function of rats; effects of upper lethal temperature on thyroid of tadpoles. *Mailing Add:* Dept Biol Edgecliff Col Xavier Univ 2220 Victory Pkwy Cincinnati OH 45206

CHARTOCK, MICHAEL ANDREW, b Palo Alto, Calif, May 25, 43; m 71; c 1. ECOLOGY, SCIENCE POLICY. *Educ:* Univ Calif, Berkeley, AB, 65; San Jose State Univ, MA, 71; Univ Southern Calif, PhD(biol), 72. *Prof Exp:* Asst prof, 71-77, ASSOC PROF ZOOL, UNIV OKLA, 77- *Concurrent Pos:* Res fel sci & pub policy, Univ Okla, 71-; consult, BDM Corp, 74-75. *Mem:* AAAS; Ecol Soc Am; Am Inst Biol Sci. *Res:* Technology assessment and policy oriented research in energy development including coal, oil, gas, uranium, geothermal and other sources; energy flow in aquatic ecosystems; role of detritus in coral reefs. *Mailing Add:* Dept of Zool Univ of Okla Norman OK 73019

CHARTON, MARVIN, b Brooklyn, NY, May 1, 31; m 55; c 3. PHYSICAL ORGANIC CHEMISTRY, QUANTITATIVE STRUCTURE. *Educ:* City Col New York, BS, 53; Brooklyn Col, MA, 56; Stevens Inst Technol, PhD(chem), 62. *Prof Exp:* Res chemist, Evans Res & Develop Corp, 55-56; instr, 56-61, from asst prof to assoc prof, 61-67, chmn dept, 69-71, PROF CHEM, PRATT INST, 67- *Concurrent Pos:* Fel, Intrasci Res Found, 69- *Mem:* AAAS; Am Chem Soc; Brit Chem Soc; NY Acad Sci. *Res:* Linear free energy relationships in organic chemistry; quantitative treatment of proximity effects; quantitative treatment of bioactivity as a function of molecular structure and activity relationships. *Mailing Add:* Dept of Chem Pratt Inst Ryerson St Brooklyn NY 11205

CHARTRAND, GARY, b Sault Ste Marie, Mich, Aug 24, 36; m 68. MATHEMATICS. *Educ:* Mich State Univ, BS, 58, MS, 60, PhD(math), 64. *Prof Exp:* From asst prof to assoc prof, 64-70, PROF MATH, UNIV WESTERN MICH, 70- *Concurrent Pos:* Res grants, US Air Force Off Sci Res, Univ Mich, 65-66 & NIMH, Res Ctr Group Dynamics, 66; NSF grant, 68-69; Off Naval Res fel, 70-71; vis math scholar, Univ Calif, Santa Barbara, 70-71; managing ed, J Graph Theory, 75-78; vis prof, San Jose State Univ, 78. *Mem:* Am Math Soc; Math Asn Am. *Res:* Theory of graphs; connectivity and line-connectivity; graphical partitions; traversability; line, total and permutation graphs; planarity; colorability; graphs and matrices; reconstruction of graphs. *Mailing Add:* Dept of Math Western Mich Univ Kalamazoo MI 49008

CHARTRAND, MARK RAY, III, b Miami, Fla, Aug 2, 43; div. ASTRONOMY. *Educ:* Case Inst Technol, BS, 65; Case Western Reserve Univ, PhD(astron), 70. *Prof Exp:* Asst to dir astron, Ralph Mueller Planetarium, Cleveland Mus Natural Hist, 65-66; asst astronr & dir educ, Am Mus, 70-74, chmn & assoc astron, Hayden Planetarium, 74-80; EXEC DIR, NAT SPACE INST, 80- *Concurrent Pos:* Adj asst prof, Fordham Univ, Lincoln Ctr Campus, 72-80; mem fac, New Sch, 80-81. *Mem:* AAAS; sr mem Am Astron Soc; fel Brit Interplanetary Soc; Am Inst Aeronaut & Astronaut. *Res:* Galactic structure; photoelectric and photographic photometry. *Mailing Add:* 2801 Park Center Dr Apt A1602 Alexandria VA 22302

CHARVAT, F(EDIA) R(UDOLF), b Pilsen, Czech, Mar 11, 31; US citizen; m 56; c 2. CERAMICS. *Educ:* Univ Leeds, BSc, 53; Mass Inst Technol, DSc(ceramics), 56. *Prof Exp:* Res ceramist, Metals Div, Union Carbide Corp, NY, 56-57, sect leader, 57-59, sect mgr, 59-63, supvr crystal prod, Linde Div, Ind, 63-67, mgr res & develop, Crystal Prod Electronic Div, 67-68, mgr opers, Crystal Prod Dept, San Diego, 68-69, asst gen mgr, 69-71, gen mgr, 71-77, GEN MGR ELECTRONICS DIV, UNION CARBIDE CORP, 77- *Mem:* Am Inst Mining, Metall & Petrol Engrs; Am Ceramic Soc. *Res:* Solid-state materials; thermal properties of dielectrics; properties of liquid oxides; growth of metallic and non-metallic single crystals. *Mailing Add:* Electronics Div Union Carbide Corp Old Ridgebury Rd Danbury CT 06817

CHARVONIA, DAVID ALAN, b Denver, Colo, July 19, 29; m 53; c 2. DYNAMICS, SYSTEMS CONCEPTS. *Educ:* Univ Colo, BS, 51; Purdue Univ, MS, 53, PhD(propulsion), 59. *Prof Exp:* Div mgr & other positions in electronics & space syst, Aerojet-Gen Corp, 61-68; sr staff mem radar syst, ITT Gilfillan, 68; vpres & tech dir res & develop admin, Telluron, 68-72; staff specialist res & develop prog admin, Off Dir Defense Res & Eng, Dept Defense, 72-75, actg asst dir electronic technol, 75, spec asst to dep dir res & advan technol, 75-77; DIR, EUROP REGIONAL OFF, DEFENSE ADVAN RES PROJS AGENCY, STUTTGART, WGER, 77- *Mem:* Sigma Xi. *Res:* Exploratory development pertinent to military applications. *Mailing Add:* Defense Advan Res Projs Agency Hq Europ Command Box 1118 APO New York NY 09128

CHARWAT, ANDREW F(RANCISZEK), b Tallin, Estonia, Feb 10, 25; nat US; m 48; c 1. MECHANICAL ENGINEERING. *Educ:* Stevens Inst Technol, ME, 48; Univ Calif, PhD(mech eng), 52. *Prof Exp:* Lectr, Univ Calif, 49-51, instr, 51-52; aerodynamicist, Propulsion Res Corp, 52-54; preliminary designer, Northrop Aircraft, 54-55; assoc prof, 55-63, PROF ENG & APPL SCI, UNIV CALIF, LOS ANGELES, 63- *Concurrent Pos:* Consult, 58-; Fulbright fel, 61-62; assoc prof, Univ Paris, 61-63; Guggenheim fel, 62-63. *Res:* Aerodynamics and propulsion; heat transfer; energy systems. *Mailing Add:* Dept of Eng & Appl Sci Univ of Calif Los Angeles CA 90024

CHARYK, JOSEPH VINCENT, b Canmore, Alta, Can, Sept 9, 20; nat US; m 45; c 4. AERONAUTICS. *Educ:* Univ Alta, BSc, 42; Calif Inst Technol, MS, 43, PhD(aeronaut), 46. *Hon Degrees:* LLD, Univ Alta, 64; DEng, Univ Bologna, 74. *Prof Exp:* Res engr, Calif Inst Technol, 43-45; instr appl math, 44-46, chief hydrodyn sect, Jet Propulsion Lab, 46; from asst prof to assoc prof aeronaut, Princeton Univ, 46-55; dir aerophys & chem lab, Missile Systs Div, Lockheed Aircraft Corp, 55-56; dir, Aeronaut Lab, Aeronutronics Systs, Inc, 56-58, gen mgr, Space Tech Div, 58-59; chief scientist & Asst Secy Res & Develop, US Dept Air Force, 59, Under Secy of Air Force, 60-63; PRES & DIR, COMMUN SATELLITE CORP, 63-, CHIEF EXEC OFFICER, 79- *Concurrent Pos:* Gen ed, aeronaut pub prog, Princeton Univ, 51-56. *Honors & Awards:* Guglielmo Marconi Int Award, Marconi Found, 74; Theodore Von Karman Award, Am Inst Aeronaut & Astronaut, 77 & Goddard Astronaut Award, 78. *Mem:* Nat Acad Eng; Int Acad Astronaut; fel Am Inst Aeronaut & Astronaut; fel Inst Elec & Electronic Engrs. *Res:* Jet propulsion, space technology and communications. *Mailing Add:* Communications Satellite Corp 950 L'Enfant Plaza SW Washington DC 20024

CHARYULU, KOMANDURI K N, b Hanamkonda, India, May 24, 24; US citizen; m 44; c 6. ONCOLOGY, RADIOLOGY. *Educ:* Andhra Univ, BSc, 45, MD, 51; Royal Col Physicians & Surgeons, dipl med radiation therapy, 60, FFR, 61; Am Bd Radiol, dipl radiation therapy, 70; FRCR. *Prof Exp:* Radium registr & asst surgeon radiother, Radium Inst & Cancer Hosp, India, 55-57; tutor radiol, Osmania Med Col, India, 57-58; hon clin asst, London Hosp, Eng, 59-60, registr, 60-61; locum consult, St Mary's Hosp, Portsmouth, Eng, 62; asst prof radiol, Univ Minn Hosps, Minneapolis, 64-67, assoc prof, 67-70; dir radiation ther, 70-80, PROF RADIOL, SCH MED, UNIV MIAMI, 70-; CHIEF, DEPT RADIATION THER, VET ADMIN MED CTR, 80- *Concurrent Pos:* Spec vis res fel, Mem Hosp & Sloan-Kettering Cancer Inst, 62-63. *Mem:* Radiation Res Soc; Am Soc Therapeut Radiol; Am Soc Clin Oncol; fel Am Col Radiol; Am Radium Soc. *Res:* Oxygenation of tissues and study of radiation sensitivity; modification of radio sensitivity by heat and microwaves; endocrine relationships in carcinoma; dose distribution in electron and x-ray therapeutic regimens. *Mailing Add:* Radiation Ther Dept Vet Admin Med Ctr 1201 NW l6th St Miami FL 33136

CHASALOW, IVAN G, b New York, NY, Mar 6, 30; m 54; c 6. OPERATIONS RESEARCH. *Educ:* Mass Inst Technol, BS, 51; Columbia Univ, MA, 52, PhD(chem), 57. *Prof Exp:* Opers analyst, opers eval group, Mass Inst Technol, 56-59; opers analyst, Bell Tell Labs, 59-76, opers analyst, Am Bell Int Inc, 76-78, OPERS ANALYST, BELL TEL LABS, 78- *Mem:* Sigma Xi; Am Chem Soc; Opers Res Soc Am. *Res:* Military operations research and applied research in underwater sound. *Mailing Add:* 3C332B Bell Tel Labs Whippany NJ 07981

CHASANOV, MARTIN GERSON, b Philadelphia, Pa, Aug 23, 27; m 54; c 3. PHYSICAL CHEMISTRY. *Educ:* Univ Del, BS, 49, MS, 50, PhD(chem), 52. *Prof Exp:* Res chemist, Rohm and Haas Co, 52-54; chemist, Chem Corps, US Army, 54-56; staff chemist, Mil Prod, Int Bus Mach Corp, 56-59; chemist, 59-80, CHEM ENGR, ARGONNE NAT LAB, 80- *Mem:* Am Chem Soc; Sigma Xi. *Res:* Chemical kinetics; heterogeneous catalysis; nuclear radiation effects on electronic materials; nuclear dosimetry; thermodynamics; surface chemistry; semiconductors; ion exchange; high temperature chemistry and batteries; nuclear reactor materials and waste treatment processes; toxic materials. *Mailing Add:* Argonne Nat Lab Argonne IL 60439

CHASE, ANDREW J(ACKSON), b Sebec Station, Maine, Feb 16, 16; m 44; c 1. CHEMICAL ENGINEERING. *Educ:* Univ Maine, BS, 49, MS, 51. *Prof Exp:* From instr to assoc prof, 50-65, PROF CHEM ENG, UNIV MAINE, 65- *Honors & Awards:* Forest Prod Div Award, Am Inst Chem Engrs, 79. *Mem:* Am Inst Chem Engrs; Am Tech Asn Pulp & Paper Indust; Am Soc Eng Educ. *Res:* Surface properties of natural fibers; fluid flow (non-Newtonian); pulp and paper technology. *Mailing Add:* Dept of Chem Eng Univ of Maine Orono ME 04473

CHASE, ANN RENEE, b San Bernardino, Calif, Dec 28, 54. ORNAMENTAL PLANT DISEASE. *Educ:* Univ Calif, Riverside, BS, 76, PhD(plant path), 79. *Prof Exp:* ASST PROF PLANT PATH, AGR RES CTR, UNIV FL, 79- *Mem:* Am Phytopath Soc. *Res:* Diseases of ornamental plants, especially foliage plants; description of new diseases and investigation of the role of nutrition, light and temperature in plant disease; importance of cultural controls in disease control. *Mailing Add:* Agr Res Ctr Rt 3 Box 580 Apopka FL 32703

CHASE, ARLEEN RUTH, b Boston, Mass, Aug 21, 45. IMMUNOCHEMISTRY, PHARMACOLOGY. *Educ:* Boston State Col, BS, 67; Northeastern Univ, MS, 71; Boston Univ, PhD(pharmacol), 82. *Prof Exp:* Immunochemist, Leary Labs, Inc, Boston, Mass, 71-72; supvr, Radioimmunoassay Develop Prog, Collab Res Inc, Waltham, Mass, 72-76; SR SCIENTIST IMMUNOCHEM, INSTRUMENTATION LAB, INC, LEXINGTON, MASS, 80- *Concurrent Pos:* Consult, Collab Res Inc, 76-79; prin investr, Pharmaceut Mfg Assoc Found Inc, 79-80. *Mem:* Am Chem Soc. *Res:* Pharmacological investigations of hypertension and aging in animal models; development of state of the art nonisotopic immunoassay for application to existing and future instrumentation. *Mailing Add:* Instrumentation Lab Inc 113 Hartwell Ave Lexington MA 02173

CHASE, CHARLES ELROY, JR, b Lyndonville, Vt, May 16, 29; m 54; c 2. LASERS. *Educ:* Mass Inst Technol, BS, 50; Camridge Univ, PhD(physics), 54. *Prof Exp:* Staff mem physics, Lincoln Lab, Mass Inst Technol, 54-63 & Francis Bitter Nat Magnet Lab, 63-75; pres, Tachisto Inc, 75-79; SR ENGR, RAYTHEON CO, 80- *Concurrent Pos:* Fulbright award, Univ Leiden, 62-63; adj assoc prof physics, Boston Univ, 70-71. *Mem:* Fel Am Phys Soc. *Res:* Low temperature physics; ultrasonics in solids and liquids; nonlinear optics; plasmas; quantum electronics; laser development; microelectronics. *Mailing Add:* 141 Paul Revere Rd Needham MA 02194

CHASE, CLEMENT GRASHAM, b Phoenix, Ariz, Mar 27, 44; m 66; c 2. MANTLE KINEMATICS, PLATE TECTONICS. *Educ:* Calif Inst Technol, BS, 66; Univ Calif, San Diego, PhD(oceanog), 70. *Prof Exp:* NSF fel, Dept Geod & Geophysics, Univ Cambridge, 70-71; asst prof, 71-75, ASSOC PROF, DEPT GEOL & GEOPHYSICS, UNIV MINN, 75- *Concurrent Pos:* Vis assoc prof, Bd Earth Sci, Univ Calif, Santa Cruz, 78-79. *Mem:* Am Geophys Union; Geol Soc Am. *Res:* Use of geoid and of isotopic systematics to constrain models of mantle kinematics and convection patterns; plate tectonic analysis of structures in western North America. *Mailing Add:* Dept Geol & Geophysics Pillsbury Hall 310 Pillsbury Dr SE Minneapolis MN 55455

CHASE, CURTIS ALDEN, JR, b Palatka, Fla, Mar 20, 36; m 63. CHEMICAL ENGINEERING. *Educ:* Univ Fla, BS, 59; Ill Inst Technol, PhD(chem eng), 69. *Prof Exp:* Engr, Am Oil Co, Ind, 63-65 & Shell Develop Co, 68-77; engr, Intercomp, 77-78; ENGR, TODD, DIETRICH & CHASE, INC, 79- *Mem:* Am Inst Mining, Metall & Petrol Engrs; Soc Indust & Appl Math; Soc Petrol Eng. *Res:* Applied mathematics as related to solving the partial differential equations describing heat and mass transfer processes. *Mailing Add:* 2903 Redbud Katy TX 77449

CHASE, DAVID BRUCE, b Quincy, Mass, June 17, 49; m 71; c 1. OPTICAL SPECTROSCOPY. *Educ:* Williams Col, BA, 70; Princeton Univ, PhD(phys chem), 75. *Prof Exp:* RES CHEMIST, E I DU PONT DE NEMOURS & CO, INC, 75- *Mem:* Soc Appl Spectros; Am Chem Soc; Optical Soc Am; Coblentz Soc. *Res:* Applications of infrared interferometry to industrial problems and development of laser raman microprobe techniques. *Mailing Add:* Exp Sta E328/126 E I du Pont de Nemours & Co Inc Wilmington DE 19898

CHASE, DAVID MARION, b Denver, Colo, Jan 20, 30; m 63; c 1. FLOW-INDUCED NOISE, MATHEMATICAL MODELING. *Educ:* Univ Colo, BS, 51; Princeton Univ, AM, 53, PhD(physics), 55. *Prof Exp:* Staff mem, Los Alamos Sci Lab, 54-57; sr physicist, TRG, Inc, Melville, 57-68; sr scientist, Bolt Beranek & Newman, Inc, 68-79; SR SCIENTIST, CHASE INC, 79- *Concurrent Pos:* Vis asst prof, Iowa State Univ, 56. *Mem:* Am Phys Soc; Am Finance Asn; Acoust Soc Am. *Res:* Analytical modeling in fluid dynamics and structural vibration, especially turbulence and acoustics of flow-induced noise in sonar applications; nuclear models and scattering; acoustics; turbulence; stochastic financial economics. *Mailing Add:* 14 Pinckney St Boston MA 02114

CHASE, FRED LEROY, b Dedham, Mass, Nov 30, 14; m 45; c 2. CHEMISTRY, RESEARCH ADMINISTRATION. *Educ:* Harvard Univ, AB, 37; Mass Inst Technol, ScD(chem eng), 42. *Prof Exp:* Instr chem eng, Mass Inst Technol, 39-40; res chemist, Dewey & Almy Chem Div, 41-44, lab mgr, 44-58, asst dir res, Container & Chem Spec Div, 58-62, mgr compounding tech ctr, Overseas Chem Div, Eng, 62-64, asst dir res, Container & Chem Spec Div, 64, res dir can & drum sealing compounds, Dewey & Almy Chem Div, 64-70, assoc dir res, 70-73, assoc dir res, 73-79, CONSULT CHEMIST, INDUSTRIAL CHEM GROUP, W R GRACE & CO, 80- *Mem:* Am Chem Soc. *Res:* Rubber; colloid chemistry; canning technology; sealing compounds for containers for food preservation and industrial packaging. *Mailing Add:* 30 Lake Shore Dr Arlington MA 02174

CHASE, GARY ANDREW, b New York, NY, Jan 5, 45; m 68, 80; c 2. PUBLIC HEALTH, STATISTICS. *Educ:* Harvard Univ, AB, 66; Johns Hopkins Univ, PhD(statist), 70. *Prof Exp:* NIH fel, Sch Med, Johns Hopkins Univ, 70-71, asst prof med & biostatist, 71-77, ASSOC PROF HEALTH SERV ADMIN & BIOSTATIST, SCH HYG & PUB HEALTH, JOHNS HOPKINS UNIV, 78-, CHIEF STATISTICIAN, LIPID RES CLIN, 72- *Concurrent Pos:* Consult, Nat Heart & Lung Inst Collab Lipid Res Prog, 72- *Mem:* Am Statist Asn. *Res:* Statistical methods in public health. *Mailing Add:* Dept Health Serv Admin Johns Hopkins Univ Baltimore MD 21205

CHASE, GERALD ROY, b Janesville, Wis, Oct 16, 38; m 61, 73; c 4. BIOSTATISTICS, COMPUTER BASED HEALTH SURVEILLANCE. *Educ:* Beloit Col, BS, 61, Stanford Univ, MS, 63, PhD(statist), 66. *Prof Exp:* From asst prof to assoc prof statis & community health, Univ Mo-Columbia, 66-73; vis scientist, environ biomet, Nat Inst Environ Health Sci, 73-74; assoc prof statist & community health, Univ Mo-Columbia, 74-75; BIOSTATISTICIAN/EPIDEMIOLOGIST, DEPT HEALTH, SAFETY & ENVIRON, JOHNS-MANVILLE CORP, 75- *Mem:* Inst Math Statist; Am Statist Asn; Biomet Soc. *Res:* Applications of statistics in health related fields; occupational health surveillance. *Mailing Add:* Johns-Manville Corp PO Box 5108 Denver CO 80217

CHASE, GRAFTON D, b NJ, May 2, 21; m 53; c 3. PHYSICAL CHEMISTRY. *Educ:* Philadelphia Col Pharm, BSc, 43; Temple Univ, MA, 51, PhD(chem), 55. *Prof Exp:* Instr chem, Philadelphia Col Pharm, 46-48; res scientist, Johnson & Johnson, 48-49; from instr to assoc prof, 49-65, PROF CHEM, PHILADELPHIA COL PHARM & SCI, 65-, DIR RADIOCHEM LABS, 67-, DIR DEPT CHEM, 81- *Concurrent Pos:* Assoc canning technologist, Crown Can Co, 45-47; consult, Clinica Quintero Venezuela, 55-56; ed, Remington's Pharmaceut Sci; consult, US Food & Drug Admin, 75- *Mem:* Am Chem Soc. *Res:* Fundamentals of radiochemistry; investigation of antigen-antibody interactions and radioimmunoassay. *Mailing Add:* Dept of Chem Philadelphia Col of Pharm & Sci Philadelphia PA 19104

CHASE, HAROLD FREDERICK, b Nanuet, NY, June 20, 12; m 40; c 3. ANESTHESIOLOGY. *Educ:* Colby Col, BS, 33; Boston Univ, MD, 38. *Prof Exp:* From instr to asst prof pharmacol, Med Sch, Wayne State Univ, 39-44; from asst prof to assoc prof, Western Reserve Univ, 44-48; Commonwealth Fund fel, Hartford Hosp, 48, resident anesthesia, 48-49; anesthesiologist in-chg, Univ Va Hosp, 49-55; prof clin & res anesthesiol, Thomas Jefferson Univ, 55-65; anesthesiologist, Lankenau Hosp, Philadelphia, Pa, 65-68; PROF CLIN & RES ANESTHESIOL, THOMAS JEFFERSON UNIV, 68- *Concurrent Pos:* Consult, Univ Hosp, Cleveland, 45-48. *Res:* Pharmacology of curare and curare-like drugs and anesthetic drugs; clinical usefulness of newer analgesics; carbon dioxide absorption; relationship of intrathoracic and intercranial pressures; humidity in anesthesia systems. *Mailing Add:* 1732 Old Gulph Rd Villanova PA 19085

CHASE, HELEN CHRISTINA (MATULIC), b New York, NY, Mar 21, 17; m 42. BIOSTATISTICS. *Educ:* Hunter Col, AB, 38; Columbia Univ, MSc, 51; Univ Calif, DrPH, 61. *Prof Exp:* Jr statistician, NY State Dept Health, 48-50, from biostatistician to prin biostatistician, 50-63; chief mortality statist br, Nat Ctr Health Statist, US Dept Health, Educ & Welfare, 63-65, statistician, Off Health Statist Anal, 65-69; dir res, Asn Schs Allied Health Prof, 69-71; staff assoc biostatist, Inst Med, Nat Acad Sci, 71-72; statistician, Off Res & Statist, Social Security Admin, Va, 73-75, dep chief, Epidemiol Studies Br, Bur Radiol Health, HEW, Md, 75-80; CONSULT, FOOD & DRUG ADMIN, 80-81. *Concurrent Pos:* Lectr biostatist, Grad Sch Nursing, Cath Univ Am, 66-76; consult, US Dept Health, Educ & Welfare, 61-62, White House Conf Food, Nutrit & Health, 69, Nat Acad Sci, 70 & Maternal & Child Health Proj, George Washington Univ, 70-73; mem radiation bioeffects & epidemiol adv comt, Food & Drug Admin, 71-75; mem, Task Force Ionizing Radiation, US Interagency, 78. *Mem:* Fel AAAS; fel Am Pub Health Asn; fel Am Statist Asn; Soc Epidemiol Res; Pop Asn Am. *Res:* Public health; health planning; epidemiology; infant mortality. *Mailing Add:* 6417 15th St Alexandria VA 22307

CHASE, HERMAN BURLEIGH, b New Hampton, NH, May 7, 13; m 37, 67; c 5. ANIMAL GENETICS. *Educ:* Dartmouth Col, AB, 34; Univ Chicago, PhD(zool), 38. *Prof Exp:* Asst zool, Univ Chicago, 35-38; instr, Univ Ill, 38-41, assoc, 41-45, asst prof, 45-48; assoc prof biol, 48-52, chmn dept, 63-67, dir, Inst Life Sci, 67-75, prof biol, 52-78, EMER PROF BIOL, BROWN UNIV, 78- *Concurrent Pos:* Nat Cancer Inst spec fel, Radiobiol Unit, Mt Vernon Hosp, Eng, 56-57; USPHS spec fel, Commonwealth Sci & Indust Res Orgn, Australia, 64-65 & 72-73. *Res:* Genetics Soc Am; Am Soc Zoologists; Soc Study Evolution; Soc Develop Biol; Radiation Res Soc. Res: Genetics of mice; physiological genetics; radiation biology. *Mailing Add:* RFD New Hampton NH 03256

CHASE, IVAN DMITRI, b Syracuse, NY, Feb 1, 43. ETHOLOGY, SOCIOLOGY. *Educ:* Univ SC, BS, 65; Harvard Univ, MA, 70, PhD(sociol), 72. *Prof Exp:* Vis fel math, Dartmouth Col, 71-73, vis scholar math & soc sci, 73-74, vis scholar sociol, 74-75; hon fel zool, Univ Wis-Madison, 75-78; ASST PROF SOCIOL, STATE UNIV NY STONY BROOK, 78- *Concurrent Pos:* Fel Soc Sci Res Coun, 71-73. *Mem:* Animal Behav Soc; Am Sociol Asn. *Res:* Social inequality in animals and humans; formation and maintenance of dominance hierarchies; cooperative and non-cooperative behavior. *Mailing Add:* Dept Sociol State Univ NY Stony Brook NY 11794

CHASE, JAY BENTON, b Los Angeles, Calif, July 18, 40; m 63; c 2. RESEARCH ADMINISTRATION. *Educ:* Linfield Col, BA, 62, Iowa State Univ, PhD(physics), 70. *Prof Exp:* Jr physicist, Lawrence Livermore Lab, 62-65; physicist, Ames Lab, 66-70; physicist, 70-78, group leader, 78-81, DEP DIV LEADER, LAWRENCE LIVERMORE NAT LAB, 81- *Mem:* Sigma Xi; Am Defense Preparedness Asn. *Res:* Nuclear weapons; continuum mechanics; equations of state; charged particle and neutron transport; radiative transfer. *Mailing Add:* PO Box 808 L-35 Livermore CA 94550

CHASE, JOHN DONALD, b Port Williams, NS, Dec 27, 35; m 63; c 1. CHEMICAL ENGINEERING. *Educ:* Acadia Univ, BSc, 56; McGill Univ, BEng, 58; Univ London, PhD(chem eng), 62. *Prof Exp:* Lectr, W Ham Col Tech, Eng, 59-61; sr res asst combustion, Imp Col, London, 63-64; res engr, Cent Res Div, Am Cyanamid Co, 65-72, sr res engr, 73-74; PROJ LEADER, GULF OIL CAN, 74- *Concurrent Pos:* Admiralty fel, 63-64. *Mem:* Sr mem Chem Inst Can; Am Inst Chem Engrs; Combustion Inst. *Res:* Flame kinetics; acetylene decomposition; heterogenous combustion; high temperature inorganic synthesis; plasma physics; crystal growth; plasma chemistry; fuel engineering; oxygenated gasoline components. *Mailing Add:* Gulf Oil of Can 2489 N Sheridan Way Sheridan Park ON L5K 1A8 Can

CHASE, JOHN WILLIAM, b Baltimore, Md, May 30, 44; m 67. BIOCHEMICAL GENETICS, MOLECULAR BIOLOGY. *Educ:* Drew Univ, BA, 66; Johns Hopkins Univ, PhD(biochem), 71. *Prof Exp:* Res fel biol chem, Harvard Med Sch, 71-74, res assoc, 74-75; asst prof, 75-81, ASSOC PROF MOLECULAR BIOL, ALBERT EINSTEIN COL MED, 81- *Concurrent Pos:* NIH fels, 71-72 & 74-75; Am Cancer Soc fel, 72-73. *Mem:* NY Acad Sci; Am Soc Microbiol. *Res:* Enzymology of DNA replication, recombination and repair including biochemical and genetic studies of the functions of nucleases in these processes. *Mailing Add:* Albert Einstein Col of Med 1300 Morris Park Ave Bronx NY 10461

CHASE, LARRY EUGENE, b Wadsworth, Ohio, Sept 23, 43; m 64; c 2. ANIMAL NUTRITION, ANIMAL PHYSIOLOGY. *Educ:* Ohio State Univ, BS, 66; NC State Univ, Raleigh, MS, 69; Pa State Univ, University Park, PhD(animal nutrit), 75. *Prof Exp:* Dairy supvr, NC Dept Agr, Willard, 68-69; res aide animal nutrit & physiol, Pa State Univ, 69-74; asst prof, 75-81, ASSOC PROF ANIMAL SCI, CORNELL UNIV, 81- *Mem:* Am Dairy Sci Asn; Am Soc Animal Sci. *Res:* Improvement of intake and utilization of foodstuffs by ruminants with emphasis on forage utilization and nitrogen metabolism. *Mailing Add:* 112 Christopher Circle Ithaca NY 14850

CHASE, LLOYD FREMONT, JR, b San Francisco, Calif, Feb 1, 31; m 52; c 3. PHYSICS. *Educ:* Stanford Univ, BS, 53, PhD(physics), 57. *Prof Exp:* Res assoc physics, Stanford Univ, 57-58; res scientist, Res Labs, Lockheed Missiles & Space Co, 58-64, sr staff scientist & sr mem labs, 64-76, MGR NUCLEAR SCI, LOCKHEED PALO ALTO RES LAB, 76- *Concurrent Pos:* Res collabr, Brookhaven Nat Lab, 61-62; vis sr res officer, Univ Oxford, 62-63. *Mem:* Am Phys Soc. *Res:* Low energy nuclear physics; nuclear structure and nuclear reaction mechanisms; space physics. *Mailing Add:* Lockheed Air Craft Corp 3251 Hanover St Palo Alto CA 94304

CHASE, LLOYD LEE, b Milwaukee, Wis, Oct 24, 39; m 68. PHYSICS. *Educ:* Univ Ill, BS, 61; Cornell Univ, PhD(physics), 66. *Prof Exp:* Mem tech staff, Bell Tel Labs, NJ, 66-69; asst prof physics, 69-74, assoc prof, 74-76, PROF PHYSICS, IND UNIV, BLOOMINGTON, 76- *Mem:* Am Phys Soc. *Res:* Electron spin resonance; optical pumping in solids; Raman scattering. *Mailing Add:* Dept of Physics Ind Univ Bloomington IN 47405

CHASE, MERRILL WALLACE, b Providence, RI, Sept 17, 05; m 61; c 3. IMMUNOLOGY, MICROBIOLOGY. *Educ:* Brown Univ, AB, 27, MA, 29, PhD(immunol), 31. *Hon Degrees:* Md, Univ Munster, 74; ScD, Brown Univ, 77. *Prof Exp:* Instr bact, Brown Univ, 31-32; asst immunol, Rockefeller Univ, 32-43, assoc, 43-53, assoc mem & assoc prof, 53-65, prof, 65-76, EMER PROF IMMUNOL, ROCKEFELLER UNIV, 76- *Concurrent Pos:* Mem sci & educ coun, Allergy Found Am, 55-; mem sci adv bd, St Jude Hosp, Memphis, 62-65 & 66-67; mem, Nat Inst Allergy & Infectious Dis, 70-73, consult, sci adv comt, 74-76; mem sci adv comt, Ore Regional Primate Ctr, 71-77. *Honors & Awards:* Distinguished Sci Award, Am Acad Allergy, 69. *Mem:* Nat Acad Sci; Am Asn Immunologists (pres, 56-57); Am Soc Microbiol; Am Asn Lab Animal Sci; fel Am Acad Arts & Sci. *Res:* Hypersensitivity to simple chemical allergens; cellular transfer of contactant and tuberculin hypersensitivities; immunologic unresponsiveness to chemical allergens; study of native mycobacterial antigens; Kveim antigen in sarcoidosis. *Mailing Add:* Rockefeller Univ 1230 York Ave New York NY 10021

CHASE, NORMAN E, b Cincinnati, Ohio, June 29, 26; m 54; c 2. MEDICINE. *Educ:* Univ Cincinnati, BS, 49, MD, 53. *Prof Exp:* Instr radiol, Col Physicians & Surgeons, Columbia Univ, 59-61, assoc, 61; assoc attend, 61, from asst prof to assoc prof, 61-66, PROF RADIOL, MED CTR, NY UNIV, 66-, CHMN DEPT, 69- *Concurrent Pos:* Dir radiol, Bellevue Hosp, NY, 64-74, assoc dir, 74-; sr consult, Manhattan Vet Admin Hosp, 69- *Mem:* AMA; Am Soc Neuroradiol (secy-treas, 62, pres elect, 71); Asn Univ Radiol; NY Acad Sci; Am Col Radiol. *Res:* Cerebrovascular disease; radiology; neuroradiology. *Mailing Add:* NY Univ Med Ctr 550 First Ave New York NY 10016

CHASE, RANDOLPH MONTIETH, JR, b Brooklyn, NY, Aug 10, 28; m 55; c 2. MEDICINE, IMMUNOLOGY. *Educ:* NY Univ, AB, 50, MD, 58. *Prof Exp:* Asst med, Sch Med, NY Univ, 59-61, instr, 61-62; asst physician, Rockefeller Inst Hosp, 62-64; asst prof, 64-70, ASSOC PROF MED, SCH MED, NY UNIV, 70-, DIR MICROBE LAB, UNIV HOSP, 64- *Concurrent Pos:* Nat Inst Allergy & Infect Dis fel, Rockefeller Inst, 62-64; clin asst, Bellevue Hosp, 62-64, asst attend physician, 62-, asst vis physician, 65- *Mem:* AAAS; Transplantation Soc. *Res:* Infectious disease and allergy, including the effect of antibiotics on streptococcal cell wall, particularly the effect of prophylactic antibiotics in RHD and the appearance of given streptoccal strains in SBE; cross reacting antigens existing between bacteria and mammalicin tissues, especially tissue transplants. *Mailing Add:* NY Univ Med Ctr 560 First Ave New York NY 10016

CHASE, RICHARD CONANT, physics, see previous edition

CHASE, RICHARD L, b Perth, Australia, Dec 25, 33; m 65; c 2. GEOLOGY. *Educ:* Univ Western Australia, BSc, 56; Princeton Univ, PhD(geol), 63. *Prof Exp:* Geologist, WAustralian Petrol Ltd, 54-55; asst geologist, Geosurv Australia Ltd, 56-57; sr asst geologist, Ministry Mines, Que, 59; geologist, Ministry Mines & Hydrocarbons, Venezuela, 60-61; Ford Found fel, Woods Hole Oceanog Inst, 63-64, asst scientist, 64-68; asst prof geol, 68-74, assoc prof, 74-78, PROF GEOL SCI, UNIV BC, 78- *Mem:* Geol Soc Am; Am Geophys Union; Geol Asn Can. *Res:* Petrology and structural geology; origin of oceanic igneous rocks; history of ocean floors; marine geology, geotectonics and petrology in the northeastern Pacific. *Mailing Add:* Dept of Geol Sci Univ of BC Vancouver BC V6T 2B4 Can

CHASE, RICHARD LYLE, Nampa, Idaho, Feb 9, 45; m 67; c 5. WEED SCIENCE. *Educ:* Brigham Young Univ, BS, 69; Utah State Univ, MS, 72; Ore State Univ, PhD(weed sci), 79. *Prof Exp:* Area agt, Utah State Univ Exten Serv, 72-74; weed specialist, Int Plant Protection Ctr, Ore State Univ, 74-78; county agt, 78-81, EXTEN WEED SPECIALIST, UTAH STATE UNIV EXTEN SERV, 81- *Mem:* Weed Sci Soc Am; Int Weed Sci Soc. *Mailing Add:* Plant Sci Dept UMC 48 Utah State Univ Logan UT 84322

CHASE, ROBERT A, b Keene, NH, Jan 6, 23; m 46; c 3. RECONSTRUCTIVE SURGERY. *Educ:* Univ NH, BS, 45; Yale Univ, MD, 47; Am Bd Surg, dipl, 55; Am Bd Plastic Surg, dipl, 60. *Prof Exp:* Intern, New Haven Hosp, 47-48; asst resident surg path, bact & cancer clin & asst surg path & bact, Sch Med, Yale Univ, 48-49; asst resident, New Haven Hosp, 49-50, sr asst resident surg, 52-53, chief res surgeon, 53-54; res plastic surgeon, Univ Pittsburgh Hosp, 57-59; from asst prof to assoc prof surg, Sch Med, Yale Univ, 59-63; prof surg & chmn dept, Sch Med, Stanford Univ, 63-73; pres & dir, Nat Bd Med Examr, 73-76; EMILE HOLMAN PROF SURG & PROF ANAT, SCH MED, STANFORD UNIV, 76- *Concurrent Pos:* Teaching fel plastic surg, Univ Pittsburgh Hosp, 57-59; asst, Sch med, Yale Univ, 53-54; attend surgeon, US Vet Admin Hosp, West Haven, Conn, 59-62, consult, 62-63; attend surg, Grace New Haven Community Hosp, 59-63; consult, Christian Med Col & Hosp, India, 62 & Vet Admin Hosp, Palo Alto, Calif; mem med staff, Santa Clara County Hosp; mem, Plastic Surg Res Coun. *Mem:* Inst of Med of Nat Acad Sci; Asn Am Med Cols; fel Am Col Surg; Am Soc Plastic & Reconstruct Surg; Am Soc Surg of the Hand. *Res:* Nerve pedicle regeneration in anterior ocular chamber; objective evaluation of palatopharyngeal function. *Mailing Add:* Dept of Surg Stanford Univ Sch of Med Stanford CA 94305

CHASE, ROBERT L(LOYD), b Brooklyn, NY, Mar 19, 26; m 50, 70; c 3. ELECTRONICS. *Educ:* Columbia Univ, BSEE, 45; Cornell Univ, MEE, 47; Univ Uppsala, PhD(elec eng), 73. *Prof Exp:* From assoc head to head instrumentation div, Brookhaven Nat Labs, 47-77; SR ENGR, ACCELERATOR LINEAR LAB, ORSAY, FRANCE, 77- *Mem:* Fel Inst Elec & Electronics Engrs. *Res:* Nuclear instrumentation. *Mailing Add:* Accelerator Linear Lab Bldg 200-91405 Orsay France

CHASE, ROBERT SILMON, JR, b Abington, Pa, June 9, 30; m 55; c 4. VERTEBRATE ZOOLOGY. *Educ:* Haverford Col, AB, 52; Univ Ark, MS, 55; Bryn Mawr Col, PhD(biol), 67. *Prof Exp:* From instr to assoc prof biol, 58-68, asst dean, 61-64, dean studies, 68-69, dean col, 69-70, 75-78, provost, 70-72, PROF BIOL, LAFAYETTE COL, 74-, HEAD DEPT, 78- *Mem:* Fel AAAS. *Res:* Amphibian development, vertebrate behavior and ecology. *Mailing Add:* Dept Biol Lafayette Col Easton PA 18042

CHASE, RONALD, b Chicago, Ill, Sept 12, 40; m 68; c 2. NEUROBIOLOGY. *Educ:* Stanford Univ, BSc, 62; Mass Inst Technol, PhD(psychol), 69. *Prof Exp:* Asst prof biol, 71-75, ASSOC PROF BIOL, McGILL UNIV, 75- *Mem:* Am Soc Zoologists; Soc Neurosci; AAAS. *Res:* Cellular basis of behavior in gastropod molluscs; development of the nervous system; olfaction. *Mailing Add:* Dept of Biol 1205 McGregor Ave Montreal PQ H3A 1B1 Can

CHASE, SHERRET SPAULDING, b Toledo, Ohio, June 30, 18; m 43; c 5. GENETICS, BOTANY. *Educ:* Yale Univ, BS, 39; Cornell Univ, PhD(bot cytol, genetics), 47. *Prof Exp:* Assoc prof bot, Iowa State Col, 47-54; res geneticist & mgr foreign seed opers, DeKalb Agr Asn, Inc, 54-66, dir, Dekalb-Italiana, 65-66; Bullard fel, Bot Mus, Harvard Univ, 66-67, Cabot fel, Forest Res, 67-69, res assoc econ bot, Bot Mus, 69-70; PROF BIOL, STATE UNIV NY OSWEGO, 70- *Concurrent Pos:* Pres, Catskill Ctr Conserv & Develop,

Inc; dir, Hanford Mills Mus Corp, 73- *Mem:* AAAS; Bot Soc Am; Am Soc Agron; Genetics Soc Am. *Res:* Plant breeding; cytotaxonomy of Najas; parthenogenesis in maize; corn breeding; forest genetics. *Mailing Add:* Dept Biol State Univ NY Col Oswego Oswego NY 13126

CHASE, THEODORE, JR, b Boston, Mass, Aug 20, 38; m 65; c 1. ENZYMOLOGY. *Educ:* Harvard Univ, AB, 60; Univ Calif, Berkeley, PhD(biochem), 66. *Prof Exp:* Res assoc biol, Brookhaven Nat Lab, 67-69; asst prof, 69-74, ASSOC PROF BIOCHEM & MICROBIOL, RUTGERS UNIV, 74- *Mem:* Am Soc Microbiol; Am Chem Soc; Sigma Xi; Am Ornith Union; Brit Ornith Union. *Res:* Mechanism of enzyme action; practical utilization of enzymes and enzyme inhibitors. *Mailing Add:* Dept of Biochem & Microbiol Cook Col Rutgers Univ New Brunswick NJ 08903

CHASE, THOMAS NEWELL, b Westfield, NJ, May 23, 32; m 59; c 2. NEUROLOGY, NEUROPHARMACOLOGY. *Educ:* Mass Inst Technol, BS, 54; Yale Univ, MD, 62. *Prof Exp:* Engr, Singer Mfg Co, Conn, 54-55; res technician, Col Physicians & Surgeons, Columbia Univ, 57-58; intern internal med, Yale-New Haven Med Ctr, 62-63; from asst resident to resident neurol, Mass Gen Hosp, 63-66; guest worker, Lab Clin Sci, 66-68, chief neurol unit, NIMH, 68-74, chief exp therapeut, 70-74; chief, Lab Neuropharmacol, 74-76, dir intramural res, 74-81, CHIEF PHARMACOL SECT, NAT INST NEUROL DIS & STROKE, 76- *Concurrent Pos:* Fel neuropath, Mass Gen Hosp & Harvard Sch Med, 64-65; Nat Inst Neurol Dis & Stroke spec fel, 66-68; clin assoc prof neurol, Sch Med, Georgetown Univ, 71-; consult lectr, Nat Naval Med Ctr, 78-; mem neurol adv comt, Food & Drug Admin; res group Huntington's chorea, World Fedn Neurol; mem sci adv bd & comt to combat Huntington's dis, Huntington's Chorea Found; mem Hereditary Dis Found & Nat Parkinson's Found; mem ed adv bd, Neuropharmacol, Arch Neurol, Progress Neuro-Psychopharmacol & Psychopharmacol Commun. *Honors & Awards:* Winternitz Prize Path, Yale Univ, 60, Ramsay Prize Clin Med, 61; Dipl of Merit, Govt Bolivia, 74; USPHS Meritorious Serv Medal. *Mem:* Am Soc Neurochem; Soc Neurosci; Asn Res Nerv & Ment Dis; Am Neurol Asn; Am Col Neuro-Psychopharmacol. *Res:* Neuropharmacology; clinical and experimental neurology; neurochemistry; neurohumoral mechanisms; research administration. *Mailing Add:* Nat Inst Neurol Dis & Stroke 9000 Rockville Pike Bldg 36 Rm 5A-05 Bethesda MD 20205

CHASE, VERNON LINDSAY, b Baltimore, Md, Mar 20, 20; m 43; c 4. TEXTILE CHEMISTRY. *Educ:* Western Md Col, BA, 41. *Prof Exp:* Res chemist electrochem, Am Smelting & Refining Co, 41-46; res chemist org chem, Ridbo Labs, 47; dir res & develop textile colors, Color & Chem Div, Interchem Corp, 48-57, prog mgr org coatings, Cent Res Labs, 58-66; RES ASSOC POLYMERS, TECH CTR, J P STEVENS & CO, INC, 67- *Mem:* Am Asn Textile Chemists & Colorists. *Res:* Polymeric systems for elastic fabrics; acrylic binders for pigment printing and non-woven fabrics; foam-backcoating; systems for carpet backing and flame retardancy; dyeing systems for new fiber blends. *Mailing Add:* 303 Edgewood Ave Clemson SC 29631

CHASE, WILLIAM HENRY, b Montreal, Que, June 15, 27. IMMUNOPATHOLOGY, NEPHROPATHOLOGY. *Educ:* McGill Univ, BSc, 48, MD & CM, 52. *Prof Exp:* Resident path, Vancouver Gen Hosp, 52-56; from asst prof to assoc prof, 58-74, PROF PATH, UNIV BC, 74-, ASSOC DIR LABS, 79- *Concurrent Pos:* Res fel anat, Univ Chicago, 56-58. *Mem:* Am Asn Path; Can Soc Immunol. *Res:* Electron microscopy, nephropathology, immunophathology. *Mailing Add:* Dept of Path Univ of BC Vancouver BC V6T 1W5 Can

CHASEN, SYLVAN HERBERT, b Richmond, Va, May 19, 26; m 47; c 4. COMPUTER SCIENCES, OPERATIONS RESEARCH. *Educ:* Ga Inst Technol, BChE, 47; Emory Univ, MS, 51. *Prof Exp:* Instr math, Ga Inst Technol, 47-50; mathematician, Naval Air Test Ctr, Md, 51-54 & 56-58, math statistician, 54-56; math specialist, 58-61, assoc scientist, 61-64, staff scientist & head man-comput systs res, Res Lab, 64-68, SR STAFF SCIENTIST, RES LAB, LOCKHEED-GA CO, 68- *Concurrent Pos:* Lectr, Ga Inst Technol, 66, Univ Mich, 66-70, NSF, 67 & Tech Univ Norway, Univ Edinburgh, Tech Univ Delft, Univ Warwick, Brunel Univ, Univ Wis, Univ Ill & Univ Tenn, 68-69; tech prog chmn, Integrated Info Systs Conf, 71. *Mem:* Inst Math Statist; Asn Comput Mach; assoc fel Am Inst Aeronaut & Astronaut. *Res:* Numerical methods; interactive computation; computer techniques in application to systems problems relative to aircraft, missiles and rockets; use of operation techniques in reliability, marketing and war gaming. *Mailing Add:* 760 Starlight Ct NE Atlanta GA 30342

CHASENS, ABRAM I, b Woodbine, NJ, Sept 7, 12; m 42. PERIODONTICS, DENTISTRY. *Educ:* Temple Univ, DDS, 36; NY Univ, cert, 52; Am Bd Periodont, dipl, 54; Am Bd Oral Med, dipl, 66. *Prof Exp:* Asst prof periodont & oral med, Col Dent, NY Univ, 53-57; PROF PERIODONT & ORAL MED & CHMN DEPT, SCH DENT, FAIRLEIGH DICKINSON UNIV, 57- *Concurrent Pos:* Consult, Muhlenberg Hosp, Plainfield, NJ, VA Hosp, Lyons, NJ, St Joseph's Hosp, Paterson, NJ & Holy Name Hosp, Teaneck, NJ, 54-; consult, Dent Educ & Hosp Dent Serv Coun; dir, Am Bd Oral Med, 72-80 & Am Bd Periodont, 80- *Honors & Awards:* Samuel Charles Miller Mem Award, 71; Hirschfeld Medal, Northeastern Soc Periodont, 72. *Mem:* Fel Am Col Dent; fel Am Acad Oral Med (pres, 67-68); fel Int Col Dentists; Am Acad Periodont; fel Royal Soc Health; fel NY Acad Sci. *Res:* Periodontology; oral medicine; occlusion diseases and disturbances of the temporo-mandibular joint; periodontal surgery. *Mailing Add:* Fairleigh Dickinson Univ Sch Dent 110 Fuller Pl Hackensack NJ 07601

CHASIN, LAWRENCE ALLEN, b Willimantic, Conn, July 2, 41; m 61, 75; c 2. BIOCHEMICAL GENETICS. *Educ:* Brown Univ, BS, 62; Mass Inst Technol, PhD(biol), 67. *Prof Exp:* Res assoc microbiol, Lab Enzymol, Ctr Nat Sci Res, 66-68; sr instr cell genetics, Univ Colo Med Ctr, 68-70; from asst prof to assoc prof, 70-81, PROF BIOL SCI, COLUMBIA UNIV, 81- *Concurrent Pos:* Mem genetics study sect, Div Res Grants, NIH, 75-79. *Mem:* AAAS; Genetics Soc Am; Am Soc Cell Biol. *Res:* Application of somatic cell genetic techniques to the study of the regulation of gene expression; biochemical characterization of regulatory variants of cultured mammalian cells. *Mailing Add:* Dept of Biol Sci Columbia Univ New York NY 10027

CHASIN, MARK, b New York, NY, Feb 20, 42; m 63; c 3. BIOCHEMISTRY, ENZYMOLOGY. *Educ:* Cornell Univ, AB, 63; Mich State Univ, PhD(biochem), 67. *Prof Exp:* Sr res investr biochem pharmacol, Squibb Inst Med Res, 67-74; group leader molecular biol, Ortho Res Found, 74-75, sect head biochem res, 75-77, DIR, DIV BIOCHEM RES, ORTHO PHARMACEUT CORP, 77- *Mem:* AAAS; Am Chem Soc; NY Acad Sci; Am Soc Biol Chemists; Am Soc Pharmacol & Exp Therapeut. *Res:* Enzymology and enzyme inhibitors; enzymology concerned with 3', 5'-cyclic adenosine monophosphate; biochemical pharmacology; cardiovascular, hypersensitivity, control nervous system and reproductive research. *Mailing Add:* Ortho Pharmaceut Corp Raritan NJ 08869

CHASIN, WERNER DAVID, b Danzig, Feb 29, 32; US citizen; m 63; c 3. OTOLARYNGOLOGY. *Educ:* Harvard Univ, AB, 54; Tufts Univ, MD, 58. *Prof Exp:* Rotating intern, Mt Sinai Hosp, New York, 58-59; resident otolaryngol, Mass Eye & Ear Infirmary, 59-62, asst otolaryngologist, 62-64; chief otolaryngol, Beth Israel Hosp, 64-68; CHMN DEPT OTOLARYNGOL, SCH MED, TUFTS UNIV, 68-; OTOLARYNGOLOGIST-IN-CHIEF, TUFTS-NEW ENG MED CTR, 68- *Concurrent Pos:* Vis surgeon, Boston City Hosp, 68-; secy-treas, New Eng Otolaryngol Soc, 69-72. *Mem:* Fel Am Acad Ophthal & Otolaryngol. *Mailing Add:* New Eng Med Ctr Hosp 171 Harrison Ave Boston MA 02111

CHASIS, HERBERT, b New York, NY, Nov 9, 05; m 43; c 2. MEDICINE. *Educ:* Syracuse Univ, AB, 26; NY Univ, MD, 30, ScD(med), 37. *Prof Exp:* From instr to assoc prof, 35-64, PROF MED, COL MED, NY UNIV, 64-, ATTEND PHYSICIAN, UNIV HOSP & CLIN, 55- *Concurrent Pos:* Asst vis physician, Bellevue Hosp, 38-43, assoc attend physician, 44-54, attend physician, 57-; chief, Cardiac Clin, French Hosp, 46-64, consult physician, 64-68; consult, St Lukes Hosp, Newburg, NY & Vet Admin, 51-; consult physician, Phelps Mem Hosp, Tarrytown, NY. *Mem:* Am Soc Clin Invest; Am Physiol Soc; Harvey Soc; Soc Exp Biol & Med; fel Am Col Physicians. *Res:* Cardiovascular and renal physiology; physiological and clinical investigation of renal and hypertensive diseases. *Mailing Add:* Dept of Med NY Univ Med Sch New York NY 10016

CHASMAN, CHELLIS, b New York, NY, Feb 11, 32. NUCLEAR PHYSICS. *Educ:* Harvard Univ, BA, 53; Columbia Univ, PhD(physics), 61. *Prof Exp:* SR SCIENTIST PHYSICS, BROOKHAVEN NAT LAB, 61- *Mem:* Am Phys Soc. *Mailing Add:* Brookhaven Nat Lab Upton NY 11973

CHASON, JACOB LEON, b Monroe, Mich, May 12, 15; m 42; c 3. PATHOLOGY, NEUROPATHOLOGY. *Educ:* Univ Mich, AB, 37, MD, 40. *Prof Exp:* Chmn dept, 64-78, CLIN PROF PATH, SCH MED, WAYNE STATE UNIV, 51- *Concurrent Pos:* Neuropathologist, Henry Ford Hosp, 78-; assoc dean, Wayne State Univ Sch Med, 70-72. *Mem:* Am Soc Clin Path; Col Am Path; Am Acad Neurol; Int Acad Path. *Res:* Pathology of the nervous system. *Mailing Add:* 4862 Keithdale Lane Bloomfield Hills MI 48013

CHASSAN, JACOB BERNARD, b New York, NY, Oct 16, 16; m 52; c 3. PSYCHOLOGY, STATISTICS. *Educ:* City Col New York, BS, 39; George Washington Univ, MA, 49, PhD, 58. *Prof Exp:* Statistician, Air Tech Serv Command, Wright Field, Ohio, 42-48; statistician, Med Statist Div, Off Surgeon Gen, US Dept Army, 46-47, chief health reports br, 47-49; chief div tuberc, USPHS, 49-50; chief clin eval & follow-up studies unit, Dept Med & Surg, Vet Admin, 50-53; sci analyst, Mass Inst Tech Opers Eval Group, 53-55; chief statistician, St Elizabeths Hosp, DC, 55-60; math statistician, Off Educ, US Dept Health, Educ & Welfare, 60-61; head statistician, Hoffmann-La Roche, Inc, 61-66; dir statist serv, Sandoz, Inc, NJ, 66-67; assoc dir med res planning, Hoffmann-La Roche Inc, 67-69, psychiat res planner, 69-73, clin res scientist, 73-79; DIR, J B CHASSAN CONSULTS, 80- *Concurrent Pos:* Mem fac, USDA Grad Sch; asst clin prof psychiat, George Washington Univ, 61-73, spec lectr psychiat & behav sci, Sch Med, 73-; lectr biostatist, Seton Hall, 64-65; clin assoc prof statist in psychiat, Med Col, Cornell Univ, 71-73; fac mem, NY Ctr Psychoanal Training, 72-; pvt pract psychother. *Mem:* Fel AAAS; fel Am Statist Asn; Am Acad Psychother; Am Asn Marriage & Family Counrs; Math Asn Am. *Res:* Design of clinical research; applied statistics in epidemiology, psychiatry and psychoanalysis; mathematical statistics. *Mailing Add:* 763 Bloomfield Ave Montclair NY 07042

CHASSON, ROBERT LEE, b Cincinnati, Ohio, May 30, 19; m 42; c 2. EXPERIMENTAL PHYSICS. *Educ:* Univ Calif, Berkeley, AB, 40, AM, 50, PhD(physics), 51. *Prof Exp:* Sr res asst, Elec Resistance Welding Processes, Lockheed Aircraft Corp, 40-42; sr eng aide radar, SigC, Spec Tech Sch, 42-43; asst physics, Univ Calif, 46-50, jr physicist, Off Naval Res & AEC Cosmic-Ray Proj, 50-51; from asst prof to prof, Univ Nebr, 51-62, chmn dept, 56-62; chmn dept, 62-77, dir physics res, Denver Res Inst, 62-77, PROF PHYSICS, UNIV DENVER, 62- *Concurrent Pos:* Fac res fel, Nebr Res Coun, 54; mem comt cosmic rays, Int Geophys Year & Int Geophys Coop, 55-; fel mem vis scientist prog, Am Inst Physics, 58-; Guggenheim fel, sr vis fel, UK Dept Sci & Indust Res & vis prof, Imp Col, London, 62-63 & 76-77; lectr, Univ Denver, 66-67; mem rep, Univ Corp Atmospheric Res, 66-, trustee, 70-79, vchmn trustees, 71-72; mem atmospheric sci adv panel, NSF, 68-70; vis prof, Space Res Lab, Astron Inst, Univ Utrecht, 70; resident vis scientist, Haleakala Observ, Univ Hawaii, 70; mem geophys res bd, Nat Acad Sci-Nat Res Coun, 73-76; Rockefeller fel environ affairs, 78-79. *Mem:* Fel AAAS; fel Phys Soc; Am Geophys Union; Am Asn Univ Prof. *Res:* Cosmic rays; fields and particles in space. *Mailing Add:* Dept of Physics Univ of Denver Denver CO 80208

CHASSON, ROBERT MORTON, b St Louis, Mo, Mar 3, 30; m 54; c 4. PLANT PHYSIOLOGY. *Educ:* Univ Mo, AB, 52, PhD(plant physiol), 59. *Prof Exp:* Asst prof biol, Ill State Univ, 59-60; from asst prof to assoc prof bot, Iowa State Univ, 60-65; ASSOC PROF BOT, ILL STATE UNIV, 65- *Concurrent Pos:* NSF res grant, 62-64; Univ Found res grant, Ill State Univ, 66-71. *Mem:* Bot Soc Am; Am Soc Plant Physiol. *Res:* Cytological and biochemical changes associated with aging of plant storage tissues. *Mailing Add:* Dept of Biol Sci Ill State Univ Normal IL 61761

CHASSY, BRUCE MATTHEW, b Ft Jackson, SC, Oct 22, 42; m 64; c 2. BIOCHEMISTRY, MOLECULAR BIOLOGY. *Educ:* San Diego State Col, AB, 62; Cornell Univ, NIH fel & PhD(biochem), 66. *Prof Exp:* Fel biochem, Albert Einstein Med Ctr, 65-67; fel biochem, 68-69, RES CHEMIST, NAT INST DENT RES, 69- *Concurrent Pos:* Prof lectr, Am Univ, 69-72. *Mem:* AAAS; NY Acad Sci; Am Soc Biol Chem; Am Soc Microbiol. *Res:* Enzyme mechanisms and specificity; plasmids; nucleic acids; nucleotides. *Mailing Add:* Nat Inst Dent Res NIH Bldg 30 Bethesda MD 20014

CHASTAGNER, GARY A, b Woodland, Calif, Sept 9, 48. PLANT PATHOLOGY. *Educ:* Calif State Univ, Fresno, BA, 71; Univ Calif, Davis, MS, 73, PhD(plant path), 76. *Prof Exp:* Res plant pathologist, Univ Calif, Davis, 77-78; ASST PLANT PATHOLOGIST, WESTERN WASH RES & EXTEN CTR, WASH STATE UNIV, 78- *Mem:* Am Phytopath Soc; Sigma Xi. *Res:* Epidemiology and control of diseases on turf, christmas trees, and ornamental bulbs. *Mailing Add:* Western Wash Res & Exten Ctr Wash State Univ Puyallup WA 98371

CHASTAIN, BENJAMIN BURTON, b Tuscaloosa, Ala, Dec 21, 36; m 79; c 2. INORGANIC CHEMISTRY. *Educ:* Birmingham-Southern Col, BS, 56; Columbia Univ, MA, 57, PhD(inorg chem), 67. *Prof Exp:* Assoc chemist, Southern Res Inst, 57-58; pub sch teacher, Ala, 58-59; from instr to assoc prof chem, 59-70, PROF CHEM, SAMFORD UNIV, 70- *Concurrent Pos:* Mem secretary's adv comt coal mine safety res, US Dept Interior, 71-74; vis assoc, Calif Inst Technol, 78. *Mem:* Am Chem Soc; Sigma Xi. *Res:* Synthesis and electronic structures of coordination complexes on transition metals; crystal and molecular structures of complexes of biological interest. *Mailing Add:* Dept of Chem Samford Univ Birmingham AL 35229

CHASTAIN, JACK B, US citizen. ELECTRICAL ENGINEERING. *Educ:* Ga Inst Technol, BSEE, 58, MSEE, 60. *Prof Exp:* Mem staff, Dun & Bradstreet, Inc, Atlanta, Ga, 50-51; res asst, Eng Exp Sta, Ga Inst Technol, 57-60; sr engr, 60-63, mgr elec eng dept, 63-66, group engr, 66-69, PRIN ENGR, SCI-ATLANTA INC, 69- *Res:* Electronic circuitry; radar systems; microwave instrumentation; receiving systems; communications systems. *Mailing Add:* Sci-Atlanta Inc 3845 Pleasantdale Rd Atlanta GA 30340

CHASTAIN, MARIAN FAULKNER, b Sept 9, 22; US citizen; m 56; c 2. FOOD CHEMISTRY, NUTRITION. *Educ:* Cedar Crest Col, BS, 44; Fla State Univ, MS, 53, PhD(food, nutrit), 55. *Prof Exp:* Jr chemist, Hoffmann-La Roche, Inc, NJ, 44-52; asst prof foods & nutrit, Purdue Univ, 55-56; ASSOC PROF FOODS & NUTRIT, AUBURN UNIV, 56-59, 62- *Mem:* AAAS; Am Home Econ Asn; Am Dietetic Asn; Inst Food Technologists; Sigma Xi. *Res:* Improvement of nutritional value of protein foods; effects of microwave heating on palatability and nutritive value; oxidative changes in stored foods and their prevention. *Mailing Add:* 1104 S Gay St Auburn AL 36830

CHASTEEN, NORMAN DENNIS, b Flint, Mich, Oct 6, 41; m 67. BIOINORGANIC CHEMISTRY. *Educ:* Univ Mich, AB, 65; Univ Ill, Urbana-Champaign, MS, 66, PhD(chem), 69. *Prof Exp:* NIH fel, 69-70; asst prof chem, Lawrence Univ, 70-74; assoc prof, 74-79, PROF CHEM, UNIV NH, 79- *Mem:* AAAS; Am Chem Soc; NY Acad Sci. *Res:* Proteins of iron storage and transport. *Mailing Add:* Dept of Chem Univ of NH Durham NH 03824

CHASTON, PETE, meteorology, oceanography, see previous edition

CHASZEYKA, MICHAEL A(NDREW), b Youngstown, Ohio, July 28, 20; m 46. MECHANICAL ENGINEERING, RESEARCH ENGINEERING. *Educ:* Ohio State Univ, BME, 43; Ill Inst Technol, MS, 59. *Prof Exp:* Apprentice engr, US Steel Corp, 46-47; draftsman, Lombard Corp, 47; designer, Youngstown Steel Tank Co, 47; jr engr, Truscon Steel Div, Repub Steel Corp, 47; sr detailer design, Electromotive Div, Gen Motors Corp, 47-51, jr process engr, 51; res engr, Armour Res Found, 53-61; phys sci coordr phys, Mat & Math Sci, Off Naval Res, Chicago, 61-81; CONSULT RES & DEVELOP, 81- *Concurrent Pos:* Organizer & coordr govt groups eval tech qual of independent res & develop progs. *Mem:* Am Soc Mech Engrs; assoc fel Am Inst Aeronaut & Astronaut; fel Marine Technol Soc. *Res:* Energy conversion; theoretical and applied fluid mechanics; underwater propulsion; structural mechanics; numerical methods; tribology. *Mailing Add:* 4147 Grove Ave Western Springs IL 60558

CHATELAIN, JACK ELLIS, b Ogden, Utah, July 17, 22; m 46; c 2. THEORETICAL PHYSICS. *Educ:* Utah State Univ, BS, 47, MS, 48; Lehigh Univ, PhD(physics), 57. *Prof Exp:* Instr physics, Univ Wyo, 50-52; physicist, Dugway Proving Ground, 53; instr physics, Lehigh Univ, 53-57; physicist, Phillips Atomic Energy Div, Phillips Petrol Co, 58; from asst prof to assoc prof physics, 57-71, PROF PHYSICS, UTAH STATE UNIV, 71- *Concurrent Pos:* Physicist, White Sands Proving Ground, 54-55; sci specialist & consult, Edgerton, Germeshausen & Grier, Inc, Nev, 61-63. *Mem:* Am Phys Soc. *Res:* Theoretical aspects of radiation and its interaction with matter. *Mailing Add:* Dept of Physics Utah State Univ Logan UT 84321

CHATENEVER, ALFRED, b New York, NY, May 1, 16; m 40; c 3. PHYSICAL CHEMISTRY, PETROLEUM ENGINEERING. *Educ:* City Col New York, BS, 36; Columbia Univ, MA, 37; NY Univ, PhD(phys chem), 48. *Prof Exp:* Chief chemist & head res & develop sects, Aquatic Chem Labs, New York, 38-42, tech dir, 46-47; sr chemist, Matam Corp, 42-43; res scientist & group leader, Manhattan Dist Proj, 44-46; pvt chem consult, 48-49; res engr & prof petrol eng, Res Inst, Univ Okla, 49-58; sr res assoc, Sinclair Res, Inc, 58-69; INDEPENDENT CONSULT, 69- *Mem:* AAAS; Am Chem Soc; Nat Asn Corrosion Engrs; Am Inst Mining, Metall & Petrol Engrs. *Res:* Kinetics of ionic reactions in solution; gaseous diffusion; physical chemical measurements; water conditioning; corrosion; fluid behavior in porous systems; thermal conductivity; free radicals; research evaluation. *Mailing Add:* 4615 S Florence Ave Tulsa OK 74105

CHATFIELD, DALE ALTON, b Pontiac, Mich, Apr 5, 47. ANALYTICAL CHEMISTRY. *Educ:* Oakland Univ, BA & MS, 69; Univ NC, Chapel Hill, PhD(anal chem), 75. *Prof Exp:* Assoc chem, Univ Utah, 74-77, asst res prof mat sci, 77-78; ASST PROF CHEM, SAN DIEGO STATE UNIV, 78- *Concurrent Pos:* Asst ed, Fire Res, Elsevier Sequoia SA, 78- *Mem:* Am Chem Soc; Am Soc Mass Spectrometry. *Res:* Ionization techniques in mass spectrometry; analytical uses and fundamental studies of ion-molecule reactions in gas phase; chromatographic separation science; thermal degradation of polymeric materials. *Mailing Add:* Dept of Chem San Diego State Univ San Diego CA 92182

CHATIGNY, MARK A, b Can, Sept 19, 20; nat US; m 45; c 5. BIOENGINEERING. *Educ:* Univ Calif, BSEE, 49. *Prof Exp:* From jr res engr to assco res engr, 49-62, chmn, Dept Environ Biol, 68, asst dir, 73, RES ENGR, NAVAL BIOSCI LAB, UNIV CALIF, OAKLAND, 62- *Concurrent Pos:* Consult var agencies, US Dept Defense & univs; mem, Biohazards work group, Nat Cancer Inst, 63-74, Planetary Quarantine Adv Panel, 68-76, Am Inst Biol Sci & Air Sampling Comt & Am Conf Govt Indust Hyg; lectr, Univ Minn, 71-76. *Mem:* Inst Environ Sci; Int Soc Contamination Control; Int Aerobiol Asn. *Res:* Aerosols; biohazards; contamination control in biological facilities; facility design for biohazards and contamination control; modeling risk assessment procedures in microbiology laboratories, hospitals and pharmaceutical plants; studies in development and demonstration of medically acceptable energy conservation techniques in hospitals and laboratories. *Mailing Add:* Naval Biosci Lab Univ Calif Oakland CA 94625

CHATLAND, HAROLD, b Hamilton, Can, Nov 13, 11; nat US; m 37; c 3. MATHEMATICS. *Educ:* McMaster Univ, BA, 34; Univ Chicago, MS, 35, PhD(math), 37. *Prof Exp:* Asst prof math, Univ Mont, 39-46 & Ohio State Univ, 46-49; prof, Univ Mont, 49-59, dean col arts & sci, 54, dean fac, 56-57, acad vpres, 57-59; eng specialist, Sylvania Elec Prod, Inc, 59-62; acad dean, Western Wash State Col, 62-64; sr eng specialist, Electronic Defense Labs, 64-68; mem staff, Sylvania Electronics Systs, 68-71; CONSULT, 71- *Mem:* Soc Indust & Appl Math; Math Asn Am. *Res:* Number theory; decision-making techniques. *Mailing Add:* 10566 Blandor Way Los Altos Hills CA 94022

CHATO, JOHN C(LARK), b Budapest, Hungary, Dec 28, 29; nat US; m 54; c 3. MECHANICAL ENGINEERING, BIOENGINEERING. *Educ:* Univ Cincinnati, ME, 54; Univ Ill, MS, 55; Mass Inst Technol, PhD, 60. *Prof Exp:* Asst mech eng, Mass Inst Technol, 56-57, from instr to asst prof, 57-64; assoc prof, 64-69, PROF MECH ENG, UNIV ILL, URBANA, 69- *Concurrent Pos:* Engr & consult indust & govt, 54-; NSF fel, Europe, 61-62; Fogarty sr int fel, Fogarty Found, NIH & Inst Biomed Technol, Zürich, Switz, 78-79. *Honors & Awards:* Charles Russ Richards Mem Award, Am Soc Mech Engrs & Pi Tau Sigma, 78. *Mem:* Fel Am Soc Mech Engrs; Am Soc Heating, Refrig & Air-Conditioning Eng; Inst Elec & Electronics Engrs; Am Soc Eng Educ; Int Inst Refrig. *Res:* Heat transfer and fluid mechanics; bio-medical engineering; two phase flows; environmental controls and refrigeration; cryogenics. *Mailing Add:* Dept of Mech & Indust Eng Univ of Ill Urbana IL 61801

CHATT, ALLEN BARRETT, b Phoenix, Ariz, July 17, 49; m 71. EPILEPTOLOGY, ELECTROPHYSIOLOGY. *Educ:* State Univ NY, Buffalo, BS, 71; Fla State Univ, MS, 74, PhD(psychol), 78. *Prof Exp:* Res assoc, Marine Biomed Inst, Univ Tex Med Br, 77; fel assoc, 79-80, RES ASST PROF, DEPT NEUROL, SCH MED, YALE UNIV, 80-; RES PSYCHOLOGIST, NEUROL SERV, EPILEPSY CTR, VET ADMIN MED CTR, 79- *Mem:* Soc Neurosci; Int Asn Study Pain; NY Acad Sci; AAAS. *Res:* Small focus neocortical model of penicillin epilepsy; monitoring of neuronal responses early in seisure development, used to identify epileptic responses mediated by neural pathways; transmitters different from those of normal responses and site of focus generation. *Mailing Add:* Dept Neuro Sch Med Yale Univ 333 Cedar St New Haven CT 06510

CHATTEN, LESLIE GEORGE, b Calgary, Alta, May 10, 20; m 43; c 3. PHARMACEUTICAL CHEMISTRY. *Educ:* Univ Alta, BSc, 47, MSc, 49; Ohio State Univ, PhD(pharmaceut chem), 61. *Prof Exp:* Head pharmaceut chem sect, Food & Drug Directorate, Dept Nat Health & Welfare, Govt Can, 49-61; assoc prof, 61-65, PROF PHARMACEUT CHEM, UNIV ALTA, 65- *Concurrent Pos:* Mem comt assay tablets & capsules, Brit Pharmacopoeia, 53-63 & comt org synthetic substances, 58-63; vis scientist, Med Res Coun Can, 70-71. *Mem:* Am Chem Soc; Sigma Xi; Acad Pharmaceut Sci; Chem Inst Can; fel Royal Soc Chem. *Res:* Qualitative and quantitative pharmaceutical chemistry; application of nonaqueous titrimetry to analysis of drugs and pharmaceuticals; identification of organic medicinal agents; polarography and other electroanalytical techniques; absorption spectrophotometry; fluorimetry; high performance liquid chromatography; redox titrimetry. *Mailing Add:* Fac Pharm & Pharmaceut Sci Univ Alta Edmonton AB T6G 2E8 Can

CHATTERJEE, NANDO KUMAR, b W Bengal, India, Nov 1, 38; US citizen; m 69; c 1. BIOCHEMISTRY, MOLECULAR BIOLOGY. *Educ:* Univ Calcutta, India, PhD(bot), 62; Univ Nebr, PhD(genetics biochem), 69. *Prof Exp:* Res assoc genetics, Univ Nebr, 65-67, fel biochem, 69-71; guest scientist biochem, Roche Inst Molecular Biol, 71-74; molecular biologist virol, Plum Island Animal Dis Ctr, Agr Res Serv, USDA, 74-75; SR RES SCIENTIST VIROL, DIV LABS & RES, NY DEPT HEALTH, 75- *Concurrent Pos:* 10th Int Cong Biochem travel grant; res grants, NIH & NY State Health Res Coun. *Mem:* AAAS; Am Soc Biol Chemists; Genetics Soc Am. *Res:* Molecular biology of viruses, cells; mechanisms of gene expression in uninfected and virus-infected cells using the parameters of RNA and protein synthesis. *Mailing Add:* Div of Labs & Res IDC Empire State Plaza Albany NY 12201

CHATTERJEE, PRONOY KUMAR, b Varanasi, India, Oct 26, 36; m 62; c 2. POLYMER SCIENCE, PHYSICAL CHEMISTRY. *Educ:* Banaras Hindu Univ, BS, 56, MS, 58; Calcutta Univ, PhD(chem), 63, DSc(chem), 74. *Prof Exp:* Sr res asst polymers, Indian Asn Cultivation Sci, Calcutta, 59-63; Nat

Acad Sci-Nat Res Coun res assoc chem, Southern Regional Res Labs, USDA, La, 63-65; res assoc polymers, Princeton Univ, 65-66; sr res chemist, 66-74, MGR, MAT RES DEPT, PERSONAL PROD CO DIV, JOHNSON & JOHNSON, 74- *Honors & Awards:* P B Hofman Res Scientist Award, Johnson & Johnson, 73; Educ Serv Award, Plastic Inst Am, 74. *Mem:* AAAS; Am Chem Soc; fel Am Inst Chemists; Tech Asn Pulp & Paper Indust; Int Confederation Thermal Anal. *Res:* Rubber vulcanization mechanism; analysis of rubber chemicals; polymer characterization; reaction kinetics; thermal analysis; reaction mechanism of polysulfides; polymerization; inter-fiber bonding mechanism of cellulose; characterization and preparation of chemically modified wood pulp. *Mailing Add:* Mat Res Dept Personal Prod Co Div Johnson & Johnson Milltown NJ 08850

CHATTERJEE, RAMANANDA, b India, Mar 1, 36; m 65; c 2. SOLID STATE PHYSICS. *Educ:* Calcutta Univ, BS, 54, MS, 56, PhD(physics), 63. *Prof Exp:* Fel, Inst Theoret Physics, Univ Alta, 63-65; from asst prof to assoc prof physics, 65-74, PROF PHYSICS, UNIV CALGARY, 74- *Res:* Theoretical aspects of electron paramagnetic resonance and electron-nuclear double resonance spectrum. *Mailing Add:* Dept of Physics Univ of Calgary Calgary AB T2N 1N4 Can

CHATTERJEE, SAMPRIT, b Calcutta, India, June 3, 38; US citizen; m. STATISTICS, OPERATIONS RESEARCH. *Educ:* Univ Calcutta, BS & MS, 60; Univ Cambridge, DStat, 62; Harvard Univ, PhD(statist), 66. *Prof Exp:* Instr statist, Boston Univ, 62-63; res asst, Harvard, 63-65; asst prof statist & opers res, 66-69, assoc prof statist, 69-74, PROF STATIST, NY UNIV, 74- *Concurrent Pos:* Consult, Mass Ment Health Ctr, 63-65, Coun Drug Abuse, 75-76 & Montefiore Hosp, 76-; res fel, Univ Col, London, 73-74; res scholar, Rand Corp, 68-70, Inst Appl Systs Anal, Vienna, 74 & Environ Protection Res Inst, 81-; vis fel, Stat Dept, Govt New Zealand, 80; vis prof, Auckland Univ, 81 & statist, Stanford Univ, 81. *Mem:* Am Statist Asn; Biomet Soc; Royal Statist Soc; Opers Res Soc Am; AAAS. *Res:* Environmental problems; ecology; linear models; sample survey; systems analysis; public policy; market research; data analysis. *Mailing Add:* Dept of Quantitative Anal NY Univ New York NY 10006

CHATTERJEE, SANKAR, b Calcutta, India, May 28, 43; m 71; c 1. PALEONTOLOGY. *Educ:* Jadavpur Univ, India, BS, 62, MS, 64; Calcutta Univ, PhD(geol), 70. *Prof Exp:* Sr lectr geol, Indian Statist Inst, India, 68-75; asst lectr paleont, Univ Calif, Berkeley, 76; asst lectr geol, George Washington Univ, DC, 76-77; fel paleont, Smithsonian Inst, DC, 77-78; asst lectr geol, George Mason Univ, Va, 78-79; ASST LECTR & CUR PALEONT, TEX TECH UNIV, 79- *Concurrent Pos:* Prin investr, Explor Triassic Vertebrates at WTex, Nat Geog Soc, 80-81; prin investr, Geol Marie Byrd land, Antarctic, NSF, Tex Tech, 79-; prin investr, stratig & paleont, S Victoria Land, Antarctic, NSF, Tex Tech, 79- *Mem:* Soc Vertebrate Paleont; Am Geol Inst. *Res:* Fossil vertebrates of Indian Gondwana rocks; Gondwana reassembly; geology of Antarctica; triassic fossils from Texas. *Mailing Add:* The Museum Tex Tech Univ Lubbock TX 79409

CHATTERJEE, SUNIL KUMAR, b Calcutta, India, Aug 7, 40; m 72; c 2. BIOCHEMISTRY. *Educ:* Presidency Col, Calcutta, BS, 59; Univ Calcutta, MS, 61, PhD(biochem), 66. *Prof Exp:* Fel protein biosynthesis, Univ Pa, 66-68; res assoc, Inst Cancer Res, 68-70; asst res officer, Univ Calcutta, 70-71; res fel, Max-Planck Inst, Ger, 71-72; SR CANCER RES SCIENTIST, ROSWELL PARK MEM INST, 72- *Mem:* AAAS; Am Asn Cancer Res; NY Acad Sci. *Res:* Biochemistry of cancer cells. *Mailing Add:* Roswell Park Mem Inst 666 Elm St Buffalo NY 14263

CHATTERJI, DEBAJYOTI, b Puri, India, Aug 4, 44; m 68; c 3. METALLURGICAL ENGINEERING, PHYSICAL CHEMISTRY. *Educ:* Utkal Univ, India, BS, 63; Indian Inst Technol, India, BTech, 66; Purdue Univ, MS, 68, PhD(metall eng), 71. *Prof Exp:* Asst lectr metall, Indian Inst Technol, India, 66-67; asst, Purdue Univ, 67-71; vis scientist, Wright-Patterson AFB, Ohio, 71-73; metall engr, 73-74, tech adminr tech liaison, 74-75, mgr electrochem br, 75-79, mgr chem systems & technol lab, 79-80, MGR, INORGANIC MATERIALS & STRUCTURES LAB, GEN ELEC CORP & DEVELOP CTR, 80- *Concurrent Pos:* Nat Res Coun resident res fel, 71-73; mem nat battery adv comt, Dept of Energy, 76-79. *Honors & Awards:* Geisler Award, Am Soc Metals, 80. *Mem:* Electrochem Soc; Am Soc Metals; Sigma Xi. *Res:* High temperature corrosion and oxidation; batteries; fuel cells; thermochemistry; thermodynamics; mass transfer; electrochemistry; coatings; ceramics; superalloys. *Mailing Add:* Gen Elec Corp Res & Develop PO Box 8 Bldg K-1 Rm 5B39 Schenectady NY 12301

CHATTERTON, BRIAN DOUGLAS EYRE, b Khartoum, Sudan, July 31, 43; Irish & Can citizen; m 70; c 2. PALEONTOLOGY. *Educ:* Trinity Col, Dublin, BA, 65; Australian Nat Univ, PhD(paleont), 70. *Prof Exp:* Sr demonstr paleont, Australian Nat Univ, 69-70; asst prof, 70-76, ASSOC PROF PALEONT, UNIV ALTA, 76- *Mem:* Geol Asn Can; Paleont Soc; Palaeont Asn; Int Palaeont Asn. *Res:* Ontogenetic, paleoecologic and systematic studies of trilobites from Western and Arctic Canada; systematics, paleoecology and biostratigraphy of conodonts from Western and Arctic Canada; Paleoezoic paleontology. *Mailing Add:* Dept of Geol Univ of Alta Edmonton Can

CHATTERTON, NORMAN JERRY, b Mapleton, Idaho, Feb 11, 39; m 63; c 4. PLANT PHYSIOLOGY. *Educ:* Utah State Univ, BS, 66; Univ Calif, MS, 68, PhD(plant physiol), 70. *Prof Exp:* Plant physiologist crops, 70-81, AGR ADMINR, AGR RES SERV, USDA, 81- *Mem:* Am Soc Agron; Crop Sci Soc Am. *Res:* Whole plant photosynthesis; photosynthate partitioning and utilization in crop plants including forages. *Mailing Add:* Agr Res Serv USDA Utah State Univ UMC 48 Logan UT 84322

CHATTERTON, ROBERT TREAT, JR, b Catskill, NY, Aug 9, 35; m 56; c 4. ENDOCRINOLOGY, BIOCHEMISTRY. *Educ:* Cornell Univ, BS, 58, PhD(physiol biochem), 63; Univ Conn, MS, 60. *Prof Exp:* Res fel biol chem, Harvard Univ, 63-65; res assoc, Div Neoplastic Med, Montefiore Hosp & Med Ctr, 65-70; from asst prof to assoc prof obstet & gynec, physiol & biol chem, Univ Ill Med Ctr, 70-79; PROF OBSTET & GYNEC, NORTHWESTERN UNIV MED SCH, 79- *Mem:* Am Chem Soc; Endocrine Soc; Soc Study Reproduction; Soc Gynec Invest; Am Physiol Soc. *Res:* Physiology, biochemistry and histology of mammary gland development and ovarian function; steroid biosynthesis; contraceptive development. *Mailing Add:* Prentice Hosp Maternity Ctr Suite 1130 Northwestern Univ Med Sch Chicago IL 60611

CHATTHA, MOHINDER SINGH, b Gurdaspur, India, Oct 15, 40; m 67; c 2. POLYMER CHEMISTRY. *Educ:* Sikh Nat Col, India, BSc, 60; Banaras Hindu Univ, MSc, 63; Tulane Univ, PhD(chem), 71. *Prof Exp:* Teacher sci, Khalsa High Sch, Wadala, India, 60-61; lectr chem, Sikh Nat Col, 63-65; res fel, Coun Sci & Indust Res, New Delhi, 65-67; fel, Tulane Univ, 71-72; Nat Res Coun fel polymer chem, Wright-Patterson AFB, Ohio, 72-73; SR RES SCIENTIST POLYMER CHEM, RES & DEVELOP, FORD MOTOR CO, 73- *Mem:* Am Chem Soc. *Res:* Organophosphorus chemistry; synthesis and chemistry of new polymers of potential use in coatings, adhesives and elastomers. *Mailing Add:* 33466 Vargo Livonia MI 48152

CHATTOPADHYAY, KAMANIO, b India, Mar 3, 50; m 79; c 1. PHASE TRANSFORMATION, RAPID SOLIDIFICATION. *Educ:* Baharas Hindu Univ, India, BS, 71, MS, 73, PhD(metall), 78. *Prof Exp:* Asst prof, Baharas Hindu Univ, 76-80; VIS RES PROF METALL, CARNEGIE-MELLON UNIV, 80- *Honors & Awards:* Young Scientist of the year, Indian Nat Sci Acad, 79. *Mem:* Am Metals Soc; Am Inst Mining; Indian Inst Metals. *Res:* Study of metastable crystalline alloys formed by rapid solidification processing; the nature of growth interface during phase transformation using high resolution electon microscopy. *Mailing Add:* 5440 Claybourne St Pittsburgh PA 15232

CHATTORAJ, SATI CHARAN, b WBengal, India, Aug 1, 34; m 61; c 1. REPRODUCTIVE ENDOCRINOLOGY. *Educ:* Univ Calcutta, BS, 54, MS, 56; Boston Univ, PhD(biochem), 65. *Prof Exp:* Asst prof obstet & gynec, Chicago Med Sch, 65-69; asst prof, 69-71, ASSOC PROF BIOCHEM OBSTET & GYNEC, SCH MED, BOSTON UNIV, 71- *Concurrent Pos:* Nat Inst Child Health & Human Develop grant, Sch Med, Boston Univ, 74-77; asst dir gynecic endocrinol, Michael Reese Hosp & Med Ctr, 65-69. *Honors & Awards:* Morris L Parker Award, Chicago Med Sch, 67. *Mem:* AAAS; Am Inst Biol Sci; Endocrine Soc; Soc Study Reproduction; Am Chem Soc. *Res:* Reproductive endocrinology; control of steroidogenesis during pregnancy; contraception; breast and endometrial cancer. *Mailing Add:* Dept of Obstet & Gynec Boston Univ Sch of Med Boston MA 02118

CHATURVEDI, MAHESH CHANDRA, b Unnao, India, May 3, 40. METALLURGY, MATERIALS SCIENCE. *Educ:* Banaras Hindu Univ, BSc, 60; Univ Sheffield, MMet, 62, PhD(metall), 66. *Prof Exp:* Res fel, 66-69, asst prof, 69-70, assoc prof, 70-75, PROF METALL, METALL SCI LAB, UNIV MAN, 75- *Mem:* Am Soc Metals; Am Inst Mining, Metall & Petrol Engrs; Electron Micros Soc Am; Can Inst Mining & Metall. *Res:* Precipitation strengthening of metallic materials; electron microscopic studies of phase transformations in metals and alloys; alloy development work; corrosion of metals and alloys. *Mailing Add:* Dept of Mech Eng Univ of Man Winnipeg MB R3B 2E9 Can

CHATURVEDI, RAM PRAKASH, b India, Dec 15, 31; m 64; c 1. ATOMIC PHYSICS. *Educ:* Agra Univ, BSc, 53, MSc, 55; Univ BC, PhD(nuclear spectros), 63. *Prof Exp:* Lectr physics, Agra Univ, 55-59; fel & lectr, Panjab Univ, India, 63-64; fel, State Univ NY Buffalo, 64-65; assoc prof, 65-70, PROF PHYSICS, STATE UNIV NY COL CORTLAND, 70- *Concurrent Pos:* Mem users group, Oak Ridge Nat Lab, 70; mem, Res Participation Team, Brookhaven Nat Lab. *Mem:* Am Phys Soc; Am Asn Physics Teachers. *Res:* Nuclear level schemes. *Mailing Add:* Dept of Physics State Univ of NY Col Cortland NY 13045

CHATURVEDI, RAMA KANT, b Kanker, India, July 7, 33; m 58; c 3. BIO-ORGANIC CHEMISTRY. *Educ:* Agra Univ, India, BSc, 54, MSc, 56, PhD(chem), 60. *Prof Exp:* Lectr chem, H B Technol Inst, India, 60-64 & St Stephen's Col, Univ Delhi, 64-65; res assoc, Ind Univ, 65-66; res assoc biochem, Yale Univ, 66-70; assoc prof, 70-76, PROF CHEM, GTR HARTFORD COMMUNITY COL, 76-, CHMN DEPT SCI, 77- *Concurrent Pos:* Fulbright Award, US Educ Found in India, 65; asst instr, Yale Univ, 70-74; lectr, Cent Conn State Col, 73 & 75- *Mem:* AAAS; Am Chem Soc. *Res:* Mechanism of acyl transfer reactions with special attention to the formation and partitioning of tetrahedral intermediates involved in these reactions. *Mailing Add:* 39 Beacon St Newington CT 06111

CHATY, JOHN CULVER, b San Francisco, Calif, Sept 12, 25; m 51; c 1. CHEMICAL ENGINEERING. *Educ:* Univ Ala, BS, 57; Univ Va, DSc(chem eng), 62. *Prof Exp:* Prod supvr, Calabama Plant, Olin-Mathieson Chem Corp, 50-53, tech asst, 53-54; engr develop, Esso Res & Eng Co, 57-59; engr res & develop, Chem Div, 61-75, technol mgr, 75-81, LARGE SCALE PILOT PLANT MGR, ETHYLENE OXIDE/GLYCOL DIV, UNION CARBIDE CORP, 81- *Mem:* Am Inst Chem Engrs. *Res:* Application of fundamentals of chemical engineering in development of chemical process facilities; polymer systems. *Mailing Add:* 1001 Rustling Rd South Charleston WV 25303

CHAU, ALFRED SHUN-YUEN, b Hong Kong, Nov 20, 41; Can citizen; m 66; c 1. ANALYTICAL CHEMISTRY. *Educ:* Univ BC, BSc, 61; Carleton Univ, MSc, 66. *Prof Exp:* Pesticide analyst, Dept Agr, Ottawa, 65-70; chemist, 70-73, head, Spec Serv Sect, 73-80, HEAD QUAL ASSURANCE & METHODS SECT, DEPT ENVIRON, CAN 80- *Concurrent Pos:* Sci reviewer, J Asn Off Anal Chemists, 70- *Mem:* Can Inst Chem; Asn Off Anal Chemists. *Res:* Design quality controls studies for trace organics; development of methodology for the analysis and positive confirmation of organic pollutants, particularly biocides, by chemical derivatization-gas chromatographic techniques; development of standard reference materials for environmental analysis. *Mailing Add:* Water Qual Br PO Box 5050 Burlington ON L7R 4A6 Can

CHAU, CHEUK-KIN, b Hong Kong, Sept 25, 41; m 68. SOLID STATE PHYSICS, CRYOGENICS. *Educ:* MacMurray Col, BA, 62; Univ Ill, Urbana, MS, 63, PhD(physics), 68. *Prof Exp:* Vis asst prof, Ill Inst Technol, 68-69, asst prof physics, 69-75; vis assoc prof, 75-76, assoc prof, 76-80, PROF PHYSICS, CALIF STATE UNIV, CHICO, 80- *Mem:* Am Phys Soc; Am Asn Physics Teachers; Sigma Xi. *Res:* Apply cryogenic technology to investigate heat transport, electrical transport, optics and radiation damages in condensed materials such as insulators, semiconductors, semi-metal and superconductors. *Mailing Add:* Dept of Physics Calif State Univ Chico CA 95926

CHAU, LING-LIE, b Hunan, China, Jan 18, 39; US citizen; m 64; c 1. HIGH ENERGY PHYSICS. *Educ:* Nat Taiwan Univ, BS, 61; Univ Calif, Berkeley, PhD(physics), 66. *Prof Exp:* Fel physics, Lawrence Radiation Lab, Berkeley, 67; mem, Inst Advan Study, 67-69; vis fel, Europe Cttr High Energy Physics, 69; from asst physicist to assoc physicist, 69-74, PHYSICIST, BROOKHAVEN NAT LAB, 74- *Mailing Add:* Dept Physics Brookhaven Nat Lab Upton NY 11973

CHAU, MICHAEL MING-KEE, b Hong Kong, Nov 14, 47; m 75; c 2. PHYSICAL ORGANIC CHEMISTRY, POLYMER CHEMISTRY. *Educ:* Calif State Univ Fresno, BS, 71; Univ Ill, Urbana, PhD(chem), 75. *Prof Exp:* res assoc org chem, Tex Tech Univ, 75-77; SR RES CHEMIST, PPG INDUST, INC, 77- *Mem:* Am Chem Soc. *Res:* Polymer design, synthesis and characterization; organic synthesis; mechanistic studies of organosulfur compounds; anchimeric acceleration of bond homolyses of peresters; coatings and resins research. *Mailing Add:* 141 Carters Grove Dr Gibsonia PA 15044

CHAU, THUY THANH, b Cantho, Vietnam, June 8, 44; m 75; c 3. PHARMACOLOGY, PHARMACY. *Educ:* Univ Saigon, BS, 66; Univ Hawaii, MS, 68; Univ NC, Chapel Hill, PhD(pharmacol), 72. *Prof Exp:* Assoc prof pharmacol, Sch Pharm, Univ Saigon, 72-75; res assoc, 75-77, ASST PROF PHARMACOL, MED COL VA, 77- *Concurrent Pos:* Chmn dept pharmacol, Sch Med, Univ Minh Duc, 72-75; dir qual control, Tenamyd Labs, Vietnam, 73-75. *Mem:* Sigma Xi; Am Soc Pharmacol & Exp Therapeut. *Res:* Agents that affect the central nervous system and their interactions with neurochemical transmitter systems; opiates and their endogenous ligands. *Mailing Add:* Dept of Pharmacol Med Col of Va Richmond VA 23298

CHAU, YIU-KEE, b Canton, China, Dec 6, 27; m 56; c 2. CHEMICAL OCEANOGRAPHY, LIMNOLOGY. *Educ:* Lingnan Univ, BS, 49; Univ Hong Kong, MS, 61; Univ Liverpool, PhD(chem oceanog), 65. *Prof Exp:* Sci master, Mid Sch, Macau, 50-54; res officer chem oceanog, Fisheries Res Unit, Univ Hong Kong, 54-59; assoc prof chem, Chinese Univ Hong Kong, 59-68; RES SCIENTIST, NAT WATER RES INST, 68- *Concurrent Pos:* UNESCO fel, Commonwealth Sci & Indust Res Orgn, Australia, 57; Brit Coun fel, Univ Liverpool, 63-65. *Mem:* AAAS; assoc Royal Australian Chem Inst; Am Chem Soc; Spectros Soc Can: Am Soc Limnol & Oceanog. *Res:* Chemical and biological processes of trace metals in the aquatic environment; interaction of metals and organics in natural water; transformation of elements by biotic and abiotic processes. *Mailing Add:* Can Ctr for Inland Waters PO Box 5050 Burlington Can

CHAUBAL, MADHUKAR GAJANAN, b Nasik City, India, May 15, 30; m 66. PHARMACOGNOSY, CHEMISTRY. *Educ:* Univ Poona, BSc, 51; Univ Bombay, BSc, 54; Univ Toronto, MSc, 60; Univ RI, PhD(pharmaceut sci), 64. *Prof Exp:* Demonstr pharm, Dept Chem Technol, Univ Bombay, 56-58; demonstr pharm, Univ Toronto, 58-60; res asst, Univ RI, 60-64; from asst prof to assoc prof, 64-74, PROF MED CHEM, UNIV OF THE PAC, 74- *Mem:* Acad Pharmaceut Sci; Am Pharmaceut Asn; Am Soc Pharmacog; NY Acad Sci; fel Am Inst Chem. *Res:* Phytochemistry of medicinal plants; biosynthesis of plant constituents; essential oils from plants; constituents of the Saururaceae and pharmacology of the constituents. *Mailing Add:* Sch of Pharm Univ of the Pac 751 Brookside Rd Stockton CA 95211

CHAUDHARI, BIPIN BHUDHARLAL, b Taloda, India, Aug 31, 35; m 65. MEDICINAL CHEMISTRY. *Educ:* Univ Bombay, BS, 57 & 59; Univ Iowa, MS, 62, PhD(med chem), 65. *Prof Exp:* Anal chemist, Oriental Chem Industs, Bombay, India, 59-60; res assoc chem, Ill Inst Technol, 65; res chemist, Bauer & Black-Polyken Res Ctr, Kendall Co, 65-69; SR RES CHEMIST, MED CHEM SECT, BIOMED RES LABS, ICI AMERICAS INC, 69- *Mem:* Am Chem Soc. *Mailing Add:* ICI Americas Inc Biomed Res Labs Concord Pike & New Murphy Wilmington DE 19897

CHAUDHARI, PRAVEEN, b Ludhiana, India, Nov 30, 37; m 64; c 2. PHYSICAL METALLURGY, PHYSICS. *Educ:* Indian Inst Technol, Kharagpur, BTech, 61; Mass Inst Technol, SM, 63, ScD(metall), 66. *Prof Exp:* Res asst phys metall, Mass Inst Technol, 61-65, res assoc metall, 65-66; mem res staff, 66-80, DIR, PHYS SCI DEPT, INT BUS MACH CORP, 80- *Concurrent Pos:* Mem res staff, Danish Atomic Energy Comn, Denmark, 64. *Mem:* Am Phys Soc. *Res:* Amorphous solids; radiation damage; defects in crystalline solids; crystal plasticity; electron localization. *Mailing Add:* Thomas J Watson Res Ctr PO Box 218 Yorktown Heights NY 10598

CHAUDHARY, RABINDRA KUMAR, b India; Can citizen. MEDICAL MICROBIOLOGY. *Educ:* Bihar Vet Col, BVSc, 58; Guelph Univ, MSc, 65; Univ Toronto, dipl bacteriol, 66; Univ Ottawa, PhD(microbiol), 71. *Prof Exp:* Res scientist microbiol, Bell & Craig Pharmaceut Co, 66-67; res assoc, Univ Ottawa, 71-75; BIOLOGIST, LAB CTR DIS CONTROL, BUR VIRAL DIS, 75- *Mem:* Am Soc Microbiologists. *Res:* Biophysical studies of hepatitis B antigen. *Mailing Add:* Lab Ctr Dis Control Bur Viral Dis Tunney's Pasture Ottawa ON K1A 0K9 Can

CHAUDHARY, SOHAN SINGH, b Pakistan, Oct 15, 30; m 61; c 4. PHYSICAL ORGANIC CHEMISTRY. *Educ:* Univ Punjab, India, BSc, 52, Hons, 54, MSc, 56; Univ Calif, Davis, PhD(phys org chem), 65. *Prof Exp:* Chemist, Indian Coun Med Res, 56; res asst, Coun Sci Indust Res, India, 56-60, sr res asst, 60-61; res asst aroma of Calif wines, Univ Calif, Davis, 61-63,

teaching asst chem, 63-65; NIH fel syntheses & reaction mech, Case Inst Technol, 65-66; res chemist, Res Dept, 66-70, PROJ SCIENTIST, ARCO/ POLYMER, INC, 70- *Mem:* Am Chem Soc; Am Soc Enol; NY Acad Sci; Sigma Xi. *Res:* Isolation and structural elucidation of active principals of herbs; organic syntheses and reaction mechanism; thermoplastics; polyurethanes. *Mailing Add:* 2451 Saunders Station Rd Monroeville PA 15146

CHAUDHRY, ANAND P, b WPunjab, India, Oct 19, 22; US citizen; m 57; c 2. ORAL PATHOLOGY. *Educ:* Panjab Univ, India, BS, 42, BDS, 47; Univ Mich, MS, 53; Univ Minn, PhD(path), 56; Am Bd Oral Path, dipl. *Prof Exp:* From instr to prof, Univ Minn, 56-61; prof path & chmn dept, Sch Dent, Univ Pittsburgh, 61-66; PROF PATH, STATE UNIV NY BUFFALO, 67- *Concurrent Pos:* Consult, Children's Hosp, Millard Fillmore Hosp, Buffalo Gen Hosp & Vet Admin Hosp. *Mem:* Am Acad Oral Path; Am Asn Dent Res. *Res:* Experimental carcinogenesis of the oral cavity, skin and the salivary glands; experimental teratology with special interest in the study of embryogenesis and pathogenesis of cleft lip and palate. *Mailing Add:* Dept of Path State Univ of NY Sch of Med Buffalo NY 14214

CHAUDHURI, TUHIN, b Bengal, India, Jan 3, 42; m 69. NUCLEAR MEDICINE, HEMATOLOGY. *Educ:* Univ Calcutta, MB & BS, 64. *Prof Exp:* Intern med, Med Col & Hosp, Univ Calcutta, 64-65; resident surg, RKM Seva Pratishthan, Calcutta, 65-66; res assoc radiol & nuclear med, Yale Univ, 66-67; from asst prof to assoc prof radiol, Univ Iowa, 69-75, assoc dir nuclear med, 69-75; CHIEF NUCLEAR MED, AUDIE MURPHY VET ADMIN MED CTR, UNIV TEX HEALTH SCI CTR, SAN ANTONIO, 75- *Concurrent Pos:* Fel nuclear med, Yale Univ, 67-68; James Picker fel, Nat Acad Sci-Nat Res Coun, 67-70; fel, Donner Lab, Univ Calif, Berkeley, 68-69; guest scientist, Lawrence Radiation Lab, Berkeley, 68-69. *Mem:* AAAS; Am Fedn Clin Res; Biophys Soc; Soc Nuclear Med. *Res:* Gastro-intestinal nuclear medicine; Oesophagal and gastric motility; cardio-vascular nuclear medicine; non-invassive cardiac function studies; diagnosis and therapeutic efficiency studies in cancer. *Mailing Add:* Audi Murphy Mem Vet Admin Hosp Dept of Nuclear Med San Antonio TX 78284

CHAUFFE, LEROY, b Freetown, La, Dec 26, 36; m 69. ORGANIC CHEMISTRY. *Educ:* Xavier Univ, La, BS, 59; Howard Univ, MS, 64; Univ Calif, Davis, PhD(chem), 66. *Prof Exp:* Chemist, Shell Chem Co, 65-66; fel, Univ Calif, Davis, 66-67; asst prof chem, State Col Long Beach, 67-68; asst prof, 68-74, assoc dean instr, 70-71, actg dean grad studies, 71-72, assoc prof, 74-80, PROF CHEM, CALIF STATE UNIV, HAYWARD, 80- *Mem:* Am Chem Soc; Royal Chem Soc. *Res:* Physical organic chemistry; biochemical kinetics and mechanism. *Mailing Add:* Dept of Chem Calif State Univ Hayward CA 94542

CHAUVIN, ROBERT S, b West Beekmantown, NY, Nov 20, 20; m 46; c 2. GEOLOGY, GEOGRAPHY. *Educ:* NY Univ, BS, 43; Columbia Univ, MA, 50, PhD(geol, geog), 55. *Prof Exp:* Head dept geol & geog, 50-68, dean sci, 68-70, assoc prof geol, 50-55, PROF GEOL, STETSON UNIV, 55-, DEAN COL LIB ARTS, 70- *Mem:* Am Geog Soc. *Res:* Arctic flora, fauna and glaciation. *Mailing Add:* Col of Lib Arts Stetson Univ De Land FL 32721

CHAVE, CHARLES TRUDEAU, b New York, NY, Apr 4, 05; m 40; c 1. MECHANICAL & CHEMICAL ENGINEERING. *Educ:* Columbia Univ, AB, 27, BS, 28, ME, 29. *Prof Exp:* Engr, Foster Wheeler Corp, NY, 29-31 & Alco Prods Div, Am Locomotive Co, 31-39; process engr, Stone & Webster Eng Corp, 39-51, asst chief engr, Badger Process Div, 51-56, chief nuclear engr, 56-69, consult engr, 69-70; INDEPENDENT CONSULT ENGR, 70- *Mem:* Fel Am Soc Mech Engrs; Am Inst Chem Engrs; Nat Soc Prof Engrs. *Res:* Design and construction of nuclear power plants. *Mailing Add:* 4 Waterbury Ave Madison CT 06443

CHAVE, KEITH ERNEST, b Chicago, Ill, Jan 18, 28; m 51; c 2. GEOLOGY. *Educ:* Univ Chicago, PhB, 48, MS, 51, PhD, 52. *Prof Exp:* Asst, State Geol Surv, Ill, 48; res geologist, Calif Res Corp, 52-59; from asst prof to prof geol, Lehigh Univ, 59-67, assoc dir marine sci ctr, 62-67; chmn dept, 70-73, PROF OCEANOG, UNIV HAWAII, 67- *Concurrent Pos:* Trustee, Bermuda Biol Sta, 62-68; Alexander von Humboldt sr scientist, Univ Kiel, 73-74. *Mem:* Fel AAAS; Soc Econ Paleont & Mineral; Geochem Soc; Am Geophys Union; Am Soc Limnol & Oceanog. *Res:* Geochemistry; marine geology. *Mailing Add:* Dept Oceanog Univ Hawaii Honolulu HI 96822

CHAVEL, ISAAC, b Louisville, Ky, Apr 2, 39. GEOMETRY. *Educ:* Brooklyn Col, BA, 61; NY Univ, MS, 64; Yeshiva Univ, PhD(math), 66. *Prof Exp:* Teaching asst math, Brooklyn Col, 61-64; asst prof, Univ Minn, 66-70; asst prof, 70-73, assoc prof, 73-80, PROF MATH, CITY COL NEW YORK, 80- *Mem:* Am Math Soc. *Res:* Interplay of Riemannian geometry with mathematical analysis, especially as relates to the Laplace operator. *Mailing Add:* Dept of Math City Col of New York New York NY 10031

CHAVIN, WALTER, b US, Dec 6, 25 ENDOCRINOLOGY, RADIOBIOLOGY. *Educ:* City Col New York, BS, 46; NY Univ, MS, 49, PhD(zool), 54. *Prof Exp:* Instr biol, City Col New York, 46-47; asst, NY Aquarium, 48-49; instr zool, Univ Ariz, 49-51; res specialist, Am Mus Natural Hist, 51-53; assoc prof biol, 53-68, prof radiol, 74-80, PROF BIOL SCI, WAYNE STATE UNIV, 68- *Concurrent Pos:* Res assoc, Div Biol & Med Res, Argonne Nat Lab, 55, 56, consult, 57-58; NSF sr fel, 60-61; Sigma Xi fac res award, 68; coordr, US-Japan Seminar Responses of Fish to Environ Changes, Tokyo, 70; consult, Great Lakes Lab, Bur Com Fisheries, US Dept Interior. *Mem:* Fel AAAS (secy, Biol Sci Sect, 78-82); Am Soc Cell Biol; Am Physiol Soc; fel NY Acad Sci; Radiation Res Soc; Soc Exp Biol & Med. *Res:* Comparative endocrinology; pigment cell physiology; environmental biology; radiation biology. *Mailing Add:* Dept Biol Sci Wayne State Univ Detroit MI 48202

CHAVKIN, LEONARD THEODORE, b New York, NY, Dec 2, 25; m 44; c 4. PHARMACY. *Educ:* Columbia Univ, BS, 44; Philadelphia Col Pharm, MS, 47; NY Univ, PhD, 60. *Prof Exp:* Assoc pharm, Col Pharm, Columbia Univ, 47-49, assoc prof, 49-59; dir develop, 59-63, dir res develop, 63, asst vpres res develop, 63-67, VPRES RES & DEVELOP, BRISTOL-MYERS CO, 67- *Mem:* AAAS; Am Pharmaceut Asn; Soc Cosmetic Chem. *Res:* Industrial pharmaceutical manufacturing. *Mailing Add:* Res & Develop Dept Bristol-Myers Co 1350 Liberty Ave Hillside NJ 07207

CHAWNER, WILLIAM DONALD, b Calif, May 13, 03; wid; c 2. PETROLEUM GEOLOGY. *Educ:* Occidental Col, BS, 25; Calif Inst Technol, MS, 34; La State Univ, PhD(geol), 37. *Prof Exp:* Geologist, Atlantic Refining Co, 27-33, State Geol Surv, La, 34-36, Australasian Petrol Co, 36-41, Carter Oil Co, 41-58 & Humble Oil & Refining Co, 58-68; geol consult, 68-75; RETIRED. *Mem:* Am Asn Petrol Geol; fel Geol Soc Am; Am Inst Mining, Metall & Petrol Eng; Am Inst Prof Geol. *Res:* Petroleum geology; stratigraphy; mineral exploration; uranium deposits. *Mailing Add:* PO Box 608 Del Mar CA 92014

CHAY, DONG MYUNG, ceramic engineering, inorganic chemistry, see previous edition

CHAYES, FELIX, b New York, NY, May 10, 16; m 41. PETROLOGY. *Educ:* NY Univ, BA, 36; Columbia Univ, MA, 39, PhD(geol), 42. *Prof Exp:* Chemist, Gillis & Pawel Metal Co, NC, 41; bus analyst, War Prod Bd, Washington, DC, 41-42; chemist-petrographer, US Bur Mines, 42-46; mineralogist, Mass Inst Technol, 46-47; PETROLOGIST, GEOPHYS LAB, CARNEGIE INST, 47- *Mem:* Fel Mineral Soc Am; fel Geol Soc Am; Am Geophys Union. *Res:* Petrology of alkali intrusion of Bancroft, Ontario; quantitative analysis by fragment counting; precision of linear analysis; application of statistics to chemical petrography; petrography of granite; geochemical data. *Mailing Add:* Carnegie Inst Geophys Lab 2801 Upton St NW Washington DC 20008

CHAYKIN, STERLING, b New York, NY, Sept 18, 29; m 54; c 4. BIOCHEMISTRY. *Educ:* NY Univ, AB, 50; Univ Wash, PhD(biochem), 54. *Prof Exp:* Runyon fel, Harvard, 56-59; from asst prof to assoc prof biochem, 59-69, chmn dept biochem & biophys, 68-70, assoc dean resident instr, Col Agr & Environ Sci, 70-74, PROF BIOCHEM, UNIV CALIF, DAVIS, 74- *Concurrent Pos:* Fulbright fel, Ger, 66-67; Guggenheim fel, 66-67. *Mem:* AAAS; Am Chem Soc; Am Soc Biol Chemists. *Res:* Enzymology; biochemistry of development, vitamins and mammalian genetics. *Mailing Add:* Dept of Biochem & Biophys Univ of Calif Davis CA 95616

CHAYKOVSKY, MICHAEL, b Mayfield, Pa, Sept 19, 34; m 66; c 2. ORGANIC CHEMISTRY, BIOCHEMISTRY. *Educ:* Pa State Univ, BS, 56; Univ Mich, MS, 59, PhD(org chem), 61. *Prof Exp:* Res fel chem, Harvard Univ, 61-64; asst prof, State Univ NY Buffalo, 64-65; res fel, Labs of Chem, Nat Inst Arthritis & Metab Dis, 65-66; sr res chemist, Hoffmann-La Roche Inc, 66-69; res assoc chem, Harvard Med Sch, 69-80; res chemist, Naval Surface Weapons Ctr, 80-82; RES CHEMIST, WALTER REED ARMY INST RES, 82- *Mem:* Am Chem Soc. *Res:* Synthetic organic chemistry; steroids, terpenes, sulfur ylides and carbanions; photochemistry; organophosphorous chemistry; heterocycles; carbenes; nitrenes; diborane reductions; cancer chemotherapy. *Mailing Add:* Bldg 310A Naval Surface Weapon Ctr Silver Springs MD 20910

CHAZEN, PATRICIA LYNNE, b Detroit, Mich, Sept 20, 46; m 71. SEDIMENTOLOGY, GEOCHEMISTRY. *Educ:* Mich State Univ, BS, 68, PhD(geol), 71. *Prof Exp:* Asst prof geol, Cent Mich Univ, 71-73; chemist environ, Environ Health Lab, Kelsey-Seybold Clin, NASA, 74-75; asst prof geol, Univ Houston, Clear Lake City, 75-78; GEOLOGIST, GETTY OIL CO, 78- *Mem:* Soc Econ Paleontologists & Mineralogists; Int Asn Sedimentologists. *Res:* Deltaic sedimentation; carbonate geochemistry; silica geochemistry as it pertains to the formation of chert. *Mailing Add:* 111 Ferndale Bellaire TX 77401

CHE, STANLEY CHIA-LIN, b Amoy, China, Sept 11, 46; m 72; c 2. FUEL SCIENCE. *Educ:* Cheng Kung Univ, Taiwan, BS, 68; Univ Utah, PhD(fuels eng), 74. *Prof Exp:* Fel coal gasification, Argonne Nat Lab, 74-75; res engr coal conversion, 75-78, SR RES ENGR COAL CONVERSION, OCCIDENTAL RES CORP, OCCIDENTAL PETROL CORP, 79- *Mem:* Am Chem Soc; Am Inst Chem Engrs. *Res:* Development of novel chemistry to improve the yield and quality of coal tar by flash pyrolysis; upgrading of pyrolysis coal tar; pyrolysis of coals; analytical method development for characterization of coal liquids; catalyst deactivation; characterization and upgrading of shale oil. *Mailing Add:* Occidental Res Corp PO Box 19601 Irvine CA 92713

CHEADLE, VERNON IRVIN, b Salem, SDak, Feb 6, 10; m 39; c 1. BOTANY. *Educ:* Miami Univ, AB, 32; Harvard Univ, AM, 34, PhD(biol bot), 36. *Hon Degrees:* LLD, Miami Univ & Univ RI, 64. *Prof Exp:* Austin teaching fel bot, Harvard Univ, 33-36; from instr to asst prof, RI State Col, 36-42, prof & head dept, 42-52, dir grad div, 43-52; botanist, Exp Sta & prof bot, Univ Calif, Davis, 52-60, chmn dept, 52-60, actg vchancellor, 61-62; chancellor, Univ Calif, Santa Barbara, 62-77. *Concurrent Pos:* Fulbright fel, 59. *Mem:* Fel AAAS; fel Am Acad Arts & Sci; Am Soc Plant Taxon; Bot Soc Am (pres, 61); Torrey Bot Club. *Res:* Anatomy; morphology of vascular plants. *Mailing Add:* 891 Cieniguitas Rd Santa Barbara CA 93110

CHEAL, MARYLOU, b St Clair Co, Mich. PSYCHOBIOLOGY. *Educ:* Oakland Univ, BA, 69; Univ Mich, Ann Arbor, PhD(psychobiol), 73. *Prof Exp:* Res investr taste regeneration, Dept Zool, Univ Mich, 73-75, res investr taste develop, Dept Oral Biol, Sch Dent, 75-76; asst psychologist, 76-81, ASSOC PSYCHOLOGIST, NEUROPSYCHOL LAB, MCLEAN HOSP, 81- *Concurrent Pos:* Lectr psychol, Univ Mich, 73-76 & Dept Psychiat, Harvard Med Sch, 77- *Mem:* AAAS; Sigma Xi; Soc Neurosci; Am Psychol Asn; Am Women in Sci. *Res:* Neuropharmacoloy of attention and habituation; reproduction and behavior of gerbils; social behavior mediated by olfactory stimuli. *Mailing Add:* Neuropsychol Lab McLean Hosp Belmont MA 02178

CHEANEY, EDGAR S, b Petersburg, Ill, Apr 24, 22; m 44; c 4. MECHANICAL ENGINEERING, SYSTEMS ENGINEERING. *Educ:* Univ Ill, BSME, 44. *Prof Exp:* Jr engr, Allis Chalmers Mfg Co, 46-51, designer, 53-58; res engr, 58-59, proj leader, 59-61, res group dir, 61-63, div chief tech planning, 63-68, div chief mech products & mfg, 69-72, ASSOC MGR TRANSP SYSTS, BATTELLE MEM INST, 73- *Mem:* Soc Automotive Engrs; Int Syst Safety Soc. *Res:* Systems involving flow and modulation of mechanical energy; transmission design; technical planning; technology of transportation systems; safety analysis in transportation equipment. *Mailing Add:* Battelle Mem Inst 505 King Ave Columbus OH 43201

CHEATHAM, DANIEL W(ASHINGTON), JR, aerodynamics, gas dynamics, see previous edition

CHEATHAM, JOHN B(ANE), JR, b Houston, Tex, June 29, 24; m 47; c 2. MECHANICAL ENGINEERING. *Educ:* Southern Methodist Univ, BS, 48, MS, 53; Mass Inst Technol, ME, 54; Rice Univ, PhD, 60. *Prof Exp:* Test engr, Gen Elec Co, 48; design engr, Link Belt Co, 49-50; engr, Atlantic Ref Co, 50-53; res assoc, Shell Develop Co, 54-63; assoc prof mech eng, 63-66, chmn dept mech & aerospace eng & mat sci, 69-73, PROF MECH ENG, RICE UNIV, 66- *Concurrent Pos:* Lectr, Univ Houston, 60-63; pres, Cheatham Eng Inc, 77-; pres, Techaid Corp, 77-; founding tech ed, Am Soc Mech Engrs Trans J Energy Resources Tech, 79-80. *Honors & Awards:* Ralph James Award, Am Soc Mech Engrs, 80. *Mem:* Fel Am Soc Mech Engrs; Am Inst Mining, Metall & Petrol Engrs; Am Soc Eng Educ. *Res:* Rock mechanics; plasticity; machine design; oil well drilling research. *Mailing Add:* Dept Mech Eng & Mat Sci Rice Univ Houston TX 77001

CHEATHAM, ROBERT GRAY, b Guam Naval Base, Mariana Islands, Oct 30, 26; m 57; c 2. MATERIALS SCIENCE ENGINEERING. *Educ:* The Citadel, BS, 47; Mass Inst Technol, SM, 50, ScD, 57. *Prof Exp:* Res asst plastic mat, Plastic Lab/Colloid & Rubber Lab, Mass Inst Technol, 48-54; dir res, WASCO Chem, 54-57; dir, Plastic Div, D S Kennedy & Co, 57-59; pres mat res, Mat Technol Inc, 59-64; prin scientist polymeric mat, United Aircraft Res Lab, 64-67; unit chief chem mat, The Boeing Co, 67-77; CHIEF COMPOSITE MAT, SIKORSKY AIRCRAFT DIV, UNITED TECHNOL CORP, 78- *Concurrent Pos:* Consult, Stanford Res Int, 68-77; fel, Mass Inst Technol Colloid Lab. *Mem:* Sigma Xi; Am Inst Aeronaut & Astronaut; Am Helicopter Soc. *Res:* Development and application of polymeric materials to high performance vehicles in extreme environments; development of required suitable process techniques; published thirty-five technical papers. *Mailing Add:* Seven Beech Tree Circle Trumbull CT 06611

CHEATHAM, THOMAS J, b Campbellsville, Ky, Oct 8, 44; m 66; c 1. MATHEMATICS. *Educ:* Campbellsville Col, BS, 66; Univ Ky, MS, 68, PhD(math), 71. *Prof Exp:* From asst prof to assoc prof math, Samford Univ, 71-77; vis assoc prof, Univ Ky, 77-78; prof math, Samford Univ, 78-81; PROF MATH & COMPUT SCI, WESTERN KY UNIV, 81- *Concurrent Pos:* Samford Univ Res Fund fels, 74, 75 & 77. *Mem:* Am Math Soc. *Res:* Nonsingular ring and module; numerous publications and journals. *Mailing Add:* Dept Math & Comput Sci Western Ky Univ Bowling Green KY 42101

CHEAVENS, THOMAS HENRY, b Dallas, Tex, May 19, 30; m 55; c 3. INDUSTRIAL CHEMISTRY, PETROLEUM CHEMISTRY. *Educ:* Univ Tex, BS, 50, PhD(chem), 55. *Prof Exp:* Res chemist, Org Pigments, Res Div, Am Cyanamid Co, 55-56, develop chemist, Org Chem Div, 56, develop chemist, Intermediates & Rubber Chem, 57, group leader, process develop dept, NJ, 58-61, group leader, Refinery Catalysts Group, Conn, 61-67; supvr indust catalysts res, W R Grace & Co, 67-70, dir indust catalysts res dept, 71-75; sr prog mgr, Div Fossil Energy Res, US Energy Res & Develop Admin, 75-77; res dir, 77-80, PRES, QUEST RES INT, INC, 80-; VPRES, IMPROTEE, INC, 80- *Mem:* Am Chem Soc; Catalysis Soc; AAAS. *Res:* Catalysis in fossil fuel production and refining, industrial chemical processes; distillation technology. *Mailing Add:* Quest Res Int Inc PO Box 478 Tyler TX 75710

CHECHIK, BORIS, b Kislovodsk, USSR, Mar 31, 31; Can citizen; m 58; c 1. TUMOR IMMUNOLOGY, IMMUNOCHEMISTRY. *Educ:* Second Med Sch, Moscow, MD, 56; P A Gertzen Oncol Inst, Moscow, PhD(tumor immunol), 63. *Prof Exp:* Gen practitioner med, Hosp N33, Moscow, 56-59; res investr tumor immunol, P A Gertzen Oncol Inst, 59-71 & Hadassah Med Sch, Jerusalem, 71-73; res assoc, Hosp Sick Children, Toronto, 74-76; res investr tumor immunol, 77-81, SR STAFF MEM, MT SINAI HOSP, TORONTO, 81-; ASSOC PROF, UNIV TORONTO, 81- *Mem:* Int Asn Comparative Res Leukemia & Related Dis; Am Asn Cancer Res. *Res:* Immunochemistry of differentiation antigens of human normal and leukemic hematopoietic cells; immunobiology of adenosine deminase. *Mailing Add:* Res Dept Mount Sinai Hosp 600 University Ave Toronto ON M5G 1X5 Can

CHEEKE, PETER ROBERT, b Duncan, BC, Oct 19, 41; m 70; c 2. ANIMAL SCIENCE, NUTRITION. *Educ:* Univ BC, BSA, 63, MSA, 65; Ore State Univ, PhD(animal nutrit), 69. *Prof Exp:* from asst prof to assoc prof, 69-79, PROF ANIMAL SCI, ORE STATE UNIV, 79- *Concurrent Pos:* Ed, J Appl Rabbit Res. *Mem:* Am Inst Nutrit; Am Soc Animal Sci. *Res:* Nutrition of rabbits; pyrrolizidine alkaloid toxicity; nutritional toxicology interrelationships. *Mailing Add:* Dept Animal Sci Ore State Univ Corvallis OR 97331

CHEEMA, MOHINDAR SINGH, b Sialkot, Panjab, India, Jan 15, 29; m 51; c 4. MATHEMATICS. *Educ:* Univ Panjab, BA, 48, MA, 50; Univ Calif, Los Angeles, MA, 60, PhD(math), 61. *Prof Exp:* Res scholar math, Univ Panjab, 51-54, instr, 54-58; jr res mathematician, Univ Calif, Los Angeles, 58-61; from asst prof to assoc prof, 61-68, PROF MATH, UNIV ARIZ, 68- *Mem:* Am Math Soc; Math Asn Am; Asn Comput Mach. *Res:* Number theory; pure mathematics; numerical analysis. *Mailing Add:* Dept of Math Univ of Ariz Tucson AZ 85721

CHEEMA, ZAFARULLAH K, b Gakkhar, WPakistan, Apr 21, 34; US citizen; m 62; c 2. ORGANIC CHEMISTRY, PHARMACEUTICAL CHEMISTRY. *Educ:* Panjab Univ, WPakistan, BPharm, 54; Univ Tubingen, Dr rer nat(chem), 57. *Prof Exp:* Res assoc, Univ Kans, 57-58 & Univ Tübingen, 58-59; chmn dept chem, Knoxville Col, 59-63, assoc prof chem, 61-63; adv chemist, Health Dept, Govt Pakistan, 60-61; lectr chem, Univ Del, 63-64; res chemist, Gen Chem Div, Allied Chem Corp, 64-65, sr res chemist agr div, 66, res assoc, Plastics Div, 66-69, tech supvr res, 69-71; group leader, Am Hoechst Corp, 71-75, mgr res, Keuffel & Esser Co, 75-78; V PRES RES, RICHARDSON GRAPHICS CO, 78- *Concurrent Pos:* Consult, Oak Ridge Nat Lab, 62-63; res fel, Univ Tenn, 63; adj prof & chmn chem dept, Fairleigh Dickinson Univ, 66-67. *Mem:* Am Chem Soc; Soc Photog Scientists & Engrs; Tech Asn Graphic Arts; NY Acad Sci. *Res:* Terpenes; conformational analysis; reaction mechanisms such as epimerization and pinnacol rearrangement; synthesis of pesticides; oxidation; photopolymers, diazo, graphic arts and engineering product development. *Mailing Add:* Richardson Graphics Co 2701 Lake St Melrose Park IL 60160

CHEER, CLAIR JAMES, b Lakewood, Ohio, May 16, 37; m 62; c 2. ORGANIC CHEMISTRY. *Educ:* Kenyon Col, BA, 59; Wayne State Univ, PhD(org chem), 64. *Prof Exp:* Res asst chem, Parma Res Lab, Union Carbide Corp, 59; res assoc org chem, Frank J Seiler Res Lab, off aerospace res, US Air Force Acad, 64-67; res assoc chem, Univ Ariz, 67-68; asst prof, 68-74, ASSOC PROF CHEM, UNIV RI, 74- *Mem:* Am Chem Soc; Royal Soc Chem; Am Inst Physics; Am Crystallog Asn; NY Acad Sci. *Res:* Organic reactions and mechanisms; organic synthetic methods; natural products; use of x-ray crystallography in solution of organic chemical problems, especially geometrical relationships in trigonal-pyramidal centers. *Mailing Add:* Dept of Chem Univ of RI Kingston RI 02881

CHEETHAM, RODGER PRICE, electrical engineering, see previous edition

CHEETHAM, RONALD D, b Duluth, Minn, Oct 8, 43; m 65; c 3. PHYCOLOGY, AQUATIC MICROBIOLOGY. *Educ:* Univ Minn, Duluth, BA, 65; Univ Minn, St Paul, MS, 67; Purdue Univ, PhD(plant ecol & physiol), 70. *Prof Exp:* Asst prof biol & plant physiol, Minn State Univ, 70-73; asst prof, 73-78, ASSOC PROF BIOL & ECOL, WORCESTER POLYTECH INST, 78- *Concurrent Pos:* Agr ecol advisor, New Eng Res, Inc, 73-; advisor, Worcester Consortium Water Quality, 73- *Mem:* AAAS; Nat Wildlife Soc; Am Ecol Soc; Sigma Xi. *Res:* Aquatic ecology; nitrogen relationships of blue-green algae; public health significance of macroinvertebrates in potable waters. *Mailing Add:* Biol Dept Worcester Polytech Inst Inst Rd Worcester MA 01609

CHEEVERS, WILLIAM PHILLIP, b Tallulah, La, Nov 10, 41. MOLECULAR BIOLOGY. *Educ:* Univ Colo, BA, 63; Univ Miss, PhD(microbiol), 68. *Prof Exp:* Sci staff molecular virol, Cancer Res Lab, Univ Western Ont, Can, 70-76; asst prof, 76-80, ASSOC PROF, DEPT VET MICROBIOL & PATH, WASH STATE UNIV, 80- *Res:* Molecular mechanisms of viral persistence in retrovirus diseases. *Mailing Add:* Dept Vet Microbiol & Pathol Wash State Univ Pullman WA 99164

CHEH, ALBERT MEI-CHU, b New York, NY, Mar 8, 47; m 70; c 2. TOXICOLOGY. *Educ:* Columbia Univ, BA, 67; Univ Calif, Berkeley, PhD(biochem), 74. *Prof Exp:* Res assoc, Univ Ill, 74; res assoc, Univ Minn, 74-77, NIH fel, 77-78, scientist, 78-80; ASST PROF CHEM, AM UNIV, 80- *Mem:* Am Chem Soc; AAAS; Environ Mutagen Soc; Fedn Am Scientists. *Res:* Detection, analysis and study of the formation of mutagenic electrophiles in environmental samples; study of the mechanisms for the mutagenicity and carcinogenicity of natural products. *Mailing Add:* Dept Chem Am Univ Washington DC 20016

CHEIN, ORIN NATHANIEL, b New York, NY, Aug 29, 43; m 65; c 2. MATHEMATICS. *Educ:* NY Univ, BA, 64, MS, 66, PhD(math), 68. *Prof Exp:* from asst prof to assoc prof, 68-79, PROF MATH, TEMPLE UNIV, 79- *Mem:* Am Math Soc; Math Asn Am. *Res:* Automorphisms of free and free metabelian groups; Moufang loops; combinatorics; math recreations. *Mailing Add:* Dept Math Temple Univ Philadelphia PA 19122

CHEITLIN, MELVIN DONALD, b Wilmington, Del, Mar 25, 29; m 52; c 3. INTERNAL MEDICINE, CARDIOLOGY. *Educ:* Temple Univ, BA, 50, MD, 54. *Prof Exp:* Chief cardiovasc serv, Madigan Gen Hosp, US Army, 60-64, Tripler Gen Hosp, 64-68 & Letterman Gen Hosp, 68-71, asst clin prof med, Univ Calif, San Francisco, 69-71, chief cardiovasc serv, Walter Reed Army Hosp, 71-74; prof, 74-77, clin prof, 77-79, PROF MED, UNIV CALIF, SAN FRANCISO, 79- *Concurrent Pos:* Consult, Queen's Hosp, Honolulu, 65-68 & Letterman Gen Hosp, 75-; fel, Coun Clin Cardiol, Am Heart Asn, 66-68; cardiovasc consult to surgeon gen, Walter Reed Gen Hosp, 71-74; assoc dir cardiopulmonary unit, San Francisco Gen Hosp, 74- *Mem:* AMA; fel Am Col Physicians; fel Am Col Cardiol; Am Heart Asn; Am Fedn Clin Res. *Mailing Add:* Dept Med Sch Med Univ Calif San Francisco CA 94143

CHELAPATI, CHUNDURI V(ENKATA), b Eluru, Andhra State, India, Mar 11, 33. CIVIL ENGINEERING, ENGINEERING MECHANICS. *Educ:* Andhra Univ, India, BE, 54; Indian Inst Sci, dipl, 56; Univ Ill, MS, 59, PhD(civil eng), 62. *Prof Exp:* Asst prof struct eng, Birla Eng Col, India, 56-57; asst civil eng, Univ Ill, 57-62; asst prof, Calif State Col, Los Angeles, 62-65, NSF instnl grant, 63-65; assoc prof, 65-70, vchmn dept, 71-73, chmn dept, 73-80, PROF CIVIL ENG, CALIF STATE UNIV, LONG BEACH, 70- *Concurrent Pos:* Consult, US Naval Civil Eng Lab, Calif, 63-68; vis scholar, Univ Calif, Los Angeles, 68-69; consult & proj mgr, Holmes & Narvar, Inc, Calif, 68-73; consult, Civil Eng Lab, Naval Construct Battalion Ctr, Port Hueneme, Calif, 75- *Mem:* Am Soc Civil Engrs; Seismol Soc Am; Am Soc Eng Educ; Earthquake Engrs Res Inst. *Res:* Dynamics of structures subjected to earthquakes and blasts; arching in soils; soil structure interaction; buckling of structures; nuclear reactor structures; earthquake hazard mitigation; professional review courses; seismic design; computer methods. *Mailing Add:* Dept of Civil Eng Calif State Univ Long Beach CA 90840

CHELEMER, HAROLD, b Green Bay, Wis, Nov 28, 28; m 57; c 3. CHEMICAL ENGINEERING, STATISTICS. *Educ:* Univ Mo, BSc, 49, MSc, 51; Univ Tenn, PhD(chem eng), 55. *Prof Exp:* Sr engr, Reactor Eng & Mat Dept, Westinghouse Atomic Power Div, 57-64, fel engr, PWR Plant Div, 64-70, ADV ENGR, NUCLEAR FUEL DIV, WESTINGHOUSE NUCLEAR ENERGY SYSTS, 70- *Res:* Pressurized water reactor core thermal and hydraulic design analysis; computer program development; statistical evaluation of limiting parameters. *Mailing Add:* Nuclear Fuel Div PO Box 3912 Westinghouse Nuclear Energy Systs Pittsburgh PA 15230

CHELIKOWSKY, JAMES ROBERT, b Manhattan, Kans, June 1, 48. SOLID STATE PHYSICS. *Educ:* Kans State Univ, BS, 70; Univ Calif, Berkeley, PhD(physics), 75. *Prof Exp:* Mem tech staff, Bell Tel Lab, Murray Hill, NJ, 76-78; asst prof physics, Univ Ore, 78-80; STAFF PHYSICIST, EXXON RES & ENG CO, 80- *Mem:* Am Phys Soc. *Res:* Electronic structure of solids; band structures; optical properties of solids; phase stability of intermetallic alloys; surface properties of semiconductors and metals; cohesion in metals. *Mailing Add:* Exxon Res & Eng Co PO Box 45 Linden NJ 07036

CHELLEW, NORMAN RAYMOND, b Aurora, Minn, June 17, 17; m 43. INORGANIC CHEMISTRY. *Educ:* Univ Minn, BS, 39. *Prof Exp:* Teacher, Breitung Twp Schs Mich, 40-41; chemist & supvr, E I du Pont de Nemours & Co, 41-46; jr chemist, 47-49, ASSOC CHEMIST, ARGONNE NAT LAB, 49- *Mem:* Sci Res Soc Am; Am Chem Soc; Am Nuclear Soc. *Res:* Research and development of inorganic chemistry; radiochemistry; development of fission product monitors for nuclear reactor systems. *Mailing Add:* 811 Winthrop Ave Joliet IL 60435

CHELLO, PAUL LARSON, b New Haven, Conn, Nov 11, 42. BIOCHEMICAL PHARMACOLOGY. *Educ:* Johns Hopkins Univ, BA, 64; Univ Vt, PhD(pharmacol), 71. *Prof Exp:* Res assoc molecular therapeut, 74-75, ASSOC, MEM SLOAN KETTERING INST CANCER RES, 75- *Concurrent Pos:* asst prof, Grad Sch Med Sci, Cornell Univ, 75- *Mem:* Am Asn Cancer Res; Am Soc Pharmacol & Exp Therapeut; Am Soc Cell Biol; NY Acad Sci; Sigma Xi. *Res:* Cancer chemotherapy; drug transport; mechanisms of drug resistance; mechanism of action of antifolates; folic acid, vitamin B12 and methionine metabolism. *Mailing Add:* 710 Boston Post Rd Guilford NY 06437

CHELTON, DUDLEY B(OYD), b Baltimore, Md, July 17, 28; m 47; c 2. CRYOGENIC ENGINEERING. *Educ:* Ohio State Univ, BSME, 48; Mass Inst Technol, SM, 49. *Prof Exp:* Instr mech eng, Mass Inst Technol, 49-50; mech engr, Los Alamos Sci Lab, 50-51; chief, Cryogenics Div, Nat Bur Standards, 68-74, mech engr, 51-77, sr eng consult, 74-77; CRYOGENIC ENGR CONSULT, 77- *Honors & Awards:* Gold Medal Award, US Dept Commerce, 53. *Mem:* Sigma Xi. *Res:* Liquefaction of gases; refrigeration techniques; measurement science; materials; liquid hydrogen bubble chambers; cryogenic processes; cryogenic and liquified natural gas technology. *Mailing Add:* 500 Mohawk Dr #308 Boulder CO 80303

CHEMSAK, JOHN A, b Ambridge, Pa, Feb 19, 32; m 59; c 3. ENTOMOLOGY. *Educ:* Pa State Univ, BS, 54, MS, 56; Univ Calif, Berkeley, PhD(entom), 61. *Prof Exp:* Biol aide plant path, USDA, 56; from jr res entomologist to asst res entomologist, 61-62, SPECIALIST ENTOM, UNIV CALIF, BERKELEY, 62- *Res:* Biosystematics and zoogeography of North and central American cerambycid beetles; biologies of insects. *Mailing Add:* Div of Entom 201 Wellman Hall Univ of Calif Berkeley CA 94720

CHEN, ALBERT TSU-FU, b Fukien, China, Sept 2, 37; m 61; c 2. SOIL MECHANICS, APPLIED MATHEMATICS. *Educ:* Taiwan Univ, BSCE, 58; Univ Mass, MSCE, 62; Rensselaer Polytech Inst, PhD(soil mech), 67. *Prof Exp:* Instr, Rensselaer Polytech Inst, 65-67; RES CIVIL ENGR, US GEOL SURV, 67- *Mem:* Earthquake Eng Res Inst; Am Soc Civil Engrs. *Res:* Dynamic soil behavior; consolidation theory; response of soil layers during earthquakes. *Mailing Add:* US Geol Surv 345 Middlefield Rd Menlo Park CA 94025

CHEN, AN-BAN, b Chiayi, Taiwan, Oct 10, 42; m 69; c 2. SOLID STATE PHYSICS. *Educ:* Taiwan Norm Univ, BS, 66; Col William & Mary, MS, 69, PhD(physics), 71. *Prof Exp:* Res assoc, Col William & Mary, 71-72; res assoc, Case Western Reserve Univ, 72-74; asst prof, 74-78, ASSOC PROF PHYSICS, AUBURN UNIV, 78- *Mem:* Am Phys Soc. *Res:* Study of electronic structures and related properties in crystalline solids and in disordered condensed matters. *Mailing Add:* Dept of Physics Auburn Univ Auburn AL 36830

CHEN, ANDREW TAT-LENG, b Kedah, Malaysia, June 17, 38; m 70; c 2. CYTOGENETICS, GENETICS. *Educ:* Chinese Univ Hong Kong, BSc, 61; McGill Univ, MSc, 63; Univ Western Ont, PhD(human cytogenetics), 69. *Prof Exp:* Assoc psychiat, Emory Univ, 69-70, asst prof, 70-72; asst prof genetics & pediat & dir cytogenetics lab, Med Col Va, 72-74; CHIEF CELLULAR GENETICS LAB, CTR DIS CONTROL, 74- *Concurrent Pos:* Res geneticist, Ga Ment Health Inst, 69-72. *Mem:* AAAS; Tissue Cult Asn; Sigma Xi; Am Soc Human Genetics. *Res:* Human cytogenetics; tissue culture of mammalian cells. *Mailing Add:* Cellular Genetics Lab Path Div Ctr for Dis Control Atlanta GA 30333

CHEN, ANTHONY HING, b China, July 10, 45; US citizen; m 71. FOOD ENGINEERING. *Educ:* Univ Calif, Berkeley, BS, 69; Ohio State Univ, MS, 71, PhD(food sci), 78. *Prof Exp:* Assoc process develop engr, Res & Develop, Miles Lab, Inc, 71-75, supvr process develop, 75-78; mgr process develop, 78-81, DIR NEW TECHNOL, RES & DEVELOP, ANDERSON CLAYTON CO, 81- *Concurrent Pos:* Lectr food chem & chem eng, Univ Tex, Dallas, 79- *Mem:* Am Inst Chem Engrs; Int Food Technologists; Am Oil Chemist Soc. *Res:* Vegetable oil hydrogenation; process development; process optimization; protein texturization; food rheology; fats and oils processing. *Mailing Add:* 3333 N Central Expressway Richardson TX 75080

CHEN, ARTHUR CHIH-MEI, b Boston, Mass, Apr 19, 39; m 63; c 2. ELECTRICAL ENGINEERING, COMPUTER SCIENCES. *Educ:* Mass Inst Technol, BS, 61, MS, 62, PhD(elec eng), 66. *Prof Exp:* Elec engr comput memories, 66-75, WBS proj mgr comput tomography, 75-77, mgr, Energy Progs-Energy Syst Management, 77-80, Energy Systs Management Br, 80, MGR, ELEC SYSTS & TECHNOL LAB, GEN ELEC CORP RES & DEVELOP, 80- *Mem:* Inst Elec & Electronics Engrs. *Res:* Development of computerized control and distributed computer architechture to automate the control of electrical power and drive systems and to computerized tomography for medical diagnostics. *Mailing Add:* Gen Elec Corp Res & Develop 1 River Rd Schenectady NY 12301

CHEN, B(IH) H(WA), b Foochow, China, Sept 24, 33; m 66. CHEMICAL ENGINEERING. *Educ:* Nat Taiwan Univ, BSc, 54; McGill Univ, MEng, 61, PhD(chem eng), 65. *Prof Exp:* Asst res officer, Appl Chem Div, Nat Res Coun Can, 65-66; from asst prof to assoc prof, 66-81, PROF CHEM ENG, TECH UNIV NS, 81- *Concurrent Pos:* Nat Res Coun Can res grant. *Mem:* Chem Inst Can. *Res:* Transport phenomena. *Mailing Add:* Dept Chem Eng Tech Univ NS Halifax NS B3J 2X4 Can

CHEN, B(ENJAMIN) T(EH-KUNG), b Shanghai, China. CHEMICAL ENGINEERING, PHOTOGRAPHY. *Educ:* Nat Taiwan Univ, BS, 58; Univ Miss, MS, 63; Univ Rochester, PhD(chem eng), 68. *Prof Exp:* Res asst, Dept Chem Eng, Univ Rochester, 65-67; SR RES CHEMIST, MAT COATING & ENG DIV, RES LABS, EASTMAN KODAK CO, 67- *Mem:* Soc Photog Sci & Eng. *Res:* Making and coating photographic emulsions. *Mailing Add:* Mat Coating & Eng Div Eastman Kodak Co 343 State St Rochester NY 14650

CHEN, BANG-YEN, b Ilan, Taiwan, Oct 3, 43; m 68; c 2. GEOMETRY. *Educ:* Tamkang Col, Taiwan, BS, 65; Nat Tsinghua Univ, MS, 67; Univ Notre Dame, PhD(math), 70. *Prof Exp:* Res assoc math, 70-72, assoc prof, 72-76, PROF MATH, MICH STATE UNIV, 76- *Concurrent Pos:* Ed, Tamkang J Math, 70-, Soochow J Math, 78- & Bull Inst Math Acad Sinica, 79- *Mem:* Am Math Soc. *Res:* Differential geometry, global analysis and algebraic geometry. *Mailing Add:* Dept of Math Mich State Univ East Lansing MI 48824

CHEN, C(HIH) W(EN), b Changsha, Hunan, China, Jan 2, 22; m 58. METALLURGY, MATERIALS SCIENCE. *Educ:* Chiaotung Univ, BS, 44; Ill Inst Technol, MS, 50; Columbia Univ, PhD(phys metall), 54. *Prof Exp:* Res assoc, Columbia Univ, 55-57; fel scientist, Westinghouse Res Lab, 57-66; assoc prof metall, 66-71, PROF METALL, IOWA STATE UNIV, 71- *Concurrent Pos:* Metallurgist, Ames Lab, US Atomic Energy Comn, 66-70, sr metallurgist, Ames Lab, US Dept Energy, 71- *Mem:* Am Phys Soc. *Res:* Crystal defects and radiation effects; magnetism and magnetic materials; thin films and amorphous alloys; electron microscopy. *Mailing Add:* 1528 Meadowlane Ave Ames IA 50010

CHEN, CARL W(AN-CHENG), b Tainan, Taiwan, Feb 22, 36; US citizen; m 66; c 2. SANITARY ENGINEERING, POWER PLANT IMPACTS. *Educ:* Nat Taiwan Univ, BS, 58; Univ Calif, Berkeley, MS, 63, PhD(eng), 67. *Prof Exp:* Jr engr, Taiwan Pub Works Bur, 60-61, asst engr, 61-62; res asst, Univ Calif, Berkeley, 62-63, res specialist, 63-66, teaching asst, 66-67; assoc engr, Water Resources Engrs, Inc, 67-69, sr engr, 69-73; assoc dir, 73-75, dir, 75-78, V PRES, TETRA TECH, INC, 78- *Concurrent Pos:* Vis scholar, The Swedish Univ Agr Sci, Uppsala, Sweden, 80. *Mem:* Am Soc Civil Engrs; Am Soc Limnol & Oceanog. *Res:* Data analyses and interpretation of water quality-ecologic responses of water resources systems to wastewater discharges, water resources development, and energy development projects such as power plants and coal mining; hydrodynamic-water quality-ecological simulation of Lake Ontario. *Mailing Add:* Tetra Tech Inc 3746 Mt Diablo Blvd Lafayette CA 94549

CHEN, CATHERINE S H, b Chungking, China; US citizen. POLYMER CHEMISTRY. *Educ:* Barnard Col, BA, 50; Columbia Univ, MA, 52; Polytech Inst New York, PhD(polymer chem), 55. *Prof Exp:* Res assoc, Dept Chem, Columbia Univ, 54-56, Celanese Res Co, Celanese Corp, 64-70; sr res chemist, Cent Res Div, Am Cyanamid Co, 56-64; res scientist, Corp Res & Develop Lab, Singer Co, 72-75; res assoc, 75-78, mgr resources chem, Cent Res Div, 78-79, PROG LEADER, ENHANCED OIL RECOVERY, MOBIL RES & DEVELOP CORP, 79- *Mem:* Am Chem Soc; Soc Petrol Engrs. *Res:* All aspects of polymer science; tertiary oil recovery chemicals; surfactants and mobility control agents, including polymers. *Mailing Add:* Mobil Res & Develop Corp PO Box 1025 Princeton NJ 08540

CHEN, CHANG-HWEI, b Taiwan, Oct 12, 41; m 70; c 2. PHYSICAL CHEMISTRY. *Educ:* Nat Taiwan Univ, BS, 64; Univ Conn, PhD(phys chem), 70. *Prof Exp:* Res assoc chem, Univ Pittsburgh, 70-73; fel, 73-74, res scientist I, 74-75, res scientist II, 75-76, res scientist III, 77-80, RES SCIENTIST IV, CHEM, DIV LABS & RES, NY STATE DEPT HEALTH, 80- *Mem:* Am Chem Soc. *Res:* Physical chemical properties of protein and lipid solutions; thermodynamics and transport processes; calorimetry and structure of water. *Mailing Add:* Div Labs & Res NY State Dept Health Albany NY 12201

CHEN, CHAO LING, b Tsaotun, Taiwan, Sept 28, 37; m 66. VETERINARY PHYSIOLOGY, ENDOCRINOLOGY. *Educ:* Nat Taiwan Univ, DVM, 60; Iowa State Univ, MS, 66; Mich State Univ, PhD(neuroendocrinol), 69. *Prof Exp:* Instr histol, Taipei Med Col, 61-63; asst vet, US Naval Med Res Unit, 63-64; res asst reproductive physiol, Iowa State Univ, 64-66; asst neuroendocrinol, Mich State Univ, 66-69; from asst prof to assoc prof physiol, Col Vet Med, Kans State Univ, 69-76; ASSOC PROF REPRODUCTION, UNIV FLA, 76- *Mem:* Soc Study Reproduction; Am Soc Animal Sci; Endocrine Soc; Int Soc Neuroendocrinol. *Res:* Hypothalamic regulation of the pituitary gonadotropin secretion by hypothalamic stimulation, lesion and sectioning and by radioimmunoassay; relationship between the uterus and luteal function. *Mailing Add:* Dept of Reproduction J-135 JHMHC Col Vet Med Univ Fla Gainesville FL 32611

CHEN, CHAO-HSING STANLEY, engineering mechanics, applied mathematics, see previous edition

CHEN, CHARLES CHIN-TSE, b Taipei, Taiwan, May 22, 29. SOLID STATE PHYSICS. *Educ:* Nat Taiwan Univ, BS, 51; Univ Md, PhD(physics), 62. *Prof Exp:* Instr physics, Nat Taiwan Univ, 51-57; asst, Univ Md, 57-62, res assoc, 63; from res asst prof to assoc prof, 63-77, PROF PHYSICS, OHIO UNIV, 77- *Mem:* Am Phys Soc; Phys Soc Japan. *Res:* Statistical mechanics. *Mailing Add:* Dept of Physics Ohio Univ Athens OH 45701

CHEN, CHARLES SHIN-YANG, b Changhua, Taiwan, Dec 25, 34; US citizen; m 63; c 2. MECHANICAL ENGINEERING, ENERGY CONVERSION. *Educ:* Purdue Univ, BS, 57; Univ Wash, MS, 65; Univ Wis, PhD(mech eng), 68. *Prof Exp:* Res engr bldg prod & insulation, Johns-Manville Corp, 57-60; sr res engr aircrafts, Boeing Co, 61-65; assoc prof mech eng, Univ Va, 68-72; prog mgr solar energy, NSF, 72-75; prog mgr solar energy & conserv, US Dept of Energy, 75-77; dir, Ctr Eng Res, Univ Hawaii, 77-80; VPRES PAC OPERS, ULTRASYSTEMS, INC, 80- *Concurrent Pos:* NASA grant hybrid rocket, 68-72; US Dept Interior grant water res, 68-72; consult air pollution, US Environ Protection Agency, 70-75; adj prof mech eng, Univ Miami, 75-76. *Honors & Awards:* Ralph R Teetor Award, Soc Automotive Engrs, 69; Dirs Commendation, NSF, 74. *Mem:* Assoc fel Am Inst Aeronaut & Astronaut; Am Soc Mech Engrs; Soc Automotive Engrs; Combustion Inst; Int Solar Energy Soc. *Res:* Alternative energy fields of solar, wind, ocean thermal, biomass and geothermal energy; combustion phenomena of hydrocarbon fuels; energy conservation in transportation; development of automotive gas turbine and Stirling engines; development of alternative fuels. *Mailing Add:* Ctr for Eng Res 2540 Dole St Honolulu HI 96822

CHEN, CHEN HO, b Kiangsu, China, Sept 9, 29; US citizen; m 60; c 3. PLANT CYTOLOGY, PLANT PHYSIOLOGY. *Educ:* Nat Taiwan Univ, BS, 54; La State Univ, MS, 60; SDak State Univ, PhD(plant sci), 64. *Prof Exp:* Fel, SDak State Univ, 63-64 & Argonne Nat Lab, US Atomic Energy Comn, 64-65; lectr & head biol, Hong Kong Baptist Col, 65-68; from asst prof to assoc prof, 68-75, PROF BIOL & PLANT SCI, SDAK STATE UNIV, 75- *Mem:* Bot Soc Am; Tissue Cult Asn. *Res:* Development of cell and tissue culture techniques for use in breeding monocotyledonous species. *Mailing Add:* Dept of Bot & Biol SDak State Univ Brookings SD 57007

CHEN, CHENG-LIN, b Mukden, China, Aug 14, 29; m 48; c 3. ELECTRICAL ENGINEERING. *Educ:* Taiwan Univ, BS, 53; Univ Ill, MS, 56, PhD(elec eng), 59. *Prof Exp:* Res assoc gaseous electronics, Univ Ill, 58-59, res asst prof plasma physics, Coord Sci Lab, 59-63; SR RES SCIENTIST, WESTINGHOUSE RES LABS, 63- *Mem:* Am Phys Soc. *Res:* Gaseous electronics; plasma physics; atomic physics; magnetohydrodynamics and laser physics. *Mailing Add:* Westinghouse Res Labs Churchill Borough Pittsburgh PA 15235

CHEN, CHENG-LUNG, b Taichung, Taiwan, Nov 1, 31; m 70. HYDRAULIC ENGINEERING, WATER RESOURCES. *Educ:* Nat Taiwan Univ, BS, 54; Mich State Univ, MS, 60, PhD(hydraul), 62. *Prof Exp:* Res assoc civil eng, Mich State Univ, 62-63; assoc res engr, Utah State Univ, 63-64, from asst prof to assoc prof civil eng, 64-66; assoc prof, Univ Ill, Urbana-Champaign, 66-69; prof civil eng, Utah State Univ, 69-80; MEM STAFF, GULF COAST HYDROSCI CTR, US GEOL SURV, 80- *Mem:* Am Soc Civil Engrs; Am Geophys Union; Int Asn Hydraul Res. *Res:* Sprinkler and surface irrigation; watershed hydraulics; soil moisture and ground water; sediment transportation; hydraulic transients; soil and thermal pollution; drainage and porous media flow; geohydrology and biohydrology; hydrosystems analysis. *Mailing Add:* Gulf Coast Hydrosci Ctr NSTL Station MS 39529

CHEN, CHIADAO, b Peiping, China, Dec 7, 13; nat US. BIOCHEMISTRY. *Educ:* Shanghai Univ, BS, 36; Dresden Tech Univ, Dipl Ing, 39; Berlin Tech, DSc(biochem), 41. *Prof Exp:* Res chemist, Ciba Pharmaceut, Inc, 42-44; sr res fel, Univ Pittsburgh, 44-48; res assoc & asst prof biochem, Univ Notre Dame, 48-49; assoc prof, 49-67, PROF BIOCHEM, MED SCH, NORTHWESTERN UNIV, CHICAGO, 67- *Concurrent Pos:* Biochemist & sect chief, Vet Admin Res Hosp, 54-56. *Mem:* AAAS; Am Chem Soc; NY Acad Sci; Am Soc Biol Chem; Brit Biochem Soc. *Res:* Steroid chemistry; oxygenation mechanism; chemical carcinogenesis; liver function. *Mailing Add:* Dept of Biochem Northwestern Univ Med Sch Chicago IL 60611

CHEN, CHIH SHAN, b Chekiang, China, Oct 1, 29; m 62; c 1. STRATIGRAPHY, SEDIMENTOLOGY. *Educ:* Nat Taiwan Univ, BS, 54; Fla State Univ, MS, 60; Northwestern Univ, PhD(geol), 64. *Prof Exp:* Asst geol, Nat Taiwan Univ, 54-57 & Fla State Univ, 60; res geologist, Pure Oil Co, 64-65; SR RES SCIENTIST, UNION OIL CO CALIF, 65- *Mem:* Am Asn Petrol Geol; Soc Econ Paleontologists & Mineralogists; Int Asn Sedimentologists; Sigma Xi; Geol Soc Am. *Res:* Sedimentology; regional lithostratigraphic analysis; reservoir geology. *Mailing Add:* Union Oil Co of Calif Res Ctr PO Box 76 Brea CA 92621

CHEN, CHI-HAU, b Fukien, China, Dec 22, 37; m 66; c 2. INFORMATION & COMMUNICATION SCIENCES. *Educ:* Nat Taiwan Univ, BS, 59; Univ Tenn, Knoxville, MS, 62; Purdue Univ, PhD(elec eng), 65. *Prof Exp:* Res engr, Radio Wave Res Lab, Taiwan, 61; teaching asst elec eng, Univ Tenn, Knoxville, 61-62; instr, Purdue Univ, 62; sr res engr, ADCOM, Inc, Mass, 65-66; staff mem, Systs Div, AVCO Corp, 66-68; assoc prof elec eng, 68-73, PROF ELEC ENG, SOUTHEASTERN MASS UNIV, 73- *Concurrent Pos:* Lectr, Northeastern Univ, 68-69; consult, Systs Div, AVCO Corp, Mass, 68-74; chmn elec group, Southeastern Mass Univ, 78- *Mem:* AAAS; Inst Elec & Electronics Engrs. *Res:* Pattern recognition; information theory; communication theory and systems; adaptive and learning systems; digital signal processing; mathematical statistics. *Mailing Add:* Dept of Elec Eng Southeastern Mass Univ North Dartmouth MA 02747

CHEN, CHI-HONG BETTY, b Ching-King, China, Dec 10, 45; m 69; c 1. ORGANIC CHEMISTRY. *Educ:* Nat Taiwan Univ, BS, 68; NY Univ, PhD(org chem), 76. *Prof Exp:* Res fel, Am Health Found, 74-77, res assoc, 77-79; RES CHEMIST, OCCIDENTAL RES CORP, 79- *Mem:* Am Chem Soc. *Res:* Metabolism and mechanisms of action of chemical carcinogens. *Mailing Add:* 33771 Avenida Calita San Juan Capistrano CA 92675

CHEN, CHIN HSIN, b Che-Kiang, China, Feb 7, 43; m 69. SYNTHETIC ORGANIC CHEMISTRY. *Educ:* Tunghai Univ, Taiwan, BS, 64; Okla State Univ, PhD(org chem), 71. *Prof Exp:* Fel org chem, Ohio State Univ, 71-72 & Harvard Univ, 72-73; sr res chemist, 73-80, RES ASSOC SYNTHETIC ORG CHEM, EASTMAN KODAK CO RES LAB, 80- *Mem:* Am Chem Soc; Sigma Xi. *Res:* Exploratory organic synthesis in the field of organosulfur and organophosphorus heterocyclic chemistry. *Mailing Add:* Eastman Kodak Co Res Lab 1669 Lake Ave Rochester NY 14650

CHEN, CHING-CHIH, b Foochow, China, Sept 3, 37; US citizen; m 61; c 3. INFORMATION SCIENCE. *Educ:* Nat Taiwan Univ, BA, 59; Univ Mich, AMLS, 61; Case Western Reserve Univ, PhD(info sci), 74. *Prof Exp:* Serv librn, Univ Mich, 61-62; sci ref librn, Windsor Pub Libr, Ont, 62; ref librn, McMaster Univ, 62-63; head sci librn, 63-64; sr sci librn, Univ Waterloo, 64-65; head librn, Eng, Math & Sci Libr, 65-68; assoc head sci libr, Mass Inst Technol, 68-71; from asst prof to assoc prof libr sci, 71-79, asst dean acad affairs, 77-79, PROF LIBR SCI & ASSOC DEAN, SIMMONS COL, 79- *Concurrent Pos:* Consult, Sci & Tech Doc Ctr, Nat Sci Coun, Repub of China, 73-77; consult, WHO; vpres, Chen & Chen Consults, Inc. *Mem:* Am Soc Info Sci; Am Libr Asn; Med Libr Asn; Spec Libr Asn; Am Asn Univ Prof. *Res:* Scientific management, especially the application of modern analytic techniques in library problems; systems analysis; biomedical, scientific and technical library and information services and systems; author of numerous books and scholarly articles. *Mailing Add:* Sch of Libr Sci 300 The Fenway Boston MA 02115

CHEN, CHING-JEN, b Taipei, Taiwan, July 6, 36; m 65; c 2. MECHANICAL ENGINEERING, APPLIED MATHEMATICS. *Educ:* Taipei Inst Technol, Taiwan, Dipl, 57; Kans State Univ, MS, 62; Case Inst Technol, PhD(mech eng), 67. *Prof Exp:* Design engr, Ta-Tong Grinding Co, Taipei, 59-60; res asst heat transfer, Kansas State Univ, 60-62; res asst fluid mech & heat transfer, Case Inst Technol, 62-67; from asst prof to assoc prof, 67-76, PROF MECH ENG, UNIV IOWA, 77- *Concurrent Pos:* US Sr Scientist Award, Alexander von Humboldt Found, Ger, 74-75. *Mem:* Am Soc Mech Engrs; Am Inst Aeronaut & Astronaut; Am Soc Eng Educ; Am Phys Soc. *Res:* Fluid mechanics and heat transfer such as melting phenomena, two phase flow, turbulent flow, hydrodynamic instability, heat convection, condensation and boundary layer phenomenon. *Mailing Add:* EB 2208 Eng Div Univ of Iowa Iowa City IA 52242

CHEN, CHING-LING CHU, b Taipei, Taiwan, May 8, 48; m 76; c 1. MOLECULAR BIOLOBY, ENDOCRINOLOGY. *Educ:* Nat Taiwan Univ, BS, 71; Columbia Univ, MA, 75, PhD(biochem), 79. *Prof Exp:* fel, 79, FEL RES, COLUMBIA UNIV, 80- *Mem:* Am Chem Soc. *Res:* Isolation and characterization of proopimelanocortin (precursor for adrenocorticortropic hormone-B-Endorphin) genes in rodent and human pituitanes; hormonal regulation of expression of these genes in rat pituitary and possible mechanisms involved in the hormone action. *Mailing Add:* Dept Biochem Col Physicians Surgeons Columbia Univ New York NY 10032

CHEN, CHING-NIEN, b China, 45. IMAGE RECONSTRUCTION ALGORITHMS. *Educ:* Nat Taiwan Univ, BS, 67; Nat Tsing-Hua Univ, MS, 69; State Univ NY at Stony Brook, PhD(chem), 80. *Prof Exp:* Lectr, Gen Chem Lab, Nat Tsing-Hua Univ, Taiwan, 69-73; fel nuclear magnetic resonance imaging res, State Univ NY at Stony Brook, 80; vis fel, 80-81, EXPERT NUCLEAR MAGNETIC RESONANCE IMAGING, NIH, 81- *Concurrent Pos:* Lectr gen chem, Fu-Jen Catholic Univ, 68-69. *Mem:* Sigma Xi; Asn Comput Mach; Soc Magnetic Resonance Med. *Res:* Nuclear magnetic resonance imaging techniques; three-dimensional image reconstruction from plane-integrals; reconstruction algorithms; computer software in nuclear magnetic resonance imaging. *Mailing Add:* Bldg 13 Rm 3W-13 Biomed Eng & Instrumentation Br NIH Bethesda MD 20205

CHEN, CHIN-LIN, b Honan, China, Mar 27, 37; m 67; c 2. ELECTRICAL ENGINEERING. *Educ:* Taiwan Univ, BS, 58; NDak State Univ, MS, 61; Harvard Univ, PhD(appl physics), 65. *Prof Exp:* Res fel electronics, Harvard Univ, 65-66; from asst prof to assoc prof, 66-78, PROF ELEC ENG, PURDUE UNIV, 78- *Mem:* Inst Elec & Electronics Engrs. *Res:* Electromagnetic theory; antennas and diffraction of waves; surface acoustic wave devices, integrated optics. *Mailing Add:* Sch of Elec Eng Purdue Univ West Lafayette IN 47907

CHEN, CHIOU SHIUN, b Taipei, Taiwan, Jan 22, 38; m 63; c 1. ELECTRICAL ENGINEERING, AUTOMATIC CONTROL SYSTEMS. *Educ:* Taiwan Univ, BS, 60; Univ Rochester, MS, 64, PhD(elec eng), 67. *Prof Exp:* Assoc engr, Taylor Instrument Co, 64-66; Nat Acad Sci-Nat Res Coun res assoc, Ames Res Ctr, NASA, 67-68; from asst prof to assoc prof, 68-78, PROF ELEC ENG, UNIV AKRON, 78- *Mem:* Inst Elec & Electronics Engr; Sigma Xi. *Res:* Dispersion and attenuation compenstion by cepstral processing for better and more accurate identification of echo signals; microprocessor application in digital control; spectral estimation. *Mailing Add:* Dept of Elec Eng Univ of Akron Akron OH 44325

CHEN, CHI-PO, b Taiwan, China, May 14, 40; US citizen; m 68; c 2. PHARMACOLOGY, PHARMACY. *Educ:* Kaohsiung Med Col, Taiwan, BSc, 63; Queen's Univ, Ont, MSc, 69; Univ Ky, PhD(pharmacol), 73. *Prof Exp:* Chief pharmacist, Heng Hsin Pharmaceut Co, 64-67; res asst pharmacol, Univ Ky, 69-73; res assoc biochem, Vanderbilt Univ, 73-74; asst prof pharmacol, Univ Conn, Storrs, 74-80; ASSOC PROF PHARMACOL, OHIO COL PODIATRIC MED, CLEVELAND, 80- *Concurrent Pos:* Fac fel, Univ Conn, 75. *Mem:* AAAS; NY Acad Sci; Acad Pharmaceut Sci; Am Pharmaceut Asn; Am Soc Pharmacol & Exp Therapeut. *Res:* Transport through biological membranes with special interests in the area of drug transport in isolated liver cells, perfused liver, the choroid plexus and intestine. *Mailing Add:* Ohio Col Podiatric Med 10515 Carnegie Ave Cleveland OH 44106

CHEN, CHI-TSONG, b Taiwan, China, Jan 7, 36; m 63; c 3. SYSTEMS THEORY, CONTROL SYSTEMS. *Educ:* Univ Calif, Berkeley, PhD(elec eng), 66. *Prof Exp:* From asst prof to assoc prof, 66-74, PROF ELEC SCI, STATE UNIV NY, STONY BROOK, 74- *Mem:* Inst Elec & Electronics Engrs. *Res:* Systems and control theory; digital signal processing. *Mailing Add:* Dept of Elec Eng State Univ of NY Stony Brook NY 11794

CHEN, CHONG MAW, b Taoyuan, Taiwan; m 66; c 2. PLANT BIOCHEMISTRY. *Educ:* Taiwan Norm Univ, BS, 58; Univ Kans, MA, 64, PhD(plant biochem), 67. *Prof Exp:* Teaching asst biol, Taiwan Norm Univ, 61-62; fel biochem, McMaster Univ, 67-69; res fel, Roche Inst Molecular Biol, 69-71; asst prof life sci, 71-73, assoc prof, 73-77, PROF LIFE SCI, UNIV WIS-PARKSIDE, 77- *Mem:* AAAS; Am Chem Soc; Am Soc Biol Chemists; Am Soc Plant Physiol. *Res:* Mechanism of action of plant hormones; nucleic acid and protein biosynthesis. *Mailing Add:* Sci Div Univ Wis-Parkside Kenosha WI 53141

CHEN, CHUAN FANG, b Tientsin, China, Nov 15, 32; nat US; m 57:; c 3. MECHANICAL & AEROSPACE ENGINEERING. *Educ:* Univ Ill, BSc, 53, MSc, 54; Brown Univ, PhD(eng), 60. *Prof Exp:* Res scientist, Hydronautics, Inc, 60-61; sr res scientist, 61-62; asst to chief engr, 62-63; from asst prof to prof mech eng, Rutgers Univ, 63-80, chairperson, Dept Mech, Indust & Aerospace Eng, 76-80; HEAD, DEPT AEROSPACE & MECH ENG, UNIV ARIZ, 80- *Concurrent Pos:* Consult, Hydronautics, Inc, Vitro Labs & Bard Inc; sr visitor, Dept Appl Math & Theoretical Physics, Cambridge Univ, England, 71-72; vis fel, Res Sch Earth Sci, Australian Nat Univ, 78. *Mem:* Am Inst Aeronaut & Astronaut; Am Phys Soc; Am Soc Eng Educ. *Res:* Supersonic interference; supercavitating flow past hydrofoils; heat transfer to gas-solid suspensions; stratified flows; hydrodynamic stability; double diffusive convection. *Mailing Add:* Dept Aerospace & Mech Eng Univ Ariz Tucson AZ 85721

CHEN, CHUAN JU, b Tainan, Taiwan, Mar 21, 47; m 72; c 1. POLYMER SCIENCE ENGINEERING. *Educ:* Chung Yuan Univ, BE, 70; Worcester Polytech Inst, MS, 74; Univ Mich, PhD(polymer sci & eng), 80. *Prof Exp:* SR ENGR RES, MONSANTO CO, 80- *Mem:* Sigma Xi; Am Chem Soc; Soc Plastics Engrs. *Res:* Products in styrenic polymers; structure-property-processing relationships of polymers. *Mailing Add:* Monsanto Co 730 Worcester St Indian Orchard MA 01151

CHEN, CHUNG WEI, b Hunan, China, Dec 25, 21; US citizen; m 65; c 2. APPLIED STATISTICS. *Educ:* Nat Chengchi Univ, China, BA, 46, LLB, 48; La State Univ, MBA, 54, PhD(statist), 57. *Prof Exp:* Secy, Human Prov Govt, 46-47; judge, Hunan Changsha Dist Ct, 47-48; statistician, Haloid-Xerox, Inc, 56-61; chief statistician, 61-72, mgr statist serv, 72-76, sr consult corp staff, 76-80, PRIN CONSULT, XEROX CORP, 80- *Concurrent Pos:* Instr, Rochester Inst Technol, 59-67. *Mem:* Am Statist Asn; Am Econ Asn. *Mailing Add:* 310 Orchard Park Blvd Rochester NY 14609

CHEN, CHUNG-HO, b Kaohsiung, Taiwan, Dec 1, 37; US citizen; m 65; c 4. BIOCHEMISTRY. *Educ:* Chung-Hsing Univ, BS, 62; Okla State Univ, PhD(biochem), 69. *Prof Exp:* Res asst pharmacol, Kaohsiung Med Col, 63-64; asst biochem, Okla State Univ, 64-69; ASST PROF OPHTHALMIC BIOCHEM, SCH MED, JOHNS HOPKINS UNIV, 73- *Concurrent Pos:* Fel biochem, Okla State Univ, 69; fel, Sch Med, Johns Hopkins Univ, 69-73, consult ophthal, 72-73; Nat Eye Inst res grant, 75-; Am Diabetes Asn grant, 75- *Honors & Awards:* Mayers Award, 75. *Mem:* AAAS; Am Chem Soc; Asn Clin Scientists; NY Acad Sci; Asn Res Vision & Ophthal. *Res:* Ocular biochemistry; enzymatic activities in mitochondria; metabolic regulations and disorders; angiogenesis; membrane chemistry; active transport. *Mailing Add:* Dept of Ophthal Johns Hopkins Univ Med Sch Baltimore MD 21205

CHEN, DAVID HOU-CHUNG, b Quayang, June 8, 41; US citizen; m 71; c 1. MEDICAL PARASITOLOGY, IMMUNOLOGY. *Educ:* Univ Md, BS, 67; Am Univ, MS, 72; NY Univ, PhD(med sci), 74; Johns Hopkins Univ, MPH, 79. *Prof Exp:* Res entomologist, Walter Reed Army Inst Res, 67-69; trainee, Dept Prev Med, Sch Med, NY Univ, 71-74; staff fel parasite immunol, Lab Parasitic Dis, Nat Inst Allergy & Infectious Dis, 74-77, sr staff fel, 77-78; ENVIRON HEALTH SCIENTIST, AM PETROL INST, 81- *Mem:* NY Acad Sci; Am Pub Health Asn. *Res:* Mechanisms of parasite induced immunity; malaria in rodent and primate models. *Mailing Add:* Am Petrol Inst 2101 P St Northwest Washington DC 20037

CHEN, DAVID HSIAO TSUNG, chemical engineering, see previous edition

CHEN, DAVID J, b China, Dec 6, 44; m 71; c 1. GENETIC TOXICOLOGY, CELL GENETICS. *Educ:* Nat Taiwan Univ, BS, 68; Univ Mo, PhD(genetics), 78. *Prof Exp:* Fel, 78-80, MEM STAFF, LOS ALAMOS NAT LAB, 80- *Concurrent Pos:* Prin investr, Los Alamos Nat Lab, 80- *Mem:* Am Soc Cell Biol; Environ Mutagen Soc; Tissue Culture Asn; Radiation Res Soc. *Res:* Study of mechanisms of cell cycle progression in mammalian cells in culture using temperature-sensitive cell cycle mutants; development of human cell mutagenesis and transformation assays for detection of chemical and physical mutagens-carcinogens; study of mechanisms of mutation and transformation induction by radiations. *Mailing Add:* Genetics Group MS886 Life Sci Div Los Alamos Nat Lab Los Alamos NM 87545

CHEN, DAVIDSON TAH-CHUEN, b Wenling, China, Apr 1, 42; US citizen; m 66; c 2. PHYSICAL OCEANOGRAPHY, REMOTE SENSING. *Educ:* Nat Taiwan Univ, BS, 63; Univ Calif, Berkeley, MS, 66; NC State Univ, PhD(phys oceanog), 72. *Prof Exp:* Consult engr struct dynamics, John A Blume & Assoc Engrs, 66-67; Nat Res Coun resident res assoc phys oceanog & remote sensing, Wallops Flight Ctr, NASA, 72-74; PHYS OCEANOGR, NAVAL RES LAB, 74- *Concurrent Pos:* Organizer, John W Wright Mem Lect, 80- *Mem:* Am Geophys Union. *Res:* Developing mathematical models, based upon fluid dynamics and physics of electromagnetic waves,, for physical parameters which describe important and meaningful phenomena geophysically; developing microwave remote sensors for inferring the measurements of these physical parameters. *Mailing Add:* Code 7112 C Naval Res Lab Washington DC 20375

CHEN, DI, b Chekiang, China, Mar 15, 29; m 58; c 2. ELECTRICAL ENGINEERING, MAGNETISM. *Educ:* Nat Taiwan Norm Univ, BS, 53; Univ Minn, Minneapolis, MS, 56; Stanford Univ, PhD(elec eng), 59. *Prof Exp:* Teaching asst elec eng, Nat Taiwan Univ, 53-54; asst prof, Univ Minn, Minneapolis, 59-62; sr res scientist, Honeywell Corp Tech Ctr, 62-65, sr prin re scientist, 66-69, staff scientist & group leader, 69-79, fel, 79-80; TECHNOL DIR, ADVAN MEM LAB, MAGNETIC PERIPHRALS INC, 80- *Honors & Awards:* Honeywell Sweatt Eng & Scientist Award, 72. *Mem:* Am Phys Soc; Inst Elec & Electronics Engrs. *Res:* Ferrites; ferromagnetic resonance of magnetic films; microwave magnetron research; lasers; magneto-optic effects; microwave modulation of light; optical memory; optical communication and integrated optics. *Mailing Add:* Magnetic Periphals Inc 2766 Janitell Rd Colorado Springs CO 80906

CHEN, DILLION TONG-TING, b Tayu, China, Nov 1, 34; US citizen; m 65; c 2. PLANT ANATOMY, HERBS. *Educ:* Nat Taiwan Univ, BS, 57; Atlanta Univ, MS, 71, PhD(bot & phytopath), 78. *Prof Exp:* Lab asst, Col Agr, Nat Chung Hsing Univ, 59-61; teacher, Taoyuan Agr Acad, Taiwan Prov, 62-63; teaching demonstr, New Asia Col, Chinese Univ Hong Kong, 63-68; RES ASSOC BOT & PHYTOPATH, ATLANTA UNIV, 81- *Res:* Histological appearance or pathological anatomy of bud tissue in balsam fir before or following an attack of the budworm. *Mailing Add:* 2915 Porter Glade Ct Doraville GA 30360

CHEN, EDWIN HUNG-TEH, b Tainan, Taiwan, Aug 23, 34; US citizen; m 66; c 2. BIOSTATISTICS. *Educ:* Nat Taiwan Univ, BS, 57; Mich State Univ, MS, 64; Univ Calif, Los Angeles, PhD(biostatist), 69. *Prof Exp:* Systs analyst statist, Union Am Comput Corp, 64-65; asst res statistician & lectr biostatist, Univ Calif, Los Angeles, 69-72; assoc prof biomet, 72-78, PROF BIOMET, UNIV ILL MED CTR, 78- *Mem:* Am Statist Asn; Inst Math Statist; Biomet Soc; AAAS. *Res:* Data analysis; robust statistical procedures; statistical computing; computer simulation. *Mailing Add:* Sch Pub Health Univ of Ill PO Box 6998 Chicago IL 60680

CHEN, ERH-CHUN, b Kwangtung, China, Nov 11, 34; Can citizen; m 64; c 2. CHEMICAL ENGINEERING, ENVIRONMENTAL ENGINEERING. *Educ:* Nat Taiwan Univ, BEng, 57; McGill Univ, MEng, 64, PhD(chem eng), 68. *Prof Exp:* Shift supvr mfg process, Taiwan Fertilizer Corp, 59-62; res engr hydrometall, Que Iron & Titanium Corp, 62-71; res scientist environ pollution, 71-80, DIR WATER POLLUTION CONTROL ENG, FISHERIES & ENVIRON CAN, 80- *Mem:* Chem Inst Can; Can Soc Chem Eng. *Res:* Oil pollution in cold environment; wastewater treatment and interfacial phenomena. *Mailing Add:* Environ Protection Serv Fisheries & Environ Can Ottawa Can

CHEN, ER-PING, b Kansu, China, May 19, 44; US citizen; m 73; c 2. APPLIED MECHANICS. *Educ:* Chung-Hsing Univ, Taiwan, BS, 66; Lehigh Univ, MS, 69, PhD(appl mech), 72. *Prof Exp:* Asst prof mech, Lehigh Univ, 72-77, assoc prof, 77-78; MEM TECH STAFF, SANDIA LABS, 78- *Mem:* Sigma Xi; Am Soc Mech Engrs; Am Soc Testing & Mat; Soc Exp Stress Anal; Soc Eng Sci. *Mailing Add:* 3917 Mary Ellen Pl NE Albuquerque NM 87111

CH'EN, EUGENE, b Peking, China, Aug 15, 45; US citizen. PHYSICS, MATHEMATICS. *Educ:* Univ Ore, BS, 66; Univ Calif, MA, 68, PhD(physics), 71. *Prof Exp:* Mathematician, Res Dept, US Naval Ord Test Sta, 65-; physicist, Res Dept, Naval Weapons Ctr, 66; res mgr, Off Res, US Dept Transp, 72-74; sr scientist, Systs Group, 74-76, dep mgr, Energy & Environ Sci Div, 76-78, corp sci adv, off chief scientist, 78-80, ADV, ADVAN CONCEPTS CTR, SCI APPLNS, INC, 80- *Concurrent Pos:* Physicist, Inst Theoret Sci, Univ Ore, 71-72; adv, Transp Res Bd, 72-74 & Nat Acad Sci, 74-; consult physics, Lawrence Livermore Lab, 74-75. *Mem:* AAAS; Am Phys Soc. *Res:* Perturbative techniques; risk analysis; nuclear effects; directed energy systems; strategic and tactical C3I; non-acoustic acoustic surface wave; technology assessment; relativity. *Mailing Add:* Sci Applns Inc 1200 Prospect St La Jolla CA 92038

CHEN, FANG SHANG, b Taipeh, Formosa, Feb 25, 28; m 61. ELECTRICAL ENGINEERING. *Educ:* Taiwan Univ, BSEE, 51; Purdue Univ, MSEE, 55; Ohio State Univ, PhD(elec eng), 59. *Prof Exp:* Engr, Taiwan Power Co, 51-54; asst, Electron Devices Lab, Ohio State Univ, 55-57, res assoc, 57-59; MEM TECH STAFF, BELL LABS, 59- *Mem:* Am Phys Soc; Inst Elec & Electronics Engrs. *Res:* Microwave electron tubes; solid state devices, especially ferrite devices and masers; optical communication devices. *Mailing Add:* Rm 2D 320 Bell Labs Murray Hill NJ 07974

CHEN, FRANCIS F, b Canton, China, Nov 18, 29; US citizen; m 56; c 3. PLASMA PHYSICS. *Educ:* Harvard Univ, AB, 50, MA, 51, PhD(physics), 54. *Prof Exp:* Res assoc physics, Brookhaven Nat Lab, 53-54; res staff mem, Plasma Physics Lab, Princeton Univ, 54-64, res physicist, 64-69, sr res physicist, 69; PROF ENG & APPL SCI, UNIV CALIF, LOS ANGELES, 69- *Concurrent Pos:* Attend physicist, Nuclear Res Ctr, Fontenay, France, 62-63; chmn fusion adv comt, Elec Power Res Inst, 73-; consult, TRW Inc, 77- *Mem:* Fel Am Phys Soc; fel Inst Elec & Electronics Engrs. *Res:* Basic plasma physics; fusion reactors; laser-plasma interactions. *Mailing Add:* Boelter Hall 7731 Univ of Calif Los Angeles CA 90024

CHEN, FRANCIS HAP-KWONG, b Shanghai, China, Mar 14, 48. STRUCTURAL ANALYSIS, NOISE & VIBRATIONS. *Educ:* Lafayette Col, BS, 71; Univ Ill, Urbana, MS, 73, PhD(theoret & appl mech), 76. *Prof Exp:* Assoc sr res engr, 76-79, STAFF RES ENG, GEN MOTORS RES LAB, GEN MOTORS CORP, 79- *Mem:* Am Soc Mech Engrs; Soc Automotive Engrs; Sigma Xi. *Res:* Analytical and experimental structural mechanics, with emphasis on: structural dynamics, system modeling and applications of digital signal processing techniques to noise and vibration problems. *Mailing Add:* 6106 Atkins Rd Troy MI 48098

CHEN, FRANKLIN F K, mechanical engineering, nuclear engineering, see previous edition

CHEN, FRANKLIN M, b Chang-Hua, Taiwan, Sept 19, 46; m 74; c 1. PHYSICAL CHEMISTRY, BIOCHEMISTRY. *Educ:* Taiwan Univ, BS, 70; Princeton Univ, MS, 73, PhD(phys chem), 76. *Prof Exp:* Res assoc enzyme chem, Rutgers Univ, 76-77; RES CHEMIST RES & DEVELOP, COLGATE & PALMOLIVE CO, 77- *Mem:* AAAS; Am Chem Soc; Sigma Xi. *Res:* Colloid and surface chemistry. *Mailing Add:* 909 River Rd Piscataway NJ 08854

CHEN, FRED FEN CHUAN, b Hukou, Taiwan, Nov 20, 34; m 60; c 2. CHEMICAL ENGINEERING. *Educ:* Taiwan Norm Univ, BS, 57; Ga Inst Technol, MS, 61; Va Polytech Inst, PhD(chem eng), 67. *Prof Exp:* Jr process engr, Taiwan Fertilizer Co, 57-59; engr, Celanese Fibers Co Div, Celanese Corp Am, 60-62, develop engr, 62-64, sr develop engr, 64; res chem engr, 66-68, sr res chem engr, 68-71, res assoc, 72-76, asst supt, 76-79, sr res assoc, 79-81, ASST SUPT, TENN EASTMAN CO DIV, EASTMAN KODAK CO, 81- *Mem:* Am Chem Soc; Am Inst Chem Engrs; Am Asn Textile Technol; Sigma Xi. *Res:* Polymer engineering; rheology; polymerization kinetics; synthetic fiber technology. *Mailing Add:* Tenn Eastman Co Eastman Rd Kingsport TN 37662

CHEN, FREEMAN PHILIP, b San Fernando, Trinidad, Feb 27, 47; US citizen; m 70; c 2. CHEMICAL PHYSICS. *Educ:* Brooklyn Polytech Inst, BS, 69; State Univ NY Stony Brook, MS, 73, PhD(chem physics), 75. *Prof Exp:* Vis prof & teaching assoc chem, State Univ NY Buffalo, 75-77; SCIENTIST, POLAROID CORP, 77- *Res:* Thermodynamic properties of polymers; Dember effect and electronic spectroscopy of photographic systems; studies of molecules and molecular crystals using Stark spectroscopy; laser Raman and electronic spectroscopy of solid state organic charge transfer complexes; dynamic laser scattering of polymers and colloids. *Mailing Add:* Res Labs 750 Main St Cambridge MA 02139

CHEN, H R, b Puten, Fukien, China, June 13, 29; m 60; c 3. DNA, RNA. *Educ:* Taiwan Normal Univ, BS, 52; Univ SC, MS, 60; Yale Univ, PhD(biol), 64. *Prof Exp:* Res assoc biol, Yale Univ, 64-66; asst prof, WVa Univ, 66-69; assoc prof, Univ SC, 70-74; programmer & analyst database, Duke Power Co, 78-79; SR RES SCIENTIST DNA & RNA, NAT BIOMED RES FOUND, GEORGETOWN UNIV MED CTR, 80- *Concurrent Pos:* Vis prof, NC State Univ, 76-77. *Res:* Analyzing sequence data of nucleic acids and proteins in the computerized databases. *Mailing Add:* Nat Biomed Res Found Georgetown Univ Med Ctr 3900 Reservoir Rd Washington DC 20007

CHEN, HAO-CHIA, b Taiwan, China, Feb 3, 35; US citizen; m 65; c 2. BIOCHEMISTRY, ENDOCRINOLOGY. *Educ:* Nat Taiwan Univ, BS, 57, MS, 59; Emory Univ, PhD(biochem), 64. *Prof Exp:* Guest investr biochem, Rockefeller Univ, 64-65, res assoc, 65-69, asst prof, 69-72; SR INVESTR CHEM, NAT INST CHILD HEALTH & HUMAN DEVELOP, 72- *Concurrent Pos:* Joseph B Whitehead fel, Emory Univ Sch Med, 64-65. *Mem:* Am Soc Biol Chemists; Endocrine Soc; Am Chem Soc. *Res:* Chemistry of polypeptides important on reproductive biology; structure and function of primate chorionic gonadotropins; production and characterization of specific anti-sera to gonadotropins and development of immunoassay methods for diagnostic uses. *Mailing Add:* Endocrinol & Reproduction Res Br Human Develop Bethesda MD 20014

CHEN, HAO-LIN, physical chemistry, chemical physics, see previous edition

CHEN, HARRY WU-SHIONG, b Kaohsiung, Taiwan, June 17, 37; m 69. CELL BIOLOGY, BIOCHEMISTRY. *Educ:* Nat Chengchi Univ, BA, 60; Univ Kans, PhD(biochem), 69. *Prof Exp:* Fel, 69-70, assoc res biochem, 70-74, staff scientist, 74-79, SR STAFF SCIENTIST, JACKSON LAB, 79- *Res:* Regulation of cell growth; function of cholesterol in the surface membranes of mammalian cells. *Mailing Add:* Jackson Lab Bar Harbor ME 04609

CHEN, HERBERT HWA-SEN, b China, Mar 16, 42; US citizen; m 69; c 1. PARTICLE PHYSICS. *Educ:* Calif Inst Technol, BS, 64; Princeton Univ, MA, 65, PhD(physics), 68. *Prof Exp:* Asst res physicist, 68-71, asst prof, 71-74, assoc prof physics, 74-78, PROF PHYSICS, UNIV CALIF, IRVINE, 78- *Concurrent Pos:* Co-prin investr, NSF grant, 72-77, prin investr, 77-; Co-prin invest, Dept Energy contract, 80- *Mem:* AAAS; Am Phys Soc. *Res:* Experimental research in high energy and particle physics with emphasis on neutrinos. *Mailing Add:* Dept of Physics Univ of Calif Irvine CA 92717

CHEN, HO SOU, b Taiwan, Nov 24, 32; US citizen; c 2. SOLID STATE PHYSICS. *Educ:* Nat Taiwan Univ, BS, 56; Brown Univ, MS, 63; Harvard Univ, PhD(appl physics), 67. *Prof Exp:* Mem tech staff mat, Bell Tel Labs, 68-70; asst prof chem, Yeshiva Univ, 70-71; physicist, Allied Chem Corp, 71-72; MEM TECH STAFF MAT, BELL LABS, 72- *Honors & Awards:* George W Morey Award, Am Ceramic Soc, 78. *Res:* Structure, thermal and physical properties of metallic glasses. *Mailing Add:* 600 Mountain Ave Murray Hill NJ 07974

CHEN, HOLLIS C(HING), b Chekiang, China, Nov 17, 35; m 61; c 2. ELECTRICAL ENGINEERING, APPLIED MATHEMATICS. *Educ:* Nat Taiwan Univ, BSEE, 57; Ohio Univ, MS, 61; Syracuse Univ, PhD(elec eng), 65. *Prof Exp:* Teaching asst physics, Taiwan Univ, 57-60; res asst, Ohio Univ, 60-61; instr, Syracuse Univ, 61-62; res assoc, 62-65, res fel, 65-67; from asst prof to assoc prof, 67-75, PROF ELEC ENG, OHIO UNIV, 75- *Concurrent Pos:* Mem Comn B, Int Sci Radio Union; NSF grant; Ohio Univ res comts grants. *Mem:* AAAS; Inst Elec & Electronics Engrs; Soc Indust & Appl Math; Math Asn Am; Am Soc Eng Educ. *Res:* Electromagnetic radiation in a moving or plasma medium; applied mathematics; electromagnetic theory; plasma physics; applied optics. *Mailing Add:* Dept Elec Eng Ohio Univ Athens OH 45701

CHEN, HSIEN-JEN JAMES, b Kwangtung, China, June 19, 31; m 71; c 1. NEUROENDOCRINOLOGY. *Educ:* Nat Taiwan Normal Univ, BS, 65, Nat Taiwan Univ Med Col, MS, 69; Mich State Univ, PhD(physiol), 76. *Prof Exp:* Res asst physiol, Mich State Univ, 71-76; fel neuroendocrinol, Mt Sinai Hosp, 76-78, dept anat, Univ Tex Health Sci Ctr, 78-79; ASST NEUROENDOCRINOLOGIST, DEPT NEUROBIOL, BARROW NEUROL INST, ST JOSEPH HOSP MED CTR, 79- *Concurrent Pos:* Adj asst prof, dept anat, Univ Ariz Health Sci Ctr, 79- *Mem:* Endocrine Soc; Am Physiol Soc; Soc Neurosci; Soc Study Reproduction. *Res:* Neuroendocrine control of pituitary thyroid and pituitary testicular function; effects of pituitary and ovarian hormone on mammary cancers; pineal control of reproduction. *Mailing Add:* Barrow Neurol Inst 350 W Thomas Rd Phoenix AZ 85013

CHEN, HSING-HEN, b Yun Kang, Chekiang, China, May 7, 47; m 71; c 2. PHYSICS, ASTRONOMY. *Educ:* Nat Taiwan Univ, BS, 68; Columbia Univ, MA, 70, PhD(physics), 73. *Prof Exp:* Mem, Sch Natural Sci, Inst Advan Study, 73-75; vis asst prof, 75-78, asst prof, 78-80, ASSOC PROF, PHYSICS & ASTRON, UNIV MD, COLLEGE PARK, 80- *Mem:* Am Phys Soc. *Res:* Nonlinear plasma physics; solitons; inverse scattering methods; laser fusions; plasma astrophysics. *Mailing Add:* Dept of Physics & Astronomy Univ of Md College Park MD 20742

CHEN, HSUAN, b Shanghai, China, Jan 10, 36; US citizen; m 66; c 2. OPTICS, PARTICLE PHYSICS. *Educ:* Nat Taiwan Univ, BS, 57; Univ Minn, PhD(physics), 70; Univ Mich, MS, 75. *Prof Exp:* assoc prof, 69-80, PROF PHYSICS, SAGINAW VALLEY STATE COL, 80- *Concurrent Pos:* Res assoc physics, Univ Mich, 72, fel, 74; vis res scientist optics, Univ Mich, 77-78, 79 & 80. *Mem:* Am Phys Soc; Am Optical Soc. *Res:* White light transmission holography and optical processes; high energy neutrino physics. *Mailing Add:* Dept of Physics Saginaw Valley State Col University Center MI 48710

CHEN, HUBERT JAN-PEING, b Kiangsu Prov, China, Oct 29, 42; m; c 1. STATISTICS. *Educ:* Nat Taiwan Univ, BA, 67; Univ Rochester, MA, 71, PhD(statist), 73. *Prof Exp:* Asst teacher statist, Nat Taiwan Univ, 67-69; teaching asst, Univ Rochester, 69-72; lectr, Ohio State Univ, 72-73; asst prof statist, Memphis State Univ, 73-76; asst prof statist, 76-79, dir consult serv, 78-80, ASSOC PROF, UNIV GA, 79- *Concurrent Pos:* Mem staff, Math Rev, 72- *Mem:* Am Statist Asn; Inst Math Statist; Am Soc Qual Control. *Res:* Estimation of ranked parameters; ranking and selections; multiple comparisons; regression analysis; scientific computations; simulation and Monte Carlo methods. *Mailing Add:* Dept Statist & Comput Sci Univ Ga Athens GA 30602

CHEN, HUNG T, chemical engineering, deceased

CHEN, INAN, b Tainan, Taiwan, Oct 9, 33; m 59; c 2. SOLID STATE PHYSICS, SPECTROSCOPY. *Educ:* Nat Taiwan Univ, BS, 56; Tsinghua Univ, China, MS, 58; Univ Mich, PhD(nuclear sci), 64. *Prof Exp:* Res assoc nuclear sci, Univ Mich, 64-65; from scientist to sr scientist, 65-71, PRIN SCIENTIST, RES LABS, XEROX CORP, 71- *Mem:* Am Phys Soc; Soc Photog Scientists & Engrs. *Res:* Theoretical studies of electronic states in solids; theoretical studies of electronic properties of amorphous and molecular solids, and their applications to electrophotographic processes. *Mailing Add:* Res Labs Xerox Corp Xerox Sq Rochester NY 14644

CHEN, I-NGO, computer science, deceased

CHEN, I-WEN, b Tokyo, Japan, Aug 3, 34; US citizen; m 64; c 3. RADIOBIOLOGY, BIOCHEMISTRY. *Educ:* Nat Taiwan Univ, BS, 56; Univ Pa, PhD(biochem), 64. *Prof Exp:* Asst prof, 66-72, ASSOC PROF RADIOL, UNIV CINCINNATI, 72- *Concurrent Pos:* NIH fel, 64-66; adj affil mem, Jewish Hosp, Cincinnati, 73- *Mem:* AAAS; Radiation Res Soc. *Res:* Biochemical effect of radiation; radioimmunoassays for various hormones. *Mailing Add:* 9270 Long Lane Cincinnati OH 45231

CHEN, JAMES CHE WEN, b Taipei, Taiwan, Nov 21, 30; m 59; c 3. DEVELOPMENTAL BIOLOGY, BOTANY. *Educ:* Taiwan Prov Norm Univ, BS, 55; Univ Pa, PhD(bot), 63. *Prof Exp:* Asst instr bot, Taiwan, 56-58; asst instr biol, Univ Pa, 61-62; res assoc, Princeton Univ, 63-65; from asst prof to assoc prof, Washington & Jefferson Col, 65-68; ASSOC PROF BOT, DOUGLASS COL, RUTGERS UNIV, 68- *Mem:* AAAS; Soc Develop Biol; Bot Soc Am. *Res:* Investigations of growth and differentiation of plants and quantitative description of growth processes of plants. *Mailing Add:* Dept of Biol Sci Douglass Col Rutgers Univ New Brunswick NJ 08903

CHEN, JAMES L, b Nanking, China, Nov 3, 14; nat US; m 46; c 2. PHARMACEUTICAL CHEMISTRY. *Educ:* Sino-French Univ, China, BS, 39; Purdue Univ, MS, 40, PhD, 47. *Prof Exp:* Chemist, Merck & Co, 42-45; res chemist, Arlington Chem Co, 47-49; res assoc, 49-69, res fel, 69-79, SR RES FEL, E R SQUIBB & SONS, 79- *Mem:* Am Pharmaceut Asn; NY Acad Sci; fel Am Inst Chem; AAAS. *Res:* Phytochemistry; biological adhesives; pharmaceutical research; analytical chemistry. *Mailing Add:* 30 Fairview Ave East Brunswick NJ 08816

CHEN, JAMES PAI-FUN, b Fengyuan, Taiwan, May 1, 29; nat US; m 64; c 3. BIOCHEMISTRY, IMMUNOLOGY. *Educ:* Houghton Col, BS, 55; St Lawrence Univ, MS, 57; Pa State Univ, PhD(biochem), 62. *Prof Exp:* Instr chem, Houghton Col, 60-62, assoc prof, 62-64; res assoc, Div Exp Med, Col Med, Univ Vt, 64-65; res assoc med, Sch Med, State Univ NY Buffalo, 65-68; res asst prof internal med, Univ Tex Med Br Galveston, 68-70, asst prof human genetics, 70-75; sr res assoc, Biomed Res Div, NASA Johnson Space Ctr, 75-76; res assoc prof, Mem Res Ctr, 76-78, ASSOC PROF MED BIOL, UNIV TENN COL MED, KNOXVILLE, 78- *Mem:* AAAS; Am Soc Biol Chemists; Am Asn Immunologists; Int Soc Hematol; Soc Exp Biol Med. *Res:* Immunoassay of biologically active materials; animal models of intravascular coagulation and fibrinolysis; immunochemical distinction of variable region subgroups of immunoglobulin heavy chains. *Mailing Add:* Mem Res Ctr Univ Tenn Knoxville TN 37920

CHEN, JAMES RALPH, b Kingston, Jamaica, Sept 22, 39; US citizen; m; c 3. PARTICLE PHYSICS, ATOMIC PHYSICS. *Educ:* Brandeis Univ, BA, 62; Harvard Univ, MA, 64, PhD(physics), 69. *Prof Exp:* Res asst physics, Harvard Univ, 67-68; res assoc & fel, Univ Pa, 68-69, asst prof, 69-73; asst prof, 72-73, ASSOC PROF PHYSICS, STATE UNIV NY COL GENESEO, 73- *Concurrent Pos:* Res consult, Los Alamos Sci Lab, 72, spokesman-scientist, Los Alamos Meson Physics Facil, 74-75; spokesman-scientist, Brookhaven Nat Lab, 72-73; State Univ NY Res Found res fels, 74-76; res consult, Ctr Dis Control, 76; NSF panelist, 77 & 81; Alexander von Humboldt fel & vis scientist, Max Planck Inst Nuclear Physics, Heidelberg, WGer, 79-80; US rep, Int Comt Develop Proton-Induced X-Ray Emission, 80- *Mem:* Am Phys Soc; AAAS; Am Asn Physics Teachers. *Res:* Particle physics experiments; atomic physics x-ray spectroscopic calculations and measurements; elemental analysis using proton-induced x-ray emission and synchrotron radiation. *Mailing Add:* 6 Elm St Geneseo NY 14454

CHEN, JEFFREY CHUANG-FEI, b China, Mar 1, 46; m 69. NUCLEAR PHYSICS, COMPUTER SCIENCE. *Educ:* Nat Taiwan Univ, BS, 68; Univ Wis-Madison, PhD(exp nuclear physics), 77. *Prof Exp:* Sect mgr comput sci, Comput Sci Corp, 74-77; PRES COMPUT SCI, INFO PROCESSING & SPACE SCI, GEN SOFTWARE CORP, 77- *Res:* Software system design and implementation; image processing; information graphic display; space sciences; remote sensing with satellites; data base management. *Mailing Add:* Gen Software Corp 8401 Corporate Dr Landover MD 20785

CHEN, JOHN CHUN-CHIEN, b China, Feb 6, 34; US citizen; m 60; c 3. CHEMICAL ENGINEERING, MECHANICAL ENGINEERING. *Educ:* Cooper Union, BChE, 56; Carnegie-Mellon Univ, MS, 58; Univ Mich, PhD(chem eng), 61. *Prof Exp:* Res sr engr thermal sci, Brookhaven Nat Lab, 60-70; prof mech eng, 70-80, ANDERSON PROF CHEM ENG, LEHIGH UNIV, 81- *Concurrent Pos:* Consult, Brookhaven Nat Lab, 75-, Air Prod & Chem, 75-, Exxon Res & Eng Co, 76-78 & Argonne Nat Lab, 77- *Honors & Awards:* Melville Medal, Am Soc Mech Engrs, 80. *Mem:* Am Inst Chem Engrs; Am Soc Mech Engrs. *Res:* Thermo-fluid sciences; boiling heat transfer and two-phase flows; fluidization and heat transfer; nuclear reactor safety. *Mailing Add:* Dept Chem Eng Lehigh Univ Bethlehem PA 18015

CHEN, JOHN HENG, biochemistry, see previous edition

CHEN, JOSEPH CHENG YIH, b Nanking, China, Nov 12, 33; nat US; m 59; c 1. THEORETICAL PHYSICS, THEORETICAL CHEMISTRY. *Educ:* St Anselm's Col, BA, 57; Univ Notre Dame, PhD(theoret chem), 61. *Prof Exp:* Res assoc theoret chem, Brookhaven Nat Lab, 61-63, assoc chemist, 63-65; vis fel, Joint Inst Lab Astrophys, Univ Colo, 65-66; from asst prof to assoc prof physics, 66-74, PROF PHYSICS, UNIV CALIF, SAN DIEGO, 74- *Concurrent Pos:* Vis lectr, Univ Manchester, 64; Nordic Inst Theoret Atomic Physics vis prof, Univ Oslo, 70. *Mem:* Fel Am Phys Soc. *Res:* Scattering problem; reaction theories; atomic and molecular systems; many body theory; history of science in China. *Mailing Add:* Dept of Physics Univ of Calif La Jolla CA 92093

CHEN, JOSEPH H, b Tientsin, China, Mar 22, 31; m 56; c 2. PHYSICS. *Educ:* St Procopius Col, BS, 54; Univ Notre Dame, PhD(physics), 58. *Prof Exp:* Instr physics, Univ Notre Dame, 57-58; from asst prof to assoc prof, 58-77, PROF PHYSICS, BOSTON COL, 77- *Mem:* Am Phys Soc. *Res:* Dielectric relaxation phenomena; electron spin resonance and optical properties of solids; Mossbauer effect and high pressure studies in solids. *Mailing Add:* Dept of Physics Boston Col Chestnut Hill MA 02167

CHEN, JOSEPH KE-CHOU, b Hupei, China, May 27, 36; m 67; c 2. MEDICAL MICROBIOLOGY. *Educ:* Nat Taiwan Univ, BS, 59; Univ Pittsburgh, PhD(microbiol), 72. *Prof Exp:* Res asst microbiol, Sch Med, Univ Pittsburgh, 66-72, res assoc biochem, 72-74; cancer res scientist viral oncol, Roswell Park Mem Inst, 75-76; sr staff fel, Lab Gen & Comp Biochem, NIMH, 77-79; STAFF SCIENTIST, BIONETIC LAB PRODS, LITTON BIONETIC INC, 79- *Mem:* Am Soc Microbiol; Am Chem Soc. *Res:* Immunodiagnosis techniques development. *Mailing Add:* 7901 Declaration Lane Potomac MD 20854

CHEN, JUEI-TENG, b Taiwan, May 9, 38; US citizen; m 66; c 2. LOW TEMPERATURE PHYSICS. *Educ:* Tunghai Univ, Taiwan, BS, 62; Univ Waterloo, MS, 66, PhD(physics), 69. *Prof Exp:* Res assoc physics, Univ Pa, 68-70; from asst prof to assoc prof, 70-79, PROF PHYSICS, WAYNE STATE UNIV, 79- *Concurrent Pos:* Res grants, NSF, 74-83; consult, Energy Conversion Devices, Inc, 77- *Mem:* Am Phys Soc; Am Asn Univ Professors. *Res:* Superconductivity; electron tunneling; microwave absorption and emission; Josephson effects; proximity effect; nonequilibrium effect; flux flow. *Mailing Add:* Dept of Physics Wayne State Univ Detroit MI 48202

CHEN, JUH WAH, b Shanghai, China, Nov 10, 28; m 58; c 3. CHEMICAL ENGINEERING, PHYSICAL CHEMISTRY. *Educ:* Nat Taiwan Univ, BS, 53; Univ Ill, MS, 57, PhD(chem eng, phys chem), 59. *Prof Exp:* Asst prof chem eng, Bucknell Univ, 59-65; assoc prof & prof-in-chg transfer & rate processes, 65-69, PROF THERMAL & ENVIRON ENG & CHMN DEPT, SCH ENG & TECHNOL, SOUTHERN ILL UNIV, CARBONDALE, 70- *Concurrent Pos:* Res consult engr, Upjohn Co, 60-65. *Mem:* AAAS; Am Inst Chem Engrs; Am Chem Soc; Soc Eng Educ; Am Soc Mech Eng. *Res:* Kinetics; coal conversion; applied mathematics. *Mailing Add:* Dept Thermal & Environ Eng Southern Ill Univ Carbondale IL 62901

CHEN, KAN, b Hong Kong, China, Aug 28, 28; nat US; m 53; c 4. ELECTRICAL ENGINEERING, COMPUTER ENGINEERING. *Educ:* Cornell Univ, BEE, 50; Mass Inst Technol, SM, 51, ScD, 54. *Prof Exp:* Asst elec eng, Mass Inst Technol, 52-54; res mgr, Westinghouse Elec Corp, 54-65; res dir, SRI Int, 66-70; prof environ systs eng & elec eng, Univ Pittsburgh, 70-71; PROF ELEC & COMPUT ENG & PROF INDUST & OPERS ENG, UNIV MICH, 71-, DIR, PHD PROG, URBAN & REGIONAL PLANNING, 81- *Concurrent Pos:* From lectr to adj prof, Univ Pittsburgh,

55-66; vis prof, Stanford Univ, 62-63; sr lectr, Carnegie Inst Technol, 64-65 & Paul Goebel Prof, Univ Mich, 71-73; chief scientist, Acumenics Res & Technol, Inc, 78- *Mem:* Fel Inst Elec & Electronics Engrs; fel AAAS. *Res:* Systems technology; operations research; automatic control; computer coordinated systems; systems planning; urban and environmental systems; technology assessment and science policy. *Mailing Add:* Col of Eng Univ of Mich Ann Arbor MI 48109

CHEN, KAO-WEI WENDELL, physics, see previous edition

CHEN, KENNETH YAT-YI, b Chunghwa, Taiwan, Rep of China, Feb 12, 41; US citizen; m 67; c 2. ENVIRONMENTAL ENGINEERING, CIVIL ENGINEERING. *Educ:* Nat Taiwan Univ, BS, 63; Univ RI, MS, 66; Harvard Univ, PhD(environ sci & eng), 70. *Prof Exp:* From asst prof to assoc prof, 70-78, assoc prof & dir, 76-78, PROF & DIR ENVIRON ENG PROG, UNIV SOUTHERN CALIF, 78-, CHMN PROG, 80-, PROF CIVIL ENG, 80- *Concurrent Pos:* Consult, var indust orgn & consult co, 70-; prin investr many grants, 70-; chmn joint task group, Atomic Absorption Method Metals, Water Pollution Control Fedn, 76-78; consult, Dept Eng, Argonne Nat Lab, 77-78 & Dept of Com, Off Energy Related Invention, Nat Bur Standards, 77- *Mem:* Am Soc Civil Engrs; Am Chem Soc; Water Pollution Control Fedn; Am Soc Limnol & Oceanog; Am Water Works Asn. *Res:* Chemical behavior of trace contaminants in environment, chemical and biological processes in environmental engineering. *Mailing Add:* Environ Eng Prog Univ of Southern Calif Los Angeles CA 90007

CHEN, KUEI-LIN, b Chungwha, Taiwan, Jan 25, 45; m 78. OPERATIONS RESEARCH, STATISTICAL ANALYSIS. *Educ:* Tunghai Univ, Taiwan, BS, 67; Ore State Univ, MS, 74, PhD(indust eng), 77. *Prof Exp:* Indust engr, China Productivity Ctr, 68-70; assoc res engr technol forecasting & assessment, Res Inst, 77-81, ASST PROF, DEPT MGT, UNIV DAYTON, 81- *Mem:* Inst Mgt Sci; AAAS; Sigma Xi. *Res:* Technological forecasting; technology assessment; systems analysis; optimization; financial analysis; corporate planning; quantitative business analysis; production management. *Mailing Add:* Univ Dayton Dayton OH 45469

CHEN, KUN-MU, b Taipei, Taiwan, Feb 3, 33; nat US; m 62; c 4. ELECTRICAL ENGINEERING. *Educ:* Taiwan Univ, BS, 56; Harvard Univ, MS, 58, PhD(appl physics), 60. *Prof Exp:* Res assoc, Radiation Lab, Univ Mich, 60-64; assoc prof, 64-67, PROF ELEC ENG, MICH STATE UNIV, 67- *Concurrent Pos:* Air Force Cambridge Res Labs res grant, 66-; NSF grant, 66-; Army Res Off grant, 76-78; Navy res grant, 78- *Mem:* Fel AAAS; fel Inst Elec & Electronics Engrs; Sigma Xi. *Res:* Electromagnetic theory; antenna theory; applied plasma physics; biological effects of EM waves. *Mailing Add:* Dept of Elec Eng Mich State Univ East Lansing MI 48823

CHEN, KUO-KUANG, b Tientsin, China, Jan 30, 38; m 67; c 2. ENGINEERING SCIENCE, APPLIED MATHEMATICS. *Educ:* Nat Taiwan Univ, BS, 60; Pratt Inst, MME, 64; State Univ NY Buffalo, PhD(eng sci), 69. *Prof Exp:* Instr mech eng, Nat Taiwan Univ, 66-67 & State Univ NY Buffalo, 67-68; ASSOC SR RES ENGR, GEN MOTORS RES LABS, 68- *Res:* Stochastic processes with applications to analysis of engineering systems and environmental sciences; structural mechanics. *Mailing Add:* Dept of Math Gen Motors Res Labs Warren MI 48090

CHEN, KUO-TSAI, b Chekiang, China, July 15, 23; m 53; c 3. MATHEMATICS. *Educ:* Southwest Assoc Univ, China, BS, 46; Columbia Univ, Phd(math), 50. *Prof Exp:* Instr math, Princeton Univ, 50-51; res assoc, Univ Ill, 51-52; lectr, Univ Hong Kong, 52-58; assoc prof, Tech Inst Aeronaut, Brazil, 58-60, prof, 60-61; from assoc prof to prof, Rutgers Univ, 62-65; prof, State Univ NY Buffalo, 65-67; PROF MATH, UNIV ILL, URBANA-CHAMPAIGN, 67- *Concurrent Pos:* Mem, Inst Advan Study, 60, 62, 71 & 79. *Mem:* Am Math Soc. *Res:* Differential topology and global analysis on path spaces. *Mailing Add:* Dept Math Univ Ill Urbana IL 61801

CHEN, KWAN-YU, b Shanghai, China, Aug 29, 30; m 61; c 3. ASTRONOMY. *Educ:* Ill Inst Technol, BS, 53, MS, 56; Univ Pa, PhD(astron), 63. *Prof Exp:* Asst prof astron, 63-68, from asst prof to assoc prof astron & phys sci, 68-78, PROF ASTRON, UNIV FLA, 78- *Mem:* Am Astron Soc; Int Astron Union. *Res:* Photometric study of variable stars. *Mailing Add:* Dept Astron Univ of Fla Gainesville FL 32611

CHEN, LAWRENCE CHIEN-MING, b Ping-Yang, China, Oct 9, 33; Can citizen. PHYCOLOGY. *Educ:* Nat Taiwan Normal Univ, BSc, 60; Univ NB, MSc, 67, PhD(bot), 77. *Prof Exp:* Teaching asst biol, Biol Dept, Nat Taiwan Normal Univ, 60-64; res officer hydrabiol, 67-74, RES OFFICER MARINE BOT, ATLANTIC RES LAB, NAT RES COUN CAN, 74- *Mem:* Can Bot Asn; Int Phycological Soc; Phycological Soc Am; Phycological Soc Japan; Phycological Soc China. *Res:* Study of the ontogeny, development and growth of marine phycocolloid plants; tissue or cell culture of marine plants. *Mailing Add:* Atlantic Res Lab Nat Res Coun 1411 Oxford St Halifax NS B3H 3Z1 Can

CHEN, LESLIE H(UNG), b Canton, China, Nov 22, 23; nat US; m 47; c 4. MECHANICAL ENGINEERING. *Educ:* Chiaotung Univ, China, BS, 46; Univ Del, MME, 48; Harvard Univ, MS, 49, ScD(mech eng), 50. *Prof Exp:* Mech engr, Jackson & Moreland, Inc, 50-51; asst prof mech eng, Univ Notre Dame, 51-52; sr engr mech sect, Sverdrup & Parcel, Inc, 52-56; head appl mech sect, Gen Dynamics Corp, 56-62, mgr basic eng, 62-72, mgr technol develop, Elec Boat Div, 72-77; chmn, Ocean Eng Br, 78-81, ASST CHMN RES & DEVELOP, MARINE TECHNOL DIV, US COAT GUARD OFF, 81- *Concurrent Pos:* Lectr, Univ Conn, 56-77. *Mem:* Am Soc Mech Engrs; Am Soc Naval Engrs. *Res:* Marine/ocean technology; nuclear submarine technology. *Mailing Add:* 5408 Richenbacher Ave Apt 101 Alexandria VA 22304

CHEN, LILY CHING-CHUN, b China, Feb 17, 46; m 69. NUCLEAR PHYSICS, COMPUTER SCIENCE. *Educ:* Nat Taiwan Univ, BS, 68; Univ Cincinnati, MS, 69; Univ Wis-Madison, PhD(nuclear physics), 74. *Prof Exp:* Task leader comput sci, Comput Sci Corp, 74-78; VPRES COMPUT SCI, GEN SOFTWARE CORP, 78- *Res:* Orbit and attitude determination for satellites; spacecraft navigation; image processing and data base management. *Mailing Add:* Gen Software Corp 8401 Corp Dr Landover MD 20785

CHEN, LINDA LI-YUEH HUANG, b Tokyo, Japan, Mar 22, 37; m 61; c 2. BIOCHEMISTRY, NUTRITION. *Educ:* Nat Taiwan Univ, BS, 59; Univ Louisville, PhD(biochem), 64. *Prof Exp:* Res assoc biochem, Univ Louisville, 64-66; asst prof nutrit, 67-72, assoc prof, 72-79, PROF NUTRIT, UNIV KY, 79- *Concurrent Pos:* Mem, Cancer Res Manpower Rev Comt, Nat Cancer Inst. *Mem:* AAAS; Gerontol Soc; Am Chem Soc; Am Inst Nutrit; Nutrit Today Soc. *Res:* Vitamin K and oxidative phosphorylation; physiological function of vitamin E and its interaction with other nutrients; tissue antioxidant status; nutrition and aging; nutrient-drug interaction. *Mailing Add:* Dept of Nutrit & Food Sci Univ of Ky Lexington KY 40506

CHEN, LIU, b Hanchow, China, Jan 3, 46; m 69; c 1. PLASMA PHYSICS, SPACE PHYSICS. *Educ:* Nat Taiwan Univ, BS, 66; Wash State Univ, MS, 69; Univ Calif, Berkeley, PhD(elec eng, comput sci), 72. *Prof Exp:* Mem tech staff plasma physics & space physics, Bell Labs, Murray Hill, NJ, 72-74; res assoc plasma physics, 74-75, mem res staff, 75-77, RES PHYSICIST, PLASMA PHYSICS LAB, PRINCETON UNIV, 77- *Mem:* Am Phys Soc. *Res:* Plasma physics, especially parametric instabilities, rf plasma heating, nonlinear theories and microinstabilties; space physics, especially magnetic pulsations and very low frequency emissions. *Mailing Add:* Plasma Physics Lab Princeton Univ Princeton NJ 08544

CHEN, LO-CHAI, b Kwang-Tung, China, Dec 9, 39; m 65. ICHTHYOLOGY. *Educ:* Nat Taiwan Univ, BS, 61; Univ Alaska, MS, 65; Univ Calif, San Diego, PhD(marine biol), 69. *Prof Exp:* From asst prof to assoc prof, 69-77, PROF ZOOL, SAN DIEGO STATE UNIV, 77- *Mem:* Am Soc Ichthyologists & Herpetologists. *Res:* Systematics and zoogeography of fishes, especially Sebastes Scorpaenidae; growth and meristic determination in fishes. *Mailing Add:* Dept of Zool San Diego State Univ San Diego CA 92182

CHEN, MAYNARD MING-LIANG, b Shanghai, China, June 14, 50. QUANTUM CHEMISTRY. *Educ:* Univ Calif, Berkeley, BS, 71; Cornell Univ, PhD(chem), 76. *Prof Exp:* SCIENTIST, POLAROID CORP, 80- *Res:* Quantum chemistry programs to help understand and design molecules used in a photographic context. *Mailing Add:* 20 Fresh Pong Pl Cambridge MA 02138

CHEN, MICHAEL CHIA-CHAO, b Shanghai, China, Jan 13, 47. PHYSICAL CHEMISTRY, POLYMER SCIENCE. *Educ:* Univ Minn, BChem, 69; Mass Inst Technol, PhD(phys chem), 73. *Prof Exp:* Res assoc, Mass Inst Technol, 73-75; res assoc, Univ Mass, 75-76; chemist, 76-80, SR CHEMIST, EXXON CHEM CO, 80- *Concurrent Pos:* Sloan res trainee, Mass Inst Technol, 72. *Mem:* Am Chem Soc. *Res:* Morphology, optical and mechanical properties of polymers; polymer physics; polymer characterization; structure-function correlation of nucleic acids, proteins and their model compounds; spectroscopy. *Mailing Add:* Plastics Technol Div Exxon Chem Co PO Box 4255 Baytown TX 77520

CHEN, MICHAEL MING, b Hankow, China, Mar 10, 32; m 61; c 3. MECHANICAL ENGINEERING, BIOENGINEERING. *Educ:* Univ Ill, BS, 55; Mass Inst Technol, SM, 57, PhD(mech eng), 61. *Prof Exp:* Sr staff scientist, Res & Adv Develop Div, Avco Corp, Mass, 60-63; asst prof eng & appl sci, Yale Univ, 63-69; assoc prof, NY Univ, 69-73; PROF MECH & INDUST ENG, UNIV ILL, URBANA-CHAMPAIGN, 73- *Concurrent Pos:* Consult, A D Little Co, 56-58, Bell Tel Labs, 66-69 & Argonne Nat Lab, 76-; assoc ed, J Biomech Eng, Am Soc Mech Engrs. *Mem:* Am Phys Soc; Am Soc Mech Engrs; AAAS. *Res:* Fluid mechanics and heat transfer in energy, manufacturing, and bioengineering. *Mailing Add:* 144 Mech Eng Bldg Univ of Ill Urbana IL 61801

CHEN, MICHAEL S K, b Taipei, Formosa, May 18, 41; m 66; c 1. CHEMICAL & BIOCHEMICAL ENGINEERING. *Educ:* Nat Taiwan Univ, BS, 63; Kans State Univ, PhD(chem eng), 69. *Prof Exp:* From lectr to asst prof chem eng, Univ Pa, 69-72; sr process engr, 72-75, staff engr, 75-77, res mgr, 77-78, staff assoc, 78-79, actg res dir, 81, SECT HEAD, AIR PROD & CHEM, 79- *Mem:* Am Inst Chem Engrs. *Res:* Wastewater treatments; flue gas scrubbing; gas separation; mass transfer; air separation. *Mailing Add:* RD1 Box 140A Zionsville PA 18092

CHEN, MING CHIH, b China, Aug 15, 20; m 43; c 3. ORGANIC CHEMISTRY. *Educ:* Fukien Christian Univ, BS, 42; Univ Buffalo, PhD, 50. *Prof Exp:* Asst, Univ Buffalo, 48-50; res fel, Purdue Univ, 50-52; res assoc, O-Cel-O Div, Gen Mills Inc, 52-57; group leader, Simoniz Co, 57-62; mgr urethane develop, Sheller Labs, Sheller Mfg Corp, 62-67, dir prod develop, 67-73, dir mfg develop, 73-80, DIR ANAL SERV, SHELLER GLOBE CORP, 80- *Mem:* Chem Soc; Soc Plastics Engrs; Soc Plastics Indust; Soc Automotive Engrs; NY Acad Sci. *Res:* Cyanogen in the formation of oxamidine; halogenated hydrocarbon for non-inflammable hydraulic fluid and additives; cellulose and its derivatives; organic coating and polymeric foams. *Mailing Add:* Tech Ctr Sheller Globe Corp 4444 N Detroit Toledo OH 43612

CHEN, MING M, b Fukien, China, Apr 23, 19; US citizen; m 48; c 2. STRUCTURAL DYNAMICS. *Educ:* Wuhan Univ, BS, 41; Univ Ill, MS, 48, PhD(appl mech), 52; Univ Wash, MS, 52. *Prof Exp:* Res engr, airframe struct, Repub Aviation Corp, 52-53; mem res staff aeroelasticity & struct, Mass Inst Technol, 53-60; assoc prof, 60-66, PROF AEROSPACE ENG, BOSTON UNIV, 66-, CHMN DEPT, 68- *Concurrent Pos:* Vis prof, Cheng Kung Univ, Taiwan, 66-67, actg dean acad affairs, 67; actg dir, Eng Sci Res Ctr, Taiwan, 67; gen engr, Transp Syst Ctr, Dept Transp, 75- *Honors & Awards:* NASA Tech Brief Award, 75. *Mem:* Am Inst Aeronaut & Astronaut; Am Soc Eng Educ; Soc Exp Stress Anal; AAUP. *Res:* Flight structures; structural dynamics; high temperature structures; collision dynamics. *Mailing Add:* Dept of Aerospace Eng Boston Univ 110 Cummington St Boston MA 02215

CHEN, MIN-SHIH, b Kiangsu, China, Nov 13, 42; m 69; c 1. THEORETICAL HIGH ENERGY PHYSICS. *Educ:* Nat Taiwan Univ, BSc, 64; Yale Univ, MPhil, 67, PhD(physics), 70. *Prof Exp:* Res assoc physics, Brookhaven Nat Lab, 70-72; res assoc, Stanford Linear Accelerator Ctr, 72-74; lectr, 74-75, scholar physics, 75-76, ADJ ASSOC PROF, UNIV MICH, ANN ARBOR, 76-; proj mgt specialist, 76-79, SOFTWARE DEVELOP MGR, ADP NETWORK SERV, 79- *Mem:* Proj Mgt Inst; Am Phys Soc. *Res:* Phenomenology in multiparticle production and weak interactions; atomic physics and computational science. *Mailing Add:* 2730 Hampshire Rd Ann Arbor MI 48104

CHEN, MO-SHING, b Chekiang, China, Aug 20, 31; m 59. ELECTRICAL ENGINEERING. *Educ:* Taiwan Norm Univ, BS, 54; Univ Tex, MS, 58, PhD(elec eng), 62. *Prof Exp:* Elec engr, Taiwan Power Co, 54-56; from asst prof to assoc prof, 62-69, PROF ELEC ENG & DIR ENERGY SYSTS RES CTR, UNIV TEX, ARLINGTON, 69- *Honors & Awards:* Power Eng Educr Award, Edison Elec Inst & Western Elec Award, Am Soc Eng Educ, 76. *Mem:* Fel Inst Elec & Electronics Engrs; Am Soc Eng Educr. *Res:* Electric power generation, transmission, and distribution; system analysis; computer applications; power system load modeling and voltage reduction research. *Mailing Add:* Energy Systs Res Ctr Univ of Tex Arlington TX 76019

CHEN, NING HSING, b Kweihsien, Kwangsi, China, Apr 21, 18; US citizen; m 57. CHEMICAL ENGINEERING. *Educ:* Nat Chekiang Univ, China, BS, 41; Polytech Inst New York, BChE, 49, DChE, 61; Univ Mo, MS, 50. *Prof Exp:* Chem engr, First Chem Co, China, 41-48; engr, Allied Chem & Dye Corp, 50-54; process engr, Bechtel Corp, 54-56; proj engr, Indust Process Engrs, 56-58; heat transfer engr, M W Kellogg Co, 58-59; develop & res engr, Aerojet Gen Corp, 59-62; mem tech staff, Aerospace Corp, 62-63; staff engr, Lockheed Missiles & Space Co, 63-64; prin engr, Space Booster Div, Thiokol Chem Corp, Brunswick, 64-65; staff engr, Space Div, Chrysler Corp, Ala, 65-66; assoc prof, 66-77, PROF CHEM ENG, UNIV LOWELL, 78- *Concurrent Pos:* Vis res prof chem eng, Nat Tsing Hua Univ, Taiwan, 76-77; hon lectr, Univ China, Tianjin, 79 & Univ China, Zhejiang, 81. *Mem:* AAAS; Am Chem Soc; Am Inst Chem Engrs; NY Acad Sci; AAUP. *Res:* Heat transfer; thermodynamics; fluid dynamics; transport and physical properties; distillation; leaching; absorption; extraction; rockets and missiles; optimization. *Mailing Add:* 36 Elliott Dr Lowell MA 01852

CHEN, PAUL EAR, b Hangchow, China, June 29, 25; US citizen; m 49; c 2. APPLIED MECHANICS, APPLIED MATHEMATICS. *Educ:* Chiao Tung Univ, BS, 47; Purdue Univ, MS, 53; Washington Univ, DSc(appl mech), 62. *Prof Exp:* Instr civil eng, Nat Taiwan Univ, 47-51; struct engr, Mississippi Valley Struct Steel Co, 53-55; sr struct engr, Sverdrup & Parcel Eng Co, 55-59; proj engr, Cent Res Dept, Monsanto Co, 59-66, res scientist, Adv Res Proj Agency Proj, 66-70; SUPVR ADVAN PHYS DESIGN, BELL LABS, NAPERVILLE, 70- *Concurrent Pos:* Affil prof mat sci, Washington Univ, 66-70; dir bd, Unisysts, Inc, 69-; adj prof, Ill Inst Technol, 75- *Mem:* AAAS; Am Soc Civil Eng; Am Soc Mech Eng; Am Soc Eng Educ; Soc Rheol. *Res:* Structural engineering. *Mailing Add:* 22W131 Glen Park Glen Ellyn IL 60137

CHEN, PHILIP STANLEY, JR, b St Johns, Mich, July 3, 32; m 55; c 2. PHARMACOLOGY, PHYSIOLOGY. *Educ:* Clark Univ, BA, 50; Univ Rochester, PhD(pharmacol), 54. *Prof Exp:* Res assoc, Atomic Energy Proj, Univ Rochester, 50-54, jr scientist, 54-56; sr asst scientist, Nat Heart Inst, 56-59; asst prof radiation biol & biophys & pharmacol, Univ Rochester, 59-66; Guggenheim fel, Copenhagen, Denmark, 66-67; grants assoc, 67-68, spec asst to asst dir prog planning & eval, 68-70, chief spec projs br, Off Prog Anal, 70-71, chief anal & eval br, Prog Planning & Eval, 71-72, assoc dir prog planning & eval, Nat Inst Gen Med Sci, 72-74, ASST DIR INTRAMURAL AFFAIRS, NIH, 74- *Concurrent Pos:* NSF fel, Copenhagen, Denmark, 54-55. *Mem:* Am Chem Soc; Am Physiol Soc; Radiation Res Soc. *Res:* Radioactive tracer techniques in biology; microanalytical chemistry; bone and mineral metabolism; vitamin D; renal excretion. *Mailing Add:* Bldg 1 Rm 103 Off of Dir NIH Bethesda MD 20205

CHEN, PI-FUAY, b Taipei, Taiwan, Aug 17, 30; m 64; c 2. ELECTRICAL ENGINEERING, AUTOMATIC CONTROL SYSTEMS. *Educ:* Taipei Inst Technol, Taiwan, BS, 56; Va Polytech Inst, MS, 63; Univ Va, DSc(elec eng), 69. *Prof Exp:* Asst engr, Taipei Telecommun Off, 56-60; engr, Int Tel & Tel Corp, 63-65, sr engr, 66; asst prof, George Washington Univ, 68-69; RES ENGR ELECTRONICS, RES INST, US ARMY ENGR TOPOG LABS, 69- *Honors & Awards:* Outstanding Achievement Award, US Army Sci Conf, Spec Act and Serv Award and Outstanding Performance Award, Res Inst, US Army Engr Topog Labs, Spec Act and Serv Award, 70. *Mem:* Inst Elec & Electronics Engrs; Pattern Recognition Soc. *Res:* Various automated and semi-automated techniques for aerial and radar image analysis and cartographic feature extraction and recognition using pattern recognition and image understanding principles. *Mailing Add:* US Army Topographic Labs Ft Belvoir VA 22060

CHEN, PING-FAN, b Kiangyin, China, May 13, 17; div; c 3. GEOLOGY. *Educ:* Nat Cent Univ, China, BS, 38; Univ Cincinnati, MS, 57; Va Polytech Inst, PhD(geol), 59. *Prof Exp:* From jr to sr geologist, Nat Geol Surv China, 38-46; from sr geologist to chief petrol geol, Chinese Petrol Corp, 46-55; petrol geologist & head petrol div, 60-66, STRATIGRAPHER, WVA GEOL & ECON SURV, 67- *Concurrent Pos:* Adj prof geol, WVa Univ, 75-; Hwakang prof, Univ Chinese Cult. *Mem:* sr fel China Acad. *Res:* Geological exploration work for petroleum, ground water, coal and other mineral deposits in China; detail stratigraphic and structural geology studies in Central Appalachian for oil and gas possibilities in Lower Paleozoic rocks. *Mailing Add:* 1277 Dogwood Morgantown WV 26505

CHEN, ROBERT CHIA-HUA, b Shanghai, China, Oct 26, 46; m 71; c 1. COMPUTER SCIENCE, ELECTRICAL ENGINEERING. *Educ:* Rensselaer Polytech Inst, BEE, 66; Mass Inst Technol, SM, 68; Carnegie-Mellon Univ, PhD(comput sci), 74. *Prof Exp:* Eng programmer comput sci, Burroughs Corp, 68-69; ASST PROF COMPUT & INFO SCI, UNIV PA, 74- *Concurrent Pos:* Staff engr, Burroughs Corp, 74- *Mem:* Asn Comput Mach; Inst Elec & Electronics Engrs. *Res:* Concurrency and modularity in computer systems. *Mailing Add:* Dept of Comput & Info Sci Univ of Pa Philadelphia PA 19174

CHEN, ROBERT LONG WEN, b Shanghai, China, Aug 23, 25; US citizen; m 58; c 2. PLASMA PHYSICS. *Educ:* Nanking Univ, BS, 47; Univ Syracuse, MA, 57, PhD(physics), 60. *Prof Exp:* Res assoc physics, Syracuse Univ, 60-61, asst prof, 61-62; res assoc, Goddard Inst Space Studies, 62-64; assoc prof, 64-70, PROF PHYSICS, EMORY UNIV, 70- *Mem:* Am Phys Soc. *Res:* Nonequilibrium statistical mechanics; plasma theory; molecular biophysics. *Mailing Add:* Dept of Physics Emory Univ Atlanta GA 30322

CH'EN, SHANG-YI, b China, Mar 4, 10; nat US; m 31; c 5. SPECTROSCOPY. *Educ:* Yenching Univ, BS, 32, MS, 34; Calif Inst Technol, PhD(physics), 40. *Prof Exp:* Asst, Inst Physics, Nat Acad Peiping, 34-37 & Norman Bridge Physics Lab, Calif Inst Technol, 38-39; lectr physics, Yenching Univ, 39-41, asst prof optics & spectros, 41-43, prof optics & chmn dept physics, 43-46; res prof, Inst Physics, Nat Acad Peiping, 46-49; from assoc prof to prof physics, 49-75, EMER PROF PHYSICS, UNIV ORE, 75- *Concurrent Pos:* Res grants, NSF, 52-75, Off Ord Res, 57-60 & Air Force Off Sci Res, 63-70; vis prof, High Pressure Lab, Nat Ctr Sci Res, Bellevue, France, 61 & Clarendon Lab, Oxford, 68; assoc ed, J Quant Spectros & Radiative Transfer, 72-84. *Mem:* Fel Am Phys Soc; Am Asn Physics Teachers; French Phys Soc. *Res:* Atomic spectroscopy; spectral line shape; pressure and temperature effects. *Mailing Add:* Dept of Physics Univ of Ore Eugene OR 97403

CHEN, SHAO LIN, b China, Aug 15, 18; nat; m 50; c 2. BIOCHEMISTRY. *Educ:* Nanking Univ, BS, 40; Cornell Univ, PhD(plant physiol, biochem), 49. *Prof Exp:* Fel plant biochem, Carnegie Inst, 49-50; res assoc, Am Smelting & Refining Co, 50-52; biochemist, Red Star Yeast Co, 52-56, sr scientist, 56-60; dir microbiol chem lab, 60-65, DIR BIOCHEM LAB, UNIVERSAL FOODS CORP, 66- *Concurrent Pos:* Res fel, China Found, 43; Rockefeller Found fel, 46-49; vis assoc prof, Univ Wis-Milwaukee, 65-67. *Mem:* AAAS; Am Chem Soc; fel Am Inst Chemists; fel Royal Soc Health; Sigma Xi. *Res:* Fermentation; enzymology; metabolism; cereal chemistry; food technology. *Mailing Add:* Universal Foods Corp Tech Ctr 6143 N 60th St Milwaukee WI 53218

CHEN, SHEPLEY S, b Taipei, Taiwan, Mar 28, 38; m 67; c 2. BIOLOGY, PLANT PHYSIOLOGY. *Educ:* Nat Taiwan Univ, BSc, 61; Harvard Univ, PhD(biol), 66. *Prof Exp:* Res assoc biochem, Mich State Univ-AEC Plant Res Lab, 65-69; asst prof, 69-73, ASSOC PROF BIOL SCI, UNIV ILL, CHICAGO CIRCLE, 73- *Concurrent Pos:* Jane Coffin Childs Mem Fund med res fel, 65-66; Nat Coun Sci Develop lectr, Repub of China, 67 & 69. *Mem:* Am Soc Plant Physiologists. *Res:* Physiology and biochemistry of seed germination; plant growth hormones; single-cell protein; algal physiology; algae as human food; food science and technology; microbiology. *Mailing Add:* Dept of Biol Sci Univ of Ill at Chicago Circle Chicago IL 60680

CHEN, SHI-HAN, b Che-Kiang, China, June 29, 36; US citizen; m 68; c 2. BIOCHEMICAL GENETICS, MEDICAL GENETICS. *Educ:* Taiwan Norm Univ, BS, 59; Nat Taiwan Univ, MS, 63; Univ Tex, Austin, PhD(zool), 68. *Prof Exp:* Instr biol, Taiwan Norm Univ, 63-64; teaching & res asst, Univ Tex, Austin, 64-68; res assoc & fel, King County Blood Bank, 69-71; res asst prof, 72-74, RES ASSOC PROF, DEPT PEDIAT, SCH MED, UNIV WASH, 74- *Mem:* Am Soc Human Genetics; AAAS. *Res:* Genetic variation of enzyme systems in man; biochemical causes of immunodeficiency diseases. *Mailing Add:* Dept Pediat Univ Wash Sch Med Seattle WA 98195

CHEN, SHIOU-SHAN, b Tao-yuan, Taiwan, Feb 22, 38; m 69; c 2. CHEMICAL ENGINEERING, PHYSICAL CHEMISTRY. *Educ:* Taipei Inst Technol, BS, 58; Calif Inst Technol, MS, 62, PhD(chem eng & chem), 65. *Prof Exp:* Asst prof chem eng, Mass Inst Technol, 65-67 & Tufts Univ, 67-71; process engr, sr process engr & mgr process eng, Velsicol Chem Corp, 71-74; DIR, RES & DEVELOP LABS, BADGER CO, INC, 74- *Concurrent Pos:* Ford Found fel eng, 65-67. *Mem:* Am Inst Chem Engrs; Sigma Xi. *Res:* Fluid mechanics; heat and mass transfer; thermodynamics; chemical reactors; chemical and petrochemical processes. *Mailing Add:* Badger Co Inc 1 Broadway Cambridge MA 02142

CHEN, SOW-HSIN, b Taiwan, Mar 5, 35; m 61; c 3. EXPERIMENTAL FLUID PHYSICS, RADIATION PHYSICS. *Educ:* Nat Taiwan Univ, BS, 56; Nat Tsing-Hua Univ Taiwan, MS, 58; Univ Mich, MNS, 62; McMaster Univ, PhD(physics), 64. *Prof Exp:* Asst reactor physics, Argonne Nat Lab, 59-60; from asst prof to assoc prof physics, Univ Waterloo, 64-68; res assoc, Harvard Univ, 67-68; from asst prof to assoc prof nuclear eng, 68-74, PROF NUCLEAR ENG, MASS INST TECHNOL, 74- *Concurrent Pos:* Res assoc & fel, Atomic Energy Res Estab, Harwell, Eng, 64-65; vis scientist, Solid State Sci Div, Argonne Nat Lab, 75; distinguished vis prof, Univ Guelph, Can, 81; vis scientist, Lab Leon Brillouin, Centre d'Etudes Nucleaires, Saclay, France, 81. *Mem:* Fel Am Phys Soc; Am Nuclear Soc; AAAS. *Res:* Study of molecular dynamics in solids and fluids by thermal neutron and laser light scattering. *Mailing Add:* 24-209 Dept of Nuclear Eng Mass Inst of Technol Cambridge MA 02139

CHEN, SOW-YEH, b Chang-Hwa, Taiwan, Aug 28, 39; m 72; c 2. ORAL PATHOLOGY. *Educ:* Nat Taiwan Univ, BMD, 65; Univ Ill Med Ctr, MS, 70, PhD(path), 72. *Prof Exp:* Nat Inst Dent Res spec fel, 71-73; asst prof, 73-78, ASSOC PROF PATH, SCH DENT, TEMPLE UNIV, 78- *Mem:* Am Acad Oral Path; Int Asn Dent Res; Am Asn Cancer Educ; Sigma Xi; AAAS. *Res:* Ultrastructural study of tumors in the oral region and cell biology of oral squamous cell carcinoma. *Mailing Add:* 3223 N Broad St Philadelphia PA 19140

CHEN, STANLEY SHIAO-HSIUNG, b Chekiang, China, Feb 24, 37; US citizen; m 59; c 2. ENGINEERING MECHANICS, BIOMECHANICS. *Educ:* Taipei Inst Technol, dipl mech eng, 57; Ohio Univ, MS, 60; Univ Wis-Madison, PhD(eng mech), 67. *Prof Exp:* Exp engr res & develop, A O Smith Corp, Milwaukee, Wis, 60-64; instr eng, Univ Wis, 66-67; asst prof, 67-71, assoc prof, 71-76, PROF ENG, ARIZ STATE UNIV, 76- *Concurrent Pos:* Vis prof eng, Chung Cheng Inst Technol, 73-74; consult, Flui Dyne Eng Corp, 73-; dir, SEM-TEC Labs Inc, 76- *Mem:* Sigma Xi; Am Inst Aeronaut & Astronaut; Am Soc Mech Engrs; Aeronaut & Astronaut Soc Repub China. *Res:* Applied mechanics; biomechanics in human major joint replacement such as knee and hip; gait analysis and application in sport medicine. *Mailing Add:* Dept of Aerospace Eng & Eng Sci Ariz State Univ Tempe AZ 85281

CHEN, STEPHEN P K, b Shanghai, China, June 19, 42. CHEMISTRY. *Educ:* Chung Chi Col, Hong Kong, Dipl, 63; Univ Wis, PhD(chem), 68. *Prof Exp:* SR RES CHEMIST, EASTMAN KODAK CO, 68- *Mem:* Am Chem Soc; Soc Rheol. *Res:* Rheological behavior of polymers; molecular mobilities in both rubbery and glassy polymers; polymer physical chemistry. *Mailing Add:* 142 Ledgewood Circle Rochester NY 14615

CHEN, STEPHEN SHIOWSHIUNG, physical chemistry, deceased

CHEN, SUNG JEN, b Chia-yi, Taiwan, Mar 31, 39; US citizen; m 71. CHEMICAL ENGINEERING, MINERAL PROCESSING. *Educ:* Nat Taiwan Univ, BS, 62; Calif Inst Technol, MS, 67; Kans State Univ, PhD(chem eng), 71. *Prof Exp:* Syst analyst, Atlantic Richfield Co, 67-69; vpres res & develop, Kenics Corp, 71-81; ASSOC PROF, UNIV LOWELL, 81- *Mem:* Am Inst Chem Engrs; Am Chem Soc. *Res:* Mixing; Polymerization and two-phase flow; solvent extraction; polymer processing. *Mailing Add:* 36 Algonquin Ave Andover MA 01810

CHEN, T R, b Kaohsiung, Taiwan. TISSUE CULTURE, SOMATIC CELL GENETICS. *Educ:* Nat Taiwan Univ, BS, 58; Yale Univ, PhD(biol), 67. *Prof Exp:* Res assoc, Dept Biol, Yale Univ, 67-71; asst prof tissue cult, Grad Sch Biomed Sci, Univ Tex, Houston, 72-77; dir, Cytogenetic Lab, EKS Ctr Mental Retardation Inc, 77-80; CYTOGENETICIST, AM TYPE CULT COLLECTION, ROCKVILLE, MD, 80- *Mem:* Genetic Soc Am; Tissue Cult Asn. *Res:* Cytogenetic aspect of degrees of diversity in human cancer cells in vitro and in vivo; drug induction of karyotypic changes and stemline evoltuion; mapping of cancer genes. *Mailing Add:* Am Type Cult Collection 12301 Parklawn Dr Rockville MD 20852

CHEN, T(IEN) Y(OU), b China, Jan 18, 23; nat US. ENGINEERING. *Educ:* St John's Univ, Shanghai, BS, 45; Polytech Inst Brooklyn, MCE, 51; Univ Ill, PhD(civil eng), 54. *Prof Exp:* Res assoc civil eng, Univ Ill, 54, asst prof, 54-58; assoc prof, Darmouth Col, 58-62; assoc prof, 62-69, PROF CIVIL ENG, OHIO STATE UNIV, 70- *Mem:* Am Soc Civil Engrs; Am Concrete Inst. *Res:* Structural engineering and mechanics; numerical methods of stress analysis. *Mailing Add:* Dept Civil Eng Ohio State Univ Columbus OH 43210

CHEN, TA-SHEN, b Lung-ching, Taiwan, Feb 5, 32; m 64; c 2. CONVECTIVE HEAT TRANSFER, FLUID MECHANICS. *Educ:* Nat Taiwan Univ, BS, 54; Kans State Univ, MS, 61; Univ Minn, PhD(mech eng), 66. *Prof Exp:* Mech engr, Taiwan Shipbldg Corp, 55-57 & Engalls-Taiwan Shipbldg & Dry Dock Co, 57-59; mech engr, Twin Cities Mining Res Ctr, US Bur Mines, 63-66, res engr, 66-67; res fel, Univ Minn, 66; from asst prof to assoc prof, 67-73, PROF MECH ENG, UNIV MO-ROLLA, 73- *Concurrent Pos:* NSF grants, 69-70, 75-77, 77-79 & 80-82. *Honors & Awards:* Spec Serv Award, US Bur Mines, 66. *Mem:* Am Soc Mech Engrs; Am Soc Eng Educ; Am Inst Aeronaut & Astronaut; Sigma Xi. *Res:* Heat and mass transfer; fluid mechanics; mixed convection; wave and thermal instability of flows. *Mailing Add:* Dept of Mech & Aerospace Eng Univ of Mo Rolla MO 65401

CHEN, TCHAW-REN, b Kaohsiung, Taiwan, June 2, 35; US citizen; m 68; c 2. CELL BIOLOGY, CYTOGENETICS. *Educ:* Nat Taiwan Univ, BA, 58; Yale Univ, PhD(biol), 67. *Prof Exp:* Res staff ichthyol, Taiwan Fisheries Res Inst, Keelung, 58; res asst ichthyol, Inst Fisheries Biol, Nat Taiwan Univ, 60, asst zool, 60-61; cur asst ichthyol, Dept Zool, Yale Univ, 61-63; technician I & II ichthyol, Univ Calif, Santa Barbara, 63-67; res assoc, Biol Dept, Yale Univ, 67-71; asst prof biol, Grad Sch Biomed Sci, Univ Tex Health Sci Ctr Houston, 72-77; DIR CYTOGENETICS LAB, E K SHRIVER CTR MENT RETARDATION, WALTHAM MEM, 77- *Mem:* AAAS; Tissue Cult Asn; Am Genetic Asn; Genetics Soc Can. Herpetologists; AAAS; Am Soc Cell Biol; Am Genetic Asn; Genetics Soc Can. *Res:* Chemically, physically, and virally induced human cell alteration in vitro; cytogenetics of human and other vertebrate cells in vitro and in natural populations; amniocentesis; somatic cell genetics; carcinogenetics; factors influencing cell growth of in vitro cells. *Mailing Add:* E K Shriver Ctr for Ment Retardation Inc 200 Trapelo Rd Waltham MA 02154

CHEN, TIEN CHI, b Hong Kong, Nov 12, 28; US citizen; m 67. COMPUTER SCIENCE. *Educ:* Brown Univ, SB, 50; Duke Univ, MA, 52, PhD(physics), 57. *Prof Exp:* Assoc physicist res ctr, 56-58, staff mathematician, 58-59, mathematician data systs div, 59-61, develop engr, 61-62, sr programmer & mgr problem-oriented programming, 62-67, tech staff mem, Advan Comput Systs, 67-68, STAFF MEM RES CTR, INT BUS MACH CORP, 68-; PROF COMPUT SCI & ELECTRONICS & HEAD, UNITED COL, CHINESE UNIV, HONG KONG, 80- *Concurrent Pos:* Vis scientist, Univ Uppsala, 65-66; mgr technol & systs, Int Bus Mach San Jose fel Res Lab, 73; vis prof electronics, Chinese Univ Hong Kong, 79-80. *Mem:* Am Phys Soc; Asn Comput Mach; fel Inst Elec & Electronics Engrs. *Res:* Eigenvalue problems in chemical physics; digital computer design and applications; numerical analysis; computer algorithms; magnetic bubbles. *Mailing Add:* United Col Chinese Univ Hong Kong Shatin NT Hong Kong

CHEN, TIEN-WEI, b Taipei, Taiwan, Nov 17, 47; m 73; c 1. STRUCTURAL DYNAMICS, VIBRATION. *Educ:* Cheng Kung Univ, BS, 70; Univ Nebr, MS, 75; Univ Tex, PhD(eng mech), 80. *Prof Exp:* SR RES ENGR, RES LABS, GEN MOTORS CORP, 79- *Concurrent Pos:* Asst instr, Univ Tex, 77-78. *Mem:* Am Soc Mech Engrs. *Res:* Identification of various paths through which vibration can transmit from a source to other parts of a complex system and also the contribution to the output through each path; coupling effect of a structural-acoustic interaction system on the overall response; flow-induced vibrations. *Mailing Add:* Eng Mech Dept Gen Motors Res Labs Gen Motors Tech Ctr Warren MI 48090

CHEN, TIMOTHY LIANG-CHU, b Taipei, Taiwan; m 76. ENGINEERING, COMPOSITE MATERIAL MECHANICS. *Educ:* Tatung Inst Technol, Taipei, BS, 70; Univ Okla, MS, 76, PhD(mech eng), 78. *Prof Exp:* Grad res assoc composite flywheel res, Sch Aerospace, Mech & Nuclear Eng, Univ Okla, 78; assoc sr res engr, 78-80, SR RES ENGR RES IN COMPOSITES, ENG MECH DEPT, RES LAB, GEN MOTORS TECH CTR, 80- *Mem:* Am Soc Mech Engrs; Am Acad Mech. *Res:* Plate and shell structures; dynamics; optimization of composite structure; finite element analysis. *Mailing Add:* Dept Eng Mech Gen Motors Res Lab Warren MI 48090

CHEN, TIMOTHY SHIEH-SHENG, b Taipei, Taiwan, Feb 8, 49; m 75; c 2. CHEMISTRY, SURFACE CHEMISTRY. *Educ:* Cheng Kung Nat Univ, BS, 71, Univ Notre Dame, MS, 76, PhD(chem), 78. *Prof Exp:* Res assoc, Mich Molecular Inst, 78-79; RES ASSOC, AMES RES CTR, NASA, 79- *Mem:* Am Chem Soc. *Res:* Surfactans behaviors in aqueous and nonaqueos solutions; radiation effects on polymeric materials; ultra high molecular weight, polymer synthesis and characteriation; elastomer, expoxy, polimide and composite research; organic synthesis and characterization. *Mailing Add:* 223-6 NASA Ames Res Ctr Moffett Field CA 94035

CHEN, TSAI HWA, b Wenling Chekiang, China, Oct 14, 23; US citizen; m 54; c 4. ELECTRONIC SYSTEMS, COMPUTERS. *Educ:* Pei Yang Univ, China, BSEE, 46; Chiao Tung Univ, MSEE, 61; Univ Calif, Los Angeles, MS, 65, PhD(eng), 68. *Prof Exp:* Asst prof & assoc res fel radio & radar var univ in China & Ord Res Inst, China, 47-59; tech specialist comput circuit design, Electronics Div, Nat Cash Regist Co, 63-69; mem tech staff airborne comput, Guid & Control Systs Div, Litton Indust, 69-70; proj engr comput memory, Res Dept, Data Processing Div, NCR Corp, 70-73; sr proj engr automatic test systs, Support Systs Div, 73-79, SR PROJ ENGR, ENG DIV, RADAR SYSTS GROUP, HUGHES AIRCRAFT CO, 79- *Mem:* AAAS; Inst Elec & Electronics Engrs. *Res:* Automatic electronic test systems and applications of transmission line theory in large electronic systems; radar systems. *Mailing Add:* 8010 Bobbyboyar Ave Canoga Park CA 91304

CHEN, TSANG JAN, b Taiwan, China, Nov 13, 34; m 61; c 3. POLYMER CHEMISTRY. *Educ:* Nat Taiwan Univ, BS, 57; NDak State Univ, PhD(polymer chem), 67. *Prof Exp:* SR CHEMIST, RES LABS, EASTMAN KODAK CO, 67- *Mem:* Am Chem Soc. *Res:* Emulsion polymerization; anionic polymerization. *Mailing Add:* 475 Warren Ave Rochester NY 14618

CHEN, TSEH-AN, b Shanghai, China, Oct 26, 28; US citizen; m 54; c 4. BOTANY. *Educ:* Nat Taiwan Univ, BS, 51; Univ Wis, MS, 53; Univ NH, PhD(bot), 62. *Prof Exp:* Res analyst bot, Univ NH, 60-62; from asst prof to assoc prof biol, Fairleigh Dickinson Univ, 62-69; assoc prof entom & econ zool, 69-74, PROF PLANT PATHOL, RUTGERS UNIV, 74-, DIR GRAD PROG NEMATOL, 70- *Concurrent Pos:* Res grants, NIH, 64-66, NJ Dept Health, 65 & NSF, 70-; res assoc, Cornell Univ, 63-66; mem, US-Repub China Prog, NSF, 78-82, USDA Competetive, 79-, NSF, 81-82 & sci proj rev bd, Nat Sci Coun, Repub China. *Mem:* Am Phytopath Soc; Soc Nematologists; Am Soc Microbiol; Int Orgn Mycoplasmologists. *Res:* Interaction of soil fungi and plant parasitic nematodes on development of root rots; mechanism of plant virus transmission by nematodes; myco-plasma-like organisms that cause plant diseases; corn stunt spiro-plasma; nutrition and pathogenesis of spiroplasma; ultrastructures of nematodes. *Mailing Add:* Dept of Plant Biol Rutgers Univ New Brunswick NJ 08903

CHEN, TSONG MENG, b Yunlin, Taiwan, July 1, 35; US citizen; m 63; c 3. PLANT PHYSIOLOGY. *Educ:* Nat Taiwan Univ, BS, 58, MS, 62; Univ Calif, Davis, PhD(plant physiol), 66. *Prof Exp:* Res assoc plant physiol, Mich State Univ, 66-68 & Univ Ga, 68-70; assoc prof crop physiol, Nat Taiwan Univ, 70-72; res assoc plant physiol, Univ Ga, 72-73; biologist, Union Carbide Corp, 73-76; assoc plant physiol, Mobil Chem Co, 76-81; SR RES ASSOC, FMC CORP, 81- *Mem:* Am Soc Plant Physiologists; Weed Sci Soc Am; Am Agron Soc. *Res:* Natural and synthetic plant growth regulators which will increase the yield of the major agronomic crops. *Mailing Add:* Res & Develop PO Box 240 Edison NJ 08817

CHEN, TSONG-MING, b Chia-Yi, Taiwan, China, Nov 25, 34; m 64; c 2. SOLID STATE ELECTRONICS, ELECTRICAL ENGINEERING. *Educ:* Nat Taiwan Univ, BS, 56; Univ Minn, PhD(elec eng), 64. *Prof Exp:* From asst prof to assoc prof eng sci, Fla State Univ, 64-72; assoc prof, 72-74, PROF ELEC ENG, UNIV SFLA, 74- *Concurrent Pos:* Tech consult electronic indust. *Mem:* Inst Elec & Electronics Engrs; Int Soc Hybrid Minoelectronics; Am Vacuum Soc. *Res:* Noise in electronic devices; semiconductor electronics. *Mailing Add:* Dept of Elec Eng Univ of SFla Tampa FL 33602

CHEN, TU, b I-Lan, Taiwan, Mar 19, 35; US citizen; m 61; c 2. MAGNETISM, MATERIALS SCIENCE. *Educ:* Cheng Kung Univ, Taiwan, BS, 58; Univ Minn, Minneapolis, MS, 64, PhD(metall eng, mat sci), 67. *Prof Exp:* Teacher math & physics, Nan-Yiang Girls High Sch, Taiwan, 61-62; staff engr mat sci res, IBM Corp, 67-68; prin scientist mat sci, Corp Res Ctr, Northrop Corp, 68-71; res scientist, 71-75, PRIN SCIENTIST MAT SCI, XEROX PALO ALTO RES CTR, 75- *Mem:* Am Asn Crystal Growth; Inst Elec & Electronics Engrs; Am Chem Soc; Mat Res Soc. *Res:* Solid state physics and magnetism; crystal growth, structure and phase equilibria; inorganic chemistry. *Mailing Add:* Gen Sci Lab 3333 Coyote Hill Rd Palo Alto CA 94304

CHEN, TUAN WU, b Taiwan, China, Mar 26, 36; m 63; c 2. THEORETICAL PHYSICS. *Educ:* Nat Taiwan Univ, BS, 58; Tsing Hua Univ, Taiwan, MS, 60; Syracuse Univ, PhD(physics), 66. *Prof Exp:* Instr physics, Univ Guelph, 67-68; from asst prof to assoc prof, 68-79, PROF PHYSICS, NMEX STATE UNIV, 79- *Concurrent Pos:* Fel physics, Univ Toronto, 66-68; vis scientist, Los Alamos Sci Lab, 74-; vis prof, Nat Tsing Hua Univ, 74-75. *Mem:* Am Phys Soc. *Res:* Formalism of asymptotic quantum field theory in functional derivatives; effect of masses of gauge fields on chiral symmetry; high energy behaviors of scattering processes; nucleus scattering at medium energy; nonperturbative method for bound state problems. *Mailing Add:* Dept of Physics NMex State Univ Las Cruces NM 88001

CHEN, TUNG-SHAN, b April 17, 39; US citizen; m 64; c 2. FOOD CHEMISTRY. *Educ:* Nat Taiwan Univ, Taipei, BS, 60; Univ Calif, Berkeley, MS, 64, PhD(comp biochem), 69. *Prof Exp:* From asst to assoc prof, 69-78, PROF FOOD SERV, CALIF STATE UNIV, NORTHRIDGE, 78- *Concurrent Pos:* Chmn, Food Sci & Nutrit Div, Calif State Univ, Northridge, 70-74; vis assoc prof, Univ Calif, Los Angeles, 74; consult, State Sch Food Surv Proj, Calif State Dept Educ, 79-80; plan IV prog rep, Am Dietetic Asn, 80- *Mem:* Am Chem Soc; Am Dietetic Asn; fel Am Inst Chemists; Sigma Xi. *Res:* Chemistry of pectic substances; kinetics of enzyme induction; effects of processing and packaging on food qualities; stability of vitamins. *Mailing Add:* 10400 Irondale Ave Chatsworth CA 91311

CHEN, W(AI) K(AI), b Nanking, China, Dec 23, 36; m 62; c 2. ELECTRICAL ENGINEERING. *Educ:* Ohio Univ, BSEE, 60, MS, 61; Univ Ill, Urbana-Champaign, PhD(elec eng), 64. *Prof Exp:* Asst electronics, Ohio Univ, 60-61; asst graph theory, Co-ord Sci Lab, Univ Ill, 62-63, res assoc topology, 64; from asst prof to prof, Ohio Univ, 64-78, distinguished prof elec eng & grad chmn dept, 78-81; PROF & HEAD, DEPT INFO ENG, UNIV ILL, CHICAGO CIRCLE, 81- *Concurrent Pos:* Vis assoc prof, Purdue, Univ, 70-71; vis prof, Univ Hawaii, Manoa, 79. *Honors & Awards:* Lester R Ford Award, Math Asn Am, 67; Inst Elec & Electronics Engrs Fel Award, 77; AAAS Fel Award, 78. *Mem:* AAAS; Inst Elec & Electronics Engrs; Math Asn Am; Asn Comput Mach; Tensor Soc; Sigma Xi. *Res:* Communication nets; network topology; graph and network theory; switching circuits. *Mailing Add:* Univ Ill Chicago Circle Chicago IL 60680

CHEN, WAYNE H(WA-WEI), b Soochow, China, Dec 13, 22; m 57. ELECTRICAL ENGINEERING, MATHEMATICS. *Educ:* Chiao Tung Univ, BS, 44; Univ Wash, Seattle, MS, 49, PhD(math), 52. *Prof Exp:* Eng staff, Applied Physics Lab & Cyclotron Proj, Univ Wash, Seattle, 49-50, assoc dept math, 50-52; from asst prof to assoc prof elec eng, 52-57, chmn dept, 65-73, PROF ELEC ENG, UNIV FLA, 57-, DEAN COL ENG & DIR ENG & INDUST EXP STA, 73- *Concurrent Pos:* Vis prof, Nat Univ Taiwan & Chiao Tung Univ, 64; vis scientist & lectr, Nat Acad Sci to USSR, 67; nat chmn, Elec Eng Dept Heads Asn, 69-70; mem accreditation team, Inst Elec & Electronics Engrs-Eng Coun Prof Develop, 68-72. *Honors & Awards:* Outstanding Publ Award, Chia Hsin Cement Co Cult Fund, Taiwan, 69. *Mem:* Am Soc Eng Educ; fel Inst Elec & Electronics Engrs; Am Asn Univ Prof. *Res:* Switching circuits and theory; network theory; applied mathematics. *Mailing Add:* Col of Eng Univ of Fla Gainesville FL 32611

CHEN, WEI LEE, Taipei, Taiwan. GEOPHYSICAL FLUID DYNAMICS. *Educ:* Nat Cent Univ, Taiwan, BS, 73, MS, 75; Univ Calif, Los Angeles, PhD(atmospheri sci), 81. *Prof Exp:* Res asst, Inst Geophys, Nat Cent Univ, Taiwan, 74-75; res asst, Inst Geophys & Planetary Physics, Univ Calif, Los Angeles, 76-81; ASST SCIENTIST, APPL RES CORP, 81- *Mem:* Am Meterol Soc. *Res:* Developing a spectral general circulation model to study the coupling of chemistry and dynamics in the stratosphere; linear and nonlinear stability analysis of shear flows in a rotating system. *Mailing Add:* 223 Lakeside Dr T-4 Greenbelt MD 20770

CHEN, WEN SHERNG, b Taiwan; US citizen. MEDICINAL CHEMISTRY, BIOCHEMISTRY. *Educ:* Taipei Med Col, BS, 66, Univ NC, PhD(med chem), 74. *Prof Exp:* Fel biochem, Dept Chem, Univ Colo, 74-75; fel, Dept Biochem, Col Med, Univ Iowa, 75-79; SR RES SCIENTIST PROTEIN PROD LAB, KRAFT RES & DEVELOP, DART & KRAFT, INC, 79- *Mem:* Am Chem Soc. *Res:* Physicochemical properties of proteins; isolation and purification of enzymes; enzyme kinetics; chemical modification of enzymes and proteins; design and synthesis of new compounds for biological evaluation, structure-activity relationship. *Mailing Add:* 213 Flora Ave Glenview IL 60025

CHEN, WEN-LAN, b Hsiaohsien, Kiangsu, China, Nov 15, 17; m 45; c 3. MINING. *Educ:* Nat Northwestern Eng Col, China, BS, 40; Pa State Univ, MS, 47, PhD(mining), 50. *Prof Exp:* Asst mining, Nat Northwestern Eng Col, China, 40-41; asst engr, Yunnan Tin Corp, 41-43; assoc engr, Tein-Fu Coal Mining Co, 43-45; training engr, Int Training Admin, Wash, 45-46; asst fuel technol, Pa State Univ, 47-50; asst prof mining, Ore State Col, 50-52; design engr, O W Walvood, Inc, 52-53; res engr, Link-Belt Co, 54-58; prep engr, 59-69, mgr process develop, 69-78, DIR PREP, ROBERTS & SCHAEFER CO, DIV ELGIN NAT INDUST, INC, 79- *Mem:* Am Inst Mining, Metall & Petrol Engrs. *Res:* Coal preparation; mineral dressing. *Mailing Add:* Div Elgin Nat Indust Inc 120 S Riverside Plaza Chicago IL 60606

CHEN, WENPENG, b Ta-Chi, Taiwan. PHYSICS, OPTICS. *Educ:* Nat Tsing-Hwa Univ, Taiwan, BS, 70; Univ Pa, PhD(physics), 77. *Prof Exp:* SCIENTIST PHYSICS, MARTIN MARIETTA LABS, 77- *Mem:* Am Phys Soc; Optical Soc Am. *Res:* Metal surface and adsorbed layer; surface plasmon and surface plariton; visible and infrared spectroscope using attentuated total reflection technique; wave guide and electromagnetic wave propagation; interface of metal and semiconductor; gallium arsenide Impatt diodes; IR switch. *Mailing Add:* Martin Marietta Labs 1450 S Rolling Rd Baltimore MD 21227

CHEN, WILLIAM KWO-WEI, b Shanghai, China, July 18, 28; US citizen; m 51; c 2. POLYMER CHEMISTRY, CHEMICAL ENGINEERING. *Educ:* Mass Inst Technol, BSc, 51; Polytech Inst Brooklyn, PhD(chem), 58. *Prof Exp:* Chem engr, Quaker Chem Prod Co, 51-52; chem engr, Am Mach & Foundry Co, 52-53, sr chem engr, 53-54, group leader plastic prod, 54-56, sect mgr desalination & membranes, 56-61, asst mgr chem lab, 61-63, mgr liquid processing lab, 63-64; mgr res & develop, Celanese Plastic Co, 64-68, VPRES AMCEL CO & GEN EXPORT MGR, CELANESE PLASTIC CO, 68- *Mem:* Am Chem Soc; Soc Plastics Eng. *Res:* Membranes, films and battery separators; desalination and liquid processing; plastic and resins; marketing; international trade. *Mailing Add:* 102 Pinegrove Rd Berkeley Heights NJ 07922

CHEN, YANG-JEN, b Tainan, Taiwan, June 16, 47; c 1. BIOFLUIDDYNAMICS, ENERGY. *Educ:* Chung Yuan Christian Col Sci & Eng, BS, 69; La State Univ, MS, PhD(physics). *Prof Exp:* Res assoc physics, Lehigh Univ, 77-78; sr prod develop engr air pollution control technol, C-E Walther, Inc, 78-79; supvr develop & testing air pollution control technol, Combustion Eng Environ Syst Div, 79-80; SR RES ENGR AIR POLLUTION CONTROL TECHNOL, WESTERN PRECIPITATION DIV, JOY MFG CO, 80- *Mem:* Air Pollution Control Asn; Am Phys Soc; Am Asn Aerosol Res. *Res:* Develop and evaluate the emerging air pollution control technologies including precipitator, fabric filter and scrubber; bench scale research; full scale demonstration research project. *Mailing Add:* 24049 Avenida Crescenta Valencia CA 91355

CHEN, YI-DER, b Taipei, Taiwan, May 29, 40; m 69. THEORETICAL CHEMISTRY, BIOPHYSICS. *Educ:* Nat Taiwan Univ, BS, 63; Nat Tsing Hua Univ, MS, 65; Pa State Univ, PhD(chem), 70. *Prof Exp:* Res chemist biophys Univ Calif, Santa Cruz, 69-72; res assoc, Theoret Biol, 72-78, RES CHEMIST, NAT INST ARTHRITIS, DIGESTIVE DIS, KIDNEYS, NIH, 78- *Mem:* Biophys Soc; Am Chem Soc. *Res:* Statistical mechanics of nonspherical molecules; fluctuations and noise in chemical and biological systems; theoretical studies of membrane transports, muscle contractions, conformational transitions in biopolymers, statistical mechanics of ring polymers and circular DNA. *Mailing Add:* Bldg 2 Rm 319 NIH Bethesda MD 20014

CHEN, YOK, b Soochow, China, July 27, 31; US citizen; m 61; c 3. PHYSICS. *Educ:* Univ Wis, BSc, 52; Purdue Univ, PhD(physics), 65. *Prof Exp:* Electron microscopist, Univ Chicago, 53-55; physicist, Hoffman Semiconductor Prod, Evanston, Ill, 55-58; RES PHYSICIST, OAK RIDGE NAT LAB, 65- *Honors & Awards:* Indust Res 100 Award, 75. *Mem:* Fel Am Phys Soc; Am Ceramic Soc. *Res:* Radiation damage in semiconductors; impurities and defects in insulators; radiation effects and ion implantation in oxides; optical and magnetic resonance spectroscopy. *Mailing Add:* 132 Windham Rd Oak Ridge TN 37830

CHEN, YOUNG CHANG, b Shin-Chu, Taiwan, Feb 28, 35; US citizen; m 67; c 2. TUMOR VIROLOGY, MICROBIOLOGY. *Educ:* Nat Chung-Hsing Univ Taiwan, BS, 57; Univ Tokyo, Japan, MS, 63; Univ Utah, AM, 68; Univ Southern Calif, PhD(virol), 73. *Prof Exp:* Lectr chem, Taiwan Prov Shin-Chu Sch Polytech, 59-61; sr lectr microbiol, Univ Southern Calif, 73-76; ASST PROF MICROBIOL & VIROL, N TEX STATE UNIV, 76- *Concurrent Pos:* Fel, Nat Cancer Inst, 73-76; consult, Monogram Industs, Inc, 76-; fac res grants, N Tex State Univ, 76-79. *Mem:* Am Soc Microbiol; AAAS. *Res:* Animal virology and oncogenic virology; somatic cell genetics and viral genetics; antiviral and anti-tumor substances; cell cultures and biology of aging; public health and water pollution microbiology. *Mailing Add:* Dept of Biol Sci N Tex State Univ Denton TX 76203

CHEN, YU, b June 8, 21; US citizen; m 51; c 2. MECHANICS. *Educ:* Chiao Tung Univ, BS, 42; Harvard Univ, MS, 47, ScD, 50. *Prof Exp:* Sr develop engr, Burroughs Corp, 52-56; sr res engr, Ford Motor Co, 56-59; assoc prof mech eng, NY Univ, 59-64; assoc prof, 64-66, PROF MECH, RUTGERS UNIV, 66-, CHMN, DEPT MECH & MAT SCI, 81- *Concurrent Pos:* Consult, Bell Tel Labs, Inc, 60-63 & Goddard Space Flight Ctr, 64-67, Arradcom, 73- *Mem:* Fel Am Soc Mech Engrs; Am Soc Eng Educ; Sigma Xi. *Res:* Fluid mechanics; elasticity; structural mechanics; space flight dynamics. *Mailing Add:* Dept of Mech Col of Eng Rutgers Univ New Brunswick NJ 08903

CHEN, YU WHY, b Nantungchow, China, Apr 1, 10; m 38; c 1. MATHEMATICS. *Educ:* Univ Gottingen, PhD, 34. *Prof Exp:* Prof math, Peking Univ, 36-45; res assoc, NY Univ, 46-49; res fel, Inst Adv Study, 49-50; assoc prof, Univ Okla, 50-52; from assoc prof to prof, Wayne State Univ, 52-65; PROF MATH, UNIV MASS, AMHERST, 65- *Mem:* Am Math Asn; Soc Indust & Appl Math; Am Math Soc. *Res:* Partial differential equations and applications. *Mailing Add:* Dept Math Univ Mass Amherst MA 01003

CHEN, YUH-CHING, b Fukien, China, May 20, 30; m 55; c 3. PURE MATHEMATICS. *Educ:* City Univ New York, PhD(math), 66. *Prof Exp:* Asst math, Taiwan Norm Univ, 54-59; asst, Nanyang Univ, Singapore, 59-60; teacher high sch, Malaya, 60-62; asst prof, Univ Minn, Morris, 64-65 & Wesleyan Univ, 66-71; asst prof, 71-72, chmn dept, 74-78, ASSOC PROF MATH, FORDHAM UNIV, 72- *Concurrent Pos:* Vis prof, Peking Normal Univ, 78-79. *Mem:* Sigma Xi. *Res:* Homology and homotopy theories and their applications. *Mailing Add:* Dept of Math Fordham Univ Bronx NY 10458

CHEN, YUNG MING, b China, Dec 30, 35; US citizen; m 62. APPLIED MATHEMATICS. *Educ:* Univ Md, BS, 56; Drexel Inst, MS, 58; Univ Calif, Berkeley, MA, 60; NY Univ, PhD(appl math), 63. *Prof Exp:* Res engr, Radio Corp Am, NJ, 56-58; asst, Electronics Res Labs, Univ Calif, Berkeley, 58-59; asst, Dept Math, 59-60; asst appl math, Courant Inst Math Sci, NY Univ, 60-63; asst prof, Purdue Univ, 63-65; assoc prof, Univ Fla, 65-67; assoc prof, 67-72, PROF APPL MATH, STATE UNIV NY STONY BROOK, 72- *Mem:* Am Phys Soc; Soc Indust & Appl Math. *Res:* Wave propagation; approximation methods in initial and boundary value problems; numerical analysis and stochastic process numerical methods for inverse problems. *Mailing Add:* Dept of Appl Math State Univ of NY Stony Brook NY 11790

CHENEA, PAUL F(RANKLIN), b Milton, Ore, May 17, 18; m 41; c 2. ENGINEERING MECHANICS. *Educ:* Univ Calif, BS, 40; Univ Mich, MS, 47, PhD(eng mech), 49. *Hon Degrees:* DSc, Rose Polytech Inst, 68; DEng, Purdue Univ, 68; DEngSc, Tri-State Col, 68; DH Clarkson Col Technol, 71; DEng, Drexel Univ, 71. *Prof Exp:* Proj engr, Contractors Pacific Naval Air Bases, 40 & US Army Ord Dept, 41; from instr to assoc prof, Univ Mich, 46-52; asst dean & head div eng sci, Purdue Univ, 52-55, assoc dean eng, 56-58, actg head, Sch Elec Eng, 57-58; Webster vis prof elec eng, Mass Inst Technol, 58-59, head, Sch Mech Eng, 59-61, head div math sci, 60-61, vpres acad affairs, 61-63, actg dean, Sch Sci Educ & Humanities, 62-63; vpres acad affairs, Purdue Univ, 63-67; sci dir, 67-69, V PRES RES LABS, TECH CTR, GEN MOTORS CORP, 69- *Concurrent Pos:* Consult, Gen Motors Corp, E I du Pont de Nemours & Co, Inc & RCA Corp; dir, Comn Eng Educ. *Mem:* Nat Acad Eng; AAAS; Am Soc Mech Engrs; Am Soc Eng Educ; Nat Soc Prof Engrs; fel Am Acad Arts & Sci. *Res:* Administration; continuum physics; applied mechanics; electromagnetic field theory. *Mailing Add:* Res Labs Gen Motors Corp 12 Mile & Mound Rd Warren MI 48090

CHENEY, CHARLES BROOKER, b New Haven, Conn, Mar 2, 12; m 34; c 5. OBSTETRICS & GYNECOLOGY. *Educ:* Yale Univ, BA, 34, MD, 41; Am Bd Obstet & Gynec, dipl, 52. *Prof Exp:* Asst surg obstet & gynec, 41-43, asst obstet & gynec, 46-47, instr, 47-49, clin instr, 49-52, asst clin prof, 52-69, sr clin assoc, 69-74, assoc clin prof, 74-80, CLIN PROF OBSTET & GYNEC, SCH MED, YALE UNIV, 80-; ASST ASSOC CHIEF OBSTET & GYNEC & ATTEND OBSTETRICIAN & GYNECOLOGIST, YALE-NEW HAVEN HOSP, 57- *Concurrent Pos:* Former pres, Conn Med Exam Bd. *Mem:* AMA; Am Col Obstet & Gynec. *Mailing Add:* 111 Park St New Haven CT 06511

CHENEY, CLARISSA M, b Sanford, Maine, Oct 22, 46. DEVELOPMENTAL GENETICS. *Educ:* Goucher Col, AB, 69; Yale Univ, MPhil, 70; Univ Pa, PhD(biol), 79. *Prof Exp:* Teach sci, private high sch, New Haven, Conn & Boston, Mass, 70-74; teaching asst embryol, Marine Biol Lab, Woods Hole, Mass, 78; NIH NAT RES SERV AWARD FEL, DEPT BIOL, JOHNS HOPKINS UNIV, 79- *Mem:* Am Soc Cell Biol; Soc Develop Biol; Int Soc Develop Biol. *Res:* The role of tubulin in control of growth and determination in Drosophila imaginal discs; extracellular matrix and somite formation in chick embryos; mechanisms of determination and differentiation during early development. *Mailing Add:* Dept Biol Johns Hopkins Univ 3400 N Charles St Baltimore MD 21218

CHENEY, ELLIOTT WARD, (JR), b Gettysburg, Pa, June 28, 29; m 52; c 3. MATHEMATICS. *Educ:* Lehigh Univ, BA, 51; Univ Kans, PhD(math), 57. *Prof Exp:* Instr math, Univ Kans, 52-56; design specialist & mathematician, Convair-Astronaut Div, Gen Dynamics Corp, 56-59; mem tech staff, Space Tech Labs, Inc, 59-61; asst prof math, Iowa State Univ, 61-62; from asst prof to assoc prof, Univ Calif, Los Angeles, 62-65; assoc prof, 65-66, PROF MATH, UNIV TEX, AUSTIN, 66- *Concurrent Pos:* Vis assoc prof, Univ Tex, 64; guest prof, Univ Lund, 66-67; vis prof, Mich State Univ, 69-70; assoc ed, J Approximation Theory; assoc ed, J Numerical Anal, Soc Indus & Appl Math & Numerical Function Anal & Optimization. *Mem:* Am Math Soc; Math Asn Am; Soc Indust & Appl Math. *Res:* Approximation theory; linear inequalities; numerical analysis. *Mailing Add:* Dept of Math Univ of Tex Austin TX 78712

CHENEY, ERIC SWENSON, b New Haven, Conn, Nov 17, 34; m 58; c 4. ECONOMIC GEOLOGY. *Educ:* Yale Univ, BS, 56, PhD(geol), 64. *Prof Exp:* Instr sci, Southern Conn State Col, 63-64; asst prof geol, 64-69, ASSOC PROF GEOL, UNIV WASH, 69- *Concurrent Pos:* Consult, Maine Geol Surv, 63-69, Amoco Minerals Co, 70-71, Texasgulf Inc, 72, Urangesellschaft-USA, 74, Continental Oil Co Inc, 75, Chevron Resources Co, 76-77, Wold Nuclear Co, 78, Seattle City Light, 79-80 & B/T Enterprises, 81. *Mem:* AAAS; Geol Soc Am; Am Inst Mining, Metall & Petrol Eng; Sigma Xi; Geochem Soc. *Res:* Geology and geochemistry of ore deposits; mineral and energy resources; siting of nuclear power plants; geology of Pacific northwest. *Mailing Add:* Dept of Geol Sci Univ of Wash Seattle WA 98195

CHENEY, FREDERICK WYMAN, b Ayer, Mass, Jan 17, 35; m 59; c 2. ANESTHESIOLOGY. *Educ:* Tufts Univ, BS, 56, MD, 60. *Prof Exp:* Instr anesthesiol, 64-66, from asst prof to assoc prof, 66-74, PROF ANESTHESIOL, SCH MED, UNIV WASH, 74- *Concurrent Pos:* NIH res fel, Sch Med, Univ Wash, 66-67. *Mem:* Am Physiol Soc; Am Soc Anesthesiologists; Am Thoracic Soc; Soc Critical Care Med. *Res:* Pulmonary edema; pulmonary vasculature; clinical respiratory care. *Mailing Add:* Dept Anesthesiol Mail Stop RN10 Univ of Wash Sch of Med Seattle WA 98195

CHENEY, HORACE BELLATTI, b Emerson, Iowa, Dec 15, 13; m 40; c 3. SOIL FERTILITY. *Educ:* Iowa State Univ, BS, 35; Ohio State Univ, PhD(soil fertility). *Prof Exp:* Jr soil surveyor, Soil Conserv Serv, USDA, Iowa, 35-37; exten assoc agron, Iowa State Univ, 37-39; res assoc, Ohio State Univ, 39-41; exten & res asst prof agron, econ & sociol, Iowa State Univ, 41-43, exten asst prof agron, 43-44, from assoc prof to prof, 45-52; prof & head dept, 52-77, EMER PROF SOILS, ORE STATE UNIV, 77- *Mem:* Fel AAAS; fel Soil Sci Soc Am (pres, 64); fel Soil Conserv Soc Am; fel Am Soc Agron (pres, 73). *Res:* Soil management. *Mailing Add:* Dept Soil Sci Ore State Univ Corvallis OR 97331

CHENEY, JAMES A, b Los Angeles, Calif, Feb 2, 27; m 51; c 6. SOIL MECHANICS. *Educ:* Univ Calif, Los Angeles, BS, 51, MS, 53; Stanford Univ, PhD(eng mech), 63. *Prof Exp:* Asst engr struct mech, Univ Calif, Los Angeles, 51-53; assoc engr, L T Evans Found Eng Co, 53-55; struct engr, Missile & Syst Div, Lockheed Aircraft Corp, 55-58, head strength group, Lockheed Missile & Space Co, 58-59, grad study engr, 59-62; asst prof, 62-66, assoc prof, 66-80, PROF CIVIL ENG, UNIV CALIF, DAVIS, 80- *Concurrent Pos:* Staff engr & consult, Lockheed Missile & Space Co, 62-66. *Mem:* Am Soc Civil Engrs; Am Soc Eng Educ. *Res:* Structural mechanics; buckling of structures and structural elements; dynamic response of structure and soil; geotechnical centrifuge model testing; structural properties of bone, constitutive relations in soil mechanics; soil-structure interaction. *Mailing Add:* Dept of Civil Eng Univ of Calif Davis CA 95616

CHENEY, MONROE G, b Ft Worth, Tex, Mar 10, 19; m 52; c 3. PHYSICS, GEOPHYSICS. *Educ:* Rice Univ, BA, 41; Univ Tex, MA, 50; Columbia Univ, MA, 52. *Prof Exp:* Radio physicist, US Naval Res Lab, DC, 42-47; asst prof physics, Hardin-Simmons Univ, 47-49; physicist, US Bur Mines, Pa, 52; reservoir engr, Anzac Oil Corp, Tex, 52-55 & Socony Mobil, Venezuela, 55-59; asst prof physics, Arlington State Col, 59-67, ASST PROF PHYSICS, UNIV TEX, ARLINGTON, 67- *Concurrent Pos:* Mem, Byrd Antarctic Exped, 46-47; consult, Anzac Oil Corp, 55-74. *Mem:* Am Inst Mining, Metall & Petrol Eng; Am Geophys Union. *Res:* Ground constants at radio frequency; gas resaturation of oil; seismic surface-waves; fracturing limestone with crude oil; seismic waves in ice; radiowave patterns; water conservation; underground housing; oil secondary recovery. *Mailing Add:* 1217 W Cedar Arlington TX 76012

CHENEY, PAUL DAVID, b Jamestown, NY, Oct 10, 47; m 66; c 2. PHYSIOLOGY, NEUROPHYSIOLOGY. *Educ:* State Univ NY Col Fredonia, BS, 69; State Univ NY Upstate Med Ctr, PhD, 75. *Prof Exp:* Fel physiol, Univ Wash Sch Med, 74-77; res asst prof, Dept Physiol & Biophysics, Univ Wash, 77-78; ASST PROF PHYSIOL, UNIV KANS MED CTR, 78- *Mem:* Soc Neurosci; Sigma Xi. *Res:* Motor control; muscle receptors; spinal cord; role of cerebral cortex and brainstem in movement. *Mailing Add:* Dept of Physiol 39th & Rainbow Blvd Kansas City KS 66103

CHENG, ANDREW FRANCIS, b Princeton, NJ, Oct 15, 51; m 79. ASTROPHYSICS. *Educ:* Princeton Univ, AB, 71; Columbia Univ, MPhil, 74, PhD(physics), 77. *Prof Exp:* Fel physics, Bell Tel Labs, 76-78; ASST PROF PHYSICS, RUTGERS UNIV, 78- *Mem:* Am Phys Soc; Am Astron Soc; Am Geophys Union; NY Acad Sci. *Res:* Physics of magnetospheres, pulsars, Jupiter, and Saturn. *Mailing Add:* Dept of Physics & Astron Rutgers Univ Piscataway NJ 08854

CHENG, BOB B, b Tainan, Taiwan, July 16, 40; US citizen; m 70; c 2. PHYSICAL CHEMISTRY, POLYMER CHEMISTRY. *Educ:* Nat Taiwan Univ, BS, 62; Syracuse Univ, MS, 67, PhD(chem), 70. *Prof Exp:* Res chemist colloid chem, 69-73, SR RES CHEMIST COLLOID & SURFACE CHEM, COLGATE-PALMOLIVE CO, 73- *Res:* Detergent chemistry and development of non-phosphorus-built detergents. *Mailing Add:* 12 Peter Ave Kendall Park NJ 08824

CHENG, CHENG-YIN, b Shinpu, Formosa, Jan 29, 30; nat US; m 61. ANALYTICAL CHEMISTRY, ENVIRONMENTAL CHEMISTRY. *Educ:* Berea Col, BS, 55; Univ Ill, MS, 56, PhD(soil chem), 60. *Prof Exp:* Instr chem, Wilson Col, 60-61; from asst prof to assoc prof, Shippensburg State Col, 61-65; from asst prof to assoc prof, Ithaca Col, 65-68; PROF CHEM, EAST STROUDSBURG STATE COL, 68- *Mem:* Am Chem Soc; Sigma Xi; Am Soc Agron. *Res:* Cation diffusion in soils; radioisotope technology; instrumental methods of analysis; precipitation from homogeneous solution; ion selective electrodes; air and water quality. *Mailing Add:* Dept of Chem East Stroudsburg State Col East Stroudsburg PA 18301

CHENG, CHIA-CHUNG, b China, May 5, 25; m 53; c 4. ORGANIC CHEMISTRY. *Educ:* Chekiang Univ, BS, 48; Univ Tex, MA, 51, PhD, 54. *Prof Exp:* Res assoc org res, NMex Highlands Univ, 54-57 & Princeton Univ, 57-59; head, Cancer Chemother Sect, Midwest Res Inst, 59-66, head, Med Chem Sect, 66-78; DIR, MID-AM CANCER CTR & PROF PHARMACOL, UNIV KANS MED CTR, 78- *Concurrent Pos:* Mem med chem A study sect, NIH, 73-77. *Honors & Awards:* Sci Award, Midwest Res Inst, 74. *Mem:* AAAS; Am Chem Soc; NY Acad Sci; The Chem Soc. *Res:* Synthesis, identification and reaction mechanism study of organic compounds; synthesis and evaluation of antimetabolites, antibiotics, alkylating agents, vitamin analogs and natural products. *Mailing Add:* Mid-Am Cancer Ctr Univ Kans Med Ctr Kansas City KS 64103

CHENG, CHIANG-SHUEI, b Sinchu, Taiwan, Sept 22, 35; US citizen; m 60; c 1. PLASMA PHYSICS. *Educ:* Nat Taiwan Univ, BS, 58; Nat Tsing Hua Univ, MS, 60; Lehigh Univ, PhD(physics), 68. *Prof Exp:* Instr physics, Lehigh Univ, 65-69; assoc prof, 69-73, PROF PHYSICS, EAST STROUDSBURG STATE COL, 73- *Mem:* Am Phys Soc; Sigma Xi. *Res:* Scattering function and transport theory of a plasma. *Mailing Add:* Dept of Physics East Stroudsburg State Col East Stroudsburg PA 18301

CHENG, CHING-CHI CHRIS, b Kaohsiung, Taiwan, Dec 30, 46; m 72; c 3. PHYSICAL CHEMISTRY, INORGANIC CHEMISTRY. *Educ:* Fu-Jen Cath Univ, Taiwan, BS, 68; Brandeis Univ, PhD(chem), 76. *Prof Exp:* Res assoc solid state chem, Northeastern Univ, 75-76; res assoc laser chem, Brandeis Univ, 76-77, lectr phys chem, 77-78; ASSOC NUCLEAR MED, HARVARD MED SCH & CHILDREN'S HOSP, 78- *Concurrent Pos:* Res assoc, Brandeis Univ, 77-78; vis scientist, Nuclear Reactor Lab, Mass Inst Technol, 78-; res collabr, Brookhaven Nat Lab, 78- *Mem:* Am Chem Soc; Optical Soc Am; Soc Nuclear Med. *Res:* Development of ultra-short-lived radionuclide generators for angiography; laser induced chemistry; solid-state chemistry; magneto-chemistry; mossbauer spectroscopy. *Mailing Add:* Nuclear Med Res Enders Res Bldg SB 22 300 Longwood Ave Boston MA 02115

CHENG, CHUEN HON, b Hong Kong, Oct 4, 50. GEOPHYSICS. *Educ:* Cornell Univ, BSc, 73; Mass Inst Technol, ScD(geophys), 78. *Prof Exp:* RES ASSOC GEOPHYS, MASS INST TECHNOL, 78- *Mem:* Am Geophys Union; Soc Explor Geophysicists; Seismol Soc Am; Acoust Soc Am. *Res:* Borehole geophysics; elastic wave propagation in porous rocks; planetary interiors. *Mailing Add:* 54-512 Mass Inst of Technol Cambridge MA 02139

CHENG, CHUNG-CHIEH, b Chungking, China; US citizen. SOLAR PHYSICS. *Educ:* Nat Taiwan Univ, BS, 60; Harvard Univ, MA, 63, PhD(astron & astrophys), 70. *Prof Exp:* Res assoc solar physics, Nat Res Coun, 70-72; solar physicist, Naval Res Lab & Ball Brothers Res, 73-79; astrophysicist, Marshall Space Fight Ctr, NASA, 79-81; ASTROPHYSICIST, NAVAL RES LAB, 81- *Mem:* Am Astron Soc. *Res:*

Interpretation of the ultraviolet, extra ultraviolet and x-ray spectra of the sun; theoretical studies of solar activities; applications of magnetohydrodynamic theory and plasma physics to interpretations of solar phenomena. *Mailing Add:* Code 4175 CC Naval Res Lab Washington DC 20375

CHENG, DAVID, b Chungking, China, July 21, 41; US citizen; c 2. EXPERIMENTAL PHYSICS. *Educ:* Univ Calif, Berkeley, BS, 62, MS, 63, PhD(exp high energy physics), 65. *Prof Exp:* Physicist exp physics, Lawrence Radiation Lab, Univ Calif, 65-67; assoc physicist, Brookhaven Nat Lab, 67-70; mem tech staff, Bell Labs, 70-74; PROJ LEADER, XEROX RES CTR, 74- *Mem:* Optical Soc Am; Am Phys Soc; Inst Elec & Electronics Engrs; Soc Photog Scientists & Engrs; Soc Photo-Optical Instrumentation Engrs. *Res:* High speed and high density optical recording technique; laser physics and applications; integrated circuit pattern generation techniques; laser and CCD image recording; acousto-optical devices and electro optics. *Mailing Add:* Xerox Res Ctr 3333 Coyote Hill Rd Palo Alto CA 94304

CHENG, DAVID H(ONG), b I-Shing, China, Apr 19, 20; nat US; m 49; c 2. ENGINEERING MECHANICS. *Educ:* Franco-Chinese Univ, BS, 42; Univ Minn, MS, 47; Columbia Univ, PhD(mech), 50. *Prof Exp:* Instr civil eng, Rutgers Univ, 49-50; struct eng, Ammann & Whitney, 50-52; struct & develop engr, M W Kellogg Co, 53-55; from asst prof to assoc prof, 55-66, dir grad studies, Sch Eng, 77-78, exec off PhD prog eng, Grad Ctr, 77-78, PROF CIVIL ENG, CITY COL NEW YORK, 66-, DEAN, SCH ENG, 79- *Concurrent Pos:* Am Soc Eng Educ-NASA fel, 64; NASA fel, 64-65; hon res assoc, Harvard Univ, 67-68; consult, M W Kellogg Co & Inst Defense Anal. *Mem:* Am Soc Mech Engrs; Am Soc Civil Engrs; Am Soc Eng Educ. *Res:* Structural dynamics and vibrations; wind engineering and stability of suspended bridges; stress in pressure vessels and pipings for nuclear power. *Mailing Add:* Sch of Eng City Col of New York New York NY 10031

CHENG, DAVID H S, b Shanghai, China; US citizen. SUBMARINE ANTENNAS, COMPUTER GRAPHICS. *Educ:* St John's Univ, BA, 43; Univ Mo, MA, 49, BS, 56, MS, 58, PhD(elec eng), 64. *Prof Exp:* Scientist, NASA-Am Soc Elec Engrs, Goddard Space Flight Ctr, 65, fel, 67 & 68; elec engr, Naval Underwater Systs Ctr, New London Lab, 70-79; from asst prof to assoc prof, PROF ELEC ENG, UNIV MO-COLUMBIA, 57-; CONSULT, NAVAL UNDERWATER SYSTS CTR, NEW LONDON LAB, 80- *Concurrent Pos:* Vis scientist, Radiation Lab, Univ Mich, 67-68. *Mem:* Inst Elec & Electronics Engrs; Am Phys Soc; Am Geophys Union; NY Acad Sci; Sigma Xi. *Res:* Research and development in connection with submarine antenna systems. *Mailing Add:* Code 342 Naval Underwater Systs Ctr New London Lab New London CT 06320

CHENG, DAVID KEUN, b China, Jan 10, 18; US citizen; m 48; c 1. ELECTRICAL ENGINEERING, ELECTROMAGNETICS. *Educ:* Chiao Tung Univ, BSEE, 38; Harvard Univ, SM, 44, ScD, 46. *Prof Exp:* Engr, Cent Radio Corp, China, 38-43; electronics & proj engr, US Air Force Cambridge Field Sta, 46-48; from asst prof to assoc prof, 48-55, PROF ELEC ENG, SYRACUSE UNIV, 55- *Concurrent Pos:* Dir electromagnetics & antennas res proj, Syracuse Univ Res Inst, 49-; consult, IBM, 52-53, Gen Elec Co, 57-60 & Syracuse Res Corp, 61-65; John Simon Guggenheim Mem Found fel, 60-61; consult ed elec sci, Addison-Wesley Publ Co, 61-; centennial prof, Syracuse Univ, 70; Nat Acad Sci exchange scientist, Hungary, 72, Yugoslavia, 74, Poland & Romania, 78; European distinguished lectr, Inst Elec & Electronics Engrs Antennas & Propagation Soc, 75-76; liaison scientist, US Off Naval Res, London Br, 75-76; mem, US Nat Comn Comts, Int Union Radio Sci. *Honors & Awards:* Ann Achievement Award, Chinese Inst Engrs, 72; Ann Res Award, Sigma Xi, 72. *Mem:* Fel AAAS; fel Inst Elec & Electronics Engrs; fel Brit Inst Elec Engrs; Sigma Xi; Am Soc Eng Educ. *Res:* Electromagnetic theory; synthesis and optimization of antenna arrays; theory and applications of Walsh functions; communication systems. *Mailing Add:* Dept of Elec & Comput Eng Syracuse Univ Syracuse NY 13210

CHENG, DAVID KUOHO, b Foochow, China, Nov 25, 25; m 55; c 2. SEED TECHNOLOGY. *Educ:* Fukien Christian Univ, BS, 47; Miss State Univ, MS, 66, PhD(vegetable crops), 69. *Prof Exp:* Teacher hort, Tainan Voc Agr Sch, 47-48; head, Agr Div, Pingtung Voc Agr Sch, 48-57; agr educ specialist, Mutual Security Mission China, Agency Int Develop, 57-60, Mich State Univ Adv Team 60-64; PLANT BREEDER, DESERT SEED CO, INC, 69- *Mem:* Am Soc Hort Sci; Am Orchid Soc. *Res:* Onion and lettuce breeding; develop types that meet the requirements of different consumers; incorporate resistance to various diseases and also improve seed production. *Mailing Add:* Desert Seed Co PO Box 181 El Centro CA 92243

CHENG, FRANCIS SHENG-HSIUNG, US citizen. PHYSICAL CHEMISTRY, POLYMER SCIENCE. *Educ:* Cheng-kung Univ, Taiwan, BS, 59; Baylor Univ, PhD(phys chem), 67; Washington Univ, DSc(polymer sci), 70. *Prof Exp:* Eng consult, Robertson & Assocs, Inc, 71-72; res scientist polymer anal & qual control, United Merchants & Mfg, Inc, 72-75; res specialist injection molding processes, Monsanto, Inc, 75-77; PROCESS ENGR & ASST TO V PRES FOREIGN TRADE, R T VANDERBILT CO, INC, 77- *Concurrent Pos:* NSF res assoc, Wash Univ, 66-67; res engr, Esso Res & Eng Co, 70-71; chem abstractor, Chem Abstr Serv, 65-75. *Honors & Awards:* Chem Abstr Serv Award, 76. *Mem:* Am Chem Soc; Am Inst Chem Engrs. *Res:* Organic systhesis; physical and thermodynamic characterizations of organic and inorganic sulfur compounds and polymeric substances; implementation of computerized fail-proof process and quality control systems. *Mailing Add:* 42 Mohegan St West Hartford CT 06117

CHENG, FRANK HSIEH FU, b Shanghai, China, Nov 16, 23; US citizen; m 58; c 3. BIOCHEMISTRY, IMMUNOCHEMISTRY. *Educ:* St John's Univ, China, BS, 46; Univ Tenn, MS, 50; Ind Univ, PhD(biochem), 57. *Prof Exp:* Chemist & assoc supt pharmaceut lab, T W Wu & Co, China, 46-49; asst, Ind Univ, 53-56; biochemist, Toledo Hosp Inst Med Res, Ohio, 58-63; asst prof, 64-69, assoc prof, 69-80, PROF RADIOL, UNIV IOWA, 80- *Concurrent Pos:* Fel, Univ Wis, 56-58. *Mem:* AAAS; Am Chem Soc; Am Acad Allergy; Soc Nuclear Med. *Res:* Radiobiology. *Mailing Add:* Dept of Nuclear Med Univ of Iowa Hosp Iowa City IA 52242

CHENG, FRANKLIN YIH, b Shanghai, China, July 1, 36; m 63; c 2. STRUCTURAL ENGINEERING, ENGINEERING MECHANICS. *Educ:* Cheng Kung Univ, Taiwan, BSc, 60; Univ Ill, Champaign, MSc, 62; Univ Wis-Madison, PhD(civil eng), 66. *Prof Exp:* Struct engr, C F Murphy Architects & Engrs, Ill, 62-63 & Sargent & Lundy Engrs, 63; from asst prof to assoc prof struct eng, 66-76, PROF STRUCT ENG, UNIV MO-ROLLA, 76-; STRUCT ENGR, LOS ALAMOS NAT LAB, NMEX, 81- *Concurrent Pos:* Res grant, Nat Sci Found, Univ Mo-Rolla, 67-81; Hon prof, Horbin Civil Eng Inst; hon fel, Univ Wis. *Mem:* Am Soc Civil Engrs; Am Soc Eng Educ; Am Concrete Inst; Sigma Xi. *Res:* Dynamics in elastic earthquake structures; finite element method in continuum mechanics; plastic behavior of tall buildings; dynamic instability of stochastic excitations; nonlinear and random vibrations; optimum structeral design. *Mailing Add:* Dept of Civil Eng Univ of Mo Rolla MO 65401

CHENG, GEORGE CHIWO, b China, Sept 7, 29; US citizen; m 70; c 1. BIOMEDICAL ENGINEERING, ELECTRICAL ENGINEERING. *Educ:* South China Univ, BA, 53; Mont State Univ, MS, 60. *Prof Exp:* Res assoc, Electronics Res Lab, Mont State Univ, 59-61; asst prof elec eng, Southeastern Mass Tech Inst, 61-62; sr res scientist, 63-68, head biomath div, Nat Biomed Res Found, 68-71; consult, Toshiba Res & Develop Ctr, Japan, 71-72; assoc prof, 73-74, EXEC STAFF, COMP SCI CORP, UNIV FLA, 80-; CONSULT AUTOMATIC MED DATA PROCESSING & INT TECHNOL EXCHANGE, 74- *Concurrent Pos:* Vis lectr, Southeastern Mass Tech Inst, 62-; managing ed, Pattern Recognition Soc Jour. *Mem:* AAAS; Am Soc Eng Educ; Pattern Recognition Soc. *Res:* Information processing; pattern recognition; microelectronics and billiongate computer design; nervous system simulation; automatic medical data processing; pictorial data processing by computers; innovation management; international technology exchange. *Mailing Add:* 1177 Janaf Pl Norfolk VA 23502

CHENG, H(SIEN) K(EI), b Macau, South China, June 13, 23; nat US; m 56; c 1. FLUID MECHANICS, APPLIED MATHEMATICS. *Educ:* Chiao Tung Univ, BSc, 47; Cornell Univ, MSc, 50, PhD(aeronaut eng), 52. *Prof Exp:* Aerodynamic engr, Bell Aircraft Corp, 52-56; res aerodynamicist, Cornell Aeronaut Lab Inc, Cornell Univ, 56-57, prin aerodynamicist, 57-63; lectr, Stanford Univ, 63-64; spec lectr, 64-65, PROF AEROSPACE ENG, UNIV SOUTHERN CALIF, 65- *Mem:* Am Inst Aeronaut & Astronaut; Am Phys Soc. *Res:* Theory of subsonic, transonic, supersonic and hypersonic flows; theoretical gas dynamics; geophysical fluid dynamics; mechanics of animal swimming, flying and soaring; singular-perturbation problems in fluid mechanics. *Mailing Add:* Dept Aerospace Eng Univ Southern Calif Univ Park Los Angeles CA 90007

CHENG, HAZEL PEI-LING, b Hong Kong; Can citizen. GASTROENTEROLOGY, CELL BIOLOGY. *Educ:* McGill Univ, BSc, 67, MSc, 69, PhD(anat), 72. *Prof Exp:* Lectr anat, McGill Univ, 72-73; res staff cell biol, Yale Univ, 73-75; ASST PROF ANAT, UNIV ILL, URBANA, 75- *Concurrent Pos:* Adj res assoc cell biol, Rockefeller Univ, 73. *Mem:* Am Asn Anatomists; Am Soc Cell Biol; Am Asn Cell Biologists. *Res:* Biological mechanism involved in the origin, differentiation and renewal of the four main epithelial cell types in the mouse small intestine. *Mailing Add:* Sch of Basic Med Sci Med Sci Bldg Univ Ill Urbana IL 61801

CHENG, HSIANG-SHOU, nuclear engineering, electrical engineering, see previous edition

CHENG, HSIEN HUA, b Shantung, China, Jan 3, 35; Canadian citizen; m 63; c 4. ENTOMOLOGY, INSECT ECOLOGY. *Educ:* Nat Taiwan Univ, BSc, 59; McGill Univ, MSc, 65, PhD(insect ecol), 67. *Prof Exp:* Coordr, Taiwan Sugar Corp, 61-63; instr entom, Nat Taiwan Univ, 63; RES SCIENTIST ENTOM, RES STA AGR CAN, 67- *Mem:* Entom Soc Can; Entom Soc Am. *Res:* Ecology, bionomics and control of tobacco insects. *Mailing Add:* Res Sta Agr Can PO Box 186 Delhi ON N4B 2W9 Can

CHENG, HUNG-YUAN, Taipei, Taiwan, May 12, 50; China citizen; m 75; c 1. ELECTROCHEMISTRY, NEUROCHEMISTRY. *Educ:* Nat Tsing Hua Univ, Taiwan, BS, 72, Ohio State Univ, PhD(anal chem), 78. *Prof Exp:* Teaching asst chem, Ohio State Univ, 74-76, res asst, 76-78; res assoc anal & neuro chem, Univ Kans, 78-80; ASST PROF CHEM, UNIV MD, COLLEGE PARK, 80- *Mem:* Am Chem Soc. *Res:* Development of electroanalytical techniques for neurochemical applications, especially in the field of brain research. *Mailing Add:* Dept Chem Univ Md College Park MD 20742

CHENG, HWEI-HSIEN, b Shanghai, China, Aug 13, 32; US citizen; m 62; c 2. SOIL CHEMISTRY, BIOCHEMISTRY. *Educ:* Berea Col, BA, 56; Univ Ill, MS, 58, PhD(agron), 61. *Prof Exp:* Res assoc soil chem, Univ Ill, 61-62; soil biochem, Iowa State Univ, 62-63, asst prof, 64-65; Fulbright res scholar & collab soil chem, soils res ctr, State Agr Univ, Belgium, 63-64; from asst prof to assoc prof soils, 65-77, chmn, prog environ sci & regional planning, 77-79, PROF SOILS & CHMN PROG ENVIRON SCI, WASH STATE UNIV, 77- *Concurrent Pos:* Guest scientist, Julich Nuclear Res Ctr, Ger, 72-73, 74 & 79-80, Acad Sinica, Repub China, 78 & Fed Agr Res Ctr, Braunschweig, Ger, 80. *Mem:* AAAS; Soc Environ Toxicol Chem; Soil Sci Soc Am; Am Chem Soc; Am Soc Agron. *Res:* Fractionation and distribution of nitrogen in soils; methods for use of nitrogen-15 and carbon-14 in soils research; movement and transformation of pesticides in soils; soil organic matter turnover. *Mailing Add:* Dept of Agron & Soils Wash State Univ Pullman WA 99164

CHENG, KANG, b Kwei-Young, China, Feb 17, 46; m 71; c 1. ENDOCRINOLOGY, DIABETES. *Educ:* Nat Taiwan Univ, BS, 68; State Univ NY Albany, MS, 72; Mt Sinai Sch Med, PhD(biochem), 77. *Prof Exp:* Res fel, Sloan-Kettering Inst Cancer Res, 77-79; RES ASST PROF, DEPT PHARMACOL, UNIV VA, 79- *Mem:* Sigma Xi. *Res:* Effect of insulin, extracellular ions and membrane potential on amino acid transport; glycogen synthane and pyruvate dehydrogenase in isolated rat adipocytes. *Mailing Add:* Dept Pharmacol Univ Va Charlottesville VA 22908

CHENG, KIMBERLY MING-TAK, b Hong Kong, Feb 22, 48; Brit citizen; m 76. AVIAN BEHAVIOR, POULTRY BREEDING. *Educ:* Tenn Technol Univ, BS, 69; Southern Ill Univ, MS, 71; Univ Minn, PhD(poultry breeding), 78. *Prof Exp:* Res specialist waterfowl behav, James Ford Bell Mus Natural Hist, Univ Minn, 78-80; ASST PROF POULTRY GENETICS & BEHAV, DEPT POULTRY SCI, UNIV BC, 80- *Mem:* Animal Behavior Soc; Poultry Sci Asn; Sigma Xi; AAAS; Am Ornothologists Union. *Res:* Evolution of waterfowl reproductive behavior; genetic changes affecting behavior associated with domestication; early imprinting and mate preference; development of animal models for research; propagation of endangered waterfowl species. *Mailing Add:* Dept Poultry Sci Univ BC Vancouver BC V6T 2A2 Can

CHENG, KUANG LIU, b Chuhsien, Chekiang, China, July 9, 19; nat US; m 49; c 2. MECHANICS, PHYSICS. *Educ:* Ordnance Eng Col, China, BS, 47; Va Polytech Inst, MS, 58, PhD(eng mech), 61. *Prof Exp:* From asst to assoc engr, Chinese Govt Arsenal, 47-56; sr engr, Burroughs Res Ctr, 60-64; res physicist, Cent Res Dept, Lord Corp, 64-66, sr physicist, 66-67, res assoc, 67-72, sr tech assoc, 72-75. *Mem:* AAAS; Soc Rheol. *Res:* Solid state magnetic ink; superconductivity and cryotronics; thermoelasticity; viscoelasticity; electroelasticity; mechanical properties of high polymers. *Mailing Add:* 2432 W 36th St Erie PA 16506

CHENG, KUANG LU, b Yangchow, China, Sept 14, 19; nat US. ANALYTICAL CHEMISTRY. *Educ:* Northwestern Col, BS, 41; Univ Ill, MS, 49, PhD(soil chem), 51. *Prof Exp:* Fel, Univ Ill, 51-52; microchemist, Com Solvents Corp, 52-53; instr chem, Univ Conn, 53-55; engr, Westinghouse Elec Corp, 55-57; assoc dir res, Metals Div, Kelsey-Hayes Co, 57-59; mem tech staff, Labs, Radio Corp Am, 59-66; PROF CHEM, UNIV MO-KANSAS CITY, 66- *Mem:* Fel AAAS; Am Chem Soc; Electrochem Soc; Soc Appl Spectros. *Res:* Photoelectron spectroscopy; ion selective electrodes; ligand chromatography. *Mailing Add:* Dept of Chem Univ of Mo Kansas City MO 64110

CHENG, KUANG-FU, b Taipei, Taiwan. NONPARAMETRIC INFERENCE, APPLIED PROBABILITY. *Educ:* Nat Tsing-Hua Univ, Taipei, Taiwan, BS, 74; Fla State Univ, MS, 77, PhD(statist), 79. *Prof Exp:* ASST PROF STATIST, STATE UNIV NY BUFFALO, 79- *Concurrent Pos:* Prin investr, State Univ NY Res Found, 80-82. *Mem:* Inst Math Statist; Am Statist Asn. *Res:* Nonparametric regression methods; density estimation; inference based on censored data; jackknifed statistics; nonparametric inference from fragmentary samples. *Mailing Add:* Dept Statist State Univ NY Buffalo 4230 Ridge Lea Rd Amberst NY 14226

CHENG, KUO-JOAN, b Taiwan, China, Dec 9, 40; m 68; c 2. AGRICULTURAL MICROBIOLOGY. *Educ:* Nat Taiwan Univ, BS, 63; Univ Sask, MS, 66, PhD(microbiol), 69. *Prof Exp:* Res asst dairy & food sci, Univ Sask, 64-66; Nat Res Coun Can fel microbiol, MacDonald Col, McGill Univ, 69-71; RUMINANT MICROBIOLOGIST, ANIMAL SCI SECT, RES STA, CAN DEPT AGR, 71- *Concurrent Pos:* Vis scientist, Rowett Res Inst, Scotland, 78-79. *Mem:* Am Soc Microbiol; Can Soc Microbiol; Am Soc Animal Sci; Can Soc Animal Sci; Agr Inst Can. *Res:* Coliform bacteria in Canadian diary products; degradation of rutin and related flavonoids by anaerobic rumen bacteria; studies on the localization and the role of periplasmic enzymes in bacterial cell; microbiology and biochemistry of digestion in the rumen; ecomicrobiology of digestive tracts of ruminant animals; microbial adhesion in nature and disease. *Mailing Add:* Animal Sci Sect Res Sta of Can Dept of Agr Lethbridge AB T1J 4B1 Can

CHENG, KWOK-TSANG, b Hong Kong, May 5, 50; m 75. ATOMIC PHYSICS. *Educ:* Chinese Univ Hong Kong, BSc, 71; Univ Notre Dame, PhD(physics), 77. *Prof Exp:* RESEARCHER PHYSICS, ARGONNE NAT LAB, 77- *Mem:* Am Phys Soc. *Res:* Relativistic atomic structure calculations; interactions between atoms and radiation fields. *Mailing Add:* Physics Bldg 203 Argonne Nat Lab Argonne IL 60439

CHENG, LANNA, b Singapore, Apr 27, 41; m 69. MARINE ZOOLOGY, MARINE BIOLOGY. *Educ:* Univ Singapore, BSc, 63, hons, 64, MSc, 66; Oxford Univ, DPhil(entom), 69. *Prof Exp:* Nat Res Coun Can fel biol, Univ Waterloo, 68-69; Am Asn Univ Women fel, 69-70; res assoc, 70-72, asst res biologist, 72-77, ASSOC RES BIOLOGIST, SCRIPPS INST OCEANOG, UNIV CALIF, SAN DIEGO, 77- *Mem:* Orgn Trop Studies; fel Royal Entom Soc London; Western Soc Naturalists; Am Soc Limnol & Oceanog; Entom Soc Am. *Res:* Taxonomic and biological studies of aquatic insects especially Gerridae, Hemiptera; population ecology; host-parasite relationships; physiological adaptations of insects to marine environments; ecology of marine insects; pleuston; animals of the sea-air interface; entomology. *Mailing Add:* A-002 Scripps Inst of Oceanog Univ of Calif San Diego La Jolla CA 92093

CHENG, LAWRENCE KAR-HIU, b Hong Kong, July 25, 47. PHARMACEUTICS. *Educ:* Univ Calif, Santa Barbara, BS, 71; State Univ NY Buffalo, PhD(pharmaceut), 75. *Prof Exp:* Anal chemist pharmaceut, Stuart Pharmaceut, ICI US Inc, 75-80; GROUP MGR, DRUG METAB DEPT, A H ROBINS CO, 81- *Mem:* Am Pharmaceut Asn; AAAS; NY Acad Sci; Am Chem Soc. *Res:* Analytical methods development for drugs and metabolites in the biological tissues and dosage forms; pharmacokinetics of drugs and other pharmacologically active chemicals; bioequivalency studies of new formulations in vivo-in vitro biotransformation of drugs. *Mailing Add:* Drug Metab Dept A H Robbins Co 1211 Sherwood Ave Richmond VA 23220

CHENG, LESTER (LE-CHUNG), b China, Apr 20, 44; US citizen; m 69; c 2. THERMAL SCIENCE, BIOENGINEERING. *Educ:* Nat Taiwan Univ, BS, 65; NDak State Univ, MS, 68; Univ Ill, Urbana, PhD(mech), 71. *Prof Exp:* Res assoc mech, Dept Theoret & Appl Mech, Univ Ill, Urbana, 70-71; sr engr analyst mech eng, Sargent & Lundy Engrs, Chicago, 71-74; sr engr, Gen Atomic Co, San Diego, 74-76; asst prof, 76-79, ASSOC PROF MECH ENG, WICHITA STATE UNIV, 79- *Concurrent Pos:* Consult, Dept Theoret & Appl Mech, Univ Ill, Urbana, 74-76; prin investr NSF grant, 77-80; consult, Vet Admin Ctr, Wichita, Kans, 78-; consult, Kans Energy & Environ Lab, Wichita, 78- *Honors & Awards:* Ralph R Teetor Award, Soc Automotive Eng, 80. *Mem:* Am Acad Mech; Sigma Xi; Am Soc Mech Engr; Am Soc Engr Educ. *Res:* Bio-fluid mechanics; mechanical system analysis; energy. *Mailing Add:* Dept of Mech Eng Wichita State Univ Wichita KS 67208

CHENG, LI-JEN, experimental solid state physics, see previous edition

CHENG, PAUL J(IH) T(IEN), b Hsilo, Taiwan, Dec 13, 35; m 66. CHEMICAL ENGINEERING. *Educ:* Nat Taiwan Univ, BS, 58; Univ Utah, PhD(chem eng), 67. *Prof Exp:* Res asst, Univ Utah, 61, 62-67; res engr, 67-68; SR RES ENGR, PHILLIPS PETROL CO, 68- *Mem:* Am Inst Chem Engrs; Am Chem Soc. *Res:* Non-Newtonian behaviors of solid-liquid mixtures; reaction behaviors of solid composite propellants; pyrolysis of polymers; carbon black process innovations; improvements, optimization and exploration of new reaction process technology; process models and computer simulation. *Mailing Add:* 2901 SE Greenwood Ct Bartlesville OK 74003

CHENG, PING, b Canton, China; US citizen; c 2. HEAT TRANSFER, FLUID MECHANICS. *Educ:* Okla State Univ, BS, 58; Mass Inst Technol, MS, 60; Stanford Univ, PhD(aeronaut & astronaut), 65. *Prof Exp:* Res assoc aeronaut & astronaut, Stanford Univ, 64-65; res scientist aeronaut & astronaut, NY Univ, 65-67; res assoc, NASA Ames Res Ctr, 67-68; vis prof mech eng, Nat Taiwan Univ, 68-70; assoc prof, 70-74, PROF MECH ENG, UNIV HAWAII, 74- *Concurrent Pos:* Vis prof petrol eng, Stanford Univ, 76-77; prin investr, NSF grants, 77- *Honors & Awards:* Chungshan Award, Chungshan Found, Taipei, Taiwan, 69. *Mem:* Am Soc Mech Engrs; Sigma Xi. *Res:* Convective and boiling heat transfer in porous media and geothermal systems; well test analyses and geothermal reservoir engineering; radiative heat transfer and solar energy. *Mailing Add:* 717 Olohena St Honolulu HI 96825

CHENG, R(ICHARD) K(UO-WEI), electrical engineering, see previous edition

CHENG, RALPH T(A-SHUN), b Shanghai, China, Sept 26, 38; m 63; c 2. FLUID DYNAMICS, APPLIED MATHEMATICS. *Educ:* Nat Taiwan Univ, BS, 61; Univ Calif, Berkeley, MS, 64, PhD(mech eng), 67. *Prof Exp:* Asst prof mech eng, State Univ, NY Buffalo, 67-77; MEM STAFF, US GEOL SURV, 77- *Concurrent Pos:* Proj dir, NSF res grant, 69-; consult, Cornell Aeronaut Lab, 68-70. *Mem:* Am Inst Aeronaut & Astronaut; Am Phys Soc; Am Geophys Union. *Res:* Fluid dynamics, especially numerical modeling; thermodynamics; numerical solutions of nonlinear differential equations; geophysical fluid dynamics; transport processes in the atmosphere. *Mailing Add:* Calif Dist Off US Geol Surv Menlo Park CA 94025

CHENG, RICHARD M H, b Hong Kong; Can citizen. CONTROL ENGINEERING, INDUSTRIAL AUTOMATION. *Educ:* Hong Kong Univ, BSc, 61; Univ Manchester Inst Sci & Technol, MSc, 67; Birmingham Univ, PhD(control eng), 71. *Prof Exp:* Lectr mech eng, Birmingham Univ, Eng, 69-72; assoc prof, 72-78, PROF MECH ENG, CONCORDIA UNIV, CAN, 78- *Concurrent Pos:* Grad engr, Brit Leyland Motor Corp, Longbridge, Birmingham, Eng, 65-66; air advan systs, Dynamic Sci Ltd, St Laurent, Can, 79-80; consult, var govt bodies & corps including Can Nat Railways. *Mem:* Brit Inst Mech Engrs; Am Soc Mech Engrs; Inst Elec & Electron Engrs; sr mem Inst Soc Am; Can Indust Comput Soc. *Res:* Applying fluid mechanics, electronics, mini & microcomputer to industrial control & automation problems; pneumatic brake systems of freight trains; microprocessor-based fuel control of small gas turbines; micro-computer based simulation of process control circuits; computer-aided design using interactive colour graphics. *Mailing Add:* Fluid Control Ctr H833 Concordia Univ De Maisonneuve Blvd W Montreal PQ H3G 1M8 Can

CHENG, SHANG I, b Chiete, Chekiang, China, June 5, 20; US citizen; m 41; c 5. CHEMICAL ENGINEERING. *Educ:* Chekiang Univ, BS, 45; Univ Fla, MS, 59, PhD(chem eng), 61. *Prof Exp:* Chem engr, Hsinchu Res Inst, Taiwan, 45-54; supvr res & develop, Union Indust Res Inst, 54-58; develop scientist, B F Goodrich Chem Co, 61-65; from asst prof to assoc prof, 65-70, PROF CHEM ENG, COOPER UNION, 70- *Concurrent Pos:* Consult, Nat Sci Coun, Repub of China, 74- *Honors & Awards:* Award Syst Design, NASA, 74. *Mem:* Am Inst Chem Engrs; Am Chem Soc. *Res:* Mass transfer and reactor engineering; computer simulation; polymerization kinetics; air pollution abatement; solid waste recycle; energy conservation. *Mailing Add:* 17 Woodsend Dr Matawan NJ 07747

CHENG, SHEUE-YANN, chemistry, biology, see previous edition

CHENG, SHUN, b China, July 10, 19; US citizen; m 47. ENGINEERING MECHANICS. *Educ:* Univ Wis-Madison, PhD(eng mech), 59. *Prof Exp:* Asst prof mech, Univ Dayton, 54-56; from instr to assoc prof eng mech, 56-72, PROF ENG MECH, UNIV WIS-MADISON, 72- *Mem:* AAAS; Am Soc Mech Engrs; Am Inst Aeronaut & Astronaut. *Res:* Solid mechanics; structures. *Mailing Add:* Dept Eng Mech Col Eng Univ Wis Madison WI 53706

CHENG, SHU-SING, b Kwangtung, China, Sept 7, 23. ORGANIC CHEMISTRY, MICROBIOLOGY. *Educ:* Nat Col Pharm, Nanking, BS, 47; Univ NC, MS, 59, PhD(pharmaceut chem), 61. *Prof Exp:* Res assoc virol, Sch Med, Univ NC, 60-62; res fel steroid biochem, Worcester Found Exp Biol, 62-63; res asst prof med chem & biochem, Univ NC, 63-65; HEAD MICROBIOL RES, KENDALL RES CTR, KENDALL CO, 66- *Mem:* AAAS; Am Chem Soc; Am Pharmaceut Asn; Am Soc Microbiol. *Res:* Design and synthesis of organic compounds of medicinal interest; chemistry and biochemistry of steroids; tissue culture and microbiology; screening of antimicrobial agents; process research in cold sterilization and monitoring devices. *Mailing Add:* 1820 Laurel Ave Hanover Park IL 60103

CHENG, SIN-I, b China, Dec 28, 21; US citizen; m 49; c 3. AERONAUTICS. *Educ:* Chiao Tung Univ, BS, 46; Univ Mich, MS, 49; Princeton Univ, MA & PhD(aeronaut eng), 52. *Prof Exp:* From instr to assoc prof, 51-60, PROF AERONAUT ENG, PRINCETON UNIV, 60- *Concurrent Pos:* Fel, Chinese Ministry Educ, 48-49; Guggenheim fel, 49-51. *Mem:* Assoc fel Am Inst Aeronaut & Astronaut; Combustion Inst. *Res:* Rocketry; combustion; fluid mechanics; propulsion; aerodynamics. *Mailing Add:* Dept of Mech & Aerospace Eng Princeton Univ Princeton NJ 08540

CHENG, SZE-CHUH, b Soochow, China, Nov 11, 21; US citizen; m; c 3. NEUROCHEMISTRY, BIOLOGY. *Educ:* Southwest Assoc Univ, China, BSc, 43; Brown Univ, MSc, 49; Univ Pa, PhD(gen physiol), 54. *Prof Exp:* Res asst gen physiol, Tsinghua Univ, Peking, 43-47; res assoc neurophysiol, Rockefeller Univ, 55-60; sr res scientist neurochem, NY State Psychiat Inst, 60-64; sr res scientist neurochem, NY State Res Inst Neurochem & Drug Addiction, 65-71; ASSOC PROF ANESTHESIOL, SCH MED, NORTHWESTERN UNIV, CHICAGO, 71- *Concurrent Pos:* Fel, McCollum-Pratt Inst, Johns Hopkins Univ, 53-55; Pub Health Serv spec fel, Agr Res Coun Inst Animal Physiol, Babraham, Eng, 64-65. *Mem:* Am Soc Neurochem; Soc Neurosci. *Res:* Metabolism and function of nervous tissue including drug effects. *Mailing Add:* Dept of Anesthesia Northwestern Univ Sch of Med Chicago IL 60611

CHENG, TAI CHUN, b Shanghai, China; US citizen; m 64; c 2. ORGANIC POLYMER CHEMISTRY, ORGANOMETALLIC CHEMISTRY. *Educ:* Tunghai Univ, BS, 60; Wash State Univ, PhD(chem), 68. *Prof Exp:* Res assoc chem, Univ Notre Dame, 67-68; res scientist, Firestone Tire & Rubber, 68-75, sr res scientist polymers, 75-81; MEM SR STAFF, RAYCHEM CORP, 81- *Mem:* Am Chem Soc; Sigma Xi. *Res:* Basic understanding of polymers and fillers; synthesis of specialty polymer such as phosphazene polymer; new polymers and monomers synthesis; mechanism study of radical anion and aryl halides; synthesis and kinetic study of organoboron compounds; conductive polymer synthesis and application. *Mailing Add:* Res & Develop Raychem Corp 300 Constitution Menlo Park CA 94025

CHENG, TA-PEI, b Shanghai, China; US citizen. THEORETICAL PHYSICS. *Educ:* Dartmouth Col, AB, 64; Rockefeller Univ, PhD(physics), 69. *Prof Exp:* Mem, Inst Advan Study, 69-71; res assoc, Rockefeller Univ, 71-73; from asst prof to assoc prof, 73-78, chmn, Physics Dept, 78-79, PROF PHYSICS, UNIV MO-ST LOUIS, 78- *Concurrent Pos:* Vis assoc prof physics, Princeton Univ, 77-78; mem, Inst Advan Study, 77-78; vis prof physics, Univ Minn, 79-80. *Mem:* Am Phys Soc. *Res:* Gauge theories of weak, electromagnetic and strong interactions. *Mailing Add:* Dept of Physics Univ of Mo St Louis MO 63121

CHENG, THOMAS CLEMENT, biology, see previous edition

CHENG, TSEN-CHUNG, b Shanghai, China, Dec 24, 44; US citizen; m 74; c 1. ELECTRIC POWER SYSTEMS, DIELECTRIC MATERIALS. *Educ:* Mass Inst Technol, BS, 69, MS, 70, ScD, 74. *Prof Exp:* Asst prof, 74-80, ASSOC PROF & DIR ELEC POWER ENG, UNIV SOUTHERN CALIF, 80- *Concurrent Pos:* Sr consult, Southern Calif Edison Co, 79-, Failure Anal Assocs, 80- & Pac Gas & Elec Co, Idaho Power Co & Portland Gen Elec Co, 81-; pres, T C Cheng, ScD, Inc, 81-; prin investr, Res Proj, Dept Water & Power, Elec Power Res Inst, Elec Utilities, 75- *Mem:* Inst Elec & Electronics Engrs; Sigma Xi; Conf Int des Grands Reseaux Electriques. *Res:* High voltage insulation and breakdown, dielectrics and materials properties; author or coauthor of over 40 papers. *Mailing Add:* Dept Elec Eng Univ Southern Calif Los Angeles CA 90007

CHENG, TSUNG O, b Shanghai, China, Mar 30, 25; nat US; m; c 2. CARDIOLOGY. *Educ:* St Johns Univ, China, BS, 47; Pa Med Sch, China, MD, 50; Univ Pa, MMedSc, 56; Am Bd Internal Med, dipl, 61; Am Bd Cardiovasc Dis, dipl, 63. *Prof Exp:* Intern, Hosp St Barnabas, NJ, 50-51; resident internal med, Cook County Hosp, Ill, 52-55; asst cardiol, Mass Gen Hosp, 56-57; asst physician, Cardiac Clin, Johns Hopkins Hosp, 57-59; dir cardiopulmonary lab, Brooklyn Hosp & asst prof med, State Univ NY Downstate Med Ctr, 59-70; dir cardiovasc lab & chief cardiol, Vet Admin Hosp, Brooklyn, 66-70; assoc prof, Sch Med, 70-72, PROF MED, SCH MED & DIR CARDIAC CATHETERIZATION LAB, MED CTR, GEORGE WASHINGTON UNIV, 72- *Concurrent Pos:* Fel Northwestern Univ, 54-55; fel cardiol, Sch Med, George Washington Univ, 55-56; res fel cardiopulmonary physiol, Johns Hopkins Univ & Hosp, 57-59, Am Heart Asn advan res fel, 58-59; consult & chief pediat cardiac clin, Cumberland Hosp, 63-66; asst vis physician, Kings County Hosp, 64-70; fel coun clin cardiol, Am Heart Asn, 64-; consult, Beth Israel Hosp, New York, 70-; chief cardiol, DC Gen Hosp, 71-72. *Mem:* Fel Am Col Physicians; fel Am Col Cardiol; AMA; fel Am Col Chest Physicians; fel Int Col Angiol. *Res:* Clinical investigations in cardiopulmonary pathophysiology in health and diseases. *Mailing Add:* Med Ctr George Washington Univ Washington DC 20037

CHENG, WILLIAM J(EN) P(U), b Changsha, China, Sept 26, 15; m 54; c 4. CHEMICAL ENGINEERING. *Educ:* Tsing Hua Univ, China, BS, 39; Washington Univ, St Louis, MS, 51. *Prof Exp:* Asst, Tsing Hua Inst, China, 39-40; asst chem engr, China Veg Oil Corp, 40-41, chem engr & plant supt, 42-44; chem engr, arsenal, Chinese Army, 45-47; sr res chem engr, Petrolite Corp, 53-58, group leader, 58-60, head pilot plant, 60-63, mgr eng res, 63-67, DIR ENG, TRETOLITE DIV, PETROLITE CORP, 67- *Mem:* Am Chem Soc; Am Inst Chem Engrs; NY Acad Sci. *Res:* Petroleum and demulsification; chemicals for petroleum production; synthetic resin and high polymers; industrial surfactants; organic unit process; process development, design and

optimization. *Mailing Add:* Tretolite Div Petrolite Corp 369 Marshall St St Louis MO 63119

CHENG, WU-CHIEH, b Shanghai, China, Aug 11, 22; US citizen; m 63; c 1. PHYSICAL CHEMISTRY, PHYSICS. *Educ:* St John's Univ, China, BS, 44; Kans State Col, MS, 49; Ga Inst Technol, PhD(phys chem), 54. *Prof Exp:* From asst prof to prof chem, Union Univ, 55-66, head dept, 58-66; assoc prof, George Peabody Col, 66-72; teacher rank I, Lyman High Sch, Longwood Fla, 72-75; asst prof, 75-76, ASSOC PROF PHYSICS, PAINE COL, 76- *Concurrent Pos:* Vis instr, Ga Inst Technol, 56. *Mem:* AAAS; Am Chem Soc; Am Inst Chem; Sigma Xi; Am Asn Physics Teachers. *Res:* Molecular structure; chemical education; spectroscopy; ion-exchange equilibria; starch derivatives; metabolism of unsaturated fatty acids; synthetic resins and plastics. *Mailing Add:* Paine Col Box 115 1235 15th St Augusta GA 30910

CHENG, YEAN FU, b Foochow, China, Oct 19, 24; nat US; m 53; c 2. MECHANICS, MECHANICAL ENGINEERING. *Educ:* Nat Amoy Univ, China, BS, 46; Univ Wash, Seattle, MS, 57; Ill Inst Technol, PhD(mech), 61. *Prof Exp:* Engr, Ministry Commun, China, 46-56; res assoc, Ill Inst Technol, 61; mem res staff, Boeing Sci Res Labs, Wash, 61-71; mech engr, Benet Res & Eng Lab, Watervliet Arsenal, 71-77; MECH ENGR, BENET WEAPONS LAB, LARGE CALIBER WEAPON SYSTS LAB, ARMAMENT RES & DEVELOP COMMAND, US ARMY, 77- *Mem:* Am Soc Mech Engrs; Am Acad Mech; Soc Exp Stress Anal. *Res:* Photoelasticity; strength of materials; solid mechanics. *Mailing Add:* Benet Weapons Lab Watervliet Arsenal Watervliet NY 12189

CHENG, YIU CHUNG PATRICK, solid state physics, semiconductor physics, see previous edition

CHENG, YUNG-CHI, b Eng, Dec 29, 44; Chinese citizen; m 69; c 2. BIOCHEMICAL PHARMACOLOGY. *Educ:* Tunghai Univ, Taiwan, BSc, 66; Brown Univ, PhD(biochem pharmacol), 72. *Prof Exp:* Fel pharmacol, Yale Univ, 72-73, res assoc, 73-74; asst prof, 74-77, ASSOC PROF PHARMACOL, STATE UNIV NY BUFFALO, 77-; CANCER RES SCIENTIST V, ROSWELL PARK MEM RES INST, 76- *Concurrent Pos:* Am leukemia scholar, 76-81; Am Leukemia Scholar, 76-81; prof, Dept Pharmacol, Univ NC, Chapel Hill, 78- *Honors & Awards:* Rhoads Mem Award, 81. *Mem:* Am Soc Biochem; Am Soc Microbiol; Am Soc Pharmacol & Exp Therapeut. *Res:* Development and use of nucleoside analogs for cancer and viral chemotherapy. *Mailing Add:* Dept of Exp Therapeut Roswell Park Mem Res Inst Buffalo NY 14263

CHENGALATH, RAMA, b Calicut, India; Can citizen. HYDROBIOLOGY. *Educ:* Univ Kerala, India, BSc, 62, MSc, 64; Univ Waterloo, Can, MSc, 71. *Prof Exp:* Res biologist, Can Aquatic Identification Ctr, 76; special lectr biol, Trent Univ, Ont, 76; prin investr res, Sci Ctr, Supply & Serv Can, 76-80; INVERT ZOOLOGIST, NAT MUS NATURAL SCI, 80- *Mem:* Can Soc Zoologists; Soc Int Limnologists; Can Soc Environ Biologists; Crustacean Soc; Can Soc Limnologists. *Res:* Taxonomy, ecology and distribution of rotifera and cladocera. *Mailing Add:* Invert Zool Div Nat Mus Natural Sci Ottawa ON K1A 0M8 Can

CHENIAE, GEORGE MAURICE, b Mounds, Ill, Aug 27, 28; m 52; c 3. PLANT BIOCHEMISTRY. *Educ:* Univ Ill, BS, 50; NC State Col, MS, 57, PhD(plant physiol), 59. *Prof Exp:* Asst, Oak Ridge Nat Lab, 50-52; Nat Sci fel, 59-60; res scientist, Res Inst Advan Study, 60-75; PROF AGRON, UNIV KY, 75- *Mem:* Am Soc Plant Physiologists; Am Soc Biol Chemists. *Res:* Lipid metabolism; respiration; photosynthesis. *Mailing Add:* Dept Agron Univ Ky Lexington KY 40546

CHENICEK, ALBERT GEORGE, b Chicago, Ill, Dec 15, 13; m 43; c 3. POLYMER CHEMISTRY. *Educ:* Univ Chicago, BS, 34, PhD(org chem), 37. *Prof Exp:* Res chemist, Columbis Chem Div, Pittsburgh Plate Glass Co, Ohio, 37-41 & Interchem Corp, 41-53; actg dir develop, Standard Coated Prods, Inc, 53-56; mgr res, Stoner-Mudge Co, 56-61; PRES, UNIFILM CORP, 61- *Mem:* AAAS; Am Chem Soc. *Res:* Chlorination of organic compounds; synthetic resins; coated fabrics; protective coatings; inks. *Mailing Add:* Unifilm Corp 60 Cornell Blvd Somerville NJ 08876

CHENOT, CHARLES FREDERIC, b Canton, Ohio, Sept 16, 38; m 62; c 4. SOLID STATE CHEMISTRY. *Educ:* Col Wooster, BA, 60; Univ Cincinnati, PhD(phys chem), 64. *Prof Exp:* ENG SPECIALIST, CHEM & METALL DIV, GTE SYLVANIA INC, 64- *Mem:* Am Ceramic Soc; Am Chem Soc; Electrochem Soc. *Res:* Physical chemical studies of diffusion in the solid state; research and development of solid state luminescent materials including phase equilibrium relationships, solid state reactions and associated luminescence spectroscopy. *Mailing Add:* Chem & Metall Div GTE Sylvania Inc Box 70 Towanda PA 18848

CHENOWETH, DARREL LEE, b Indianapolis, Ind, Nov 6, 41; m 63; c 2. CONTROL SYSTEMS. *Educ:* Auburn Univ, MS, 64, PhD(elec eng), 69; Gen Motors Inst, BEE, 65. *Prof Exp:* Instr elec eng, Auburn Univ, 67-68; eng specialist, Vought Aeronaut Div, Ling-Temco-Vought Corp, Tex, 69-70; from asst prof to assoc prof, 70-78, PROF ELEC ENG, UNIV LOUISVILLE, 78- *Mem:* Sr mem Inst Elec & Electronics Engrs; Am Soc Elec Engrs. *Res:* Optimal control systems; application of optimal control theory to coupled hydraulic winch systems; sampled data control systems for space vehicles; quantization in digital control systems; digital control systems; microprocessors; digital signal processing. *Mailing Add:* Dept of Elec Eng Univ of Louisville Louisville KY 40208

CHENOWETH, JAMES MERL, b Dayton, Ohio, May 22, 24; m 49; c 2. MECHANICAL ENGINEERING. *Educ:* Purdue Univ, BS, 49, MS, 50, PhD(mech eng), 52. *Prof Exp:* Sr res engr two-phase flow, C F Braun & Co, 52-59; sr staff heat transfer, Nat Eng Sci Co, 59-66; sr staff mech eng, Survival Systs, Inc, 66-70; ASST TECH DIR, HEAT TRANSFER RES, INC, 70- *Mem:* Am Soc Mech Engrs; Sigma Xi; Survival & Flight Equip Asn. *Res:* Heat transfer and fluid mechanics; two-phase flow; flow-induced tube vibration. *Mailing Add:* Heat Transfer Res Inc 1000 S Fremont Ave Alhambra CA 91802

CHENOWETH, MAYNARD BURTON, b Chicago, Ill, Nov 25, 17; m 40; c 5. CLINICAL PHARMACOLOGY. *Educ:* Columbia Univ, BA, 38; Cornell Univ, MD, 42. *Prof Exp:* Asst prof pharmacol, Cornell Univ, 46-48; assoc prof, Univ Mich, 48-53; res scientist pharmacol, Dow Chem Co, 53-81. *Concurrent Pos:* Adj prof pharmacol, Mich Molecular Inst, 81- *Mem:* Am Soc Pharmacol & Exp Therapeut; Soc Toxicol; Soc Exp Biol & Med. *Res:* Study of new drugs or chemicals in man. *Mailing Add:* Dow Chem Co Midland MI 48640

CHENOWETH, PHILIP ANDREW, b Chicago, Ill, Aug 21, 19; m 52; c 2. GEOLOGY, STRATIGRAPHY. *Educ:* Columbia Univ, BA, 46, MA, 47, PhD, 49. *Prof Exp:* Instr geol, Amherst Col, 49-51; sr geologist, Sinclair Oil & Gas Co, 51-54; assoc prof geol, Univ Okla, 54-60; staff geologist, Sinclair Oil & Gas Co, 60-65; res assoc, Sinclair Res Ctr, 65-68; CONSULT GEOLOGIST, 54-60, 68- *Honors & Awards:* Prof Award, Univ Okla, 55. *Mem:* AAAS; fel Geol Soc Am; Am Asn Petrol Geologists; Am Inst Prof Geologists; Am Inst Mining, Metall & Petrol Eng. *Res:* Petroleum and exploration geology. *Mailing Add:* 1000 Petrol Club Bldg Sixth at Boulder Tulsa OK 74119

CHENOWETH, R(OBERT) D(EAN), b San Angelo, Tex, Oct 17, 26; m 47; c 4. ELECTRICAL ENGINEERING, POWER SYSTEM ANALYSIS. *Educ:* Agr & Mech Col, Tex, BS, 46, MS, 51; Ga Inst Technol, PhD, 55. *Prof Exp:* Student engr, Westinghouse Elec Corp, 46-47; asst prof & res asst, Agr & Mech Col, Tex, 47-52; asst prof elec eng, Ga Inst Technol, 53-55 & Case Inst Technol, 55-60; prof, Univ Mo, Rolla, 60-67; PROF ELEC ENG, TEX A&M UNIV, 67- *Concurrent Pos:* NSF fel, 52-53. *Mem:* Inst Elec & Electronics Engrs; Am Soc Eng Educ; Simulation Coun. *Res:* Power in electrical engineering; computers; control. *Mailing Add:* Dept Elec Eng Tex A&M Univ College Station TX 77843

CHENOWETH, WANDA L, b Salt Lake City, Utah. NUTRITION. *Educ:* Univ Utah, BS, 56; Univ Iowa, MS, 59; Univ Calif, Berkeley, PhD(nutrit), 72. *Prof Exp:* Res dietitian, Univ Iowa Hosps, 57-59 & Mayo Clin, 59-64; head therapeut dietitian, Univ Iowa Hosps, 64-67; teaching assoc nutrit, Univ Calif, Berkeley, 72; asst prof, 72-76, ASSOC PROF NUTRIT, MICH STATE UNIV, 76- *Concurrent Pos:* Consult, Diet, Nutrit & Cancer Prog, Nat Cancer Inst, 76-78. *Mem:* Am Dietetic Asn; Soc Nutrit Educ; Inst Food Technol. *Res:* Clinical nutrition; effect of diet and nutrition on gastrointestinal function; mineral metabolism; lipid metabolism. *Mailing Add:* Dept Food Sci & Human Nutrit Mich State Univ East Lansing MI 48824

CHENOWETH, WILLIAM LYMAN, b Wichita, Kans, Sept 16, 28; m 55; c 4. GEOLOGY. *Educ:* Univ Wichita, AB, 51; Univ NMex, MS, 53. *Prof Exp:* Area geologist, Div Raw Mat, Atomic Energy Comn, 55-58, chief geol engr, Sect Off, Flagstaff, Ariz, 58-62, proj geologist, Resource Appraisal Br, 62-70, Chief, 70-74, staff geologist, US Energy Res & Develop Admin, 75-77, STAFF GEOLOGIST, US DEPT ENERGY, 78- *Mem:* Fel Geol Soc Am; Am Inst Mining, Metall & Petrol Eng; Am Asn Petrol Geologists. *Res:* Uranium geology; Mesozoic stratigraphy; depositional environment of uranium ore deposits. *Mailing Add:* 707 Brassie Dr Grand Junction CO 81501

CHEO, BERNARD RU-SHAO, b Nanking, China, May 29, 30; m 57; c 2. ELECTRICAL ENGINEERING. *Educ:* Taiwan Univ, BSc, 53; Univ Notre Dame, MS, 56; Univ Calif, Berkeley, PhD(elec eng), 61. *Prof Exp:* Mem tech staff, Bell Tel Labs, Inc, 60-62; from asst prof to assoc prof elec eng, New York Univ, 62-73; PROF ELEC ENG, POLYTECH INST NY, 73- *Mem:* Inst Elec & Electronics Engrs. *Res:* Electromagnetic theory; plasmas. *Mailing Add:* Dept of Elec Eng Polytech Inst NY Brooklyn NY 11201

CHEO, PEN CHING, b Ho-Fei, China, Mar 28, 19; m 49. PLANT VIROLOGY. *Educ:* Nanking Univ, China, BS, 41; WVa Univ, MS, 49; Univ Wis, PhD(plant path), 51. *Prof Exp:* Fel, Plant Indust Sta, USDA, 51-53; res assoc, Univ RI, 53-55; fel, Tree Fruit Exp Sta, Wash State Col, 55-57; res fel, Div Biol, Calif Inst Technol, 57-61; asst plant pathologist, Wash State Univ, Wenatchee, 61-66; plant pathologist, Dept Arboreta & Bot Gardens, 66, CHIEF RES DIV, DEPT ARBORETA & BOT GARDENS, LOS ANGELES STATE & COUNTY ARBORETUM, 66- *Mem:* Am Phytopath Soc; Sigma Xi. *Res:* Resistance of different plant species to virus infection in correlation with their differences in physiological responses to extrinsic factors such as light, darkness, and growth hormones; investigation on factors of virus survival in soil. *Mailing Add:* Los Angeles State & Co Arboretum 301 N Baldwin Ave Arcadia CA 91006

CHEO, PETER K, b Nanking, China, Feb 2, 30; US citizen; m 56; c 5. OPTICAL ENGINEERING, COMMUNICATIONS. *Educ:* Aurora Col, BS, 51; Va Polytech Inst, MS, 53; Ohio State Univ, PhD(physics), 64. *Prof Exp:* Instr physics, Bethany Col, 54-57; asst prof, Aurora Col, 57-61; mem prof staff, Bell Tel Labs, 63-70; mgr laser appln res, Aerojet-Gen Corp, 70-71; SR RES SCIENTIST, UNITED TECHNOLOGIES RES CTR, 71- *Concurrent Pos:* Adj prof elec eng, Hartford Grad Ctr, 78- *Mem:* Am Phys Soc; fel Optical Soc Am; sr mem Inst Elec & Electronics Eng. *Res:* Laser and device research; optical communication; non-linear and coherent phenomena; atomic and molecular spectroscopy; integrated optics; submillimeterwaves. *Mailing Add:* United Technologies Res Silver Lane East Hartford CT 06108

CHEPENIK, KENNETH PAUL, b Jacksonville, Fla, Mar 14, 38; m 63; c 2. DEVELOPMENTAL BIOLOGY. *Educ:* Univ Fla, BSAdv, 61, MS, 65, PhD(human anat, biochem, physiol), 68. *Prof Exp:* Instr anat, Bowman Gray Sch Med, Wake Forest Univ, 68-70, asst prof, 70-73; ASSOC PROF ANAT, JEFFERSON MED COL, THOMAS JEFFERSON UNIV, 73- *Mem:* Sigma Xi; NY Acad Sci; Teratology Soc; Am Asn Anatomists; Soc Develop Biol. *Res:* Biochemical mechanisms underlying normal and abnormal mammalian embryogenesis. *Mailing Add:* Dept Anat Jefferson Med Col Philadelphia PA 19107

CHER, MARK, b Buenos Aires, Arg, June 14, 32; nat US; m 56; c 4. PHYSICAL CHEMISTRY. *Educ:* Calif Inst Technol, BS, 54; Harvard Univ, AM, 55; PhD(chem), 58. *Prof Exp:* Instr chem, Univ Calif, Los Angeles, 57-59, asst prof, 59-60; res specialist, Atomics Int, Calif, 60-63; mem tech staff, NAm Aviation Sci Ctr, 63-69; assoc prof chem & chmn dept, Wis State Univ, River Falls, 69-71; sr chemist, Addressograph-Multigraph Corp, 71-74; mgr qual assurance, 74-80, PROG MGR, PLUME MODEL VALIDATION STUDY-FIELD MEASUREMENTS, ENVIRON PROTECTION RES INST, AIR MONITORING CTR, ROCKWELL INT CORP, 80- . *Mem:* Am Chem Soc; Am Phys Soc. *Res:* Fast reaction kinetics; atoms and free radicals in gas phase; application of ultrasonics to chemical kinetics; shock waves and detonations; photochemistry; radiation chemistry; air pollution monitoring; data quality assurance; program management. *Mailing Add:* Rockwell Int 2421 W Hillcrest Newbury Park CA 91320

CHERASKIN, EMANUEL, b Philadelphia, Pa, June 9, 16; m 44; c 1. ORAL MEDICINE. *Educ:* Univ Ala, AB, 39, MA, 41, DMD, 52; Univ Cincinnati, MD, 43; Am Bd Oral Med, dipl. *Prof Exp:* Intern med, Hartford Munic Hosp, 43-44; resident, St Mary's Hosp, Ind, 46-47; asst prof physiol, 50-52, assoc prof oral med, Sch Dent, 52-56, prof oral surg & oral med & chmn dept, 56-62, prof oral med & chmn dept, 62-79, EMER PROF, MED CTR, UNIV ALA, BIRMINGHAM, 79- *Concurrent Pos:* Consult, Vet Admin Hosps, 52-79 & Southeastern Area, Vet Admin, 55-64; mem staff, Univ Hosp, Univ Ala & Hillman Clin, 57- *Mem:* Am Acad Oral Med; Am Dent Asn; AMA; hon mem Circle Odontol Paraguay; hon mem Dom Odontol Soc. *Res:* Predictive medicine; nutrition; metabolism. *Mailing Add:* Univ of Ala University Sta Birmingham AL 35294

CHERAYIL, GEORGE DEVASSIA, b Kothamangalam, India, Dec 17, 29; m 57; c 3. BIOCHEMISTRY, CHEMISTRY. *Educ:* Univ Madras, BSc, 49, Hons, 52, MA, 55; St Louis Univ, PhD(biochem), 62. *Prof Exp:* Demonstr chem, St Xavier's Col, India, 49-50; lectr, Fatima Mata Nat Col, India, 52-54; lectr, Med Col, Univ Mysore, 54-55; chmn chem dept, Andhra Loyola Col, 55-58; ASSOC PROF PATH, MED COL WIS, 62- *Mem:* AAAS; Am Chem Soc; Am Soc Neurochem. *Res:* Metabolism of steroids, especially bile acids; lipid metabolism in central nervous system disorders; biochemistry of phospholipids, sphingolipids and glycolipids; levo-dihydroxyphenylalanine and catecholamines. *Mailing Add:* Dept of Path Med Col of Wis 8700 W Wisconsin Ave Milwaukee WI 53226

CHERBAS, LUCY FUCHSMAN, developmental biology, see previous edition

CHERBAS, PETER THOMAS, b Bryn Mawr, Pa, Mar 26, 46; m 68; c 1. DEVELOPMENTAL BIOLOGY, INSECT ENDOCRINOLOGY. *Educ:* Harvard Col, BA, 67; Harvard Univ, PhD(biol), 73. *Prof Exp:* Res fel genetics, Cambridge Univ, 73-74; res fel, 74-77, asst prof, 77-81, ASSOC PROF BIOL, HARVARD UNIV, 81- *Mem:* Genetics Soc Am; Soc Develop Biol. *Res:* Molecular analysis of the action of steroid hormones especially the insect molting hormones, the ecdysteroids; insect cell culture and its applications in the study of development. *Mailing Add:* Biol Labs Harvard Univ 16 Divinity Ave Cambridge MA 02138

CHERENACK, PAUL FRANCIS, b Hazleton, Pa, June 19, 42. MATHEMATICS. *Educ:* Villanova Univ, BS, 63; Univ Pa, PhD(math), 68. *Prof Exp:* Teaching asst, Univ Pa, 63-68; instr, Villanova Univ, 68; asst prof, Ind Univ, Bloomington, 68-74; MEM FAC MATH, UNIV CAPE TOWN, SAFRICA, 74- *Mem:* Am Math Soc; Math Asn Am. *Res:* Nature of singularities on algebraic varieties via their analytic homotopy groups; algebraic geometry. *Mailing Add:* Dept of Math Univ Cape Town Private Bag Rondebasch South Africa

CHERIAN, SEBASTIAN K, b Palai, India, Sept 23, 38; m 67; c 2. ZOOLOGY. *Educ:* Univ Kerala, BSc, 59; Duquesne Univ, MS, 63; St Bonaventure Univ, PhD(physiol), 67. *Prof Exp:* USPHS res grant, 61-63; teaching asst physiol, Duquesne Univ, 60-63 & zool, St Bonaventure Univ, 63-66; asst prof biol, St Francis Col, Pa, 66-69; asst prof, 69-74, PROF BIOL, JAMESTOWN COL, 74-, ACTG CHMN DEPT, 70- *Mem:* Am Soc Zoologists. *Res:* Ovarian and uterine responses to exogenous hormone administration in the immature rat; concentration and distribution of uterine glycogen in unilaterally pregnant rats. *Mailing Add:* Dept of Biol Jamestown Col Jamestown ND 58401

CHERIN, PAUL, b Brooklyn, NY, Oct 14, 34; m 57; c 3. SOLID STATE PHYSICS, ANALYTICAL CHEMISTRY. *Educ:* Brooklyn Col, BS, 55; Polytech Inst Brooklyn, PhD(phys chem), 63. *Prof Exp:* Staff scientist, Int Bus Mach Corp, 60-61; scientist, 62-66, sr scientist, 66-76, TECH SPEC PROG MGR, XEROX CORP, 77- *Mem:* Am Chem Soc; Am Crystallog Asn; Sigma Xi; NY Acad Sci. *Res:* Relating structural properties of photoreceptors to electrical properties. *Mailing Add:* 30 Whitney Ridge #B9 Fairport NY 14450

CHERITON, DAVID ROSS, b Vancouver, BC, Mar 29, 51. COMPUTER SCIENCE, SOFTWARE ENGINEERING. *Educ:* Univ BC, BSc, 73; Univ Waterloo, MMath, 74, PhD(comput sci), 78. *Prof Exp:* ASST PROF COMPUT SCI, UNIV BC, 78- *Mem:* Asn Comput Mach; Inst Elec & Electronics Engrs. *Res:* Logical design of mini computer operating systems for portability, reliability and configurability. *Mailing Add:* Dept of Comput Sci Univ of BC Vancouver Can

CHERKASKY, MARTIN, b Philadelphia, Pa, Oct 6, 11; m 41; c 2. PUBLIC HEALTH. *Educ:* Temple Univ, MD, 36. *Prof Exp:* Pvt pract, 39-40; exec, Home Care Dept, 47, dir med group, 48-51, chief, Div Social Med, 50, dir, 51-75, pres, 75-81, CONSULT, MONTEFIORE HOSP & MED CTR, 81-; ATRAN PROF COMMUNITY HEALTH, ALBERT EINSTEIN COL MED, 67- *Concurrent Pos:* Consult, NY State Joint Hosp Rev & Planning Coun; consult, Comnr Hosps, New York City Dept Hosps, 61-62; mem exec comt, Health Res Coun New York City, 69-70; mem regional health adv bd, Region II, HEW, 70-71; mem, Gov Steering Comt Social Probs, 70-72. *Mem:* Inst of Med of Nat Acad Sci; NY Acad Med; Am Pub Health Asn; Asn Am Med Cols. *Mailing Add:* Montefiore Hosp & Med Ctr 111 E 210th St Bronx NY 10467

CHERKIN, ARTHUR, b Latrobe, Pa, July 24, 13; m 43; c 2. BIOCHEMISTRY. *Educ:* Univ Calif, Los Angeles, BA, 33, PhD(biochem), 53. *Prof Exp:* Res chemist, Max Factor & Co, Calif, 33; co-owner, Synthetics, 34; chemist, Don Baxter, Inc, 34-36, chief chemist, 36-43, dir res, 43-48, vpres, 48-63; CHIEF PSYCHOBIOL RES LAB, 65-, DIR, GERIAT RES, EDUC & CLIN CTR, SEPULVEDA VET ADMIN MED CTR, 75- *Concurrent Pos:* Res chemist, Univ Calif, Los Angeles, 33, lectr anesthesiol, Sch Med, 66-, res biochemist, Dept Psychiat, 73-; res fel, Calif Inst Technol, 62-66; consult, Don Baxter, Inc, 63-65. *Mem:* Geront Soc; Int Brain Res Orgn; Soc Neurosci; Am Geriat Soc; Am Soc Pharmacol & Exp Therapeut. *Res:* Amino acids and peptides; pyrogens; parenteral alimentation and therapy; mechanism of general anesthesia; aging, learning and memory; experimental amnesias; memory enhancement. *Mailing Add:* Geriat Res Educ & Clin Ctr Vet Admin Hosp Sepulveda CA 91343

CHERKOFSKY, SAUL CARL, b Lynn, Mass, June 2, 42; m 62; c 3. ORGANIC CHEMISTRY. *Educ:* Mass Inst Technol, BS, 63; Harvard Univ, MA, 64, PhD(org chem), 67. *Prof Exp:* res chemist, Cent Res Dept, 66-80, PRES & RES SUPVR, BIOCHEM DEPT, E I DU PONT NEMOURS & CO, INC, 80- *Mem:* Am Chem Soc. *Res:* Anthracene photodimers; carbonium ion rearrangements; bicyclobutane synthesis and polymers; aromatic substitutions; heterocyclic chemistry; medicinal chemistry. *Mailing Add:* 1013 Woodstream Dr Ramblewood Wilmington DE 19810

CHERLIN, GEORGE (YALE), b New Haven, Conn, Feb 21, 24; m 45; c 2. MATHEMATICS. *Educ:* Rutgers Univ, MSc, 49, PhD(math), 51. *Prof Exp:* Asst instr, Rutgers Univ, 47-51; asst mathematician, Mutual Benefit Life Ins Co, 51-62; vpres-actuary, Nat Health & Welfare Retirement Asn, Inc, 62-72; second vpres & actuary, Mutual Benefit Life Ins Co, 72-77; pres, APL Bus Consults, Inc, 77-81; CONSULT ACTUARY, STSC, INC, 81- *Mem:* Casualty Actuarial Soc; Soc Actuaries; Am Acad Actuaries; Sigma Xi. *Res:* Actuarial science; computer science; mathematical logic; complex variable. *Mailing Add:* 9 Porter Pl Newark NJ 07112

CHERMACK, EUGENE E A, b New York, NY, Aug 31, 34; m 56; c 4. PHYSICAL METEOROLOGY. *Educ:* Queens Col, NY, BS, 56; Univ Wash, BS, 58; NY Univ, MS, 62, PhD(meteorol), 70. *Prof Exp:* Weather officer, US Air Force, 56-59; asst res scientist, NY Univ, 59-62, instr meteorol, 62-67; ASSOC PROF METEOROL, STATE UNIV NY COL OSWEGO, 67- *Mem:* Am Meteorol Soc; Am Geophys Union; Int Asn Gt Lakes Res. *Res:* Development of indirect sounding techniques applied to the atmosphere; infrared radiation and atmospheric optics; surface temperature of lakes and rivers. *Mailing Add:* Dept Earth Science State Univ NY Col Oswego NY 13126

CHERMS, FRANK LLEWELLYN, JR, b Warwick, RI, June 4, 30; m 52; c 2. POULTRY PHYSIOLOGY. *Educ:* Univ RI, BS, 52; Univ NH, MS, 54; Univ Md, PhD, 58. *Prof Exp:* Instr & asst geneticist, Univ NH, 54-55; from asst prof to prof, Univ Wis, 57-69; REPROD PHYSIOLOGIST, NICHOLAS TURKEY BREEDING FARMS, INC, 69- *Mem:* AAAS; Poultry Sci Asn; Soc Study Reprod; World Poultry Sci Asn. *Res:* Improving the reproductive performance of the turkey through breeding and physiology. *Mailing Add:* 19449 Riverside Dr PO Box Y Sonoma CA 95476

CHERN, M MYRA, b Soochow, Kiangsu, Apr 19, 46; US citizen; m 69; c 1. GENETIC EPIDEMIOLOGY, DATABASE MANAGEMENT. *Educ:* Nat Taiwan Univ, BS, 67; Univ Minn, MS, 70, PhD(biomet), 73. *Prof Exp:* Fel biomet & health computer sci, Univ Minn, 71-73, res assoc, 73-74, asst prof, 74-80; ASST PROF BIOSTATISTICS, SCH PUB HEALTH, UNIV CALIF, LOS ANGELES, 80- *Concurrent Pos:* Mem tech Staff, Logicon, Inc, 80. *Mem:* Am Satist Asn; Biomet Soc; Am Soc Human Genetics; Asn Comput Mach. *Res:* Family and epidemiological studies of heterogeneous disease such as epilepsy or diabetes; study design and statistical methodology development related to multivariate survival data analysis; linkage analysis and segregation analysis. *Mailing Add:* Div Biosatist Sch Pub Health Univ Calif Los Angeles CA 90024

CHERN, SHIING-SHEN, b Kashing, China, Oct 26, 11; US citizen; m 39; c 2. GEOMETRY. *Educ:* Nankai Univ, China, BS, 30; Tsing Hua Univ, China, MS, 34; Univ Hamburg, DSc, 36. *Hon Degrees:* LLD, Chinese Univ Hong Kong & DSc, Univ Chicago, 69, Univ Hamburg, 69. *Prof Exp:* Prof math, Tsing Hua Univ, China, 37-43, Acad Sinica, 46-48 & Univ Chicago, 49-59; prof, 60-80, EMER PROF MATH, UNIV CALIF, BERKELEY, 80- *Concurrent Pos:* Guggenheim fel, 54-55 & 67; colloquium lectr, Am Math Soc, 60. *Honors & Awards:* Chauvenet Prize, Math Asn Am, 70; Nat Medal Sci, 76. *Mem:* Nat Acad Sci; Am Acad Arts & Sci; Am Math Soc (vpres, 63-64); Math Asn Am; Acad Sinica. *Res:* Differential geometry; integral geometry; topology. *Mailing Add:* Dept of Math Univ of Calif Berkeley CA 94720

CHERNA, JOHN C(HARLES), b Budapest, Hungary, Apr 6, 21; Can citizen; m 56; c 4. INDUSTRIAL ENGINEERING, ENGINEERING GRAPHICS.

Educ: Swiss Fed Inst Technol, Dipl Ing, 47. *Prof Exp:* Lectr mech technol, Swiss Fed Inst Technol, 45-49; indust engr, Paris, France & Montreal, Can, 49-51; lectr mech eng, 51-54, asst prof, 54-58, ASSOC PROF MECH ENG, McGILL UNIV, 58- *Concurrent Pos:* Training consult, Bathurst Power & Paper Co Ltd, 64- *Honors & Awards:* Ralph R Teetor Award, Soc Automotive Engrs, 79. *Mem:* Soc Automotive Engrs; Am Soc Metals; Eng Inst Can; Can Soc Mech Eng. *Res:* Metal cutting and working. *Mailing Add:* 5511 Westbourne Montreal PQ H4V 2G9 Can

CHERNAK, JESS, b Brooklyn, NY, Aug 30, 28; m 55; c 2. ELECTRICAL ENGINEERING, COMPUTER SCIENCE. *Educ:* Brooklyn Polytech Inst, BEE, 60; NY Univ, MEE, 61. *Prof Exp:* Mem tech staff comput, 60-63, supvr, 63-68, head dept technol, 68-70, dir technol, 70-75, dir, Digital Transmission Lab, 75-79, EXEC DIR, LOOP TRANSMISSION DIV, BELL LABS, 79- *Concurrent Pos:* Mem tech prog comt, Spring Joint Comput Conf, 67-68, steering comt, 69-70. *Mem:* Inst Elec & Electronics Engrs. *Res:* Systems engineering and development of the communications network including cables, electronics, installation, protection and maintenance systems; characterization of solid state components; thin film and magnetic component design; network design; digital transmission system design; digital terminals; digital regenerators; system analysis. *Mailing Add:* Bell Labs Whippany NJ 07981

CHERNESKY, MAX ALEXANDER, b Inglis, Man, Aug 1, 38; m 65. MEDICAL VIROLOGY. *Educ:* Univ Guelph, BS, 65; Univ Toronto, MS, 67; Univ BC, PhD(virol), 69. *Prof Exp:* From instr to asst prof, 70-76, ASSOC PROF PEDIAT, McMASTER UNIV, 77-; DIR, HAMILTON REG VIROL LAB, ST JOSEPH'S HOSP, 78- *Mem:* Am Soc Microbiol; Am Soc Trop Med & Hyg; Can Soc Microbiol. *Res:* Pathogenesis of viral infections; rapid viral diagnosis technology. *Mailing Add:* Dept of Pediat Fac of Med McMaster Univ Hamilton ON L8S 4L8 Can

CHERNIACK, LOUIS, b Winnipeg, Man, Nov 23, 08. PULMONARY DISEASES. *Educ:* Univ Man, MD, 32, BSc, 34; FRCP(C); FRCP(London). *Prof Exp:* Asst prof, 50-60, ASSOC PROF INTERNAL MED, FAC MED, UNIV MAN, 60-, MEM, JOINT RESPIRATORY PROG, 68- *Concurrent Pos:* Physician, Health Sci Ctr, 47-78, mem hon attend staff, 78. *Mem:* Fel Am Col Physicians; fel Am Col Chest Physicians; Am Thoracic Soc; Can Med Asn; Can Thoracic Soc. *Res:* Cinical investigation. *Mailing Add:* 206-333 Wellington Cresent Winnipeg MB R3M 0A1 Can

CHERNIACK, NEIL S, b Brooklyn, NY, May 28, 31; m 55; c 3. INTERNAL MEDICINE. *Educ:* Columbia Univ, AB, 52; State Univ NY, MD, 56. *Prof Exp:* Intern med, Univ Ill Med Ctr, 56-57, res fel, 57-58, resident, 60-62; res fel pulmonary dis, Columbia Univ, 62-64; from asst prof to assoc prof med, Univ Ill Med Ctr, 64-69; assoc prof, 69-73, prof med & assoc dir pulmonary serv, Univ Pa, 73-77; PROF & DIR PULMONARY SERV, CASE WESTERN RESERVE UNIV, 77- *Concurrent Pos:* Consult, Chicago State Tuberc Sanitarium, Ill, 64-69; assoc attend physician, Cook County Hosp, 65-69; assoc attend physician & sr res assoc, Michael Reese Hosp, 67-69; sr attend physician, Philadelphia Gen Hosp, Pa, 69-76; vis scholar, Karolinska Inst, Stockholm, 76-77; chief pulmonary serv, Cleveland & Brecksville Vet Admin Hosp, 77-; attending physician, Univ Hosp, Cleveland, 77-; assoc ed, J Appl Physiol, 81- *Mem:* Am Thoracic Soc; Am Physiol Soc; Am Soc Clin Invest; Am Asn Physicians Bioeng Soc. *Res:* Control of ventilation and circulation; pulmonary disease; oxygen and carbon dioxide stores of the body; bioengineering; sleep disorders. *Mailing Add:* Dept of Med Case Western Reserve Univ Cleveland OH 44106

CHERNIACK, REUBEN MITCHELL, b Can, June 15, 24; m 52; c 3. MEDICINE. *Educ:* Univ Man, MD, 48, MSc, 51; FRCP(C). *Prof Exp:* Lectr, Dept Physiol & Med Res, Univ Man, 54-56, from asst prof to prof med, 56-76, chmn fac med, 74-78; PROF MED, UNIV COLO, 76-, VCHMN, FAC MED, 78-; CHMN DEPT MED, NAT JEWISH HOSP & RES CTR, 78- *Concurrent Pos:* Fel med, Columbia Univ, 52-54; Life Ins fel & Markle scholar, 54; dir, Cardiorespiratory Unit, Winnipeg Gen Hosp, 54, Inhalation Ther Unit, 61, consult physician in respiratory dis, 58, dir respiratory div, Clin Invest Unit; dir, Joint Respiratory Prog, Sanatorium Bd Man & Univ Man; med dir, D A Stewart Ctr Study & Treat Respiratory Dis; consult, Man Rehab Hosp & Munic Hosps, 58. *Honors & Awards:* Prowse Prize, 52; Drewery Prize, 53. *Mem:* Fel Am Col Physicians; Am Soc Clin Invest; Am Physiol Soc; Can Col Physicians & Surg; Can Soc Clin Invest (secy, 61-63, pres, 63, past pres, 64). *Res:* Internal medicine; respiratory function and diseases. *Mailing Add:* Dept Med 3800 E Colfax Ave Denver CO 80206

CHERNIAK, EUGENE ANTHONY, b Windsor, Ont, Dec 17, 30; m 55; c 2. PHYSICAL CHEMISTRY. *Educ:* Queen's Univ, Ont, BA, 53, MA, 56; Univ Leeds, PhD(radiation chem), 59. *Prof Exp:* Sci master, Pickering Col, Can, 53-55; Nat Res Coun Can fel, 59-60; lectr chem, Carleton Univ, Can, 60-61, asst prof, 61-65; chmn dept, 65-69, PROF CHEM, BROCK UNIV, 65- *Mem:* AAAS; Int-Am Photochem Soc; fel Chem Inst Can; Am Chem Soc. *Res:* Chemical kinetics; photochemistry (including flash photochemistry); radiation chemistry. *Mailing Add:* 7 Wychwood Rd St Catharines ON L2R 3S1 Can

CHERNIAK, ROBERT, b New York, NY, June 26, 36; m 61; c 2. BIOCHEMISTRY. *Educ:* City Col New York, BS, 59; Duke Univ, PhD(biochem), 64. *Prof Exp:* Arthritis Found fel biochem, Univ Newcastle, 64 & Albert Einstein Col Med, 65; assoc res biologist, Sterling-Winthrop Res Inst Div, Sterling Drug, Inc, 66-68; from asst prof to assoc prof, 68-81, PROF CHEM, GA STATE UNIV, 81- *Res:* Structure and biosynthesis of polysaccharides of biological origin. *Mailing Add:* Dept of Chem Ga State Univ University Plaza Atlanta GA 30303

CHERNIAVSKY, ELLEN ABELSON, b Philadelphia, Pa. OPERATIONS RESEARCH. *Educ:* Stanford Univ, BS, 68; Cornell Univ, MS, 71, PhD(opers res), 73. *Prof Exp:* Assoc scientist, Brookhaven Nat Lab, 73-81; ANALYST, THE ANAL SCI CORP, 81- *Concurrent Pos:* Adj prof, State Univ NY, Stony Brook, 73-75; consult, Brookhaven Nat Lab, 81-; assoc ed, Opers Res Letters, 81- *Mem:* Opers Res Soc Am; AAAS; Int Asn Energy Economists. *Res:* Cost and performance trends over time for tactical aircraft; formulation and evaluation of energy system models, particularly those pertaining to hydrocarbon supplies; multiobjective analysis. *Mailing Add:* 5512 Massachusetts Ave Bethesda MD 20816

CHERNIAVSKY, JOHN CHARLES, b Boston, Mass, Feb 15, 47; m 68; c 2. THEORY, SOFTWARE SYSTEMS. *Educ:* Stanford Univ, BS, 69; Cornell Univ, MS, 71, PhD(comput sci), 72. *Prof Exp:* Asst prof comput sci, State Univ NY, Stony Brook, 72-80, assoc prof, 80-81; PROG DIR THEORET COMPUT SCI, NAT SCI FOUND, 80- *Concurrent Pos:* Vis fel, Johns Hopkins Univ, 78-79. *Mem:* Asn Comput Mach; Am Math Soc; Soc Indust & Appl Math; AAAS; Asn Symbolic Logic. *Res:* Theoretical computer science; software engineering; mathematical logic. *Mailing Add:* Comput Sci Sect Nat Sci Found Washington DC 20550

CHERNICK, SIDNEY SAMUEL, b Winnipeg, Man, Mar 6, 21; US citizen. BIOCHEMISTRY. *Educ:* Univ Calif, Los Angeles, AB, 43; Univ Calif, MA, 45, PhD(physiol), 48. *Prof Exp:* Physiologist, Med Sch, Univ Calif, 48-51; prof pharmacol & physiol, NDak State Col, 51-52; scientist, 52-63, SCIENTIST DIR, NAT INST ARTHRITIS, METAB & DIGESTIVE DIS, 63- *Concurrent Pos:* Vis scientist, Med Clin, Munich, 63-64. *Honors & Awards:* Purkinje Medal, Czech Med Soc, 69. *Mem:* Soc Exp Biol & Med; Am Soc Biol Chem. *Res:* Metabolic defects in endocrine and nutritional diseases; in vitro metabolism; diabetes; mechanisms of hormone action. *Mailing Add:* Lab Nutrit & Endocrinol Metab & Digestive Dis Bethesda MD 22014

CHERNICK, VICTOR, b Winnipeg, Man, Dec 31, 35; m 57; c 4. PEDIATRICS, PHYSIOLOGY. *Educ:* Univ Man, MD, 59; Am Bd Pediat, dipl, 65. *Prof Exp:* Rotating intern, Winnipeg Gen Hosp, Man, 59-60; Nat Inst Neurol Dis & Blindness perinatal fel, Johns Hopkins Univ, 60, from jr asst resident to asst resident pediat, 60-62, univ fel environ med & pediat, 62-64, from instr to asst prof pediat, 64-66; from asst prof to assoc prof pediat & physiol, 66-71, head dept, 71-79, PROF PEDIAT, UNIV MAN, 71- *Concurrent Pos:* Resident, Vet Admin Hosp, Baltimore, 64; attend physician, 64-65, consult, 66; chief respiratory dis & perinatal physiol, Children's Hosp, 67-71; pediatrician in chief, Health Sci Ctr, 71-79. *Honors & Awards:* Queen Elizabeth II Scientist Award, 67; Medal, Can Pediat Soc, 70. *Mem:* Fel Am Thoracic Soc; fel Am Acad Pediat; Soc Pediat Res; Can Soc Clin Invest; Am Physiol Soc. *Res:* Pulmonary physiology; neonatology. *Mailing Add:* Children's Ctr 685 Bannatyne Ave Winnipeg MB R3E 0W1 Can

CHERNICK, WARREN SANFORD, b Providence, RI, Oct 6, 29. PHARMACOLOGY. *Educ:* RI Col Pharm, BS, 52; Philadelphia Col Pharm, MS, 54, DSc, 56. *Prof Exp:* From instr to asst prof pharmacol, Philadelphia Col Pharm, 54-64; from asst prof to assoc prof, 64-68, PROF PHARMACOL & CHMN DEPT, HAHNEMANN MED COL & HOSP, 68- *Concurrent Pos:* Res assoc, Children's Hosp & Med Sch, Univ Pa, 57-64. *Mem:* Am Pharmaceut Asn; Am Soc Pharmacol & Exp Therapeut. *Res:* Salivary secretion; psychopharmacology; cystic fibrosis. *Mailing Add:* Dept of Pharmacol Hahnemann Med Col & Hosp 230 N Broad St Philadelphia PA 19102

CHERNIN, ELI, b New York, NY, Sept 12, 24; m 56; c 3. MEDICAL PARASITOLOGY, TROPICAL PUBLIC HEALTH. *Educ:* City Col New York, BS, 44; Univ Mich, MA, 48; Johns Hopkins Univ, ScD(parasitol), 51. *Hon Degrees:* AM, Harvard Univ, 70. *Prof Exp:* Asst zool, Univ Mich, 47-48; asst parasitol, Sch Med, Johns Hopkins Univ, 48-49, 50-51 & Sch Hyg & Pub Health, 49-51; res assoc, 51-52, from instr to assoc prof, 52-69, PROF TROP PUB HEALTH, SCH PUB HEALTH, HARVARD UNIV, 70- *Concurrent Pos:* Consult, Ludlow Mfg & Sales Co, Calcutta & Boston, 51-53, trop med & parasitol study sect, USPHS, 66-70 & parasitic dis panel, US-Japan Coop Med Sci Prog, 70-74; sr res fel, USPHS, 56-61, career develop award, 61-64, res career award, 64-; China Med Bd-La State Univ travel fel, Cent Am, 57; asst ed, Jour Parasitol, 68-72; adv, WHO, 70; mem ed bd, Am J Trop Med & Hyg, 71-72; consult, Ctr Dis Control, USPHS, PR, 71-72, mem training grant comt, Nat Inst Allergy & Infectious Dis, 72-73; coun mem, Am Soc Trop Med & Hyg, 74-77; vchmn & mem bd dir, Coun Biol Ed, 75-76, chmn, 76-77; coun mem, Am Soc Parasitol, 75-78; assoc ed, New Eng J Med, 78-79, rev ed, 78-80; instr, Marine Biol Lab, Woods Hole, 80; vis Franklin prof biomed writing, Auburn Univ, 81. *Honors & Awards:* Bailey K Ashford Res Award, Am Soc Trop Med & Hyg, 61. *Mem:* AAAS; Am Soc Parasitol; Am Soc Trop Med & Hyg; Coun Biol Ed; Royal Soc Trop Med & Hyg. *Res:* Incidence and epidemiology of malaria and other parasitic infections in industrial workers in India; biology and biological control of disease-carrying snails, especially of vectors of human schistosmiasis; transmission and biology of filariasis; biomedical communications; history of medicine. *Mailing Add:* Dept of Trop Pub Health Harvard Sch of Pub Health Boston MA 02115

CHERNOCK, WARREN PHILIP, b Fall River, Mass, Jan 12, 26; m 47; c 4. METALLURGY, NUCLEAR ENGINEERING. *Educ:* Columbia Univ, BS, 49; NY Univ, MS, 55. *Prof Exp:* Metall engr, Argonne Nat Lab, 49-51; sr metall engr, Sylvania Elec, 51-56; mgr metall, 56-64, mgr nuclear labs, 64-69, dir nuclear labs, 69-74, V PRES DEVELOP, COMBUSTION ENG, INC, 74- *Concurrent Pos:* Adj prof & chmn dept metall, Hartford Grad Ctr, Rensselaer Polytech Inst, 56-; vis assoc prof nuclear eng, Mass Inst Technol, 61-62. *Mem:* Fel Am Nuclear Soc; fel Am Soc Metals; Am Soc Testing & Mat; Metal Properties Coun; Atomic Indust Forum. *Res:* Irradiation effects; nuclear fuels and materials; anisotropy and preferred orientation; corrosion. *Mailing Add:* 14 Bainton Rd West Hartfield CT 06117

CHERNOFF, AMOZ IMMANUEL, b Malden, Mass, Mar 17, 23; m 53; c 3. HEMATOLOGY. *Educ:* Yale Univ, BS, 43, MD, 47. *Prof Exp:* Intern med, Mass Gen Hosp, 47-48; asst resident, Barnes Hosp, St Louis, Mo, 48-49; res fel hemat, Michael Reese Hosp, Chicago, 49-51; from instr to asst prof, Wash Univ, 51-56; assoc prof, Duke Univ, 56-58; res prof, Univ Tenn, Knoxville, 58-78, dir, Mem Res Ctr, 64-77, prof med, Sch Med, 66-78, assoc vice chancellor, Ctr Health Sci, 77-78; DIR, DIV BLOOD DIS & RESOURCES, NAT HEART, LUNG & BLOOD INST, NIH, BETHESDA, MD, 79- *Concurrent Pos:* Asst dir hemat res lab, Michael Reese Hosp, 50-51; Am Col Physicians fel med, Sch Med, Wash Univ, 51-52, USPHS fel, 52-53; consult, City Hosp, St Louis, 52-56; asst physician, Barnes Hosp, 52-56; chief hemat sect, Vet Admin Hosp, Durham, NC, 56-58; mem cancer chemother study sect, USPHS, 58-63; USPHS res career award, 62-77; med dir, Cystic Fibrosis Found, Atlanta, 75-77; attend physician, Univ Tenn Mem Res Ctr & Hosp, 58-78. *Mem:* AAAS; fel Am Col Physicians; Am Soc Hemat; Int Soc Hemat; Am Soc Clin Invest. *Res:* Hemolytic anemias; abnormal hemoglobins; biochemical genetics. *Mailing Add:* Nat Heart Lung & Blood Inst Div of Blood Dis & Resources Bethesda MD 20205

CHERNOFF, HERMAN, b New York, NY, July 1, 23; m 47; c 2. MATHEMATICAL STATISTICS. *Educ:* City Col New York, BS, 43; Brown Univ, ScM, 45, PhD(appl math), 48. *Prof Exp:* Res assoc, Cowles Comn Res Econ, Chicago, 47-49; asst prof statist & math, Univ Ill, 49-52; from assoc prof to prof statist, Stanford Univ, 52-74; PROF APPL MATH, MASS INST TECHNOL, 74- *Concurrent Pos:* Fel, Ctr Advan Study Behav Sci, 59-60. *Mem:* Nat Acad Sci; Am Math Soc; Inst Math Statist (pres, 68-69); Am Statist Asn; Am Acad Arts & Sci. *Res:* Statistical problems in econometrics; sequential design of experiments; rational selection of decision functions; large sample theory; pattern recognition. *Mailing Add:* Dept of Math 2-381 Mass Inst Technol Cambridge MA 02139

CHERNOFF, PAUL ROBERT, b Philadelphia, Pa, June 21, 42. MATHEMATICS. *Educ:* Harvard Univ, BA, 63, MA, 65, PhD(math), 68. *Prof Exp:* Lectr, 69-71, asst prof, 71-74, assoc prof, 74-80, PROF MATH, UNIV CALIF, BERKELEY, 80- *Concurrent Pos:* Fel NSF, Univ Calif, Berkeley, 68-69; consult, Inst Defense Analyses, Princeton, 79- *Mem:* Am Math Soc; Math Asn Am; AAAS. *Res:* Functional analysis; operator theory; mathematical physics. *Mailing Add:* Dept of Math Univ of Calif Berkeley CA 94720

CHERNOSKY, EDWIN JASPER, b Rosenberg, Tex, May 21, 14; wid; c 3. ENVIRONMENTAL PHYSICS, SPACE PHYSICS. *Prof Exp:* Chemist, Champion Paper Co, Tex, 37-42; observer, Huancayo Magnetic Observ, Peru, Carnegie Inst, 42-45, res geophysicist, 45-46; mem tech staff physics res dept, Naval Ord Lab, Washington, DC, 46-52; physicist & actg chief geomagnetics unit, 52-55; chief geomagnetic activity sect, Air Force Cambridge Res Labs, 55-67, res physicist, 67-76; mem staff, Visidyne, Inc, 76-78; CONSULT, 79- *Concurrent Pos:* Deleg, Int Asn Geomagnetism & Aeronomy, Toronto, 57, Helsinki, 60, Berkeley, 63, Zurich, 67, Madrid, 69, Moscow, 71, Kyoto, 73, Grenoble, 75, Seattle, 77, Canberra, 79, Edinburgh, 81 & mem comn IV, IX & lunar variations, chmn interdiv comn of hist; mem organizing comt & deleg, Int Symp Equatorial Aeronomy, Huaychulo, Peru, 62, San Jose do Campos, Brazil, 65 & Ahmedabad, India, 69. *Mem:* AAAS; Am Geophys Union; Am Phys Soc; Inst Elec & Electronics Engrs; Sigma Xi. *Res:* Solar geomagnetic relationships, morphology of solar activity and geomagnetic variations, characterization of geomagnetic time variations, recurrence phenomena of geomagnetic variations; 22 year geomagnetic cycle, dichotomy in geomagnetic activity; solar-terrestrial physics. *Mailing Add:* 48 Berkley St Waltham MA 02154

CHERNOW, FRED, b Brooklyn, NY, Sept 13, 32; m 56; c 3. ELECTRICAL ENGINEERING. *Educ:* Brooklyn Col, BA, 55; NY Univ, PhD(ejection polarization), 62. *Prof Exp:* Fel solid state, Lab Insulation Res, Dept Elec Eng, Mass Inst Technol, 61-62, Ford asst prof elec eng, 62-64, asst prof, 64-66; assoc prof, 66-70, PROF ELEC ENG, UNIV COLO, BOULDER, 70- *Mem:* Am Phys Soc; Am Vacuum Soc. *Res:* Transport properties of II-VI compounds; thin film research studies of II-VI compounds and insulators; ion implantation of II-VI compounds. *Mailing Add:* Dept of Elec Eng Univ of Colo Boulder CO 80302

CHERNY, WALTER B, b Montreal, Que, Apr 13, 26; nat US; m 55; c 2. OBSTETRICS & GYNECOLOGY. *Educ:* McGill Univ, BSc, 48, MD, CM, 50. *Prof Exp:* Instr obstet & gynec, Sch Med, Duke Univ, 55, assoc, 55-57, from asst prof to prof, 57-70; DIR RESIDENCY, POST-GRAD TRAINING IN OBSTET & GYNEC, GOOD SAMARITAN HOSP, 70- *Concurrent Pos:* Chief serv obstet, Lincoln Hosp, 58; consult, Watts Hosp, 58-70. *Mem:* AAAS; AMA; Am Col Obstet & Gynec. *Res:* Obstetrics and gynecology affecting physical and emotional health; reproductive physiology. *Mailing Add:* Dept of Obstet & Gynec Good Samaritan Hosp Phoenix AZ 85006

CHERRICK, HENRY M, b Brooklyn, NY, Dec 4, 39; m 61; c 1. ORAL SURGERY, ORAL PATHOLOGY. *Educ:* Univ Fla, Gainesville, AA, 61; Med Col Va, Va Commonwealth Univ, DDS, 65; Ind Univ, MSD, 70; Am Bd Oral Path, dipl. *Prof Exp:* Resident oral surg, Univ Cincinnati Med Ctr, 68; chmn sect oral diag, med & path, Sch Dent, Univ Calif, Los Angeles, 72-76, assoc prof, 73-77, chmn, Div Biol Dent Sci, 74-78, prof sect oral diag, med & path, 76-78, asst dean hosp affairs, 77-78; DEAN & PROF, SCH DENT MED, SOUTHERN ILL UNIV, EDWARDSVILLE, 78- *Concurrent Pos:* Consult oral path & oral surg var hosps & univs, 70-78; ed consult, J Oral Surg, 73- *Mem:* Am Dent Asn; Am Asn Dent Schs; Am Acad Oral Med; Am Soc Oral Surg. *Res:* Chemical carcinogenesis; chemical topical chemotherapy. *Mailing Add:* Sch of Dent Med Southern Ill Univ Edwardsville IL 62026

CHERRINGTON, BLAKE EDWARD, b Belleville, Ont, Mar 16, 37; m 60; c 2. ELECTRICAL ENGINEERING, PHYSICS. *Educ:* Univ Toronto, BASc, 59, MASc, 61; Univ Ill, PhD(elec eng), 65. *Prof Exp:* Res assoc elec eng, Univ Ill, Urbana-Champaign, 65-66, from asst prof to assoc prof, 66-74, asst dean eng, 69-70, prof elec & nuclear eng, 74-79; PROF & CHMN ELEC ENG,

UNIV FLA, 79- *Concurrent Pos:* Consult, Zenith Radio, 72-77; Am Coun Educ fel acad admin, 77-78. *Mem:* Inst Elec & Electronics Engrs; Am Phys Soc; Am Soc Eng Educ. *Res:* Gaseous electronics, plasmas and gas lasers; basic electronic and atomic processes occuring in gas lasers and gas discharges. *Mailing Add:* Dept Elec Eng Univ Fla Gainesville FL 32611

CHERRY, DONALD STEPHEN, b Paterson, NJ, Sept 23, 43; m 66; c 2. AQUATIC ECOLOGY. *Educ:* Furman Univ, BSc, 65; Clemson Univ, MSc, 70, PhD(zool), 73. *Prof Exp:* Teacher biol & football coach, J L Mann High Sch, SC, 65-68; instr human ecol, Clemson Univ, 72-73; res assoc & fel, 73-74, asst prof biol, 74-76, ASSOC PROF, CTR ENVIRON STUDIES, VA POLYTECH INST & STATE UNIV, 80- *Concurrent Pos:* Consult, Dept Microbiol, Clemson Univ, 73; investr, Facil Use Agreement, Savannah River Proj, 72-75, co-investr, AEC contract, 73-75; consult, Am Elec Power Serv Corp, Canton, Ohio, 74-75, co-investr, 74-76; co-prin investr, Dept Energy, 79-81. *Mem:* Ecol Soc Am; Am Water Works Asn; Int Water Resources Asn. *Res:* Impact of power production discharges upon aquatic food chains in the drainage systems by site-specific field laboratory and field biomonitoring activities; validation of aquatic field and laboratory data of organisms (bacteria, algae, aquatic insects, micro-invertebrates and fish) for hazard evaluation; correlation of physiological-biochemical to ecological mechanisms of fish to heavy metal toxicity responses from power effluents. *Mailing Add:* Ctr Environ Studies Dept of Biol Va Polytech Inst & State Univ Blacksburg VA 24061

CHERRY, EDWARD TAYLOR, b Gainesboro, Tenn, Nov 12, 41; m 67; c 4. ENTOMOLOGY. *Educ:* Tenn Polytech Inst, BS, 63; Univ Tenn, MS, 66, PhD(entom), 70. *Prof Exp:* Res assoc appl entom, Miss State Univ, 70-71; asst prof agr biol, Univ Tenn, 71-74; RES SPECIALIST PLANT PROTECTANTS, CIBA-GEIGY CORP, 74- *Mem:* Entom Soc Am; Sigma Xi. *Res:* Chemical insecticides both from a potential nature and extension of existing compounds; subject areas of pest management, biological control. *Mailing Add:* Ciba-Geigy Corp Box 11422 Greensboro NC 27409

CHERRY, JAMES DONALD, b Summit, NJ, June 10, 30; m 54; c 3. PEDIATRICS, INFECTIOUS DISEASES. *Educ:* Springfield Col, BS, 53; Univ Vt, MD, 57; Am Bd Pediat, dipl, 62. *Prof Exp:* Intern pediat, Boston City Hosp, 57-58, asst resident, 58-59; resident, Kings County Hosp, Brooklyn, NY, 59-60; instr, Col Med, Univ Vt, 60-61; NIH fel med, Harvard Med Sch & Thorndike Mem Lab, 61-62; from asst prof to assoc prof, Med Sch, Univ Wis, 63-66; from assoc prof to prof pediat, Sch Med, St Louis Univ, 68-73, assoc prof microbiol, 68-73, vchmn dept pediat, 70-73; PROF PEDIAT, SCH MED, UNIV CALIF, LOS ANGELES, 73- *Concurrent Pos:* Asst attend physician, Mary Fletcher Hosp & DeGoesbriand Hosp, Burlington, Vt, 61-62; asst pediat, Boston City Hosp, 61-62; assoc attend physician, Madison Gen Hosp, 62-67; dir, John A Hartford Res Found, 62-67; Markle scholar, 64; mem med staff, Cardinal Glennon Mem Hosp Children, 66-67; vis worker, Common Cold Res Unit & Clin Res Ctr, Salisbury, Eng, 69. *Mem:* Am Soc Microbiol; Am Fedn Clin Res; Am Acad Pediat; AAAS; Soc Pediat Res. *Res:* Clinical manifestations of viral diseases; viral vaccines; interaction of infectious agents in the pathogenesis of disease. *Mailing Add:* Div Infectious Dis Dept Pediat Univ Calif Sch Med Los Angeles CA 90024

CHERRY, JERRY ARTHUR, b Dayton, Tex, Feb 5, 42; m 65; c 3. POULTRY NUTRITION. *Educ:* Sam Houston State Univ, BS, 64; Univ Mo, PhD(poultry nutrit), 72. *Prof Exp:* Asst prof, 72-77, ASSOC PROF NUTRIT, DEPT POULTRY SCI, VA POLYTECH INST & STATE UNIV, 77- *Mem:* Poultry Sci Asn; Sigma Xi; Nutrit Res Coun; AAAS. *Res:* Lipid metabolism; food intake control mechanisms; energy metabolism. *Mailing Add:* Dept of Poultry Sci Va Polytech Inst & State Univ Blacksburg VA 24061

CHERRY, JESSE THEODORE, b St Louis, Mo, Sept 22, 31; m 55; c 4. GEOPHYSICS, SEISMOLOGY. *Educ:* St Louis Univ, BS, 53, MS, 56, PhD(geophys), 60. *Prof Exp:* Instr eng, St Louis Univ, 57-60; group leader explor geophys, Continental Oil Co, 60-63; group leader geophys comput, Lawrence Radiation Lab, 63-71; sr vpres geophys opers, 71-80, SR VPRES, GEOPHYS & SEISMIC PROGS, SYSTS SCI & SOFTWARE, 80- *Mem:* Seismol Soc Am; Am Geophys Union. *Res:* Rock fracturing from explosive sources; exploration geophysics; computer simulation of non linear material behavior; earthquake hazards. *Mailing Add:* Systs Sci & Software PO Box 1620 La Jolla CA 92038

CHERRY, JOE H, b Newbern, Tenn, June 3, 34; m 55; c 3. PLANT PHYSIOLOGY, BIOCHEMISTRY. *Educ:* Univ Tenn, BS, 57; Univ Ill, MS, 59, PhD(agron, biochem), 61. *Prof Exp:* Res assoc biochem, Seed Protein Pioneering Res Lab, USDA, La, 61-62; from asst prof to assoc prof hort, 62-67, PROF HORT, PURDUE UNIV, WEST LAFAYETTE, 67- *Mem:* AAAS; Am Soc Plant Physiol; Am Soc Biol Chemists. *Res:* Nucleic acid metabolism during seed germination and plant growth; induction of enzymes during cell differentation; effects of ionizing radiation on plants; mechanism of action of plant hormones. *Mailing Add:* Dept of Hort Purdue Univ West Lafayette IN 47907

CHERRY, JOHN PAUL, b Rhinebeck, NY, Jan 31, 41; m 64; c 2. BIOCHEMICAL GENETICS, PROTEIN CHEMISTRY. *Educ:* Furman Univ, BS, 63; WVa Univ, MS, 66; Univ Ariz, PhD(genetics & biochem), 71. *Prof Exp:* Res chemist, USDA, 71-72; res assoc biochem & biophys, Tex A&M Univ, 72-73; asst prof food sci, Univ Ga, 73-75; SUPVRY RES CHEMIST/RES LEADER PROTEIN CHEM, SOUTHERN REGIONAL RES CTR, AGR RES SERV, USDA, 76- *Concurrent Pos:* Res chemist, Southern Res Ctr, Sci Educ Admin-Fed Res, USDA, 70-72; res grant, Univ Ga, 74-75, S Res Ctr, USDA. *Mem:* Inst Food Technologists; Am Chem Soc; Am Asn Cereal Chemists; Am Peanut Res & Educ Asn; Sigma Xi. *Res:* Discovery, isolation, fractionation, purification and modification of proteins and related constituents and their interaction chemistry and deterioration from conventional and nonconventional food sources; characterization of biochemical, functional nutritional and organoleptic properties of proteins for use as food and feed ingredients. *Mailing Add:* Food Lab Southern Regional Res Ctr Agr Res Serv USDA PO Box 19687 New Orleans LA 70179

CHERRY, LEONARD VICTOR, b Los Angeles, Calif, May 3, 23; m 53; c 1. SOLID STATE PHYSICS. *Educ:* City Col New York, BS, 47; Duke Univ, PhD(chem), 53. *Prof Exp:* Prin chemist, Battelle Mem Inst, 51-53; from asst prof to assoc prof chem, Hampton Inst, 53-57; instr & res assoc, Univ Pittsburgh, 57-61; asst prof, 61-65, ASSOC PROF PHYSICS, FRANKLIN & MARSHALL COL, 65- *Mem:* AAAS; Am Phys Soc; Am Asn Physics Teachers; Fedn Am Sci; Bioelec Repair & Growth Soc. *Res:* Kerr effect in aromatic fluorine compounds; physicochemical problems connected with photoengraving and electrophotography; properties of intermetallic compounds; Mossbauer effect; electrical properties of bone. *Mailing Add:* Dept of Physics Franklin & Marshall Col Lancaster PA 17604

CHERRY, MARIANNA, b Hartford, Conn, Dec 28, 24. IMMUNOGENETICS. *Educ:* Wheaton Col, BA, 46; Bryn Mawr Col, MA, 51; Yale Univ, PhD(biophys chem), 64. *Prof Exp:* Res biologist, Univ Calif, San Diego, 62; vis asst prof chem, Mt Holyoke Col, 62-63; asst prof chem, State Univ NY Albany, 63-65; from assoc staff scientist to staff scientist, 65-75, SR STAFF SCIENTIST, JACKSON LAB, 75- *Mem:* AAAS. *Res:* Genetic control in mice of histocompatibility antigens and other cell membrane alloantigens; genetic control of immune response. *Mailing Add:* 41 Rodick Bar Harbor ME 04609

CHERRY, S(HELDON), b Winnipeg, Man, Mar 28, 28; m 62; c 2. EARTHQUAKE ENGINEERING, STRUCTURAL DYNAMICS. *Educ:* Univ Man, BSc, 49; Univ Ill, MS, 51; Bristol Univ, PhD(civil eng), 56. *Prof Exp:* Asst, Univ Ill, 49-52; asst prof civil eng, Univ Man, 55-56; from asst prof to assoc prof, 56-69, asst to head dept, 70-78, PROF CIVIL ENG, UNIV BC, 69- *Concurrent Pos:* Sr res fel, Calif Inst Technol, 63-64; chmn, Can Nat Comt Earthquake Eng, 64-75. *Mem:* Seismol Soc Am; Am Soc Civil Engrs; Eng Inst Can; Earthquake Eng Res Inst. *Res:* Structures; applied mechanics; earthquake engineering, particularly dynamic characteristics of structures and influence of site conditions on ground response. *Mailing Add:* Dept of Civil Eng Univ of BC Vancouver BC V6T 1W5 Can

CHERRY, WILLIAM BAILEY, b Bowling Green, Ky, Apr 27, 16; m 44; c 2. BACTERIOLOGY. *Educ:* Western Ky State Teachers Col, BS, 37; Univ Ky, MS, 42; Univ Wis, PhD(bact), 49; Am Bd Med Microbiol, dipl, 62. *Prof Exp:* Bacteriologist, Univ Ky, 41-43 & Nat Naval Med Ctr, Md, 43-46; asst prof bact, Univ Tenn, 49-51; res microbiologist, Ctr Dis Control, USPHS, 51-81; RETIRED. *Concurrent Pos:* Assoc prof, Sch Pub Health, Univ NC. *Honors & Awards:* Meritorious Serv Award, USPHS, 63; Kimble Award, 67; P R Edwards Award, 68; Difco Award, 74; Distinguished Serv Award, USPHS, 77. *Mem:* AAAS; Am Soc Microbiol; fel Am Acad Microbiol; Fedn Am Scientists. *Res:* Enteric bacteriology; bacteriology of anthrax; listeriosis; Legionnaires' disease; fluorescent antibody techniques. *Mailing Add:* 2857 Talisman Ct NE Atlanta GA 30345

CHERRY, WILLIAM HENRY, b New York, NY, Oct 9, 19; m 47; c 3. PHYSICS. *Educ:* Mass Inst Technol, BS, 41; Princeton Univ, MA, 48, PhD, 58. *Prof Exp:* RES PHYSICIST, LABS, RCA CORP, 41- *Honors & Awards:* Levy Medal, Franklin Inst. *Mem:* Am Phys Soc; Inst Elec & Electronics Engrs. *Res:* Electrodynamics in magnetron, betatron and velocity modulated tubes; gas and ultra high frequency discharge; colorimetry in color television; time division multiplex, communications systems; information theory; multiplex, color television systems; cable television education systems; secondary electron emission from surfaces bombarded by positrons; time dependent effects; superconductivity; electromechanical phenomena in accelerated reference frames; special relativity. *Mailing Add:* 24 Dempsey Ave Princeton NJ 08540

CHERRY, WILLIAM RICHARD, b Santa Rosa, Calif, Dec 15, 49. PHOTOCHEMISTRY, THEORETICAL CHEMISTRY. *Educ:* Univ San Francisco, BS, 72; Univ Wash, PhD(chem), 76. *Prof Exp:* Assoc chem, Columbia Univ, 76-78; asst prof chem, WVa Univ, 78-81; ASST PROF CHEM, LA STATE UNIV, 81- *Mem:* Am Chem Soc. *Res:* Photochemistry of charge transfer complexes; synthesis of unusual intermediates by photochemical techniques and matrix isolation; potential energy surfaces and their relation to chemical reactivity. *Mailing Add:* Dept Chem La State Univ Baton Rouge LA 70803

CHERTKOFF, MARVIN JOSEPH, b Baltimore, Md, Nov 20, 30; m 63. PHARMACEUTICAL CHEMISTRY, PHYSICAL PHARMACY. *Educ:* Univ Md, BS, 51, MS, 54; Purdue Univ, PhD(pharm), 58. *Prof Exp:* Chemist chem warfare labs, Army Chem Ctr, Md, 56; mgr tech unit, Qual Stand Sect, Merck Sharp & Dohme, 58-59, corp trainee, 59-61, mgr qual control, Pharm Prod, 61-63, supt, Sterile Opers, 63-65, qual motivation coordr, 65-67; planning mgr, Hoffmann-La Roche Inc, 67-68; dir bus develop, Givaudan Corp, 68-69, dir, Aroma Chem Div, 69-70, vpres chem div, 70-73; PRES, BIOZEST LABS, 73- *Mem:* Am Chem Soc; Am Pharmaceut Asn; Am Soc Qual Control. *Res:* Quality control and pharmaceutical production; physical pharmacy. *Mailing Add:* 202 Beechwood Dr Ridgewood NJ 07450

CHERTOCK, GEORGE, b New York, NY, Aug 1, 14; m 37; c 2. PHYSICS. *Educ:* City Col New York, BS, 39; George Washington Univ, MA, 43; Cath Univ Am, PhD(physics), 52. *Prof Exp:* Instr physics, City Col New York, 39; phys sci aide to physicist, Bur Standards, 40-46; PHYSICIST, NAVAL SHIP RES & DEVELOP CTR, 46- *Concurrent Pos:* Lectr, Univ Md, 53-54 & Cath Univ Am, 64-66; sr vis, Dept Appl Math, Cambridge Univ, 66-67. *Mem:* NY Acad Sci; fel Acoust Soc Am. *Res:* Underwater acoustics; interaction of elastic structures and hydrodynamic pressures; stellar structure. *Mailing Add:* Naval Ship Res & Develop Ctr Bethesda MD 20084

CHERTOK, BENSON T, nuclear physics, particle physics, deceased

CHERTOK, ROBERT JOSEPH, b Spartanburg, SC, Sept 5, 35; m 59; c 3. PHYSIOLOGY. *Educ:* Univ SC, BS, 57; Univ Miami, PhD(renal physiol), 65. *Prof Exp:* Sr scientist, Lawrence Livermore Lab, Univ Calif, 64-73; assoc prof, Jackson State Univ, 73-75; ASSOC PROF, COMP ANIMAL RES LAB,

OAK RIDGE ASSOC UNIVS, 76- *Mem:* Am Physiol Soc; Am Soc Nephrol; Soc Exp Biol & Med. *Res:* Renal transport; metabolism of environmental pollutants. *Mailing Add:* Univ Tenn Comp Animal Res Lab 1299 Bethel Valley Rd Oak Ridge TN 37830

CHERTOW, BERNARD, b Brooklyn, NY, Dec 30, 19; m 47; c 5. CHEMICAL ENGINEERING. *Educ:* Ill Inst Technol, BS, 42, MS, 43; Mass Inst Technol, ScD(chem eng), 48. *Prof Exp:* Asst chem eng, Mass Inst Technol, 43-44; staff engr, Off Sci Res & Develop, 44-45; instr chem eng & consult climatic res lab, Mass Inst Technol, 45-47, asst prof chem eng & dir Parlin Field Sta, 47-49; develop engr, 49-64, mgr chem develop pilot plants, 64-74, gen mgr, Bristol Labs, 74-80, VPRES OPERS, INDUST DIV, BRISTOL-MYERS CO, 80- *Concurrent Pos:* Consult, Godfrey Cabot Co, 46-47 & Tuscarora Chem Works, Inc, 71-74. *Mem:* Am Chem Soc; Am Inst Chem Engrs; Sigma Xi. *Res:* Manufacture of antibiotics and anticancer agents; adsorption of gas mixtures; process development for antibiotics and other pharmaceuticals. *Mailing Add:* 139 Sunnyside Park Rd Syracuse NY 13214

CHERVENICK, PAUL A, b Pittsburgh, Pa, Apr 20, 32; m 54; c 3. HEMATOLOGY, ONCOLOGY. *Educ:* Univ Pittsburgh, BS, 57, MD, 61. *Prof Exp:* From intern to resident med, Univ Pittsburgh, 61-64; fel hemat, Univ Utah, 64-67; asst prof med, Rutgers Med Sch, 67-69; assoc prof, 69-73, PROF MED, SCH MED, UNIV PITTSBURGH, 73-, DIR, DIV HEMATOL-ONCOL, 79- *Concurrent Pos:* Consult, Nat Cancer Inst, Am Cancer Soc & NIH; Leukemia Soc Am scholar, 70. *Mem:* Am Soc Clin Invest; Am Soc Clin Res; Am Soc Hemat; fel Am Col Physicians. *Res:* Study of factors controlling the proliferation and maturation of blood leukocytes in health and diseases, such as leukemia; proliferation of cells in an in vitro culture system; internal medicine. *Mailing Add:* 922 Scaife Hall Univ Pittsburgh Sch Med Pittsburgh PA 15261

CHERVENKA, CHARLES HENRY, b Howe, Okla, July 3, 21; m 47; c 2. BIOCHEMISTRY. *Educ:* Univ Okla, BS, 49, MS, 50; Univ Wash, PhD(biochem), 55. *Prof Exp:* Anal org chemist, Dow Chem Co, 50-52; res chemist, Reichhold Chems, Inc, 55-56; res assoc enzyme chem, Palo Alto Med Res Found, 56-60; APPLN CHEMIST, BECKMAN INSTRUMENTS, INC, 60- *Mem:* AAAS; Am Chem Soc. *Res:* Structure of proteins and enzymes; biomedical instrumentation. *Mailing Add:* Beckman Instruments Inc Appln Res Dept 1117 Calif Ave Palo Alto CA 94304

CHERVIN, MIRA, marine biology, ecology, see previous edition

CHERY, DONALD LUKE, JR, b Denver, Colo, Sept 16, 37; c 1. HYDROLOGY. *Educ:* Univ Ariz, BS, 60; Utah State Univ, MS, 65, PhD(civil eng), 76. *Prof Exp:* Res hydrol engr, Agr Res Serv, USDA, 65-80; sr hydrologist, Dames & Moore, 80-82; HYDROLOGIST, US NUCLEAR REGULATORY COMN, 82- *Mem:* Am Soc Civil Engrs; Am Geophys Union; AAAS; Sigma Xi. *Res:* Watershed surface water flow; complex watershed models. *Mailing Add:* US Nuclear Regulatory Comn Mail Stop P-214 Washington DC 20555

CHESBRO, WILLIAM RONALD, b Cohoes, NY, Oct 6, 28; m 50; c 2. MICROBIOLOGY. *Educ:* Ill Inst Technol, BS, 51, MS, 55, PhD(bact), 59. *Prof Exp:* Plant bacteriologist, Wanzer Dairy, Ill, 51-55; asst bacteriologist, Am Meat Inst Found, 55-59; from asst prof to assoc prof, 59-68, PROF MICROBIOL, UNIV NH, 68- *Concurrent Pos:* NIH res grants, 60- *Mem:* Am Soc Microbiol. *Res:* Microbial physiology and pathogenic microbiology. *Mailing Add:* Dept of Microbiol Univ of NH Durham NH 03824

CHESEBROUGH, HARRY E, b Ludington, Mich, 1909. MECHANICAL ENGINEERING. *Educ:* Univ Mich, BSE, 30; Chrysler Inst Eng, MAE, 32. *Hon Degrees:* DrEng, Univ Mich. *Prof Exp:* Mem staff, Chrysler Corp, 32-58, vpres, 58-73; RETIRED. *Concurrent Pos:* Trustee, Rackham Eng Found, 65-68. *Mem:* Nat Acad Eng; Soc Automotive Engrs (pres, 60). *Mailing Add:* 471 Dunston Rd Bloomfield Hills MI 48013

CHESEMORE, DAVID LEE, b Janesville, Wis, Nov 3, 39; m 61; c 1. WILDLIFE ECOLOGY. *Educ:* Univ Wis-Stevens Point, BS, 61; Univ Alaska, College, MS, 67; Okla State Univ, PhD(wildlife ecol), 75. *Prof Exp:* Res asst, Wildlife Res Unit, Univ Alaska, College, 61-63; res asst, Dept Wildlife Mgt, 63-64; forester, US Peace Corps, Nepalese Forestry Dept, Birganj, 64-65; res biologist, US Fish & Wildlife Serv, Univ Alaska, College, 67-68; res asst, Wildlife Res Unit, Okla State Univ, 68-72; asst prof, 72-77, assoc prof biol, 77-80, PROF BIOL, CALIF STATE UNIV, FRESNO, 80- *Mem:* Wildlife Soc; Am Soc Mammalogists; Sigma Xi. *Res:* Population dynamics and ecology of big game; canid ecology; biometrics and computer applications to field ecology; ecology of rare and endangered species; aspects of scientific photography. *Mailing Add:* Dept of Biol Calif State Univ Fresno CA 93740

CHESICK, JOHN POLK, b New Castle, Ind, Aug 8, 33; m 56; c 2. PHYSICAL CHEMISTRY. *Educ:* Purdue Univ, BS, 54; Harvard Univ, PhD(chem), 57. *Prof Exp:* From instr to asst prof chem, Yale Univ, 57-62; assoc prof, 62-71, PROF CHEM, HAVERFORD COL, 71- *Mem:* Am Chem Soc. *Res:* Chemical kinetics; Molecular structure; photochemistry. *Mailing Add:* Dept of Chem Haverford Col Haverford PA 19041

CHESKY, JEFFREY ALAN, b Lynn, Mass, May 11, 46; m 70; c 1. MUSCULAR PHYSIOLOGY, GERONTOLOGY. *Educ:* Cornell Univ, AB, 67; Univ Miami, PhD(physiol, biophys), 74. *Prof Exp:* NIH trainee & res instr physiol & biophys, Sch Med, Univ Miami, 74-77; ASST PROF, SANGAMON STATE UNIV, 77- *Concurrent Pos:* Adj asst prof, Fla Int Univ, 76-77 & Sch Med, Southern Ill Univ, 78- *Mem:* Geront Soc; AAAS; Am Physiol Soc; Am Aging Asn; Sigma Xi. *Res:* Physiology of aging; age related changes in cardiac and skeletal muscle; contractile protein age changes; exercise and aging. *Mailing Add:* Dept of Geront Sangamon State Univ Springfield IL 62708

CHESLER, DAVID ALAN, b New York, NY. MEDICAL PHYSICS. *Educ:* Mass Inst Technol, SB, 55, SM, 55, ScD(elec eng), 60. *Prof Exp:* Engr, Gen Tel & Electronics, 60-70; ASSOC PHYSICIST RADIOL, MASS GEN HOSP, 70- *Concurrent Pos:* NIH res fel, Mass Gen Hosp, 70-72. *Mem:* Sigma Xi; Inst Elec & Electronics Engrs. *Res:* Tomography and computer processing of medical x-ray and radionuclide images. *Mailing Add:* Physics Res Lab Mass Gen Hosp Fruit St Boston MA 02114

CHESLEY, LEON CAREY, b Montrose, Pa, May 22, 08; m 34; c 5. BIOCHEMISTRY. *Educ:* Duke Univ, PhD(physiol), 32. *Prof Exp:* Asst biophysicist, Mem Hosp, New York, 32-35; biochemist, Margaret Hague Maternity Hosp, 35-53; from assoc prof to prof, 53-79, EMER PROF OBSTET & GYNEC, STATE UNIV NY DOWNSTATE MED CTR, 79- *Concurrent Pos:* Instr eve session, City Col New York, 33-35. *Mem:* AAAS; Am Physiol Soc; hon mem Am Gynec Soc; Soc Gynec Invest. *Res:* Toxemias of pregnancy. *Mailing Add:* Dept of Obstet & Gynec State Univ NY Downstate Med Ctr Brooklyn NY 11203

CHESNEY, RUSSELL WALLACE, b Knoxville, Tenn, Aug 25, 41; m 68; c 2. PEDIATRICS, NEPHROLOGY. *Educ:* Harvard Col, AB, 63; Univ Rochester, MD, 68. *Prof Exp:* Intern & resident pediat, Johns Hopkins Hosp, Baltimore, 68-70; clin assoc renal biochem, Nat Inst Child Health & Human Develop, NIH, 70-72; sr asst resident pediat, Johns Hopkins Hosp, 72-73; fel nephrology, Montreal Children's Hosp, McGill Univ, 73-74, fel biochem genetics, DeBelle Lab Biochem Genetics, 74-75; from asst prof to assoc prof, 75-81, PROF PEDIAT, UNIV WIS, 81- *Concurrent Pos:* Med Res Coun Can fel, 74-75. *Mem:* Soc Pediat Res; Am Soc Nephrology; Am Fedn Clin Res. *Res:* Renal metabolism and transport; pediatric renal metabolic bone disease; renal tubular disease. *Mailing Add:* Univ of Wis Hosps 600 N Highland Ave Madison WI 53792

CHESNIN, LEON, b New York, NY, Mar 28, 19; m 40; c 4. SOIL CHEMISTRY, PLANT NUTRITION. *Educ:* Univ Ky, BS, 40; Rutgers Univ, PhD(soils), 48. *Prof Exp:* Jr soil surveyor, Soil Conserv Serv, USDA, Ind, 41-42; chemurgic res supvr, Joseph E Seagram & Sons, Inc, Ky, 42-44; asst, NJ Exp Sta, 44-47; asst prof agron, 47-54, ASSOC PROF AGRON & AGRONOMIST, UNIV NEBR, LINCOLN, 54- *Concurrent Pos:* Consult fertilizer co; mem, Nat Micronutrient Comt, Am Coun Fertilizer Appln; consult, Fed Drug Admin, US Congress. *Honors & Awards:* Environ Award, Eviron Protective Agency, 79 & 80. *Mem:* Am Soc Agron; Soil Sci Soc Am. *Res:* Micronutrients for crop production; micronutrient and major nutrient interrelations for crop growth; nutrition of crop varieties; influence of soil management on nutrient availability; composting, recycling and disposal of animal, municipal and industrial wastes in soil for crop production as influenced by soil management and waste management practices; waste management and recycling in soils. *Mailing Add:* Dept Agron Univ Nebr Lincoln NE 68583

CHESNUT, DONALD BLAIR, b Richmond, Ind, Dec 27, 32; m 54. PHYSICAL CHEMISTRY. *Educ:* Duke Univ, BS, 54; Calif Inst Technol, PhD(chem), 58. *Prof Exp:* Res assoc & instr physics, Duke Univ, 57-58; res chemist, Cent Res Dept, Exp Sta, E I du Pont de Nemours & Co, Inc, 58-65; assoc prof, 65-71, PROF CHEM, DUKE UNIV, 71- *Mem:* Am Phys Soc. *Res:* Quantum mechanics; magnetic resonance. *Mailing Add:* Dept of Chem Duke Univ Durham NC 27706

CHESNUT, DWAYNE A(LLEN), b Stephenville, Tex, Mar 8, 36; m 55; c 3. PETROLEUM ENGINEERING, PHYSICAL CHEMISTRY. *Educ:* Rice Univ, BS, 59, PhD(phys chem), 63. *Prof Exp:* NASA res asst, Rice Univ, 61-63; chemist, Explor & Prod Res, Shell Develop Co, 63-64, res chemist, 64-65, sect leader phys chem, 65-68, staff reservoir engr, Shell Oil Co, 68-73, sr staff reservoir engr, 73-74; pres, Energy Consult Assocs, Inc, 74-81; PRES, CRITICAL RESOURCES, INC, 81- *Concurrent Pos:* Consult, Dept Chem, Rice Univ, 63-64 & Lawrence Radiation Lab, 64-65; lectr, Univ Houston, 68; honorarium teacher, Univ Colo, Denver Ctr, 70-72. *Mem:* NY Acad Sci; fel Am Inst Chemists; Int Solar Energy Soc; Am Inst Chem Engrs; Soc Petrol Engrs. *Res:* Enhanced oil and gas recovery, computer applications and mathematical modeling in petroleum reservoir engineering, risk analysis. *Mailing Add:* Critical Resources Inc 425 S Cherry Suite 300 Denver CO 80222

CHESNUT, THOMAS LLOYD, b Pulaski, Miss, June 14, 42; m 61; c 2. ENTOMOLOGY, FRESH WATER ECOLOGY. *Educ:* Miss State Univ, BS, 65, MS, 66, PhD(entom), 69. *Prof Exp:* Res technologist insect ecol, Boll Weevil Res Lab, Agr Res Serv, 64-68; asst prof biol sci, Fla Technol Univ, 69-72, dir fresh water ecol, 70-72; assoc prof & dir ctr environ study & planning, 72-74, dir off res serv, 74-75, dir off grad studies, 75-76, PROF BIOL & DEAN GRAD SCH, GA COL, 77- *Mem:* Entom Soc Am. *Res:* Effects of competitive displacement between natural populations of insects; biological control of insect populations using insect parasites; effects of eutrophication on the aquatic habitat. *Mailing Add:* Grad Sch Ga Col Milledgeville GA 31061

CHESNUT, WALTER G, b Montclair, NJ, July 20, 28; m 51; c 5. ENGINEERING PHYSICS. *Educ:* Lehigh Univ, BS, 50, MS, 52; Univ Rochester, PhD(physics), 56. *Prof Exp:* Res assoc high energy physics, Cosmotron Dept, Brookhaven Nat Lab, 56-58; sr assoc appl physics, G C Dewey Corp, NY, 58-62; sr physicist, Radio Physics Lab, 62-63, STAFF SCIENTIST, STANFORD RES INST, 63- *Concurrent Pos:* Consult, Stanford Res Inst, 58-61 & Los Alamos Sci Lab, 68-; vis lectr elec eng, Stanford Univ, 73. *Mem:* AAAS; Am Phys Soc. *Res:* Utilization of radio and radar waves as a probe of the upper atmosphere or space environments. *Mailing Add:* Stanford Res Inst 333 Ravenswood Ave Menlo Park CA 94025

CHESS, DANIEL S, b New York, NY, May 12, 52. TOPOLOGY. *Educ:* Harvard Col, AB, 74; Princeton Univ, PhD(math), 79. *Prof Exp:* Instr math, Princeton Univ, 79-80; INSTR MATH, COURANT INST, NY UNIV, 80- *Res:* Relations between singularity theory and the algebraic topology of smooth manifolds. *Mailing Add:* Courant Inst Math Sci 251 Mercer St New York NY 10012

CHESS, KARIN V T, b Hobbs, NMex, Dec 17, 39; m 60. MATHEMATICS. *Educ:* Univ Kans, BS, 62, MA, 64, PhD(math), 68. *Prof Exp:* Instr, Univ Kans, 64-65 & 66-69; asst prof, 69-78, PROF MATH, UNIV WIS-EAU CLAIRE, 78- *Mem:* Am Math Soc; Math Asn Am. *Res:* Generalized nilpotent groups. *Mailing Add:* Dept of Math Univ Wis Eau Claire WI 54701

CHESSER, NANCY JEAN, b Albany, NY, Aug 31, 46; m 75. EXPERIMENTAL SOLID STATE PHYSICS. *Educ:* Cornell Univ, BA, 67; State Univ NY Stony Brook, PhD(physics), 72. *Prof Exp:* Asst physicist & instr physics, Ames Lab & Iowa State Univ, 72-73, assoc physicist & asst prof, 73-75; resident res assoc physics, Feltman Res Lab, 75-77; proj scientist, 77-80, PRIN SCIENTIST, B-K DYNAMICS INC, 80- *Mem:* Am Phys Soc. *Res:* Investigation of the dynamical properties of various solids through inelastic and quasielastic neutron scattering. *Mailing Add:* B-K Dynamics Inc 15825 Shady Grove Rd Rockville MD 20850

CHESSICK, RICHARD D, b Chicago, Ill, June 2, 31; m 53; c 3. PSYCHIATRY. *Educ:* Univ Chicago, PhB, 49, SB & MD, 54; Calif Western Univ, PhD(philos), 77. *Prof Exp:* Asst chief psychiat, USPHS Hosp, Lexington, Ky, 58-60; staff psychiatrist, Michael Reese Hosp, Chicago, 60-61; instr psychiat, 60-61; assoc, 61-62, from asst prof to assoc prof, 62-72, PROF PSYCHIAT, NORTHWESTERN UNIV, EVANSTON, 73- *Concurrent Pos:* Pvt pract, 60-; chief, Vet Admin Res Hosp, Chicago, 61-65, assoc dir res training prog, 64; sr attend psychiatrist, Evanston Hosp & Northwestern Mem Hosp, Chicago; adj prof philos, Loyola Univ, 79- *Honors & Awards:* Merck Award, 54. *Mem:* Fel Am Psychiat Asn; Am Psychosom Soc; Ger Psychoanal Soc; fel Am Orthopsychiat Asn; Asn Advan Psychother. *Res:* Psychoanalytic psychotherapy. *Mailing Add:* Suite 628 636 Church St Evanston IL 60201

CHESSIN, HENRY, b Cleveland, Ohio, Dec 8, 19; m 50; c 3. PHYSICS. *Educ:* Western Reserve Univ, BS, 47; Purdue Univ, MS, 50; Polytech Inst Brooklyn, PhD(physics), 59. *Prof Exp:* Instr physics, Polytech Inst Brooklyn, 51-57; res physicist, US Steel Corp, 57-64; PROF PHYSICS, STATE UNIV NY ALBANY, 64- *Mem:* Am Crystallog Asn; Am Inst Mining, Metall & Petrol Engrs; Am Phys Soc. *Res:* X-ray crystallography; crystal physics. *Mailing Add:* Dept of Physics State Univ of NY Albany NY 12222

CHESSIN, HYMAN, b Cleveland, Ohio, Sept 27, 20; m 42; c 4. PHYSICAL CHEMISTRY. *Educ:* Western Reserve Univ, BS, 47, MS, 49, PhD(phys chem), 51. *Prof Exp:* Anal chemist, Harshaw Chem Co, 41-43, 46-47; asst phys chem, Western Reserve Univ, 47-50; asst prof phys & anal chem & res assoc, Kenyon Col, 50-52; asst prof phys chem, Univ Ark, 52-54; dir res, Vander Horst Corp, NY, 54-62; sr res chemist, 62-68, res assoc, 68-73, SR RES ASSOC, M&T CHEM, INC, RAHWAY, 73- *Mem:* Am Chem Soc; Electrochem Soc; Am Electroplaters Soc. *Res:* Electrochemistry; physical chemistry. *Mailing Add:* 110 Rochester Dr Brick NJ 08723

CHESSIN, MEYER, b New York, NY, Feb 5, 21; m 45; c 5. PLANT PHYSIOLOGY, STRESS PHYSIOLOGY. *Educ:* Univ Calif, BS, 41, PhD(plant physiol), 50. *Prof Exp:* Asst bot, Univ Calif, 47-48; from instr to assoc prof, 49-61, PROF BOT, UNIV MONT, 61- *Concurrent Pos:* Res fel, USPHS, Rothamsted Exp Sta, Eng, 56-57; travel awards, Int Photobiol Cong, Copenhagen, 60, Oxford, 64; AEC fel, Univ Minn, 64-65; consult, Nat Libr Med, 70; Nat Acad Sci mem sci exchange, Romania, 71 & 75 & Bulgaria, 80. *Mem:* AAAS; Am Phytopath Soc. *Res:* Virology; biological effects of radiation. *Mailing Add:* Dept of Bot Univ of Mont Missoula MT 59801

CHESSON, EUGENE, JR, b Sao Paulo, Brazil, Dec 1, 28; US citizen; m 54; c 2. CIVIL ENGINEERING, FORENSIC ENGINEERING. *Educ:* Duke Univ, BSCE, 50; Univ Ill, MS, 56, PhD(civil eng), 59. *Prof Exp:* Inspection engr oil refinery, Standard Oil Co, Ind, 53; asst civil eng, Univ Ill, 53-56, res assoc, 56-59, from asst prof to assoc prof, 59-66; Prof civil eng, Univ Del, 66-80, chmn dept, 66-75; PRES, CHESSON ENG, INC, 80- *Concurrent Pos:* Mem res coun riveted & bolted struct joints, Eng Found. *Honors & Awards:* W E Wickenden Award, Am Soc Eng Educ, 79-80. *Mem:* Am Soc Civil Engrs; Am Soc Testing & Mat; Am Soc Eng Educ; Nat Soc Prof Engrs; Am Inst Steel Construct. *Res:* Static and fatique properties of structural joints; behavior of metal structures; failure analysis. *Mailing Add:* 130 Du Pont Hall Univ Del Newark DE 19711

CHESSON, PETER LEITH, b Medindie, SAustralia, Nov 7, 52; m 74. THEORETICAL ECOLOGY, ECOLOGICAL STATISTICS. *Educ:* Univ Adelaide, BSc, 74, PhD(statist & zool), 78. *Prof Exp:* Fel res biologist, biometry & theoret ecol, Univ Calif, Santa Barbara, 77-81; ASST PROF, DEPT ZOOL, OHIO STATE UNIV, 81- *Concurrent Pos:* Lectr, Univ Calif, Santa Barbara, 78. *Mem:* Inst Math Statist. *Res:* Development of stochastic population and behavior models, of an analytical nature, for competition, predation and host-parasitoid relationships; models for animal movements; theory of bivariate distributions; random probability measures. *Mailing Add:* Dept Zool Ohio State Univ 1735 Neil Ave Columbus OH 43210

CHESTER, ALEXANDER JEFFREY, b Davenport, Iowa, Feb 4, 50. STATISTICAL CONSULTING, ESTUARINE ECOLOGY. *Educ:* Rutgers Col, AB, 72; Univ Wash, MS, 75. *Prof Exp:* Asst biol oceanog, Univ Wash, 72-75, oceanogr, 75-76; oceanogr, Pac Marine Environ Lab, 76-79, BIOMETRICIAN, BEAUFOR LAB, NAT MARINE FISHERIES SERV, NAT OCEANIC & ATMOSPHERIC ADMIN, 79- *Mem:* Am Soc Limnol & Oceanog; Am Inst Fishery Res Biologists. *Res:* Application of statistical methods to problems in estuarine and fisheries ecology, including community analysis, larval fish growth and distribution, production and fate of organic matter, and microzooplankton ecology. *Mailing Add:* Beaufort Lab Nat Marine Fisheries Serv Beaufort NC 28516

CHESTER, ARTHUR NOBLE, b Seattle, Wash, Aug 5, 40; m 69. THEORETICAL PHYSICS. *Educ:* Univ Tex, Austin, BS, 61; Calif Inst Technol, PhD(theoret physics), 65. *Prof Exp:* Physicist, Bell Tel Labs, NJ, 65-69; mem tech staff physics, 69-71, head chem laser sect, 71-73, mgr, Laser Dept, 73-75, asst dir, 75-79, assoc dir, Res Labs, 79-80, MGR HIGH SPEED INTEGRATED CIRCUITS & ASST MGR, STRATEGIC SYSTS DIV, HUGHES AIRCRAFT CO, 80- *Concurrent Pos:* Consult, Dept Defense Adv Group, 75- *Mem:* AAAS; Am Phys Soc; fel Inst Elec & Electronics Engrs; Optical Soc Am; Quantum Electronics & Appln Soc (pres, 80). *Res:* laser physics; microelectronics; research management. *Mailing Add:* Bldg E 51 Mail Sta A 269 Hughes Aircraft Co PO Box 902 El Segundo CA 90245

CHESTER, ARTHUR WARREN, b Brooklyn, NY, Jan 9, 40; m 61; c 3. INORGANIC CHEMISTRY. *Educ:* Brooklyn Col, BS, 61; Mich State Univ, PhD(inorg chem), 66. *Prof Exp:* Res chemist, 66-70, sr res chemist, 70-75, assoc, 75-78, res assoc, 78-81, MGR EXPLOR PROCESS RES, MOBIL RES & DEVELOP CORP, 81- *Mem:* Am Chem Soc. *Res:* Metal complexes in non-aqueous solvents; metals in hydrocarbon autoxidations; catalysis by inorganic solids; zeolite chemistry and catalysts; cracking catalysts; chemisorption on metal catalysts; synthesis gas conversion; aromatics processing; processes for synthetic fuels production. *Mailing Add:* Mobil Res & Develop Corp Paulsboro NJ 08066

CHESTER, BRENT, b New York, NY, Apr 19, 42; m 67; c 2. CLINICAL MICROBIOLOGY. *Educ:* City Col New York, BS, 62; Long Island Univ, MS, 70; NY Univ, PhD(microbiol), 75. *Prof Exp:* Jr bacteriologist, Bur Labs, New York City Dept Health, 65-68; supvr clin microbiol res, Kings County Res Lab, New York, 68-70; sr supvr microbiol, Mt Sinai Serv, Elmhurst Hosp, New York, 70-74; hosp microbiologist, Vet Admin Hosp, Gainesville, Fla, 74-75, HOSP MICROBIOLOGIST, VET ADMIN HOSP, MIAMI, 75- *Mem:* Am Soc Microbiol. *Res:* Isolation and identification procedures for bacteria in clinical specimens with emphasis on Yersinia, Klebsiella and nonfermentative Bacilli. *Mailing Add:* Vet Admin Hosp Lab Serv 1201 NY 16th St Miami FL 33155

CHESTER, CLARENCE LUCIAN, b Cabot, Vt, Jan 5, 15; m 47; c 2. PATHOLOGY, ANATOMY. *Educ:* Univ Vt, BS, 37, MD, 40. *Prof Exp:* Intern, Burbank Hosp, Mass, 40-42; res path, St Elizabeth's Hosp, 47-48; asst path med col, Tufts Col, 48-49, instr, 53, lectr path & bact, 53-55; pathologist, Vet Admin Hosp, Little Rock, Ark, 55-59 & Portland, Ore, 59-74; asst clin prof path, Med Sch, Univ Ore, 62-74; chief anat path serv, Vet Admin Hosp, Portland, 74-79; assoc prof path, Med Sch, Univ Ore, 74-79; RETIRED. *Concurrent Pos:* Asst pathologist, Mt Auburn Hosp, 49-53, assoc pathologist, 53-55. *Mem:* NY Acad Sci; Col Am Path; Asn Advan Med Instrumentation. *Res:* Cancer. *Mailing Add:* Anat Path Serv Vet Admin Hosp Sam Jackson Park Portland OR 97207

CHESTER, CLIVE RONALD, b Brooklyn, NY, Apr 6, 30. MATHEMATICS. *Educ:* NY Univ, AB, 50, MS, 51, PhD(math), 55. *Prof Exp:* Asst math, Inst Math Sci, NY Univ, 51-56; instr, Queens Col, NY, 56-61; from asst prof to assoc prof, Polytech Inst Brooklyn, 61-68; ASSOC PROF MATH, NY INST TECHNOL, 68- *Mem:* Am Math Soc. *Res:* Applied mathematics; wave propagation; partial differential equations. *Mailing Add:* 5928 Flushing Ave Maspeth NY 11378

CHESTER, DANIEL LEON, b Albany, Calif, Feb 26, 43. COMPUTER SCIENCES. *Educ:* Univ Calif, Berkeley, BA, 66, MA, 68, PhD(math), 73. *Prof Exp:* Asst prof math, Univ Tex, Austin, 73-76, asst prof comput sci, 73-80; ASST PROF COMPUT SCI, UNIV DEL, 80- *Concurrent Pos:* Vis scientist, T J Watson Res Ctr, Int Bus Mach, 78-79. *Mem:* Asn Comput Mach; Asn Comput Ling; Inst Elec & Electronics Engrs; Am Asn Artificial Intel; Cognitive Sci Soc. *Res:* Software engineering methodology; natural language question answering systems; artificial intelligence. *Mailing Add:* Dept Comput & Info Sci Univ Del Newark DE 19711

CHESTER, EDWARD HOWARD, b New York, NY, Mar 10, 31; m 59; c 1. PULMONARY MEDICINE, RESPIRATORY PHYSIOLOGY. *Educ:* Ohio Wesleyan Univ, BA, 52; NY Univ, MD, 56. *Prof Exp:* Sr instr med, 62-65, from asst prof to assoc prof med, 65-78, from asst prof to assoc prof biomed eng, 66-78, PROF BIOMED ENG & PROF MED, CASE WESTERN RESERVE UNIV, 79- *Concurrent Pos:* Chief pulmonary serv, US Naval Hosp, Philadelphia, 60-62. *Mem:* Am Thoracic Soc; Am Acad Allergy; Am Col Chest Physicians; Am Fed Clin Res; Inst Elec & Electronics Engrs. *Res:* Pulmonary disease; respiratory physiology; pulmonary mechanics; pulmonary gas transport. *Mailing Add:* Vet Admin Med Ctr 10701 East Boulevard Cleveland OH 44106

CHESTER, EDWARD M, b Queens Co, NY, Jan 12, 12; m 38; c 2. INTERNAL MEDICINE. *Educ:* NY Univ, BS, 32; State Univ Iowa, MD, 36; Am Bd Internal Med, dipl, 44. *Prof Exp:* From clin instr to sr clin instr, 43-49, asst clin prof, 49-54, assoc prof, 54-74, prof, 74-80, EMER PROF MED & ADJ PROF, DIV RES MED EDUC, CASE WESTERN RESERVE UNIV, 80- *Concurrent Pos:* Vis in med & med dir out-patient clins, Cleveland Metrop Gen Hosp, 59-63; dir ambulatory teaching clin, Case Western Reserve Univ. *Mem:* Am Fedn Clin Res; fel Am Col Physicians. *Res:* Vertebral column acromegaly; infarction of the lung; lung abscess secondary to aseptic pulmonary infarction; diabetes and medical education; retinal changes in systemic disease; hypertensive encephalopathy; nervous system, including optic nerve changes, in Vitamin B12 deficient monkeys. *Mailing Add:* PO Box 304 Bearea OH 44017

CHESTER, MARVIN, b New York, NY, Dec 29, 30; m; c 3. SOLID STATE PHYSICS, CRYOGENICS. *Educ:* City Col New York, BS, 52; Calif Inst Technol, PhD(physics), 61. *Prof Exp:* From asst prof to assoc prof, 61-74, PROF PHYSICS, UNIV CALIF, LOS ANGELES, 74- *Concurrent Pos:* Alexander von Humboldt Award, 74. *Mem:* Am Phys Soc. *Res:* Configurational emf, a transport property in semiconducting materials; second sound, a thermal wave which exists in certain solids at low temperatures; electric field effects on the infrared absorption of silicon; superfluidity in almost-two-dimensional liquid helium; adsorption phenomena. *Mailing Add:* Dept of Physics Univ of Calif Los Angeles CA 90024

CHESTNUT, ALPHONSE F, b Stoughton, Mass, Nov 20, 17; m 43; c 2. MARINE ECOLOGY, ZOOLOGY. *Educ:* Col William & Mary, BSc, 41; Rutgers Univ, MSc, 43, PhD, 49. *Prof Exp:* Asst zool, Rutgers Univ, 41-43; res assoc oyster culture, NJ Agr Exp Sta, 43-48; specialist, Inst Marine Sci, 48-49, asst to dir, 49-55, assoc prof, 49-59, dir, 55-80, PROF MARINE SCI & ZOOL, INST MARINE SCI, UNIV NC, 59- *Mem:* Am Soc Limnol & Oceanog; Nat Shellfisheries Asn (vpres, 51-53, pres, 53); Sigma Xi; Atlantic Estuarine Res Soc (secy-treas, 52-53); Nat Shellfisheries Asn. *Res:* Food and feeding mechanism of lamellibranchia; estuarine ecology of pelecypods. *Mailing Add:* Inst of Marine Sci Univ of NC Morehead City NC 28557

CHESTNUT, H(AROLD), b Albany, NY, Nov 25, 17; m 44; c 3. ELECTRICAL ENGINEERING, SYSTEMS SCIENCE. *Educ:* Mass Inst Technol, BSEE, 39, MSEE, 40. *Hon Degrees:* DEE, Case Western Reserve Univ, 66; DEng, Villanova Univ, 72. *Prof Exp:* Mgr, systs eng & anal, 40-66, Info Sci Lab, 66-67 & Systs Eng & Anal Br, 67-71, CONSULT SYSTS ENG, RES & DEVELOP CTR, GEN ELEC CO, 71- *Concurrent Pos:* Lectr, exten div, Union Col, 47-49; ed, Systs Eng & Anal Ser, John Wiley & Sons; mem, NRC Comn Sociotech Systs, 75-78. *Mem:* Nat Acad Eng; Int Fedn Automatic Control (pres, 57-59); fel Instrument Soc Am; Am Automatic Control Coun (pres, 62-63); fel AAAS. *Res:* Control systems and systems engineering; systems research in control and other systems; supplemental ways for improving international stability. *Mailing Add:* Gen Elec Co One River Rd Schenectady NY 12345

CHESTON, CHARLES EDWARD, b Princeton, NJ, Nov 23, 11; m 38; c 2. FORESTRY. *Educ:* Syracuse Univ, BS, 33; Yale Univ, MF, 40. *Prof Exp:* Asst forester, NJ, 33-42; PROF FORESTRY & CHMN DEPT, UNIV OF THE SOUTH, TENN, 42- *Concurrent Pos:* Asst, Univ Mich, 57-58; mem, Tenn Conserv Comn, 63- *Mem:* Soc Am Foresters. *Res:* Forest economics; management of hardwood forest lands; rehabilitation of devastated forest lands on the Cumberland plateau. *Mailing Add:* Dept of Forestry Univ of the South Sewanee TN 37375

CHESTON, WARREN BRUCE, b Rochester, NY, Mar 15, 26; m 50; c 4. PHYSICS. *Educ:* Harvard Univ, BS, 47; Univ Rochester, PhD(physics), 51. *Prof Exp:* Asst prof physics, Washington Univ, 51-52; from assoc prof to prof, Univ Minn, Minneapolis, 53-71, dir space sci ctr, 65-68, dean inst technol, 68-71; chancellor, Univ Ill, Chicago Circle, 71-75; ASSOC DIR, WISTAR INST, 75- *Concurrent Pos:* Fulbright lectr, Univ Utrecht, 58-59; dept sci attache, Am Embassy, London, 63-65. *Mem:* Am Phys Soc. *Res:* Theoretical nuclear and meson physics. *Mailing Add:* Wistar Inst 36 & Spruce Sts Philadelphia PA 19104

CHETSANGA, CHRISTOPHER J, b Chetsanga Village, Zimbabwe, Aug 22, 35; m 70. MOLECULAR BIOLOGY, BIOCHEMISTRY. *Educ:* Pepperdine Univ, BS, 64; Univ Toronto, MS, 67, PhD(biochem & molecular biol), 69. *Prof Exp:* Tutor biochem, Harvard Univ, 70-72; from asst prof to assoc prof, 72-81, PROF BIOCHEM, UNIV MICH, DEARBORN, 81- *Concurrent Pos:* Res fel biochem, Harvard Univ, 69-72. *Mem:* AAAS; Am Soc Biol Chemists; Biophys Soc. *Res:* Mechanisms of repair of DNA modified by alkylating agents. *Mailing Add:* Dept Natural Sci Univ Mich Dearborn MI 48128

CHEUNG, ALBERT CHI-TONG, b Macau, Nov 15, 47; UK citizen. ASTROPHYSICS, QUANTUM ELECTRONICS. *Educ:* Stanford Univ, AB, 65; Univ Calif, Berkeley, MA, 66, PhD(physics), 76. *Prof Exp:* From res asst to res assoc physics, Univ Calif, Berkeley, 68-75; ASST PROF PHYSICS, UNIV CALIF, DAVIS, 75- *Concurrent Pos:* Res astronomer, Radio Astron Lab, Univ Calif, Berkeley, 72- *Mem:* Am Astron Soc. *Res:* Radio astrophysics; microwave spectroscopy; interstellar molecules; star formation; masers and low noise microwave receivers. *Mailing Add:* Dept of Physics Univ of Calif Davis CA 95616

CHEUNG, HARRY, b Oxnard, Calif, May 5, 31; m 54; c 3. CHEMICAL ENGINEERING. *Educ:* Ga Inst Technol, BS, 53, MS, 55. *Prof Exp:* Engr, 55-59, proj engr, 59-62, sect engr, 62-65, div engr, 65-67, div mgr, 67-69, eng assoc, 69-71, SR ENG ASSOC, LINDE DIV, UNION CARBIDE CORP, 71- *Mem:* Am Chem Soc; Am Mgt Asn. *Res:* Distillation; mass exchange; heat transfer; process development; hydrogen purification and production; air separation and cryogenics. *Mailing Add:* Linde Div Union Carbide Corp 61 E Park Dr Tonawanda NY 14150

CHEUNG, HERBERT CHIU-CHING, b Canton, China, Dec 19, 33; nat US; m 66; c 2. BIOPHYSICS, PHYSICAL CHEMISTRY. *Educ:* Rutgers Univ, AB, 54, PhD(phys chem, physics), 60; Cornell Univ, MS, 56. *Prof Exp:* Asst chem, Cornell Univ, 54-56; asst scientist, Fundamental Res Labs, US Steel Corp, 56-57; asst instr chem, Rutgers Univ, 58-60; res chemist res & develop dept, Am Viscose Div, FMC Corp, 60-63 & Gen Chem Div Res Labs, Allied Chem Corp, 63-66; sr fel biophys, Cardiovasc Res Inst, Med Ctr, Univ Calif, San Francisco, 66-69; assoc prof biophys, 69-73 & biomath, 73-74, ASSOC PROF BIOCHEM, UNIV ALA MED CTR, 69-, PROF BIOMATH & HEAD, BIOPHYSICS SECT, 74-, SR SCIENTIST, COMPREHENSIVE CANCER CTR, 76- *Concurrent Pos:* Lectr eve div, Pa Mil Col, 61-63; USPHS res career develop award, 71-76. *Mem:* Am Chem Soc; Biophys Soc; Am Soc Biol Chemists. *Res:* Molecular basis of contractility; relationship between macromolecular conformation and biological function; fluorescence spectroscopy. *Mailing Add:* Dept Biomath Univ Ala Univ Sta Birmingham AL 35294

CHEUNG, HOU TAK, b Shanghai, China, Sept 14, 50; m 77. LYMPHOCYTE CELL BIOLOGY. *Educ:* Univ Wis, Oshkosh, BS, 72, MS, 74, PhD(med microbiol), 77. *Prof Exp:* Res assoc, Immunobiol Res Ctr, 77-79; ASST PROF MICROBIOL & IMMUNOL, ILL STATE UNIV, 79- *Mem:* Am Asn Immunologists; Reticuloendothelial Soc; Am Soc Microbiol. *Res:* Cell biology of lymphocytes, particularly the molecular mechanism and regulation of lymphocyte mobility; the immunology of aging, especially interested in the mechanism of the age-related decline of the immune system. *Mailing Add:* Dept Biol Sci Ill State Univ Normal IL 61761

CHEUNG, JEFFREY TAI-KIN, b Shanghai, China, Apr 26, 46; US citizen; m 68. PHYSICAL CHEMISTRY, SEMICONDUCTOR PHYSICS. *Educ:* Univ Calif, Los Angeles, BSc, 69; Harvard Univ, PhD(chem), 74. *Prof Exp:* Res staff chem, Oak Ridge Nat Lab, 75-77; MEM TECH STAFF SEMICONDUCTOR PHYSICS, ROCKWELL INT, 77- *Res:* Gas phase kinetics; semiconductor material research. *Mailing Add:* 1049 Camino Dos Rios Thousand Oaks CA 91360

CHEUNG, MO-TSING MIRANDA, b Hong Kong, Nov 13, 42; Can citizen. ANALYTICAL CHEMISTRY, ECOLOGY. *Educ:* McGill Univ, BSc, 63, PhD(anal chem), 69. *Prof Exp:* Chemist org chem, United Aircraft Co Ltd, Quebec, 69-70; lectr, 72-77, SR LECTR ANAL CHEM, HONG KONG BAPTIST COL, 77- *Concurrent Pos:* Grant org chem, McGill Univ, 70-71; grant anal chem, 75-76; dep supvr & consult, Chem Testing Lab, Hong Kong Baptist Col, 73-75; dir, 76-; publ & res comt grants, 74, 76, 77-79, 81, secy, 76-79, ed, Acad J, 76-78; chmn, Comt Standardization Methodology Water Pollution, 78-82; Univ Outreach Comt grant, United Bd Christian Higher Educ in Asia, 78 & 80; sr res analyst, Dow Chem Hong Kong, Ltd, 80-81. *Mem:* Asian Ecol Soc (vpres, 77-); Asian Women Inst; Hong Kong Chem Soc. *Res:* Development of new analytical methods for the determination of trace metals by high performance liquid chromatography and investigation of the degree of water pollution in Hong Kong Harbour; air pollution; ion selective electrodes. *Mailing Add:* Dept Chem 224 Waterloo Rd 2nd Floor Kowloon Hong Kong

CHEUNG, PAUL JAMES, b Hong Kong, May 6, 42; US citizen; m 69; c 2. MARINE BIOLOGY. *Educ:* Iona Col, BS, 66; NY Univ, MS, 69, PhD(marine biol), 73. *Prof Exp:* Res staff marine 67-76, FISH PATHOLOGIST, OSBORN LABS MARINE SCI, NEW YORK ZOOL SOC, 76- *Mem:* Am Micros Soc; NY Acad Sci; Am Soc Zoologists. *Res:* Mass rearing of marine invertebrates; evaluation of anti-fouling paints; fish diseases in salt water fishes; biogenesis and biochemistry of barnacle adhesive and neuroendocrine physiology of barnacle. *Mailing Add:* Osborn Labs Marine Sci W Eighth St Coney Island Brooklyn NY 11224

CHEUNG, PETER PAK LUN, b China, Feb 2, 39; m 65; c 2. DENTAL MATERIALS. *Educ:* Colo State Univ, BS, 64; Okla State Univ, PhD(chem), 67. *Prof Exp:* Instr chem, Okla State Univ, 67-68; investr, N J Zinc Co, 68-69; res chemist, 69-70, sr chemist, 70-80, PROJ LEADER, PENWALT CHEM CORP, 80- *Mem:* Am Chem Soc; Int Asn Dent Res. *Res:* Surface chemistry of titanium dioxide; properties and compositions of dental materials; composite resin filling materials; alginate and silicone impression materials; x-ray opaque materials; cavity varnishes. *Mailing Add:* Pennwalt Corp 900 First Ave King of Prussia PA 19406

CHEUNG, SHIU MING, b Canton, China, Dec 31, 42; m 73; c 3. MATHEMATICAL STATISTICS, ELECTRICAL ENGINEERING. *Educ:* Polytech Inst NY, PhD(math), 74. *Prof Exp:* MATHEMATICIAN, FED AVIATION ADMIN TECH CTR, US GOVT, 76- *Mem:* Inst Elec & Electronic Engrs. *Res:* Theories, techniques and procedures which can be used to analyze, design and implement digital filters; construction of algorithms that can be used to filter recorded signals. *Mailing Add:* 143 W Rutgers Court College Park Egg Harbor NJ 08215

CHEUNG, WAI YIU, b Canton, China, July 15, 33; US citizen; m 62; c 3. BIOCHEMISTRY. *Educ:* Chung Hsing Univ, Taiwan, BS, 56; Univ Vt, MS, 60; Cornell Univ, PhD(biochem), 64. *Prof Exp:* USPHS trainee, 64-67; asst mem, 67-70, assoc mem, 70-71, MEM, DEPT BIOCHEM, ST JUDE CHILDREN'S RES HOSP, 71- *Concurrent Pos:* Prof biochem, Univ Tenn Ctr Health Sci; USPHS res career develop award, 71-76. *Honors & Awards:* Gairdner Award, 81. *Mem:* AAAS; Am Chem Soc; Am Soc Biol Chem. *Res:* Biological regulatory mechanisms; hormonal action; cyclic nucleotides; calcium and calmodulin. *Mailing Add:* Dept of Biochem St Jude Children's Res Hosp Memphis TN 38101

CHEVALIER, HOWARD L, b Beaumont, Tex, Sept 14, 31; m 51; c 2. FLIGHT MECHANICS, AIRCRAFT DESIGN. *Educ:* Tex A&M Univ, BS, 57, MS, 71. *Prof Exp:* Res engr, Aro Inc, 56-63; res scientist, NASA Ames Res Ctr, 63-69; from asst prof to prof, 69-81, DRESSER INDUST PROF AEROSPACE ENG, TEX A&M UNIV, 81- *Concurrent Pos:* Prin investr, NASA, Dept Energy, Fed Aviation Admin & indust, 69-81; consult, Challenge Eng Inc, 81- *Res:* Aerodynamic; wind tunnel testing; dynamics; stability; control and aircraft design; aircraft design research include canard configurations and remotely controlled aircraft. *Mailing Add:* Aerospace Eng Dept Tex A&M Univ College Station TX 77843

CHEVALIER, PEGGY, b Green Bay, Wis. PLANT PHYSIOLOGY, PLANT BREEDING. *Educ:* Univ Ill, Urbana, BS, 71; Univ Wis-Madison, MS, 76, PhD(agron, plant breeding & genetics), 78. *Prof Exp:* ASST PROF AGRON, WASH STATE UNIV, 78- *Mem:* Crop Sci Soc Am; Am Soc Plant Physiologists; Am Soc Agron. *Res:* Sucrose and starch synthesis in leaves and endosperm of crop plants; use of physiological and biochemical tools in plant breeding programs. *Mailing Add:* Dept of Agron & Soils Wash State Univ Pullman WA 99164

CHEVALIER, PETER ANDREW, b Chicago, Ill, Mar 4, 40; m 64; c 2. PHYSIOLOGY. *Educ:* Univ Minn, BA, 62, PhD(physiol), 67. *Prof Exp:* Asst prof physiol, Univ Del, 67-73; asst prof, 73-77, ASSOC PROF PHYSIOL & MED, MAYO MED SCH, 77- *Mem:* AAAS; Am Physiol Soc; Am Thoracic Soc; Sigma Xi; Am Heart Asn. *Res:* Respiratory and circulatory physiology; dynamic regional lung mechanics; Roentgen videodensitometry and computer-based three-dimensional reconstruction techniques; cardiac pacing and electrophysiology. *Mailing Add:* Medtronic Inc 3055 Old Hwy Eight Minneapolis MN 55369

CHEVILLE, NORMAN F, b Rhodes, Iowa, Sept 30, 34; m 58; c 4. VETERINARY PATHOLOGY. *Educ:* Iowa State Univ, DVM, 59; Univ Wis, MS, 63, PhD(path), 64. *Prof Exp:* Res vet virol, US Army Biol Lab, 59-61; proj assoc path, Univ Wis, 61-63; PATHOLOGIST, NAT ANIMAL DIS LAB, USDA, 63-, PROF VET PATH, IOWA STATE UNIV, 69- *Concurrent Pos:* Res pathologist, Nat Inst Med Res, London, 68. *Mem:* Am Vet Med Asn; Am Col Vet Path (secy-treas, 74-, pres, 81); Conf Res Workers Animal Dis (vpres, 78, pres, 79). *Res:* Pathology of disease of infectious origin and domesticated animals. *Mailing Add:* Nat Animal Dis Lab Ames IA 50010

CHEVONE, BORIS IVAN, b Lynn, Mass, Aug 25, 43; m 69; c 1. INSECT PHYSIOLOGY. *Educ:* Univ Mass, Amherst, BA, 65, MS, 68; Univ Minn, St Paul, PhD(entom), 74. *Prof Exp:* Res scientist virol, 74-77, RES FEL PLANT PATH, UNIV MINN, ST PAUL, 77- *Mem:* Entom Soc Am; Sigma Xi. *Res:* Physiology of insect vectors of plant viruses. *Mailing Add:* Dept of Plant Path Univ of Minn St Paul MN 55108

CHEVRAY, RENE, b Paris, France, Feb 6, 37; m 64; c 2. FLUID MECHANICS. *Educ:* Univ Toulouse, BS, 62; Nat Sch Advan Electrotech & Hydraul, Toulouse, dipl Ing, 62; Univ Iowa, MS, 64, PhD(fluid mech), 67. *Hon Degrees:* ScD, Univ Claude Bernard, Lyon, France, 78. *Prof Exp:* Res engr, Worthington Co, France, 63-64; fel & lectr, Johns Hopkins Univ, 67-69; from asst prof to assoc prof, 69-79, PROF FLUID MECH, STATE UNIV NY STONY BROOK, 79-, ACTG CHMN, DEPT MECH ENG, 80- *Concurrent Pos:* State Univ NY Res Found grant in aid, 70-71, fac res fel, 71; fac assoc, NSF res grants, 70-71, 73 & 75, prin investr, 71-73, 75-77, 77-79, 78-80 & 79-81; prin investr, Dept Energy contract, 79-82. *Mem:* Am Phys Soc; Fr Eng Asn; Int Asn Hydraul Res; Sigma Xi; NY Acad Sci. *Res:* Turbulence; two-dimensional and axisymmetric turbulent wakes; electronic instrumentation in turbulence research; preferential transport of heat over momentum in intermittent regions of turbulent shear flows; history of science. *Mailing Add:* Dept of Mech State Univ of NY Stony Brook NY 11790

CHEW, FRANCES SZE-LING, b Los Angeles, Calif, May 11, 48. BIOLOGY, ENTOMOLOGY. *Educ:* Stanford Univ, AB, 70; Yale Univ, PhD(biol), 74. *Prof Exp:* Fel, Dept Biol Sci, Stanford Univ, 74-75; asst prof, 75-81, ASSOC PROF BIOL, TUFTS UNIV, 81- *Concurrent Pos:* managing ed, J Lepid Soc, 78-81. *Mem:* Soc Study Evolution; Lepidopterists Soc; AAAS. *Res:* Plant-herbivore interactions, especially evolution of pierid butterflies and their cruciferous food plants. *Mailing Add:* Dept of Biol Tufts Univ Medford MA 02155

CHEW, FRANK, b San Francisco, Calif, Aug 17, 16; m 46; c 3. OCEANOGRAPHY. *Educ:* Univ Calif, Los Angeles, BA, 43, MA, 50; Univ Miami, PhD(oceanog), 73. *Prof Exp:* Asst prof oceanog, Univ Miami, 52-59; res assoc, Gulf Coast Lab, Miss, 59-62; res scientist, Lockheed-Calif Co, 62-65 & Bissett-Berman Corp, 65-66; RES OCEANOGR, ATLANTIC OCEANOG & METEOROL LABS, NAT OCEANIC & ATMOSPHERIC ADMIN, 66- *Mem:* Am Meteorol Soc; Am Geophys Union. *Res:* Accelerative process in ocean currents and its relation to horizontal sea level and change. *Mailing Add:* 901 Sistina Ave Coral Gables FL 33146

CHEW, GEOFFREY FOUCAR, b Washington, DC, June 5, 24; m 45, 71; c 5. THEORETICAL HIGH ENERGY PHYSICS. *Educ:* George Washington Univ, BS, 44; Univ Chicago, PhD(physics), 48. *Prof Exp:* Jr theoret physicist, Los Alamos Sci Lab, NMex, 44-46; Nat Res fel, Univ Chicago, 46-48; theoret physics res radiation lab, Univ Calif, 48-49, asst prof physics, 49-50; from asst prof to prof, Univ Ill, 50-57; theoret group leader, 70-74, chmn dept, 74-78, Miller Prof, 81-82, PROF PHYSICS, UNIV CALIF, BERKELEY, 57-, THEORET GROUP LEADER, 79- *Concurrent Pos:* Fulbright lectr, Les Houches, 53, 60 & 65; fel, Churchill Col, Cambridge, 62-63; lectr, Tata Inst, Nainital, 69; vis prof, Princeton Univ, 70-71; consult, Los Alamos & Brookhaven Nat Labs. *Honors & Awards:* Hughes Prize, Am Phys Soc, 62; E O Lawrence Award, 69. *Mem:* Nat Acad Sci; fel Am Phys Soc; Am Acad Arts & Sci. *Res:* Theoretical particle physics; scattering matrix theory; strong interactions. *Mailing Add:* 10 Maybeck Twin Dr Berkeley CA 94708

CHEW, HERMAN W, b China; US citizen. ELECTROMAGNETISM. *Educ:* Univ Chicago, SM, 58, PhD(physics), 61. *Prof Exp:* Res assoc physics, Univ Pa, 61-62; res scientist, Columbia Univ, 62-63; instr, Princeton Univ, 63-64; asst prof, Case-Western Reserv Univ, 64-67; assoc prof, 67-80, PROF PHYSICS, CLARKSON COL, 80- *Mem:* Am Phys Soc; Sigma Xi. *Res:* Weak and electromagnetic interactions; scattering theory. *Mailing Add:* Dept Physics Clarkson Col Postdam NY 13676

CHEW, JU-NAM, b China, Oct 8, 23; nat US; m 47; c 3. PETROLEUM RESERVOIR ENGINEERING, ENHANCED OIL RECOVERY. *Educ:* Univ Tex, BSChE, 44, MSChE, 47, PhD(chem eng), 53; Univ Mich, MSE, 49. *Prof Exp:* Chemist, Phelps Dodge Refining Corp, 44; tutor & instr chem, Univ Tex, 44-45; asst chem eng, Eng Res Inst, Univ Mich, 46-49, res assoc, 49; res scientist, Univ Tex, 49-50; sr res engr, Socony Mobil Oil Co, 53-66, SR RES ENGR, MOBIL RES & DEVELOP CORP, 66- *Concurrent Pos:* Lectr, Univ Tex, Arlington, 57-71. *Mem:* Am Inst Chem Engrs; Am Chem Soc; Sigma Xi; Am Inst Mining, Metall & Petrol Engrs. *Res:* Phase equilibria; fluid mechanics; petroleum reservoir engineering; enhanced oil recovery processes; in-situ coal recovery. *Mailing Add:* Mobil Field Res Lab PO Box 900 Dallas TX 75221

CHEW, KENNETH KENDALL, b Red Bluff, Calif, Oct 29, 33; m 58; c 2. MARINE BIOLOGY. *Educ:* Chico State Col, BA, 55; Univ Wash, MS, 58, PhD(fisheries), 61. *Prof Exp:* Sr fisheries biologist, Fisheries Res Inst, 61-62, from res asst prof to res assoc prof, 62-67, assoc prof, 67-71, PROF FISHERIES, UNIV WASH, 71- *Mem:* Am Fisheries Soc; Nat Shellfisheries Asn; World Mariculture Soc; AAAS. *Res:* Shellfish biology; marine ecology; growth, condition and survival of Pacific oysters; shellfish toxicity studies in Washington and Southeast Alaska; clam and mussel culture studies; ecological baseline studies. *Mailing Add:* Col of Fisheries Univ of Wash Seattle WA 98105

CHEW, ROBERT MARSHALL, ecology, see previous edition

CHEW, VICTOR, b Djakarta, Indonesia, July 9, 23; m 49; c 3. MATHEMATICAL STATISTICS, BIOMETRICS. *Educ:* Univ Western Australia, BSc, 44; Univ Melbourne, BA, 53. *Prof Exp:* Tech officer, Commonwealth Sci & Indust Res Orgn, Melbourne, Australia, 47-49, res officer, Sydney, 53-55; instr math, Univ Melbourne, 49-53; res asst, Univ Fla, 55-56, asst prof, 56-57; asst statistician, NC State Col, 57-60; math statistician, US Naval Weapons Lab, 60-62; sr engr, RCA Serv Co, 62-70; MATH STATISTICIAN, BIOMET SERV STAFF, AGR RES SERV, USDA, 71- *Concurrent Pos:* Lectr, Am Univ, 60-61, 62-63, Johns Hopkins Univ, 61-62, Brevard Eng Col, 63-67 & Fla State Univ, 67-70. *Mem:* Biomet Soc; Am Statist Asn; Int Asn Statist in Phys Sci; fel Royal Statist Soc. *Res:* Experimental designs; mathematical modeling; statistical inference; regression analysis; biometry. *Mailing Add:* Biomet Serv Staff Agr Res Serv USDA Univ of Fla Gainesville FL 32611

CHEW, WILLIAM HUBERT, JR, b Macon, Ga, Sept 21, 33; m 57; c 3. INTERNAL MEDICINE, INFECTIOUS DISEASES. *Educ:* Med Col Ga, MD, 58. *Prof Exp:* Asst med, Sch Med, Tufts Univ, 62-63, instr, 63-64; from instr to assoc prof, 64-72, chief infectious dis sect, 67-70, dir & coordr, Physician Augmentation Prog, 70-75, PROF MED, MED COL GA, 72- *Concurrent Pos:* Res fel infectious dis, Pratt Clin, New Eng Ctr Hosp, 63-64; Markle scholar acad med, 64; dir, NIH Training Grant, 67. *Mem:* Am Fedn Clin Res. *Res:* Candida-host defense interactions, specifically what alterations in host defense occur to permit either local or disseminated candidiasis. *Mailing Add:* Sch of Med Med Col of Ga Augusta GA 30901

CHEW, WOODROW W(ILSON), b Burlington, Okla, Jan 29, 13; m 39; c 1. CHEMICAL ENGINEERING. *Educ:* NMex State Univ, BS, 36; Okla State Univ, MS, 38. *Prof Exp:* Asst chem & chem eng, Okla State Univ, 36-38; engr & asst engr, Pub Works Admin, Tex, 38-39; instr chem & physics, Northeastern Okla Jr Col, 39-40; asst prof chem eng, La Polytech Inst, 40-41, from asst prof & head dept to prof & head dept, 41-52; chem engr, Monsanto Chem Co, 45; plant engr & consult, Magnolia Petrol Co, 52; prof chem eng & head dept, La Tech Univ, 52-75; RETIRED. *Concurrent Pos:* Pres, Woodrow W Chew & Assocs, Inc, 75- *Mem:* Am Chem Soc; Am Soc Eng Educ; Nat Soc Prof Engrs; Am Inst Chem Engrs. *Res:* Vapor-liquid equilibrium; mutual solubility in ternary systems; chemical plant economic evaluations and designs. *Mailing Add:* Box 5166 Tech Sta Ruston LA 71272

CHEYDLEUR, BENJAMIN FREDERIC, b Grenoble, France, Oct 22, 12; US citizen; m 43; c 5. COMPUTER SCIENCE, ELECTRONICS. *Educ:* Univ Wis, BA, 38. *Prof Exp:* Statistician, US Civil Serv Comn, Washington, DC, 40-42; chief numerical anal, Appl Math Div, Naval Ord Lab, Silver Spring, Md, 46-54; dir systs anal comput design, Remington Rand Univac, St Paul, Minn, 55-58; mgr advan prog comput design, Electronic Data Div, RCA, Camden, NJ, 58-60; staff & prin scientist info sci, Philco-Ford, Willow Grove, Pa & Dearborn, Mich, 60-68; PROF ENG COMPUT SCI, OAKLAND UNIV, 68- *Concurrent Pos:* Mem aeroballistics comt, Bur Ord, Dept Defense, 52-54; mem comt data lang systs, Asn Comput Mach, 59-60; mem adv comt info retrieval, Moore Sch, Univ Pa, 62-63; mem, Pa Gov Scranton's Tech Adv Comn, 64; contribr, Merrill Flood Report, Cong Cont Automation, 65; mem int adv bd, Ctr Res & Lang Behavior, Univ Mich, 66-68. *Mem:* Asn Comput Mach; Am Soc Info Sci; Inst Elec & Electronics Engrs; Am Math Soc; Pattern Recognition Soc. *Res:* Computer architecture; information retrieval hardware and switching theory. *Mailing Add:* Sch of Eng Oakland Univ Rochester MI 48063

CHEZEM, CURTIS GORDON, b Eugene, Ore, Jan 28, 24; div; c 2. PHYSICS, NUCLEAR ENGINEERING. *Educ:* Univ Ore, BA, 51, MA, 52; Ore State Univ, PhD(physics), 60. *Prof Exp:* Flight radio officer, Alaska Div, Pan Am World Airways, 42-43, Pac Div, 43-44; chief radio officer, Hammond Steamship Lines, 44-45; telegrapher, Western Union Tel Co, Ore, 46; announcer & engr, Radio Stas KUGN & KASH, 46-51; staff mem, Los Alamos Sci Lab, 52-67; prof physics & nuclear eng, Los Alamos Grad Ctr, NMex, 62-67; chief systs studies br, Off Safeguards & Mat Mgt, US AEC, 67-69; prof nuclear eng & head dept, Kans State Univ, 69-72; dir, Nuclear Activ, Mid South Servs, New Orleans, 72-77; gen mgr, Waterman Inc, 77-79; PRES, THE SEVEN SEAS GIFTS INC, 79- *Concurrent Pos:* Asst, Univ Ore, 50-51 & Ore State Univ, 55-57; reactor prog supvr, AEC, Bogota, Colombia, 63; vis prof, Tex A&M Univ, 66-67; mem, Kans Nuclear Energy Coun, 70- & Kans State Univ rep, Atomic Indust Forum, 69-72. *Mem:* Inst Nuclear Mat Mgt. *Res:* Nuclear materials control and safeguards; nuclear Power; interacting critical and sub-critical nuclear systems; computer programming; data analysis; navigation and communications. *Mailing Add:* 46 Center St PO Box 396 Nantucket Island MA 02554

CHHABRA, RAJENDRA S, b India, Mar 4, 39; m 66; c 2. PHARMACOLOGY, TOXICOLOGY. *Educ:* Vet Col, Mhow, India, BVSc&AH, 62; Univ London, PhD(pharmacol), 70. *Prof Exp:* Res asst pharmacol, Vet Col, Mhow, India, 62-64, asst res officer, 64-66; res pharmacologist, Biorex Labs, London, Eng, 66-67; vis assoc pharmacol, 70-73, sr staff fel, Pharmacol Br, 73-77, pharmacologist, Environ Biol & Chem Br, 78-80, SUPERVISORY PHARMACOLOGIST, TOXICOL RES & TESTING PROG, NAT TOXICOL PROG, NAT INST ENVIRON HEALTH SCI, 80- *Mem:* Soc Toxicol; Am Soc Pharmacol & Exp Therapeut. *Res:* Transport and biotransformation of foreign chemicals; species and strain variations in enzymatic biotransformation of xenobiotics. *Mailing Add:* Nat Inst of Environ Health Sci Research Triangle Park NC 27709

CHHEDA, GIRISH B, b Kutch, India, Mar 4, 34; m 62. MEDICINAL CHEMISTRY, BIOCHEMISTRY. *Educ:* Univ Bombay, BSc, Hons 55, BS, 57; Univ Mich, MS, 59; State Univ NY Buffalo, PhD(med chem), 63. *Prof Exp:* Apprentice drug anal, Glaxo Labs, Bombay, India, 56; pharmaceut chemist, Castophene Mfg Co, 57; fel, State Univ NY Buffalo, 63-64; cancer res scientist, 64-65, sr cancer res scientist, 65-68, assoc cancer res scientist, 68-73, PRIN CANCER RES SCIENTIST, ROSWELL PARK MEM INST, 73- *Concurrent Pos:* Res prof, Niagara Univ, 68- & State Univ NY Buffalo, 68. *Mem:* Am Chem Soc. *Res:* Anti-metabolites and enzyme inhibitors; synthesis of oligonucleotides; investigation of human urinary nucleic acid constituents. *Mailing Add:* Roswell Park Mem Inst 666 Elm St Buffalo NY 14263

CHI, BENJAMIN E, b Tientsin, China, June 18, 33; US citizen. COMPUTER OPERATING SYSTEMS, DATA COMMUNICATIONS. *Educ:* Antioch Col, BS, 55; Rensselaer Polytech Inst, PhD(physics), 62. *Prof Exp:* Fel & lectr physics, Western Reserve Univ, 62-63; instr, 63-65; asst prof, 65-69, chmn dept, 70-73, ASSOC PROF PHYSICS, STATE UNIV NY ALBANY, 69-, ASSOC DIR, COMPUT CTR, 82- *Mem:* AAAS; Am Phys Soc; Asn Comput Mach; Am Asn Physics Teachers. *Res:* Efficiency in operating systems; new methodologies in real time data handling; high-volume delivery of interactive computing; experimental data, acquisition and processing. *Mailing Add:* Comput Ctr State Univ NY Albany NY 12222

CHI, CHAO SHU, b Naking, China, Sept 12, 36; US citizen; m; c 3. ELECTRONICS, COMPUTER DESIGN. *Educ:* Nat Cheng-Kung Univ, Taiwan, BS, 61; Worcester Polytech Inst, MS, 65, PhD(elec eng), 74. *Prof Exp:* Engr power syst, Northeast Utilities Serv Co, 63-66; prin mem tech staff advan develop, RCA, Camden, NJ & Marlboro, Mass, 66-71; proj engr comput develop, Digital Equip Corp, Mass, 71-77; prin investr data trans, 77-78, MGR MAGNETIC RES, RES CTR, SPERRY CORP, 78- *Concurrent Pos:* Reviewer trans magnetics, Inst Elec & Electronics Engrs, 78. *Mem:* Inst Elec & Electronics Engrs. *Res:* High density magnetic recording process and identificaon of linear and nonlinear distortions, their origins and solutions to advance the art of computer mass storage technology. *Mailing Add:* 4 Wiltshire Dr Shrewsbury MA 01545

CHI, CHE, b Peking, China, Feb 6, 49; US citizen; m 77; c 1. NEUROSCIENCE. *Educ:* Nat Taiwan Univ, BS, 70; Okla State Univ, MS, 72; Univ Wis, PhD(neurosci), 76, MS, 81. *Prof Exp:* Res asst, Okla State Univ, 71-72 & Univ Wis, 72-76; res fel, Univ Minn, Minneapolis, 76-77; res fel, 77-78, ASST SCIENTIST, UNIV WIS, 79- *Concurrent Pos:* Vis instr, Univ Ore, 75. *Mem:* Sigma Xi; Entom Soc Am. *Res:* Scanning and transmission electron microscopy (high-voltage electron microscopy) of the house fly ommatidium and first optic neuropile and blood brain barrier; intrafusal muscles of "wobbler" mice; developing computer programs for 3-D reconstruction of neural networks. *Mailing Add:* Dept of Entom Univ of Wis Madison WI 53706

CHI, CHENG-CHING, b Canton, China, Feb 15, 39; US citizen; m 67; c 1. MECHANICAL SYSTEMS ANALYSIS. *Educ:* Nat Taiwan Univ, BS, 62; Kans State Univ, MS, 65; Univ Calif, Berkeley, PhD(appl mech), 69. *Prof Exp:* Engr, 69-71, sr engr, 71-74, sr eng specialist, 74-80, ENG SUPVR, GARRETT CORP, 80- *Concurrent Pos:* Lectr, Calif State Univ, Northridge, 71. *Res:* Nonlinear oscillations; dynamic analysis of high speed trains; computer simulations of jet engine dynamics; vibration signature techniques for machine health monitoring and diagnosis. *Mailing Add:* 6454 Parklynn Dr Rancho Palos Verdes CA 90274

CHI, CHIEN CHEN, b Shang-tung, China, Feb 16, 15; m 50; c 4. PLANT PATHOLOGY. *Educ:* Western China Union Univ, BS, 42; Nanking Univ, MS, 47; Univ Wis, PhD(plant path), 59. *Prof Exp:* Plant pathologist sugar cane, Taiwan Sugar Exp Sta, 47-56; proj assoc plant path, Univ Wis, 59-60; fel, 60-62; PLANT PATHOLOGIST FORAGE CROPS, CAN DEPT AGR, 62- *Mem:* Am Phytopath Soc. *Res:* Diseases of forage crops host-pathogen relationships of soil-inhabiting fungi in forage crops. *Mailing Add:* 30 Beaverton Ave Neplan K2E 5K4 Can

CHI, DONALD NAN-HUA, b Medan, Indonesia, June 28, 39; US citizen; m 68; c 2. APPLIED MATHEMATICS. *Educ:* Willamette Univ, BA, 62; Carnegie Inst Technol, MS, 65; Univ Pittsburgh, PhD(math), 70. *Prof Exp:* Instr math, Univ Pittsburgh, 68-70, res physicist, 70-75; supvry res physicist numerical anal & aerodynamics, 75-80, SUPVRY SYSTS ANALYST, PITTSBURGH RES CTR, US BUR MINES, 80- *Concurrent Pos:* Mem comt Masters & PhD degrees, Dept Mech Eng, Univ Pittsburgh, 73-; reviewer, Appl Mech Rev, Am Soc Mech Engrs, 74- *Mem:* Soc Indust & Appl Math. *Res:* Transient phenomena of flame propagation in coal mine networks via computer simulation; numerical techniques in solving gas-dynamic and heat transfer problems and in solving nonlinear algebraic equations and nonlinear least square problems; computer applications ranging from process control, data-reduction to administrative applications; data-base management system and management information system. *Mailing Add:* Pittsburgh Res Ctr PO Box 18070 Pittsburgh PA 15236

CHI, HENRY HSI-KUANG, b Peking, China, Aug 27, 31; US citizen; m 62; c 3. CHEMICAL ENGINEERING, POLYMER SCIENCE. *Educ:* Univ Wis, BS, 54, MS, 58. *Prof Exp:* Res engr dry cells, Ray-O-Vac Co, Madison, Wis, 54-57; SR RES TECHNOLOGIST POLYMERS, MONSANTO CO, 58- *Mem:* Am Inst Chem Engrs. *Res:* Polymer synthesis; polymer product and process designs. *Mailing Add:* 200 Birch Rd Longmeadow MA 01106

CHI, JOHN WEN HUA, b Nanking, China, July 20, 34; US citizen; m 58; c 3. NUCLEAR ENGINEERING. *Educ:* Willamette Univ, BA, 58; Carnegie-Mellon Univ, BS, 58, MS, 60; Univ Pittsburgh, PhD(chem eng), 68. *Prof Exp:* Engr coal processes, Res Dept, Consol Coal Co, 56-58; res engr metall processes, Res Div, Jones & Laughlin Steel Corp, 59-62; sr engr heat transfer res, Astronuclear Lab, 62-68, fel engr thermal design, 68-76, ADV ENGR THERMAL DESIGN, FUSION POWER SYSTS DEPT, WESTINGHOUSE ELEC CORP, 76- *Mem:* Am Nuclear Soc; Am Inst Chem Engrs; Am Inst Aeronaut & Astronaut. *Res:* Cryogenic heat transfer; two-phase flow; advanced heat transfer techniques; heat pipes; advanced energy systems; fusion power. *Mailing Add:* Fusion Power Systs Dept Westinghouse Elec Corp Large PA 15236

CHI, L K, b Shanghai, China, Dec 12, 33; US citizen; m; c 3. SOFTWARE DEVELOPMENT, MATHEMATICAL APPLICATIONS. *Educ:* Nat Taiwan Univ, BS, 56; Univ Md, MA, 60; Drexel Univ, PhD(appl mech), 68. *Prof Exp:* Res scientist, Spau Sci, Inc, Waltham, Mass, 62-65; instr math, Community Col Philadelphia, 65-66; asst prof, Widener Col, 66-68; res assoc elec eng, Drexel Univ, 68-69; sr software specialist, RCA, 69-71; prin syst programer, Sperry Univac, 72-77; asst prof, 77-81, ASSOC PROF COMPUT

SCI, US NAVAL ACAD, 82- *Mem:* Asn Comput Mach; Am Phys Soc; Am Acad Mech. *Res:* Kinetic theory; boundary layer theory; plasma physics; numerical solutions to various physical problems. *Mailing Add:* Appl Sci Dept US Naval Acad Annapolis MD 21402

CHI, LOIS WONG, b Foochow, Fukien, China; m 45; c 3. PARASITOLOGY. *Educ:* Wheaton Col, Ill, BS, 45; Univ Southern Calif, MS, 48, PhD, 53. *Prof Exp:* Res assoc & instr, Loma Linda Univ, 52-56; from instr to assoc prof biol, Immaculate Heart Col, 57-66, chmn dept, 63-66; assoc prof biol sci, 66-70, chmn dept, 71-72, PROF BIOL SCI, CALIF STATE COL, DOMINGUEZ HILLS, 70- *Concurrent Pos:* Prin investr, NIH grant, 67-75; prog dir, Minority Biomed Support Prog, 77- *Mem:* Am Soc Parasitol; Am Soc Trop Med & Hyg; AAAS; NY Acad Sci. *Res:* Host and parasite relationship; control of Schistosoma parasites through snail vector Oncomelania; hybrid snail reproduction and susceptibility to schistosome infection and host immune response. *Mailing Add:* Dept of Biol Sci Calif State Col Dominguez Hills CA 90747

CHI, MICHAEL, mechanical engineering, see previous edition

CHI, MINN-SHONG, b Taichung, Taiwan, Dec 11, 40; US citizen; m 71; c 2. CHEMISTRY, PSYCHOLOGY. *Educ:* Nat Taiwan Univ, BS, 65; Univ Louisville, MS, 69; Univ Mich, PhD(chem), 72. *Prof Exp:* Fel, Univ Mich, 72-74; res chemist org & polymer chem, Witco Chem Corp, 74-77; STAFF CHEMIST ORG, POLYMER & SOLID PROPELLANT CHEM, ALLEGANY BALLISTICS LAB, HERCULES, 77- *Mem:* Am Chem Soc. *Res:* Polymer chemistry; polyurethanes, poly amino acids, polyesters; organic chemistry; explosive materials; photochemistry; azo compounds. *Mailing Add:* Allegany Ballistics Lab PO Box 210 Cumberland MD 21502

CHI, MYUNG SUN, nutrition, nutritional biochemistry, see previous edition

CHI, TSUNG-CHIN, b Pukiang, China, Dec 1, 43; m 72; c 2. SOLID STATE PHYSICS, ULTRASONICS. *Educ:* Cheng Kung Univ, BS, 65; Purdue Univ, MS, 69, PhD(physics), 72. *Prof Exp:* Res assoc physics, Purdue Univ, 73-75, sr res asst, 75-78, sr res assoc physics, Ctr Info & Numerical Data Anal, 78-81; RES PHYSICIST, NAVAL SURFACE WEAPONS CTR, 81- *Mem:* Sigma Xi. *Res:* Experimental solid state physics. *Mailing Add:* 100 Old Landing Court Fredricksburg VA 22401

CHIA, FU-SHIANG, b Shantung, China, Jan 15, 31; m 63; c 2. ZOOLOGY. *Educ:* Taiwan Norm Univ, BS, 55; Univ Wash, MS, 62, PhD(zool), 64. *Prof Exp:* Lab instr biol, Tunghai Univ, 57-58; asst zool, Univ Wash, 58-64; asst prof life sci, Sacramento State Col, 64-66; sr res officer zool, Univ Newcastle, 66-69; assoc prof, 69-75, PROF ZOOL, UNIV ALTA, 75-, CHMN DEPT, 78- *Mem:* Am Soc Zoologists. *Res:* Developmental biology; marine invertebrate zoology. *Mailing Add:* Dept of Zool Univ of Alta Edmonton ON T6G 2E8 Can

CHIACCHIERINI, RICHARD PHILIP, b Elmira, NY, Mar 21, 43; m 65; c 2. RISK ASSESSMENT, MODELLING. *Educ:* St Bonaventure Univ, BS, 65; NC State Univ, MES, 67; Va Polytech Inst & State Univ, PhD(statist), 72. *Prof Exp:* Jr statistician, Biometry Sect, Nat Ctr Radiol Health, 67-70; trainee, Bur Radiol Health, Food & Drug Admin, 70-72, chief, Statist Sect, Off Radiol Prog, Environ Protection Agency, 72-73, sr statistician, Epidemiol Br, Bur Radiol Health, Food & Drug Admin, 73-79, chief, Statist Sect, 79-82, CHIEF, IONIZING RADIOL BR, BUR RADIOL HEALTH, FOOD & DRUG ADMIN, 82- *Concurrent Pos:* Adj prof, Va Polytech Inst & State Univ, 81- *Mem:* Biomet Soc; Am Statist Asn. *Res:* Design, analysis, and interpretation of categorical data; modelling of risks and benefits from the use of ionizing radiation; derivation of risk assessment information from experimental and epidemiologic studies. *Mailing Add:* Bur Radiol Health FDA 5600 Fishers Lane Rockville MD 20857

CHIAKULAS, JOHN JAMES, b Chicago, Ill, Aug 3, 15; m 49; c 1. ANATOMY. *Educ:* Northwestern Univ, BS, 40, MA, 47; Univ Chicago, PhD(zool), 51. *Prof Exp:* Spec lectr zool, Grinnell Col, 46-47; instr biol, Roosevelt Univ, 51-52; asst prof anat, Chicago Col Optom, 52-53; instr, 53-55, assoc, 56-57, from asst prof to assoc prof, 58-66, PROF ANAT, CHICAGO MED SCH, 66-, ACTG CHMN, ANAT DEPT, 80- *Mem:* Int Soc Chronobiol; Am Soc Zool; Am Asn Anat; Soc Develop Biol. *Res:* Wound healing; tissue specificity; organ regeneration; biorythmicity. *Mailing Add:* Dept of Anat Univ Health Sci Chicago Med Sch Chicago IL 60612

CHIANELLI, RUSSELL ROBERT, b Newark, NJ, May 22, 44; m 71; c 3. INORGANIC CHEMISTRY. *Educ:* Polytech Inst Brooklyn, BS, 70, PhD(chem), 74. *Prof Exp:* Res chemist, 73-76, SR RES CHEMIST & GROUP HEAD CATALYTIC MAT GROUP, EXXON RES & ENG CO, 76- *Mem:* AAAS; NY Acad Sci; Am Chem Soc; Am Phys Soc; Electrochem Soc. *Res:* Physics and chemistry of solids particularly transition metal chalcogenides, metallic non-metals and related compounds which are studied with x-ray crystallography, optical microscopy and spectroscopy. *Mailing Add:* Exxon Res & Eng Co Corp Res Labs Linden NJ 07036

CHIANG, ALICE M F, solid state physics, see previous edition

CHIANG, ANNE, b Canton, China, Oct 3, 42; US citizen; m 67; c 1. PHYSICAL CHEMISTRY, DISPLAY TECHNOLOGY. *Educ:* Nat Taiwan Univ, BS, 64; Univ Southern Calif, PhD(phys chem), 68. *Prof Exp:* Sr chemist photochem & colloid chem, Memorex Corp, 69-71; MEM RES STAFF & PROJ LEADER EXPLOR DISPLAYS, XEROX PALO ALTO RES CTR, 72- *Mem:* Am Chem Soc; Soc Photographic Scientists & Engrs; Soc Info Display. *Res:* Viscoelasticity of polymers; non-aqueous colloid chemistry; photochemistry of coordination compounds; laser annealed silicon devices, very large scale integration, flat panel displays. *Mailing Add:* Xerox Palo Alto Res Ctr 3333 Coyote Hill Rd Palo Alto CA 94304

CHIANG, BIN-YEA, b China. FOOD SCIENCE & TECHNOLOGY. *Educ:* Chung-Hsing Univ, Taiwan, BS, 66; Kansas State Univ, MS, 72, PhD(food sci), 75. *Prof Exp:* Sr res scientist, Modern Maid Food Prod, Inc, 75-81; PROJ LEADER, NABISCO BRAND INC, 81- *Mem:* Am Asn Cereal Chemists; Inst Food Technol. *Res:* Baking technology; flour quality; cereal grains; cake mixes batter; cookies and crackers. *Mailing Add:* 57-46 Hewlett St Little Neck NY 11362

CHIANG, CHAO-WANG, b Ann-Hui, China, May 21, 25; m 60; c 4. MECHANICAL ENGINEERING. *Educ:* Chiao Tung Univ, BS, 48; Univ Wis, PhD(mech eng), 60. *Prof Exp:* Mech engr, Taiwan Hwy Bur, 48-50, 52-56, heavy equip div, 50-52; sr engr, Corning Glass Works, NY, 60-64; from assoc prof to prof mech eng, Univ Denver, 69-74; PROF MECH ENG & HEAD DEPT, SDAK SCH OF MINES & TECHNOL, 74- *Concurrent Pos:* Mem staff, Nat Comn Space Res, 70-71. *Mem:* Am Soc Mech Engrs; Am Soc Eng Educ; Sigma Xi. *Res:* Diesel engine combustion; heat transfer and viscous flow problems of glass; conductive, convective and boiling heat transfer; solar energy, geothermal energy and thermoscience. *Mailing Add:* SDak Sch of Mines & Technol Rapid City SD 57701

CHIANG, CHIH-SHU, b Taiwan, Repub China, Sept 29, 50; m 74; c 3. ORGANIC SYNTHESIS, CATALYSIS. *Educ:* Nat Taiwan Univ, BS, 71; Princeton Univ, PhD(chem), 77. *Prof Exp:* Res chemist, Gen Elec Corp Res & Develop, 77-78, res chemist, Oxirane Tech Ctr, 78-79; RES CHEMIST, E I DU PONT DE NEMOURS & CO INC, 79- *Mem:* Am Chem Soc. *Res:* Process research. *Mailing Add:* 107 Banbury Dr Wilmington DE 19803

CHIANG, CHIN LONG, b Ningpo, China, Nov 12, 16; US citizen; m 45; c 3. BIOSTATISTICS. *Educ:* Tsing Hua Univ, China, BA, 40; Univ Calif, Berkeley, MA, 48, PhD(statist), 53. *Prof Exp:* Instr pub health, 53-55, from asst prof to assoc prof biostatist, chmn div measurement sci, 70-75, chmn fac, 75-76, PROF BIOSTATIST, UNIV CALIF, BERKELEY, 66- *Concurrent Pos:* Consult, State Dept Health, Calif, 58 & 64, State Dept Hyg, 61-62, NY State Dept Health, 62, Nat Ctr Health Statist, 62-64, 73-75 & 78, Rand Corp, 73; Nat Ctr Health Serv Res, 73-, WHO, 70-, Nat Inst Neurol Dis & Stroke & Nat Ctr Health Serv Res & Develop, 73- & Bur Manpower, 78; spec res fel, Nat Heart Inst, 59-60; vis asst prof, Univ Mich, 59; vis lectr, Univ Minn, Minneapolis, 60, 61; spec consult, Nat Vital Statist, 62-64; vis assoc prof, Univ NC, 63, vis prof, 70; Fulbright fel, Gt Brit, 64; vis prof, Yale Univ, 65 & 66, Emory Univ, 67, Univ Pittsburgh, 68, Univ Wash, 69, Univ Tex, 73, Vanderbilt Univ, 75 & Harvard Univ, 77; assoc ed, Biometrics, 70-75 & Math Biosci, 75- *Mem:* AAAS; Am Pub Health Asn; Am Statist Asn; Inst Math Statist; Biomet Soc. *Res:* Stochastic studies of the life table; competing risks; illness and death processes. *Mailing Add:* 844 Spruce St Berkeley CA 94707

CHIANG, DONALD C, b Kaohsiung, Formosa, Jan 29, 31; m 55; c 2. FLUID MECHANICS. *Educ:* Taiwan Col Eng, BS, 53; Univ Minn, PhD(fluid mech), 65. *Prof Exp:* Engr, Taiwan Aluminum Co, 54-55 & Kaohsiung Oil Refinery, 57-59; asst prof mech eng, 65-68, assoc prof, 68-72, PROF MECH ENG, ROSE-HULMAN INST TECHNOL, 72- *Concurrent Pos:* Tech transl Japanese & Chinese. *Mem:* Am Soc Mech Engrs; Am Inst Aeronaut & Astronaut; Am Soc Eng Educ. *Res:* Heat transfer. *Mailing Add:* Dept of Mech & Aerospace Eng Rose-Hulman Inst of Technol Terre Haute IN 47803

CHIANG, FU-PEN, b Checkiang, China, Oct 10, 36; m 63; c 3. SOLID MECHANICS, EXPERIMENTAL MECHANICS. *Educ:* Univ Taiwan, BS, 57; Univ Fla, MS, 63, PhD(mech), 66. *Prof Exp:* Civil engr, Mil Construct Bur, Taiwan, China, 58-59, Shihmen Dam Construct Comn, 59-61; res asst, Univ Fla, 62-66; res fel mech, Cath Univ Am, 66-67; from asst prof to assoc prof mech, 67-70, PROF ENG, STATE UNIV NY STONY BROOK, 74- *Concurrent Pos:* NSF eng res initiation grant, 68-70, grants, 70-73, 76-79 & 79-82; res found fac fel & grant-in-aid, 68 & 70; vis prof, Swiss Fed Inst Technol, Lausanne, 73-74; consult to various indust & govt agencies & labs; sr vis fel, Cavendish Lab, Univ Cambridge, Eng, 80-81. *Mem:* Am Acad Mech; AAAS; Soc Exp Stress Anal; Optical Soc Am; Soc Photo-optical Instrumentation Engrs. *Res:* Theory and applications of photoelasticity; Moire methods; holographic inteferometry; laser speckle and white light speckle methods for stress analysis. *Mailing Add:* Dept Mech Eng State Univ NY Stony Brook NY 11794

CHIANG, GEORGE C(HIHMING), b Nanking, China, Sept 12, 31; US citizen; m 59; c 3. STRUCTURAL ENGINEERING, ENGINEERING MECHANICS. *Educ:* Nat Taiwan Univ, BS, 54; Univ Southern Calif, MS, 58 & 63; Stanford Univ, PhD(solid mech), 67. *Prof Exp:* Proj engr, Richard R Bradshaw Inc, 59-62, vpres, 62-64; asst prof eng, 67-69, assoc prof eng & chmn fac civil eng & eng mech, 69-74, PROF ENG, CALIF STATE UNIV, FULLERTON, 74- *Mem:* Am Inst Aeronaut & Astronaut; Am Concrete Inst. *Res:* Stability of elastic thin shells; stability problems involving viscoelastic materials and dynamics of structures. *Mailing Add:* Sch of Eng Calif State Univ Fullerton CA 92634

CHIANG, HUAI C, b Sunkiang, China, Feb 15, 15; m 46; c 3. ENTOMOLOGY. *Educ:* Tsing Hua Univ, China, BS, 38; Univ Minn, MS, 46, PhD(entom), 48. *Hon Degrees:* DSc, Bowling Green State Univ, 79. *Prof Exp:* Asst entom, Tsing Hua Univ, China, 38-40, instr, 40-44; asst, 45-48, res fel, 48-53, from asst prof to prof biol, 54-61, PROF ENTOM, UNIV MINN, ST PAUL, 61- *Concurrent Pos:* Guggenheim fel, 56-57. *Mem:* Entom Soc Am; Ecol Soc Am; Can Entom Soc; fel Royal Entom Soc London; Int Asn Ecol. *Res:* Insect biology and ecology. *Mailing Add:* Dept Entom Univ Minn St Paul MN 55108

CHIANG, JOSEPH FEI, b Hunan, China, Feb 22, 38; m 63; c 1. PHYSICAL CHEMISTRY, APPLIED PHYSICS. *Educ:* Tunghai Univ, Taiwan, BS, 60; Cornell Univ, MS, 64, PhD(phys chem), 67. *Prof Exp:* Asst prof chem, Hudson Valley Community Col, 64-65; fel, Cornell Univ, 67-68; asst prof, 68-74, ASSOC PROF CHEM, STATE UNIV NY COL ONEONTA, 74- *Concurrent Pos:* NIH fel, 75. *Mem:* Am Chem Soc; Am Phys Soc. *Res:* Use of electron diffraction technique and spectroscopic techniques to study molecular structures in gas phase. *Mailing Add:* Dept of Chem State Univ of NY Col Oneonta NY 13820

CHIANG, KWEN-SHENG, b Shanghai, China, Feb 12, 39. MOLECULAR BIOLOGY. *Educ:* Nat Taiwan Univ, BS, 59; PhD(biochem Princeton Univ, PhD(biochem sci), 65. *Prof Exp:* Res assoc biochem, Princeton Univ, 65-66; asst prof, 66-72, assoc prof biophys, 72-76, ASSOC PROF BIOCHEM & THEORET BIOL, UNIV CHICAGO, 76- *Concurrent Pos:* USPHS res career develop award, 70-75; ed bd, Plant Sci Letters J, 73-; vis prof, Inst Bot, Acad Sinica, 74-75; mem, Comn Genetics, Univ Chicago. *Mem:* Genetics Soc Am; Am Soc Microbiol; Biophys Soc; Am Soc Cell Biol. *Res:* Molecular mechanisms of meiosis and sexual reproduction; molecular biology of cellular organelles; chloroplast and mitochondria; biochemical mechanisms of non-Mendelian genetics. *Mailing Add:* Dept of Biophys & Theoret Biol Univ of Chicago Chicago IL 60637

CHIANG, MORGAN S, b Kiangsu, China, Dec 30, 26; m 65; c 1. GENETICS. *Educ:* Nat Taiwan Univ, BSc, 50; McGill Univ, MSc, 59; Tex A&M Univ, PhD(genetics), 65. *Prof Exp:* Asst genetics, Nat Taiwan Univ, 50-55 & lectr, 55-57; res asst, Jackson Mem Lab, 59-61; RES SCIENTIST, RES STA, CAN DEPT AGR, 65- *Mem:* Agr Inst Can; Genetics Soc Can; Can Soc Hort Sci; Sigma Xi; Am Soc Hort Sci. *Res:* Discovery of mutant Careener in mice; breeding cabbage variety resistant to clubroot disease; development of hybrid cabbage variety Chateauguay; cabbage pollen physiology; breeding grain corn resistant to corn borer. *Mailing Add:* Can Dept of Agr PO Box 457 Res Sta St Jean PQ J3B 6Z8 Can

CHIANG, PETER K, b Hong Kong, China, Oct 20, 41; US citizen; m 67; c 2. BIOCHEMISTRY. *Educ:* Univ San Francisco, BSc, 65; Univ Alta, MSc, 67, PhD(biochem), 71. *Prof Exp:* Fel, John Hopkins Univ, 71-72; vis fel, NIH, 72-74; sr staff fel, NIMH, 74-80, res scientist, 80-81; RES CHEMIST, WALTER REED ARMY INST RES, 81- *Mem:* Am Soc Biol Chemists; Am Soc Pharmacol & Exp Therapeut; Acad Pharm & Pharmaceut Sci; NY Acad Sci; Am Chem Soc. *Res:* Methylation reactions; methylases; s-adenosylmethionine; s-adenosylhomocysteine; inhibitors of methylation; neurobiology; cholinergic system; differentiation. *Mailing Add:* Div Biochem Walter Reed Army Inst & Res Washington DC 20012

CHIANG, S(HIAO) H(UNG), b Soochow, China, Oct 10, 29; US citizen; m 58; c 3. CHEMICAL ENGINEERING. *Educ:* Nat Univ Taiwan, BS, 52; Kans State Univ, MS, 55; Carnegie Inst Technol, PhD(chem eng), 58. *Prof Exp:* Proj engr chem eng, Linde Co, Union Carbide Corp, 58-60; from asst prof to assoc prof, 60-70, PROF CHEM ENG, UNIV PITTSBURGH, 70- *Mem:* Am Inst Chem Engrs; Am Chem Soc; Am Inst Chemists; Am Soc Eng Educ. *Res:* Mass transfer processes; interface phenomena; cryogenic engineering; phase equilibrium; energy conversion. *Mailing Add:* Dept Chem & Petrol Eng Univ Pittsburgh Pittsburgh PA 15213

CHIANG, SCHUMANN, b Shanghai, China, May 27, 44; Can citizen; m 70; c 1. CHEMISTRY. *Educ:* Queen's Univ, Ont, BSc, 68; Univ Waterloo, PhD(polymer chem), 74. *Prof Exp:* RES SCIENTIST, FIBERGLAS CAN LTD, 74- *Mem:* Chem Inst Can; Am Chem Soc; N Am Thermal Anal Soc; Fedn Soc Coating Technol. *Mailing Add:* Fiberglas Can Ltd PO Box 3005 Sarnia ON N7S 4H8 Can

CHIANG, SHEAU-HWA, b Taitung, Taiwan, Oct 28, 52. CHEMISTRY. *Educ:* Nat Cheng Kung Univ, Taiwan, BS, 74; Boston Univ, PhD(chem), 79. *Prof Exp:* Fel, Princeton Univ, 80-81; RES CHEMIST, E I DU PONT DE NEMOURS & CO, INC, 81- *Mem:* Am Chem Soc; Sigma Xi. *Res:* Mechanistic and applied photochemistry; photochemical conversion of solar energy; photopolymer; quantitative luminescence techniques; reaction mechanism; synthetic methodology. *Mailing Add:* Apt 6-3D 2515 Cedar Tree Dr Wilmington DE 19810

CHIANG, SOONG TAO, b Shanghai, China, Nov 14, 37; US citizen; m 66; c 2. BIOMATHEMATICS, PHYSICS. *Educ:* Univ Calif, Los Angeles, BS, 64, MS, 66, PhD(physics), 70. *Prof Exp:* Teaching asst physics, Univ Calif, Los Angeles, 64-70; res assoc, Univ Nfld, 70-71; instr & systs analyst med physics, Thomas Jefferson Univ, 71-73; SR BIOMATHEMATICIAN BIOSTATIST & PHARMACOKINETICS, WYETH LABS, INC, 73- *Mem:* Am Statist Asn. *Res:* Applied multivariate statistical analyses and pharmacokinetics. *Mailing Add:* Dept of Biostatist & Pharmacokinetics Wyeth Labs Inc Radnor PA 19087

CHIANG, TAI-CHANG, b Taipei, Rep China, Aug 28, 49; m 79; c 1. SURFACE PHYSICS, PHOTOELECTRON SPECTROSCOPY. *Educ:* Nat Taiwan Univ, BS, 71; Univ Calif, Berkeley, PhD(physics), 78. *Prof Exp:* Fel, T J Watson Res Ctr, IBM, 78-80; ASST PROF PHYSICS, UNIV ILL, URBANA-CHAMPAIGN, 80- *Mem:* Am Phys Soc. *Res:* Electronic properties and atomic structure of bulk materials, surfaces and interfaces using synchrotron radiation photoemission and related techniques. *Mailing Add:* Dept Physics Univ Ill 1110 W Green Urbana IL 61801

CHIANG, TOM CHUAN-HSIEN, b Chungking, China, April 1, 44; US citizen; m 71. MOLECULAR BIOLOGY, VIROLOGY. *Educ:* Tunghai Univ, Taiwan, BS, 67; Ill State Univ, MS, 71; UUniv Tex, PhD(molecular biol), 75. *Prof Exp:* Res fel, Univ Tex, Dallas, 76-78; res assoc, Tex A&M Univ, 78-79, asst prof, Med Sch, 80-81; ASST RES CHEMIST RES & DEVELOP, TEX A&M AGR EXP STA, 81- *Mem:* Sigma Xi; Biophhysics Soc; Asn Official Anal Chemists Soc. *Res:* DNA repair and chemical carcinogens in bacterial viruses and mammalian tissue culture systems; interaction between single-stranded DNA and proteins studied by electron microscopy; molecular mechanism of antibiotic action and study of pesticide degrading genes from microorganism. *Mailing Add:* Agr Anal Serv Dept Tex A&M Univ College Station TX 77843

CHIANG, TZE I, b Foochow, Fukien, China, Apr 19, 23; US citizen; m 29; c 3. ECONOMIC FEASIBILITY, ECONOMIC ANALYSIS. *Educ:* Fukien Christian Univ, BA, 46; Okla State Univ, MA, 55; Univ Fla, PhD(agr econ),58. *Prof Exp:* Teacher chinese, Sin-Ding Jr Girls High Sch, 46-47; mem staff, China Textile Indust Inc, 47-53; teaching asst land use, Okla State Univ,

54-55; res asst agr mkt, Univ Fla, 55-58; PRIN RES SCIENTIST ECON STUDIES, GA INST TECHNOL, 58- *Mem:* Am Agr Econ Soc; Forest Prod Res Soc. *Res:* Economic studies concerning manufacturing processes; input-output relationships; investment requirements; financial returns; author of over fifty formal reports. *Mailing Add:* Econ Develop Lab Eng Exp Sta Ga Inst Technol Atlanta GA 30332

CHIANG, YUEN-SHENG, b Tsingtao, China, Feb 2, 36. PHYSICAL CHEMISTRY, TECHNICAL MANAGEMENT. *Educ:* Nat Taiwan Univ, BS, 56; Univ Louisville, MChE, 60; Princeton Univ, PhD(phys chem), 64; Rutgers Univ, MBAC, 79. *Prof Exp:* Res assoc phys chem, Princeton Univ, 63; from scientist to sr scientist, Xerox Corp, NY, 64-69; MEM TECH STAFF, RCA LABS, 69- *Mem:* AAAS; Am Chem Soc; Electron Micros Soc Am; Electrochem Soc; Inst Elec & Electronics Engrs. *Res:* Physics and chemistry of surfaces; crystal growth and dislocation studies; electron paramagnetic resonance; electron microscopy; organic semiconductors; metal physics; ultra high vacuum technology. *Mailing Add:* RCA Labs Princeton NJ 08540

CHIAO, RAYMOND YU, b Hong Kong, Oct 9, 40; US citizen; m 68; c 3. PHYSICS. *Educ:* Princeton Univ, AB, 61; Mass Inst Technol, PhD(physics), 65. *Prof Exp:* Asst prof physics, Mass Inst Technol, 65-67; asst prof, 67-70, assoc prof, 70-77, PROF PHYSICS, UNIV CALIF, BERKELEY, 77- *Concurrent Pos:* Alfred P Sloan fel, 67-72. *Mem:* Am Phys Soc. *Res:* Lasers; non-linear optics; spontaneous and stimulated Brillouin scattering; stimulated Raman scattering; self-trapping of optical beams; superconductivity; astrophysics. *Mailing Add:* Dept of Physics Univ of Calif Berkeley CA 94720

CHIAO, TANG, atomic physics, see previous edition

CHIAO, WEN BIN, b Chang Hua, Taiwan, Sept 21, 48; US citizen; m 75; c 2. ORGANIC POLYMER CHEMISTRY. *Educ:* Nat Tsing Hua Univ, BS, 71; Univ Rochester, PhD(chem), 77. *Prof Exp:* Fel, Univ Md, 76-78; proj supvr, 78-81, RES ASSOC, NAT STARCH & CHEM CORP, 81- *Mem:* Am Chem Soc. *Res:* Synthesis of monomers and polymers; water soluble polymers; adhesives; mechanisms of organic reactions. *Mailing Add:* 6 Welles Ct Piscataway NJ 08854

CHIAO-YAP, LUNG WEN, theoretical nuclear physics, see previous edition

CHIAPPINELLI, VINCENT A, b Pawtucket, RI, Mar 16, 51. NEUROPHARMACOLOGY, DRUG RECEPTORS. *Educ:* Boston Univ, AB, 73; Univ Conn, PhD(neuropharm), 77. *Prof Exp:* Res fel, Dept Pharmacol, Harvard Med Sch, 77-80; ASST PROF NEUROPHARM, DEPT PHARMACOL, SCH MED, ST LOUIS UNIV, 80- *Mem:* Soc Neurosci; AAAS. *Res:* Nicotinic cholinergic receptors in chick autonomic ganglia, both during development and in mature birds; role of neurotransmission in the biochemical development of nervous system. *Mailing Add:* Dept Pharmacol Sch Med St Louis Univ 1402 S Grand Blvd St Louis MO 63104

CHIARANDINI, DANTE JULIO, b Punta Alta, Argentina, Mar 1, 37; US citizen; c 1. PHYSIOLOGY, BIOPHYSICS. *Educ:* Univ Buenos Aires, MD, 62. *Prof Exp:* Asst prof exp ophthal, 72-77, ASSOC PROF EXP OPHTHAL, SCH MED, NY UNIV, 77-, ASSOC PROF PHYSIOL, 79- *Mem:* Asn Res Vision & Ophthal; Biophys Soc. *Res:* Neurophysiology; experimental ophthalmology; muscle contraction; synaptic function. *Mailing Add:* Dept of Ophthal Med Ctr 550 First Ave New York NY 10016

CHIARAPPA, LUIGI, b Rome, Italy, Dec 12, 25; US citizen; m 51; c 3. PHYTOPATHOLOGY. *Educ:* Univ Florence, Gen Agr Laurea, 50; Univ Calif, PhD(plant path), 58. *Prof Exp:* Agronomist tech comn, Ital Colonization in Chile, 50-51; entomologist, Di Giorgio Corp, 52-55, plant pathologist, Res Dept, 59-62; from tropical plant pathologist to SR PLANT PATHOLOGIST, RES DEPT, FOOD & AGR ORGN, UN, 62- *Concurrent Pos:* Vis prof, Univ Calif, Davis, 75-76. *Mem:* Am Phytopath Soc; Int Orgn Citrus Virol. *Res:* Diseases of fruit, nut and vine crops; epidemiology; disease loss appraisal. *Mailing Add:* Via San Lucio 38 Rome Italy

CHIARODO, ANDREW, b New York, NY, June 26, 34. m 69. DEVELOPMENTAL BIOLOGY, CELL BIOLOGY. *Educ:* Fordham Univ, AB, 56, MS, 59; Washington Univ, PhD(zool), 63. *Prof Exp:* NIH fel, Med Col, Cornell Univ, 63; from instr to assoc prof biol, Georgetown Univ, 63-73; grants assoc, Div Res Grants, NIH, 73-74; PROG DIR, NAT ORGAN SITE PROGS, NAT CANCER INST, 74- *Mem:* AAAS; Soc Develop Biol; Am Soc Zoologists. *Mailing Add:* Nat Cancer Inst Bethesda MD 20014

CHIARULLI, PETER, applied mathematics, mechanics, deceased

CHIASSON, BERTRAND ARNOLD, organic chemistry, see previous edition

CHIASSON, LEO PATRICK, b Cheticamp, NS, May 14, 18; m 48; c 5. GENETICS. *Educ:* St Francis Xavier Univ, BA, 38, BSc, 40; Univ Toronto, PhD(genetics), 44. *Prof Exp:* Assoc prof biol, 44-49, PROF BIOL, ST FRANCIS XAVIER UNIV, 49- *Concurrent Pos:* Assoc scientist, Fisheries Res Bd Can, 44-55; sr researcher zool, Columbia Univ, 63-64. *Mem:* AAAS; Genetics Soc Am; Genetics Soc Can. *Res:* Tomato species hybrids; relative growth in mice; blood groups and dermatoglyphics in Micmac Indians; distribution of scallops; species hybrids of Abies; mutagenic effects of heat in bacteria. *Mailing Add:* Dept of Biol St Francis Xavier Univ Antigonish NS B2G 1C0 Can

CHIASSON, ROBERT BRETON, b Griggsville, Ill, Oct 9, 25; m 44; c 8. COMPARATIVE ANATOMY, COMPARATIVE ENDOCRINOLOGY. *Educ:* Ill Col, AB, 49; Univ Ill, MS, 50; Stanford Univ, PhD(biol sci), 56. *Prof Exp:* Spec supvr, Ill State Mus, 50-51; from instr zool to prof biol sci, 51-75, PROF VET SCI, UNIV ARIZ, 75- *Concurrent Pos:* Fulbright lectr, Univ Sci & Technol, Ghana, 69-70. *Mem:* Am Soc Zoologists; Am Physiol Soc; Int Soc

Stereology; Soc Vert Paleont; World Asn Vet Anatomists. *Res:* Regulation of pituitary function in the chicken and anatomy of vertebrates; anatomy of the eye of doves and skin of snakes. *Mailing Add:* Dept of Vet Sci Univ of Ariz Tucson AZ 85721

CHIAZZE, LEONARD, JR, b Falconer, NY, June 19, 34; m 54; c 4. BIOSTATISTICS, EPIDEMIOLOGY. *Educ:* Univ Buffalo, BS, 55, MBA, 57; Univ Pittsburgh, ScD(biostatist), 64. *Prof Exp:* Asst health serv officer, Nat Cancer Inst, 57-60, sr asst health serv officer, 60-63, health serv officer, 63-64, scientist, 64-66; res assoc ctr pop res, 66-68, dir cerebrovasc dis follow-up & surveillance syst, 68-71, assoc prof community med & int health, 68-77, PROF COMMUNITY & FAMILY MED, SCH MED, GEORGETOWN UNIV, 77- DIR, GRAD PROG BIOSTATIST, 71-, DIR DIV BIOSTATIST & EPIDEMIOL, 66- *Concurrent Pos:* Chief biomet br, Nat Cancer Inst, 75-76; consult epidemiol & biostatist to pvt & pub orgn. *Mem:* Fel Am Pub Health Asn; Am Statist Asn; Pop Asn Am; Soc Epidemiol Res; fel Am Col Epidemiol. *Res:* Chronic disease epidemiology, especially cancer; occupational and environmental epidemiology; morbidity survey and case register methodologies; population research; delivery of medical services; clinical trials; occupational health surveillance systems. *Mailing Add:* Dept Community & Family Med 3900 Reservoir Rd Washington DC 20007

CHIBA, MIKIO, b Miyagi-Ken, Japan, Aug 4, 29; m 56; c 2. ANALYTICAL CHEMISTRY. *Educ:* Hokkaido Univ, BSc, 53, DSc(anal chem), 62. *Prof Exp:* Chemist, Hokkaido Police Hq, 54-56; res chemist, Sci Police Res Inst, 56-64; RES SCIENTIST, CAN DEPT AGR, 64- *Concurrent Pos:* Nat Res Coun Can fel, 62-64; hon res prof, Brock Univ, 73-; fel Japan Soc for Prom Sci. *Mem:* Am Chem Soc; Chem Inst Can; Chem Soc Japan; Food Hyg Soc Japan. *Res:* Method development for pesticide analysis and to find better ways of applying pesticides. *Mailing Add:* Res Sta Agr Can ON Vineland Station ON L0R 2E0 Can

CHIBNIK, SHELDON, b New York, NY, Dec 20, 25; m 45; c 2. ORGANIC CHEMISTRY. *Educ:* Cornell Univ, AB, 44; Polytech Inst Brooklyn, MS, 51; Temple Univ, PhD(chem), 55. *Prof Exp:* Lab instr chem, Hunter Col, 46-48; from chemist to sr chemist, Nat Lead Co, 48-55, group leader indust finishes, 55-61; sr res chemist, Mobil Chem Co, Edison, 61-70, sr res chemist, Mobil Res & Develop Corp, Paulsboro, 71-81, assoc chem, 75-80, RES ASSOC, MOBIL RES & DEVELOP CORP, 81- *Mem:* Am Chem Soc. *Res:* Polymer chemistry; protective coatings; monomer synthesis; liquid phase oxidations; heterogeneous catalysis; lubricating oil and fuel additives. *Mailing Add:* 7 Glen View Pl Cherry Hill NJ 08034

CHIBURIS, EDWARD FRANK, b Omaha, Nebr, July 31, 33; m 54; c 5. GEOPHYSICS. *Educ:* Tex A&M Univ, BS, 60, MS, 62; Ore State Univ, PhD(geophys), 65. *Prof Exp:* Res geophysicist, Seismic Data Lab, Teledyne, Inc, 65-68 & dir res, 68-69; assoc prof geophys & asst dir, Marine Sci Inst, Univ Conn, 69-77; assoc prof geophys & asst dir, Weston Observ, Boston Col, 77-80; MGR, FLA LABS, TELEDYNE GEOTECH, 80- *Mem:* Am Geophys Union; Seismol Soc Am; Soc Explor Geophys. *Res:* Hypocenter location techniques; seismic network and array analyses; focal mechanism studies; gravity and magnetic methods; crustal studies; computer modeling; geophysical data processing. *Mailing Add:* Teledyne Geotech Box 2630 Indian Harbour Beach FL 32937

CHIBUZO, GREGORY ANENONU, b Abor, Nigeria, July 25, 43; m 72; c 1. VETERINARY ANATOMY. *Educ:* Tuskegee Inst, BS, 68, DVM, 70, MS, 75; Cornell Univ, PhD, 79. *Prof Exp:* From instr to assoc prof, 70-79, PROF ANAT, SCH VET MED, TUSKEGEE INST, 79- *Concurrent Pos:* Consult bio-med studies, Southern Voc Col, Tuskegee, 74-75. *Mem:* World Asn Vet Anatomists; Am Asn Vet Anatomists; Soc Study Reproduction; Am Vet Med Asn; Am Asn Anatomists. *Res:* Influence of neurohumoral substances on uterine motility; effect of progesterone and/or estrogen on the integrity of intra-ovarian vascular growth and distribution at birth, maturity and menopause; central projection of lingual structures. *Mailing Add:* Dept Anat Tuskegee Inst Sch of Vet Med Tuskegee Institute AL 36088

CHICHESTER, CLINTON OSCAR, b New York, NY, Feb 11, 25; m 47; c 3. FOOD TECHNOLOGY. *Educ:* Mass Inst Technol, SB, 49; Univ Calif, MS, 51, PhD, 54. *Prof Exp:* From asst prof to prof food technol, Univ Calif, Davis, 53-70, chmn dept, 67-70; prof food & resource chem, 70-77, PROF FOOD SCI & TECHNOL & ASSOC DIR, INT CTR MARINE RESOURCE DEVELOP, UNIV RI, 77- *Concurrent Pos:* Mem, NIH, 57-, Coun Foods & Nutrit, AMA, 62- & Space Sci Bd, Nat Acad Sci, 63-; vpres res, Nutrit Found, New York, 72-74. *Honors & Awards:* Bernardo O'Higgins Award, Govt Chile, 69; Medal, Czech Acad Sci; Babcock Hart Award, Inst Food Technologists, 73. *Mem:* Fel Inst Food Technologists; Am Chem Soc; Optical Soc Am; Am Inst Chem Eng; Am Soc Biol Chemists. *Res:* Pigment biochemistry; food processing. *Mailing Add:* Dept of Food & Resource Chem Univ of RI Kingston RI 02881

CHICHESTER, FREDERICK WESLEY, b New Haven, Conn, Apr 28, 29; m 58; c 4. SOIL CHEMISTRY, PLANT PHYSIOLOGY. *Educ:* Colo State Univ, BS, 52; Univ Conn, MS, 60; Ore State Univ, PhD(soils), 66. *Prof Exp:* Asst soils, Ore State Univ, 63-66; RES SCIENTIST, AGR RES SERV, USDA, 66- *Mem:* Am Soc Agron; Soil Sci Soc Am; Crop Sci Soc Am. *Res:* Mineral nutrition of forage grasses; nutrient cycling in grasslands; soil nitrogen and phosphorus transformations; reclamation of mined lands. *Mailing Add:* Agr Res Serv Southern Region USDA PO Box 748 Temple TX 76503

CHICHESTER, LYLE FRANKLIN, b Albany, NY, Nov 5, 31; m 54; c 3. ZOOLOGY. *Educ:* Univ Conn, BS, 54, PhD(zool), 68; Cent Conn State Col, MS, 61. *Prof Exp:* From instr to assoc prof biol, 60-74, PROF BIOL, CENT CONN STATE COL & CHMN DEPT BIOL SCI, 74- *Mem:* AAAS; Ecol Soc Am. *Res:* Distribution, ecology and systematics of terrestrial slugs, especially introduced European species; application of biochemical methods to systematic problems involving mollusks. *Mailing Add:* Dept of Biol Sci Cent Conn State Col New Britain CT 06050

CHICK, ERNEST WATSON, mycology, preventive medicine, see previous edition

CHICK, THOMAS WESLEY, b Martin, Tenn, May 1, 40; m 72; c 3. PULMONARY PHYSIOLOGY. *Educ:* Univ Cent Ark, BS, 61; Univ Ark, Little Rock, MD, 65. *Prof Exp:* From intern to resident internal med, Univ Tex Southwestern Med Sch Dallas, 65-68, fel pulmonary med, 68-70, from instr to asst prof internal med, 70-72; asst prof, 72-78, ASSOC PROF INTERNAL MED, SCH MED, UNIV N MEX, 78- *Res:* Clinical pulmonary physiology of obstructive airway disease; effects of bronchodilators, oxygen and exercise. *Mailing Add:* Univ NMex Albuquerque NM 87131

CHICKOS, JAMES S, b Buffalo, NY, Oct 27, 41; m 66; c 2. ORGANIC CHEMISTRY, PHYSICAL ORGANIC CHEMISTRY. *Educ:* Univ Buffalo, BA, 63; Cornell Univ, PhD(org chem), 66. *Prof Exp:* NIH vis fel, Princeton Univ, 66-67; NIH fel & res assoc, Univ Wis, 67-69; asst prof 69-80, ASSOC PROF ORG CHEM, UNIV MO-ST LOUIS, 80- *Mem:* Am Chem Soc; Royal Soc Chem. *Res:* Role of tautomeric catalysis in organic and enzymatic systems; small ring, non-benzenoid aromatics; chemistry for the non-major. *Mailing Add:* Dept Chem Univ Mo 80001 Natural Bridge Rd St Louis MO 63121

CHICKS, CHARLES HAMPTON, b Sandpoint, Idaho, Nov 10, 30; m 56; c 4. MATHEMATICS. *Educ:* Linfield Col, BA, 53; Univ Ore, MA, 56, PhD(math), 60. *Prof Exp:* Adv res engr, Sylvania Electronic Defense Labs, Gen Tel & Electronics Corp, 60-62, engr specialist, 62-69; SR MEM TECH STAFF, ESL INC, 69- *Concurrent Pos:* Lectr, Univ Santa Clara, 64- *Mem:* Am Math Soc. *Res:* Periodic automorphisms on banach algebras; military operations research; arms control and disarmament. *Mailing Add:* Tech Staff ESL Inc 495 Java Dr Sunnyvale CA 94086

CHICO, RAYMUNDO JOSE, b Hernando, Arg, Sept 17, 30; m 59; c 4. MINING GEOLOGY, ECONOMIC GEOLOGY. *Educ:* Univ Cordoba, dipl geol, 53; Mo Sch Mines, MS, 58; Harvard Univ, MA, 63. *Prof Exp:* Asst, Univ Cordoba, 53; geologist, Direccion Gen de Ingenieros, Arg, 54; geologist, Peruvian Mines, Cerro de Pasco Corp, 54-55, off geologist, NY, 58-59; geol engr, Four Corners Uranium Corp, Colo, 56-57; consult, Nat Lead Co, Arg, 59, Int Basic Econ Corp, NY, 60 & Air Force Cambridge Res Labs, 60; geologist, Ltd War Lab, Aberdeen, Md, 63-65; oceanogr, Nat Oceanog Data Ctr, DC, 65-66; consult econ mining & eng geol indust, US & Latin Am, 66-68; PRES, RAYMUNDO J CHICO, INC, 68- *Concurrent Pos:* Guest crystallog lab, Johns Hopkins Univ, 65; US deleg, NATO Advan Study Inst Uranium, London, 72; pres & chmn bd, Am Gold Minerals Corp. *Honors & Awards:* State of Md Gov Citation, 69. *Mem:* Am Inst Mining, Metall & Petrol Eng; Geol Soc Am; Sigma Xi; Am Mining Cong. *Res:* Engineering earth sciences; inter-American mineral industry; applied geology and mining for business development and economic growth; ore genesis; minerals; field economic geology. *Mailing Add:* 110 Inverness Circle E-Unita Englewood CO 80112

CHICOINE, LUC, b Montreal, Que, Apr 19, 29; m 53; c 1. PEDIATRICS. *Educ:* Univ Montreal, BA, 48, MD, 53; FRCP(C), 60. *Prof Exp:* From asst prof to assoc prof, 61-71, PROF PEDIAT, UNIV MONTREAL, 71-, CHMN DEPT, 75- *Concurrent Pos:* Dir, Poison Control Ctr. *Mem:* Am Acad Pediat; Can Med Asn; Can Pediat Soc. *Res:* Pediatric water and electrolyte problems. *Mailing Add:* Ste Justine Hosp 3175 Cote Ste Catherine Montreal Can

CHICOYE, ETZER, b Jacmel, Haiti, Nov 4, 26; US citizen; m 54; c 2. FOOD CHEMISTRY. *Educ:* Univ Haiti, BS, 48; Univ Wis-Madison, MS, 54, PhD(food sci), 68. *Prof Exp:* Grader & cup tester, Nat Coffee Bur, Haiti, 48-52; res asst, Univ Wis-Madison, 52-54, 64-67; anal chemist, Chicago Pharmacol Co, 54-56; res chemist, Julian Labs, Ill, 56-64; chem res supvr, 67-72, MGR RES, MILLER BREWING CO, 72-, DIR RES, 78- *Mem:* Am Chem Soc; Inst Food Technol; Master Brewers Asn Am; Am Soc Brewing Chemists. *Res:* Steroid chemistry; steroid hormones and vitamin D; cholesterol and degradation products of cholesterol in food; brewing chemistry; flavor chemistry. *Mailing Add:* Miller Brewing Co Res Lab 4000 W State St Milwaukee WI 53208

CHIDAMBARASWAMY, JAYANTHI, b Hamsavaram, India, Nov 14, 27; m 46; c 5. MATHEMATICS. *Educ:* PR Col, Kakinada, India, BA, 50; Andhra Univ, India, MA, 53; Univ Calif, Berkeley, PhD(math), 64. *Prof Exp:* Lectr math, Andhra Univ, India, 53-62; teaching asst, Univ Calif, Berkeley, 62-64, instr, 64-65; asst prof, Univ Kans, 65-66; assoc prof, 66-69, PROF MATH, UNIV TOLEDO, 69- *Mem:* Am Math Soc; London Math Soc; Indian Math Soc. *Res:* Theory of numbers. *Mailing Add:* Dept of Math Univ of Toledo Toledo OH 43606

CHIDDIX, MAX EUGENE, b Palestine, Ill, Apr 13, 18; m 44; c 2. ORGANIC CHEMISTRY. *Educ:* Ill State Norm Univ, BEd, 40; Univ Ill, PhD(org chem), 43. *Prof Exp:* Res chemist, Gen Aniline & Film Corp, 43-49, group leader, 50-53, res fel, 53-55, prog mgr acetylene derivatives res, 55-60 & chem & polymer res, 60-68; chief chemist amiben, 68-69, CHIEF PROJ CHEMIST, GAF CORP, 69- *Mem:* AAAS; NY Acad Sci; Am Chem Soc. *Res:* Polymers; plastics; resins; polyamide fibers and film; acetylene and textile chemicals; surfactants; alkylphenols; chelating agents; corrosion inhibitors; reactive dyes; lube oil additives; bactericides; fungicides; herbicides; analytical methods; pollution control. *Mailing Add:* Apt 103 310 Waco St League City TX 77573

CHIDESTER, ALFRED HERMAN, b East Moline, Ill, Sept 23, 14; m 37; c 3. GEOLOGY. *Educ:* Augustana Col, AB, 42; Univ Chicago, PhD, 59. *Prof Exp:* Geologist, US Geol Surv, 43-46; instr mapping, Univ Chicago, 47-48; geologist, Br Rocky Mountain Natural Resources, 48-72, CHIEF BR LATIN AM & AFRICAN GEOL, US GEOL SURV, 72- *Mem:* Mineral Soc Am; Geol Soc Am; Soc Econ Geologists; Am Geophys Union; Geochem Soc. *Res:* Geology and petrology of talc and asbestos bearing ultramafic rocks of Vermont; petrology and mineralogy; structure; pyrite, sulfure and barite resources of Japan; astronaut training in geology; regional geology of Liberia. *Mailing Add:* US Geol Surv Mail Stop 917 Nat Ctr Reston VA 22092

CHIDSEY, JANE LOUISE, b Wilkes-Barre, Pa, Apr 1, 08. PHYSIOLOGY. *Educ:* Wellesley Col, AB, 29; Brown Univ, AM, 31; Cornell Univ, PhD(physiol), 34. *Prof Exp:* Demonstr biol, Brown Univ, 29-31; Coxe fel, Yale Univ, 34-35; instr zool, Smith Col, 35-39; from asst prof to prof biol, 39-73, Fund Adv Educ fac fel, 52-53, actg dean, 61-62, EMER PROF BIOL, WHEATON COL, MASS, 73- *Concurrent Pos:* Mem corp, Mt Desert Island Biol Lab. *Res:* Carbohydrate and fat metabolism; general animal and cellular physiology. *Mailing Add:* W Bare Hill Rd Harvard MA 01451

CHIEN, CHIA-LING, b China, Nov 10, 42; US citizen; m 72; c 2. AMORPHOUS SOLIDS, MOSSBAUER SPECTROSCOPY. *Educ:* Tunghai Univ, Taiwan, BS, 65; Carnegie-Mellon Univ, MS, 68, PhD(physics), 73. *Prof Exp:* Res assoc, 73-74, assoc res scientist, 74-75, vis asst prof, 75-76, asst prof, 76-79, ASSOC PROF PHYSICS, JOHNS HOPKINS UNIV, 79- *Mem:* Am Phys Soc; Sigma Xi. *Res:* Magnetic, hyperfine interaction, conductivity, structural and superconductivity in amorphous and crystalline solids; hyperfine interactions in rare earth solids; mossbauer spectroscopy. *Mailing Add:* Dept Physics Johns Hopkins Univ Baltimore MD 21218

CHIEN, CHIH-YUNG, b Chungking, China, Aug 5, 39; m 63; c 3. EXPERIMENTAL HIGH ENERGY PHYSICS. *Educ:* Nat Taiwan Univ, BS, 60; Yale Univ, MS, 63, PhD(physics), 66. *Prof Exp:* Asst res physicist, Univ Calif, Los Angeles, 66-67, asst prof in residence, 67-68, asst prof, 68-69; asst prof, 69-73, assoc prof, 73-77, PROF PHYSICS, JOHNS HOPKINS UNIV, 77- *Concurrent Pos:* Ed, Sci & Technol Review; hon prof, Nanjing Univ, China, 80- *Mem:* Am Phys Soc. *Res:* Experimental research on particle physics; development and application of data processing and nuclear physics detection devices. *Mailing Add:* Dept of Physics Johns Hopkins Univ Baltimore MD 21218

CHIEN, HENRY H(UNG-YEH), b Shanghai, China, Sept 28, 35; m 61; c 2. CHEMICAL ENGINEERING. *Educ:* Univ Minn, PhD(chem eng), 63. *Prof Exp:* Sr chem engr, 63-67, eng supt, Cent Eng Dept, 67-75, MONSANTO FEL, CORP ENG DEPT, MONSANTO CO, 75- *Mem:* Am Inst Chem Engrs. *Res:* System modeling, simulation, optimization and control; applied mathematics. *Mailing Add:* Corp Eng Dept Monsanto Co 800 N Lindbergh Blvd St Louis MO 63166

CHIEN, JAMES C W, b Shanghai, China, Nov 4, 29; US citizen; m 53; c 3. PHYSICAL CHEMISTRY. *Educ:* St John's Univ, China, BS, 49; Univ Ky, MS, 51; Univ Wis, PhD(phys chem), 54. *Prof Exp:* Sr res chemist, Hercules Powder Co, Del, 54-69; PROF CHEM, UNIV MASS, AMHERST, 69- *Mem:* Am Chem Soc. *Res:* Metalloenzymes and metalloproteins; äelectron paramagnetic resonance crystallography; electrical conducting polymers, polymerization catalysts; oxidation, stabilization and flame retarding polymers; radiation chemistry; oxidation; ultraviolet spectroscopy; electron spin resonance. *Mailing Add:* Dept Chem Univ Mass Amherst MA 01003

CHIEN, LUTHER C, b China, Dec 30, 23; US citizen; m 49; c 2. CHEMICAL ENGINEERING, ORGANIC CHEMISTRY. *Educ:* Harvard Univ, BS, 44; Mass Inst Technol, MS, 47. *Prof Exp:* Res engr, 47-55, supvr, 55-57, chief supvr, 57-78, res fel, 79-80, RES MGR FLUORO CHEM PROCESS RES & DEVELOP, E I DU PONT DE NEMOURS & CO, INC, 81- *Mem:* Am Chem Soc; Am Inst Chem Engrs. *Res:* Fluoro chemical processes. *Mailing Add:* E I du Pont de Nemours & Co Inc PO Box 525 Wilmington DE 19898

CHIEN, PING-LU, b China, Nov 5, 28; m 57; c 3. ORGANIC CHEMISTRY. *Educ:* Nat Taiwan Univ, BS, 52; Univ Kans, PhD(org chem), 64. *Prof Exp:* Chemist, Union Indust Res Inst, 55-59; res assoc med chem, Univ Kans, 64-65; assoc chemist, 65-68, SR CHEMIST, MIDWEST RES INST, 68- *Mem:* Am Chem Soc. *Res:* Synthetic organic and medicinal chemistry; absorption spectroscopy; radiolabeling. *Mailing Add:* Midwest Res Inst 425 Volker Blvd Kansas City MO 64110

CHIEN, R(OBERT) T(IENWEN), b Wusih, China, Nov 20, 31; m 57; c 4. ELECTRICAL ENGINEERING. *Educ:* Univ Ill, BS, 54, AM, 57, PhD(elec eng), 58. *Prof Exp:* Asst, Univ Ill, 54-58; res staff mem, Int Bus Mach Corp, 58-64, assoc mgr, 60-65; assoc prof elec eng, 65-66, PROF ELEC ENG, UNIV ILL, URBANA-CHAMPAIGN, 66-, DIR COORD SCI LAB, 73- *Concurrent Pos:* Adj assoc prof, Columbia Univ, 62-65; consult, IBM Corp, Borroughs, UNIVAC, Hewlett Packard & Control Data. *Mem:* Inst Elec & Electronics Engrs; Asn Comput Mach. *Res:* Information and computer sciences. *Mailing Add:* Coord Sci Lab Univ of Ill Urbana-Champaign Urbana IL 61801

CHIEN, SEN HSIUNG, b Taiwan, China, Aug 31, 41; m 70; c 1. SOIL CHEMISTRY. *Educ:* Nat Taiwan Univ, BS, 63; Univ NH, MS, 68; Iowa State Univ, PhD(soil chem), 72. *Prof Exp:* Assoc, Iowa State Univ, 72-73 & Washington Univ, 73-75; RES CHEMIST SOIL CHEM, INT FERTILIZER DEVELOP CTR, 75- *Mem:* Soil Sci Soc Am; Am Soc Agron; Int Soil Sci Soc. *Res:* Dissolution of phosphate rock in relation to the utilization of phosphate rock for direct application to soils. *Mailing Add:* Int Fertilizer Develop Ctr PO Box 2040 Muscle Shoals AL 35660

CHIEN, SHU, b Peiping, China, June 23, 31; m 57; c 2. PHYSIOLOGY. *Educ:* Nat Taiwan Univ, MD, 53; Columbia Univ, PhD(physiol), 57. *Prof Exp:* Intern, Taiwan Univ Hosp, 52-53; asst, 54-56, from instr to assoc prof, 56-69, PROF PHYSIOL, COL PHYSICIANS & SURGEONS, COLUMBIA UNIV, 69- *Mem:* AAAS; Harvey Soc; Am Physiol Soc; Soc Exp Biol & Med; NY Acad Sci. *Res:* Blood viscosity; red cell membrane; microcirculation; blood flow and volume; hemorrhage; endotoxin shock; body fluids; autonomic nervous system. *Mailing Add:* Dept of Physiol Columbia Univ Col Physicians & Surgeons New York NY 10032

CHIEN, SZE-FOO, b China, Aug, 1929; m 61; c 2. MECHANICAL ENGINEERING. *Educ:* Univ Taiwan, BS, 53; Univ Minn, MS, 56, PhD(mech eng), 61. *Prof Exp:* Instr mech eng, Univ Minn, 56-61; RES ENGR, TEXACO BELLAIRE RES LABS, 61- *Concurrent Pos:* Consult, G

H Tennant Co & Furcura Co. *Mem:* Am Soc Mech Engrs; Sigma Xi. *Res:* Non-Newtonian fluid mechanics; oil-well drilling hydraulics and mechanics; multi-phase flow; secondary and tertiary oil recovery; tar-sands oil technology; product research and development; enchanced gas recovery. *Mailing Add:* 5027 S Braeswood Blvd Houston TX 77096

CHIEN, YIE W, pharmaceutics, see previous edition

CHIEN, YI-TZUU, b Shanghai, China, Aug 21, 38; m 65; c 1. ELECTRICAL ENGINEERING, COMPUTER SCIENCE. *Educ:* Nat Taiwan Univ, BSEE, 60; Purdue Univ, MSEE, 64, PhD, 67. *Prof Exp:* Mem tech staff, Bell Tel Labs, Inc, NJ, 66-67; from asst prof to assoc prof elec eng, 67-77, PROF ELEC ENG & COMPUT SCI, UNIV CONN, 77- *Mem:* Inst Elec & Electronics Engrs; Asn Comput Mach; Pattern Recognition Soc; Am Statist Asn. *Res:* Automatic pattern recognition; adaptive and learning systems; artificial intelligence; computer programming languages. *Mailing Add:* Dept of Elec Eng Univ of Conn Storrs CT 06268

CHIERI, P(ERICLE) A(DRIANO), b Mokanshan, China, Sept 6, 05; nat US; m 38. AERONAUTICAL & MECHANICAL ENGINEERING. *Educ:* Univ Genoa, Dr Ing, 27; Univ Naples, ME, 27; Univ Rome, Dr AeroE, 28. *Prof Exp:* Naval architect & marine engr, Res & Exp Div Submarines, Ital Navy Yard, La Spezia, 29-31; naval archit marine eng supt ship hulls & engines, Libera Shipping Corp, Trieste & Genoa, 31-35; aeronaut engr & tech adv to govt, Chinese Comn Aeronaut Affairs, 35-37; dir mat test lab & supt tech voc instruct, Chinese Govt Cent Mil Aircraft Factory, Nanchang, 37-39; aeronaut engr & tech writer, Off Air Attache, Ital Embassy, Washington, DC, 39-41; mem fac aeronaut eng, Tri-State Col, 42; aeronaut engr design & develop, Aeronaut Prod, Inc, 43-44; sr aeronaut engr aerodyn & struct stress anal, Eng & Res Corp, 44-46; assoc prof mech eng, Univ Toledo, 46-47; assoc prof, Newark Col Eng, 47-52; prof mech eng & chmn, Dept Mech & Eng, Univ Southwestern La, 52-72; CONSULT ENGR, 72- *Mem:* AAAS; assoc fel Am Inst Aeronaut & Astronaut; Am Soc Mech Engrs; Soc Exp Stress Anal; Instrument Soc Am. *Res:* Naval architecture; propulsion; turbomachinery; gas dynamics; aerothermodynamics; aeronautical structures; machine design; vibrations; hydrodynamics; marine engineering; internal combustion engines; turbines. *Mailing Add:* 142 Oak Crest Dr Lafayette LA 70503

CHIERICI, GEORGE J, b Napa, Calif, Nov 8, 26; m 56; c 4. PROSTHODONTICS. *Educ:* Univ Pac, DDS, 50. *Prof Exp:* Asst clin prof, 63-68, asst prof, 68-70, assoc prof, 70-76, PROF, UNIV CALIF, SAN FRANCISCO, 77- *Mem:* Int Asn Dent Res; Am Cleft Palate Asn. *Res:* Normal and abnormal growth and development; morphologic and physiologic interrelationships in the orofacial complex. *Mailing Add:* Ctr for Craniofacial Anomalies Univ of Calif San Francisco CA 94143

CHIGA, MASAHIRO, b Tokyo, Japan, Mar 6, 25; nat US; m 62; c 2. PATHOLOGY. *Educ:* Univ Tokyo, MD, 50. *Prof Exp:* Asst, Inst Infectious Dis, Univ Tokyo, 54; resident, Med Ctr, Univ Kans, 54-58; from asst prof to assoc prof path, Sch Med, Univ Utah, 60-69; assoc prof, 69-72, PROF PATH, SCH MED, UNIV KANS, 72- *Concurrent Pos:* Childs Mem Fund fel, 56-57; Nat Found fel, Metab Lab, Univ Utah, 58-60. *Mem:* Int Acad Path; Am Soc Exp Path. *Res:* Viral and rickettsial infection; experimental oncology; enzymes. *Mailing Add:* Dept of Path Univ of Kans Med Ctr Kansas City KS 66103

CHIGNELL, COLIN FRANCIS, b London, Eng, Apr 7, 38; US citizen; m 66; c 2. ORGANIC CHEMISTRY, PHARMACOLOGY. *Educ:* Univ London, BPharm, 59, PhD(med chem), 62. *Prof Exp:* Vis fel, Nat Inst Arthritis, Metab & Digestive Dis, 62-65; vis assoc, Nat Health & Lung Inst, 65-70, res pharmacologist, 70-77; CHIEF, LAB ENVIRON BIOPHYS, NAT INST ENVIRON HEALTH SCI, 77- *Concurrent Pos:* Res assoc, Nat Inst Gen Med Sci, 66-69. *Honors & Awards:* J J Abel Prize, Am Soc Pharmacol & Exp Therapeut, 73. *Mem:* Am Chem Soc; Am Soc Pharmacol & Exp Therapeut; Am Soc Biol Chemists; Biophys Soc; Soc Exp Biol & Med. *Res:* Spectroscopic studies of drug interactions with biological systems at a molecular level; structure and function of biological membranes and their interaction with drug molecules; mechanisms of drug photo toxicity. *Mailing Add:* Lab of Environ Biophys PO Box 12233 Research Triangle Park NC 27709

CHIGNELL, DEREK ALAN, b London, Eng, July 4, 43; m 70; c 3. BIOCHEMISTRY. *Educ:* Kings Col, Univ London, BS, 64, PhD(biophys chem), 68; Wheaton Col, MA, 77. *Prof Exp:* Fel, Univ Calif, Los Angeles, 68-71; asst prof biochem, Univ Dundee, Scotland, 71-75; ASSOC PROF CHEM, WHEATON COL, ILL, 75- *Concurrent Pos:* Lectr, Med Sch, Loyola Univ, 76- *Mem:* Am Sci Affil; Am Chem Soc. *Res:* Mechanism of action of local anesthetics, specifically their interaction with membrane proteins. *Mailing Add:* Dept Chem Wheaton Col Wheaton IL 60187

CHIH, CHUNG-YING, b China, Dec 11, 16; nat US; m 55. PHYSICS. *Educ:* Nat Tsing Hua Univ, China, BSc, 37; Univ Calif, Berkeley, PhD(physics), 54. *Prof Exp:* Instr physics, Fukien Med Col, 37-40; assoc prof, Fukien Teachers Col, 40-44; prof, Nat Chi-nan Univ, 44-45 & Kiangsu Col, 45-48; physicist radiation lab, Univ Calif, 48-54; from asst prof to prof physics, Middlebury Col, 54-68; SCI CONSULT, 68- *Concurrent Pos:* NSF res grant, 57-60. *Mem:* Am Phys Soc. *Res:* Neutron proton scattering; elementary particles. *Mailing Add:* PO Box 2556 Noble Sta Bridgeport CT 06608

CH'IH, JOHN JUWEI, b Tsingtao, China, Oct 29, 33; US citizen; m 62; c 1. BIOLOGICAL CHEMISTRY. *Educ:* Southern Ill Univ, BA, 60; Univ Del, MS, 63; Thomas Jefferson Univ, PhD(biochem), 68. *Prof Exp:* Res technician, Biochem Res Found, Newark, Del, 60-63; clin chemist, St Mary's Hosp, Philadelphia, 63-65; teaching asst biochem, Thomas Jefferson Univ, 65-68, instr, 68-69; sr instr biol chem, 69-71, from asst prof to assoc prof, 71-81, PROF BIOL CHEM, HAHNEMANN MED COL, 81- *Concurrent Pos:* Sr int fel, Fogarty Int Ctr, 78-79. *Mem:* Am Soc Biol Chemists; Sigma Xi; AAAS; Am Chem Soc; Am Soc Cell Biol. *Res:* Regulatory mechanisms in nucleic acids and protein biosynthesis of the eukaryotic cells; biogenesis of mammalian cell organelles. *Mailing Add:* Dept of Biol Chem Hahnemann Med Col Philadelphia PA 19102

CHIHARA, CAROL JOYCE, b New York, NY, Oct 31, 41; m 64; c 1. DEVELOPMENTAL GENETICS. *Educ:* Univ Calif, Berkeley, BA, 62, PhD(develop genetics), 72; San Francisco State Univ, MA, 67. *Prof Exp:* NIH fel genetics, Cambridge Univ, 72-73; RESEARCHER DEVELOP BIOL, UNIV CALIF, BERKELEY, 74- *Concurrent Pos:* Lectr cell & molecular biol, San Francisco State Univ, 74. *Mem:* AAAS. *Res:* Genetic control mechanisms in Drosophila as expressed by the phenomena of transdetermination in imaginal discs; effect of environmental factors and hormones as well as developmental capacities of the discs. *Mailing Add:* 567 Cragmont Ave Berkeley CA 94708

CHIHARA, THEODORE SEIO, b Seattle, Wash, Mar 14, 29; m 56; c 5. MATHEMATICAL ANALYSIS. *Educ:* Seattle Univ, BS, 51; Purdue Univ, MS, 53, PhD(math), 55. *Prof Exp:* Asst math, Purdue Univ, 52-55; from asst prof to prof, Seattle Univ, 55-69, actg head dept, 58-59, head, 59-66; prof assoc, Univ Alta, 69-70; vis prof, Univ Victoria, BC, 70-71; chmn dept, 71-77, PROF MATH, PURDUE UNIV, CALUMET CAMPUS, 71- *Mem:* Am Math Soc; Math Asn Am; Soc Indust Appl Math. *Res:* Theory of orthogonal polynomials; moment problems; special functions. *Mailing Add:* Dept Math Purdue Univ Hammond IN 46322

CHIKALLA, THOMAS D(AVID), b Milwaukee, Wis, Sept 9, 35; m 60; c 3. PHYSICAL METALLURGY, CERAMICS. *Educ:* Univ Wis, BS, 57, PhD(metall), 66; Univ Idaho, MS, 60. *Prof Exp:* Res engr plutonium metall, Gen Elec Co, 57-62; sr res scientist ceramics, 64-67, res assoc 67-72, mgr, Ceramics & Graphite Sect, 72-80, MGR NUCLEAR WASTE TECHNOL, BATTELLE MEM INST, 80- *Mem:* Am Inst Mining, Metall & Petrol Engrs; fel Am Ceramic Soc; Sigma Xi; AAAS; Am Soc Metals. *Res:* High temperature phase equilibria in actinide oxide and carbide systems; vaporization behavior and thermodynamics of actinide oxides; crystal structures of nonstoichiometric compounds; materials development for nuclear waste management; nuclear fuels development. *Mailing Add:* 2108 Harris Richland WA 99352

CHIKO, ARTHUR WESLEY, b Yorkton, Sask, Feb 15, 38. PLANT VIROLOGY. *Educ:* Univ BC, BSc, 61; Univ Idaho, MS, 67, PhD(plant path), 70. *Prof Exp:* Res officer forest path, Can Dept Forestry, Forest Entom & Path Lab, Fredericton, NB, 61-63; res scientist, Plant Virol, Res Sta, Winnipeg, Manitoba, 70-79, RES SCIENTIST, PLANT VIROLOGY, SAANICHTON RES & PLANT QUARANTINE STA, AGR CAN, SIDNEY, BC, 80- *Mem:* Am Phytopath Soc. *Res:* Virus diseases of oranamentals. *Mailing Add:* Saanichton Res & Plant Quarantine Sta Agr Can 8801 E Saanich Rd Sidney BC V8L 1H3 Can

CHILCOTE, DAVID OWEN, b Sask, Can, July 8, 31; m 53; c 2. c 2. AGRONOMY, PLANT PHYSIOLOGY. *Educ:* Ore State Univ, BS, 53, MS, 57; Purdue Univ, PhD(agron), 61. *Prof Exp:* From instr to assoc prof farm crops, 53-70, PROF CROP SCI, ORE STATE UNIV, 70- *Mem:* Am Soc Plant Physiol; Am Soc Agron; Crop Sci Soc Am. *Res:* Herbicides and growth regulators; crop physiology and ecology. *Mailing Add:* Dept of Crop Sci Ore State Univ Corvallis OR 97331

CHILCOTE, MAX ELI, b Bemidji, Minn, Sept 1, 17; m 43; c 3. CLINICAL CHEMISTRY, LABORATORY MEDICINE. *Educ:* Univ Minn, BS, 38, MS, 41; Univ Mich, PhD(biol chem), 44. *Prof Exp:* Asst biochem, Univ Mich, 40-44; instr, Med Sch, Loyola Univ, Ill, 44-46; Nutrit Found res fel, Pa State Col, 46-48; from asst prof to assoc prof biochem, Sch Med State Univ NY Buffalo, 48-60, asst dir biochem lab, 59-66, dir clin biochem, 66-69, assoc dir, 69-70, DIR ERIE COUNTY LABS, 70- *Concurrent Pos:* Clin assoc prof, 60-70, clin prof biochem, 70- & Dept of Pathol, Sch Med, State Univ NY Buffalo, 74- *Honors & Awards:* Educ Award, Am Asn Clin Chem, 75. *Mem:* Am Asn Clin Chem; Can Soc Clin Chem; Am Chem Soc; Acad Clin Lab Physicians & Scientists (pres, 73-75). *Res:* Clinical chemistry. *Mailing Add:* Erie County Labs 462 Grider St Buffalo NY 14215

CHILCOTE, WILLIAM W, b Washington, Iowa, Mar 6, 18; m 46; c 2. PLANT ECOLOGY. *Educ:* Iowa State Col, BS, 43, PhD(bot), 50. *Prof Exp:* Instr forestry, Iowa State Col, 46-50; asst prof bot & asst ecologist, 50-56, assoc prof bot & assoc ecologist, 56-62, PROF BOT, AGR EXP STA, ORE STATE UNIV, 62- *Concurrent Pos:* Fulbright grant, Finland, 58-59. *Mem:* Ecol Soc Am; Soc Am Foresters. *Res:* Forest and range ecology; autecology; community dynamics. *Mailing Add:* Dept of Bot Ore State Univ Corvallis OR 97331

CHILD, CHARLES GARDNER, III, b New York, NY, Feb 1, 08; m 41; c 6. SURGERY. *Educ:* Yale Univ, AB, 30; Cornell Univ, MD, 34; Am Bd Surg, dipl, 42. *Prof Exp:* Attend surgeon, NY Hosp, 47-53; assoc prof clin surg, Med Col, Cornell Univ, 47-53; prof surg & chmn dept, Med Sch, Tufts Univ, 53-58; prof surg & chmn dept, Med Sch, Univ Mich, Ann Arbor, 59-78; CLIN PROF SURG, EMORY UNIV, ATLANTA, 77- *Concurrent Pos:* Surgeon in chief, Boston Dispensary & surgeon, Boston Floating Hosp, Infants & Children, 53-58; dir first surg serv, Boston City Hosp, 54-58; consult to Surg Gen, Liver Study Sect, US Army, 56-62; consult, Vet Admin, 57-62, mem adv comt res, Dept Med & Surg, 60-68; mem, Am Bd Surg, 59-65, chmn, 64-65; mem surg study sect, NIH, 59-63, mem gen clin res ctr comt, 63-66; ed, J Surg Res, 60-66; mem surg test comt, Nat Bd Med Exam, 61-68, mem ad hoc comt study & improv part II exam, 62-64, mem at large, 65-; mem halothane anesthesia comt, NSF, 63-67; mem sci adv comt, United Health Founds, 63-, mem grants rev subcomt, 63-; mem study comt, USPHS Hosps, 65; mem bd med, Nat Acad Sci, 67-; chmn differences in postoperative mortality policy comt, Nat Res Coun, 70-; actg dir, Study Instnl Differences in Postoperative Mortality, Nat Acad Sci-Inst Med-Nat Res Coun, 71- *Mem:* Am Surg Asn; Soc Clin Surg; fel Am Col Surg; Soc Surg Alimentary Tract; NY Acad Sci. *Res:* Portal hypertension, liver diseases and pancreatic duodenal physiology and neoplasia. *Mailing Add:* Vet Admin Med Ctr 1670 Clairmont Rd Decatur GA 30033

CHILD, EDWARD T(AYLOR), b Richmond, Va, July 9, 30; m 55; c 5. CHEMICAL ENGINEERING. *Educ:* Yale Univ, BE, 52; Univ Del, MS, 54, PhD(chem eng), 57; Pepperdine Univ, MBA, 72. *Prof Exp:* Res chem engr, Texaco Res Ctr, NY, 56-62, group leader process develop, Texaco Montebello Res Lab, 62-67, asst supvr, 67-68, supvr res, 68-73, ASST MGR, TEXACO DEVELOP CORP, 73- *Mem:* Am Inst Chem Engrs; Sci Res Soc Am; Am Mgt Asn. *Res:* Process development research and engineering of technology for conversion of coal and heavy petroleum residues to clean gaseous products and technical liaison with contractors building these plants. *Mailing Add:* Texaco Develop Corp 2000 Westchester Ave White Plains NY 10650

CHILD, FRANK MALCOLM, b Jersey City, NJ, Nov 30, 31; m 60; c 3. CELL BIOLOGY. *Educ:* Amherst Col, AB, 53; Univ Calif, PhD(zool), 57. *Prof Exp:* Instr zool, Univ Chicago, 57-60, asst prof, 60-65; assoc prof biol, 65-73, chmn dept, 74-78, PROF BIOL, TRINITY COL, CONN, 73- *Mem:* Soc Protozool; Am Soc Cell Biol; Am Soc Zoologists. *Res:* Protozoan physiology; developmental and cellular biology; cilia and flagella. *Mailing Add:* Dept of Biol Trinity Col Hartford CT 06106

CHILD, HARRY RAY, b Bedford, Ind, Oct 30, 28; m 54; c 1. SOLID STATE PHYSICS, MAGNETISM. *Educ:* Univ Tex, BS, 56; Univ Tenn, PhD(physics), 65. *Prof Exp:* PHYSICIST, OAK RIDGE NAT LAB, 56- *Mem:* Am Phys Soc. *Res:* Neutron scattering studies of solids, mostly magnetic properties. *Mailing Add:* 1034 W Outer Dr Oak Ridge TN 37830

CHILD, JEFFREY JAMES, b Gateshead, Eng, June 26, 36; m 58; c 2. MICROBIOLOGY. *Educ:* Univ Durham, BSc, 58, PhD, 62. *Prof Exp:* Fel, Prairie Regional Lab, Nat Res Coun Can, 62-63; asst lectr biol, Univ Salford, 63-64, lectr microbiol, 64-67; assoc res officer, 67-76, sr res officer, 76-80, EXEC SECY, TACTICAL STUDIES COMT, PRAIRIE REGIONAL LAB, NAT RES COUN CAN, OTTAWA, 80- *Concurrent Pos:* Vis scientist, Commonwealth Sci & Indust Res Orgn, Australia, 74-75. *Honors & Awards:* Medal Award, Can Soc Microbiol, 79. *Mem:* Can Soc Microbiol; Brit Soc Gen Microbiol; Am Soc Microbiol. *Res:* Physiology of fungi; microbiological degradation of natural products; symbiotic nitrogen fixation. *Mailing Add:* Nat Res Coun Prairie Regional Lab Saskatoon SK S7N 0W9 Can

CHILD, PROCTOR LOUIS, b Brooklyn, NY, Nov 29, 25; m 52; c 3. PATHOLOGY. *Educ:* Long Island Col Med, MS, 49. *Prof Exp:* Intern, St Agnes Hosp, White Plains, NY, US Army, 49-50, gen med officer, 155th Sta Hosp, Japan, 50, battalion & regimental surgeon, 1st Cavalry Div, Korea, 50-51, gen med officer, Army Hosp, Camp Pickett, Va, 51-52, path resident, Fitzsimons Gen Hosp, Denver, 52-56, chief path serv, 5th Gen Hosp, Stuttgart, 56-58, 130th Sta Hosp, Heidelberg, 58-60, chief path, William Beaumont Gen Hosp, El Paso, 60-64, mem geog path div, Armed Forces Inst Path, 64-66, chief viro-path br & asst chief geog path div, 67; assoc prof path, Sch Med, Temple Univ, 68-80; ASSOC PATHOLOGIST, ALLENTOWN GEN HOSP, PA, 80- *Concurrent Pos:* Mem staff, Roxborough Mem Hosp, Philadelphia, 70- *Mem:* AMA; Am Soc Clin Path; Col Am Path; Int Acad Path. *Res:* Geographic pathology and infectious disease, especially viropathology and study of hemorrhagic fevers. *Mailing Add:* 1819 Saratoga Court Allentown PA 18104

CHILD, RALPH GRASSING, b New York, NY, Oct 7, 19; m 44; c 3. MEDICINAL CHEMISTRY. *Educ:* Hofstra Col, BA, 41; George Washington Univ, MA, 48; Univ Iowa, PhD(org chem), 50. *Prof Exp:* Res chemist, 50-74, SR RES CHEMIST, LEDERLE LABS, AM CYANAMID CO, 74- *Mem:* Am Chem Soc. *Res:* Medicinal organic chemistry; chemotherapy of virus and neoplastic diseases; chemistry of antibacterial compounds; immune response inhibitors and stimulators; antiinflamatory-analgesics. *Mailing Add:* Lederle Labs Pearl River NY 10965

CHILD, WILLIAM CLARK, JR, b Elizabeth, NJ, Sept 2, 27; m 60; c 3. PHYSICAL CHEMISTRY. *Educ:* Oberlin Col, AB, 50; Univ Wis, PhD(chem), 55. *Prof Exp:* Proj assoc chem, Univ Wis, 55-56; from instr to assoc prof, 56-69, PROF CHEM, CARLETON COL, 69- *Concurrent Pos:* NSF fac fel, Univ Calif, Santa Barbara, 71-72; res fac mem, Oak Ridge Sci Semester, Oak Ridge Nat Lab, 79-80; Fac res participant, Argonne Nat Lab, 81. *Mem:* Am Chem Soc. *Res:* Raman spectroscopy of motten salts. *Mailing Add:* Dept of Chem Carleton Col Northfield MN 55057

CHILDERS, DONALD GENE, b The Dalles, Ore, Feb 11, 35; m 53; c 2. ELECTRICAL ENGINEERING. *Educ:* Univ Southern Calif, BS, 58, MS, 59, PhD(elec eng), 64. *Prof Exp:* Mem tech staff res & develop, Aeronutronic Div, Philco Corp, 58-60 & 61-64 & Hughes Aircraft Co, 60-61; asst prof elec eng, Univ Calif, Davis, 64-65; assoc prof, 65-68, PROF ELEC ENG, UNIV FLA, 68- *Concurrent Pos:* Lectr, Univ Southern Calif, 62-64. *Mem:* Inst Elec & Electronics Engrs. *Res:* Communication and information theory; telemetry; array detection; random fields and processes; biomedical engineering; visual evoked responses; vision research. *Mailing Add:* Dept of Elec Eng Univ of Fla Gainesville FL 32601

CHILDERS, NORMAN FRANKLIN, b Moscow, Idaho, Oct 29, 10; c 4. HORTICULTURE. *Educ:* Univ Mo, BS, 33, MS, 34; Cornell Univ, PhD(pomol), 37. *Prof Exp:* Asst pomol, Cornell Univ, 34-37; asst prof hort, Ohio State Univ, 37-44, assoc, Ohio Exp Sta, 39-44; asst dir & sr plant physiologist, PR Exp Sta, USDA, 44-47; prof, res specialist & chmn, Dept Hort & Forestry, 48-66, Blake prof hort, Agr Exp Sta, 66-80, EMER PROF, RUTGERS UNIV, 80- *Concurrent Pos:* Adj prof, Univ Fla, Gainesville, 81- *Mem:* AAAS; Am Soc Plant Physiologists; Am Soc Agron; fel Am Soc Hort Sci. *Res:* Photosynthesis; transpiration; respiration; nutrition of fruits and other horticultural plants; tropical and temperate pomology; tropical vegetables; nightshades effects on arthritis. *Mailing Add:* Dept of Hort & Forestry Rutgers Univ New Brunswick NJ 08903

CHILDERS, RAY FLEETWOOD, b Los Angeles, Calif, Apr 16, 45; m 71; c 1. PHARMACEUTICAL CHEMISTRY, ANALYTICAL CHEMISTRY. *Educ:* Univ Calif, Los Angeles, BS, 67; Ind Univ, PhD(inorg chem), 72. *Prof Exp:* Res assoc biophys chem, Ind Univ, 72-74; sr anal chemist, 74-78, RES SCIENTIST, ELI LILLY & CO, 79- *Mem:* Am Chem Soc. *Res:* Automated flow analysis of pharmaceuticals; activity and structure of biological molecules using nuclear magnetic resonance; pharmaco-kinetics. *Mailing Add:* Eli Lilly & Co Indianapolis IN 46285

CHILDERS, RICHARD LEE, b Birmingham, Ala, Dec 10, 30; m 60; c 2. PHYSICS. *Educ:* Presby Col, SC, BS, 53; Univ Tenn, MS, 56, PhD(particle physics), 62. *Prof Exp:* Res assoc physics, Univ Tenn, 61-63; asst prof, 63-66, ASSOC PROF PHYSICS, UNIV SC, 66- *Concurrent Pos:* Consult, Neutron Physics Div, Oak Ridge Nat Lab, 62-64; dir, Honors Prog, 67-69. *Mem:* Am Phys Soc; Am Asn Physics Teachers; Am Inst Physics. *Res:* Electron-position colliding beam experiment; acoustics of musical instruments. *Mailing Add:* Dept Physics Univ SC Columbia SC 29208

CHILDERS, ROBERT LEE, b Parkersburg, WVa, May 3, 36; m 62; c 2. PHOTOGRAPHIC CHEMISTRY. *Educ:* WVa Univ, BS, 60, MS, 61; Ohio State Univ, PhD(org chem), 65. *Prof Exp:* Sr res chemist, 65-71, RES ASSOC, EASTMAN KODAK CO, 71- *Mem:* Am Chem Soc; Soc Photog Sci & Eng. *Res:* Chemistry of photographic emulsions and photographic processing. *Mailing Add:* Res Labs B-59 Eastman Kodak Co Rochester NY 14650

CHILDERS, ROBERT WAYNE, b Ft Worth, Tex, May 25, 37; m 62; c 3. THEORETICAL PHYSICS. *Educ:* Howard Payne Col, BA, 60; Vanderbilt Univ, PhD(physics), 63. *Prof Exp:* Res fel, Argonne Nat Lab, 63-65; asst prof, 65-72, ASSOC PROF PHYSICS, UNIV TENN, KNOXVILLE, 65- *Concurrent Pos:* Consult, Oak Ridge Nat Lab, 66- *Mem:* Am Phys Soc. *Res:* Elementary particle physics; theory of infinitely rising Regge trajectories and local duality; Veneziano model; quantum field theory; symmetries of elementary particles. *Mailing Add:* Dept of Physics & Astron Univ of Tenn Knoxville TN 37916

CHILDERS, RODERICK W, b Paris, France, 31; m; c 1. MEDICINE, CARDIOLOGY. *Educ:* Univ Dublin, BA, 53, MD, 54, MA, 58; Am Bd Cardiovasc Dis, cert, 69. *Prof Exp:* Intern med, St Andrew's Hosp, London, Eng, 54-55; intern surg, May Day Hosp, Croydon, 55-56; chief cardiologist, Royal City of Dublin Hosp, Ireland, 59-63; asst prof cardiol, 63-69, ASSOC PROF MED, UNIV CHICAGO, 69-, HEAD HEART STA, 66- *Concurrent Pos:* Fel, Harvard Univ & WRoxbury Vet Admin Hosp, Mass, 58-59; res assoc nutrit, Sch Pub Health, Harvard Univ, 59-62; med tutor cardiol, Med Sch, Univ Dublin, 59-63; cardiac asst, Nat Children's Hosp, Dublin & vis pediat cardiologist, Rotunda Maternity Hosp, 59-63. *Mailing Add:* 5725 S Kenwood Ave Chicago IL 60637

CHILDERS, STEVEN ROGER, b Houston, Tex, Sept 28, 50; m 76. NEUROPHARMACOLOGY, NEUROCHEMISTRY. *Educ:* Univ Tex, Austin, BS, 72; Univ Wis, Sch Med, PhD(physiol chem), 76. *Prof Exp:* Fel pharmacol, Sch Med, Johns Hopkins Univ, 76-79; ASST PROF PHARMACOL, COL MED, UNIV FLA, 79- *Mem:* Soc Neurosci; AAAS. *Res:* Neuropharmacology and neurochemistry; characterization of opioid and other neuropeptide systems in mammalian brain. *Mailing Add:* Dept Pharmacol Col Med Univ Fla Gainesville FL 32610

CHILDERS, WALTER ROBERT, b Kelowna, BC, Mar 29, 16; m 53; c 2. PLANT BREEDING, PLANT GENETICS. *Educ:* McGill Univ, BSc, 38; Univ Wis, MS, 47, PhD(plant breeding & genetics), 51. *Prof Exp:* Asst corn & soybeans, Forage Crop Div, 38-40, CHIEF FORAGE SECT, OTTAWA RES STA, CAN DEPT AGR, 46- *Mem:* Am Soc Agron; Agr Inst Can; Can Soc Genetics; Can Soc Agron; Can Phytopath Soc. *Res:* Orchard and brome grass; timothy; cytology and genetics; alfalfa. *Mailing Add:* Ottawa Res Sta Bldg 12 Cent Exp Farm Can Dept Agr Ottawa ON K1A 0C6 Can

CHILDRESS, CHARLES CURTIS, b Pittsburg, Kans, Nov 10, 39; m 60; c 3. BIOCHEMISTRY, BIOMEDICAL ENGINEERING. *Educ:* Col Great Falls, BS, 61; Kans State Univ, MS, 64; Johns Hopkins Univ, PhD(biochem), 69. *Prof Exp:* Res asst biol, Kans State Univ, 62-64; res biochemist, US Army Chem Res & Develop Labs, Md, 64-67; biochemist, NIH, 67-69; dir of labs, Upsher Labs, Kansas City, Mo, 69-71; PRES, MIDWEST SCI LABS, INC, 71-; PRES, MIDWEST SCI INSTRUMENTS, INC, 72-; PRES, LIBRA SYSTS, INC, 74- *Honors & Awards:* Qual Performance Award, US Army, 65. *Mem:* AAAS; Am Chem Soc; Am Asn Clin Chem; Am Asn Off Anal Chemists; Am Acad Clin Toxicol. *Res:* Plant physiology; insect biochemistry; clinical biochemistry; computerized diagnosis; laboratory computer systems. *Mailing Add:* 1203 Willow Dr Olathe KS 66061

CHILDRESS, DENVER RAY, b Alcoa, Tenn, Feb 5, 37; m 57; c 2. PURE MATHEMATICS. *Educ:* Maryville Col, Tenn, BS, 59; Univ Tenn, Knoxville, MMath, 64, EdD(math educ), 75. *Prof Exp:* Teacher math, Powell High Sch, Knox County, Tenn, 59-60; Maryville Jr High Sch, Maryville, Tenn, 60-62 & Maryville High Sch, 62-65; from asst prof to assoc prof, 67-81, PROF MATH, CARSON-NEWMAN COL, 81- *Mem:* Am Asn Univ Prof; Nat Coun Teachers Math; Math Asn Am. *Res:* Factors which influence student ratings of mathematics teaching and teachers, especially attitudes. *Mailing Add:* Rte 1 Box 46 New Market TN 37820

CHILDRESS, DUDLEY STEPHEN, b Cass Co, Mo, Sept 25, 34; m 59; c 2. BIOMEDICAL ENGINEERING. *Educ:* Univ Mo-Columbia, BS, 57, MS, 58; Northwestern Univ, PhD(elec eng), 67. *Prof Exp:* From instr to asst prof elec eng, Univ Mo-Columbia, 59-63; res asst, Physiol Control Syst Lab, Northwestern Univ, Evanston, 64-66, from asst prof to assoc prof elec eng & orthoped surg, 72-77, PROF ELEC ENG, TECHNOL INST & PROF ORTHOPED SURG RES, MED SCH, NORTHWESTERN UNIV, CHICAGO, 77-, DIR, PROSTHETICS RES LAB, 71-, CO-DIR, REHAB ENG PROG, 72- *Concurrent Pos:* Mem comt prosthetics res & develop, Nat

Acad Sci-Nat Res Coun, 69-72, mem sub-comt design, 70-73, chmn upper-extremity prosthetics panel, 71-73; Nat Inst Gen Med Sci res career develop award, 70-75; mem appl physiol & bioeng study sect, NIH, 74-78. *Honors & Awards:* Goldenson Award Res in Med & Technol, United Cerebral Palsy Found. *Mem:* AAAS; Inst Elec & Electronics Eng; Biomed Eng Soc; Rehab Eng Soc NAm; Int Soc Prosthetics & Orthotics. *Res:* Rehabilitation engineering, design and development of modern technological systems for disabled people and scientific approach to analysis and description of problems of these people. *Mailing Add:* Prosthetics Res Lab Rm 1441 345 E Superior St Chicago IL 60611

CHILDRESS, EVELYN TUTT, b Joplin, Mo, Feb 8, 26; m 67. MICROBIOLOGY, IMMUNOLOGY. *Educ:* Lincoln Univ, Mo, BS, 47; Univ Mich, MS, 48, MS, 56; Stanford Univ, PhD(med microbiol), 67. *Prof Exp:* Instr biol, Fla Agr & Mech Univ, 48-49; instr, Lincoln Univ, Mo, 49-52, asst prof, 52-63; mem fac, Fullerton Jr Col, 67-69; asst prof, 69-72, assoc prof biol, 72-77, CALIF STATE UNIV, DOMINGUEZ HILLS, 77- *Mem:* Am Soc Microbiol; Sigma Xi; AAAS; Am Asn Univ Prof. *Res:* Aging in the immune system; origin of naturally occuring antibodies, particularly with their specificity and the question of necessity of antigenic stimulation for their appearance; schistosome immunology. *Mailing Add:* Dept of Biol Calif State Univ Dominguez Hills Carson CA 90747

CHILDRESS, JAMES J, b Kokomo, Ind, Nov 17, 42; div. COMPARATIVE PHYSIOLOGY, BIOLOGICAL OCEANOGRAPHY. *Educ:* Wabash Col, BA, 64; Stanford Univ, PhD(biol), 69. *Prof Exp:* Asst prof, 69-77, assoc prof zool, 77-80, PROF UNIV CALIF, SANTA BARBARA, 81- *Concurrent Pos:* Prin investr, NSF grant, 70-72; NSF grants, 70- *Mem:* AAAS; Am Soc Zoologists; Am Soc Limnol & Oceanog; Sigma Xi. *Res:* Ecological physiology of marine invertebrates and fishes; respiratory physiology; deep-sea biology; effects of hydrostatic pressure on organisms; biology of hydrothermal vent animals; physiology of locomotion in fishes and crustaceans. *Mailing Add:* Dept of Zool Univ of Calif Santa Barbara CA 93106

CHILDRESS, NOEL A, b Lafayette Co, Miss, Jan 12, 20; m 46; c 2. GEOMETRY. *Educ:* Univ Miss, BAE, 41, MA, 47; Univ Fla, PhD(math), 54. *Prof Exp:* Pub sch teacher, Miss, 41-42; from instr to assoc prof, 48-57, PROF MATH, UNIV MISS, 57- *Mem:* Math Asn Am; Am Math Soc. *Res:* Projective transformations in algebraic geometry; involutions. *Mailing Add:* Dept of Math Univ of Miss University MS 38677

CHILDRESS, OTIS STEELE, JR, b Richmond, Va, Dec 27, 36; m 62; c 2. ENGINEERING MANAGEMENT, SYSTEMS ENGINEERING. *Educ:* Va Polytech Inst, BSEE, 62. *Prof Exp:* Aero-decelerator engr, Advan Missions Studies Off, Langley Res Ctr, 67-68, sterilization engr bioeng, Viking Proj Off, 68-70, orbiter sci instruments mgr eng mgt, 70-73, Viking orbiter mgr, 73-76, head, Proj Integration Off Systs Eng, Projs Directorate, 76-78, dep prof mgr & chief engr, Rotor Systs Res Aircraft Proj, 78-80, MGR, PROPFAN NOISE PROG, LANGLEY RES CTR, NASA, 80- *Concurrent Pos:* Exec mem, Orbiter Imaging Team, Mars Atmospheric Water Detection Team & Mars Infrared Thermal Mapping Team, 70-73. *Res:* Management and engineering research and development efforts in aeronautics and space. *Mailing Add:* 119 National Lane Williamsburg VA 23185

CHILDRESS, SCOTT JULIUS, b Greenville, SC, Apr 6, 26; m 75. ORGANIC CHEMISTRY. *Educ:* Furman Univ, BS, 47; Univ NC, PhD(chem), 51. *Prof Exp:* Res chemist catalysis, Tenn Eastman Co, 51-52 & pharmaceut, Wallace & Tiernan, Inc, 52-58; res chemist pharmaceut, 59-60, group leader, 60-61, mgr med chem sect, 61-68, asst to vpres res & develop, 68-74, ASST VPRES RES & DEVELOP, WYETH LABS, 74- *Mem:* Fel NY Acad Sci; Am Chem Soc. *Res:* Design, synthesis and testing of organic compounds of possible therapeutic value. *Mailing Add:* Wyeth Labs PO Box 8299 Philadelphia PA 19101

CHILDRESS, WILLIAM STEPHEN, b Houston, Tex, Oct 5, 34; m 60; c 2. FLUID MECHANICS, APPLIED MATHEMATICS. *Educ:* Princeton Univ, BSE, 56, MSE, 58; Calif Inst Technol, PhD(aeronaut, math), 61. *Prof Exp:* Assoc res Scientist, Jet Propulsion Lab, 61-64; res assoc magneto-fluid dynamics, Courant Inst Math Sci, 64-66, asst prof, 66-70, assoc prof, 70-76, PROF MATH, NY UNIV, 76- *Concurrent Pos:* Assoc, Inst Henri Poincare, Univ Paris, 67-68; Guggenheim fel, 76-77. *Mem:* Am Math Soc; Soc Indust & Appl Math. *Res:* Singular perturbation problems in fluid dynamics and applied mathematics; magnetohydrodynamics; dynamo theory of geomagnetism; viscous flow theory; biomathematics. *Mailing Add:* Dept of Math Col of Arts & Sci NY Univ New York NY 10003

CHILDS, BARTON, b Chicago, Ill, Feb 29, 16; m 50; c 2. PEDIATRICS. *Educ:* Williams Col, AB, 38; Johns Hopkins Univ, MD, 42. *Prof Exp:* Intern, asst resident & resident pediat, Johns Hopkins Hosp, 42-43, 46-48; res fel, Children's Hosp, Boston, 48-49; mem fac, 49-62, PROF PEDIAT, SCH MED, JOHNS HOPKINS UNIV, 62- *Concurrent Pos:* Commonwealth Fund fel, Univ Col, Univ London, 52-53; Markle scholar, 53-58; mem, NIH Consult Comts, 59-; Grover F Powers distinguished scholar, 60-62; mem res adv comt, United Cerebral Palsy Found, 60-63; NIH res career award, 62. *Honors & Awards:* Meade Johnson Award Pediat, NIH, 59. *Mem:* Inst of Med of Nat Acad Sci; Am Pediat Soc; Soc Pediat Res; Am Acad Pediat; Am Acad Arts & Sci. *Mailing Add:* Dept of Pediat Charles & 34th St Baltimore MD 21218

CHILDS, DANA PITT, b Herington, Kans, Mar 24, 26; m 50; c 2. ENTOMOLOGY. *Educ:* Kans State Univ, BS, 49. *Prof Exp:* RES ENTOMOLOGIST, SCI & EDUC ADMIN, USDA, 49- *Mem:* Entom Soc Am. *Res:* Biological and chemical control of insect pests attacking stored products. *Mailing Add:* Sci & Educ Admin USDA PO Box 10125 Richmond VA 23240

CHILDS, DONALD RAY, b Lynn, Mass, May 31, 30; m 64; c 2. MATHEMATICAL PHYSICS. *Educ:* Univ NH, BS, 52, MS, 54; Vanderbilt Univ, PhD(physics), 58. *Prof Exp:* Scientist, Westinghouse Elec Corp, 57-59; sr scientist, Allied Res Assocs, 59-60; prin res scientist, Avco-Everett Res Lab, 60-64; sr scientist, Lab of Electronics, 64-66 & Quincy Div, Elec Boat Co, 66-69; PHYSICIST, NAVAL UNDERWATER SYST CTR, 69- *Concurrent Pos:* Spec lectr, Northeastern Univ, 67-69. *Res:* Multivariate analysis; signal processing; non-linear mechanics; non-linear control systems; non-linear differential equations. *Mailing Add:* Naval Underwater Systs Ctr Hq Newport Lab Newport RI 02840

CHILDS, GEORGE RICHARD, b Terra Alta, WVa, Oct 9, 24; m 49; c 4. NUTRITION. *Educ:* WVa Univ, BS, 50; Purdue Univ, MS, 51; Univ Md, PhD(nutrit), 64. *Prof Exp:* Poultry res specialist, Cent Soya Co, Inc, 51-61; animal husbandman, Bur Commercial Fisheries, 61-64; mgr poultry res, 64-68, DIR FEED RES, CENT SOYA CO, INC, 68- *Mem:* Poultry Sci Asn. *Res:* Amino acid requirements of growing chicks and laying hens. *Mailing Add:* Res Dept Cent Soya Co Inc 1230 N Second St Decatur IN 46733

CHILDS, JAMES FIELDING LEWIS, b Tucson, Ariz, Jan 3, 10; m 36; c 4. PLANT PATHOLOGY. *Educ:* Univ Calif, BS, 37, PhD(plant path), 41. *Prof Exp:* Agent, USDA, 41-43, from asst pathologist to prin pathologist, 43-66, res pathologist, Agr Res Serv, 66-76; RETIRED. *Concurrent Pos:* Consult, Egypt, 55, Morroco, 59, Surinam, 63 & Sudan, 64; ed proc, Int Orgn Citrus Virol, 66. *Mem:* Am Phytopath Soc; Int Orgn Citrus Virol. *Res:* Etiology, virus indexing procedures and programs; control of virus diseases; Rio Grande gummosis, its nature and control; citrus blight (YTD, RLD, SHD), its nature and control. *Mailing Add:* 1206 Nottingham St Orlando FL 32803

CHILDS, LINDSAY NATHAN, b Boston, Mass, Apr 17, 40. MATHEMATICS. *Educ:* Wesleyan Univ, BA, 62; Cornell Univ, PhD(math), 66. *Prof Exp:* Asst prof math, Northwestern Univ, 66-68; assoc prof, 71-80, PROF MATH, STATE UNIV NY, ALBANY, 71- *Mem:* Am Math Soc; Math Asn Am. *Res:* Algebra. *Mailing Add:* Dept of Math State Univ of NY Albany NY 12222

CHILDS, MARIAN TOLBERT, b Twin Falls, Idaho, Nov 18, 25; m 52; c 4. LIPID METABOLISM. *Educ:* Univ Calif, Berkeley, BS, 46, PhD(nutrit), 50. *Prof Exp:* Teaching & res asst nutrit, Univ Calif, Berkeley, 46-50; asst prof nutrit, Univ Ill, 50-54; lab technician lipid biochem, 66-68, actg asst prof, 68-71, asst prof, 73-81, ASSOC PROF NUTRIT, UNIV WASH, 81- *Concurrent Pos:* NIH fel nutrit & atherosclerosis, Dept Med, Univ Wash, 76-78. *Mem:* Sigma Xi; Am Inst Nutrit. *Res:* Lipid metabolism, primarily the interaction of nutrients with lipids; phosphatide choline turnover studies; lecithin feeding to humans; hyperlipidemia of pregnancy in rats used turnover and removal studies; oyster feeding in rats. *Mailing Add:* Dept Nutrit Sci DL10 Univ Wash Seattle WA 98195

CHILDS, MORRIS E, b Yellville, Ark, Mar 30, 23; m 52; c 4. MECHANICAL ENGINEERING. *Educ:* Univ Okla, BS, 44; Univ Ill, MS, 47, PhD(mech eng), 56. *Prof Exp:* Res assoc mech eng, Univ Ill, 47-54; from asst prof to assoc prof, 54-61, chmn dept, 73-80, PROF MECH ENG, UNIV WASH, 61-, . *Mem:* Am Soc Eng Educ; Am Soc Mech Engrs; Am Inst Aeronaut & Astronaut. *Res:* Thermodynamics; fluid flow; heat transfer; turbulent boundary layer flow; separated flows. *Mailing Add:* Dept Mech Eng FU-10 Univ of Wash Seattle WA 98195

CHILDS, RONALD FRANK, b Liss, Eng, Nov 30, 39; m 65; c 2. PHYSICAL ORGANIC CHEMISTRY. *Educ:* Bath Univ Technol, BSc, 63; Univ Nottingham, PhD(org chem), 66. *Prof Exp:* Fel, Univ Calif, Los Angeles, 66-68; asst prof, 68-72, assoc prof, 72-78, PROF CHEM, McMASTER UNIV, 78- *Mem:* Am Chem Soc; The Chem Soc; sr mem Chem Inst Can. *Res:* Physical organic chemistry, particularly thermal and photochemical rearrangements of carbonium ions. *Mailing Add:* Dept of Chem McMaster Univ Hamilton ON L8S 4L8 Can

CHILDS, S(ELMA) BART, b Magnolia, Ark, Jan 3, 38; m 70. COMPUTER SCIENCE, ENGINEERING. *Educ:* Okla State Univ, BS, 59, MS, 60, PhD(eng mech), 66. *Prof Exp:* Instr civil eng, Okla State Univ, 61-64; res engr, Space & Info Systs Div, NAm Aviation, Inc, Okla, 64-65; asst prof mech eng, Univ Houston, 65-68, assoc prof & assoc chmn dept, 68-71; prof appl math & comput sci & chmn dept, Speed Sci Sch, Univ Louisville, 71-74; PROF COMPUT SCI, TEX A&M UNIV, 74- *Mem:* Am Inst Aeronaut & Astronaut; Soc Indust & Appl Math; Asn Comput Mach; Am Soc Mech Engrs. *Res:* Hydraulics, elasticity; numerical and applied mathematics; boundary value problems, codes for analysis. *Mailing Add:* Dept of Indust Eng Tex A&M Univ College Station TX 77843

CHILDS, WILLIAM HENRY, b Princeton, Ill, Jan 1, 07; m 34; c 4. POMOLOGY. *Educ:* Univ Ill, BS, 30, MS, 31; Cornell Univ, PhD(pomol), 40. *Prof Exp:* Instr hort univ & asst agr exp sta, 31-38, from asst prof hort & asst horticulturist to prof hort & horticulturist, 40-74, actg chmn dept hort univ, 60-62, EMER PROF HORT, WVA AGR EXP STA, WVA UNIV, 72- *Mem:* Am Soc Hort Sci. *Res:* Small fruits; cultural studies with strawberries, raspberries, blackberries and grapes; blueberry selection, hybridization and propagation. *Mailing Add:* 936 Virginia St Apt 309 Dunedin FL 33528

CHILDS, WILLIAM JEFFRIES, b Boston, Mass, Nov 9, 26; m 51; c 2. ATOMIC PHYSICS. *Educ:* Harvard Univ, AB, 48; Univ Mich, MS, 49, PhD(physics), 56. *Prof Exp:* PHYSICIST, ARGONNE NAT LAB, 56- *Concurrent Pos:* Vis prof, Univ Bonn, Ger, 72-73. *Mem:* Am Phys Soc; Optical Soc Am. *Res:* Atomic-beam magnetic resonance; hyperfine structure; laser spectroscopy; atomic and molecular structure. *Mailing Add:* Argonne Nat Lab 9700 S Cass Ave Argonne IL 60439

CHILDS, WILLIAM VES, b Cale, Ark, Sept 14, 35; m 62; c 3. FLUORINE CHEMISTRY, ELECTROCHEMISTRY. *Educ:* Southern State Col, BS, 56; Univ Ark, MS, 60, PhD(phys chem), 63. *Prof Exp:* SR CHEMIST, PHILLIPS PETROL CO, 62- *Concurrent Pos:* Vis scientist, Univ Tex, 69-70; consult, NIH, Lung & Heart Inst, 75. *Mem:* AAAS: Am Chem Soc (treas, 75); Am Inst Chem Engrs. *Res:* Fluorine chemistry; kinetics; computer simulations; application of small, dedicated computers to data acquisition and processing; synthetic electrochemistry; combustion processes; organic syntheses. *Mailing Add:* 1504 Harris Dr Bartlesville OK 74003

CHILDS, WYLIE J(ONES), metallurgy, see previous edition

CHILENSKAS, ALBERT ANDREW, b Chicago, Ill, Nov 7, 27; m 63. CHEMICAL ENGINEERING. *Educ:* Univ Ill, BS, 49. *Prof Exp:* Asst chem engr, 49-51 & 53-60, assoc chem engr, 60-75, MGR ADV BATTERY TECHNOL DEVELOP, ARGONNE NAT LAB, 77- *Honors & Awards:* Indust Res-100 Award, Nat Battery Adv Comt, 81. *Mem:* Am Nuclear Soc; Sigma Xi; Am Inst Chem Engrs; Commercial Develop Asn; AAAS. *Res:* Nuclear fuel reprocessing; high-temperature lithium-chalcogen batteries; lithium/metal sulfide battery technology. *Mailing Add:* Argonne Nat Lab Bldg 205 Argonne IL 60439

CHILGREEN, DONALD RAY, b Jenkins, Ky, Nov 8, 39; m 64; c 3. SOIL MICROBIOLOGY. *Educ:* Marion Col, AB, 64; Kans State Univ, MS, 67, PhD(microbiol), 74. *Prof Exp:* Asst prof biol, Marion Col, 67-68; instr microbiol, Kans State Univ, 68-69; from asst prof to assoc prof, 70-81, PROF BIOL, MARION COL, 81- *Mem:* Am Soc Microbiol; Sigma Xi. *Res:* Diversity of the indigenous thermophilic microorganism in prairie soils; growth curves and respiratory activity of thermophilic bacteria from soil. *Mailing Add:* Dept of Biol Marion Col 4201 S Washington St Marion IN 46952

CHILGREN, JOHN DOUGLAS, b New Ulm, Minn, Sept 14, 43. PHYSIOLOGY. *Educ:* Gonzaga Univ, BS, 65; Wash State Univ, MS, 68, PhD(zoophysiol), 75. *Prof Exp:* Res assoc psychobiol, US Army Human Eng Lab, 68-69; opers & training adminr, Eighth US Army, UN Command, 69-70; asst prof zool, Ore State Univ, 75-78; ASST PROF PHYSIOL, NAT COL NATUROPATHIC MED, 78- *Mem:* AAAS; Am Soc Zoologists; Am Ornithologists Union; Cooper Ornith Soc; Am Physiol Soc. *Res:* Ecological energetics of vertebrates; avian and mammalian annual cycles and periodicities; air pollution effects in terrestrial vertebrates. *Mailing Add:* Basic Sci Div 11231 SE Market Portland OR 97204

CHILINGAR, GEORGE V(AROS), b Tiflis, Ga, July 22, 29; m 53; c 3. PETROLEUM ENGINEERING. *Educ:* Univ Southern Calif, BE, 49, MS, 50, PhD(geol), 56. *Prof Exp:* Proj engr & chief petrol & chem qual control lab, Wright-Patterson AFB, 54-56; from asst prof to assoc prof, 56-70, actg chmn dept, 65-67, PROF PETROL ENG, UNIV SOUTHERN CALIF, 70- *Concurrent Pos:* Pres, Electroosmotics, Inc, 64-67; sr UN consult, 67-; vpres, Inst Resources Consult, Inc, 68-72 & Global Oil Corp, 75- *Mem:* NY Acad Sci; Am Soc Eng Educ; Am Inst Mining, Metall & Petrol Engrs; Am Asn Petrol Geol; Am Geophys Union. *Res:* Petroleum products and analysis; geochemical methods of exploration for petroleum; carbonate rocks; porosity, permeability and compaction of sediments; drilling fluids and clays; electrokinetics. *Mailing Add:* Dept of Eng University Park Los Angeles CA 90007

CHILTON, A(RTHUR) B(OUNDS), b Montgomery, Ala, Sept 22, 18; m 42; c 3. NUCLEAR TECHNOLOGY. *Educ:* US Naval Acad, BS, 39; Rensselaer Polytech Inst, BCE, 42, MCE, 43; Ohio State Univ, MSc, 51, PhD(physics), 53. *Prof Exp:* Mgr atomic energy br, Res Div, Bur Yards & Docks, Dept Navy, 53-57, dir Res & Develop Div, 58-59, commanding officer & dir, Naval Civil Eng Lab, 59-62; assoc prof civil & nuclear eng, 62-65, PROF CIVIL & NUCLEAR ENG, UNIV ILL, URBANA-CHAMPAIGN, 65- *Concurrent Pos:* Indust & govt consult, 62- *Mem:* Am Phys Soc; Health Phys Soc; Am Nuclear Soc; Radiation Res Soc. *Res:* Radiation shielding; interaction of radiation with matter; radiation protection. *Mailing Add:* 214 Nuclear Eng Lab Univ of Ill Urbana IL 61801

CHILTON, BRUCE L, b Buffalo, NY, June 14, 35. MATHEMATICS. *Educ:* Univ Buffalo, BA, 58, MA, 60; Univ Toronto, PhD(math), 62. *Prof Exp:* Asst prof math, State Univ NY Buffalo, 62-68; dean dept, 68-74, ASSOC PROF MATH, STATE UNIV NY COL FREDONIA, 68- *Mem:* Math Asn Am; Am Math Soc. *Res:* Geometry, especially properties of regular and semiregular figures in Euclidean n-spaces. *Mailing Add:* Dept of Math State Univ of NY Fredonia NY 14063

CHILTON, ERNEST G(UNTHER), b Gladbach, Ger, May 3, 19; nat US; m 42; c 3. DESIGN MECHANISMS. *Educ:* Mass Inst Technol, BS, 40; Calif Inst Technol, MS, 41; Stanford Univ, PhD(appl mech), 47. *Prof Exp:* Instr mech eng, Ill Inst Technol, 41-42; asst prof eng & res engr, Guggenheim Airship Inst, Ohio, 42-44; res engr, Firestone Industs Prod Co, Ohio, 45-46; acting instr civil eng, Stanford Univ, 46-47; res engr, Shell Develop Co, 47-54, supvr develop, 54-59; mgr mech, Stanford Res Inst, 59-69; prof eng sci, Ariz State Univ, 69-73; PROF DESIGN DIV, MECH ENG DEPT, STANFORD UNIV, 73- *Mem:* Fel Am Soc Mech Engrs; Am Soc Eng Educ. *Res:* Elasticity; behavior of rubber; instrumentation; pressure pulsations; product liability; air pollution. *Mailing Add:* Design Div-Mech Eng Dept Stanford Univ Stanford CA 94305

CHILTON, JOHN MORGAN, b Tuscaloosa, Ala, Apr 20, 21; m 45; c 3. INORGANIC CHEMISTRY. *Educ:* Univ Ala, AB, 42; Univ Va, MS, 47, PhD(chem), 50. *Prof Exp:* Jr chemist, Gen Anal Lab, Tenn Valley Authority, 42-45; asst prof anal chem, Ala Polytech Inst, 49-51; chemist, Ionic Develop Group, Anal Chem Div, 51-54, CHEMIST, CHEM DEVELOP SECT, CHEM TECH DIV, OAK RIDGE NAT LAB, 54- *Mem:* Am Chem Soc. *Res:* Structure of metal ions in solution; spectrophotometric methods of analysis; chemistry of actinides; radioactive waste disposal. *Mailing Add:* Oak Ridge Nat Lab X-10 Area Oak Ridge TN 37830

CHILTON, MARY-DELL MATCHETT, b Indianapolis, Ind, Feb 2, 39; m 66; c 2. MOLECULAR BIOLOGY, BIOCHEMISTRY. *Educ:* Univ Ill, Urbana, BSc, 60, PhD(chem), 67. *Prof Exp:* Fel microbiol, Univ Wash, 67-69, fel biochem, 69-70, asst biologist, 71-73, res asst prof biol, 73-77, res assoc prof, 77-79; ASSOC PROF BIOL, WASHINGTON UNIV, 79- *Honors & Awards:* Bronze Medal, Am Inst Chemists, 60. *Mem:* Am Soc Microbiol. *Res:* Crown gall tumorigenesis; bacterial plasmids; plant genome organization; satellite DNA; DNA and RNA hybridization; bacterial genetics. *Mailing Add:* Dept of Microbiol Washington Univ St Louis MO 63130

CHILTON, NEAL WARWICK, b New York, NY, June 24, 21; m 47; c 5. ORAL MEDICINE. *Educ:* City Col New York, BSc, 39; NY Univ, DDS, 43; Columbia Univ, MSc, 46; Am Bd Endodont & Am Bd Periodont, dipl. *Prof Exp:* Intern, Lincoln Hosp, New York, 43; from instr to asst clin prof pharmacol & therapeut, NY Univ, 44-50; res assoc dent & asst prof dent pub health pract, Columbia Univ, 49-54; from asst prof to assoc prof periodont, Sch Dent, Temple Univ, 52-63, assoc prof prev med, Sch Med, 59-66, clin prof periodont, Sch Dent, 63-76, prof oral med, Sch Med, 66-76; res prof oral med & assoc dir, Clin Res Ctr, Sch Dent Med, Univ Pa, 76-80; RES CONSULT, 80- *Concurrent Pos:* Lectr, Seton Hall Univ, 47-52 & Temple Univ, 52-53; guest lectr, Evans Dent Inst, Univ Pa, 50-; clin prof, Univ Kansas City, 54-55; res assoc, Fac Med, Columbia Univ, 57-70, sr res assoc biostatist, Sch Pub Health & sr res assoc prev med, Sch Dent & Oral Surg, 70-; asst prof, Grad Sch Med, Univ Pa, 57-70, lectr, Sch Dent Med, 70-; asst chief, Bur Dent Health, State Dept Health, NJ; consult, Coun Dent Therapeut, Am Dent Asn & Surgeon Gen, USPHS; mem comt res manpower, Nat Inst Dept Res & mem dent study sect, Div Res Grants, NIH; ed-in-chief, J Pharmacol & Therapeut Dent; res prof periodont, NY Univ, 79- *Mem:* Am Asn Endodont; fel Am Col Dent; Am Acad Periodont; Am Acad Oral Path; Int Asn Dent Res. *Res:* Diseases of the mouth and gums, etiology, pathology, treatment and prevention; dental public health; design and statistical analysis of agents in clinical trial; clinical therapeutics. *Mailing Add:* 2975 Princeton Pike Lawrenceville NJ 08648

CHILTON, ST JOHN POINDEXTER, b Philadelphia, Pa, Feb 3, 09; m 35. PLANT PATHOLOGY. *Educ:* La State Univ, BS, 35, MS, 36; Univ Minn, PhD(plant path), 38. *Prof Exp:* Instr, Univ Minn, 37-38; agent, USDA, 38-40; from asst prof to assoc prof, La State Univ, Baton Rouge, 40-48, from asst pathologist to pathologist, 42-50, prof bot & plant path & chmn dept, 50-76, plant pathologist & head agr exp sta, 50-76; RETIRED. *Mem:* AAAS; Am Soc Sugar Cane Technologists (past pres); Int Soc Sugar Cane Technologists. *Res:* Genetics of fungi; sugar cane breeding and pathology. *Mailing Add:* Rt 2 PO Box 431 Boyce LA 71409

CHILTON, WILLIAM SCOTT, b Philadelphia, Pa, Aug 29, 33; m 65; c 2. ORGANIC CHEMISTRY. *Educ:* Duke Univ, BS, 55; Univ Ill, Urbana-Champaign, PhD(org chem), 63. *Prof Exp:* Asst prof, 63-68, assoc prof, 68-80, PROF CHEM, UNIV WASH, 80- *Concurrent Pos:* Sci adv, Food & Drug Admin, 67- *Mem:* AAAS; Am Chem Soc; Ger Chem Soc; Royal Soc Chem. *Res:* Structure of natural products; new naturally occurring amino acids; synthesis of higher carbon sugars; applications of circular dichroism. *Mailing Add:* Dept of Chem Univ of Wash Seattle WA 98105

CHIMENTI, DALE EVERETT, b Chicago, Ill, July 26, 46; m 70; c 1. PHYSICS. *Educ:* Cornell Col, Iowa, BA, 68; Cornell Univ, MS, 72, PhD(physics), 74. *Prof Exp:* Res assoc, Argonne Nat Lab, 74-76; vis asst prof physics, Univ Tuebbingen, WGer, 76-78; RES PHYSICIST, AIR FORCE MAT LAB, 78- *Concurrent Pos:* Fel, Alexander von Humboldt Found, 76-78. *Mem:* Am Phys Soc. *Res:* Transport properties of metals (helicon waves, electromagnetic generation of ultrasound) on superconductivity (current-induced flux flow); acoustics (critical angle phenomena). *Mailing Add:* Air Force Wright Aeronaut Labs Wright Patterson AFB Dayton OH 45433

CHIMENTI, FRANK A, b Erie, Pa, May 3, 39; m 64; c 2. MATHEMATICAL ANALYSIS. *Educ:* Gannon Col, BA, 61; John Carroll Univ, MS, 63; Pa State Univ, PhD(math), 70. *Prof Exp:* Res asst appl math, Lord Mfg Co, Pa, 63-65 & Ord Res Lab, Pa State Univ, 65-67; asst prof, 69-74, ASSOC PROF MATH, STATE UNIV NY COL FREDONIA, 74- *Mem:* Math Asn Am; Am Math Soc; Soc Indust & Appl Math. *Res:* General topology; convergence of sequences of sets; multivalued functions; convergence formulas; mathematical modeling and simulation. *Mailing Add:* Dept Math & Comput Sci State Univ of NY Fredonia NY 14063

CHIMOSKEY, JOHN EDWARD, b Traverse City, Mich, Apr 15, 37; div; c 2. PHYSIOLOGY. *Educ:* Univ Mich, MD, 63. *Prof Exp:* Intern internal med, Univ Calif, 64; USPHS fel, Harvard Med Sch, 64-66 & Retina Found, Boston, 66-67; assoc prof physiol, Hahnemann Med Col, 69-70; actg instr dermat, Med Ctr, Stanford Univ, 70-71; asst prof bioeng, Univ Wash, 71-75; assoc prof physiol & surg & dir, Taub Labs Mech Circulatory Support, Baylor Col Med, 75-78; PROF PHYSIOL, MICH STATE UNIV, 78- *Concurrent Pos:* Guest scientist, US Naval Air Develop Ctr, 69-70; NIH spec fel, Hahnemann Med Col, 70; guest lectr, Hahnemann Med Col & Calif Col Podiatric Med, 70-71; NIH spec fel & Dermat Found fel, Stanford Univ, 70-71; NIH grant, 73-75; adj assoc prof bioeng, Rice Univ, 75-78. *Mem:* AAAS; Am Physiol Soc. *Res:* Cardiovascular physiology. *Mailing Add:* Dept of Physiol Mich State Univ East Lansing MI 48824

CHIN, BYONG HAN, b Shanghai, China, Nov 27, 34; US citizen; m 61; c 3. BIOCHEMISTRY. *Educ:* Yonsei Univ, Korea, BS, 57; Univ Hawaii, MS, 64, PhD(hort), 67. *Prof Exp:* Marine biochemist, Hawaii Marine Lab, Univ Hawaii, 63-64; fel, Mellon Inst, Carnegie-Mellon Univ, 67-79; biochem toxicologist, Diamond Shamrock Corp, 79-81; BIOCHEM TOXICOLOGIST, MITRE CORP, 81- *Mem:* Am Chem Soc; Soc Toxicol; Am Asn Clin Chem. *Res:* The metabolism of pesticides by plants and animals; bioassay of poisonous fishes; methodology development in clinical biochemistry. *Mailing Add:* Mitre Corp W810 1820 Dolley Madison McLean VA 22102

CHIN, CHARLES L(EE) D(ONG), b New York, NY, Feb 4, 23; m 46; c 1. ENGINEERING MECHANICS, MATERIAL SCIENCE ENGINEERING. *Educ:* Tri-State Col, BS, 41; Polytech Inst Brooklyn, MAE, 48; Harvard Univ, SM, 49, ScD(eng), 65. *Prof Exp:* Engr, Curtiss-Wright Corp, 41-43; sr engr, Chance Vought Aircraft, 43-44; sr res asst aerodyn, Polytech Inst Brooklyn, 46-48; asst prof aeronaut eng, Univ RI, 50-52; head anal res, Jackson & Church Co, 52-55; asst prof aeronaut eng, Boston Univ, 55-58, prof & chmn dept, 58-68; dir eng & res mach div, Borg-Warner Corp, 68-70, res fel chem & plastics group, 70-71; SR ENG SPECIALIST, MONSANTO CO, 72- *Concurrent Pos:* Staff engr & consult, Res & Advan Design Div, Avco Corp, 62-63; res specialist, NAm Aviation, Inc, Calif, 66; adj fac mech eng, Univ Hartford, 73- *Mem:* Am Inst Aeronaut & Astronaut; Am Soc Eng Educ; Soc Plastics Engrs. *Res:* Structural analysis; aerodynamics of sweat cooling; aerodynamic ablation of reentry vehicles; stress concentration around holes; aerodynamics of supersonic wings; atmospheric gust velocity determination; rheology of plastics; mechanics of polymer processing; plastics processing equipment and apparatus. *Mailing Add:* Monsanto Co 101 Granby St Bloomfield CT 06002

CHIN, DAVID, b Boston, Mass. CHEMISTRY. *Educ:* Boston Univ, BA, 64; Purdue Univ, PhD(chem), 71. *Prof Exp:* Teaching asst chem, Purdue Univ, 64-68; Sr Chemist, 70-80, GROUP LEADER, CONSTRUCTION PROD DIV, W R GRACE & CO, 81- *Mem:* Am Chem Soc; Am Ceramics Soc; Am Soc Testing & Mats. *Res:* Develop chemical admixtures for concrete; hardened concrete analysis; technical service work involving admixtures, cement, hardened concrete, concrete trial mixes. *Mailing Add:* W R Grace & Co 62 Whittemore Ave Cambridge MA 02140

CHIN, DER-TAU, b Chekiang, China, Sept 14, 39. ELECTROCHEMISTRY, CHEMICAL ENGINEERING. *Educ:* Chung Yuan Col Sci & Eng, BS, 62; Tufts Univ, MS, 65; Univ Pa, PhD(chem eng), 69. *Prof Exp:* Process engr, Taiwan Sugar Corp, 62-63; sci programmer, US Air Force Cambridge Res Labs, 65; sr res engr, Res Labs, Gen Motors Corp, 69-75; assoc prof, 75-80, PROF CHEM ENG, CLARKSON COL TECHNOL, 80- *Concurrent Pos:* Vis scientist, Brookhaven Nat Lab, 77 & 80; consult, Hooker Chemicals & Plastics Corp, 80-; vis prof, Eidgenoessische Tech Hochschule, Zurich, Switz, 81 & Univ Calif, Berkeley, 81; consult, Los Alamos Nat Lab, 81-; vis prof, Nat Univ Singapore, 82. *Mem:* Electrochem Soc; Am Inst Chem Eng; Am Electroplaters Soc; Inst Colloid Surface Sci. *Res:* Electrolytic mass transfer; electrochemical study of flow turbulence; electrochemical machining; high current density electrode process; electrochemical waste treatment; potential and current distribution; engineering analysis of electrochemical systems; corrosion; fuel cells; batteries; electroplating. *Mailing Add:* Dept of Chem Eng Clarkson Col Technol Potsdam NY 13676

CHIN, EDWARD, b Boston, Mass, Sept 4, 26; m 52; c 4. BIOLOGY. *Educ:* Harvard Univ, BS, 48; Univ NH, MS, 53; Univ Wash, PhD, 61. *Prof Exp:* Biol aide clam invest, US Fish & Wildlife Serv, 49-51; fishery res biologist king crab studies, 54-55 & gulf shrimp studies, 55-61; asst sci dir, US Prog Biol Int Indian Ocean Exped, 62-65; assoc prof biol, Tex A&M Univ, 65-68; dir biol oceanog prog, NSF, 68-70; assoc dir, Inst Natural Resources, 70-76, DIR, MARINE SCI, UNIV GA, 77- *Mem:* Am Fisheries Soc; Am Inst Fishery Res Biol; Brit Marine Biol Asn. *Res:* Marine invertebrates; marine ecology. *Mailing Add:* Marine Sci Ecol Bldg Univ of Ga Athens GA 30602

CHIN, GILBERT YUKYU, b Toishan, China, Sept 21, 34; US citizen; m 60; c 4. PHYSICAL METALLURGY, MATERIALS SCIENCE. *Educ:* Mass Inst Technol, BS, 59, ScD(ductile fracture), 63. *Prof Exp:* Mem tech staff, 62-73, head, phys metall & crystal growth res dept, 73-75, HEAD, PHYS METALL & CERAMICS RES & DEVELOP DEPT, BELL TEL LABS, 75- *Concurrent Pos:* Mem prog comt, Conf Magnetism & Magnetic Mat, 66, 72 & 75; mem adv comt, Conf Magnetism & Magnetic Mat, 69-74. *Honors & Awards:* New Eng Regional Conf Award, 65 & Mathewson Gold Medal, 74, Am Inst Mining, Metall & Petrol Engrs. *Mem:* AAAS; NY Acad Sci; fel Am Inst Mining, Metall & Petrol Engrs; Am Soc Metals; Am Ceramic Soc. *Res:* Relationship between metallurgical structure and magnetic and mechanical properties, particularly the effect of plastic deformation on such properties; development of crystallographic texture during plastic deformation; magnetic alloys. *Mailing Add:* Bell Tel Labs Murray Hill NJ 07974

CHIN, (JIN) H(AM), b Kwangtung, China, Oct 15, 28; nat US; m 60; c 2. COMPUTATIONAL ENGINEERING ANALYSIS. *Educ:* Stanford Univ, BS, 50; Univ Mich, MSE, 51, PhD(chem eng), 55. *Prof Exp:* Asst, Univ Mich, 54, res assoc, 55-57; heat transfer specialist, Flight Propulsion Div, Gen Elec Co, 57-60; staff engr, 60-80, SR STAFF ENGR, LOCKHEED MISSILES & SPACE CO, 80- *Concurrent Pos:* Consult, Armed Forces Spec Weapons Proj, 57 & Dept Aeronaut Eng, Princeton Univ, 59. *Mem:* AAAS; fel Am Inst Chemists; Am Inst Aeronaut & Astronaut. *Res:* Light scattering; particle size determination; applied mathematics; radiative transport; aircraft component cooling; boundary layer theory; computer analyses; chemical kinetics; thermodynamics; cryogenics; propellant behaviors; missiles and space vehicle thermal environments; superorbital entry thermal environments; reentry physics; finite element methods; solid rocket propulsion nozzles. *Mailing Add:* Lockheed Missiles & Space Co 3251 Hanover Palo Alto CA 94304

CHIN, HSIAO-LING M, b Shanghai, China, Aug 2, 47; m 74; c 1. ORGANIC CHEMISTRY. *Educ:* Nat Taiwan Univ, BS, 68; Univ Southern Calif, PhD(chem), 74. *Prof Exp:* res chemist, 73-81, SR RES CHEMIST ORG SYNTHESIS, STAUFFER CHEM CO, 81- *Mem:* Am Chem Soc. *Res:* Synthesis of novel organic compounds as agricultural chemicals. *Mailing Add:* Stauffer Chem Co 1200 S 47th St Richmond CA 94804

CHIN, JANE ELIZABETH HENG, b Augusta, Ga, Nov 20, 33; m 60; c 2. PHARMACOLOGY. *Educ:* Univ Ga, BS, 54; Univ Mich, MS, 56, PhD(pharmacol), 60. *Prof Exp:* USPHS fel neuropharmacol, Univ Ill, 59-60; USPHS fel neuropharmacol, Sch Med, 60-68, USPHS fel biosci, Univ, 68-71, res assoc, 71-75, SR RES ASSOC PHARMACOL, SCH MED, STANFORD UNIV, 75- *Mem:* Res Soc Alcoholism; Am Soc Pharmacol & Exp Therapeut. *Res:* Neuropharmacology; pain and analgesics; psychopharmacology; neuropsychology; biophysics; high pressure physiology; drug effects on membranes; drug tolerance. *Mailing Add:* Dept of Pharmacol Stanford Univ Sch of Med Stanford CA 94305

CHIN, SEE LEANG, b Padang Rengas, Malaya, May 24, 42; Can citizen; m 71. LASERS. *Educ:* Nat Taiwan Univ, BSc, 64; Univ Waterloo, MSc, 66, PhD(physics), 69. *Prof Exp:* Teacher math, Hua Lian High Sch, Taiping, Malaya, 60; fel physics, 69-70, res assoc, 71-72, asst prof, 72-77, ASSOC PROF PHYSICS, LAVAL UNIV, 78-, DIR, OPTICS & LASER RES LAB, 81- *Concurrent Pos:* Sci consult, K A Mace Ltd, Kitchener, Ont, 73-79; vis scientist, Nuclear Study Ctr, Saclay, France, 75; vis scientist, Ctr Interdisciplinary Studies, Univ Bielefeld, WGer. *Mem:* Can Asn Physicists; Optical Soc Am. *Res:* Pulse compression in a dye medium; multiphoton interaction of high power lasers with atoms and molecules. *Mailing Add:* Dept Physics Laval Univ Quebec PQ G1K 7P4 Can

CHIN, TOM DOON YUEN, b Kwangtung, China, May 29, 22; US citizen; m 50; c 1. EPIDEMIOLOGY. *Educ:* Univ Mich, MD, 46; Tulane Univ, MPH, 50; Am Bd Prev Med & Am Bd Med Microbiol, dipl. *Prof Exp:* Intern, Binghamton City Hosp, 47; intern, Western Pa Hosp, 47-48; resident, Sea View Hosp, 48-49; dir health unit, State Dept Health, La, 50-51; asst chief epidemiol, Kansas City Field Sta, USPHS, 54-64, chief, 64-66, dir ecol invests prog, Ctr Dis Control, Kansas City, 67-73; PROF MED & COMMUNITY HEALTH, UNIV KANS MED CTR, KANSAS CITY, 73-, CHMN DEPT COMMUNITY HEALTH, 74- *Concurrent Pos:* Assoc ed, Am J Epidemiol, 66-; control study sect, Nat Inst Health, 74-78; vis prof, Univ Minn Sch Pub Health, 80 & 81; mem, Biometry & Epidemiol Contract Rev Comt, 80-83. *Mem:* Fel Am Col Prev Med; fel Am Pub Health Asn; Am Epidemiol Soc; Soc Epidemiol Res; NY Acad Sci. *Res:* Infectious diseases. *Mailing Add:* Dept Community Health Univ of Kans Med Ctr Kansas City KS 66103

CHIN, WEI TSUNG, b Loo-Yee, China, July 5, 28; m 63; c 4. AGRICULTURAL CHEMISTRY. *Educ:* Nat Taiwan Univ, BS, 52, MS, 57; Va Polytech Inst, PhD(agron), 62, MS, 63. *Prof Exp:* Res chemist pesticides, Niagara Chem Div, FMC Corp, 62-66; sr res chemist, Uniroyal Chem Corp, 66-72; sr res chemist, 73-80, SR RES ASSOC, DIAMOND SHAMROCK CORP, 80- *Mem:* Am Chem Soc. *Res:* Chemistry of soils, fertilizers and pesticides. *Mailing Add:* Diamond Shamrock Corp T R Evans Res Ctr Painesville OH 44077

CHIN, WILLIAM W, b New York, NY, Nov 20, 47. ENDOCRINOLOGY. *Educ:* Columbia Univ, AB, 68; Harvard Univ, MD, 72. *Prof Exp:* ASST PROF MED, HARVARD MED SCH, 73-; ASSOC INVESTR, HOWARD HUGHES MED INST, 73- *Concurrent Pos:* Mem staff, Lab Molecular Endocrinol, Mass Gen Hosp. *Mem:* Endocrine Soc; Am Thyroid Asn; Am Fedn Clin Res; AAAS. *Res:* Regulation of expression of anterior pituitary gland and central-nervous-system polypeptide hormones. *Mailing Add:* Lab Molecular Endocrinol Bulfinch 3 Mass Gen Hosp Boston MA 02114

CHIN, YU-REN, b Shanghai, China, Mar 6, 38; m 66; c 1. CHEMICAL ENGINEERING, CHEMISTRY. *Educ:* Nat Taiwan Univ, BS, 60; Purdue Univ, MS, 65, PhD(chem eng), 69. *Prof Exp:* Sr chem engr, Chem Div, Uniroyal, Inc, 68-73; sr chem engr, SRI Int, 73-79; PROCESS ECONOMICS CONSULT, 80- *Concurrent Pos:* Lectr process design & eval, Taiwan & Beijin, China. *Mem:* Am Chem Soc; Am Inst Chem Engrs; Sigma Xi. *Res:* Process design and development in chemical industries; chemical kinetics; operations research; technoeconomic evaluation of chemical processes for petrochemicals, inorganochemicals and polymers. *Mailing Add:* 4185 Georgia Ave Palo Alto CA 94306

CHINARD, FRANCIS PIERRE, b Berkeley, Calif, June 30, 18; m 43; c 3. PHYSIOLOGICAL CHEMISTRY, INTERNAL MEDICINE. *Educ:* Univ Calif, AB, 37; Johns Hopkins Univ, MD, 41. *Prof Exp:* Intern, Presby Hosp, New York, 41-42; Nat Res Coun fel, Rockefeller Inst, 45-46, asst Rockefeller Inst Hosp, 46-49; instr med & physiol chem, Sch Med, Johns Hopkins Univ, 49-51, asst prof physiol chem, 51-56, asst prof med, 52-56, assoc prof physiol chem & med, 59-63; prof exp med, Fac Med, McGill Univ, 63-64; prof med, Sch Med, NY Univ, 64-68; prof med & chmn dept, 68-74, prof exp med, 75-77, PROF RES MED NJ MED SCH, COL MED & DENT NJ, 77-, PROF PHYSIOL, 78- *Concurrent Pos:* Markle scholar, 49-54; asst chief med, Baltimore City Hosps, Md, 53-60, physiciant in chief, 60-63; chief med, Goldwater Mem Hosp, 66-68; adj prof, NY Univ, 68-70; career scientist, Health Res Coun, New York; prin investr grant on pulmonary transport & metabolism in vivo NIH, 70; chmn ad hoc rev comt, Spec Ctr Res prog on adult respiratory distress syndrome, NIH, 78 & pulmonary vascular disease, 80-81. *Honors & Awards:* Landis Award, Microcirculatory Soc, 78. *Mem:* Am Chem Soc; Am Soc Biol Chem; Am Soc Clin Invest; Soc Exp Biol & Med; fel Am Col Physicians. *Res:* Membrane permeability; renal and pulmonary physiology and metabolism. *Mailing Add:* Col of Med & Dent of NJ NJ Med Sch 100 Bergen St Newark NJ 07103

CHIN-BING, STANLEY ARTHUR, b New Orleans, La, Nov 3, 42. ACOUSTICS, ELECTRO-OPTICS. *Educ:* Tulane Univ, BS, 64; Univ New Orleans, MS, 68, PhD(physics), 73. *Prof Exp:* Systs analyst mech eng, Martin Marietta Corp, 74-76; sr engr electro-optics, Space Div, Chrysler Corp, 76-77; RES PHYSICIST ACOUST, NAVAL OCEAN RES & DEVELOP ACTIV, 78- *Concurrent Pos:* Asst prof physics & eng, Univ New Orleans, 75-80. *Mem:* Am Phys Soc; Optical Soc Am; Am Asn Physics Teachers; Am Inst Physics; NY Acad Sci. *Res:* Theoretical underwater acoustics; electro-optical systems; electric and magnetic fields; radiative lifetimes of excited electronic atomic levels. *Mailing Add:* Naval Ocean Res & Develop Activ Code 321 NSTL Station MS 39529

CHINCARINI, GUIDO LUDOVICO, b Venice, Italy, Jan 24, 38; c 2. ASTROPHYSICS. *Educ:* Liceo Scientifico G B Genedetti, Maturity in sci, 56; Univ Padua, Italy, PhD(physics), 61. *Prof Exp:* Astronr, Asiago Observ, Univ Padua, 61-68; res assoc, Wesleyan Univ, 69-71; res scientist & engr,

McDonald Observ, Univ Tex, 71-74; vis assoc prof, 75 & 76-77, assoc prof, 77-79, PROF PHYSICS & ASTRON, UNIV OKLA, 79- *Concurrent Pos:* Res assoc Lick Observ, Univ Calif, 64-66; astronr, Hoherlist Observ, Univ Bonn, 68; res assoc, Johnson Space Ctr, NASA, Houston; chair prof astron, Univ Bologna, Italy, 76-78. *Mem:* Int Astron Union; Am Astron Soc; Sigma Xi. *Res:* Extragalactic astronomy; observational cosmology. *Mailing Add:* Dept of Physics & Astron Univ of Okla Norman OK 73069

CHING, HILDA, b Honolulu, Hawaii, June 30, 34; m 60; c 3. PARASITOLOGY. *Educ:* Ore State Univ, BA, 56, MS, 57; Univ Nebr, PhD(zool), 59. *Prof Exp:* Asst parasitol, Agr Exp Sta, Univ Hawaii, 59-60; lectr invert zool, 74-77, lectr biol, Douglas Col, 76-79, RES ASSOC, DEPT ZOOL, UNIV BC, 60- *Mem:* Am Soc Parasitol. *Res:* Trematodes of fishes and birds. *Mailing Add:* 3912 Lewister Univ of BC North Vancouver BC V7R 4C2 Can

CHING, JASON KWOCK SUNG, b Honolulu, Hawaii, Dec 18, 40; m 64; c 3. ENVIRONMENTAL SCIENCE. *Educ:* Univ Hawaii, BS, 62; Pa State Univ, MS, 64; Univ Wash, PhD(meteorol), 74. *Prof Exp:* Res asst meteorol, Pa State Univ, 62-64; Woods Hole Oceanog Inst, 64-66 & Univ Wash, 66-70; res meteorologist, Barbados Oceanog & Meteorol Anal Proj, 70-75, METEOROLOGIST, METEOROL DIV, AIR RES LAB, NAT OCEANIC & ATMOSPHERIC ADMIN, ENVIRON SCI RES LAB, ENVIRON PROTECTION AGENCY, 75- *Mem:* Am Meteorol Soc; Sigma Xi. *Res:* Numerical-theoretical modelling and field studies leading to documentation of the dynamics, thermodynamics and transport characteristics in the planetary boundary layer of the atmosphere. *Mailing Add:* Meteorol Div Environ Sci Res Lab Environ Protection Agency Research Triangle Park NC 27711

CHING, MELVIN CHUNG HING, b Honolulu, Hawaii, Feb 11, 35; m 65; c 2. ANATOMY. *Educ:* Univ Nebr, AB, 57, MSc, 60; Univ Calif, Berkeley, PhD(anat), 71. *Prof Exp:* Instr anat, Sch Med & Dent, Univ Rochester, 71-73, asst prof, 73-77; ASSOC PROF ANAT, MED COL VA, 78- *Mem:* Am Asn Anat; Sigma Xi; Endocrinol Soc; Neurosci Soc; AAAS. *Res:* Neuroendocrinology; endocrinology; neuroendocrine control mechanisms; hypothalamic-pituitary-thyroid gonadal axis. *Mailing Add:* Dept Anat PO Box 709 Med Col Va Richmond VA 23298

CHING, STEPHEN WING-FOOK, b Canton, China, May 6, 36; m 64. COMPUTER ENGINEERING, COMPUTER SCIENCE. *Educ:* Nat Univ Taiwan, BSEE, 58; Univ Pa, MSEE, 61, PhD(elec eng), 66. *Prof Exp:* Electronic engr, Burroughs Corp, Pa, 60-64; sr electronic engr, 65-67; res asst appl math, Johnson Res Found, Univ Pa, 64-65; asst prof elec eng, 67-69, ASSOC PROF ELEC ENG, VILLANOVA UNIV, 69- *Mem:* Inst Elec & Electronics Engrs; Am Math Soc; Math Asn Am; Soc Indust & Appl Math; Sigma Xi. *Res:* Scientific computation; electronic engineering. *Mailing Add:* Dept of Elec Eng Villanova Univ Villanova PA 19085

CHING, TA YEN, b Peking, China, Mar 23, 47; m 75. ORGANIC CHEMISTRY. *Educ:* Fu-Jen Univ, BS, 69; Baylor Univ, MS, 72; Univ Calif, Los Angeles, PhD(chem), 76. *Prof Exp:* Res assoc chem, Yale Univ, 76-77; STAFF CHEMIST, CORP RES & DEVELOP, GEN ELEC CO, 77- *Mem:* Am Chem Soc; AAAS. *Res:* Organic photochemistry; chemistry of singlet oxygen; photostabilization of engineering plastics; chemistry of silicone and silica. *Mailing Add:* Corp Res & Develop Gen Elec Co Schenectady NY 12301

CHING, TE MAY, b Soochow, China, Jan 9, 23; US citizen; m 46; c 2. PLANT PHYSIOLOGY. *Educ:* Nat Cent Univ, China, BS, 44; Mich State Col, MS, 50; Mich State Univ, PhD(cytol), 54. *Prof Exp:* Asst wood chem, Nat Cent Univ, China, 44-48; asst plant anat, hist & cytol, Mich State Univ, 50-52, asst plant physiol & cytol, 52-54, instr, 54-56; from asst prof to assoc prof seed physiol, 56-71, PROF SEED PHYSIOL, ORE STATE UNIV, 71- *Mem:* AAAS; Am Soc Plant Physiol; Genetics Soc Am; Am Soc Agron; Am Oil Chem Soc. *Res:* Seed physiology; cytology; lipid metabolism; structure and function of cellular organelles; developmental biology. *Mailing Add:* Dept of Crop Sci Ore State Univ Corvallis OR 97331

CHINITZ, WALLACE, b Brooklyn, NY, Mar 13, 35; m 60; c 2. MECHANICAL ENGINEERING. *Educ:* City Col New York, BME, 57; Polytech Inst Brooklyn, MME, 59, PhD(mech eng), 62. *Prof Exp:* Res engr, Fairchild Engine & Airplane Corp, 57-59; sr sci res engr, Plasma Propulsion Proj, Repub Aviation Corp, 59-60; res asst prof mech eng, Polytech Inst Brooklyn, 60-63; proj engr gas dynamic & combustion res, Gen Appl Sci Labs, Inc, 63-67; PROF MECH ENG, SCH ENG & SCI, COOPER UNION, 67- *Mem:* Am Soc Mech Engrs; assoc fel Am Inst Aeronaut & Astronaut; Combustion Inst. *Res:* High-temperature gas dynamics and combustion; thermodynamics; transport processes; air pollution control; energy. *Mailing Add:* Sch Eng & Sci Cooper Union Cooper Sq New York NY 10019

CHINN, AUSTIN BROCKENBROUGH, b Warsaw, Va, May 8, 08; m 38; c 3. MEDICINE. *Educ:* Univ Va, MD, 32. *Prof Exp:* Instr med, George Washington Univ, 36-38, assoc, 38-41; asst clin prof, Sch Med, Western Reserve Univ, 46-53, assoc prof, 53-62, assoc dean, 60-62; CHIEF GERONT BR, DIV CHRONIC DIS, USPHS, 62- *Concurrent Pos:* Prof & dir rehab res & training ctr, Univ Southern Calif, 67-69. *Mem:* AMA; Am Col Physicians; Am Fedn Clin Res. *Res:* Gastrointestinal disease. *Mailing Add:* 422 E Beverley St Staunton VA 24401

CHINN, CLARENCE EDWARD, b Cheney, Wash, Dec 1, 25; m 53; c 3. CHEMISTRY. *Educ:* Walla Walla Col, BA, 51; Ore State Col, MS, 53, PhD(soils), 56; Univ Tenn, PhD(inorg chem), 69. *Prof Exp:* From asst prof to assoc prof chem & math, Southern Missionary Col, 56-67; assoc prof, 67-74, PROF CHEM, WALLA WALLA COL, 74- *Mem:* Am Chem Soc. *Res:* Soil moisture measurement; effect of herbicides on plant enzymes; solvent extraction of metal chelates. *Mailing Add:* 649 SW 3rd College Place WA 99324

CHINN, HERMAN ISAAC, b Connellsville, Pa, Apr 8, 13; m 45; c 4. BIOCHEMISTRY. *Educ:* Pa State Col, BS, 34; Northwestern Univ, MS, 35, PhD(biochem), 38. *Prof Exp:* Instr biochem, Med Sch, Northwestern Univ, 38-42; prin chemist, Fla State Bd Health, 46-47; chief dept biochem, Sch Aviation Med, 47-55; sci liaison officer, Off Naval Res, London, 55-57; biochemist, Air Force Off Sci Res, 57-60; dep sci attache, Am Embassy, Ger, 60-63; sci officer, Off Int Sci Affairs, US Dept State, DC, 63-65; sci attache, Am Embassy, Tehran, Iran, 65-67; sci officer, US Dept State, 67-70; sci attache, Am Embassy, Stockholm, Sweden, 70-73; sci attache, Am Embassy, Tel Aviv, Israel, 73-75; CONSULT, US DEPT STATE, WASHINGTON, DC, 75-; SR STAFF SCIENTIST, FED AM SOC EXP BIOL, BETHESDA, MD, 76- *Mem:* AAAS; Soc Exp Biol & Med; Am Physiol Soc; Am Soc Pharmacol & Exp Therapeut; Am Chem Soc. *Res:* Biochemistry of the eye; aviation physiology; motion sickness. *Mailing Add:* 9907 Wildwood Rd Kensington MD 20795

CHINN, JAMES, civil engineering, deceased

CHINN, LELAND JEW, b Sacramento, Calif, Oct 19, 24; m 59; c 1. MEDICINAL CHEMISTRY. *Educ:* Univ Calif, BS, 48; Univ Wis, PhD(chem), 51. *Prof Exp:* Asst to prof, Univ Wis, 48-51; res chemist, 52-70, group leader, 70-72, RES FEL, G D SEARLE & CO, 72- *Concurrent Pos:* Vis scientist, Univ Southern Calif, 68. *Mem:* AAAS; Am Chem Soc. *Res:* Natural products; stereochemistry of polycyclic compounds; medicinal chemistry. *Mailing Add:* 6141 Elm St Morton Grove IL 60053

CHINN, PHYLLIS ZWEIG, b Rochester, NY, Sept 26, 41; m 68. MATHEMATICS. *Educ:* Brandeis Univ, BA, 62; Harvard Univ, MAT, 63; Univ Calif, San Diego, MA, 66; Univ Calif, Santa Barbara, PhD(math), 69. *Prof Exp:* Teacher jr high sch, Mass, 63-64; instr math, Mass State Col Salem, 64; asst prof math, Towson State Col, 69-75; asst prof, 75-79, ASSOC PROF MATH, HUMBOLDT STATE UNIV, 79- *Concurrent Pos:* Coordr, Annual Conf Nat Womens Studies Asn, 82. *Mem:* Math Asn Am; Nat Coun Teachers Math; Asn Women Sci; Asn Women Math. *Res:* Graph reconstruction problems; frequency partition of graphs; means of improving the teaching of mathematics to prospective teachers; graph coloring problems; coding; discovery learning of mathematics; graphical operations and properties; band width in graphs; women in science and math; graph theory models for wildlife management. *Mailing Add:* Dept of Math Humboldt State Univ Arcata CA 95521

CHINN, STANLEY H F, b Vancouver, BC, Apr 9, 14; m 44; c 2. SOIL MICROBIOLOGY. *Educ:* Iowa State Col, BS, 40, MSc, 42, PhD, 46. *Prof Exp:* Lectr, Univ Sask, 49-51; BACTERIOLOGIST, RES BR, CAN DEPT AGR, 51- *Concurrent Pos:* Adj prof, Univ Sask. *Mem:* Can Soc Phytopath; Can Soc Microbiol. *Res:* Soil microbiology as related to common rootrot of wheat. *Mailing Add:* Res Br Can Dept of Agr Univ Campus Saskatoon SK S7N 0W0 Can

CHINNERY, MICHAEL ALISTAIR, b London, Eng, Sept 27, 33; m 64. GEOPHYSICS, SEISMOLOGY. *Educ:* Cambridge Univ, BA, 57, MA, 61, DSc, 77; Univ Toronto, MA, 59, PhD(geophys), 62. *Prof Exp:* Geophysicist, Seismol Serv, Ltd, Eng, 57-58 & Hunting Surv Corp, 59; lectr geophys, Univ Toronto, 61-62; instr, Univ BC, 62-63, asst prof, 63-65; res assoc geol & geophys, Mass Inst Technol, 65-66; from assoc prof to prof, Dept Geol Sci, Brown Univ, 66-73; GROUP LEADER, LINCOLN LAB, MASS INST TECHNOL, 73- *Concurrent Pos:* Assoc ed, J Geophys Res, Am Geophys Union, 70-72; chmn adv subcomt geophys & geol, NASA, 78-81; chmn study on geophys data & pub policy, Nat Acad Sci, 80-; chmn coord comt, Data Exchange & Data Ctr, Int Comn Lithosphere, 81-; solid earth rep, Panel World Data ctr, Int Coun Sci Unions, 81- *Mem:* Am Geophys Union; Seismol Soc Am; fel Royal Astron Soc. *Res:* Displacements and stresses in faulting; strength of earth's crust; earthquake mechanism; geotectonics; elasticity theory; earthquake risk; seismic discrimination. *Mailing Add:* Lincoln Lab 42 Carleton St Mass Inst Technol Cambridge MA 02142

CHINNICI, JOSEPH (FRANK) PETER, b Philadelphia, Pa, Oct 12, 43; m 65; c 3. GENETICS, EVOLUTIONARY BIOLOGY. *Educ:* La Salle Col, AB, 65; Univ Va, PhD(biol), 70. *Prof Exp:* asst prof, 70-79, ASSOC PROF BIOL, VA COMMONWEALTH UNIV, 79-; ASSOC PROF HUMAN GENETICS, MED COL VA, 81- *Honors & Awards:* Andrew Fleming Award, Univ Va, 70. *Mem:* Genetics Soc Am; AAAS; Soc Study Evolution; Sigma Xi. *Res:* Genetic control of crossing-over in Drosophila melanogaster; genetic control of aflatoxin and caffeine toxicity resistance in Drosophila melanogaster; effects on crossing-over; genetic aspects of human birth weight. *Mailing Add:* Dept Biol Va Commonwealth Univ Richmond VA 23284

CHINOWSKY, WILLIAM, b New York, NY, Feb 24, 29; m 50; c 2. PHYSICS. *Educ:* Columbia Univ, AB, 49, AM, 51, PhD(physics), 55. *Prof Exp:* Res assoc physics, Brookhaven Nat Lab, 54-56, assoc physicist, 56-61; assoc prof, 61-67, PROF PHYSICS, UNIV CALIF, BERKELEY, 67- *Mem:* Am Phys Soc. *Res:* High energy physics. *Mailing Add:* Dept of Physics Univ of Calif Berkeley CA 94720

CHIO, (EDDIE) HANG, b Macao, Portugal, Mar 25, 48; m 73; c 2. ENTOMOLOGY, TOXICOLOGY. *Educ:* Nat Taiwan Univ, BS, 70; Univ Ill, MS, 76, PhD(entom), 77. *Prof Exp:* SR ENTOMOLOGIST, ELI LILLY & CO, 77-, CHMN, ENTOM RES COMT, 79- *Mem:* Entom Soc Am; AAAS. *Res:* Insect pest management and insect growth regulator development. *Mailing Add:* Lilly Res Labs PO Box 708 Greenfield IN 46140

CHIOGIOJI, MELVIN HIROAKI, b Hiroshima, Japan, Aug 21, 39; US citizen; m 60; c 2. ENGINEERING, OPERATIONS RESEARCH. *Educ:* Purdue Univ, BSEE, 61; Univ Hawaii, MBA, 68; George Washington Univ, DBA, 72. *Prof Exp:* Head weapons component div eng, Qual Eval & Eng Lab, US Navy, 65-69; dir weapons eval & eng div test & eval, Naval Ord Systs Command, Washington, DC, 69-73; dir, Off Indust Anal Energy Conserv, Fed Energy Admin, 73-75, dir, Div Commercialization, 75-80, DEP ASST

SECY, US DEPT OF ENERGY, 80- *Concurrent Pos:* Prof, George Washington Univ, 72-; mem, Md State Adv Comt Civil Rights, 75- & Nat Naval Reserve Policy Bd, 77-; consult ed, Marcel Dekker, Inc Publs, 78- *Mem:* Inst Elec & Electronics Engrs; Nat Soc Prof Engrs; Acad Mgt; Soc Am Mil Engrs; Asn Sci Technol & Innovation (pres). *Res:* Research and development management theory; energy supply and conservation; industrial energy conservation; buildings energy conservation; management of innovation and technology. *Mailing Add:* 15113 Middlegate Rd Silver Spring MD 20904

CHIOLA, VINCENT, b Bayonne, NJ, May 7, 22; m 52; c 2. INORGANIC CHEMISTRY, LUMINESCENT MATERIALS & CHEMICALS. *Educ:* Wagner Col, BS, 47; Univ Tex, MA, 50. *Prof Exp:* Chemist, Gen Aniline & Film Corp, 50-51; asst, Plastics Lab, Princeton Univ, 51; eng chemist, Chem & Metall Div, 51-60, from develop engr to adv develop engr, 60-68, sect head, Chem Develop Lab, 68-69, SECT HEAD, CHEM & METALL DIV, PHOSPHOR DEVELOP LAB & PHOSPHOR PILOT PLANT, GTE SYLVANIA INC, 69- *Mem:* AAAS; Am Chem Soc; Am Inst Chem; Electrochem Soc. *Res:* Allyl compounds reaction rates; polyurethane polymerization; protective coatings; chemistry of tungsten and molybdenum; electronic grade chemicals; inorganic luminescent chemicals; phosphors. *Mailing Add:* Chem & Metall Div GTE Prod Corp Inc Towanda PA 18848

CHIONG, MIGUEL ANGEL, b Havana, Cuba, Dec 20, 25; Can citizen. INTERNAL MEDICINE, CARDIOLOGY. *Educ:* Univ Havana, MD, 50; Queen's Univ, Ont, MSc, 64, PhD(cardiovasc physiol), 65; FRCPS(C), 63. *Prof Exp:* Assoc prof med & physiol, 66-76, PROF PHYSIOL, FAC MED, QUEEN'S UNIV, ONT, 76- *Concurrent Pos:* Sr fel, Ont Heart Found, 66-75; attend staff, Kingston Gen Hosp, 66-; mem Am group, Int Group Study Myocardial Metab, 70- *Mem:* AAAS; Can Med Asn; Can Physiol Soc; Can Cardiovasc Soc; Am Col Cardiol. *Res:* Study of myocardial metabolism and hemodynamics in response to cardiovascular drugs and hypoxia or ischemia in isolated hearts and in patients with coronary artery disease. *Mailing Add:* Dept Med Etherington Hall Queen's Univ Kingston ON K7L 3N6 Can

CHIOTTI, PREMO, b Cuba, Ill, Feb 18, 11; m 42. PHYSICAL CHEMISTRY. *Educ:* Univ Ill, BS, 38; Iowa State Univ, PhD(phys chem), 50. *Prof Exp:* Supt finishing dept, Otsego Falls Paper Mills, Inc, Mich, 39-42 & Manhattan Project, US Army, 42-46; jr chemist, 44-50, from asst prof to assoc prof, 50-61, prof, 61-78, sr chemist, 62-78, EMER PROF CHEM, DEPT MAT SCI & ENG, IOWA STATE UNIV, 78- *Mem:* AAAS; Metall Soc; Am Chem Soc; Am Soc Metals. *Res:* Physical and chemical metallurgy; thermodynamic properties and high temperature properties of metals and alloys. *Mailing Add:* 2230 S State Ames IA 50010

CHIOU, C(HARLES), b Kashing, China, July 15, 24; nat US; m 60; c 2. PHYSICAL METALLURGY, MATERIALS SCIENCE. *Educ:* Pei-Yang Univ, China, BS, 48; Mo Sch Mines, MS, 54; Northwestern Univ, PhD, 59. *Prof Exp:* Asst eng, Taiwan Indust & Mining Corp, 48-52; asst, Northwestern Univ, 55-58; mem res staff, Res Ctr, 58-64, adv metallurgist, 64-65, mgr joining technol dept, 66-68, mgr thin film develop, 63-69, adv engr, 69-77, sr engr & mgr inorg mat, 72-75, sr engr & mgr film process develop, 76-81, PROG COORDR, TECHNICAL STAFF, IBM CORP, 81- *Honors & Awards:* Invention achievement award, Int Bus Mach Corp. *Mem:* Am Soc Metals; Am Inst Mining, Metall & Petrol Engrs; Am Vacuum Soc; Sigma Xi; Electro Chem Soc. *Res:* Vacuum deposited thin films; superconductivity metals; metallurgy; insulation and interconnection technology of integrated circuits; photoconductor materials and electrophotography; thin film technology; ink jet technology; magnetic bubble device fabrication. *Mailing Add:* IBM Corp H58/282 Monterey & Cottle Rds San Jose CA 95193

CHIOU, CARY TSAIR, b Maioli, Taiwan, Nov 22, 40; US citizen; m 68; c 2. PHYSICAL CHEMISTRY, SURFACE CHEMISTRY. *Educ:* Cheng Kung Univ, Taiwan, BSE, 65; Kent State Univ, MS, 70, PhD(phys chem), 73. *Prof Exp:* Grad asst phys chem, Kent State Univ, 68-73; fel chem kinetics, Brown Univ, 73-74; fel phys chem, Univ Ky, 74-75; res assoc, 75-78, asst prof, 78-81, ASSOC PROF ENVIRON CHEM, ORE STATE UNIV, 81- *Mem:* Am Chem Soc; AAAS. *Res:* Chemodynamics of environmental chemicals; evaporation from aqueous and nonaqueous systems; partition equilibria in solvent (lipid)-water mixtures; sorptive mechanisms with soils and activated carbons; transport models. *Mailing Add:* Dept of Agr Chem Ore State Univ Corvallis OR 97331

CHIOU, CHII-SHYOUNG, b Tainan, Taiwan, Mar 7, 48; m 73; c 1. CHEMICAL ENGINEERING. *Educ:* Nat Taiwan Univ, MS, 72; Univ Fla, MS, 74, PhD(chem eng), 76. *Prof Exp:* Res engr, 77-80, SR RES ENGR ENHANCED RECOVERY, CITIES SERV CO, 80- *Mem:* Am Inst Chem Engrs; Soc Petrol Engrs. *Res:* Surfactant-polymer flooding process; fluid flow in porous media; polymer theology; mathematical reservoir simulation. *Mailing Add:* Cities Serv Co PO Box 3908 Tulsa OK 74119

CHIOU, GEORGE CHUNG-YIH, b Taoyuan, Taiwan, July 11, 34; US citizen; m 61; c 2. PHARMACOLOGY, BIOCHEMISTRY. *Educ:* Nat Taiwan Univ, BS, 57, MS, 60; Vanderbilt Univ, PhD(pharmacol), 67. *Prof Exp:* Pharmacist, William Pharmaceut Works, Taiwan, 60-61; pharmacist, Chinese Air Force Hosp, 61-62; instr pharmacol, China Med Col, Taiwan, 62-64; from res asst to res assoc, Col Med, Vanderbilt Univ, 64-68; fel pharmacol, Univ Iowa, 68-69; asst prof, 69-73; assoc prof, pharmacol, Col Med, Univ Fla, 73-77, prof, 77-78; PROF & HEAD DEPT PHARMACOL, COL MED, TEX A&M UNIV, 78- *Concurrent Pos:* NIH health sci advan award pharmacol, Vanderbilt Univ, 67-68; NIH res grant, Univ Fla, 69-71; Nat Inst Neurol Dis & Stroke res grant, 71-74; Nat Cancer Inst, res grant, 75-77; Am Cancer Soc res grant, 77-79; Nat Eye Inst res grants, 76-78 & 81-; res grant, Cooper Vision Labs, 80-81. *Mem:* NY Acad Sci; Am Soc Pharmacol & Exp Therapeut; Sigma Xi; Soc Exp Biol Med; Asn Res Vision & Ophthalmol. *Res:* Autonomic pharmacology; calcium antagonists; neurochemistry; enzymology; structure-activity relationships of cholinergic and cholinolytic agents; enzyme kinetics of acetylcholinesterase and butyrylcholinesterase; action mechanisms of nicotinic responses; nature of cholinergic receptor; cytolysis of neuroblastomas; treatment of glaucoma; aqueous humor dynamics. *Mailing Add:* Dept of Med Pharmacol & Toxicol Tex A&M Univ Col of Med College Station TX 77843

CHIOU, MINSHON JEBB, b China, Feb 1, 51. CHEMICAL ENGINEERING, APPLIED MATHEMATICS. *Educ:* Univ Del, PhD(chem eng), 79. *Prof Exp:* CHEM ENGR ENERGY CONVERSION PROGS, JAYCOR, 79- *Mem:* Am Inst Chem Engrs. *Res:* Catalysis, reaction engineering, process simulation, transport phenomena and fossil energy conversion processes. *Mailing Add:* 7104 Columbine Dr Carlsbad CA 92008

CHIOU, WIN LOUNG, b Hsinchu, Taiwan, Aug 29, 38; m 63; c 2. PHARMACOLOGY. *Educ:* Nat Taiwan Univ, BS, 61; Univ Calif, San Francisco, PhD(pharmaceut chem), 69. *Prof Exp:* From res assoc to asst prof pharm, Wash State Univ, 69-71; asst prof pharm, 71-73, assoc prof pharm & occup & environ med, 73-75, dir, Clin Pharmacokinetics Lab, Col Pharm, 75-79, PROF PHARM, MED CTR, UNIV ILL, 76- *Concurrent Pos:* Consult, Med Lett on Drugs & Therapeut, 74-75; mem pharmacol study sect, NIH, 81. *Mem:* Acad Pharmaceut Sci; Am Pharmaceut Asn. *Res:* Biopharmaceutics and clinical pharmacokinetics of drugs; drug interactions; solid dispersion formulation of dosage forms; blood level monitoring; liquid chromatography in drug analysis; renal function; formulation of dosage forms. *Mailing Add:* Univ Ill Med Ctr 833 S Wood St 60612

CHIPAULT, JACQUES ROBERT, b La Vernelle, France, May 13, 14; nat US; m 41; c 2. BIOCHEMISTRY. *Educ:* Carleton Col, BA, 35; Univ Minn, MS, 41, PhD(biochem), 46. *Prof Exp:* Res fel, Hormel Inst, Univ Minn, 46-48, res assoc, 48-51, from asst prof to assoc prof biochem, 51-60, prof biochem, Univ Minn, 60-79, asst to dir, Hormel Inst, 76-79; RETIRED. *Mem:* Am Chem Soc. *Res:* Fat antioxidants; fat oxidation; fat metabolism; infrared spectroscopy; effect of high-energy radiation on fats; lipid deterioration; lipids of the eye; intestinal sterols and bile acids. *Mailing Add:* 511 9th St SW Austin MN 55912

CHIPLEY, JOHN RAYMOND, microbiology, see previous edition

CHIPLEY, ROBERT MACNEILL, b Cincinnati, Ohio, Nov 20, 39; m 67; c 2. ORNITHOLOGY. *Educ:* Yale Univ, BA, 61; Cornell Univ, PhD(ecol), 74. *Prof Exp:* Sci ed, Dover Publ, 65-68; DIR, ECOL RES FOR HERITAGE PROGS, THE NATURE CONSERVANCY, 74- *Mem:* Ecol Soc Am; Am Ornithologists Union; Cooper Ornith Soc. *Res:* Inventory and preservation of natural areas; conservation of endangered species. *Mailing Add:* 703 Ware St SW Vienna VA 22180

CHIPMAN, DAVID MAYER, b New York, NY, Oct 7, 40; m 62; c 3. ENZYMOLOGY, BIO-ORGANIC CHEMISTRY. *Educ:* Columbia Univ, BA, 62; PhD(org chem), 65. *Prof Exp:* Nat Acad Sci-Nat Res Coun res fel biophys, Weizmann Inst, 65-66; NIH res fel, 66-67; asst prof chem, Mass Inst Technol, 67-71; sr lectr biochem, 71-74, chmn dept biol, 74-77, ASSOC PROF BIOCHEM, BEN GURION UNIV OF THE NEGEV, 74- *Concurrent Pos:* Vis assoc prof chem, Univ Ore, 77-78. *Mem:* AAAS; Am Chem Soc; Israel Biochem Soc. *Res:* Mechanisms of chemical reactions of biological interest; enzyme mechanisms; physical organic chemistry; bioenergetics. *Mailing Add:* Ben Gurion Univ of the Negev PO Box 653 Beersheva Israel

CHIPMAN, DAVID RANDOLPH, b Atlanta, Ga, Jan 23, 28; m 52; c 2. X-RAY CRYSTALLOGRAPHY. *Educ:* Mass Inst Technol, BS, 49, ScD(metall), 55; Univ Ill, MS, 50. *Prof Exp:* Fulbright fel, Stuttgart Tech Univ, Ger, 55-56; SOLID STATE PHYSICIST, US ARMY MAT & MECH RES CTR, 56- *Mem:* Am Phys Soc; Am Crystallog Asn. *Res:* X-ray and neutron diffraction studies of the structure of metals and alloys; magnetic studies of hard magnetic materials; x-ray studies of amorphous metals. *Mailing Add:* Army Mat & Mech Res Ctr Watertown MA 02172

CHIPMAN, GARY RUSSELL, b Berlin, Wis, Feb 27, 43; m 67; c 2. ORGANIC CHEMISTRY. *Educ:* Univ Wis, BS, 65; Univ Mich, MS, 67, PhD(org chem), 70. *Prof Exp:* Res chemist, Amoco Chem Corp, 70-76, res chemist, 76-81, SR RES CHEMIST, STANDARD OIL CO, IND, 81- *Mem:* Am Chem Soc. *Res:* Product and process research on random olefin copolymers, polyesters, and block copolymers; organic analysis; mass spectrometry. *Mailing Add:* Standard Oil Co Amoco Res Ctr PO Box 400 Naperville IL 60566

CHIPMAN, JOHN, b Tallahassee, Fla, Apr 25, 97; m 23; c 2. METALLURGY, PHYSICAL CHEMISTRY. *Educ:* Univ of the South, BS, 20; Univ Iowa, MS, 22; Univ Calif, PhD, 26. *Hon Degrees:* ScD, Univ of the South, 40; DSc, Univ Pa, 62; DrIngEh, Aachen Inst Technol, 70. *Prof Exp:* Asst prof chem, Ill Wesleyan Univ, 22-24 & Ga Inst Technol, 26-29; res engr, Univ Mich, 29-35; assoc dir res labs, Am Rolling Mill Co, Ohio, 35-37; prof metall, 37-62, head dept, 46-62, EMER PROF & LECTR METALL, MASS INST TECHNOL, 62- *Concurrent Pos:* Mem, Manhattan Proj, Metall Lab, Univ Chicago & Mass Inst Technol, 42-45; Schwab mem lectr, Am Iron & Steel Inst, 53; Priestly lectr, Pa State Univ, 57; hon mem, Japanese Iron & Steel Inst. *Honors & Awards:* Howe Medal, Am Soc Metals, 34, Sauvenur Award, 51; Gold Medal, 57; Hunt Award, Am Inst Mining, Metall & Petrol Engrs, 39; Clamer Medal, Franklin Inst, 51; Losana Gold Medal, Italian Asn Metall, 52; Brinell Gold Medal, Royal Swedish Acad Eng Sci, 54; Bessemer Medal, Brit Iron & Steel Inst, 55; Benjamin Fairless Award, Metall Soc, 63. *Mem:* Nat Acad Sci; fel Metall Soc; Am Soc Metals (pres, 52); hon mem Indian Inst Metals; hon mem Fr Soc Metall. *Res:* Chemical equilibrium at high temperatures; reactions in liquid metals and slags; process metallurgy; steel-making. *Mailing Add:* 19 Lorena Rd Winchester MA 01890

CHIPMAN, R(OBERT) A(VERY), b Winnipeg, Man, Apr 28, 12; m 38; c 3. ELECTRICAL ENGINEERING. *Educ:* Univ Man, BSc, 32; McGill Univ, MEng, 33; Cambridge Univ, PhD(physics), 39. *Prof Exp:* Asst prof physics, Acadia Univ, 38-40; res asst & asst prof, Queen's Univ, Ont, 40-46; from asst McGill prof to assoc prof elec eng, McGill Univ, 46-57; prof, 57-78, chmn dept, 59-65, EMER PROF ELEC ENG, UNIV TOLEDO, 78- *Mem:* Fel Am Inst Elec & Electronics Engrs; Soc Hist Technol. *Res:* Electrical measurement at very high frequencies; history of science and technology; dielectric and magnetic materials. *Mailing Add:* Dept of Elec Eng Univ of Toledo Toledo OH 43606

CHIPMAN, ROBERT K, b New York, NY, Nov 16, 31; m 54; c 2. ZOOLOGY. *Educ:* Amherst Col, AB, 53; Tulane Univ, MS, 58, PhD(zool), 63. *Prof Exp:* From instr to asst prof biol, State Univ NY Col Plattsburgh, 61-62; from asst prof to assoc prof zool, Univ Vt, 62-68, asst dean grad sch, 67-68; chmn dept, 68-74, PROF ZOOL, UNIV RI, 68- *Mem:* Am Soc Mammal; Am Soc Zool. *Res:* Morphological variation of fish; vertebrate ecology; rodent population dynamics; vertebrate physiological ecology; physiology of reproduction of rodents. *Mailing Add:* Dept of Zool Univ of RI Kingston RI 02881

CHIPMAN, WILMON B, b Reading, Mass, July 6, 32; m 60; c 3. ORGANIC CHEMISTRY, BIOCHEMISTRY. *Educ:* Harvard Univ, AB, 54; Dartmouth Col, AM, 56; Univ Ill, PhD(org chem), 60. *Prof Exp:* Instr chem, Colby Col, 60-62, asst prof, 62-65; assoc prof, 65-67, PROF CHEM, BRIDGEWATER STATE COL, 67-, CHMN DEPT, 65- *Concurrent Pos:* Vis lectr, NSF Inst, Mt Hermon Sch, 61-64; NSF vis lectr, 63-65; lectr, NSF in-serv inst, Bridgewater State Col, 66-71, 75-78 & 80-81. *Mem:* Am Chem Soc; Asn Comput Mach. *Res:* Heterocyclic chemistry; infrared and ultraviolet spectroscopy; transannular interactions; natural products; nuclear magnetic resonance spectrometry; microcomputers in chemistry; computer-aided instruction. *Mailing Add:* 64 Pleasant Dr Bridgewater MA 02324

CHIQUOINE, A DUNCAN, b Upland, Pa, May 3, 26; m 50; c 4. CELL BIOLOGY. *Educ:* Swarthmore Col, AB, 47; Cornell Univ, PhD(zool), 52. *Prof Exp:* Asst, Cornell Univ, 47-52; instr anat, Univ Wash, 52-53; from instr to asst prof biol, Princeton Univ, 53-57; from asst prof to assoc prof anat, Wash Univ, 57-67; PROF BIOL & CHMN DEPT, HAMILTON COL, 72- *Mem:* AAAS; Histochem Soc. *Res:* Histochemistry and cytochemistry; mammalian embryology; electron microscopy of mammalian embryos; germ cells. *Mailing Add:* Dept of Biol Hamilton Col Clinton NY 13323

CHIRIGOS, JOHN N, b Pittsburgh, Pa, June 3, 27; m 53; c 2. METALLURGY. *Educ:* Carnegie Inst Technol, BS, 51, PhD(metall), 57. *Prof Exp:* Engr, 51-61, fel engr, 61-63, supvr reactor vessels, 63-65, mgr eng mech, 65-67, MGR NAVAL FUEL ELEMENT DEVELOP, BETTIS ATOMIC POWER LAB, WESTINGHOUSE ELEC CORP, 67- *Res:* Oxidation and hot water corrosion of nuclear materials; irradiation of structural materials; brittle fractures; fracture mechanics; fatigue; shock and vibration; fuel element design. *Mailing Add:* 16 Lewin Lane Pittsburgh PA 15235

CHIRIGOS, MICHAEL ANTHONY, b Wierton, WVa; Sept 14, 24; c 3. BIOCHEMISTRY. *Educ:* Western Md Col, BS, 52; Univ Del, MS, 54; Rutgers Univ, PhD(biochem), 57. *Prof Exp:* Asst bact, Univ Del, 52-54; fel, Nat Heart & Lung Inst, 57-59, pharmaceut chemist, 59-67; head viral chemother sect, Drug Eval Br, 66-67, HEAD VIRUS & DIS MODIFICATION SECT, NAT CANCER INST, 67-, ASSOC BR CHIEF VIRAL BIOL BR, 70-, CHIEF, IMMUNOPHARMACOL SECT, 81- *Mem:* AAAS; Am Asn Cancer Res; Soc Exp Biol & Med. *Res:* Chemotherapy of cancer and oncogenic viruses; oncogenic virology; transport mechanisms in vitro and in vivo; immune modifiers. *Mailing Add:* Bldg 37 Rm 5A-15 Nat Cancer Inst Div Cancer Treat Bethesda MD 20014

CHIRIKJIAN, JACK G, b Dec 10, 40; US citizen; m 64; c 2. BIOLOGICAL CHEMISTRY. *Educ:* Trenton State Col, BA, 63; Rutgers Univ, MS, 66, PhD(biochem), 69. *Prof Exp:* Nat Cancer Inst fel biochem, Princeton Univ, 69-71, res assoc, 71-72; from asst prof to assoc prof, 72-81, PROF BIOCHEM, SCHS MED & DENT, GEORGETOWN UNIV, 81- *Concurrent Pos:* Sr consult & dir bd, BRL, Inc, 75- & Pharmacia Fine Chem, 74-; Leukemia Soc Am scholar, 75-80. *Mem:* Am Soc Biol Chemists; Am Soc Microbiol; Am Chem Soc; Sigma Xi; Am Asn Univ Professors. *Res:* Studies dealing with protein-nucleic acid interactions using sequence specific endonucleases as model systems; emphasis is placed on structure and function and uses of the various enzymes. *Mailing Add:* Molecular Genetics Div Vincent T Lombardi Cancer Ctr Washington DC 20007

CHIRINO, FERNANDO PORFIRIO, b Havana, Cuba, Sept 15, 18; US citizen; m 40; c 2. MEDICINE. *Educ:* Tulane Univ, BS, 40, MD, 43; Univ Havana, MD, 46. *Prof Exp:* Indust physician, Hershey Corp, Cuba, 46-59; PROF MED, SCH MED, TULANE UNIV, 63-; DIR MED EDUC, CHARITY HOSP LA, 76- *Concurrent Pos:* Vpres & mem vis staff, Charity Hosp La, 82; vis prof, Lallie-Kemp Charity Hosp & Huey P Long Mem Hosp, La. *Res:* Internal medicine; geriatrics. *Mailing Add:* 1415 Tulane Ave New Orleans LA 70112

CHIRLIAN, PAUL M(ICHAEL), b New York, NY, Apr 29, 31; m 61; c 2. ELECTRICAL ENGINEERING, ELECTRONICS. *Educ:* NY Univ, BEE, 50, MEE, 52, EngScD, 56. *Hon Degrees:* ME, Stevens Inst Technol, 65. *Prof Exp:* Asst elec eng, NY Univ, 50-51, from instr to asst prof, 51-60; assoc prof, 60-65, PROF ELEC ENG, STEVENS INST TECHNOL, 65- *Concurrent Pos:* Consult, Anesthesia Assoc, 57-58 & Radio Corp Am, 62-63; consult ed, Dilithium Press & Matrix Publ, Inc, 78- *Mem:* Fel Am Inst Elec & Electronics Engrs; Am Soc Eng Educ. *Res:* Electronic circuits; network theory; physical and medical electronics; digital signal processing; filter synthesis; analog and digital electronics. *Mailing Add:* Dept Elec Eng Stevens Inst Technol Hoboken NJ 07030

CHISARI, FRANCIS VINCENT, b New York, NY, April 5, 42; m 67; c 2. IMMUNOPATHOLOGY, LIVER DISEASES. *Educ:* Fordham Univ, AB, 63; Cornell Univ Med Col, MD, 68. *Prof Exp:* Fel anat path, Mayo Grad Sch, Rochester, 69-70; staff assoc exp path, NIH, Md, 70-72; resident internal med, Dartmouth Med Sch, 72-73; res fel exp path, 73-75; asst staff mem molecular immunol, 75-81, DIR IMMUNOL CORE LAB, SCRIPPS CLIN & RES FOUND, 80-, ASSOC MEM CLIN RES, 81- *Concurrent Pos:* Consult, Naval Regional Med Ctr, San Diego, 75-; adj assoc prof, Dept Path, Univ Calif, San Diego, 76-, Diag Immunol Lab, Orange, Calif, 78- *Mem:* Am Asn Immunologists; Am Soc Exp Path; AAAS; NY Acad Sci; Am Fedn Clin Res. *Res:* Immunopathogenetic mechanisms responsible for liver disease in hepatitis B virus infection; modulation of immune response by hepatic bioregulatory molecules. *Mailing Add:* Scripps Clin & Res Found 10666 N Torrey Pines Rd LaJolla CA 92037

CHISCON, J ALFRED, b Kingston, Pa, Feb 18, 33; m 69. GENETICS, EVOLUTION. *Educ:* Bloomsburg State Col, BS, 54; Purdue Univ, MS, 56, PhD(biol), 61. *Prof Exp:* From instr to assoc prof, 61-70, PROF BIOL, PURDUE UNIV, 70- *Concurrent Pos:* Carnegie fel, 68-69. *Mem:* AAAS. *Res:* Social impact of biology; molecular evolution; nucleic acid reassociation studies; DNA relationships between primates; rate of nucleotide sequence change during evolution. *Mailing Add:* Dept of Biol Sci Purdue Univ Lafayette IN 47907

CHISCON, MARTHA OAKLEY, b Chicago, Ill, Aug 27, 35; m 69; c 2. PLANT CELL BIOLOGY. *Educ:* Western Ill Univ, BSEd, 56; Purdue Univ, PhD(immunobiol), 71. *Prof Exp:* High sch teacher biol, chem & physics, Ill & Alaska, 56-64; instr biol, 64-70, NIH fel immunol, 71-72, asst prof, 72-77, ASSOC PROF BIOL, PURDUE UNIV, 77- *Mem:* Soc Develop Biol; Genetics Soc; Tissue Cult Asn; Sigma Xi; AAAS. *Res:* Plant cell biology, tissue culture and genetics. *Mailing Add:* Dept of Biol Sci Purdue Univ West Lafayette IN 47907

CHISHOLM, ALEXANDER JAMES, b Minnedosa, Man, July 28, 41; m 66; c 3. CLOUD PHYSICS. *Educ:* Univ Alta, BSc, 62; McGill Univ, MSc, 66, PhD(radar meteorol), 70. *Prof Exp:* Meteorol officer forecast div, Can Meteorol Serv, 62-66, meterologist, 66-70, res scientist, Res & Training Div, 70-74, chief, Cloud Physics Res Div, 74-79, DIR, ATMOSPHERIC PROCESSES RES BR, ATMOSPHERIC RES ENVIRON SERV, 79- *Honors & Awards:* President's Prize, Can Meteorol Soc, 74. *Mem:* Am Meteorol Soc; Can Meteorol Soc. *Res:* Hailstorm airflow; hail suppression concepts; rainfall enhancement of cumuliform clouds by weather modification. *Mailing Add:* Atmospheric Environ Serv 4905 Dufferin St Downsview Toronto ON M3H 5T4 Can

CHISHOLM, DAVID R, b Chippewa Falls, Wis, Sept 24, 23; c 4. INFECTIOUS DISEASES. *Educ:* Univ Minn, BS, 50; Univ Mich, PhD(bacteriol), 58. *Prof Exp:* Microbiologist, Pfizer & Co, 58-64; MICROBIOLOGIST, BRISTOL LABS, 65- *Res:* Immunolgoy and chemotherapy of infectious diseases. *Mailing Add:* 5100 Highbridge St #26 Fayetteville NY 13066

CHISHOLM, DONALD ALEXANDER, b Waltham, Mass, Oct 27, 36; m 58; c 4. METEOROLOGY, APPLIED STATISTICS. *Educ:* Tufts Univ, BS, 58; NY Univ, MS, 69. *Prof Exp:* Res assoc meteorol, Travelers Res Ctr Inc, 61-69; res scientist solar physics, Geomet Inc, 69-71; res physicist meteorol, Air Force Cambridge Res Labs, 71-75, sci adminr geophys, Air Force Systs Command Hq, 75-77, SUPVR PHYSICIST METEOROL, AIR FORCE GEOPHYS LAB, 78- *Concurrent Pos:* US Air Force rep, Interdept Comt Atmospheric Sci Subgroup, Nat Climate Prog Plan, 76-77. *Mem:* Am Meteorol Soc. *Res:* Mesoscale meteorology including sensor development for observations, objective analysis procedures and mesoscale weather prediction based on physical and dynamical processes. *Mailing Add:* Air Force Geophys Lab/LYP Hanscom AFB MA 01731

CHISHOLM, DOUGLAS BLANCHARD, b Bay City, Mich, Mar 1, 43. ENGINEERING MECHANICS, FRACTURE MECHANICS. *Educ:* Cornell Univ, BME, 66, MME, 67; George Washington Univ, DSc, 75. *Prof Exp:* Engr scientist vibration shock, Missile & Space Systs Div, McDonnell-Douglas, 66-68; mem tech staff systs anal, Comput Sci Corp, 68-70; sr mech engr vibration shock, Div Litton Industs, Amecom, 70-71; res mech engr transp struct safety, Fed Hwy Admin, 71-80; DIR, RES & SPEC PROGS ADMIN, NAT TESTING LAB, US DEPT TRANSP, 80- *Concurrent Pos:* Res fel, George Washington Univ, 75-; consult patent develop, Aluminum Corp Am, 76-, Transpo Safety, Inc, 76- & Pole-Lite Ltd, 76- *Honors & Awards:* Bronze Medal, Fed Hwy Admin, 76; Award, Indust Res Mag, 77. *Mem:* Nat Soc Prof Engrs; Am Soc Mech Engrs; Soc Exp Stress Anal; Am Soc Metals; Am Soc Testing & Mat. *Res:* Structural and transportation safety; fatigue and fracture mechanics; materials testing and evaluation. *Mailing Add:* 2865 Sutton Oaks Lane Vienna VA 22180

CHISHOLM, JAMES JOSEPH, b Natick, Mass, May 29, 36; c 3. OPTICS, SPECTROSCOPY. *Educ:* Boston Col, BS, 58; Univ Rochester, MS, 65. *Prof Exp:* Res physicist, Air Force Cambridge Res Ctr, 57-58; from physicist to prog mgr spectrophotom, Bausch & Lomb Inc, 58-75, dir spectrophotom res & develop, 75-77; dir eng, Hack Chem Co, 77-78, vpres corp eng & develop, 78-79; eng mgr, Anal Chem Lab & Mat Anal Lab, 79-81, PROD ASSURANCE MGR, HEWLETT PACKARD CO, 81- *Concurrent Pos:* Pres & gen mngr, Spectra Technol Inc, 79- *Mem:* Optical Soc Am; Soc Photo-Optical Instrumentation Engrs; Am Soc Testing & Mat. *Res:* Monochromators, spectrophotometers, radiometry and photometry; color measurements; atomic absorption spectroscopy; ultraviolet and infrared optics; light sources and detectors; interferometry; diffraction gratings; photometric standards; water analysis; RF treatment of cancer in animals; photolithography & micrometrology; semiconductor materials analysis. *Mailing Add:* 2730 Logan Dr Loveland CO 80537

CHISHOLM, SALLIE WATSON, b Marquette, Mich, Nov 5, 47. AQUATIC ECOLOGY, PHYTOPLANKTON PHYSIOLOGY. *Educ:* Skidmore Col, BA, 69; State Univ NY Albany, PhD(biol), 74. *Prof Exp:* Res assoc phytoplankton ecol, Inst Marine Resources, Univ Calif, San Diego, 74-76; asst prof, 76-79, ASSOC PROF ENVIRON ENG, MASS INST TECHNOL, 79-, HENRY L DOHERTY PROF OCEAN UTILIZATION, 80- *Mem:* Am Soc Limnol & Oceanog; Ecol Soc Am; Phycol Soc Am; Int Asn Limnol. *Res:* Diel periodicity in physiological processes in phytoplankton. *Mailing Add:* Dept Civil Eng Bldg 48-425 Mass Inst Technol Cambridge MA 02139

CHISLER, JOHN ADAM, b Daybrook, WVa, Feb 25, 37; m 59; c 2. BACTERIOLOGY, GENETICS. *Educ:* Ohio State Univ, BSc, 59, MSc, 61, PhD(plant path), 62. *Prof Exp:* Asst prof bot, Marshall Univ, 62-65; PROF BIOL & CHMN DIV SCI & MATH, GLENVILLE STATE COL, 65- *Mem:* AAAS; Am Inst Biol Sci; Sigma Xi. *Mailing Add:* Div of Sci & Math Glenville State Col Glenville WV 26351

CHISM, GRADY WILLIAM, III, b Tampa, Fla, June 18, 46; m 72; c 1. FOOD SCIENCE. *Educ:* Univ Fla, BS, 68; Univ Mass, Amherst, PhD(food sci), 73. *Prof Exp:* Fel food sci, Cook Col, Rutgers Univ, 73-74; asst prof, 74-79, ASSOC PROF FOOD SCI, OHIO STATE UNIV & OHIO RES & DEVELOP CTR, 80- *Mem:* Inst Food Technologists; Am Soc Plant Physiologists. *Res:* Biochemical control mechanisms of enzymatic processes important in the development and maintenance of quality in plant tissues used as food; enzymatic regulation of cytokinin levels in tomato fruits. *Mailing Add:* Dept of Food Sci & Nutrit Ohio State Univ Columbus OH 43210

CHISMAN, JAMES ALLEN, b Ravenna, Ohio, Mar 4, 35; m 57, 78. INDUSTRIAL & ELECTRICAL ENGINEERING. *Educ:* Univ Akron, BS, 58; Univ Iowa, MS, 60, PhD(mgt eng), 63. *Prof Exp:* Res & develop engr, Firestone Tire & Rubber Co, 58-59; instr indust eng, Univ Iowa, 62-63; from asst prof to assoc prof, 63-76, head, Eng Technol Dept, 74-80, PROF SYST ENG, CLEMSON UNIV, 77-; PRES, CLEMSON INVEST & DEVELOP CO, 64- *Concurrent Pos:* Consult, Consumer Power Co, 63-72 & E I du Pont de Nemours & Co, 77-78; coordr, systs eng prog, Clemson Univ, 68-73; adj prof, Overseas Grad Mgt Prog, Boston Univ, 80-81. *Mem:* Am Inst Indust Engrs; Inst Mgt Sci; Am Soc Eng Educ; Sigma Xi. *Res:* Operations research; production control. *Mailing Add:* Sch of Eng Clemson Univ Clemson SC 29631

CHISOLM, JAMES JULIAN, JR, b Baltimore, Md, July 24, 21; m 48; c 2. MEDICINE. *Educ:* Princeton Univ, AB, 44; Johns Hopkins Univ, MD, 46; Am Bd Pediat, dipl, 52. *Prof Exp:* Intern pediat, Johns Hopkins Hosp, 46-47, asst resident, Johns Hopkins Hosp & asst in pediat, Sch Med, Johns Hopkins Univ, 48; sr asst resident, Babies Hosp, New York, 50-51; resident, Johns Hopkins Hosp, 51-52, asst pediat, Sch Med, Johns Hopkins Univ, 53-55, from instr to asst prof, 55-63, ASSOC PROF PEDIAT, SCH MED, JOHNS HOPKINS UNIV, 63-, PEDIATRICIAN, JOHNS HOPKINS HOSP, 52- *Concurrent Pos:* Fel pediat, Sch Med, Johns Hopkins Univ, 51-53; hosp physician, Baltimore City Hosp, 53-56, asst chief hosp physician, 56-61, assoc chief hosp physician, 61-74, sr staff pediat, 74-; mem panel on lead, Nat Res Coun, 70-71; pediat consult, USPHS, 71. *Mem:* AAAS; Soc Pediat Res; Am Acad Pediat; Am Pediat Soc. *Res:* Renal tubular function; biochemical effects of lead poisoning; porphyrin metabolism. *Mailing Add:* Dept of Pediat Baltimore City Hosp Baltimore MD 21224

CHISWIK, HAIM H, b Russia, Nov 29, 15; nat US; m 42; c 3. METALLURGY. *Educ:* Harvard Univ, ScB & ScD(phys metall), 41. *Prof Exp:* Res engr metall, Battelle Mem Inst, 42-44 & Air Reduction Co, 44-48; sr metallurgist & assoc dir, Metall Div, Atomic Energy, Argonne Nat Lab, 48-81; CONSULT, 81- *Mem:* Fel Am Soc Metals; Am Inst Mining, Metall & Petrol Engrs. *Res:* Physical metallurgy in atomic energy fields. *Mailing Add:* 1525 Thornwood Dr Downers Grove IL 60515

CHITGOPEKAR, SHARAD SHANKARRAO, b Raichur, India, Jan 3, 38. STATISTICS, OPERATIONS RESEARCH. *Educ:* Osmania Univ, India, BA, 57; Univ Poona, MA, 59; Fla State Univ, PhD(statist), 68. *Prof Exp:* Lectr statist, Osmania Univ, India, 59-63; res asst, Fla State Univ, 63-68; vis asst prof, Univ Wis, 70-71 & 72-74; asst prof quant methods, Univ Ill, Chicago Circle, 74-78; ASSOC PROF QUANT METHODS, ILL STATE UNIV, 78- *Concurrent Pos:* Fulbright Travel Award, 63. *Mem:* Am Statist Asn; Am Inst Decision Sci; Opers Res Soc Am. *Res:* Dynamic programming; Markovian decision processes. *Mailing Add:* Dept of Mgt & Mkt Ill State Univ Normal IL 61761

CHITHARANJAN, D, b Madras, India, May 25, 40; c 3. ORGANIC CHEMISTRY. *Educ:* Annamalai Univ, Madras, BSc, 60, MSc, 61; Wayne State Univ, PhD(org chem), 69. *Prof Exp:* Asst prof, 68-70, assoc prof, 73-76, PROF CHEM, UNIV WIS-STEVENS POINT, 77-, DIR MED TECHNOL, 74- *Mem:* Am Chem Soc; Sigma Xi. *Res:* Synthesis of 4-amino-4, 6-dideoxy hexoses and unsaturated derivatives of carbohydrates. *Mailing Add:* Dept of Chem Univ of Wis Stevens Point WI 54481

CHITTENDEN, DAVID H, b Chicago, Ill, July 30, 35; m 61; c 2. CHEMICAL ENGINEERING. *Educ:* Ill Inst Technol, BS, 56; Univ Wis, MS, 57, PhD(chem eng), 61. *Prof Exp:* Teaching asst chem eng, Univ Wis, 59-60, instr, 60-61; process engr, Calif Res Corp, 61-63; asst prof chem eng, Univ NH, 63-70, consult eng exp sta, 63-68; sr tech systs analyst, 70-74, SPECIALIST, OCCIDENTAL SYSTS, 75- *Concurrent Pos:* Lectr, Univ Calif, Santa Barbara, 74-75. *Mem:* Am Inst Chem Engrs; Asn Comput Mach. *Res:* Diffusive mass tranfer in solids; computer application in engineering; chemical process simulation. *Mailing Add:* PO Box 19601 Irvine CA 92713

CHITTENDEN, MARK EUSTACE, JR, b Jersey City, NJ, July 30, 39; m 68; c 2. FISHERIES ECOLOGY. *Educ:* Hobart Col, BA, 60; Rutgers Univ, MS, 65, PhD(aquatic biol), 69. *Prof Exp:* Fisheries biologist, NJ Div Fish & Game, 60-64; res fel, Dept Environ Sci, Rutgers Univ, 64-67, res asst, 67-68, res assoc fisheries, 68-69; asst prof marine fisheries, Col William & Mary & Univ Va, 69-72; assoc marine scientist, Va Inst Marine Sci, 69-72; asst prof, 73-77, ASSOC PROF FISHERIES, DEPT WILDLIFE & FISHERIES SCI, TEX A&M UNIV, 77- *Mem:* Am Fisheries Soc; Am Soc Ichthyologists & Herpetologists; AAAS; Am Inst Fishery Res Biologists. *Res:* Marine, estuarine and anadromous fishes and fisheries; life histories, population dynamics, ecology and factors affecting distributions of fishes and fisheries communities; stock assessments and effects of harvesting fishes and statistics. *Mailing Add:* Dept Wildlife & Fisheries Sci Tex A&M Univ College Station TX 77840

CHITTICK, DONALD ERNEST, b Salem, Ore, May 3, 32; m 57; c 1. PHYSICAL CHEMISTRY. *Educ:* Willamette Univ, BS, 54; Ore State Univ, PhD(chem), 60. *Prof Exp:* Instr chem, Univ Puget Sound, 58-59, from asst prof to assoc prof, 59-68; prof chem, George Fox Col, 68-79, chmn, Dept Sci & Math, 74-79; DIR RES, PYRENCO, INC, 79- *Mem:* Am Chem Soc; NY Acad Sci; AAAS; Creation Res Soc. *Res:* Photochemistry; electrochemistry; fuels; programmed instruction. *Mailing Add:* Rte 2 Box 194 Newberg OR 97132

CHITTICK, K(ENNETH) A, b NJ, Nov 6, 03; m 28. RADIO & TELEVISION ENGINEERING. *Educ:* Rutgers Univ, BS, 25. *Prof Exp:* Radio engr, Gen Elec Co, 25-30; radio engr, Victor Div, RCA Corp, 30-39, mgr, TV eng, 39-41, mgr, airborne radar & TV, 41-45 & TV eng, 45-60, mgr eng admin, Indianapolis Consumer Prod Div, 60-68; CONSULT, 68- *Concurrent Pos:* Mem, Nat TV Systs Comt. *Mem:* Fel Inst Elec & Electronics Engrs; Electronics Industs Asn. *Res:* Television and other electronic devices for the consumer market and industry. *Mailing Add:* 8020 College Ave Indianapolis IN 76240

CHITTIM, RICHARD LEIGH, b Easthampton, Mass, Dec 2, 15; m 49; c 3. MATHEMATICS. *Educ:* Bowdoin Col, AB, 41; Oxford Univ, BA, 50, MA, 55. *Prof Exp:* From instr to prof, 42-77, WING PROF MATH, BOWDOIN COL, 77- *Concurrent Pos:* Dir, NSF In-Serv Inst, 59-61; NSF fac fel, Univ London, 61-62. *Mem:* Am Math Soc. *Res:* Algebra and analysis; complex function theory. *Mailing Add:* Dept of Math Bowdoin Col Brunswick ME 04011

CHITTY, DENNIS HUBERT, b Bristol, Eng, Sept 18, 12; m 36; c 3. POPULATION ECOLOGY. *Educ:* Univ Toronto, BA, 35; Oxford Univ, MA, 47, DPhil(zool), 49. *Prof Exp:* From res officer to sr res officer ecol, Bur Animal Pop, 35-61; prof zool, 61-78, EMER PROF ZOOL, UNIV BC, 78- *Concurrent Pos:* NSF sr foreign scientist fel, Smith Col, 68-69. *Mem:* Ecol Soc Am; Brit Ecol Soc (vpres, 60); Can Soc Zool; fel Royal Soc Can. *Res:* Regulation of numbers in natural populations; control of rats; history and principles of scientific methodology. *Mailing Add:* Dept of Zool Univ of BC Vancouver BC V6T 1W5 Can

CHITWOOD, DAVID JOSEPH, b Baltimore, Md, April 29, 50. NEMATOLOGY. *Educ:* Univ Md, BS, 72, MS, 75, PhD(plant path), 80. *Prof Exp:* fel nematologist, 81-82, ZOOLOGIST, INSECT PHYSIOL LAB, AGR RES SERV, USDA, 82- *Mem:* AAAS; Am Phytopath Soc; Soc Nematologists. *Res:* Biochemistry, physiology and endocrinology of free-living and plant-parasitic nematodes. *Mailing Add:* Insect Physiol Lab B-467 Beltsville Agr Res Ctr East Beltsville MD 20705

CHITWOOD, HOWARD, b Creekmore, Ky, Feb 4, 32; m 53; c 2. MATHEMATICS. *Educ:* Carson-Newman Col, BS, 53; Univ Fla, MS, 55; Univ Tenn, PhD, 71. *Prof Exp:* PROF MATH, CARSON-NEWMAN COL, 57- *Mem:* Math Asn Am. *Res:* Differential equations. *Mailing Add:* Rt 1 Laurel Hills Jefferson City TN 37760

CHITWOOD, JAMES LEROY, b St Petersburg, Fla, Mar 17, 43; m 64; c 2. ORGANIC CHEMISTRY. *Educ:* Emory Univ, BS, 65; Univ Calif, Berkeley, PhD(org chem), 68. *Prof Exp:* Res chemist, 68-69, sr res chemist, 70-72, res assoc, 72-74, div head phys & anal chem res, 74, staff asst to exec vpres develop, Res & Develop Admin, 74-75, dir chem res div, 76-78, asst div supt, Org Chem Div, 79, asst div head, Chem Div, Res Labs, 80, DIR DEVELOP, CHEM DIV, EASTMAN KODAK CO, 81- *Mem:* AAAS; Am Chem Soc; Sigma Xi; Am Asn Textile Chemists & Colorists; Am Inst Chemists. *Res:* Organic synthesis; reaction mechanisms; radiation induced reactions; structure-property relationships. *Mailing Add:* Bldg 150 Tenn Eastman Co Kingsport TN 37662

CHITWOOD, PAUL H(ERBERT), b Riverside, Calif, July 15, 15; m 40; c 3. ELECTRONIC ENGINEERING, COMPUTER SCIENCE. *Educ:* Ore State Col, BS, 60; Chico Calif State Col, MS, 72. *Prof Exp:* Technician, Western Elec Co, Inc, 36-41; technician airframe & engine mech, Lockheed Aircraft Corp, 41-45; owner-mgr, Paul's Radio-TV Serv, 46-56; instr electronics technol, 56-58, asst prof & curric chmn dept, 58-66, assoc prof electro-mech eng technol, 66-76, chmn dept, 66-77, prof, 76-81, EMER PROF COMPUT SYSTS ENG TECHNOL, ORE INST TECHNOL, 81- *Concurrent Pos:* NSF consult, Wentworth Tech Inst, 65; mem, Technol Educ Consortium, 66- *Mem:* Am Soc Eng Educ; Inst Elec & Electronics Engrs; Asn Comput Mach. *Res:* Adaption and application of computer science techniques to the education of engineering technicians at the college level. *Mailing Add:* 6738 Eberlein Ave Klamath Falls OR 97601

CHIU, ARTHUR NANG LICK, b Singapore, Mar 9, 29; US citizen; m 52; c 2. STRUCTURAL ENGINEERING, WIND ENGINEERING. *Educ:* Ore State Univ, BA & BS, 52; Mass Inst Technol, SM, 53; Univ Fla, PhD(struct eng), 61. *Prof Exp:* From instr to assoc prof civil eng, Univ Hawaii, 53-62; res specialist struct mech, NAm Aviation, Inc, 62-63; assoc prof civil eng, 63-64, chmn dept, 63-66, assoc dean res, training & fels, Grad Div, 72-76, PROF CIVIL ENG, UNIV HAWAII, MANOA, 64- *Concurrent Pos:* Consult var struct engrs; on leave prof struct eng, Colo State Univ-Asian Inst Technol, Bangkok, 66-68; vis res scientist, Naval Civil Eng Lab, 76-77. *Mem:* Am Soc Civil Engrs; Am Soc Eng Educ; Nat Soc Prof Engrs; Int Asn Bridge & Struct Eng; Am Concrete Inst. *Res:* Dynamic response of structures to wind loads and earthquake forces; computer applications to structural analysis. *Mailing Add:* Dept of Civil Eng 2540 Dole St Honolulu HI 96822

CHIU, CHAO-LIN, b Kaohsiung, China, Nov 9, 34; m 65. HYDRAULICS, HYDROLOGY. *Educ:* Univ Taiwan, BS, 57; Univ Toronto, MS, 61; Cornell Univ, PhD(hydraulics), 64. *Prof Exp:* Asst, Cornell Univ, 61-64; from asst prof to assoc prof civil eng, 64-71, PROF CIVIL ENG, UNIV PITTSBURGH, 72-, CHMN WATER RESOURCES PROG, 69- *Concurrent Pos:* NSF res initiation grant, 65-66; hydrologist, US Geol Surv, 74-78; vis prof, Univ Karlsruhe, Ger, 80. *Mem:* Am Soc Civil Engrs; Int Asn Hydraul Res; Am Geophys Union. *Res:* Mechanics of secondary flow; open channel hydraulics; three-dimensional mathematical modeling of open channel flow. *Mailing Add:* Dept of Civil Eng Univ of Pittsburgh Pittsburgh PA 15261

CHIU, CHARLES BIN, b Foochow, China, May 19, 40; m 64; c 1. ELEMENTARY PARTICLE PHYSICS, HIGH ENERGY PHYSICS. *Educ:* Seattle Pac Col, BSc, 61; Univ Calif, Berkeley, PhD(physics), 66. *Prof Exp:* Fel theoret particle physics, Theoret Group, Lawrence Radiation Lab, Calif, 65-67; vis scientist theory div, Europ Orgn Nuclear Res, Switz, 67-68; sr res fel, Cavendish Lab, Cambridge, 68-69; res fel, Calif Inst Technol, 69-70, Tolman sr res fel, 70-71; asst prof physics, 71-74, ASSOC PROF PHYSICS, UNIV TEX, AUSTIN, 74-; RES SCIENTIST, CTR FOR PARTICLE THEORY, 80- *Concurrent Pos:* Co-organizer, Conf Phenomenology Particle Physics, 71; Alexander von Humboldt Found sr US scientist award, Max Planck Inst Physics & Astrophys, Munich, WGer, 78-79. *Mem:* Am Phys Soc; Sigma Xi; Am Asn Univ Prof; AAAS. *Res:* Participation of measurements on particle scattering cross sections; high energy scattering phenomenon; Regge theory; theory of strong interactions and general theory of elementary particle physics. *Mailing Add:* Dept of Physics Univ of Tex Austin TX 78712

CHIU, CHING CHING, b Manila, Philippines; US citizen; m 73; c 2. ORGANIC CHEMISTRY, CHEMICAL ENGINEERING. *Educ:* Univ Santo Tomas, BS, 63; Univ Calif, Santa Barbara, MA, 65; Iowa State Univ, PhD(org chem), 69. *Prof Exp:* Res chemist high temperature polymer chem, Marshall Lab, E I du Pont de Nemours & Co, Inc, 69; res assoc barnacle cement chem, Univ Akron, 69-70; prof chem, Claflin Col, 70-74; asst prof, Frederick Community Col, 74-75; fel, 75-77, res scientist chemother, Frederick Cancer Res Ctr, 77-80; SR SCI ASSOC, ANTIBIOTIC REF STANDARDS EVAL, US PHARMACOPEIA CONV, INC, 80- *Concurrent Pos:* Res coordr, Phelps-Stokes Found Consortium Res Training, Claflin Col, 72-73 & 73-74. *Mem:* Am Chem Soc; Sigma Xi. *Res:* Chemotherapy fermentation; thin-layer chromatography and high performance liquid chromatograph assay of antibiotics; pyrolysis of organic compounds; free radical reaction mechanisms; quantitative and qualitative assay of antibiotics; isolation of antibiotics; structural elucidation of natural products; analysis of pharmaceutical products. *Mailing Add:* 9369 Highlander Blvd Walkersville MD 21793

CHIU, CHU JENG (RAY), b Tokyo, Japan, Mar 13, 34; Can citizen; m 62; c 2. CARDIOVASCULAR THORACIC SURGERY, EXPERIMENTAL SURGERY. *Educ:* Nat Taiwan Univ, MD, 59; FRCS (C), 69; McGill Univ, PhD(exp surg), 70; Am Col Surgeons, FACS, 73. *Prof Exp:* From asst prof to assoc prof, 71-81, PROF SURG, MCGILL UNIV, 81- *Concurrent Pos:* Scholar, Med Res Coun Can, 71-76; attending surgeon, Montreal Gen Hosp, 71-, Royal Victoria Hosp, Montreal, 73-; consult, Montreal Chinese Hosp, 73-; vis prof, Univ Manitoba, 74 & Nat Taiwan Univ, 75; lectr, Surg Asn Repub China, 75; assoc, Artificial Organs Res Ctr, McGill Univ, 78- *Mem:* Am Asn Thoracic Surg; Soc Univ Surgeons; Coun Cardiovascular Surg, fel Am Heart Asn; NY Acad Sci; Soc Int Surgeons. *Res:* Cardiovascular research related to myocardial protection in cardiac surgery and myocardial infarction; shock and trauma endocrinology. *Mailing Add:* Montreal Gen Hosp 1650 Cedar Ave Montreal PQ H3G 1A4 Can

CHIU, HONG-YEE, b Shanghai, China, Oct 4, 32; m 66; c 3. ASTROPHYSICS. *Educ:* Okla State Univ, BSc, 56; Cornell Univ, PhD(physics), 59. *Prof Exp:* Nat Acad Sci res assoc physics, Theoret Div, NASA, 60-62, physicist, Goddard Inst Space Studies, 62-78; ADJ PROF PHYSICS, CITY COL OF NEW YORK, 66-; ADJ PROF PHYSICS, COLUMBIA UNIV, 78- *Concurrent Pos:* Mem, Inst Advan Study, 59-61; asst prof physics, Yale Univ, 61-62; adj asst prof, Columbia Univ, 62-65, adj assoc prof, 65-68. *Mem:* Inst Elec & Electronics Engrs; Optical Soc Am; Am Phys Soc; Am Astron Soc; fel Royal Astron Soc. *Res:* Nuclear physics; strange particles; stellar evolution; neutrino astrophysics; x-ray astronomy. *Mailing Add:* 828 Mudd Hall Columbia Univ New York NY 10027

CHIU, HUEI-HUANG, b Formosa, China, Dec 29, 30; m 61; c 1. AEROSPACE & MECHANICAL ENGINEERING. *Educ:* Taiwan Univ, BS, 54; Kans State Univ, MS, 56; Princeton Univ, PhD(aeronaut eng), 62. *Prof Exp:* Res assoc aeronaut eng, Princeton Univ, 62-63; from asst prof to assoc prof aeronaut & astronaut, New York Univ, 63-74; PROF, UNIV ILL, 74- *Concurrent Pos:* NASA res grant, 65-66; consult proj engr, Curtiss Wright Co, 65-; res grant, Argonne Nat Lab, 75-81. *Mem:* Am Inst Aeronaut & Astronaut. *Res:* Energy conversion; energy conservation; combustion; fluid dynamics; applied mathematics. *Mailing Add:* Univ Ill PO Box 4348 Chicago IL 60680

CHIU, JEN, b China, June 22, 24; US citizen; m; c 4. ANALYTICAL CHEMISTRY, POLYMER CHEMISTRY. *Educ:* Hunan Univ, BS, 46; Univ Ill, MS, 59, PhD(anal chem), 61. *Prof Exp:* Res chemist, 60-65, sr res chemist, 65-72, res assoc, 72-79, RES FEL, E I DU PONT DE NEMOURS & CO, INC, 79- *Mem:* Am Chem Soc; Int Confedn Thermal Anal; fel NAm Thermal Anal Soc (vpres, 75-76, pres, 77); Sigma Xi. *Res:* Analytical research in polymer characterization using chromatographic, spectroscopic, and thermal methods. *Mailing Add:* E I du Pont de Nemours & Co Inc Exp Sta Wilmington DE 19898

CHIU, JEN-FU, b Taiwan, China, Sept 30, 40; m 70; c 2. BIOCHEMISTRY. *Educ:* Taipei Med Col, Taiwan, BPharm, 64; Nat Taiwan Univ, MSc, 67; Univ BC, PhD(biochem), 72. *Prof Exp:* Teaching asst chem, Taipei Med Col, 65-67; lectr biochem, Chung Shan Med Col, 67-68; proj investr, Univ Tex M D Anderson Hosp & Tumor Inst Houston, 72-74, asst biochemist, 74-75; asst prof biochem, Sch Med, Vanderbilt Univ, 75-78; ASSOC PROF BIOCHEM, COL MED, UNIV VT, 78- *Concurrent Pos:* Rosalie B Hite fel, Univ Tex, 72-73. *Mem:* Am Soc Cell Biol; Am Asn Cancer Res; Can Biochem Soc; Biophys Soc; Am Soc Biol Chem. *Res:* Role of nuclear nonhistone proteins in the regulation of genetic activity; biochemistry of chromatin; macromolecular mechanism of carcinogenesis; antibodies to tumor associated antigens. *Mailing Add:* Dept of Biochem Univ of Vt Col Med Burlington VT 05401

CHIU, JOHN SHIH-YAO, b Soochow, China, Sept 8, 28; US citizen; m 59; c 2. APPLIED STATISTICS, ECONOMETRICS. *Educ:* Nat Taiwan Univ, BA, 52; Univ Ky, MS, 55; Univ Ill, PhD(econ & statist), 60. *Prof Exp:* Adv economet, Coun Int Econ Coop, Taiwan Cent Govt, 67-68, adv statist, Bur Statist, 67-68; PROF STATIST, GRAD SCH BUS, UNIV WASH, 69- *Mem:* Am Statist Asn. *Res:* Applied statistics in business and economics. *Mailing Add:* Grad Sch Bus Univ Wash Seattle WA 98195

CHIU, KUO CHENG, chemical engineering, see previous edition

CHIU, LUE-YUNG CHOW, b Kiang-su, China, Sept 14, 31; m 60; c 2. THEORETICAL CHEMISTRY, ATOMIC PHYSICS. *Educ:* Nat Taiwan Univ, BS, 52; Bryn Mawr Col, MA, 54; Yale Univ, PhD(phys chem), 57. *Prof Exp:* Fel atomic physics, Yale Univ, 57-60; res physicist, Radiation Lab, Columbia, 60-62; res assoc, Lab Molecular Struct & Spectra, Univ Chicago, 62-63 & Inst for Studies of Metals, 63-64; res asst prof chem, Cath Univ Am, 64-65; Nat Res Coun-Nat Acad Sci sr resident res assoc, Lab Theoret Studies, Goddard Space Flight Ctr, NASA, 65-67, sr resident res assoc, Astrochem Sect, 67-68; assoc prof quantum chem, 68-72, PROF PHYS CHEM, HOWARD UNIV, 72- *Mem:* Am Phys Soc. *Res:* Photochemistry; atomic beam magnetic resonances; theoretical studies on magnetic interactions in molecules; atomic and molecular collisions; interaction of radiation with atoms and molecules. *Mailing Add:* Dept of Chem Howard Univ Washington DC 20059

CHIU, PETER JIUNN-SHYONG, b Miao-Li, Taiwan, June 9, 42; m 67; c 3. PHARMACOLOGY. *Educ:* Taipei Med Col, BS, 64; Nat Taiwan Univ, MS, 66; Columbia Univ, PhD(pharmacol), 72. *Prof Exp:* Res fel nephrology, Sch Med, Univ Pa, 72-74; sr scientist, 74-77, PRIN SCIENTIST RENAL PHARMACOL, RES DIV, SCHERING CORP, 77- *Mem:* Am Soc Pharmacol & Exp Therapeut; Int Soc Nephrology; Am Soc Nephrology; Am Fedn Clin Res; AAAS. *Res:* Effect of antihypertensive agents on fluid and electrolytes balance; renal handling of antibiotics and their effects on kidney function; evaluation of new cytoprotective agents for anti-nuclear and other uses. *Mailing Add:* Schering Corp Res Div 60 Orange St Bloomfield NJ 07003

CHIU, TAI-WOO, b China, May 18, 44. PHYSICAL CHEMISTRY. *Educ:* Chinese Univ Hong Kong, BSc, 66; Univ Miami, PhD(phys chem), 71. *Prof Exp:* Res assoc polymers, Mat Res Ctr, Lehigh Univ, 71-73 & Univ Cincinnati, 73-74; phys chemist rubber res, Polyfibron Div, W R Grace & Co, 75-77; SR RES CHEMIST PAPER RES, SCOTT PAPER CO, 77- *Mem:* Am Chem Soc; Tech Asn Pulp & Paper Indust. *Res:* Mastism and efficiency of non-woven binder. *Mailing Add:* Dept of New Technol Scott Plaza Philadelphia PA 19113

CHIU, THOMAS T, b Shanghai, China, Jan 24, 33; m 60; c 4. CHEMICAL ENGINEERING, PHYSICAL CHEMISTRY. *Educ:* Nat Univ Taiwan, BS, 56; Case Inst Technol, MS, 60, PhD(chem eng), 62. *Prof Exp:* Res chem engr, 62-66, sr res engr, 66-77, RES MGR, DOW CHEM CO, 77- *Mem:* Am Inst Chem Engrs; Am Tech Asn Pulp & Paper Indust; Sigma Xi. *Res:* Physical properties of polyelectrolytes and thermal plastics. *Mailing Add:* Dow Chem USA 1712 Bldg Midland MI 48640

CHIU, TIN-HO, b Kiang Si Prov, China, June 22, 42; m 69; c 2. SURFACE CHEMISTRY. *Educ:* Chung Chi Col, Chinese Univ Hong Kong, BSc, 64; Lehigh Univ, PhD(chem), 72. *Prof Exp:* High sch teacher chem, Fai Yuen Col, Hong Kong & sci teacher biol, South Western Col, Hong Kong, 64-66; teaching asst chem, Lehigh Univ, 67-69, res asst, Ctr Surface & Coatings Res, 69-72; res assoc, AVCO Everett Res Lab, Subsid AVCO Corp, 72-76, sr staff mem microcalorimetry, 76-79; PROJ MGR RES & DEVELOP, BIOMAT INSTRUMENTATION LAB INC, 80- *Mem:* Am Chem Soc; Am Soc Artifical Internal Organs. *Res:* The interaction of solid/gas, solid/liquid, gas/liquid and protein/surface interaction including surface, biophysical, colloid, corrosion, polymer and pollution chemistry; biodegradable nerve channels. *Mailing Add:* 22 Bolton St Reading MA 01867

CHIU, WAN-CHENG, b Meihsien, China, Nov 1, 19; US citizen; m 54; c 3. METEOROLOGY. *Educ:* Nat Cent Univ, China, BS, 41; NY Univ, MS, 47, PhD(meteorol), 51. *Prof Exp:* Technician, Fukein Weather Bur, China, 41-42; teacher math, Pungshan Model Sch, China, 42-43; asst teacher meteorol, Nat Cent Univ, China, 44-45; res assoc, NY Univ, 51-54, from assoc meteorologist to meteorologist, 54-60, res scientist, 60-61; actg chmn dept, 81, PROF METEOROL, UNIV HAWAII, 61- *Concurrent Pos:* Vis scientist, Nat Ctr Atmospheric Res, 67-68, sr fel, 75; res academician, Chung Hwa Acad Cult, Repub China. *Mem:* Am Meteorol Soc; Am Geophys Union; Royal Meteorol Soc. *Res:* Atmospheric energy and circulation; study effect of Southeastern Pacific sea surface warming on the momentum and heat transport in the atmosphere. *Mailing Add:* Dept of Meteorol Univ of Hawaii Honolulu HI 96822

CHIU, YAM-TSI, b Canton, China, Sept 5, 40; US citizen; m 68. ATMOSPHERIC PHYSICS, PLASMA PHYSICS. *Educ:* Yale Univ, BS, 61, MS, 63, PhD(physics), 65. *Prof Exp:* Res assoc elem particle physics, Yale Univ, 65 & Enrico Fermi Inst Nuclear Studies, Univ Chicago, 65-67; mem tech staff, 67-74, staff scientist, 74-79, SR SCIENTIST, AEROSPACE CORP, 79- *Concurrent Pos:* Mem Upper Atmosphere Comn, Int Asn Geomagnetism & Aeronomy, 72-73; prin invest contracts, NASA & Dept of Energy, 78- *Mem:* Am Phys Soc; Am Geophys Union. *Res:* Atmospheric dynamics; ionospheric and solar coronal dynamics-nonlinear waves in gas dynamic and magneto gas dynamic media; space plasma physics. *Mailing Add:* Space Sci Lab Aerospace Corp Box 92957 Los Angeles CA 90009

CHIU, YING-NAN, b Canton, China, Nov 25, 33; m 60; c 2. PHYSICAL CHEMISTRY. *Educ:* Berea Col, BA, 55; Yale Univ, MS, 56, PhD(phys chem), 60. *Prof Exp:* Fel chem, Columbia Univ, 60-62; res assoc physics, Univ Chicago, 62-64; from asst prof to assoc prof, 64-70, chmn chem dept, 72-80, PROF QUANTUM CHEM, CATH UNIV AM, 70- *Concurrent Pos:* A P Sloan fel, Harvard & Princeton Univs, 69-71. *Mem:* Am Chem Soc. *Res:* Spin-spin and spin-orbit interaction in molecules; quantum theory of molecular structure and valence; theory of optical and magnetic resonance spectra, molecular interactions, chemical reaction dynamics, molecular quantum mechanics; Ligand field theory; electron transfer; energy transfer. *Mailing Add:* Dept of Chem Cath Univ Am Washington DC 20017

CHIVERS, HUGH JOHN, b Frome, Eng, June 26, 32; m 56; c 2. MANAGEMENT ENGINEERING, ATMOSPHERIC SCIENCES. *Educ:* Univ Manchester, BSc, 56, PhD(physics), 59. *Prof Exp:* Res asst radio astron, Univ Manchester, 60-61; proj leader ionospheric physics, Environ Sci Serv Admin, 61-62, sect chief, 62-64, dir, Space Disturbance Monitoring Sta, 65-67, mem staff, Tropospheric Wave Propagation, Colo, 67-68; MEM FAC, DEPT ELEC ENG & COMP SCI, UNIV CALIF, SAN DIEGO, 68- *Concurrent Pos:* Mem Comn G & H, Int Sci Radio Union, 61-; owner, La Jolla Sci, 73- *Mem:* Am Geophys Union; fel Explorers Club. *Res:* Earth-space research using scintillations and absorption caused by charged particles from space; very high frequency radio noise instrumentation. *Mailing Add:* Dept Elec Eng & Comput Sci Univ Calif at San Diego La Jolla CA 92093

CHIVIAN, JAY SIMON, b Newark, NJ, Mar 17, 31; m 56; c 2. PHYSICS. *Educ:* Franklin & Marshall Col, BS, 52; Lehigh Univ, MS, 54, PhD(physics), 60. *Prof Exp:* Res asst, Brookhaven Nat Lab, 56; instr physics, Lafayette Col, 59-60; res physicist, Texas Instruments Inc, 60-67; res scientist, Ling-Temco-Vought Res Ctr, 67-71; sr scientist, Vought Advan Technol Ctr Inc, 71-81, SR ENG SPECIALIST, VOUGHT CORP, 81- *Mem:* Am Phys Soc; sr mem Inst Elec & Electronics Engrs; Sigma Xi. *Res:* Laser applications, holography and nonlinear optics; physical electronics; plasma and neutron physics; thermionic energy conversion; signal detection in antisubmarine warfare; thin film physics; infrared detection; quantum electronics. *Mailing Add:* 919 Warfield Way Richardson TX 75080

CHIVUKULA, RAMAMOHANA RAO, b Vijayavada, India, June 20, 33; m 57; c 3. MATHEMATICS. *Educ:* Andra Univ, BA, 53, MA, 55, PhD(math), 60; Univ Ill, PhD, 62. *Prof Exp:* Lectr math, Andhra Univ, 53-59 & Univ Mich, 62-63; from asst prof to assoc prof, 63-80, chmn grad comt, 76-80, PROF MATH, UNIV NEBR, LINCOLN, 80- *Mem:* Am Math Soc; Math Asn Am; Indian Math Soc. *Res:* Functional analysis. *Mailing Add:* Dept of Math Univ of Nebr Lincoln NE 68588

CHIYKOWSKI, LLOYD NICHOLAS, b Garson, Man, July 26, 29; m 53; c 4. ENTOMOLOGY, DISEASE TRANSMISSION. *Educ:* Univ Man, BSA, 53, MSc, 54; Univ Wis, PhD(entomol), 58. *Prof Exp:* Asst entomol, Univ Wis, 54-58; res officer, Plant Res Inst, 58-67, res scientist, Cent Exp Farm, Cell Biol Res Inst, 67-71, res scientist, 71-80, SR RES SCIENTIST, CENT EXP FARM, CHEM & BIOL RES INST, CAN DEPT AGR, 80- *Mem:* Entom Soc Am; Am Phytopath Sco; Entom Soc Can; Agr Inst Can; Can Phytopath Soc. *Res:* Leafhopper transmission of plant viruses; leafhopper transmission of plant viruses and mycoplasmas. *Mailing Add:* Chem & Biol Res Inst Res Br Can Dept Agr Ottawa ON K1A 0C6 Can

CHIZINSKY, WALTER, b Springfield, Mass, Nov 27, 26; m 53; c 3. REPRODUCTION & HUMAN SEXUALITY. *Educ:* Univ Mass, BS, 49; Univ Chicago, SM, 50; NY Univ, PhD(biol), 60. *Prof Exp:* Instr & assoc prof biol, Bennett Col, NY, 54-67, chmn dept sci & math, 60-67; assoc prof & prof biol, Briarcliff Col, 67-74, acad dean, 70-74, chmn dept sci & math, 71-73, distinguished prof sci, 74-77; vpres & dean fac, Stephens Col, 78-79; ASST DEAN, DIV NAT SCI & MATH, BERGEN COMMUNITY COL, 81- *Concurrent Pos:* Shell Merit fel, Stanford Univ, 69. *Mem:* AAAS; Am Asn Univ Prof; Am Asn Sex Educr Counr & Therapists; Soc Sci Study Sex; Sex Info & Educ Coun US. *Res:* Human sexuality, especially behavior; anatomy, physiology and behavior of sex and reproduction, especially in vertebrates. *Mailing Add:* Off Asst Dean Nat Sci & Math Bergen Community Col Paramus NJ 07652

CHLANDA, FREDERICK P, b Poughkeepsie, NY, July 26, 43; m 64; c 2. POLYMER CHEMISTRY. *Educ:* Clarkson Col Technol, BS, 65, PhD(org chem), 70. *Prof Exp:* Res scientist chem, Columbia Univ, 69-70; sr res chemist, 70-80, RES ASSOC, ALLIED CORP, 80- *Mem:* Am Chem Soc. *Res:* Synthetic membranes, polyelectrolytes, and ion exchange. *Mailing Add:* Allied Corp PO Box 1021R Morristown NJ 07960

CHLAPOWSKI, FRANCIS JOSEPH, b Newport, RI, Feb 28, 44; m 65; c 4. CELLULAR MEMBRANES, CELL CULTURE. *Educ:* Univ Mass, BS, 65; Mich State Univ, PhD(zool), 69. *Prof Exp:* Res fel cell biol, Harvard Univ, 69-70; asst prof anat, 70-73, asst dean admin affairs, 76-78, ASSOC PROF BIOCHEM, MED SCH, UNIV MASS, 73-, DIR, INTERDEPT ELECTRON MICROS FACIL, 74- *Concurrent Pos:* Prin investr, NIH res grant, Univ Mass, 70- *Mem:* Am Soc Cell Biol; Tissue Cult Asn; AAAS; NY Acad Sci. *Res:* Growth differentiation and carcinogenesis of urinary bladder epithelium in vitro. *Mailing Add:* Biochem Dept Med Sch Univ Mass Worcester MA 01605

CHLEBOWSKI, JAN F, b Toledo, Ohio, Dec 20, 43. ENZYMOLOGY, PROTEIN STRUCTURE. *Educ:* St Marys Col, Minn, BA, 65; Case Western Reserve Univ, PhD(chem), 69. *Prof Exp:* Res fel chem, Univ Col, London, 69-71; res assoc biochem, Yale Univ, 71-79; ASST PROF, VA COMMONWEALTH UNIV, 79- *Mem:* Am Chem Soc; Biophys Soc; AAAS; Sigma Xi. *Res:* Factors controlling and modulating protein-enzyme structure and function employing differential scanning calorimetry and magnetic resonance methods; systems include alkaline phosphatase deuterium-macroglobulin and aminoaspartate transaminase. *Mailing Add:* Dept Biochem Box 614 Va Commonwealth Univ Richmond VA 23298

CHMIELEWSKI, MARGARET ANN, b Cleveland, Ohio. STATISTICS. *Educ:* Cleveland State Univ, BA, 70, MS, 71; Va Polytech Inst & State Univ, PhD(statist), 78. *Prof Exp:* Instr math, Va State Col, 72-73 & Richard Bland Col, 73-74; ASST PROF STATIST, INST STATIST, TEX A&M UNIV, 78- *Concurrent Pos:* Consult statistician, US Dept Energy grant, 78-81. *Mem:* Am Statist Asn; Inst Math Statist; Biomet Soc; Asn Women Sci. *Res:* Multivariate statistical inference when the underlying distribution belongs to the class of elliptically symmetric distributions; invariant test procedures; path analysis; graphical techniques for multivariate distributions. *Mailing Add:* Inst of Statist Tex A&M Univ College Station TX 77843

CHMURA, NORMAN WALTER, b Cleveland, Ohio, May 28, 28; m 53; c 2. MICROBIOLOGY. *Educ:* Western Reserve Univ, BS, 49; Univ NH, MS, 55; Univ Md, PhD(microbiol), 58. *Prof Exp:* Res asst bovine mastitis & disinfectants, Univ NH, 53-55; asst bacter & virol, Univ Md, 55-57; res bacteriologist meat microbiol & food poisoning, Swift & Co, 57-59; from asst prof to assoc prof biol sch, Carnegie Inst Technol, 59-65; assoc prof biol & chmn dept, 65-70, prof biol & provost, 70-74, Mary Helen Marks prof biol, 74-77, PROF BIOL & HEALTH PROF ADV, CHATHAM COL, 77-, CHMN, DEPT BIOL, 79- *Mem:* AAAS; Am Soc Microbiol. *Res:* Microbial associations and genetics; ultraviolet resistance and sensitivity; biological aging. *Mailing Add:* Dept of Biol Chatham Col Pittsburgh PA 15232

CHMURA-MEYER, CAROL A, b Chicopee, Mass, Sept 22, 39. GEOLOGY. *Educ:* Smith Col, BA, 61; Univ NMex, MS, 63; Stanford Univ, PhD(geol), 70. *Prof Exp:* Lectr geol, Muhlenberg Col, 67-72; sr paleontologist, Mobil Oil Corp, 72-74; res geologist, 74-80, SR RES GEOLOGIST PALYNOLOGY GEOL, CHEVRON OIL FIELD RES CO, 80- *Concurrent Pos:* Res assoc geol, Lehigh Univ, 67-72. *Mem:* Sigma Xi; Am Asn Stratig Palynologists. *Res:* Palynology and sedimentology. *Mailing Add:* Chevron Oil Field Res Co PO Box 446 La Habra CA 90631

CHMURNY, ALAN BRUCE, b Oak Park, Ill, May 31, 44; m 66; c 1. ORGANIC CHEMISTRY. *Educ:* Univ Ill, Urbana, BS, 66; Univ Calif, Los Angeles, PhD(org chem), 71. *Prof Exp:* NIH fel, Mass Inst Technol, 72-73; res scientist, Pfizer Inc, Groton, 73-77, sr scientist org chem, 77-81; DIR ORG CHEM, BETHESDA RES LABS, ROCKVILLE, MD, 81- *Mem:* Sigma Xi; AAAS; Am Chem Soc. *Res:* Application of enzyme catalyzed reactions to the production of fine organic chemicals on an industrial scale. *Mailing Add:* 6211 White Oak Dr Frederick MD 21701

CHMURNY, GWENDOLYN NEAL, b Gulfport, Miss, Oct 22, 37; m 66; c 1. NUCLEAR MAGNETIC RESONANCE, ORGANIC CHEMISTRY. *Educ:* Memphis State Univ, BA, 59; Univ Ill, Urbana, MS, 61, PhD(phys org chem), 66. *Prof Exp:* Res chemist org chem, E I du Pont de Nemours & Co, 65-66; fel nuclear magnetic resonance, Univ Calif, Los Angeles, 67-68 & spectroscopist, 68-71; fel nuclear magnetic resonance, Ohio State Univ, 71-72 & Mass Inst Technol, 72-73; assoc scientist, 75-81, RES SCIENTIST NUCLEAR MAGNETIC RESONANCE, PFIZER, INC, 81- *Mem:* Am Chem Soc; Sigma Xi. *Res:* Carbon-13 and proton nuclear magnetic resonance applied to physical organic and medicinal chemistry; instrumentation and adaption of new techniques. *Mailing Add:* 6211 White Oak Dr Frederick MD 21701

CHO, ALFRED CHIH-FANG, b Shanghai, China, Dec 31, 21; US citizen; m 57; c 2. ACOUSTICS, AEROSPACE SCIENCES. *Educ:* Univ Shanghai, BSc, 43; Univ Tex, MA, 50, PhD(physics), 58. *Prof Exp:* Asst engr, Shanghai Tel Co, 44-48; teaching fel physics, Univ Tex, 49-53, spec instr math, 53-57; sr struct engr, Gen Dynamics/Ft Worth, 57-60, sr physicist, 60-62; sr tech specialist acoust & vibration, res & eng, Space Div, NAm Rockwell, 62-63, supvr, 63-67, mem tech staff, 67-69; sr res specialist antisubmarine warfare & shock & vibration dir, Lockheed-Calif Co, 69-71; eng supvr specialist, Litton Ship Syst, 71-72; mem tech staff, Hughes Aircraft, Space & Commun Group, 72-73; MEM TECH STAFF, SPACE DI, ROCKWELL INT, 73- *Concurrent Pos:* Adj prof physics, Tex Christian Univ, 58-62; translr, Am Inst Physics, 64-69. *Mem:* Acoust Soc Am; Brit Acoust Soc. *Res:* Acoustics and vibration of aircraft and launch vehicle; dynamic responses of spacecraft; aeromechanics in aeronautics; pulse statistical analysis in architectural acoustics. *Mailing Add:* 6263 S Roundhill Dr Whittier CA 90601

CHO, ALFRED Y, b Peking, China, July 10, 37; m 68; c 4. MICROWAVE & OPTOELECTRONIC DEVICES. *Educ:* Univ Ill, BSEE, 60, MS, 61, PHD(elec eng), 68. *Prof Exp:* Tech staff res, Ion Physics Corp, 61-62, TRW-Space Tech Lab, 62-65; res asst elec eng, Univ Ill, 65-68; TECH STAFF RES, BELL LABS, 68- *Concurrent Pos:* Vis prof, Univ Ill, 77-78, adj prof, 78- *Honors & Awards:* Int Prize New Mat, Am Phys Soc, 82; Morris N Liebmann Award, Inst Elec & Electronic Engrs, 82. *Mem:* Inst Elec & Electronics Engrs; Am Phys Soc; Am Vacuum Soc; Electrochem Soc; NY Acad Sci. *Res:* Thin film technology called molecular beam epitaxy--this ultra high vacuum process grows semiconductor, insulator, and metal layers measured in depths as thin as a few atoms, used for fabrication of microwave and optoelectronic devices. *Mailing Add:* IC-323 Bell Labs Murray Hill NJ 07974

CHO, ARTHUR KENJI, b Oakland, Calif, Nov 7, 28; m 53; c 2. PHARMACOLOGY, ORGANIC CHEMISTRY. *Educ:* Univ Calif, BS, 52; Ore State Univ, MS, 53; Univ Calif, Los Angeles, PhD(chem), 58. *Prof Exp:* Asst res pharmacologist, Univ Calif, Los Angeles, 58-61; res chemist, Don Baxter Inc, 61-65; res pharmacologist, Nat Heart & Lung Inst, 65-70; assoc prof, 70-74, PROF PHARMACOL, UNIV CALIF, LOS ANGELES, 74- *Mem:* Am Chem Soc; Am Soc Pharmacol & Exp Therapeut. *Res:* Drug metabolism; adrenergic mechanisms. *Mailing Add:* Dept Pharmacol Med Sch Univ Calif Los Angeles CA 90024

CHO, BYONG KWON, b Seoul, Keora, March 29, 44; m 75; c 2. REACTOR DESIGN, CATALYSIS. *Educ:* Seoul Nat Univ, Korea, BS, 68; Univ Alta, Can, MS, 75; Univ Minn, PhD(chem eng), 80. *Prof Exp:* Res officer, Army Chem Lab, Korea, 68-70; proces engr, Korea Explosives Co, 70-71 & Korea Inst Sch & Technol, 71-73; SR RES ENGR, GEN MOTORS RES LABS, 79-

Mem: Am Inst Chem Engrs; Catalysis Soc; Sigma Xi. *Res:* Theoretical and experimental application of catalysis; catalytic kinetics and mathematical modeling technique to emission control systems such as the automobile catalytic converters; chromatography and catalyst poisoning problem. *Mailing Add:* Phys Chem Dept Gen Motors Res Labs Warren MI 48090

CHO, BYUNG-RYUL, b Seoul, Korea, Feb 3, 26; m 48; c 3. VETERINARY MEDICINE, MICROBIOLOGY. *Educ:* Seoul Nat Univ, DVM, 50; Univ Minn, MS, 59, PhD(vet microbiol), 61. *Prof Exp:* Instr animal infectious dis, Col Vet Med, Seoul Nat Univ, 57-58, from asst prof to assoc prof poultry dis, 61-64; from res assoc to assoc prof avian tumors, 64-72, PROF AVIAN DISEASES, WASH STATE UNIV, 76- *Mem:* AAAS; Am Asn Avian Pathologists; Am Soc Microbiologists; Conf Res Workers Animal Dis. *Res:* Viral diseases of poultry, particularly in avian tumor research. *Mailing Add:* 1405 Deane NW Pullman WA 99163

CHO, CHENG T, b Kaohsiung, Taiwan, Dec 2, 37; US citizen; m 68; c 2. PEDIATRICS, INFECTIOUS DISEASES. *Educ:* Kaohsiung Med Col, Taiwan, MD, 62; Am Bd Pediat, Dipl, 69; Univ Kans, PhD(microbiol), 70. *Prof Exp:* Asst prof pediat & microbiol, 70-74, assoc prof, 74-78, actg chmn, 78-79, CHIEF PEDIAT INFECTIOUS DIS, MED CTR, UNIV KANS, 72-, VCHMN, 79-, PROF PEDIAT & MICROBIOL, 78- *Concurrent Pos:* Pediat resident, Med Ctr, Univ Kans, 65-67; fel infectious dis, 67-70; vis prof, Tri-Serv Gen Hosp & Nat Defense Med Sch, Taiwan, 80. *Mem:* Am Acad Pediat; Soc Pediat Res; Soc Exp Biol & Med; fel Infectious Dis Soc Am; Am Pediat Soc. *Res:* Pathogenesis; immunity and control of viral infection; clinical pediatric infectious diseases. *Mailing Add:* 10215 Howe Lane Leawood KS 66206

CHO, CHUNG WON, b Seoul, Korea, Feb 7, 31; m 58; c 3. MOLECULAR PHYSICS. *Educ:* Seoul Nat Univ, BSc, 53; Univ Toronto, MA, 55, PhD(physics), 58. *Prof Exp:* Asst, Univ Toronto, 58; from asst prof to assoc prof, 58-67, PROF PHYSICS, MEM UNIV NFLD, 67-, HEAD DEPT, 76- *Concurrent Pos:* Vis assoc prof, Pa State Univ, 66-68. *Mem:* Europ Phys Soc; Can Asn Physicists; Am Phys Soc; Optical Soc Am. *Res:* Lasers; laser spectroscopy; stimulated laser light scattering; pressure-induced infrared absorption; dye lasers. *Mailing Add:* Dept of Physics Mem Univ of Nfld St John's NF A1B 3X7 Can

CHO, HAN-RU, b Peking, China, Feb 4, 45; m 71; c 1. DYNAMIC METEOROLOGY. *Educ:* Nat Taiwan Univ, BS, 67; Univ Ill, MS, 70, PhD(atmospheric sci), 72. *Prof Exp:* Res assoc meteorol, Lab Atmospheric Res, Univ Ill, 72-74; asst prof, 74; asst prof meteorol, 74-78, ASSOC PROF METEOROL, DEPT PHYSICS, UNIV TORONTO, 78- *Mem:* AAAS; Am Meteorol Soc; Can Meteorol & Oceanog Soc; Can Asn Physicists; NY Acad Sci. *Res:* Interactions of cumulus cloud ensembles with large scale convective weather systems and tropical meterology. *Mailing Add:* Dept of Physics Univ of Toronto Toronto ON M5S 1A1 Can

CHO, KON HO, b Kangwha, Korea, May 3, 37; m 68. PHYSICAL CHEMISTRY, BIOCHEMISTRY. *Educ:* Seoul Nat Univ, BS, 62; Auburn Univ, MS, 65; Princeton Univ, MA & PhD(chem), 70. *Prof Exp:* Proj engr, Hyosung Moolsan Co, Ltd, 62-63; MEM RES STAFF, WESTERN ELEC CO, INC, 69- *Mem:* Am Chem Soc. *Res:* Mechanisms of enzyme catalysis; conformation and conformational changes of proteins; radiation chemistry of polymers. *Mailing Add:* Western Elec Co Inc Eng Res Ctr PO Box 900 Princeton NJ 08540

CHO, SANG HA, b Korea, Nov 25, 36; m 63; c 2. CHEMICAL ENGINEERING. *Educ:* Univ Seoul, BS, 58; Univ Ala, MSE, 61; Princeton Univ, PhD(chem eng), 65. *Prof Exp:* Fel, Univ Toronto, 65-67; ASST PROF CHEM ENG, QUEEN'S UNIV, ONT, 67- *Concurrent Pos:* Nat Res Coun Can res grants, 67- *Mem:* Chem Inst Can; Can Soc Chem Eng. *Res:* Mass and heat transfer in chemical reactors; turbulence and mixing; high temperature reactions in a shock tube. *Mailing Add:* Dept Chem Eng Queen's Univ Kingston ON K7L 3N6 Can

CHO, YONGOCK, b Seoul, Korea, Mar 20, 35; US citizen; m 61; c 2. HISTOLOGY, HEALTH SCIENCE. *Educ:* Ewha Womans Univ, Korea, BS, 55, MD, 59, MS, 61. *Prof Exp:* Asst histol, Dept Anat, Col Med, Ewha Womans Univ, 59-62, instr, 63-68; res assoc anat & physiol, Ind Univ, Bloomington, 68-71; RES ASSOC & ASST PROF ANAT, UNIV CHICAGO, 71- *Concurrent Pos:* Intern, Dept Surg, Pusan Nat Univ, 61; student dir, Med Col, Ewha Womans Univ, 67-68. *Mem:* Am Asn Anatomists; Sigma Xi; Am Soc Cell Biol. *Res:* Structure of hematopoietic organs under normal and abnormal conditions. *Mailing Add:* Dept of Anat 1025 E 57th St Chicago IL 60637

CHO, YOUNG WON, b Seoul, Korea, Mar 3, 31; US citizen; m 59, 72; c 3. CLINICAL PHARMACOLOGY, INTERNAL MEDICINE. *Educ:* Seoul Nat Univ, MD, 56; Emory Univ, MS, 62; Nihon Univ, Tokyo, 72. *Prof Exp:* Instr physiol, Sch Med, Emory Univ, 63-64; chief cardiovasc res lab, Philadelphia Gen Hosp, 64-68; group dir cardiol, William S Merrell Co, Cincinnati, 68-71; assoc prof med & pharmacol, Sch Med, La State Univ, 71-73; asst prof clin pharmacol, Univ NC, Chapel Hill, 73-76; head cardiopulmonary clin res, Burroughs Wellcome Co, 73-76; assoc dir med res, Riker Lab, St Paul, Minn, 76; MED DIR, COOPER LAB, INC, 77- *Concurrent Pos:* NIH fel, Emory Univ, 60-64; instr pharmacol, Sch Med, Univ Pa, 64-70; consult, US Eighth Army Korea, 75- & US Vet Admin Hosp, Castle Point, NY, 68-; ed-in-chief, Int J Clin Pharmacol & Biopharm, 77- *Honors & Awards:* Prin Senatum, Int Soc Clin Pharmacol, 78. *Mem:* Fel Am Col Angiol; Int Soc Clin Pharmacol (vpres, 78-); Int Acad Clin Pharmacol (vpres, 78-); Am Soc Pharmacol & Exp Therapeut; fel Am Col Chest Physicians. *Res:* Development of new compounds in cardiopulmonary medicine; clinical pharmacology of cardiopulmonary drugs. *Mailing Add:* Cooper Labs Inc 110 E Hanover Ave Cedar Knolls NJ 07927

CHO, YOUNG-CHUNG, b Kyung-nam, Korea, Nov 19, 40; US citizen; m 72; c 2. PHYSICS, ACOUSTICS. *Educ:* Seoul Nat Univ, Korea, BS, 63; Mass Inst Technol, PhD(physics), 72. *Prof Exp:* Res scientist nuclear eng, Atomic Energy Res Inst, Korea, 65-66; teaching asst physics, Mass Inst Technol, 66-72; assoc res scientist, NY Univ, 73; res assoc acoustics, Mass Inst Technol, 74-75; consult acoustics, Sonotech, Inc, 76-77; vis scientist, Joint Inst Advan Flight Sci, George Washington Univ, 77-79, AEROSPACE ENGR ACOUSTICS, NASA LEWIS RES CTR, 79- *Mem:* Am Phys Soc; Acoust Soc Am; Sigma Xi; Am Inst Aeronaut & Astronaut. *Res:* Duet acoustics; turbomachinery noise generation. *Mailing Add:* Mail Stop 500-208 NASA Lewis Res Ctr Cleveland OH 44136

CHOATE, JERRY RONALD, b Bartlesville, Okla, Mar 21, 43; m 63; c 1. MAMMALOGY, EVOLUTIONARY BIOLOGY. *Educ:* Kans State Col, Pittsburg, BA, 65; Univ Kans, PhD(zool), 69. *Prof Exp:* Asst prof biol, Univ Conn, 69-71; dir, Mus High Plains, 71-80, assoc prof, 76-80, PROF ZOOL & DIR MUS, FT HAYS STATE UNIV, 80- *Concurrent Pos:* Guest lectr, Yale Univ, 70; spec consult, Snyecol Corp, 70-, Harvard Univ, 77, US Fish & Wildlife Serv, 77, Asn Systematics Collections, 78-, Am Mus Natural Hist, 78, Oregon State Univ, 79, Sunflower Elec Coop, 80 & Kans Fish & Game, 81- *Mem:* AAAS; Am Soc Mammalogists (recording sec, 74-); Soc Study Evolution; Soc Syst Zool; Southwestern Asn Naturalists (pres, 79-). *Res:* Systematics and natural history of mammals; speciation and evolutionary biology of insectivores, bats and rodents; biogeography of mammals on the Great Plains. *Mailing Add:* Mus of the High Plains Ft Hays State Univ Hays KS 67601

CHOATE, W CLAY, b Miami, Fla, Sept 24, 34; div; c 1. ELECTRICAL & CHEMICAL ENGINEERING. *Educ:* Univ Fla, BSChE, 57, BSEE, 61, PhD, 66; Univ Wis, MSChE, 58. *Prof Exp:* Sr mem tech staff res & develop, Esso Res & Eng Co, NJ, 59-61; mem tech staff res, Sandia Corp, NMex, 62 & Bell Tel Labs, NJ, 63; mgr control & data systs, 66-70, mgr anal & simulation, 70-73, MGR SYSTS RES, CENT RES LABS, TEX INSTRUMENTS, INC, 73- *Mem:* Inst Elec & Electronics Engrs. *Res:* Geophysical signal processing; digital methods for the processing of information; image processing; interactive computer graphics. *Mailing Add:* Tex Instruments Inc PO Box 226015 MS 238 Dallas TX 75266

CHOBANIAN, ARAM V, b Pawtucket, RI, Aug 10, 29; m 55; c 3. CARDIOVASCULAR DISEASES, INTERNAL MEDICINE. *Educ:* Brown Univ, AB, 51; Harvard Med Sch, MD, 55. *Prof Exp:* Intern & chief resident med, Univ Hosp, Boston, 55-59; assoc prof, 60-71, prof med, 71-77, PROF PHARMACOL, SCH MED, BOSTON UNIV, 77-, DIR CARDIOVASCULAR INST, MED CTR, 73-, DIR HYPERTENSION CTR, 75- *Concurrent Pos:* NIH cardiovascular fel, Univ Hosp, Boston, 59-62; Nat Heart & Lung Inst grants, Sch Med, Boston Univ, 68-; lectr, Harvard Med Sch, 71; mem coun arteriosclerosis and high blood pressure res, Am Heart Asn; mem cardiovasc & renal adv comt, Food & Drug Admin, 75-80, chmn, 78-80; mem hypertension & arteriosclerosis adv comt, Nat Heart & Lung Inst, 75-79, chmn, 77-79. *Mem:* Am Soc Clin Invest; Am Heart Asn; Am Physiol Soc; Am Fedn Clin Res; Asn Am Physicians. *Res:* Hypertension; arterial metabolism. *Mailing Add:* Dept of Med Boston Univ Sch of Med Boston MA 02118

CHOBOTAR, BILL, b Vita, Man, Sept 2, 34; m 56; c 3. ZOOLOGY, ANIMAL PARASITOLOGY. *Educ:* Walla Walla Col, BA, 63, MA, 65; Utah State Univ, PhD(zool), 69. *Prof Exp:* from asst to assoc prof biol, 68-76, PROF BIOL, ANDREWS UNIV, 76- *Concurrent Pos:* Alexander von Humboldt fel, Univ Bonn, 74. *Mem:* Am Soc Parasitol; Soc Protozool; Wildlife Dis Asn. *Res:* Biology, development and pathology of parasitic infections, especially of parasitic protozoa; life cycles and fine structure of coccidia. *Mailing Add:* Dept Biol Andrews Univ Berrien Springs MI 49104

CHO-CHUNG, YOON SANG, b Korea, June 11, 32; US citizen; m 65; c 2. BIOCHEMISTRY, MOLECULAR BIOLOGY. *Educ:* Seoul Womens Med Sch, Korea, MD, 56; Univ Wis-Madison, MS, 60, PhD(biochem), 63. *Prof Exp:* Res asst biochem, Dept Biochem, Univ Wis, 57-60, McArdle Lab, 60-63, fel, 63-66; res assoc, Dept Biol Sci, Purdue Univ, 67-70; vis scientist, Lab Biochem, 70-74, res biochemist, 74-80, CHIEF CELLULAR BIOCHEMISTRY SECT, LAB PATHOPHYSIOL, NAT CANCER INST, BETHESDA, MD, 81. *Mem:* Am Soc Biol Chemists; Am Asn Cancer Res; AAAS; Soc Exp Biol & Med; NY Acad Sci. *Res:* Mechanisms of actions of hormones in metabolic regulation and development; significance and control mechanism of cyclic nucleotides in growth regulation. *Mailing Add:* Lab Pathophysiol Cellular Biochem Sect Nat Cancer Inst Bethesda MD 20205

CHOCK, ERNEST PHAYNAN, b Medan, Indonesia, Oct 27, 37; US citizen; m 65; c 2. PHYSICAL INORGANIC CHEMISTRY, POLYMER CHEMISTRY. *Educ:* Univ Calif, Santa Barbara, MA, 63, PhD(surface chem), 66. *Prof Exp:* Asst chem, Univ Calif, Santa Barbara, 61-66; consult, Bell & Howell Res Ctr, Calif, 66-67; researcher dept physics, Univ Calif, Santa Barbara, 67-68 & Los Angeles, 67-70, RES PHYSICIST, UNIV CALIF, LOS ANGELES, 70- *Mem:* Am Chem Soc; Am Phys Soc. *Res:* General material science, inorganic syntheses, preparation of single crystals, intermetallic compounds and alloys, thin films and ultrafine particles; physical properties of solids by x-ray spectroscopy, magnetic susceptibility, conductivity, surface adsorption and catalytic activity; polymerization of organic and inorganic molecules; electrochemical systems for batteries. *Mailing Add:* 1048 24th St Santa Monica CA 90403

CHOCK, JAN SUN-LUM, b Honolulu, Hawaii, Jan 22, 44; m 68. PHYCOLOGY. *Educ:* Univ Hawaii, BA, 67; Univ NH, PhD(bot), 75. *Prof Exp:* Res asst marine phycol, Univ Hawaii, 67-68; inspector, Animal & Plant Health Inspection Serv, Agr Res Serv, USDA, 68-70; ASST PROF BIOL, KING'S COL, PA, 75- *Mem:* AAAS; Phycol Soc Am. *Res:* Marine algal ecology, specifically in the estuarine intertidal environment; productivity of brown algae and salt marsh grass. *Mailing Add:* Dept of Biol King's Col Wilkes Barre PA 18711

CHODOROW, MARVIN, b Buffalo, NY, July 16, 13; m 37; c c 2. ACOUSTICS, ELECTRONICS. *Educ:* Univ Buffalo, AB, 34; Mass Inst Technol, PhD(physics), 39. *Hon Degrees:* DL, Univ Glasgow, 72. *Prof Exp:* Asst, Carnegie Inst, 39-40; res assoc physics, Pa State Col, 40-41; instr, City Col, 41-43; res physicist, Gen Elec Industs, Conn, 43; sr proj engr, Sperry Gyroscope Corp, NY, 43-47; assoc prof physics, 47-54, chmn dept appl physics, 62-69, dir, Ginzton Lab, 59-78, prof, 54-78, EMER PROF APPL PHYSICS & ELEC ENG, STANFORD UNIV, 78- *Concurrent Pos:* Vis lectr, Ecole Normale Superieure, Univ Paris, 55-56; Fulbright fel, Univ Cambridge, 62-63; vis res assoc, Univ Col, Univ London, 69-70; consult, Rand Corp & Lincoln Lab; mem, US Nat Comt, Int Sci Radio Union; mem adv comt on USSR & Eastern Europe, Nat Acad Sci, 69-71, chmn, 71-73. *Honors & Awards:* Baker Award, Inst Elec & Electronics Engrs, 62. *Mem:* Nat Acad Sci; Nat Acad Eng; fel Am Phys Soc; fel Inst Elec & Electronics Engrs; fel Am Acad Arts & Sci. *Res:* Electronic devices and microwave acoustics. *Mailing Add:* Ginzton Lab Stanford Univ Stanford CA 94305

CHODOS, ARTHUR A, b New York, NY, Oct 27, 22; m 43; c 2. GEOCHEMISTRY, ANALYTICAL CHEMISTRY. *Educ:* City Col NY, BS, 43; Polytech Inst Brooklyn, MS, 69. *Prof Exp:* Org chemist, Fed Telecommun Lab, NJ, 43-48; anal chemist, Gen Serv Admin, Fed Supply Serv, NY, 48-50; chemist spectros, US Geol Surv, 50-51, spectroscopist, Anal Labs Br, Colo, 51-52; sr spectroscopist, 52-70, sr res spectroscopist, 70-77, MEM PROF STAFF, DIV GEOL SCI, CALIF INST TECHNOL, 77- *Concurrent Pos:* Consult, US Geol Surv, 54-64; co-investr lunar samples. *Honors & Awards:* Presidential Award, Microbeam Anal Soc, 80. *Mem:* Microbeam Anal Soc (treas, Electron Probe Anal Soc Am, 68-69, pres, 71, treas, 77-78); Soc Appl Spectros; Sigma Xi. *Res:* Application of instrumental analysis to problems in geochemistry and petrology; electron microprobe analysis of lunar materials. *Mailing Add:* Dept of Geol 170-25 Calif Inst of Technol Pasadena CA 91125

CHODOS, ROBERT BRUNO, b Gap, Pa, July 12, 18; m 50; c 4. MEDICINE. *Educ:* Franklin & Marshall Col, BS, 39; Univ Pa, MD, 43; Am Bd Internal Med, dipl, 53; Am Bd Nuclear Med, dipl, 72. *Prof Exp:* Intern, US Naval Hosp, Philadelphia, 43-44; asst med, Sch Med, Boston Univ, 47-49, instr, 52-53; from instr to assoc prof, State Univ NY Upstate Med Ctr, 53-69; PROF MED & RADIOL, ALBANY MED COL, 69-; HEAD NUCLEAR MED DIV, RADIOL DEPT, ALBANY MED CTR, 69- *Concurrent Pos:* Fel med, Evans Mem Hosp, Boston, 47-48, asst resident, 48-49; resident, Cushing Vet Admin Hosp, Framingham, 49-50, physician med serv & radioisotope unit, 50-52; resident, Vet Admin Hosp, Boston, 52-53, asst chief med & dir radioisotope unit, 53-57, assoc chief staff, 57-65, chief radioisotope serv, 57-69; from asst attend physician to assoc attend physician, State Univ NY Upstate Med Ctr, 53-59; attend physician med & radiol, Albany Med Ctr, 69-; chief nuclear med serv, Vet Admin Hosp, 69-71, physician, 71-75; assoc ed, J Nuclear Med, 70-75. *Mem:* AMA; fel Am Col Physicians; Am Fedn Clin Res; Soc Nuclear Med. *Res:* Radioisotopes; human iron absorption; pathologic physiology of anemias; human thyroid metabolism; renal function in hypertension; blood volume in man in health and disease. *Mailing Add:* Nuclear Med Div Albany Med Ctr Hosp Albany NY 12208

CHODOSH, SANFORD, b Carteret, NJ, Jan 14, 28; m 50; c 3. PULMONARY MEDICINE, INTERNAL MEDICINE. *Educ:* Univ Va, BA, 48; Johns Hopkins Univ, MD, 52. *Prof Exp:* Asst prof med, Sch Med, Tufts Univ, 62-70, assoc prof, 70-74; fel pulmonary med, 58-59, DIR, SPUTUM LAB, BOSTON CITY HOSP, 59-, ASSOC VIS PHYSICIAN, 73- & CHMN, HUMAN STUDIES COMT, 74-; ASSOC PROF MED, SCH MED, BOSTON UNIV, 74- *Concurrent Pos:* Consult pulmonary med, Mead Johnson Res Ctr, 68-79, Hoffmann-LaRoche, Inc, 73-76 & Smith Kline & French, 74-77; chief, Pulmonary Clin, Vet Admin Outpatients Clin, 79-; pres, Pub Responsibility Res & Med, Inc, 79- *Mem:* fel Am Col Chest Physicians; Am Thoracic Soc; Sigma Xi; Am Col Clin Pharmacol; Am Therapeut Soc. *Res:* Inflammatory process as it relates to bronchopulmonary disease; clinical pharmacology in pulmonary medicine; methods for detecting patients with early chronic bronchial disease. *Mailing Add:* Sputum Lab ACC Bldg Boston City Hosp Boston MA 02118

CHODROFF, SAUL, b Brooklyn, NY, Apr 29, 14; m 39; c 2. CHEMISTRY. *Educ:* Brooklyn Col, BS, 38, MA, 42; Polytech Inst Brooklyn, PhD(org chem), 48. *Prof Exp:* Asst res chemist, Weiss & Downs, Inc, NY, 39-40; res chemist, Nat Oil Prods Co, NJ, 41-48; assoc res dir, Nopco Chem Co, 48-50; res dir, Norda Essential Oil & Chem Co, 50-65, vpres res & develop, Norda Inc, 65-79; CONSULT, 79- *Honors & Awards:* Am Inst Chem Award. *Mem:* Am Chem Soc. *Res:* Chemistry of organic sulfur; catalytic oxidation; organic synthesis in vitamins, hormones and pharmaceuticals; essential oils, aromatics, perfumes and flavors. *Mailing Add:* Norda Inc 140 Hwy Ten East Hanover NJ 07936

CHOE, BYUNG-KIL, b Taegu, Korea, Feb 15, 33; m 60; c 2. MICROBIOLOGY, CELL BIOLOGY. *Educ:* Kyungpook Nat Univ, Korea, MD, 58, MS, 60; Ind Univ, Bloomington, PhD(microbiol), 70. *Prof Exp:* Res assoc med microbiol, Med Sch, Kyungpook Nat Univ, Korea, 59-62; res assoc microbial genetics, Karolinska Inst, 62-68; res assoc microbiol, Ind Univ, Bloomington, 70-71; res asst prof immunol, Med Sch, State Univ NY, Buffalo, 71-73; asst prof, 73-78, ASSOC PROF IMMUNOL & MICROBIOL, MED SCH, WAYNE STATE UNIV, 78- *Concurrent Pos:* Boswell fel, NY Res Found, 71-72. *Mem:* Am Soc Microbiol; Tissue Cult Asn; Am Soc Cell Biol. *Res:* Growth regulation of mammalian cells; tumor immunology. *Mailing Add:* Dept Immunol & Microbiol Wayne State Univ Med Sch Detroit MI 48202

CHOE, HYUNG TAE, b Seoul, Korea, Apr 27, 27; m 64; c 2. PLANT PHYSIOLOGY, HORTICULTURE. *Educ:* Seoul Nat Univ, BS, 54, MSc, 57; Ohio State Univ, PhD(plant physiol, hort), 63. *Prof Exp:* Instr agr, UNESCO Fundamental Educ Ctr, Ministry of Educ, Korea, 56-59; from asst prof to assoc prof, 63-72, PROF BIOL, MANKATO STATE UNIV, 72- *Concurrent Pos:* Res biologist & NSF fel, Thimann Labs, Univ Calif, Santa Cruz, 73-74. *Mem:* AAAS; Am Soc Plant Physiol; Am Soc Hort Sci; Int Soc Hort Sci; Bot Soc Am. *Res:* Senescence of isolated chloroplasts and metabolic functions during the senescence in oat leaves; the effect of growth regulators, light qualities on the senescence of chloroplasts and leaves of oat seedlings. *Mailing Add:* Dept of Biol Mankato State Univ Mankato MN 56001

CHOGUILL, HAROLD SAMUEL, b Humboldt, Kans, Jan 12, 07; m; c 1. CHEMISTRY. *Educ:* Col of Emporia, AB, 27; Univ Kans, AM, 31, PhD(chem), 38. *Prof Exp:* Teacher high sch, Kans, 27-30, prin, 28-30; instr math, Garden City Jr Col, 32-37; instr chem, Independence Jr Col, 37-43, ground instr, Civilian Pilot Training, 37-43; prof chem, 46-76, EMER PROF CHEM, FT HAYS STATE UNIV, 76- *Concurrent Pos:* NSF res fel, Univ Col, London, 59-60; vis lectr, Div Chem Educ, Am Chem Soc. *Mem:* Am Chem Soc; Sigma Xi. *Res:* Iodination of phenols and ethers; kinetics of deiodination; halogenated nitroparaffins. *Mailing Add:* 602 S Evergreen Chanute KS 66720

CHOI, BYUNG CHANG, b Changsung, Korea, July 24, 40; m 72; c 2. CATALYSIS, COMBUSTION. *Educ:* Tex A&M Univ, BS, 68; Univ Pa, PhD(chem eng), 79. *Prof Exp:* Syst analyst statist, Int Latex Corp, 68-71; res engr, 76-79, SR RES ENGR CHEM ENG, MOBIL RES & DEVELOP, 79- *Mem:* Combustion Inst; Am Chem Soc; Am Inst Chem Engrs. *Res:* Modeling various refining processes such as reforming, visbreaking and coking; modeling deactivation phenomenon of reforming catalyst; thermodynamics of colloid stability. *Mailing Add:* Mobil Res & Develop Corp Billingsport Rd Paulsboro NJ 08066

CHOI, BYUNG HO, b Hwang Hae Do, Korea, Oct 16, 28; m; c 2. PATHOLOGY, NEUROPATHOLOGY. *Educ:* Yonsei Univ, Korea, MD, 53, MSD, 63. *Prof Exp:* Asst in path, Yonsei Univ, Korea, 53-54; resident, Inst Path, Western Reserve Univ, 54-57, demonstr, 56-57; from instr to assoc prof, Yonsei Univ, Korea, 59-65; res assoc path, Albany Med Col, 65-67, asst prof, 67-69; assoc prof path, Sch Med, St Louis Univ, 69-72; assoc prof path, Sch Med & Dent, Univ Rochester, 72-77, prof, 77-81; PROF & DIR NEUROPATH, CALIF COL MED, UNIV CALIF, IRVINE, 81- *Concurrent Pos:* Univ fel, Western Reserve Univ, 57-59; consult pathologist, Cuyahoga County Hosp, Cleveland, 57-59; attend pathologist, Vet Admin Hosp, Albany, NY, 68-69; assoc pathologist, Cardinal Glennon Mem Hosp, St Louis, 69-72; pathologist, Firmin-Desloge Hosp, 69-72; pathologist, Strong Mem Hosp, Rochester, 72-; Neuropathologist-in-chg, Irvine Med Ctr, Univ Calif, 81- *Mem:* Am Soc Clin Path; Col Am Path; Am Asn Neuropath. *Res:* Kinetics of cell proliferation in arterial intimal cells under different experimental conditions; developmental neurobiology; effects of methylmercury and other environmental agents on developing nervous system. *Mailing Add:* 1109 Debra Drive Costa Mesa CA 92626

CHOI, DUK-IN, b Inchon, Korea, Apr 30, 36; m 65; c 1. PLASMA PHYSICS. *Educ:* Seoul Nat Univ, Korea, BS, 59; Univ Colo, PhD(physics), 68. *Prof Exp:* Fel statist mech, Univ Brussels, 68-70; res assoc, Ctr Statist Mech, Univ Tex, Austin, 70-73; RES SCI ASSOC PLASMA PHYSICS, FUSION RES CTR, UNIV TEX, AUSTIN, 73- *Mem:* Am Phys Soc. *Res:* Theory and application of plasma physics in the thermonuclear fusion research. *Mailing Add:* Fusion Res Ctr Univ Tex Austin TX 78712

CHOI, KEEWHAN, b Seoul, Korea, Jan 26, 31; US citizen; m 56; c 3. STATISTICS. *Educ:* Case Inst, BS, 58; Harvard Univ, PhD(statist), 63. *Prof Exp:* Asst prof statist, Cornell Univ, 62-66; res assoc, Atomic Bomb Casualty Comn, 68-72; PROF MATH, GA STATE UNIV, 72- *Concurrent Pos:* Consult clin cancer invest rev comt, Nat Cancer Inst, 75-78. *Mem:* Math Asn Am; Inst Math Statist; Am Statist Asn. *Res:* Classification; pattern recognition; application of statistics to biological and societal problems. *Mailing Add:* 1122 Springdale Rd NE Atlanta GA 30306

CHOI, NUNG WON, b Pyong Yong, Korea, Nov 1, 31; m 62; c 3. EPIDEMIOLOGY, ONCOLOGY. *Educ:* Seoul Nat Univ, MD, 58; Univ Minn, MPH, 61, PhD(epidemiol), 66. *Prof Exp:* Assoc prof social & prev med, 66-72, PROF EPIDEMIOL & CHIEF SECT EPIDEMIOL & BIOSTATIST, FAC MED, UNIV MAN, 72-; DIR EPIDEMIOL & BIOSTATIST, MAN CANCER TREAT & RES FOUND, 68- *Concurrent Pos:* Med fel epidemiol, Univ Minn, 60-65, fel epidemiol & med statist, Mayo Grad Sch Med, 65-66; USPHS traineeship epidemiol, 62-65; Am Pub Health Asn associateship for prep vital & health statist monogr, 65-66; Can Nat Health Dept positionship epidemiol, 66-72; mem adv comt statist studies, Nat Cancer Inst Can, 69-72; mem nat adv comt epidemiol, Dept Nat Health & Welfare, 74- *Mem:* Fel Am Pub Health Asn; Am Acad Neurol; Can Pub Health Asn; NY Acad Sci. *Res:* Epidemiologies of toxoplasmosis; brain tumor, cardiovascular, cerebrovascular and other neurological diseases; cancer of gastrointestinal tract; childhood and female breast and genital tract congenital malformation; cancer epidemiology. *Mailing Add:* Dept of Social & Prev Med Univ of Man Winnipeg MB R3T 2N2 Can

CHOI, SANG-IL, b Korea, Sept 1, 31; m 61; c 2. SOLID STATE PHYSICS, THEORETICAL CHEMISTRY. *Educ:* Seoul Nat Univ, BSc, 53; Brown Univ, PhD(chem), 61. *Prof Exp:* Res assoc theoret chem, Univ Chicago, 61-63; from asst prof to assoc prof, 63-72, PROF PHYSICS, UNIV NC, CHAPEL HILL, 72- *Concurrent Pos:* Consult, Res Ctr, Am Optical Corp, 67-69; guest lectr, Res Inst Fund Physics, Kyoto Univ, 70. *Mem:* fel Am Phys Soc. *Res:* Transport phenomena of gases; semiclassical scattering theory; physics of organic solids; theoretical study of solid electrolytes and organic crystals. *Mailing Add:* Dept of Physics & Astron 039A Univ of NC Chapel Hill NC 27514

CHOI, SOOK Y, b Seoul, Korea, Dec 13, 38; nat US; m 60; c 3. PHYSIOLOGY, BIOCHEMISTRY. *Educ:* Seton Hall Univ, BS, 64; Rutgers Univ, MS, 70, PhDPhD(physiol), 73. *Prof Exp:* ASST PROF BIOL, UPSALA COL, 73- *Mem:* Am Physiol Soc; Sigma Xi; Am Asn Univ Profs. *Res:* Cellular respiration; oxidative phosphorylation of mitochondria. *Mailing Add:* Dept of Biol Upsala Col East Orange NJ 07019

CHOI, SUNG CHIL, b Seoul, Korea, Dec 30, 30; m 67. BIOSTATISTICS. *Educ:* Univ Wash, Seattle, BS, 57, MA, 60; Univ Calif, PhD(biostatist), 66. *Prof Exp:* Mathematician, Boeing Co, 59-62; mem tech staff, Aerospace Corp, 63-64; asst prof math, Calif State Col, 64-66; mem sci staff, Measurement Anal Corp, 66-67; asst prof, Washington Univ, 67-73, assoc prof biostatist, Med Sch, 73-78, prof, 78; PROF BIOSTATIST, MED COL OF VA, 78- *Mem:* Am Pub Health Asn; Am Statist Asn; Biomet Soc. *Res:* Biostatistical methodology. *Mailing Add:* Dept of Biostatist Med Col of Va Richmond VA 23298

CHOI, TAI-SOON, b Seoul, Korea, Dec 29, 35; US citizen; m 65; c 3. MEDICINE. *Educ:* Seoul Nat Univ, Korea, MD, 61. *Prof Exp:* Resident pediat, Children's Hosp, Buffalo, 67-69; res asst & instr, Dept Pediat, 71-72, CLIN ASST PROF PEDIAT, STATE UNIV NEW YORK, BUFFALO, 72-; RES ASST & INSTR DEPT PEDIAT, PHARMACOL & NEONATOLOGY, CHILDREN'S HOSP, BUFFALO, 71-; DIR NURSERY, BUFFALO MERCY HOSP, 73- *Concurrent Pos:* Fel neonatology, Jewish Gen Hosp, Montreal, 69-70 & Hosp Sick Children, Toronto, 70-71. *Res:* Newborn medicine, especially the prevention of Hyaline Membrane disease; utilizing human plasminogen injections immediately after birth to premature infants. *Mailing Add:* Buffalo Mercy Hosp 565 Abbott Rd Buffalo NY 14220

CHOI, WON KIL, b Kangwon, Korea, Feb 15, 43; m 73; c 3. ELECTRONICS ENGINEERING. *Educ:* Yon-Sei Univ, Seoul, Korea, BSEE, 69; Iowa State Univ, MSEE, 74, PhD(elec eng), 78. *Prof Exp:* Asst prof, Elec Eng Dept, Mich Technol Univ, 78-80; STAFF ENGR, IRT CORP, 80- *Mem:* Inst Elec & Electronics Engrs. *Res:* Electromagnetic pulse hardening for various electronics equipments; analysis of electromagnetic field coupling to enclosures, cables, connectors, gaskets, apertures and slots. *Mailing Add:* 13211 Pageant Ave San Diego CA 92129

CHOI, YE-CHIN, b Chunchon, Korea, Mar 13, 29; m 50; c 5. VIROLOGY. *Educ:* Univ Tex El Paso, BS, 71; La State Univ, PhD(microbiol), 76. *Prof Exp:* Fel virol, Sch Med, Yale Univ, 76-77; res assoc biochem, State Univ NY Stony Brook, 78-80; STAFF ASSOC GENETICS, COLUMBIA UNIV, 80- *Mem:* Am Soc Microbiol. *Res:* Isolation and characterization of ribosome RNA genes of animals; cloning of intact 18S-28S (45 kb) in cosmid vectors. *Mailing Add:* 701 W 168th St HSC 1424 Columbia Univ New York NY 10032

CHOI, YONG CHUN, b Sunchun, Korea, Dec 25, 35; US citizen; c 2. MOLECULAR BIOLOGY, CANCER RESEARCH. *Educ:* Seoul Nat Univ, MD, 59; Univ Rochester, PhD(biochem), 67. *Prof Exp:* Asst prof, 69-72, ASSOC PROF, BAYLOR COL MED, 72- *Mem:* Am Asn Cancer Res; Am Soc Cell Biol. *Res:* Mechanisms of gene expression in cancer cells; molecular biology of nuclear RNAs of cancer cells; structures of eukaryotic RNAs. *Mailing Add:* Dept Pharmacol Baylor Col Med 1200 Moursund Ave Houston TX 77030

CHOI, YONG SUNG, b Korea, Sept 11, 36; US citizen; m 66. IMMUNOBIOLOGY. *Educ:* Seoul Nat Univ, BMS, MD, 61; Univ Minn, Minneapolis, PhD(biochem), 65. *Prof Exp:* Intern & resident pediat, Univ Minn, Minneapolis, 65-67, med fel, 67-70; res assoc biochem, Salk Inst, La Jolla, Calif, 67-69; asst prof pediat, biochem & path, Univ Minn, Minneapolis, 69-73; MEM, SLOAN-KETTERING INST & PROF BIOL, SLOAN-KETTERING DIV, CORNELL UNIV GRAD SCH MED SCI, 73- *Concurrent Pos:* NIH spec res fel, 69-70; fac res award, Am Cancer Soc, 70; USPHS career develop award, 71. *Mem:* Harvey Soc; Am Asn Exp Path; Am Asn Immunol; Sigma Xi; NY Acad Sci. *Res:* Immunological studies of thymus-derived lymphocytes; synthesis and secretion of immunoglobulins; biochemical studies of lymphocyte membranes. *Mailing Add:* Sloan-Kettering Inst Walker Lab 145 Boston Post Rd Rye NY 10580

CHOLAK, JACOB, b Elsass, Russia, Aug 23, 00; nat US; m 32; c 2. ANALYTICAL CHEMISTRY. *Educ:* Univ Cincinnati, ChE, 24; Am Acad Sanit Engrs, dipl; Environ Eng Intersoc, dipl, 57; Am Bd Indust Hyg, dipl, 62. *Prof Exp:* Asst appl physiol, Col Med, Univ Cincinnati, 26-40, res assoc, 40-42, from asst prof to prof, 42-65, prof environ health eng, 65-70, EMER PROF, ENVIRON HEALTH ENG, UNIV CINCINNATI, 70- *Honors & Awards:* Eminent Chemist Award, Am Chem Soc, 55. *Mem:* Am Chem Soc; Am Indust Hyg Asn. *Res:* Industrial hygiene; atmospheric pollution; field surveys; instrumental and physical analytical methods. *Mailing Add:* 3115 S Whitetree Circle Cincinnati OH 45236

CHOLETTE, A(LBERT), b Quebec, Que, Oct 12, 18; m 43. CHEMICAL ENGINEERING. *Educ:* McGill Univ, BEng, 42; Mass Inst Technol, SM, 43, ScD(chem eng), 45. *Prof Exp:* HEAD DEPT CHEM ENG, LAVAL UNIV, 46-, PROF, 66- *Concurrent Pos:* Mem, Corp Prof Engrs Que. *Mem:* Am Inst Chemists; Chem Inst Can; Eng Inst Can. *Res:* Mixing; reactor design; heat transfer; evaporation. *Mailing Add:* Dept of Chem Eng Laval Univ Quebec PQ G1K 7P4 Can

CHOLICK, FRED ANDREW, b Portland, Ore, Mar 27, 50; m 70. GENETICS, PLANT BREEDING. *Educ:* Ore State Univ, BS, 72; Colo State Univ, MS, 75, PhD(genetics), 77. *Prof Exp:* Grad asst plant breeding, Colo State Univ, 72-77; res assoc plant breeding, Ore State Univ, 77-81; ASSOC PROF PLANT BREEDING, SOUTH DAKOTA STATE UNIV, 81- *Mem:* Am Soc Agron; Sigma Xi. *Res:* The development of superior cultivars for increased world food production, with emphasis on the genetic control of yielding ability. *Mailing Add:* Dept of Crop Sci Ag Hall 138 Corvallis OR 97331

CHOLLET, RAYMOND, b Flushing, NY, Oct 4, 46; m 69; c 3. PLANT BIOCHEMISTRY, PHYSIOLOGY. *Educ:* Colgate Univ, AB, 68; Univ Ill, MS, 69, PhD(bot), 72. *Prof Exp:* Res assoc plant physiol, Univ Ill, 71-72; res scientist plant physiol, E I du Pont de Nemours & Co, Inc, 72-77; ASSOC PROF PLANT BIOCHEM, DEPT AGR BIOCHEM, UNIV NEBR-LINCOLN, 77-

Mem: Am Soc Plant Physiologists; Crop Soc Am. *Res:* Photosynthetic and photorespiratory carbon metabolism in higher plants, involving studies with isolated enzymes, organelles, protoplasts, cells and intact leaf tissue; related studies with isolated enzymes in photosynthetic bacteria and cyanobacteria. *Mailing Add:* Dept Agr Biochem Univ Nebr Lincoln NE 68583

CHOLVIN, NEAL R, b Chippewa Falls, Wis, Sept 8, 28; m 57; c 3. BIOMEDICAL ENGINEERING. *Educ:* Wayne State Univ, BS, 49; Mich State Univ, DVM, 54, MS, 58; Iowa State Univ, PhD, 61. *Prof Exp:* Instr vet surg & med, Mich State Univ, 55-59; asst prof vet physiol & pharmacol, Iowa State Univ, 59-60; assoc prof vet surg & med, Mich State Univ, 61-63; chmn, Dept Vet Anat, Pharmacol & Physiol, 74-79, biomed chmn, Biomet Eng Prog, 63-74, PROF VET PHYSIOL & PHARMACOL, IOWA STATE UNIV, 63-, BIOMED CHMN, BIOMED ENG PROG, 80- *Concurrent Pos:* Nat Heart Inst fel, 60-61. *Mem:* AAAS; Am Physiol Soc; Am Vet Med Asn; Am Soc Vet Physiol & Pharmacol; Am Heart Asn. *Res:* Cardiopulmonary physiology; experimental surgery. *Mailing Add:* 2008 Vet Med Bldg Iowa State Univ Ames IA 50011

CHOMA, JOHN, JR, b Sewickley, Pa, Nov 6, 41. ELECTRICAL ENGINEERING. *Educ:* Univ Pittsburgh, BSEE, 63, MSEE, 65, PhD(elec eng), 69. *Prof Exp:* From instr to asst prof elec eng, Univ Pittsburgh, 65-69; assoc prof, Sacramento State Col, 69-71 & Ill Inst Technol, 71-76; sr res engr, TRW Defense & Space Systs Group, 76-81; VIS ASSOC PROF, UNIV SOUTHERN CALIF, 81- *Concurrent Pos:* Consult, Nat Acad Sci, 66-67 & Radio Corp Am, Pa, 67-68; co-investr, NSF grant, 68-69, prin investr, 70-71; consult, Allis-Chalmers Corp, Pa, 69-70, Compact Eng, Jet Propulsion Lab, Aerospace & Acrian, 81- *Mem:* Inst Elec & Electronics Engrs; Am Soc Eng Educ. *Res:* Stability of large signal electronic systems; active device models for computer-aided analysis and design. *Mailing Add:* TRW Defense & Space Systs Group One Space Park Redondo Beach CA 90278

CHOMAN, BOHDAN RUSSELL, b Cass Twp, Pa, May 17, 26; m 56; c 2. MICROBIOLOGY. *Educ:* Pa State Univ, BS, 49, MS, 50, PhD(bact), 54. *Prof Exp:* Res biochemist, Union Carbide Co, 50-57; res assoc, Lever Bros Co, NJ, 57-63; microbiol expert, Lederle Labs, 63-67, supt, 67-73, MGR, QUAL ASSURANCE, LEDERLE LABS, AM CYANAMID CO, 78- *Mem:* Am Chem Soc; Am Soc Microbiol; fel Am Acad Microbiol; NY Acad Sci. *Res:* Immunology; virology; biologicals. *Mailing Add:* 574 Blauvelt Dr Oradell NJ 07649

CHOMCHALOW, NARONG, b Bangkok, Thailand, Aug 26, 35; m 60; c 3. AGRONOMY, PLANT GENETICS. *Educ:* Kasetsart Univ, Bangkok, BS, 57; Univ Hawaii, MS, 61; Univ Chicago, PhD(bot), 64. *Prof Exp:* Instr agr, Kasetsart Univ, 57-59; res asst bot, Univ Chicago, 61-64; asst prof biol, Northern Ill Univ, 64-66; res dir, Agr Prod Res Inst, 71-76, RES OFFICER AGR, APPL SCI RES CORP THAILAND, BANGKOK, 66-, DEP GOV, THAI INST SCI TECH RES, 76- *Concurrent Pos:* Exec & vchmn, Int Bd Plant Genetic Resources. *Honors & Awards:* Ratnabhorn Medal. *Mem:* Agr Sci Soc Thailand; Sigma Xi; Orchid Soc Thailand; Ornamental Plant Soc Thailand; Sci Soc Thailand. *Res:* Agronomic investigation and plant improvement of kenaf, jute, peanut, sunflower, banana, basil, Japanese mint and other essential oil crops; genetics and cytogenetics research on banana, mint and Ocimum species; winged bean and fast growing nitrogen fixing trees. *Mailing Add:* Thai Inst Sci Tech Res 196 Phahonyothin Rd Bang Khen Bangkok 9 Thailand

CHOMPFF, ALFRED J(OHAN), b Malang, Indonesia, Oct 26, 30; m 52; c 2. PHYSICAL CHEMISTRY, POLYMER SCIENCE. *Educ:* Delft Univ Technol, MS, 62, PhD(phys chem). 65. *Prof Exp:* Chemist, TNO Paint Res Inst, Delft Univ Technol, 54-62; res scientist, Delft Univ Technol, 62-66; staff scientist, Sci Res Staff, Ford Motor Co, 66-75; assoc prof chem eng, Univ Southern Calif, 75-79; mgr, Intermedics Intraocular Inc, 79-80; SR RES ASSOC, AVERY INT, 80- *Concurrent Pos:* Consult, self employed, 75-79. *Mem:* Am Chem Soc; Am Soc Rheol; Brit Soc Rheol; Am Inst Physics. *Res:* Viscoelasticity; rubberelasticity; composites; polymerization engineering; kinetics. *Mailing Add:* 6192 Point Loma Dr Huntington Beach CA 92647

CHON, CHOON TAIK, b Seoul, Korea, Oct 4, 46; m 71; c 1. SOLID MECHANICS, MECHANICAL ENGINEERING. *Educ:* Seoul Nat Univ, BSME, 70; Brown Univ, MS, 73, PhD(solid mech), 75. *Prof Exp:* Res assoc dynamic plasticity, Brown Univ, 75-76; assoc sr engr dynamic plasticity & mech composite mat, Gen Motors Res Labs, 76-78, sr res engr, 78-80, PRINC RES ENGR STRUCT DYNAMICS & MECH COMPOSITE MAT & COMPUT-AIDED ENG, FORD MOTOR RES STAFF, 80- *Mem:* Am Soc Mech Engrs; Am Acad Mech. *Res:* Structural dynamics for elastic-viscoplastic materials with large deformations; mechanics of composite materials, especially for fiber-reinforced plastics; computer-aided engineering. *Mailing Add:* Metall Dept PO Box 2053 Dearborn MI 48121

CHONACKY, NORMAN J, b Cleveland, Ohio, Oct 14, 39; m 64; c 2. PHYSICS. *Educ:* John Carroll Univ, BS, 61; Univ Wis, PhD(physics), 67. *Prof Exp:* Asst prof, 67-74, ASSOC PROF PHYSICS, SOUTHERN CONN STATE COL, 74- *Concurrent Pos:* Vis res scientist, Max Planck Inst Biophys Chem, Gottingen, W Ger, 77; vis instr physics, Univ Nebr-Lincoln. *Mem:* Am Asn Physics Teachers. *Res:* Physics of organic and biologically important materials, including water. *Mailing Add:* Dept of Physics Southern Conn State Col New Haven CT 06515

CHONG, BERNI PATRICIA, b West Palm Beach, Fla, Aug 29, 45; div; c 2. SYNTHETIC ORGANIC CHEMISTRY. *Educ:* Swarthmore Col, AB, 67; Univ Mich, PhD(org chem), 71. *Prof Exp:* Fel org chem, Cornell Univ, 71-72; fel org chem, Univ Calif, San Diego, 72-73; RES CHEMIST FLUID PROCESS CHEM, ROHM AND HAAS CO, 74- *Mem:* Am Chem Soc. *Res:* Synthesis of ion exchange resins and adsorbents. *Mailing Add:* Rohm and Haas Co Spring House PA 19477

CHONG, CALVIN, b Jamaica, Dec 12, 43; Can citizen; m 66; c 3. AGRICULTURE, HORTICULTURE. *Educ:* McGill Univ, BSc, 68, MSc, 70, PhD(hort), 72. *Prof Exp:* Res asst, Dept Hort, McGill Univ, 68-72, res assoc hort, 73-74; tech info officer, Info Div, Agr Can, 74, res scientist, Res Br, 74-77; asst prof, 77-80, ASSOC PROF, DEPT PLANT SCI, MCGILL UNIV, 80- *Concurrent Pos:* Assoc ed, Can J Plant Sci, 78-81. *Mem:* Int Plant Propagators' Soc; Int Asn Plant Tissue Cult; Agr Inst Can; Can Soc Hort Sci. *Res:* Physiology of ornamental and horticultural crops; clonal multiplication of woody species; tissue culture; nursery management; floricultural crops; naturaltoxicants (goitrogens) in vegetables of the cruciferae. *Mailing Add:* Dept Plant Sci Macdonald Col McGill Univ Ste-Anne-de-Bellevue PQ H9X 1C0 Can

CHONG, CLYDE HOK HEEN, b Honolulu, Hawaii, Mar 6, 33; m 64; c 3. ANALYTICAL CHEMISTRY, INORGANIC CHEMISTRY. *Educ:* Wabash Col, BA, 54; Mich State Univ, PhD(chem), 58. *Prof Exp:* Asst chem, Mich State Univ, 54-57; group leader develop, 61-68, RES SPECIALIST, MOUND LAB, 68- *Mem:* Am Chem Soc. *Res:* Some reactions and properties of tetralithium peroxydiphosphate tetrahydrate; nuclear chemistry. *Mailing Add:* Monsanto Res Corp Mound Facil Miamisburg OH 45342

CHONG, JOSHUA ANTHONY, b Kingston, Jamaica, May 15, 43; US citizen; m 68; c 2. SYNTHETIC ORGANIC CHEMISTRY. *Educ:* Univ Calif, Berkeley, BS, 67; Univ Mich, PhD(org chem), 71. *Prof Exp:* Fel org synthesis, Cornell Univ, 71-74; RES CHEMIST HEALTH PROD, ROHM AND HAAS CO, 74- *Mem:* Am Chem Soc. *Res:* Synthesis of physiologically active compounds; polymers and monomers synthesis. *Mailing Add:* Rohm and Haas Co Spring House PA 19477

CHONG, KEN PIN, b Linpin, China, Sept 22, 42; US citizen; m 67; c 2. STRUCTURAL ENGINEERING, SOLID MECHANICS. *Educ:* Cheng Kung Univ, Taiwan, BS, 64; Univ Mass, MS, 66; Princeton Univ, MSE, MA & PhD(struct & mech), 69. *Prof Exp:* Sr proj engr res & develop, Nat Steel Prod Co, Bldg Syst, Nat Steel Corp, 69-74; assoc prof, 74-79, PROF STRUCT & MECH, DEPT CIVIL & ARCHIT ENG, UNIV WYO, 79- *Concurrent Pos:* Lectr, Dept Civil Eng, Univ Houston, 72-74; prin investr energy res & develop admin, Dept of Energy, 76-; adv, Tech Adv Comt, Am Inst Timber Construct, 77-; hon prof, Univ Hong Kong, 81. *Honors & Awards:* Dow Outstanding Young Fac Award, Am Soc Eng Educ, 77. *Mem:* Am Soc Civil Engrs; Am Soc Eng Educ; Am Soc Mech Engrs; Am Acad Mech. *Res:* Solid mechanics and structural engineering; light-gage steel structures; composite structures; static and dynamic mechanical behavior of oil shale; author of over 100 technical papers and publications. *Mailing Add:* Dept of Civil & Archit Eng Univ of Wyo Laramie WY 82071

CHONG, SHUANG-LING, b Kiangtu, China, July 4, 43; US citizen; m 67; c 2. PHYSICAL CHEMISTRY, ORGANIC CHEMISTRY. *Educ:* Taiwan Nat Cheng Kung Univ, BS, 64; Rutgers Univ, MS, 66, PhD(phys chem), 69. *Prof Exp:* Fel, Rice Univ, 69-72; chemist, Energy Res & Develop Admin, 75-76; RES CHEMIST, DEPT ENERGY, 76- *Mem:* Am Chem Soc; Sigma Xi. *Res:* Research in gas phase photochemistry; ion-molecule reaction; fractionation and characterization of organic materials in oil shale. *Mailing Add:* Laramie Energy Technol Ctr Box 3395 Univ Sta Laramie WY 82071

CHOO, THIN-MEIW, b Tapah, Malaysia, May 15, 47; Can citizen; m 77. PLANT GENETICS, PLANT BREEDING. *Educ:* Nat Taiwan Univ, BSc, 71; McGill Univ, PhD(plant breeding), 76. *Prof Exp:* Res assoc, Dept Crop Sci, Univ Guelph, Ont, 76-78; RES SCIENTIST, RES STA, AGR CAN, 78- *Mem:* Crop Sci Soc Am; Am Soc Agron; Genetics Soc Can; Agr Inst Can. *Res:* Genetics and breeding of forage legumes. *Mailing Add:* Res Sta Agr Can PO Box 1210 Charlottetown PE C1A 7M8 Can

CHOONG, ELVIN T, b Jakarta, Indonesia, Oct 20, 32; US citizen; m 60; c 2. WOOD TECHNOLOGY, FORESTRY. *Educ:* Mont State Univ, BS, 56; Yale Univ, FM, 58; State Univ NY Col Forestry, Syracuse, PhD(wood technol), 62. *Prof Exp:* Instr wood sci & technol, State Univ NY Col Forestry, Syracuse, 61-63; asst prof, Humboldt State Col, 64-65; from asst prof to assoc prof, 65-73, prof forestry, 73-77, PROF FORESTRY & WILDLIFE MGT, LA STATE UNIV, 77- *Concurrent Pos:* Vis res fel, Commonwealth Sci & Indust Res Orgn, Australia, 72. *Mem:* Forest Prod Res Soc; Soc Wood Sci & Technol. *Res:* Physical and mechanical properties of wood and wood products; nondestructive testings of wood; wood drying and preservation; wood quality. *Mailing Add:* Sch of Forestry La State Univ Baton Rouge LA 70803

CHOONG, HSIA SHAW-LWAN, b China, July 12, 45; m 71; c 2. ORGANIC CHEMISTRY, POLYMER CHEMISTRY. *Educ:* Nat Taiwan Univ, BS, 66; Mass Inst Technol, PhD(chem), 71. *Prof Exp:* Teaching asst chem, Mass Inst Technol, 67-68, res asst, 68-71; sr chemist, Gen Foods Corp, 72-73; MEM TECH STAFF, HEWLETT PACKARD CO, 73- *Mem:* Am Chem Soc; Electrochem Soc; Sigma Xi. *Res:* Liquid crystals for displays and electronic devices; polymers for optical fiber coating and high resolution lithography; electron beam and x-ray lithography. *Mailing Add:* Hewlett Packard Co 1501 Page Mill Rd Palo Alto CA 94304

CHOPPIN, GREGORY ROBERT, b Eagle Lake, Tex, Nov 9, 27; m 51; c 4. INORGANIC CHEMISTRY, NUCLEAR CHEMISTRY. *Educ:* Loyola Univ La, BS, 49; Univ Tex, PhD(chem), 53; Loyola Univ, DSc, 69. *Prof Exp:* Mem staff, Radiation Lab, Univ Calif, 53-56; from asst prof to assoc prof, 56-63, chmn dept, 68-77, PROF CHEM, FLA STATE UNIV, 63- *Concurrent Pos:* Vis scientist, Ctr Study Nuclear Energy, Belgium, 62-63; Fulbright lectr, Uruguay, 65 & Portugal, 69; vis prof, Sci Univ Tokyo, 78; Alexander von Humboldt US sr scientist award, 79; vis scientist, Europ Tranuranium Inst, Karlsruhe, WGer, 79-80. *Mem:* AAAS; Am Chem Soc (chmn, Div Nuclear Chem Technol, 76). *Res:* Nuclear chemistry; physical chemistry of the actinides and lanthanides; environmental behavior of actinedes. *Mailing Add:* Dept Chem Fla State Univ Tallahassee FL 32306

CHOPPIN, PURNELL WHITTINGTON, b Baton Rouge, La, July 4, 29; m 59; c 1. VIROLOGY, INTERNAL MEDICINE. *Educ:* La State Univ, MD, 53; Am Bd Internal Med, dipl. *Prof Exp:* Intern ward med, Barnes Hosp & Sch Med, Wash Univ, 53-54, asst resident, 56-57; vis investr, 57-59, res assoc, 59-60, from asst prof to assoc prof, 60-70, PROF VIROL & MED, ROCKEFELLER UNIV, 70- *Concurrent Pos:* Nat Found fel, 57-59; asst physician, Rockefeller Univ Hosp, 57-60, res assoc physician, 60-62, from assoc physician to physician, 62-70, sr physician, 70-; mem virol study sect, NIH, 68-72, chmn, 75-78; mem, Nat Allergy & Infectious Dis Adv Coun, NIH, 80- *Mem:* Nat Acad Sci; Am Soc Microbiol; Am Soc Cell Biol; Am Asn Immunol; Am Soc Clin Invest; Asn Am Physicians. *Res:* Animal virology; myxoviruses and paramyxoviruses; virus multiplication, structure, and pathogenesis. *Mailing Add:* Rockefeller Univ New York NY 10021

CHOPRA, BALDEO K, b Multan, W Pakistan, Aug 10, 42; m 64; c 1. PLANT PATHOLOGY, MICROBIOLOGY. *Educ:* Benares Hindu Univ, BSc, 60, MSc, 62; Auburn Univ, PhD(plant path, microbiol), 68. *Prof Exp:* Res asst plant path, Univ Allahabad, 62-65; res asst, Auburn Univ, 65-68, tech res asst, 68-69; assoc prof biol, Prairie View Agr & Mech Col, 69-73; actg head dept, 76-77, ASSOC PROF BIOL, J C SMITH UNIV, 73- *Concurrent Pos:* Proj leader, USDA soybean study grant, Prairie View Agr & Mech Col, 69-72; proj dir, Minority Access Res Career Prog, 78-; prin investr, Minority Biomed Support Proj & Antimicrobiol Susceptibility Anal, 78-81 & A Comp Study Susceptibility Clin Isolates of Bacteria to Cefoxitin, Cefamandole & Cephalothin, 82- *Mem:* Am Phytopath Soc; Am Soc Microbiol. *Res:* Mycology; taxonomy of Aspergilli and Xylaria; interaction of pesticides and soil microflora; nutritional physiology of Fusarium and Aspergillus flavus. *Mailing Add:* 1023 Worthley Ct Charlotte NC 28211

CHOPRA, DEV RAJ, b Jullundur City, Punjab, Apr 14, 30; m 56; c 1. EXPERIMENTAL SOLID STATE PHYSICS, SURFACE PHYSICS. *Educ:* Punjab Univ, MS, 52; Univ Nebr, MA, 60; NMex State Univ, PhD(physics), 64. *Prof Exp:* Demonstr physics, Punjab Univ, 51-52, lectr, 52-58; asst, Univ Nebr, 58-60; res assoc, NMex State Univ, 60-64; assoc prof, 64-71, res grants, 66-68, 70-75, 77-80, PROF PHYSICS, EAST TEX STATE UNIV, 71- *Concurrent Pos:* Prin investr, East Tex State Univ res award, 70-80 & Robert A Welch Found, 76-82; consult surface sci, mat characterization & nondestructive eval, 79-81. *Mem:* Am Asn Physics Teachers; Am Phys Soc; Sigma Xi; Am Vacuum Soc. *Res:* Soft x-ray spectroscopy; valence band studies of transition and rare-earth elements using photo-absorption and appearance potential spectroscopy techniques; nondestructive evaluation; material characterization of solid surfaces; author of several technical publications. *Mailing Add:* Dept of Physics East Tex State Univ Commerce TX 75428

CHOPRA, DHARAM PAL, b India, Feb 2, 44; m 68; c 1. CELL BIOLOGY. *Educ:* Univ Delhi, BS, 63; Univ London, MS, 67; Univ Newcastle, Eng, PhD(cell biol, path), 71. *Prof Exp:* Res assoc cellular develop biol, Univ Newcastle, Eng, 67-71; asst prof dermat, Skin & Cancer Hosp, Temple Univ, 71-74; SR SCIENTIST CELL BIOL, SOUTHERN RES INST, 74- *Concurrent Pos:* Nat Cancer Inst & Nat Inst Arthritis & Metab Dis grant, Temple Univ, 71-72. *Mem:* AAAS; Soc Invest Dermat; Tissue Cult Asn; Am Asn Cell Biol; Am Asn Cancer Res. *Res:* Regulation of growth and differentiation in normal and neoplastic tissues. *Mailing Add:* Kettering-Meyer Lab Southern Res Inst PO Box 3307-A Birmingham AL 35255

CHOPRA, DHARAM-VIR, b Jullundur, India, Oct 15, 30; m 69. STATISTICS, MATHEMATICS. *Educ:* Panjab Univ, MA, 53; Univ Mich, MS, 61, MA, 63; Univ Nebr, PhD(statist), 68. *Prof Exp:* Lectr math, DAV Col, India, 53-59; instr, Univ Nebr, 63-66; asst prof, SC State Col, 66-67; asst prof, 67-71, assoc prof, 71-77. PROF MATH, WICHITA STATE UNIV, 77- *Concurrent Pos:* Statist consult dent sch, Univ Nebr, 64-65. *Mem:* Am Statist Asn; Inst Math Statist; Indian Math Soc; Int Asn Surv Statisticians; Indian Statist Asn. *Res:* Design of experiments and their analysis; combinatorial mathematics; application of statistics to social sciences; psychology. *Mailing Add:* Dept of Math Wichita State Univ Wichita KS 67208

CHOPRA, INDER JIT, b Gujranwala, India, Dec 15, 39; m 66; c 3. ENDOCRINOLOGY, INTERNAL MEDICINE. *Educ:* All India Inst Med Sci, New Delhi, MB, BS, 61, MD, 65; Am Bd Internal Med, dipl, 72, cert endocrinol, 73. *Prof Exp:* Intern, All India Inst Med Sci, New Delhi, 62, resident med, 63-65; res officer, Indian Coun Med Res, New Delhi, 66; registr med, All India Inst Med Sci, 66-67; resident med, Queen's Med Ctr, Honolulu, Hawaii, 67-68; fel endocrinol, Harbor Gen Hosp, Sch Med, Univ Calif, Los Angeles, Torrance, 68-71; from asst prof to assoc prof, 71-78, PROF MED, SCH MED, UNIV CALIF, LOS ANGELES, 78- *Concurrent Pos:* Staff physician, Harbor Gen Hosp, Torrance, 71-72 & Ctr Health Sci, Univ Calif, Los Angeles, 72-; NIH res career develop award, 72-77 & grant, 72- *Mem:* Sigma Xi; Am Soc Clin Invest; Am Thyroid Asn; Endocrine Soc; fel Am Col Physicians. *Res:* Thyroid physiology and disease; nature of biologically active thyroid hormones, thyroid hormone metabolism, pathogenesis of Graves' disease, nature of thyroid stimulators, radioimmunoassay, pituitary-thyroid axis. *Mailing Add:* Dept of Med Ctr Health Sci Univ of Calif Sch of Med Los Angeles CA 90024

CHOPRA, JOGINDER GURBUX, b Punjab, India, June 3, 32; US citizen. PEDIATRICS, PUBLIC HEALTH. *Educ:* Univ Bombay, MS, 54; Columbia Univ, MPH & MS(nutrit), 61. *Prof Exp:* Resident physician pediat med, NY Polyclin Med Sch & Hosp, 57-58; fel nutrit & metab dis, Tulane Univ, 58-59; adv nutrit, Pan Am Health Org, WHO, 61-67, reg adv nutrit res, 68-73; act dir nutrit, 73-74, SPEC ASST MED, BUR FOODS, FOOD & DRUG ADMIN, 75- *Concurrent Pos:* Assoc prof clin pediat, George Washington Univ & Georgetown Univ, 70-; consult, Food & Nutrit Bd, Comt Int Nutrit Prog, Subcomt Nutrit & Fertil, Washington, DC & Comt Res, George Washington Univ Med Ctr, 73-74. *Mem:* Am Soc Clin Nutrit; Am Acad Pediat; Am Pub Health Asn; Brit Med Asn. *Mailing Add:* Food & Drug Admin 200 C St SW Washington DC 20204

CHOPRA, KULDIP P, b Srinagar, Kashmir, Mar 25, 32; m 68. ENVIRONMETNAL PHYSICS, SPACE PHYSICS. *Educ:* Univ Delhi, BSc, 51, MSc, 53, PhD(physics), 60. *Prof Exp:* Res assoc & res asst, Univ Md, 57-58; vis asst prof physics & res scientist, Univ Southern Calif, 58-60; res asst prof astronaut, Polytech Inst Brooklyn, 60-63; sr scientist, Melpar Inc, 63-65, head space physics, 64-65; assoc prof atmospheric sci, Univ Miami, 65-67; prof appl physics, Nova Univ, 67-69; PROF PHYSICS, OLD DOM UNIV, 69- *Concurrent Pos:* Vis prof, Va Inst Marine Sci, 71-; sci consult, NASA Wallops Flight Ctr, 75-; sci adv to gov, 76-77; ed-in-chief, Va J Sci, 78- *Honors & Awards:* Melpar Award, 64. *Mem:* AAAS; fel Am Inst Physics; Am Inst Aeronaut & Astronaut; Am Geophys Union; Am Meteorol Soc. *Res:* Cosmical magnetism; space vehicles in ionized media; plasma physics and magneto-fluidynamics; low speed aerodynamics; mesometeorology; mathematical physics; urban coastal environment, atmospheric and oceanic flow problems caused by islands. *Mailing Add:* Dept of Physics Old Dom Univ PO Box 6173 Norfolk VA 23508

CHOPRA, NAITER MOHAN, b Amritsar, India, Nov 23, 23; US citizen; m 53; c 4. ORGANIC CHEMISTRY. *Educ:* Punjab Univ, Lahore, BSc, 44, MSc, 45; Trinity Col, Dublin, PhD(chem), 55. *Prof Exp:* Demonstr chem, Forman Christian Col, Lahore, 46-47; asst lectr, Allahabad Agr Inst, India, 47-49; res fel, Univ Toronto, 55-57; res officer, Can Dept Agr Res Sta, Man, 57-65; assoc prof chem, 65-67, PROF CHEM, NC AGR & TECH STATE UNIV, 67-, DIR TOBACCO RES PROJ, 67- *Concurrent Pos:* Dir & prin investr, US Dept Agr grants, 72-77, 78-81 & 79- *Mem:* Am Chem Soc; Chem Inst Can; Nat Geog Sci. *Res:* Chemistry of wheat rust and pesticides; chemistry of viricides and antibiotics which could be employed in cure of cereal disease; breakdown of pesticides in tobacco and cigaret smokes. *Mailing Add:* Dept of Chem NC Agr & Tech State Univ Greensboro NC 27411

CHOQUETTE, PHILIP WHEELER, b Utica, NY, Aug 16, 30; m 59; c 2. GEOLOGY. *Educ:* Allegheny Col, BS, 52; Johns Hopkins Univ, MA, 54, PhD(geol), 57. *Prof Exp:* Geologist, US Geol Surv, 56-58; from res geologist to adv res geologist, 58-72, SR RES GEOLOGIST, MARATHON OIL CO, 72- *Concurrent Pos:* Assoc ed, J Sedimentary Petrol, 78- & Geol Soc Am Bulletin, 78-80. *Mem:* Fel AAAS; fel Geol Soc Am; Am Asn Petrol Geologists; Soc Econ Paleontologists & Mineralogists; Am Inst Prof Geologists. *Res:* Physical stratigraphy, petrology and geochemistry of sedimentary carbonate rocks; diagenesis and porosity in limestones and dolomites. *Mailing Add:* Denver Res Ctr Marathon Oil Co PO Box 269 Littleton CO 80160

CHORPENNING, FRANK WINSLOW, b Marietta, Ohio, Aug 17, 13; m 42; c 4. IMMUNOLOGY, MICROBIOLOGY. *Educ:* Marietta Col, AB, 39; Ohio State Univ, MSc, 50, PhD(microbiol), 63. *Prof Exp:* Admin asst typhus comn, US Army, Philippines & Japan, 45-46, bacteriologist, 4th Army Area Lab, 48-49; serologist & dir blood bank, Med Lab, Ger, 52-55; chief clin path & dir blood bank, Brooke Army Hosp, 55-61; from asst prof to prof, 63-81, EMER PROF MICROBIOL & IMMUNOL, OHIO STATE UNIV, 81- *Concurrent Pos:* Mem coop study group, WHO, 53-55. *Mem:* Sigma Xi; fel Am Acad Microbiol; Am Soc Microbiol; Am Asn Immunol; Asn for Genotobiotics. *Res:* Mechanisms and development of immune responses; immunochemical specificity of bacterial antigens. *Mailing Add:* Dept Microbiol Ohio State Univ 484 W 12th Ave Columbus OH 43210

CHORVAT, ROBERT JOHN, b Chicago, Ill, Aug 16, 42; m 64; c 3. MEDICINAL CHEMISTRY. *Educ:* Ill Benedictine Col, BS, 64; Ill Inst Technol, PhD(org Chem), 68. *Prof Exp:* Sr res investr, 68-74, res scientist I, 74-79, res scientist II, 79-81, SR RES SCIENTIST, G D SEARLE & CO, 81- *Mem:* Am Chem Soc. *Res:* Four-membered, single phosphorus atom heterocycles; synthesis; chemistry; physical properties; synthesis of steroids and nucleo-hetero steroids; synthesis of pyridone heterocycles; oxygenated sterol synthesis; mevalonolactone derivatives; small peptide/synthesis. *Mailing Add:* G D Searle & Co PO Box 5110 Chicago IL 60680

CHOSY, JULIUS J, internal medicine, psychosomatic medicine, see previous edition

CHOU, ALBERT CHUNG-HO, b Hainan, China, Mar 14, 43; m 70; c 1. BIOCHEMISTRY, HEMATOLOGY. *Educ:* Nat Taiwan Univ, BS, 66; WVa Univ, MS, 69; Mich State Univ, PhD(biochem), 73. *Prof Exp:* Res assoc biochem, Mich State Univ, 73-74; res assoc hemat, Sch Med, St Louis Univ, 75-78, res asst prof hemat & biochem, 78-80; ASST PROF, DEPT NUTRIT, SCH PUB HEALTH & TROPIC MED, TULANE UNIV, 80-; ASST DIR, RES DEPT, TOURO INFIRMARY, NEW ORLEANS, 81- *Mem:* Sigma Xi; Fedn Clin Res. *Res:* Role of oxidized heme in hemolytic anemia; role of vitamin E in iron metabolism; purification and characterization of enzyme; drug receptors in malaria-infected animals. *Mailing Add:* Dept Nutrit Sch Pub Health & Tropic Med Tulane Univ New Orleans LA 70112

CHOU, CHEN-LIN, b Kiangsu, China, Oct 8, 43; m 70; c 2. GEOCHEMISTRY, COAL GEOLOGY. *Educ:* Nat Taiwan Univ, BS, 65; Univ Pittsburgh, PhD(geochem), 71. *Prof Exp:* Scholar geochem, Univ Calif, Los Angeles, 71-72, asst res geochemist, 72-75; sr res assoc geol, Univ Toronto, 75-76, asst prof geol, 76-79; fel geol, McMaster Univ, 79-80; ASST GEOLOGIST, ILL STATE GEOL SURV, 80- *Concurrent Pos:* Lectr earth sci, Calif State Univ, Fullerton, 73-74; mem, Assoc Comt on Meteorites, Can Nat Res Coun, 78-80. *Mem:* Geochem Soc; Meteoritical Soc; Am Geophys Union; Geol Soc Am; Mineral Soc. *Res:* Geochemistry of earth's crust and mantle, lunar samples, meteorites and coal; neutron activation analysis. *Mailing Add:* Ill State Geol Surv 615 E Peabody Dr Champaign IL 61820

CHOU, CHING, b Szechwan, China, Oct 23, 41; US citizen; m 68; c 2. ABSTRACT HARMONIC ANALYSIS. *Educ:* Nat Taiwan Univ, BA, 63; Univ Rochester, PhD(math), 67. *Prof Exp:* Asst prof, 67-72, ASSOC PROF MATH, STATE UNIV NY, BUFFALO, 72- *Mem:* Am Math Soc. *Res:* Abstract harmonic analysis on locally compact groups, especially inveriant means, weakly almost periodic functions; Fourier algebras and Von Neumann algebras of locally compact groups. *Mailing Add:* Dept Math State Univ NY Buffalo NY 14214

CHOU, CHING-CHUNG, b Taipei, Taiwan, June 25, 32; m 62; c 3. PHYSIOLOGY, INTERNAL MEDICINE. *Educ:* Nat Taiwan Univ, BM, 58; Northwestern Univ, MS, 64; Univ Okla, PhD(physiol), 66. *Prof Exp:* Intern, Nat Taiwan Univ Hosp, Taipei, 57-58; resident radiol, Chinese Air Force Gen Hosp, 59-60; intern, Washington Hosp Ctr, DC, 60-61; resident internal med, Northwestern Univ, 61-64; instr physiol, Univ Okla, 65-66; from asst prof to assoc prof, 66-73, PROF PHYSIOL & MED, MICH STATE UNIV, 73- *Concurrent Pos:* Pres, Splanchnic Circulation Group, 79- *Mem:* Am Fedn Clin Res; Cent Soc Clin Res; Am Physiol Soc; Am Gastroenterol Asn; fel Am Heart Asn. *Res:* Gastroenterology; gastrointestinal physiology; cardiovascular physiology. *Mailing Add:* Dept Physiol Mich State Univ East Lansing MI 48824

CHOU, CHUNG-CHI, b Taiwan, Dec 24, 36; US citizen; m 61; c 3. PHYSICAL CHEMISTRY, CHEMICAL ENGINEERING. *Educ:* Chen-Kung Univ, BS, 59; Baylor Univ, PhD(phys chem), 68. *Prof Exp:* Process supt, Taiwan Sugar Corp, 59-65; teaching asst, Baylor Univ, 65-68; res assoc res & develop, Amstar Corp, 68-72, mgr, Opers Lab, 72-75, mgr process develop, 75-81, MGR TECH DIV, AM SUGAR DIV, AMSTAR CORP, 81- *Concurrent Pos:* Mem exec comt, US Nat Comt Sugar Anal, 78-; referee, Int Comn Uniform Method Sugar Anal, 78-; mem bd dir, Sugar Processing Res Inst, 81- & NT Sugar Trade Lab,, Inc, 81- *Honors & Awards:* George & Eleanore Meade Award, Sugar Indust Technologists, 71 & 78. *Mem:* Sigma Xi; Am Chem Soc; Sugar Indust Technologists. *Res:* Thermal energy utilization improvement in unit operations; application of interfaces physical chemical principles to process design and development; analytical method development for sugar analysis and process control. *Mailing Add:* Amstar Corp 1251 Ave of Americas New York NY 10021

CHOU, CHUNG-KWANG, b Chung-King, China, May 11, 46; US citizen; m 73; c 2. BIOELECTROMAGNETICS. *Educ:* Nat Taiwan Univ, BSEE, 68; Washington Univ, MS, 71; Univ Wash, PhD(elec eng & physiol), 75. *Prof Exp:* Res trainee, Dept Elec Eng, Washington Univ, 69-70, teaching asst, 70-71; res asst, Dept Rehab Med, 71-75, res assoc, 76, fel, Dept Physiol & Biophysics, Regional Primate Res Ctr, 76-77, asst prof, 77-81, RES ASSOC PROF, DEPT REHAB MED & CTR BIOENG & ASSOC DIR, BIOELECTROMAGNETICS RES LAB, DEPT REHAB MED, UNIV WASH, 81- *Concurrent Pos:* Consult, Nat Coun Radiation Protection & Measurement, 78- *Honors & Awards:* Special Decade Award, Int Microwave Power Inst, 81. *Mem:* Inst Elec & Electronic Engrs; Bioelectromagnetics Soc; Int Microwave Power Inst. *Res:* Study the biological effects of microwave radiation, especially on the nervous system and cardiovascular system; develop methods for cancer hyperthermia treatment in combination with radiation and chemotherapy. *Mailing Add:* Bioelectromagnetics Res Lab BB805 Univ Hosp RJ 30 Univ Wash Seattle WA 98055

CHOU, DAVID YUAN PIN, b Shantung, China, Mar 5, 22; US citizen; m 53; c 3. PHYSICAL CHEMISTRY. *Educ:* Tokyo Inst Technol, BE, 48; Ohio State Univ, PhD(soil chem), 54. *Prof Exp:* Assoc prof chem, St Augustine's Col, 54-56; GLENN FRYE PROF CHEM & HEAD DEPT, LENOIR RHYNE COL, 56- *Concurrent Pos:* Am Chem Soc Petrol Res Fund fac award advan sci study, 63; res fel, Univ Kans, 64-65. *Honors & Awards:* R M Bost Distinguished Prof Award, 71. *Mem:* AAAS; Am Chem Soc; fel Am Inst Chem. *Res:* Nonaqueous solvents; phase equilibria; colloidal properties of silicates. *Mailing Add:* 768 Eighth St N E Hickory NC 28601

CHOU, DORTHY T C T, b Taiwan, Feb 6, 40; m 65; c 2. NEUROPHARMACOLOGY. *Educ:* Nat Taiwan Univ, Taipei, BS, 62, MS, 64; Columbia Univ, New York, PhD(pharmacol), 71. *Prof Exp:* Res fel, Dept Pathobiol, Sch Hyg & Pub Health, Johns Hopkins Univ, Baltimore, 71-72; res assoc, Dept Pharmacol, Col Physicians & Surgeons, Columbia Univ, New York, 72-76; proj specialist, 76-79, RES SPECIALIST, DEPT PHYSIOL & PHARMACOL, GEN FOODS CORP TECH CTR, CRANBURY, NJ, 79- *Concurrent Pos:* Adj asst prof, Dept Pharmacol, NY Med Col, Valhalla, 76-81. *Mem:* Soc Neurosci; Am Soc Pharmacol & Exp Therapeut; AAAS; NY Acad Sci. *Res:* Neurochemical and electrophysiological techniques to study the mechanism and sites of foods or food components' effects on the central nervous system. *Mailing Add:* Gen Foods Corp Tech Ctr Prospect Plains Rd Cranbury NJ 08512

CHOU, JAMES C S, b Kiangsu, China, Jan 13, 20; US citizen; m 48; c 2. MECHANICAL ENGINEERING. *Educ:* Nat Inst Technol, China, BS, 41; Ga Inst Technol, MS, 49; Okla State Univ, PhD(mech eng), 68. *Prof Exp:* Gen design engr, Hawaiian Commercial & Sugar Co, 51-57; partner, Zuckermann & Chou, 58-59; from asst prof to assoc prof mech eng, 60-70, PROF MECH ENG, UNIV HAWAII, 70- *Mem:* Am Soc Mech Engrs; Am Soc Eng Educ. *Res:* Thermal properties of sea water. *Mailing Add:* 3232 Ahinahina Pl Honolulu HI 96822

CHOU, LARRY I-HUI, b Hunan Province, China, May 5, 36; m; c 1. SOLID MECHANICS, FLUID MECHANICS. *Educ:* Cheng Kung Univ, Taiwan, BS, 58; Colo State Univ, MS, 63; Univ Utah, PhD(civil eng), 79. *Prof Exp:* Anal engr stress, Clark Brothers Co, New York, 66-68; res engr shell stress, Metal Indust Res Inst, Taiwan, 69-72; ENGR, NUCLEAR POWER PLANT, BECHTEL POWER CO, 80- *Res:* Stress analysis in a conical shell theory and technics; prediction of viscoelastic pavement roughness growth. *Mailing Add:* 3343 Puente Ave Baldwin Park CA 91706

CHOU, LIBBY WANG, b China; US citizen; m 63; c 1. ORGANIC CHEMISTRY. *Educ:* Brooklyn Col, BS, 60; Univ Ill, MA, 62; Wayne State Univ, PhD(org chem), 67. *Prof Exp:* PROF CHEM, ALA A&M UNIV, 67- *Mem:* Am Chem Soc. *Res:* Natural products; isolation and identification of compounds from Chinese medicinal herbs. *Mailing Add:* Dept of Chem Ala A&M Univ Normal AL 35762

CHOU, MEI-IN MELISSA LIU, b Taiwan, Oct 4, 47; m 71; c 1. ORGANOMETALLIC CHEMISTRY & ANALYTICAL CHEMISTRY. *Educ:* Nat Taiwan Normal Univ, BS, 70; Mich State Univ, PhD(chem), 77. *Prof Exp:* Asst, Mich State Univ, 73-74, res asst organometallic chem, 74-77; res asoc hydrocarbon shale & coal, Ill State Geol Surv, 78-80; ASST ORGANIC CHEMIST, DEPT ENERGY & NAT RESOURCES, ILL INST, 80- *Mem:* Am Chem Soc. *Mailing Add:* 371 Natural Resource Bldg Ill Inst Dept Energy & Natural Resource Champaign IL 61820

CHOU, PEI CHI (PETER), b China, Dec 1, 24; nat US; m 56; c 4. ENGINEERING, MECHANICS. *Educ:* Nat Cent Univ, China, BS, 46; Harvard Univ, MS, 49; NY Univ, PhD(aeronaut eng), 51. *Prof Exp:* Asst, NY Univ, 49-51; designer, Devenco Inc, 51-52; aerodynamicist, Repub Aviation Corp, 52-53; from asst prof to prof aerospace eng, 53-73, dir wave propagation res ctr, 67-73, chmn mech & struct advan study group, 69-73, J HARLAND BILLINGS PROF AEROSPACE ENG, DREXEL UNIV, 73- *Concurrent Pos:* Sr stress analyst, Budd Co, 55-57; dynamicist, Prewitt Aircraft Corp, 57-58; staff res scientist, Kellet Aircraft Co, 58-62; consult, Alleghany Ballistics Lab, 61-63, Air Force Mat Lab, 66-, Army Ballistic Res Labs, 70-71 & Dyna East Corp, 71- *Mem:* Am Soc Mech Engrs; Am Inst Aeronaut & Astronaut; Am Soc Eng Educ; Am Acad Mech; Am Defense Prep Asn. *Res:* Elasticity and plasticity; rotary wing aircraft; impacts; continuum mechanics; wave propagation; structural dynamics; mechanics of composite materials; explosive-metal interaction; material fatigue; mechanical reliability. *Mailing Add:* Dept of Mech Eng & Mech 32nd & Chestnut Sts Philadelphia PA 19104

CHOU, SHELLEY NIEN-CHUN, b Chekiang, China, Feb 6, 24; nat US; m 56; c 3. NEUROSURGERY. *Educ:* St John's Univ, China, BS, 46; Univ Utah, MD, 49; Univ Minn, MS, 54, PhD, 64. *Prof Exp:* Intern, Providence Hosp, 49-50; univ fel, Univ Minn, 50-53, res fel, 53-55, AEC grant, 54-55; clin asst neurosurg, Univ Utah, 56-58; vis scientist, NIH, 59-60; from instr to assoc prof, 60-68, PROF NEUROSURG, MED SCH, UNIV MINNEAPOLIS, 68-, HEAD DEPT, 74- *Concurrent Pos:* Mem, Am Bd Neurol Surg, 74- *Mem:* Soc Neurol Surg; Am Col Surg; Soc Nuclear Med; Neurosurg Soc Am; Am Acad Neurol Surg. *Res:* Experimental neurosurgery and neurophysiology; isotopic tracer investigation in neurophysiology. *Mailing Add:* Dept of Neurosurg Univ of Minn Med Sch Minneapolis MN 55455

CHOU, TING-CHAO, b Taiwan, Sept 9, 38; nat US; m 65; c 2. PHARMACOLOGY, CHEMOTHERAPHY. *Educ:* Kaohsiung Med Col, Taiwan, BS, 61; Nat Taiwan Univ, MS, 65; Yale Univ, PhD(pharmacol), 70. *Prof Exp:* Teaching asst pharmacol, Col Med, Nat Taiwan Univ, 64-65; res asst, Yale Univ, 65; fel, Sch Med, Johns Hopkins Univ, 69-72; assoc pharmacol, 72-78, ASSOC MEM, SLOAN-KETTERING INST CANCER RES, 79-; asst prof, 73-78, ASSOC PROF PHARMACOL, SLOAN-KETTERING DIV, GRAD SCH MED SCI, CORNELL UNIV, 79- *Mem:* AAAS; Am Asn Cancer Res; Am Soc Pharmacol Exp Therapeut; Am Soc Prev Oncol; Am Soc Biol Chem. *Res:* Pharmacology and biochemistry of cancer chemotherapeutic agents; enzyme kinetics; theoretical biology of dose-effect relationships. *Mailing Add:* Sloan-Kettering Inst Cancer Res Lab Pharmacol 1275 York Ave New York NY 10021

CHOU, TSONG-WEN, b Tokyo, Japan, Feb 10, 33; US citizen; m 58; c 4. FERMENTATION, ENVIRONMENTAL SCIENCE. *Educ:* Nat Taiwan Univ, BS, 55; Utah State Univ, PhD(food sci & technol), 70. *Prof Exp:* Res assoc, Wei-Chaun Foods Co, 59-64, Mass Inst Technol, 69-70; res biochemist, Univ Calif, Davis, 71-72; sr microbiologist, Rachelle Labs, Inc, 72-75; SR MICROBIOLOGIST & BIOCHEMIST, SRI INT, 75- *Mem:* Am Chem Soc; Am Soc Microbiologists; Soc Indust Microbiol. *Res:* Biotechnology; fermentation technology; enzyme technology; biodegradation of chemicals; microbial physiology and genetics; food science; environmental science. *Mailing Add:* Life Sci SRI Int Menlo Park CA 94025

CHOU, TSU-TEH, b Shanghai, China, Mar 10, 34; m 73. ELEMENTARY PARTICLE PHYSICS, HIGH ENERGY PHYSICS. *Educ:* Nat Taiwan Univ, BS, 56; Tsing Hua Univ, MS, 58; Univ Iowa, PhD, 65. *Prof Exp:* Res assoc, State Univ NY Stony Brook, 65-70; asst prof physics, Univ Denver, 70-74; asst prof, 74-77, ASSOC PROF PHYSICS, UNIV GA, 77- *Mem:* Am Phys Soc. *Mailing Add:* Dept Physics Univ Ga Athens GA 30602

CHOU, TSU-WEI, b Shanghai, China, June 2, 40; m 68; c 1. METALLURGY, SOLID MECHANICS. *Educ:* Nat Taiwan Univ, BS, 63; Northwestern Univ, MS, 66; Stanford Univ, PhD(mat sci), 69. *Prof Exp:* Res assoc, Mat Res Ctr, Allied Chem Corp, 69; from asst prof to assoc prof mech eng, 69-78, PROF MECH ENG, UNIV DEL, 78- *Concurrent Pos:* Frederick Gardner Cottrell fel, 70-71; vis scientist, Argonne Nat Lab, 75-76; sr vis res fel, Brit Sci Res Coun, 76; vis prof, Univ Witwatersrand, SAfrica, 77 & Comt Nat Invest Sci & Technol, Argentina, 81. *Mem:* Am Soc Metals. *Res:* Fiber composite materials; crystal defect theory; fracture and wear of materials; elasticity; plasticity; microbiomechanics. *Mailing Add:* Dept Mech & Aerospace Eng Univ Del Newark DE 19711

CHOU, TZI SHAN, b Taipei, Mar 21, 42; m 69; c 3. PHYSICAL CHEMISTRY, NUCLEAR PHYSICS. *Educ:* Nat Taiwan Univ, BS, 64; Univ SC, MS, 68; Univ Calif, Berkeley, PhD(nuclear chem), 74. *Prof Exp:* Asst gen chem, Nat Taiwan Univ, 65-66; res asst comput, Univ SC, 66-68; res asst low temp, Univ Calif, Lawrence Berkeley Lab, 68-74; res assoc x-ray photoelectron, 74-76, assoc chemist fustion vacuum, 76-78, ACTG HEAD INTERSECTING STORAGE ACCELERATOR, BROOKHAVEN NAT LAB, 81- *Res:* Surface chemistry of fusion reactor environment; ultra high vacuum technology in accelerator; structure of matter; beam profile instrumentation for storage ring. *Mailing Add:* Bldg 902 Brookhaven Nat Lab Upton NY 11973

CHOU, WUSHOW, b Shanghai, China, Feb 12, 39; m 65. COMPUTER SCIENCE, ELECTRICAL ENGINEERING. *Educ:* Chen Kung Univ, Taiwan, BS, 61; Univ NMex, MS, 65; Univ Calif, Berkeley, PhD(elec eng), 68. *Prof Exp:* Asst elec eng, Univ NMex, 63-65; asst elec eng, Univ Calif, Berkeley, 66-67, teaching fel, 67-68, actg asst prof, 68-69; sr tech staff mem, Network Anal Corp, 69-71, vpres telecommun, 71-75; PROF COMPUT SCI & ELEC ENG & DIR COMPUT STUDIES, NC STATE UNIV, 76- *Concurrent Pos:* Vis prof, State Univ NY, Stony Brook, 76; consult, Page Commun Eng, 76-; pres, ACK Comput Appln, Inc, 77-; gen chmn, 7th Data Com Symp, 79-81; tech prog chmn, 6th Data Com Symp, 77-79; ed in chief, J Telecommunication Networks, 82- *Mem:* Asn Comput Mach; Inst Elec & Electronics Engrs. *Res:* Computer communications; network analysis and optimization; computer performance evaluation. *Mailing Add:* Comput Studies Prog PO Box 5490 Raleigh NC 27650

CHOU, Y(E) T(SANG), b Kingsu, China, Mar 20, 24; US citizen; m 58; c 2. METALLURGY, MATERIALS SCIENCE. *Educ:* Nat Chungking Univ, BS, 45; Carnegie Inst Technol, MS, 54, PhD(math), 57. *Prof Exp:* Jr res metallurgist, Metals Res Lab, Carnegie Inst Technol, 52-54, proj mathematician, 56-57; scientist, Edgar C Bain Lab for Fundamental Res, US Steel Corp, 57-62, supvr scientist, 62-64, sr scientist, 65-68; vis assoc prof, Brown Univ, 64-65; assoc prof metall & mat sci, 68-70, PROF METALL & MAT SCI, LEHIGH UNIV, 70- *Concurrent Pos:* US Steel Corp fel, Cambridge Univ, 60-61; vis prof, Mass Inst Technol, 75-76. *Mem:* Am Soc Metals; Metall Soc Am; Phys Soc. *Res:* Mechanical properties of metals; flow and fracture of metals; theory of dislocations; superconductivity. *Mailing Add:* Dept of Metall & Mat Eng Lehigh Univ Bethlehem PA 18015

CHOUDARY, JASTI BHASKARARAO, b Jalipudi, India, Jan 15, 33; m 73; c 4. REPRODUCTIVE PHYSIOLOGY, ENDOCRINOLOGY. *Educ:* Madras Vet Col, BVSc, 54; Kans State Univ, MS, 64, PhD, 66. *Prof Exp:* Vet surgeon, India, 54-61; res asst reproductive physiol, Kans State Univ, 63-66; Ford Found fel, Univ Kans Med Ctr, Kansas City, 66-68; sect head reproductive physiol, William S Merrell Co Div, Richardson-Merrell, Inc, 68-71; RES SCIENTIST ENDOCRINOL & METAB REGULATION, G D SEARLE & CO, 71- *Mem:* Soc Study Reproduction; Endocrine Soc; Am Fertil Soc; Am Asn Anat; NY Acad Sci. *Res:* In vitro storage of spermatozoa; pituitary-ovarian relationships; ovarian follicular development and atresia; luteotropic mechanisms; luteolytic mechanisms; control of fertility; drugs; endocrinology of pregnancy; biology of gonadal steroids; biosynthesis of progesterone; radioimmunoassays of steroid hormones; slow-reacting substance anaphylaxis and leukotriene antagonism. *Mailing Add:* Searle Labs PO Box 5110 Chicago IL 60680

CHOUDHURY, ABDUL LATIF, b Dacca, Bangladesh, Jan 1, 33; m 60; c 2. THEORETICAL HIGH ENERGY PHYSICS. *Educ:* Univ Dacca, BS, 53, MS, 54; Free Univ Berlin, PhD(theoret physics), 60. *Prof Exp:* Asst to prof physics, Univ Dacca, 55, sr lectr, 61-66 & 68, reader, 69; asst to prof theoret physics, Free Univ Berlin, 58-60; res fel, Fritz-Haber Inst Ger, 60; Brit Coun-Colombo Plan res asst, Imp Col, Univ London, 60-61; consult, Nat Bur Standards-Univ Dacca proj, 63-66; assoc prof, 66-73, PROF PHYSICS & MATH, ELIZABETH CITY STATE UNIV, 73- *Concurrent Pos:* Vis physicist, Int Ctr Theoret Physics, Italy, 68. *Mem:* Am Phys Soc; Am Asn Univ Prof. *Res:* Quantum field theory; atomic physics; symmetry principles and group theoretical approach to particle physics; magnetic properties of the proposed charmed particles. *Mailing Add:* Dept of Phys Sci & Math Box 287 Elizabeth City State Univ Elizabeth City NC 27909

CHOUDHURY, DEO C, b Darbhanga, India, Feb 1, 26; m 63; c 1. NUCLEAR PHYSICS. *Educ:* Univ Calcutta, BS, 44, MS, 46; Univ Calif, Los Angeles, PhD(physics), 59. *Prof Exp:* Asst physics, Univ Rochester, 55-56 & Univ Calif, Los Angeles, 56-59; asst prof, Univ Conn, 59-62; assoc prof, 62-67, PROF PHYSICS, POLYTECH INST NY, 67- *Concurrent Pos:* Sabbatical leave, Niels Bohr Inst, Copenhagen, 78-79. *Mem:* Am Phys Soc; NY Acad Sci; Indian Phys Soc. *Res:* Theoretical investigations of nuclear structure and reactions; theory of B-decay; theory of strong interactions in nuclear physics; theory of high energy nuclear scattering. *Mailing Add:* Dept Physics Polytech Inst NY 333 Jay St Brooklyn NY 11201

CHOUDHURY, P ROY, b Calcutta, India, Aug 27, 30. MECHANICAL ENGINEERING. *Educ:* Univ Wash, BS, 51, BS, 52, MS, 53; Northwestern Univ, PhD(mech eng), 58. *Prof Exp:* Instr mech eng, Northwestern Univ, 56-58; asst prof, 58-76, ASSOC PROF MECH ENG, UNIV SOUTHERN CALIF, 76- *Res:* Thermodynamics of combustion phenomena and aerothermochemistry; heat transfer. *Mailing Add:* Dept of Mech Eng Univ of Southern Calif Los Angeles CA 90007

CHOUDRY, AMAR, nuclear physics, see previous edition

CHOUINARD, LEO GEORGE, II, b Waterbury, Conn, Oct 18, 49. COMMUTATIVE SEMIGROUP RINGS, COMBINATORIAL DESIGNS. *Educ:* Mass Inst Technol, BS, 70; Princeton Univ, PhD(math), 75. *Prof Exp:* Instr, Univ Kans, 74-76; asst prof math, 76-81, ASSOC PROF MATH, UNIV NEBR-LINCOLN, 81- *Mem:* Am Math Soc; Sigma Xi; Math Asn Am. *Res:* Modules over commutative semigroup rings; applications of finite group actions to combinatorial design problems. *Mailing Add:* Dept of Math & Statist Univ of Nebr Lincoln NE 68588

CHOUKAS, NICHOLAS C, b Chicago, Ill, Sept 5, 23; m 51; c 5. ORAL & MAXILLOFACIAL SURGERY. *Educ:* Loyola Univ, Ill, DDS, 50, MS, 58; Am Bd Oral Surg, dipl, 61. *Prof Exp:* Fel, 53, from instr to assoc prof oral & maxillofacial surg, 56-70, assoc prof oral biol & chmn dept oral surg, 63-69, PROF ORAL BIOL, GRAD SCH & PROF ORAL & MAXILLOFACIAL SURG, SCH DENT, LOYOLA UNIV CHICAGO, 69- *Concurrent Pos:* Attend oral & maxillofacial surgeon, Hines Vet Admin Hosp, 58-60, consult, 60-; NIH teachers training grant, 61, res grant, 61-64; chief oral surg, Loyola Univ Hosp, 69- *Mem:* Am Asn Oral & Maxillofacial Surg; fel Int Asn Oral Surg; fel Am Col Dent; fel Int Col Dent; fel Am Col Stomatologic Surgeons. *Res:* Growth changes of the temporomandibular joint and mandible of the Macca rhesus monkey following various experimentally induced environments. *Mailing Add:* Sch of Dent Loyola Univ Med Ctr Maywood IL 60153

CHOULES, GEORGE LEW, b Salt Lake City, Utah, Mar 5, 33; m 60; c 3. BIOCHEMISTRY. *Educ:* Utah State Agr Col, BS, 55, MS, 57; Johns Hopkins Univ, PhD(biochem), 64. *Prof Exp:* Fel protein chem, Univ Calif, San Diego, 64-67; ASST RES PROF BIOL, UNIV UTAH, 67-, MEM LIFE SCI DIV, 74- *Mem:* AAAS; Biophys Soc; Am Soc Microbiol. *Res:* Protein chemistry; nitrogen fixation; subcellular particles; structure of membranes and antibodies; animal physiology, ecology and toxicology. *Mailing Add:* Life Sci Div Dugway Proving Ground Dugway UT 84112

CHOUNG, HUN RYANG, b Seoul, Korea, Aug 4, 49; m 76; c 2. POLYMER CHEMISTRY. *Educ:* Hanyang Univ, Korea, BS, 71; Calif State Univ, Long Beach, BS, 75. *Prof Exp:* Develop chemist, Essex Chem Corp, 74-78; sr chemist, Sealant Oper, Norton Co, 78-79; RES MGR, DAP INC, 79- *Mem:* Am Chem Soc; Am Soc Testing & Mat; Soc Advan Mat & Process Eng; Soc Automotive Engrs. *Res:* Research polymers; building construction sealants; caulks and construction adhesives; aerospace sealants and adhesives; insulating glass sealants. *Mailing Add:* PO Box 277 Dayton OH 45401

CHOVAN, JAMES PETER, b Bethlehem, Pa, April 16, 48. ENZYMOLOGY. *Educ:* Clemson Univ, BS, 70; Lehigh Univ, MS, 77, PhD(biochem), 80. *Prof Exp:* RES ASSOC, STATE UNIV NY, STONY BROOK, 80- *Mem:* Am Chem Soc; NY Acad Sci; AAAS. *Res:* Interactions of biomolecules and drugs with cell membranes and the resulting alterations in ion (specifically calcium) movements induced by these interactions. *Mailing Add:* 8A Wendover Rd East Setauket NY 11733

CHOVER, JOSHUA, b Detroit, Mich, Mar 26, 28; m 52. MATHEMATICS. *Educ:* Univ Mich, PhD(math), 52. *Prof Exp:* Res mathematician, Bell Tel Labs, 52-56; from instr to assoc prof, 56-65, chmn dept, 77-79, PROF MATH, UNIV WIS-MADISON, 65- *Concurrent Pos:* Mem, Inst Advan Study, 55-56. *Mem:* Am Math Soc. *Res:* Probability and analysis. *Mailing Add:* Dept of Math Univ of Wis Madison WI 53706

CHOVITZ, BERNARD H, b Norfolk, Va, Nov 10, 24; m 49; c 3. GEODESY, CARTOGRAPHY. *Educ:* Col William & Mary, BS, 44; Harvard Univ, MA, 47. *Prof Exp:* Mathematician, Army Map Serv, 48-60; Geod Intel, Mapping Res & Develop Agency, 60-61; prin scientist, Autometric Oper, Raytheon Co, 61-64; geodesist, Off Res & Develop, US Coast & Geod Surv, 64-65; geodesist, Environ Sci Serv Admin, 65-70; geodesist, 70-74, dir, Geod Res & Develop Lab, 74-81, CHIEF GEODESIST, NAT OCEANIC & ATMOSPHERIC ADMIN, 81- *Concurrent Pos:* Pres sect II, Int Asn Geod, 75-79; pres, Geodesy Sect, Am Geophys Union, 78-80. *Honors & Awards:* Meritorious Civilian Serv Award, US Dept Army, 57. *Mem:* Am Math Asn; Math Soc; Am Geophys Union; Int Asn Geod. *Res:* Mathematical analysis of map projections; determination of size of earth; application of artificial satellites to the determination of the earth's gravitational field and its size and shape. *Mailing Add:* 8813 Clifford Chevy Chase MD 20815

CHOVNICK, ARTHUR, b New York, NY, Aug 2, 27; m 49; c 2. GENETICS. *Educ:* Ind Univ, AB, 49, MA, 50; Ohio State Univ, PhD(genetics), 53. *Prof Exp:* Asst physiol genetics, Ohio State Univ, 51-53; instr zool, Univ Conn, 53-57, asst prof genetics, 57-59; asst dir, Long Island Biol Asn, 59-60, dir, 60-62; PROF GENETICS, UNIV CONN, 62- *Concurrent Pos:* Assoc ed, Genetics, 72-82; mem genetics study sect, Div Res Grants, NIH, 72-76. *Mem:* Fel AAAS; Genetics Soc Am (treas, 81-83); Am Genetic Asn; Am Soc Naturalists; Am Soc Cell Biol. *Res:* Gene structure, function, regulation, mutation, mechanism of recombination. *Mailing Add:* Dept Genetics & Cell Biol Univ Conn Storrs CT 06268

CHOW, ALFRED WEN-JEN, b Peiping, China, Jan 11, 24; m 57. MEDICINAL CHEMISTRY, ORGANIC CHEMISTRY. *Educ:* Univ Mich, BS, 46; Univ Minn, PhD(med chem), 50. *Prof Exp:* Res chemist, Bjorksten Res Lab, 51 & Kremers Urban Co, 52-56; sr res chemist, Pabst Res Lab, 56-59; sr med chemist, Smith Kline & French Lab, 59-71, SR INVESTR, SMITH KLINE CORP, 71- *Mem:* AAAS; Am Chem Soc; Royal Soc Chem. *Res:* Preparation of organic compounds of antimicrobial and antiviral interest; synthetic organic chemistry; animal health products; ruminant nutrition. *Mailing Add:* Smith Kline Corp 1600 Paoli Pike West Chester PA 19380

CHOW, ARTHUR, b Meaford, Ont, Oct 23, 36; m 63. ANALYTICAL CHEMISTRY. *Educ:* Univ Toronto, BSc, 61, MA, 62, PhD(anal chem), 66. *Prof Exp:* Lectr chem, Univ Toronto, 62-64, instr, 64-66; Nat Res Coun Can fel, 66-68; from asst prof to assoc prof, 68-79, PROF CHEM, UNIV MAN, 79- *Mem:* Am Chem Soc; Chem Inst Can. *Res:* Analytical chemistry of the noble metals; analytical uses of polyurethane foam for extraction and separation; analysis of inorganic pollutants. *Mailing Add:* Dept Chem Univ Manitoba Winnipeg MB R3T 2N2 Can

CHOW, BRIAN GEE-YIN, b Macau, Aug 10, 41; US citizen; m 69; c 2. PHYSICS, ASTRONOMY. *Educ:* Chung Chi Col, Hong Kong, BSc, 63; Case Western Reserve Univ, PhD(physics), 69; Univ Mich, MBA, 77, PhD(finance), 80. *Prof Exp:* Instr physics, Chung Chi Col, 63-64; from asst prof to prof physics, Saginaw Valley State Col, 69-78, chmn dept, 70-74, dir observ, 74-76; SR RES SPECIALIST, PAN HEURISTICS RES & DEVELOP ASSOCS, 78- *Concurrent Pos:* Res grant, Nat Energy Proj, Am Enterprise Inst Pub Policy, 74-75; consult, Trippensee Planetarium Co, 76-78; Sci Appl Inc, 78, US Dept Energy, Arms Control & Disarmament Agency & US Dept Defense, 78- *Mem:* Am Phys Soc. *Res:* National and international nuclear energy policies, national security and defense. *Mailing Add:* 926 Harvard Santa Monica CA 90403

CHOW, BRYANT, b Peking, China, Dec 24, 36; nat US; m 59; c 2. MATHEMATICS, STATISTICS. *Educ:* Franklin & Marshall Col, BS, 59; Rutgers Univ, MS, 61; Va Polytech Inst, PhD(statist), 66. *Prof Exp:* Instr statist, Va Polytech Inst, 64-65; asst prof appl math statist, Rutgers Univ, 65-69; assoc prof, 69-75, PROF MATH, UNIV SOUTHWESTERN LA, 75- *Mem:* Am Soc Qual Control; Am Statist Asn; Biomet Soc. *Res:* Non-parametric statistics; biometrics. *Mailing Add:* Dept of Math Univ of Southwestern La Lafayette LA 70501

CHOW, CHAO K, b Hong Kong, Dec 28, 28; US citizen; m 53; c 2. ELECTRICAL ENGINEERING. *Educ:* Utopia Univ & Tsing Hua Univ, China, BEE, 49; Cornell Univ, MEE, 50, PhD(elec eng), 53. *Prof Exp:* Asst prof elec eng, Pa State Univ, 53-55; sr staff scientist, Burroughs Corp, Pa, 55-64; mem res staff & mgr, 64-81, MGR COMPUT ENG, T J WATSON RES CTR, IBM, 81- *Concurrent Pos:* Mem fac grad ctr, Pa State Univ, 61-64; vis prof, Mass Inst Technol, 68-69; assoc ed, J Pattern Recognition, 68- *Mem:* Fel Inst Elec & Electronics Engrs; Soc Pattern Recognition. *Res:* Image processing and pattern recognition; switching theory; medical applications; storage hierarchies; computer sciences; recognition systems; medical ultrasound. *Mailing Add:* Res Div IBM Corp PO Box 218 Yorktown Heights NY 10598

CHOW, CHE CHUNG, b Shanghai, China, Feb 6, 35; m 60. PHYSICAL CHEMISTRY. *Educ:* Univ Hong Kong, BSc, 58; Brown Univ, PhD(chem), 64. *Prof Exp:* Asst chem, Brown Univ, 58-63; res chemist, Cent Res Dept, E I du Pont de Nemours & Co, Inc, Del, 63-69; chemist, East Lab, NJ, 69-70; SCIENTIST, XEROGRAPHIC TECHNOL DEPT, XEROX CORP, 70- *Mem:* Am Chem Soc. *Res:* Chemical reactions in shock waves; molecular energy transfer; growth kinetics of inorganic fibers; electrical and magnetic properties of solids; magneto-optics; laser-magnetic memories and imaging systems; coagulation mechanism of polymer solutions; mechanism of detonation in solid explosives; imaging and reproduction systems. *Mailing Add:* Xerographic Technol Dept Xerox Corp 800 Phillips Rd W147 Webster NY 14580

CHOW, CHING KUANG, b Chiayi, Taiwan, May 7, 40; m 67; c 3. NUTRITIONAL BIOCHEMISTRY. *Educ:* Nat Taiwan Univ, BS, 63; Univ Ill, Urbana, MS, 66, PhD(nutrit sci), 69. *Prof Exp:* From res asst to res assoc nutrit biochem, Univ Ill, Urbana, 64-69; assoc res scientist biochem, NY Univ Med Ctr, 69-70; Nat Vitamin Found fel biochem, 71-72, asst res biochemist, Univ Calif, Davis, 72-76; asst prof, 76-78, ASSOC PROF DEPT NUTRIT & FOOD SCI, UNIV KY, 78- *Mem:* Am Inst Nutrit; NY Acad Sci. *Res:* Metabolism and function of vitamin E; intrinsic antioxidant defense mechanism; nutritional and environmental stresses on normal and pathological processes. *Mailing Add:* Dept of Nutrit & Food Sci Univ of Ky Lexington KY 40506

CHOW, CHRISTOPHER N, b Nanking, China, Dec 23, 46. ELECTROOPTICS. *Educ:* Calif Lutheran Col, BA, 68; Univ Minn, PhD(physics), 74. *Prof Exp:* RES SPECIALIST ELECTROOPTICS, 3M CO, 74- *Res:* Electrophotography; electro-optical information processing and display; laser technology. *Mailing Add:* 3M Ctr 235-2E St Paul MN 55101

CHOW, CHUEN-YEN, b Nanchang, China, Dec 5, 32; m 60; c 3. AEROSPACE ENGINEERING. *Educ:* Univ Taiwan, BS, 55; Purdue Univ, MS, 58; Mass Inst Technol, SM, 61; Univ Mich, PhD(aeronaut & astronaut eng), 64. *Prof Exp:* Fel, inst sci & tech, Univ Mich, 64-65; asst prof aerospace eng, Univ Notre Dame, 65-67, assoc prof, 67-68; assoc prof, 68-76, PROF AEROSPACE ENG, UNIV COLO, 76- *Concurrent Pos:* Distinguished vis prof, US Air Force Acad, 79-80. *Mem:* Sigma Xi; Am Inst Aeronaut & Astronaut. *Res:* Radiative gasdynamics; magnetohydrodynamics; hydromagnetic instability; aerodynamics; computational fluid mechanics. *Mailing Add:* Dept of Aerospace Eng Sci Univ of Colo Boulder CO 80309

CHOW, KAO LAING, b Tientsin, China, Apr 21, 18; US citizen; m 64. NEUROSCIENCES, NEUROANATOMY. *Educ:* Yenching Univ China, BA, 43; Harvard Univ, PhD(psychol), 50. *Prof Exp:* Asst, Yerkes Labs Primate Biol, 47-54; asst prof physiol, Univ Chicago, 54-60; assoc prof med, 60-65, PROF NEUROL, MED SCH, STANFORD UNIV, 65- *Concurrent Pos:* Mem, Int Brain Res Orgn. *Mem:* AAAS; Am Physiol Soc; Soc Neurosci. *Res:* Neurophysiology of learning and vision; neuroanatomy of vision and central nervous system. *Mailing Add:* Dept of Neurol Stanford Univ Sch Med Palo Alto CA 94305

CHOW, LAURENCE CHUNG-LUNG, b Taipei, Taiwan, Feb 8, 43; US citizen; m 67; c 3. PHYSICAL CHEMISTRY, DENTAL RESEARCH. *Educ:* Chen-Kung Univ, Taiwan, BS, 64; Georgetown Univ, PhD(chem), 70. *Prof Exp:* Res assoc, 69-75, CHIEF RES SCIENTIST, DENT CHEM DIV, AM DENT ASN HEALTH FOUND RES UNIT, NAT BUR STANDARDS, 76- *Mem:* Am Chem Soc; Int Asn Dent Res. *Res:* Dental research; dental caries prevention; topical fluoridation of teeth; thermodynamics; solution theories; transport of ions through membranes. *Mailing Add:* Am Dent Asn Health Found Res Unit Nat Bur of Standards Washington DC 20234

CHOW, LOUISE TSI, b Hunan, China, Sept 30, 43; m 74. MOLECULAR GENETICS, TUMOR VIROLOGY. *Educ:* Nat Taiwan Univ, BS, 65; Calif Inst Technol, PhD(chem), 73. *Prof Exp:* Res fel biochem, Univ Calif Med Ctr, San Francisco, 73-74; res fel chem, Calif Inst Technol, 74-75; res fel, 75, staff investr, 76, sr staff investr, 77-79, SR STAFF SCIENTIST ELECTRON MICROSCOPY, COLD SPRING HARBOR LAB, 79- *Mem:* Am Soc Microbiol. *Res:* Electron microscopic studies of gene arrangements in bacterial, viral and eucaryotic chromosomes; adenovirus RNA transcription and splicing patterns. *Mailing Add:* Cold Spring Harbor Lab PO Box 100 Cold Spring Harbor NY 11724

CHOW, PAO LIU, b Fukien, China, Nov 28, 36; m 65; c 2. APPLIED MATHEMATICS, STOCHASTIC DIFFERENTIAL EQUATIONS. *Educ:* Cheng Kung Univ, Taiwan, BS, 59; Rensselaer Polytech Inst, MS, 64, PhD(mech), 67. *Prof Exp:* Asst prof math, Rensselaer Polytech Inst, 66-67; asst prof, NY Univ, 67-72; assoc prof, 72-77, PROF MATH, WAYNE STATE UNIV, 77- *Concurrent Pos:* Vis scholar, Univ Calif, Berkeley, 78; vis prof, Inst Nat Recherche Infomatique & Automatique, France, 79. *Mem:* Am Mat Soc; Mem: Soc Indust & Appl Math. *Res:* Stochastic differential equations; wave propagation in random medium; stochastic analysis; fluid mechanics. *Mailing Add:* Dept of Math Wayne State Univ Detroit MI 48202

CHOW, PAUL C, b Peking, China, Aug 1, 26; m 65; c 3. SOLID STATE PHYSICS, THEORETICAL PHYSICS. *Educ:* Univ Calif, Berkeley, BS, 60; Northwestern Univ, PhD(physics), 65. *Prof Exp:* Res assoc physics, Northwestern Univ, 65; res assoc, Univ Southern Calif, 65-66, asst prof, 66-67; res scientist, Univ Tex, 67-68; assoc prof, 68-80, PROF PHYSICS & ASTRON, CALIF STATE UNIV, NORTHRIDGE, 80- *Concurrent Pos:* Vis asst prof, Univ Tex, 70; consult, Control Data Corp, 81- *Mem:* Am Phys Soc. *Res:* Theoretical solid state physics; computer used as a teaching tool. *Mailing Add:* Dept Physics & Astron Calif State Univ Northridge CA 91330

CHOW, RICHARD H, b Vancouver, BC, Sept 6, 24; nat US; m 48; c 5. PHYSICS. *Educ:* Univ BC, BA, 47, MA, 49; Univ Calif, Los Angeles, PhD(nuclear physics), 55. *Prof Exp:* Asst physics, Univ BC, 46-49; from asst to assoc, Univ Calif, Los Angeles, 50-54; asst res officer reactor physics, Atomic Energy Can, Ltd, 54-58; from asst prof to assoc prof, 58-65, PROF PHYSICS, CALIF STATE UNIV, LONG BEACH, 65- *Concurrent Pos:* Richland fac appointment, NWCol & Univ Asn Sci, 68-69. *Mem:* Am Asn Physics Teachers; Am Phys Soc; Am Nuclear Soc. *Res:* Reactor physics; nuclear physics; energy sources. *Mailing Add:* Dept of Physics & Astron Calif State Univ Long Beach CA 90840

CHOW, RITA K, b Aug 19, 26. NURSING. *Educ:* Columbia Univ, EdD, 68. *Prof Exp:* CHIEF, QUAL ASSURANCE BR, DIV LONG TERM CARE, OFF STANDARDS & CERT, HEALTH STANDARDS & QUAL BUR, HEALTH CARE FINANCING ADMIN, DEPT HEALTH & HUMAN SERV, 78- *Mem:* Inst Med, Nat Acad Sci. *Mailing Add:* Dogwood East Bldg 1849 Gwynn Oak Ave Baltimore MD 21207

CHOW, SHIN-KIEN, b Shan-Tan, China, June 12, 35; m 65; c 3. FLUID MECHANICS, MATHEMATICS. *Educ:* Nat Univ Taiwan, BS, 57; Calif Inst Technol, MS, 61; Univ Iowa, PhD(fluid mech), 67. *Prof Exp:* Sr engr, 65-70, supvr, 70-71, MGR, WESTINGHOUSE RES LABS, 71- *Res:* Hydrodynamics; hydraulic systems; fluidics. *Mailing Add:* 106 Chatam Lane Monroeville PA 15146

CHOW, TAI-LOW, b Yencheng, China, May 18, 37; m 63; c 2. ASTROPHYSICS. *Educ:* Nat Taiwan Univ, BS, 58; Case Western Reserve Univ, MS, 63; Univ Rochester, PhD(physics, astron), 70. *Prof Exp:* Instr physics, Cheng Kung Univ, 60-61; from asst prof to assoc prof, 69-77, PROF PHYSICS, CALIF STATE COL, STANISLAUS, 77-, CHMN DEPT, 73- *Mem:* AAAS; Am Phys Soc; Am Astron Soc; Am Asn Physics Teachers. *Res:* Scattering of high-energy electrons by nucleons; x-ray and gamma-ray astronomy; electron gas in ultraintense magnetic fields and the astrophysical applications; high-velocity neutral hydrogen gases at high galactic latitudes; interstellar medium; pulsar and gravitation radiations. *Mailing Add:* Dept of Physics Calif State Col Turlock CA 95380

CHOW, TAT-SING PAUL, b China, July 26, 53; US citizen. INTEGRATED CIRCUIT PROCESSING. *Educ:* Augustana Col, BA, 75; Columbia Univ, MS, 77; Rensselaer Polytech Inst, PhD(elec eng), 82. *Prof Exp:* INTEGRATED CIRCUITS PROCESS ENGR, RES & DEVELOP, GEN ELEC CO, 77- *Mem:* Inst Elec & Electronics Engrs; Electrochem Soc. *Res:* Thin film processes for m,etal oxide silicon integrated-circuits; application of refractory metal and metal silicides to microcircuits. *Mailing Add:* Rm 207 Bldg 37 Corp Res & Develop Gen Elec Co Schenectady NY 12301

CHOW, THIEN LIEN, b Malaysia, Nov 25, 44; Can citizen; m 67; c 2. SOIL PHYSICS, MICROMETEOROLOGY. *Educ:* Chung-Hsing Univ, Taiwan, 67; Univ BC, PhD(soil physics), 73. *Prof Exp:* Res assoc hydrol, Univ BC, 73-74; res scientist soil physics, Can Forestry Serv, 74-78; RES SCIENTIST HYDROL, AGR CAN, 78- *Mem:* Soil Sci Soc Am; Int Soc Soil Sci. *Res:* Soil-water management in crop production; environmental impact of forestry and agricultural practices. *Mailing Add:* Res Sta Agr Can PO Box 20280 Fredericton E3B 4Z7 Can

CHOW, TSAIHWA JAMES, b Shanghai, China, Oct 13, 24; US citizen. ANALYTICAL CHEMISTRY, GEOCHEMISTRY. *Educ:* Nat Chiaotung Univ, BS, 46; Wash State Univ, MS, 49; Univ Wash, PhD(anal chem), 53. *Prof Exp:* Instr, Nat Chiaotung Univ, 46-47; res asst, Univ Wash, 50-52, asst, 52-53, res assoc oceanog, 53-55; res fel geochem, Calif Inst Technol, 55-60; MEM STAFF, SCRIPPS INST OCEANOG, 60- *Concurrent Pos:* Vis researcher, Royal Inst Technol, Sweden, 62-63. *Mem:* AAAS; Am Geophys Union. *Res:* Microanalytical chemistry; mass spectrometry; chemical oceanography; trace elements in the sea; strontium-calcium ratio in marine organisms; geochemistry of lead isotopes; geochronology; solution chemistry; lead pollution. *Mailing Add:* Scripps Inst of Oceanog Univ of Calif La Jolla CA 92037

CHOW, TSENG YEH, b Shanghai, China, July 22, 21. MATHEMATICS. *Educ:* Nat Chiao-Tung Univ, BS, 42; Mass Inst Technol, SM, 48; Cornell Univ, PhD(math), 53. *Prof Exp:* From asst prof to assoc prof math, Rensselaer Polytech Inst, 52-63; assoc prof, 64-67, PROF MATH, CALIF STATE UNIV, SACRAMENTO, 67- *Mem:* Am Math Soc; Math Asn Am. *Res:* Mathematical analysis; applied mathematics. *Mailing Add:* Dept of Math Calif State Univ Sacramento CA 95819

CHOW, TSU LING, b China, Apr 4, 15; nat US; m 50. ANIMAL VIROLOGY. *Educ:* Nat Cent Univ, China, BVS, 40; Mich State Univ, PhD(animal path), 50. *Prof Exp:* Asst, Nat Cent Univ, China, 40-42; vet, Ministry Agr & Forestry, 42-45; res assoc, Univ Wis, 50-53; assoc prof path & bact, Sch Vet Med, 54-69, prof, 69-75, EMER PROF PATH & BACT, SCH VET MED, COLO STATE UNIV, 75- *Mem:* Am Vet Med Asn; Am Soc Microbiol; Conf Res Workers Animal Dis; NY Acad Sci; Int Acad Path. *Res:* Virus diseases of domestic animals such as rinderpest, contagious ecthyma, vesicular stomatitis; infectious bovine rhinotracheitis; blue tongue. *Mailing Add:* 923 Valleyview Rd Ft Collins CO 80521

CHOW, TSU-SEN, b China, Nov 8, 39; US citizen; m 67; c 1. POLYMER PHYSICS, MECHANICS. *Educ:* Cheng Kung Univ, Taiwan, BS, 62; Rensselaer Polytech Inst, MS, 66; Carnegie-Mellon Univ, PhD(math, mech), 68. *Prof Exp:* Teaching asst thermodyn, Nat Cheng Kung Univ, 63-64; res assoc polymer/composite, Univ NC, Chapel Hill, 68-72; scientist mat, Wilson Ctr Technol, 72-79, SR SCIENTIST POLYMER PHYSICS & COMPOSITE MAT, XEROX WEBSTER RES CTR, XEROX CORP, 79- *Mem:* Am Phys Soc; Soc Rheology; Am Acad Mech; Am Chem Soc. *Res:* Mechanical and thermal properties of polymers and composites; rheology and stability of disperse systems; adhesion and surface sciences; statistical and continuous mechanics. *Mailing Add:* Wilson Ctr Technol Xerox Corp 800 Phillips Rd Webster NY 14580

CHOW, VEN TE, water resources, hydrology, deceased

CHOW, WEN MOU, b Peiping, China, Apr 2, 19; m 51; c 2. COMPUTER SCIENCE. *Educ:* Chiao-Tung Univ, Shanghai, BS, 41; Mass Inst Technol, MS, 42, DSc, 45. *Prof Exp:* Asst prof, Lafayette Col, 47-51 & Cath Univ, 51-52; chem engr, Calco Chem Div, Am Cyanamid Co, 45-47 & 52-56; statistician, Union Carbide Plastics Co, 56-68; Mead Johnson prof mgt & chmn dept, Univ Evansville, 68-69; PROF QUANT METHODS, CALIF STATE UNIV, FULLERTON, 69- *Mem:* Asn Comput Mach; Inst Mgt Sci; Am Statist Asn. *Res:* Applied mathematics; digital computers; applied statistics; operations research. *Mailing Add:* Dept of Quant Methods Calif State Univ Fullerton CA 92634

CHOW, WENG WAH, b Singapore, April 22, 48; m 79. LASER PHYSICS. *Educ:* Colo State Univ, BS, 68; Univ Ariz, MS, 74, PhD(physics), 75. *Prof Exp:* physicist, Max-Planck-Inst fur Biophys Chemie, 75-77, physicist, Max-Planck-Inst fur Plasmaphysik, 77; physicist, Optical Sci Ctr, Univ Ariz, 78-80; ASST PROF, DEPT PHYSICS & ASTRON, UNIV NMEX, 80- *Mem:* Optical Soc Am; Am Phys Soc; Inst Elec & Electronics Soc. *Res:* Laser theory; laser gyros; short wavelength lasers and high power lasers. *Mailing Add:* Dept Physics & Astron Univ NMex Albuquerque NM 87131

CHOW, YUAN LANG, b Formosa, May 28, 29; m 58; c 3. ORGANIC CHEMISTRY. *Educ:* Nat Taiwan Univ, BSc, 51; Duquesne Univ, PhD(chem), 57. *Prof Exp:* Engr, Chinese Petrol Co, 51-54; fel, Ill Inst Technol, 57-58; res fel, Royal Inst Technol, Sweden, 58-59, asst lectr, 59-61; res assoc, Imp Col, Univ London, 61-62; lectr, Univ Singapore, 62-63; asst prof org chem, Univ Alta, 63-65; assoc prof, 65-69, PROF CHEM, SIMON FRASER UNIV, 69- *Mem:* Fel Chem Inst Can; The Chem Soc; Am Chem Soc; Sigma Xi. *Res:* Photochemistry in solution, synthetic and mechanistic studies of free radical reaction; carcinogen chemistry. *Mailing Add:* Dept of Chem Simon Fraser Univ Burnaby Can

CHOW, YUAN SHIH, b Hupeh, China, Sept 1, 24; m 63; c 3. MATHEMATICS. *Educ:* Chekiang, China, BS, 49; Univ Ill, MA, 55, PhD(math), 58. *Prof Exp:* Res assoc, Univ Ill, 58-59; staff mathematician, Inst Bus Mach Corp, 59-62; vis assoc prof statist, Columbia Univ, 62-63; from assoc prof to prof, Purdue Univ, 63-68; PROF STATIST, COLUMBIA UNIV, 68- *Mem:* Am Math Soc; Soc Indust & Appl Math; Inst Math Statist. *Res:* Probability; Fourier series. *Mailing Add:* Dept of Math Statist Columbia Univ New York NY 10027

CHOW, YUNG LEONARD, b Foochow, Fukien, China, Dec 29, 36; Can citizen; m 72; c 2. STATIC COMPUTATION, DYNAMIC FIELD COMPUTATION. *Educ:* McGill Univ, BE, 60; Univ Toronto, MASc, 61, PhD(elec eng), 65. *Prof Exp:* Res assoc array design, Nat Radio Astron Observ, 64-66; from asst prof to assoc prof, 66-81, PROF ELEC ENG, UNIV WATERLOO, 81- *Mem:* Inst Elec & Electronics Engrs; Can Astron Soc; Can Soc Elec Engrs. *Res:* Microstrip; electromagnetic scattering; antenna array for radio astronomy; transient frequency modulation fields; static electric fields; field simplification by optimization routine. *Mailing Add:* Dept Elec Eng Univ Waterloo Waterloo ON N2L 3G1 Can

CHOW, YUTZE, b Shanghai, China, Sept 29, 27; m 54; c 3. THEORETICAL PHYSICS, MATHEMATICS. *Educ:* Chin-Kung Univ, Taiwan, 52; Univ RI, MS, 57; Brandeis Univ, MA, 64, PhD(physics), 65. *Prof Exp:* Res asst elec eng, Univ RI, 55-57; asst prof, Inst Tech Aeronaut, Brazil, 57-61; asst prof elec eng, Univ Waterloo, 61-62; teaching asst physics, Brandeis Univ, 62-63, res asst, 63-64; from asst prof to assoc prof, 64-67, PROF PHYSICS, UNIV WIS-MILWAUKEE, 67- *Concurrent Pos:* Vis assoc prof, Syracuse Univ, 57. *Mem:* Am Phys Soc. *Res:* Quantum field theory and elementary particle symmetries; Lie groups and Lie algebras. *Mailing Add:* Dept of Physics Univ of Wis Milwaukee WI 53201

CHOWDHRY, UMA, b Bombay, India, Sept 14, 47; m 70. HETEROGENEOUS CATALYSIS, CATALYST MICROSTRUCTURE. *Educ:* Inst Sci, Bombay, BSc, 68; Calif Inst Technol, MS, 70; Mass Inst Technol, PhD(mat sci), 76. *Prof Exp:* Fel, Mass Inst Technol, 76-77; res scientist, 77-80, GROUP LEADER PHYS SCI, E I DU PONT DE NEMOURS & CO, INC, 80-, RES SUPVR, CENT RES & DEVELOP DEPT, 81- *Mem:* Am Ceramic Soc. *Res:* Synthesis and characterization of heterogeneous catalysts; correlation of catalyst microstructure with catalytic properties; defects in inorganic solids; mass transport in ceramics; microstructural evolution during ceramic fabrication. *Mailing Add:* E356/301 Cent Res & Develop Dept Du Pont Exp Sta Wilmington DE 19898

CHOWDHURI, PRITINDRA, b Calcutta, India, July 12, 27; US citizen; m 62; c 4. ELECTRICAL ENGINEERING. *Educ:* Univ Calcutta, BSc, 45, MSc, 47; Ill Inst Technol, MS, 51; Rensselaer Polytech Inst, DEng(eng sci), 66. *Prof Exp:* Jr engr, Lightning Arresters Sect, Westinghouse Elec Corp, 51-52; elec engr, High Voltage Lab, Maschinenfabrik Oerlikon, Switz, 52-53; res engr, High Voltage Res Comn, Swiss Electrotech Soc, 53-56; developer, High Voltage Lab, Gen Elec Co, 56-59, elec engr, Advan Technol Labs, 59-62, engr elec invests, Transp Systs Div, 62-75; STAFF MEM, LOS ALAMOS NAT LAB, 75- *Concurrent Pos:* Lectr, Grad Ctr, Pa State Univ,

Behrend Campus, 69-75. *Honors & Awards:* Invention Disclosure Award, Westinghouse Elec Corp, 51. *Mem:* Sr mem Inst Elec & Electronics Engrs; Int Conf Large High-Voltage Elec Systs; fel Inst Elec Engrs (Eng); AAAS. *Res:* Dielectrics; electrical transients; high voltage engineering; power semiconductor devices; power system engineering. *Mailing Add:* 510 Bryce Ave White Rock NM 87544

CHOWDHURY, AJIT KUMAR, b Calcutta, India, Apr 6, 28; m 61; c 2. REPRODUCTIVE PHYSIOLOGY, REPRODUCTIVE ENDOCRINOLOGY. *Educ:* Univ Calcutta, BSc, 51, MSc, 53, PhD(reprod physiol), 58. *Prof Exp:* Asst prof pharmacol, Bengal Vet Col, Calcutta, 54-64, prof physiol, 64-68; asst mem reprod endocrinol, Albert Einstein Med Ctr, Philadelphia, 68-71; asst prof, 71-80, ASSOC PROF REPROD BIOL & ENDOCRINOL, UNIV TEX MED SCH HOUSTON, 80-, ASSOC MEM, GRAD SCH BIOMED SCI, 74- *Concurrent Pos:* Pop Coun grant, Albert Einstein Med Ctr, 61-63. *Mem:* Soc Study Reprod; Am Soc Andrology; Indian Physiol Soc. *Res:* Morphology and kinetics of spermatogenesis in man, monkey and rodents; endocrine control and effect of noxious agents. *Mailing Add:* Dept Reprod Med & Biol Univ of Tex Med Sch Houston TX 77025

CHOWDHURY, DIPAK KUMAR, b Jhargram, India, Nov 15, 36; m 65; c 2. GEOPHYSICS, TECTONICS. *Educ:* Indian Inst Technol, Kharagpur, BS, 56, MTechnol, 58; Tex A&M Col, PhD(geophys), 61. *Prof Exp:* Lectr geophys, Indian Sch Mines & Appl Geol, Dhanabad, 61-63, asst prof, 63-67; Nat Res Coun fel, Univ BC, 67-69; physicist, Shell Develop Co, Tex, 69-70; asst prof geol, 70-73, ASSOC PROF GEOL, IND UNIV, FT WAYNE, 73-, CHMN, DEPT EARTH & SPACE SCI, 74- *Concurrent Pos:* Geophys consult, Law Eng & Testing Co, Ga, 70-74 & Gen Portland Cement, 75-77. *Mem:* Am Geophys Union; Am Geol Inst; European Geophys Soc. *Res:* Interpretation of self potential data for tabular shaped ore bodies; elastic wave propagations along layers in two-dimensional models; elastic wave velocities and attenuations in rocks and plastics; variations in azimuths and incident angles due to dipping interfaces; studies on earthquake seismology, upper mantle heterogenity, core-mantle boundary. *Mailing Add:* Dept of Earth & Space Sci Ind Univ Ft Wayne IN 46805

CHOWDHURY, IKBALUR RASHID, b Dacca, Pakistan, Feb 12, 39; m 67; c 1. SOIL FERTILITY, AGRONOMY. *Educ:* Univ Dacca, BSc, 60, MS, 63; NDak State Univ, PhD(soil fertil), 70. *Prof Exp:* Sr res asst bact, Pak-SEATO Cholera Res Inst, 64; sr lectr soil microbiol, Univ Dacca, 64-65; res asst soil fertil, NDak State Univ, 65-70, fel soil chem, 70-72; asst prof agr, 72-75, ASSOC PROF AGR, LINCOLN UNIV, 75- *Mem:* Am Soc Agron; Soil Sci Soc Am; Int Soc Soil Sci. *Res:* Soil testing; soil chemistry; plant physiology; environmental quality; soybean fertilization with respect to oil and protein. *Mailing Add:* Lincoln Univ Jefferson City MO 65101

CHOWDHURY, MRIDULA, b Calcutta, India, Feb 22, 38; m 61; c 2. REPRODUCTIVE BIOLOGY. *Educ:* Presidency Col, Calcutta, BS, 57; Calcutta Univ, MS, 59, PhD(reproductive physiol), 68. *Prof Exp:* NIH fel reproductive biol, Albert Einstein Med Ctr, 69-71; res assoc, 71-74, sr res scientist reproductive biol, 74-77, ASST PROF DEPT REPRODUCTIVE MED & BIOL, SCH MED, UNIV TEX, HOUSTON, 77- *Mem:* Am Endoctrine Soc; AAAS. *Res:* Feedback control of gonadotropins in male with special emphasis on the control mechanism of synthesis of gonadotropins in the pituitary. *Mailing Add:* Dept of Reproductive Med & Biol Sch of Med Univ of Tex Houston TX 77025

CHOWDHURY, PARIMAL , b Chittagong, Bangladesh, Dec 31, 40; US citizen; m 71; c 2. BIOCHEMISTRY, TOXICOLOGY. *Educ:* Dacca Univ, Bangladesh, BSc, 60, MSc, 62; McGill Univ, Can, PhD(immunochem & physiol), 70. *Prof Exp:* Lectr chem, BPC Inst, West Bengal, India, 64-65; lectr med chem, Calcutta Med Col, India, 65-67; fel immunochem, McGill Univ, Can, 67-70; instr med, NJ Med Sch, 70-74, adj instr, 74-76, asst prof med, 76-80; ASST PROF PHYSIOL & BIOPHYS, UNIV ARK MED SCI, 80- *Concurrent Pos:* Co-investr, NIH Funded Res, 70-80; prin investr, Inst Pilot Study, GRS grant, NJ, 74-77 & Little Rock, Ark, 80-82. *Mem:* Am Physiol Soc; Am Chem Soc; AAAS; Am Asn Univ Professors; Sigma Xi. *Res:* Structure-function relationship of proteins specially immunoglobulins; heavy metal toxicity and mechanism of lung injury; cigarette smoking, pulmonary emphysema, its relationship with seran anti-taypsin activity; blood coagulation, demonstration of a method of gastroin intestinal physiology. *Mailing Add:* 5 New Haven Ct Little Rock AR 72207

CHOWN, EDWARD HOLTON, b Kingston, Ont, Feb 24, 32; m 65; c 3. PETROLOGY, ECONOMIC GEOLOGY. *Educ:* Queen's Univ, Ont, BSc, 55; Univ BC, MASc, 57; Johns Hopkins Univ, PhD(geol), 63. *Prof Exp:* Geologist, Dept Natural Resources, Que, 63-66; asst prof geol, Loyola Col Montreal, 66-70, assoc prof, 70-75; assoc prof, 75-79, PROF SCI, UNIV QUE, CHICOUTIMI, 79- *Mem:* Geol Soc Am; Geol Asn Can; Can Inst Mining & Metall; Mineral Asn Can. *Res:* Proterozoic clastics and carbonates in central Quebec; weathered profile beneath carbonate sequence; origin and metamorphism of archaen volcanogenic gold deposit. *Mailing Add:* Dept of Earth Sci Univ of Que Chicoutimi Can

CHOYKE, WOLFGANG JUSTUS, b Berlin, Ger, July 24, 26; nat US; m 49; c 2. SOLID STATE PHYSICS. *Educ:* Ohio State Univ, BSc, 48, PhD(physics), 52. *Prof Exp:* Res physicist, 52-60, fel physicist, 60-62, adv physicist, 62-77, CONSULT PHYSICIST, WESTINGHOUSE RES LABS, 78- *Concurrent Pos:* Adj prof physics, Univ Pittsburgh, 74- *Mem:* Am Phys Soc. *Res:* Experimental nuclear physics; radiative recombination processes; optical absorption; silicon carbide; reflectivity and ellipsometry of metals and semiconductors; ion implantation; ion beam simulation of neutron damage in solids. *Mailing Add:* 5424 Kipling Rd Pittsburgh PA 15217

CHRAPLIWY, PETER STANLEY, b Pulaski, Wis, Oct 20, 23; m 47; c 4. HERPETOLOGY. *Educ:* Univ Kans, BA, 53, MA, 56; Univ Ill, PhD(zool), 64. *Prof Exp:* From instr to asst prof, 60-64, ASSOC PROF BIOL, UNIV TEX, EL PASO, 64- *Mem:* Am Soc Ichthyologists & Herpetologists. *Res:* Taxonomy of modern amphibians and reptiles; biology of desert flora and fauna. *Mailing Add:* Dept of Biol Sci Univ of Tex El Paso TX 79968

CHRAPLYVY, ANDREW R, b St Louis, Mo, June 5, 50; m 75; c 2. FIBER OPTICS, NONLINEAR OPTICS. *Educ:* Washington Univ, St Louis, BA, 72; Cornell Univ, MS, 75, PhD(physics), 77. *Prof Exp:* Res scientist, Gen Motors Res Lab, 77-80; MEM TECH STAFF, BELL LABS, 80- *Mem:* Am Phys Soc; Optical Soc Am. *Res:* Nonlinear spectroscopy; fiber optics; high resolution infrared spectroscopy; solid state physics. *Mailing Add:* 25 Colonial Dr Matawan NJ 07747

CHRENKO, RICHARD MICHAEL, b Gillette, NJ, July 16, 30; m 63; c 2. SPECTROSCOPY, SOLID STATE PHYSICS. *Educ:* NY Univ, BA, 52; Harvard Univ, MA, 54. *Prof Exp:* Physicist, Knolls Atomic Power Lab, 56, physicist, Res Lab, 56-65, PHYSICIST, RES & DEVELOP CTR, GEN ELEC CO, 65- *Mem:* Soc Exp Stress Anal. *Res:* Molecular and solid state spectroscopy; nuclear physics and reactors; physical properties of diamonds; residual stress. *Mailing Add:* Gen Elec Res & Develop Ctr PO Box 8 Schenectady NY 12301

CHREPTA, STEPHEN JOHN, b Watervliet, NY, May 19, 21. ANALYTICAL CHEMISTRY. *Educ:* Fordham Univ, MS, 51. *Prof Exp:* Instr, 46-53, ASST PROF CHEM & DEAN, ST BASIL'S COL, 53- *Mem:* NY Acad Sci; AAAS; Am Chem Soc. *Res:* Spectroscopy; x-ray diffraction. *Mailing Add:* Dept Chem St Basil's Col Stamford CT 06902

CHRESTENSON, HUBERT EDWIN, b Grandview, Wash, Oct 21, 27; m 47; c 3. MATHEMATICS. *Educ:* State Col Wash, BA, 49, MA, 51; Univ Ore, PhD(math), 53. *Prof Exp:* Instr math, Purdue Univ, 53-54; asst prof, Whitman Col, 54-57; from asst prof to assoc prof, 57-80, PROF MATH, REED COL, 80- *Mem:* Am Math Soc; Math Asn Am. *Res:* Fourier analysis. *Mailing Add:* Dept of Math Reed Col Portland OR 97202

CHRETIEN, MAX, b Basel, Switz, Feb 29, 24; m 58; c 1. PHYSICS. *Educ:* Univ Basel, Switz, PhD(physics), 49. *Prof Exp:* Fels, Univ Birmingham, Eng, 51-53 & Columbia Univ, 53-54, from instr to asst prof, 53-58, ASSOC PROF HIGH ENERGY PHYSICS, BRANDEIS UNIV, 58- *Concurrent Pos:* Swiss Nat Fund fel, 63 & 69. *Mem:* Am Physical Soc. *Res:* Theory of elementary particles. *Mailing Add:* 39 Florence Rd Waltham MA 02154

CHRETIEN, MICHEL, b Shawinigan, Que, Mar 26, 36; m 60; c 2. ENDOCRINOLOGY. *Educ:* Univ Montreal, BA, 55, MD, 60; McGill Univ, MSc, 62. *Hon Degrees:* DSc, Univ de Liege, 80. *Prof Exp:* Med Res Coun Can fel, McGill Univ, 60-62; resident med, Peter Bent Brigham Hosp, 62-63, clin fel endocrinol, 63-64; Childs Mem Fund fel biochem, Hormone Res Lab, Univ Calif, Berkeley, 64-66, Med Res Coun Can fel, 66-67; SR INVESTR ENDOCRINOL, CLIN RES INST MONTREAL, 67-; PROF MED, UNIV MONTREAL & HOTEL-DIEU HOSP, 67- *Concurrent Pos:* Res fel endocrinol, Hotel Dieu Hosp, 60-62; asst prof exp med, McGill Univ, 67- *Honors & Awards:* Basic Res Award, Asn Fr Speaking Physicians Can, 71; Clarke Inst Psychiat Award, 77; Medaille Archambault, Fr-Can Asn Advan Sci, 78. *Mem:* Can Soc Clin Invest; Endocrine Soc; NY Acad Sci; Can Biomed Soc; AAAS. *Res:* Purification, isolation, chemical characterization, biosynthesis and physiology of pituitary hormones related to beta-LPH, beta-MSH and beta-endorphin. *Mailing Add:* Clin Res Inst Montreal 110 Pine Ave W Montreal PQ H2W 1R7 Can

CHRIEN, ROBERT EDWARD, b Cleveland, Ohio, Apr 15, 30; m 53; c 4. NUCLEAR PHYSICS. *Educ:* Rensselaer Polytech Inst, BS, 52; Case Inst Technol, MS, 55, PhD(physics), 58. *Prof Exp:* Res assoc physics, 57-59, from asst physicist to physicist, 59-72, group leader, Neutron Physics, 70-81, SR PHYSICIST, BROOKHAVEN NAT LAB, 72-, GROUP LEADER, MEDIUM ENERGY PHYSICS, 81- *Concurrent Pos:* Past secy & past chmn nuclear cross sect adv comt, US AEC; mem, Nuclear Data Comt, Nuclear Energy Agency, 72-, Tech Adv Panel, Los Alamos Meson Physics Facil, 72-, Nuclear Physics Div, Comt Nuclear Data & Prog Comt, Am Phys Soc, 73, chmn, 78-79 & Nuclear Data Comt, Energy Res & Develop Admin, 75- *Mem:* Fel Am Phys Soc; AAAS; Sigma Xi; NY Acad Sci; Am Chem Soc. *Res:* Neutron physics; neutron resonance parameters; capture gamma rays from neutron resonances; neutron total cross sections; applications of on-line computers in nuclear physics; nuclear detectors; photonuclear reactions; intermediate energy physics; hypernuclear physics; kaon and proton scattering. *Mailing Add:* Dept of Physics Brookhaven Nat Lab Upton NY 11973

CHRISMAN, CHARLES LARRY, b St Joseph, Mo, Mar 1, 41; m 62; c 2. CYTOGENETICS. *Educ:* Univ Mo-Columbia, BS, 67, MS, 69, PhD(cytogenetics), 71. *Prof Exp:* ASSOC PROF GENETICS & CYTOGENETICS, PURDUE UNIV, 71- *Mem:* AAAS; Am Soc Animal Sci; Am Genetic Asn; Genetics Soc Can; Genetics Soc Am. *Res:* Investigations involving the effects of chemicals, drugs, hormones and environmental stress on the chromosomes of domestic animals; investigations of animals with birth defects as possibly caused by chromosomal aberrations or detrimental genes. *Mailing Add:* Dept of Animal Sci Lilly Hall Purdue Univ West Lafayette IN 47907

CHRISMAN, NOEL JUDSON, b Visalia, Calif, July 30, 40; m 62; c 1. MEDICAL ANTHROPOLOGY. *Educ:* Univ Calif, Riverside, BA, 62, Univ Calif, Berkeley, PhD(anthrop), 66, MPH, 67. *Prof Exp:* NIMH fel pub health, Sch Pub Health, Univ Calif, Berkeley, 66-67; asst prof anthrop, Pomona Col, 67-73; asst prof, 73-79, ASSOC PROF COMMUNITY HEALTH CARE SYSTS, SCH NURSING, UNIV WASH, 79- *Concurrent Pos:* Nat Endowment Humanities Younger Humanist fel, Univ Calif, Berkeley, 71. *Mem:* Fel Am Anthrop Asn; fel Soc Appl Anthrop; Soc Med Anthrop. *Res:* Urban studies, particularly the role of social networks in urban adaptation; class and ethnic variation in health seeking behaviors; working class Americans; network analysis. *Mailing Add:* Sch of Nursing Univ of Wash Seattle WA 98195

CHRISPEELS, MAARTEN JAN, b Kortenberg, Belg, Feb 10, 38; m 66; c 2. PLANT PHYSIOLOGY. *Educ:* Univ Ghent, Engr, 60; Univ Ill, Urbana, PhD(agron), 64. *Prof Exp:* Res asst agron, Univ Ill, 63-64; res assoc plant biochem, Res Inst Advan Studies, 64-65; plant res lab, AEC, 65-67; res assoc microbiol, Purdue Univ, 67; from asst prof to assoc prof, 67-79, PROF BIOL, UNIV CALIF, SAN DIEGO, 79- *Concurrent Pos:* John S Guggenheim Found fel, 73-74; prog mgr, Competitive Res Grant Off, USDA, 79. *Mem:* AAAS; Am Soc Plant Physiol; Am Soc Cell Biol. *Res:* Biochemistry of plant development, especially seed formation and seedling growth; structure-function relationships in cells (secretion, lysosomes, protein bodies). *Mailing Add:* C-016 Dept Biol Univ Calif San Diego La Jolla CA 92093

CHRISS, TERRY MICHAEL, b Vallejo, Calif, Dec 10, 45. BOUNDARY LAYER TURBULENCE, SEDIMENT TRANSPORT. *Educ:* Univ Calif, Los Angeles, BS, 68, MS, 71, Ore State Univ, PhD(oceanog), 81. *Prof Exp:* Prof geol, Los Angeles Community Col Dist, 69-74; RES ASSOC, DEPT OCEANOG, DALHOUSIE UNIV, 81- *Mem:* Am Geophys Union. *Res:* Field investigation of boundary layer turbulence in the region just above the sediment-water interface (viscous sublayer and lower portion of the turbulent logarithmic layer). *Mailing Add:* Dept Oceanog Dalhousie Univ Halifax NS B3H 4J1 Can

CHRIST, ADOLPH ERVIN, b Reedley, Calif, May 13, 29; m 51; c 4. CHILD PSYCHIATRY. *Educ:* Univ Calif, Berkeley, AB, 51; Univ Calif, San Francisco, MD, 54; Am Bd Psychiat & Neurol, dipl, 62, cert child psychiat, 67. *Prof Exp:* Intern univ hosp, Univ Calif, San Francisco, 54-55; resident psychiat, Langley Porter Neuropsychol Inst, 58-60; child psychiat, 60-62; instr med sch, Univ Wash, 62-65, asst prof, 65-67; dir psychol inst Scivia children, 62-67; asst prof child psychiat & dir inpatient child psychiat, Albert Einstein Col Med, 68-69; dir training clin psychol, 69-72, EXEC DIR DIV CHILD PSYCHIAT, STATE UNIV NY DOWNSTATE MED CTR, 72- *Mem:* Am Psychiat Asn; Am Orthopsychiat Asn; Am Col Psychiat; World Fedn Ment Health. *Res:* Treatment of childhood psychosis, especially milieu treatment. *Mailing Add:* 853 Seventh Ave Apt 6C New York NY 10019

CHRIST, CHARLES LOUIS, physical chemistry, deceased

CHRIST, DARYL DEAN, b Buffalo Center, Iowa, Nov 3, 42; m 66; c 1. PHARMACOLOGY, PHYSIOLOGY. *Educ:* Loyola Univ, BS, 64; Loyola Univ Chicago, PhD(pharmacol), 69. *Prof Exp:* NIH fel, Loyola Univ Chicago, 69-70; asst prof, 71-75, ASSOC PROF PHARMACOL, SCH MED, UNIV ARK, LITTLE ROCK, 75- *Concurrent Pos:* Vis assoc prof physiol, Sch Med, Kurume Univ, Japan, 81. *Mem:* Am Soc Pharmacol & Exp Therapeut; Soc Neurosci. *Res:* Effects of adrenergic drugs on ganglionic transmission; pharmacology and physiology of synaptic transmission. *Mailing Add:* 2417 Gristmill Rd Little Rock AR 72207

CHRISTE, KARL OTTO, b Ulm, Ger, July 24, 36; nat US; m 62; c 3. INORGANIC CHEMISTRY, PHYSICAL CHEMISTRY. *Educ:* Stuttgart Tech Univ, BS, 57, MS, 60, PhD(inorg chem), 61. *Prof Exp:* Teaching asst anal chem, Stuttgart Tech Univ, 56-60, res assoc inorg polymer chem, 60-61; mem res staff, Stauffer Chem Co, 62-67; mem tech staff, Rocketdyne Div, 67-79, MGR EXPLOR CHEM, ROCKWELL INT, 79- *Mem:* Am Chem Soc. *Res:* Inorganic and organic fluorine chemistry; high energy oxidizers and explosives; structural studies; vibrational spectroscopy; low-temperature matrix isolation; chlorinated hydrocarbons; inorganic polymers; boron hydrides; water treatment chemicals. *Mailing Add:* Rocketdyne Div Rockwell Int 6633 Canoga Ave Canoga Park CA 91304

CHRISTEN, ALICE ANN, b Albany, Minn, Dec 7, 50. PLANT PATHOLOGY, MYCOLOGY. *Educ:* St Cloud State Col, BA, 72; Wash State Univ, Pullman, MS, 74, PhD(plant path), 78. *Prof Exp:* RES ASSOC PLANT PATH, IRRIGATED AGR RES & EXTEN CTR, 77- *Mem:* Am Phytopath Soc; Mycol Soc Am; Am Entom Soc; Sigma Xi. *Res:* Soil borne fungal diseases of field crops. *Mailing Add:* Irrigated Agr Res & Exten Ctr PO Box 30 Prosser WA 99350

CHRISTEN, DAVID KENT, b Paris, Ill, Aug 16, 45; m 70; c 2. SOLID STATE PHYSICS. *Educ:* Univ Ill, BS, 67; Mich State Univ, MS, 70, PhD(physics), 74. *Prof Exp:* Res assoc physics, 74-78, RES STAFF PHYSICS, OAK RIDGE NAT LAB, 78- *Mem:* Am Phys Soc; Sigma Xi. *Res:* Low temperature physics; superconductivity; small-angle neutron scattering. *Mailing Add:* Solid State Div PO Box X Oak Ridge TN 37830

CHRISTENA, RAY CLIFFORD, b Indianapolis, Ind, Aug 17, 15; m 47; c 5. INDUSTRIAL CHEMISTRY. *Educ:* Univ Tex, BS, 39; Ind Univ, MA, 48, PhD(phys chem), 51. *Prof Exp:* Lab asst, Allison Div, Gen Motors Corp, 40-42 & Calco Div, Am Cyanamid, Ind, 46-51; res chemist, Benger Lab, E I du Pont de Nemours & Co, 51-58, Thiokol Chem Corp, NJ, 58-62, Brigham City, Utah, 62-63 & Celanese Corp Am, 63-67; res assoc res & develop, Chem Div, Vulcan Mat Co, 67-80; RETIRED. *Mem:* Am Chem Soc; Soc Rheol. *Res:* Research and development in area of sodium hydroxide, chlorine and chlorinated hydrocarbons. *Mailing Add:* 18 Conasuagua Dr Hardy AR 72542

CHRISTENBERRY, GEORGE ANDREW, b Macon, Ga, Sept 3, 15; m 37; c 3. MYCOLOGY, ACADEMIC ADMINISTRATION. *Educ:* Furman Univ, BS, 36; Univ NC, AM, 38, PhD(bot), 40. *Prof Exp:* Asst, Univ NC, 36-40; asst prof biol, Meredith Col, 40-41, assoc prof & head dept, 41-43, prof, 43; instr pre-flight prog, Furman Univ, 43-44; instr voc appraiser, Vet Guid, 46, assoc prof biol, 46-48, prof & dean men's col, 48-53; pres, Shorter Col, Ga, 53-58; admin dir, Furman Univ, 58-64; prof biol & chmn dept, Ga Col Milledgeville, 64-65, dean, 65-70; PRES, AUGUSTA COL, 70- *Concurrent Pos:* Carnegie Found grant, 48; bd dir, Asn State Cols & Univs, 73- *Mem:* Am Inst Biol Sci. *Res:* Taxonomic study of Mucorales in southeastern United States. *Mailing Add:* Augusta Col 2500 Walton Way Augusta GA 30904

CHRISTENSEN, A(LBERT) KENT, b Washington, DC, Dec 3, 27; m 52; c 5. ANATOMY, CELL BIOLOGY. *Educ:* Brigham Young Univ, AB, 53; Harvard Univ, PhD(biol), 58. *Prof Exp:* NIH fel, Col Med, Cornell Univ, 58-59; NIH fel, Harvard Med Sch, 59-60, instr anat, 60-61; from asst prof to assoc prof, Sch Med, Stanford Univ, 61-71; prof anat & chmn dept, Sch Med, Temple Univ, 71-78; PROF ANAT & CHMN DEPT, UNIV MICH MED SCH, 78- *Mem:* Am Soc Cell Biol; Am Asn Anat; Soc Study Reprod; Am Soc Zool; Electron Micros Soc Am. *Res:* Ultrastructure and cytochemistry of testis and of steroid-secreting cells; reproductive biology; macrophages. *Mailing Add:* Dept of Anat Med Sci II Bldg Univ of Mich Med Sch Ann Arbor MI 48109

CHRISTENSEN, ANDREW BRENT, b Salt Lake City, Utah, Feb 8, 40; c 4. ATMOSPHERIC PHYSICS, AERONOMY SPACE SCIENCES. *Educ:* Univ Utah, BS, 62; Univ Calif, Berkeley, MA, 64; Univ Denver, PhD(physics), 69. *Prof Exp:* Res assoc shock wave physics, Stanford Res Inst, 64-66; res scientist atmospheric & space sci, Univ Tex, Dallas, 69-79; RES SCIENTIST, AEROSPACE CORP, EL SEGUNDO, CALIF, 79- *Mem:* Am Geophys Union; Int Union Geod & Geophys. *Res:* Atmospheric and space sciences; airglow and auroral physics; atomic and molecular physics; radiation transfer; EUV spectroscopy; low light level photometry. *Mailing Add:* PO Box 92957 Los Angeles CA 90009

CHRISTENSEN, BENT AKSEL, b Copenhagen, Denmark, Mar 22, 28; m 58; c 2. CIVIL ENGINEERING, HYDRAULICS. *Educ:* Copenhagen Univ, Filosofikum, 48; Tech Univ Denmark, MS, 51; Univ Minn, PhD(hydraul), 61. *Prof Exp:* Asst prof hydraul, Tech Univ Denmark, 51-55, assoc prof, 55-59, 61-63; assoc prof, 63-65, PROF CIVIL ENG & HYDRAUL, UNIV FLA, 65- *Concurrent Pos:* Govt supvr, Hydraul Lab, Polytech Sch, Lausanne, 53; Danish Mil Acad, NATO, 55-62; mem bd dirs, Fluid Mech Inst, Univ Fla, 65- *Mem:* Am Soc Civil Engrs; Am Soc Eng Educ; Am Water Resources Asn; Danish Inst Civil Engrs; Int Asn Hydraul Res. *Res:* Hydraulics; pipe and open channel flow; water resources engineering; hydrology; sediment transport; fluid dynamics; ground water flow and soil mechanics. *Mailing Add:* Dept of Civil Eng Univ of Fla Gainesville FL 32601

CHRISTENSEN, BERT EINAR, b Duluth, Minn, Oct 20, 04; m 32; c 3. SYNTHETIC ORGANIC CHEMISTRY. *Educ:* Wash State Univ, BS, 27; Univ Wash, PhD(chem), 32. *Prof Exp:* Chemist, Atmospheric Nitrogen Corp, Syracuse, 27-28; from instr to prof chem, 31-70, chmn dept, 56-70, EMER PROF CHEM, ORE STATE UNIV, 70- *Mem:* AAAS; Am Chem Soc. *Res:* Organic synthesis of quinazoline, purine, pyrimidine and other related heterocyclic compounds. *Mailing Add:* 337 NW 23rd Corvallis OR 97330

CHRISTENSEN, BURGESS NYLES, b San Francisco, Calif, Oct 4, 40; m 61; c 2. NEUROPHYSIOLOGY. *Educ:* Univ Utah, BA, 63, PhD(biophys, bioeng), 67. *Prof Exp:* Fel physiol, Univ Utah, 67-68; fel, Yale Univ, 68-70; asst prof neurosci, Brown Univ, 70-76; ASST PROF PHYSIOL, UNIV TEX MED BR, 76- *Mem:* AAAS; Soc Neurosci. *Res:* Synaptic transmission in the central nervous system. *Mailing Add:* Dept of Physiol & Biophys Univ of Tex Med Br Galveston TX 77550

CHRISTENSEN, BURTON GRANT, b Waterloo, Iowa, Apr 8, 30; m 61, 81; c 2. BIO-ORGANIC CHEMISTRY, MEDICINAL CHEMISTRY. *Educ:* Iowa State Univ, BS, 52; Harvard Univ, AM, 54, PhD(chem), 56. *Prof Exp:* Chemist, 56-71, asst dir, 71-73, dir synthetic chem res, 73-76, EXEC DIR SYNTHETIC CHEM RES, MERCK, SHARP & DOHME RES LABS, 76- *Mem:* Am Chem Soc; Royal Soc Chem. *Res:* Organic chemistry, with emphasis on antibacterial synthesis. *Mailing Add:* Merk & Co Inc R 80 M 113 PO Box 2000 Rahway NJ 07065

CHRISTENSEN, CHARLES RICHARD, b Florence, Ala, Oct 18, 38; m 59; c 3. OPTICAL PHYSICS, SOLID STATE PHYSICS. *Educ:* Vanderbilt Univ, BE, 60; Calif Inst Technol, PhD(chem), 66. *Prof Exp:* Res chemist, 67-68; RES PHYSICIST, PHYS SCI LAB, US ARMY MISSILE COMMAND, 69- *Mem:* Am Phys Soc; Am Chem Soc; Optical Soc Am. *Res:* Coherent optics with applications in signal processing and correlation; coherent optical imaging, optical synthetic aperture methods; magnetic resonance and magnetic materials. *Mailing Add:* 1400 Levert Ave Athens AL 35611

CHRISTENSEN, CHRISTIAN MARTIN, b Ft Collins, Colo, Sept 24, 46; m 68; c 2. ECONOMIC ENTOMOLOGY. *Educ:* Rutgers Univ, BS, 68; Purdue Univ, MS, 70, PhD(entom), 74. *Prof Exp:* Livestock & forage entom exten specialist, 74-80, ASST EXTEN PROF ENTOM, UNIV KY, 80- *Mem:* Entom Soc Am. *Res:* Practical application techniques and control methods for controlling livestock insect pests; development and implementation of a practical integrated pest management system for Kentucky alfalfa producers. *Mailing Add:* Dept of Entom Univ of Ky Lexington KY 40506

CHRISTENSEN, CLARK G, b Spanish Fork, Utah, June 17, 43; m 67; c 5. ASTRONOMY. *Educ:* Brigham Young Univ, BS, 66; Calif Inst Technol, PhD(astron). 72. *Prof Exp:* ASSOC PROF PHYSICS & ASTRON, BRIGHAM YOUNG UNIV, 72- *Mem:* Am Astron Soc; Astron Soc Pac. *Res:* Luminosity function of galaxies; metal poor stars; variable stars; population syntheses of stellar systems. *Mailing Add:* 410 ESC Brigham Young Univ Provo UT 84602

CHRISTENSEN, CLYDE MARTIN, b Sturgeon Bay, Wis, Aug 8, 05; m 35; c 3. PLANT PATHOLOGY. *Educ:* Univ Minn, BS, 29, MS, 30, PhD(plant path), 37. *Prof Exp:* Instr plant path, Univ Minn, 30-32 & 34-40, asst prof, 40-47; asst pathologist, Forest Prod Lab, US Forest Serv, Wis, 43; assoc prof plant path, 47-48, PROF PLANT PATH, UNIV MINN, ST PAUL, 48- *Concurrent Pos:* Rockefeller Found Agr Prog, Mex, 59-63 & 64; consult, Cargill, Inc, 62- *Mem:* Am Asn Cereal Chemists; Mycol Soc Am; Am Phytopath Soc; Am Soc Microbiol. *Res:* Deterioration of stored grains caused by molds; mycotoxins. *Mailing Add:* 12619 Skyview Dr Sun City W AZ 85375

CHRISTENSEN, CRAIG MITCHELL, b Chicago, Ill, Jan 25, 32; m 58; c 2. CHEMICAL ENGINEERING, INDUSTRIAL ENGINEERING. *Educ:* Univ Ill, Urbana, BS, 53; Cornell Univ, PhD(chem eng), 61. *Prof Exp:* Res engr, B F Goodrich Res Ctr, 60-63, sr res engr, 63-66, mgr qual assurance, 66-73, MGR, INVENTORY & DISTRIB METHODS, TIRE DIV, B F GOODRICH CO, AKRON, 73- *Mem:* Am Soc Qual Control; Am Chem Soc; Am Inst Chem Engrs; Am Statist Asn. *Res:* Industrial statistics; liquid-liquid extraction; applied statistical design and analysis of experiments; physical distribution. *Mailing Add:* 5919 Bradford Way Hudson OH 44236

CHRISTENSEN, D(ON) C(OY), b Richfield, Utah, Aug 26, 29; m 54; c 4. EXTRUSION ENGINEERING, PLASTIC PROCESSING. *Educ:* Univ Utah, BS, 51, MS, 53. *Prof Exp:* Tech man chem eng, B F Goodrich Co, Ohio, 56-60; develop engr, 60-65, SECT MGR PLASTICS EXTRUSION, PHILLIPS PETROL CO, 65- *Mem:* Soc Plastics Engrs. *Res:* Plastics extrusion; heat transfer. *Mailing Add:* Phillips Res Ctr Phillips Petrol Co Bartlesville OK 74004

CHRISTENSEN, DOUGLAS ALLEN, b Bakersfield, Calif, Dec 14, 39; m 62; c 3. ELECTRICAL ENGINEERING, BIOENGINEERING. *Educ:* Brigham Young Univ, BS, 62; Stanford Univ, MS, 63; Univ Utah, PhD(elec eng), 67. *Prof Exp:* Sr res engr elec eng, Gen Motors Res Lab, 66-70; asst prof elec eng & bioeng, 70-78, ASSOC PROF ELEC ENG & BIOENG, UNIV UTAH, 78- *Concurrent Pos:* NIH fel, Ctr Bioeng, Univ Washington, 71-73. *Mem:* Inst Elec & Electronics Engrs. *Res:* Bioinstrumentation, especially optical and ultrasound interaction in biological material; microwave hyperthermia. *Mailing Add:* 8520 Top of World Circle Salt Lake City UT 84121

CHRISTENSEN, EDWARD RICHARDS, b Salt Lake City, Utah, Dec 21, 24; m 49; c 1. PETROLEUM CHEMISTRY. *Educ:* Univ Utah, BS, 48, MS, 49; Union Col, MS, 74. *Prof Exp:* Chemist, Beacon Res Labs, 49-56, group leader fuels process develop, 56-58, admin asst to dir res, 58-59, asst supvr petrochem res, 60-65, supvr, 65-67, res dir chem & process res, 67-75, asst mgr res & tech dept, Beacon Res Labs, 75-77, asst mgr, Port Arthur Res Labs, Tex, 77-78, MGR SCI PLANNING, RES, ENVIRON & SAFETY DEPT, TEXACO, INC, 78- *Mem:* Am Chem Soc; Am Inst Chem Eng; Sigma Xi. *Res:* Synthesis and applications testing of chemicals derived from petroleum and development of pilot scale processes for their manufacture; development of new or improved catalysts and processes for the conversion of crude oil to marketable products; development of improved methods and equipment for carrying out process development. *Mailing Add:* Beacon Res Labs Texaco Inc PO Box 509 Beacon NY 12508

CHRISTENSEN, ERIC, b Brooklyn, NY, Sept 18, 14; m 39; c 2. BIOLOGY. *Educ:* NY State Col Forestry, BS, 47; Hofstra Col, MA, 58. *Prof Exp:* Res assoc & tech specialist, Brookhaven Nat Lab, 47-53; from assoc prof to prof biol, 55-76, EMER PROF BIOL, STATE UNIV NY AGR & TECH COL FARMINGDALE, 76- *Mem:* Am Inst Biol Sci; Bot Soc Am. *Res:* Radiobiology; microtechnique teaching sciences; Ginkgo biloba specialist. *Mailing Add:* 295 S Howard St Ventura CA 93003

CHRISTENSEN, ERIK REGNAR, b Copenhagen, Denmark, Apr 17, 43; m 68; c 3. WATER CHEMISTRY. *Educ:* Tech Univ Denmark, MS, 67; Univ Calif, Irvine, PhD(Environ Eng), 77. *Prof Exp:* Res asst, Danish Defense Res Bd, 67-69; asst prof applied nuclear physics & reactor physics, Dept Electrophysics, Tech Univ Denmark, 69-73, assoc prof, 73-74; teaching asst water qual & teaching assoc radioisotope, Dept Chem, Sch Eng, Univ Calif, Irvine, 74-77; ASST PROF CIVIL & ENVIRON ENG, DEPT CIVIL ENG, COL ENG & APPLIED SCI, UNIV WIS, MILWAUKEE, 77- *Mem:* Am Nuclear Soc; Int Asn Water Pollution Res; Asn Environ Eng Professors; AAAS. *Res:* Multiple toxicity of various compounds to algal growth; sources and pathways of pollutants (metals and organics) in sediments using, for example, radiometric geochronologic methods. *Mailing Add:* Dept Civil Eng Univ Wis Milwaukee WI 53201

CHRISTENSEN, GEORGE CURTIS, b New York, NY, Feb 21; m 47; c 4. VETERINARY ANATOMY. *Educ:* Cornell Univ, DVM, 49, MS, 50, PhD(mammal anat, higher educ), 53. *Hon Degrees:* DSc, Purdue Univ, 78. *Prof Exp:* Instr vet anat, Cornell Univ, 49-53; assoc prof, Iowa State Univ, 53-58; prof vet anat & head dept, Purdue Univ, 58-63; dean col vet med & dir vet med res inst, 63-65, V PRES FOR ACAD AFFAIRS, IOWA STATE UNIV, 65- *Concurrent Pos:* Comnr, NIH & NCent Asn Cols & Sec Schs; mem comt educ & res, Nat Acad Sci, 70-72; mem bd dirs, Iowa State Hyg Lab & Ctr Res Libr, Chicago; mem, Iowa Bd Health; mem exec comt, Nat Asn State Univs & Land-Grant Cols, 73-, chmn coun acad affairs, 73-74; chmn, Comt Educ Telecommun, vpres, Mid-Am State Univs Asn, 75-76. *Mem:* Nat Acad Sci; Am Vet Med Asn; Conf Res Workers Animal Dis; Am Asn Vet Anatomists (pres, 63); World Asn Vet Anatomists (vpres, 63-65). *Res:* University administration; comparative cardiovascular anatomy and physiology; comparative vasculature of urogenital and central nervous systems; history of veterinary medical education; higher education. *Mailing Add:* 110 Beardshear Hall Iowa State Univ Ames IA 50010

CHRISTENSEN, GERALD M, b Pocatello, Idaho, Dec 23, 28; m 49; c 2. BIOCHEMISTRY, RADIOBIOLOGY. *Educ:* Univ Utah, BS, 51; Emory Univ, PhD, 58. *Prof Exp:* Fel, Virus Lab, Univ Calif, Berkeley, 58-59; sr biochemist, Boeing Co, Wash, 59-64; from asst prof to assoc prof radiol, 64-80, ASSOC PROF ENVIRON SCI, UNIV WASH, 80- *Res:* Biological effects of ionizing radiation; enzyme and protein chemistry; amino acid and nucleotide metabolism. *Mailing Add:* Dept of Radiol Univ of Wash Seattle WA 98195

CHRISTENSEN, GLEN C, wildlife management, see previous edition

CHRISTENSEN, GLENN MARVIN, biochemistry, see previous edition

CHRISTENSEN, H(ARVEY) D(EVON), b Challis, Idaho, Apr 6, 20; m 51; c 5. AEROSPACE & MECHANICAL ENGINEERING. *Educ:* Univ Wash, Seattle, BS, 43; Ore State Univ, MS, 50; Stanford Univ, PhD(eng mech), 60. *Prof Exp:* Eng designer, Boeing Airplane Co, 43-46; from instr to assoc prof mech eng, Ore State Univ, 47-51, head, aeronaut option, 51-58; head dept, 58-70, PROF AEROSPACE & MECH ENG, UNIV ARIZ, 58- *Concurrent Pos:* NSF grant, 57-58. *Mem:* Am Soc Mech Engrs; Soc Automotive Engrs; Am Soc Eng Educ. *Res:* Engineering mechanics and analysis dynamics; structures; aerodynamics; experimental stress analysis; aerospace engineering; interactive learning systems. *Mailing Add:* 5714 E South Wilshire Dr Tucson AZ 85711

CHRISTENSEN, HALVOR NIELS, b Cozad, Nebr, Oct 24, 15; m 39; c 3. BIOCHEMISTRY, BIOPHYSICS. *Educ:* Kearney State Col, BS, 35; Purdue Univ, MS, 37; Harvard Univ, PhD(biol chem), 40. *Prof Exp:* Fel chem, Harvard Univ, 40-41; res biochemist, Lederle Labs, 41-42; instr biol chem, Harvard Med Sch, 42-44; dir chem labs, Mary-Imogene Bassett Hosp, Cooperstown, NY, 44-47; asst prof biochem, Harvard Med Sch, 47-49; prof biochem & nutrit & head dept, Sch Med, Tufts Univ, 49-55; chmn dept biol chem, 55-70, PROF BIOL CHEM, UNIV MICH, ANN ARBOR, 55- *Concurrent Pos:* Dir lab biochem res, Childrens Hosp, Boston, 47-49; Guggenheim fel, Carlsberg Lab, Copenhagen, 52; consult, NIH, 61-68; Nobel guest prof, Univ Uppsala, 68. *Honors & Awards:* Russel lectr, 80. *Mem:* Fel Am Acad Arts & Sci; Am Soc Biol Chem; Am Chem Soc; Am Inst Nutrit; Biophys Soc. *Res:* Amino acid transport; intravenous amino acid nutrition; peptide metabolism and antibiotics. *Mailing Add:* Dept of Biol Chem Univ of Mich Ann Arbor MI 48109

CHRISTENSEN, HOWARD ANTHONY, b Oakland, Calif, Apr 26, 28; m 52. MEDICAL ENTOMOLOGY, MEDICAL PARASITOLOGY. *Educ:* San Francisco State Col, BA, 63, MA, 66; Univ Calif, Davis, PhD(entom), 68. *Prof Exp:* MED ENTOMOLOGIST, GORGAS MEM LAB, 68- *Mem:* Am Soc Parasitol; Am Soc Trop Med & Hyg; Am Mosquito Control Asn. *Res:* Bionomics of arthropod vectors of medical importance and the epidemiology of arthropod borne diseases; leishmaniasis. *Mailing Add:* Gorgas Mem Lab PO Box 935 APO Miami FL 34002

CHRISTENSEN, HOWARD DIX, b Logan, Utah, Mar 30, 40; m 66; c 3. NEUROPHARMACOLOGY. *Educ:* Univ Nev, Reno, BS, 61; Univ Calif, Los Angeles, PhD(biophys, nuclear med), 66. *Prof Exp:* Fel pharmacol, Univ Calif, San Francisco, 66-68 & Columbia Univ, 68-69; pharmacologist, Res Triangle Inst, 69-74; ASSOC PROF PHARMACOL, SCHS MED & DENT, UNIV OKLA, 74- *Mem:* Am Soc Pharmacol & Exp Therapeut; NY Acad Sci; Sigma Xi; Soc Neurosci; Soc Exp Biol & Med. *Res:* Central nervous system mechanisms of cannabinoids, anticonvulsants, central nervous system depressants and stimulants and contraceptive steroids; antihypertensives and antiglaucoma drugs; correlations between drug development of analytical methodologies; kinetics and physiological or behavioral response. *Mailing Add:* 416 NW 17th Oklahoma City OK 73103

CHRISTENSEN, JAMES, b Ames, Iowa, Jan 4, 32; m 58; c 3. PHYSIOLOGY, GASTROENTEROLOGY. *Educ:* Univ Nebr, BS, 53, MS & MD, 57. *Prof Exp:* From instr to assoc prof, 65-72, PROF INTERNAL MED, UNIV IOWA, 72- *Concurrent Pos:* Lectr, Univ Alta, 65-66; Markle scholar, 65-70; USPHS career develop award, 69-74; mem eval comt gastroenterol, Vet Admin Res, 69- *Mem:* Am Fedn Clin Res; Asn Am Physicians; Am Gastroenterol Asn; Am Soc Clin Invest. *Res:* Gastrointestinal motility; autonomic and smooth muscle physiology. *Mailing Add:* Dept of Internal Med Univ of Iowa Hosps Iowa City IA 52242

CHRISTENSEN, JAMES HENRY, b Beaver Dam, Wis, Apr 9, 42; m 63; c 2. PROGRAMMABLE CONTROLLERS, DATA COMMUNICATIONS. *Educ:* Univ Wis, BS, 63, MS, 65, PhD(chem eng), 67. *Prof Exp:* Fel eng design, Dartmouth Col, 67-68; asst prof chem eng, Univ Okla, 68-71, assoc prof, 71-76; pres, Strider Syst, Inc, 76-79; sr syst engr, Tex Instruments, Inc, 79-82; MGR ADVAN RES & DEVELOP, SYST DIV, ALLEN-BRADLEY CO, 82- *Concurrent Pos:* Mem, Comput Aids Chem Eng Educ Comt, Nat Acad Sci, 69-73; consult, Chemshare, Ltd, 69-70; ac fel, Ames Lab, US Atomic Energy Comn, 72; chmn, US Task Force Prog Language, Int Electrotech Comn, 81. *Mem:* Am Inst Chem Eng. *Res:* Advanced research in digital systems for industrial control, commmunication and automation. *Mailing Add:* Syst Div Allen-Bradley Co 747 Alpha Dr Highland Heights OH 44143

CHRISTENSEN, JAMES J, b Salt Lake City, Utah, Apr 30, 31; m 52; c 5. CHEMICAL ENGINEERING. *Educ:* Univ Utah, BS, 53, MS, 55; Carnegie Inst Technol, PhD(chem eng), 57. *Prof Exp:* From asst prof to assoc prof, 58-66, annual fac lectr, 70, PROF CHEM ENG, BRIGHAM YOUNG UNIV, 66- *Concurrent Pos:* NIH spec fel, Oxford, 64-65 & career develop award, 67-72; mem bd dirs, Calorimetry Conf, 70-73, chmn, 73-74. *Honors & Awards:* Karl G Maeser Res Award, Brigham Young Univ, 67. *Mem:* AAAS; Am Soc Eng Educ; Am Inst Chem Engrs; Am Chem Soc. *Res:* Thermochemistry and thermometric titrations; heats of formation of complex ions in aqueous solutions; metal binding and transport with macrocyclic compounds. *Mailing Add:* Dept of Chem Eng Brigham Young Univ Provo UT 84601

CHRISTENSEN, JAMES ROGER, b Des Moines, Iowa, Oct 28, 25; m 51; c 2. VIROLOGY. *Educ:* Iowa State Col, BS, 49; Cornell Univ, PhD(biochem), 53. *Prof Exp:* Fel biophysics, Sch Med, Univ Colo, 53-55; from instr to assoc prof, 55-70, actg chmn, 67-70, PROF MICROBIOL, SCH MED & DENT, UNIV ROCHESTER, 70- *Mem:* Am Soc Microbiologists; Genetics Soc. *Res:* Bacteriophage; DNA replication and recombination; gene function; mutual exclusion. *Mailing Add:* Dept of Microbiol Univ of Rochester Sch of Med Rochester NY 14642

CHRISTENSEN, JOHN, b Mahtowa, Minn, June 19, 08; m 32, 64; c 3. BIOCHEMISTRY. *Educ:* Union Col, Nebr, BA, 39; Univ Nebr, MA, 46; Mich State Univ, PhD, 56. *Prof Exp:* Teacher, Shelton Acad, 39-41; asst chem, Union Col, Nebr, 41-45; from instr to asst prof chem, Emmanuel Missionary Col, 45-55; prof, 55-75, EMER PROF CHEM, SOUTHERN MISSIONARY COL, 75- *Mem:* Am Chem Soc RES: Periodate oxidations of sugars and related organic compounds; chemistry of 1,3-diketones. *Mailing Add:* Box 507 Collegedale TN 37315

CHRISTENSEN, JOHN BERT, anatomy, see previous edition

CHRISTENSEN, KENNER ALLEN, b Duluth, Minn, July 18, 43; m 68; c 2. NUCLEAR MAGNETIC RESONANCE, ORGANIC CHEMISTRY. *Educ:* Univ Minn-Duluth, BA, 65; Ohio State Univ, MS, 68, PhD(chem), 71. *Prof Exp:* Fel chem, Univ Utah, 70-73; asst prof, Univ Notre Dame, 73-76; NUCLEAR MAGNETIC RESONANCE SPECIALIST, NORTHWESTERN UNIV, 76- *Mem:* Am Chem Soc; AAAS. *Res:* Development of instrumentation and techniques in nuclear magnetic resonance; studies of organometallic compounds by nuclear magnetic resonance. *Mailing Add:* Dept of Chem Northwestern Univ Evanston IL 60201

CHRISTENSEN, LARRY WAYNE, b Elkhart, Ind, Sept 1, 43; m 65; c 2. ORGANIC CHEMISTRY. *Educ:* Goshen Col, BA, 65; Purdue Univ, PhD(chem), 69. *Prof Exp:* Assoc prof, 69-76, PROF CHEM & CHMN DEPT, HOUGHTON COL, 76- *Concurrent Pos:* Vis fac mem, Univ Ariz, 75. *Mem:* Am Chem Soc; Am Sci Affil. *Res:* Mechanistic and synthetic organosulfur chemistry; applications of mass spectrometry to organic chemistry. *Mailing Add:* Dept of Chem Houghton Col Houghton NY 14744

CHRISTENSEN, MARK NEWELL, b Green Bay, Wis, July 16, 30; m 55. GEOLOGY. *Educ:* Univ Alaska, BS, 52; Univ Calif, PhD, 59. *Prof Exp:* From actg instr to instr geol, Univ Calif, Berkeley, 59-60, from asst prof to assoc prof, 60-74; prof geol & geophys, Univ Calif, Santa Cruz, 60-76, chancellor, 74-76; PROF ENERGY & RESOURCES, UNIV CALIF, BERKELEY, 76- *Concurrent Pos:* Asst dean, Col Letters & Sci, Univ Calif, Berkeley, 65-74. *Mem:* AAAS; Geol Soc Am; Am Geophys Union. *Res:* Structural geology; deformation of rocks; stratigraphy; tectonics. *Mailing Add:* 230 Fall Creek Dr Felton CA 94720

CHRISTENSEN, MARTHA, b Ames, Iowa, Jan 4, 32. MYCOLOGY, ECOLOGY. *Educ:* Univ Nebr, BSc, 53; Univ Wis, MS, 56, PhD(bot), 60. *Prof Exp:* Proj assoc mycol, Univ Wis, 60-63; asst prof, 63-68, assoc prof, 68-75, PROF BOT, UNIV WYO, 75- *Honors & Awards:* Weber-Ernst Award, 53. *Mem:* Mycol Soc Am; Ecol Soc Am; Brit Mycol Soc. *Res:* Ecology and taxonomy of soil microfungi. *Mailing Add:* Dept of Bot Univ of Wyo Laramie WY 82070

CHRISTENSEN, N(EPHI) A(LBERT), b Provo, Utah, Jan 19, 03; m 29; c 4. CIVIL ENGINEERING, MATHEMATICS. *Educ:* Brigham Young Univ, BS, 25; Univ Wis, BS, 28; Calif Inst Technol, MS, 34, PhD(civil eng), 39. *Prof Exp:* Teacher high sch, Utah, 25-26; prof exact sci, Ricks Col, Idaho, 28-33; instr, Calif Inst Technol, 33-35; hydraul res lab, Soil Conserv Serv, US Dept Agr, 35-38; dean eng, Colo State Univ, 38-48, dir eng div, exp sta, 39-48; dir, Sch Civil Eng, Cornell Univ, 48-68, emer prof, 68-81; ENG CONSULT, EPITAXY INC, 73-; PRES, GAS SCRUBBERS, INC, 80- *Concurrent Pos:* Spec lectr, Univ Southern Calif, 36; engr, State Hwy Comn, Wis, 27-28; chief engr, Ballistics Res Lab, Aberdeen Proving Ground, Md, 43-44; chief Rocket Res Div, Ord Res & Develop Ctr, 44-45; consult, Brookhaven Nat Lab & Argonne Nat Lab Atomic Energy Comn; office ord res, US Army, 53-54; mem, NY State Flood Control Comn, 54-60; trustee, Cayuga Heights Village, 56; coordr four eng firms to develop comprehensive sewerage plan for Monroe County, NY, 66-68; col admin adv, Near East Found, Rezaiyeh Agr Col, Iran, 68-72. *Mem:* Am Soc Civil Engrs; Am Soc Eng Educ; Am Geophys Union. *Res:* Rocket research; hydraulics; structures; erosion and sedimentation; irrigation. *Mailing Add:* 7801 Pickard Ave NE Albuquerque NM 87110

CHRISTENSEN, NED JAY, b Clarkston, Utah, June 23, 29; m 51; c 3. AUDIOLOGY. *Educ:* Brigham Young Univ, BA, 54, MA, 55; Pa State Univ, PhD, 59. *Prof Exp:* Instr, Pa State Univ, 55-59; asst prof speech & clin supvr, WVa Univ, 59-62; from asst prof to assoc prof, 62-74, asst dir, 62-70, dir speech path-audiol prog, 72-76, PROF SPEECH, UNIV ORE, 74-, COORDR, COM DISORDERS, 76- *Mem:* Am Speech & Hearing Asn. *Res:* Audiological rehabilitation. *Mailing Add:* Dept of Speech Path-Audiol Univ of Ore Col of Educ Eugene OR 97403

CHRISTENSEN, NIELS GUNNAR, electrooptics, see previous edition

CHRISTENSEN, NIKOLAS IVAN, b Madison, Wis, Apr 11, 37; m m 60; c 1. GEOPHYSICS, MINERALOGY. *Educ:* Univ Wis, BS, 59, MS, 61, PhD(geol), 63. *Prof Exp:* Res fel geophys, Harvard Univ, 63-64; assoc prof geol, Univ Southern Calif, 64-67; PROF GEOL, UNIV WASH, 67- *Mem:* Fel Geol Soc Am; Am Geophys Union; Seismol Soc Am. *Res:* Elasticity of rocks and minerals; crystal physics, nature of the earth's interior. *Mailing Add:* Dept of Geol Univ of Wash Seattle WA 98105

CHRISTENSEN, NORMAN LEROY, JR, b Fresno, Calif, Dec 28, 46; m 68; c 2. PLANT ECOLOGY. *Educ:* Calif State Univ, Fresno, BA, 68, MA, 70; Univ Calif, Santa Barbara, PhD(biol), 73. *Prof Exp:* asst prof, 73-80, ASSOC PROF BOT, DUKE UNIV, 80- *Mem:* Ecol Soc Am; AAAS; Sigma Xi; Brit Ecol Soc. *Res:* Effects of disturbance on plant community structure and function; effects of fire on community nutrient relations; forest demography. *Mailing Add:* Dept of Bot Duke Univ Durham NC 27706

CHRISTENSEN, ODIN DALE, b Duluth, Minn, Dec 12, 47; m 71. MINERALOGY, GEOCHEMISTRY. *Educ:* Univ Minn, BA, 70; Stanford Univ, PhD(geol), 75. *Prof Exp:* Asst prof geol, Univ NDak, 75-78; res geochemist, Univ Utah Res Inst, 78-81; RES GEOLOGIST, NEWMONT EXPLOR LTD, 81- *Mem:* Geol Soc Am; Mineral Soc Am; Soc Mining Engrs; Mineral Asn Can; Am Geophys Union. *Res:* Defining the mineralogic and petrographic changes which occur during diagenesis of pelitic rocks and using these criteria as indicators of low-grade metamorphism; geochemistry of geothermal systems; exploration geologic techniques. *Mailing Add:* Newmont Explor Ltd 327 Freeport Blvd Sparks NV 89431

CHRISTENSEN, RALPH CHRESTEN, b San Mateo, Calif, Dec 11, 39; m 78; c 3. RADIOLOGICAL HEALTH, MEDICAL PHYSICS. *Educ:* Stanford Univ, BS, 61, MA, 62; Univ Calif, Berkeley, MBiorad, 65, PhD(biophysics), 71. *Prof Exp:* Res fel biophysics, Pa State Univ, 71-73, asst prof radiobiol, Hershey Med Ctr, 73-76; asst prof, 76-80, ASSOC PROF RADIOL HEALTH, UNIV KY, 80- *Concurrent Pos:* co-ed, Selected Topics in Reactor Health Physics; mem, Educ & Training Comt, Am Assoc Physicists Med, 81- *Mem:* Health Physics Soc; Am Assoc Physicists Med; Biophys Soc; Sigma Xi. *Res:* Radiation dosimetry; applied health physics; applied medical physics; radiation biophysics. *Mailing Add:* Dept of Health Radiation Sci Univ Ky Med Ctr Rm 130 Annex 2 Lexington KY 40536

CHRISTENSEN, RICHARD MONSON, b Idaho Falls, Idaho, July 3, 32; m 58; c 2. COMPOSITE MATERIALS, VISCOELASTICITY. *Educ:* Univ Utah, BSc, 55; Yale Univ, MEng, 56, DEng, 61. *Prof Exp:* Struct engr, Convair Div, Gen Dynamics, 56-58; mem tech staff, TRW Systs, 61-64; asst prof mech eng, Univ Calif, Berkeley, 64-67; staff res engr, Shell Develop Co, 67-74; prof mech eng, Washington Univ, 74-76; MEM TECH STAFF, LAWRENCE LIVERMORE NAT LAB, 76- *Concurrent Pos:* Lectr, Univ Southern Calif, 62-64, Univ Calif, Berkeley, 69-70, 78 & 80, Univ Houston, 73; chmn, Appl Mech Div, Am Soc Mech Engrs, 80-81; mem, US Nat Comt Theoret & Appl Mech, 80- *Mem:* Fel Am Soc Mech Engrs; Soc Rheology; Am Chem Soc. *Res:* Properties of polymers, wave propagation, failure theories, crack kinetics, composite materials. *Mailing Add:* Lawrence Livermore Nat Lab PO Box 808 Livermore CA 94550

CHRISTENSEN, RICHARD W, soil mechanics, foundation engineering, see previous edition

CHRISTENSEN, ROBERT LEE, b Orange, NJ, July 23, 29; m 52; c 3. ATOMIC PHYSICS, COMPUTER SCIENCE. *Educ:* Princeton Univ, AB, 50, MA, 54, PhD(physics), 57. *Prof Exp:* Asst reactor dept, Brookhaven Nat Lab, 53; asst physics dept, Princeton Univ, 57-58; physicist res lab, Int Bus Mach Corp, 58-61, eng mgt, 61-65; vpres, Quantum Sci Corp, 66-67; VPRES, A G BECKER INC, 68- *Mem:* Am Phys Soc; Inst Elec & Electronics Engrs; Inst Chartered Financial Analysts. *Res:* Nuclear and atomic resonance; ultra-high vacuum; photoelectric effect; application of digital computers to image and language processing; management information systems, applied statistics and econometrics; technological forecasting. *Mailing Add:* A G Becker Inc 55 Water St New York NY 10041

CHRISTENSEN, SABINUS HOEGSBRO, b New York, NY, May 20, 15; m 46. PHYSICS. *Educ:* Pratt Inst, BME, 41; Harvard Univ, MS, 48, ScD(math physics), 51. *Prof Exp:* Lab asst, Pratt & Whitney Aircraft Div, United Aircraft Corp, 33-37; jr res engr, Sperry Gyroscope Co, 41-42; res engr, Fairchild Aircraft Corp, 42-44; physicist in chg aerodynamic res, Carrier Corp, 44-47; res assoc prof, Ga Inst Technol, 51-53; prof & chmn dept physics, Clark & Morehouse Cols, 53-60; prof physics, Deep Springs Col, 60-61; prof physics, Hobart & William Smith Cols, 61-64; prof & chmn, Physics Dept, Bard Col, 64-66; chmn, Physics Dept, 75-, PROF PHYSICS, LINCOLN UNIV, PA, 66- *Concurrent Pos:* Consult, Oak Ridge Assoc Univs, 63- & Goddard Space Flight Ctr, NASA, 69. *Mem:* Am Asn Physics Teachers; Sigma Xi. *Res:* Radiation physics. *Mailing Add:* RD 1 Box 224 New Providence PA 17560

CHRISTENSEN, STANLEY HOWARD, b Boone, Iowa, Mar 6, 35; m 56; c 4. SOLID STATE PHYSICS. *Educ:* Iowa State Univ, BS, 57; Cornell Univ, PhD(physics), 63. *Prof Exp:* Jr physicist, Iowa State Univ, 57; asst prof, 63-67, assoc prof, 67-78, PROF PHYSICS, KENT STATE UNIV, 78- *Mem:* Am Phys Soc; Am Asn Physics Teachers. *Res:* Electron paramagnetic resonance; laser light scattering. *Mailing Add:* Dept of Physics Kent State Univ Kent OH 44242

CHRISTENSEN, STEVEN MARK, theoretical physics, see previous edition

CHRISTENSEN, THOMAS GASH, b Richmond, Va, Sept 16, 44. EXPERIMENTAL BIOLOGY, LUNG PATHOLOGY. *Educ:* Rutgers Univ, BS, 66; Univ Vt, PhD(bot), 71. *Prof Exp:* Res assoc med biochem, Sch Med, Univ Vt, 71-74; res assoc pulmonary path, 74-77, asst res prof, 77-80, ASST PROF PATH, SCH MED, BOSTON UNIV, 80-; res assoc, 74-79, SR RES ASSOC, MALLORY INST PATH, 79- *Concurrent Pos:* Vis lectr biol, Univ Vt, 71-74; prin investr, Nat Heart, Lung & Blood Inst grant, 78- *Mem:* Sigma Xi; AAAS; Electron Micros Soc Am. *Res:* Response of airway epithelium to foreign proteins; distribution and function of peroxidase in respiratory epithelium. *Mailing Add:* Mallory Inst Path Boston MA 02118

CHRISTENSON, CHARLES O, b Oakland, Calif, Sept 17, 36; m 60; c 4. TOPOLOGY. *Educ:* Univ Kans, BA, 58, MA, 60; NMex State Univ, PhD(math), 64. *Prof Exp:* From asst prof to assoc prof, 64-80, PROF MATH, UNIV IDAHO, 80- *Concurrent Pos:* Vis prof math, Col VI, 81-82. *Mem:* AAAS; Am Math Soc; Math Asn Am. *Res:* Knot theory; study of the knotting number; topology of manifolds. *Mailing Add:* Dept of Math Univ of Idaho Moscow ID 83843

CHRISTENSON, DONALD ROBERT, b Terry, Mont, Mar 31, 37; m 59; c 3. SOIL SCIENCE, PLANT PHYSIOLOGY. *Educ:* Mont State Col, BS, 60, MS, 64; Mich State Univ, PhD(soil sci), 68. *Prof Exp:* From asst prof to assoc prof, 68-79, PROF SOIL SCI, MICH STATE UNIV, 79- *Honors & Awards:* Scarseth Award, Am Soc Agron, 67. *Mem:* Am Soc Agron; Am Soc Sugar Beet Technol. *Res:* Soil-plant nutrient relationships; response of plants to applied nutrients; soil test correlations; mechanisms of nutrient release from soil minerals. *Mailing Add:* Dept Crop & Soil Sci Mich State Univ East Lansing MI 48824

CHRISTENSON, PAUL JOHN, b Watervliet, NY, Aug 13, 21; m 48; c 9. MEDICINE, PREVENTIVE MEDICINE. *Educ:* Siena Col, NY, BS, 43; Marquette Univ, MD, 46; Columbia Univ, MPH, 55. *Prof Exp:* Pvt pract med, NY, 49-52; dir pub health, Tri County Unit, Va, 52-53 & Mich, 53-54; dir pub health, Utica City Dept Health, NY, 55-57; mem med staff, Eaton Labs, Norwich Pharmacol Col, 57-59, dir clin res, 59-60, med dir, Norwich Prod Div, 60-65; med dir, Quinton Div, Merck & Co, Inc, NJ, 65-69; med dir, S E Massengill Co, 69-71; med dir, Semed Pharmaceut, 69-71; med dir, Ottawa Coun Health Dept, 71-79; HEALTH OFFICER & MED DIR, DISTRICT HEALTH DEPT #2, 79- *Concurrent Pos:* Chief med examr, Ottawa Co, Mich; mem Mich Gov comt med manpower. *Mem:* AAAS; Am Pub Health Asn; Am Col Prev Med; World Med Asn; AMA. *Res:* Clinical pharmaceutical research, especially chemotherapeutic agents; public health. *Mailing Add:* 3061 One-Eight Line Rd West Branch MI 48661

CHRISTENSON, ROGER MORRIS, b Sturgeon Bay, Wis, Sept 28, 19; m 47; c 3. CHEMISTRY. *Educ:* Univ Wis, BS, 41, MS, 42, PhD(food chem), 44. *Prof Exp:* Asst, Univ Wis, 41-44; res chemist, 44-52, res supvr, Synthetic Vehicles, 52-56, mgr new prods res, 58-65, div dir resin res, 65-76, assoc dir res, 76-80, DIR RES, PPG INDUSTS, 80- *Mem:* Am Chem Soc; Fedn Socs Paint Technol. *Res:* Polymer chemistry related to coatings and adhesives; thermosetting and thermoplastic acrylic polymers, alkyd and epoxy resins, melamine and urea resins, polymer dispersions, electrocoating. *Mailing Add:* PPG Industs Res Ctr PO Box 9 Allison Park PA 15101

CHRISTIAN, CHARLES DONALD, b Parker, Kans, Nov 28, 30; m 56; c 3. OBSTETRICS & GYNECOLOGY. *Educ:* Univ Kans, AB, 52; Duke Univ, PhD, 56, MD, 58. *Prof Exp:* Instr anat, Sch Med, Duke Univ, 55-59; resident obstet & gynec, Columbia-Presby Med Ctr, 59-62; asst prof, Col Med, Univ Fla, 62-64; assoc prof obstet & gynec & dir endocrine div, Med Ctr, Duke Univ, 64-69; PROF OBSTET & GYNEC & HEAD DEPT, SCH MED, UNIV ARIZ, 69- *Concurrent Pos:* Macy Found fel, Columbia-Presby Med Ctr, 59-62. *Res:* Neuro-endocrine relationships in reproductive processes. *Mailing Add:* Dept of Obstet & Gynec Univ of Ariz Sch of Med Tucson AZ 85721

CHRISTIAN, CHARLES L, b Wichita, Kans, July 10, 26; m 54; c 3. IMMUNOLOGY. *Educ:* Univ Wichita, BS, 49; Western Reserve Univ, MD, 53. *Prof Exp:* From instr to prof med, Col Physicians & Surgeons, Columbia Univ, 58-70; PROF MED, COL MED, CORNELL UNIV, 70-; PHYSICIAN IN CHIEF, HOSP SPEC SURG, 70- *Concurrent Pos:* Consult, USPHS, 63- *Mem:* AAAS; Soc Exp Biol & Med; Am Asn Immunol; Am Rheumatism Asn (pres 77-78). *Res:* Immunochemistry; experimental pathology. *Mailing Add:* The Hosp for Spec Surg 535 E 70th St New York NY 10021

CHRISTIAN, CURTIS GILBERT, b Norwich, NY, Nov 16, 17; m 46; c 2. ORGANIC CHEMISTRY. *Educ:* Univ Calif, BS, 49, MS, 50. *Prof Exp:* Res chemist, Ansco Div, Gen Aniline & Film Corp, 50-52 & Union Oil Co, Calif, 52-55; res assoc, Gasparcolor, Inc, 55-58, prod mgr, 58-60; mgr photo prod pilot plant, 60-63, mgr photo prod tech serv, 63-66, mgr tech serv, Photo Film Div, 66-70, mgr prof photog prod lab, Photog Prod Div, 70-72, tech mgr, Dynacolor Subsidiary, 74-78, SR SPECIALIST, PHOTOG PROD DIV, MINN MINING & MFG CO, 72- *Mem:* Am Chem Soc; Soc Photog Sci & Eng; Royal Photog Soc; Soc Motion Picture & TV Engrs. *Res:* Photographic chemistry; organic synthesis. *Mailing Add:* Box 3064 St Paul MN 55165

CHRISTIAN, DONALD PAUL, b Akron, Ohio, Mar 16, 49; m 70. POPULATION ECOLOGY, PHYSIOLOGICAL ECOLOGY. *Educ:* Mich State Univ, BS, 71, MS, 73, PhD(zool), 77. *Prof Exp:* ASST PROF BIOL, UNIV MINN, DULUTH, 78- *Mem:* Am Soc Mammal; Ecol Soc Am. *Res:* Mammalian population ecology; physiological ecology, especially water metabolism and bioclimatology. *Mailing Add:* Dept of Biol Univ of Minn Duluth MN 55812

CHRISTIAN, FREDERICK ADE, b Lagos, Nigeria, July 8, 37; US citizen; m 71; c 2. HELMINTH PHYSIOLOGY, MEDICAL ENTOMOLOGY. *Educ:* Allen Univ, BS, 62; Wayne State Univ, MS, 64; Ohio State Univ, PhD(parasitol), 69. *Prof Exp:* Teaching asst zool, Wayne State Univ, 62-64; teaching asst & instr zool, Ohio State Univ, 65-69; from asst prof to assoc prof, 69-74, PROF BIOL & DIR, HEALTH RES CTR, SOUTHERN UNIV, 75-, DIR RES, COL SCI, 76- *Concurrent Pos:* Prin investr, US Dept Agr, 72-77, NIH, 72- & NSF, 80-; Coun mem, La Univ Marine Consortium, 78-; extramural assoc, NIH, 79; chmn, Univ Res Coun, Southern Univ, 79-, Res Incentive Comt, 81- *Mem:* Am Soc Parasitologists; Am Micros Soc; Nat Minority Health Affairs Assoc; Am Inst Biol Sci. *Res:* Physiology of host-parasite relationships of Fasciola hepatica liver fluke of cattle and man; the effects of environmental pollution pesticides on parasites physiology and occurrences. *Mailing Add:* Southern Br Post Off PO Box 9882 Baton Rouge LA 70813

CHRISTIAN, GARY DALE, b Eugene, Ore, Nov 25, 37; m 61; c 2. ANALYTICAL CHEMISTRY. *Educ:* Univ Ore, BS, 59; Univ Md, MS, 62, PhD(anal chem), 64. *Prof Exp:* Res anal chemist, Walter Reed Army Inst Res, 61-67; from asst prof to assoc prof, Univ Ky, 67-72; PROF CHEM, UNIV WASH, 72- *Concurrent Pos:* Asst prof, Univ Md, 65-66; guest lectr, Walter Reed Army Inst Res, 66; consult electroanal chem, 68-; consult, Miles Labs, Inc, 68-72 & Beckman Instruments, Inc, 70-; Fulbright/Hays scholar, 78-79; vis prof, Univ Libre de Bruxelles, 78-79; invited prof, Univ Geneva, 79. *Mem:* Am Chem Soc; Soc Appl Spectros; fel Am Inst Chemists; Spectros Soc Can. *Res:* Atomic spectroscopy; electroanalytical chemistry; fluorometric analysis; competitive protein binding assays; clinical chemistry; enzyme assay; catalytic analysis; flow injection analysis; chromatography detectors. *Mailing Add:* Dept of Chem Univ of Wash Seattle WA 98195

CHRISTIAN, HOWARD HARRIS, b Philadelphia, Pa, Sept 30, 26; m 55. BIOLOGY, DATA PROCESSING. *Educ:* DePauw Univ, BA, 50; Univ Mass, MA, 52. *Prof Exp:* Instr biol, Susquehanna Univ, 53-54; res biochemist, Smith Kline & French Labs, 54-57; lit scientist, 57-65, SUPVR TECH RECORDS SECT, WYETH LABS, 65- *Res:* Biological sciences; pharmaceutics; experimental pharmacology and therapeutics. *Mailing Add:* Tech Rec Sect Sci Info Sect Wyeth Labs Box 8299 Philadelphia PA 19101

CHRISTIAN, HOWARD J, b Cambridge, Mass, Sept 17, 23; m 45; c 8. PATHOLOGY. *Educ:* Tufts Univ, BS, 49, MD, 52. *Prof Exp:* Intern path, Boston City Hosp, 52-53, resident, 53-56; from instr to asst prof, 56-70, assoc prof, 70-74, CLIN PROF PATH, SCH MED, TUFTS UNIV, 74-; PATHOLOGIST, CARNEY HOSP, BOSTON, 57- *Concurrent Pos:* Instr, Sch Med, Boston Univ, 54-56; asst pathologist, St Elizabeth's Hosp, Brighton, Mass, 56-57; jr vis pathologist, Lemuel Shattuck Hosp, Boston, 57-; attend pathologist, Vet Admin Hosp, 61-; hon sr lectr, Aberdeen Univ, 63-64; Commonwealth Fund fel, 63-; assoc prof, Boston Univ Sch Med, 71. *Mem:* AMA; Col Am Pathologists. *Res:* Electron microscopy; cancer and diabetes. *Mailing Add:* Carney Hosp 2100 Dorchester Ave Boston MA 02124

CHRISTIAN, JAMES A, b Kansas City, Mo, June 20, 35; m 55; c 4. BOTANY, GENETICS. *Educ:* Univ Mo-Columbia, BS, 58, MA, 62, PhD(biosysts), 71. *Prof Exp:* Teacher, St Clair Sch Dist, Mo, 58-60 & Mehlville Sch Dist, 60-61; asst bot, Univ Mo, 61-64; asst prof biol, Tarkio Col, 64-66; from asst prof to assoc prof, 66-80, PROF BOT, LA TECH UNIV, 80- *Mem:* Am Soc Plant Taxonomists; Int Asn Plant Taxonomists; Genetics Soc Am; Bot Soc Am; Torrey Bot Club. *Res:* Biosystematics and genetics of the genus Lupinus; taxonomy and phylogeny of vascular plants. *Mailing Add:* Dept Bot & Bact La Tech Univ Ruston LA 71272

CHRISTIAN, JOE CLARK, b Marshall, Okla, Sept 12, 34; m 60; c 2. MEDICAL GENETICS. *Educ:* Okla State Univ, BS, 56; Univ Ky, MS, 59, PhD(genetics), 60, MD, 64. *Prof Exp:* From intern to resident internal med, Vanderbilt Univ Hosp, 64-66; from asst prof to assoc prof, 66-74, PROF MED GENETICS, MED SCH, IND UNIV, INDIANAPOLIS, 74-, CHMN, 78- *Mem:* Am Soc Human Genetics; Am Fedn Clin Res; Am Oil Chem Soc. *Res:* Quantitative genetics of cardiovascular diseases; clinical genetics. *Mailing Add:* Dept of Med Genetics Ind Univ Med Sch Indianapolis IN 46223

CHRISTIAN, JOHN JERMYN, b Scranton, Pa, Apr 12, 17; m 42, 58; c 1. ENDOCRINOLOGY, PATHOBIOLOGY. *Educ:* Princeton Univ, AB, 39; Johns Hopkins Univ, ScD, 54. *Prof Exp:* Asst res pharmacologist, Wyeth Inst Appl Biochem, 48-51; head animal labs, US Naval Med Res Inst, 51-56; physiologist exp med, 56-59; assoc prof comp path, Univ Pa, 59-62; mem div endocrinol, Albert Einstein Med Ctr, 62-69, PROF BIOL SCI, STATE UNIV NY BINGHAMTON, 69- *Concurrent Pos:* Res assoc pathobiol, Johns Hopkins Univ, 54-59; assoc dir, Penrose Res Lab, Philadelphia Zool Soc, 59-62; mem ad hoc comt comp path, Nat Res Coun, Nat Acad Sci, 63-70. *Honors & Awards:* Mercer Award, Ecol Soc Am, 57. *Mem:* AAAS; Am Asn Path; Am Ornithologists Union; Soc Exp Biol & Med; Wildlife Dis Asn (vpres, 63-64, pres, 65-67). *Res:* Relationship of population density and social factors to endocrine adaptive mechanisms; reproduction; adrenal cortex; pathogenesis of renal disease. *Mailing Add:* Dept Biol Sci State Univ NY Binghamton NY 13901

CHRISTIAN, JOSEPH RALPH, b Chicago, Ill, June 15, 20; m 44; c 2. PEDIATRICS. *Educ:* Loyola Univ, Ill, MD, 44; Am Bd Pediat, dipl, 50. *Prof Exp:* Clin asst pediat, Stritch Sch Med, Loyola Univ, Ill, 48-50, clin instr, 50-51, asst clin prof, 51-52; from asst prof to prof, 53-61, asst chmn dept & dir res, 53-61; prof, Col Med, Univ Ill, 61-71; PROF PEDIAT & CHMN DEPT, RUSH MED COL, 71-; CHMN DEPT PEDIAT, PRESBY-ST LUKE'S HOSP, 61- *Concurrent Pos:* Dir med educ & sr pediatrician, Mercy Hosp, 48-61, dir pediat cardiac clin & cardiac in patient serv, 48-61, dir pediat out patient clin, 49-61, dir pediat residency training prog, 54-61; attend pediatrician, Loyola Serv, La Rabida Sanitarium, 48-61; chief pediat, Lewis Mem Hosp, 51-61; sr attend pediatrician, Cook County Hosp, 59-65. *Mem:* Fel Am Acad Pediat; fel Am Col Chest Physicians; fel Am Col Physicians; Am Fedn Clin Res; fel Am Pub Health Asn. *Res:* Infant nutrition; fluid and electrolyte balance; accidental poisoning in children; pediatric cardiology. *Mailing Add:* Rush-Presby-St Luke's Med Ctr 1753 Congress Pkwy Chicago IL 60612

CHRISTIAN, LARRY OMAR, b Kalamazoo, Mich, Aug 20, 36; c 3. PHYSICS, SOLAR ENERGY. *Educ:* Albion Col, BA, 58; Univ Ariz, MS, 64, PhD(physics), 66. *Prof Exp:* Res physicist atmospheric physics, White Sands Missile Range, 65-67; asst prof physics, Willamette Univ, 67-68; RESEARCHER SOLAR ENERGY, ENERGY CONVERSION DEVICES INC, 76- *Res:* Materials research with emphasis toward solar devices. *Mailing Add:* 1063 Kirts Rd 221 Troy MI 48084

CHRISTIAN, PAUL JACKSON, b Barre, Vt, Sept 9, 20; m 46; c 4. SYSTEMATIC ENTOMOLOGY. *Educ:* Wheaton Col, AB, 47; Univ Kans, PhD(entom), 52. *Prof Exp:* Asst instr biol, Univ Kans, 48-51; from asst prof to assoc prof, Univ Louisville, 52-61; assoc prof, 61-63, chmn dept, 63-77, PROF BIOL, BETHEL COL, MINN, 63- *Concurrent Pos:* Consult, Louisville & Jefferson County Dept Pub Health, 60-61. *Mem:* Soc Study Evolution; Soc Syst Zool. *Res:* Classification of leaf hoppers. *Mailing Add:* Dept of Biol Bethel Col St Paul MN 55112

CHRISTIAN, ROBERT ROLAND, b Meriden, Conn, Nov 10, 24. MATHEMATICS. *Educ:* Yale Univ, BS, 47, MA, 49, PhD(math), 54. *Prof Exp:* Instr math, New Haven Col, 46-49; asst instr, Yale Univ, 48-49; instr, Clark Univ, 49-51; from asst to asst prof, 52-62, ASSOC PROF MATH, UNIV BC, 62- *Concurrent Pos:* Pvt sch teacher, 47; vis lectr, Univ Ill, 59-60; consult math, Int Develop Asn Educ Proj, Inst Educ, Univ Sierra Leone, 71-72. *Mem:* Nat Coun Teachers Math; AAAS; Math Asn Am. *Res:* Mathematics education; integration; partially ordered vector spaces. *Mailing Add:* Dept of Math Univ of BC Vancouver BC V6T 1W5 Can

CHRISTIAN, ROBERT THOMAS, virology, see previous edition

CHRISTIAN, ROBERT VERNON, JR, b Wichita, Kans, Mar 1, 19; m 44; c 3. CHEMISTRY. *Educ:* Munic Univ Wichita, BS, 40; Iowa State Col, PhD(chem), 46. *Prof Exp:* Asst, Nat Defense Res Comt Proj, Iowa State Col, 42-43; from asst prof to assoc prof, 46-60, PROF CHEM, WICHITA STATE UNIV, 60- *Mem:* AAAS; Am Chem Soc. *Res:* Mass spectroscopy; volatile metal chelates; metal dithiocarbamates; trace metal analysis; chemical instrumentation. *Mailing Add:* Dept of Chem Wichita State Univ Wichita KS 67208

CHRISTIAN, ROSS EDGAR, b DuBois, Pa, Nov 1, 25; m 46; c 2. PHYSIOLOGY, GENETICS. *Educ:* Pa State Univ, BS, 47; Univ Wis, MS, 49, PhD(genetics), 51. *Prof Exp:* Asst genetics, Univ Wis, 47-50, instr & agt, Bur Dairy Indust, USDA, 50-51; asst prof animal husb, Wash State Univ, 51-56; from asst prof to assoc prof, 56-67, PROF ANIMAL SCI, UNIV IDAHO, 67- *Mem:* AAAS; Am Soc Animal Sci; Am Dairy Sci Asn; Am Genetic Asn. *Res:* Sterility in farm animals; genetics of fertility. *Mailing Add:* Dept of Animal Sci Univ of Idaho Moscow ID 83843

CHRISTIAN, SAMUEL TERRY, b Huntington, WVa, Dec 4, 37; m 58; c 3. BIOPHYSICS, ORGANIC CHEMISTRY. *Educ:* Marshall Univ, BA, 60; Univ Tenn, PhD(biochem), 66. *Prof Exp:* Res biochemist, Addiction Res Ctr, NIMH, Ky, 68-69, chief biochem pharmacol sect, 69-72; chief neurochem sect, neurosci prog & assoc prof psychiat & biochem, 72-76, PROF NEUROBIOL PSYCHIAT, ASSOC PROF BIOCHEM, PHYSIOL & BIOPHYSICS, MED CTR, UNIV ALA, BIRMINGHAM, 76-, SR SCIENTIST, COMPREHENSIVE CANCER CTR, 76-, ASSOC PROF PHARMACOLOGY, 81-, SCIENTIST, CYSTIC FIBROSIS CTR, 81- *Concurrent Pos:* Fel med chem, Univ Tenn, Memphis, 66-67; fel pharmacol, Univ Ky, 67-68; consult, NMiss Res Found, 66-72; adj asst prof, Depts Community Med & Pharmaceut Chem, Univ Ky, 69-72; consult, Pierce Chem Co, 75- *Mem:* Sigma Xi; NY Acad Sci; Am Soc Biol Chem; Am Soc Neurochem; Soc Neurosci. *Res:* Neurochemistry and molecular pharmacology; investigation of events produced by psychoactive agents on central nervous system macromolecular or subcellular organelles and their relevance to behavioral or physiological parameters; basic neurochemistry of the brain and its relevance to brain function. *Mailing Add:* Neurosci Prog Univ Ala Med Ctr Univ Sta-CDLD Birmingham AL 35294

CHRISTIAN, SHERRIL DUANE, b Estherville, Iowa, Sept 28, 31; m 56; c 3. PHYSICAL CHEMISTRY. *Educ:* Iowa State Univ, BS, 52, PhD, 56. *Prof Exp:* From asst prof to prof, 56-69, asst dean, Col Arts & Sci, 63-66, chmn dept chem, 68-69, GEORGE LYNN CROSS RES PROF CHEM, UNIV OKLA, 69- *Concurrent Pos:* Okla Found res award, 56-57; guest prof chem, Univ Oslo, 66-67 & 74-75 & Univ Trondheim, 79-80; res grants, NSF, Off Saline Water, Dept Interior, PRF Res Corp & Dept Energy; pres, CET Res Group, Norman, Okla. *Mem:* Am Chem Soc; Sigma Xi. *Res:* Physical chemistry of molecular complexes; spectral and thermodynamic properties of hydrogen-bonded and charge-transfer complexes; effect of solvents on complex equilibria; effects of pressure on conformational equilibria. *Mailing Add:* Univ of Okla Dept of Chem 620 Parrington Oval Rm 211 Norman OK 73069

CHRISTIAN, WALTER, microbiology, immunology, see previous edition

CHRISTIAN, WAYNE GILLESPIE, b King City, Mo, Oct 28, 18; m 43; c 2. GEOPHYSICS. *Educ:* WTex State Univ, BS, 39; Univ Denver, MS, 48, EdD(sci ed), 51. *Prof Exp:* Mus technician, WTex State Teachers Col, 36-37, hist geol lab supvr, 36-39, field & lab supvr paleont & archeol, Mus, 39-40; chief computer, Western Geophys Los Angeles, 40-44; supt schs, Mo, 43-44 & 46-48; teacher pub schs, 44-46; dept dir, Colo State Home Children, 51-52; geophysicist, Sun Oil Co, 52-77; coordr environ affairs, 77-78, MGR ENVIRON AFFAIRS, SUNOCO ENERGY DEVELOP CO, 78- *Concurrent Pos:* Supvr, Ground Water Surv & Mineral Surv, US Dept Interior & State Tex, 37-39; instr & teaching fel, Univ Denver, 48-56. *Mem:* Soc Vert Paleont; Soc Explor Geophys. *Mailing Add:* Sunoco Energy Develop Co 12700 Park Central Pl Dallas TX 75251

CHRISTIANO, JOHN G, b Falerna, Italy, Aug 29, 17; nat US; m 43; c 3. APPLIED MATHEMATICS. *Educ:* Univ Pittsburgh, BS, 39, MS, 42, PhD(math), 50. *Prof Exp:* From instr to assoc prof math, Univ Pittsburgh, 42-59; asst prof & actg head dept, Duquesne Univ, 46-47; PROF MATH, NORTHERN ILL UNIV, 59- *Mem:* Fedn Am Scientists; Math Asn Am; Am Math Soc. *Res:* Mathematics; mechanics. *Mailing Add:* Dept of Math Northern Ill Univ DeKalb IL 60115

CHRISTIANS, CHARLES J, b Parkersburg, Iowa, Apr 15, 34; m 57; c 2. ANIMAL BREEDING. *Educ:* Iowa State Univ, BS, 55; NDak State Univ, MS, 58; Okla State Univ, PhD(animal breeding), 62. *Prof Exp:* Asst animal husb, NDak State Univ, 56-58 & Okla State Univ, 58-61; from asst prof to assoc prof, Miss State Univ, 61-64; from asst prof to assoc prof, 64-71, PROF ANIMAL HUSB, UNIV MINN, ST PAUL, 71- *Mem:* Am Soc Animal Sci; Sigma Xi; Am Inst Biol Sci. *Res:* Beef breeding; swine breeding; factors affecting various beef carcass traits. *Mailing Add:* Animal Sci & Agr Exten Dept Agr Univ of Minn St Paul MN 55108

CHRISTIANSEN, ALFRED W, b Chicago, Ill, Nov 12, 40. ADHESION. *Educ:* Univ Ill, BS, 63; Case Western Reserve Univ, MS, 65, PhD(macromolecular sci), 70. *Prof Exp:* Res fel, Dept Metall, Univ Liverpool, 70-73; res chemist, Plastics Div, Exxon Chem Co, 73-75; CHEM ENGR, FOREST PROD LAB, USDA, 75- *Mem:* Adhesion Soc; Am Chem Soc; Forest Prods Res Soc. *Res:* Acid catalysis of phenolic resins; conversion of carbohydrates to exterior-durable wood adhesives; characterization and testing of wood adhesives. *Mailing Add:* 50 Whitcomb Circle Apt 4 Madison WI 53711

CHRISTIANSEN, DAVID ERNEST, b Salt Lake City, Utah, Jan 19, 37; m 62; c 5. CHEMICAL ENGINEERING. *Educ:* Univ Utah, BS, 62; Princeton Univ, MA, 64, PhD(chem eng), 67. *Prof Exp:* Vis res fel, Sloan Found, 67-68; staff mem, Los Alamos Sci Lab, 68-74; sr res engr, Stauffer Chem Co, 75-78; CHEM ENGR, LAWRENCE LIVERMORE LAB, 78- *Mem:* Am Chem Soc; Am Inst Chem Engrs. *Res:* Turbulent flow and mixing; photon transport; very high pressure phenomena including explosive initiation and detonation; fluid flow; crystallization; process simulation; fluidized bed processing. *Mailing Add:* Lawrence Livermore Lab PO Box 808 Livermore CA 94550

CHRISTIANSEN, E A, b Shellbrook, Sask, Sept 20, 28; m 59. GEOLOGY. *Educ:* Univ Sask, BSA, 52, MSc, 56; Univ Ill, PhD(geol), 59. *Prof Exp:* Asst res officer, Sask Res Coun, Univ Sask, 59-63, assoc res officer geol, 63-75, adj prof geol sci, 74, prin res scientist, 75-77; CONSULT GEOLOGIST, 77- *Mem:* Fel Geol Soc Am. *Res:* Glacial and groundwater geology; occurrence of groundwater in drift, Tertiary and upper Cretaceous sediments. *Mailing Add:* E A Christiansen Consult Ltd Box 3087 Saskatoon SK S7K 3S9 Can

CHRISTIANSEN, E(RNEST) B(ERT), b Richfield, Utah, July 31, 10; m 35; c 7. CHEMICAL ENGINEERING. *Educ:* Univ Utah, BS, 37; Univ Mich, MS, 39, PhD(chem eng), 41. *Prof Exp:* Chem engr, E I du Pont de Nemours & Co, NY, 41, Del, 42-43, Ill, 43, Manhattan Dist, Tenn, 43-45 & Del, 45-46; prof chem eng, Univ Idaho, 46-47; PROF CHEM ENG, UNIV UTAH, 47- *Concurrent Pos:* Nat dir, Am Inst Chem Engrs, 65-68. *Honors & Awards:* Founder's Award, Am Inst Chem Engrs, 78. *Mem:* Fel Am Inst Chem Engrs; Am Chem Soc; Soc Eng Educ; Soc Rheol. *Res:* Fluid flow; rheology; particle dynamics; coal gasification; heat transmission; crystallization; bioengineering. *Mailing Add:* Dept of Chem Eng Univ of Utah Salt Lake City UT 84112

CHRISTIANSEN, FRANCIS WYMAN, b Richfield, Utah, Feb 19, 12; m 33; c 6. GEOLOGY. *Educ:* Univ Utah, BS, 35, MS, 37; Princeton Univ, PhD(struct ecol geol), 48. *Prof Exp:* Mining geologist, Sierra Consol Mines, Inc, Nev, 37-38; instr geol, Univ Utah, 39-40; indust specialist, War Prod Bd, Washington, DC, 42, asst dep dir mining div, 42-43, chief metals sect, 43-46; from asst prof to prof, 46-76, PROF GEOL & GEOPHYS UNIV UTAH, 76- *Mem:* AAAS; Geol Soc Am; Am Geophys Union; Am Inst Mining, Metall & Petrol Engrs; Am Asn Petrol Geologists. *Res:* Structural geology and ore deposit; polygonal yielding of tabular bodies; magasutures of the earth and continental genesis. *Mailing Add:* Dept Geol & Geophys Sci Univ Utah Salt Lake City UT 84112

CHRISTIANSEN, J(ERALD) E(MMETT), b Hyrum, Utah, Apr 9, 05; m 29; c 2. IRRIGATION, CIVIL ENGINEERING. *Educ:* Utah Agr Col, BS, 27; Univ Calif, MS, 28, CE, 35. *Hon Degrees:* DSc, Utah State Univ, 76. *Prof Exp:* Jr irrig engr, exp sta, Univ Calif, 28-36, asst irrig engr, 36-42; irrig & drainage engr, Regional Salinity Lab, Bur Plant Indus, USDA, 42-46; dean sch eng & tech, 46-57, prof, 57-70, EMER PROF CIVIL ENG, UTAH STATE UNIV, 70- *Concurrent Pos:* Consult, Resettlement Admin, 36, Rocky Ford Irrig Co, 52-54, Food & Agr Orgn, UN, Uruguay, 57, Italy, Spain, Greece, Turkey, Syria & Iraq, 58, Peru, 68, lectr, Arg, 61; consult, US Agency Int Develop, Spain, 60-61, NC State Agr Mission, Peru, 64, Hydrotechnic Corp, NY & Morocco, 64, Spain, 64 & 65, Utah State Univ-Interam Ctr Integral Develop Waters & Lands, Orgn Am States, Venezuela, 65-70, Arg, 67 & 68, Uruguay, 69, Colombia, 69 & 70 & AID & World Bank, Washington, DC, 75; vis prof, Univ Calif, Davis, 57-58; consult eng sci, Peru, 75 & Chas Main Inc, Boston, 75-76. *Honors & Awards:* Outstanding serv award, Irrig Sprinkler Asn, 68; Royce J Tipton Award, Am Soc Civil Engrs, 76. *Mem:* Am Soc Civil Engrs; fel Am Soc Agr Engrs; Nat Soc Prof Engrs; Am Soc Eng Educ. *Res:* Irrigation and drainage; water measurement; irrigation structures; irrigation by sprinkling; drainage investigations; irrigation water requirements; administration. *Mailing Add:* 544 E 500 N Logan UT 84321

CHRISTIANSEN, JAMES BRACKNEY, b Alden, Minn, Mar 14, 11; m 37; c 2. BIOLOGICAL CHEMISTRY. *Educ:* Carroll Col, Wis, BA, 32; Univ Wis, MA, 34, PhD(biol chem), 39. *Hon Degrees:* DSc, Buena Vista Col, 76. *Prof Exp:* Res assoc, Larrowe Div, Gen Mills Inc, Mich, 39-50; prof & head dept chmn, 54-76, EMER PROF CHEM, BUENA VISTA COL, 76- *Concurrent Pos:* Pvt res, 50- *Mem:* Fel AAAS; Am Chem Soc; World Poultry Sci Asn; Poultry Sci Asn; Am Dairy Sci Asn. *Res:* Chemical measurements of vitamins and other nutrient factors; nutritional requirements of poultry and dogs; livestock feed. *Mailing Add:* Dept of Chem Buena Vista Col Storm Lake IA 50588

CHRISTIANSEN, JAMES LEARNED, ecology, herpetology, see previous edition

CHRISTIANSEN, JERALD N, b Arimo, Idaho, July 21, 31; m 54; c 4. ENGINEERING MECHANICS. *Educ:* Utah State Univ, BS, 53, MS, 55; Stanford Univ, PhD(eng mech), 58. *Prof Exp:* Instr eng mech, Cornell Univ, 54-56; from instr to asst prof, US Air Force Acad, 58-60; res specialist, 60-61, staff scientist, 61-63, asst resident dir, 63-64, sr staff scientist, 64-65, resident mgr, 65-66, mgr data systs, 66-67, consult scientist, 67-70, SR CONSULT SCIENTIST & PROG MGR, SPACE SYST DIV, LOCKHEED MISSILES & SPACE CO, 70- *Concurrent Pos:* Partner, J E Christiansen & Sons, 52- *Mem:* Am Soc Civil Engrs; Am Inst Aeronaut & Astronaut. *Res:* Structural dynamics; difference equations; data processing; computer utilization for engineering problems; information systems; signal processing systems. *Mailing Add:* 2068 Cynthia Way Los Altos CA 94022

CHRISTIANSEN, KENNETH ALLEN, b Chicago, Ill, June 24, 24; m 47; c 4. EVOLUTIONARY BIOLOGY, SPELEOLOGY. *Educ:* Boston Univ, BA, 48; Harvard Univ, PhD(biol), 51. *Prof Exp:* Asst prof biol, Am Univ Beirut, 51-54; instr, Smith Col, 54-55; from asst prof to assoc prof, 55-62, PROF BIOL, GRINNELL COL, 62- *Concurrent Pos:* Correspondent, Mus Paris; Iowa Gov's sci adv coun. *Mem:* Fel AAAS; Soc Study Evolution; Soc Syst Zool; fel Nat Speleol Soc; fel Explorers Club. *Res:* Taxonomy and evolution; Collembola. *Mailing Add:* Dept of Biol Grinnell Col Grinnell IA 50112

CHRISTIANSEN, MARJORIE MINER, b Canton, Ill, Feb 28, 22; m 51; c 1. NUTRITION, BIOCHEMISTRY. *Educ:* Univ NMex, BS, 49, MA, 55; Utah State Univ, PhD(nutrit, biochem), 67. *Prof Exp:* Chemist, Carnegie-Ill Steel Co, Ind, 42-44; control chemist, Blockson Chem Co, Ill, 44-47; asst dietitian, St Joseph Hosp, Albuquerque, NMex, 48-50; instr sci, Regina Sch Nursing, 50-64, instr nutrit, 52-64, proj dir utilization of basic sci prin in solving nursing care probs, 66-69; PROF HOME ECON, JAMES MADISON UNIV, VA, 69- *Concurrent Pos:* USPHS div nursing training grant, 66-68; proj dir dietary sem, Va Regional Med Prog proj grant, 73-76. *Mem:* Am Dietetic Asn; Am Home Econ Asn; Soc Nutrit Educ; Nutrit Today Soc. *Res:* Serum alpha-tocopherol, cholesterol and lipids in adults on self-selected diets at different levels of polyunsaturated fat. *Mailing Add:* Dept of Home Econ James Madison Univ Harrisonburg VA 22807

CHRISTIANSEN, MERYL NAEVE, b Gooselake, Iowa, Sept 5, 25; m 50. PLANT PHYSIOLOGY. *Educ:* Univ Ark, BS, 50, MS, 55; NC State Univ, PhD(crop sci), 60. *Prof Exp:* Asst, Univ Ark, 51-54; agronomist crops res div, USDA, 55-58; asst, NC State Univ, 58-60; plant physiologist, Crops Res Div, USDA, 60-75, plant physiologist & chief plant stress lab, Sci & Educ Admin, 73-80, PLANT PHYSIOLOGIST & CHMN PLANT PHYSIOL INST, AGR RES SERV, USDA, 80- *Mem:* Am Soc Plant Physiol; Crop Sci Soc Am; Phytochem Soc NAm; NY Acad Sci. *Res:* Seed germination physiology; environmental influences on seedling development and metabolism. *Mailing Add:* Plant Stress Lab Physiol Inst USDA Beltsville Agr Res Ctr Beltsville MD 20705

CHRISTIANSEN, PAUL ARTHUR, b Mitchell Co, Iowa, June 7, 32; m 55; c 2. BOTANY, PLANT ECOLOGY. *Educ:* Univ Iowa, BA, 59; Univ Ore, MS, 64; Iowa State Univ, PhD(plant ecol), 67. *Prof Exp:* Teacher, Humboldt Community Schs, Iowa, 59-64; from asst prof to assoc prof, 74-81, PROF BIOL, CORNELL COL, 81- *Concurrent Pos:* Vis prof, Ore State Univ, 69-70. *Mem:* AAAS; Sigma Xi. *Res:* Establishment of prairie species; management of natural areas. *Mailing Add:* Dept Biol Cornell Col Mt Vernon IA 52314

CHRISTIANSEN, RICHARD LOUIS, b Denison, Iowa, Apr 1, 35; m 56; c 3. ORTHODONTICS, PHYSIOLOGY. *Educ:* Univ Iowa, DDS, 59; Ind Univ, Indianapolis, MSD, 64; Univ Minn, Minneapolis, PhD(physiol), 70. *Prof Exp:* Intern dent, USPHS Hosp, San Francisco, 59-60; chief dent officer, USPHS Outpatient Clin, St Louis, 60-62; NIH trainee, Sch Dent, Ind Univ, Indianapolis, 62-64; staff orthodontist, Oral Med & Surg Br, Nat Inst Dent Res, 64-66; staff lectr orthod, Sch Dent & NIH trainee grad sch, Univ Minn, Minneapolis, 66-70; prin investr, Oral Med & Surg Br, 70-81, chief, Craniofacial Anomalies Prog Br, 73-81, ASSOC DIR EXTREME PRESSURE, NAT INST DENT RES, 81-, . *Concurrent Pos:* NIH res fel physiol, Univ Minn, Minneapolis, 66-70; mem & originator numerous state of the art planning comt, Nat Inst Dent Res, 69-; vis prof orthod, Sch Dent, Georgetown Univ, 70-; vis lectr, Univ Md, 70- *Mem:* Am Dent Asn; Am Asn Orthod; Int Asn Dent Res; AAAS; Int Union Physiol Sci. *Res:* Craniofacial malformations; oral physiology, especially intra-oral pressures and motor function, hemodynamics of oral-facial tissues, equilibrium of the dentition and biophysics of orthodontic tooth movement. *Mailing Add:* Rm 503 Westwood Bldg Nat Inst Dent Res NIH Bethesda MD 20205

CHRISTIANSEN, ROBERT GEORGE, b Sangudo, Alta, Apr 23, 24; m 48. ORGANIC CHEMISTRY. *Educ:* Univ Alta, BSc, 46, MSc, 48; Univ Wis, PhD(chem), 52. *Prof Exp:* Lectr org chem, Univ Alta, 46-48; asst, Univ Wis, 48-50; res assoc, 51-61, sr res assoc & group leader, 61-78, RES FEL, STERLING-WINTHROP RES INST, 78- *Mem:* Am Chem Soc. *Res:* Steroids; medicinal chemistry; modified steroidal hormones. *Mailing Add:* Sterling-Winthrop Res Inst Rensselaer NY 12144

CHRISTIANSEN, ROBERT LORENZ, b Kingsburg, Calif, June 13, 35; m 62; c 3. VOLCANOLOGY, IGNEOUS PETROLOGY. *Educ:* Stanford Univ, BS, 56, MS, 57, PhD(geol), 61. *Prof Exp:* Geologist explor geol, Utah Construct & Mining Co, 57-58; geologist mineral, Stanford Res Inst, 60-61; GEOLOGIST VOLCANIC GEOL & PETROL, US GEOL SURV, 61- *Concurrent Pos:* Coord geothermal res prog, US Geol Surv, 76-79. *Mem:* AAAS: Geol Soc Am; Mineral Soc Am; Am Geophys Union. *Res:* Igneous petrology; volcanology; geothermal energy; geology of cordilleran region of the United States. *Mailing Add:* US Geol Surv 345 Middlefield Rd Menlo Park CA 94025

CHRISTIANSEN, ROBERT M(ILTON), b Chicago, Ill, Nov 5, 24; m 52; c 3. CHEMICAL ENGINEERING. *Educ:* Northwestern Technol Inst, BS, 47; Northwestern Univ, MS, 49; Univ Pa, PhD(chem eng), 55. *Prof Exp:* Jr engr, Universal Oil Prod Co, 48; asst, Am Petrol Inst Res Proj, Northwestern Univ, 48-49; jr engr, Shell Develop Co, 49-52; instr chem eng, Univ Pa, 52-54; proj mgr, Owens-Corning Fiberglas Corp, 55-56, mgr physics res lab, 56-59; chief process engr, 59-70, MGR, ENVIRON SCI DIV, STEARNS-ROGER ENG CORP, 70-, VPRES, STEARNS-ROGER SERV INC, 76- *Concurrent Pos:* Lectr, Dept Chem Eng, Ohio State Univ, 56-57. *Mem:* Air Pollution Control Asn; Am Chem Soc; Am Inst Chem Engrs. *Res:* Fluid and particle mechanics; chemical and metallurgical plant design; industrial plant design for environmental protection; air pollution control; water pollution control; solids waste handling. *Mailing Add:* 4081 S Holly St Englewood CO 80111

CHRISTIANSEN, WALTER HENRY, b McKees Rocks, Pa, Dec 14, 34; m 60; c 2. GAS DYNAMICS, LASER PHYSICS. *Educ:* Carnegie Inst Technol, BS, 56; Calif Inst Technol, MS, 57, PhD(aeronaut & physics), 61. *Prof Exp:* Sr scientist gas dynamics, Jet Propulsion Lab, 61-62 & 64-67; res assoc prof, 67-70, PROF AERONAUT & ASTRONAUT, UNIV WASH, 70- *Mem:* Am Inst Aeronaut & Astronaut; Am Phys Soc. *Res:* Laser and gas physics; associated with high power gas lasers; gas dynamics; rarefied gas flows. *Mailing Add:* Dept of Aeronaut & Astronaut Univ of Wash Seattle WA 98105

CHRISTIANSEN, WAYNE ARTHUR, b Ft Collins, Colo; c 2. RADIO ASTRONOMY. *Educ:* Univ Colo, BS, 62; Univ Calif, Santa Barbara, MA, 66, PhD(physics), 68. *Prof Exp:* Scientist physics, E G & G Inc, 62-64; fel astrophys, Joint Inst Lab Astrophys, Univ Colo, 68-70; asst prof, 70-76, ASSOC PROF ASTRON, UNIV NC, CHAPEL HILL, 76- *Mem:* Am Astron Soc; Royal Astron Soc. *Res:* Origin and evolution of radio galaxies and quasars and the interaction between these objects and their surroundings. *Mailing Add:* Dept of Physics & Astron Univ of NC Chapel Hill NC 27514

CHRISTIANSON, CLINTON CURTIS, b Deer Park, Wis, Sept 25, 28; m 52; c 4. ELECTRICAL ENGINEERING. *Educ:* Univ Minn, BEE & BS, 51. *Prof Exp:* Engr, Aeronaut & Ord Dept, Gen Elec Co, 54-58 & Aircraft Accessory Turbine Dept, 58-63, team leader fuel cell develop, Direct Energy Conversion Oper, 63-65, mgr prototype design, 65-66, mgr design eng, 66-67, mgr appln eng, 67-68; mgr systs & elec eng, Energy Technol Lab, Gould Labs, 68-76, assoc dir energy res, 76-80; MEM STAFF, ARGONNE NAT LAB, 80- *Mem:* Inst Elec & Electronics Engrs; Am Inst Aeronaut & Astronaut. *Res:* Power systems; static power converters and inverters; control systems; batteries; fuel cells; thermoelectrics. *Mailing Add:* Argonne Nat Lab 9700 S Cass Ave Argonne IL 60439

CHRISTIANSON, DONALD DUANE, b Fertile, Minn, May 26, 31; c 4. PLANT BIOCHEMISTRY. *Educ:* Concordia Col, BA, 55; NDak State Univ, MS, 57. *Prof Exp:* PRIN RES CHEMIST BIOCHEM, NORTHERN REGIONAL LAB, USDA, 57- *Mem:* Int Asn Cereal Chemists; Am Chem Soc. *Res:* The formation of complexes between food carbohydrates (starch, hemicelluloses, sugars) and additive hydrophilic colloids, pectic substances, lipids, and proteins as a basis for developing improved texture and stability in processed foods. *Mailing Add:* 1010 N Summit Blvd Peoria IL 61606

CHRISTIANSON, GEORGE, b Volga, SDak, May 7, 17; m 47; c 2. FOOD SCIENCE. *Educ:* SDak State Col, BS, 39; Univ Tenn, MS, 40; Univ Minn, MS, 51, PhD(biochem), 53. *Prof Exp:* Asst blood lipids, Univ Minn, 41-42, asst dairy chem, 50-53; res chemist cereal chem, Gen Mills, Inc, 46-48; res scientist meats & meat prod, Rath Packing Co, 53-63; RES ASSOC, JAMES FORD BELL TECH CTR, GEN MILLS, INC, 63- *Mem:* Inst Food Technologists. *Res:* Milk stability; meat preservation studies; cereal chemistry; freezing and storage of meats; meat processing equipment; ready to eat cereals; physical chemistry of sugars; confectionary development; cereal snack development. *Mailing Add:* Gen Mills Inc 9000 Plymouth Ave N Minneapolis MN 55427

CHRISTIANSON, LEE (EDWARD), b Dayton, Ohio, May 5, 40; m 63; c 2. MAMMALOGY, ECOLOGY. *Educ:* Univ NDak, BS, 63; Southern Ill Univ, MA, 65; Univ Ariz, PhD(zool), 67. *Prof Exp:* From asst prof to assoc prof, 67-78, PROF BIOL SCI, UNIV OF THE PAC, 78- *Mem:* Am Soc Mammalogists; AAAS; Am Inst Biol Sci. *Res:* Mammalian systematics and ecology. *Mailing Add:* Dept of Biol Sci Univ of the Pac Stockton CA 95211

CHRISTIE, BERTRAM RODNEY, b Moorefield, Ont, Mar 22, 33; m 60; c 3. CROP BREEDING. *Educ:* Ont Agr Col, BSA, 55, MSA, 56; Iowa State Univ, PhD(crop breeding), 59. *Prof Exp:* From asst prof to assoc prof crop sci, Ont Agr Col, 59-70, PROF CROP SCI, ONT AGR COL, UNIV GUELPH, 70- *Mem:* Am Soc Agron; Agr Inst Can. *Res:* Forage crop breeding. *Mailing Add:* Dept of Crop Sci Ont Agr Col Univ of Guelph Guelph ON N1G 2W1 Can

CHRISTIE, BRUCE ROBERT, b Colac, Australia, Sept 22, 32; m; c 4. PHARMACOPATHOLOGY. *Educ:* Univ Sydney, BVSc, 57; Mich State Univ, MS, 67, PhD(path), 69. *Prof Exp:* Sr res pathologist agr, Victoria Dept Agr, Australia, 64-70; sr vet res officer, Attwood Res Lab, Westmeadows, 70-72; vis sr scientist path, Ill Inst Technol Res, 72-73; dir path, Specialized Ctr Res, Rancho Los Amigos Hosp, 73-76; sr res pathologist, Schering Corp, Lafayette, NJ, 76-79; MGR PATHOL, DUPONT PHARMACEUT, GARDEN CITY, NY, 79- *Concurrent Pos:* Lectr vet med, Longerenong Col, Dooen, Australia, 57-61; asst instr path, Mich State Univ, 64-69; traveling fel, Australian Commonwealth Serv Grant, 69-70; asst prof path, Univ Southern Calif, 74-; consult, Prof Staff Assoc, Rancho Los Amigos Hosp, 74-76, Div Lab Animal Med, Univ Calif, Los Angeles, 76- & Cancer Ctr, Univ Calif, Los Angeles, 77- *Mem:* Royal Col Vet Surgeons; Australian Col Vet Scientists; Australian Vet Asn; Am Col Toxicol; Am Vet Med Asn. *Res:* Antibiotics; bagonists; sedatives/hypnotics; pulmonary pathology; chronic obstructive lung disease; morphometrics; pathology of radio therapy. *Mailing Add:* 1000 Stewart Ave Garden City NY 11530

CHRISTIE, JOHN MCDOUGALL, b Calcutta, India, Dec 4, 31; m 57; c 3. STRUCTURAL GEOLOGY, ELECTRON MICROSCOPY. *Educ:* Univ Edinburgh, BSc, 53, PhD, 56. *Prof Exp:* Instr geol, Pomona Col, 56-58; from asst prof to assoc prof, 58-68, PROF GEOL, UNIV CALIF, LOS ANGELES, 68- *Concurrent Pos:* Guggenheim fel, 64-65; hon fel, Australian Nat Univ, 64-65. *Mem:* Geol Soc Am; Am Geophys Union; Electron Micros Soc Am. *Res:* Structural geology and petrology; electron microscopy of minerals; experimental deformation of minerals and rocks. *Mailing Add:* Dept of Geol Univ of Calif Los Angeles CA 90024

CHRISTIE, JOSEPH HERMAN, b Magnolia, Ark, Aug 30, 37. ANALYTICAL CHEMISTRY. *Educ:* Rensselaer Polytech Inst, BS, 59; La State Univ, MS, 62; Colo State Univ, PhD(chem), 74. *Prof Exp:* Mem tech staff chem, Rockwell Int, 62-69; asst prof, Colo State Univ, 74-75; SUPVRY

CHEMIST, US GEOL SURV, 75- *Concurrent Pos:* Fac affil chem, Colo State Univ, 75- *Mem:* Am Chem Soc; Electrochem Soc; Soc Appl Spectros. *Res:* Electrochemical and spectroscopic trace analysis; computer applications in analytical chemistry and instrumentation. *Mailing Add:* Br Anal Labs US Geol Survey MS 928 Box 25046 Denver Fed Ctr Denver CO 80225

CHRISTIE, PETER ALLAN, b Englewood, NJ, Feb 2, 40; m 62. ORGANIC POLYMER CHEMISTRY. *Educ:* Juniata Col, BS, 62; Univ Del, PhD(org chem), 67. *Prof Exp:* Res chemist, 67-74, res scientist, 74-76, SR RES SCIENTIST, RES & DEVELOP CTR, ARMSTRONG CORK CO, 76- *Mem:* Sigma Xi; Am Chem Soc. *Res:* Heterocyclic synthesis; organophosphorus chemistry; application of nuclear magnetic resonance spectroscopy to stereochemistry; condensation, addition, and ring-opening polymerization; reactions on polymers; organic-inorganic polymer systems; photochemistry. *Mailing Add:* Res & Develop Ctr Armstrong Cork Co Lancaster PA 17604

CHRISTIE, ROBERT WILLIAM, b Mineola, NY, Sept 22, 23; m 48; c 5. PATHOLOGY. *Educ:* Norwich Univ, Northfield, Vt, AB, 47; State Univ NY, MD, 51. *Prof Exp:* Surgeon, Norwich Univ, 53-54; gen practice, Green Mt Clin, Northfield, Vt, 53-54; asst pathologist, Med Ctr, Brookhaven Nat Lab, 56-57; assoc pathologist, Ball Mem Hosp, Muncie, Ind, 58-61; ASST PROF PATH, DARTMOUTH MED SCH, 77- *Concurrent Pos:* Asst scientist exp path, Brookhaven Nat Lab, 56-57; pathologist & lab dir, Androscoggin Valley Hosp, 61-, B D Weeks Mem Hosp, 61- & Upper Conn Valley Hosp, 61- *Mem:* Am Soc Exp Path; AAAS; Am Col Nuclear Med; Am Soc Clin Pathologists; Col Am Pathologists. *Res:* Preventive medicine; problem oriented autopsy; clinical pathology; parasitology. *Mailing Add:* Diag Serv Prof Asn Middle St Lancaster NH 03584

CHRISTIE, STEPHEN ROLLAND, b Dunedin, Fla, Nov 5, 29; m 68; c 1. PLANT VIROLOGY. *Prof Exp:* Lab technician food sci, Dept Food Technol, 58-60, lab technician plant path, 60-64, sr lab technician plant virol, 64-68, electron micros technician, 68-73, PLANT PATHOLOGIST PLANT VIROL, UNIV FLA, 73- *Mem:* Am Phytopath Soc. *Res:* Hybridizes nicotiana species for use in plant virus research; characterizes new plant viruses by host ranges, serology, and electron microscopy; tests crops for plant viruses; identifies them and considers control. *Mailing Add:* Dept of Plant Path Univ of Fla Plant Virus Lab Gainesville FL 32611

CHRISTIE, WARNER HOWARD, b Brooklyn, NY, Oct 29, 29; m 66; c 3. MASS SPECTROMETRY. *Educ:* Univ Miami, Fla, BS, 51, MS, 53; Univ Fla, PhD(chem), 58. *Prof Exp:* CHEMIST, MASS SPECTROMETRY, ANAL CHEM DIV, OAK RIDGE NAT LAB, 59- *Mem:* Am Soc Mass Spectrom; Sigma Xi. *Res:* Synthesis and reactions of organic fluorine containing materials; isotope exchange reactions of fluorocarbons; mass spectrometry; application of small computers to mass spectrometry; research development and applications of secondary ion mass spectrometry. *Mailing Add:* 952 W Outer Dr Oak Ridge TN 37830

CHRISTISON, GEORGE IAIN, swine husbandry, nutrition, see previous edition

CHRISTMAN, ARTHUR CASTNER, JR, b North Wales, Pa, May 11, 22; m 45; c 6. PHYSICS. *Educ:* Pa State Univ, BS, 44, MS, 50. *Prof Exp:* Instr physics, George Washington Univ, 48-51; physicist opers res off, Johns Hopkins Univ, 51-58; sr physicist, Stanford Res Inst, 58-62, head opers res group, 62-64, mgr opers eval dept, 65-66, mgr opers res dept, 66-69, dir opers res dept, 69-71, dir tactical systs, 71-75; SCI ADV, HQ US ARMY TRAINING & DOCTRINE COMMAND, 75- *Concurrent Pos:* Consult, US Navy, 50-51. *Mem:* Am Phys Soc; Sigma Xi; Opers Res Soc Am; fel AAAS. *Res:* Operations research; systems analysis; weapons, information, traffic, postal and health systems; analytic modeling; simulation; field experimentation; reconnaissance; surveillance; target acquisition; interdiction; close support; air defense; countermeasures; x-rays. *Mailing Add:* 102 Sherwood Dr Williamsburg VA 23185

CHRISTMAN, DAVID R, b Columbus, Ohio, Oct 14, 23; m 52; c 3. ORGANIC CHEMISTRY, PHARMACEUTICAL CHEMISTRY. *Educ:* Ohio State Univ, BSc, 47; Carnegie Inst Technol, MSc, 50, DSc(chem), 51. *Prof Exp:* Asst, Carnegie Inst Technol, 47-51; assoc chemist, 51-64, CHEMIST, BROOKHAVEN NAT LAB, 64- *Concurrent Pos:* Lectr, Columbia Univ, 58-64. *Mem:* Am Chem Soc; The Chem Soc; Soc Nuclear Med. *Res:* Organic radioactivity analysis and syntheses; organic radiation chemistry; organic radiopharmaceuticals with isotopes of short half-life; data processing; use of position emission tomography. *Mailing Add:* Dept of Chem Brookhaven Nat Lab Upton NY 11973

CHRISTMAN, EDWARD ARTHUR, b Lakewood, Ohio, Aug 3, 43. RADIATION PHYSICS, HEALTH PHYSICS. *Educ:* Ohio Univ, BS, 65; Rutgers Univ, MS, 74, PhD(radiation sci), 76. *Prof Exp:* Mech engr aerospace, Missile Syst Div, Avco Corp, Mass, 65-71; instr radiation sci, Busch Campus, 73-76, SUPV RADIOL PHYSICIST, RUTGERS UNIV, 77-, ASSOC GRAD FAC, 80- *Concurrent Pos:* Fel, Lawrence Berkeley Lab, 76-77. *Mem:* Health Physics Soc; Sigma Xi; Radiation Res Soc. *Res:* Radiation chemistry of tritium, heavy ions and radiological health and protection. *Mailing Add:* Dept of Radiation Environ Health Safety PO Box 1178 Piscataway NJ 08854

CHRISTMAN, JUDITH KERSHAW, b Teaneck, NJ, Apr 8, 41; m 59. BIOCHEMISTRY, MOLECULAR BIOLOGY. *Educ:* NY Univ, AB, 62; Columbia Univ, PhD(biochem), 67. *Prof Exp:* Res fel, Nucleic Acid Dept, NY Blood Ctr, 67-71; asst mem dept enzym, Inst Muscle Dis, 71-74; asst prof, 74-75, assoc prof, 75-80, RES PROF, DEPT PEDIAT, MT SINAI SCH MED, 80-, ASSOC PROF BIOCHEM, 77- *Mem:* Am Soc Biol Chemists; Am Soc Cell Biol; Sigma Xi; Harvey Soc; Am Soc Cancer Res. *Res:* Role of DNA methylation in regulating gene activity and the mechanisms by which tumor promoters and oncogenic viruses enhance and/or fix expression of the transformed phenotype. *Mailing Add:* Dept Biochem Mt Sinai Sch of Med New York NY 10029

CHRISTMAN, LUTHER P, b Summit Hill, Pa, Feb 26, 15; m 39; c 3. NURSING. *Educ:* Temple Univ, BS, 48, EdM, 52; Mich State Univ, PhD(anthrop & sociol), 65. *Hon Degrees:* DHL, Thomas Jefferson Univ, 80. *Prof Exp:* Dir nursing, Yankton State Hosp, SDak, 53-56; nursing consult, Mich Dept Ment Health, 56-63; assoc prof psychol nursing, Univ Mich, 63-67, res assoc, 64-67; dir nursing, Vanderbilt Univ Hosp, 67-72, dean, Sch Nursing, Vanderbilt Univ, 67-72; JOHN L & HELEN KELLOGG DEAN, COL NURSING, RUSH UNIV, 72-, PROF SOCIOL, 76-; VPRES NURSING AFFAIRS, RUSH-PRESBY-ST LUKES MED CTR, 72-, PROF SOCIOL, 72- *Concurrent Pos:* Vis prof, Col NSW, 78, Nordic Sch Pub Health, Sweden, 79 & Univ Lund, Sweden, 81; lectr, Nat Ziekenhuistitut, Netherlands, 79; consult, Univ Mich, Ann Arbor, 79, & Univ Alberta, 80; mem Rev Comt, Psychol Nursing Educ, Dept Health & Human Servs, NIMH, 80- *Mem:* Inst Med-Nat Acad Sci; Am Nurses Asn; NY Acad Sci; fel AAAS; fel Soc Appl Anthorp. *Mailing Add:* Col Nursing Rush Univ 600 S Paulina Chicago IL 60612

CHRISTMAN, ROBERT ADAM, b Ann Arbor, Mich, May 16, 24; m 53; c 4. GEOLOGY. *Educ:* Univ Mich, BS, 46, MS, 47; Princeton Univ, PhD(geol), 50. *Prof Exp:* Geologist, US Geol Surv, 50-54; asst prof geol, Cornell Univ, 54-60; ASSOC PROF GEOL, WESTERN WASH UNIV, 60- *Mem:* AAAS; Nat Asn Geol Teachers; Geol Soc Am. *Res:* Petrology; mineralogy; earth science for teachers. *Mailing Add:* Dept of Geol Western Wash Univ Bellingham WA 98225

CHRISTMAN, RUSSELL FABRIQUE, b June 20, 36; m 58; c 3. CHEMISTRY. *Educ:* Univ Fla, BS, 58, MS, 60, PhD(chem), 62. *Prof Exp:* Res asst prof sanit chem, Univ Wash, 62-66, asst prof civil eng, 66-68, assoc prof appl sci, 68-74, asst to provost & dir div environ affairs, 70-74; PROF ENVIRON SCI, UNIV NC, CHAPEL HILL, 74-, CHMN DEPT ENVIRON SCI & ENG, 77- *Mem:* AAAS; Water Pollution Control Fedn; Am Water Works Asn; Am Soc Limnol & Oceanog. *Res:* Chemical structures of natural product organic materials in water; methods of organic analysis in water samples; mechanisms of colloidal destabilization with hydrolysis products of aluminum III. *Mailing Add:* Dept of Environ Sci & Eng Univ of NC Chapel Hill NC 27514

CHRISTMAN, STEVEN PHILIP, b Grass Valley, Calif, May 21, 45; m 68. ECOLOGY, HERPETOLOGY. *Educ:* Univ Fla, BS, 71, PhD(zool), 75. *Prof Exp:* Contract biologist, Fla Game & Fish Comn, 75-76; RES BIOLOGIST, US FISH & WILDLIFE SERV, 76- *Concurrent Pos:* Sci consult, Fla Comn Rare & Endangered Plants & Animals, 73-; Fla rep, Soc Study Amphibians & Reptiles, Legis Alert Comn, 77- *Honors & Awards:* Austin Award, Fla State Mus, 74. *Mem:* Soc Study Syst Zool; Am Soc Ichthyologists & Herpetologists; Herpetologist's League; Soc Study Amphibians & Reptiles. *Res:* Biogeography; herpetology; wildlife management. *Mailing Add:* Nat Fish & Wildlife Lab 412 NE 16th Ave Gainesville FL 32601

CHRISTMANN, MARVIN HENRY, b Petrel, NDak, July 3, 34; m 60; c 2. SOLID STATE PHYSICS, MATHEMATICS. *Educ:* SDak Sch Mines & Technol, BS, 56; Iowa State Univ, MS, 60. *Prof Exp:* Consult, Minneapolis-Honeywell Res Ctr, 56-57; rea physicist, 60-61 & 63-66, sr res physicist, 66-71, res specialist, 71-76, patent liaison, Central Res Labs, 76-81, MGR, DIV INTELLECTUAL PROPERTIES, MAGNETIC AUDIOVIDEO DIV, MINN MINING & MFG CO, 81- *Mem:* Inst Elec & Electronic Engrs; Metall Soc; Am Inst Mining, Metall & Petrol Engrs. *Res:* Interact with inventors, business and technical management, and patent counsel to secure proctection for intellectual property. *Mailing Add:* 15398 S Afton Hills Dr Afton MN 55001

CHRISTMAS, ELLSWORTH P, b Warrick Co, Ind, Nov 5, 35; m 58; c 2. AGRONOMY. *Educ:* Purdue Univ, BS, 58, MS, 61, PhD(agr ed, agron), 64. *Prof Exp:* Teacher sec sch, Ind, 58-60; from asst prof to assoc prof, 64-74, PROF AGRON, PURDUE UNIV, 74-, ASST DIR, IND COOP EXT SERV, 74- *Concurrent Pos:* Agronomist, Int Progs Agr, Purdue-Brazil Proj, Brazil, 69-73. *Mem:* Am Soc Agron; Soil Sci Soc Am; Crop Sci Soc Am. *Res:* Teaching methods in agriculture; soil characterization and conservation. *Mailing Add:* Coop Ext Serv Agr Admin Bldg Purdue Univ West Lafayette IN 47906

CHRISTOFFERSEN, DONALD JOHN, b Ogema, Wis, July 27, 34; m 51; c 4. ANALYTICAL CHEMISTRY. *Educ:* Wis State Univ-Stevens Point, BS, 56; Univ Wis, PhD(anal chem), 66. *Prof Exp:* Chemist, Pure Oil Co, 61-63, group leader gas chromatography, 63-65, sr res chemist, 64-69, SUPVR, SPECTRAL ANAL CHEM, UNION OIL CO, 69- *Mem:* Am Chem Soc; Am Soc Testing Mat. *Res:* Gas chromatography with petroleum oriented applications. *Mailing Add:* Union Oil Co Res Ctr Box 76 Brea CA 92621

CHRISTOFFERSEN, RALPH EARL, b Elgin, Ill, Dec 4, 37; m 61; c 3. PHYSICAL CHEMISTRY. *Educ:* Cornell Col, BS, 59; Ind Univ, PhD(phys chem), 64. *Prof Exp:* NIH fel quantum chem, Univ Nottingham, 64-65 & Iowa State Univ, 65-66; from asst prof to prof phys chem, Univ Kans, 66-81, assoc vchancellor, 78-79, vchancellor, 79-81; PRES, COLO STATE UNIV, 81- *Concurrent Pos:* Alfred P Sloan res fel, 71-73; consult, Lawrence Livermore Lab, 78- & Upjohn Co, Mich. *Honors & Awards:* Am Inst Chemists Award, 59; Outstanding Scientist of the Year Award, Inst Soc Quantum Biol, 81. *Mem:* AAAS; Am Inst Chemists; Am Chem Soc; Am Phys Soc. *Res:* Quantum chemistry; theory of chemical bonds; ab initio calculations on large molecules; development of algorithms and associated software/hardware to perform large-scale numerical calculations; investigation of geometric and electronic structural features of chlorophyll and related molecular systems and their relationship to photosynthesis. *Mailing Add:* Off of Pres Colo State Univ Ft Collins CO 80523

CHRISTOFFERSON, ERIC, b Newburyport, Mass, May 29, 39; m 61; c 2. GEOLOGICAL OCEANOGRAPHY. *Educ:* Princeton Univ, AB, 61; Univ RI, PhD(oceanog), 73. *Prof Exp:* Instr oceanog, Univ RI, 73-74, res assoc, 74-75; ASST PROF GEOL, RUTGERS UNIV, 75- *Mem:* Sigma Xi; Am Geophys Union. *Res:* Geologic history of the Caribbean Sea Basin. *Mailing Add:* Dept of Geol Sci Rutgers Univ New Brunswick NJ 08903

CHRISTOFFERSON, GLEN DAVIS, b Tacoma, Wash, Feb 7, 31; m 51; c 2. PHYSICAL CHEMISTRY. *Educ:* Univ Wash, BS, 53; Univ Calif, Los Angeles, PhD(chem), 58. *Prof Exp:* Asst, Univ Calif, Los Angeles, 53-57; res chemist, Calif Res Corp, 57-63, sr res chemist, 64-68, SR RES ASSOC, CHEVRON RES CO, 68- *Mem:* Soc Appl Spectros; Am Chem Soc; Am Crystallog Asn. *Res:* Organic and inorganic crystal structure determination; x-ray emission and absorption spectroscopy; x-ray low angle scattering; electron diffraction and microscopy. *Mailing Add:* Chevron Res Co 576 Standard Ave Richmond CA 94802

CHRISTOPH, FRANCIS THEODORE, JR, b Alexandria, La, Jan 1, 43; m 68. TOPOLOGY. *Educ:* St Peter's Col, NJ, BS, 64; Rutgers Univ, MS, 66, PhD(math), 69. *Prof Exp:* asst prof, 69-77, ASSOC PROF MATH, TEMPLE UNIV, 77- *Mem:* Math Asn Am; Am Math Soc. *Res:* Decompositions and extensions of topological semigroups; embedding topological semigroups in topological groups. *Mailing Add:* Dept of Math Temple Univ Philadelphia PA 19122

CHRISTOPH, GREG ROBERT, b Chicago, Ill, Dec 10, 49; m 70; c 1. NEUROPHARMACOLOGY, NEUROBIOLOGY. *Educ:* Univ Chicago, AB, 71; Ind Univ, PhD(exp psychol), 76. *Prof Exp:* Assoc instr psychol, Ind Univ, 74-75; NIMH fel neurosci, Princeton Univ, 76-78; res scientist neuropharmacol, 78-81, PRIN INVESTR NEUROBIOL, EXP STA, E I DU PONT DE NEMOURS & CO, INC, 81- *Res:* Behavioral pharmacology of psychoactive drugs; neurophysiology and neuropharmacology of monoamine containing neurons in brain. *Mailing Add:* Exp Sta CRDD 328/236 E I du Pont de Nemours & Co Inc Wilmington DE 19898

CHRISTOPHER, JOHN, b Chicago, Ill, Oct 15, 23; m 47; c 3. MATHEMATICS. *Educ:* Knox Col, AB, 46; Univ Ore, MA, 50, PhD(math), 52. *Prof Exp:* Instr math, Univ Ore, 50-52 & Knox Col, 52-54; asst prof, Univ of the Pac, 54-55; instr, Fresno State Col, 55-56; sr mathematician, Electrodata Corp, Calif, 56-58; asst prof math, Sacramento State Col, 58-60; dir comput ctr, Univ Nebr, 60-63; assoc prof, 63-67, PROF MATH, CALIF STATE UNIV, SACRAMENTO, 67- *Mem:* Am Math Soc. *Res:* Number theory and numerical analysis. *Mailing Add:* Dept of Math Sacramento State Col 600 Jay St Sacramento CA 95819

CHRISTOPHER, ROBERT A(RTHUR), b Port Deposit, Md, Jan 31, 29; m 53; c 3. MECHANICAL ENGINEERING, BIOENGINEERING. *Educ:* Univ Colo, Boulder, BA, 51, BS, 57, MS, 58, PhD(mech eng), 71. *Prof Exp:* From instr to assoc prof mech eng, 56-78, PROF MECH ENG, UNIV COLO, BOULDER, 78- *Concurrent Pos:* Consult, Automotive Specialists, Denver, 76-; chmn mech eng, 80. *Mem:* Am Soc Mech Engrs; Soc Automotive Engrs; Acad Forensic Sci; Sigma Xi. *Res:* Contact problems of cylindrical shells using a shear deformation theory; prosthetic heart valves; modeling of vehicular collisions; echo cardiology. *Mailing Add:* Dept of Mech Eng Univ of Colo Boulder CO 80309

CHRISTOPHER, ROBERT PAUL, b Cleveland, Ohio, Apr 27, 32; m 62; c 3. PHYSICAL MEDICINE & REHABILITATION. *Educ:* Northwestern Univ, BS, 54; St Louis Univ, MD, 59. *Prof Exp:* US Off Voc Rehab fel phys med & rehab, Univ Mich, Ann Arbor, 60-63, from instr to asst prof, 63-67; assoc prof, 67-71, PROF PHYS MED & REHAB, UNIV TENN, MEMPHIS, 71-; ASSOC MED DIR, LES PASSEES REHAB CTR, 70- *Concurrent Pos:* Chief phys med & rehab, Vet Admin Hosp, Ann Arbor, 63-67; consult, St Jude Children's Res Hosp, 67-, Le Bonheur Children's Hosp, 68-, Vet Admin Hosps, Memphis, 67- & Nashville, 70-, Coun Med Educ, AMA, 69- & Comn Accreditation Rehab Facil, 73- *Mem:* Fel Am Acad Phys Med & Rehab; Am Cong Rehab Med; Am Asn Electromyog & Electrodiag. *Res:* Electrodiagnostic studies in collagen vascular disease; habilitation programs for brain damaged children; primary muscle disease. *Mailing Add:* Div of Phys Med & Rehab Univ Tenn 800 Madison Ave Memphis TN 38163

CHRISTOPHERSON, WILLIAM MARTIN, b Salt Lake City, Utah, July 2, 16; m 43; c 1. MEDICINE. *Educ:* Univ Louisville, MD, 42. *Prof Exp:* Ewing fel, Mem Cancer Ctr, NY, 49-50; from asst prof to assoc prof, 50-56, chmn dept, 56-74, PROF PATH, SCH MED, UNIV LOUISVILLE, 56- *Concurrent Pos:* Pathologist, Louisville Gen Hosp, 56-; consult, Med Div, Nat Cancer Inst, Vet Admin Hosp & Ireland Army Hosp, Ky; mem adv comt & spec consult, Cancer Control Prog, USPHS. *Mem:* Int Acad Path (past pres); Am Soc Cytol (past pres); Soc Exp Path; Am Asn Cancer Educ (past pres); Am Cancer Soc. *Res:* Cancer. *Mailing Add:* Dept of Path Univ Louisville Health Sci Ctr Louisville KY 40202

CHRISTOPHOROU, LOUCAS GEORGIOU, b Limassol, Cyprus, Jan 21, 37; m 63; c 2. ATOMIC PHYSICS, MOLECULAR PHYSICS. *Educ:* Nat Univ Athens, BSc, 60; Manchester, dipl adv physics, 61, PhD(physics), 63, DSc(physics), 69. *Prof Exp:* Res physicist, Health Physics Div, Oak Ridge Nat Lab, 63-64; from asst prof to assoc prof, 64-68, PROF PHYSICS, UNIV TENN, KNOXVILLE, 69-; HEAD ATOMIC & MOLECULAR & HIGH VOLTAGE PHYSICS, HEALTH & SAFETY RES DIV, OAK RIDGE NAT LAB, 76- & DISTINGUISHED RES STAFF MEM, 81- *Concurrent Pos:* Consult, Oak Ridge Nat Lab, 64-66, head atomic & molecular radiation physics group, Health Physics Div, 66-76. *Mem:* Am Phys Soc; Radiation Res Soc; Health Physics Soc; AAAS. *Res:* Radiation physics; chemical physics; low-energy electron-molecule interactions; electron scattering; electron motion in gases; negative ions; gaseous and liquid dielectrics; photophysical processes. *Mailing Add:* 121 Nebraska Ave Oak Ridge TN 37830

CHRISTOPOULOS, GEORGE NICK, b Kokkino, Greece, Sept 13, 38; US citizen; m 64; c 2. TOXICOLOGY. *Educ:* Roosevelt Univ, BS, 66; Univ Ill Med Ctr, MS, 71, PhD(med chem), 72. *Prof Exp:* Lab technician, Dearborn Chem Co, 60-63, Div Corn Prod, Best Foods, 63-65 & Durkee's Famous Food, 65-66; CHIEF TOXICOLOGIST, COOK COUNTY CORONER, 66- *Concurrent Pos:* Consult, Dept Pub Health, State of Ill, 74-75. *Mem:* Am Chem Soc; NY Acad Sci; Am Acad Forensic Sci. *Res:* Isolation and identification of toxic gases other than carbon monoxide in fire victims. *Mailing Add:* Off Coroner Chicago Civic Ctr Chicago IL 60607

CHRISTY, ALFRED LAWRENCE, b Pittsburgh, Pa, Mar 15, 45; m 67; c 1. PHOTOSYNTHESIS, TRANSLOCATION. *Educ:* Univ Dayton, BS, 67, MS, 69; Ohio State Univ, PhD(bot), 72. *Prof Exp:* Fel plant physiol, Univ Ga, 72-74; sr res biologist, 74-77, res specialist, 77-78, sr res group leader, 78-81, SCI FEL, MONSANTO CO, 81- *Mem:* Am Soc Plant Physiol; Am Soc Agron; Crop Sci Soc Am. *Res:* Photosynthesis and translocation in crop plants in relationship to grain yield; development of screening systems for evaluation of plant growth regulators on crop plants. *Mailing Add:* Monsanto Co 800 N Lindbergh Blvd St Louis MO 63167

CHRISTY, JAMES WALTER, b Milwaukee, Wis, Sept 15, 38; m 75; c 4. ASTRONOMY, PHYSICS. *Educ:* Univ Ariz, BS, 65. *Prof Exp:* ASTRONR, US NAVAL OBSERV, 62- *Honors & Awards:* Credited with discovering first satellite of Pluto (Charon), Int Astron Union, 78. *Mem:* Am Astron Soc; Int Astron Union. *Res:* Astrometry and spectrography of low luminosity stars; radial velocities for galactic structure; color astrophotography; conceptual basis of cosmology. *Mailing Add:* Explor Develop Staff US Naval Observ Washington DC 20390

CHRISTY, JOHN HARLAN, b Ft Smith, Ark, Aug 13, 37; m 60; c 2. MATHEMATICS. *Educ:* Mass Inst Technol, BS, 59; Vanderbilt Univ, PhD(math), 64. *Prof Exp:* Res asst physics, Los Alamos Sci Lab, 59-60; asst prof math, Southwestern at Memphis, 63-66; assoc prof, Hendrix Col, 66-67; PROF MATH & CHMN DEPT MATH & PHYSICS, TEX WOMAN'S UNIV, 67- *Concurrent Pos:* Vis prof, Univ Ark, 64. *Mem:* Math Asn Am. *Res:* Topological dynamics; expansive transformation groups. *Mailing Add:* Dept of Math & Physics Tex Woman's Univ Denton TX 76204

CHRISTY, NICHOLAS PIERSON, b Morristown, NJ, June 18, 23; m 47; c 2. MEDICINE. *Educ:* Yale Univ, AB, 45; Columbia Univ, MD, 51; Am Bd Internal Med, 58. *Prof Exp:* from instr to assoc prof med, Columbia Univ, 56-65, assoc clin prof, 65-72, prof med, Col Physicians & Surgeons, 72-79; chmn dept med, Roosevelt Hosp, 70-79; PROF MED, STATE UNIV NY, DOWNSTATE MED CTR, 79- *Concurrent Pos:* Markle scholar, 56; asst physician, Presby Hosp, 54-60, asst attend physician, 60-62, assoc attend physician, 62-; asst vis physician, Francis Delafield Hosp, 54- & first med div, Bellevue Hosp, 58-; ed, J Clin Endocrin & Metab, 63-67; chief staff, Brooklyn Vet Admin Med Ctr, 79-; lectr med, Columbia State Univ, 79- *Honors & Awards:* Borden Award, 51. *Mem:* AAAS; Am Physiol Soc; Soc Exp Biol & Med; Fedn Clin Res; Endocrine Soc (secy-tres, 78-). *Res:* Clinical disorders of the adrenal cortex; adrenal cortical physiology of animals and man; mechanisms of action of adrenal cortical and gonadal steroids at a cellular level; metabolism of estrogens in hepatic disease. *Mailing Add:* Brooklyn Vet Admin Med Ctr 800 Poly Pl Brooklyn NY 11209

CHRISTY, ROBERT FREDERICK, b Vancouver, BC, May 14, 16; nat US; m 73; c 3. THEORETICAL PHYSICS, THEORETICAL ASTROPHYSICS. *Educ:* 0niv BC, BA, 35, MA, 37; Univ Calif, PhD(theoret physics), 41. *Prof Exp:* Instr physics, Ill Inst Technol, 41-42; res assoc, Univ Chicago, 42-43 & AEC, Los Alamos, NMex, 43-46; from asst prof to assoc prof, 46-50, chmn fac, 69-70, actg pres, 77-78, PROF PHYSICS, CALIF INST TECHNOL, 50-, VPRES & PROVOST, 70- *Concurrent Pos:* Chmn comt nat acad to surv risks of nuclear power. *Mem:* Int Astron Union; Am Phys Soc; Am Astron Soc; Nat Acad Sci. *Res:* Cosmic rays; nuclear physics; astrophysics; variable stars. *Mailing Add:* Calif Inst of Technol Pasadena CA 91125

CHRISTY, ROBERT WENTWORTH, b Chicago, Ill, Nov 2, 22. PHYSICS. *Educ:* Univ Chicago, MS, 49, PhD(physics), 53. *Prof Exp:* Consult, Motorola, Inc, 52-53; from instr to assoc prof, 53-62, chmn dept, 63-67 & 78-80, prof physics, 62-80, APPLETON PROF PHYSICS, DARTMOUTH COL, 80- *Concurrent Pos:* Consult, TRW Space Technol Labs, 58-68. *Mem:* AAAS; Am Phys Soc. *Res:* Ionic crystals; plastic flow; thermoelectric power; color centers; luminescence; thin films; metal optics. *Mailing Add:* Dept of Physics & Astron Dartmouth Col Hanover NH 03755

CHRISTY, WILLIAM O(LIVER), b Barberton, Ohio, Oct 4, 07; m 32; c 1. MECHANICAL ENGINEERING. *Educ:* Houghton Col, AB, 28; Mass Inst Technol, BS, 31. *Prof Exp:* Instr, Houghton Col, 29; draftsman, Goodyear Tire & Rubber Co, Akron, 31-35, designer, Goodrich Tire & Rubber Co, 35-36; develop engr, 36-61, SUPT ENG & CONTROL DEPT, E I DU PONT DE NEMOURS & CO, 61- *Res:* Design and development of rayon processing equipment; selection of metals. *Mailing Add:* 2010 Robin Rd North Augusta SC 29841

CHROMEY, FRED CARL, b Philadelphia, Pa, June 30, 18; m 43; c 4. APPLIED PHYSICS. *Educ:* St Josephs Col, Pa, BS, 40; Cornell Univ, PhD(physics), 44. *Prof Exp:* Asst physics, Ind Univ, 40-42 & Cornell Univ, 42-44; res assoc, Mass Inst Technol contract, res physicist, Los Alamos Sci Lab, NMex, 44-46; RES PHYSICIST, E I DU PONT DE NEMOURS & CO, INC, 46- *Concurrent Pos:* Instr univ exten, Purdue Univ, 41-42, supvr studies, 41. *Mem:* Am Phys Soc. *Res:* Measurement of radio-activity; cyclotron construction and operation; cosmic rays; theory of scattering by colored bodies; viscoelasticity; digital computer programs; statistical experimental designs; explosion hazards. *Mailing Add:* 6 N Cliffe Dr Wycliffe Wilmington DE 19809

CHRONES, JAMES, b Weyburn, Sask, Sept 6, 25; Can citizen; m 51; c 3. CHEMICAL ENGINEERING. *Educ:* Univ Sask, BSc, 46, MSc, 48; Mass Inst Technol, SM, 50. *Prof Exp:* Res engr, Atomic Energy of Can Ltd, 50-53; M W Kellogg Co Div, Pullman, Inc, 53-55, process engr, 56-58, process mgr, 61-64; sr process engr, Kellogg Int Corp, 58-60; chem engr & head dept design, Underwood McLellan & Assocs, 65; pres, Cambrian Eng Ltd, 66-70; assoc, Hatch Assocs, Ltd, 71-73; vpres & gen mgr, Pullman Kellogg Can, Ltd, 73-79; pres, Dynawest Projs Ltd, 79-80; CONSULT, 80- *Concurrent Pos:* Gen mgr, Deuterium of Can Ltd, 70. *Mem:* Am Inst Chem Engrs; Can Soc Chem Eng; fel Chem Inst Can. *Res:* Heavy water production processes; hydrocarbon pyrolysis for olefins production; synthesis gas preparation; distillation; vegetable oil refining; design of olefins, petrochemical, sodium sulphate, and vegetable oil refining plants; nuclear fuel reprocessing; bitumen and heavy oil upgrading processes; petrochemical feasibility studies. *Mailing Add:* 111 Lord Seaton Rd Willowdale ON M2P 1K8 Can

CHRONIC, JOHN, b Tulsa, Okla, June 3, 21; m 48; c 4. INVERTEBRATE PALEONTOLOGY, STRATIGRAPHY. *Educ:* Univ Tulsa, BS, 42; Univ Kans, MS, 47; Columbia Univ, PhD(geol), 49. *Prof Exp:* Instr geol, Univ Mich, 49-50; asst prof, 50-65, prof geol, 65-80, EMER PROF GEOL, UNIV COLO, BOULDER, 80- *Concurrent Pos:* Exchange lectr, Univ Edinburgh, 58-59; NSF lectr, State Univ NY Col Oneonta, 62; prof & chmn dept, Haile Sellassie Univ, 65-66; exchange prof, Univ PR, 78-79. *Mem:* AAAS; Geol Soc Am; Soc Econ Paleontologists & Mineralogists; Am Asn Petrol Geologists; Paleont Soc. *Res:* Colorado paleozoic geology; economic geology. *Mailing Add:* Dept of Geol Univ Colo Boulder CO 80309

CHRONISTER, ROBERT BLAIR, b Huntingdon, Pa, Aug 24, 42; m 68; c 2. NEUROANATOMY, NEUROBIOLOGY. *Educ:* Juniata Col, Pa, BS, 65; Univ Vt, Burlington, PhD(exp psychol), 72. *Prof Exp:* Fel neurosci, Univ Fla, 71-73; asst prof neurol & psychol, 74-76, asst prof, 76-81, ASSOC PROF ANAT, UNIV SOUTH ALA, MOBILE, 81- *Mem:* Soc Neurosci; Am Asn Anatomists. *Res:* Organization of basal forebrain structures; effects of DNA alkylating agents on brain and retinal development. *Mailing Add:* Dept Anat Col Med Univ South Ala Mobile AL 36688

CHRYSANT, STEVEN GEORGE, b Gargaliani, Greece, Feb 22, 34; US citizen; m 69; c 2. CARDIOVASCULAR DISEASES, HYPERTENSION. *Educ:* Univ Athens, MD, 59, PhD(biochem), 68; Am Bd Internal Med. *Prof Exp:* From instr to asst prof med, Stritch Sch Med, Loyola Univ, 70-72; from asst prof to assoc prof med, Health Sci Ctr, Univ Okla, 72-81, dir div hypertension, 76-81; PROF MED & CHIEF HYPERTENSION, KANSAS UNIV MED CTR, 81- *Concurrent Pos:* Res assoc nephrology, Hines Vet Admin Hosp, Ill, 70-71; staff physician, 71-72; asst sect chief renal hypertension & in-chg-hemodialysis unit, 72; dir hypertension screening & treatment prog, Oklahoma City Vet Admin Hosp, 72-; fel, Hypertension Res Coun, Am Heart Asn. *Mem:* Am Heart Asn; Am Soc Nephrology; Int Soc Nephrology; fel Am Col Cardiol; fel Am Col Physicians. *Res:* Systemic and renal hemodynamics effects of hypertension in the rat, dog, and man; role of salt in hypertension; role of prostaglandins in hypertension; pharmacotherapy of hypertension. *Mailing Add:* 4801 Linwood Blvd Kansas City MO 64128

CHRYSOCHOOS, JOHN, b Icaria, Greece, Feb 27, 34; nat US; m 64; c 3. PHYSICAL CHEMISTRY. *Educ:* Athens Tech Univ, dipl, 57; Univ BC, MSc, 62, PhD(phys chem), 64. *Prof Exp:* Instr chem, Univ BC, 60-64; res fel chem physics, Harvard Univ, 64-65; res assoc biophys, Michael Reese Hosp, 65-66; res assoc phys chem, Ill Inst Technol, 66-67; from asst prof to assoc prof, 67-76, PROF CHEM, UNIV TOLEDO, 76- *Concurrent Pos:* Sr vis fel, Univ Western Ont, 80. *Mem:* AAAS; Am Chem Soc; Radiation Res Soc; Soc Appl Spectros; NY Acad Sci. *Res:* Molecular luminescence; spectroscopy; lasers; flash spectroscopy; radiation chemistry; luminescence of duped glasses and crystals; spectroscopy of biomolecules; magnetic circular dichroism. *Mailing Add:* Dept of Chem Univ of Toledo Toledo OH 43606

CHRYSSAFOPOULOS, HANKA WANDA SOBCZAK, b Porto Alegre, Brazil, Sept 24, 26; m 56. GEOTECHNICAL ENGINEERING, GLACIAL GEOLOGY. *Educ:* Univ Rio Grande do Sul, CEng, 51, MEE, 52; Univ Ill, MS, 54, PhD(civil eng), 64. *Prof Exp:* Head Res & Soils Lab, Tech Inst Rio Grande do Sul, 52-55; geotech res engr, Woodward-Clyde-Sherard & Assocs, 64-65; asst prof civil eng, Calif State Col, Long Beach, 65-67; private res, 67-77; SR ENGR, DAMES & MOORE, 78- *Concurrent Pos:* Mem, Regional Coun Eng & Archit, Brazil, 51-; Fulbright scholar; mem, Am Arbit Asn; consult UN Develop Prog. *Mem:* Am Soc Civil Engrs; Int Soc Soil Mech & Found Engrs; fel Geol Soc Am; Sigma Xi; Soc Women Engrs. *Res:* Basic soil mechanics; engineering geology; information retrieval. *Mailing Add:* Dames & Moore 301 W Camino Gardens Bl Bora Raton FL 33432

CHRYSSAFOPOULOS, N(ICHOLAS), b Istanbul, Turkey, Apr 23, 19; nat US; m 56. CIVIL ENGINEERING, SOIL MECHANICS. *Educ:* Robert Col, Istanbul, BS, 40; Univ Ill, MS, 52, PhD, 56. *Prof Exp:* Res engr construct, Turkey, 40-51; asst civil eng, Univ Ill, 52-55, res assoc, 55-56, asst prof, 56-59; chief engr, Greer Eng Assocs Div, Woodward-Clyde-Sherard & Assocs, 59-60, vpres, 60-66, exec vpres in charge, Southern Calif, 66-68; assoc, 68-69, PARTNER, REGIONAL MGR-LATIN AM, DAMES & MOORE, 69- *Concurrent Pos:* US Nat Comn, Union Panamericana de Asociaciones de Ingenieros. *Mem:* Fel Am Soc Civil Engrs; fel Am Consult Engrs Coun; Am Soc Testing & Mat; Am Asn Eng Soc. *Res:* Airphoto interpretation and soil mapping for highway purposes; subgrade oils; pavements for highways and airports; foundation problems in refineries, heavy industrial plants, offshore facilities. *Mailing Add:* 301 W Camino Gardens Blvd Suite A Boca Raton FL 33432

CHRYSSANTHOU, CHRYSSANTHOS, b Thessalonika, Greece, Oct 15, 25; m 58; c 2. EXPERIMENTAL PATHOLOGY. *Educ:* Aristotelean Univ Thessalonika, MD, 53. *Hon Degrees:* Dipl, Fac Arias Schreiber Central Hosp, Lima, Peru, 78. *Prof Exp:* Pathologist, Gynec-Obstet Clin, Med Sch, Univ Thessalonika, 53-54; instr path, Sch Med, NY Univ, 57; fel, 58-59, res asst path, 59-60, assoc exp path, 60-63, assoc pathologist, assoc dir path acad affairs, 69-76, PATHOLOGIST, DEPT LABS & RES, BETH ISRAEL MED CTR, 68-, ASSOC DIR DEPT, 64-; assoc prof, 67-80, PROF PATH, MT SINAI SCH MED, CITY UNIV NEW YORK, 80- *Concurrent Pos:* Vis prof, Claude Bernard Inst, Univ Montreal, 66; NIH res grants hypertension, 67-72; US Naval res grants decompression sickness & shock, Off Naval Res, 68-82; lectr, Sch Nursing, Beth Israel Hosp. *Honors & Awards:* Am Soc Clin Pathologists-Col Am Pathologists Award, 75 & 78. *Mem:* Soc Exp Biol & Med; Am Soc Exp Path; Am Asn Path & Bact; Am Asn Cancer Res; NY Acad Sci. *Res:* Mechanism; mechanism and prevention of decompression sickness; aseptic bone necrosis; pathophysiology of vasoactive polypeptides; tolerance and addiction to narcotics; endotoxin induced reactions; coagulation-fibrinolysis; laser photocoagulation. *Mailing Add:* Dept Labs & Res Beth Israel Med Ctr 10 Nathan D Perlman Pl New York NY 10003

CHRZANOWSKI, ADAM, b Cracow, Poland, Dec 22, 32; Can citizen; m 56; c 2. ENGINEERING. *Educ:* Acad Mining & Metall, Kracow, Engr, 54, MEng, 56, DEngSc, 62. *Prof Exp:* Sr asst surv, Acad Mining & Metall, Cracow, 55-61, asst prof, 62-66; fel, 64-66, assoc prof, 66-71, PROF SURV, UNIV NB, 71- *Concurrent Pos:* Mem, Mt Kennedy Exped, Yukon, Alaska, 65; vis prof, Eidgenoessische Tech Hochschule, Zurich, 80. *Mem:* Am Cong Surv & Mapping; Can Inst Surv; Int Soc Mine Surv; Am Geophys Union. *Res:* New methods and instruments in engineering and mining surveying; use of laser in surveying; tectonic movements; mining subsidence. *Mailing Add:* 85 Rankine St Fredericton NB E3B 4S2 Can

CHRZANOWSKI, ROBERT LAWRENCE, b Philadelphia, Pa, Oct 3, 41; m 69. BIO-ORGANIC CHEMISTRY, AGRICULTURAL CHEMISTRY. *Educ:* Drexel Inst Technol, BS, 64; Univ Nev, MS, 67; Pa State Univ, PhD(bio-org chem), 71. *Prof Exp:* RES CHEMIST AGRICHEM, E I DU PONT DE NEMOURS & CO, INC, 73- *Mem:* Am Chem Soc. *Res:* Agricultural metabolism chemistry and environmental degradation of pesticides and agrichemical products. *Mailing Add:* Exp Res Sta 324/333 E I du Pont de Nemours & Co Inc Wilmington DE 19898

CHRZANOWSKI, THOMAS HENRY, b Irvington, NJ, April 11, 52; m 75. MICROBIOL ECOLOGY, MYCOLOGY. *Educ:* Bloomfield Col, BA, 74; Univ SC, 76, PhD(microbiol), 81. *Prof Exp:* ASST PROF MICROBIOL, UNIV TEX, ARLINGTON, 81- *Mem:* Am Soc Microbiol; Mycol Soc Am; AAAS; Sigma Xi. *Res:* Quantifying microbiol biomass exchanges between a salt marsh and the Atlantic Ocean; use of filamentous fungi as an indicator of water masses. *Mailing Add:* Dept Biol Univ Tex Arlington TX 76019

CHU, AN-SHEK (ARTHUR S), b Peking, China, Sept 18, 22; US citizen; c 3. CHEMICAL ENGINEERING. *Educ:* Ta Tung Univ, China, BS, 46; Univ Pittsburgh, MS, 48; Okla State Univ, PhD(chem eng), 53. *Prof Exp:* Foreman, Ammonium Sulfate Dept, Yungli Chem Indust, China, 46-47; res chem engr res & develop, Gen Chem Div, 53-55, sr res chem engr, 55-57, tech supvr, 57-60, sr res technologist, 61-66, RES SUPVR, SPEC CHEM DIV, ALLIED CHEM CORP, 66- *Mem:* Am Inst Chem Engrs. *Res:* Fluorinated compounds. *Mailing Add:* 118 Fox Hunt Lane East Amherst NY 14051

CHU, BENJAMIN PENG-NIEN, b Shanghai, China, Mar 3, 32; m 59; c 3. PHYSICAL CHEMISTRY. *Educ:* St Norbert Col, BS, 55; Cornell Univ, PhD(phys chem), 59. *Prof Exp:* Res asst nuclear eng, Brookhaven Nat Lab, NY, 57; res assoc chem, Cornell Univ, 58-62; from asst prof to assoc prof, Univ Kans, 62-68; PROF CHEM, STATE UNIV NY STONY BROOK, 68-, CHMN DEPT, 78- *Concurrent Pos:* Sloan res fel, 66-68; Guggenheim fel, 68-69; vis prof & fel, Univ New South Wales & Australian Nat Univ, 74, Wayne State Univ & Hokkaido Univ 75, Univ Koln, 77 & Beijing Univ, 79. *Honors & Awards:* Humboldt Award for Sr US Scientist, 77. *Mem:* Am Chem Soc; Am Phys Soc. *Res:* Critical phenomena; molecular configuration and dynamics of macromolecules in solution; structure of non-crystalline media; light scattering and small angle x-ray scattering; ion exchange. *Mailing Add:* Dept Chem State Univ NY Stony Brook NY 11794

CHU, BOA-TEH, b Peiping, China, Sept 26, 24. AERONAUTICAL ENGINEERING. *Educ:* Nat Cent Univ, China, BSc, 45; Johns Hopkins Univ, PhD(aeronaut eng), 54. *Prof Exp:* Asst aeronaut eng, Johns Hopkins Univ, 49-54; res staff asst, 54-56; from asst prof to assoc prof eng, Brown Univ, 56-59; PROF ENG & APPL SCI, YALE UNIV, 64- *Res:* Fluid mechanics; thermodynamics; combustion aerodynamics; magnetohydrodynamics; elasticity; viscoelasticity. *Mailing Add:* Dept of Eng & Appl Sci Yale Univ New Haven CT 06520

CHU, CHANG-CHI, b Yentai, Shantung, China, Sept 9, 33; m 68; c 1. CROP PHYSIOLOGY, CROP PRODUCTION. *Educ:* Taiwan Chung-Hsing Univ, BS, 54; Kans State Univ, MS, 73; Cornell Univ, PhD(bot), 76. *Prof Exp:* Asst agronomist & prod mgr, Taiwan Sugar Corp, 55-60, res assoc sugar cane, 60-70; res asst agron, Kans State Univ, 71-73; res asst bot, Cornell Univ, 73-76, res support specialist nitrate pollution, 76-77; CROPS RES & DEVELOP SPECIALIST & BIOMETRICIAN, AGWAY, INC, 77- *Mem:* Am Soc Agron; Crop Sci Soc Am; Am Soc Hort Sci; Am Soc Plant Physiologists; Coun Agr Sci & Technol. *Res:* Crop production and physiology. *Mailing Add:* Agway Farm Res Ctr RD 2 Tully NY 13159

CHU, CHAUNCEY C, b Shanghai, China, Oct 17, 24; nat US; m 44; c 2. MECHANICAL ENGINEERING, DESIGN ENGINEERING. *Educ:* Purdue Univ, BSME, 43; Univ Toronto, MASc, 46; Harvard Univ, MS, 47. *Prof Exp:* Sr res assoc, Fabric Res Labs Inc, 51-67; vpres, Kybe Corp, 67-70; mgr & sr staff engr, 70-72, pres, Puerto Rico Br, 78, SR VPRES MFG, WANG LABS, INC, 72-, PRES, TAIWAN BR, 79- *Concurrent Pos:* Sr consult, Cybetronics, Inc, 60-67. *Mem:* Am Soc Mech Engrs; Am Inst Aeronaut & Astronaut. *Res:* Dynamic and thermal behaviors of polymeric re-entry decelerator materials; development of magnetic tape transports and disc-pack drives; mechanical design of electronic calculators and mini-computers. *Mailing Add:* 1 Industrial Ave Lowell MA 01851

CHU, CHI HSUIN ULLI, anatomy, deceased

CHU, CHIA-KUN, b Shanghai, China, Aug 14, 27; m 52; c 3. APPLIED MATHEMATICS. *Educ:* Chiao-Tung Univ, China, BS, 48; Cornell Univ, MME, 50; NY Univ, PhD(math), 59. *Prof Exp:* Develop engr, Gen Elec Co, 50-53; asst prof mech eng, Stevens Inst Technol, 53-57; assoc prof eng sci, Pratt Inst, 57-59; assoc prof aero eng, NY Univ, 59-63; vis res assoc, Plasma Res Lab, 63-65, assoc prof, 65-68, PROF ENG SCI, COLUMBIA UNIV, 68- *Concurrent Pos:* Guggenheim fel, 71-72. *Mem:* Am Math Soc; Am Inst Aeronaut & Astronaut; Am Phys Soc. *Res:* Fluid dynamics; plasma physics; numerical methods and computing. *Mailing Add:* Appl Physics Dept Columbia Univ New York NY 10027

CHU, CHIEH, b Chekiang, China, Jan 17, 22; US citizen; m 48; c 3. CHEMICAL ENGINEERING. *Educ:* Chekiang Univ, BS, 47; Univ Wis, MS, 59, PhD(chem eng), 61. *Prof Exp:* Assoc engr, Chinese Petrol Corp, 47-58; res scientist, Sinclair Res, Inc, 61-65, sr res scientist, Sinclair Oil & Gas Co, 65; asst prof eng & appl sci, Univ Calif, Los Angeles, 65-72; res scientist, 72-80, SR RES SCIENTIST, GETTY OIL CO, 80- *Mem:* Am Inst Mining, Metall & Petrol Engrs; Am Inst Chem Engrs. *Res:* Enhanced oil recovery processes, thermal recovery, and chemical flood; reservoir engineering and simulation; aquifer simulation; chemical kinetics; catalysis; combustion; chemical reactor analysis and design; air and water pollution control; seawater desalination. *Mailing Add:* Getty Oil Co PO Box 42214 Houston TX 77042

CHU, CHING-WU, b Hodnam, China, Dec 2, 41; US citizen; m 68; c 2. MATERIALS SCIENCE. *Educ:* Cheng-king Univ, BS, 62; Fordham Univ, MS, 65; Univ Calif, La Jolla, PhD(physics), 68. *Prof Exp:* Mem tech staff physics, Bell Labs, Am Tel & Tel, 68-70; asst prof, 70-73, assoc prof, 73-75, prof, Cleveland State Univ, 75-79; PROF PHYSICS, UNIV HOUSTON, 79- *Concurrent Pos:* Resident res assoc, Argonne Nat Lab, 73; consult, Bell Labs, 73; vis staff mem, Los Alamos Sci Lab, 75-80. *Mem:* fel Am Phys Soc. *Res:* High pressure low temperature studies; superconductivity, magnetism, dielectrics and novel materials. *Mailing Add:* Physics Dept Univ Houston Cent Campus Houston TX 77004

CHU, CHUNG K, b Seoul, Korea, May 18, 41; US citizen; m 73; c 2. CHEMOTHERAPY. *Educ:* Seoul Nat Univ, BS, 64; Idaho State Univ, MS, 70; State Univ NY, Buffalo, PhD(med chem), 74. *Prof Exp:* Fel med chem, Sloan-Kettering Inst Cancer Res, 74-75, res assoc, 76-80; asst prof med chem, Idaho State Univ, 80-82; ASST PROF MED CHEM, UNIV GA, 82- *Mem:* Am Chem Soc; NY Acad Sci. *Res:* Design and synthesis of anticancer and antiviral agents; heterocyclic carbohydrates; nucleosides chemistry. *Mailing Add:* Sch Pharm Univ Ga Athens GA 30602

CHU, CHUN-LUNG, b Hong Kong, Apr 29, 50; Brit citizen; m 80. POSTHARVEST PHYSIOLOGY. *Educ:* Nat Chung-Hsing, BSc, 72; Univ Guelph, MSc, 77; Wash State Univ, PhD(hort), 80. *Prof Exp:* Teaching asst postharvest physiol, Wash State Univ, 77-78, res asst, 77-80, teaching asst pomol, 80; RES SCIENTIST APPLE STORAGE, ONT MINISTRY AGR & FOOD, 80- *Honors & Awards:* Joseph Harvey Gourley Award. *Mem:* Am Soc Hort Sci. *Res:* Fruit maturity indices; storage and handling techniques to enhance efficiency of apple production and marketing systems. *Mailing Add:* Hort Exp Sta Ont Ministry Agr & Food PO Box 587 Simcoe ON N3Y 4N5 Can

CHU, ELIZABETH WANN, b Shanghai, China, Oct 29, 21; US citizen; m 46; c 1. CYTOLOGY, PATHOLOGY. *Educ:* Univ Hong Kong, BS & BM, 46; Shanghai Med Col, MD, 46; Am Bd Path, dipl, 65. *Prof Exp:* Resident internal med, Beekman Hosp, New York, 48-49; resident internal med, Cambridge City Hosp, Mass, 50-51 & path, 51-52; resident, Boston City Hosp, 52-53; med officer cytol, Washington Cytol Unit, 56-58, MED OFFICER CYTOL, PATH LAB, NAT CANCER INST, 58- *Mem:* Am Soc Cytol. *Res:* Exfoliative cytology, its value in experimental carcinogenesis, metastases and endocrine factors. *Mailing Add:* Path Lab Nat Cancer Inst Bethesda MD 20014

CHU, ERNEST HSIAO-YING, b Haining, China, June 3, 27; US citizen; m 54; c 3. GENETICS. *Educ:* St John's Univ, China, BS, 47; Univ Calif, Berkeley, MS, 51, PhD(genetics), 54. *Prof Exp:* From res asst to res assoc bot, Yale Univ, 54-59, lectr anat, Sch Med, 58-59; biologist genetics, Oak Ridge Nat Lab, 59-72; PROF HUMAN GENETICS, MED SCH, UNIV MICH, ANN ARBOR, 72- *Concurrent Pos:* Prof zool & biomed sci, Univ Tenn, Knoxville, 67-72. *Mem:* Genetics Soc Am; Am Soc Human Genetics; Am Soc Cell Biol; Tissue Cult Asn; Environ Mutagen Soc. *Res:* Somatic cell genetics; mammalian cytogenetics; radiation biology. *Mailing Add:* Dept of Human Genetics Univ of Mich Med Sch Ann Arbor MI 48109

CHU, FLORENCE CHIEN-HWA, b China, May 20, 18; nat US; m 43; c 2. RADIOLOGY. *Educ:* Nat Med Col, Shanghai, MD, 42; Am Bd Radiol, dipl, 50. *Prof Exp:* Instr radiol, 53-55, asst prof clin, 56-61, clin asst prof, 61-69, assoc prof, 69-73, clin prof, 73-77, PROF RADIOL, MED COL, CORNELL UNIV, 77-; PROF RADIOL & CHMN DEPT RADIATION THERAPY, MEM HOSP, 76- *Concurrent Pos:* Fel radiol, Mem Hosp, 49-50, clin asst radiation therapist, 50-53, asst attend radiation therapist, 55-65, assoc attend radiation therapist, 65-69, attend radiation therapist, 69-, actg chmn dept radiation therapy, 76; res assoc, Sloan-Kettering Inst, 55, assoc mem, 77-; assoc attend radiologist, New York Hosp, 70-74. *Mem:* AMA; Am Col Radiol; Radiol Soc NAm; Am Radium Soc. *Res:* Ionizing radiation. *Mailing Add:* Mem Sloan-Kettering Cancer Ctr 1275 York Ave New York NY 10021

CHU, FUN SUN, b China, May 7, 33; m 58; c 3. BIOCHEMISTRY. *Educ:* Nat Chung-Hsin Univ, BS, 54; WVa Univ, MS, 59; Univ Mo, PhD(biochem), 64. *Prof Exp:* Res assoc, Food Res Inst, Univ Chicago, 63-67; asst prof, Food Res Inst, 67-72, assoc prof, Dept Food Sci & Food Res Inst, 72-77, PROF, DEPT FOOD MICROBIOL & TOXICOL, UNIV WIS-MADISON, 78- *Mem:* Am Soc Microbiol. *Res:* Protein chemistry; biochemistry of microorganisms; mycotoxins; biochemistry of microbial toxins. *Mailing Add:* Food Res Inst Univ of Wis 1925 Willow Dr Madison WI 53706

CHU, GORDON P K, b Kiangsi, China, Jan 29, 15; m 41; c 3. CERAMICS, METALLURGY. *Educ:* Shanghai Univ Sci & Technol, BS, 38; Pa State Univ, MS, 49; Mo Sch Mines, PhD(ceramic eng), 64. *Prof Exp:* Res engr enamel & glass-metals, Nat Resources Comn, Chinese Nationalist Govt, 38-47; res asst ceramics & metals, Pa State Univ, 47-53; res engr, Res Lab, Pfaudler Co, 53-57, mgr basic res, 57-59, sr res fel, 59-60; supvr ceramics & metall sect, Res Div, Am Radiator & Standard Sanit Corp, 61-62, actg mgr ceramics & metall res dept, 63-67; res assoc, Tech Staffs Div, Corning Glassworks, 67-69 & mat res, Gen Tel Elec Lab, 69-76; MEM STAFF, GTF SYLVANIA, INC, 76- *Mem:* AAAS; fel Am Ceramic Soc; Am Inst Ceramic Engrs; Am Soc Metals; Brit Inst Metals. *Res:* Composition and chemico-physical properties of glasses and enamels; crystalized glasses; glass-metal reactions; gases in ceramic-metal systems; whitware ceramics; metallic and ceramic coatings on refractory materials; vapor deposition through halides reactions. *Mailing Add:* GTF Sylvania Inc 100 Endicott St Danvers MA 01923

CHU, HORN DEAN, b Tientsin, China, Sept 9, 33; US citizen; m 62. CHEMICAL ENGINEERING. *Educ:* Waseda Univ, Japan, BS, 59, MS, 61; Univ Pa, MS, 63; Univ Ala, PhD(chem eng), 65. *Prof Exp:* Proj engr, Selas Corp of Am, 65-72; adj prof & asst prof food sci, Cook Col, Rutgers Univ, 72-79; SR ENGR, MACANDREWS & FORBES CO, 79- *Mem:* AAAS; Am Inst Chem Engrs; Am Chem Soc; Inst Food Technologists; fel Am Inst Chemists. *Res:* Combustion instability; heat and fluid processing; thermodynamics and kinetics of heterogeneous reaction; heat and mass transfer; immobilized enzyme reactor; energy conservation in food processing; utlization of biomass; food processing development. *Mailing Add:* 105 The Mews Haddonfield NJ 08033

CHU, HSIEN-KUN, b Shanghai, China, Oct 14, 47; m 76; c 1. ORGANIC CHEMISTRY. *Educ:* Nat Taiwan Univ, BS, 70; Vanderbilt Univ, PhD(chem), 76. *Prof Exp:* Vis instr, Univ Tex-Arlington, 76-77; res assoc chem, Tex Christian Univ, 77-80; PROJ CHEMIST, DOW CORNING CORP, 80- *Concurrent Pos:* Fel, Tex Christian Univ, 77- *Mem:* Am Chem Soc; Sigma Xi. *Res:* Mechanisms of organic reactions; photooxygenation; reactions involving thermally generated singlet oxygen. *Mailing Add:* Dow Corning Corp Midland MI 48640

CHU, HUAI-PU, b Hsin-Yeh, Honan, China, Nov 11, 27; US citizen; m 56; c 2. METALLURGY, MECHANICAL ENGINEERING. *Educ:* Ordnance Eng Col, Taipei, BS, 53; Colo Sch Mines, MS, 63, DSc(metall), 65. *Prof Exp:* SR RES METALLURGIST, NAVAL SHIP RES & DEVELOP CTR, 64- *Mem:* Am Soc Metals; Am Soc Testing & Mat; Am Soc Mech Engrs; Soc Exp Stress Anal; Am Inst Mining, Metall & Petrol Engrs. *Res:* Physical and mechanical metallurgy including fracture, fatigue, creep and stress corrosion of engineering alloys. *Mailing Add:* Naval Ship Res & Develop Ctr Code 2814 Annapolis MD 21402

CHU, IRWIN Y E, b Taipei, Taiwan, Sept 28, 37; m 66; c 2. PLANT GENETICS. *Educ:* Chung-Shin Univ, BS, 61; Tokyo Univ, MS, 65, PhD(plant genetics), 68. *Prof Exp:* Fel appl genetics, Nat Inst Genetics, Japan, 68-69; assoc res fel plant genetic, Acad Sinica, Taiwan, 69-72, head lab, Inst Bot, 71-72; asst res prof, Univ Utah, 72-74, res assoc, 74-76; SR PLANT GENETICIST, GREENFIELD RES LAB, ELI LILLY & CO, 76- *Concurrent Pos:* Vis assoc prof, Inst Food Crops, Chung-Shing Univ, 71; asst ed newsletter, Soc Advan Breeding Res in Asia & Oceania, 70-72. *Mem:* Sigma Xi; Genetic Soc Am; Crop Soc Am; Japanese Soc Genetics; Chinese Soc Agron. *Res:* Genetical studies on plant tissue, cell and protoplast culture; application of tissue culture techniques for plant breeding. *Mailing Add:* Lilly Res Labs PO Box 708 Greenfield IN 46140

CHU, JOSEPH YUNG-CHANG, b Anhwei, China, Aug 16, 40; US citizen; m 67. ORGANIC CHEMISTRY, PHOTOCHEMISTRY. *Educ:* Nat Taiwan Univ, BS, 61; Fla State Univ, MS, 67; Univ Rochester, PhD(org chem), 72. *Prof Exp:* Res chemist, Sinclair Res, Inc, 67-68; assoc scientist, 71-73, scientist, 73-78, sr scientist chem, Webster Res Ctr, 78-80, MGR, CHINA ADMIN, XEROX CORP, 80- *Mem:* Am Chem Soc; The Chem Soc; Inter-Am Photochem Soc; AAAS; Soc Photog Scientists & Engrs. *Res:* Synthesis; thermal and photochemical reactions of organic compounds; electrical and photoconductive properties of organic materials; reprographic materials and processes. *Mailing Add:* Webster Res Ctr Xerox Sq-114 Rochester NY 14644

CHU, JU CHIN, b Taitsang, China, Dec 14, 19; m. CHEMICAL ENGINEERING. *Educ:* Tsing Hua Univ, BSc, 40; Mass Inst Technol, ScD(chem eng), 46. *Prof Exp:* Asst chem, Tsing Hua Univ, 40-43; instr, Yunan Army Med Acad, 42-43; petrol technologist, Shell Chem Corp, Calif, 46; asst prof chem eng, Wash Univ, 46-49; from assoc prof to prof, Polytech Inst Brooklyn, 49-67; tech adv, Strategic Missile Systs Div, NAm Rockwell Corp, 66-70; TRUSTEE & CHMN BD, TECHNOL RESOURCES, INC, 70- *Concurrent Pos:* Consult, Sun Oil Co, 52, Am Cyanamid Co, 53, Rohm and Haas, 55, Curtiss Wright Corp, 55-57, Union Carbide Nuclear Co, 55-58, Argonne Nat Lab & US Dept Agr, 56-61, Gen Elec Co, 58, Space Technol Labs, 59, Rocketdyne, NAm Aviation, 60-62, space info & systs div, 52-53, Aerospace Corp & Erie Resistor Corp, 62, ARO, Inc, 62-64, Huyck Corp, 62-65, W R Grace, 63, Grumman Aircraft Eng Corp, 64, Gen Motors Corp, 65 & Sandia Corp, 66-67; tech dir, Chem Construct Corp, 56-57; global lectr, Univs & Sci Socs, 62-63; prof, Va Polytech Inst & State Univ, 69-72. *Honors & Awards:* Ann Achievement Award, Chinese Inst Eng, 61; Medal of Honor, Univ Liege, 63; Gold Medal, Chinese Educ Ministry, 63. *Mem:* Fel AAAS; Am Chem Soc; Am Petrol Inst; fel Am Inst Chem Engrs; fel Chinese Acad Sci. *Res:* Advanced weapon systems; nuclear technology and hardening; environment control and industrial waste recycle; process design; unit operation. *Mailing Add:* 21 Yorktown Irvine CA 92714

CHU, KAI-CHING, b Szechwan, China, Nov 19, 44; m 72; c 2. APPLIED MATHEMATICS, SYSTEM THEORY. *Educ:* Nat Taiwan Univ, BS, 66; Harvard Univ, MS, 68, PhD(appl math), 71. *Prof Exp:* Res asst appl math, Harvard Univ, 68-71; mathematician, Systs Control, Inc, 71-72; res staff mem appl math, 73-75, MGR SOCIAL SCI GROUP, DEPT GEN SCI, T J WATSON RES CTR, IBM CORP, 75- *Concurrent Pos:* Assoc ed, Trans on Automatic Control, 71- *Mem:* Sr mem Inst Elec & Electronics Engrs; Opers Res Soc Am. *Res:* Decision and control theories, optimization and estimation techniques; communication networks; computer applications to urban and industrial problems; image processing. *Mailing Add:* T J Watson Res Ctr PO Box 218 Yorktown Heights NY 10598

CHU, KEH-CHANG, b Feng-Yang, China, May 19, 33; m 63; c 2. MAGNETIC RESONANCE, RADIATION PHYSICS. *Educ:* Nat Taiwan Univ, BS, 55; Univ Mich, MS, 62, PhD(nuclear sci), 67. *Prof Exp:* Instr nuclear sci, Nat Tsing Hua Univ, 60-62; asst prof, 68-72, PROF PHYSICS, WESTERN ILL UNIV, 74- *Mem:* Am Phys Soc. *Res:* Electron spin resonance; electron nuclear double resonance; radiation effects in solids. *Mailing Add:* Dept of Physics Western Ill Univ Macomb IL 61455

CHU, KUANG-HAN, b Chekiang, China, Nov 13, 19; m 62. CIVIL ENGINEERING. *Educ:* Nat Cent Univ, China, BS, 42; Univ Ill, MS, 47, PhD(civil eng), 50. *Prof Exp:* Struct designer, Ammann & Whitney, 50-51 & D B Steinman, 51-55; actg assoc prof civil eng, Univ Iowa, 55-56; assoc prof, 56-63, PROF CIVIL ENG, ILL INST TECHNOL, 63- *Honors & Awards:* Collingwood Prize, Am Soc Civil Engrs, 53. *Mem:* Fel Am Soc Civil Engrs; Am Concrete Inst; Int Asn Bridge & Struct Engrs. *Res:* Structural analysis and design; stability and dynamics of structures; computer techniques. *Mailing Add:* Dept of Civil Eng Technol Ctr Ill Inst of Technol Chicago IL 60616

CHU, KWO RAY, b Human, China, Oct 10, 42; US citizen; m 68. GYROTRON. *Educ:* Cornell Univ, PhD(physics), 72. *Prof Exp:* Res physicist, Sci Applications, Inc, 73-77; SUPVR RES PHYSICIST, NAVAL RES LAB, 77- *Mem:* Am Phys Soc. *Res:* Plasma physics; relativistic electronics. *Mailing Add:* 4916 Andrea Ave Annandale VA 22003

CHU, MAMERTO LOARCA, b Philippines, Oct 15, 33; US citizen; m 62; c 5. VIBRATIONS, ACOUSTICS. *Educ:* Iloilo City Univ, Philippines, 56; Univ Houston, MSME, 64, PhD(mech eng), 67. *Prof Exp:* Plant engr, Int Steel, 58-67; res assoc, Univ Houston, 67-68, lectr mech eng, 68-69; asst prof, 69-71, assoc prof, 71-80, PROF MECH ENG, UNIV AKRON, 80- *Concurrent Pos:* Prin investr, NIH, 72-76, Babcock & Wilcox Co, 77-79; adj prof, Akron City Hosp, 77- *Mem:* Am Soc Mech Engrs; Sigma Xi; Acoust Soc Am; Am Soc Eng Educ. *Res:* Acoustics and vibrations as applied to both mechanical and bio-engineering systems, such as audiometric studies of pathological joints, diagnostic applications, modal analysis, random data statistical analysis. *Mailing Add:* Mech Eng Dept Univ Akron Akron OH 44325

CHU, MARILYN WEI-SHI, inorganic chemistry, see previous edition

CHU, NORI YAW-CHYUAN, b Taipei, Taiwan, Mar 31, 39; US citizen; m 67; c 2. PHYSICAL CHEMISTRY, CHEMICAL ENGINEERING. *Educ:* Cheng-Kung Univ, Tainan, Taiwan, BS, 61; Univ Chicago, PhD(phys chem), 68. *Prof Exp:* Fel chem, Univ Calif, Riverside, 68-71; res assoc chem, Northeastern Univ, 71-73; SR RES CHEMIST CHEM & MAT SCI, AM OPTICAL CORP, 73- *Concurrent Pos:* Pub health serv fel, Univ Calif, Riverside, 69-70. *Mem:* Am Chem Soc. *Res:* Basic and applied research in photochromic materials; photophysical processes and energy-transfer mechanisms in molecules and solids; synthesis of photosensitive materials; crosslinking polymers and networks. *Mailing Add:* Am Optical Corp Res Ctr 14 Mechanic St Southbridge MA 01550

CHU, PAUL TAI, chemical engineering, mathematics, see previous edition

CHU, SHERWOOD CHENG-WU, b Shanghai, China, Aug 30, 37; US citizen; m 59; c 1. MATHEMATICS. *Educ:* Harvard Univ, BA, 59; Univ Md, MA, 61, PhD(math), 63. *Prof Exp:* Res asst, Inst Fluid Dynamics & Appl Math, Univ Md, 60-63; Nat Acad Sci-Nat Res Coun resident res assoc, US Naval Ord Lab, 63-64; mem tech staff, Bellcomm, Inc, 64-66; asst prof math, Univ Del, 66-68; mem tech staff, Bellcomm, Inc, Washington, DC, 68-72; res mathematician, NIH, 72-76; GEN ENGR, US DEPT TRANSP, 76- *Concurrent Pos:* Asst prof lectr, George Washington Univ, 65-66. *Mem:* Am Math Soc; Soc Indust & Appl Math. *Res:* Applied mathematics. *Mailing Add:* 7012 Marbury Rd Bethesda MD 20034

CHU, SHIH I, b Taipei, Taiwan, Jan 8, 43. LASER INDUCED CHEMISTRY, ATOMIC COLLISIONS. *Educ:* Nat Taiwan Univ, BS, 65, MS, 68; Nat Tsing Hua Univ, DSc, 71; Harvard Univ, PhD(chem physics), 74. *Prof Exp:* Res assoc, Joint Inst Lab Astrophysics, 74-76; J W Gibbs Lectr atomic physics, Yale Univ, 76-78; asst prof, 78-81, ASSOC PROF PHYS CHEM, UNIV KANS, 81- *Concurrent Pos:* vis scientist, Int Bus Machines Res Lab, San Jose, Calif, 74; consult, Ctr Astrophysics, Harvard Univ, 77 & 80; vis assoc, Calif Inst Tech, 81; prin investr, Dept Energy, Chem Sciences, 80- *Honors & Awards:* Alfred P Sloan Found Award, 80. *Mem:* Am Phys Soc; AAAS. *Res:* Theoretical chemistry and molecular astrophysics; atomic and molecular collisions; intense field multiphoton processes; laser-induced chemical dynamics, complex-coordinate method; interstellar chemistry; application of quantum mechanics to chemical, physical and astronomical problems of current interest. *Mailing Add:* Dept Chem Univ Kans Lawrence KS 66045

CHU, SHIRLEY SHAN-CHI, b Peking, China, Feb 16, 29; US citizen; m 54; c 3. SOLID STATE SCIENCE. *Educ:* Taiwan Nat Univ, BS, 51; Duquesne Univ, MS, 54; Univ Pittsburgh, PhD(phys chem), 61. *Prof Exp:* Res assoc x-ray crystallog, Crystallog Lab, Univ Pittsburgh, 61-67; asst prof, 68-73, assoc prof, 73-81, PROF ELEC ENG, SOUTHERN METHODIST UNIV, 81- *Mem:* Am Crystallog Asn; Am Chem Soc; Electrochem Soc; Inst Elec & Electronics Engrs. *Res:* X-ray crystallography; crystal structures of organic compounds and electronic materials by x-ray diffraction; crystallographic computer programming; characterization of electronic materials; photovoltaic solar enerrgy conversion. *Mailing Add:* Sch of Eng & Appl Sci Southern Methodist Univ Dallas TX 75275

CHU, SHU TUNG, water resources & agricultural engineering, see previous edition

CHU, SOU YIE, b Taipei, Taiwan, Feb 17, 42; m 67; c 1. DRUG METABOLISM. *Educ:* Nat Taiwan Univ, BS, 64; Univ Ill, Chicago, PhD(pharmaceut chem), 70. *Prof Exp:* Res asst chem pharmacol, Univ Ill Med Ctr, 70, trainee, 70-74; vis fel, Nat Cancer Inst, 72-73, Nat Inst Arthritis, Metab & Digestive Dis spec fel, Roche Inst, 73-74; PHARMACOLOGIST, DRUG METAB DEPT, ABBOTT LABS, 74- *Mem:* Sigma Xi; Am Pharmaceut Asn; NY Acad Sci; Am Chem Soc. *Res:* Synthesis of biologically active compounds; analysis of drugs in biological fluids; pharmacokinetic studies. *Mailing Add:* Drug Metab Dept Abbott Labs North Chicago IL 60064

CHU, SUNG GUN, b Seoul, Korea; m 75; c 2. RHEOLOGY, PHYSICALPOLYMER CHEMISTRY. *Educ:* HanYang Univ, BS, 73; Univ Tex, Austin, MS, 75, PhD(chem), 78. *Prof Exp:* Fel rheology, Carnegie-Mellon Univ, 78-79; res chemist, Polymer Res Inst, Univ Dayton, 79-81; RES CHEMIST ADHESIVE POLYMER, HERCULES RES CTR, 81- *Mem:* Am Chem Soc; Soc Rheology. *Res:* Characterization of polymer; modification of polymers; adhesive formulation development; viscoelastic properties of polymers as well as lower molecular weight resins. *Mailing Add:* Res Ctr Hercules Inc Wilmington DE 19899

CHU, T(ING) Y(E), engineering, see previous edition

CHU, TAK-KIN, b Kwang Tung, China, Dec 14, 38; US citizen; m 74; c 2. PHYSICS. *Educ:* Chung Chi Col, Hong Kong, BS, 61; Dartmouth Col, PhD(physics), 69. *Prof Exp:* Instr & res assoc, Univ Conn, 68-76; asst sr researcher, Physics & Eng, Ctr Info & Numerical Data Anal & Synthesis, Purdue Univ, 76-80; MEM STAFF, NAVAL SURFACE WEAPONS CTR, 80- *Mem:* Am Phys Soc; Sigma Xi. *Res:* Thermal and electrical properties of materials; relationship of these properties to the fundamental physical processes and to the structural constitution of materials. *Mailing Add:* Naval Surface Weapons Ctr Code R45 White Oak Lab Silver Spring MD 20910

CHU, TA-SHING, b Shanghai, China, July 18, 34; m 62; c 2. ELECTRICAL ENGINEERING, APPLIED MATHEMATICS. *Educ:* Univ Taiwan, BSc, 55; Ohio State Univ, MSc, 57, PhD(elec eng), 60. *Prof Exp:* Res assoc, Antenna Lab, Ohio State Univ, 57-61; res assoc, Div Electromagnetic Res, Courant Inst Math Sci, 61-63; MEM TECH STAFF, RADIO RES LAB, BELL LABS, 63- *Concurrent Pos:* Mem, Comn Bell & Flange, Int Sci Radio Union. *Mem:* Fel Inst Elec & Electronics Engrs. *Res:* Surface wave diffraction; precision gain standard; propagation through precipitation; dual-polarization radio transmission; Crawford Hill 7-meter millimeter antenna. *Mailing Add:* Dept Radio Commun Res Bell Labs Holmdel NJ 07733

CHU, TING LI, b Peking, China, Dec 26, 24; m 54; c 3. PHOTOVOLTAICS, ELECTRONIC MATERIALS. *Educ:* Catholic Univ Peking, BS, 45, MS, 48; Washington Univ, St Louis, PhD(chem), 52. *Prof Exp:* From asst prof chem to assoc prof, Duquesne Univ, 52-56; res scientist, fel scientist & mgr electronic mat, Westinghouse Res Labs, 56-67; PROF ELEC ENG, SOUTHERN METHODIST UNIV, 67- *Concurrent Pos:* Consult, Westinghouse Res Labs, 67-69; Tex Instruments, 69-75; Monsanto, NCR Corp, & Union Carbide, 75-78, Poly Solar Incorp, 78- *Mem:* Electrochem Soc; Inst Elec & Electronics Engrs; Am Soc Eng Educ. *Res:* Electronic materials and devices, including photovoltaic solar energy conversion, growth and characterization of crystals and films, and fabrication and characterization of junction devices, dielectric-semiconductor devices. *Mailing Add:* Dept Elec Eng Southern Methodist Univ Dallas TX 75275

CHU, TSANN MING, b Kaoh-siung, Formosa, Apr 18, 38; m 67. BIOCHEMISTRY. *Educ:* Nat Taiwan Univ, BS, 61; NC State Univ, MS, 65; Pa State Univ, PhD(biochem), 67. *Prof Exp:* Clin chemist, Buffalo Gen Hosp, 69-70; sr cancer res scientist & asst dir clin chem, 70-71, prin cancer res scientist, 71-72, assoc chief cancer res scientist & dir clin chem, 72-76, DIR DIAG IMMUNOL RES & BIOCHEM, ROSWELL PARK MEM INST, 76- *Concurrent Pos:* Res fel biochem, Med Found Buffalo, 67-69; United Health Found Western NY fel, 68-69; asst prof exp path, State Univ NY Buffalo, 71-74, assoc prof, 74-77, prof, 77-; mem, Comt Cancer Immunodiagnosis, Nat Cancer Inst, 78-79, Tumor Immunol Comt, 79-81. *Mem:* Am Asn Cancer Res; Am Chem Soc; Am Soc Biol Chemists; Am Asn Immunologists; Am Asn Pathologists. *Res:* Biochemistry of steroids and its conjugates; clinical endocrinology; clinical enzymology; tumor antigen and antibody; bichemical and immunological markers for cancer. *Mailing Add:* Roswell Park Mem Inst 666 Elm St Buffalo NY 14263

CHU, VICTOR FU HUA, b Hankow, China, Jan 22, 18; nat US; m 47; c 3. PHYSICAL CHEMISTRY. *Educ:* Cent China Univ, BS, 38; Yale Univ, PhD(phys chem), 50. *Prof Exp:* Chemist, Chungking Saltpeter Ref, 38-39; chemist & plant supt, Kweichow Saltpeter Ref, 39-42; chemist, Hunan Oil Ref, 42-43; plant supt, Pai-Yeh Oil Ref, 43-44; instr chem, Cent China Univ, 44-47; from res chemist to sr res chemist, 50-65, res assoc, 65-75, RES FEL, PHOTO PRODS DEPT, E I DU PONT DE NEMOURS & CO, INC, 75- *Honors & Awards:* Journal Award, Photog Soc Am, 53. *Mem:* Am Chem Soc. *Res:* Color photography; conductance of electrolytes; photographic chemistry and systems. *Mailing Add:* 2502 Garth Rd Chalfonte Wilmington DE 19810

CHU, VINCENT HAO KWONG, b Shanghai, China, Oct 20, 18; m 50; c 1. INORGANIC CHEMISTRY, PHYSICAL CHEMISTRY. *Educ:* Sun Yat-Sen Univ, BSc, 44; Lehigh Univ, MSc, 57, PhD(inorg chem), 62. *Prof Exp:* Asst engr, Cent Indust Res Inst, China, mfg head, Taiwan Camphor Bur & supt res & mfg, Taipei Chem Works, 44-52; ENGR RAW MAT, HOMER RES LABS, BETHLEHEM STEEL CORP, 57- *Mem:* AAAS; Am Chem Soc; Am Inst Mining, Metall & Petrol Engrs; Sigma Xi; Chinese Inst Engrs (pres, 81-83). *Res:* Organo-metal compound; coordination in aprotic media; reduction kinetics of iron ore; iron ore agglomeration; crystal field theory; powder metallurgy; pyrometallurgy; coal gasification; coking coal immprovement. *Mailing Add:* 1310 Woodland Circle Bethlehem PA 18017

CHU, WEI-KAN, b Yunnan, China, Apr 1, 40. EXPERIMENTAL ATOMIC PHYSICS, ENGINEERING PHYSICS. *Educ:* Cheng-Kung Univ, BS, 62; Baylor Univ, 63, MS, 65, PhD(physics), 69. *Prof Exp:* Fel, Baylor Univ, 69-72; res fel, Calif Inst Technol, 72-73, sr res fel, 73-75; eng ion implantation & backscattering, IBM Corp, 75-81; PROF, UNIV NC, 81- *Mem:* Am Phys Soc; Electrochem Soc; Sigma Xi; Bohmische Phys Soc. *Res:* Energy loss of ions in matter; ion beam surface layer analysis; ion implantation in semiconductors; thin film interactions. *Mailing Add:* Dept Physics & Astron Univ NC Chapel Hill NC 27514

CHU, WESLEY W(EI-CHIN), b Shanghai, China, May 5, 36; US citizen; m 60; c 2. COMPUTER SCIENCE, ELECTRICAL ENGINEERING. *Educ:* Univ Mich, BSE, 60, MSE, 61; Stanford Univ, PhD(elec eng), 66. *Prof Exp:* Engr, Comput Dept, Gen Elec Co, Ariz, 61-62 & Int Bus Mach Corp, Calif, 64-66; res engr, Stanford Electronics Labs, 66; mem tech staff, Bell Tel Labs, NJ, 66-69; assoc prof comput sci, 69-75, PROF COMPUT SCI, UNIV CALIF, LOS ANGELES, 75- *Concurrent Pos:* Consult govt agencies & pvt industs; ed text bk, Advances in Comput Commun, 1st ed, 74, 2nd ed, 76, 77; prog chmn, Fourth Data Commun Symp & chmn, Interprocess Commun Workshop, 75; ed, J Comput Networks, 75- & J Comput & Elec Eng, 78-; assoc ed, Inst Elec & Electronic Engrs Trans Comput, 78-80. *Honors & Awards:* ACM Serv Award, Asn Comput Mach, 77. *Mem:* Fel Inst Elec & Electronics Engrs; Asn Comput Mach Spec Interest Group on Data Commun. *Res:* Computer communications and computer networking, distributed processing, and distributed data bases. *Mailing Add:* Dept of Comput Sci Univ of Calif Los Angeles CA 90024

CHU, WILLIAM HOW-JEN, b Shanghai, China, July 9, 37; US citizen; c 3. POLYMER PHYSICS. *Educ:* Nat Taiwan Univ, BS, 59; Univ Mass, MS, 65 & 67, PhD(chem), 69. *Prof Exp:* Sr phys chemist, Plastic Coating Corp, 62-67; res mem staff polymer physics, 69-80, MGR, PRINTER TECHNOL MAT, INT BUS MACH CORP, 80- *Mem:* Am Chem Soc. *Res:* Structural-property relationship of polymers; electrophotography. *Mailing Add:* 70E/071 Int Bus Mach Corp Tucson AZ 85744

CHU, WILLIAM PETER, optical physics, see previous edition

CHU, WILLIAM TONGIL, b Seoul, Korea, Apr 16, 34; m 62; c 2. RADIATION PHYSICS. *Educ:* Carnegie Inst Technol, BS, 57, MS, 59, PhD(physics), 63. *Prof Exp:* Res assoc high energy physics, Brookhaven Nat Lab, 63-64; asst prof physics, Ohio State Univ, 64-70; asst prof radiol, Sch Med, Loma Linda Univ, 71-75, assoc prof radiol, 75-78, prof radiol, 78-79; SCIENTIST III, DIV ACCELERATOR & FUSION RES, LAWRENCE BERKELEY LAB, UNIV CALIF, BERKELEY, 79- *Concurrent Pos:* Res collabr, Brookhaven Nat Lab, 72-73; res consult, Lawrence Berkeley Lab, 76-79. *Mem:* Am Phys Soc; Radiation Res Soc; Am Asn Physicists Med; Sigma Xi; AAAS. *Res:* Experimental elementary particle physics; radiation physics and radiation biology; radiation physics for biomedical use of accelerated heavy ions; heavy ion imaging; experimental elementary particle physics. *Mailing Add:* Lawrence Berkeley Lab Univ Calif Berkeley CA 94720

CHU, WILLIAM WEI-LING, b Shanghai, China, June 27, 38; US citizen; m 70. APPLIED MECHANICS, APPLIED MATHEMATICS. *Educ:* Northeastern Univ, MS, 65; Cornell Univ, PhD(theoret & appl mech), 69. *Prof Exp:* Engr, Beacon Brass Co, Mass, 62-63; asst prof mech eng, Northeastern Univ, 69-76; DEVELOP ENGR, LARGE STEAM TURBINE-GENERATOR DEPT, GEN ELEC CO, 76- *Concurrent Pos:* Assoc, Abacus Intersysts, Inc, 69- *Mem:* Am Acad Mech; NY Acad Sci; Am Soc Mech Engrs. *Res:* Numerical method for the solution of problems in three dimensional elasticity; bond stresses in fiber reinforced composites; stress concentrations in composite materials; dynamic analysis of turbine blade. *Mailing Add:* 1016 Tomahawk Trail Scotia NY 12302

CHU, WING TIN, b Hong Kong, Oct 22, 35; Can citizen; m 68; c 2. AERODYNAMICS, ACOUSTICS. *Educ:* Univ BC, BASc, 61; Univ Toronto, MASc, 63, PhD(aerospace eng), 66. *Prof Exp:* Sr res fel aerospace eng, Inst Aerospace Studies, Univ Toronto, 66-69; asst prof, Univ Southern Calif, 69-73, sr res assoc aerospace eng, 73-75; assoc res officer, 75-80, SR ASSOC RES OFFICER, NAT RES COUN CAN, 80- *Mem:* Acoust Soc Am. *Res:* Room acoustics and noise control engineering. *Mailing Add:* Nat Res Coun of Can Div of Bldg Res Montreal Rd Ottawa ON K1A 0R6 Can

CHU, YUNG YEE, b Hangchow, China, Aug 18, 33; m 67. NUCLEAR CHEMISTRY. *Educ:* Nat Taiwan Univ, BSc, 54; Univ Calif, Berkeley, PhD(chem), 60. *Prof Exp:* Res assoc nuclear chem, 59-61, assoc chemist, 61-65, CHEMIST, BROOKHAVEN NAT LAB, 65- *Mem:* Am Chem Soc; Am Phys Soc. *Res:* Nuclear fission; high energy nuclear reactions; nuclear spectroscopy. *Mailing Add:* Chem Dept Brookhaven Nat Lab Upton NY 11973

CHUA, LEON O(NG), b Tarlac, Philippines, June 28, 36; m 61; c 2. ELECTRICAL ENGINEERING, MATHEMATICS. *Educ:* Mapua Inst Technol, BSEE, 59; Mass Inst Technol, MSEE, 62; Univ Ill, PhD(elec eng), 64. *Prof Exp:* Prof elec eng, Mapua Inst Technol, 59-60; res engr, Data Syst Div, Int Bus Mach Corp, 62; from asst prof to assoc prof elec eng, Purdue Univ, 64-71; assoc prof,X71-72,XPROF prof elec eng & comput sci, 71-72, PROF ELEC ENG & COMPUT SCI, UNIV CALIF, BERKELEY, 72- *Honors & Awards:* Browder J Thompson Mem Prize, Inst Elec & Electronics Engrs, W R G Baker Prize, 73; Frederick E Terman Award, Am Soc Eng Educ, 74. *Mem:* Inst Elec & Electronics Engrs. *Res:* Analysis and synthesis of nonlinear networks; general stability theory; distributed networks; modelling. *Mailing Add:* Dept of Elec Eng & Comput Sci Univ of Calif Berkeley CA 94720

CHUAN, RAYMOND LU-PO, b Shanghai, China, Mar 4, 24; US citizen; m 51; c 2. GAS DYNAMICS. *Educ:* Pomona Col, BA, 44; Calif Inst Technol, MS, 45, PhD(aeronaut), 53. *Prof Exp:* Res assoc aeronaut, Eng Ctr, Univ Southern Calif, 53-57, dir & adj prof, 57-64; pres, Celestial Res Corp, 64-68; mgr adv technol, Missile Syst Div, Atlantic Res Corp, 68-72; staff asst technol, Celesco Indust Inc, 72-76; STAFF SCIENTIST, DEFENSE DIV, BRUNSWICK CORP, 76- *Concurrent Pos:* Consult, Adv Group Aero Res & Develop, NATO, 60-64 & Nat Aero & Space Admin, 67- *Mem:* Assoc fel Am Inst Aeronaut & Astronaut; Am Phys Soc; Am Meteorol Soc; AAAS. *Res:* Rarefied gasdynamics; vacuum technology; analytical instrumentation for air quality; aerosol technology. *Mailing Add:* 1457 E Altadena Dr Altadena CA 91001

CHUANG, HANSON YII-KUAN, b Nanking, China, Sept 24, 35; US citizen; m 66; c 2. BIOCHEMISTRY, PATHOLOGY. *Educ:* Nat Taiwan Univ, BS, 58; Univ NC, PhD(biochem), 68. *Prof Exp:* Res asst chem, Acad Sinica, China, 60-63; res assoc path, 72-73, instr path & biochem, 73-74, asst prof path & biochem, Univ NC, Chapel Hill, 74-75; asst prof path, Brown Univ, 75-77; asst prof path, Univ S Fla, 77-79; RES ASSOC PROF PATH, UNIV UTAH, 79- *Concurrent Pos:* Res fel physiol chem, Johns Hopkins Univ, 68-71. *Mem:* Am Chem Soc; Am Asn Pathologists; NY Acad Sci; Int Soc Artificial Organs. *Res:* Enzyme and protein isolation, purification and characterization; protein biosynthesis; drug metabolism; metabolism and function of biogenic and cholinergic amines; blood enzymology; platelet function in blood; blood-artificial surface interaction; endothelium function in thrombosis and hemostasis. *Mailing Add:* 3427 E Brockbank Dr Salt Lake City UT 84117

CHUANG, HENRY NING, b Nanking, China, July 5, 37; m 65; c 3. MECHANICAL ENGINEERING, ENERGY ENGINEERING. *Educ:* Nat Taiwan Univ, BSME, 58; Univ Md, MSAeroE, 62; Carnegie Inst Tech, PhD(mech eng), 66. *Prof Exp:* From instr to assoc prof, 65-78, Univ Energy Coord, 77-80, PROF MECH ENG, UNIV DAYTON, 78- *Mem:* Am Soc Mech Engrs; Am Soc Eng Educ; Am Soc Heating, Refrigerating & Air Conditioning Engrs. *Res:* Energy conservation/conversion and energy engineering. *Mailing Add:* Dept of Mech Eng Univ of Dayton Dayton OH 45469

CHUANG, KUEI, b Shanghai, China, June 26, 26; US citizen; m 60. ELECTRICAL ENGINEERING. *Educ:* Nat Taiwan Univ, BSE, 50; Univ Mich, MSE, 52, PhD(elec eng), 58. *Prof Exp:* Spec instr elec eng, Wayne State Univ, 54-55; res assoc, 58-59, from asst prof to assoc prof, 59-69, PROF ELEC ENG, UNIV MICH, ANN ARBOR, 69- *Honors & Awards:* First Prize Indust Div, Inst Elec & Electronics Engrs, 59. *Mem:* Inst Elec & Electronics Engrs. *Res:* Control engineering; stochastic processes; optimal control systems. *Mailing Add:* Dept of Elec & Comput Eng Univ of Mich Ann Arbor MI 48104

CHUANG, KUEN-PUO, b Ilan, Formosa, Jan 20, 33; m 63; c 3. FINITE ELEMENT. *Educ:* Nat Taiwan Univ, BS, 55; Univ Ill, MS, 59, PhD(civil eng), 62. *Prof Exp:* Asst prof civil eng, Univ Okla, 62-66; assoc prof, 66-73, PROF CIVIL ENG, LOYOLA MARYMOUNT UNIV, 73- *Concurrent Pos:* Consult, Agbabian Assocs, El Segundo, Calif, 77- *Mem:* Am Soc Civil Engrs; Sigma Xi. *Res:* Structural analysis using finite elements; code development and applications. *Mailing Add:* Dept of Civil Eng 7101 W 80th St Los Angeles CA 90045

CHUANG, MING CHIA, b Taiwan, China, Feb 13, 37; m 64; c 3. ENGINEERING, COMPUTER SCIENCE. *Educ:* Cheng Kung Univ, Taiwan, BSc, 59, MSc, 61; Univ Rochester, PhD(mech & aerospace sci), 67. *Prof Exp:* Teaching asst fluid mech & eng math, Cheng Kung Univ, Taiwan, 62-63; SR ENGR, WESTINGHOUSE RES LABS, 66- *Mem:* Am Soc Mech Engrs. *Res:* Refrigeration and air conditioning; microrheological study of flow behavior of thixotropic suspensions; reactor heat transfer and fluid flow problems; bubble dynamics; heat exchanger design; solar energy utilization; computer code development; heat transfer; fluid dynamics. *Mailing Add:* Westinghouse Res Labs Pittsburgh PA 15235

CHUANG, RONALD YAN-LI, b Szuchuan, China, Feb 12, 40; m 67; c 3. BIOCHEMISTRY, PHARMACOLOGY. *Educ:* Nat Taiwan Univ, BS, 61; Univ Calif, Davis, MS, 66, PhD(biochem), 71. *Prof Exp:* Res assoc cancer res, Columbia Univ, 71-72; asst prof pharmacol, Med Ctr, Duke Univ, 72-76; asst res biochemist, Calif Primate Res Ctr, Univ Calif, Davis, 76-78; asst prof biochem, Sch Med, Oral Roberts Univ, 78-81; ASST PROF PHARMACOL, UNIV CALIF, DAVIS, 81- *Concurrent Pos:* NIH fel, Col Physicians & Surgeons, Columbia Univ, 71-72; chemist, Vet Admin Hosp, Durham, NC, 73-76; NIH res grant, Med Ctr, Duke Univ, 74-76 & Univ Calif, Davis, 76-78. *Mem:* AAAS; Am Soc Biol Chemists; Am Asn Cancer Res. *Res:* Study of the control mechanism of gene expression in leukemic cells; study of the biochemical mechanism of the action of antineoplastic agents. *Mailing Add:* Dept Pharmacol Univ Calif Davis CA 95616

CHUANG, TSAN IANG, b Hsin-Chu, Taiwan, Apr 21, 33; US citizen; m 58; c 3. SYSTEMATIC BOTANY. *Educ:* Taiwan Normal Univ, BS, 56; Nat Taiwan Univ, MS, 59; Univ Calif, Berkeley, PhD(bot), 66. *Prof Exp:* Asst res fel & cur herbarium, Inst Bot, Academia Sinica, Taiwan, 59-62; asst prof, Univ RI, 66-67; asst prof, 67-71, assoc prof bot, 71-77, CUR HERBARIUM, DEPT BIOL SCI, ILL STATE UNIV, 71-, PROF BOT, 77- *Concurrent Pos:* NSF res grants, 72 & 75. *Mem:* Bot Soc Am; Am Soc Plant Taxonomists; Int Asn Plant Taxon; Int Orgn Plant Biosystematists. *Res:* Systematics and evolution of genera cordylanthus, castilleia, orthocarpus; cytotaxonomy of umbelliferae; pollen morphology and its taxonomic significance of hydrophyllaceae, Campanulaceae and scrophulariaceae. *Mailing Add:* Dept of Biol Sci Ill State Univ Normal IL 61761

CHUANG, TZE-JER, b Chiayi, Taiwan, July 19, 43; US citizen; m 74; c 1. FRACTURE MECHANICS, MECHANICAL PROPERTIES OF MATERIALS. *Educ:* Nat Cheng Kung Univ, BSc, 65; Duke Univ, ScM, 70; Brown Univ, PhD(eng), 75. *Prof Exp:* Civil engr, Taiwan Power Co, 66, 68; sr engr, Westinghouse Elec Corp, 74-80; PHYSICIST, NAT BUR STANDARDS, 80- *Mem:* Am Soc Mech Engrs; Am Soc Metals; Am Ceramic Soc. *Res:* Fracture and deformation of crystalline materials, especially crack tip growth processes at both microstructural and atomic (lattics) levels. *Mailing Add:* 9 Manette St Gaithersburg MD 20878

CHUBB, CHARLES F(RISBIE), JR, b Pittsburgh, Pa, Jan 31, 20; m 48; c 2. ELECTRICAL ENGINEERING. *Educ:* Princeton Univ, BA, 41; Mass Inst Technol, BS, 43; Polytech Inst Brooklyn, MEE, 50. *Prof Exp:* Mem staff, Radiation Lab, Mass Inst Technol, 43-46; proj engr, Sperry Gyroscope Co, 46-50, sr proj engr, 50-53, res engr, 53-54, head eng sect, 54-57, head eng dept, 58-63; vpres, Dynell Electronics Corp, 63-66, sr vpres, 66-78; vpres technol, 78-81, MGR SHIPBOARD TECHNOL, NORDEN SYSTS, INC, 81- *Mem:* Sr mem Inst Elec & Electronics Engrs. *Res:* Servomechanisms and radar. *Mailing Add:* 25 Meadowood Lane Brookville NY 11545

CHUBB, CURTIS EVANS, b Fort Worth, Tex, Feb 19, 45; m 76. REPRODUCTIVE BIOLOGY. *Educ:* Okla State Univ, BS, 68; Johns Hopkins Univ, PhD(reprod biol), 78. *Prof Exp:* NIH fel, male reprod biol, Johns Hopkins Univ, 72-78 & Univ Tex, Austin, 78-80; ASST PROF CELL BIOL, UNIV TEX HEALTH SCI CTR, DALLAS, 80- *Concurrent Pos:* Prin investr, Univ Tex Health Sci Ctr, Dallas, 81- *Mem:* Soc Study Reprod; Am Soc Andrology; AAAS. *Res:* Control strategies of mammalian testis function; research in male-sterile mice to decipher hormonal requirements for spermatogenesis and to study male infertility. *Mailing Add:* Dept Cell Biol Univ Tex Health Sci Ctr Dallas TX 75235

CHUBB, FRANCIS LEARMONTH, b Que, June 26, 13; m 44. ORGANIC CHEMISTRY. *Educ:* McGill Univ, BSc, 35; Univ Southern Calif, MSc, 49, PhD, 52. *Prof Exp:* Chemist, Dom Oilcloth & Linoleum Co, 35-46; lab asst, Univ Southern Calif, 46-50; Can Cancer Soc fel, Univ Alta, 51-54; sr chemist, Merck & Co, Ltd, 54-55; dir org chem res, Frank W Horner Ltd, 55-75; RES ASSOC CHEM, McGILL UNIV, 75- *Mem:* Am Chem Soc; fel Chem Inst Can. *Res:* Pharmaceutical chemistry; five and six-membered heterocyclic compounds; six-membered alicyclic compounds. *Mailing Add:* Dept of Chem McGill Univ Montreal PQ H3A 2T5 Can

CHUBB, TALBOT ALBERT, b Pittsburgh, Pa, Nov 5, 23; m; c 4. GEOPHYSICS, ASTROPHYSICS. *Educ:* Princeton Univ, AB, 44; Univ NC, PhD(physics), 50. *Prof Exp:* head, upper air physics br, Naval Res Lab, 59-81; PRES, RES SYSTEMS INC, 81- *Honors & Awards:* E O Hulburt Award, Naval Res Lab, 63. *Mem:* Am Geophys Union; Am Astron Soc; Am Phys Soc; Int Solar Energy Soc. *Res:* Aeronomy; optical geophysics; x-ray astronomy; solar thermal processes for energy recovery. *Mailing Add:* 5038 N 38th St Arlington VA 22207

CHUBB, WALSTON, b Washington, DC, July 23, 23; m 51; c 2. MATERIALS ENGINEERING, RADIOCHEMISTRY. *Educ:* Harvard Univ, AB, 44; Univ Mo, BS, 48, MS, 49. *Prof Exp:* Asst engr, Brush Beryllium Co, 49-51; res engr, Battelle Mem Inst, 51-57, asst div consult, 57-62, res assoc, 62-66, fel, Dept Mat Eng, 66-72; PRIN ENGR, NUCLEAR FUEL DIV, WESTINGHOUSE ELEC CORP, 72- *Mem:* Am Soc Metals; Am Nuclear Soc; Nat Soc Prof Engrs; Sigma Xi. *Res:* Refractory nuclear fuels and other high temperature materials. *Mailing Add:* Nuclear Fuel Div PO Box 355 Pittsburgh PA 15230

CHUBBUCK, EDWIN R(ICHARD), b San Francisco, Calif, Apr 6, 23; m 45; c 1. ENGINEERING MECHANICS. *Educ:* Kans State Univ, BS, 47, MS, 50; Iowa State Univ, PhD(theoret & appl mech), 58. *Prof Exp:* Instr agr eng, Kans State Univ, 48-51, asst prof appl mech, 53-56; assoc prof, 58-63, PROF ENG MECH, LA STATE UNIV, 63- *Mem:* Am Soc Eng Educ. *Res:* Dynamics; elasticity. *Mailing Add:* 1128 Verdun Dr Baton Rouge LA 70803

CHUBER, STEWART, b Queens Village, NY, Dec 22, 30; m 53; c 2. PETROLEUM GEOLOGY. *Educ:* Colo Sch Mines, GeolE, 52; Stanford Univ, MS, 53, PhD(geol), 61. *Prof Exp:* Subsurface geologist, Magnolia Petrol Corp, 53-54; field geologist, Mobil Oil Co Can, Ltd, 54-56; party chief, 56; subsurface geologist, Western Div, Mobil Oil Co, Calif, 57-60 & Franco Western Oil Co, Calif & Tex, 61-65; consult geologist, 65-68; div geologist, Buttes Gas & Oil Co, 68-70; consult geologist, 71; vpres, Cantrell, Wheeler, Lewis & Chuber Geologists & Engrs, 71-72; CONSULT, 73- *Mem:* Am Asn Petrol Geol; Geol Soc Am; Sigma Xi; Soc Econ Paleontologists & Mineralogists. *Res:* Stratigraphy; stratigraphic nomenclature; geologic history, especially Permian and Pennsylvanian cyclic sedimentation. *Mailing Add:* Drawer J Schulenburg TX 78956

CHUCKROW, VICKI G, b Brooklyn, NY, July 26, 41. MATHEMATICS. *Educ:* City Col NY, BS, 62; NY Univ, MS, 64, PhD(math), 66. *Prof Exp:* Asst prof, 66-72, ASSOC PROF MATH, CITY COL NY, 72- *Concurrent Pos:* NSF grant, 66-67. *Mem:* Am Math Soc; Math Asn Am. *Res:* Riemann surfaces; Schottky groups, a special subclass of Kleinian groups. *Mailing Add:* Dept of Math City Col of NY New York NY 10031

CHUDD, CLETUS CHARLES, b Cleveland, Ohio, May 5, 11. ORGANIC CHEMISTRY. *Educ:* Univ Dayton, BS, 35; Western Reserve Univ, PhD(chem), 52. *Prof Exp:* Teacher private sch, Hawaii, 35-45 & Ohio, 45-46; instr, 47-50, chmn dept, 55-64, PROF CHEM, UNIV DAYTON, 52-, CHEM DISTINGUISHED SERV PROF, 80- *Honors & Awards:* Distinguished Serv Prof, Univ Dayton, 75. *Mem:* Am Chem Soc. *Res:* Conjugated and non-conjugated diene systems; organic synthesis; polymers. *Mailing Add:* Dept of Chem Univ of Dayton Dayton OH 45469

CHUDNOVSKY, GREGORY V, b Kiev, USSR, April 17, 52. TRANSCENDENTAL NUMBERS, SOLVABLE MODELS. *Educ:* Kiev State Univ, Dipl Math, 74; Inst Math, Kiev, PhD(math), 75. *Prof Exp:* Res fel, Kiev State Univ, 74-76; MAITRE DE RECHERCHE, NAT CTR SCI RES, 79-; RES ASSOC DEPT MATH, COLUMBIA UNIV, 78- *Concurrent Pos:* Vis prof, Inst Higher Sci Studies, France, 77-78; John D & Catherine MacArthur Found fel, 81. *Mem:* Am Math Soc; Am Phys Soc; French Math Soc; Math Asn Am. *Res:* Pure mathematics; number theory, especially theory of transcendental numbers; mathematical physics with emphasis on classical and quantum dynamical systems of physical origin. *Mailing Add:* Dept Math Columbia Univ New York NY 10027

CHUEH, CHUN FEI, b Chaochow, China, Sept 17, 32; m 61; c 2. CHEMICAL ENGINEERING, THERMODYNAMICS. *Educ:* Nat Taiwan Univ, BS, 55; Kans State Univ, MS, 57; Ga Inst Tech, PhD(chem eng), 62. *Prof Exp:* Sr chem engr, 62-67, sect head, 67-78, process mgr, Halcon Int Inc, 78-81, TECH DIR, HALCON SD GROUP, INC, 81- *Mem:* Am Chem Soc; Am Inst Chem Engrs; Nat Asn Corrosion Engrs. *Res:* Theory and application of gas chromatography; thermodynamics of phase equilibria; correlation and prediction of physical properties; distillation. *Mailing Add:* 187-16 Cambridge Rd Jamaica NY 11432

CHUEY, CARL FRANCIS, b Youngstown, Ohio, Mar 19, 44; div; c 1. PLANT TAXONOMY. *Educ:* Youngstown Univ, BS, 66; Ohio Univ, MS, 69. *Prof Exp:* Instr, 67-74; asst prof, 74-81, ASSOC PROF BIOL, YOUNGSTOWN STATE UNIV, 81- *Concurrent Pos:* Cur herbarium, Youngstown State Univ, 68- *Mem:* Am Fern Soc; Am Soc Plant Taxon; Brit Pteridological Soc. *Res:* Pteridophyte flora of Ohio, western Pennsylvania, and West Virginia. *Mailing Add:* 214 Wildwood Dr Youngstown OH 44512

CHUGH, YOGINDER PAUL, b Multan, India, Oct 6, 40; m 70; c 3. ROCK MECHANICS, PRODUCTION ENGINEERING. *Educ:* Banaras Hindu Univ, BS, 61; Pa State Univ, MS, 68, PhD(mining eng), 71. *Prof Exp:* Mgr coal mining, Andrew Yule Coal Co, 61-65; res asst, Pa State Univ, 65-70; res assoc, Columbia Univ, 71; res engr soil-rock mech, IIT Res Inst, 72-74; planning engr, Amax Coal Co, 74-76; actg chmn, Dept Mining, 80-81, PROF MINING ENG, SOUTHERN ILL UNIV, 77- *Concurrent Pos:* Prin investr, US Bur Mines, US Dept Energy, 73-82; consult, US Dept Commerce, 78-82. *Mem:* Am Inst Mining Engrs. *Res:* Surface coal mining; roof control in underground excavations; planning improved mining and reclamation operations; assessing roof conditions prior to mining; effects of moisture on roof control; author or coauthor of over 35 publications. *Mailing Add:* Dept Mining Eng Southern Ill Univ Carbondale IL 62966

CHUI, CHARLES KAM-TAI, b Macao, China, May 7, 40; m 64; c 2. MATHEMATICS. *Educ:* Univ Wis-Madison, BS, 62, MS, 63, PhD(math), 67. *Prof Exp:* Asst prof math, State Univ NY Buffalo, 67-70; assoc prof, 70-74, PROF MATH, TEX A&M UNIV, 74- *Concurrent Pos:* Vis prof, Nat Res Coun, Italy, 80-81. *Mem:* Math Asn Am; Am Math Soc; Soc Indust Appl Math; Int Elec & Electronic Engrs. *Res:* Analysis; approximation theory. *Mailing Add:* Dept of Math Tex A&M Univ College Station TX 77843

CHUI, GRANGER K, b Macau, SChina, June 1, 42; m 66; c 1. HEAT TRANSFER, FLUID MECHANICS. *Educ:* Univ Wis, Madison, BS, 62; Stanford Univ, MS, 63, PhD(mech eng), 67. *Prof Exp:* Engr, Walkers Mfg Co, 62; asst fluid mech, Stanford Univ, 63-67; RES STAFF, FORD MOTOR CO, 67- *Concurrent Pos:* Lectr, Wayne State Univ, 68. *Mem:* Am Soc Mech Engrs. *Res:* Thermal radiation; viscous fluid flow; manufacturing processes; internal combustion engines; fuels and lubricants; alternative fuels for transportation. *Mailing Add:* Dept of Fuels & Lubricants Ford Motor Co PO Box 2053 Dearborn MI 48121

CHUI, SIU-TAT, b Hong Kong, Apr 20, 49; Chinese citizen. THEORETICAL SOLID STATE PHYSICS. *Educ:* McGill Univ, BSc, 69; Princeton Univ, PhD(physics), 72. *Prof Exp:* Instr physics, Princeton Univ, 72-73; mem tech staff, Bell Tel Lab, 73-75; asst prof physics, State Univ NY Albany, 75-79; ASSOC PROF, BARTOL FOUND, FRANKLIN INST, UNIV DEL, 79- *Mem:* Am Phys Soc; Sigma Xi. *Res:* Superconductivity; one-dimensional physics; lattice dynamics; metal-insulator transition; surface physics. *Mailing Add:* Dept Physics State Univ NY Albany NY 12222

CHULICK, EUGENE THOMAS, b Jackson, Calif, Jan 8, 44; m 66; c 2. WATER TECHNOLOGY. *Educ:* Univ of the Pac, BS, 65; Wash Univ, PhD(nuclear chem), 69. *Prof Exp:* Res assoc nuclear chem, Cyclotron Inst, Tex A&M Univ, 69-74; instr, Physics Dept, 74; sr res chemist, 74-77; supvr radiochem group, 77-79; mgr nuclear & radiohem sec, 79-80, MGR, WATER TECHNOL BUS DEVELOP, RES & DEVELOP DIV, LYNCHBURG RES CTR, BABCOCK & WILCOX, 80- *Concurrent Pos:* Tex Res Coun fel, 70-; Tech expert, Int Atomic Energy Agency, 73-74; mem subcomt, Nuclear & Radiochem Sect, Nat Acad Sci, 81-84. *Mem:* AAAS; Am Chem Soc; Am Phys Soc; Am Nuclear Soc. *Res:* Delayed neutrons from fission products; nuclear reactions; internal ionization during beta decay; radiochemistry of pressurized water reactors; water technology and management. *Mailing Add:* Res & Develop Div Babcock & Wilcox 1562 Beeson St Alliance OH 44601

CHULSKI, THOMAS, b Grand Rapids, Mich, Aug 6, 21; m 47; c 6. ANALYTICAL CHEMISTRY. *Educ:* Mich State Univ, PhD(chem), 53. *Prof Exp:* Chemist, Lindsay Chem Co, 47-50; chemist, Upjohn Co, 53-63; ASSOC PROF CHEM, FERRIS STATE COL, 63- *Mem:* AAAS; Am Chem Soc; NY Acad Sci. *Res:* Analytical chemistry of drugs in biological systems; drug dosage in relation to metabolism and mode of degradation. *Mailing Add:* 258 Mill Big Rapids MI 49307

CHUMLEA, WILLIAM CAMERON, b Ft Worth, Tex, Mar 10, 47; m 73. HUMAN GROWTH, HUMAN NUTRITION. *Educ:* Washington & Lee Univ, BS, 69; Univ Tex, Austin, MA, 76, PhD(anthrop), 78. *Prof Exp:* RES SCIENTIST, SECT GROWTH & GENETICS, FELS RES INST & ASST PROF, DEPT PEDIAT & SCH MED, WRIGHT STATE UNIV, 78- *Mem:* Soc Study Human Biol; Human Biol Coun; Am Asn Phys Anthrop. *Res:* Human growth and development; human nutrition; pediatrics; body composition; longitudinal studies. *Mailing Add:* Fels Res Inst & Dept Pediat Sch Med Wright State Univ Yellow Springs OH 45387

CHUN, ALEXANDER HING CHINN, b Wahiawa, Hawaii, Jan 15, 28; m 57; c 4. PHYSICAL PHARMACY. *Educ:* Purdue Univ, BS, 54, MS, 56, PhD, 59. *Prof Exp:* Res pharmacist, 58-62, pharmacologist, 62-71, ASSOC RES FEL BIOPHARMACEUT, ABBOTT LABS, 71- *Mem:* Am Pharmaceut Asn; Am Chem Soc; Sigma Xi; fel Acad Pharmaceut Sci. *Res:* Drug absorption and distribution; chemical pharmacology; application of physical and colloidal chemistry to pharmaceuticals; biopharmaceutics. *Mailing Add:* 1908 Linden Ave Waukegan IL 60087

CHUN, BYUNGKYU, b Korea, Apr 10, 28; US citizen; m 57; c 2. SURGICAL PATHOLOGY. *Educ:* Seoul Nat Univ, MD, 52. *Prof Exp:* From instr to asst prof, 61-69, ASSOC PROF PATH, MED CTR, GEORGETOWN UNIV, 69- *Concurrent Pos:* Consult, Glen Dale Hosp, Glen Dale, Md, 64 & Children's Hosp, DC, 65. *Honors & Awards:* Achievement Award, Angiol Res Found, 66. *Mem:* Col Am Path. *Res:* Oncology. *Mailing Add:* 12606 Eldrid Ct Silver Spring MD 20004

CHUN, EDWARD HING LOY, b Wahiawa, Hawaii, Nov 2, 30. CHEMISTRY. *Educ:* Univ Hawaii, BA, 52, MA, 54; Harvard Univ, PhD(chem), 58. *Prof Exp:* Res assoc biol, Mass Inst Technol, 58-63; res investr chem, Univ Pa, 63-68, res investr, Sch Vet Med, 68-70, asst prof biochem, Sch Vet Med, 70-73; CHEMIST, ABBOTT LABS, 74- *Mem:* Am Chem Soc. *Res:* Research and development of radioimmunoassay test systems; molecular structure of biological macromolecules. *Mailing Add:* Abbott Labs 14th & Sheridan North Chicago IL 60064

CHUN, KEE WON, b Korea; US citizen. THEORETICAL PHYSICS. *Educ:* Univ Pa, AB, 51, PhD(physics), 60; Princeton Univ, AM, 55. *Prof Exp:* Res assoc theoret physics, Columbia Univ, 59-62 & Yale Univ, 62-65; assoc prof physics, 65-69, PROF PHYSICS, UNIV NEW HAVEN, 69-, CHMN DEPT, 71- *Mem:* Am Phys Soc; Am Asn Physics Teachers. *Res:* Field theory and nuclear physics; quantizied field in general theory of relativity and astrophysics. *Mailing Add:* Dept of Physics Univ of New Haven West Haven CT 06516

CHUN, MYUNG K(I), b Seoul, Korea, Mar 19, 32; US citizen; m 62. QUANTUM ELECTRONICS. *Educ:* Yonsei Univ, Korea, BSEE, 56, MSEE, 58; Yale Univ, MEng, 62; Rensselaer Polytech Inst, PhD(electrophysics), 69. *Prof Exp:* From engr to chief engr, Christian Broadcasting System, Korea, 56-61; engr rectifier component dept, Gen Elec Co, NY, 62-64; res asst solid state phys, Syracuse Univ, 64-66; physicist, Res & Develop Ctr, Gen Elec Co, Binghamton, 66-69, develop engr, Aerospace Controls Dept, 69-73; SR PHYSICIST, ELECTRONICS LAB, GEN ELEC CO, SYRACUSE, NY, 73- *Concurrent Pos:* Instr, Yonsei Univ, Korea, 58-61; adj prof, Sch Advan Technol, State Univ NY Binghamton, 69-70. *Mem:* Am Phys Soc; sr mem Inst Elec & Electronics Engrs; Sigma Xi; Korean Scientist & Engrs Asn Am; Optical Soc Am. *Res:* Laser device areas; optically pumped solid-host lasers; Q-switched lasers; laser resonators; nonlinear optics; uv preionized gas discharge lasers; computer modeling of various laser features: resonators, optical pumping, dynamic gain, and gas discharge. *Mailing Add:* Gen Elec Co Electronics Lab Syracuse NY 13221

CHUN, PAUL W, b Repub of Korea, Dec 14, 28; US citizen; m 64; c 1. PHYSICAL BIOCHEMISTRY. *Educ:* Northwestern State Col, Okla, 55; Okla State Univ, MS, 57; Univ Mo-Columbia, PhD(biochem), 65. *Prof Exp:* Chemist, Worcester Found Exp Biol, 61-63; fel biochem, Univ Mo-Columbia, 65-66; fel, 66-67, asst prof, 67-70, assoc prof, 70-80, PROF BIOCHEM & MOLECULAR BIOL, UNIV FLA, 80- *Mem:* AAAS; Am Chem Soc; Am Soc Biol Chemists; Biophys Soc. *Res:* Protein-protein interaction; molecular exclusion. *Mailing Add:* Dept of Biochem Univ of Fla Gainesville FL 32601

CHUN, PEGGY ANN DAVIS, b Duluth, Minn, Aug 2, 47; m 78. ATMOSPHERIC PHYSICS, SOLAR ENERGY. *Educ:* Univ Minn, Duluth, BS & BA, 69. *Prof Exp:* Physicist atmospheric, 71-76, PHYSICIST ENERGY, NAVAL WEAPONS CTR, 76- *Res:* Fair weather and thunderstorm atmospheric research; effects of pollutants in the atmosphere and in energy research and development, especially solar and photo voltaic. *Mailing Add:* Code 3246 Naval Weapons Ctr China Lake CA 93555

CHUN, RAYMOND WAI MUN, b Honolulu, Hawaii, Jan 21, 26; m 60; c 3. PEDIATRICS, NEUROLOGY. *Educ:* St Joseph's Col, BS, 51; Georgetown Univ, MD, 55. *Prof Exp:* Intern med, Philadelphia Gen Hosp, Pa, 55-56; resident pediat, Univ Hosp, Georgetown Univ, 56-58; resident neurol, 58-59 & 60-61, from asst prof to assoc prof, 61-72, PROF PEDIAT NEUROL, UNIV WIS-MADISON, 72- *Concurrent Pos:* Fel pediat neurol, Columbia-Presby Hosp, New York, 59-60; consult, Wis Diag Ctr, 61- *Mem:* Fel Am Acad Pediat; Am Acad Neurol. *Res:* Epilepsy; neurophysiology; clinical research; transillumination of skull of infants. *Mailing Add:* 600 Highland Ave H4/450 Madison WI 53792

CHUN, SUN WOONG, b Seoul, Korea, Mar 30, 34; m 60; c 2. CHEMICAL ENGINEERING, THERMODYNAMICS. *Educ:* Ohio State Univ, BChE & MS, 59, PhD(chem eng), 64. *Prof Exp:* Res asst chem thermodyn, Goodyear Res Proj, Ohio State Univ, 59-63, res fel, Univ, 63-64; res scientist, Union Bag-Camp Paper Corp, 64-69; sr res engr, Gulf Res & Develop Co, 67, sect supvr, 69-75; supvr pyrolysis, Dept Energy, Pittsburgh Energy Res Ctr, 75-76, mgr, Process Sci Div, 76-77, dep dir, 77-78, DIR, PITTSBURGH ENERGY TECHNOL CTR, 78- *Honors & Awards:* Benjamin & Lamme Medal, 81. *Res:* Petroleum refining; cool liquefaction and synthetic fuels processing. *Mailing Add:* 3304 Hermar Dr Murrysville PA 15668

CHUNG, ALBERT EDWARD, b Jamaica, West Indies, Dec 18, 36; m 58; c 3. BIOCHEMISTRY. *Educ:* Univ West Indies, BS, 57, MS, 59; Johns Hopkins Univ, PhD(biochem), 62. *Prof Exp:* Res fel, Harvard Univ, 62-64; asst prof biochem, Med Ctr, Univ Colo, 64-67; assoc prof, 67-74, PROF BIOCHEM, UNIV PITTSBURGH, 74- *Concurrent Pos:* Fulbright sr res scholar, France, 74-75. *Mem:* AAAS; Am Chem Soc; Am Soc Biol Chemists. *Res:* Regulation of enzymes; basement membrane structure and assembly; cellular differentiation. *Mailing Add:* Dept of Biol Sci Fac Arts & Sci Univ of Pittsburgh Pittsburgh PA 15260

CHUNG, BENJAMIN T, b China; US citizen. HEAT TRANSFER, FLUID MECHANICS. *Educ:* Kans State Univ, MS, 62, PhD(mech eng), 68; Univ Wisc, MS, 65. *Prof Exp:* Res engr mech eng, Allis-Chalmers Mfg Co, 62-69; from asst prof to assoc prof, 70-80, PROF MECH ENG, UNIV AKRON, 80- *Concurrent Pos:* Sr eng analyst consult, Babcock & Wilcox, 77-79. *Mem:* Am Soc Mech Eng; Sigma Xi. *Res:* Nonlinear heat transfer with phase change; turbulent and laminar boundary layer flow with heat transfer; radiative view factor computations. *Mailing Add:* Dept Mech Eng Univ Akron Akron OH 44325

CHUNG, CHI HSIANG, b Taiwan, Rep China, Feb 19, 49; m 79; c 1. ELECTRO-OPTIC MATERIALS, THIN FILM TECHNOLOGY. *Educ:* Nat Tsing Hua Univ, BS, 71; Syracuse Univ, MS, 76; Univ Calif Los Angeles, PhD(mat sci), 79. *Prof Exp:* Mat scientist, Kylex Div, Exxon Corp, 80-81, sr mat scientist, 81; RES SPECIALIST, INFO STORAGE, 3M CO, 81- *Mem:* Am Ceramic Soc. *Res:* Structure and properties of simple and interacted thin and thick film materials and their application in the electronic and optic devices. *Mailing Add:* 420 Bernardo Ave Mountain View CA 94043

CHUNG, CHIN SIK, b Taejon, Korea, May 6, 24; nat US; m 57; c 3. HUMAN GENETICS, BIOSTATISTICS. *Educ:* Ore State Univ, BS, 51; Univ Wis, MS, 53, PhD, 57. *Prof Exp:* Asst genetics, Univ Wis, 52-57, res assoc med genetics, 57-61; vis scientist, NIH, 61-64, res biologist, 64-65; chmn, Dept Pub Health Sci, Sch Pub Health, 73-77, chmn, Biomed Sci Grad Prog, 75-78, PROF PUB HEALTH, UNIV HAWAII, 65-, PROF GENETICS, 69-, CHMN DEPT PUB HEALTH SCI, SCH PUB HEALTH, 81- *Concurrent Pos:* Res grants, NSF & NIH, Hawaii, 73-; consult, NIH, 74. *Mem:* Am Soc Human Genetics; Am Statist Asn; Biomet Soc; Am Pub Health Asn; Soc Study Social Biol. *Res:* Genetic epidemiology of human conditions, including muscular dystrophy, blood groups, dental carics, oral clefts, periodontal disease, birth defects and interracial crosses; epidemiologic studies of long-term effects of induced abortion; genetic epidemiology. *Mailing Add:* Dept Pub Health Sci Sch Pub Hlth Univ of Hawaii Honolulu HI 96822

CHUNG, CHOONG WHA, b Korea, Aug 14, 18; nat US; m 49; c 2. MICROBIOLOGY, MEDICINE. *Educ:* Keio Univ, Japan, MD, 46; Rutgers Univ, PhD(microbiol), 53. *Prof Exp:* Asst microbiol, Med Sch, Seoul Nat Univ, 46-49; res fel microbial biochem, Inst Microbiol, Rutgers Univ, 49-53; instr biochem, Dept Pediat, Sch Med, Johns Hopkins Univ, 53-55; instr, Med Sch, Univ Colo, 55-56; instr chem, Ind Univ, 57-60; chief med chem sect, Med Lab Br, Nat Commun Dis Ctr, Atlanta, Ga, 60-67, asst chief dermal toxicity Br, 67-77, RES CHEMIST, DIV TOXICOL, FOOD & DRUG ADMIN, USPHS, 77- *Mem:* AAAS; Am Chem Soc; Sigma Xi; Am Soc Microbiol; Brit Biochem Soc. *Res:* Delayed and immediate hypersensitivity; chemical allergens; photoallergy; skin biochemistry; immunological aspects of neoplasia. *Mailing Add:* Dermal Toxicity Br Div Toxicol HFF 164 Food & Drug Admin 200 C St SW Washington DC 20204

CHUNG, DAE HYUN, b Jungup, Korea, Dec 6, 34; US citizen; m 63; c 2. GEOPHYSICS, MATERIALS SCIENCE. *Educ:* Alfred Univ, AB, 59, MS, 61; Pa State Univ, PhD(solid state sci), 66. *Prof Exp:* Fel geophys, Mass Inst Technol, 67-68, res assoc geophys, 68-72; prof geophysics, Boston Col, Chestnut Hill, Mass, 72-74; dir, Weston Observ, Mass, 72-74; STAFF GEOPHYSICIST, LAWRENCE LIVERMORE NAT LAB, 74- *Concurrent Pos:* Consult, Lincoln Lab, Mass Inst Technol, 68-72, US Nuclear Regulatory Comn, 78- & US Dept Energy, 79-; mem, Korea Sci & Technol Develop Bd, 69-71, sci adv to minister sci & technol, Korea; ed, Earthquake Notes, Seismol Soc Am, 72-74; coordr geophys prog, Dept Appl Sci, Univ Calif, Livermore, 75-80. *Honors & Awards:* Geol Surv of Korea Achievement Award, 70. *Mem:* AAAS; Am Geophys Union; Seismol Soc Am; NY Acad Sci. *Res:* Seismic wave propagation; physical state and constitution of the earth's interior; elasticity and equation of state; engineering seismology; earthquake hazard analysis. *Mailing Add:* 4150 Colgate Way Livermore CA 94550

CHUNG, DAVID YIH, b Shanghai, China, Nov 14, 36; m 67; c 1 5OLID STATE PHYSICS, LOW TEMPERATURE PHYSICS. PHYSICS, SOLID STATE PHYSICS. *Educ:* Nat Taiwan Univ, BSc, 58; Univ BC, MSc, 62, PhD(physics), 66. *Prof Exp:* Res physicist, Heat Div, Nat Bur Standards, 66-67; asst prof, 67-71, assoc prof, 71-77, PROF PHYSICS, HOWARD UNIV, 78- *Concurrent Pos:* Vis prof, Dept Appl Physics & Electronics, Univ Durham, Brit Sci Res Coun vis fel, 73-74; vis fel, Cavendish Lab, Univ Cambridge, 78-79. *Mem:* Am Phys Soc. *Res:* Second sound propagation in solids; superfluid flow in liquid helium; ultrasonic waves in solids; optical property of solids; non-linear acoustics in liquids and solids; magnetic properties of solids at low temperature; properties of magnetic fluids. *Mailing Add:* Dept of Physics Howard Univ Washington DC 20001

CHUNG, DEBORAH DUEN LING, b Hong Kong, Sept 12, 52; UK citizen; m 76. MATERIALS SCIENCE, SOLID STATE PHYSICS. *Educ:* Calif Inst Technol, BS & MS, 73; Mass Inst Technol, SM, 75, PhD(mat sci), 77. *Prof Exp:* Res asst mat sci, Mass Inst Technol, 73-77; asst prof, 77-82, ASSOC PROF METALL, MAT SCI & ELEC ENG, CARNEGIE-MELLON UNIV, 82- *Concurrent Pos:* Vis scientist, Francis Bitter Nat Magnet Lab, 74-77; prin investr res proj, Air Force Off Sci Res, 77- & NSF, 80-; consult res & develop ctr, Westinghouse Elec Corp, 78- *Honors & Awards:* Ladd Award, Carnegie-Mellon Univ, 79; Hardy Gold Medal, Am Inst Mining, Metall & Petrol Engrs, 80. *Mem:* Am Inst Mining, Metall & Petrol Engrs; Am Phys Soc; Am Chem Soc; Am Carbon Soc; Mat Res Soc. *Res:* Graphite intercalation compounds; interfacial reactions between metals and semiconductors; coal conversion catalysts; thermal analysis; x-ray crystallography. *Mailing Add:* 3812 Henley Dr Pittsburgh PA 15235

CHUNG, DO SUP, b Inchon, Korea, Mar 20, 35; m 61; c 2. CHEMICAL ENGINEERING, FOOD SCIENCE. *Educ:* Purdue Univ, BS, 58; Kans State Univ, MS, 60, PhD(chem eng, food sci), 66. *Prof Exp:* From instr to assoc prof, 65-80, PROF AGR ENG, KANS STATE UNIV, 80- *Concurrent Pos:* Agr Res Serv, US Dept Agr res contract, 67-70. *Mem:* Am Soc Agr Engrs; Am Inst Chem Engrs; Inst Food Technol; Am Asn Cereal Chemists. *Res:* Adsorption, desorption and absorption of water by cereal products; heat transfer in grain investigations; physical properties of grains and handling of grain for minimizing damage investigations. *Mailing Add:* Dept of Agr Eng Kans State Univ Manhattan KS 66502

CHUNG, ED BAIK, b Seoul, Korea, Mar 16, 28; US citizen; m 58; c 5. MEDICINE, PATHOLOGY. *Educ:* Severance Union Med Col, MD, 51; Georgetown Univ, MS, 56, PhD(path), 58; Am Bd Path, cert anat path & clin path. *Prof Exp:* Resident path, Med Ctr, Georgetown Univ, 54-58, from instr to asst prof, 58-63; assoc prof, 64-70, PROF PATH, COL MED, HOWARD UNIV, 70-, PROF ONCOL, 76- *Concurrent Pos:* Attend pathologist, Howard Univ Hosp, 64-; consult path, Glenn Dale Hosp, Md, 68-74 & Coroner's Off, Washington, DC, 69-71; spec res fel, Nat Cancer Inst, 71-72. *Mem:* Int Acad Path; Am Soc Clin Path; Col Am Path; NY Acad Sci. *Res:* Orthopedic and renal pathology; oncologic pathology; tumor immunology. *Mailing Add:* Dept of Path Howard Univ Col of Med Washington DC 20001

CHUNG, FAN RONG KING, b China, Oct 9, 49; m 70; c 2. MATHEMATICS. *Educ:* Nat Taiwan Univ, BS, 70; Univ Pa, MA, 72, PhD(math), 74. *Prof Exp:* MEM TECH STAFF MATH, BELL LABS, 74- *Mem:* Am Math Soc. *Res:* Combinatories; graph theory; switching networks; mathematical algorithms. *Mailing Add:* Bell Labs 600 Mountain Ave Murray Hill NJ 07974

CHUNG, HOAN MOSES, geochemistry, see previous edition

CHUNG, HUI-YING, b China, Nov 23, 27; m 60; c 2. ELECTRICAL ENGINEERING. *Educ:* Nat Taiwan Univ, BS, 51; Iowa State Univ, MS, 60, PhD(elec eng), 64. *Prof Exp:* Engr, Taiwan Power Co, Formosa, 51-57; instr & assoc elec eng, Iowa State Univ, 59-65; asst prof, 65-73, ASSOC PROF ELEC ENG, UNIV NEBR, LINCOLN, 73- *Mem:* Am Soc Eng Educ. *Res:* Power system analysis; power electronics. *Mailing Add:* Dept of Elec Eng Univ of Nebr Lincoln NE 68588

CHUNG, JING-YAU, b Miao-Li, Taiwan, Oct 31, 39; US citizen; m 67; c 2. ACOUSTICS, FLUID MECHANICS. *Educ:* Nat Taiwan Univ, BS, 64; Kans State Univ, MS, 68; Purdue Univ, PhD, 74. *Prof Exp:* staff res engr noise control, Gen Motors Res Labs, Gen Motors Corp, Warren, 74-81; SR SPECIALIST, EXXON PROD RES CO, EXXON CORP, HOUSTON, 81- *Mem:* Acoustical Soc Am. *Res:* Digital signal analysis; new measurement techniques in acoustical engineering. *Mailing Add:* PO Box 2189 Houston TX 77001

CHUNG, JIWHEY, b Korea, Feb 26, 36; m 64; c 2. BIOCHEMISTRY, FOOD SCIENCE. *Educ:* Seoul Nat Univ, BS, 61; Univ Ill, MS, 66; Univ Tenn, PhD(biochem), 69. *Prof Exp:* Res assoc, Albert Einstein Med Ctr, 69-71; RES ASSOC BIOCHEM, UNIV CHICAGO, 71- *Concurrent Pos:* NIH fel, 71-72 & spec res fel, 72-73; Ill & Chicago Heart Asn grant-in-aid, 75. *Mem:* Sigma Xi. *Res:* Lipid metabolism; mechanism of action of lipoprotein lipase and lecithin cholesterol acyl transferase; synthesis and metabolism of plasma; very low density lipoproteins. *Mailing Add:* 1464 Lori Lyn Lane Northbrook IL 60062

CHUNG, KAI LAI, b Shanghai, China, Sept 19, 17; nat US; m; c 3. MATHEMATICS. *Educ:* Princeton Univ, MA & PhD(math), 47. *Prof Exp:* Instr math, Princeton Univ, 47-48; asst prof, Cornell Univ, 48-50, vis assoc prof, 51-52; from assoc prof to prof, Syracuse Univ, 53-61; PROF MATH, STANFORD UNIV, 61- *Concurrent Pos:* Vis prof, Columbia Univ, 50-51 & 59, Univ Chicago, 56-57, Univ Strasbourg, 68-69 & Swiss Fed Inst Technol, 70; G A Miller vis prof, Univ Ill, 70-71; Guggenheim fel, 75-76; fel, Churchill Col, Cambridge Univ, 76; ed, Zeitschrift für Wahrscheinlichkeitstheorie und Verwandte Gebiete. *Mem:* Am Math Soc; Inst Math Statist. *Res:* Probability. *Mailing Add:* Dept of Math Stanford Univ Stanford CA 94305

CHUNG, KUK SOO, b Kyungpuk, Korea, Nov 15, 35; US citizen. ASTROPHYSICS, PARTICLE PHYSICS. *Educ:* Yale Univ, BA, 59; Princeton Univ, MA, 61, PhD(physics), 69. *Prof Exp:* Asst prof physics, State Univ NY, 62-68; res assoc, Princeton Univ, 69-70; res scientist, Watson Res Ctr, Int Bus Mach Corp, 70-72; resident res assoc astrophys, Columbia Univ, 72-73; from asst prof to assoc prof, 73-80, PROF PHYSICS, LEHMAN COL, 80- *Concurrent Pos:* Consult, McNulty Assoc, 67-69. *Mem:* Am Phys Soc. *Res:* Theoretical work on gravitational radiations from black holes; dispersion-theoretic approach to pion-pion interactions. *Mailing Add:* Herbert Lehman Col Bedford Park Blvd Bronx NY 10468

CHUNG, KYUNG WON, b Seoul, Korea, Aug 15, 38; US citizen; m 66; c 2. REPRODUCTIVE ENDOCRINOLOGY. *Educ:* Yonsei Univ, Korea, BS, 64, MS, 66; St Louis Univ, MS, 69; Univ Okla, PhD(anat), 71. *Prof Exp:* Instr biol, Yonsei Univ, 66; fel endocrinol, Hershey Med Ctr, Pa State Univ, 71-72; instr, State Univ NY Downstate Med Ctr, 72-75, asst prof anat, 75-77; asst prof, 77-79, ASSOC PROF ANAT SCI, COL MED, UNIV OK, 79- *Mem:* Sigma Xi; Am Asn Anatomists; Endocrine Soc. *Res:* Ultrastructural and biochemical studies on the testes in mice and rats with testicular feminization. *Mailing Add:* 8233 NW 100 Oklahoma City OK 73132

CHUNG, OKKYUNG KIM, b Seoul, Korea, Apr 11, 36; m 61; c 2. CEREAL CHEMISTRY. *Educ:* Ewha Womens Univ, Korea, BS, 59; Kans State Univ, MS, 65, PhD(grain sci), 73. *Prof Exp:* Res asst lipids, Kans State Univ, 64-66, res assoc lipids & surfactants, 73-74; RES CHEMIST LIPIDS & SURFACTANTS, US GRAIN MKT RES LAB, AGR RES SERV, USDA, 74- *Concurrent Pos:* Assoc ed, Cereal Chem, 78- *Mem:* Am Asn Cereal Chemists; Sigma Xi; Am Chem Soc; Am Oil Chem Soc. *Res:* Functionality of wheat flour lipids and lipid related surfactants in breadmaking; interaction of lipids and surfactants with other flour components during processing into bread; fractionation of wheat flour components; characterization of lipids in cereal grains. *Mailing Add:* US Grain Mkt Res Lab 1515 College Ave Manhattan KS 66502

CHUNG, PAUL M(YUNGHA), b Seoul, Korea, Dec 1, 29; nat US; m 52; c 2. COMBUSTION, FLUID MECHANICS. *Educ:* Univ Ky, BS, 52, MS, 54; Univ Minn, PhD(mech eng), 57. *Prof Exp:* From instr to asst prof mech eng, Univ Minn, 55-58; aeronaut res scientist, Ames Res Ctr, NASA, 58-61; head fluid dynamics dept, Aerospace Corp, 61-66; head, Energy Eng Dept, 74-79, PROF FLUID MECH, UNIV ILL, CHICAGO CIRCLE, 66-, DEAN, ENG COL, 79- *Concurrent Pos:* Consult, Sandia Lab, 66-74, Argonne Nat Lab, 75-81 & Aerospace Corp, 80- *Mem:* Am Inst Aeronaut & Astronaut; Am Inst Chem Engrs. *Res:* Combustion; turbulence; fluid mechanics; heat transfer; plasma. *Mailing Add:* Dean Col Eng Univ Ill Chicago Circle Chicago IL 60680

CHUNG, RACK HUN, b Seoul, Korea, Dec 8, 39; US citizen; m 68; c 1. ORGANIC CHEMISTRY. *Educ:* Han Yang Univ, BE, 64; Howard Univ, MS, 68; Yale Univ, PhD(chem), 72. *Prof Exp:* Res assoc med chem, Wesleyan Univ, 72-74; sr res chemist dye chem, GAF Corp, 74-77; SR RES SCIENTIST MED CHEM, USV PHARMACEUT CORP, 77- *Mem:* Am Chem Soc; Korea Scientists & Engrs Asn. *Res:* Medicinial, agricultural, and dyestuff chemistry. *Mailing Add:* Dept Med Chem 1 Scarsdale Rd Tuckahoe NY 10707

CHUNG, RAYMOND, b San Francisco, Calif, Apr 5, 20; m 48; c 2. CHEMICAL ENGINEERING. *Educ:* Univ Calif, BS, 42; Univ Okla, MChE, 43; Mass Inst Tech, MS, 47. *Prof Exp:* Asst res engr, Calif Res Corp, Standard Oil Co Calif, 43-45 & Armour Res Found, 48-49; self-employed, 50-55; from res asst to res assoc solar energy, Univ Wis, 55-62; from res scientist to sr res scientist, 63-80, RES ASSOC, KIMBERLY-CLARK CORP, 81- *Mem:* Am Chem Soc; Am Inst Chem Engrs. *Res:* Cooling and refrigeration with solar energy; dispersion flash drying; unusual methods for forming paper, paper making without water. *Mailing Add:* 208 Alcott Dr Neenah WI 54956

CHUNG, RILEY M, b Peoples Repub China; US citizen; m 72; c 1. SOIL MECHANICS, FOUNDATION ENGINEERING. *Educ:* Nat Taiwan Univ, BSCE, 68; Rensselaer Polytech Inst, 70; Northwestern Univ, PhD(civil eng), 76. *Prof Exp:* Engr, Westenhoff & Norvicle, 70-72; proj eng, Harza Eng Co, 72-77; srproj eng, Schnekel Eng Asn, 77-79; RES CIVIL ENGR, NAT BUR STANDARDS, 79- *Mem:* Am Soc Civil Engrs; Am Soc Testing Mat; Am Soc Agron; Mat Res Soc. *Res:* Soils dynamic properties under earthquake loadings; use of soils as the barrier to isolate radioactive wastes in underground geologic waste isolation system. *Mailing Add:* Rm B150 Bldg 226 Nat Bur Standards Washington DC 20234

CHUNG, RONALD ALOYSIUS, b Christiana, Jamaica, Sept 30, 36; m 63; c 3. FOOD SCIENCE. *Educ:* Col Holy Cross, BSc, 59; Purdue Univ, MS, 61, PhD(food technol), 63. *Prof Exp:* Asst food technol, Purdue Univ, 61-63; PROF FOOD SCI & NUTRIT & PROG COORDR, TUSKEGEE INST, 63- *Concurrent Pos:* Res assoc, Carver Res Found, 63-70; consult, 70- *Honors & Awards:* Res Award, Poultry Sci Asn, 66. *Mem:* Fel AAAS; Am Chem Soc; Inst Food Technol; Poultry Sci Asn. *Res:* Lipid metabolism in poultry and livestock; biochemical activity of food additives in mammalian cell systems; new food product development; dietary related toxemia in pregnancy. *Mailing Add:* Sch Appl Sci Food Sci & Nutrit Tuskegee Institute AL 36088

CHUNG, SHIAU-TA, b Taiwan, Aug 21, 34; m 63; c 3. MICROBIAL GENETICS. *Educ:* Chung-Shin Univ, BS, 57; Univ Tokyo, PhD(microbiol), 67. *Prof Exp:* Res asst microbiol, Univ Manitoba, 67-70; res assoc genetics, Univ Mich, 70-73; RES SCIENTIST, MICROBIAL GENETICS, THE UPJOHN CO, 73- *Mem:* Am Soc Microbiol. *Res:* Genetics of streptomyces which produced antibiotics. *Mailing Add:* Fermentation Res & Develop The Upjohn Co Kalamazoo MI 49001

CHUNG, SUH URK, b Pyongyang, Korea, Nov 11, 36; US citizen; m 63; c 2. HIGH ENERGY PHYSICS. *Educ:* Univ Fla, BES, 61; Univ Calif, Berkeley, PhD(physics), 66. *Prof Exp:* Assoc physicist, 66-74, PHYSICIST, BROOKHAVEN NAT LAB, 74- *Mem:* Am Phys Soc. *Res:* Experimental high energy physics. *Mailing Add:* Dept Physics Brookhaven Nat Lab Upton NY 11973

CHUNG, SUNG-KEE, b Andong, Korea, Dec 14, 45. BIOORGANIC MECHANISMS, SYNTHETIC METHODOLOGIES. *Educ:* Yonsei Univ, Korea, BSc, 68; Univ Ill, Urbana, PhD(org chem), 72. *Prof Exp:* Asst org chem, Univ Ill, Urbana, 68-72; fel, Yale Univ, 72-75, sr assoc, 75-77; ASST PROF ORG CHEM, TEX A&M UNIV, COLLEGE STATION, 77- *Concurrent Pos:* Prin Investr, NIH Grants. *Mem:* Am Chem Soc; NY Acad Sci; AAAS. *Res:* Natural products chemistry-antibiotics; bioorganic models; synthetic methods; mechanistic organic chemistry. *Mailing Add:* Dept Chem Tex A&M Univ College Station TX 77843

CHUNG, VICTOR, b Vancouver, BC, Sept 7, 40; m 64; c 1. PHYSICS. *Educ:* Mass Inst Technol, SB, 61, SM, 62; Univ Calif, Berkeley, PhD(physics), 66. *Prof Exp:* Asst res physicist, Univ Calif, San Diego, 66-68; asst prof, 68-78, ASSOC PROF PHYSICS, CITY COL NEW YORK, 78- *Mem:* Am Phys Soc. *Res:* Theoretical high energy physics; quantum electrodynamics; medical physics. *Mailing Add:* Dept of Physics City Col of New York New York NY 10031

CHUNG, YIP-WAH, b Hong Kong. SURFACE SCIENCE, SOLID STATE PHYSICS. *Educ:* Univ Hong Kong, BSc, 71, MPhil, 73; Univ Calif, Berkeley, PhD(physics), 77. *Prof Exp:* ASST PROF MAT SCI & ENG, NORTHWESTERN UNIV, 77- *Mem:* Am Phys Soc. *Res:* Metal semiconductor interfaces; energy conversion; chemisorption and catalysis; alloy and grain boundary segregation; fatigue enhanced photoemission; multiple technique surface analysis. *Mailing Add:* Dept of Mat Sci & Eng Northwestern Univ Evanston IL 60201

CHUPKA, WILLIAM ANDREW, b Pittston, Pa, Feb 12, 23; m 55; c 2. PHYSICAL CHEMISTRY. *Educ:* Univ Scranton, BS, 43; Univ Chicago, MS, 49, PhD(chem), 51. *Prof Exp:* Instr chem, Harvard Univ, 51-54; consult, Argonne Nat Lab, 52-54, assoc physicist, 54-68, sr physicist, 68-75; PROF CHEM, YALE UNIV, 75- *Concurrent Pos:* Guggenheim fel, 61-62. *Mem:* Am Chem Soc; fel Am Phys Soc. *Res:* Mass spectrometry; molecular and atomic structure; high temperature thermodynamics; chemical kinetics; photoionization; vacuum ultraviolet spectroscopy; photoelectron spectroscopy; ion-molecular reactions. *Mailing Add:* Sterling Chem Lab Yale Univ New Haven CT 06520

CHUPP, EDWARD LOWELL, b Lincoln, Nebr, May 14, 27; m 50; c 3. PHYSICS. *Educ:* Univ Calif, Berkeley, AB, 50, PhD(physics), 54. *Prof Exp:* Staff mem physics, Lawrence Radiation Lab, Univ Calif, 54-59; unit chief geospace physics, Aerospace Div, Boeing Co, 59-62; assoc prof physics, 62-67, PROF PHYSICS, UNIV NH, 67- *Concurrent Pos:* Consult, Lawrence Radiation Lab, Univ Calif, 59-63 & Geophys Corp Am, Mass, 63-65; mem, State of NH Radiation Adv Comt, 66; consult, Solar Physics Subcomt, NASA, 67; mem sci balloon panel, Nat Ctr Atmospheric Res, 70; NATO sr res fel, Max Planck Inst, Munich, 70, Alexander von Humboldt sr award, 72-73, Fulbright-Hayes hon sr fel, Max Planck Inst Extraterrestrial Physics, 72-73. *Honors & Awards:* Exceptional Sci Achievement Medal, NASA, 72. *Mem:* Fel Am Phys Soc; Am Geophys Union; Am Asn Physics Teachers; Am

Astron Soc. *Res:* Cosmic radiation time variations; gamma ray spectroscopy and gamma ray astronomy; neutron and gamma ray detectors; solar flare physics; solar terrestrial relations; measurements of atomic transition probabilities. *Mailing Add:* Dept of Physics Univ of NH Durham NH 03824

CHURCH, ALONZO, b Washington, DC, June 14, 03; wid; c 3. MATHEMATICS. *Educ:* Princeton Univ, AB, 24, PhD(math), 27. *Hon Degrees:* DSc, Case Western Reserve Univ, 69. *Prof Exp:* Nat Res fel math, Harvard Univ, 27-28, Univ Gottingen, 28-29 & Univ Amsterdam, 29; from asst prof to prof, Princeton Univ, 29-67; PROF PHILOS & MATH, UNIV CALIF, LOS ANGELES, 67- *Mem:* Nat Acad Sci; AAAS; Am Math Soc; Asn Symbolic Logic; Am Acad Arts & Sci. *Res:* Mathematical logic. *Mailing Add:* Dept of Philos Univ of Calif Los Angeles CA 90024

CHURCH, BROOKS DAVIS, b Youngstown, Ohio, May 6, 18; c 2. MICROBIOLOGY. *Educ:* Univ Mich, BS, 47, MS, 52, PhD(bact), 55. *Prof Exp:* Res bacteriologist, Ft Detrick, Md, 49-50; asst med, Univ Chicago, 50-52; sr res assoc, Warner Res Inst, 55-60; asst prof, Univ Wash, 60-62; from asst prof to assoc prof microbiol, Univ Minn, 62-66; sr microbiologist, North Star Res Inst, 66-72; sr microbiologist, Denver Res Inst, Univ Denver, 72-76, prof biol sci, 72-77; PRES BIO-SEARCH ASSOC, INC, 81- *Concurrent Pos:* Mem comt safe drinking water, Nat Acad Sci, 76-77; consult, Inpro Inc, 77-, Marathon Oil, 78-, Allied Mills Starches Australia, 80-, Ralston-Purina, 81-, URS Corp, 81- *Mem:* AAAS; Am Soc Microbiol; Sigma Xi. *Res:* Biochemistry of bacterial spores and cell walls; fungal digestion of food processing wastes; biosynthesis of heteropolysaccharides. *Mailing Add:* 329 W Caley Dr Littleton CO 80120

CHURCH, CHARLES ALEXANDER, JR, b Rock Hill, SC, Oct 29, 32; m. MATHEMATICS. *Educ:* Va Polytech Inst, BS, 57; Duke Univ, PhD(math), 65. *Prof Exp:* Instr math, Roanoke Col, 59-62; asst prof, WVa Univ, 65-66; asst prof biomet, Med Col Va, 66-67; ASSOC PROF MATH, UNIV NC, GREENSBORO, 67- *Mem:* AAAS; Am Math Soc; Math Asn Am. *Res:* Combinatorial mathematics. *Mailing Add:* Dept of Math Univ of NC Greensboro NC 27412

CHURCH, CHARLES HENRY, b Phoenix, Ariz, May 15, 29; m 56; c 3. OPTICAL PHYSICS, ENGINEERING PHYSICS. *Educ:* Univ Mo-Rolla, BS, 50; Pa State Univ, MS, 51; Univ Mich, PhD(physics), 59. *Prof Exp:* Assayer anal chem, Bradley Mining Co, Idaho, 50; asst physics, Pa State Col, 50-51; jr physicist, Res Labs Div, Gen Motors Corp, 51-52; res assoc, Eng Res Inst, Univ Mich, 56-58; assoc physicist, Cent Res Lab, Crucible Steel Co Am, 58-59; sr physicist, Westinghouse Res Labs, 59-63, fel physicist, 63-65, adv physicist, 65-68; staff specialist laser technol & systs, Advan Res Projs Agency, US Dept Defense, Va, 68-71, dep dir, Res & Develop Ctr, Thailand, 71, staff specialist laser technol & syst, Va, 71-72, asst dir target acquisition, identification & advan delivery concepts, 72-74, sr prog mgr, 74-75; ASST DIR ARMY RES TECHNOL, OFF DEP CHIEF STAFF RES, DEVELOP & ACQUISITION, US ARMY, 75- *Concurrent Pos:* Teacher, Univ Calif Far East Exten, 53-54; lectr, Univ Pittsburgh, 58-59 & Carnegie Inst Technol, 64. *Mem:* Soc Automotive Engrs; Am Phys Soc; fel Optical Soc Am; Inst Elec & Electronics Eng; Am Inst Aeronaut & Astronaut. *Res:* Lasers; atomic and molecular plasmas; optical intrumentation and design; spectroscopy; weapons systems; solid state physics, energy. *Mailing Add:* Hq DA DAMA-ARZ-E Pentagon Washington DC 20310

CHURCH, CLIFFORD CARL, b Carmen, Okla, Oct 4, 99; m 27; c 2. GEOLOGY, PALEONTOLOGY. *Educ:* Univ Okla, AB, 23; Stanford Univ, MA, 25. *Prof Exp:* Heavy mineral res, Marland Oil Co, San Francisco, 26; micropaleontologist, Assoc Oil Co, 26-48; sr micropaleontologist, Getty Oil Co, 48-60; CONSULT MICROPALEONTOL, 60-; CUR PALEONTOL, KERN COUNTY OIL MUS, 74- *Concurrent Pos:* Optical worker, Calif Acad Sci, 43-45; lectr, Stanford Univ, 46-48; consult, Western Geothermal, Inc, 62; adj instr paleontol, Calif State Col, Bakersfield, 76. *Mem:* Am Asn Petrol Geol; Paleont Soc; Soc Econ Paleontologists & Mineralogists (vpres, 30, pres, 52); fel Geol Soc Am; fel Am Inst Prof Geologists. *Res:* Micropaleontology; malacology; mineralogy; Mesozoic and Cenozoic Foraminifera in California. *Mailing Add:* 15 Montrose St Bakersfield CA 93305

CHURCH, DAVID ARTHUR, b Berlin, NH, Apr 3, 39. PHYSICS. *Educ:* Dartmouth Col, BA, 61; Univ Wash, MS, 63, PhD(physics), 69. *Prof Exp:* Res assoc physics, Univ Bonn, Ger, 69, Univ Mainz, Ger, 69-71 & Univ Ariz, 71-72; physicist, Lawrence Berkeley Lab, Univ Calif, 72-75; asst prof, 75-81, ASSOC PROF PHYSICS, TEX A&M UNIV, 81- *Mem:* Am Phys Soc. *Res:* Stored multi-charged ion collisions and precision spectroscopy; fast ion coherence spectroscopy, collisional orientation and alignment; laser spectroscopy and x-ray polarization spectroscopy. *Mailing Add:* Dept of Physics Tex A&M Univ College Station TX 77843

CHURCH, DAVID CALVIN, b Iola, Kans, Nov 1, 25; m 52. ANIMAL NUTRITION, ANIMAL PHYSIOLOGY. *Educ:* Kans State Univ, BS, 50; Univ Idaho, MS, 52; Okla State Univ, PhD(animal nutrit), 56. *Prof Exp:* From asst prof to assoc prof, 56-70, PROF ANIMAL NUTRIT, ORE STATE UNIV, 70- *Mem:* Am Soc Animal Sci; Am Dairy Sci Asn. *Res:* Nutrition of the ruminant animal; rumen physiology; feedstuff and forage evaluation. *Mailing Add:* Dept of Animal Sci Ore State Univ Corvallis OR 97331

CHURCH, EUGENE LENT, b Yonkers, NY, July 30, 25; m 48; c 2. NUCLEAR PHYSICS, OPTICAL PHYSICS. *Educ:* Princeton Univ, AB, 48; Harvard Univ, PhD(physics), 53. *Prof Exp:* Res assoc, Princeton Univ, 48; res assoc, Brookhaven Nat Lab, 50-52; guest scientist, Argonne Nat Lab, 52-55; guest scientist, Brookhaven Nat Lab, 55-59; Secy of Army fel, Univ Inst Theoret Physics, Copenhagen, 59-61; guest scientist, Brookhaven Nat Lab, 61-71; physicist, Frankford Arsenal, US Army, 71-77; PHYS SCIENTIST, ARRADCOM, 77- *Concurrent Pos:* Mem solid state adv panel, Nat Res Coun, 73-78; res collabr, Nat Synchrotron Light Source, 81- *Mem:* Fel Am Phys Soc; sr mem Inst Elec & Electronics Engr; Optical Soc Am; Soc Photo-Optical Inst Engrs; Sigma Xi. *Res:* Experimental and theoretical optics; surface metrology; signal processing. *Mailing Add:* USA ARRADCOM Dover NJ 07801

CHURCH, GEORGE LYLE, b Boston, Mass, Dec 19, 03; m 34; c 1. BOTANY. *Educ:* Mass Col, BS, 25; Harvard Univ, AM, 27, PhD(bot), 28. *Prof Exp:* Teaching fel bot, Harvard Univ, 26-28; instr, Brown Univ & RI Col Pharm, 28-34; from asst prof to prof bot, 34-59, cur herbarium, 40-72, chmn dept bot, 58-66, Stephen Olney prof, 59-72, EMER PROF BOT, BROWN UNIV, 72- *Mem:* AAAS; Bot Soc Am; Soc Develop Biol; Soc Study Evolution; Am Soc Plant Taxonomists. *Res:* Cytology and taxonomy; cytotaxonomy and cytogenetics of Gramineae. *Mailing Add:* 278 Doyle Ave Providence RI 02906

CHURCH, JAMES M(ARION), polymer science & technology, deceased

CHURCH, JOHN ARMISTEAD, b Richmond, Va, Apr 3, 37; m 64; c 3. CELLULOSE CHEMISTRY, BIOMASS CONVERSION. *Educ:* Univ Va, BA, 59; Inst Paper Chem, MS, 61, PhD(org chem), 64. *Prof Exp:* Sr scientist, 64-70, res assoc, 70-78, SR RES ASSOC, PRINCETON RES CTR, AM CAN CO, 78- *Mem:* Am Chem Soc. *Res:* Cellulose, wood and sugar chemistry; fuels and chemicals from biomass; continuous lignocellulose hydrolysis; autoxidation; chemical kinetics; paper deterioration; graft copolymers; pulp and paper science and technology; history of optics. *Mailing Add:* Princeton Lab Am Can Co PO Box 50 Princeton NJ 08540

CHURCH, JOHN PHILLIPS, b Columbus, Ohio, July 14, 34; m 59; c 2. REACTOR PHYSICS. *Educ:* Univ Cincinnati, ChE, 57; Univ Fla, MSc, 60, PhD(nuclear eng), 63. *Prof Exp:* Chem engr, Nat Cash Register Co, 58-59; res engr, 63-77, STAFF PHYSICIST, E I DU PONT DE NEMOURS & CO, INC, 77- *Mem:* Am Nuclear Soc; Nat Soc Prof Engrs. *Res:* Reactor kinetics; core design; reactor safety analysis; radiation shielding. *Mailing Add:* Savannah River Lab Aiken SC 29801

CHURCH, JOSEPH AUGUST, b Plainfield, NJ, Sept 4, 46. ALLERGY, IMMUNOLOGY. *Educ:* Johns Hopkins Univ, BA, 68; NJ Col Med, MD, 72. *Prof Exp:* Fel allergy & immunol, Med Ctr, Georgetown Univ, 74-76; intern-resident pediat, Childrens Hosp Nat Med Ctr, 72-74; ASST PROF PEDIAT, SCH MED, UNIV SOUTHERN CALIF, 76- *Concurrent Pos:* Asst attend physician & consult, Dept Path, Childrens Hosp Los Angeles, 76- *Mem:* Am Col Allergists; Am Acad Allergy; Am Acad Pediat. *Res:* Recognition, management and investigation of immune deficiencies; management and investigation of mechanisms of severe allergic disease. *Mailing Add:* Childrens Hosp of Los Angeles PO Box 54700 Los Angeles CA 90054

CHURCH, LARRY B, b St Louis, Mo, Apr 19, 39; m 62. ANALYTICAL CHEMISTRY, NUCLEAR CHEMISTRY. *Educ:* Univ Rochester, BS, 61; Carnegie Inst Technol, MS, 64, PhD(chem), 66. *Prof Exp:* Fel chem, Univ Calif, Irvine, 66-68; asst prof, State Univ NY Buffalo, 68-73; assoc prof chem, Reed Col, 73-80; ANAL SCIENTIST, TEKTRONIX, INC, 80- *Concurrent Pos:* Consult, Fabric Flammability Res. *Mem:* Am Chem Soc; Electrochem Soc. *Res:* Nuclear reactions; surface and material science phosphors and semi-conductor materials. *Mailing Add:* Tektronix Inc Reed Col Beaverton OR 97077

CHURCH, LLOYD EUGENE, b Littleton, WVa, Sept 25, 19; m 64. ANATOMY, DENTISTRY. *Educ:* WVa Univ, AB, 42; Univ Md, DDS, 44; George Washington Univ, MS, 51, PhD(anat), 59. *Prof Exp:* Intern oral surg, Bellevue Hosp, New York, 44-45; resident & instr, Med Col Va, 45-46; clin instr, George Washington Univ, 52-62; sr res scientist, Nat Biomed Res Found, 63-67; ASSOC RES PROF ANAT & SURG, SCH MED, GEORGE WASHINGTON UNIV, 67- *Concurrent Pos:* Mem staff, Dept Oral Path, Armed Forces Inst Path, DC, 59-62, vis scientist, 62; mem attend staff, Suburban Montgomery County Gen, Prince Georges Gen Hosp, Sibley Shady Grove, Holy Cross, George Wash Med Ctr, Nat Orthop & Rehab, Capital Hill, Fairfax, St Mary's Hosp. *Mem:* Fel AAAS; Am Asn Anat; fel Am Col Dent; Am Acad Oral Path; Am Acad Oral Roentgenol. *Res:* Anatomy of temporo-mandibular joint; salivary glands; growth and function of mandible; bone growth; aid to handicapped. *Mailing Add:* 8218 Wisconsin Ave Bethesda MD 20014

CHURCH, MARSHALL ROBBINS, b Richmond, Va, Mar 23, 48; m 76. PHYSIOLOGICAL LIMNOLOGY, CHEMICAL LIMNOLOGY. *Educ:* Univ Va, BA, 71, PhD(environ sci), 80. *Prof Exp:* Phys sci technician, Denver Wildlife Res Ctr, US Dept Interior, 71-72; teaching asst ecol & aquatic ecol, Dept Environ Sci, Univ Va, 72-75; phys scientist, Waterways Exp Sta, US Army Engrs, 77-78; instr, 79, RES ASSOC AQUATIC ECOL, DEPT ENVIRON SCI, UNIV VA, 80- *Mem:* AAAS; Am Soc Limnol & Oceanog; Ecol Soc Am; NAm Benthological Soc. *Res:* Effects of nutrients and light on primary productivity in aquatic ecosystems; physiology and biochemistry of algae; effects of acid precipitation on the chemistry and ecology of surface waters. *Mailing Add:* Dept Environ Sci Clark Hall Univ Va Charlottesville VA 22903

CHURCH, PHILIP THROOP, b Winchester, Conn, Mar 18, 31; m 54; c 3. TOPOLOGY. *Educ:* Wesleyan Univ, BA, 53; Harvard Univ, MA, 54; Univ Mich, PhD, 59. *Prof Exp:* From asst prof to prof, 58-76, FRANCIS H ROOT PROF MATH, SYRACUSE UNIV, 76- *Concurrent Pos:* NSF grants, 59-62 & 63-69; mathematician, Inst Defense Anal, 62-63; mem, Inst Advan Study, 62 & 65-66; NSF sr fel, 65-66; ed topol, Transactions of & Memoirs of Am Math Soc, 74-77, chmn, Ed Comt, 77. *Mem:* Am Math Soc; Math Asn Am. *Res:* Singularities of differentiable maps; nonlinear elliptic partial differential equations. *Mailing Add:* Dept Math Syracuse Univ Syracuse NY 13210

CHURCH, RICHARD LEE, b Escondido, Calif. ENVIRONMENTAL ENGINEERING, OPERATIONS RESEARCH. *Educ:* Lewis & Clark Col, BS, 70; Johns Hopkins Univ, PhD(environ systs), 74. *Prof Exp:* Asst prof, 74-80, ASSOC PROF ENVIRON ENG, UNIV TENN, 80- *Concurrent Pos:* Consult, LBJ Sch, Univ Tex, 76-, Brookhaven Nat Lab, 76-77 & Oak Ridge Nat Lab, 78- *Mem:* Opers Res Soc Am; Regional Sci Asn; Asn Am Geographers; Water Pollution Control Fedn. *Res:* Modelling of environmental systems engineering problems; location model development for public and private facilities; water resources systems. *Mailing Add:* Dept of Civil Eng Univ of Tenn Knoxville TN 37916

CHURCH, ROBERT BERTRAM, b Calgary, Alta, May 7, 37; m 57; c 2. DEVELOPMENTAL BIOLOGY. *Educ:* Univ Alta, BSc, 62, MSc, 63; Univ Edinburgh, PhD(animal genetics), 65. *Prof Exp:* NIH fel cancer biol, Med Sch, Univ Wash, 65-66, res assoc, 66-67; mem fac develop biol, 67-68, asst prof, 67-69, assoc prof, 68-69, PROF MED BIOCHEM & HEAD DIV, UNIV CALGARY, 69- *Concurrent Pos:* Nat Res Coun grant develop biol, Univ Calgary, 67-; pres, Church Livestock Consult, Ltd, 70-; Med Res Coun grant, 72-; dir, Highfield Stock Farms & Connaught Labs, Ltd, Toronto, 79; Exec mem, Natural Sci & Eng Res Coun Can, Ottawa, 78. *Mem:* Soc Study Reprod; AAAS; Genetics Soc Am; Can Biochem Soc. *Res:* Analysis of genetic transcription in developing mammalian systems utilizing biochemical parameters; synthesis of ribonucleic acid and control at the transcription and translational levels; evolution of desoxyribonucleic acid base sequences in mammals; bovine embryo transplants. *Mailing Add:* Div of Med Biochem Univ of Calgary Fac of Med Calgary AB T2N 1N4 Can

CHURCH, ROBERT FITZ (RANDOLPH), b Philadelphia, Pa, Mar 27, 30; m 53; c 3. ORGANIC CHEMISTRY. *Educ:* Amherst Col, BA, 51; Univ Mich, MS, 61, PhD(chem), 62. *Prof Exp:* Sales serv rep, Am Cyanamid Co, 51-53, chemist, 55-57; instr, Univ Mich, 60-61; res chemist, Am Cyanamid Co, 61-62; RES CHEMIST, LEDERLE LABS, PEARL RIVER, NY, 63- *Concurrent Pos:* Instr, Bridgeport Eng Inst, 56-57 & 62-68. *Mem:* Am Chem Soc; Sigma Xi. *Res:* Chemistry of steroids and other natural products; pharmaceutical and synthetic organic chemistry; chemistry of small ring compounds; process research. *Mailing Add:* 201 Sheephill Rd Riverside CT 06878

CHURCH, RONALD L, b Monterey, Calif, Nov 19, 30. ZOOLOGY, POLLUTION BIOLOGY. *Educ:* San Jose State Col, BA, 53; Univ Calif, Berkeley, MA, 61, PhD(zool), 64. *Prof Exp:* Asst prof biol, San Jose State Col, 63-65; asst prof, Univ Nev, Reno, 65-70, res assoc, Desert Res Inst, 68-70; environ specialist, Div Water Qual, State Water Resources Control Bd, 70-72, ENVIRON SPECIALIST, NORTH COAST REGION, CALIF REGIONAL WATER QUAL CONTROL BD, 72- *Concurrent Pos:* NSF grant, 65-66; adj prof, Pac Marine Sta, Univ of the Pac, 74-79. *Mem:* AAAS; Ecol Soc Am; Wildlife Soc; Am Ornith Union; Am Soc Mammal. *Res:* Water quality biology; vertebrate biology; animal ecology. *Mailing Add:* Calif Region Water Qual Control Bd 1000 Coddingtown Ctr Santa Rosa CA 95401

CHURCH, SHEPARD EARLL, (JR), b Syracuse, NY, Dec 4, 21; m 43; c 3. PHYSICAL CHEMISTRY. *Educ:* NY State Col Forestry, Syracuse Univ, BS, 43, MS, 50; Syracuse Univ, PhD(chem), 58. *Prof Exp:* Res chemist, Rohm and Haas Co, Pa, 43-47; from instr to assoc prof pulp & paper technol, State Univ NY Col Forestry, 47-57; tech serv rep, ITT Rayonier, Inc, 57-59, mgr tech serv, 59-69, gen mgr tech serv & prod develop, 69-76, dir, Mkt Serv, 76-79; MGR, BRITISH COLUMBIA LIAISON OFF, 80- *Mem:* Am Chem Soc; Tech Asn Pulp & Paper Indust; Can Pulp & Paper Asn. *Res:* Pulp and paper technology; cellulose chemistry; kinetics of organic redox reactions; photochemistry; urea formaldehyde and melamine formaldehyde resins; plywood adhesives; paper wet strength. *Mailing Add:* Indust Can 1111 W Georgia St Vancouver BC V6E 3H1 Can

CHURCH, STANLEY EUGENE, b Oakland, Calif, Sept 13, 43; m 66; c 2. GEOCHEMISTRY. *Educ:* Univ Kans, BS, 65, MS, 67; Univ Calif, Santa Barbara, PhD(geochem), 70. *Prof Exp:* Res asst geochem, Univ Calif, Santa Barbara, 69-70; res assoc, Carnegie-Mellon Univ, 70-71; Nat Res Coun Assoc, Johnson Space Ctr, NASA, 71-73; res assoc geochem, Univ Calif, Santa Barbara, 73-75; res assoc geochem, Hasler Res Ctr, Appl Res Lab, Goleta, Ca, 75-79; MEM STAFF US GEOL SURV BR EXPLOR RES, FED CTR, DENVER COLO, 79- *Mem:* Fel Geol Soc Am; Am Geophys Union; Geochem Soc; Sigma Xi; Soc Econ Geologists. *Res:* The application of isotopic and trace element geochemical methods to the problem of the genesis of calc-alkaline magma and the evolution of the earth's mantle; trace element abundance distributions and the effect of micrometeorite bombardment of the lunar soils to form agglutinites; investigations of elemental dispersion patterns and interpretation of these patterns as clues to the occurrance of economic deposits. *Mailing Add:* US Geol Surv Fed Ctr Mail Stop 955 PO Box 25046 Denver CO 80225

CHURCH, WILLIAM RICHARD, b Tonyrefail, Glamorgan, UK, July 10, 36; m 63; c 4. GEOLOGY. *Educ:* Univ Wales, BSc, 57, PhD(geol), 61. *Prof Exp:* Boese fel, Columbia Univ, 61-62; lectr, 62-63, asst prof, 63-68, ASSOC PROF GEOL, UNIV WESTERN ONT, 68- *Mem:* Fel Geol Soc London; fel Geol Asn Can; Geol Soc Am; Can Inst Mining & Metall. *Res:* Geology of northeast Newfoundland, northwest Ireland, Huronian and Grenvillian of northern Ontario; eclogites; ophiolites of the Appalachian and Pan African systems. *Mailing Add:* Dept of Geol Univ of Western Ont London Can

CHURCHER, CHARLES STEPHEN, b Aldershot, Eng, Mar 21, 28; Can citizen; m 59; c 3. VERTEBRATE PALEONTOLOGY, MAMMALOGY. *Educ:* Univ Natal, BSc, 50, Hons, 52, MSc, 54; Univ Toronto, PhD, 57. *Prof Exp:* Lectr zool, 57-59, from asst prof to assoc prof, 60-70, assoc dean, Arts & Sci, 75-78, PROF ZOOL, UNIV TORONTO, 70-, ASSOC PROF DENT, 69- *Concurrent Pos:* Res assoc, Royal Ont Mus, Toronto, 59-; consult, Geol Surv Can, 66- *Mem:* Am Soc Mammalogists; Soc Vert Paleont; Can Soc Zoologists; Australian Mammal Soc. *Res:* Pleistocene mammals, especially Canadian and African. *Mailing Add:* Dept of Zool Univ of Toronto Toronto ON M5S 1A1 Can

CHURCHILL, ALGERNON COOLIDGE, b Aug 15, 37; US citizen; m 59; c 3. PHYCOLOGY, PLANT ECOLOGY. *Educ:* Harvard Univ, BA, 59; Univ Ore, MS, 63, PhD(biol), 68. *Prof Exp:* From instr to asst prof, 66-74, ASSOC PROF BIOL, ADELPHI UNIV, 74- *Concurrent Pos:* Sr investr, NY Ocean Sci Lab grant, 70-71. *Mem:* AAAS; Phycol Soc Am; Am Inst Biol Sci; Am Soc Limnol & Oceanog; Int Phycol Soc. *Res:* Physiological ecology of algae; growth and differentiation of marine algae; culturing of algae. *Mailing Add:* Adelphi Inst of Marine Sci Adelphi Univ Garden City NY 11530

CHURCHILL, CONSTANCE LOUISE, b Los Angeles, Calif, May 10, 41. ORGANIC CHEMISTRY. *Educ:* Baylor Univ, BS, 63, PhD(org chem), 69. *Prof Exp:* From asst prof to prof chem, Dakota State Col, 68-77, chmn, Div Sci, Math & Health Serv, 74-77; CHMN DIV SCI, MATH & TECHNOL, BURLINGTON COUNTY COL, 78- *Mem:* AAAS; Am Chem Soc; Royal Soc Chem; Sigma Xi. *Res:* Decomposition of ozonides; water pollution. *Mailing Add:* Div of Sci Math & Technol Burlington County Col Pemberton NJ 08068

CHURCHILL, DEWEY ROSS, JR, b Blackwell, Okla, May 19, 26; m 53; c 4. PHYSICS. *Educ:* Univ Kans, BS, 48, MS, 53. *Prof Exp:* Comput-observer geophys, Seismograph Serv Corp, 50-53; physicist, Res & Develop Lab, Phillips Petrol, 54-55; staff mem physics, Los Alamos Sci Lab, 55-60; sr res engr, 60-61, RES SCIENTIST THEORET PHYSICS, LOCKHEED MISSLES & SPACE CO, 61- *Mem:* AAAS; Am Phys Soc. *Res:* Radiative processes in molecules and atoms; radiative transfer; nuclear weapons effects; shock hydrodynamics; ion ballistics; aeronomy. *Mailing Add:* 1711 Karameos Dr Sunnyvale CA 94087

CHURCHILL, DON W, b Seattle, Wash, Feb 5, 30; m 55; c 3. PSYCHIATRY. *Educ:* Lawrence Col, BS, 51; Univ Wis, MS, 56, MD, 57; Am Bd Psychiat & Neurol, dipl psychiat, 63, dipl child psychiat, 66. *Prof Exp:* Instr path, Univ Wis, 53-56; intern, King County Hosp, Seattle, 57-58; resident psychiat, Cincinnati Gen Hosp, 58-60, fel child psychiat, 60-62; from asst prof to assoc prof, 64-73, PROF PSYCHIAT, MED CTR, IND UNIV-PURDUE UNIV, INDIANAPOLIS, 73-, DIR, RILEY CHILD GUID CLIN, 73- *Concurrent Pos:* Consult, Ind Boys' Sch, 64-69 & Ind Sch for Deaf, 69- *Mem:* AAAS; Am Psychiat Asn. *Res:* Pathology of connective tissue and histochemistry of mucomucopolysaccharides; childhood psychosis; language development and its relation to performance and cognitive levels; relationship of success-failure level to affect mood and specific behavioral measures; language and learning abilities. *Mailing Add:* Dept of Psychiat Ind Univ Sch of Med Indianapolis IN 46202

CHURCHILL, EDMUND, b Chelsea, Mass, Nov 10, 12; m 38; c 1. MATHEMATICS. *Educ:* Univ Md, BS, 43; Columbia Univ, AM, 44. *Prof Exp:* Instr math, Rutgers Univ, 45-47; from asst prof to prof, Antioch Col, 47-70, dir anthrop res proj, 50-70; MEM STAFF, WEBB ASSOCS, 70-, DIR ANTHROP RES PROJ, 77- *Concurrent Pos:* Lectr, Grad Ctr, Ohio State Univ, Wright Field, 48. *Mem:* Am Math Soc; Am Statist Asn; Am Asn Phys Anthrop; Am Anthrop Asn. *Res:* Statistics; anthropometry. *Mailing Add:* Webb Assocs Yellow Springs OH 45387

CHURCHILL, GEOFFREY BARKER, b Glen Cove, NY, July 10, 50; m 77; c 2. POLYMER SCIENCE, PLASTICS ENGINEERING. *Educ:* Mass Inst Technol, SB & SM, 74. *Prof Exp:* Res engr plastics, 74-79, SR TECHNOL ENGR, MONSANTO CO, 79- *Mem:* Am Chem Soc. *Res:* Incompatible species in polymer systems, polyblends and polymer alloys; extrusion fundamentals and extruder screw design; adhesion and fiber reinforcement of polymers; polymer formulation and product development for use in major appliances. *Mailing Add:* Monsanto Co 730 Worcester St Indian Orchard MA 01151

CHURCHILL, HELEN MAR, b Lawrence, Kans, Nov 14, 07. BIOLOGY. *Educ:* Univ Kans, AB, 28; Univ Mich, MA, 36, PhD(zool), 51. *Prof Exp:* Instr biol, William Jewell Col, Mo, 31-36 & Hibbing Jr Col, Minn, 37-38; teaching asst, Univ Mich, 39-40, 41, teaching fel, 40, 41-42; bacteriologist, Patuxent Res Refuge, US Fish & Wildlife Serv, Md, 42-45; protozoologist, NIH, 45; instr biol, Cornell Col, Iowa, 45-47; from asst prof to assoc prof, 47-73, EMER ASSOC PROF BIOL, HOLLINS COL, VA, 73- *Concurrent Pos:* Res parasitologist, Univ Philippines, 64-65. *Mem:* AAAS. *Res:* Germ cell cycle; digenetic trematode; cercaricides; preventive ointments and fabrics for control of schistosomiasis; methods for culturing parasites. *Mailing Add:* 515 Strand Rd NE Roanoke VA 24012

CHURCHILL, JOHN ALVORD, b Boston, Mass, Mar 25, 20; c 1. NEUROLOGY, PEDIATRIC NEUROLOGY. *Educ:* Trinity Col, BS, 42; Univ Pa, MD, 45. *Prof Exp:* Kirby-McCarthy fel, Johnston Found, Univ Pa, 46-50, asst prof neurol, Sch Med, 49-50; mem staff, Hartford Hosp, 50-53; assoc, Henry Ford Hosp, 53-60; chief dept child neurol, Lafayette Clin & assoc prof neurol, Wayne State Univ, 60-67; head sect neuropediat, Perinatal Br, Nat Inst Neurol Dis & Blindness, 67-72; PROF NEUROL & CHIEF CHILD NEUROL, SCH MED, WAYNE STATE UNIV, 72- *Concurrent Pos:* Res consult, pediat, Guys Hosp & Spastic Soc, UK, 60; mem comt ment retardation, Dept Ment Health State of Mich, 64-67; res fel bot, Mus Natural Hist, Smithsonian Inst, 70-; res fel, Cranbrook Inst Sci, 72- *Mem:* AAAS; Am Acad Neurol; Asn Res Nerv & Ment Dis; Am Acad Cerebral Palsy. *Res:* Relationships of perinatal events to neurological disabilities in the child. *Mailing Add:* Dept of Neurol Wayne State Univ Sch Med Detroit MI 48201

CHURCHILL, LYNN, b Sacramento, Calif, Mar 27, 47. NEUROCHEMISTRY. *Educ:* Univ Houston, BS, 69; Univ Calif, Irvine, PhD(biol sci), 73. *Prof Exp:* Teaching asst psychobiol, Univ Calif, Irvine, 69-73; res assoc pharmacol, Univ Wis-Madison, 74-77, NIH fel pharmacol, 74-77, proj assoc, 77-79, asst scientist, 79-80; res assoc neurobiol & anat, Med Sch, Univ Tex, Houston, 80-81; RES ASSOC ANAT, MED CTR, UNIV KANS, KANSAS CITY, 81- *Mem:* Soc Neurosci; Am Soc Neurochem. *Res:* Modifications in neurotransmitter receptor proteins with drug treatments or physiological stimulation, modifiability of retinal neurotransmitter proteins. *Mailing Add:* Dept Anat Univ Kans Med Ctr Kansas City KS 66103

CHURCHILL, MELVYN ROWEN, b London, Eng, June 2, 40; m 66; c 2. INORGANIC CHEMISTRY, CRYSTALLOGRAPHY. *Educ:* Univ London, BSc, 61, PhD(inorg chem), 64. *Prof Exp:* From instr to assoc prof chem, Harvard Univ, 64-71; prof, Univ Ill, Chicago Circle, 71-75; assoc provost, Fac Natural Sci & Math, 76-78, PROF CHEM, STATE UNIV NY BUFFALO, 75-, ACTG CHMN, 81- *Concurrent Pos:* Alfred P Sloan fel, 68-70; assoc ed, Inorg Chem, 70- *Honors & Awards:* Corday-Morgan Medal,

Chem Soc, London, 76. *Mem:* Am Chem Soc; Am Crystallog Asn; Royal Soc Chem. *Res:* Crystallographic studies on inorganic compounds particularly organometallic and transition metal complexes; synthetic organometallic chemistry. *Mailing Add:* Dept of Chem State Univ NY Buffalo NY 14214

CHURCHILL, PAUL CLAYTON, b Carson City, Mich, Feb 23, 41; m 70. PHYSIOLOGY. *Educ:* Univ Mich, Ann Arbor, BS, 63, PhD(physiol), 69. *Prof Exp:* NSF fel pharmacol, Univ Lausanne, 69-70; asst prof physiol, Sch Med, Univ Mich, Ann Arbor, 70-72; asst prof, 72-80, ASSOC PROF PHYSIOL, SCH MED, WAYNE STATE UNIV, 80- *Mem:* Am Physiol Soc; Int Soc Nephrology; Am Soc Nephrology. *Res:* Physiology of kidney, excretory function, transport; control or renin secretion from kidney. *Mailing Add:* Dept of Physiol Sch Med Wayne State Univ 540 E Canfield Detroit MI 48201

CHURCHILL, RALPH JOHN, b Pittsburgh, Pa, July 16, 44; m 66; c 2. WATER CHEMISTRY, ENVIRONMENTAL CHEMISTRY. *Educ:* Univ Ky, BS, 66; Univ Houston, MS, 70; Univ Calif, Berkeley, PhD(civil eng), 73. *Prof Exp:* Engr pollution control, Shell Oil Co, 66-71; consult, Eng-Sci Inc, 73-75; group leader water res, Tretolite Div, Petrolite Corp, 75-81; CONSULT, 81- *Mem:* Am Inst Chem Engr; Am Water Works Asn; Water Pollution Control Fedn. *Res:* Water and wastewater investigation; oil-water separation; water and wastewater treatment technology; mineral scale deposition-inhibition; municipal and industrial wastewater management. *Mailing Add:* 524 Warren Ave St Louis MO 63130

CHURCHILL, STUART W(INSTON), b Imlay City, Mich, June 13, 20; m 46, 74; c 4. COMBUSTION, HEAT TRANSFER. *Educ:* Univ Mich, BSE(chem eng), 42, BSE(math), 42, MSE, 48, PhD(chem eng), 52. *Hon Degrees:* MA, Univ Pa, 72. *Prof Exp:* Tech asst petrol refining, Shell Oil Co, Inc, 42-46; tech supvr, Electrochem Mfg, Frontier Chem Co, 46-47; res asst, Chem & Metall Eng, Univ Mich, 48-49, res assoc, 49-50, instr chem eng, 50-52, asst prof, 52-55, assoc prof, 55-57, prof, 57-67, chmn, Dept Chem & Metall Eng, 62-67; CARL V S PATTERSON PROF CHEM ENG, UNIV PA, 67- *Concurrent Pos:* Vis res, Okayama, Japan, 77. *Honors & Awards:* Prof Progress Award, Am Inst Chem Engrs, 65, William H Walker Award, 69, Warren K Lewis Award, 78 & Founders Award, 80; Max Jakob Mem Award, Am Soc Mech Engrs & Am Inst Chem Engrs, 79. *Mem:* Am Chem Soc; fel Am Inst Chem Engrs (vpres, 65, pres, 66); Combustion Inst. *Res:* Radiantly stabilized combustion, natural convection in enclosures, solar heating, migration of moisture in porous materials. *Mailing Add:* 311A Towne Bldg D3 Univ Pa 220 S 33rd St Philadelphia PA 19104

CHURCHWELL, EDWARD BRUCE, b Sylva, NC, July 9, 40; m 64; c 2. ASTRONOMY, SPECTROSCOPY. *Educ:* Earlham Col, BA, 63; Ind Univ, MS, 67, PhD(astrophys), 70. *Prof Exp:* Scientist radio astron, Max Planck Inst Radio Astronomy, 70-77; ASST PROF ASTRON, UNIV WIS, MADISON, 77- *Concurrent Pos:* Heinrich Hertz Found fel, 70-72. *Mem:* Am Astron Soc; Astronomische Gesellschaft. *Res:* Interstellar molecular clouds; star formation; molecular and atomic spectroscopy at microwave frequencies, and the physics of HII regions. *Mailing Add:* Washburn Osberv 475 N Charter St Madison WI 53706

CHURG, JACOB, b Dolhinow, Poland, July 16, 10; US citizen; m 42; c 2. PATHOLOGY, ENVIRONMENTAL HEALTH. *Educ:* Univ Wilno, MD, 33, DMedSc, 36. *Prof Exp:* Asst path, Sch Med, Univ Wilno, 34-36; asst bact, 38, fel path, 41-43, res assoc, 46-62, assoc attend pathologist, 62-75, ATTEND PATHOLOGIST, MT SINAI HOSP, 76-; PROF PATH & RES PROF COMMUNITY MED, MT SINAI SCH MED, 66- *Concurrent Pos:* Resident, Beth Israel Hosp, Newark, NJ, 39-40; pathologist, Barnert Mem Hosp, Paterson, 46-; chmn, US Mesothelioma Ref Panel, Int Union Against Cancer, 65-; chmn, Comt Histol Class Renal Dis, WHO, 75- *Mem:* Am Asn Path; NY Acad Med; Int Acad Path; Int Soc Nephrology. *Res:* Vascular diseases; renal structure and diseases; pneumoconioses; syndrome of allergic granulomatosis. *Mailing Add:* 711 Ogden Ave Teaneck NJ 07666

CHURKIN, MICHAEL, JR, b San Francisco, Calif, Jan 6, 32; m 60; c 2. GEOLOGY. *Educ:* Univ Calif, Berkeley, BA, 57, MA, 58; Northwestern Univ, PhD, 61. *Prof Exp:* Fel geol, Columbia Univ, 61-62; GEOLOGIST, ALASKAN GEOL BR, US GEOL SURV, 62- *Mem:* AAAS; Geol Soc Am. *Res:* Iectonostratigraphic terranes of north Pacific and Arctic; accretion tectonics of north Pacific and Arctic; geology of North-East USSR; graptolites. *Mailing Add:* US Geol Surv 345 Middlefield Rd Menlo Park CA 94025

CHURNSIDE, JAMES H, b Seattle, Wash, Aug 29, 51; m 72; c 1. OPTICS. *Educ:* Whitworth Col, BS, 74; Ore Grad Ctr, PhD(physics), 78. *Prof Exp:* Fel, Ore Grad Ctr, 78-79; MEM TECH STAFF, AEROSPACE CORP, 79- *Mem:* Optical Soc Am; Soc Photo-Optical Instrumentation Engrs. *Res:* Speckle statistics of laser light backscattered from atmospheric aerosols; laser speckle velocimetry and laser Dappler velocimetry techniques for wind measurement. *Mailing Add:* Aerospace Corp PO Box 92957 Los Angeles CA 90009

CHUSED, THOMAS MORTON, b St Louis, Mo, Mar 29, 40; m 65; c 2. IMMUNOLOGY. *Educ:* Harvard Col, BA, 62; Harvard Med Sch, MD, 67. *Prof Exp:* Clin assoc immunol, Arthritis Br, Nat Inst Arthritis & Metab Dis, 69-71; sr staff fel, 71-74, sr investr immunol, Lab Microbiol & Immunol, Nat Inst Dent Res, 74-78, SR INVESTR IMMUNOL, LAB MICROBIOL IMMUNITY, NAT INST ALLERGY & INFECTIOUS DIS, 78- *Mem:* Am Asn Immunologists. *Res:* Understanding the mechanism of autoimmune disease in autoimmune mice and applying this to human autoimmune disease. *Mailing Add:* Bldg 5 Rm 235 Nat Inst Health Bethesda MD 20014

CHUSID, JOSEPH GEORGE, b Newark, NJ, Aug 23, 14; m 42; c 2. NEUROLOGY. *Educ:* Univ Pa, AB, 34, MD, 38; Am Bd Psychiat & Neurol, dipl. *Prof Exp:* Asst instr neurol, Univ Pa, 41-45; resident & fel, Neuropsychiat Inst, Univ Ill, 46-47; from asst attend neurologist to attend neurologist, 48-59, assoc dir dept neurol & neurosurg, 59-64, chief neurol

serv, 64-70, DIR DEPT NEUROL, ST VINCENT'S HOSP & MED CTR, 70- *Concurrent Pos:* Clin assoc prof med, NJ Col Med & Dent, 61-72; assoc clin prof neurol, Col Physicians & Surgeons, Columbia Univ, 65-, assoc attend neurologist, Columbia Presby Med Ctr, 65-77; prof neurol, NY Med Col, 77- *Mem:* Am Physiol Soc; fel Am Acad Neurol; Asn Res Nerv & Ment Dis; Soc Exp Biol & Med; Am Epilepsy Soc. *Res:* Neurological sciences; cortical connections and functions in the monkey; chronic experimental epilepsy; electroencephalographic studies on humans; cerebral angiography; clinical neurology; effects of major cerebral arterial ligations in monkeys; neuropharmacology; effects of metals on the brain. *Mailing Add:* St Vincent's Hosp & Med Ctr 145 W 11th St New York NY 10011

CHUSID, MICHAEL JOSEPH, b Coral Gables, Fla, Aug 23, 44; m 72; c 2. IMMUNOLOGY. *Educ:* Yale Col, BA, 66; Sch Med, Yale Univ, MD, 70. *Prof Exp:* Intern pediat, Yale New Haven Hosp, 70-71, asst resident, 71-72; clin assoc infectious dis, Lab Clin Invest, Bethesda, 72-75; fel, Children's Hosp Med Ctr, Boston, 75-76; asst prof, 76-79, ASSOC PROF PEDIAT, MED COL WIS, 79- *Concurrent Pos:* Dir postgrad med educ, Med Col Wis, 78- *Mem:* Am Soc Microbiol; Am Fedn Clin Res; AAAS; fel Infectious Dis Soc Am. *Res:* Leukocyte physiology. *Mailing Add:* Milwaukee Children's Hosp 1700 W Wisconsin Ave Milwaukee WI 53233

CHUTE, HAROLD LEROY, b Winnipeg, Ont, Sept 4, 21; nat US; m 54; c 3. ANIMAL PATHOLOGY. *Educ:* Univ Toronto, DVM, 49, DVSc, 55; Ont Vet Col, VS, 49; Ohio State Univ, MSc, 53. *Prof Exp:* Animal pathologist, Nova Scotia Agr Col, 49; asst prof, 49-52, assoc prof & assoc animal pathologist, 52-55, dir develop, 69-77, PROF ANIMAL PATH & ANIMAL PATHOLOGIST, UNIV MAINE, ORONO, 55- *Concurrent Pos:* Dir develop, Pullorum-Typhoid Agency, 58-69; pres, Chute Chem Co, Bangor, Maine, 77- *Mem:* AAAS; fel Am Vet Med Asn; Am Soc Microbiol; Am Asn Avian Path (pres, 63). *Res:* Virology in poultry diseases; veterinary bacteriology. *Mailing Add:* Off Dir Develop Alumni Ctr Univ Maine Orono ME 04473

CHUTE, JOHN LAWRENCE, JR, b Biddeford, Maine, June 12, 38; m 60; c 2. GEOLOGY, OCEANOGRAPHY. *Educ:* Univ Notre Dame, BS, 60; Ind Univ, MA, 62; Columbia Univ, PhD(geol), 69. *Prof Exp:* ASST PROF GEOL, LEHMAN COL, 63-; RES ASSOC, LAMONT-DOHERTY GEOL OBSERV, 69- *Mem:* AAAS; Am Geophys Union. *Res:* Physical oceanography of coastal waters, especially the Hudson Estuary and New York Bight; lunar studies, including the Apollo lunar heat flow experiments. *Mailing Add:* 680 Piermont Ave Piermont NY 10968

CHUTE, ROBERT MAURICE, b Naples, Maine, Feb 13, 26; m 46; c 2. ENVIRONMENTAL PHYSIOLOGY, LIMNOLOGY. *Educ:* Univ Maine, AB, 50; Johns Hopkins Univ, ScD, 53. *Prof Exp:* From instr to asst prof biol, Middlebury Col, 53-58; asst prof, San Fernando Valley State Col, 58-60; assoc prof & chmn, Lincoln Univ, Pa, 60-61; prof & chmn, 61-62, PROF BIOL & CHMN DEPT, BATES COL, 62- *Concurrent Pos:* Dir, Bates-Morse Mt Res Area, 78- *Mem:* AAAS. *Res:* Human ecology; estimation of cultural impact on lake and coastal ecosystems. *Mailing Add:* Dept of Biol Bates Col Lewistown ME 04240

CHUTJIAN, ARA, b New York, NY, Apr 23, 41; m 77; c 1. ATOMIC & MOLECULAR PHYSICS. *Educ:* Brown Univ, BSc, 62; Univ Calif, Berkeley, PhD(chem physics), 66. *Prof Exp:* Res assoc light diffraction, Holography, Bell Labs, 66-67; res assoc molecular spectros, Univ Southern Calif, 67-68; sr scientist, 69-76, MEM TECH STAFF ELECTRON SCATTERING, JET PROPULSION LAB, CALIF INST TECHNOL, 76- *Concurrent Pos:* Calif Inst Technol Pres Fund grant, 73-74 & 77-78; Planetary Atmospheres Br & Astron/Relativity Br, NASA grant, 78- *Mem:* Am Phys Soc. *Res:* Low-energy electron scattering from positive ions; low-energy electron scattering from neutral atoms and molecules; threshold (zero-energy). *Mailing Add:* Jet Propulsion Lab 4800 Oak Grove Dr Pasadena CA 91103

CHUTKOW, JERRY GRANT, b Denver, Colo, June 14, 33; m 57; c 4. NEUROLOGY, INTERNAL MEDICINE. *Educ:* Univ Chicago, AB, 52, SB, 55, MD, 58. *Prof Exp:* Intern med, Presbyterian Hosp, City New York, 58-59; resident, Univ Chicago Hosp & Clin, Univ Chicago, 59-62, instr, 62-64, resident neurol, 64-67, asst prof, 67; captain to lt colonel, US Army Med Corps, 67-69; asst prof, Mayo Med Sch, Univ Minn, 70-74, assoc prof, 74-77; PROF & CHMN NEUROL, STATE UNIV NY, BUFFALO, 77- *Concurrent Pos:* Res asst, Argonne Cancer Res Hosp, 62-64; spec fel, Nat Inst Neurol Dis & Stroke, 65-67; fel med, Schweppe Found, 67-69; chief neurol serv, Martin Army Hosp, 67-69; consult, Mayo Clinic, 69-77; dir, Dept Neurol, Erie Co Med Ctr, 79-; chief, Neurol Serv, Vet Admin Med Ctr, 79- *Mem:* Am Neurol Asn; Am Acad Neurol; Am Col Physicians; Am Psychiat Asn; Am Col Nutrit. *Res:* Metabolism of divalent cations in the central and peripheral nervous systems. *Mailing Add:* Dept Neurol Sch Med State Univ NY, 3495 Bailey Ave Buffalo NY 14215

CHVAPIL, MILOS, b Kladno, Czech, Sept 29, 28; m 53; c 2. PHYSIOLOGICAL CHEMISTRY, EXPERIMENTAL PATHOLOGY. *Educ:* Charles Univ, Prague, MD, 52, DSc(exp path), 66; Czech Acad Sci, PhD(biochem), 55. *Prof Exp:* Scientist, Inst Indust, Hyg & Occup Dis, Prague, 52-68; fel sci, Max Planck Inst Protein & Leather Res, Ger, 68-69; vis prof med, Sch Med, Univ Miami, 69-70; PROF SURG BIOL, COL MED, UNIV ARIZ, 70- *Concurrent Pos:* Consutl scientist, Ministry of Light Indust & Ministry of Food Indust, 58-68; fel surg, Med Sch, Univ Ore, 63; assoc prof exp path, Med Sch, Charles Univ, Prague, 65. *Honors & Awards:* Laureate of State Prize, Czech Repub, 66; Ministry of Health Award & Sci Bd, Czech Acad Sci Award, 68. *Mem:* Am Soc Exp Path. *Res:* Connective tissue physiology; biochemistry control of collagen biosynthesis by chelating agents; oxygen effect on collagen synthesis. *Mailing Add:* Dept of Surg Univ of Ariz Col of Med Tucson AZ 85724

CHWANG, ALLEN TSE-YUNG, b Shanghai, China, Nov 7, 44; US citizen; m 68; c 3. FLUID MECHANICS. *Educ:* Chu Hai Col, BS, 65; Univ Sask, MS, 67; Calif Inst Technol, PhD(mech eng), 71. *Prof Exp:* Res fel eng sci, Calif Inst Technol, 71-73, sr res fel, 73-76, res assoc, 76-78; assoc prof, 78-81, PROF MECH ENG, UNIV IOWA, 81- *Concurrent Pos:* Sr vis fel, Dept Appl Math & Theoret Physics, Univ Cambridge, John Simon Guggenheim fel, 74-75. *Mem:* Sigma Xi; Am Acad Mech; Am Phys Soc; Am Soc Civil Engrs; Am Soc Mech Engrs. *Res:* Low-Reynolds-number hydromechanics; nonlinear water waves; hydrodynamic pressures on dams; general fluid mechanics and applied mathematics. *Mailing Add:* Inst Hydraulic Res Univ Iowa Iowa City IA 52242

CHYATTE, SAMUEL BARUCH, physical medicine, deceased

CHYLEK, PETR, b Ostrava, Czech, Nov 6, 37; US citizen. ATMOSPHERIC PHYSICS, OPTICS. *Educ:* Charles Univ, Prague, dipl, 66; Univ Calif, Riverside, PhD(physics), 70. *Prof Exp:* Res assoc physics, Ind Univ, Bloomington, 70-72; fel, Nat Ctr Atmospheric Res, Boulder, 72-73; asst prof, State Univ NY Albany, 73-75; ASSOC PROF GEOSCI, PURDUE UNIV, 75- *Mem:* Am Geophys Union; Am Meteorol Soc; Am Optical Soc. *Res:* Light scattering in the atmosphere, effects of air pollution on climate, radiative transfer and atmospheric optics. *Mailing Add:* Dept of Geosci Purdue Univ West Lafayette IN 47907

CHYNOWETH, ALAN GERALD, b Harrow, Eng, Nov 18, 27; m 50; c 2. SOLID STATE PHYSICS, MATERIALS SCIENCE. *Educ:* King's Col, Univ London, BSc, 48, PhD(physics), 50. *Prof Exp:* Demonstr physics, King's Col, Univ London, 48-50; res fel, Nat Res Coun Can, 50-52; mem tech staff, 53-60, head crystal electronics res dept, 60-65, asst dir mat res, 65-73, dir mat res, 73-76, EXEC DIR, ELECTRONIC DEVICE, PROCESS & MAT DIV, BELL LABS, 76- *Concurrent Pos:* Surv dir, Nat Acad Sci Comt on Surv Mat Sci & Eng, 70-75; mem & panel chmn, Nat Acad Sci Comt on Mineral Resources & Environ, 73-75; mem, Nat Mat Adv Bd, 76-78; mem, NATO Spec Prog Panel Mat Sci, 77-81, chmn, 78; assoc ed, Ann Rev Mat Sci, 74-78 & Solid State Commun, 74- *Honors & Awards:* Baker Prize, Inst Elec & Electronics Engrs, 67. *Mem:* Fel Am Phys Soc; fel Inst Physics London; fel Inst Elec & Electronics Engrs; Am Inst Mining, Metall & Petrol Engrs; Mat Res Soc. *Res:* Transport properties of semiconductors and insulators; electrical breakdown; ferroelectrics; tunnelling; solid state plasmas; materials research; national materials policies; electronic and photonic devices. *Mailing Add:* Bell Labs Murray Hill NJ 07974

CHYTIL, FRANK, b Prague, Czech, Aug 28, 24; m 49; c 3. BIOCHEMISTRY, PHYSIOLOGY. *Educ:* Col Chem Tech, Prague, Ing, 49, PhD(biochem), 52, CSc(physiol chem), 56. *Prof Exp:* Res biochemist, Charles Univ, Prague, 49-51; Czech Acad Sci res fel biochem, Inst Human Nutrit, Prague, 52-55; sr scientist physiol, Czech Acad Sci, 56-62, sr scientist microbiol, 63-64; sr res fel biochem, Brandeis Univ, 64, sr res assoc, 65-66; from asst prof to assoc prof, 66-75, PROF BIOCHEM, SCH MED, VANDERBILT UNIV, 75- *Concurrent Pos:* Sect head, Southwest Found Res & Educ, 66-72. *Mem:* Am Inst Nutrit; Am Soc Biol Chem; Endocrine Soc; Am Chem Soc; Sigma Xi. *Res:* Metabolic regulations; mechanism of vitamin A action. *Mailing Add:* Dept Biochem Vanderbilt Univ Sch Med Nashville TN 37232

CHYUNG, DONG HAK, b Pyungyang, Korea, Aug 5, 37. ELECTRICAL & COMPUTER ENGINEERING. *Educ:* Seoul Nat Univ, BS, 59; Univ Minn, MS, 61, PhD(elec eng), 65. *Prof Exp:* Asst prof elec eng, Univ Minn, 65-66 & Univ SC, 66-68; assoc prof, 68-73, PROF ELEC ENG, UNIV IOWA, 73- *Mem:* Am Math Soc. *Res:* Control theory; computer-based systems. *Mailing Add:* Dept of Elec & Comput Eng Univ of Iowa Iowa City IA 52242

CHYUNG, KENNETH, b Seoul, Korea, Mar 16, 36; m 65; c 2. METALLURGY. *Educ:* Mich State Univ, BS, 60, PhD(metall), 65. *Prof Exp:* Res fel metall, Mich State Univ, 66; RES SUPVR, CORNING GLASS WORKS, 66- *Mem:* Am Soc Metals; Am Ceramic Soc. *Res:* Mechanical twinning of zinc bicrystals; crystal growth; metal fiber-ceramic composite materials; physical and mechanical properties of glass-ceramics: strengthening, fracture, crystallization and grain growth; creep and stress relaxation. *Mailing Add:* Sullivan Park Corning Glass Works Painted Post NY 14870

CIACCIO, EDWARD I, biochemistry, see previous edition

CIALDELLA, CATALDO, b Rochester, NY, Aug 26, 26; m 59; c 4. ORGANIC CHEMISTRY, POLYMER CHEMISTRY. *Educ:* Clarkson Col Technol, BS, 50; Case Inst Technol, MS, 54, PhD(org chem), 56. *Prof Exp:* Chemist, Bausch & Lomb Optical Co, 50-52; res chemist, Esso Res & Eng Co, 56-58, res dir, 58-60, dir res & develop, 60-61; VPRES, HYSOL DIV, DEXTER CORP, 61- *Mem:* Am Chem Soc. *Res:* Polymers, especially epoxy, urethane silicones. *Mailing Add:* Hysol Div Dexter Corp 211 Franklin St Olean NY 14760

CIALELLA, CARMEN MICHAEL, b Trenton, NJ, Apr 18, 25; m 51; c 5. NUCLEAR PHYSICS, BALLISTICS. *Educ:* Pa State Univ, BS, 50. *Prof Exp:* Physicist x-ray physics, Nat Bur Standards, 49-53; res physicist nuclear physics, US Geol Surv, 53-57; res physicist, Ballistic Res Labs, 57-79; RETIRED. *Res:* First laboratory experiments to determine neutron and gamma ray transmission through armored vehicles; developed single crystal spectrometer to measure neutron and gamma ray spectra simultaneously. *Mailing Add:* 622 Southgate Rd Aberdeen MD 21001

CIANCANELLI, EUGENE VINCENT, b Beacon, NY, July 6, 39; m 64; c 2. ECONOMIC GEOLOGY, VOLCANOLOGY. *Educ:* Univ Ariz, BS, 63, MS, 65. *Prof Exp:* Geologist, Phelps Dodge Corp, 66-68; chief geologist, Geothermal Resources Int, 68-73; vpres, Can Geothermal Oil Ltd, 73-75; consult geologist, Eugene V Ciancanelli Consult Geologists, 75-79; PRES, CASCADIA EXPLOR CORP CONSULT GEOLOGISTS, 79- *Concurrent Pos:* Lectr, geol explor methods, First SINO-US Geothermal Conf, Tianjin, China, 81r,. *Mem:* Geol Soc Am; Soc Mining Engrs; Geothermal Resources Coun; AAAS; Int Asn Volcanol & Chem Earth's Interior. *Res:* Geothermal energy; volcanogenic ore deposits; hydrothermal systems; petrology of volcanic rocks; structural geology of volcanic regions. *Mailing Add:* Eugene V Ciancanelli 3358 Apostol Rd Escondido CA 92025

CIANCIO, SEBASTIAN GENE, b Jamestown, NY, June 21, 37; m 63; c 1. PHARMACOLOGY, PERIODONTOLOGY. *Educ:* Univ Buffalo, DDS, 61; Am Bd Periodont, dipl. *Prof Exp:* Fel pharmacol & periodont, 63-65, from asst prof to assoc prof periodont & chmn dept, 65-73, assoc prof pharmacol, Sch Med, 65-73, PROF PERIODONT & CHMN DEPT, SCH DENT, STATE UNIV NY BUFFALO, 73-, CLIN PROF PHARMACOL, SCH MED, 73- *Concurrent Pos:* Res grants, United Health Found of Western NY, 65-66 & 70-71, Nat Inst Dent Res, 67-69 & Merrill Nat Labs, 73-; consult, Vet Admin Hosp, Buffalo, 70-, Pharmaceut Mfrs Asn, 73-, US Pharmacopae, Nat Formulary, 75-, Am Cyanamid Corp, 78-, Dupont Co, 81- & Erie County Med Ctr; chmn, Coun Dent Therapeut, Am Dent Asn, 76-78; pres, Pharmacol, Toxicol & Therapeut Group, Int & Am Asn Dent Res, 79; chmn, US Pharm Dent Comt Rev, 80-85; dir, Chautauqua Dent Cong, 79. *Mem:* Am Dent Asn; fel Int Col Dentists; Am Acad Periodont; Int Asn Dent Res. *Res:* Papain induced changes in rabbit tissues; local hemostasis; principal fibers of the periodontium; plaque control agents; periodontal observations in twins; acid mucopolysaccharides in gingivitis and periodontitis; antibiotics in periodontal therapy. *Mailing Add:* Dept Periodont-Endodont State Univ NY Sch Dent Buffalo NY 14214

CIAPPENELLI, DONALD JOHN, b Worcester, Mass, Dec 4, 43. CHEMISTRY. *Educ:* Univ Mass, BSc, 66; Brandeis Univ, MSc, 67, PhD(chem), 71. *Prof Exp:* Dir, Chem Dept, Brandeis Univ, 72-77; DIR CHEM DEPT, HARVARD UNIV, 77- *Mem:* Am Chem Soc; AAAS. *Mailing Add:* Dept Chem Harvard Univ Cambridge MA 02138

CIARAMITARO, DAVID A, b Detroit, Mich, Apr 15, 46. CHEMISTRY, ORGANIC CHEMISTRY. *Educ:* Oakland Univ, BA, 68; Univ Ariz, PhD(org chem), 74. *Prof Exp:* Res assoc wood chem, Univ Ariz, 74-75, res assoc pharmacol, Health Sci Ctr, 75-77; res chemist, 78-80, CHIEF CHEMIST, EXPLOSIVES, APACHE POWDER CO, 80- *Concurrent Pos:* Mem tech comt, Inst Makers Explosives, 81- *Mem:* Am Chem Soc; Soc Explosives Engrs. *Res:* New product development in dynamites; water gels; emulsion explosives and detonating cord; organic synthesis, including synthesis of radiolabeled compounds; investigation of biochemical and pharmacologic phenomena in experimental animals. *Mailing Add:* PO Box 700 Benson AZ 85602

CIARLONE, ALFRED EDWARD, b Reading, Pa, May 2, 32; m 59; c 2. PHARMACOLOGY, DENTISTRY. *Educ:* Univ Pittsburgh, DDS, 59, PhD(pharmacol), 74. *Prof Exp:* Gen pract resident dent, Vet Admin Hosp, Pittsburgh, 59-60; self-employed dentist, 60-69; asst prof oral biol & pharmacol, Sch Dent, 73-77, asst prof, 73-79, ASSOC PROF PHARMACOL, SCH MED, MED COL GA, 79-, ASSOC PROF ORAL BIOL & PHARMACOL, SCH DENT, 77- *Concurrent Pos:* Nat Inst Dent Res trainee fel, 69-73; consult, Doctors Hosp of Augusta, Ga, 77, J Am Dent Asn, 76- & Nat Bd Test Construct Comt, Dent Examr, 78-82; prin investr, Nat Inst Dent Res, 78-81; mem, Adv Panel Dent, rev US Pharmacopeia, 75-80 & rev cycle 80-85. *Mem:* Int Asn Dent Res; AAAS; Am Asn Dent Schs; Am Soc Pharmacol & Exp Therapeuts. *Res:* Pain control; anticaries efficacy of food additives and patented and nonpatented antiplaque agents; changes in brain amines induced by dental local anesthetics. *Mailing Add:* Dept Oral Biol & Pharmacol Sch Dent Med Col Ga 1120 15th St Augusta GA 30912

CIBILS, LUIS ANGEL, b Yuty, Paraguay, Mar 22, 27; m 61; c 3. OBSTETRICS & GYNECOLOGY. *Educ:* Col San Jose, BA, 42; Univ Paraguay, MD, 50. *Prof Exp:* Scholar, Span Inst Cult, 51-52; vis asst gynec, Univ Paris, 52-53; res fel obstet & gynec, Univ of Repub Uruguay, 57-60; res consult, Western Reserve Univ, 60, from instr to asst prof, 60-66; assoc prof, 66-70, PROF OBSTET & GYNEC, UNIV CHICAGO, 70- *Honors & Awards:* Found Prize, Am Asn Obstet & Gynec, 65. *Res:* Physiology of reproduction. *Mailing Add:* Dept of Obstet & Gynec Univ of Chicago Chicago IL 60637

CIBULA, ADAM BURT, b Salem, Ohio, June 4, 34; m 77; c 2. BIOLOGY, ENTOMOLOGY. *Educ:* Kent State Univ, BS, 56, MA, 58; Ohio State Univ, PhD(entom), 65. *Prof Exp:* Asst biol, Kent State Univ, 56-58, instr, 58-60; asst zool, Ohio State Univ, 60-64; asst prof, 64-69, assoc prof biol, 69-77, PROF BIOL SCI, KENT STATE UNIV, 77- *Mem:* AAAS; Entom Soc Am; Nat Asn Biol Teachers; Am Inst Biol Sci. *Res:* Insect nutrition; relationship of free amino acid composition in plants and insect growth and development. *Mailing Add:* Dept of Biol Sci Kent State Univ Kent OH 44242

CIBULA, WILLIAM GANLEY, b Cleveland, Ohio, Jan 16, 32; m 56; c 5. REMOTE SENSING, AGARIC TAXONOMY. *Educ:* John Carroll Univ, BS, 56, MS, 65; Univ Mass, PhD(bot), 76. *Prof Exp:* Physicist, Wright Patterson AFB, 56-60 & Picker X-ray Corp, 60-68; BOTANIST, NAT SPACE TECHNOL LABS, NASA, 71- *Concurrent Pos:* Adj prof, Univ S Miss, 78- *Mem:* Mycol Soc Am; AAAS; NAm Mycol Asn. *Res:* Development, analysis and specification of computer processed land cover classifications from Landsat and other multi-spectral scanners; Austroriparian agaric and bolete taxonomy; chromatography and chemical analysis of fungal pigments and other metabolites to exemplify their taxonomy and phylogeny. *Mailing Add:* 700 Idlewild Dr Picayune MS 39466

CIBULSKY, ROBERT JOHN, b Johnson City, NY, Feb 4, 46; m 72. ENTOMOLOGY, MICROBIOLOGY. *Educ:* Hamilton Col, BA, 68; Auburn Univ, MS, 71, PhD(entom), 75. *Prof Exp:* MGR FIELD RES & DEVELOP, CHEM & AGR PRODS DIV, ABBOTT LABS, 75- *Mem:* Sigma Xi; Entomol Soc Am; Am Soc Microbiol; Soc Invert Path; Am Soc Hort Sci. *Res:* Development of microbial products for agricultural uses; organisms include bacterial, fungal, and viral entomopathogens, plant pathogen antagonists, and soil inoculants. *Mailing Add:* Abbott Labs W Rosegarden Blvd Mechanicsburg PA 17055

CICCARELLI, ROGER N, b Rochester, NY, Dec 23, 34; m 60; c 2. POLYMER CHEMISTRY. *Educ:* St Bonaventure Univ, BS, 56; Syracuse Univ, MS, 58, PhD(org chem), 61; State Univ NY, PhD(org chem), 61. *Prof Exp:* Chemist, Exxon Res & Eng Co, 61-62; scientist, 62-70, SR SCIENTIST, XEROX CORP, 70- *Mem:* Am Chem Soc; Sigma Xi; The Chem Soc. *Res:* Synthetic and polymer chemistry; structure versus electrical properties of polymers; toners and carriers; electrostatics; photoconductors; reaction mechanisms; rocket fuels. *Mailing Add:* 145 Hibiscus Dr Rochester NY 14618

CICCHINELLI, ALEXANDER L, b Waterford, NY, Oct 13, 34; m 59; c 7. BIOSTATISTICS, ACADEMIC ADMINISTRATION. *Educ:* Cornell Univ, AB, 56; Univ Mich, MA, 59, PhD(biostatist), 62. *Prof Exp:* Asst prof biostatist, Western Reserve Univ, 62-64; dir comput ctr, Clark Col Technol, 64-70; dir anal studies & mgt anal, 70-77, assoc provost, 77-79, ASST VCHANCELLOR POLICY ANAL, CENT ADMIN, STATE UNIV NY, ALBANY, 79- *Res:* Development, assessment and advocacy of university-wide policy, development, organization and maintenance of university-wide data bases; projection, monitoring and interpretation of enrollment trends; management Management of higher education; faculty productivity analysis; program cost estimation and analysis; enrollment projection, long range planning. *Mailing Add:* State Univ NY Cent Admin Univ Plaza Albany NY 12246

CICCOLELLA, JOSEPH A, b Albany, NY, Sept 3, 09; m 46; c 7. NAVIGATION. *Educ:* Rensselaer Polytech Inst, ME, 31, DME, 34. *Prof Exp:* Asst examr, State Civil Serv Comn, NY, 34-35; engr, Fred Page Construct Co, NY, 35-36; field serv, US Lighthouse Serv, 36-39; comn officer, US Coast Guard, 39-61, chief, Testing & Develop Div, 59-61; dir eng signal prod, Amerace-Esna Corp, 61-72; RETIRED. *Concurrent Pos:* Lectr, US Coast Guard Training Sta; mem night visibility comt, Nat Res Coun; secy, US Indust Comt Lighthouse Conf. *Mem:* Am Soc Naval Engrs; Marine Technol Soc. *Res:* Pharology; search and rescue; maritime safety; aids to navigation. *Mailing Add:* PO Box 143 Bethania NC 27010

CICCONE, PATRICK EDWIN, b Newark, NJ, Nov 20, 44; m 78; c 2. PSYCHOPHARMACOLOGY, PSYCHIATRY. *Educ:* Harvard Col, BA, 66; Univ Pa, MD, 70; Hosp Univ Pa, residency dipl psychiat, 74; Am Bd Psychiat, 76. *Prof Exp:* Staff psychiatrist, Erich Lindemann Ment Health Ctr, 74-75; asst dir & clin investr psychopharmacol, McNeil Labs, Inc, 75-77, assoc dir, 78, DIR CLIN RES, MCNEIL CONSUMER PROD CO, 79- *Concurrent Pos:* Clin assoc psychiat, Mass Gen Hosp, 74-75; dir & staff psychiatrist, Revere Community Ment Health Ctr, 74-75; clin assoc psychiat, Med Sch, Univ Pa, 76-; vis asst prof, Temple Univ, 78-79. *Mem:* Am Psychiat Asn; AAAS; Am Soc Clin Pharmacol & Therapeut. *Res:* Potential over the counter drugs with emphasis on analgesics. *Mailing Add:* Plymouth Rd Gwynedd Valley PA 19437

CICERO, ARTHUR BENNETT, physics, computer science, see previous edition

CICERO, THEODORE JAMES, b Niagara Falls, NY, Aug 14, 42; m 66; c 4. BIOCHEMICAL PHARMACOLOGY. *Educ:* Villanova Univ, BS, 64; Purdue Univ, MS, 66, PhD(physiol psychol), 69. *Prof Exp:* Fel neurochem, 68-70, from asst prof to assoc prof, 70-78, PROF NEUROPHARMACOL, SCH MED, WASH UNIV, 78- ASSOC PROF NEUROBIOL, 76- *Concurrent Pos:* Consult, Nat Inst Alcoholism & Alcohol Abuse, 71-75 & NIMH, 72-73; consult, Nat Inst Drug Abuse, 77- *Mem:* Soc Neurosci; Soc Biol Psychiat; Am Psychopath Asn; Soc Neurochem. *Res:* Neurochemical, neurobiological and neuroendocrinological correlates of tolerance to and dependence on narcotics and alcohol; developmental neurochemistry. *Mailing Add:* Dept of Psychiat Sch Med Wash Univ 4940 Audubon Ave St Louis MO 63110

CICERONE, CAROL MITSUKO, Olaa, Hawaii, July 16, 43; m 67; c 1. NEUROPHYSIOLOGY OF THE VISUAL SYSTEM, VISION. *Educ:* Univ Ill, Urbana, BS, 65, MS, 67, Univ Mich, Ann Arbor, PhD(psychol), 74. *Prof Exp:* Res scientist psychol, Univ Mich, Ann Arbor, 76-78; ASST PROF PSYCHOL, UNIV CALIF, SAN DIEGO, 78- *Mem:* AAAS; Asn Res Vision & Opthal. *Res:* Psychophysical studies of sensitivity regulation and color vision in humans; neurophysiological studies of the vertebrate visual system involving retino-tectal connections in goldfish, retinal degenerations in rats & sensitivity regulation in the mammilian visual system. *Mailing Add:* Univ Calif San Diego La Jolla CA 92093

CICERONE, RALPH JOHN, b New Castle, Pa, May 2, 43; m 67; c 1. ATMOSPHERIC CHEMISTRY, AERONOMY. *Educ:* Mass Inst Technol, SB, 65; Univ Ill, MS, 67, PhD(elec eng & physics), 70. *Prof Exp:* Physicist, US Dept Com, 67; res asst aeronomy, Univ Ill, 67-70; assoc res scientist aeronomy, Space Physics Res Lab, Univ Mich, Ann Arbor, 70-78; assoc res chemist, Ocean Res Div, 78-80, RES CHEMIST, SCRIPPS INST OCEANOG, UNIV CALIF, SAN DIEGO, 80-; SR SCIENTIST & DIR, ATMOSPHERIC CHEM DIV, NAT CTR ATMOSPHERIC RES, BOULDER, COLO, 80- *Concurrent Pos:* Consult, Aeronomy Corp, 70-71 & NSF, 75; lectr & asst prof elec eng, Univ Mich, Ann Arbor, 73-75; assoc ed, J Geophys Res, 77-79; ed, J Geophys Res, 79-; mem comt atmospheric sci, Nat Acad Sci, 80- *Honors & Awards:* Macelwane Award, Am Geophys Union, 79. *Mem:* Fel AAAS; fel Am Geophys Union; Am Chem Soc; Am Meteorol Soc. *Res:* Theoretical and experimental studies of the earth's atmosphere. *Mailing Add:* Nat Ctr Atmospheric Res PO Box 3000 Boulder CO 80307

CICHELLI, MARIO T(HOMAS), b Baltimore, Md, Jan 28, 20; m 43; c 4. CHEMICAL ENGINEERING. *Educ:* Loyola Col, Md, BS, 40; Johns Hopkins Univ, PhD(chem eng), 45. *Prof Exp:* Process engr, Kellex Corp, New York, 44-45 & Carbide & Carbon Chem Corp, Manhattan Dist Proj, Oak Ridge, 45-46; res eng fel, Mellon Inst, 46-50; res engr, 50-53, res supvr & res mgr, 54-79, MGR, PATENT LIAISON DIV, TEXTILE FIBERS DEPT, E

I DU PONT DE NEMOURS & CO, INC, 79- *Mem:* Am Chem Soc; Am Inst Chem Engrs. *Res:* Heat transmission; diffusional separation processes; high temperature technology. *Mailing Add:* G101 Centre Rd Bldg E I du Pont de Nemours & Co Inc Wilmington DE 19898

CICHOCKI, FREDERICK PAUL, evolutionary biology, ichthyology, see previous edition

CICHOWSKI, ROBERT STANLEY, b Lakewood, Ohio, Feb 28, 42; m 66; c 3. HETEROGENEOUS CATALYSIS, CHILDREN'S SCIENCE EDUC. *Educ:* Purdue Univ, BSChE, 64; State Univ NY Col Ceramics, Alfred Univ, PhD(ceramic sci), 68. *Prof Exp:* Res chemist, Phillips Petrol Co, Okla, 68-71; lectr, 71, asst prof, 71-75, assoc prof, 76-80, PROF CHEM, CALIF POLYTECH STATE UNIV, SAN LUIS OBISPO, 80- *Concurrent Pos:* Actg dir sci, Pac Sci Ctr, Seattle, Wash, 80. *Mem:* Am Chem Soc; Catalysis Soc; Am Ceramic Soc; Nat Sci Teachers Asn. *Res:* Chemistry of glazes; surface chemistry of solids and solid state chemistry related to heterogeneous catalysis. *Mailing Add:* Dept of Chem Calif Polytech State Univ San Luis Obispo CA 93407

CIEGLER, ALEX, microbiology, see previous edition

CIER, H(ARRY) E(VANS), b Monroe, La, Sept 16, 12; m 31; c 3. CHEMICAL ENGINEERING. *Educ:* La State Univ, BS, 33. *Prof Exp:* Chem engr develop div, Esso Standard Oil Co, 34-36; res chem engr res & develop div, Humble Oil & Ref Co, 36-42, 46-48, sr res chem engr, 48-55, res specialist, 55-60, sr res specialist, 60-63, res assoc, 64-65; staff adv to vpres chem, Esso Res & Eng Co, 65-66, eng assoc chem raw mat staff, Esso Res Labs, La, 66-67, res assoc res planning, Baytown Chem Res Labs, 67-71; chief process engr, Jovan Consult Engrs, Tehran, Iran, 71, consult, 72; sr engr, C F Braun & Co, 75; RETIRED. *Mem:* Fel Am Inst Chem; Am Inst Chem Engrs. *Res:* Development of petroleum processes; petrochemical processes; research planning. *Mailing Add:* 2027 Lakeview Dr Baytown TX 77520

CIERESZKO, LEON STANLEY, b Holyoke, Mass, July 30, 17; m 43; c 1. BIOCHEMISTRY. *Educ:* Mass State Col, BS, 39; Yale Univ, PhD(physiol chem), 42. *Prof Exp:* Lab asst physiol chem, Yale Univ, 39- 42; res biochemist, Med Res Div, Sharp & Dohme, Inc, Pa, 42-45; instr biol chem, Sch Med, Univ Utah, 45-46; instr chem, Univ Ill, 46-48; from asst prof to assoc prof, 48-56, chmn dept, 69- 70, PROF CHEM, UNIV OKLA, 56- *Concurrent Pos:* Fulbright fel, Zool Sta, Naples, Italy, 55-56; res fel, Yale Univ, 59; off partic, US Prog Biol, Int Indian Ocean Exped, 63; fel & vis investr, Friday Harbor Labs, Seattle, 64; consult prof biochem, Sch Med, Univ Okla, 67-79; vis investr, Dept Marine Sci, Univ PR, 70 & 74-75, Caribbean Res Inst, VI, 71 & Marine Sci Inst, Univ Tex, 74; consult, Caribbean Res Inst, 70-; vis lectr, Col VI, 71; vis prof, Marine Lab, Univ Tex, Port Aransas, 78. *Mem:* AAAS; Am Chem Soc; Geochem Soc; The Chem Soc. *Res:* Comparative biochemistry; chemistry of natural products from marine animals; chemistry of coelenterates and their zooxanthellae; toxic substances of marine origin; biogeochemistry of coral reefs. *Mailing Add:* Dept of Chem Univ of Okla 620 Parrington Oval 211 Norman OK 73069

CIFONELLI, JOSEPH ANTHONY, b Utica, NY, Mar 19, 16; m 49; c 2. CARBOHYDRATE CHEMISTRY. *Educ:* Univ Minn, PhD(biochem), 52. *Prof Exp:* Res assoc carbohydrate chem, Univ Minn, 53; res assoc pediat, Bobs Roberts Hosp, 53-64, RES ASSOC BIOCHEM, LA RABIDA INST, 64-; PROF PEDIAT, UNIV CHICAGO, 71- *Concurrent Pos:* Assoc prof pediat, Univ Chicago, 67-71. *Mem:* Am Chem Soc; Am Soc Biol Chemists. *Res:* Biosynthesis of mucopolysaccharides; enzyme chemistry. *Mailing Add:* Dept of Pediat Pritzker Sch of Med Univ of Chicago Chicago IL 60637

CIFTAN, MIKAEL, b Istanbul, Turkey, Aug 12, 35; US citizen; m 57; c 1. THEORETICAL PHYSICS. *Educ:* Robert Col, Istanbul, BSc, 57; Mass Inst Technol, MSc, 59; Duke Univ, PhD(physics), 67. *Prof Exp:* Res physicist, Raytheon Co, 60-65; res assoc physics, Ind Univ, Bloomington, 68-70; DIR THEORET PHYSICS, US ARMY RES OFF-DURHAM, 70- *Concurrent Pos:* Adj prof physics, Duke Univ, 70- *Mem:* Am Phys Soc. *Res:* Symmetry principles in physics and representation theory; elementary particle phenomenology; special functions via group theory; theoretical and experimental laser physics, spectroscopy; biomethematical approach to experimental histocompatibility and genetic mapping; theoretical solid state physics; statistical physics. *Mailing Add:* US Army Res Off PO Box 12211 Research Triangle Park NC 27709

CIGNETTI, JESS A, science education, see previous edition

CIHACEK, LARRY JOSEPH, b North Bend, Nebr, Apr 21, 48; m 73; c 1. SOIL CHEMISTRY, PLANT NUTRITION. *Educ:* Univ Nebr-Lincoln, BS, 70, MS, 72; Iowa State Univ, PhD(soil fertil), 79. *Prof Exp:* Res asst agron, Univ Nebr, Lincoln, 70-72; res asst soil, Iowa State Univ, 73-75, res assoc, 75-78; ASST PROF AGRON, NMEX STATE UNIV, 78- *Mem:* Soil Sci Soc Am; Am Soc Agron; AAAS; Int Soc Soil Sci; Coun Agr Sci & Technol. *Res:* Correction of micronutrient deficiencies in grain sorghum; evaluation of the status of nitrogen in cropland soils; evaluation of the mineral nutrition requirements of field crops grown under irrigation. *Mailing Add:* Southeastern Br Agr Sta NMex State Univ Rte 1 Box 121 Artesia NM 88210

CIHONSKI, JOHN LEO, b Butler, Pa, Oct 24, 48; m 72. INORGANIC CHEMISTRY. *Educ:* Slippery Rock State Col, BA, 71; Tex A&M Univ, PhD(chem), 75. *Prof Exp:* Res assoc chem eng, Tex A&M Univ, 75; SR RES CHEMIST CATALYSIS, EL PASO PROD CO, 75- *Mem:* Am Chem Soc; AAAS. *Res:* Solid waste disposal by microbal decomposition; industrial heterogeneous catalysis with continued interests in organometallic photochemistry and molecular spectroscopy. *Mailing Add:* El Paso Prod Co PO Box 3986 Odessa TX 79760

CIMBERG, ROBERT LAWRENCE, b New York, NY, Nov 15, 44. MARINE BENTHIC ECOLOGY, ENVIRONMENTAL IMPACTS. *Educ:* Southern Ill Univ, BS, 67; Calif State Univ, MS, 75; Univ Southern Calif, PhD(biol), 78. *Prof Exp:* Res asst, Calif State Univ, Humboldt, 68-69; res asst, Univ Southern Calif, 69-74, lab instr embryol, Catalina Marine Sci Ctr, 71-74; lectr ecology, Univ Calif, Irvine, 78-80; SR MARINE BIOL, VTN ORE INC, 80- *Concurrent Pos:* Lectr biol, Calif State Univ, Los Angeles, 79. *Mem:* Sigma Xi; AAAS; Am Soc Zoologists. *Res:* Marine benthic ecology from Alaska to Baja California, including ecology of intertidal and subtidal habitats and impacts of environmental factors and pollutants on physiological and community processes. *Mailing Add:* 232 SW Hamilton St Portland OR 97201

CIMENT, MELVYN, b New York, NY, Sept 23, 41; m 66; c 2. NUMERICAL ANALYSIS. *Educ:* Univ Miami, Fla, BS, 62; NY Univ, MS, 64, PhD(math), 68. *Hon Degrees:* JD, Am Univ, 78. *Prof Exp:* From instr to asst prof math, NY Univ, 67-69; asst prof, Univ Mich, 69-70; vis lectr, Tel Aviv Univ, 70-71; asst prof, Univ Mich, 71-72; mathematician, Naval Surface Weapons Ctr, Silver Spring, Md, 72-77; SR APPL MATHEMATICIAN, NAT BUR STANDARDS, 77- *Concurrent Pos:* Courant Inst Math Sci fel, NY Univ, 62-66; cong sci fel, US Senate Comt Com Sci & Transp, 80-81; fel, Dept Com Sci & Technol, 80-81. *Honors & Awards:* Group Super Achievement Award, Naval Surface Weapons Ctr, 76. *Mem:* Am Math Soc; Soc Indust & Appl Math. *Res:* Numerical solution of partial differential equations; design and analysis higher order compact implicit methods; computer resources and technology policy issues. *Mailing Add:* 11208 Bybee St Silver Spring MD 20902

CIMINERA, JOSEPH LOUIS, b Philadelphia, Pa, Dec 4, 17; m 45; c 2. PHARMACY, BIOSTATISTICS. *Educ:* Philadelphia Col Pharm & Sci, BSc, 38; Villanova Univ, MSc, 60. *Hon Degrees:* DSc, Philadelphia Col Pharm & Sci, 69. *Prof Exp:* Pharmaceut worker, 31-38; res assoc, 38-49, mgr statist serv, 49-71, res fel, 71-72, sr res fel, 72-77, sr invest, 77-81, DIR BIOMET RES, MERCK SHARP & DOHME RES LABS, 81- *Concurrent Pos:* Mem clin guidelines comt, FDA-Pharmaceut Mfrs Asn, 70-; mem panel on drug bioavailability studies, US Pharmacopoeia, 70- *Mem:* Am Pharmaceut Asn; Am Statist Asn; Biomet Soc (secy-treas, 78-); Acad Pharmaceut Sci. *Res:* Biometry; pharmaceutical chemistry. *Mailing Add:* Merck Sharp & Dohme Res Lab West Point PA 19486

CINADER, BERNHARD, b Vienna, Austria, Mar 30, 19; c 1. IMMUNOCHEMISTRY. *Educ:* Univ London, BSc, 45, PhD, 48, DSc, 58. *Prof Exp:* Asst, Lister Inst Prev Med, Eng, 45-46, Beit Mem fel, 49-53, Agr Res Coun grantee, 53-56; fel immunochem, Inst Path, Western Reserve Univ, 48-49; prin sci officer, Dept Exp Path, Agr Res Coun Inst Animal Physiol, Eng, 56-58; head subdiv immunochem div biol, Ont Cancer Inst, 58-69; assoc prof, 58-69, dir, Inst Immunol, 71-81, PROF MED BIOPHYS & MED GENETICS, UNIV TORONTO, 69-, PROF, DEPT CLIN BIOCHEM, 70- *Concurrent Pos:* Lectr & medallist, Fr Soc Biol Chemists, 54; joint chmn sect immunochem, Int Cong Biochem, Belgium, 55; dir, Austria, 58; spec lectr, Pasteur Inst, 60; pub lectr, Univ Col, Univ London, 63; Enrique E Ecker lectr, Western Reserve Univ, 64; vis prof, Univ Alta, 68 & Univ Manitoba; Pfizer fel, Inst Clin Res, Montreal, 72; A Harrington lectr, State Univ NY, Buffalo, 74; guest lectr, Acads Sci, Czech & Hungary & Acad Med, Rumania, 74. Mem grant panel epidemiol, immunol, microbiol, path & virol, Nat Cancer Inst; mem comt on antilymphocytic serum, Med Res Coun, chmn grants panel immunol & transplantation, 70; mem expert adv panel on immunol, WHO, 70-, mem task force standardization immune reagents, 73-; mem spec comt clin immunol, Royal Col Physicians & Surgeons; pres, Int Union Immunol Socs, 69-74; chmn immunol comt, Biol Coun Can; mem, Adv Bd, Human Reprod Task Force Steering Comt, WHO, Med Univ SC, Centre Immunol, Buffalo & Amsterdam chmn, Int Union Immunol Socs-WHO Inst, 71-79; mem, Can Sci Deleg to USSR, 75; mem, Can Nat Comt Immunol, 77; alt rep IUIS, Int Coun Sci Unions, 78-; vis prof, Inst Res Reprod, 81; mem gov coun, Univ Toronto, 82. *Mem:* Am Asn Immunologists; Brit Soc Immunologists; Can Soc Immunol (pres, 66-69 & 79-81); fel Royal Soc Can; Can Fedn Biol Socs (vchmn, 75-76, chmn, 76-77). *Res:* Immunochemistry and genetics of mammalian polymorphic proteins; antibodies to enzymes; regulation of the immune response; acquired immunological tolerance; allotypes; age dependent changes in cellular interactions of immune system, antibody synthesis; tumor immunology. *Mailing Add:* Inst Immunol Med Sci Bldg Univ of Toronto Toronto ON M5S 1A1 Can

CINADR, BERNARD F(RANK), b Brecksville, Ohio, June 5, 33; m 61; c 1. CHEMICAL ENGINEERING. *Educ:* Case Inst Technol, BS, 55, PhD(phys chem), 60. *Prof Exp:* Asst polymer chem, Case Inst Technol, 59-60; res chemist, 60-61, res engr, 61-63, sr res engr, 63-69, sect leader, 69-76, SR RES & DEVELOP ASSOC, CHEM DIV, B F GOODRICH RES CTR, 76- *Mem:* Am Inst Chem Engrs; Am Chem Soc. *Res:* Polymerization chemistry; polymerization process research, including monomer purification, polymerization and isolation and drying of polymers; process design and cost estimation. *Mailing Add:* 9921 Brecksville Rd Brecksville OH 44141

CINCOTTA, JOSEPH JOHN, b Queens, NY, Sept 15, 31; m 55; c 3. ANALYTICAL CHEMISTRY. *Educ:* Columbia Univ, BS, 53; City Univ New York, MS, 66. *Prof Exp:* Anal chemist, Am Molasses Co, 53-59; anal res chemist, Am Cyanamid Co, 59-68 & M W Kellogg Co, 68-69; SR ANAL CHEMIST, CONOCO INC CO, 69- *Mem:* Am Chem Soc; fel Am Inst Chemists. *Res:* Gas chromatography; coulometry; spectrophotometry; atomic absorption spectrometry and liquid chromatography. *Mailing Add:* 5025 Cloudburst Hill Columbia MD 21044

CINK, CALVIN LEE, b Valley City, NDak, March 1, 47; m 70; c 2. BEHAVIORAL ECOLOGY. *Educ:* NDak State Univ, Fargo, BS, 69; Univ Nebr, Lincoln, MS, 71; Univ Kans, Lawrence, PhD(biol), 77. *Prof Exp:* ASST PROF BIOL, BAKER UNIV, 76- *Concurrent Pos:* Vis instr, Biol Dept, Univ Nebr at Omaha, 79, Creighton Univ, Omaha, 80; ed, Winter Bird Pop Studies, 80- *Mem:* Ecol Soc Am; Animal Behav Soc; Am Ornithologists Union; Wildlife Soc; Sigma Xi. *Res:* Vertebrate ecology and behavior; structure of bird communities; population ecology; determinants of territory size; philopatry; dispersal; breeding biology; comparative ethology; animal communication including song dialects. *Mailing Add:* Biol Dept Baker Univ Baldwin City KS 66006

CINLAR, ERHAN, b Divrigi, Turkey, May 28, 41; US citizen. MATHEMATICAL STATISTICS, OPERATIONS RESEARCH. *Educ:* Univ Mich, BSE, 63, MA, 64, PhD(indust eng), 65. *Prof Exp:* From asst prof to assoc prof opers res, Northwestern Univ, 65-71; vis prof, Stanford Univ, 71-72; PROF OPERS RES, NORTHWESTERN UNIV, EVANSTON, 72- *Concurrent Pos:* Assoc ed, J Stochastic Processes & Their Applns, Res & Mgt Sci; vis prof statist, Princeton Univ, 79-80. *Mem:* Am Math Soc; fel Inst Math Statist; Inst Mgt Sci. *Res:* Stochastic processes; theory of regeneration; Markov processes and boundary theory; Markov renewal theory; point processes; random measures. *Mailing Add:* Dept of Indust Eng Northwestern Univ Evanston IL 60201

CINO, PAUL MICHAEL, b New York, NY, Dec 8, 46; m 73; c 1. INDUSTRIAL MICROBIOLOGY. *Educ:* Hunter Col, BA, 68; Rutgers Univ, MS, 70, PhD(microbiol), 73. *Prof Exp:* Res fel, Waksman Inst Microbiol, Rutgers Univ, 73-75; res investr, 75-81, SR RES INVESTR MICROBIOLOGIST, E R SQUIBB & SONS INC, 81- *Mem:* Am Soc Microbiol; Soc Indust Microbiol. *Res:* Microbial bioconversions and enzymatic synthesis of microbial products; new screening techniques. *Mailing Add:* Squibb Inst for Med Res Georges Rd New Brunswick NJ 08903

CINOTTI, ALFONSE A, b Jersey City, NJ, Jan 1, 23; m 46; c 5. MEDICINE, OPHTHALMOLOGY. *Educ:* Fordham Univ, BS, 43; Long Island Univ, MD, 46; Am Bd Ophthal, dipl. *Prof Exp:* From asst prof surg & ophthal to assoc prof ophthal, 57-73, PROF OPHTHAL & CHMN DEPT, COL MED NJ, 73- *Concurrent Pos:* Assoc examr, Am Bd Ophthal, 53-63; dir resident training ophthal, New York Eye & Ear Infirmary, 55-63, asst dir inst ophthal, 57-63, attend ophthalmologist & dir glaucoma, 63-70, consult glaucoma, 70-; chmn eye health screening prog, State of NJ, 58-76; dir ophthal, Jersey City Med Ctr, 63 & Col Hosp, Newark, 71-; med dir, Eye Inst NJ, 74-; mem bd joint comn, Allied Health Personnel Ophthal. *Mem:* Fel Am Col Surg; Asn Res Vision & Ophthal; Am Asn Ophthal; Am Asn Ophthal (pres, 78-); Am Acad Ophthal. *Res:* Influence of hormones and methods of case finding of glaucoma; optic nerve in glaucoma; secondary glaucomas diabetic cataracts; scanning electron microscopy of human cataract; trace metals in retinitis pigmentosa; color field studies in retinitis pigmentosa; comparative studies of biomicroscopy of cataracts in vivo with scanning electron microscopy. *Mailing Add:* Dept of Ophthal 15 S Ninth St Newark NJ 07107

CINOTTI, WILLIAM RALPH, b Jersey City, NJ, Sept 14, 26; m 54; c 2. PROSTHODONTICS, PERIODONTICS. *Educ:* Georgetown Univ, BS, 46, DDS, 51; NY Univ, cert periodont, 64. *Prof Exp:* Intern oral surg, Martland Med Ctr, 51-52; pvt pract, 52-60; from clin instr to clin asst prof dent, Sch Dent, Seton Hall Univ, 60-67; clin assoc prof, 67-68, assoc prof, 68-71, PROF DENT, NJ DENT SCH, COL MED & DENT NJ, 71-, ACTG CHAIRPERSON, DEPT REMOVABLE PROSTHODONTICS, 77- *Concurrent Pos:* Dir dept dent serv, Hudson County, NJ, 70-; pres, Hudson County Ment Health Asn, 75-77, pres emer, 77-; mem bd dirs, Ment Health Asn NJ & Hudson County Men Health Asn. *Mem:* Am Prosthodont Soc; fel Am Col Dent; Am Geriat Soc; Royal Soc Health; fel Int Col Dent. *Res:* Termporomandibular joint dysfunction; desensitization of teeth; psychologic evaluation of dental patients; evaluation of efficacy of denture adhesive and denture cleanser; evaluation of oral appliances in treatment of reflex spasm of the masticatory muscles; evaluation of cost control procedures for the fabrication of overlay complete dentures. *Mailing Add:* NJ Dent Sch 100 Bergen St Newark NJ 07103

CINQUINA, CARMELA LOUISE, b Philadelphia, Pa, Mar 11, 36. BACTERIOLOGY. *Educ:* West Chester State Teachers Col, BS, 57; Villanova Univ, MS, 63; Rutgers Univ, PhD(bact), 68. *Prof Exp:* Instr biol & phys educ, York Jr Col, 57-61; from instr to asst prof biol, 61-68, assoc prof, 68-69, prof bact, 69-77, PROF BIOL, WEST CHESTER STATE COL, 77- *Mem:* AAAS; Am Soc Microbiol. *Res:* The effect of caffeine on growth in bacterial cells particularly on morphological changes, variation in lipid composition and changes in cyclic adenosine monophosphate phosphodiesterase activity. *Mailing Add:* Dept of Biol West Chester State Col West Chester PA 19380

CINTI, DOMINICK LOUIS, b Wilkes-Barre, Pa, Dec 16, 39; m 67. PHYSIOLOGY, PHARMACOLOGY. *Educ:* Univ Scranton, BS, 61; Jefferson Med Col, MS, 66, PhD(physiol), 68; Drexel Inst Technol, MSBmE, 69. *Prof Exp:* Sr med technician, Jefferson Med Col, 62-63, asst, 64-66; instr physiol, Sch Med, Temple Univ, 66-67; Nat Heart Inst fel, 67-69; res assoc pharmacol, Sch Med, Yale Univ, 69-72; vis scientist, Karolinska Inst, Stockholm, 72-73; asst prof, 73-77, ASSOC PROF PHARMACOL, HEALTH CTR, UNIV CONN, FARMINGTON, 77- *Res:* Hepatic membrane bound enzymes, such as mixed function oxidase system; microsomal electron transport system; microsomal fatty acid elongation system. *Mailing Add:* Dept of Pharmacol Univ of Conn Health Ctr Farmington CT 06032

CINTRON, CHARLES, cell biology, biochemistry, see previous edition

CIOCHON, RUSSELL LYNN, b Altadena, Calif, Mar 11, 48. PALEOANTHROPOLOGY, PRIMATE PALEONTOLOGY. *Educ:* Univ Calif, Berkeley, BA, 71, MA, 74, PhD(anthrop), 82. *Prof Exp:* Lectr sociol & anthrop, 78-81, RES ASSOC BIOL, UNIV NC, 81- *Mem:* Am Anthrop Asn; Am Asn Physical Anthropologists; AAAS; Soc Syst Zool; Soc Vert Paleont. *Res:* Paleoanthropology, primarily primate paleontology; documenting the Tertiary evolutionary history of the primates through both field collecting and museum analysis. *Mailing Add:* 415 Ridgeway Ave Charlotte NC 28204

CIOFFI, PAUL PETER, b Cervinara, Italy, June 29, 96; nat US; m 26; c 2. MAGNETISM. *Educ:* Cooper Union, BS, 19, EE, 22; Columbia Univ, AM, 24. *Prof Exp:* Mem tech staff, Bell Tel Labs, 17-61; consult, Arnold Eng Co, Ill, 61-65; MAGNETICS TECHNOL CONSULT, 65- *Mem:* AAAS; fel Am Phys Soc; Inst Elec & Electronics Engrs; NY Acad Sci; Sigma Xi. *Res:* Magnetic measurements, materials and circuits; ideal magnetic circuit through superconductivity; electromagnets for intense magnetic fields. *Mailing Add:* 132 Kent Pl Blvd Summit NJ 07901

CIONCO, RONALD MARTIN, b Erie, Pa, Dec 4, 34; m 55; c 3. MICROMETEOROLOGY, METEOROLOGY. *Educ:* Pa State Univ, BS, 57; Cornell Univ, MS, 71. *Prof Exp:* Meteorologist, Army Res & Develop, Meteorol Dept, Electronics Command, 57-58; weather forecaster, Army Res & Develop, Signal Corps, Evans Labs, US Army, 58-60; res meteorologist micro-meteorol, Atmospheric Sci Lab, ERDA, 60-70; RES METEOROLOGIST MICRO- & MESO-METEOROL, ATMOSPHERIC SCI LAB, ERADCOM, 71- *Mem:* Am Meteorol Soc; Sigma Xi. *Res:* Micrometeorological modeling of air flow within and above vegetative canopies including their turbulence and energy budget aspects; mesometeorological modeling of the wind field over complex terrain. *Mailing Add:* 1012 Cedardale Las Cruces NM 88002

CIOSEK, CARL PETER, JR, b Montclair, NJ, Oct 9, 43; m 66; c 1. CELL BIOLOGY, RHEUMATOLOGY. *Educ:* Univ Mass, BS, 66; Univ Vt, PhD(med microbiol), 73. *Prof Exp:* Res assoc microbiol, Hazelton Labs, 66-68; res assoc rheumatology, Col Med, Univ Vt, 73-77; fel, 77-79, RES INVESTR RHEUMATOLOGY, INST MED RES, E R SQUIBB & SONS, 79- *Concurrent Pos:* Nat Arthritis Found fel, 75-77. *Mem:* Am Rheumatism Asn; NY Acad Sci; Tissue Cult Asn; Am Soc Microbiol. *Res:* Connective tissue diseases, especially rheumatoid arthritis; inflammation; autoimmunity; cell defense mechanisms; collagenase, especially proteolytic enzymes; prostaglandins, especially cyclic nucleotides; membrane receptors; cell culture; virology. *Mailing Add:* Inst of Med Res Box 4000 Princeton NJ 08540

CIPAU, GABRIEL R, b June 18, 41. CHEMICAL ENGINEERING, COMPUTER SCIENCE. *Educ:* Timisoara Polytech Inst, BS, 64, PhD(chem eng), 68; ECarolina Univ, MS, 73. *Prof Exp:* Asst prof chem eng, Timisoara Polytech Inst, 64-70; dir tech serv, 70-78, VPRES PROD & ENG, BURROUGHS WELLCOME CO, 78- *Concurrent Pos:* Res grant, Timisoara Polytech Inst, 64-68. *Mem:* Am Chem Soc; Am Mgt Asn; Int Soc Pharmaceut Enrs. *Res:* Applications of computers in process control, laboratory automation and engineering design. *Mailing Add:* Burroughs Wellcome Co 3030 Cornwallis Rd Research Triangle Park NC 27709

CIPERA, JOHN DOMINIK, b Czech, Aug 7, 23. ORGANIC BIOCHEMISTRY. *Educ:* Tech Univ, Czech, Ing, 48; Univ Toronto, MSA, 51; McGill Univ, PhD(chem), 54. *Prof Exp:* Asst chem, Col Forestry, State Univ NY, 55-56; res assoc, Univ Pittsburgh, 56-58; RES SCIENTIST, ANIMAL RES INST, CAN DEPT AGR, 58- *Honors & Awards:* Eddy Found Award, 52. *Mem:* Am Chem Soc; Biochem Soc; Chem Inst Can. *Res:* Organic chemistry of naturally occurring polymers; peptides; glycosaminoglycans; chemistry and physiology of connective tissues; role of organic matrix in calcification processes. *Mailing Add:* Dept Poultry Nutrit Can Dept Agr K W Neattey Bldg Ottawa ON K1A 0C6 Can

CIPOLLA, JOHN WILLIAM, JR, b Clifton Heights, Pa, Aug 7, 42; m 67. KINETIC THEORY OF GASES, RADIATIVE TRANSFER. *Educ:* Drexel Univ, BSME, 65; Brown Univ, ScM, 67, PhD(eng), 69. *Prof Exp:* Res scientist, Inst Physics, Univ Milan, 69-70; res scientist, Max-Planck-Inst Fluid Mech, 70-71; from asst prof to assoc prof, 71-81, PROF MECH ENG, NORTHEASTERN UNIV, 81- *Concurrent Pos:* Res scientist, Max-Planck-Inst Fluid Mech, 73-75; vis asst prof, Brown Univ, 78-79. *Mem:* Sigma Xi; Am Phys Soc; Am Soc Mech Engrs; Soc Eng Sci. *Res:* Theoretical research of non-equilibrium problems areas in the thermal sciences, particularly with respect to heat and mass transfer, interfacid phenomena, plasma physics and radiative transfer. *Mailing Add:* Dept Mech Eng 435 LA Northeastern Univ Boston MA 02115

CIPOLLA, SAM J, b Chicago, Ill, July 24, 40; m 66; c 2. ATOMIC PHYSICS, NUCLEAR PHYSICS. *Educ:* Loyola Univ Chicago, BS, 62; Purdue Univ, MS, 65, PhD(nuclear physics), 69. *Prof Exp:* Asst, Purdue Univ, 62-69; res assoc, 69; asst prof, 69-72, ASSOC PROF PHYSICS, CREIGHTON UNIV, 72- *Concurrent Pos:* Res partic, Oak Ridge Nat Lab, 71-80; Cottrell Col sci grant, Res Corp, USA, 72-75 & 78-80; consult, Omaha Pub Power Dist, 74- *Mem:* Am Phys Soc; Am Asn Physics Teachers. *Res:* Radioactivity measurement; operation of nuclear instrumentation; nuclear spectroscopy measurements; radioactive source preparation; vacuum technology; ion-induced inner-shell ionization measurements in atoms; radiation dosimetry in nuclear power plants. *Mailing Add:* Dept of Physics Creighton Univ Omaha NE 68178

CIPOLLINI, NED EMIDIO, b New Haven, Conn, Oct 8, 49; m 71; c 3. CHEMICAL PHYSICS. *Educ:* Stevens Inst Technol, BS & MS, 71; Dartmouth Col, PhD(chem physics), 76. *Prof Exp:* Fel, Brookhaven Nat Lab, 75-77; SR SCIENTIST, CHEM PHYSICS, SPRAGUE ELEC CO, 77- *Concurrent Pos:* Instr, North Adams State Col, 78-79. *Res:* Ionic and electronic conduction in solids and liquids; charge transfer across interfaces; dielectric breakdown; photo-electro chemical energy conversion. *Mailing Add:* Sprague Elec Co Res & Develop Marshall St North Adams MA 01247

CIPPARONE, JOSEPH ROBERT, pathology, deceased

CIPRIANI, CIPRIANO, b Venezia, Italy, Aug 25, 23; m 54; c 5. MATERIALS SCIENCE ENGINEERING, TECHNICAL MANAGEMENT. *Educ:* Univ Bologna, Italy, PhD(indust chem), 49. *Prof Exp:* Res chemist, Snia Viscosa, Italy, 48-52 & Courtaulds Can Ltd, Ont, 52-57; sr res chemist, Celanese Corp Am, 57-62; supvr res, Fibers Div, Allied Chem Corp, 62-68, dep sci dir, Allied Chem SA, Brussels, 68-72; prin chemist, Fiber Div, FMC Corp, 72-76; prin prod develop chemist, 77-78, mgr prod develop, 78-79, DIR PROD DEVELOP, EL PASO POLYOLEFINS CO, PARAMUS, NJ, 79- *Mem:* Am Chem Soc. *Res:* Etherogeneous catalysis; polymerization of olefins; condensation polymerization; polyamides; polyesters; polymers modification, stabilization, processing and applications. *Mailing Add:* 9 Sunderland Dr Morristown NJ 07960

CIPRIANO, LEONARD FRANCIS, b New York, NY, Feb 26, 38; m 62; c 1. PHYSIOLOGY. *Educ:* City Col New York, BS, 59; Univ Calif, Berkeley, PhD(physiol), 70. *Prof Exp:* Res physiologist, US Army Res Inst Environ Med, Natick, Mass, 70-72; lab dir cardiovasc & pulmonary physiol, Lovelace Found Med Educ & Res, Albuquerque, NMex, 72-76; asst prof physiol dept, Baylor Univ Col Med, Houston, Tex, 76-77; prof, Antelope Valley Col, Lancaster, Calif, 77-80; MEM STAFF, MIL AIRCRAFT TECH SYSTS CO, GEN ELEC CO, 80- *Concurrent Pos:* Instr, Calif State Col, Bakersfield, 73-75; consult space life sci, physiol & biol, 78- *Mem:* Am Physiol Soc; Can Physiol Soc; AAAS; Sigma Xi. *Res:* Cellular and systemic physiology; acclimatization and adaptation to altitude; thermoregulation; exercise physiology; pulmonary and cardiovascular physiology; man's interaction with the environment. *Mailing Add:* Matsco Gen Elec Co PO Box 138 Moffett Field CA 94035

CIPRIANO, RAMON JOHN, b Warsaw, NY. AIR-SEA INTERACTION, CLOUD PHYSICS. *Educ:* State Univ, NY at Geneseo, BA, 67, MS, 69, at Albany, MS, 75, PhD(atmospheric sci), 79. *Prof Exp:* RES ASSOC, ATMOSPHERIC SCI RES CTR, 79- *Concurrent Pos:* Prin investr, 79- *Mem:* Sigma Xi. *Res:* Role played by the oceans in the production of marine aerosol--this aerosol can be highly enriched in various pollutants, and is largely formed by bursting bubbles from breaking waves. *Mailing Add:* Atmospheric Sci Res Ctr Earth Sci Rm 324 State Univ NY 1400 Washington Ave Albany NY 12222

CIPRÍOS, GEORGE, b New York, NY, June 30, 31; m 64. CHEMICAL ENGINEERING. *Educ:* Columbia Univ, BS, 53, MS, 60. *Prof Exp:* Res assoc chem eng, 56-62; sr engr, 62-69, res assoc, 69-77, SR RES ASSOC, EXXON RES & ENG CO, 77- *Mem:* Am Inst Chem Engrs; Am Chem Soc. *Res:* Energy conversion, particularly fuel cells; chemical and refinery process research and development. *Mailing Add:* Govt Res Lab Exxon Res & Eng Co PO Box 8 Linden NJ 07036

CIRIACKS, JOHN A(LFRED), b Milwaukee, Wis, Mar 10, 36; m 60; c 4. CHEMICAL ENGINEERING, PHYSICAL CHEMISTRY. *Educ:* Univ Wis, Madison, BS, 58; Inst Paper Chem, MS, 64, PhD(phys chem), 67. *Prof Exp:* Process engr, Neenah Mill, Wis, 58-59, Niagara Falls Mill, NY, 59-61 & Coosa River Mill, Ala, 63, res chem engr, Res & Eng Div, Wis, 67-75, SR RES SCIENTIST & PROJ LEADER, CONSUMER PROD RES & DEVELOP, KIMBERLY-CLARK CORP, WIS, 75- *Mem:* Tech Asn Pulp & Paper Indust. *Res:* Chemistry and physics of wood pulp fibers; electrokinetic phenomena, mainly charge transport from fibrous networks. *Mailing Add:* 1029 Pembrook Dr Neenah WI 54956

CIRIACKS, KENNETH W, b West Bend, Wis, May 7, 38; c 2. GEOLOGY. *Educ:* Univ Wis, BS, 58; Columbia Univ, PhD(geol), 62. *Prof Exp:* Res scientist, Pan Am Petrol Corp Res Ctr, Stand Oil Co Ind, 62-65, sr res scientist, 65-71, staff res scientist, Res Ctr, 71-72; proj geologist, Amoco Prod Co, Houston, 72-73, dist geologist, 73-75, div geologist, Amoco Prod Co, Denver, 76-77, chief geologist, Amoco Int Oil Co, Chicago, 77-79, mgr, Dept Exploration, Gupco, Cairo, 79-81, MGR REGIONAL EXPLORATION, AMOCO PROD CO INT, HOUSTON, 81- *Concurrent Pos:* NSF fel, Columbia Univ, 62. *Mem:* Geol Soc Am; Am Paleont Soc; Asn Econ Paleont & Mineral; Brit Paleont Asn. *Res:* Late Paleozoic biostratigraphy; taxonomy, evolution and ecology of fossil and living pelecypods; geological aspects of physical and biological processes in modern marine carbonate environments. *Mailing Add:* Amoco Prod Co Int PO Box 4381 Houston TX 77210

CIRIACY, EDWARD W, b Philadelphia, Pa, Feb 12, 24; c 4. FAMILY MEDICINE. *Educ:* Pa State Col, BS, 48; Temple Univ, MD, 52. *Prof Exp:* Intern, Frankford Hosp, Philadelphia, 52-53, resident surg, Frankford & Temple Univ Hosps, 53-54; pvt pract, 54-71; PROF FAMILY PRACT & HEAD DEPT, UNIV MINN MINNEAPOLIS, 71- *Concurrent Pos:* Mem bd & mem res & develop comt, Am Bd Family Pract, 72-75, mem recert exam panel, 74-76; mem adv bd, Mod Med Publ, 74- *Mem:* Am Acad Family Physicians; AMA; Asn Am Med Cols; Pan-Am Med Asn; Soc Teachers Family Med. *Mailing Add:* Dept Fam Pract & Community Hlth Univ Minn Mayo Mem Bldg Box 381 Minneapolis MN 55455

CIRIC, JULIUS, b Kragujevac, Yugoslavia, Nov 10, 22; nat US; m 56; c 4. PHYSICAL CHEMISTRY, CHEMICAL ENGINEERING. *Educ:* Darmstadt Tech Univ, Dipl, 49; Univ Toronto, MASc, 52, PhD, 56. *Prof Exp:* Instr, Univ Toronto, 50-52; jr chem engr, Ont Paper Co, 52-53; chem engr, Shawinigan Chems, Ltd, 56-57; asst res specialist, Sch Chem, Rutgers Univ, 57-59 & Ont Res Found, 59-62; SR RES CHEMIST, MOBIL RES & DEVELOP CORP, 62- *Res:* Ion-exchange; chemical engineering unit operations; inorganic preparative and physical chemistry. *Mailing Add:* Mobil Res & Develop Corp Paulsboro NJ 08066

CIRIELLO, JOHN, b Sannicandro, Italy, Oct 18, 50; Can citizen; m 77; c 2. NEUROPHYSIOLOGY, NEUROANATOMY. *Educ:* Univ Western Ont, BBA, 74, MSc, 77, PhD(physiol), 79. *Prof Exp:* Fel physiol, Can Heart Found, Dept Physiol, Univ Western Ont, 79-80 & McGill Univ, 80-81; ASST PROF PHYSIOL, UNIV WESTERN ONT, 81- *Concurrent Pos:* Instr, Dept Zool, Univ Western Ont, 73-75, univ, 74-80, lectr, Dept Physiol, 78-80, sr res scholar, 81-; instr, Dept Physiol, McGill Univ, 80-81. *Mem:* Am Physiol Soc; Can Hypertension Soc; Can Physiol Soc; Soc Neurosci. *Res:* Peripheral and central neural mechanisms in the pathogenesis of hypertension; central regulation of the circulation. *Mailing Add:* Dept Physiol & Health Sci Ctr Univ Western Ont London ON N6A 5C1 Can

CIRILLO, VINCENT PAUL, b New York, NY, Oct 16, 25; m 49; c 4. BIOCHEMISTRY. *Educ:* Univ Buffalo, BA, 47; NY Univ, MS, 52; Univ Calif, Los Angeles, PhD(biol), 53. *Prof Exp:* Asst biol, Univ Buffalo, 46-47 & NY Univ, 48-50; asst zool, Univ Calif, Los Angeles, 50-53; asst prof prev med & pub health, Sch Med, Univ Okla, 53-56; sr res microbiologist, Anheuser-Busch, Inc, Mo, 56-59; asst prof microbiol, Col Med & Dent, Seton Hall Univ, 59-62, assoc prof biochem, 62-64; assoc prof, 64-69, PROF BIOCHEM, STATE UNIV NY STONY BROOK, 69- *Concurrent Pos:* Fulbright travel award, Israel, 78. *Mem:* Am Soc Biol Chemists; Am Soc Microbiol. *Res:* Mechanisms of sugar transport. *Mailing Add:* Dept Biochem State Univ NY Stony Brook NY 11794

CIRINO, ELIZABETH FAHEY, b Taunton, Mass, Oct 28, 17; m 53; c 1. MARINE ECOLOGY. *Educ:* Mass State Teachers Col, BS, 40; Boston Univ, AM, 51, PhD(biol), 58. *Prof Exp:* From instr to assoc prof, 52-59, prof biol, 59-76, PROF ZOOL, BRIDGEWATER STATE COL, 76- *Mem:* AAAS; NY Acad Sci; Am Soc Limnol & Oceanog; Phycol Soc Am; Ecol Soc Am. *Res:* Intertidal and subtidal communities. *Mailing Add:* Dept of Biol Sci Bridgewater State Col Bridgewater MA 02324

CISIN, IRA HUBERT, b New York, NY, Sept 1, 19; m 46; c 3. STATISTICS. *Educ:* NY Univ, BS, 39; Am Univ, MA, 51, PhD(statist), 57. *Prof Exp:* Asst res dir, Samuel E Gill, 41-42; res technician, Off War Info, 42 & Res Br, War Dept, 42-45; res assoc, Columbia Broadcasting Syst, 45-46; co-chief prof staff, Attitude Res Br, Defense Dept, 46-52; sr res scientist, Human Resources Res Off, George Washington Univ, 52-53; dir res, motivation, morale & leadership, 53-54, adv res design, 54-59; res specialist, Calif Dept Pub Health, 59-62; PROF SOCIOL & DIR SOCIAL RES GROUP, GEORGE WASHINGTON UNIV, 62- *Concurrent Pos:* Consult, Bur Social Sci Res, 54-, Calif Dept Pub Health, 62-81 & Columbia Broadcasting Syst, 64-, Social Res Group, Univ Calif, Berkeley, 70-81, Nat Inst Drug Abuse, 74-81; mem, Surg Gen Adv Comt TV & Social Behav, 69-70. *Mem:* AAAS; Am Asn Pub Opinion Res; Am Statist Asn; Inst Math Statist. *Res:* Development of mathematical models and improvement of measurement techniques for social science; devising statistical procedures for application in problem areas not previously amenable to quantitative approaches. *Mailing Add:* Dept of Sociol George Washington Univ Washington DC 20037

CISLER, WALKER L(EE), b Marietta, Ohio, Oct 8, 97; m 39; c 2. MECHANICAL ENGINEERING. *Educ:* Cornell Univ, ME, 22. *Hon Degrees:* LLD, Univ Detroit, 55, Wayne State Univ, 57, Marietta Col, 58 & Univ Akron, 61; DE, Univ Mich, 56; DSc, Univ Toledo, 59, Ind Tech Col, 59 & Mich Technol Univ, 64; EE, Stevens Inst Technol, 59. *Prof Exp:* Asst gen mgr, Pub Serv Elec & Gas Co, 43; chief engr power plants, Detroit Edison Co, 43-48, exec vpres, 48-51, pres & dir, 51-64, chmn bd, 64-77; pres, 77-81, CHMN, OVERSEAS ADV ASSOCS, INC, 81- *Honors & Awards:* Washington Award; George Westinghouse Gold Medal. *Mem:* Nat Acad Eng; fel Inst Elec & Electronics Engrs; fel Am Soc Mech Engrs; Soc Am Mil Engrs. *Mailing Add:* 1249 Washington Blvd Detroit MI 48226

CISNE, JOHN LUTHER, b Summit, NJ, Apr 27, 47; m 78. PALEOBIOLOGY, STRATIGRAPHY. *Educ:* Yale Univ, BS, 69; Univ Chicao, PhD(geol), 73. *Prof Exp:* asst prof, 73-79, ASSOC PROF GEOL & BIOL, DEPT GEOL SCI, DIV BIOL SCI, CORNELL UNIV, 79- *Concurrent Pos:* Trustee, Paleontol Res Inst, 76-83. *Mem:* Ecol Soc Am; Geol Soc Am; Int Paleontol Asn; Paleontol Soc; Soc Study Evolution. *Res:* Invertebrate biology and paleontology; marine ecology and paleoecology; evolutionary biology; biostratigraphy. *Mailing Add:* Dept Geol Sci Cornell Univ Ithaca NY 14853

CISTONE, FRANK, b Philadelphia, Pa, Sept, 4, 53. ENGINEERING THERMOPLASTICS. *Educ:* Drexel Univ, BS, 76, MS, 79, PhD(org chem), 80. *Prof Exp:* RES CHEMIST, ARCO CHEM CO, 81- *Concurrent Pos:* Adj asst prof chem, Drexel Univ, 81- *Mem:* Planetary Soc. *Res:* Stereoselective reduction of carbon-nitrogen pi systems via complex metal hydrides; polyolefin catalysis chemistry; free radical polymerization of styrene and co-monomers; expandable polystyrene. *Mailing Add:* 3801 W Chester Pike Neutown Square PA 19073

CISZEK, TED F, b Midland, Mich, Jan 26, 42; m 64; c 3. CRYSTAL GROWTH, MATERIALS CHARACTERIZATION. *Educ:* Case Inst Technol, BS, 64; Iowa State Univ, MS, 66. *Prof Exp:* Physicist, Dow Corning Corp, 66-71; consult crystal growth, 71-72; assoc physics, IBM Corp, 72-78; PRIN SCIENTIST, SOLID STATE RES BR, SOLAR ENERGY RES INST, GOLDEN, 78- *Mem:* Am Asn Crystal Growth; Am Phys Soc; Electrochem Soc. *Res:* New crystal growth techniques for photovoltaic materials including silicon, copper indium diselenide and indium phosphide and electrical and structural characterization of these materials. *Mailing Add:* Solar Energy Res Inst 1617 Cole Blvd Golden CO 80401

CITRON, IRVIN MEYER, b Atlanta, Ga, May 5, 24; m 65; c 1. ANALYTICAL CHEMISTRY, SCIENCE EDUCATION. *Educ:* Hebrew Univ, Jerusalem, 58; Emory Univ, MS, 61; NY Univ, PhD(sci educ), 69. *Prof Exp:* Chem lab asst, Israel Defense Dept Labs, Weizmann Inst Sci, 54-56; res asst inorg chem, Hebrew Univ, Jerusalem, 56-58; res asst anal chem, Emory Univ, 58-61; asst prof anal & inorg chem, Troy State Col, 61-62; asst prof, 62-69, asst chmn dept chem, 67-69, assoc prof, 69-74, chmn dept, 75-78, PROF ANAL & INORG CHEM, FAIRLEIGH DICKINSON UNIV, 74- *Concurrent Pos:* Deleg, Colloquium Spectroscopicum Int, Ottawa, 67 & Spectros Symp Can, 69 & Pittsburgh Conf, Anal Chem & Appld Spectros, Cleveland, 79; fac res leave appointment, Argonne Nat Lab, Ill, 81-82. *Mem:* Am Chem Soc; Soc Appl Spectros; Nat Sci Teachers Asn; Nat Asn Res Sci Teaching. *Res:* Use of organometallic complexes for analytical purposes; methods of teaching science at high school and college levels; rare earth metals analysis by x-ray fluorescence and atomic absorption spectroscopy. *Mailing Add:* Dept of Chem Fairleigh Dickinson Univ Rutherford NJ 07070

CITRON, JOEL DAVID, b Brooklyn, NY, Apr 19, 41. ORGANIC CHEMISTRY, POLYMER CHEMISTRY. *Educ:* Polytech Inst Brooklyn, BS, 62; Univ Calif, Davis, PhD(org chem), 67. *Prof Exp:* Teaching assoc chem, Univ Calif, Davis, 67-68; res chemist, Elastomer Chem Dept, 69-80, SR RES CHEMIST, POLYMER PROD DEPT, E I DU PONT DE NEMOURS & CO, INC, 80- *Mem:* Am Chem Soc. *Res:* Elastomers. *Mailing Add:* Elastomer Chem Dept E I du Pont de Nemours & Co Inc Wilmington DE 19898

CITRON, STEPHEN J, b New York, NY, July 3, 33; m 57; c 3. APPLIED MATHEMATICS, SPACE MECHANICS. *Educ:* Rensselaer Polytech Inst, BS, 54, MS, 55; Columbia Univ, PhD(mech), 59. *Prof Exp:* Asst prof, Div Eng Sci, 59-62, from assoc prof to prof aeronaut eng sci, 62-76, exec asst to head sch aeronaut, astronaut & eng sci, 62-65, asst to vpres acad affairs, 68-69, asst vpres acad affairs, 69-76, PROF MECH ENG, PURDUE UNIV, 76- *Concurrent Pos:* Ford Found fel, Harvard Univ, 60-61; sr staff consult, Hughes Aircraft Corp, 62; consult, Off Manned Space Flight, NASA, 62-63 & Res & Develop Div, Avco Corp, 62-65. *Mem:* Am Soc Mech Engrs; Am Soc Eng Educ; fel Am Inst Aeronaut & Astronaut. *Res:* Mathematical techniques in engineering problems; control and application of optimization techniques; orbit mechanics and guidance; industrial management; operations research. *Mailing Add:* Dept of Mech Eng Purdue Univ West Lafayette IN 47907

CIULA, RICHARD PAUL, b Lorain, Ohio, Dec 8, 33; m 59; c 3. ORGANIC CHEMISTRY. *Educ:* Bowling Green State Univ, BA, 55; Univ Calif, MS, 57; Univ Wash, PhD, 60. *Prof Exp:* From asst prof to assoc prof, 60-68, chmn dept, 66-71, PROF CHEM, CALIF STATE UNIV, FRESNO, 68- *Mem:* Am Chem Soc; The Chem Soc. *Res:* Synthesis and properties of small ring compounds, particularly in the cyclobutane series; kinetics and mechanism of the nitrile exchange reaction; synthesis of bicyclic amines. *Mailing Add:* Dept of Chem Calif State Univ Fresno CA 93740

CIVAN, MORTIMER M, b New York, NY, Nov 13, 34; m 61; c 3. PHYSIOLOGY. *Educ:* Columbia Univ, AB, 55, MD, 59. *Prof Exp:* Intern, Presby Hosp, 59-60, asst resident, 60-62; staff assoc biophys, NIH, 62-64; instr med, Harvard Med Sch, 65-68, assoc, 68-69, asst prof, 69-72; assoc prof physiol, 72-77, PROF PHYSIOL, SCH MED, UNIV PA, 77-, ASSOC PROF MED, 72- *Concurrent Pos:* USPHS clin & res fel, Mass Gen Hosp & Harvard Univ, 64-65 & USPHS spec fel, Weizmann Inst Sci, 70-71; Am Heart Asn grant-in-aid, 71-73; NSF grant, 73-; NIH grant, 74-; asst, Mass Gen Hosp, 65-72; estab investr, Am Heart Asn, 71-76; fac scholar, Macy Found, 78-79; overseas fel, Churchill Col, Cambridge Univ, 78-79. *Mem:* Am Soc Clin Invest; Am Physiol Soc; Biophys Soc; Am Soc Nephrology; Soc Gen Physiol (secy, 81-84). *Res:* Kinetics of muscle contraction; transport of solutes and water across membranes. *Mailing Add:* Dept of Physiol Richards Bldg G4 Univ of Pa Sch of Med Philadelphia PA 19174

CIVARDI, FRANK P, b Piacenza, Italy, Sept 20, 30; US citizen; m 57; c 1. CHEMICAL ENGINEERING. *Educ:* Univ Milan, PhD(chem eng), 55. *Prof Exp:* Engr, Nuove Reggiano, 55-57; chemist, Penick & Ford, 57-58; proj engr, Pfaudler Permutit, Inc, 58-63; eng coordr, Chem Develop Corp Div, Gen Elec Co, 63-64, mgr eng, Chem Develop Oper, 64-67; TECH DIR, FOOTWEAR & ALLIED PROD, INMONT CORP, 67- *Res:* Chemical process development; project engineering; product development of polymer film and sheeting; coated fabrics. *Mailing Add:* 1255 Broad Clifton NJ 07013

CIVELLI, OLIVER, b Fribourg, Switzerland, May 8, 49. MOLECULAR BIOLOGY. *Educ:* Swiss Inst Technol, Zurich, Dipl, 73, Dr Natural Sci, 79. *Prof Exp:* Res asst, Swiss Inst Cancer Res, Luasanne, 73-74, Inst Res Molecular Biol, Univ Paris, 74-79; RES ASSOC, DEPT CHEM, UNIV ORE, 79-82. *Res:* Genetic regulation in eucaryotic cells; post transcriptional regulation; gene expression of hormones; neurotransmitters. *Mailing Add:* Dept Chem Univ Ore Eugene OR 97403

CIVEN, MORTON, b Boston, Mass, June 20, 29; m 54; c 2. BIOCHEMISTRY. *Educ:* Harvard Univ, MSc, 53, PhD(biochem), 57. *Prof Exp:* Fel, Harvard Med Sch, 58-59; USPHS fel, Nat Inst Med Res, London, 59-61; RES BIOCHEMIST, US VET ADMIN HOSP, LONG BEACH, 62- *Concurrent Pos:* Asst prof biochem, Univ Southern Calif, 62-68, adj asst prof, 68-; adj assoc prof physiol, Univ Calif, Irvine, 72- *Mem:* AAAS; Brit Biochem Soc; Am Soc Biol Chemists. *Res:* Mechanism of enzyme induction, especially effects of peptide hormones on target cell membranes; mechanisms of action of gonadotropins; enzymatic regulation of amino acid metabolism; biochemistry of adrenal cells; effect of toxic chemicals on adrenocortical secretion. *Mailing Add:* Med Res 151 Vet Admin Hosp Long Beach CA 90822

CIVEROLO, EDWIN LOUIS, plant pathology, plant virology, see previous edition

CIVIAK, ROBERT L, b Brooklyn, NY, Nov 18, 47. NUCLEAR ENERGY POLICY. *Educ:* Rensselaer Polytech Inst, BS, 68; Univ Pittsburgh, MS, 70, PhD(physics), 74; Univ Chicago, MLS, 77. *Prof Exp:* Fel res assoc, Mat Res Prog, Brown Univ, 74-76; ref librarian, Nat Oceanic & Atmospheric Admin, 77-78; ANALYST ENERGY TECHNOL, SCI POLICY RES DIV, CONG RES SERV, LIBRARY CONG, 78- *Mem:* AAAS; Am Nuclear Soc. *Res:* Nuclear energy development and national nuclear energy policy. *Mailing Add:* Cong Res Serv Libr of Cong Washington DC 20540

CIVIN, PAUL, b Rochester, NY, April 29, 19; m 39; c 2. MATHEMATICS. *Educ:* Univ Buffalo, BA, 39; Duke Univ, MA, 41, PhD(math), 42. *Prof Exp:* Instr math, Univ Mich, 42-43 & Univ Buffalo, 43-46; from asst prof to assoc prof, 46-57, PROF MATH, UNIV ORE, 57-, ASSOC PROVOST FOR PLANNING, 77- *Concurrent Pos:* Mem, Inst Advan Study, 53-54; vis res prof, Univ Fla, 60-61; vis prof, Copenhagen Univ, 61-62 & 68-69; consult, Pres, Univ Ore, 73- *Mem:* Am Math Soc. *Res:* Fourier series; topology; two-to-one mappings of manifolds; Banach algebra. *Mailing Add:* Dept of Math Univ of Ore Eugene OR 97403

CIZEK, LOUIS JOSEPH, b New York, NY, Apr 11, 16; m 41; c 2. PHYSIOLOGY. *Educ:* Fordham Univ, BS, 37; Columbia Univ, MD, 41. *Prof Exp:* Intern med serv, Beekman Hosp, NY, 41-42; from instr to asst prof, 46-56, ASSOC PROF PHYSIOL, COL PHYSICIANS & SURGEONS, COLUMBIA UNIV, 56- *Concurrent Pos:* Managing ed, Proc, Soc Exp Biol & Med. *Mem:* Fel AAAS; Am Physiol Soc; Harvey Soc; Soc Exp Biol & Med (secy-treas); Am Soc Zool. *Res:* Water and electrolyte balance. *Mailing Add:* Dept of Physiol Columbia Univ Col Physicians & Surgeons New York NY 10032

CLAASSEN, E(DWIN) J(ACK), JR, b St Joseph, Mo, June 20, 20; m 42; c 3. CHEMICAL ENGINEERING. *Educ:* Mo Sch Mines, BS, 42; Univ Tex, MS, 44, PhD(chem eng), 48. *Prof Exp:* Instr chem eng, Univ Tex, 43-44; res scientist, Bur Indust Chem, 44-50; mgr res & develop, Sid Richardson Carbon Co, 50-69; plant supt, 70-74, ENG DIR, CHAMPION CHEM, INC, 75- *Mem:* Am Inst Chem Engrs; Am Chem Soc; Nat Asn Corrosion Engrs; Soc Petrol Engrs. *Res:* Electric discharge through gases; production and uses of carbon black; production and uses of oil field chemicals. *Mailing Add:* Champion Chem Inc Box 4513 Odessa TX 79760

CLAASSEN, RICHARD STRONG, b Ithaca, NY, May 10, 22; m 45; c 3. MATERIALS SCIENCE ENGINEERING. *Educ:* Cornell Univ, AB, 43; Columbia Univ, MA, 47; Univ Minn, PhD(physics), 50. *Prof Exp:* Asst, Substitute Alloy Material Labs, 44-46 & Univ Minn, 47-50; physicist, 51-53, supvr, 53-57, mgr phys sci res dept, 57-60, dir phys res, 60-68, dir electronic component develop, 68-75, DIR MATERIALS & PROCESS SCI, SANDIA LABS, 75- *Concurrent Pos:* Chmn Nat Sci Seminar, 63; mem, Rocky Mountain Sci Coun, 61-76, chmn, 65-66; mem solid state sci comt, Nat Acad Sci-Nat Res Coun, 65-78, chmn, 74, mem nat material adv bd, 73-76; panel chmn surv mat sci, Nat Acad Sci, 71; mem, Mat Res Adv Comt, NSF, 79, chmn, 81; chmn, Tech Eval Panel, Dept Energy, 80. *Mem:* Fel Am Phys Soc. *Res:* Physics of solids; research and development administration. *Mailing Add:* Sandia Labs Albuquerque NM 87185

CLABAUGH, STEPHEN EDMUND, b Carthage, Tex, Apr 2, 18; m 45; c 3. GEOLOGY. *Educ:* Univ Tex, BS, 40, MA, 41; Harvard Univ, PhD(geol), 50. *Prof Exp:* Asst geol, Univ Tex, 40-41; geologist, US Geol Surv, 42-54; from asst prof to assoc prof, 47-55, chmn dept, 62-66, prof geol, 55-77, Fred M Bullard prof geol sci, 77-80, EMER PROF, UNIV TEX, AUSTIN, 80- *Concurrent Pos:* Nat Res Coun fel, Harvard Univ, 46-47; Piper prof geol, 58. *Mem:* AAAS; fel Geol Soc Am; Am Geophys Union; fel Mineral Soc Am; Geochem Soc. *Res:* Geology of Montana corundum deposits; tungsten deposits of Osgood Range, Nevada; igneous and metamorphic rocks of Cornudas Peaks; Texas and New Mexico, and Christmas Mountains, Texas; vermiculite deposits and metamorphic rocks, central Texas; volcanic rocks of western Texas and Mexico. *Mailing Add:* Dept of Geol Sci Univ of Tex Austin TX 78712

CLADIS, JOHN BAROS, b Dawson, NMex, June 21, 22; m 47; c 4. NUCLEAR PHYSICS, PLASMA PHYSICS. *Educ:* Univ Colo, BS, 44; Univ Calif, Berkeley, PhD(nuclear physics), 52. *Prof Exp:* Asst, Univ Colo, 46-47; physicist, Lawrence Radiation Lab, Univ Calif, 48-52; mem res staff, Los Alamos Sci Lab, 52-55; sr staff scientist, Lockheed Missiles & Space Co, 55-65; CONSULT SCIENTIST & SR MEM RES LAB, THEORET SPACE PHYSICS, LOCKHEED PALO ALTO RES LAB, 65- *Mem:* Am Phys Soc; Am Geophys Union. *Res:* High energy nuclear scattering experiments; nuclear weapons diagnostic measurements; Van Allen radiation belt measurements; plasma-magnetic field interactions; magnetospheric physics. *Mailing Add:* Lockheed Palo Alto Res Lab Dept 52-12 Bldg 255 3251 Hanover St Palo Alto CA 94304

CLADIS, PATRICIA ELIZABETH RUTH, b Shanghai, China, July 13, 37; US citizen; m 62; c 2. CHEMICAL PHYSICS, FLUID DYNAMICS. *Educ:* Univ BC, BA, 59; Univ Toronto, MA, 60; Univ Rochester, PhD(physics), 68. *Prof Exp:* Meteorologist, Govt Can, 59-62; programmer-analyst, Katz, Casciato & Shapiro, Ltd, Can, 62; instr physics, Western Conn State Col, 63-64; res asst, Univ Rochester, 64-68, consult, 68; consult, Univ Toronto, 68-69; research, Fac Sci, Lab Physics of Solids, Univ Paris South, Orsay, 69-72, MEM TECH STAFF, BELL LABS, 72- *Concurrent Pos:* Kreeger Wolf distinguished prof, Northwestern Univ, Evanston, 76. *Mem:* Am Phys Soc. *Res:* Liquid crystal defects; static and dynamic properties of liquid crystals. *Mailing Add:* Bell Labs 600 Mountain Ave Murray Hill NJ 07970

CLAESSENS, PIERRE, b Brussels, Belg, Sept 5, 39; m 68; c 2. ELECTROCHEMISTRY. *Educ:* Univ Louvain, Lic, 63, Dr(electrochem), 67. *Prof Exp:* Asst prof chem, Univ Montreal, 67-68; res chemist, 68-70, group leader, 70-73, head dept, 73-81, CHIEF DIV SCIENTIST, NORANDA RES CTR, 81- *Mem:* Am Inst Mining & Petrol Engrs; Can Inst Mining & Metall; Electrochem Soc; Nat Asn Corrosion Engrs. *Res:* Electrodeposition of metals; cathodic process; study of the physical properties of solutions. *Mailing Add:* Noranda Res Ctr 240 Hymus Blvd Pointe Claire PQ H9R 1G5 Can

CLAFF, CHESTER ELIOT, JR, b Brockton, Mass, Apr 17, 28; m 52; c 2. ORGANIC CHEMISTRY. *Educ:* Mass Inst Technol, BS, 50, PhD(org chem), 53. *Prof Exp:* Chemist polymerization, B B Chem Co, Inc, 55-60; gen mgr, Mark Co, 60-64; vpres, M B Claff & Sons, Inc, 64-71; transl mgr, 74-78, TECH TRANSLR, LINGUISTIC SYSTS, INC, 78- *Concurrent Pos:* Res assoc, Mass Inst Technol; partic, Rubber Reserve Prog, Reconstruction Corp, 53-55. *Res:* Preparation and reaction of organosodium compounds; leather technology; acrylic polymerization technology. *Mailing Add:* PO Box 2038 Brockton MA 02403

CLAFLIN, ALICE J, b River Falls, Wis, Feb 12, 32. IMMUNOBIOLOGY. *Educ:* Northern State Col, BS, 53; Univ Wis, PhD(med genetics), 70. *Prof Exp:* Instr med, 70-73, RES ASSOC PROF SURG, SCH MED, UNIV MIAMI, 73- *Mem:* Reticuloendothelial Soc; Am Asn Tissue Banks; Tissue Cult Asn. *Res:* Immune mechanisms of tumor-bearing animals; cellular and humoral immune response with immunosuppressive therapy and transplantation immunology. *Mailing Add:* 8377 Southwest 62nd Ave Miami FL 33143

CLAFLIN, ROBERT MALDEN, b Flint, Mich, Nov 11, 21; m 57; c 3. VETERINARY PATHOLOGY. *Educ:* Mich State Univ, DVM, 52; Purdue Univ, MS, 56, PhD(vet path), 58. *Prof Exp:* Instr res animal dis, 52-58, assoc prof vet path, 58-59, PROF & HEAD DEPT VET MICROBIOL, PATH & PUB HEALTH, SCH VET MED, PURDUE UNIV, 59- *Mem:* Am Vet Med Asn; Conf Res Workers Animal Dis; Int Acad Path. *Res:* Etiology, pathology and epizoology of respiratory diseases of swine, particularly atrophic rhinitis and mucosal diseases of cattle. *Mailing Add:* Vet Microbiol Path & Pub Health Purdue Univ West Lafayette IN 47906

CLAFLIN, TOM O, b Ripon, Wis, Apr 1, 39; m 61; c 1. BIOLOGY. *Educ:* Northern State Col, BS, 61; Univ SDak, MA, 63, PhD(zool), 66. *Prof Exp:* From asst prof to assoc prof, 66-74, PROF BIOL, UNIV WIS-LA CROSSE, 69- *Mem:* AAAS; Am Fisheries Soc. *Res:* Ecology of the benthos of river and lake systems. *Mailing Add:* Dept of Biol Univ of Wis La Crosse WI 54601

CLAGETT, DONALD CARL, b Madison, Wis, Dec 31, 39; m 68; c 4. ORGANIC CHEMISTRY. *Educ:* Pa State Univ, BS, 61; Yale Univ, MS, 63, PhD(chem), 66. *Prof Exp:* Asst res scientist, NY Univ, 67-68; asst prof chem, Northeastern Univ, 68-73; group leader, Dewey & Almy Div, W R Grace & Co, 73-75, sr group leader, 75-78; prod develop specialist, Plastics Bus Div, 78-81, SUPVR, PROCESS DEVELOP, GEN ELEC CO, 81- *Mem:* AAAS; Am Chem Soc; The Chem Soc; NY Acad Sci. *Res:* Chemistry of small ring organic compounds; chemistry of nucleic acids; chemical mutagens; chemistry of arthropod venoms; rubber latex formulations; powdered coatings; urethane foam systems; thermoset molding compounds; melt-polymerization of thermoplastics, process development. *Mailing Add:* Gen Elec Co Plastics Bus Div 1 Plastics Ave Pittsfield MA 01201

CLAGUE, WILLIAM DONALD, b Mobile, Ala, Nov 29, 20; m 44; c 2. SCIENCE EDUCATION. *Educ:* Bridgewater Col, AB, 41; Univ Va, MEd, 52, EdD, 60. *Prof Exp:* Teacher high sch, Ala, 41-43; from asst prof to assoc prof chem, Bridgewater Col, 43-60, dean students, 52-66, prof natural sci, 60-66; PROF EDUC & DEAN GRAD & PROF STUDIES, UNIV LA VERNE, 66-, VPRES ACAD AFFAIRS, 75- *Res:* Choline; methods of laboratory instruction in college chemistry; sources of teaching personnel for church related colleges; development leading to accreditation of a new institution of higher education in a frontier. *Mailing Add:* Univ of La Verne 1950 Third St La Verne CA 91750

CLAIBORNE, H(ARRY) C(LYDE), b New Orleans, La, July 13, 21; m 49; c 4. NUCLEAR & CHEMICAL ENGINEERING. *Educ:* La State Univ, BS, 41; Univ Tenn, MS, 49. *Prof Exp:* From jr engr to asst chem engr, Tenn Valley Authority, 42-46; instr chem eng, Univ Tenn, 46-49; develop engr, 49-52, tech engr, Atomic Energy Comn, 52-53, DEVELOP ENGR, RES STAFF, OAK RIDGE NAT LAB, 53- *Mem:* Am Nuclear Soc. *Res:* Nuclear waste management and the design of geologic waste repositories. *Mailing Add:* Oak Ridge Nat Lab PO Box X Oak Ridge TN 37830

CLAIBORNE, LEWIS T, JR, b Holly Grove, Ark, Sept 17, 35; m 62. ACOUSTICS. *Educ:* Baylor Univ, BS, 57; Brown Univ, PhD(physics), 61. *Prof Exp:* Res assoc physics, Brown Univ, 61-62; res physicist, 62-69, br mgr, Cent Res Labs, 69-74, lab dir, Advan Technol Lab, 75-79, LAB DIR, SYSTS COMPONENTS LAB, CENT RES LABS, TEX INSTRUMENTS, INC, 79- *Mem:* Am Inst Physics; Inst Elec & Electronics Engrs. *Res:* Ultrasonic attenuation; lattice-electron interactions in both normal and superconducting metals; surface acoustic wave devices; charge-coupled devices; microwave devices; infrared detectors. *Mailing Add:* Tex Instruments Inc PO Box 225936 Dallas TX 75265

CLAISSE, FERNAND, b Quebec, Que, Apr 2, 23; m 49; c 2. PHYSICS, METALLURGY. *Educ:* Laval Univ, BSc, 47, DSc(physics), 57. *Prof Exp:* Physicist, Que Dept Natural Resources Labs, 47-54, chief physicist, 54-58; PROF PHYSICS OF METALS, LAVAL UNIV, 58- *Concurrent Pos:* Pres, Claisse Sci Corp, Inc, 76- *Honors & Awards:* Prov Que Sci Award, 58. *Mem:* French-Can Asn Adv Sci; Spectros Soc Can; Soc Appl Spectros. *Res:* Order-disorder reaction; phase transformations; diffusion of atoms in metals; twinning in explosively shocked metals; x-ray fluorescence. *Mailing Add:* Dept of Mining & Metall Laval Univ Quebec PQ G1K 7P4 Can

CLAITOR, L(ILBURN) CARROLL, b Plainview, Tex, July 1, 18; m 46. CHEMICAL ENGINEERING. *Educ:* Tex Tech Col, BS, 41; Agr & Mech Col Tex, MS, 48. *Prof Exp:* Instr chem eng, Agr & Mech Col Tex, 42-45; from engr to supvr, Elliott Co Inc, 45-53, asst to vpres eng, 53-55; asst chief engr, 55-63, mgr, Mgt Info Dept, 63-80, SR CORP ADV, AIR PROD INC, 80- *Mem:* Am Inst Chem Engrs; Asn Comput Mach; Opers Res Soc Am; Am Mgt Asn; Soc Mgt Info Systs. *Res:* Thermodynamics; heat transfer; distillation. *Mailing Add:* Air Prod & Chem Inc PO Box 538 Allentown PA 18105

CLAMAN, HENRY NEUMANN, b New York, NY, Dec 13, 30; m 56; c 3. INTERNAL MEDICINE, IMMUNOLOGY. *Educ:* Harvard Univ, AB, 52; NY Univ, MD, 55. *Prof Exp:* Intern, Barnes Hosp, St Louis, Mo, 55-56, asst resident, 56-57; from asst resident to resident, Mass Gen Hosp, Boston, 57-61; from instr to assoc prof, 62-73, assoc dean fac affairs, 69-71, PROF MED & MICROBIOL & IMMUNOL, UNIV COLO MED CTR, DENVER, 73- *Concurrent Pos:* Fel allergy, Sch Med, Univ Colo, 61-62; consult, Fitzsimons Gen Hosp, 68-; mem immunobiol study sect, NIH, 68-72, mem allergy immunol res comn, 73-77. *Honors & Awards:* Heidelberger lectr, Colo Univ, 74. *Mem:* Fel Am Acad Allergy; Am Asn Immunol; Soc Exp Biol & Med. *Res:* Immunological tolerance to protein antigens; roles of the thymus and bone marrow cells in immunocompetence; effect of corticosteroids on immunocompetence; graft-versus-host reactions; cell interaction in immune responses; immunology of contact allergy; human vasculitis. *Mailing Add:* Univ of Colo Med Ctr Denver CO 80262

CLAMANN, H PETER, b Berlin, Ger, Nov 18, 39; US citizen; m 67; c 2. NEUROPHYSIOLOGY, BIOMEDICAL ENGINEERING. *Educ:* St Mary's Univ, Tex, BS, 61; Johns Hopkins Univ, PhD(biomed eng), 67. *Prof Exp:* Res physiologist, Walter Reed Army Inst Res, 68-70; res fel neurophysiol, Harvard Med Sch, 70-72, instr physiol, 72-73; asst prof physiol, 73-78, ASSOC PROF PHYSIOL, MED COL VA, 78- *Concurrent Pos:* NIH res grant, 75-81. *Mem:* Biomed Eng Soc; Soc Neurosci; Am Physiol Soc; Inst Elec & Electronics Engrs. *Res:* Motor systems neurophysiology; statistical properties of neuronal spike trains; biomedical instrumentation; electromyography. *Mailing Add:* Dept Physiol Med Col Va Box 608 MCU Sta Richmond VA 23298

CLAMBEY, GARY KENNETH, b Fergus Falls, Minn, Feb 27, 45; m 69; c 2. PLANT ECOLOGY. *Educ:* NDak State Univ, BS, 67, MS, 69; Iowa State Univ, PhD(bot), 75. *Prof Exp:* Instr nat sci, Fergus Falls Jr Col, Minn, 68-69; specialist prev med, US Army Med Dept, 69-71; ASST PROF BOT, N DAK STATE UNIV, 74- *Mem:* AAAS; Am Inst Biol Sci; Ecol Soc Am; Sigma Xi. *Res:* Analysis of plant community structure and dynamics in forest and wetland vegetation. *Mailing Add:* Dept of Bot NDak State Univ Fargo ND 58105

CLANCY, EDWARD PHILBROOK, b Beloit, Wis, July 3, 13; m 43; c 5. PHYSICS. *Educ:* Beloit Col, BS, 35; Harvard Univ, AM, 37, PhD(physics), 40. *Prof Exp:* Instr physics, Harvard Univ, 37-43; asst prof, Hamilton Col, 43-44; res assoc, Underwater Sound Lab, Harvard Univ, 44-45, lectr, 46; from asst prof to assoc prof, 46-57, PROF PHYSICS, MT HOLYOKE COL, 57- *Mem:* Am Phys Soc; Am Asn Physics Teachers. *Res:* Radiation physics; optics. *Mailing Add:* Dept of Physics Mt Holyoke Col South Hadley MA 01075

CLANCY, JOHN, b Dungarvan, Ireland, Oct 27, 22; US citizen; m 52; c 6. PSYCHIATRY. *Educ:* Nat Univ Ireland, MB & ChB, 46; FRCPS(C). *Prof Exp:* Intern med, St Vincents Hosp, Dublin, Ireland, 46; pvt pract, 47-51; resident psychiat, Iowa, 51-54; dir psychiat, Union Hosp, Moosejaw, Sask, 55-59; from asst prof to assoc prof, 59-66, PROF PSYCHIAT, UNIV IOWA, 66- *Concurrent Pos:* Mem Gov Comn Alcoholism, Iowa, 60-61 & 66-; consult, Vet Admin Hosp, Iowa City, 66-; dir outpatient & psychiat consult serv, Univ Iowa Hosps, 78. *Mem:* AMA; fel Am Psychiat Asn; Am Psychopath Asn. *Res:* Psychopathology and treatment of alcoholism; psychophysiological relationships; psychotherapy. *Mailing Add:* Dept Psychiat Univ Iowa Psychopathic Hosp Iowa City IA 52242

CLANCY, RICHARD L, b Hardy, Iowa, Dec 26, 33; m 56; c 2. PHYSIOLOGY. *Educ:* Univ Minn, BA, 56, MSc, 61; Univ Kans, PhD(physiol), 65. *Prof Exp:* Asst prof physiol, Ohio State Univ, 67-69; PROF PHYSIOL, SCH MED, UNIV KANS, 69- *Concurrent Pos:* Nat Heart Inst fel, 65-67. *Mem:* AAAS; Am Physiol Soc. *Res:* Acid-base and cardiovascular physiology. *Mailing Add:* Dept of Physiol Univ Kans Med Ctr Kansas City KS 66103

CLANDININ, DONALD ROBERT, b Vandura, Sask, Jan 19, 14; m 38; c 3. POULTRY NUTRITION. *Educ:* Univ BC, BSA, 35, MSA, 36; Univ Wis, PhD(biochem, poultry), 48. *Prof Exp:* Poultry geneticist, Govt Alta, 36-38; from lectr to assoc prof poultry nutrit, 38-53, prof poultry nutrit, 53-79, EMER PROF, UNIV ALTA, 79- *Honors & Awards:* Queen's Silver Jubilee Medal; McHenry Award. *Mem:* Agr Inst Can; fel Poultry Sci Asn; World Poultry Sci Asn; Animal Nutrition Res Coun; Can Soc Nutrit Sci. *Res:* Nutrient requirements of chickens and turkeys; factors affecting protein quality. *Mailing Add:* Dept of Animal Sci Univ Alta Poultry Div Edmonton Can

CLANTON, DONALD CATHER, b Belle Fourche, SDak, Dec 22, 26; m 50; c 2. ANIMAL NUTRITION. *Educ:* Colo State Univ, BS, 49; Mont State Univ, MS, 54; Utah State Univ, PhD(animal nutrit), 57. *Prof Exp:* From asst prof to assoc prof, 58-66, PROF ANIMAL SCI, UNIV NEBR, 66- *Mem:* AAAS; Am Soc Animal Sci; Am Soc Range Mgt. *Res:* Ruminant nutrition, particularly nutrition of reproduction; range nutrition. *Mailing Add:* North Platte Exp Sta Univ Nebr Rt 4 Box 46-A North Platte NE 69101

CLANTON, DONALD HENRY, b Hickory, NC, Sept 3, 26; m 49; c 3. MATHEMATICS. *Educ:* Baylor Univ, BS, 50, MA, 52; Auburn Univ, PhD(math), 64. *Prof Exp:* Teacher high sch, Tex, 50-51; instr math, Allen Mil Acad, 51-53; Univ SC, 53-56 & Auburn Univ, 56-60; Oak Ridge Inst Nuclear Studies fel, Oak Ridge Nat Lab, Tenn, 60-62; from asst prof to assoc prof, 62-70, PROF MATH, FURMAN UNIV, 70-, CHMN DEPT, 76- *Concurrent Pos:* Eve instr, Baylor Univ, 50-51. *Mem:* Math Asn Am; Am Math Soc; Nat Coun Teachers Math. *Res:* Characteristic roots and values, and inclusion regions of matrices. *Mailing Add:* Dept of Math Furman Univ Greenville SC 29613

CLANTON, UEL S, JR, b Brownwood, Tex, June 23, 31; m 56; c 2. GEOCHEMISTRY, ASTROGEOLOGY. *Educ:* Univ Tex, Austin, BS, 55, MA, 60, PhD(geol), 68. *Prof Exp:* Chief computer, United Geophys Corp, 55-56; teaching asst, Univ Tex, Austin, 58-61; res scientist, Environ Health Eng Res Lab, 62-63; PHYS SCIENTIST & GEOLOGIST, GEOL BR, NASA JOHNSON SPACE CTR, 63- *Mem:* AAAS; Geol Soc Am; Microbeam Anal Soc. *Res:* Vapor-phase crystallization in lunar breccias; morphology and chemistry of impact and volcanic glassy droplets; faulting and subsidence along the Texas Gulf Coast. *Mailing Add:* Geol Br NASA Johnson Space Ctr SN 6 Houston TX 77058

CLAPHAM, WENTWORTH B, JR, ecology, environmental management, see previous edition

CLAPP, CHARLES EDWARD, b Holden, Mass, Aug 29, 30; m 53; c 4. SOIL BIOCHEMISTRY. *Educ:* Univ Mass, BS, 52; Cornell Univ, MS, 54, PhD(soil chem), 57. *Prof Exp:* Asst soil chemist, Cornell Univ, 52-56; org chemist, Agr Res Serv, USDA, 56-61; from asst prof to assoc prof, 61-76, PROF SOIL SCI, UNIV MINN, ST PAUL, 76-; RES CHEMIST, AGR RES SERV, USDA, 61- *Mem:* Am Chem Soc; Am Soc Agron; Soil Sci Soc Am; Int Soil Sci Soc; Sigma Xi. *Res:* Chemistry of soil organic matter; clay-organic complexes; electrophoresis; polysaccharide chemistry; ethylenimine chemistry; viscosity; soil structure; sewage, sludge and wastewater chemistry; soil and crop residue management; nitrogen transformation and modeling; nitrogen 15 in soil-plant-water biosystem. *Mailing Add:* 2847 N Griggs St Paul MN 55113

CLAPP, CHARLES H, b Stamford, Conn, Oct 4, 48. BIO-ORGANIC CHEMISTRY, ENZYMOLOGY. *Educ:* Bowdoin Col, AB, 70; Harvard Univ, PhD(chem), 75. *Prof Exp:* Res fel biochem, Harvard Univ, 75; ASST PROF CHEM, BROWN UNIV, 77- *Mem:* Am Chem Soc; AAAS. *Res:* Mechanisms of enzymatic and related chemical reactions; design of specific enzyme inhibitors. *Mailing Add:* Chem Dept Box H Brown Univ Providence RI 02912

CLAPP, J(OHN) W(ILLIAM), JR, b Greensboro, NC, May 17, 25; m 48; c 4. CHEMICAL ENGINEERING. *Educ:* Elon Col, AB, 46; NC State Col, BChE, 48. *Prof Exp:* Chem engr, 48-53, sr chem engr, 53-61, chief chem engr, 61-66, dept supt, Kodel Develop & Control, 66-77, DEPT SUPT, KODEL FIBER SPINNING, TENN EASTMAN CO, 77- *Mem:* Inst Chem Engrs; Am Asn Textile Tech; Am Soc Qual Control. *Res:* Fiber manufacturing, including acetate, acrylic, modified acrylic, polyester, and polyolefin fibers. *Mailing Add:* Tenn Eastman Co Kingsport TN 37660

CLAPP, JAMES L, b Madison, Wis, Mar 14, 33; m 61; c 3. CIVIL ENGINEERING, REMOTE SENSING. *Educ:* Univ Wis, BS(civil eng) & BS(naval sci), 56, MS, 61, PhD(civil eng), 64. *Prof Exp:* From asst prof to prof civil eng, Univ Wis, Madison, 64-78; DEAN COL ENG & SCI, UNIV MAINE, ORONO, 78- *Concurrent Pos:* Keuffel & Esser fel surv, 61-62; res & study grants, 65- *Honors & Awards:* Emil Steiger Award & Cong Medal for Antarctic Serv, 68. *Mem:* Am Soc Civil Engrs; Am Cong Surv & Mapping; Am Soc Photogram; Nat Soc Prof Engrs. *Res:* Applications of remote sensing to environmental monitoring; multipurpose land information systems. *Mailing Add:* Col of Eng & Sci Univ of Maine Orono ME 04473

CLAPP, JAMES R, b Siler City, NC, Sept 3, 31; m 53; c 2. INTERNAL MEDICINE. *Educ:* Univ NC, MD, 57. *Prof Exp:* Intern & resident med, Parkland Mem Hosp, Dallas, Tex, 57-59; investr kidney & electrolytes, NIH, 61-63; assoc, 63-66, asst prof, 66-70, assoc prof internal med, Sch Med 70-77, PROF NEPHROL & ASSOC PROF PHYSIOL, DUKE UNIV MED CTR, 77- *Concurrent Pos:* USPHS trainee, 59-61 & grant, 63-; fel renol, Southwestern Med Sch, Univ Tex, 59-61; estab investr, Am Heart Asn. *Mem:* Am Physiol Soc; Am Fedn Clin Res. *Res:* Renal physiology and pathophysiology. *Mailing Add:* Dept of Physiol Duke Univ Med Ctr Durham NC 27710

CLAPP, JOHN GARLAND, JR, b Greensboro, NC, Oct 27, 36; m 59; c 3. AGRONOMY. *Educ:* NC State Univ, BS, 59, MS, 61, PhD(crop sci), 69. *Prof Exp:* Asst agr exten agent, NC State Univ, 61-62; exten agronomist, Clemson Univ, 62-63 & NC State Univ, 63-75; SCI AGRONOMIST, ALLIED CHEM CORP, 75- *Concurrent Pos:* Exten agronomist, Nat Soybean Resource Comt, 70- *Honors & Awards:* Geigy Award in Agron, Am Soc Agron, 72; Meritorious Serv Award, Am Soybean Asn, 74. *Mem:* Am Soc Agron. *Res:* Applied on-farm evaluation of fertilizers, herbicides, growth regulators, nematocides, plant population and tillage methods for soybean production. *Mailing Add:* PO Box 2120 Houston TX 77001

CLAPP, JOHN T, b Beech Grove, Ind, Sept 29, 12; m 50; c 4. COMPUTER SYSTEMS ENGINEERING. *Educ:* Purdue Univ, BS, 33; Univ Ill, MS, 40, PhD(chem eng), 42. *Prof Exp:* Chemist, R P Mallory & Co, Indianapolis, 33-38; chem engr, Standard Oil Co, Ind, 42-46; lectr chem, Univ Southern Calif, 46; asst, Calif Inst Technol, 46-47; asst prof, Ore State Col, 47-51; prin engr, Aerojet Gen Corp, 51-68; aerospace engr, Command & Control Sect, 68-69, gen engr comput systs eng, 69-70, ELECTRONIC ENGR, COMPUT SYSTS ENG, SMAMA/MMEEF, McCLELLAN AIR FORCE BASE, 70- *Concurrent Pos:* Consult, Bonneville Power Admin, 50. *Mem:* Am Inst Aeronaut & Astronaut; Asn Comput Mach. *Res:* Heat transfer; thermodynamics; fluid dynamics; metallurgy; solid propellant rockets; aerospace, chemical, electronic, general and mechanical engineering, mathematics and computer programming. *Mailing Add:* 3157 Ellington Circle Sacramento CA 95825

CLAPP, LEALLYN BURR, b Paris, Ill, Oct 13, 13; m 40. ORGANIC CHEMISTRY. *Educ:* Eastern Ill Univ, BEd, 35; Univ Ill, AM, 39, PhD(chem), 41. *Hon Degrees:* PdD, Eastern Ill Univ, 56; LLD, RI Col, 64. *Prof Exp:* Instr high sch, Ill, 35-38; asst chemist, Univ Ill, 39-41; from instr to assoc prof org chem, 41-56, exec officer dept chem, 55-59, PROF ORG CHEM, BROWN UNIV, 56- *Honors & Awards:* Sci Apparatus Makers Award in Chem Educ, Am Chem Soc, 76. *Mem:* Am Chem Soc. *Res:* Chemistry of ethylenimines and other heterocyclic nitrogen compounds. *Mailing Add:* Dept of Chem Brown Univ Providence RI 02912

CLAPP, NEAL K, b Shelby Co, Ind, Oct 14, 28; m 53; c 3. RADIOBIOLOGY, PATHOLOGY. *Educ:* Purdue Univ, BS, 50; Ohio State Univ, DVM, 60; Colo State Univ, MS, 62, PhD, 64. *Prof Exp:* Instr surg, Vet Clins, Colo State Univ, 60-61; EXP PATHOLOGIST, OAK RIDGE NAT LAB, 64-, EXP PATHOLOGIST, OAK RIDGE ASSOC UNIVS, 81- *Mem:* AAAS; Am Vet Med Asn; Radiation Res Soc; Am Asn Cancer Res. *Res:* Radiation pathology; chemical carcinogenesis. *Mailing Add:* Biol Div Oak Ridge Nat Lab Y-12 Oak Ridge TN 37830

CLAPP, PHILIP CHARLES, b Belleville, Ont, Oct 14, 35; US citizen; m 61; c 3. SOLID STATE PHYSICS. *Educ:* Queen's Univ, BS, 57; Mass Inst Technol, PhD(physics), 63. *Prof Exp:* Lectr magnetism, Mass Inst Technol, 63; physicist, Ledgemont Lab, Kennecott Copper Corp, 63-75; head physics & metall group, 75-77; vis assoc prof mat sci, Mass Inst Technol, 77-78; PROF METALL & HEAD DEPT, UNIV CONN, 78- *Concurrent Pos:* Sr vis scientist, Oxford Univ, 69-70; vis prof, Nat Comn Atomic Energy, Buenos Aires, Arg, 72; adj prof physics, Boston Col, 73-78. *Mem:* Metallurgical Soc; Am Phys Soc. *Res:* Alloy research; Martensitic phase transformations; theories of order-disorder phenomena; low temperature physics and magnetism. *Mailing Add:* PO Box 274 Storrs CT 06268

CLAPP, RICHARD CROWELL, b Boston, Mass, July 25, 15; m 46; c 2. ORGANIC CHEMISTRY. *Educ:* Bowdoin Col, AB, 37; Harvard Univ, MA, 39, PhD(org chem), 41. *Prof Exp:* Sr chemist, Am Cyanamid Co, 41-54; res chemist, US Army Natick Res & Develop Command, 54-74, head, Org Chem Group, 74-79; RETIRED. *Concurrent Pos:* Chemist, Nat Defense Res Comt, 40-41. *Mem:* Fel AAAS; Am Chem Soc; Sigma Xi. *Res:* Synthesis of carcinogenic hydrocarbons; synthesis of chemotherapeutic agents; antitubercular compounds; sulfur compounds; heterocyclic compounds; natural products; cyanogenetic glycosides; laser dyes; anthraquinone dyes. *Mailing Add:* 194 Bacon St Natick MA 01760

CLAPP, ROGER EDGE, b Cleveland, Ohio, Oct 9, 19; m 57; c 2. THEORETICAL PHYSICS, BIOPHYSICS. *Educ:* Harvard Univ, AB, 41, AM, 42, PhD(physics), 49. *Prof Exp:* Mem staff microwaves, Radiation Lab, Mass Inst Technol, 42-46, AEC fel, 49-50; sr physicist, Snow & Schule, Inc, 50-52; consult, Ultrasonic Corp, 52-57; staff consult, Adv Industs, Inc, 57-61; staff consult, Air Tech Corp, 61-67; PRES, BASIC RES ASSOC INC, 70-; DEPT STAFF, MITRE CORP, 78- *Concurrent Pos:* Res contractor, US Off Naval Res, 52-54; consult, Airborne Instruments Lab Div, Cutler-Hammer, Inc, NY, 59-75, Carter's Ink Co, 66-76, EPP Corp, 77- & Integral Data Systs, 79- *Mem:* AAAS; Am Phys Soc; Am Geophys Union; Inst Elec & Electronics Eng. *Res:* Nuclear three-body problem; radar ground reflections; electromagnetic radiation from nuclear detonations in the lower atmosphere; electron and muon structure; gravitational theory; entropy flow in biology; photosynthesis; vision; central nervous system. *Mailing Add:* 19 Copley St Cambridge MA 02183

CLAPP, ROGER WILLIAMS, JR, b Tampa, Fla, Aug 31, 29; m 59; c 4. PHYSICS. *Educ:* Davidson Col, BS, 50; Univ Va, MS, 52, PhD(physics), 54. *Prof Exp:* Res physicist, Army Missile Command, Redstone Arsenal, 56-63; asst prof, 63-66, ASSOC PROF PHYSICS, UNIV S FLA, 66- *Mem:* Am Phys Soc; Am Asn Physics Teachers. *Res:* Surface physics; thin films; history of physics. *Mailing Add:* Dept of Physics Univ of SFla Tampa FL 33620

CLAPP, THOMAS WRIGHT, b Fulton, Ky, Sept 3, 37; m 69; c 1. BOTANY, SOIL SCIENCE. *Educ:* Murray State Univ, BS, 63; NDak State Univ, MS, 65; Tex A&M Univ, PhD(range sci), 68. *Prof Exp:* Asst prof, 67-80, ASSOC PROF BIOL, ST CLOUD STATE UNIV, 80- *Mem:* Soc Econ Bot. *Res:* Allelopathy, seed germination; hormonal regulation of plant growth; plant physiology; plant ecology. *Mailing Add:* Dept of Biol St Cloud State Univ St Cloud MN 56301

CLAPP, WILLIAM LEE, b Memphis, Tenn, Feb 16, 43; m 65; c 2. ANALYTICAL CHEMISTRY. *Educ:* Wake Forest Col, BS, 64; Duke Univ, MA, 66, PhD(chem), 69. *Prof Exp:* Res chemist anal chem, R J Reynolds Tobacco Co, 68-69; chem officer, Weapons Develop & Eng Lab, Edgewood Arsenal, US Army, 69-71; res chemist anal chem, 71-72, sect head proj mgt, 72-80, MGR, ANAL TECHNOL DIV, R J REYNOLDS TOBACCO CO, 80- *Mem:* Am Chem Soc; Sigma Xi. *Res:* Research project management. *Mailing Add:* Res Dept R J Reynolds Tobacco Co Winston-Salem NC 27102

CLAPPER, MUIR, b Detroit, Mich, May 26, 13; m 62. INTERNAL MEDICINE. *Educ:* Wayne State Univ, AB, 33, MD, 36, MS, 40. *Prof Exp:* From instr to assoc prof, 40-53, PROF MED, SCH MED, WAYNE STATE UNIV, 53- *Concurrent Pos:* Consult, Dearborn Vet Hosp, 51-, Detroit Mem Hosp, 57-; emer, Harper Hosp, 62- & Detroit Receiving Hosp. *Mem:* AMA; Am Heart Asn; Am Col Physicians; Asn Univ Cardiol; Am Col Cardiol. *Res:* Cardiology. *Mailing Add:* Wayne State Univ Sch of Med 540 E Canfield Ave Detroit MI 48201

CLAPPER, THOMAS WAYNE, b McKean, Pa, Oct 15, 15; m 41; c 3. ORGANIC CHEMISTRY. *Educ:* St Vincent Col, BS, 37; Pa State Univ, MS, 38, PhD(org chem), 42. *Prof Exp:* Res chemist, Pharmaceut Div, Calco Chem Div, Am Cyanamid Co, 40-44, from asst chief chemist to chief chemist, Pharmaceut Dept, 44-48, prod mgr, 48-51, tech dir, Atomic Energy Div, 51-52, gen supt, Chem Processing Plant, 52, asst gen mgr, 52-53; asst to gen mgr, Atomic Energy Div, Phillips Petrol Co, 54; plant mgr, Calera Ref, Chem Construct Corp, 54-56; res mgr, Am Potash & Chem Corp, 56-63, tech dir res, 63-68; dir res, Kerr-McGee Corp, 68-75, mgr technol assessment & planning, 75-81; PRES, CLAPPER ENTERPRISES INC, 81- *Mem:* Am Chem Soc; Electrochem Soc; Am Tech Asn Pulp & Paper Indust; Am Soc Metals; Am Inst Mining, Metall & Petrol Engrs. *Res:* Sulfa drugs; vitamins; chemical processing of uranium; cobalt; high energy fuels; electrochemistry; rare earths; boron compounds; maganese metal and compounds. *Mailing Add:* 12104 Camelot Pl Oklahoma City OK 73120

CLARDY, JON CHRISTEL, b Washington, DC, May 16, 43; m 66; c 2. STRUCTURAL CHEMISTRY, ORGANIC CHEMISTRY. *Educ:* Yale Univ, BS, 64; Harvard Univ, PhD(chem), 69. *Prof Exp:* From instr to prof, Iowa State Univ, 69-78; PROF CHEM, CORNELL UNIV, 78- *Concurrent Pos:* Camille & Henry Dreyfus Found fel, 72; Alfred P Sloan Found fel, 73. *Mem:* Am Chem Soc; Am Crystallog Asn. *Res:* Application of x-ray diffraction to problems of biological and chemical interest; natural products chemistry. *Mailing Add:* Dept Chem Cornell Univ Ithaca NY 14853

CLARDY, LEROY, b Ft Worth, Tex, July 16, 10; m 38; c 1. PHYSICAL CHEMISTRY. *Educ:* Tex Christian Univ, BS, 31, MS, 34. *Prof Exp:* Anal chemist, Armour & Co, Tex, 34-36; chief chemist, Terrell's Labs, 36-37; chemist, Swift & Co, 37-43, physicist, 43-70, mgr control eng div, Eng Res Dept, 70-75; CONSULT, 75- *Res:* Application of instrumentation and automatic control systems to meat packing and allied processes. *Mailing Add:* 835 Edgewater Dr Naperville IL 60540

CLARE, STEWART, b Montgomery Co, Mo, Jan 31, 13; m 36. SOILS & SOIL SCIENCE. *Educ:* Univ Kans, BA, 35; Iowa State Univ, MS, 37; Univ Chicago, PhD(zool), 49. *Prof Exp:* Tech consult, White-Fringed Beetle Proj, Bur Entom & Plant Quarantine, US Civil Serv Comn, 41-42, instr meteorol, Army Air Force Weather Sch, 42-43; res biologist, Midwest Res Inst, Mo, 45-46; mem spec res proj, Univ Mo-Kansas City, Midwest Res Inst & Kansas City Art Inst, 46-49; instr zool, Univ Alta, 49-50, asst prof zool & lectr sci of color, 50-53; asst prof physiol & pharmacol, Kansas City Col Osteop & Surg, Univ Health Sci, 53; lectr, Univ Adelaide, 54-55; sr res officer entom, Ministry Agr & Gezira Res Sta, Sudan Govt, NAfrica, 55-56; sr entomologist, Klipfontein Org Prod Corp, SAfrica, 57; prof biol & head dept, Union Col, Ky, 58-59, chmn div sci, 59-61; prof biol & head dept, Mo Valley Col, 61-62; Buckbee Found prof biol & lectr, Eve Col, Rockford Col, 62-63; prof biochem & chmn dept & mem res div, Kansas City Col Osteop & Surg, Univ Health Sci, 63-67; prof biol, 67-72, dir biol res, 72-74, EMER PROF BIOL, COL EMPORIA, 74-; RES BIOLOGIST & CONSULT, 74- *Concurrent Pos:* Entomologist, US Bur Entom, 37-40; res & study grants, Alta Res Coun, 51-53, Union Col, Ky, 59-61, Mo Valley Col, 61-62, Rockford Col, 62-63, Adirondack Res Sta, 63-66, NIH, 63-65 & Col Emproia, 67-74; consult, Vols for Tech Assistance, 62- & Info Resource, Nat Referral Ctr for Sci & Technol, Libr of Cong, 70-; lectr & consult, Adirondack Res Sta, NY State Univ, Plattsburgh, 62-66. *Mem:* NY Acad Sci; Am Entom Soc; Brit Asn Advan Sci; Arctic Inst NAm; Nat Asn Biol Teachers. *Res:* Comparative physiology-biochemistry; circulation of the Arthropoda; trace elements in invertebrates; capillary movement in porous materials; gums, extractives and extraneous materials of plants; biometeorology; chromatology; history of science; science of color. *Mailing Add:* 405 NW Woodland Rd Indian Hills in Riverside Kansas City MO 64150

CLARENBURG, RUDOLF, b Utrecht, Holland, May 3, 31; US citizen; m 59; c 1. PHYSIOLOGICAL CHEMISTRY. *Educ:* Univ Utrecht, Drs, 59, DSc(chem), 65. *Prof Exp:* Res physiologist, Univ Calif, Berkeley, 59-66; assoc prof, 66-74, PROF PHYSIOL, KANS STATE UNIV, 74- *Mem:* AAAS; Am Physiol Soc; Soc Exp Biol Med. *Res:* Membrane receptors; transport across biological membranes; physiologic significance of asialoglycoprotein receptors in liver; transport of bilirubin and sulfobromophthalein from blood to bile. *Mailing Add:* Dept of Physiol Sci VMS Bldg Kans State Univ Manhattan KS 66502

CLARIDGE, CHARLES ALFRED, b Victoria, BC, Sept 5, 21; m 47; c 4. MICROBIOLOGY. *Educ:* Univ BC, BA, 43; Iowa State Col, PhD(physiol bact), 53. *Prof Exp:* Microbiologist, Merck & Co, Inc, 54-56; microbiologist, Fisheries Res Bd Can, 56-59; MICROBIOLOGIST, BRISTOL LAB, INC DIV, BRISTOL-MYERS CO, 59- *Mem:* AAAS; Am Soc Microbiol; Am Chem Soc. *Res:* Microbial metabolism; microbial transformation of organic compounds; antibiotic fermentations; mutational biosynthesis of new antibiotics by idiotrophic cultures. *Mailing Add:* Silverwood Lane Manlius NY 13104

CLARIDGE, E(LMOND) L(OWELL), b Delaplaine, Ark, June 5, 17; m 39; c 2. CHEMICAL ENGINEERING. *Educ:* Mo Sch Mines, BS, 39, MS, 41, Univ Houston, PhD, 79. *Prof Exp:* Jr res chemist, Wood River Res Lab, Shell Oil Co, 41-43, oper asst, Wood River Ref, 43-47, technologist & asst head exp lab, 47-48, res group leader, Houston Res Lab, 48-51, asst chief res chemist, process res supvr, 51-55, sect leader, Royal Dutch Labs, Amsterdam, 55-57, asst chief res technologist res lab, Shell Oil Co, 57-60, sr technologist mfg res dept head off, NY, 60-64, res assoc, 64-66, sr res assoc, 66-70, sr staff res engr, 70-79, ASSOC PROF CHEM ENG & DIR GRAD PROG PETROL ENG, SHELL DEVELOP CO, 79- *Concurrent Pos:* Petrol eng consult, Conoco & Gulf Univ Res Consortium & Todd, Dietrich & Chase, 81- *Mem:* AAAS; Am Chem Soc; Am Inst Chem Engrs; Soc Petrol Engrs. *Res:* Crude oil recovery processes. *Mailing Add:* 5439 Paisley Houston TX 77096

CLARK, A GAVIN, b Warrington, Eng, Nov 18, 38. MICROBIOLOGY. *Educ:* Univ Edinburgh, BSc, 63, PhD(microbiol), 66. *Prof Exp:* Res asst bact, Med Sch, Univ Edinburgh, 61-62, res asst microbiol, Sch Agr, 63-66; fel soil sci, Univ Alta, 66-68; asst prof, 68-78, ASSOC PROF MICROBIOL, UNIV TORONTO, 78- *Mem:* Brit Soc Appl Bact; Brit Soc Gen microbiol. *Res:* Microbial degradation of crude oil; pathogenicity of Vibro parahaemolyticus. *Mailing Add:* Dept of Microbiol & Parasitol Univ of Toronto St George Campus Toronto ON M5S 1A3 Can

CLARK, ALAN CURTIS, b Springfield, Mass, May 6, 44; m 70; c 2. ORGANIC CHEMISTRY. *Educ:* Bowdoin Col, AB, 66; Ind Univ, PhD(org chem), 70. *Prof Exp:* Vis res assoc chem, Ohio State Univ, 70-71; fel, Univ Cincinnati, 71-73, lectr, 73-74; RES CHEMIST, LUBRIZOL CORP, 74- *Mem:* Am Chem Soc; Sigma Xi. *Res:* Organic synthesis; polymer chemistry; lubricant additive chemistry. *Mailing Add:* 8246 Fairfax Dr Mentor OH 44060

CLARK, ALAN FRED, b Milwaukee, Wis, June 29, 36; m 57; c 4. PHYSICS, MATERIALS SCIENCE. *Educ:* Univ Wis, BS, 58, MS, 59; Univ Mich, PhD(nuclear sci), 64. *Prof Exp:* Nat Acad Sci-Nat Res Coun res assoc low temperature physics, 64-66, staff physicist low temperature physics & mat sci, 66-78, chief thermophys properties of solids, 78-80, CHIEF SUPERCONDUCTORS MAGNETIC MAT, NAT BUR STANDARDS, 81- *Concurrent Pos:* Asst prof mat sci, Colo State Univ, Ft Collins, 65-68; tech ed, Rev Sci Instruments, 74-76; adv ed, Cryogenics, 77-; titanium combustion, mem adv panel, Joint NASA, US Air Force & Fed Aviation Admin panel on titanium combustion, 75- & magnetic energy storage panel, Dept Energy, 77-; chmn, Int Cryog Mat Conf Bd, 79-83. *Honors & Awards:* Superior Accomplishment Award, Nat Bur Standards, 67. *Mem:* Am Nuclear Soc; Am Phys Soc; Combustion Inst; Int Cryogenic Mat Conf. *Res:* Thermophysical properties of materials at low temperatures; transport properties of high purity metals; combustion of metals; critical properties of superconductors. *Mailing Add:* Electromagnetic Technol Nat Bur of Standards Boulder CO 80303

CLARK, ALAN RODERICK, experimental high energy physics, see previous edition

CLARK, ALFRED, b Beverly, Mass, Aug 5, 09; m 35; c 1. PHYSICAL CHEMISTRY, CHEMICAL ENGINEERING. *Educ:* Purdue Univ, BS, 30; Mich State Univ, MS, 32; Univ Ill, PhD(phys chem), 35. *Prof Exp:* Res chemist viscose, North Am Rayon Corp, 35-36; sr res chem catalysis, Battelle Mem Inst, 36-42; div mgr, Res Catalysis, Publicker Com Alcohol Co, 42-44; br mgr res, Phillips Petrol Co, 44-59, sr res scientist, 59-71; prof chem eng, Univ Okla, 71-79; CONSULT, 79- *Honors & Awards:* Mod Pioneer Creative Indust Award, Nat Asn Mfrs, 66; E V Murphree Award, Am Chem Soc, 67. *Mem:* Sigma Xi. *Res:* Heterogeneous catalysis; polymerization; kinetics of catalytic reactions. *Mailing Add:* 1722 S Carson Apt 2600 Tulsa OK 74119

CLARK, ALFRED, JR, b Elizabethton, Tenn, May 5, 36; m 60; c 1. APPLIED MATHEMATICS. *Educ:* Purdue Univ, BS, 58; Mass Inst Technol, PhD(appl math), 63. *Prof Exp:* NSF fel, 63-64; from asst prof to assoc prof, 64-74, chmn dept, 72-77, PROF MECH ENG, UNIV ROCHESTER, 74- *Concurrent Pos:* Vis fel, Joint Inst Lab Astrophys, Univ Colo, 70-71. *Mem:* Am Soc Mech Engrs; Int Astron Union; Am Phys Soc. *Res:* Fluid dynamics; bioengineering. *Mailing Add:* Dept Mech Eng Univ of Rochester Rochester NY 14627

CLARK, ALLAN H, b Cincinnati, Ohio, July 16, 35; c 3. MATHEMATICS. *Educ:* Mass Inst Technol, BS, 57; Princeton Univ, MA, 59, PhD(math), 61. *Prof Exp:* From instr to prof math, Brown Univ, 61-75; DEAN, SCH SCI, PURDUE UNIV, WEST LAFAYETTE, 75- *Concurrent Pos:* NSF grant, 62-; vis mem, Inst Advan Study, Princeton Univ, 65-66; vis prof, Math Inst, Aarhus Univ, 70-71; trustee, Univs Res Asn, Inc, 76- *Mem:* Am Asn Higher Educ; Am Coun Educ; Am Math Soc. *Res:* Algebraic topology. *Mailing Add:* Sch of Sci Purdue Univ West Lafayette IN 47907

CLARK, ALLEN KEITH, b Bridgeton, NJ, June 25, 33; m 57; c 2. ORGANIC CHEMISTRY. *Educ:* Catawba Col, AB, 55; Univ NC, PhD(org chem), 60. *Prof Exp:* From asst prof to assoc prof, 62-66, actg chmn dept, 68-69, asst provost, 72-79, PROF CHEM, OLD DOM UNIV, 66-, CHMN DEPT, 69-, DEP VPRES ACAD AFFAIRS, 81- *Concurrent Pos:* Sigma Xi res grant-in-aid, 63-64. *Mem:* Am Chem Soc; Am Inst Chemists. *Res:* Chemistry of ferrocene; aromatic nitroso compounds. *Mailing Add:* 1050 Manchester Ave Norfolk VA 23508

CLARK, ALLEN LEROY, b Delaware, Iowa, Sept 29, 38; m 55, 81; c 3. ECONOMIC GEOLOGY, GEOCHEMISTRY. *Educ:* Iowa State Univ, BS, 61; Univ Idaho, MS, 63, PhD(geol), 68. *Prof Exp:* Instr geol, Univ Idaho, 65-66; geologist, Bear Creek Mining Co, Kennecott Copper Corp, 66-67; res geologist, US Geol Surv, 67-72, chief, Off Resource Anal, 72-78, sr staff coordr, 78-80; DIR GEN, INT INST RESOURCE DEVELOP, 80- *Concurrent Pos:* Co-investr, Apollo 12-14, NASA, 70-73. *Mem:* Am Asn Petrol Geol; Geol Soc Am; Soc Econ Geologists; Int Asn Genesis of Ore Deposits. *Res:* Economics of international development; economic analysis of exploration and resource availability; wallrock alteration and trace element distributions associated with base metal deposits; platinum group metals distribution in ultramafic rocks; structural analysis of lunar samples; international resource assessment; resource data systems. *Mailing Add:* Int Inst Resource Develop #2 Belvederegasse Vienna A1040 22091 Austria

CLARK, ALLEN VARDEN, b Attleboro, Mass, Nov 1, 41; m 63; c 3. FOOD SCIENCE. *Educ:* Mass Inst Technol, BS, 63, MS, 65, PhD(food sci & technol), 69. *Prof Exp:* Prin investr, Corp Res & Develop Lab, 68-80, MGR, CITRUS RES & DEVELOP, FOODS DIV, THE COCA-COLA CO, 80- *Mem:* AAAS; Am Chem Soc; Inst Food Technologists. *Res:* Isolation and characterization of pigments from protein carbonyl browning systems; tea; food processing; citrus processing; product development; management. *Mailing Add:* 1044 Golfside Dr Winter Park FL 32792

CLARK, ALTON HAROLD, b Bangor, Maine, Oct 10, 39; m 61; c 2. SOLID STATE PHYSICS. *Educ:* Univ Maine, BA, 61; Univ Wis, Madison, MS, 63; Cornell Univ, PhD(physics), 67. *Prof Exp:* Physicist, Sprague Elec Co, 66-68; from asst prof to prof physics, Univ Maine, Orono, 68-81; GROUP LEADER, STANDARD OIL CO, 81- *Concurrent Pos:* Vis scientist, Xerox Palo Alto Res Ctr, 74-75. *Mem:* Am Phys Soc. *Res:* Electrical and optical properties of crystalline and amorphous semiconductors. *Mailing Add:* Res & Develop Lab Standard Oil Co Cleveland OH 49115

CLARK, ALVIN JOHN, b Oak Park, Ill, Apr 13, 33; div. GENETICS, BACTERIOLOGY. *Educ:* Univ Rochester, BS, 55; Harvard Univ, PhD(chem), 59. *Prof Exp:* Asst prof bact, 62-64, asst prof bact & molecular biol, 64-67, assoc prof, 67-72, PROF MOLECULAR BIOL, UNIV CALIF, BERKELEY, 72- *Concurrent Pos:* Am Cancer Soc fel, 59-61; fel, Yale Univ, 62; John Simon Guggenheim Mem Found fel, 69. *Mem:* Am Soc Microbiol; Genetics Soc Am. *Res:* Enzymological and genetic analysis of genetic recombination; bacterial conjugation. *Mailing Add:* Dept of Molecular Biol Univ of Calif Berkeley CA 94720

CLARK, ARMIN LEE, b Huntington, WVa, June 16, 28; m 51; c 2. GEOLOGY. *Educ:* Marshall Univ, BA, 51; Ohio State Univ, MSc, 58; Univ Tenn, PhD(geol), 73. *Prof Exp:* Teacher sci, Cabell & Mingo Counties, WVa Schs, 58-60 & Jefferson County, Ky Schs, 60-61; assoc prof, 61-80, PROF GEOL, MURRAY STATE UNIV, 80- *Mem:* Geol Soc Am. *Res:* Petrology of the Eocene sediments in western Kentucky and Tennessee. *Mailing Add:* 1504 Oak Dr Murray KY 42071

CLARK, ARNOLD FRANKLIN, b Madison, Wis, Apr 27, 16; m; c 3. X-RAY DIFFRACTION, EXPERIMENTAL DESIGNS. *Educ:* Swarthmore Col, AB, 37; Ind Univ, AM, 39, PhD(physics), 41. *Prof Exp:* Asst math & physics, Univ Wis, 37-38; asst physics, Ind Univ, 38-41; res fel & physicist, Univ Calif, 41-46; res assoc, Univ Rochester, 46-47; asst prof physics, 47-49; asst prof physics, Carnegie Inst Technol, 49-54; PHYSICIST, LAWRENCE LIVERMORE NAT LAB, UNIV CALIF, 54- *Mem:* Fel Am Phys Soc; Sigma Xi; Int Solar Energy Soc. *Res:* Nuclear physics; engineering physics; design of electromagnetic accelerators; nuclear emulsions; radiation effects; cloud chambers; solar energy research and development; shallow solar ponds; x-ray diffraction with bent crystal spectrometers. *Mailing Add:* Lawrence Livermore Nat Lab PO Box 808 Livermore CA 94550

CLARK, ARNOLD M, b Philadelphia, Pa, Jan 28, 16; m 53; c 2. GENETICS. *Educ:* Pa State Col, AB, 37; Univ Pa, MA, 39, PhD(zool), 43. *Prof Exp:* Res biologist, Smyth Labs, Philadelphia, 40-46; asst instr zool, Univ Pa, 44-45; instr, Philadelphia Col Pharm, 45-46; from instr to assoc prof, 46-56, PROF BIOL, UNIV DEL, 56- *Concurrent Pos:* Radiation biologist, Brookhaven Nat Lab, 53-54. *Mem:* AAAS; Am Soc Naturalists; Radiation Res Soc; Am Genetics Soc; Genetic Asn Am. *Res:* Genetics of Habrobracon; toxicological studies on insecticides; resins; pharmaceuticals; gene dosage; radiation damage; action of cell poisons; oxygen poisoning; genetics of aging; studies of genetic mosaics in insects and their use in the analysis of development and behavior; analysis of chromosomal aberrations in man. *Mailing Add:* Sch of Arts & Sci Univ of Del Newark DE 19711

CLARK, ARTHUR EDWARD, b Scranton, Pa, July 9, 32; m 58; c 4. SOLID STATE PHYSICS. *Educ:* Univ Scranton, BS, 54; Univ Del, MS, 56; Cath Univ, PhD(physics), 60. *Prof Exp:* RES PHYSICIST, US NAVAL SURFACE WEAPONS CTR, 59- *Mem:* AAAS; Am Phys Soc. *Res:* Magnetic, elastic and magnetoelastic properties of solids; ultrasonics and hypersonics. *Mailing Add:* US Naval Surface Weapons Ctr White Oak Lab Silver Spring MD 20910

CLARK, BARRY GILLESPIE, b Happy, Tex, Mar 5, 38; m 63; c 4. ASTRONOMY. *Educ:* Calif Inst Technol, BS, 59, PhD(astron), 64. *Prof Exp:* Asst scientist, 64-69, SCIENTIST, NAT RADIO ASTRON OBSERV, 69- *Mem:* Am Astron Soc. *Res:* Radio astronomy interferometry and array design and use. *Mailing Add:* Nat Radio Astron Observ PO Box O 1000 Bullock Blvd Socorro NM 87801

CLARK, BENJAMIN CATES, JR, b Knoxville, Tenn. FLAVOR REACTIONS, ANALYTICAL FLAVOR CHEMISTRY. *Educ:* Duke Univ, BA, 63; Emory Univ, MS & PhD(org chem), 67. *Prof Exp:* Fel, Univ Ga, 67-69; prin staff chemist, 69-75, SR RES SCIENTIST, CORP RES & DEVELOP DEPT, COCA-COLA CO, 75- *Mem:* Am Chem Soc; Inst Food Technol; Am Soc Testing & Mat; Sigma Xi. *Res:* analytical organic chemistry; flavor research, particularly terpene chemistry; the reactions of flavors in dilute aqueous systems and micelles; photochemistry; flavor analysis-carbonated beverages, citrus and other essential oils; beverage technology. *Mailing Add:* Corp Res & Develop Dept PO Drawer 1734 Coca-Cola Co Atlanta GA 30301

CLARK, BENJAMIN EDWARD, b Southampton, NY, Oct 3, 14; m 47; c 2. AGRONOMY. *Educ:* Cornell Univ, BS, 40, MS, 46; Mich State Col, PhD(hort), 49. *Prof Exp:* From asst prof to assoc prof, 48-56, head dept, 52-68, prof seed invests, 56-80, asst dir, 68-77, EMER PROF, DEPT SEED & VEGETABLE SCI, AGR EXP STA, NY STATE COL AGR & LIFE SCI, CORNELL UNIV, 80- *Mem:* Am Soc Agron; Am Soc Hort Sci. *Res:* Seed germination and seed vigor testing. *Mailing Add:* 75 Highland Ave Geneva NY 14456

CLARK, BENTON C, b Oklahoma City, Okla, Aug 4, 37; m 65; c 2. GEOCHEMISTRY, BIOPHYSICS. *Educ:* Univ Okla, BS, 59; Univ Calif, MA, 61; Columbia Univ, PhD(biophys), 69. *Prof Exp:* Res asst radiation instrumentation res & develop, Los Alamos Sci Lab, 59-60; assoc electronic speech recognition, Advan Systs Develop Div, Int Bus Mach Corp, 61; sr staff scientist res & develop, Avco Corp, 68-71; SR RES SCIENTIST, MARTIN-MARIETTA CORP, 71- *Concurrent Pos:* Dep team leader, NASA Viking Inorg Chem Team, 72- *Mem:* AAAS; Am Geophys Union; Am Inst Aeronaut & Astronaut. *Res:* Radiobiological effects of very soft x-rays; space radiation research; detection of life on Mars; geochemical analysis of planetary and comet surfaces by x-ray fluorescence spectrometry. *Mailing Add:* 10890 Park Range Rd Littleton CO 80123

CLARK, BILL PAT, b Bartlesville, Okla, May 15, 39. SEMICONDUCTORS, SOLID STATE PHYSICS. *Educ:* Okla State Univ, BS, 61, MS, 64, PhD(physics), 68. *Prof Exp:* Asst physics, Okla State Univ, 61-68; res fel, Dept Theoret Physics, Univ Warwick, Eng, 68-69; sr mem tech staff, Booz Allen Appl Res, 69-70; sr mem tech staff & analyst, Comput Sci Corp, 70-77; sect mgr data qual assurance, NASA Landsat Proj, 77-79, SR STAFF SCIENTIST, IMAGE PROCESSING OPER, COMPUT SCI TECHNICOLOR ASSOCS, GODDARD SPACE FLIGHT CTR, 79- *Mem:* AAAS; Am Phys Soc; NY Acad Sci. *Res:* Quantum field theory; instabilities and transport properties in solids; mathematical models; systems analysis; analysis of electro optical remote sensors; computer simulations of solar cells, injection lasers, and other devices; digital image processing, and mathematical models for biochemical systems. *Mailing Add:* 5811 Barwood Place Columbia MD 21044

CLARK, BRIAN ROGER, biochemistry, see previous edition

CLARK, BRUCE R, b Pittsburgh, Pa, June 17, 41; m 67; c 2. GEOLOGY. *Educ:* Yale Univ, BS, 63; Stanford Univ, PhD(geol), 68. *Prof Exp:* Res assoc geol, Stanford Univ, 67-68; asst prof, 68-73, assoc prof geol, Univ Mich, Ann Arbor, 73-77; DIR ROCK MECH, LEIGHTON & ASSOCS, 77- *Concurrent Pos:* Vis lectr, Monash Univ, Australia, 74-75; mem, US Nat Comt on Rock Mech. *Mem:* Fel Geol Soc Am; Am Geophys Union; Int Soc Rock Mech; Asn Eng Geologist; Seismol Soc Am. *Res:* Structural geology; rock mechanics; landslide and earthquake hazard evaluation; earthquake prediction, in vito stress measurements in rock. *Mailing Add:* Leighton and Assocs 17975 Sky Park Circle Irvine CA 92714

CLARK, BURR, JR, b Howell, Mich, Jan 20, 24; m 47; c 3. AGRICULTURAL BIOCHEMISTRY. *Educ:* Mich State Univ, BS, 52; Univ NH, MS, 60; WVa Univ, PhD(agr biochem), 66. *Prof Exp:* Self-employed in agr, 47-49 & 52-56; from asst ed to assoc ed, 63-69, SR ED BIOCHEM, CHEM ABSTRACTS SERV, 69- *Mem:* AAAS; Am Chem Soc. *Res:* Volatile fatty acids metabolism in ruminants and forage quality in relation to volatile fatty acids metabolism in ruminants. *Mailing Add:* Chem Abstracts Serv PO Box 3012 Columbus OH 43210

CLARK, BYRON BRYANT, b Temple, Tex, Apr 5, 08; m 31; c 3. PHARMACOLOGY. *Educ:* Baylor Univ, AB, 30; Univ Iowa, MS, 32, PhD, 34. *Prof Exp:* Asst biochem, Univ Iowa, 30-31; asst path chemist, Gen Hosp Univ Iowa, 31-36; from instr to assoc prof physiol & pharmacol, Albany Med Col, 36-47; prof pharmacol & chmn dept, Med Sch, Tufts Univ, 47-57; dir pharmacol & chemother, Mead Johnson & Co, Ind, 57-62, vpres res ctr, 62-68; dir, Pharmacol & Toxicol Progs, Nat Inst Gen Med Sci, 68-79; RETIRED. *Concurrent Pos:* Consult pharmacologist, Albany Hosp, NY, 37-47 & New Eng Ctr Hosp, 47-57; mem comt drug safety, Drug Res Bd, Nat Acad Sci-Nat Res Coun. *Mem:* Fel AAAS; Am Soc Pharmacol & Exp Therapeut; Soc Exp Biol & Med; Soc Toxicol; NY Acad Sci. *Res:* Insulin and carbohydrate metabolism; ethyl and methyl alcohol pharmacology and metabolism; drugs on blood and hemoglobin; gastric secretion; antacids; antispasmodics; autonomic drugs; cardiovascular drugs. *Mailing Add:* 9612 Linfield Dr Cincinnati OH 45242

CLARK, C(HARLES) C(ANFIELD), b Paterson, NJ, Aug 19, 28; m 59; c 2. METALLURGY. *Educ:* Rensselaer Polytech Inst, BMetE, 50. *Prof Exp:* Res metallurgist, Res Lab, Int Nickel Co, 50-57, metallurgist, 57-61, appln engr aerospace & power industs, 61-69, nickel alloy group mgr prod develop, 70-72; proj mgr, Inco, Inc, 72-75; mgr high temperature alloy develop, Climax Molybdenum Co, 75-80; MGR, MARKET DEVELOP, AMAX TUNGSTEN, 80- *Mem:* Am Soc Metals; Am Inst Mining, Metall & Petrol Engrs; Am Soc Testing & Mat; Am Soc Mech Engrs. *Res:* Properties and uses of alloy and stainless steels; research and development of nickel base alloys; development of superalloys and chromium-molybdenum steels for energy conversion, petroleum, automotive and aerospace industries. *Mailing Add:* AMAX Tungsten 1 Greenwich Plaza Greenwich CT 06830

CLARK, C ELMER, b Tooele, Utah, Mar 5, 21; m 51; c 4. PHYSIOLOGY, BIOCHEMISTRY. *Educ:* Utah State Univ, BS, 50; Univ Md, MS, 60, PhD(poultry physiol), 62. *Prof Exp:* Asst prof poultry sci, Utah State Univ, 52-57 & Univ Md, 57-61; assoc prof, 62-70, asst dir agr exp sta, 70-75, ASSOC DIR AGR EXP STA, UTAH STATE UNIV, 75-, PROF POULTRY SCI, 70- *Mem:* AAAS; Poultry Sci Asn; World Poultry Sci Asn; Soc Exp Biol & Med. *Res:* Neurohumoral factors in ovulation in chickens; environmental-physiology relationships in the avian species. *Mailing Add:* Agr Exp Sta Utah State Univ Logan UT 84322

CLARK, CARL CYRUS, b Manila, Philippines, Apr 23, 24; US citizen; m 47; c 4. BIOPHYSICS. *Educ:* Worcester Polytech Inst, BS, 44; Columbia Univ, PhD(zool), 50. *Prof Exp:* Res assoc physiol & infrared spectrophotom, Med Col, Cornell Univ, 47-51; asst prof zool, Univ Ill, 51-55; head biophys div, Naval Aviation Med Acceleration Lab, 55-61; mgr, Lift Sci Dept, Martin Co, 61-66; assoc chief, Sci & Technol Div, Libr of Cong, 66-68; chief, Task Group on Indust Self-Regulation, Nat Comn Prod Safety, 68-70; staff consult prod safety, Prod Eval Technol Div, Nat Bur Standards, 70-72; head dept life sci, Worcester Polytech Inst, 72-74; exec dir, comn advan pub interest orgn, dir, Health Satellite Proj & Community Health Resources Proj, Monsour Med Found, 74-77; OCCUPANT PACKAGING STAFF, NAT HIGHWAY TRAFFIC SAFETY ADMIN, 77- *Concurrent Pos:* From assoc physiol to asst prof, Sch Med, Univ Pa, 55-61; pres, Safety Systs Co, 68-; prof, Master of Sci in Safety Prog, Univ Southern Calif Eastern Off, 78- *Mem:* AAAS; Systs Safety Soc; Am Inst Aeronaut & Astronaut; Aerospace Med Asn; Human Factors Soc. *Res:* Infrared spectrophotometry and x-ray diffraction studies of biochemicals; microbiospectrophotometry; human centrifuge dynamic flight simulation; airbag restraint development; flight physiology; auto and home safety; information systems and satellite teleconferences; public interest organizations. *Mailing Add:* 23 Seminole Ave Baltimore MD 21228

CLARK, CARL HERITAGE, b Los Angeles, Calif, Nov 18, 25; m 48; c 1. PHARMACOLOGY. *Educ:* State Col Wash, BS & DVM, 47; Ohio State Univ, MS, 49, PhD(physiol), 53. *Prof Exp:* Asst, State Col Wash, 45-47; instr physiol, Ohio State Univ, 47-53; assoc head, Dept Animal Dis Res, 60-67, PROF PHYSIOL & PHARMACOL & HEAD DEPT, SCH VET MED, AUBURN UNIV, 53- *Mem:* Am Vet Med Asn; Am Soc Vet Physiologists & Pharmacologists (pres, 61). *Res:* Pharmacology of antibiotics in animals; pharmacology of body fluids and fluid therapy. *Mailing Add:* Dept of Physiol & Pharmacol Auburn Univ Sch of Vet Med Auburn AL 36830

CLARK, CHARLES AUSTIN, b Owego, NY, Dec 18, 15; m 37; c 4. ORGANIC CHEMISTRY. *Educ:* Cornell Univ, BS, 37. *Prof Exp:* Bacteriologist, NY State Dept Health Labs, 37-42; org res chemist, GAF Corp, 42-50, mgr, Org Prep Lab Unit, Ansco Div, 50-80; CONSULT, 80- *Mem:* Am Chem Soc; Soc Photog Scientists & Engrs; Am Inst Chemists. *Res:* Optical photographic sensitizing dyes photographic color formers, stabilizers and related intermediates. *Mailing Add:* 14 Westwood Ct Binghamton NY 13905

CLARK, CHARLES CHRISTOPHER, b Erie, Pa, Feb 17, 43; m. BIOCHEMISTRY. *Educ:* Gannon Col, BA, 65; Northwestern Univ, PhD(biochem), 70. *Prof Exp:* Asst prof, 72-77, ASSOC PROF BIOCHEM, MED SCH, UNIV PA, 77- *Concurrent Pos:* NIH grant, Univ Wash, 70-72 & res career develop award, 75-80. *Mem:* Soc Complex Carbohydrates. *Res:* Structure and biosynthesis of connective tissue macromolecules with particular emphasis on interstitial collagens, and basement membrane collagen and noncollagen glycoprotein(s). *Mailing Add:* Univ City Sci Ctr 3624 Market St Philadelphia PA 19104

CLARK, CHARLES KITTREDGE, b Berkeley, Calif, Oct 15, 06; m 35; c 2. NATURAL PRODUCTS CHEMISTRY. *Educ:* Stanford Univ, AB, 28, MA, 29; Univ Fla, PhD(chem), 40. *Prof Exp:* Res chemist, Hercules Powder Co, 30-31; res chemist petrochems, Shell Develop Co, 32; res chemist naval stores, USDA, 33-37; res chemist tall oil, Quaker Chem Prods Corp, 40-42; res chemist terpenes, Naval Stores Div, Glidden Co, 43-45; res chemist wood prods, Weyerhaeuser Timber Co, 46-47; res chemist naval stores, Crosby Chem Inc, 48-52; res chemist wood prods, Crossett Co, 53-62; res chemist chem prod div, Union Camp Corp, 62-73; RETIRED. *Mem:* Am Chem Soc. *Res:* Rosin; terpenes and tall oil products. *Mailing Add:* 231 Andover Dr Savannah GA 31405

CLARK, CHARLES LESTER, b San Jose, Calif, Nov 17, 17; m 40; c 3. MATHEMATICS. *Educ:* Stanford Univ, AB, 39, MA, 40; Univ Va, PhD(math), 44. *Prof Exp:* Asst math, Stanford Univ, 39-40; instr, Univ Va, 42-44; from asst prof to prof, Ore State Col, 44-57; dir comput ctr, 61-71, dir inst res, 64-71, head dept, 57-64 & 71-77, PROF MATH, CALIF STATE UNIV, LOS ANGELES, 57- HEAD DEPT. *Concurrent Pos:* Vis prof, Univ Va, 55-56; consult to educ, indust & legislative groups, 58- *Mem:* Sigma Xi; Am Math Soc; Math Asn Am; Asn Comput Mach. *Res:* Topology; analysis; arc reversing transformations; computer science; privacy and security. *Mailing Add:* Dept of Math Calif State Univ Los Angeles CA 90032

CLARK, CHARLES MALCOLM, JR, b Greensburg, Ind, Mar 12, 38; m 63; c 2. MEDICINE. *Educ:* Ind Univ, AB, 60, MD, 63. *Prof Exp:* Intern, St Vincent's Hosp, Indianapolis, Ind, 63-64; resident internal med, Ind Univ, 64-65; staff assoc metab res, Nat Inst Arthritis & Metab Dis, 67-69; from asst prof to assoc prof med & pharmacol, Med Sch, Ind Univ, Indianapolis, 69-75; res & educ assoc, 69-71, clin investr endocrinol & metab, 71-74, assoc chief staff educ, 74-78, CHIEF DIABETES SERV, VET ADMIN HOSP, 78-; PROF MED & PHARMACOL, MED SCH, IND UNIV, INDIANAPOLIS, 76- *Concurrent Pos:* Clin fel diabetes, Joslin Clin, Boston, Mass, 65-66, NIH fel, Joslin Res Lab, 66-67; fel med, Peter Bent Brigham Hosp, Boston, 66-67; Robert Woods Johnson health policy fel, 75-76; dir, Diabetes Res & Training Ctr, 77- *Mem:* AMA; Am Diabetes Asn; Endocrine Soc; fel Am Col Physicians; Am Fedn Clin Res. *Res:* Metabolic control mechanisms; regulation of intermediary metabolism in fetal development. *Mailing Add:* Vet Admin Hosp 1481 W Tenth St Indianapolis IN 46202

CLARK, CHARLES RICHARD, b Burbank, Calif, Jan 22, 47; m 72; c 1. TOXICOLOGY, ENVIRONMENTAL TOXICOLOGY. *Educ:* Univ Calif, Davis, BS, 73, PhD(toxicol), 77. *Prof Exp:* MAT ASSESSMENT TOXICOLOGIST & GENETIC TOXICOLOGIST, INHALATION TOXICOL RES INST, 77- *Mem:* Soc Toxicol; Environ Mutagen Soc. *Res:* Toxicological evaluation of materials used in solar energy; mutagenicity evaluation of coal combustion effluents and diesel exhaust emissions. *Mailing Add:* Inhalation Toxicol Res Inst PO Box 5890 Albuquerque NM 87185

CLARK, CHESTER WILLIAM, b San Francisco, Calif, July 18, 06; m 30; c 2. PHYSICS. *Educ:* Univ Calif, BS, 27, MS, 29; State Univ Leiden, PhD(physics), 35. *Prof Exp:* Res chemist, Standard Oil Co, Calif, 29-33; instr chem, Univ Calif, 35-37 & San Francisco City Col, 37-41; res assoc, Johns Hopkins Univ, 46-47; low temp consult & physicist, Naval Res Lab, US Army, Washington, DC 47, sci asst to dir, Ballistic Res Lab, Aberdeen Proving Ground, 47-51, chief res & develop div & dep comdr, Picatinny Arsenal, 51-54, chief ord res & develop, 55-61, dir army res, 61-63, Commanding Gen, US Army-Japan, 63-65; vpres res, Res Triangle Inst, NC, 65-71; special sci & technol asst to ambassador, Am Embassy, Taiwan, 73-75; corp secy & admin dir, Microelectronics Ctr, NC, 80-81. *Concurrent Pos:* Am Comnr, Joint US-Rep China Comn Rural Reconstruction, Taipei, 73-75. *Mem:* Soc Rheol; AAAS; Am Phys Soc. *Res:* Low temperature specific heats of inorganic substances; superconductivity of metals and alloys; preparation of interstitial alloys; attainment of temperatures below 1K. *Mailing Add:* 52 Glenmore Dr Durham NC 27707

CLARK, CHRISTOPHER ALAN, b Geneva, NY, Jan 27, 49; m 71; c 2. PLANT PATHOLOGY, AGRICULTURE. *Educ:* Cornell Univ, BS, 70, MS, 73, PhD(plant path), 76. *Prof Exp:* Res assoc, NC State Univ, 76-77; asst prof, 77-81, ASSOC PROF PLANT PATH, LA STATE UNIV, 81- *Mem:* Am Phytopath Soc; Soc Nematologists. *Res:* Ecology of soil-borne plant pathogens; biological control of plant pathogens; post-harvest pathology; sweet potato diseases. *Mailing Add:* Dept of Plant Path & La State Univ Baton Rouge LA 70803

CLARK, CLARENCE FLOYD, b Briceton, Ohio, May 26, 12; m 34; c 1. ZOOLOGY. *Educ:* Miami Univ, BS, 34; Ohio State Univ, MS, 42. *Prof Exp:* Teacher, High Sch, Ohio, 35-37; fish mgt agent, Ohio Div Wildlife, 37-57, asst supvr fish mgt, 57-60, supvr fish invest, 60-63, asst supvr fish mgt, 63-69; asst fisheries res, 69-71, PROF RES & FISH CULT, SCH NAT RESOURCES, OHIO STATE UNIV, 71- *Concurrent Pos:* Consult, Environ Consult, 72-75 & Dept Nat Resources, Ohio Div Wildlife, 74-75; consult, environ fisheries & freshwater mussels probs, 72-80. *Mem:* Fel Am Inst Fishery Res Biol; Am Fisheries Soc; Int Acad Fishery Sci; Am Soc Ichthyologists & Herpetologists; Sigma Xi. *Res:* Management and propagation of northern pike, minnows, muskelluge, creek chubs; status of freshwater naiads in relation to environmental impacts from man made changes in the environment. *Mailing Add:* 2625 E Southern #214 Green Valley AZ 85282

CLARK, CLAYTON, b Hyde Park, Utah, Mar 9, 12; m 33; c 2. ELECTRICAL ENGINEERING. *Educ:* Utah State Univ, BS, 33; Stanford Univ, EE, 47, PhD(elec eng), 58. *Prof Exp:* Instr elec eng, Utah State Univ, 37-40; res engr, Douglas Aircraft, 47; prof elec eng, 48-77, dir eng exp sta & dir ctr res aeronomy, 64-77, EMER PROF ELEC ENG, UTAH STATE UNIV, 77- *Concurrent Pos:* Mem comn III, Int Sci Radio Union. *Mem:* Am Soc Eng Educ; Am Geophys Union; fel Inst Elec & Electronics Engrs. *Res:* Radio propagation; microwaves. *Mailing Add:* 798 N 1500 E Logan UT 84321

CLARK, CLIFTON BOB, b Ft Smith, Ark, July 8, 27; m 50; c 3. SOLID STATE PHYSICS. *Educ:* Univ Ark, BA, 49, MA, 51; Univ Md, PhD(physics), 57. *Prof Exp:* Asst prof sci & math, Florence State Teachers Col, Ala, 50-51; asst prof physics, US Naval Acad, 51-55; physicist, US Naval Res Lab, 55-56; assoc prof physics, US Naval Acad, 56-57; from assoc prof to prof, Southern Methodist Univ, 57-65, chmn dept, 62-65; head dept, 65-75, PROF PHYSICS, UNIV NC, GREENSBORO, 65- *Concurrent Pos:* Vis prof physics, Fla State Univ, 75-76. *Mem:* AAAS; Am Asn Physics Teachers; Am Phys Soc; Sigma Xi. *Res:* Electron-lattice interactions in metals; lattice dynamics. *Mailing Add:* 800 Montrose Dr Greensboro NC 27410

CLARK, COLIN WHITCOMB, b Vancouver, Can, June 18, 31; m 55; c 3. APPLIED MATHEMATICS, RESOURCE ECONOMICS. *Educ:* Univ BC, BA, 53; Univ Wash, PhD(math), 58. *Prof Exp:* Instr math, Univ Calif, Berkeley, 58-60; from asst prof to assoc prof, 60-69, PROF MATH, UNIV BC, 69- *Concurrent Pos:* Investr, US Air Force Off Sci Res, 60-67; vis res scholar, Univ Calif, Berkeley, 65-66; vis res prof, NMex State Univ, 70-71; vis scientist, Commonwealth Sci & Indust Res Orgn, Australia, 75-76; Killam res fel, Univ BC, 75-76 & 81-82; prin investr, US Nat Oceanic & Atmospheric Admin, Nat Marine Fisheries Serv, 77-78. *Honors & Awards:* Jacob Biely Res Prize, Univ BC, 77. *Mem:* Soc Indust & Appl Math; Can Appl Math Soc (pres, 81-84); Asn Environ & Resource Economists. *Res:* Spectral theory of partial differential equations; mathematical models in renewable resource economics. *Mailing Add:* Dept of Math Univ of BC Vancouver Can

CLARK, CORODON SCOTT, b Rochester, NY, Feb 1, 38. PUBLIC HEALTH, ENVIRONMENTAL HEALTH ENGINEERING. *Educ:* Antioch Col, BS, 61; Johns Hopkins Univ, MS, 63, PhD(eng sci), 65. *Prof Exp:* Sanit engr, Ohio River Valley Water Sanit Comn, 65-67; sr res assoc, 67-70, asst prof, 71-75, ASSOC PROF ENVIRON HEALTH, UNIV CINCINNATI, 76- *Concurrent Pos:* Consult, Am Pub Works Asn, 69, Ohio River Valley Water Sanit Comn, 71-73 & Environ Protection Agency, Cincinnati, 72-74. *Mem:* Am Pub Health Asn; Am Water Works Asn; Water Pollution Control Fedn. *Res:* Epidemiologic-Serologic study of health risks of wastewater exposure; sources of lead in pediatric lead absorption; development of potability indicator for direct reuse water. *Mailing Add:* Dept of Environ Health Kettering Lab 3223 Eden Ave Cincinnati OH 45267

CLARK, CROSMAN JAY, b Jackson, Mich, Mar 6, 25; m 45; c 3. ELECTROMAGNETISM, COMPUTER SCIENCES. *Educ:* Okla State Univ, BA, 46, MS, 48, PhD(math), 53. *Prof Exp:* Res engr, Curtiss-Wright Corp, 48; instr elec eng, Ohio State Univ, 49; instr & res asst, Okla State Univ, 49-52; mathematician, Stanolind Gas & Oil Co, 51; res mathematician, Continental Oil Co, 53-56; mathematician, Lockheed Missile & Space Corp, 56-61; eng specialist, Sylvania Electronic Defense Lab, Gen Tel & Electronics Corp, 61-64; staff scientist, Apparatus Res Dept, Tex Instruments Inc, Dallas, 64-66; dir advan studies, Northrop Corp, Calif, 66-70; vpres res & develop, Underwater Sci, Inc, Calif, 70-72; PRES, INTERSCI SYSTS, INC, 72-; DIR, INTERDISCIPLINARY SYSTS INST, 78- *Concurrent Pos:* Instr, Okla State Univ, 46-48 & 50-53, Foothill Col, 61-63 & Univ Santa Clara, 64; lectr, Calif State Col, Hayward, 71-72; consult, Nat Endowment Arts, 72-; adj prof cybernetic syst & mgt sci, San Jose State Univ, 73-; lectr, Univ Calif, Santa Cruz, 78- *Mem:* Environ Design Res Asn; Soc Gen Systs Res; Math Asn Am; Soc Indust & Appl Math. *Res:* Topology; set theory; logic; wave theory; automata; operations research; stochastic processes; decision theory; general systems theory; mathematical-statistical model building; behavioral cybernetics; humanistic measures of design; business-management systems. *Mailing Add:* 15555 Old Ranch Rd Los Gatos CA 95030

CLARK, DALE ALLEN, b Munden, Kans, Sept 14, 22; m 48; c 2. BIOCHEMISTRY. *Educ:* Hastings Col, BA, 44; Univ Colo, MA, 47; Univ Utah, PhD(biochem), 50. *Prof Exp:* Asst prof biochem, Sch Med, Univ Okla, 50-52, assoc prof, 53-54; res biochemist, Vet Admin Hosp, Dallas, 54-59; BIOCHEMIST, CLIN SCI DIV, US AIR FORCE SCH AEROSPACE MED, BROOKS AFB, 59- *Mem:* Fel AAAS; Am Chem Soc; Am Oil Chemists Soc; Aerospace Med Asn; Soc Exp Biol & Med. *Res:* Atherosclerosis; steroid and sterol metabolism. *Mailing Add:* Clin Path Br US Air Force Sch Aerospace Med Brooks AFB TX 78235

CLARK, DAVID BARRETT, b Glen Ellyn, Ill, Nov 1, 13; m 48; c 2. NEUROLOGY, NEUROPATHOLOGY. *Educ:* Univ Chicago, PhD(neuroanat), 40, MD, 46. *Prof Exp:* Asst anat, Univ Chicago, 38-47; intern med, Johns Hopkins Hosp, 47-48, asst resident neurol, 48-49; Fulbright lectr, Nat Hosp, Queen Sq, Eng, 50-51; from asst prof to assoc prof neurol & pediat, Johns Hopkins Hosp, 51-65; chmn dept, 65-79, PROF NEUROL, SCH MED, UNIV KY, 65-; CHIEF, NEUROL SERV, VET ADMIN CTR, LEXINGTON, KY, 79- *Concurrent Pos:* Fel neurol, Johns Hopkins Hosp, 49-50; attend neurologist, Baltimore City Hosp, 51-59, Johns Hopkins Hosp, 51-65 & Rosewood State Training Sch, 52-65; adv, Epilepsy Found, 66-; Teale lectr, Royal Col Physicians, 67-; mem field study sect, Nat Inst Neurol Dis & Blindness, 58-60, prog proj study sect, 60-64, neurol res & training sect, 65-69 & residency rev comt, 67- *Mem:* Am Acad Neurol; Am Neurol Asn; Am Asn Neuropath; AMA; Royal Soc Med. *Res:* Pediatric neurology; pathology of cerebral birth injuries; developmental defects of the central nervous system. *Mailing Add:* Univ of Ky Col of Med Lexington KY 40506

CLARK, DAVID C, b Woodland, Calif, May 19, 41. MATHEMATICAL ANALYSIS. *Educ:* Calif Inst Technol, BS, 63; Stanford Univ, MS, 65, PhD(math), 67. *Prof Exp:* Vis mem, Courant Inst Math Sci, 67-68; asst prof math, Rutgers Univ, 68-72; asst prof math, Univ PR, Mayaguez, 72-78; instr dept comput sci, Univ Tenn, 77-79; mathematician, Naval Weapons Sta, Corona, Calif, 80; SR STAFF MEM, PAR TECHNOL, 81- *Mem:* Am Math Soc. *Res:* Ordinary and partial differential equations; pattern analysis. *Mailing Add:* 4359 Van Gold Ave Lakewood CA 90712

CLARK, DAVID DELANO, b Austin, Tex, Feb 10, 24; m 49; c 3. NUCLEAR PHYSICS. *Educ:* Univ Calif, Berkeley, AB, 48, PhD(physics), 53. *Prof Exp:* Asst physics, Univ Calif, Berkeley, 48-51, physicist, 53; res assoc, Brookhaven Nat Lab, 53-55; from asst prof to assoc prof eng physics, 55-64, PROF APPL PHYSICS, CORNELL UNIV, 64-, DIR WARD LAB NUCLEAR ENG, 60- *Concurrent Pos:* Euratom fel, Italy, 62; Guggenheim fel, Niels Bohr Inst, Copenhagen, Denmark, 68-69; vis prof, Tech Univ Munich, Ger, 76. *Mem:* Am Phys Soc. *Res:* Nuclear structure physics, especially isomers; nuclear instrumentation; reactor physics. *Mailing Add:* Ward Lab Cornell Univ Ithaca NY 14853

CLARK, DAVID ELLSWORTH, b Paso Robles, Calif, Nov 22, 22; m 47; c 2. ORGANIC CHEMISTRY. *Educ:* Univ Redlands, BA, 47; Stanford Univ, MS, 48, PhD(org chem), 53. *Prof Exp:* Instr chem, Fresno State Col, 50-51 & 53-54, from asst prof to prof, 54-65; assoc acad planning, Chancellor's Off, Calif State Cols, 65-67; acad admin internship, Brown Univ, 67-68; ASSOC VPRES ACAD AFFAIRS, CALIF STATE UNIV, FRESNO, 70- *Concurrent Pos:* NSF sci fac fel, Harvard Univ, 62-63. *Mem:* Am Chem Soc. *Res:* Organic synthesis; chemical therapeutics. *Mailing Add:* Assoc VPres Acad Affairs Calif State Univ Fresno CA 93740

CLARK, DAVID LEE, b Gallipolis, Ohio, Feb 17, 42; m 67; c 1. PHYSICS. *Educ:* Ohio State Univ, BS, 65; Univ Minn, PhD(physics), 77. *Prof Exp:* Res assoc, Williams Lab of Nuclear Physics, Univ Minn, 70-76; fel, Stanford Univ, 76-77, asst prof nuclear physics, Dept Physics, 77-80; ASST PROF PHYSICS, DEPT PHYSICS, UNIV ROCHESTER, 80- *Mem:* Am Phys Soc; Sigma Xi. *Res:* Experimental nuclear physics research with emphasis on weak interactions; properties of nuclear states; heavy-ion reactions; application of lasers to nuclear physics. *Mailing Add:* Nuclear Structure Res Lab Univ Rochester Rochester NY 14627

CLARK, DAVID LEE, b Detroit, Mich, Apr 7, 39; m 67; c 3. VESTIBULAR THERAPY, EYE MOVEMENTS. *Educ:* Kalamazoo Col, BA, 62; Univ Okla, MS, 63; Mich State Univ, PhD(zool), 67. *Prof Exp:* ASSOC PROF ANAT, COL MED, OHIO STATE UNIV, 68- *Concurrent Pos:* Great Lakes Cols Asn teaching fel, Kenyon Col, 67-68. *Mem:* AAAS; Am Anat Asn; Animal Behav Soc. *Res:* Effects of vestibular stimulation therapy applied to developmentally delayed children (cerebral palsied, Down's syndrome, autistic, hyperactive); control of eye movements in children. *Mailing Add:* Dept Anat Ohio State Univ Columbus OH 43210

CLARK, DAVID LEIGH, b Albuquerque, NMex, June 15, 31; m 51; c 4. PALEONTOLOGY. *Educ:* Brigham Young Univ, BS, 53, MS, 54; Univ Iowa, PhD(geol), 57. *Prof Exp:* Geologist, Standard Oil Co, 54; asst geol, Columbia Univ, 54-55; asst, Univ Iowa, 55-57; asst prof, Southern Methodist Univ, 57-59; from asst prof to assoc prof, Brigham Young Univ, 59-63; assoc prof geol, 63-68, prof geol & geophys, 68-74, chmn dept, 71-74, W H TWENHOFEL PROF, UNIV WIS-MADISON, 74- *Concurrent Pos:* Sr Fulbright fel & vis prof, Univ Bonn, 65-66. *Mem:* Geol Soc Am; Am Asn Petrol Geologists; Paleont Soc; Soc Econ Paleontologists & Mineralogists. *Res:* Artic Ocean geology and paleoecology; Paleozoic and Mesozoic conodonts. *Mailing Add:* Dept of Geol & Geophys Weeks Hall Univ of Wis Madison WI 53706

CLARK, DAVID SEDGEFIELD, b St Stephen, NB, Nov 13, 29; m 52; c 3. FOOD MICROBIOLOGY. *Educ:* McGill Univ, MS, 53, PhD(physiol), 57. *Prof Exp:* Lectr agr bact, MacDonald Col, McGill Univ, 53-57; tech sales, Buckman Labs Can, Ltd, 57-58; from asst res officer to assoc res officer, 58-70, sr res officer, Nat Res Coun Can, 70-76; chief, Div Microbial Res, 76-78, DIR, BUR MICROBIAL HAZARDS, HEALTH PROTECTION BR, DEPT NAT HEALTH & WELFARE, 78- *Concurrent Pos:* Secy-treas, Int Standing Comn Microbiol Specifications Foods, Int Asn Microbiol Socs; hon mem expert panel on food microbiol & hyg, WHO. *Mem:* Can Soc Microbiol; Can Inst Food Technologists (pres, 75-76). *Res:* Industrial fermentations; bacterial physiology; meat microbiology; microbiol methodology; effect of the gaseous environment on microorganisms. *Mailing Add:* 1 Kaymar Dr Ottawa ON K1J 7C8 Can

CLARK, DAVID THURMOND, b Topeka, Kans, Aug 3, 25; m 47; c 2. PARASITOLOGY, IMMUNOLOGY. *Educ:* Univ Nebr, BA, 49, MA, 51; Univ Ill, PhD, 55. *Prof Exp:* Asst zool, Univ Nebr, 49-51 & Univ Ill, 51-55; from instr to prof microbiol & pub health, Mich State Univ, 56-65, asst vpres res & develop, 65-69; staff assoc univ sci & develop, Instnl Rels, NSF, Washington, DC, 69-70; Dean Grad Studies & Res, 70-76, PROF BIOL, PORTLAND STATE UNIV, 76- *Concurrent Pos:* Mem subcomt prenatal & postnatal mortality in swine, Comt Animal Health, Nat Res Coun, 59- *Mem:* Am Soc Parasitologists; Am Micros Soc; NY Acad Sci; Soc Protozool. *Res:* Parasites of wildlife; physiological studies on nematodes; immunology of parasitic infections; science policy. *Mailing Add:* Dept of Biology Portland State Univ Portland OR 97207

CLARK, DENNIS RICHARD, b Palo Alto, Calif, Mar 13, 44. TOXICOLOGY, ANALYTICAL CHEMISTRY. *Educ:* Univ Ore, BA, 66; Stanford Univ, PhD(org chem), 70. *Prof Exp:* Fel chem, Stanford Univ, 70-71, fel pharmacol, 71-73; asst dir, Drug Assay Lab, 73-80, CLIN CHEMIST, STANFORD UNIV HOSP, 80- *Mem:* Am Asn Clin Chem. *Res:* Development of methods for drug analysis in biological fluids; study of relationships between drug blood levels and clinical effects of drugs. *Mailing Add:* Drug Assay Lab C-214 Stanford Univ Med Ctr Stanford CA 94305

CLARK, DONALD LYNDON, b Lyndon, Vt, Feb 17, 20; m 44; c 3. APPLIED PHYSICS, ELECTRICAL ENGINEERING. *Educ:* Univ Vt, BS, 43; Univ Rochester, PhD(physics), 52. *Prof Exp:* Elec engr, Stromberg Carlson Co, 43-46; res assoc physics, Univ Rochester, 52; STAFF MEM & GROUP LEADER, DEFENSE ELECTRONICS, LINCOLN LAB, MASS INST TECHNOL, 52- *Mem:* AAAS; Am Phys Soc; Am Asn Physics Teachers; Inst Elec & Electronics Engrs; Sigma Xi. *Res:* Radar and optical measurements of hyper-velocity vehicles outside and within the atmosphere, and their implications for strategic offense and defense systems. *Mailing Add:* Lincoln Lab Mass Inst Technol Lexington MA 02173

CLARK, DONALD RAY, JR, b Garrett, Ind, Jan 20, 40; m 58; c 3. POLLUTION BIOLOGY. *Educ:* Univ Ill, Urbana, BS, 61; Tex A&M Univ, MS, 64; Univ Kans, PhD(zool), 68. *Prof Exp:* Asst prof wildlife sci, Tex A&M Univ, 68-72; RES BIOLOGIST, PATUXENT WILDLIFE RES CTR, US FISH & WILDLIFE SERV, DEPT INTERIOR, 72- *Concurrent Pos:* Prin investr, Tex Agr Exp Sta, 68-72. *Mem:* Ecol Soc Am; Am Soc Ichthyologists & Herpetologists; Soc Study Amphibians & Reptiles; Am Soc Mammalogists; AAAS. *Res:* Understanding the relationships between environmental contaminants and declining populations of bats. *Mailing Add:* Patuxent Res Ctr US Fish & Wildlife Res Ctr Laurel MD 20811

CLARK, DOUGLAS NAPIER, b New York, NY, Jan 24, 44; m 68. MATHEMATICAL ANALYSIS. *Educ:* Johns Hopkins Univ, AB, 64, PhD(math), 67. *Prof Exp:* Fel math, Univ Wis-Madison, 67-68; asst prof, Univ Calif, Los Angeles, 68-73; assoc prof, 73-77, PROF MATH, UNIV GA, 77- *Concurrent Pos:* Res assoc, Off Naval Res, Nat Res Coun, 67-68; vis prof, Univ Va, 79-80 & State Univ NY, Stony Brook, 81. *Mem:* Am Math Soc. *Res:* Operator theory and its applications to complex variables, chiefly Toeplitz and Hankel matrices and the study of invariant subspaces; analytic functions in polydiscs; interpolation problems. *Mailing Add:* Dept of Math Univ of Ga Athens GA 30602

CLARK, DUNCAN WILLIAM, b New York, NY, Aug 31, 10; m 43, 71; c 3. MEDICINE. *Educ:* Fordham Col, AB, 32; Long Island Col Med, MD, 36. *Prof Exp:* Intern, Brooklyn Hosp, 36-38; resident med, Kings County Hosp, 38-40; dir student health, Long Island Col Med, 41-49, instr med, 42-47, from asst dean to assoc dean, 43-48, asst prof med, actg chmn prev med & dean, 48-50; chmn dept, 51-78, PROF PREV MED & COMMUNITY HEALTH, STATE UNIV NY DOWNSTATE MED CTR, 51- *Concurrent Pos:* Fel, Yale Univ, 40-41; traveling fel, WHO, 52; Commonwealth Found fel, 61; vis prof, Univ Birmingham, 61; consult, Health Serv Res Study Sect, US Pub Health Serv, 61-65 & 73-77, consult & chmn community health res training, 65-69, consult, Nat Ctr Health Serv Res & Develop, 70-81, mem tech adv group on med care effectiveness, 71-74; res scientist, Fel Rev Comt, 70-72; consult, Nat Acad Sci-Nat Res Coun, 65-68. *Mem:* Am Col Prev Med; Am Col Physicians; Harvey Soc; Am Pub Health Asn; NY Acad Med (vpres, 76-78). *Res:* Medical education; public health and medical care; preventive medicine. *Mailing Add:* Dept of Prev Med State Univ NY Downstate Med Ctr Brooklyn NY 11203

CLARK, EDWARD ALOYSIUS, b Jersey City, NJ, Jan 28, 34; m 55; c 4. THEORETICAL PHYSICS. *Educ:* Col Holy Cross, BS, 55; Fordham Univ, MS, 60, PhD(physics), 66. *Prof Exp:* From instr to assoc prof physics, 60-70, chmn dept, 66-70, asst to pres, Univ, 70-71, acad vpres, Brooklyn Ctr, 74-75, PROF PHYSICS, LONG ISLAND UNIV, BROOKLYN CTR, 70-, DEAN COL LIB ARTS & SCI, 71-, PRES, BROOKLYN CTR, 75- *Concurrent Pos:* Consult, State NY Dept Educ, 66- *Mem:* Am Phys Soc; Am Asn Physics Teachers. *Res:* Calculation of molecular vibration-rotation spectra. *Mailing Add:* Long Island Univ Brooklyn Ctr Brooklyn NY 11201

CLARK, EDWARD MAURICE, b Edinburgh, Scotland, Feb 16, 20; div; c 1. PLANT BREEDING. *Educ:* Univ Minn, BS, 49, MS, 55, PhD(plant breeding), 56. *Prof Exp:* From asst botanist to assoc botanist, 56-62, ASSOC PROF BOT, AUBURN UNIV, 62- *Mem:* AAAS; Genetics Soc Am; Am Genetics Asn; Am Phytopath Soc. *Res:* Diseases of forage legumes and grasses. *Mailing Add:* Dept of Bot Auburn Univ Auburn AL 36830

CLARK, EDWARD SHANNON, b Schenevus, NY, Apr 26, 30. POLYMER CHEMISTRY. *Educ:* Union Col, NY, BS, 51; Univ Calif, PhD(chem), 56. *Prof Exp:* Res phys chemist, E I du Pont de Nemours & Co, Inc, 55-62, sr res chemist, 62-72; PROF, DEPT CHEM & METALL & POLYMER ENG, UNIV TENN, KNOXVILLE, 72- *Concurrent Pos:* Fulbright scholar, Aarhus Univ, 62-63. *Mem:* Am Chem Soc; Am Crystallog Asn; Am Phys Soc; Soc Plastics Eng; Am Inst Chem Engr. *Res:* Structure-property relationships in polymers. *Mailing Add:* Dept of Chem & Metall Eng Univ of Tenn Knoxville TN 37916

CLARK, ELOISE ELIZABETH, b Grundy, Va, Jan 20, 31. BIOCHEMISTRY, BIOPHYSICS. *Educ:* Mary Washington Col, BA, 51; Univ NC, PhD(zool), 58. *Hon Degrees:* DSc, King Col, 76. *Prof Exp:* Instr biol, Women's Col, Univ NC, Greensboro, 52-53; res asst physiol, Univ NC, Chapel Hill, 53-55; from instr to assoc prof biol & biochem, Columbia Univ, 59-69; prog dir, Develop Biol Prog, 69-70, prog dir, Biophysic Prog, 70-73, sect head, Molecular Biol Sect, 71-73; div dir, Biol & Med Sci Div, 73-75, dep asst dir, 75-76, ASST DIR, BIOL, BEHAV & SOC SCI DIRECTORATE, NSF, 76- *Mem:* AAAS; Am Soc Cell Biol; Soc Gen Physiologists (secy, 65-67); Biophysical Soc; Sigma Xi. *Res:* Physical biochemistry of muscle protein and enzymes; science administration. *Mailing Add:* Biol Behav & Social Sci Nat Sci Found Washington DC 20550

CLARK, ERVIL DELWYN, biology, deceased

CLARK, EUGENIE, b New York, NY, May 4, 22; div; c 4. ZOOLOGY. *Educ:* Hunter Col, BA, 42; NY Univ, MS, 46, PhD(zool), 50. *Prof Exp:* Asst ichthyol, Scripps Inst Oeanog, 46-47 & NY Zool Soc, 47-48; asst animal behavior, Am Mus Natural Hist, 48-49; res assoc, 50-66; dir marine biol, Cape Haze Marine Lab, 55-66; assoc prof biol, City Col New York, 66-67; assoc prof, 69-73, PROF ZOOL, UNIV MD, COLLEGE PARK, 73- *Concurrent Pos:* AEC fel, 50; Fulbright scholar, Egypt, 51; Saxton fel & Breadloaf Writer's fel, 52; instr, Hunter Col, 54. *Honors & Awards:* Gold Medal, Soc Women Geogr, 75. *Mem:* Am Soc Ichthyologists & Herpetologists; Soc Women Geogr; fel AAAS. *Res:* Ichthyology; reproductive behavior of fishes; morphology and taxonomy of plectognath fishes; isolating mechanisms of poeciliid fishes; behavior of sharks; Red Sea fishes. *Mailing Add:* Dept of Zool Univ of Md College Park MD 20742

CLARK, EVELYN GENEVIEVE, b Brooksville, Ky, Jan 8, 22. MICROBIOLOGY. *Educ:* Georgetown Col, AB, 47; Univ Ky, MS, 53. *Prof Exp:* From instr to asst prof, 47-64, ASSOC PROF BIOL, GEORGETOWN COL, 64- *Concurrent Pos:* Consult microbiologist, Cent Baptist Hosp, Ky, 53-64; bacteriologist, Ford Mem Hosp, Ky, 67-71. *Mem:* AAAS; Nat Asn Biol Teachers; Am Soc Microbiol; Am Inst Biol Sci. *Res:* Clinical mycology. *Mailing Add:* Dept of Biol Georgetown Col Georgetown KY 40324

CLARK, EZEKAIL LOUIS, b Gomel, Russia, June 29, 12; US citizen; m 33; c 2. CHEMICAL ENGINEERING. *Educ:* Northeastern Univ, BSChE, 37. *Prof Exp:* Chemist, Mass State Dept Pub Health, 37-40; jr engr, Stone & Webster Eng Corp, 40-43; sr engr, Cities Serv Ref Corp, La, 43-45; chem engr, US Bur Mines, Pa & DC, 45-54; dir lab, Israel Mining & Industs, 54-56; pvt

consult, 56-64; pres, Pressure Chem Co, 64-74; asst div dir, ERDA, 74-77 & Dept Energy, 77-78; INDEPENDENT CONSULT, 78- *Concurrent Pos:* Assoc prof, Univ Pittsburgh, 51-52 & Israel Inst Technol, 55-56; lectr, Cath Univ Am, 53-54 & Pa State Univ, 65-67. *Mem:* Fel Am Inst Chem Engrs; Am Chem Soc. *Res:* Pilot plant experimentation; high pressure technology; coal science; process development; waste disposal. *Mailing Add:* 4615 N Park Ave Chevy Chase MD 20815

CLARK, FLORA MAE, b Houston Co, Ala, Nov 19, 33. GENETICS. *Educ:* Ala Col, BS, 60, MAT, 65; Univ Tenn, PhD(zool), 70. *Prof Exp:* Teacher biol, Rehobeth High Sch, Ala, 60-62 & Dependent Educ Group, US Army, France, 62-64; instr, Jacksonville State Univ, 65-67; res assoc genetics, Univ Ga, 70-71; assoc prof, 71-81, PROF BIOL, COLUMBUS COL, 81- *Concurrent Pos:* Consult, St Francis Hosp Lab, 75. *Mem:* AAAS; Am Inst Biol Sci. *Res:* Human chromosome abnormalities. *Mailing Add:* Fac Off Bldg Columbus Col Columbus GA 31907

CLARK, FLOYD BRYAN, b Akron, Ohio, Nov 15, 25; m 49; c 2. FORESTRY, RESEARCH ADMINISTRATION. *Educ:* Purdue Univ, BSF, 49; Univ Mo, MSF, 54; Univ Southern Ill, PhD(bot), 68. *Prof Exp:* Res forester silvicult, 49-59, proj leader, 59-68, asst dir, NCent Forest Exp Sta, 68-74, dir, Northeastern Forest Exp Sta, 74-79, dir, Timber Mgt Res, 79-80, ASSOC DEP CHIEF, US FOREST SERV, 80- *Mem:* Am Soc Foresters; Am Forestry Asn. *Res:* Forest management; silviculture; silvics; natural and artificial regeneration. *Mailing Add:* US Dept Agr Forest Serv PO Box 2417 Washington DC 20013

CLARK, FRANCIS JOHN, b Chicago, Ill, May 30, 33. NEUROPHYSIOLOGY. *Educ:* Northwestern Univ, BSEE, 56; Purdue Univ, MSEE, 57, PhD(elec eng), 65. *Prof Exp:* Engr, Cook Res Labs, Ill, 57-59; proj mgr, Advan Res Dept, Sunbeam Corp, 59-61; instr elec eng, Purdue Univ, West Lafayette, 64, asst prof, Sch Elec Eng & Dept Vet Anat, 64-68, assoc prof, 68-72; assoc prof, 72-77, PROF PHYSIOL & BIOPHYS, UNIV NEBR MED CTR, OMAHA, 77- *Concurrent Pos:* Nat Inst Neurol Dis & Stroke spec fel, Nobel Inst Neurophysiol, Karolinska Inst, Sweden, 69-71; fel, Lab Physiology, Oxford Univ, Eng, 79-80. *Mem:* AAAS; Am Phys Soc; Soc Neurosci; fel Muscular Dytrophy Asn. *Res:* Mammalian nervous system. *Mailing Add:* Dept Physiol & Biophys Univ Nebr Med Ctr Omaha NE 68105

CLARK, FRANCIS MATTHEW, b Augusta, Ill, Sept 26, 00; m 25. MICROBIOLOGY. *Educ:* Univ Ill, BS, 23, MS, 26, PhD(bact), 33. *Prof Exp:* Asst soil fertility, 23-25, asst soil biol, 25-29, asst bact, 29-33, instr, 33-37, assoc, 37-39, from asst prof to assoc prof, 39-57, prof, 57-70, EMER PROF BACT, UNIV ILL, URBANA-CHAMPAIGN, 70- *Mem:* Am Soc Microbiologists; Am Chem Soc; Inst Food Technologists. *Res:* Thermophilic organisms and food spoilage; bacterial nutrition; yeast nutrition; vitamin and nitrogen requirements. *Mailing Add:* 726 S Foley St Champaign IL 61820

CLARK, FRANK EUGENE, b St Louis, Mo, Sept 16, 19; m 48. MATHEMATICS. *Educ:* Dartmouth Univ, BA, 41; Duke Univ, MA, 46, PhD(math), 48. *Prof Exp:* Vis instr math, Duke Univ, 47-48; instr, Tulane Univ, 48-50; from asst prof to assoc prof, 50-61, chmn dept, Univ Col, 59-75, PROF MATH, RUTGERS UNIV, 61- *Concurrent Pos:* Vis prof, Univ Nairobi, Kenya, 75-76. *Mem:* Am Math Soc; Math Asn Am. *Res:* Combinatorial problems; linear programming. *Mailing Add:* Dept of Math Univ Col Rutgers Univ New Brunswick NJ 08903

CLARK, FRANK S, b San Mateo, Calif, Sept 27, 33. ORGANIC CHEMISTRY. *Educ:* Stanford Univ, BS, 55; Purdue Univ, PhD(org chem), 60. *Prof Exp:* Res chemist, 60-68, RES SPECIALIST, MONSANTO CO, 68- *Mem:* AAAS; Am Chem Soc. *Res:* Development of high temperature gas turbine engine oils; organic synthesis; synthesis of synthetic lubricants; boundary lubrication, corrosion and wetting of synthetic lubricants. *Mailing Add:* Corp Res Dept Monsanto Co 800 N Lindbergh Blvd St Louis MO 63166

CLARK, GARY EDWIN, b Lees Summit, Mo, Jan 5, 39. NUCLEAR STRUCTURE. *Educ:* Park Col, BA, 61; Kans State Univ, MS, 66; Iowa State Univ, PhD(nuclear physics), 72. *Prof Exp:* Instr physics, Kans State Univ, 66-; asst prof, Cent Mo State Col, 66-68; teaching & res, Iowa State Univ, 69-72; INTERN, NAT BUR STANDARDS, 72-; STAFF OFFICER, NAT ACAD SCI, 72- *Mem:* Am Phys Soc; AAAS; Sigma Xi. *Res:* Photnuclear physics; neutron detectors. *Mailing Add:* Nat Acad Sci 2101 Constitution Ave NW Washington 20418

CLARK, GEORGE, b Sunnyside, Wash, May 18, 05; m 34; c 4. NEUROPHYSIOLOGY. *Educ:* Univ Wash, BS, 36; Northwestern Univ, MS, 37, PhD(neurophysiol), 39. *Prof Exp:* Instr neurol, Northwestern Univ, 39-40; assoc anat, Med Col SC, 40-42, asst prof, 42; asst prof psychobiol, Yerkes Labs Primate Biol, 43-47; assoc prof neuroanat, Chicago Med Sch, 47-53; assoc prof physiol, Univ Buffalo, 53-59; res physiologist, US Army Med Res Lab, Ky, 59-61 & Inst Environ Med, Mass, 61-64; res physiologist, Civil Aeromed Res Inst, Fed Aviation Agency, 64-70; vis prof anat, Med Univ SC, 70-77; MEM STAFF VET ADMIN HOSP, 70- *Concurrent Pos:* Consult anat, Med Univ SC, 77-81; consult path, 81- *Mem:* Am Acad Neurol; Am Asn Anat; Soc Exp Biol & Med; Am Physiol Soc; Biol Stain Comn. *Res:* Functions of hypothalamus; temperature regulation; staining mechanisms. *Mailing Add:* Vet Admin Hosp Charleston SC 29403

CLARK, GEORGE ALFRED, JR, b Camden, NJ, May 6, 36; m 61. ORNITHOLOGY. *Educ:* Amherst Col, BA, 57; Yale Univ, PhD(biol), 64. *Prof Exp:* Res assoc zool, Univ Wash, 63-64, actg instr, 64-65; asst prof, 65-70, ASSOC PROF ZOOL, UNIV CONN, 70- *Mem:* Soc Study Evolution; Am Ornith Union; Am Soc Naturalists; Cooper Ornith Soc; Wilson Ornith Soc. *Res:* Integumental structure, behavior and evolution of birds. *Mailing Add:* Biol Sci Group Univ Conn Storrs CT 06268

CLARK, GEORGE BROMLEY, b Pleasant Grove, Utah, June 5, 12; m 54; c 7. MINING ENGINEERING. *Educ:* Univ Utah, BS, 35, MS, 46; Univ Ill, EM, 49, PhD(mining eng), 52. *Prof Exp:* Jr engr, Tintic Standard Mining Co, 35-40; sampling foreman, US Bur Mines, 40-41; prof mining eng, Univ Ill, 46-54; prof, Sch Mines, Univ Mo-Rolla, 54-64, chmn dept, 54-61, dir, Res Ctr, 61-64 & Rock Mech & Explosives Res Ctr, 64-76; adj prof mining eng, Colo Sch Mines, 76-81. *Concurrent Pos:* Actg chmn dept & instr, Univ Utah, 38-39. *Honors & Awards:* Citation, Outstanding Contrib to Rock Mech, US Nat Comt Rock Mech, Nat Acad Sci. *Mem:* Am Inst Mining, Metall & Petrol Engrs; Am Geophys Union; Am Soc Testing & Mat; Am Soc Civil Engrs. *Res:* Teaching and research; detonation and blasting of high explosives; dynamic and static rock mechanics; mine ventilation and related fields. *Mailing Add:* Dept Mining Eng Colo Sch of Mines Golden CO 80401

CLARK, GEORGE C(HARLES), b Battle Creek, Mich, June 26, 30. CHEMICAL ENGINEERING. *Educ:* Univ Mich, BSE, 52, MSE, 53, PhD, 60. *Prof Exp:* Res engr reservoir eng res, 57-64, res group leader, 64-67, RES ASSOC, CONTINENTAL OIL CO, 67- *Mem:* AAAS; Am Inst Chem Engrs; Soc Petrol Engrs; Sigma Xi. *Res:* Application of mathematics and computers to reservoir engineering; solution of systems of linear and non-linear partial differential equations. *Mailing Add:* 2309 E Hartford Ponca City OK 74601

CLARK, GEORGE RICHMOND, II, b Princeton, Maine, Mar 23, 38; m 61; c 3. PALEOECOLOGY, MARINE BIOLOGY. *Educ:* Cornell Univ, AB, 61; Calif Inst Technol, MS, 66, PhD(geobiol), 69. *Prof Exp:* Asst prof geol, Univ NMex, 69-74, State Univ NY Col Geneseo, 74-76 & Edinboro State Col, Pa, 76-77; asst prof, 77-81, ASSOC PROF GEOL, KANS STATE UNIV, 81- *Mem:* AAAS; Am Soc Zoologists; Soc Econ Paleont & Mineral; Geol Soc Am; Paleont Soc. *Res:* Growth lines; environmental variations in shell morphology; invertebrate calcification and shell structure; paleopopulation dynamics. *Mailing Add:* Dept Geol Kans State Univ Manhattan KS 66506

CLARK, GEORGE WHIPPLE, b Evanston, Ill, Aug 31, 28; m 54; c 2. PHYSICS. *Educ:* Harvard Univ, AB, 49; Mass Inst Technol, PhD(physics), 52. *Prof Exp:* From instr to assoc prof, 52-65, PROF PHYSICS, MASS INST TECHNOL, 65- *Concurrent Pos:* Guggenheim fel & Fulbright res scholar, 63; bd dir, AURA, Inc, 78-; mem, Astron Surv Comt, Nat Acad Sci, 79-81, chmn, Panel High Energy Astrophysics; prin investr, Solar Array Syst-3 X-ray Observ, 72-82. *Mem:* Nat Acad Sci; Am Astron Soc; Int Astron Union; Am Acad Arts & Sci; Am Phys Soc. *Res:* Cosmic rays; x-ray astronomy. *Mailing Add:* Dept Physics Mass Inst Technol Cambridge MA 02139

CLARK, GLEN HOWARD, b McGill, Nev, Nov 14, 25; m 64; c 2. COMPUTER SCIENCE, ELECTRICAL ENGINEERING. *Educ:* Univ Nev, BSEE, 51, MAEd, 59; Univ Colo, MSEE, 62. *Prof Exp:* Develop engr, Gen Elec Advan Elec Lab, 52-58; from instr to asst prof elec, 59-68, ASST DIR, COMPUT CTR, UNIV NEV, 68- *Honors & Awards:* Prof Engr Award, State Nev, 60. *Mem:* Asn Comput Mach; Inst Elec & Electronics Engrs; Sigma Xi. *Res:* Computer interfacing; computer software and processors; switching circuit theory; feedback control systems; error correcting codes. *Mailing Add:* Comput Ctr PO Box 9068 Reno NV 89507

CLARK, GLEN W, b Newdale, Idaho, Apr 17, 31; m 51; c 5. PARASITOLOGY, PROTOZOOLOGY. *Educ:* Ricks Col, BS, 56; Utah State Univ, MS, 58; Univ Calif, Davis, PhD(zool), 62. *Prof Exp:* Instr life sci, Am River Jr Col, 62-64; from asst prof to assoc prof, 64-71, prof zool, 71-77, PROF BIOL, CENT WASH UNIV, 77- *Mem:* Soc Protozool; Wildlife Dis Asn. *Res:* Blood parasites of the class Aves; coccidial parasites of reptiles. *Mailing Add:* Dept of Biol Cent Wash Univ Ellensburg WA 98926

CLARK, GORDON MEREDITH, b Akron, Ohio, Nov 21, 34; m 57; c 2. OPERATIONS RESEARCH, INDUSTRIAL ENGINEERING. *Educ:* Ohio State Univ, BIE, 57, PhD(opers res), 69; Univ Southern Calif, MSc in IE, 65. *Prof Exp:* Engr mfg, Lamp Div, Gen Elec Co, 60-61; sr reliability engr reliability anal, Rocketdyne Div, NAm Aviation, 61-65; res assoc indust & syst eng, 65-68, from asst prof to assoc prof, 69-79, PROF INDUST & SYSTS ENG, OHIO STATE UNIV, 79- *Concurrent Pos:* Consult, Army Res Off, 70-76, Comput Sci Corp, 70-73 & Battelle Mem Inst, 78-; ed, Phalanx, Newslett Opers Res Soc Am, 71-73, assoc ed, J Opers Res Soc Am, 75-78. *Mem:* Opers Res Soc Am; Soc Comput Simulation; Mil Opers Res Soc; Inst Mgt Sci; Am Inst Indust Engrs. *Res:* Development of improved methods for designing and analyzing simulation of complex systems, improved procedures for predicting and analyzing system reliability and more reliable methods for forecasting system performance. *Mailing Add:* Dept of Indust & Systs Eng 1971 Neil Ave Columbus OH 43210

CLARK, GORDON MURRAY, b Montreal, Que, July 9, 25; m 51; c 6. RADIATION BIOLOGY. *Educ:* Sir George Williams Univ, BSc, 48; McGill Univ, MSc, 51; Emory Univ, PhD(radiation biol), 54. *Prof Exp:* Asst, McGill Univ, 50-51 & Univ Miami, 51-52; res, Emory Univ, 54-55 & Univ Mich, 55-57; asst prof zool & radiation biol, 57-64, assoc prof radiobiol, 64-68, prof radiobiol, 68-77, PROF ZOOL, UNIV TORONTO, 77- *Mem:* Soc Protozool; Royal Astron Soc Can; Can Genetic Soc. *Res:* Radiation effects on the cellular level; chemistry of the cell; dose and dose-rate studies in plant and animal cells; fallout studies; hyperbaric oxygen studies; x-ray and gamma ray irradiation; molecular biology; radiation injury and recovery; molecular level. *Mailing Add:* Dept of Zool St George Campus Toronto ON M5S 1A1 Can

CLARK, GRADY WAYNE, b Candler, NC, Nov 29, 22; m 52. PHYSICS. *Educ:* Clemson Col, BS, 44; Univ Va, PhD(physics), 51. *Prof Exp:* Res engr, Univ Va, 51-52, Linde Air Prod, 52-55 & Va Inst Sci Res, 55-58; res engr, 58-59, LAB HEAD, OAK RIDGE NAT LAB, 59- *Mem:* Am Phys Soc; Am Soc Metals; Am Ceramics Soc. *Res:* Crystal physics; crystal growth; eutetic solidification; biomagnetism. *Mailing Add:* 107 E Morningside Dr Oak Ridge TN 37830

CLARK, H(AROLD) B(LACK), b Huntingdon, Pa, May 20, 28; m 58. CHEMICAL ENGINEERING. *Educ:* Pa State Univ, BS, 50; Univ Ill, MS, 51, PhD(chem eng), 57. *Prof Exp:* ENGR, E I DU PONT DE NEMOURS & CO, INC, 57- *Mem:* Am Chem Soc; Am Inst Chem Engrs; Tech Asn Pulp & Paper Indust. *Res:* White pigment. *Mailing Add:* 2026 Floral Dr Wilmington DE 19810

CLARK, HARLAN EUGENE, b Bloomington, Ill, July 29, 41; m 67; c 2. CUSTOMIZED SOFTWARE, X-RAY PHYSICS. *Educ:* Univ Ill, BS, 63; Univ Mich, MS, 64, PhD(chem), 68. *Prof Exp:* Sr res chemist, Res Ctr, Sherwin-Williams Co, 68-73, sr scientist, Sherwin-Williams Chem, Chicago, 73-77, mem staff, 77-81, PROGRAMMER & CONSULT, E S INDUST, 81- *Mem:* Am Chem Soc. *Res:* Molecular vibrations; infrared and Raman spectroscopy; titanium dioxide pigments; zinc and barium chemicals; x-ray fluorescence; x-ray diffraction. *Mailing Add:* E S Indust 8 S Maple Ave Marlton NJ 08053

CLARK, HAROLD ARTHUR, b East Jordan, Mich, Apr 10, 10; m 38; c 2. POLYMER CHEMISTRY. *Educ:* Mich State Univ, BS, 31. *Prof Exp:* Analyst, Monolith Portland Midwest Co, 37-40 & Dow Chem Co, 42-43; anal supt, 43-48, res chemist, 48-53, res group leader, 53-60, res supvr, 60-64, tech dir, Eng Prod Div, 64-69, asst dir corp develop, 69-70, res scientist, 70-75, CONSULT, DOW CORNING CORP, 75- *Mem:* Am Chem Soc; Sigma Xi. *Res:* Silicone resins and polymers; abrasion resistant coatings for plastics and solar collectors. *Mailing Add:* 7081 Cedarhurst Dr SW Ft Meyers FL 33907

CLARK, HAROLD EUGENE, b Sunderland, Mass, Feb 21, 06; m 38; c 2. PLANT PHYSIOLOGY. *Educ:* Mass Col, BS, 28; Rutgers Univ, MS, 31, PhD(plant physiol), 33. *Prof Exp:* Nat Res Coun fel, Yale Univ & Univ Conn Exp Sta, 33-35; assoc biochemist, Exp Sta, Pineapple Res Inst, Hawaii, 35-38, head dept physiol & soil, 38-46, head dept chem, 46-47; from assoc prof to prof plant physiol, 47-74, EMER PROF PLANT PHYSIOL, RUTGERS UNIV, 74- *Mem:* Am Soc Plant Physiol; Am Chem Soc; Am Inst Biol Sci. *Res:* Mineral nutrition. *Mailing Add:* 24 E Lawrence St Milltown NJ 08850

CLARK, HELEN EDITH, b Edam, Sask, Feb 4, 12; nat US. NUTRITION. *Educ:* BHSc, Univ Sask, 39; Iowa State Col, MS, 45, PhD(nutrit), 50. *Prof Exp:* Res assoc, Iowa State Col, 45-50; from asst prof to assoc prof nutrit, Kans State Col, 50-54; assoc prof, 54-59, prof nutrit, Purdue Univ, 59-77. *Honors & Awards:* Borden Award, Am Home Econ Asn, 68. *Mem:* Am Bd Nutrit; Am Home Econ Asn; Am Inst Nutrit. *Res:* Factors influencing utilization of proteins and amino acids; amino acid requirements of man. *Mailing Add:* 2550 Yeager Rd 19-8 West Lafayette IN 47906

CLARK, HERBERT MOTTRAM, b Derby, Conn, Sept 3, 18. RADIOCHEMISTRY. *Educ:* Yale Univ, BS, 40, PhD(phys chem), 44. *Prof Exp:* Lab asst, Yale Univ, 40-42, instr chem, 42-46; asst prof phys chem, 46-49, assoc prof phys nuclear chem, 49-51, PROF PHYS & NUCLEAR CHEM, RENSSELAER POLYTECH INST, 51- *Concurrent Pos:* Res assoc, Monsanto Chem Co & Clinton Labs, Oak Ridge, 46-47; consult, Union Carbide & Carbon Corp, 55-58 & US AEC, 65-70; mem subcomt radiochem, Comt Nuclear Sci, Nat Acad Sci-Nat Res Coun, 61-72; consult radiol health, USPHS, 67-69. *Mem:* Fel AAAS; fel NY Acad Sci; Am Chem Soc; Am Phys Soc; Am Soc Eng Educ. *Res:* Radiochemistry applied to the environment; radiological health, nuclear power, nuclear medicine; radiochemical separations; Mossbauer spectrometry. *Mailing Add:* Dept of Chem Rensselaer Polytech Inst Troy NY 12181

CLARK, HOWARD CHARLES, b Auckland, NZ, Sept 4, 29; m 54; c 2. INORGANIC CHEMISTRY. *Educ:* Univ Auckland, BSc, 51, MSc, 52, PhD, 54; Cambridge Univ, PhD, 57, ScD(chem), 72. *Prof Exp:* Jr lectr chem, Univ Auckland, 54-55; res fel, Cambridge Univ, 55-57; from asst prof to prof, Univ BC, 57-65; sr prof, Univ Western Ont, 65-76, head dept, 67-76; PROF INORG CHEM & V PRES ACAD, UNIV GUELPH, 76- *Concurrent Pos:* Mem chem grant selection comt, Nat Res Coun Can, 68-70, chmn, 70; chmn comt chem dept chmn, Ont Univs, 69-; consult, E I du Pont de Nemours & Co, Inc, Del, 70-71. *Honors & Awards:* Noranda Lectr Award, Chem Inst Can. *Mem:* The Chem Soc; Am Chem Soc; fel Chem Inst Can; fel Royal Soc Can. *Res:* Chemistry of inorganic fluorides and organometallic compounds; coordination chemistry; organometallic and coordination compounds. *Mailing Add:* Off of the VPres Acad Univ of Guelph Guelph Can

CLARK, HOWARD CHARLES, JR, b Wichita, Kans, June 4, 37; m 57; c 5. GEOPHYSICS, GEOENVIRONMENTAL SCIENCE. *Educ:* Univ Okla, BS, 59; Stanford Univ, MS, 65, PhD(geophys), 67. *Prof Exp:* Teaching asst, Stanford Univ, 59-60; instr physics, Kansas City Jr Col, 61-62; res asst geophys, Stanford Univ, 65; instr geol, Menlo Col, 62-66; asst prof, 66-73, ASSOC PROF GEOL, RICE UNIV, 73- *Mem:* Geol Soc Am; Am Geophys Union; Soc Explor Geophys. *Res:* Marine geophysics; paleomagnetism. *Mailing Add:* Dept of Geol Rice Univ Houston TX 77001

CLARK, HOWARD GARMANY, b Birmingham, Ala, Feb 25, 28; m 47; c 3. BIOMEDICAL ENGINEERING. *Educ:* Howard Col, AB, 47; Univ Notre Dame, MS, 49; Univ Md, PhD(org chem), 54. *Prof Exp:* Chemist, Chemstrand Corp, 54-59; group leader, Peninsular Chem Res, Inc, 60; sr chemist, Camille Dreyfus Lab, Res Triangle Inst, 60-67; assoc prof textiles, Clemson Univ, 67-68; assoc prof biomed eng, 68-75, PROF BIOMED ENG & MECH ENG, DUKE UNIV, 75-, CHMN BIOMED ENG DEPT, 79- *Mem:* AAAS; Am Chem Soc. *Res:* Medical applications of polymer materials; coagulation of blood. *Mailing Add:* Dept Biomed Eng Duke Univ Durham NC 27706

CLARK, HOWELL R, b Dexter, Ky, Aug 9, 26; m 58; c 2. INORGANIC CHEMISTRY, ANALYTICAL CHEMISTRY. *Educ:* Murray State Univ, BS, 56; Vanderbilt Univ, MS, 58, PhD(inorg chem), 70. *Prof Exp:* Chemist, Shell Oil Co, 58-63; from asst prof to assoc prof 63-73, PROF CHEM, MURRAY STATE UNIV, 73- *Mem:* Am Chem Soc; Sigma Xi. *Res:* Kinetics of catalyzed organic fluoride hydrolysis; factors affecting acid formation in spoils from surface mining. *Mailing Add:* Dept of Chem Murray State Univ Murray KY 42071

CLARK, HUGH, b Pawling, NY, Apr 15, 14; m 39; c 4. EMBRYOLOGY. *Educ:* Clark Univ, AB, 34; Univ Mich, PhD(zool), 41. *Prof Exp:* Asst zool, Univ Mich, 35-39; prof physiol, Des Moines Still Col Osteop, 39-45; assoc zool, Univ Iowa, 45-46, asst prof, 46-47; from asst prof to assoc prof, 47-59, PROF ZOOL, UNIV CONN, 59-, ASSOC DEAN, GRAD SCH, 63- *Concurrent Pos:* Dir mus reconstruct, Southern Ill State Norm Univ, 39. *Mem:* AAAS; Soc Develop Biol. *Res:* Embryology of hemipenis in North American snakes; homogamy in the earthworm; respiration in reptile embryos; nitrogen metabolism in embryonic development; factors in embryonic differentiation. *Mailing Add:* Dept of Biol Sci Univ of Conn Storrs CT 06268

CLARK, HUGH KIDDER, b St Louis, Mo, Jan 22, 18; m 42; c 2. REACTOR PHYSICS. *Educ:* Oberlin Col, AB, 39; Cornell Univ, PhD(phys chem), 43. *Prof Exp:* Res assoc, Radio Res Lab, Harvard Univ, 43-45; res chemist, 45-62, RES ASSOC, E I DU PONT DE NEMOURS & CO, INC, 62- *Mem:* AAAS; Am Chem Soc; fel Am Nuclear Soc. *Res:* X-ray crystallography; radar direction finding; spinning of synthetic fibers; nuclear reactor physics; criticality safety. *Mailing Add:* Savannah River Lab E I du Pont de Nemours & Co Inc Aiken SC 29801

CLARK, IRWIN, b Boston, Mass, Apr 28, 18; m 49; c 4. BIOCHEMISTRY. *Educ:* Harvard Univ, AB, 39; Columbia Univ, PhD(biochem), 50. *Prof Exp:* Head isotope dept, Merck Inst, 51-59; from asst prof to prof biochem, Col Physicians & Surgeons, Columbia Univ, 59-71; prof biochem & surg, Sch Med, Univ NC, 71-74; PROF SURG (BIOCHEM), COL MED & DENT NJ-RUTGERS MED SCH, 74- *Concurrent Pos:* Sr Fulbright scholar, Cambridge Univ, 50-51; res career develop award, 62-69; consult, Merck, Sharpe & Dohme, 59-60 & Squibb Inst Med Res, 60-62; vis prof, Rice Univ, 63; ed, Proc, Soc Exp Biol & Med, 67- *Mem:* Soc Exp Biol & Med; Am Soc Biol Chem; Am Inst Nutrit; Endocrine Soc; Brit Biochem Soc. *Res:* Metabolism of bone; hormonal effects on bone; tRNA and cancer. *Mailing Add:* Dept of Surg Col Med Dent NJ-Rutgers Med Sch Piscataway NJ 08854

CLARK, J(OHN) B(EVERLEY), b Port Dalhousie, Ont, July 13, 24; nat US; m 51; c 3. METALLURGICAL ENGINEERING. *Educ:* Univ Toronto, BASc, 48; Carnegie Inst Tech, MS, 51, PhD(metall eng), 53. *Prof Exp:* Res engr, Dow Chem Co, 52-61; sr res scientist sci lab, Ford Motor Co, 61-66; assoc grad dean, 73-79, asst dean mines & metall, 79-81, PROF METALL ENG, UNIV MO-ROLLA, 66- *Concurrent Pos:* Assoc prog dir metall & mat prog, NSF, 72-73, consult, 73-76. *Honors & Awards:* Henry Marion Howe Medal, 60. *Mem:* Am Soc Metals; Am Inst Mining, Metall & Petrol Engrs; AAAS; Nat Coun Univ Adminr. *Res:* Physical metallurgy; phase equilibria and precipitation processes in metal alloy systems. *Mailing Add:* Grad Sch Univ of Mo Rolla MO 65401

CLARK, J(AMES) EDWIN, b Winnsboro, SC, Mar 3, 33; m 56; c 3. CIVIL ENGINEERING. *Educ:* Univ SC, BSCE, 57, ME, 64; Univ NC, PhD(civil eng), 67. *Prof Exp:* Engr, Union-Bag-Camp Paper Corp, 57-60; sr bridge designer, Smith-Pollite & Assoc, 60-62; instr civil eng, Univ SC, 62-63, res asst, 63-64; instr, NC State Univ, 64-65; asst prof, Miss State Univ, 67-70; assoc prof, 70-81, PROF CIVIL ENG, CLEMSON UNIV, 81- *Res:* Elements of highway safety; emergency medical care and theory of traffic flow. *Mailing Add:* Dept Civil Eng Clemson Univ Clemson SC 29631

CLARK, JAMES BENNETT, b Shamrock, Tex, Aug 24, 23; m 44; c 2. MICROBIAL PHYSIOLOGY. *Educ:* Univ Tex, BA, 47, MA, 48, PhD(bact), 50. *Prof Exp:* Res asst bact, Univ Tex, 46-48, res scientist bact genetics, 48-50; asst prof biol, Univ Houston, 50-51; PROF MICROBIOL, UNIV OKLA, 51- *Mem:* Am Soc Microbiol; Am Acad Microbiol. *Res:* Control mechanisms during morphogenesis in procaryotic cells. *Mailing Add:* Dept of Bot & Microbiol Univ of Okla Norman OK 73069

CLARK, JAMES D'ARGAVILLE, b Beith, Scotland, Jan 21, 01; nat US; m 30. PULP PAPER & BOARD TECHNOLOGY. *Educ:* Univ Cape Town, BSc, 18; Univ London, BSc, 22; Lawrence Col, PhD(chem), 41. *Prof Exp:* Apprentice, Masson Scott & Co, London, 22 & Hendon Paper Works Co, Ltd, 23; asst elec engr, Edward Lloyd, Ltd, 24-25; chief chemist, Bowater's Paper Mills, Ltd, 26-30; develop engr, Mead Corp, Ohio, 30-32; tech dir, Scott Paper Co, Pa, 32-35, eng & tech mgr, 35-39; res assoc, Inst Paper Chem, Lawrence Col, 41-42; CONSULT, 46-; HON RES ASSOC, WESTERN WASH UNIV, 64- *Concurrent Pos:* Prof pulp & paper sci, Ore State Univ, 59-63. *Honors & Awards:* Gold Medal, Tech Asn Pulp & Paper Indust, 63. *Mem:* Hon mem Can Pulp & Paper Tech Asn; hon mem Papermakers Asn Gt Brit & Ireland; Hon mem Australian Pulp & Paper Indust Tech Asn. *Res:* Fundamental properties of pulps; cellulose-water relationships; pulp, paper and board manufacture; paper and board quality evaluation; originator of waferboard and process; manufacture of structural boards by dry processes; manufacture of non-woven fabrics. *Mailing Add:* Chuckanut Point Bellingham WA 98225

CLARK, JAMES DERRELL, b Atlanta, Ga, Mar 8, 37; m 60; c 3. LABORATORY ANIMAL MEDICINE. *Educ:* Univ Ga, DVM, 61, MS, 64; Tulane Univ, DSc(microbiol), 69. *Prof Exp:* Asst prof lab animal med, Sch Med, Tulane Univ, 67-72; res asst vet med, 61-62, DIR LAB ANIMAL MED, COL VET MED, UNIV GA, 72- *Concurrent Pos:* Vet consult, Audubon Park Zoo, New Orleans, 66-72; consult, Am Asn Accreditation Lab Animal Care, 70- *Mem:* Am Vet Med Asn; Am Asn Lab Animal Sci; Am Asn Zoo Vets; Am Asn Vet Med Cols; Am Col Lab Animal Med. *Res:* Study the effects of mycotoxins upon the health of laboratory and domestic animals; development of new and innovative teaching methods. *Mailing Add:* Lab Animal Med Univ of Ga Col of Vet Med Athens GA 30602

CLARK, JAMES DONALD, b Plainville, Ind, Jan 1, 18; m 44; c 4. PETROLEUM ENGINEERING & TECHNOLOGY. *Educ:* NMex Sch Mines, BS, 47; Univ Okla, MPE, 49. *Prof Exp:* Asst instr petrol eng, Univ Okla, 47-48; petrol engr, Stanolind Oil & Gas Co, 48-52; chief reservoir engr, 52-66, regional reservoir engr, 66-80, CONSULT RESERVOIR ENGR, UNION OIL CO CALIF, 80- *Concurrent Pos:* Mem, Nat Petrol Council Comt Geothermal-Geopressure Studies, 79-80; reservoir eng test, Dept Energy Geothermal-Geopressure Well Testing, Gulf Coast, 80, 81 & 82. *Mem:* Soc Petrol Engrs; Soc Petrol Eval Engrs (pres, 73); Soc Prof Well Log Analysts(vpres, 68-69). *Res:* Secondary recovery; oil field evaluation; natural gas and oil reserves; reservoir limit tests, geopressured-geothermal sands. *Mailing Add:* 5423 Queensloch Houston TX 77096

CLARK, JAMES EDWARD, b Elkins, WVa, Nov 19, 26; m 49, 77; c 3. INTERNAL MEDICINE. *Educ:* WVa Univ, AB, 48; Jefferson Med Col, MD, 52; Am Bd Internal Med, dipl, 59. *Prof Exp:* Intern, Jefferson Med Col Hosp, 52-53, resident med, 53-55, chief resident, 55-56, asst, 56-58, instr, 58-62, assoc, 62-64; asst prof clin med, Jefferson Med Col & dir artificial kidney unit & dialysis unit, Hosp, 64-68; CHIEF MED, CROZER-CHESTER MED CTR, 68-; PROF MED, HAHNEMANN MED COL, 69- *Concurrent Pos:* Vis lectr, Univ Pa; lectr, US Naval Hosp, Philadelphia; courtesy med staff, Pa Hosp, 62-; consult, Jefferson Med Col Med Serv, Philadelphia Gen Hosp & Riddle Mem Hosp; chmn nat adv coun, Nat Kidney Dis Found, 62-64; chmn pharm comt, Riddle Mem Hosp, 62-64; dir health serv, Swarthmore Col; med dir, The Franklin Mint, Franklin Ctr, Pa; mem bd dirs, Kidney Found Southeastern Pa, Inc; mem bd trustees, Thomas Jefferson Univ. *Mem:* AAAS; fel Am Col Physicians; AMA; NY Acad Sci; Am Heart Asn. *Res:* Kidney disease and electrolyte metabolism. *Mailing Add:* Crozer-Chester Med Ctr 15th & Upland Sts Chester PA 19013

CLARK, JAMES HENRY, b Earlington, Ky, June 17, 32; m 57; c 2. REPRODUCTIVE PHYSIOLOGY, ENDOCRINOLOGY. *Educ:* Western Ky State Univ, BS, 59; Purdue Univ, MS, 66, PhD(endocrinol), 68. *Prof Exp:* Instr develop biol, Purdue Univ, 64-68, asst prof endocrinol, 70-73; assoc prof, 73-77, PROF CELL BIOL, BAYLOR COL MED, 77- *Concurrent Pos:* NIH fel biochem endocrinol, Univ Ill, Urbana, 68-70; NIH res grants, 70, 73, 76 & 79; Nat Cancer Inst res grant, 77 & 78; Am Cancer Soc res grant, 72-78; mem rev panel for contraceptive devices, NIH, 73, mem endocrinol study sect, 74-78; mem sci adv bd, Nat Ctr Toxicol Res. *Mem:* AAAS; Endocrine Soc; Soc Study Reprod; AAAS; Sigma Xi. *Res:* Mechanism of steroid hormone action; the control of reproductive function and the control of hormone indued growth. *Mailing Add:* Dept of Cell Biol Baylor Col of Med Houston TX 77030

CLARK, JAMES RICHARD, b New Brunswick, NJ, Oct 23, 51; m 78. HORTICULTURE. *Educ:* Rutgers Univ, BS, 73, MS, 75; Univ Calif, PhD(plant physiol), 79. *Prof Exp:* Res asst hort, Rutgers Univ, 73-75; res asst environ hort, Univ Calif-Davis, 75-78; asst prof hort, Mich State Univ, 78-81; ASST PROF ENVIRON HORT, CTR URBAN HORT, UNIV WASH, 81- *Mem:* Am Soc Hort Sci; Int Soc Arboricult; Int Plant Propagator's Soc. *Res:* Growth and development of woody plants, specifically phase change, assimilate partitioning and the development of crown form. *Mailing Add:* AR-10 Ctr Urban Hort Univ Wash Seattle WA 98195

CLARK, JAMES WILLIAM, b Beaumont, Tex, Nov 28, 24; m 49; c 3. DENTISTRY. *Educ:* Univ Tex, DDS, 47; Univ Toronto, dipl, 52; Am Bd Periodont, dipl, 55. *Prof Exp:* Pvt pract, 47-64; assoc prof periodont, Med Ctr, Univ Ala, 64-69; prof periodont & chmn dept, Col Dent, Univ Tenn, Memphis, 69-77; PROF PERIODONT & DIR CLIN NUTRIT, MED COL GA SCH DENT, 77- *Concurrent Pos:* Co-founder, Rowe Smith Mem Found; ed-in-chief, Clin Dent. *Mem:* Am Acad Periodont. *Res:* Clinical investigation of etiology and treatment of periodontal disease. *Mailing Add:* Med Col of Ga Sch of Dent Augusta GA 30912

CLARK, JASPER ARNOLD, b Kansas City, Mo, Sept 4, 09; m 31; c 2. BOTANY. *Educ:* William Jewell Col, AB, 31; Univ Okla, MS, 33; Univ Mo, PhD(bot), 56. *Prof Exp:* Asst bot, Univ Okla, 31-33 & Univ Mo, 34-35; prof biol, Hannibal-LaGrange Col, 35-38; chmn natural sci div, 65-75, PROF BIOL SCI, SOUTHWEST BAPTIST COL, 38- *Concurrent Pos:* Instr bot, Univ Mo, 56; NSF partic, Ore Inst Marine Biol, 58; res partic, Okla State Univ, 61; environ consult, Clark, Dietz & Assocs-Engrs, Inc, 72-75. *Mem:* Am Inst Biol Sci; Am Soc Plant Physiologists. *Res:* Drought resistance by plants; plant physiology. *Mailing Add:* Southwest Baptist Col 233 W College Bolivar MO 65613

CLARK, JEFFREY LEE, biochemistry, see previous edition

CLARK, JIMMY DORRAL, b Hobart, Okla, Feb 21, 39. MYCOLOGY. *Educ:* Wayne State Univ, BS, 65, MS, 66; Univ Calif, Berkeley, PhD(bot), 72. *Prof Exp:* Res assoc, Univ Calif, Berkeley, 72-74; asst prof, 75-80, ASSOC PROF BIOL, UNIV KY, 81- *Mem:* Mycol Soc Am; Bot Soc Am; Am Inst Biol Sci. *Res:* Genetic control of senescence and agametic cell fusion in the true slime molds and the associated physiological aspects of aging and incompatible reactions. *Mailing Add:* Sch of Biol Sci Univ of Ky Lexington KY 40506

CLARK, JIMMY HOWARD, b Sedalia, Ky, Feb 22, 41; m 74. RUMINANT NUTRITION, NITROGEN METABOLISM. *Educ:* Murray State Univ, BS, 63; Univ Tenn, PhD(animal sci), 67. *Prof Exp:* Res assoc fel ruminant nutrit, Clemson Univ, 67-68; from asst prof to assoc prof, 68-80, PROF NUTRIT & DAIRY SCI, UNIV ILL, 80- *Concurrent Pos:* Mem Comt Animal Nutrit, Nat Acad Sci, 82-85. *Honors & Awards:* Am Feed Mfrs Award, Am Dairy Sci Asn, 80. *Mem:* Am Dairy Sci Asn; Am Inst Nutrit; Nutrit Soc; Am Soc Animal Sci. *Res:* Ruminant nutrition and metabolism; limiting nutrients for milk production; amino acid metabolism; rumen fermentation; gluconeogenesis and nutritional hormonal interactions; nonprotein nitrogen utilization. *Mailing Add:* Dept Dairy Sci Rm 315 Univ Ill 1207 W Gregory Dr Urbana IL 61801

CLARK, JOAN ROBINSON, b Madison, Wis, Jan 22, 20; wid. CRYSTALLOGRAPHY. *Educ:* Barnard Col, BA, 45; Johns Hopkins Univ, PhD(crystallog), 58. *Prof Exp:* Jr sci aide phys chem, Eastern Regional Res Lab, USDA, 43; math asst, Manhattan Proj, Carbide & Carbon Chem Corp,

45; jr proj engr develop eng, Brown Instruments Div, Minneapolis-Honeywell Regulator Corp, 46-49; asst physics, Inst for Cancer Res, 49-53; mathematician, 53-56, physicist crystallog, 56-72, dep chief geochem, 72-75, PHYS SCIENTIST, US GEOL SURV, DEPT INTERIOR, 75- *Concurrent Pos:* Fulbright res scholar, Univ Sydney, 62; co-investr, Apollo Lunar Samples, NASA, 69-72. *Mem:* AAAS; fel Geol Soc Am; fel Mineral Soc Am (secy, 72-75); Am Crystallog Asn; Am Phys Soc. *Res:* X-ray diffraction studies of crystal structure; borates, silicates, and other minerals. *Mailing Add:* US Geol Surv Stop 18 345 Middlefield Rd Menlo Park CA 94025

CLARK, JOHN A(LDEN), b Ann Arbor, Mich, July 9, 23; m 45; c 3. MECHANICAL ENGINEERING. *Educ:* Univ Mich, BSE, 48; Mass Inst Technol, SM, 49, ScD(mech eng), 53. *Prof Exp:* Res engr res dept, United Aircraft Corp, 48; asst dept mech eng, Mass Inst Technol, 49-50, from instr to asst prof, 50-57; prof-in-charge heat transfer lab, 57-65, chmn dept mech eng, 66-74, PROF MECH ENG, UNIV MICH, ANN ARBOR, 57-; bd chmn & sr partner, Solarco, Inc, 76-78; pres, 78-80, CONSULT, CENT SOLAR ENERGY RES CORP, 80- *Concurrent Pos:* Consult, Corps Engrs, US Army, 52-57, E I du Pont de Nemours & Co, 53-59, Westinghouse Atomic Power Dept, 60-, Kelsey-Hayes Corp, 61- & Babcock & Wilcox Co, 64-; guest prof, Inst Thermodyn Technol, Munich Tech, 65-66 & Inst Thermodyn, Tech Univ Berlin, 72-73; NSF sr fel, 65-66. *Honors & Awards:* Gold Medal Award, 56 & Mem Award, Heat Transfer Div, 78, Am Soc Mech Engrs; Cent Medallion, Am Soc Mech Engrs, 81. *Mem:* Am Soc Mech Engrs; fel Am Soc Mech Engrs. *Res:* Heat and mass transfer; thermodynamics; fluid mechanics; temperature measurement; cryogenic heat transfer; solar energy; economics of energy. *Mailing Add:* Dept of Mech Eng Univ of Mich Ann Arbor MI 48104

CLARK, JOHN F, b Reading, Pa, Dec 12, 20; m 43, 74; c 2. SPACE APPLICATIONS & TECHNOLOGY, COMMUNICATIONS. *Educ:* Lehigh Univ, BS, 42, EE, 47; George Washington Univ, MS, 46; Univ Md, PhD(physcis), 56. *Prof Exp:* Engr, US Naval Res Lab, 42-47; asst prof elec eng, Lehigh Univ, 47-48; unit head ionospheric physics, US Naval Res Lab, 48-54, br head atmospheric elec, 54-58; dir physics & astron progs, NASA, 58-63, dep assoc adminr space sci & appln & chmn space sci steering comt, Goddard Space Flight Ctr, NASA, 63-65, dir, 65-76; DIR SPACE APPLN & TECHNOL, RCA CORP, PRINCETON, NJ, 76- *Concurrent Pos:* Lectr, George Washington Univ, 56-58, res assoc atmospheric physics, Grad Coun, 60-66; mem, Joint Comt Atmospheric Elec, Int Union Geod & Geophys, 60-63; mem, US Nat Comt, Int Sci Radio Union, 62-64; indust & prof adv coun, Pa State Univ, 63-65; mem vis comt physics, Lehigh Univ, 66-74, mem Comt Fed Labs, 71-75; mem, Md Gov Sci Adv Coun, 72-76; mem study panel, Off Telecommunications, Nat Assembly Eng, 76-77. *Honors & Awards:* NASA Medals for Distinguished Serv, Outstanding Leadership & Except Serv; Collier Trophy, Nat Aeronaut Asn, 75. *Mem:* Fel Inst Elec & Electronics Engrs; fel Am Astron Soc; fel Explorers Club; fel Am Inst Aeronaut & Astronaut; Sigma Xi. *Res:* Space applications-earth resources survey, meteorology, communications; upper atmospheric physics; ionospheric physics; atmospheric potential gradient and polar conductivities; algebraic ring theory; weather radar and radar beacon development. *Mailing Add:* 157 Hun Rd Princeton NJ 08540

CLARK, JOHN HARLAN, b Helena, Mont, Aug 30, 48; m 67; c 2. FISHERIES. *Educ:* Carroll Col, BA, 71; Colo State Univ, MS, 74, PhD(fisheries), 75. *Prof Exp:* Fisheries biologist III, 75-79, CHIEF FISHERIES SCIENTIST, ALASKA DEPT FISH & GAME, 79- *Mem:* Am Fisheries Soc; Nat Audubon Soc; Sigma Xi. *Res:* Production capabilities of lakes used for nursery areas by sockeye salmon. *Mailing Add:* 333 Raspberry Rd Anchorage AK 99502

CLARK, JOHN JEFFERSON, b Shrewsbury, Mass, Dec 30, 22; m 43; c 3. VETERINARY PATHOLOGY. *Educ:* Univ Ga, DVM, 53; Univ Minn, PhD(vet path), 59. *Prof Exp:* Res fel vet path, Univ Minn, 53-57; res assoc, 57-70, RES SECT HEAD VET PATH, UPJOHN CO, 70- *Mem:* Am Vet Med Asn; Am Soc Clin Path. *Res:* Cancer embryology, histology, chemotherapy and immunity; immunology, bacteriology and pathology of leptospirosis and other infectious diseases; parasitology of domesticated animals; hematology; clinical chemistry. *Mailing Add:* Upjohn Co Kalamazoo MI 49001

CLARK, JOHN M, JR, b San Antonio, Tex, Oct 5, 16; m 41; c 3. MECHANICAL ENGINEERING. *Educ:* Rice Inst, BS, 40; Mass Inst Technol, MS, 41. *Prof Exp:* Res & design engr, Douglas Aircraft, 41-47; pres, John Clark Indust, 47-53; plant mgr, Mathes Co, 53-55; sect mgr, 55-59, dir dept automotive res, 59-74, VPRES AUTOMOTIVE RES DIV, SOUTHWEST RES INST, 74- *Concurrent Pos:* Mem, Blue Ribbon Comt, Main Battle Tank, US Army, 68-69, mem engine selection comt, 76. *Mem:* Soc Automotive Engrs; Sigma Xi. *Res:* Engine design, research and development; air bags and seat belt restraint systems; vehicle accident research; vehicle handling and performance; vehicle soil mobility studies; soil mass movement techniques. *Mailing Add:* Southwest Res Inst 6220 Culebra Rd San Antonio TX 78284

CLARK, JOHN MAGRUDER, JR, b Ithaca, NY, June 10, 32; m 57; c 2. BIOCHEMISTRY. *Educ:* Cornell Univ, BS, 54; Calif Inst Technol, PhD(biochem), 58. *Prof Exp:* From instr to assoc prof, 58-79, PROF BIOCHEM, UNIV ILL, URBANA, 80- *Mem:* Am Soc Biol Chemists; Am Chem Soc. *Res:* Enzymology related to protein biosynthesis. *Mailing Add:* Roger Adams Lab 1209 W Calif St Urbana IL 61801

CLARK, JOHN PETER, b Philadelphia, Pa, May 6, 42; m 68; c 2. CHEMICAL ENGINEERING, PROCESS DEVELOPMENT. *Educ:* Univ Notre Dame, BSChE, 64; Univ Calif, Berkeley, PhD(chem eng), 68. *Prof Exp:* Res engr chem eng, Agr Res Serv, USDA, Berkeley, 68-71, indust engr, Hyattsville, Md, 71-72; from asst prof to assoc prof, Va Polytech & State Univ, 72-78; dir process develop, Int Tel & Tel Continental Baking Co, 78-81; PRES, EPSTEIN PROCESS ENG, INC, 81- *Concurrent Pos:* Consult, Gen Foods Corp, 75-78. *Mem:* Am Inst Chem Engrs; Inst Food Technologists; Am Chem Soc; Soc Rheology. *Res:* Food engineering; food rheology; food extrusion; cellulose hydrolysis; renewable resources; waste water treatment; fermentation. *Mailing Add:* Epstein Process Eng 2011 W Pershing Rd Chicago IL 60609

CLARK, JOHN R(AY), b Chester, WVa, May 4, 18; m 49; c 2. ELECTRICAL ENGINEERING. *Educ:* Purdue Univ, BS, 39, MSE, 41; Ohio State Univ, PhD(elec eng), 52. *Prof Exp:* Asst elec engr, Radio Lab, Purdue Univ, 39-40; res engr, Continental Elec Co, Ill, 40-41; instr elec eng, Purdue Univ, 41-44, from asst prof to assoc prof, 46-58; prin engr, Electronic Corp, 58-60; head dept, 60-70, PROF ELEC ENG, MICH TECHNOL UNIV, 60- *Mem:* Inst Elec & Electronics Engrs; assoc mem Acoust Soc Am; assoc mem Am Soc Eng Educ. *Res:* Radio; electronic circuits; installation and maintenance of fire control radar; a telemetering device. *Mailing Add:* Dept of Elec Eng Mich Technol Univ Houghton MI 49931

CLARK, JOHN R(OBERT), b Schenectady, NY, July 30, 11; m 42; c 2. METALLURGY. *Educ:* Union Col, NY, BS, 35; Mass Inst Technol, ScD(metall), 42. *Prof Exp:* Engr, Gen Elec Co, 35-39; asst, Mass Inst Technol, 39-42, res assoc, 43-44; metallurgist, Metall Lab, Univ Chicago, 44; supt metall lab, Clinton Eng Works, Tenn Eastman Corp, Oak Ridge, 45; res assoc, Carnegie-Ill Steel Co, Pa, 45-47; from assoc prof to prof metall, 47-76, EMER PROF METALL, NAVAL POSTGRAD SCH, 76- *Concurrent Pos:* Instr metall, Stanford Univ, 42-43. *Mem:* Am Phys Soc; Am Inst Mining, Metall & Petrol Engrs; Am Soc Metals; Am Crystallog Soc. *Res:* Magnetic and low temperature studies of metals and alloys; x-ray diffraction of the structure of metals and alloys; deformation and recrystallization in metals and alloys; radiation damage; physics of metals. *Mailing Add:* Dept of Physics Naval Postgrad Sch Monterey CA 93941

CLARK, JOHN S, b Tientsin, N China, Oct 1, 25; m 51; c 2. SOIL CHEMISTRY. *Educ:* Univ BC, BSA, 48, MSA, 50; Cornell Univ, PhD(soil chem), 53. *Prof Exp:* Res officer soil chem, Can Dept Agr, 53-55; asst prof, Cornell Univ, 55-56 & Univ BC, 56-60; res officer, 60-69, DIR SOIL RES INST, CAN DEPT AGR, 69- *Res:* Ion equilibria and phosphate fixation in soils; mineralogical and chemical properties of soil clays. *Mailing Add:* Soil Res Inst Can Dept of Agr Ottawa Can

CLARK, JOHN W, sanitary engineering, deceased

CLARK, JOHN W(OOD), b Jacksonville, Ill, July 17, 22; m 49, 68; c 3. CIVIL ENGINEERING. *Educ:* Purdue Univ, BS, 46, MS, 47; Univ Pittsburgh, PhD(math), 54. *Prof Exp:* Res Engr, Alcoa Res Labs, 47-52, from asst chief to chief, Eng Design Div, 57-75, mgr, Eng Properties & Design Div, 75-78, tech adv, 78-80; RETIRED. *Honors & Awards:* Rowland Prize, Am Soc Civil Engrs, 57, Res Prize, 58, Croes Medal, 66. *Mem:* Am Soc Civil Engrs; Structural Stability Res Coun; Sigma Xi. *Res:* Strength and design of aluminum structures. *Mailing Add:* 904 Farragut St Pittsburgh PA 15206

CLARK, JOHN WALTER, b Lockhart, Tex, Apr 7, 35. THEORETICAL NUCLEAR PHYSICS, THEORETICAL ASTROPHYSICS. *Educ:* Univ Tex, BS, 55, MA, 57; Wash Univ, PhD(physics), 59. *Prof Exp:* Res assoc physics, Wash Univ, 59; NSF fel, Princeton Univ, 59-61; assoc res scientist, Denver Div, Martin Co, 61; NATO fel, 62-63; from asst prof to assoc prof, 63-72, PROF PHYSICS, WASH UNIV, 72- *Concurrent Pos:* Alfred P Sloan Found fel, 65-67; guest prof, Swed Univ Abo, 71-72. *Mem:* Fel Am Phys Soc. *Res:* Quantum mechanics of many-body systems; nuclear interactions and nuclear structure; hypernuclear physics; neutron stars; quantum fluids and solids; theoretical neurophysics. *Mailing Add:* Dept of Physics Wash Univ St Louis MO 63130

CLARK, JOHN WHITCOMB, b Walkerton, Ind, Aug 14, 18; m 61. RADIOLOGY. *Educ:* Harvard Univ, MD, 43. *Prof Exp:* From instr to prof radiol, Univ Ill, 48-70, PROF RADIOL, RUSH MED COL, 70- *Concurrent Pos:* Resident, Presby-St Luke's Hosp, 46-49, from asst attend radiologist to attend radiologist, 49-; assoc scientist, Argonne Nat Lab, 52-56, consult, 56-62. *Mem:* AMA; fel Am Col Radiol; Radiation Res Soc; Radiol Soc NAm; Am Roentgen Ray Soc. *Res:* Clinical radiology; radiobiology. *Mailing Add:* Dept Radiol Presby-St Luke's Hosp 1753 W Congress Pkwy Chicago IL 60612

CLARK, JOSEPH E(DWARD), b Philadelphia, Pa, Oct 2, 35; m 59; c 5. POLYMER SCIENCE, PHYSICAL CHEMISTRY. *Educ:* Villanova Univ, MS, 60; Univ Windsor, PhD(polymer chem), 63. *Prof Exp:* Chemist, Res & Develop Div, Villanova Univ, 57-58; sr res chemist, Res Ctr, W R Grace & Co, 63-65; res assoc weathering of plastics, Mfg Chemists Asn, 65-67, prog mgr, 67-69; tech coordr textile flammability standards, Nat Bur Standards, 69, chief div textile flammability standards, Off Flammable Fabrics, 70-73; prof eng & fel pub affairs, Princeton Univ, 73-74; assoc adminr fire safety res, US FIRE ADMIN, 75-79; SR POLICY ANALYST & EXEC SECY, INTERGOVT SCI, ENG & TECHNOL ADV PANEL, OFF SCI & TECHNOL POLICY, EXEC OFF OF THE PRESIDENT, 79- *Mem:* Am Chem Soc; Nat Fire Protection Asn; Am Soc Testing & Mat; Technol Transfer Soc; AAAS. *Res:* Natural and synthetic polymer synthesis, properties, characterization and degradation; materials problems including durability, weatherability and flammability; analysis of science and technology policy issues. *Mailing Add:* 14607 Westbury Rd Rockville MD 20853

CLARK, JULIA BERG, b Moline, Ill, June 7, 40; m 63; c 2. BIOCHEMISTRY, PHARMACOLOGY. *Educ:* Radcliffe Col, BA, 62; Ind Univ, PhD(biochem), 66. *Prof Exp:* Res assoc, 70-71, asst prof, 71-77, ASSOC PROF PHARMACOL & DIR GRAD STUDIES, DEPT OF PHARMACOL, SCH MED, IND UNIV, INDIANAPOLIS, 77- *Concurrent Pos:* USPHS fels, Harvard Univ, 66-67, NIH, 67-68, Ind Univ, 70-71; Nat Inst Arthritis & Metab Dis fel, 67-69. *Res:* Enzymology; endocrinology. *Mailing Add:* Dept of Pharmacol Ind Univ Med Sch Indianapolis IN 46202

CLARK, JULIAN JOSEPH, b Brooklyn, NY, June 21, 35. PSYCHOSOMATIC MEDICINE. *Educ:* Princeton Univ, AB, 56; Columbia Univ, Col Physicians & Surgeons, MD, 60. *Prof Exp:* Sr psychiatrist, Kings Co Hosp, New York City, 71-; CLIN ASSOC PROF PSYCHIAT, DOWNNSTATE MED CTR, STATE UNIV NY, 78- *Concurrent Pos:* Attend physician liaison psychiat, Dept Psychiat & Med, State Univ Hosp, NY, 71- *Mem:* Am Psychosom Asn; Am Psychosom Soc; Sigma Xi. *Res:* Influence of environmental factors on hyperactive behavior in childrren; study of inflammatory bowel disease in patients; study of hemodialysis and renal transplant patients. *Mailing Add:* 335 E 17th St Brooklyn NY 11226

CLARK, KENNETH COURTRIGHT, b Austin, Tex, Sept 30, 19; m 47; c 2. ATOMIC PHYSICS, MOLECULAR PHYSICS. *Educ:* Univ Tex, BA, 40; Harvard Univ, AM, 41, PhD(physics), 47. *Prof Exp:* Tutor physics, Harvard Univ, 41-42, spec res assoc, Nat Defense Res Comt Proj, Electro-Acoustic Lab, 41-45, instr physics, 47-48; from asst prof to assoc prof, 48-60, PROF PHYSICS, UNIV WASH, 60- *Concurrent Pos:* Actg head physics div & res assoc prof, Geophys Inst, Univ Alaska, 57-58; consult, US Agency Int Develop, India, 64 & 66 & Battelle Northwest Labs, Battelle Mem Inst, 71-; prog dir aeron, NSF, Washington, DC, 69-70; mem adv comt, Geophys Inst, Univ Alaska, 73-77; vis prof space physics, Latrobe Univ, Melbourne, Australia, 79-80. *Mem:* Fel Am Phys Soc; fel Optical Soc Am; Am Asn Physics Teachers; Am Geophys Union. *Res:* Auroral physics; optical excitation processes in upper atmosphere; afterglow spectra; laboratory aeronomy; extreme ultraviolet spectroscopy. *Mailing Add:* Dept Physics FM-15 Univ of Wash Seattle WA 98195

CLARK, KENNETH FREDERICK, b Liverpool, Eng, Apr 4, 33; m 62. ECONOMIC GEOLOGY. *Educ:* Univ Durham, BSc, 56, Univ NMex, MS, 62, PhD(geol), 66. *Prof Exp:* Geologist, Anglo Am Corp of SAfrica, Ltd, 56-60; asst prof geol sci, Cornell Univ, 66-71; from assoc prof to prof geol, Univ Iowa, 71-80; PROF GEOL SCI, UNIV TEX, 80- *Concurrent Pos:* Consult, Mexican Govt, 69- *Mem:* Geol Soc Am; Mex Geol Soc; Mex Asn Mining Engrs, Metallurgists & Geologists; Am Inst Mining, Metall & Petrol Eng. *Res:* Exploration and development of mineral resources; geophysical and geochemical exploration. *Mailing Add:* Dept Geol Sci Univ Tex El Paso TX 79968

CLARK, KERRY BRUCE, b Woodbury, NJ, Aug 22, 45; m 66; c 1. INVERTEBRATE ZOOLOGY, MARINE ECOLOGY. *Educ:* Rutgers Univ, BA, 66; Univ Conn, MS, 68, PhD(invert zool), 71. *Prof Exp:* from asst prof to assoc prof, 71-80, PROF BIOL SCI, FLA INST TECHNOL, 80- *Mem:* Ecol Soc Am; Am Inst Biol Sci; Am Soc Zoologists; Sigma Xi. *Res:* Taxonomy and ecology of opisthobranch molluscs; ecology of fouling communities; physiology of chloroplast and algal symbioses. *Mailing Add:* Dept of Biol Sci Fla Inst of Technol Melbourne FL 32901

CLARK, L(YLE) G(ERALD), b Gratiot Co, Mich, July 12, 24; m 49; c 4. MECHANICAL ENGINEERING. *Educ:* Univ Mich, BS(eng) & BS(math), 48, MS, 49, PhD(eng), 55. *Prof Exp:* Instr eng mech, Univ Mich, 48-55; dir res eng, Aro Equip Corp, 55-56; chmn mech eng, Univ Del, 56-60; PROF AEROSPACE ENG & ENG MECH, UNIV TEX, AUSTIN, 60- *Mem:* Am Soc Mech Engrs; Am Soc Eng Educ. *Res:* Theoretical mechanics; analytical dynamics; vibrations; nonlinear analysis. *Mailing Add:* Dept of Eng Mech Univ of Tex Austin TX 78712

CLARK, LARRY P, b Chicago, Ill, June 18, 36; m 59; c 2. ORGANIC CHEMISTRY, MEDICINAL CHEMISTRY. *Educ:* Univ Mich, BS, 58; Univ Notre Dame, PhD(org chem), 66. *Prof Exp:* Control chemist, Abbott Labs, 58-62 & Miles Labs, 62-63; res assoc org chem, Col Pharm, Univ Mich, 66-67; asst prof chem, Univ Pittsburgh, Bradford, 67-69; group leader drug anal, Pharmaco Inc, Schering Corp, 69-71, GROUP LEADER DRUG ANAL, PLOUGH, INC, SCHERING-PLOUGH CORP, 71- *Mem:* AAAS; Am Chem Soc. *Res:* Analysis of drugs in dosage forms and in vivo; determination of drug stability. *Mailing Add:* Res Dept Plough Inc 3022 Jackson Ave Memphis TN 38101

CLARK, LEIGH BRUCE, b Seattle, Wash, Sept 9, 34; c 1. SPECTROCHEMISTRY. *Educ:* Univ Calif, Berkeley, BS, 57; Univ Wash, PhD(chem), 63. *Prof Exp:* Asst prof, 64-72, ASSOC PROF CHEM, UNIV CALIF, SAN DIEGO, 72- *Res:* Molecular spectroscopy; reflection spectroscopy of molecular crystals. *Mailing Add:* Dept of Chem Univ of Calif at San Diego La Jolla CA 92037

CLARK, LELAND CHARLES, JR, b Rochester, NY, Dec 4, 18; m 39; c 4. BIOCHEMISTRY. *Educ:* Antioch Col, BS, 41; Univ Rochester, PhD(biochem), 44. *Prof Exp:* Chmn biochem dept, Fels Res Inst, 44-58; asst prof biochem, Antioch Col, 44-56, prof, 56-58; from assoc prof to prof surg, Med Ctr, Univ Ala, 58-68; PROF RES PEDIAT, CHILDREN'S HOSP RES FOUND, MED COL, UNIV CINCINNATI, 68- *Concurrent Pos:* Sr res assoc surg & pediat, Univ Cincinnati, 55-58; consult, Wright-Patterson AFB, 56-58 & NIH, 61-; NIH res career award, 62-68; vis prof, Cardiovasc Res Inst San Francisco, 67; fel, coun cerebrovascular dis, Am Heart 67-; ed, Symp Oxygen Transport. *Honors & Awards:* Distinguished Lect Award, Am Col Chest Physicians, 75. *Mem:* AAAS; NY Acad Sci; Sigma Xi; Artificial Organs Soc; Am Heart Asn. *Res:* Vitamin, steroid and oxygen metabolism; polarography; cardiovascular disease; hydrogen and oxygen electrodes in diagnosis; ion exchange resins in biology; glucose electrode; surgical monitoring; intermediary metabolism and synthesis of psychotomimetic drugs; fluorocarbon liquid breathing; artificial blood; enzyme electrode. *Mailing Add:* Children's Hosp Res Found Elland Ave & Bethesda Cincinnati OH 45229

CLARK, LINCOLN DUFTON, b Andover, Mass, Jan 18, 23; m 49; c 2. MEDICINE. *Educ:* Harvard Univ, MD, 47. *Prof Exp:* Asst instr psychiat, Med Sch, Harvard Univ, 49-50, asst physician, 51-53; from asst prof to assoc prof psychiat, 55-64, dir, Behav Sci Lab, 64-76, asst prof pharmacol & psychol, 76-80, PROF PSYCHIAT, DEPT OF PSYCHIAT, UNIV UTAH, 76-, ADJ PROF PHARMACOL & PSYCHOL, 80- *Concurrent Pos:* NIMH res career award, 63-67 & res scientist award, 67-72; asst physician, Mass Gen Hosp, 51-53; sci assoc, Roscoe B Jackson Mem Lab; chmn adv comt preclin psychopharmacol, NIMH, 61-66, res scientist, 68- *Mem:* Am Psychiat Asn; Am Col Neuropsychopharmacol; Psychiat Res Soc; Sigma Xi. *Res:* Experimental psychiatry; psychopharmacology; animal behavior; Forensic psychiatry. *Mailing Add:* Dept of Psychiat Univ of Utah Salt Lake City UT 84112

CLARK, LLEWELLYN EVANS, b Brunswick, Maine, July 30, 32; m 56; c 4. MECHANICAL & CIVIL ENGINEERING. *Educ:* Univ Maine, BS, 55, MS, 56; Univ Colo, PhD(civil eng), 66. *Prof Exp:* From instr to asst prof mech eng, Univ Maine, 55-63; assoc civil eng, Univ Colo, 63-64; assoc prof mech eng, Univ Maine, 65-67; proj engr, Jones Div, Beloit Corp, 67-68, mgr res, 68-79; VPRES ENG, VICON RECOVERY SYSTS, 82- *Concurrent Pos:* Proj mgr, Vicon Recovery Assoc, 79-81. *Mem:* Am Soc Eng Educ; Soc Exp Stress Anal; Tech Asn Pulp & Paper Inst; Am Inst Plant Eng. *Res:* Research and development in pulp stock preparation equipment; secondary fiber processing; contaminant removal; deinking systems; thermomechanical pulping systems; dewatering characteristics of pulp and food products; project development refuse to energy systems design; development, construction, start-up and operation of resource recovery plants. *Mailing Add:* 1133 Barker Rd Pittsfield MA 01201

CLARK, LLOYD ALLEN, b North Battleford, Sask, Mar 17, 32; m 55; c 4. ECONOMIC GEOLOGY, MINERAL EXPLORATION. *Educ:* Univ Sask, BE, 54, MSc, 55; McGill Univ, PhD(geol), 59. *Prof Exp:* Fel geochem, Carnegie Inst Geophys Lab, 58-60; from asst prof to assoc prof econ geol, McGill Univ, 60-70; chief geochem res & lab div, Kennecott Explor, Inc, 70-76; explor mgr, 76-81, CHIEF GEOLOGIST, SASK MINING DEVELOP CORP, SASKATOON, 81- *Concurrent Pos:* Nat Res Coun Can res grants, 60-70, fel, 65-66; guest investr, Univ Tokyo & Univ Florence, 65-66. *Mem:* Soc Econ Geol; fel Geol Asn Can; fel Mineral Asn Can; Can Inst Mining & Metall; Soc Geol Appl Mineral Depostis. *Res:* Phase equilibrium and related studies in synthetic systems; studies of naturally occurring minerals and ores to yield quantitative information about environment of ore formation; exploration programs for uranium and base metals. *Mailing Add:* Sask Mining Develop Corp 122 Third Ave N Saskatoon SK S7K 2H6 Can

CLARK, LLOYD DOUGLAS, b Ventura, Calif, Oct 30, 40. ELECTRICAL ENGINEERING, MATERIALS SCIENCE. *Educ:* Stanford Univ, BS, 63, MS, 67, PhD(mat sci), 70; Carnegie-Mellon Univ, MS, 65. *Prof Exp:* Res scientist, Xerox Corp, 70-71; res assoc mat sci, Stanford Univ, 71-72; res scientist & mgr, Med Ultrasound, Varian Assocs, 80; NEW PROD RES & DEVELOP MGR, XEROX CORP, 80- *Concurrent Pos:* Consult, Rodder Instrument, 63-71; proprietor & pvt inventor, Clark Systs, 70- *Mem:* Am Inst Ultrasound in Med. *Res:* Medical ultrasound imaging; nuclear magnetic resonance; x-ray computed tomography imaging. *Mailing Add:* 15 Conrad St San Francisco CA 94131

CLARK, MALCOLM A, b Ottawa, Ont, May 30, 25; m 47; c 2. SPACE PHYSICS, AEROSPACE TECHNOLOGY. *Educ:* Queen's Univ, Ont, BSc, 47, MSc, 48; Mass Inst Technol, PhD(physics), 52. *Prof Exp:* Mem tech staff acoustics res, Bell Tel Labs, Inc, 52-54; assoc res officer, Physics Div, Atomic Energy Can Ltd, 54-62; staff scientist, Space Physics Lab, 62-69, systs eng dir, Space Exp Support Prog, 69-72, GROUP DIR, SPACE TEST TECHNOL DIV, AEROSPACE CORP, 72- *Res:* Cosmic ray balloon experiments; beta and gamma ray spectroscopy; short nuclear lifetimes; night airglow and aurora; ultraviolet dayglow; far ultraviolet sky radiance; experimental spacecraft. *Mailing Add:* Off for Technol Aerospace Corp Box 95085 Los Angeles CA 90045

CLARK, MALCOLM JOHN ROY, b Bournemouth, Eng, May 22, 44; m 68. ENVIRONMENTAL CHEMISTRY. *Educ:* Univ Victoria, BSc, 66; Univ NB, PhD(chem), 71. *Prof Exp:* BR ENVIRON CHEMIST, BC MINISTRY ENVIRONMENT, 71- *Concurrent Pos:* Vis scientist, Univ Victoria, 75- *Mem:* Am Chem Soc; Am Fisheries Soc; Am Soc Limnol & Oceanog; Am Soc Testing & Mat; Chem Inst Can. *Res:* Investigation of various problems in pollution and environmental chemistry, particularly regarding metals, color and dissolved gases; environmental data storage and retrieval. *Mailing Add:* 336 Foul Bay Rd Victoria BC V8S 4G7 Can

CLARK, MALCOLM MALLORY, b Palo Alto, Calif, Sept 21, 31; c 5. QUATERNARY GEOLOGY, TECTONICS. *Educ:* Univ Calif, Berkeley, BS, 57; Stanford Univ, PhD(geol), 67. *Prof Exp:* Engr, Temescal Metall Corp, 57-60; lab mgr, Dumont Mfg Co, 60-61; mfg mgr, Monitor Plastics Co, 61-63; GEOLOGIST, US GEOL SURV, 67- *Mem:* Geol Soc Am; Seismol Soc Am; Glaciol Soc; Am Geophys Union. *Res:* Geology of active faults; glacial geology; glaciation of the Sierra Nevada, California. *Mailing Add:* US Geol Surv MS 77 345 Middlefield Rd Menlo Park CA 94025

CLARK, MARION THOMAS, b Hapeville, Ga, Aug 20, 17; m 42; c 3. CHEMISTRY. *Educ:* Emory Univ, AB, 38, AM, 39; Univ Va, PhD(org chem), 46. *Prof Exp:* Instr chem, Emory Jr Col, 39-43; asst, Univ Va, 43-46; assoc prof, Birmingham-Southern Col, 46-48; asst prof, Emory Univ, 48-51; asst & actg chmn, Univ Rel Div, Oak Ridge Inst Nuclear Studies, 51-53; assoc prof chem, Emory Univ, 53-63; PROF CHEM, AGNES SCOTT COL, 63- *Mem:* Am Chem Soc; Sigma Xi. *Res:* Synthesis of quinoline methanols and aminomethyl benzyl alcohols as possible antimalarials. *Mailing Add:* Dept of Chem Agnes Scott Col Decatur GA 30030

CLARK, MARTIN RALPH, US citizen. REPRODUCTIVE ENDOCRINOLOGY, BIOLOGICAL CHEMISTRY. *Educ:* Univ Mich, Ann Arbor, BS, 72, PhD(biol chem), 76. *Prof Exp:* Fel reproduction endocrinol, Ford Found, 76-77, NIH individual fel reproduction endocrinol, 77-79, ASST PROF OBSTET/GYNEC & BIOCHEM, UNIV MIAMI, 79- *Mem:* AAAS; Soc Study Reprod; Endocrine Soc. *Res:* Biochemistry of hormone action; ovulation. *Mailing Add:* Endocrine Lab D5 PO Box 016960 Miami FL 33101

CLARK, MARY ELEANOR, b San Francisco, Calif, Apr 28, 27. CELL BIOPHYSICS, COMPARATIVE PHYSIOLOGY. *Educ:* Univ Calif, Berkeley, AB, 49, MA, 51, PhD(zool), 60. *Prof Exp:* USPHS fel zool, Bristol Univ, 61-63; Sci Res Coun Gt Brit fel, Bristol & Newcastle Univs, 63-66; vis prof zool, Univ Lund, 67; res asst organismic biol, Univ Calif, Irvine, 67-68; NSF fel environ health eng, Calif Inst Technol, 68-69; asst prof, 69-70, assoc prof biol, 70-73, PROF BIOL, SAN DIEGO STATE UNIV, 73- *Mem:* Fel AAAS; NY Acad Sci; Am Soc Zoologists; Am Soc Cell Biol; Biophys Soc. *Res:* Culture of normal and malignant fibroblasts; polychaete neurosecretion; monoamine histochemistry; regeneration; biochemistry of amino acids in marine invertebrates; osmoregulation; marine pollution and kelp-bed ecology; biophysics of cell osmolytes. *Mailing Add:* Dept of Biol San Diego State Univ San Diego CA 92182

CLARK, MARY JANE, b McKeesport, Pa, Sept 18, 25. BIOCHEMISTRY. *Educ:* Univ Pittsburgh, BS, 47, PhD(biochem), 57. *Prof Exp:* Jr chemist, Koppers Co, Inc, Pa, 52-54; res assoc biochem, Sch Pub Health, Univ Pittsburgh, 54-58; res assoc biochem, Col Physicians & Surgeons, Columbia Univ, 58-64; chmn dept chem, 73-78, asst prof, NY Med Col, Flower & Fifth Ave Hosps, 64-68; ASSOC PROF BIOCHEM, JERSEY CITY STATE COL, 68-, ASSOC PROF CHEM, 73-, DEAN ARTS & SCI, 78- *Mem:* Am Chem Soc. *Res:* Synthesis of peptides and their enzymic hydrolysis; aromatic biosynthesis in bacteria; general intermediary metabolism of amino acids and derivatives; coenzymes in intermediary metabolism; folic acid and leukemia. *Mailing Add:* Dean Arts & Sci 2039 Kennedy Blvd Jersey City NJ 07305

CLARK, MELVILLE, JR, b Syracuse, NY, Dec 19, 21. PHYSICS, ELECTRICAL ENGINEERING. *Educ:* Mass Inst Technol, SB, 43; Harvard Univ, AM, 47, PhD(physics), 49. *Prof Exp:* Mem staff microwaves, Radiation Lab, Mass Inst Technol, 42-45; mem staff electronics, Los Alamos Sci Lab, 45-46; mem staff reactors, Brookhaven Nat Lab, 49-53; mem staff neutronics, Radiation Lab, Univ Calif, 53-55; assoc prof nuclear eng, Mass Inst Technol, 55-62; sr eng specialist, Appl Res Lab, Sylvania Elec Prod, Inc, 62-64; sr consult scientist, Res & Advan Develop Div, Avco Corp, 64-67; sr scientist, NASA Electronics Ctr, 67-70; sr develop engr, Thermo Electron Eng Corp, 70-73; MEM STAFF, COMBUSTION ENG, 73- *Concurrent Pos:* Lectr, United Shoe Mach Corp, 56; consult, Raytheon Mfg Co, 55-58 & Arthur D Little, 57-58; pres, Melville Clark Assocs, 55-; vpres, Clark Music Co, 57-60; dir, 416 S Salina St Corp, 57-60; vpres & dir, Meldor Corp, 60-65, pres, 65-67. *Mem:* AAAS; Am Phys Soc; Acoust Soc Am; Inst Elec & Electronics Engrs; Am Inst Physics. *Res:* Microwave radiation; quantum mechanics; nuclear and plasma physics; reactor engineering; neutral particle transport; musical acoustics; ionospheric propagation; speech research; electric space propulsion; auditory perception; electronics; numerical analysis; mathematical methods of physics; software. *Mailing Add:* 8 Richard Rd Wayland MA 01778

CLARK, MERVIN LESLIE, b Baltimore, Md, May 18, 21; m 49; c 4. MEDICINE. *Educ:* Va Polytech Inst, BS, 42; Northwestern Univ, MD, 48. *Prof Exp:* From asst prof to assoc prof psychiat, 60-69, from asst prof to assoc prof med, 62-69, actg dir, Div Clin Pharmacol, 70-75, adj assoc prof psychiat, 77-79, PROF MED, SCH MED, UNIV OKLA, 69-, ADJ PROF PSYCHIAT, 79- *Concurrent Pos:* Res fel, Exp Therapeut Unit, Sch Med, Univ Okla, 55-56; chief med serv & dir res unit, Cent State Griffin Mem Hosp, Norman, Okla, 56-; mem sci rev panel, Drug Interactions Eval Prog, Am Pharmaceut Asn, 74. *Mem:* Am Soc Pharmacol & Exp Therapeut; Am Soc Clin Pharmacol & Therapeut; fel Am Col Neuropsychopharmacol. *Res:* Clinical pharmacology and therapeutics; psychopharmacology; controlled clinical trials of new antipsychotic agents; metabolism and kinetics of chlorpromazine. *Mailing Add:* Univ Okla Health Sci Ctr PO Box 26901 Oklahoma City OK 73190

CLARK, NANCY BARNES, b Hamden, Conn, July 1, 39; m 61; c 1. COMPARATIVE ENDOCRINOLOGY, COMPARATIVE PHYSIOLOGY. *Educ:* Mt Holyoke Col, BA, 61; Columbia Univ, MA, 62, PhD(endocrinol), 65. *Prof Exp:* Asst prof zool, 65-70, assoc prof biol, 70-76, PROF BIOL, UNIV CONN, 77- *Mem:* Am Soc Bone & Mineral Res; Am Physiol Soc; Am Soc Zool; Endocrine Soc. *Res:* Parathyroid function, and calcium and phosphate regulation in non-mammalian vertebrates; comparative studies of thyroid function. *Mailing Add:* Biol Sci Group Univ of Conn Storrs CT 06268

CLARK, NATHAN EDWARD, b Milford, Conn, Feb 26, 40; m 80. OCEANOGRAPHY, CLIMATOLOGY. *Educ:* Brown Univ, ScB, 62; Mass Inst Technol, PhD(oceanog), 67. *Prof Exp:* Meteorologist, Southwest Fisheries Ctr, Nat Marine Fisheries Serv, Nat Oceanic & Atmospheric Admin, 67-76; ASST RES OCEANOGRAPHER, SCRIPPS INST OCEANOG, 77- *Concurrent Pos:* Res assoc, Scripps Inst Oceanog, 74- *Mem:* Am Meteorol Soc; Am Geophys Union. *Res:* Large scale air-sea heat transfer processes and fluctuations in the North Pacific Ocean; effects of large scale changes of ocean and atmosphere on northeastern Pacific fisheries. *Mailing Add:* Scripps Inst Oceanog NORPAX A-030 La Jolla CA 92093

CLARK, NERI ANTHONY, b New Haven, Conn, Apr 19, 18; m 43; c 1. AGRONOMY. *Educ:* Univ Md, BS, 54, PhD(agron), 59. *Prof Exp:* From asst prof to prof, 58-78, EMER PROF AGRON, UNIV MD, COLLEGE PARK, 79-; CONSULT, 78- *Concurrent Pos:* Consult, 78- *Mem:* Am Soc Agron. *Res:* Agronomy; forage management. *Mailing Add:* RD 1 Halpin Rd Middlebury VT 05753

CLARK, PATRICIA ANN, b Dubuque, Iowa, Mar 28, 40. PHYSICAL CHEMISTRY. *Educ:* Univ NC, Greensboro, AB, 62; Univ Mass, PhD(chem), 67. *Prof Exp:* Fel, Cornell Univ, 67-68; asst prof, 68-73, ASSOC PROF CHEM, VASSAR COL, 73-, CHMN DEPT, 77- *Mem:* AAAS; Am Phys Soc; Am Chem Soc. *Res:* Molecular electronic absorption spectroscopy; semi-empirical molecular orbital theory calculations; molecular charge-transfer complexes. *Mailing Add:* Dept of Chem Vassar Col Poughkeepsie NY 12601

CLARK, PATRICIA ANN ANDRE, b Leadville, Colo, Mar 23, 38; m 60; c 1. ASTROPHYSICS. *Educ:* Mass Inst Technol, SB, 61, SM, 64; Univ Rochester, PhD(astrophys), 69. *Prof Exp:* Instr eng, Univ Rochester & instr math, Rochester Inst Technol, 73-74; asst chief, Int Field Year Great Lakes, US Environ Protection Agency, 74-76; instr eng, Univ Rochester, 76-78; VIS ASST PROF, ROCHESTER INST TECHNOL, 78- *Mem:* Am Astron Soc. *Res:* Solar hydrodynamics. *Mailing Add:* 210 Chelmsford Rd Rochester NY 14618

CLARK, PAUL ENOCH, b Cambridge, Ohio, Nov 24, 05; m 41; c 2. PHYSICAL CHEMISTRY. *Educ:* Muskingum Col, AB, 27; Ohio State Univ, MS, 31, PhD(phys chem), 38. *Prof Exp:* From instr to assoc prof chem, Muskingum Col, 27-42, prof chem & chmn div nat sci, 42-43; prof chem & head dept, Washington & Jefferson Col, 43-49; chemist, Appl Physics Lab, Johns Hopkins Univ, 49-75. *Concurrent Pos:* Chemist, Armstrong Cork Co, 44-46. *Honors & Awards:* Cert of Achievement Award, Int Publ Competition, Soc Tech Commun, Boston, 72, Award of Merit, Houston, 73. *Mem:* Am Chem Soc; fel Am Inst Chemists. *Res:* Heat capacities of oils; photovoltaic effect; threshold values for silver, gold and copper electrodes in electrolytic solutions; monomolecular surface films. *Mailing Add:* 2505 Eccleston St Silver Spring MD 20902

CLARK, PETER O(SGOODE), b Ottawa, Ont, June 5, 38; m 61; c 2. ELECTRICAL ENGINEERING, PHYSICS. *Educ:* McGill Univ, BEng, 60; Calif Inst Technol, MSc, 61, PhD(elec eng, physics), 64. *Prof Exp:* Mem tech staff, Hughes Res Labs, 64-68, tech sect head, 68-69, assoc dept mgr, 69-70, mgr laser dept, 70-76; ASST DIR TECHNOL, DEFENSE ADVAN RES PROJ AGENCY, 76- *Concurrent Pos:* Mem adv comt, Group on Electronic Devices, 69; mem, Quantum Electronics Coun, 70. *Mem:* Am Phys Soc; Inst Elec & Electronics Engrs; Can Asn Physicists. *Res:* Electromagnetic theory; electron devices; lasers and laser systems. *Mailing Add:* Defense Advan Res Proj Agency Sto 1400 Wilson Blvd Arlington VA 22209

CLARK, RALPH B, b Farmington, Utah, Sept 12, 33; m 57; c 6. PLANT PHYSIOLOGY, MINERAL NUTRITION. *Educ:* Brigham Young Univ, BS, 57; Utah State Univ, MS, 59; Univ Calif, Los Angeles, PhD(plant sci), 62. *Prof Exp:* Res assoc, Ore State Univ, 63; res chemist, NCent Region, Agr Res, USDA, 63-78; MEM FAC, DEPT AGRON, UNIV NEBR-LINCOLN, 75- *Mem:* AAAS; Am Soc Plant Physiologists; Am Soc Agron; Crop Sci Soc Am; Soil Sci Soc Am. *Res:* Physiology and biochemistry of mineral nutrition and metabolism in sorghum. *Mailing Add:* Dept Agron Univ Nebr Lincoln NE 68583

CLARK, RALPH LEIGH, b East Jordan, Mich, June 2, 08; m 30; c 4. ELECTRICAL ENGINEERING, TELECOMMUNICATIONS. *Educ:* Mich State Col, BS, 30. *Prof Exp:* Radio inspector, Radio Div, US Dept Com, Fed Radio Comn & Fed Commun Comn, Detroit & Washington, DC, 30-35, radio engr, Fed Commun Comn, Washington, DC, 35-41; partner, Ring & Clark Consult Eng Firm, 41-42; contract engr, Bur Aeronaut, US Dept Navy, 42; contract employee, Res & Develop Bd, 46, dir prog div, 46-49; consult govt agencies, 49-57; off mgr, Stanford Res Inst, Washington, DC, 57-59; asst dir defense res & eng for commun, 59-62; spec asst to dir, Telecommun Mgt, 62-70; telecommun consult, 70-72; dir Washington off, 72-76, CONSULT, INST ELEC & ELECTRONICS ENGRS, 76- *Concurrent Pos:* Mem, Coun Foreign Rels. *Mem:* Fel AAAS; life fel Inst Elec & Electronics Engrs. *Res:* Radio wave propagation measurement and frequency measurement; electronics, including radar navigation systems and countermeasures; research administration; telecommunications policy and management. *Mailing Add:* 4307 N 39th St Arlington VA 22207

CLARK, RALPH M, b Stowe, Vt, Dec 12, 26; m 59; c 1. ZOOLOGY. *Educ:* Univ Vt, AB, 50, MEd, 51; Wash State Univ, MS, 61; Univ Mass, PhD(zool), 63. *Prof Exp:* Teacher, Vt High Sch, 51-56, USAF High Sch, Ger, 56-58 & NY High Sch, 58-59; from asst prof to assoc prof, 63-72; PROF BIOL, STATE UNIV NY COL PLATTSBURGH, 72- *Concurrent Pos:* NY Res Found grants-in-aid, 63-66. *Mem:* AAAS; Am Soc Cell Biol. *Res:* Developmental biology. *Mailing Add:* Dept of Biol Sci State Univ of NY Col Plattsburgh NY 12901

CLARK, RALPH O, b Broken Bow, Nebr, Aug 17, 12; m 34. CHEMISTRY. *Educ:* Univ Nebr, BS, 34, MS, 35. *Prof Exp:* Control chemist, Kendall Ref Co, 36-37; head anal sect, 37-55, asst dir, Gulf Res & Develop Co, 55-78, tech assoc, 61-78; RETIRED. *Mem:* Am Chem Soc; Am Soc Testing & Mat; Am Petrol Inst. *Res:* Microanalysis; polarography as applied to analysis; chromatography of petroleum products; absorption analysis; analysis by x-ray fluorescence; emission spectroscopy; process analyzers. *Mailing Add:* 7126 Shannon Rd Verona PA 15147

CLARK, RANDOLPH LEE, b Hereford, Tex, July 2, 06; m 32; c 2. SURGERY. *Educ:* Univ SC, BS, 27; Med Col Va, MD, 32; Univ Minn, MSc, 38. *Hon Degrees:* DSc, Med Col Va, 54. *Prof Exp:* Intern, Garfield Mem Hosp, Washington, DC, 33; chief resident, Am Hosp, Paris, France, 33-35; first asst, Mayo Clin, Minn, 35-39, asst surgeon, 39; chief surgeon, Shands Clin, Jackson, Miss, 39-42; dir & surgeon-in-chief, 46-68, prof surg, Univ Tex M D Anderson Hosp & Tumor Inst, 65-68, UNIV TEX M D ANDERSON HOSP & TUMOR INST, pres, 68-78, EMER PRES, UNIV TEX SYST CANCER CTR, 78- *Concurrent Pos:* Actg dean, Univ Tex Grad Sch Biomed Sci, 48-50, prof surg, 48-65; consult, Surgeon Gen, US Dept Air Force, 48-53 & consult med div, Oak Ridge Inst Nuclear Studies, 50-56; med ed, Cancer Bull; co-ed, Bk of Health, 53- & Year Bk of Cancer, 56-; mem, Nat Adv Cancer Coun, 61-65 & President's Comn Heart Dis, Cancer & Stroke, 64-65; co-chmn senate panel, Consult for Conquest Cancer, 70-71; mem, President's Cancer Panel, 72-77; chmn comt int collab activities, Int Union Against Cancer, 75- *Honors & Awards:* Nat Award, Am Cancer Soc, 64; Distinguished Serv Award, Am Col Surgeons, 69; Rodman E & Thomas G Sheen Award, AMA, 74. *Mem:* Fel AMA; Am Cancer Soc (vpres & pres-elect, 75-76, (pres, 76-77); fel Am Col Surg; Asn Am Cancer Insts (pres, 61-62 & 75-76). *Res:* Cancer. *Mailing Add:* Univ of Tex Syst Cancer Ctr M D Anderson Hosp & Tumor Inst Houston TX 77030

CLARK, RAYMOND DONALD, organic chemistry, see previous edition

CLARK, RAYMOND LOYD, b Tacoma, Wash, Jan 23, 35; m 55; c 4. PLANT PATHOLOGY. *Educ:* Wash State Univ, BS, 57, PhD(plant path), 61. *Prof Exp:* Res plant pathologist, Crops Res Div, 61-67, RES PLANT PATHOLOGIST, N CENT REGIONAL PLANT INTROD STA, AGR RES, SCI & EDUC ADMIN, USDA, 65- *Mem:* Am Phytopath Soc; Sigma Xi. *Res:* Diplodia stalk rot of corn; tomato fruit rots; leptosphaerulina leafspot on alfalfa; root knot nematode; disease resistance; evaluation of foreign and wild germplasm. *Mailing Add:* NCent Regional Plant Intro Sta USDA Agr Res Sci & Educ Admin Ames IA 50011

CLARK, REDMOND ROBERT, climatology, physical geography, see previous edition

CLARK, REGINALD HAROLD, b London, Eng, June 11, 28. CHEMICAL ENGINEERING. *Educ:* Univ London, BSc, 48, PhD(chem eng), 51. *Prof Exp:* Tech supvr, Murgatroyds Salt & Chem Co, Eng, 50-55; from asst prof to assoc prof, 55-69, chmn & head dept, 62-71, PROF CHEM ENG, QUEEN'S UNIV, ONT, 69- *Mem:* Chem Inst Can; Brit Inst Chem Engrs. *Res:* Fluid and process dynamics; mass transfer; chemical engineering processes; environmental studies; solid waste management. *Mailing Add:* Middle Rd R R 2 Kingston Can

CLARK, REX L, b Houston, Tex, Nov 9, 41; m 62; c 3. AGRICULTURAL & BIOLOGICAL ENGINEERING. *Educ:* Univ Ark, BS, 64; NC State Univ, MS, 65; Miss State Univ, PhD(eng), 68. *Prof Exp:* Asst prof, 68-76, ASSOC PROF AGR ENG, UNIV GA, 76- *Honors & Awards:* Outstanding Paper Award, Am Soc Agr Engrs, 70. *Mem:* Am Soc Agr Engrs. *Res:* Physical properties, mechanical, electrical, optical and sonic, of biological materials; mechanical harvesting of fruits and vegetables. *Mailing Add:* Agr Eng Ctr Univ Ga Athens GA 30602

CLARK, RICHARD BENNETT, b Charleston, WVa, Nov 1, 20; m 49; c 2. CHEMISTRY. *Educ:* WVa Univ, BS, 42; Yale Univ, PhD(chem), 51. *Prof Exp:* Chemist, 50-54, sr chemist, 54-65, DEPT SUPT ORG CHEM DEVELOP, TENN EASTMAN CO, 65- *Mem:* Am Chem Soc. *Res:* Processes for manufacture of organic chemicals with particular reference to dyestuffs and chemicals used in photographic processing. *Mailing Add:* 1821 E Sevier Ave Kingsport TN 37664

CLARK, RICHARD JAMES, b Lockport, NY, July 15, 35; m 58; c 3. VERTEBRATE ZOOLOGY, ORNITHOLOGY. *Educ:* State Univ NY, Buffalo, BS, 59, MS, 63; Cornell Univ, PhD(vert zool), 70. *Prof Exp:* Teacher biol, Lewiston-Porter Cent Sch, 60-66; researcher vert zool, Cornell Univ, 66-71; instr ethol, 71, from asst prof to assoc prof, 71-81, PROF EHTOL ENVIRON BIOL, YORK COL, PA, 81- *Concurrent Pos:* Fel, NY Unit, Cooperative Wildlife Res Prog, 70-71; publ grants from var wildlife orgn, 71-; F M Chapman Mem grant, Am Mus Natural Hist, 69 & 76; current staff reviewer, J Field Ornthology; reviewer instrumentation prog, NSF, 80; invited partic, XVII Congressus Int Ornithologici, Berlin, WGer, 78. *Mem:* Am Ornithologists Union; Wildlife Soc; Ecol Soc Am; Wilson Ornithol Soc; Raptor Res Found. *Res:* Autoecological studies of raptors, especially nocturnal; avifaunal population studies relative to habitat and land-use changes; ecological parameters affecting bird song. *Mailing Add:* Dept of Biol York Col of Pa York PA 17405

CLARK, ROBERT, b New York, NY, Apr 19, 33; m 55; c 3. TOXICOLOGY. *Educ:* Columbia Univ, AB, 54; Columbia Univ, AM, 55, PhD(psychol), 58. *Prof Exp:* Asst psychol, Columbia Univ, 54-58, lectr, 56-58; res psychologist, Walter Reed Army Inst Res, 58-62; dir behav res, Hazleton Labs, Va, 62-63; res pharmacologist, 63-66, res supvr, 66-71, res assoc, Stine Lab, 71-73, asst dir toxicol, 73-74, DIR TOXICOL, ENDO LAB, E I DU PONT DE NEMOURS & CO, INC, 74- *Mem:* AAAS; Am Psychol Asn; Soc Toxicol; Am Soc Pharmacol & Exp Therapeut. *Mailing Add:* E I du Pont de Nemours & Co Inc Endo Lab 1000 Stewart Ave Garden City NY 11530

CLARK, ROBERT ALFRED, b Boston, Mass, Oct 28, 08; m 37; c 3. PSYCHIATRY. *Educ:* Harvard Univ, AB, 30, MD, 34. *Prof Exp:* Resident physician neurol, Boston City Hosp, 34-35; intern med, Univ Hosps, Cleveland, 35-37; resident physician psychiat, Boston Psychopathic Hosp, 37-39; sr physician, RI State Hosp, 39-42; sr physician, Western Psychiat Inst, Pittsburgh, 42-44, clin dir, 44-55; clin dir, Friends Hosp, 55-58; med dir, 58-70, chief outpatient serv, 70-71, asst to med dir med educ & res, 71-74, psychiatrist, Northeast Community Ment Health Ctr, 74-78; dir student training, Friends Hosp, 68-78, CLIN PROF, HAHNEMANN MED COL, 74- *Concurrent Pos:* Rockefeller fel, C G Jung Inst, Zurich, 48-49, Bollingen fel, 54; from instr to assoc prof, Sch Med, Univ Pittsburgh, 42-55; asst, Harvard Med Sch, 38-39; asst prof, Jefferson Med Col, 61-; clin assoc prof, Hahnemann Med Col, 74- *Mem:* Life fel Am Psychiat Asn. *Res:* Psychiatry and religion. *Mailing Add:* 8301 Forest Ave Elkins Park PA 19117

CLARK, ROBERT ALFRED, b Smith Center, Kans, Aug 18, 24; m 52; c 2. METEOROLOGY, CIVIL ENGINEERING. *Educ:* Kans State Univ, BS, 48; Tex A&M Univ, MS, 59, PhD(meteorol), 64. *Prof Exp:* Hydraul engr, US Bur Reclamation, 48-50, 52-60; from assoc prof to prof meteorol, Tex A&M Univ, 60-73; ASSOC DIR, OFF HYDROL, NAT WEATHER SERV, 73- *Mem:* Am Meteorol Soc; Am Soc Civil Eng; Am Geophys Union; Royal Meteorol Soc. *Res:* Hydrology; hydrometeorology; physical meteorology. *Mailing Add:* Off of Hydrol Nat Weather Serv Silver Spring MD 20910

CLARK, ROBERT AMOS, b Oswego, NY, Jan 14, 42; m 65; c 3. INFECTIOUS DISEASES. *Educ:* Syracuse Univ, AB, 63; Columbia Univ, MD, 67. *Prof Exp:* Intern med, 67-68; asst resident, Columbia Presby Med Ctr, 68-69; clin assoc, Nat Inst Allergy & Infectious Dis, 69-71, sr staff fel, 71-72; from instr to asst prof med, Univ Wash, 73-77; assoc prof, 77-82, PROF MED, BOSTON UNIV, 82-; CHIEF, SECT INFECTIOUS DIS, UNIV HOSP, BOSTON, 77- *Concurrent Pos:* Consult infectious dis, Nat Naval Med Ctr, 70-72; chief resident, Harborview Med Ctr, Univ Wash, 72-73, attend physician, 73-77; Nat Cancer Inst res career develop award, 75.

Mem: Am Col Physicians; Am Fedn Clin Res; AAAS; Am Soc Clin Invest. *Res:* Mechanisms of host defense against microorganisms and neoplasia, with emphasis on the function of polymorphonuclear leukocytes. *Mailing Add:* Dept Med Univ Hosp 75 E Newton St Boston MA 02118

CLARK, ROBERT ARTHUR, b Melrose, Mass, May 3, 23; m 66. APPLIED MATHEMATICS. *Educ:* Duke Univ, AB, 44; Mass Inst Technol, MS, 46, PhD(math), 49. *Prof Exp:* Instr math, Mass Inst Technol, 46-49, res assoc, 49-50; from instr to prof, Case Inst Technol, 50-67, PROF MATH, CASE WESTERN RESERVE UNIV, 67- *Mem:* Am Math Soc; Math Asn Am; Soc Indust & Appl Math. *Res:* Elasticity, shell theory; asymptotic theory of differential equations. *Mailing Add:* Dept of Math Case Western Reserve Univ Cleveland OH 44106

CLARK, ROBERT BECK, b Rock Springs, Wyo, July 18, 41; m 59; c 4. ELEMENTARY PARTICLE PHYSICS. *Educ:* Yale Univ, BA, 63, MPhil, 67, PhD(physics), 68. *Prof Exp:* Fac assoc physics, Ctr Particle Theory, Univ Tex, Austin, 68-70, asst prof, Dept Physics, 70-73; asst prof, 73-76, ASSOC PROF PHYSICS, TEX A&M UNIV, 76- *Mem:* Am Phys Soc; Am Asn Physics Teachers (treas, 78-); Am Inst Physics (mem gov bd, 78-). *Res:* Investigations of the electromagnetic and weak interactions of elementary particles. *Mailing Add:* Dept of Physics Tex A&M Univ College Station TX 77843

CLARK, ROBERT EDWARD HOLMES, b July 8, 47; m 70; c 2. ELECTRON IMPACT EXCITATIONS. *Educ:* Frostburg State Col, BS, 69; Pa State Univ, MS, 78, PhD(astron), 80. *Prof Exp:* FEL, LOS ALAMOS NAT LAB, 80- *Mem:* Sigma Xi. *Res:* Theoretical calculations of electron impact excitation cross sections; rates for positively charged atomic ions. *Mailing Add:* Rte 4 Box 94L Santa Fe NM 87501

CLARK, ROBERT H, b Winnipeg, Man, Dec 25, 21; m 43; c 2. HYDROLOGY. *Educ:* McGill Univ, BEng, 43, MEng, 45. *Prof Exp:* Demonstr civil eng, McGill Univ, 43-44; hydraul design engr, Hydraul Div, Dominion Eng Works, Ltd, Montreal, 46-48; lectr civil eng, Univ Man, 48-52, asst prof, 52; chief hydraul engr, Red River Invest, Winnipeg, Can Dept Resources & Develop, 50-53; asst chief water resources br, 53-57; chief hydraul engr, Can Dept Northern Affairs & Nat Resources, 57-66, chief planning div, Dept Energy, Mines & Resources, 66-68, spec adv, 68-74, dir, Inland Waters Br, 74-80, SR ENG ADV, DEPT ENVIRON, 81- *Concurrent Pos:* Mem, Prairie Prov Water Bd, 53-69; mem, Souris-Red River Eng Bd, 53-; mem subcomt hydrol, Nat Res Coun Can, 57-66; mem, Greater Winnipeg Floodway Adv Bd, 62-69; secy, Can Nat Comt, Int Hydrol Decade, 64-68; chmn working group on guide & tech regulations, Comn Hydrometeorol, World Meteorol Orgn, 64-72 & mem adv working group, 68-72; chmn, Can Sect, Int Great Lakes Working Comt, 65-; chmn, Atlantic Tidal Power Eng & Mgt Comt, 66-70; chmn, Can Sect, Int Niagara Bd Control, 69-73; mem for Can, Int Lake Superior Bd of Control & Int Niagara Comt, 69-73; chmn, Mgt Comt Bay Fundy Fed Power Reassessment Studies, 75-78; vpres, Comn Hydrol World Meteorol Orgn, 72-76; pres, Comn Hydrol, 76-84. *Mem:* Am Geophys Union; Int Asn Sci Hydrol. *Res:* Snowmelt floods and river flow under ice conditions; water resources planning and development; tidal power engineering. *Mailing Add:* 1461 McRobie Ave Ottawa ON K1H 7E3 Can

CLARK, ROBERT M, b Canton, Ohio. PATHOLOGY. *Educ:* Muskingum Col, BS, 44; Case Western Reserve Univ, MD, 48. *Prof Exp:* From instr to asst prof, Case Western Reserve Univ, 50-62; ASSOC PROF PATH, UNIV MIAMI, 62-; CHIEF LAB PATH, VET ADMIN HOSP, MIAMI, 62- *Concurrent Pos:* Staff physician, Vet Admin Hosp, Cleveland, Ohio, 50-62. *Mem:* Am Soc Clin Path; Int Acad Path. *Res:* Blood coagulation. *Mailing Add:* Vet Admin Hosp Miami FL 33125

CLARK, ROBERT NEWHALL, b Ann Arbor, Mich, Apr 17, 25; m 49; c 4. ELECTRICAL ENGINEERING. *Educ:* Univ Mich, BSE, 50, MSE, 51; Stanford Univ, PhD, 69. *Prof Exp:* Res engr, Honeywell, Inc, Minn, 51-57; from asst prof to assoc prof elec eng, 57-66, consult, Appl Physics Lab, 57-77 NSF fac fel, 66-67, PROF ELEC ENG, UNIV WASH, 66- *Concurrent Pos:* Consult, Boeing Co, Wash, 58-66 & 71-82 & Perspective, Inc, 64-66; gen chmn, Joint Automatic Control Conf, 66; lectr, Stanford Univ, 68; vis scientist, Fraunhofer Gesellschaft Inst Informationsverarbeitung Technik & Biologie, Karlsruhe, Ger, 76-77. *Mem:* Am Inst Aeronaut & Astronaut; Inst Elec & Electronics Engrs. *Res:* Automatic control system theory; guidance and control of aerospace vehicles; electromechanical servomechanisms; inertial systems and component development. *Mailing Add:* Dept of Elec Eng Univ of Wash FT-10 Seattle WA 98195

CLARK, ROBERT PAUL, b Jackson, Mich, July 19, 35; m 59; c 4. ANALYTICAL CHEMISTRY, PHYSICAL CHEMISTRY. *Educ:* Univ Mich, BS, 57; Univ Ill, MS, 59, PhD(anal chem), 62. *Prof Exp:* Staff mem, Power Sources Div, 62-69, mem tech staff, Explor Battery Div, 69-80, SUPVR, STORAGE BATTERIES DIV, SANDIA NAT LABS, 80- *Mem:* Am Chem Soc; Electrochem Soc; Int Confederation Thermal Anal; NAm Thermal Anal Soc. *Res:* Batteries; energy conversion; thermal batteries; power sources; electrochemistry; fused salts; phase equilibria; thermal analysis; storage batteries; utility load leveling; electric vehicles; alternative energy sources. *Mailing Add:* Div 2525 Sandia Nat Labs Albuquerque NM 87185

CLARK, ROBERT VERNON, b PEI, Aug 9, 26; m 54; c 4. PLANT PATHOLOGY. *Educ:* McGill Univ, BSc, 49, MSc, 52; Univ Wis, PhD(plant path), 56. *Prof Exp:* Res officer, Plant Path, Bot & Plant Path Lab, 49-59, Cereal Dis, Res Br, Genetics & Plant Breeding Inst, 59-64, RES OFFICER, CEREAL DIS, RES BR, OTTAWA RES STA, CAN DEPT AGR, 64- *Mem:* Am Phytopath Soc; Can Phytopath Soc (secy-treas, 62-64). *Res:* Plant pathology and mycology of cereal diseases. *Mailing Add:* Res Br Ottawa Res Sta Can Dept of Agr Ottawa Can

CLARK, ROGER WILLIAM, b Oxford, Nebr, Nov 23, 42; m 67; c 2. MOLECULAR BIOLOGY, GENETICS. *Educ:* Colo State Univ, BS, 65, MS, 67; Univ Ill, PhD(genetics), 71. *Prof Exp:* Instr, 74-77, ASST PROF MOLECULAR GENETICS, SCH MED & DENT, UNIV ROCHESTER, 77- *Concurrent Pos:* NIH fel gen med sci, Fla State Univ, 71-72; Nat Cancer Inst fel, Univ Tex, Houston, 72-74. *Res:* Chromosome structure; biochemistry and biophysics of nucleic acids. *Mailing Add:* Dept of Exp Radiol Univ Rochester Sch Med & Dent Rochester NY 14642

CLARK, RONALD DAVID, b Leeds, Eng, July 18, 38; m 64; c 1. ORGANIC CHEMISTRY, ACADEMIC ADMINISTRATION. *Educ:* Univ Leeds, BSc, 59, PhD(chem), 62. *Prof Exp:* Fel, Univ Nebr, 62-65; sci officer chem, Radiochem Ctr, UK Atomic Energy Authority, 65-67; assoc prof chem, Jamestown Col, 67-75; DEAN, SCH NATURAL & SOCIAL SCI, KEARNEY STATE COL, 75- *Mem:* Am Chem Soc; Royal Soc Chem. *Res:* Steroid synthesis; synthesis of small ring compounds and isotopically labelled polypeptides. *Mailing Add:* Sch Natural & Social Sci Kearney State Col Kearney NE 68847

CLARK, RONALD DUANE, b Hollywood, Calif, Nov 21, 38; m 67; c 4. ORGANIC CHEMISTRY, ENVIRONMENTAL CHEMISTRY. *Educ:* Univ Calif, Los Angeles, BS, 60; Univ Calif, Riverside, PhD(org chem), 64. *Prof Exp:* Fel, Mich State Univ, 64-65; sr res chemist, Standard Oil Co, Ohio, 65-69; from asst prof to assoc prof chem, 69-78, PROF CHM, NMEX HIGHLANDS UNIV, 78-, CHMN DIV SCI & MATH, 77- *Mem:* Am Chem Soc. *Res:* catalysis; studies of coal fly ash. *Mailing Add:* Div Sci & Math NMex Highlands Univ Las Vegas NM 87701

CLARK, RONALD GREY, neuroanatomy, see previous edition

CLARK, RONALD JENE, b Hutchinson, Kans, July 11, 32; m 56; c 2. INORGANIC CHEMISTRY. *Educ:* Univ Kans, BS, 54, PhD(chem), 58. *Prof Exp:* Asst, Univ Kans, 54-57; res chemist, Linde Co, NY, 58-61; instr & assoc, Iowa State Univ, 61-62; from instr to assoc prof, 62-72, PROF CHEM, FLA STATE UNIV, 72- *Mem:* Am Chem Soc; The Chem Soc; AAAS; Sigma Xi. *Res:* Metal coordination compounds-phosphorus triflouride substitution products of metal carbonyls; lower oxidation state compounds of transition and actinide elements. *Mailing Add:* Dept of Chem Fla State Univ Tallahassee FL 32306

CLARK, RONALD KEITH, b Los Angeles, Calif, Aug 28, 41; m 60; c 2. PHYSICAL CHEMISTRY. *Educ:* Univ Calif, Riverside, BA, 63, PhD(phys chem), 66. *Prof Exp:* NIH fel, Cornell Univ, 66-67; chemist, 67-74, sr res chemist, 74-79, STAFF RES CHEMIST, SHELL DEVELOP CO, 79- *Mem:* Sigma Xi; Am Chem Soc; Soc Petrol Engrs. *Res:* Statistical thermodynamics and mechanics of nonelectrolyte solutions; theory of phase transitions, particularly in the critical region; oil-well drilling fluids; phase behavior of polymer solutions. *Mailing Add:* Shell Develop Co PO Box 481 Houston TX 77001

CLARK, RONALD ROGERS, b Percy, NH, Jan 7, 35; m 56; c 4. ELECTRICAL ENGINEERING. *Educ:* Univ NH, BS, 56; Yale Univ, MEng, 57; Syracuse Univ, PhD(elec eng, automatic control), 63. *Prof Exp:* Assoc prof, 57-67, PROF ELEC & COMPUT ENG, UNIV NH, 67- *Mem:* Inst Elec & Electronic Engrs; Am Geophys Union. *Res:* Communication and control systems; meteor wind radar system; digital signal processing; ionospheric propagation and antenna systems. *Mailing Add:* Dept of Elec & Comput Eng Kingsbury Hall Univ of NH Durham NH 03824

CLARK, RUSSELL NORMAN, b Norwood, Ohio, Mar 23, 21; c 7. ORGANIC CHEMISTRY. *Educ:* Xavier Univ, BS, 42; Univ Detroit, MS, 43; Iowa State Univ, PhD(org chem), 45. *Prof Exp:* Tech supt, E I du Pont de Nemours & Co, Inc, 45-60; vpres res & com develop, Celanese Plastic Co, 60-67; exec vpres, Inmont Corp, 67-70; vpres & gen mgr, Polyester Div, 70-75, VPRES TECH, ECUSTA PAPER & FILM GROUP, OLIN CORP, 75- *Mem:* Am Chem Soc. *Res:* Polymer chemistry; cellulose chemistry; film fabrication; plastics fabrication; aquaculture; hydroponics. *Mailing Add:* Olin Corp Pisgah Forest NC 28768

CLARK, SALEM THOMAS, b Mokane, Mo, June 26, 27; m 47; c 4. PHYSICAL CHEMISTRY. *Educ:* Univ Mo, BS, 54, MS, 56, PhD(phys chem), 58. *Prof Exp:* Res chemist, Linde Co, 57-59; infrared spectroscopist, Celanese Corp, 59-60; prod mgr, Union Carbide Corp, 60-63; anal group leader, Celanese Fibers Co, 63-66, tech planning coordr, 66-69; DIR UNIV RELS, CELANESE CORP, 69- *Mem:* Am Chem Soc; Instrument Soc Am; Am Soc Qual Control. *Res:* Gas chromatography; instrumental analysis. *Mailing Add:* Celanese Corp 1211 Ave of Americas New York NY 10036

CLARK, SAM LILLARD, JR, b St Louis, Mo, June 9, 26; m 74; c 6. ANATOMY. *Educ:* Harvard Univ, MD, 49. *Prof Exp:* Intern med, Mass Gen Hosp, 49-50; from instr to assoc prof anat, Wash Univ, 54-68; chmn dept, 68-77, PROF ANAT, MED SCH, UNIV MASS, 68-, DIR, CTR FOR EDUC RESOURCES, 77- *Concurrent Pos:* Nat Res Coun fel med sci biochem & nutrit, Med Sch, Vanderbilt Univ, 50-52; Palmer sr res fel; USPHS sr res fel; USPHS career develop award anat, Wash Univ; mgr ed, Am J Anat, 74-80. *Mem:* AAAS; Asn Am Med Cols; Am Asn Anat (vpres, 77-79); Am Soc Cell Biol. *Res:* Cellular differentiation; immunology; electron microscopy of tissues, relating structure to function. *Mailing Add:* Ctr Educ Resources Univ of Mass Med Ctr Worcester MA 01605

CLARK, SAMUEL FRIEND, b Danville, Ky, Jan 16, 14; m 46; c 2. ORGANIC CHEMISTRY. *Educ:* Univ WVa, AB, 34, MS, 37; Univ NC, PhD(org chem), 39. *Prof Exp:* Asst org chem, Univ WVa, 34-36, Johns Hopkins Univ, 36-37 & Univ NC, 37-39; res chemist, Union Carbide Chem Co, WVa, 39-42, group leader, 42-46; from assoc prof to prof chem, Univ Miss, 46-63, chmn, 55-63; chmn dept chem & phys sci, 63-67, chmn dept chem, 68-77, PROF CHEM, FLA ATLANTIC UNIV, 63- *Concurrent Pos:* Summer sr scientist, Union Carbide Nuclear Co, Tenn, 51-56; temporary chem liaison & field rep, NSF-AID Prog to Asn Cent Am Univs, Costa Rica, 67-68; US AID consult, Pedag Insts & Simon Bolivar Univ, Venezuela, 69. *Mem:* Am Chem Soc. *Res:* Constitution of natural tannins; synthesis of vinyl monomers and polymers, azo dyes and insecticides; reaction kinetics in radiology; molecular rearrangements. *Mailing Add:* Dept of Chem Fla Atlantic Univ Boca Raton FL 33431

CLARK, SAMUEL KELLY, b Ypsilanti, Mich, Nov 3, 24; m 51; c 5. APPLIED MECHANICS, MECHANICAL ENGINEERING. *Educ:* Univ Mich, BSE, 46, MSE, 48, PhD(appl mech), 51. *Prof Exp:* Staff engr, Douglas Aircraft Co, 46-47, Borg Warner Corp, 48-50 & Ford Motor Co Sci Lab, 50-52; asst prof, Case Inst Technol, 52-55; PROF APPL MECH, UNIV MICH, 55- *Mem:* Soc Automotive Engrs; Am Soc Mech Engrs; Soc Exp Stress Anal; Am Soc Testing & Mat. *Res:* Applied mechanics as applied to problems in the rubber industry, with particular attention to pneumatic tires. *Mailing Add:* Dept Mech Eng & Appl Mech Univ Mich Ann Arbor MI 48109

CLARK, SANDRA HELEN BECKER, b Kansas City, Mo, July 27, 38; div; c 2. GEOLOGY. *Educ:* Univ Idaho, BS, 63, MS, 64, PhD(geol), 68. *Prof Exp:* Geologist, Cominco Am, Inc, 66-67; geologist, Alaska Mineral Resources Br, Calif, 67-72, staff geologist, Off Mineral Resources, US Geol Surv, 72-74, equal employ opportunity officer & spec asst to dir, 78-80, GEOLOGIST, EASTERN MINERAL RESOURCES BUR, US GEOLOGICAL SURV, RESTON, VA, 80- *Concurrent Pos:* Coord staff mem, Alaska Natural Gas EIS Task Force, Dept of Interior, Washington, DC, 74-75, partic, Mgr Develop Prog, 75-76. *Mem:* AAAS; Geol Soc Am. *Res:* Geologic mapping; field and laboratory studies of structure and petrology of metamorphic and igneous terranes in northern Idaho, east central and south central Alaska; zinc, lead, barite in east-central US. *Mailing Add:* 11910 Barrel Cooper Ct Reston VA 22092

CLARK, SIDNEY GILBERT, b Wolfsburg, Pa, Sept 2, 30; m 57; c 2. ORGANIC CHEMISTRY. *Educ:* Juniata Col, BS, 53; Pa State Univ, MS, 56, PhD(org chem), 58. *Prof Exp:* Res chemist, 57-62, res specialist, 62-64, group leader sulfonation-sulfation, 64-66, sr res group leader, 66-69, sect mgr detergents & phosphates res & develop, 69-78, PROJ MGR COM DEVELOP, MONSANTO INDUST CHEM CO, 78- *Mem:* Am Chem Soc; Sigma Xi; Am Oil Chemists' Soc. *Res:* Alkylation; sulfonation; ethoxylation; surfactant intermediates; anionic and nonionic surfactants; enzymes. *Mailing Add:* Com Develop Dept Monsanto Indust Chem Co 800 N Lindbergh Blvd St Louis MO 63166

CLARK, STANLEY JOE, b McPherson, Kans, Sept 22, 31; m 58; c 5. AGRICULTURAL ENGINEERING. *Educ:* Kans State Univ, BS, 54, MS, 59; Purdue Univ, PhD(agr eng), 66. *Prof Exp:* Instr agr eng, Purdue Univ, 60-64; asst prof, Colo State Univ, 64-66; assoc prof, 66-75, PROF AGR ENG, KANS STATE UNIV, 75- *Concurrent Pos:* Actg br chief, Agr Prod & Food Processing Br, Indust Energy Conserv & Solar Applications, Dept of Energy, Washington, DC, 77-78, consult, Dept of Energy, 78- *Mem:* Am Soc Agr Engrs; Am Soc Eng Educ; Int Soc Terrain Vehicle Systs. *Res:* Crop production mechanization; traction and tillage mechanics; alternative energy sources for agricultural production; energy conservation in agricultural production and food processing; farm equipment product liability and safety; farm equipment design. *Mailing Add:* Dept of Agr Eng Kans State Univ Manhattan KS 66506

CLARK, STANLEY PRESTON, b Colby, Kans, June 24, 17; m 42; c 4. CHEMICAL ENGINEERING, GENERAL ENGINEERING. *Educ:* Park Col, AB, 39; Univ Kans, BS, 41; Tex A&M Univ, MS, 58. *Prof Exp:* Chemist, Jones-Dabney Paint Co, 41-42; jr chem engr, Tenn Valley Authority, 42-44; chem engr, Cent Soya Co, 44-48; assoc res engr, Food Protein Res & Develop Ctr, 48-80, PROCESS ENG CONSULT, TEX A&M UNIV, 80- *Concurrent Pos:* Consult, UN Children's Fund, 63 & 65. *Mem:* Am Inst Chem Engrs; Am Chem Soc; Am Oil Chem Soc. *Res:* Processing of oilseeds and products from oilseeds. *Mailing Add:* Rte 4 Box 440 College Station TX 77840

CLARK, STANLEY ROSS, b Berwyn, Alta, Mar 8, 37; m 62; c 2. COMPUTER SCIENCE. *Educ:* Univ BC, BASc, 59; Aberdeen Univ, MSc, 61; Univ Manchester, PhD(comput sci), 67. *Prof Exp:* Chief programmer math, Pac Naval Lab, Dept Nat Defence, 62-64; res assoc comput sci, Inst Comput Studies, Univ Man, 67-68, asst prof, 68-69; ASSOC PROF COMPUT SCI, UNIV VICTORIA, BC, 69- *Concurrent Pos:* Nat Res Coun Can grants, 68-70. *Mem:* Asn Comput Mach; Brit Comput Soc. *Res:* Design and implementation of programming languages; simulation studies of computer systems. *Mailing Add:* Dept of Math Univ of Victoria Victoria Can

CLARK, STEPHEN DARROUGH, b Seattle, Wash, Apr 10, 45; m 68; c 3. INDUSTRIAL WASTE TREATMENT, WATER MANAGEMENT. *Educ:* Seattle Univ, BS, 68; Mass Inst Technol, PhD(org chem), 72. *Prof Exp:* Fel chem, Syntex Res Inc, Calif, 72-73; res chemist, Arapahoe Chem Inc, 73-75, group leader chem, Arapahoe-Newport Div, Syntex Inc, Ind, 75-78, group leader, Process Develop, Arapahoe Chem Inc, 78-79, mgr, 79; DIST REP, NALCO CHEM CO, 79- *Mem:* Am Chem Soc; Sigma Xi; Tech Asn Pulp & Paper Indust. *Res:* Process development research in pharmaceutical intermediates fine chemicals; pilot plant management; secondary waste treatment operation, fuels and combustion; applications for corrosion control; energy management. *Mailing Add:* 1010 Chippewa St Mount Vernon WA 98273

CLARK, STEPHEN HOWARD, b Boston, Mass, May 3, 40; m 65; c 2. FISH BIOLOGY, MARINE SCIENCE. *Educ:* Univ Maine, BS, 66, MS, 68; Univ Miami, PhD(marine sci), 70. *Prof Exp:* Asst prof biol, Grand Valley State Col, 70-73; fishery biologist, Galveston Lab, Tex, 73-74, FISHERY BIOLOGIST, NAT MARINE FISHERIES SERV, WOODS HOLE LAB, MASS, 74- *Concurrent Pos:* US rep, Shellfish Comt, Int Coun Explor of Sea, 78-; mem working group, Int Coun Exploration of the Sea, Homaus, 78-80, Saithe, Pandalus, & European Lake 78- *Mem:* Am Fisheries Soc; Nat Shellfisheries Asn. *Res:* Fishery science; oceanography; limnology; evaluation of the effects of fising on marine finfish and crustacean stocks both single and multispecies assessments; biological and environmental aspects. *Mailing Add:* Nat Marine Fisheries Serv Northeast Fisheries Ctr Woods Hole MA 02543

CLARK, SYDNEY P, JR, b Philadelphia, Pa, July 26, 29; m 63; c 4. GEOPHYSICS. *Educ:* Harvard Univ, AB, 51, MA, 53, PhD(geol), 55. *Prof Exp:* Res fel geophys, Harvard Univ, 55-57; geophysicist, Geophys Lab, Carnegie Inst, 57-62; WEINBERG PROF GEOPHYS, YALE UNIV, 62-, DIR UNDERGRAD STUDIES, 81- *Concurrent Pos:* Fulbright scholar, Australian Nat Univ, 63. *Mem:* Fel Am Geophys Union. *Res:* Terrestrial and lunar heat flow; high pressure phase equilibria; constitution of earth's interior. *Mailing Add:* Box 2161 Yale Sta New Haven CT 06520

CLARK, T(HOMAS) F(RANCIS), chemical engineering, deceased

CLARK, T(HELMA) K, b Pa, Aug 11, 30; m 54; c 1. PSYCHOLOGICAL PHYSICS. *Educ:* Ind Univ, Pa, BS, 52; Univ Pittsburgh, PhD(biol & psychol), 79. *Prof Exp:* RES ASSOC, BIOL SCI DEPT, UNIV PITTSBURGH, 80- *Mem:* Soc Neurosci; Parapsychol Asn. *Res:* Function of the locus coeruleus-dorsal noradrenaline system; organizational patterns in psychokinetic behavior. *Mailing Add:* Biol Sci Dept Univ Pittsburgh Pittsburgh PA 15260

CLARK, TERRY LESTER, b Penticton, BC, Mar 26, 43; m 66; c 3. ATMOSPHERIC SCIENCE. *Educ:* Univ BC, BASc, 67; Univ Toronto, MSc, 69, PhD(physics), 71. *Prof Exp:* Fel, Geophys Fluid Dynamics Lab, 71-73; res scientist, Atmospheric Environ Serv, 73-77; RES SCIENTIST METEOROL, NAT CTR ATMOSPHERIC RES, 77- *Res:* Numerical modeling of convective clouds; numerical fluid dynamics. *Mailing Add:* Nat Ctr Atmospheric Res PO Box 3000 Boulder CO 80307

CLARK, THOMAS ALAN, b Leicestershire, Eng, Mar 14, 38; m 60; c 2. ASTRONOMY. *Educ:* Univ Leeds, BSc, 59, PhD(cosmic ray physics), 63. *Prof Exp:* Fel physics, Univ Calgary, 62-64, sessional lectr, 64-65; vis scientist, Defence Res Telecommun Estab, Defence Res Bd Can, 65; lectr physics, Univ Col, Univ London, 66-69, tutor, 68-69; from asst prof to assoc prof, 69-81, PROF PHYSICS, UNIV CALGARY, 81-, EXEC ASST DEAN SCI, PHYSICS/ASTRON, 80- *Concurrent Pos:* Mem, Assoc Comt Astron, Nat Res Coun, Can, 72-80; mem, Adv Comt Stratospheric Pollution, Atmospheric Environ Serv, Can, 74- *Honors & Awards:* Killah res fel, Univ Calgary, 79. *Mem:* Royal Astron Soc Can; assoc Brit Inst Physics & Phys Soc; Am Astron Soc; Can Astron Soc; Can Asn Physicists. *Res:* Infrared astronomy; far infrared solar spectral studies by balloon-borne and mountain altitude instrumentation; stratospheric emission; spectral measurements in the Far Infra Red as an aid in pollution studies; Infra Red Solar measurements. *Mailing Add:* Physics Dept Univ Calgary 2500 University Dr NW Calgary Can

CLARK, THOMAS ARVID, b Durango, Colo, Aug 23, 39; m 67. RADIO ASTRONOMY, GEODESY. *Educ:* Univ Colo, BS, 61, PhD(astrophys), 67. *Prof Exp:* Staff scientist astron, Boulder Labs, Environ Sci Serv Admin, Colo, 61-66 & NASA Marshall Space Flight Ctr, 66-68; RADIO ASTRONR, NASA GODDARD SPACEFLIGHT CTR, 68-; ASSOC PROF ASTRON, UNIV MD, 69- *Concurrent Pos:* Exec vpres, 74-81, pres, Radioamateur Satellite Corp, 81-; mem study group 2nd radio astron, Int Consultative Radio Comn, 74-79; mem radio astron subcomt, Comt Radio Frequencies, Nat Res Coun-Nat Acad Sci, 74-79; co-chmn serv working group radio astron, Fed Commun Comn, 75-79. *Mem:* Int Astron Union; Am Astron Soc; Int Sci Radio Union; Am Geophys Union; AAAS. *Res:* Development of very long baseline interferometry for high accuracy astronomical and geophysical measurements; development of astronomical instrumentation; radio frequency spectrum management; education. *Mailing Add:* Crustal Dynamics Proj Code 974 NASA Goddard Space Flight Ctr Greenbelt MD 20771

CLARK, THOMAS HENRY, b London, Eng, Dec 3, 93; m 27; c 1. STRATIGRAPHY, PALEONTOLOGY. *Educ:* Harvard Univ, AB, 17, AM, 21, PhD(geol, paleont), 23. *Prof Exp:* Instr, Harvard Univ, 15-17 & 20-24; 20-24; from asst prof to assoc prof paleont, 24-29, Logan prof, 29-62, prof, 62-64, dir univ mus, 25-52, chmn dept geol sci, 52-59, EMER PROF PALEONT, McGILL UNIV, 64- *Concurrent Pos:* Geologist, Geol Surv Can, 28-31 & 35 & Dept Mines, Que, 38-64; consult, Dept Natural Resources, Que, 64-69; consult geologist, 62-; adv geol, Redpath Mus, 64- *Honors & Awards:* Logan Medal, 71. *Mem:* Paleont Soc; Geol Soc Am; Royal Soc Can (pres sect IV, 53-54); Geol Asn Can (pres, 58-59); Can Inst Mining & Metal. *Res:* Invertebrate paleontology; Paleozoic stratigraphy. *Mailing Add:* Dept of Geol Sci McGill Univ Montreal Can

CLARK, TREVOR H, b Haviland, Kans, July 16, 09; m 33, 66; c 4. PHYSICS. *Educ:* Friends Univ, AB, 30, Univ Mich, MS, 33. *Prof Exp:* Serv mgr, Geo E Marshall Co, Kans, 29-32; serviceman, Int Radio, Mich, 33-34; lab asst, Univ Mich, 34; engr, Radio Corp Am Mfg Co, NJ, 34-38; engr, Les Laboratoires LMT, Int Tel & Tel Co, France, 38-40, dept head, Fed Telecommunication Labs, NJ, 40-45, div head, 45-47, mgr tech servs, 47-48, mgr eng servs & special projs, 49-51; asst to pres, Fed Tel & Radio Corp, 48-49; assoc dir, Southwest Res Inst, 51-55; asst to eng mgr, Air Arm Div, Westinghouse Elec Corp, 55-61, mgr underwater launch prog, Aerospace Div, 61-64, mgr deep submergence prog, 64-65, mgr prog opers, 65-67, asst div mgr, 67-69, mgr info serv, 70-71; CONSULT, 71- *Mem:* Fel Inst Elec & Electronics Engr; Acoustical Soc Am; assoc fel Am Inst Aeronaut & Astronaut; Am Inst Physics. *Res:* High vacuum; sound; thermionics; microwaves; wave propagation; telephony; electron emission; navigation; vacuum tubes; photocells; multipliers; beam tubes; switching systems; direction finders; antennas; communications; countermeasures; radar; research administration. *Mailing Add:* 684 Blue Crab Cove Annapolis MD 21401

CLARK, TRUMAN BENTON, b Pine City, Minn, Jan 13, 28; m 51; c 3. INSECT PATHOLOGY. *Educ:* Univ Minn, BA, 51, MS, 53, PhD(zool), 58. *Prof Exp:* Res specialist parasitol, Minn State Bd Health, 56-58; res asst, Univ Minn, 58-59; asst prof zool, Iowa State Univ, 59-61; specialist I insect path, Calif Pub Health Dept, 61-66 & Univ Calif, Berkeley, 66-67; res entomologist, Entom Res Div, 67-70, RES ENTOMOLOGIST, AGR RES SERV, USDA, 72- *Concurrent Pos:* Assoc prof biol, Calif State Univ, Fresno, 70-72. *Mem:* Soc Protozoologists; Soc Invert Path; Entom Soc Am; Am Mosquito Control Asn; Am Soc Microbiol. *Res:* Microbial control of mosquitoes and honey bee pathology and disease control; microbiological control of coleopterous plant pests; spiroplasma ecology. *Mailing Add:* Insect Path Lab Agr Res Serv USDA Beltsville MD 20705

CLARK, VIRGINIA, b Grand Rapids, Mich, Nov 18, 28; m 53. BIOSTATISTICS. *Educ:* Univ Mich, BA, 50, MA, 51; Univ Calif, Los Angeles, PhD(biostatist), 63. *Prof Exp:* Statistician, Gen Elec Co, 51-54; appl mathematician, Econ Res Proj, Harvard Univ, 54-56, res assoc biostatist, Med Sch, 60-61; statistician, Systs Lab Corp, 56-57; from asst prof to assoc prof biostatist, 63-74, assoc prof biomath, 71-74, PROF BIOSTATIST & PROF BIOMATH, SCH PUB HEALTH, UNIV CALIF, LOS ANGELES, 74- *Mem:* Inst Math Statist; Biomet Soc; fel Am Statist Asn. *Mailing Add:* Dept of Biostatist Sch of Pub Health Univ of Calif Los Angeles CA 90024

CLARK, VIRGINIA LEE, b Washington, DC, Aug 30, 45. MICROBIAL PHYSIOLOGY, MEDICAL MICROBIOLOGY. *Educ:* Carleton Col, BA, 67; Univ Rochester, PhD(microbiol), 77. *Prof Exp:* Fel biol, Mass Inst Technol, 76-78, instr, 79; ASST PROF MICROBIOL, UNIV ROCHESTER, 79- *Mem:* Am Soc Microbiol; AAAS; NY Acad Sci. *Res:* Genetic engineering and molecular biology of pathogenicity in Neisseria gonorrhoeae; molecular biology of antibiotic resistance in Bacteroides fragilis; regulation of translation in prokaryotes. *Mailing Add:* Dept Microbiol Sch Med Univ Rochester Rochester NY 14642

CLARK, WALLACE HENDERSON, JR, b LaGrange, Ga, May 16, 24; m; c 5. MEDICINE, PATHOLOGY. *Educ:* Tulane Univ, BS, 44, MD, 47. *Prof Exp:* From instr to prof path, Sch Med, Tulane Univ, 49-62; asst prof, Harvard Univ, 62-68, assoc clin prof, 68-69; prof path, Sch Med, Temple Univ, 69-78, chmn dept, 74-78; RES PROF DERMAT & PATH, SCH MED, UNIV PA, 78- *Concurrent Pos:* Markle scholar, 54-60; consult pathologist, Orleans Parish Coroner's Off, 50-52, 54-56 & Armed Forces Inst Path, Washington, DC; assoc path, Mass Gen Hosp, 62-68. *Mem:* Am Asn Path & Bact; Am Asn Cancer Res; Am Soc Exp Path; Am Acad Dermat. *Res:* Dermal pathology; electron microscopy; correlation of ultrastructural changes with known changes in cellular function; tumor progression in human neoplastic systems; immunology and fine structure of primary human cutaneous malignant melanomas; induction of animal model of human malignant melanoma in the guinea pig. *Mailing Add:* Dept of Dermat 3400 Spruce St Philadelphia PA 19104

CLARK, WALLACE LEE, b St Joseph, Mo, June 12, 44. ATMOSPHERIC PHYSICS. *Educ:* Univ Colo, BA, 67. *Prof Exp:* PHYSICIST, AERONOMY LAB, NAT OCEANIC & ATMOSPHERIC ADMIN, DEPT COM, 67- *Mem:* Am Geophys Union; Am Meteorol Soc. *Res:* Radar studies of the atmosphere. *Mailing Add:* Aeronomy Lab Nat Oceanic & Atmospheric Admin Boulder CO 80302

CLARK, WALTER ERNEST, b Stuart, Va, Sept 25, 16; m 39; c 3. APPLIED CHEMISTRY. *Educ:* Va Mil Inst, BS, 37; George Washington Univ, MA, 39; Univ Wis, PhD(chem & chem eng), 49. *Prof Exp:* Instr chem, Va Mil Inst, 39-41; asst prof chem eng, Mo Sch Mines, 49-51; sr res chemist, Oak Ridge Nat Lab, 51-56, group leader, 56-79; RETIRED. *Concurrent Pos:* Lectr, Univ Tenn, 63-64; Fulbright lectr, Tribhuvan Univ, Nepal, 67-68. *Mem:* Am Chem Soc; fel Am Inst Chem. *Res:* Electrochemistry; polarography; corrosion; nuclear fuel processing; nuclear waste disposal. *Mailing Add:* Rte 1 Box 95 Stuart VA 24171

CLARK, WALTER LEIGHTON, III, b Springfield, Pa, Feb 3, 21; m 45; c 1. FOOD SCIENCE. *Educ:* Pomona Col, BA, 42; Georgetown Univ, MS, 46; Cornell Univ, PhD(biochem), 53. *Prof Exp:* Res assoc, Food Sci & Tech Div, NY State Agr Exp Sta, Cornell Univ, 48-50, asst, 50-53, asst prof biochem, Grad Sch Nutrit, 53-56; sr res biologist, Dept Nutrit & Food Technol, Lederle Labs, Agr Ctr, Am Cyanamid Co, 56-58, group leader food res, 58-61, group leader food res & develop, 61-64; tech mgr new prod develop refrig foods, Res Ctr, Pillsbury Co, 65-67; assoc dir res-explor, Quaker Oats Co, Ill, 67-73; CORP DIR SCI & NUTRIT, HUNT-WESSON FOODS, INC, 73- *Concurrent Pos:* Lectr on US Food Legislation & Regulations by Japan External Trade Relations Orgn, Tokyo, 78; adj prof food sci, Chapman Col, Orange, Calif, 79-; consult & lectr, 79- *Mem:* Am Oil Chemists Soc; Am Chem Soc; Inst Food Technologists (pres-elect, 78-79, pres, 79-80); Am Asn Cereal Chemists. *Res:* Teaching food science; food additives; diet and nutrition; protein sources and technology; food fabrication; heavy metals; food regulations; tomato processing; edible fats and oils; research management. *Mailing Add:* Hunt-Wesson Foods Inc 1645 W Valencia Dr Fullerton CA 92634

CLARK, WAYNE ELDEN, b Lehi, Utah, May 2, 43; m 66; c 4. SYSTEMATICS. *Educ:* Brigham Young Univ, BS, 68, MS, 70; Tex A&M Univ, PhD(entom), 75. *Prof Exp:* Res assoc, Tex A&M Univ, 74-75, fel, 76; fel, Smithsonian Inst, 75-76 & Univ Pa, 76-77; sr scientist, Technassociats, Inc, 77; mgr, Gypsy N Tech Info Proj, Libr Cong, 77-78; ASST PROF ENTOM, AUBURN UNIV, 78- *Mem:* Coleopterists Soc; Entom Soc Am; Sigma Xi; Soc Syst Zool. *Res:* Taxonomy, phylogeny and biogeography of weevils (insecta, coleoptera, curculionidae); studies on natural history and host plant relationships. *Mailing Add:* Dept Zool & Entom Auburn Univ Auburn AL 36849

CLARK, WESLEY GLEASON, b Wadsworth, Ohio, July 1, 33; m 65; c 3. PHARMACOLOGY. *Educ:* Univ Colo, BA, 55, MS, 58; Univ Utah, PhD(pharmacol), 62. *Prof Exp:* Instr, 62-63, asst prof, 63-72, ASSOC PROF PHARMACOL, UNIV TEX HEALTH SCI CTR DALLAS, 72- *Concurrent Pos:* USPHS grant, Nat Inst Allergy & Infectious Dis, 64-66 & Nat Inst Neurol Dis & Stroke, 70-78. *Mem:* Am Physiol Soc; Am Soc Pharmacol & Exp Therapeut; Soc Exp Biol & Med; Soc Neurosci; NY Acad Sci. *Res:* Neuropharmacology; effects of drugs on thermoregulation; bacterial pyrogens; food poisoning; vomiting. *Mailing Add:* Dept of Pharmacol Univ Tex Health Sci Ctr Dallas TX 75325

CLARK, WILBURN O, b Farber, Mo, Feb 9, 38; m 64. ELECTRICAL ENGINEERING, INFORMATION SCIENCE. *Educ:* Univ Kans, BSEE, 60, MSEE, 61, PhD(elec eng), 64. *Prof Exp:* Staff consult comput, Gen Elec Co, Ala, 64-66, consult specialist info serv, Ariz, 66-67; from asst prof to prof eng, Ariz State Univ, 67-80; consult, US Air Force, 80-81; SR STAFF ENGR, MOTOROLA, INC, 81- *Concurrent Pos:* Consult, Vendo Co, Mo, 62-64 & Goodyear Aerospace Corp, Ariz, 74-80; in-plant training instr, Motorola Inc, Ariz, 67. *Mem:* Inst Elec & Electronics Engrs; Asn Comput Mach; NY Acad Sci; Sigma Xi. *Res:* Translation and programming language specification and implementation; special purpose digital systems; x-band traveling wave tube experimentation instrumentation; systems engineering. *Mailing Add:* 603 E Carson Dr Tempe AZ 85282

CLARK, WILLIAM ARTHUR, b Chicago Heights, Ill, Nov 6, 23; m 46; c 3. BACTERIOLOGY. *Educ:* Univ Colo, BA, 50; Cornell Univ, MS, 51, PhD(bact), 53. *Prof Exp:* Asst prof bact, Cornell Univ, 53-54; asst cur, Am Type Cult Collection, 54-60, dir, 60-73; mem fac, Dept Microbiol, Queensland Univ, 73-74, vis scientist, Ctr Dis Control, 74-77; DIR CLIN MICROBIOL, GA DEPT HUMAN RESOURCES, 77- *Concurrent Pos:* Exec secy, Int Comn Syst Bact, 58-74. *Mem:* Am Soc Microbiol. *Res:* Taxonomy of myxobacteria; preservation of bacteria, bacteriophage and other microorganisms; taxonomy of bacteria and bacteriophage. *Mailing Add:* Lab Serv Sect Rm 116-H 47 Trinity Ave SW Atlanta GA 30334

CLARK, WILLIAM B, b Delanco, NJ, Aug 27, 17; m 39; c 2. CHEMICAL ENGINEERING. *Educ:* Lehigh Univ, BS, 38, MS, 39. *Prof Exp:* Chem engr, Ammonia Dept, E I Du Pont de Nemours & Co, Inc, 39-49, supvr, Polychem Dept, 49-53, sr supvr, 53-58, sect mgr, 58-60, lab mgr, Plastics Dept, 60-69, P&C Div, 69-71, lab div res admin, 69-72; RETIRED, 72- *Mem:* Am Chem Soc; AAAS. *Res:* Research and development on nylon intermediates, polyolefins and other plastics. *Mailing Add:* 241 Cheltenham Rd Newark DE 19711

CLARK, WILLIAM CUMMIN, b Greenwich, Conn, Dec 20, 48. POLICY ANALYSIS, SOCIOLOGY OF SCIENCE. *Educ:* Yale Univ, BSc, 71; Univ BC, PhD(ecol), 79. *Prof Exp:* res scholar, Int Inst Appl Syst Anal, 73-74 & 78-79; vis fac, Inst Resource Ecol, Univ BC, 79-80; SCIENTIST, INST ENERGY ANAL, OAK RIDGE ASSOC UNIVS, 81- *Concurrent Pos:* Consult, Spruce Budworm Prog, Can Forestry Serv, 73-80. *Res:* Basic studies on stability & resilience of ecosystems; policy analysis for resource management; social dimensions of risk assessment; development strategies for third world; carbon dioxide-climate impact assessment. *Mailing Add:* Inst Energy Anal Oak Ridge Assoc Univ PO Box 117 Oak Ridge TN 37830

CLARK, WILLIAM DEAN, b Guthrie, Okla, Feb 1, 36; m 54; c 2. MATHEMATICAL ANALYSIS. *Educ:* Cent State Col, Okla, BSEd, 62; Univ Tex, Austin, MA, 64, PhD(math), 68. *Prof Exp:* NSF Acad Year Inst partic, Univ Tex, Austin, 62-63; assoc prof math, 66-74, res grant, 68-69, PROF MATH, STEPHEN F AUSTIN STATE UNIV, 74- *Concurrent Pos:* NSF res grant, 70-73. *Mem:* Soc Indust & Appl Math; Math Asn Am. *Res:* Summability of series. *Mailing Add:* Dept of Math Stephen F Austin State Univ Nacogdoches TX 75962

CLARK, WILLIAM DEMPSEY, b Buffalo, NY, July 15, 21; m 80; c 3. PHYSICAL CHEMISTRY. *Educ:* Univ Miami, BS, 50, MS, 51; Univ Ore, MS, 54, PhD(phys chem), 58. *Prof Exp:* Staff mem, Los Alamos Sci Lab, NMex, 56-61; proj mgr, Phys Sci Corp, 61-62; consult, Aerosols, Mass Spectrometry, Radiation, 62-63; staff mem, Hughes Aircraft Co, 63-64; eng specialist, Garret Corp, 64-65; tech dir, Dyna-Therm Corp, 65-66; founder, Ropat Co, 63, pres, 68-69; pres, Ropat-Caslon Inc, 69-75; FOUNDER, FOUR-ZERO CO, 77- *Concurrent Pos:* Consult, Pub Utilities & Foreign Co. *Mem:* AAAS; Am Chem Soc; Fedn Am Scientists; Am Inst Aeronaut & Astronaut; Am Inst Physics. *Res:* Chemical kinetics; mass and optical spectroscopy; high temperature measurement; gravitation; nuclear propulsion; cryogenics; specialized analytical and space instrumentation; energy systems development; aerosols; horology; nuclear weapons and reactors. *Mailing Add:* PO Box 634 El Segundo CA 90245

CLARK, WILLIAM DENNIS, b Redding, Calif, Jan 20, 48; m 69, 81. PLANT TAXONOMY, NATURAL PRODUCTS CHEMISTRY. *Educ:* Sacramento State Col, BA, 70; Univ Tex-Austin, PhD(bot), 77. *Prof Exp:* asst prof, 76-81, ASSOC PROF BOT, ARIZ STATE UNIV, 81- *Mem:* Bot Soc Am; Am Soc Plant Taxonomists; Phytochem Soc NAm; Int Asn Plant Taxon; Soc Study Evolution. *Res:* Chemical taxonomy of flowering plants, especially compositae; chemical ecology of plants; coevolution, especially plant-insect interactions; plant natural products chemistry, especially flavonoids. *Mailing Add:* Dept of Bot & Microbiol Ariz State Univ Tempe AZ 85281

CLARK, WILLIAM E(UGENE), b Kingman, Kans, July 19, 24; m 54; c 3. CHEMICAL ENGINEERING. *Educ:* Marquette Univ, BChE, 45; Univ Chicago, BS, 50; Univ Kans, MS, 59, PhD(chem eng), 63. *Prof Exp:* Process engr, Mobil Oil Co, 50-53; chem engr, Midwest Res Inst, 53-58; instr fluid mech, Univ Kans, 58-61; sr chem engr, Midwest Res Inst, 61-66; PROCESS ENGR, CONOCO COAL DEVELOP CO, 66- *Concurrent Pos:* Process engr, J F Pritchard & Co, 59-61. *Mem:* Am Inst Chem Engrs. *Res:* Liquid fuel from coal; drying; thermodynamics; kinetics. *Mailing Add:* Res Div Conoco Coal Develop Co Library PA 15129

CLARK, WILLIAM EDWIN, b Brunswick, Ga, Dec 7, 34; m 60; c 1. MATHEMATICS. *Educ:* Sam Houston State Col, BA, 60; Tulane Univ, PhD(math), 64. *Prof Exp:* Ford Found res fel math, Calif Inst Technol, 64-65; from asst prof to assoc prof, Univ Fla, 65-70; PROF MATH, UNIV S FLA, 70- *Concurrent Pos:* NSF res grant, 67- *Mem:* Am Math Soc; Math Asn Am. *Res:* Arithmetic coding theory. *Mailing Add:* Dept of Math Univ of SFla Tampa FL 33620

CLARK, WILLIAM GILBERT, b Los Angeles, Calif, May 26, 30; m 59; c 2. MAGNETIC RESONANCE, EXPERIMENTAL SOLID STATE PHYSICS. *Educ:* Stanford Univ, BS, 52; Cornell Univ, PhD(physics), 61. *Prof Exp:* Asst, Stanford Univ, 52-53; asst, Cornell Univ, 54-60; jr res physicist, Univ Calif, San Diego, 60-62, asst res physicist, 62-64; from asst prof to assoc prof, 64-73, PROF PHYSICS, UNIV CALIF, LOS ANGELES, 73- *Concurrent Pos:* Nat Ctr Sci Res fel, Fac Sci, Orsay, France, 69-70, exchange prof, 70; assoc prof, Sci & Med Univ, Univ Grenoble, France, 75-76. *Mem:* Am Phys Soc. *Res:* Low temperature physics; physical properties of pseudo one-dimensional solids at very low temperatures. *Mailing Add:* Dept of Physics Univ of Calif Los Angeles CA 90024

CLARK, WILLIAM GREER, b Waltham, Mass, Aug 6, 45; m 69; c 3. MARINE STOCK ASSESSMENT. *Educ:* Univ Calif, BA, 67; Univ Wash, PhD(fisheries), 75. *Prof Exp:* Fishery officer, Food & Agr Orgn UN, 75-79; RES ASSOC, UNIV WASH, 79- *Mem:* AAAS; Am Fisheries Soc. *Res:* Dynamics of exploited marine populations; mathematical problems in estimating population sizes and parameters. *Mailing Add:* Ctr Quant Sci HR-20 Univ Wash Seattle WA 98195

CLARK, WILLIAM HILTON, b Caldwell, Idaho, Dec 17, 44; m 68; c 2. ENTOMOLOGY, ECOLOGY. *Educ:* Col Idaho, BS, 67; Univ Nev-Reno, MS, 71. *Prof Exp:* Teaching asst bot, Univ Nev-Reno, 67-69, res asst ecol, 68 & 72-73; res assoc, 76-80, ASST DIR, O J SMITH MUS NATURAL HIST & ADJ PROF BIOL, COL IDAHO, 80-; SR ENVIRON QUAL SPECIALIST, WATER POLLUTION, DIV ENVIRON, IDAHO DEPT HEALTH & WELFARE, 74- *Concurrent Pos:* Consult, Nev Archaeol Surv, 72; asst investr, Res Adv Bd, Univ Nev, 72; prin investr, Sigma Xi, 73-74 & 76, Found Environ Educ, 74, Am Philos Soc, 74 & Ctr Field Res & Earthwatch, 79, 80 & 81. *Mem:* AAAS; Brit Ecol Soc; Ecol Soc Am; Entomol Soc Am; NAm Benthological Soc. *Res:* Entomology; ants of Idaho and Baja California, ant ecology; aquatic biology; pollution ecology; desert ecology; natural history of Baja California; ecology of Yucca, especially in Southwest United States and Mexico. *Mailing Add:* Div Environ 801 Reserve St Boise ID 83702

CLARK, WILLIAM JESSE, b Salt Lake City, Utah, Sept 29, 23; m 51; c 2. LIMNOLOGY, AQUATIC ECOLOGY. *Educ:* Utah State Univ, BS, 50, MS, 56, PhD(aquatic biol), 58. *Prof Exp:* From asst prof to assoc prof biol, 57-68, assoc prof biol & wildlife sci, 68-75, ASSOC PROF WILDLIFE & FISHERIES SCI, TEX A&M UNIV, 75- *Mem:* Am Soc Limnol & Oceanog; Ecol Soc Am; Int Asn Theoret & Appl Limnol. *Res:* Ecology of ponds; regional limnology; limnology and ecology of rivers. *Mailing Add:* Dept of Wildlife & Fisheries Sci Tex A&M Univ College Station TX 77843

CLARK, WILLIAM KEMP, b Dallas, Tex, Sept 2, 25; m; c 6. NEUROSURGERY. *Educ:* Univ Tex, BA, 45, MD, 48. *Prof Exp:* From asst prof to assoc prof, 56-69, PROF SURG, UNIV TEX HEALTH SCI CTR DALLAS, 69-, CHMN DIV NEUROSURG, 56- *Concurrent Pos:* Dir serv neurosurg, Parkland Mem Hosp, 56-; attend neurol surg, Vet Admin Hosp, 56-, consult, 64-; consult, Children's Med Ctr, 56-; chmn, Am Bd Neurolog Surg, 76-78. *Mem:* Am Neurol Asn; Am Acad Neurol Surg; Soc Neurol Surg (secy, 79-82); Neurol Soc Am. *Res:* Injuries to the nervous system; ultrastructure of nervous system. *Mailing Add:* Div of Neurosurg Univ of Tex Health Sci Ctr Dallas TX 75235

CLARK, WILLIAM MELVIN, JR, b Baldwin, Kans, Apr 17, 22; m 45; c 2. MEDICAL EDUCATION ADMINISTRATION. *Educ:* Baker Univ, AB, 46; Univ Chicago, MD, 49; Am Bd Pediat, dipl. *Prof Exp:* From instr to assoc prof, 54-67, PROF PEDIAT, SCH MED, ORE HEALTH SCI UNIV, 67-, DIR GRAD MED EDUC, 77-, ASSOC MED DIR, UNIV HOSPS & CLINS, 72- *Mem:* Am Acad Pediat; Am Acad Neurol. *Res:* Pediatric neurology. *Mailing Add:* Ore Health Sci Univ Portland OR 97201

CLARK, WILLIAM MERLE, JR, b Amarillo, Tex, Apr 23, 37; m 62; c 2. ELECTRICAL ENGINEERING. *Educ:* Stanford Univ, BS, 58; Univ Calif, Berkeley, MS, 66, PhD(elec eng), 68. *Prof Exp:* Engr, Microwave Components Lab, Sylvania Elec Prod Inc, Calif, 58-59; res asst elec eng, Univ Calif, Berkeley, 65-68; from asst prof to assoc prof elec eng, Univ Tex, Austin, 68-73; MEM TECH STAFF, HUGHES RES LABS, MALIBU, 73- *Mem:* Am Phys Soc; Inst Elec & Electronics Engrs. *Res:* Quantum electronics; nonlinear optics. *Mailing Add:* Res Lab 3011 Malibu Canyon Rd Malibu CA 90265

CLARK, WILLIAM R, b Detroit, Mich, Aug 18, 38. IMMUNOLOGY, BIOCHEMISTRY. *Educ:* Univ Calif, Los Angeles, BS, 63; Univ Ill, MS, 65; Univ Wash, PhD(biochem), 68. *Prof Exp:* Trainee cellular immunol, Weixmann Inst Sci, Rehovot, Israel, 68-70; asst prof cell biol, 70-74, assoc prof molecular biol, 74-78, PROF MOLECULAR BIOL, UNIV CALIF, LOS ANGELES, 78- *Concurrent Pos:* Career develop award, NIH, 75-80; asst dir, Univ Calif, Los Angeles Cancer Ctr, 75-78; head, Parvin Cancer Res Labs, 75-; vis scholar, Stanford Univ, 77-78; assoc dir, Molecular Biol Inst, Univ Calif, Los Angeles, 78- *Mem:* Am Asn Immunologists. *Res:* Structure-function relationships in plasma membranes of cells involved in cell-mediated cytotoxic immune reactions; fetal pancreas transplantation in diabetes. *Mailing Add:* Molecular Biol Inst Univ of Calif Los Angeles CA 90024

CLARK, WILLIAM RICHARD, b New Brunswick, NJ, Oct 25, 49; m 74; c 2. POPULATION DYNAMICS, COMPUTER SIMULATION. *Educ:* Rutgers Univ, BS, 71; Utah State Univ, MS, 74, PhD(ecol), 79. *Prof Exp:* Instr forestry, Rutgers Univ, 74; instr wildlife, Utah State Univ, 78-79; ASST PROF ECOL, IOWA STATE UNIV, 79- *Mem:* Wildlife Soc; Am Soc Ecol; Am Soc Mammalogists; Sigma Xi. *Res:* Statistical analysis of wildlife populations with emphasis on impact of herbivory or revegetated rangelands and crop fields; simulation of effects of sport exploitation and economic control on population. *Mailing Add:* Dept Animal Ecol Iowa State Univ 124 Sci II Ames IA 50011

CLARK, WILSON FARNSWORTH, b Schenectady, NY, Feb 25, 21; m 45; c 4. ENVIRONMENTAL SCIENCES, CONSERVATION. *Educ:* Middlebury Col, BA, 42; Cornell Univ, PhD(conserv educ), 49. *Prof Exp:* Asst prof & exten conservationist, Cornell Univ, 49-54; prof & head div sci & math, 54-76, prof, 76-80, EMER PROF PHYS SCI, EASTERN MONT COL, 80- *Concurrent Pos:* Res chemist, Manhattan Proj, 45-47; mem, Mont State Bd Natural Resources & Conserv; writer-ed, Bilboys Off of Custer Nat Forest, 80- *Mem:* Soc Am Foresters; Wildlife Soc; Soil Conserv Soc Am; Conserv Educ Asn (pres, 65-69). *Res:* Broad interpretation of methods, results, development, concepts and implications of environmental science and education. *Mailing Add:* Dept of Phys Sci Eastern Mont Col Billings MT 59101

CLARKE, ALEXANDER MALLORY, b Richmond, Va, Mar 29, 36; m 59; c 3. BIOPHYSICS, BIOMEDICAL ENGINEERING. *Educ:* Va Mil Inst, BS, 58; Univ Va, MS, 60, PhD(physics), 63. *Prof Exp:* Asst prof, 64-69, ASSOC PROF BIOPHYS, MED COL VA, 69- *Concurrent Pos:* Mem subcomt ocular effects, Am Nat Stand Inst, 69-; mem tech comt, 76, Int Electrotech Comn, 73- *Mem:* Asn Res Vision & Ophthal; Am Phys Soc. *Res:* Biomedical instrumentation; physical chemistry of macromolecules; effects of intense optical sources on the pupil and retina. *Mailing Add:* Dept Biophys Box 877 Med Col Va Richmond VA 23298

CLARKE, ALLAN JAMES, b Adelaide, Australia, Oct 10, 49; m 78; c 1. PHYSICAL OCEANOGRAPHY, GEOPHYSICAL FLUID DYNAMICS. *Educ:* Adelaide Univ, BSc, 71, Hons, 72; Cambridge Univ, PhD(oceanog), 76. *Prof Exp:* Res assoc, Mass Inst Technol, 75-77, phys oceanog, Univ Wash, 78-81; ASST PROF PHYS OCEANOG, FLA STATE UNIV, 81- *Concurrent Pos:* Guest investr, Woods Hole Oceanog Inst, 79-80; prin investr, NSF, 79-, NASA, 81-82. *Mem:* Am Geophys Union. *Res:* Wind driven and tidal motions on continental shelves; equatorial ocean dynamics; climatic fluctuations; fluctuations in the large scale wind driven circulation of the antartic circumpolar current; wind driven motions near ice edges. *Mailing Add:* Dept Oceanog Fla State Univ Tallahassee FL 32306

CLARKE, ALLEN BRUCE, b Saskatoon, Sask, Sept 8, 27; nat US; m 49; c 3. MATHEMATICS. *Educ:* Univ Sask, BA, 47; Brown Univ, MS, 49, PhD(math), 51. *Prof Exp:* From instr to prof math, Univ Mich, 51-67; chmn dept, 67-78, PROF MATH, WESTERN MICH UNIV, 67-, DEAN, COL ARTS & SCI, 78- *Concurrent Pos:* Fulbright lectr, Univ Turku & Abo Acad, Finland, 59-60. Mem. Am Math Soc; Inst Math Statist; Math Asn Am. *Res:* Probability theory; theory of waiting lines. *Mailing Add:* Col of Arts & Sci Western Mich Univ Kalamazoo MI 49008

CLARKE, ANN NEISTADT, b Philadelphia, Pa, July 27, 46; m 72. PHYSICAL CHEMISTRY, ENVIRONMENTAL ENGINEERING. *Educ:* Drexel Inst Technol, BS, 68; Johns Hopkins Univ, MA, 70 & 71; Vanderbilt Univ, PhD(phys chem), 75. *Prof Exp:* Res chemist, protein chem, Easter Utilization Res & Develop Div, USDA, 64-68; consult engr, Indust Environ, Sheppard T Powell Assocs; res engr, Ctr Indust Water Qual Mgt, 74-75; asst prof environ eng & chem, Vanderbilt Univ, 75-81; proj mgr, Assoc Water & Air Resources Engrs, Inc, 78-81; DIR TRAINING & PROF DEVELOP, RECRA RES INC, 81- *Concurrent Pos:* Consult, Assoc Water & Air Resources Engrs, Inc, Resources Consult, Environ Sci Eng, Gerry Shell Environ Engr & Stauffer Chem Co, 72- *Mem:* Am Chem Soc; Water Pollution Control Fedn; Am Soc Testing & Mat; Sigma Xi; Nat Environ Trainers Asn. *Res:* Environmental research-resources management, especially water, toxics, land, air, solids, noise; mathematical modelling in particular waste water treatment unit operations; bioassays; adsorbing colloid flotation (heavy metals and anions removal). *Mailing Add:* Recra Res Inc 4248 Ridgelea Rd Amherst NY 14226

CLARKE, BRUCE LESLIE, b Toronto, Ont, Aug 4, 42; m 68; c 2. THEORETICAL CHEMISTRY. *Educ:* Univ Toronto, BSc, 65; Univ Chicago, PhD(chem), 69. *Prof Exp:* Res asst chem, Univ Calif, Santa Cruz, 69-70; asst prof, 70-76, ASSOC PROF CHEM, UNIV ALTA, 76- *Mem:* Am Phys Soc. *Res:* Diagrammatic stability analysis of oscillatory chemical reaction systems; topological properties of self-organizing chemical networks; non-equilibrium statistical mechanics, fluctuations, phase transitions and critical phenomena. *Mailing Add:* Dept of Chem Univ of Alta Edmonton AB T6G 2E8 Can

CLARKE, DAVID BRUCE, industrial organic chemistry, see previous edition

CLARKE, DAVID HARRISON, b Jamestown, NY, Aug 14, 30; m 52; c 3. HUMAN PHYSIOLOGY. *Educ:* Springfield Col, BS, 52, MS, 53; Univ Ore, PhD(phys educ), 59. *Prof Exp:* Asst prof phys educ, Univ Calif, Berkeley, 58-64; from assoc prof to prof phys educ, Univ Md, College Park, 64-80, dir grad studies, Dept Phys Educ, 73-80; CHMN, DEPT PHYS EDUC, IND UNIV, BLOOMINGTON, 80- *Concurrent Pos:* Chmn res sect, Nat Col Phys Educ Asn, 65-66; Pres, Res Consortium, Am Asn Health, Phys Educ & Recreation, 78-80. *Mem:* Asn Health, Phys Educ & Recreation; fel Am Acad Phys Educ; fel Am Col Sports Med. *Res:* Physiology of exercise, especially in the area of muscular fatigue and the strength debt of exercise. *Mailing Add:* Dept of Phys Educ Ind Univ Bloomington IN 47405

CLARKE, DONALD ALSTON, b Mansfield, Pa, Aug 27, 15; m 51; c 3. PHARMACOLOGY. *Educ:* Philadelphia Col Pharm, BS, 37, AM, 46, PhD(pharmacol), 50. *Prof Exp:* Apothecary-in-chief, NY Hosp, 37-49, lectr pharmacol, Sch Nursing, 43-49; instr, Sloan-Kettering Div, Grad Sch Med Sci, Cornell Univ, 51-53, from asst prof to assoc prof, 53-62; med dir, Clairol Inc, 63-71; nutrit consult, Wright Tech Inst, 71-73; prof sci chem & biol, St Basil's Prep Sch, 73-76; prof sci physics & chem, Sacred Heart Acad, 78-80; instr chem & math, Parkway Acad, 80-81. *Concurrent Pos:* Asst, Sloan-Kettering Inst Cancer Res, 50-51, assoc mem, 51-60, head solid tumor screening sect, 51-62, mem, 60-62; vpres, treas & dir opers, Cancirco Inc, 62-64; consult, Nash Eng, 76-77. *Mem:* AAAS; Soc Pharmacol; Asn Cancer Res; Soc Exp Biol; NY Acad Sci. *Res:* Pharmacology of diuretics; cardiac glycosides, vasodepressants and fluoroacetic acid; experimental cancer chemotherapy; toxicology. *Mailing Add:* 25 Geneva Rd Norwalk CT 06850

CLARKE, DONALD DUDLEY, b Kingston, BWI, Mar 20, 30; US citizen; m 53; c 7. BIOCHEMISTRY. *Educ:* Fordham Univ, BS, 50, MS, 51, PhD(org Chem, enzym), 55. *Prof Exp:* Nat Res Coun Can fel, Banting Inst, 55-57; res scientist neurochem, NY State Psychiat Inst, 57-62; assoc prof, 62-70, PROF BIOCHEM, FORDHAM UNIV, 70-, CHMN DEPT CHEM, 78- *Concurrent Pos:* Res assoc biochem, Col Physicians & Surgeons, Columbia Univ, 59-61; adj assoc prof, Fordham Univ, 61-62; spec fel, NIH, 72-73; mem adv comt, NIMH, 73-77. *Mem:* AAAS; Am Chem Soc (counr, 80-82); Am Soc Biol Chemists; Int Soc Neurochem; Am Soc Neurochem. *Res:* Neurochemistry, glutamic acid metabolism and related compounds with special reference to brain; mold metabolites, structure and biosynthesis. *Mailing Add:* Dept Chem Fordham Univ New York NY 10458

CLARKE, DONALD WALTER, b Vermilion, Alta, Apr 12, 20; m 51. BIOCHEMISTRY. *Educ:* Univ Alta, BSc, 41, MSc, 43; Calif Inst Technol, PhD(chem), 51. *Prof Exp:* Asst fuels, Res Coun Alta, 41-43; from asst prof to assoc prof, 51-64, prof, Banting & Best Dept Med Res, 64-68, actg chmn, Dept Physiol, 80-81, PROF PHYSIOL, UNIV TORONTO, 68-, ASSOC DEAN, FAC MED, 81- *Mem:* Can Physiol Soc. *Res:* Intermediate metabolism of carbohydrates; protein complexes with other larger molecules; electrophoresis. *Mailing Add:* Dept of Physiol Univ of Toronto Med Sci Bldg Toronto ON M5S 1A8 Can

CLARKE, DUANE GROOKETT, b Philadelphia, Pa, Jan 7, 18; m 49. CHEMISTRY. *Educ:* Fla Southern Col, BS, 40; Pa State Univ, MS, 42, PhD(org chem), 44. *Prof Exp:* From res chemist to develop chemist, 43-67, head, Pollution Abatement Lab, 67-69, asst to mgr, Environ Control Dept, 70-78, TECH ASSOC ENVIRON AFFAIRS, ROHM AND HAAS CO, 78- *Mem:* Am Chem Soc; Sigma Xi. *Res:* Heavy hydrocarbons synthesis and properties; synthesis of insecticides, fungicides and monomers; process development; pollution abatement. *Mailing Add:* Rohm and Haas Co Independence Mall W Philadelphia PA 19105

CLARKE, EDWARD NIELSEN, b Providence, RI, Apr 25, 25; m 49; c 4. RESEARCH ADMINISTRATION. *Educ:* Brown Univ, BS, 45, PhD(physics), 51, Harvard Univ, MS, 47, MES, 48. *Prof Exp:* Physicist solid state physics, res lab, Sylvania Elec Prod, 50-56 & Sperry Semiconductor Div, Sperry Rand Corp, 56-59; founder & vpres opers, Nat Semiconductor Corp, 59-64, vpres corp develop & diversification, 64-65; assoc dean fac, 65-74, DIR RES, WORCESTER POLYTECH INST, 65-, ASSOC DEAN GRAD STUDIES, 74- *Concurrent Pos:* Consult, Semiconductor Indust; mem, Nat Coun Univ Res Adminr; tri-col res coordr, Clark Univ, Holy Cross Col & Worcester Polytech Inst, 74-; mgr, Urban Technol Syst Backup Site, 74-78; dir, Eng Res Coun, 76-79. *Mem:* AAAS; Sigma Xi; Am Phys Soc; Inst Elec & Electronics Engrs; Am Soc Eng Educ. *Res:* Semiconductors; solar energy; technology transfer. *Mailing Add:* 85 Richards Ave Paxton MA 01612

CLARKE, FRANK ELDRIDGE, b Brunswick, Md, Dec 26, 13; m 34; c 2. HYDROLOGY. *Educ:* Western Md Col, AB, 35. *Prof Exp:* Head chem process br, Chem Eng Lab, US Naval Eng Exp Sta, 51-57, head chem engr div, 57-61; res engr, US Geol Surv, 61-62, chief water qual res, 62, chief gen hydrol br, 62-65, asst chief hydrologist, 65-67, assoc chief hydrologist, 67-68, asst dir, 68-71; dep undersecy, US Dept Interior, 71-72, sr scientist, US Geol Surv, 72-76; CONSULT, 76- *Concurrent Pos:* Consult, US State Dept, 62- & Univ Queensland, 67- *Honors & Awards:* Am Chem Soc Cert Merit, 53; Am Soc Testing & Mat Merit Award, 61; Max Hecht Award, 64; Cert Award, Gordon Res Conf, 66. *Mem:* AAAS; Am Inst Chem Eng; Am Chem Soc; Am Soc Testing & Mat (pres, 74-75). *Res:* Geochemical controls of water quality; environmental sciences; corrosion and encrustation processes, particularly in water wells; systems for environmental impact assessment. *Mailing Add:* 165 Williams Dr Annapolis MD 21401

CLARKE, FRANK HENDERSON, b Newcastle, NB, Can, Dec 6, 27; m 54; c 2. ORGANIC CHEMISTRY, MEDICINAL CHEMISTRY. *Educ:* Univ NB, BSc, 49, MS, 50; Harvard Univ, PhD(org chem), 54. *Prof Exp:* Fel, Columbia Univ, 53-55; sr res chemist, med chem, Schering Corp, 55-62; res supvr, Geigy Chem Corp, 62-65 assoc dir med chem, 65-67, dir med chem, 67-71, dir med chem, 71-80, DISTINGUISHED RES FEL, GIBA-GEIGY CORP, 80- *Concurrent Pos:* Ed-in-chief, Ann Reports Med Chem, Am Chem Soc, 75-78; mem comn on med chem, Int Union Pure & Appl Chem. *Mem:* AAAS; Harvey Soc; NY Acad Sci. *Res:* Design and synthesis of medicinal agents; calculator programming; designer of molecular models. *Mailing Add:* 14 Long Pond Rd Windmill Farms Armonk NY 10504

CLARKE, FREDERIC B, III, b Portsmouth, NH, Aug 31, 42; m 62; c 2. PHYSICAL ORGANIC CHEMISTRY, PHYSICAL CHEMISTRY. *Educ:* Wash Univ, AB, 66; Harvard Univ, AM, 68, PhD(chem), 71. *Prof Exp:* Res chemist fire retardants, Monsanto Co, 71-73, prod supvr mkt, 73-74; asst to dir, 74-77, dep dir, 77-78, DIR FIRE RES, CTR FIRE RES, NAT BUR STANDARDS, 78- *Concurrent Pos:* Cong fels, 76-77. *Mem:* Nat Fire Protection Asn; Am Chem Soc. *Res:* Fire retardant chemical mechanisms; organophosphorous chemistry; high-temperature reactions. *Mailing Add:* US Dept of Com Nat Bur of Standards Washington DC 20234

CLARKE, FREDERICK JAMES, b Little Falls, NY, Mar 1, 15; m 38; c 3. CIVIL ENGINEERING. *Educ:* US Mil Acad, BS, 37; Cornell Univ MSCE, 40. *Prof Exp:* Mgr, Hanford Eng Works, US Army, 45-47, exec, Sandia Base, NMex, 47-49, chief, Atomic Res & Develop Sect, 52-53, commandant, US Army Eng Sch, Ft Belvoir, 65-66, chief engrs, US Army, 69-73; exec dir, Nat Comn on Water Qual, 73-76; ENERGY & WATER CONSULT, TIPPETTS-ABBETT-McCARTHY-STRATTON, 76- *Honors & Awards:* Nat Soc Prof Engrs Award, 78. *Mem:* Nat Acad Engrs; Am Soc Civil Engrs; Nat Soc Prof Engrs; Am Acad Environ Eng; Am Pub Works Asn. *Mailing Add:* Tippetts-Abbett-McCarthy-Stratton 1101 15th St NW Washington DC 20005

CLARKE, GARRY K C, b Hamilton, Ont, Oct 6, 41. GLACIOLOGY. *Educ:* Univ Alta, BSc, 63; Univ Toronto, MA, 64, PhD(physics), 67. *Prof Exp:* Assoc prof, 67-76, PROF GEOPHYS, UNIV BC, 76- *Concurrent Pos:* Partic glaciol expeds, Can & Greenland. *Mem:* Soc Explor Geophys; Am Geophys Union; Int Glaciological Soc. *Res:* Geophysical applications of statistical communication theory; glacier flow theory. *Mailing Add:* Dept of Geophys Univ of BC Vancouver Can

CLARKE, GARY ANTHONY, b Washington, DC, May 31, 46; m 75. MICROBIAL PHYSIOLOGY. *Educ:* Indiana Univ, Pa, BS, 68; St Bonaventure Univ, PhD(biol), 73. *Prof Exp:* asst prof, 73-80, ASSOC PROF BIOL, ROANOKE COL, 80- *Mem:* Am Soc Microbiol. *Res:* Chemostatic growth of nitrogen fixing bacteria and the effect of environmental variables on this growth; carbon dioxide fixation. *Mailing Add:* Dept of Biol Roanoke Col Salem VA 24153

CLARKE, GEORGE, b Readfield, Maine, Mar 10, 15; m 38; c 4. ANALYTICAL CHEMISTRY. *Educ:* Univ Maine, AB, 36. *Prof Exp:* Chemist, 43-51, group leader anal chem, Reactor Testing Sta, Chem Processing Plant, 51-54, res chemist, 54-62, group leader anal chem, 62-70, GROUP LEADER ANAL CHEM, CENT RES DIV, AM CYANAMID CO, 70- *Mem:* Am Microchem Soc. *Mailing Add:* Stamford Res Lab Am Cyanamid Co 1937 W Main St Stamford CT 06904

CLARKE, GEORGE A, b New York, NY, Apr 4, 33; m 66; c 2. PHYSICAL CHEMISTRY. *Educ:* City Col New York, BS, 55; Pa State Univ, PhD(phys chem), 60. *Prof Exp:* Res assoc theoret chem, Columbia Univ, 60-62; asst prof chem, State Univ NY Buffalo, 62-68; assoc prof, Drexel Inst Technol, 68-70 & Drexel Univ, 70-71; ASSOC PROF CHEM, UNIV MIAMI, 71-, ASSOC DEAN COL ARTS & SCI, 78- *Concurrent Pos:* USPHS grants, 64-66; co-sr investr, AEC Proj Grant, 64-68. *Mem:* Am Chem Soc; Am Phys Soc. *Res:* Intermolecular interactions in gaseous and condensed media; studies on molecular complexes; inter-and intramolecular energy transfer processes; electrolyte effects on solvent structure and reactive species; approximation methods in quantum chemistry. *Mailing Add:* Dept of Chem Univ of Miami Coral Gables FL 33124

CLARKE, JAMES, b New York, NY, Jan 17, 27; m 56; c 3. CHEMICAL ENGINEERING, ORGANIC CHEMISTRY. *Educ:* Cornell Univ, BChE, 53; Univ SC, PhD(chem eng), 69. *Prof Exp:* Process engr, Textile Fibers Dept, E I du Pont de Nemours & Co, Inc, 53-58; res engr, Rock Hill Lab, Chemetron Corp, 59-64; gen mgr biochem, Southeastern Biochem Inc, 63-69; pvt consult, 69-71; DIR, CAROSYN RES ASSOC, 71- *Mem:* AAAS; Am Chem Soc. *Res:* Fine chemicals production with specialization in steroid synthesis and pharmaceuticals; industrial waste treatment; modification of steroids to enhance biological activity. *Mailing Add:* Carosyn Res Assoc 3905 Kenilworth Rd Columbia SC 29205

CLARKE, JAMES NEWTON, b Montreal, Que, Mar 9, 48; m 69; c 2. COMPUTER SCIENCE, ASTRONOMY. *Educ:* McGill Univ, BSc, 68; Univ Toronto, MSc, 69; Univ Sydney, PhD(physics, radio astron), 75. *Prof Exp:* Res assoc radio astron, Dept Physics, Queen's Univ, 74-76; res fel, Nuffield Radio Astron Labs, Jodrell Bank, 76-77; res assoc radio astron, Dept Astron, 77-80, ASST PROF, DEPT COMPUT SCI, UNIV TORONTO, 80- *Mem:* Fel Royal Astron Soc; Asn Comput Mach. *Res:* Computer architecture, operating systems; extraterrestrial intelligence. *Mailing Add:* Dept Comput Sci Univ of Toronto Toronto ON M5S 1A7 Can

CLARKE, JOHN, b Cambridge, Eng, Feb 10, 42; m 79; c 1. PHYSICS. *Educ:* Cambridge Univ, BS, 64, MS, 68, PhD(physics), 68. *Prof Exp:* Scholar, 68-69, from asst prof to assoc prof, 69-73, PROF PHYSICS, UNIV CALIF, BERKELEY, 73- *Concurrent Pos:* Alfred P Sloan fel, 70-72; John Simon Guggenheim fel, 78-79. *Honors & Awards:* Charles Vernon Boys Prize for Physics, 77. *Mem:* Am Phys Soc; AAAS. *Res:* Superconductivity; Josephson tunneling application to measurement of low voltages and magnetic fields and detection of electromagnetic radiation; experimental and theoretical study of low frequency electrical noise in solids; geophysics; magnetotellurics. *Mailing Add:* Dept of Physics Univ of Calif Berkeley CA 94720

CLARKE, JOHN F, b Hempstead, NY, Sept 5, 39. PHYSICS. *Educ:* Fordham Univ, BS, 61; Mass Inst Technol, MS, 64, PhD(nuclear eng), 66. *Prof Exp:* Res staff mem plasma physics, Oak Ridge Nat Lab, 66-73, group leader confinement physics, 73-74, dir thermonuclear div, 74-77; DEP DIR, OFF FUSION ENERGY, DEPT ENERGY, 77- *Concurrent Pos:* Mem fusion power coord comt, Div Controlled Thermonuclear Res, Energy Res & Develop Admin, 74; mem, Joint US/USSR Fusion Power Coord Comt, 74- & Fusion Power Coord Comt, US Dept Energy, 77- *Mem:* Fel Am Phys Soc; fel AAAS. *Res:* Thermonuclear fusion; plasma heating and confinement; MHD equilibrium; neutral particle and heavy ion transport in plasmas. *Mailing Add:* Dept of Energy G-234 Washington DC 20545

CLARKE, JOHN FREDERICK GATES, b Victoria, BC, Feb 22, 05; nat US; m 29; c 2. ENTOMOLOGY. *Educ:* State Col Wash, PhC, 26, BS, 30, MS, 31; Univ London, PhD(entom), 53. *Prof Exp:* Pharmacist, Red Cross Pharm, Wash, 26-29; fel, State Col Wash, 30-32, instr, 33-35; assoc entomologist, Bur Entom & Plant Quarantine, USDA Nat Mus, 36-40, entomologist, 40, entom res br, Agr Res Serv, 53-54; cur insects, 54-63, chmn dept entom, 63-65, sr entomologist, 65-75, RES ASSOC, SMITHSONIAN INST, 75- *Honors & Awards:* Karl Jordan Medal, 79. *Mem:* Fel Royal Entom Soc London. *Res:* Insect gall-formation; life histories and habits of Microlepidoptera; morphology and classification of Microlepidoptera. *Mailing Add:* Dept of Entom Smithsonian Inst Washington DC 20560

CLARKE, JOHN FREDERICK GATES, JR, b Pullman, Wash, Nov 11, 33; m 56; c 2. ANALYTICAL CHEMISTRY. *Educ:* Wash State Univ, BS, 55; Purdue Univ, MS, 58, PhD(anal chem), 60. *Prof Exp:* Res chemist, 60-70, sr res chemist & group leader gas chromatography sect, 70-78, RES CHEMIST & GROUP LEADER SEPARATIONS & MASS SPECTROSCOPY SECT,

HERCULES RES CTR, HERCULES, INC, 78- *Mem:* Am Chem Soc. *Res:* Automation of analytical instrumentation, particularly gas chromatography; glass capillary. *Mailing Add:* Hercules Res Ctr Hercules Inc Wilmington DE 19899

CLARKE, JOHN MILLS, b June 7, 49. PLANT PHYSIOLOGY. *Educ:* Univ BC, BSc, 71, MSc, 73; Univ Sask, PhD(crop physiol), 77. *Prof Exp:* RES SCIENTIST, AGR CAN RES BR, 77- *Concurrent Pos:* Assoc ed, Can J Plant Sci, 82-84. *Mem:* Am Soc Agron; Crop Sci Soc Am. *Res:* Pre-harvest sprouting and weathering in wheat; physiological and morphological changes associated with maturation of cereals; cereal harvest methods; cereal harvesting losses; drought physiology, wheat. *Mailing Add:* Res Sta Agr Can Box 1030 Swift Current SK S9H 3X2 Can

CLARKE, JOHN ROSS, b Martinsville, Va, Mar 23, 41; m 65; c 2. SOLID STATE ELECTRONICS. *Educ:* Univ Va, BEE, 64, MS, 67, PhD(elec eng), 70. *Prof Exp:* Elec engr, Warrenton Training Ctr, 64-65; PHYSICIST, EASTMAN KODAK CO RES LABS, 70- *Mem:* Am Vacuum Soc. *Res:* Vacuum deposition preparation and characterization of photoconductive films; low pressure chemical vapor deposition of films for integrated circuit manufacture. *Mailing Add:* Eastman Kodak Co Res Labs 1669 Lake Ave Rochester NY 14650

CLARKE, JOSEPH H(ENRY), b New York, NY, July 28, 27; m 50; c 2. GAS DYNAMICS. *Educ:* Polytech Inst New York, BAE, 50, MAE, 51, PhD(appl mech), 54. *Hon Degrees:* AM, Brown Univ, 58. *Prof Exp:* From res asst to res assoc appl mech, Polytech Inst New York, 50-54, asst prof, 54-57; assoc prof eng, 57-63, PROF ENG, BROWN UNIV, 63- *Concurrent Pos:* Consult, NAm Aircraft, 54-55; Gen Appl Sci Labs, 56-57; Norden-Ketay Co, 57; Boeing Co, 59-62; Goodyear Aircraft Co, 61-62; Douglas Aircraft Co & Northrup Co, 62 & Clevepak Corp, 70-73; NSF sr fel & vis prof, Turin Polytech, 63-64 & 80-81. *Mem:* AAAS; Am Inst Aeronaut & Astronaut; Am Phys Soc; Am Soc Mech Engrs; Combustion Inst. *Res:* Physical gas dynamics with nonequilibrium rate processes; phase changes; physics of fluids; fluid mechanics; aeronautics; applied mathematics; chemical kinetics; radiation transfer; transport properties; applied mechanics. *Mailing Add:* Div of Eng Brown Univ Box D Providence RI 02912

CLARKE, JOY HAROLD, b Lafayette, Ind, June 12, 99; m 77; c 2. HORTICULTURE. *Educ:* Purdue Univ, BSA, 21; Univ Del, MS, 23; Columbia Univ, PhD(bot), 42. *Prof Exp:* Asst horticulturist, Exp Sta, Univ Del, 21-23; from instr to prof pomol, Rutgers Univ, 23-46; from asst pomologist to assoc pomologist, NJ Exp Sta, 23-46; gen mgr, Cranguyma Farms, 46-54; NURSERYMAN, HORT CONSULT & WRITER, 54- *Concurrent Pos:* Owner, Clarke Nursery. *Mem:* Am Soc Hort Sci; Royal Hort Soc; Int Plant Propagator's Soc. *Res:* Culture and breeding of small fruits; rhododendrons and azaleas. *Mailing Add:* 9750 Edward Dr Sun City AZ 85341

CLARKE, LEMUEL FLOYD, zoology, deceased

CLARKE, LILIAN A, b Humboldt, Iowa, Aug 9, 15; m 42. INORGANIC CHEMISTRY. *Educ:* Grinnell Col, BA, 36; Pa State Univ, MS, 39, PhD(inorg chem), 42. *Prof Exp:* Instr chem, Pa State Univ, 37-42; ASST PROF CHEM, VILLANOVA UNIV, 63- *Concurrent Pos:* Consult, Berks Assoc, Inc, 68- & Basic Inc, 69- *Mem:* AAAS; Am Chem Soc. *Res:* Studies of properties of surface active agents; identification of chemical and biological warfare agents; rerefining of crankcase oils; water pollution abatement; solvent extraction of lubricating oils; chemistry of carbon black. *Mailing Add:* Dept of Chem Villanova Univ Villanova PA 19085

CLARKE, LORI A, b New York, NY, Feb 11, 47; m 74; c 2. SOFTWARE ENGINEERING. *Educ:* Univ Rochester, BA, 69; Univ Colo, Phd(conput sci), 76. *Prof Exp:* Programmer, Sch Med, Univ Rochester, 70-71; Nat Ctr Atmospheric Res, 71-75; asst prof, 75-81, ASSOC PROF, COMPUT SCI, UNIV MASS, 81- *Concurrent Pos:* Consult var high technol corps, 75-; prin investr, NSF & NASA grants. *Mem:* Asn Comput Mach. *Res:* Design of a software development environment to support all phases of the software lifecycle. *Mailing Add:* Dept Comput & Info Sci Univ Mass Amherst MA 01003

CLARKE, LUCIEN GILL, b Eagle Grove, Iowa, Mar 11, 21; m 48. ENGINEERING, ELECTRONICS. *Educ:* Iowa State Col, BS, 42. *Prof Exp:* Engr, Naval Res Labs, 43, physicist & proj officer, Off Naval Res, 46-47; engr, Raytheon Mfg Co, 47-48; asst gen mgr eng, 48-64, exec dir admin, 64-69, SR RES ENGR, SRI INT, 69- *Mem:* Inst Elec & Electronics Engrs. *Res:* Communications engineering; radio electronics; research management. *Mailing Add:* 12550 La Cresta Dr Los Altos Hills CA 94022

CLARKE, MARGARET BURNETT, b Enid, Okla. BIOCHEMISTRY, CELL BIOLOGY. *Educ:* Mills Col, BA, 65; Univ Calif, Berkeley, PhD(molecular biol), 71. *Prof Exp:* Res assoc biochem, Univ Calif, San Francisco, 72-76; ASST PROF DEPT MOLECULAR BIOL, ALBERT EINSTEIN COL MED, 76- *Concurrent Pos:* NIH fel, 72-74; Nat Res Serv Award, 75-76; co-investr, NIH prog proj grant, 76-83; estab investr, Am Heart Asn, 77-82; prin investr, Am Cancer Soc Res grant, 78-80; prin investr, NIH res grant, 81-84. *Mem:* Am Soc Cell Biol. *Res:* Molecular basis of motility in eukaryotic cells. *Mailing Add:* Dept Molecular Biol Albert Einstein Col Med 1300 Morris Park Ave Bronx NY 10461

CLARKE, MICHAEL J, b St Louis, Mo, Dec 30, 46; m 68; c 3. BIO-INORGANIC CHEMISTRY, ELECTROCHEMISTRY. *Educ:* Catholic Univ Am, AB, 68; Stanford Univ, MS, 70, PhD(inorg chem), 74. *Prof Exp:* Instr chem, City Col San Francisco, 70; asst prof chem, Wheaton Col, 74-75; asst prof chem, Wheaton Col, 75-76; asst prof, 76-80, ASSOC PROF CHEM, BOSTON COL, 80- *Concurrent Pos:* Ed, Structure & Bonding, 80- *Mem:* Am Chem Soc. *Res:* Interactions of metal ions with nucleotides and coenzymes; chemistry of ruthenium and metal-containing anticancer pharmaceuticals; chemistry of ruthenium and technetium. *Mailing Add:* Dept Chem Boston Col Chestnut Hill MA 02167

CLARKE, NORMAN ARTHUR, b Waterbury, Conn, May 20, 22; m 47; c 3. MICROBIOLOGY. *Educ:* Univ Conn, BS, 47; Yale Univ, PhD(microbiol), 51; dipl. *Prof Exp:* DIR, TOXICOL DIV, HEALTH EFFECTS RES LAB, ENVIRON PROTECTION AGENCY, 50- *Mem:* AAAS; Am Soc Microbiol; fel Am Pub Health Asn; Am Water Works Asn; Am Acad Microbiol. *Res:* Enteric viruses; chemical and physical disinfection; water and sewage treatment; mobile source air pollution; chemical toxicology and carcinogenicity. *Mailing Add:* Environ Protection Agency 26 St Clair St Cincinnati OH 45268

CLARKE, RAYMOND DENNIS, b King's Lynn, Eng, May 13, 46; m 69; c 2. ECOLOGY, MARINE BIOLOGY. *Educ:* McGill Univ, BSc, 67; Yale Univ, MFS, 69, MPhil, 71, PhD(ecol), 73. *Prof Exp:* PROF BIOL, SARAH LAWRENCE COL, 72- *Concurrent Pos:* Res grants, Am Philos Soc, 74, Nat Geog Soc, 74 & Sigma Xi, 76; mission chief scientist, Nat Oceanic & Atmospheric Admin, 78-81; vis scientist, West Indies Lab, Fairleigh Dickinson Univ, 79-80. *Mem:* Ecol Soc Am; Sigma Xi; Am Inst Biol Sci; Am Philos Soc. *Res:* Coral reef fish ecology; species diversity; interspecific competition. *Mailing Add:* Dept Biol Sarah Lawrence Col Bronxvi' NY 10708

CLARKE, RICHARD HENRY, physical chemistry, see previous edition

CLARKE, RICHARD PENFIELD, b Baltimore, Md, Jan 30, 19; m 46; c 4. PHYSICAL CHEMISTRY. *Educ:* Princeton Univ, AB, 41, MA, 48, PhD(phys chem), 50. *Prof Exp:* Asst, Manhattan Proj, Princeton Univ, 43-45; chemist, Air Reduction Co, 46; asst, Princeton Univ, 47-50; chemist, res dept, Standard Oil Co Ind, 50-51; proj leader, Exp, Inc, 51-56; mgr res, Okonite Co, 56-59; vpres, Hasche Eng Co, Tenn, 59-64; from vpres to pres, Kalamazoo Spice Extraction Co, 64-70; consult chem engr, Fuel Gas Prod & Econ, 70-73; ASSOC PROF CHEM, LAKE MICH COL, 73- *Concurrent Pos:* Vpres, Thermo Time Corp, 53-59, pres, 59-69. *Mem:* Am Chem Soc; NY Acad Sci. *Res:* Dielectric increments of amino acid and polypetide solutions; kinetics; decomposition diborane; heterogeneous catalysis; oxidation hydrocarbons; combustion; chemical engineering. *Mailing Add:* 2124 Aberdeen Dr Kalamazoo MI 49008

CLARKE, ROBERT FRANCIS, b Portsmouth, Va, Oct 8, 19; m 47; c 2. ZOOLOGY, ANIMAL BEHAVIOR. *Educ:* Kans State Teachers Col, BSEd, 55, MS, 57; Okla Univ, PhD(zool), 63. *Prof Exp:* Instr educ, 56-58, from instr to assoc prof biol, chmn dept, 72-79, 58-68, PROF BIOL, EMPORIA STATE UNIV, 68- *Mem:* Am Soc Ichthyol & Herpet. *Res:* Display behavior of lizards, particularly the family Iguanidae; ecology of reptiles; color change in gravid lizards. *Mailing Add:* Div of Biol Sci Emporia State Univ Emporia KS 66801

CLARKE, ROBERT LA GRONE, b Tullahoma, Tenn, Mar 10, 17; m 43; c 2. PHARMACEUTICAL CHEMISTRY. *Educ:* Ga Inst Technol, BS, 38; Emory Univ, MS, 39; Univ Wis, PhD(org chem), 47. *Prof Exp:* Instr chem, Young Harris Jr Col, Ga, 39-40; org chemist, Sterling-Winthrop Res Inst, 47-81; RETIRED. *Mem:* Am Chem Soc. *Res:* Ketene acetals; nitrogen heterocycles; steroids; mercurial diuretics; alkaloids. *Mailing Add:* 5 Sunset Dr Delmar NY 12054

CLARKE, ROBERT LEE, b Vermilion, Alta, Apr 17, 22; m 45; c 4. MEDICAL PHYSICS. *Educ:* Univ Alta, BSc, 43; McGill Univ, PhD(physics), 48. *Prof Exp:* Asst physics, Nat Res Coun, Can, 43-45; from asst res officer to assoc res officer, Atomic Energy Can, Ltd, 48-68; PROF PHYSICS, CARLETON UNIV, 68- *Mem:* Can Asn Physicist. *Res:* Nuclear reactions; neutrons, low to medium energy; radiography; medical physics; radiography, ultrasonic imaging. *Mailing Add:* Dept of Physics Carleton Univ Ottawa ON K1S 5B6 Can

CLARKE, ROBERT TRAVIS, b Brooklyn, NY, Nov 17, 37; m 58; c 4. PALYNOLOGY, PALEONTOLOGY. *Educ:* Univ Okla, MS, 61, PhD(geol), 63. *Prof Exp:* Res tech palynology, Socony Mobil Oil Co, Inc, 63-69, SR RES GEOLOGIST, FIELD RES LAB, MOBIL OIL CORP, 69-, TRAINING COORDR EXPLOR COURSES, 78- *Mem:* Geol Soc Am; Am Asn Stratig Palynologists. *Res:* Research in the field of palynology applicable to resolving problems in stratigraphic zonation and correlation; paleoecologic and environmental interpretations and age determinations. *Mailing Add:* Field Res Lab Mobil Res & Develop Corp PO Box 900 Dallas TX 75221

CLARKE, ROY, b Bury, Eng, May 9, 47; m 73; c 2. PHYSICS, MATERIALS SCIENCE. *Educ:* Univ London, BS, 69, PhD(physics), 73. *Prof Exp:* Res asst, Cavendish Lab, Univ Cambridge, 73-78; James Franck fel physics, James Franck Inst, Univ Chicago, 78-79; PROF PHYSICS, UNIV MICH, 79- *Mem:* Am Phys Soc; Brit Inst Physics. *Res:* Structural phase transitions; x-ray scattering; ferroelectrics; disordered materials, intercalation compounds, photovoltaics, artificial heterostructures. *Mailing Add:* Dept Physics Univ Mich Ann Arbor MI 48109

CLARKE, ROY SLAYTON, JR, b Philadelphia, Pa, Jan 23, 25; m 51; c 3. GEOCHEMISTRY. *Educ:* Cornell Univ, AB, 49; George Washington Univ, MS, 57, PhD, 76. *Prof Exp:* Chemist, USDA, 49-51; res assoc chem, George Washington Univ, 51-52; chemist, USDA, 52-53; anal chemist, US Geol Surv, 53-57; chemist, Div Meteorites, Smithsonian Inst, 57-66, assoc cur, 66-70, CUR, NAT MUS NATURAL HIST, 70- *Mem:* AAAS; Am Chem Soc; Mineral Soc Am; Geochem Soc. *Res:* Geochemistry and metallography of meteorites. *Mailing Add:* Div Meteorites Smithsonian Inst Washington DC 20560

CLARKE, STEVEN DONALD, b Brockton, Mass, Dec 22, 48; m 69; c 2. BIOCHEMISTRY, NUTRITION. *Educ:* Univ Maine, BS, 70; Wash State Univ, MS, 72; Mich State Univ, PhD(human nutrit), 76. *Prof Exp:* Instr, Univ Mich, 75-76; asst prof, Johns Hopkins Univ, 76-78; asst prof nutrit, Ohio State Univ, 78-80; ASST PROF NUTRIT, UNIV MINN, 81- *Concurrent Pos:* NIH trainee fel, Mich State Univ, 74-76; mem, Comt Nutrit Surveillance, State

Mich, 75-76; assoc, Health & Weight Prog, Johns Hopkins Univ, 77-78; assoc, Proj Prevention, 77- *Mem:* Am Inst Nutrit; Am Oil Chemists. *Res:* Intracellular regulation of carbohydrate and lipid metabolism as affected by dietary fat and carbohydrate intake and composition. *Mailing Add:* Dept Food Sci & Nutrit Univ Minn 1334 Eckles Ave St Paul MN 55108

CLARKE, STEVEN GERARD, b Los Angeles, Calif, Nov 19, 49. BIOCHEMISTRY. *Educ:* Pomona Col, BA, 70; Harvard Univ, PhD(biochem & molecular biol), 76. *Prof Exp:* Instr biochem & molecular biol, Harvard Univ, 73-74; Miller fel, Univ Calif, Berkeley, 76-78; ASST PROF CHEM, UNIV CALIF, LOS ANGELES, 78- *Mem:* Am Soc Biol Chemists. *Res:* Structure and function of membrane proteins; detergent protein interactions; protein carboxyl methylation reactions; biosynthesis of mitochondrial matrix proteins. *Mailing Add:* Dept of Chem 405 Hilgard Ave Los Angeles CA 90024

CLARKE, THOMAS ARTHUR, b Peoria, Ill, Aug 13, 40. OCEANOGRAPHY, ECOLOGY. *Educ:* Univ Chicago, BS, 62; Univ Calif, San Diego, PhD(oceanog), 68. *Prof Exp:* Asst prof oceanog, 68-74, ASST MARINE BIOLOGIST, HAWAII INST MARINE BIOL, 68-, ASSOC PROF OCEANOG, UNIV HAWAII, 74- *Mem:* AAAS; Ecol Soc Am; Am Soc Limnol & Oceanog; Brit Ecol Soc. *Res:* Behavior and population dynamics of pomacentrid fish; shark ecology; fisheries ecology. *Mailing Add:* Hawaii Inst Marine Biol PO Box 1067 Univ of Hawaii Kaneohe HI 96744

CLARKE, W T W, b Toronto, Ont, Nov 6, 20; m 47; c 4. INTERNAL MEDICINE. *Educ:* Univ Toronto, MD, FRCP(C), 50. *Prof Exp:* PROF MED, UNIV TORONTO, 66- *Concurrent Pos:* Dep physician-in-chief, Toronto Gen Hosp, 69-74; mem drug qual & therapeut comt, Govt of Ont. *Mem:* Fel Am Col Physicians; Am Soc Nephrology; Am Diabetes Asn; Can Diabetic Asn; Can Med Asn. *Res:* Diabetes; nephrology. *Mailing Add:* Rm 228 Floor 13 Eaton Wing Toronto Gen Hosp Toronto ON M5G 1L7 Can

CLARKE, WILBUR BANCROFT, b Colon, Panama, July 22, 29; US citizen; m 59; c 1. ORGANIC CHEMISTRY. *Educ:* Xavier Univ, BS, 50, MS, 53; Univ Ind, PhD(chem), 62. *Prof Exp:* Instr chem, Xavier Univ, 50-53; asst neurol, US Army Chem Ctr, Md, 53-55; asst chem, Ind Univ, 56-58; chemist, Northern Regional Labs, 58-59; PROF CHEM, SOUTHERN UNIV, 60-, CHMN DEPT, 70- *Concurrent Pos:* Res grants, NSF & Sigma Xi, 63-64, NIH, 64-66; res specialist, Miss Test Facil, NASA-Gen Elec Co, 66 & 67; fel, La State Univ, 67-68; consult, NSF, 64. *Mem:* AAAS; Am Chem Soc; Brit Chem Soc. *Res:* Heterocyclics; preparation and elucidation of antiviral and anti-carcinogenic agents; infrared spectroscopy. *Mailing Add:* 1357 Balsam Ave Baton Rouge LA 70807

CLARKSON, ALLEN BOYKIN, JR, b Augusta, Ga, July 1, 43; m 67; c 1. PARASITOLOGY. *Educ:* Univ of the South, BS, 65; Univ Ga, PhD(zool), 75. *Prof Exp:* Instr biol, Univ Ga, 72-74; fel parasitol, Rockefeller Univ, 74-77; ASST PROF PARASITOL, SCH MED, NY UNIV, 77- *Concurrent Pos:* Adv, WHO, 77- *Mem:* AAAS; Am Soc Trop Med & Hyg; Soc Protozoologists; Sigma Xi. *Res:* Parasitic protozoa, particularly trypanosomatids; chemotherapy related to carbohydrate pathways for energy production; antigenic variation; immunological response and host parasite interactions at the parasite cell surface; host-parasite-drug interactions. *Mailing Add:* Div Parasitol 550 First Ave New York NY 10016

CLARKSON, BAYARD D, b New York, NY, July 15, 26; c 4. HEMATOLOGY, ONCOLOGY. *Educ:* Yale Univ, BA, 48; Columbia Univ, MD, 52. *Prof Exp:* From intern to resident, NY Hosp, 52-58; instr clin med, Med Col, Cornell Univ, 58-62, from asst prof to assoc prof med, 62-74; res fel, 58-59, res assoc, 59-61, assoc, 61-65, assoc mem, 65-71, MEM, SLOAN-KETTERING INST CANCER RES, 71-; PROF MED, MED COL, CORNELL UNIV, 74- *Concurrent Pos:* Mem adv comt ther, Am Cancer Soc, 65-68; mem pharmacol B study sect, NIH, 67-71; mem bd trustees, Cold Spring Harbor Lab, 68; mem ed adv bd, Cancer Res, 70; mem chemother adv comt, Nat Cancer Inst, 71-74; attend physician & chief hemat & lymphoma serv, Mem Hosp, NY, 71-; assoc ed, Cancer Res, 73-76 & 76-81. *Mem:* NY Acad Sci; Am Asn Cancer Res (pres, 80-81); fel Am Col Physicians; Am Soc Clin Oncol (pres, 73-74); Am Soc Clin Invest. *Res:* Cancer chemotherapy; leukemia; cell kinetics and regulation of cell growth as related to control of cancer. *Mailing Add:* Mem Sloan-Kettering Cancer Ctr 1275 York Ave New York NY 10021

CLARKSON, JACK E, b Provo, Utah, June 17, 36; m 63; c 3. ANALYTICAL CHEMISTRY, NUCLEAR CHEMISTRY. *Educ:* Brigham Young Univ, BS, 60; Univ Calif, Berkeley, PhD(chem), 65. *Prof Exp:* SR CHEMIST, LAWRENCE LIVERMORE NAT LAB, UNIV CALIF, 65- *Mem:* Am Chem Soc. *Res:* Trace impurity analysis by gas chromatography; gas chromatographic analysis of explosives; gel permeation chromatography of polymers and explosives; helium ionization detector utilization part-per-million analysis; high pressure liquid chromatography; shale oil analysis; capillary column gas chromatography. *Mailing Add:* 1541 Roselli Dr Livermore CA 94550

CLARKSON, MARK H(ALL), b Lafayette Co, Mo, Sept 27, 17; m 42; c 3. AEROSPACE ENGINEERING. *Educ:* Univ Minn, BAeroEng, 39; Univ Tex, MA, 48, PhD, 53. *Prof Exp:* Shop training, Douglas Aircraft Co, Calif, 39-40, stress analyst, 40-41; aerodynamicist, Consol Vultee Aircraft Co, 41-42, Tenn, 42-43, Tex, 43-45; res engr, Defense Res Lab, Univ Tex, 45-51, res mathematician, 52-54; res & develop proj engr, Chance Vought Aircraft, Tex, 53-59, sr scientist, Res Ctr, 59-60; chmn, Aerospace Eng Dept, 61-72, PROF ENG SCI, UNIV FLA, 61- *Concurrent Pos:* Sr Nat Res Coun fel, NASA Ames Res Ctr, 73-74. *Mem:* Assoc fel Am Inst Aeronaut & Astronaut; Sigma Xi. *Res:* Theoretical and experimental work in fluid mechanics and aerodynamics. *Mailing Add:* Dept of Eng Sci Univ of Fla Gainesville FL 32605

CLARKSON, MERTON ROBERT, b Ferndale, Wash, July 25, 08; m 30; c 3. VETERINARY MEDICINE. *Educ:* Wash State Univ, BS & DVM, 30; Georgetown Univ, LLB, 42. *Prof Exp:* Jr vet, meat inspection div, Bur Animal Indust, USDA, SDak, 30-32, NY, 32-35, inspector, Ind, 35-39, asst chief, trade label sect, 39-42 & war food admin, 42-44, chief, 44, asst chief, meat inspection div, 44-47, chief inspection & quarantine div, Agr Res Admin, 47-51, asst to adminr, defense progs, Agr Res Serv, 51-52, dep adminr, 52-59, assoc adminr, 59-64; *Concurrent Pos:* Consult, Nat Security Resources Bd, 50-51; mem comt animal health, Nat Acad Sci-Nat Res Coun, chmn, 63-69, mem agr bd, vchmn, 65-70; dir, Am Vet Med Asn, 66-71, trustee, Prof liability ins trust, 66-71 & group ins trust, 67-; dir, Bur Vet Med, Food & Drug Admin, 66; dir, prof exam serv, 70-71; mem adv coun, NY State Vet Col, 73-78; dir, Monadnock Community Col, 72-77. *Honors & Awards:* Distinguished Serv Award, USDA, 56; Prizes, Am Vet Med Asn, 62 & 72; Award, Am Meat Inst, 64. *Mem:* Fel AAAS; Am Vet Med Asn (pres elect, 63, pres, 64); Am Animal Hosp Asn; Conf Res Works Animal Dis. *Res:* Prevention, control and eradication of diseases and pests of livestock, crops and agricultural products with inspection and research programs to improve and safeguard the quality of agricultural products. *Mailing Add:* PO Box 388 Peterborough NH 03458

CLARKSON, QUENTIN DEANE, b Eugene, Ore, Sept 26, 25; m 47; c 4. BIOSTATISTICS. *Educ:* Univ Ore, BS, 49, MS, 50; Ore State Col, PhD(bot), 55. *Prof Exp:* Instr bot, Ore State Col, 52-54; from asst prof to assoc prof, Portland State Col, 55-68; assoc prof neurol, Med Sch, Univ Ore, 69-74; mem fac, Portland State Univ, 74-77, assoc prof, Dept Social Work, 70-77; MEM STAFF, ORE HEALTH SCI UNIV, 78- *Concurrent Pos:* Assoc prof, NC State Univ, 65-69. *Res:* Biostatistics; systematics. *Mailing Add:* 5203 SE 38th Portland OR 97202

CLARKSON, ROBERT BRECK, b Buffalo, NY, Apr 19, 43; m 65; c 2. PHYSICAL CHEMISTRY, SURFACE CHEMISTRY. *Educ:* Hamilton Col, BA, 65; Princeton Univ, MA, 68, PhD(chem), 69. *Prof Exp:* asst prof phys chem, Univ Wis-Milwaukee, 69-76; head, Electron Paramagnetic Resonance Applications Lab, Varian Assocs, 76-81; DIR, LAB MOLECULAR SPECTROS, SCH CHEM SCI, UNIV ILL, 82- *Concurrent Pos:* NSF Indust Res Participation Prog, Exxon Res Corp, 76. *Honors & Awards:* Norton Found Prize. *Mem:* Am Chem Soc; Am Phys Soc; Catalysis Soc. *Res:* Applications of electron paramagnetic resonance and nuclear magnetic resonance characterization of gas-solid interactions; electron paramagnetic resonance and electron-nuclear double resonance studies of polymer systems; solid state nuclear magnetic resonance of catalytic systems. *Mailing Add:* Sch Chem Sci Univ Ill 505 S Mathews Urbana IL 61801

CLARKSON, ROY BURDETTE, b Cass, WVa, Oct 25, 26; m 52; c 3. BOTANY. *Educ:* Davis & Elkins Col, BS, 51; WVa Univ, MA, 54, PhD, 60. *Prof Exp:* Teacher, pub sch, WVa, 51-56; from instr to assoc prof, 56-69, assoc chmn dept, 69-74, actg chmn, 74-75, PROF BIOL, W VA UNIV, 69-, CUR HERBARIUM, 75- *Res:* Plant taxonomy and geography; chemosystematics, especially comparison of macromolecules utilizing electrophoretic and serologic techniques. *Mailing Add:* Dept of Biol WVa Univ Morgantown WV 26506

CLARKSON, THOMAS BOSTON, b Decatur, Ga, June 13, 31; m 50; c 3. VETERINARY MEDICINE. *Educ:* Univ Ga, DVM, 54. *Prof Exp:* Res assoc pharmacol & exp therapeut sect, S E Massengill Co, 54-57; from asst prof to assoc prof exp med & dir vivarium, 57-64, assoc prof lab animal med & head dept, 64-65, PROF COMP MED & CHMN DEPT, BOWMAN GRAY SCH MED, WAKE FOREST UNIV, 65-, DIR ARTERIOSCLEROSIS RES CTR, 71- *Concurrent Pos:* Mem comt coronary artery lesions & myocardial infarctions, Am Heart Asn, 70-; mem sci adv comt, Univ Wash Regional Primate Res Ctr, 71-; mem adv comt, Cerbrovascular Res Ctr, 73-; mem comt vet med sci, Nat Acad Sci-Nat Res Coun, 75-; mem clin sci panel study nat needs biomed & behav res personnel comt & task force animal models atherosclerosis, Nat Acad Sci, 76- *Honors & Awards:* Griffin Award, Am Asn Lab Animal Sci, 77; Charles River Prize, Am Vet Med Asn, 78. *Mem:* Am Vet Med Asn; Am Asn Advan Lab Animal Sci; Am Asn Pathologists; Am Heart Asn; Am Soc Exp Path. *Res:* Comparative and experimental atherosclerosis, particularly factors affecting susceptibility and resistance to the disease and the mechanisms by which risk factors affect the pathogenesis. *Mailing Add:* Arteriosclerosis Res Ctr Wake Forest Univ Winston-Salem NC 27103

CLARKSON, THOMAS WILLIAM, b UK, Aug 1, 32; m 57; c 2. TOXICOLOGY. *Educ:* Univ Manchester, BSc, 53, PhD(biochem), 56. *Prof Exp:* Med Res Coun fel, Univ Manchester, 56-57; instr radiation biol, Univ Rochester, 57-61, asst prof, 61-62; sci officer, Med Res Coun, UK, 62-64; sr fel, Weizmann Inst, 64-65; assoc prof biophys, pharmacol, radiation biol & toxicol, 65-71, PROF TOXICOL, UNIV ROCHESTER, 71-, DIR ENVIRON HEALTH SCI CTR, 75-, HEAD, DIV TOXICOL, 80- *Concurrent Pos:* Mem comt food protection, Nat Acad Sci-Nat Acad Eng, 73-76, subcomt toxicol, 72-76; mem toxicol adv bd, Food & Drug Admin, 75-77; mem toxicol study sect, NIH, 76-77 & WHO, 75 & 80; mem water reuse, Nat Acad Sci, 80- *Mem:* AAAS; Health Physics Soc; Brit Pharmacol Soc; Soc Toxicol; Royal Soc Chem. *Res:* Cellular physiology; reabsorption mechanisms in intestine and kidney; heavy metal toxicology; action of metals on cellular level in intestine, kidney and red blood cells. *Mailing Add:* Sch of Med Box RB & B Univ of Rochester Rochester NY 14642

CLARKSON, VERNON A, b Tacoma, Wash, Apr 19, 21; m 47; c 3. HORTICULTURE. *Educ:* Wash State Univ, BS, 49; Ore State Univ, MS, 51. *Prof Exp:* Asst, Inst Hort, Ore State Univ, 50-57; horticulturist, Plastics Div, Union Carbide Corp, 57-60 & Olefins Div, 60-70; HORTICULTURIST, AGR CHEM DIV, CIBA-GEIGY CHEM CORP, 70- *Mem:* Am Soc Hort Sci. *Res:* Agricultural uses of plastic materials; agricultural pesticides. *Mailing Add:* 15 Trinity Pl Rhinebeck NY 12572

CLARY, BOBBY LELAND, b Jesup, Ga, Aug 14, 38; m 57; c 3. AGRICULTURAL ENGINEERING. *Educ:* Univ Ga, BSAE, 60; Okla State Univ, PhD(agr eng), 69. *Prof Exp:* Asst prof agr eng, State Univ NY Agr & Tech Col Alfred, 60-65; prof, Polk Jr Col, Fla, 65-66; res asst, 66-68, from asst prof to assoc prof, 68-78, PROF AGR ENG, OKLA STATE UNIV, 78- *Concurrent Pos:* Actg chief agr & food processes br, Energy Res & Develop Admin, Washington, DC, 75-76. *Honors & Awards:* Young Eng of the Year Award, Okla Soc Prof Engrs, 74; Young Educr Award, 75 & Distinguished Young Agr Engr Award, Southwest Region, 76, Am Soc Agr Engrs. *Mem:* Am Soc Agr Engrs; Am Soc Eng Educ; Inst Food Technol; Nat Soc Prof Engrs. *Res:* Heat and mass transfer in biological materials; agricultural energy. *Mailing Add:* Dept of Agr Eng Okla State Univ Stillwater OK 74074

CLASE, HOWARD JOHN, b Salisbury, Eng, June 14, 38; m 63; c 2. INORGANIC CHEMISTRY. *Educ:* Cambridge Univ, BA, 60, PhD(inorg chem), 63, MA, 65. *Prof Exp:* Fel, McMaster Univ, 63-65; asst chem, Univ Oulu, 65-66; tutorial fel, Univ Sussex, 66-68; asst prof, 68-74, ASSOC PROF CHEM, MEM UNIV NFLD, 74- *Mem:* Royal Soc Chem; Chem Inst Can. *Res:* Application of Raman spectroscopy to problems in inorganic chemistry. *Mailing Add:* Dept of Chem Mem Univ Nfld St John's NF AIB 3X7 Can

CLASEN, RAYMOND ADOLPH, b Chicago, Ill, June 28, 26; m 50; c 1. PATHOLOGY. *Educ:* Univ Ill, BS, 50, MD, 52. *Prof Exp:* Intern, Cook County Hosp, 52-53; resident, Presby Hosp, Chicago, 53-57; Nat Inst Neurol Dis & Blindness fel, 57-59, asst prof 59-73, ASSOC PROF PATH, RUSH-PRESBY-ST LUKE'S MED CTR, CHICAGO, 73- *Mem:* AAAS; Am Asn Neuropath; Am Asn Pathologists & Bacteriologists; Am Soc Exp Path; Int Acad Path. *Res:* Experimental neuropathology. *Mailing Add:* 3440 Parthenon Way Olympia Fields IL 60461

CLASS, CALVIN MILLER, b Baltimore Co, Md, Jan 27, 24; m 48; c 1. NUCLEAR PHYSICS. *Educ:* Johns Hopkins Univ, AB, 43, PhD(physics), 51. *Prof Exp:* Physicist hydrodyn, Nat Adv Comt Aeronaut, 44-46; asst nuclear physics, Johns Hopkins Univ, 49-52; from instr to assoc prof, 52-63, PROF PHYSICS, RICE UNIV, 63- *Concurrent Pos:* Guggenheim fel, 55-56. *Mem:* Fel Am Phys Soc. *Res:* Spectroscopy of light and medium nuclei. *Mailing Add:* Dept Physics Rice Univ Houston TX 77001

CLASS, JAY BERNARD, b Baltimore, Md, Apr 14, 28; m 58; c 2. ADHESIVES, ELASTOMERS. *Educ:* Univ Md, BS, 49; Pa State Univ, PhD(org chem), 52. *Prof Exp:* Res chemist, 52-66, res supvr, 66-78, RES SCIENTIST & GROUP LEADER, ADHESIVES LAB RES CTR, HERCULES INC, 78- *Mem:* Am Chem Soc; Sigma Xi. *Res:* Studies on the use of low molecular weight hydrocarbon and rosin-based resins in pressure sensitive and hot melt adhesives; the effects of these resins on polymer properties. *Mailing Add:* Hercules Res Ctr Hercules Inc Wilmington DE 19899

CLASS, WALTER, b New York, NY, Mar 1, 36; m 60; c 2. METALLURGY, CERAMICS. *Educ:* NY Univ, BMetEng, 57; Univ Ill, MS, 60; Columbia Univ, PhD(metall), 64. *Prof Exp:* Sr scientist, 63-66, mgr adv develop, 66-67, gen mgr ceramic prod div, 67-76, CHIEF RES OFFICER, MAT RES CORP, 76- *Mem:* Am Vacuum Soc. *Res:* Growth of high purity inorganic compound single crystals; synthesis and hot pressing of highly pure materials; manufacture of very smooth surface alumina substrates by the tape process; research and development in high rate sputtering and high rate thin-film coating process; management of corporate long range development activities. *Mailing Add:* Mat Res Corp 35 Jefferson Ave Pearl River NY 10965

CLATOR, IRVIN GARRETT, b Huntington, WVa, Nov 2, 41. NUCLEAR PHYSICS, EXPLOSIVES. *Educ:* WVa Univ, BS, 63, MS, 65, PhD(physics), 69. *Prof Exp:* From physicist to res physicist, US Naval Weapons Lab, 65-70; asst prof, 70-74, ASSOC PROF PHYSICS, UNIV NC, WILMINGTON, 74-, CHMN DEPT, 71- *Mem:* AAAS. *Res:* Neutron induced reaction in the 10 to 20 mev energy range with medium A nuclei; explosive material properties. *Mailing Add:* Dept of Physics Univ of NC PO Box 3725 Wilmington NC 28401

CLATWORTHY, WILLARD HUBERT, b Auxier, Ky, Oct 16, 15; div; c 2. STATISTICS. *Educ:* Berea Col, BA, 38; Univ Ky, MA, 40; Univ NC, PhD(math statist), 52. *Prof Exp:* Asst, Univ Ky, 38-40; prof, Louisburg Col, 40-42; tool designer, Wright Automatic Packing Mach Co, 42 & Bell Aircraft Corp, 42-43; instr math, Wayne State Univ, 46-49; statistician math & probability, Nat Bur Standards, 52-55; statistician, Bettis Atomic Power Div, Westinghouse Elec Corp, 55-62; prof statist, State Univ NY, Buffalo, 62-81; RETIRED. *Mem:* Fel AAAS; Inst Math Statist; fel Am Statist Asn; Int Asn Statist in Phys Sci; fel Royal Statist Soc. *Res:* Mathematics of statistical design of experiments; combinatorial aspects of design of experiments; regression and least squares; analysis of variance. *Mailing Add:* 378 Cottonwood Dr Williamsville NY 14221

CLAUDE, PHILIPPA, b New York, NY, Jan 21, 36; m 75. CELL BIOLOGY, NEUROBIOLOGY. *Educ:* Cornell Univ, BA, 57; Univ Pa, PhD(zool), 68. *Prof Exp:* Instr, Harvard Med Sch, 69-72, prin res assoc neurobiol, 72-75; ASST SCIENTIST, WIS REGIONAL PRIMATE RES CTR, 75-; LECTR BIOL, CORE CURRIC, UNIV WIS-MADISON, 76-, MEM NEUROSCI TRAINING PROG, 77- *Concurrent Pos:* NIH fel, Harvard Med Sch, 69-72, NIH spec fel, 72-73. *Mem:* Am Soc Cell Biol; AAAS; Soc Neurosci; Electron Micros Soc Am. *Res:* Intercellular junctions; neuronal development and neurospecificity; neuronal tissue culture; membrane specializations; cell surface receptors; internalization and processing of growth factors and hormones; neuronal cell culture; electron microscopic autoradiography; surface replicas; scanning electron microscopy. *Mailing Add:* Regional Primate Res Ctr Univ Wis-Madison 1223 Capitol Ct Madison WI 53706

CLAUDSON, T(HOMAS) T(UCKER), b Pratt, Kans, Apr 25, 33; m 55; c 4. MECHANICAL ENGINEERING, METALLURGICAL ENGINEERING. *Educ:* Univ Wash, BS, 55; Ore State Univ, MS, 58, PhD(metall eng), 62. *Prof Exp:* Engr, Gen Elec Co, 55-59, sr engr, 61-67; mgr mech metall, Pac Northwest Lab, Battelle Mem Inst, 67-68, asst dept mgr fast flux test facil fuels dept, 68-70; mgr, Reactor Assembly Sub-Dept, Westinghouse Hanford Co, Westinghouse Elec Corp, 70-79; GROUP VPRES, CRITON CORP, 79- *Mem:* Fel Am Soc Metals; Am Nuclear Soc; Am Soc Mech Engrs. *Res:* Physical metallurgy; heat transfer. *Mailing Add:* Criton Corp 10800 NE 8th St Bellevue WA 98004

CLAUER, ALLAN HENRY, b Milwaukee, Wis, Nov 3, 36; m 56; c 3. MECHANICAL METALLURGY, PHYSICAL METALLURGY. *Educ:* Univ Wis-Madison, BSc, 58, MSc, 61; Ohio State Univ, Columbus, PhD(metall eng), 68. *Prof Exp:* Instr metall, Dept Mining & Metals, Univ Wis, 59; RES SCIENTIST & ASSOC SECT MGR, PROCESS METALL SECT, BATTELLE MEM INST, COLUMBUS, 60- *Concurrent Pos:* Vis scientist, Danish AEC Lab, Riso, Denmark, 72-73. *Mem:* Sigma Xi; Am Soc Metals; Am Inst Mining, Metall & Petrol Engrs; Am Ceramics Soc. *Res:* High temperature strength properties of metals and ceramics; the relation between strength and microstructure; laser processing of metals utilizing both shockwave and thermal effects; powder metallurgy; hot isostatic processing. *Mailing Add:* Battelle Columbus Labs 505 King Ave Columbus OH 43201

CLAUER, C ROBERT, b Wooster, Ohio, Aug 18, 48; m 75. SPACE PLASMA PHYSICS. *Educ:* Miami Univ, Ohio, BA, 70; Univ Calif, Los Angeles, MS, 74, PhD(geophys space physics), 80. *Prof Exp:* Res geophysicist, Univ Calif, Los Angeles, 73-79, res assoc, 79-80; RES ASSOC, STANFORD UNIV, 80- *Concurrent Pos:* Res assoc, Stanford Univ, 80-; mem, Magnetic Fields Subgroup Coord Data Anal Workshop, Nat Space Flight Data Ctr, 81- *Mem:* Am Geophys Union; Sigma Xi. *Res:* Ground based and satellite based experimental data for research in solar terrestrial and magnetospheric space plasma physics and auroral dynamics. *Mailing Add:* Radio Sci Lab Stanford Univ Durand 206 Stanford CA 94305

CLAUS, ALFONS JOZEF, b Belg, May 21, 32; US citizen; m 63; c 3. COMPUTER SCIENCES, OCEAN SCIENCES. *Educ:* Univ Ghent, BS, 56; Univ Mich, PhD(eng mech), 61. *Prof Exp:* Mem tech staff commun satellites, 61-65, SUPVR SPACE PROG OCEAN ACOUST & DATA ANAL, BELL LABS, 65- *Res:* Application of computer science and technology to the study of ocean acoustic phenomena. *Mailing Add:* Post House Rd Morristown NJ 07960

CLAUS, GEORGE WILLIAM, b Council Bluffs, Iowa, Aug 15, 36; m 58; c 3. BACTERIAL PHYSIOLOGY. *Educ:* Iowa State Univ, BS, 59, PhD(physiol bact), 64. *Prof Exp:* Bacteriologist & biochemist, US Army Med Unit, Ft Detrick, Md, 64-66; asst prof microbiol, Pa State Univ, University Park, 66-73; asst prof, 73-76, ASSOC PROF MICROBIOL, VA POLYTECH INST & STATE UNIV, 76- *Concurrent Pos:* Consult, Hoffmann-La Roche, Inc, 74-78. *Mem:* AAAS; Am Soc Microbiol; Soc Indust Microbiol; Sigma Xi; US Fedn Cult Collections. *Res:* Physiology and fine-structure of acetic acid bacteria; intracytoplasmic membrane development in nonphotosynthetic gram-negative bacteria; limited oxidation of Gluconobacter; biochemical cytology. *Mailing Add:* Dept Biol Va Polytech Inst & State Univ Blacksburg VA 24061

CLAUS, RICHARD OTTO, b Baltimore, Md, May 29, 51. ACOUSTOOPTICS, ULTRASONICS. *Educ:* Johns Hopkins Univ, BES, 73, PhD(elec eng), 77. *Prof Exp:* Instr elec eng, Johns Hopkins Univ, 73-76; asst prof, 77-81, ASSOC PROF ELEC ENG, VA POLYTECH INST & STATE UNIV, 81- *Mem:* Inst Elec & Electronics Engrs; Optical Soc Am; Soc Photo-optical Instrumentation Engrs; Am Soc Eng Educ. *Res:* Applied optics; nondestructive evaluation; interferometry; ultrasonic transducer characterization; optical fiber instrumentation. *Mailing Add:* Elec Eng Dept Va Polytech Inst & State Univ Blacksburg VA 24061

CLAUS, THOMAS HARRISON, medical physiology, see previous edition

CLAUSEN, CHRIS ANTHONY, b New Orleans, La, Dec 7, 40; m 62; c 2. INORGANIC CHEMISTRY. *Educ:* La State Univ, Baton Rouge, BS, 63; La State Univ, New Orleans, PhD(inorg chem), 69. *Prof Exp:* Chemist, Standard Oil Co Calif, 63-66; from asst prof to assoc prof, 69-77, PROF CHEM UNIV CENTRAL FLA, 77- *Concurrent Pos:* AEC res grant, 69-70; tour speaker, Am Chem Soc, 74; res scientist, Dow Chem Co, 77. *Honors & Awards:* Excellence in Sci Res Award, Sigma Xi, 77. *Mem:* Am Chem Soc; Am Soc Appl Spectros. *Res:* Mossbauer spectroscopy as applied in bonding and structural studies; molecular vibrations in the far infrared; coordination chemistry in marine environments; petroleum development and catalysis studies. *Mailing Add:* Dept of Chem Fla Technol Univ PO Box 25000 Orlando FL 32816

CLAUSEN, CONRAD DUANE, b Takoma Park, Md, May 18, 43; m 75. INVERTEBRATE ZOOLOGY. *Educ:* Columbia Union Col, BA, 66; Loma Linda Univ, PhD(biol), 72. *Prof Exp:* asst prof, 72-79, ASSOC PROF BIOL, LOMA LINDA UNIV, 79- *Mem:* AAAS; Sigma Xi. *Res:* The effect of environmental and other factors on growth line formation in bivalve mollusc shells. *Mailing Add:* Dept Biol Loma Linda Univ Loma Linda CA 92354

CLAUSEN, EDGAR CLEMENS, b St Louis, Mo, Dec 15, 51; m 74; c 1. CHEMICAL ENGINEERING. *Educ:* Univ Mo-Rolla, BS, 74, MS, 75, PhD(chem eng), 78. *Prof Exp:* Process design engr, Monsanto Co, 74; asst prof chem eng, Tenn Tech Univ, 77-81; ASSOC PROF CHEM ENG, UNIV ARK, 81- *Concurrent Pos:* Prof, E I du Pont de Nemours & Co, 78; process design consult, Oak Ridge Nat Lab, 80-81. *Mem:* Am Inst Chem Engrs; Am Soc Eng Educ; Sigma Xi. *Res:* Conversion of biomass to chemicals and energy: methane production by anaerobic digestion, conversion of lignocellulosics to sugars by acid hydrolysis, fermentation of hydrolyzates to chemicals. *Mailing Add:* Dept Chem Eng Univ Ark Fayetteville AR 72701

CLAUSEN, ERIC NEIL, b Ithaca, NY, July 2, 43. GEOMORPHOLOGY. *Educ:* Columbia Univ, BS, 65; Univ Wyo, PhD(geol), 69. *Prof Exp:* Asst prof geol, 68-75, dir acad comput serv, 75-79, ASSOC PROF EARTH SCI, MINOT STATE COL, 75- *Mem:* Geol Soc Am; Nat Asn Geol Teachers; Am Asn Quaternary Environ. *Res:* Badland geomorphology; geologic history of northern great plains; earth science education. *Mailing Add:* Dept of Earth Sci Minot State Col Minot ND 58701

CLAUSEN, KNUD ERIK, b Sakskobing, Denmark, Nov 20, 27; US citizen; m 56. FOREST GENETICS. *Educ:* Univ Minn, MS, 59, PhD(forest genetics), 61. *Prof Exp:* Asst forester, Horsholm Forestry Dist, Denmark, 50-51; field asst, Gaävleborgs Laäns Skogsvardsstyrelse, Sweden, 51; trainee, Skoghallsverken, Uddeholm Co, 51; field asst, genetics, Forest Res Inst, Sweden, 52-53; res asst, Univ Wis, 53-54; field asst genetics, Forest Res Inst Sweden, 55-56; res forester, 61-62, GENETICIST, N CENT FOREST EXP STA, US FOREST SERV, 62- *Concurrent Pos:* Nat Acad Sci travel grant, Poland & Ger Acad Exchange Serv study grant, 70; consult, Inst Forest Improvement, Sweden, 70; adj prof forestry, Southern Ill Univ, 78. *Mem:* AAAS; Am Genetic Asn; Soc Study Evolution. *Res:* Genetics of Betula, Fraxinus, Juglans. *Mailing Add:* NCent Forest Exp Sta Southern Ill Univ Carbondale IL 62901

CLAUSEN, ROBERT THEODORE, b New York, NY, Dec 26, 11; m 42; c 4. PLANT TAXONOMY. *Educ:* Cornell Univ, AB, 33, AM, 34, PhD(plant taxon), 37. *Prof Exp:* Asst, Univ, 33-35, from asst to assoc prof, Bailey Hortorium, 35-41, from asst prof to prof bot, 41-77, EMER PROF BIOL, CORNELL UNIV, 77- *Concurrent Pos:* Collabr, USDA, 43. *Mem:* Am Inst Bio Sci; Bot Soc Am; Am Soc Plant Taxonomists; Torrey Bot Club; Am Fern Soc (pres, 39-42). *Res:* Taxonomy of vascular plants; phytogeography; monograph of Ophioglossaceae; Crassulaceae; Sedum; ecology. *Mailing Add:* PO Box 579 Ithaca NY 14850

CLAUSEN, WILLIAM E(ARLE), b Rochester, Pa, Mar 11, 38; m 64. ENGINEERING MECHANICS. *Educ:* Lehigh Univ, BS, 60; Ohio State Univ, MSc, 61, PhD(eng mech), 65. *Prof Exp:* Asst prof, 65-69, ASSOC PROF ENG MECH, OHIO STATE UNIV, 69- . *Concurrent Pos:* Consult, Battelle Mem Inst, 66- *Mem:* Am Inst Aeronaut & Astronaut. *Res:* Elasticity; dynamics; composite materials; shells; numerical techniques. *Mailing Add:* Dept of Eng Mech Ohio State Univ Columbus OH 43210

CLAUSER, FRANCIS HETTINGER, b Kansas City, Mo, May 25, 13; m 37; c 2. AERONAUTICS. *Educ:* Calif Inst Technol, BS, 34, MS, 35, PhD(aeronaut), 37. *Prof Exp:* Engr in charge aerodyn & design res, Douglas Aircraft Co, 37-46; prof aeronaut & chmn dept, Johns Hopkins Univ, 46-60, prof mech, 60-64; prof eng & vchancellor, Univ Calif, Santa Cruz, 65-69; chmn, Div Eng & Appl Sci, 69-74, Clark B Millikan prof eng, 69-80, EMER CLARK B MILLIKAN PROF ENG, CALIF INST TECHNOL, 80- *Mem:* AAAS; Nat Acad Eng; fel Am Inst Aeronaut & Astronaut. *Res:* Aerodynamics; fluid mechanics; non-linear mechanics. *Mailing Add:* Calif Inst Technol Pasadena CA 91109

CLAUSER, JOHN FRANCIS, b Pasadena, Calif, Dec 1, 42; m 64. QUANTUM MECHANICS, EXPERIMENTAL PHYSICS. *Educ:* Calif Inst Technol, BS, 64; Columbia Univ, MA, 66, PhD(physics), 69. *Prof Exp:* Res physicist quantum physics, Univ Calif & Lawrence Berkeley Lab, 69-75, RES PHYSICIST PLASMA PHYSICS, UNIV CALIF & LAWRENCE LIVERMORE LAB, 75- *Mem:* Am Phys Soc. *Res:* Reconciliation of everyday notions of objectivity, space and time with the observed and predicted behavior of quantum mechanical systems; understanding fundamental processes in magnetic-mirror-confined plasmas; development of computer systems for experimental physics research. *Mailing Add:* Lawrence Livermore Lab L 637 PO Box 808 Livermore CA 94550

CLAUSER, MILTON JOHN, b Santa Monica, Calif, June 17, 40; m 61; c 2. NUCLEAR ENGINEERING. *Educ:* Mass Inst Technol, SB, 61; Calif Inst Technol, PhD(physics), 66. *Prof Exp:* NSF res fel physics, Munich Tech Univ, 66-67; mem tech staff, 67-79, SUPVR, ADVAN REACTOR SAFETY ANAL, SANDIA NAT LABS, 80- *Mem:* Am Phys Soc; Am Nuclear Soc. *Res:* Electron and ion beam fusion; target behavior; laser created plasmas; reactor safety. *Mailing Add:* Div 4424 Sandia Nat Labs Albuquerque NM 87185

CLAUSER, MILTON URE, aeronautical engineering, deceased

CLAUSING, A(RTHUR) M(ARVIN), b Palatine, Ill, Aug 17, 36; m 64; c 2. SOLAR ENERGY, HEAT TRANSFER. *Educ:* Valparaiso Univ, BS, 58; Univ Ill, MS, 60, PhD(mech eng), 63. *Prof Exp:* ASSOC PROF MECH ENG, UNIV ILL, URBANA-CHAMPAIGN, 62- *Concurrent Pos:* Consult, Environ Protection Res Inst & Off Energy Rel Inventions. *Mem:* Int Solar Energy Soc; Am Soc Mech Engrs; Am Soc Heating Refrig & Airconditioning Engrs. *Res:* Field of solar energy utilization; heat transfer; numerical methods. *Mailing Add:* 144 Mech Eng Bldg Univ Ill Urbana IL 61801

CLAUSON, W(ARREN) W(ILLIAM), b Chicago, Ill, Mar 9, 26; m 63. CHEMICAL ENGINEERING. *Educ:* Ill Inst Technol, BS, 49, MS, 52, PhD(chem eng), 55. *Prof Exp:* Draftsman, NuWay Refrig Co, 46-47; chem engr, L R Kerns Co, 49-51; eng instr, Bell & Howell Co, 51-52; asst, Chem Eng Dept, Ill Inst Technol, 54-55; asst prof chem eng, Rose Polytech Inst, 55-58; heat transfer specialist rocket appln res sect, Flight Propulsion Lab Dept, Gen Elec Co, Ohio, 58; supvr heat transfer sect, Appl Mech Div, Aerojet-Gen Corp Div, Gen Tire & Rubber Co, 58-65; mgr, Eng Anal Dept, Wright Aeronaut Div, Curtiss-Wright Corp, 65-68; proj dir, Gries Reprod Co, 68-69; mgr papermaking develop, Scott Paper Co, 69-71; independent consult, 71-74; PROJ & PROCESS ENGR, AMOCO CHEM CORP, 74- *Concurrent Pos:* Consult, Aircraft Gas Turbine Div, Gen Elec Co, 56-58; lectr exten, Univ Calif, Berkeley, 59-61 & Sacramento State Col, 61-65. *Mem:* Inst Chem Engrs. *Res:* Thermodynamics; heat transfer; fluid dynamics; applied mathematics. *Mailing Add:* Amoco Chem Corp PO Box 8640A Chicago IL 60680

CLAUSS, JAMES K, b Cambridge, Mass, Aug 3, 20; m 44; c 3. ANALYTICAL CHEMISTRY, PHYSICAL CHEMISTRY. *Educ:* Reed Col, BA, 41; Ore State Univ, MS, 43, PhD(anal chem), 55. *Prof Exp:* Sr analyst, Gen Chem Div, Allied Chem Corp, 43-46, chief chemist, 46-52; from assoc chemist to chemist, Stanford Res Inst, 54-58; chief chemist display devices, Electron Tube Div, Litton Indust Inc, 58-64; MEM SR STAFF CHEM, DEPT RES & DEVELOP, SIGNETICS CORP, 64- *Mem:* Electrochem Soc; Sigma Xi. *Res:* Analytical methods; plant stream and effluent analyzers; emission spectrography trace elements; vacuum technology; cathode-ray tube materials and fabrication techniques; xerographic materials; electrophoretic coatings; integrated circuit process development. *Mailing Add:* 744 Coastland Dr Palo Alto CA 94303

CLAUSS, N(ATHAN) W(AGNER), b Jackson, Mich, Aug 22, 13; m 41; c 2. CHEMICAL ENGINEERING, SAFETY ENGINEERING. *Educ:* Univ Mich, BS, 41. *Prof Exp:* Agr chemist, McLaughlin-Ward & Co, Mich, 35-37; lab supvr, Goodyear Tire & Rubber Co, 37-39; instr chem gas anal, Univ Mich, 39-40, instr eng res, 39-41; head prod dept, Chem & Plastics Div, Union Carbide Corp, 41-70, sr eng specialist reliability eng, 70-71; sr staff engr, 71-75, sr staff safety engr & process safety adminr, Chem & Plastics Div, 75-78; CONSULT, 78- *Mem:* Am Chem Soc; Am Inst Chem Engrs; fel Am Inst Chem. *Res:* Manufacture of acetic anhydride, acetic acid and glycol ethers; synthetic alcohol production; concentration and manufacture of sulfuric acid; ethylene oxide; plasticizers; esters; organics solids; phosphates and agricultural chemicals; chemical equipment and process safety technology. *Mailing Add:* 512 Superior Ave South Charleston WV 25303

CLAUSS, ROY H, b Ill, Feb 8, 23; m 45; c 3. CARDIOVASCULAR SURGERY. *Educ:* Northwestern Univ, BS, 43, MD, 46; Am Bd Surg, dipl, 56; Am Bd Thoracic Surg, dipl, 57. *Prof Exp:* Instr surg, Col Physicians & Surgeons, Columbia Univ, 55-57; asst, Harvard Med Sch, 57-58; asst prof, Col Med, Univ Cincinnati, 58-60; assoc prof, Sch Med, NY Univ, 60-69; PROF SURG, NEW YORK MED COL, 69- *Concurrent Pos:* Am Trudeau Soc teaching fel, 54-55; USPHS spec fel, Harvard Med Sch, 57-58; consult, Cabrini Health Care Ctr, 66-; attend surgeon, Lenox Hill Hosp, 76-, St Vincent's Hosp, 77-; courtesy surgeon, Doctor's Hosp, 78- vis surgeon, Metrop & Coler Hosps; mem coun circulation, Am Heart Asn. *Mem:* Am Col Chest Physicians; Am Heart Asn; Am Col Surg; Am Asn Thoracic Surg; Int Cardiovasc Soc. *Res:* Cardiovascular and pulmonary surgery and physiology. *Mailing Add:* 1021 Park Ave New York NY 10028

CLAUSSEN, DENNIS LEE, b Pender, Nebr, Sept 23, 41; m 64; c 2. PHYSIOLOGICAL ECOLOGY. *Educ:* Pomona Col, BA, 63; Univ Calif, Riverside, MA, 66; Univ Mont, PhD(zool), 71. *Prof Exp:* Entomologist, Nutrilite Prod Inc, Calif, 66-68; res asst biol control, Univ Calif, Riverside, 68; asst prof, 71-75, ASSOC PROF ZOOL, MIAMI UNIV, 75- *Mem:* AAAS; Sigma Xi; Am Soc Zoologists. *Res:* The metabolism, thermal relations and water relations of arthropods, amphibians and reptiles. *Mailing Add:* Dept of Zool Miami Univ Oxford OH 45056

CLAUSSEN, MARK J, b Whitter, Calif, April 20, 52; m 76; c 2. RADIOASTRONOMY. *Educ:* Mo Southern State Col, BS, 74; NMex State Univ, MS 76; Univ Iowa, PhD(physics), 81. *Prof Exp:* RES FEL, CALIF INST TECHNOL, 81- *Mem:* Am Astron Soc. *Res:* Radio interferometry of molecular lines in star-forming regions and evolved stars; continuum interferometry of galactoc H II regions and planetary nebulae. *Mailing Add:* Calif Inst Technol MC 105-24 Pasadena CA 91125

CLAUS-WALKER, JACQUELINE LUCY, b Paris, France, Dec 13, 15; US citizen; m 65. ENDOCRINOLOGY. *Educ:* Univ Paris, BA, 35; Sorbonne, MS, 46; Union Col, BS, 51; Univ Houston, MS, 55; Baylor Univ, PhD(physiol), 66. *Prof Exp:* Lab technician, Robert Packer Hosp, 47-48; chief pharmacist, James Walker Mem Hosp, 51-53; res asst, Univ Tex M D Anderson Hosp & Tumor Inst, 55-58; res asst, 61-66, from instr to asst prof physiol chem, Dept Biochem & Med Rehab, 66-71, ASSOC PROF PHYSIOL, DEPTS REHAB & PHYSIOL & ASST PROF BIOCHEM, BAYLOR COL MED, THE INST NEUROENDOCRINE LAB, THE INST REHAB & RES, 66- *Mem:* AAAS; NY Acad Sci; Am Soc Bone & Mineral Res; Endocrine Soc; Am Physiol Soc. *Res:* Pharmacology of spinal cord injury; biochemistry and histology of skin in spinal cord injury; bone and collagen metabolism in man with section of the cervical spinal cord. *Mailing Add:* The Inst for Rehab & Res 1333 Moursund Ave Houston TX 77025

CLAUSZ, JOHN CLAY, b Hackensack, NJ, Oct 5, 40; m 63; c 2. MYCOLOGY, MICROBIOLOGY. *Educ:* Ohio Wesleyan Univ, BA, 62; Univ NC, Chapel Hill, MA, 66, PhD(bot), 70. *Prof Exp:* Asst prof biol, St Andrews Presby Col, 69-76; asst prof biol, State Univ NY Geneseo, 76-79; ASST PROF BIOL, CARROLL COL, WAUKESHA, WIS, 79- *Mem:* Mycol Soc Am; Am Soc Microbiol; Sigma Xi. *Res:* Physiology and ecology of fungi, especially the aquatic fungi; lipids in water molds; heavy metal uptake by water mold achlya. *Mailing Add:* Dept Biol Carroll Col Waukesha WI 53186

CLAVAN, WALTER, b Philadelphia, Pa, Apr 6, 21; m 45; c 2. ANALYTICAL CHEMISTRY. *Educ:* Univ Pa, BS, 42, MS, 47, PhD(anal chem), 49. *Prof Exp:* Anal chemist, E J Lavino & Co, 42-44; group leader, anal dept, 49-70, dir anal serv, 70-74, MGR, ANAL CHEM DEPT, KING OF PRUSSIA TECHNOL CTR, PENNWALT CORP, 74- *Concurrent Pos:* Lectr, eve div, La Salle Col, 60-70. *Mem:* AAAS; Am Chem Soc; Geochem Soc; Sigma Xi. *Mailing Add:* Benson E 620 Jenkintown PA 19046

CLAVEAU, ROSARIO, b Chicoutimi, Que, Dec 13, 24; m 51; c 2. HEMATOLOGY, INTERNAL MEDICINE. *Educ:* Chicoutimi Sem, BA, 45; Laval Univ, MD, 50; FRCP(C). *Prof Exp:* CHIEF DEPT HEMAT, HOPITAL DE CHICOUTIMI, LAVAL UNIV, 60-, HON PROF, FAC MED, 64- *Mem:* Am Soc Hemat; fel Am Col Physicians; NY Acad Sci; Can Med Asn. *Mailing Add:* Hemat Lab Hopital de Chicoutimi Chicoutimi PQ G7H 5H6 Can

CLAVENNA, LEROY RUSSELL, b Joliet, Ill, May 12, 43; m 68; c 3. CHEMICAL ENGINEERING. *Educ:* Univ Ill, BS, 66; Univ Minn, PhD(chem eng), 71. *Prof Exp:* Res engr solid state chem, NJ, 71-74, res engr coal gasification, Tex, 74-78, staff engr, 78-80, proj leader gasification, 80-81, PROJ LEADER, COAL GASIFICATION & INDIRECT LIQUEFACTION, EXXON RES & ENG CO, 81- *Mem:* Am Inst Chem Engrs. *Res:* Surface physics; solid state inorganic chemistry; coal science. *Mailing Add:* Exxon Res & Eng Co PO Box 4255 Baytown TX 77520

CLAWSON, ALBERT J, b Curtis, Nebr, Feb 15, 24; m 48; c 6. ANIMAL NUTRITION. *Educ:* Univ Nebr, BS, 49; Kans State Univ, MS, 51; Cornell Univ, PhD(nutrit), 55. *Prof Exp:* Asst, Kans State Univ, 49-51; animal husbandman, Exp Sta, North Platte, Nebr, 51-52; asst, Cornell Univ, 52-55; assoc prof, 55-69, PROF ANIMAL SCI, NC STATE UNIV, 69- *Concurrent Pos:* Res fel, Centro Internacional Agricultura Tropical, Cali, Colombia, 72-73. *Mem:* Am Inst Nutrit; Am Soc Animal Sci. *Res:* Nutrient requirements for reproduction in swine; amino acid requirements of pig as determined by manipulation of dietary ingredients; indirect methods of determining live animal composition and factors influencing carcass composition. *Mailing Add:* Dept of Animal Sci NC State Univ Raleigh NC 27607

CLAWSON, DAVID KAY, b Salt Lake City, Utah, Aug 8, 27; m 52; c 2. ORTHOPEDIC SURGERY. *Educ:* Harvard Univ, MD, 52; Am Bd Orthop Surg, dipl, 61. *Prof Exp:* Intern surg, Stanford Univ Hosp, 52-53, resident, 53-54, resident orthop, 54-55; resident, San Francisco City & County Hosp, 54-57; mem bd fel adv, Orthopedic Rev, 72-75; assoc ed, J Bone & Joint Surg, 73-75. resident orthop, Stanford Univ Hosp, 56-57; asst prof surg, Univ Calif, Los Angeles, 58; head div surg & from asst prof to assoc prof surg, Univ Wash, 58-65, prof orthop & chmn dept, 65-75; DEAN, COL MED, UNIV KY, 75-, ASSOC VPRES CLIN AFFAIRS, 82- *Concurrent Pos:* Nat Found Infantile Paralysis fels orthop, 55-57 & advan orthop, 57-58; hon sr registr, Royal Nat Orthop Hosp & clin res asst, Univ London, 57-58. *Mem:* Am Acad Orthop Surg; Royal Soc Med; Asn Bone & Joint Surgeons (secy, 72-75, pres, 77); fel Am Geriat Soc; AMA. *Res:* Infections of bone and joints; bone implants; health care delivery; orthopedic manpower. *Mailing Add:* Sch Med Univ Ky Lexington KY 40506

CLAWSON, ROBERT CHARLES, b South Haven, Mich, May 10, 29; m 58; c 5. HISTOLOGY, EMBRYOLOGY. *Educ:* Spring Hill Col, BS, 50; St Louis Univ, MS, 53; Loyola Univ Chicago, PhD(anat), 62. *Prof Exp:* From instr to asst prof anat, Stritch Sch Med, 64-68; from asst prof to assoc prof, 68-77, PROF ANAT, SCH MED, LA STATE UNIV, SHREVEPORT, 77- *Concurrent Pos:* NIH fel, Loyola Univ Chicago, 62-64. *Mem:* Am Soc Zool; Am Asn Anat. *Res:* Structure of defensive glands of arthropods. *Mailing Add:* Dept Anat La State Univ Sch of Med Shreveport LA 71103

CLAXTON, WILLIAM EUGENE, b Hartville, Mo, Oct 27, 23; m 52; c 4. STATISTICS, COMPUTER APPLICATIONS. *Educ:* Harvard Univ, BS, 48; Univ Cincinnati, MS, 50. *Prof Exp:* Res physicist, 51-73, res assoc, 73-75, SR RES ASSOC, CENT RES LAB, FIRESTONE TIRE & RUBBER CO, 75- *Mem:* Am Chem Soc. *Res:* Applications of experimental design and statistical analysis; applied computer applications; development of special purpose computers; instrument development; microprocessor applications. *Mailing Add:* Cent Res Lab Firestone Tire & Rubber Co Akron OH 44317

CLAY, CLARENCE SAMUEL, b Kansas City, Mo, Nov 2, 23; m 45; c 4. GEOPHYSICS. *Educ:* Kans State Univ, BA, 47, MS, 48; Univ Wis, PhD(physics), 51. *Prof Exp:* Asst prof physics, Univ Wyo, 50-51; res physicist, Carter Oil Co, 51-55; sr res scientist, Hudson Lab, Columbia Univ, 55-67; PROF GEOL & GEOPHYS, UNIV WIS-MADISON, 68- *Mem:* Fel Acoust Soc Am; Am Geophys Union; Soc Explor Geophys. *Res:* Wave propagation in inhomogeneous media; scattering at rough interfaces; ocean acoustics; electrical geophysics; acoustic measurements of fish populations. *Mailing Add:* Weeks Hall Dept Geol & Geophys Univ of Wis Madison WI 53706

CLAY, FORREST PIERCE, JR, b Sutherland, Va, Nov 15, 27. PHYSICS. *Educ:* Randolph-Macon Col, BS, 48; Univ Va, MS, 50, PhD(physics), 52. *Prof Exp:* With Atlantic Res Corp, 52; asst prof physics, Georgetown Univ, 52-54 & Rutgers Univ, 54-61; from asst prof to assoc prof, 57-61, chmn, Dept Physics, 79-80, PROF PHYSICS, OLD DOMINION UNIV, 61- *Concurrent Pos:* Vis prof, Randolph-Macon Col, 57-58. *Mem:* Am Phys Soc; Am Asn Physics Teachers; Sigma Xi. *Res:* Positronium decay; quadrupole mass spectrometry electronics. *Mailing Add:* Dept of Physics Old Dom Univ Norfolk VA 23508

CLAY, GEORGE A, b Cambridge, Mass, June 24, 38; m 65; c 4. NEUROPHARMACOLOGY. *Educ:* Dartmouth Col, AB, 61; Boston Univ, MA, 64, PhD, 68. *Prof Exp:* Nat Heart & Lung Inst fel, 67-68, Nat Inst Gen Med Sci Res Assocs Pharmacol Training Prog fel, 68-70; asst prof pharmacol, Bowman Gray Sch Med, 70-72; from res investr to sr res investr, 72-74, group leader, 74-80, SECTION HEAD, CENT NERV SYST PHARMACOL, G D SEARLE & CO, 80- *Mem:* Am Soc Pharmacol & Exp Therapeut; AAAS. *Res:* Biochemical mechanisms of action of drugs affecting the central nervous system. *Mailing Add:* Searle Labs PO Box 5110 Chicago IL 60680

CLAY, JAMES RAY, b Burley, Idaho, Nov 5, 38; m 59; c 3. MATHEMATICS. *Educ:* Univ Utah, BS, 60; Univ Wash, MS, 62, PhD(math), 66. *Prof Exp:* Assoc engr, Boeing Co, 60-63; phys scientist, US Govt, 64-66; from asst prof to assoc prof, 66-74, assoc head dept, 69-72, PROF MATH, UNIV ARIZ, 74- *Concurrent Pos:* Humboldt Found spec award, 72; guest prof, Univ Tübingen, 72-73, Univ London, 73, Tech Univ, Munich, 79-80 & Univ Edinburgh, 80. *Mem:* Am Math Soc; Math Asn Am. *Res:* Abstract algebra; computer science; algebraic structures arising from endomorphism and mappings of groups. *Mailing Add:* Dept of Math Univ of Ariz Tucson AZ 85721

CLAY, JOHN PAUL, b Dawson, Ga, Oct 2, 10; m 33; c 3. PHYSICAL CHEMISTRY. *Educ:* Univ Ga, BS, 32, MS, 34; Columbia Univ, PhD(chem), 38. *Prof Exp:* Asst chem, Univ Ga, 32-34 & Columbia Univ, 34-38; res chemist, Interchem Corp, 38; from instr to assoc prof, 39-55, prof, 55-76, chmn dept, 68-76, EMER PROF CHEM, LEHMAN COL, 76- *Concurrent Pos:* Chem adv, Europ Command, 49-50; sci dir, Dugway Proving Ground, 52-55. *Res:* Complex ion exchange; catalysis; aerosols; fuels; wood chemistry; lignin; reaction rates; organo-phosphorous compounds. *Mailing Add:* Dept Chem Herbert H Lehman Col Bedford Park Blvd W Bronx NY 10468

CLAY, MARY ELLEN, b Freeport, Ohio, July 28, 40. ENTOMOLOGY, BIOLOGY. *Educ:* Muskingum Col, BS, 63; Ohio State Univ, MS, 66, PhD(entom), 69. *Prof Exp:* Res assoc mosquito biol, 69-73, lectr introd biol prog, 73-74, asst prof, 74-79, ASSOC PROF ENTOM, OHIO STATE UNIV, 79- *Mem:* Am Inst Biol Sci; Am Mosquito Control Asn; AAAS; Arctic Inst NAm; Entom Soc Am. *Res:* Insect biology; structural and functional aspects of the mosquito crop; insect diapause; mosquito neuroendocrine system; internal and external factors controlling diapause processes; biology of phychodids. *Mailing Add:* 1474 F Neil Ave Columbus OH 43210

CLAY, MICHAEL M, b Cleveland, Ohio, Aug 10, 20; m 55; c 2. PHARMACOLOGY. *Educ:* Ohio State Univ, BA, 41, PhD(pharmacol), 53; Univ Toledo, BS, 50, MS, 51. *Prof Exp:* Res assoc endocrinol, Ohio State Univ, 52-53; from asst to assoc prof pharmacol, Col Pharm, Columbia Univ, 53-64; guest prof, Med Clin, Univ Münster, 64-68; PROF PHARMACOL, UNIV HOUSTON, 68- *Mem:* Am Pharmaceut Asn; Am Geront Soc; NY Acad Sci. *Res:* Connective tissue physiology; cardiovascular disease. *Mailing Add:* 1926 Norfolk Houston TX 77004

CLAY, ROBERT EDWARD, mathematical logic, see previous edition

CLAYBAUGH, GLENN ALAN, b Lincoln, Nebr, Dec 10, 27; m 50; c 2. BACTERIOLOGY. *Educ:* Univ Nebr, BSc, 49; Mich State Univ, MSc, 50; Iowa State Univ, PhD(dairy bact), 53. *Prof Exp:* Sr bacteriologist, 53-60, sect leader, 60-63, prod mgr, 63-65, assoc, Mkt Div, 65-69, mkt dir, 69-72, DIR PROF SERV, MEAD JOHNSON NUTRIT DIV, MEAD JOHNSON & CO, 72- *Mem:* AAAS; Am Soc Microbiol; Am Dairy Sci Asn; fel Royal Soc Health; fel Am Pub Health Asn. *Res:* Infant feeding; dairy and food bacteriology; antibiotics and non-sporulating anaerobic bacteria in dairy products; quality control of milk products, infant formulas and other specialized food products; hospital consulting. *Mailing Add:* Mead Johnson Nutrit Div Mead Johnson & Co Evansville IN 47721

CLAYBERG, CARL DUDLEY, b Tacoma, Wash, Mar 1, 31; m 77; c 2. GENETICS. *Educ:* Univ Wash, BS, 54; Univ Calif, PhD(genetics), 58. *Prof Exp:* Asst genetics, Univ Calif, 54-56; asst geneticist, Conn Agr Exp Sta, 57-61, assoc geneticist, 61-74; assoc prof hort & forestry, 74-77, PROF HORT, KANS STATE UNIV, 77- *Mem:* Am Genetic Asn; Soc Study Evolution; Bot Soc Am; Am Soc Hort Sci. *Res:* Plant genetics, especially in Gesneriaceae, Lycopersicon, and Phaseolus. *Mailing Add:* Dept Hort Kans State Univ Manhattan KS 66506

CLAYBROOK, JAMES RUSSELL, b Cleburne, Tex, Aug 24, 36; m 63. MOLECULAR PHYSIOLOGY. *Educ:* Univ Tex, BS, 57, PhD(chem), 63. *Prof Exp:* Asst prof biochem, Med Sch, Univ Ore, 63-66; asst scientist, Ore Regional Primate Res Ctr, 63-66; NIH res fel microbiol, Univ Ill, Urbana-Champaign, 66-68; researcher, Int Lab Genetics & Biophys, Naples, Italy, 68-69; ASSOC PROF PHYSIOL, MED COL OHIO, TOLEDO, 69-; ASSOC DEAN RES, 74- *Mem:* AAAS; Am Chem Soc; Soc Gen Physiol; NY Acad Sci. *Res:* Role of nucleic acids in development and cell differentiation. *Mailing Add:* Med Col of Ohio CS 10008 Toledo OH 43699

CLAYCOMB, CECIL KEITH, b Twin Falls, Idaho, Oct 19, 20; m 43; c 2. BIOCHEMISTRY. *Educ:* Univ Ore, PhD(biochem), 51. *Prof Exp:* AEC res asst, Med Sch, 49-51, asst prof, 51-61, head dept, 51-81, asst to pres Health Sci Ctr for Minority Student Affairs, 75-78, PROF BIOCHEM, SCH DENT, ORE HEALTH SCI UNIV, 61-, DIR MINORITY STUDENT AFFAIRS, 80- *Concurrent Pos:* Vis res scientist, Inst Dent Res, United Dent Hosp, NSW, Australia, biol sci coordr, 72-76, chmn, Biol Sci Comt, 77-79. *Mem:* AAAS; Am Chem Soc; NY Acad Sci; Int Asn Dent Res. *Res:* Oral collagen metabolism using proline labeled with tritium and/or radiocarbon. *Mailing Add:* Dept Biochem Sch Dent Univ Ore Health Sci Ctr Portland OR 97201

CLAYCOMB, WILLIAM CREIGHTON, b Cincinnati, Ohio, Dec 20, 42; m 65; c 1. BIOLOGICAL CHEMISTRY. *Educ:* Ind Univ, AB, 66, PhD(pharmacol), 69. *Prof Exp:* asst prof cell biophys, Baylor Col Med, 72-76; ASSOC PROF BIOCHEM, SCH MED, LA STATE UNIV, 76- *Concurrent Pos:* Res fel biol chem, Harvard Med Sch, 69-72 & NIH fel differentiation, 70-72. *Mem:* AAAS; Soc Develop Biol; Am Soc Cell Biol; Am Soc Zool; Am Soc Biol Chemists. *Res:* Regulation of cell differentiation and cell proliferation; developmental biology; DNA replication. *Mailing Add:* Dept of Biochem Sch of Med La State Univ New Orleans LA 70112

CLAYMAN, BRUCE PHILIP, b New York, NY, Sept 2, 42; m 62; c 1. SOLID STATE PHYSICS. *Educ:* Rensselaer Polytech Inst, BS, 64; Cornell Univ, PhD(physics), 69. *Prof Exp:* Asst prof, 68-73, assoc prof, 73-80, assoc dean grad studies, 76-79, actg dean sci, 80, PROF PHYSICS PHYSICS, SIMON FRASER UNIV, 80- *Concurrent Pos:* Consult, Xerox Palo Alto Res Ctr, 79-80; vis prof physics, Emory Univ, 81. *Mem:* Am Phys Soc; Can Asn Physicists. *Res:* Far-infrared spectroscopic study of pure and doped materials. *Mailing Add:* Dept of Physics Simon Fraser Univ Burnaby BC V5A 1S6 Can

CLAYPOOL, DON PEARSON, b Salt Lick, Ky, Sept 20, 19; m 43; c 4. ORGANIC CHEMISTRY. *Educ:* Tulane Univ, BS, 46; Univ Ky, MS, 50, PhD(chem), 52. *Prof Exp:* Instr chem, Morehead State Col, 46-47 & Univ Ky, 47-52; res chemist, Monsanto Chem Co, WVa, 52-56; assoc prof, 56-63, PROF CHEM, MEMPHIS STATE UNIV, 63- *Mem:* AAAS; Am Chem Soc (treas, 61-62). *Res:* Fats and oils; organosulfur compounds; sulfonium salts; reactions of dimethyl sulfoxide; organonitrogen compounds; other syntheses and mechanisms of reactions. *Mailing Add:* Dept of Chem Memphis State Univ Memphis TN 38152

CLAYPOOL, GEORGE EDWIN, b Shenandoah, Iowa, Nov 20, 39; m 62; c 3. GEOCHEMISTRY, GEOLOGY. *Educ:* Colo State Univ, BS, 63; Univ Calif, Los Angeles, PhD(geochem), 74. *Prof Exp:* Lab technician chem, United Testing Labs, Monterey Park, 61-62; chemist geol, Denver Res Ctr, Marathon Oil Co, 63-69; res asst geochem, Inst Geophys & Planetary Physics, Univ Calif, Los Angeles, 69-74; RES CHEMIST GEOCHEM, US GEOL SURV, DENVER, 74- *Concurrent Pos:* Teaching asst chem, Univ Calif, Los Angeles, 70-71. *Mem:* Geochem Soc. *Res:* Research in geochemistry of sedimentary organic substances and petroleum; investigation of chemical reactions in earth's crust linked to the decomposition of organic matter; geochemistry of light stable isotopes. *Mailing Add:* US Geol Surv Box 25046 Denver Fed Ctr Denver CO 80225

CLAYPOOL, LAWRENCE LEONARD, b Pueblo, Colo, Dec 30, 07; m 29, 41; c 4. POMOLOGY. *Educ:* Univ Calif, BS, 28; State Col Wash, PhD(hort), 35. *Prof Exp:* Asst horticulturist, State Col Wash, 30-34; supvr, Prod Credit Corp, Wash, 34-37; from instr to prof pomol, 37-75, from jr pomologist to pomologist, Exp Sta, 37-75, EMER PROF POMOL, UNIV CALIF, DAVIS, 75- *Concurrent Pos:* Prof, Univ Ankara, Turkey, 57-58. *Mem:* Fel AAAS; fel Am Soc Hort Sci; Int Soc Hort Sci. *Res:* Maturity, handling and physiology of fruits in relation to fresh shipment, canning and drying; mechanical harvesting. *Mailing Add:* Col of Agr & Environ Sci Univ of Calif Davis CA 95616

CLAYTON, ANTHONY BROXHOLME, b Solihull, Eng, Jan 14, 40; m 63; c 4. ORGANIC CHEMISTRY. *Educ:* Univ Aston, ARIC, 62; Univ Birmingham, PhD(org chem), 65. *Prof Exp:* Res assoc, Cornell Univ, 65-67; res chemist, 67-78, SR RES CHEMIST, HERCULES INC, 78- *Mem:* Am Chem Soc; Royal Soc Chem. *Res:* Organic Fluorine chemistry; agricultural chemistry; polymer chemistry; general organic chemistry. *Mailing Add:* Hercules Inc Res Ctr Wilmington DE 19899

CLAYTON, CARL CLEVELAND, b Texarkana, Tex, May 23, 19; m 51; c 1. CHEMICAL ENGINEERING, COST ENGINEERING. *Educ:* Univ Tex, BS, 42. *Prof Exp:* Chem engr, 42-44, proj leader, 46-51, group leader econ eval, 53-66, SR PROJ ENGR, DEVELOP DEPT, PPG INDUSTS, CORPUS CHRISTI, 66- *Mem:* Am Asn Cost Engrs (secy, 63-66). *Res:* Computer applications in design and cost estimation of chemical plants. *Mailing Add:* PPG Industs PO Box 4026 Corpus Christi TX 78408

CLAYTON, CARLYLE NEWTON, b Liberty, SC, Dec 20, 12; m 35; c 2. PLANT PATHOLOGY. *Educ:* Clemson Agr Col, BS, 34; Univ Wis, PhD(plant path, physiol), 40. *Prof Exp:* Asst plant path, Univ Wis, 35-40; asst & assoc plant pathologist, SC Truck Exp Sta, 40-45; assoc prof, 45-50, prof, 50-80, EMER PROF PLANT PATH, NC STATE UNIV, 80- *Mem:* AAAS; Am Phytopath Soc. *Res:* Fruit diseases. *Mailing Add:* Dept of Plant Path NC State Univ Raleigh NC 27607

CLAYTON, CLIVE ROBERT, b Croydon, Eng, Oct 26, 49. CORROSION SCIENCE, ELECTRON SPECTROSCOPY. *Educ:* Univ Surrey, BSc, 73, PhD(surface chem), 76. *Prof Exp:* Res assoc, 76-78, ASST PROF MAT SCI, STATE UNIV NY, STONY BROOK, 78- *Mem:* Electrochem Soc; Inst Metallurgists. *Res:* Corrosion of metals and alloys; electron spectroscopy; surface analysis; modification of surface properties of metals and alloys by ion implantation. *Mailing Add:* Dept of Mat Sci & Eng State Univ NY Stony Brook NY 11794

CLAYTON, DALE LEONARD, b Harrisville, Mich, Apr 16, 39; m 61; c 2. ZOOLOGY. *Educ:* Andrews Univ, BA, 62; Loma Linda Univ, MA, 64; Mich State Univ, PhD(zool), 68. *Prof Exp:* Teaching asst biol sci, Mich State Univ, 64-67, dir human biol labs, 67-69, from instr to asst prof physiol, 67-69, asst prof, 70-77, prof biol, Walla Walla Col, 77-81; PROF BIOL & CHMN, DEPT BIOL, SOUTHWESTERN ADVENTIST COL, KEENE, TEX, 81- *Concurrent Pos:* Vis prof, Philippine Union Col, 78-80. *Mem:* AAAS; Int Soc Chronobiol; Sigma Xi; Animal Behav Soc. *Res:* Physiological basis of animal behavior, especially the interaction of internal circadian rhythms, homeostatic mechanisms, development rates and external variables of photoperiod, twilight, temperature and other environmental perturbations. *Mailing Add:* Dept of Biol Walla Walla Col College Place WA 99324

CLAYTON, DAVID WALTON, b Leicester, Eng; m 55; c 3. ORGANIC CHEMISTRY, WOOD CHEMISTRY. *Educ:* Univ London, BSc, 45, MSc, 51; Cambridge Univ, BA, 50, PhD(org chem), 53. *Prof Exp:* Res asst chem, Brit Leather Mfrs Res Asn, London, 45-48; Nat Res Coun Can fel, 53-55; sr scientific officer, Radiochem Ctr, United Kingdom Atomic Energy Authority, Amersham, Eng, 55-58; res chemist, 58-68, dir process res div, 68-76, asst dir res, 77-79, DIR RES, PULP & PAPER RES INST CAN, 79- *Concurrent Pos:* Mem, Task Force Biotechnol, Ministry State Sci & Technol, Ottawa, 80-81. *Mem:* Royal Soc Chem; Chem Inst Can; Am Chem Soc; Can Pulp & Paper Asn. *Res:* Chemistry of alkaline pulping; chemistry of pulp bleaching; carbohydrate and wood chemistry. *Mailing Add:* PO Box 358 24 Westwood Dr Hudson PQ J0P 1H0 Can

CLAYTON, DONALD DELBERT, b Shenandoah, Iowa, Mar 18, 35. ASTROPHYSICS, NUCLEAR PHYSICS. *Educ:* Southern Methodist Univ, BS, 56; Calif Inst Technol, MS, 59, PhD(physics), 62. *Prof Exp:* Res fel physics, Calif Inst Technol, 61-63; asst prof space sci, 63-65, from assoc prof to prof physics & space sci, 65-75, A H BUCHANAN PROF ASTROPHYS, RICE UNIV, 75- *Concurrent Pos:* Vis fel, Inst Theoret Astron, Cambridge, UK, 67-72; mem panel astrophys & relativity, astron & physics surv comt, Nat Res Coun, 70-; Fulbright fel, 80. *Honors & Awards:* George Darwin lectr, Royal Astron Soc, 81. *Mem:* Fel Am Phys Soc; Meteoritical Soc; Am Astron Soc. *Res:* Nucleosynthesis; space science; stellar evolution; geochemistry; cosmology; origin of solar system. *Mailing Add:* Dept of Space Physics & Astron Rice Univ Houston TX 77001

CLAYTON, EUGENE DUANE, b Ravena, Nebr, Mar 20, 23; m 47; c 3. NUCLEAR ENGINEERING, PHYSICS. *Educ:* Whitman Col, BA, 47; Univ Ore, MS, 49, PhD(physics), 52. *Prof Exp:* Res physicist appl res reactors, Gen Elec Co, 51-56, supvr reactor lattice physics, 56-57, supvr critical mass physics, 57-65; mgr criticality res & anal, 65-81, MGR CRITICAL MASS LAB, BATTELLE-NORTHWEST, 81- *Concurrent Pos:* Res assoc prof, Dept Nuclear Eng, Univ Wash, 64-78. *Honors & Awards:* Nuclear Criticality Safety Achievement Award, Am Nuclear Soc. *Mem:* Fel Am Nuclear Soc; Am Phys Soc. *Res:* Criticality measurements and studies; nuclear criticality safety in fuel recycle operations; criticality safety evaluations; techniques for criticality prevention and control; fissionability and criticality of actinide elements; anomalies of nuclear criticality. *Mailing Add:* Battelle-Northwest Div Battelle Blvd Richland WA 99352

CLAYTON, FRANCES ELIZABETH, b Texarkana, Tex, Nov 6, 22. GENETICS. *Educ:* Tex State Col Women, BA, 44; Univ Tex, MA, 47, PhD(zool, genetics), 51. *Prof Exp:* Teacher, high sch, Ark, 44-45; tutor & fel, Univ Tex, 45-50; instr zool, Univ Ark, 50-51 & Univ Tex, 51-52, Hite fel, 52-53, res scientist, Genetics Found, 53-54; from asst prof to assoc prof, 54-62, PROF ZOOL, UNIV ARK, FAYETTEVILLE, 62- *Concurrent Pos:* Vis colleague, Univ Hawaii, 63-64. *Mem:* Soc Exp Biol & Med; Am Soc Zoologists; Genetics Soc Am; Am Genetic Asn; Am Soc Cell Biol. *Res:* Developmental and irradiation genetics; cytogenetics in Drosophila. *Mailing Add:* Dept Zool SE 632 Univ of Ark Fayetteville AR 72701

CLAYTON, FRED RALPH, JR, b Knoxville, Tenn, Dec 22, 40; m 62; c 1. ANALYTICAL CHEMISTRY, INORGANIC CHEMISTRY. *Educ:* Univ Tenn, BS, 66, PhD(chem), 72. *Prof Exp:* Chem technician nuclear res, Oak Ridge Nat Lab, Union Carbide Nuclear Co, 59-62; process engr nylon prod, Firestone Synthetic Fibers Co, Firestone Tire & Rubber Co, 64-66; asst prof chem, 71-76, ASSOC PROF CHEM, FRANCIS MARION COL, 76- *Mem:* Am Chem Soc; Sigma Xi. *Res:* Electroanalytical chemistry in non-aqueous solvents; environmental analysis in waste water systems; surfactant and detergent analysis and synthesis. *Mailing Add:* Dept of Chem & Physics PO Box F7500 Florence SC 29501

CLAYTON, GLEN TALMADGE, b Elmo, Ark, Jan 30, 29; m 50; c 2. PHYSICS. *Educ:* Univ Ark, BS, 53, MS, 54; Univ Mo, PhD, 60. *Prof Exp:* Instr physics, Univ Ark, 53-54; asst prof, William Jewell Col, 54-56; instr, Univ Mo, 56-58; res assoc, Argonne Nat Lab, 58-60; from asst prof to prof, Univ Ark, Fayetteville, 60-72; PROF PHYSICS & DEAN SCH SCI & MATH, STEPHEN F AUSTIN STATE UNIV, 72- *Mem:* Am Asn Physics Teachers; Am Phys Soc. *Res:* X-ray; neutron diffraction; electronics. *Mailing Add:* Sch of Sci & Math Stephen F Austin State Univ Nacogdoches TX 75961

CLAYTON, HARRY HENDRICKS, JR, b Lewisville, Ark, Oct 30, 17; m 46; c 2. AERONAUTICAL ENGINEERING. *Educ:* Univ Ark, BSME, 41. *Prof Exp:* Proj engr exhaust flame damping, US Air Force, 41-42, field proj engr jet aircraft, 43-45, tech asst to chief test engr, Muroc Air Force Base, 46-48, chief eng lab, Flight Test Ctr, 49-53, spec asst to dir nuclear systs, Wright Air Develop Ctr, Convair Plant, Tex, 53-57; head test opers, Hughes Aircraft Co, NMex, 58-61, sr tech staff asst, Tucson Eng Lab, 61-66, mgr proj mgt staff, 66-68; PRES & GEN MGR, IOTA ENG, INC, 68- *Mem:* Am Inst Aeronaut & Astronaut; Am Mgt Asn. *Res:* Aeromechanical engineering; propulsion; aircraft; missiles; rockets. *Mailing Add:* IOTA Eng Inc 1735 E Ft Lowell Rd Tucson AZ 85719

CLAYTON, J(OE) T(ODD), b Etowah, Tenn, Oct 2, 24; m 46; c 3. FOOD ENGINEERING & TECHNOLOGY. *Educ:* Univ Tenn, BSAE, 49; Univ Ill, MS, 51; Cornell Univ, PhD, 62. *Prof Exp:* Asst agr eng, Univ Ill, 50-51, instr, 51-54, asst prof, 55-57; asst prof, Univ Conn, 54-55; assoc prof, 57-61, PROF AGR ENG, UNIV MASS, AMHERST, 61-, HEAD DEPT FOOD & AGR ENG, 66- *Concurrent Pos:* NSF fel, Cornell Univ, 60-62; vis prof, Univ Reading, 70-71; NSF-NATO sr fel sci, Univ Reading & Nat Col Food Technol, Eng, 71; Japan Soc Prom Sci fel, Univ Tokyo, 81. *Mem:* AAAS; Am Soc Agr Engrs; Int Soc Biometeorol; Inst Food Technol; NY Acad Sci. *Res:* Design of food production and preservation structures and processes; food and biological engineering; engineering properties of food and other biological materials. *Mailing Add:* Dept Food Eng Univ Mass Amherst MA 01002

CLAYTON, JAMES WALLACE, b New Westminster, BC, Nov 4, 33; m 57; c 4. BIOCHEMISTRY. *Educ:* Univ BC, BA, 55; Univ Sask, PhD(phys & org chem), 62. *Prof Exp:* Chemist wood pulp bleaching, Res Div, MacMillan & Bloedel, Ltd, BC, 56-58 & cereal protein chem, Grain Res Lab, Bd Grain Comnrs, Can, 62-66; RES SCIENTIST, FRESHWATER INST, CAN DEPT FISHERIES & OCEANS, FISHERIES & MARINE SERV, 67- *Mem:* Chem Inst Can; Can Biochem Soc. *Res:* Protein chemistry of freshwater fish; genetics of fish proteins and enzymes; population genetics; systematics and evolution of freshwater fishes. *Mailing Add:* Freshwater Inst 501 University Crescent Winnipeg MB R3T 2N6 Can

CLAYTON, JOE EDWARD, b Tillar, Ark, Sept 17, 32; m 52; c 3. AGRICULTURAL ENGINEERING. *Educ:* Univ Ark, BS(agr) & BS(agr eng), 59; Clemson Univ, MS, 60. *Prof Exp:* Agr engr, Allis-Chalmers Mfg Co, 59; AGR RES ENGR, USDA, 60- *Mem:* Am Soc Agr Engrs. *Res:* Design and field testing of harvesting and farm processing machinery. *Mailing Add:* Sugarcane Harvesting Res Unit PO Box 758 Belle Glade FL 33430

CLAYTON, JOHN CHARLES (HASTINGS), b Pittston, Pa, June 15, 24; m 68. PHYSICAL INORGANIC CHEMISTRY. *Educ:* St Joseph's Col, Philadelphia, BS, 49; Univ Pa, MS, 50, PhD(chem), 53. *Prof Exp:* Asst chem, Univ Pa, 52, fel, 53-54; sr res chemist, 54-81, FEL SCIENTIST, BETTIS ATOMIC POWER LAB, WESTINGHOUSE ELEC CORP, 81- *Mem:* AAAS; Am Chem Soc; Am Ceramic Soc; Am Nuclear Soc; Sigma Xi; Am Soc Metals. *Res:* Inorganic chemistry of solids; physical and inorganic chemistry of nuclear materials; thermodynamics and material properties. *Mailing Add:* Bettis Atomic Power Lab Westinghouse Elec Corp PO Box 79 West Mifflin PA 15122

CLAYTON, JOHN MARK, b Kevil, Ky, Aug 6, 45; m 70; c 3. MEDICINAL CHEMISTRY, MEDICAL RESEARCH. *Educ:* Tenn Technol Univ, BS, 68; Univ Tenn, PhD(pharmaceut sci), 71. *Prof Exp:* Res assoc drug design, Dept Chem, Pomona Col, 71-72; res biologist chem carcinogenesis, Nat Ctr Toxicol Res, Food & Drug Admin, 72-73; clin res assoc, 74-75, dir clin & regulatory serv, 75-78, VPRES QUAL CONTROL & CLIN & REGULATORY SERV, CONSUMER OPERS-HQ, SCHERING-PLOUGH CO, 78- *Concurrent Pos:* Asst prof pharmacol, Col Med, Univ Ark, 73-77; asst prof molecular biol, Col Pharm, Univ Tenn, 74. *Mem:* Acad Pharmaceut Sci; Am Chem Soc; Am Acad Dermat; NY Acad Sci; AAAS. *Res:* Quantitative structure-activity relationship approach to drug design; contact dermatitis; evaluations of sunscreens. *Mailing Add:* Plough Inc 3030 Jackson Ave Memphis TN 38151

CLAYTON, JOHN WESLEY, JR, b Philadelphia, Pa, Sept 1, 24. TOXICOLOGY, RESPIRATORY PHYSIOLOGY. *Educ:* Wheaton Col, AB, 48; Univ Pa, AM, 50, PhD(parasitol), 54. *Prof Exp:* Toxicologist, Haskell Lab, E I du Pont de Nemours & Co, Inc, 54-60, asst dir labs, 60-69; dir environ sci lab, Hazleton Labs, TRW Inc, 69-71; dir toxicol ctr, Univ Wis, 71-73; chief toxicol br & dir health effects div, US Environ Protection Agency, 73-74; PROF PHARMACOL, TOXICOL, MICROBIOL & DIR TOXICOL PROG, UNIV ARIZ, 74- *Concurrent Pos:* Mem tech adv bd, State Air Pollution Control Bd, Va, 70-71 & policy bd, Nat Ctr Toxicol Res, 73-74; consult, Wis Dangerous Substances Bd, 72-73, Reese & Schluechter, Ill, 72-73, Kennecott Copper Corp, 74- & Food & Drug Admin, 74-; mem sci adv bd, Food & Drug Admin; mem adv bd, Inhalation Toxicol Res Inst, Electronic Resources Develop Agency; mem ed bd, Am Indust Hyg Asn, 67-; mem ed bd, Soc Toxicol, 69-, chmn tech comt, 70-71. *Mem:* Am Indust Hyg Asn; Soc Toxicol. *Res:* Toxicology of fluorocarbons, including cardiac effects; action of fluoro-olefins on renal function; pyrolysis products of fluoropolymers. *Mailing Add:* Toxicol Prog Biol Sci W Univ of Ariz Tucson AZ 85721

CLAYTON, NEAL, b Ripley, Miss, Aug 23, 13; m 40; c 1. SEISMOLOGY, GEOPHYSICS. *Educ:* Miss Col, BA, 34; La State Univ, MS, 37. *Prof Exp:* Eng trainee, Schlumberger Well Surv, Tex, 37; seismic helper, Humble Oil Co, 37, seismic computer, 37-39 & seismic Explor, Inc, 40-41; assoc physicist, US Navy, 42-43; seismic observer, Magnolia Petrol Co, 43-44; seismic party chief, NAm Geophys Co, 44-46 & Repub Explor Co, 46-51; asst mgr domestic opers, Century Geophys Corp, 51-54; pres & supvr, Liberty Explor Co, 54-56; mem staff & dist geophysicist, Sohio Petrol Co, La, 56-60; supvr, Index Explor Co, Tex, 60-61; Gulf Coast geophysicist, Cosden Petrol Co, 61-64; CONSULT GEOPHYSICIST, 64- *Mem:* Soc Explor Geophys; Am Asn Petrol Geologists. *Res:* Application of seismology to exploration for oil and gas; geophysical prospecting. *Mailing Add:* PO Box 3637 Corpus Christi TX 78404

CLAYTON, PAULA JEAN, b St Louis, Mo, Dec 1, 34; m 58; c 3. PSYCHIATRY. *Educ:* Univ Mich, Ann Arbor, BS, 56; Washington Univ, MD, 60. *Prof Exp:* Intern, St Luke's Hosp, St Louis, 60-61; asst resident & chief resident psychiat, Barnes & Renard Hosps, St Louis, 61-65; from instr to assoc prof psychiat, 65-74, PROF PSYCHIAT, SCH MED, WASHINGTON UNIV, 74- *Concurrent Pos:* Consult psychiatrist, Malcolm Bliss Ment Health Ctr, St Louis, 72- & dir training & res, 75; dir, Barnes & Renard Hosp Psychiat Inpatient Serv, 75-81; PROF & HEAD, DEPT PSYCHIAT, UNIV MINN, 81- *Mem:* Fel Am Psychiat Asn; Psychiat Res Soc; Asn Res Nerv Ment Dis; Am Psychopath Asn; Soc Biol Psychiat. *Res:* Studies dealing with nosology, course and treatment of patients with psychiatric diagnosis; also the symptomatology and course of normal bereavement. *Mailing Add:* Dept of Psychiat Univ Minn Box 393 Mayo Minneapolis MN 55455

CLAYTON, RAYMOND BRAZENOR, b Manchester, Eng, Sept 16, 25; m 62; c 2. BIOCHEMISTRY, ENDOCRINOLOGY. *Educ:* Univ Manchester, BSc, 49, MSc, 50, PhD(chem), 52. *Prof Exp:* Res fel org chem, Univ Manchester, 52-53; res fel biochem, Univ Chicago, 53-54, res fel chem, Harvard Univ, 54-55; Imp Chem Indust fel, Oxford Univ, 55-56; res dir, Manchester Cancer Res Trust Fund, 56-58; res fel chem, Harvard Univ, 59-63; assoc prof, 63-68, PROF BIOCHEM, DEPT PSYCHIAT & BEHAV SCI, STANFORD UNIV. *Concurrent Pos:* Hon lectr, Univ Manchester, 56-58; estab investr, Am Heart Asn, 60-65. *Mem:* AAAS; Am Soc Biol Chemists; Endocrine Soc; Am Soc Zoologists; Royal Soc Chem. *Res:* Steroid biosynthesis; comparative aspects of steroid and terpenoid metabolism; genetics of steroid hormone metabolism and hormonal effects; action of steroid hormones in the central nervous system. *Mailing Add:* Dept of Psychiat & Behav Sci Stanford Univ Stanford CA 94305

CLAYTON, ROBERT ALLEN, b Milwaukee, Wis, Nov 21, 22; m 47; c 3. BIOCHEMISTRY. *Educ:* Univ Wis, BS, 49, MS, 51, PhD(biochem), 53. *Prof Exp:* Instr, Univ Wis, 52-53; asst prof biochem, Med Sch, George Washington Univ, 53-56; res assoc, Am Tobacco Co, 56-57, sr res assoc, 57-58, head biochem sect, 59; head, Fundamental Food Res Dept, Gen Mills, Inc, 59-61 & Explor Food Res Dept, 61-63, dir food sci activity, 64-67; dir res, Anheuser-Busch Inc, 67-75; PRES, ROBERT A CLAYTON & ASSOCS, 75- *Mem:* Am Chem Soc; Inst Food Technologists; Am Asn Cereal Chemists. *Res:* Industrial biochemistry and food science. *Mailing Add:* 1370 Forest Ave Kirkwood MO 63122

CLAYTON, ROBERT NORMAN, b Hamilton, Ont, Mar 20, 30; m 71; c 1. GEOCHEMISTRY. *Educ:* Queen's Univ, Ont, BSc, 51, MS, 52; Calif Inst Technol, PhD(chem), 55. *Prof Exp:* Res fel geochem, Calif Inst Technol, 55-56; asst prof geochem, Pa State Univ, 56-58; from asst prof to assoc prof chem, 58-66, master phys sci col div, assoc dean col & assoc dean phys sci, 69-72, chmn, Dept Geophys Sci, 76-79, PROF CHEM & GEOPHYS, UNIV CHICAGO, 66- *Concurrent Pos:* Guggenheim fel, 64-65; Sloan fel, 64-66. *Honors & Awards:* NASA Excep Sci Achievement Medal, 77; George P Merrill Award, Nat Acad Sci, 80; Goldschmidt Medal, Geochem Soc, 81. *Mem:* AAAS; fel Am Geophys Union; fel Meteoritical Soc; fel Am Acad Arts & Sci; fel Royal Soc Can. *Res:* Natural variations of stable isotope abundances. *Mailing Add:* Enrico Fermi Inst Univ of Chicago Chicago IL 60637

CLAYTON, RODERICK KEENER, b Tallin, Estonia, Mar 29, 22; US citizen; m 44; c 2. BIOPHYSICS. *Educ:* Calif Inst Technol, BS, 47, PhD(physics, biol), 51. *Prof Exp:* Merck fel, Stanford Univ, 51-52; assoc prof physics, US Naval Post Grad Sch, 52-57; NSF sr fel, 57-58; sr biophysicist, biol div, Oak Ridge Nat Lab, 58-62; vis prof microbiol, Dartmouth Col Med Sch, 62-63; sr investr, C F Kettering Res Lab, 63-66; PROF PLANT BIOL & APPL & ENG PHYSICS, CORNELL UNIV, 66- *Concurrent Pos:* Lalor fel, Woods Hole Marine Biol Lab, 55; consult, Firestone Res & Develop Lab, 56-57. *Mem:* Nat Acad Sci; Am Soc Biol Chemists; Am Acad Arts & Sci; Soc Gen Physiol; Am Soc Plant Physiol. *Res:* Physical aspects of photosynthesis; biochemistry of photosynthetic bacteria. *Mailing Add:* Ithaca NY

CLAYTON, WILLIAM HOWARD, b Dallas, Tex, Aug 16, 21; c 2. PHYSICAL OCEANOGRAPHY. *Educ:* Bucknell Univ, BSc, 49; Tex A&M Univ, PhD(phys oceanog), 56. *Prof Exp:* Instr physics, Bucknell Univ, 47-49; asst, Ohio State Univ, 49 & Univ NMex, 50; asst oceanog & meterorol, 50-51, oceanog, 51-54, assoc & instr math, 54-56, micrometeorologist & prin investr oceanog & meteorol res for US Air Force & US Army, 56-58, from asst prof to assoc prof, 58-65, dir micrometeoral res, 58-61, provost & dean, Col Marine Sci & Maritime Resources, 74-77, PROF OCEANOG & METEOROL, TEX A&M UNIV, 65-, DEAN, COL GEOSCI, 71-, PRES, 79- *Concurrent Pos:* Vis prof, Univ Hawaii, 63-64; pres, Moody Col, 77-79. *Mem:* Am Meteorol Soc; Am Geophys Union. *Res:* Micrometeorology; numerical analysis; water level variations; air-sea interchange; oceanographic and meteorological instrumentation; machine computational methods. *Mailing Add:* Tex A&M Univ PO Box 1675 Galveston TX 77553

CLAYTON-HOPKINS, JUDITH ANN, b Santa Monica, Calif, Sept 17, 39; c 1. ENDOCRINOLOGY. *Educ:* Univ Calif, Los Angeles, BA, 60, MA, 63, PhD(zool), 66. *Prof Exp:* Staff physiologist, Worcester Found Exp Biol, 68-70; res assoc, Dept Biol Sci & Dept Nutrit Sci, Univ Conn, Storrs, 70-71, asst prof physiol, 71-72; DIR, RADIOISOTOPE/ENDOCRINE LAB, DEPT PATH & LAB MED, ST FRANCIS HOSP & MED CTR, HARTFORD, 72-; ASST PROF LAB MED, HEALTH CTR, UNIV CONN, FARMINGTON, 73-; MEM STAFF, ABBOTT LABS, CHICAGO, 81- *Concurrent Pos:* Res assoc NIH grant, Harvard Med Sch & Beth Israel Hosp, Boston, 67-68; consult, Automation Med Lab Sci Rev Comt, NIH, 73-77; consult radioimmunoassay, Bur Med Devices & Diag Prod, Food & Drug Admin, 76-79; ed, Selected Methods Clin Chem, Am Asn Clin Chemists, 74-; chief oncofelt antigen & endocrine physiol, Ctr Dis Contrl, Atlanta, Ga, 80-81. *Mem:* Am Soc Zool; Endocrine Soc; NY Acad Sci; Am Physiol Soc; Am Asn Clin Chem. *Res:* Radioimmunochemistry; biochemical and molecular mechanisms of hormone action. *Mailing Add:* Dept Path & Lab Med 114 Woodland St Hartford CT 06105

CLAYTOR, THOMAS NELSON, b Tulsa, Okla, Aug 17, 49; m 69; c 1. ACOUSTIC LEAK DETECTION, ACOUSTIC NOISE ANALYSIS. *Educ:* Okla State Univ, BS, 71; Purdue Univ, MS, 73, PhD(physics), 76. *Prof Exp:* SCIENTIST, ARGONNE NAT LAB, 77- *Mem:* Am Phys Soc; Inst Elec & Electronics Engrs; Sigma Xi. *Res:* Acoustic instrumentation for processes related to energy production; measurements and modeling of the ultrasonic properties of metals and composite materials; development of signal processing techniques for acoustic and ultrasonic noise analysis. *Mailing Add:* Argonne Nat Lab B 308 9700 S Cass Ave Argonne IL 60439

CLAZIE, RONALD N(ORRIS), b Oakland, Calif, Apr 17, 38; m 61; c 2. CHEMICAL ENGINEERING. *Educ:* Univ Calif, BS, 60, PhD, 67; Calif Inst Technol, MS, 61. *Prof Exp:* Process engr, Dow Chem Co, 61-63; asst, Univ Calif, 63-67; mgr chem process develop, 67-70, supvr chem prod, 70-71, mgr chem process eng, 71-73, mgr eng, Mat Div, 73-74, mgr eng, Wire & Cable Div, 74-76, mgr eng, Thermofit Div, 76-78, tech servs mgr, 78-79, tech mgr, AME Div, 79-81, MFG MGR, THERMOFIT DIV, RAYCHEM CORP, 81- *Mem:* Am Inst Chem Engrs; Soc Plastics Eng; Sigma Xi. *Res:* Product design and application of heat shrinkable plastic tubing and molded parts. *Mailing Add:* 300 Constitution Dr Menlo Park CA 94025

CLEALL, JOHN FREDERICK, b Birmingham, Eng, Feb 6, 34; m 56; c 2. ORTHODONTICS. *Educ:* Otago Univ, Dunedin, NZ, BDS, 56, MDS, 60, DDS, 64; FRCP, 67. *Prof Exp:* Prof & chmn orthod, Dept Orthod, Fac Dent & Dept Dent Sci, Fac Grad Studies & Res, Univ Man, 64-74; PROF & HEAD, DEPT ORTHOD, MED CTR, UNIV ILL, 74- *Concurrent Pos:* Dir res exec coordr, Eastman Dent Dispensary, 60-64; res assoc, Res Dept, Winnipeg Children's Hosp, 64-74. *Honors & Awards:* Milo Hellman Res Award, 64. *Mem:* Int Asn Dent Res; Am Asn Orthodontists. *Res:* Bone growth of the craniofacial complex, oral physiology, clinical research, including growth of the craniofacial region in humans and physiologic aspects of muscle function; computer-aided diagnostic systems and orthodontic appliance systems. *Mailing Add:* Dept Orthod Col Dent Univ Ill 801 S Paulina St Chicago IL 60612

CLEARE, HENRY MURRAY, b Dalton, Ga, Aug 5, 28; m 50; c 3. MEDICAL PHYSICS. *Educ:* Ga Inst Technol, BS, 51. *Prof Exp:* Physicist, 51-58, res physicist, 58-62, res assoc, 62-79, head, Radiography Lab, 64-78, SR RES ASSOC, RES LABS, EASTMAN KODAK CO, 79-, TECH ADV, BLACK & WHITE DIV, 78- *Concurrent Pos:* Clin prof, Dept Radiol, Univ Mo. *Mem:* Health Physics Soc. *Res:* Image-forming properties of medical and industrial radiographic systems; properties of quantum limited radiographic systems; photographic radiation dosimetry; photographic effects of radiations in space. *Mailing Add:* 291 Hemlock Trail Webster NY 14580

CLEARFIELD, ABRAHAM, b Philadelphia, Pa, Nov 9, 27; m 49; c 2. INORGANIC CHEMISTRY. *Educ:* Temple Univ, BA, 48, MA, 50; Rutgers Univ, PhD(phys chem, crystallog), 54. *Prof Exp:* Assoc chemist, Titanium Alloy Mfg Div, Nat Lead Co, 54-56, sr chemist, 56-58, asst chief chem res, 58-63; from asst prof to prof chem, Ohio Univ, 63-74; assoc prog dir thermodyn, NSF, 74-75; PROF CHEM, TEX A&M UNIV, 76- *Concurrent Pos:* Lectr, Niagara Univ, 57-60; consult, Bio-Rad Labs, Tizon Chem Co & Magnesium Elektron, Manchester, Eng, 75- *Mem:* Am Chem Soc; Am Crystallog Asn. *Res:* Chemistry of transition metals, especially titanium and zirconium; solid state chemistry; x-ray diffraction and crystal structure, inorganic ion exchangers; heterogeneous catalysis. *Mailing Add:* Dept of Chem Tex A&M Univ College Station TX 77843

CLEARY, EDWARD J(OHN), b Newark, NJ, June 16, 06; m 34; c 4. ENVIRONMENTAL ENGINEERING. *Educ:* Rutgers Univ, BS, 29, MS, 32, Civil Engr, 33. *Hon Degrees:* DSc, Rutgers Univ, 59; DEng, Rose-Hulman Inst Technol, 72. *Prof Exp:* Field engr, Utilities Power & Light Corp, Ill, 29-30; asst, Dept Sanit, Rutgers Univ, 31-34; exec ed, Eng News-Record, McGraw-Hill Publ Co, 35-49; exec dir & chief engr, Ohio River Valley Water Sanit Comn, 49-67, consult engr, 67-76; EMER PROF ENVIRON HEALTH, UNIV CINCINNATI, 76- *Concurrent Pos:* Lectr, Col Eng, NY Univ, 37-41; consult, Inst Inter-Am Affairs, 43-50, Ministry Water Econ, Fed Repub Ger, 59, Del River Basin Comn, 63, World Bank, 69- & US Army Med Res & Develop Command, 75-; lectr, Grad Sch Med, Univ Cincinnati, 55-67, adj prof environ health, 67-76; dir, Resources for the Future, Inc. *Honors & Awards:* Hemispheric Sanit Eng Award, Inter-Am Asn Sanit Eng, 54; Centennial Award, US Geol Surv. *Mem:* Nat Acad Eng; hon mem Am Pub Works Asn (pres, 52); hon mem Am Water Works Asn; hon mem Water Pollution Control Fedn; hon mem Am Soc Civil Engrs. *Res:* Sanitary engineering and water resources development, particularly the practice and administration of water pollution control. *Mailing Add:* 32088 Waterside Lane Westlake Village CA 91361

CLEARY, HAROLD J, b Boston, Mass, Dec 6, 29; m 62; c 2. MATERIALS ENGINEERING. *Educ:* Mass Inst Technol, BS, 54; Rensselaer Polytech Inst, PhD(mat eng), 67. *Prof Exp:* Metallurgist, Nuclear Metals, Inc, 54-57 & Mass Steel Treating Corp, 58-62; ENGR, BETHLEHEM STEEL CORP, 67- *Mem:* Am Soc Metals; Nat Asn Corrosion Engrs. *Res:* Effects of composition and structure of steel alloys on electrolytic corrosion properties; microelectrode techniques; electrochemistry of palladium-hydrogen diffusion electrode. *Mailing Add:* RD 2 Coopersburg PA 18036

CLEARY, JAMES WILLIAM, b Evanston, Ill, Apr 13, 26; m 60; c 4. ORGANIC CHEMISTRY, POLYMER CHEMISTRY. *Educ:* Loyola Univ, Ill, BS, 50; State Col Wash, MS, 53, PhD, 56. *Prof Exp:* Sr exp aide agr chem, State Col Wash, 51-53, asst chem, 53-55; res chemist, 56-68, SR RES CHEMIST, PHILLIPS PETROL CO, 68- *Mem:* AAAS; Am Chem Soc. *Res:* Peppermint oil; a-ketobutyrolactones; synthesis and modification of synthetic rubber; sulfur compounds; polyolefins; polymerization catalysts; condensation polymers; polyamides; polyesters; polyvinyl pyridines; polyphenylene sulfides; polymer blends. *Mailing Add:* 1215 S Dewey Ave Bartlesville OK 74003

CLEARY, LAURENCE TWOMEY, b Andover, Mass, 23; m 47; c 4. TEXTILES, CHEMISTRY. *Educ:* Tufts Col, BS, 47; Inst Textile Technol, MS, 49; Columbia Univ, MA, 52, PhD(chem eng), 54. *Prof Exp:* Res engr, synthetic fiber process develop, 53-59, sr res engr & group supvr, 59, res supvr, 59-63, tech serv rep, 63-68, tech serv specialist, 69-79, SR TECH SERV SPECIALIST, E I DU PONT DE NEMOURS & CO, 79- *Res:* Solution properties of surface active agents; fire retardant investigations of cellulose structures; synthetic fiber process development; new process scouting; product improvement and development. *Mailing Add:* 323 Spalding Rd Wilmington DE 19803

CLEARY, MARGOT PHOEBE, b Lawrence, Mass, Mar 8, 48. NUTRITIONAL BIOCHEMISTRY. *Educ:* Regis Col, BA, 70; Columbia Univ, MS, 71, MPhil, 73, PhD(nutrit), 76. *Prof Exp:* Instr, Teachers Col, Columbia Univ, 76, NIH fel, Inst Human Nutrit, 76-78; ASST PROF, DEPT NUTRIT & FOOD SCI, DREXEL UNIV, 78- *Concurrent Pos:* Res assoc, Vassar Col, 77-78. *Res:* Adipose tissue development; obesity; nutrition and women; nutrition, growth and development. *Mailing Add:* Dept of Nutrit & Food Sci Nesbit Col Drexel Univ Philadelphia PA 19104

CLEARY, MICHAEL, b Co Mayo, Ireland, Aug 16, 50. APPLIED MECHANICS. *Educ:* Nat Univ Ireland, BE, 72; Brown Univ, MS, 74, PhD(mech solids & struct), 75. *Prof Exp:* Asst prof, 76-79, ASSOC PROF MECH ENG, MASS INST TECHNOL, 79- *Concurrent Pos:* Indust fel, Marathon Oil Co, 78. *Mem:* Am Soc Mech Engrs; Am Soc Civil Engrs; Soc Eng Sci; Soc Petrol Engrs; Int Soc Rock Mech. *Res:* Constitutive relations for porous fluid-infiltrated media; fracture in geophysical and geotechnical applications; material microstructural modelling; recovery of oil and gas; mining; structural analysis; energy and material resources. *Mailing Add:* Bedford Lane Lincoln MA 01773

CLEARY, PAUL PATRICK, b Watertown, NY, July 9, 41; m 63; c 2. MOLECULAR BIOLOGY, MEDICAL MICROBIOLOGY. *Educ:* Univ Cincinnati, BS, 65; Univ Rochester, MS, 69, PhD(microbiol genetics), 71. *Prof Exp:* ASSOC PROF MICROBIOL & PEDIAT, UNIV MINN, MINNEAPOLIS, 72- *Concurrent Pos:* Trainee biol sci, Univ Calif, Santa Barbara, 71-72. *Mem:* Am Soc Microbiol; Sigma Xi. *Res:* Regulation of the biotin gene cluster in Escherichia coli; regulation of the arabinose operon in Escherichia coli; genetic determinants for resistance to phagocytosis in group A streptococci; epidemiology of plasmid coded antibiotic resistance. *Mailing Add:* Dept of Microbiol Box 196 Univ of Minn Minneapolis MN 55400

CLEARY, ROBERT WILLIAM, b Lowell, Mass, Mar 4, 43. CIVIL ENGINEERING, CHEMICAL ENGINEERING. *Educ:* Univ Lowell, BS, 64; Univ Mass, MS, 68, PhD(chem eng), 71. *Prof Exp:* From lectr to asst prof civil eng, Princeton Univ, 72-79; PARTNER, HIDROSISTEM CONSULTS, SAO PAULO, BRAZIL, 79- *Concurrent Pos:* Proposal reviewer, Fed Environ Protection Agency, 73-74; mem, Water Qual Comt, Pinchot Inst Consortium, US Forestry Serv, 75- *Mem:* Am Soc Civil Engrs; Am Water Resources Asn; Am Geophys Union. *Res:* Groundwater pollution and hydrology; multi-dimensional, analytical modeling of mass and energy transport phenomena in water resources systems; ecosystem simulation; applied mathematics. *Mailing Add:* Dept of Civil Eng Princeton Univ Princeton NJ 08540

CLEARY, STEPHEN FRANCIS, b New York, NY, Sept 28, 36; m 59; c 3. BIOPHYSICS, RADIOBIOLOGY. *Educ:* NY Univ, BSChE, 58, PhD(biophys), 64; Univ Rochester, MS, 60. *Prof Exp:* Res engr sterio-specific polymers, Texus-US Chem Co, 58-59; teaching asst radiation biol, Inst Environ Med, NY Univ, 60-62, res assoc biophys, 62-64; from asst prof to assoc prof, 64-77, PROF BIOPHYS, MED COL VA, VA COMMONWEALTH UNIV, 77- *Concurrent Pos:* Consult, Environ Biophys Br, Nat Inst Environ Health Sci, NIH, 74- *Mem:* Biophys Soc; NY Acad Sci; Am Soc Photobiol. *Res:* Biological effects of non-ionizing radiation; lasers, light, microwave and radiofrequency radiation; effects of ionizing radiation on the mammalian eye; structural bonding forces in viruses. *Mailing Add:* Dept of Biophys Box 877 Med Col of Va Richmond VA 23298

CLEARY, TIMOTHY JOSEPH, b Philadelphia, Pa, Aug 8, 42; m 65; c 2. MEDICAL MICROBIOLOGY. *Educ:* Mt St Mary's Col, BS, 64; Univ Cincinnati, MS, 68, PhD(microbiol), 69; Am Bd Med Microbiol, dipl, 74. *Prof Exp:* Asst prof biol, Duquesne Univ, 69-71; fel, Ctr Dis Control, 71-73; asst prof path, 73-78, asst prof microbiol, 75-79, ASSOC PROF PATH, UNIV MIAMI, 78-, ASSOC PROF MICROBIOL, 79- *Mem:* Am Soc Microbiol; Sigma Xi. *Res:* Antimicrobial drug interactions and assays; immuno-assay procedures for the diagnosis of infectious diseases. *Mailing Add:* Dept of Path Univ of Miami Jackson Mem Hosp Miami FL 33161

CLEARY, WILLIAM JAMES, b St Louis, Mo, Dec 10, 43; m 67; c 1. MARINE GEOLOGY, SEDIMENTARY PETROLOGY. *Educ:* Southern Ill Univ, BA, 65; Duke Univ, MA, 67; Univ SC, PhD(geol), 72. *Prof Exp:* Geologist, Pan Am Petrol Corp, 67-68; asst prof, 72-76, ASSOC PROF GEOL, UNIV NC, WILMINGTON, 76- RES ASSOC MARINE SCI, 74- *Mem:* Geol Soc Am; Sigma Xi; Soc Econ Paleontologists & Mineralogists; Am Asn Geol Teachers. *Res:* Continental margin sedimentation off Southeastern United States; barrier island sedimentation; turbidite sedimentation on the Hatteras Abyssal Plain; deep sea sedimentation on the Balearic Abyssal Plain. *Mailing Add:* Dept of Marine Sci Box 3725 Univ of NC Wilmington NC 28406

CLEASBY, JOHN LEROY, b Madison, Wis, Mar 1, 28; m 50; c 3. SANITARY & CIVIL ENGINEERING. *Educ:* Univ Wis, BS, 50, MS, 51; Iowa State Univ, PhD(sanit eng), 60. *Prof Exp:* Inspection engr refinery construct, Standard Oil Co, Ind, 51-52; proj engr, Consoer, Townsent & Assoc, Ill, 52-54; from instr to assoc prof civil eng, 54-65, PROF CIVIL ENG, IOWA STATE UNIV, 65- *Honors & Awards:* G W Fuller Award, Am Water Works Asn, 78; Norman Medal, Am Soc Civil Engrs, 80. *Mem:* Am Water Works Asn; Water Pollution Control Fedn; Am Soc Civil Engrs; Nat Soc Prof Engrs. *Res:* Water treatment research for economy of plant design and operation, particularly sand and diatomite filtration, softening, disinfection and sedimentation. *Mailing Add:* Dept of Civil Eng Iowa State Univ Ames IA 50010

CLEATOR, IAIN MORRISON, b Edinburgh, Scotland, Oct 18, 39; m 61; c 3. SURGERY, MEDICINE. *Educ:* Univ Edinburgh, MBChB, 62; FRCS(E), 66; FRCS, 67; FRCS(C), 72; FACS, 74. *Prof Exp:* Resident surg, Edinburgh Teaching Hosps, 62-72; fel, 70-71; asst prof surg, 72-80, ASSOC PROF SURG, UNIV BC, 80-; DIR, GASTROINTESTINAL CLIN, ST PAUL'S HOSP, VANCOUVER, 74- *Concurrent Pos:* Clin instr surg, Univ Edinburgh, 68-72. *Mem:* Can Asn Gastroenterol. *Res:* Gastrointestinal hormones in relation to physiology, obesity, diabetes; peptic ulcer disease. *Mailing Add:* Dept of Surg 1081 Burrard Vancouver BC V6T 1W5 Can

CLEAVER, CHARLES E, b Paris, Ky, Mar 14, 38; m 59; c 3. MATHEMATICS. *Educ:* Eastern Ky Univ, BS, 60; Univ Ky, MS, 63, PhD(math), 68. *Prof Exp:* Instr math, Murray State Univ, 62-64, asst prof, 64-65; asst prof, 68-73, asst chmn math, 75-76, ASSOC PROF MATH, KENT STATE UNIV, 73-, ASST DEAN, COL ARTS & SCI, 76- *Mem:* Am Math Soc; Math Asn Am. *Res:* Operator theory in Banach spaces; functional analysis. *Mailing Add:* Dept of Math Kent State Univ Kent OH 44242

CLEAVER, FRANK L, b Palm, Pa, Feb 3, 25; m 53; c 2. MATHEMATICS. *Educ:* Pa State Univ, BS, 48; Univ Miami, MS, 55; Tulane Univ, PhD(math), 60. *Prof Exp:* Instr math, Tulane Univ, 55-60; asst prof, Univ Ky, 61-62; from asst prof to assoc prof, 60-66, PROF MATH, UNIV S FLA, 66- *Mem:* Am Math Soc; Math Asn Am. *Res:* Topology and geometry of numbers. *Mailing Add:* Dept of Math Univ of S Fla Tampa FL 33620

CLEAVER, JAMES EDWARD, b Portsmouth, Hants, Eng, May 17, 38; m 64. CANCER. *Educ:* St Catharine's Col, Cambridge Univ, BA, 61, PhD(radiobiol), 64. *Prof Exp:* Res fel neurosurg, Mass Gen Hosp, Boston & surg, Harvard Med Sch, 64-66; asst res biophysicist, lab radiobiol, 66-68, from asst prof to assoc prof radiobiol, 68-74, PROF RADIOL, SCH MED, UNIV CALIF, SAN FRANCISCO, 74- *Honors & Awards:* Research Award, Radiation Res Soc, 73. *Mem:* Radiation Res Soc; Photobiol Soc. *Res:* Effects of ultraviolet light on mammalian cells and mechanisms of recovery from radiation damage; dermatology; mutagenesis; xeroderma pigmentosum; radiobiology of tritium decays. *Mailing Add:* Lab of Radiobiol Univ of Calif Sch of Med San Francisco CA 94143

CLEAVES, DUNCAN WORSTER, b Bangor, Maine, Aug 23, 19; m; c 3. PHYSICAL CHEMISTRY. *Educ:* Brown Univ, BS, 40; Univ Calif, PhD(chem), 51. *Prof Exp:* Jr chemist, E I du Pont de Nemours & Co, 40-41; jr engr, Chile Explor Co, 41-44; jr chemist, Shell Develop Co, 44-46 & Int Minerals & Chem Corp, 46-48; asst, Univ Calif, 48-50; instr chem, Univ Ore, 50-51; sr res engr, Titanium Metals Corp, 51-56; assoc prof chem & physics, southern regional div, Univ Nev, 56-63; sr res scientist, astropower lab, Douglas Aircraft Co, Inc, 63-64; instr sci, high sch, 64-68; instr chem, Santa Rosa Jr Col, 68; PROF CHEM & MATH, CERRO COSO COMMUNITY COL, 68- *Mem:* AAAS. *Res:* Polymerization of alkenes in sulfuric acid; vacuum fusion analysis; lactam formation of glutamic acid. *Mailing Add:* Cerro Coso Community Col Ridgecrest CA 93555

CLEAVES, EMERY TAYLOR, b Easton, Pa, May 11, 36; m 60; c 4. GEOMORPHOLOGY, ENVIRONMENTAL GEOLOGY. *Educ:* Harvard Col, BA, 60; John Hopkins Univ, MA, 64, PhD(geog), 73. *Prof Exp:* Assoc geologist, 63-65, geologist IV, 65-73, asst dir, 73-80, DEP DIR & PRIN GEOLOGIST, MD GEOL SURV, 81- *Mem:* Fel Geol Soc Am. *Res:* Chemical weathering of crystalline rocks; role of chemical weathering in landform development; landform mapping and its application to environmental geology. *Mailing Add:* Md Geol Surv Johns Hopkins Univ Baltimore MD 21218

CLEBNIK, SHERMAN MICHAEL, b Lynn, Mass, Nov 15, 43. GLACIAL GEOLOGY. *Educ:* Ind Univ, MA, 67, Univ Mass, Amherst, BA, 65, PhD(geol), 75. *Prof Exp:* PROF EARTH SCI, EASTERN CONN STATE COL, 73- *Mem:* Geol Soc Am ; AAAS; Am Asn Univ Prof. *Res:* Glacial geology of eastern Connecticut. *Mailing Add:* Earth Sci Dept Eastern Conn State Col Willimantic CT 06226

CLEBSCH, ALFRED, JR, b Clarksville, Tenn, Jan 20, 21; m 48; c 2. HYDROGEOLOGY, HYDROLOGY. *Educ:* Univ Chicago, SB, 47, SM, 48. *Prof Exp:* Geologist mil geol, 49-54, hydrologist ground water, 54-73, REGIONAL HYDROLOGIST MGT, US GEOL SURV, 73- *Mem:* Geol Soc Am;· Am Geophys Union; AAAS. *Res:* Geothermal energy; ground disposal of radioactive wastes. *Mailing Add:* 50 Hoyt St Lakewood CO 80225

CLEBSCH, EDWARD ERNST COOPER, b Clarksville, Tenn, June 6, 29; m 56; c 3. PLANT ECOLOGY. *Educ:* Univ Tenn, AB, 55, MS, 57; Duke Univ, PhD(bot), 60. *Prof Exp:* Res assoc, 60-63, from asst prof to assoc prof bot, 63-75, PROF BOT & ECOL, UNIV TENN, KNOXVILLE, 75- *Mem:* Fel AAAS; Ecol Soc Am; Bot Soc Am; Asn Trop Biol. *Res:* Mineral cycling in Southern Appalachian ecosystems; radiation ecology; physiological ecology of Arctic-Alpine plants; flora and vegetation of Tennessee; mountain environments; ecology of the Aleutian Islands. *Mailing Add:* Dept of Bot Univ of Tenn Knoxville TN 37916

CLEEK, GEORGE KIME, b Warm Springs, Va, Aug 27, 26; m 48; c 3. CHEMISTRY. *Educ:* Va Polytech Inst, BS, 48. *Prof Exp:* Res chemist, Nitrogen Div, Allied Chem Corp, 48-55, res chemist, Tech Serv, 55-63, res chemist, Appln Res, 63-66, tech serv prod supvr, Plastics Div, 66-69; mgr res lab, Caradco Div, Scovill Mfg Co, 69-70; develop chemist, Chem Div, 70-73, mgr res & develop, Lab Resins Div, TECH SPECIALIST, GEORGIA PACIFIC CORP, 80- *Mem:* Am Chem Soc; Forest Prod Res Soc. *Res:* Ureaformaldehyde resins. *Mailing Add:* 2883 Miller Rd Decatur GA 30035

CLEEK, GIVEN WOOD, b Warm Springs, Va, Nov 6, 16; m 41; c 3. CHEMISTRY, GLASS TECHNOLOGY. *Educ:* George Washington Univ, BS, 54. *Prof Exp:* Lab apprentice, Nat Adv Comt Aeronaut, 35-36; lab apprentice, Nat Bur Standards, 36-41, glassworker, 46-49, technologist, 49-57, phys chemist, 58-67, res chemist, 67-73; RETIRED. *Concurrent Pos:* Consult, 74-80. *Honors & Awards:* Silver Medal, US Dept Commerce, 73. *Mem:* Am Chem Soc; Am Ceramic Soc; Optical Soc Am; Am Soc Test & Mat. *Res:* Development of special optical glasses having higher refractive indices and special dispersions; development of infrared transmitting glasses; determination of physical properties of glass as a function of chemical composition. *Mailing Add:* 421 Palmary Dr El Paso TX 79912

CLEELAND, CHARLES SAMUEL, b Jacksonville, Ill, Sept 23, 38; m 81; c 1. NEUROPSYCHOLOGY, PSYCHOLOGY. *Educ:* Wesleyan Univ, BS, 60; Wash Univ, PhD(psychol), 66. *Prof Exp:* Instr psychiat, Med Sch, Univ Mo, 64-65; from instr to asst prof, 66-72, ASSOC PROF NEUROL, MED SCH, UNIV WIS, MADISON, 72- *Concurrent Pos:* Consult, Dept Ment Health, State of Wis, 68- & Dept Corrections, 72- *Mem:* AAAS; Soc Psychophysiol Res; Soc Neurosci; Pavlovian Soc NAm. *Res:* Cancer pain, its impact and treatment; behavioral treatment in illness. *Mailing Add:* 600 Highland Ave Madison WI 53792

CLEERE, ROY LEON, b Madisonville, Tex, Dec 20, 05; m 31. PUBLIC HEALTH. *Educ:* Agr & Mech Col Tex, BS, 27; Univ Tex, MD, 29; Johns Hopkins Univ, MPH, 36; Am Bd Prev Med & Pub Health, cert, 50. *Prof Exp:* Intern, Kansas City Gen Hosp, 29-30; resident, Presby Hosp, 30-31; pvt pract, Denver, Colo, 31-35; exec dir, State Dept Pub Health, Colo, 35-74; asst prof pub health & lab diag, Sch Med, Univ Colo, Denver, 47-74; dir, Colo-Wyo Regional Arthritis Dept, 74-76; EXEC DIR, COLO DEPT PUB HEALTH, 76-; ASST CLIN PROF PREV MED & PUB HEALTH, UNIV COLO, 76- *Concurrent Pos:* Deleg, World Health Assembly, Geneva, 51. *Mem:* Fel Am Pub Health Asn; AMA. *Mailing Add:* 4210 E 11th Ave Denver CO 80220

CLEGG, DAVID JOHN, toxicology, teratology, see previous edition

CLEGG, FREDERICK WINGFIELD, b Atlanta, Ga, Oct 9, 44; div; c 1. COMPUTER SCIENCE, ELECTRICAL ENGINEERING. *Educ:* Oakland Univ, BS, 65; Stanford Univ, MS, 67, PhD(elec eng, comput sci), 70. *Prof Exp:* Develop engr eng software, Ford Motor Co, 67; res asst elec eng, Stanford Univ, 67-69, instr, 69-70; asst prof, Univ Santa Clara, 70-75; SECT MGR SOFTWARE RES & DEVELOP, HEWLETT-PACKARD CO, 75- *Concurrent Pos:* Consult various pvt & govt agencies, 67- *Mem:* Sigma Xi; Inst Elec & Electronics Engrs. *Res:* Software engineering; computer architecture; microprocessors; digital systems reliability. *Mailing Add:* Hewlett-Packard Co 11000 Wolfe Rd Cupertino CA 95014

CLEGG, JAMES S, b Aspinwall, Pa, July 27, 33; div; c 3. PHYSIOLOGY, BIOCHEMISTRY. *Educ:* Pa State Univ, BS, 57; Johns Hopkins Univ, PhD(biol), 61. *Prof Exp:* Res assoc biol, Johns Hopkins Univ, 61-62; asst prof zool, 62-64, assoc prof biol, 64-70, PROF BIOL, UNIV MIAMI, 70- *Concurrent Pos:* Wilson fel, 58-59; Fulbright sr res award, Univ London, 78. *Mem:* AAAS; Am Soc Zoologists; Am Soc Cell Biol. *Res:* Comparative biochemistry; mechanisms of cryptobiosis; properties and role of water in cellular metabolism; biophysics and biochemistry of dried but viable organisms. *Mailing Add:* Dept of Biol Univ of Miami Coral Gables FL 33124

CLEGG, JOHN C(ARDWELL), b Heber, Utah, Sept 19, 27; m 53; c 8. ELECTRICAL ENGINEERING. *Educ:* Univ Utah, BS, 49, MS, 54, PhD(elec eng, physics), 57. *Prof Exp:* Test engr, Gen Elec Co, 49-50, develop engr, 50-53; mem tech staff, Space Tech Labs, 57-61; from asst prof to assoc prof elec eng, 61-70, PROF ELEC ENG, BRIGHAM YOUNG UNIV, 70- *Concurrent Pos:* Consult, TRW Systs, 62- *Mem:* Inst Elec & Electronics Engrs; Am Soc Eng Educ; Sigma Xi; Nat Soc Prof Engrs. *Res:* Nonlinear control systems; high velocity projectiles; inertial instruments; ultra-high pressure; clinical instruments; power electronics. *Mailing Add:* 1785 N 1500 East Provo UT 84604

CLEGG, JOHN W(ILLIAM), b Atlanta, Ga, Feb 8, 16; m 49; c 3. CHEMICAL ENGINEERING. *Educ:* Ga Inst Technol, BS, 37; Univ Minn, PhD, 42. *Prof Exp:* Res chemist, Nylon Div, E I du Pont de Nemours & Co, Inc, 41-44; res engr, Battelle Mem Inst, 44-47, div chief, 47-53, mgr, Chem Eng Dept, 53-63; pres, North Star Res & Develop, 63-73; pres, Heat Transfer Res, Inc, 73-81; CONSULT CHEM ENGR, 81- *Mem:* Fel Am Inst Chem Engrs. *Res:* Chemical process development; research administration; heat transfer. *Mailing Add:* 1104 Kewen Dr San Marino CA 91108

CLEGG, MICHAEL TRAN, b Pasadena, Calif, Aug 1, 41; c 4. POPULATION GENETICS, EVOLUTION. *Educ:* Univ Calif, Davis, BS, 69, PhD(genetics), 72. *Prof Exp:* Res asst genetics, Univ Calif, Davis, 70-72; from instr to asst prof biol, Div Biol Med Sci, Brown Univ, 72-76; assoc prof bot, 76-80, PROF BOT & GENETICS, UNIV GA, 80- *Concurrent Pos:* Prin investr, NSF grants, 74-79; assoc ed, Am Naturalist; Guggenheim Fel, 81-82. *Mem:* Soc Study Evolution (secy, 79-82); Genetics Soc Am; Am Soc Naturalists; Am Genetic Asn. *Res:* Dynamics of multilocus genetic systems; genetic demography of plant populations and selection component analysis; biochemical variation in populations. *Mailing Add:* Dept Bot Univ Ga Athens GA 30602

CLEGG, ROBERT EDWARD, b Providence, RI, July 29, 14; m 41; c 3. BIOCHEMISTRY. *Educ:* Univ RI, BS, 36; NC State Col, MS, 39; Iowa State Univ, PhD(phys chem, nutrit), 48. *Prof Exp:* Assoc prof, 48-54, PROF BIOCHEM, BIOCHEM AGR EXP STA, KANS STATE UNIV, 54- *Mem:* AAAS; Am Chem Soc; Am Soc Biol Chemists. *Res:* Hormone influence on lipoprotein level; application of trace techniques to biochemical problems; enzyme kinetics; in vivo protein formation. *Mailing Add:* Dept of Biochem Kans State Univ Manhattan KS 66506

CLEGG, THOMAS BOYKIN, b Emory University, Ga, Jan 6, 40; m 68. EXPERIMENTAL NUCLEAR PHYSICS. *Educ:* Emory Univ, BA, 61; Rice Univ, MA, 63, PhD(physics), 65. *Prof Exp:* Res assoc physics, Rice Univ, 65 & Univ Wis-Madison, 65-68; from asst prof to assoc prof, 68-76, PROF PHYSICS, UNIV NC, CHAPEL HILL, 76- *Concurrent Pos:* Staff mem, Triangle Univ Nuclear Lab, Durham, 68-; Fulbright grant, 75-76; vis physicist, Ctr Nuclear Res, Saclay, France, 75-76, Ctr Nuclear Res, Bruyeres-le-Chatel, France, 81; res assoc, Inst Fundamental Electronics, Univ Paris, 76. *Mem:* Am Phys Soc. *Res:* Elastic scattering of polarized protons and deuterons from nuclei; development of polarized ion beams for nuclear physics experiments. *Mailing Add:* Dept of Physics Phillips Hall Univ of NC Chapel Hill NC 27514

CLEGHORN, ROBERT ALLEN, b Cambridge, Mass, Oct 6, 04; m 32, 77; c 3. PSYCHIATRY. *Educ:* Univ Toronto, MD, 28; Aberdeen Univ, DSc(physiol), 32; FRC Psych, 71. *Prof Exp:* Jr rotating intern, Toronto Gen Hosp, 28-29; demonstr physiol, Aberdeen Univ, 29-32; demonstr med & asst attend physician, Toronto Gen Hosp, 33-46; from asst to prof psychiat, 46-64, prof & chmn dept, 64-70, EMER PROF PSYCHIAT, McGILL UNIV, 71-; MEM STAFF, PSYCHIAT DEPT, SUNNYBROOK HOSP, 78- *Concurrent Pos:* Dir therapeut res lab, Allan Mem Inst, 46-64, dir, 64-70, hon consult, 70-; res assoc, Harvard Univ Med Sch, 53-54; psychiatrist in chief, Royal Victoria Hosp, 64-70. *Mem:* Am Psychiat Asn; Can Physiol Soc; Can Med Asn; Can Psychiat asn; fel Royal Col Psychiatrists. *Res:* Physiology and clinical aspects of the adrenal cortex; clinical endocrinology; autonomic nervous system in adrenal insufficiency; shock and blood substitutes; physiological correlates and psychoanalytic studies in psychosomatic states and psychopharmacology; study of schizo-affective psychoses and lithium therapy. *Mailing Add:* Psychiat Dept Sunnybrook Hosp 2075 Bayview Ave Toronto ON M4N 3M5 Can

CLELAND, CHARLES FREDERICK, b Indianapolis, Ind, July 1, 39; m 78. PLANT PHYSIOLOGY. *Educ:* Wabash Col, BA, 61; Stanford Univ, PhD(plant physiol), 67. *Prof Exp:* NSF fels, 66-68; Milton Fund res grant, Harvard Univ, 68; asst prof biol, Harvard Univ, 68-73, lectr, 73-74; vis asst prof bot, Univ NC, Chapel Hill, 74-75; PLANT PHYSIOLOGIST, RADIATION BIOL LAB, SMITHSONIAN INST, 75- *Concurrent Pos:* NSF res grants, 69 & 72; prof lectr, dept biol, George Washington Univ, 79-; NATO grant, 78. *Mem:* Bot Soc Am; Am Soc Plant Physiologists; AAAS; Am Inst Biol Sci; Japanese Soc Plant Physiologists. *Res:* Plant growth and development, especially hormonal basis for the photoperiodic control of flowering; biology and physiology of Lemnaceae. *Mailing Add:* 9506 Culver Kensington MD 20895

CLELAND, FRANKLIN ANDREW, b St Francis, Kans, Oct 7, 28; m 56; c 2. CHEMICAL ENGINEERING. *Educ:* Tex A&M Univ, BS, 50; Princeton Univ, PhD(chem eng), 54. *Prof Exp:* Engr, Shell Develop Co, 54-62, supvr chem eng res, 62-63, supvr process eng, 63-66, dept head process develop, 66-67, mgr process develop, Synthetic Rubber Div, Shell Chem Co, 67-69, mgr tech dept, Polymer Div, 70-72, mgr chem eng dept, Shell Develop Co, 72-74, mgr physics & systs dept, 74-76, mgr process eng, chem, Shell Oil Co, 76-77, DIR CORP RES & DEVELOP ENG, SHELL DEVELOP CO, 77- *Mem:* Am Inst Chem Engrs; Am Chem Soc. *Res:* Coordination, planning and guidance of engineering research programs aimed at developing improved engineering procedures for use during process development, process design and mechanical design of oil and petrochemical processes. *Mailing Add:* Westhollow Res Ctr PO Box 1380 Houston TX 77001

CLELAND, GEORGE HORACE, b Pasadena, Calif, July 19, 21; m 53; c 1. ORGANIC CHEMISTRY. *Educ:* Occidental Col, BA, 42; Calif Inst Technol, PhD(chem), 51. *Prof Exp:* Res assoc, Nat Defense Res Comn, 43-45; res chemist org chem, Naval Ord Test Sta, 52-54; assoc prof, 54-70, PROF CHEM, OCCIDENTAL COL, 70- *Mem:* AAAS; Am Chem Soc. *Res:* Reactions of amino acids; reaction mechanisms. *Mailing Add:* Dept of Chem Occidental Col Los Angeles CA 90041

CLELAND, JOHN GREGORY, b Middlesboro, Ky, Feb 10, 46; m 69; c 1. SYNTHETIC FUELS, ENERGY SYSTEMS. *Educ:* Univ Tenn, BS, 70; Univ Ala, Huntsville, MS, 75; NC State Univ, PhD(mech eng), 81. *Prof Exp:* Naval architect, Charleston Naval Shipyard, 69; mech eng asst, US Army Missile Command, 70-72; res teaching asst, Univ Ala, Huntsville, 72-74; sr engr, Sperry Rand Corp, 73-75; SR ENGR & SECT HEAD, RES TRIANGLE INST, 75- *Concurrent Pos:* Consult, Univ Ala, Huntsville, 72-74. *Mem:* Am Inst Chem Eng. *Res:* Fossil energy systems experimentation and modeling; design of measurement devices; studies of industrial environmental problems and control technologies; management or projects and personnel. *Mailing Add:* Res Triangle Inst 807 Bacon St Durham NC 27703

CLELAND, JOHN W, b New Concord, Ohio, Oct 29, 21; m 47; c 2. EXPERIMENTAL SOLID STATE PHYSICS. *Educ:* Monmouth Col, BS, 43; Purdue Univ, MS, 49. *Prof Exp:* PHYSICIST, SOLID STATE DIV, OAK RIDGE NAT LAB, 49- *Honors & Awards:* Radiation Indust Award, Am Nuclear Soc, 79. *Mem:* Sigma Xi; Am Asn Crystal Growers; AAAS. *Res:* Electrical properties of semiconductors; radiation effects research; low temperature work, thermal properties; reactor research; crystal growth materials. *Mailing Add:* 7101 Stockton Dr Knoxville TN 37919

CLELAND, LAURENCE LYNN, b Defiance, Ohio, Oct 22, 39; m 61; c 1. ENGINEERING SCIENCES, PHYSICS. *Educ:* Purdue Univ, BS, 61, MS, 64, PhD(elec eng), 68. *Prof Exp:* Proj engr, Univ Calif, 63-64; asst prof, Purdue Univ, 68-69; group leader, 69-70, div leader, 70-71, dep dept head, 78-79, PROF MGR, NUCLEAR SAFETY, LAWRENCE LIVERMORE LAB, UNIV CALIF, 79- *Concurrent Pos:* Consult, Midwest Appl Sci Corp, 66-69, CTS Microelectronics Inc, 69; NSF grant, 64-68. *Mem:* Sr mem Inst Elec & Electronics Engrs; AAAS; Am Nuclear Soc. *Res:* System and management sciences applied to energy issues; nuclear safeguards, waste management, safety analyses and methodology development. *Mailing Add:* Lawrence Livermore Nat Lab Univ Calif Livermore CA 94550

CLELAND, ROBERT E, b Baltimore, Md, Apr 30, 32; m 57; c 2. PLANT PHYSIOLOGY. *Educ:* Oberlin Col, AB, 53; Calif Inst Technol, PhD(biochem), 57. *Prof Exp:* USPHS fels plant physiol, Lund, 57-58 & King's Col, London, 58-59; asst prof bot, Univ Calif, Berkeley, 59-64; assoc prof, 64-68, PROF BOT, UNIV WASH, 68- *Concurrent Pos:* Guggenheim fel, Univ Leeds, 67-68. *Mem:* Am Soc Plant Physiol (pres, 74-75); Bot Soc Am. *Res:* Mechanism of auxin action; cell extension. *Mailing Add:* Dept of Bot Univ of Wash Seattle WA 98195

CLELAND, ROBERT LINDBERGH, b St Francis, Kans, June 10, 27; m 56; c 4. PHYSICAL CHEMISTRY. *Educ:* Agr & Mech Col Tex, BS, 48; Mass Inst Technol, SM, 51, PhD(phys chem), 56. *Prof Exp:* Res asst chem, Mass Inst Technol, 48-50, res employee, div indust coop, 50-52, res asst, 52-56; res assoc chem, Cornell Univ, 56-58; from asst prof to assoc prof, 60-71, PROF CHEM, DARTMOUTH COL, 71- *Concurrent Pos:* Fulbright res scholar, State Univ Leiden, 58-59; USPHS spec res fel, Retina Found, Mass, 59-60; res fel, Univ Uppsala, 68; vis prof, Univ Strasbourg, 68-69; assoc ed, Macromolecules, 74-76; guest researcher, Univ Uppsala, 77-78. *Mem:* AAAS. *Res:* Physical chemistry of solutions of ionic polysaccharides. *Mailing Add:* Dept of Chem Dartmouth Col Hanover NH 03755

CLELAND, WILFRED EARL, b St Francis, Kans, Aug 10, 37; m 66; c 2. ELEMENTARY PARTICLE PHYSICS. *Educ:* Agr & Mech Col Tex, BS, 59; Yale Univ, MS, 60, PhD(physics), 64. *Prof Exp:* Instr physics, Yale Univ, 63-64; vis scientist, Europ Orgn Nuclear Res, Geneva, 64-67; from asst prof to assoc prof physics, Univ Mass, Amherst, 67-70; assoc prof, 70-78, PROF PHYSICS, UNIV PITTSBURGH, 78- *Concurrent Pos:* NATO fel, 64-65; NSF fel, 65-66. *Mem:* Am Phys Soc. *Res:* Studies of interactions of elementary particles using electronic techniques at high energy accelerators, including muonium, lambda decay, muon tridents and K Mesons systems. *Mailing Add:* Dept of Physics Univ Pittsburgh 4200 Fifth Ave Pittsburgh PA 15260

CLELAND, WILLIAM WALLACE, b Baltimore, Md, Jan 6, 30; m 67. BIOCHEMISTRY. *Educ:* Oberlin Col, AB, 50; Univ Wis, MS, 53, PhD(biochem), 55. *Prof Exp:* NSF fel, Univ Chicago, 57-59; from asst prof to assoc prof, 59-66, PROF BIOCHEM, UNIV WIS-MADISON, 66- *Mem:* Am Chem Soc; Am Soc Biol Chemists; Am Acad Arts & Sci. *Res:* Use of enzyme kinetics to deduce enzymatic mechanisms. *Mailing Add:* Dept of Biochem Univ of Wis Madison WI 53706

CLELLAND, RICHARD COOK, b Camden, NY, Aug 23, 21; m 63; c 2. APPLIED STATISTICS. *Educ:* Hamilton Col, BA, 44; Columbia Univ, AM, 49; Univ Pa, PhD(statist), 56. *Prof Exp:* Instr math, Syracuse Univ, 46-47; instr, Hamilton Col, 50-53; from asst prof to assoc prof statist, 56-66, chmn dept statist & opers res, 66-71, actg dean, 71-72, assoc dean, Wharton Sch, 75-81, PROF STATIST, UNIV PA, 66-, ATG ASSOC PROVOST, 81- *Mem:* Fel Am Statist Asn; Inst Math Statist; Opers Res Soc Am; Inst Mgt Sci. *Res:* Experimental design; statistical methodology; operations research. *Mailing Add:* Dept of Statist & Opers Res E-111 Dietrich Hall Univ of Pa Philadelphia PA 19104

CLEM, JOHN RICHARD, b Waukegan, Ill, Apr 24, 38; m 60; c 2. THEORETICAL SOLID STATE PHYSICS, SUPERCONDUCTIVITY. *Educ:* Univ Ill, Urbana, BS, 60, MS, 62, PhD(physics), 65. *Prof Exp:* Res assoc physics, Univ Md, 65-66; vis res fel, Tech Univ Munich, 66-67; from asst prof to assoc prof, 67-75, PROF PHYSICS, IOWA STATE UNIV, 75- *Concurrent Pos:* Consult, Argonne Nat Lab, 71-76; vis staff mem, Los Alamos Sci Lab, 71-; Fulbright-Hayes sr res scholar, Inst Solid State Res, Juelich, Ger, 74-75; consult, Brookhaven Nat Lab, 80-81. *Mem:* AAAS; Am Phys Soc; Sigma Xi. *Res:* Theoretical research in solid state physics, low-temperature solid state physics; electrodynamic and thermal properties of superconductors subjected to electrical currents and magnetic fields. *Mailing Add:* Dept of Physics Iowa State Univ Ames IA 50011

CLEM, LESTER WILLIAM, b Frederick, Md, June 23, 34; m 57; c 5. IMMUNOLOGY, IMMUNOCHEMISTRY. *Educ:* Western Md Col, BS, 56; Univ Del, MS, 60; Univ Miami, PhD(microbiol), 63. *Prof Exp:* From instr to assoc prof microbiol, 64-71, prof immunol & med microbiol, Col Med, Univ Fla, 71-79; PROF MICROBIOL & CHMN DEPT, UNIV MISS MED CTR, 79- *Concurrent Pos:* Res assoc immunol, Variety Children's Res Found, Miami, 63-66; WHO consult immunol, India, 70; instr physiol course, Marine Biol Lab, Woods Hole, 72 & 74. *Mem:* AAAS; Am Asn Immunol; Soc Exp Biol & Med; Am Asn Zool; Am Soc Microbiol. *Res:* Phylogenetic development of immunological competency and immunoglobulin structure and function; cholera immunity. *Mailing Add:* Dept of Immunol & Med Microbiol Univ of Fla Gainesville FL 32601

CLEM, WILLIAM HENRY, b Champaign, Ill, Dec 8, 32; m 59; c 1. ENDODONTICS, ORAL MICROBIOLOGY. *Educ:* Northwestern Univ, DDS, 56; Univ Wash, MSD, 65. *Prof Exp:* Instr endodont, Dent Sch, Northwestern Univ, 60-63; asst prof, Sch Dent, Univ Wash, 65-67; ASSOC PROF ENDODONT, COL DENT, UNIV ILL, 67- *Concurrent Pos:* Nat Inst Dent Res fel, Univ Wash, 63-65; res assoc & consult, USPHS Hosp, Seattle, 65-; consult, Coun Dent Educ, Am Dent Asn, 74- & Am Bd Endodont, 78-; pvt pract endodont, 66- *Mem:* Am Dent Soc; Am Soc Microbiol; Am Asn Endodont. *Res:* Antibacterial factors in saliva; role of peroxidase; glutamic acid isotope transport in lactobacillus; dental caries in rat; pathogenic potential of root canal bacteria, streptococci; post-treatment endodontic pain. *Mailing Add:* 111 N Wabash Ave Suite 2022 Chicago IL 60602

CLEMANS, GEORGE BURTIS, b Huntington, NY, May 11, 38; m 61. ORGANIC CHEMISTRY, BIOCHEMISTRY. *Educ:* Va Polytech Inst, BS, 60; Duke Univ, MA, 63, PhD(chem), 64. *Prof Exp:* Res assoc chem, Ind Univ, 64-65; res assoc chem, Univ Ark, 65-66, asst prof, 66-74, assoc prof, 74-76, PROF CHEM, BOWLING GREEN STATE UNIV, 76- *Res:* Stereospecific reactions of dicyclopentadiene derivatives; synthesis of diterpenes. *Mailing Add:* Dept of Chem Bowling Green State Univ Bowling Green OH 43403

CLEMANS, KERMIT GROVER, b Adrian, NDak, Apr 14, 21; m 44; c 3. MATHEMATICAL STATISTICS. *Educ:* Jamestown Col, BS, 43; Univ Minn, MA, 48; Univ Ore, PhD(math statist), 53. *Prof Exp:* Instr math, Willamette Univ, 48-50 & Univ Ore, 50-53; math & statist consult, US Naval Test Sta, 53-59; dean div sci & technol, 60-67, PROF MATH STUDIES, SOUTHERN ILL UNIV, EDWARDSVILLE, 59- *Mem:* Am Math Soc; Math Asn Am; Am Soc Qual Control. *Res:* Nonparametric statistics; extreme value statistics. *Mailing Add:* Fac of Math Studies Southern Ill Univ Edwardsville IL 62025

CLEMANS, STEPHEN D, b Gloversville, NY, Apr 1, 39; m 61; c 2. STRUCTURAL CHEMISTRY. *Educ:* Rensselaer Polytech Inst, BS, 61, MS, 64, PhD(org chem), 67. *Prof Exp:* Asst res chemist, 63-69, res chemist, 69-76, sr res chemist & group leader, 76-77, SECT HEAD ANAL CHEM, STERLING WINTHROP RES INST, RENSSELAER, 77- *Concurrent Pos:* Fel, Harvard Univ, 67. *Mem:* Am Chem Soc. *Res:* Pharmaceutical research; structure determination by spectroscopic methods of compounds of pharmaceutical interest. *Mailing Add:* Box 149 RD 4 Troy NY 12180

CLEMENCE, SAMUEL PATTON, b Knoxville, Tenn, May 23, 39; m 67; c 2. CIVIL ENGINEERING. *Educ:* Ga Inst Technol, BS, 62, MS, 64, PhD(civil eng), 73. *Prof Exp:* Res asst civil eng, Ga Inst Technol, 63-64; Lieutenant construct, US Navy Civil Eng Corps, 64-69; res asst civil & geotech eng, Ga Inst Technol, 69-73; asst prof, Civil Eng Dept, Univ Mo, Rolla, 73-77; ASSOC PROF CIVIL & GEOTECH ENG, CIVIL ENG DEPT, SYRACUSE UNIV, 77-, CHMN DEPT, 82- *Concurrent Pos:* Expert witness, Construct contractors, 77-; consult, O'Brien & Gere, Dames & Moore, & Mobil Oil, 77-; prin investr res contracts, Niagara Mohawk Power Corp, 80- *Mem:* Am Soc Civil Engrs; Int Soc Soil Mech & Found Eng; Asn Eng Geologists; Sigma Xi; Int Soc Rock Mech. *Res:* Uplift capacity of helical anchors; bearing capacity of drilled piers; hydraulic fracturing of soils; hazard waste contaminents in clay. *Mailing Add:* 132 Hinds Hall Dept Civil Eng Syracuse Univ Syracuse NY 13210

CLEMENCY, CHARLES V, b New York, NY, Feb 12, 29; m 54; c 3. GEOCHEMISTRY, CLAY MINERALOGY. *Educ:* Polytech Inst Brooklyn, BS, 50; NY Univ, MS, 58; Univ Ill, PhD(geol), 61. *Prof Exp:* Chemist, Sylvania Elec Prod Inc, 53-58; asst prof, 61-67, ASSOC PROF GEOL, STATE UNIV NY BUFFALO, 67- *Concurrent Pos:* Ford Found for study grant, Univ Sao Paulo, Brazil, 69; sr exchange scientist, Nat Acad Sci, Czech, 74. *Mem:* Fel Mineral Soc Am; AAAS; Geochem Soc; Clay Minerals Soc. *Res:* Analytical geochemistry; rock weathering; low temperature water-rock interactions. *Mailing Add:* Dept of Geol Sci State Univ of NY Buffalo NY 14226

CLEMENS, ANTON HUBERT, b Gerolstein, Ger, Nov 19, 28; m 52; c 3. BIOINSTRUMENTATION. *Educ:* Polytech Inst Bingen, MScEE, 51. *Prof Exp:* Europ res rep, Picker Int Corp, Switz, 59-62, consult res & develop nuclear instr patient monitoring, 62-65; dir instrument res & develop, Ames Co Div, 65-72, V PRES LIFE SCI INSTRUMENTS, MILES LABS, INC, 72- *Mem:* Asn Advan Med Instrumentation; NY Acad Sci; Ger Soc Nuclear Med; Ger Soc Data Processing & Automation Med. *Res:* Patient monitoring; nuclear medicine systems; spectrophotometry; laboratory automation; research instrumentation for endocrinology and metabolism; artificial endocrine pancreas. *Mailing Add:* 3435 Calumet Ave Elkhart IN 46514

CLEMENS, CARL FREDERICK, b Elkland, Pa, Nov 24, 24; m 53; c 8. CHEMISTRY. *Educ:* Ohio Univ, BS, 55; Univ Rochester, MBA, 66. *Prof Exp:* Asst biochem, Univ Rochester, 52-53; jr chemist, Haloid Co, 55-56, chemist, Haloid-Xerox, Inc, 56-58, proj chemist, 58-59; sr proj chemist, 59-64, scientist, 64-66, mgr instrumental anal, 66-67, mgr mat appln & develop, 67-69, tech prog mgr, Advan Develop Dept, 69-72, technol prog mgr, Xerographic Technol Dept, 72-77, mgr mats processing area, 77-79, MGR ENVIRON HEALTH & SAFETY AREA, XEROX CORP, 79- *Mem:* Am Chem Soc; Am Mgt Asn; fel Am Inst Chemists. *Res:* Xerography; application of polymer science to xerographic materials; polymer characterization and analytical chemistry; technical management. *Mailing Add:* 1119 Lake Rd Ontario NY 14519

CLEMENS, CHARLES HERBERT, b Dayton, Ohio, Aug 15, 39; m 66; c 2. MATHEMATICS. *Educ:* Holy Cross Col, AB, 61; Univ Calif, Berkeley, PhD(math), 66. *Prof Exp:* From asst prof to assoc prof math, Columbia Univ, 70-75; assoc prof, 75-76, PROF MATH, UNIV UTAH, 76- *Mem:* Am Math Soc. *Res:* Complex geometry. *Mailing Add:* Dept of Math Univ of Utah Salt Lake City UT 84112

CLEMENS, DAVID HENRY, b Newton, Mass, Nov 8, 31; m 53; c 3. ORGANIC CHEMISTRY. *Educ:* Middlebury Col, AB, 53; Univ Wis, PhD(chem), 57. *Prof Exp:* Head ion exchange & pollution control synthesis, 57-75, proj leader coatings res, 75-76, MGR POLYMERS & RESINS SYNTHESIS, ROHM AND HAAS CO, 76- *Mem:* Am Chem Soc; Royal Soc Chem. *Res:* Organic synthesis; vinyl polymers; plasticizers; ion exchange; adsorbents; membrane processes; organic coatings; chemicals for textiles, leather, paper, non-wovens and chemical specialties. *Mailing Add:* Spring House Res Labs Rohm and Haas Co Spring House PA 19477

CLEMENS, G(EORGE) W(ILLIAM), JR, electronic & quality engineering, deceased

CLEMENS, HOWARD PAUL, b Arthur, Ont, May 31, 23; nat US; m; c 4. ZOOLOGY. *Educ:* Univ Western Ont, BS, 46, MS, 47; Ohio State Univ, PhD(zool), 49. *Prof Exp:* Asst zool, Univ Western Ont, 47; from instr to assoc prof, 49-72, PROF ZOOL, UNIV OKLA, 72-, MEM GRAD FAC, 80- *Mem:* AAAS; Am Soc Limnol & Oceanog; Am Fisheries Soc; Am Soc Zoologists; Am Soc Ichthyologists & Herpetologists. *Res:* Limnology; fishery biology; aquatic invertebrates; fish endocrines. *Mailing Add:* Dept of Zool Univ of Okla Norman OK 73019

CLEMENS, JAMES ALLEN, b Windsor, Pa, Feb 4, 41; m 64; c 2. NEUROENDOCRINOLOGY, NEUROPHYSIOLOGY. *Educ:* Pa State Univ, BS, 63, MS, 65; Mich State Univ, PhD(physiol), 68. *Prof Exp:* RES ASSOC, ELI LILLY & CO, 69- *Concurrent Pos:* Nat Inst Neurol Dis & Blindness fel, Univ Calif, Los Angeles, 68-69. *Mem:* AAAS; Endocrine Soc; Soc Neurosci; Int Soc Psychoneuroendocrinol. *Res:* Neural mechanisms that control anterior pituitary hormone secretion. *Mailing Add:* Dept of Physiol Res Lilly Res Labs Indianapolis IN 46206

CLEMENS, JON K(AUFMANN), b Sellersville, Pa, May 10, 38; m 59; c 3. VIDEO SYSTEMS, ELECTRICAL ENGINEERING. *Educ:* Goshen Col, BA, 60; Mass Inst Technol, BS & MS, 63, PhD(elec eng), 65. *Prof Exp:* Mem tech staff, 65-75, head, Signal Systs Res Group, 75-80, DIR, VIDEO-DISC SYSTS RES, DAVID SARNOFF RES CTR, RCA CORP, 80- *Honors & Awards:* Edward Rhine Prize, 80. *Mem:* Inst Elec & Electronics Engrs; Sigma Xi. *Res:* Video disc; image processing; digital recording of video, audio and data; communication transmission and video systems. *Mailing Add:* David Sarnoff Res Ctr RCA Corp Rte 1 Princeton NJ 08540

CLEMENS, LAWRENCE MARTIN, b Chicago, Ill, Nov 14, 37; m 63. ORGANIC CHEMISTRY. *Educ:* Ill Inst Technol, BS, 59; Carnegie Inst Technol, PhD(org chem), 64. *Prof Exp:* NIH fel chem, Univ Notre Dame, 63-64; res chemist, Archer Daniels Midland Co, 64-69; res specialist, 69-80, RES MGR, MINN MINING & MFG CO, 80- *Mem:* Am Chem Soc. *Res:* Ultraviolet curing coatings; polymer chemistry; product development and applied chemistry. *Mailing Add:* Minn Mining & Mfg Co 3M Ctr Bldg 236-1 St Paul MN 55101

CLEMENS, STANLEY RAY, b Souderton, Pa, May 11, 41; m 62; c 4. MATHEMATICS. *Educ:* Bluffton Col, AB, 63; Ind Univ, MA, 65; Univ NC, PhD(math), 68. *Prof Exp:* Instr, Univ NC, 67-68; asst prof, 68-76, ASSOC PROF MATH, ILL STATE UNIV, 76- *Mem:* Am Math Soc; Math Asn Am. *Res:* Topology. *Mailing Add:* Dept of Math Ill State Univ Normal IL 61761

CLEMENS, WILLIAM ALVIN, b Berkeley, Calif, May 15, 32; m 55; c 4. PALEONTOLOGY. *Educ:* Univ Calif, Berkeley, BA, 54, PhD(zool), 60. *Prof Exp:* NSF fel, 60-61; from asst prof & asst cur to assoc prof zool & assoc cur fossil higher vert, Univ Kans, 61-67; assoc prof, 67-71, PROF PALEONT, UNIV CALIF, BERKELEY, 71- *Concurrent Pos:* NSF fel, 68-69; John Simon Guggenheim Found fel, 74; Alexander von Humboldt fel, 78-79; vis prof, Miller Inst, 82- *Mem:* Soc Syst Zool; Soc Vert Paleont; Geol Soc Am; Palaeont Asn; Zool Soc London. *Res:* Evolution of Mesozoic and Cenozoic mammals. *Mailing Add:* Dept Paleont Univ Calif Berkeley CA 94720

CLEMENS, WILLIAM BRYSON, b Milton, Pa, Sept 28, 16; m 42. BACTERIOLOGY. *Educ:* Bucknell Univ, BS, 37, MS, 38. *Prof Exp:* High sch head dept sci, Pa, 38-42; sr supvr, Acid Dept, Pa Ord Works, US Rubber Co, 42-43, supvr acid area 3, Kankakee Ord Works, 43-45; high sch head dept sci, Ga, 45-46; from instr to prof bact, 46-73, chmn dept sci, 58-61, sci bldg coordr, 62-64, exec chmn div & chmn dept biol, 64-68, EMER PROF BACT, STATE UNIV NY COL CORTLAND, 73- *Mem:* AAAS; Am Nature Study Soc; Nat Asn Biol Teachers; Nat Sci Teachers Asn; Am Forestry Asn. *Res:* Subject matter and methods used in introductory bacteriology courses in colleges and universities. *Mailing Add:* E River Rd RD 1 Cortland NY 13045

CLEMENST, JAMES LEE, b Salt Lake City, Utah, Apr 17, 50. HYDROMETALLURGY, EXTRACTIVE METTALLURGY. *Educ:* Univ Utah, BA, 74; Wash State Univ, MS, 77; Univ Idaho, MS, 79, PhD(metall eng), 81. *Prof Exp:* Res asst, Wash State Univ, 74-76, Univ Idaho, 76-81; RES ENGR, CONOCO INC, 81- *Mem:* Am Inst Mining Metall & Petrol Engrs. *Res:* Chemical desulfurization of coal; mathematical modelling of metallurgical reactions and the leaching of uranium, vanadium and phosphorus from phosphate ore. *Mailing Add:* Conoco Inc PO Box 1267 MRB 50 Ponca City OK 74603

CLEMENT, ANTHONY CALHOUN, b Spartanburg, SC, Nov 24, 09; m 59. EMBRYOLOGY. *Educ:* Univ SC, BS, 30; Princeton Univ, AM, 33, PhD(biol), 35. *Prof Exp:* From asst prof to prof biol, Col Charleston, 35-49; assoc prof, 49-56, prof, 56-77, EMER PROF BIOL, EMORY UNIV, 77- *Concurrent Pos:* Guggenheim fel, 54-55; prog dir develop biol, NSF, 58-59, mem adv panel develop biol, 59-62; trustee, Marine Biol Lab, Woods Hole, 64-72; vis assoc, Calif Inst Technol, 67. *Mem:* AAAS; Am Soc Zoologists; Soc Develop Biol. *Res:* Molluscan embryology; cytoplasmic localization and embryonic determination; deletion experiments. *Mailing Add:* Dept of Biol Emory Univ Atlanta GA 30322

CLEMENT, CHRISTINE MARY (COUTTS), b Chatham, Ont; m 75; c 1. ASTRONOMY. *Educ:* Univ Toronto, BSc, 63, MA, 64, PhD(astron), 67. *Prof Exp:* Fel astron, Asiago Astrophys Observ, Italy, 67-68; res assoc, David Dunlap Observ, 69-74, LECTR ASTRON, UNIV TORONTO, 74- *Mem:* Am Astron Soc; Can Astron Soc; Am Asn Variable Star Observers; Royal Astron Soc Can. *Res:* Study of variable stars in globular clusters. *Mailing Add:* Dept of Astron Univ of Toronto Toronto ON M5S 1A1 Can

CLEMENT, DUNCAN, b Pittsfield, Mass, Oct 22, 17. SCIENCE ADMINISTRATION. *Educ:* Mt St Mary's Col, Md, BS, 40; Harvard Univ, MA, 42, PhD(bot), 48. *Prof Exp:* Econ botanist, Atkins Garden, Harvard Univ, Cuba, 48-53, in chg, 49-53, dir, 53-60, dir, US, 61-63; consult, Off Int Sci Activities, NSF, 62-63, prog dir, 63-64, head sci liaison staff, Costa Rica, 64-68, prof assoc, Off Int Progs, 68-74; sci attache, US Embassy, Madrid, Spain, 74-79; RETIRED. *Res:* International science cooperation. *Mailing Add:* 620 SW 70th Ave Pembroke Pines FL 33023

CLEMENT, GERALD EDWIN, b Austin, Minn, Nov 5, 35; m 57; c 2. CLINICAL CHEMISTRY. *Educ:* Univ Minn, BA, 57; Purdue Univ, PhD(org chem), 61; Am Bd Clin Chemists, cert, 75. *Prof Exp:* NIH fel, Northwestern Univ, 61-63; asst prof org chem, Harpur Col, 63-68; assoc prof chem, Kenyon Col, 68-74; CLIN CHEMIST, ALLENTOWN SACRED HEART HOSP, 74- *Concurrent Pos:* Fel, Hahnemann Hosp, 72-74. *Mem:* Am Asn Clin Chemists; Am Chem Soc; Am Soc Biol Chemists. *Res:* Organic reaction mechanisms, especially acid, base and enzyme catalysis. *Mailing Add:* Allentown Sacred Heart Hosp 1200 S Cedar Crest Blvd Allentown PA 18105

CLEMENT, JACOB JAMES, b Chicago, Ill, Feb 28, 44. RADIOBIOLOGY. *Educ:* St Mary's Col, BA, 66; Roosevelt Univ, MS, 69; Univ NC, MSPH, 70, PhD(radiol health), 73. *Prof Exp:* Instr, 73-75, asst prof radiobiol, Dept Therapeut Radiol, Univ Minn Hosps, 75-78; STAFF SCIENTIST, ARTHUR D LITTLE CO, 78- *Mem:* Radiation Res Soc; AAAS; Am Asn Cancer Res; Int Soc Study Xenobiotics. *Res:* Radiation effects on tumors and normal tissue; development of hypoxic cell radiosensitizers; combined chemotherapy and radiotherapy; characterization of radioprotectant compounds. *Mailing Add:* Arthur D Little Co Inc Acorn Park Cambridge MA 02140

CLEMENT, JOHN REID, JR, b East Spencer, NC, Apr 14, 21; m 45; c 2. PHYSICS. *Educ:* Catawba Col, AB, 43. *Prof Exp:* Proj physicist low temp thermomet & calorimet, 46-53, head, Cryogenic Properties, Matter & cryogenic Devices Sect, 53-59, asst head, Cryogenics Br, 59-62, head, 62-69, assoc supt, Solid State Div, 69-74, head, High Magnetic Field Facil, 74-80, SR RES PHYSICIST, US NAVAL RES LAB, 80- *Mem:* Fel Am Phys Soc; Sigma Xi. *Res:* High voltage electricity; low temperature thermometry and calorimetry; cryogenic devices; high magnetic fields. *Mailing Add:* 3410 Weltham St Suitland MD 20746

CLEMENT, JOSEPH D(ALE), b Kalamazoo, Mich, Jan 7, 28; m 56; c 2. PHYSICS, NUCLEAR ENGINEERING. *Educ:* Western Mich Univ, BS, 49; Univ Wis, MS, 53, PhD(physics), 57. *Prof Exp:* Jr scientist, inst atomic res, Iowa State Univ, 49-52; sr scientist, Bettis Atomic Power Lab, Westinghouse Elec Corp, 57-59, group leader, Astronuclear Lab, 60-62; supvry engr reactor physics, Nuclear Div, Martin Co, 59-60; dept mgr nuclear eng, Nuclear Mat & Equip Corp, 62-65; assoc prof, 65-68, PROF NUCLEAR ENG, GA INST TECHNOL, 68- *Mem:* Am Phys Soc; Am Nuclear Soc. *Res:* Nuclear physics; interactions of neutrons with complex nuclei; nuclear engineering; reactor physics; shielding; radioisotope utilization; nuclear power economics. *Mailing Add:* Dept of Nuclear Eng Ga Inst of Technol Atlanta GA 30332

CLEMENT, MAURICE JAMES, b Vancouver, BC, Sept 11, 38; m 75; c 1. THEORETICAL ASTROPHYSICS. *Educ:* Univ BC, BSc, 60, MSc, 61; Univ Chicago, PhD(astrophys), 65. *Prof Exp:* From asst prof to assoc prof, 67-81, PROF ASTRON, UNIV TORONTO, 81- *Concurrent Pos:* Fel, Princeton Univ, 65-66; Nat Res Coun Can fel, 66-67. *Mem:* Am Astron Soc; Can Astron Soc; Int Astron Union. *Res:* Equilibrium and stability of rotating stars; differential rotation and meridian circulation in stars. *Mailing Add:* Dept of Astron Univ of Toronto Toronto ON M5S 1A7 Can

CLEMENT, ROBERT ALTON, b Brockton, Mass, Aug 12, 29; m 55; c 4. INDUSTRIAL ORGANIC CHEMISTRY. *Educ:* Mass Inst Technol, BS, 50; Univ Calif, Los Angeles, PhD(chem), 54. *Prof Exp:* Proj assoc chem, Univ Wis, 54-55; from instr to asst prof, Univ Chicago, 55-62; RES CHEMIST, E I DU PONT DE NEMOURS & CO, INC, 62- *Mem:* Am Chem Soc; Royal Soc Chem. *Res:* Synthetic methods in organic chemistry; polymer chemistry. *Mailing Add:* Cent Res & Develop Dept Exp Sta E I du Pont de Nemours & Co Inc Wilmington DE 19898

CLEMENT, STEPHEN LEROY, b Ventura, Calif, Aug 25, 44. ENTOMOLOGY. *Educ:* Univ Calif, Davis, BS, 67, MS, 72, PhD(entom), 76. *Prof Exp:* Fel & res entomologist pheromones, Univ Calif, Davis, 77; asst prof entom, Ohio Agr Res & Develop Ctr, Ohio State Univ, 77-81; RES ENTOMOLOGIST, BIOL CONTROL WEEDS, AGR RES SERV, USDA, ALBANY, CALIF, 81- *Concurrent Pos:* Environ Protection Agency grant pest mgt, Ohio Agr Res & Develop Ctr, 77-81. *Mem:* Entom Soc Am; Sigma Xi; AAAS. *Res:* Applied ecology with emphasis on insects and weeds; pollination ecology; aquatic entomology; pest management. *Mailing Add:* USDA Biol Control Weeds 1050 San Pablo Ave Albany CA 94706

CLEMENT, WILLIAM GLENN, b Denver, Colo, Apr 11, 31; m 52; c 2. GEOPHYSICS, ELECTRICAL ENGINEERING. *Educ:* Stanford Univ, BS, 56, PhD(geophys), 63. *Prof Exp:* Geophysicst, Pan Am Petrol Corp, Tex, 63-65, sr geophysicist, Res Lab, Okla, 65-68, staff res engr, 68-74, sr res engr, Amoco Prod Res Ctr, 74-76; MGR GEOPHYS RES, CITIES SERV OIL CO, 76- *Mem:* Soc Explor Geophys; Europ Asn Explor Geophys. *Res:* Application of communication theory to the analysis of seismic and potential field data. *Mailing Add:* Cities Serv Co Box 3908 4500 S 129th East Ave Tulsa OK 74102

CLEMENT, WILLIAM H, b Johnstown, Pa, Dec 17, 31; m 65; c 2. ORGANIC CHEMISTRY, ENVIRONMENTAL CHEMISTRY. *Educ:* Gettysburg Col, AB, 54; Univ Del, MS, 57, PhD(chem), 60. *Prof Exp:* Chemist, E I du Pont de Nemours & Co, 55 & Pittsburgh Plate Glass Co, 56-57; res chemist, Gulf Oil Corp, 59-62; asst prof chem, Waynesburg Col, 62-63; NSF fel, Univ Buffalo, 63; USDA fel, Univ Cincinnati, 63-65; asst prof, Ithaca Col, 65-70, prof, 70-71; res assoc environ sci, Rutgers Univ, 71-81; ENVIRON CONSULT, 81- *Mem:* Am Chem Soc; Sigma Xi. *Res:* Oxidation reactions and mechanisms; organometallics; catalysis; organic synthesis; environmental chemistry; water quality. *Mailing Add:* 1186 Wothington Heights Bl Worthington OH 43085

CLEMENT, WILLIAM MADISON, JR, b Rome, Ga, Dec 15, 28; m 50. GENETICS. *Educ:* Univ Ga, BSA, 50; Univ Calif, PhD, 58. *Prof Exp:* Lab technician agron, Univ Calif, 52-57; res geneticist, Forage & Range Br, Agr Res Serv, USDA, 58-65; ASSOC PROF CYTOL & CYTOGENETICS, VANDERBILT UNIV, 65-, DIR UNDERGRAD STUDIES, DEPT GEN BIOL. *Concurrent Pos:* Asst prof, Univ Minn, 61-65. *Mem:* Crop Sci Soc Am; Am Genetics Soc; Genetics Soc Can; Am Soc Naturalists. *Res:* Cytogenetics of medicago sativa and related species; chromosome structure. *Mailing Add:* Dept of Gen Biol Vanderbilt Univ Nashville TN 37240

CLEMENTE, CARMINE DOMENIC, b Penns Grove, NJ, Apr 29, 28; m 68. NEUROANATOMY. *Educ:* Univ Pa, AB, 48, MS, 50, PhD, 52. *Prof Exp:* From instr to assoc prof, 52-63, chmn dept, 63-73, PROF ANAT, SCH MED, UNIV CALIF, LOS ANGELES, 63-, DIR, BRAIN RES INST, 76- *Concurrent Pos:* Gianinni Found fel, 53-54; hon res assoc, Univ Col, Univ London, 53-54; consult, Vet Admin Hosp, Sepulveda, Calif & Martin Luther King Mem Hosp; ed, Gray's Anat & Exp Neurol; vis scientist & spec consult, NIH, 58; mem, Biol Stain Comn; mem subcomt neuropath, Nat Acad Sci; mem med adv bd, Bank of Am-Gianinni Found; mem admin bd, Asn Am Med Cols, 73-; Japan Soc Prom Sci res award, 78. *Honors & Awards:* Res Award, Pavlovian Soc NAm, 68; Award of Merit in Sci, Nat Paraplegic Found, 73. *Mem:* Am Asn Anat (vpres, 70-72, pres, 76-77); Am Acad Neurol; Am Physiol Soc; Am Acad Cerebral Palsy; Pavlovian Soc NAm (vpres, 70-72, pres, 72-73). *Res:* Regeneration of nerve fibers; effects of x-irradiation on brain; neurocytology; basic neurology; sleep and wakefulness. *Mailing Add:* Brain Res Inst Univ of Calif Sch of Med Los Angeles CA 90024

CLEMENTS, BURIE WEBSTER, b Pierce, Fla, Dec 16, 27; m 52; c 3. MEDICAL ENTOMOLOGY. *Educ:* Univ Fla, BS, 54, MSA, 56. *Prof Exp:* Entomologist, stored prod insects, Ga Lab, USDA, 56-58, Savannah, Ga Lab, 58-60; Vero Beach Lab, Entom Res Ctr, 60-64, ENTOMOLOGIST & ADMINR, W FLA ARTHROPOD RES LAB, DIV HEALTH, 64- *Mem:* Entom Soc Am; Am Mosquito Control Asn; Sigma Xi. *Res:* Development of effective and economical methods for controlling insects of public health importance. *Mailing Add:* WFla Arthropod Res Lab Div of Health PO Box 2326 Panama City FL 32401

CLEMENTS, GEORGE FRANCIS, b Colfax, Wash, Apr 17, 31; m 52; c 4. MATHEMATICS. *Educ:* Univ Wis, BSME, 53; Syracuse Univ, MA, 57, PhD(math), 62. *Prof Exp:* Asst math, Syracuse Univ, 55-62; asst prof appl math, 62-68, assoc prof math, 68-76, PROF MATH, UNIV COLO, BOULDER, 76-, FAC GRAD SCH, 80- *Mem:* Am Math Soc. *Res:* Combinatorial theory. *Mailing Add:* Dept of Math Univ Colo Boulder CO 80302

CLEMENTS, GREGORY LELAND, b Lincoln, Nebr, Apr 5, 49; m 74; c 3. ASTRONOMY. *Educ:* Univ Iowa, BA, 71, MS, 76, PhD(physics), 78. *Prof Exp:* ASST PROF PHYSICS & ASTRON, DICKINSON COL, 78- *Mem:* Am Astron Soc; Am Asn Physics Teachers. *Res:* Spectrophotometry of planets, satellites, asteroids and eclipsing binary stars. *Mailing Add:* Dept of Physics & Astron Dickinson Col Carlisle PA 17013

CLEMENTS, JOHN ALLEN, b Auburn, NY, May 16, 23; m 49; c 2. PHYSIOLOGY. *Educ:* Cornell Univ, MD, 47. *Prof Exp:* Res asst physiol, Med Sch, Cornell Univ, 47-49; physiologist, Med Labs, Army Chem Ctr, Md, 51-62, asst chief clin invest br, 52-61; res assoc physiol & assoc prof pediat, 61-64, PROF PEDIAT & AM HEART ASN CAREER INVESTR, SCH MED, UNIV CALIF, SAN FRANCISCO, 64- *Concurrent Pos:* Res assoc physiol, Sch Med, Univ Pa, 52-58; lectr, Sch Med, Johns Hopkins Univ, 55-61; consult, Baltimore City Hosp, 57-61, Roswell Park Mem Inst, 58-61 & Surgeon Gen, USPHS, 64-68; sci counr, Nat Heart & Lung Inst, 72; assoc ed, Am Rev Respiratory Dis, 73-80. *Honors & Awards:* Modern Med Distinguished Achievement Award, 73. *Mem:* Nat Acad Sci; Am Physiol Soc; hon fel Am Col Chest Physicians. *Res:* Biophysics; respiration; membrane and cardiovascular physiology. *Mailing Add:* Cardiovasc Res Inst Univ of Calif Med Ctr San Francisco CA 94143

CLEMENTS, JOHN B(ELTON), b Dillwyn, Va, May 25, 29; m 56; c 2. AIR POLLUTION. *Educ:* Hampden-Sydney Col, BS, 50; Univ Va, PhD(org chem), 55. *Prof Exp:* Res chemist, Summit Res Labs, Celanese Corp Am, 55-60; res chemist, Chemstrand Res Ctr, Monsanto Co, 60-63, sr res chemist, 63-68; chief bioanal sect, 68-70, chemist, off criteria & standards, 70-72, chief, Methods Standardization Br, 72-75, chief, Quality Assurance Br, 75-79, DIR, ENVIRON MONITORING DIV, ENVIRON PROTECTION AGENCY, 79- *Mem:* Am Chem Soc; Am Soc Testing & Mat; Air Pollution Control Asn. *Res:* Measurement of air pollutants; methods of handling air pollution data; quality assurance for air pollution monitoring data. *Mailing Add:* Environ Protection Agency Research Triangle Park NC 27711

CLEMENTS, JOHN RICHARD, environmental sciences, see previous edition

CLEMENTS, REGINALD MONTGOMERY, b Vancouver, BC, Apr 13, 40; m 64. PLASMA PHYSICS. *Educ:* Univ BC, BASc, 63, MASc, 64; Univ Sask, PhD(plasma physics), 67. *Prof Exp:* Fel plasma physics, Univ Alta, 67-68; from asst prof to assoc prof, 68-79, PROF PLASMA PHYSICS, UNIV VICTORIA, 79- *Mem:* Can Asn Physicists; Combustion Inst. *Res:* Gas discharge physics; plasma diagnostic methods, specifically electrostatic and rf probes; microwave-plasma interactions; electrical phenomena in combustion. *Mailing Add:* Dept Physics Univ Victoria PO Box 1700 Victoria BC V8W 2Y2 Can

CLEMENTS, REX S, JR, b Philadelphia, Pa, Nov 3, 38; m 70; c 5. DIABETES MELLITUS, INSULIN SECRETION. *Educ:* Amherst Col, BA, 60; Univ Pa, MD, 64. *Prof Exp:* Instr med, Sch Med, Univ Pa, 66-70, asst prof, 70-73; assoc prof & dir, Clin Res Ctr, 73-80, PROF MED, SCH MED, UNIV ALA BIRMINGHAM, 80- *Concurrent Pos:* prin investr grants, NIH, Vet Admin, Am Diabetes Asn & Juvenile Diabetes Found, 73-; consult, NIH, 76-; vis prof, Univ Nottingham, Eng, 80 & Univ Rome & Univ Naples, 81. *Honors & Awards:* Mary Jane Kugel Award, Juvenile Diabetes Found, 78. *Mem:* Am Soc Clin Invest; Am Diabetes Asn; AAAS; Endocrine Soc. *Res:* Role of polyols and of disordered myo-inositol metabolism in the pathogenesis of diabetic complications as well as their role in insulin secretion. *Mailing Add:* 414 Diabetes Hosp Univ Ala Univ Sta Birmingham AL 35294

CLEMENTS, RICHARD GERALD, soil science, ecology, see previous edition

CLEMENTS, ROBERT LAWRENCE, food biochemistry, see previous edition

CLEMENTS, WILLIAM EARL, b Temple, Tex, Mar 8, 42; m 64; c 2. PHYSICS, ATMOSPHERIC PHYSICS. *Educ:* Tex A&I Univ, BS, 65, MA, 66; NMex Inst Mining & Technol, PhD(physics), 74. *Prof Exp:* Asst prof physics, Calif Polytech State Univ, San Luis Obispo, 66-70; STAFF PHYSICIST ATMOSPHERIC PHYSICS, LOS ALAMOS SCI LAB, UNIV CALIF, 74- *Mem:* Am Geophys Union; Am Meteorol Soc. *Res:* Complex terrain meteorology; natural atmospheric radioactivity; radon transport on the ground. *Mailing Add:* Los Alamos Sci Lab PO Box 1663 Mail Stop 588 Los Alamos NM 87545

CLEMENTSON, GERHARDT C, b Black Earth, Wis, May 3, 17; m 43; c 3. COMPUTER SCIENCES, OPERATIONS RESEARCH. *Educ:* US Mil Acad, BS, 42; Calif Inst Technol, MS, 45; Mass Inst Technol, MSAE, 48, ScD, 50. *Prof Exp:* Asst prof elec eng, US Air Force Inst Technol, 54-55, prof aeronaut & head dept, US Air Force Acad, 55-61; asst to exec vpres-tech, Space & Info Syst Div, NAm Aviation, Inc, 64-68; dir opers res, Auto-Tronix Universal Corp, 68-70; PROF COMPUT & MGT SCI & DIR ACAD COMPUT CTR, METROP STATE COL, 70- *Mem:* Asn Comput Mach. *Res:* Guidance and control; education; management sciences. *Mailing Add:* 6423 Sycamore St Littleton CO 80120

CLEMENTZ, DAVID MICHAEL, b Cleveland, Ohio, Sept 4, 45; m 67; c 2. CLAY MINERALOGY, PETROLEUM ENGINEERING. *Educ:* Univ Ariz, BS, 67; Purdue Univ, MS, 69; Mich State Univ, PhD(clay mineral), 73; Pepperdine Univ, MBA, 80. *Prof Exp:* Res chemist surface chem, 73-76, sr res chemist org geochem, 77-79, petrol prod engr, 80-81, SR RES CHEMIST, ENHANCED OIL RECOVERY, CHEVRON OIL FIELD RES CO, 81- *Concurrent Pos:* Mem coun, Clay Minerals Soc, 80-82. *Mem:* Clay Minerals Soc; Soc Petrol Engrs; Am Chem Soc. *Res:* Enhanced oil recovery; surface chemistry of minerals especially clays; clay organic interactions; petroleum source rock characterization; organic geochemistry. *Mailing Add:* Chevron Oil Field Res Co PO Box 446 La Habra CA 90631

CLEMETSON, CHARLES ALAN BLAKE, b Canterbury, Eng, Oct 31, 23; m 47; c 4. OBSTETRICS & GYNECOLOGY. *Educ:* Oxford Univ, BM & BCh, 48, MA, 50; FACOG, FRCOG, FRCSC. *Prof Exp:* Res asst obstet, Univ Col Hosp, London, 50-52, lectr obstet & gynec, 56-58; house surgeon, London Hosps, 52-54; registr, Ashton-under-Lyne Hosp, 54-56; asst prof, Univ Sask Hosp, 58-61; asst prof, Med Ctr, Univ Calif, San Francisco, 61-67; lectr maternal health, Univ Calif, Berkeley, 63-67; assoc prof obstet & gynec, State Univ NY Downstate Med Ctr, 67-72, prof, 72-81; dir obstet & gynec, Methodist Hosp Brooklyn, 67-81; PROF OBSTET & GYNEC, TULANE UNIV, 81- *Mem:* Fel Am Col Obstet & Gynec. *Res:* Obstetric and menstrual physiology. *Mailing Add:* Dept Obstet & Gynec Huey P Long Mem Hosp Pineville LA 71360

CLEMMENS, RAYMOND LEOPOLD, b Baltimore, Md, Apr 2, 22; m 52; c 3. MEDICINE, PEDIATRICS. *Educ:* Loyola Col, Md, BS, 47; Univ Md, MD, 51; Am Bd Pediat, dipl, 56. *Prof Exp:* From instr to assoc prof, 54-70, PROF PEDIAT, UNIV MD, BALTIMORE, 70- *Concurrent Pos:* Pediat consult, USPHS & Md State Health Dept, 62-; mem adv comt, Crippled Children's Prog, Md State Health Dept, 62-; mem adv coun ment hyg, State Bd Health & Ment Hyg, 62-67; mem task force, Nat Inst Neurol Dis & Stroke, 65- *Mem:* Fel Am Acad Pediat; Am Pediat Soc; Am Acad Ment Deficiency. *Res:* Handicapped children's diagnostic and evaluation clinic. *Mailing Add:* 522 Goucher Blvd Towson MD 21204

CLEMMONS, JACKSON JOSHUA WALTER, b Beloit, Wis, Mar 24, 23; m 52; c 4. BIOCHEMISTRY, PATHOLOGY. *Educ:* Univ Wis, BS, 48, MS, 49, PhD, 56; Western Reserve Univ, MD, 59; Am Bd Path, dipl, 64. *Prof Exp:* Res assoc path, Univ Wis, 51-56; univ fel, Western Reserve Univ, 57-60, Helen Hay Whitney fel, 60-62; asst prof, 62-64, assoc prof, 64-77, PROF PATH, SCH MED, UNIV VT, 77- *Mem:* Am Soc Exp Path; NY Acad Sci; Int Acad Path; Am Asn Clin Chem. *Mailing Add:* Dept of Path Univ of Vt Med Sch Burlington VT 05401

CLEMMONS, JOHN B, b Rome, Ga, Apr 11, 18; m 47; c 2. MATHEMATICS, PHYSICS. *Educ:* Morehouse Col, AB, 37; Univ Atlanta, MS, 39. *Prof Exp:* Admin prin high sch, Ky, 40-43; asst prin high sch, Md, 43-47; assoc prof, 47-74, PROF MATH, SAVANNAH STATE COL, 74-, HEAD DEPT MATH & PHYSICS, 47- *Concurrent Pos:* Lectr, Univ Southern Calif, 50; chmn acad adv comt to Bd Regents, State of Ga. *Mem:* Am Math Soc; Nat Inst Sci. *Res:* Special properties of convex sets. *Mailing Add:* Dept of Math & Physics Savannah State Col Savannah GA 31404

CLEMONS, GISELA KAETHE, physiology, endocrinology, see previous edition

CLEMONS, RUSSELL EDWARD, b Warner, NH, Oct 1, 30; m 68. ECONOMIC GEOLOGY. *Educ:* Univ NMex, BS, 60, MS, 62; Univ Tex, Austin, PhD(geol), 66. *Prof Exp:* From instr to asst prof geol, Univ Tex, Arlington, 65-69; assoc prof, 69-74, PROF GEOL, N MEX STATE UNIV, 74- *Mem:* Fel Geol Soc Am; Am Asn Petrol Geologists; Asn Prof Geologists; Mineral Soc Am. *Res:* Areal field geology and geologic mapping in Mexico and New Mexico; igneous petrography and associated mineral deposits of plutons in northeastern Mexico and southern New Mexico. *Mailing Add:* Dept of Earth Sci N Mex State Univ Las Cruces NM 88003

CLEMSON, HARRY C, b Pawtucket, RI, Aug 12, 34; m 57; c 3. BIOCHEMISTRY, CLINICAL CHEMISTRY. *Educ:* Univ RI, BS, 58, PhD(pharmaceut chem), 66; Univ NH, MS, 61. *Prof Exp:* Instr chem, Rochester Inst Technol, 60-63; USPHS fel pharmacol, Yale Univ, 66-68; asst prof med chem, Northeastern Univ, 68-70; HEAD BIOCHEM, LYNN HOSP, 70- *Mem:* AAAS; Am Chem Soc; Am Asn Clin Chemists; Am Inst Chemists. *Res:* Diagnostic enzymology; drug analysis. *Mailing Add:* Path Lab Lynn Hosp 212 Boston St Lynn MA 01904

CLENCH, MARY HEIMERDINGER, b Louisville, Ky, Jan 18, 32; wid. ORNITHOLOGY. *Educ:* Wheaton Col, Mass, BA, 53; Yale Univ, MS, 55 & 59, PhD(biol), 64. *Prof Exp:* Instr biol & conserv, Am Mus Natural Hist, 55-56; instr biol, Wittenberg Col, 56-57; asst zool, Yale Univ, 57-58, instr, 58-59, asst, 60; asst ornith, Peabody Mus, Yale Univ, 59-63; from res asst to asst cur, Carnegie Mus Natural Hist, 63-67, assoc cur ornith, 68-80; RES ASSOC & ADJ CUR BIRDS, FLA STATE MUS, UNIV FLA, 80- *Concurrent Pos:* Frank M Chapman Mem Fund grant, Am Mus Natural Hist, 64-65; asst prof, Univ Fla, 67-68; dir, Nat Audobon Soc, 78-; ed, The Living Bird, Cornell Univ, 81- *Mem:* Fel Am Ornith Union; Wilson Ornith Soc; Cooper Ornith Soc; Brit Ornith Union. *Res:* Avian anatomy; pterylography of passerines; passerine systematics and taxonomy; migration patterns; other banding-related studies. *Mailing Add:* Fla State Mus Univ Fla Gainesville FL 32611

CLENCH, WILLIAM JAMES, b Brooklyn, NY, Oct 24, 97; m 24; c 2. ZOOLOGY. *Educ:* Mich State Col, BS, 21; Harvard Univ, MS, 23; Univ Mich, PhD, 53. *Hon Degrees:* Dsc, Mich State Univ, 53. *Prof Exp:* Custodian, Grand Rapids Pub Mus, 25-26; lectr zool, 30-36, cur mollusks, 26-66, HON CUR MALACOL, MUS COMP ZOOL, HARVARD UNIV, 66- *Concurrent Pos:* Res assoc, Bishop Mus, 41 & Am Mus Natural Hist, New York, 47-; mem, Pac Sci Cong, 46; field expeds, Ky, Tenn, Ala, Ga, Fla, West Indies & Hawaiian Islands; collab, Univ Fla, 53-; sr res assoc, mus zool, Ohio State Univ, 68-71; cur mollusks, 71-; adj prof zool, 71-74; field assoc, Fla State Mus, 78- Spec ed, Webster's New Int Dict, 32-34; ed, Johnsonia & Occasional Paper on Mollusks, 41-; collab, World Bk Encycl, 44-46; spec ed, Encycl Americana, 53- *Mem:* Am Malacol Union (pres, 34); Conchol Soc Gt Brit & Ireland. *Res:* Taxonomy of western Atlantic mollusks; medically important mollusks; marine boring mollusks; land mollusks of western Pacific Islands and of the West Indies. *Mailing Add:* 26 Rowena St Dorchester MA 02124

CLENDENIN, JAMES EDWIN, b Paris, Tenn, June 10, 39; m 62; c 1. PHYSICS. *Educ:* Univ Va, BEE, 62; Columbia Univ, PhD(physics), 75. *Prof Exp:* res assoc physics, Yale Univ, 75-79; STAFF PHYSICIST, STANFORD LINEAR ACCELERATOR CTR, STANFORD UNIV, 79- *Mem:* Am Phys Soc. *Res:* Atomic physics; high energy physics; accelerator physics. *Mailing Add:* Slac-Bin 31 PO Box 4349 Stanford CA 94305

CLENDENIN, MARTHA ANNE, b Salem, Ohio, Jan 26, 44. NEUROSCIENCES. *Educ:* Med Col Va, Richmond, BS, 65, MS, 70, PhD(anat), 72. *Prof Exp:* NIH fel, Sweden, 72-73; asst prof anat, 73-78, ASSOC PROF ANAT, EASTERN VA MED SCH, 79- *Honors & Awards:* Dorothy Briggs Mem Award for Res, Am Phys Ther Asn, 72. *Mem:* Soc Neurosci; Am Asn Anatomists; Sigma Xi; Am Phys Ther Asn; AAAS. *Res:* Investigations of normal mechanisms of movement and posture utilizing intra and extracellular recording techniques in animals and electromyography in human subjects. *Mailing Add:* Dept of Anat Eastern Va Med Sch PO Box 1980 Norfolk VA 23501

CLENDENING, JOHN ALBERT, b Martinsburg, WVa, Mar 6, 32; m 54; c 3. PALYNOLOGY. *Educ:* WVa Univ, BS, 58, MS, 60, PhD(palynology), 70. *Prof Exp:* Asst coal geologist, WVa Geol & Econ Surv, 60-64, palynologist, 64-66, coal geologist & palynologist, 66-68; geologist, Pan Am Petrol Corp, 68-71; sr geologist, 71-75, SR STAFF PALEONTOLOGIST, AMOCO PROD CO, 75- *Mem:* Fel Geol Soc Am; Am Asn Stratig Palynologists (vpres, 76-77, secy-treas, 78-). *Res:* Applied Paleozoic stratigraphic palynology with emphasis on the Pennsylvanian and Permian systems of North America. *Mailing Add:* Amoco Prod Co Box 3092 Houston TX 77001

CLENDENNING, WILLIAM EDMUND, b Waynesburg, Pa, June 23, 31; m 58; c 4. DERMATOLOGY. *Educ:* Allegheny Col, BS, 52; Jefferson Med Col, MD, 56. *Prof Exp:* Instr dermat, Case Western Reserve Univ, 60-61; sr investr, Dermat Br, Nat Cancer Inst, 61-63; sr instr dermat, Case Western Reserve Univ, 63-66, asst prof, 66-67; clin assoc prof, 67-72, PROF CLIN DERMAT, DARTMOUTH MED SCH, 72- *Concurrent Pos:* Nat Cancer Inst fel, Sch Med, Case Western Reserve Univ, 63-66 & 67-69; mem gen med A study sect, NIH, 65-69; assoc ed, J Invest Dermat, 67-72; mem, Path & Chemother Panels-Mycosis Fungoides Coop Study Group, 72- *Mem:* Am Acad Dermat; Soc Invest Dermat; Am Dermat Asn; Am Soc Dermatopath; Am Fedn Clin Res. *Res:* Immunoglobulin E in atopic dermatitis; mycosis fungoides; contact dermatitis. *Mailing Add:* Dartmouth Med Sch 2 Maynard Rd Hanover NH 03755

CLENDENON, NANCY RUTH, b Ahoskie, NC, July 27, 33. NEUROCHEMISTRY. *Educ:* Old Dom Univ, BS, 62; Univ NC, Chapel Hill, PhD(biochem), 68. *Prof Exp:* From instr to asst prof, 69-81, ASSOC PROF NEUROCHEM, COL MED, OHIO STATE UNIV, 81- *Concurrent Pos:* Res fel neurochem, Ohio State Univ Hosp, 68-69; Ohio State Univ Res Found-Charles R Kistler Mem Found, 69- *Mem:* AAAS; Int Soc Neurochem; Am Chem Soc; Soc Neurosci; Am Soc Neurochem. *Res:* Cerebral hydrolytic enzyme localization in subcellular fractions of normal and pathologic tissues; combined modalities in the treatment of experimentally induced brain tumors in rats and their effects on lysosomal enzymes; response of hydrolytic, mitochondrial and plasma membrane enzymes in dog spinal cord and cerebrospinal fluid to experimental injury; fluid and electrolyte alterations in experimental spinal cord trauma. *Mailing Add:* 10573 Riverside Dr Powell OH 43065

CLENDINNING, ROBERT ANDREW, b Schenectady, NY, Dec 12, 31; m 57; c 2. ORGANIC CHEMISTRY, POLYMER CHEMISTRY. *Educ:* Union Col, BS, 53; Rensselaer Polytech Inst, PhD(org chem), 59. *Prof Exp:* Asst, Rensselaer Polytech Inst, 53-58; chemist, 58-68, PROJ SCIENTIST, UNION CARBIDE CHEM & PLASTICS, 68- *Mem:* Am Chem Soc. *Res:* Synthetic organic chemistry; monomer synthesis and polymerization; mechanism of polymerization reactions; condensation polymerization reactions; polyolefin and olefin copolymers research and development; polymer evaluation. *Mailing Add:* Union Carbide Bldg 200 PO Box 670 New Providence NJ 07974

CLERMONT, YVES WILFRED, b Montreal, Can, Aug 14, 26; m 50; c 3. MICROSCOPIC ANATOMY. *Educ:* Univ Montreal, BSc, 49; McGill Univ, PhD(anat), 53. *Prof Exp:* From lectr to assoc prof, 53-63, chmn dept, 75, PROF ANAT, MCGILL UNIV, 63-, CHMN, 75- *Concurrent Pos:* Anna Fuller fel, 54-55; Lalor Found award, 62; consult, WHO, Geneva, 72-78; mem adv comt, Ford Found, 76-79. *Honors & Awards:* S L Siegler Award, Am Fertility Soc, 66. *Mem:* Am Asn Anat (2nd vpres, 70-73); Soc Study Reproduction; Can Asn Anat; Microsc Soc Can; fel Royal Soc Can. *Res:* Histology and histophysiology of mammalian testes; cytological studies of spermatogenesis with light and electron microscopes. *Mailing Add:* Strathcona Anat & Dent Bldg 3640 University St Montreal PQ H3A 2B3 Can

CLESCERI, LENORE STANKE, b Chicago, Ill, Aug 9, 35; m 57; c 5. BIOCHEMISTRY, MICROBIOLOGY. *Educ:* Loyola Univ, BS, 57; Marquette Univ, MS, 61; Univ Wis, PhD(biochem), 63. *Prof Exp:* NIH res fel, 63-65; asst prof, 66-74, ASSOC PROF MICROBIAL BIOCHEM, RENSSELAER POLYTECH INST, 74- *Mem:* Soc Environ Toxicol & Chem; Am Chem Soc; Soc Int Limnol; Am Soc Microbiol. *Res:* Kinetics of microbial growth; biochemical ecology. *Mailing Add:* Dept Biol Rensselaer Polytech Inst Troy NY 12181

CLESCERI, NICHOLAS LOUIS, b Chicago, Ill, Sept 13, 36; m 57; c 5. ENVIRONMENTAL ENGINEERING. *Educ:* Marquette Univ, BCE, 58; Univ Wis, MSCE, 61, PhD(sanit eng), 64. *Prof Exp:* Foreman construct, A L Clesceri & Co, Ill, 54-58 & Hahn Plumbing Co, Wis, 58; civil engr, sewer eng div, City of Milwaukee, 58-59; NIH res fel sanit eng, Swiss Fed Inst Technol, 63-65; from asst prof to assoc prof environ eng, 65-75, PROF ENVIRON ENG, RENSSELAER POLYTECH INST, 75- *Concurrent Pos:* NSF res grants, 66-67; res & teaching asst, Univ Wis, 61 & 62; mem, Environ Adv Bd, Army Corp Engrs; chmn, Joint Task Group Phosphorus Anal, 16th Ed Standard Methods for Water Pollution Control Fedn. *Mem:* Water Pollution Control Fedn; Am Chem Soc. *Res:* Chemical limnology; problems of eutrophication by nutrient discharges; inorganic nutrition of algae; chemical methods of nutrient removal from wastewaters; acid precipitation research. *Mailing Add:* Dept Chem & Environ Eng Rensselaer Polytech Inst Troy NY 12181

CLEVELAND, ANNE STACK, b Chicago, Ill, Oct 7, 08; m 40; c 2. BIOCHEMISTRY. *Educ:* Univ Chicago, SB, 30, SM, 48, PhD(org chem), 54. *Prof Exp:* From asst to res assoc instr cancer res, Univ Chicago, 47-55; res biochemist, Univ Calif, 55-56; instr biochem, Med Sch, Northwestern Univ, 56-57; res biochemist cancer res, Donner Lab, Univ Calif, Berkeley, 57-74; consult, Endocrine Div, Alta Bates Hosp, Berkeley, 74-75; biochemist, Fac Med, Atma Jaya Cath Univ, Jakarta, Indonesia, 76; clin investr & vis prof, Sch pharm, Nat Defense Med Ctr, Taipei, Taiwan, 77-79. *Concurrent Pos:* Commonwealth fel, Gt Brit, 61-62; biochemist in chg metab res lab, Chicago Wesley Mem Hosp, 56-57; consult, Cancer Res Inst, Sch Med, Univ Calif, San Francisco, 60-66; consult, St Joseph Hosp, Kaohsiung, Taiwan, 67-69; vis prof, Dept Chem, Fu Jen Univ, Taiwan, 71-74; Bur Med consult, US Naval Med Res Unit-2, Taiwan, 71-74. *Mem:* Sigma Xi; Am Chem Soc; Endocrine Soc; Brit Soc Endocrinol. *Res:* Steroid studies in cancer and pituitary-adrenal pathologies; chromatography; carbohydrates; enzymes; clinical chemistry. *Mailing Add:* Apt 7 1221 Kennedy Pl Davis CA 95616

CLEVELAND, BRUCE TAYLOR, b Boston, Mass, Aug 6, 37; m 64. NUCLEAR STRUCTURE. *Educ:* Johns Hopkins Univ, PhD(physics), 70. *Prof Exp:* Lectr physics, State Univ NY Buffalo, 70-72; res assoc, Columbia Univ, 72-75; sr res assoc, 76-78, assoc scientist, 79-80, SCIENTIST, BROOKHAVEN NAT LAB, 81- *Mem:* Am Phys Soc. *Res:* Experimental nuclear physics; studies of double beta decay and solar neutrinos. *Mailing Add:* Dept of Chem Brookhaven Nat Lab Upton NY 11973

CLEVELAND, DONALD EDWARD, b Seattle, Wash, May 25, 28; m 55; c 3. CIVIL ENGINEERING. *Educ:* Mass Inst Technol, SB, 49; Yale Univ, cert, 50, MEng, 59; Tex A&M Univ, PhD(civil eng), 62. *Prof Exp:* Res asst, Bur Hwy Traffic, Yale Univ, 50-51, res assoc, 56-59; consult engr, Ramp Bldgs Corp, 54-56; assoc prof civil eng, Tex A&M Univ, 59-64 & Univ Va, 64-65, assoc prof, 65-68, PROF CIVIL ENG, UNIV MICH, 68- *Concurrent Pos:* Mem tech comts, Transp Res Bd, Nat Acad Sci-Nat Res Coun; consult, Detroit & Philadelphia; sr Fulbright res fel, Tech Univ, Aachen, WGer, 71-72; sr Fulbright lectr, Helsinki Tech Univ, Finland, 78-79. *Honors & Awards:* President's Award, Inst Transp Eng, 61. *Mem:* Am Soc Civil Engrs; Opers Res Soc Am; Inst Transp Eng. *Res:* Analytic techniques in transportation. *Mailing Add:* Dept of Civil Eng Univ of Mich Ann Arbor MI 48109

CLEVELAND, GREGOR GEORGE, b San Jose, Calif, Sept 21, 48; m 69; c 1. BIOPHYSICS, MAGNETIC RESONANCE. *Educ:* La Tech Univ, BS, 70; Rice Univ, MA, 73, PhD(physics), 75. *Prof Exp:* Instr physics, Univ Houston, Downtown, 75; asst prof, 75-80, ASSOC PROF PHYSICS, UNIV NC, GREENSBORO, 80- *Mem:* Am Phys Soc; Biophys Soc. *Res:* Investigation of the physicochemical state of water and ions in various biological or model systems utilizing pulsed nuclear magnetic resonance. *Mailing Add:* Dept Physics Univ NC Greensboro NC 27412

CLEVELAND, JAMES PERRY, b Charlotte, NC, Feb 20, 42; m 65. ORGANIC CHEMISTRY. *Educ:* Ga Inst Technol, BS, 63, PhD(org chem), 67. *Prof Exp:* NIH fel org chem, Ore State Univ, 69-70; mem staff, Res Labs, 70-77, RES ASSOC, TENN EASTMAN CO, 77- *Mem:* Am Chem Soc; The Chem Soc. *Res:* Mechanisms of reactions of organo-phosphorus and organo-sulfur compounds. *Mailing Add:* Res Labs Tenn Eastman Co Kingsport TN 37662

CLEVELAND, JOHN H, b Bloomington, Ind, Nov 12, 32; m 53; c 3. ECONOMIC GEOLOGY. *Educ:* Univ Ind, BA, 54, PhD(geol), 63; Univ Wis, MS, 61. *Prof Exp:* From asst prof to assoc prof, 62-70, PROF GEOL, IND STATE UNIV, 70- *Mem:* AAAS; Nat Asn Geol Teachers; Mineral Soc Am; Geol Soc Am. *Res:* Geology and geochemistry of magnesite deposits; lead-zinc deposits of the upper Mississippi Valley; economic geology of Indiana; computer utilization. *Mailing Add:* Dept of Geol Ind State Univ Terre Haute IN 47809

CLEVELAND, LAURENCE F(ULLER), b Worcester, Mass, May 6, 05; m 33; c 2. ELECTRICAL ENGINEERING. *Educ:* Worcester Polytech Inst, BS, 29; Mass Inst Technol, MS, 35. *Hon Degrees:* DSc, Northeastern Univ, 74. *Prof Exp:* Tech engr, Westinghouse Elec Co, 29; from instr to prof elec eng, 29-73, supvr, Elec Eng Labs, 57-58, exec officer, dept, 59-61, actg chmn, 62-63, dir power systs eng, 63-73, EMER PROF ELEC ENG, NORTHEASTERN UNIV, 73- *Concurrent Pos:* Teacher, 42-46; chmn dept elec eng, Lincoln Col, 38-73. *Mem:* Sr mem Inst Elec & Electronics Engrs; Am Soc Eng Educ. *Res:* Power systems engineering. *Mailing Add:* 24 Fairfield St Newtonville MA 02160

CLEVELAND, MERRILL L, b Orleans, Ind, Feb 29, 28; m 50; c 1. ENTOMOLOGY. *Educ:* Ind State Teachers Col, BS, 50; Purdue Univ, MS, 54, PhD, 64. *Prof Exp:* Pub sch teacher, 50-52; entomologist, Fruit Insects Sect, Entom Res Div, 55-68, asst chief fruit insects res br, 68-72, STAFF SCIENTIST, NAT PROG STAFF, FRUIT & VEG INSECTS, SCI EDUC ADMIN, USDA, 72- *Mailing Add:* 1220 Burton St Silver Spring MD 20910

CLEVELAND, RICHARD WARREN, b Santa Ana, Calif, Dec 4, 24; m 52; c 2. PLANT BREEDING. *Educ:* Univ Calif, BS, 49, PhD(genetics), 53. *Prof Exp:* Asst agron, Univ Calif, 49-53; from asst prof to assoc prof, 53-74, PROF AGRON, PA STATE UNIV, STATE COLLEGE, 74- *Mem:* Am Soc Agron. *Res:* Breeding and cytogenetics of forage plants. *Mailing Add:* 361 Laurel Lane State College PA 16801

CLEVELAND, THOMAS HILBURN, b Anniston, Ala, Dec 1, 19; m 50; c 4. ORGANIC CHEMISTRY, POLYMER CHEMISTRY. *Educ:* Birmingham Southern Col, BS, 42. *Prof Exp:* From chemist to group leader, Monsanto Chem Co, 47-54; group leader res, 54-69, ASST DIR RES, MOBAY CHEM CO, 69- *Mem:* Am Chem Soc; Soc Plastics Engrs. *Res:* Isocyanate and isocyanate polymer chemistry; polyether and polyester chemistry; polycarbonate polymer chemistry. *Mailing Add:* Res Dept Mobay Chem New Martinsville WV 26155

CLEVELAND, WILLIAM SWAIN, b Sussex, NJ, Jan 24, 43; c 2. STATISTICS. *Educ:* Princeton Univ, AB, 65; Yale Univ, MS, 67, PhD(statist), 69. *Prof Exp:* Asst prof statist, Univ NC, Chapel Hill, 69-72; MEM TECH STAFF, BELL LABS, 72- *Mem:* Am Statist Asn. *Res:* Data analysis; psychophysics; graphical methods in statistics; time series analysis; seasonal adjustment of economic data. *Mailing Add:* Bell Labs 600 Mountain Ave Murray Hill NJ 07974

CLEVENGER, IMA FUCHS, b Mayfield, Okla, Jan 24, 03; m 35; c 4. SPEECH PATHOLOGY, AUDIOLOGY. *Educ:* Abilene Christian Univ, BA, 24; Univ Iowa, MA, 28; Univ Okla, PhD(speech), 55. *Prof Exp:* Prof speech & Eng & chmn dept, Oklahoma City Univ, 46-56; prof & dir dept, 56-71, EMER PROF SPEECH PATH & AUDIOL, ABILENE CHRISTIAN UNIV, 71- *Concurrent Pos:* Consult, WTex Rehab Ctr, 57-71 & Abilene State Sch, 62-71; asst dir, Sch Speech Path, Lang & Audiol, Univ PR, San Juan, 71-76. *Mem:* Am Speech & Hearing Asn; Speech Asn Am; Coun Except Children. *Mailing Add:* 815 Park Dr Benton AR 72051

CLEVENGER, RICHARD LEE, b Columbus, Ind, May 16, 31. ORGANIC CHEMISTRY, BIOCHEMISTRY. *Educ:* Univ Ind, BS, 59; Univ Louisville, PhD(org chem), 63. *Prof Exp:* Instr chem, Univ Louisville, 62-63; from asst prof to assoc prof chem, Easts Tex State Univ, 63-81, dir forensic chem, 73-81; CONSULT, DALCHEM, 80- *Mem:* Am Chem Soc. *Res:* Thiadiazoles; hydrazones; geometrical isomerism; cyclopentane derivatives; azasteroids; neuro-biochemistry; B vitamins; drug metabolites; forensic chemistry. *Mailing Add:* 112 Briarwood Dr Commerce TX 75428

CLEVENGER, SARAH, b Indianapolis, Ind, Dec 19, 26. PLANT BIOCHEMISTRY. *Educ:* Miami Univ, AB, 47; Ind Univ, PhD(plant physiol), 57. *Prof Exp:* Asst prof biol, Berea Col, 57-59, Wittenburg Col, 59-60, Eastern Ill Univ, 60-61 & Berea Col, 61-63; from asst prof to assoc prof, 63-78, PROF LIFE SCI, IND STATE UNIV, TERRE HAUTE, 78- *Concurrent Pos:* Contrib ed, Book Forum, 74-79. *Mem:* AAAS; Am Soc Plant Taxonomists; Int Asn Plant Taxon; Phytochem Soc NAm (secy, 67-68); Am Inst Biol Sci. *Res:* Flower pigments; gene control of flower pigments and simulation of population biology. *Mailing Add:* 717 S Henderson St Bloomington IN 47401

CLEVENGER, THOMAS R(USSELL), JR, b Camden, NJ, Mar 14, 30; m 56; c 2. CERAMICS, RESEARCH ADMINISTRATION. *Educ:* Rutgers Univ, BSc, 56; Mass Inst Technol, ScD(ceramics), 61. *Prof Exp:* Res asst ceramics, Mass Inst Technol, 56-59, instr, 59-60, asst prof, 61-64; res adv elec & magnetic oxides, Consumer & Tech Prod Div, Owens-Ill Glass Co, Inc, 64-65, mgr tech admin, Consumer & Tech Prod Div, 65-68, vpres & tech dir consumer & tech prod, 68-77, VPRES, TECH DIR & GEN MGR, FAR EAST-PAC OPERS, OWENS-ILL, INC, 77- *Concurrent Pos:* Vis mem, Wireless Div, Matsushita Elec Co Ltd, Japan, 61-62; Ford fel, 61-63. *Mem:* Am Ceramic Soc. *Res:* Characterization and development of dielectric, ferroelectric and ferromagnetic ceramics; electronic and electro-optic applications of glass; research management. *Mailing Add:* Owens-Ill Inc 1700 N Westwood Ave Toledo OH 43607

CLEVER, HENRY LAWRENCE, b Mansfield, Ohio, June 14, 23; m 56; c 1. PHYSICAL CHEMISTRY. *Educ:* Ohio State Univ, BSc, 45, MS, 49, PhD(chem), 51. *Prof Exp:* Jr chemist, Shell Develop Co, 45-47; asst, Res Found, Ohio State Univ, 47-50; instr & res assoc, Duke Univ, 51-54; from instr to assoc prof, 54-65, PROF CHEM, EMORY UNIV, 65-, DIR SOLUBILITY DATA, 81- *Concurrent Pos:* Partic, Oak Ridge Nat Lab, 57; res assoc, Univ Mich, 63-64; res assoc, Polymer Res Inst, Univ Mass, Amherst, 72-73. *Mem:* AAAS; Am Chem Soc. *Res:* Thermodynamics; solubility; surface tension; heat capacity; thermal properties; light scattering; compilation and evaluation of solubility and other data. *Mailing Add:* Dept Chem Emory Univ Atlanta GA 30322

CLEWE, THOMAS HAILEY, b San Francisco, Calif, Sept 9, 25; m 52; c 3. DERMATOLOGY, MEDICAL RESEARCH. *Educ:* Stanford Univ, BS, 49, MD, 55. *Prof Exp:* Res assoc reprod, Stanford Univ, 55-56; instr anat, Sch Med, Yale Univ, 57-58; asst res prof obstet & gynec & anat, Sch Med, Univ Kans, 58-61; asst res prof obstet & gynec, Sch Med, Vanderbilt Univ, 61-66; res assoc, Div Reprod Physiol, Delta Regional Primate Res Ctr, 66-73; asst clin res dir, Squibb Inst Med Res, 73-75, assoc clin res dir, 75-76; ASSOC MED DIR, SYNTEX RES, 76- *Concurrent Pos:* Pop Coun med res fel, Sch Med, Yale Univ, 56-57; assoc prof anat, Tulane Univ, 66-73, clin assoc prof obstet & gynec, Med Sch, 68-73. *Honors & Awards:* Rubin Award, Am Fertil Soc, 59. *Mem:* Am Asn Anatomists; Am Acad Dermat; Int Soc Trop Dermat; Soc Invest Dermat; Soc Clin Trials. *Res:* Structure and function of mammalian oviduct; physiology of early stages of mammalian reproduction; fertility and sterility; comparative reproduction, especially of primates; fertility control devices; physiology of skin; design of clinical investigations. *Mailing Add:* Inst of Clin Med 3401 Hillview Ave Palo Alto CA 94304

CLEWELL, ANDRE F, systematic botany, plant ecology, see previous edition

CLEWELL, DAYTON HARRIS, b Berwick, Pa, Dec 15, 12; m 38; c 2. PHYSICS. *Educ:* Mass Inst Technol, BS, 33, PhD(physics), 36. *Prof Exp:* Physicist, C K Williams Co, 35-38 & Magnolia Petrol Co, 38-42, supvr physics res, 42-46, from asst dir to dir field res labs, 46-56; gen mgr res dept, Mobil Oil Corp, 56-62, gen mgr res & eng, 62-64, sr vpres, 64-77; CONSULT, 77- *Mem:* Nat Acad Eng; Am Phys Soc; Soc Explor Geophys; Am Asn Petrol Geologists; Inst Elec & Electronics Engrs. *Res:* Design of spectrophotometers; gravity meters; seismographs; terrestrial magnetism; propagation of electric waves through earth; research administration in areas of petroleum exploration, production, processing and product development; engineering administration. *Mailing Add:* 34 Driftway Lane Darien CT 06820

CLEWELL, DON BERT, b Dallas, Tex, Sept 5, 41; m 68. BIOCHEMISTRY, MICROBIOLOGY. *Educ:* Johns Hopkins Univ, AB, 63; Ind Univ, Indianapolis, PhD(biochem), 67. *Prof Exp:* Biologist, Univ Calif, San Diego, 69-70; from asst prof to assoc prof, 70-77, PROF ORAL BIOL, SCH DENT & MICROBIOL, SCH MED, UNIV MICH, ANN ARBOR, 77-, RES SCIENTIST, DENT RES INST, 80- *Concurrent Pos:* Nat Cancer Inst fel molecular genetics, Univ Calif, San Diego, 67-69; USPHS res career develop award, 75-80. *Mem:* AAAS; Am Chem Soc; Biophys Soc; Am Soc Biol Chem; Int Asn Dent Res. *Res:* Molecular biology; molecular genetics; nucleic acid chemistry; streptococci; transposons. *Mailing Add:* Dept of Oral Biol Univ of Mich Sch of Dent Ann Arbor MI 48104

CLIATH, MARK MARSHALL, b Palo Alto, Calif, July 6, 35; m 64; c 1. SOIL SCIENCE, CHEMISTRY. *Educ:* Univ Calif, Riverside, AB, 63, PhD(soil sci), 78. *Prof Exp:* CHEMIST SOIL-PESTICIDE INTERACTIONS, SOIL & WATER MGT RES, SCI & EDUC ADMIN, USDA, RIVERSIDE, 66- *Mem:* Am Chem Soc. *Res:* Soil-pesticide interactions; volatilization of pesticides from agricultural soil and water surfaces; vapor behavior of pesticides in soil, water and air. *Mailing Add:* Dept of Soil & Environ Sci Univ of Calif Riverside CA 92521

CLIBURN, JOSEPH WILLIAM, b Hazlehurst, Miss, Jan 20, 26; m 50; c 2. ZOOLOGY, BOTANY. *Educ:* Millsaps Col, BS, 47; Univ Southern Miss, MA, 53; Univ Ala, PhD(zool), 60. *Prof Exp:* Instr, pub schs, Miss, 47-53; instr biol, Copiah-Lincoln Jr Col, 53-55; instr, pub schs, Miss, 55-58; assoc prof, 60-64, PROF BIOL, UNIV SOUTHERN MISS, 64- *Concurrent Pos:* Prof zool, Gulf Coast Res Lab, 70- *Mem:* Am Soc Ichthyologists & Herpetologists; Soc Study Amphibians & Reptiles. *Res:* Taxonomy and zoogeography of southeastern amphibians, reptiles and fishes. *Mailing Add:* Dept of Biol Univ of Southern Miss Hattiesburg MS 39401

CLICK, ROBERT EDWARD, b Wenatchee, Wash, Mar 22, 37; m 56; c 2. IMMUNOBIOLOGY. *Educ:* Wash State Univ, BS, 60; Univ Calif, Berkeley, PhD(biochem), 64. *Prof Exp:* NIH fels, Columbia Univ, 64-65 & Sloan-Kettering Cancer Inst, 65-66; NIH fel, Univ Wis, 66-68, asst prof immunol, 68-72; scientist, Wis Alumni Res Inst, Madison, 72-73; assoc, Sloan-Kettering Cancer Inst, 73-74; ASST PROF IMMUNOL, DEPT MICROBIOL, UNIV MINN, MINNEAPOLIS, 74- *Mem:* AAAS; Soc Develop Biol; Soc Plant Physiol; Am Asn Immunol. *Res:* Genetic control of immune responses, primarily in vitro. *Mailing Add:* Dept Microbiol Univ Minn Minneapolis MN 55455

CLIETT, CHARLES BUREN, b Montpelier, Miss, July 10, 24; m 46; c 2. AEROSPACE ENGINEERING. *Educ:* Ga Inst Technol, BS, 45, MS, 50. *Prof Exp:* Instr aeronaut eng, Miss State Univ, 47-49; asst, Ga Inst Technol, 49-50; from asst prof to assoc prof, 50-60, PROF AEROSPACE ENG, MISS STATE UNIV, 60-, HEAD DEPT AEROSPACE ENG, 60- *Mem:* Am Soc Eng Educ; Am Inst Aeronaut & Astronaut; Nat Soc Prof Engrs. *Res:* Engineering mechanics; stress analysis and structural dynamics. *Mailing Add:* Dept of Aerospace Eng Drawer A Mississippi State MS 39762

CLIFF, FRANK SAMUEL, b Carson City, Nev, Apr 3, 28; m 55; c 3. VERTEBRATE ZOOLOGY. *Educ:* Stanford Univ, AB, 51, PhD, 54. *Prof Exp:* Herpetologist, Sefton-Stanford exped, Gulf of Calif, 52-53; asst comp anat & gen biol, Natural Hist Mus, Stanford Univ, 52, 53-56; from instr to asst prof, Colgate Univ, 56-59; from asst prof to assoc prof, 59-69, PROF COMP ANAT & GEN BIOL, CALIF STATE UNIV, CHICO, 69- *Mem:* Am Soc Ichthyologists & Herpetologists. *Res:* Reptiles of islands adjacent to Baja California and Mexico; reptiles of western North America and Mexico; insular evolution; osteology of reptiles. *Mailing Add:* Dept of Biol Calif State Univ Chico CA 95929

CLIFFORD, ALAN FRANK, b Natick, Mass, June 8, 19; m 49; c 2. INORGANIC CHEMISTRY, FLUORINE CHEMISTRY. *Educ:* Harvard Univ, AB, 41; Univ Del, MS, 47, PhD(inorg chem), 49. *Prof Exp:* Anal chemist & lab supvr, Kankakee Ord Works, Ill, 41-43; asst, Manhattan Dist Proj, Radiation Lab, Univ Chicago, 43; anal res chemist, Clinton Labs, Tenn, 43-44; res chemist, Hanford Eng Works, Wash, 44-45; develop chemist, Exp Sta, E I du Pont de Nemours & Co, Del, 45-47; instr chem, Univ Del, 47-49; asst prof inorg chem, Ill Inst Technol, 49-51; from asst prof to assoc prof, Purdue Univ, 53-66; PROF INORG CHEM & HEAD DEPT CHEM, VA POLYTECH INST & STATE UNIV, 66- *Concurrent Pos:* Guggenheim fel, Cambridge Univ, 51-53; mem subcomt solubility data, Comt Equilibrium Data, Int Union Pure & Appl Chem, 73- *Mem:* AAAS; Am Chem Soc; fel NY Acad Sci; The Chem Soc. *Res:* Rare earth, inorganic fluoride chemistry; hydrogen fluoride system; acid theory; inorganic polymers; oxidations in liquid ammonia; multiple bonding in inorganic compounds; hypofluorites; Mossbauer spectrometry of rare earths and biological materials. *Mailing Add:* Dept of Chem Va Polytech Inst & State Univ Blacksburg VA 24061

CLIFFORD, ALFRED HOBLITZELLE, b St Louis, Mo, July 11, 08; m 42; c 2. MATHEMATICS. *Educ:* Yale Univ, AB, 29; Calif Inst Technol, PhD(math), 33. *Prof Exp:* Mem, Inst Advan Study, 33-36, asst, 36-38; instr math, Mass Inst Technol, 38-41, asst prof, 41-42; assoc prof math, Johns Hopkins Univ, 46-55; prof, 55-74, EMER PROF MATH, NEWCOMB COL, TULANE UNIV, 74- *Mem:* Am Math Soc; Math Asn Am. *Res:* Algebraic theory of semigroups and ordered groups. *Mailing Add:* Dept of Math Tulane Univ New Orleans LA 70118

CLIFFORD, DONALD H, b Burlington, Vt, June 7, 25; m 54; c 4. VETERINARY SURGERY. *Educ:* Univ Montreal, DVM, 50; Univ Minn, MPH, 55, PhD(vet med), 59; Am Col Lab Animal Med, dipl, 60; Am Col Vet Surgeons, dipl. *Prof Exp:* Intern vet med, Angell Mem Hosp, Boston, Mass, 50-51, intern res, 51-52; from instr to assoc prof vet surg, Col Vet Med, Univ Minn, 52-65; med assoc lab animal care, Brookhaven Nat Lab, 62-63; assoc prof med, sci & technol, Col Med, Baylor Univ, 65-71, lectr exp surg, 66-71; chief animal res facil, Vet Admin Hosp, Houston, Tex, 65-71; DIR DIV LAB ANIMAL MED, MED COL OHIO AT TOLEDO, 71- *Concurrent Pos:* Consult, dept pharmacol, Boston Univ, 51 & St Paul Como Zoo; ed, Minn Vet, 64-65; mem subcomt dog & cat standards, Nat Res Coun, Nat Acad Sci; exec comt & exam comt, Am Col Lab Med; consult, Am Asn Accreditation of Lab Animal Care. *Mem:* Fel Am Col Vet Surgeons; Am Vet Med Asn; Am Asn Lab Animal Sci; Am Asn Lab Animal Practitioners. *Res:* Veterinary surgery, especially comparative restraint and anesthesiology in laboratory, zoological and domestic animals; pathology and surgery of the canine mouth and esophagus; pathogenesis and treatment of achalasia of the esophagus in dogs and cats; effect of acupuncture on the cardiovascular system of dogs. *Mailing Add:* Div Lab Animal Med Med Col Ohio CS 1008 Toledo OH 43699

CLIFFORD, GEORGE O, b Akron, Ohio, Apr 30, 24; m 48; c 3. INTERNAL MEDICINE, HEMATOLOGY. *Educ:* Tufts Univ, MD, 49; Am Bd Internal Med, dipl, 57. *Prof Exp:* Intern Henry Ford Hosp, Detroit, 49-50; resident med, Detroit Receiving Hosp, 54-55; from instr to assoc prof, Col Med, Wayne State Univ, 55-63; assoc prof, Med Col, Cornell Univ, 63-72; PROF MED & CHMN DEPT, SCH MED, CREIGHTON UNIV, 72- *Concurrent Pos:* Res fel, Detroit Receiving Hosp, 50-52; res fel, Med Sch, Univ NC, 54; Markle scholar, 59; dir blood bank med lab serv, Mem Hosp, Sloan-Kettering Inst, 63-72, dir hemat, 63-70, assoc chmn dept med, 70-72. *Mem:* AMA; Am Fedn Clin Res; Am Soc Hemat; NY Acad Sci; fel Am Col Physicians. *Res:* Clinical and research hematology; hemaglobiopathies; megaloblastic anemias; leukemias. *Mailing Add:* Dept of Med Creighton Univ Sch of Med Omaha NE 68131

CLIFFORD, HOWARD JAMES, b Binghamton, NY, May 29, 39; m 62; c 3. PHYSICAL CHEMISTRY, MOLECULAR SPECTROSCOPY. *Educ:* Univ NMex, BS, 63; Wash State Univ, PhD(chem), 71. *Prof Exp:* Lab technician, Vet Admin Hosp, Albuquerque, 63-64; instr, Regina Sch Nursing, Univ Albuquerque, 64-66; teaching asst chem, Univ NMex, 66-67; res asst, Wash State Univ, 67-70; assoc prof chem, 70-76, ADMIN VPRES, UNIV PUGET

SOUND, 76- *Concurrent Pos:* Lab technician, Med Sch, Univ NMex, 65. *Mem:* AAAS; Sigma Xi; Am Chem Soc. *Res:* Synthesis, purification and spectroscopic investigation of six-coordinated metal complexes containing ions from the second and third transition series group VIII elements; examination of effects due to differences in molecular symmetries using absorption and emission spectroscopy. *Mailing Add:* Off of Admin VPres Univ of Puget Sound Tacoma WA 98416

CLIFFORD, HUGH FLEMING, b Warren, Pa, Dec 9, 31; m 61; c 2. LIMNOLOGY, INVERTEBRATE ZOOLOGY. *Educ:* Mich State Univ, BS, 58, MS, 59; Ind Univ, PhD(limnol), 65. *Prof Exp:* Fishery biologist, Mo Conserv Comn, 60-62; from asst prof to assoc prof, 65-78, PROF ZOOL, UNIV ALTA, 78- *Mem:* Am Soc Limnol & Oceanog; Int Asn Theoret & Appl Limnol; Ecol Soc Am; Can Soc Zoologists. *Res:* Stream ecology; ecology of mayflies. *Mailing Add:* Dept of Zool Univ of Alta Edmonton AB T6G 2C2 Can

CLIFFORD, JOSEPH MICHAEL, b Oak Park, Ill, Nov 11, 25; m 59; c 5. PHYSICS. *Educ:* Harvard Univ, AB, 48; Lehigh Univ, MS, 49, PhD(physics), 55. *Prof Exp:* Analyst, Inst Res, Lehigh Univ, 53-54; sci warfare adv, Off Asst Secy Defense Res & Eng, US Dept Defense, 55; mem staff, weapons systs eval group, Inst Defense Anal, 56-61; chief missions anal, Martin Co, Colo, 61-63; head, Opers Anal Dept, Aerospace Corp, San Bernadino, Calif, 63-69; sr staff scientist, 69-80, dir mission analysis, 80-81, SYST ENG DIR, TEST & OPERS, NAVIGATION SATELLITE DIRECTORATE, EL SEGUNDO, CALIF, 81- *Mem:* Opers Res Soc Am. *Res:* Operations research; mathematical physics. *Mailing Add:* 30907 Rue de la Pierre Palos Verdes Peninsula CA 90274

CLIFFORD, PAUL CLEMENT, b Bismarck, NDak, Nov 23, 10; m 36; c 7. STATISTICS, QUALITY CONTROL. *Educ:* Columbia Univ, AB, 31, AM, 34. *Prof Exp:* Instr math, Columbia Univ, 32-35; from instr to prof, 35-77, chmn dept, 63-72, EMER PROF MATH, MONTCLAIR STATE COL, 77- *Concurrent Pos:* Lectr, NY Univ, 44-45, Newark Col Eng, 46-47, Rutgers Univ, 48-64, Univ Mich, 57-69 & Univ Wis, 62-70; indust consult, Nat Broadcasting Co Continental Classroom, 44-49, instr, 61-62; indust consult, UN, 53, Int Coop Admin, 54-59 & AID, 59-64. *Honors & Awards:* Shewhart Medal, Am Soc Qual Control, 65 & Ott Award, 73. *Mem:* Fel AAAS; fel Am Soc Qual Control; fel Am Statist Asn; Inst Math Statist; hon mem Europ Orgn Qual Control. *Res:* Application of statistics and industrial quality control. *Mailing Add:* 39 Norman Rd Upper Montclair NJ 07043

CLIFFORD, STEVEN FRANCIS, b Boston, Mass, Jan 4, 43. WAVE PROPALATION, GEOPHYSICS. *Educ:* Northeastern Univ, BSEE, 65; Dartmouth, PhD(eng sci), 69. *Prof Exp:* Physicist environ res, 69-70, SUPVR PHYSICIST, WAVE PROPALATION LAB, NAT OCEANIC & ATMOSPHERIC ADMIN, BOULDER, 70- *Concurrent Pos:* Assoc ed, J Optical Soc Am, 80-83; topical adv atmospheric optics, Optical Soc Am, 82-85. *Mem:* Fel Optical Soc Am; Int Radio Sci Union; Acoust Soc; Am Meteorol Soc; Am Geophys Union. *Res:* Engaged in theoretical research in the field of optical acoustical & microwave propagation through turbulent geophysical flows. *Mailing Add:* Environ Res Lab R45X1 Nat Oceanic & Atmospheric Admin 325 Broadway Boulder CO 80303

CLIFFTON, MICHAEL DUANE, b Hastings, Nebr, Feb 28, 52. SYNTHETIC ORGANIC CHEMISTRY. *Educ:* Univ Nebr, Omaha, 74, Lincoln, PhD(chem), 80. *Prof Exp:* Fel, Georgia Inst Technol, 80-81; RES CHEMIST, PHILLIPS PETROL CO, 81- *Mem:* Am Chem Soc. *Res:* Engineering plastics; unsaturated polyester resins. *Mailing Add:* Phillips Petrol Co Res Ctr 110 CPL Bartlesville OK 74003

CLIFT, WILLIAM ORRIN, b Flint, Mich, Mar 27, 14; m 51; c 2. GEOLOGY, STRATIGRAPHY-SEDIMENTATION. *Educ:* Univ Mich, BS, 38; Columbia Univ, PhD, 56. *Prof Exp:* Stratigrapher, Sinclair Refining Co, Venezuela, 46-49, stratigr-paleontologist, Sinclair Petrol Co, 49, chief geologist, Ethiopia, 49-52, gen supt, 53-56, mgr, Sinclair Somal Corp, Somalia, 56-59, pres, Sinclair & BP Explor Co, NY, 59-62, vpres, Sinclair Int Oil Co, 62-69; vpres, Podesta, Meyers, Rominger & Clift, Inc, 69-74; DIR EXPLOR SCI, FOREST OIL CORP, DENVER, 74- *Mem:* Fel Geol Soc Am; Asn Petrol Geologists; Paleont Soc. *Res:* Eocene stratigraphy and paleontology. *Mailing Add:* Forest Oil Corp 950-17th St Denver CO 80202

CLIFTON, CARL MOORE, b Greenup Co, Ky, Sept 18, 14; m 47; c 3. DAIRY HUSBANDRY. *Educ:* Eastern Ky State Col, BS, 36; Univ Ky, MS, 39; Ohio State Univ, PhD(dairy sci), 54. *Prof Exp:* Supt dairy, Univ Ky, 45-46, field agt, 46-50; co-op agt, Dairy Husb Res Br, Agr Res Serv, USDA, 50-55; asst prof dairy, Univ Minn, 55-59; from asst prof to assoc prof dairy, Univ Ga, 60-76, mem fac, Dept Dairy Sci, 76-80; RETIRED. *Mem:* Am Dairy Sci Asn. *Res:* Dairy cattle breeding and management. *Mailing Add:* Rt 3 Box 277 Danielsville GA 30633

CLIFTON, DAVID GEYER, b Pomeroy, Ohio, Mar 20, 24; m 56. PHYSICAL CHEMISTRY. *Educ:* Miami Univ, Ohio, BA, 48, MA, 50; Ohio State Univ, PhD, 55. *Prof Exp:* Res chemist, Film Dept, E I du Pont de Nemours & Co, Inc, 55-56; staff mem, Los Alamos Sci Lab, Univ Calif, 57-64; sr res chemist, Gen Motors Defense Res Labs, 64-68; STAFF MEM, LOS ALAMOS SCI LABS, UNIV CALIF, 68- *Mem:* Am Chem Soc; Am Inst Physics; AAAS; Am Nuclear Soc. *Res:* Thermodynamics; rocket propellant systems; advanced breeder reactor fuels; aerophysics; plutonium chemistry. *Mailing Add:* Los Alamos Sci Labs Univ of Calif Los Alamos NM 87544

CLIFTON, DONALD F(REDERIC), b Pella, Iowa, Apr 28, 17; m 52; c 2. METALLURGY. *Educ:* Mich Col Mining & Technol, BS, 40; Univ Utah, PhD(metall), 57. *Prof Exp:* Metallurgist, Globe Steel Tubes Co, 40-45 & Inst Study of Metals, Chicago, 46-50; asst prof metall, Univ Ky, 54-57; from asst prof to assoc prof, 57-68, PROF METALL, UNIV IDAHO, 68- *Mem:* Am Phys Soc; Am Crystallog Asn; Am Soc Metals. *Res:* Crystallography and kinetics of phase changes; crystal growth; electrometallurgy. *Mailing Add:* Col of Mines Univ of Idaho Moscow ID 83843

CLIFTON, HUGH EDWARD, b Prospect, Ohio, July 29, 34; m 57; c 3. GEOLOGY. *Educ:* Ohio State Univ, BSc, 56; Johns Hopkins Univ, PhD(geol), 63. *Prof Exp:* GEOLOGIST, US GEOL SURV, 63- *Mem:* AAAS; Geol Soc Am; Soc Econ Paleont & Mineral; Int Soc Sedimentol. *Res:* Sedimentary petrography; sedimentology. *Mailing Add:* US Geol Surv 345 Middlefield Rd Menlo Park CA 94025

CLIFTON, JAMES ALBERT, b Fayetteville, NC, Sept 18, 23; m 49; c 3. INTERNAL MEDICINE. *Educ:* Vanderbilt Univ, BA, 44, MD, 47; Am Bd Internal Med, dipl, 55; Am Bd Gastroenterol, dipl, 62. *Prof Exp:* Intern, Univ Hosps, Univ Iowa, 47-48, resident dept med, 48-51; mem staff, Vet Admin Hosp, Tenn, 52-53; assoc internal med, 53-54, from asst prof to assoc prof, 54-63, vis prof dept physiol, 64, vchmn dept med, 67-70 & head dept, 70-75, actg head dept, 75-76, PROF MED, UNIV IOWA, 63- *Concurrent Pos:* Fel med, Mass Mem Hosp, 55-56; NIH spec res fel, 55-56; attend physician, Vet Admin Hosp, Iowa, 53-; consult, Surgeon Gen, USPHS, 64-; mem, Nat Adv Arthritis & Metab Dis, 70-73; mem exec comt, Am Bd Internal Med, 78-81. *Mem:* Inst Med-Nat Acad Sci; AMA; Am Col Physicians (pres, 76-77); Am Gastroenterol Asn (pres, 70-71); AAAS. *Res:* Patho-physiology of the gastrointestinal system; liver disease and mechanisms of intestinal absorption. *Mailing Add:* Dept of Med Univ of Iowa Iowa City IA 52241

CLIFTON, KELLY HARDENBROOK, experimental biology, see previous edition

CLIFTON, RODNEY JAMES, b Orchard, Nebr, July 10, 37; m 58; c 4. SOLID MECHANICS. *Educ:* Univ Nebr, BS, 59; Carnegie Inst Technol, MS, 61, PhD(civil eng), 64. *Prof Exp:* Fel, 64-65, from asst prof to assoc prof, 65-71, PROF ENG, BROWN UNIV, 71- *Concurrent Pos:* NSF sci fac fel, Univ Southampton, Eng, 71-72; consult, Terra Tek Inc, Salt Lake City, 73-; chmn exec comt, Div Eng, Brown Univ, 74-79; consult, Sandia Nat Labs, Albuquerque, 79-; vis prof mat sci & eng, Stanford Univ, 79-80. *Honors & Awards:* Melville Medal, Am Soc Mech Engrs. *Mem:* Am Soc Civil Engrs; fel Am Acad Mech; AAAS; Soc Eng Sci. *Res:* Stress waves; plate impact theory and experiments; dynamic plasticity; dislocation dynamics; mechanics of hydraulic fracturing; rock mechanics; numerical methods. *Mailing Add:* Div Eng Brown Univ Providence RI 02912

CLIMENHAGA, JOHN LEROY, b Delisle, Sask, Nov 7, 16; m 43; c 2. ASTROPHYSICS. *Educ:* Univ Sask, BA, 45, MA, 49; Univ Mich, MA, 56, PhD, 60. *Prof Exp:* Instr physics, Regina Col, 46-48; from asst prof to assoc prof, 49-63, head dept physics, 56-69, dean Fac Arts & Sci, 69-72, PROF PHYSICS, UNIV VICTORIA, BC, 63- *Concurrent Pos:* Mem, Nat Comt Can, Int Astron Union, 67-71; mem scholar comt, Nat Res Coun, 69-72, mem radio & elec eng div adv bd, 71-74. *Mem:* Am Astron Soc; Can Asn Physicists; Royal Astron Soc Can; Int Astron Union; Astron Soc Pac. *Res:* Abundance ratio C-12/C-13 in carbon stars; spectral studies of late type supergiants; cometary spectra. *Mailing Add:* Dept of Physics Univ of Victoria Victoria BC V8W 2Y2 Can

CLINARD, FRANK WELCH, JR, b Winston-Salem, NC, Aug 4, 33; m 68. MATERIALS SCIENCE. *Educ:* NC State Univ, BME, 55, MS, 57; Stanford Univ, PhD(mat sci), 65. *Prof Exp:* Staff mem metallurgist, Sandia Corp, 57-61; MAT SCIENTIST & PRIN INVESTR, LOS ALAMOS NAT LAB, UNIV CALIF, 64- *Mem:* AAAS; Am Soc Metals; Am Ceramic Soc; Am Nuclear Soc. *Res:* Structural defects in crystalline solids; phase transformations; physical properties of rare earths; behavior of crystalline materials at cryogenic temperatures; radiation damage; rare gases in ceramic fuels; fusion reactor materials; ceramic nuclear waste. *Mailing Add:* 2940 Arizona Ave Los Alamos NM 87544

CLINE, CARL F, b Detroit, Mich, Nov 25, 28; m 54; c 4. METALLURGY, CERAMICS. *Educ:* Ga Inst Technol, BS, 53; Niagara Univ, MS, 58. *Prof Exp:* Develop engr, Nat Carbon Co, 53-55; prin ceramist, Battelle Mem Inst, 55-56; sr engr, Res Div, Carborundum Co, 56-58; group leader mat res, Chem Div, Lawrence Radiation Lab, Univ Calif, Livermore, 58-70; dep mgr mat dynamics dept, Physics Int Co, 70-72; mgr strength physics dept, Mat Res Ctr, Allied Chem Co, 72-74; SECT LEADER, METALS & CERAMICS DIV, LAWRENCE LIVERMORE NAT LAB, 74-, DEP DIV LEADER, MAT SCI DIV, 81- *Concurrent Pos:* Panel mem, Solid State Sci Comn, 76-; chmn, Tungsten Comt, Nat Acad Sci, 77-78, dynamic compaction metal & ceramic powders, 81. *Honors & Awards:* IR-100 Award, Indust Res Mag, 77. *Mem:* Am Phys Soc; fel Am Ceramic Soc; Am Soc Metals. *Res:* Crystal growth of oxides; advanced materials for ceramic armor and cutting tools; ferroelectrics for high strain applications; management of materials research and development; crystal growth; physical ceramics; hard compounds; properties and processing of amorphous metals; high rate forming; rapid solification technology. *Mailing Add:* Mat Sci Div Lawrence Livermore Nat Lab Livermore CA 94550

CLINE, DOUGLAS, b York, Eng, Aug 28, 34. NUCLEAR PHYSICS. *Educ:* Univ Manchester, BSc, 57, PhD(physics), 63. *Prof Exp:* Res fel physics, Univ Manchester, 60-63; res assoc, 63-65, from asst prof to assoc prof, 65-76, PROF PHYSICS, UNIV ROCHESTER, 76- *Concurrent Pos:* Assoc dir, Nuclear Structure Res Lab & mem prog adv comt, Brookhaven Nat Lab, 74-78; chmn exec comt, Holifield Fac, Oak Ridge Nat Lab. *Mem:* Am Phys Soc. *Res:* Heavy ion physics, including coulomb excitation, electromagnetic moments and transition strengths; collective model interpretation of nuclear properties. *Mailing Add:* Nuclear Structure Res Lab Univ of Rochester Rochester NY 14627

CLINE, EDWARD TERRY, b Ischua, NY, Aug 20, 14; m 39, 67; c 3. ORGANIC CHEMISTRY, POLYMER CHEMISTRY. *Educ:* Antioch Col, BS, 36; Ohio State Univ, PhD(chem), 39. *Prof Exp:* Asst, Ohio State Univ, 36-39; res org chemist, E I du Pont de Nemours & Co, Inc, 39-66, res assoc, 66-79; RETIRED. *Mem:* Am Chem Soc; Sigma Xi. *Res:* Textile treatments; new textile fibers; polymers; specialty film; chemical development. *Mailing Add:* 209 Lewis Ave Penney Farms FL 32079

CLINE, GEORGE BRUCE, b McConnellsburg, Pa, Sept 30, 36; m 61. PHYSIOLOGY, BIOPHYSICS. *Educ:* Juniata Col, BS, 58; State Univ NY, PhD(physiol), 67. *Prof Exp:* Consult molecular anat sect, Oak Ridge Nat Lab, 64-66, res assoc, 66-67; from asst prof to assoc prof, Univ Ala, Birmingham, 67-75, prof biol, 75-79, chmn dept, 75-80, asst prof physiol & biophys, Sch Med, 67-79. *Concurrent Pos:* Consult, Electro-Nucleonics, Inc, NJ, 67-75 & Argonne Nat Lab, 77-79; vis prof, Univ Brussels, 73-74; adj prof, Col Virgin Islands, 82-83; mem adv bd, Wolfson Bioanalyt Ctr, Univ Surrey, Guildford, Gt Brit, 78- *Mem:* AAAS; Soc Invert Path; Soc Study Reproduction. *Res:* Isoenzyme distributions of products of structural genes in Scyllarid lobsters from the Gulf of Mexico and the Caribbean Sea; Scyllarid lobster larvae rearing and development. *Mailing Add:* Dept of Biol Univ Col Univ of Ala Univ Sta Birmingham AL 35294

CLINE, HARVEY ELLIS, b Cambridge, Mass, Aug 15, 40; m 62; c 1. METALLURGY. *Educ:* Mass Inst Technol, BS, 62, MS, 64, PhD(metall), 65. *Prof Exp:* RES METALLURGIST, GEN ELEC RES & DEVELOP CTR, 65- *Concurrent Pos:* Coolidge fel, Gen Elec Corp. *Mem:* Am Inst Mining, Metall & Petrol Engrs; Am Inst Physics; Inst Elec & Electronics Engrs. *Res:* Solidification and properties of eutectics; magnetic properties of type II superconductors; semiconductor processing; developed the thermomogration process. *Mailing Add:* Gen Elec Res & Develop Ctr One River Rd Schenectady NY 12305

CLINE, J(ACK) F(RIBLEY), b Cadillac, Mich, June 19, 17; m 41; c 2. ELECTRICAL ENGINEERING. *Educ:* Univ Mich, BS, 38, MS, 41, PhD, 50. *Prof Exp:* From instr to asst prof elec eng, Univ Mich, 42-57; sr res eng, Stanford Res Inst, 57-76, STAFF ENGR, SRI INT, 76- *Concurrent Pos:* Design specialist, Antenna Lab, Douglas Aircraft Co, 53-54. *Mem:* Inst Elec & Electronics Eng. *Res:* Radio transmitters, receivers, antennas; electronic and microwave circuits and measurements; wave propagation; filters; multicouplers; radar; radio navigation; multilateration tracking; signal population analysis; systems evaluation. *Mailing Add:* SRI Int 333 Ravenswood Ave Menlo Park CA 94025

CLINE, JACK HENRY, b Columbus, Ohio, Feb 27, 27; m 48; c 8. ANIMAL NUTRITION. *Educ:* Ohio State Univ, BS, 50, MS, 52, PhD(animal sci), 56. *Prof Exp:* Asst animal nutrit, Exp Sta, 51-56, from instr to assoc prof, 56-69, PROF ANIMAL SCI, OHIO STATE UNIV, 69- *Concurrent Pos:* With Ohio Agr Res & Develop Ctr, Wooster; consult feed comp. *Mem:* Am Soc Animal Sci; Sigma Xi. *Res:* Ruminant and non-ruminant nutrition; feeding and metabolism studies with sheep and swine; mineral metabolism. *Mailing Add:* Dept of Animal Sci Ohio State Univ Columbus OH 43210

CLINE, JAMES E, b Detroit, Mich, Mar 10, 31; m 53; c 4. EXPERIMENTAL NUCLEAR PHYSICS. *Educ:* Univ Mich, BSE, 53, MS, 54, PhD(physics), 58. *Prof Exp:* Res assoc synchrotron proj, Univ Mich, 54-57; physicist, Atomic Energy Div, Phillips Petrol Co, 57-64, group leader, Decay Schemes Group, 64-66; group leader exp physics, Nat Reactor Test Sta, Aerojet Nuclear Co, 66-70, sect chief, 70-73; lab dir, 73-81, DIV MGR, NUCLEAR ENVIRON SERV, DIV SCI APPLICATIONS, INC, 81- *Concurrent Pos:* Lectr nuclear physics, Idaho State Univ, 58-59 & Univ Idaho, 58-73; asst prof & collab physics, Utah State Univ, 65-73. *Mem:* Am Phys Soc; Am Nuclear Soc; Inst Elec & Electronics Eng. *Res:* Gamma ray spectroscopy and automatic data analysis, measurement and study of various molecular forms of radioiodine in ventilation air in nuclear power plants; study of transuranics in Radwaste systems; develop instrumentation and techniques and provide services for radioactive effluent monitoring. *Mailing Add:* Suite 100 Nuclear Environ Serv No 3 Choke Cherry Rd Rockville MD 20850

CLINE, JAMES EDWARD, b Glens Falls, NY, Nov 13, 13; m 37; c 3. OPERATIONS RESEARCH. *Educ:* Cornell Univ, AB, 34; Harvard Univ, AM, 35, PhD(phys chem), 37. *Prof Exp:* Asst photochem, Harvard Univ, 37-41; asst chemist, Tenn Valley Authority, Wilson Dam, Ala, 41-42, assoc chemist, 42-45; chief res chemist, Beacon Co, Boston, 45-48; phys chemist & proj leader, Mass Inst Technol, 48-52; engr specialist, Sylvania Elec, 52-58; eng group leader, Raytheon Mfg Co, 58-61; staff scientist, Kearfott Semiconductor Corp, 61-62; eng specialist, Sylvania Electronic Syst Div, Gen Tel & Electronics Corp, 62-64; eng specialist aerospace technol, Electronic Res Ctr, NASA, 64-70; OPERS RES, US DEPT TRANSP, CAMBRIDGE, 70- *Res:* Instrumentation for vapor trace detection; computer interfacing; microelectronics. *Mailing Add:* 23 Stetson St Brookline MA 02146

CLINE, KENNETH CHARLES, b Ann Arbor, Mich, May 12, 48; m 71; c 1. PLANT MEMBRANE BIOGENESIS. *Educ:* Univ Mich, Ann Arbor, BS & BSE, 71; Univ Colo, Boulder, PhD(biochem), 79. *Prof Exp:* Quality control engr, Ford Motor Co, Rawsonville, Mich, 71-72; technician, Great Western Sugar, Longmont, Colo, 72-73; FEL, DEPT BOT, UNIV WIS-MADISION, 79- *Mem:* Am Soc Plant Physiol. *Res:* Structure function, and biogenesis of chloroplast membranes; mechamisms of synthesis and incorporation of chloroplast envelope membrane lipids and proteins. *Mailing Add:* Dept Bot Univ Wis Madison WI 53706

CLINE, MARLIN GEORGE, b Bertha, Minn, Dec 31, 09; m 36; c 3. SOIL MORPHOLOGY. *Educ:* NDak State Col, BS, 35; Cornell Univ, PhD(soils), 42. *Hon Degrees:* DSc, NDak State Univ & Trinity Col, Dublin, 65. *Prof Exp:* Jr soil surveyor, 35-38, assoc soil scientist, 41-42, soil scientist, 44-45, AGT CORRELATION SOILS, USDA, 46-; EMER PROF SOIL SCI, CORNELL UNIV, 74- *Concurrent Pos:* From instr to prof soils, State Univ NY Col Agr, Cornell Univ, 42-46, head dept agron, 63-70; soil scientist, Econ Coop Admin, Brit Africa, 49; Cornell contract, Philippines, 54-56; mem US mission soil & water, USSR, 58. *Mem:* Soil Sci Soc Am; Am Soc Agron; Soil Conserv Soc Am; Int Soc Soil Sci. *Res:* Morphology, genesis and cartography of soils; soil management. *Mailing Add:* 107 Brandywine Rd Ithaca NY 14850

CLINE, MICHAEL CASTLE, b Richmond, Va, Apr 3, 45; m 69; c 1. FLUID DYNAMICS. *Educ:* Va Polytech Inst & State Univ, BS, 67; Purdue Univ, MS, 68, PhD(mech eng), 71. *Prof Exp:* Nat Acad Sci res assoc, Langley Res Ctr, NASA, 71-73; STAFF MEM FLUID DYNAMICS, LOS ALAMOS NAT LAB, 73- *Mem:* Am Inst Aeronaut & Astronaut. *Res:* Computation of high speed, compressible fluid flows. *Mailing Add:* Gp T-3 MS-216 Los Alamos Nat Lab Los Alamos NM 87545

CLINE, MORRIS GEORGE, b Los Angeles, Calif, Aug 10, 31; m 59; c 6. PLANT PHYSIOLOGY, ECOLOGY. *Educ:* Univ Calif, Berkeley, BS, 53; Brigham Young Univ, MS, 61; Univ Mich, PhD(bot), 64. *Prof Exp:* Asst plant physiologist, Colo State Univ, 64-66; res fel environ plant physiol, Calif Inst Technol, 66-68; asst prof, 68-74, ASSOC PROF BOT, OHIO STATE UNIV, 74- *Res:* Effects of temperature, low and high intensity visible and ultraviolet radiation on plants; mechanisms in apical dominance; effects of soil environment on root growth of mountain shrubs; hormone action and nucleic acid metabolism. *Mailing Add:* Fac of Bot Ohio State Univ Columbus OH 43210

CLINE, RANDALL EUGENE, b Marietta, Ohio, Oct 4, 31; m 56; c 3. APPLIED MATHEMATICS. *Educ:* Marietta Col, BA, 53; Purdue Univ, MS, 55, PhD(math), 63. *Prof Exp:* Res asst & instr math, Purdue Univ, 55-59; res assoc, Inst Sci & Technol, Mich, 59-63, assoc res mathematician, 63-65, res mathematician, 65-68; from assoc prof to prof math & comput sci, 68-77, PROF MATH, UNIV TENN, KNOXVILLE, 77- *Concurrent Pos:* Mem staff, Math Res Ctr, US Army-Univ Wis, 64-65. *Mem:* AAAS; Soc Indust & Appl Math. *Res:* Matrix theory; algorithms. *Mailing Add:* Dept of Math Univ of Tenn Knoxville TN 37916

CLINE, SYLVIA GOOD, b Atlantic City, NJ, Dec 27, 28; m 50; c 3. CELL PHYSIOLOGY, CYTOLOGY. *Educ:* Bryn Mawr Col, PhD(biol), 65. *Prof Exp:* Res asst physiol chem, Univ Pa, 50-51; res asst biol, Bryn Mawr Col, 60-64, fel, 65-66; res assoc biochem, Queens Col, NY, 66-67, lectr chem & biochem, 67-68; from asst prof to assoc prof, 68-78, asst dean acad affairs, 73-76, PROF BIOL, QUEENSBOROUGH COMMUNITY COL, 78- *Concurrent Pos:* Guest investr, Biochem Cytol Lab, Rockefeller Univ, 66-67. *Mem:* AAAS; Am Chem Soc; Am Soc Cell Biol; Sigma Xi. *Res:* Glucose metabolism; RNA catabolism; growth of protozoa. *Mailing Add:* Dept of Biol Queensborough Community Col Bayside NY 11364

CLINE, THOMAS L, b Peiping, China, May 14, 32; US citizen; m 54; c 3. PHYSICS. *Educ:* Hiram Col, BA, 54; Mass Inst Technol, PhD(physics), 61. *Prof Exp:* Res assoc, lab nuclear sci, Mass Inst Technol, 60-61; PHYSICIST, SPACE SCI LAB, GODDARD SPACE FLIGHT CTR, NASA, 61- *Concurrent Pos:* Mem solar physics subcomt, Space Sci Steering Comt, DC, 62-64; actg chief, high energy astrophys prog, NASA, DC, 70-71, asst head, cosmic radiation br, 70- *Mem:* AAAS; fel Am Phys Soc; Am Astron Soc. *Res:* Cosmic rays; solar particle production; astrophysics. *Mailing Add:* Lab High-Energy Astrophys NASA-Code 661 Greenbelt MD 20771

CLINE, THOMAS WARREN, b Oakland, Calif, May 6, 46; div. DEVELOPMENTAL GENETICS. *Educ:* Univ Calif, Berkeley, AB, 68; Harvard Univ, PhD(biochem), 73. *Prof Exp:* Fel develop genetics, Helen Hay Whitney Found, Univ Calif, Irvine, 73-76; ASST PROF BIOL, PRINCETON UNIV, 76- *Concurrent Pos:* Guest scientist, Zool Inst, Univ Zürich. *Mem:* Genetics Soc Am; Soc Develop Biol; AAAS. *Res:* Developmental regulation of gene expression and pattern formation in Drosophila melanogaster with emphasis on oogenesis, sex determination, and X-chromosome dosage compensation. *Mailing Add:* Dept Biol Gugot Hall Princeton Univ Princeton NJ 08544

CLINE, WARREN KENT, b Bluefield, Va, July 28, 21; m 46; c 2. ORGANIC CHEMISTRY. *Educ:* Va Polytech Inst, BS, 42; Ohio State Univ, PhD(chem), 50. *Prof Exp:* Chemist, Gen Chem Defense Corp, 42-43; res chemist, Magnolia Petrol Co, 43-46; asst, Ohio State Univ, 46-50; res org chemist, Olin Mathieson Chem Corp, 50-59, res assoc, 59-60, supvr res group, Film Opers, 60-69, mgr polymer res group, Film Div, 69-76, SR RES ASSOC, TOBACCO INDUST RES GROUP, OLIN CORP, 76- *Mem:* Am Chem Soc. *Res:* Organic synthesis; polymer chemistry. *Mailing Add:* Olin Corp Film Div Box 200 Pisgah Forest NC 28768

CLINE, WILLIAM H, JR, b Elkins, WVa, Dec 28, 40; m 59; c 3. AUTONOMIC NERVOUS SYSTEM, CARDIOVASCULAR. *Educ:* Davis & Elkins Col, BS, 62; WVa Univ, MS, 64, PhD(pharmacol), 65. *Prof Exp:* Fel pharmacol, Sch Med, WVa Univ, 65-66; asst prof, Sch Med, Univ Mo, 66-71, assoc prof, 71-73; dir, Dept Med Sci, Div Pharmacol, 73-79, PROF PHARMACOL, SCH MED, SOUTHERN ILL UNIV, 73- *Concurrent Pos:* Adj prof, Sagamon State Univ, 73-77 & 81-; prof, Dept Physiol, Col Sci, Southern Ill Univ, Carbondale, 74-78. *Mem:* Sigma Xi; NY Acad Sci; AAAS. *Res:* Pharmacology of the involvement of antiotensin II in blood pressure control including interactions with the autonomic nervous system and adrenal medulla in hypertension. *Mailing Add:* Dept Pharmacol Sch Med Southern Ill Univ PO Box 3926 Springfield IL 62708

CLINESCHMIDT, BRADLEY VAN, b Redding, Calif, Dec 11, 41. NEUROPHARMACOLOGY. *Educ:* Ore State Univ, BS, 64; Univ Wash, PhD(pharmacol), 68. *Prof Exp:* Res assoc pharmacol, Exp Therapeut Br, Nat Heart & Lung Inst, NIH, 69-71, sr staff fel, 71-72; res fel, 72-75, dir neuropsychopharmacol, 75-80, SR DIR PHARMACOL, MERCK INST THERAPEUT RES, 80- *Mem:* Am Soc Pharmacol & Exp Therapeut; Soc for Neuroscience. *Res:* Neuropharmacological, behavioral and neurochemical actions of drugs affecting the central nervous system. *Mailing Add:* Merck Inst Therapeut Res West Point PA 19486

CLINGMAN, WILLIAM HERBERT, JR, b Grand Rapids, Mich, May 5, 29; m 51; c 2. PHYSICAL CHEMISTRY. *Educ:* Univ Mich, BS, 51; Princeton Univ, MA & PhD(phys chem), 54. *Prof Exp:* Res chemist, Am Oil Co, 54-57, group leader, 57-59; sect head, Tex Instruments Inc, 59-61, dir energy res lab,

61-62, mgr res exploitation dept, 62-64, corporate res & develop mkt, 64-67; PRES, W H CLINGMAN & CO, 67- *Mem:* Am Chem Soc; Inst Elec & Electronics Eng. *Res:* Radiation chemistry; catalysis; organic reaction mechanism; energy conversion; thermodynamics. *Mailing Add:* W H Clingman & Co 2001 Bryan St Suite 2265 Dallas TX 75201

CLINNICK, MANSFIELD, b Somerville, NJ, Jan 21, 22; m 42; c 6. MATHEMATICS. *Educ:* Calif State Polytech Col, BS, 47; Univ Calif, Berkeley, AB, 53, MA, 55. *Prof Exp:* Prin programmer, Lawrence Radiation Lab, Univ Calif, 55-58; proj mgr, Broadview Res Corp, 58-60; from asst prof to assoc prof math, Calif State Polytech Col, 60-67; COMPUT SCIENTIST, LAWRENCE BERKELEY LAB, UNIV CALIF, BERKELEY, 67- *Mem:* Sigma Xi; Math Asn Am; Asn Comput Mach. *Res:* Digital computer programming; algebra. *Mailing Add:* Real-Time Systs Group Lawrence Berkeley Lab Univ Calif Berkeley CA 94720

CLINTON, BRUCE ALLAN, b Jackson Heights, NY, Apr 27, 37; m 67; c 1. CELLULAR IMMUNOLOGY, MONOCLONAL ANTIBODY. *Educ:* Hofstra Univ, NY, BA, 61, MA, 62; Rutgers Univ, NJ, PhD(immunol), 69. *Prof Exp:* Instr immunol, Hofstra Univ, 62-63; res fel immunopath, Scripps Clinic Res Found, 69-72; WHO fel cellular immunol, Univ Autonoma De Mexico, Mexico City, 72; res scientist immunol, G D Searle & Co, 72-73, sr res scientist, 73-76, group leader, 76-77; dir immunohematol, 77-81, DIR IMMUNOLOGY RES & DEVELOP, DIV AM HOSP SUPPLY CORP, AM DADE, 81- *Mem:* Sigma Xi; Am Asn Parasitol; Am Asn Immunol. *Res:* Lymphokines and delayed hypersensitivity publications; immunochemistry of parasites; immune response to parasitic infection and auto immune disease; monoclonal antibody production; allergic response; blood-bank immunology. *Mailing Add:* Am Dade PO Box 520672 Miami FL 33152

CLINTON, GAIL M, b Klamath Falls, Ore, Jan 23, 46. CELL BIOLOGY, VIROLOGY. *Educ:* Univ Calif, San Diego, BA, 69, MS, 71, PhD(virol), 75. *Prof Exp:* Fel, Harvard Med Sch, 75-77, res assoc, 77-79; res assoc, Children's Hosp Med Ctr, Boston, 79-81; ASST PROF, DEPT BIOCHEM, LA STATE UNIV MED CTR, 81- *Mem:* AAAS; Am Soc Microbiol. *Res:* Role of protein modifications in growth regulation of animal cells and viruses. *Mailing Add:* Dept Biochem 1901 Perdido St La State Univ Med Ctr New Orleans LA 70112

CLINTON, RAYMOND OTTO, b Burbank, Calif, Apr 12, 18; m 38; c 2. MEDICINAL CHEMISTRY. *Educ:* Calif Inst Technol, BS, 40; Univ Calif, Los Angeles, MA, 41, PhD(org chem), 43. *Prof Exp:* Jr chemist, C F TenEyck & Co, Calif, 35-38; asst, Calif Inst Technol, 36-40; asst inorg chem, Univ Calif, Los Angeles, 41; chemist, Union Oil Co, Calif, 41-42; instr org chem, Marymount Col, 42; sr res chemist, Gasparcolor, Inc, Calif, 46-47 & Sterling-Winthrop Res Inst, 43-46, group leader, 47-56, head org sect, 56-60, dir res admin, 60-67; asst to chmn, Sterling Drug, Inc, 67-74, dir corp serv, 74-79; CONSULT, 79- *Concurrent Pos:* Chemist, Black Diamond Oil Co, Calif, 39-40; res chemist, Nat Defense Res Comt proj, Univ Calif, Los Angeles, 41-43; adj prof Rensselaer Polytech Inst, 52-62. *Mem:* Am Chem Soc; NY Acad Sci; Royal Soc Chem. *Res:* Chemistry of plant pigments; antitubercular agents; local anesthetics; antimalarials; sulfur-containing amines; anti-virus agents; color photography dyes; flavonones and related plant pigments; synthesis of acids related to vitamin A; steroids; structural activity relationships. *Mailing Add:* 110 W Mora Dr Green Valley AZ 85614

CLINTON, WILLIAM L, b St Louis, Mo, Sept 17, 30; m 52; c 9. THEORETICAL PHYSICS. *Educ:* St Louis Univ, PhD(chem), 59. *Prof Exp:* Teacher chem, St Louis Univ, 55-58; res assoc, Brookhaven Nat Lab, 58-60; asst prof chem, 60-63, from asst prof to assoc prof physics, 64-70, PROF PHYSICS, GEORGETOWN UNIV, 70- *Concurrent Pos:* Consult, Nat Bur Standards, Brookhaven Nat Lab, Oak Ridge Nat Lab & Lawrence Berkeley Lab. *Mem:* Am Phys Soc. *Res:* Application of quantum mechanics to molecular and solid state physics and theoretical chemistry; electronic structure. *Mailing Add:* Dept of Physics Georgetown Univ Washington DC 20007

CLIPPINGER, FRANK WARREN, JR, b Appleton, Wis, Oct 27, 25; m 50; c 2. ORTHOPEDIC SURGERY. *Educ:* Drury Col, Mo, AB, 48; Wash Univ, St Louis, MD, 52. *Prof Exp:* From instr to assoc prof, 57-70, PROF ORTHOP SURG, SCH MED, DUKE UNIV, 70- *Concurrent Pos:* Chmn, Prosthetics Res & Develop Comt, Nat Acad Sci, 75-76; med dir, Duke Hosp W-Duke Univ Med Sch, 75-, dir rehab, Duke Univ Med Ctr, 75-; chmn, Orthop Surg Adv Coun, Am Col Surgeons, 73-76, mem bd gov, 75- *Mem:* Am Orthop Asn; Am Acad Orthop Surgeons; Am Col Surgeons; Am Soc Surg Hand. *Res:* Research and development of artificial limbs; socket design and sensory feedback mechanism. *Mailing Add:* Box 3435 Duke Univ Med Ctr Durham NC 27710

CLISE, RONALD LEO, b Westernport, Md, Aug 19, 23; m; c 3. GENETICS, ZOOLOGY. *Educ:* Marietta Col, BA, 49; Mich State Univ, MS, 52; Western Reserve Univ, PhD(genetics), 60. *Prof Exp:* From instr to assoc prof, 55-72, chmn dept, 60-62, PROF BIOL, CLEVELAND STATE UNIV, 72- *Mem:* AAAS. *Res:* Population studies with Drosophila. *Mailing Add:* Dept of Biol Cleveland State Univ Euclid Ave at 24th St Cleveland OH 44115

CLITHEROE, H JOHN, b Hornchurch, Eng, Jan 2, 35; m 68; c 1. ENDOCRINOLOGY, GYNECOLOGY. *Educ:* Univ Sheffield, BSc, 59, MIBiol & PhD(med), 62; Royal Soc Health, FRSH, 74. *Prof Exp:* Johnson & Johnson fel, Rutgers Univ, 62-63; NIH fel pharmacol, 63-65, asst prof, 66-70, CLIN ASST PROF OBSTET & GYNEC, NJ COL MED, 70-; PROF BIOL SCI, COL STATEN ISLAND, CITY UNIV NEW YORK, 75- *Concurrent Pos:* Consult cytol, St Elizabeth's Hosp, Elizabeth, NJ, 67-75 & St Vincent's Med Ctr, New York, 67-80; assoc prof biol sci, Staten Island Community Col, New York Univ, 70-75. *Mem:* Brit Soc Endocrinol; Brit Inst Biol; Pan-Am Cancer Cytol Soc; NY Acad Sci; World Population Soc. *Res:* Uterine physiology; cytology of reproductive organs; sex selection of offspring; sexual therapy. *Mailing Add:* Dept of Biol Sci Col Staten Island Staten Island NY 10301

CLIVER, DEAN OTIS, b Berwyn, Ill, Mar 2, 35; m 60; c 4. VIROLOGY. *Educ:* Purdue Univ, BS, 56, MS, 57; Ohio State Univ, PhD(agr), 60. *Prof Exp:* Fel, Ohio State Univ, 60; resident res assoc virus serol, US Army Chem Corps Biol Labs, Ft Detrick, Md, 61-62; res assoc virol, food res inst & dept microbiol, Univ Chicago, 62-66; from asst prof to assoc prof, 66-76, PROF VIROL, FOOD RES INST & DEPT BACT, UNIV WIS-MADISON, 76- *Concurrent Pos:* Resident res assoc, Nat Acad Sci-Nat Res Coun, 61-62; consult, WHO, 69- *Mem:* Am Soc Microbiol; Sigma Xi. *Res:* Food research; studies on virus contamination of foods and water; animal virology. *Mailing Add:* Food Res Inst Univ of Wis 1925 Willow Dr Madison WI 53706

CLOGSTON, ALBERT MCCAVOUR, b Boston, Mass, July 13, 17; m; c 2. SOLID STATE PHYSICS. *Educ:* Mass Inst Technol, SB, 38, PhD(physics), 41. *Prof Exp:* Teaching fel physics, Mass Inst Technol, 38-41, mem staff, radiation lab, 41-46; res physicist, Bell Tel Labs, 46-63, asst dir mat res lab, 63-65, dir, phys res lab, 65-71; vpres res, Sandia Labs, 71-73; EXEC DIR RES, PHYSICS & ACAD AFFAIRS DIV, BELL TEL LABS, 73- *Mem:* Nat Acad Sci; fel Am Phys Soc. *Res:* Magnetism; theory of metals; superconductivity; nuclear magnetic resonance; alloys and intermetallic compounds. *Mailing Add:* Bell Tel Labs Murray Hill NJ 07974

CLOKE, PAUL LEROY, b Orono, Maine, Feb 6, 29; m 55; c 2. GEOCHEMISTRY. *Educ:* Harvard Univ, AB, 51; Mass Inst Technol, PhD(geol), 54. *Prof Exp:* Res geologist, mining & explor geol, Anaconda Co, 54-57; res fel geochem, Harvard Univ, 57-59; from asst prof to assoc prof, 59-69, PROF GEOCHEM, UNIV MICH, ANN ARBOR, 69- *Concurrent Pos:* Chemist, Dept Sci & Indust Res, Gracefield, NZ, 66-67; ed, The Geochem News, 65-73. *Mem:* AAAS; Soc Econ Geologists; Geochem Soc; Am Inst Mining, Metall & Petrol Engrs; Mineral Soc Can. *Res:* Application of chemistry to geologic problems, such as hydrothermal solutions, ore deposits, mineral-solution equilibria at low to high temperature and pressure, and recent sediments. *Mailing Add:* Dept of Geol & Mineral Univ of Mich Ann Arbor MI 48109

CLONEY, RICHARD ALAN, b Port Angeles, Wash, Feb 12, 30; m 52; c 3. DEVELOPMENTAL BIOLOGY, HISTOLOGY. *Educ:* Humboldt State Col, AB, 52, MA, 54; Univ Wash, PhD(zool), 59. *Prof Exp:* NIH fel anat, Sch Med, 59-61, from asst prof to assoc prof zool, 61-72, PROF ZOOL, UNIV WASH, 72- *Concurrent Pos:* Consult, Develop Biol Sect, Educ Develop Ctr, Mass; NSF grant; instr, Fri Harbor Labs, 63, 68-73, 75, 78 & 80; assoc ed, Cell & Tissue Res, 76- *Mem:* Am Soc Zoologists; AAAS; Am Soc Cell Biol. *Res:* Electron microscopic, cinemicrographic and experimental analyses of metamorphosis in ascidians; microfilaments and morphogenesis; fine structure of ascidian larvae; chaetogenesis in polychaetes; structure of chromatophore organs and iridophores in cephalopods; cinemicrography of marine invertebrate larvae. *Mailing Add:* Dept Zool Univ Wash Seattle WA 98105

CLONEY, ROBERT DENNIS, b Boston, Mass, May 6, 27. PHYSICAL CHEMISTRY. *Educ:* Spring Hill Col, BS, 52; Cath Univ Am, PhD(chem), 57; Woodstock Col, STB, 61. *Prof Exp:* Instr, pvt sch, NY, 52-53; res assoc chem, Woodstock Col, 57-62; from instr to asst prof, 62-71, ASSOC PROF CHEM, FORDHAM UNIV, 71- *Mem:* Am Chem Soc. *Res:* Quantum chemistry; molecular structure. *Mailing Add:* Dept of Chem Fordham Univ Bronx NY 10458

CLONINGER, CLAUDE ROBERT, b Beaumont, Tex, Apr 4, 44; m 69; c 2. PSYCHIATRY, POPULATION GENETICS. *Educ:* Univ Tex, Austin, BA, 62; Washington Univ, St Louis, MD, 70. *Prof Exp:* Resident psychiat, 70-73, from asst prof to assoc prof psychiat, 73-80, assoc prof genetics, 79-80, PROF PSYCHIAT & GENETICS, SCH MED, WASH UNIV, 81- *Concurrent Pos:* NIMH res scientist develop award, 75-; vis assoc prof, Pop Genetics Lab, Univ Hawaii, 78-79; consult, Am Psychiat Asn Task Force on Nomenclature, 78-80; vis prof psychiat & genetics, Umea Univ, Sweden, 80; psychiatrist, Jewish Hosp St Louis, 76-; mem res rev comt psychopath & clin biol, NIMH, 80-; assoc ed, Am J Human Genetics, 80- & J Clin Psychiat, 81- *Mem:* Am Psychiat Asn; Am Psychopath Asn; Am Soc Human Genetics; Behav Genetics Asn; Soc Biol Psychiat. *Res:* Genetic epidemiology of psychiatric disorders and classification of psychiatric disorders. *Mailing Add:* Sch Med Washington Univ 4940 Audubon St St Louis MO 63110

CLOPPER, HERSCHEL, b Winthrop, Mass, May 11, 41; m 63; c 2. CHEMICAL ENGINEERING, RHEOLOGY. *Educ:* Mass Inst Technol, BS, 62, MS, 63; Rice Univ, PhD(chem eng), 68. *Prof Exp:* Res engr, Plastics Dept, Res & Develop Div, E I du Pont de Nemours & Co, 67-68 & Fluorocarbons Div, 68-70; asst prof chem eng, Cath Univ Am, 70-71; develop engr, 71-77, prod develop engr, 77-81, PRIN ENGR, BATTERY DIV, POLAROID CORP, 81- *Mem:* Am Inst Chem Engrs; Am Chem Soc. *Res:* Rheology of and reactor design for non-Newtonian fluids; materials development. *Mailing Add:* 4 Ford Lane Framingham MA 01701

CLORE, WALTER JOSEPH, b Tecumseh, Okla, July 1, 11; m 34; c 3. HORTICULTURE. *Educ:* Okla Agr & Mech Col, BS, 33; State Col Wash, PhD, 47. *Prof Exp:* Asst hort, 37-46, assoc horticulturist, 46-51, horticulturist, 51-76, EMER HORTICULTURIST, IRRIG AGR RES & EXTEN CTR, WASH STATE UNIV, 76- *Mem:* Am Soc Hort Sci. *Res:* Production of grapes for juice and wine and asparagus production under irrigation. *Mailing Add:* 1317 Paterson Rd Prosser WA 99350

CLOSE, CHARLES M(OLLISON), b Ilion, NY, Mar 15, 27; m 57; c 3. ELECTRICAL ENGINEERING. *Educ:* Lehigh Univ, BS, 50; Stevens Inst Technol, MS, 53; Rensselaer Polytech Inst, PhD(network theory), 62. *Prof Exp:* Engr, Westinghouse Elec Corp, 50-52; asst, Stevens Inst Technol, 52-54; from instr to assoc prof, 54-67, PROF ELEC ENG, RENSSELAER POLYTECH INST, 67-, CURRIC CHMN COMPUT & SYSTS ENG & CURRIC CHMN ELEC ENG, 76- *Mem:* Inst Elec & Electronics Engrs; Am Soc Eng Educ. *Res:* Network theory. *Mailing Add:* Dept of Elec Eng Rensselaer Polytech Inst Troy NY 12181

CLOSE, DAVID MATZEN, b Plainfield, NJ, Mar 9, 42. RADIATION BIOLOGY, COMPUTER INTERFACING. *Educ:* Franklin & Marshall Col, AB, 64; WVa Univ, MS, 67; Clark Univ, PhD(physics), 72. *Prof Exp:* Fel physics, Univ Conn, 73-74; fel radiation biol, Univ Rochester, 74-78; ASST PROF PHYSICS, EAST TENN STATE UNIV, 78-, ADJ PROF, COL MED, 79- *Mem:* Am Phys Soc; fel Radiation Res Soc; Sigma Xi. *Res:* Electron spin resonance and electron-nuclear double resonance studies of radiation damage to nucleic acid constituents; theoretical calculations of free radical structors. *Mailing Add:* Physics Dept East Tenn State Univ Box 22060A Johnson City TN 37614

CLOSE, DONALD ALAN, b Tucson, Ariz, Nov 19, 46. NUCLEAR PHYSICS. *Educ:* Hastings Col, BA, 68; Univ Kans, MA, 70, PhD(physics), 72. *Prof Exp:* NSF presidential internship, 72-73, staff mem, 73, STAFF PHYSICIST NUCLEAR PHYSICS, LOS ALAMOS SCI LAB, UNIV CALIF, 73- *Mem:* Am Phys Soc; Sigma Xi. *Res:* Muonic atoms, gamma-ray spectroscopy and nuclear structure; proton induced x-ray fluorescence; development of assay instrumentation for fissionable material; application of Monte Carlo and discrete ordinates transport calculations to problems in nuclear science and geophysics. *Mailing Add:* Los Alamos Sci Lab Los Alamos NM 87545

CLOSE, DONALD HENRY, optics, see previous edition

CLOSE, PERRY, b Chicago, Ill, May 20, 21; m 61; c 2. GENETICS, PHYSIOLOGY. *Educ:* Univ Calif, Berkeley, AB, 47, MA, 48; Univ Tex, PhD(zool), 55. *Prof Exp:* Asst prof biol, Univ Southwestern La, 48-49; asst human genetics, Univ Tex, 54-55; aviation physiologist, med dept, US Naval Air Sta, Va, 55-57 & US Naval Sch Aviation Med, 57-62; mem res staff, Northrop Space Labs, Calif, 62-64; res biologist, Vet Admin Hosp, Long Beach, Calif, 64-65; head life sci, Chrysler Space Div, 65-68; PROF BIOL, CITY COL SAN FRANCISCO, 68- *Mem:* Am Soc Human Genetics; assoc fel Aerospace Med Asn; Soc Study Social Biol. *Res:* Genetics of longevity; hereditary deafness; low pressure and impact patho-physiology and the effects of radiation in combination with aerospace stresses; evaluation of radiotherapy procedures; genetics of mental retardation. *Mailing Add:* 272 Dennis Dr Daly City CA 94015

CLOSE, R(ICHARD) N(ORCROSS), b Philadelphia, Pa, Apr 20, 23; m 52; c 4. ELECTRONICS. *Educ:* Univ Rochester, BS, 43. *Prof Exp:* Proj engr, Radiation Lab, Mass Inst Technol, 43-45; prog dir reconaissance systs, Airborne Instruments Lab Div, Cutler Hammer, Inc, 45-60, dir, Indust Electronics Div, 60-68; progs mgr, Raytheon Co, 68-74, pres, Raytheon Europe Electronics Co, 74-75; PRES, R N CLOSE ASSOCS INC, 75- *Concurrent Pos:* Sci consult, USAF, 45; consult, Air Navig Develop, 50. *Mem:* Inst Elec & Electronics Engrs. *Res:* Military electronics; reconnaissance systems; radar data processing. *Mailing Add:* 85 Highland Circle Wayland MA 01778

CLOSE, RICHARD THOMAS, b New York, NY, Dec 24, 34; m 58; c 7. COMPUTER SCIENCE, ELECTROMAGNETIC THEORY. *Educ:* Iona Col, BS, 56; Cath Univ Am, PhD(physics), 67. *Prof Exp:* Res physicist, Naval Res Lab, Washington, DC, 59-68; assoc prof physics, St Bonaventure Univ, 68-71; dir comput ctr, State Univ NY Agr & Tech Col, Alfred Univ, 71-76; assoc prof, 76-80, PROF COMPUT SCI, US COAST GUARD ACAD, 80- *Concurrent Pos:* Lectr, Univ Md, 60-68; adj fac, Grad Sch, Univ New Haven, 76-80 & Hartford Grad Ctr, 80-; lectr, Data Processing Res Corp. *Mem:* Data Processing Mgt Asn; Asn Comput Mach. *Res:* Antenna research with particular emphasis on frequency independent scanning arrays; intense electron beam studies including both theoretical and experimental studies; solution of elliptic partial differential equations using various numerical methods; environmental remote sensing and its military uses; computer simulation; computer programming languages; computer literacy. *Mailing Add:* Comput Sci Dept US Coast Guard Acad New London CT 06320

CLOSMANN, PHILIP JOSEPH, b New Orleans, La, July 28, 25; m 56; c 6. PHYSICS, CHEMICAL PHYSICS. *Educ:* Tulane Univ, BE, 44; Mass Inst Technol, SM, 48; Calif Inst Technol, MS, 50; Rice Inst, PhD(physics), 53. *Prof Exp:* PHYSICIST, SHELL DEVELOP CO, 53- *Mem:* Am Phys Soc; Soc Petrol Engrs. *Res:* Fluid flow; heat flow; low temperature physics; fluidized solids; thermal recovery of hydrocarbons; oil shale recovery. *Mailing Add:* 27 Williamsburg Houston TX 77024

CLOSS, GERHARD LUDWIG, b Wuppertal, Ger, May 1, 28. ORGANIC CHEMISTRY. *Educ:* Univ Tubingen, Dipl Chem, 53, PhD(chem), 55. *Prof Exp:* Fel, Harvard Univ, 55-57; from asst prof to assoc prof, 57-63, PROF CHEM, UNIV CHICAGO, 63- *Concurrent Pos:* A P Sloan Found fel, 62-66. *Honors & Awards:* James Flack Norris Award, Am Chem Soc, 74. *Mem:* Nat Acad Sci; AAAS; Am Chem Soc; Royal Soc Chem; Am Acad Arts & Sci. *Res:* Chemistry of reactive intermediates; carbenes; carbanions; porphyrins; magnetic resonance. *Mailing Add:* Dept of Chem Univ of Chicago Chicago IL 60637

CLOSSON, WILLIAM DEANE, b Remus, Mich, Feb 3, 34; m 69. ORGANIC CHEMISTRY. *Educ:* Wayne Univ, BS, 56; Univ Wis, PhD(org chem), 60. *Prof Exp:* Asst org chem, Univ Wis, 56-60; NSF res fel, Harvard Univ, 60-61; from instr to asst prof, 61-66; assoc prof, 66-71, PROF CHEM, STATE UNIV NY ALBANY, 71- *Concurrent Pos:* Res grants, Petrol Res Fund, 62-65, USPHS, 63-66 & 67- & NSF, 65-67; Alfred P Sloan res fel, 68-70; Nat Acad Sci-Nat Res Coun travel grant, IVPAC Cong, Jerusalem, 75. *Mem:* AAAS; Am Chem Soc; Royal Soc Chem. *Res:* Solvolytic reactions of organic compounds; electronic absorption spectra of ketones, esters and alkyl azides; reactions of organic anion radicals; mecuration reactions and silver pi complexes of substituted alkenes. *Mailing Add:* Dept of Chem State Univ NY at Albany Albany NY 12222

CLOTFELTER, BERYL EDWARD, b Prague, Okla, Mar 23, 26; m 51; c 3. PHYSICS. *Educ:* Okla Baptist Univ, BS, 48; Univ Okla, MS, 49, PhD(physics), 53. *Prof Exp:* Instr math & physics, Okla Baptist Univ, 49-50; res physicist, Phillips Petrol Co, 53-55; assoc prof physics, Univ Idaho, 55-56; from asst prof to assoc prof physics, Okla Baptist Univ, 56-63; assoc prof, 63-68, PROF PHYSICS, GRINNELL COL, 68- *Concurrent Pos:* NSF sci fac fel, 68-69. *Mem:* Am Phys Soc; Am Asn Physics Teachers. *Res:* Astrophysics; cosmology. *Mailing Add:* Dept of Physics Grinnell Col Grinnell IA 50112

CLOTHIER, GALEN EDWARD, b Stafford, Kans, Nov 7, 33; m 55; c 3. CELL BIOLOGY, DEVELOPMENTAL BIOLOGY. *Educ:* Fresno State Col, AB, 55; Ore State Univ, MS, 57, PhD(biol), 60. *Prof Exp:* Asst prof zool, Los Angeles State Col, 60-62; from asst prof to assoc prof, 62-68, PROF BIOL, CALIF STATE UNIV, SONOMA, 68- *Mem:* Am Soc Zoologists; AAAS; Sigma Xi. *Res:* Physiology of mitosis; developmental biology of sea urchins. *Mailing Add:* Dept of Biol Calif State Univ Sonoma Rohnert Park CA 94928

CLOTHIER, ROBERT FREDERIC, b Pocatello, Idaho, Sept 15, 25. MECHANICAL ENGINEERING, PHYSICS. *Educ:* Univ Southern Calif, BE, 42, MSc, 43; Univ Montpellier, Dr Univ & DSc(physics), 65. *Prof Exp:* Asst chem, Univ Southern Calif, 41-42, asst physics, 42-43, lectr math, 45-46, instr mech eng, 49; instr physics, Ariz State Univ, 43-44; staff tech supvr, Electromagnetic Div, Manhatten Eng Dist, 44-45; instr math, Univ Okla, 46-47; assoc prof mech eng, Auburn Univ, 50-55; sr engr & adminstr, Atomic Power Div, Westinghouse Elec Corp, 55-57; prof eng & in chg nuclear eng, 57-77, chmn dept mech eng, 70-77, PROF MECH ENG, SAN JOSE STATE UNIV, 77- *Concurrent Pos:* Prof indust nuclear eng, Atomic Power Div, Westinghouse Elec Corp, 54, consult, Atomic Power Div, 54-55; consult, US Atomic Energy Comn, 59-; vis prof, London Polytech, 64-65 & 70. *Mem:* Am Soc Mech Engrs; Am Soc Eng Educ. *Res:* Dielectric properties of glass and cellulose materials; electrochemical isolation of isotopes; nuclear engineering; thermodynamics. *Mailing Add:* Dept of Mech Eng San Jose State Univ San Jose CA 95192

CLOTHIER, RONALD RAYMOND, b Cimarron, Kans, June 8, 24; m 46; c 1. MAMMALOGY. *Educ:* Fresno State Col, AB, 48; Univ Mont, MA, 50; Univ NMex, PhD, 57. *Prof Exp:* Asst zool, Univ Mont, 48-50; asst biol, Univ NMex, 50-52; asst prof biol, Kans Wesleyan Univ, 52-55; asst prof, 55-80, EMER ASSOC PROF ZOOL, ARIZ STATE UNIV, 80- *Mem:* Am Soc Mammalogists; Wildlife Soc; Soc Syst Zool. *Res:* Mammal life history; mammalian systematics. *Mailing Add:* Dept of Zool Ariz State Univ Tempe AZ 85281

CLOTHIER, WILLIAM DELBERT, b Potlatch, Idaho, Feb 11, 25; m 48; c 3. FISH & WILDLIFE MANAGEMENT, AQUATIC BIOLOGY. *Educ:* Mont State Col, BS, 51, MS, 52. *Prof Exp:* Fisheries res fieldman, Mont Fish & Game Dept, 49-50, lab supvr, 50, jr fishery biologist, 51-52; leader fishery invests, SDak Dept Game, Fish & Parks, 53-58; proj leader, Coastal Rivers Invests, Ore State Fish Comn, 58-60, water resources analyst, 60-62, asst state fisheries dir, 62-65; aquatic biologist, Nat Coastal Pollution Res Prog, Marine Sci Ctr, Pac Northwest Water Lab, Fed Water Qual Admin, 65-69, regional res & develop prog specialist, 69-70, regional res & monitoring rep, Environ Protection Agency, 71-73, chief, Region X Silvicult Proj, 73-76, supvry ecologist, Nonpoint Source Pollution Control, 76-81, REGIONAL SPECIALIST, FOREST PRACT & WATER QUAL & URBAN STORM WATER RUNOFF, ENVIRON PROTECTION AGENCY, 81- *Mem:* Am Fisheries Soc; Inst Fishery Res Biol. *Res:* Loss and movement of trout in irrigation diversions; ecological field investigations involving warm water fishes and salmonids; administration in sport and commercial fisheries, marine and fresh water; water pollution control. *Mailing Add:* Environ Protection Agency 1200 Sixth Ave Seattle WA 98101

CLOUD, JAMES DOUGLAS, b Dover, Ohio, Mar 29, 28; m 46; c 5. ELECTRICAL ENGINEERING. *Educ:* Purdue Univ, BS, 51, MS, 52. *Prof Exp:* Mem tech staff, Hughes Aircraft Co, 52-56, group head, 56-57, proj engr, 57-58, sect head, 58-59, head computs & integration, 59-60, head guid & controls, 60-61, mgr, Surveyor Syst Anal Lab, 61-68, asst mgr advan systs, 68-70, mgr advan systs, 70-71, asst mgr advan systs div, 71-76, mgr, Technol Div, Space & Commun Group, 76-79; asst group exec, Electro-Optical & Data Systs Group, 79-80, MGR, SPACE SENSORS DIV & CHMN OF BD, SANTA BARBARA RES CTR, 79-, GROUP VPRES, 80- *Mem:* Fel Am Inst Aeronaut & Astronaut; sr mem Inst Elec & Electronics Engrs. *Mailing Add:* Electro-Optical & Data Systs Group Centinela & Teale Sts Culver City CA 90230

CLOUD, JOSEPH GEORGE, b Phoenixville, Pa, Nov 27, 44; m 70; c 3. OOGENESIS, ENDOCRINOLOGY. *Educ:* WVa Univ, BS, 66; Univ Wis, Madison, MS, 68, PhD(physiol), 74. *Prof Exp:* Asst fel reproductive biol, John Hopkins Univ, 74-76, asst prof, 76-77; ASST PROF ZOOL, UNIV IDAHO, 77- *Mem:* Soc Study Reproduction; Am Soc Zoologists. *Res:* Hormonal control of the reinitiation of meiosis in oocytes at the time of ovulation. *Mailing Add:* Dept Biol Sci Univ Idaho Moscow ID 83843

CLOUD, PRESTON, JR, b West Upton, Mass, Sept 26, 12; m 72; c 3. GEOLOGY, INVERTEBRATE PALEONTOLOGY. *Educ:* George Washington Univ, BS, 38; Yale Univ, PhD, 40. *Prof Exp:* Instr geol, Mo Sch Mines, 40-41; Sterling res fel, Yale Univ, 41-42; geologist, US Geol Surv, 42-61, chief, paleont & stratig br, 49-59; prof geol & geophys, Univ Minn, 61-65, chmn dept, 61-63, head, sch earth sci, 62-63; prof geol, Univ Calif, Los Angeles, 65-68; geologist, US Geol Surv, 74-79; prof biogeol & environ studies, 68-74, EMER PROF, UNIV CALIF, SANTA BARBARA, 74- *Concurrent Pos:* Asst prof, Harvard Univ, 46-48; mem exec comt, earth sci div, Nat Res Coun, 52-56; vis prof, Univ Tex, 62 & 78; H R Luce prof cosmology, Mt Holyoke Col, 79-80; Queen Elizabeth II sr res fel, Australian Dept Sci, 81. *Honors & Awards:* Morrison Prize, NY Acad, 40; Rockefeller Pub Serv Award, 56; Distinguished Serv Award & Gold Medal, US Dept Interior, 59; Medal, Paleont Soc Am, 71; Lucius Wilbur Cross Medal, Yale

Univ Grad Sch, 73; Penrose Medal, Geol Soc Am, 76; Walcott Medal, US Nat Acad Sci, 77. *Mem:* Nat Acad Sci, (mem coun, 72-75, exec comt, 73-75); Am Acad Arts & Sci; Geol Soc Am; Paleont Soc Am; Soc Study Evolution. *Res:* Biogeology; sedimentology; marine geology; historical geology. *Mailing Add:* US Geol Surv & Dept of Geol Sci Univ of Calif Santa Barbara CA 93106

CLOUD, WILLIAM K, b Tucson, Ariz, May 7, 10; m 40; c 4. SEISMOLOGY, MECHANICAL ENGINEERING. *Educ:* Univ Ariz, BS, 34. *Prof Exp:* Irrig engr, Exten Serv, Univ Ariz, 35-37; state engr, Agr Adjust Admin, Ariz, 37-42; geophysicist, US Coast & Geod Surv, 46-52, chief seismol field surv, 52-71; sr seismologist, Univ Calif, Berkeley, 71-76; PVT PRACTICE, 76- *Honors & Awards:* Colbert Medal, Soc Am Mil Engrs, 58. *Mem:* Seismol Soc Am (secy, 71); Soc Am Mil Engrs; Earthquake Eng Res Inst. *Res:* Engineering seismology; natural and artificial earthquake vibrations of engineering significance; vibration characteristics of structures. *Mailing Add:* 1920 8th Ave San Francisco CA 94116

CLOUD, WILLIAM MAX, b Wilmot, Kans, Mar 27, 23; m 47; c 3. ATOMIC SPECTROSCOPY. *Educ:* Southwestern Col, BA, 47; Univ Wis, MS, 49, PhD(physics), 55. *Prof Exp:* Instr physics, Southwestern Col, 49-50, asst prof physics & counr men, 50-53; from asst prof to assoc prof, Kans State Teachers Col, 55-62; assoc prof, 62-66, PROF PHYSICS & CHMN DIV PRE-ENG STUDIES, EASTERN ILL UNIV, 66- *Mem:* Am Asn Physics Teachers; Sigma Xi; Am Phys Soc. *Res:* High resolution atomic spectroscopy using an atomic beam. *Mailing Add:* Dept of Physics Eastern Ill Univ Charleston IL 61920

CLOUGH, DAVID EDWARDS, b New Brunswick, NJ, Apr 12, 46; wid; c 2. CHEMICAL ENGINEERING. *Educ:* Case Western Reserve Univ, BS, 68; Univ Colo, MS, 69, PhD(chem eng), 75. *Prof Exp:* Chem engr, E I du Pont de Nemours & Co, 69-72; instr, 75, ASST PROF CHEM ENG, UNIV COLO, 75- *Concurrent Pos:* Consult, E I du Pont de Nemours & Co, 72- & Latin Am Scholar Prog, Am Univ, 75- *Mem:* Am Inst Chem Engrs; Instrument Soc Am; Am Soc Eng Educ. *Res:* Optimization and control of chemical processes; application of real time computers; mathematical modeling and applied mathematics in chemical engineering. *Mailing Add:* Dept of Chem Eng Univ of Colo Boulder CO 80309

CLOUGH, DONALD J, operations research, see previous edition

CLOUGH, FRANCIS BOWMAN, b Boise, Idaho, Feb 4, 24; m 62. PHYSICAL INORGANIC CHEMISTRY. *Educ:* Univ Wyo, BS, 44; Princeton Univ, MA, 48, PhD(chem), 51. *Prof Exp:* Chemist org res, Distillation Prod, Inc, 44-46; asst, Princeton Univ, 46-50; from instr to asst prof chem, Va Polytech Inst & State Univ, 50-55; asst prof chem, Stevens Inst Technol, 55-59, assoc prof, 59-80; CONSULT & PROPRIETOR, CHEM CRITERIA, 81- *Concurrent Pos:* Vis scientist, Nat Ctr Atmospheric Res, 79. *Mem:* AAAS; Am Chem Soc; fel Am Inst Chemists. *Res:* Optical rotatory power; solvent interactions; energy transfer in inorganic reactions. *Mailing Add:* 8451 Allison Ct Arvado CO 80005

CLOUGH, GARRETT CONDE, b Mystic, Conn, Dec 25, 31; m 61; c 2. ECOLOGY, CONSERVATION. *Educ:* Union Col, BS, 53; Univ Mich, MS, 54; Univ Wis, PhD(zool), 62. *Prof Exp:* Asst zool, Univ Wis, 58-62; asst prof, Dalhousie Univ, 61-63; NIMH res fel, Norweg State Game Res Inst, 63-64; vis res fel ecol, Cornell Univ, 64-65; asst prof zool, Univ RI, 65-74; sci dir, Ctr Natural Areas, 74-76; ASSOC PROF BIOL, NASSON COL, 76- *Concurrent Pos:* Nat Res Coun Can grant, 61-63; vis res prof, Univ Oslo, 69-70; NIH spec res fel, Univ Wis, 69-70. *Mem:* Am Inst Biol Sci; Sigma Xi; Am Soc Mammalogists; Ecol Soc Am; Animal Behav Soc. *Res:* Ecology and animal behavior; population dynamics; arctic ecology. *Mailing Add:* Dept Biol Nasson Col Springvale ME 04083

CLOUGH, JOHN WENDELL, b Oak Bluffs, Mass, Jan 3, 42; m 68; c 1. GEOPHYSICS. *Educ:* Northeastern Univ, BS, 65; Univ Wis, Madison, MS, 70, PhD(geophys), 74. *Prof Exp:* Proj assoc geophys, Geophys & Polar Res Ctr, Univ Wis, 74-75; sci dir & asst prof geophysics, Ross Ice Shelf Proj, Univ Nebr, Lincoln, 75-79; asst prof geophysics, NC State Univ, Raleigh, 79-81; GEOPHYSICIST, MARATHON OIL CO, CASPER, WY, 81- *Mem:* Sigma Xi; Am Geophys Union; Soc Explor Geophys; Int Glaciol Soc. *Res:* Radar echo sounding of polar ice thickness; geophysical survey of Ross Ice Shelf, Antartica. *Mailing Add:* 751 Goodstein Dr Casper WY 82601

CLOUGH, RAY W(ILLIAM), b Seattle, Wash, July 23, 20; m 42; c 3. STRUCTURAL ENGINEERING. *Educ:* Univ Wash, BS, 42; Calif Inst Technol, MS, 43; Mass Inst Technol, MS, 47, ScD, 49; Techn Dr, Chalmers Univ Technol, Grottenburg, Sweden, 79. *Prof Exp:* From asst prof to assoc prof, 49-59, PROF CIVIL ENG, UNIV CALIF, BERKELEY, 59- *Concurrent Pos:* Fulbright fel, res ship vibrations, Norway, 56-57; overseas fel, Churchill Col, Cambridge Univ, 63-64; consult struct dynamics and earthquake engineering. *Honors & Awards:* Res Award, Am Soc Civil Engrs, 61, Howard Award, 70, Moisseiff Award, 80; Newmark Medal, 79. *Mem:* Nat Acad Sci; Nat Acad Eng; Seismol Soc Am; Earthquake Eng Res Inst; Am Soc Civil Engrs. *Res:* Application of electronic digital computers to problems of structural analysis; response of structures to earthquake loads. *Mailing Add:* Dept of Civil Eng Univ of Calif Berkeley CA 94720

CLOUGH, RICHARD H(UDSON), b Springer, NMex, Aug 25, 22; m 45; c 2. CIVIL ENGINEERING, CONSTRUCTION MANAGEMENT. *Educ:* Univ NMex, BS, 43; Univ Colo, MS, 49; Mass Inst Technol, ScD(civil eng), 51. *Prof Exp:* Instr & asst prof, Univ NMex, 46-49, assoc prof, 51-52; res assoc, Mass Inst Technol, 49-51; vpres & owner, Lembke, Clough & King, Inc, 52-57; from assoc prof civil eng to prof & chmn dept, 57-60, dean, col eng, 60-68, PROF CIVIL ENG, UNIV N MEX, 68- *Honors & Awards:* SIR Award, NMex Bldg Br, Assoc Gen Contractors Am. *Mem:* Am Soc Civil Engrs; Nat Soc Prof Engrs; Am Soc Eng Educ; Am Soc Testing & Mat. *Res:* Metrication of construction industry; bidding strategies; construction project time control; construction forensics. *Mailing Add:* Dept of Civil Eng Univ of NMex Albuquerque NM 87131

CLOUGH, ROBERT RAGAN, b Sibley, Iowa, Feb 25, 42. MATHEMATICS. *Educ:* Univ Md, AB, 64; Northwestern Univ, MS, 66, PhD(math), 67. *Prof Exp:* Asst prof math, Univ Notre Dame, 67-73; systs rep, 73-77, SOFTWARE SPECIALIST, BURROUGHS CORP, 77- *Mem:* Am Math Soc; Math Asn Am. *Res:* Algebraic topology; fiber spaces; homotopy theory. *Mailing Add:* 753 Juniper Dr Palatine IL 60067

CLOUGH, ROGER LEE, b Salt Lake City, Utah, Aug 24, 49; m 70. ORGANIC CHEMISTRY. *Educ:* Univ Utah, BA, 71; Calif Inst Technol, PhD(chem), 75. *Prof Exp:* NATO fel, Tech Univ Munich, Ger, 75-76; NSF fel, Univ Calif, Los Angeles, 76-77; STAFF SCIENTIST CHEM, SANDIA LABS, 77- *Mem:* Am Chem Soc. *Res:* Organic chemistry; photochemistry and radiation chemistry; polymer degradation and stabilization; free radical chemistry; molecular conformational studies; nuclear magnetic resonance; transition metal organometallics. *Mailing Add:* Sandia Labs Org 5811 Albuquerque NM 87115

CLOUGH, STUART BENJAMIN, b Tisbury, Mass, Mar 16, 37; m 61; c 3. PHYSICAL CHEMISTRY, POLYMER CHEMISTRY. *Educ:* Univ Mass, Amherst, BS, 59, PhD(chem), 66; Univ Del, MChE, 61. *Prof Exp:* Chemist, Dewey & Almy Chem Div, W R GRace Co, 61-62; res fel chem, Univ Mass, Amherst, 62-65; chemist, US Army Natick Labs, 65-68 & US Army Mat & Mech Res Ctr, 68-70; from asst prof to assoc prof, 70-78, PROF CHEM, UNIV LOWELL, 78-, CHMN, CHEM DEPT, 81- *Mem:* Am Chem Soc; Am Phys Soc. *Res:* Structure and physical properties of bulk polymers. *Mailing Add:* Dept Chem Univ Lowell Lowell MA 01854

CLOUGH, STUART CHANDLER, b Richmond, Va, July 29, 43; m 68; c 2. ORGANIC CHEMISTRY. *Educ:* Univ Richmond, BS; Univ Fla, PhD(chem), 69. *Prof Exp:* Res assoc chem, State Univ NY Buffalo, 69-71; res assoc, Philip Morris, Inc, 71-73; ASST PROF CHEM, UNIV RICHMOND, 73- *Mem:* Am Chem Soc. *Res:* Thermal and photochemical rearrangements and reactions of small organic molecules with particular interest in the formation and characterization of reactive intermediates. *Mailing Add:* Dept of Chem Univ of Richmond Richmond VA 23173

CLOUGH, WENDY GLASGOW, b Salem, NJ, Sept 7, 42. ANIMAL VIROLOGY. *Educ:* Harvard Univ, BA, 64; Dartmouth Med Sch, BMS, 66; Harvard Med Sch, MD, 68. *Prof Exp:* Fel molecular biol, Dept Microbiol, Sch Med, Tufts Univ, 68-71; NIH spec fel molecular biol, Dept Biol, John Hopkins Univ, 71-73; fel biochem, Dept Biochem & Molecular Biol, Harvard Univ, 73-74; res assoc molecular biol, Basic Sci Div, Sidney Faber Cancer Inst, Harvard Med Sch, 74-75, instr, 75-77; asst prof, 77-81, ASSOC PROF MOLECULAR BIOL, DEPT BIOL SCI, MOLECULAR BIOL DIV, UNIV SOUTHERN CALIF, 81- *Concurrent Pos:* Fel, Med Found Boston, 76-77; res career develop award, Nat Cancer Inst, 80. *Mem:* AAAS; Am Soc Microbiol; Sigma Xi; Asn Women Sci. *Res:* Molecular biology and biochemistry of herpes viruses, specifically Epstein-Barr virus; eucaryotic and viral DNA replication; mechanism of action of anti-viral drugs; viral DNA methylation; molecular genetics of bacterial viruses. *Mailing Add:* ACBR 126 Molecular Biol Univ Southern Calif Los Angeles CA 90007

CLOUSER, WILLIAM SANDS, b Atlantic City, NJ, Feb 8, 21; m 51; c 1. ENGINEERING MECHANICS, MATERIALS SCIENCE. *Educ:* Univ NMex, BSME, 55; Univ Wis, MS, 57, PhD(eng mech), 58. *Prof Exp:* Draftsman, Los Alamos Sci Lab, 49-53; asst prof eng mech, Univ Wis, 58-63; STAFF MEM ENG MECH, LOS ALAMOS NAT LAB, 63- *Concurrent Pos:* Vis asst prof & Ford Found res grant, Univ Mich, 60; adv prof, Univ NMex, 71- *Mem:* Am Soc Mech Engrs. *Res:* Properties of wood and wood products; graphite and metals behavior; research and development for weapons systems and reactor components; stress analysis. *Mailing Add:* 126 Rover Blvd Los Alamos NM 87544

CLOUTIER, CONRAD FRANCOIS, b Chateau-Richer, Que, July 11, 48. ENTOMOLOGY. *Educ:* Laval Univ, BA, 70, MSc, 72; Simon Fraser Univ, PhD(entom), 78. *Prof Exp:* Lectr, 76-78, asst prof, 78-81, ASSOC PROF ENTOM, DEPT BIOL, LAVAL UNIV, 81- *Mem:* Entom Soc Can; Entom Soc Am; Can Soc Zoologists. *Res:* General entomology; aphid biology and ecology; host-parasite interactions. *Mailing Add:* Dept of Biol Fac of Sci & Eng Laval Univ Quebec PQ G1K 7P4 Can

CLOUTIER, ELMER JOSEPH, entomology, deceased

CLOUTIER, GILLES GEORGES, b Quebec City, Que, June 27, 28; m 54; c 1. PHYSICS. *Educ:* Laval Univ, BA, 49, BASc, 53; McGill Univ, MSc, 56, PhD(physics), 59. *Prof Exp:* Tech officer, Defence Res Bd Can, 53-54; sr mem sci staff, plasma physics, res labs, RCA Victor Co, Ltd, Can, 59-64; assoc prof physics, Univ Montreal, 64-68; sci dir, Hydro-Quebec Inst Res, 68-71, dir res, 71-74, asst dir, 74-78; PRES, ALTA RES COUN, 78- *Concurrent Pos:* Mem comn, Int Sci Radio Union, Can, 64-68; assoc comt space res, Nat Res Coun Can, 64-69, mem Coun, 73- *Mem:* Sr mem Inst Elec & Electronics Engrs; Am Phys Soc; Can Asn Physicists (pres, 72-73); Royal Soc Can. *Res:* Plasma physics; microwave optics; electron impact phenomena; electric propulsion; electromagnetic waves and plasmas; arc physics. *Mailing Add:* Alta Res Coun 11315 87th Ave Edmonton AB T6G 2E8 Can

CLOUTIER, LEONCE, b Quebec City, Que, Feb 5, 28; m 51; c 3. CHEMICAL ENGINEERING. *Educ:* Laval Univ, BScA, 50, DSc(chem eng), 63. *Prof Exp:* Plant engr, Can Packers Ltd, 50-52; design engr atomic reactor, C D Howe Co, 52-55; lectr, 55-59, assoc prof, 59-67, chmn dept, 69-75, PROF CHEM ENG, LAVAL UNIV, 67- *Concurrent Pos:* Tech consult, Aluminum Co Can Ltd; vis prof, Univ Calif, Berkeley, 75-76. *Mem:* Chem Inst Can; Can Soc Chem Engrs. *Res:* Efficiency and mechanism of mixing for liquid continuous systems; process instrumentation and control; chemical kinetics; applications of computers to chemical engineering. *Mailing Add:* Dept Chem Eng Laval Univ Quebec PQ G1K 7P4 Can

CLOUTIER, PAUL ANDREW, b Opelousas, La, Feb 7, 43; m 64; c 2. SPACE SCIENCE, PLASMA PHYSICS. *Educ:* Univ Southwestern La, BS, 64; Rice Univ, PhD(space sci), 67. *Prof Exp:* Res assoc space sci, 67, asst prof, 67-76, PROF SPACE PHYSICS & ASTRON, RICE UNIV, 76- *Res:* Experimental research in ionospheric currents and fields, especially rocketborne magnetometers; theoretical research in macroscopic plasma phenomena, especially interaction of the solar wind with planetary atmospheres. *Mailing Add:* Dept of Space Physics & Astron Rice Univ Houston TX 77001

CLOUTIER, PAUL FREDERICK, biochemistry, see previous edition

CLOUTIER, ROGER JOSEPH, b North Attleboro, Mass, July 25, 30; m 54; c 5. HEALTH PHYSICS. *Educ:* Univ Mass, BS, 56; Univ Rochester, MS, 57. *Prof Exp:* Assoc engr, Westinghouse Elec Corp, 57-59; scientist, Med Div, 59-74, chmn, Spec Training Div, 74-77, DIR PROF TRAINING, OAK RIDGE ASSOC UNIVS, 77- *Mem:* Health Physics Soc; Am Asn Physicists in Med; Soc Nuclear Med. *Res:* Radiation safety and dosimetry; medical use of radioisotopes. *Mailing Add:* Mert Div Oak Ridge Assoc Univs Oak Ridge TN 37830

CLOUTMAN, LAWRENCE DEAN, b Pratt, Kans, Nov 5, 44; m 69; c 1. ASTROPHYSICS, FLUID DYNAMICS. *Educ:* Univ Kans, BS, 68; Ind Univ, MA, 71, PhD(astrophys), 72. *Prof Exp:* STAFF MEM NUMERICAL FLUID DYNAMICS, LOS ALAMOS SCI LAB, 72- *Mem:* Am Astron Soc; Sigma Xi. *Res:* Methodology development in numerical fluid dynamics; theoretical performance studies on gas centrifuges and internal combustion engines; theoretical astrophysics. *Mailing Add:* Group T3 MS 216 Los Alamos Nat Lab Los Alamos NM 87545

CLOVER, RICHMOND BENNETT, b Johnson City, NY, Jan 30, 43; m 66; c 2. MAGNETISM. *Educ:* Cornell Univ, BS, 65; Yale Univ, MS, 67, PhD(appl physics), 69. *Prof Exp:* Mem tech staff, RCA Labs, 69-72; mem tech staff, Hewlett-Packard Lab, 72-73; dept mgr, 72-77; VPRES ENG & MKT, INTEL MAGNETICS, INC, 77- *Mem:* Inst Elec & Electronic Engrs. *Res:* Investigation of magnetic bubble domain materials, devices and memory systems. *Mailing Add:* Intel Magnetics 3000 Oakmead Village Dr Santa Clara CA 95051

CLOVIS, JAMES S, b Waynesburg, Pa, Aug 14, 37; m 70. PHYSICAL ORGANIC CHEMISTRY. *Educ:* Waynesburg Col, BS, 59; Calif Inst Technol, PhD(chem), 63. *Prof Exp:* Fel, Univ Munich, 62-63; mem staff, Rohm & Haas Co, 63-70, lab head, process chem, 70-74, proj leader, Pollution Control Res, 74-76, res & develop mgr, Indust Chem & Plastics, 76-79; mgr res & develop, Indust Chem, 79-81, DIR INDUST CHEM RES, NAM REGION, 82- *Mem:* Am Chem Soc. *Res:* Benzidine rearrangement; 1, 3-dipolar addition; phosphorus chemistry; plastics research; process research; pollution control research; ion exchange research; oil additive research. *Mailing Add:* 207 Pen Valley Terrace Morrisville PA 19067

CLOVIS, JESSE FRANKLIN, b Clarksburg, WVa, Jan 31, 21; m 48; c 3. SYSTEMATIC BOTANY. *Educ:* WVa Univ, BSF, 47, MS, 52; Cornell Univ, PhD, 55. *Prof Exp:* Instr bot, Univ Conn, 55-57; from asst prof to assoc prof biol, 57-72, pre-med adv, 63-70, PROF BIOL, WVA UNIV, 72- *Mem:* Bot Soc Am; Am Soc Plant Taxonomists. *Res:* Aquatic plants; speciation. *Mailing Add:* Dept Biol W Va Univ Morgantown WV 26506

CLOWER, DAN FREDERIC, b Crystal Springs, Miss, Mar 9, 28; m 51; c 4. ENTOMOLOGY. *Educ:* La State Univ, BS, 49; Cornell Univ, PhD(econ entom), 55. *Prof Exp:* Asst entom, Cornell Univ, 50-55; asst entomologist, 55-58, assoc prof entom, 58-63, PROF ENTOM, LA STATE UNIV, BATON ROUGE, 63- *Mem:* Entom Soc Am. *Res:* Cotton entomology; ecological relationships; forest entomology. *Mailing Add:* Dept of Entom Life Sci Bldg La State Univ Baton Rouge LA 70803

CLOWERS, CHURBY CONRAD, JR, b Little Rock, Ark, Mar 23, 34; m 59; c 2. ANALYTICAL CHEMISTRY. *Educ:* Univ Mo, Kansas City, BS, 57; Univ Mo, Columbia, PhD(anal chem), 66. *Prof Exp:* Res chemist, Textile Fibers Dept, Nylon Tech Div, E I du Pont de Nemours & Co, Inc, 66-68; ANAL RES CHEMIST, ANAL CHEM DEPT, MERRELL DOW PHARMACEUTICALS, INC, 68- *Mem:* Am Chem Soc. *Res:* Pharmaceutical, biochemical and metabolic analytical research; chemical instrumentation; physicochemical studies of drug degradation; chromatographic separations; spectra-structure relationships. *Mailing Add:* 3 Revel Ct Cincinnati OH 45217

CLOWES, RONALD MARTIN, b Calgary, Alta, Mar 18, 42; m 68. SEISMOLOGY, MARINE GEOPHYSICS. *Educ:* Univ Alta, BSc, 64, MSc, 66, PhD(geophys), 69. *Prof Exp:* Nat Res Coun Can postdoctoral & hon res fel geophys, Australian Nat Univ, 69-70; asst prof, 70-77, ASSOC PROF GEOPHYS, UNIV BC, 77- *Concurrent Pos:* Consult, Horton Maritime Explor Ltd, 75-76; vis assoc prof, Inst Geophys, Copenhagen Univ, 79-80 & Lab Geophys, Aarhus Univ, Denmark, 79-80. *Honors & Awards:* Soc Explor Geophysicists Award, 68. *Mem:* Am Geophys Union; Soc Explor Geophysicists; Seismol Soc Am; Can Soc Explor Geophysicists; Can Geophys Union. *Res:* Structure and properties of the earth's crust and upper mantle, at sea and on land, from detailed analysis of reflected and refracted seismic waves generated by chemical explosions; relationship of seismic results with tectonics and geology. *Mailing Add:* Dept of Geophys & Astron Univ of BC Vancouver BC V6T 1W5 Can

CLOWES, ROYSTON COURTENAY, b Swansea, Wales, Sept 11, 21; m 52; c 3. MICROBIOLOGY, GENETICS. *Educ:* Univ Birmingham, BSc, 48, PhD(physiol), 51, DSc(genetics), 65. *Prof Exp:* Res assoc microbiol, Wright-Fleming Inst, St Mary's Hosp, London, Eng, 51-57; staff mem, Microbial Genetics Res Unit, Med Res Coun, Hammersmith Hosp, London, 57-65; prof biol, Grad Res Ctr Southwest, 65-69, head div, 68-69, chmn biol, 69-74, PROF BIOL, UNIV TEX, DALLAS, 69-, CHMN BIOL, 79- *Concurrent Pos:* Damon Runyon Cancer Res fel, 55-56; vis prof, virus lab, Univ Calif, Berkeley, 61; mem, Microbial Chem Study Sect, NIH, 71-73, chmn, 73-75. *Mem:* Am Soc Microbiol; Genetics Soc Am; Brit Soc Gen Microbiol; Brit Genetical Soc. *Res:* Microbial genetics; molecular biology; biology of bacterial plasmids; genetic engineering. *Mailing Add:* Div of Biol Univ Tex at Dallas PO Box 688 Richardson TX 75080

CLOYD, GROVER DAVID, b Mosheim, Tenn, Oct 25, 18; m 74; c 3. VETERINARY MEDICINE. *Educ:* Auburn Univ, DVM, 42. *Prof Exp:* Self employed, Vet Med Pract, 47-55; dir vet serv, Ky Chem Indust, 55-57; asst dir field res pharmaceut prod, Richardson-Merrell Inc, 57-59, dir field res, 59-62, asst dir res, 62-65, sci develop aide gen mgr, 65-68; vet med dir, 68-71, dir vet med, 71-72, DIR VET MED & CONSUMER PROD RES & DEVELOP, A H ROBINS CO, INC, 72- *Mem:* Indust Vets Asn (secy, 70-74, pres, 75-76). *Res:* Pharmaceutical products research and development, veterinary and human. *Mailing Add:* 2024 Floyd Ave Richmond VA 23220

CLOYD, JAMES C, III, b Louisville, Ky, July 1, 48. PHARMACY, CLINICAL PHARMACOLOGY. *Educ:* Purdue Univ, BS, 71; Univ Ky, DPharm, 76. *Prof Exp:* asst prof, 76-80, ASSOC PROF & CLIN PHARMACIST, COL PHARM, ST PAUL RAMSEY MED CTR, 80- *Concurrent Pos:* Resident, Hosp Pharm, Univ Hosp, Univ Ky Med Ctr, 73-76; consult, licensure examr, Nat Asn Bds Pharm, 77- *Mem:* Am Asn Cols Pharm; Am Soc Hosp Pharmacists; Am PharmaPharmaceut Asn; Am Epilepsy Soc. *Res:* Clinical pharmacology of anticonvulsant drugs; physical-chemical compatibility of drugs in intravenous solutions. *Mailing Add:* Health Sci Unit F Col Pharm Univ Minn Minneapolis MN 55455

CLUFF, CARWIN BRENT, b Central, Ariz, Feb 20, 35; m 68; c 5. HYDROLOGY. *Educ:* Univ Ariz, BS, 59, MS, 61; Colo State Univ, PhD, 77. *Prof Exp:* Asst engr civil eng, Calif Dept Water Resources, 61-62; res assoc hydrol, Water Resources Res Ctr, Univ Ariz, 62-63; from asst hydrologist to assoc hydrologist, 63-75; expert in hydrol, Food & Agr Orgn, UN, 75-76; ASSOC HYDROLOGIST, WATER RESOURCES RES CTR, UNIV ARIZ, 76- *Mem:* Am Soc Civil Engrs; Am Water Resources Asn. *Res:* Evaporation and seepage control; water harvesting; reuse of municipal waste water; solar energy. *Mailing Add:* Water Resources Res Ctr Univ of Ariz Tucson AZ 85721

CLUFF, EDWARD FULLER, b Dedham, Mass, Feb 14, 28; m 56; c 2. ORGANIC CHEMISTRY. *Educ:* Mass Inst Technol, BS, 49, PhD(org chem), 52. *Prof Exp:* Res chemist, 52-69, develop supvr, 69-70, res div head, 70-74, develop supt, 74-77, gen process supt, 77-80, RES MGR, E I DU PONT DE NEMOURS & CO, INC, 80- *Res:* Polymer chemistry; elastomers, including polyurethanes and fluoroelastomers; hydrocarbon elastomers and olefin polymerization via transition metal catalysts. *Mailing Add:* Elastomer Div PPO E I du Pont de Nemours & Co Inc Wilmington DE 19899

CLUFF, LEIGHTON EGGERTSEN, b Salt Lake City, Utah, June 10, 23; m 44; c 2. ALLERGY, INFECTIOUS DISEASES. *Educ:* George Washington Univ, MD, 49. *Prof Exp:* House officer med, Johns Hopkins Hosp, Baltimore, 49-50; asst res physician, Hosp, Duke Univ, 50-51; asst res physician, Johns Hopkins Hosp, 51-52; asst physician & vis investr, Rockefeller Inst, 52-54; res physician, Johns Hopkins Hosp, 54-55, from instr to prof, 54-66; prof med & chmn dept, Col Med, Univ Fla, Gainesville, 66-76; vpres, 76-80, EXEC VPRES, ROBERT WOOD JOHNSON FOUND, PRINCETON, 80- *Concurrent Pos:* Markle scholar, 55-62; consult, Food & Drug Admin; consult ed, Dermatol Dig; chmn training grant comn, Nat Inst Allergy & Infectious Dis; mem, Nat Res Coun-Nat Acad Sci Drug Res Bd; mem, Nat Comn Pharm & Pharm Educ; chmn comt biomed res & patient care in the Vet Admin, Nat Acad Sci-Nat Res Coun; expert adv panel on bact dis, WHO. *Honors & Awards:* Ordronaux Award, 49. *Mem:* Am Fedn Clin Res; Am Soc Clin Invest; Soc Exp Biol & Med; Am Acad Allergy; Am Phys Asn. *Res:* Elucidation of the role of psychologic factors in convalescence from acute infection; studies of the epidemiology of staphylococcal infections; pathogenesis of fever due to bacterial pyrogens; mechanism of host injury in infection; studies of the epidemiology of adverse drug reactions. *Mailing Add:* Robert Wood Johnson Found PO Box 2316 Princeton NJ 08540

CLUFF, LLOYD STERLING, b Provo, Utah, Sept 29, 33; c 2. GEOLOGY. *Educ:* Univ Utah, BS, 60. *Prof Exp:* Geologist, Lottridge Thomas & Assoc, 60; staff geologist, 60-65, assoc & chief eng geologist, 65-71, VPRES, PRIN & DIR, WOODWARD-CLYDE CONSULT, 71- *Concurrent Pos:* Consult, Venezuelan Pres Earthquake Comn, 67-; mem consult bd, San Francisco Bay Conserv & Develop Comn, 68-73; mem consult panel to President & Secy Interior for Santa Barbara Oil Leak, 69; mem state Calif joint comt, Seismic Safety & Gov Earthquake Coun, 72-75; mem US Geol Surv earthquake adv panel, Nat Acad Sci comt seismol & SRI Int oversight comt earthquake prediction, 75-; mem consult bd, Int Atomic Energy Agency, Vienna. *Honors & Awards:* Hogentogler Award, Am Soc Testing & Mat, 65. *Mem:* Nat Acad Eng; Asn Eng Geologists (pres, 68-69); Earthquake Eng Res Inst; Int Asn Eng Geologists (vpres, 70-74); Seismol Soc Am; Struct Engrs Asn. *Res:* Active faults, earthquake and geologic hazards; engineering geology. *Mailing Add:* 3 Embarcadero Suite 700 San Francisco CA 94111

CLUFF, ROBERT MURRI, b Buenos Aires, Argentina, Jan 17, 53; US citizen. GEOLOGY. *Educ:* Univ Calif, Riverside, BS, 74; Univ Wis-Madison, MS, 76. *Prof Exp:* ASST GEOLOGIST PETROL GEOL, ILL STATE GEOL SURV, 76- *Concurrent Pos:* Consult petrol geologist, Denver, 81- *Honors & Awards:* A I Levorsen Award, Am Asn Petrol Geologists, 80. *Mem:* Am Asn Petrol Geologists; Soc Econ Paleontologists & Mineralogists. *Res:* Sedimentology and diagenesis of carbonate rocks; sedimentology, paleoecology and depositional environments of shales. *Mailing Add:* c/o Kerr Jain & Assoc 1550 Security Life Bldg Denver CO 80202

CLUM, HAROLD HAYDN, b Cleveland, Ohio, Feb 16, 94; m 24; c 2. PLANT PHYSIOLOGY. *Educ:* Oberlin Col, AB, 17; Cornell Univ, PhD(plant physiol), 24. *Prof Exp:* Asst bot, Cornell Univ, 19-23; instr, Univ Mich, 23-24; prof, Univ PR, 24-26; asst prof, Syracuse Univ, 26-27; from instr to assoc prof, Hunter Col, 27-52, chmn dept, 44-56, prof biol sci, 53-63; hon plant physiologist, NY Bot Garden, New York, 63-67; HON RES ASSOC, KITCHAWAN RES STA, BROOKLYN BOT GARDEN, 67- *Mem:* AAAS; Bot Soc Am; Am Phytopath Soc; Am Soc Plant Physiologists. *Res:* Effects of cytokinins in plant tissues. *Mailing Add:* 40 Smith St Chappaqua NY 10514

CLUM, JAMES AVERY, b Sidney, NY, July 7, 37; m 62; c 1. PHYSICAL METALLURGY. *Educ:* Ohio State Univ, BMetE, 60; Carnegie Inst Technol, MSc, 63, PhD(metall eng), 68. *Prof Exp:* Res metallurgist, Battelle Mem Inst, 64-67; fel metall eng, Ohio State Univ, 67-68; res fel metall, Cambridge Univ, 68-69; ASST PROF PHYS METALL, UNIV WIS, MADISON, 69-, ASSOC DIR UNIV-INDUST RES PROG, 70- *Mem:* AAAS; Am Soc Metals; Am Inst Mining, Metall & Petrol Engrs; Am Soc Eng Educ; fel Am Inst Chemists. *Res:* Surface physics; diffusion; nucleation; solid-solid phase transformations; relation of material properties and microstructure. *Mailing Add:* Dept of Metall & Eng Extension Univ of Wis Madison WI 53706

CLUMP, CURTIS WILLIAM, b Reading, Pa, May 27, 23; m 44; c 2. CHEMICAL ENGINEERING. *Educ:* Bucknell Univ, BS, 47, MS, 49; Carnegie Inst Technol, PhD(chem eng), 54. *Prof Exp:* Res engr, Air Reduction, 47-48; instr, Univ Rochester, 48-50; res engr, Gen Foods, 53-55; from asst prof to assoc prof chem eng, 55-65, chmn dept, 69-70, PROF CHEM ENG, LEHIGH UNIV, 65-, ASSOC DEAN, COL ENG, 75- *Concurrent Pos:* Consult. *Mem:* Am Inst Chem Engrs; Am Soc Eng Educ. *Res:* Fluid mechanics; thermodynamics; dry blending. *Mailing Add:* Dept of Chem Eng Lehigh Univ Bethlehem PA 18015

CLUNIE, THOMAS JOHN, b Racine, Wis, Mar 8, 40; m 70. CHEMICAL ENGINEERING, APPLIED MATHEMATICS. *Educ:* Northwestern Univ, BS, 63; Univ Notre Dame, PhD(chem eng), 68. *Prof Exp:* Engr new investments develop, 67-69, sr proj engr, 69-72, group leader, 72-77, SECT HEAD, EXXON RES & ENG CO, TEX, 77- *Concurrent Pos:* Tech adv, Esso Res & Eng Co/Imp Oil Enterprises Ltd, 68-69. *Mem:* AAAS; Am Chem Soc; Am Inst Chem Engrs. *Res:* Unsteady state heat transfer; direct reduction of iron ore; liquified natural gas technology. *Mailing Add:* Exxon Co USA 5011 Baker Rd Baytown TX 77520

CLUTTER, JEROME LEE, b Washington, Pa, Mar 19, 34; m 54; c 3. BIOMETRICS, OPERATIONS RESEARCH. *Educ:* Mich State Univ, BS, 56; Duke Univ, MF, 57, DF(biomet), 61. *Prof Exp:* Math statistician, Southeastern Forest Exp Sta, US Forest Serv, 57-58 & 59-63; prog analyst, Comput Ctr, Duke Univ, 58-59; opers analyst, Res Anal Corp, 63; assoc prof biomed & opers res, 63-76, PROF FOREST RESOURCES & STATIST, SCH FORESTRY, UNIV GA, 76- *Mem:* Biomet Soc; Opers Res Soc Am; Soc Am Foresters. *Res:* Prediction of growth and yield of forests; applications of operations research techniques in forest management. *Mailing Add:* Sch of Forest Resources Univ of Ga Athens GA 30602

CLUTTER, MARY ELIZABETH, b Charleroi, Pa; m. BOTANY. *Educ:* Allegheny Col, BS, 53; Univ Pittsburgh, MS, 57, PhD(bot), 60. *Prof Exp:* Res assoc, Yale Univ, 61-73, lectr biol, 65-78, sr res assoc, 73-78; prog dir, 76-81, SECT HEAD, NSF, 81- *Mem:* AAAS; Am Soc Cell Biol; Am Soc Plant Physiologists; Scand Soc Plant Physiol; Soc Develop Biol. *Res:* Function of polytene chromosomes in plant embryo development. *Mailing Add:* Nat Sci Found Washington DC 20550

CLUTTERHAM, DAVID ROBERT, b Chicago, Ill, Feb 10, 22; m 45; c 4. MATHEMATICS. *Educ:* Cornell Col, BA, 45; Univ Ariz, MS, 48; Univ Ill, PhD(math), 53. *Prof Exp:* Asst Math, Univ Ariz, 46-48 & Univ Ill, 48-49, asst digital comput, 50-53; design specialist, Convair Div, Gen Dynamics Corp, 53-59, sect chief comput design, Martin-Orlando, 59-63, mgr, Info Sci Dept, 63-64; mem tech staff, Bunker-Ramo Corp, Calif, 64-65; sr scientist, Radiation Inc, Fla, 65-68; PROF MATH SCI & HEAD DEPT, FLA INST TECHNOL, 68- *Mem:* Am Math Soc; Asn Comput Mach; Inst Elec & Electronics Eng. *Res:* Digital computers and computing techniques. *Mailing Add:* Dept of Math Sci Fla Inst of Technol Melbourne FL 32901

CLUXTON, DAVID H, b Martinsville, Ohio, 1943. EXPERIMENTAL PHYSICS, SCIENCE EDUCATION. *Educ:* Wilmington Col, AB, 65; Mich State Univ, MS, 67; Kent State Univ, PhD(physics), 72. *Prof Exp:* Asst prof, 72-77, ASSOC PROF PHYSICS, RUSSELL SAGE COL, 77- *Concurrent Pos:* Consult, Gen Elec Res & Develop Ctr, Schenectady, 75- *Mem:* Am Phys Soc; AAAS. *Res:* Applications of physics techniques to biological systems; intensity fluctuation spectroscopy. *Mailing Add:* 23 Grissom Dr Clifton Park NY 12065

CLYDE, CALVIN G(EARY), b Springville, Utah, Sept 5, 24; m 48; c 8. GROUND WATER HYDROLOGY, FLUID MECHANICS. *Educ:* Univ Utah, BS, 51; Univ Calif, Berkeley, MS, 52, CE, 53, PhD(civil eng), 61. *Prof Exp:* From instr to assoc prof civil eng, Univ Utah, 53-63; from asst dir to assoc dir, Utah Water Res Lab, 65-77, PROF CIVIL ENG, UTAH STATE UNIV, 63- *Concurrent Pos:* Sr develop engr, Hercules Inc, 61-63, consult, 62-63. *Mem:* Am Soc Civil Engrs; Am Soc Eng Educ; Am Inst Aeronaut & Astronaut; Nat Water Well Asn. *Res:* Turbulence, instrumentation; hydraulics; sediment transport; ground water hydrology; water resources planning; systems analysis; simulation of water resources systems; hydrology; hydroelectric power development. *Mailing Add:* Utah Water Res Lab Utah State Univ Logan UT 84322

CLYDE, WALLACE ALEXANDER, JR, b Birmingham, Ala, Nov 7, 29; m 53; c 3. PEDIATRICS, INFECTIOUS DISEASES. *Educ:* Vanderbilt Univ, BA, 51, MD, 54. *Prof Exp:* Intern pediat, Univ Hosp, Vanderbilt Univ, 54-55; asst resident, NC Baptist Hosp, 55-56; resident, Univ Hosp, Vanderbilt Univ, 56-57; trainee infectious dis, 61-62, from instr to assoc prof pediat, 62-72, assoc prof bact, 68-72, PROF PEDIAT & BACT, UNIV NC, CHAPEL HILL, 72- *Concurrent Pos:* Nat Inst Allergy & Infectious Dis fel prev med, Case Western Reserve Univ, 59-61, career develop award, 63-73; assoc mem comn acute respiratory dis, Armed Forces Epidemiol Bd, 63-72; mem bact-mycol study sect, Div Res Grants, NIH, 66-70; vis assoc prof path, Yale Univ, 71-72. *Mem:* Am Soc Microbiol; Soc Pediat Res; Am Soc Clin Invest; Infectious Dis Soc Am; Am Pediat Soc. *Res:* Infectious diseases of children, especially nonbacterial respiratory infections; relationship of Mycoplasmataceae to human disease; respiratory disease pathogenesis. *Mailing Add:* Dept Pediat Sch Med Univ NC 535 Burnett Womack Bldg 229H Chapel Hill NC 27514

CLYDESDALE, FERGUS MACDONALD, b Toronto, Ont, Feb 19, 37; m 79; c 2. CHEMISTRY, FOOD SCIENCE. *Educ:* Univ Toronto, BA, 60, MA, 62; Univ Mass, PhD(food sci), 66. *Prof Exp:* Chemist, Can Industs Ltd, 60; physiol chemist, Can Defence Res Med Lab, 62; from fel to asst prof food sci, 66-72, assoc prof, 72-76, PROF FOOD SCI & NUTRIT, UNIV MASS, AMHERST, 76- *Honors & Awards:* William V Cruess Award, Inst Food Technologists, 76; Distinguished Scientist Year Award, Inst Food Technol, 78. *Mem:* AAAS; Inst Food Technologists; Am Chem Soc; Inter-Soc Color Coun; Am Inst Nutrit. *Res:* Basic chemical changes in processed foods and their effect on quality and nutrition; basic color measurement problems involved with foods; chemistry of iron and its relationship to bioavailability. *Mailing Add:* Dept of Food Sci & Nutrit Univ of Mass Amherst MA 01003

CLYNE, ROBERT MARTIN, b Bridgeport, Conn, July 23, 18; m 43; c 3. INDUSTRIAL MEDICINE. *Educ:* Fordham Univ, BS, 39; Cornell Univ, MD, 43. *Prof Exp:* Intern med, Lenox Hill Hosp, 43-44; from asst resident to resident internal med, Lincoln Hosp, 44-45; resident, Bronx Vet Admin Hosp, 46-47; physician, Am Cyanamid Co, 48-50, chief physician clin, 50-55, asst to the med dir, 55-56, asst med dir, 56-58, dir employee health, 58-67, corp med dir, 67-81; RETIRED. *Concurrent Pos:* Lectr alcoholism, Rutgers Univ, Univ Utah & Univ Miami; lectr occup health, Colby Col; consult occup health, 81- *Honors & Awards:* Spec Award, Indust Med Asn, 72. *Mem:* Fel Am Col Physicians; fel Am Acad Occup Med; fel Am Occup Med Asn; fel Am Col Prev Med; fel AMA. *Mailing Add:* 18 Kitchell Lake Dr West Milford NJ 07480

CLYNES, MANFRED, b Vienna, Austria, Aug 14, 25; US citizen; div; c 3. NEUROPSYCHOLOGY, SENTICS. *Educ:* Univ Melbourne, BEngSci, 46, DSc(neurosci), 64; Juilliard Sch Music, MS, 49. *Prof Exp:* Chief study teacher pianoforte, Univ Melbourne, 50-52; instr music, Princeton Univ, 52-53; chief mathematician & comput specialist, Bogue Elec Mfg Co, 54-56; chief res scientist & dir biocybernetic labs, Rockland State Hosp, 56-73; dir, Biocybernetic Inst, 73-78; res assoc, Western Behav Sci Inst, 78-81; LECTR, SCH MED, UNIV CALIF, SAN DIEGO, 77-; RES PROF & HEAD, MUSIC RES CTR, NSW STATE CONSERVATORIUM MUSIC, SYDNEY, 81- *Concurrent Pos:* Consult, Sonomedic Corp; staff consult, Feedback Syst Dynamics & Electronics, Bogue Elec Mfg Co, 56-; pres & chmn bd, Mnemotron Corp, 60-62; vpres, Tech Measurement Corp, 61-62. *Mem:* Soc Neurosci; Am Sentic Asn (pres, 74-); Inst Elec & Electronics Engrs; Am Phys Soc; Asn Hosp Psychologists. *Res:* Brain function; application of automatic control system theory to biological systems, neurophysiology, circulation, sentics; biologic basis of dynamic communication of emotions and qualities, neurophysiology of musical language, evolution of communication. *Mailing Add:* Res Ctr NSW State Conservatorium Music Sydney 2000 Australia

CMEJLA, HOWARD EDWARD, b Milwaukee, Wis, Dec 25, 26; m 48; c 6. PARASITOLOGY, ENTOMOLOGY. *Educ:* Univ Wis, BS, 50, MS, 51, PhD(entom, zool), 54. *Prof Exp:* Collabr, Div Apicult & Biol Control, USDA, Wis, 51-54; parasitologist, Parasitol Dept, Abbott Labs, 54-58, Food & Drug Admin liaison, 58-63; dir regulatory liaison, 63-70, vpres & dir prod planning & develop, 69-79, DIR, RES & DEVELOP ADMIN, AYERST LABS, 79- *Concurrent Pos:* Food & Drug Admin liaison. *Mem:* Am Soc Parasitologists; Entom Soc Am; Am Soc Trop Med & Hyg. *Res:* Drugs-product planning and development, and research and development administration; amebiasis; apiculture; bee diseases and colony management. *Mailing Add:* Ayerst Labs 685 Third Ave New York NY 10017

COACHMAN, LAWRENCE KEYES, b Rochester, NY, Apr 25, 26; m 81; c 4. PHYSICAL OCEANOGRAPHY. *Educ:* Dartmouth Col, AB, 48; Yale Univ, MF, 51; Univ Wash, PhD(oceanog), 62. *Prof Exp:* Hydrographer & oceanogr, Dartmouth Col Blue Dolphin Labrador Expeds, 50-55; sr scientist gases in glacier ice, Univ Oslo, 55-57; asst, 57-62, from asst prof to assoc prof, 62-72, PROF OCEANOG, UNIV WASH, 72- *Concurrent Pos:* Sr scientist, Arctic Inst NAm Expeds, Greenland, 58 & 63, Bering & Chukchi Seas, 64, 66 & 69-78, Cent Arctic Ocean, 70-72; mem Saronikos Systs Proj, Athens, 73-75; chmn, US-USSR Oceanog Exchange Deleg, 64; Arctic Inst NAm/McGill Univ vis prof, 67; vis lectr, AARI, Leningrad, 76. *Mem:* Am Geophys Union; fel Arctic Inst NAm. *Res:* Physical oceanography of Arctic Ocean and peripheral seas; oceanography of coastal, fjord and ice-covered waters. *Mailing Add:* Dept of Oceanog WB-10 Univ of Wash Seattle WA 98195

COAD, BRIAN WILLIAM, b England, Oct 19, 46; m 73; c 1. ICHTHYOLOGY, ZOOGEOGRAPHY. *Educ:* Univ Manchester, Eng, BSc, 70; Univ Waterloo, Ontario, MSc, 72; Univ Ottawa, PhD(biol), 76. *Prof Exp:* Assoc prof ichthyol & zool, Pahlavi Univ, Shiraz, Iran, 76-79; res assoc, 79-81, ASSOC CUR, NAT MUS NATURAL SCI, OTTAWA, CAN, 81- *Mem:* Am Soc Ichthyologists & Herpetologists; Soc Syst Zoologists; Japanese Soc Ichthyol; Indian Soc Ichthyol; French Soc Ichthyol. *Res:* Systematics and zoogeography of the fresh water fishes of Southwest Asia and of North America. *Mailing Add:* Ichthyol Sect Nat Mus Natural Sci Ottawa ON K1A 0M8 Can

COADY, LARRY B, b Ottumwa, Iowa, Mar 4, 33; m 56; c 10. ELECTRICAL ENGINEERING. *Educ:* Iowa State Univ, BS, 59, MS, 63, PhD(elec eng), 65. *Prof Exp:* Jr res engr, Collins Radio Co, 59-62; from instr to asst prof, 62-75, ASSOC PROF ELEC ENG, IOWA STATE UNIV, 75- *Mem:* Inst Elec & Electronics Engrs. *Res:* Circuit and systems theory. *Mailing Add:* Dept of Elec Eng Iowa State Univ Ames IA 50010

COAKER, A(NTHONY) WILLIAM, b Johannesburg, SAfrica, Oct 8, 27; m 54; c 5. CHEMICAL ENGINEERING. *Educ:* Univ Witwatersrand, BSc, 49, PhD(chem eng), 53. *Prof Exp:* Demonstr chem, Univ Witwatersrand, 49-50; asst works chemist chem eng, Masonite Africa, Ltd, 51-52; asst res officer chem, SACSIR, 52-53; chemist plastics technol, Monsanto Co, 53-56, group leader vinyl plastics, 57-64, group leader plasticizer applns, 64-66, sr group leader, Org Chem Div, 66-71, mkt supvr plasticizers, Monsanto Indust Chem Co, 71-75; vpres, Triple R Indust, 76-77; DIR, MGF SERV, TENNECO CHEMICALS INC, 78- *Mem:* Soc Plastics Engrs; Am Chem Soc; Am Inst Chem Engrs. *Res:* Polymerization; thermoplastics processing; plastisol technology; compounding of vinyl plastics; industrial wastes treatment; rheology. *Mailing Add:* 4 Redwood Rd Morristown NJ 07960

COAKLEY, CHARLES SEYMOUR, b Washington, DC, July 4, 14; m; c 5. ANESTHESIOLOGY. *Educ:* George Washington Univ, MD, 37; Am Bd Anesthesiol, dipl, 48. *Prof Exp:* From instr to assoc prof, 39-49, PROF ANESTHESIOL & CHMN DEPT, SCH MED, GEORGE WASHINGTON UNIV, 49- *Concurrent Pos:* Consult, Walter Reed Army Med Ctr, Vet Admin Hosp, Washington, DC & NIH; med consult, CARE-Medico. *Mem:* AMA; Am Col Anesthesiol; Asn Am Med Cols; Am Soc Anesthesiol; Asn Univ Anesthetists. *Res:* Use of monitors for anesthetized and critically ill patients; applications of computer of continuous automated monitoring. *Mailing Add:* 910-23rd St NW Washington DC 20037

COAKLEY, JAMES ALEXANDER, JR, b Long Beach, Calif, Dec 14, 46; m 71; c 2. ATMOSPHERIC SCIENCES, CLIMATE THEORY. *Educ:* Univ Calif, Los Angeles, BS, 68; Univ Calif, Berkeley, MA, 70, PhD(physics), 72. *Prof Exp:* SCIENTIST CLIMATE, NAT CTR ATMOSPHERIC RES, 74- *Concurrent Pos:* Nat Ctr Atmospheric Res fel, 72-73; res assoc, Nat Acad Sci-Nat Res Coun-Nat Environ Satellite Serv, 73-74; affil prof & vis asst prof, Univ Corp Atmospheric Res, Dept Earth Sci, Iowa State Univ, 76-78. *Mem:* AAAS; Am Geophys Union; Am Meteorol Soc. *Res:* Energy balance climate models; radiative transfer in planetary atmospheres; remote sensing of atmospheres from space. *Mailing Add:* Nat Ctr for Atmospheric Res PO Box 3000 Boulder CO 80307

COAKLEY, JOHN PHILLIP, b Nassau, Bahamas, Jan 7, 40; m 68; c 2. SEDIMENTOLOGY, COASTAL ENGINEERING. *Educ:* St Francis Xavier Univ, BSc, 64; Univ Ottawa, MSc, 67. *Prof Exp:* Sci officer quant geol limnogeol, Inland Waters Br, Geol Surv Can, 66-67; sci officer, 67-72, RES SCI NEARSHORE SEDIMENTOLOGY, DEPT ENVIRON, 72- *Concurrent Pos:* Dir environ control, Bahamas Develop Corp, 75-76. *Mem:* Int Asn Great Lakes Res. *Res:* Processes and response of coastal systems in the Great Lakes; palaeoenvironments and long-term post-glacial evolution of Great Lakes shorelines. *Mailing Add:* 23 Lower Horning Rd Hamilton ON L8S 3E9 Can

COAKLEY, MARY PETER, b South Amboy, NJ. PHYSICAL CHEMISTRY, INORGANIC CHEMISTRY. *Educ:* Georgian Court Col, AB, 47; Univ Notre Dame, MS, 53, PhD, 55. *Prof Exp:* Parochial high sch teacher, 42-47; TEACHER CHEM & CHMN DEPT, GEORGIAN COURT COL, 47- *Concurrent Pos:* Mem atomic energy proj, Univ Notre Dame, 54-55; res grants, AEC, 57-60 & 61-63, Petrol Res Fund, 66-68 & NSF, 68-70; res, Univ Calif, Berkeley, 68. *Mem:* Am Chem Soc; NY Acad Sci. *Res:* Nuclear magnetic resonance studies of tin complexes; spectroscopy; ultraviolet and infrared absorption; spectra of metal chelates. *Mailing Add:* Dept Chem Georgian Court Col Lakewood NJ 08701

COALE, CECIL ROBERTS, b Beaumont, Tex, June 19, 36. ELECTRICAL ENGINEERING. *Educ:* Tex Tech Col, BS, 57; Southern Methodist Univ, MS, 59; Univ Tex, PhD(elec eng), 62. *Prof Exp:* Engr, Gen Dynamics/Ft Worth, 57-59; res engr, Electro-Mech Corp, Tex, 61-62; asst prof elec eng, Tex Technol Col, 62-67; ENGR, EQUIP GROUP, TEX INSTRUMENTS, INC, 67- *Res:* Infrared systems; signal processing. *Mailing Add:* Equip Group PO Box 226015 Dallas TX 75266

COALSON, JACQUELINE JONES, b Oklahoma City, Okla, Mar 12, 38; div; c 3. PATHOLOGY. *Educ:* Okla Baptist Univ, BS, 60; Univ Okla, MS, 63, PhD(path), 65. *Prof Exp:* Teaching asst histol & embryol, Med Ctr, Univ Okla, 60-63, from res asst to prof path, 63-79; PROF PATH, UNIV TEX MED CTR, SAN ANTONIO, 79- *Concurrent Pos:* Mem, Pulmonary Dis Adv Comt, Div Lung Dis, NIH, 76-81. *Mem:* Am Thoracic Soc; Am Asn Path; Electron Micros Soc Am. *Res:* Electron microscopy and histochemistry of normal and diseased lungs of both human and experimental animals. *Mailing Add:* Univ Tex Med Ctr San Antonio TX 78284

COALSON, ROBERT ELLIS, b Hobart, Okla, Dec 7, 28; m 62; c 3. ANATOMY. *Educ:* Univ Okla, BS, 49, MS, 51, PhD(med sci), 55. *Prof Exp:* Instr anat, Sch Nursing, Univ Okla, 52-54; instr, Sch Med, Vanderbilt Univ, 57-60; from asst prof to assoc prof, 60-70, PROF ANAT, SCH MED, UNIV OKLA, 70-, ASST PROF PATH, 68- *Concurrent Pos:* Consult, Meharry Med Col, 58-60. *Mem:* Am Soc Zool; Tissue Cult Asn. *Res:* Comparative embryology, anatomy and histology; tissue transplantation. *Mailing Add:* Dept of Anat Univ of Okla Med Ctr Oklahoma City OK 73104

COAN, EUGENE VICTOR, b Los Angeles, Calif, Mar 26, 43. ENVIRONMENTAL SCIENCES, MALACOLOGY. *Educ:* Univ Calif, Santa Barbara, AB, 64; Stanford Univ, PhD(biol sci), 69. *Prof Exp:* Dir polit activ, Zero Pop Growth, 69-70; consult, 70-75, major issues specialist, 75-76, ASST CONSERV DIR, THE SIERRA CLUB, 77- *Concurrent Pos:* Ed, Western Soc Malacol. *Mem:* Am Malacol Union. *Res:* Public lands; international aspects of environmental movement; history of natural sciences; taxonomy and distribution of northwest American bivalves. *Mailing Add:* 891 San Jude Ave Palo Alto CA 94306

COAN, STEPHEN B, b New York, NY, Apr 8, 21; m 42; c 2. ORGANIC CHEMISTRY. *Educ:* Univ Mich, BS, 41; Polytech Inst Brooklyn, MS, 50, PhD(chem), 54. *Prof Exp:* Anal chemist, Gen Chem Co, 41-42, TNT control chemist, 42-43, res chemist, 46; develop chemist, 46-51, res chemist, 51-54, patents-res liaison, 51-63, from assoc dir to dir, Patent Dept, 63-78, STAFF VPRES LICENSING, SCHERING CORP, 78- *Mem:* Am Chem Soc; Licensing Exec Asn. *Res:* Organic and medicinal research; organic synthesis; pharmaceuticals. *Mailing Add:* 72 Sykes Ave Livingston NJ 07039

COARTNEY, JAMES S, b Coles Co, Ill, Sept 3, 38; m 64; c 2. PLANT PHYSIOLOGY, WEED SCIENCE. *Educ:* Eastern Ill Univ, BSEd, 60; Purdue Univ, MS, 63, PhD(plant physiol), 67. *Prof Exp:* Res asst plant physiol, Purdue Univ, 60-66; from asst prof to, assoc prof plant physiol, 66-79, ASSOC PROF HORT, VA POLYTECH INST & STATE UNIV, 79- *Mem:* Weed Sci Soc Am; Am Soc Hort Sci; Int Plant Propagators Soc. *Res:* Plant growth regulation and mode of action of herbicides. *Mailing Add:* Dept Hort Va Polytech Inst & State Univ Blacksburg VA 24061

COASH, JOHN RUSSELL, b Denver, Colo, Sept 24, 22; m 48; c 3. GEOLOGY. *Educ:* Colo Col, BA, 47; Univ Colo, MA, 49; Yale Univ, PhD, 54. *Prof Exp:* From asst prof to assoc prof geol, Bowling Green State Univ, 49-61, chmn dept, 54-64, prof, 61-64, asst to provost & dir hon prog, 63-65, dir res, 65-66; assoc prog dir, NSF, 66-68; DEAN SCH ARTS & SCI, CALIF STATE COL, BAKERSFIELD, 68- *Concurrent Pos:* NSF vis lectr, 62, 63, 64 & 65; consult, geostudy & earth sci teacher training panel, Am Geol Inst; panelist, NSF, 68- & NIH, 72-73. *Mem:* Fel AAAS; fel Geol Soc Am; Am Asn Petrol Geol; Nat Asn Geol Teachers (pres, 81); Nat Sci Teachers Asn. *Res:* Field geology of northern Nevada and central Rocky Mountains; stratigraphic and structural geology; science administration. *Mailing Add:* Sch of Arts & Sci Calif State Col Bakersfield CA 93309

COATE, WILLIAM BLEECKER, b Pasadena, Calif, Sept 23, 21; m 41; c 2. INHALATION TOXICOLOGY. *Educ:* Cornell Univ, AB, 47, PhD(psychol), 50. *Prof Exp:* Asst prof psychol, Harpur Col, 50-55, chmn dept, 53-54; from asst prof to assoc prof, Wellesley Col, 55-63; assoc dir div pharmacol, 63-68, proj dir, 68-72, DIR INHALATION TOXICOL, HAZLETON LABS AM, INC, 72- *Mem:* Am Psychol Asn; Psychonomic Soc; Am Indust Hyg Asn. *Res:* Psychopharmacology; method development; impairment of pulmonary function by inhalants. *Mailing Add:* Hazleton Labs Am Inc 9200 Leesburg Turnpike Vienna VA 22180

COATES, ANTHONY GEORGE, b Staines, Eng, May 20, 36; m 61; c 1. PALEONTOLOGY, STRATIGRAPHY. *Educ:* Univ London, BSc, 59, PhD(geol), 63. *Prof Exp:* Geologist, Jamaican Geol Surv, 62-64; lectr geol, Univ West Indies, 64-67; assoc prof, 67-74, PROF GEOL, GEORGE WASHINGTON UNIV, 74- *Concurrent Pos:* Extra-mural lectr, Univ West Indies, 63-67, external examr, 70-; res assoc, Smithsonian Inst, 68-; NSF sci equip grant, 70; ed jour, Geol Soc Jamaica, 64-66. *Mem:* Paleont Soc Am; fel Geol Soc London; Geol Soc France; fel Geol Soc Jamaica. *Res:* Paleontology, stratigraphy and sedimentation of ordovician of Normandy; cretaceous Caribbean corals and biostratigraphy; Jamaican cretaceous stratigraphy. *Mailing Add:* Dept of Geol George Washington Univ Washington DC 20006

COATES, ARTHUR DONWELL, b Steubenville, Ohio, June 14, 28; m 57; c 3. PHYSICAL CHEMISTRY, FUEL SCIENCE. *Educ:* Col Steubenville, BS, 50; Univ Del, MS, 61. *Prof Exp:* Practice engr chem & metall, Wheeling Steel Corp, 50-51; chemist, 51-55, chief ignition sect, Combustion & Incendiary Effects Br, 55-57, Spec Prob Sect, Nuclear Physics Br, 57-59 & Radiation Damage Sect, 60-70, chief, Methodology Sect, Combustion & Incendiary Effects Br, 70-75, tech asst to chief detonation & deflagration dynamics lab, 75-76, tech asst to chief, Terminal Ballistics Div, 76-78, SPEC ASST TO DIR, BALLISTIC RES LABS, ABERDEEN PROVING GROUND, 79- *Mem:* AAAS; Am Chem Soc; fel Am Inst Chem; Combustion Inst; NY Acad Sci. *Res:* Fuels; combustion; powdered metals; pyrophoric materials; propellants; explosives; mass spectrometry; thin film physics; ignition; chemistry of exothermic reactions; thermal analysis. *Mailing Add:* 311 N Osborn Lane Aberdeen MD 21001

COATES, CLARENCE L(EROY), JR, b Hastings, Nebr, Nov 5, 23; m 43, 69; c 3. COMPUTER ENGINEERING. *Educ:* Univ Kans, BS, 44, MS, 48; Univ Ill, PhD(elec eng), 53. *Prof Exp:* Instr elec eng, Univ Kans, 46-48; from instr to assoc prof, Univ Ill, 48-56; res engr, Info Studies Sect, Gen Elec Res Lab, 56-63; prof elec eng, Univ Tex, Austin, 63-67, prof elec eng & comput sci, 67-71, chmn dept elec eng, 64-66, dir electronics res ctr, 67-71; prof elec eng & dir, Coord Sci Lab, Univ Ill, Urbana-Champaign, 71-73; PROF & HEAD SCH ELEC ENG, PURDUE UNIV, 73- *Concurrent Pos:* Adj prof, Rensselaer Polytech Inst, 58-63; mem, Comput Elec Eng Comt, Comn Educ, Nat Acad Eng, 68-73, chmn, 71-73. *Mem:* Fel AAAS; fel Inst Elec & Electronics Engrs. *Res:* Switching theory; adaptive systems; computer organization; recognition systems. *Mailing Add:* Sch of Elec Eng Purdue Univ West Lafayette IN 47907

COATES, DONALD ALLEN, b Sonoma, Calif, Apr 10, 38. STRATIGRAPHY, ENVIRONMENTAL GEOLOGY. *Educ:* Univ Colo, BA, 61, MS, 64; Univ Calif, Los Angeles, PhD(geol), 69. *Prof Exp:* Geologist, Texaco Inc, 63-64 & CRA Explor, 64-65; res assoc, Inst Polar Studies, Ohio State Univ, 69-71; asst prof geol, Cleveland State Univ, 71-75; GEOLOGIST, US GEOL SURV, 75- *Concurrent Pos:* Adj asst prof, Calif State Univ, Los Angeles, 69, Ohio State Univ, 69-71; consult, 69-75. *Mem:* Geol Soc Am; AAAS; Sigma Xi. *Res:* Stratigraphy of Gondwana and lacial deposits in South America and Antarctica; natural burning of coal beds and structure, petrology, paleomagnetism, and relation to landscape development of the baked rocks clinker produced. *Mailing Add:* US Geol Surv Fed Ctr MS-913 Denver CO 80033

COATES, DONALD FRANCIS, soil mechanics, deceased

COATES, DONALD ROBERT, b Grand Island, Nebr, July 23, 22; m 44; c 3. GEOLOGY, GEOMORPHOLOGY & GLACIOLOGY. *Educ:* Col Wooster, BA, 44; Columbia Univ, MA, 48, PhD(geol), 56. *Prof Exp:* Asst geol, Columbia Univ, 46-48; asst prof & head dept, Earlham Col, 48-51, geologist, Ground Water Br, US Geol Surv, 51-54; chmn dept, 54-63, from instr to assoc prof, 54-63, PROF GEOL, STATE UNIV NY BINGHAMTON, 63- *Concurrent Pos:* Party chief, Ind Geol Surv, 49; lectr, Ind Univ, 50; res geologist, Off Naval Res, 54; consult, Chernin & Gold, NY, 55-; geologist, Gen Hydrol Br, US Geol Surv, 58-60; vis prof, Cornell Univ, 58, 60 & 61; State Univ NY Res Found fels, 61 & 66, grants-in-aid, 62-65; vis prof, Univ Ill, 63; assoc prof dir, NSF, 63-64, consult, 64-69; vis geoscientist for Am Geol Inst, 63-65; consult, US Army Corps Engrs, 65-68, NY State Attorney Gen, 65-, US Dept Com, 72-75 & Consol Edison of New York, 75-76; proj dir, NY State Atomic & Space Develop Authority, 75; consult, US Nat Park Serv, 71-77, NY Dept Transp, 76- & Niagara Mohawk Power Corp, 76-; Consult, Town of Islip, 74-77, Town of Vestal, 81- & Broome County, 81- *Honors & Awards:* Award for Sustained Superior Performance, NSF, 64. *Mem:* Nat Asn Geol Teachers; Asn Eng Geologists; Geol Soc Am; Asn Prof Geol Scientists; AAAS. *Res:* Geomorphology; environmental geology and environmental lawsuits; glacial geology of eastern United States; analysis of man's changes of rivers and coasts; evaluation of water and earth surface resources; landslides; geomorphology and engineering; urban, glacial & coastal geomorphology. *Mailing Add:* Dept of Geol Sci State Univ of NY Binghamton NY 13901

COATES, GEOFFREY EDWARD, b London, Eng, May 14, 17; m 51; c 2. ORANOMETALLIC CHEMISTRY, INORGANIC CHEMISTRY. *Educ:* Oxford Univ, BA, 38, BSc, 39, MA, 42; Bristol Univ, DSc(chem), 54. *Prof Exp:* Res chemist, Magnesium Metal Corp, Eng, 40-45; lectr chem, Bristol Univ, 45-53; prof chem & head dept, Univ Durham, 53-68; head dept, 68-77, PROF CHEM, UNIV WYO, 68- *Concurrent Pos:* Consult, Rio Tinto Zinc Corp, 47-71; Imp Chem Indust, 55-68; Clarke, Chapman & Co, 55-69 & Ethyl Corp, 57-69. *Mem:* Am Chem Soc; The Chem Soc; Royal Inst Chem. *Res:* Beryllium chemistry; organometallic compounds. *Mailing Add:* 1801 Rainbow Ave Laramie WY 82070

COATES, JESSE, b Baton Rouge, La, Mar 12, 08; m 39; c 2. CHEMICAL ENGINEERING. *Educ:* La State Univ, BS, 28; Univ Mich, MS & PhD(chem eng), 36. *Prof Exp:* Chemist & treating engr, Nat Lumber & Creosoting Co, 28; chemist, Int Paper Co, 28-29, Meeker Sugar Refining, 30-31 & Punta Alegre Sugar Co, 31; chem engr, Tex Pac Coal & Oil Co, 32-33; chem engr, United Gas Pub Serv, 33-36; from asst prof to prof, 36-69, chmn dept, 55-67, 69-70, EMER ALUMNI PROF CHEM ENG, LA STATE UNIV, BATON ROUGE, 69- *Concurrent Pos:* Consult, Nat Gas Odorizing Co, 45-56. *Honors & Awards:* Coates Mem Award, Am Chem Soc, 58. *Mem:* Am Chem Soc; Am Inst Chem Engrs; fel Am Inst Chemists; Nat Coun Eng Exam; Am Soc Eng Educ. *Res:* Thermodynamics of solutions; thermal conductivity of liquids; mass transfer; distillation; evaporation; process development. *Mailing Add:* 2320 Terrace Ave Baton Rouge LA 70806

COATES, JOSEPH FRANCIS, b Brooklyn, NY, Jan 3, 29; m 52; c 5. TECHNOLOGY ASSESSMENT, FUTURES RESEARCH. *Educ:* Polytech Inst Brooklyn, BS, 51; Pa State Univ, MS, 53. *Prof Exp:* Res chemist, Atlantic Refining Co, Philadelphia, 53-60; chief chemist, Onyx Chem Co, Jersey City, 60-61; staff scientist, Inst Defense Anal, Arlington, 61-70; proj mgr, NSF, Washington, DC, 70-74; asst to dir, Off Technol Assessment, US Cong, 74-78, sr assoc, 78-79; PRES, J F COATES INC, WASHINGTON, DC, 79- *Concurrent Pos:* Adj prof, Am Univ, 71-73 & George Washington Univ, 72- *Mem:* AAAS; World Future Soc; Am Chem Soc. *Res:* Impacts of science and technology on society and on the future. *Mailing Add:* 3738 Kanawha St NW Washington DC 20015

COATES, R(OBERT) J(AY), b Lansing, Mich, May 8, 22; m 46. PHYSICS, ELECTRICAL ENGINEERING. *Educ:* Mich State Univ, BSEE, 43; Univ Md, MSEE, 48; Johns Hopkins Univ, PhD(physics), 57. *Prof Exp:* Radio engr, US Naval Res Lab, 43-46, electronic scientist, 46-56, head, solar physics sect, 56-59; consult, 59-60, assoc chief, tracking systs div, 60-62, chief, space data acquisition div, 62-63, chief, Advan Develop Div, 63-71, chief, Advan Data Systs Div, 71-74, sr scientist applns, 74-79, PROJ MGR CRUSTAL DYNAMICS, GOODARD SPACE FLIGHT CTR, 79- *Concurrent Pos:* Jr instr, Johns Hopkins Univ, 49-52; del, Int Sci Radio Union, 57, 60 & 63. *Honors & Awards:* Exceptional Performance Award, Goddard Space Flight Ctr, 71. *Mem:* Am Phys Soc; fel Inst Elec & Electronics Engrs; Am Geophys Union; AAAS; Sigma Xi. *Res:* Microwave; radio astronomy; telemetry; satellite tracking; geophysics; satellite communications. *Mailing Add:* Goddard Space Flight Ctr NASA Code 904 Greenbelt MA 20771

COATES, RALPH L, b Moroni, Utah, July 24, 34; m 51; c 3. CHEMICAL ENGINEERING. *Educ:* Univ Utah, BSChE, 59, PhD(chem eng), 62. *Prof Exp:* Res assoc chem eng, Univ Utah, 60-62; sr engr, Hercules Powder Co, 62-63; tech specialist propellant combustion, Lockheed Propulsion Co, 63-67; assoc prof, 67-77, PROF CHEM ENG, BRIGHAM YOUNG UNIV, 77- *Mem:* Am Inst Aeronaut & Astronaut; Am Chem Soc; Am Inst Chem Engrs. *Res:* Combustion; fluid mechanics; heat transfer; thermodynamics. *Mailing Add:* Dept of Chem Eng Brigham Young Univ Provo UT 84602

COATES, ROBERT MERCER, b Evanston, Ill, May 21, 38; m 64. ORGANIC CHEMISTRY. *Educ:* Yale Univ, BS, 60; Univ Calif, Berkeley, PhD(chem), 64. *Prof Exp:* NIH fel, Stanford Univ, 63-65; asst prof, 65-77, PROF CHEM, UNIV ILL, URBANA-CHAMPAIGN, 77- *Concurrent Pos:* A P Sloan Found fel, 71-73. *Mem:* Am Chem Soc; The Chem Soc. *Res:* Synthesis and biosynthesis of natural products; synthetic methods; biogenetic-like rearrangement of terpenes; synthesis and reactions of polycyclic compounds. *Mailing Add:* Dept of Chem Univ of Ill Urbana IL 61801

COATS, ALFRED CORNELL, b Portland, Ore, Mar 12, 36; m 63; c 2. NEUROPHYSIOLOGY. *Educ:* Stanford Univ, BA, 59; Baylor Univ, MD, 62, MS, 63. *Prof Exp:* From instr to assoc prof, 62-72, PROF PHYSIOL & OTOLARYNGOL, BAYLOR COL MED, 72- *Concurrent Pos:* Dir electronystagmography lab & mem consult staff, Methodist Hosp, 63-, St Luke's Hosp, 73- & Hermann Hosp, 75-; mem consult staff, Ben Taub Hosp, 65- *Mem:* Am Neuro-Otologic Asn; Soc Neurosci. *Res:* Physiology of peripheral auditory system; clinical vestibulometry; study of balance-and-equilibrium system in humans. *Mailing Add:* Dept Otolaryngol Baylor Col of Med Houston TX 77025

COATS, JOEL ROBERT, b Kenton, Ohio, Apr 24, 48; m 71; c 3. TOXICOLOGY. *Educ:* Ariz State Univ, BS, 70; Univ Ill, MS, 72, PhD(entom), 74. *Prof Exp:* Res assoc environ toxicol, Univ Ill, Urbana, 74-76; vis prof, Univ Guelph, Ont, 76-78; asst prof, 78-81, ASSOC PROF TOXICOL, IOWA STATE UNIV, 81- *Mem:* AAAS; Am Chem Soc; Entom Soc Am; Coleopterists Soc; Soc Environ Toxicol & Chem. *Res:* Toxicology and chemistry of pesticides, especially insecticides; mode of action, selectivity, metabolism, degradation, uptake mechanisms, environmental fate and effects. *Mailing Add:* Dept Entom Iowa State Univ Ames IA 50011

COATS, JOHN H(ENRY), b Templeton, Ind, Apr 16, 30; m 57. MICROBIOLOGY. *Educ:* DePauw Univ, AB, 52; Purdue Univ, MS, 57, PhD(mycol), 59. *Prof Exp:* MICROBIOLOGIST, UPJOHN CO, 59- *Mem:* Am Soc Microbiol. *Res:* Methodology of screening for antibiotics. *Mailing Add:* Pharm Res & Develop Lab Upjohn Co 301 Henrietta St Kalamazoo MI 49001

COATS, KEITH HAL, b Ann Arbor, Mich, Nov 14, 34; m 56; c 3. PETROLEUM ENGINEERING, APPLIED MATHEMATICS. *Educ:* Univ Mich, BS, 56, MS, 57 & 58, PhD(chem eng), 59. *Prof Exp:* Lectr chem eng, Univ Mich, 59, asst prof, 59-61; sr res engr, Jersey Prod Res Co, 61-64; res assoc, Esso Prod Res Co, 64-66; assoc prof petrol eng, Univ Tex, Austin, 66-70; BD CHMN, INTERCOMP RESOURCE DEVELOP & ENG, 70- *Concurrent Pos:* Consult, Northern Natural Gas Co, Nebr, 66- & Chevron Res Corp, 67- *Mem:* Am Inst Mining, Metall & Petrol Engrs; Am Inst Chem Engrs. *Res:* Computer simulation of oil and gas reservoir performance through numerical solution of partial differential equations. *Mailing Add:* INTERCOMP Inc 1201 Dairy Ashford Suite 200 Houston TX 77079

COATS, RICHARD LEE, b Madill, Okla, Feb 14, 36; m 59; c 4. NUCLEAR PHYSICS, REACTOR PHYSICS. *Educ:* Univ Okla, BS, 59, MS, 63, PhD(nuclear eng), 66. *Prof Exp:* Mem tech staff, 66-69, DIV SUPVR, NUCLEAR ENG & SUPVR, REACTOR CONTAINMENT SAFETY STUDIES DIV, 4422, SANDIA LABS, 69- *Mem:* Am Nuclear Soc. *Res:* Experimental and theoretical nuclear reactor physics; coupled reactor dynamics; stochastic reactor kinetics; Monte Carlo reactor physics calculations; advanced reactor safety research. *Mailing Add:* Reactor Containment Safety Sandia Labs Albuquerque NM 87115

COATS, ROBERT ROY, b Toronto, Ont, Nov 22, 10; US citizen; m 37; c 3. GEOLOGY. *Educ:* Univ Wash, BS, 31, MS, 32; Univ Calif, PhD(geol), 38. *Prof Exp:* Geologist, Storey County Mines, 37; asst prof geol, Univ Alaska, 37-39; from jr geologist to geologist, US Geol Surv, 39-64, res geologist, 64-81; RETIRED. *Mem:* Fel Mineral Soc Am; Soc Econ Geologists; fel Geol Soc Am; Sigma Xi. *Res:* Tin deposits of Alaska; alteration by hydrothermal solutions; Aleutian volcanoes; geology of the northeastern Great Basin; tectonics and Mesazoic and Tertiary plutonism and vulcanism in northeastern Nevada and their relation to ore deposition. *Mailing Add:* 3836 La Selva Dr Palo Alto CA 94306

COBB, CAROLUS M, b Lynn, Mass, Jan 22, 22; m 66; c 1. PHYSICAL CHEMISTRY. *Educ:* Mass Inst Technol, SB, 44, PhD(phys chem), 51. *Prof Exp:* Chemist, Tenn Eastman Corp, 44-46 & Ionics, Inc, 51-55; prin scientist, Allied Res Assocs, Inc, 55-60; CHIEF CHEMIST, AM SCI & ENG, INC, CAMBRIDGE, MASS, 60- *Concurrent Pos:* Affil in bioeng, Forsyth Dent Ctr, Harvard Sch Pub Health, 64- *Mem:* Am Chem Soc; Am Phys Soc. *Res:* Titanium and solution chemistry; ion exchange chromatography; atmospheric and physical optics; fluorescent materials; nuclear phenomena; high temperature and electronic materials; thermodynamics. *Mailing Add:* Am Sci & Eng Inc 955 Massachusetts Ave Cambridge MA 02139

COBB, CHARLES MADISON, b Kansas City, Mo, Sept 20, 40; m 64; c 1. DENTISTRY, PERIODONTICS. *Educ:* Univ Mo-Kansas City, DDS, cert periodont & MS, 64; Georgetown Univ, PhD(anat), 71. *Prof Exp:* Prof periodont, Sch Dent, La State Univ, 71-72; asst prof periodont, 73-74, investr periodont, Inst Dent Res, 73-76, ASSOC PROF ANAT & PERIODONT, SCH DENT, UNIV ALA, BIRMINGHAM, 74-; CLIN ASSOC PROF DENT, UNIV MO-KANSAS CITY, 78- *Honors & Awards:* Balant Orban Prize, Am Acad Periodont, 66. *Mem:* Int Asn Dent Res; Am Acad Periodont; Am Dent Asn. *Res:* Ultrastructure and histopathology of periodontal disease; ultrastructure and biochemistry of developing salivary glands; basic enzymology of mammalian type. *Mailing Add:* 6301 N Oak Trafficway Kansas City MO 64118

COBB, DONALD D, b Atlantic, Iowa, May 4, 43. PHYSICS. *Educ:* Northern Ill Univ, BS, 65; Univ Iowa, MS, 68, PhD(physics), 70. *Prof Exp:* Sect leader, E G & G, Inc, Los Alamos, 70-75; GROUP LEADER ATMOSPHERIC SCI, LOS ALAMOS NAT LAB, 81- *Concurrent Pos:* Staff mem nuclear safeguards, Los Alamos Nat Lab, 76-81, assoc group leader, 81. *Mem:* Am Phys Soc. *Res:* Aeronomy; nuclear test detection; statistical analysis of data. *Mailing Add:* MS D466 Los Alamos Nat Lab Los Alamos NM 87545

COBB, EDWARD HUNTINGTON, b Great Barrington, Mass, Apr 23, 16; m 53. GEOLOGY. *Educ:* Yale Univ, BS, 38, MS, 41. GEOLOGIST, ALASKAN GEOL BR, US GEOL SURV, 46- *Mem:* AAAS; Geol Soc Am; Am Asn Petrol Geologists. *Res:* Mineral deposits geology; indices; bibliographies; collecting and synthesizing data on Alaskan mineral resources. *Mailing Add:* 1140 Cotton St Menlo Park CA 94025

COBB, EMERSON GILLMORE, b Slaughters, Ky, Nov 28, 07; m 29; c 2. ORGANIC CHEMISTRY. *Educ:* Union Col, Ky, AB, 28; Univ Ky, MS, 31; Univ NC, PhD(org chem), 41. *Hon Degrees:* LHD, Union Col, Ky, 61. *Prof Exp:* High sch instr, Ky, 28-29 & 32-40; asst prof chem, La Polytech Inst, 40-42; prof & head dept, Dakota Wesleyan Univ, 42-48; chmn dept, 48-74, prof, 48-78, EMER PROF CHEM, UNIV OF THE PAC, 78- *Concurrent Pos:* Fulbright vis lectr, Univ Peshawar, 61-62; vis lectr, Univ Baja Calif & Univ Ciencias Marinas, 74-75. *Mem:* Am Chem Soc. *Res:* Natural plant products; protective coatings; constitution of tannins. *Mailing Add:* PO Box 228 Burson CA 95225

COBB, FIELDS WHITE, JR, b Key West, Fla, Feb 16, 32; m 58; c 3. PLANT PATHOLOGY. *Educ:* NC State Univ, BS, 55; Yale Univ, MF, 56; Pa State Univ, PhD(plant path), 63. *Prof Exp:* Res forester, Southeastern Forest Exp Sta, US Forest Serv, 55-57; plant pathologist, Southern Forest Exp Sta, 57; statist clerk agr econ, Agr Mkt Serv, USDA, 57-58; instr plant path, Pa State Univ, 63; asst prof, 63-70, ASSOC PROF PLANT PATH, UNIV CALIF, BERKELEY, 70- *Mem:* AAAS; Soc Am Foresters; Am Phytopath Soc. *Res:* Diseases of forest trees, particularly those of roots and the vascular system, their causes, epidemiology, development and control; interactions with insects, air pollutants and activities of humans. *Mailing Add:* Dept of Plant Path Univ of Calif Berkeley CA 94720

COBB, GLENN WAYNE, b Jonesboro, La, Dec 1, 36; m 58; c 2. PLANT MORPHOGENESIS, PLANT PATHOLOGY. *Educ:* La Polytech Inst, BS, 58; Purdue Univ, MS, 61, PhD(plant morphol), 62. *Prof Exp:* Asst prof biol, Stephen F Austin State Univ, 62-65; from assoc prof to prof biol, 65-77, PROF BOT, McNEESE STATE UNIV, 77- *Concurrent Pos:* Fac res grants, 63-64 & 65. *Res:* Plant disease research. *Mailing Add:* Dept of Biol McNeese State Univ Lake Charles LA 70609

COBB, GROVER CLEVELAND, JR, b Atlanta, Ga, Feb 6, 35; m 54; c 2. NUCLEAR PHYSICS. *Educ:* Univ Ga, BS, 56, MS, 57; Univ Va, PhD(physics), 60. *Prof Exp:* Asst prof, 60-69, ASSOC PROF PHYSICS, NC STATE UNIV, 69- *Mem:* Am Phys Soc. *Res:* Neutron scattering; optical spectroscopy; gaseous discharge experiments; nuclear cross sections; plasma oscillations. *Mailing Add:* Dept of Physics NC State Univ Raleigh NC 27607

COBB, HOWELL DEE, JR, b San Antonio, Tex, Sept 12, 30; m 52; c 5. CELL PHYSIOLOGY, MICROBIAL PHYSIOLOGY. *Educ:* Trinity Col, Tex, BS, 53, MS, 58; Univ Tex, PhD(nitrogen fixation), 63. *Prof Exp:* Asst prof physiol, Baylor Univ, 62-63; from asst prof to assoc prof physiol, 63-77, PROF BIOL, TRINITY UNIV, TEX, 77- *Concurrent Pos:* Res fel, Univ Tex, 63. *Mem:* AAAS; Am Soc Plant Physiologists; Am Soc Microbiol. *Res:* Relationships between photosynthesis and nitrogen metabolism in algae; study of microecological systems involved in the biodegradation of cresol; genetic control of cresol degradation by bacteria. *Mailing Add:* Dept of Biol Trinity Univ San Antonio TX 78284

COBB, JAMES TEMPLE, JR, b Cincinnati, Ohio, Mar 9, 38; m 64; c 2. CHEMICAL ENGINEERING. *Educ:* Mass Inst Technol, SB, 60; Purdue Univ, MS, 63, PhD(chem eng), 66. *Prof Exp:* Engr, Esso Res Lab, 67-70; asst prof chem eng, 70-75, ASSOC PROF CHEM ENG, UNIV PITTSBURGH, 75- *Concurrent Pos:* Consult, A-C Valley Corp, Goodyear Tire & Rubber Co & Gulf Res & Develop Co. *Honors & Awards:* Navy Commendation Medal, 67. *Mem:* Am Inst Chem Engrs; Am Soc Eng Educ. *Res:* High temperature fuel cells; warm fog dispersal; chemical process development; enzyme engineering; coal conversion processes; zeolite catalysis. *Mailing Add:* 141 Deerfield Dr Pittsburgh PA 15235

COBB, JEWEL PLUMMER, b Jan 17, 24; US citizen; div; c 1. CELL BIOLOGY. *Educ:* Talladega Col, AB, 44; NY Univ, MS, 47, PhD(cell biol), 50. *Hon Degrees:* LLD, Wheaton Col, Mass, 71; ScD, Lowell Technol Inst, 72. *Prof Exp:* Instr anat, Col Med, Univ Ill, 52-54; from instr to asst prof res surg, Post Grad Med Sch, NY Univ, 55-60; prof biol, Sarah Lawrence Col, 60-69; prof zool & dean, Conn Col, 69-76; prof biol & dean, Douglass Col, Rutgers Univ, 76-81; PRES, CALIF STATE UNIV, FULLERTON, 81- *Concurrent Pos:* Nat Cancer Inst grant, 69-74 & 74-77; Am Cancer Soc grant, 71-73; vis lectr res assoc prog, Hunter Col, 56-57; mem bd, Nat Sci Bd, NSF, 74-; mem bd, Am Coun Educ, 74-; mem bd dirs, Nat Inst Med. *Mem:* Nat Inst Med; AAAS; fel NY Acad Sci; Tissue Cult Asn; Am Asn Cancer Res. *Res:* Research on mechanisms controlling differentiation and growth in malignant pigment cells. *Mailing Add:* Calif State Univ 800 N College Blvd Fullerton CA 92631

COBB, JOHN CANDLER, b Boston, Mass, July 8, 19; m 46; c 4. PREVENTIVE MEDICINE. *Educ:* Harvard Univ, BA, 41; MD, 48; Johns Hopkins Univ, MPH, 54. *Prof Exp:* Asst malaria control, Friends Serv Comt, 41-42; instr maternal & child health, Sch Hyg & Pub Health, Johns Hopkins Univ, 51-54; instr pediat, Sch Med, 51-56 & psychiat, 52-56; asst prof maternal & child health, Sch Hyg, 54-56; area consult, USPHS, Div Indian Health, N Mex, 56-60; Johns Hopkins Univ & Ford Found dir med social res proj, Lahore, Pakistan, 60-64; chmn dept, 66-72, PROF PREV MED, SCH MED, UNIV COLO, DENVER, 65- *Concurrent Pos:* Mem comt peace educ & family planning, Am Friends Serv Comt, 64-74; WHO short term consult maternal & child health & family planning, Indonesia, 69-70 & family health educ, Western Pac Region, 71-72; mem gov sci adv coun, Colo; mem environ coun; mem air pollution control comn, Colo, 76-; mem gov's task force Nuclear Energy Plant, 75; mem bd dirs, Rocky Mountain Ctr Environ & Colo Coalition Full Employ, 78-; mem, Colo Gov Task Force Health Effects of Air Pollution, 78. *Mem:* AAAS; Int Solar Energy Soc. *Res:* Environmental health. *Mailing Add:* Dept of Prev Med Univ of Colo Sch of Med Denver CO 80220

COBB, JOHN IVERSON, b Marianna, Fla, Feb 9, 38. TOPOLOGY. *Educ:* Fla State Univ, BA, 60; Univ Wis, MA, 61, PhD(math), 66. *Prof Exp:* Instr math, Racine Ctr, Univ Wis, 66; asst prof, Rutgers Univ, 66-69; asst prof, 69-74, ASSOC PROF MATH, UNIV IDAHO, 74- *Mem:* Am Math Soc; Math Asn Am. *Res:* Point-set topology; piece-wise linear topology. *Mailing Add:* Dept of Math Univ of Idaho Moscow ID 83843

COBB, JOSEPH R, JR, b Atoka, Okla, Nov 21, 24; m 51; c 2. CHEMICAL ENGINEERING. *Educ:* Mass Inst Technol, BS, 49, MS, 50. *Prof Exp:* Pilot plant engr, M W Kellogg Co, 50-52; res engr, 52-55, supvr process calculations, 55-64, MGR TECH SYSTS DEVELOP DIV, PHILLIPS PETROL CO, 64- *Mem:* Am Inst Chem Engrs; Opers Res Soc Am; Inst Mgt Sci. *Res:* Corrosion resistance of titanium; reforming catalyst research; hydrocarbon processing; analysis of engineering data. *Mailing Add:* Phillips Petrol Co 415 Info Ctr Bartlesville OK 74004

COBB, LOREN, b Boston, Mass, May 8, 48; m 75. STATISTICAL CATASTROPHE THEORY, MATHEMATICAL STATISTICS. *Educ:* Cornell Univ, BA, 70, MA, 71, PhD(sociol), 73. *Prof Exp:* Asst prof sociol, Univ NH, 72-77; fel psychiat, Med Sch, Univ SFla, 77-79; asst prof, 79-81, ASSOC PROF BIOMET, MED UNIV SC, 81- *Concurrent Pos:* Res assoc, Cornell Univ, 73-77. *Mem:* Inst Math Statist; Soc Indust & Appl Math; Am Statist Asn; Am Sociol Asn. *Res:* Estimation and hypothesis testing for stochastic nonlinear dynamical systems; statistical catastrophe theory and its applications in the biological and social sciences. *Mailing Add:* Dept Biomet Med Univ SC Charleston SC 29425

COBB, R M KARAPETOFF, b Winthrop, Mass; m 36. PAPER CHEMISTRY. *Educ:* Tufts Col, BS, 22; Mass Inst Technol, MS, 23. *Prof Exp:* Asst, Mass Inst Technol, 23-24; res chemist, Larkin Co, Inc, 24 & Hunt-Rankin Leather Co, 24-26; res dir, 26-51, tech adv, 51-65, consult, Lowe Paper Co, Ridgefield, NJ, 65-80; RETIRED. *Concurrent Pos:* Mem lithograph adv comt, Nat Bur Standards, 29-55, res assoc, Lithograph Tech Found, 31. *Honors & Awards:* Coating & Graphic Arts Div Award, Tech Asn Pulp & Paper Indust, 68. *Mem:* Am Chem Soc; Soc Rheol; fel Tech Asn Pulp & Paper Indust. *Res:* Paper sizing and coating; adhesives; lithography; emulsions. *Mailing Add:* 77 Grozier Rd Cambridge MA 02138

COBB, RAYMOND LYNN, b Ochelata, Okla, Dec 10, 29; m 66; c 1. ORGANIC CHEMISTRY. *Educ:* Ottawa Univ, BS, 51; Univ Kans, PhD(org chem), 55. *Prof Exp:* RES CHEMIST & RES ASSOC, PHILLIPS PETROL CO, 55- *Mem:* Am Chem Soc. *Res:* Organic nitrogen compounds; catalytic organic processes; thermal reactions; organosulfur compounds; reaction mechanisms. *Mailing Add:* Res & Develop Dept Phillips Petrol Co Bartlesville OK 74004

COBB, SIDNEY, b Cambridge, Mass, June 1, 16; m 41; c 4. EPIDEMIOLOGY. *Educ:* Harvard Univ, BS, 38, MD, 42, MPH, 51. *Prof Exp:* Intern med, Johns Hopkins Hosp, 42-43; chief resident, Sydenham Hosp Infectious Dis, 46-47; dir, Nashoba Assoc Bds Health, 48-52; from asst prof to assoc prof biostatist & epidemiol, Univ Pittsburgh, 52-61; assoc, Ment Health Res Inst, Univ Mich, Ann Arbor, 61-68; prog dir, Surv Res Ctr & lectr, Sch Pub Health, 61-73; PROF COMMUNITY HEALTH & PSYCHIAT, BROWN UNIV, 73- *Concurrent Pos:* Fel biochem, Harvard Med Sch, 47-48; NIH career develop award, 63-68; instr, Med Sch, Johns Hopkins Univ, 46-47 & Sch Pub Health, Harvard Univ, 48-52; res scientist, NIH, 68-73, consult, NIMH, 69-; chief psychiat epidemiol, Butler Hosp, Providence, 73-74. *Mem:* Am Pub Health Asn; Am Rheumatism Asn; Am Psychosom Soc; Am Heart Asn; Am Epidemiol Soc. *Res:* Epidemiology of non-communicable diseases, especially psychosomatic disease and mental health. *Mailing Add:* Box G Brown Univ Providence RI 02912

COBB, THOMAS BERRY, b Atlanta, Ga, Nov 4, 39; m 64. PHYSICS, CHEMISTRY. *Educ:* Southern Missionary Col, BA, 60; Univ SC, MS, 63; NC State Univ, PhD(physics), 68. *Prof Exp:* Instr physics, Western Md Col, 63-65; res assoc chem, Univ NC, 68-69; asst prof, 69-74, ASSOC PROF PHYSICS & ASST VPROVOST RES, BOWLING GREEN STATE UNIV, 74- . *Mem:* AAAS; Am Asn Physics Teachers. *Res:* Nuclear magnetic resonance. *Mailing Add:* Dept of Physics Bowling Green State Univ Bowling Green OH 43402

COBB, WILLIAM EDWARD, b Chicago, Ill, Apr 2, 24; m 64; c 2. METEOROLOGY, ATMOSPHERIC ELECTRICITY. *Prof Exp:* RES METEOROLOGIST, NAT OCEANIC & ATMOSPHERIC ADMIN, 53- *Mem:* Am Meteorol Soc; Am Geophys Union. *Res:* Atmospheric electricity and air pollution; solar terrestrial links with atmospheric electricity; atmospheric electric measurements from the South Pole, ocean research vessels and Mauna Loa Observatory in Hawaii. *Mailing Add:* Nat Oceanic & Atmospheric Admin RX8 Boulder CO 80303

COBB, WILLIAM MONTAGUE, b Washington, DC, Oct 12, 04; m 29; c 2. ANATOMY, PHYSICAL ANTHROPOLOGY. *Educ:* Amherst Col, AB, 25; Howard Univ, MD, 29; Western Reserve Univ, PhD, 32. *Hon Degrees:* ScD, Amherst Col, 55, Georgetown Univ, 78, Med Col Wis, 79; LLD, Morgan State Col, 64 & Univ Witwatersrand, 77; LHD, Howard Univ, 80. *Prof Exp:* Instr embryol, 28-29, from asst prof to prof anat, 32-69, mem exec comt, Med Sch, 41 & 45-69, head dept anat, 47-69, distinguished prof, 69-73, EMER PROF, HOWARD UNIV, 73- *Concurrent Pos:* Fel, Western Reserve Univ, 33-39, Rosenwald fel, 41-42, assoc, 42-44; jr med officer, USDA, 35; chmn nat med comt, Nat Asn Advan Colored People, 44-77, nat pres, 76-; health specialist, Nat Urban League, 46 & 47; mem exec comt, White House

Conf Health, 65; ed, J Nat Med Asn, 49-77; assoc ed, J Am Asn Phys Anthrop, 44-48, ed, 49- *Honors & Awards:* Distinguished Serv Medal, Nat Med Asn, 55; US Navy Distinguished Pub Serv Award, 78. *Mem:* AAAS (vpres, 55); Am Asn Anat; Am Soc Mammal; Nat Med Asn (pres, 64-65); Am Asn Phys Anthrop (vpres, 48-50 & 54-56, pres, 57-59). *Res:* Physical anthropology; collections of human materials; growth and development of the American Negro; aging in the adult skeleton; graphic method of anatomy; history of American Negro in medicine. *Mailing Add:* 1219 Girard St NW Washington DC 20009

COBB, WILLIAM THOMPSON, b Spokane, Wash, Nov 10, 42; m 64; c 4. PLANT PATHOLOGY, WEED SCIENCE. *Educ:* Eastern Wash Univ, BA, 64; Ore State Univ, PhD(plant path), 73. *Prof Exp:* Mgr agron, Sun Royal Co, 70-74; sr scientist plant path, 74-78, RES SCIENTIST, LILLY RES LABS, 78- *Concurrent Pos:* Plant pathol instr, Columbia Basin Col, 71, 73, 75, & 77. *Mem:* Sigma Xi; Am Phytopath Soc; Weed Sci Soc Am; Am Soc Agron; Ctr Applications Sci Technol. *Res:* Field screening of experimental pesticides; crop fertility and disease interactions. *Mailing Add:* 815 S Kellogg Kennewick WA 99336

COBBAN, WILLIAM AUBREY, b Anaconda, Mont, Dec 31, 16; m 42; c 3. GEOLOGY. *Educ:* Univ Mont, BA, 40; Johns Hopkins Univ, PhD(geol), 49. *Prof Exp:* Geologist, Carter Oil Co,Tulsa, 39-45; PALEONTOLOGIST & STRATIGRAPHER, US GEOL SURV, 46- *Mem:* Soc Econ Paleontologists & Mineralogists; Paleont Soc; Am Asn Petrol Geol; Geol Soc Am. *Res:* Upper Cretaceous stratigraphy and paleontology of the Rocky Mountain area. *Mailing Add:* US Geol Surv Fed Ctr Bldg 25 Mail Stop 919 Denver CO 80225

COBBE, THOMAS JAMES, b Cincinnati, Ohio, July 18, 18; m 44; c 2. FOREST ECOLOGY. *Educ:* Univ Cincinnati, BA, 40, MA, 41; Univ Mich, PhD(bot), 53. *Prof Exp:* Asst prof biol, Am Univ, 48-49; instr, Oberlin Col, 49-52; from instr to asst prof, Capital Univ, 52-57; asst prof, 57-71, ASSOC PROF BOT, MIAMI UNIV, 71- *Mem:* AAAS; Ecol Soc Am; Am Soc Photogram. *Res:* Secondary forest successions; Dutch elm disease. *Mailing Add:* Dept of Bot Miami Univ Oxford OH 45056

COBBLE, JAMES WIKLE, b Kansas City, Mo, Mar 15, 26; m 49; c 2. PHYSICAL CHEMISTRY, INORGANIC CHEMISTRY. *Educ:* Ariz State Univ, AB, 46; Univ Southern Calif, MS, 49; Univ Tenn, PhD(phys chem), 52. *Prof Exp:* Chemist, Oak Ridge Nat Lab, 49-52 & Lawrence Berkeley Lab, Univ Calif, 52-54; from asst prof to prof chem, Purdue Univ, 55-73; PROF CHEM & DEAN GRAD DIV & RES, SAN DIEGO STATE UNIV, 73- *Concurrent Pos:* Instr, Univ Calif, 53; consult, Gen Elec Co, 72-, Great Lakes Chem Corp, 73- & Squibb Corp, 73-; vpres, San Diego State Univ Found, 75- *Honors & Awards:* E O Lawrence Award, AEC, 70; Robert A Welch Found lectr, 71. *Mem:* Am Chem Soc; fel Am Phys Soc; Sigma Xi. *Res:* Radiochemistry; physical-inorganic chemistry; correlation of thermodynamic properties with structures; high temperature solutions; nuclear chemistry; mechanisms of nuclear reactions. *Mailing Add:* Dept Chem San Diego State Univ San Diego CA 92182

COBBLE, MILAN HOUSTON, b St Paul, Minn, Mar 13, 22; m 49; c 4. MECHANICAL ENGINEERING. *Educ:* Univ Mich, BSME, 48, PhD(mech eng), 58; Wayne State Univ, MSME, 52. *Prof Exp:* Instr eng drawing, Bowling Green State Univ, 49-51, asst prof, 51-54; res assoc fluids lab, Univ Mich, 55-56; from asst prof to assoc prof, 56-62, PROF MECH ENG, N MEX STATE UNIV, 62- *Concurrent Pos:* NSF fac fel, 59-62; Western Elec Fund Award, 67. *Mem:* Fel AAAS; Am Soc Mech Engrs; Soc Rheol; Am Soc Eng Educ; Am Acad Mech. *Res:* Nonlinear mathematics; solar energy; heat transfer. *Mailing Add:* Dept of Mech Eng NMex State Univ Las Cruces NM 88003

COBBOLD, R S C, b Worcester, Eng, Dec 10, 31; Can citizen; m 63; c 3. BIOMEDICAL ENGINEERING. *Educ:* Univ London, BSc, 56; Univ Sask, MSc, 61, PhD(elec eng), 65. *Prof Exp:* Asst exp officer electronics, Ministry of Supply, Eng, 49-53; sci officer, Defence Res Bd, Ottawa, Can, 56-59; from lectr to assoc prof elec eng, Univ Sask, 60-66; from assoc prof to prof elec eng, 66-75, DIR INST BIOMED ENG, UNIV TORONTO, 75- *Mem:* Inst Elec & Electronics Engrs; Int Fedn Med & Biol Eng; fel Royal Soc Can. *Res:* Medical ultrasonics; biomedical transducers; physics of semiconductor devices. *Mailing Add:* Inst of Biomed Eng Univ of Toronto Toronto ON M5S 1A4 Can

COBERLY, CAMDEN ARTHUR, b Elizabeth, WVa, Dec 21, 22; m 46; c 4. CHEMICAL ENGINEERING, ACADEMIC ADMINISTRATION. *Educ:* WVa Univ, BS, 44; Carnegie Inst Technol, MS, 47; Univ Wis-Madison, PhD(chem eng), 49. *Prof Exp:* Chief chem engr & supvr, Mallinckrodt Chem Works, 49-65; chmn dept, 68-71, PROF CHEM ENG, UNIV WIS-MADISON, 64-, ASSOC DEAN ENG, 71- *Mem:* Fel Am Inst Chem Engrs; AAAS; Am Soc Eng Educ; Am Chem Soc; Nat Asn Corrosion Engrs. *Res:* Chemical engineering transfer operations; chemical plant design. *Mailing Add:* 4114 N Sunset Ct Madison WI 53705

COBINE, J(AMES) D(ILLON), electrical engineering, deceased

COBLE, ANNA JANE, b Raleigh, NC, July 12, 36. PHYSICAL PROPERTIES OF MEMBRANES. *Educ:* Howard Univ, BS, 58, MS, 61; Univ Ill, Urbana, PhD(biophysics), 73. *Prof Exp:* Instr physics, NC Agr & Tech State Univ, 60-64; assoc, Ctr Biol Nat Syst, Washington Univ, 69-71; lectr, 71-74, ASST PROF PHYSICS & BIOPHYSICS, HOWARD UNIV, 74- *Concurrent Pos:* MARC fac fel, NIH, 79-80. *Mem:* AAAS; Am Asn Physics Teachers; Sigma Xi. *Res:* Biological effects and properties of ultrasound; physical studies of membranes and membrane transport. *Mailing Add:* 1000 Fairview Ave Takoma Park MD 20912

COBLE, HAROLD DEAN, b Burlington, NC, Feb 3, 43; m 65; c 3. WEED SCIENCE, AGRONOMY. *Educ:* NC State Univ, BS, 65, MS, 67; Univ Ill, Urbana, PhD(weed sci), 70. *Prof Exp:* Asst prof, 70-74, assoc prof weed sci, 74-80, PROF CROP SCI, NC STATE UNIV, 80- *Concurrent Pos:* Consult, Union Carbide Corp, 74-77, Monsanto Chem Co, 73- & Velsicol Chem Corp, 76- *Honors & Awards:* Meritorious Serv Award, Am Soybean Asn, 77. *Mem:* Am Soc Agron; Weed Sci Soc Am; Plant Growth Regulator Group; Am Peanut Res & Educ Asn. *Res:* Weed-crop interactions as related to integrated pest management; herbicide effects on crops and weeds; crop yield enhancement with plant growth regulators. *Mailing Add:* Dept of Crop Sci NC State Univ Raleigh NC 27650

COBLE, R(OBERT) L(OUIS), b Uniontown, Pa, Jan 22, 28; m 52; c 5. CERAMICS. *Educ:* Bethany Col, WVa, BS, 50; Mass Inst Technol, ScD(ceramics), 55. *Prof Exp:* Res asst ceramics, Mass Inst Technol, 50-55; ceramist, Gen Elec Res Lab, 55-60; from asst prof to assoc prof, 60-69, PROF CERAMICS, MASS INST TECHNOL, 69- *Concurrent Pos:* Sosman lectr, Am Ceramic Soc, 79. *Honors & Awards:* Award, Nat Inst Chem Engrs, 60 & Ross Coffin Purdy Award, Am Ceramic Soc, 70. *Mem:* Fel Am Ceramic Soc; Nat Inst Ceramic Engrs; AAAS; Nat Acad Eng. *Res:* High temperature creep; thermodynamics of solid solutions and defect equilibria in ceramics; diffusion in non-metals; modeling of diffusion-controlled phenomena; creep rupture; powder metallurgy and ceramics processing. *Mailing Add:* Dept of Mat Sci & Eng Mass Inst of Technol Cambridge MA 02139

COBLER, JOHN GEORGE, b Conneaut Lake, Pa, Sept 15, 18; m 41; c 2. ORGANIC POLYMER CHEMISTRY. *Educ:* Col Wooster, BA, 40. *Prof Exp:* Lab asst, Col Wooster, 38-39; control chemist, Ohio Exp Sta, 39-40; asst, Purdue Univ, 40-41; res chemist, Distillation Prod, Inc, NY, 42-45; lab dir, Bordon Co, NJ, 45-47; head spec prod develop, Bordens Soy Processing Co, 47-49; group leader, Anal Dept, Dow Chem Co, 49-59, tech expert, 59-69, tech consult, 69-70, assoc anal scientist, 70-75, ASSOC SCIENTIST, HEALTH & ENVIRON DEPT, DOW CHEM CO, 75- *Concurrent Pos:* Asst, Manhattan Proj, Univ Rochester, 44-45. *Mem:* Am Chem Soc; Sigma Xi; Am Soc Testing & Mat; NY Acad Sci. *Res:* Structure and composition of polymers; stability and degradation of polymers. *Mailing Add:* 2008 Rapanos Dr Midland MI 48640

COBURN, CORBETT BENJAMIN, JR, b Lake Providence, La, Dec 7, 40; m 61; c 1. ENVIRONMENTAL PHYSIOLOGY, PHYSIOLOGICAL ECOLOGY. *Educ:* La Polytech Inst, BS, 62, MS, 64; Univ Southern Miss, PhD(zool), 70. *Prof Exp:* Instr biol, Calif Baptist Col, 64-65 & East Central Jr Col, 66-68; instr, Wesleyan Col, 70-71; asst prof, West Liberty State Col, 71-72; asst prof, 72-80, ASSOC PROF BIOL, TENN TECHNOL UNIV, 80- *Mem:* Am Fisheries Soc; AAAS. *Res:* Vertebrate hematology; metabolic responses of aquatic animals to pollutants; RNA/DNA ratio as affected by season and water quality; histological and physiological responses of fish to nitrogen supersaturation; environmental assessment of highway impact on organisms in flood plain. *Mailing Add:* Dept of Biol Tenn Technol Univ Cookeville TN 38501

COBURN, EVERETT ROBERT, b Manchester, NH, Aug 10, 15; m 39; c 2. ORGANIC CHEMISTRY. *Educ:* Harvard Univ, SB, 38, AM, 40, PhD(org chem), 41. *Prof Exp:* Lilly fel polarog studies of quinones, Harvard Univ, 41-42; res chemist, Nat Defense Res Comt, 42-43; prof chem, Bennington Col, 43-80; RETIRED. *Concurrent Pos:* Lectr, Middlebury Col, 44; consult, Sprague Elec Co, 52- *Mem:* Am Chem Soc. *Res:* Diels-Alder reactions on quinones; polarographic work on quinones and related compounds; incendiary mixtures and design of apparatus for use. *Mailing Add:* 43 Spindle Point Mededith NH 03253

COBURN, FRANK EMERSON, b Toronto, Ont, Apr 25, 12; m 40; c 4. PSYCHIATRY. *Educ:* Univ Toronto, BA, 36, MD, 39; RCPS(C), cert psychiat. *Prof Exp:* Assoc prof psychiat, Univ Iowa, 50-55; assoc prof, 55-58, prof, 58-80, EMER PROF PSYCHIAT, UNIV SASK, 80- *Concurrent Pos:* Baker lectr, Univ Mich, 54; mem, Am Bd Psychiat & Neurol, 47- *Mem:* Fel Am Psychiat Asn; Am Psychosom Soc; Can Psychiat Asn; Can Med Asn. *Res:* Teaching; therapy; community psychiatry. *Mailing Add:* 1302 Colony St Saskatoon S7N 0S7 Can

COBURN, HORACE HUNTER, b Cambridge, Mass, May 10, 22; m 47; c 3. PHYSICS. *Educ:* Ohio State Univ, BS, 43; Univ Ill, MS, 47; Univ Pa, PhD(physics), 56. *Prof Exp:* Assoc prof physics, Moravian Col, 50-51; from asst prof to assoc prof, 54-69, PROF PHYSICS, NMEX STATE UNIV, 69- *Concurrent Pos:* Physicist, Manhattan Proj, Tenn, 44-46; consult, Los Alamos Sci Lab, 62-; mem fac, Univ Inst Optics, Univ Rochester, 64-65. *Mem:* AAAS; Am Phys Soc; Am Asn Physics Teachers; Optical Soc Am. *Res:* Optics; biophysics. *Mailing Add:* NMex State Univ Box 3D Las Cruces NM 88001

COBURN, JACK WESLEY, b Fresno, Calif, Aug 6, 32; m 58; c 3. INTERNAL MEDICINE, NEPHROLOGY. *Educ:* Univ Redlands, BS, 53; Univ Calif, Los Angeles, MD, 57; Am Bd Internal Med, dipl, 65. *Prof Exp:* Intern med, Med Ctr, Univ Calif, Los Angeles, 57-58; asst res physician, Univ Wash Hosp Syst, Seattle, 58-60; assoc res physician, Med Ctr, Univ Calif, Los Angeles, 60-61; sect chief gen med, Wadsworth Hosp, Los Angeles, 68-69; from asst prof to assoc prof, 65-73, PROF MED, SCH MED, UNIV CALIF, LOS ANGELES, 73-; CHIEF NEPHROLOGY SECT, VET ADMIN WADSWORTH HOSP CTR, 70- *Concurrent Pos:* Nat Inst Arthritis & Metab res fel, Vet Admin Hosp & Univ Calif, Los Angeles, 61-63, clin investr award, Vet Admin Ctr, 65-67; chief metab res ward, Vet Admin Ctr, Los Angeles, 67-70. *Mem:* Am Fedn Clin Res; AMA; Am Soc Nephrology; fel Am Col Physicians; Am Physiol Soc. *Res:* Renal physiology, especially renal handling of divalent ions; pathophysiology of uremia; renal osteodystrophy; vitamin D and calcium metabolism. *Mailing Add:* Vet Admin Wadsworth Hosp Ctr Wilshire & Sawtelle Blvds Los Angeles CA 90073

COBURN, JOHN WYLLIE, b Vancouver, BC, Nov 9, 33; m 66; c 2. PLASMA CHEMISTRY. *Educ:* Univ BC, BASc, 56, MASc, 58; Univ Minn, Minneapolis, PhD(elec eng), 67. *Prof Exp:* Fel physics, Simon Fraser Univ, 67-68; RES STAFF MEM, MAT SCI DEPT, RES LAB, INT BUS MACH CO, 68- *Mem:* Am Vacuum Soc. *Res:* Particle diagnostics in glow discharges; thin film formation by sputtering and by plasma polymerization; physics and chemistry of dry etching processes. *Mailing Add:* IBM Res Lab K33/281 5600 Cottle Rd San Jose CA 95193

COBURN, MICHAEL DOYLE, b Houston, Tex, Aug 6, 39; m 60; c 2. ORGANIC CHEMISTRY. *Educ:* Univ Tex, Austin, BS, 62, PhD(chem), 64. *Prof Exp:* STAFF MEM, LOS ALAMOS SCI LAB, UNIV CALIF, 64- *Mem:* Am Chem Soc; Int Soc Heterocyclic Chem. *Res:* Synthesis of energetic organic compounds, predominantly in the heterocyclic field. *Mailing Add:* PO Box 1633 MS 920 Los Alamos NM 87544

COBURN, RICHARD KARL, b Salt Lake City, Utah, Feb 24, 20; m 42; c 16. APPLIED MATHEMATICS. *Educ:* Utah State Univ, BS, 42 & 43; Univ Wash, MS, 56; Univ Ill, MA, 62. *Prof Exp:* Instr math & physics, Pa State Univ, 46-48; prof chem & physics, Ricks Col, 48-58; chmn dept, 58-80, PROF MATH, BRIGHAM YOUNG UNIV, HAWAII CAMPUS, 58- *Concurrent Pos:* Math consult, Lockheed Airplane Co, 60-62; pres, Hawaii Coun Teachers Math; assoc dir, Hawaii Sci Fair; lectr, Nat Coun Teachers Math. *Mem:* Am Chem Soc. *Res:* Analytical methods of solving inequalities of order two and higher. *Mailing Add:* 55-521 Naniloa Loop Laie Oahu HI 96762

COBURN, ROBERT A, b Akron, Ohio, Dec 31, 38; m 66; c 2. MEDICINAL CHEMISTRY, PHYSICAL ORGANIC CHEMISTRY. *Educ:* Univ Akron, BS, 60; Harvard Univ, AM, 62, PhD(org chem), 66. *Prof Exp:* Res chemist, US Army Natick Labs, Mass, 65-66; asst prof, 68-73, ASSOC PROF MED CHEM, SCH PHARM, STATE UNIV NY BUFFALO, 73- *Mem:* Am Chem Soc; Royal Soc Chem. *Res:* Synthesis and molecular structure studies of heterocyclic compounds of biological and/or pharmacological significance. *Mailing Add:* 35 Chestnut Hill Lane S Williamsville NY 14221

COBURN, RONALD F, b Grand Rapids, Mich, Dec 10, 31; m 62; c 2. PHYSIOLOGY. *Educ:* Northwestern Univ, BS, 54, MD, 57. *Prof Exp:* Intern, Presby-St Luke's Hosp, Chicago, 57-58; resident internal med, Vet Admin Res Hosp, Chicago, 58-60; from instr to assoc med, 63-66 & asst prof, 67-68, from asst prof to assoc prof physiol, 66-75, PROF PHYSIOL & MED, SCH MED, UNIV PA, 75- *Concurrent Pos:* Fel physiol, Sch Med, Univ Pa, 60-63; mem, Vet Admin Respiratory Syst Res Eval Comt, 69-71. *Mem:* Am Physiol Soc; Am Soc Clin Invest; Am Fedn Clin Res. *Res:* Pulmonary and carbon monoxide physiology; heme catabolism; pulmonary gas exchange; tissue oxygenation; airway physiology. *Mailing Add:* Dept of Physiol Sch Med Univ Pa Philadelphia PA 19174

COBURN, STEPHEN PUTNAM, b Orange, NJ, Nov 10, 36. BIOCHEMISTRY. *Educ:* Rutgers Univ, BS, 58; Purdue Univ, MS, 61, PhD(biochem), 64. *Prof Exp:* DIR DEPT BIOCHEM, FT WAYNE STATE HOSP & TRAINING CTR, 63- *Concurrent Pos:* Instr, Ind Univ-Purdue Univ, Ft Wayne; dipl, Am Bd Clin Chem. *Mem:* Am Chem Soc; Am Asn Ment Deficiency; Am Asn Clin Chem; Brit Biochem Soc; Am Inst Nutrit. *Res:* Biochemistry of mental retardation and other metabolic diseases; vitamin B6. *Mailing Add:* Ft Wayne State Hosp & Training Ctr Dept Biochem 4900 St Joe Rd Ft Wayne IN 46815

COBURN, THEODORE JAMES, b Newton, Mass, June 11, 26; m 49; c 3. SOLID STATE PHYSICS. *Educ:* Ohio State Univ, BSc, 47, PhD(physics), 57. *Prof Exp:* Contract administr, Armaments Br, Off Naval Res, DC, 53-55; proj engr, Apparatus & Optical Div, 57-60, sr res physicist, 60-80, SR STAFF RES ASSOC, RES LABS, EASTMAN KODAK CO, NY, 80- *Mem:* Inst Elec & Electronic Engrs; Am Phys Soc; Electrochem Soc. *Res:* Surface state physics as applied to electrostatics; infrared spectroscopy; military applications of infrared; solid state silicon photosensor and integrated circuit very large scale integration fabrication and testing. *Mailing Add:* Eastman Kodak Co Res Labs Rochester NY 14650

COBURN, WILLIAM CARL, JR, b Duluth, Minn, Nov 2, 26; m 51; c 2. PHYSICAL ORGANIC CHEMISTRY. *Educ:* Univ Colo, BA, 48; Fla State Univ, MA, 51, PhD(phys chem), 54. *Prof Exp:* Phys chemist, 54-59, sr phys chemist, 59-67, HEAD MOLECULAR SPECTROS SECT, SOUTHERN RES INST, 67- *Mem:* AAAS; Coblentz Soc; Am Chem Soc; Sigma Xi. *Res:* Kinetics and mechanisms of organic reactions; molecular complexing; hydrogen bonding; theoretical and applied infrared spectroscopy; ultraviolet spectroscopy; nuclear magnetic resonance spectroscopy; mass spectroscopy. *Mailing Add:* Southern Res Inst 2000 Ninth Ave S Birmingham AL 35255

COCANOWER, R(OBERT) D(UNLAVY), b Hoehne, Colo, Dec 6, 20; m 47; c 2. PETROLEUM ENGINEERING. *Educ:* Univ Okla, BS, 46. *Prof Exp:* Chemist, Mercury Refining Co, 38-41; dist mgr, West Co, 46-52, supvr res, 53-65, mgr eng & develop, 65-77; DIR MKT, CRC WIRELINE, 77- *Mem:* Am Inst Mining, Metall & Petrol Engrs; Am Petrol Inst; Am Soc Petrol Engrs; Independent Petrol Assoc Am. *Res:* Radioactivity; explosives; detection of radiation in oil well bores; use of radioactive isotopes in tracing fluids in oil wells; design of oil well perforating guns; design of electronic instruments for oil wells. *Mailing Add:* 500 W 13th Suite 210 Fort Worth TX 76102

COCCA, M(ICHAEL) A(NTHONY), b Green Island, NY, Mar 27, 25; m 48; c 4. METALLURGY. *Educ:* Rensselaer Polytech Inst, BMet, 51, MMetE, 59. *Prof Exp:* Metallurgist, Res Lab, Gen Elec Co, 51-54; supvr heat treating & surfaces, 54-57, admin asst, 57-59, metallurgist, 59-70, mgr struct mat appln, 70-76, prog mgr, Int Mat Progs, Gas Turbine Dept, 76-81. *Mem:* Am Soc Metals; Am Vacuum Soc (secy-treas, 61-); Am Inst Mining, Metall & Petrol Engrs; Am Welding Soc. *Res:* Physical metallurgy of refractory and reactive metals, including high purity atmosphere technology in refining and processing; thin film technology; reactor structural materials; pressure vessel steels; nickel base alloys; process control, forging, casting, fabrication of alloy steels and superalloys. *Mailing Add:* Bldg 53 Gen Elec Co One River Rd Schenectady NY 12345

COCCODRILLI, GUS D, JR, b Peckville, Pa, July 28, 45; m 67; c 2. NUTRITION. *Educ:* Pa State Univ, BS, 67, PhD(food sci), 71; Va Polytech Inst, MS, 69. *Prof Exp:* Sr chemist, 71-74, prof leader nutrit, 74-76, group leader nutrit, 76-80, lab mgr dent res, 80-81, SR LAB MGR, NUTRIT SCI, GEN FOODS CORP, 81- *Mem:* Inst Food Technologists; Nutrit Today Soc; assoc mem Am Inst Nutrit. *Res:* Mineral nutrition research; trace element metabolism; vitamin nutrition; dental health research; cereal nutrition. *Mailing Add:* Tech Ctr 250 North St Gen Foods Corp White Plains NY 10625

COCEANI, FLAVIO, b Trieste, Italy, Jan 3, 37; m 69. NEUROPHYSIOLOGY. *Educ:* Univ Bologna, MD, 61, Docent(human physiol), 68. *Prof Exp:* Asst prof, Univ Bologna, 65-66; vis scientist neurochem, Montreal Neurol Inst, 66-68; asst prof, 68-70, asst prof pediat, 69-77, ASSOC PROF PHYSIOL, UNIV TORONTO, 70-, ASSOC PROF PEDIAT, 77-; PROG DIR, RES INST, HOSP SICK CHILDREN, 77- *Concurrent Pos:* Nat Res Coun fel & res fel, Dept Physiol, Univ Bologna, 61-62; res fel neurophysiol, Montreal Neurol Inst, 62-64; asst scientist, Res Inst, Hosp Sick Children, 68-77. *Mem:* AAAS; Am Soc Neurochem; Can Soc Clin Invest; NY Acad Sci; Can Physiol Soc. *Res:* Role of prostaglandins in brain function; role of prostaglandins in fetal and neonatal cardiovascular homeostasis. *Mailing Add:* Res Inst Hosp for Sick Children Toronto ON M5G 1X8 Can

COCH, NICHOLAS KYROS, b New York, NY, Mar 30, 38; m 71. SEDIMENTOLOGY, ENVIRONMENTAL GEOLOGY. *Educ:* City Col New York, BS, 59; Univ Rochester, MS, 61; Yale Univ, PhD(geol), 65. *Prof Exp:* Asst prof, Southampton Col, Long Island Univ, 65-67; from asst prof to assoc prof, 67-75, PROF GEOL, QUEENS COL, CITY UNIV NEW YORK, 76- *Concurrent Pos:* Consult geologist, Va Div Mining Resources, 65-71; prin investr, NASA grant, 75-77. *Mem:* Nat Asn Geol Teachers; fel Geol Soc Am; Am Asn Petrol Geologists; Int Asn Sedimentol. *Res:* Coastal and estuarine sedimentology; Atlantic Coastal Plain stratigraphy; environmental geology; pollution studies in Hudson Estuary and adjacent waters; determination of sedimentary structures and dispersal patterns in lunar cores. *Mailing Add:* Dept of Earth & Environ Sci Queens Col Flushing NY 11367

COCHIN, JOSEPH, b Winnipeg, Man, July 17, 16; nat US; m 51; c 3. PHARMACOLOGY. *Educ:* Wayne State Univ, BS, 37; Univ Mich, MD, 53, PhD(pharmacol), 55. *Prof Exp:* Chemist, Keystone Oil Refining Co, 37-39; teacher, Detroit Bd Educ, 39-41; asst pharmacol, Univ Mich, 47-53, intern, Univ Hosp, 53-54; pharmacologist, Sect Analgesics, Nat Inst Arthritis & Metab Dis, 54-62; assoc prof, 62-66, PROF PHARMACOL, SCH MED, BOSTON UNIV, 66-, PROF PSYCHIAT, 70- *Concurrent Pos:* Consult, Coun Drugs, AMA; mem sci rev comt, Ctr for Study Narcotic & Drug Abuse, NIMH, 67-70, chmn, 70-72; mem, Nat Acad Sci-Nat Res Coun Comt on Probs of Drug Dependence, 68-73; chmn sci consults, Alcohol & Drug Dependence Merit Rev Bd, Vet Admin, 72; mem ad hoc rev comt drug abuse training & educ, Nat Inst Drug Abuse, 72-; consult, Spec Action Off Drug Abuse Prev & Ctr Dis Control; specific field ed, J Pharmacol & Exp Therapeut. *Mem:* Fel AAAS; Am Soc Pharmacol & Exp Therapeut; Am Col Neuropsychopharmacol. *Res:* Tolerance, habituation and physical dependence to drugs; psychopharmacology; mode of action of analgesic drugs; drug metabolism. *Mailing Add:* Dept of Pharmacol Boston Univ Sch of Med Boston MA 02218

COCHIS, THOMAS, b Boston, Mass, June 24, 36; m 60; c 1. BOTANY, HORTICULTURE. *Educ:* McNeese State Col, BS, 60; La State Univ, MS, 62, PhD(hort, bot), 64. *Prof Exp:* Asst hort, La State Univ, 60-62, instr, 62-64; asst prof bot, Millsaps Col, 64-66; asst prof hort, Univ Fla, 66-68; PROF BOT, JACKSONVILLE STATE UNIV, 68- *Mem:* AAAS; Am Soc Hort Sci; Am Inst Biol Sci; Int Soc Hort Sci. *Res:* Horticultural and botanical research and teaching. *Mailing Add:* Dept of Biol Ayers Hall Jacksonville State Univ Jacksonville AL 36265

COCHKANOFF, O(REST), b Homeglen, Alta, Mar 14, 26; m 53; c 2. MECHANICAL ENGINEERING. *Educ:* Univ BC, BASc, 49; Univ Toronto, MASc, 52; Iowa State Univ, PhD(theoret & appl mech), 63. *Prof Exp:* Instr mach design, Univ Toronto, 49-53; from asst prof to assoc prof, 53-63, prof mech eng & head dept, 63-76, dean eng, 71-78, PROF MECH ENG, TECH UNIV NS, 79- *Concurrent Pos:* Consult, indust, 52- & Defense Res Bd Can, 54- *Mem:* Can Aeronaut & Space Inst; Am Soc Eng Educ; Am Soc Automotive Engrs; Can Soc Mech Engrs; fel Eng Inst Can. *Res:* Applied mechanics; experimental methods; fundamental studies and applications of dynamics, stress analysis and fluid mechanics; ocean engineering and aerospace operations. *Mailing Add:* Dept Mech Eng Tech Univ NS Halifax NS B3J 2X4 Can

COCHRAN, ALLAN CHESTER, b Long Beach, Calif, Jan 23, 42; m 62; c 2. TOPOLOGY. *Educ:* E Cent State Col, BS, 62; Univ Okla, MA, 64, PhD(math), 66. *Prof Exp:* Asst prof, 66-71, assoc prof, 71-77, PROF MATH, UNIV ARK, FAYETTEVILLE, 77-, VCHMN DEPT, 79- *Mem:* Am Math Soc; Math Asn Am. *Res:* Convergence space theory; theory of topological algebras. *Mailing Add:* SE 301 Dept Math Univ Ark Fayetteville AR 72701

COCHRAN, ANDREW AARON, b West Plains, Mo, Sept 28, 19; m 42; c 3. BIOPHYSICS, QUANTUM PHYSICS. *Educ:* Univ Mo-Rolla, BS, 41, MS, 63. *Prof Exp:* Chem engr, Phillips Petrol Co, Kans, 41-46; org res chemist, Mallinckrodt Chem Works, Mo, 46-52; chemist, Metall Res, Rolla Metall Res Ctr, US Bur Mines, 52-60, supvry phys chemist, 60-62, supvry res chemist, 62-80. *Mem:* Am Inst Mining, Metall & Petrol Eng; Sigma Xi. *Res:* The fundamental theory of biophysics; development of new processes for recovering titanium, tin, and manganese from their respective ores; development of processes for treating industrial wastes to recover metals and reduce pollution. *Mailing Add:* College Hills RFD 4 Box 99 Rolla MO 65401

COCHRAN, BILLY JUAN, b Dec 10, 33; m 55; c 2. AGRICULTURAL ENGINEERING. *Educ:* Miss State Univ, BS, 58; Tex A&M Univ, MS, 62; Okla State Univ, PhD(agr eng), 73. *Prof Exp:* Instr, Tex A&M Univ, 58-64; from asst prof to assoc prof, 64-78, PROF AGR ENG, LA STATE UNIV, 78- *Concurrent Pos:* Proj leader, Agr Res Serv, USDA, 64-67, Am Sugar Cane League, 72-73, La Dept Conserv, 76-77, Battelle Columbus Labs, 77- & Dept Energy, 78- *Mem:* Am Soc Agr Engrs; Am Soc Sugarcane Technologists; Int Soc Sugarcane Technologists. *Res:* Development of system and machinery for biomass production as an alternate energy resource; development of systems and machinery for sugarcane production. *Mailing Add:* Dept of Agr Eng La State Univ Baton Rouge LA 70803

COCHRAN, CHARLES NORMAN, b Pittsburgh, Pa, Mar 24, 25; m 46; c 3. PHYSICAL CHEMISTRY. *Educ:* Westminster Col, Pa, BS, 45; Ohio State Univ, MS, 47. *Prof Exp:* Scientist, Phys Chem Div, 47-58, sect head, 58-63, MGR, PHYS CHEM DIV, ALCOA LABS, 63- *Honors & Awards:* Dr Rene Wasserman Award, Am Welding Soc, 72. *Mem:* Am Chem Soc; Metall Soc; Electrochem Soc. *Res:* Oxidation of metals; gas in light metals; gas sorption; high temperature chemistry of aluminum; aluminum smelting; joining of aluminum; energy involvement of aluminum industry; technology forecasting. *Mailing Add:* Phys Chem Div Alcoa Labs Alcoa Center PA 15069

COCHRAN, DAVID L(EO), b New York, NY, Dec 17, 29; m 56; c 3. MECHANICAL ENGINEERING. *Educ:* Univ Nev, BSME, 51; Stanford Univ, MSME, 52, PhD(mech eng), 57. *Prof Exp:* Asst mech eng, Stanford Univ, 51-57; sr mech engr, Aerojet-Gen Nucleonics, Gen Tire & Rubber Co, 57-61, asst mgr space power dept, 61-63; SR VPRES & DIR ENG, MB ASSOCS, SAN RAMON, 63- *Mem:* Am Soc Mech Engrs; Am Inst Aeronaut & Astronaut; Am Ord Asn. *Res:* Heat transfer; aerodynamics; mechanics; thermodynamics; research, development and manufacture of passive electronic warfare systems, miniature and rocket signaling and marking systems. *Mailing Add:* 472 Constitution Dr Danville CA 94526

COCHRAN, DONALD GORDON, b New Hampton, Iowa, July 5, 27; m 52; c 3. INSECT PHYSIOLOGY. *Educ:* Iowa State Univ, BS, 50; Va Polytech Inst, MS, 52; Rutgers Univ, PhD(entom), 55. *Prof Exp:* Entomologist, Chem Ctr, US Army, 55-57; assoc entomologist, Agr Exp Sta, 57-59, assoc prof, 59-64, PROF ENTOM, DEPT ENTOM, VA POLYTECH INST & STATE UNIV, 64- *Mem:* AAAS; Entom Soc Am. *Res:* Physiological and genetical aspects of insect resistance to insecticides; cockroach genetics and cytogenetics; biochemistry of insect excretion. *Mailing Add:* Dept Entom Va Polytech Inst & State Univ Blacksburg VA 24061

COCHRAN, DONALD ROY FRANCIS, b San Francisco, Calif, Oct 6, 26; m 60; c 3. NUCLEAR SCIENCE. *Educ:* Univ Calif, Berkeley, BS, 48; Johns Hopkins Univ, PhD(nuclear chem), 54. *Prof Exp:* Instr chem, Johns Hopkins Univ, 52-54; mem staff physics, 54-68, group leader, 68-73, ASST DIV LEADER, MESON PHYSICS DIV, LOS ALAMOS SCI LAB, 73- *Concurrent Pos:* Mem adv panel on accelerator radiation safety, US AEC, 70-73 & US DOE, 76- *Mem:* Am Phys Soc; Am Inst Physics; Am Nuclear Soc; Am Chem Soc. *Res:* Medium energy physics; nuclear chemistry and physics; accelerators. *Mailing Add:* PO Box 1663 MPDO-MS850 Los Alamos NM 87545

COCHRAN, GEORGE THOMAS, b Washington, DC, Dec 28, 38. INORGANIC CHEMISTRY, ANALYTICAL CHEMISTRY. *Educ:* Univ Richmond, BS, 60; Univ Tenn, MS, 63; Clemson Univ, PhD(chem), 67. *Prof Exp:* Teacher high sch, Va, 60-61; asst prof, Rollins Col, 67-71, assoc prof chem, 71-78; QUAL ASSSURANCE SCIENTIST, BURROUGHS WELLCOME PHARMACEUT CO, 78-, HEAD, DPET QUAL ASSURANCE & AUDITING, 81- *Mem:* Am Chem Soc. *Res:* Coordination chemistry of univalent metal ions; high pressure liquid chromatography; organic polarography. *Mailing Add:* Burroughs Wellcome Co Box 1887 Greenville NC 27834

COCHRAN, GEORGE VAN BRUNT, b New York, NY, Jan 20, 32; m 70; c 2. MEDICINE, BIOMEDICAL ENGINEERING. *Educ:* Dartmouth Col, AB, 53; Columbia Univ, MD, 56, ScD(med, physiol), 67. *Prof Exp:* DIR ORTHOP RES LAB, ST LUKES HOSP, 70-; DIR, BIOMED RES UNIT, HELEN HAYES HOSP, DIR, ORTHOP ENG & RES CTR, 81- *Concurrent Pos:* Assoc prof clin orthop surg, Col Physicians & Surgeons, Columbia Univ, 75-, prof, 81-; adj assoc prof biomed eng, Rensselaer Polytech Inst, 75-; chmn res comt, Helen Hayes Hosp. *Honors & Awards:* Nicholas Andry Award, Asn Bone & Joint Surgeons, 75. *Mem:* Orthop Res Soc; Am Acad Orthop Surgeons; fel NY Acad Sci; fel Explorers Club (pres, 81-); Sigma Xi. *Res:* Biomechanics and electrophysiology of bone and soft tissues; gait analysis in musculoskeletal disabilities. *Mailing Add:* Orthop Eng & Res Ctr Helen Hayes Hosp West Haverstraw NY 10993

COCHRAN, HENRY DOUGLAS, JR, b Plainfield, NJ, Sept 13, 43; m 73; c 2. CHEMICAL ENGINEERING, COAL CONVERSION. *Educ:* Princeton Univ, BSE, 65; Mass Inst Technol, SM, 67, PhD(chem eng), 73. *Prof Exp:* Instr chem eng, Mass Inst Technol, 67-68; develop engr, Oak Ridge Nat Lab, 68-69; res asst, Dept Chem Eng, Mass Inst Technol, 69-72; develop engr, 72-74, group leader, 74-77, MGR COAL CONVERSION, OAK RIDGE NAT LAB, UNION CARBIDE CORP, 77- *Mem:* Am Inst Chem Engrs. *Res:* Effluent control technology; catalysis; fluid dynamics; physical properties; vapor-liquid equilibria; pyrolysis. *Mailing Add:* Oak Ridge Nat Lab PO Box X Oak Ridge TN 37830

COCHRAN, JAMES ALAN, b San Francisco, Calif, May 12, 36; m 58; c 2. APPLIED MATHEMATICS. *Educ:* Stanford Univ, BS, 56, MS, 57, PhD(math), 62. *Prof Exp:* Res mathematician, Stanford Res Inst, 55-58; asst math, Stanford Univ, 58-61; mem tech staff, Bell Tel Labs, 62-65, supvr, Electromagnetic Res Dept, 65-68, supvr, Appl Math & Statist Dept, 69-72; prof math, Va Polytech Inst & State Univ, 72-78; PROF MATH & CHMN DEPT PURE & APPL MATH, WASH STATE UNIV, 78- *Concurrent Pos:* Vis prof math, Stanford Univ, 68-69 & Wash State Univ, 77. *Mem:* Am Math Soc; Soc Indust & Appl Math; Math Asn Am; Sigma Xi. *Res:* Applied research in electromagnetic theory and microwave propagation; basic research in special functions, asymptotics, differential and integral equations, and operator theory. *Mailing Add:* Dept of Math Wash State Univ Pullman WA 99164

COCHRAN, JOHN CHARLES, b Akron, Ohio, Feb 10, 35; m 58; c 3. ORGANIC CHEMISTRY. *Educ:* Col Wooster, BA, 57; Univ NC, MA, 60; Univ NH, PhD(org chem), 67. *Prof Exp:* Instr chem, Randolph-Macon Women's Col, 60-62; asst prof, 66-71, ASSOC PROF CHEM, COLGATE UNIV, 71-, CHMN DEPT, 81- *Concurrent Pos:* vis prof, State Univ NY Albany, 81. *Mem:* Am Chem Soc. *Res:* Preparation and reactions of organotin compounds; structure of allylic carbanions; reactions of sulfite esters; Reimer-Tiemann reaction. *Mailing Add:* Dept Chem Colgate Univ Hamilton NY 13346

COCHRAN, JOHN EUELL, JR, b Dawson, Ala, May 22, 44; m 65; c 2. AEROSPACE ENGINEERING, AIRCRAFT ACCIDENT ANALYSIS. *Educ:* Auburn Univ, BAE, 66, MS, 67; Univ Tex, Austin, PhD(aerospace eng), 70; Jones Law Inst, JD, 76. *Prof Exp:* Res engr, Dept Aerospace Eng & Eng Mech, Univ Tex, 69; from instr to assoc prof, 69-80, PROF AEROSPACE ENG, AUBURN UNIV, 80- *Concurrent Pos:* Am Soc Elec Engrs/NASA fel, Marshall Space Flight Ctr, 70 & 71; consult, Northrop Serv Inc, 72-73, Battelle Mem Labs, 74-, Cooper & Cooper, Atty at Law, 77- & Accident Prev, Invest & Anal Co, 77-; vis assoc prof eng sci & systs, Univ Va, 75. *Mem:* Assoc fel Am Inst Aeronaut & Astronaut; Nat Soc Prof Engrs; Sigma Xi. *Res:* Dynamics of spacecraft and aircraft; stability and control; dynamics of rocket launchers; products liability. *Mailing Add:* Dept of Aerospace Eng Auburn Univ Auburn AL 36830

COCHRAN, JOHN FRANCIS, b Saskatoon, Sask, Jan 29, 30; m 57; c 2. SOLID STATE PHYSICS. *Educ:* Univ BC, BASc, 50, MASc, 51; Univ Ill, PhD(physics), 55. *Prof Exp:* Res assoc physics, Univ Ill, 55-56; Nat Res Coun Can fel, Clarendon Lab, Eng, 56-57; asst prof physics, Mass Inst Technol, 57-65; PROF PHYSICS, SIMON FRASER UNIV, 65-, DEAN SCI, 81- *Concurrent Pos:* Sloan fel, 58-60. *Mem:* Am Phys Soc; Can Asn Physicists. *Res:* Electronic properties of very pure metals; ferromagnetic metals. *Mailing Add:* Dept of Physics Simon Fraser Univ Burnaby BC V5A 1S6 Can

COCHRAN, JOHN RODNEY, b St Joseph, Mo, Feb 7, 20; m 41; c 2. SPEECH PATHOLOGY. *Educ:* Utah State Univ, BS, 49, MS, 50; Univ Utah, PhD(speech path), 59. *Prof Exp:* Asst speech path, Univ Utah, 54-59; assoc prof speech path & psychol, Southwest Tex State Col, 59-61; assoc prof speech & speech path, chmn dept speech path & audiol & dir speech & hearing clin, Eastern NMex Univ, 61-70; prof & dir speech & hearing clin, Univ Alaska, 70-71; assoc prof & dir speech & hearing clin, Lehman Col, 71-73; PROF SPEECH & PATH, KEARNEY STATE COL, 73- *Mem:* Am Psychol Asn; Am Speech & Hearing Asn; Nat Educ Asn. *Res:* Communication abilities of air force personnel. *Mailing Add:* Speech & Hearing Clin Kearney State Col Kearney NE 68847

COCHRAN, KENNETH E(DWARD), b Columbus, Ohio, May 14, 21; m 46; c 2. ELECTRICAL ENGINEERING. *Educ:* Ohio State Univ, BEE, 48. *Prof Exp:* Res engr, Semiconductor & Dielec Div, 48-51, asst chief, Solid State Devices Div, 51-55, chief, Reliability Eng Div, 55-62, asst mgr, Eng Physics Dept, 62-66, gen mgr, Battelle Pesquisas Cientificas, Ltd, Brazil, 66-68, asst dir, BMI-Int, 68-70, asst mgr int opers, 70-76, PROG MGR ENERGY CONSERV, BATTELLE MEM INST, 76- *Mem:* AAAS; Inst Elec & Electronics Engrs. *Res:* Small electrical machinery; electronics; semiconductors; solid state physics; reliability engineering; quality control. *Mailing Add:* Battelle Mem Inst 505 King Ave Columbus OH 43201

COCHRAN, KENNETH WILLIAM, JR, b Chicago, Ill, Nov 2, 23; m 45; c 2. PHARMACOLOGY. *Educ:* Univ Chicago, SB, 47, PhD(pharmacol), 50; Am Bd Med Microbiol, dipl virol; Am Bd Indust Hyg, cert toxicol. *Prof Exp:* Res asst toxicity lab, Univ Chicago, 48-50, res assoc, US Air Force Radiation Lab & Dept Pharmacol, 50-52; from instr to asst prof pharmacol, Sch Med, 52-76, res assoc epidemiol, Sch Pub Health, 52-55, from asst prof to assoc prof, 55-68, secy fac, 70-73, ASSOC PROF PHARMACOL, SCH MED, UNIV MICH, ANN ARBOR, 76-, PROF EPIDEMIOL, SCH PUB HEALTH, 68- *Concurrent Pos:* Mem, pharmacol & endocrinol fel rev panel, NIH, 60-64. *Mem:* AAAS; Am Soc Microbiol; Am Acad Indust Hyg; Am Soc Pharmacol; Mycol Soc Am. *Res:* Virus chemotherapy; toxicology. *Mailing Add:* 3556 Oakwood Ann Arbor MI 48104

COCHRAN, LEWIS WELLINGTON, b Perryville, Ky, Oct 12, 15; m 40; c 2. PHYSICS. *Educ:* Morehead State Col, BS, 36; Univ Ky, MS, 39 & 40, PhD(physics), 52. *Prof Exp:* Instr math & physics, Morehead State Col, 39-41 & Cumberland Univ, 41; from asst prof to prof physics, Univ Ky, 46-81, actg head dept, 56-58, assoc dean, 63-66, provost, 65-67, actg dean, Grad Sch, 66-67, dean, Grad Sch & vpres res, 67-70, vpres acad affairs, 70-81; RETIRED. *Mem:* Am Phys Soc; Am Asn Physics Teachers. *Res:* Proton induced nuclear reactions; interaction of radiation with matter; experimental nuclear physics; nuclear structure physics; gaseous electronics. *Mailing Add:* 305 Kinkead Hall Univ Ky Lexington KY 40506

COCHRAN, PATRICK HOLMES, b Guthrie Center, Iowa, Oct 14, 37; m 61; c 3. FOREST SOILS. *Educ:* Iowa State Univ, BSc, 59; Ore State Univ, MSc, 63, PhD(soils), 66. *Prof Exp:* Asst soils, Ore State Univ, 64-65; asst prof silvicult, State Univ NY Col Forestry, Syracuse Univ, 65-67; SOIL SCIENTIST, PAC NORTHWEST FOREST & RANGE EXP STA, US FOREST SERV, 67- *Mem:* Am Soc Agron; Soc Am Foresters. *Res:* Relationships of physical, thermal and chemical soil properties to the distribution of wild land vegetation and tree growth. *Mailing Add:* Silvicult Lab 1027 Trenton Ave Bend OR 97701

COCHRAN, PAUL TERRY, b Sullivan, Ind, Jan 27, 38; m 72; c 2. CARDIOLOGY, MEDICAL EDUCATION. *Educ:* DePauw Univ, BA, 60; Western Reserve Univ, MD, 64; Am Bd Internal Med, dipl; Am Bd Cardiovasc Dis, dipl. *Prof Exp:* Staff cardiologist, Malcolm Grow US Air Force Hosp, 69-71; clin cardiologist, Gallatin Med Group, Downey, Calif, 71-72; asst prof med, 72-77, CLIN ASSOC PROF MED, SCH MED, UNIV NMEX, 77-; clin cardiologist, Albuquerque Cardiovascular Assocs, 77-81; CLIN CARDIOLOGIST, SOUTHWEST CARDIOL ASN, 81- *Concurrent Pos:* Dir cardiac diag lab, Bernalillo County Med Ctr, 72-77; staff cardiologist, Vet Admin Hosp, Albuquerque, 72-77; fel coun clin cardiol, Am Heart Asn. *Mem:* Fel Am Col Cardiol; fel Am Col Physicians; Am Heart Asn. *Res:* Clinical investigations of the hemodynamics of heart disease; research in teaching methods in cardiovascular medicine. *Mailing Add:* 201 Cedar SE Suite 604 Albuquerque NM 87106

COCHRAN, ROBERT GLENN, b Indianapolis, Ind, July 12, 19; m 44; c 1. PHYSICS. *Educ:* Ind Univ, AB, 48, MS, 50; Pa State Univ, PhD(nuclear physics), 57. *Prof Exp:* Res asst cyclotron group, Ind Univ, 47-50; nuclear physicist & group leader chg swimming pool reactor fac, Physics Div, Oak Ridge Nat Lab, 50-54; assoc prof nuclear eng & dir res reactor facil, Pa State Univ, 54-59; PROF NUCLEAR ENG & HEAD DEPT & DIR NUCLEAR SCI CTR, TEX A&M UNIV, 59- *Concurrent Pos:* Consult, Nat Regulatory Comn; US Air Force; Sandia Corp & Watertown Arsenal. *Mem:* Am Nuclear Soc; Am Phys Soc; Am Soc Eng Educ; Nat Soc Prof Engrs. *Res:* Nuclear physics; decay schemes and isomeric states of short half-life nuclids; nuclear reactor physics and nuclear engineering; power reactors and their environmental effects. *Mailing Add:* Dept Nuclear Eng Tex A&M Univ College Station TX 77843

COCHRAN, STEPHEN G, b Indianapolis, Ind, Aug 19, 47; m 69; c 3. PHYSICS, COMPUTER SCIENCE. *Educ:* Loyola Univ, BS, 69; Cornell Univ, MS, 73, PhD(physics), 74. *Prof Exp:* PHYSICIST, DEPT ENERGY, LAWRENCE LIVERMORE LAB, UNIV CALIF, 74- *Mem:* Am Phys Soc. *Res:* Continuum dynamics; materials properties; numerical simulation; creation of models of material behavior exhibited in experiments. *Mailing Add:* 5440 Arlene Way Livermore CA 94550

COCHRAN, THOMAS HOWARD, Aliquippa, Pa, Apr 6, 40; m 62; c 4. COMBUSTION, PROPULSION. *Educ:* Renesselaer Polytech Inst, BME, 62, Case Inst Tech, MSME, 67. *Prof Exp:* Proj engr exp res, 62-73, sect head res & tech, 74-79, br chief syst anal, 79-80, BR CHIEF ELEC PROPULSION & SPACE EXP, LEWIS RES CTR, NASA, 81- *Res:* Technology efforts in electric propulsion; definition of fundamental experiments to be conducted in space; analytical and experimental research on gravitational effects on fundamental combustion and fluid physics phenomena as applied to spacecraft fire safety and propellant handling systems. *Mailing Add:* 31115 Nantucket Row Bay Village OH 44140

COCHRAN, VERLAN LEYERL, b Declo, Idaho, Feb 19, 38; m 69; c 2. SOIL MANAGEMENT, SOIL FERTILITY. *Educ:* Calif State Polytech Univ, BS, 66; Wash State Univ, MS, 71. *Prof Exp:* SOIL SCIENTIST, LAND MGT & WATER CONSERV RES UNIT, US DEPT AGR, 66- *Concurrent Pos:* Asst soil scientist, Wash State Univ, 73-; affil fac, Univ Idaho, 81- *Mem:* Am Soc Agron; Soil Sci Soc Am; Soil Conserv Soc Am. *Res:* Soil management and fertility problems associated with reduced tillage systems in small grain production with emphasis on water use efficiency and nutrient cycling. *Mailing Add:* 215 Johnson Hall Wash State Univ Pullman WA 99164

COCHRAN, WILLIAM GEMMELL, applied statistics, deceased

COCHRAN, WILLIAM RONALD, b Kalamazoo, Mich, May 24, 40. PHYSICS. *Educ:* Univ Calif, Los Angeles, BA, 62, MS, 64, PhD(physics), 69. *Prof Exp:* Asst prof, 69-74, assoc prof, 74-81, PROF PHYSICS, YOUNGSTOWN STATE UNIV, 81- *Mem:* Am Phys Soc; Optical Soc Am. *Res:* Spectroscopy of ions in crystals; heterodyne spectroscopy of solids; optical physics. *Mailing Add:* Dept Physics Youngstown State Univ Youngstown OH 44555

COCHRANE, CHAPPELLE CECIL, b Conway, SC, Oct 28, 13; m 40; c 3. ORGANIC CHEMISTRY. *Educ:* Howard Univ, BS, 38, MS, 40; Ohio State Univ, PhD(chem), 51. *Prof Exp:* Assoc, Howard Univ, 40-41; instr chem, Morgan State Col, 41-42 & Cent State Col, 46-47; res chemist, Glidden co, 51-58, Armour & Co, 58-60, US Army Chem Ctr, 60-62 & Nalco Chem Co, 62-74; asst prof, 74-80, ASSOC PROF CHEM, CHICAGO STATE UNIV, 80- *Concurrent Pos:* Assoc, Ohio State Univ, 51. *Honors & Awards:* Lloyd Hall Award, Howard Univ, 38. *Mem:* Am Chem Soc. *Res:* Polynuclear aromatic hydrocarbons; steroids; fatty acids. *Mailing Add:* Dept of Chem 95th St at King Dr Chicago IL 60628

COCHRANE, DAVID EARLE, b Coldspring, NY, July 16, 44; c 2. PHYSIOLOGY, NEUROBIOLOGY. *Educ:* Cornell Univ, BS, 66; Univ Vt, MS, 68, PhD(physiol & biophys), 71. *Prof Exp:* Res assoc electrophys, Univ Vt, 71-72; NIH fel cellular aspects of secretion, Dept Pharm, Yale Univ, Pharmacol, Yale Univ, 72-76; ASST PROF BIOL, TUFTS UNIV, 76- *Res:* Cellular aspects of secretion, specifically calcium mobilization and channel mechanisms; mast cell physiology. *Mailing Add:* Dept of Biol Tufts Univ Medford MA 02155

COCHRANE, HECTOR, b Stowmarket, Eng, Mar 16, 40; m 65; c 3. PHYSICAL CHEMISTRY. *Educ:* Univ Nottingham, BSc, 61, PhD(chem), 64. *Prof Exp:* Fel fuel sci, Pa State Univ, 64-66; res chemist, 66-73, group leader, 73-80, TECH DIR, CAB-O-SIL RES & DEVELOP, CABOT CORP, 80- *Mem:* Am Chem Soc. *Res:* Formation of fine particles in flames; study of the surface chemistry and aggregate morphology of particles and how these properties affect their theological properties in liquids and reinforcement properties in rubber. *Mailing Add:* Cabot Corp Cab-O-Sil Div Tuscola IL 61953

COCHRANE, ROBERT LOWE, b Morgantown, WVa, Feb 10, 31. REPRODUCTIVE PHYSIOLOGY, ENDOCRINOLOGY. *Educ:* WVa Univ, BA, 53; Univ Wis, MS, 54, PhD(genetics), 61. *Prof Exp:* Animal husb agent, USDA, 54-61; biologist, US Food & Drug Admin, 61-62; sr res fel primate reproduction, Med Sch, Univ Birmingham, 62-65; proj assoc, Sch Med, Univ Pittsburgh, 65-66; sr endocrinologist, Lilly Res Labs, 66-80; RES ASSOC, G D SEARLE & CO, 80- *Concurrent Pos:* Res asst zool, Univ Wis, 57-60. *Mem:* AAAS; Am Soc Animal Sci; Soc Study Reproduction; Endocrine Soc. *Res:* Contraception; ovoimplantation; control of corpus luteum and ovary function; immunological tolerance, hormonal control of growth and effects of estrogens on reproduction in mustelids. *Mailing Add:* Grand View Park Lot 17 RFD 1 Neillsville WI 54456

COCHRANE, VINCENT WINNER, b Plainfield, NJ, Aug 21, 16; m 45; c 2. MICROBIOLOGY. *Educ:* Cornell Univ, BS, 39, PhD(plant path), 44. *Hon Degrees:* MA, Wesleyan Univ, 57. *Prof Exp:* Asst, Cornell Univ, 41-44; microbiologist, Lederle Labs, NY, 44-45; asst plant pathologist, Exp Sta, Conn, 45-47; from asst prof to assoc prof, 47-57, PROF BIOL, WESLEYAN UNIV, 57- *Mem:* AAAS; fel Am Phytopath Soc; Bot Soc Am; Am Soc Microbiol; Mycol Soc Am. *Res:* Physiology of fungi and actinomycetes; ecology of soil microorganisms. *Mailing Add:* Dept of Biol Hall-Atwater Lab Wesleyan Univ Middletown CT 06457

COCHRANE, WILLIAM, b Toronto, Ont, Mar 18, 26; m 51; c 3. PEDIATRICS. *Educ:* Univ Toronto, MD, 49; FRCP(C), 56. *Prof Exp:* Clinician, Hosp Sick Children, Toronto, 56-58; assoc prof pediat, Fac Med, Dalhousie Univ, 58-63, prof & head dept, 63-67; dean fac med, Univ Calgary, 67-73, pres & vchancellor, 74-78; CHMN & CHIEF EXEC OFFICER, CONNAUGHT LABS LTD, 78- *Concurrent Pos:* Dep minister health serv, Govt Alta, 73-74. *Mem:* Soc Pediat Res; fel Am Col Physicians; Can Pediat Soc; Can Soc Clin Invest. *Res:* Metabolic diseases of children; biochemical relationship of protein and amino acid metabolism to mental disease. *Mailing Add:* Connaught Labs Ltd 1755 Steeles Ave W Willowdale ON M2N 5T8 Can

COCIVERA, MICHAEL, b Pittsburgh, Pa, Jan 21, 37; m 69. PHYSICAL CHEMISTRY. *Educ:* Carnegie-Mellon Univ, BSc, 59; Univ Calif, Los Angeles, PhD(phys chem), 63. *Prof Exp:* Mem tech staff chem, Bell Tel Labs, 63-69; assoc prof, 69-74, PROF CHEM, UNIV GUELPH, 74- *Res:* Nuclear magnetic resonance studies of fast thermal and photochemical reactions; electrodeposition of organometallic compounds on CDS films. *Mailing Add:* Dept Chem Univ Guelph Guelph ON N1G 2W1 Can

COCK, LORNE M, b Tatamagouche, NS, June 1, 32; m 57; c 2. ANIMAL NUTRITION. *Educ:* McGill Univ, BSc, 54; Univ Wis, MS, 60; Univ Maine, PhD(animal nutrit), 66. *Prof Exp:* From instr to asst prof animal sci, Univ Maine, 65-69; assoc prof, 69-74, PROF ANIMAL SCI, NS AGR COL, 74-, HEAD DEPT, 69- *Mem:* Am Soc Animal Sci; Am Dairy Sci Asn; Agr Inst Can. *Res:* Energy metabolism of ruminants; influence of dietary nitrogen on ruminant heat increment; fasting metabolism of sheep. *Mailing Add:* Dept of Animal Sci NS Agr Col Truro NS B2N 5E3 Can

COCKERELL, GARY LEE, b Fort Dodge, Iowa, Dec 20, 45; m 69; c 2. ONCOLOGY. *Educ:* Univ Calif, Davis, BS, 68, DVM, 70; Ohio State Univ, PhD(vet path), 76. *Prof Exp:* Vet lab admin officer res, US Army Med Res Inst Infectious Dis, 70-73; veterinarian, McClellan Vet Clinic, 71-73; grad res assoc path, Ohio State Univ, 73-76; asst prof, 76-81, ASSOC PROF, DEPT PATH, NY STATE COL VET MED, CORNELL UNIV, 81- *Concurrent Pos:* Res fel, NIH, 75-76; prin investr, Nat Cancer Inst contract, 76-81; mem bd dirs, Cornell Veterinarian, 81- *Mem:* Am Col Vet Path; Int Asn Comparative Leukemia Res; Am Vet Med Asn; Int Acad Path; Vet Cancer Soc. *Res:* Comparative pathology and the immunobiology of naturally occurring neoplasms in domestic animals; chemical and viral induced neoplasms in domestic and laboratory species of animals. *Mailing Add:* Dept Path NY State Col Vet Med Cornell Univ Ithaca NY 14853

COCKERHAM, COLUMBUS CLARK, b Mountain Park, NC, Dec 12, 21; m 44; c 3. POPULATION & QUANTATIVE GENETICS. *Educ:* NC State Col, BS, 43, MS, 49; Iowa State Univ, PhD(animal breeding & genetics), 52. *Prof Exp:* Asst prof biostatist, Sch Pub Health, Univ NC, 52-53; from assoc prof to prof exp statist, 53-72, WILLIAM NEAL REYNOLDS PROF STATIST & GENETICS, NC STATE UNIV, 72- *Concurrent Pos:* Prin investr, NIH Grant, 60-63, proj dir, 63-; mem genetics study sect, 65-69; consult, adv comt protocols for safety eval, Food & Drug Admin, 67-69; mem Nat Acad Sci, 74; ed, Theoret Pop Biol, 75-81, assoc ed, 82-; assoc ed, Am J Human Genetics, 78-80. *Honors & Awards:* Recipient, NC Award in Field of Sci; Max Gardner Award. *Mem:* AAAS; Biomet Soc; Am Soc Animal Sci; Genetics Soc Am; fel Am Soc Agron. *Res:* Population and quantitative genetic theory; estimation of genetic parameters in populations; development of mating and experimental designs for estimation; selection theory; applications to plant and animal breeding. *Mailing Add:* Dept Statist NC State Univ Raleigh NC 27650

COCKERHAM, LORRIS GAY, b Denham Springs, La, Sept 27, 35; c 4. NEUROTOXICOLOGY, NEUROPHYSIOLOGY. *Educ:* La Col, Ba, 57; Colo State Univ, Ms, 73, PhD(physiol toxicol), 79. *Prof Exp:* Instr biol sci, US Air Force Acad, 73-75, asst prof & div chief, 75-77; DIV CHIEF PHYSIOL, ARMED FORCES RADIOBIOL RES INST, DEFENSE NUCLEAR AGENCY, 80-; ASST PROF NEUROPHYSIOL, UNIFORMED SERV UNIV HEALTH SCI, 81- *Concurrent Pos:* Consult, Orgn Concerned Toxicity Agent Orange & Assoc Chlorinated Dioxins, 79-; prin investr, Armed Forces Radiobiol Res Inst, 80-, comdr, Air force Element, 81- *Mem:* Sigma Xi; AAAS; NY Acad Sci. *Res:* Effect of selected chemicals on radiation induced early transient incapacitation and performance decrement; chemicals of special interest are neurotoxins and their antidotes. *Mailing Add:* Physiol Dept Armed Forces Radiobiol Res Inst Nat Naval Med Ctr Bethesda MD 20814

COCKERLINE, ALAN WESLEY, b Toronto, Ont, Oct 2, 26; m 51; c 3. CYTOLOGY. *Educ:* Univ Mich, BS, 52, MS, 53; Mich State Univ, PhD(bot), 61. *Prof Exp:* Asst prof, 61-66, ASSOC PROF BIOL, TEX WOMAN'S UNIV, 66-, DIR MED TECHNOL PROG, 75- *Concurrent Pos:* Proj dir undergrad res partic, NSF, 64-72. *Mem:* AAAS; Am Chem Soc; Am Asn Plant Physiologists; Mycol Soc Am; Tissue Cult Asn. *Res:* Mycotoxins; plant embryo culture; related callus formations. *Mailing Add:* Dept Biol Tex Woman's Univ PO Box 22847 Denton TX 76204

COCKETT, ABRAHAM TIMOTHY K, b Maui, Hawaii, Sept 4, 28; m; c 4. UROLOGY, PHYSIOLOGY. *Educ:* Brigham Young Univ, BS, 50; Univ Utah, MD, 54. *Prof Exp:* Res fel, Dept Med, Univ Southern Calif, 57-58; assoc prof urol, Univ Calif, Los Angeles, 62-69; PROF UROL SURG, SCH MED, UNIV ROCHESTER, 69- *Concurrent Pos:* Chief urol, Harbor Gen Hosp, Torrance, Calif, 62-69; urologist in chief, Strong Mem Hosp, Rochester, NY, 69- *Mem:* AAAS; Soc Univ Surgeons; Am Urol Asn; Soc Univ Urologists; Undersea Med Soc. *Res:* Kidney physiology and transplantation; underwater physiology related to problems in decompression sickness and treatment of these alterations; support of man in outer space; studies related to renal, urinary and testicular physiology. *Mailing Add:* Div of Urol Univ of Rochester 601 Elmwood Ave Rochester NY 14642

COCKING, W DEAN, b San Diego, Calif, Oct 27, 40; m. PLANT ECOLOGY. *Educ:* Pomona Col, BA, 62; Cornell Univ, MS, 67; Rutgers Univ, PhD(bot & ecol), 73. *Prof Exp:* Instr, Mohawk Valley Community Col, Utica, 66-69; asst prof biol, 73-79, ASSOC PROF BIOL, JAMES MADISON UNIV, 80- *Concurrent Pos:* Dir, Madison Fire Ecol Res Proj, Shenandoah Nat Park, 75-80. *Mem:* Ecol Soc Am; Brit Ecol Soc; Sigma Xi. *Res:* Ecosystem and physiological ecology; stability of systems in response to stress; ecosystem development; practical application of ecological concepts; plant community pattern in Shenandoah National Park. *Mailing Add:* Dept of Biol James Madison Univ Harrisonburg VA 22807

COCKRELL, BEVERLY YVONNE, b Harrisonville, Mo, Feb 1, 37. VETERINARY PATHOLOGY, ELECTRON MICROSCOPY. *Educ:* Rockford Col, BA, 59; Univ Ill, Urbana-Champaign, BS, 63, DVM, 65, PhD(path), 69. *Prof Exp:* Res asst, Ben May Lab Cancer Res, Univ Chicago, 59-61; asst prof, Ctr Lab Animal Resources, Col Vet Med, Mich State Univ, 69-72; sr scientist, Litton Bionetics, Inc, 72-75; DIR, ELECTRON MICROS, EXP LABS, INC, HERNDON, VA, 75- *Mem:* Sigma Xi; Am Vet Med Asn; Soc Toxicol; Int Acad Path; Am Thoracic Soc. *Res:* Ultrastructure of drug-induced changes in animals. *Mailing Add:* 9320 Marseille Dr Potomac MD 20854

COCKRELL, ROBERT ALEXANDER, b Yonkers, NY, Aug 11, 09; m 33; c 3. DENDROLOGY, WOOD SCIENCE & TECHNOLOGY. *Educ:* Syracuse Univ, BS, 30, MS, 31; Univ Mich, PhD(wood technol), 34. *Prof Exp:* Asst, NY State Col Forestry, Syracuse Univ, 30-32; asst, Sch Forestry & Conserv, Univ Mich, 32-34; jr forester, 34-35; assoc prof forestry, Clemson Col, 35-36; from asst prof to prof, Univ Calif, Berkeley, 36-77, assoc forester, Exp Sta, 45-62, assoc dean, Grad Div Univ, 56-67, secy, Acad Senate, 68-78, wood technologist, Exp Sta, 62-77, EMER PROF FORESTRY, UNIV CALIF, BERKELEY, 77- *Concurrent Pos:* Technologist, Forest Prod Lab, US Forest Serv, 42-45; forestry res specialist, US Army, Japan, 50; Orgn Europ Econ Coop sr vis fel, 61. *Mem:* AAAS; Soc Am Foresters; Forest Prod Res Soc. *Res:* Anatomy of tropical woods; mechanical properties of wood; gluing of wood; wood shrinkage; cell wall structure. *Mailing Add:* Forestry Dept Univ Calif Berkeley CA 94720

COCKRELL, RONALD SPENCER, b Kansas City, Mo, June 26, 38; m 60; c 2. BIOCHEMISTRY. *Educ:* Univ Mo, BS, 63, BMedS, 64; Univ Pa, PhD(molecular biol), 68. *Prof Exp:* Asst prof, 69-74, ASSOC PROF BIOCHEM, SCH MED, ST LOUIS UNIV, 74- *Concurrent Pos:* USPHS fel, Cornell Univ, 68-69. *Mem:* AAAS; Am Soc Biol Chem. *Res:* Bioenergetics; ion transport and metabolism. *Mailing Add:* Dept Biochem St Louis Univ Sch Med St Louis MO 63104

COCKRUM, ELMER LENDELL, b Sesser, Ill, May 29, 20; m 43; c 3. VERTEBRATE ZOOLOGY. *Educ:* Univ Kans, PhD(zool), 51. *Prof Exp:* Asst cur mammal, Mus Natural Hist, Univ Kans, 46-48, res assoc, 51-52, fel embryol & gen zool, Univ, 48-49; from asst prof to assoc prof, 52-60, dir, Desert Biol Sta, 65-68, mammalogist, Agr Exp Sta 74-80, PROF ZOOL, UNIV ARIZ, 60-, CUR MAMMALS, 57-, HEAD, DEPT ECOL & EVOLUTIONARY BIOL, 76- *Mem:* AAAS; Am Soc Zool; Am Soc Mammal. *Res:* Mammals of Kansas and Arizona; microtine rodents; life history studies of bats. *Mailing Add:* Dept of Ecol & Evolutionary Biol Univ of Ariz Tucson AZ 85721

COCKS, FRANKLIN H, b Staten Island, NY, Oct 1, 41; m 66; c 2. MATERIALS SCIENCE, PHYSICAL METALLURGY. *Educ:* Mass Inst Technol, BS, 63, MS, 64; ScD(phys metall), 65. *Prof Exp:* Fulbright fel, Imp Col, Univ London, 65-66; staff scientist, Tyco Labs, Inc, 66-67; asst head, Mat Sci Dept, 70-72; assoc prof mech eng & mat sci, 72-75, PROF MECH ENG & MAT SCI, DUKE UNIV, 75- *Concurrent Pos:* Consult, Los Alamos Nat Lab, 79-; vis scholar, Div Appl Physics, Harvard Univ, 81. *Mem:* Nat Asn Corrosion Engrs; Am Inst Mining, Metall & Petrol Engrs; Brit Inst Metall. *Res:* Corrosion; stress corrosion; corrosion fatigue; hydrogen embrittlement; failure analysis; x-ray diffraction; photovoltaic materials; amorphous materials; positron annihilation; non-destructive testing. *Mailing Add:* Dept of Mech Eng & Mat Sci Duke Univ Durham NC 27706

COCKS, GEORGE GOSSON, b Sioux City, Iowa, Mar 22, 19; m 42; c 4. CHEMICAL MICROSCOPY. *Educ:* Iowa State Col, BS, 41; Cornell Univ, PhD(chem micros), 49. *Prof Exp:* Chemist, Allison Div, Gen Motors Corp, 41; asst chem micros, Cornell Univ, 46-49; asst chief physics solids div, Battelle Mem Inst, 49-64; assoc prof, 64-81, EMER PROF CHEM MICROS, CORNELL UNIV, 81-; STAFF MEM, SCI LAB, LOS ALAMOS NAT LAB, 81- *Concurrent Pos:* Vis staff mem, Sci Lab, Los Alamos Nat Lab, 80-81. *Mem:* AAAS; Am Chem Soc; Optical Soc Am; Electron Micros Soc Am (exec secy, 59-75); Electron Microscopy Soc Can. *Res:* Light and electron microscopy; chemical microscopy; optical crystallography; structure of polymer gels; growth of crystals in gels; crystallization of ice; cement. *Mailing Add:* 549 Todd Loop Los Alamos NM 87544

COCKSHUTT, E(RIC) P(HILIP), b Brantford, Ont, May 30, 29; m 54; c 5. ENERGY, MECHANICAL ENGINEERING. *Educ:* Univ Toronto, BASc, 50; Mass Inst Technol, SM, 51, ME, 52, ScD(mech eng), 54. *Prof Exp:* Res officer, 53-67, prin res officer & sect head, Engine Lab, 67-75, MEM STAFF ENERGY RES & DEVELOP, NAT RES COUN CAN, 75- *Concurrent Pos:* Sessional lectr, Carleton Univ, 59-73. *Honors & Awards:* Casey Baldwin Award, Can Aeronaut & Space Inst, 61 & 65; Turnbull lectr, Can Aeronaut & Space Inst, 76. *Mem:* Can Aeronaut & Space Inst; Can Soc Mech Eng; Solar Energy Soc Can Inc. *Res:* Renewable energy including solar, wind, bioenergy and hydraulic; conservation including heat pumps, building use, storage and hydrogen systems; fusion. *Mailing Add:* Energy Res & Develop Nat Res Coun of Can Ottawa ON K1A 0R6 Can

COCOLAS, GEORGE HARRY, b Flushing, NY, July 9, 29; m 53; c 4. MEDICINAL CHEMISTRY. *Educ:* Univ Conn, BS, 52; Univ NC, PhD(pharm), 56. *Prof Exp:* Org res chemist, Res Labs, Nat Drug Co, 56-58; from asst prof to assoc prof, 58-73, PROF MED CHEM, UNIV NC, CHAPEL HILL, 73-, HEAD DIV MED CHEM, SCH PHARM, 75- *Mem:* Am Chem Soc; Am Pharmaceut Asn. *Res:* Stereochemistry and biological activity; cholinergic mechanisms. *Mailing Add:* Sch of Pharm Univ of NC Chapel Hill NC 27514

COCOZELLA, ROBERT ANTHONY, b Swampscott, Mass, Sept 1, 28; m 55. MECHANICAL ENGINEERING. *Educ:* Tufts Univ, BSME, 52. *Prof Exp:* Res engr, Automotive Engine Dept, Gen Motors Corp, 52-57; res engr, Res Dept, Res & Adv Develop Div, 57-64, sr scientist, Appln Dept, 64-65, sect chief, Mat Develop Dept, 65-66, asst mgr, Mat Develop Dept, Space Systs Div, 66-69, mgr, Mat Appln Dept, Systs Div, 69-76, mgr, Fire & Thermal Properties Lab, Elec & Laser Mat Lab & Mech Eval Lab, 76-80, DIR, MAT MFG DIRECTORATE SYST DIV, AVCO CORP, 80- *Res:* Development of advanced materials for structural use and for use in thermal protection systems, particularly advanced composites; high temperature measurement techniques. *Mailing Add:* Avco Corp 201 Lowell St Wilmington MA 01887

CODD, JOHN EDWARD, b Spokane, Wash, Oct 13, 36; m 64; c 5. TRANSPLANTATION IMMUNOLOGY, THORACIC SURGERY. *Educ:* Gonzaga Univ, BA, 58; St Louis Univ, MD, 63. *Prof Exp:* Asst prof, 71-74, assoc prof, 75-80, PROF SURG, MED SCH, ST LOUIS UNIV, 80- *Concurrent Pos:* Chief, Unit II Surg, John Cochran Vet Admin Hosp, 71- *Mem:* Am Col Surgeons; Soc Transplant Surgeons; Asn Acad Surg. *Res:* Organ preservation for transplantation. *Mailing Add:* Dept Surg St Louis Univ Med Sch 1325 S Grand Blvd St Louis MO 63104

CODDING, EDWARD GEORGE, b Ionia, Mich, Jan 17, 42; m 68; c 1. ANALYTICAL CHEMISTRY. *Educ:* Cent Mich Univ, BSc, 65; Mich State Univ, PhD(chem), 71. *Prof Exp:* Asst prof chem, Kent State Univ, 74-77; ASST PROF CHEM, UNIV CALGARY, 77- *Mem:* Am Chem Soc; Soc Appl Spectroscopy. *Res:* Application of solid state image sensors as spectrochemical detectors; digital data handling techniques; incorporation of digital and analog instrumentation techniques for the measurement of chemical information. *Mailing Add:* Dept of Chem Univ of Calgary Calgary Can

CODDING, PENELOPE WIXSON, b Emporia, Kans, Sept 18, 46; m 68; c 2. X-RAY DIFFRACTION. *Educ:* Mich State Univ, BSc, 68, PhD(x-ray crystallog), 71. *Prof Exp:* Fel, Dept Biochem, Univ Alta, 71-73, Dept Chem, 73-74; asst prof, Dept Chem, Kent State Univ, 74-76; res assoc, 76-81, ASST PROF, DEPT CHEM, UNIV CALGARY, 81- *Mem:* Am Crystallog Asn; Am Chem Soc. *Res:* Structural aspects of the activity of drugs, neurotoxins and peptides using single crystal X-ray diffraction; correlation of conformational and pharmacological data to determine the molecular basis for binding to receptors. *Mailing Add:* Dept Chem Univ Calgary Calgary AB T2N 1N4 Can

CODDINGTON, EARL ALEXANDER, b Washington, DC, Dec 16, 20; m 45; c 3. MATHEMATICS. *Educ:* Johns Hopkins Univ, PhD(math), 48. *Prof Exp:* Physicist, Naval Ord Lab, Washington, DC, 42; mathematician, Navy Dept, 42-46; instr, Johns Hopkins Univ, 48-49; instr math, Mass Inst Technol, 49-52; from asst prof to assoc prof, 52-59, chmn dept, 68-71, PROF MATH, UNIV CALIF, LOS ANGELES, 59- *Mem:* AAAS; Math Asn Am; Am Math Soc. *Res:* Differential equations; analysis. *Mailing Add:* Dept of Math Univ of Calif Los Angeles CA 90024

CODE, ARTHUR DODD, b Brooklyn, NY, Aug 13, 23; m 43; c 4. ASTRONOMY, ASTROPHYSICS. *Educ:* Univ Chicago, MS, 47, PhD(astron & astrophysics), 50. *Prof Exp:* Asst, Yerkes Observ, Univ Chicago, 46-49; instr, Univ Va, 50; from instr to asst prof astron, Univ Wis, 51-56; assoc prof & mem staff, Mt Wilson & Palomar Observs, Calif Inst Technol, 56-58; prof, 58-69, JOEL STEBBINS PROF ASTRON, WASHBURN OBSERV, UNIV WIS-MADISON, 69-, DIR, 58- *Concurrent Pos:* Chmn bd dirs, Asn Univs Res Astron, 76- *Honors & Awards:* Pub Serv Award, Nat Aeronaut & Space Admin, 69; Prof Achievement Award, Univ Chicago Alumni Asn, 70. *Mem:* Nat Acad Sci; Am Astron Soc; Int Acad Astronaut. *Res:* Photoelectric photometry of stars and nebulae; stellar spectroscopy; development of instruments; satellite astronomy. *Mailing Add:* Washburn Observ Univ of Wis Madison WI 53706

CODE, CHARLES FREDERICK, b Can, Feb 1, 10; nat US; m 35; c 3. PHYSIOLOGY. *Educ:* Univ Man, MD & BSc, 34; Univ Minn, PhD, 39. *Prof Exp:* Lectr physiol, Univ London, 35-36; asst exp surg, Mayo Grad Sch Med, Univ Minn, 37, from instr to prof physiol, 38-75, dir med educ & res, 66-72;

assoc dir & sr res scientist, Ctr Ulcer Res & Educ, Wadsworth Vet Admin Hosp & Univ Calif, Los Angeles, 75-80; PROF MED & SURGERY, UNIV CALIF, SAN DIEGO, 80- Concurrent Pos: Mem staff & consult, Mayo Clin, 40-75; staff physician, Vet Admin Med Ctr, San Diego, 80- Honors & Awards: Theobald Smith Award, AAAS, 38; Friedenwald Medal, Am Gastroenterol Asn, 74. Mem: AAAS; Am Physiol Soc; Brit Physiol Soc; Am Soc Pharmacol & Exp Therapeut; Am Soc Clin Invest. Res: Metabolism of histamine, relationship to gastric secretion; hypersensitive state; physiology of gastrointestinal tract; motor action of the alimentary canal, secretion and absorption from the stomach, small and large bowel. Mailing Add: Gastroenterol Sect Vet Admin Med Ctr 3350 La Jolla Village Dr San Diego CA 92161

CODEN, MICHAEL H, b New York, NY, Mar 6, 47. HIGH SPEED FIBER OPTIC COMMUNICATIONS. Educ: Mass Inst Technol, BS, 67; Columbia Univ, MS, 75; Courant Inst Math Sci, MS, 79. Prof Exp: Prod mgr, Hewlett Packard Co, Inc, 67-69; mkt mgr, Digital Equip Corp, 69-72; asst vpres, Maher Terminals Incorp, 72-75; div mgr, Exxon Corp, 75-79; PRES, CODENOLL TECHNOL CORP, 79- Concurrent Pos: Preceptor, Columbia Univ, 74-75; lectr, Farleigh-Dickinson Univ, 79. Mem: AAAS; NY Acad Sci; Inst Elec & Electronics Engrs; Optical Soc Am; Soc Photo-Optical Instrumentation. Res: In computer hardware architecture: data business and multiprocessor; development of semiconductor laser sources and systems; fiber optic components and systems for very high speed data communications, including development of compound semiconductor components, microelectronics and electromagnetic wave theory. Mailing Add: Codenoll Technol Corp 1086 N Broadway Yonkers NY 10701

CODINGTON, JOHN F, b Macon, Ga, Feb 9, 20; m 52; c 3. BIOCHEMISTRY. Educ: Emory Univ, AB, 41, MA, 42; Univ Va, PhD(org chem), 45. Prof Exp: Res asst, Joint Off Sci Res & Develop & Comt Med Res Proj, Univ Va, 43-45; chemist, NIH, Md, 45-49; res biochem, Columbia Univ, 51-55; asst, Sloan-Kettering Inst Cancer Res, 55-59, assoc, 59-67; asst biochemist, 67-74, ASSOC BIOCHEMIST, DEPT MED, MASS GEN HOSP, 74-; PRIN RES ASSOC BIOL CHEM, HARVARD MED SCH, 67- Concurrent Pos: Asst prof, Cornell Med Col, 62-67. Res: Amino-alcohols; stilbenes; thiamine analogs; peptide antibiotics; nucleosides and sugars as potential anti-cancer agents; isolation, structures and immunological properties of glycoproteins of tumor cell surfaces. Mailing Add: 1725 Commonwealth Ave West Newton MA 02165

CODISPOTI, LOUIS ANTHONY, b Brooklyn, NY, June 6, 40; m 68. CHEMICAL OCEANOGRAPHY. Educ: Fordham Univ, BS, 62; Univ Wash, MS, 65, PhD(oceanog), 73. Prof Exp: Oceanogr, US Naval Hydrographic Off, 66-69; actg asst prof chem oceanog, Univ Wash, 73-74, fel, 74-75, prin oceanogr, 75-80; RES SCIENTIST, BIGELOW LAB, 80- Mem: Arctic Inst NAm; Am Soc Limnol & Oceanog; Sigma Xi. Res: Upwelling and marine identification; upwelling; chemical oceanography of the Arctic Ocean; marine denitrification; global nutrient budgets, cycles and feedback mechanisms; marine carbon dioxide system. Mailing Add: Bigelow Lab Ocean Sci W Boothbay Harbor ME 04575

CODRINGTON, ROBERT SMITH, b Victoria, BC, Dec 11, 25; nat US; m 48; c 1. PHYSICS. Educ: Univ BC, BA, 46, MA, 48; Univ Notre Dame, PhD(physics), 51. Prof Exp: Asst physics, Univ BC, 45-47; res assoc, Univ Notre Dame, 48-51; asst res specialist, Rutgers Univ, 51-54; physicist, Schlumberger, Ltd, 54-62; mgr eng, 62-79, MGR RES & DEVELOP INSTRUMENTS DIV, VARIAN ASSOCS, 79- Honors & Awards: Nat Telemetry Prize, 62. Mem: Am Phys Soc; Inst Elec & Electronic Engrs; Inst Soc Am. Res: Magnetic instrumentation; geophysics; radar and telemetry synchronization; high resolution nuclear magnetic resonance; optical instruments. Mailing Add: Varian Assocs D-317 611 Hansen Way Palo Alto CA 94304

CODY, D THANE, b St John, NB, June 23, 32; m 63; c 2. OTOLARYNGOLOGY, PHYSIOLOGY. Educ: Dalhousie Univ, MD & CM, 57; Univ Minn, PhD(otolaryngol), 66. Prof Exp: Asst to staff otorhinolaryngol, Mayo Clin, 62-63, consult, 63-68, from instr to assoc prof otolaryngol & rhinol, Mayo Grad Sch Med, 63-74, PROF OTOLARYNGOL, MAYO MED SCH, UNIV MINN, 74-, CHMN DEPT OTORHINOLARYNGOL, MAYO CLIN, 68- Concurrent Pos: Edward John Noble travel award, Mayo Found, 61; Am Acad Ophthal & Otolaryngol res award, 61. Honors & Awards: Dr John Black Award surg, Dalhousie Univ, 55. Mem: Fel Am Acad Ophthal & Otolaryngol; fel otolaryngol Am Col Surg; Am Laryngol, Rhinol & Otol Soc; Asn Res Otolaryngol; Am Otol Soc. Res: Labyrinthine otosclerosis. Mailing Add: Mayo Clin Rochester MN 55901

CODY, GEORGE DEWEY, b New York, NY, May 16, 30. SOLID STATE PHYSICS. Educ: Harvard Univ, AB, 52, MA, 54, PhD(physics), 57. Prof Exp: Asst, Harvard Univ, 52-57; staff physicist, RCA Labs, 57-69, dir, Solid State Lab, 69-78; sr res assoc, 78-80, SCIENTIFIC ADV, CORP RES LABS, EXXON RES & ENG CO, 80- Concurrent Pos: Harvard Univ Parker fel, Clarendon Lab, Oxford Univ, 57-58; regents prof, Univ Calif, San Diego, 69. Mem: Fel, Am Phys Soc. Res: Low temperature physics; superconductivity; high temperature thermal conductivity; thin films; magnetic properties of metals. Mailing Add: Corp Res Labs Exxon Res & Eng PO Box 45 Linden NJ 07030

CODY, MARTIN LEONARD, b Peterborough, Eng, Aug 7, 41; c 3. COMMUNITY ECOLOGY, ECOLOGICAL BIOGEOGRAPHY. Educ: Edinburgh Univ, MA, 63; Univ Pa, PhD(zool), 66. Prof Exp: asst prof zool, 66-72, PROF BIOL, UNIV CALIF, LOS ANGELES, 72- Concurrent Pos: John Simon Guggenheim Fel, 78-79. Mem: Soc Study Evolution; Ecol Soc Am; Am Soc Naturalists; Cooper Ornith Soc; Bot Soc Am. Res: Population biology; community ecology; patterns of competition and coexistence of plant and animal communities; convergent and divergent evolution; ecological biogeography; Mediterranean-climate ecosystems in California, Chile, Europe and South Africa; island biogeography; theoretical ecology. Mailing Add: Dept Biol Univ Calif Los Angeles CA 90024

CODY, REGINA JACQUELINE, b Steubenville, Ohio, May 13, 43. PHYSICAL CHEMISTRY. Educ: West Liberty State Col, BS, 65; Univ Pittsburgh, PhD(phys chem), 72. Prof Exp: Nat Acad Sci/Naval Res Labs res assoc IR laser res, Naval Res Lab, Washington, DC, 72-74; ASTROPHYSICIST PHOTOCHEM, LASER SPECTROS, GODDARD SPACE FLIGHT CTR, NASA, 74- Mem: Am Chem Soc; Am Phys Soc; AAAS; Sigma Xi. Res: Photochemistry of small molecules; laser spectroscopy, especially laser induced fluorescence spectroscopy; chemistry of comets and interstellar clouds. Mailing Add: NASA Bldg 2 Rm 161 Goddard Space Flight Ctr Code 691 Greenbelt MD 20771

CODY, REYNOLDS M, b Asheville, NC, Apr 17, 29; m 58; c 2. MICROBIOLOGY. Educ: Univ Tenn, BA, 56; Miss State Univ, MS, 61, PhD(microbiol), 64. Prof Exp: Instr microbiol, Miss State Univ, 58-61, res asst, 61-64; asst prof bact, 64-65, ASSOC PROF MICROBIOL & BOT, SCH VET MED, AUBURN UNIV, 65- Mem: Am Soc Microbiol; Am Indust Microbiol. Res: Biochemistry and physiology of pathogenic microorganisms including viruses; elucidation of metabolic pathways in Serratia indica. Mailing Add: Sch of Agr Med Auburn Univ Auburn AL 36830

CODY, TERENCE EDWARD, b Orrville, Ohio, June 3, 38; m 61; c 2. ENVIRONMENTAL HEALTH. Educ: Mt Union Col, BS, 60; Case Western Reserve Univ, MS, 68; Ohio State Univ, PhD(bot), 72. Prof Exp: Asst ed biochem, Chem Abstracts Serv, 64-68; fel environ health, 72-73, ASST PROF ENVIRON HEALTH, UNIV CINCINNATI, 73- Mem: Am Inst Biol Sci; Am Soc Limnologists & Oceanogr; Ecol Soc Am; Int Asn Water Pollution Res; Sigma Xi. Res: The applicability of bioassays and bioindicators for evaluating environmental impacts and health effects of organic chemicals and heavy metals in aquatic systems. Mailing Add: Inst Environ Health 3223 Eden Ave Univ of Cincinnati Med Ctr Cincinnati OH 45267

CODY, VIVIAN, b San Diego, Calif, Jan 28, 43. CRYSTALLOGRAPHY. Educ: Univ Mich, BS, 65; Univ Cincinnati, PhD(chem), 69. Prof Exp: Res asst chem, Univ Mich, 63-65; teaching asst, Univ Cincinnati, 65-67, NSF fel, 67-69; fel, Univ Mo, St Louis, 69-70; fel endocrinol trainee, 70-72, res scientist crystallog, 72-78, ASSOC RES SCIENTIST, MED FOUND OF BUFFALO, 79-; ASSOC PROF MED, STATE UNIV NY BUFFALO, 79- Mem: Endocrine Soc; Am Thyroid Asn; Am Crystallog Asn; Am Chem Soc; Biophys Soc. Res: Structure-function analysis of thyroid, steroid and polypeptide hormones as well as antifolate antineoplastic agents using the techniques of x-ray crystallography. Mailing Add: Med Found of Buffalo 73 High St Buffalo NY 14203

CODY, WILLIAM JAMES, b Hamilton, Ont, Dec 2, 22; m 50; c 5. BOTANY. Educ: McMaster Univ, BA, 46. Prof Exp: ASSOC BOTANIST, CAN DEPT AGR, 46-, CUR, VASCULAR PLANT HERBARIUM, 59- Mem: Am Soc Plant Taxon; Int Asn Plant Taxon; Can Bot Asn. Res: Floristics of Mackenzie district, Northwest Territories and Yukon Territory; Canadian ferns. Mailing Add: Dept of Agr Biosysts Res Inst Cent Exp Farm Ottawa ON K1A 0C6 Can

CODY, WILLIAM JAMES, JR, b Melrose Park, Ill, Nov 28, 29; m 53; c 5. NUMERICAL ANALYSIS. Educ: Elmhurst Col, BS, 51; Univ Okla, MA, 56. Hon Degrees: ScD, Elmhurst Col, 77. Prof Exp: Instr math, Univ Okla, 57-58 & Northwestern Univ, 58-59; asst mathematician, 59-66, assoc mathematician, 66-79, SR MATHEMATICIAN, ARGONNE NAT LAB, 79- Concurrent Pos: Consult, Int Math & Statist Libr, Inc, 73-81. Mem: Am Math Soc; Math Asn Am; Inst Elec & Electronic Engrs; Soc Indust & Appl Math; Asn Comput Mach. Res: Approximation of functions; computer arithmetic. Mailing Add: Appl Math Div Bldg 221 Argonne Nat Lab 9700 S Cass Ave Argonne IL 60439

COE, BERESFORD, b Philadelphia, Pa, May 4, 19; m 45; c 3. ORGANIC CHEMISTRY. Educ: Earlham Col, AB, 41. Prof Exp: Res chemist, Barrett Div, Allied Chem & Dye Corp, 41-46; res chemist, Rohm & Haas Co, 46-81; RETIRED. Mem: Am Chem Soc. Res: Adhesives technical service. Mailing Add: 17029 106th Ave Sun City AZ 85373

COE, CHARLES GARDNER, b Philadelphia, Pa, Nov 13, 50; m 72; c 1. INORGANIC CHEMISTRY, ORGANIC CHEMISTRY. Educ: Thiel Col, BA, 72; Carnegie-Mellon Univ, PhD(inorg chem), 76. Prof Exp: Teaching asst, Carnegie-Mellon Univ, 72-76; res chemist, 76-81, GROUP LEADER, MAT RES, AIR PROD & CHEM INC, 81- Mem: Am Chem Soc; Sigma Xi. Res: Synthetic inorganic chemistry; studying the interaction and activation of small molecules by metalions; heterogeneous and homogeneous catalysis. Mailing Add: Air Prod & Chem Inc PO Box 538 Marcus Hook PA 19061

COE, EDWARD HAROLD, JR, b San Antonio, Tex, Dec 7, 26; m 49; c 2. GENETICS. Educ: Univ Minn, BS, 49, MS, 51; Univ Ill, PhD(bot), 54. Prof Exp: Res fel genetics, Calif Inst Technol, 54-55; res assoc field crops, 55-58, assoc prof, 59-63, PROF AGRON, UNIV MO, 64-, GENETICIST, USDA, 55-, RES LEADER, CEREAL GENETICS, USDA, 77- Concurrent Pos: Ed, Maize Genetics Coop Newslett, 75- Mem: AAAS; Genetics Soc Am; Am Genetic Asn; Crop Sci Soc Am; Am Soc Naturalists. Res: Genetics of maize; anthocyanin synthesis; extramendelian inheritance; fertilization and development. Mailing Add: 206 Heather Lane Columbia MO 65201

COE, ELMON LEE, b Phoenix, Ariz, Mar 6, 31; m 61. BIOCHEMISTRY. Educ: Harvard Univ, AB, 52; Univ Calif, Los Angeles, PhD(physiol chem), 61. Prof Exp: Res assoc biochem, Univ Ind, 60-61; from instr to asst prof, 61-68, ASSOC PROF BIOCHEM, MED SCH, NORTHWESTERN UNIV, CHICAGO, 68- Concurrent Pos: NIH grant, 64-67. Res: Interactions between metabolic pathways and metabolic control mechanisms; carbohydrate metabolism; biochemistry of tumors. Mailing Add: Dept of Biochem Northwestern Univ Med Sch Chicago IL 60611

COE, FREDRIC LAWRENCE, b Chicago, Ill, Dec 25, 36; m 65; c 2. INTERNAL MEDICINE, NEPHROLOGY. *Educ:* Univ Chicago, BA & BS, 57, MD, 61. *Prof Exp:* From asst prof to prof med, 69-80, PROF PHYSIOL, UNIV CHICAGO, 80-; DIR & CHMN RENAL DIV, MICHAEL REESE HOSP, 72- *Concurrent Pos:* USPHS fel, Univ Tex Southwestern Med Sch Dallas, 67-69; mem renal prog, Michael Reese Hosp, 69-72, chmn prog, 72- *Mem:* Am Physiol Soc; Am Soc Nephrology; Am Fedn Clin Res; Cent Soc Clin Res; Am Soc Clin Invest. *Res:* Renal physiology; causes of renal calculi; computer medicine. *Mailing Add:* Michael Reese Hosp 2900 Ellis Ave Chicago IL 60616

COE, GERALD EDWIN, b Granville, Ill, Apr 21, 22; m 41; c 3. GENETICS, CYTOLOGY. *Educ:* Tex Col Arts & Indust, BS, 42; Univ Tex, PhD(bot), 52. *Prof Exp:* Asst, Univ Tex, 52; GENETICIST, SCI & EDUC ADMIN, USDA, 52- *Mem:* Bot Soc Am. *Res:* Cytology and genetics in the genus Beta. *Mailing Add:* 4300 Maple Place Beltsville MD 20705

COE, GORDON RANDOLPH, b Cincinnati, Ohio, Aug 10, 33; m 60; c 1. POLYMER CHEMISTRY, PHYSICAL ORGANIC CHEMISTRY. *Educ:* Centre Col, Ky, AB, 55; Univ Tenn, MS, 60; Univ Cincinnati, PhD(inorg chem), 64. *Prof Exp:* Assoc prof chem, Univ Southern Miss, 64-67; chemist, E I du Pont, 67-70 & Joseph E Seagrams, 70-72; PROG MGR POLYMER CHEM, GEN ELEC CO, 72- *Mem:* Soc Plastics Engrs. *Res:* Polymer characterization, stabilizer and additive analysis. *Mailing Add:* 3132 Trinity Rd Louisville KY 40206

COE, JOHN EMMONS, b Evanston, Ill, Sept 1, 31; m 54; c 3. IMMUNOLOGY. *Educ:* Oberlin Col, BA, 53; Hahnemann Med Col, MD, 57. *Prof Exp:* Intern, Univ Ill Res & Educ Hosp, 57-58; resident internal med, Med Ctr, Univ Colo, 58-60; surgeon, Rocky Mountain Lab, Nat Inst Allergy & Infectious Dis, NIH, 60-63; fel path, Scripps Clin & Res Found, 63-65; MED OFFICER, ROCKY MOUNTAIN LAB, NAT INST ALLERGY & INFECTIOUS DIS, NIH, 65- *Concurrent Pos:* Affil prof microbiol & zool, Univ Mont, 74- *Mem:* Am Asn Immunologists. *Res:* Selective induction of antibody formation in immunoglobulin classes of rodents, especially Syrian hamsters; immunity in lower vertebrates, especially amphibians and reptiles. *Mailing Add:* Rocky Mountain Lab Hamilton MT 59840

COE, JOHN IRA, b Chicago, Ill, Jan 21, 19; m 42. PATHOLOGY. *Educ:* Carleton Col, AB, 40; Univ Minn, MB, 44, MD, 45. *Prof Exp:* Fel, Univ Minn, 45-46 & 48-49; chief path, Vet Admin Hosp, Minneapolis, 49-50; from asst prof to assoc prof, 52-72, PROF PATH, UNIV MINN, MINNEAPOLIS, 72-; CHIEF PATH, HENNEPIN COUNTY MED CTR, 50-, MED EXAMR, 64- *Concurrent Pos:* Pathologist, Drs Mem Hosp, 52-57. *Mem:* Am Soc Clin Path; Col Am Pathologists; Am Acad Forensic Sci; Int Acad Path; Nat Asn Med Examr (pres, 79-80). *Res:* forensic pathology postmortem biochemistry. *Mailing Add:* 5108 Tifton Dr Minneapolis MN 55435

COE, KENNETH LOREN, b Omaha, Nebr, Apr 16, 27. CHEMISTRY, INFORMATION SCIENCE. *Educ:* Tarkio Col, BA, 49. *Prof Exp:* From asst ed to assoc ed chem abstr, 51-58, head ed dept, 59-61, managing ed, abstr issues, 62-69, MANAGING ED, PUBL, CHEM ABSTR, 69- *Mem:* AAAS; Am Chem Soc; Coun Biol Ed; Asn Earth Sci Ed. *Res:* Chemical documentation. *Mailing Add:* 1631 Roxbury Rd Apt D1 Columbus OH 43212

COE, RICHARD HANSON, b Stamford, Conn, Jan 29, 20; m 55; c 6. CHEMISTRY. *Educ:* Wesleyan Univ, BA, 41, MA, 42; Stanford Univ, PhD(chem), 47. *Prof Exp:* Chemist, Conn State Water Comn, 41-42; actg instr chem, Stanford Univ, 43, asst, Nat Defense Res Comt, 44; asst res chemist, Calif Res Corp, 45-46; instr chem, Wesleyan Univ, 46-48; sr technologist, 49-64, sr res chemist, 64-67, supvr, 67-69, staff res chemist, 69-71; sr staff res chemist, 71-77, MGR OSH REGULATIONS, SAFETY & INDUST HYG, SHELL OIL CO, 77- *Honors & Awards:* Indust Wastes Medal, Fed Sewage & Indust Wastes Asn, 52. *Mem:* AAAS; Am Chem Soc; Am Inst Chem. *Mailing Add:* Shell Oil Co One Shell Plaza PO Box 4320 Houston TX 77210

COE, ROBERT STEPHEN, b Toronto, Ont, Feb 20, 39; m 69. GEOPHYSICS, GEOCHEMISTRY. *Educ:* Harvard Univ, BA, 61; Univ Calif, Berkeley, MS, 64, PhD(geophys), 66. *Prof Exp:* Asst prof, 68-74, assoc prof, 74-78, PROF EARTH SCI & CHMN DEPT, UNIV CALIF, SANTA CRUZ, 78- *Concurrent Pos:* Fel, Australian Nat Univ, 66-68; starter grant, Petrol Res Fund, Am Chem Soc, 69-70; NSF grants, 70-72. *Mem:* AAAS; Am Geophys Union; Geol Soc Am; Soc Terrestrial Magnetism & Elec Japan. *Res:* Paleomagnetism, especially paleointensities of the geomagnetic field; effects of shear stress on polymorphic transitions in minerals. *Mailing Add:* Dept of Earth Sci Univ of Calif Santa Cruz CA 95064

COELHO, ANTHONY MENDES, JR, b Danbury, Conn, May 26, 47; m 74. PRIMATOLOGY, AUXOLOGY. *Educ:* Western Conn State Col, BS, 70; Univ Tex, Austin, MA, 73, PhD(anthrop), 74. *Prof Exp:* Asst prof anthrop, Tex Tech Univ, 74-75; ASSOC FOUND SCIENTIST & HEAD PRIMATE ETHOLOGY LAB, SW FOUND RES & EDUC, 75- *Concurrent Pos:* Adj asst prof, Univ Tex Health Sci Ctr San Antonio, 76-, Univ Tex, San Antonio, 77- & Univ Tex, Austin, 78- *Mem:* Am Asn Phys Anthrop; Int Primatological Soc; Am Anthrop Asn; Soc Study Human Biol; Am Soc Primatologists. *Res:* Primate behavior; ecology and socio-bioenergetics; behavioral correlates of atherosclerosis; human and nonhuman primate physical growth, development, nutrition and evolution; quantitative ethology; behavioral medicine. *Mailing Add:* NW Loop 410 PO Box 28147 San Antonio TX 78284

COELING, KENNETH JAMES, mechanical engineering, see previous edition

COEN, GERALD MARVIN, b Camrose, Alta, Mar 26, 39; m 64; c 2. SOIL SCIENCE, PEDOLOGY. *Educ:* Univ Alta, BSc, 63, MSc, 65; Cornell Univ, PhD(agron), 70. *Prof Exp:* Res scientist, 69-74, BIOL SCIENTIST, AGR CAN, 74- *Concurrent Pos:* Assoc asst prof, Univ Alta, 71-; assoc ed, Can J Soil Sci, 75-77. *Mem:* Agr Inst Can; Can Soc Soil Sci; Am Soc Agron; Int Soc Soil Sci; Soil Conserv Soc Am. *Res:* Soil survey and resource inventories including research on soil genesis, classification and interpretation necessary to carry out the inventory programs. *Mailing Add:* Agr Can Soil Surv 4445 Calgary Trail S Edmonton Can

COESTER, FRITZ, b Berlin, Ger, Oct 16, 21; nat US; m 52; c 6. PHYSICS. *Educ:* Univ Zurich, PhD(theoret physics), 44. *Prof Exp:* Res, Sulzer Bros, Inc, Switz, 44-46; instr, Univ Geneva, 46-47; from asst prof to prof physics, Univ Iowa, 47-63; SR PHYSICIST, ARGONNE NAT LAB, 63- *Concurrent Pos:* Mem, Inst Advan Study, 53-54. *Mem:* Fel Am Phys Soc; Switz Phys Soc; Europ Phys Soc. *Res:* Quantum theory of fields; theoretical nuclear physics; theoretical physics. *Mailing Add:* Argonne Nat Lab Argonne IL 60439

COETZEE, JOHANNES FRANCOIS, b Bloemfontein, Union SAfrica, Nov 25, 24; m 54; c 1. ANALYTICAL CHEMISTRY. *Educ:* Univ Orange Free State, SAfrica, BSc, 44, MSc, 49; Univ Minn, PhD(chem), 55. *Prof Exp:* Instr chem, Univ Orange Free State, 45-48, lectr, 49-51 & Univ Witwatersrand, 56-57; from asst prof to assoc prof, 57-66, PROF CHEM, UNIV PITTSBURGH, 66- *Concurrent Pos:* Titular mem Int Union Pure & Appl Chem. *Res:* Non-aqueous solutions; electroanalytical chemistry; kinetics of fast ligand-substitution reactions. *Mailing Add:* Dept of Chem Univ of Pittsburgh Pittsburgh PA 15260

COFER, HARLAND E, JR, b Atlanta, Ga, Dec 28, 22; m 45; c 6. ECONOMIC GEOLOGY, MINERALOGY. *Educ:* Emory Univ, AB, 47, MS, 48; Univ Ill, Urbana-Champaign, PhD(geol), 57. *Prof Exp:* Asst prof geol, Emory Univ, 48-58; sr geologist, Indust Chem Div, Am Cyanamid Co, Ga, 58-66; PROF GEOL & CHMN DIV SCI & MATH, GA SOUTHWESTERN COL, 66- *Concurrent Pos:* Geologist, Groundwater Div, US Geol Surv, Ga, 53-54; consult, Consol Quarries Inc, Ga, 52-53 & Indust Chem Div, Am Cyanamid Co, 52-58. *Mem:* Geol Soc Am; Clay Minerals Soc. *Res:* Clay mineral research, especially utilization of kaolin group minerals as sources for alumina; mechanism of dissolution of clay minerals in natural and artificial environments. *Mailing Add:* Dept of Geol Ga Southwestern Col Americus GA 31709

COFFEE, ROBERT DODD, b East Orange, NJ, Dec 18, 20; m 71; c 2. CHEMICAL SAFETY, INSTRUMENTATION. *Educ:* Newark Col Eng, BS, 42; Univ Wis, Madison, MS, 47, PhD(chem eng), 49. *Prof Exp:* Develop engr, Plastics Div, Monsanto Chem Co, Mass, 42-46; develop engr, 49-53, sr develop engr, 53-63, supvr tech safety, 63-81, TECH ASST, EASTMAN KODAK CO, 81- *Concurrent Pos:* Safety consult, US Dept Transportation, 71-; lectr, Nat Safety Coun, 75-78. *Mem:* Am Chem Soc; Nat Fire Protection Asn; Am Soc Testing & Mat; Am Inst Chem Engrs; Instrument Soc Am. *Res:* Plastics manufacture and processing; equipment design; chemical safety; hazard evaluation and protection. *Mailing Add:* Eastman Kodak Co Kodak Park Bldg 320 Rochester NY 14650

COFFEEN, W(ILLIAM) W(EBER), b Champaign, Ill, Aug 13, 14; m 45; c 2. CERAMICS. *Educ:* Univ Ill, BS, 35, MS, 37, prof degree, 49; Rutgers Univ, PhD, 69. *Prof Exp:* Assoc, Univ Ill, 35-37; ceramic engr, Canton Stamping & Enameling Co, Ohio, 37-39; asst prof ceramics eng, Ga Inst Technol, 40-41; res assoc, porcelain enamel inst, Nat Bur Standards, 41-42; glass technologist, 42-45; res supvr, Metal & Thermit Corp, 45-62, dir res M&T Chem, Inc, 63-67, tech adv to pres, 67-68; assoc prof ceramic eng, 69-78, PROF CERAMIC ENG, CLEMSON UNIV, 78- *Honors & Awards:* Greaves-Walker Award, 80. *Mem:* Fel Am Ceramic Soc (vpres, 68-69); Nat Inst Ceramic Engrs (pres, 63-64). *Res:* Vitreous enamels; optical glass; opacification in vitreous media; electronic ceramics, especially capacitors; tin, antimony and zirconium compounds in ceramics; arc welding equipment; thermite reactions; mineral beneficiation; ceramic prosthetics. *Mailing Add:* Dept of Ceramic Eng Olin Hall Clemson Univ Clemson SC 29631

COFFEY, CHARLES EUGENE, b Bristol, Va, Feb 12, 31; m 54; c 3. PHYSICAL CHEMISTRY. *Educ:* King Col, AB, 52; Univ NC, PhD(phys chem), 56. *Prof Exp:* Fel phys chem, Univ Wash, 56-57; chemist, E I du Pont de Nemours & Co, Inc, 57-62, sr res chemist, 62-70, res supvr, 70-75, lab dir, 75-77, res mgr, 78-80; RES MGR, SAVANNAH RIVER LAB, AIKEN, SC, 78- *Concurrent Pos:* Fel inorg chem, Univ London, 61. *Res:* Extractive metallurgy; molecular structure; metal-organic and inorganic chemistry; explosives; roof support systems; polyesters; nuclear engineering. *Mailing Add:* 1774 Huntsman Rod Aiken SC 29801

COFFEY, CHARLES WILLIAM, II, b Somerset, Ky, July 28, 49; m 71. MEDICAL PHYSICS, HEALTH PHYSICS. *Educ:* Univ Ky, BS, 71, MS, 72; Purdue Univ, PhD(bionucleonics), 75; Am Bd Radiol, cert therapeut radiol physics, 77. *Prof Exp:* Asst med physicist & asst prof clin physics, 75-78, CHIEF CLIN PHYSICS & ASST PROF MED PHYSICS, DEPT RADIATION THER, MED CTR, UNIV KY, 78- *Mem:* Am Asn Physicists Med; Health Physics Soc; Sigma Xi. *Res:* Applied and clinical physics in radiation medicine; high energy electron beams, used in radiotherapy; the use of linear accelerators in radiotherapy; computer techniques in radiotherapy. *Mailing Add:* Dept of Radiation Med Rm C-21 Univ of Ky Med Ctr Lexington KY 40506

COFFEY, DEWITT, JR, b Gilmer, Tex, Apr 12, 35; m 68. CHEMICAL PHYSICS. *Educ:* Abilene Christian Col, BS(chem), 58; Univ Tex, BS(chem eng), 58, PhD(chem), 67. *Prof Exp:* Res asst drilling & well completion, Mobil Oil Field Res Lab, Tex, 58-61; McBean fel, Stanford Res Inst, 66-68; assoc prof, 68-77, PROF CHEM, SAN DIEGO STATE UNIV, 77- *Concurrent Pos:* Res Corp Frederick Gardner Cottrell grants-in-aid, 69-; consult, Stanford Res Inst, Calif, 69-; San Diego State Univ Found fac res grant, 69-; vis prof, Kyushu Univ, Fukuoka City, Japan, 75. *Mem:* AAAS; Am Chem Soc; Am Phys Soc. *Res:* infrared laser; microwave spectroscopy; stark-shifted spectroscopy. *Mailing Add:* Dept of Chem San Diego State Univ San Diego CA 92182

COFFEY, DONALD STRALEY, b Bristol, Va, Oct 10, 32; m 53; c 2. PHARMACOLOGY, BIOCHEMISTRY. *Educ:* ETenn State Univ, BS, 57; Johns Hopkins Univ, PhD(biochem), 64. *Hon Degrees:* DSc, King Col, 77. *Prof Exp:* Chemist, NAm Rayon Corp, Tenn, 55-57; chem engr, Westinghouse Corp, Md, 57-59; actg dir James B Brady Urol Res Lab, Johns Hopkins Hosp, 59-60, instr physiol chem, 65-66, from asst prof to assoc prof pharmacol, 66-74, assoc prof, The Oncol Ctr, Sch Med, 73-74, dir, James Buchanan Brady Lab Reprod Biol, Johns Hopkins Hosp, 64-74, actg chmn, Dept Pharmacol & Exp Therapeut, Sch Med, 73-74, DIR, DEPT UROL RES LABS, JOHNS HOPKINS HOSP, 74-, PROF PHARMACOL & EXP THERAPEUT, SCH MED, JOHNS HOPKINS UNIV & PROF, ONCOL CTR, 74-, PROF UROL, 75- *Concurrent Pos:* USPHS res career award, 66-72; asst ed, J Molecular Pharmacol, 67-71 & Cancer Res, 81. *Honors & Awards:* D R Edwards Award, 81. *Mem:* Am Soc Pharmacol & Exp Therapeut; Am Soc Biol Chemists; Cell Biol. *Res:* Control of cell replication and DNA synthesis; biochemistry of mammalian nuclei; growth and development of the prostate gland; control of reproduction; cancer chemotherapy. *Mailing Add:* Dept Urol Johns Hopkins Univ Sch Med Baltimore MD 21205

COFFEY, HOWARD THOMAS, low temperature physics, see previous edition

COFFEY, JAMES CECIL, JR, b Salisbury, NC, July 2, 38; m 57; c 2. ENDOCRINOLOGY, PARASITOLOGY. *Educ:* Catawba Col, BA, 63; Univ NC, MSPH, 66, PhD(parasitol, biochem), 70. *Prof Exp:* Res assoc, Dent Res Ctr, 71-72, asst prof pediat & oral biol, Sch Med & Dent Res Ctr, 72-78, ASSOC PROF ORAL BIOL & PEDIAT, SCH DENT & MED, UNIV NC, CHAPEL HILL, 78- *Concurrent Pos:* Fel pediat endocrinol, Sch Med, Univ NC, 70-71; NIH res career develop award. *Mem:* Endocrine Soc. *Res:* Androgen metabolism; physiology of submaxillary glands. *Mailing Add:* Dent Res Ctr Univ NC Chapel Hill NC 27514

COFFEY, JANICE CARLTON, b Lenoir, NC, July 8, 41. SYSTEMATIC BOTANY. *Educ:* Appalachian State Univ, BS, 62; Univ SC, MS, 64, PhD(biol), 66. *Prof Exp:* Asst prof biol, Clemson Univ, 66-67; assoc prof biol, Queens Col, NC, 67-78; ASSOC PROF BIOL, ST MARY'S COL, NC, 79- *Concurrent Pos:* Nat Acad Sci exchange scientist, USSR, 73 & 75; Fulbright scholar, Egypt, 80. *Mem:* Am Soc Plant Taxonomists (secy, 75-76); Am Inst Biol Sci; Bot Soc Am; Int Asn Plant Taxon; Sigma Xi. *Res:* Systematics of the Juncaceae, emphasis on Luzula. *Mailing Add:* c/o Dallas D Carlton 671 East Blvd Lenoir NC 28645

COFFEY, JOHN JOSEPH, b Cambridge, Mass, Apr 24, 40. BIOCHEMISTRY, BIOCHEMICAL PHARMACOLOGY. *Educ:* Harvard Univ, AB, 61; Johns Hopkins Univ, PhD(biochem), 67. *Prof Exp:* NSF fel, Virus Lab, Univ Calif, Berkeley, 67-68; BIOCHEMIST, ARTHUR D LITTLE, INC, 68- *Mem:* Am Chem Soc; AAAS. *Res:* Kinetics of regulatory processes; enzyme induction; allosteric properties of proteins; drug distribution and metabolism; protein binding of drugs; pharmacokinetics; cancer chemotherapy. *Mailing Add:* One President Rd West Roxbury MA 02132

COFFEY, JOHN WILLIAM, b Sedalia, Mo, Jan 20, 37; m 63; c 3. BIOCHEMISTRY. *Educ:* Rockhurst Col, BS, 59; Tulane Univ, PhD(biochem), 63. *Prof Exp:* Res fel biochem, Touro Res Inst, 63-65 & Rockefeller Univ, 65-67; asst prof, Tulane Med Sch, 67-69, sr scientist, 69-75; asst group leader, 76-78, GROUP LEADER, HOFFMANN-LA ROCHE INC, 79- *Mem:* AAAS; NY Acad Sci; Am Soc Biol Chemists. *Res:* Arachidome acid metabolism; lysosomal functions; vitamin B12 metabolism; collagen metabolism. *Mailing Add:* Dept Pharmacol Hoffmann-La Roche Inc Nutley NJ 07110

COFFEY, JOSEPH FRANCIS, b East St Louis, Ill, June 6, 17; m 44; c 5. CHEMISTRY, CHEMICAL ENGINEERING. *Educ:* Mass Inst Technol, BS, 39, MS, 42; St Louis Univ, PhD(chem), 70. *Prof Exp:* Res staff mem, Standard Oil Co Ind, 39-40; asst, Mass Inst Technol, 40-42; res staff mem, Standard Oil Co Ind, 42-45; group leader process develop, 45-47, sect leader process design develop, 48-53; develop dir, Indoil Chem Co, 53-55; mgr commercial develop, Am Viscose Corp, 55-57; pvt consult, 57-62; asst prof chem, Westminster Col, 62-63; asst prof & actg chmn dept, Florrissant Valley Community Col, 63-65; PROF CHEM, FOREST PARK COMMUNITY COL, 65- *Res:* Petrochemicals; organic chemistry. *Mailing Add:* 7156 Kingsbury Blvd University City MO 63130

COFFEY, MARVIN DALE, b Midvale, Idaho, Apr 25, 30; m 52; c 5. ENTOMOLOGY, ZOOLOGY. *Educ:* Brigham Young Univ, AB, 52, MA, 53; Wash State Univ, PhD(entom), 57. *Prof Exp:* From instr to assoc prof zool & entom, 57-67, chmn dept biol, 65-70, PROF ZOOL & ENTOM, SOUTHERN ORE STATE COL, 67- *Concurrent Pos:* Asst prof, Fresno State Col, 64-65; vis prof, Tex A&M Univ, 69-70 & Univ Ky, 76-77. *Mem:* AAAS; Entom Soc Am; Am Inst Biol Sci. *Res:* Taxonomy, ecology and medical importance of parasitic arthropods and of the Diptera. *Mailing Add:* Dept of Biol Southern Ore State Col Ashland OR 97520

COFFEY, MICHAEL THOMAS, atmospheric physics, molecular spectroscopy, see previous edition

COFFEY, MITCHAEL DEWAYNE, b Ada, Okla, Feb 2, 44; m 65; c 3. ORGANIC CHEMISTRY. *Educ:* ECent State Col, BS, 66; Purdue Univ, PhD(org chem), 72. *Prof Exp:* RES SPECIALIST, DOW CHEM CO, 71- *Mem:* Am Chem Soc. *Res:* Development of products and services for the oilfield industry; synthetic-organosulfur, organonitrogen and organophosphorus; surface-scale inhibitors, corrosion inhibitors, electrophoretic mobilities and polarization studies. *Mailing Add:* Dowell Div of Dow Chem Co PO Box 21 Tulsa OK 74102

COFFEY, RONALD GIBSON, b Monte Vista, Colo, Dec 29, 36; m 59; c 3. BIOCHEMISTRY, PHARMACOLOGY. *Educ:* Colo State Univ, BS, 58; Ore State Univ, PhD(biochem), 63. *Prof Exp:* Res asst biochem, Ore State Univ, 58-63; chief div chem, Fifth US Army Med Lab, St Louis, Mo, 63-65; res assoc biochem, Univ Ore, 65-68; head div biochem, Children's Asthma Res Inst & Hosp, Denver, Colo, 68-73; ASSOC IMMUNOPHARMACOL, SLOAN-KETTERING INST CANCER RES, 73- *Concurrent Pos:* NIH grant, Children's Asthma Res Inst & Hosp, Denver, Colo, 70-73. *Mem:* Am Soc Biol Chemists; NY Acad Sci. *Res:* Regulation of cell membrane enzymes, especially adenylate cyclase, guanylate cyclase and ATPase by hormonal and pharmacologic agents and its application to immunology, allergy and cancer. *Mailing Add:* Dept of Immunopharmacol Sloan-Kettering Inst Cancer Res Rye NY 10580

COFFEY, TIMOTHY, b Washington, DC, June 27, 41; m 63; c 3. TECHNICAL MANAGEMENT. *Educ:* Mass Inst Technol, BS, 62; Univ Mich, MS, 63, PhD(physics), 67. *Prof Exp:* Physicist, Air Force Cambridge Res Lab, 64-65; res asst physics, Univ Mich, 65-66; physicist, EG&G, Inc, 66-71; br head, 71-75, div head plasma physics, 75-82, ASSOC DIR RES, GEN SCI, NAVAL RES LAB, 80- *Mem:* Fel Am Phys Soc; AAAS; Int Union Radio Sci; NY Acad Sci. *Res:* Theoretical non-linear mechanics; theoretical plasma physics; relativistic electron beam theory; ionospheric and space plasma theory. *Mailing Add:* Naval Res Lab Washington DC 20375

COFFIN, DAVID L, b Neshameny, Pa, Feb 24, 13; m 40; c 1. ENVIRONMENTAL HEALTH, EXPERIMENTAL PATHOLOGY. *Educ:* Univ Pa, VMD, 38. *Prof Exp:* Asst prof clin path, Univ Pa, 40-46; pathologist, Angell Mem Hosp, 46-56; prof path, Univ Pa, Philadelphia, 57-61; res adv air pollution, Robert Taft Eng Ctr, 61-71; SR RES ADV AIR POLLUTION, US ENVIRON PROTECTION AGENCY, 71- *Concurrent Pos:* Res assoc path, Harvard Med, Calif, 46-56; dir res path, Caspary Inst, New York City, 56-61; vis prof, Los Alamos Lab, Univ Calif, 78-80; consult mem, Comt Refining Syn Fuels, Nat Acad Sci, 80-81. *Mem:* Am Asn Path & Bact; Soc Toxicol; Int Acad Path; Am Col Vet Path; AAAS. *Res:* Environmental health; interaction of toxicants with infectious agents; influence of environmental factors on pulmonary defense to infectious disease and cancer; role of organics and mineral fibers in elicitation of cancer. *Mailing Add:* 1023 Sycamore St Durham NC 27707

COFFIN, HAROLD GLEN, b Nanning, China, Apr 9, 26; US citizen; m 47; c 2. PALEONTOLOGY. *Educ:* Walla Walla Col, BA, 47, MA, 52; Univ Southern Calif, PhD, 55. *Prof Exp:* Head dept biol, Can Union Col, 47-52; res fel, Univ Southern Calif, 52-54; head div sci & math, Can Union Col, 54-56; assoc prof, Walla Walla Col, 56-58, head dept, 58-64; prof zool, Geosci Res Inst, Andrews Univ, 64-65; prof paleont, 65-80; SR RES SCIENTIST, GEOSCI RES INST, LOMA LINDA UNIV, 80- *Mem:* AAAS; Sigma Xi; Geol Soc Am. *Res:* Marine invertebrates; science and religion, especially as related to geology and biology. *Mailing Add:* Geosci Res Inst Loma Linda Univ Loma Linda CA 92350

COFFIN, JOHN MILLER, b Boston, Mass, Apr 20, 44; m 68; c 2. VIROLOGY, MOLECULAR BIOLOGY. *Educ:* Wesleyan Univ, BA, 67; Univ Wis, PhD(molecular biol), 72. *Prof Exp:* Trainee oncol, Univ Wis, 67-72; fel, Inst Molecular Biol, Univ Zurich, 72-75; asst prof, 75-78, ASSOC PROF MOLECULAR BIOL, SCH MED, TUFTS UNIV, 78- *Concurrent Pos:* Jane Coffin Childs Mem Fund Med Res fel, 72-74; prin investr, Nat Cancer Inst, 75- & Am Cancer Soc, 75-; fac award, Am Cancer Soc, 78-83, mem virol study sect, 80- *Mem:* Am Soc Microbiol. *Res:* Viral oncology; genome structure and gentics of avian RNA tumor viruses. *Mailing Add:* Dept of Molecular & Microbiol 136 Harrison Ave Boston MA 02111

COFFIN, LAURENCE HAINES, b Buenos Aires, Arg, June 4, 33; US citizen; m 58; c 3. THORACIC SURGERY, CARDIAC SURGERY. *Educ:* Mass Inst Technol, BS, 55; Case Western Reserve Univ, MD, 59; Am Bd Surg & Bd Thoracic Surg, dipl, 68. *Prof Exp:* From instr to sr instr thoracic surg, Case Western Reserve Univ, 67-69; assoc prof surg, 69-75, PROF SURG, COL MED, UNIV VT, 75-, CHIEF SECT THORACIC & CARDIAC SURG, 69-, ATTEND & CHIEF THORACIC SERV, MED CTR HOSP VT, 70-, DIR THORACIC & CARDIOVASC SURG, 77- *Concurrent Pos:* Surg intern, Univ Hosps Cleveland, 59-60, resident, 60-61 & 63-67, asst thoracic surgeon, 67-69; chief thoracic surg, Vet Admin Hosp Cleveland, 67-69; mem coun cardiovasc surg, Am Heart Asn, 70- *Mem:* Soc Thoracic Surgeons; As Am Acad Surg; fel Am Col Surg; Am Asn Thoracic Surgeons. *Res:* Pathophysiology of burn shock; cardiovascular physiology. *Mailing Add:* 1 S Prospect St Med Ctr Hosp Vt Burlington VT 05401

COFFIN, LOUIS F(USSELL), JR, b Schenectady, NY, Aug 30, 17; m 42; c 8. MECHANICAL METALLURGY. *Educ:* Swarthmore Col, BS, 39; Mass Inst Technol, ScD(mech eng), 49. *Prof Exp:* Instr mech eng, Mass Inst Technol, 41-46, asst prof, 46-49; res assoc gen physics unit, Knolls Atomic Power Lab, 49-55, MECH ENGR, GEN ELEC RES LAB, GEN ELEC CO, 55- *Concurrent Pos:* Adj assoc prof, Dept Metall, Rensselaer Polytech Inst, 56-59; mem comt, Mat Adv Bd, Nat Acad Sci, 60-62 & 65-; adj prof, Union Col, 67-; Gen Elec Coolidge fel, 74; vis fel, Clare Hall, Cambridge Univ, Eng, 76; mem adv comt, Dept Metall, Univ Pa, 77-80. *Honors & Awards:* Hunt Award, 58; Award Excellence, Carborundum Co, 74; Dudley Award, Am Soc Testing & Mat, 75, Award Merit, 78; Nadai Award, Am Asn Mech Engrs, 79. *Mem:* Nat Acad Eng; fel Am Soc Mech Engrs; Am Inst Mining, Metall & Petrol Engrs; fel Am Soc Metals; fel Am Soc Testing & Mat. *Res:* Behavior of materials under stress; lubrication and friction; plasticity; metal working; fatigue. *Mailing Add:* 1178 Lowell Rd Schenectady NY 12308

COFFIN, PERLEY ANDREWS, b Newburyport, Mass, Oct 8, 08; m 39; c 1. RUBBER CHEMISTRY, POLYMER CHEMISTRY. *Educ:* Northeastern Univ, BChE, 31; Mass Inst Technol, MS, 33. *Prof Exp:* Lab asst, Simplex Wire & Cable Co, Mass, 30-31; control chemist, Vultex Chem Co, 33-37; develop chemist, Gen Latex & Chem Corp, 37-42; lab mgr, Gen Tire & Rubber Co, Tex, 43-45; sect head qual control, Gen Latex & Chem Corp, 46-61, lab mgr, 62-78; RETIRED. *Mem:* Am Chem Soc; Am Soc Testing & Mat. *Res:* Polymerization; rubber; synthetic resin and plastics; latex. *Mailing Add:* 4 Hammond St Gloucester MA 01930

COFFINO, PHILIP, b New York, NY, Sept 7, 42. CELL BIOLOGY, GENETICS. *Educ:* Univ Calif, Berkeley, BA, 63; Einstein Col Med, PhD, 71, MD, 72. *Prof Exp:* Resident, Cancer Res Inst, 73-74, ASST PROF MICROBIOL, UNIV CALIF, 74-, ASST PROF RESIDENCE, DEPT MED, 75- *Concurrent Pos:* Am Cancer Soc fac res award; NIH res career develop award. *Honors & Awards:* Trygve Tuve Mem Award, NIH, 77. *Mem:* Am Soc Clin Invest; Am Soc Biol Chemists. *Res:* Genetics of animal cells, mutagenesis; hormone and cyclic nucleotide mediated regulation; growth regulation. *Mailing Add:* Dept of Microbiol & Immunol Univ of Calif San Francisco CA 94143

COFFMAN, CHARLES BENJAMIN, b Baltimore, Md, Dec 19, 41; m 71; c 2. AGRONOMY. *Educ:* Univ Md, BS, 66, MS, 69, PhD(soil mineral), 72. *Prof Exp:* Asst geol, Univ Md, 66-71, instr 72; RES AGRONOMIST, AGR ENVIRON QUAL INST, AGR RES SERV, USDA, 72- *Concurrent Pos:* Instr geol, Frederick Community Col, 73-; Ed, Northeastern Weed Soc. *Mem:* Am Soc Agron; Soil Sci Soc Am; Clay Mineral Soc; AAAS; Weed Sci Soc Am. *Res:* Evaluation of potential new herbicides and controlled release formulations of existing herbicides; weed control in no-till agriculture; herbicide-narcotic plant relationships. *Mailing Add:* AEQI Agr Res Serv USDA Bldg 050 ARC-West Beltsville MD 20705

COFFMAN, CHARLES VERNON, b Hagerstown, Md, Oct 23, 35; m 63; c 2. MATHEMATICS. *Educ:* Johns Hopkins Univ, BES, 57, PhD(math), 62. *Prof Exp:* Assoc engr, Appl Physics Lab, Johns Hopkins Univ, 57; vis mem res staff math, Res Inst Advan Study, Martin Co, Md, 60; from asst prof to assoc prof, 62-71, PROF MATH, CARNEGIE-MELLON UNIV, 71- *Mem:* Am Math Soc. *Res:* Differential equations and functional analysis. *Mailing Add:* Dept Math Carnegie-Mellon Univ Pittsburgh PA 15213

COFFMAN, HAROLD H, b Overbrook, Kans, Feb 16, 15; m 46; c 4. CHEMISTRY. *Educ:* Kans State Univ, BS, 40. *Prof Exp:* Res chemist, Bareco Oil Co, 40-42, 46-52, dir res, 52-55; dir, Barnsdall Res Group, 55-66, asst dir, Appln Res Lab, 66-70, MGR QUAL CONTROL, BARECO DIV, PETROLITE CORP, 70- *Mem:* Am Chem Soc; Am Soc Testing & Mat. *Res:* Microcrystalline petroleum waxes in regard to their properties; end use applications and processes of manufacturing. *Mailing Add:* Bareco Div Petrolite Corp PO Box 669 Barnsdall OK 74002

COFFMAN, JAMES BRUCE, b Cheyenne, Wyo, July 15, 25; m 50; c 4. GEOLOGY. *Educ:* Univ Nebr, BC, 50. *Prof Exp:* Gen mgr geol res, Exxon Prod Res Co, 67-70, explor mgr, Esso Explor, Inc, 70-72, mgr, Prod Dept, Esso Europe, 72-74, exec vpres, Esso Explor & Prod UK, Inc, 73-74, VPRES EXPLOR RES, EXXON PROD RES CO, 74- *Mem:* Am Asn Petrol Geologists; Soc Explor Geophysicists; Am Petrol Inst; Am Geol Inst; Geol Soc Am. *Mailing Add:* Exxon Prod Res Co PO Box 2189 Houston TX 77001

COFFMAN, JAY D, b Quincy, Mass, Nov 17, 28; m 55; c 4. INTERNAL MEDICINE. *Educ:* Harvard Col, BA, 50; Boston Univ, MD, 54. *Prof Exp:* From asst to assoc prof, 60-70, PROF MED, MED CTR, BOSTON UNIV, 70- *Mem:* Am Physiol Soc; Am Fedn Clin Res; Am Heart Asn; Am Soc Clin Invests. *Res:* Peripheral vascular physiology and disease. *Mailing Add:* Peripheral Vascular Lab Univ Hosp 75 E Newton St Boston MA 02118

COFFMAN, JOHN W, b El Dorado, Kans, Dec 19, 31; m 54; c 3. PHYSICS. *Educ:* Univ Kans, BS, 54, MS, 56. *Prof Exp:* Res asst, Univ Kans, 54-56; physicist atmospheric acoustics, Missile Geophys Div, White Sands Missile Range, 58-60, supvry physicist, Missile Meteorol Div, 60-63, res atmospheric physicist, Environ Sci Dept, 63-67; WITH GODDARD SPACE FLIGHT CTR, NASA, 67- *Mem:* Am Phys Soc. *Res:* Polarizable dielectrics; atmospheric infrared absorption and emission spectra; low frequency sound propagation in the atmosphere. *Mailing Add:* 11004 Hunt Club Dr Potomac MD 20854

COFFMAN, MICHAEL S, forest ecology, plant physiology, see previous edition

COFFMAN, MOODY LEE, b Abilene, Tex, July 25, 25; m 47; c 4. THEORETICAL PHYSICS, ACOUSTICS. *Educ:* Abilene Christian Col, BA, 47; Univ Okla, MA & MS, 49; Agr & Mech Col Tex, PhD(physics), 54. *Prof Exp:* Instr physics, E Tex State Col, 49-51; instr, Agr & Mech Col Tex, 51-53, instr math, 53-54; sr nuclear engr, Convair, Tex, 54-55; from asst prof to assoc prof physics & math, Abilene Christian Col, 55-60, head dept, 56-60; sr physicist, Missile & Space Systs Dept, Hamilton Standard Div, United Aircraft Corp, Conn, 60-61; prof physics & head dept, Oklahoma City Univ, 61-69; PROF PHYSICS, CENT STATE UNIV, OKLA, 69- *Concurrent Pos:* Adj prof, Tex Christian Univ, 54-55; adj assoc prof physics, Hartford Grad Ctr, Rensselaer Polytech Inst, 60-61; consult, Convair, 55-57; consult physics, 69-; vpres res, Acoustic Controls, Inc, Tex, 69- *Mem:* Am Phys Soc; Am Math Soc; Am Asn Physics Teachers; Am Geophys Union; Sigma Xi. *Res:* Electromagnetic theory and quantum mechanics related to molecular and atomic structure; mechanics of charged particles; geomagnetism. *Mailing Add:* 3612 Ann Arbor Ave Oklahoma City OK 73122

COFFMAN, ROBERT EDGAR, b Grosse Pointe Farms, Mich, Jan 5, 31; m 59; c 3. CHEMICAL PHYSICS. *Educ:* Univ Ill, BS, 53; Univ Calif, Berkeley, MS, 55; Univ Minn, PhD(chem physics), 64. *Prof Exp:* Chemist, Hanford Atomic Prod Oper, Gen Elec Co, Wash, 55-56; chemist, Chemet Prog, NY, 56-57, phys chemist, Advan Semiconductor Prod Dept, 57-60; NSF fel physics, Nottingham Univ, 64-65; asst prof chem, Augsburg Col, 65-67; from asst prof to assoc prof, 67-79, PROF CHEM, UNIV IOWA, 79- *Concurrent Pos:* NATO sr fel, Cambridge Univ, 73. *Mem:* AAAS; Am Phys Soc; Am Chem Soc. *Res:* Quantum chemistry; electron paramagnetic resonance in inorganic, metal-ligand and biological molecules. *Mailing Add:* Dept of Chem Univ of Iowa Iowa City IA 52242

COFFMAN, WILLIAM PAGE, b Vandergrift, Pa, Jan 7, 42; m 65; c 2. ECOLOGY, LIMNOLOGY. *Educ:* Thiel Col, BS, 63; Univ Pittsburgh, PhD(biol), 67. *Prof Exp:* Hydrobiologist, Karlsruhe, Ger, 68-69; asst prof, 69-74, ASSOC PROF ECOL, UNIV PITTSBURGH, 74- *Res:* Energy flow in aquatic ecosystems; ecology and taxonomy of aquatic insects, particularly the Dipteran family Chironomidae. *Mailing Add:* Dept of Biol Sci Univ of Pittsburgh Pittsburgh PA 15260

COFRANCESCO, ANTHONY J, b New Haven, Conn, Feb 24, 10; m 41; c 3. INDUSTRIAL ORGANIC CHEMISTRY. *Educ:* Wesleyan Univ, BA, 33, MA, 34; Yale Univ, PhD(org chem), 39. *Prof Exp:* Res chemist, Calco Chem Co, NJ, 39-44; chief chemist, Arnold & Hofmann, RI, 44-45 & Carwin Chem Co, Conn, 45-50; group leader, 50-54, sect mgr, TPM Dyes, 54-58 & Intermediates, 58-62, mgr, Chem Specialty Sect, GAF Corp, Rensselaer, 62-75; CONSULT INDUST ORG CHEM, 75- *Res:* Anthraquinone intermediates and dyes; industrial organic chemicals. *Mailing Add:* Knight Road Delanson NY 12053

COGAN, DAVID GLENDENNING, b Fall River, Mass, Feb 14, 08; m 34; c 3. OPHTHALMOLOGY. *Educ:* Dartmouth Col, AB, 29; Harvard Univ, MD, 32. *Prof Exp:* Asst ophthal, 34-40, from asst prof to prof ophthalmic res, 40-63, Henry Willard Williams prof ophthal, 63-70, prof, 70-74, actg dir lab, 40-42, dir, Howe Lab Ophthal, 43-74, EMER HENRY WILLARD WILLIAMS PROF OPHTHAL, HARVARD MED SCH, 74-; CHIEF, NEURO-OPHTHAL SECT, NAT EYE INST, NIH, 76- *Concurrent Pos:* Moseley traveling fel, Harvard Med Sch, 37-38; asst ophthal, Mass Eye & Ear Infirmary, 34-40, clin asst, 35-39, from asst surgeon to surgeon, 39-74, dir, Ophthal Labs, 47-74, chief ophthal, 60-66; consult, Los Alamos Med Ctr; mem comt ophthalmic consults, Nat Res Coun; coun inst neurol & blindness, USPHS; mem coun, Nat Eye Inst, 70-73; ed-in-chief, AMA, Arch of Ophthal, 60-67; med officer USPHS, 74-76. *Mem:* AAAS; AMA; Am Soc Clin Invests; Am Neurol Soc; Can Ophthal Soc. *Res:* Clinical physiology of the eye; neuro-ophthalmology. *Mailing Add:* Bldg 10 Rm 1355261 Nat Insts of Health Bethesda MD 22014

COGAN, EDWARD J, b Milwaukee, Wis, Jan 18, 25; m 47; c 1. MATHEMATICAL LOGIC. *Educ:* Univ Wis, BA, 46, MA, 48; Pa State Univ, PhD(math philos), 55. *Prof Exp:* Instr math, Pa State Univ, 48-50, 51-55 & Dartmouth Col, 55-57; MEM FAC, SARAH LAWRENCE COL, 57- *Concurrent Pos:* Dir, NSF Insts, 59-64, co-dir, Upward Bound Prog, 66-69; consult, Metrop Sch Study Coun, 59-60; co-dir, Spec Prog, Sarah Lawrence Col, 74-78. *Mem:* Math Asn Am; Asn Symbolic Logic. *Res:* Foundations of mathematics; theory of sets; combinatory logic; automatic programming languages for computers. *Mailing Add:* Dept of Math Sarah Lawrence Col Bronxville NY 10708

COGAN, HAROLD LOUIS, b Framingham, Mass, May 30, 31; m 55; c 2. PHYSICAL CHEMISTRY. *Educ:* Univ Mass, BS, 54; Yale Univ, MS, 56, PhD(phys chem), 58. *Prof Exp:* Asst, Yale Univ, 54-56, NSF asst phys chem of electrolytes, 56-57; PRES, HAROLD L COGAN, INC, 57- *Mem:* Am Chem Soc. *Res:* Thermodynamic studies of the effect of pressure upon ionic equilibria; pressure and temperature dependence of the dielectric constant of water; use of coaxial cavity resonators for dielectric constant measurements. *Mailing Add:* 2600 Hampshire Rd SE Grand Rapids MI 49506

COGAN, ILIE ADRIAN, b Bucharest, Romania, Feb 11, 46; m 70; c 2. ELECTRONICS, SOLID STATE PHYSICS. *Educ:* Polytech Inst, Bucharest, BS, 68, MS, 69, PhD(solid state physics), 75. *Prof Exp:* Res electronics, Inst Semiconductor Res, 69-73; group leader, 73-75, lab chief, 75-77; TECH STAFF MEM SEMICONDUCTOR DEVICES, GTE LABS, WALTHAM, 78- *Concurrent Pos:* Mem, Nat Romanian Comn for Microwave Applns, 75-76. *Mem:* Inst Elec & Electronics Engrs; Sigma Xi; Electrochem Soc. *Res:* Microwave semiconductor devices; metal-semiconductor devices and contacts; electrical field analysis in planar microwave structures; semiconductor devices processing. *Mailing Add:* GTE Labs 40 Sylvan Rd Waltham MA 02154

COGAN, JERRY ALBERT, JR, b Flushing, NY, Jan 22, 35; m 58; c 3. CHEMICAL ENGINEERING. *Educ:* Amherst Col, BA, 56; Mass Inst Technol, SM, 58. *Prof Exp:* Instr chem eng, Mass Inst Technol, 57-58; chem engr, E I du Pont de Nemours & Co, Inc, 58-61; chem engr, Deering Milliken Res Corp, 61, prod supvr, Deering Milliken, Inc, 62, new prod mgr, 62, exec vpres, 63, PRES, MILLIKEN RES CORP, 64- *Mem:* Inst Chem Engrs; Am Asn Textile Chem & Colorists. *Res:* Research and development management. *Mailing Add:* Milliken Res Corp PO Box 1927 Spartanburg SC 29301

COGBILL, BELL A, b Marianna, Ark, Mar 18, 09; m 43; c 4. ELECTRICAL ENGINEERING. *Educ:* Univ Tenn, BSEE, 31, MS, 36. *Prof Exp:* Instr elec eng, Univ Tenn, 34-36; engr, Gen Elec Co, 36-64; from assoc prof to prof elec eng, Northeastern Univ, 64-74; RETIRED. *Mem:* AAAS; fel Inst Elec & Electronics Engrs; Am Soc Eng Educ; Nat Soc Prof Engrs. *Res:* Electromagnetic characteristics of large power transformers; power system engineering; electric power circuits; power transformers design. *Mailing Add:* 51 Jackson Rd Wellesley Hills MA 02181

COGBURN, ROBERT RAY, b Weatherford, Tex, Mar 3, 35; m 58; c 4. ENTOMOLOGY. *Educ:* Univ Tex A&M Univ, BS, 58, MS, 61. *Prof Exp:* Entomologist, Agr Res Serv, USDA, Tex, 59-63; res entomologist, Stored Prod Insects Br, Calif, 63-66, Ga, 66-69, RES ENTOMOLOGIST, AGR RES SERV, USDA, STORED RICE INSECTS LAB, BEAUMONT, TEX, 69- *Mem:* Entom Soc Am. *Res:* Research with insects affecting stored rice. *Mailing Add:* Stored-Rice Insects Lab USDA Rte 7 Box 999 Beaumont TX 77706

COGDELL, THOMAS JAMES, b Quanah, Tex, Aug 19, 34; m 61; c 4. ORGANIC CHEMISTRY. *Educ:* Midwestern Univ, BA, 55; Univ Tex, MA, 62; Harvard Univ, PhD(chem), 65. *Prof Exp:* Chemist, Dow Chem Co, 55-58; mem tech staff, Bell Tel Labs, 65-66; asst prof, 66-74, ASSOC PROF CHEM,

UNIV TEX, ARLINGTON, 74- *Mem:* AAAS; Am Chem Soc. *Res:* Organic reaction mechanisms; carbonium ion rearrangements; stable free radicals; benzyne intermediates. *Mailing Add:* Dept of Chem Univ of Tex Arlington TX 76019

COGEN, WILLIAM MAURICE, b Chicago, Ill, Mar 30, 09; m 41; c 2. GEOLOGY. *Educ:* Calif Inst Technol, BS, 31, MS, 33, PhD(geol), 37. *Prof Exp:* Petrol geologist, Superior Oil Co, Tex, 36-37 & Shell Oil Co, 37-62; consult, 63-67; supvr tech writers, Lockheed Electronics Co, 67-74; GEOL CONSULT, 74- *Mem:* Geol Soc Am; Am Asn Petrol Geologists. *Res:* Heavy minerals of Gulf Coast sediments; mechanics of landslides; geology of Texas Gulf coast; petroleum geology. *Mailing Add:* 11 Hawks Hill Ct Oakland CA 94618

COGGESHALL, NORMAN DAVID, b Ridgefarm, Ill, May 15, 16; m 40; c 4. PHYSICS. *Educ:* Univ Ill, BA, 37, MS, 39, PhD(physics), 42. *Prof Exp:* Asst physics, Univ Ill, 37-41, instr, 42-43; dir, Phys Sci Div, Gulf Res & Develop Co, 43-66, dir, Proc Sci Dept, 66-70, dir, Explor & Prod Dept, 70-74, vpres, Explor & Prod, 74-76, vpres, Govt-Technol Coordr, 76-80; CONSULT, 81- *Concurrent Pos:* Mem adv bd, Nat Bur Stand. *Honors & Awards:* Recipient of Resolution of Appreciation, Div Refining, Am Petrol Inst; Award, Am Chem Soc, 69. *Mem:* Am Chem Soc; Am Phys Soc. *Res:* Mass, infrared and ultraviolet spectroscopy; molecular physics; general research management; separation processes; process instrumentation. *Mailing Add:* 701 Driftwood Dr Lynn Haven FL 32444

COGGESHALL, RICHARD E, b Chicago, Ill, May 29, 32; m 59; c 4. ANATOMY. *Educ:* Univ Chicago, BA, 51; Harvard Med Sch, MD, 56. *Prof Exp:* Instr anat, Harvard Med Sch, 64-65, assoc, 65-67, from asst prof to assoc prof, 67-71; PROF ANAT, PHYSIOL & BIOPHYS, UNIV TEX MED BR, GALVESTON, 71- *Concurrent Pos:* USPHS career develop award, 66-; NIH fels, Univ Tex Med Br, Galveston, 71-74 & 75-79, NIH grant, 71- *Mem:* Am Asn Anatomists; Am Soc Cell Biol; Am Soc Neurosci; Sigma Xi; AAAS. *Res:* Neurobiology and the structure of the nervous system. *Mailing Add:* Marine Biomed Inst 200 University Blvd Galveston TX 77550

COGGIN, JOSEPH HIRAM, b Birmingham, Ala, Feb 4, 38; m 57; c 4. MICROBIOLOGY, VIROLOGY. *Educ:* Vanderbilt Univ, BA, 59; Univ Tenn, MS, 61; Univ Chicago, PhD(midrobiol), 65. *Prof Exp:* Sr bacteriologist, Tenn Dept Pub Health, 59-60; sr res virologist virus & cell biol div, Merck Inst; therapeut res, 65-67; asst prof & virologist, Univ Tenn, Knoxville, 67-68, assoc prof microbiol, 68-73, prof microbiol, 73-77; PROF & CHMN, UNIV SOUTH ALA, 77- *Concurrent Pos:* Sect chief & consult, Molecular Anat Prog, Tumor transplanation Study, Oak Ridge Nat Labs, 68-; mem immunol sci study sect, Nat Cancer Inst, 75. *Mem:* AAAS; Tissue Culture Asn; Soc Exp Biol & Med; Am Soc Microbiol; Am Asn Immunol. *Res:* Drug resistance in microorganisms; tumor immunology; virology of cancer. *Mailing Add:* Dept Microbiol/Immunol Univ So Ala Mobile AL 36688

COGGINS, CHARLES WILLIAM, JR, b NC, Nov 17, 30; m 51; c 3. PLANT PHYSIOLOGY. *Educ:* NC State Col, BS, 52, MS, 54; Univ Calif, PhD(plant physiol), 58. *Prof Exp:* Asst plant physiologist, 57-64, assoc plant physiologist, 64-70, PLANT PHYSIOLOGIST, DEPT BOT & PLANT SCI, CITRUS RES CTR, UNIV CALIF, RIVERSIDE, 70-, PROF PLANT PHYSIOL & CHMN DEPT BOT & PLANT SCI, 75- *Honors & Awards:* Am Soc Hort Sci Award, 66. *Mem:* AAAS; Am Soc Hort Sci; Am Soc Plant Physiologists; Am Inst Biol Sci; Int Soc Citricult. *Res:* Evaluation of vegetative, reproductive and fruit quality responses of citrus, avocado and other subtropical fruit to plant regulators. *Mailing Add:* Dept of Bot & Plant Sci Univ of Calif Riverside CA 92521

COGGINS, JAMES RAY, b Denton, NC, Dec 2, 47; m 70; c 2. PARASITOLOGY, ELECTRON MICROSCOPY. *Educ:* E Carolina Univ, BA, 70, MA, 72; Wake Forest Univ, PhD(biol), 75. *Prof Exp:* Res assoc parasitol, Univ Notre Dame, 75-77; ASST PROF ZOOL, UNIV WIS-MILWAUKEE, 77- *Concurrent Pos:* NIH trainee fel, 75-77. *Mem:* Am Soc Parasitologists; Electron Micros Soc Am; Am Micros Soc; AAAS. *Res:* Growth and development of parasitic helminths. *Mailing Add:* 8644 N 56th Milwaukee WI 53223

COGGINS, LEROY, b Thomasville, NC, July 29, 32; m 56; c 5. VETERINARY VIROLOGY. *Educ:* NC State Col, BS, 55; Okla State Univ, DVM, 57; Cornell Univ, PhD(vet virol), 62. *Prof Exp:* Vet res officer virus res, Ft Detrick, Md, 57-59; asst, NY State Col Vet Med, Cornell Univ, 59-62; res assoc, Cornell Univ, 62-63; vet res officer, EAfrican Vet Res Orgn, USDA, 63-68; prof virol, NY State Col Vet Med, Cornell Univ, 68-80; PROF & HEAD DEPT MICROBIOL, PATH & PARASITOL, SCH VET MED, NC STATE UNIV, 80- *Mem:* Am Vet Med Asn; US Livestock Sanit Asn; Conf Res Workers Animal Dis; Am Asn Equine Practrs. *Res:* Virus research; viruses of variola, hog cholera, bovine virus diarrhea and African swine fever and the host response to these agents; equine infectious anemia; equine influenza. *Mailing Add:* Dept of Path NY State Col Vet Med Cornell Univ Ithaca NY 14853

COGGON, PHILIP, b Kirkby, Eng, Mar 22, 42; US citizen; m 65; c 1. FOOD CHEMISTRY. *Educ:* Univ Nottingham, BS, 63, PhD(chem), 66. *Prof Exp:* Res fel chem, Univ Sussex, 66-68; res assoc crystallog, Duke Univ, 68-70; group leader tea res, Thomas J Lipton, Inc, 70-76, mgr bev res & process develop, 76-78; MGR TECH SERV, ROYAL ESTATE TEA CO, 79- *Mem:* Royal Soc Chem; Am Chem Soc; Inst Food Technologists. *Res:* Organic chemistry of natural products from food sources; process and product development of beverage products. *Mailing Add:* 800 Sylvan Ave Royal Estate Tea Co Englewood Cliffs NJ 07632

COGHLAN, ANNE EVELINE, b Boston, Mass, Mar 29, 27. MICROBIOLOGY. *Educ:* Simmons Col, BS, 48; Boston Univ, MEd, 53; Univ Vt, MS, 57; Univ RI, PhD(biol sci), 65. *Prof Exp:* Instr bact, Colby Jr Col, 49-59; NSF fel, 59-61; chmn dept, 72-78, PROF BIOL, SIMMONS COL, 62-, DEAN SCI, 78- *Mem:* AAAS; Am Soc Microbiol; Am Soc Cell Biol. *Res:* General microbiology; basic bacteriology; immunology; host-parasite relationships. *Mailing Add:* Simmons Col Boston MA 02115

COGHLAN, DAVID B(UELL), b Cleveland, Ohio; m 42, 69; c 5. CHEMICAL ENGINEERING. *Educ:* Yale Univ, BChE, 41. *Prof Exp:* Chemist, Gen Chem Co, 41-42, TNT mfg foreman, 42-43, res engr, 43-46; res engr, E I du Pont de Nemours & Co, 46-49; head res eng div, 49-57, asst dir res, 57-62, mgr contract res, 62-65, MGR SPEC PROJ, FOOTE MINERAL CO, 65- *Mem:* Soc Indust & Appl Math; Am Inst Chem Engrs; Am Chem Soc; Am Inst Mining, Metall & Petrol Engrs. *Res:* Fluosulfonic acid; lithium chemical processes. *Mailing Add:* 124 Grubbs Mill Rd West Chester PA 19380

COGLEY, ALLEN C, b Grinnell, Iowa, Apr 16, 40; m 63; c 2. AERONAUTICAL ENGINEERING, ATMOSPHERIC SCIENCES. *Educ:* Iowa State Univ, BSAE, 62; Univ Va, MSAE, 64; Stanford Univ, PhD(aeronaut sci), 68. *Prof Exp:* Res scientist, Langley Res Ctr, NASA, 62-63; from asst prof to assoc prof, 68-79, PROF FLUID MECH, UNIV ILL, CHICAGO CIRCLE, 79- *Concurrent Pos:* NASA and NSF res grants. *Mem:* Am Inst Aeronaut & Astronaut; Am Meteorol Soc. *Res:* Wave propagation; radiative gas dynamics; radiative transfer; fluid mechanics. *Mailing Add:* Dept of Energy Eng Univ of Ill Chicago Circle Chicago IL 60680

COGLIANO, JOSEPH ALBERT, b Brooklyn, NY, Mar 4, 30. ORGANIC CHEMISTRY. *Educ:* Polytech Inst Brooklyn, BS, 51; Princeton Univ, MA, 56, PhD, 58; George Washington Univ, MS, 57. *Prof Exp:* Chemist, Nat Bur Stand, 51-53; res assoc, George Washington Univ, 53-54; asst, Princeton Univ, 54-57; RES ASSOC, W R GRACE & CO, 57- *Concurrent Pos:* Staff mem, Nat Acad Sci, 55. *Mem:* Am Chem Soc. *Res:* Organic research and synthesis; process development; organophosphorous chemistry; physico-chemical measurements; permeability; foams-preparation and properties; technical trouble shooting; technical program management; bound enzymes. *Mailing Add:* 1268 Maple Ave Baltimore MD 21227

COGSWELL, GEORGE WALLACE, b New York, NY, Feb 8, 23; m 49; c 4. ORGANIC CHEMISTRY. *Educ:* City Col New York, BS, 53; Fordham Univ, MS, 55, PhD(org chem), 60. *Prof Exp:* Chemist indust detergents, Colgate-Palmolive Co, NJ, 50-53; lab asst, Fordham Univ, 54-57; res assoc, Dept Pharmacol, Med Col, Cornell Univ, 57-58; sr develop chemist-proj coord, A E Staley Mfg Co, 58-64; sect mgr, A-U Proj, Armour & Co, 64-65; mkt develop mgr, Hooker Chem Co, Inc, 65-68; vpres, Woodburn Anal Lab & Vanguard Chem Co, 68-72; pres, Arlington Serv Corp, 72-78; PRES, FIELDING CHEM CO, INC, 78- *Concurrent Pos:* Pres, Woodburn Anal Lab, 68-; instr chem, Anderson Col, SC, 74- *Mem:* Am Chem Soc; Am Oil Chem Soc; Am Asn Textile Chem & Colorists; Am Pharmaceut Asn; Tech Asn Pulp & Paper Indust. *Res:* Synthetic and natural polymers; specialty and fine chemicals; coatings; paper; detergents, ozonolysis; structure activity studies; instrumental and wet analyses. *Mailing Add:* Fielding Chem Co PO Box 282 Anderson SC 29621

COGSWELL, HOWARD LYMAN, b Susquehanna Co, Pa, Jan 19, 15; m 38; c 1. ORNITHOLOGY, ECOLOGY. *Educ:* Whittier Col, BA, 48; Univ Calif, Berkeley, MA, 51, PhD(zool), 62. *Prof Exp:* Asst prof biol sci, Mills Col, 52-64; assoc prof, 64-69, prof, 69-80, EMER PROF BIOL SCI, CALIF STATE UNIV, HAYWARD, 80- *Concurrent Pos:* NSF sci fac fel, 63-64. *Mem:* Am Ornith Union; Cooper Ornith Soc; Ecol Soc Am; Wilson Ornith Soc. *Res:* Habits, phenology and populations of birds of California; territory size in birds of chaparral; habitat distribution and selection in birds; biology of shorebirds in relation to tides; solid waste disposal; bird hazard to aircraft. *Mailing Add:* Dept of Biol Sci Calif State Univ Hayward CA 94542

COGSWELL, HOWARD WINWOOD, b Sherman, Tex, Apr 22, 23; m 47; c 1. ANALYTICAL CHEMISTRY. *Educ:* Austin Col, BS, 47. *Prof Exp:* Jr chemist, Cities Serv Refining Corp, 48-49, anal chemist, Cities Serv Res & Develop Co, 49-53, sr anal chemist, 53-56, sect leader, 56-60, sr res chemist, 58-60, res assoc, 60-61; head anal res group, Petro-Tex Chem Corp, 61-77; SUPT, ANAL SERV & QUAL CONTROL, DENKA CHEM CORP, 77- *Mem:* Am Chem Soc. *Res:* Catalytic petroleum processing; catalyst reactivation and development; research, design, and construction in gas chromatography; analytical instrumentation and methods development. *Mailing Add:* 526 Shawnee Houston TX 77034

COHART, EDWARD MAURICE, b New York, NY, Dec 8, 09; m 33; c 2. PUBLIC HEALTH. *Educ:* Columbia Univ, AB, 28, MD, 33, MPH, 47; Am Bd Prev Med & Pub Health, dipl. *Hon Degrees:* MA, Yale Univ, 56. *Prof Exp:* Assoc prof, 48-56, chmn dept epidemiol & pub health, 66-68, prof pub health, 56-78, EMER PROF PUB HEALTH, SCH MED, YALE UNIV, 78- *Concurrent Pos:* Cancer control consult, USPHS, 47-48; dep comnr, Dept Health, NY, 55-56, mem adv coun, Nat Inst Environ Health Sci, 69-73. *Mem:* AAAS; AMA; Am Cancer Asn; Am Col Prev Med (vpres pub health, 73-74); Am Pub Health Asn. *Res:* Epidemiology of chronic disease; public health practice. *Mailing Add:* 625 Ellsworth Ave New Haven CT 06511

COHEE, GEORGE VINCENT, b Indianapolis, Ind, Feb 4, 07; m 30. PETROLEUM GEOLOGY. *Educ:* Univ Ill, BS, 31-33, MS, 32, PhD(geol), 37. *Prof Exp:* Asst geologist, Oil & Gas Div, State Geol Surv, Ill, 36-42; asst state geologist, State Geol Surv, Ind, 42-43; petrol analyst, Petrol Admin for War, 43; geologist, Fuels Br, US Geol Surv, 43-47, sr geologist, 47-51, chmn geol names comt, 52-77. *Concurrent Pos:* Chmn geol dept, Univ Ark, 51-52. *Mem:* Fel Geol Soc Am; Soc Econ Paleontologists & Mineralogists; hon mem Am Asn Petrol Geologists (secy-treas, 60-62). *Res:* Stratigraphy and petroleum geology. *Mailing Add:* 5508 Namakagan Rd Bethesda MD 20816

COHEN, ABRAHAM BERNARD, b Philadelphia, Pa, July 19, 22; m 53; c 2. ORGANIC CHEMISTRY, PHOTOCHEMISTRY. *Educ:* Temple Univ, AB, 48; Cornell Univ, PhD(chem), 52. *Prof Exp:* Asst, Temple Univ, 47-48 & Cornell Univ, 48-50; sr res chemist, Photo Prod Dept, 51-55, res supvr, 55-65, res fel, 65-66, res mgr, 66-69, mgr new prod develop, 69-70, mgr photopolymer systs, 70-72, dir res, 72-80, DIR RES ELECTRONICS, E I DU PONT DE NEMOURS & CO, INC, 81- *Concurrent Pos:* Gen chmn, First Int Symp Photpolymerization, Washington, DC, 78. *Honors & Awards:*

Indust Res Mag IR 100 Award, 69, 74 & 75; Kosar Mem Award, Soc Photog Sci & Eng, 79; Com Develop Asn Honor Award, 81. *Mem:* Am Chem Soc; Soc Photog Sci & Eng. *Res:* Correlation of structure and properties of polymers; mechanism of polymer reactions; photopolymerization; nonconventional photographic systems; dimensionally stable film bases and coatings; photoresist films and equipment; photopolymer printing plates, color proofing systems and graphic arts systems; new venture management. *Mailing Add:* 33 Hemlock Terr Springfield NJ 07081

COHEN, ADOLPH IRVIN, b New York, NY, Apr 7, 24; m 55; c 2. NEUROBIOLOGY. *Educ:* City Col New York, BS, 48; Columbia Univ, MA, 50, PhD(zool), 54. *Prof Exp:* From instr to asst prof anat, 55-64, res assoc prof ophthal, 64-70, chmn univ comt neurobiol, 70-74, PROF ANAT & NEUROBIOL IN OPHTHAL, SCH MED, WASH UNIV, 70-, PROF ANAT & NEUROBIOL, 70- *Concurrent Pos:* USPHS fel, Univ Calif, Berkeley, 53-54 & Wash Univ, 54-55; mem bd trustees, Asn Res Vision & Ophthal, 73-78. *Mem:* AAAS; Soc Neurosci; Am Soc Cell Biol; Asn Res Vision & Ophthal; Am Asn Anat. *Res:* Vision; cell biology; receptor physiology. *Mailing Add:* 4550 Scott Ave St Louis MO 63110

COHEN, ALAN MATHEW, b Chicago, Ill, Mar 22, 43. BIOLOGY, EMBRYOLOGY. *Educ:* Univ Ill, BSc, 64; Univ Va, PhD(biol), 69. *Prof Exp:* ASST PROF ANAT, SCH MED, JOHNS HOPKINS UNIV, 71- *Concurrent Pos:* USPHS fel anat, Harvard Med Sch, 69-71 & grant, 74-77; Nat Found March Dimes Basil O'Conner grant, 74-76; Nat Found March Dimes res grant, 77-80; USPHS grant, 78-81. *Mem:* AAAS; Am Soc Zoologists; Soc Develop Biol. *Res:* Regulation of cellular events during embryogenesis; neural crest as a model system for the study of development. *Mailing Add:* Dept of Cell Biol & Anat Johns Hopkins Univ Sch of Med Baltimore MD 21205

COHEN, ALAN SEYMOUR, b Boston, Mass, Apr 9, 26; m 54; c 3. MEDICINE. *Educ:* Harvard Univ, AB, 47; Boston Univ, MD, 52. *Prof Exp:* Instr, Harvard Med Sch, 58-60; from asst prof to prof, 60-72, CONRAD WESSELHOEFT PROF MED, SCH MED, BOSTON UNIV, 72-, DIR ARTHRITIS & CONNECTIVE TISSUE DIS SECT, UNIV HOSP, 60-; CHIEF MED, HOSP & DIR THORNDIKE MEM LAB, BOSTON CITY HOSP, 73- *Concurrent Pos:* Fel med, Harvard Med Sch, 53; res fel, 56-58; consult, USPHS, 66-70; Bernadine Becker Mem lectr, 69; consult, Food & Drug Admin, 70-; mem gen med study sect A, Nat Inst Arthritis, Metab & Digestive Dis, 72-76; Wallace-Graham Mem lectr, Queen's Univ, Ont, 73; chmn med & sci comt, Mass Arthritis Found (pres, 81-82); mem House Deleg & bd trustees, Arthritis Found, 76-, mem budget & finance comt, 77-78; Tyndale vis prof, Univ Utah Sch Med, 78. *Honors & Awards:* Maimonides Award, Boston Med Soc, 52. *Mem:* Am Soc Clin Invest; Am Fedn Clin Res; Asn Am Physicians; Am Soc Cell Biol; Am Soc Exp Path. *Res:* Internal medicine; rheumatology; electron microscopy. *Mailing Add:* Thorndike 314 Boston City Hosp 818 Harrison Ave Boston MA 02118

COHEN, ALEX, b New York, NY, Feb 7, 31. ORGANIC CHEMISTRY, CLINICAL CHEMISTRY. *Educ:* Brooklyn Col, 54. *Prof Exp:* ORG CHEMIST, NAT BUR STANDARDS, 57- *Mem:* Am Chem Soc. *Res:* Synthesis and reaction mechanisms of carbohydrates and nitrogen mustards; clinical standard characterization-cholesterol; anticancer agents; fluorinated compounds; stable isotope-labeled clinical compounds. *Mailing Add:* 5811 14th St NW Washington DC 20011

COHEN, ALLEN IRVING, b New York, NY, May 26, 32; m 54; c 3. ANALYTICAL CHEMISTRY, STRUCTURAL CHEMISTRY. *Educ:* City Col New York, BS, 54; Syracuse Univ, PhD(chem), 58. *Prof Exp:* Asst instr, Syracuse Univ, 54, AEC asst, 54-57; res chemist anal chem, Gulf Res & Develop Co, 57-59; sr res chemist, 59-66, res assoc, 66-69, res group leader, 69-72, SECT HEAD MOLECULAR SPECTROS, SQUIBB INST MED RES, 72- *Mem:* Am Chem Soc; The Chem Soc; Am Soc Mass Spectrometry. *Res:* Structure determination of organic compounds and natural products by physicochemical methods; nuclear magnetic resonance and ultraviolet spectroscopy; organic polarography; radio chemistry, coprecipitation phenomena; developmental analytical methods; mass spectrometry and development of computer data acquisition programs. *Mailing Add:* Squibb Inst for Med Res PO Box 4000 Princeton NJ 08540

COHEN, ALONZO CLIFFORD, JR, b Stone Co, Miss, Sept 4, 11; m 34; c 3. STATISTICS, QUALITY CONTROL. *Educ:* Ala Polytech Univ, BS, 32, MS, 33; Univ Mich, MA, 40, PhD(statist), 41. *Prof Exp:* Student engr, Westinghouse Elec & Mfg Co, 33-34; instr math, Ala Polytech Univ, 34-40; from instr to asst prof, Mich State Univ, 40-47; assoc prof, 47-52, prof math, 52-64, dir, Inst Statist, 59-65, prof, 64-78, EMER PROF STATIST, UNIV GA, 78- *Concurrent Pos:* Consult, Opers Anal Off Hq, US Air Force, 50-72. *Honors & Awards:* Michael Award, Univ Ga, 54. *Mem:* Fel AAAS; fel Am Soc Qual Control; Inst Math Statist; fel Am Statist Asn; Math Asn Am. *Res:* Truncated frequency distributions; statistical methods of quality control; mathematical statistics. *Mailing Add:* Dept of Statist Univ of Ga Athens GA 30602

COHEN, ALVIN JEROME, b Louisville, Ky, July 21, 18; m 43, 69; c 4. GEOCHEMISTRY. *Educ:* Univ Fla, BS, 40; Univ Ill, PhD(inorg chem), 49. *Prof Exp:* Anal chemist, Tenn Valley Authority, Wilson Dam, Ala, 41; physicist closed bomb ballistics, Ind Ord Works, 42; chemist war alcohol prod, Joseph Seagram & Sons, 43; asst, Purdue Univ, 46-47 & Univ Ill, 47-49; fel, Calif Inst Technol, 49-50; chemist phys chem, Naval Ord Test Sta, China Lake, 50-53; from fel to sr fel, Mellon Inst, 53-62; PROF GEOCHEM, UNIV PITTSBURGH, 63- *Concurrent Pos:* Distinguished vis prof, Am Univ, Cairo, Egypt, 79. *Mem:* Am Mineral Soc; Am Geochem Soc; Meteoritical Soc; AAAS. *Res:* Radiation effects in silicate minerals and glasses; geochemistry of meteorites; vacuum UV spectra of minerals and meteorites. *Mailing Add:* Dept Earth & Planetary Sci Univ Pittsburgh Pittsburgh PA 15260

COHEN, ARNOLD A, b Duluth, Minn, Aug 1, 14; m 42; c 2. COMPUTER SCIENCE, PHYSICS. *Educ:* Univ Minn, BEE, 35, MS, 38, PhD(physics), 47. *Prof Exp:* Develop engr electron tubes, RCA Corp, 42-46; various tech mgt positions comput develop, Sperry Univac, 46-71; asst dean, Inst Technol, 71-81, SR FEL, CHARLES BABBAGE INST, UNIV MINN, 81- *Concurrent Pos:* Consult & mem sci adv bd, Dept Defense, 60-74; mem adv bd, Chem Abstr Serv, 70-73; mem bd trustees, Charles Babbage Inst, 78- *Honors & Awards:* Valuable Invention Citation, Am & Minn Patent Law Asns, 61. *Mem:* Fel Inst Elec & Electronics Engrs. *Res:* History of computing; gaseous conduction devices; mass spectrometry; magnetic drum information storage; digital computer systems; education technology; history of computing. *Mailing Add:* 3517 W 39th St Minneapolis MN 55410

COHEN, ARTHUR DAVID, b Wilmington, Del, Feb 26, 42; m 70; c 2. COAL & PEAT PETROLOGY, PALYNOLOGY. *Educ:* Univ Del, BS, 64; Pa State Univ, PhD(geol), 68. *Prof Exp:* Asst prof geol, Univ Ga, 68 & Southern Ill Univ, Carbondale, 69-74; geologist, Coal Resources Br, US Geol Surv, 74-75; assoc prof, 75-80, PROF GEOL, UNIV SC, 80- *Concurrent Pos:* Nat Sci Found grants, 69, 71, 73, 75, 77 & 79; Dept Energy grants, 79, 80 & 81; consult, projects dealing with peat and coal. *Mem:* AAAS; Geol Soc Am (chmn, coal geol div, 75-76); Bot Soc Am; Am Asn Stratig Palynologists; Am Asn Petrol Geologists. *Res:* Petrologic investigation of the peats of southern Florida with special reference to the origin of coal; coal petrology and geologic history of the Okefenokee Swamp from study of its peat sediments; economic characteristics of North Carolina, South Carolina and Georgia coastal peats. *Mailing Add:* Dept Geol Univ SC Columbia SC 29208

COHEN, ARTHUR LEROY, b Newport News, Va, Jan 22, 16; m 43; c 4. ELECTRON MICROSCOPY, RESEARCH ADMINISTRATION. *Educ:* Stanford Univ, AB, 37; Harvard Univ, MA, 39, PhD(bot), 40. *Prof Exp:* Sheldon traveling fel from Harvard Univ, Hopkins Marine Sta, 40-41; res fel, Calif Inst Technol, 42-47; prof biol, Oglethorpe Univ, 47-62; assoc prof biol & dir, Electron Micros Ctr, 62-79, prof bot & biol sci, 68-79, EMER PROF BOT & BIOL SCI, WASH STATE UNIV, 80- *Concurrent Pos:* Res assoc, Cedars of Lebanon Hosp, Los Angeles, 45-47; Guggenheim fel, Delft Univ Technol, 56-57; vis prof, Yale Sch Med, 71. *Mem:* Fel Royal Micros Soc; Electron Micros Soc Am; Electron Micros Soc Can; Soc Cell Biologists. *Res:* Experimental morphogenesis of Myxomycetes; general biology, ultrastructure; critical point drying; enzymatic and chemical subcellular dissection. *Mailing Add:* Electron Micros Ctr Rt 1 Box 468 Wash State Univ Pullman WA 99163

COHEN, AVIS HOPE, b Chicago, Ill, Nov 29, 41; m 61; c 2. NEUROPHYSIOLOGY, MOTOR PHYSIOLOGY. *Educ:* Univ Mich, BS, 64; Cornell Univ, PhD(neurobiol), 77. *Prof Exp:* Fel, Karolinska Inst, 77-79; res assoc, Washington Univ, 79-80; RES ASSOC, CORNELL UNIV, 80- *Mem:* Soc Neurosci. *Res:* Organization of systems of neurons which are responsible for generating temporally patterned activity; the spinal neurons of lampreys which generate swimming. *Mailing Add:* Sect Neurobiol Behavior Cornell Univ Ithaca NY 14853

COHEN, BARRY GEORGE, b New York, NY, June 2, 30; m 51; c 4. ELECTRICAL ENGINEERING, SEMICONDUCTOR PHYSICS. *Educ:* Brown Univ, ScB, 51; Johns Hopkins Univ, DEng, 59. *Prof Exp:* Mem tech staff, Bell Tel Labs, Inc, 59-68; Fulbright fel & vis prof elec eng, Israel Inst Technol, 68-69; PRES, RES DEVICES INC, 69- *Mem:* Am Phys Soc; Inst Elec & Electronics Engrs. *Res:* Infrared and optical properties of solids; semiconductor devices, including cryogenic and microwave devices. *Mailing Add:* Res Devices Inc 616 Springfield Ave Berkeley Heights NJ 07922

COHEN, BENNETT J, b Brooklyn, NY, Aug 2, 25; m 52; c 2. LABORATORY ANIMAL MEDICINE, COMPARATIVE MEDICINE. *Educ:* Cornell Univ, DVM, 49; Northwestern Univ, MS, 51, PhD(physiol), 53; Am Col Lab Animal Med, dipl, 58. *Prof Exp:* Veterinarian, Northwestern Univ, 49-53; statewide veterinarian, Univ Calif, Berkeley, 53-57; veterinarian, Univ Calif, Los Angeles, 54-62; from instr to asst prof, 56-62; assoc prof physiol & dir animal care unit, 62-67, PROF LAB ANIMAL MED & DIR UNIT FOR LAB ANIMAL MED, UNIV MICH, ANN ARBOR, 67- *Concurrent Pos:* Mem, Nat Adv Comn, Calif Primate Res Ctr, Univ Calif, Davis, 77-81; assoc ed, J Geront, 80. *Mem:* Am Vet Med Asn; Am Asn Lab Animal Sci (pres, 58-60); Am Physiol Soc; fel Geront Soc. *Res:* Pathology of aging in laboratory animals; diseases of laboratory animals. *Mailing Add:* Unit for Lab Animal Med Univ Mich Animal Res Facil Ann Arbor MI 48109

COHEN, BENNETT NATHANIEL, b New Haven, Conn, July 30, 48; m 73; c 1. RECOMBINANT DNA, PLANT MOLECULAR BIOLOGY. *Educ:* Univ Miami, Coral Gables, BS, 71; Ohio Univ, Athens, PhD(chem), 79. *Prof Exp:* Sr scientist, Dade Div, Am Hosp Supply Corp, Miami, 71-73; grad teaching asst chem, Ohio Univ, Athens, 73-79; fel, Dept Cell Biol, 79-80, ASST MEM, DEPT BIOCHEM, ROCHE INST MOLECULAR BIOL, 81- *Concurrent Pos:* vis asst prof, Dept Biochem Sci, Princeton Univ, 82. *Mem:* Sigma Xi. *Res:* Cloning and expression of photoinduced plant genes to elucidate the mechanism of photoinduced gene expression; tumor-virus bases recombinant mammalian cell vectors. *Mailing Add:* Dept Biochem Roche Inst Molecular Biol 340 Kingsland St Nutley NJ 07110

COHEN, BERNARD, b Wilmington, Del, Nov 2, 33; m 55; c 2. INORGANIC CHEMISTRY. *Educ:* Temple Univ, AB, 55; Univ Pa, MS, 57, PhD(chem), 63. *Prof Exp:* Chemist, Geol Surv, US Dept Interior, 55-57; res chemist, Pennsalt Chem Corp, 57-59 & Foote Mineral Co, 59-61; res fel chem, Univ Birmingham, 63-65; sr res chemist, 65-70, mgr process res, 70-74, dir specialty chem, 74-76, dir prod res, 76-78, dir prod & process develop, 78-79, DIR TECHNOL DEVELOP, FMC CORP, 79-81. *Mailing Add:* Indust Chem Group FMC Corp PO Box 8 Princeton NJ 08540

COHEN, BERNARD, b Newark, NJ, Apr 30, 29; m 55; c 3. NEUROLOGY, NEUROPHYSIOLOGY. *Educ:* Middlebury Col, AB, 50; NY Univ, MD, 54; Am Bd Psychiat & Neurol, dipl, 61. *Prof Exp:* Asst attend neurologist, Mt Sinai Hosp, New York, 61-66; assoc prof neurol & physiol, 66-69, prof neurol, 69-76, MORRIS B BENDER PROF NEUROL, MT SINAI SCH MED, 76-, DIR, NEUROBIOL GRAD PROG, 80- *Concurrent Pos:* Res fel neurophysiol, Col Physicians & Surgeons, Columbia Univ, 60-61; trainee, Nat Inst Neurol Dis & Blindness, 60-62; Nat Inst Neurol Dis & Stroke career res develop award, 67-73; assoc attend neurologist, Mt Sinai Hosp, New York, 66-69, attend neurologist, 69-; attend neurol, Elmhurst Gen Hosp; mem neurol study sect A, NIH, 77-82; expert in neurol, Food & Drug Admin, 75-80. *Mem:* Am Physiol Soc; Am Acad Neurol; Am Neurol Asn; Barany Soc; Asn Res Nervous & Mental Dis (secy-treas, 80). *Res:* Physiology of oculomotor and vestibular systems. *Mailing Add:* Mt Sinai Sch of Med One E 100th St New York NY 10029

COHEN, BERNARD ALLAN, b Fond du Lac, Wis, Oct 6, 46; m 69; c 4. BIOMEDICAL ENGINEERING, NEUROSCIENCE. *Educ:* Milwaukee Sch Eng, BSEE, 71; Marquette Univ, MSEE, 73, MSBME, 73, PhD(biomed eng), 75. *Prof Exp:* Res asst neurosci, Vet Admin Ctr, Wood, Wis, 72-75; sr res investr rehab, Emory Univ Rehab Res & Training Ctr, 75-78, asst prof rehab med, Sch Med, 75-78; DIR BIOMED ENG SECT, NEUROL, VET ADMIN CTR, WOOD WIS, 78-; ASST PROF NEUROL, MED COL WIS, 78-, DIR, ELECTRODIAG LABS, 79- *Concurrent Pos:* Instr eng, Milwaukee Sch Eng, 74-75; clin fel rehab med, Vet Admin Hosp, Atlanta, 75-76; curric consult, DeKalb Community Col, Decatur, 75-78; adj sr res engr, Ga Inst Technol, 77-78, adj asst prof mech eng, 77-78; consult biomed eng, Tech Adv Serv for Attys, Ft Washington, 77-; asst prof biomed eng, Marquette Univ, 78-; asst prof elec eng, Milwaukee Sch Eng, 78- *Mem:* Inst Elec & Electronics Engrs; Asn Advan Med Instrumentation; Am Soc Eng Educ; Instrument Soc Am; Sigma Xi. *Res:* Biomedical engineering involved with data acquisition and analysis aimed at the target population of patients suffering from neurological diseases. *Mailing Add:* 3264 N 50th St Milwaukee WI 53226

COHEN, BERNARD LEONARD, b Pittsburgh, Pa, June 14, 24; m 50; c 4. NUCLEAR PHYSICS, NUCLEAR ENGINEERING. *Educ:* Case Western Reserve Univ, BS, 44; Univ Pittsburgh, MS, 48; Carnegie Inst Technol, DSc(physics), 50. *Prof Exp:* Asst, Carnegie Inst Technol, 47-49; physicist & group leader, Oak Ridge Nat Lab, 50-58; assoc prof, 58-61, dir, Scaife Nuclear Physics Lab, 65-78, PROF PHYSICS, UNIV PITTSBURGH, 61- *Concurrent Pos:* Consult, Oak Ridge Nat Lab, 58-66, Nuclear Sci Eng Corp, 59-61, Gen Atomic, 59-60, NSF, 62, Inst Defense Anal, 62, Brookhaven Nat Lab, 65, Los Alamos Sci Lab, 68, World Publ Co, 69-70, Elec Power Res Inst, 75, Gen Accounting Off, 76-, Pac Legal Fedn, 77-78 & McGraw-Hill Energy Systs, 78- mem Nat Coun, Am Asn Physics Teachers, 73-76; mem exec comt, 71-73, chmn, Div of Nuclear Physics, Am Phys Soc, 74-75; vis staff, Inst Energy Anal, 74-75 & Argonne Nat Lab, 78-79. *Honors & Awards:* Bonner Prize, Am Phys Soc, 81. *Mem:* Fel Am Phys Soc; fel AAAS; Am Nuclear Soc; Health Physics Soc; Soc Risk Anal. *Res:* Nuclear structure; nuclear reactions and scattering; applied nuclear physics; environmental impacts of nuclear power; health effects of radiation and risk analysis. *Mailing Add:* 5414 Albemarle Ave Pittsburgh PA 15217

COHEN, BERNICE HIRSCHHORN, b Baltimore, Md, Apr 25, 24; m; c 2. HUMAN GENETICS, EPIDEMIOLOGY. *Educ:* Goucher Col, AB, 44; Johns Hopkins Univ, PhD(human genetics), 58, MPH, 59. *Prof Exp:* Nat Heart Inst fel, Div Med Genetics, Sch Med, 59-60, from asst prof to assoc prof, 60-70, PROF EPIDEMIOL, DEPT CHRONIC DIS, SCH HYG, JOHNS HOPKINS UNIV, 70-, PROF, DEPT MED, SCH MED & DEPT BIOL, 73-, DIR HUMAN GENETICS, GENETIC EPIDEMIOL PROG, 73- *Concurrent Pos:* Nat Inst Gen Med Sci res career develop award, Dept Chronic Dis, Johns Hopkins Univ, 60-70; assoc, Univ Sem in Genetics & Evolution of Man, Columbia Univ, 64-70; consult, Baltimore City Hosps, Md, 66-; asst prof, Sch Med, Johns Hopkins Univ, 70- *Mem:* AAAS; Am Soc Human Genetics; Am Pub Health Asn; Genetics Soc Am; fel Am Col Epidemiol. *Res:* Human epidemiological genetics, especially the role of genetic factors in chronic diseases, differential fertility, aging and mortality; congenital anomalies; genetically determined marker traits and disease; maternal-fetal blood group incompatibility. *Mailing Add:* Dept of Epidemiol Johns Hopkins Univ Sch of Hyg Baltimore MD 21205

COHEN, BRUCE IRA, b Los Angeles, Calif, Oct 26, 48; m 75. PLASMA PHYSICS. *Educ:* Harvey Mudd Col, BS, 70; Univ Calif, Berkeley, MA, 72, PhD(physics), 75. *Prof Exp:* Res assoc, Plasma Physics Lab, Princeton Univ, 75-76; PHYSICIST, LAWRENCE LIVERMORE NAT LAB, UNIV CALIF, 76- *Concurrent Pos:* Jr staff scientist, Phys Dynamics, Inc, Calif, 73- *Mem:* Am Phys Soc. *Res:* Theoretical plasma physics and physical oceanography; computational plasma physics and fluid mechanics. *Mailing Add:* Lawrence Livermore Nat Lab L630 PO Box 808 Livermore CA 94550

COHEN, BURTON D, b Waterbury, Conn, Aug 10, 26; m 51; c 3. INTERNAL MEDICINE. *Educ:* Yale Univ, AB, 50; Columbia Univ, MD, 54; Am Bd Internal Med, dipl, 63. *Prof Exp:* From clin asst prof to assoc prof, 70-79, PROF MED, ALBERT EINSTEIN COL MED, 79; CHIEF METAB SECT, BRONX-LEBANON HOSP, 62- DIR, DEPT MED, 80- *Concurrent Pos:* Asst vis physician, Bellevue Hosp, 59-68; clin investr, Vet Admin, 59-62; career scientist, Health Res Coun New York, 65-73. *Mem:* Am Fedn Clin Res; Am Diabetes Asn; fel Am Col Physicians. *Res:* Metabolism and renal disease. *Mailing Add:* 1276 Fulton Ave Bronx NY 10456

COHEN, CARL, b Brooklyn, NY, Nov 15, 20; m 49; c 3. IMMUNOGENETICS. *Educ:* Ohio State Univ, BSc, 46, MSc, 48, PhD(bact), 51. *Prof Exp:* Asst bact, Ohio State Univ, 46-50; mem staff immunogenetics, Jackson Mem Lab, 51-57; proj leader, Battelle Mem Inst, 57-62; prof biol & assoc prof exp path, Case Western Reserve Univ, 62-70; prof genetics & dir, Ctr Genetics, Univ Ill Med Ctr, 70-77; chief, Genetics & Transplantation Biol Br, Nat Inst Allergy & Infectious Dis, NIH, 77-79; PROF GENETICS & SURG, CHIEF DIV SURG IMMUNOL, DEPT SURG, UNIV ILL MED CTR, 79- *Mem:* Fel AAAS; Am Asn Immunol; Genetics Soc Am; Am Soc Human Genetics. *Res:* Immunology; mammalian genetics. *Mailing Add:* 122 Wright Lane Oak Park IL 60302

COHEN, CAROLYN, b Long Island City, NY, June 18, 29. BIOPHYSICS. *Educ:* Bryn Mawr Col, AB, 50; Mass Inst Technol, PhD(biophys), 54. *Prof Exp:* Fulbright scholar, King's Col, Univ London, 54-55; res assoc, Children's Cancer Res Found, 55-56; instr biol, Mass Inst Technol, 57-58; res assoc path, Children's Cancer Res Found, Children's Hosp Med Ctr, 58-74; PROF BIOL & MEM ROSENSTIEL BASIC MED SCI RES CTR, BRANDEIS UNIV, 72- *Concurrent Pos:* Res assoc biol, Mass Inst Technol, 55-58; res assoc biochem, Harvard Med Sch, 58-64, Harvard Med Sch lectr biophys, Children's Hosp, 64-74. *Mem:* Am Crystallog Asn; Am Soc Biol Chemists; Soc Gen Physiol; AAAS; Biophys Soc. *Res:* Structure of protein assemblies in the cell as determined by x-ray diffraction and electron microscopy; muscle structure and the contractile mechanism; morphogenesis; structural aspects of blood coagulation. *Mailing Add:* Rosenstiel Ctr Brandeis Univ Waltham MA 02154

COHEN, CLARENCE B(UDD), b Monticello, NY, Feb 7, 25; m 47; c 2. FLUIDS, ENGINEERING PHYSICS. *Educ:* Rensselaer Polytech Inst, BAE, 45, MAE, 47; Princeton Univ, MA, 52, PhD, 54. *Prof Exp:* Aeronaut engr, Nat Adv Comt Aeronaut, Ohio, 47-56, head propulsion aerodyn sect, 53-55, assoc chief spec proj br, 56; head hypersonics res sect, Ramo-Wooldridge Corp, 57, asst dir, Aerosci Lab, Thompson-Ramo-Woolridge Space Technol Labs, 58-65, mgr, Aerosci Lab, 65-69, dir technol appln, TRW systs Energy, 70-81, DIR TECHNOL COORD, TRW ELEC & DEFENSE, 81- *Concurrent Pos:* Guggenheim fel, Princeton Univ, 50-52. *Mem:* Assoc fel Am Inst Aeronaut & Astronaut; Sigma Xi; Indust Res Inst; Lic Exec Soc. *Res:* Viscous flow; heat transfer; gas dynamics; hypersonics; aerodynamics; ballistic missiles and space vehicles; technology administration. *Mailing Add:* TRW Elec & Defense One Space Park Redondo Beach CA 90248

COHEN, DANIEL, b Brooklyn, NY, June 22, 24; m 47; c 3. PUBLIC HEALTH, EPIDEMIOLOGY. *Educ:* Univ Ill, BS, 53, DVM, 55; Univ Pittsburgh, MPH, 60. *Prof Exp:* Vet officer, Commun Dis Ctr, USPHS, 55-60, assigned to Southern Health Dist, NJ, 55-56, NJ State Dept Health, 56-57,, Cancer Control Prog, 57-58 & fel, Grad Sch Pub Health, Univ Pittsburgh, 58-60; assoc mem, Lab Res Virol, Wistar Inst, Univ Pa, 60-61; dir, Vet Res Inst, Beit Dagan, Israel, 61-62; dir grad training prog epidemiol, Univ Pa, 62-71, from asst prof to prof vet pub health, Sch Vet Med, 63-71; pub health vet, Div Commun Dis, WHO, Switz, 71-73; PROF COMP MED, BEN GURION UNIV, ISRAEL, 73- *Concurrent Pos:* Consult, WHO & Pan Am Health Orgn, 65- & US AID, 66-; Am Pub Health Asn fel, Univ Pittsburgh, 66-; pres, Conf Pub Health Vets, 68. *Mem:* AAAS; Am Pub Health Asn; Am Vet Med Asn; Am Asn Cancer Res; Asn Teachers Vet Pub Health & Prev Med. *Res:* Epidemiology of acute and chronic disease of animals of comparative interest to man, zoonoses, and international aspects of veterinary public health; animal neoplasia; animal influenza; respiratory and enteric diseases of domestic animals. *Mailing Add:* Dept of Comp Med Ben Gurion Univ Beersheva Israel

COHEN, DANIEL MORRIS, b Chicago, Ill, July 6, 30; m 55; c 2. ICHTHYOLOGY, MARINE BILOGY. *Educ:* Stanford Univ, AB, 52, MA, 53, PhD, 58. *Prof Exp:* Asst gen biol, Stanford Univ, 53-55, actg instr, 55-57; asst prof, Univ Fla, 57-58; syst zoologist fishes, 58-60, lab dir, Ichthyol Lab, 60-70, dir, Systs Lab, 70-81, SR FISHERIES SCIENTIST, NAT MARINE FISHERIES SERV, 81- *Concurrent Pos:* Vis researcher, Brit Mus Natural Hist, 64-65; mem, Nat Acad Sci Comn Ecol Res Interocean Canal, 69-70; res assoc, Smithsonian Inst, 69-; Ed-in-chief, Fishes of West NAtlantic, pt 6; mem oceanog deleg, Nat Acad Sci, People's Repub China, 78. *Mem:* AAAS; Am Soc Ichthyologists & Herpetologists (vpres, 69-70); Japanese Soc Ichthyologists; Soc Syst Zool; Soc Syst Zool. *Res:* Biology of fishes, particularly systematics; deepsea fishes; general marine biology; museum collections; systematics and biology of deep benthic fishes and other coldwater fishes, especially in gadiform, ophidiiform and argentinoid fishes. *Mailing Add:* Northwest & Alaska Fisheries Ctr Nat Marine Fisheries Serv 2725 Montlake Blvd E Seattle WA 98112

COHEN, DAVID, b Winnipeg, Man, Dec 1, 27; US citizen. MAGNETISM. *Educ:* Univ Man, BA, 48; Univ Calif, Berkeley, PhD(exp nuclear physics), 55. *Prof Exp:* Assoc physicist, Defence Res Bd Can, 55-57; res assoc physics, Univ Rochester, 57-58; assoc physicist, Argonne Nat Lab, 58-65; assoc prof physics, Univ Ill, Chicago Circle, 65-68; SR SCIENTIST BIOPHYS, FRANCIS BITTER NAT MAGNET LAB, MASS INST TECHNOL, 68- *Mem:* AAAS; Am Phys Soc. *Res:* Measuring magnetic fields produced by organs of the human body, including magnetocardiography and magnetoencephalography. *Mailing Add:* Nat Magnet Lab Mass Inst Technol Cambridge MA 02139

COHEN, DAVID HARRIS, b Springfield, Mass, Aug 26, 38; m 60, 81; c 4. NEUROBIOLOGY. *Educ:* Harvard Univ, AB, 60; Univ Calif, Berkeley, PhD(psychol), 63. *Prof Exp:* Asst prof physiol, Sch Med, Case Western Reserve Univ, 64-68; assoc prof physiol, Sch Med, Univ Va, 68-71, prof, 71-79, dir neurosci prog, 75-79; LEADING PROF & CHMN NEUROBIOL & BEHAV, STATE UNIV NY, STONY BROOK, 79-, PROF ANAT SCI, 79- & PROF PSYCHOL, 80- *Concurrent Pos:* NSF fel neurophysiol, Med Sch, Univ Calif, Los Angeles, 63-64; Nat Heart & Lung Inst career develop award, 69-74; mem adv panel neurobiol, NSF, 72-75; mem ed bd, Brain Res Bull, 75-; Nat Sci Adv Comt, Brain Info Serv, 75-79; mem neurol A study sect, NIH, 77-81; assoc ed, Exp Neurol, 77-; bd dir, Nat Soc Med Res, 81-; assoc ed, J Neurosci, 80- *Mem:* Sigma Xi; Am Asn Anat; Am Physiol Soc; Pavlovian Soc NAm (pres, 78-79); Soc Neurosci (secy, 75-80, pres, 81-82). *Res:* Neural mechanisms of learning; neural control of the cardiovascular system; comparative neurology. *Mailing Add:* Dept Neurobiol & Behav Grad Biol Bldg State Univ NY Stony Brook NY 11794

COHEN, DAVID WALTER, b Philadelphia, Pa, Dec 15, 26; m 48; c 3. DENTISTRY. *Educ:* Univ Pa, DDS, 50; Hebrew Univ, PhD, 77. *Hon Degrees:* DSc, Boston Univ, 75. *Prof Exp:* From asst instr to assoc oral med & oral path, Sch Dent, 51-55, asst prof periodont, Dent Sch & Grad Sch Med & vchmn dept, Grad Sch Med, 55-59, assoc prof periodont, Dent Sch & Grad Sch Med & chmn dept, Grad Sch Med, 59-64, prof periodont & chmn depts, 69-72, DEAN, SCH DENT MED, UNIV PA, 72-; PROF DENT MED, MED COL PA, 73- *Concurrent Pos:* Res fel path & periodont, Beth Israel Hosp, Boston, 50-51; asst vis chief oral med, Philadelphia Gen Hosp, 51-; clin asst periodont, Albert Einstein Med Ctr, 53-; nat consult periodont, US Air Force, 65-69, nat emer consult, 69-; dir, Am Bd Periodont, 68, vchmn, 70-, chmn, 71; vis prof, Col Dent, Univ Ill; consult, Vet Admin Hosp, Philadelphia, Ft Dix Army Base & Walter Reed Army Med Ctr. *Honors & Awards:* Spec Citation Periodont, Boston Univ, 69; Israel Peace Award, 70; Gold Medal Award, Am Acad Periodont, 71; William J Gies Found Periodont Award, 75. *Mem:* Fel AAAS; fel Am Acad Oral Path; Int Asn Dent Res; Inst Med-Nat Acad Sci; fel AAAS. *Res:* Vascular plexus of oral tissues; periodontal disease; treatment planning in dentistry; periodontal therapy. *Mailing Add:* Dept of Periodont Univ of Pa Sch of Dent Med Philadelphia PA 19104

COHEN, DAVID WARREN, b Hartford, Conn, Feb 28, 40; m 64; c 1. MATHEMATICS. *Educ:* Worcester Polytech Inst, BS, 62; Univ NH, MS, 64, PhD(math), 68. *Prof Exp:* Instr math, Exten Serv, Univ NH, 65-68 & Univ, 67-68; asst prof, 68-74, ASSOC PROF MATH, SMITH COL, 74- *Mem:* Math Asn Am. *Res:* Quantum theory; mathematical physics. *Mailing Add:* Dept of Math Smith Col Northampton MA 01063

COHEN, DONALD, b Tom's River, NJ, Feb 9, 20; m 43; c 4. RADIOCHEMISTRY. *Educ:* Univ Buffalo, BS, 41; Purdue Univ, MS, 48, PhD(chem), 50. *Prof Exp:* Assoc chemist, 49-72, CHEMIST, ARGONNE NAT LAB, 72- *Mem:* Sigma Xi; Am Chem Soc. *Res:* Electrode potentials; chemistry of the transuranium elements; Xenon chemistry and chemistry of molten copper. *Mailing Add:* Chem Div Argonne Nat Lab 9700 S Cass Ave Argonne IL 60439

COHEN, DONALD SUSSMAN, b Providence, RI, Nov 30, 34; m 58; c 2. APPLIED MATHEMATICS. *Educ:* Brown Univ, ScB, 56; Cornell Univ, MS, 59; NY Univ, PhD(math), 62. *Prof Exp:* Preceptorship, Dept Eng Mech & Inst Flight Struct, Columbia Univ, 62-63; asst prof math, Rensselaer Polytech Inst, 63-65; asst prof math, 65-67, assoc prof appl math, 67-71, PROF APPL MATH, CALIF INST TECHNOL, 71- *Concurrent Pos:* Ed, SIAM Rev. *Mem:* AAAS; Am Math Soc; Soc Indust & Appl Math. *Res:* Wave propagation and vibration problems; partial differential equations; special functions; variational techniques; non-linear boundary value problems; bifurcation theory; perturbation and asymptotic methods; differential equations. *Mailing Add:* Dept of Appl Math Calif Inst of Technol Pasadena CA 91125

COHEN, E RICHARD, b Philadelphia, Pa, Dec 14, 22; m 53; c 1. MATHEMATICAL PHYSICS, REACTOR PHYSICS. *Educ:* Univ Pa, AB, 43; Calif Inst Technol, MS, 46, PhD(physics), 49. *Prof Exp:* Asst instr physics, Univ Pa, 43-44; jr physicist acoust-electronic res, Calif Inst Technol, 44-45; theoret physicist, NAm Rockwell Corp, 49-56, res adv, 56-61, assoc dir, Res Dept, 61-62 & Sci Ctr, 62-69, mem tech staff, 69-75, DISTINGUISHED FEL, SCI CTR, ROCKWELL INT CORP, 75- *Concurrent Pos:* Sr lectr, Calif Inst Technol, 62-63, res assoc, 63-72; comn, Symbols, Units, Nomenclature, Atomic Masses & Fundamental constants, 78- *Mem:* Fel AAAS; fel Am Phys Soc; fel Am Nuclear Soc; Asn Comput Mach; Sigma Xi. *Res:* Evaluation of the fundamental physical constants; nuclear reactor theory; molecular spectroscopy. *Mailing Add:* Sci Ctr Rockwell Int Corp 1049 Camino Dos Rios Thousand Oaks CA 91360

COHEN, EDWARD, b Glastonbury, Conn, Jan 6, 21; m 81; c 3. CIVIL ENGINEERING. *Educ:* Columbia Univ, BS, 46, MS, 54. *Prof Exp:* Eng aide, Conn Hwy Dept, 40-41; asst engr, Dept Pub Works, East Hartford, Conn, 42-44; struct engr, Hardesty & Hanover, New York, 45-47 & Sanderson & Porter, New York, 47-49; consult engr, 49-63, partner, 63-74, sr partner, 74-77, MANAGING PARTNER, AMMANN & WHITNEY INC, 77-, CHMN & CHIEF EXEC OFFICER IN-CHG BLDGS, TRANSP, COMMUN, MIL & PLANNING PROJS, 78-; PRES, SAFEGUARD CONSTRUCT MGT CORP, 73- *Concurrent Pos:* Lectr archit, Columbia Univ, 48-51; consult, Rand Corp, Santa Monica, 58-72, Dept Defense, 62-63 & Hudson Inst, NY, 67-71; vpres, Ammann & Whitney Int Ltd, 63-73; exec vpres bldgs, transp, commun, mil & planning projs, Ammann & Whitney Inc, 63-78. *Honors & Awards:* I B Laskowitz Aerospace Res Medal, 70; Civil Eng State-of-the-Art Award, Am Soc Civil Engrs, 74; Egleston Medal, Columbia, 81. *Mem:* Nat Acad Eng; fel Am Soc Civil Engrs; hon mem Am Concrete Inst; Am Nat Standards Inst; hon mem NY Acad Sci. *Res:* Structural design; seismic design; hardened design; sind forces; dynamic analysis of structures; ultimate strength and plastic design; tower analysis and shell structures. *Mailing Add:* Ammann & Whitney Inc Consult Engrs Two World Trade Ctr New York NY 10048

COHEN, EDWARD DAVID, b Haverhill, Mass, Mar 12, 37; m 58; c 3. PHYSICAL CHEMISTRY, CHEMICAL ENGINEERING. *Educ:* Tufts Univ, BSChE, 58; Univ Del, PhD(phys chem), 64. *Prof Exp:* Jr engr, Elkton Div, Thiokol Chem Corp, 58-60; res chemist, 64-67, sr res chemist, 67-72, res assoc, 72-77, RES FEL, PHOTOPROD DEPT, E I DU PONT DE NEMOURS & CO, INC, 77- *Mem:* Am Chem Soc; Soc Photog Sci & Eng. *Res:* Rheology; radiation and polymer chemistry; analytical chemistry; gelatin and bio-polymers; emulsion chemistry. *Mailing Add:* Du Pont Photo Prod Photosystems Res Lab Parlin NJ 08859

COHEN, EDWARD HIRSCH, b Seattle, Wash, Aug 28, 47. CELL BIOLOGY. *Educ:* Univ Chicago, BS, 68; Yale Univ, MPhil, 70, PhD(biol), 73. *Prof Exp:* asst prof biol, Princeton Univ, 74-81; ASST STAFF SCIENTIST, FRED HUTCHINSON CANCER RES CTR, SEATTLE, 81- *Concurrent Pos:* Fel zool, Univ Wash, 72-74. *Mem:* Am Soc Cell Biol; Genetics Soc Am. *Res:* Organization of DNA sequences in eukaryote chromosomes; structure and evolution of satellite DNAs of Drosophila. *Mailing Add:* Div Biol Fred Hutchinson Cancer Res Ctr 1124 Columbia St Seattle WA 98104

COHEN, EDWARD MORTON, b New York, NY, May 12, 36; m 59; c 3. PHARMACEUTICAL CHEMISTRY, ANALYTICAL CHEMISTRY. *Educ:* Columbia Univ, BS, 57; Rutgers Univ, MS, 60, PhD(pharmaceut chem), 65. *Prof Exp:* Res chemist, Johnson & Johnson Res Ctr, 62-65; res assoc, 65-70, sr res fel anal chem, 70-78, dir, 76-81, SR DIR PHARMACEUT RES, MERCK SHARP & DOHME RES LABS, WEST POINT, 81- *Mem:* AAAS; Am Chem Soc; Am Pharmaceut Asn. *Res:* Development of analytical methods for pharmaceutical dosage forms; measurement of physical properties of compounds; polarography and other electroanalytical methods; thin layer chromatography; thermal analysis; pharmaceutical foundations. *Mailing Add:* 3008 Eisenhower Dr Norristown PA 19401

COHEN, EDWARD P, b Glen Ridge, NJ, Sept 28, 32; m 63; c 4. IMMUNOLOGY, ALLERGY. *Educ:* Washington Univ, MD, 57; Am Bd Allergy & Immunol, cert, 74. *Prof Exp:* Intern med, Univ Chicago, 57-58; USPHS fel, NIH, 58-60; res fel, Univ Colo, 60-63, asst prof microbiol, 63-65; assoc prof, Rutgers Univ, 65-68; assoc prof, Univ Chicago, 68-76, prof microbiol, 76-79; dean Sch Basic Med Sci & prof microbiol & immunol, 79-82, DIR OFF RES & DEVELOP & PROF MICROBIOL & IMMUNOL, UNIV ILL MED CTR, 82- *Mem:* Am Asn Immunol; Am Soc Cell Biol; Am Acad Allergy. *Res:* Immune resistance to cancer. *Mailing Add:* Dept Microbiol Rm 109 Univ Ill Med Ctr Chicago IL 60612

COHEN, EDWIN, b Cairo, Egypt, July 3, 34; US citizen; m 60; c 2. ELECTRICAL ENGINEERING, APPLIED MATHEMATICS. *Educ:* Cairo Univ, Egypt, BS, 57; Newark Col Eng, MS, 64; Polytech Inst New York, PhD(systs sci, elec eng), 70. *Prof Exp:* Engr elec power, Sadelmi, Ltd, Milan, 57-60; engr res & develop, Weston Instruments, 60-61; engr thermistors, Victory Eng, 61-62; mem fac, 62-81, ASSOC PROF ELEC ENG, NJ INST TECHNOL, 71- *Concurrent Pos:* Consult, Calculagraph Co, 66, Kahle Eng Co, 73-74, Vector Eng, 78-80 & Systematics, 80-; NASA fel, 81. *Mem:* Inst Elec & Electronics Engrs; Sigma Xi; Conf Int Grande Res Elec. *Res:* Computer application to analysis of power systems; approximation theory applied to electric filter design; programmable logic controllers for manufacturing machines. *Mailing Add:* NJ Inst of Technol 323 High St Newark NJ 07102

COHEN, ELAINE, b NJ, July 17, 46; m 74. MATHEMATICAL ANALYSIS, SYSTEMS THEORY. *Educ:* Vassar Col, BA, 68; Syracuse Univ, MA, 70, PhD(math), 74. *Prof Exp:* Vis instr math, 74-75, RES ASST PROF COMPUT SCI, UNIV UTAH, 74-, ASSOC INSTR MATH, 75- *Concurrent Pos:* Adj asst prof math, Univ Utah, 76- *Mem:* Am Math Soc; Asn Comput Mach; Inst Elec & Electronics Engrs. *Res:* Mathematical structures in sensory information processing; Fourier analysis. *Mailing Add:* Comput Sci Univ of Utah Salt Lake City UT 84112

COHEN, ELIAS, b Baltimore, Md, Sept 17, 20; m 46; c 2. IMMUNOLOGY. *Educ:* Univ Md, BSc, 42; Johns Hopkins Univ, MA, 49; Rutgers Univ, PhD(immunol), 52. *Prof Exp:* Biologist, Sch Hyg & Pub Health, Johns Hopkins Univ, 46, jr instr biol & asst, 47-49; jr instr, Rutgers Univ, 49-50, asst genetics & physiol, 50-52; instr clin path & asst dir clin labs, Sch Med, Univ Okla, 52-54, res assoc clin path, 54-56; assoc cancer res scientist immunohemat, 56-69, prin cancer res scientist, 69-72, ASSOC CHIEF CANCER RES SCIENTIST, ROSWELL PARK MEM INST, 72-; RES ASSOC PROF MICROBIOL & IMMUNOL, SCH MED, STATE UNIV NY BUFFALO, 68-, RES ASST PROF PATH, 77- *Concurrent Pos:* Lectr, Okla City Univ, 53-54; prin investr, S R Noble Found, Inc, 54-56; lab consult, Erie County Lab, 57-64; lectr med genetics, Sch Med, State Univ NY Buffalo, 57-72; lab consult, Erie County Lab, 57-64; lectr, Queen's Univ, 58; mem acute leukemia task force & proj dir, Platelet Transfusion Eval Prog, Nat Cancer Inst, 64-; immunohemat consult, Children's Hosp, Buffalo, NY, 67-; US-USSR exchange scientist, 69, 73, 75 & 76; pres, NY Publ Health Lab Asn, 74-75. *Mem:* Am Soc Exp Path; Am Soc Hemat; Am Asn Immunol; Int Soc Blood Transfusion; Int Soc Hemat. *Res:* Immunobiology and immunogenetics; comparative and mammalian immunohematology; physiology and biochemistry; biomedical applications of erythrocytes and serum proteins of human and other species; clinical immunology. *Mailing Add:* Roswell Park Mem Inst 666 Elm St Buffalo NY 14263

COHEN, ELLIOTT, b New York, NY, Apr 14, 30; m 58; c 3. MEDICINAL CHEMISTRY. *Educ:* Syracuse Univ, BA, 51; Columbia Univ, PhD(chem), 56. *Prof Exp:* Chemist, NY State Psychiat Inst, 56-57; res chemist, 57-61, group leader org chem, 61-74, dept head, Cent Nerv Syst Dis Ther Sect, 74-77, DEPT HEAD, CARDIOVASCULAR-CNS RES SECT, MED RES DIV, LEDERLE LABS, DIV AM CYANAMID CO, 77- *Mem:* Am Chem Soc. *Res:* Organic synthetic work in heterocyclic and cardiovascular drugs, anti-inflammatory agents and central nervous systems agents; mechanism of action and structure activity relationships. *Mailing Add:* Lederle Labs Div of Am Cyanamid Co Pearl River NY 10965

COHEN, ELLIS N, b Des Moines, Iowa, June 5, 19; m 47; c 3. ANESTHESIOLOGY. *Educ:* Univ Minn, BS, 41, MD, 43, MS, 49. *Prof Exp:* From Clin instr to assoc clin prof anesthesiol, Univ Minn, 49-60; assoc prof, 60-65, prof, 65-79, EMER PROF ANESTHESIOL, STANFORD UNIV, 79- *Mem:* AMA; Am Soc Anesthesiol. *Res:* Clinical pharmacology; toxicology; uptake and distribution and metabolism of drugs; analytic methods. *Mailing Add:* Dept Anesthesia Stanford Univ Stanford CA 94305

COHEN, EZECHIEL GODERT DAVID, b Amsterdam, Neth, Jan 16, 23; m 50; c 2. PHYSICS. *Educ:* Univ Amsterdam, BS, 47, PhD(physics), 57. *Prof Exp:* First asst physics, Univ Amsterdam, 50-61, assoc prof, 61-63; PROF, ROCKEFELLER UNIV, 63- *Concurrent Pos:* Netherlands Orgn Pure Sci Res scholar, Univ Mich, 57-58 & Johns Hopkins Univ, 58-59; Van der Waals prof, Univ Amsterdam, 69; vis prof, Col France, Paris, 69 & 72; Lorentz prof, Univ Leiden, Neth, 79. *Mem:* Fel Am Phys Soc; Neth Phys Soc. *Res:* Statistical mechanics, particularly applied to equilibrium and nonequilibrium properties of gases and liquids at normal and low temperatures. *Mailing Add:* Rockefeller Univ 1230 York Ave New York NY 10021

COHEN, FLOSSIE, b Calcutta, Brit India, May 10, 25; US citizen; m 58; c 1. IMMUNOLOGY, PEDIATRICS. *Educ:* Med Col, Calcutta, MB, 45; Univ Buffalo, MD, 50. *Prof Exp:* Hematologist, 56-58, from asst pediatrician & assoc hemat to assoc pediatrician, 58-73, DIR CLIN IMMUNOL & RHENMATOL, CHILDREN'S HOSP MICH, DETROIT, 69- *Concurrent Pos:* Res assoc, Child Res Ctr Mich, Detroit, 58-60, sr res assoc, 60-; univ assoc, Dept Affil-Pediat, Hutzel Hosp, Detroit, 64-; attend pediatrician, Dept Pediat Med, Children's Hosp Mich, 71-, attend pediatrician, Dept Lab Med, Immunol Sect, 74-; immunol consult, William Beaumont Hosp, Royal Oak, Mich, 73-; mem biomet & epidemiol contract rev comt, Nat Cancer Inst, 74-78, chmn biomet & epidemiol contract rev comt, 77-78. *Mem:* Am Pediat Soc; Am Soc Hemat; Am Soc Human Genetics; Soc Pediat Res; Am Asn Immunologists. *Res:* Immunodeficiency diseases; immunology of pregnancy; transplacental passage of cells. *Mailing Add:* 3901 Beaubien Blvd Detroit MI 48201

COHEN, FREDRIC SUMNER, b Boston, Mass, Dec 17, 35; m 81; c 2. POLYMER CHEMISTRY, OPTICS. *Educ:* Oberlin Col, AB, 57; Brandeis Univ, PhD, 63; Mass Inst Technol, MSM, 76. *Prof Exp:* Res chemist, US Indust Chem Co, 59-60; sr res chemist, Diamond Alkali Co, 63-65; res chemist, Stauffer Chem Co, 65-67, sr res chemist, 67-69; scientist, 69-70, res group leader, 71-80, TECH SERV MGR, POLAROID CORP, 80- *Mem:* Am Chem Soc; Soc Plastics Eng; Soc Rheol. *Res:* Physical polymer chemistry, especially related to optical systems and light polarizers; correlation of molecular and gross properties of synthetic polymers; polymer orientation and dyeing; electrochemical systems and materials. *Mailing Add:* Battery Div Polaroid Corp 784 Memorial Dr Cambridge MA 02139

COHEN, GARY H, b Brooklyn, NY, May 7, 34; m 59; c 2. MICROBIOLOGY, VIROLOGY. *Educ:* Brooklyn Col, BS, 56; Univ Vt, PhD(microbiol), 64. *Prof Exp:* assoc prof, 67-81, PROF MICROBIOL, SCH DENT MED, UNIV PA, 81- *Concurrent Pos:* USPHS fel virol, Univ Pa, 64-67; USPHS res career develop award, 69-74; vis scientist, Swiss Inst Exp Cancer Res, Lausanne, 76-77. *Mem:* AAAS; Sigma Xi; Am Soc Microbiol. *Res:* soluble antigens of vaccinia virus-infected mammalian cells; antigens of herpes simplex virus; DNA synthesis in herpes-infected mammalian cells; ribonucleotide reductase; herpes simplex glycoproteins synthesis, processing and function; herpes infection in synchronized human cells. *Mailing Add:* Dept of Microbiol Univ of Pa Sch of Dent Med Philadelphia PA 19104

COHEN, GEORGE LESTER, b Brooklyn, NY, Dec 24, 39; m 62; c 3. PHYSICAL CHEMISTRY. *Educ:* Clarkson Col Technol, BS, 61, MS, 63; Univ Md, PhD(phys chem), 67. *Prof Exp:* Chemist, US Naval Ord Lab, Md, 62-67; proj supvr, Gillette Res Inst, 67-69; head phys chem res dept, Prod Div, 67-76, MGR, CHEM SCI, BRISTOL-MYERS, INC, 76- *Concurrent Pos:* Adj asst prof, Rutgers Univ, Newark, 70-75; co-res dir, Ctr Prof Advan, 78- *Mem:* Am Chem Soc; Soc Cosmetic Chemists. *Res:* Chemistry of silver oxides, pharmaceutical, cosmetic, polymer, surface and colloid chemistry; laboratory computers. *Mailing Add:* Bristol-Myers Inc Prod Div 225 Long Ave Hillside NJ 07207

COHEN, GEORGE S(OL), b Far Rockaway, NY, Jan 10, 25; m 50; c 5. ELECTRICAL ENGINEERING. *Educ:* Univ Dayton, BEE, 53; Univ Mich, MSE, 55, PhD(elec eng), 62. *Prof Exp:* Res asst electronic defense group, Univ Mich, 53-55, res assoc, 56-59; engr, Bendix Systs Div, 59-61; assoc res engr & res engr, Univ Mich, 61-67; sr eng specialist, EDL Sylvania, 67-69; from assoc prof to prof elec eng, Univ Akron, 69-74; SR ENG SPECIALIST, GTE SYLVANIA INC, 74- *Concurrent Pos:* Instr elec eng, Univ Kans, 55-56; fel, Univ Mich Eng Res Inst, 55. *Mem:* AAAS; Inst Elec & Electronics Engrs. *Res:* Radar signal enhancement techniques; electronic countermeasures; signal systems. *Mailing Add:* GTE Sylvania Inc Box 188 Mountain View CA 94043

COHEN, GERALD, b New York, NY, Feb 1, 30. NEUROCHEMISTRY. *Educ:* City Col New York, BS, 50; Columbia Univ, MA, 52, PhD(chem), 55. *Prof Exp:* Assoc biochem, Col Physicians & Surgeons, Columbia Univ, 54-65, asst prof, 65-73; RES PROF NEUROL, MT SINAI SCH MED, 73- *Honors & Awards:* Claude Bernard Sci Jour Award, Nat Soc Med Res, 68. *Mem:* Am Soc Biol Chem; Am Soc Pharmacol & Exp Therapeut; Am Chem Soc. *Res:* Biochemical pharmacology. *Mailing Add:* Dept of Neurol Mt Sinai Sch of Med New York NY 10029

COHEN, GERALD H(OWARD), b Milwaukee, Wis, Oct 11, 22; m 46; c 2. ELECTRICAL ENGINEERING. *Educ:* Univ Wis, BS, 48, MS, 49, PhD(elec eng), 50. *Prof Exp:* Mem staff, Radiation Lab, Mass Inst Technol, 43; asst instr, Univ Wis, 49; res engr, Taylor Instrument Co, 50-58; PROF ELEC ENG, UNIV ROCHESTER, 58- *Concurrent Pos:* Consult, Gen Dynamics, Worthington Corp, Bausch & Lomb, Inc, Transmation, Inc, Rochester Appl Sci Asn & Friden Corp. *Mem:* AAAS; NY Acad Sci; Inst Elec & Electronics Engrs. *Res:* Non-linear circuit analysis; ultrasonic physics; industrial automatic controls; biomedical engineering. *Mailing Add:* Dept of Elec Eng Univ of Rochester Rochester NY 14627

COHEN, GERALD STANLEY, b New York, NY, Nov 29, 26; m 51; c 2. BIOMEDICAL ENGINEERING. *Educ:* City Col New York, BS, 50; Univ Md, MS, 67; Univ NC, PhD, 79. *Prof Exp:* Electronic engr, Philco-Ford Corp, 50-58; electronic engr, Army Ord, Harry Diamond Labs, 58-60; chief electronic & elec eng sect, Div Res Servs, 60-68, CHIEF, MED INFO SYSTS, NAT CTR HEALTH SERVS, RES & DEVELOP, USPHS, 68- *Mem:* Instrument Soc Am; Inst Elec & Electronics Eng; Opers Res Soc Am. *Res:* Design and development of electronic instrumentation for medical research; computer applications in the delivery of health services. *Mailing Add:* Nat Ctr Health Serv Res FCB-2 8-41A 3700 East West Hwy Hyattsville MD 20782

COHEN, GERSON H, b Philadelphia, Pa, July 8, 39; m 63; c 3. PHYSICAL CHEMISTRY. *Educ:* Temple Univ, AB, 61; Cornell Univ, PhD(phys chem), 65. *Prof Exp:* RES CHEMIST, NIH, 65- *Mem:* AAAS; Am Chem Soc; Am Crystallog Asn. *Res:* Chemical crystallography with emphasis in protein structure. *Mailing Add:* NIH Bldg 2 Rm 312 Bethesda MD 20205

COHEN, GLENN MILTON, b Elizabeth, NJ, Sept 8, 43; m 68. PHYSIOLOGY. *Educ:* Rutgers Univ, BA, 65; Fla State Univ, PhD(physiol), 70. *Prof Exp:* Asst res scientist electron micros, Inst Rehab Med, New York Univ, 70-72; res fel motion sickness, NASA, 76-77; MEM STAFF, FLA INST TECHNOL, 77- *Mem:* Asn Res Otolaryngol; Electron Micros Soc Am; Southeast Electron Micros Soc; Soc Neurosci; Am Soc Zool. *Res:* Normal and abnormal development of the ear and the effects of drugs on the ear during development; causes of genetic & congenital deafness and impaired balance. *Mailing Add:* Dept Biol Sci Fla Inst Technol 150 W University Blvd Melbourne FL 32901

COHEN, GLORIA, b Leeds, Eng, Jan 2, 30; m 51; c 3. INFORMATION SCIENCE. *Educ:* Univ Birmingham, Eng, DDS, 52. *Prof Exp:* Dental res fel, London Hosp Med Col, 52-53, clin asst, 53-55; gen dent practr, London, 55-67; info scientist, Data & Info Ctr, Res & Develop Div, 68-69, supvr biomed doc, 69-70, from asst mgr to mgr, 70-72, dir, Info Serv Dept, 72-76, dir, Corp Bus Res & Eval Dept, 76-80, CONSULT, INFO SERV, G D SEARLE & CO, 80- *Concurrent Pos:* Prog evaluator, NSF, 74-; mem task force sci & technol, Indust Res Inst, 74- *Mem:* AAAS; Am Soc Info Sci; Drug Info Asn; Am Rec Mgt Asn; Int Asn Dent Res. *Mailing Add:* 200 Kilpatrick Ave Wilmette IL 60091

COHEN, GORDON MARK, b Chicago, Ill, Jan 7, 48; US & Can citizen; m 78; c 1. SYNTHETIC POLYMER CHEMISTRY, MONOMER SYNTHESIS. *Educ:* McGill Univ, BSc, 69; Harvard Univ, AM, 70, PhD(chem), 74. *Prof Exp:* RES CHEMIST, E I DU PONT DE NEMOURS & CO INC, 74- *Mem:* Am Chem Soc. *Res:* Preparative polymer chemistry and organic chemistry in polymer systems, mechanistic and synthetic aspects. *Mailing Add:* Polymer Prod Dept Exp Sta E I du Pont de Nemours & Co Inc Wilmington DE 19898

COHEN, HARLEY, b Winnipeg, Manitoba, May 12, 33; m 56; c 3. THEORETICAL & APPLIED MECHANICS. *Educ:* Univ Manitoba, BSc, 56; Brown Univ, ScM, 58; Univ Minn, PhD(theory of elastic surfaces), 64. *Prof Exp:* Res engr, Boeing Airplane Co, 58-60; sr develop engr, Aeronaut Div, Honeywell Inc, 60-63, sr scientist, Corp Res Ctr, 64-65; asst prof aeronaut & eng mech, Univ Minn, 65-66; assoc prof, 66-68, PROF CIVIL ENG, UNIV MANITOBA, 68- *Concurrent Pos:* Nat Res Coun Can res grant, 66-82; James L Record vis prof, Univ Minn, 79; Killam vis scholar, Univ Calgary, 82. *Mem:* Am Acad Mech; Soc Eng Sci; Soc Natural Philos. *Res:* Non-linear theories of shells; directed elastic continua and high order theories of elasticity; continuum mechanics in general; wave propagation in rods, plates and shells. *Mailing Add:* Dept Civil Eng Univ Manitoba Winnipeg MB R3D 2E4 Can

COHEN, HAROLD KARL, b Trenton, NJ, Mar 12, 15; m 60; c 2. VETERINARY PATHOLOGY. *Educ:* City Col New York, BS, 38; Kans State Col, DVM, 47; Univ Wis, MS, 52, PhD(path), 55. *Prof Exp:* Instr vet path, Univ Wis, 50-55; vet pathologist, Ralph M Parsons Co, 55; vet, Eli Lilly & Co, 55-73, vet pathologist, 73-77; RETIRED. *Mem:* Am Col Vet Path. *Res:* Virology. *Mailing Add:* 6302 Brookline Dr Indianapolis IN 46220

COHEN, HAROLD P, b Brooklyn, NY, Sept 6, 24; m 57; c 3. BIOLOGICAL CHEMISTRY. *Educ:* City Col New York, BS, 48; Univ Iowa, MS, 51, PhD(biochem), 53. *Prof Exp:* Res assoc, Albert Einstein Med Ctr, 52-53; res assoc neurol, Med Sch, 53-55, asst prof, 55-63, ASSOC PROF NEUROL, COL MED SCI, UNIV MINN, MINNEAPOLIS, 65- *Mem:* AAAS; Am Soc Neurochem; Int Soc Neurochem; Am Soc Biol Chem. *Res:* Central nervous system metabolism; amino acid metabolism; biogenic amine detection and metabolism in CNS. *Mailing Add:* Col of Med Sci Univ of Minn Minneapolis MN 55455

COHEN, HARRY, b Chicago, Ill, May 17, 16; m 44; c 1. CHEMISTRY. *Educ:* Univ Ill, BS, 38, MS, 39; Univ Wis, PhD(org chem), 41. *Prof Exp:* Fel, Univ Wis, 42-43; res chemist, Upjohn Co, Mich, 43-44; lectr org chem, 46-52, from asst prof to assoc prof chem, 52-65, PROF CHEM, ROOSEVELT UNIV, 65- *Concurrent Pos:* Res chemist, Armour & Co, 44-49. *Mem:* Am Chem Soc. *Res:* Organic synthesis; reactions of ketene diethylacetal; formation of heterocyclic compounds; formation of unsaturated compounds. *Mailing Add:* Dept of Chem Roosevelt Univ Chicago IL 60605

COHEN, HASKELL, b Omaha, Nebr, Sept 12, 20; m 45; c 3. MATHEMATICS. *Educ:* Univ Omaha, AB, 42; Univ Chicago, SM, 47; Tulane Univ, PhD(math), 52. *Prof Exp:* Instr math, Univ Ala, 46-50; asst, Off Naval Res contract, Tulane Univ, 51-52; instr, Univ Tenn, 52-55; from asst prof to prof, La State Univ, 55-67; PROF MATH, UNIV MASS, AMHERST, 67- *Concurrent Pos:* Partic, US Air Force res contract, La State Univ, 56-57; consult, US Naval Ord Testing Sta, Calif, 58; mem, Inst Advan Study, 62. *Mem:* Am Math Soc; Math Asn Am. *Res:* Topology; fixed point theorems; dimension theory; topological semigroups. *Mailing Add:* Dept of Math Univ of Mass Amherst MS 01002

COHEN, HERBERT DANIEL, b New York, NY, Apr 27, 37; m 59. PHYSICS. *Educ:* Antioch Col, BS, 59; Stanford Univ, PhD(physics), 66. *Prof Exp:* Res assoc low temperature physics, Stanford Univ, 66-67; asst prof physics, Brandeis Univ, 67-72; assoc prof physics, Univ Vt, 72-77; ASSOC PROF PHYSICS & ASSOC DEAN, ARTS & SCI, STATE UNIV NY, BINGHAMTON, 77- *Concurrent Pos:* NSF fel, 66-67. *Mem:* AAAS; Am Asn Physics Teachers; Am Phys Soc. *Res:* Low temperature physics. *Mailing Add:* LN2430 State Univ of NY Binghamton NY 13901

COHEN, HERMAN, b New York, NY, Mar 1, 15; m 42; c 2. BIOCHEMISTRY. *Educ:* City Col New York, BS, 40; NY Univ, MS, 42, PhD, 51. *Prof Exp:* Res assoc, E R Squibb & Sons, 46-53; dir prod develop, 53-71, vpres & dir res, 71-76, SR V PRES, WAMPOLE LABS, CARTER-WALLACE DIV, PRINCETON LABS, INC, 76- *Mem:* Fel AAAS; Soc Exp Biol & Med; Am Chem Soc; fel NY Acad Sci; Am Physiol Soc. *Res:* Endocrinology; estrogenic hormones, pituitary hormones; enzymes. *Mailing Add:* Wampole Labs Half-Acre Rd Cranbury NJ 08512

COHEN, HERMAN JACOB, b New York, NY, Sept 18, 22. MATHEMATICS. *Educ:* City Col New York, BA, 43; Univ Wis, MA, 46, PhD(math), 49. *Prof Exp:* Jr physicist, Nat Bur Stand, 43-44; asst math, Univ Wis, 45-49; instr, Tulane Univ, 49-50; Fulbright scholar, Univ Paris, 50-51; from instr to assoc prof, 54-70, PROF MATH, CITY COL NEW YORK, 70- *Mem:* Am Math Soc; Math Asn Am. *Res:* General topology; plane continua; uniform spaces; theory of numbers; combinatorics. *Mailing Add:* 90 La Salle St Apt 11 H New York NY 10027

COHEN, HIRSH G, b St Paul, Minn, Oct 6, 25; m 52; c 3. APPLIED MATHEMATICS. *Educ:* Univ Wis, BS, 47; Brown Univ, MS, 48, PhD(appl math), 50. *Prof Exp:* Asst prof eng res, Pa State Univ, 50-51; res assoc aeronaut eng, Israel Inst Technol, 51-53; asst prof math, Carnegie Inst Technol, 53-55; sr engr, NAm Aviation Co, 55; from assoc prof to prof math, Rensselaer Polytech Inst, 55-59; mgr appl math, 61-65, from asst dir to dir math sci dept, IBM Res Ctr, 65-68, asst dir res, IBM Res Div, 69-72, consult to dir, 72-74, chmn res rev bd, 74-81, dir, Yorktown Lab Opers, 81, RES MEM STAFF, IBM CORP, 59- *Concurrent Pos:* Fulbright vis res prof, Delft Univ Technol, 58-59; assoc scientist, Sloan-Kettering Inst Cancer Res, 64-70; consult biostatistician, Mem Hosp, 64-70; vis prof biomath, Med Col, Cornell Univ, 65-70; vis assoc appl math, Calif Inst Technol, 68-69; vis prof, Hebrew Univ, Jerusalem, 73-74; actg dir, IBM Res, Zurich, 74 & 81. *Mem:* AAAS; Am Math Soc; Biophys Soc; Soc Indust & Appl Math. *Res:* Applied mathematical investigations in acoustics, vibration theory, hydrodynamics, cavitation, nonlinear differential equations; superconductivity theory; mathematical biology. *Mailing Add:* IBM Corp PO Box 218 Yorktown Heights NY 10598

COHEN, HOWARD DAVID, b San Francisco, Calif, Jan 10, 40; m 62; c 2. CHEMICAL PHYSICS, ENERGY CONVERSION. *Educ:* Univ Calif, Berkeley, BS, 62; Univ Chicago, PhD(chem), 65. *Prof Exp:* Res scientist, Nat Bur Standards, 65-66; corp appointee chem, Harvard Univ, 66-67; mem tech staff, NAm Rockwell Corp, 67-69; res scientist, Systs Sci & Software Corp, 69-74; res scientist, STD Res Corp, 74-75; sr staff mem, Mass Inst Technol 75-78; SR APPLN SPECIALIST, ANALOGIC CORP, WAKEFIELD, MASS, 78- *Concurrent Pos:* Instr chem, Univ Calif Exten, 68. *Mem:* AAAS; Am Phys Soc; Soc Exploration Geophysicists; Inst Elec & Electronic Engrs. *Res:* Hartree-Fock wave functions; polarizabilities; photoionization phenomena; molecular collisions; plasmas; numerical analysis; group theory; finite element methods; computers; magnetohydrodynamics power systems; array processors. *Mailing Add:* 4 Hastings Rd Lexington MA 02173

COHEN, HOWARD JOSEPH, b New York, NY, Jan 12, 28; m 52; c 2. CHEMISTRY. *Educ:* City Col New York, BS, 54; George Washington Univ, MSA, 75. *Prof Exp:* Technician powder metall & inorg synthesis, Sylvania Elec Prod Inc, 52-55; res chemist, Nat Lead Co, 55-56 & US Indust Chem Co, 56-61; proj leader corp res, Glidden Co, 61-64 & chem res ctr, 64, sr chemist pigments & color group, 64-69, mkt res, 69-71, prod, 72-73, SR CHEMIST PROCESS & PROD DEVELOP, GLIDDEN DURKEE DIV OF SCM CORP, 73- *Concurrent Pos:* Ed, The Chesapeake Chemist, 73-76; consult organometallic compounds. *Mem:* Am Chem Soc; Inst Food Technologists. *Res:* Organometallics; polymers; inorganics; metal organics; catalysts; pigments; process and product development of silica gels as pigments, desiccants, catalysts and additives for food, cosmetics and pharmaceuticals. *Mailing Add:* Chem/Metall Div SCM Corp 3901 Glidden Rd Baltimore MD 21226

COHEN, HOWARD LIONEL, b New York, NY, May 27, 40; m 62; c 2. ASTRONOMY, ASTROPHYSICS. *Educ:* Univ Mich, BS, 62; Ind Univ, AM, 64, PhD(astron), 68. *Prof Exp:* From asst prof to assoc prof phys sci & astron, 68-79, ASSOC PROF ASTRON, UNIV FLA, 79- *Honors & Awards:* Res Award, 70. *Mem:* AAAS; Am Astron Soc; Royal Astron Soc; Astron Soc Pac; Int Planetarium Soc. *Res:* Photoelectric and photographic photometry of stars; spectroscopic and eclipsing binaries, variable stars; computer applications in astronomy; planetarium education. *Mailing Add:* Dept Astron Univ Fla Space Sci Res Bldg 211 Gainesville FL 32611

COHEN, HOWARD MELVIN, b Ft Wayne, Ind, May 22, 36; m 57; c 2. SOLID STATE CHEMISTRY. *Educ:* George Washington Univ, BS, 58; Pa State Univ, PhD(geochem), 62. *Prof Exp:* Mem tech staff, 62-64, SUPVR, BELL LABS, INC, 65- *Mem:* Inst Elec & Electronic Engrs. *Res:* Glass technology; thermodynamics; defects in solids; phase equilibrium; high temperature chemistry of solids; magnetic oxides; thick film technology; printed wiring board technology. *Mailing Add:* Whippany Rd Bell Telephone Lab Whippany NJ 07981

COHEN, HYMAN L, b New York, NY, Apr 11, 19; m 49; c 1. ORGANIC CHEMISTRY. *Educ:* City Col New York, BS, 39; Brooklyn Col, MA, 48; Univ Toronto, PhD(chem), 52. *Prof Exp:* Chemist, Felton Chem Co, NY, 46-47; res assoc, Jewish Hosp, Brooklyn, 47-48; chief chemist, Bell Craig, Ltd, Can, 48-49; res chemist, Glidden Co, Ill, 52-55; sr res chemist, 55-62, RES ASSOC, RES LABS, EASTMAN KODAK CO, 62- *Mem:* Am Chem Soc. *Res:* Organometallic compounds; reactions of polymers. *Mailing Add:* Res Labs Eastman Kodak Co Rochester NY 14650

COHEN, I BERNARD, b New York, NY, Mar 1, 14; m 44; c 1. HISTORY OF SCIENCE. *Educ:* Harvard Univ, SB, 37, PhD(hist sci), 47, LLD, 64. *Prof Exp:* Librn, Eliot House, 37-42, instr physics, 42-46 & hist sci, 46-49, from asst prof to assoc prof, 49-59, PROF HIST SCI, HARVARD UNIV, 59-, VICTOR S THOMAS PROF, 77- *Concurrent Pos:* Guggenheim fel, 56; NSF sr fel, 60-61; vis fel, Clare Hall, Cambridge Univ, 65; spec lectr, Univ London, 59; Lowell lectr, Boston Univ, 61; chmn, US Nat Comt Hist & Philos Sci, 61-62; vpres, Int Union Hist & Philos Sci. *Mem:* Fel AAAS; Int Acad Hist Sci; Asn Hist Med; Am Acad Arts & Sci; Am Hist Sci Soc (pres, 61-62). *Res:* Newtonian science; science in America; effects of science on society. *Mailing Add:* Harvard Univ Cambridge MA 02138

COHEN, IRA M, b Chicago, Ill, July 18, 37; m 60; c 2. FLUID MECHANICS. *Educ:* Polytech Inst Brooklyn, BAeroEng, 58; Princeton Univ, MA, 61, PhD(aeronaut eng, plasma physics), 63. *Hon Degrees:* MA, Univ Pa, 69. *Prof Exp:* Asst prof eng, Brown Univ, 63-66; from asst prof to assoc prof mech eng, 66-76, PROF MECH ENG, UNIV PA, 76- *Concurrent Pos:* Fulbright travel grant, 66; guest ord prof, Technische Hochschule Aachen, W Ger, 66; consult, Joseph Oat Corp & Nat AirOil Burner Co, 78-; expert witness indust accidents, prod liability & mach safety, INCO Safety Prod. *Mem:* Assoc fel Am Inst Aeronaut & Astronaut; Am Phys Soc; Sigma Xi; Am Asn Univ Prof. *Res:* Fluid mechanics; heat transfer; ionized gases; magnetohydrodynamics. *Mailing Add:* Dept Mech Eng & Appl Mech Univ Pa Philadelphia PA 19104

COHEN, IRVING DAVID, b Brooklyn, NY, May 12, 45; m 66; c 4. ENVIRONMENTAL ENGINEERING, CHEMICAL ENGINEERING. *Educ:* City Col New York, BE, 67; NY Univ, ME, 70. *Prof Exp:* Sr process engr process design, Crawford & Russell, Inc, 67-71; assoc chem engr process design, Hoffmann-LaRoche, 71-72; sr proj mgr environ consult, Woodward-Envicon, Inc, 72-75; PRES ENVIRON CONSULT, ENVIRO-SCI INC, 75-; PRES ATMOSPHERIC MONITORING, AERO-INSTRUMENTATION RESOURCES, INC, 78- *Mem:* Am Inst Chem Engrs; Am Indust Hyg Asn; Asn Environ Prof; Air Pollution Control Asn; Int Asn Pollution Control. *Res:* Atmospheric emission treatment for submicron hydrocarbons; activated carbon in wastewater treatment; the environmental impacts associated with energy development and processes. *Mailing Add:* 19 Copeland Rd Denville NJ 07834

COHEN, IRWIN, b Cleveland, Ohio, Feb 28, 24; m 45; c 3. ORGANIC CHEMISTRY, STRUCTURAL CHEMISTRY. *Educ:* Case Western Reserve Univ, AB, 44, MS, 48, PhD(chem), 50. *Prof Exp:* From asst prof to assoc prof, 49-58, PROF CHEM, YOUNGSTOWN STATE UNIV, 58- *Mem:* Am Chem Soc; Sigma Xi. *Res:* Molecular structure through molecular orbital results by localization, density difference methods and population analysis; development of non-arbitrary bond order definition based on molybdenum theory. *Mailing Add:* Dept of Chem Youngstown State Univ Youngstown OH 44555

COHEN, IRWIN A, b New York, NY, Apr 28, 39; m 64; c 3. INORGANIC CHEMISTRY. *Educ:* Boston Univ, BA, 60; Northwestern Univ, PhD(inorg chem), 64. *Prof Exp:* Fel, Med Sch, Johns Hopkins Univ, 64-66; from asst prof to assoc prof chem, Polytech Inst New York, 66-74; assoc prof, 74-76, PROF CHEM, BROOKLYN COL, 76- *Mem:* Am Chem Soc. *Res:* Biochemically significant reactions of inorganic metal complexes, metalloporphyrins, organometallics; mechanisms of inorganic and biochemical reactions. *Mailing Add:* Dept of Chem Brooklyn Col Brooklyn NY 11210

COHEN, J(EROME) B(ERNARD), b Brooklyn, NY, July 16, 32; m 57; c 2. MATERIALS SCIENCE, CRYSTALLOGRAPHY. *Educ:* Mass Inst Technol, BS, 54, ScD(metall), 57. *Prof Exp:* Asst & res engr metall, Mass Inst Technol, 54, asst, 57; Fulbright scholar, Univ Paris, 57-58, sr scientist mat, Avco Corp, 58-59; from asst prof to assoc prof mat sci, 59-65, PROF MAT SCI, NORTHWESTERN UNIV, 65- *Honors & Awards:* Hardy medal, Am Inst Mining, Metall & Petrol Engrs, 60; Henry Marion Howe Medal, Am Soc Metals, 81. *Mem:* Fel Am Inst Mining, Metall & Petrol Engrs; Am Crystallog Asn; Am Ceramic Soc; Royal Inst Gr Brit; fel Am Soc Metals. *Res:* X-ray diffraction; thermodynamics; physical metallurgy; ceramics; physics of solids; ordering; plastic deformation; clustering; catalysis. *Mailing Add:* Dept of Mat Sci & Eng Northwestern Univ Evanston IL 60201

COHEN, JACK, b New York, NY, Jan 31, 37; m 59; c 3. PHARMACY, ANALYTICAL CHEMISTRY. *Educ:* Columbia Univ, BS, 57; Univ Iowa, MS, 59, PhD(pharm, anal chem), 61. *Prof Exp:* Sr res chemist anal res, Lakeside Lab, Inc, 61-62; res chemist, Chas Pfizer & Co, Inc, Conn, 62-65; asst dir, Inst Pharmaceut Sci, 73-78, head, Pharmaceut Anal Dept, 65-78, dir, 78-81, VPRES & DIR, QUALITY CONTROL, SYNTEX LABS, INC, 81- *Mem:* Am Chem Soc; Am Pharmaceut Asn; Am Soc Quality Control. *Res:* Pharmaceutical analysis; drug stability; quality control systems for pharmaceutical products. *Mailing Add:* Syntex Labs Inc Stanford Indust Park Palo Alto CA 94304

COHEN, JACK SIDNEY, b London, Eng, Sept 6, 38; m 61; c 2. PHYSICAL BIOCHEMISTRY. *Educ:* Univ London, BSc, 61; Cambridge Univ, PhD(chem), 64. *Prof Exp:* Sci Res Coun UK fel, Weizman Inst, Israel, 64-66; fel, Harvard Med Sch, 66-67; sr res chemist, Merck Inst, 67-69; sr staff fel, Phys Sci Lab, Div Comput Res & Technol, 69-73, SR INVESTR, NAT INST CHILD HEALTH & HUMAN DEVELOP, NIH, 73- *Mem:* Am Soc Biol Chemists; Am Chem Soc; Biophys Soc. *Res:* Studies of proteins, nucleic acids and cells using nuclear magnetic resonance; biophysical applications of stable isotopes, such as carbon-13; nucleotide and phosphorus chemistry; history of biochemistry. *Mailing Add:* 6045 Rossmore Dr Bethesda MD 20014

COHEN, JACOB ISAAC, b Boston, Mass, Sept 8, 41; m 63; c 1. PHOTOGRAPHIC CHEMISTRY. *Educ:* Harvard Univ, BA, 63; Brandeis Univ, MA, 65, PhD(org chem), 67. *Prof Exp:* NIH fel, Dept Chem, Univ Chicago, 67-69; RES CHEMIST, EASTMAN KODAK CO, 69- *Mem:* Am Chem Soc; Soc Photog Sci & Eng. *Res:* Photographic research and development. *Mailing Add:* Res Chem Dept 343 State Eastman Kodak Co Rochester NY 14608

COHEN, JACOB ORTLIEB, b Jacksonville, Fla, Feb 17, 30; m 52; c 2. MEDICAL MICROBIOLOGY. *Educ:* Univ Fla, BS, 52, MS, 55; Purdue Univ, PhD(bact), 59. *Prof Exp:* MICROBIOLOGIST COMMUN DIS CTR, USPHS, 59- *Mem:* Sigma Xi; Am Soc Microbiol; fel Am Acad Microbiol. *Res:* Production and coagglutinatio/identification of the O-antigens of Salmonelta immunogenicity of M protein of group A streptococci; natural antibodies for staphylococci in nonimmunized animals; serological relationships of strains of staphylococci; epidemiology of staphyloccus disease; scientific writing and editing. *Mailing Add:* USPHS Ctr for Dis Control Atlanta GA 30333

COHEN, JAMES SAMUEL, b Houston, Tex, July 29, 46; m 68; c 1. ATOMIC & MOLECULAR PHYSICS. *Educ:* Rice Univ, BA, 68, MA, 70, PhD(physics), 73. *Prof Exp:* STAFF MEM, LOS ALAMOS NAT LAB, UNIV CALIF, 72- *Concurrent Pos:* Co-investr, New Res Initiative Prog, Los Alamos Sci Lab, 76-78; vis assoc prof, Physics Dept, Rice Univ, 79-80. *Honors & Awards:* H A Wilson Award, Rice Univ, 73. *Mem:* Am Phys Soc; Sigma Xi. *Res:* Theoretical atomic and molecular physics, especially atom and molecule scattering, molecular structure, meson-molecule interactions, chemical kinetics. *Mailing Add:* Theoret Div T-12 Los Alamos Nat Lab Los Alamos NM 87545

COHEN, JEFFREY M, b Elizabeth, NJ, Aug 30, 40; m 64; c 3. ASTROPHYSICS, THEORETICAL PHYSICS. *Educ:* Newark Col Eng, BS, 62; Yale Univ, MS, 63, PhD(physics), 66. *Prof Exp:* Res staff physicist, Yale Univ, 65-66, vis fel physics, 66-67; resident res assoc gravitation & astrophys, Inst Space Studies, New York, 67-69; mem physics, Inst Advan Study, NJ, 69-71; ASSOC PROF PHYSICS, UNIV PA, 71- *Concurrent Pos:* Fel, Inst Space Studies, 66 & US AEC, 66-67; assoc, Nat Acad Sci-Nat Res Coun, 67-69; NSF grant, 70-76 & 77-; vis scientist, Max Planck Inst, 71; consult, Naval Res Lab, 74-; Air Force Off Sci Res grant, 78-; sr assoc, Nat Acad Sci & Lab High Energy Astrophys, NASA, 72-73. *Mem:* Int Astron Union; fel Am Phys Soc; Am Astron Soc; fel NY Acad Sci; Int Soc Gen Relativity & Gravitation. *Res:* Theoretical astrophysics; rotating bodies in general relativity; neutron star models and pulsars; gravitational collapse; relativistic astrophysics; cosmology. *Mailing Add:* Dept of Physics Univ of Pa Philadelphia PA 19104

COHEN, JOEL EPHRAIM, b Washington, DC, Feb 10, 44; m 70; c 2. POPULATION BIOLOGY, APPLIED MATHEMATICS. *Educ:* Harvard Univ, BA, 65, MA, 67, PhD(appl math), 70, MPH, 70, DrPH, 73. *Hon Degrees:* MA, Univ Cambridge, Eng, 74. *Prof Exp:* Asst & assoc prof biol, Harvard Univ, 71-75; PROF POPULATIONS, ROCKEFELLER UNIV, 75- *Concurrent Pos:* Consult, Dept Math, Rand Corp, 68-74 & Computer Sci & Eng Bd, Nat Acad Sci, 69-73; mem comt conserv nonhuman primates, Nat Res Coun, 71-74; lectr pop sci, Harvard Sch Pub Health, 71-73; chmn bd dirs, Inst Math, Soc Indust & Appl Math, 73-; fel King's Col, Cambridge, Eng, 74-75; fel, Ctr Advan Study Behav Sci, 81-82; John Simon Guggenheim fel, 81-82. *Honors & Awards:* Mercer Award, Ecol Soc Am, 72. *Mem:* AAAS; Am Soc Naturalists; Math Asn Am; Am Statist Asn; Soc Indust & Appl Math. *Res:* Populations, especially molecular and cellular populations, demography, social groups and ecology; applied mathematics especially stochastic processes, combinatorics, statistics and computing. *Mailing Add:* Rockefeller Univ 1230 York Ave New York NY 10021

COHEN, JOEL M, b Worcester, Mass, Sept 27, 41. ALGEBRA. *Educ:* Brown Univ, ScB, 63; Mass Inst Technol, PhD(math), 66. *Prof Exp:* Instr math, Univ Chicago, 66-68; asst prof, Univ Pa, 68-75; assoc prof, 75-78, PROF MATH, UNIV MD, 78- *Concurrent Pos:* Vis prof, Univ Perugia, Italy, 77, 78 & 81 & Univ Rome, 80. *Mem:* Am Math Soc; Math Asn Am; Ital Math Union. *Res:* Algebraic topology, chiefly low dimensional complexes and group theory; algebra and operator algebras, chiefly analysis on the free group. *Mailing Add:* Dept of Math Univ of Md College Park MD 20742

COHEN, JOEL RALPH, b Chelsea, Mass, Oct 20, 26; m 47; c 3. CLINICAL MICROBIOLOGY. *Educ:* Univ Mass, BS, 49, MS, 50, PhD(microbiol), 75. *Prof Exp:* Microbiologist & supvr labs, Springfield Hosp, 50-64, chief clin labs, 64-68; assoc prof, 68-75, PROF BIOSCI, SPRINGFIELD COL, 75- *Concurrent Pos:* Lectr microbiol, Sch Nursing, 51-53; vis lectr, Univ Mass, 52-62 & Springfield Col, 54-68; consult, Ludlow Hosp, 52-68, Noble Hosp, 52-74, Baystate Med Ctr, 55-, Wesson Maternity Hosp, 56-68, Springfield Munic Hosp, Vet Admin Hosp, Northampton & Springfield Health Dept; regist & specialist microbiologist, Am Bd Microbiol. *Mem:* Fel AAAS; Am Soc Microbiol; Sigma Xi; fel Am Pub Health Asn; NY Acad Sci. *Res:* Methods in clinical microbiology in area of incidence of intrahospital infections and microbial susceptibility to antibiotics; rapid identification of bacterial agents. *Mailing Add:* Dept Biol Springfield Col 263 Alden St Springfield MA 01109

COHEN, JOEL SEYMOUR, b Baltimore, Md, Aug 27, 41. MATHEMATICS. *Educ:* Univ Md, BSEE, 64, PhD(math), 70. *Prof Exp:* ASST PROF MATH, UNIV DENVER, 69- *Mem:* Am Math Soc; Math Asn Am. *Res:* Functional analysis; Banach spaces; absolutely p-summing operators. *Mailing Add:* Dept of Math Univ of Denver Denver CO 80208

COHEN, JOHN DAVID, solid state physics, see previous edition

COHEN, JONATHAN BREWER, b Akron, Ohio, Dec 17, 44. MOLECULAR PHARMACOLOGY. *Educ:* Harvard Col, BA, 66; Harvard Univ, MA, 67, PhD(chem), 72. *Prof Exp:* Res assoc neurobiol, Pasteur Inst, Paris, 71-74; asst prof, 75-80, ASSOC PROF PHARMACOL, HARVARD MED SCH, 80- *Concurrent Pos:* Lectr neurobiol, Ecole Normale Superieure, Paris, 73-74. *Mem:* Am Soc Pharmacol & Exp Therapeut; Biophys Soc; AAAS. *Res:* Molecular basis of synaptic function; mechanism of permeability control by acetycholine receptors; mode of action of drugs acting at cholinergic synapses; structural and functional properties of synaptic membranes. *Mailing Add:* Dept of Pharmacol Harvard Med Sch 250 Longwood Ave Boston MA 02115

COHEN, JORDAN J, b St Louis, Mo, June 18, 34; m 56; c 3. INTERNAL MEDICINE, NEPHROLOGY. *Educ:* Yale Univ, BA, 56; Harvard Univ, MD, 60. *Prof Exp:* Assoc physician, assoc div med res & dir div renal dis, RI Hosp, Providence, 65-71; PROF MED, MED SCH, TUFTS UNIV & DIR RENAL DIV, TUFTS-NEW ENG MED CTR, 71- *Concurrent Pos:* From asst prof to assoc prof, Brown Univ, 65-71; instr med, Harvard Med Sch, 67-71. *Mem:* Fedn Clin Res; Am Soc Nephrology; Am Soc Internal Med. *Res:* Renal mechanisms involved in acid-base homeostasis; application of computer techniques to simulation analyses of body fluid; electrolyte physiology. *Mailing Add:* Tufts-New Eng Med Ctr 171 Harrison Ave Boston MA 02111

COHEN, JOSEPH, b Pittsburgh, Pa, Nov 11, 16; m 47; c 3. INORGANIC CHEMISTRY. *Educ:* Univ Pittsburgh, BSChem, 38. *Prof Exp:* Res fel chem & physics, Mellon Inst Indust Res, 45-47; salesman restaurant equip, Interstate Restaurant Supply, Calif, 47-48; res chemist, Naval Ord Test Sta, China Lake, Calif, 48-50, unit leader solid propellant res, combustion mech & heterogeneous interactions, 50-53; prin chemist, 53-58, dept mgr process control eng, 58-60, div mgr solid rocket prod, 60-62, prog mgr solid propellant develop, 63-79, PROG MGR, AEROJET SOLID PROPULSION CO & AEROJET STRATEGIC PROPULSION CO, AEROJET-GEN CORP, 80- *Mem:* Am Chem Soc; Sigma Xi; fel Am Inst Chemists. *Res:* Synthesis of high energy tetrazole and guanidine derivatives; formulated low flame-temperature gun propellants; crystallization control of inorganic compounds; solid propellant research; internal ballistics of solid rockets. *Mailing Add:* 888 Campus Commons Rd Sacramento CA 95825

COHEN, JUDITH GAMORA, b NY, May 5, 46; m 73. ASTROPHYSICS. *Educ:* Radcliffe Col, BA, 67; Calif Inst Technol, MS, 69, PhD(astron), 71. *Prof Exp:* Miller fel astron, Univ Calif, Berkeley, 71-73; asst astronomer, Kitt Peak Nat Observ, 73-77, assoc astronomer, 77-79; ASSOC PROF ASTRON, CALIF INST TECHNOL, 79- *Mem:* Am Astron Soc; Int Astron Union. *Res:* Nucleosynthesis, interstellar medium, globular clusters. *Mailing Add:* Calif Inst of Technol 1201 E California Blvd Pasadena CA 91101

COHEN, JULES, b Brooklyn, NY, Aug 26, 31; m 56; c 3. INTERNAL MEDICINE, CARDIOLOGY. *Educ:* Univ Rochester, AB, 53, MD, 57. *Prof Exp:* Intern, Beth Israel Hosp, 57-58; resident, Strong Mem Hosp, 58-59; res assoc, NIH, 60-62; res asst, Royal Postgrad Md Sch London, 62-63; sr instr med, 64-65, from asst prof to assoc prof, 66-73, PROF MED, UNIV ROCHESTER, 73- *Concurrent Pos:* USPHS trainee med, Med Ctr, Univ Rochester, 59-60, res fel, 64-65; USPHS res grants, 63-69 & 75-; Am Heart Asn res grant, 70-72. *Mem:* Am Physiol Soc; Am Fedn Clin Res; Royal Soc Med; Am Heart Asn; Am Col Physicians. *Res:* Cardiac hypertrophy; hemoglobin function and tissue oxygenation; cardiomyopathies. *Mailing Add:* Dept of Med Strong Mem Hosp Rochester NY 14642

COHEN, JULES BERNARD, b New York, NY, June 12, 33; m 56; c 2. ENVIRONMENTAL HEALTH ENGINEERING. *Educ:* City Col New York, BCE, 55; Univ Colo, MS, 58; Calif Inst Technol, PhD(environ health eng), 65. *Prof Exp:* Lectr civil eng, City Col New York, 55-56; staff engr, USPHS, Colo, 56-59 & Ohio, 59-62, sr staff engr, 65-66; sect chief environ eng, Arctic Health Res Ctr, 66-71, br chief environ sci, 71-73; tech coordr, Nat Enforcement Invests Ctr, Environ Protection Agency, 73-78, dep asst dir, 78-79; LAB DIR & VPRES, ENVIRON LAB, SVERDRUP TECHNOL INC, 79- *Concurrent Pos:* Assoc prof, Univ Alaska, 71-73; consult, Environ Protection Agency Sci Adv Bd. *Honors & Awards:* Bronze Medal, US Environ Protection Agency, 78. *Mem:* Am Soc Civil Engrs; Water Pollution Control Fedn; Air Pollution Control Asn; Sigma Xi. *Res:* Water and air pollution control; stream sanitation; environmental health engineering aspects of the adaptation of man to life in the Arctic and sub-Arctic. *Mailing Add:* 202 Meadowbrook Dr Tullahoma TN 37388

COHEN, JULIUS, b Brooklyn, NY, Apr 16, 26. PHYSICS. *Educ:* NY Univ, AB, 50; Syracuse Univ, MS, 53. *Prof Exp:* Res assoc thin films, Syracuse Univ, 51-52; jr engr transistor physics, Gen Tel & Electronics Labs, 52-53, adv res engr emission & thin films, 54-67, eng specialist, 67-69; PHYSICIST, NAT BUR STAND, 69- *Concurrent Pos:* Assoc physicist thermistor bolometers, Bulova Res & Develop Labs, 53-54; Japanese Ministry Educ guest scholar tunnel emission, Japan & Osaka Univs, 64-65. *Mem:* Am Phys Soc; Sigma Xi. *Res:* Thin films; semiconductors; electrical conductivity; emission; vacuum techniques; photoconductivity; piezoeletricity and pyroelectricity in polymers; systems analysis; optical instrumentation; physics engineering; infared; noise. *Mailing Add:* MET B306 Nat Bur Standards Washington DC 20234

COHEN, JULIUS JAY, b Newark, NJ, Apr 26, 23; m 52; c 2. PHYSIOLOGY. *Educ:* Rutgers Univ, BS, 45; NY Univ, MD, 48. *Prof Exp:* Intern, Cincinnati Gen Hosp, 48-49; from jr to sr resident, Dept Med, Col Med, Univ Cincinnati, 49-51, res fel dept clin physiol, 51 & dept physiol, 53-54, instr physiol, 54-55, asst prof physiol & instr med, 55-59; assoc prof physiol, 59-66, actg chmn dept physiol, 67-68, PROF PHYSIOL, SCH MED & DENT, UNIV ROCHESTER, 66- *Concurrent Pos:* Markle Found med sci scholar, 55-60; mem physiol study sect, NIH, 65-70. *Mem:* AAAS; Soc Exp Biol & Med; Am Heart Asn; Am Physiol Soc. *Res:* Renal physiology and metabolism; relationships between intermediary metabolism of the kidney and its excretory function; comparative physiology; pathological physiology; isotopes. *Mailing Add:* Dept Physiol Box 642 Sch Med & Dent Univ Rochester Rochester NY 14642

COHEN, KARL (PALEY), b New York, NY, Feb 5, 13; m 38; c 3. NUCLEAR SCIENCE. *Educ:* Columbia Univ, AB, 33, AM, 34, PhD(phys chem), 37. *Prof Exp:* From asst to prof, Columbia Univ, 38-40, dir, Theoret Div SAM Labs, 40-44; head theoret physics group, Standard Oil Develop Co, 44-48; tech dir, H K Ferguson Co, 48-52; vpres, Walter Kidde Nuclear Labs, Inc, 52-55; mgr adv eng, Atomic Power Equip Dept, Gen Elec Co, 55-65, gen mgr, Breeder Reactor Dept, 65-71, mgr, Oper Planning, 71-73, chief scientist, Nuclear Energy Div, 73-78; CONSULT NUCLEAR ENERGY, 78- *Concurrent Pos:* Regents lectr, Univ Calif, Berkeley, 70; dir, US Nat Comt, World Energy Conf, 72-78; mem adv comt, Energy Proj, Int Inst Appl Systs Anal, Vienna, 76-81; mem adv coun, Ctr Theoret Studies, Univ Miami, 77-; consult prof, Stanford Univ, 78-81. *Honors & Awards:* Krupp Prize for Energy Res, 77; Chem Pioneer Award, 79. *Mem:* Fel AAAS; Am Phys Soc; fel Am Nuclear Soc (treas, 55-57, pres, 68-69); Nat Acad Eng. *Res:* Applied nuclear energy; isotope separation; gaseous diffusion; gas centrifuges; fast breeder reactors. *Mailing Add:* 928 N California Ave Palo Alto CA 94303

COHEN, KENNETH SAMUEL, b Los Angeles, Calif, May 30, 37; m 61; c 4. INDUSTRIAL HYGIENE, TOXICOLOGY. *Educ:* San Diego State Univ, BS, 65; Calif Western Univ, PhD(occup health), 76. *Prof Exp:* Lab mgr, clin path, NIH Primate Res Colony, 63-65; mgr safety & qual anal, Biol Assocs, Inc, 67-72; dir indust hyg, Micronomics Int, Inc, 72-76; acting head indust hyg, Naval Regional Med Ctr, 76-78; TOXICOLOGIST & LECTR, OCCUP HEALTH, CONSULT HEALTH SERVS, 78- *Concurrent Pos:* Mem Toxicol & Textbook Comts, Am Indust Hyg Asn, 76-; mem educ comt, Am Soc Safety Engrs, 76-; mem Am Col Toxicol, 78- *Mem:* Am Pub Health Asn; Soc Occup Environ Health; Nat Fire Protection Asn; Am Conf Govt Indust Hygienists. *Res:* Toxic vapor simulation of industrial ventilation systems using SF6 as an inert tracer gas to model emissions which are very toxic or difficult to measure. *Mailing Add:* PO Box 1625 El Cajon CA 92022

COHEN, LARRY WILLIAM, b Winnipeg, Man, Dec 24, 36; US citizen; m 59; c 2. GENETICS, MOLECULAR BIOLOGY. *Educ:* Univ Calif, Los Angeles, BA, 60, MA, 62, PhD(zool), 64. *Prof Exp:* NIH fel, Univ Calif, San Diego & Med Sch Univ Mich, 63-65; asst prof, Dept Biol Sci, Douglass Col, Rutgers Univ, 65-67; asst prof zool, 67-70, assoc prof zool, 70-76, chmn dept, 73-76, PROF BIOL, POMONA COL, 76-, CHMN, BIOL DEPT, 81- *Concurrent Pos:* NIH spec fel, Univ Calif, Riverside, 71; vis prof, Dept Molecular Virol, Hadassah Med Sch, Hebrew Univ Jerusalem, 74; vis scientist, City of Hope Nat Med Ctr, 78 & 81. *Mem:* AAAS; Am Soc Microbiol. *Res:* Microbial genetics; cell to cell agglutination phenomena; lysis in salmonella phage P22; recombinant DNA - directed mutagenesis. *Mailing Add:* Dept of Biol Pomona Col Claremont CA 91711

COHEN, LAWRENCE, b Leeds, Eng, Nov 23, 26; m 51; c 3. ORAL MEDICINE, ORAL PATHOLOGY. *Educ:* Univ Leeds, BChD, 49, Univ London, MD, 56, PhD(histochem), 66. *Prof Exp:* Resident oral surg, Middlesex Hosp, London, Eng, 57-59; sr resident, Plastic & Jaw Unit, Stoke Mandeville Hosp, Buckinghamshire, 60-61; sr resident, Univ Col Hosp Dent Sch, 61-62; lectr oral path, Inst Dent Surg, London, 62-63, sr lectr oral med, 63-67; prof oral diag & head dept, Univ Ill Med Ctr, 67-76; CHMN DEPT DENT, ILL MASONIC MED CTR, 76- *Concurrent Pos:* Consult, West Side Vet Admin Hosp, Chicago, Ill, 68-74; vis prof med, Univ Chicago, 74-75; chmn panel rev of oral cavity drug preparations, Food & Drug Admin, 74-80. *Honors & Awards:* Samuel Charles Miller Award, Am Acad Oral Med, 80. *Mem:* Fel Royal Soc Med; Brit Bone & Tooth Soc; Int Asn Dent Res. *Res:* Keratinization and histochemistry of the oral mucosa. *Mailing Add:* Dept Dent 927 W Wellington Ave Chicago IL 60657

COHEN, LAWRENCE BARUCH, b Indianapolis, Ind, June 18, 39; c 2. NEUROPHYSIOLOGY. *Educ:* Univ Chicago, BS, 61; Columbia Univ, PhD(zool), 65. *Prof Exp:* Asst prof, 68-71, ASSOC PROF PHYSIOL, SCH MED, YALE UNIV, 71- *Concurrent Pos:* NSF fel, Agr Res Coun Inst Physiol, Cambridge, Eng, 66-68. *Honors & Awards:* McMaster Award, Columbia Univ, 65. *Mem:* Soc Neurosci; Soc Gen Physiol; Biophys Soc. *Res:* Optical methods for measuring activity in invertebrate central nervous systems. *Mailing Add:* Dept of Physiol Yale Univ Sch of Med New Haven CT 06510

COHEN, LAWRENCE SOREL, b New York, NY, Mar 27, 33; m 61; c 2. INTERNAL MEDICINE, CARDIOLOGY. *Educ:* Harvard Col, AB, 54; NY Univ, MD, 58. *Hon Degrees:* MA, Yale Univ, 70. *Prof Exp:* Fel cardiol, Harvard Univ, 62-64; sr investr cardiol, NIH, 65-68; assoc prof med, Univ Tex Southwestern Med Sch Dallas, 68-70; PROF MED, SCH MED, YALE UNIV, 70- *Concurrent Pos:* Attend physician, Yale-New Haven Med Ctr, 70- *Honors & Awards:* NY Univ Sch Med Award, 58. *Mem:* Am Fedn Clin Res; fel Am Col Cardiol; fel Am Col Physicians; Am Heart Asn. *Res:* Coronary artery disease; hemodynamics; radionuclide myocardial perfusion. *Mailing Add:* Dept of Med Yale Univ Sch of Med New Haven CT 06510

COHEN, LEONARD A, b New York, NY, Mar 21, 39; m 67; c 2. CELL BIOLOGY. *Educ:* Univ Wis-Madison, BS, 60; City Univ New York, PhD(biol), 72. *Prof Exp:* Res asst microbiol, Kingsbrooke Jewish Med Ctr, 60-62; res asst cell biol, Albert Einstein Col Med, 63-66; instr biol, City Univ New York, 67-72; res assoc cell biol, 73-78, RES ASSOC, DIV NUTRIT, AM HEALTH FOUND, 78- *Mem:* AAAS; Sigma Xi. *Res:* The influence of dietary fat on mammary tumor development in rodent models; analysis of intracellular response systems in cultured mammal and neoplastic mammary epithelial cells. *Mailing Add:* Naylor Dana Inst for Dis Prev Am Health Found Dana Rd Valhalla NY 10595

COHEN, LEONARD ARLIN, b Brooklyn, NY, May 4, 24; m 50; c 3. PHYSIOLOGY. *Educ:* Univ Conn, BA, 48; Yale Univ, PhD(physiol), 52. *Prof Exp:* From instr to asst prof physiol & pharmacol, Sch Med, Univ Pittsburgh, 51-61; head dept physiol, Albert Einstein Med Ctr, 61-67; prof phys med & rehab, Sch Med, Temple Univ, 67-70; pres, 70-74, PROF PHYSIOL, MICH STATE UNIV, 70- *Concurrent Pos:* Fulbright fel, Oxford Univ, 56-57, NSF fel, 57-58; pres, Human Capability Charitable Corp, 76- & Human Capability Charitable Corp. *Mem:* AAAS; Am Physiol Soc; Aerospace Med Asn; fel Royal Soc Med; physiology of cervical, vestibular, joint, muscle and tactile receptors; mechanisms for body orientation and interraction with motor coordination; vision dynamics, including postural and other non-retinal inputs; visually centered performance; disability evaluation; clinical physiology; hallucinogens and body-environment orientation. *Res:* Neurophysiology; proprioception. *Mailing Add:* 15951 Harden Circle Southfield MI 48075

COHEN, LEONARD DAVID, b Philadelphia, Pa, Aug 7, 32; m 57; c 3. NUCLEAR PHYSICS, REACTOR PHYSICS. *Educ:* Univ Pa, BA, 54, MS, 56, PhD(physics), 59. *Prof Exp:* Reactor physicist, Knolls Atomic Power Lab, Gen Elec Co, 59-62, geophysicist, Space Sci Lab, 62-64; asst prof, 64-73, ASSOC PROF PHYSICS, DREXEL UNIV, 73- *Mem:* Am Phys Soc; Am Nuclear Soc; Am Geophys Union. *Res:* Space radiation physics; atmospheric physics using radon gas as a tracer of atmospheric turbulence. *Mailing Add:* Dept Physics Drexel Univ Philadelphia PA 19104

COHEN, LEONARD GEORGE, b Brooklyn, NY, Feb 28, 41. COMMUNICATIONS, PLASMA PHYSICS. *Educ:* City Col New York, BEE, 62; Brown Univ, ScM, 64, PhD(plasma physics), 68. *Prof Exp:* Res asst eng, Brown Univ, 64-66, plasma physics, 66-68; MEM TECH STAFF, GUIDED WAVE RES LAB, BELL TEL LABS, 68- *Mem:* Sr mem Inst Elec & Electronics Engrs; Optical Soc Am. *Res:* Experimental and theoretical studies of the interaction between collisionless plasmas and electromagnetic fields; measured attenuation and depolarization of light transmitted along glass fibers; optical communications. *Mailing Add:* 69 Longstreet Rd Holmdel NJ 07733

COHEN, LEONARD HARVEY, b Winnipeg, Man, Mar 19, 25; m 49; c 2. BIOCHEMISTRY. *Educ:* Univ Man, BSc, 48, MSc, 51; Univ Toronto, PhD(biochem), 54. *Prof Exp:* Asst pharmacol, Yale Univ, 54-55; res scientist, Roswell Mem Inst, 55-59; from asst prof pharmacol to prof biochem, Univ Man, 59-65; SR MEM, INST CANCER RES, 65- *Concurrent Pos:* Assoc prof phys biochem, Univ Pa, 65-81, adj prof, 81- *Mem:* Am Soc Biol Chemists; Am Soc Cell Biol; AAAS; Am Soc Develop Biol. *Res:* Nucleic acid and nucleotide metabolism; development, differentiation; enzymology; chromosomal proteins; histones, gene regulation. *Mailing Add:* Inst for Cancer Res 7701 Burholme Ave Philadelphia PA 19111

COHEN, LESLIE, b Baltimore, Md, Jan 14, 23; m 67; c 1. NUCLEAR PHYSICS. *Educ:* Johns Hopkins Univ, BA, 44, PhD(physics), 52. *Prof Exp:* Physicist, Bur Standards, 44-45; instr physics, Loyola Col, 47-48; jr instr, Johns Hopkins Univ, 48-51, asst, 51-52; res assoc, Knolls Atomic Power Lab, Gen Elec Co, 53-55; res assoc, Nuclear Physics Div, 55-81, EXP PHYS, CONDENSED MATTER & RADIATION SCI DIV, NAVAL RES LAB, 81- *Concurrent Pos:* Vis scientist, Optical Sci Ctr, Univ of Ariz, 75-76. *Mem:* Am Phys Soc. *Res:* Nuclear spectroscopy; nuclear reactors; photonuclear and charged particle reactions; lasers. *Mailing Add:* 4555 Overlook Ave SW Naval Res Lab Nuclear Physics Div Washington DC 20032

COHEN, LEWIS H, b Dallas, Tex, Jan 2, 37. GEOCHEMISTRY. *Educ:* Mass Inst Technol, BS, 58; Univ Calif, Berkeley, MS, 61; Univ Calif, San Diego, PhD(earth sci), 65. *Prof Exp:* Asst prof geophys eng, Univ Calif, Berkeley, 65-66; asst prof geol, 66-69, assoc prof, 69-76, PROF GEOL, UNIV CALIF, RIVERSIDE, 76- *Mem:* Am Geophys Union; Geochem Soc; Mineral Soc Am. *Res:* Chemistry and physics at elevated temperatures and pressures; physical properties of rocks; radioactive waste disposal. *Mailing Add:* Dept of Earth Sci Univ of Calif Riverside CA 92521

COHEN, LOUIS, b Chicago, Ill, Dec 5, 28; m 52; c 3. INTERNAL MEDICINE, CARDIOLOGY. *Educ:* Univ Chicago, BS, 48, MD, 53. *Prof Exp:* Res asst, 49-53, from intern to resident med, 53-55 & 57-58, instr, 59-61, asst prof, 61-68, assoc prof, 68-75, PROF MED UNIV CHICAGO, 75-, ATTEND PHYSICIAN, UNIV CHICAGO HOSPS & CLINS, 61- *Concurrent Pos:* Nat Heart Inst trainee, 55; Am Heart Asn res fel, 58-60, advan res fel, 60-62; vis prof, Shaare Zedek Hosp, Jerusalem, Israel, 66, Sacred Heart Hosp, Eugene, Ore, 68, Univ Hawaii, 68, Pahlavi Univ, Iran, 77 & Hasharon Hosp, 78 & 80; fel coun arteriosclerosis & coun clin cardiol, Am Heart Asn; panelist, Nat Acad Sci & Sigma Xi. *Mem:* Tissue Cult Asn; Am Soc Human Genetics; fel Am Col Physicians; fel Am Col Cardiol; fel Am Col Clin Pharmacol. *Res:* Lipoproteins structure; experimental and clinical atherosclerosis; diagnostic enzymology; tissue culture; treatment and basic mechanisms in muscular dystrophy; myocardial infarction and salvage. *Mailing Add:* Sch Med Univ Chicago 950 E 59th St Chicago IL 60637

COHEN, LOUIS ARTHUR, b Boston, Mass, July 12, 26; m 55; c 1. PHYSICAL ORGANIC CHEMISTRY, BIO-ORGANIC CHEMISTRY. *Educ:* Northeastern Univ, BS, 49; Mass Inst Technol, PhD(chem), 52. *Prof Exp:* Instr biochem, Med Sch, Yale Univ, 52-54; asst scientist, 54-57, from scientist to sr scientist, 57-64, CHIEF CHEM, SECT BIOCHEM MECHANISMS, NAT INST ARTHRITIS & METAB DIS, NIH, 65-, DIR GRAD SCH, FOUND ADVAN EDUC SCI, 70- *Concurrent Pos:* USPHS scientist, 54- *Mem:* Am Chem Soc. *Res:* Steroid synthesis; veratrum alkaloids; peptide synthesis; phosphorylation; oxidation of nitrogen compounds; amino acid metabolism and interconversion; protein structure; reaction kinetics and mechanism; nuclear magnetic resonance spectroscopy; biochemical mechanisms; drug design; antiviral antibiotics. *Mailing Add:* Lab of Chem Nat Inst Arthritis & Metab Dis NIH Bethesda MD 20205

COHEN, MAIMON MOSES, b Baltimore, Md, Jan 24, 35; m 55; c 3. CYTOGENETICS. *Educ:* Johns Hopkins Univ, AB, 55; Univ Md, MS, 59, PhD(agron), 63. *Prof Exp:* Jr asst health serv officer, NIH, 60-62; NSF fel human genetics, Univ Mich, 62-64, instr, 64-65; from asst prof to assoc prof pediat & assoc res prof microbiol, Med Sch, State Univ NY Buffalo, 68-72; prof human genetics & chmn dept, Hadassah-Hewbrew Univ Med Ctr, 72-78; prof pediat & assoc chief genetics, Children's Mem Hosp, Northwestern Univ Med Sch, 78-82; PROF OBSTET, PEDIAT & BIOL CHEM & CHIEF, DIV GENETICS & DIR, CTR HUMAN GENETICS, SCH MED, UNIV MD, 82- *Concurrent Pos:* Dir cytogenetics, Buffalo Children's Hosp, 67-72. *Mem:* AAAS; Genetics Soc Am; Soc Pediat Res; Am Soc Human Genetics; Tissue Cult Asn. *Res:* Structure and function of human chromosomes; effect of various mutagenic agents on chromosomes of cultured tissues; chromosome instability syndromes. *Mailing Add:* Sch Med Univ Md 600 W Redwood St Baltimore MD 21201

COHEN, MARC SINGMAN, b Charleston, WVa, Feb 22, 50; m 75; c 2. UROLOGY. *Educ:* Univ SFla, BA, 72; Univ Miami, MD, 75. *Prof Exp:* Resident surg, Boston Univ Affil Hosp, 75-76; resident urol, 76-80, instr, 80-81 & ASST PROF UROL, UNIV TEX MED BR, 81- *Concurrent Pos:* Res award, Mead Johnson Nat Student Res Forum, 79; Res award, Am Soc Pediat Nephrologists, 79; Res fel, AUA Res Scholar, 80-82. *Mem:* Am Med Asn; Sigma Xi. *Res:* Investigating the etiologies of urinary calculi, particularly the role of bacteria and bacterial byproducts; bacterial-urothelial interactions and urothelial replacement. *Mailing Add:* Div Urol Univ Tex Med Br Galveston TX 77550

COHEN, MARGO NITA PANUSH, b Detroit, Mich, Oct 28, 40; m 61; c 3. INTERNAL MEDICINE, ENDOCRINOLOGY. *Educ:* Univ Mich, BS, 60, MD, 64; Univ Buenos Aires, PhD(biochem), 70; Am Bd Internal Med & Subspecialty Bd Endocrinol & Metab, Dipl. *Prof Exp:* Intern, Sinai Hosp, Detroit, 64-65; resident internal med, Henry Ford Hosp, 65-66; instr physiol, Univ Buenos Aires, 68-70; investr, Arg Nat Res Coun, 70-71; asst prof, 71-75, assoc prof med & physiol, 75-78, PROF MED, SCH MED, WAYNE STATE UNIV, 78- *Concurrent Pos:* USPHS diabetes trainee, Wayne State Univ & Sinai Hosp, Detroit, 66-68; NIH spec fel, Wayne State Univ, 68-69; vis scientist, Univ Manchester, 79; mem bd sci coun, Nat Inst Dent Res, NIH, 76-80; mem coun, Midwest Am Fedn Clin Res, 79-81. *Mem:* Am Fedn Clin Res; Am Physiol Soc; Am Diabetes Asn; Endocrine Soc; fel Am Col Physicians. *Res:* Diabetes, complications of; glomerular disease; basment membrane metabolism. *Mailing Add:* Dept of Med Wayne State Univ Sch of Med Detroit MI 48201

COHEN, MARION DEUTSCHE, b Perth Amboy, NJ, Jan 2, 43; m 64; c 2. MATHEMATICAL ANALYSIS. *Educ:* NY Univ, BA, 64; Wesleyan Univ, MA, 66, PhD(math), 70. *Prof Exp:* From asst prof to assoc prof math, NJ Inst Technol, 69-80. *Concurrent Pos:* Adj assoc prof, Temple Univ, 75- & Drexel Univ, 76-77 & 78-79. *Mem:* Am Math Soc. *Res:* Schwartz distribution theory, particularly the concepts of order and value of a distribution at a point. *Mailing Add:* Rm 310 Temple Univ 1616 Walnut St Philadelphia PA 19103

COHEN, MARLENE LOIS, b New Haven, Conn, May 5, 45; m 76; c 1. PHARMACOLOGY. *Educ:* Univ Conn, Storrs, BS, 68; Univ Calif, San Francisco, PhD(pharmacol), 73. *Prof Exp:* Fel, Roche Inst Molecular Biol, 73-75; sr pharmacologist, 75-80, RES SCIENTIST, LILLY RES LABS, ELI LILLY & CO, 80- *Concurrent Pos:* Adj asst prof, Dept Pharmacol, Ind Univ Sch Med, 76- *Mem:* Soc Exp Biol & Med; Am Soc Pharmacol & Exp Therapeuts. *Res:* Pharmacology, physiology and biochemistry of vascular and other smooth muscle. *Mailing Add:* Lilly Res Labs Div Eli Lilly & Co Indianapolis IN 46206

COHEN, MARSHALL HARRIS, b Manchester, NH, July 5, 26; m 48; c 3. ASTRONOMY. *Educ:* Ohio State Univ, BEE, 48, MSc, 49, PhD(physics), 52. *Prof Exp:* Res assoc, Antenna Lab, Ohio State Univ, 52-54; from asst prof to assoc prof, Sch Elec Eng, Cornell Univ, 54-64, assoc prof astron, 64-66; prof, Dept Appl Electrophys, Univ Calif, San Diego, 66-68; PROF RADIO-ASTRON, CALIF INST TECHNOL, 68-, EXEC OFFICER ASTRON, 81- *Concurrent Pos:* Guggenheim fel, 60-61 & 80-81. *Honors & Awards:* Rumford Medal, Am Acad Arts & Sci, 71. *Mem:* Am Astron Soc; Int Union Radio Sci; Int Astron Union. *Res:* Radio astronomy. *Mailing Add:* Dept of Astron Calif Inst of Technol Pasadena CA 91125

COHEN, MARSHALL JAY, solid state physics, see previous edition

COHEN, MARTIN ALLEN, inorganic chemistry, textile technology, see previous edition

COHEN, MARTIN GILBERT, b Brooklyn, NY, Jan 13, 38; div; c 3. LASERS. *Educ:* Columbia Col, AB, 57; Harvard Univ, MA, 58, PhD(appl physics), 64. *Prof Exp:* Mem tech staff, Bell Tel Labs, 64-69; DIR APPL RES, QUANTRONIX CORP, 69- *Mem:* Am Phys Soc. *Res:* Optical modulation and deflection; interaction of materials and laser light, solid state lasers, laser Q-switching and mode-locking. *Mailing Add:* Quantronix Corp 225 Engineers Rd Smithtown NY 11788

COHEN, MARTIN JOSEPH, b Brooklyn, NY, May 6, 21; m 49; c 3. ELECTRONIC PHYSICS. *Educ:* Brooklyn Col, BA, 42; Princeton Univ, MA, 48, PhD(physics), 51. *Prof Exp:* Staff mem, Radiation Lab, Mass Inst Technol, 42-45; res assoc electronics, Princeton Univ, 45-49; staff physicist, Princeton Lab, Radio Corp Am, 49-52; sr physicist, Radiation Res Corp, 52-55; consult physicist, 55-57; vpres, Franklin Systs, Inc, 57-63, vpres, Franklin GNO Corp, 63-74; PRES, PCP, INC, 75- *Mem:* Am Phys Soc; Inst Elec & Electronics Engrs; Am Chem Soc. *Res:* Solid state electronics; ion dynamics applications in gaseous chemistry. *Mailing Add:* PCP Inc 2155 Indian Rd West Palm Beach FL 33409

COHEN, MARTIN O, b New York, NY, Jan 15, 40; m 63; c 2. PHYSICS, COMPUTER SCIENCE. *Educ:* Cooper Union, BEE, 60; Columbia Univ, MSNE, 61, DEngSc(nuclear sci & eng), 65. *Prof Exp:* Proj scientist, United Nuclear Corp, 65-68; asst mgr, 68-76, MGR RES & DEVELOP, MATH APPLN GROUP, INC, 76- *Mem:* Am Nuclear Soc; Mil Opers Res Soc. *Res:* Development of sophisticated computer software packages to solve radiation transport, computer generated imagery, mass properties, and other scientific problems. *Mailing Add:* Math Applications Group Inc 3 Westchester Plaza Elmsford NY 10523

COHEN, MARTIN WILLIAM, b Brooklyn, NY, Feb 18, 35; m 62. IMMUNOLOGY, HUMAN PATHOLOGY. *Educ:* Columbia Col, AB, 56; State Univ NY, MD, 60. *Prof Exp:* Intern, NY Hosp, 60-61; instr, Albert Einstein Col Med, 67-68, asst prof, 69-70; assoc attend pathologist, Beth Israel Med Ctr, 70-78; STAFF PATHOLOGIST, BROOKLYN VET ADMIN HOSP, 78- *Concurrent Pos:* Fel, NY Univ Med Ctr, 61-65; spec fel, Nat Inst Allergy & Infectious Dis, 65; asst attend pathologist, Bronx Munic Hosp Ctr, 67-70; asst prof, Mt Sinai Med Sch, 70-78; clin assoc prof, NY Univ Med Sch, 76- *Mem:* Int Acad Path. *Res:* Cellular aspects of hormonal immunity; immunopathology. *Mailing Add:* Brooklyn Vet Admin Hosp Lab Serv Brooklyn NY 11209

COHEN, MARVIN LOU, b Montreal, Que, Mar 3, 35; US citizen; m 58; c 2. PHYSICS. *Educ:* Univ Calif, Berkeley, AB, 57; Univ Chicago, MS, 58, PhD(theoret solid state physics), 64. *Prof Exp:* Mem tech staff, Bell Tel Labs, 63-64; from asst prof to assoc prof, 64-68, PROF PHYSICS, UNIV CALIF, BERKELEY, 69- *Concurrent Pos:* A P Sloan fel, Cambridge Univ, Eng & Univ Calif, Berkeley, 65-67; prof, Miller Inst Basic Res Sci, Univ Calif, Berkeley, 69-70 & 76-77; exchange prof, Univ Paris, 72-73; Guggenheim fel, Univ Hawaii, 78-79; US rep semiconductor comn, Int Union Pure & Appl Physics, 75-81. *Honors & Awards:* Oliver E Buckley Prize Solid State Physics, Am Phys Soc, 79. *Mem:* Nat Acad Sci; fel Am Phys Soc. *Res:* Theoretical solid state physics; superconductivity; semiconductors; optical bonding and electronic properties of solids; surfaces of solids. *Mailing Add:* Dept Physics Univ Calif Berkeley CA 94720

COHEN, MARVIN MORRIS, b New York, NY, Apr 24, 40; m 61; c 4. SOLID STATE PHYSICS. *Educ:* Brooklyn Col, BA, 62; Am Univ, MS, 65, PhD(solid state physics), 67. *Prof Exp:* Res physicist, Harry Diamond Labs, 62-74; PHYSICIST, ENERGY RES & DEVELOP ADMIN, 74- *Concurrent Pos:* Adj prof, Am Univ, 67- *Mem:* AAAS; Am Phys Soc. *Res:* Impurity band conduction in solids; tunneling in solids; radiation damage in a fusion environment. *Mailing Add:* 14116 Bauer Dr Rockville MD 20853

COHEN, MAYNARD, b Regina, Sask, May 17, 20; US citizen; m 45; c 2. NEUROSCIENCES. *Educ:* Univ Mich, AB, 41; Wayne Univ, MD, 44; Univ Minn, PhD(path), 53. *Prof Exp:* Res assoc, Riks Hosp, Oslo, Norway, 51-52; from asst prof to prof neurol, Univ Minn, 53-63; prof & head div neurol & prof pharmacol, Col Med, Univ Ill, 63-71; PROF & HEAD, DEPT NEUROL SCI & PROF BIOCHEM, RUSH MED COL, 71-, CHMN, DEPT NEUROL SCI, PRESBY-ST LUKE'S HOSP, 63- *Concurrent Pos:* NIH spec fel, Univ London, 57-58; consult, Nat Inst Neurol Dis & Blindness, 59-63 & NIMH, 68-72; mem prof adv bd, Epilepsy Founds; Fulbright lectr, Univ Oslo, 77. *Honors & Awards:* Distinguished Serv Award, Col Med, Wayne State Univ, 64. *Mem:* Biochem Soc; Am Acad Neurol (past vpres, pres, 81-83); Am Asn Neuropath; Int Soc Neurochem; Asn Univ Prof Neurol (past pres). *Res:* Nervous and mental diseases; biochemistry of the nervous system; cerebrovascular disease; neurotoxic agents; phosphorylated compounds in the brain; amino acid and carbohydrate interrelationships in the brain. *Mailing Add:* Dept of Neurol Sci Rush Med Col Chicago IL 60612

COHEN, MELVIN JOSEPH, b Los Angeles, Calif, Sept 28, 28; m 63; c 4. NEUROBIOLOGY. *Educ:* Univ Calif, Los Angeles, BA, 49, MA, 52, PhD(zool), 54. *Prof Exp:* NSF fel, Stockholm, Sweden, 54-55; instr biol, Harvard Univ, 55-57; from asst prof to prof, Univ Ore, 57-69; PROF BIOL, YALE UNIV, 69- *Concurrent Pos:* Guggenheim Found fel, 64-65. *Mem:* Nat Acad Sci; Am Soc Zool; Soc Gen Physiol. *Res:* Comparative neurophysiology; growth and regeneration of nerve cells. *Mailing Add:* Dept of Biol Yale Univ New Haven CT 06520

COHEN, MERRILL, b Boston, Mass, Feb 5, 26; m 50; c 3. POLYMERS, ENGINEERING MATERIALS. *Educ:* Boston Univ, BA, 48; Univ Chicago, MS, 49, PhD(chem), 51. *Prof Exp:* Res assoc, Res Lab, Gen Elec Co, 51-52, Specialist org chem, Thomson Lab, 52-55, mgr chem & insulat- ion eng, Medium Steam Turbine Generator Dept, 55-70, MGR MAT & PROCESSES LAB, MEDIUM STEAM TURBINE GENERATOR DEPT, GEN ELEC CO, 70- *Concurrent Pos:* Jr chemist, Ionics Inc, 49, 50; mem tech adv comt, Nat Geothermal Info Resource Proj, Lawrence Berkeley Lab, Univ Calif, 74- *Mem:* Am Chem Soc; fel Am Inst Chem; Geothermal Res Coun. *Res:* Organic resin and polymer chemistry; epoxy, polyester, silicone resins; electrical insulation; laminated plastics; adhesives; protective coatings, high temperature synthetic lubricants; gas chromatography, air, water pollution; geothermal energy and steam turbine materials. *Mailing Add:* 8 May St Marblehead MA 01945

COHEN, MICHAEL, b New York, NY, May 9, 30; m 58. THEORETICAL PHYSICS. *Educ:* Cornell Univ, AB,51; Calif Inst Technol, PhD(physics), 56. *Prof Exp:* Res fel theoret physics, Calif Inst Technol, 55-57; mem, Inst Advan Study, NJ, 57-58; from asst prof to assoc prof, 58-75, assoc chmn grad affairs, 68-71, PROF PHYSICS, UNIV PA, 75- *Concurrent Pos:* Consult, Los Alamos Sci Lab. *Mem:* Am Phys Soc. *Res:* Quantum and statistical mechanics; theory of liquid helium. *Mailing Add:* Dept Physics Univ Pa Philadelphia PA 19104

COHEN, MITCHELL S(IMMONS), b Schenectady, NY, Nov 8, 30. ENGINEERING PHYSICS. *Educ:* Rensselaer Polytech Inst, BS, 52; Cornell Univ, PhD(eng physics), 58. *Prof Exp:* Staff mem, Lincoln Lab, Mass Inst Technol, 58-69; staff scientist, Micro-Bit Corp, 69-74; RES STAFF MEM, WATSON RES CTR, IBM CORP, 74- *Mem:* Am Phys Soc; Inst Elec & Electronics Engrs. *Res:* Magnetic bubbles; electron optics. *Mailing Add:* IBM Corp Watson Res Ctr PO Box 218 Yorktown Heights NY 10598

COHEN, MONROE W, b Montreal, Que, May 3, 40; m 65; c 2. NEUROSCIENCES. *Educ:* McGill Univ, BSc, 61, PhD(neurophys), 65. *Prof Exp:* Res fel neurobiol, Harvard Med Sch, 65-68; asst prof, 68-74, ASSOC PROF PHYSIOL, MCGILL UNIV, 74- *Concurrent Pos:* NATO sci fel, Nat Res Coun Can, 66-68; Med Res Coun Can scholar, 71-76; ed, The J Physiol, 75-77; Sci Res Coun Que res fel, 76-79. *Mem:* Can Physiol Soc; Soc Neurosci; Physiol Soc; AAAS. *Res:* Formation and development of nerve-muscle synapses; regulation of the distribution of acetylcholine receptors in skeletal muscle. *Mailing Add:* Dept of Physiol McGill Univ 3655 Drummond Montreal PQ H3G 1Y6 Can

COHEN, MONTAGUE, b London, Eng, July 24, 25; m 47; c 3. MEDICAL PHYSICS. *Educ:* Univ London, BSc, 46, PhD(physics), 58; ARCS, 46; FCCPM. *Prof Exp:* Physicist, Royal Aircraft Estab, 46-47 & Gen Elec Co Res Labs, 47-48; physicist med physics, London Hosp, 48-61, chief physicist, 66-75; prof officer, Int Atomic Energy Agency, 61-66; PROF RADIO PHYSICS, MCGILL UNIV, 75-, PROF MED PHYSICS, 79- *Concurrent Pos:* Consult radiother physics, Int Comn Radiation Units & Measurements, 64- & WHO, 70-; consult med physics, Int Atomic Energy Agency, 66-; dep ed, Brit J Radiol, 70-74, assoc ed, 79- *Honors & Awards:* Roentgen Prize, Brit Inst Radiol, 74. *Mem:* Inst Physics; Brit Inst Radiol (secy, 73-75); Hosp Physicists Asn; Am Asn Physicists in Med; Can Asn Physicists. *Res:* Clinical dosimetry applied to radiotherapy, with special reference to the acquisition of patient data and the use of such data in computerized dosimetry systems; medical imaging with special reference to quality control in diagnostic radiology. *Mailing Add:* Med Physics Unit Royal Victoria Hosp Montreal PQ H3A 1A1 Can

COHEN, MORREL HERMAN, b Boston, Mass, Sept 10, 27; m 50; c 4. THEORETICAL PHYSICS. *Educ:* Worcester Polytech Inst, BS, 47; Dartmouth Col, MA, 48; Univ Calif, Berkeley, PhD(physics), 52. *Hon Degrees:* DSc, Worcester Polytech Inst, 73. *Prof Exp:* Res assoc physics, Dartmouth Col, 47-48; from instr to assoc prof theoret physics, Univ Chicago, 52-60, prof, Dept Physics, Univ Chicago & James Franck Inst, 60-72, actg dir, 65-66, dir, James Franck Inst, 68-71, prof theoret biol, 68-72, Louis Block prof physics & theoret biol, 72-82, dir, Mat Res Lab, NSF, 77-81; SR SCI ADV, RES LABS, EXXON RES & ENG CO, EXXON CORP, 81- *Concurrent Pos:* Guggenheim fel, Cambridge Univ, 57-58; vis scientist, Nat Res Coun Can, 60; NSF sr fel, Univ Rome, 64-65; consult, Westinghouse Res Labs, 53, Chicago Midway Labs, 54, 55, Gen Elec Co Res Labs, 57-65, Argonne Nat Lab, 59-81, Boeing Sci Res Labs, 60, Hughes Res Lab, 60 & 62, Basic Sci Ctr, NAm Aviation Co, 62, Energy Conversion Devices Inc, 67-71 & 74-81, Monsanto Co, 72-78, Union Carbide Co, 76-79, Xerox Corp, 77 & 78 & Schlumberger Technol Corp, 78-81; NASA mem, Adv Panel Electrophysics, 62-66; mem adv comt, Nat Magnet Lab, 63-66; review comt, Solid State Sci & Metall Div, Argonne Nat Lab, 64-66, chmn, 66; chmn, Gordon Conf Chem & Physics of Solids, NH, 68 & chmn, Fourth Int Conf Amorphous & Liquid Semiconductors, 71; assoc ed, J Chem Physics, 60-63; publ bd, Univ Chicago, 69-70 & bd eds, J Statist Physics, 70-75; NIH spec fel, 72-73; vis fel, Cambridge Univ, 72-73, assoc, 73- *Honors & Awards:* Shrum lectr, Simon Fraser Univ, 73. *Mem:* Nat Acad Sci; AAAS; Am Inst Physics; fel Am Phys Soc; Sigma Xi. *Res:* Theoretical physics of condensed matter; developmental biology; quantum theory of solids; general physics of solids. *Mailing Add:* Exxon Res & Eng Co 1900 Linden Ave Linden NJ 07036

COHEN, MORRIS, b Santa Ana, Calif, July 20, 21. CELL BIOLOGY, MEDICAL RESEARCH. *Educ:* Univ Calif, BS, 47, PhD(plant path), 51. *Prof Exp:* Asst plant path, Univ Calif, Berkeley, 48-51; res assoc bot, Univ Calif, Los Angeles, 51-54, asst res botanist, 54-57; electron microscopist, St Joseph Hosp, Burbank, Calif, 57-62, res assoc, 62; res biologist, 62-81, RES AFFIL, WADSWORTH VET ADMIN HOSP, 81- *Concurrent Pos:* Am Cancer Soc fel, 51-54. *Mem:* AAAS; Am Soc Cell Biol; Electron Micros Soc Am; NY Acad Sci; Am Soc Microbiol. *Res:* Submicroscopic morphology, pathogenesis of inflammatory diseases; bacteria; fungi; adipose tissue fine structure and function. *Mailing Add:* Electron Micros Res Lab Rm 209 Wadsworth Vet Admin Hosp Bldg 114 Los Angeles CA 90073

COHEN, MORRIS, b Regina, Can, July 10, 15; m 40; c 2. PHYSICAL CHEMISTRY. *Educ:* Brandon Col, BA, 34; Univ Toronto, MA, 35, PhD, 39. *Prof Exp:* Chemist, Monarch Battery Mfg Co, 40-43; prin res officer metallic corrosion & oxidation & head, Corrosion Lab, Nat Res Coun Can, 43-79; RETIRED. *Concurrent Pos:* Vis prof metall, Univ New South Wales, 66; chmn, Gordon Conf Corrosion, 61. *Honors & Awards:* Willis Rodney Whitney Award, Asn Corrosion Eng, 60; Outstanding Achievement Award, Electrochem Soc, 73. *Mem:* Fel Chem Inst Can. *Res:* Reactions of metal surfaces with their environment, oxidation of iron and its alloys; passivity; electrochemistry. *Mailing Add:* Div of Chem Nat Res Coun Can Montreal Rd Ottawa ON K1A 0R6 Can

COHEN, MORRIS, b Chelsea, Mass, Nov 27, 11; m 37; c 2. MATERIALS SCIENCE & ENGINEERING. *Educ:* Mass Inst Technol, BS, 33, ScD, 36. *Hon Degrees:* DTech, Royal Inst Technol, Sweden, 77. *Prof Exp:* Asst phys metall, 34-36, from instr to prof, 36-62, Ford prof mat sci & eng, 62-75, INST PROF METALL & MAT SCI, MASS INST TECHNOL, 75- *Concurrent Pos:* Official investr, Off Sci Res & Develop, 42-43; assoc dir, Manhattan Proj, Mass Inst Technol, 43-46; Campbell Mem lectr, 48; Inst Metals lectr, 57; Burgess Mem lectr, Carnegie Mem lectr & Sauveur lectr, 58; Woodside lectr, 59; Coleman lectr, Franklin Inst, 60; Houdremont Mem lectr, Int Inst Welding, 61; Howe Mem lectr, Metall Soc, 62; Hatfield Mem lectr, Brit Iron & Steel Inst, 62; Rockwell Mem lectr, 65; Robert S Williams lectr, Mass Inst Technol, 70. *Honors & Awards:* Howe Medal, Am Soc Metals, 45, 49, Sauveur Award, 47, 77, Gold Medal, 68; Mathewson Gold Medal, Am Inst Mining, Metall & Petrol Engrs, 53; Kamani Medal, Indian Inst Metals, 53; Gold Medal, Japan Inst Metals, 70; Pierre Chevenard Medal, Fr Soc Metall, 71; Procter Prize, Res Soc NAm, 76; Nat Medal Sci, President Carter, 77; Kraner Award, Am Soc Testing Mat, 79. *Mem:* Nat Acad Eng; AAAS; hon mem Am Soc Metals; fel NY Acad Sci; fel Am Acad Arts & Sci. *Res:* Materials science and engineering; materials policy; physical metallurgy; phase transformations; strengthening mechanisms; mechanical behavior of metals. *Mailing Add:* 491 Puritan Rd Swampscott MA 01907

COHEN, MORTIMER, b New York, NY, Mar 7, 16; m 43; c 2. PLANT PATHOLOGY. *Educ:* City Col New York, MSEd, 42; Univ Minn, Minneapolis, PhD(plant path), 51. *Prof Exp:* Plant pathologist, Div Plant Path, Calif Dept Agr, 51-52 & Fla State Plant Bd, 52-56; PROF & PLANT PATHOLOGIST, UNIV FLA, 56- *Mem:* Am Phytopath Soc. *Res:* Diseases of citrus trees. *Mailing Add:* Agr Res Ctr Univ of Fla PO Box 248 Ft Pierce FL 33450

COHEN, MORTON IRVING, b New York, NY, July 11, 23; m 58; c 2. NEUROPHYSIOLOGY. *Educ:* City Col New York, BS, 42; Columbia Univ, AM, 50, PhD(physiol), 57. *Prof Exp:* From instr to assoc prof, 57-73, prof physiol, 73-76, PROF NEUROSCI, ALBERT EINSTEIN COL MED, 76- *Mem:* Am Physiol Soc; Soc Neurosci. *Res:* Neural regulation of respiration and circulation; spontaneous activity of neurons in central nervous system; patterns of synaptic excitation and inhibition; computer analysis of neuroelectric data. *Mailing Add:* Albert Einstein Col of Med Yeshiva Univ New York NY 10461

COHEN, MOSES E, US citizen. APPLIED MATHEMATICS. *Educ:* Univ London, BSc, 63; Univ Wales, PhD(theoret physics, appl math), 67. *Prof Exp:* Res fel astrophys, French Atomic Energy Comn, 68; asst prof math, Mich Technol Univ, 68-69; from asst prof to assoc prof, 69-74, PROF MATH, CALIF STATE UNIV, FRESNO, 74- *Mem:* Am Math Soc; assoc fel Brit Inst Math & Appln; assoc Brit Inst Physics & Phys Soc. *Res:* Astrophysics, especially cosmic radiation; applied mathematics, especially generating functions, combinatorial identities; solid state physics, especially solar cells. *Mailing Add:* Dept Math Calif State Univ Fresno CA 93710

COHEN, MURRAY SAMUEL, b Brooklyn, NY, May 19, 25; m 48; c 2. ORGANIC CHEMISTRY. *Educ:* Univ Mo, BS, 48, MA, 50, PhD(chem), 52. *Prof Exp:* Res chemist, Schenley Labs, 52-53; res chemist reaction motors div, Thiokol Chem Corp, 53-54, proj leader synthetic org & inorg res, 54-56, chief propellant synthesis sect, 56-62, mgr chem dept, 62-67; staff adv advan planning, Esso Res & Eng Co, 67-68, dir new ventures & dir fuel additives labs, 68-73; vpres res, Weston Chem Div & tech dir chem, Borg Warner Corp, 73-78; dir govt liason, 78-80, DIR RES & DEVELOP, APOLLO TECHNOL, SUBSID ECON LABS, INC, 80- *Mem:* Am Chem Soc; Soc Plastics Indust. *Res:* Solid and liquid propellants; light weight metal hydrides and derivatives; organometallic polymers; additive research, antioxidants, heat and ultra violet stabilizers, copper deactivators; pollution control, fuel additives. *Mailing Add:* Symor Dr Convent St Morristown NJ 07960

COHEN, MYRON LESLIE, b New York, NY, March 7, 34; m 55; c 3. MEDICAL DEVICE DESIGN. *Educ:* Purdue Univ, BSME, 55; Univ Ala, MSE, 58; Polytech Inst Brooklyn, PhD(mech eng), 66. *Prof Exp:* Res engr, Allegany Ballistics Lab, Hercules Powder Co, 55-56; sr thermodynamics engr, Repub Aviation Corp, 58-60; instr mech eng, Polytech Inst Brooklyn, 60-66; asst prof mech eng, Stevens Inst Technol, 66-69, assoc prof mech eng, 69-77, dir, Med Eng Lab, 75-78, prof mech eng, Dept Mech Eng, 77-78; DIR RES & DEVELOP, HOSP PROD DIV, CHESEBOROUGH-POND'S, INC, 78- *Concurrent Pos:* prof & sr US scientist, Inst Bioeng & Biomed Tech, Univ Karlsruhe, WGer, 74-75; pres, CAS Inc, NJ, 75-78; vpres & ed dir, Freshet Press, 70-78; consult, US Navy, Johnson & Johnson, Vitro Corp Am; adj assoc prof surg, Sect Orthopedic Surg, Col Med & Dent NJ, 78- *Mem:* Am Soc Mech Engrs; Sigma Xi; Cadiovasc Systs Dynamics Soc; Soc Biomat; Am Inst Advan Med Instrumentation. *Res:* The use of engineering technologies in the design and development of products to be used in clinical medicine including wound management, blood pressure measurement and medical device development. *Mailing Add:* Cheseborough-Ponds Inc Res Labs Trumbull Indust Park Trumbull CT 06611

COHEN, NADINE DALE, b Yonkers, NY, Sept 15, 49; m 68. BIOCHEMISTRY. *Educ:* Rensselaer Polytech Inst, 70; Univ Rochester, 74. *Prof Exp:* Res assoc biochem, Case Western Reserve Univ, 73-76, sr res assoc, 76-79; ASST PROF BIOCHEM, WRIGHT STATE UNIV, 79- *Mem:* Sigma Xi; AAAS. *Res:* Vitamin biotin including its transport, metabolism and role as the prosthetic group of the carborylase enzymes. *Mailing Add:* Biol Chem Dept Wright State Univ Colonel Glen Hwy Dayton OH 45435

COHEN, NATALIE SHULMAN, b New York, NY, Jan 16, 38; m 58; c 2. CELL PHYSIOLOGY, BIOCHEMISTRY. *Educ:* Cornell Univ, BA, 59; NY Univ, MS, 61, PhD(biol), 65. *Prof Exp:* Res fel biol, Calif Inst Technol, 66-70; res assoc biochem, 70-77, SR RES ASSOC, BIOCHEM, SCH MED, UNIV SOUTHERN CALIF, 77- *Concurrent Pos:* Res assoc biochem, Col Med, Univ Ariz, 73-74. *Res:* Physiological and biochemical aspects of cellular functions; relation to cellular structure; kinetics and regulation of the enzymes of the urea cycle; behavior of enzymes in the mitochondria. *Mailing Add:* 1725 Homet Rd Pasadena CA 91106

COHEN, NATHAN WOLF, b Richmond, Va, Oct 3, 19; m 46; c 2. HERPETOLOGY. *Educ:* Univ Calif, Los Angeles, AB, 44; Univ Calif, Berkeley, MA, 50; Ore State Univ, PhD(zool), 55. *Prof Exp:* Asst physiol & zool, Univ Calif, 48-50, res zoologist, San Joaquin Exp Range, 50-51; instr zool, Fresno State Col, 51-52; instr physiol & biol, Modesto Jr Col, 55-63; sci coordr, Lib Arts Dept, Univ Calif Exten, Berkeley, 63, head, Letters & Sci Exten, 64-70 & Continuing Educ Sci & Math, 70-72, dir curric develop sci, 72-79. *Concurrent Pos:* Res assoc herpet, Los Angeles, County Mus Natural Hist & Mus Vert Zool, Univ Calif, Berkeley. *Mem:* Fel AAAS; Am Soc Ichthyologists & Herpetologists; fel Herpet League; Sigma Xi. *Res:* Environmental physiology of terrestrial cold-blooded vertebrates; color photography of amphibians and reptiles; environmental physiology and behavior of amphibians and reptiles. *Mailing Add:* 1324 Devonshire Ct El Cerrito CA 94530

COHEN, NICHOLAS, b New York, NY, Nov 20, 38; m 74; c 4. IMMUNOLOGY, DEVELOPMENTAL BIOLOGY. *Educ:* Princeton Univ, AB, 59; Univ Rochester, PhD(biol), 66. *Prof Exp:* USPHS scholar med microbiol & immunol, Univ Calif, Los Angeles, 65-67; asst prof, 67-73, assoc prof, 73-80, PROF MICROBIOL & IMMUNOL, SCH MED & DENT, UNIV ROCHESTER, 80- *Concurrent Pos:* Mem, Basel Inst Immunol, Switz, 75-76; USPHS career develop award, 73-77; mem, Immunol Study Sect, NIH, 76-80. *Mem:* AAAS; Transplantation Soc; Am Soc Zool; Am Asn Immunol; Int Soc Develop Comp Immunol. *Res:* Comparative and developmental immunology; transplantation and psychoneuroimmunology. *Mailing Add:* Dept Microbiol Sch Med & Dent Univ Rochester Rochester NY 14642

COHEN, NOAL, b Rochester, NY, Dec 29, 37; m 60; c 2. SYNTHETIC ORGANIC CHEMISTRY, NATURAL PRODUCTS CHEMISTRY. *Educ:* Univ Rochester, BS, 59; Northwestern Univ, PhD(org chem), 65. *Prof Exp:* Chemist, Eastman Kodak Co, 59-61; sr chemist, Dept Chem Res, 67-75, res fel, 75-80, RES GROUP CHIEF, HOFFMAN-LA ROCHE, INC, 80- *Concurrent Pos:* NSF fel, Stanford Univ, 65-67. *Mem:* Am Chem Soc; Sigma Xi; AAAS; NY Acad Sci; Int Soc Heterocyclic Chem. *Res:* Synthesis of natural products and other organic compounds possessing biological activity. *Mailing Add:* Hoffmann-La Roche Inc Nutley NJ 07110

COHEN, NOEL LEE, b New York, NY, Sept 20, 30; m 57; c 1. OTOLARYNGOLOGY. *Educ:* NY Univ, BA, 51; State Univ Utrecht, MD, 57. *Prof Exp:* From instr to assoc prof, 62-72, prof clin otolaryngol, 72-80, PROF & ACTG CHMN OTOLORYNGOL, SCH MED, NY UNIV, 80- *Concurrent Pos:* Consult, Manhattan Vet Admin Hosp, 74-; assoc attend physician, Univ Hosp, 68- & Bellevue Hosp, NY, 70- *Mem:* Am Neurotology Soc; Am Acad Ophthal & Otolaryngol; Am Col Surg; Soc Univ Otolaryngol; Am Laryngol, Rhinol & Otol Soc. *Res:* Neurotology. *Mailing Add:* Dept Otolaryngol NY Univ Sch Med New York NY 10016

COHEN, NORMAN, b New York, NY, Dec 13, 36; m 59. PHYSICAL CHEMISTRY. *Educ:* Reed Col, AB, 58; Univ Calif, Berkeley, MA, 60, PhD(chem), 63. *Prof Exp:* Mem tech staff phys chem, 63-69, staff scientist, 69-73, HEAD CHEM KINETICS DEPT, AEROSPACE CORP, 73- *Concurrent Pos:* Asst ed, Int J Chem Kinetics, 76- *Mem:* Am Chem Soc; Am Phys Soc. *Res:* Gas phase chemical kinetics and photochemistry; reactions of free radicals and atoms; kinetics of chemical lasers; decomposition of hydrogen halides; vibrational energy transfer. *Mailing Add:* Aerospace Corp PO Box 92957 Los Angeles CA 90009

COHEN, NORMAN, b Brooklyn, NY, Nov 6, 38; m 62; c 1. RADIOLOGICAL PHYSICS, RADIOBIOLOGY. *Educ:* Brooklyn Col, BS, 60; NY Univ, MS, 65, PhD(environ sci), 70. *Prof Exp:* Chemist, Columbia Presby Hosp, NY, 60-61; res assoc radiobiol & radiochem, 66-74, ASSOC PROF ENVIRON MED, MED CTR, NY UNIV, 74- *Mem:* AAAS; Am Indust Hyg Asn; Health Physics Soc; Radiation Res Soc; Sigma Xi. *Res:* Radiobiological research of the metabolism of various radionuclides and elements in man and other primates; research and evaluation of toxicological properties of heavy metals in man. *Mailing Add:* Inst Environ Med A J Lanza Lab NY Univ Med Ctr Tuxedo NY 10987

COHEN, PAUL, b New York, NY, Aug 11, 12; m 37; c 1. NUCLEAR ENGINEERING. *Educ:* City Col, New York, BS, 34; Carnegie Inst Technol, MS, 41. *Prof Exp:* Fuel engr heat transfer rheology slags, US Bur Mines, Dept Interior, 36-49; mgr chem develop water coolant technol, Bettis Atomic Power Lab, Westinghouse Elec Co, 49-59; mgr chem develop, Westinghouse Atomic Power Dept, 59-67; consult, Westinghouse Advan Reactors Div, 67-77; CONSULT WATER TECHNOL, 77- *Honors & Awards:* Special award, Am Nuclear Soc, 67; Merit Award, Pittsburgh Water Conference, 75. *Mem:* Fel Am Soc Mech Eng; fel Am Nuclear Soc; Am Chem Soc; Nat Asn Corrosion Eng. *Mailing Add:* 3024 Beechwood Blvd Pittsburgh PA 15217

COHEN, PAUL JOSEPH, b Long Branch, NJ, Apr 2, 34; m 63; c 2. MATHEMATICS. *Educ:* Univ Chicago, MS, 54, PhD(math), 58. *Prof Exp:* Instr math, Univ Rochester, 57-58 & Mass Inst Technol, 58-59; fel, Inst Advan Study, 59-61; from asst prof to assoc prof, 61-64, PROF MATH, STANFORD UNIV, 64- *Honors & Awards:* Bocher prize & Res Corp Award, 64; Fields Medal, Int Math Union, 66; Nat Medal Sci, 67. *Mem:* Am Math Soc. *Res:* Axiomatic set theory; harmonic analysis; partial differential equations. *Mailing Add:* Dept of Math Stanford Univ Palo Alto CA 94305

COHEN, PAUL SIDNEY, b Boston, Mass, Jan 20, 39. MOLECULAR BIOLOGY. *Educ:* Brandeis Univ, AB, 60; Boston Univ, AM, 62, PhD(genetics), 64. *Prof Exp:* USPHS trainee, St Jude Hosp, 64-66, asst prof microbiol, 66-69; assoc prof, 69-75, PROF MICROBIOL, UNIV RI, 75- *Mem:* Am Soc Biol Chemists; Am Soc Microbiol. *Res:* Regulation of protein synthesis in virus infected cells; molecular basis of E coli cologization. *Mailing Add:* Dept Microbiol Univ RI Kingston RI 02881

COHEN, PHILIP, b New York, NY, Dec 13, 31; m 54; c 1. HYDROGEOLOGY, GROUNDWATER GEOLOGY. *Educ:* Univ Rochester, MS, 56. *Prof Exp:* Asst, Univ Rochester, 54-56; geologist, 56-67, res hydrologist, 67-68, hydrologist in charge LI prog, 68-72, staff scientist, Off of the Dir, 72-74, actg chief res & tech coord, 74-76, assoc chief res & tech coord, Land Info & Anal Off, 76-79, ASST CHIEF HYDROLOGIST, SCIENTIFIC PUBLICATIONS & DATA MANAGEMENT, & CHIEF HYDROLOGIST, WATER RESOURCES DIV, US GEOL SURV, 79- *Honors & Awards:* Ward Medal, 54; Meritorious Serv Award, Dept of the Interior, 75. *Mem:* Fel Geol Soc Am; Am Water Resources Asn; Am Inst Prof Geologists; Sigma Xi. *Res:* Artificial groundwater recharge; seawater encroachment; land-use planning implications of earth sciences. *Mailing Add:* US Geol Surv Nat Ctr MS 703 12201 Sunrise Valley Dr Reston VA 22092

COHEN, PHILIP IRA, b Baltimore, Md, Oct 27, 48. SURFACE PHYSICS. *Educ:* Johns Hopkins Univ, BA, 69; Univ Wis-Madison, PhD(physics), 75. *Prof Exp:* Teaching asst, Univ Wis, 70, res asst, 70-75; res assoc physics & chem, Ctr Mat Res, Univ Md, College Park, 76-78; ASST PROF ELEC ENG, UNIV MINN, MINNEAPOLIS, 78- *Concurrent Pos:* Guest worker, Nat Bur Standards, 76- *Mem:* Sigma Xi; Am Inst Physics. *Res:* Surface physics and chemistry, surface crystallography, electron diffraction, and molecular beam epitaxy. *Mailing Add:* Dept of Elec Eng Univ of Minn Minneapolis MN 55455

COHEN, PHILIP PACY, b Derry, NH, Sept 26, 08; m 35; c 4. PHYSIOLOGICAL CHEMISTRY, ENZYMOLOGY. *Educ:* Tufts Col, BS, 30; Univ Wis, PhD(physiol chem), 37, MD, 38. *Hon Degrees:* DSc, Univ Mex, 78. *Prof Exp:* From asst prof to assoc prof, 43-47, prof physiol chem & chmn dept, 48-75, H C Bradley prof physiol chem, 68-79, EMER PROF, UNIV WIS-MADISON, 79- *Concurrent Pos:* Nat Res Coun fel, Univ Sheffield, 38-39 & Yale Univ, 39-40; Commonwealth Fund fel, Oxford Univ, 58; mem comt growth, Nat Res Coun, 54-56; mem bd sci counr, Nat Cancer Inst, 57-61, mem adv cancer coun, 63-67; mem adv comt biol & med, US AEC, 63-71; mem adv coun to dir, NIH, 66-70, mem adv coun arthritis, metab & digestive dis, 70-74; mem adv comt med res, Pan-Am Health Orgn, 67-75; mem, Nat Comn Res, 78-80; vis prof, Univ Calif, Los Angeles, 76 & Univ Mexico, 79. *Honors & Awards:* Hon mem fac, Univ Chile, 66. *Mem:* Nat Acad Sci; Am Soc Biol Chem (treas, 51-55); Brit Biochem Soc; hon mem Harvey Soc; hon mem Mex Nat Acad Med. *Res:* Intermediary nitrogen metabolism; action of thyroxine; differentiation and development; comparative biochemistry. *Mailing Add:* 694 Med Sci Bldg Univ of Wis Madison WI 53706

COHEN, PINYA, b Burlington, Vt, Dec 23, 35; div. BIOCHEMISTRY, IMMUNOLOGY. *Educ:* Del Valley Col, BS, 57; Univ Ga, MS, 59; Purdue Univ, PhD(microbiol), 64. *Prof Exp:* Res microbiologist, NIH, 64-68, chief plasma derivatives sect, Lab Blood & Blood Prod, 68-72; dir plasma derivatives br, Bur Biologics, Food & Drug Admin, 72-76; dir, 76-78, VPRES QUAL CONTROL & REGULATORY AFFAIRS, MERIEUX INST, 79- *Mem:* AAAS; Am Soc Microbiol; Am Asn Immunologists; Int Soc Blood Transfusion; NY Acad Sci. *Res:* Immunology and biochemistry of plasma proteins. *Mailing Add:* Merieux Inst Suite 109 1200 NW 78th Ave Miami FL 33126

COHEN, RAYMOND, b St Louis, Mo, Nov 30, 23; m 48; c 3. MECHANICAL ENGINEERING. *Educ:* Purdue Univ, BSME, 47, MSME, 50, PhD, 55. *Prof Exp:* From instr to assoc prof, 47-60, asst dir, R W Herrick Labs, 70-71, PROF MECH ENG, PURDUE UNIV, 60-, DIR, R W HERRICK LABS, 71- *Concurrent Pos:* Consult, Gen Elec Co, 56-60 & Bendix Corp, 62-72; dept ed, Encycl Britannica, 57-62; consult, Gen Motors Res Labs, 74-78. *Mem:* Am Soc Mech Engrs; Am Soc Eng Educ; Nat Soc Prof Engrs; Am Soc Heating, Refrig & Air Conditioning Engrs; Int Inst Refrig. *Res:* Machine design; noise and vibration problems. *Mailing Add:* R W Herrick Labs Purdue Univ West Lafayette IN 47907

COHEN, RICHARD LAWRENCE, b Philadelphia, Pa, Oct 6, 22; m 50; c 2. CHILD PSYCHIATRY. *Educ:* Univ Pa, AB, 43, MD, 47; Am Bd Psychiat & Neurol, cert psychiat, 53, cert child psychiat, 60. *Prof Exp:* Clin dir psychiat, Embreeville State Hosp, 51-52; dir child psychiat, Oakburne Hosp, 57-62; dir training, Philadelphia Child Guid Clin, 62-64; assoc prof child psychiat, Col Med, Univ Nebr, 64-67; assoc prof, 67-70, PROF CHILD PSYCHIAT, SCH MED, UNIV PITTSBURGH, 70-, CHIEF CHILD PSYCHIAT, DEPT PSYCHIAT, 72-; DIR CHILDREN'S SERV, WESTERN PSYCHIAT INST & CLIN, 72-; EXEC DIR, PITTSBURGH CHILD GUID CTR, 72- *Concurrent Pos:* Psychiat consult, Univ Settlement House, Jewish Family Serv Philadelphia, Asn Jewish Children, Nat Teacher Corps & Student Health Serv & Univ Nebr; mem deans comt psychiat residency, 48-51; exec dir, Pittsburgh Child Guid Ctr, 72-79. *Mem:* AAAS; Am Acad Child Psychiat; Am Orthopsychiat Asn; Am Psychiat Asn; Am Pub Health Asn. *Res:* Prenatal prevention of developmental disorders in children; operations research into systems of delivery of medical service. *Mailing Add:* Child Psychiat Serv 3811 O'Hara Street Pittsburgh PA 15261

COHEN, RICHARD LEWIS, b New York, NY, Sept 8, 36; m 59; c 1. SOLID STATE SCIENCE. *Educ:* Haverford Col, BS, 57; Calif Inst Technol, MS, 59, PhD(physics), 62. *Prof Exp:* MEM TECH STAFF PHYSICS, BELL LABS, 62- *Concurrent Pos:* Res fel, Inst Physics, Munich Tech Univ, 64-65; mem ed bd, Rev Sci Instruments, 75-78. *Honors & Awards:* Gold Medal, Electroplaters Soc, 76. *Mem:* Fel AAAS; fel Am Phys Soc. *Res:* Use of Mossbauer effect to study nuclear and solid state physics, especially with rare-earth isotopes; x-ray photoelectric spectroscopy in solids; fiber optics; colloidal catalysts; gold electrodeposits; pulsed annealing. *Mailing Add:* Bell Labs Murray Hill NJ 07974

COHEN, ROBERT, b Indianapolis, Ind, Oct 15, 24; m 63; c 2. ENERGY CONVERSION. *Educ:* Wayne Univ, BS, 47; Univ Mich, MS, 48; Cornell Univ, PhD(elec eng), 56. *Prof Exp:* Res asst, Univ Mich, 47-48, Purdue Univ, 48-51 & Cornell Univ, 51-56; physicist, Aeronomy Lab, Environ Res Labs, Nat Oceanic & Atmospheric Admin, 56-73, prog mgr ocean thermal energy conversion, NSF Res Appl to Nat Needs, 73-75; br chief ocean thermal energy conversion, Div Solar Energy, Energy Res & Develop Admin, 75-76; PROG MGR, OCEAN SYSTS BR, DIV CENT SOLAR TECHNOL, US DEPT ENERGY, 77- *Honors & Awards:* Boulder Scientist Award, 64. *Mem:* Sigma Xi; Inst Elec & Electronics Eng; Am Geophys Union; Int Solar Energy Soc; fel AAAS. *Res:* Ionospheric radio-wave propagation; irregularities in the ionosphere; equatorial ionosphere; ionospheric modification; aeronomy; program management of the ocean thermal energy conversion program. *Mailing Add:* Div Ocean Energy Systs US Dept of Energy Washington DC 20585

COHEN, ROBERT ABRAHAM, b Chicago, Ill, Nov 13, 09; m 33; c 2. PSYCHIATRY. *Educ:* Univ Chicago, SB, 30, PhD(physiol) & MD, 35. *Prof Exp:* Clin dir, Chestnut Lodge Sanatorium, 47-53; dir clin invests, 53-68, DIR DIV CLIN & BEHAV RES, NIMH, 68- *Concurrent Pos:* Training & supv analyst, Wash Psychoanal Inst, 50-, chmn educ comt, 54-59, dir, 59-62; dir, Found Fund Res Psychiat, 60-63, chmn, 62-63; pres, Wash Sch Psychiat, 73- *Honors & Awards:* Distinguished Serv Award, Dept Health, Educ & Welfare; Salmon Medal, NY Acad Med, 78. *Mem:* Fel Am Psychiat Asn; Am Psychoanal Asn; Am Psychopathol Asn; Asn Res Nerv & Ment Dis. *Res:* Social psychiatry; nature of the psychotherapeutic process; research administration. *Mailing Add:* Div of Clin & Behav Res NIMH Bethesda MD 20205

COHEN, ROBERT JAY, b Milwaukee, Wis, May 31, 42; m 68; c 3. BIOPHYSICS, BIOCHEMISTRY. *Educ:* Univ Wis, BS, 64; Yale Univ, PhD(biophys chem), 69. *Prof Exp:* NIH fel, Calif Inst Technol, 69-71; asst prof, 71-76, ASSOC PROF BIOCHEM, COL MED, UNIV FLA, 76- *Concurrent Pos:* Vis prof, Univ Freiburg, 80. *Mem:* Am Chem Soc; AAAS; Biophysics Soc. *Res:* Sensory and hormonal transduction in model system phycomyces; physical chemistry of nucleic acids; electrokinetics, biomathematics, receptor physiology. *Mailing Add:* Dept of Biochem & Molecular Biol Univ of Fla Col of Med Gainesville FL 32610

COHEN, ROBERT ROY, b Duluth, Minn, June 3, 39. VERTEBRATE ZOOLOGY, ORNITHOLOGY. *Educ:* Univ Minn, Duluth, BA, 61; Univ Colo, PhD(zool), 65. *Prof Exp:* Asst prof biol, Univ Sask, 65-67 & N Mex Inst Mining & Technol, 67-69; assoc prof, 69-74, PROF BIOL, METROP STATE COL, DENVER, 74- *Mem:* AAAS; Sigma Xi; Wilson Ornithological Soc; Am Ornith Union; Am Soc Zool. *Res:* Breeding biology and population dynamics of the tree swallow; avian erythrocyte and hemoglobin kinetics. *Mailing Add:* Dept of Biol Metrop State Col Denver CO 80204

COHEN, ROBERT SONNE, b New York, NY, Feb 18, 23; m 44; c 3. THEORETICAL PHYSICS, PHILOSOPHY OF SCIENCE. *Educ:* Wesleyan Univ, AB, 43; Yale Univ, MS, 43, PhD(physics), 48. *Prof Exp:* Instr physics, Yale Univ, 43-44; mem sci staff, Div War Res, Columbia Univ, 44-46; Am Coun Learned Socs fel philos of sci, Yale Univ, 48-49, instr philos, 49-51;

asst prof physics & philos, Wesleyan Univ, 49-57; assoc prof physics, 57-59, chmn dept, 58-73, actg dean, Col Lib Arts, 71-73, PROF PHYSICS & PHILOS, BOSTON UNIV, 59- *Concurrent Pos:* Mem tech staff, Joint Commun Bd, US Joint Chiefs of Staff, 44-46; consult, Fund Advan Educ, 51-53 & Nat Woodrow Wilson Found, 59-64; Ford fac fel, 55-56; vis prof, Mass Inst Technol, 58-59, Brandeis Univ, 59-60 & Univ Calif, San Diego, 69; chmn, Ctr Philos & Hist of Sci, Boston Univ, 61-; vis lectr, Polish & Czech Acad Sci, 62, Yugoslav Philos Asn, 63 & Hungarian Acad Sci, 64; ed, Boston Studies in Philos of Sci, 63-, Vienna Circle Collection, 70- & Studies Hist Mod Sci, 76-; mem staff, Oak Ridge Conf Sci & Contemporary Social Probs, 64; chmn, Am Inst Marxist Studies, 64-; trustee, Inst Unity of Sci, 66- & Wesleyan Univ, 68-; chmn US nat comt, Int Union Hist & Philos of Sci, 67-75. *Mem:* Am Phys Soc; Am Asn Physics Teachers; Hist of Sci Soc; Am Philos Asn; Philos Sci Asn (vpres, 73-75, pres, 82-84). *Res:* Concept and theory formation in physical sciences; science and the social order; logical empiricism and natural science; dialectical materialism and science; general education in science; history of scientific concepts; comparative historical sociology of science. *Mailing Add:* Dept Physics Boston Univ Boston MA 02215

COHEN, ROCHELLE SANDRA, b Brooklyn, NY, June 20, 45. ENDOCRINOLOGY, NEUROBIOLOGY. *Educ:* Rutgers Univ, AB, 67; Univ Conn, MS, 70, PhD(physiol, endocrinol), 73. *Prof Exp:* Res asst endocrinol, Univ Conn, 68, teaching asst biol, 68-72; asst prof, State Univ NY Col Purchase, 72-74; NIH fel cell biol, Rockefeller Univ, 74-76, res assoc cell biol, 76-77; RES ASSOC, DEPT ANAT, RUDOLF MAGNUS INST PHARMACOL, UNIV ILL MED CTR, 77- *Concurrent Pos:* Asst prof biol, Empire State Col, 73-74; res assoc biochem genetics, Rockefeller Univ, 73-74. *Mem:* Am Soc Cell Biol; NY Acad Sci. *Res:* Characterization of the synaptic junction by the use of biochemical, ultra structural and immunological techniques to find the relationship between its structure and function. *Mailing Add:* Dept Anat PO Box 6998 Chicago IL 60680

COHEN, RONALD R H, b Philadelphia, Pa, Jan 14, 47; m 70. ESTUARINE ECOLOGY, PHYTOPLANKTON ECOLOGY. *Educ:* Temple Univ, BA, 71; Univ Va, PhD(environ sci), 78. *Prof Exp:* Instr ecol, Univ Va, 77; ECOLOGIST-HYDROLOGIST ESTUARINE ECOL, DEPT INTERIOR, US GEOL SURV, 78- *Mem:* Am Soc Limnol & Oceanog; Ecol Soc Am; AAAS; Am Soc Plant Physiol. *Res:* Interaction between nutrients, light and primary productivity; estuarine phytoplankton dynamics and modelling; effect of invertebrates on phytoplankton biomass; statistical techniques in phytoplankton research. *Mailing Add:* 12204 Nutmeg Lane Reston VA 22091

COHEN, SAMUEL ALAN, b Brooklyn, NY, Feb 3, 47; m 73. PLASMA PHYSICS, SURFACE PHYSICS. *Educ:* Mass Inst Technol, BS, 68, PhD(physics), 72. *Prof Exp:* Teaching asst physics, Mass Inst Technol, 68-72; mem res staff, 73-78, RES PHYSICIST, PLASMA PHYSICS LAB, PRINCETON UNIV, 78- *Concurrent Pos:* Consult, Res Lab Electronics, Mass Inst Technol, 73- & Dept Energy-ETM Task Group on Plasma-Wall Interactions, 76- *Mem:* Am Phys Soc; Am Vacuum Soc. *Res:* Experimental work on surface physics and plasma physics related to controlled thermonuclear fusion. *Mailing Add:* Plasma Physics Lab Princeton Univ Forrestal Campus Princeton NJ 08540

COHEN, SAMUEL MONROE, b Milwaukee, Wis, Sept 24, 46; m 68; c 4. PATHOLOGY. *Educ:* Univ Wis-Madison, BS, 67, MD & PhD(oncol), 72. *Prof Exp:* instr path, Med Sch, Univ Mass, 74-77, assoc prof, 77-81; PROF RES, EPPLEY INST CANCER RES & PROF & VCHMN PATH & LAB MED, UNIV NEBR MED CTR, 81- *Concurrent Pos:* Staff pathologist, St Vincent Hosp, 75-76 & 77-81; vis prof path, Nagoya City Univ Med Sch, 76-77; assoc ed, Cancer Res, 82. *Mem:* Am Asn Path; Am Asn Cancer Res; Japanese Cancer Asn; AAAS. *Res:* Mechanisms of carcinogenesis, including carcinogen metabolism, evaluation of factors influencing the different stages and development of a generalized computer-based model of carcinogenesis; diagnostic application of electron microscopy. *Mailing Add:* Dept Path & Lab Med Univ Nebr Med Ctr 42nd & Dewey Ave Omaha NE 68105

COHEN, SANFORD I, b New York, NY, Sept 5, 28; m 52; c 3. PSYCHIATRY, PSYCHOPHYSIOLOGY. *Educ:* NY Univ, AB, 48; Chicago Med Sch, MD, 52; Am Bd Psychiat, dipl, 59. *Prof Exp:* Resident psychiat, Med Ctr, Univ Colo, 54 & Med Ctr, Duke Univ, 55, instr, 56-58, assoc, 58-59, from asst prof to assoc prof, 59-61, head div psychophysiol res, 60-65, prof & chmn exec comt inter-dept res training prog nerv syst sci, 64-68, head div psychosom med & psychophysiol res, 65-68; prof psychiat & biobehav sci & chmn dept, Med Ctr, La State Univ, New Orleans, 68-70; PROF PSYCHIAT & CHMN DIV, MED SCH, BOSTON UNIV, 70-, PSYCHIATRIST-IN-CHIEF, UNIV HOSP, 70- *Concurrent Pos:* Markle scholar, 57-62; fel psychoanal, Found Fund Res Psychiat, 58-63; instr, Wash Psychoanal Inst, 64-; mem ment health small grants comt, NIMH, 63-66; supt, Dr Solomon Carter Fuller Ment Health Ctr, 70-75. *Mem:* AAAS; fel Am Psychiat Asn; Am Psychosom Soc; Am Fedn Clin Res; Soc Biol Psychiat. *Res:* Psychosomatic medicine; psychophysiology of emotions and behavior; neuroendocrinology and physiology of conditioned reflexes; effects of altered sensory environments; perceptual mode, personality and Pavlovian typology; life stress, hopelessness, and voodoo; death. *Mailing Add:* Div of Psychiat Boston Univ Med Sch Boston MA 02118

COHEN, SANFORD NED, b Bronx, NY, June 12, 35; m 58; c 1. PHARMACOLOGY, DEVELOPMENTAL BIOLOGY. *Educ:* Johns Hopkins Univ, AB, 56, MD, 60. *Prof Exp:* Res physician, Walter Reed Army Inst Res, 63-65; from instr to asst prof pharmacol, Sch Med, NY Univ, 65-71, asst prof pediat, 68-71, assoc prof pharmacol & pediat, 71-74; pediatrician-in-chief, Children's Hosp Mich, 74-81; prof pediat & chmn dept, 74-81, PROF PEDIAT & ASST DEAN, SCH MED, WAYNE STATE UNIV, 81- *Concurrent Pos:* Nat Inst Child Health & Human Develop spec fel, 63-65; Markle Found scholar acad med, 68; physician-in-chg nurseries & assoc dir pediat, Bellevue Hosp, 69-74. *Mem:* Am Pediat Soc; Am Acad Pediat; Soc Pediat Res (vpres, 80-81); Am Soc Pharmacol & Exp Therapeut. *Res:* Developmental pharmacology; how developmental phenomena alter the rate of metabolism or the biological effects of drugs in the immature animal. *Mailing Add:* Dept of Pediat Wayne State Univ Sch Med Detroit MI 48202

COHEN, SAUL G, b Boston, Mass, May 10, 16; m 41; c 2. ORGANIC CHEMISTRY. *Educ:* Harvard Univ, AB, 37, MA, 38, PhD(org chem), 40. *Prof Exp:* Pvt asst, Harvard Univ, 39-40, instr chem, 40-41; res assoc, Nat Defense Res Comt, 41, res fel, 41-43; Nat Res fel & lectr chem, Univ Calif, Los Angeles, 43-44; res chemist, Pittsburgh Plate Glass Co, 44-45; sr chemist, Polaroid Corp, 45-50; assoc prof chem, 50-52, prof, 52-74, chmn dept, 59-72, dean fac, 55-58, UNIV PROF CHEM, BRANDEIS UNIV, 74- *Concurrent Pos:* Fulbright sr scholar & Guggenheim fel, UK, 58-59; consult, Polaroid Corp. *Honors & Awards:* James F Norris Award, Am Chem Soc, 72. *Mem:* Am Chem Soc; Am Acad Arts & Sci; Royal Soc Chem. *Res:* Mechanisms of organic reactions; free radicals; polymerization; stereochemistry; photography; enzyme reactions; photochemistry. *Mailing Add:* Dept of Chem Brandeis Univ Waltham MA 02154

COHEN, SAUL ISRAEL, b Boston, Mass, Feb 15, 26; m 52; c 2. NUTRITION. *Educ:* Northeastern Univ, BS, 45; Boston Univ, MA, 46; Harvard Univ, MS, 51; Columbia Univ, PhD, 56. *Prof Exp:* Asst, Harvard Med Sch, 44-45; jr chemist & jr bacteriologist, State Dept Pub Health, Mass, 46-48; asst, Sch Pub Health, Harvard Univ, 49-52; instr, NY Med Col, 55; res assoc, Harvard Med Sch, 56-64; assoc prof, NEssex Community Col, 65-66; RES ASST, RETINA FOUND, 67- *Concurrent Pos:* Teacher high sch, Boston, 67-68. *Mem:* AAAS. *Res:* Chemical interactions of the protein components of blood plasma; amino acids and proteins in liver repair. *Mailing Add:* 67 Cricket Lane West Roxbury MA 02132

COHEN, SAUL LOUIS, b Regina, Sask, May 10, 13; m 38; c 3. BIOCHEMISTRY, ENDOCRINOLOGY. *Educ:* Brandon Col, BA, 32; Univ Toronto, PhD(biochem, physiol), 36. *Prof Exp:* Exhib of 1851 fel, Swiss Fed Inst Technol, 36-37; instr physiol, Med Sch, Ohio State Univ, 37-42; asst prof, Med Sch, Univ Mich, 42-46; from asst prof to assoc prof biochem, Univ Minn, 46-56; res asst, 62-67, asst prof, 67-76, ASSOC PROF PATH CHEM, OBSTET & GYNEC, MED SCH, UNIV TORONTO, 76- *Honors & Awards:* Ortho Award, Soc Obstetricians & Gynaecologists Can, 67. *Mem:* AAAS; Am Soc Biol Chem; Endocrine Soc; Can Fedn Biol Sci. *Res:* Biochemical endocrinology; hydrolysis, assay, concentration, isolation identification, metabolism and significance of conjugate steroids. *Mailing Add:* Rm 6366 Med Sci Bldg Univ of Toronto Toronto ON M5S 1H1 Can

COHEN, SAUL MARK, b Springfield, Mass, Oct 6, 24; m 53; c 1. ORGANIC CHEMISTRY, COATINGS. *Educ:* Univ Mass, BS, 48; Univ Ill, MS, 49, PhD(org chem), 52. *Prof Exp:* Asst, Univ Ill, 50-52; res chemist, Eastman Kodak Co, 52-55; res chemist, Shawinigan Resins Corp, 55-60, res group leader, 60-65; res specialist, 65-69, SR RES SPECIALIST, MONSANTO CO, 69- *Honors & Awards:* Arthur K Doolittle Award, Div Org Coatings & Plastic Chem, Am Chem Soc, 72. *Mem:* AAAS; NY Acad Sci; Am Chem Soc; fel Am Inst Chemists; Sigma Xi. *Res:* Organic synthesis; polymerization; polymer properties; mechanism studies; automotive safety glass windshields. *Mailing Add:* 15 Lindsay Rd Springfield MA 01128

COHEN, SEYMOUR STANLEY, b New York, NY, Apr 30, 17; m 40; c 2. BIOCHEMISTRY. *Educ:* City Col New York, BS, 36; Columbia Univ, PhD(biochem), 41. *Hon Degrees:* Dr, Univ Louvain, 72. *Prof Exp:* Res assoc biochem, Columbia Univ, 42-43; instr pediat, Univ Pa, 45-47, assoc prof physiol chem, Dept Pediat, 47-54, prof, 54-57, Am Cancer Soc Charles Hayden prof biochem, 57-71, Hartzell prof therapeut res & chmn dept, 63-71; prof, 71-72, Am Cancer Soc prof microbiol, Sch Med, Univ Colo, Denver, 71-76; AM CANCER SOC PROF PHARMACOL SCI & DISTINGUISHED PROF, STATE UNIV NY STONY BROOK, 76- *Concurrent Pos:* Abbott Lab fel, Columbia Univ, 40-41; Nat Res Found fel plant viruses, Rockefeller Inst, 41-42; Johnson Found fel, Univ Pa, 43-45; Guggenheim fel, Pasteur Inst, Paris, 47-48; Lalor fel, Marine Biol Lab, 50-51; Fogarty scholar, Nat Cancer Inst, 73-74; ed, Virology, 54-59, J Biol Chem, 60-65 & J Bact Rev, 69-73; vis prof, Radium Inst, 67, Col France, 70, Hadassah Med Sch, 74 & Univ Tokyo, 74; Smithsonian scholar, 73-74; trustee, Marine Biol Lab; mem bd sci consult, Sloan-Kettering Inst; mem, Coun for Anal & Proj, Am Cancer Soc, 71-75. *Honors & Awards:* Eli Lilly Award, 51; Mead Johnson Award, 52; Cleveland Award, AAAS, 55; Borden Award, Am Asn Med Cols, 68; Passano Award, 74; Townsend Harris Medal, City Col New York, 78; French Soc Biol Chem Medal, 64; Forster Prize, Mainz Acad Sci & Letters, 78. *Mem:* Nat Acad Sci; Inst of Med of Nat Acad Sci; fel AAAS; fel Am Acad Arts & Sci; Soc Gen Physiol (pres, 68). *Res:* Chemistry of viruses and nucleoproteins; metabolism of bacteria and virus infected cells; nucleic acids and phosphate compounds; polyamines; cancer research and infectious disease. *Mailing Add:* Dept of Pharmacol Sci State Univ of NY Stony Brook NY 11794

COHEN, SHELDON GILBERT, b Pittston, Pa, Sept 21, 18. IMMUNOLOGY, ALLERGY. *Educ:* Ohio State Univ, BA, 40; NY Univ, MD, 43. *Hon Degrees:* DSc, Wilkes Col, 76. *Prof Exp:* Intern, Bellevue Hosp, 44; resident internal med, Vet Admin Hosp, Md, 47-48; resident allergy, Vet Admin Hosp & Univ Med Ctr, Univ Pittsburgh, 48-49; res fel, Addison H Gibson Lab of Appl Physiol, Univ Pittsburgh, 49-50, res assoc, 50-51; res assoc immunol, Dept Biol, Wilkes Col, 51-56, from assoc prof to prof biol res, 57-68, prof exp biol, 68-72; consult, Inst, 72-73, chief extramural prog, Allergy & Immunol Br, 73-76, DIR, IMMUNOL, ALLERGIC & IMMUNOL DIS PROG, NAT INST ALLERGY & INFECTIOUS DIS, 77- *Concurrent Pos:* Attend physician, Vet Admin Hosp, 51-60, consult internal med, 60-72, consult res, 61-72; chief allergy, Mercy Hosp, 51-72; exec vpres, Lupus Found Am, 81- *Honors & Awards:* M Peshkin Award, Asn Care Asthma, 81; Clemens von Pirquet Award, Georgetown Univ, 81. *Mem:* Am Asn Immunol; Am Soc Exp Biol; fel Am Acad Allergy; fel Am Col Physicians; Asn Am Physicians. *Res:* Immunologic basis of hypersensitivity reactions; experimental eosinophilia; histopathogenesis of allergic inflammation. *Mailing Add:* Bldg 31 Rm 7A52 NIAID Nat Inst Health Bethesda MD 20205

COHEN, SHELDON H, b Milwaukee, Wis, May 21, 34; m 62; c 3. INORGANIC CHEMISTRY. *Educ:* Univ Wis, BS, 56; Univ Kans, PhD(chem), 62. *Prof Exp:* From asst prof to assoc prof, 60-70, PROF CHEM & CHMN DEPT, WASHBURN UNIV, 70- *Concurrent Pos:* Feature ed, J Chem Educ. *Mem:* Am Chem Soc; AAAS. *Res:* Polarography of inorganic systems; preparation of compounds with unusual oxidation states; preparation and stability of inorganic complexes; chemical education. *Mailing Add:* Dept of Chem Washburn Univ Topeka KS 66621

COHEN, SIDNEY, b Boston, Mass, June 3, 28; m 62; c 2. ORGANIC CHEMISTRY. *Educ:* Northeastern Univ, BS, 51; Tufts Univ, MS, 52; Univ Colo, PhD(org chem), 59. *Prof Exp:* Develop engr, Chem Div, Gen Elec Co, NY, 52-55; res assoc fluorine chem, Univ Colo, 60-61; from asst prof to assoc prof chem, Ft Lewis Col, 61-66; assoc prof, 66-69, PROF CHEM, STATE UNIV NY COL BUFFALO, 69- *Mem:* Am Chem Soc. *Res:* Small ring compounds; oxycarbons; fluorine chemistry; photochemistry. *Mailing Add:* Dept of Chem State Univ of NY Col Buffalo NY 14222

COHEN, SIDNEY, b Malden, Mass, Jan 29, 13; m 54; c 2. MEDICINE, MICROBIOLOGY. *Educ:* Harvard Univ, AB, 33; Harvard Med Sch, MD, 37; Am Bd Internal Med, dipl. *Prof Exp:* Intern, Mt Sinai Hosp, 37-40; resident med, Beth Israel Hosp, 40-41; res assoc, 41-42, assoc path & med & in chg bact lab, 46-51, dir clin labs, 51-56, from assoc vis physician to vis physician, 49-58; DIR DEPT MICROBIOL, MICHAEL REESE HOSP, 58-; PROF MED, PRITZKER SCH MED, UNIV CHICAGO, 71- *Concurrent Pos:* Res fel bact, Harvard Med Sch, 40; asst bact & med, Harvard Med Sch, 41-42, instr med, 45-51, assoc, 51-58. *Mem:* Infectious Dis Soc Am; Am Soc Microbiol; Am Col Physicians; Brit Soc Gen Microbiol. *Res:* Medical microbiology with relation to staphylococcal infection; action of antibiotics and mechanism of microbial resistance to antibiotics. *Mailing Add:* Dept of Microbiol Michael Reese Hosp Chicago IL 60616

COHEN, SIMON SEBAN, b Gersif, Morocco, Apr 1, 43; Israeli citizen; m 68; c 3. LATTICE DYNAMICS, SEMICONDUCTOR PHYSICS. *Educ:* Technion-Israel Inst Technol, BSc, 68, MSc, 70, DSc, 73. *Prof Exp:* Res asst phys chem, Technion-Israel Inst Technol, 68-73; res fel solid state physics, Nat Res Coun Can, 73-75; Welch fel condensed matter, Tex Tech Univ, 76-77; sr lectr phys chem, Technion-Israel Inst Technol, 77-80; STAFF PHYSICIST SEMICONDUCTOR PHYSICS, RES & DEVELOP, GEN ELEC CORP, 80- *Concurrent Pos:* Vis prof, Dept Physics, Portland State Univ, 75; vpres eng, Solarex Systs Am, Lubbock, 77-78. *Res:* Problems in solid state physics, including studies on the dynamical properties of impure solids, light absorption and neutron scattering from condensed matter, molecular motion in liquid systems and physics of semiconductors. *Mailing Add:* Gen Elec Cent Res & Develop Signal Electronics Lab PO Box 8 Schenectady NY 12309

COHEN, STANLEY, b Brooklyn, NY, Nov 17, 22; m 51, 80; c 2. BIOCHEMISTRY. *Educ:* Brooklyn Col, BA, 43; Oberlin Col, MA, 45; Univ Mich, PhD(biochem), 48. *Prof Exp:* Instr pediat res, Univ Colo, 48-52; Am Cancer Soc fel, Wash Univ, 52-53, res assoc biochem, Dept Biol, 53-59; sr res fel, 59-62, assoc prof, 62-67, Am Cancer Soc res prof, 76, PROF BIOCHEM, VANDERBILT UNIV, 67- *Honors & Awards:* William Thomson Wakeman Award, Nat Paraplegia Found; Earl Sutherland Res Prize; Albion O Bernstein, M D Award, Med Soc NY; H P Robertson Mem Award. *Mem:* Nat Acad Sci; Am Soc Biol Chem; Am Chem Soc. *Res:* Structure and function of growth factors; mechanism of hormone actin. *Mailing Add:* Dept of Biochem Vanderbilt Univ Sch of Med Nashville TN 37203

COHEN, STANLEY, b New York, NY, June 4, 37; m; c 3. IMMUNOLOGY, PATHOLOGY. *Educ:* Columbia Univ, BA, 57, MD, 61. *Prof Exp:* Asst attend pathologist, Med Ctr, NY Univ, 65-66; capt immunochem, Walter Reed Army Inst Res, 66-68; from assoc prof to prof path, State Univ NY Buffalo, 68-74, assoc dir, Ctr Immunol, 71-74; PROF PATH, UNIV CONN HEALTH CTR, 74- *Concurrent Pos:* Buswell fel, 68-70; NIH grants, 69-; instr, NY Univ, 66-68; lectr, Cath Univ, 68. *Honors & Awards:* Parke-Davis Award, 77. *Mem:* Am Asn Immunol; Am Asn Path; Reticuloendothelial Soc; Int Union Immunol Sci. *Res:* Biological activities of lymphokines; mechanism of delayed hypersensitivity; lymphocyte activation; regulation of cellulor immunity. *Mailing Add:* Dept of Path Univ of Conn Health Ctr Farmington CT 06032

COHEN, STANLEY NORMAN, b Perth Amboy, NJ, Feb 17, 35; m 61; c 2. MOLECULAR GENETICS, MICROBIOLOGY. *Educ:* Rutgers Univ, BS, 56; Sch Med, Univ Pa, MD, 60. *Prof Exp:* PROF MED, STANFORD UNIV, 75-, PROF GENETICS, 77-, CHMN DEPT GENETICS, SCH MED, 78- *Concurrent Pos:* US Pub Health Serv grant, 69-74; head Div Pharmacol, Sch Med, Stanford Univ, 70-78; Josiah Macy Found fel, 75-76; Guggenheim Found fel, 75; mem comt on genetic eng, Int Coun Sci Unions, 75. *Honors & Awards:* Burroughs-Wellcome Scholar Award, 70; V D Mattia Award, Roche Inst Molecular Biol, 70; Lasker Award, 80; Wolf Prize, 81. *Mem:* Nat Acad Sci; Genetics Soc Am; Am Soc Biol Chemists; Am Soc Microbiol; fel Am Acad Arts & Sci. *Res:* Molecular genetics biology and evolution of bacterial plasmids; structural evolution of genes encoding neuropeptide hormones; expression of DNA in heterogenic environments. *Mailing Add:* Dept Genetics Sch Med Stanford Univ Stanford CA 94305

COHEN, STEPHEN ROBERT, b New York, NY, May 7, 28; m 54; c 2. NEUROCHEMISTRY, PHYSICAL CHEMISTRY. *Educ:* Cornell Univ, BChE, 51, PhD(phys chem), 56. *Prof Exp:* Asst phys chem, Cornell Univ, 51-55; instr chem, Brown Univ, 56-58; phys chemist, Itek Corp, 58-59; asst prof chem, Northeastern Univ, 59-61; asst prof, City Col New York, 61-64; res assoc, Col Physicians & Surgeons, Columbia Univ, 64-66; sr res scientist, NY State Res Inst Neurochem & Drug Addiction, 66-70, assoc res scientist, 70-76; RES SCIENTIST V, NY STATE INST BASIC RES MENT RETARDATION, 76- *Mem:* Int Soc Neurochem; Am Chem Soc; Am Soc Neurochem; Royal Soc Chem; Fedn Am Socs Exp Biol. *Res:* Kinetics and reaction mechanisms; neurochemistry; active transport; extracellular spaces; mass spectrometry. *Mailing Add:* NY State Inst Basic Res 1050 Forest Hill Rd Staten Island NY 10314

COHEN, STEVEN CHARLES, b New Kensington, Pa, Aug 27, 47; m 70; c 2. TECTONOPHYSICS, GEODYNAMICS. *Educ:* Drexel Univ, BS, 70; Univ Md, MS, 72, PhD(physics), 73. *Prof Exp:* GEOPHYSICIST/PHYSICIST, GODDARD SPACE FLIGHT CTR, NASA, 70- *Mem:* Am Geophys Union; Am Phys Soc. *Res:* Research activities on crustal deformation; mechanisms of earthquakes, geodynamic processes; application of space geodetic techniques to earth science studies. *Mailing Add:* Goddard Space Flight Ctr Code 921 Greenbelt MD 20771

COHEN, STEVEN DONALD, b Boston, Mass, Nov 22, 42; m 65; c 2. TOXICOLOGY, PHARMACOLOGY. *Educ:* Mass Col Pharm, BS, 65, MS, 67; Harvard Univ, DSc(toxicol), 70. *Prof Exp:* Res assoc toxicol, Harvard Univ, 70-72; asst prof, 72-77, ASSOC PROF TOXICOL, UNIV CONN, 77- *Mem:* AAAS; Soc Toxicol; Am Asn Cols Pharm; Am Conf Govt Indust Hyg. *Res:* Biochemical actions of toxicants; special emphasis on toxicologic interactions involving organophosphate insecticides. *Mailing Add:* Sect of Pharmacol & Toxicol Univ Conn Sch of Pharm Storrs CT 06268

COHEN, STUART COLIN, b London, Eng, Apr 13, 44; m 66; c 3. ORGANIC POLYMER CHEMISTRY. *Educ:* Univ London, BSc, 65, PhD(chem), 68. *Prof Exp:* Res assoc chem, Va Polytech Inst, 68-69; asst prof, Syracuse Univ, 69-73; sr chemist, Borg-Warner Chem, 73-75; prin scientist, Leeds & Northrup Co, 75-76; prod develop specialist, Gen Elect Co, 76-77, mgr qual control & anal, 77-79, mgr tech mkt, 79-80; SR GROUP LEADER, RUBICON CHEMICALS, 80- *Concurrent Pos:* Petrol Res Fund grant, 69-72. *Mem:* Am Chem Soc; Soc Plastics Engrs. *Res:* Development and evaluation of MDI isocyanates for use in polyurethane foams, RIM elastomers and as adhesives for wood. *Mailing Add:* Rubicon Chemicals Inc PO Box 900 Woodbury NJ 08096

COHEN, THEODORE, b Arlington, Mass, May 11, 29; m 54; c 2. ORGANIC CHEMISTRY. *Educ:* Tufts Univ, BS, 51; Univ Southern Calif, PhD(chem), 55. *Prof Exp:* Asst chem, Univ Southern Calif, 52-55; asst lectr, Glasgow Univ, 55-56; from instr to assoc prof, 56-66, PROF CHEM, UNIV PITTSBURGH, 66- *Concurrent Pos:* Fulbright grant & Ramsay fel, Glasgow Univ, 55-56; consult, FMC Corp, Gulf & Technol Co. *Mem:* Am Chem Soc; The Chem Soc. *Res:* New synthetic methods involving sulfur and/or copper; the biosynthesis of cyclopropane rings. *Mailing Add:* Dept of Chem Univ of Pittsburgh Pittsburgh PA 15260

COHEN, WILLIAM, b Brooklyn, NY, Apr 19, 31; m 63. BIOCHEMISTRY. *Educ:* Long Island Univ, BS, 51; Purdue Univ, MS, 54; Fordham Univ, PhD(biochem), 58. *Prof Exp:* Asst, Purdue Univ, 51-54; assoc dept microbiol, Col Physicians & Surgeons, Columbia, 58-63; from asst prof to assoc prof, 63-74, PROF BIOCHEM, SCH MED, TULANE UNIV, 74- *Mem:* Am Soc Biol Chem. *Res:* Enzyme therapy. *Mailing Add:* Dept of Biochem Tulane Univ New Orleans LA 70112

COHEN, WILLIAM C(HARLES), b Brooklyn, NY, May 30, 33; m 55; c 5. CHEMICAL ENGINEERING. *Educ:* Pratt Inst Technol, BChE, 54; Princeton Univ, MSE, 57, PhD(chem eng), 60. *Prof Exp:* From asst prof to assoc prof chem eng, Univ Pa, 58-72, dir continuing eng studies, 69-72; PROF CHEM ENG, & ASSOC DEAN INDUST & ACAD AFFAIRS, NORTHWESTERN UNIV, 72- *Concurrent Pos:* Consult, Systs Anal Dept, Leeds & Northrup Co, 60; NSF fac fel sci, Univ Calif, Berkeley, 65-66. *Mem:* Am Inst Chem Engrs; Instrument Soc Am. *Res:* Dynamics, control and optimization of process systems. *Mailing Add:* Tech Inst Rm 2804 Northwestern Univ Evanston IL 60201

COHEN, WILLIAM DAVID, b Brooklyn, NY, Feb 24, 28; m 48; c 6. BIOCHEMISTRY. *Educ:* Univ Iowa, BS, 47; Univ Minn, MS, 50, PhD(biochem), 52. *Prof Exp:* Damon Runyan sr res fel, 52-53; chief biochemist, Mem Hosp, Worcester, Mass, 53-61; consult chemist, Minn State Dept Health, 62; asst prof obstet & gynec, Med Col, Univ Minn, 62-68; CHIEF BIOCHEMIST LAB, ST JOHN'S GEN HOSP, 70- *Concurrent Pos:* Clin assoc prof path, Mem Univ Nfld, 71- *Mem:* Am Asn Clin Chem; Can Soc Clin Chemists. *Res:* Chemistry and metabolism of lipids and steroid hormones. *Mailing Add:* St John's Gen Hosp St John's NF A1B 3V6 Can

COHICK, A DOYLE, JR, b Nevada, Mo, July 14, 39; m 61; c 2. ECONOMIC ENTOMOLOGY, INFORMATION SCIENCE. *Educ:* Cent Mo State Col, BSEd, 61, MA, 64; Cornell Univ, PhD(entom), 68. *Prof Exp:* Teacher pub schs, Raytown, Mo, 61-65; asst entom, Cornell Univ, 65-68; res biologist, Chemagro Corp, 68-72, mgr data documentation, 72-81, MGR INSECTICIDE RES, AGR DIV, MOBAY CHEM CORP, 81- *Mem:* Entom Soc Am. *Res:* Odonate ethology; mammalian and insect ecology; stored products insect behavior and control; information storage and data processing systems. *Mailing Add:* Agr Div Mobay Chem Corp Box 4913 Kansas City MO 64120

COHICK, SUSAN MARY, acoustics, see previous edition

COHLAN, SIDNEY QUEX, b New York, NY, July 31, 15; m 51; c 2. PEDIATRICS. *Educ:* Brooklyn Col, AB, 34; NY Med Col, MD, 39; Am Bd Pediat, dipl, 52. *Prof Exp:* From asst prof to assoc prof clin pediat, 53-70, PROF PEDIAT, MED SCH, NY UNIV-BELLEVUE MED CTR, 70- *Concurrent Pos:* Adj pediatrician, Beth Israel Hosp, 50-56, assoc pediatrician, 56-; vis physician, Children's Med Serv, Bellevue Hosp, 53-58, vis physician, Hosp, 58-; asst vis physician, NY Univ Hosp, 53-, pediat in chg, Dept Pediat, 58-; mem med bd, Irvington House, 59-; study sect child health & human develop, NIH. *Mem:* AAAS; Am Pediat Soc; Am Acad Pediat; Soc Pediat Res. *Res:* Vitamin A metabolism; developmental malformations. *Mailing Add:* NY Univ 550 First Ave New York NY 10016

COHLBERG, JEFFREY ALLAN, b Philadelphia, Pa, Geb 26, 43. BIOCHEMISTRY. *Educ:* Cornell Univ, AB, 66; Univ Calif, Berkeley, PhD(biochem), 72. *Prof Exp:* NIH fel, Inst Enzyme Res, Univ Wis, 72-75; ASST PROF CHEM, CALIF STATE UNIV, LONG BEACH, 75- *Res:* Interactions among protein and RNA molecules in ribosomes; quaternary structure of macromolecules; mechanism of protein synthesis. *Mailing Add:* Dept of Chem Calif State Univ Long Beach CA 90840

COHN, CHARLES ERWIN, b Chicago, Ill, Apr 25, 31; m 76. EXPERIMENTAL PHYSICS. *Educ:* Univ Chicago, PhD(physics), 57. *Prof Exp:* Asst physicist, 56-59, PHYSICIST, ARGONNE NAT LAB, 59- *Mem:* Am Phys Soc. *Res:* Nuclear reactor experimental physics; reactor kinetics, noise and computer-aided experimentation. *Mailing Add:* 445 Ridge Ave Clarendon Hills IL 60514

COHN, DANIEL ROSS, b Berkeley, Calif, Nov 28, 43. LASERS, PLASMA PHYSICS. *Educ:* Univ Calif, Berkeley, AB, 66; Mass Inst Technol, PhD(physics), 71. *Prof Exp:* Staff physicist, 71-74, tech asst to dir, 74-75, assoc group leader quantum optics & plasma physics, 75-77, GROUP LEADER PLASMA & LASER SYSTS, FRANCIS BITTER NAT MAGNET LAB, MASS INST TECHNOL, 77- *Res:* Laser plasma interactions; infrared and submillimeter lasers; plasma diagnostics; controlled thermonuclear fusion; controlled thermonuclear fusion. *Mailing Add:* Francis Bitter Nat Magnet Lab 170 Albany St Cambridge MA 02139

COHN, DAVID L(ESLIE), b Highland Park, Ill, Apr 20, 43; m 65; c 1. ELECTRICAL ENGINEERING. *Educ:* Mass Inst Technol, SB, 66, SM, 66, PhD(elec eng), 70. *Prof Exp:* Consult, Sylvania, Farrel Lines, 66-70; asst prof elec eng, Southern Methodist Univ, 70-76; ASSOC PROF ELEC ENG, UNIV NOTRE DAME, 76- *Mem:* Inst Elec & Electronics Engrs. *Res:* Information theory; communication theory and coding. *Mailing Add:* Dept of Elec Eng Univ of Notre Dame Notre Dame IN 46556

COHN, DAVID VALOR, b New York, NY, Nov 8, 26; m 47; c 2. BIOCHEMISTRY, ENDOCRINOLOGY. *Educ:* City Col New York, BS, 48; Duke Univ, PhD, 52. *Prof Exp:* USPHS fel, Western Reserve Univ, 52-53; prin scientist & actg chief radioisotope serv, Vet Admin Hosp, 53-68, assoc chief staff & dir, Calcium Res Lab, 68-81; from instr to prof biochem, 53-81, assoc dean, Col Health Sci, Univ Kans Med Ctr, Kansas City, 74-81; DIR RES & DEVELOP, IMMUNO NUCLEAR CORP, 81- *Concurrent Pos:* From asst prof to assoc prof, Sch Dent, Univ Mo, 62-70, prof, 71-81; mem gen med B study sect, USPHS, 71-75; chmn, Gordon Res Conf Chem, Physiol & Structure Bones & Teeth, 74; mem exec comt, Int Parathyroid Conf, 74-; pres, Int Conf on Calcium Regulating Hormones, Inc; mem bd sci coun, Nat Inst Dent Res, NIH, 81- *Mem:* AAAS; Am Chem Soc; Am Soc Biol Chem; Endocrine Soc. *Res:* Chemistry and physiology of peptide hormones including parathyroid hormone and calcitonin; biology of bone growth and resorption; calcium binding proteins; radioimmunoassay technology. *Mailing Add:* Immuno Nuclear Corp PO Box 285 Stillwater MN 55082

COHN, DEIRDRE ARLINE, b New York, NY. ANDROGENS, IMMUNE RESPONSE. *Educ:* Hunter Col, BA, 48, MA, 65; State Univ NY, Downstate Med Ctr, PhD(anat), 71. *Prof Exp:* Lectr physiol, Hunter Col, 65-66; instr anat & cell biol, State Univ NY, Downstate Med Ctr, 70-76, asst prof, 76-77, lectr, 77-78; ASSOC PROF BIOL, YORK COL, CITY UNIV NY, 77- *Concurrent Pos:* Prin investr, NIH Androgen Sensitivity as a Factor in Immunocompetence, 77-; consult & site vis, Minority Access to Res Careers Prog, NIH, 78-81; prog dir, Minority Biomed Support Prog, York Col, NIH, 78- *Mem:* Am Asn Immunologists; Am Asn Anatomists; Reticuloendothelial Soc; Asn Women Sci; NY Acad Sci. *Res:* The influence of sensitivity to adrogens; aging and splenectomy on host variability, particularly sex differences in the immune response. *Mailing Add:* Div Natural Sci York Col City Univ NY Jamaica NY 11451

COHN, ELLEN RASSAS, b Long Branch, NJ, Jan 12, 53; m 82. SPEECH PATHOLOGY. *Educ:* Douglass Col, Rutgers Univ, BA, 74; Vanderbilt Univ, MS, 76; Univ Pittsburgh, PhD(speech path), 81. *Prof Exp:* RES ASSOC, CLEFT PALATE CTR, UNIV PITTSBURGH, 80-, CLIN ASST PROF, DEPT SPEECH PATH, 81- *Concurrent Pos:* Prin investr, Fac Develop Grant & Teaching Develop Grants, Univ Pittsburgh, 81 & Nat Inst Dent Res Grants. *Mem:* Am Cleft Palate Educ Fedn; Am Speech & Hearing Asn. *Res:* Cleft palate and craniofacial disorders; velopharyngeal inadequacy; non-verbal communication; speech in relationship to orthodontic problems; video fluoroscopy and ultrasound. *Mailing Add:* 5436 Northumberland St Pittsburgh PA 15217

COHN, ERNST M, b Mainz, Ger, Mar 31, 20; nat US; m 49. PHYSICAL CHEMISTRY. *Educ:* Univ Pittsburgh, BS, 42, MS, 52. *Prof Exp:* Chemist minimum ignition energies gas mixtures, US Bur Mines, 42-44, chemist Fischer-Tropsch synthesis & magnetochem, 46-53; chemist, Bituminous Coal Res Br, Dept Interior, 53-60; phys chemist, US Army Res Off, 60-62; mgr solar & chem power, NASA, 62-76; CONSULT & COLUMNIST, 76- *Mem:* Am Chem Soc. *Res:* Kinetics of reactions in solids; carbides of iron, cobalt and nickel; Fischer-Tropsch synthesis; magnetochemistry; chemistry and physics of coal; batteries; fuel cells; bioelectrochemistry; electrocatalysis; photovoltaics and solar-cell arrays. *Mailing Add:* 1138 Appian Way Dothan AL 36303

COHN, GEORGE I(RVING), b Lake Forest, Ill, Jan 29, 21; m 53; c 4. ELECTRICAL ENGINEERING. *Educ:* Calif Inst Technol, BS, 42; Ill Inst Technol, MS, 47, PhD(elec eng), 51. *Prof Exp:* Instr elec eng, Ill Inst Technol, 47-49, from asst prof to prof, 49-61; chief scientist fluid physics div & mgr exploding mat lab, Electro-Optical Systs, Inc, 61-62; mgr penetration aids prog & electromagnetics group, Nat Eng Sci Co, 62-63; consult, 64-68; PROF ENG, CALIF STATE UNIV FULLERTON, 68- *Concurrent Pos:* Consult, Cook Res Co, Bendix Prod Div, Space Tech Labs, Inc, Motorola, Southwest Res Found, Armour Res Found, Jet Propulsion Lab, Autonetics Div, NAm Aviation, Inc & Magnavox Co. *Mem:* AAAS; Am Math Soc; Am Phys Soc; Am Soc Eng Educ; Optical Soc Am. *Res:* Electromagnetic theory; propagation; antennas; microwaves; tubes; accelerators; network theory; applied analysis; transform techniques; nonlinear differential equations; integration; electronics; teaching techniques; worktexts; lasers; plasmas; scattering. *Mailing Add:* Dept of Eng Calif State Univ Fullerton CA 92631

COHN, GERALD EDWARD, b Buffalo, NY, June 10, 43; m 69; c 3. MOLECULAR BIOPHYSICS. *Educ:* Columbia Univ, AB, 65; Univ Wis-Madison, MA, 68, PhD(physics), 72. *Prof Exp:* Trainee biophys, Pa State Univ, 71-72, scholar, 73; ASST PROF PHYSICS, ILL INST TECHNOL, 73- *Concurrent Pos:* Cottrell Res Corp res grant, 74; fac res grant, Ill Inst Technol, 74, 75 & 77. *Mem:* Am Phys Soc; Biophys Soc; Am Asn Physics Teachers. *Res:* Electron spin resonance studies of the photobiology of natural and model membrane systems; photodynamic damage in yeast. *Mailing Add:* Dept of Physics Siegel Hall Ill Inst of Technol Chicago IL 60616

COHN, HANS OTTO, b Berlin, Ger, Dec 27, 27; Nat US; m 60; c 3. PHYSICS, ELEMENTARY PARTICLE PHYSICS. *Educ:* Ind Univ, BS, 49, MS, 50, PhD(physics), 54. *Prof Exp:* Asst physics, Ind Univ, 49-51, res asst, 52-54; PHYSICIST, OAK RIDGE NAT LAB, 54- *Mem:* Fel Am Phys Soc. *Res:* Strange particles; nuclear and high energy physics. *Mailing Add:* Oak Ridge Nat Lab PO Box X Oak Ridge TN 37830

COHN, HARVEY, b New York, NY, Dec 27, 23; m 51; c 2. MATHEMATICS. *Educ:* City Col New York, BS, 42; NY Univ, MS, 43; Harvard Univ, PhD(math), 48. *Prof Exp:* Asst prof math, Wayne Univ, 48-54; vis assoc prof, Stanford Univ, 54-55; assoc prof, Wayne Univ, 55-56; assoc prof, Wash Univ, 56-57; prof math & dir comput ctr, 57-58; prof math, Univ Ariz, 58-71, head dept, 58-67; DISTINGUISHED PROF MATH, CITY UNIV NEW YORK, 71- *Concurrent Pos:* Consult, Gen Motors Corp, 53, AEC, NY, 54, Nat Bur Standards, 56, Int Bus Mach Corp, 57 & Argonne Nat Lab, 58-68; mem comt regional develop for math, Nat Res Coun, 62-65; mem adv comt, Autonomous Univ Guadalajara, 63-65; vis mem, Inst Advan Study, Princeton, 70-71; vis lectr, Univ Copenhagen, 76-77. *Mem:* Am Math Soc; Asn Comput Mach; Math Asn Am. *Res:* Number theory and modular functions, particularly use of computer techniques. *Mailing Add:* Dept Math City Col New York 138th St & Convent Ave New York NY 10031

COHN, ISIDORE, JR, b New Orleans, La, Sept 25, 21; m 44; c 2. SURGERY. *Educ:* Tulane Univ, BS, 42; Univ Pa, MD, 45, MSc, 52, DSc(med), 55; Am Bd Surg, dipl, 53. *Prof Exp:* From instr to assoc prof, 52-59, PROF SURG, SCH MED, LA STATE UNIV MED CTR, NEW ORLEANS, 59-, CHMN DEPT, 62- *Concurrent Pos:* Surgeon-in-chief, La State Univ Serv, Charity Hosp; mem Am Bd Surg, 69-75; chmn, clin invest adv comt, Am Cancer Soc, 69-73; mem ed staff, Am Surg, Rev Surg, Am J Surg & Surg Digest; dir, Nat Pancreatic Cancer Proj, 75- *Mem:* Am Surg Asn; Am Col Surgeons; Am Gastroenterol Asn; Soc Univ Surgeons; Int Soc Surg. *Res:* Gastrointestinal surgery, strangulation intestinal obstruction and secondary interest in problems involving biliary, pancreatic and tumor problems associated with antibacterial agents; surgical research in germ-free animals. *Mailing Add:* Dept of Surg La State Univ Med Ctr New Orleans LA 70112

COHN, J GUNTHER E, b Berlin, Ger, May 6, 11; nat US; m 40; c 1. CHEMISTRY. *Educ:* Univ Berlin, PhD(chem), 34. *Prof Exp:* Asst, Nobel Inst, Sweden, 34-36; asst & instr, Chalmers Tech Univ, Sweden, 37-41; Carnegie fel, Univ Minn, 41-42, Welsh fel, 43; vpres, Engelhard Industs Div, 43-63, vpres & dir, Res & Develop Dept, 63-72, vpres res & technol, Engelhard Industs Div, Engelhard Minerals & Chem Corp, 72-76; CONSULT, 76- *Mem:* Am Chem Soc; Electrochem Soc. *Res:* Corrosion of metals and reactions in solid state; catalytic properties of solids; photochemistry of solids; powder metallurgy; instrumentation of chemical processes; precious metals; electrochemistry. *Mailing Add:* 20 Lincoln Ave West Orange NJ 07052

COHN, JACK, b Rock Island, Ill, May 6, 32; m 53; c 4. THEORETICAL PHYSICS, ELECTRODYNAMICS. *Educ:* Univ Iowa, BA, 53, MS, 56, PhD(statist mech), 62. *Prof Exp:* From asst prof to assoc prof, 60-71, PROF PHYSICS, UNIV OKLA, 71- *Res:* Statistical mechanics; general relativity. *Mailing Add:* Dept of Physics Univ of Okla Norman OK 73069

COHN, JAY BINSWANGER, b Pelham, NY, Feb 22, 22; m 45; c 2. PSYCHIATRY. *Educ:* Amherst Col, BA, 42; Yale Univ, MD, 45; Univ Calif, Irvine, PhD(psychol), 74. *Prof Exp:* Intern, St Elizabeth's Hosp, Washington, DC, 45-46; resident, Crile Hosp, Cleveland, Ohio, 48-49 & Cleveland Receiving Hosp, 51-53; lectr psychiat, Western Reserve Univ, 54-59; instr, Univ Calif, Los Angeles, 59-65; asst clin prof, Univ Southern Calif, 65-68, assoc prof, 68-71; PROF PSYCHIAT & SOC SCI, UNIV CALIF, IRVINE, 71- *Concurrent Pos:* Consult, res projs, State Dept Ment Hyg, Ohio, 53-58, Vet Admin, Calif, 59-65, Indust Accident Comn, 60- & US Fed Court, Panel, 61- *Mem:* AAAS; fel Am Psychiat Asn; Am Psychol Asn; Am Acad Neurol; AMA; Acad Psychoanal. *Res:* Counter-transference and pharmacology; electrical measurement of counter-transference as measured in electrocardiogram. *Mailing Add:* Dept of Psychiat & Human Behav Univ of Calif Irvine CA 92664

COHN, JAY NORMAN, b Schenectady, NY, July 6, 30; m 53; c 3. CARDIOVASCULAR DISEASES. *Educ:* Union Univ, NY, BS, 52; Cornell Univ, MD, 56; Am Bd Internal Med, dipl. *Prof Exp:* Intern med, Beth Israel Hosp, Boston, Mass, 56-57, asst resident, 57-58; chief resident, Vet Admin Hosp, 61-62, clin investr cardiovasc, 62-65; from instr to prof med, Georgetown Univ, 62-74; PROF MED & HEAD CARDIOVASC DIV, MED SCH, UNIV MINN, MINNEAPOLIS, 74- *Concurrent Pos:* Res fel cardiovasc, Georgetown Univ Hosp, 60-61; chief hypertension & clin hemodynamics, Vet Admin Hosp, DC, 65-74; chmn, Coun on Circulation, Am Heart Asn, 79-81, chmn, Sci Sessions Prog Comt, 79-82. *Honors & Awards:* Arthur S Flemming Award, 69. *Mem:* Am Col Cardiol; Am Heart Asn; Asn Am Physicians; Am Soc Clin Invest; Am Soc Pharmacol & Exp Therapeut. *Res:* Hemodynamics of myocardial infarction; pathophysiology and treatment of hypertension and congestive heart failure in man; hemodynamic factors in clinical hypotension and shock; dynamics of regional blood flow in man. *Mailing Add:* Med Sch Univ of Minn Minneapolis MN 55455

COHN, JONA, b Chicago, Ill, June 19, 26; m 49; c 3. ELECTRICAL ENGINEERING. *Educ:* Ill Inst Technol, BS, 48, MS, 51; Northwestern Univ, PhD, 57. *Prof Exp:* Sect head & asst chief engr, 58-61, chief engr, 61-71, DIR RES, SYSTS & STAS, MOTOROLA, INC, 71- *Res:* Threshold reception of radio signals; application of digital computer techniques to communication systems development. *Mailing Add:* Motorola Inc Commun Group 1301 E Algonquin Rd Schaumburg IL 60196

COHN, KIM, b New York, NY, Jan 25, 39; m 62, 82; c 1. INORGANIC CHEMISTRY. *Educ:* Queens Col, NY, BS, 60; Univ Mich, PhD(chem), 67. *Prof Exp:* Asst prof chem, Mich State Univ, 67-72; assoc prof, 72-80, PROF CHEM, CALIF STATE COL, BAKERSFIELD, 80- *Mem:* Am Chem Soc; Royal Soc Chem. *Res:* Synthesis, structure and bonding of non-transition elements. *Mailing Add:* Calif State Col 9001 Stockdale Hwy Bakersfield CA 93309

COHN, LESLIE, b Philadelphia, Pa, Feb 3, 43. MATHEMATICS. *Educ:* Univ Pa, BA, 65; Univ Chicago, MS, 67, PhD(math), 69. *Prof Exp:* Asst prof, Univ Ill, Chicago Circle, 69-70; vis mem, Inst Advan Study, 70-71; asst prof, 71-77, ASSOC PROF MATH, JOHNS HOPKINS UNIV, 77- *Mem:* Am Math Soc. *Res:* Number theory; automorphic forms; representations of live groups. *Mailing Add:* Dept of Math Johns Hopkins Univ Baltimore MD 21218

COHN, MILDRED, b New York, NY, July 12, 13; m 38; c 3. BIOCHEMISTRY, BIOPHYSICS. *Educ:* Hunter Col, BA, 31; Columbia Univ, PhD(phys chem), 38. *Hon Degrees:* ScD, Women's Med Col Pa, 66, Radcliffe Col, 78, Washington Univ, 81. *Prof Exp:* Res assoc biochem, George Washington Univ, 37-38, Cornell Univ, 38-46 & Harvard Med Sch, 50-51; res assoc, Wash Univ, 46-58, assoc prof, 58-60; prof biophys & phys biochem, 61-78, BENJAMIN RUSH PROF PHYSIOL CHEM, UNIV PA, 78- *Concurrent Pos:* Career investr, Am Heart Asn, 64-78; vis prof biochem, Inst Biol Phys Chem, Paris, 66-67; chancellor's distinguished vis prof, Univ Calif, Berkeley, 81. *Honors & Awards:* Garvan Medal, Am Chem Soc, 63; Cresson Medal, Franklin Inst, 75; Biochemists Award, Int Orgn Women, 79. *Mem:* Nat Acad Sci; Am Philos Soc; Am Acad Arts & Sci; Am Soc Biol Chem (pres, 78-79); Am Chem Soc (chmn, Div Biol Chem, 73-74). *Res:* Metabolic studies with isotopes, stable and radioactive; mechanisms of enzymatic reactions; electron spin and nuclear magnetic resonance. *Mailing Add:* Univ of Pa G4 Dept Biochem Biophys Richards Bldg Philadelphia PA 19104

COHN, NAOMI KENDA, b Syracuse, NY. CELL BIOLOGY, CANCER. *Educ:* Syracuse Univ, BS, 52; Univ Wis-Madison, MS, 54. *Prof Exp:* Microbiologist, Rocky Mountain Lab, NIH, USPHS, 57-61; res asst oncol & med genetics, MacArdle Lab, Univ Wis-Madison, 61-68, microbiologist III, Dept Radiobiol, 68-70; RES SCIENTIST CELL BIOL, BURROUGHS-WELLCOME CO, 70- *Mem:* Tissue Cult Asn; Am Soc Microbiol; AAAS; Sigma Xi. *Res:* Mouse mammary carcinoma; drug resistance. *Mailing Add:* Burroughs-Wellcome Co 3030 Cornwallis Rd Research Triangle Park NC 27709

COHN, NATHAN, b Hartford, Conn, Jan 2, 07; m 40; c 5. ELECTRICAL ENGINEERING. *Educ:* Mass Inst Technol, SB, 27. *Prof Exp:* Trainee, Leeds & Northrop Co, Pa, 27-28, field engr, 28-29, dist mgr, Calif, 29-37, regional mgr, 51-55, mgr mkt develop div, Pa, 55-58, vpres tech affairs, 58-65, mem bd dirs, 63-75, sr vpres tech affairs, 65-67, exec vpres res & corp develop, 67-71, exec vpres corp develop, 71-72; CONSULT ENGR, 72- *Concurrent Pos:* Pres, Nat Electronics Conf, 49-50; mem, US State Dept Automatic Control Group Exchange Visit to USSR, 58 & 65; co-rep, Indust Res Inst, 62-72; chmn educ & accreditation, Engrs Comt Prof Develop, 64; mem vis comt libr, Mass Inst Technol, 64-69; mem staff, Div Eng & Indust Res, Nat Res Coun, 64-67; US deleg, Cong Int Fedn Automatic Control, 60, 63, 66, 69, 72, 75, 78 & 81; chmn adv panel Time & Frequency Div, Nat Bur Standards, 68-71; mem adv comt eng & phys sci, Univ City Sci Ctr, Philadelphia, 68-70; bd dirs, Pa Environ Coun, 70-72. *Honors & Awards:* John Price Wetherill Medal Award, Franklin Inst, Philadelphia, 68; Lamme Medal Award, Inst Elec & Electronics Engrs, 68; Albert F Sperry Medal Award, Instrument Soc Am, 68; Sci Apparatus Makers Award, 78. *Mem:* Nat Acad Eng; fel AAAS; fel Inst Elec & Electronics Engrs; fel Instrument Soc Am (pres, 63). *Res:* Measurement and automatic control, including automatic control of generation and power flow on interconnected electric power systems. *Mailing Add:* 1457 Noble Rd Jenkintown PA 19046

COHN, NORMAN STANLEY, b Philadelphia, Pa, June 26, 30; m 56; c 3. CYTOLOGY, CYTOCHEMISTRY. *Educ:* Univ Pa, AB, 52; Univ Ky, MS, 53; Yale Univ, PhD(bot), 57. *Prof Exp:* Asst biol, Yale Univ, 53-56; NSF res fel, Johns Hopkins Univ, 57-59; from asst prof to assoc prof, 59-68, chmn dept, 69-70, dean, Grad Col & dir res, 70-79, DISTINGUISHED PROF BOT, OHIO UNIV, 68- *Concurrent Pos:* Fulbright res scholar, State Univ Leiden, 65-66 & 68-69; Nat Acad Sci vis lectr, Czech & Yugoslavia, 68 & 73; head cellular & physiol biosci, NSF, 79-81. *Mem:* AAAS; Am Soc Cell Biol; Sigma Xi; Genetics Soc Am; Am Inst Biol Sci. *Res:* Radiation cytology; chromosome breakage and chemistry; cell nucleus and cytochemical techniques; developmental plant biology. *Mailing Add:* Dept Bot Ohio Univ Athens OH 45701

COHN, PAUL DANIEL, b Portland, Ore, July 14, 36. NUCLEAR ENGINEERING, ECONOMICS. *Educ:* Ore State Univ, BS, 58, MS, 59. *Prof Exp:* Proj mgr, space systs, N Am Rockwell Corp, 62-65; mgr, fast flux test facility core & fuels design, Pac Northwest Div, Battelle Mem Inst, 65-70; dep mgr nuclear proj, Battelle Northwest, 70-72, mgr nuclear projs, 72-73, mgr safety res, 73-74; CONSULT, ENERGY ENG ASSOCS, 74- *Concurrent Pos:* Consult, reactor safety anal, United Nuclear Industs, 76-, energy econ, Pac Northwest Div, Battelle Mem Inst, 77-, prod eval, Exxon Nuclear, 77- & fuel cycle econ, Westinghouse-Hanford, 78- *Res:* Nuclear safety; fuel design; thermal hydraulics; economic modeling and analysis; production analysis. *Mailing Add:* Energy Eng Assocs 1818 SE Oakland Richland WA 99352

COHN, RICHARD MOSES, b New York, NY, Sept 2, 19. ALGEBRA. *Educ:* Columbia Univ, BA, 39, MA, 41, PhD(math), 47. *Prof Exp:* Engr, Inspection Agency, Signal Corps, US Army, 42-44; lectr elem math, Columbia Univ, 46-47; from instr to assoc prof, 47-59, PROF MATH, RUTGERS UNIV, 59- *Mem:* Am Math Soc. *Res:* Difference algebra; differential algebra; electrical networks. *Mailing Add:* Dept Math Rutgers Univ New Brunswick NJ 08903

COHN, ROBERT, b Washington, DC, Feb 25, 09; m 37. NEUROLOGY. *Educ:* George Washington Univ, BS, 32, MD, 36. *Prof Exp:* Fel neurophysiol, St Elizabeth's Hosp, Washington, DC, 36-38; mem staff neurol & electroencephalog, St Elizabeth's Hosp, 38-43; dir neurol res, US Naval Hosp, Bethesda, 46-71; PROF NEUROL, HOWARD UNIV, 71- *Concurrent Pos:* Clin prof, Howard Univ, 60-65; prof lectr, Mt Sinai Med Sch, NY, 69-; vis prof, Boston Univ, 70- *Mem:* Am Neurol Asn; Am Electroencephalog Soc; Asn Res Nerv & Ment Dis. *Res:* Clinical and experimental neurology and electroencephalography; physiology of sensation. *Mailing Add:* 7221 Pyle Rd Bethesda MD 20817

COHN, SEYMOUR B(ERNARD), b Stamford, Conn, Oct 21, 20; m 48; c 3. ENGINEERING. *Educ:* Yale Univ, BE, 42; Harvard Univ, MS, 46, PhD(electromagnetic theory), 48. *Prof Exp:* Spec res assoc, Radio Res Lab, Harvard Univ, 42-45; Nat Res Coun fel, 46-48; res engr, Sperry Gyroscope Co, 48-53; lab mgr, Stanford Res Inst, 53-60, vpres & tech dir, Rantec Corp, 60-67; MICROWAVE CONSULT, S B COHN ASSOCS, 67- *Mem:* Fel Inst Elec & Electronics Engrs. *Res:* Ultra high frequency and microwave transmission apparatus. *Mailing Add:* 5021 Palomar Dr Tarzana CA 91356

COHN, SIDNEY ARTHUR, b Toronto, Ont, May 8, 18; US citizen; m 46; c 2. BIOLOGY. *Educ:* Univ Conn, BS, 40, MS, 48; Brown Univ, PhD(biol), 51. *Prof Exp:* From instr to assoc prof, 51-66, PROF ANAT, UNIV TENN, MEMPHIS, 66-, ACTG CHMN DEPT, 80- *Mem:* Am Asn Anat; Int Asn Dent Res; Sigma Xi; Am Asn Dent Sch. *Res:* Developmental and histological studies of teeth; long-term effects of non-function on supportive tissues of teeth; temporomandibular joint; attachment of fibers of periodontal ligament; study of the supportive tissues of the teeth. *Mailing Add:* Dept of Anat Univ Tenn Ctr Health Sci Memphis TN 38163

COHN, STANLEY HOWARD, b Toronto, Ont, Aug 23, 26; m 49; c 5. INFORMATION SYSTEMS, INDUSTRIAL ENGINEERING. *Educ:* Univ Toronto, BA, 48, MA, 50. *Prof Exp:* Instr appl math, Fournier Inst Technol, 52-55; specialist, Avro Aircraft Ltd, Ont, 55-59; head digital comput, Space Task Group, NASA, 59-62; mgr sci comput, Int Bus Mach Can, Ltd, 62-68; ASSOC PROF INDUST ENG, UNIV TORONTO, 68- *Concurrent Pos:* Nat Res Coun Can grant-in-aid res, 68-81; vis fel, Gen Pract Res Unit, UK, 77-78. *Mem:* Asn Comput Mach; Can Info Processing Soc. *Res:* Information systems engineering in primary health care; organizational information systems. *Mailing Add:* Dept of Indust Eng Univ of Toronto Toronto ON M5S 1A1 Can

COHN, STANTON HARRY, b Chicago, Ill, Aug 25, 20; m 49; c 5. PHYSIOLOGY, RADIOBIOLOGY. *Educ:* Univ Chicago, SB, 46, SM, 49; Univ Calif, Berkeley, PhD(physiol, radiobiol), 52. *Prof Exp:* Chemist, Kankakee Ord Works, 41-42; chemist, Sherwin Williams, 42-43; jr scientist biochem, Argonne Nat Lab, Univ Chicago, 46-49; asst radiobiol, Crocker Radiation Lab, Univ Calif, 49-50; head internal toxicity br, Biomed Div, US Naval Radiation Lab, 50-58; scientist, 58-70, SR SCIENTIST & HEAD MED PHYSICS DIV, MED RES CTR, BROOKHAVEN NAT LAB, 70- *Concurrent Pos:* Mem subcomt inhalation hazards, Path Effects Atomic Radiation Comt, Nat Acad Sci; mem, Nat Coun Radiation Protection subcomt II, Int Radiation Dose, 61-; prof med, Med Sch, State Univ NY, Stony Brook. *Mem:* Radiation Res Soc; Am Physiol Soc. *Res:* Chemical dynamics of the mineral metabolism of bone; distribution and biological effects of internally deposited radioisotopes; whole-body neutron activation analysis and whole-body counting; application of nuclear technology to medical problems. *Mailing Add:* Med Res Ctr Brookhaven Nat Lab Upton NY 11973

COHN, VICTOR HUGO, b Reading, Pa, July 9, 30; m 53; c 3. BIOCHEMICAL PHARMACOLOGY. *Educ:* Lehigh Univ, BS, 52; Harvard Univ, AM, 54; George Washington Univ, PhD(biochem), 61. *Prof Exp:* Pharmacologist, Army Chem Ctr, 55-56; neuropharmacologist, Vet Admin Res Labs, 56-57; biochem pharmacologist, Nat Heart Inst, 57-61; from asst prof to assoc prof, 61-71, actg chmn dept, 70-71 & 78-79, PROF PHARMACOL, MED CTR, GEORGE WASHINGTON UNIV, 71- *Concurrent Pos:* Vis investr, Jackson Labs, 66; drug policy adv, The White House, 79-80; mem, Bd Toxicol & Environ Health Hazards, Nat Res Coun-Nat Acad Sci, 80- *Mem:* Fel AAAS; Am Soc Pharmacol & Exp Therapeut; Am Chem Soc; Int Soc Biochem Pharmacol; Am Pub Health Asn. *Res:* Drug metabolism; drug abuse; fluorometric methods of analysis of biochemicals; histamine metabolism; pharmacogenetics. *Mailing Add:* Dept Pharmacol George Washington Univ Med Ctr Washington DC 20037

COHN, WALDO E, b San Francisco, Calif, June 28, 10; m 38, 43; c 2. BIOCHEMISTRY. *Educ:* Univ Calif, BS, 31, MS, 32, PhD(biochem), 38. *Prof Exp:* Asst biochem, Huntington Labs, Harvard Med Sch, 39-42; tutor biochem sci, Harvard Univ, 39-42; biochem group leader, Plutonium Proj, Univ Chicago, 42-43; group leader, Manhattan Proj, Oak Ridge, 43-47; sr biochemist, Oak Ridge Nat Lab, 47-75; CONSULT, 75- *Concurrent Pos:* Fulbright scholar, Cambridge Univ, 55-56; Guggenheim fel, 55-56, 62-63; secy, Comn Biochem Nomenclature, Int Union Pure & Appl Chem-Int Union Biochem, 65-76; dir off biochem nomenclature, Nat Acad Sci-Nat Res Coun, 65-76. *Honors & Awards:* Chromatography Award, Am Chem Soc, 63. *Mem:* Fel AAAS; fel Am Acad Arts & Sci; Am Chem Soc; Am Soc Biol Chemists (treas, 59-64). *Res:* Ion-exchange separations of rare earth elements and fission products, also of nucleic acid constituents and related biochemical substances; chemistry and structure of nucleic acids; biochemical nomenclature and editing. *Mailing Add:* Biol Div Oak Ridge Nat Lab Box Y Oak Ridge TN 37830

COHOON, DANIEL FRED, plant pathology, see previous edition

COHOON, DAVID KENT, b Terre Haute, Ind, June 4, 40; m 64; c 5. APPLIED MATHEMATICS. *Educ:* Mass Inst Technol, SB, 62; Purdue Univ, MS, 64, PhD(math), 69. *Prof Exp:* Teaching asst, Purdue Univ, 62-63, res assoc, 63-65; res assoc, Inst Henri Poincare, Paris, 65-66 & Purdue Univ, 66-67; asst prof, Bucknell Univ, 67-68; res assoc math, Purdue Univ, 68; mem tech staff, Bell Tel Labs, 69-70; Off Naval Res res assoc, Univ Wis-Madison, 69-70; asst prof math, Univ Minn, Minneapolis, 70-74; MATHEMATICIAN, BIOMETRICS DIV, SCH AEROSPACE MED, BROOKS AFB, 74- *Concurrent Pos:* Consult, Electromagnetic Compatibility Lab, Southwest Res Inst, 81- *Mem:* Math Asn Am; Am Math Soc. *Res:* The general theory of linear partial differential operators heat transfer; electromagnetic scattering; RFR effects on biochemical reactions. *Mailing Add:* Biomet Div Sch Aerospace Med Brooks AFB San Antonio TX 78235

COIL, WILLIAM HERSCHELL, b Ft Wayne, Ind, July 6, 25; m 46; c 3. PARASITOLOGY. *Educ:* Purdue Univ, BS, 48, MS, 49; Ohio State Univ, PhD(zool), 53. *Prof Exp:* Asst zool, Univ Tenn, 49-50; instr, Purdue Univ, 53-54; asst prof, Univ Nebr, 56-64; assoc prof, 64-69, assoc chmn, Dept Systs & Ecol, 68-72, PROF ZOOL, UNIV KANS, 69- *Concurrent Pos:* Mem exped, Oaxaca & Chiapas, Mex, 54 & 55; Muellhaupt scholar, Ohio State Univ, 54-56; NSF fel, Ore Inst Marine Biol, 57; res fel, Biol Sta, Univ Okla, 58; fac fel, Univ Nebr, 59; res assoc, Duke Marine Lab, 62-65; vis prof, Kans State Univ, 75-76. *Mem:* Am Soc Zool; Soc Syst Zool; Am Micros Soc; Am Soc Parasit. *Res:* Histochemistry and electron microscopy of cestodes and trematodes, fascioliasis, life histories and bionomics. *Mailing Add:* Dept of Syst & Ecol Univ of Kans Lawrence KS 66045

COILE, RUSSELL CLEVEN, b Washington, DC, Mar 11, 17; m 51; c 3. OPERATIONS RESEARCH, INFORMATION SCIENCE. *Educ:* Mass Inst Technol, SB, 38, SM, 39, EE, 50; City Univ, London, PhD(info sci), 78. *Prof Exp:* Asst, Mass Inst Technol, 38-39; magnetician, Carnegie Inst, 39-42; engr, Colton & Foss, Inc, 46-47; opers analyst, Opers Eval Group, Mass Inst Technol, 47-62; dir Marine Corps Opers anal group, Ctr Naval Anal, Franklin Inst, 62-67; opers analyst, Univ Rochester, 67-78; opers analyst, Ketron, Inc, 78-81; CONSULT ENGR, 81- *Concurrent Pos:* Dir res, Opers Res Group, Off Naval Res, 53-54 & 56-57; Am del, Int Fedn Oper Res Socs Conf, Oslo, Norway, 63; mem small arms adv comt, Advan Res Proj Agency, Dept Defense, 68-70; fel, Brit Fel Oper Res. *Mem:* Inst Elec & Electronics Eng; Opers Res Soc Am; Brit Oper Res Soc; Am Soc Info Sci. *Res:* Acoustics; electronics, radar; nomography; documentation; information retrieval; operational research; information science. *Mailing Add:* 4323 Rosedale Ave Bethesda MD 20814

COISH, HAROLD ROY, b Bronte, Ont, Aug 20, 18; m 42; c 4. THEORETICAL PHYSICS. *Educ:* Mt Allison Univ, BA, 38, BSc, 39; Dalhousie Univ, MSc, 42; Univ Toronto, MA, 46, PhD(appl math), 52. *Prof Exp:* Jr res scientist physics, Nat Res Coun Can, 40-42, jr engr theoret physics, 48-49; jr engr electronics, Can Marconi Co, 42-45; from asst prof to assoc prof, 49-55, PROF MATH PHYSICS, UNIV MAN, 55- *Mem:* Am Phys Soc; Can Asn Physicists; Can Math Cong. *Res:* Theory of internal conversion; physical geometry as a finite geometry and application to elementary particles. *Mailing Add:* Dept of Physics Univ of Man Winnipeg R3T 2N2 Can

COKE, C(HAUNCEY) EUGENE, b Toronto, Ont; m 41. POLYMER CHEMISTRY. *Educ:* Univ Man, BSc, MSc; Univ Toronto, MA; Univ Leeds, PhD(polymer chem), 38. *Prof Exp:* Asst org chem, Yale Univ; asst phys chem, Univ Toronto; res fel, Ont Res Found; dir res, Courtaulds Can, Ltd, 39-42, several exec res & develop posts, 48-59; dir res & develop & mem exec comt, Hartford Fibres Co Div 59-62; tech dir, Drew Chem Corp, 62-63; dir new prod, Fibers Div, Am Cyanamid Co, NJ, 63-70; pres, 70-78, CHMN BD, COKE & ASSOC CONSULT, 79-; VIS RES PROF, STETSON UNIV, 79- *Concurrent Pos:* Chmn, Can Adv Comt on Int Orgn for Stand, 57-59, mem Can Nat Comt, 59; dir, Textile Technol Fedn Can, 58-59; pres, Aqua Vista Corp, Inc, 72-74. *Honors & Awards:* Bronze Medal, Can Asn Textile Colorists & Chem, 63; Bronze Medal, Am Asn Textile Technol, 71. *Mem:* Fel AAAS; NY Acad Sci; Am Asn Textile Technol (vpres, 61-62, pres, 63-65, secy, 69-70); fel Royal Inst Chem; Can Asn Textile Colorists & Chem (vpres, 54, pres, 57-59). *Res:* Basic organic and physical chemistry; equilibrium; manufacture of cellulosic and acrylic fibers; performance and end-use properties; physical characteristics of man-made fibers. *Mailing Add:* 26 Aqua Vista Dr Ormond Beach FL 32074

COKE, JAMES LOGAN, b Brownwood, Tex, Nov 1, 33; m 58; c 3. ORGANIC CHEMISTRY, BIOCHEMISTRY. *Educ:* Wash State Univ, BS, 56; Wayne State Univ, PhD(chem), 61. *Prof Exp:* Res assoc, Univ Wis, 60-61; from instr to asst prof, 61-67, assoc prof, 67-77, PROF ORG CHEM, UNIV NC, CHAPEL HILL, 77- *Concurrent Pos:* Res assoc, Univ Minn, 64. *Mem:* Am Chem Soc. *Res:* Physical organic chemistry; organic chemistry of natural products; plant biochemistry. *Mailing Add:* Dept of Chem Univ of NC Chapel Hill NC 27514

COKELET, EDWARD DAVIS, b Bremerton, Wash, Aug 9, 47; m 69; c 2. WATER WAVES, GEOPHYSICAL FLUID DYNAMICS. *Educ:* Univ Wash, BSc, 70, MSc, 71; Cambridge Univ, PhD(appl math), 76. *Prof Exp:* Oceanogr, Inst Oceanog Sci, UK, 75-78; OCEANOGR, PAC MARINE ENVIRON LAB, NAT OCEANIC & ATMOSPHERIC ADMIN, 78- *Mem:* Challenger Soc; Am Geophys Union. *Res:* Dynamics of steep and breaking water waves. *Mailing Add:* Pac Marine Environ Lab/NOAA 3711 15th Ave NE Seattle WA 98105

COKELET, GILES R(OY), b New York, NY, Jan 7, 32; m 63; c 2. CHEMICAL ENGINEERING. *Educ:* Calif Inst Technol, BS, 57, MS, 58; Mass Inst Technol, ScD(blood rheol), 63. *Prof Exp:* Chem engr, Dow Chem Co, 58-60; asst prof chem eng, Mass Inst Technol, 63-64 & Calif Inst Technol, 64-68; from assoc prof to prof, Mont State Univ, 68-78; PROF, SCH MED & DENT, UNIV ROCHESTER, 78- *Mem:* AAAS; Am Inst Chem Engrs; Microcirc Soc; Soc Rheol. *Res:* Rheology of disperse systems; applications of chemical engineering to medical problems. *Mailing Add:* Dept of Radiation Biol & Biophys Med Sch Univ of Rochester Rochester NY 14642

COKER, EARL HOWARD, JR, b Cottonwood, Calif, May 4, 34; m 60; c 4. PHYSICAL CHEMISTRY. *Educ:* Ore State Univ, PhD(phys chem), 62. *Prof Exp:* From asst prof to assoc prof, 61-71, PROF PHYS CHEM, UNIV SDAK, 71- *Mem:* Am Chem Soc; Am Sci Affil. *Res:* Spectroscopy of complex ions in dilute solid solution; internal forces in ionic solids; point defects in ionic solids. *Mailing Add:* Dept of Chem Univ of SDak Vermillion SD 57069

COKER, SAMUEL TERRY, b Evergreen, Ala, Nov 29, 26; m 54; c 4. PHARMACOLOGY. *Educ:* Auburn Univ, BS, 51; Purdue Univ, MS, 53, PhD(pharmacol), 55. *Prof Exp:* Instr pharmacol, Univ Pittsburgh, 53-54; assoc prof, Univ Miss, 55-56 & Univ Mo, Kansas City, 56-59; dean, Sch Pharm, 59-73, PROF PHARMACOL, AUBURN UNIV, 73- *Mem:* Am Pharmaceut Asn; Acad Pharmaceut Sci. *Res:* Toxicology, especially drug detoxification. *Mailing Add:* Rte 3 Box 99 Auburn AL 36830

COKER, WILLIAM RORY, b Athens, Ga, Dec 20, 39. THEORETICAL NUCLEAR PHYSICS, EXPERIMENTAL NUCLEAR PHYSICS. *Educ:* Univ Ga, BS, 61, MS, 64, PhD(physics), 66. *Prof Exp:* Res fel nuclear physics, Ctr Nuclear Studies, 66-68, from asst prof to assoc prof, 68-80, PROF PHYSICS, UNIV TEX, AUSTIN, 80- *Mem:* Am Phys Soc. *Res:* Mechanisms of direct nuclear reactions; reactions to particle-unstable states; several-nucleon transfer reactions; nuclear spectroscopy; low and medium energy nuclear physics. *Mailing Add:* Dept of Physics Univ of Tex Austin TX 78712

COKINOS, DIMITRIOS, US citizen. NUCLEAR PHYSICS, NUCLEAR ENGINEERING. *Educ:* Cent State Col, BS, 59; NC State Univ, MS, 60; Columbia Univ, PhD(nuclear sci & eng), 69. *Prof Exp:* Physics lectr, City Col of City Univ NY, 61-64; asst prof nuclear eng, Stevens Inst Technol, 61-70; lectr physics, City Col NY, 69-70; adj assoc prof physics, Hunter Col, 70-73; group leader, Gen Elec Co, 73-78; NUCLEAR ENGR, BROOKHAVEN NAT LAB, 78- *Concurrent Pos:* US Atomic Energy Comn fel, Columbia Univ, 64-67, res scientist, 69-70. *Mem:* Am Nuclear Soc; Sigma Xi. *Res:* Nuclear and reactor physics; neutron physics; neutron thermalization; pulsed neutron source experiments; neutron cross sections; nuclear fuel cycles, core management; reactor dynamics and control, transient behavior; nuclear safety. *Mailing Add:* Brookhaven Nat Lab Upton NY 11973

COLAIZZI, JOHN LOUIS, b Pittsburgh, Pa, May 10, 38. PHARMACEUTICS, PHARMACY. *Educ:* Univ Pittsburgh, BS, 60; Purdue Univ, MS, 62, PhD(pharm), 65. *Prof Exp:* Asst prof pharm, WVa Univ, 64-65; asst prof pharm, 65-68, assoc prof pharmaceut, 68-72, prof pharmaceut & chmn dept, Sch Pharm, Univ Pittsburgh, 72-78; DEAN COL PHARM, RUTGERS, STATE UNIV NJ, 78- *Concurrent Pos:* Mem comt revision, US Pharmacopeial Convention, 75- *Mem:* Am Pharmaceut Asn; Acad Pharmaceut Sci; Am Soc Hosp Pharmacists; Am Asn Cols Pharm. *Res:* Bioequivalency and biavailability of drugs; sterile dosage forms technology; drug formulation factors related to pharmacological response. *Mailing Add:* Col of Pharm Rutgers State Univ of NJ Piscataway NJ 08854

COLAS, ANTONIO E, b Muel, Spain, June 22, 28; US citizen; m 55; c 4. BIOCHEMISTRY, REPRODUCTIVE PHYSIOLOGY. *Educ:* Univ Zaragoza, Lic, 51; Univ Madrid, MD, 53; Univ Edinburgh, PhD(biochem), 55. *Prof Exp:* Prof in chg physiol & biochem, Lit Univ Salamanca, 55-57; prof biochem, Univ Valle, Colombia, 57-62, dir grad div, 60-62; assoc prof biochem, obstet & gynec, Med Sch, Univ Ore, 62-66, prof obstet & gynec, 66-68, prof biochem, 68; PROF OBSTET & GYNEC & PHYSIOL CHEM, SCH MED, UNIV WIS-MADISON, 68- *Concurrent Pos:* Rockefeller Found grants, 57-62. *Mem:* AAAS; Am Chem Soc; Endocrine Soc; Soc Gynec Invest; Am Soc Biol Chemists. *Res:* Biochemistry and metabolism of steroid hormones; in vitro and in vivo studies during pregnancy; steroid hydroxylases; steroid hormone receptors. *Mailing Add:* Dept of Obstet & Gynec Sch Med Univ Wis 600 Highland Ave Madison WI 53792

COLASANTI, BRENDA KAREN, b Charleston, WVa, Dec 5, 45; m 68. NEUROPHARMACOLOGY. *Educ:* WVa Univ, BS, 66, PhD(pharmacol), 70. *Prof Exp:* NIMH fel neurol & psychopharmacol, Mt Sinai Sch Med, 70-72; from asst prof to assoc prof, 72-80, PROF PHARMACOL & SURG OPHTHAL, WVA UNIV, 80- *Mem:* Sigma Xi; Asn Psychophys Study Sleep; Am Soc Pharmacol & Exp Therapeut; Asn Res Vision & Ophthalmol; Am Soc Neurochem. *Res:* Mechanisms underlying the effects of autonomic drugs on intraocular pressure after selective alteration of adrenergic or cholinergic input to the eye. *Mailing Add:* Dept Pharmacol WVa Univ Med Ctr Morgantown WV 26506

COLASITO, DOMINIC JAMES, b Denver, Colo, July 10, 25; m 51; c 4. INDUSTRIAL MICROBIOLOGY. *Educ:* Purdue Univ, BS, 49, MS, 52, PhD(microbiol), 56. *Prof Exp:* Microbiologist, Swift & Co, 56-57; bact group leader, Chicago Div, Kendall Co, 57-61; actg chmn dept microbiol, Stanford Res Inst, 61-64; sr res microbiologist, Bioferm Div, Int Minerals & Chem Corp, 64-71; LAB DIR, BIO-CON, 72- *Concurrent Pos:* Lectr biol, Calif State Univ, Bakersfield, 73- *Mem:* Am Soc Microbiol; AAAS. *Res:* Hydrocarbon microbiology; enzymatic attack on lignins; microbiological treatment of waste streams. *Mailing Add:* Bio-Con 3601 Gibson Bakersfield CA 93308

COLBERT, CHARLES, b Minneapolis, Minn, Feb 19, 19; m 45; c 5. ELECTRICAL ENGINEERING. *Educ:* Univ Minn, BEE, 40; Union Grad Sch, Cincinnati, PhD, 74. *Prof Exp:* Jr engr equip develop, Gen Develop Lab, Signal Corps, US Army, 41, field engr, 41-43, engr, Aircraft Signal Agency, Ohio, 44; proj engr, Mil TV Aerial Reconnaissance Lab, Wright Air Develop Ctr, 46-48, sect chief res & develop, 48-54; consult engr & pres, Westgate Lab, Inc, 54-62; asst to dean faculty for sponsored res, Antioch Col, 64-70, assoc prof eng, 66-70, sr investr, Fels Res Inst, 66-70, mem res staff, 64-66; dir radiol res lab, Res Inst & adj assoc prof eng, 71-77, ASST CLIN PROF RADIOL SCI, SCH MED, WRIGHT STATE UNIV, 79- *Concurrent Pos:* Consult engr, 54-66; exec dir, Ohio Res & Develop Found; consult, Goodyear Aircraft Corp, Martin Co, Appl Physics Lab, Johns Hopkins Univ, Autometric Corp, Aero Serv Corp, Philco Corp, Motorola, Inc, Harris-

Intertype Corp, SINTRA, France Westgate Lab, Inc & Miami Valley Consortium of Col; dir, Radiol Res Lab, Greene Mem Hosp, 77-81; dir, Clin Radiol Testing Lab, Miami Valley Hosp, Dayton, 81- *Mem:* AAAS; Am Soc Artificial Internal Organs; Inst Elec & Electronics Engrs; Am Asn Physics in Med; fel Royal Numis Soc. *Res:* Radar mapping; ancient numismatics; ancient languages; archeology; computer analysis of normal and diseased bone and forensic analyses from radiographic films. *Mailing Add:* Radiol Res Lab Wright State Univ Res Inst Dayton OH 45431

COLBERT, EDWIN HARRIS, b Clarinda, Iowa, Sept 28, 05; m 33; c 5. VERTEBRATE PALEONTOLOGY. *Educ:* Univ Nebr, AB, 28; Columbia Univ, AM, 30, PhD(vert paleont), 35. *Hon Degrees:* DSc, Univ Nebr, 73 & Univ Ariz, 76. *Prof Exp:* Asst, Univ Nebr, 26-29; asst, Am Mus Natural Hist, 30-33, asst cur paleont, 33-42, cur fossil reptiles & amphibians, 43-70; prof, 45-69, EMER PROF VERT PALEONT, COLUMBIA UNIV, 70-; EMER CUR FOSSIL REPTILES & AMPHIBIANS, AM MUS NATURAL HIST, 70-; CUR VERT PALEONT, MUS NORTHERN ARIZ, 70- *Concurrent Pos:* Assoc cur, Acad Natural Sci, Philadelphia, 37-40, res assoc, 40-; lectr, Bryn Mawr Col, 39-42 & Univ Calif, 45; assoc cur, Mus Northern Ariz, 49-69. *Honors & Awards:* Elliot Medal, Nat Acad Sci, 35; Am Mus Natural Hist Medal, 69. *Mem:* Nat Acad Sci; fel Geol Soc Am; fel Am Paleont Soc (vpres, 63); Soc Vert Paleont (secy & treas, 44, pres, 46-47); Soc Study Evolution (pres, 58). *Res:* Evolution of fossil vertebrates, particularly fossil amphibians, reptiles and mammals; fossil reptiles of North and South America and Asia; fossil mammals of North America and Asia; past distribution and intercontinental migrations of land-living vertebrates; paleoecology as based upon study of fossil vertebrates; fossil amphibians and reptiles of Antarctica. *Mailing Add:* Mus of Northern Ariz Rte 4 Box 720 Flagstaff AZ 86001

COLBERT, MARVIN J, b Spokane, Wash, Nov 6, 23; m 51; c 3. INTERNAL MEDICINE. *Educ:* Yale Univ, BS, 46; Boston Univ, MD, 49; Am Bd Internal Med, dipl, 58. *Prof Exp:* Intern, Presby Hosp, Chicago, Ill, 49-50, asst resident internal med, 50; indust physician, Pub Serv Co Northern Ill, 52; asst resident internal med, Vet Admin Hosp, Boston, Mass, 53-54; resident, Univ Ill Res & Educ Hosps, Chicago, 54-55, instr, Dept Med, 56-58; physician, Steele Mem Clin, Belmond, Iowa, 55-56; from instr to assoc prof, 56-65, dir health serv, 59-78, PROF MED, COL MED, UNIV ILL MED CTR, 65-; DIR EMPLOYEE HEALTH SERV, EVANGEL HOSP ASN, OAKBROOK, 78- *Concurrent Pos:* Vis prof, Chiengmai Med Sch & Hosp, Thailand, 65-66; lectr, Ill Acad Gen Pract, 67-68 & 77-78; attend physician, West Side Vet Admin Hosp & Univ Ill Hosp, Chicago. *Mem:* Am Fed Clin Res; Am Asn Automotive Med; Am Col Physicians. *Res:* Medical aspects of automotive safety; smallpox vaccination during pregnancy; nutritional studies of Eskimoes. *Mailing Add:* 3815 Highland Ave Downers Grove IL 60516

COLBORN, GENE LOUIS, b Springfield, Ill, Nov 23, 35; m 56; c 3. ANATOMY. *Educ:* Ky Christian Col, BA, 57; Milligan Col, BS, 62; Bowman Gray Sch Med, MS, 64, PhD(anat), 67. *Prof Exp:* Asst prof, 68-71, assoc prof anat, Univ Tex Health Sci Ctr San Antonio, 71-75; ASSOC PROF ANAT, MED COL GA, 75-, DIR GROSS ANAT, 75- *Concurrent Pos:* Fel, Dept Anat, Sch Med, Univ NMex, 67-68; grants, Med Res Found Tex, 68-69 & Am Heart Asn, 70-; consult dept surg, Ft Sam Houston, 69-75; secy-treas, State Anat Bd Ga, 75- *Mem:* AAAS; Am Asn Anat; Am Soc Zool; Am Soc Cell Biol. *Res:* Morphology and cytochemistry of atrioventricular conduction system and autonomic ganglia; gross anatomy, especially primate; cardiac tissue culture and organ culture; effects of heavy metals on fetal malformation. *Mailing Add:* Dept Anat Med Col of Ga Augusta GA 30904

COLBORNE, WILLIAM GEORGE, b Carleton Place, Ont, Feb 18, 26; nat US; m 55; c 4. MECHANICAL ENGINEERING. *Educ:* Queen's Univ, Ont, BSc, 48, MSc, 51. *Prof Exp:* Researcher thermodyn, Nat Res Coun Can, 50; researcher combustion, Queen's Univ, Ont, 50-55, asst prof thermodyn, 54-58; assoc prof eng, 58-66, head, Dept Mech Eng, 59-78, PROF MECH ENG, UNIV WINDSOR, 66- *Mem:* Fel Am Soc Heat, Refrig & Air-Conditioning Engrs; Am Soc Mech Engrs. *Res:* Bistable fluidic amplifiers; computer aided design; computer simulation of buildings; energy conservation. *Mailing Add:* Dept Mech Eng Univ Windsor Windsor ON N9B 3P4 Can

COLBOURN, JOSEPH LEASON, b Baltimore, Md, Oct 29, 29; m 52; c 6. BIOCHEMISTRY. *Educ:* Loyola Col, Md, AB, 51; Univ Md, PhD(biochem), 63. *Prof Exp:* Instr biochem, Sch Med, Univ Md, 63; res assoc, Sch Hyg & Pub Health, Johns Hopkins Univ, 63-67, asst prof, 67-71; res scientist, 71-73, mgr prod & product develop, 73-78, MGR PROD & PROCESS DEVELOP, ENZYMES, RES PROD DIV, MILES LABS, 78-, TECH DIR, RES PROD DIV, ELKHART, 81- *Mem:* Am Soc Microbiol; Am Chem Soc; Am Asn Clin Chem. *Res:* Toxicology of military chemicals; polyamines; kinetics of M luteus RNA polymerase; purification of polynucleotide polymerizing enzymes; enzyme synthesis of polyribonucleotides and polydeoxyribonucleotides; purification of restriction enzymes and recombinant DNA reagents; clin electrophoresis, clin reagents. *Mailing Add:* 3216 Cherry Tree Lane Elkhart IN 46514

COLBOW, KONRAD, b Bremen, Ger, May 23, 35; Can citizen; m 60; c 2. SOLID STATE PHYSICS. *Educ:* McMaster Univ, BSc, 59, MSc, 60; Univ BC, PhD(physics), 63. *Prof Exp:* Mem tech staff, Bell Tel Labs, 63-65; assoc prof, 65-75, PROF PHYSICS, SIMON FRASER UNIV, 75- *Mem:* Am Phys Soc. *Res:* Light interaction with matter; physics of biological membranes. *Mailing Add:* Dept of Physics Simon Fraser Univ Burnaby Can

COLBURN, CHARLES BUFORD, b Harrisonville, Mo, July 6, 23; m 50; c 5. PHYSICAL INORGANIC CHEMISTRY. *Educ:* Kans State Col, BS, 44; Univ Utah, PhD(phys chem), 51. *Prof Exp:* Develop chemist, Lederle Labs, 44; res assoc, Univ Utah, 51-52; group leader phys chem, Restone Res Div, Rohm and Haas Co, 52-68; PROF CHEM & HEAD DEPT, AUBURN UNIV, 68- *Concurrent Pos:* Centenary lectr, 65. *Mem:* Am Chem Soc; Am Phys Soc; fel Am Inst Chem; Brit Chem Soc. *Res:* Chemistry of nitrogen and fluorine; inorganic free radicals; physical chemistry of combustion and ignition. *Mailing Add:* 235 Cary Dr Auburn AL 36830

COLBURN, IVAN PAUL, b San Diego, Calif, June 5, 27; m 58; c 3. STRUCTURAL GEOLOGY, STRATIGRAPHY. *Educ:* Pomona Col, BA, 51; Claremont Grad Sch, MA, 53; Stanford Univ, PhD(geol), 61. *Prof Exp:* Exploration engr, Shell Oil Co, 53-56; Am Asn Petrol Geol res grant, 58-59; from asst prof to assoc prof geol, Calif State Col, Hayward, 61-64; assoc prof, 64-70, PROF GEOL, CALIF STATE UNIV, LOS ANGELES, 70- *Concurrent Pos:* NSF res grant, 63-65; Nat Sci grant, 69-71. *Mem:* Am Asn Petrol Geol; Soc Econ Paleont & Mineral; Geol Soc Am; Nat Asn Geol Teachers. *Res:* California Coast Range structure and stratigraphy; sedimentation and paleocurrent analysis of Jurassic-Cretaceous sediments in California Coast Ranges; statistical analysis of clastic rock fabrics. *Mailing Add:* Dept of Geol Calif State Univ Los Angeles CA 90032

COLBURN, JOEL CLARK, b Bronx, NY, Oct 31, 50; m 73; c 1. ORGANIC CHEMISTRY, INORGANIC CHEMISTRY. *Educ:* City Col New York, BS, 72; Univ Mich, MS, 75, PhD(chem), 78. *Prof Exp:* Res chemist phosphates, FMC Corp, 77-79; RES CHEMIST LUBRICANTS & GASOLINE, EXXON RES & ENG CO, 79- *Mem:* Am Chem Soc. *Res:* Synthesis and properties of pi and sigma heterobenzene complexes; catalysis; phosphorus chemistry. *Mailing Add:* 16 New York Ave Metuchen NJ 08840

COLBURN, NANCY HALL, b Wilmington, Del, May 15, 41; m 81; c 2. BIOCHEMISTRY, CELL BIOLOGY. *Educ:* Swarthmore Col, BA, 63; Univ Wis, PhD(oncol), 67. *Prof Exp:* Asst prof molecular biol, Univ Del, 68-72; spec res fel dermat/carcinogenesis, Univ Mich, 72-74, asst prof biochem, Depts Biol Chem & Dermat, 74-75, vis scientist carcinogenesis, Dept Environ & Indust Health, 75-76; expert chem carcinogenesis in vitro, Lab Exp Path, 76-79, CHIEF, CELL BIOL SECT, LAB VIRAL CARCINOGENESIS, NAT CANCER INST, 79- *Concurrent Pos:* NIH spec res fel, 72-74. *Mem:* AAAS; Am Asn Cancer Res; NY Acad Sci; Sigma Xi. *Res:* Molecular and cellular mechanism of chemical carcinogenesis; use of epithelial cell culture model systems to test the somatic mutation theory and to study tumor promotion and preneoplastic progression. *Mailing Add:* Lab Viral Carinogenesis-FCRF Nat Cancer Inst Frederick MD 21701

COLBURN, ROBERT WARREN, biochemistry, see previous edition

COLBY, CLARENCE, biochemical genetics, virology, see previous edition

COLBY, DAVID ANTHONY, b Brookline, Mass, Feb 21, 46; m 68; c 1. LIQUID CHROMATOGRAPHY. *Educ:* Va Polytech Inst, BA, 68, PhD(chem), 78; Clemson Univ, BS, 69. *Prof Exp:* Chemist, Dept Agr Chem Serv, Clemson Univ, 69-70; teaching asst, Chem Dept, Va Polytech Inst, 71-77; tech mkt chemist, Autolab Div, Spectra Physics Inc, 74-76, mgr tech support group, 77-78; SR RES & DEVELOP CHEMIST, R J REYNOLDS TOBACCO CO, 78- *Concurrent Pos:* Lectr, Am Chem Soc, 72-; admin tech asst, Process Control Div, Honeywell Inc, 74. *Mem:* Am Chem Soc; Am Soc Testing Mat. *Res:* High performance liquid chromatography; advancing the use and understanding of this powerful separation technique in pure and applied research area including instrument design and automation. *Mailing Add:* 4310 Mill Creek Rd Winston Salem NC 27106

COLBY, EDWARD EUGENE, b Aberdeen, SDak, June 8, 29; m 53; c 4. CHEMICAL ENGINEERING. *Educ:* Princeton Univ, BS, 51. *Prof Exp:* Engr, 54-56, group leader process develop, 56-65, sect head, 65-66, sect head food tech packaging, 66-77, ASSOC DIR, FOOD PACKAGING & TECH SERV, PROCTER & GAMBLE CO, 77- *Res:* New packages and package materials. *Mailing Add:* Proctor & Gamble Co 6071 Center Hill Rd Cincinnati OH 45224

COLBY, FRANK GERHARDT, b Muhlhausen, Ger, Apr 10, 15; m 52; c 2. CHEMISTRY. *Educ:* Univ Geneva, ChemEng, 39, DSc, 41. *Prof Exp:* Consult chemist, Havana, Cuba, 42-46; res chemist, Indust Tape, NJ, 46-47; chem lit specialist, Com Solvents Corp, 47-51; dir res info, R J Reynolds Tobaco Co, 51-70, mgr sci info, 70-79, ASSOC DIR SCI ISSUES, R J REYNOLDS INDUSTS, INC, 79- *Mem:* Fel AAAS; Am Chem Soc. *Res:* Chemical, bioscience and technological literature; tobacco; research analysis. *Mailing Add:* Res Dept R J Reynolds Indust Inc 115 Chestnut St SE Winston-Salem NC 27102

COLBY, GEORGE VINCENT, JR, b Montpelier, Vt, Sept 4, 31; m 55; c 3. ELECTRICAL ENGINEERING. *Educ:* Mass Inst Technol, SB & SM, 54. *Prof Exp:* Tech engr, test equip, Measurements Lab, Gen Elec Co, 54-55; proj engr, US Army Signal Corps, 55-57; eng mgr, LFE Corp, 57-60; mem tech staff radar & commun, Lincoln Lab, Mass Inst Technol, 70-80; SR CONSULT, ENG SYSTS DIV, AVCO CORP, 80- *Mem:* Inst Elec & Electronics Engrs. *Res:* Military voice and digital data communications systems; air traffic control radar and radar transponders; digital and analog circuit design; electronic missle guidance systems. *Mailing Add:* Mass Inst Technol Lincoln Lab 244 Wood St Lexington MA 02173

COLBY, HOWARD DAVID, b New York, NY, June 16, 44; m 70. ENDOCRINOLOGY. *Educ:* City Col New York, BS, 65; State Univ NY Buffalo, PhD(endocrinol), 70. *Prof Exp:* NIH fel physiol, Med Sch, Univ Va, 70-72; from asst prof to assoc prof, 72-78, PROF PHYSIOL, MED SCH, W VA UNIV, 78- *Mem:* Am Physiol Soc; Endocrine Soc; Am Soc Pharmacol & Exp Therapeut; AAAS; Soc Toxicol. *Res:* Hormonal regulation of adrenocortical secretion; hormonal control of hepatic steroid and drug metabolism; endocrine toxicology. *Mailing Add:* Dept Physiol WVa Univ Sch Med Morgantown WV 26506

COLBY, PETER J, b Grand Rapids, Mich, Mar 26, 33; m; c 3. AQUATIC BIOLOGY, FISHERIES. *Educ:* Mich State Univ, BS, 55, MS, 58; Univ Minn, PhD(fishery biol), 66. *Prof Exp:* Food technologist, Gen Foods Corp, 57-62; res asst fishery biol, Univ Minn, 62-66; aquatic biologist & proj leader, US Bur Com Fisheries, 66-70, US Bur Sport Fisheries, 70-71; RES SCIENTIST, ONT MINISTRY NATURAL RESOURCES, 71- *Concurrent Pos:* Res assoc environ & indust health, Sch Pub Health, Univ Mich, 70-71.

Mem: Am Soc Zool; Am Fisheries Soc; Int Asn Gt Lakes Res; fel Am Inst Fisheries Res Biologists. Res: Physiological and behavioral responses of fish to environmental stress; response of fish communities to perturbations. Mailing Add: Fish & Wildlife Res Fisheries Sect Box 5000 Thunder Bay ON P7C 5G6 Can

COLCLASER, ROBERT GERALD, b Wilkinsburg, Pa, Sept 21, 33; m 58; c 3. ELECTRICAL ENGINEERING, POWER ENGINEERING. Educ: Univ Cincinnati, BS, 56; Univ Pittsburgh, MS, 61, DSc(elec eng), 68. Prof Exp: Design engr circuit breakers, Westinghouse Elec Co, 56-63, test engr, 63-66, supvr eng training, 66-67, adv engr power systs, 67-70; from asst prof to assoc prof, 70-80, assoc dean, 74-80, PROF ELEC ENG & CHMN, DEPT ELEC ENG, UNIV PITTSBURGH, 80- Concurrent Pos: Mid Atlantic Power Res Comt res grant, 71-; consult, Gould-Brown Boverri, 75-80, Nuclear Regulatory Comn, 78- & Westinghouse Elec, Sharon, Pa, 80- Mem: Fel Inst Elec & Electronics Engrs; Am Soc Eng Educ. Res: Transient recovery voltage; arc interruption; system overvoltages; insulation coordination. Mailing Add: Dept of Elec Eng Univ of Pittsburgh Pittsburgh PA 15261

COLCORD, J E, b Portland, Maine, June 15, 22; m 47; c 1. PHOTOGRAMMETRY, GEODESY. Educ: Univ Maine, BS, 47; Univ Minn, MS, 49. Prof Exp: Instr & surveyor summer camp, Maine, 47; instr surv, Univ Minn, 47-49; from instr to assoc prof, 49-68, PROF SURV, UNIV WASH, 68- Concurrent Pos: Vis prof, Univ Calif, Berkeley, 64 & Univ Ill; sci fac fel, NSF, 59-60. Mem: Am Soc Civil Engrs; Am Cong Surv & Mapping; Am Soc Photogram; Can Inst Surv; Photogram Soc London. Res: Geometronics; surveying; remote sensing. Mailing Add: Dept Civil Eng 121 More Hall Univ of Wash Seattle WA 98195

COLDREN, CLARKE L(INCOLN), b Uniontown, Pa, Jan 24, 26; m 49; c 4. CHEMICAL ENGINEERING. Educ: Pa State Univ, BS, 48; Univ Ill, MS, 50, PhD(chem eng), 54. Prof Exp: Engr chem & mech eng, Shell Develop Co, 52-54, 55-59, Koninklijke Shell Lab, Delft, 54-55, mgr tech develop lab, Shell Pipe Line Corp, 59-64, asst to gen mgr transp & supplies, Shell Oil Co, 64-68, mgr planning & anal unconventional raw mat, 68-69, mgr econ & financial res, Shell Chem Co, 69-72, mgr, Resins Bus Ctr, 72-78, strategic planner, 78-79, MGR TRANSP SUPPORT & PLANNING, SHELL OIL CO, 79- Mem: Am Chem Soc; Am Inst Chem Engrs; NAm Soc Corp Planners. Res: Fluid mechanics; non-Newtonian and multiphase flow; atomization; research administration; business economics; business administration; futurity; transportation. Mailing Add: Shell Oil Co One Shell Plaza Houston TX 77001

COLDWELL, ROBERT LYNN, b Woodland, Wash, May 27, 41; m 62; c 2. STATISTICAL MECHANICS, COMPUTATIONAL PHYSICS. Educ: Univ Wash, BS, 63, PhD(physics), 69. Prof Exp: Fel & teacher physics, Washington & Lee Univ, 69-71; res, Northwestern Univ, 71-72; RES PHYSICS, UNIV FLA, 72- Mem: Am Phys Soc. Res: Developing Monte Carlo and nonlinear optimization procedures for finding accurate ground and excited state eigen functions for systems of nuclei and electrons. Mailing Add: 1520 NW 40th Dr Gainesville FL 32605

COLE, ALAN L, b Battle Creek, Mich, May 23, 22; m 46; c 2. METEOROLOGY, PHYSICS. Educ: Univ Mich, BSE, 48, MS, 49 & 60, PhD(physics), 61. Prof Exp: Res meteorologist, Univ Mich, 61-69; ASSOC PROF GEOG, NORTHERN ILL UNIV, 69- Mem: Am Meteorol Soc; Air Pollution Control Asn. Res: Mesoscale winds in the Great Lakes; wave hindcasting and forecasting; air pollution; wind energy. Mailing Add: Dept of Geog Northern Ill Univ DeKalb IL 60115

COLE, AVEAN WAYNE, b Smithville, Miss, June 23, 34; m 60; c 2. WEED SCIENCE. Educ: Miss State Univ, BS, 62; Iowa State Univ, PhD(hort & plant physiol), 66. Prof Exp: Asst prof hort, Univ Wis, 66-68; PROF WEED SCI, MISS STATE UNIV, 68- Mem: Weed Sci Soc Am. Res: Weed control and related responses of both weed and crop plants to herbicides. Mailing Add: Clarence Dorman Forestry Plant Sci Bldg Miss State Univ Mississippi State MS 39762

COLE, BARBARA RUTH, b Hope, Kans, May 14, 41. PEDIATRIC NEPHROLOGY. Educ: Doane Col, AB, 63; Univ Kans, MD, 67. Prof Exp: Inst pediat, 72-73, asst prof, 73-81, ASSOC PROF PEDIAT, SCH MED, WASHINGTON UNIV, 81-; ASST PEDIATRICIAN, ST LOUIS CHILDREN'S HOSP, 72- Concurrent Pos: Spec fel, NIH, 71-73; asst prof pediat, Univ Calif, San Diego, 77; exec comt, Network Coord Coun 9, 78-81; clin investr award, NIH, 79-82. Mem: Am Soc Nephrol; Am Soc Clin Res; Am Soc Pediat Nephrology; Int Soc Nephrology. Res: Tubular diseases; amino acidurias; study of kidney tubular function, transport and metabolism in adult and developing kidneys, employing quantitative histochemical techniques; pediatric dialysis techniques. Mailing Add: St Louis Children's Hosp PO Box 14871 St Louis MO 63178

COLE, BENJAMIN THEODORE, b New Brunswick, NJ, May 24, 21; m 43; c 2. PHYSIOLOGY. Educ: Duke Univ, BS, 49, MA, 51, PhD(physiol), 54. Prof Exp: Instr physiol, Sch Med, Duke Univ, 53-54; from asst prof to assoc prof zool, La State Univ, 54-58; res partic cell physiol & biol, Oak Ridge Nat Lab, 59-60; assoc prof, 60-63, head dept, 64-73, PROF BIOL, UNIV SC, 63- Concurrent Pos: Consult, Cell Physiol Sect, Biol Div, Oak Ridge Nat Lab. Mem: Fel AAAS; Soc Exp Biol & Med; Am Physiol Soc. Res: Digestion; absorption and metabolism of unsaturated fatty acids; in vitro autoxidation of unsaturated fatty acids; effects of sodium fluoroacetate on carbohydrate metabolism in cold-blooded animals. Mailing Add: Dept Biol Univ SC Columbia SC 29208

COLE, CHARLES DANIEL, b Lockport, NY, Apr 14, 25; m 51; c 4. PHYSICS. Educ: Univ Buffalo, BA, 49, PhD(physics), 61. Prof Exp: Asst physics, Univ Buffalo, 48-54; mem appl math group, Bell Aerosysts Co, 54-56, group leader, 56-59, supvr math anal, 59-61; prof physics & chmn dept, Parsons Col, 61-62; PROF PHYSICS, UNIV LOWELL, 62-, ASST CHMN DEPT, 75- Concurrent Pos: Consult, Lowell Tech Inst Res Found, 62-66.

Mem: AAAS; Am Phys Soc; Am Asn Physics Teachers; Optical Soc Am. Res: Atomic spectra; forbidden lines; mathematical modeling; applied mathematics; theoretical physics; philosophy of physics; biophysics. Mailing Add: Dept Physics Univ Lowell Lowell MA 01854

COLE, CHARLES F(REDERICK), JR, b Shidler, Okla, July 31, 26; m 55; c 2. ELECTRICAL ENGINEERING. Educ: Okla State Univ, BS, 50, MS, 56. Prof Exp: Radio-activity engr, Lane-Wells Co, Okla & Venezuela, 50- 52; field engr & systs engr, Western Elec Co, NY, 53-55; asst prof elec eng, La Polytech Inst, 56-60; radio engr & instr elec eng, Univ Tex, 60-61; reliability engr, Radio Corp Am Serv Co, NJ & Alaska, 61-63; res scientist, 63-70, SR RES ENGR, CONTINENTAL OIL CO, 70- Mem: Inst Elec & Electronics Engrs. Res: Transistor and solid state devices; solid state physics; nuclear microwave systems; electronic instrumentation; physics. Mailing Add: 400 North Irving Ponca City OK 74601

COLE, CHARLES FRANKLYN, b Beaver Falls, Pa, Aug 3, 28; m 52; c 3. FISH BIOLOGY. Educ: Cornell Univ, BA, 50, PhD(vert zool), 57. Prof Exp: Instr zool, Univ Ark, 57-60; asst prof biol, Univ SFla, 60-62, assoc prof zool & chmn prog, 62-64; from assoc prof to prof fishery biol, Univ Mass, Amherst, 64-80; PROF & CHMN, DIV FISH & WILDLIFE, SCH NATURAL RESOURCES, OHIO STATE UNIV, 80- Mem: AAAS; Am Soc Ichthyol & Herpet; Am Fisheries Soc; Ecol Soc Am; Am Soc Limnol & Oceanog. Res: Percid and sciaenid biology; ecology of estuarine fishes. Mailing Add: 365B ANRPP Bldg Ohio State Univ Columbus OH 43210

COLE, CHARLES N, b New York, NY, Oct 28, 46; m 69; c 2. MOLECULAR VIROLOGY. Educ: Oberlin Col, AB, 68; Mass Inst Technol, PhD(cell biol), 72. Prof Exp: Instr virol, Mass Inst Technol, 72-73; fel biochem, Stanford Univ, 74-77; ASST PROF HUMAN GENETICS, SCH MED, YALE UNIV, 78- Concurrent Pos: Fel virol, Mass Inst Technol, 72-73. Mem: Am Soc Microbiol; AAAS; Union Concerned Scientists. Res: Molecular biology with emphasis on regulation of eucaryotic gene expression and molecular virology; molecular biology of the DNA tumor virus, SV40, and the regulation of transcription termination and processing in animal cells; recombinant DNA technology. Mailing Add: Dept Human Genetics Sch Med Yale Univ PO Box 3333 New Haven CT 06510

COLE, CHARLES RALPH, b Canfield, Ohio, Aug 31, 42; c 2. HYDROLOGY, COMPUTER SCIENCE. Educ: Kent State Univ, BS, 64; Wash State Univ, MS, 75. Prof Exp: Res scientist, Monsanto Res Corp, 64-66; SR RES SCIENTIST, PAC NORTHWEST DIV, BATTELLE MEM INST, 66- Mem: Am Geophys Union. Res: Surface and groundwater hydrology; development of a compatible set of research and management simulation models for surface and groundwater which are used to study and manage water resources. Mailing Add: Battelle Northwest PO Box 999 Richland WA 99352

COLE, CLARENCE RUSSELL, b Crestline, Ohio, Nov 20, 18; m 45; c 3. VETERINARY PATHOLOGY, MEDICAL ADMINISTRATION. Educ: Ohio State Univ, DVM, 43, MSc, 44, PhD(comp path), 47. Prof Exp: Instr vet path, 44-46, prof, 46-71, chmn dept, 47-67, from asst dean to dean col vet med, 60-72, REGENTS PROF VET PATH, OHIO STATE UNIV, 71- Concurrent Pos: Assoc vet res, Ohio Agr Res & Develop Ctr, 47-; consult, US Air Force, 43-, Walter Reed Med Ctr, 51-, Armed Forces Inst Path, 53- & USPHS, 53-; mem spec bd, Am Col Vet Pathologists, 59 & Am Col Toxicol, 78; lectr, Auburn Univ, 53. Mem: AAAS; Am Vet Med Asn; Am Asn Lab Animal Sci; Am Col Vet Path (vpres, 56, pres, 57); Int Acad Path. Res: Toxicologic pathology; lab animal diseases; animal infectious diseases; animal neoplasms; metabolic diseases, comparative pathology. Mailing Add: Col of Vet Med Ohio State Univ Columbus OH 43210

COLE, DALE WARREN, b Everett, Wash, May 28, 31; m 56; c 4. FOREST SOILS. Educ: Univ Wash, BSF, 55, PhD(forest soils), 63; Univ Wis, MS, 57. Prof Exp: Res assoc, 60-63, res instr, 63-64, from instr to assoc prof, 64-74, PROF FOREST SOILS, COL FOREST RESOURCES, UNIV WASH, 74-, DIR CTR ECOSYST STUDIES, 72- Mem: AAAS; Soil Sci Soc Am; Am Geophys Union; Am Inst Biol Sci; Ecol Soc Am. Res: Mineral cycling in a forest ecosystem; processes of elemental leaching in forest soils; forest ecosystem response to fertilizers and municipal wastewater and sludge; soils and land-use planning. Mailing Add: 6114 164th Ave SE Issaquah WA 98027

COLE, DAVID EDWARD, b Detroit, Mich, July 20, 37; m 65; c 2. MECHANICAL ENGINEERING. Educ: Univ Mich, BS(mech eng) & BS(math), 60, MS, 61, PhD(mech eng), 66. Prof Exp: From instr to asst prof, 65-71, ASSOC PROF MECH ENG, UNIV MICH, 71-, DIR CTR STUDY AUTOMOTIVE TRANSP, 78- Concurrent Pos: Consult, Ford Motor Co, 65-78, Outboard Marine Corp, 67-70, Gen Motors Corp, 69-70, Alcoa, Exxon, ICS, Dow Chem, DOT, 78-, Aluminum Assoc, Environ Protection Agency, Aisin Seiki, Bendix, NASA & Panhandle Eastern, 81-; chmn bd, Environ Dynamics Inc, 70-; pres, Appl Theory, Inc, 80- Honors & Awards: Ralph Teetor educ award, 67. Mem: Soc Automotive Engrs. Res: Exhaust emission and fuel consumption research on the 2 and 4-stroke spark ignited reciprocating and rotating engines; investigation of mixture motion in combustion bombs and reciprocating engines; advanced power plants and total vehicle design; future automotive technology trends; strategic planning in automotive industry. Mailing Add: Dept Mech Eng Univ Mich Ann Arbor MI 48109

COLE, DAVID F, b Childress, Tex, Mar 3, 33. PHYSICAL CHEMISTRY, SURFACE CHEMISTRY. Educ: Univ Tex, Austin, BS, 57, PhD(phys chem), 64; Southern Methodist Univ, MBA, 78. Prof Exp: Jr chemist, Oak Ridge Nat Lab, 57; vis asst prof chem, La State Univ, 63-64; mem tech staff, Cent Res Labs, Tex Instruments, 65-82. Mem: Electrochem Soc; Am Chem Soc. Res: Advanced processes and yield improvement studies for the manufacture of semiconductor and other electronic devices; fuel cells; surface properties of solids. Mailing Add: MS 944 Tex Instruments PO Box 225936 Dallas TX 75265

COLE, DAVID LE ROY, b Preston, Idaho, Aug 6, 39; m 65; c 2. PHYSICAL CHEMISTRY, CHEMICAL KINETICS. *Educ:* Univ Utah, BS, 66, PhD(phys chem), 70. *Prof Exp:* SR RES CHEMIST, RES LABS, EASTMAN KODAK CO, 69- *Mem:* Am Chem Soc. *Res:* Kinetic studies of group III metal ion hydrolysis using E-jump perturbation techniques; investigation of fundamental reaction kinetics between metal ions and organic and inorganic ligands. *Mailing Add:* Bldg 59 Res Lab Eastman Kodak Co Kodak Park Freeport NY 14650

COLE, EDMOND RAY, b Huntington, WVa, Dec 17, 28; m 55; c 3. BIOCHEMISTRY. *Educ:* WVa Univ, BS, 52, MS, 55; Purdue Univ, PhD(biochem), 61. *Prof Exp:* NIH grants, Purdue Univ, 60-61 & Wayne State Univ, 61-63; res assoc coagulation, 63-69, asst dir coagulation, 69-73, DIR COAGULATION, RUSH-PRESBY-ST LUKE'S MED CTR, 73-, ASSOC PROF BIOCHEM, RUSH MED COL, 73- *Concurrent Pos:* Assoc scientist, Presby-St Luke's Hosp, 73- *Mem:* AAAS; Int Soc Thrombosis & Haemostasis; Am Soc Hemat. *Res:* Coagulation; fibrinolysis; tissue activators of plasminogen; enzymology. *Mailing Add:* Sect of Hemat Dept of Med Rush-Presby-St Luke's Med Ctr Chicago IL 60612

COLE, EDWARD ANTHONY, b Boston, Mass, Oct 16, 32; m 64; c 3. MICROBIOLOGY, PHYSIOLOGY. *Educ:* Univ Notre Dame, BS, 56, PhD(microbiol), 67. *Prof Exp:* Teacher, St Charles High Sch, Wis, 54-56, Vincentian Inst, NY, 56-57, Boysville High Sch, Mich, 57-62 & Bradley High Sch, NH, 62-63; teaching asst biol, Univ Notre Dame, 63-64; from asst prof to assoc prof, 66-72, PROF BIOL, ANNA MARIA COL WOMEN, 72- *Mem:* AAAS; NY Acad Sci. *Res:* Experimental hematology; transplantation. *Mailing Add:* Dept of Biol Anna Maria Col Paxton MA 01612

COLE, EVELYN, b Aberdeen, Miss, June 10, 10. ZOOLOGY. *Educ:* Miss Univ Women, AB, 32; Duke Univ, MA, 43; Vanderbilt Univ, PhD(biol), 66. *Prof Exp:* From instr to asst prof biol, Greensboro Col, 45-57; from asst prof to prof, 60-75, EMER PROF BIOL, MURRAY STATE UNIV, 75- *Res:* Taxonomy and ecology of freshwater Ostracoda; taxonomy of invertebrates. *Mailing Add:* 1703 Ryan Ave Murray KY 42071

COLE, FRANCIS TALMAGE, b Lynbrook, NY, Oct 6, 25; m 55; c 4. PHYSICS. *Educ:* Oberlin Col, AB, 47; Cornell Univ, PhD(physics), 53. *Prof Exp:* Asst physics, Cornell Univ, 47-51; from instr to assoc prof, Univ Iowa, 51-64; physicist, Lawrence Radiation Lab, 64-67; PHYSICIST, NAT ACCELERATOR LAB, 67- *Concurrent Pos:* Physicist, Midwestern Univs Res Asn, 55-59, head theory sect, 59-60, head physics div, 60-64. *Mem:* AAAS; Am Phys Soc. *Res:* High energy particle accelerators. *Mailing Add:* PO Box 500 Batavia IL 60510

COLE, FRANKLIN RUGGLES, b Newton, Mass, Aug 16, 25; m 47; c 2. PHARMACOGNOSY. *Educ:* Mass Col Pharm, BS, 51, MS, 53; Univ Utah, PhD(pharmacog), 56. *Prof Exp:* From asst prof to assoc prof, 56-65, PROF PHARMACOG, IDAHO STATE UNIV, 65- *Concurrent Pos:* Fulbright lectr, Cairo Univ, 65. *Mem:* AAAS; Am Soc Pharmacog; Am Pharmaceut Asn; Sigma Xi. *Res:* Re-evaluation of ethnobotanical drugs of the Bannock-Shoshone Indians. *Mailing Add:* Col of Pharm Idaho State Univ Pocatello ID 83201

COLE, GARRY THOMAS, b Toronto, Ont, June 26, 41; m 64; c 2. MEDICAL MYCOLOGY, ELECTRON MICROSCOPY. *Educ:* Carleton Univ, Ottawa, BA, 63; Univ Waterloo, Ont, PhD(biol), 69. *Prof Exp:* Teacher Sci, Clarke High Sch, Newcastle, Ont, 64-65; teaching fel biol, Univ Waterloo, Ont, 66-69; fel mycol, Univ Fla, Gainesville, 70-71; fac assoc, 70-71, asst prof, 71-75, assoc prof, 75-82, PROF BOT, UNIV TEX, AUSTIN, 82- *Concurrent Pos:* Vis asst prof, Lehrstühl für Zellenlehre, Universitat Heidelburg, 74; vis assoc prof, 81; Humboldt fel, Inst für Meeres forschung, Bremerhaven, WGer, 75; Nat Sci Found fel, Biochem Dept, Gifu Sch Med, Japan, 77-78. *Mem:* Am Soc Microbiol; Bot Soc Am; Mycol Soc Am; Med Mycol Soc Am; Electron Microscope Soc Am. *Res:* Taxonomy and biology of conidial fungi, including morphogenetic, ultrastructural, cytological, host-parasite interaction, wall chemistry and immunological studies. *Mailing Add:* Dept Bot Univ Tex Austin TX 78712

COLE, GEORGE CHRISTOPHER, b Brooklyn, NY, Oct 12, 29; m 55; c 5. MICROBIOLOGY. *Educ:* St John's Univ, NY, BS, 50, MS, 52; Univ Wis, PhD(bact), 57. *Prof Exp:* Lab asst parasitol, NY Univ-Bellevue Med Ctr, 51-52; asst virol, Univ Wis, 54-57; sr res scientist microbiol, E R Squibb & Sons, 57-66; sr res microbiologist, Parke, Davis & Co, Detroit, 66-80; RES ASSOC, SCH MED, WAYNE STATE UNIV, 81- *Mem:* AAAS; Am Soc Microbiol. *Res:* Chemotherapy of viral, bacterial and parasitic infections; pleuropneumonia-like organisms of swine and chickens; viral interference; Rubella vaccines; bacterial vaccines; viral and bacterial serology and immunology; malaria cultivation in vitro; alpha and gamma human interferon. *Mailing Add:* 3834 Quarton Rd Bloomfield Hills MI 48013

COLE, GEORGE DAVID, b Minden, La, June 23, 25; m 47; c 3. CHEMICAL PHYSICS. *Educ:* Northwestern State Col, La, BS, 50; Univ Ala, PhD(physics), 63. *Prof Exp:* Asst prof physics & math, Nicholls State Col, 54-60; from asst prof to assoc prof, 64-72, from actg head to head dept, 68-72, PROF PHYSICS & CHMN, DEPT PHYSICS & ASTRON, UNIV ALA, 72-, ACTG ASST VPRES ACAD AFFAIRS, 80- *Concurrent Pos:* Physics consult, Insts Int Educ, E & W Pakistan, 67-70. *Mem:* Am Phys Soc; Am Asn Physics Teachers. *Res:* Positron annihilation in liquid crystalline compounds; partial L- and M-shell fluorescence yields; polymorphic and mesomorphic behavior in organic compounds. *Mailing Add:* Dept Physics & Astron Univ Ala Box 1921 University AL 35486

COLE, GEORGE ROLLAND, b Lincoln, Kans, Dec 12, 25; m 50; c 4. SOLID STATE SCIENCE. *Educ:* Univ Kans, BS, 49, MA, 54, PhD(physics), 57. *Prof Exp:* Asst instr physics, Univ Kans, 51-56; res engr, Savannah River Lab, 56-65; res physicist, Electrochem Dept, Wilmington, Del, 65-69, qual control supvr, Electronic Prod Div, Niagara Falls, 69-73, SR RES PHYSICIST,

PHOTO PROD DEPT, E I DU PONT DE NEMOURS & CO, INC, 73- *Mem:* Sigma Xi; Am Phys Soc. *Res:* Color centers in alkali halides; properties and irradiation behavior of uranium oxide; solid actinide compounds; thick film electronic components; photographic science; electron spectroscopy; chromium dioxide magnetic tape. *Mailing Add:* Exp Sta 352 E I du Pont de Nemours & Co Inc Wilmington DE 19898

COLE, GEORGE WILLIAM, b Ridgewood, NJ, Oct 20, 33; m 55; c 4. INTERNAL MEDICINE, HEMATOLOGY. *Educ:* Univ Pa, BA, 54; Univ Miami, MD(med), 58. *Prof Exp:* Fel hemat, Dept Hemat, Jackson Mem Hosp, Miami, 61-63; instr hemat & internal med, Univ Miami, 63-66; from asst prof to assoc prof clin pathol, 66-73, ASST PROF INTERNAL MED, UNIV ALA, BIRMINGHAM, 66-, PROF PATH, 73-, PROF & MED DIR CLIN LAB SCI, SCH COMMUNITY & ALLIED HEALTH, 76-, VCHMN, DEPT PATH, 78- *Concurrent Pos:* Consult, Vet Admin Hosp, Birmingham, 66-; dir, Hemat Sect, Dept Clin Path, Univ Ala & Vet Admin Hosp Clin Labs, 66-76; dir, Lab Opers, CLin Labs, Univ Ala Hosp, 67-70, dir, Outpatient Oper, 70-72, dir, Gen Hemat & Chem, 74-; lab inspector, Col Am Pathologists, 70-74, adv, Clin Path Comt, 80-81. *Mem:* Acad Clin Lab Physicians & Scientists; AMA; Am Soc Clin Pathologists; Col Am Pathologists; Nat Comt Clin Lab Standards. *Res:* Medical laboratory system engineering: construction of testing panels, analysis of test results, test reporting systems in health care systems. *Mailing Add:* Dept Path Med Ctr Univ Ala Birmingham AL 35294

COLE, GERALD AINSWORTH, b Hartford, Conn, Dec 25, 17; m 44; c 5. LIMNOLOGY. *Educ:* Middlebury Col, AB, 39; St Lawrence Univ, MS, 41; Univ Minn, PhD(zool), 49. *Prof Exp:* Teaching fel biol, St Lawrence Univ, 40-41; teacher chem, Milton Acad & instr biol, Phillips Acad, 42; asst zool, Univ Minn, 46-49; from asst prof to assoc prof biol, Univ Louisville, 49-58; from lectr to prof, 58-80, EMER PROF ZOOL, ARIZ STATE UNIV, 80- *Concurrent Pos:* Res, Douglas Lake State Biol Sta, Mich, 50; mem teaching staff, Lake Itasca Biol Sta, Minn, 64-66, 68 & 70; res, Coahuila, Mex, 67 & 68. *Mem:* Am Soc Limnol & Oceanog; Int Asn Theoret & Appl Limnol. *Res:* Microcrustacea and regional limnology. *Mailing Add:* Rt 4 Box 892 Flagstaff AZ 86001

COLE, GERALD ALAN, b West New York, NJ, June 11, 31; m 58; c 3. VIROLOGY, IMMUNOLOGY. *Educ:* Wilson Teachers Col, BS, 52; Univ Md, PhD(microbiol), 66. *Prof Exp:* Med bacteriologist, Walter Reed Army Inst Res, 55-59; virologist, Sch Med, Univ Md, 59-60, res assoc microbiol, 66-67; from asst prof to assoc prof, 67-74, PROF EPIDEMIOL, SCH HYG & PUB HEALTH, JOHNS HOPKINS UNIV, 74-, PROF MICROBIOL, 81- *Concurrent Pos:* USPHS res grant, Sch Hyg & Pub Health, Johns Hopkins Univ, 70-78, res career develop award, 71-76; Josiah Macy Jr Found fac scholar award, John Curtin Sch Med Res, Australian Nat Univ, 74-75; mem ed hoc study group virus & rickettsial dis, US Army Res & Develop Command, 73-77; consult to Surgeon Gen, 73-77. *Mem:* AAAS; Am Soc Microbiol; Am Asn Immunol; Am Soc Trop Med & Hyg. *Res:* Role of the immune response in the outcome of viral infections. *Mailing Add:* Sch Med Univ Md 655 W Balt St Baltimore MD 21201

COLE, GERALD SIDNEY, b Toronto, Ont, Mar 29, 36; m 69; c 1. PHYSICAL METALLURGY. *Educ:* Univ Toronto, BASc, 59, MA, 60, PhD(metall), 63. *Prof Exp:* Res scientist, Res Labs, Ford Motor Co, 64-67; French Atomic Energy Comn res fel, Grenoble Nuclear Res Ctr, 67-68; PRIN STAFF ENGR, SCI RES STAFF, FORD MOTOR CO, 68- *Concurrent Pos:* Foundry expert, UN Indust Develop Orgn, Mex, 75-76. *Mem:* AAAS; Am Inst Mining, Metall & Petrol Engrs; Am Soc Metals; Am Foundrymens Soc; Soc Mfg Engrs. *Res:* Foundry technology; manufacturing, solidification; foundry sand and binders; ferrous metallurgy; aluminum. *Mailing Add:* Ford Motor Co 24500 Glendale Detroit MI 48239

COLE, HAROLD S, b Brooklyn, NY, Apr 20, 16. MEDICINE. *Educ:* Univ Md, BS, 37; NY Univ, MD, 42; Am Bd Pediat, dipl, 49. *Prof Exp:* Assoc prof, 48-74, PROF PEDIAT & CHIEF, SECT METAB, DEPT PEDIAT, NY MED COL, 74-, PROF COMMUNITY & PREV MED, 79- *Concurrent Pos:* Assoc attend pediatrician, Flower & Fifth Ave Hosps, New York, 48-74, attend pediatrician, 74-80; assoc vis pediatrician, Metrop Hosp, 48-73, vis pediatrician, 73-, head, pediat diabetes clin; attend physician, Bird S Coler Mem Hosp, NY, 76-; med dir, Flower Hosp, 78-80. *Mem:* Fel Am Acad Pediat; Lawson Wilkins Pediat Endocrine Soc; Am Pediat Soc; Am Diabetes Asn. *Res:* Adolescent medicine; diabetes mellitus in children; the infant of the diabetic mother; developmental disabilities. *Mailing Add:* 185 E 85th St New York NY 10028

COLE, HARVEY M, b North Weymouth, Mass, June 1, 20; m 46; c 4. CHEMICAL ENGINEERING. *Educ:* Northeastern Univ, BSchE, 43. *Prof Exp:* Chem engr, Godfrey L Cabot, Inc, 46-51, leader anal group, 51-57, head anal res & serv sect, 57-62, assoc dir res & develop, anal res & serv, 62-68, MGR CARBON BLACK RES SECT, CABOT CORP, 68- *Mem:* Am Chem Soc; Soc Appl Spectros. *Res:* Combustion; carbon formation in flames; radical reactions. *Mailing Add:* Billerica Res Ctr Cabot Corp Concord Rd Billerica MA 01821

COLE, HENDERSON, b Wilmington, NC, Oct 2, 24; m 50; c 4. PHYSICS. *Educ:* Mass Inst Technol, BS, 50, PhD(physics), 52. *Prof Exp:* Asst physics, Mass Inst Technol, 49-52, instr, 53-55; Fulbright fel, Col France, 52-53; staff physicist, Res Ctr, Brooklyn Heights, NY, 55-78, SR SCIENTIST, IBM INSTRUMENTS, IBM CORP, 78- *Mem:* Am Phys Soc; Sigma Xi; Am Crystallog Asn. *Res:* Supervising service work; solid state physics; x-ray diffraction; computer control of instruments. *Mailing Add:* IBM Instruments Inc PO Box 332 Danbury CT 06810

COLE, HERBERT, JR, b Long Island, NY, Mar 29, 33. PLANT PATHOLOGY, AGRICULTURAL CHEMISTRY. *Educ:* Pa State Univ, BS, 54, MS, 55, PhD(plant path, agr biochem), 57. *Prof Exp:* From asst prof to assoc prof plant path, 57-66, agr chem coord, Col Agr, 64-66, assoc prof plant path & chem pesticides, 66-70, PROF PLANT PATH & CHEM PESTICIDES, PA STATE UNIV, 70- *Concurrent Pos:* Consult pesticide litigation, Agr Chem Indust. *Mem:* Am Phytopath Soc; Can Phytopath Soc; Am Soc Testing & Mat. *Res:* Side effects of pesticides; control of plant diseases. *Mailing Add:* 131 W Marylyn Ave State Col PA 16801

COLE, JACK ROBERT, b Milwaukee, Wis, Dec 28, 29; m 52; c 3. MEDICINAL CHEMISTRY. *Educ:* Univ Ariz, BS, 53; Univ Minn, PhD(pharmaceut chem), 57. *Prof Exp:* From asst prof to assoc prof, 57-62, head, Dept Pharmaceut Sci, 75-79, PROF MED CHEM, UNIV ARIZ, 62-, DEAN, COL PHARM, 77- *Res:* Chemistry of natural medicinal products; chromatography; synthetic organic medicinals. *Mailing Add:* Col of Pharm Univ of Ariz Tucson AZ 85721

COLE, JACK WESTLEY, b Portland, Ore, Aug 28, 20; m 43; c 4. EXPERIMENTAL SURGERY. *Educ:* Univ Ore, AB, 41; Wash Univ, MD, 44; Am Bd Surg, dipl, 53. *Prof Exp:* From jr instr to sr instr surg, Western Reserve Univ, 52-54, asst surgeon, Univ Hosps, 54-56, from assoc prof to prof surg, Sch Med, 56-63; prof & chmn dept, Hahnemann Med Col & Hosp, 63-66; chmn dept surg, 66-74, ENSIGN PROF, DEPT SURG, YALE UNIV SCH MED, 66-; DIR, DIV ONCOL & YALE COMPREHENSIVE CANCER CTR, 75- *Concurrent Pos:* Chief, Hahnemann Serv, Div B, Dept Surg, Philadelphia Gen Hosp, 63-66; consult, Vet Admin Hosp, Philadelphia, 63-66; chief surg, Yale New Haven 66-74; attend surgeon, 74-; 66-74; consult, West Haven Vet Hosp, 66-; vis fel, Woodrow Wilson Found, 81- *Mem:* Soc Exp Biol & Med; Am Fedn Clin Res; fel Am Col Surg; Soc Univ Surg; Am Surg Asn. *Res:* Cellular kinetics of gastrointestinal epithelium, normal and neoplastic. *Mailing Add:* Yale Comprehensive Cancer Ctr 333 Cedar St New Haven CT 06510

COLE, JAMES A, b Albany, NY, Nov 18, 39; m 63; c 2. SYSTEMS ENGINEERING. *Educ:* Union Col, NY, BS, 61; Johns Hopkins Univ, PhD(physics). *Prof Exp:* Instr physics, Johns Hopkins Univ, 65-66; res assoc, State Univ NY Stony Brook, 66-67, asst prof, 67-71; mgr systs eng, Elsytec Inc, NY, 71-74; mgr systs eng, 74-80, DIR RES & DEVELOP, MEGADATA INC, BOHEMIA, NY, 80- *Concurrent Pos:* Guest res assoc, Brookhaven Nat Lab, 63-71. *Mem:* AAAS; Am Phys Soc; Inst Elec & Electronics Engrs. *Res:* Elementary particle physics; sound and vibration analysis. *Mailing Add:* 20 Upper Sheep Pasture Rd East Setauket NY 11733

COLE, JAMES CHANNING, b Oakland, Calif, May 22, 48; m 70. REGIONAL GEOLOGY, PETROLOGY. *Educ:* Univ Calif, Santa Barbara, BA, 69; Univ Colo, Boulder, PhD(geol), 77. *Prof Exp:* Geologist, Br Cent Environ Geol, 78-80, geologist, 80-81, CHIEF GEOLOGIST, SAUDI ARABIAN MISSION, US GEOL SURV, 81- *Concurrent Pos:* Vis lectr, Dept Geol Sci, Univ Colo, Boulder, 78-79. *Mem:* Geol Soc Am. *Res:* Structure and petrology of Precambrian rocks of the central United States; emplacement mechanisms of igneous bodies; uranium occurrences in igneous and metamorphic rocks; regional geology, petrology and structure of the Arabian Shield; metallogenesis of stockwork tungsten deposit. *Mailing Add:* US Geol Surv New York NY 09697

COLE, JAMES EDWARD, b Detroit, Mich, Sept 10, 40; m 60; c 2. ETHOLOGY, VERTEBRATE ZOOLOGY. *Educ:* Western Mich Univ, BA, 62; Ill State Univ, PhD(zool), 69. *Prof Exp:* Instr biol, Highland Park Col, 63-64; fac asst zool, Ill State Univ, 65-67; assoc prof, 68-71, prog coordr health sci, 73-79, PROF BIOL, BLOOMSBURG STATE COL, 71-, CHAIRPERSON DEPT, 79- *Mem:* AAAS; Am Soc Zool; Animal Behav Soc; Am Inst Biol Sci. *Res:* Parent-young interactions of Cichlid fishes; behavior of lower vertebrates; allied health sciences. *Mailing Add:* Dept Biol & Allied Health Sci Bloomsburg State Col Bloomsburg PA 17815

COLE, JAMES WEBB, JR, b Norfolk, Va, July 22, 10; m 36; c 2. CHEMISTRY. *Educ:* Univ Va, BS, 32, MS, 34, PhD(phys chem), 36. *Prof Exp:* Res chemist, Exp Sta, E I du Pont de Nemours & Co, 36-37; from asst prof to prof, 37-75, dean, 58-75, EMER PROF CHEM, UNIV VA, 75- *Concurrent Pos:* Instr, USN, 44; prog dir, NSF, 52-53, mem adv panel, 53-; consult, Off Sci Res & Develop; investr, Nat Defense Res Comt. *Mem:* AAAS; fel Am Inst Chem; Am Chem Soc. *Res:* Thermal measurements; adsorption of gases on solids; vapor phase catalytic oxidation and hydrolysis; new analytical methods; gas analysis; synthesis of complex inorganic compounds and of organo metallic compounds; spectrophotometer used in analysis and in problems of structure; mechanisms of antioxidants and anticorrosion agents. *Mailing Add:* 900 Rosser Lane Charlottesville VA 22903

COLE, JERRY JOE, b Kansas City, Mo, May 22, 38; m 61; c 2. ANALYTICAL CHEMISTRY. *Educ:* Univ Kansas City, BS, 60; Univ Iowa, MS, 63, PhD(anal chem), 65. *Prof Exp:* Asst prof chem, Ft Hays Kans State Col, 64-67; PROF CHEM, ASHLAND COL, 74-, CHMN DEPT, 80- *Mem:* Am Chem Soc. *Res:* Complexing of metal ions with organic and inorganic moieties; organic precipitants as a means of gravimetric estimation; amperometric titrations of inorganic ions. *Mailing Add:* Dept of Chem Ashland Col Ashland OH 44805

COLE, JOHN E(MERY), III, b Upper Darby, Pa, May 20, 42; m 68. ACOUSTICS, FLUID MECHANICS. *Educ:* Drexel Univ, BSME, 65; Brown Univ, ScM, 67, PhD(fluid mech), 70. *Prof Exp:* Asst prof mech eng, Tufts Univ, 70-77; scientist, 77-80, SR SCIENTIST, CAMBRIDGE ACOUST ASSOCS, INC, 80- *Mem:* Am Soc Mech Engrs; Acoust Soc Am. *Res:* Vibrations; applied mathematics. *Mailing Add:* Cambridge Acoust Assoc 54 Rindge Ave Ext Cambridge MA 02138

COLE, JOHN OLIVER, b Jamestown, NY, Apr 15, 15; m 44; c 2. CHEMISTRY. *Educ:* Bethany Col, Kans, BS, 39; Univ Colo, MS, 41, PhD(org chem), 43. *Prof Exp:* Asst chem, Univ Colo, 40-43, asst chem eng, 43; res chemist, Goodyear Tire & Rubber Co, 43-57, head anal sect, 57-65, mgr anal chem, 65-77, mgr spec projs, Org Chem Dept, 77-81. *Mem:* Am

Chem Soc. *Res:* Organic and analytical chemistry; reaction of phenyl glyoxal with aliphatic amidines; autoxidation of elastomers; rubber chemicals; kinetics of autoxidation of hydrocarbons. *Mailing Add:* 1883 Glengary Rd Akron OH 44313

COLE, JOHN RUFUS, JR, b Baconton, Ga, Oct 27, 38; m 64; c 2. VETERINARY MICROBIOLOGY. *Educ:* Univ Ga, BS, 60, MS, 63, PhD(microbiol), 66. *Prof Exp:* Res asst microbiol, Poultry Dis Res Ctr, 61-63, microbiologist, Diag & Res Labs, 66-80, ASSOC PROF, COL VET MED, UNIV GA, 80- *Mem:* Am Soc Microbiol. *Res:* Blood chemistry of chicks infected or endointoxicated with Escherichia coli; fat absorption from the small intestine of gnotobiotic chicks; efficacy of Pasteurella multocida bacterins in turkeys; fluorescent antibody tests for animal diseases; Leptospirosis; Mycobacteriosis. *Mailing Add:* Vet Diag & Investigational Labs Univ of Ga PO Box 1389 Tifton GA 31794

COLE, JON A(RTHUR), b Chicago, Ill, Apr 14, 39; m 60; c 4. SANITARY ENGINEERING. *Educ:* Ill Inst Technol, BSCE, 61; Univ Wis, Madison, MS, 64, PhD(civil eng), 70. *Prof Exp:* Consult civil engr, Harold F Steinbrecher, Ill, 60-63; from asst prof to assoc prof, 64-77, PROF ENG, WALLA WALLA COL, 77- *Mem:* Am Soc Civil Engrs; Water Pollution Control Fedn; Am Water Works Asn. *Res:* Physical processes in sanitary engineering; gravity thickening of compressible slurries. *Mailing Add:* Dept of Eng Walla Walla Col College Place WA 99324

COLE, JULIAN D(AVID), b Brooklyn, NY, Apr 2, 25; m 49; c 3. AERODYNAMICS. *Educ:* Cornell Univ, BME, 44; Calif Inst Technol, MS & AE, 46, PhD(aeronaut & math), 49. *Prof Exp:* Asst prof aeronaut & appl mech, Calif Inst Technol, 51-59, prof, 59-69; chmn dept, 69-76, PROF APPL SCI & ENG, UNIV CALIF, LOS ANGELES, 69-, PROF MATH, 76- *Mem:* Nat Acad Sci; Nat Acad Eng; Am Inst Aeronaut & Astronaut. *Res:* Aeronautics and applied mechanics. *Mailing Add:* Sch of Eng Mech & Struct Univ of Calif Los Angeles CA 90024

COLE, KENNETH STEWART, b Ithaca, NY, July 10, 00; wid; c 2. BIOPHYSICS. *Educ:* Oberlin Col, AB, 22; Cornell Univ, PhD(exp physics), 26. *Hon Degrees:* ScD, Oberlin Col, 54 & Univ Chicago, 67; MD, Univ Uppsala, 67. *Prof Exp:* Instr, Cornell Univ, 22-26, Nat Res Coun fel, 26-29; from asst prof to assoc prof physiol, Col Physicians & Surgeons, Columbia Univ, 29-46; prin biophysicist, Metall Lab, Univ Chicago, 42-46, prof biophys, 46-49; dir, Naval Med Res Inst, 49-54; chief lab biophys, Nat Inst Neurol Dis & Blindness, NIH, 54-66; sr res biophysicist, 66-78, EMER BIOPHYSICIST, NAT INST NEUROL & COMMUN DISORDERS & STROKE, NIH, 78- *Concurrent Pos:* Mem staff, Cold Spring Harbor, 34-37, mem bd, 40-45; Guggenheim fel, Inst Advan Study, 42; trustee, Marine Biol Lab, Woods Hole, 47-55, 56-64, emer trustee, 66-, mem exec comt, 56-59, 60-64; Regents prof, Univ Calif, Berkeley, 63-64, prof, 65-; Priestley lectr, Pa State Col, 39; Tennant lectr, Bryn Mawr Col, 41; guest lectr, Pa State Univ, 61 & Yale Univ, 62; Whitehead lectr, Nat Acad Sci-Nat Res Coun Conf Elec Insulation, 64; vis prof, Univ Tex Med Br Galveston, 74-; adj prof neurosci, Univ Calif, San Diego, 78- *Honors & Awards:* Order of the Southern Cross, Brazil, 66; Nat Medal Sci, 67; Bicentennial Medal, Col Physicians & Surgeons, Columbia Univ, 67. *Mem:* Nat Acad Sci; fel Am Phys Soc; Biophys Soc (pres elect, 62-63, pres, 63-64); fel Am Acad Arts & Sci; for mem Royal Soc London. *Res:* Photographic action of electrons; heat production and surface force of Arbacia eggs; electrical impedance of tissues, cells, natural and artificial membrane; electrical analysis of nerve impulse; ionic conductances of squid axon membrane. *Mailing Add:* 2404 Loring St San Diego CA 92109

COLE, LARRY KING, b Grundy, Va, July 11, 39; c 2. TOXICOLOGY, ENTOMOLOGY. *Educ:* WVa Univ, BA, 61; Univ Utah, MS, 68; Univ Ga, PhD(entom), 73. *Prof Exp:* Instr molecular biol, Juniata Col, 68-70; vis lectr entom, Univ Ill, Urbana, 73-74; res coordr, environ toxicol, 74-77; ASST PROF ENTOM, UNIV MASS, AMHERST, 77- *Concurrent Pos:* Res assoc, Ill Natural Hist Surv, 74-77; US rep, NATO Workshop on Ecotoxicol, 77. *Mem:* Entom Soc Am; Am Chem Soc; AAAS. *Res:* Environmental toxicology; pesticide toxicology; model ecosystems. *Mailing Add:* Dept of Entom Fernald Hall Univ Mass Amherst MA 01002

COLE, LARRY S, b Logan, Utah, Aug 31, 06; m 29; c 2. ELECTRICAL ENGINEERING. *Educ:* Univ Utah, BS, 40; Utah State Univ, MS, 45; Stanford Univ, DEng, 50. *Prof Exp:* Instr, 39-50, head dept, 50-65, prof, 50-76, actg dean col eng, 65-66, asst dean, 66-69, assoc dean col eng, 69-71, EMER PROF ELEC ENG, UTAH STATE UNIV, 76- ; CONSULT ENGR, 79- *Concurrent Pos:* Consult, Cole & Clark, 47-49. *Mem:* Sr mem Inst Elec & Electronics Engrs; Nat Soc Prof Engrs. *Res:* Electronic ckt design; electroacoustics. *Mailing Add:* 1692 E 1030 N Logan UT 84321

COLE, MADISON BROOKS, JR, b Worcester, Mass, Aug 30, 40; m 67; c 1. CELL BIOLOGY, ORTHOPEDICS. *Educ:* Colgate Univ, AB, 62; Univ Tenn, PhD(zool), 69. *Prof Exp:* Res asst biol, Brown Univ, 62-63 & Univ Tenn, 64-68; from instr to asst prof biol sci, Oakland Univ, 68-74; spec trainee biophys, NY Univ, 74-75; ASST PROF ORTHOPEDIC SURG, LOYOLA UNIV MED CTR, 75- *Mem:* AAAS; Orthop Res Soc; Electron Micros Soc Am; Am Soc Cell Biol; Am Asn Anat. *Res:* Electron microscopy; cytochemistry; growth and differentiation of bone and cartilage; electro-magnetic effects on living systems. *Mailing Add:* Dept of Orthopedic Surg Loyola Univ Med Ctr 2160 S1st Ave Maywood IL 60153

COLE, MICHAEL ALLEN, b Denver, Colo, Dec 15, 43. MICROBIAL GENETICS, SOIL MICROBIOLOGY. *Educ:* Cornell Univ, BS, 67; NC State Univ, Raleigh, MS, 71, PhD(microbiol), 72. *Prof Exp:* Asst prof microbiol, Southern Ill Univ, Edwardsville, 72-73; ASST PROF SOIL MICROBIOL, UNIV ILL, 74- *Mem:* Sigma Xi; Am Soc Microbiol. *Res:* Genetics of Rhizobium, particularly plasmid genetics; effects of agricultural chemicals and pollutants on soil micro-organisms. *Mailing Add:* Dept of Agron Univ of Ill Urbana IL 61801

COLE, MILTON WALTER, b Washington, DC, Dec 14, 42. SOLID STATE PHYSICS, LOW TEMPERATURE PHYSICS. *Educ:* Johns Hopkins Univ, BA, 64; Univ Chicago, MS, 65, PhD(physics), 70. *Prof Exp:* Fel physics, Univ Toronto, 70-72; res assoc, Univ Wash, 72-74; asst prof, Pa State Univ, 74-75; assoc prof physics, Brooklyn Col, 75-76; assoc prof, 75-81, PROF PHYSICS, PA STATE UNIV, 81- *Concurrent Pos:* Consult, Jet Propulsion Lab, Calif Inst Technol, 74-; vis assoc, Calif Inst Technol, 81-82; vis prof physics & chem, Brown Univ, 82. *Mem:* Sigma Xi; Am Vacuum Soc; Am Phys Soc. *Res:* Surface physics, especially thin films, liquid helium and electronic properties; inhomogenous quantum systems; absorption statistical mechanics and kinetics. *Mailing Add:* 104 Davey Lab Pa State Univ University Park PA 16802

COLE, MONROE, neurology, see previous edition

COLE, MORTON S, b Chicago, Ill, June 16, 29; m 52; c 3. FOOD TECHNOLOGY. *Educ:* Univ Ill, BS, 51, MS, 53; Iowa State Univ, PhD(food technol), 61. *Prof Exp:* Scientist grocery prod develop, Pillsbury Co, 59-61, dried prod develop, 61-63; food technologist, Archer-Daniels-Midland Co, 63-64, group leader edible prod, 64-68; dir res, Paniplus Co, Div ITT Continental Baking Co, 68-74; assoc dir res, 74-76, DIR RES, ARCHER-DANIELS-MIDLAND CO, 76- *Mem:* Inst Food Technologists; Am Asn Cereal Chem; Am Oil Chem Soc. *Res:* Porphyrin pigments in fresh and processed meats; lipid oxidation; pectic enzymes; vegetable dehydration; edible oxygen and moisture barriers; fabricated foods from vegetable proteins; bakery ingredients; chemical surfactants. *Mailing Add:* 2506 Ivy Lane Decatur IL 62521

COLE, NANCY, b Boston, Mass, Oct 15, 02. MATHEMATICS. *Educ:* Vassar Col, AB, 24; Radcliffe Col, AM, 29, PhD(math), 34. *Prof Exp:* Instr, Oxford Sch, 24-26 & Vassar Col, 27-28; tutor, Radcliffe Col, 28-29; instr, Wells Col, 31-32; instr math, Sweet Briar Col, 33-42; from vis asst prof to vis assoc prof, Kenyon Col, 43-44; asst prof, Conn Col, 44-47; from asst prof to assoc prof, 47-71, EMER ASSOC PROF MATH, SYRACUSE UNIV, 71- *Concurrent Pos:* Actg head dept, Sweet Briar Col, 34-35 & 41-42. *Mem:* AAAS; Am Math Soc; Math Asn Am. *Res:* Calculus of variations; index form associated with an extremaloid. *Mailing Add:* 1214 Westcott St Syracuse NY 13210

COLE, NOEL ANDY, b Pampa, Tex, Feb 16, 49. RUMINANT NUTRITION, ANIMAL SCIENCE. *Educ:* W Tex State Univ, BS, 71; Okla State Univ, MS, 73, PhD(animal nutrit), 75. *Prof Exp:* Vis asst prof, Dept Animal Sci, Tex Tech Univ, 75-76; RESEARCHER ANIMAL NUTRIT, CONSERV & PROD RES LAB, AGR RES SERV, USDA, 76- *Mem:* Am Soc Animal Sci; Coun Agr Sci & Technol; Am Dairy Sci Asn. *Res:* Beef cattle nutrition, especially as it relates to reducing environmental and physiological stresses occurring during the marketing and transporting of calves. *Mailing Add:* Conserv & Prod Lab Agr Res Serv USDA PO Drawer 10 Bushland TX 79012

COLE, NYLA J, b Wasco, Calif, Dec 5, 25; m 55. PSYCHIATRY. *Educ:* Univ Calif, Berkeley, BA, 47; Univ Rochester, MD, 51. *Prof Exp:* Intern, 52, resident psychiat, 55, instr, 56-60, dir outpatient div, 56-62, asst prof, 60-68, dir adult psychiat, 62-65, ASSOC PROF PSYCHIAT, COL MED, UNIV UTAH, 68-, DIR PSYCHIAT OUTPATIENT DEPT, 70- *Concurrent Pos:* Lectr, Dept Social Work, 61-; mem, President's Comt Employ Handicapped, 67-72; chmn med subcomt, Gov Comt Employ Handicapped, 68-72. *Mem:* Fel Am Psychiat Asn; AMA. *Res:* Natural history of psychiatric disease; mental health care delivery systems; social survival of discharged patients. *Mailing Add:* Dept Psychiat Univ Utah Col Med Salt Lake City UT 84112

COLE, PATRICIA ELLEN, b New York, NY, July 27, 44. BIOPHYSICAL CHEMISTRY. *Educ:* Brown Univ, AB, 66; Yale Univ, MPhil, 69, PhD(biophys chem), 72. *Prof Exp:* Fel biochem, Inst Cancer Res, Columbia Univ, 72-73, asst prof chem, 74-78; Res assoc biochem, Dept Molecular Biophys & Biochem, Yale Univ, 78-80; SPEC FEL, AM CANCER SOC, ALBERT EINSTEIN COL MED, 82- *Concurrent Pos:* Damon Runyon fel, Damon Runyon Mem Fund Cancer Res, 72-73; NIH career develop award, 76-80. *Mem:* Am Chem Soc; Biophys Soc. *Res:* Biophysical studies of gene expression using fast reaction kinetics, NMR, fluorescence; promoter recognition and RNA transcription; molecular mechanisms of RNA replication by RNA viral replicases; RNA conformational changes. *Mailing Add:* Albert Einstein Col Med Box 16A 1300 Morris Park Ave Bronx NY 10461

COLE, RALPH I(TTLESON), b St Louis, Mo, Aug 17, 05; m 31; c 2. ENGINEERING. *Educ:* Washington Univ, St Louis, BS, 27; Rutgers Univ, MS, 36. *Prof Exp:* Proj engr, Sig Corps Labs, Ft Monmouth, NJ, 29-31, asst chief radio sect, 31-38, engr in charge radio receiver work, 32-35, radio receiver, installation & direction finding, 35-38, chief radio sect, 38-40; chief radio direction finding sect, Eatontown Sig Lab, 40-42; chief Eng Div, Watson Labs, NJ, 45-47, chief engr, 47-52; mgr mil projs planning, Melphar, Inc, 52-63; mgr & tech consult, 63-73; prof lectr & adj prof, 63-69, dir insts & spec projs, 64-69, assoc prof eng & dir grad res & develop prog, 69-72, ADJ PROF, AM UNIV, 73-; CONSULT, INDEPENDENT RES & DEVELOP MGT, 73- *Concurrent Pos:* Guest lectr, Air Univ, 47-49; mgr, WABCO Govt Serv, Washington, DC, 61-63; mem, Eng Manpower Comn, 64-69; resident prof, Univ Southern Calif, Patuxent River Naval Base, 80. *Mem:* Fel AAAS; Am Inst Aeronaut & Astronaut; fel Inst Elec & Electronics Engrs. *Res:* Systems effectiveness; education research and development management; obsolescence and the engineer; technology transfer. *Mailing Add:* 3431 Blair Rd Falls Church VA 22041

COLE, RANDAL HUDIE, b Clinton, Ont, Nov 6, 08; m 40; c 3. MATHEMATICS. *Educ:* Univ Western Ont, BA, 36; Univ Wis, AM, 37, PhD(math), 40. *Prof Exp:* Asst math, Univ Wis, 38-40; from instr to prof, 40-74, EMER PROF MATH, UNIV WESTERN ONT, 74- *Concurrent Pos:* Res assoc, Princeton Univ, 48-49. *Mem:* Am Math Soc; Inst Math Statist; Math Asn Am. *Res:* Analysis; statistics. *Mailing Add:* RR1 Arva Can

COLE, RANDALL KNIGHT, b Putnam, Conn, Sept 21, 12; m 39; c 3. ANIMAL GENETICS. *Educ:* Mass State Col, BS, 34; Cornell Univ, MS, 37, PhD(animal breeding), 39. *Prof Exp:* Asst animal dis, Univ Conn, 34-35; instr poultry husb, 35-40, asst prof poultry sci & animal genetics, 40-48, from assoc prof to prof, 48-73, EMER PROF POULTRY SCI & ANIMAL GENETICS, CORNELL UNIV, 73- *Concurrent Pos:* Animal geneticist, Exp Sta, NY State Col Agr, Cornell Univ, 40-73; consult, Shaver Poultry Breeding Farms, Ltd, Cambridge, Ont, 56-; hon mem, 1st World Cong Genetics Appl to Livestock Prod, Madrid, 74. *Honors & Awards:* Poultry Sci Asn Res Award, 49; Tom Newman Mem Int Award, 69. *Mem:* AAAS; Am Genetic Asn; Poultry Sci Asn; World Poultry Sci Asn; Am Inst Biol Sci. *Res:* Genetics of disease resistance in poultry, especially to neoplasms; avian genetics; animal models of specific diseases. *Mailing Add:* Dept Poultry Sci Cornell Univ Ithaca NY 14853

COLE, RICHARD, b New York, NY, Apr 16, 24; m 47; c 2. PHYSICAL CHEMISTRY, ENVIRONMENTAL MANAGEMENT. *Educ:* City Col New York, BChE, 44; Univ Ill, MS, 48, PhD(phys chem), 52. *Prof Exp:* Asst phys chem, Univ Ill, 47-49, 50-51; radiol chemist, US Naval Radiol Defense Lab, 52-61, head countermeasures eval br, 61-64, chem tech div, 64-66 & nuclear tech div, 66-69; sr res assoc, 69-74, VPRES, ENVIRON SCI ASSOCS, FOSTER CITY, 74- *Mem:* Am Chem Soc; Opers Res Soc Am; Asn Environ Prof. *Res:* Formation, transport, deposition and removal of radioactive and other contamination; on-site inspection for clandestine nuclear operations; radioactivity in the oceans; environmental impact analysis and mitigation. *Mailing Add:* 1431 Tarrytown St San Mateo CA 94402

COLE, RICHARD ALLEN, b Suffern, NY, Oct 27, 42. AQUATIC ECOLOGY. *Educ:* State Univ NY Col Forestry, Syracuse Univ, BS, 64, MS, 66; Pa State Univ, PhD(zool), 69. *Prof Exp:* Res assoc, Mich State Univ, 69-73, asst prof aquatic ecol, 73-78; ASST PROF FISHERY SCI, NMEX STATE UNIV, 78- *Mem:* Am Soc Limnologists & Oceanogr; Am Fisheries Soc; Int Soc Limnol; Ecol Soc Am; NAm Benthological Soc. *Res:* Aquatic community ecology, particularly as influenced by eutrophication, thermal discharge and other watershed disturbances. *Mailing Add:* Dept of Fisheries & Wildlife Sci NMex State Univ Las Cruces NM 88001

COLE, RICHARD H, b Woodstock, Maine, Mar 2, 30; m 53; c 4. AGRONOMY. *Educ:* Univ Maine, BS, 52; Pa State Univ, PhD, 60. *Prof Exp:* Assoc county agent crops, Mass Exten Serv, 54-55; asst prof agron & agr eng, Univ Del, 60-65, chmn dept, 65-68, assoc prof plant sci, 68-70; assoc prof int agron, 70-76, POTATO PROD EXTEN SPECIALIST, PA STATE UNIV, 76- *Mem:* Potato Asn Am; Am Soc Agron; Crop Sci Soc Am; Weed Sci Soc Am. *Res:* Crop management; seed quality; weed control. *Mailing Add:* 103 Tyson Bldg Pa State Univ University Park PA 16802

COLE, ROBERT, b Bridgeport, Conn, Dec 31, 28; m 55; c 3. CHEMICAL ENGINEERING, HEAT TRANSFER. *Educ:* Clarkson Col Technol, BChE, 54, MChE, 59, PhD(chem eng), 65. *Prof Exp:* Res engr heat transfer, Nat Adv Comt Aeronaut, 54-56; from asst to assoc prof, 56-77, PROF CHEM ENG, CLARKSON COL TECHNOL, 77- *Concurrent Pos:* Vis prof, Technische Hogeschool Eindhoven, Nederland, 71-72 & 78-79. *Mem:* Am Inst Chem Engrs; Am Soc Mech Engrs; Am Optical Soc; Am Ceramic Soc. *Res:* Adsorption on to dry ion exchange resins; liquid film flows; boiling heat transfer; nucleation, growth, and detachment; glass processing in space; bubble migration phenomena; bubble dynamics. *Mailing Add:* Dept of Chem Eng Clarkson Col of Technol Potsdam NY 13676

COLE, ROBERT HUGH, b Oberlin, Ohio, Oct 26, 14; m 43. CHEMICAL PHYSICS. *Educ:* Oberlin Col, AB, 35; Harvard Univ, AM, 36, PhD(physics), 40. *Prof Exp:* Instr & tutor physics, Harvard Univ, 39-41; res supvr underwater explosives, Oceanog Inst, Woods Hole, 41-46; asst prof physics, Univ Mo, 46-47; from assoc prof to prof, 47-60, chmn dept, 49-61, JESSE H & LOUISA D SHARPE METCALF PROF CHEM, BROWN UNIV, 60- *Concurrent Pos:* Fulbright lectr & Guggenheim fel, State Univ Leiden, 55-56; NSF sr fel & Guggenheim fel, Oxford Univ, 61-62; vis prof, Univ Paris, Orsay, 69-70. *Honors & Awards:* Langmuir Prize Chem Physics, Am Phys Soc, 75. *Mem:* Fel Am Phys Soc; fel Am Acad Arts & Sci; Am Chem Soc. *Res:* Dielectric properties of matter; intermolecular forces. *Mailing Add:* Dept of Chem Brown Univ Providence RI 02912

COLE, ROBERT KLEIV, b San Francisco, Calif, Dec 19, 28; m 53; c 4. PHYSICS. *Educ:* Univ Calif, Berkeley, AB, 52; Univ Wash, PhD(physics), 59. *Prof Exp:* Physicist, Hanford Works, Gen Elec Corp, Wash, 52-54; vis asst prof, Univ Calif, Los Angeles, 59-62; asst prof, 62-66, ASSOC PROF PHYSICS, UNIV SOUTHERN CALIF, 66- *Mem:* Am Phys Soc. *Res:* Nuclear scattering; nuclear reactions studies; nuclear physics instrumentation. *Mailing Add:* Dept of Physics Univ of Southern Calif Los Angeles CA 90007

COLE, ROBERT STEPHEN, b Los Angeles, Calif, Apr 10, 43; m 65; c 2. SOLAR PHYSICS, QUANTUM PHYSICS. *Educ:* Univ Calif, Berkeley, AB, 65; Univ Wash, MS, 67; Mich State Univ, PhD(physics), 72. *Prof Exp:* Instr physics, St Martins Col, 67-69; asst prof, 72-77, ASSOC PROF PHYSICS, UNIV NC, ASHEVILLE, 72- *Concurrent Pos:* Consult solar energy, Asheville Orthop Hosp & Rehab Ctr, 75- *Mem:* Am Asn Physics Teachers; Nat Asn Environ Educ; Int Solar Energy Soc. *Res:* Solar energy research, especially passive systems for residential heating and cooling. *Mailing Add:* Dept of Physics Univ of NC Asheville NC 28804

COLE, ROGER DAVID, b Berkeley, Calif, Nov 17, 24; m 44; c 3. PROTEIN CHEMISTRY. *Educ:* Univ Calif, BS, 48, PhD(biochem), 54. *Prof Exp:* Asst phys chem, Atomic Res Inst, Univ Iowa, 48-49; chemist, Tidewater Oil Co, Calif, 49-51; jr res biochemist, Univ Calif, 54-55; fel, Nat Inst Med Res, London & Nat Found Infantile Paralysis, 55-56; res assoc biochem, Rockefeller Inst, 56-58; from asst prof to assoc prof, 58-65, chmn dept, 68-73, PROF BIOCHEM, UNIV CALIF, BERKELEY, 65-, DIR, ELECTRON MICROS LAB, 79- *Concurrent Pos:* Guggenheim fel, Cambridge Univ,

66-67. *Mem:* AAAS; Am Soc Biol Chem; Am Chem Soc. *Res:* Protein and peptide isolation and structural determination; relation of structure and biological activity of enzymes and hormones; histones; microtubules. *Mailing Add:* Dept of Biochem Univ of Calif Berkeley CA 94720

COLE, ROGER M, b Akron, Ohio, Nov 5, 34; m 58; c 2. INORGANIC CHEMISTRY, RESEARCH ADMINISTRATION. *Educ:* Kent State Univ, BS, 56; Univ Minn, MS, 58. *Prof Exp:* From res chemist to sr res chemist, 58-69, head Processing Res Lab, 69-73, asst dir, black & white photog res, 73-78, asst to dir res, 78-80, ASST DIR, RES ADMIN DIV, EASTMAN KODAK CO, 80- *Concurrent Pos:* Secy bd dir, Coun Chem Res, 80- *Mem:* Soc Photog Sci & Eng; Am Inst Chemists. *Res:* Mechanism of photographic development; photographic chemistry of silver ion complexes; mechanism and application of physical development; methods to simplify photographic processing. *Mailing Add:* 225 Imperial Ct Rochester NY 14617

COLE, RONALD SINCLAIR, molecular biology, radiobiology, see previous edition

COLE, STEPHEN H(ERVEY), b New Brunswick, NJ, Dec 16, 42; m 70; c 2. METALLURGY, CHEMICAL ENGINEERING. *Educ:* Univ Del, BChE, 64; Alfred Univ, MS, 66; Columbia Univ, DEng, 71- *Prof Exp:* Scientist, Metal Mining Div, Kennecott Res Ctr, 71-76; res engr, 77-81, GEN MGR, ENG & CONSTRUCT, TEXASGULF, INC, 81- *Mem:* Am Inst Mining, Metall & Petrol Engrs; Am Inst Chem Engrs. *Res:* Hydrometallurgy; determination of rate-limiting factors in oxidation of copper sulfide through electrochemical techniques; air pollution abatement. *Mailing Add:* Texasgulf Inc High Ridge Park Stamford CT 06904

COLE, TERRY, b Albion, NY, Mar 28, 31; m 55; c 3. CHEMICAL PHYSICS. *Educ:* Univ Minn, BS, 54; Calif Inst Technol, PhD(chem), 58. *Prof Exp:* Asst, Calif Inst Technol, 54-57; res scientist, Ford Motor Co, 59-71, mgr chem dept, 71-75, mgr chem eng dept, 75-76, sr staff scientist res staff, 76-80; CHIEF TECHNOLOGIST & RES ASSOC ENERGY TECHNOL, JET PROPULSION LAB, CALIF INST TECHNOL, 80- *Concurrent Pos:* Adj prof, Univ Mich; Fairchild scholar, Calif Inst Technol, 76-77. *Mem:* Am Phys Soc; Am Chem Soc. *Res:* Electron spin and nuclear magnetic resonance; radiation damage; free radical chemistry; quasielastic light scattering; thermo-electric energy conversion; solar energy. *Mailing Add:* Div Chem & Chem Eng Calif Inst Technol 127-72 Pasadena CA 91125

COLE, THOMAS A, b Harrisburg, Ill, Jan 9, 36; div; c 2. BIOCHEMISTRY, GENETICS. *Educ:* Wabash Col, BA, 58; Calif Inst Technol, PhD(biochem), 63. *Prof Exp:* From asst prof to assoc prof, 62-76, chmn dept, 68-79, NORMAN E TREVES PROF BIOL, WABASH COL, 76- *Concurrent Pos:* Comnr, Comn Undergrad Educ Biol Sci, 68-71; panelist, Educ Directorate, NSF, 75- *Mem:* Fel AAAS; NY Acad Sci. *Res:* Biochemistry of metamorphosing Drosophila; nutrition of paramecia; centrifugation techniques; identification of hydrolytic enzymes in substrate-included gels for electrophoresis; liposomen. *Mailing Add:* Dept of Biol Wabash Col Crawfordsville IN 47933

COLE, THOMAS EARLE, b Winter Park, Fla, Dec 13, 22; m 44; c 3. NUCLEAR ENGINEERING, PHYSICS. *Educ:* Rollins Col, BS, 46. *Prof Exp:* Physicist, 46-69, DEVELOP STAFF MEM NUCLEAR REACTORS, OAK RIDGE NAT LAB, 69-, MGR LIGHT WATER REACTOR TECHNOL PROG, 80- *Concurrent Pos:* Consult, various companies and countries, 56-62, Repub SAfrica, 62-65, US Energy Res & Develop Admin, 73-74. *Mem:* Am Phys Soc; Am Nuclear Soc; Sigma Xi. *Res:* Nuclear research reactors - all aspects; reactor safety and control; probabilistic reactor safety studies; nuclear energy centers, energy parks. *Mailing Add:* Oak Ridge Nat Lab Box X Oak Ridge TN 37830

COLE, THOMAS WINSTON, JR, b Vernon, Tex, Jan 11, 41; m 64. ORGANIC CHEMISTRY. *Educ:* Wiley Col, BS, 61; Univ Chicago, PhD(chem), 66. *Prof Exp:* Asst prof, 66-69, FULLER E CALLAWAY PROF CHEM, ATLANTA UNIV, 69-, CHMN DEPT, 71- *Concurrent Pos:* Vis prof, Dept Chem, Mass Inst Technol, 73-74. *Mem:* AAAS; Am Chem Soc; Nat Inst Sci. *Res:* Chemistry of cubane; small ring compounds; photochemistry; application of gas chromatography-mass spectrometry to problems in clinical chemistry; bio-organic chemistry. *Mailing Add:* Dept of Chem Atlanta Univ Atlanta GA 30314

COLE, VERNON C, b Wenatchee, Wash, Nov 12, 22; m 48; c 3. SOIL SCIENCE. *Educ:* Univ Mass, BS, 47, MS, 48; PhD(soil sci), 50. *Prof Exp:* RES SOIL SCIENTIST, SOIL & WATER CONSERV RES DIV, AGR RES SERV, USDA, 50- *Mem:* Am Soc Agron; Soil Sci Soc Am; Am Soc Plant Physiol. *Res:* Soil physical chemistry; plant mineral nutrition. *Mailing Add:* Dept Agron Colo State Univ Ft Collins CO 80521

COLE, W STORRS, b Albany, NY, July 16, 02; m 26. GEOLOGY. *Educ:* Cornell Univ, BS, 25, MS, 28, PhD(micropaleont), 30. *Prof Exp:* Asst instr hist geol, Cornell Univ, 26; paleontologist, Huasteca Petrol Co, Mex, 26-27; instr physiog & com geog, Cornell Univ, 28-30; paleontologist, Sun Oil Co, Tex, 30-31; from instr to prof geomorphol, Ohio State Univ, 31-45; prof paleont & stratig, 46-68, chmn dept geol, 47-62, EMER PROF PALEONT & STRATIG, CORNELL UNIV, 68- *Concurrent Pos:* Mem div geol & geog, Nat Res Coun, 44-47; geologist, US Geol Surv, Wash, 47-75; mem, NY State Mus Coun, 58-63. *Mem:* AAAS; fel Asn Am Geog; fel Am Geol Soc (3rd vpres, 54); fel Paleont Soc (pres, 53); Paleont Res Inst (vpres, 54). *Res:* Micropaleontology; geomorphology; fossil larger Foraminifera of Florida, Mexico, Trinidad, Panama, Cuba, Guam, Saipan, Bikini and Fiji Islands; stratigraphy and micropaleontology of the Tampico Embayment, Mexico and of Florida; erosion surfaces of the Appalachians. *Mailing Add:* 310 Fall Creek Dr Ithaca NY 14850

COLE, WALTER EARL, b Hunter, Ark, Aug 5, 21; m 47; c 2. ORGANIC CHEMISTRY. *Educ:* Ark State Teachers Col, BS, 43; Vanderbilt Univ, MS, 48, PhD(chem), 57. *Prof Exp:* Instr chem, Vanderbilt Univ, 48-51, asst, 52-53; res chemist tech sect, Film Dept, E I du Pont de Nemours & Co, Inc, Tenn, 53-55, develop group leader, 55-56, develop supvr, Iowa, 56-57, coating area supvr, 57-59, mfg supt, Spruance Film Plant, 59-62, tech supt, 62-64, acetate supt, 64-72; mgr, Tee-Pak Inc, 72-74; dir licensing, Paper & Film Group, Olin Corp, NC, 74-75, dir process eng, 75-76; vpres, S P Assocs, NC, 76-77; dir opers, Penta Corp, Tenn, 77-79; PRES, DUNHILL OF NUECES BAY, INC, PORTLAND, TEX, 79- *Mem:* Am Chem Soc; Am Inst Chemists; Sigma Xi. *Res:* Synthesis of quinolines; halogenation of heterocyclic compounds; preparation of oximes; Beckman rearrangement; cellulose chemistry; manufacture of packaging films. *Mailing Add:* 701 Moore Ave Portland TX 78374

COLE, WALTER ECKLE, b Muskogee, Okla, Sept 2, 28; m 55; c 3. ENTOMOLOGY, MATHEMATICAL BIOLOGY. *Educ:* Colo State Univ, BSc, 50, MSc, 55; NC State Univ, PhD, 72. *Prof Exp:* Entomologist forest insect res, 54-60, actg proj leader pop dynamics res, 60-65, PROJ LEADER POP DYNAMICS RES, US FOREST SERV, 65-, PRIN ENTOMOLOGIST, 70- *Concurrent Pos:* Counr, Western Forest Insect Work Conf, 70-73; chmn working party, Int Union Forest Res Orgns. *Honors & Awards:* Superior Serv Award, Forest Serv, US Dept Agr, 55. *Mem:* Am Statist Asn; Biomet Soc; Entom Soc Am; Japanese Soc Pop Ecol. *Res:* Population dynamics of forest insects; mensurational aspects of behavioral sampling; analysis and modeling of populations. *Mailing Add:* Forest Serv Bldg 507 25th St Ogden UT 84401

COLE, WAYNE, b Indianapolis, Ind, Nov 5, 13; m 36; c 5. NATURAL PRODUCTS CHEMISTRY. *Educ:* DePauw Univ, AB, 35; Univ Ill, AM, 36, PhD(org chem), 38. *Prof Exp:* Asst chem, Univ Mich, 38-39; res chemist, Glidden Co, 39-46, from asst dir to dir res, 46-58; proj leader steroid res, Abbott Labs, 58-72, res fel, 72-79; CONSULT, 79- *Mem:* Fel AAAS; Am Chem Soc; Am Oil Chem Soc; Soc Chem Indust; Swiss Chem Soc. *Res:* Synthesis of carcinogenic hydrocarbons, protein derivatives; sterols and hormones; steroid and lipid research; peptide synthesis. *Mailing Add:* 1224 Norman Lane Deerfield IL 60015

COLE, WILBUR VOSE, b Waterville, Maine, Jan 19, 13; m 36; c 3. NEUROANATOMY. *Educ:* Univ NH, BS, 35; Kirksville Col Osteop, DO, 43; Northeast Mo State Teachers Col, MA, 54. *Prof Exp:* Lab asst histol, Kirksville Col Osteop, 43-44, instr histol & embryol, Dept Anat, 44, asst prof histol & neuroanat, 44-51; assoc prof anat, Kansas City Col Osteop Med, 51-79, prof clin neurol, 69-79, dean, 73-79. *Mem:* AAAS; Photog Biol Asn; Nat Asn Biol Teachers; Sigma Xi; Am Micros Soc. *Res:* Histopathology; polarized light in photomicroscopy; gallocyanin as a nuclear stain; comparative anatomy and physiology of motor and sensory endings in striated muscle. *Mailing Add:* Box 6 Star Route Prospect Harbor ME 04669

COLE, WILFRED Q, b Jackson, Miss, Nov 28, 24; m 49; c 3. PEDIATRICS. *Educ:* Univ Va, MD, 51; Am Bd Allergy & Immunol, dipl, 74. *Prof Exp:* From intern to resident pediat, Univ Hosp, Birmingham, Ala, 51-54; from clin instr to clin asst prof, 55-68, asst dir pediat allergy clin, 62-77, CLIN ASSOC PROF PEDIAT, SCH MED, UNIV MISS, 68-, ASST DIR CYSTIC FIBROSIS RES CTR, 62- *Concurrent Pos:* Pediat allergy fel, Duke Med Ctr, 61; co-chmn clin comt, Nat Cystic Fibrosis Res Found, 66-70. *Mem:* Am Acad Pediat; Am Col Allergists; Am Acad Allergy. *Res:* Cystic fibrosis; pediatric allergy. *Mailing Add:* 940 N State St Jackson MS 39201

COLEBROOK, LAWRENCE DAVID, b Helensville, NZ, Dec 29, 30; m 59. PHYSICAL ORGANIC CHEMISTRY. *Educ:* Univ NZ, BSc, 54, MSc, 55, PhD(chem), 61. *Prof Exp:* From jr lectr to lectr chem, Univ Auckland, 57-60; fel, Univ Rochester, 61-63, from asst prof to assoc prof, 69-74, PROF CHEM, SIR GEORGE WILLIAMS CAMPUS, CONCORDIA UNIV, 74- *Concurrent Pos:* Vis prof, Univ BC, 77-78. *Mem:* Brit Chem Soc; assoc NZ Inst Chem; Am Chem Soc; Chem Inst Can. *Res:* Nuclear magnetic resonance spectroscopy; computers in chemistry; natural products. *Mailing Add:* Dept of Chem Concordia Univ 1455 de Maisonneuve Blvd W Montreal PQ H3G 1M8 Can

COLEGROVE, FORREST DONALD, b Madeira, Ohio, Nov 21, 29; m 56; c 2. APPLIED PHYSICS. *Educ:* Purdue Univ, BS, 51; Univ Mich, MS, 54, PhD(physics), 60. *Prof Exp:* mem tech staff, 59-80, SR MEM TECH STAFF PHYSICS, TEX INSTRUMENTS, INC, 80- *Concurrent Pos:* Vis scientist, Southwest Ctr Advan Studies, 65-69. *Mem:* AAAS; Am Phys Soc. *Res:* Superconducting device research; magnetic resonance; infrared systems; physics of the upper atmosphere. *Mailing Add:* 15022 N Lakes Dr Dallas TX 75240

COLELLA, DONALD FRANCIS, b Utica, NY, Mar 22, 38; m 69; c 1. PHARMACOLOGY. *Educ:* Rensselaer Polytech Inst, BS, 61; Col St Rose, MS, 68; Drexel Univ, MBA, 75. *Prof Exp:* Assoc res biologist pharmacol, Sterling-Winthrop Res Inst, 61-68; assoc pharmacologist, 68-69, pharamacologist, 69-72, sr pharmacologist, 72-76, Int Mkt Mgr, 76-77, sr mkt res analyst, 77-78, prod mgr, 78-80, MGR NEW PROD DEVELOP, SMITH KLINE & FRENCH LABS, 80- *Mem:* NY Acad Sci; Am Chem Soc. *Res:* Cardiovascular and respiratory pharmacology; pharmacology of cardiac and smooth muscle; adrenergic mechanisms; theory of drug-receptor interactions; structure-activity relationships of medicinal agents. *Mailing Add:* Smith Kline & French Labs PO Box 7929 Philadelphia PA 19101

COLELLA, ROBERTO, b Milano, Italy, May 22, 35; m 60; c 3. SOLID STATE PHYSICS. *Educ:* Univ Milano, Laurea(physics), 58. *Prof Exp:* Trainee physics, Nat Nuclear Energy Comt, Casaccia, Rome, Italy, 60-61; staff scientist, Europe Atomic Energy Comn, Common Ctr Res, Ispra, Italy, 61-67; res assoc physics, Cornell Univ, 67-70 & Catholic Univ, Washington, DC, 70-71; asst prof to assoc prof, 71-77, PROF PHYSICS, PURDUE UNIV, WEST LAFAYETTE, 77- *Concurrent Pos:* USA co ed, Acta

Crystallographica, 80. *Mem:* Am Phys Soc; Am Crystallog Asn; Italian Phys Soc. *Res:* Diffraction physics in perfect and imperfect crystals; phonons, charge densities and interferometry. *Mailing Add:* Dept of Physics Purdue Univ West Lafayette IN 47907

COLEMAN, ALBERT JOHN, b Toronto, Ont, Can, May 20, 18; m 53; c 2. APPLIED MATHEMATICS. *Educ:* Univ Toronto, BA, 39, PhD, 43; Princeton Univ, MA, 43. *Prof Exp:* Lectr math, Queen's Univ, Can, 43-45; travelling secy, World's Student Christian Fedn, 45-49; from lectr to assoc prof math, Univ Toronto, 49-60; head dept, 60-80, PROF MATH, QUEEN'S UNIV, ONT, 80- *Concurrent Pos:* Mem, Sci Coun Can, 73-77 & Lambeth Conf, 78. *Mem:* Am Math Soc; Math Asn Am. *Res:* Eddington's fundamental theory; group theory; quantum mechanics. *Mailing Add:* 1001-185 Ontanco St Kingston ON K7L 2Y7 Can

COLEMAN, ANNA M, b New Concord, Ohio, Jan 5, 13. INFORMATION SCIENCE. *Educ:* Geneva Col, BS, 33; Univ Pa, MS, 34; Univ Pittsburgh, PhD(chem), 58. *Prof Exp:* Teacher high sch, Pa, 34-42; Koppers Co res asst, Mellon Inst, 42-44, jr fel, 44-50; chem librn, Dow Corning Corp, 50-60, supvr res info serv, 60-67, mgr tech info serv, 67-78; RETIRED. *Mem:* Am Chem Soc; Sigma Xi. *Res:* Chemical documentation; dipole moments. *Mailing Add:* Tech Info Servs Dow Corning Corp Midland MI 48640

COLEMAN, ANNETTE WILBOIS, b Des Moines, Iowa, Feb 28, 34; m 58; c 3. CELL BIOLOGY. *Educ:* Barnard Col, AB, 55; Univ Ind, PhD(bot), 58. *Prof Exp:* NSF res fel, Johns Hopkins Univ, 58-61; res assoc, Univ Conn, 62-63; res assoc, 63-72, asst prof biol, 72-80, ASSOC PROF BIOL, BROWN UNIV, 81- *Mem:* Bot Soc Am; Soc Protozool; Phycol Soc Am; Soc Gen Physiol; NY Acad Sci. *Res:* Physiological control of mating in algae, inheritance of mating type; geographical distribution and speciation in algae; genetics; structure of chloroplast desoxyribonucleic acid; problems of cell fusion. *Mailing Add:* Div of Biol & Med Sci Brown Univ Dept of Biol Providence RI 02912

COLEMAN, BERNARD DAVID, b New York, NY, July 5, 30; m 65; c 2. CONTINUUM MECHANICS, MATHEMATICAL ANALYSIS. *Educ:* Ind Univ, BS, 51; Yale Univ, MS, 53, PhD(chem), 54. *Prof Exp:* Res chemist, E I du Pont de Nemours & Co, 54-57; sr fel, 57-77, PROF MATH & BIOL, CARNEGIE-MELLON UNIV, 67- *Concurrent Pos:* Visitor, Inst Math, Univ Bologna, 60-61; vis prof, Johns Hopkins Univ, 62-63; adj prof, Univ Pittsburgh, 64-65; ed-in-chief, Springer Tracts in Natural Philos, 67-; lectr, Univ Pisa, 66, 68, 69, 74 & 78, Scuola Normale Superiore, Italy, 69 & 70 & Int Ctr Mech Sci, Udine, Italy, 71 & 73. *Mem:* Soc Natural Philos (treas, 67-68). *Res:* Viscoelasticity; foundations of thermodynamics; functional analysis; differential equations; mathematical biology; theories of visual perception; population dynamics. *Mailing Add:* Dept of Math Carnegie-Mellon Univ Pittsburgh PA 15213

COLEMAN, BERNELL, b Lorman, Miss, Apr 26, 29; m 62; c 2. PHYSIOLOGY. *Educ:* Alcorn Agr & Mech Col, BS, 52; Loyola Univ, Ill, PhD(physiol), 64. *Prof Exp:* Asst path, Med Ctr, Univ Kans, 52-53; asst biochem, Univ Chicago, 56-57; asst cancer res, Hines Vet Admin Hosp, Ill, 57-59; instr physiol, Sch Med St Louis Univ, 63-65, asst prof, 65-69; assoc prof physiol & cardiovasc res, Chicago Med Sch, 69-76, prof physiol, 76; actg chmn physiol, 79-80, PROF PHYSIOL, COL MED, HOWARD UNIV, 76- *Concurrent Pos:* Mem coun basic sci, Am Heart Asn; mem Clin Sci Review Group B, NIH, 81- *Mem:* AAAS; Am Heart Asn; Am Physiol Soc; Sigma Xi; Sci Res Soc. *Res:* Myocardial catecholamines in hemorrhagic hypotension; electrolytes and water metabolism of the heart in hemorrhagic shock; effects of norepinephrine on electrolytes and water content of cardiac muscle; cardiodynamics in irreversible hemorrhagic shock; cardiodynamic and circulatory responses to heat; angiotensin II and cardiac function; carotid sinus reflex control of the heart; systolic stress and strain relation in normal and hypertrophied hearts. *Mailing Add:* Dept Physiol & Biophys 520 W St NW Washington DC 20059

COLEMAN, CHARLES CLYDE, b York, Eng, July 31, 37; US citizen; m 76; c 2. SOLID STATE PHYSICS. *Educ:* Univ Calif, Los Angeles, BA, 59, MA, 61, PhD(physics), 68. *Prof Exp:* Assoc prof, 68-77, PROF PHYSICS, CALIF STATE UNIV, LOS ANGELES, 77-, EXEC DIR, APPL PHYSICS INST, 81-, DIR, ACCELERATOR FACIL & TRUSTEE FOUND, 81- *Concurrent Pos:* Sr res fel, Cavendish Lab, Cambridge Univ, 75-76; NSF res grant, 76-79. *Mem:* Am Phys Soc; fel Brit Interplanetary Soc. *Res:* Semiconductors; superconductors; crystal growth; thin films; interfaces; simulated bioluminescence; modulation spectroscopy; ion implantation. *Mailing Add:* Dept of Physics Calif State Univ Los Angeles CA 90032

COLEMAN, CHARLES FRANKLIN, b Burley, Idaho, Dec 30, 17; m 52; c 3. SEPARATIONS CHEMISTRY, PHASE EQUILIBRIA. *Educ:* Univ Utah, BS, 41; Purdue Univ, MS, 43, PhD(phys chem), 48. *Prof Exp:* Asst chem, Univ Utah, 39-41 & Purdue Univ, 42-44; chemist, Substitute Alloy Mat Labs, Columbia Univ, 44, Tenn Eastman Corp & Clinton Eng Works, Oak Ridge, 44-46; asst chem, Purdue Univ, 46-47; chemist, Y-12 Plant, Carbide & Carbon Chem Corp, 48-51, chemist, Union Carbide Corp, 51-67, asst sect chief, 67-76, MGR CHEM DEVELOP, SEPARATIONS CHEM PROGS, UNION CARBIDE CORP, OAK RIDGE NAT LAB, 76- *Mem:* AAAS; Am Chem Soc; Sigma Xi. *Res:* Calorimetry; phase equilibria; solution chemistry; separations chemistry; solvent extraction reagents, equilibria, kinetics, applications; actinide-lanthanide chemistry. *Mailing Add:* Union Carbide Corp-ORNL PO Box X Oak Ridge TN 37830

COLEMAN, CHARLES MOSBY, b New York, NY, Oct 14, 25; m 51; c 5. CLINICAL CHEMISTRY, MICROBIOLOGY. *Educ:* Univ Mich, BS, 49; Univ Chicago, MS, 54; Univ Colo, PhD(microbiol), 56. *Prof Exp:* Asst med bact & virol, Univ Chicago, 52; biochemist, Nat Jewish Hosp, Denver, Colo, 56-58, chief clin labs, 58-60, res biochemist, 60-62; biochemist, Warner-Lambert Res Inst NJ, 63-64; chief clin chem, Vet Admin Hosp, Pittsburgh, 64-69; INVENTOR & CONSULT, 69-; PRES, COLEMAN LABS, 77- *Mem:* AAAS; Am Chem Soc; Am Asn Clin Chem; NY Acad Sci. *Res:* Clinical laboratory diagnostic devices; analytical and organic chemistry; instrumentation and automation; biochemistry of trace metals and chelates; chemistry of mycobacteria. *Mailing Add:* 958 Washington Rd Pittsburgh PA 15228

COLEMAN, COURTNEY (STAFFORD), b Ventura, Calif, July 19, 30; m 54; c 3. MATHEMATICAL ANALYSIS. *Educ:* Univ Calif, BA, 51; Princeton Univ, MA, 53, PhD, 55. *Prof Exp:* Instr math, Princeton Univ, 54-55; from instr to asst prof, Wesleyan Univ, 55-59; from asst prof to assoc prof, 59-66, PROF MATH, HARVEY MUDD COL, 66- *Concurrent Pos:* Vis scientist, Res Inst Advan Studies, 58-59 & 63-64; mem fac, Claremont Grad Sch, 68- *Mem:* Am Math Soc; Soc Indust & Appl Math; Math Asn Am. *Res:* Ordinary differential equations. *Mailing Add:* 675 Northwestern Dr Claremont CA 91711

COLEMAN, DAVID COWAN, b Bennington, Vt, Nov 7, 38; m 65; c 2. ECOLOGY, SOILS SCIENCE. *Educ:* Reed Col, BA, 60; Univ Ore, MA, 63, PhD(biol), 64. *Prof Exp:* Demonstr, Univ Col Swansea, Wales, 64-65; res assoc & fel, Savannah River Ecol Lab, Univ Ga, 65-72, asst prof zool, 67-72; res assoc agron, Natural Res Ecol Lab, 72-75, asst prof, 75-77, ASSOC PROF ZOOL, COLO STATE UNIV, 78- *Concurrent Pos:* Sr fel, Nat Res Adv Comt, Dept Sci & Indust Res, Soil Bureau & Inst Nuclear Sci, Lower Hutt, New Zeland, 79-80. *Mem:* AAAS; Ecol Soc Am; Am Soc Microbiol; Brit Ecol Soc; Sigma Xi. *Res:* Decomposition and nutrient cycles; terrestrial ecosystems; flora-fauna interactions in the soil; nutrient cycling in reclaimed and agricultural lands. *Mailing Add:* Natural Resource Ecol Lab Colo State Univ Ft Collins CO 80523

COLEMAN, DAVID MANLEY, b Duluth, Minn, Mar 24, 48; m 69; c 2. ANALYTICAL CHEMISTRY, PHYSICAL CHEMISTRY. *Educ:* Southern Ill Univ, BA, 70; Univ Wis, MS, 72, PhD(anal chem), 76. *Prof Exp:* Proj assoc chem, Univ Wis, 76-77; ASST PROF CHEM, WAYNE STATE UNIV, 77- *Concurrent Pos:* Consult, Baird Atomic Corp, 77-, Jarrell-Ash Div, Fisher Sci, 77- & Detroit Edison Corp, 80-; Wayne State fac res fel, 78-79. *Mem:* Am Chem Soc; Soc Appl Spectros; Sigma Xi; Asn Anal Chemists. *Res:* Optical emission spectroscopy; analytical spectroscopy; excitation mechanisms in atmospheric pressure; plasmas; excitation sources; optics; instrumentation. *Mailing Add:* Dept of Chem Chem Bldg 175 Wayne State Univ Detroit MI 48202

COLEMAN, DENIS, b Manchester, Eng, Dec 2, 15; nat US; m 51; c 5. ORGANIC CHEMISTRY. *Educ:* Univ London, BSc, 39, PhD(protein chem), 44. *Prof Exp:* Res officer natural silk, Shirley Inst, Brit Cotton Indust Res Asn, 39-47; sr res chemist, Imp Chem Industs, 47-57; head dept polymers, Monsanto Can, Ltd, 57-61; sr res chemist, Fibers Div, 61-79, SR RES CHEMIST, CENT RES DIV, AM CYANAMID CO, 79- *Mem:* Sr mem Am Chem Soc. *Res:* High polymers; chemistry of silk fibroin; synthesis of polypeptides and block polymers; new polyamides, polyesters and acid-dyeable acrylic fibers; novel flame-retardants. *Mailing Add:* 223 Glenbrook Rd Stamford CT 06906

COLEMAN, DONALD BROOKS, b Russellville, Ky, June 18, 34; m 54; c 4. MATHEMATICS. *Educ:* Union Univ, BA, 56; Purdue Univ, MS, 58, PhD(math), 61. *Prof Exp:* Asst instr math, Mich State Univ, 60-61; from asst prof to assoc prof, Vanderbilt Univ, 61-66; assoc prof, 66-75, PROF MATH, UNIV KY, 75- *Mem:* Am Math Soc; Math Asn Am; Nat Coun Teachers Math. *Res:* Algebra. *Mailing Add:* 1146 Athenia Dr Lexington KY 40504

COLEMAN, DONALD JAMES, JR, physics, solid state electronics, see previous edition

COLEMAN, ERNEST, b Detroit, Mich, Aug 31, 43; m 64; c 2. NUCLEAR PHYSICS, HIGH ENERGY PHYSICS. *Educ:* Univ Mich, BS & MS, 63, PhD(physics), 66. *Prof Exp:* Instr physics, Univ Mich, 66-67; from asst prof to assoc prof, Univ Minn, Minneapolis, 68-77, spec asst to actg vpres, 73-74; HEAD CENT LAB RES, OFF ENERGY RES, US DEPT ENERGY, 77- *Concurrent Pos:* Deutsches Elektronen-Synchrotron fel, Hamburg, Ger, 67-68; vis assoc prof, Stanford Univ, 71-72; NSF award, 62; vis prof, Univ Heidelberg, Ger, 72 & Univ Tel-Aviv, 73; head, Cent Lab Res, High Energy Phys Prog, AEC, 74-75; mem, Coun Int Exchange Scholars, Grad Records Exam Comt & exec secy, US High Energy Phys Adv Panel; head cent lab res, Div Phys Res, Energy Res & Develop Admin, 75-77; mem, Interagency Coord Comt Astron, 75-77, mem solar subcomt, 75-76. *Honors & Awards:* Aldrich Sci Award, US Am, 62; A P Sloan Res Award in Physics, 73; Distinguished Serv Award, Am Asn Physics Teachers, 77. *Mem:* Europ Phys Soc; fel Am Phys Soc; Am Asn Phys Teachers; Math Asn Am; AAAS. *Res:* Experimental particle physics; theoretical nuclear physics; quantum electrodynamics; boundary layer problems; education of gifted students; research management; complex analysis; decision theory; fluid flow; econometric models. *Mailing Add:* G-256 Res US Dept Energy Washington DC 20545

COLEMAN, GEOFFRY N, b Dover, Ohio, Oct 12, 46. SPECTROCHEMISTRY, TRACE ANALYSIS. *Educ:* De Pauw Univ, BA, 70, MA, 72; Colo State Univ, PhD(chem), 76. *Prof Exp:* Fel, Colo State Univ, 76; ASST PROF CHEM, UNIV GA, 76- *Concurrent Pos:* Instr, Ctr Prof Advan, 81 & 82. *Mem:* Am Chem Soc; Soc Appl Spectros; Optical Soc Am; AAAS. *Res:* Trace analysis primarily by spectrochemical means; atomic emission, atomic absoprtion and atomic fluorescence; development and application of photoacoustic spectroscopy; applications of computers in chemistry. *Mailing Add:* Dept Chem Univ Ga Athens GA 30602

COLEMAN, GEORGE HUNT, b San Gabriel, Calif, Oct 15, 28; m 53; c 3. NUCLEAR CHEMISTRY. *Educ:* Univ Calif, Berkeley, AB, 50; Univ Calif, Los Angeles, PhD(chem), 58. *Prof Exp:* Chemist, Calif Res & Develop Co, Livermore, 51-53; sr chemist, Lawrence Radiation Lab, 57-69; assoc prof, 69-77, head dept, 76-79, PROF CHEM, NEBR WESLEYAN UNIV, 77- *Mem:* Am Chem Soc. *Res:* Radiocarbon dating; activation analysis. *Mailing Add:* Dept of Chem Nebr Wesleyan Univ Lincoln NE 68504

COLEMAN, GEORGE W(ILLIAM), b Watertown, Mass, July 4, 00; m 44; c 1. CHEMISTRY, METALLURGY. *Educ:* Tufts Col, BS, 23; Mass Inst Technol, MS, 37; Temple Bar, ScD(metall), 39. *Prof Exp:* Res chemist & metallurgist, Waltham Watch Co, 23-33; res assoc, Mass Inst Technol, 35-37; chief metallurgist & chemist, Parker Mfg Co, 38-57, dir res, 57-75; CONSULT, 75- *Mem:* AAAS; Am Chem Soc; fel Am Inst Chem; Am Inst Mining, Metall & Petrol Engrs; NY Acad Sci. *Res:* Hair springs; forgings; electroplating; heat treating of steel; electropolishing. *Mailing Add:* 10 Meadow Lane PO Box 284 Southborough MA 01772

COLEMAN, HOWARD S, b Everett, Pa, Jan 10, 17; m 41; c 4. ELECTROOPTICS, RENEWABLE ENERGY. *Educ:* Pa State Univ, BS, 38, MS, 39, PhD(physics), 42. *Prof Exp:* Asst, Pa State Univ, 39-40, instr phys sci, 40-42; dir optical inspection lab, 42-47; assoc prof physics & tech dir optical res lab, Univ Tex, 47-51; dir, Sci Bur, Bausch & Lomb Optical Co, NY, 51-56, vpres in charge res & eng, 56-62; head physics res & tech asst to vpres for res, Melpar, Inc, Va, 62-64; dean, Col Eng, Univ Ariz, 64-68; res engr, Schellinger Res Labs, Univ Tex, El Paso, 68-69, dir spec projs, 69-75; DIR, HOWARD S COLEMAN & ASSOCS, 75-; dir, Div Cent Solar Technol, 76-81, DEP ASST SECY CONSERV & RENEWABLE ENERGY, DEPT ENERGY, 81- *Concurrent Pos:* Consult, Xerox Corp, Burr-Brown Co, Kollsman Instrument Co, Melpar, Inc, Singer Co, NSF, NASA & Univ Calif, San Diego. *Honors & Awards:* Serv Tech Award, Depts Army & Navy-Am Acad Motion Picture Arts & Sci, 42. *Mem:* Nat Soc Prof Eng; Am Asn Physics Teachers; Am Soc Metals; Am Soc Eng Educ; fel Optical Soc Am. *Res:* Properties of optical instruments; guided missiles; atmospheric physics; solar energy; lasers; hydrology; optical radiometry; night vision; countermeasures; camouflage; topography; simulation and consulting assistance in test and evaluation of weapon systems. *Mailing Add:* PO Box 26368 El Paso TX 79926

COLEMAN, JAMES ANDREW, b Niagara Falls, NY, Mar 11, 21; m 47; c 2. THEORETICAL PHYSICS. *Educ:* NY Univ, BA, 46; Columbia Univ, MA, 47. *Prof Exp:* Assoc physicist, Appl Physics Lab, Johns Hopkins Univ, 47-50; instr physics & astron, Conn Col Women, 50-57; PROF PHYSICS & CHMN DEPT, AM INT COL, 57- *Concurrent Pos:* Mem guided missile subcomt, Res & Develop Bd, 48-50; NSF fac fel, 58- *Mem:* AAAS; Am Phys Soc; Am Astron Soc; Am Asn Physics Teachers; Nat Asn Sci Writers. *Res:* Astronomy; relativity; cosmology. *Mailing Add:* Dept Physics Am Int Col 1000 State St Springfield MA 01109

COLEMAN, JAMES EDWARD, b Newport, Ark, Oct 6, 28; m 54; c 3. PHYSICAL CHEMISTRY. *Educ:* La State Univ, BS, 50, MS, 52; Ohio State Univ, PhD(chem), 59. *Prof Exp:* Lab asst, La State Univ, 50-52; asst boron chem, Ohio State Univ, 52-58; chemist long range fuels, Esso Stand Oil Co, La, 59-60 & spec proj unit, Esso Res & Eng Co, NJ, 60-63, sr chemist, 63-64, sr chemist, Process Res Div, 64-68; assoc prof, 68-72, PROF CHEM, FAIRMONT STATE COL, 72- *Mem:* Am Chem Soc. *Res:* Boron chemistry; rocket propellants; synthesis and thermal stability of high energy fuels. *Mailing Add:* Dept Chem Fairmont State Col Fairmont WV 26554

COLEMAN, JAMES MALCOLM, b Vinton, La, Nov 19, 35; m 58. GEOMORPHOLOGY. *Educ:* La State Univ, BS, 58, MS, 62, PhD(geol), 66. *Prof Exp:* Assoc researcher geol, 60-66, asst dir, Coastal Studies Inst, 70-75, from asst prof to prof sedimentol, 66-80, BOYD PROF, LA STATE UNIV, BATON ROUGE, 80-, DIR, COASTAL STUDIES INST, 75- *Concurrent Pos:* Leader of numerous clastic sandstone seminars for industry; dir recent & ancient deltaic deposits seminar, NSF grants, 67, 69 & 71; mem sedimentary processes panel, Gulf Univs Res Consortium, 67; mem ad hoc comt on EPakistan, Nat Acad Sci; mem, Prog Develop Coun, Gulf Univs Res Consortium, 80. *Honors & Awards:* A I Levorsen Award, Am Asn Petrol Geologists, 74; Shepard Award, Soc Econ Paleontologists & Mineralogists, 80. *Res:* Relationships between process and form and sedimentary characteristics of recent environments, especially in deltaic and offshore regions. *Mailing Add:* Coastal Studies Inst La State Univ Baton Rouge LA 70803

COLEMAN, JAMES R, b New York, NY, Nov 24, 37; m 59; c 2. ANALYTICAL CHEMISTRY. *Educ:* St Peter's Col, BS, 59; NY Univ, MS, 61; Duke Univ, PhD(cytol), 64. *Prof Exp:* Asst cytol, Inst Muscle Dis, 60; asst zool, Duke Univ, 61-62, res assoc cell biol, Dept Anat, 64; NIH fel, 64-65; from asst prof to assoc prof, Dept Radiation Biol & Biophys, Sch Med & Dent, Univ Rochester, 65-81; SR SCIENTIST, EASTMAN KODAK CO, 81- *Concurrent Pos:* Assoc dir educ, Univ Rochester. *Honors & Awards:* Nat lectr, Microbeam Soc, 79. *Mem:* Am Soc Cell Biol; Histochem Soc; Sigma Xi; Microbean Anal Soc; AAAS. *Res:* Cytology; histochemistry; light and electron microscopy; electron probe analysis. *Mailing Add:* 154 Mareeta Rd Rochester NY 14605

COLEMAN, JAMES ROLAND, b Kansas City, Mo, Oct 12, 46; m 71. NEUROSCIENCE, PHYSIOLOGICAL PSYCHOLOGY. *Educ:* Univ Calif, Los Angeles, BA, 69, MA, 71, PhD(psychol), 74. *Prof Exp:* MHTP trainee, Brain Res Inst, Univ Calif, Los Angeles, 69-73, res asst dept psychol, 73-74; fel neurosci, Duke Univ, 74-76; asst prof, 77-81, ASSOC PROF PSYCHOL, UNIV SC, 81- *Concurrent Pos:* Adj asst prof physiol, Sch Med, Univ SC, 78-81, adj assoc prof physiol, 81- *Mem:* AAAS; Am Asn Anatomists; Asn Res Otolaryngol; Soc Neurosci. *Res:* Developmental mechanism in central auditory structures; organization of central auditory and visual pathways; organization and function of limbic pathways. *Mailing Add:* Dept of Psychol Univ of SC Columbia SC 29208

COLEMAN, JAMES STAFFORD, b CleElum, Wash, May 8, 28; m 64; c 6. ENERGY RESEARCH. *Educ:* Wash State Univ, BS, 50; Mass Inst Technol, PhD(physical chem), 53. *Prof Exp:* Mem staff, Los Alamos Nat Lab, 53-67; chemist, Div Res, Atomic Energy Comn, 67-69, tech adv, Off Gen Mgr, 69-75; asst div dir, Div Physical Res, Energy Res & Develop Admin, 75-77; DIV DIR, OFF ENERGY RES, DEPT ENERGY, 77- *Mem:* Sigma Xi; AAAS. *Res:* Engineering; mathematics; computer sciences; earth sciences. *Mailing Add:* 12416 Deoudes Rd Boyds MD 20841

COLEMAN, JOHN DEE, b Dozier, Tex, Oct 2, 32; m 54; c 3. ANIMAL NUTRITION. *Educ:* Tex A&M Univ, DVM, 56; Auburn Univ, MS, 62. *Prof Exp:* Vet prev med, US Army, 60-62; sr res scientist feedlot dis, Abbott Labs, 64-68; pvt pract vet med, 68-70; assoc prof dis res, Tex A&M Univ, 70-76; ASST V PRES BACTERIN PROD, FRANKLIN LABS, DIV AM HOME PROD CORP, 76- *Mem:* Am Vet Med Asn; Am Soc Animal Sci; Am Asn Vet Nutritionists (secy-treas, 67-69); Am Asn Bovine Practitioners. *Res:* Diseases of feedlot cattle; nutrition of feedlot cattle; immunology of clostridial bacterin-toxoids. *Mailing Add:* 705 15th St Canyon TX 79015

COLEMAN, JOHN FRANKLIN, b Akron, Ohio, July 15, 39; m 61; c 3. ORGANIC CHEMISTRY, POLYMER CHEMISTRY. *Educ:* Univ Akron, BS, 61; Univ Ill, MS, 63, PhD(org chem), 66. *Prof Exp:* Asst gen chemist inorg chem, Univ Ill, 61-62, res asst org chem, 62-65; polymer res chemist, 65-67, 69-70, sr adhesives res chemist, 70-73, group leader, 73-74, sect leader mat, 74-77, res & develop mgr, New Plastics, B F Goodrich Res & Develop Ctr, 77-79, GEN MGR, NEW PLASTICS, B F GOODRICH CHEM GROUP, 79- *Mem:* Am Chem Soc. *Res:* Polymerization of vinyl monomers; polymer modifications; condensation polymerization; adhesives; fire retardant additives; thermally stable polymers; materials technology. *Mailing Add:* 2465 Olentangy Dr Akron OH 44313

COLEMAN, JOHN HOWARD, b Danville, Va, Aug 21, 25; m 64; c 5. PHYSICAL ELECTRONICS, LASER CHEMISTRY. *Educ:* Univ Va, BEE, 46. *Prof Exp:* Res physicist electronics, RCA Labs, NJ, 46-50; pres physics, Radiation Res Corp, 50-67; PRES PHYSICS, PLASMA PHYSICS CORP, 67- *Mem:* Am Phys Soc; AAAS; NY Acad Sci; Inst Elec & Electronics Engrs; Am Inst Metall Engrs. *Res:* Plasma deposition of semiconductor films and laser isotope separation. *Mailing Add:* Plasma Physics Corp PO Box 548 Locust Valley NY 11560

COLEMAN, JOHN RUSSELL, b Medford, Ore, Nov 4, 33; m 58; c 3. DEVELOPMENTAL BIOLOGY. *Educ:* Univ Minn, AB, 55; Ind Univ, MA, 57; Johns Hopkins Univ, PhD(biol), 61. *Prof Exp:* Res assoc develop biol, Univ Conn, 62-63; asst prof, 63-69, assoc prof, 69-78, PROF BIOL, BROWN UNIV, 78-, CHMN DEVELOP BIOL SECT, 80- *Concurrent Pos:* NIH spec res fel, Univ Calif, San Diego, 69-70; mem cell biol study sect, NIH, 74-78; Fogarty int fel, Karolinska Inst, Stockholm, Sweden, 76-77. *Mem:* AAAS; Am Soc Cell Biol; Am Soc Zool; Int Soc Develop Biologists. *Res:* Differentiation of chicken embryo cells in culture-myogenesis, protein and RNA synthesis, genome organizations and expression, physiological maturation, hormone function; cell reconstitution. *Mailing Add:* Div of Biol & Med Sci Brown Univ Providence RI 02912

COLEMAN, JOHN SHERRARD, b Honolulu, Hawaii, Jan 15, 14; m 44; c 2. PHYSICS. *Educ:* Col William & Mary, BS, 35; Mass Inst Technol, SM, 40. *Prof Exp:* Construct supt, Washington, DC, 36-37; tech aide, Nat Defense Res Comt, Mass, 40-43; res assoc, Harvard Univ, 43-44; tech aide, Off Sci Res & Develop, London, 44-45; asst dir summary reports group, Columbia Univ, 45-46; exec secy, Comt Undersea Warfare, 47-53, exec secy, Div Phys Sci, 53-65, EXEC OFFICER, DIV PHYS SCI, NAT ACAD SCI-NAT RES COUN, 65- *Concurrent Pos:* Prof, Pa State Univ, 53. *Honors & Awards:* Meritorious Pub Serv Award, US Navy, 58. *Res:* Systems analysis; research and development administration. *Mailing Add:* Nat Acad of Sci 2101 Constitution Ave Washington DC 20418

COLEMAN, JOSEPH EMORY, b Iowa City, Iowa, Oct 11, 30; m 61; c 1. BIOCHEMISTRY, BIOPHYSICS. *Educ:* Univ Va, BA, 53, MD, 57; Mass Inst Technol, PhD(biophys), 63. *Prof Exp:* Intern med, Peter Bent Brigham Hosp, Harvard Sch Med, 57-58, Nat Acad Sci fel biophys, 48-59, NIH fel, 59-62, univ res fel, Biophys Res Lab, 58-63, sr resident med, Peter Bent Brigham Hosp, 63-64; from asst prof to assoc prof biochem, 64-74, PROF MOLECULAR BIOPHYS & BIOCHEM, YALE UNIV, 74- *Mem:* Am Chem Soc; Am Soc Biol Chemists. *Res:* Physical chemistry of proteins; mechanisms of enzyme action; metalloenzymes. *Mailing Add:* Dept of Molecular Biophys & Biochem Yale Univ New Haven CT 06510

COLEMAN, JULES VICTOR, b Brooklyn, NY, Nov 2, 07; m 32; c 2. PSYCHIATRY. *Educ:* Cornell Univ, AB, 28; Univ Vienna, MD, 34; Am Bd Psychiat & Neurol, dipl, 46. *Prof Exp:* Dir, East Harlem Unit, Delinquency Proj, Bur Child Guid, 41-42; head ment hyg div, Med Ctr, Univ Colo, 46-50; psychiatrist, Dept Univ Health, 50-52, clin prof psychiat, Sch Med, 52-62, chief ment health sect, Dept Epidemiol & Pub Health, 62-74, dir social & community psychiat training prog, 70-73, CLIN PROF PUB HEALTH & PSYCHIAT, SCH MED, YALE UNIV, 62- *Concurrent Pos:* Lectr, Sch Social Work, Univ Denver, 46-50; consult, Community Serv Comn, USPHS, 47-49, State Dept Health, Colo, 47-50 & Health Dept, New York, 49; mem nat tech fact finding comt, Mid-Century White House Conf Children & Youth, 50; assoc dir, Bur Ment Hyg, State Dept Health, Conn, 50-52; physician-in-chief, Psychiat Clin, New Haven Hosp, 52-56; consult, Vet Admin Hosp, West Haven, 53-; mem psychiat training rev comt, NIH, 65-69, chmn, 67-69; mem, Conn State Bd Ment Health, 65-71, chmn, 69-71; chief ment health & psychiat, Community Health Care Ctr Plan, New Haven, 71-78. *Mem:* Am Psychiat Asn; Am Orthopsychiat Asn; Asn Psychiat Clins Children (pres, 49-51); Am Psychoanal Asn. *Res:* Psychotherapy; health management organization psychiatry. *Mailing Add:* 135 Whitney Ave New Haven CT 06510

COLEMAN, LAMAR WILLIAM, b Philadelphia, Pa, Feb 19, 34; m 62; c 2. INERTIAL CONFINEMENT FUSION, DIAGNOSTICS. *Educ:* Va Mil Inst, 55; Ore State Univ, MS, 58, PhD(physics), 63. *Prof Exp:* Res assoc, nuclear physics, Ore State Univ, 63-64; physicist, 64-69, group leader, 69-79, dep assoc prog leader, 79-81, ASSOC PROG LEADER FUSION EXP, LAWRENCE LIVERMORE NAT LAB, 81- *Mem:* Am Phys Soc. *Res:* Inertial confinement fusion and high resolution diagnostics development and applications; high energy density physics and pulsed power systems. *Mailing Add:* L-473 Lawrence Livermore Nat Lab Livermore CA 94550

COLEMAN, LAWRENCE BRUCE, b Baltimore, Md, Feb 29, 48; m 71. SOLID STATE PHYSICS. *Educ:* Johns Hopkins Univ, BA, 70; Univ Pa, PhD(physics), 75. *Prof Exp:* Fel physics, Univ Pa, 75-76; ASST PROF PHYSICS, UNIV CALIF, DAVIS, 76- *Concurrent Pos:* Regent's jr fac fel, Univ Calif, Davis, 77-78. *Mem:* Am Phys Soc. *Res:* Experimental solid state physics; far infrared spectroscopy and transport properties of quasi-one dimensional solids and superionic conductors. *Mailing Add:* Dept of Physics Univ of Calif Davis CA 95616

COLEMAN, LESLIE CHARLES, b Toronto, Ont, Oct 22, 26; m 52; c 2. GEOLOGY. *Educ:* Queen's Univ, Can, BA, 50, MA, 52; Princeton Univ, PhD(geol), 55. *Prof Exp:* Instr geol, Tulane Univ, 55-56; vis asst prof, Lafayette Col, 56-57; asst prof mineral, Ohio State Univ, 57-60; from asst prof to assoc prof, 60-70, PROF GEOL, UNIV SASK, 70- *Mem:* Geol Soc Am; Mineral Soc Am; Geochem Soc; Geol Asn Can; Mineral Asn Can. *Res:* Distribution of trace metals in bedrock and relationship to the geology of the Hanson Lake area in Saskatchewan; mineralogy, petrology and geochemistry of meteorites and volcanic rocks. *Mailing Add:* Dept of Geol Sci Univ of Sask Saskatoon Can

COLEMAN, LESTER EARL, (JR), b Akron, Ohio, Nov 6, 30; m 51; c 2. ORGANIC CHEMISTRY, POLYMER CHEMISTRY. *Educ:* Univ Akron, BS, 52; Univ Ill, MS, 53, PhD(chem), 55. *Prof Exp:* Chemist, Polymer Res Div, Goodyear Tire & Rubber Co, 51-52; asst gen chem, Univ Ill, 52-53, chemist res, Govt Synthetic Rubber Prog, 53-55; chemist, Lubrizol Corp, 55; proj engr, Polymer Sect, Mat Lab, Wright Air Develop Ctr, US Air Force, 55-57; proj leader additive res dept, 59-64, dir org res, 64-68, asst div head res & develop, 68-72, asst to the pres, 72-73, exec vpres, 74-76, DIR, LUBRIZOL CORP, 77-, PRES, 76-, CENT EXEC OFFICER, 78- *Concurrent Pos:* Dir, Ferro Corp, 76-81, Soc Corp & Soc Nat Bank, 78-, Norfolk & Western Rwy Co, 80-, S C Johnson & Son, Inc, 81- *Mem:* Am Chem Soc; Chem Mfrs Asn; Soc Chem Indust. *Res:* Synthesis and polymerization of vinyl monomers; synthetic organic chemistry; lubricant additives. *Mailing Add:* 35850 Eddy Rd Willoughby Hills OH 44094

COLEMAN, LESTER F, b Burrwood, La, Jan 30, 22; m 53; c 3. CHEMICAL & NUCLEAR ENGINEERING. *Educ:* Tulane Univ, BE, 43. *Prof Exp:* Foreman & tech supvr, Y12 Plant, Tenn Eastman Corp, 43-45; from asst chem engr to assoc chem engr, 46-68, CHEM ENGR, ARGONNE NAT LAB, 68- *Mem:* Instrument Soc Am; Sigma Xi. *Res:* Nuclear fuel processing; radiation shielding design; process instrumentation; glovebox and gas purification system design; safety engineering; criticality hazards control. *Mailing Add:* Argonne Nat Lab 9700 S Cass Ave Argonne IL 60439

COLEMAN, MARCIA LEPRI, b New Haven, Conn. CHEMICAL PHYSICS, POLYMER PHYSICS. *Educ:* Mt Holyoke Col, BA, 69; Mass Inst Technol, PhD(chem physics), 73. *Prof Exp:* res chemist polymer physics & chem, Elastomer Chem Dept, 73-79, SR RES SUPVR, POLYMER PROD DEPT, E I DU PONT DE NEMOURS & CO, INC, 79- *Mem:* AAAS; Am Chem Soc; Am Inst Physics. *Res:* Polymer chemistry and physics. *Mailing Add:* Exp Sta Bldg 353 E I du Pont de Nemours & Co Inc Wilmington DE 19803

COLEMAN, MARILYN A, b Lancaster, SC, March 27, 46; m 68; c 2. GROWTH PHYSIOLOGY, REPRODUCTIVE PHYSIOLOGY. *Educ:* Univ SC, BS, 68; Auburn Univ, PhD(physiol), 76. *Prof Exp:* Teaching asst hist, Univ SC, 67-68; instr biol, Brunswick Co Schs, 68-69; teaching asst biol, Va Polytech Inst & State Univ, 70-72; res asst physiol, Auburn Univ, 73-76; asst prof poultry sci, physiol & mgt, 77-82, ASSOC PROF PHARMACOL, OHIO STATE UNIV, 82-; PRES POULTRY PHYSIOL & MGT, MAC ASSOCS, 82- *Concurrent Pos:* Consult, poultry co allied indust, 77-; guest lectgr, Regional Poultry Hatchability Schs, 77- *Mem:* Am Physiol Soc; Poultry Sci Asn; World Poultry Sci Asn; Sigma Xi. *Res:* Effects of environment and management on reproductive performance and hatchability of poultry; instrumental in development of computerized incubation system, software and other equipment for poultry incubation and reproductive management. *Mailing Add:* MAC Assocs 2532 Zollinger Rd Columbus OH 43221

COLEMAN, MARY SUE, b Richmond, Ky, Oct 2, 43; m 65; c 1. ENZYMOLOGY, PROTEIN STRUCTURE. *Educ:* Grinnell Col, BA, 65; Univ NC, PhD(biochem), 69. *Prof Exp:* Fel, Univ NC, 69-70, Univ Tex, 70-71; fel, 71-72, instr biochem, 72-75, asst prof, 75-80, ASSOC PROF BIOCHEM, UNIV KY, 80- *Concurrent Pos:* Actg dir basic sci, McDowell Cancer Ctr, Univ Ky, 80-; PBC study sect, NIH, 80-84. *Mem:* Am Chem Soc; AAAS; Am Soc Biol Chemists. *Res:* Purified human enzymes, their structure-function relationships and regulation of expression of these enzymes at genetic level. *Mailing Add:* Dept Biochem Univ Ky Lexington KY 40536

COLEMAN, MICHAEL MURRAY, b Herne Bay, Eng, Jan 24, 38. POLYMER SCIENCE. *Educ:* Borough Polytech, Eng, BSc, 68; Case Western Reserve Univ, MS, 71, PhD(polymer sci), 73. *Prof Exp:* Assayer chem, Rhokana Corp Ltd, Zambia, 55-61; anal chemist, Johnson Mathey Ltd, Eng, 63-64; res chemist polymers, Revertex Ltd, Eng, 68-69 & E I du Pont de Nemours & Co, 73-75; asst prof, 75-78, ASSOC PROF POLYMERS, PA STATE UNIV, UNIVERSITY PARK, 78- *Mem:* Am Chem Soc; Royal Inst Chem; Am Phys Soc. *Res:* Polymer physical chemistry; polymer characterization; infrared, Raman and NMR spectroscopy as applied to polymers; vulcanization elastomers. *Mailing Add:* Dept of Mat Sci Pa State Univ University Park PA 16802

COLEMAN, MORTON, b Norfolk, Va, Sept 15, 39; m 68; c 3. HEMATOLOGY, ONCOLOGY. *Educ:* Johns Hopkins Univ, BA, 59; Med Col Va, MD, 63. *Prof Exp:* Asst prof, 68-75, ASSOC PROF MED, MED COL, CORNELL UNIV, 75- *Concurrent Pos:* Asst attend physician, New York Hosp, 68-75, assoc attend physician, 75-; assoc dir oncol serv, New York Hosp-Cornell Med Ctr, 68-; consult, Doctors Hosp, New York, 69- & Manhattan Eye, Ear, Nose & Throat Hosp, 70-, New Rochelle Hosp, 80-;

assoc dir clin chemother prog cancer control, Nat Cancer Inst-New York Hosp, 74-; chmn new agents comt, Cancer & Leukemia Group B, 75- *Mem:* Int Soc Hemat; Am Soc Hemat; Am Soc Clin Oncol; Soc Study Blood; Harvey Soc. *Res:* Clinical research in new chemotherapeutic agents for blood and lymphatic malignancies. *Mailing Add:* 525 E 68th St New York NY 10021

COLEMAN, NEIL LLOYD, b Belvidere, Ill, Sept 3, 30; m 52. GEOLOGY, FLUID MECHANICS. *Educ:* Cornell Col, BA, 52; Univ Chicago, MS, 57, PhD(geol), 60. *Prof Exp:* GEOLOGIST, SEDIMENTATION LAB, AGR RES SERV, USDA, 59-, LAB DIR, 81- *Concurrent Pos:* Assoc prof civil eng, Univ Miss, 61- *Mem:* Am Geophys Union; Int Asn Hydraul Res. *Res:* Soil erosion; sediment transportation and deposition; mechanics of flow in natural and artificial streams or channels. *Mailing Add:* Sedimentation Lab USDA PO Box 1157 Oxford MS 38655

COLEMAN, NORMAN P, JR, b Richmond, Va, Mar 13, 42. APPLIED MATHEMATICS, ELECTRICAL ENGINEERING. *Educ:* Univ Va, BA, 65; Vanderbilt Univ, MA, 68, PhD(math), 69. *Prof Exp:* Mathematician, E I du Pont de Nemours & Co, Inc, 65; instr math, Vanderbilt Univ, 68-69; mathematician, Hq, US Army Weapons Command, 71-77, MATHEMATICIAN, US ARMY ARMAMENT RES & DEVELOP COMMAND, DOVER, 77- *Concurrent Pos:* Adj prof, Col Eng, Univ Iowa, 71- *Mem:* Soc Indust & Appl Math; Am Math Soc; Sigma Xi. *Res:* Function algebras; necessary conditions for existence of complemented subspaces; operator theory; application of the theory of perturbation for linear operations to development of algorithms in optimal design and optimal control theory; development of microprocessor based pointing and tracking systems; robotics; general engineering. *Mailing Add:* US Army Armament Res & Develop Command Dover NJ 07801

COLEMAN, OTTO HARVEY, b Denver, Colo, June 26, 05; m 35; c 3. AGRONOMY. *Educ:* Colo State Univ, BS, 34, MS, 37. *Prof Exp:* Asst agronomist, State Agr Exp Sta, Univ Colo, 35-42; asst agronomist, Sugar Plant Field Sta, Miss, 42-44 & Fla, 45-46, assoc agronomist in charge sorgo breeding, 47-54, sta supt & res agronomist, Miss, 54-70, COLLABR SUGAR CROPS FIELD STA, SCI & EDUC ADMIN-AGR RES, USDA, 70- *Mem:* AAAS; Am Soc Agron; Am Soc Sugar Cane Technol; Am Genetic Asn. *Res:* Genetics of barley and of HCN in Sudan grass; design of agricultural experiments; sugar cane breeding for sirup; breeding sorgo for sirup and sugar; sorghum genetics. *Mailing Add:* PO Box 3188 Meridian MS 39301

COLEMAN, P(AUL) D(ARE), b Stoystown, Pa, June 4, 18; m 42; c 2. ELECTRICAL ENGINEERING. *Educ:* Susquehanna Univ, BA, 40; Pa State Univ, MS, 42; Mass Inst Technol, PhD(physics), 51. *Hon Degrees:* DSc, Susquehanna Univ, 78. *Prof Exp:* Asst physics, Pa State Univ, 40-42; physicist, Wright Air Develop Command, 42-46; res assoc physics, res lab electronics, Mass Inst Tech & physicist, Cambridge Air Res Ctr, 46-51; assoc prof elec eng, 51-57, dir, microwave lab, 54-64, PROF ELEC ENG, UNIV ILL, CHAMPAIGN-URBANA, 57-, DIR ELECTRO-PHYSICS LAB, 54- *Concurrent Pos:* Consult, Ramo-Wooldridge Corp & High Voltage Corp, 58, FXR, Inc, 59-65, McDonnell-Douglas Corp, Argonne Nat Lab, 65- & Northrop Corp, 78-; mem, Nat Acad Sci-Nat Bur Standards Panel 272 & Int Sci Radio Union Comn I; treas, Electron Device Res Conf, 66-; assoc ed, J Quantum Electronics. *Mem:* Am Phys Soc; fel Inst Elec & Electronics Engrs; Sigma Xi. *Res:* Quantum electronics; chemical and molecular lasers; far infrared physics; non-linear optics; millimeter and sub-millimeter waves; megavolt electronics. *Mailing Add:* 710 Park Lane Champaign IL 61820

COLEMAN, PAUL DAVID, b New York, NY, Dec 2, 27; m 55; c 2. NEUROBIOLOGY. *Educ:* Tufts Univ, AB, 48; Univ Rochester, PhD(physiol psychol), 53. *Prof Exp:* Asst auditory physiol, Univ Rochester, 48-51, asst statist, 51-52; res psychologist, Army Med Res Lab, 54-56; asst prof & res assoc, Inst Appl Exp Psychol, Tufts Univ, 56-59; Nat Inst Neurol Dis & Stroke fel, Dept Anat, Johns Hopkins Univ, 59-62; assoc prof physiol, Sch Med, Univ Md, Baltimore County, 62-67; PROF ANAT, SCH MED, UNIV ROCHESTER, 67- *Concurrent Pos:* Assoc, Computer Ctr, Mass Inst Technol, 57-59. *Mem:* AAAS; Am Psychol Asn; Am Statist Asn; Soc Neurosci; Am Asn Anat. *Res:* Neuroanatomy; sensory physiology; brain-behavior relations; effects of early environment on quantitative aspects of brain; central nervous system aging. *Mailing Add:* Dept of Anat Univ of Rochester Sch of Med Rochester NY 14620

COLEMAN, PAUL JEROME, JR, b Evanston, Ill, Mar 7, 32; m 64; c 2. SPACE PHYSICS. *Educ:* Univ Mich, BS(eng math) & BS(eng physics), 54, MS, 58; Univ Calif, Los Angeles, PhD(space physics), 66. *Prof Exp:* Mem tech staff, Space Tech Labs, Inc, Calif, 58-61; head interplanetary sci prog, NASA, DC, 61-62; res scientist, 62-66, assoc prof, 66-71, PROF GEOPHY & SPACE PHYSICS, UNIV CALIF, LOS ANGELES, 71-; ASST DIR, LOS ALAMOS NAT LAB, 81- *Mem:* AAAS; Am Geophys Union; Am Phys Soc; Am Inst Aeronaut & Astronaut; Soc Explor Geophysicists. *Res:* Experimental space physics, including measurements of charged particles and magnetic fields in space and measurements of planetary magnetic fields. *Mailing Add:* Dept of Earth & Space Sci Univ of Calif Los Angeles CA 90024

COLEMAN, PETER STEPHEN, b New York, NY, Feb 10, 38; m 69; c 1. BIOCHEMISTRY, BIOPHYSICS. *Educ:* Columbia Univ, AB, 59, PhD(biophys, biol), 66. *Prof Exp:* Res fel mechanochem, Polymer Dept, Weizmann Inst Sci, Israel, 67-68; res fel biochem & biophys, Yale Univ, 68-70, Nat Cancer Inst fel, 68-69; asst prof, 70-75, dir grad studies, Dept Biol, 78-79, ASSOC PROF BIOCHEM, MED SCH, NY UNIV, 75-, ASSOC PROF BASIC MED SCI, 77- *Mem:* AAAS; Am Chem Soc; Am Soc Cell Biol; Biophys Soc. *Res:* Oxidative phosphorylation, mechanisms of coupling; cellular bioenergetics; tumor cell metabolism; membrane biochemistry. *Mailing Add:* Dept Biol NY Univ New York NY 10003

COLEMAN, PHILIP HOXIE, b Fredericksburg, Va, May 11, 33; m 53. VIROLOGY. *Educ:* Univ Ga, DVM, 56; Univ Wis, MS, 57, PhD(vet microbiol), 59. *Prof Exp:* Asst chief southeast rabies lab, Nat Commun Dis Ctr, USPHS, 50-60, asst chief zoonosis res unit, 60-61, in chg arbovirus lab, 61-66, asst chief biol reagents sect, 66-68, chief arbovirus infectious unit, 68-69; PROF MICROBIOL & DIR CENT ANIMAL FACIL, MED COL VA, VA COMMONWEALTH UNIV, 69- *Mem:* Am Vet Med Asn; Sci Res Soc Am; Am Soc Microbiol; Soc Exp Biol & Med; Am Soc Trop Med & Hyg. *Res:* Laboratory aspects of arthropod-borne viruses in relation to their public health significance. *Mailing Add:* Med Col of Va Health Sci Div Va Commonwealth Univ Richmond VA 23298

COLEMAN, PHILIP LYNN, b Denver, Colo, Dec 25, 44; m 68; c 2. APPLIED PHYSICS. *Educ:* Calif Inst Technol, BS, 66; Univ Wis-Madison, PhD(physics), 71. *Prof Exp:* Res assoc space physics, Univ Wis-Madison, 71-72 & Rice Univ, 72-73; SCI STAFF MEM SHOCK PHYSICS, SYSTS, SCI & SOFTWARE, 73- *Mem:* AAAS; Am Astron Soc. *Res:* Shock-wave physics; explosively induced ground motion; instrumentation for transient, high pressure shocks; applied physics. *Mailing Add:* Systs Sci & Software PO Box 1620 La Jolla CA 92038

COLEMAN, RALPH H, b Winslow, Ind, Jan 20, 12; m 46; c 3. MATHEMATICS, STATISTICS. *Educ:* Oakland City Col, AB, 31; Ind Univ, AM, 32, PhD(math, educ), 56. *Prof Exp:* Teacher & prin high sch, 32-43; army training specialist math, Ind Univ, 43-44; teacher & prin high sch, 44-46; instr math, Univ Evansville, 46-78, chmn dept, 56-77, actg vpres acad affairs, 77-78; RETIRED. *Res:* Components of success in college mathematics. *Mailing Add:* Dept of Math Univ of Evansville Evansville IN 47704

COLEMAN, RALPH ORVAL, JR, b Corvallis, Ore, Dec 9, 31; m 64; c 2. SPEECH PATHOLOGY, AUDIOLOGY. *Educ:* Ore State Univ, BS, 54; Univ Ore, MS, 60; Northwestern Univ, PhD(speech path), 63. *Prof Exp:* Asst prof speech path, Univ Nebr, 63-65; res speech pathologist, Lancaster Cleft Palate Clin, 65-66; ASSOC PROF SPEECH PATH, ORE HEALTH SCI UNIV, PORTLAND, 66- *Concurrent Pos:* Mem summer fac, Eastern Ore Col, 69 & 71; guest researcher, Speech Transmission Lab, Royal Inst Technol, Stockholm, Sweden, 73; adj assoc prof, Univ Ore, 75- & Portland State Univ, 76- *Mem:* Am Asn Univ Prof; AAAS; fel Am Speech & Hearing Asn. *Res:* Disorders of human communication; the development of language in humans; child development specifically relating to the development of communicative function; developmental disability in children. *Mailing Add:* 2923 SE Tolman Portland OR 97202

COLEMAN, RICHARD NEAL, high energy physics, see previous edition

COLEMAN, RICHARD WALTER, b San Francisco, Calif, Sept 10, 22; div; c 1. ECOLOGY, BIOLOGY. *Educ:* Univ Calif, Berkeley, BA, 45, PhD(parasitol), 51. *Prof Exp:* Asst med entom, Univ Calif, Berkeley, 46, res asst med entom & helminth, 46-47 & 49-50; pvt supported res study, 51-61; prof biol & chmn dept, Curry Col, 61-63; chmn sci & math div, Monticello Col & Preparatory Sch, Ill, 63-64; vis prof biol, Wilberforce, 64-65; head, Dept Biol, 75-81, PROF SCI, UPPER IOWA UNIV, 65- *Concurrent Pos:* Collabr nat hist div, Nat Park Serv, 52-53; spec consult, Arctic Health Res Ctr, USPHS Alaska, 54-62; appointed explorer by Comnr of Northwest Territory, Can, 66. *Mem:* AAAS; Am Asn Univ Prof; Am Bryol & Lichenol Soc; Am Soc Limnol & Oceanog; Sigma Xi. *Res:* Zoology; botany. *Mailing Add:* Dept of Biol Upper Iowa Univ Fayette IA 52142

COLEMAN, ROBERT E, b Trenton, NJ, Apr 22, 21; m 44; c 5. PLANT PHYSIOLOGY. *Educ:* Swarthmore Col, AB, 43; Univ Pa, MS, 53; Univ Hawaii, PhD(bot), 56. *Prof Exp:* Plant physiologist, Field Crops Res Br, Agr Res Serv, USDA, La, 48-54, Co-op Proj Exp Sta, Hawaiian Sugar Planters Asn, Hawaii, 54-56, Field Crops Res Br, Agr Res Serv, USDA, 56-60 & Co-op Proj Exp Sta, Hawaiian Sugar Planters Asn, 60-67; invest leader sugarcane & sweet sorghum invests, Tobacco & Sugar Res Br, Plant Sci Res Div, 67-72, staff scientist, Nat Prog Staff, Sci & Educ Admin-Agr Res, USDA, 72-80; RETIRED. *Mem:* Fel AAAS; Am Soc Plant Physiol; Soc Sugar Cane Technol; Sigma Xi; Am Inst Biol Sci. *Res:* Sugar cane physiology; post harvest deterioration; freeze injury; germination; flowering. *Mailing Add:* 4483 Foothill Dr RD 4 Doylestown PA 18901

COLEMAN, ROBERT GRIFFIN, b Twin Falls, Idaho, Jan 5, 23; m 48; c 3. GEOLOGY. *Educ:* Ore State Col, BS, 48, MS, 50; Stanford Univ, PhD(geol), 57. *Prof Exp:* Instr geol, Ore State Col, 49 & La State Univ, 51-52; mineralogist, US AEC, 52-55; br chief isotope geol, US Geol Surv, 64-68, geologist, 55-81, br chief field geochem & petrol, 76-79; PROF GEOL, STANFORD UNIV, 81- *Concurrent Pos:* Vis lectr, Stanford Univ, 60; vis geologist, NZ Geol Surv, 62; tech adv, Saudi Arabia, 70-71; consult geol, Sultanate Oman, 73-74. *Mem:* Nat Acad Sci; Mineral Soc Am; Geol Soc Am. *Res:* Mineralogy and geochemistry of uranium ore deposits; geology and mineralogy of silicate and sulfide minerals as related to their origin; glaucophane schists and ultramafic rocks of California and New Zealand; new plate tectonic theories as applied to formation of ophiolites and glaucophane schists. *Mailing Add:* Geol Dept Stanford Univ Stanford CA 94305

COLEMAN, ROBERT J(OSEPH), b Pensacola, Fla, Jan 17, 41. ELECTRICAL ENGINEERING. *Educ:* Auburn Univ, BEE, 63, MSEE, 65, PhD(elec eng), 70. *Prof Exp:* Res asst, Auburn Res Found, 64-68; instr, Auburn Univ, 68-70; asst prof, 70-77, ASSOC PROF, UNIV NC, CHARLOTTE, 77- *Mem:* Am Inst Elec & Electronics Engrs; Am Soc Eng Educ. *Res:* Electromagnetic theory; microwave antennas; antenna research; design of circular and matrix antenna arrays; transverse electromagnetic-line arrays and elements; microwave theory and devices. *Mailing Add:* Col of Eng Univ of NC Charlotte NC 28223

COLEMAN, ROBERT MARSHALL, b Bridgton, Maine, Sept 27, 25; m 47; c 2. PARASITOLOGY, IMMUNOLOGY. *Educ:* Bates Col, BS, 50; Univ NH, MS, 51; Univ Notre Dame, PhD(parasitol), 54. *Prof Exp:* From instr to assoc prof microbiol, Russell Sage Col, 54-62; assoc prof, Boston Col, 62-68; head, Dept Biol Sci, 68-80, PROF MICROBIOL, UNIV LOWELL, 80- *Concurrent Pos:* Consult, AID, India, 65 & 68, Smithsonian, Egypt, 76, WHO, 77 & NSF, 80. *Mem:* NY Acad Sci; Am Soc Parasitol; Am Soc Microbiol; Am Soc Trop Med & Hyg. *Res:* Immunology of animal parasites; helminth antigens; malaria immuno-pathology; immune complexes; cytotoxic systems malaria. *Mailing Add:* Dept of Biol Sci Univ of Lowell Lowell MA 01854

COLEMAN, ROBERT VINCENT, b Iowa City, Iowa, Oct 11, 30. PHYSICS. *Educ:* Univ Va, BA, 53, PhD(physics), 56. *Prof Exp:* Mem tech staff physics, Res Labs, Gen Elec Co, 55; sr res physicist, Res Labs, Gen Motors Corp, 56-58; asst prof physics, Univ Ill, 58-60; from assoc prof to prof, 60-76, COMMONWEALTH PROF PHYSICS, UNIV VA, 76-, CHMN DEPT, 78- *Mem:* Fel Am Phys Soc. *Res:* Solid state physics; growth and properties of crystals; magnetism and low temperature physics; metals. *Mailing Add:* Dept of Physics Univ of Va McCormick Rd Charlottesville VA 22903

COLEMAN, RONALD LEON, b Wellington, Tex, Aug 20, 34; c 3. BIOCHEMISTRY. *Educ:* Abilene Christian Col, BS, 56; Univ Okla, PhD(biochem), 63. *Prof Exp:* From instr to assoc prof biochem, 63-75, PROF BIOCHEM & ENVIRON HEALTH, SCH MED, UNIV OKLA, 75- *Mem:* Am Chem Soc; Am Pub Health Asn; Am Indust Hyg Asn; Am Conf Govt Indust Hygienists; Am Col Toxicologists. *Res:* Trace metal metabolism; toxicology of carbon monoxide, cadmium, nickel, chromium, silver and mercury; biochemical function of zinc, manganese, magnesium, iron, cadmium, nickel and chromium. *Mailing Add:* Dept of Environ Health Univ of Okla Health Sci Ctr Oklahoma City OK 73104

COLEMAN, SIDNEY RICHARD, b Chicago, Ill, Mar 7, 37. THEORETICAL PHYSICS. *Educ:* Ill Inst Technol, BS, 57; Calif Inst Technol, PhD(physics), 62. *Prof Exp:* Corning Glass Works res fel, 61-63, from asst prof to assoc prof, 63-69, PROF PHYSICS, HARVARD UNIV, 69- *Concurrent Pos:* Sloan Found fel, 64-66. *Mem:* Nat Acad Sci; Am Acad Arts & Sci; Am Phys Soc. *Res:* Theoretical high-energy physics; symmetry principles. *Mailing Add:* Lyman Lab Dept Physics Harvard Univ Cambridge MA 02138

COLEMAN, THEO HOUGHTON, b Millport, Ala, Oct 25, 21; m 49. POULTRY SCIENCE. *Educ:* Ala Polytech Inst, BS, 43, MS, 48; Ohio State Univ, PhD(poultry genetics), 53. *Prof Exp:* Instr, Dept Poultry Sci, Ohio State Univ, 51-52; with com poultry farm, 51-52; from asst prof to prof poultry sci, 55-80, PROF ANIMAL SCI, MICH STATE UNIV, 80- *Mem:* AAAS; Genetics Soc Am; Am Genetic Asn; fel Poultry Sci Asn; World Poultry Sci Asn. *Res:* Fertility and hatchability in turkeys; effective use of visual aids in teaching; genetics, reproduction and behavior of quail. *Mailing Add:* Dept of Poultry Sci Mich State Univ East Lansing MI 48824

COLEMAN, WARREN KENT, b Stratford, Ont, Dec 30, 45; m 71. PLANT PHYSIOLOGY. *Educ:* Univ Western Ont, BA, 68, PhD(plant sci), 76. *Prof Exp:* Res assoc plant physiol, Dept Biol, Univ Calgary, 75-78; res dir, Agr Res & Develop, Golden West Res, 78; RES SCIENTIST, PLANT PHYSIOL, AGR CAN RES STA, FREDERICKTON, 79- *Res:* Plant physiology and experimental morphogenesis; descriptive morphology. *Mailing Add:* Agr Can Res Sta PO Box 20280 Fredericton Can

COLEMAN, WILLIAM EARL, organic chemistry, see previous edition

COLEMAN, WILLIAM FLETCHER, b Montgomery, WVa, Sept 15, 44; m 65. PHYSICAL INORGANIC CHEMISTRY, MOLECULAR SPECTROSCOPY. *Educ:* Eckerd Col, BS, 66; Ind Univ, PhD(chem), 70. *Prof Exp:* Fel, Univ Ariz, 70-71; asst prof, 71-75, ASSOC PROF CHEM, UNIV NMEX, 75- *Concurrent Pos:* Vis prof, Stanford Univ, 78. *Mem:* Am Chem Soc; AAAS; Optical Soc Am; Soc Appl Spectros; Laser Inst Am. *Res:* Photochemistry and spectroscopy of metal complexes; laser chemistry; photoelectrochemistry; inorganic complexes of biological interest; vibrational relaxation; excited state electron spin resonance spectroscopy; nonradiative transitions; photophysics of atoms and small molecules. *Mailing Add:* Dept of Chem Univ of NMex Albuquerque NM 87131

COLEMAN, WILLIAM GILMORE, JR, b Birmingham, Ala, May 6, 42. MOLECULAR BIOLOGY. *Educ:* Talladega Col, BS, 64; Atlanta Univ, MS, 70; Purdue Univ, PhD(molecular biol), 73. *Prof Exp:* Lab instr physiol & cytol, Atlanta Univ, 64-66; high sch teacher, David T Howard Community Adult Sch & elem sch teacher, Whiteford Elem Sch, 66-69; teaching asst cell biol, Purdue Univ, 70-73, vis prof, 73-74; staff fel, 74-77, sr staff fel, 77-79, RES MICROBIOLOGIST, LAB BIOCHEM PHARMACOL, NAT INST ARTHRITIS, METAB & DIGESTIVE DIS, NIH, 79-; ASST PROF, HOWARD UNIV, WASH, DC, 79- *Concurrent Pos:* Lectr, Howard Univ, Wash, DC, 77-79; mem, Nat Inst Arthritis, Metab & Digestive Dis Equal Employ Opportunity Adv Comt, 74-, chmn employee relations subcomt, 74- *Mem:* Am Soc Microbiol. *Res:* Mode of assembly and function of the outer membrane of Escherichia coli; biosynthesis of L-glycero-D-manno heptose, a typical component of lipopolysaccharides. *Mailing Add:* 9006 Burdette Rd Bethesda MD 20014

COLEMAN, WILLIAM H, b Chestertown, Md, Mar 6, 37. MICROBIOLOGY. *Educ:* Wash Col, BS, 59; Univ Chicago, MS, 62, PhD(microbiol), 67. *Prof Exp:* Instr biol, Univ Chicago, 65-66, 67-68; sr res technologist microbiol, 66-67; fel, Univ Colo, 68-71; asst prof, 71-81, ASSOC PROF BIOL, UNIV HARTFORD, 81- *Concurrent Pos:* Lilly Found fel, Yale Univ, 75; sabbatical, Dept Microbiol & Immunol, Univ Colo Med Ctr, Denver, 79. *Mem:* AAAS; Am Soc Microbiol; Sigma Xi. *Res:* RNA, protein purifications; protein synthesis in mammalian cells. *Mailing Add:* Dept Biol Univ Hartford West Hartford CT 06117

COLEN, ALAN HUGH, b Brooklyn, NY, Jan 29, 39; m 60; c 3. BIOPHYSICAL CHEMISTRY. *Educ:* Cornell Univ, BA, 60; Univ Wis, PhD(phys chem), 67. *Prof Exp:* Great Lakes Cols Asn-Kettering Found teaching intern chem, Kalamazoo Col, 66-67, asst prof, 67-70; res biochemist, Med Sch, Univ Kans, 70-72; RES CHEMIST, VET ADMIN HOSP, KANSAS CITY, MO, 72- *Concurrent Pos:* Consult, Upjohn Co, Mich, 67-68; Res Corp grant, 70; adj asst prof, Med Sch, Univ Kans, 77-81, adj assoc prof, 81- *Mem:* Am Chem Soc; Am Soc Biol Chem; Biophys Soc; Sigma Xi. *Res:* Kinetics of fast reactions in solution; relaxation kinetics; theory of fluids; critical phenomena; enzyme kinetics. *Mailing Add:* Lab Molec Biochem Vet Admin Hosp 4801 Linwood Blvd Kansas City MO 64128

COLER, MYRON ABRAHAM, b New York, NY, Mar 30, 13; m 42; c 2. ENGINEERING. *Educ:* Columbia Univ, AB, 33, BS, 34, ChE, 35, PhD(chem eng), 37. *Prof Exp:* Res scientist, Manhattan Proj, US Govt, Columbia Univ, 43-45; asst prof chem eng, NY Univ, 45-46; founder, pres, chmn bd & dir, Markite Co, Markite Develop Co, Markite Corp, Markite Eng Co, 48-69; FOUNDER & DIR, COLER ENG CO, MARCUS & BERTHA COLER FUND, 69- *Concurrent Pos:* Adj prof & prof, dir surface technol prog, dir creative sci prog, NY Univ, 41-75; consult & comt mem, govt agencies, Naval Ordnance Lab, Oak Ridge Nat Lab, Brookhaven Nat Lab, Nat Inventors Coun, State Tech Serv Act Comt, NBS-Dept Com, Div Cult Studies, UNESCO-Dept State, NSF, indust & acad consult, 48- *Honors & Awards:* Silver Insignia, US Govt, Manhattan Proj, 45. *Mem:* AAAS; Am Ceramic Soc; Am Chem Soc; Am Math Soc; Electrochem Soc. *Res:* Research and development of high technology new materials and devices for the energy and control fields; research methodology for science-based entrepreneurship and innovation. *Mailing Add:* Pan Am Bldg Suite 303E 200 Park Ave New York NY 10017

COLER, ROBERT A, b Hartford, Conn, July 23, 28; m 53; c 5. LIMNOLOGY. *Educ:* Champlain Col, BA, 52; Col Educ, Albany, MA, 54; State Univ NY Col Forestry, Syracuse, PhD(biol), 61. *Prof Exp:* Asst prof physics, NY State Col Educ, Cortland, 55-56; res biologist, Univ Md, 60-61; asst prof comp anat, Mass State Col, Bridgewater, 61-67; fel, 67-69, sr res assoc, 69-70, lectr, 70-71, dir environ technol training prog, 70-77, ASST PROF ENVIRON SCI, UNIV MASS, 71- *Concurrent Pos:* Dir, NSF res grant, 63-65. *Mem:* AAAS; Am Soc Zoologists. *Res:* Pollution biology and ecology; rhizosphere population responses to stress. *Mailing Add:* Dept of Environ Sci Univ Mass Flint Lab Amherst MA 01002

COLERIDGE, PETER T, b Wellington, New Zealand. SOLID STATE PHYSICS. *Educ:* Victoria Univ, Wellington, BSc, 61; Univ Cambridge, Eng, PhD(physics), 66. *Prof Exp:* RES OFFICER PHYSICS, NAT RES COUN CAN, 66- *Res:* Electronic structure of metals and alloys. *Mailing Add:* Div of Physics Nat Res Coun Can Ottawa ON K1A 0R6 Can

COLES, ANNA BAILEY, b Kansas City, Kans, Jan 16, 25; m 53; c 3. NURSING. *Educ:* Avila Col, BSN, 58; Cath Univ Am, MSN, 60, PhD(higher educ), 67. *Prof Exp:* Asst dir, Freedmen's Hosp, 60-63, admin asst, 63-67, dir nursing, 67-69; DEAN COL NURSING, HOWARD UNIV, 68- *Concurrent Pos:* Consult, Gen Res Adv Comn, NIH, 72-76, Vet Admin, 76-78 & Inst Med, 77; mem bd, Nat League Nursing, 77-81. *Mem:* Nat Inst Med; Nat League Nursing; Am Nurse's Asn; Am Asn Col Nursing. *Res:* Health manpower; nursing education. *Mailing Add:* Howard Univ & Col of Nursing 2400 Sixth St NW Washington DC 20059

COLES, DONALD (EARL), b Minn, Feb 8, 24; m 47; c 4. AERONAUTICS. *Educ:* Univ Minn, BAeroE, 47; Calif Inst Technol, PhD(aeronaut), 53. *Prof Exp:* Res engr, jet propulsion lab, 50-53, res fel, 53-56, from asst prof to assoc prof, 56-64, PROF AERONAUT, CALIF INST TECHNOL, 64- *Honors & Awards:* Sperry Award, Am Inst Aeronaut & Astronaut, 54. *Mem:* fel Am Inst Aeronaut & Astronaut; fel Am Phys Soc. *Res:* Shear flows; rotating fluids; turbulence. *Mailing Add:* 1033 Alta Pine Dr Altadena CA 91001

COLES, EMBERT HARVEY, JR, b Garden City, Kans, Oct 12, 23; m 46; c 2. CLINICAL PATHOLOGY, MICROBIOLOGY. *Educ:* Kans State Univ, DVM, 45, PhD(bact, path), 58; Iowa State Univ, MS, 46. *Prof Exp:* Instr vet hyg, Iowa State Univ, 46-48; pvt pract, Kans, 48-54; from asst prof to prof path & head dept, 54-68, PROF LAB MED & HEAD DEPT, KANS STATE UNIV, 68- *Concurrent Pos:* Dean fac vet med, Ahmadu Bello Univ, Zaria, Nigeria, 70-72; chief of party, Kans State Univ-Agency Int Develop Proj, Abu, Zaria, Nigeria, 70-72; consult, Develop Planning & Res Assoc, Ethiopia, 75, Food & Agr Orgn Conference Vet Educ, 78. *Mem:* Am Vet Med Asn; Conf Res Workers Animal Dis; Am Soc Vet Clin Path (pres, 65-66); Am Soc Microbiologists. *Res:* Animal staphylococci; bovine respiratory diseases; immunology of endotoxins. *Mailing Add:* Dept of Infectious Dis Kans State Univ Manhattan KS 66506

COLES, GERALD CHRISTOPHER, b Rugby, Eng, Apr 7, 39; m 66; c 3. CHEMOTHERAPY, PHARMACOLOGY. *Educ:* Univ Cambridge, BA, 61, PhD(insect biochem), 64. *Prof Exp:* Wellcome Trust res fel, Copenhagen Univ, Denmark, 64-65, Makerere Univ, Uganda, 65-69, Univ Cambridge, 69-72; res biologist, Imperial Chem Indust, Ltd, 72-81; PROF PARASITOL, UNIV MASS, 81- *Mem:* Brit Soc Parasitol; Royal Soc Trop Med & Hyg; Am Soc Trop Med & Hyg; Am Soc Parasitol; Am Asn Vet Parasitologists. *Res:* Biochemistry; chemotherapy and mode action of drugs on parasitic nematodes, trematodes and cestodes of medical and veterinary importance; helminth drug resistance; production of helminth vaccines. *Mailing Add:* Dept Zool Morrill Sci Ctr Univ Mass Amherst MA 01003

COLES, JAMES STACY, b Mansfield, Pa, June 3, 13; m 38; c 3. PHYSICAL CHEMISTRY. *Educ:* Mansfield State Col, BS, 34; Columbia Univ, AB, 36, AM, 39, PhD(phys chem), 41. *Hon Degrees:* LLD, Brown Univ, 55, Univ Maine, 56, Colby Col, 59, Middlebury Col & Columbia Univ, 62 & Bowdoin Col, 68; DSc, Univ NB, 58; ScD, Merrimack Col, 64. *Prof Exp:* Instr chem, City Col, 36-41; from instr to asst prof, Middlebury Col, 41-43; res group leader, Underwater Explosives Res Lab, Woods Hole Oceanog Inst, Mass, 43-45, res supvr, 45-46, res consult, 46-68; from asst prof to assoc prof chem, Brown Univ, 46-52, exec off dept chem, 48-52; pres, Bowdoin Col, 52-68; dir, 58-68, PRES, RES CORP, 68- *Concurrent Pos:* Mem adv comt, NSF, 53-55; trustee, Woods Hole Oceanog Inst, 53- & Am Savings Bank, 70-; civilian aide to Secy US Dept Army, 54-57; mem adv comt educ, Int Geophys Year, 58-; dir, Coun Libr Resources, 60-; Am Coun Educ, 62-65; Chem Fund, Inc, 68-; chmn mine adv comt, Nat Res Coun-Nat Acad Sci, 68-72; dir, Res-Cottrell, Inc, 68-79; mem adv comt, US Coast Guard Acad, 69-72; trustee-at-large & treas, Independent Col Funds of Am, 70-; dir, Pennwalt Corp, 71-75, Edo Corp, 71-, Med Care Develop, Inc, Maine, 77-81 & Va Chem, Inc, 78-81; mem nat adv bd, Desert Res Inst, 77-81; emer pres, Bowdoin Col. *Mem:* Fel AAAS; Am Chem Soc; fel Am Acad Arts & Sci; NY Acad Sci; hon mem Am Inst Chem. *Res:* Physical properties of natural high polymers; ultracentrifuge; underwater explosives and measurement of shock waves. *Mailing Add:* Res Corp 405 Lexington Ave New York NY 10017

COLES, RICHARD WARREN, b Philadelphia, Pa, Sept 16, 39; m 62; c 2. PHYSIOLOGICAL ECOLOGY, ANIMAL BEHAVIOR. *Educ:* Swarthmore Col, BA, 61; Harvard Univ, MA & PhD(biol), 67. *Prof Exp:* Asst prof biol, Claremont Cols, 66-70; adj asst prof biol, 70-73, DIR, TYSON RES CTR, WASHINGTON UNIV, 70-, FAC ASSOC BIOL, 73- *Concurrent Pos:* Consult, Ealing Corp, Mass, 65; Claremont Cols grant, 67-69; dir res field exped, Colo Rockies, 67-70; dir NSF undergrad instrnl equip grant, Claremont Cols, 69-71; prin investr, NIH Animal Care Facil improvement grant, 72-73; ed consult, Nat Geog Mag, 73-74; secy-treas, Orgn Biol Field Sta, 76-79; mem bd, Open Space Coun, St Louis; prin investr, US Forest Serv grant; consult, Harland, Bartholomew & Assoc, 79-80. *Mem:* AAAS; Am Inst Biol Sci; Wilderness Soc; Nat Audubon Soc; Ecol Soc Am. *Res:* Thermoregulation of the beaver with special emphasis on the role of the beaver's expanded tail in thermoregulation; diving behavior and physiology of the dipper, or water ouzel. *Mailing Add:* Tyson Res Ctr Washington Univ PO Box 258 Eureka MO 63025

COLES, ROBERT, US citizen; c 3. PSYCHIATRY. *Educ:* Harvard Univ, AB, 50; Columbia Univ, MD, 54. *Hon Degrees:* Twenty-six from various US cols & univs, 72-81. *Prof Exp:* Intern, Hosp, 56-57; teaching fel, Harvard Med Sch, 55-58, RES PSYCHIATRIST, HARVARD UNIV HEALTH MCLEAN 63- *Concurrent Pos:* Nat Adv Comt Farm Labor, 65-; consult, Ford Found, 69-; mem adv coun, for Children Relief, 72- *Mem:* Inst Med, Nat Acad Sci, 73-78; Am Orthopsychiat Asn; Nat Hillman Migrant Children; Am Psychiat Asn. *Res:* How children in various troubled nations develop a sense of national identity, of ideological commitment. *Mailing Add:* Harvard Health Servs 75 St Cambridge MA 02138

COLES, STEPHEN LEE, b Ogden, Utah, Jan 1, 44; c 1. CORAL REEF ECOLOGY, CORAL PHYSIOLOGY. *Educ:* Dartmouth Col, BA, 66; Univ Ga, MS, 68; Univ Hawaii, PhD(zool), 73. *Prof Exp:* Res asst, marine biol, Ga Marine Inst, Univ Ga, 65-66, teaching asst zool, 66-67, res asst, 67-68; teaching asst, Univ Hawaii, 68-69, res asst marine biol, Hawaii Inst Marine Biol, 69-73; MARINE BIOLOGIST, ENVIRON DEPT, HAWAIIAN ELEC CO, 73- *Concurrent Pos:* Lectr, Windward Community Col, Univ Hawaii, 74-78. *Mem:* Sigma Xi; Ecol Soc Am; Am Soc Limnol Oceanog. *Res:* Coral reef ecology; environmental effects of power stations; physiology of reef corals; multivariate statistical analysis; biology of symbiosis; stability of marine biotic communities. *Mailing Add:* Environ Dept Hawaiian Elec Co Box 2750 Honolulu HI 96803

COLES, WILLIAM JEFFREY, b Marquette, Mich, Oct 31, 29; m 55; c 3. MATHEMATICS. *Educ:* Northern Mich Col, BA, 50; Duke Univ, MA, 52, PhD(math), 54. *Prof Exp:* Asst, Duke Univ, 50-51; instr math, Univ Wis, 54-55; analyst, Dept Defense, Washington, DC, 55-56; from asst prof to assoc prof math, Univ Utah, 56-63; vis assoc prof, Math Res Ctr, US Army, Univ Wis, 63-64; PROF MATH, UNIV UTAH, 64- *Mem:* Am Math Soc; Math Asn Am; Soc Indust & Appl Math. *Res:* Differential equations. *Mailing Add:* Dept of Math Univ of Utah Salt Lake City UT 84112

COLEY, FRANCIS H(AMILTON), chemical engineering, see previous edition

COLEY, RONALD FRANK, b Chicago, Ill, Dec 27, 41; m 62; c 4. NUCLEAR INSTRUMENTATION. *Educ:* St Procopius Col, 63; Iowa State Univ, PhD(inorg & phys chem), 69. *Prof Exp:* Asst chem, Iowa State Univ, 63-69; assoc, Biol & Med Res Div, Argonne Nat Lab, 69-70; CHEMIST, COMMONWEALTH EDISON CO, 70- *Concurrent Pos:* Res assoc, Biol & Med Res Div, Argonne Nat Lab, 70-79; mem, subcomt radioactive ref standards, Am Nat Standards Inst, 74-; consult nuclear instrumentation, 78-; adj fac, Dept Chem & Biochem, Ill Benedictine Col, 79- *Mem:* Am Chem Soc. *Res:* Neutron therapy of cancer; Monte Carlo computations of neutron and gamma interactions with matter; gamma and neutron spectrometry; chemical and radionuclide analysis of nuclear power plant systems and effluents; computerized analytical instrumentation systems and networks. *Mailing Add:* Commonwealth Edison Co PO Box 767 Chicago IL 60690

COLGATE, SAMUEL ORAN, b Amarillo, Tex, Oct 5, 33; m 55; c 2. PHYSICAL CHEMISTRY. *Educ:* West Tex State Univ, BS, 55; Okla State Univ, MS, 56; Mass Inst Technol, PhD(phys chem), 59. *Prof Exp:* Asst prof, 59-66, ASSOC PROF CHEM, UNIV FLA, 66- *Concurrent Pos:* Vis prof, Harvard & Boston Univs, 69-70. *Mem:* Am Phys Soc. *Res:* Derivation of the intermolecular potential from scattering of molecular beams. *Mailing Add:* Dept of Chem Univ of Fla Gainesville FL 32601

COLGATE, STIRLING AUCHINCLOSS, b New York, NY, Nov 14, 25; m 47; c 3. PHYSICS. *Educ:* Cornell Univ, BA, 48, PhD(physics), 52. *Prof Exp:* Physicist, Radiation Lab, Univ Calif, 51-64; pres, 65-74, ADJ PROF PHYSICS, N MEX INST MINING & TECHNOL, 75-; PHYSICIST, LOS ALAMOS NAT LAB, 76-, SR FEL, 80- *Concurrent Pos:* Mem sci adv bd, US Air Force, 58-61, gas centrifuge comt, Atomic Energy Comn, 61-69 & fluid dynamics comt, NASA, 61-63; consult, Conf Cessation Nuclear

Weapons Tests, US State Dept, 59; lectr, Univ Calif, 59-64; ed, Nuclear Fusion; trustee-at-large, Assoc Univs, Inc, 70-73; chmn subfield surv plasma physics & physics of fluids panel, Nat Acad Sci Physics Surv Comt, 70-; trustee-at-large, Assoc Univs Res Astron, Inc, 73-78; mem, Space Sci Bd, 75-78; chmn panel, Physics Sun, Space Sci Bd, 79-82. *Mem:* Fel Am Phys Soc; Am Acad Sci; Am Astron Soc; NY Acad Sci; Am Geophys Union. *Res:* Accelerators; nuclear weapon physics; controlled thermonuclear fusion; plasma physics; atmospheric physics; astrophysics. *Mailing Add:* MS210 Theoret Div Los Alamos Nat Lab Los Alamos NM 87545

COLGLAZIER, MERLE LEE, b Holyoke, Colo, Aug 6, 20; m 48; c 3. VETERINARY PARASITOLOGY. *Educ:* Univ Colo, BA, 48. *Prof Exp:* From parasitologist to sr parasitologist, Animal Parasitol Inst, Agr Res Serv, Beltsville Agr Res Ctr, USDA, 48-68, zoologist vet chemother, 68-78; RETIRED. *Mem:* Am Soc Parasitologists. *Res:* Antiparasitic investigations dealing with chemotherapy and chemical control of helminthic diseases and parasites that affect domestic animals; poultry and fur-bearing animals raised in captivity. *Mailing Add:* 2712 Philben Dr Adelphi MD 20783

COLGROVE, STEVEN GRAY, b Lancaster, Pa, Nov 5, 53. GAS CHROMATOGRAPHY, MASS SPECTROMETRY. *Educ:* Lafayette Col, BS, 75; Iowa State Univ, PhD(anal chem), 80. *Prof Exp:* RES CHEMIST, EXXON RES & ENG CO, 80- *Mem:* Am Chem Soc; Sigma Xi; Am Soc Mass Spectrometry. *Res:* Analysis of complex mixtures of organic compounds; analysis of coal liquids, shale oil, and petroleum, using gas chromatography, mass spectrometry and liquid chromatography. *Mailing Add:* Exxon Res & Eng Co PO Box 4255 Baytown TX 77520

COLI, G(UIDO) J(OHN), JR, b Richmond, Va, Sept 12, 21; m 47; c 4. CHEMICAL ENGINEERING. *Educ:* Va Polytech Inst, BS, 41, PhD(chem eng), 49. *Prof Exp:* Asst engr, Bur Indust Hyg, State Dept Health, Va, 41; assoc chemist, Naval Res Lab, 42-46; instr chem eng, Va Polytech Inst, 47-48; chem engr, Socony-Vacuum Oil Co, 49-50; mem staff, Allied Chem Corp, 50-74, group vpres, 68-74, dir, 70-74; exec vpres opers, 74-79, PRES, AM ENKA CO, 79-; DIR, AKZONA INC, 79- *Mem:* Am Chem Soc; fel Am Inst Chemists; Inst Mech Eng. *Res:* Molecular distillation; heat transfer. *Mailing Add:* Am Enka Co Enka NC 28728

COLICHMAN, EUGENE LOUIS, b Colorado City, Tex, July 11, 18; m 47; c 2. PHYSICAL CHEMISTRY. *Educ:* Univ Calif, Los Angeles, BA, 40, MA, 42, PhD(phys chem), 44. *Prof Exp:* Asst chem, Univ Calif, Los Angeles, 41-44; res chemist, Turco Prod, Inc, Calif, 44-47; instr chem, Yale Univ, 48-49; asst prof, Univ Portland, 49-52; res assoc, Stanford Res Inst, 52; supvr anal chem, Calif Res & Develop Co, 52-53; supvr radiation chem, NAm Aviation, 53-57; mem tech staff, Propulsion Res, Space Tech Labs, Inc, 57-60, staff res consult, Marquardt Corp, 60-64; INDUST CONSULT, 64- *Concurrent Pos:* Instr chem, Univ Southern Calif, 46-48. *Mem:* Am Chem Soc. *Res:* Analytical chemistry; physical chemistry of non-aqueous systems; reaction kinetics; surface active compounds; onium salt chemistry; polarography; radiation, propulsion and electrochemistry. *Mailing Add:* 509 Greencraig Rd Los Angeles CA 90049

COLIJN, H(ENDRIK), b Hague, Netherlands, July 19, 24; nat US; m 51; c 5. MECHANICAL ENGINEERING. *Educ:* Delft Inst Technol, Holland, MS, 51. *Prof Exp:* Carnegie Inst Technol staff engr, Raadgevend Efficiency Bur, Amsterdam, 51-52; trainee, Goodyear Tire & Rubber corp, Gt Brit, Ltd, 52-53, sales engr, Akron, Ohio, 53-57; sr technologist, US Steel Corp, 57-65, sr appln engr, 65-68; dir bulk handling systs, Pa Cent Co, 68-69; CONSULT ENGR, 69- *Concurrent Pos:* Adj prof, Grad Sch, Univ Pittsburgh. *Mem:* Am Soc Mech Engrs; Int Mat Mgt Soc; Asn Iron & Steel Engrs; Instrument Soc Am; Am Inst Mining, Metall & Petrol Engrs. *Res:* Raw materials processing; flow of bulk solids and materials handling engineering. *Mailing Add:* 423 Franklin Heights Dr Monroeville PA 15146

COLILLA, WILLIAM, b Shanghai, China, Sept 1, 38; US citizen; m 65; c 1. BIOCHEMISTRY. *Educ:* Univ Ill, BS, 62; Southern Ill Univ, PhD(biochem), 70. *Prof Exp:* Res scientist plastic coatings, US Gypsum, 64-65; res assoc carbohydrate metab, Sch Med, Univ NDak, 70-74; SCIENTIST ENZYMOL PROCESSES, CLINTON CORN PROCESSING CO, STANDARD BRANDS, INC, 74- *Mem:* Am Chem Soc; Sigma Xi. *Res:* Plant biochemistry; carbohydrates and carbohydrate metabolism; enzymology and enzyme kinetics. *Mailing Add:* Clinton Corn Processing Co 1251 Beaver Channel Pkwy Clinton IA 52732

COLIN, LAWRENCE, b New York, NY, Jan 19, 31; m 53; c 2. ELECTRICAL ENGINEERING. *Educ:* Polytech Inst Brooklyn, BEE, 52; Syracuse Univ, MEE, 60; Stanford Univ, PhD(elec eng), 64. *Prof Exp:* Electronic engr, Rome Air Develop Ctr, US Air Force, 52-64; AEROSPACE TECHNOLOGIST, AMES RES CTR, NASA, 64- *Concurrent Pos:* Mem comn II, US Int Sci Radio Union, 58-; mem working group, Int Satellites Ionospheric Studies, Nat Aeronaut & Space Admin, 64- *Mem:* Inst Elec & Electronics Engrs; Am Geophys Union. *Res:* Radiowave propagation; upper atmospheric physics; space physics. *Mailing Add:* Ames Res Ctr NASA Moffett Field CA 94035

COLING, FORREST L, b Lafayette, Ind, Jan 8, 24; m 47; c 3. COMPUTER SCIENCES. *Educ:* Purdue Univ, BS, 50; Ind State Univ, MS, 51. *Prof Exp:* Teacher high schs, 51-54; sr engr, NAm Aviation, Inc, 54-59; dept mgr, Raytheon Co, 59-61; group engr, Douglas Aircraft Co, 61-64; indust & govt consult, 64-66; res specialist, Lockheed Calif Co, 66-67; res engr, TRW Syst Div, 67-68; instr comput prog & technol, Hughes Aircraft Co, 68-70; CONSULT COMPUT SOFTWARE, BUDCO DATA SYSTS, 64-67 & 70- *Concurrent Pos:* Mem, Nat Comt Ceramic Mat. *Mem:* Inst Elec & Electronics Engrs; Am Inst Aeronaut & Astronaut; Math Asn Am. *Res:* Microwave devices; propagation; electromagnetic windows; testing, manufacturing and marketing; computer technology; software techniques; medical applications. *Mailing Add:* 2650 Dalemead St Torrance CA 90505

COLINGSWORTH, DONALD RUDOLPH, b Beaver Dam, Wis, June 20, 12; m 38; c 2. CHEMISTRY, BACTERIOLOGY. *Educ:* Univ Wis, BS, 34, MS, 36, PhD(bact), 38. *Prof Exp:* Biochemist, Red Star Yeast & Prod Co, 38-43; res chemist, Heyden Chem Corp, NJ, 43-44; sr res scientist, 44-56, mgr fermentation res & develop, 56-67, group mgr fermentation prod, Upjohn Co, 67-78; RETIRED. *Mem:* Am Chem Soc; Am Soc Microbiol. *Res:* Fermentation chemistry; antibiotics. *Mailing Add:* 1215 Miles Ave Kalamazoo MI 49001

COLINVAUX, PAUL ALFRED, b St Albans, Eng, Sept 22, 30; m 60; c 2. PALEOECOLOGY, PALEOCLIMATOLOGY. *Educ:* Cambridge Univ, BA, 56, MA, 60; Duke Univ, PhD(zool), 62. *Prof Exp:* Res officer pedology, Can Dept Agr, NB, 56-59; NATO fel biol, Queen's Univ, N Ireland, 62-63; res biologist, Yale Univ, 63-64; from asst prof to assoc prof, 64-71, PROF ZOOL, OHIO STATE UNIV, 71-, MEM INST POLAR STUDIES, 64- *Concurrent Pos:* Guggenheim fel, 71-72; counr for Galapagos Islands, Charles Darwin Found, 75-; chmn, Sponsoring Inst, Inst Ecol, 78-80; mem, Nat Sci Found Adv Sub-Comt Ecol, 79- & US Nat Comn Int Union Quaternary Res, Nat Acad Sci, 78- *Honors & Awards:* Ohioana Libr Asn Award Sci, 78; Tansley lectr, Brit Ecol Soc, 81. *Mem:* Am Soc Limnol & Oceanog; Arctic Inst NAm; Ecol Soc Am; Am Soc Naturalists; fel Explorers Club. *Res:* Environmental history of Bering land bridge and of equatorial South America; Galapagos limnology and ecology; pollen analysis of Galapagos, Andean, Amazonian and Arctic vegetation histories; chronology of Quaternary; ecological models of human history. *Mailing Add:* Dept of Zool Ohio State Univ 484 W12th Ave Columbus OH 43210

COLL, DAVID C, b Montreal, Que, June 17, 33; m 55; c 3. ELECTRICAL ENGINEERING. *Educ:* McGill Univ, BE, 55, ME, 56; Carleton Univ, Can, PhD(elec eng), 66. *Prof Exp:* Defence sci serv officer commun, Defence Res Bd, Can, 56-57; assoc prof, 67-73, chmn, Dept Systs Eng & Comput Sci, 75-78, PROF ELEC ENG, CARLETON UNIV, 73- *Concurrent Pos:* Sr consult, P A Lapp Ltd, 80- *Mem:* Inst Elec & Electronics Engrs; Armed Forces Commun & Electronics Asn. *Res:* Information technology: communications, computers, signal processing, digital and hybrid systems; television signals, systems and services. *Mailing Add:* Fac of Eng Carleton Univ Ottawa ON K1S 5B6 Can

COLL, HANS, b Graz, Austria, June 8, 29. CHEMISTRY. *Educ:* La State Univ, MS, 55, PhD(chem), 57. *Prof Exp:* Res assoc phys chem, Cornell Univ, 57-60; res assoc, Mass Inst Technol, 60-62; res chemist, Shell Develop Co, Calif, 62-75; RES CHEMIST, RES LABS, EASTMAN KODAK CO, 75- *Concurrent Pos:* Grants, Off of Naval Res, 57-60 & NIH, 60-62. *Mem:* Am Chem Soc. *Res:* Chemistry of metal complexes; physical chemistry of detergents and high polymers. *Mailing Add:* 2800 Oakview Dr Rochester NY 14617

COLLARD, HAROLD RIETH, b Paterson, NJ, July 29, 32; m 67; c 1. AIRBORNE INFRARED ASTRONOMY, SOLAR WIND MEASUREMENTS. *Educ:* Harvard Col, BA, 54; Stanford Univ, MS, 58, PhD(physics), 66. *Prof Exp:* Res scientist, Stanford Res Inst, 58-59, res asst, Hansen Lab Physics, 59-67; RES SCIENTIST, AMES RES CTR, NASA, 67- *Mem:* Am Geophys Union. *Res:* Electron scattering studies of structure of helium and tritium; measurement of heliocentric gradient of solar wind properties and interaction of solar wind with planetary magnetic fields; infrared astronomy instrumentation. *Mailing Add:* 496 Mariposa Ave Mountain View CA 94041

COLLAT, JUSTIN WHITE, b New York, NY, Sept 29, 28; m 60; c 3. ANALYTICAL CHEMISTRY. *Educ:* Harvard Univ, AB, 49, AM, 51, PhD(chem), 53. *Prof Exp:* Fel chem, Mass Inst Technol, 54; from asst prof to assoc prof chem, Ohio State Univ, 54-66; asst prog adminr, 66-70, prog adminr, Petrol Res Fund, 70-72, HEAD DEPT RES GRANTS & AWARDS, AM CHEM SOC, 72- *Mem:* Am Chem Soc. *Res:* Electroanalytical chemistry. *Mailing Add:* Am Chem Soc 1155 16th St NW Washington DC 20036

COLLE, RONALD, b Milwaukee, Wis, Feb 11, 46; m 68. NUCLEAR CHEMISTRY, RADIOCHEMISTRY. *Educ:* Ga Inst Technol, BS, 69; Rensselaer Polytech Inst, PhD(nuclear & radiochem), 72; George Washington Univ, MSA, 79. *Prof Exp:* Res assoc nuclear & radiochem, Dept Chem, Brookhaven Nat Lab, 72-73; fac res assoc nuclear & radiochem, Univ Md, 73-74; consult & res chemist, Radioactiv Sect, 76-77, CHEMIST RADIATION METROL, OFF RADIATION MEASUREMENTS, CTR RADIATION RES, NAT BUR STANDARDS, 77- *Concurrent Pos:* Vis res fel, Ctr Nuclear & Radiation Studies, State Univ NY, Albany, 71-72; adj fac mem & consult, Empire State Col & Albany Learning Ctr, State Univ NY, 73-75. *Honors & Awards:* Bronze Medal Award, US Dept Com, 81. *Mem:* Am Phys Soc; Am Chem Soc. *Res:* Nuclear physics; atomic physics and analytical chemistry; radiation metrology, standards development, measurement assurance for nuclear medicine, such as radiopharmaceuticals, and environmental radioactivity; research administration, environmental and technology assessment; measurement theory; radiation metrology. *Mailing Add:* Ctr for Radiation Res Nat Bur Standards Washington DC 20234

COLLEN, MORRIS F, b St Paul, Minn, Nov 12, 13; m 37; c 4. MEDICINE. *Educ:* Univ Minn, BEE, 34, MB, 38, MD, 39; Am Bd Internal Med, dipl, 46. *Prof Exp:* Intern, Michael Reese Hosp, Chicago, 38-40; resident internal med, Los Angeles County Hosp, 40-42; chief med serv, Kaiser Found Hosp, Oakland, 42-52, med dir, 52-53; med dir, West Bay Div & chmn exec comt, 53-73, dir med methods res, 61-79, DIR TECHNOL ASSESSMENT, PERMANENTE MED GROUP, 79- *Concurrent Pos:* Chief staff, Kaiser Found Hosp, San Francisco, 53-61; lectr, Sch Pub Health, Univ Calif, Berkeley, 65- & Med Sch, Univ Calif, San Francisco, 70-; consult, USPHS, 65-, mem adv comt on demonstration grants, 66-69; chmn health care systs study sect, US Dept Health, Educ & Welfare, 69-72; consult, WHO, Europe & Pan-Am Health Orgn & Tri-Serv Med Info Syst Prog, US Cong Off Technol Assessment Health Div, Dept Defense; prog chmn, 3rd Int Conf Med

Informatics, Tokyo; Centennial scholar, Johns Hopkins Univ, 76. *Mem:* Inst Med of Nat Acad Sci; fel Am Col Physicians; fel Am Col Cardiol; fel Am Col Chest Physicians; Am Pub Health Asn. *Res:* Medical research and administration; internal medicine. *Mailing Add:* Permanente Med Group 3451 Piedmont Ave Oakland CA 94611

COLLETT, EDWARD, b Bronx, NY, Sept 15, 34; m 64; c 2. PHYSICAL OPTICS, LASERS. *Educ:* City Col NY, BS, 56; NMex State Univ, MS, 61; Cath Univ Am, PhD(physics), 68. *Prof Exp:* Sr scientist microwaves, Repub Aviation, Farmingdale, LI, 61-64; proj engr optics, Booz-Allen Appl Res, Washington, DC, 64-67; proj scientist optics, US Army Res & Develop Command, Ft Monmouth, NJ, 67-80; PRES, MEASUREMENT CONCEPTS, INC, COLTS NECK, NJ, 80- *Honors & Awards:* Sam Stiber Commendation for Tech Excellence, Electronic Warfare Lab, Ft Monmouth, NJ, 78; Bronze Medallion for Sci Achievement, Dept of Army, 78 Army Sci Conf, 78. *Mem:* Optical Soc Am. *Res:* Physical optics with emphasis on classical optics and theoretical and experimental investigations of polarized light. *Mailing Add:* 1 Howard Ct Lincroft NJ 07738

COLLETTE, BRUCE BADEN, b Brooklyn, NY, Mar 14, 34; m 56; c 3. ICHTHYOLOGY. *Educ:* Cornell Univ, BS, 56, PhD(vert zool), 60. *Prof Exp:* SYST ZOOLOGIST, NAT MARINE FISHERIES SERV SYST LAB, NAT MUS NATURAL HIST, 60-, ASST LAB DIR, 63-, RES ASSOC, DEPT VERT ZOOL, SMITHSONIAN INST, 67- *Concurrent Pos:* Ichthyol ed, Copeia, Am Soc Ichthyologists & Herpetologists, 64-69; sci ed, Nat Marine Fisheries Serv, 74-77; vis prof, Marine Sci Inst, Northeastern Univ, 67-, adj prof, 80-; res assoc, Mus Comp Zool, Harvard Univ, 77- *Mem:* Ichthyol Soc Japan; fel AAAS; Am Soc Ichthyologists & Herpetologists (secy, 74-78, pres, 81); Soc Systemic Zool. *Res:* Systematics, distribution and evolution of fishes, especially Hemiramphidae, Belonidae, Percidae, Batrachoididae, and Scombridae. *Mailing Add:* Nat Marine Fish Serv Syst Lab Nat Mus of Natural Hist Washington DC 20560

COLLETTE, JOHN WILFRED, b Calgary, Alta, Can, July 20, 33; nat US; m 52; c 3. ORGANIC CHEMISTRY. *Educ:* Univ Alta, BSc, 55; Univ Calif, PhD(chem), 58. *Prof Exp:* Res chemist, 58-64, develop chemist, 64-66, res supvr, 66-69, supvr, Cent Res Dept, 69-80, ASST LAB DIR, FABRIC & FINISHES DEPT, E I DU PONT DE NEMOURS & CO, INC, 80- *Mem:* Am Chem Soc; The Chem Soc; AAAS. *Res:* Olefin polymerization; chemistry of organo metallic compounds; effect of micro structure on elastomer properties; chemistry of higher acetylenics; synthetic coatings. *Mailing Add:* 309 Brockton Rd Wilmington DE 19803

COLLEY, DANIEL GEORGE, b Buffalo, NY, Jan 21, 43; m 65. IMMUNOLOGY, MICROBIOLOGY. *Educ:* Cent Col Ky, BA, 64; Tulane Univ, PhD(microbiol), 68. *Prof Exp:* Fel, Yale Univ, 68-70; vis prof immunol, Fed Univ Pernambuco, 70-71; from asst prof to assoc prof, 71-79, PROF IMMUNOL, VANDERBILT UNIV, 79-; res immunologist, 71-79, RES CAREER SCIENTIST, VET ADMIN MED CTR, 79- *Concurrent Pos:* vis prof immunol, Fed Univ Minas Gerais, 74-81; assoc ed, J Immunol, 74-80; mem, Trop Med-Parasitol Study Sect, NIH, 74-78; vis scientist, Res & Control Dept, Ministry Health, St Lucia, W Indies, 75, 76, 77 & 78; mem, US-Japan Coop Med Sci Prog, Panel Parasitic Dis, Nat Inst Health, 78-; counr, Am Soc Trop Med & Hyg, 78-; mem, Microbiol-Infectious Dis Adv Comt, NIH, 80-; consult, Ministry of Health, Egypt, 81- *Honors & Awards:* Henry Baldwin Ward Medal, Am Soc Parasitologists, 81. *Mem:* AAAS; Am Asn Immunologists; Royal Soc Trop Med & Hygiene; Am Soc Trop Med & Hyg; Am Soc Microbiol. *Res:* Immunobiology with specific activity in the areas of immuno-regulation of cell-mediated phenomena and lymphoid-eosinophil interactions, immunopethology and resistance with specific reference to schistosomiasis; parasitology. *Mailing Add:* Vet Admin Med Ctr Rm 324 1310 24th Ave S Nashville TN 37203

COLLEY, FREDRICK CHRISTENSEN, parasitology, public health, see previous edition

COLLIAS, ELSIE COLE, b Tiffin, Ohio, Mar 24, 20; m 48; c 1. ZOOLOGY. *Educ:* Heidelberg Col, BA, 42; Univ Wis, MS, 44, PhD(zool), 48. *Prof Exp:* Asst zool, Univ Wis, 42-46, asst econ entom, 47-48; asst prof biol, Heidelberg Col, 48-49; instr, Univ Wis, 50; assoc prof, Ill Col, 53-57; res assoc entom, Univ Calif, Los Angeles, 59-62; RES ASSOC, LOS ANGELES COUNTY MUS, 62-; RES ASSOC ZOOL, UNIV CALIF, 64- *Concurrent Pos:* Entomologist, USPHS, Ga, 46-47. *Honors & Awards:* Elliott Coues Award, Am Ornithol Union, 80. *Mem:* Animal Behav Soc; Am Ornithologist Union. *Res:* Bird behavior; invertebrate zoology; insect behavior. *Mailing Add:* Dept Biol Univ Calif Los Angeles CA 90024

COLLIAS, EUGENE EVANS, b Cumberland, Wash, Feb 3, 25; m 5; c 2. OCEANOGRAPHY. *Educ:* Univ Wash, MS, 51 & Scripps Inst, Univ Calif, 59. *Prof Exp:* Res instr oceanog, Univ Wash, 48-56, sr oceanogr, 59-70, prin oceanogr, 70-80; NW CONSULT, OCEANOGRAPHERS, INC, 71- *Mem:* Marine Technol Soc; Am Geophys Union; Sigma Xi; Am Soc Limnol & Oceanog. *Res:* Descriptive and chemical oceanography; field methods of oceanography. *Mailing Add:* 4318 First NE Seattle WA 98105

COLLIAS, NICHOLAS ELIAS, b Chicago Heights, Ill, July 19, 14; m 48; c 1. ZOOLOGY. *Educ:* Univ Chicago, BS, 37, PhD(zool), 42. *Prof Exp:* Asst zool, Univ Chicago, 37-42; instr biol, Chicago City Jr Col, 46 & Amherst Col, 46-47; inst zool, Univ Wis, 47-51; conserv biologist, State Conserv Dept, Wis, 51-52; USPHS spec res fel, Cornell Univ, 52-53; prof biol, Ill Col, 53-58; from asst prof to assoc prof, 58-65, PROF ZOOL, UNIV CALIF, LOS ANGELES, 66- *Concurrent Pos:* Guggenheim fel, 62-63; hon res assoc, Los Angeles County Mus, 62-; hon res assoc, Percy Fitzpatrick Inst African Ornith, Univ Capetown, 69-70 & Nat Mus Kenya, Nairobi, 73-78. *Honors & Awards:* Elliott Coves Award, Am Ornith Union, 80. *Mem:* Am Soc Zool; Ecol Soc Am; fel Am Ornith Union; hon mem Cooper Ornith Soc; fel Animal Behav Soc. *Res:* Animal sociology and ecology; field studies of behavior and populations in birds and mammals; hormones and behavior; analysis of vocal communication in animals; nest-building in birds; ornithology; behavioral energetics. *Mailing Add:* Dept Biol Univ Calif Los Angeles CA 90024

COLLIER, BOYD DAVID, b Sacramento, Calif, Aug 14, 37; m 58; c 2. POPULATION ECOLOGY. *Educ:* Univ Calif, Berkeley, BA, 60; Cornell Univ, MST, 64, PhD(evolutionary biol), 66. *Prof Exp:* From asst prof to assoc prof, 66-72, PROF BIOL, SAN DIEGO STATE UNIV, 72-, CHMN DEPT, 78- *Mem:* Ecol Soc Am; Brit Ecol Soc. *Res:* Population ecology of terrestrial animals, particularly insects; computer simulation of ecological systems. *Mailing Add:* Dept of Biol San Diego State Univ San Diego CA 92182

COLLIER, BRIAN, b York, Eng, June 8, 40; m 65; c 3. PHARMACOLOGY, PHYSIOLOGY. *Educ:* Univ Leeds, BSc, 62, PhD(pharmacol), 65. *Prof Exp:* Brit Med Res Coun fel, Cambridge Univ, 65-66; lectr physiol, 66-67, asst prof, 67-72, assoc prof, 72-78, PROF PHARMACOL, McGILL UNIV, 78- *Concurrent Pos:* Med Res Coun Can scholar, 68-73. *Mem:* AAAS; Am Soc Pharmacol & Exp Therapeut; Can Physiol Soc; Pharmacol Soc Can. *Res:* Identity, synthesis, storage, release and fate of neurotransmitter substances in the central and peripheral nervous system of mammals; physiology and pharmacology of cholinergic synapses. *Mailing Add:* McIntyre Bldg 3655 Drummond St Montreal Can

COLLIER, CLARENCE ROBERT, b Freeport, Ill, Mar 25, 19; m 42; c 3. PHYSIOLOGY. *Educ:* Andrews Univ, BA, 40; Loma Linda Univ, MD, 49. *Prof Exp:* Instr sci, Hylandale Acad, 40-41; from instr to asst prof med, Loma Linda Univ, 52-57, assoc prof physiol, 57-64, prof physiol & biophys & chmn dept, 64-70; assoc prof med, 70-71, PROF MED & PHYSIOL, SCH MED, UNIV SOUTHERN CALIF, 71- *Concurrent Pos:* Nat Found Infantile Paralysis res fel, Sch Pub Health, Harvard Univ, 55-56; sr res fel, NIH, 59-62; res assoc, Rancho Los Amigos Hosp, 52-55, dir res, 56-57, chief med sci serv, 62-64, consult, 58-; consult, Rand Corp, 63-65; consult physiol, Christian Med Col, Vellore, India, 72- *Mem:* AAAS; Am Physiol Soc; Am Fedn Clin Res. *Res:* Pulmonary physiology; pulmonary exchange and circulation; mechanics of breathing; biological models. *Mailing Add:* Sch of Med Univ of Southern Calif Los Angeles CA 90033

COLLIER, DONALD W(ALTER), b Washington, DC, June 5, 20; m 48; c 2. CHEMICAL ENGINEERING. *Educ:* Cath Univ Am, BACh, 41; Princeton Univ, AM, 43, ChE & PhD(phys chem), 44. *Prof Exp:* Asst chem, Princeton Univ, 41-43, res assoc, Rubber Reserve Co Proj, 43-44; res chemist, Manhattan Proj contract, Sharples Corp, 44-46, res chem engr, 46-51; dir res, Thomas A Edison, Inc, 51-57, vpres, 55-57, vpres & dir res, McGraw-Edison Co Div, 57-59, pres res lab, 59-60; vpres res, 60-75, vpres technol, 75-78, SR VPRES CORP STRATEGY, BORG-WARNER CORP, 78- *Concurrent Pos:* Spec lectr, Princeton Univ, 43-44; mem adv bd nucleonics, Chem & Electronics Shares, Inc, 58-62; trustee, Rittenhouse Fund, 58-60; dir, Atomic Instruments Co, Mass, 53-56, Baird-Atomic, Inc, 56-57 & Sci and Nuclear Fund, 54-58; pres, Indust Res Inst, Inc, 66-67; dir, Alcohol Countermeasures, Inc, 76- & Tech Adv Bd, US Dept Com, 73-81. *Mem:* AAAS; Am Chem Soc; Am Inst Chem Engrs; Asn Res Dirs (pres, 58-59). *Res:* Heterogeneous catalytic kinetics; catalytic reactor design; thermodynamics and distillation in hydrocarbon rubber systems; sedimentation and classification of fine particles; solvent extraction and leaching of solids; crystal formation and growth; electrochemistry; sound recording; research administration; automotive and industrial power transmission; environment control. *Mailing Add:* Borg-Warner Corp 200 S Michigan Ave Chicago IL 60604

COLLIER, FRANCIS NASH, JR, b New York, NY, Feb 11, 17; m 47; c 3. INORGANIC CHEMISTRY. *Educ:* Howard Col, BS, 42; Ohio State Univ, MS, 49, PhD, 57. *Prof Exp:* Asst prof chem & physics, Howard Col, 43-46, assoc prof chem, 49-53, assoc prof chem & physics & chmn dept physics, 56-57; assoc prof, 57-70, PROF CHEM, UNIV NC, 70- *Mem:* Am Chem Soc. *Res:* Kinetic studies of halomines in liquid ammonia; molecular addition compounds; anhydrous metalhalides; isotope exchange studies. *Mailing Add:* Dept of Chem Venable Hall Univ of NC Chapel Hill NC 27514

COLLIER, GERALD, b Monterey Park, Calif, Nov 16, 30; m; c 1. VERTEBRATE ZOOLOGY, ANIMAL BEHAVIOR. *Educ:* Univ CAlif, Los Angeles, BA, 53, MA, 58, From asst prof to assoc prof, 61-77, PROF ZOOL, SAN DIEGO STATE UNIV, 69- *Concurrent Pos:* Grant, Mex, 65; Res Found grant, Mex & Costa Rica, 66 & 69, Sigma Xi grant, Costa Rica, 70; ecol consult, Dillingham Environ Co, 70- *Mem:* Cooper Ornith Soc; Am Ornith Union; Soc Study Evolution; Wilson Ornith Soc; Soc Syst Zool. *Res:* Avian behavior and ecology; functional vertebrate anatomy. *Mailing Add:* Dept of Zool San Diego State Univ San Diego CA 92185

COLLIER, HERBERT BRUCE, b Toronto, Ont, Oct 10, 05; m 30; c 2. BIOCHEMISTRY. *Educ:* Univ Toronto, BA, 27, MA, 29, PhD(biochem), 30. *Prof Exp:* From asst prof to assoc prof biochem, Col Med & Dent, WChina Union, 32-39; biochemist, Inst Parasitol, Macdonald Col, McGill Univ, 39-42; from asst prof to assoc prof biochem, Dalhousie Univ, 42-46; prof & head dept, Univ Sask, 46-49; head dept biochem, 49-61, prof, 49-64, prof clin biochem, 64-71, EMER PROF PATHOL, UNIV ALTA, 71- *Mem:* Am Chem Soc; Am Soc Biol Chem; Royal Soc Can; fel Int Soc Hemat. *Res:* Clinical biochemistry; chemistry of enzymes; drug action; biochemistry of erythrocytes. *Mailing Add:* Med Lab Sci Clin Sci Bldg Univ of Alta Edmonton Can

COLLIER, HERMAN EDWARD, JR, b St Louis, Mo, Aug 8, 27; m 48; c 3. ANALYTICAL CHEMISTRY, INORGANIC CHEMISTRY. *Educ:* Randolph-Macon Col, BS, 50; Lehigh Univ, MS, 52, PhD(anal chem), 55. *Hon Degrees:* LLD, Lehigh Univ, LittD, Col Charleston, 76; ScD, Randolph-Macon Col, 77. *Prof Exp:* Prof chem & chmn dept, Moravian Col, 55-57; res chemist, E I du Pont de Nemours & Co, 57-63; prof chem & chmn div natural sci & math, 63-69, PRES, MORAVIAN COL, 69- *Mem:* Am Chem Soc; fel Am Inst Chemists; Sigma Xi. *Res:* New developments in flame photometry; the hydrogenfluorine flame; quantitative analytical infrared analysis; determination of enol content; differential reaction rates as an analytical tool. *Mailing Add:* Moravian Col Main St & Elizabeth Ave Bethlehem PA 18018

COLLIER, JACK REED, b Louisville, Ky, Aug 19, 26. EMBRYOLOGY. *Educ:* Univ Ky, BS, 48, MS, 50, PhD(zool), Univ NC, 54. *Prof Exp:* USPHS fel, Tokyo Metrop Univ, 54-55 & Calif Inst Technol, 55-56; instr biol, Univ Vt, 56-57; asst prof, La State Univ, 57-59; independent investr, Marine Biol Lab, Woods Hole, 59-63; assoc prof, Rensselaer Polytech Inst, 63-66; PROF BIOL, BROOKLYN COL, 66- *Concurrent Pos:* Mem corp, Marine Biol Lab. *Mem:* Am Soc Zool; Soc Develop Biol; Biophys Soc; Soc Gen Physiol; Am Soc Cell Biol. *Res:* Invertebrate chemical embryology; molluscan and echinoderm fertilization; nucleic acid and protein metabolism of the gastropod embryo. *Mailing Add:* Dept of Biol Brooklyn Col New York NY 11210

COLLIER, JAMES BRYAN, b Portland, Maine, Apr 9, 44; m 72. GEOMETRY. *Educ:* Carleton Col, BA, 66; Univ Wash, PhD(math), 72. *Prof Exp:* Fel math, Dalhousie Univ, 72-73; asst prof math, Univ Southern Calif, 73-80; MEM TECH STAFF, JET PROPULSION LAB, CALIF INST TECHNOL, LOS ANGELES, 80- *Mem:* Am Math Soc. *Res:* Convex functions; convex sets; polytopes; graphs. *Mailing Add:* Jet Propulsion Lab Calif Inst Technol 2165 Talmadge St Los Angeles CA 90027

COLLIER, JESSE WILTON, b Killeen, Tex, Dec 20, 14; m 40; c 2. AGRONOMY, GENETICS. *Educ:* Tex A&M Univ, BS, 38, MS, 52; Rutgers Univ, PhD(agron), 57. *Prof Exp:* Jr soil surveyor, Soil Conserv Serv, USDA, 38-41; instr agr, Tex A&M Univ, 41-43; asst agr, Tex Agr Exp Sta, 43-53; res assoc, Rutgers Univ, 53-55; asst agronomist, 55-57, assoc prof, 57-72, PROF AGRON, TEX AGR EXP STA, 72-; prof, 78-79, EMER PROF AGRON, TEX A&M UNIV, 79- *Concurrent Pos:* Assoc prof agron, Tex A&M Univ, 64-77. *Mem:* Am Soc Agron; Crop Sci Soc Am. *Res:* Plant breeding methods in corn and grain sorghum; foundation seed production of several crops including small grains, corn, grain sorghum and vegetables. *Mailing Add:* 3919 Hilltop Dr Bryan TX 77801

COLLIER, JOHN ROBERT, b Indianapolis, Ind, Oct 4, 39; m 61; c 1. CHEMICAL ENGINEERING, POLYMER SCIENCE. *Educ:* SDak Sch Mines & Tech, BS, 61; Univ Ill, Urbana, MS, 62; Case Inst Technol, PhD(polymer sci, eng), 66. *Prof Exp:* Asst chem eng, Univ Ill, Urbana, 61-62; res asst polymer sci & eng, Case Inst Technol, 62-66; from asst prof to assoc prof, 66-72, assoc dean grad col, 72-78, PROF CHEM ENG, OHIO UNIV, 72- *Concurrent Pos:* Res engr plastics dept, E I du Pont de Nemours & Co, Inc, WVa, 66, res & ed consult, 67, retained res consult, 68-; mem bd dirs, Wittenberg Univ, 77- *Mem:* Soc Plastics Engrs; Am Inst Chem Engrs; Am Chem Soc. *Res:* Interrelationships between processing conditions, morphology and resultant properties of semicrystalline polymers; tailoring of properties of polymers. *Mailing Add:* Dept of Chem Eng Ohio Univ Athens OH 45701

COLLIER, MELVIN LOWELL, b Richmond, Va, Oct 17, 34; m 57; c 2. FLUID MECHANICS, MECHANICAL ENGINEERING. *Educ:* Va Polytech Inst, BS, 57, MS, 59, PhD(eng mech), 63. *Prof Exp:* Assoc prof engr mech, Va Polytech Inst, 63-66; dept mgr appl mech, Hydrospace Res Corp, 66-69; prin engr design, Litton Industs Inc, 69-71; engr fluid mech, Naval Ship Res & Develop Ctr, 71-72; dir engr, Tracor Marine Inc, 72-77; VPRES ENG DESIGN & DEVELOP, GEN OFFSHORE CORP, 77- *Mem:* Am Welding Soc; Marine Technol Soc. *Res:* Design and development of marine machinery for ocean engineering work; dynamics of cable towed and cable moored systems; design and development of dynamic oceanographic buoys; mathematics modeling of ocean engineering systems. *Mailing Add:* 7451 11th Ct NW Plantation FL 33313

COLLIER, ROBERT JACOB, b Springfield, Mass, May 27, 26; m 56; c 2. ELECTRON OPTICS. *Educ:* Yale Univ, BS, 50, MS, 51, PhD(physics), 54. *Prof Exp:* Mem tech staff res & develop, 54-59, supvr, 59-71, SUPVR ELECTRON OPTICS GROUP, BELL LABS, 71- *Mem:* Am Phys Soc; fel Optical Soc Am. *Res:* High power traveling wave tube amplifiers; optical memory devices; holography; scanning electron beam devices; design of electron optical systems for electron lithography. *Mailing Add:* Bell Labs Murray Hill NJ 07974

COLLIER, ROBERT JOHN, b Wichita Falls, Tex, Aug 6, 38; m 62; c 3. PATHOBIOLOGY, BIOCHEMISTRY. *Educ:* Rice Univ, BA, 59; Harvard Univ, MS, 61, PhD(biol), 64. *Prof Exp:* NIH fel Harvard Univ, 64; NSF fel, Inst Molecular Biol, Geneva, Switz, 64-66; from asst prof to assoc prof, 66-74, PROF BACT, UNIV CALIF, LOS ANGELES, 74- *Concurrent Pos:* Guggenheim Found fel, Pasteur Inst, Paris, France, 73-74. *Honors & Awards:* Eli Lilly & Co Award Microbiol & Immunol, Am Soc Microbiol, 72. *Mem:* AAAS; Am Soc Microbiol; Am Soc Biol Chem. *Res:* Structure and activity of bacterial toxins; selective targeting of toxin action. *Mailing Add:* Dept of Microbiol Univ of Calif Los Angeles CA 90024

COLLIER, ROBERT JOSEPH, b Madison, Ind, Feb 15, 47; c 2. PHYSIOLOGY, ENDOCRINOLGY. *Educ:* Eastern Ill Univ, BS, 69, MS, 74; Univ Ill, PhD(physiol), 76. *Prof Exp:* Res asst dairy sci, Univ Ill, 73-76; res assoc, Mich State Univ, 76-; asst prof, 76-81, PROF DAIRY SCI, UNIV FLA, 81- *Mem:* Am Dairy Sci Asn; Am Soc Animal Sci; Sigma Xi; AAAS. *Res:* Physiology of lactation and environmental effects on dairy cattle; environmental effects on endocrine system of dairy cattle. *Mailing Add:* Dept Dairy Sci Univ Fla Gainesville FL 32611

COLLIER, SUSAN S, b Washington, DC, Nov 5, 39. PHOTOCHEMISTRY. *Educ:* Cornell Univ, BA, 61; Univ Rochester, PhD(spectros), 66. *Prof Exp:* Fel, Univ Rochester, 66; D J Wilson vis res assoc, Ohio State Univ, 66-69; J G Calvert spec fel air pollution, 69; sr chemist, 69-74, RES ASSOC, RES LABS, EASTMAN KODAK CO, 74- *Concurrent Pos:* assoc ed, Photog Sci & Eng, 80- *Mem:* Am Chem Soc; Soc Photog Sci & Eng. *Res:* Chemical sensitization of photographic systems; spectral sensitization; microwave photoconductivity. *Mailing Add:* 7330 Selden Rd LeRoy NY 14482

COLLIGAN, GEORGE AUSTIN, b Far Rockaway, NY, Sept 10, 28; m 51; c 6. METALLURGICAL & CERAMIC ENGINEERING. *Educ:* Rensselaer Polytech Inst, BMetE, 50; Univ Mich, MS, 57, PhD(metall eng), 59. *Prof Exp:* Asst foundry metallurgist, Farrel-Birmingham Co, Conn, 50-52; foundry metallurgist, Turbine Div, Gen Elec Co, 52-54, proj engr, Res Lab, 54-55; instr metall eng, Col Eng & proj engr, Eng Res Inst, Univ Mich, 55-59; sr res scientist, Res Labs, United Aircraft Corp, 59-62; assoc prof, 62-66, assoc dean, 67-77, PROF ENG, THAYER SCH ENG, DARTMOUTH COL, 66- *Concurrent Pos:* Adj asst prof, Hartford Grad Div, Rensselaer Polytech Inst, 59-62; consult, United Aircraft Corp, Mass Mat Res Corp & Howmet Corp, 62- *Honors & Awards:* Thomas W Pangborn Gold Medal Award, Am Foundrymens Soc, 70. *Mem:* Am Ceramic Soc; Am Soc Metals; Am Inst Mining, Metall & Petrol Engrs; Am Foundrymens Soc; NY Acad Sci. *Res:* Solidification of metals; metal ceramic reaction studies; x-ray diffraction and fluorescence studies. *Mailing Add:* 33 Rayton Rd Hanover NH 03755

COLLIGAN, JOHN JOSEPH, b Watertown, NY, Feb 8, 37; m 58; c 3. SCIENCE POLICY, COMPUTER SCIENCE EDUCATION. *Educ:* Le Moyne Col, NY, BS, 58; Univ Notre Dame, MS, 60; State Univ NY Buffalo, PhD(policy sci), 72. *Prof Exp:* Jr engr, Int Bus Mach Corp, 60-61; from assoc engr to sr assoc engr, 61-64; asst prof physics, Broome Tech Commun Col, 64-67; admin asst, 67-68, asst dean, 68-69, assoc dean, 69-76, dir state tech serv, 67-72, DEAN, SCH ADVAN TECHNOL, STATE UNIV NY BINGHAMTON, 76- *Concurrent Pos:* Consult, Comn Col Physics Teachers, 69- *Mem:* Inst Elec & Electronics Engrs; Am Soc Eng Educ. *Res:* Marriage and family life. *Mailing Add:* Sch of Advan Technol State Univ of NY Binghamton NY 13901

COLLIN, PIERRE-PAUL, b Montreal, Que, July 23, 20; m 49; c 5. PEDIATRIC SURGERY. *Educ:* Univ Montreal, BA, 41, MD, 48. *Prof Exp:* Asst prof, 66-70, assoc prof, 70-76, PROF SURG, FAC MED, UNIV MONTREAL, 76- DIR SURG, STE JUSTINE HOSP, 66- *Concurrent Pos:* Consult, Hopital Marie-Enfant, 70- *Mem:* Fel Am Col Surg; fel Int Col Surg; fel Am Acad Pediat; fel Royal Col Surgeons Can; Am Pediat Surg Asn. *Mailing Add:* Dept of Surg Univ of Montreal Montreal Can

COLLIN, ROBERT E(MANUEL), b Donalda, Alta, Oct 24, 28; nat US; m 52; c 3. ELECTRICAL ENGINEERING. *Educ:* Univ Sask, BSc, 51; Univ London, DIC, 53, PhD(microwaves), 54. *Prof Exp:* Sci officer, Can Armament Res & Develop Estab, 54-58; from asst prof to assoc prof elec eng, 58-65, PROF ELEC ENG, CASE WESTERN RESERVE UNIV, 65-, CHMN DEPT ELEC ENG & APPL PHYSICS, 78- *Concurrent Pos:* Mem, US Comn 6, Int Sci Radio Union. *Mem:* Fel Inst Elec & Electronics Engrs. *Res:* Microwaves; antennas; electromagnetic diffraction; plasma physics. *Mailing Add:* Dept of Elec Sci & Appl Physics University Circle Cleveland OH 44106

COLLIN, WILLIAM KENT, b Los Angeles, Calif, Mar 31, 38; m 64; c 2. MEDICAL MICROBIOLOGY. *Educ:* Univ Calif, Davis, BA, 61; Univ Calif, Los Angeles, PhD(med microbiol & immunol), 68. *Prof Exp:* Fel electron micros virol, parasitol, Sch Pub Health, Univ Calif, Los Angeles, 68-70, from asst res virologist to asst res pediatrician, Dept Pediat, Sch Med, 70-74; biol res coordr dermatol, Redken Labs Inc, 74-75; lectr microbiol, 75-77, assoc, 78-80, PROF BIOL, CALIF STATE UNIV, FRESNO, 80- *Concurrent Pos:* NIH fel, 68. *Mem:* Am Soc Parasitologists; AAAS; Sigma Xi; Am Soc Microbiol. *Res:* Cytodifferentiation and histogenesis of cestode larval forms; lymphocytic responsiveness in viropathology; virol & parasitologic epidemology. *Mailing Add:* Dept of Biol Calif State Univ Fresno CA 93740

COLLINGHAM, RICHARD ELLIS, mechanical engineering, see previous edition

COLLINGS, CHARLES KENNETH, b Princeton, Mo, Apr 18, 05; m 26; c 2. DENTISTRY. *Educ:* Univ Mo, BS, 27, MA, 32; Baylor Univ, DDS, 49; Am Bd Periodont, dipl, 54. *Prof Exp:* High sch teacher, Mo, 27-31; asst zool, Univ Mo, 31-32, instr, 32-33; high sch teacher, Mo, 33-44; asst prof anat & physiol, 44-48, assoc prof, 48-49, prof, 49-51, chmn dept periodont, 51-73, EMER PROF PERIODONT, COL DENT, BAYLOR UNIV, 73- *Concurrent Pos:* Consult, William Beaumont Army Hosp, El Paso, Tex, USPHS Hosp & Carswell AFB, Ft Worth, Vet Admin Hosp, Dallas & Brooke Army Hosp, San Antonio. *Honors & Awards:* Piper Prof Tex, Minnie Stevens Piper Found, 62; Distinguished Serv Award, Tex State Dental Asn, 75, Hon Order of Good Fel, 77. *Mem:* AAAS; Am Acad Periodont; Am Dent Asn; Soc Exp Biol & Med; fel Am Col Dent. *Res:* Physiological effects of terramycin mouthwash on oral flora; rate of alveolar bone resorption in dentulous and edentulous mouths. *Mailing Add:* 2020 W Five Mile Pkwy Dallas TX 75224

COLLINGS, EDWARD WILLIAM, b New Plymouth, NZ, Jan 22, 30; m 53; c 2. EXPERIMENTAL SOLID STATE PHYSICS. *Educ:* Univ NZ, BSc, 51, MSc, 52, PhD(physics), 58; Victoria Univ Wellington, DSc(physics), 70. *Prof Exp:* mem fac physics, Victoria Univ Wellington, 52-61; sr res physicist, Franklin Inst Res Labs, Philadelphia, Pa, 62-66; SR RES PHYSICIST, COLUMBUS LABS, BATTELLE MEM INST, 66- *Concurrent Pos:* Nat Res Coun Can fel, 58-60. *Mem:* AAAS; Am Phys Soc; Metall Soc; Am Inst Mining, Metall & Petrol Engrs; Mat Res Soc. *Res:* Electronic, magnetic, and low-temperature calorimetric properties of alloys (particularly titanium alloys and stainless steels) and intermetallic compounds; applied superconductivity; relationships between electronic and mechanical properties of metals; properties of rapidly quenched alloys and metallic glasses. other electronic properties; rapidly quenched and glassy metals; superconducting materials properties, fabrication and applications. *Mailing Add:* Battelle Columbus Labs 505 King Ave Columbus OH 43201

COLLINGS, PETER JOHN, b Jamaica, NY, Jan 29, 47; m 69; c 2. SOLID STATE PHYSICS, CHEMICAL PHYSICS. *Educ:* Amherst Col, BA, 68; Yale Univ, MPh, 73, PhD(physics), 76. *Prof Exp:* Teaching fel physics, Yale Univ, 72-75, res asst, 73-75, actg instr, 75-76; ASST PROF PHYSICS,

KENYON COL, 76-, CHMN, DEPT PHYSICS, 79- *Concurrent Pos:* Res assoc, Liquid Crystal Inst, Kent State Univ, 77; NSF grant, 77-78; Res Corp Cottrell Col Sci grant, 78-81. *Mem:* Am Asn Physics Teachers; Am Phys Soc; AAAS; Sigma Xi. *Res:* Physics and chemistry of liquid crystals; order parameter measurements; thermodynamic measurements; optical measurements. *Mailing Add:* Dept of Physics Kenyon Col Gambier OH 43022

COLLINS, ALLAN CLIFFORD, b Milwaukee, Wis, June 14, 42; m 62; c 2. BIOCHEMICAL PHARMACOLOGY, BEHAVIORAL GENETICS. *Educ:* Univ Wis-Madison, BS, 65, MS, 67, PhD(pharmacol), 69. *Prof Exp:* Instr pharmacol, Univ Wis-Milwaukee, 68-69; NIH fel, Med Sch, Univ Colo, Denver, 69-71; res pharmacologist, Vet Admin Hosp, Houston, Tex, 71-72; asst prof, 72-78, ASSOC PROF PHARMACOL, UNIV COLO, BOULDER, 78-, FEL, INST BEHAV GENETICS, 73- *Mem:* Am Soc Neurochem. *Res:* Biochemical bases of tolerance to and dependence upon alcohol, barbiturates and nicotine; use of behavior genetic techniques to test hypotheses concerning mechanisms by which these drugs exert their behavioral effects. *Mailing Add:* Sch of Pharm Univ of Colo Boulder CO 80309

COLLINS, ALVA LEROY, JR, b Sanford, Fla, May 15, 40; m 67. INORGANIC CHEMISTRY, ENERGY PROGRAM MANAGEMENT. *Educ:* Oberlin Col, AB, 62; Duke Univ, MA, 66, PhD(chem), 67; Wharton Col, MBA, 77. *Prof Exp:* Res chemist, Am Cyanamid Co, 66-67; res assoc inorg chem, Ind Univ, 67-68; asst prof chem, Sam Houston State Univ, 68-75; ASSOC, RESOURCE PLANNING ASSOCS, 77- *Mem:* Am Chem Soc. *Res:* Analysis of energy supply and demand; management planning of energy programs. *Mailing Add:* Resource Planning Assocs Suite 400 1901 L St NW Washington DC 20036

COLLINS, AMY L TSUI, radiotherapy, immunology, see previous edition

COLLINS, ANITA MARGUERITE, b Allentown, Pa, Nov 8, 47. GENETICS, ANIMAL BEHAVIOR. *Educ:* Pa State Univ, BS, 69; Ohio State Univ, MSc, 72, PhD(genetics), 76. *Prof Exp:* Instr biol, Mercyhurst Col, 75-76; RES GENETICIST, BEE BREEDING & STOCK CTR LAB, AGR RES, SCI & EDUC ADMIN, USDA, 76- *Mem:* Asn Women Sci; Genetics Soc Am; Am Genetic Asn; Animal Behav Soc; Entom Soc Am. *Res:* Population, genetics and behavior of honey bees; defensive behavior and response to alarm pheromone. *Mailing Add:* Bee Breeding and Stock Ctr Lab Rte 3 Box 82-B Ben Hur Rd Baton Rouge LA 70808

COLLINS, ARLEE GENE, b Forest City, Iowa, Dec 20, 27; m 53; c 2. GEOCHEMISTRY. *Educ:* Kletzing Col, BA, 51; Kans State Col Pittsburg, MS, 55; Univ Tulsa, MS, 72. *Prof Exp:* Chemist, H C Maffitt, Consult Chemist, Iowa, 51-53 & Spencer Chem Co, Kans, 53-56; asst chief chemist, Consumers Coop Refinery, 56; proj leader geochem of petrol reservoirs, US Bur Mines, 56-75, proj leader, Bartlesville Energy Res Ctr, Energy Res & Develop Admin, 75-77; PROJ LEADER, BARTLESVILLE ENERGY TECHNOL CTR, US DEPT ENERGY, 77- *Concurrent Pos:* Mem task group, Fed Adv Comt on Water Data; mem, Adv Counc, Petrol Data Syst. *Mem:* Am Chem Soc; Geochem Soc Am; Am Soc Testing & Mat; Int Asn Geochem & Cosmochem; Am Inst Mining, Metall & Petrol Engrs. *Res:* Geochemistry of oil and gas reservoirs for the characterization of reservoirs for enhanced recovery. *Mailing Add:* Bartlesville Energy Technol Ctr US Dept of Energy Bartlesville OK 74003

COLLINS, ARLENE RYCOMBEL, b Buffalo, NY, Jan 2, 40; m 65; c 3. VIROLOGY, MICROBIOLOGY. *Educ:* D'Youville Col, BA, 61; State Univ NY, Buffalo, MA, 64, PhD(microbiol, virol), 67. *Prof Exp:* Instr microbiol, Med Col Wis, 69; asst prof, 71-78, ASSOC PROF MICROBIOL, STATE UNIV NY, BUFFALO, 78- *Concurrent Pos:* Fel Dept Microbiol, State Univ NY, Buffalo, 67-68; fel Med Col Wis, 69-70; adv comt math sci curric, Erie Community Col, 72-; vis investr, Dept Immunopath, Scripps Clin & Res Found, La Jolla, Calif, 81. *Mem:* Am Soc Microbiol; Soc Gen Microbiol; Am Asn Univ Women; Am Women Sci. *Res:* Virology, coronaviruses, mouse hepatitis virus; paramyxoviruses; Sendai virus; interferon response; persistent virus infections; monoclonal antibodies, viral antigens. *Mailing Add:* Virus Lab 218 Sherman Hall State Univ NY Buffalo NY 14214

COLLINS, ARTHUR A(NDREWS), b Kingfisher, Okla, Sept 9, 09; m 55; c 4. ELECTRONICS. *Hon Degrees:* DSc, Coe Col, 54; DEng, Brooklyn Polytech Inst, 68 & Southern Methodist Univ, 70. *Prof Exp:* PRES & CHMN BD DIR, ARTHUR A COLLINS, INC, 31- *Honors & Awards:* Distinguished Pub Serv Award, Secy Navy, 62. *Mem:* Nat Acad Eng; fel Inst Elec & Electronics Engrs. *Res:* Invention and development of electronic equipment for radio communication, navigation, flight control, data communication and computation. *Mailing Add:* 4353 Woodhollow Dr Dallas TX 75237

COLLINS, BARBARA JANE, b Passaic, NJ, Apr 29, 29; m 55; c 5. BOTANY. *Educ:* Bates Col, BS, 51; Smith Col, MS, 53; Univ Ill, PhD(geol), 55, MS, 59. *Prof Exp:* Instr geol, Univ Ill, 57, teaching asst bot, 57-59; assoc prof biol, 63-76, PROF BIOL SCI, CALIF LUTHERAN COL, 77- *Mem:* Am Soc Microbiol. *Res:* Taxonomy of gymnosperms and angiosperms; keys to the flora of regional areas; electron microscopy of clay minerals; replication. *Mailing Add:* Dept of Bot Calif Lutheran Col Thousand Oaks CA 91360

COLLINS, BILL MARTIN, speech pathology, see previous edition

COLLINS, CARL BAXTER, JR, b San Antonio, Tex, Mar 4, 40; m 60, 73; c 4. LASERS. *Educ:* Univ Tex, BS, 60, MA, 61, PhD, 63. *Prof Exp:* Instr physics, Univ Tex, 62-64; from asst prof to assoc prof, Southwest Ctr Advan Studies, 64-69, assoc prof, Univ, 69-74, head grad physics prog, 72-75, PROF PHYSICS UNIV TEX, DALLAS, 74- *Concurrent Pos:* Res asst, Univ Tex, 63-64. *Mem:* Fel Am Phys Soc. *Res:* Ion-electron recombination processes; gaseous electronics; low energy plasmas; atomic and molecular collision processes; high energy lasers; multiphoton spectroscopy; isotope separation. *Mailing Add:* Dept of Physics Univ of Tex Dallas PO Box 668 Richardson TX 75080

COLLINS, CAROL HOLLINGWORTH, b Lowell, Mass, Mar 21, 31; m 55; c 1. RADIOANALYTICAL CHEMISTRY, CHROMATOGRAPHY. *Educ:* Bates Col, BS, 52; Iowa State Univ, PhD(phys & org chem), 58. *Prof Exp:* Res scientist, Brookhaven Nat Lab, 62-63; sr res scientist, Western New York Nuclear Res Ctr, 64-67; asst prof org chem, State Univ NY Buffalo, 67-68; res scientist, Starks Assocs, 68-72; cancer res scientist, Roswell Park Mem Inst, 72-74; PROF ANAL CHEM, UNIV ESTADUAL DE CAMPINAS, 74- *Mem:* Am Nuclear Soc; Soc Nuclear Med; Radiation Res Soc; Soc Brasileira Progresso Ciencia; Soc Brasileira Quimica. *Res:* Chromatography applied to analyses of trace quantities of components generally in the presence of large quantities of similar species, using radio analytical determinations. *Mailing Add:* UNI CAMP-Quimica Cedade Univ Campinas SP 13100 Brazil

COLLINS, CAROLYN JANE, b White Plains, NY, Sept 18, 42. TUMOR VIRUSES, CELL TRANSFORMATION. *Educ:* Skidmore Col, BA, 64; Duke Univ, PhD(biochem), 70. *Prof Exp:* Fel tumor viruses, Ger Ctr Cancer Res, 70-72; fel, Dept Microbiol, Univ Mich, Ann Arbor, 73-76; asst prof microbiol, Univ Va, 76-82; MEM STAFF, SIDNEY FARBER CANCER INST, 82- *Concurrent Pos:* F G Novy fel, Univ Mich, Ann Arbor, 73-74; USPHS fel, 75-76; prin invest-grant, Nat Cancer Inst, 78-81. *Mem:* Am Soc Microbiol; Sigma Xi; NY Acad Sci; AAAS. *Res:* Molecular biology of tumor viruses; mechanism of viral integration and host cell transformation; molecular basis of reversion of viral transformed cells to normal phenotype. *Mailing Add:* Sidney Farber Cancer Inst 44 Binney St Boston MA 02115

COLLINS, CARTER COMPTON, b San Francisco, Calif, Aug 3, 25; m 61; c 2. BIOPHYSICS. *Educ:* Univ Calif, BS, 49, MS, 53, PhD(biophys), 66. *Prof Exp:* Consult biomech group, Med Ctr, Univ Calif, San Francisco, 50-54; assoc engr, Res & Develop Labs, 55, dir, 59-63; res mem, Inst Visual Sci, Pac Med Ctr, San Francisco, 63-69; assoc prof visual sci, Univ Pac, 69-71; SR SCIENTIST, SMITH-KETTLEWELL INST VISUAL SCI, INST MED SCI, 71- *Concurrent Pos:* Res & develop engr, Donner Sci Co, 53; pres, Sutter Instruments, Inc, 53-; Consult, Neurosurg Inst, Mt Zion Hosp, 54 & Dept Physiol, Univ Pa, 57-58; lectr, Cardiovasc Res Inst, 59; mem armed forces comt vision, Nat Acad Sci-Nat Res Coun. *Honors & Awards:* Hektoen Silver Medal Award, AMA, 72. *Mem:* AAAS; NY Acad Sci; Asn Res Ophthal; Inst Elec & Electronics Eng. *Res:* Conception and design of instrumentation for extracting information from physical and biological systems; basic correlates of recognition; neural information transfer codes; control of eye movements; vision substitution by tactile TV image projection. *Mailing Add:* 2232 Webster St San Francisco CA 94115

COLLINS, CHARLES THOMPSON, b Long Branch, NJ, Mar 9, 38. ZOOLOGY, ORNITHOLOGY. *Educ:* Amherst Col, AB, 60; Univ Mich, MS, 62; Univ Fla, PhD(zool), 66. *Prof Exp:* Am Mus Natural Hist Chapman res fel, 66-67; asst prof biol, Fairleigh Dickinson Univ, Florham-Madison Campus, 67-68; asst prof, 68-72, assoc prof, 72-77, PROF BIOL, CALIF STATE UNIV, LONG BEACH, 77- *Concurrent Pos:* Fulbright res scholar, India, 74-75. *Mem:* Am Ornith Union; Wilson Ornith Soc; Cooper Ornith Soc; Am Inst Biol Sci; Asn Trop Biol. *Res:* Ornithology, particularly biology and ecology of swifts. *Mailing Add:* Dept of Biol Calif State Univ Long Beach CA 90840

COLLINS, CLAIR JOSEPH, b Austin, Minn, Aug 16, 15; m 49; c 3. PHYSICAL ORGANIC CHEMISTRY. *Educ:* Univ Minn, BChemEng, 37, MS, 39; Northwestern Univ, PhD(org chem), 44. *Prof Exp:* Org chemist, Eli Lilly & Co, Ind, 39-41; asst, Northwestern Univ, 41-44; GROUP LEADER, OAK RIDGE NAT LAB, 47- *Concurrent Pos:* Fulbright lectr, Univ Tubingen, 68-69; prof chem, Univ Tenn, Knoxville, 64-80; Alexander von Humboldt Award, 82. *Honors & Awards:* Southern Chemist Award, Am Chem Soc, 79; Alexander von Humboldt Award, 82. *Mem:* Am Chem Soc. *Res:* Reaction mechanisms with deuterium, tritium and carbon-14; molecular rearrangements; isotope effects; fuel science; reactions of coal with 14C-labeled reagents; free radical reactions. *Mailing Add:* Chem Div Oak Ridge Nat Lab Oak Ridge TN 37830

COLLINS, CLIFFORD B, b Can, Nov 12, 16; nat US; m 42; c 3. PHYSICS. *Educ:* Univ Western Ont, BSc, 47; McMaster Univ, MA, 48; Univ Toronto, PhD(physics), 51. *Prof Exp:* Res assoc physics, Univ Toronto, 51-52; res assoc, Res Labs, 52-56, physicist lamp develop, 56-66, GROUP LEADER LAMP DEPT, GEN ELEC CO, 66- *Mem:* Am Phys Soc; Electrochem Soc. *Res:* Lamp development; materials liaison; technical planning. *Mailing Add:* Lamp Dept Gen Elec Co Nela Park Cleveland OH 44112

COLLINS, CURTIS ALLAN, b Des Moines, Iowa, Sept, 40; m 62; c 2. PHYSICAL OCEANOGRAPHY. *Educ:* US Merchant Marine Acad, BS, 62; Ore State Univ, PhD(oceanog), 67. *Prof Exp:* Res scientist, Pac Oceanog Group, Nanaimo, BC, 68-70; sr tech adv oceanog, Cities Serv Oil Co, Okla, 70-72; prog mgr environ forecasting, Off Int Decade Ocean Explor, 72-80, PROG MGR OCEAN DYNAMICS, OCEAN SCI, NSF, 80- *Mem:* Am Geophys Union. *Res:* Descriptive physical oceanography of the Pacific Ocean. *Mailing Add:* Int Decade Ocean Explor Rm 605 NSF Washington DC 20550

COLLINS, DEAN ROBERT, b Ft Sill, Okla, Dec 8, 35; m 62; c 3. ELECTRONICS, SOLID STATE PHYSICS. *Educ:* Mass Inst Technol, SB & SM, 59; Univ Ill, Urbana, PhD(elec eng), 67. *Prof Exp:* Coop eng studies, Int Bus Mach Corp, 56-58; mem tech staff, Bell Tel Labs, 59-60 & 62-63; asst prof elec eng, Va Polytech Inst, 61-62; asst, Univ Ill, 63-66; mem tech staff, Semiconductor Res & Develop Lab, 66-69, Cent Res Labs, 69-73, br mgr, CCD Technol Br, 73-77, dir, CCD Technol Lab, 77-79, DIR, INTERFACE TECHNOL LAB, TEX INSTRUMENTS INC, 79- *Mem:* Sr mem Inst Elec & Electronics Engrs; Am Phys Soc; Electrochem Soc; Soc Info Display. *Res:* Bucket brigade shift registers; current gain degradation; effect of gold on the silicon-silicon dioxide interface; insulating thin films; charge coupled device imagers; memory and signal processing; liquid crystal displays, electroluminescent displays; printers. *Mailing Add:* MS 119 Interface Technol Lab Tex Instruments Dallas TX 75265

COLLINS, DELWOOD C, b Cairo, Ga, Oct 7, 37; m 62; c 3. BIOCHEMISTRY, ENDOCRINOLOGY. *Educ:* Emory Univ, AB, 59; Univ Ga, MS, 63, PhD(endocrinol, physiol), 66. *Prof Exp:* Res scientist, Div Pharmacol, Food & Drug Directorate, Ottawa, Ont, 67-68; res assoc steroid biochem, Univ Ottawa, 68-69; asst prof med & instr biochem, 69-72, assoc prof med, 69-77, asst prof biochem, 72-79, PROF MED, 78- & ASSOC PROF BIOCHEM, MED SCH, EMORY UNIV, 79-; COLLAB SCIENTIST, YERKES PRIMATE CTR, 71- *Concurrent Pos:* Squibb Ayrest traveling fel, 68; Nat Inst Arthritis, Metab & Digestive Dis career develop award, 72-77. *Mem:* AAAS; Soc Study Reproduction; Endocrine Soc; Can Biochem Soc; Am Chem Soc. *Res:* Metabolism and conjugation of steroids; radioimmunoassay of steroids; gas chromatography of steroids; reproductive physiology of primates; physiological effects of estrogen; reproductive physiology. *Mailing Add:* Dept Med Emory Univ Med Sch Atlanta GA 30322

COLLINS, DESMOND H, b Daylesford, Australia, July 15, 38; m 64; c 3. PALEONTOLOGY. *Educ:* Univ Western Australia, BSc, 60; Univ Iowa, PhD(geol), 66. *Prof Exp:* Tech officer, Geol Surv Can, 64-65; sr res fel paleont, Brit Mus, London, 66-68; CUR INVERT PALEONT, ROYAL ONT MUS, 68- *Concurrent Pos:* Assoc prof zool, Univ Toronto, 70-; res assoc, McMaster Univ, 71- *Mem:* Am Paleont Soc; Brit Palaeont Asn; Brit Palaeontographical Soc; Int Paleont Union; Geol Soc Can. *Res:* Paleozoic nautiloid cephalopod systematics and shell function; burgess shale fossils. *Mailing Add:* Invert Palaeont Royal Ont Mus 100 Queen's Park Toronto ON M8X 1K1 Can

COLLINS, DON DESMOND, b Cardwell, Mont, Jan 10, 34; m 72; c 3. PLANT ECOLOGY, PLANT GENETICS. *Educ:* Mont State Univ, BS, 61, PhD(genetics), 65. *Prof Exp:* From asst prof to assoc prof, 65-78, PROF ECOL, MONT STATE UNIV, 78- *Concurrent Pos:* Nat Park Serv grant, 67-68; NSF grant, 68-73, 78; Int Biol Prog grant, 69-72; consult, Grassland Info Synthesis Proj, Int Biol Prog, Grassland Biome, 68-72; ecologist, pvt indust, 80- *Mem:* Ecol Soc Am; Bot Soc Am; Nat Parks Asn. *Res:* Ecological research on effects of weather modification and vegetational response to campground usage; mountain grasslands; impact of pipeline systems. *Mailing Add:* Dept of Bot Mont State Univ Bozeman MT 59715

COLLINS, EDWARD A, b Winnipeg, Man, Can, May 22, 28; US citizen; m 52; c 3. PHYSICAL CHEMISTRY, POLYMER CHEMISTRY. *Educ:* Univ Man, BS, 50, MS, 52, PhD(phys chem), 67. *Prof Exp:* Lectr phys chem, Royal Mil Col, Ont, 51-52; develop chemist, 52-54, assoc develop scientist, 56-59, develop scientist, 59-62, sr scientist, 62-65, develop consult, B F Goodrich Chem Co, 65-78; ASSOC DIR CORP RES, DIAMOND SHAMROCK CORP, 78- *Concurrent Pos:* Adj prof, Rensselaer Polytech Inst, 68-78; Cleveland State Univ, 69-79 & Case Western Reserve Univ, 75-82. *Mem:* Am Chem Soc; Soc Rheol; Brit Soc Rheol. *Res:* Polymer characterization and relation of molecular structure to physical and mechanical properties; rheology. *Mailing Add:* Diamond Shamrock Corp TR Evans Res Ctr PO Box 348 Painesville OH 44077

COLLINS, EDWIN BRUCE, b Conway, SC, Aug 5, 21; m 53. FOOD MICROBIOLOGY. *Educ:* Clemson Col, BS, 43; Iowa State Col, MS, 48, PhD(dairy bact), 49. *Prof Exp:* From instr dairy indust & jr dairy bacteriologist to assoc prof dairy indust & assoc dairy bacteriologist, 49-64, PROF FOOD SCI, UNIV CALIF, DAVIS & DAIRY BACTERIOLOGIST, EXP STA, 64- *Mem:* Am Soc Microbiol; Am Dairy Sci Asn. *Mailing Add:* Dept Food Sci & Technol Univ Calif Davis CA 95616

COLLINS, ELLIOTT JOEL, b New York, NY, June 12, 19; m 47; c 2. ENDOCRINOLOGY. *Educ:* Col of Charleston, BS, 49; Princeton Univ, MA, 51, PhD(biol), 52. *Prof Exp:* Res scientist, Upjohn Co, 52-62; MGR, REGULATORY AFFAIRS, SCHERING CORP, 62- *Mem:* Soc Exp Biol & Med; Endocrine Soc; affil Royal Soc Med. *Res:* Endocrine physiology; metabolic bone disease; connective tissue disease. *Mailing Add:* Schering Corp Bloomfield NJ 07003

COLLINS, F(RED) R(OBERT), b US, July 19, 26; m 50; c 5. ELECTRICAL ENGINEERING. *Educ:* Brown Univ, BS, 47. *Prof Exp:* Sect head, Alcoa Labs, Aluminum Co Am, 58-62, asst div chief, 62-67, chief elec eng div, 67-78, dir res & eng, 75-78, V PRES TECH, ALCOA CONDUCTOR PRODS CO, DIV ALCOA, 78- *Mem:* Inst Elec & Electronics Engrs; Am Welding Soc. *Res:* Aluminum reduction; welding and brazing; soldering aluminum; aluminum transmission and distribution conductors; connectors and other products used by the electrical power industry. *Mailing Add:* Alcoa Conductor Prods Co 510 One Allegheny Sq Pittsburgh PA 15212

COLLINS, FRANCIS ALLEN, b Wichita, Kans, July 24, 31. SOLID STATE PHYSICS, CHEMICAL PHYSICS. *Educ:* Univ Tex, BS, 54, MA, 57; Harvard Univ, PhD(appl physics), 64. *Prof Exp:* Physicist, Defense Res Labs, Univ Tex, 53-58; asst prof optics, Univ Rochester, 64-69; mem staff, Appl Res Labs, Univ Tex Austin, 69-77; MEM STAFF, HUGHES AIRCRAFT CO, 77- *Mem:* Am Phys Soc. *Res:* Airborne Radar. *Mailing Add:* Hughes Aircraft Co Culver City CA 90230

COLLINS, FRANK CHARLES, b Marton, NZ, Sept 18, 11; nat US; m 41; c 1. PHYSICAL CHEMISTRY. *Educ:* Univ Calif, AB, 39; Columbia Univ, AM, 47, PhD(chem), 49. *Prof Exp:* Chemist, Shell Develop Co, Calif, 39-46; lectr anal chem, Columbia Univ, 47-48; asst prof, 48-51, prof phys & environ chem, 51-77, ADJ PROF, POLYTECH INST NY, 77-; CONSULT, TECHNOL & PUB AFFAIRS, 81- *Concurrent Pos:* Consult, Oil, Chem & Atomic Workers Int Union, 75-81. *Mem:* Am Chem Soc; AAAS; Am Nuclear Soc; Fedn Am Scientists; Scientists Inst Pub Info. *Res:* Energy and public policy; nuclear policy problems; occupational health and safety. *Mailing Add:* PO Box 2186 Livermore CA 94550

COLLINS, FRANK GIBSON, b Chicago, Ill, Feb 20, 38; m 60; c 2. FLUID MECHANICS, AERODYNAMICS. *Educ:* Northwestern Univ, BS, 61; Univ Calif, Berkeley, PhD(mech eng), 68. *Prof Exp:* Res asst aeronaut sci, Univ Calif, Berkeley, 62-68; asst prof dept aeronaut eng & eng mech, Univ Tex, Austin, 68-74; ASSOC PROF AERONAUT & MECH ENG, UNIV TENN SPACE INST, 74- *Concurrent Pos:* NSF res grant, 74-75; USAF/ASEE grant, 77; consult, Eng Res Corp, Inc, & FWG Assoc, Inc, Tullahoma, Tenn, 72- *Mem:* Sigma Xi; Am Inst Aeronaut & Astronaut; Am Phys Soc. *Res:* Boundary layer stability, material processing in space, transonic viscous interactions, stall suppression, kinetic theory, development of gas diagnostic techniques, heat transfer. *Mailing Add:* Space Inst Univ of Tenn Tullahoma TN 37388

COLLINS, FRANK MILES, b Adelaide, S Australia, Mar 30, 28; US citizen; m 52; c 2. MICROBIOLOGY, IMMUNOLOGY. *Educ:* Univ Adelaide, S Australia, BSc, 49, PhD(immunochem), 61, DSc, 75. *Prof Exp:* Asst prof bacteriol, Univ Adelaide, 54-60, asst prof microbiol, 61-64; assoc mem, 65-68, MEM MICROBIOL, TRUDEAU INST INC, 68- *Concurrent Pos:* Counr-at-large, Am Thoracic Soc, 71-74; mem bacteriol & mycol study sect, NIH, 75-79; mem, US-Japan Tuberc Panel, 80- *Mem:* Am Soc Microbiol; Am Thoracic Soc; fel Am Acad Microbiol; Soc Gen Microbiol; Am Asn Immunol. *Res:* Mechanisms of immune response to infections caused by microbial intracellular parasites in rat and mouse models of human disease; cellular immunity to mycobacteria, salmonellae and listeria infections in mice. *Mailing Add:* Trudeau Inst Inc PO Box 59 Saranac Lake NY 12983

COLLINS, FRANK WILLIAM, JR, b Toronto, Ont, Mar 31, 45; m 64; c 2. PLANT BIOCHEMISTRY, BOTANY. *Educ:* Univ Toronto, BSc, 66, PhD(bot), 72. *Prof Exp:* Fel, 72-73; res assoc, Dept Bot, Univ BC, 73-75; res assoc biochem, Inst Environ Studies, Univ Toronto, 75-77, lectr Dept Bot, 76-77; RES SCIENTIST BOT, RES BR, AGR CAN, 77- *Concurrent Pos:* Consult, N Am Contact Dermatitis Group, 73-75, Working Group Environ Aspects Heavy Metals, Nat Res Coun, 76-77. *Mem:* N Am Phytochem Soc. *Res:* Chemotaxonomy of higher plants; biosystematics; phytochemistry; structure and biosynthesis of natural products including flavonoids, polyphenols, alkaloids, and phytochemical phylogeny; evolution of crop plants and grain biochemistry. *Mailing Add:* Food Res Inst Res Br Agr Can Cent Exp Farm Ottawa ON K1A 0C6 Can

COLLINS, FRANKLYN, b Toronto, Ont, Mar 13, 29; nat US; m 51; c 3. SOLID STATE PHYSICS. *Educ:* Mich State Col, BS, 50; Univ Buffalo, PhD(physics), 58. *Prof Exp:* MGR ELECTRONICS RES, RES & DEVELOP LABS, AIRCO SPEER, 57- *Mem:* Am Phys Soc; Inst Elec & Electronics Engrs. *Res:* Carbon and graphite research; electronic components. *Mailing Add:* Airco Speer Res & Develop Labs Packard Ave & 47th St Niagara Falls NY 14302

COLLINS, FREDERICK CLINTON, b Prairie Grove, Ark, May 31, 41; m 61. PLANT BREEDING, PLANT GENETICS. *Educ:* Univ Ark, Fayetteville, BSA, 63, MS, 65; Purdue Univ, PhD(plant breeding, genetics), 69. *Prof Exp:* Res asst agron, Univ Ark, 63-64; geneticist soybean invests, Agr Res Serv, USDA, 64-66; asst prof, 69-73, assoc prof, 73-78, PROF AGRON, UNIV ARK, FAYETTEVILLE, 78- *Mem:* Am Soc Agron; Crop Sci Soc Am. *Res:* Plant breeding; genetic control and physiology of yield and chemical characteristics, particularly those involved with nutritional quality of plants. *Mailing Add:* Dept of Agron Univ of Ark Fayetteville AR 72701

COLLINS, GALEN FRANKLIN, b Winona Lake, Ind, Dec 29, 27; m 56; c 4. CLINICAL BIOCHEMISTRY. *Educ:* Purdue Univ, BS, 49, MS, 52, PhD(pharmaceut chem), 54. *Prof Exp:* Asst pharm, Purdue Univ, 49-52; pharmaceut chemist, Miles Labs, Inc, 53-58, asst to dir, Miles-Ames Pharmaceut Res Lab, 58-59, head, Ames Pharmaceut Res Sect, 59-60; chief prod develop, Norwich Pharmacal Co, 60-63; mgr res div, S E Massengill Co, 63-67, dir res, 67-71; vpres res & develop, 71-75, VPRES & SCI DIR, DADE DIV, AM HOSP SUPPLY CORP, 75- *Mem:* Fel AAAS; Am Pharmaceut Asn; fel Am Inst Chem; Am Asn Clin Chemists; Asn Clin Scientists. *Res:* Clinical diagnostics which covers clinical instruments, hematology, blood coagulation, clinical chemistry, immunochemistry, immunohematology and immunology. *Mailing Add:* Dade Div Am Hosp Supply Co PO Box 5-0672 Miami FL 33152

COLLINS, GARY BRENT, b Clare, Mich, Sept 23, 40; m 62; c 2. PHYCOLOGY, AQUATIC ECOLOGY. *Educ:* Cent Mich Univ, BA, 62, MA, 64; Iowa State Univ, PhD(bot), 68. *Prof Exp:* Asst prof bot, Ohio State Univ, 68-72; RES AQUATIC BIOLOGIST, US ENVIRON PROTECTION AGENCY, 72- *Mem:* AAAS; Am Micros Soc; Int Phycol Soc; Bot Soc Am; Phycol Soc Am. *Res:* Freshwater diatom ecology and taxonomy; plankton and periphyton methods development; algal ecology; diatom paleoecology. *Mailing Add:* 8109 Woodruff Rd Cincinnati OH 45230

COLLINS, GARY SCOTT, b Plainfield, NJ, Dec 15, 44; m 78. HYPERFINE INTERACTIONS. *Educ:* Rutgers Col, BA, 66; Rutgers Univ, PhD(physics), 76. *Prof Exp:* Instr, Dept Physics, Rutgers Univ, 76-77; res assoc & instr, 77-79, RES ASST PROF, DEPT PHYSICS, CLARK UNIV, WORCESTER, MASS, 79- *Concurrent Pos:* co-prin investr, Clark Univ, NSF, 80-, prin investr, 81- *Mem:* AAAS; Am Phys Soc; Mat Res Soc. *Res:* Application of hyperfine interaction techniques to study internal fields in solids; quadrupole interactions in noncubic metals; magnetic critical phenomena in metals; lattice defects in damaged metals. *Mailing Add:* Dept Physics Clark Univ Worcester MA 01610

COLLINS, GEORGE BRIGGS, b Washington, DC, Jan 3, 06; m 34; c 3. PHYSICS. *Educ:* Johns Hopkins Univ, PhD(physics), 31. *Prof Exp:* Instr physics, Johns Hopkins Univ, 27-30; instr, Univ Notre Dame, 33-41; mem radiation lab, Mass Inst Technol, 41-46; prof physics & chmn dept, Univ Rochester, 46-50; chmn cosmotron dept, Brookhaven Nat Lab, 50-62, sr physicist, 62-71; prof physics & sr physicist, 71-76, UNIV DISTINGUISHED EMER PROF PHYSICS, VA POLYTECH INST &

STATE UNIV, 77- *Concurrent Pos:* Coun mem, State Univ NY Stony Brook, 53-70; Fulbright fel, Belg, 57; with Deutsches Elektronen-Synchrotron, 65-66; chmn, Comt on Lib Educ & Professions, Va Polytech Inst & State Univ, 80-81. *Mem:* Fel Am Phys Soc. *Res:* Raman effect; hyperfine structure of iodine; far ultraviolet spectroscope; excitation of nuclei by electrons; nuclear physics; high energy electrons and protons; particle physics; development of wire chamber spectrometers; high energy multiparticle production. *Mailing Add:* Dept Physics Va Polytech Inst & State Univ Blacksburg VA 24061

COLLINS, GEORGE EDWIN, b Stuart, Iowa, Jan 10, 28; m 54; c 3. COMPUTER ALGEBRA, ANALYSIS OF ALGORITHMS. *Educ:* Univ Iowa, BA, 51, MS, 52; Cornell Univ, PhD(math), 55. *Prof Exp:* Res mathematician, Int Bus Mach Corp, 55-66; assoc prof, 66-68, chmn dept, 70-72, PROF COMPUT SCI, UNIV WIS-MADISON, 68- *Concurrent Pos:* Res fel math, Calif Inst Technol, 63-64; vis prof, Stanford Univ, 72-73, Univ Kaiserslautern, 74-75 & Univ Karlsruhe, 78; ed, Soc Indust & Appl Math J on Comput, 77-81; vis res fel, Gen Elec Res Ctr, 81-82. *Mem:* Asn Comput Mach; Am Math Soc; Math Asn Am; Soc Indust & Appl Math. *Res:* Algebraic algorithms; computer algebra systems; polynomial factorizations; exact polynomial root calculation; quantifier elimination for the theory of real closed fields; cylindrical algebraic decomposition; resultants and subresultants. *Mailing Add:* Dept of Comput Sci Univ of Wis 1210 W Dayton St Madison WI 53706

COLLINS, GEORGE H, b Albany, NY, Sept 11, 27; m 51; c 6. PATHOLOGY, NEUROLOGY. *Educ:* Univ Vt, AB, 49, MD, 53. *Prof Exp:* From asst prof to prof path & med, Col Med, Univ Fla, 62-73; PROF PATH, COL MED, STATE UNIV NY UPSTATE MED CTR, 73- *Concurrent Pos:* Teaching fel neuropath, Harvard Med Sch, 58-59, res fel, 59-62; clin & res fel, Mass Gen Hosp, 59-62; asst resident path, Mass Gen Hosp, 58-59. *Mem:* AAAS; Am Asn Neuropath; Am Asn Pathol; Soc Neurosci. *Res:* Degeneration and regeneration in the central nervous system; glial cell function; extracellular space of the central nervous system. *Mailing Add:* Dept of Path State Univ NY Upstate Med Ctr Syracuse NY 13210

COLLINS, GEORGE W, II, b Waukegan, Ill, July 18, 37; m 61; c 1. ASTRONOMY. *Educ:* Princeton Univ, AB, 59; Univ Wis, PhD(astron), 62. *Prof Exp:* Asst prof numerical anal, Univ Wis, 62-63; from asst prof to assoc prof, 63-69, PROF ASTRON, OHIO STATE UNIV, 69- *Mem:* AAAS; Am Astron Soc; fel Royal Astron Soc. *Res:* Eclipsing binary stars; stellar atmospheres; general problems in radiative transfer; numerical analysis. *Mailing Add:* Dept Astron Smith Physics Lab Ohio State Univ Columbus OH 43210

COLLINS, GLENN BURTON, b Folsom, Ky, Aug 7, 39; m 59; c 2. PLANT GENETICS, PLANT BREEDING. *Educ:* Univ Ky, BS, 61, MS, 63; NC State Univ, PhD(genetics), 67. *Prof Exp:* Res asst plant genetics, Univ Ky, 61-63; plant cytogenetics, NC State Univ, 63-66; from asst prof to assoc prof, 66-70, PROF SOMATIC CELL GENETICS & CYTOGENETICS, UNIV KY, 75- *Concurrent Pos:* Sabbatical, John Innes Inst, Norwich, Eng, 73. *Honors & Awards:* Cooper Res Award, Col Agr, Univ Ky, 75; Univ Ky Res Found Award, 76; Philip Morris Res Award, Philip Morris Co, 80. *Mem:* Am Soc Agron; Am Genetics Soc; Tissue Culture Asn Am; Int Asn Plant Tissue & Cell Cult. *Res:* Genetics and breeding of tobacco; development and use of haploid procedures for breeding and genetic studies; use of tissue and cell culture methods in plant improvement; wide hybridization and gene transfer in crop plants. *Mailing Add:* Dept of Agron Univ of Ky Lexington KY 40506

COLLINS, HENRY A, b Machipongo, Va, Sept 21, 32; m 62; c 3. AGRONOMY, PLANT PHYSIOLOGY. *Educ:* Md State Col, BS, 55; Rutgers Univ, MS, 57, PhD(farm crops), 62. *Prof Exp:* Asst farm crops, Rutgers Univ, 59-62; from asst prof to assoc prof biol, Tuskegee Univ, 62-68; res specialist, 68-73, mkt planning specialist, 73-77, RES & SR RES SPECIALIST, AGR DIV, CIBA-GEIGY CORP, 77- *Mem:* Am Soc Agron; Crop Sci Soc Am; Weed Sci Soc Am; Aquatic Plant Mgt Soc; Southern Weed Sci Soc. *Res:* Selective absorption of strontium by plants; factors affecting weed seed germination. *Mailing Add:* 3904 Hickory Tree Lane Greensboro NC 27405

COLLINS, HERON SHERWOOD, b Charlotte, NC, Nov 17, 22; m 52; c 4. MATHEMATICS. *Educ:* Wofford Col, BS, 48; Tulane Univ, MS, 50, PhD, 52. *Prof Exp:* Asst prof math, Univ Md, 52-53; asst prof, Univ SC, 53-54; from asst prof to assoc prof, 54-62, PROF MATH, LA STATE UNIV, 62- *Mem:* Am Math Soc. *Res:* Banach spaces and algebras; measure and integration theory; analytic function theory. *Mailing Add:* Dept of Math La State Univ Univ Sta Baton Rouge LA 70803

COLLINS, HOLLIE L, b Laona, Wis, May 20, 38; m 57; c 2. ZOOLOGY. *Educ:* Wis State Univ, BS, 60; Mich State Univ, MS, 62, PhD(zool), 65. *Prof Exp:* ASSOC PROF BIOL, UNIV MINN, DULUTH, 64-, DIR GRAD STUDIES BIOL, 70- *Mem:* Animal Behavior Soc; Soc Ichthyol & Herpet. *Res:* Animal behavior of aquatic organisms, especially social behavior of fishes. *Mailing Add:* Dept of Biol Univ of Minn Duluth MN 55812

COLLINS, HORACE RUTTER, b Shawnee, Okla, Feb 4, 30. GEOLOGY. *Educ:* Ohio Univ, BS, 54; WVa Univ, MS, 59. *Prof Exp:* Instr geol, Ohio Univ, 58-59; geologist, Coal Sect, 59-60, head, 60-63, head regional sect, 63-66, asst state geologist, 66-68, asst chief Ohio Div, 67-68, STATE GEOLOGIST & CHIEF OHIO DIV, OHIO GEOL SURV, 68- *Mem:* Geol Soc Am; Asn Prof Geol Scientists; Asn Am State Geol. *Res:* Geology of Ohio; Pennsylvania stratigraphy; paleobotany; coal geology. *Mailing Add:* Ohio Div Natural Resources Div of Geol Survey Fountain Sq Columbus OH 43224

COLLINS, JACK A(DAM), b Columbus, Ohio, Nov 23, 29; m 58; c 4. MECHANICAL ENGINEERING. *Educ:* Ohio State Univ, BME, 52, MSc, 54, PhD(mech eng), 63. *Prof Exp:* From res asst to res assoc mech eng, Ohio State Univ, 52-63; assoc prof, Ariz State Univ, 63-72; assoc prof, 72-74,

PROF MECH ENG, OHIO STATE UNIV, 74-, CHMN MECH DESIGN SECT OF MECH ENG DEPT, 75- *Concurrent Pos:* Consult, Babcock & Wilcox Res Ctr, Gen Elec Co, AiResearch Mfg Co, Worthington Industs & Owens/Corning Fiberglas. *Mem:* Am Soc Mech Engrs; Am Soc Eng Educ; Am Soc Testing & Mat; Soc Exp Stress Anal. *Res:* Experimental and analytical stress and deflection analysis; experimental and analytical failure analysis, including fatigue, creep, wear and fretting. *Mailing Add:* Dept of Mech Eng 206 W 18th Ave Columbus OH 43210

COLLINS, JAMES FRANCIS, b Baltimore, Md, Jan 26, 42; m 69; c 2. BIOCHEMISTRY. *Educ:* Loyola Col, Md, BS, 63; Univ NC, Chapel Hill, PhD(genetics), 68. *Prof Exp:* Fel, Nat Inst Arthritis, Metab & Digestive Dis, NIH, 68-70, staff fel, 70-72, sr staff fel, Nat Heart & Lung Inst, 73-75; RES CHEMIST, AUDIE L MURPHY VET ADMIN HOSP & ASST PROF MED & BIOCHEM, UNIV TEX HEALTH SCI CTR, SAN ANTONIO, 75- *Concurrent Pos:* Consult, Biol & Chem Sci Degree Prog, Upward Mobility Col, Fed City Col Exp Prog, Washington, DC, 72. *Mem:* Am Fedn Clin Res; AAAS; Am Thoracic Soc; Sigma Xi. *Res:* Protein biosynthesis; connective tissue of the lung in experimental lung disease. *Mailing Add:* Dept of Med Univ of Tex Health Sci Ctr San Antonio TX 78284

COLLINS, JAMES IAN, b Birmingham, Eng, May 3, 37; US citizen; m 61; c 2. CIVIL ENGINEERING, PHYSICAL OCEANOGRAPHY. *Educ:* Univ Birmingham, BSc, 58; Queen's Univ, MSc, 60, PhD(civil eng), 62. *Prof Exp:* Staff engr, Nat Eng Sci Co, 62-63; sr engr, 63-64, assoc dir, 64-65; sr engr, 65-75, chief engr, 75-77, VPRES & CHIEF ENGR, TETRA TECH INC, 77- *Mem:* Am Geophys Union; Am Soc Civil Engrs. *Res:* Coastal engineering structures; beach processes; wave and tide dynamics. *Mailing Add:* Tetra Tech Inc 666 N Rosemead Blvd Pasadena CA 91107

COLLINS, JAMES JOSEPH, b Rochester, NY, Sept 5, 47; m 78; c 1. DEMOGRAPHY. *Educ:* Loras Col, BA, 70; Univ Mo, Kansas City, MA, 76; Univ Ill, PhD(demog), 81. *Prof Exp:* Asst scientist, Argonne Nat Lab, 79-82; STATISTICIAN, ENVIRON SERV DIV, AM CYANAMID CO, 82- *Concurrent Pos:* Consult, Argonne Nat Lab, 82- *Mem:* Pop Asn Am; Soc Epidemiol Res; Am Sociol Asn. *Res:* Development and evaluation of mathematical models for analysis of trends in disease incidence and mortality. *Mailing Add:* Environ Serv Div Am Cyanamid Co Berdan Ave Wayne NJ 07470

COLLINS, JAMES MALCOLM, b Atlanta, Ga, Mar 21, 38; m 59; c 2. BIOCHEMISTRY, MOLECULAR BIOLOGY. *Educ:* Univ Southern Miss, BS, 62; Univ Tenn, PhD(biochem), 68. *Prof Exp:* USPHS fel develop biol, Oak Ridge Nat Lab, 68-69; from asst prof to assoc prof, 69-79, PROF BIOCHEM, MED COL VA CAMPUS, VA COMMONWEALTH UNIV, 79- *Mem:* AAAS; Am Soc Biol Chemists; Am Chem Soc. *Res:* DNA synthesis; cell cycle; cancer. *Mailing Add:* Dept Biochem Box 614 Va Commonwealth Univ Richmond VA 23219

COLLINS, JAMES PAUL, b New York, NY, July 3, 47; m 70; c 2. ECOLOGY. *Educ:* Manhattan Col, BS, 69; Univ Mich, MS, 71, PhD(zool), 75. *Prof Exp:* Asst prof, 75-80, ASSOC PROF ZOOL, ARIZ STATE UNIV, 80- *Mem:* Ecol Soc Am; Am Soc Study Evolution; Am Soc Ichthyologists & Herpetologists; Sigma Xi; AAAS. *Res:* Investigation of the selective advantage of life history characters, especially in relation to the predictability of the organism's breeding habitat; the effect of competition and predation on life history characters. *Mailing Add:* Dept Zool Ariz State Univ Tempe AZ 85281

COLLINS, JANET VALERIE, b Riversdale, Jamaica, Oct 11, 39. CELL BIOLOGY, INSECT PHYSIOLOGY. *Educ:* Univ London (Univ WIndies), BSc, 63; Western Reserve Univ, PhD(biol), 67. *Prof Exp:* Res asst, Western Reserve Univ, 63-67, fel, 67-68; fel, Queen's Univ, Ont, 68-70; asst prof, 70-80, ASSOC PROF BIOL, DALHOUSIE UNIV, 80- *Mem:* Am Soc Cell Biol; Soc Develop Biol. *Res:* Effects of hormones at the cellular level, particularly on control of pinocytosis, storage and release of haemolymph proteins before and during molting; selective uptake of proteins by fat body cells. *Mailing Add:* Dept Biol Dalhousie Univ Halifax NS B3H 3J5 Can

COLLINS, JEFFERY ALLEN, b Oakland, Calif, Feb 16, 44. INDUSTRIAL CHEMICALS. *Educ:* Purdue Univ, DVM, 67; Univ Houston, MBA, 80. *Prof Exp:* Vet lab animal med, Shell Develop Co, Div Shell Oil Co, Calif, 67-68; prod develop technologist, Shell Chem Co, New York, 68-70; staff vet anthelmintic prod, 70-72, supvr vet therapeut, Shell Develop Co, 72-76, BUS MGR INDUST CHEM, SHELL CHEM CO, DIV SHELL OIL CO, 76- *Concurrent Pos:* Consult parasitol, Am Asn Zoo Animal Vet, 73-; mkt res technologist, Shell Int Chem Co, Ltd, London, 73-74. *Mem:* Am Vet Med Asn; Am Chem Soc; Indust Vet Asn. *Res:* Veterinary parasitology; administrative role re all aspects of parasiticide research and product development; industrial chemicals-manufacturing, marketing, and technical support. *Mailing Add:* Shell Develop Co PO Box 2463 Houston TX 77001

COLLINS, JEFFREY JAY, b Monroe, La, May 12, 45; m 80. TUMOR IMMUNOLOGY, TUMOR VIROLOGY. *Educ:* Cornell Univ, Ithaca, NY, BS, 66; Harvard Univ, PhD(microbiol & molecular genetics), 72. *Prof Exp:* fel tumor virol, Imperial Cancer Res Fund Lab, Lincoln's Inn Fields, London, 72-74, vis scientist, 74; asst prof exp surg, 74-81, asst prof microbiol & immunol, 75, ASSOC PROF EXP SURG, DUKE UNIV MED CTR, DURHAM, NC, 81- *Concurrent Pos:* Fac mem tumor virol, Duke Comprehensive Cancer Ctr, Durham, NC, 74; prin investr, Am Cancer Soc Res Grant, 77. *Mem:* Am Asn Immunologists; Am Soc Virol. *Res:* Use of viral structural proteins as specific antigenic targets for the passive serum therapy of virus-induced leukemias and sarcomas. *Mailing Add:* Dept Surg Duke Univ Med Ctr Box 2926 Durham NC 27710

COLLINS, JERRY DALE, b Greeneville, Tenn, June 3, 43; m 61; c 2. ORGANIC CHEMISTRY, POLYMER CHEMISTRY. *Educ:* Tusculum Col, BS, 65; Univ Ark, Fayetteville, PhD(carbene chem), 70. *Prof Exp:* Res chemist, 70-71, spec process engr, 71-73, tech supvr nylon develop, Am Enka Div, Akzona Corp, Lowland, 73-77; specialist lexan prod develop, Lexan Div, Gen Elec Co, 77-; dir res, Develop & Eng, LST Corp, 79-80; PRES, JIM WALTER PLASTICS DIV, JIM WALTER CORP, 80- *Mem:* Am Chem Soc; Soc Plastics Engrs. *Res:* Steric effects associated with insertion of carbenes into carbon-hydrogen bonds; determination of insertion reaction mechanism; modification of fiber surface by carbene insertion reactions; new process development concerning nylon textile yarns. *Mailing Add:* Rte 5 Box 292 Greeneville TN 37743

COLLINS, JIMMIE LEE, b Vicksburg, Miss, Nov 24, 34; m 59; c 3. FOOD SCIENCE. *Educ:* La State Univ, BS, 61; Univ Md, MS, 63, PhD(food tech), 65. *Prof Exp:* Asst prof, 65-69, assoc prof, 69-77, PROF FOOD TECHNOL, UNIV TENN, KNOXVILLE, 77- *Mem:* Am Inst Food Technol. *Res:* Textural characteristics of fruits and vegetables; enzymes of fresh and processed vegetables. *Mailing Add:* Dept of Food Technol Univ of Tenn Knoxville TN 37916

COLLINS, JIMMY HAROLD, b Gaffney, SC, Dec 9, 48; m 79; c 4. CELL BIOLOGY, CELL MOTILITY. *Educ:* Duke Univ, Bs, 71; Univ Tex, Austin, PhD(chem), 77. *Prof Exp:* STAFF FEL, LAB CELL BIOL, NAT HEART & LUNG INST, NIH, 77- *Mem:* Am Soc Biol Chemist; Am Soc Cell Biol; Biophys Soc; Am Chem Soc. *Res:* Biochemistry of cytoskeletal and contractile proteins, including identification, isolation, characterization and interactions of these proteins; regulation of nonmuscle myosin adenosine triphosphatase activity and assembly, especially by calcium and phosphorylation. *Mailing Add:* 17709 Shady Mill Rd Derwood MD 20205

COLLINS, JOHN A(DDISON), b Midway, Pa, Jan 6, 29; m 53; c 3. ELECTRICAL ENGINEERING, ELECTRONICS ENGINEERING. *Educ:* Washington & Jefferson Col, AB, 51; Mass Inst Technol, BS, 57. *Prof Exp:* Res engr instrumentation, Jet Propulsion Lab, Calif Inst Technol, 57-59, group supvr space photog, 61-64; staff engr, Instrumentation Lab, Mass Inst Technol, 59-61; mgr electronic systs photo-digital recorder, IBM Corp, 64-67; mgr, Electronics Div, Analog Technol Corp, Pasadena, 67-72; asst mgr, 73-81, SR SCIENTIST, HUGHES AIRCRAFT CO, 81- *Mem:* Inst Elec & Electronics Engrs. *Res:* Space qualified power conversion systems; design, development and manufacture of traveling wave tube amplifiers for satellite and satellite earth stations, electronic power conversion subsystems, high voltage system design and analysis. *Mailing Add:* Microwave Systs Div 3100 W Lomita Blvd Torrance CA 90505

COLLINS, JOHN BARRETT, b Cleveland, Ohio, Jan 25, 49; m 80. THEORETICAL ORGANIC CHEMISTRY. *Educ:* Holy Cross Col, BA, 71; Princeton Univ, MA, 73, PhD(chem), 76. *Prof Exp:* Res chemist drug design, Lederle Labs, 77-81, SYSTS ANALYST, STAMFORD RES LABS, AM CYANAMID CO, 81- *Mem:* Am Chem Soc; AAAS; Quantum Chem Prog Exchange; Inst Elec & Electronics Engrs. *Res:* Molecular orbital theory, chemistry by computer, quantitative drug design; computer software development. *Mailing Add:* Chem Res Div Am Cyanamid Co Stamford CT 06904

COLLINS, JOHN CLEMENTS, b Colchester, UK, Dec 8, 49. QUANTUM FIELD THEORY, RENORMALIZATION GROUP. *Educ:* Univ Cambridge, BA, 71, PhD(theoret physics), 75. *Prof Exp:* Res assoc, Princeton Univ, 75-76, asst prof, 76-80; ASST PROF PHYSICS, ILL INST TECHNOL, 80- *Res:* Elementary particle theory; quantum field theory. *Mailing Add:* Physics Dept Ill Inst Technol Chicago IL 60616

COLLINS, JOHN HENRY, b Peabody, Mass, Sept 6, 42; m 67; c 2. PROTEIN SEQUENCING, LIQUID CHROMATOGRAPHY. *Educ:* Northeastern Univ, AB, 65; Boston Univ, PhD(biochem), 70. *Prof Exp:* Res fel muscle res, Boston Biomed Res Inst, 69-72, res assoc, 72-74, staff scientist, 74-76; asst prof cell biophysics, Baylor Col Med, 76-77; asst prof,, 77-79, ASSOC PROF PHARMACOL & CELL BIOPHYSICS, COL MED, UNIV CINCINNATI, 79- *Concurrent Pos:* Res assoc, Harvard Col, 74-76; prin investr grants, Am Heart Asn, 75-76 & 81-84, Nat Heart Lung & Blood Inst, 76-83, Nat Inst Arthritis, Metab & Digestive Dis, 77-86. *Mem:* Am Soc Biol Chemists; Biophys Soc; NY Acad Sci; AAAS. *Res:* Protein structure and function; calcium binding, contractile and membrane proteins; chromatography; high performance liquid chromatography; amino acids; peptide isolation and characterization; sodium potassium adenosine triphatase; proteolipids; sarcoplasmic reticulum; actin, myosin and troponin; protein evolution. *Mailing Add:* Dept Pharmacol & Cell Biophysics Col Med Univ Cincinnati 231 Bethesda Ave Cincinnati OH 45267

COLLINS, JOHN JOSEPH, JR, chemical engineering, see previous edition

COLLINS, JOHN W, chemistry, see previous edition

COLLINS, JON DAVID, b Flint, Mich, Mar 14, 35; m 57; c 4. ENGINEERING MECHANICS, APPLIED MATHEMATICS. *Educ:* Univ Mich, BS, 57; Univ Colo, MS, 59; Univ Calif, Los Angeles, PhD(eng), 67. *Prof Exp:* Engr, Martin Co, 57-59; mem tech staff, Titan Prog Off, TRW Systs Group, TRW Inc, 59-63, mem tech staff, Dynamics Dept, 63-66, head, Systs Dynamics Sect, 66-67, head, Anal Dynamics Sect, 67-69; V PRES, J H WIGGINS CO, 69- *Concurrent Pos:* Res engr, Univ Calif, Los Angeles, 66-67; adj prof, Sch Bus Mgt, Northrop Univ, 75- *Honors & Awards:* New Technol Award, NASA, 76. *Mem:* Assoc fel Am Inst Aeronaut & Astronaut; Acoust Soc Am; Am Soc Mech Engrs; Am Soc Civil Engrs; Opers Res Soc Am. *Res:* Risk and safety analysis of systems (nuclear power plants and missiles) due to natural and man-made hazards; development of systems analysis models for weapon system vulnerability and effectiveness; application of statistics to problems in engineering mechanics; design of management information systems. *Mailing Add:* 27817 Longhill Dr Rancho Palos Verdes CA 90274

COLLINS, JOSEPH CHARLES, JR, b Pontiac, Mich, May 7, 31; m 53; c 4. ORGANIC CHEMISTRY. *Educ:* Wayne State Univ, BS, 53; Univ Wis, PhD(chem), 58. *Prof Exp:* Asst, Gen Motors Res, 53 & Chem Dept, E I du Pont de Nemours & Co, 56; res assoc, Univ Wis, 58 & Sterling-Winthrop Res Inst, 58-62; assoc prof chem, Ill Wesleyan Univ, 62-67; res assoc, 67-68, assoc dir chem div, 68-69, dir chem div, 69-76, V PRES CHEM, STERLING-WINTHROP RES INST, 76- *Mem:* AAAS; Am Chem Soc; The Chem Soc. *Res:* Organic synthesis and conformational analysis of biomolecular systems. *Mailing Add:* Sterling-Winthrop Res Inst Columbia Turnpike Rensselaer NY 12144

COLLINS, KENNETH ELMER, b Newcastle, Wyo, July 10, 26; m 55; c 1. RADIOCHEMISTRY, RADIATION CHEMISTRY. *Educ:* San Jose State Univ, BA, 50; Iowa State Univ, MS, 55; Univ Wis, PhD(phys chem), 62. *Prof Exp:* Res scientist, Vet Med Res Inst, Ames, 55-58, Brookhaven Nat Lab, 61-63, Centre de Physique Nucleaire, Lovain, 63-64; asst prof anal & radio chem, State Univ NY at Buffalo, 64-68; res scientist, Western NY Nuclear Res Ctr, 69-70; PROF ANAL & PHYS CHEM, UNIV ESTADUAL DE CAMPINAS, 74- *Concurrent Pos:* Adv, Int Atomic Energy Agency, 70-73; vis scientist, Centre de Recher ches Nucleaires, Strasbourg, 79. *Mem:* Am Chem Soc; AAAS; Royal Soc Chem. *Res:* Nuclear and radio chemistry with emphasis on solid state recoil studies and liquid phase radiolytic reactions. *Mailing Add:* Instituto de Quimica Univ Estadual de Campinas Campinas SP 13100 Brazil

COLLINS, LOIS COWAN, b McKeesport, Pa, July 1, 14; m 42; c 3. RADIOLOGY. *Educ:* Univ Pittsburgh, BS & MD, 37. *Prof Exp:* Instr radiol, Boston Univ, 39-42; from assoc to assoc prof, Col Physicians & Surg, Columbia Univ, 42-52; assoc prof radiol, Postgrad Sch, Univ Tex, 52-69; CLIN PROF RADIOL, COL MED, BAYLOR UNIV, 69- *Concurrent Pos:* Asst radiologist, Presby Hosp & Psychiat Inst, NY, 42-52; consult, US Marine Hosp, Staten Island, 47-52; radiologist, Ben Taub Hosp, Houston, 52-68; asst radiologist, M D Anderson Hosp, Tex, 53-62; radiologist, Methodist Hosp, 63-66, Rosewood Hosp, Tex, 68- *Mem:* Fel Am Col Radiol; Am Roentgen Ray Soc; Radiol Soc NAm. *Mailing Add:* 9200 Westheimer Ave Houston TX 77063

COLLINS, LORENCE GENE, b Vernon, Kans, Nov 19, 31; m 55; c 5. PHOTOGEOLOGY. *Educ:* Univ Ill, BS, 53, MS, 57, PhD(geol), 59. *Prof Exp:* Instr phys sci, Univ Ill, 58-59; from asst prof to prof geol, San Fernando Valley State Col, 59-74, fac res coordr, 70-78; PROF GEOSCI CALIF STATE UNIV, 74- *Res:* Mineral deposits in metamorphic terrains, particularly magnetite in granitic gneisses; refractive index studies of ferromagnesian silicates; studies of origin of myrmekite. *Mailing Add:* Dept of Geol Calif State Univ Northridge CA 91324

COLLINS, MALCOLM FRANK, b Crewe, Eng, Dec 15, 35; m 61; c 3. PHYSICS. *Educ:* Cambridge Univ, BA, 57, MA, 61, PhD(physics), 62. *Prof Exp:* Physicist, Solid State Physics Div, Atomic Energy Res Estab, Harwell, Eng, 61-69; assoc prof, 69-73, assoc chmn dept, 74-76, PROF PHYSICS, MCMASTER UNIV, 73-, CHMN DEPT, 76- *Concurrent Pos:* Guest, Brookhaven Nat Lab, 67-68, 76; fel, Alfred P Sloan Found, 70-72. *Mem:* Fel Can Asn Physicists. *Res:* Various aspects of slow neutron scattering, especially applications to magnetism, critical phenomena, transition metals, lattice vibrations and crystallography; theory of paramagnetism and order-disorder phase transitions. *Mailing Add:* Dept of Physics McMaster Univ Hamilton ON L8S 4L8 Can

COLLINS, MARY JANE, b Miami, Fla, Oct 17, 40. PSYCHOACOUSTICS, AUDIOLOGY. *Educ:* Vanderbilt Univ, BA, 61, MS, 63; Univ Iowa, PhD(hearing sci), 70. *Prof Exp:* Audiologist, Bristol Speech & Hearing Ctr, 64-65; res asst audiol, Vet Admin Hosp, Coral Gables, Fla, 65-66; audiologist, Vet Admin Hosp, HOSP, Nashville, 70-72; asst prof audiol, Univ Wis, 72-73; assoc prof audiol, Tenn State Univ, 73-77; res assoc, Speech & Hearing Sci Dept, City Univ New York, 77-80; MEM FAC, DEPT SPEECH PATH & AUDIOL, UNIV IOWA, 80- *Concurrent Pos:* Asst prof audiol, Vanderbilt Univ, 70-72; adj asst prof, Kresge Labs, La State Univ Med Ctr, 76- *Mem:* Acoust Soc Am; Am Speech & Hearing Asn. *Res:* Psychophysical phenomena in the normal and pathological human auditory system. *Mailing Add:* Dept Speech Path & Audiol Univ Iowa Iowa City IA 52242

COLLINS, MARY LYNNE PERILLE, b Evanston, Ill, May 15, 49; m 74. MICROBIAL BIOCHEMISTRY. *Educ:* Emmanuel Col, BA, 71; Rutgers Univ, PhD(microbiol), 76. *Prof Exp:* NIH fel, NY Univ Med Ctr, 76-78, res asst prof microbiol, 78-80; ASST PROF ZOOL & MICROBIOL, UNIV WIS-MILWAUKEE, 80- *Mem:* AAAS; Am Soc Microbiol. *Res:* Microbial biochemistry, membrane biogenesis and differentiation, functional organization of membranes, bacterial antigenic structure. *Mailing Add:* Dept Zool & Microbiol Univ Wis PO Box 413 Milwaukee WI 53201

COLLINS, MICHAEL, b Dayton, Ohio, Sept 18, 51; m 70; c 2. CROP SCIENCE. *Educ:* Berea Col, BS, 73; WVa Univ, MS, 75; Univ Ky, PhD(crop sci), 78. *Prof Exp:* Forestry tech strip mining, USDA Forest Serv, 72; res asst agron, WVa Univ, 73-75 & Univ Ky, 75-78; ASST PROF AGRON, UNIV WIS, MADISON, 78- *Mem:* Sigma Xi; Am Soc Agron; Crop Sci Soc Am. *Res:* Influence of management and fertility on forage chemical composition and nutritive value; chemical estimation of forage nutritive value. *Mailing Add:* Dept of Agron Univ of Wis 1575 Linden Dr Madison WI 53706

COLLINS, MICHAEL ALBERT, b Oak Park, Ill, July 6, 42; m 64; c 1. HYDRODYNAMICS. *Educ:* Ga Inst Technol, BS, 65, MS, 69; Mass Inst Technol, PhD(hydrodynamics), 70. *Prof Exp:* Teaching asst fluid mech, Ga Inst Technol, 66-67; engr hydraulics, Camp, Dresser & McKee Consult Engrs, 67-68; asst prof, 70-73, assoc prof, 73-78, PROF HYDRODYNAMICS & WATER RESOURCES, SCH ENG & APPL SCI, SOUTHERN METHODIST UNIV, 78- *Concurrent Pos:* NSF traineeship, Ga Inst Technol, 65-66, Mass Inst Technol, 66-67; res asst hydrodynamics, Mass Inst Technol, 67-80; consult, Trinity River Authority Tex, 72-74, Hydroscience,

Inc, 76-78, URS Co, Inc, 78-, Crosby, Young and Assoc, Inc, 79- & Elba, Inc, 80-; Sigma Xi res award, 82. *Mem:* Am Geophys Union; Am Soc Civil Engrs; Am Water Resources Asn; Int Asn Hydraulic Res; AAAS. *Res:* Hydrodynamics evaluation of mixing processes, with special application to waste treatment operations; mathematics of networks in physical applications, with emphasis to role of mathematical programming techniques; numerical methods in application to turbulent flows. *Mailing Add:* Dept Civil Mech Eng Sch Eng Southern Methodist Univ Dallas TX 75275

COLLINS, MICHAEL FREDERICK, developmental biology, see previous edition

COLLINS, NICHOLAS CLARK, b Ogden, Utah, Mar 2, 46. POPULATION ECOLOGY, FISH BENTHOS INTERACTIONS. *Educ:* Pomona Col, BA, 68; Univ Ga, PhD(zool), 72. *Prof Exp:* Fel acarology, Ohio State Univ, 72-73; asst prof, 73-79, ASSOC PROF ZOOL, ERINDALE COL, UNIV TORONTO, 79- *Mem:* Ecol Soc Am; AAAS; Can Soc Zoologists; NAm Benthological Soc. *Res:* Adaptive phenotypic plasticity in animals; mechanisms limiting consumer feeding in freshwater littoral zones; analyses of life history variations among brine shrimp and brine fly populations from simple environments. *Mailing Add:* Dept of Zool 3359 Mississauga Rd Mississauga ON L5L 1C6 Can

COLLINS, NORMAN EDWARD, JR, b Wilmington, Del, Mar 28, 40; m 63; c 2. AGRICULTURAL ENGINEERING, ENERGY MANAGEMENT. *Educ:* Univ Del, BS, 62; Univ Md, MS, 65; Univ Pa, PhD(civil eng), 75. *Prof Exp:* Instr, Univ Md, 64-65; asst prof, 65-76, ASSOC PROF AGR ENG, UNIV DEL, 76-, DEPT CHMN, 81- *Mem:* Am Soc Agr Engrs. *Res:* Energy use in crop and broiler production; computer modeling of on-farm broiler production. *Mailing Add:* Dept of Agr Eng Agr Hall Univ of Del Newark DE 19711

COLLINS, O'NEIL RAY, b Opelousas, La, Mar 9, 31; m 59; c 2. MYCOLOGY. *Educ:* Southern Univ, BS, 57; Univ Iowa, MS, 59, PhD(bot), 61. *Prof Exp:* Instr biol, Queens Col, 61-63; assoc prof, Southern Univ, 63-65; assoc prof, Wayne State Univ, 65-69; assoc prof, 69-73, PROF BOT, UNIV CALIF, BERKELEY, 73- *Mem:* Bot Soc Am; Mycol Soc Am. *Res:* Mating types in the Myxomycetes. *Mailing Add:* Dept of Bot Univ of Calif Berkeley CA 94720

COLLINS, PAUL EVERETT, b White Rock, Minn, Feb 22, 17; m 48; c 2. SILVICULTURE. *Educ:* Gustavus Adolphus Col, BA, 39; Univ Minn, BS, 48, MS, 49, PhD, 67. *Prof Exp:* Asst, Univ Minn, 48-49; asst prof & exten forester, Kans State Col, 49-51; from asst prof & asst forester to assoc prof & assoc forester, SDak State Univ, 52-74, prof hort & forestry, 74-82; RETIRED. *Mem:* Soc Am Foresters; Sigma Xi. *Res:* Plains windbreak and shelter belt research on matters of cultural practices, design and tree breeding. *Mailing Add:* Dept Hort & Forestry SDak State Univ Brookings SD 57007

COLLINS, PAUL WADDELL, b Greenville, SC, Feb 26, 40; m 63; c 3. MEDICINAL CHEMISTRY. *Educ:* Univ SC, BS, 62; Med Col Va, PhD(med chem), 66. *Prof Exp:* Res fel org synthesis, Univ Va, 66-67; res scientist, 67-81, SR RES SCIENTIST, G D SEARLE & CO, 81- *Mem:* Am Chem Soc. *Res:* Synthesis of heterocyclic spiro compounds; synthesis of cyclopropylogs of naturally occurring amines and amino acids; synthesis of prostaglandins, especially 16-hydroxy prostaglandins. *Mailing Add:* G D Searle & Co Chem Res Dept PO Box 5110 Chicago IL 60680

COLLINS, RALPH PORTER, b Alpena, Mich, Nov 26, 27; m 55; c 3. BOTANY. *Educ:* Mich State Univ, BA, 50, MS, 52, PhD(bot), 57. *Prof Exp:* Asst bot, Mich State Univ, 52-54 & 55-57; from instr to assoc prof, 57-69, PROF BOT, UNIV CONN, 69-, HEAD DEPT, 80- *Concurrent Pos:* NIH spec res fel, 64-65; Smithsonian Inst sr res fel, 72. *Mem:* AAAS; Mycol Soc Am; Am Chem Soc; Am Soc Pharmacog. *Res:* Fungal physiology; natural products chemistry. *Mailing Add:* Dept of Biol-Bot Sect Univ of Conn Storrs CT 06268

COLLINS, RICHARD ANDREW, b Norristown, Pa, Oct 27, 24; m 55; c 3. PATHOLOGY. *Educ:* Pa State Univ, BS, 48; Univ Wis, MS, 50, PhD(biochem), 52; Marquette Univ, MD, 62. *Prof Exp:* Asst biochem, Marquette Univ, 58-60; intern, Mary Fletcher Hosp, Burlington, Vt, 62-63; asst prof path, Med Col Wis, 65-67; pathologist, Regional Med Labs, 72-81; PATHOLOGIST, ST LUKE'S HOSP, MILWAUKEE, 81- *Concurrent Pos:* Nat Heart Inst spec fel path, Univ Vt, 63-65. *Mem:* Am Asn Pathologists; Am Asn Clin Chem; Am Soc Clin Path; Col Am Path; Int Acad Path. *Mailing Add:* St Luke's Hosp 2900 W Okla Ave Milwaukee WI 53215

COLLINS, RICHARD ARLEN, b Shaw, Miss, Aug 4, 30; m; c 5. FISHERIES BIOLOGY. *Educ:* Delta State Col, BSE, 53; Univ Southern Miss, MA, 57; Univ Southern Ill, PhD(zool), 68. *Prof Exp:* Marine biologist, Gulf Coast Res Lab, Miss, 57-59; assoc prof biol, State Col Ark, 59-65; instr zool, Univ Southern Ill, 65-68; PROF BIOL, STATE COL ARK, 68- *Mem:* AAAS; Am Fisheries Soc. *Res:* Fish culture; aquatic ecology. *Mailing Add:* Dept of Biol State Col of Ark Conway AR 72032

COLLINS, RICHARD CORNELIUS, b Phoenix, Ariz, Feb 16, 41; m 61; c 1. PARASITOLOGY, ENTOMOLOGY. *Educ:* Ariz State Univ, BS, 63; Univ Ariz, MS, 66, PhD(entom, parasitol), 70. *Prof Exp:* Res asst entom, Dept Animal Path, Univ Ariz, 64-66, parasitol, 68-70; self-employed, 66-68; fel entom & parasitol, Dept Parasitol, Tulane Univ, 70-74; RES ENTOMOLOGIST PARASITOL, CTR DIS CONTROL, BUR TROP DIS, USPHS, 74- *Mem:* Am Soc Parasitol; Entom Soc Am; Am Soc Trop Med & Hyg; AAAS. *Res:* Bionomics of parasites and insects; chemotherapy of parasitic diseases; transmission dynamics of vector-borne diseases of man and animals. *Mailing Add:* Ctr Dis Control Bur Trop Dis Atlanta GA 30333

COLLINS, RICHARD LAPOINTE, b New York, NY, May 10, 38; m 65. INVERTEBRATE ZOOLOGY, PROTOZOOLOGY. *Educ:* Boston Univ, AB, 61, MA, 62; Univ Calif, Berkeley, PhD(zool), 69. *Prof Exp:* Actg asst prof zool, Univ Calif, Berkeley, 68-69; ASST PROF ZOOL & PHYSIOL, LA STATE UNIV, BATON ROUGE, 69- *Mem:* AAAS; Am Inst Biol Sci; Soc Protozool; Am Micros Soc. *Mailing Add:* Dept of Zool & Physiol La State Univ Baton Rouge LA 70803

COLLINS, ROBERT H(ENRY), III, b Montgomery, Ala, Feb 4, 30; m 52; c 4. ELECTRONICS. *Educ:* Auburn Univ, BS, 52; US Air Force Inst Technol, MS, 58. *Prof Exp:* Assoc engr, 57-62, res engr, 62-64, HEAD ELECTRONICS SECT, SOUTHERN RES INST, 64- *Res:* Instrument development in the areas of photoelectric aerosol particle size analyzers; video tracking using vidicon pickup; particle size analysis using vidicon and flash source; microwave absorption studies. *Mailing Add:* Southern Res Inst 2000 Ninth Ave Birmingham AL 35205

COLLINS, ROBERT JAMES, b Hazel Park, Mich, July 15, 28; m 52; c 2. PHYSIOLOGY, PHARMACOLOGY. *Educ:* Alma Col, BS, 51; Mich State Univ, 54, PhD, 58. *Prof Exp:* Bacteriologist, Mich Dept Health, 51-52; lab technician, E W Sparrow Hosp, 54-56; RES HEAD, UPJOHN CO, 58- *Mem:* AAAS; Am Pharmacol Soc; Soc Exp Biol & Med. *Res:* Central nervous system. *Mailing Add:* CNS Unit Upjohn Co Kalamazoo MI 49001

COLLINS, ROBERT JOSEPH, b Philadelphia, Pa, July 23, 23; m 45; c 4. PHYSICS. *Educ:* Univ Mich, AB, 47, MS, 48; Purdue Univ, PhD(physics), 53. *Prof Exp:* Asst prof physics, Rose Polytech Inst, 49-50; asst, Purdue Univ, 50-53; mem staff, Bell Tel Lab, 53-62; Inst Defense Anal, DC, 62-63; head dept, 64-70, PROF ELEC ENG, UNIV MINN, MINNEAPOLIS, 63- *Mem:* Am Phys Soc; Optical Soc Am; fel Inst Elec & Electronics Engrs. *Res:* Optical properties of solid state; radiation effects in solids; quantum electronics. *Mailing Add:* Dept Elec Eng Univ Minn 123 Church St Minneapolis MN 55455

COLLINS, RONALD WILLIAM, b Dayton, Ohio, Feb 5, 36; m 60; c 2. INORGANIC CHEMISTRY. *Educ:* Univ Dayton, BS, 57; Ind Univ, PhD(inorg chem), 62. *Prof Exp:* Inorg res chemist, Wyandotte Chem Corp, 62-65; from asst prof to assoc prof, 65-71, dept head, 77-80, PROF CHEM, EASTERN MICH UNIV, 71-, ASSOC VPRES, ACAD AFFAIRS, 80- *Concurrent Pos:* Vis prof, Mich State Univ, 70-71. *Mem:* Am Chem Soc; Royal Soc Chem; Am Crystallog Asn; AAAS. *Res:* Inorganic compounds of group IV metals; x-ray crystallography; instructional uses of digital computers; crystal lattice energies. *Mailing Add:* Dept of Chem Eastern Mich Univ Ypsilanti MI 48197

COLLINS, ROYAL EUGENE, b Corsicana, Tex, Feb 25, 25; div; c 2. PHYSICS, PETROLEUM ENGINEERING. *Educ:* Univ Houston, BS, 49; Tex A&M Univ, MS, 50, PhD(physics), 54. *Prof Exp:* Res Mobil Field Res Lab, 50-52 & engr, Stanolind Oil Co, 54-55; sr res engr, Humble Oil Co, 55-59; assoc prof, Univ Houston, 59-71, prof, 71-79; FRANK W JESSEN PROF PETROL ENG, UNIV TEX AT AUSTIN, 79- *Concurrent Pos:* Consult, Vet Admin Hosp, Houston, 55-62; Exxon Prod Res Corp, 59-68, M D Anderson Tumor Inst, 62; Col Med, Baylor Univ, 61-78; US Bur Mines, 61-63 & Subsurface Disposal Corp, 69-79. *Mem:* Am Phys Soc; Am Asn Physics Teachers; Soc Petrol Engrs; Sigma Xi; AAAS. *Res:* Fluid flow in porous media; petroleum production operations; enhanced oil recovery; quantum theory and related topics. *Mailing Add:* Petrol Eng Univ Tex Austin TX 78712

COLLINS, RUSSELL LEWIS, b Coffeyville, Kans, Sept 21, 28; m 79; c 2. CHEMICAL PHYSICS. *Educ:* Univ Tulsa, BS, 48; Univ Okla, MS, 50, PhD(physics), 53. *Prof Exp:* Res physicist, Phillips Petrol Co, Okla, 53-58; group leader, 58-62; asst prof, 62-66, ASSOC PROF PHYSICS, UNIV TEX, AUSTIN, 66- *Concurrent Pos:* Petrol Res Fund grant, 63-66; founder & pres, Austin Sci Assocs, Inc, 64-; Robert A Welch Found grant, 65-; Off Naval Res contract, 69-; US Army Mobile Equip Res & Develop Lab contract, 70-75. *Mem:* Am Phys Soc; Weed Sci Soc Am; Am Chem Soc. *Res:* Mössbauer effect as applied to iron organometallic complexes and stresses in ferrous metals; water-degradable polymers for controlled release of pesticides and medicines; thermodynamics of kinetic temperature. *Mailing Add:* 6907 Ten Oaks Circle Austin TX 78744

COLLINS, SAMUEL CORNETTE, b Democrat, Ky, Sept 28, 98; m 29. CYROGENIC ENGINEERING. *Educ:* Univ Tenn, BSA, 20, MS, 24; Univ NC, PhD(chem), 27. *Hon Degrees:* DSc, Univ NC, 57; LLD, Univ St Andrews, 67. *Prof Exp:* Prof chem, Carson-Newman Col, 25-26; instr physics, Univ NC, 26-27; assoc prof chem, Jr Col, Univ Tenn, 27-28; prof, Tenn State Teachers Col, 28-30; res assoc, 30-36, from asst prof to prof mech eng, 36-64, EMER PROF MECH ENG, MASS INST TECHNOL, 64-; RES CHEMIST, NAVAL RES LAB, WASHINGTON, DC, 71- *Concurrent Pos:* Vpres, Cryogenic Technol, Inc, 68-71. *Honors & Awards:* Wetherill Medal, Franklin Inst, 51; Kamerlingh Onnes Gold Medal, Netherlands Soc Refrig, 58; Rumford Medal, Am Acad Arts & Sci, 65; Gold Medal, Am Soc Mech Engrs, 68. *Mem:* Nat Acad Sci; Am Soc Mech Engrs; fel Am Acad Arts & Sci; Am Soc Mech. *Res:* Thermodynamic properties of gases; production and maintenance of very low temperatures; improvement of oxygen processes of low pressure type. *Mailing Add:* 12322 Riverview Rd Fort Washington MD 20744

COLLINS, STEPHEN, b Chicago, Ill, May 14, 27; m 54; c 3. ECOLOGY. *Educ:* Cornell Univ, BS, 49; Rutgers Univ, PhD(ecol), 56. *Prof Exp:* Resident naturalist, Palisades Nature Asn, NJ, 49-51; asst forester, Conn Agr Exp Sta, 57-62; from asst prof to assoc prof, 62-71, PROF BIOL, SOUTHERN CONN STATE COL, 71- *Concurrent Pos:* Consult, McGraw-Hill Bk Co, Inc, 57. *Mem:* Ecol Soc Am; Am Soc Mammal; Wildlife Soc; Wilderness Soc; Am Nature Study Soc. *Res:* Relation of land use, climatic, biotic and fire factors on biotic communities and their successions; silvics, vertebrate ecology, biogeography and general natural history; environmental problems; natural areas; pesticides; biological photography. *Mailing Add:* Dept of Biol Southern Conn State Col New Haven CT 06515

COLLINS, STEVE MICHAEL, b Bloomington, Ind, Sept, 19, 47; c 2. BIOMEDICAL IMAGE PROCESSING. *Educ:* Univ Ill at Chicago Circle, BS, 71, MS, 74, PhD(elec eng), 77. *Prof Exp:* Consult, G D Searle Lab, 72-74; asst prof, 77-81, asst res scientist cardiol, 79, radiol, 80-81, ASSOC PROF ELEC & COMPUT ENG & DIR CARDIOVASCULAR IMAGE PROCESSING LAB, UNIV IOWA, 81- *Mem:* Inst Elec & Electronics Engrs. *Res:* Application of computer engineering techniques, including signal and image processing and real-time computers, to problems in cardiology and cardiovascular physiology. *Mailing Add:* Elec & Comput Eng Univ Iowa Iowa City IA 52242

COLLINS, SYLVA HEGHINIAN, b Aleppo, Syria, Oct 9, 48; US citizen; m 80; c 1. STATISTICAL DESIGN, ANALYSIS OF CLINICAL TRIALS. *Educ:* Am Univ Beirut, BS, 71; Boston Univ, MA, 73, PhD(statist), 77; New York Univ, MS, 82. *Prof Exp:* Res statistician, Lederle Labs, 77-79; asst dir, 79-81, ASSOC DIR BIOSTATIST, AYERST LABS, 82- *Mem:* Am Statist Asn; Biomet Soc; Soc Clin Trials. *Res:* Statistical design and analysis of clinical trials; statistical modeling of computer systems performance. *Mailing Add:* 5 Arrowhead Rd Westport CT 06880

COLLINS, TERRENCE JAMES, b Auckland, NZ, Oct 12, 52; m 75. SYNTHETIC INORGANIC & ORGANOMETALLIC CHEMISTRY. *Educ:* Univ Auckland, BSc, 74, MSc, 75, PhD(chem), 78. *Prof Exp:* Res assoc, Stanford Univ, 78-80; ASST PROF CHEM, CALIF INST TECHNOL, 80- *Mem:* Am Chem Soc; NZ Inst Chem. *Res:* Development of synthetic reagents. *Mailing Add:* Chem Lab Div Chem & Chem Eng Calif Inst Technol Pasadena CA 91125

COLLINS, VERNON KIRKPATRICK, b Advocate, NS, May 14, 17; m 39; c 2. BIOCHEMISTRY. *Educ:* Acadia Univ, BSc, 37; McGill Univ, MS, 46. *Prof Exp:* Chemist, Can Packers, Montreal, 41-43; res chemist, Ogilvie Flour Mills, 43-46; chief chemist, Vio Bin Corp, Monticello, 46-77. *Mem:* Am Chem Soc; Am Oil Chem Soc. *Res:* Food spoilage; fat deterioration. *Mailing Add:* 201 S New St Champaign IL 61820

COLLINS, VINCENT J, b Haverstraw, NY, Nov 24, 14; m 44; c 8. MEDICINE, ANESTHESIOLOGY. *Educ:* Marietta Col, BS, 36; Brown Univ, MS, 38; Yale Univ, MD, 42. *Prof Exp:* Assoc, Doctors Hosp, New York, 46-49; dir anesthesiol, St Vincent's Hosp, 49-57; asst dir, Bellevue Hosp, 57-61; assoc prof surg, 61-66, PROF ANESTHESIOL, SCH MED, NORTHWESTERN UNIV, 66-; DIR DEPT ANESTHESIOL, COOK COUNTY HOSP, CHICAGO, 61- *Mem:* Am Soc Anesthesiol; AMA (secy, 57-62), AAAS. *Res:* Investigation of drugs, shock and endocrine problems. Dept Anesthesia Northwestern Univ Sch of Med Chicago IL 60611

COLLINS, WALTER MARSHALL, b Enfield, Conn, Nov 6, 17; m 43; c 4. ANIMAL GENETICS. *Educ:* Univ Conn, BS, 40, MS, 49; Iowa State Univ, PhD(poultry breeding), 60. *Prof Exp:* Instr poultry sci, Univ Conn, 47-49; from asst prof to assoc prof, 51-63, chmn genetics prog, 65-66, PROF ANIMAL & GENETICS SCI, UNIV NH, 63- *Concurrent Pos:* NIH spec fel, Univ Calif, Davis, 64-65. *Mem:* AAAS; Am Poultry Sci Asn; Genetics Soc Am; Am Genetic Asn; Int Soc Animal Blood Group Res. *Res:* Quantitative genetics; tumor biology. *Mailing Add:* Dept Animal Sci Univ NH Durham NH 03824

COLLINS, WARREN EUGENE, b Memphis, Tenn, Jan 26, 47; m 71. NUCLEAR PHYSICS. *Educ:* Christian Bros Col, BS, 68; Vanderbilt Univ, MS, 70, PhD(physics), 72. *Prof Exp:* Assoc prof physics, Southern Univ, Baton Rouge, 72-73; asst prof, 73-74, assoc prof physics, Fisk Univ, 74; res assoc, Vanderbilt Univ, 75-77; PROF PHYSICS, SOUTHERN UNIV, BATON ROUGE, 77- ASSOC, VANDERBILT UNIV, 75- *Mem:* Am Asn Physics Teachers; Am Phys Soc. *Res:* Level structure studies of selenium and arsenic isotopes with mass numbers between 68 and 76, using various methods; singles analysis, gamma-gamma angular correlation, gamma-gamma coincidences, and life-time studies. *Mailing Add:* 11336 Perkins Rd Baton Rouge LA 70810

COLLINS, WILLIAM BECK, b Port Williams, NS, Dec 5, 26; m 50; c 1. PLANT PHYSIOLOGY, HORTICULTURE. *Educ:* McGill Univ, BSc, 48, MSc, 54; Rutgers Univ, PhD(hort, plant physiol), 61. *Prof Exp:* Res scientist, 48-73, potato physiologist, Res Sta, Can Dept Agr, 73-80, PROG SPECIALIST, ATLANTIC REGION RES BR, AGR CAN, 80- *Mem:* Int Soc Hort Sci; Am Soc Hort Sci; Can Soc Hort Sci. *Res:* Relationships of growth regulators, endogenous and applied, to growth and development in potato; growth analysis and management studies with potato. *Mailing Add:* Suite 708 1888 Brunswick St Halifax NS Can

COLLINS, WILLIAM CARRIDINE, b Henderson, NC, Jan 4, 41; m 60; c 2. SOLID STATE PHYSICS. *Educ:* NC State Univ, BS, 65; Univ NC, PhD(physics), 71. *Prof Exp:* Res assoc physics, Nat Res Coun, 71-72; RES PHYSICIST, NAVAL RES LAB, 72- *Mem:* Sigma Xi. *Res:* Optical properties of solids and optical data processing. *Mailing Add:* 4545 Wheeler Rd Oxon Hill MD 20021

COLLINS, WILLIAM E, b Beachburg, Ont, Aug 2, 15; m 42; c 1. UROLOGY. *Educ:* Queen's Univ, Ont, MD & CM, 38; FRCPS(C), 49. *Prof Exp:* PROF SURG SUB-DEPT UROL, UNIV OTTAWA, 59-; CHIEF DEPT UROL, OTTAWA CIVIC HOSP, 60- *Concurrent Pos:* Consult, Royal Ottawa Sanatorium, 50; examr urol, Royal Col Physicians & Surgeons Can, 60-64; chmn urol nucleus comt, 74-76; rep bd gov, Am Col Surgeons, 62-65; mem urol comt, 64-66; chmn urol working party, Nat Med Manpower Comn Can, 73-75. *Mem:* Fel Am Col Surg; Am Urol Asn; Can Urol Asn (pres, 62-63); Int Soc Urol; Can Acad Urol Surg (pres, 73-74). *Res:* Bladder neck obstruction; storage and transplant of urine; etiology and treatment of bladder carcinoma. *Mailing Add:* 1105 Carling Ave Suite 207 Ottawa Can

COLLINS, WILLIAM EDGAR, b Terra Alta, WVa, Mar 31, 35; m 59; c 2. ENDOCRINOLOGY. *Educ:* WVa Univ BS, 57; Univ Wis, MS, 61, PhD(endocrinol), 65. *Prof Exp:* Prog specialist, Reprod Physiol for Ford Found, Inst Agr, Gujarat, India, 65-67; from asst prof to assoc prof, 67-74, actg dean, 74-75, PROF BIOL, WVA UNIV, 74-, DEAN COL ARTS & SCI, 75- *Mem:* Brit Soc Study Fertil; Endocrine Soc. *Res:* Function of corpus luteum and control of the estrous cycle. *Mailing Add:* 201 Woodburn Hall WVa Univ Morgantown WV 26506

COLLINS, WILLIAM ERLE, b Lansing, Mich, July 9, 29; m 56. MEDICAL ENTOMOLOGY, ECONOMIC ENTOMOLOGY. *Educ:* Mich State Univ, BS, 51, MS, 52; Rutgers Univ, PhD(entom), 54. *Prof Exp:* Asst entom, Rutgers Univ, 53-54; entomologist, Diamond Alkali Chem Co, 54; med entomologist, Biol Warfare Labs, Ft Detrick, Md, 55-58; exten specialist entom, Rutgers Univ, 58-59; mem biologist, Lab Parasitic Dis, 59-74, mem biologist, Bur Trop Dis, Ctr Dis Control, 74-81, MED BIOLOGIST, PARASITIC DIS DIV, CTR INFECTIOUS DIS, USPHS, 81- *Mem:* Entom Soc Am; Am Soc Trop Med & Hyg; Am Mosquito Control Asn. *Res:* Medical entomology in field of virus and malaria transmission by arthropod vectors. *Mailing Add:* Bur Trop Dis Ctr Dis Control 1600 Clifton Rd Atlanta GA 30333

COLLINS, WILLIAM F, b Laceyville, Pa, May 9, 18; m 45; c 3. FOOD SCIENCE. *Educ:* Pa State Col, BS, 42, MS, 48, PhD(dairy sci), 49. *Prof Exp:* Dairy res chemist, Swift & Co, Chicago, 49-53, head, Ice Cream & Stabilizer Res Div, Res Labs, 53-56, mem staff, Mkt Develop, Hammond, Ind, 56-57, tech sales rep US & Can, Gen Gelatin Dept, Kearny, NJ, 57-67; mgr tech sci, Swift Chem Co, Oak Brook, Ill, 67-68; pres & gen mgr, Nutriprod Ltd & Topping Co, Can, 68-73; ASSOC PROF FOOD SCI & TECHNOL & EXTEN SPECIALIST, VA POLYTECH INST & STATE UNIV, 73- *Honors & Awards:* Award of Merit, Nat Confectioners Asn, 68. *Mem:* Am Dairy Sci Asn; Inst Food Technologists; Int Asn Milk Food & Environ Sanitarians; Am Asn Candy Technologists; AAAS. *Res:* Milk quality and flavor as affected by microbial flora and ultra high pasteurization temperatures; aseptic packaging practices. *Mailing Add:* Dept of Food Sci & Technol Va Polytech Inst & State Univ Blacksburg VA 24061

COLLINS, WILLIAM FRANCIS, JR, b New Haven, Conn, Jan 20, 24; m 51; c 3. NEUROSURGERY. *Educ:* Yale Univ, BS, 44, MD, 47; Am Bd Neurol Surg, dipl, 56. *Prof Exp:* Resident neurosurg, Barnes Hosp, St Louis, Mo, 47-49, from asst res neurosurgeon to res neurosurgeon, 51-53; from instr to assoc prof neurosurg, Sch Med, Western Reserve Univ, 54-63; prof neurol surg, dir div & neurosurgeon-in-chief, Med Col Va, 63-67; prof neurol surg & chmn dept, 67-70, CUSHING PROF SURG, SCH MED, YALE UNIV, 70- *Concurrent Pos:* Nat Found Infantile Paralysis fel, Wash Univ, 53-54; consult, West Haven Vet Admin Hosp, 67-; neurosurgeon in chief, Yale New Haven Med Ctr, 67- *Mem:* Acad Neurol Surg; Am Col Surg; Asn Res Nerv & Ment Dis; Harvey Cushing Soc; Neurosurg Soc Am. *Res:* Neurophysiology of afferent pathway systems. *Mailing Add:* Yale Univ Sch of Med 333 Cedar St New Haven CT 06510

COLLINS, WILLIAM HENRY, b Baltimore, Md, Mar 1, 30; m 51; c 2. CHEMICAL ENGINEERING, ENVIRONMENTAL SCIENCES. *Educ:* Loyola Col, BS, 52; Alexander Hamilton Inst, MBA, 65. *Prof Exp:* Chief chemist, chem mfg, John C Stalfort & Sons, 54-57; component develop supvr eng, Catalyst Res Corp, 57-60; chief engr, Miller Res Corp, 60-67; prog mgr, AAI Corp, 67-70; dir, Franklin Inst Res Labs, 70-74; BR CHIEF INSTALLATION RESTORATION, CHEM SYSTS LAB, ABERDEEN PROVING GROUND, 74- *Mem:* Sigma Xi; Am Defense Preparedness Asn; Am Chem Soc; AAAS. *Res:* Assessment of ecological stress resulting from industrial and military operations at various government installations; assessment of potential for contaminant migration; cataclysmic stress corrosion crack of steel; military ordnance design and development. *Mailing Add:* Environ Technol Div Chem Systs Lab Aberdeen Proving Ground MD 21030

COLLINS, WILLIAM JOHN, b Mt Union, Pa, July 5, 34; m 58; c 3. INSECTICIDES, ENVIRONMENTAL TOXICOLOGY. *Educ:* Juniata Col, BS, 56; Rutgers Univ, PhD(entom), 65. *Prof Exp:* Asst prof entom, Rutgers Univ, 64-66; PROF ENTOM, OHIO STATE UNIV, 67-, ASST DEAN, 80- *Mem:* Entom Soc Am; Am Chem Soc; Soc Environ Toxicol Chem. *Res:* Toxicology; insecticide resistance, especially in cockroaches; mechanisms of resistance; environmental toxicology; aquatic invertebrate toxicology. *Mailing Add:* Dept of Entom Ohio State Univ Columbus OH 43210

COLLINS, WILLIAM KERR, b Vance Co, NC, June 21, 31; m 54; c 3. PLANT BREEDING, GENETICS. *Educ:* NC State Col, BS, 54, MS, 61; Iowa State Univ, PhD(plant breeding), 63. *Prof Exp:* Res instr, Crops Dept, NC State Col, 56-60; asst agron, Iowa State Univ, 60-63; agronomist, Res Dept, R J Reynolds Tobacco Co, 63-66; tobacco exten specialist, 66-70, assoc prof, 66-70, PROF AGRON, NC STATE UNIV, 70-, PHILIP MORRIS EXTEN SPECIALIST, 78- *Honors & Awards:* Exten Educ Award, Am Soc Agron, 81. *Mem:* Am Soc Agron. *Res:* Fluecured tobacco variety evaluation for agronomic, chemical, physical and pathological properties; tobacco herbicides and sucker control chemicals; tobacco fertility; tobacco production in Greece, Iran, Afghanistan, British Honduras, Costa Rica, Uruguay, Italy and Venezuela. *Mailing Add:* Dept Crop Sci 4210 Williams Hall NC State Univ Raleigh NC 27607

COLLINSON, CHARLES WILLIAM, b Wichita, Kans, Dec 15, 23; m 78; c 2. GEOLOGY. *Educ:* Augustana Col, AB, 49; Univ Iowa, MS, 50-51, PhD(geol), 52. *Prof Exp:* Asst, Univ Iowa, 48 & 51-52; from asst geologist to geologist, 52-69, HEAD STRATIG & AREAL GEOL, STATE GEOL SURV, ILL, 69- *Concurrent Pos:* Lectr, Univ Ill, 56-57 & Stanford Univ, 60; ed, Jour Paleont, 58-64; Guggenheim fel, Gt Brit & Ger, 63-64; mem Paleont Res Inst; prof geol, Univ Ill, Urbana-Champaign, 68-77. *Mem:* Paleont Soc; fel Geol Soc Am; Am Asn Petrol Geol; Soc Econ Paleontologists &

Mineralogists (pres, 73-74); Ger Paleont Soc. *Res:* Mississippian stratigraphy of the Mississippi Valley; Devonian-Mississippian conodonts; sedimentation and paleolimnology of Lake Michigan. *Mailing Add:* Ill State Geol Survey Urbana IL 61801

COLLINSON, JAMES W, b Moline, Ill, June 24, 38; m 61; c 2. GEOLOGY. *Educ:* Augustana Col, Ill, AB, 60; Stanford Univ, PhD(geol), 66. *Prof Exp:* Asst prof, 66-71, ASSOC PROF GEOL, OHIO STATE UNIV, 71- *Honors & Awards:* Fulbright Res Award, 80. *Mem:* Geol Soc Am; Paleont Soc; Am Asn Petrol Geol; Soc Econ Paleont & Mineral. *Res:* Permian and Triassic stratigraphy and paleontology; Antarctic geology. *Mailing Add:* Dept Geol Ohio State Univ Columbus OH 43210

COLLINS-WILLIAMS, CECIL, b Toronto, Ont, Dec 31, 18; m 44; c 2. PEDIATRICS, CLINICAL IMMUNOLOGY. *Educ:* Univ Toronto, BA, 41, MD, 44. *Prof Exp:* Assoc prof, Univ Toronto, 68-74; SR STAFF PHYSICIAN, HOSP FOR SICK CHILDREN, 65-; PROF PEDIAT, UNIV TORONTO, 74- *Concurrent Pos:* Consult, Ont Crippled Children's Ctr, Toronto, 66- *Mem:* Am Col Allergists; Am Acad Allergy; Can Soc Allergy & Clin Immunol (pres, 62); Can Soc Immunol; Can Pediat Soc. *Mailing Add:* Hosp for Sick Children 555 University Ave Toronto ON M5G 1X8 Can

COLLIPP, PLATON JACK, b Niagara Falls, NY, Nov 4, 32; m 56; c 3. PEDIATRICS. *Educ:* Univ Rochester, AB, 54, MD, 57. *Prof Exp:* UPSHS trainee biochem, Univ Wash, 57-59; from intern to resident pediat, Univ Southern Calif, 59-61, asst prof, 63-65; clin prof, State Univ NY Downstate Med Ctr, 65-69; PROF PEDIAT, HEALTH SCI CTR, STATE UNIV NY STONYBROOK, 69- *Concurrent Pos:* Assoc chmn pediat, Maimonides Med Ctr, 65-67; chmn pediat, Nassau County Med Ctr, 67- *Mem:* Am Acad Pediat; Am Physiol Soc; Soc Pediat Res. *Res:* Pediatric endocrinology and metabolism, especially growth hormone, growth disorders and childhood obesity. *Mailing Add:* Nassau County Med Ctr 2201 Hempstead Trnpk East Meadow NY 11554

COLLIS, RONALD THOMAS, b London, Eng, July 22, 20; m 51; c 1. ATMOSPHERIC PHYSICS. *Educ:* Oxford Univ, MA, 51. *Prof Exp:* Meteorologist, Decca Radar Ltd, Eng, 55-58; head, Radar Aerophys Group, 58-67, dir, Atmospheric Sci Lab, 67-78, SR DIR ENG SCI, EUROPE, SRI INT, 78- *Concurrent Pos:* Consult, NASA, 74- & NSF, 70- *Mem:* Assoc fel Am Inst Aeronaut & Astronaut; fel Am Meteorol Soc; Am Geophys Union; fel Royal Meteorol Soc. *Res:* Atmospheric factors in propagation of electromagnetic energy; weather radar; lidar; instrumental and data processing aspects of air pollution, aviation, space applications and general meteorology. and general meteorology. *Mailing Add:* SRI Int 333 Ravenswood Ave Menlo Park CA 94025

COLLISON, CLARENCE H, b Battle Creek, Mich, Oct 22, 45; m 68; c 3. ENTOMOLOGY, APICULTURE. *Educ:* Mich State Univ, BS, 68, MS, 73, PhD(entom), 76. *Prof Exp:* INstr entom, Mich State Univ, 75-76; ASST PROF ENTOM, PA STATE UNIV, 76- *Honors & Awards:* Driesbach Mem Award, Mich State Univ, 75. *Mem:* Entom Soc Am; Am Beekeeping Fedn; Sigma Xi. *Res:* Pollination and nectar secretion of buckwheat, birds-foot trefoil, and lima beans; biology and control of manure breeding flies and Northern fowl mite; livestock ectoparasites. *Mailing Add:* 233 Val Verda Dr Penna Furnace PA 16865

COLLISSON, ELLEN WHITED, b Alton, Ill, Aug 13, 46; m 67; c 3. VIRAL IMMUNOLOGY, MOLECULAR VIROLOGY. *Educ:* Univ Ill, BS, 68; Univ Ala, MS, 78, PhD(microbiol), 80. *Prof Exp:* Fel researcher, Univ Ala, 80-81, instr biol, Jefferson State Jr Col, 78-81; RES ASSOC, AGR RES SERV, USDA, 81- *Mem:* Am Soc Microbiologists; Am Soc Trop Med & Hyg. *Res:* Antibody-mediated fluctuations of the immune system; fingerprint analysis of the oligonucleotides from the ten dsRNA segments of Bluetongue Virus; techniques to detect Bluetongue Virus form persistently infected cattle. *Mailing Add:* Arthropod Borne Animal Dis Res PO Box 25327 Denver Fed Ctr Denver CO 80225

COLLISTER, EARL HAROLD, b Galva, Ill, Mar 25, 23; m 45; c 3. PLANT BREEDING, GENETICS. *Educ:* Purdue Univ, BS, 47, MS, 48, PhD(plant genetics), 50. *Prof Exp:* Assoc agronomist oilseed res, Tex Res Found, 50-51, agronomist & chmn field crops dept, 51-56, from sr agronomist to prin agronomist & chmn plant sci dept, 56-59; from asst dir & chief agronomist to dir & chief agronomist, High Plains Res Found, 59-67; exec vpres res sales mkt in US & overseas, World Seeds, Inc, 67-68; PRES, INT GRAIN, INC, 68-; PRES, TRANSERA RES, INC, 71- *Concurrent Pos:* Consult, Francisco Sugar Co, Cuba, 56-58; hon trustee, Int Sesanum Found. *Mem:* Am Soc Agron; Am Genetic Asn; AAAS; NY Acad Sci. *Res:* Red clover; sesame; sunflowers; soybeans; triticale; wheat; safflower; corn; grain sorghum; millet. *Mailing Add:* 530 Park Lane Richardson TX 75081

COLLMAN, JAMES PADDOCK, b Beatrice, Nebr, Oct 31, 32; m 55. INORGANIC CHEMISTRY. *Educ:* Univ Nebr, BSc, 54, MS, 56; Univ Ill, PhD, 58. *Prof Exp:* From instr to prof chem, Univ NC, 58-67; PROF CHEM, STANFORD UNIV, 67-, DAUBERT PROF CHEM, 80- *Concurrent Pos:* A P Sloan Found fel, 64-66; Frontiers in Chem lectr, 64; Guggenheim fel, 77-78. *Honors & Awards:* Calif Sect Award, Am Chem Soc, 72, Inorg Chem Award, 75. *Mem:* Nat Acad Sci; Am Acad Sci; Am Chem Soc; The Chem Soc. *Res:* Synthesis and electron transport properties of metal-metal bonds, reactions of coordinated dioxygen, homogeneous catalysis; reactions of coordinated ligands and homogeneous catalysis; mixed-functions oxygenase models. *Mailing Add:* Dept of Chem Stanford Univ Stanford CA 94305

COLLUM, DAVID BOSHART, b Syracuse, NY, Apr 25, 55. CHEMISTRY. *Educ:* Cornell Univ, BS, 77; Columbia Univ, PhD(chem), 80. *Prof Exp:* ASST PROF CHEM, CORNELL UNIV, 80- *Mem:* Am Chem Soc. *Res:* Natural products synthesis; transition metal chemistry as applied to organic synthesis. *Mailing Add:* Dept Chem Cornell Univ Ithaca NY 14853

COLLURA, JOHN, b Waltham, Mass, Nov 11, 48; m 70; c 2. TRANSPORTATION. *Educ:* Merrimack Col, BS, 70; Villanova Univ, MS, 71; NC State Univ, PhD(civil eng), 76. *Prof Exp:* Design eng, Murphy Assocs, 69-70; field & off engr, J F White Construct & Contracting, 70; transport engr, Valley Forge Labs, 70-71; field & off engr, J F White Construct & Contracting, 71-72; teaching asst civil eng, NC State Univ, 72-73; transp analyst, NC Dept Transp, 73-76; ASST PROF TRANSP, UNIV MASS, 76- *Concurrent Pos:* Transp consult, Mass Cent RR, 77, Champagne & Assocs, 80, Cape Cod Regional Transit Authority, 80-81 & Summit Land Trust, Fall River, Mass, 81; prin investr, Cape Cod Regional Transit Authority, 78, Mass Exec Off Transp & Contruct, 78, US Dept Transp, 78-81, Nat Sci Found, 78-79, Mass Dept Pub Works, 80-81, US Dept Transp, 81-83. *Mem:* Am Soc Civil Engrs; Transp Res Bd. *Res:* Transportation systems planning; evaluation and public transportation design and operations. *Mailing Add:* Dept Civil Eng Univ Mass Marston 214C Amherst MA 01003

COLLVER, MICHAEL MOORE, b Los Angeles, Calif, Feb 9, 41; m 62; c 3. SOLID STATE PHYSICS. *Educ:* Univ Calif, Los Angeles, BA, 63; Univ Calif, Berkeley, MA, 70, PhD(mat sci), 71. *Prof Exp:* Res physicist, US Naval Radiol Lab, 68, asst superconductivity, 68-72; assoc sr res physicist, Gen Motors Res Labs, Mich, 72-76; MEM FAC PHYSICS, UNIV CAMPINAS, BRAZIL, 76- *Mem:* Am Phys Soc; Am Vacuum Soc. *Res:* Superconductivity; magnetic and semiconductor materials research; thin film physics. *Mailing Add:* Inst of Physics Univ of Campinas Campinas Brazil

COLMAN, BRIAN, b Stockport, Eng, Oct 19, 33; m 64; c 3. PLANT PHYSIOLOGY. *Educ:* Univ Keele, BA, 58; Univ Wales, PhD(plant physiol), 61. *Prof Exp:* Nat Res Coun Can fel biol, Queen's Univ, Ont, 61-62; res assoc, Univ Rochester, 62-65; from asst prof to assoc prof, 65-78, PROF BIOL, YORK UNIV, ONT, 78- *Mem:* Am Soc Plant Physiologists; Phycol Soc Am. *Res:* Photosynthesis and photorespiration in algae and higher plants; carbon metabolism in blue-green algae. *Mailing Add:* Dept Biol York Univ 4700 Keele St Downsview ON M3J 1P3 Can

COLMAN, MARTIN, b Johannesburg, SAfrica, Oct 28, 41; US citizen; m 64; c 2. RADIATION ONCOLOGY, NUCLEAR MEDICINE. *Educ:* Univ Witwatersrand, Johannesburg, MB, BCH, 64, MMed, 71; Royal Col Physicians & Royal Col Surgeons, DMRT, 71. *Prof Exp:* Instr nuclear med, Sch Med & radiologist, Div Radiother, Hosp, Johns Hopkins Univ, 72-73; assoc dir radiation oncol, Michael Reese Hosp, 73-77; asst prof, 77-80, ASSOC PROF RADIOL SCI, RADIATION ONCOL DIV, UNIV CALIF, IRVINE, 80-, CHIEF RADIATION ONCOL, 77- *Concurrent Pos:* Attend physician, Div Nuclear Med, Michael Reese Hosp, 73-77; asst prof, Dept Radiol, Univ Chicago, 73-77; consult, Radiation Therapy, Long Beach Vet Admin Hosp, 78-; asst prof, Dept Obstet & Gynec, Univ Calif, Irvine, 79-, assoc prof, 80- *Mem:* Am Soc Therapeut Radiologists; Radiol Soc NAm; Am Col Radiol; Radiation Res Soc; Royal Col Radiol. *Res:* Radiation Carcinogenesis; drug-radiation interactions; modification of radiation effects; optimization of radiation therapy of cancer. *Mailing Add:* Div Radiation Oncol Dept Radiol Sci Univ Calif Irvine CA 92717

COLMAN, NEVILLE, b Johannesburg, SAfrica, July 30, 45; m 76; c 1. HEMATOLOGY, NUTRITION. *Educ:* Univ Witwatersrand, MB, BCh, 69, PhD(hemat), 74. *Prof Exp:* Intern med & obstet, Johannesburg Gen Hosp, 70; registr hemat, Sch Path, Univ Witwatersrand & SAfrican Inst Med Res, 71-74; registr med, Edenvale Hosp, 71-73; res assoc path, Col Physicians & Surg, Columbia Univ, 74-76; RES ASSOC HEMAT, VET ADMIN HOSP, BRONX, 76-; ASST PROF MED, STATE UNIV NY, DOWNSTATE MED CTR, BROOKLYN, 76- *Concurrent Pos:* Fel med, Vets Admin Hosp, Bronx, 74-76; NIH grant, Nat Cancer Inst, 74-76. *Honors & Awards:* Watkins-Pitchford Mem Prize, SAfrican Inst Med Res, 74. *Mem:* Am Soc Hemat; Am Soc Clin Nutrit; Am Inst Nutrit; Am Fedn Clin Res; SAfrican Soc Hemat. *Res:* Hematology, nutritional anemias, folate and vitamin B12 metabolism, binding proteins for folate and vitamin B12; use of folate analogues in chemotherapy; nutrition, vitamins, food fortification. *Mailing Add:* 600 W 111th St New York NY 10025

COLMAN, ROBERTA F, b New York, NY, July 21, 38; m 57; c 2. BIOCHEMISTRY, PROTEIN CHEMISTRY. *Educ:* Radcliffe Col, AB, 59, AM, 60, PhD(biochem), 62. *Prof Exp:* NIH fel enzym, 62-64; USPHS fel, Sch Med, Wash Univ, 64-66, asst prof enzym & protein chem, 66-67; assoc enzym, Harvard Med Sch, 67-69, from asst prof to assoc prof biochem, 69-73; PROF BIOCHEM, UNIV DEL, 73- *Concurrent Pos:* USPHS career develop award & res grant, Sch Med, Wash Univ, 66-67; Med Found Boston fel, Harvard Med Sch, 67-68, USPHS res grant, 67-, career develop award, 68-, Med Found res grant, 70-; Am Soc Biol Chem travel award, Int Cong Biochem, 67, 70 & 73; assoc ed, J Protein Chem; mem, Biochem Study Sect, NIH, 74-78; mem, Cellular & Molecular Basis Dis Rev Comt, Nat Inst Gen Med Sci, 79. *Mem:* AAAS; Am Soc Biol Chemists (treas, 81); Biophys Soc; Am Chem Soc. *Res:* Mechanism of enzyme action; active sites of dehydrogenases; chemical basis of regulation of allosteric enzymes; affinity labeling of purine nucleotide sites in proteins; investigation of specific enzymes such as glutathione reductase, glutamate dehydrogenase, isocitrate dehydrogenase, pyruvate kinase. *Mailing Add:* Dept of Biochem Univ of Del Newark DE 19711

COLMAN, STEVEN MICHAEL, b New Kensington, Pa, Apr 1, 49; m 72. QUATERNARY GEOLOGY, GEOMORPHOLOGY. *Educ:* Notre Dame Univ, BS, 71; Pa State Univ, MS, 74; Univ Colo, PhD(geol), 77. *Prof Exp:* RES GEOLOGIST, US GEOL SURV, COLO, 76- *Honors & Awards:* Outstanding Paper Award, Geol Soc Am, 76. *Mem:* Geol Soc Am; Am Quaternary Asn. *Res:* Quaternary stratigraphy of Western US; Quaternary dating techniques; paleoclimatology. *Mailing Add:* US Geol Surv MS 913 Fed Ctr Denver CO 80225

COLMANO, GERMILLE, b Pola, Italy, Aug 22, 21; nat US; m 47; c 3. VETERINARY PHYSIOLOGY, MEDICAL BIOPHYSICS. *Educ:* Univ Bologna, DVM, 49, PhD(physiol, biochem), 50. *Prof Exp:* Asst physiol, Univ Bologna, 47-49, from instr to asst prof, 49-51; asst vet, Phillips Vet Hosp, Colo, 51-52; asst vet sci, Univ Wis, 52-53; proj asst, Inst Enzyme Res, Wis, 54-56; scientist biophys, Res Inst Advan Study, 56-61; Stoner fel biophys res lab, Eye & Ear Hosp, Sch Med, Univ Pittsburgh, 61-62; prof vet sci, 62-78, PROF VETBIOL, VA-MD REGIONAL COL VET MED, DIV VET BIOL, VA POLYTECH INST & STATE UNIV, 78- *Mem:* Am Asn Vet Clin; Am Soc Vet Physiol & Pharmacol; Asn Am Vet Med Cols; Biophys Soc; fel Royal Soc Health. *Res:* Lamellar function-structure; monomolecular films; absorption spectra of chromophores; trace elements; steroids and stress in health and disease; bacteriostasis of silver in intramedullary orthopedic pins; early cancer, myocandial infarction, trace and toxic minerals detection by computer analysis of spectrophotometric absorbance of body fluids. *Mailing Add:* Va Regional Col Vet Med Va Polytech Inst & State Univ Blacksburg VA 24061

COLMENARES, CARLOS ADOLFO, b Ocana, Colombia, June 17, 32; US citizen; m 56; c 2. PHYSICAL CHEMISTRY, CHEMICAL ENGINEERING. *Educ:* Univ Calif, Berkeley, BS, 53; Wash State Univ, MS, 56; Rensselaer Polytech Inst, PhD(chem eng), 60. *Prof Exp:* Actg instr chem eng, Wash State Univ, 54-56; instr, Rensselaer Polytech Inst, 56-60; CHEMIST, LAWRENCE LIVERMORE LAB, 60- *Mem:* Am Vacuum Soc. *Res:* Gas-solid interactions; surface chemistry and physics; radiation chemistry; catalysis. *Mailing Add:* 2211 Granite Dr Alamo CA 94507

COLMERY, BENJAMIN H(ERRING), JR, b Mobile, Ala, Mar 10, 21; m 44; c 3. PHYSICS, ENGINEERING MANAGEMENT. *Educ:* US Naval Acad, BS, 43; Ohio State Univ, MSc, 51; Univ Calif, Los Angeles, ME, 59. *Prof Exp:* With Armed Forces Spec Weapons Proj, 48-51, res & monitor, Nev Atomic Weapon Test Site, 51; staff radiol defense officer & staff atomic weapons selection officer, US Navy, 52-53; tech sales, Atomics Int, 55-56, 57-58, proj mgr org moderated reactor exp, 56-57, supvr component develop, 58-59; mgr nuclear sci & space power dept, Bendix Systs Div, 59-63; dir res, Indust Nucleonics Corp, 63-64, staff mgt consult, 64; chief nuclear propulsion systs, Lewis Res Ctr, NASA, 64-66; mgr advan develop, Brown Eng, Teledyne, Inc, Ala, 66-68; SUPVRY AEROSPACE ENGR, NAVAL AIR SYSTS COMMAND, NAVY DEPT, WASHINGTON, DC, 69- *Mem:* Soc Logistics Eng. *Res:* Nuclear reactor heat removal equipment; nuclear weapon effects; liquid metal technology; statistical design and evaluation of experiments; operations research; physiology; corporate management. *Mailing Add:* 6640 Midhill Pl Falls Church VA 22043

COLMEY, JOHN C, b St Louis, Mo, May 28, 30; m 53; c 2. FOOD SCIENCE. *Educ:* Colo State Univ, BS, 53, MS, 58; Univ Ill, PhD(dairy tech), 62. *Prof Exp:* Prod develop scientist, Res & Develop Lab, Pillsbury Co, Minn, 62-64, tech mgr new prod develop, 64-68; group leader, Foremost Foods Co, 68-71; dir res admin, 71-74, dir res & prod develop, ITT Continental Baking Co, 74-77, corp dir res, 77-78; V PRES RES, NABISCO INC, 78- *Mem:* Am Chem Soc; Inst Food Technologists; Am Asn Cereal Chemists; Sigma Xi. *Res:* Chromatographic identification and quantitative measurement of flavor components in cheese; identification of changes in milk during manufacture of cottage cheese; product development; development of food and bakery products; research on dairy products and functionality of protein fractions. *Mailing Add:* Nabisco World Hq East Hanover NJ 07936

COLODNY, PAUL CHARLES, b Springfield, Mass, Feb 17, 30. PHYSICAL CHEMISTRY, POLYMER CHEMISTRY. *Educ:* Univ Mass, BS, 51; Princeton Univ, MA, 53, PhD(chem), 57. *Prof Exp:* Fiber physicist, Dow Chem Co, 57-60; from res chemist to sr res chemist, Aerojet-Gen Corp, 60-63, res chem specialist, 63-65; sr res chemist, Gen Tire & Rubber Co, Ohio, 65-66; sr staff mem, Raychem Corp, 66-70; res scientist, Lockheed Missile & Space Co, 70-73; group leader, MCA Disco-Vision, 74-76; chief chemist, Reed Irrig Systs, 76-78; SR CHEM SPECIALIST, AEROJET STRATEGIC PROPULSION CO, 81- *Concurrent Pos:* Consult, Raychem Corp, 71-73 & Carson-Alexion Corp, 76-78. *Mem:* Am Chem Soc; Soc Rheol; AAAS. *Res:* Fiber physics; textile fiber spinning; elastomers; solid rocket propellants; crystalline polymers; graphite, photo-polymerization; composite materials. *Mailing Add:* 2830 Mills Park Dr #4 Rancho Cordova CA 95670

COLOMBANT, DENIS GEORGES, b Bourg, France, Feb 12, 42; US citizen; m 65; c 3. PLASMA PHYSICS. *Educ:* Nat Sch Higher Arts & Trade, Paris, Ing, 63; Mass Inst Technol, MS, 66, PhD(nuclear eng), 69. *Prof Exp:* Res scientist plasma physics, Comn Atomic Energy Saclay, France, 69-70 & Limeil France, 70-73; res scientist, SAL, McLean, Va, 73-76; RES SCIENTIST PLASMA PHYSICS, NAVAL RES LAB, WASHINGTON, DC, 76- *Mem:* Am Phys Soc; Sigma Xi. *Res:* Inertial confinement fusion. *Mailing Add:* Naval Res Lab Code 6790 Washington DC 20375

COLOMBINI, VICTOR DOMENIC, b Boston, Mass, Feb 2, 24. GEOLOGY. *Educ:* Boston Univ, AB, 50, AM, 52 & 53, PhD, 61. *Prof Exp:* Geologist, USAEC, 55; asst prof geol, La Polytech Inst, 56-61; actg asst prof, Univ Miss, 61; assoc prof earth sci & head dept, Findlay Col, 61-66; mem fac, 66-68, asst prof, 68-73, ASSOC PROF GEOG, OHIO STATE UNIV, LIMA BR, 73- *Mem:* Geol Soc Am; Mineral Soc Am; Nat Asn Geol Teachers; Asn Am Geog; Nat Coun Geog Educ. *Res:* Physical geography; introductory economic geography; economic geology; crystallography; mineralogy; geomorphology. *Mailing Add:* Dept of Geog Ohio State Univ 4240 Campus Dr Lima OH 48504

COLOMBO, JORGE A, b Buenos Aires, Arg, Mar 13, 39; c 4. ANATOMY. *Educ:* Vicente Lopez Inc Inst, Buenos Aires, BS, 55; Med Sch, Nat Univ Buenos Aires, MD, 64. *Prof Exp:* Physician endocrinol, A Peralta Ramos Maternity Inst, Buenos Aires, 65, res physician, 65-69, in chg Res Dept, 66-68, in chg Clin Lab, 68; res physician, Unidad Asistencia Medica Integral Rivadavia-Peralta Ramos, Buenos Aires, 69-73; Found Fund Res Psychiat fel, Dept Anat & Brain Res Inst, Univ Calif, Los Angeles, 73-74, Ford Found fel, 74; Nat Res Coun Arg fel, Brain Res Inst, Nat Univ Cuyo, Mendoza, Arg, 74-77; ASSOC PROF ANAT, COL MED, UNIV S FLA, 77- *Concurrent Pos:* Ford Found fel, Chile, Uruguay & Arg, 68-70; Lucio Cherny Found grant, Inst Exp Biol & Med, Buenos Aires, 70; Ford Found fel, Dept Anat & Brain Res Inst, Univ Calif, Los Angeles, 71-72, Found Fund Res Psychiat fel, 72-73; Arg Nat Coun Sci & Tech Res grants, 74-76; NIH biomed res support grant, 77-78; NSF grant, 79-82. *Mem:* Arg Med Asn; AAAS; Arg Soc Biomed Eng; Soc Neurosci; Soc Exp Biol & Med. *Res:* Neuroendocrinology; brain mechanisms controlling the release of LH and prolactin pituitary hormones; effects of sex steroids on brain function. *Mailing Add:* Dept of Anat Col of Med Univ S Fla Tampa FL 33612

COLON, FRAZIER PAIGE, b Athol, Mass, Mar 28, 34; m 60; c 3. MECHANICAL ENGINEERING, FLUID MECHANICS. *Educ:* Norwich Univ, BSME, 56; Worcester Polytech Inst, MSME, 68. *Prof Exp:* Asst engr, Allis-Chalmers Mfg Co, 56-61; proj engr, Alden Res Labs, Worcester Polytech Inst, 61-64; res observer, Nat Eng Lab, E Kilbride, Scotland, 64-66; instr fluid mech, Alden Res Lab, Worcester Polytech Inst, 66-74; proj mgr, Riley Stoker Corp, 74-76; sr mech eng, Chas T Main, Inc, 76-77; MGR, ENG CE-KSB PUMP CO, INC, 77- *Mem:* Am Soc Mech Engrs; Int Asn Hydraul Res. *Res:* Turbomachinery; design of new pumps; testing performance characteristics; optimizing design and increasing efficency; thermodynamics techniques for measuring pump efficiency. *Mailing Add:* 3 Ambler Way PO Box 594 Durham NH 03824

COLON, JOSE A, b Coamo, PR, Nov 24, 21; m 51; c 3. METEOROLOGY. *Educ:* Univ PR, BA, 44; Univ Chicago, MS, 50, PhD(air-sea interactions), 60. *Prof Exp:* Asst meteorol, Inst Trop Meteorol, PR, 45-46; instr math & meteorol, Univ PR, 46-49; instr meteorol, Univ Chicago, 51-52, res assoc, 52-54; res forecaster, US Weather Bur, PR, 54-48; supvry res meteorologist, Nat Hurricane Res Lab, Fla, 49-62, Int Meteorol Ctr, Int Indian Ocean Exped, Bombay, India, 62-64 & Nat Hurricane Res Lab, Fla, 64; METEOROLOGIST CHG, US WEATHER BUR, SAN JUAN, PR, 64- *Mem:* Am Meteorol Soc; Am Geophys Union; Royal Meteorol Soc. *Res:* Tropical cyclones, their motion and forecast problems, development, structure and evolution; air-sea interactions and atmospheric energy sources; cyclogenesis over Indian Ocean and Indian monsoon circulations. *Mailing Add:* US Weather Serv Isla Verde Int Airport San Juan PR 00913

COLON, JULIO ISMAEL, b Coamo, PR, June 19, 28; US citizen; m 55; c 2. VIROLOGY. *Educ:* Univ PR, BS, 50; Univ Chicago, PhD(microbiol), 59. *Prof Exp:* Fel, Nat Acad Sci-Nat Res Coun, 59-60; microbiologist, Ft Detrick, Md, 60-63; microbiologist, US Trop Res Med Lab, 63-65; ASSOC PROF VIROL, SCH MED, UNIV PA, SAN JUAN, 64- *Concurrent Pos:* Dir grad studies, Univ PR, San Juan, 72-74. *Mem:* Am Soc Microbiol; fel Am Acad Microbiologist; Tissue Culture Asn; Sigma Xi. *Res:* Intermediary metabolism; biochemistry and genetics of psittacosis group of microorganism; biochemistry and genetics of the arthropod-borne viruses; origin and source of viral infectious nucleic acid; radiobiology of viruses; viral and tumor immunology. *Mailing Add:* Dept of Microbiol Univ of PR Sch of Med San Juan PR 00936

COLONNIER, MARC, b Quebec, Que, May 12, 30; m 59; c 1. ANATOMY. *Educ:* Univ Ottawa, BA, 51, MD, 59, MSc, 60; Univ London, PhD(neurobiol), 63. *Prof Exp:* Med Res Coun Can fel, Univ Ottawa & Univ London, 59-63; asst prof anat, Univ Ottawa, 63-65; from asst prof to assoc prof neuroanat, Neurol Sci Lab, Univ Montreal, 65-69; prof anat & head dept, Univ Ottawa, 69-76; PROF ANAT, LAB NEUROBIOL, UNIV LAVAL, 76- *Honors & Awards:* Lederle Med Fac Award, 66; Charles Judson Herrick Award, Am Asn Anat, 67. *Mem:* Can Asn Anat; Am Asn Anat; fel Royal Soc Can; Soc Neurosci. *Res:* Cerebral cortex; synapses; visual system. *Mailing Add:* Dept of Anat Univ of Laval Fac of Med Quebec Can

COLONNO, RICHARD JAMES, b Brooklyn, NY, Nov 27, 49; m 74; c 2. VIROLOGY. *Educ:* Kans Wesleyan Univ, BA, 71; Univ Kans, PhD(microbiol), 75. *Prof Exp:* Fel Roche Inst Molecular Biol, 75-78; MEM RES STAFF, DU PONT EXP STA, DEL, 78- *Mem:* Am Soc Microbiol. *Res:* Mechanisms of viral transciption and replication; molecular virology; mechanism of interferon action. *Mailing Add:* Cent Res & Develop 328/343 Du Pont Exp Sta Wilmington DE 19898

COLOSI, NATALE, b Messina, Italy, Mar 5, 02. BACTERIOLOGY, PUBLIC HEALTH. *Educ:* St Francis Col, BS, 28; NY Univ, MS, 30, PhD, 35. *Hon Degrees:* ScD, Wagner Col, 77. *Prof Exp:* Instr bact, Col Med, NY Univ, 32-36; prof, 34-74, dean, 65-73, EMER PROF BACT & PUB HEALTH, WAGNER COL, 74-, PROF, NY POLYCLIN MED SCH & HOSP, 59-, DEAN, INST CONTINUING BIOMED EDUC, 78- *Concurrent Pos:* Dir & vpres bd trustees, Ital Hosp, 36-73; NY state comnr, Inter-State Sanit Comn, 45-, chmn, 65- *Mem:* AAAS; fel Am Pub Health Asn; Am Soc Microbiol; Air Pollution Control Asn. *Res:* Serology. *Mailing Add:* 122 Grapanche St Yonkers NY 10701

COLOVOS, GEORGE, b Thessaloniki, Greece, Oct 15, 32; m 70; c 1. ANALYTICAL CHEMISTRY, ATMOSPHERIC CHEMISTRY. *Educ:* Univ Thessaloniki, Greece, BS, 57, PhD(chem), 66. *Prof Exp:* From instr to lectr, Univ Thessaloniki, Greece, 61-69; res assoc, Univ Ariz, 67-69 & 71-73 & Utah State Univ, 69-71; mem tech staff chem, Rockwell Int, 73-74, mgr chem lab, 75-76, mgr chem, 76-77, MGR TECH OPERS, ENVIRON MONITORING & SERV CTR, ROCKWELL INT, 77- *Concurrent Pos:* Mem sci comn, Nat Inst Occupational Safety & Health, 72-73. *Mem:* Am Chem Soc. *Res:* Development of analytical methods for determination of pollutants. *Mailing Add:* Rockwell Int Environ Monitoring & Serv Ctr 2421 W Hillcrest Dr Newbury Park CA 91320

COLOWICK, SIDNEY PAUL, b St Louis, Mo, Jan 12, 16; m 43, 51; c 3. BIOCHEMISTRY. *Educ:* Wash Univ, BS, 36, MS, 39, PhD(biochem), 42. *Prof Exp:* Asst biol chem, Med Sch, Wash Univ, 36-42, from instr to asst prof pharmacol, 42-46; assoc, Div Nutrit & Physiol, Pub Health Res Inst, NY,

46-48; assoc prof biochem, Col Med, Univ Ill, 48-50; prof biol, Johns Hopkins Univ, 50-59; Harvie Branscomb Distinguished Prof, 78-79, PROF MICROBIOL & AM CANCER SOC PROF, VANDERBILT UNIV, 59- *Honors & Awards:* Eli Lilly Award, 47. *Mem:* Nat Acad Sci; Am Soc Biol Chem; Am Acad Arts & Sci. *Res:* Intermediary metabolism of carbohydrates; action of hormones. *Mailing Add:* Dept of Microbiol Vanderbilt Univ Sch of Med Nashville TN 37232

COLP, JOHN LEWIS, b Carterville, Ill; c 3. GEOLOGICAL ENGINEERING, GEOTHERMAL ENGINEERING. *Educ:* Univ Ill, BS, 49; Univ NM, MS, 66; Tex A&M Univ, PhD(civil eng), 72. *Prof Exp:* Proj engr, El Segundo Div, Douglas Aircraft Co, 42-45; transmission engr, Allison Div, Gen Motors Corp, 48-50; plant engr, Inland Container Corp, Indianapolis, 50-53; chief engr, Charles Dowd Box Co, 53-55; mem tech staff, Sandia Labs, Albuquerque, 55-69; eng res assoc, Tex Eng Exp Sta, 69-72; MEM TECH STAFF, SANDIA NAT LABS, ALBUQUERQUE, 72- *Mem:* Am Geophys Union; Soc Naval Architects & Marine Engrs; Sigma Xi. *Res:* Magma energy utilization; geothermal energy; geology and engineering interface; marine sediment instrumentation; anchor pullout forces; earth penetration by projectiles. *Mailing Add:* 1023 Washington SE Albuquerque NM 87108

COLPA, JOHANNES PIETER, b Arnhem, Netherlands, Jan 26, 26; m 51; c 1. THEORETICAL CHEMISTRY, MAGNETIC RESONANCE. *Educ:* Univ Amsterdam, PhD(chem), 57. *Prof Exp:* Res chemist, Shell Res Labs, Amsterdam, 57-66; assoc prof chem, Univ Amsterdam, 63-69; PROF CHEM, QUEEN'S UNIV, ONT, 69- *Concurrent Pos:* Fel, Cambridge Univ, 61-62; consult, Max Planck Inst, Ger, 67-69; assoc ed, Molecular Physics, 64-69. *Mem:* Am Phys Soc; Royal Netherlands Chem Soc; Netherlands Phys Soc; NY Acad Sci. *Res:* High pressure spectroscopy; pressure induced spectroscopic transitions; molecular orbital theory and magnetic resonance; theory of energy differences; reinterpretation of hunch and rules; theory of optical nuclear polarization; optical detection of magnetic resonance in paracyclophases; nuclear magnetic resonance and nuclear quadrupole resonance in excited stakes of molecules; phosphorescence. *Mailing Add:* Dept of Chem Queen's Univ Kingston ON K7L 3N6 Can

COLQUHOUN, DONALD JOHN, b Toronto, Ont, Mar 29, 32; m 56; c 2. GEOLOGY. *Educ:* Univ Toronto, BA, 53, MA, 56; Univ Ill, PhD(geol), 60. *Prof Exp:* Asst geol, Univ Ill, 58-59; from asst prof to assoc prof, 60-70, chmn dept, 70-77, PROF GEOL & MARINE BIOL 70- *Concurrent Pos:* Proj geologist, SC State Develop Bd, 60-; NSF grant, 63- *Mem:* Geol Soc Am; Am Asn Petrol Geol; Soc Econ Paleont & Mineral; Paleont Soc. *Res:* Application of sedimentalogical studies and techniques to geomorphology and stratigraphy; interpretation of coastal plain terraces; regional stratigraphy. *Mailing Add:* Dept of Geol Univ of SC Columbia SC 29208

COLQUITT, LANDON AUGUSTUS, b Ft Worth, Tex, Jan 25, 19; m 54. MATHEMATICS. *Educ:* Tex Christian Univ, BA, 39; Ohio State Univ, MA, 41, PhD(math), 48. *Prof Exp:* Instr math, Ohio State Univ, 46-48; from asst prof to assoc prof, 48-54, PROF MATH, TEX CHRISTIAN UNIV, 55- *Mem:* AAAS; Am Math Soc; Math Asn Am; Soc Indust & Appl Math. *Res:* Mathematical analysis; applied mathematics. *Mailing Add:* 2601 McPherson Ft Worth TX 76109

COLSKY, JACOB, b Memphis, Tenn, Dec 5, 21; m 53; c 3. INTERNAL MEDICINE, ONCOLOGY. *Educ:* Memphis State Col, 38-40; Univ Tenn, MD, 44; Am Bd Internal Med, dipl. *Prof Exp:* Intern med, Jackson Mem Hosp, Miami, Fla, 44-45; asst chief clin res, Nat Cancer Inst, USPHS Hosp, Baltimore, Md, 50-51, actg chief, 51-52; from instr to assoc prof med, Col Med, State Univ NY, 52-57; assoc prof, Sch Med, Univ Miami, 57-66, clin assoc prof, 66-74, clin prof med, 75-80, prof oncol, 75-80; RETIRED. *Concurrent Pos:* Fel prev med, Sch Med, Johns Hopkins Univ, 47-50; asst physician, Johns Hopkins Hosp, 47-52; instr med, Sch Med, Johns Hopkins Univ, 50-51; assoc dir med, Maimonides Hosp, Brooklyn, NY, 52-57; dir med oncol sect, Dept Med, Univ Miami & Jackson Mem Hosp, 60-70; sr investr, Eastern Co-op Group Solid Tumor Chemother, 60-; attend physician, Cedars of Lebanon Hosp & Jackson Mem Hosp, Miami, 61-; dir med oncol sect, Cedars of Lebanon Hosp, 72-, chief med, 77-; consult, Baptist Hosp, Mt Sinai Hosp & Vet Admin Hosp. *Mem:* AAAS; fel Am Col Physicians; AMA; Am Soc Clin Oncol; Am Asn Cancer Res. *Res:* Biology and chemotherapy of animal and human malignant neoplasms. *Mailing Add:* Prof Arts Ctr 1150 NW 14th St Miami FL 33136

COLSON, STEVEN DOUGLAS, b Idaho Falls, Idaho, Aug 16, 41; m 62; c 6. CHEMICAL PHYSICS. *Educ:* Utah State Univ, BS, 63; Calif Inst Technol, PhD(chem), 68. *Prof Exp:* Asst prof, 68-73, assoc prof, 73-80, PROF CHEM, YALE UNIV, 80- *Concurrent Pos:* Jr fac fel, Yale Univ, 72-73; mem, Nat Res Coun Adv Bd to US Army Res Off, 72-75; assoc ed, J Chem Physics, 80- *Res:* Intermolecular interactions and energy transfer in molecular crystals, multiphoton gas and condensed phase spectroscopy; laser, mass spectrometric and photoelectron spectroscopic techniques. *Mailing Add:* Dept of Chem Yale Univ 225 Prospect St New Haven CT 06520

COLTEN, HARVEY RADIN, b Houston, Tex, Jan 11, 39; m 59; c 3. IMMUNOLOGY, PEDIATRICS. *Educ:* Cornell Univ, BA, 59; Western Reserve Univ, MD, 63. *Prof Exp:* From intern to resident pediat, Univ Cleveland Hosps, 63-65; res assoc immunol, NIH, 65-67, sr scientist, 67-69, head molecular separations unit, 69-70; asst prof pediat, 70-73, chief, Div Allergy, 73-76, assoc prof, 73-79, PROF PEDIAT, HARVARD MED SCH, 79- *Concurrent Pos:* Assoc ed, New Eng J Med, 78-; chief div cell biol, Childrens Hosp Med Ctr, Boston; dir, Am Bd Allergy & Clin Immunol; assoc ed, J Immunol, J Allergy & Clin Immunol; Vox Sanguinis. *Honors & Awards:* E Mead Johnson Award Pediat Res, 79. *Mem:* AAAS; Am Soc Clin Invest; Am Acad Allergy; Soc Pediat Res; Am Asn Immunol. *Res:* Immunochemistry of inflamation; complement biosynthesis; genetic disorders of complement; histamine metabolism. *Mailing Add:* Div of Cell Biol Dept of Pediat 300 Longwood Ave Boston MA 02115

COLTEN, OSCAR A(ARON), b Detroit, Mich, Apr 24, 12; m 35; c 2. CHEMICAL ENGINEERING. *Educ:* Wayne State Univ, BS, 32; Univ Mich, MS, 34, ScD(phys chem), 36. *Prof Exp:* Jr technologist, Shell Petrol Co, Mo, 36-38; technologist, Shell Oil Co, Tex, 38-41, sr technologist, NY, 41-46; tech asst, Shell Develop Co, Calif, 46-49; asst mgr econ res dept, Shell Chem Corp, 49-52, asst to gen mgr mfg, 52-54, sect leader mfg develop dept, 54-58, econ & eval, Indust Chem Div, 59-67, SR STAFF ENGR, SHELL CHEM CO, 67- *Concurrent Pos:* Dep br chief, Chem Div, Nat Prod Authority, Washington, DC, 51-52. *Mem:* AAAS; Am Chem Soc; Am Inst Chem Engrs. *Res:* Reaction kinetics; petroleum refining; petrochemicals; chemical economics. *Mailing Add:* 1693 West Belt Dr Houston TX 77042

COLTER, ALLAN KENNEDY, organic chemistry, see previous edition

COLTER, JOHN SPARBY, b Bawlf, Alta, July 23, 22; m 50; c 2. VIROLOGY. *Educ:* Univ Alta, BS, 45; McGill Univ, PhD(biochem), 51. *Prof Exp:* Mem staff, Virus & Rickettsial Res Div, Lederle Labs, 51-57 & Wistar Inst, Pa, 57-61; PROF BIOCHEM & HEAD DEPT, UNIV ALTA, 61- *Mem:* Am Soc Biol Chem; Am Soc Cell Biol; Am Asn Cancer Res; Can Biochem Soc; fel Royal Soc Can. *Res:* Biochemistry of virus infection; mechanisms of viral replication and oncogenesis. *Mailing Add:* Dept of Biochem Univ of Alta Edmonton Can

COLTERYAHN, LOUIS E, physical metallurgy, see previous edition

COLTHARP, FORREST LEE, b Caney, Kans, Oct 30, 33; m 52; c 3. MATHEMATICS EDUCATION. *Educ:* Okla State Univ, BS, 57, MS, 60, EdD(higher educ), 68. *Prof Exp:* Teacher & math consult, pub schs, Okla, 57-64; asst prof math educ, Kans State Col, 64-66; instr, Okla State Univ, 66-67; PROF MATH EDUC, PITTSBURG STATE UNIV, 67- *Mem:* Nat Coun Teachers Math. *Mailing Add:* 1402 S Homer Pittsburg KS 66762

COLTHARP, GEORGE B, b Maringouin, La, Nov 28, 28; m 53; c 2. FOREST HYDROLOGY, WATER POLLUTION. *Educ:* La State Univ, BS, 51; Colo State Univ, MS, 55; Mich State Univ, PhD(forest hydrol), 58. *Prof Exp:* Proj leader watershed mgt, Rocky Mountain Forest & Range Exp Sta, US Forest Serv, NMex, 58-61; asst mgr, Coltharp's Livestock Mkt, La, 61-64; from asst prof to assoc prof range watershed mgt, Utah State Univ, 64-74; ASSOC PROF FORESTRY, UNIV KY, 75- *Mem:* Am Water Resources Asn; Soc Am Foresters; Am Soc Range Mgt; Soil Conserv Soc Am. *Res:* Forest hydrology studies; wildland water quality and watershed management. *Mailing Add:* Dept of Forestry Univ of Ky Lexington KY 40506

COLTHUP, NORMAN BERTRAM, b Paris, France, July 6, 24; nat US; m 57; c 3. SPECTROSCOPY. *Educ:* Antioch Col, BS, 49. *Hon Degrees:* DSc, Fisk Univ, 74. *Prof Exp:* INFRARED SPECTROSCOPIST, AM CYANAMID CO, 44- *Concurrent Pos:* Infrared course lectr, Fisk Univ & Asn Clin Scientists. *Honors & Awards:* Williams-Wright Award, Coblentz Soc, 79. *Mem:* Coblentz Soc. *Res:* Vibrational spectroscopy; molecular structure studies using infrared spectroscopy; infrared spectra-structure correlations. *Mailing Add:* Am Cyanamid Co Chem Res Div 1937 W Main St Stamford CT 06904

COLTMAN, CHARLES ARTHUR, JR, b Pittsburgh, Pa, Nov 7, 30; m 51; c 4. HEMATOLOGY, ONCOLOGY. *Educ:* Univ Pittsburgh, BS, 52, MD, 56; Ohio State Univ, MMS, 63; Am Bd Internal Med, dipl, 63, cert hemat, 72, cert med oncol, 73. *Prof Exp:* From intern to resident path, Del Hosp, Wilmington, 56-57; Med Corps, US Air Force, 57-77, flight surgeon, Walker AFB, NMex, 57-59, resident, Univ Hosp, Ohio State Univ, 59-63, staff hematologist, 63-66, chief hemat-oncol serv, Wilford Hall Air Force Med Ctr, 66-77, chmn dept med, 75-76; assoc prof, 77-78, PROF MED & DIR, CLIN MED ONCOL SECT, HEALTH SCI CTR, UNIV TEX, SAN ANTONIO, 78- *Concurrent Pos:* Asst med, Ohio State Univ Hosp, 59-61, from jr asst resident to sr asst resident, 59-62, asst instr med, 61-62, chief med resident & demonstr med, 62-63, attend physician & instr med, 63; mil consult to Surg Gen, US Air Force, 64-77; clin assoc prof physiol & med, Health Sci Ctr, Univ Tex, San Antonio, 70-75; med dir, Cancer Therapy & Res Ctr, San Antonio, 77-; chief, Med Oncol Sect, Med Serv, Audie Murphy Vet Admin Hosp, San Antonio, Tex, 77-; chmn, Southwest Oncol Group, 81- *Honors & Awards:* Mederi Award, Aerospace Med Div, 69; Stitt Award, Asn Mil Surg US, 70; Harold Brown Award, US Air Force, 71; Legion of Merit, 78. *Mem:* AAAS; fel Am Col Physicians; Am Asn Cancer Res; Am Fedn Clin Res; Am Soc Hemat. *Res:* Research in clinical cancer chemotherapy. *Mailing Add:* 4450 Medical Dr San Antonio TX 78229

COLTMAN, JOHN WESLEY, b Cleveland, Ohio, July 19, 15; m 41; c 2. MUSICAL ACOUSTICS, ELECTRON OPTICS. *Educ:* Case Inst Technol, BS, 37; Univ Ill, MS, 39, PhD(physics), 41. *Prof Exp:* Res engr, Res Labs, Westinghouse Elec Corp, 41-44, sect mgr, 44-49, mgr, Electronics & Nuclear Physics Dept, 49-60, assoc dir, 60-64, dir math & radiation, 64-69, res dir indust & defense prod, 69-73, dir res planning, 73-80; RETIRED. *Concurrent Pos:* Mem adv group electron devices, US Dept Defense, 62-66; mem adv comt, NASA, 64-66; mem numerical data adv bd, Nat Acad Sci, 68-71; mem, Comn on Human Resources, Nat Res Coun, 76- *Honors & Awards:* Longstreth Medal, Franklin Inst, 60; Westinghouse Order of Merit, 68; Roentgen Medal, 70. *Mem:* Nat Acad Eng; fel Am Phys Soc; fel Inst Elec & Electronics Engrs. *Res:* Slow neutrons; microwave tubes; x-ray fluorescence; scintillation counters; image amplifier tubes; energy conversion; control mechanisms; lasers; physics of wind instruments. *Mailing Add:* Westinghouse Elec Corp Res Labs Beulah Rd Pittsburgh PA 15235

COLTMAN, RALPH READ, JR, b Pittsburgh, Pa, Nov 15, 24; m 44; c 3. SOLID STATE PHYSICS. *Educ:* Carnegie Inst Technol, BS, 50. *Prof Exp:* PHYSICIST, OAK RIDGE NAT LAB, 50- *Mem:* Am Phys Soc. *Res:* Irradiation damage in metals; cryogenics. *Mailing Add:* Solid State Div Oak Ridge Nat Lab Oak Ridge TN 37830

COLTON, CLARK KENNETH, b New York, NY, July 20, 41; m 65; c 4. CHEMICAL ENGINEERING. *Educ:* Cornell Univ, BChE, 64; Mass Inst Technol, PhD(chem eng), 69. *Prof Exp:* Ford fel engr, 69-70, asst prof, 69-76, prof, 76-80, BAYER PROF CHEM ENG, MASS INST TECHNOL, 80- *Concurrent Pos:* Consult artificial kidney-chronic uremia prog, Nat Inst Arthritis & Metab Dis; mem adv bd on mil personnel supplies, Nat Res Coun; assoc ed, Am Soc Artificial Internal Organs J. *Honors & Awards:* Allan P Colburn Award, Am Inst Chem Engrs, 77; Curtis W McGraw Res Award, Am Soc Eng Educ, 80. *Mem:* AAAS; Am Inst Chem Engrs; Am Chem Soc; Am Soc Artificial Internal Organs; NY Acad Sci. *Res:* Heat and mass transfer; biomedical engineering; mass transfer in artificial organs; membrane transport phenomena; enzyme applications; quantitative physiology. *Mailing Add:* Rm 66-452 Dept Chem Eng Mass Inst of Technol Cambridge MA 02139

COLTON, DAVID L, b San Francisco, Calif, Mar 14, 43; m 68. MATHEMATICS. *Educ:* Calif Inst Technol, BS, 64; Univ Wis, MS, 65; Univ Edinburgh, PhD(math), 67, DSc(math), 77. *Prof Exp:* From asst prof to assoc prof math, Ind Univ, Bloomington, 67-75; prof math, Univ Strathclyde, 75-78; PROF MATH, UNIV DEL, 78- *Concurrent Pos:* Asst prof, McGill Univ, 68-69; assoc ed, Applicable Anal; vis res fel, Univ Glasgow, 71-72; guest prof, Univ Konstanz, 74-75; assoc ed, Complex Variables: Theory & Appln. *Mem:* Soc Indust & Applied Math. *Res:* partial differential equations; integral equations; applied mathematics. *Mailing Add:* Dept Math Univ Del Newark DE 19711

COLTON, ERVIN, b Omaha, Nebr, June 25, 27; m 55; c 4. INORGANIC CHEMISTRY. *Educ:* Ga Inst Technol, BS, 50; Univ Kans, MS, 52; Univ Ill, PhD(inorg chem), 54. *Prof Exp:* Asst prof chem, Ga Inst Technol, 54-56; prin res chemist, Int Minerals & Chem Corp, 56-58; res chemist, Allis-Chalmers Mfg Co, 58-62, mgr, Cerac Sect, New Prod Dept, 62-64, PRES, CERAC, INC, 64-, CERAC HOT-PRESSING, INC, 67- & CERAC/PURE, INC, 70- *Mem:* Am Chem Soc; Am Ceramic Soc. *Res:* Liquid ammonia and inorganic fluorine chemistry; hydrazine chemistry and synthesis; high temperature refractories; potassium chemicals. *Mailing Add:* Cerac Inc Box 1178 Milwaukee WI 53201

COLTON, FRANK BENJAMIN, b Poland, Mar 3, 23; nat US; m; c 4. CHEMISTRY. *Educ:* Northwestern Univ, BS, 45, MS, 46; Univ Chicago, PhD(chem), 49. *Prof Exp:* Fel biochem, Mayo Clin, 49-51; asst dir chem res, 51-70, RES ADV, G D SEARLE & CO, 70- *Mem:* Am Chem Soc; Royal Soc Chem. *Res:* Organic chemistry; biochemistry. *Mailing Add:* 3901 Lyons St Evanston IL 60203

COLTON, JAMES DALE, Owatonna, Minn, Sept 3, 45; m 70; c 2. SCALE MODELING, STRESS WAVE PROPAGATION. *Educ:* Univ Minn, BME, 67; Stanford Univ, MS, 68, PhD(appl math), 73. *Prof Exp:* Res eng, 68-74, asst dir eng mech, 74-81, DIR ENG MECH, POULTER LAB, SRI INT, 81- *Mem:* Am Soc Mech Eng; Sigma Xi. *Res:* Stress wave propagation in structures; scale modeling structural response; simulation of dynamic load environments. *Mailing Add:* 670 Georgia Ave Palo Alto CA 94306

COLTON, RAYMOND H, otolaryngology, communication science, see previous edition

COLTON, RICHARD J, b South Fork, Pa, Dec 12, 50; m 78. SURFACE CHEMISTRY, PHYSICAL CHEMISTRY. *Educ:* Univ Pittsburgh, BS, 72, PhD(phys chem), 76. *Prof Exp:* Teaching fel chem, Univ Pittsburgh, 72-76; Nat Res Coun res assoc, Nat Acad Sci, 76-77, RES CHEMIST, US NAVAL RES LAB, 77- *Mem:* Am Chem Soc; Am Vacuum Soc; Am Soc Mass Spectrometry. *Res:* Surface analysis by x-ray photoelectron and auger electron spectroscopy and desorption and secondary ion mass spectrometry; corrosion and contamination; thin films; organic overlayers; emission mechanisms polyatomic and molecular ions; new surface analytical tools. *Mailing Add:* Chem Div Code 6170 US Naval Res Lab Washington DC 20375

COLTON, ROGER BURNHAM, b Windsor Locks, Conn, Jan 1, 24; m 47, 73; c 5. ENVIRONMENTAL GEOLOGY. *Educ:* Yale Univ, BS, 47, MS, 49. *Prof Exp:* GEOLOGIST, US GEOL SURV, 49- *Mem:* Geol Soc Am; Am Asn Petrol Geol; Am Inst Prof Geologists; Asn Eng Geologists. *Res:* Landslides, geomorphology and photogeology. *Mailing Add:* Mail Stop 913 Box 25046 US Geol Surv Denver Fed Ctr Denver CO 80225

COLUCCI, ANTHONY VITO, b Chicago, Ill, Sept 24, 38. ENVIRONMENTAL HEALTH, TOXICOLOGY. *Educ:* Loyola Univ, Ill, BS, 61; Johns Hopkins Univ, ScD(pathobiol), 66. *Prof Exp:* Res asst bact res, Lutheran Gen Hosp, Park Ridge, Ill, 60-61; res assoc parasitol res, Loyola Univ, Ill, 61; NSF fel biol res, Univ Wis, 66-67; chemist III, R J Reynolds Tobacco Co, 67-70; chief biochem & physiol br, Human Studies Lab, US Environ Protection Agency, 70-74; vpres health progs, Greenfield, Attaway & Tyler Inc, 74-80; MEM STAFF, RES DEPT, R J REYNOLDS TOBACCO CO, 80- *Concurrent Pos:* Mem adv comt coord res coun subcomt health effect mobile source emissions, 70-; NSF consult, Dir Joint US Environ Protection Agency & NSF Spanish Am Mercury Health Effects Prog, 70-74. *Mem:* Soc Toxicol; Sigma Xi. *Res:* Parasite biochemistry; fate of smoke constituents in animals; intermediary metabolism of parasitic animals; pharmacology of helminth infections; health effects of pollutants in both occupational and environmental setting. *Mailing Add:* Res Dept R J Reynolds Tobacco Co 115 Chestnut St SE Winston-Salem NC 27102

COLUCCI, JOSEPH M(ICHAEL), b Brooklyn, NY, Aug 12, 37; m 57; c 3. MECHANICAL ENGINEERING. *Educ:* Mich State Univ, BS, 58; Calif Inst Technol, MS, 59. *Prof Exp:* Res engr, 59-63, assoc sr res engr, 63-67, sr res engr, 67-70, asst dept head, 70-72, DEPT HEAD, FUELS & LUBRICANTS DEPT, GEN MOTORS RES LABS, 72- *Mem:* Soc Automotive Engrs; AAAS. *Res:* Current and future fuels and lubricants for automotive applications; effects of fuels and lubricants on vehicle emissions; fuel economy, durability, performance; petroleum- based and non-petroleum based materials. *Mailing Add:* Fuels & Lubricants Dept Gen Motors Res Labs Warren MI 48090

COLVARD, DEAN WALLACE, b Ashe Co, NC, July 10, 13; m 39; c 3. ANIMAL SCIENCE, ANIMAL ECONOMICS. *Educ:* Berea Col, BS, 35; Univ Mo, MA, 38; Purdue Univ, PhD, 50. *Hon Degrees:* Dr, Purdue Univ, 60; Belmont Abbey Col, 79; Univ NC, Charlotte, 80. *Prof Exp:* Instr agr, Brevard Col, 35-37; res asst, Univ Mo, 37-38; supt, NC Agr Res Sta, 38-46; prof animal sci, NC State Col, 47-53, head dept, 48-53, dean agr, 53-60; pres, Miss State Univ, 60-66; chancellor, 66-78, EMER CHANCELLOR, UNIV NC, CHARLOTTE, 79- *Concurrent Pos:* Trustee, Berea Col, 56-76, & St Andrews Presby Col, 69-76; managing consult, Sci Mus Charlotte, 80-81; chmn bd trustees, NC Sch Sci & Math, 78- *Honors & Awards:* Distinguished Serv Award, US Army; Hugh McEniry Award, NC Asn of Col & Univ, 81. *Res:* Research, teaching and writing; animal physiology; economic geography and education; science education and educational administration. *Mailing Add:* Off of the Emer Chancellor Univ of NC Charlotte NC 28223

COLVER, C(HARLES) PHILLIP, b Coffeyville, Kans, Oct 21, 35; m 58; c 3. CHEMICAL ENGINEERING, FORENSIC ENGINEERING. *Educ:* Univ Kans, BS, 58, MS, 60; Univ Mich, PhD(chem eng), 63. *Prof Exp:* Engr, Gulf Oil Corp, 58-59; res assoc, Univ Mich, 61-63; from asst prof to prof chem eng, Univ Okla, 63-76, dir, Sch Chem Eng & Mat Sci, 70-74, assoc dean eng, 74-75; CONSULT ENGR, 76- *Concurrent Pos:* Vis prof chem eng, Univ Colo, 77-78. *Mem:* Am Inst Chem Engrs; Acad Forensic Sci; Nat Fire Protection Asn. *Res:* Explosions; fires; accident reconstruction; chemical and mechanical design; energy management. *Mailing Add:* 0855 Mountain Laurel Dr Aspen CO 81611

COLVIN, BURTON HOUSTON, b West Warwick, RI, July 12, 16; m 47; c 3. MATHEMATICS. *Educ:* Brown Univ, AB, 38, AM, 39; Univ Wis, PhD(math), 43. *Prof Exp:* Instr math, Univ Wis, 40-43 & 46, asst prof, 47-51; tech aid appl math panel, Nat Defense Res Comt & Off Sci Res & Develop, 44-45; mathematician, Phys Res Staff, Boeing Co, 51-55, supvr math anal, 55-58, assoc head math res lab, Boeing Sci Res Labs, 58-59, head, 59-70, head math & Info Sci Lab, 70-72; chief, Applied Math Div, 72-78, DIR, CTR APPLIED MATH, NAT BUR STANDS, 78- *Concurrent Pos:* Vis sci lectr, Soc Indust & Appl Math, 59-60 & Math Asn Am, 63-65; chmn, Conf Bd Math Scis, 75-76; mem, Comn Sci Soc Pres, 75-78; consult, NSF, 76-78. *Mem:* Fel AAAS; Soc Indust & Appl Math (pres, 71-72); Am Math Soc; Math Asn Am; Inst Math Statist. *Res:* Differential equations; applied mathematics. *Mailing Add:* Ctr Applied Math Nat Bur Stands Washington DC 20234

COLVIN, CHARLES H(ERBERT), b Sterling, Mass, Mar 4, 93; m 29; c 4. AERONAUTICS. *Educ:* Stevens Inst Tech, ME, 14. *Prof Exp:* Chief engr & mgr, Aircraft Instrument Dept, Sperry Gyroscope Co, 14-19; pres & gen mgr, Pioneer Instrument Co, 19-32; dir, Colvin Labs, 33-53, pres, Colvin Labs, Inc, 54-63; CONSULT, 63-; DIR, SQUANSET LAB, 68- *Concurrent Pos:* Asst to pres, Kollsman Instrument Co, 37-40; spec asst to chief US Weather Bur, 40-41; dir Guggenheim Sch Aeronaut, NY Univ, 41-44, coordr res, Col Eng, 42-44; res consult, Bur Aeronaut, US Navy, 44; consult engr, 44-51; adv, President's Air Policy Comn, Washington, DC, 47. *Mem:* Fel Am Inst Aeronaut & Astronaut (pres, 45); fel Am Soc Mech Engrs; fel Royal Aeronaut Soc. *Res:* Design of meteorological and aircraft instruments; turn indicator; compass; climb indicator. *Mailing Add:* Squanset Lab 222 Sierra Rd Ojai CA 93023

COLVIN, CLAIR IVAN, b Clyde, Ohio, Sept 16, 27. PHYSICAL CHEMISTRY. *Educ:* Ohio Univ, BS, 49; Univ Miami, MS, 61, PhD(phys chem), 63. *Prof Exp:* Anal chemist, Aluminum & Magnesium, Inc, 51-52 & Nat Carbon Co, 52-53; instr chem, Racine Exten Ctr, Univ Wis, 53-56; teacher high sch, 56-57; univ fel chem & USPHS grant, Sch Med, Univ Miami, 63-64; from asst prof phys chem to assoc prof chem, 64-70, PROF CHEM & CHMN DEPT, GA SOUTHERN COL, 70- *Mem:* Am Chem Soc; The Chem Soc. *Res:* Kinetics of the thermal decomposition of ammonium nitrate in the presence of catalysts; molecular orbital calculations for conjugated organic compounds of biological interest. *Mailing Add:* Dept of Chem Ga Southern Col Statesboro GA 30458

COLVIN, CURTIS A, b Provo, Utah, May 14, 28; m 54; c 4. NUCLEAR CHEMISTRY, ANALYTICAL CHEMISTRY. *Educ:* Brigham Young Univ, BS, 51. *Prof Exp:* Jr chemist, Gen Elec Co, Hanford, 51-54, chemist, 54-65, sr chemist, Isochem Inc, 65-67, sr chemist, 67-72, mgr anal chem, Atlantic Richfield Hanford Co, 72-77; mgr plutonium anal chem, 77-79, SR SCIENTIST, ENVIRON ANAL, ROCKWELL INT, 79- *Mem:* Am Chem Soc; Inst Nuclear Mat Mgt; Nat Mgt Asn. *Res:* Chemistry involved in the separation of actinide elements; analytical chemistry of the actinide elements. *Mailing Add:* 1410 Sunset Richland WA 99352

COLVIN, DALLAS VERNE, b Westport, Ore, May 30, 37; m 64. ANIMAL BEHAVIOR, ANIMAL ECOLOGY. *Educ:* Portland State Univ, BS, 63; Univ Colo, PhD(zool), 70. *Prof Exp:* Teaching asst biol, Univ Colo, Boulder, 67-68; asst prof, 70-80, ASSOC PROF BIOL, CALIF STATE COL, DOMINGUEZ HILLS, 80- *Mem:* AAAS; Am Inst Biol Sci; Am Soc Mammal. *Res:* Behavioral studies of small mammals; analysis and biological bases of ultrasounds used by Microtus as a form of communication between neonates and adults. *Mailing Add:* Dept of Biol Calif State Col Dominguez Hills CA 90246

COLVIN, HARRY WALTER, JR, b Schellsburg, Pa, Dec 5, 21; m 50; c 2. PHYSIOLOGY, ANIMAL SCIENCE. *Educ:* Pa State Univ, BS, 50; Univ Calif, Davis, PhD(comp physiol), 57. *Prof Exp:* Instr physiol, Okla State Univ, 56-57; from asst prof to assoc prof, Univ Ark, 57-65; from asst prof to assoc prof, 65-75, PROF PHYSIOL, UNIV CALIF, DAVIS, 75- *Concurrent Pos:* Coun Int Exchange Scholars Fulbright-Hays Award, 72-73. *Mem:* Sigma Xi; AAAS; Am Dairy Sci Asn; Am Soc Animal Sci; NY Acad Sci. *Res:* Rumen physiology; carbohydrate metabolism in calves; blood coagulation; animal nutrition. *Mailing Add:* Dept of Animal Physiol Univ of Calif Davis CA 95616

COLVIN, HOWARD ALLEN, b Houston, Tex, June 25, 53; m 78; c 1. CHEMISTRY. *Educ:* Univ Houston, BS, 75; Georgia Inst Technol, PhD(chem), 79. *Prof Exp:* SR RES CHEMIST, GOODYEAR TIRE & RUBBER, 79- *Mem:* Am Chem Soc. *Res:* Process development and applications of dihydroxybenzenes and derivatives; process development and applications of substituted styrenes. *Mailing Add:* 171 Hillier Ave Akron OH 44310

COLVIN, JOHN ROSS, b Regina, Sask, Jan 6, 21; m; c 2. BIOCHEMISTRY, BIOPHYSICS. *Educ:* Univ Sask, BSA, 46; Univ Alta, MSc, 48; Univ Minn, PhD(biochem), 51. *Prof Exp:* From asst res officer to sr res officer, 51-66, HEAD BIOPHYS SECT, DIV BIOL SCI, NAT RES COUN CAN, 57-, PRIN RES OFFICER, 67- *Concurrent Pos:* Spec lectr, Univ Ottawa, 61-; vis prof, Laval Univ, 69-70. *Mem:* Nat Comt Biophys Can, 61-71, mem assoc comt, 62-71. *Mem:* Biophys Soc; fel Chem Inst Can; Can Biochem Soc. *Res:* Physical chemistry of proteins; biological fibrogenesis; fine cell structure and function. *Mailing Add:* Div of Biol Sci Nat Res Coun of Can Ottawa Can

COLWELL, GENE THOMAS, b Chattanooga, Tenn, Aug 3, 37. THERMODYNAMICS, HEAT TRANSFER. *Educ:* Univ Tenn, BS, 59, MS, 62, PhD(eng sci), 66. *Prof Exp:* Res engr, Oak Ridge Nat Lab, 59-62, design specialist, 65- 66; instr mech eng, Univ Tenn, 62-65; from asst prof to assoc prof, 66-76, PROF MECH ENG, GA INST TECHNOL, 76- *Concurrent Pos:* Eng consult. *Mem:* Am Soc Mech Engrs; Sigma Xi. *Res:* Energy engineering; power plant development; gas turbines; turbomachinery. *Mailing Add:* Dept of Mech Eng Ga Inst of Technol Atlanta GA 30332

COLWELL, JACK HAROLD, b Wooster, Ohio, Dec 29, 31; m 56; c 2. EXPERIMENTAL THERMAL PHYSICS. *Educ:* Mt Union Col, BS, 53; Purdue Univ, MS, 58; Univ Wash, PhD(chem), 61. *Prof Exp:* Nat Res Coun Can fel, 61-63; chemist, Cryophysics Sect, 63-73, res chemist, Thermophysics Div, 73-81, PHYSICIST, TEMPERATURE & PRESSURE MEASUREMENTS & STANDARDS DIV, NAT BUR STANDARDS, 81- *Mem:* Am Chem Soc; Sigma Xi; Am Phys Soc. *Res:* Low temperature calorimetry; properties of molecular crystals, superconductors and magnetic insulators at low temperatures; properties of materials at high pressures; high pressure standards and instrumentation. *Mailing Add:* Temperature & Pressure Measurement Div Nat Bur Standards Washington DC 20234

COLWELL, JOHN AMORY, b Boston, Mass, Nov 4, 28; m 54; c 4. INTERNAL MEDICINE, PHYSIOLOGY. *Educ:* Princeton Univ, AB, 50; Northwestern Univ, MD, 54, MS, 57, PhD(physiol), 68; Am Bd Internal Med, dipl, 62. *Prof Exp:* Intern med, Med Sch, Western Reserve Univ, 54-55; resident, Northwestern Univ, 55-57 & 59-60; instr, Med Sch, 60-62, assoc, 62-65, from asst prof to assoc prof, 65-71; PROF MED, MED UNIV SC, 71-, DIR ENDOCRINOL & METAB, NUTRIT DIV, 72-, UNIV RES COORDR, 73- *Concurrent Pos:* NIH fel, Northwestern Univ, 56-57, Am Diabetes Asn & univ fels, 60-61, NIH res grant, 62-71; clin investr, Vet Admin Res Hosp, Chicago, 61-63, chief sect, 63-71; assoc chief staff res & develop, Vet Admin Hosp, Charleston, 71- *Mem:* AAAS; fel Am Col Physicians; Am Diabetes Asn; Am Physiol Soc; Endocrine Soc. *Res:* Insulin secretion, degradation and action in animals and man; selected clinical studies in subjects with disorder of metabolism and endocrinology; platelet function in diabetes. *Mailing Add:* Dept of Med Med Univ of SC Charleston SC 29425

COLWELL, JOSEPH F, b Brush, Colo, Mar 16, 29; m 53; c 3. SOLID STATE PHYSICS. *Educ:* Colo State Univ, BS, 51; Cornell Univ, PhD(physics), 60. *Prof Exp:* Physicist, Navy Electronics Lab, 51-53; asst physics, Cornell Univ, 53-54 & 56-60; res staff mem, Gen Atomic Div, Gen Dynamics Corp, 60-67; staff mem, Gulf Radiation Technol Div, Gulf Energy & Environ Systs, Inc, 67-74; MEM STAFF, INTELCOM/RADIATION TECHNOL, 74- *Mem:* AAAS; Am Phys Soc; Soc Explor Geophys. *Res:* Solid state theory, especially as related to direct energy conversion devices and radiation damage in solids; seismic methods of geophysical exploration. *Mailing Add:* 2030 Karren Ln Carlsbad CA 92008

COLWELL, PRISCILLA J, experimental solid state physics, quantum electronics, see previous edition

COLWELL, RITA R, b Beverly, Mass, Nov 23, 34; m 56; c 2. MICROBIOLOGY. *Educ:* Purdue Univ, BS, 56, MS, 58; Univ Wash, PhD(marine microbiol), 61. *Prof Exp:* Res asst prof, Univ Wash, 61-64; vis asst prof, Georgetown Univ, 63-64, from asst prof to assoc prof biol, 64-72; PROF MICROBIOL, UNIV MD, 72-; DIR, STATE EDUC AGENCY GRANT PROG, 78- *Concurrent Pos:* Guest scientist, Nat Res Coun Can, 61-63; mem classification res group, London; mem bd trustees, Am Type Cult Collection, chmn, 80; consult, Bur Higher Educ, Dept Health, Educ & Welfare, 68-78; consult div res grants, NIH, 70; consult adv comt sci educ & biolog oceanog, NSF, 70-81; consult, Environ Protection Agency, 75- *Honors & Awards:* Phi Sigma Serv Award; Am Chem Soc, 75. *Mem:* Fel AAAS; Am Soc Microbiol; Soc Invert Path; Soc Indust Microbiol; fel Am Acad Microbiol. *Res:* Marine microbiology; numerical taxonomy; uses of high-speed electronic computers in biology and medicine. *Mailing Add:* Dept Microbiol Univ Md College Park MD 20742

COLWELL, ROBERT KNIGHT, b Denver, Colo, Oct 9, 43; div; c 1. ECOLOGY, EVOLUTION. *Educ:* Harvard Univ, AB, 65; Univ Mich, Ann Arbor, PhD(zool), 69. *Prof Exp:* Asst to cur econ & ethnobot, Bot Mus, Harvard Univ, 66; Ford Found fel math biol, Univ Chicago, 69-70; asst prof, 70-76, ASSOC PROF ZOOL, UNIV CALIF, BERKELEY, 76- *Concurrent Pos:* Coordr, Org Trop Studies grad course in trop biol, 71. *Mem:* AAAS; Am Soc Naturalists; Asn Trop Biol; Ecol Soc Am; Soc Study Evolution. *Res:* Ecology and evolution of biological communities; tropical biology; behavioral and theoretical ecology. *Mailing Add:* 961 Hilldale Ave Berkeley CA 94708

COLWELL, ROBERT NEIL, b Star, Idaho, Feb 4, 18; m 42; c 4. FOREST MENSURATION. *Educ:* Univ Calif, BS, 38, PhD(plant physiol), 42. *Prof Exp:* Asst bot, 38-42, from asst prof to assoc prof, 47-57, PROF FORESTRY, UNIV CALIF, BERKELEY, 57-, ASSOC DIR SPACE SCI LAB, 69-, DIR BERKELEY OFF, EARTH SATELLITE CORP, 70- *Concurrent Pos:* Chmn comt crop geog & veg anal, Nat Res Coun, 53-54. *Honors & Awards:* Abrams Award, 54; Fairchild Photogram Award, 57; Photo Interpretation Award, Am Soc Photogram, 64. *Mem:* Soc Am Foresters; Am Soc Photogram (vpres, 54); Int Soc Photogram. *Res:* Identification and mapping of vegetation types from aerial and space photographs; use of radioactive tracers in biological studies; applications of remote sensing to the space sciences; aerospace and earth sciences. *Mailing Add:* 145 Mulford Hall Univ of Calif Berkeley CA 94720

COLWELL, WILLIAM MAXWELL, b Blairsville, Ga, May 28, 31; m 56; c 4. VETERINARY MICROBIOLOGY. *Educ:* Berry Col, BS, 52; Univ Ga, DVM, 59, MS, 68, PhD(microbiol), 69; Am Col Vet Microbiologists, dipl. *Prof Exp:* Vet, Vanderbilt Vet Hosp, Durham, NC, 59-60 & diag lab, Ga Poultry Lab, Oakwood, 60-64; area vet, Elanco Prod Co, Ind, 64-66; Campbell fel, Avian Dis Res Ctr, Univ Ga, 66-69; asst prof vet sci, Univ Fla, 69-70; assoc prof poultry sci, NC State Univ, 70-74, prof vet sci, 74-78; DIR VET, RES & SERV LAB, HOLLY FARMS POULTRY INDUST, INC, WILKESBORO, NC, 78- *Mem:* Am Asn Avian Pathologists; Am Vet Med Asn. *Res:* Avian disease research; epidemiology of avian tumor viruses; avian respiratory viruses; oncogenic viruses of poultry; organ culture techniques; bioassay of aflatoxins. *Mailing Add:* Holly Farms Poultry Indust Inc PO Box 88 Wilkesboro NC 28697

COLWELL, WILLIAM TRACY, b Joliet, Ill, Oct 18, 34. PHARMACEUTICAL CHEMISTRY, SYNTHETIC ORGANIC CHEMISTRY. *Educ:* Occidental Col, BA, 56; Univ Calif, Los Angeles, PhD(org chem), 62. *Prof Exp:* SR ORG CHEMIST PHARMACEUT CHEM, SRI INT, 62- *Mem:* Am Chem Soc. *Res:* Synthesis of pteridines and related heterocycles as antifolates; antiparasitic compounds; synthesis of prostaglandin metabolites and prostaglandin synthetase inhibitors. *Mailing Add:* SRI Int Menlo Park CA 94025

COLWICK, REX FLOYD, b Clifton, Tex, Mar 19, 22; m 43; c 1. AGRICULTURAL ENGINEERING. *Educ:* Tex A&M Univ, BS, 47, MS, 48. *Prof Exp:* Agr engr, USDA & Tex A&M Univ, 48-50, agr eng coordr, 51-81; invests leader crop prod systs res, USDA & prof agr & biol eng, Miss State Univ, 61-78, lab chief & location leader, Agr Res Serv, 78-80; CONSULT AGR ENG, 81- *Concurrent Pos:* Consult, Cotton Res Adv Comt & Task Force, USDA, 55-78. *Mem:* Am Soc Agr Engrs. *Res:* Agricultural engineering research in crop production and harvesting equipment. *Mailing Add:* 1006 S Montgomery Starkville MS 39759

COLWILL, JACK M, b Cleveland, Ohio, June 15, 32; m 54; c 3. INTERNAL MEDICINE. *Educ:* Oberlin Col, BA, 55; Univ Rochester, MD, 57; Am Bd Internal Med, dipl, 64; Am Bd Family Practice, dipl, 71. *Prof Exp:* Intern, Barnes Hosp, Washington Univ, 57-58; res, Univ Wash Affiliated Hosps, 58-60, chief res, Univ Hosp, 60-61; from instr to sr instr med & dir med outpatient dept, Med Sch, Univ Rochester, 61-64; asst prof, 64-70, asst dean, Sch Med, 64-67, assoc dean, 67-69, assoc prof med, 70-76, assoc dean acad affairs, 69-76, actg chmn, Dept Family & Community Med, 76-77, ASSOC PROF MED, SCH MED, UNIV MO-COLUMBIA, 70-, PROF FAMILY & COMMUNITY MED, 76-, CHMN DEPT, 77-, DIR FAMILY MED RESIDENCY PROG, MED CTR, 74- *Mem:* AMA; Asn Am Med Cols. *Mailing Add:* Dept Family & Community Med Sch Med Univ Mo Columbia MO 65201

COLWIN, ARTHUR LENTZ, b Sydney, Australia, Jan 26, 11; nat US; m 40. ZOOLOGY. *Educ:* McGill Univ, BSc, 33, MSc, 34, PhD(embryol), 36. *Prof Exp:* Moyse traveling fel, Sir William Dunn Inst Biochem & Dept Exp Zool, Univ Cambridge, 34-35; Seessel fel, Osborn Zool Lab, Yale Univ, 36-37, Royal Soc Can fel, 37-38; instr biol, NY Univ, 38-39; from instr to prof biol, Queens Col, NY, 40-73; ADJ PROF, ROSENSTEIL SCH MARINE & ATMOSPHERIC SCI, UNIV MIAMI, 73- *Concurrent Pos:* Instr embryol, Marine Biol Lab, Woods Hole, 48-50; Fulbright res scholar, Misaki Marine Biol Sta, Tokyo, 53-54; mem corp, Marine Biol Lab, Woods Hole & trustee, 62-75. *Honors & Awards:* Am Mills Gold Medal. *Mem:* Am Soc Zoologists; fel NY Acad Sci; Am Soc Cell Biol; Soc Develop Biol; Int Soc Develop Biol. *Res:* Normal and experimental embryology; cell division and differentiation; fertilization; sperm-egg association; egg cortical changes. *Mailing Add:* 320 Woodcrest Rd Key Biscayne FL 33149

COLWIN, LAURA HUNTER, b Philadelphia, Pa, July 5, 11; m 40. ZOOLOGY. *Educ:* Bryn Mawr Col, AB, 32, Univ Pa, MA, 34, PhD(protozool), 38. *Prof Exp:* Instr biol, Pa Col Women, 36-37, asst prof, 37-40; instr zool, Vassar Col, 40-43; instr biol, Pa Col Women, 45-46; lectr biol, Queens Col, NY, 47-66, prof, 66-73; ADJ PROF, ROSENSTEIL SCH MARINE & ATMOSPHERIC SCI, UNIV MIAMI, 73- *Concurrent Pos:* Morrison fel, Am Asn Univ Women, Misaki Marine Biol Sta, Tokyo, 53-54; mem corp, Marine Biol Lab, Woods Hole, 71-75. *Mem:* Am Soc Zoologists; Am Soc Cell Biol; Soc Develop Biol; Int Soc Cell Biol. *Res:* Normal and experimental embryology; cell division and differentiation; fertilization; sperm-egg association; egg cortical changes. *Mailing Add:* 320 Woodcrest Rd Key Biscayne FL 33149

COMAI-FUERHERM, KAREN, b Detroit, Mich, June 20, 46; m 75; c 1. OBESITY, ATHERSCLEROSIS. *Educ:* Wayne State Univ, BS, 69; Cornell Univ, PhD(biochem), 73. *Prof Exp:* Res asst, Med Ctr, NY Univ, 73-75; vis scientist, 75-77, sr scientist, 77-81, RES FEL, HOFFMANN LA ROCHE, NUTLEY, NJ, 81- *Mem:* AAAS; Asn Women Sci; NY Acad Sci; Am Chem Soc; Am Oil Chemists Soc. *Res:* Lipid metabolism primarily obesity; novel therapeut for obesity therapy; therapy of athersclerosis. *Mailing Add:* Hoffmann-La Roche Inc Nutley NJ 07110

COMAN, DALE REX, b Hartford, Conn, Feb 22, 06; m 37; c 2. PATHOLOGY. *Educ:* Univ Mich, AB, 28; McGill Univ, MD, 33. *Prof Exp:* Asst, Inst Path, McGill Univ, 33-34; resident, Univ Pa Hosp, 34-35; resident, Mass State Tumor Hosp, Pondville, 35-36; instr, Sch Med, NY Univ, 36-37; instr, 37-41, assoc, 41-42, from asst prof to prof exp path, 42-54, prof path, 54-72, chmn dept, 54-67, EMER PROF PATH, SCH MED, UNIV PA, 72-; RES ASSOC, JACKSON LAB, 77- *Mem:* AAAS; NY Acad Sci; Am Soc Cell Biol; Int Soc Cell Biol; Soc Exp Path & Med. *Res:* Cancer. *Mailing Add:* Sand Point Rd Bar Harbor ME 04609

COMBA, PAUL GUSTAVO, b Tunis, Tunisia, Mar 6, 26; nat US. COMPUTER SCIENCE. *Educ:* Bluffton Col, AB, 47; Calif Inst Technol, PhD(math), 52. *Prof Exp:* Asst math, Calif Inst Technol, 47-51; from asst prof to assoc prof, Univ Hawaii, 51-60; math systs analyst, 60-63, mgr advan comput technol, 63, mgr prog lang eval, 63-64, SCI STAFF MEM, IBM CORP, 65- *Concurrent Pos:* Adj prof, NY Univ, 70 & Boston Univ, 77-79; lectr, Princeton Univ, 80-81. *Mem:* Fel AAAS; Soc Indust & Appl Math; Math Asn Am. *Res:* Computer programming languages; computer graphics; computer aided design; computer applications development; design and management of data bases. *Mailing Add:* IBM Corp Cambridge Sci Ctr 545 Technol Sq Cambridge MA 02139

COMBELLACK, WILFRED JAMES, b New Gloucester, Maine, June 27, 15; m 37; c 2. MATHEMATICS. *Educ:* Colby Col, AB, 37, MA, 38; Boston Univ, PhD(physics), 44. *Prof Exp:* From instr to assoc prof math, Northeastern Univ, 38-48; head dept, 48-70, PROF MATH, COLBY COL, 48- *Mem:* Math Asn Am; Am Math Soc. *Res:* Summation of series; table of summations. *Mailing Add:* Dept of Math Colby Col Waterville ME 04901

COMBES, BURTON, b New York, NY, June 30, 27; m 48; c 3. INTERNAL MEDICINE, LIVER DISEASE. *Educ:* Columbia Univ, AB, 47, MD, 51; Am Bd Internal Med, dipl, 59. *Prof Exp:* Intern med, Columbia-Presby Med Ctr, 51-52, asst resident, 52-53, asst physician, 53-56; from instr to assoc prof, 57-67, PROF INTERNAL MED, UNIV TEX HEALTH SCI CTR DALLAS, 67- *Concurrent Pos:* Res fel, Col Physicians & Surgeons, Columbia Univ, 53-55, Am Heart Asn res fel, 55-56; Am Heart Asn res fel, Univ Col Hosp, Med Sch, Univ London, 56-57; USPHS res career develop award, 62-72; estab investr, Am Heart Asn, 57-62; consult, Dallas Vet Admin Hosp, Tex, 65-; mem adv coun, Nat Inst Arthritis, Metab & Digestive Dis, 75; chmn bd, Am Liver Found; liver ed, Gastroenterol, Am Gastroenterol Asn, 77-81; mem, Nat Digestive Dis Adv Bd, 81- *Mem:* Am Fedn Clin Res; Asn Am Physicians; Am Soc Clin Invest; Am Asn Study Liver Dis (pres, 71); Am Gastroenterol Asn. *Res:* Hepatic excretory function; liver immunology; liver function during pregnancy. *Mailing Add:* Dept of Internal Med Univ of Tex Health Sci Ctr Dallas TX 75235

COMBS, ALAN B, b Boulder, Colo, July 4, 39; m 61; c 4. PHARMACOLOGY. *Educ:* Univ of the Pac, BSc, 62, MSc, 64; Univ Calif, Davis, PhD(comp pharmacol), 70. *Prof Exp:* asst prof, 70-76, ASSOC PROF PHARMACOL, SCH PHARM, UNIV TEX, AUSTIN, 76- *Mem:* AAAS; Am Pharmaceut Asn; Am Asn Col Pharm; Soc Toxicol. *Res:* Cardiovascular pharmacology and toxicology. *Mailing Add:* Dept of Pharmacol Univ of Tex Sch of Pharm Austin TX 78712

COMBS, CLARENCE MURPHY, b Louisville, Ky, Apr 13, 25; m 46; c 3. ANATOMY. *Educ:* Transylvania Col, AB, 46; Northwestern Univ, MS, 48, PhD(anat), 50. *Prof Exp:* Instr neuroanat, Med Sch, Univ WVa, 48; from instr to prof, Northwestern Univ, 50-66; chmn dept, 66-76, PROF ANAT, CHICAGO MED SCH, 66- *Concurrent Pos:* Nat Inst Neurol Dis & Blindness career res develop award, 59-64; assoc prof, Med Sch, Univ PR, 58-60; sect chief, Perinatal Physiol Lab, Nat Inst Neurol Dis & Blindness, PR, 58-60, spec consult & trainee, 58; actg dean, Sch Grad & Postdoctoral Studies, Chicago Med Sch, Univ Health Sci, 75-76. *Mem:* Am Asn Anat; Biol Stain Comn; Int Brain Res Orgn; Soc Neurosci. *Res:* Electroanatomical studies of cerebellar connections; thalamocortical connections; spinal cord structure; neurophysiological regulation of lingual movement. *Mailing Add:* Dept Anat Chicago Med Sch 3333 Green Bay Rd North Chicago IL 60664

COMBS, GEORGE ERNEST, b Arcadia, Fla, Feb 21, 27; m 48; c 3. ANIMAL NUTRITION. *Educ:* Univ Fla, BSA, 51, MSA, 53; Iowa State Univ, PhD(animal nutrit), 55. *Prof Exp:* Asst animal husb, Univ Fla, 51-52, instr, 52-53; asst animal nutrit, Iowa State Univ, 53-55; from asst prof to assoc prof, 55-67, PROF ANIMAL NUTRIT, UNIV FLA, 67- *Mem:* Am Inst Nutrit; Am Soc Animal Sci. *Res:* Mineral, energy and amino acid metabolism with swine. *Mailing Add:* Dept of Animal Sci Univ of Fla Gainesville FL 32601

COMBS, GERALD FUSON, b Olney, Ill, Feb 23, 20; m 43; c 4. ANIMAL NUTRITION. *Educ:* Univ Ill, BS, 40; Cornell Univ, PhD(animal nutrit), 48. *Prof Exp:* Asst animal nutrit, Cornell Univ, 40-41; prof poultry nutrit, Univ Md, College Park, 68-69; dep chief nutrit prog, US Dept Health, Educ & Welfare, 69-71; nutrit & food safety coordr, USDA, 71-73; prof foods & nutrit & head dept, Univ Ga, 73-75; NUTRIT PROG DIR, NAT INST ARTHRITIS, DIABETES & DIGESTIVE & KIDNEY DIS, NIH, 75- *Honors & Awards:* Poultry Nutrit Res Award, Am Feed Mfg, 53; Man of the Year in Md Agr, 67; Cert of Appreciation, Delmarva Poultry Ind, 69; Meterious Nutritionist Award, Distillers Res Inst, 70. *Mem:* AAAS; Poultry Sci Asn; Soc Exp Biol & Med; Am Inst Nutrit; Brit Nutrit Soc. *Res:* Poultry nutrition; factors concerned in bone formation; unidentified factors; energy-protein balance; antibiotics; amino acid requirements; human and international nutrition; basic and clinical human and animal nutrition research. *Mailing Add:* Nutrit Prog NIH Nat Inst Arthritis Diabetes Dig & Kidney Dis Bethesda MD 20014

COMBS, GERALD FUSON, JR, b Ithaca, NY, June 10, 47; m 69; c 3. NUTRITION. *Educ:* Univ Md, College Park, BS, 69; Cornell Univ, MS, 71, PhD(nutrit), 74. *Prof Exp:* Asst prof biochem & nutrit, Auburn Univ, 74-75; asst prof, 75-80, ASSOC PROF NUTRIT, CORNELL UNIV, 80- *Honors & Awards:* Res Award, Poultry Sci Asn, 79. *Mem:* AAAS; Poultry Sci Asn; Am Inst Nutrit; Soc Exp Biol & Med; NY Acad Sci. *Res:* Nutrient interrelationships and mechanisms of action of selenium and vitamin E; influences of foreign compounds on selenium function. *Mailing Add:* Dept of Poultry Sci Rice Hall Cornell Univ Ithaca NY 14853

COMBS, JAMES F, b St Louis, Mo, July 27, 25; m 48; c 3. ELECTRICAL ENGINEERING, INSTRUMENTATION. *Educ:* Univ Notre Dame, BS, 46; Washington Univ, St Louis, MS, 48. *Prof Exp:* Engr, Mound Lab, Ohio, 48-53, res engr, Plastics Div Res Dept, Tex, 53-59, sr res engr, Inorg Chem Div, Mo, 59-60, res group leader, 60-64, SR RES GROUP LEADER, INORG CHEM DIV, MONSANTO CO, MO, 64- *Mem:* Instrument Soc Am. *Res:* Instrumentation for chemical process control; semiconductor instrumentation; administration of research groups; process analyzers. *Mailing Add:* Monsanto Co 800 N Lindbergh Blvd St Louis MO 63166

COMBS, L(UTHER) PAUL, b Ponca City, Okla, Sept 23, 28; m 50; c 5. TECHNICAL MANAGEMENT. *Educ:* Univ Colo, BS, 50; Univ Calif, Los Angeles, MS, 68; Univ Southern Calif, EME, 73. *Prof Exp:* Res engr, Zinc Smelting Div, St Joe Minerals Corp, Pa, 51-55 & Apache Powder Co, Ariz, 55; from res engr to proj engr, Rocketdyne Div, 55-78, PROJ ENGR, ENERGY SYSTS GROUP, ROCKWELL INT CORP, 78- *Mem:* Am Inst Chem Engrs; Am Soc Mech Engrs; Combustion Inst. *Res:* Research and development for flash hydropyrolysis of coal; combustion modification for control of air pollutant emissions; liquid rocket combustion and combustion instability. *Mailing Add:* Rockwell Int Corp 8900 DeSoto Ave Canoga Park CA 91304

COMBS, LEON LAMAR, III, b Meridian, Miss, Sept 19, 38; m 62; c 1. CHEMICAL PHYSICS. *Educ:* Miss State Univ, BS, 61; La State Univ, PhD(chem physics), 68. *Prof Exp:* Res chemist, Devoe & Reynolds Co, Inc, Ky, 61-64; from asst prof to assoc prof, 67-75, PROF CHEM & PHYSICS, MISS STATE UNIV, 75-, HEAD, DEPT CHEM, 81- *Concurrent Pos:* Vis prof quantum chem, Univ Uppsala, Sweden, 77-78. *Mem:* Am Phys Soc; Am Chem Soc; Sigma Xi. *Res:* Quantum chemistry of small molecules; application of statistical mechanics to study of phase transitions; theoretical conformational analysis; quantum mechanical studies in pharmacology. *Mailing Add:* Box CH Miss State Univ Mississippi State MS 39762

COMBS, ROBERT GLADE, b Maysville, Mo, Nov 17, 30; m 58; c 2. ELECTRICAL ENGINEERING, BIOENGINEERING. *Educ:* Univ Mo, BS, 56, MS, 59; Univ Fla, PhD(elec eng), 65. *Prof Exp:* Instr elec eng, Univ Mo, 56-58; instr, NC State Col, 58-59; asst prof, Univ Nebr, 59-65; from asst prof to assoc prof, 65-78, PROF ELEC ENG, UNIV MO-COLUMBIA, 78- *Concurrent Pos:* Teaching consult, Training Prog, Hallam Nuclear Reactor Facil, Consumers Pub Power Dist, 60-61. *Mem:* AAAS; Nat Soc Prof Engrs; Inst Elec & Electronics Engrs; Am Soc Eng Educ; Asn Advan Med Instrumentation. *Res:* Application of micro-electronic circuits to biological instrumentation; communication systems for severely physically handicapped; competency-based instructional models; grades and grading. *Mailing Add:* 209 Elec Eng Bldg Univ of Mo Columbia MO 65211

COMBS, ROBERT L, JR, b Fayetteville, Ark, Nov 6, 28; m 50; c 3. ENTOMOLOGY. *Educ:* Univ Ark, BS, 61, MS, 63; Miss State Univ, PhD(entom), 67. *Prof Exp:* Asst entom, Univ Ark, 63-64; asst entomologist, 64-70, assoc entomologist, 70-80, ENTOMOLOGIST, MISS STATE UNIV, 80- *Mem:* Entom Soc Am. *Res:* Veterinary entomology; applied and basic entomological problems. *Mailing Add:* Dept Entom Drawer EM Miss State Univ Mississippi State MS 39762

COMBS, ROBERT LEONARD, b Elizabethton, Tenn, Nov 10, 29; m 54; c 1. PHYSICAL CHEMISTRY, POLYMER CHEMISTRY. *Educ:* East Tenn State Univ, BS, 51; Univ Tenn, MS, 52, PhD(chem), 55. *Prof Exp:* Chemist, Union Carbide Corp, Tenn, 52; res chemist, 55-59, sr res chemist, 60-69, RES ASSOC, TENN EASTMAN CO DIV, EASTMAN KODAK CO, 69- *Mem:* Am Chem Soc; Soc Plastics Eng. *Res:* Characterization of polymers; rheology; kinetics and mechanisms of polymerization; polymers application requirements; adhesives; moldings; coatings. *Mailing Add:* 4509 Chickasaw Rd Kingsport TN 37664

COMEAU, ANDRE I, b Richmond, Que, Oct 8, 45; m 71; c 2. ENTOMOLOGY, VIROLOGY. *Educ:* Sherbrooke Univ, BA, 64, BS, 67; Cornell Univ, PhD(entom), 71. *Prof Exp:* RES SCIENTIST ENTOM, RES STA, AGR CAN, 71- *Mem:* Can Phytopath Soc; Entom Soc Can. *Res:* Barley yellow dwarf virus and vector aphids on oats, barley, wheat (spring and summer); insect pheromones; interspecific hybridation, cereals. *Mailing Add:* Res Sta Agr Can 2560 Boul Hochelaga Ste-Foy PQ G1V 2J6 Can

COMEAU, ROGER WILLIAM, b Quincy, Mass, Apr 22, 33; c 3. MAMMALIAN PHYSIOLOGY, MEDICAL EDUCATION. *Educ:* Boston Univ, AB, 55; State Univ NY Buffalo, PhD(physiol), 67. *Prof Exp:* Mem staff, Arthur D Little, Inc, 59-61; teaching asst physiol, State Univ NY Buffalo, 61-63, from asst instr to asst prof, 63-68; assoc dir sci info & regulatory affairs, Mead Johnson & Co, 68-69; assoc prof, Mid Ga Col, 70-75, prof biol, 75-79, chymn dept biol sci, 73-79; dir admissions, dir mat resources, 80-81, PROF PHYSIOL, MERCER UNIV SCH MED, 79-, DIR ADMIN & STUDENT AFFAIRS, 81- *Mem:* AAAS; Assoc Am Physiol Soc. *Res:* Membrane transport; teaching mammalian physiology; pharmacology and toxicology of cancer chemotherapeutic agents; meducal education. *Mailing Add:* Sch Med Mercer Univ Macon GA 31207

COMEFORD, JOHN J, b Schenectady, NY, Apr 30, 28. ANALYTICAL CHEMISTRY, PETROLEUM PRODUCT EVALUATION. *Educ:* Colo State Univ, BS, 50; Wash State Univ, MS, 53; Georgetown Univ, PhD(molecular spectros), 66. *Prof Exp:* Phys chemist, 67-68, RES CHEMIST, NAT BUR STANDARDS, 58- *Concurrent Pos:* Secy comt on spectral absorption data, Nat Res Coun-Nat Acad Sci, 59-62; vis assoc prof, Dept Mat Sci & Eng, Unit Utah, 75. *Mem:* Am Chem Soc; Soc Appl

Spectroscopy; Am Soc for Testing Mat. *Res:* Low temperature matrix-isolation spectroscopy; development of test procedures for recycled petroleum products; infrared spectra of unstable molecules; mass spectrometry of combustion products; evaluation of lubricating oils. *Mailing Add:* 3932 Wistman Lane Myersville MD 21773

COMEFORO, JAY E(UGENE), b Staten Island, NY, Aug 3, 22; m 45; c 2. CERAMICS SCIENCE & TECHNOLOGY, MINERAL SYNTHESIS. *Educ:* Rutgers Univ, BS, 44, MS, 46; Univ Ill, PhD(ceramics), 49; Rider Col, MBA, 72. *Prof Exp:* Res assoc, Rutgers Univ, 45-46; spec res assoc, Univ Ill, 46-48; ceramic engr, Electro Tech Lab, US Bur Mines, 49-53; head synthetic minerals sect, 53-54; engr in charge, Ceramics Lab, Sylvania Elec Prod, Inc, 54-55; mgr mkt & eng, Frenchtown Porcelain Co, 55-59; consult, 59-61; pres, Consol Ceramics & Metalizing Corp, 61-77; PRES, ACCURATUS CERAMIC CORP, 77- *Concurrent Pos:* Consult, Ceramic Consult & Manufacture, 77- *Mem:* Fel Am Ceramic Soc; Mineral Soc Am. *Res:* Synthesis of minerals, especially micas and asbestiform; machinable and oxide ceramics; metalizing ceramics, ceramic to metal seals. *Mailing Add:* Fox Grape Rd Flemington NJ 08822

COMENETZ, GEORGE, b New York, NY, Nov 4, 10; m 36; c 2. ENGINEERING. *Educ:* City Col NY, BS, 30; Columbia Univ, MS, 31, PhD(math), 34. *Prof Exp:* Asst math, Columbia Univ, 32-33, instr, 34-35; tutor, St John's Col Md, 37-43; math physicist, graphls lab, Carnegie Inst, 43-46; res engr metall, 46-48, adv engr, 48-75, CONSULT ENGR, WESTINGHOUSE RES LABS, 75- *Res:* Metallurgy; heat transfer; induction heating; incandescent lamps; corrosion testing equipment. *Mailing Add:* 240 Ave F Pittsburgh PA 15221

COMER, DAVID J, b Tuolumne, Calif, Jan 10, 39; m 58; c 6. ELECTRICAL ENGINEERING. *Educ:* San Jose State Col, BS, 61; Univ Calif, MS, 62; Wash State Univ, PhD(elec eng), 66. *Prof Exp:* Assoc elec eng, Int Bus Mach Corp, 59-64; asst prof elec eng, Univ Idaho, 64-66; assoc prof, Univ Calgary, 66-69; PROF ELEC ENG, CALIF STATE UNIV, CHICO, 69- *Concurrent Pos:* Asst prof, San Jose State Col, 64; consult, Int Bus Mach Corp, 66 & Mobility Systs Inc, 67-68; mem bd dir, Comput Controls, Inc, 69-72. *Mem:* AAAS; Inst Elec & Electronics Engrs; Am Soc Eng Educ. *Res:* Electronic circuit design; machine recognition of human speech; computer controlled machinery. *Mailing Add:* Dept of Eng Calif State Univ Chico CA 95926

COMER, JACK PAYNE, analytical chemistry, see previous edition

COMER, JAMES PIERPONT, b East Chicago, Ind, Sept 25, 34; m 59; c 2. CHILD PSYCHIATRY, PUBLIC HEALTH ADMINISTRATION. *Educ:* Ind Univ, AB, 56; Howard Univ, MD, 60; Univ Mich, MPH, 64. *Prof Exp:* Intern, St Catherine's Hosp, 60-61; staff physician, NIMH, 67-68; asst prof, 68-70, assoc prof, 70-75, prof, 75-76, MAURICE FALK PROF CHILD PSYCHIAT, CHILD STUDY CTR, YALE UNIV, 76- ASSOC DEAN STUDENT AFFAIRS, MED SCH, 69- *Concurrent Pos:* Fel psychiat, Med Sch, Yale Univ, 64-66 & Child Study Ctr, 66-67; NIMH fel, Hillcrest Children's Ctr, Washington, DC, 67-68; Markle scholar, 69; adv & consult, Children's Television Workshop, 70-; mem prof adv coun, Nat Asn Ment Health, 71-; mem comn, Joint Inst Judicial Admin-Am Bar Asn Juv Justice Standards Proj, 73-75; mem, Nat Adv Mental Health Coun, HEW, 76; Henry J Kaiser sr fel, Ctr Advan Studies in Behav Sci, 76-77; mem, Pub Comt Mental Health, 78-; mem, Assembly Behavioral Social Sci, Nat Res Coun, 80. *Mem:* Am Psychiat Asn; Am Orthopsychiat Asn; Am Acad Child Psychiat. *Res:* Race relations; elementary school education and mental health. *Mailing Add:* Child Study Ctr Med Sch Yale Univ 333 Cedar St New Haven CT 06510

COMER, JOSEPH JOHN, b Brooklyn, NY, Dec 8, 20; m 47; c 4. INORGANIC CHEMISTRY, ELECTRON MICROSCOPY. *Educ:* Pa State Univ, BS, 44, MS, 47. *Prof Exp:* Chemist, Naval Res Lab, 44-45; electron microscopist, Cent Res Lab, Gen Aniline & Film Corp, 46-52; res assoc, Col Mineral Indust, Pa State Univ, 52-55, from asst prof to assoc prof mineral sci, 55-62, head mineral const labs, 57-62; scientist, Res Ctr, Sperry Rand Corp, 62-67; RES CHEMIST, DEP ELECTRONIC MAT, ROME AIR DEVELOP CTR, US AIR FORCE, 67- *Mem:* AAAS; Am Chem Soc; Electron Micros Soc Am. *Res:* Electron microscope studies of electronic, electrooptic materials and thin films. *Mailing Add:* Rome Air Develop Ctr-ESM Hanscom AFB Bedford MA 01731

COMER, MARY MARGARET, b Jacksonville, Fla, Sept 11, 42. MOLECULAR GENETICS, REGULATION. *Educ:* Harvard Univ, AB, 64; Purdue Univ, PhD(biol sci), 72. *Prof Exp:* Res assoc bacteriol, Univ Wis-Madison, 72-75; res assoc microbiol, Univ Regensburg, WGer, 75-76; ASST PROF MOLECULAR BIOL, CLARK UNIV, 76- *Concurrent Pos:* NIH fel, Univ Wis-Madison, 74-75. *Mem:* AAAS; Am Soc Microbiol. *Res:* Molecular genetics of transfer RNAs and aminoacyl- tRNA synthetases in bacteria. *Mailing Add:* Dept of Biol Clark Univ Worcester MA 01610

COMER, RALPH DUDLEY, b Kansas City, Mo, Sept 28, 27; m 50; c 4. PREVENTIVE MEDICINE, ALCOHOL REHABILITATION. *Educ:* Univ Kans, BA, 50, MA, 52; Med Col SC, PhD(anat), 55, MD, 57; Johns Hopkins Univ, MPH, 65; Am Bd Prev Med, dipl gen prev med, 69. *Prof Exp:* Instr gross anat, Med Col SC, 52-55; Med officer, Rodman Naval Sta, CZ, US Navy Med Corps, 59-61, resident internal med, Naval Hosp, Oakland, 61-62, resident gen surg, 62-63, head tuberc & venereal dis control, Prev Med Div, Bur Med & Surg, DC, 63-64, officer-in-chg, Naval Med Sci Unit, Gorgas Mem Lab, 65-68, officer-in-chg, Naval Prev Med Unit 2, Va, 68-70, head community health br, Prev Med Div, Bur Med & Surg, 70-73; staff mem, Regional Dispensary, 73-77, chief alcohol rehab serv, Navy Regional Med Ctr, San Diego, 77-80. *Mem:* Am Pub Health Asn; Am Med Soc Alcoholism. *Res:* Malaria. *Mailing Add:* 6201 Highland Hills Dr Austin TX 78731

COMER, STEPHEN DANIEL, b Covington, Ky, May 2, 41; m 63; c 1. MATHEMATICAL LOGIC, ALGEBRA. *Educ:* Ohio State Univ, BSc, 62; Univ Calif, Berkeley, MA, 64; Univ Colo, Boulder, PhD(math), 67. *Prof Exp:* Asst prof math, Vanderbilt Univ, 67-74; vis asst prof, Clemson Univ, 74-75; ASSOC PROF MATH, THE CITADEL, 75- *Concurrent Pos:* Vis assoc prof, Univ Hawaii, 77-78, Oxford Univ, 80-81. *Mem:* Am Math Soc; Asn Symbolic Logic; Nat Coun Teachers Math. *Res:* Algebra and logic; algebraic logic; universal algebra; model theory; decision problems; sheaf theory; multivalued algebraic systems. *Mailing Add:* Dept of Math The Citadel Charleston SC 29409

COMER, WILLIAM TIMMEY, b Ottumwa, Iowa, Jan 11, 36; m 63; c 2. PHARMACEUTICAL RESEARCH, MEDICINAL CHEMISTRY. *Educ:* Carleton Col, BA, 57; Univ Iowa, PhD(org chem), 62. *Prof Exp:* Sr scientist, 61-67, res group leader, 67-68, sect leader chem res, 68-70, from prin investr to sr prin investr, 70-74, DIR PHARMACEUT RES, MEAD JOHNSON & CO, 75-, VPRES PHARM RES, 77- *Concurrent Pos:* Sect ed, Ann Reports Med Chem. *Mem:* AAAS; Am Chem Soc; Sigma Xi; NY Acad Sci. *Res:* Medicinal chemistry; adrenergic agents; antihypertensive agents; serotonergics; medium ring heterocycles; dopamine antagonists; cardiovascular agents; antiasthmatics. *Mailing Add:* 8234 Larch Lane Evansville IN 47710

COMERFORD, LEO P, JR, b Philadelphia, Pa, Apr 7, 47; m 73; c 3. GROUP THEORY. *Educ:* Villanova Univ, BS, 68; Univ Ill, Urbana, MS, 69, PhD(math), 73. *Prof Exp:* Teaching asst math, Univ Ill, Urbana, 68-73, Univ fel, 72-73; res assoc, Mich State Univ, 73-75; asst prof math, 75-81, ASSOC PROF MATH, UNIV WIS-PARKSIDE, 81- *Concurrent Pos:* Prin investr, NSF res grant, 77-79. *Mem:* Am Math Soc; Math Asn Am. *Res:* Combinatorial group theory, especially equations over groups and small cancellation theory for groups. *Mailing Add:* Div of Sci Univ of Wis-Parkside Kenosha WI 53141

COMERFORD, MATTHIAS F(RANCIS), b Boston, Mass, Nov 6, 25; m 56; c 5. MATERIALS SCIENCE, PHYSICS. *Educ:* Mass Inst Technol, SB, 52, SM, 57, ScD(metall), 63. *Prof Exp:* Staff mem metall, Div Sponsored Res, Mass Inst Technol, 52-56; proj supvr, Alloyd Corp, 57-60; metallurgist, Smithsonian Astrophys Observ, 62-69; prin mem tech staff, RCA Info Systs Div, 69-70, leader mat lab, RCA Systs Develop Div, 70-72; independent consult, 72-77; asst res & develop mgr, 77-78, MGR RES & DEVELOP, HOLLIS ENG, INC, 78- *Concurrent Pos:* Res assoc, Mass Inst Technol, 62-63; assoc, Harvard Col Observ, 65-69; lectr, Fitchburg State Col, 72-78. *Mem:* Am Soc Metals; Sigma Xi; AAAS; Am Soc Testing & Mat; Nat Asn Corrosion Engrs. *Res:* Mechanical and physical properties of materials; relation of properties to microstructure and environment; metallurgy of meteorites; materials and processes in computer manufacture; materials and processes in automatic soldering, cleaning and testing of printed circuit assemblies. *Mailing Add:* Hollis Eng Inc PO Box 1189 Charron Ave Nashua NH 03061

COMES, RICHARD DURWARD, b Nisland, SDak, Nov 16, 31; m 54; c 3. WEED SCIENCE. *Educ:* Univ Wyo, BS, 58, MS, 60; Ore State Univ, PhD(weed sci), 71. *Prof Exp:* Res agronomist, 60-65, PLANT PHYSIOLOGIST, AGR RES, USDA, 65- *Mem:* Aquatic Plant Mgt Soc; Weed Sci Soc Am; Int Weed Sci Soc. *Res:* Management of vegetation in aquatic and marginal areas; biology and ecology of aquatic and ditchbank vegetation; fate of herbicides in water; effect of herbicides in irrigation water on crops. *Mailing Add:* Irrigated Agr Res & Exten Ctr Agr Res USDA Prosser WA 99350

COMFORT, ALEXANDER, b London, Eng, Feb 10, 20. HUMAN BIOLOGY, GERONTOLOGY. *Educ:* Cambridge Univ, Eng, MA, MB, BCh, 44; Univ London, MRCS & LRCP, 45, DCh, 46, PhD(biochem), 49, DSc(geront), 62. *Prof Exp:* Lectr psychiat, London Hosp Med Ctr, 48-51; Nuffield res fel geront, Univ Col, Univ London, 52-65; dir res & head group on aging, 65-73; sr fel, Ctr Study Democratic Insts, Santa Barbara, Calif, 74-75; prof psychiat, Univ Calif, Irvine, 76-78; FEL, INST HIGHER STUDIES, 75-; CONSULT GERIAT PSYCHIAT, BRENTWOOD VET ADMIN HOSP, LOS ANGELES, 77- *Concurrent Pos:* Clin lectr psychiat, Stanford Univ, 74-; adj prof, Dept Psychiat, Univ Calif, Los Angeles, 77- *Honors & Awards:* Dr Heinz Karger Mem Found Prize in Geront, 69. *Mailing Add:* 683 Oak Grove Dr Santa Barbara CA 93108

COMFORT, JOSEPH ROBERT, b Fayetteville, Ark, July 18, 40. NUCLEAR PHYSICS. *Educ:* Ripon Col, AB, 62; Yale Univ, MS, 63, PhD(nuclear physics), 68. *Prof Exp:* Res physicist, Nuclear Struct Lab, Yale Univ, 67-68; fel nuclear physics, Argonne Nat Lab, 68-70; instr physics, Princeton Univ, 70-72; asst prof, Ohio Univ, Athens, 72-76; res assoc prof physics, Univ Pittsburgh, 76-81; ASSOC PROF PHYSICS, ARIZ STATE UNIV, 81- *Concurrent Pos:* Physicist, Lawrence Livermore Nat Lab, Calif, 81. *Mem:* Am Phys Soc; Am Asn Physics Teachers. *Res:* Penetration of charged particles in matter; nuclear structure physics; nuclear reaction mechanisms; medium energy nuclear physics. *Mailing Add:* Dept of Physics Ariz State Univ Tempe AZ 85281

COMFORT, WILLIAM WISTAR, b Bryn Mawr, Pa, Apr 19, 33; m 57; c 2. POINT-SET TOPOLOGY, SET THEORY. *Educ:* Haverford Col, BA, 54; Univ Wash, MSc, 57, PhD(math), 58. *Hon Degrees:* MA, Wesleyan Univ, 69. *Prof Exp:* Asst math, Univ Wash, 56-58; Benjamin Peirce instr, Harvard Univ, 58-61; asst prof, Univ Rochester, 61-65; assoc prof, Univ Mass, Amherst, 65-67; chmn dept, 69-70 & 80-82, PROF MATH, WESLEYAN UNIV, 67- *Concurrent Pos:* Managing ed proc, Am Math Soc, 74-75. *Mem:* Am Math Soc; Math Asn Am; Asn Symbolic Logic. *Res:* General topology; topological analysis; Stone-Cech compactification; the theory of ultrafilters; topological groups. *Mailing Add:* Dept of Math Wesleyan Univ Middletown CT 06457

COMINGS, DAVID EDWARD, b Beacon, NY, Mar 8, 35; m 58; c 3. MEDICAL GENETICS, CELL BIOLOGY. *Educ:* Northwestern Univ, BS, 55, MD, 58; Am Bd Internal Med, dipl. *Prof Exp:* From intern to resident internal med, Cook County Hosp, Chicago, 58-61; chief hemat, Madigan Gen Hosp, Tacoma, Wash, 62-64; DIR DEPT MED GENETICS, CITY OF HOPE MED CTR, 66- *Concurrent Pos:* Fel hemat, Cook County Hosp, Chicago, 61-62; fel med genetics, Univ Wash, 64-66; bd dirs, Am Soc Human Genetics, 74-76; genetics study sect, NIH, 75-78; co-chairman, ICN Univ Calif, Los Angeles Winter Conf Human Molecular Cytogenetics, 77; sci adv bd, Hereditary Dis Found, 75-; chmn, Symp Molecular Cytogenetics, Uruguay, 77; sci adv bd, Nat Found, March Dimes, 77-; chmn work group, Genetics, Immunol, Virol & Presymptomatic Detection Huntington's Dis Comn, 76-77; ed, Am J Human Genetics, 78-; pres med staff, City Hope Nat Med Ctr, 78-79; NIH Task Force Inborn Errors of Metab, 78-79. *Mem:* AAAS; Am Soc Human Genetics; Am Soc Cell Biol; Am Fedn Clin Res; Am Soc Clin Invest. *Res:* Human genetics; biochemistry and physiology of chromosomes; hemoglobinopathies and thalassemia; mechanisms of DNA replication; molecular aging; differentiation. *Mailing Add:* Dept of Med Genetics City of Hope Med Ctr Duarte CA 91010

COMINGS, EDWARD WALTER, b Phillipsburg, NJ, Feb 24, 08; m 31; c 3. CHEMICAL ENGINEERING, ENGINEERING ADMINISTRATION. *Educ:* Univ Ill, BS, 30; Mass Inst Technol, ScD(chem eng), 34. *Prof Exp:* Asst chem engr, Mass Inst Technol, 31-33; chem engr, Tex Co, NY, 33-35; asst prof chem eng, NC State Univ, 35-36; from asst prof to prof, Ill Univ, 36-51; prof chem eng & metall & head dept, Purdue Univ, 51-59; prof eng & dean col, 59-73, EMER PROF ENG, UNIV DEL, 73- *Concurrent Pos:* Off Sci Res & Develop official investr & assoc dir munitions develop lab, Univ Ill, 40-45; consult chem corp & other co; Fulbright lectr, Delft Technol Inst, Neth, 57; Guggenheim fel, 57; chmn, Eng Joint Coun Nominating Comt for Nat Medal of Sci; mem bd trustees, Del Tech & Community Col, 66-74; mem, Gov Coun Sci & Technol, 69-72; chmn high pressure res, Gordon Res Conf, 56, mem, Coun Gordon Res Conf; prof chem eng & chmn dept, Univ Petrol & Minerals, Saudia Arabia, 74-78. *Honors & Awards:* Naval Ord Develop Award; Army-Navy Cert Appreciation; Walker Award, Am Inst Chem Engrs, 56. *Mem:* Am Chem Soc; fel Am Inst Chem Engrs; Am Soc Eng Educ; Sigma Xi. *Res:* Author of fifty technical articles. *Mailing Add:* 509 Windsor Dr Newark DE 19711

COMINS, NEIL FRANCIS, b New York, NY, May 11, 51. ASTROPHYSICS. *Educ:* Cornell Univ, BS, 72; Univ Md, MS, 74; Univ Col, Cardiff, Wales, PhD(astrophysics), 78. *Prof Exp:* ASST PROF ASTRONOMY, UNIV MAINE, ORONO, 78- *Mem:* Fel Royal Astron Soc; Am Astron Soc. *Res:* Numerical simulation of the formation, structure and stability of galaxies, stability of rotating stars, data analysis of noise limited experiments. *Mailing Add:* Dept Physics Univ Maine Bennett Hall Orono ME 04469

COMINSKY, CATHERINE, b Las Animas, Colo, May 11, 20; m 49; c 2. ZOOLOGY, HISTOLOGY. *Educ:* Univ Colo, BA, 42, MA, 44, PhD, 46. *Prof Exp:* From instr to assoc prof, 46-54, actg head dept, 46-49, head dept, 50-51, PROF BIOL, UNIV HOUSTON, 55- *Res:* Localization of certain monoamines in the brains of the South American Caiman sclereops; mapping of fiber tracts and nuclei in brain stem. *Mailing Add:* Dept of Biol Univ of Houston Houston TX 77004

COMINSKY, LYNN RUTH, b Buffalo, NY, Nov 19, 53; m 80. X-RAY ASTRONOMY, HIGH ENERGY ASTROPHYSICS. *Educ:* Brandeis Univ, BA, 75; Mass Inst Technol, PhD(physics), 81. *Prof Exp:* RES PHYSICIST I, SPACE SCI LAB, UNIV CALIF, BERKELEY, 81- *Mem:* Am Astron Soc; Am Phys Soc; Sigma Xi; Asn Women Sci. *Res:* Optical and x-ray properties of strong galactic x-ray sources, usually believed to be neutron stars in close binary sytems. *Mailing Add:* Space Sci Lab Univ Calif Berkeley CA 94720

COMINSKY, NELL CATHERINE, b Las Animas, Colo, May 11, 20; m 49; c 3. HISTOLOGY. *Educ:* Univ Colo, BA, 42, MA, 44, PhD(zool), 46. *Prof Exp:* Asst prof comp anat, 46-69, assoc prof, 49-59, PROF HISTOL, UNIV HOUSTON, 59- *Honors & Awards:* Piper Award, Minnie Stephens Piper Found, San Antonio, 76. *Mem:* Sigma Xi. *Res:* Demonstration of monoamines in the brain of caiman sclereops; phylogenetic approach to basic sleep mechanisms. *Mailing Add:* Sci Bldg Univ Houston Houston TX 77004

COMIS, ROBERT LEO, b Troy, NY, July 16, 45; m 81; c 2. MEDICINE. *Educ:* Fordham Univ, BS, 67; State Univ NY, Upstate Med Ctr, 71. *Prof Exp:* Staff assoc oncol, Nat Cancer Inst, NIH, 72-74; oncol fel, Signey Farber Cancer Inst, Harvard, 75-76; asst med, Peter Bent Brigham Hosp, 75-76; asst prof & chief solid tumor oncol, 76-78, ASSOC PROF & CHIEF MED ONCOL, STATE UNIV NY, UPSTATE MED CTR, 78- *Concurrent Pos:* Chmn respiratory comn, Cancer & Leukemia Group B, 79-; coordr cancer res, Barbara Kopp Res Ctr, 81- *Mem:* Am Soc Clin Oncol. *Res:* Clinical pharmacology of antineoplastic agents; innovative therapies for small cell anaplastic lung cancer. *Mailing Add:* Sect Med Oncol Upstate Med Ctr State Univ NY 750 E Adams St Syracuse NY 13210

COMITA, GABRIEL WILLIAM, b Minneapolis, Minn, July 27, 15; m 51; c 2. ZOOLOGY. *Educ:* Col St Thomas, BS, 37; Univ Minn, MA, 49; Univ Wash, PhD(zool), 53. *Prof Exp:* Instr water purification, Ft Belvoir, Va, 41-43; asst chemist, Sanit Dist, Minneapolis & St Paul, 46-47; asst, Univ Minn, 48-49; jr res zoologist, Univ Wash, 51-53; from asst prof to assoc prof, 53-60, PROF ZOOL, NDAK STATE UNIV, 60- *Concurrent Pos:* Mem staff, Arctic Res Lab, Point Barrow, Alaska, 51 & 52. *Mem:* Fel AAAS; Soc Syst Zool; Am Soc Limnol & Oceanog; Am Micros Soc; Ecol Soc Am. *Res:* Limnology and invertebrate zoology; copepods, their biology, energy transformations. *Mailing Add:* Dept of Zool NDak State Univ Fargo ND 58102

COMIZZOLI, ROBERT BENEDICT, b Union City, NJ, Apr 22, 40; m 65; c 2. SEMICONDUCTORS, SOLID STATE ELECTRONICS. *Educ:* Boston Col, BS, 62; Princeton Univ, MA, 64, PhD(physics), 67. *Prof Exp:* mem tech staff res, RCA Labs, RCA Corp, 66-79, mgr qual assurance, RCA Solid State Tech Ctr, 79-81; MEM TECH STAFF, BELL LABS, 81- *Mem:* Inst Elec & Electronics Engrs; Electrochem Soc. *Res:* Semiconductor devices; integrated circuits; power devices; reliability; passivation; semiconductor processing; electrophotography. *Mailing Add:* 95 Knickerbocker Dr Belle Mead NJ 08502

COMLY, HUNTER HALL, b Denver, Colo, July 21, 19; m 41; c 5. PSYCHIATRY. *Educ:* Yale Univ, BS, 41, MD, 43. *Prof Exp:* Intern pediat, Mass Gen Hosp, Boston, 44; asst resident, Children's Hosp, Iowa City, Iowa, 44-46, resident psychiat, Psychiat Hosp, Iowa City, 46-47; asst prof pediat in psychiat, Univ Iowa, 48-56; staff psychiatrist, Children's Div, Lafayette Clin, Detroit, Mich, 56-58; dir, Children's Ctr Wayne County, Detroit, 58-67; assoc prof child psychiat, 67-71, prof child psychiat & head div, Univ Iowa, 71-76; HEAD CHILDREN'S DIV, LINN COUNTY PSYCHIAT CLIN, 76- *Concurrent Pos:* Fel child psychiat, Univ Minn Hosps, Minneapolis, 47-48; fac mem, Continuation Courses Child Psychiat, Univ Minn, 48, 54 & 61; ed, Presch study course, Nat Parent-Teacher Mag, 49-51; consult, Iowa Child Welfare Res Sta, 50-51; psychiatrist, Univ Iowa, 51-52, child psychiatrist, 52-56; workshop chmn, Psychopharmacol in Children's Learning & Behav Disorders, 63-66 & 69-70; clinician, Cedar Ctr Psychiat Clin. *Mem:* AMA; fel Am Psychiat Asn; fel Am Orthopsychiat Asn; Am Acad Child Psychiat. *Res:* Learning and behavior disorders of children; effects of psychoactive drugs on learning and behavior. *Mailing Add:* Quail Creek 2-E North Liberty IA 52317

COMLY, JAMES B, b New York, NY, Nov 28, 36; m 59; c 1. RESEARCH ADMINISTRATION. *Educ:* Cornell Univ, BEE, 59; Harvard Univ, MA, 60, PhD(appl physics), 65. *Prof Exp:* NSF fel, Atomic Energy Res Estab, Eng, 65-66; res physicist, 66-69, mgr planning & resources, 69-72, mgr, Thermal Br, 72-77, mgr, Energy Sci Br, 77-79, mgr, Combustion & Fuel Sci Br, 79-80, MGR, THERMAL & FUEL SCI BR, GEN ELEC RES & DEVELOP CTR, 80- *Concurrent Pos:* Chmn rev comt, Twin Rivers Energy Proj, Princeton Univ, 73-78; assoc ed, Int J Energy, 75-80; chmn energetics div, Am Soc Mech Engrs, 78-79; mem, Nat Res Coun eval panel, Nat Bur Standards EnCon Progs, 76-80, chmn, 80; chmn, Nat Res Coun eval panel, Nat Bur Standards Ctr Chem Eng, 81-82. *Mem:* Am Phys Soc; Inst Elec & Electronics Engrs; AAAS; Am Inst Chem Engrs; Am Soc Mech Engrs. *Res:* Energy utilization in power plants, buildings, industry, including solar energy, heat pumps, industrial processes; fluidized beds; cooling of power electronics; electrohydrodynamics; coal science. *Mailing Add:* Gen Elec Res & Develop Ctr PO Box 8 Schenectady NY 12301

COMMARATO, MICHAEL A, b Montclair, NJ, Apr 13, 40; m 67; c 1. PHARMACOLOGY. *Educ:* Rutgers Univ, BS, 62; Marquette Univ, PhD(pharmacol), 68. *Prof Exp:* USPHS fel pharmacol, Mich State Univ, 68-69; sr pharmacologist, William H Rorer, Inc, 69-71; sr scientist pharmacol, Warner Lambert Res Inst, 71-76; PHARMACOLOGIST, DIV CARDIO-RENAL DRUG PROD, FOOD & DRUG ADMIN, 76- *Mem:* Am Soc Pharmacol & Exp Therapeut; Am Heart Asn. *Res:* Review and evaluation of results of preclinical pharmacological and toxicological studies submitted in support of New Drug Applications. *Mailing Add:* Bur Drugs Food & Drug Admin Rockville MD 20857

COMMERFORD, JOHN D, b Deadwood, SDak, Aug 23, 29; m 53; c 5. ORGANIC CHEMISTRY. *Educ:* Carroll Col, Mont, AB, 50; St Louis Univ, PhD(chem), 55. *Prof Exp:* Res chemist, Callery Chem Co, 54-57; sr res scientist, Anheuser-Busch, 57-67, mgr com develop, 67-69; dir tech develop, Corn Refiners Asn, Inc, 69-77; V PRES, SHIRLO, INC, MEMPHIS, 77- *Mem:* Southern Aerosol Tech Asn; Am Asn Cereal Chem. *Res:* Carbohydrates; corn products; boron hydrides; medicinal chemistry; aerosol technology. *Mailing Add:* PO Box 18993 Memphis TN 38118

COMMERFORD, SPENCER LEWIS, b Toledo, Ohio, May 23, 30. BIOCHEMISTRY. *Educ:* Mass Inst Technol, BS & MS, 52; Harvard Univ, PhD(biochem), 59. *Prof Exp:* Res collabr biochem, 59-61, from asst scientist to assoc scientist, 61-68, SCIENTIST, BROOKHAVEN NAT LAB, 68- *Concurrent Pos:* NIH res fel, 59-61. *Mem:* Am Soc Biol Chem; Biophys Soc; Harvey Soc. *Res:* Structure and function of DNA and deoxyribonucleohistone; kinetics of cell proliferation and death; cell differentiation; chemical carcinogenesis; biological effects of exposure to radioactive isotopes. *Mailing Add:* Med Dept Brookhaven Nat Lab Upton NY 11973

COMMINS, EUGENE DAVID, b New York, NY, July 1, 32; m 58; c 2. PHYSICS. *Educ:* Swarthmore Col, BA, 53; Columbia Univ, PhD(physics), 58. *Prof Exp:* Instr physics, Columbia Univ, 58-60; from asst prof to assoc prof, 60-69, PROF PHYSICS, UNIV CALIF, 69- *Concurrent Pos:* A P Sloan Found fel, Univ Calif, Berkeley, 62-66; Guggenheim Found fel, 67-68. *Mem:* Am Phys Soc; AAAS. *Res:* Atomic spectroscopy; weak interactions. *Mailing Add:* Dept of Physics Univ of Calif Berkeley CA 94720

COMMITO, JOHN ANGELO, b Everett, Mass, Apr 23, 49; m; c 2. MARINE ECOLOGY, BENTHIC ECOLOGY. *Educ:* Cornell Univ, AB, 71; Duke Univ, PhD(zool), 76. *Prof Exp:* Teaching asst introd biol, Marine Lab, Duke Univ, 71-73, teaching asst marine sci, 72-74, teaching asst man & marine environ, 74, teaching asst invert zool, 75; asst prof biol, Univ Maine, 76-80; ASST PROF BIOL & DIR ENVIRON STUDIES PROG, HOOD COL, 80- *Concurrent Pos:* Mem search comt, Marine Sci Ctr, Dir Univ Maine, 77-78; mem selection comt marine res, Marine State Legis, 77-80; mem Washington county regional planning comn, Water Qual Rev Comt, 77-80; prin investr, Maine Sea grant, 78-80. *Mem:* AAAS; Am Soc Limnol & Oceanog; Ecol Soc Am; Am Inst Biol Sci; Atlantic Estuarine Res Soc. *Res:* Predation, competition and life history strategies of marine benthic polychaetes and bivalves; regulation of estuarine soft-bottom community structure; population biology. *Mailing Add:* Dept Biol Hood Col Frederick MD 21701

COMMON, ROBERT HADDON, b Larne, Northern Ireland, Feb 25, 07; m 35; c 6. AGRICULTURAL CHEMISTRY. *Educ:* Queen's Univ Belfast, BSc, 28, BAgr, 29, MAgr, 31, DSc, 57; Univ London, BSc, 30, PhD(biochem), 35, DSc, 44. *Hon Degrees:* LLD, Queen's Univ Belfast, 74. *Prof Exp:* Asst, Chem Res Div, Ministry Agr & instr agr chem, Queen's Univ Belfast, 29-47; prof, 47-74, chmn dept, 47-72, EMER PROF AGR CHEM, MACDONALD COL, McGILL UNIV, 75- *Honors & Awards:* E W McHenry Award, Nutrit Soc Can, 75. *Mem:* Fel Royal Soc Can; fel Can Inst Chem; fel Agr Inst Can; fel Royal Soc Chem Gt Brit. *Res:* Mineral metabolism in the domestic fowl; biochemical effects of gonadal hormones in the fowl; composition and digestibility of feedstuffs; metabolism of estrogens in the fowl. *Mailing Add:* 12A Maple Ave Ste Anne DeBellevue Quebec PQ H9X 2E4 Can

COMMONER, BARRY, b New York, NY, May 28, 17; m; c 2. BIOLOGY. *Educ:* Columbia Univ, AB, 37; Harvard Univ, MA, 38, PhD(biol), 41. *Hon Degrees:* DSc, Hahnemann Med Col, 63, Colgate Univ, 72, Clark Univ, 74, Grinnell Col, 68, Lehigh Univ, 69, Williams Col, 70 & Ripon Col, 71, Cleveland State Univ, 80; LLD, Univ Calif, 67, Grinnell Col, 81. *Prof Exp:* Asst biol, Harvard Univ, 38-40; instr, Queens Col, NY, 40-42; assoc ed, Sci Illustrated, NY, 46-47; from assoc prof to prof plant physiol, Wash Univ, 47-76, dept bot, 65-69, univ prof environ sci, 76-81, dir ctr biol natural systs, 65-81; PROF DEPT EARTH & ENVIRON SCI, QUEENS COL, CITY UNIV NY, 81- & DIR CTR BIOL NATURAL SYST, 81- *Concurrent Pos:* Naval liaison off, US Senate Comt Mil Affairs, 46; mem bd dirs, Scientists Inst Pub Info, 63-, co-chmn bd, 67-69, chmn, 69-78, chmn exec comt, 78; pres, St Louis Comt Nuclear Info, 65-66; mem bd dirs & exec comt sci div, St Louis Comt Environ Info, 66-; mem spec study group on sonic boom, US Dept Interior, 67-68; mem bd consult experts, Rachel Carson Trust for Living Environ, 67- & law ctr comn, Univ Okla, 69-70; mem bd, Univs Nat Anti-War Fund; mem adv comt, Coalition for Health of Communities, bd sponsors, In These Times, 76-; Secy's Adv Coun, US Dept Com, 76; adv comt, Ctr Develop Policy, 78; adv coun, Fund for Peace, 78; vis prof community health, A Einstein Col Med, 81- *Honors & Awards:* Newcomb Cleveland Prize, AAAS, 53; First Int Humanist Award, Int Humanist & Ethical Union, 70; Int Prize Safeguarding Environ, Cervia, Italy, 73; Comdr Order of Merit Repub Italy, 77; Premio Iglesias, Sardinia, Italy, 78, 82. *Mem:* Fel AAAS; Soc Gen Physiol; Am Inst Biol Sci; Am Chem Soc; Am Soc Plant Physiol. *Res:* Alterations in the environment in relation to modern technology; current status of the nitrogen cycle; roles of free radicals in biological processes; the origins and significance of the environmental and energy crises; environmental carcinogenesis; development of strategies to reduce the vulnerability of United States agriculture to disruptions from energy shortages. *Mailing Add:* Ctr Biol Natural Systs Queens Col Flushing NY 11367

COMNINOU, MARIA, b Athens, Greece, Aug 12, 47. THEORETICAL MECHANICS, APPLIED MECHANICS. *Educ:* Nat Tech Univ Athens, BS, 70; Northwestern Univ, MS, 71, PhD(theoret & appl mech), 73. *Prof Exp:* Instr math, Mass Inst Technol, 73-74; asst prof appl mech & eng sci, 74-79, ASSOC PROF CIVIL ENG & APPL MECH, UNIV MICH, 79- *Honors & Awards:* Alfred Noble Prize, Am Soc Civil Engrs, Am Soc Mech Engrs, Inst Elect & Electronic Engrs, Western Soc Eng & Am Inst Mining Metall & Petrol Engrs; Henry Hess Award, Am Soc Mech Engrs. *Mem:* Am Soc Mech Engrs; Am Soc Civil Engrs; Am Acad Mech; Soc Women Engrs. *Res:* Wave propagation; fracture; dislocations; contact problems; elasticity. *Mailing Add:* 314 W Eng Univ of Mich Ann Arbor MI 48109

COMPAAN, ALVIN DELL, b Hull, NDak, June 11, 43; m 69; c 4. SOLID STATE PHYSICS. *Educ:* Calvin Col, AB, 65; Univ Chicago, MS, 66, PhD(physics), 71. *Prof Exp:* Res assoc physics, NY Univ, 71-73; from asst prof to assoc prof, 73-81, PROF PHYSICS, KANS STATE UNIV, 81- *Mem:* Am Phys Soc; AAAS; Sigma Xi; Mat Res Soc; Optical Soc Am. *Res:* Raman acattering and photoluminescence studies of semiconductors; dynamics of excitons and electronphonon interactions in semiconductors; ion implantation effects in semiconductors; coherent anti-Stokes Raman scattering; laser annealing in semiconductors. *Mailing Add:* Dept of Physics Kans State Univ Manhattan KS 66506

COMPANION, AUDREY (LEE), b Tarentum, Pa, Aug 19, 32. QUANTUM CHEMISTRY. *Educ:* Carnegie Inst Technol, BS, 54, MS, 56, PhD(phys chem), 58. *Prof Exp:* From instr to assoc prof chem, Ill Inst Technol, 58-75; assoc prof, 75-76, PROF CHEM, UNIV KY, 76- *Mem:* Am Chem Soc; Am Phys Soc; AAAS. *Res:* Molecular orbital theories; electronic spectroscopy; crystal field theory; theories of chemisorption. *Mailing Add:* Dept of Chem Univ of Ky Lexington KY 40506

COMPANS, RICHARD W, b Syracuse, NY, Sept 15, 40; m 65. VIROLOGY. *Educ:* Kalamazoo Col, BA, 63; Rockefeller Univ, PhD(virol), 68. *Prof Exp:* Guest investr electron micros, Inst Sci Res Cancer, Villejuif, France, 68; Am Cancer Soc hon fel microbiol, John Curtin Sch Med Res, Australian Nat Univ, 68-69; from asst prof to assoc prof virol, Rockefeller Univ, 69-75; PROF MICROBIOL, UNIV ALA, BIRMINGHAM & SR SCIENTIST, CANCER RES & TRAINING CTR, 75-, SR SCIENTIST, DIABETES RES & TRAINING CTR, 77- *Concurrent Pos:* Vis investr, Scripps Clin & Res Found, 81; mem, Virol Study Sect, USPHS, 76-80. *Mem:* Am Soc Cell Biol; Am Soc Biol Chemists; Am Asn Immunol; Am Chem Soc; Am Soc Microbiol. *Res:* Cell biology; biochemistry; structure and assembly of viruses. *Mailing Add:* Dept of Microbiol Univ of Ala Birmingham AL 35294

COMPARIN, ROBERT A(NTON), b Hurley, Wis, July 25, 28; m 56; c 5. MECHANICAL ENGINEERING. *Educ:* Purdue Univ, BSME, 54, MSME, 58, PhD(mech eng), 60. *Prof Exp:* Instr mech eng, Purdue Univ, 54-60; staff engr, Int Bus Mach Corp, 60-62; asst prof, Univ Maine, 62-64; from assoc prof to prof, Va Polytech Inst & State Univ, 64-74; chmn, Mech Eng Dept, NJ Inst Technol, 74-77; DEAN FENN COL ENG, CLEVELAND STATE UNIV, 77- *Mem:* Am Soc Mech Engrs; Am Soc Eng Educ. *Res:* Fluid mechanics. *Mailing Add:* Fenn Col Eng Cleveland State Univ Cleveland OH 44115

COMPERE, EDGAR LATTIMORE, b Hamburg, Ark, Jan 23, 17; m 45; c 3. PHYSICAL CHEMISTRY. *Educ:* Ouachita Col, AB, 38; La State Univ, MS, 40, PhD(phys chem), 43. *Prof Exp:* Chemist, La Div, Stand Oil Co, NJ, 42-46; from asst prof to assoc prof chem, La State Univ, 46-51; sr chemist, Chem Div, 51-56, group leader corrosion sect, Reactor Exp Eng Div, 53-55, asst sect chief, 55-58, chief slurry mat sect, 58-61, sr chemist, Reactor Chem Div, 61-73, SR CHEMIST, CHEM TECHNOL DIV, OAK RIDGE NAT LAB, 73- *Concurrent Pos:* Sect ed, Nuclear Safety, 78- *Mem:* Fel AAAS; Am Chem Soc; Sigma Xi; Am Nuclear Soc; fel Am Inst Chemists. *Res:* Reaction kinetics; tritium; fractional liquid extraction; nuclear reactor chemistry; corrosion; reactor materials; fission product transport; leachability of radioactive solids. *Mailing Add:* Chem Technol Div Oak Ridge Nat Lab Oak Ridge TN 37830

COMPERE, EDWARD L, JR, b Detroit, Mich, June 22, 27; m 54; c 3. ORGANIC CHEMISTRY. *Educ:* Beloit Col, BS, 50; Univ Chicago, MS, 54; Univ Md, PhD, 58. *Prof Exp:* Asst prof chem, Univ WVa, 58-59 & Kans State Teachers Col, 59-60; from asst prof to assoc prof, Mich Tech Univ, 60-64; assoc prof, 64-67, dir state tech serv prog, 66-67, PROF CHEM, EASTERN MICH UNIV, 67- *Mem:* AAAS; Am Chem Soc; Sigma Xi. *Res:* Physical-organic chemistry; inorganic chemistry; chemistry in aquatic biology; lattice-salt structure. *Mailing Add:* Dept of Chem Eastern Mich Univ Ypsilanti MI 48197

COMPHER, MARVIN KEEN, JR, b Clifton Forge, Va, May 17, 42. DEVELOPMENTAL BIOLOGY, ENDOCRINOLOGY. *Educ:* Wake Forest Univ, BS, 64; Univ Va, PhD(biol), 68. *Prof Exp:* Asst prof biol, Col Wooster, 68-72; asst prof, 72-76, ASSOC PROF BIOL, CHATHAM COL, 76- *Res:* Regulation of the newt thyroid gland; effects of hypothalamic lesions and pituitary autotransplantations on thyroid activity. *Mailing Add:* Dept of Biol Woodland Rd Pittsburgh PA 15232

COMPTON, CHARLES (DANIEL), b Elizabeth, NJ, Jan 8, 15; m 53. CHEMISTRY. *Educ:* Princeton Univ, AB, 40; Yale Univ, PhD(org chem), 43. *Prof Exp:* Asst chemist, Calco Chem Co, NJ, 34-38, res chemist, 43; instr chem, Princeton Univ, 43-44, res assoc, Manhattan Dist proj, 44-45; instr org & gen chem, Williams Col, 46, from asst prof to prof chem, 46-74, chmn dept, 64-74, Ebenezer Fitch prof chem, 74-77; mem staff, Thomas Chem Lab, 77-81; RETIRED. *Mem:* Am Chem Soc. *Res:* Correlation of spectra and structure of organic compounds. *Mailing Add:* Thomas Chem Lab Williamstown MA 01267

COMPTON, DALE L(EONARD), b Pasadena, Calif, June 18, 35; m 59; c 2. AERONAUTICAL ENGINEERING. *Educ:* Stanford Univ, BS, 57, MS, 58, PhD, 69; Mass Inst Technol, MS, 75. *Prof Exp:* Aerospace scientist, 57-72, tech asst to dir, 72-73, dep dir, Astronaut, 73-74, CHIEF, SPACE SCI DIV, AMES RES CTR, NASA, 74- *Mem:* Am Inst Aeronaut & Astronaut; AAAS. *Res:* Vehicle aerodynamics; re-entry radiative and convective heating; ablation. *Mailing Add:* Mail Stop 245-1 NASA Ames Res Ctr Moffett Field CA 94035

COMPTON, DINSDALE MICHAEL JAMES, b London, Eng, Nov 12, 30; m 54; c 3. RADIOPHARMACEUTICALS. *Educ:* Oxford Univ, BA, 52, DPhil, 54. *Prof Exp:* Fel, Nat Res Coun, Can, 54-56; mem staff, Res Labs, IBM, 56-60; asst div dir, General Atomic, 60-70; vpres, Enviro-Med Inc, 70-74; pres, WSA, Inc, 74-81; VPRES, SYNCOR INT CORP, 81- *Mem:* Am Chem Soc; Soc Nuclear Med. *Res:* Radiation effects particularly as measured by optical phenomena; development of radiopharamaceuticals; applicaiton of epidemiological methods to safety research. *Mailing Add:* Safety Sci Div Syncor Int Corp 7586 Trade St San Diego CA 92121

COMPTON, ELL DEE, b Wilmington, Ohio, Mar 16, 16; m 44; c 1. ORGANIC CHEMISTRY, ENVIRONMENTAL MANAGEMENT. *Educ:* Univ Cincinnati, ChE, 39, MS, 40, PhD(tanning res), 42. *Prof Exp:* Monsanto Chem Co fel tanned calf skin, Univ Cincinnati, 42-43; chemist, Merrimac Div, Monsanto Chem Co, 43-46, group leader, 47-52; dir res, Eagle-Ottawa Leather Co, 52-60; res group leader, Maumee Chem Co, 60-61, appl res dir, 61-63, chem res dir, 63-69; lab dir, Sherwin-Williams Chem Div, 69-73, group dir, 73-78, dir, 78-81, CONSULT, REGULATORY AFFAIRS, SHERWIN-WILLIAMS, CO, 81- *Mem:* AAAS; Am Chem Soc; Am Inst Chem. *Res:* Applications of organic chemicals; statistics. *Mailing Add:* 8457 Whitewood Rd Brecksville OH 44141

COMPTON, JOHN LEE, b San Francisco, Calif, July 23, 47. PLANT DEVELOPMENT. *Educ:* Yale Col, AB, 69; Calif Inst Technol, MS, 71, PhD(biophysics & chem), 74. *Prof Exp:* Lectr biochem, Univ Calif, San Francisco, 78-80; RES ASSOC, BOYCE THOMPSON INST PLANT RES, CORNELL UNIV, 80- *Mem:* Plant Molecular Biol Asn; Am Soc Plant Physiol. *Res:* DNA transformation of plants; molecular biology of the regeneration of plants from protoplasts. *Mailing Add:* Boyce Thompson Inst Cornell Univ Ithaca NY 14853

COMPTON, LESLIE ELLWYN, b San Diego, Calif, Mar 24, 43; m 69; c 2. PHYSICAL CHEMISTRY, SYNTHETIC FUELS. *Educ:* Stanford Univ, BS, 66; Univ Calif, Santa Barbara, PhD(phys chem), 70. *Prof Exp:* Sr res chemist, Garrett Res & Develop Co, Occidental Petrol, 70-71; staff scientist, Sci Applications Inc, 72-75; sr res chemist, Occidental Res Corp, Occidental Petrol, 75-78; MEM TECH STAFF, JET PROPULSION LAB, CALIF INST TECHNOL, 79- *Concurrent Pos:* Fel, Univ Calif, Santa Barbara, 71-72; consult, Radiation & Environ Mat, Inc, 71-72. *Mem:* Am Phys Soc; Am Chem Soc. *Res:* Gas phase and heterogeneous reactions of chemically high energy ions, atoms and small molecules; gas phase kinetics; synthetic fuels chemistry, including oil shale, coal, tar sands, and thermochemical hydrogen; instrumental analysis and instrumentation research. *Mailing Add:* Jet Propulsion Lab Bldg 125 Rm 159 4800 Oak Grove Dr Pasadena CA 91103

COMPTON, OLIVER CECIL, b Seattle, Wash, Mar 1, 03; m 50. POMOLOGY. *Educ:* Univ Calif, BS, 31, MS, 32; Cornell Univ, PhD(pomol), 47. *Prof Exp:* Assoc, Exp Sta, Univ Calif, 32-40; from asst to instr pomol, Cornell Univ, 40-47; from asst horticulturist to assoc horticulturist, 48-60, from assoc prof to prof, 49-72, EMER PROF HORT, AGR EXP STA, ORE STATE UNIV, 72- *Mem:* Am Soc Hort Sci; Am Soc Plant Physiol. *Res:* Use of water by citrus and avocado trees; effect of aeration on absorption of nutritients by apple trees; physiological effects of fluorine on plants; response of tree and fruit to climate and nutrient level. *Mailing Add:* 1330 SW 35th St Corvallis OR 97330

COMPTON, RALPH THEODORE, JR, b St Louis, Mo, July 26, 35; m 57; c 3. ELECTRICAL ENGINEERING. *Educ:* Mass Inst Technol, SB, 58; Ohio State Univ, MSc, 61, PhD(elec eng), 64. *Prof Exp:* Jr engr, Deco Electronics, Inc, 58-59; sr engr, Battell Mem Inst, 59-62; asst supvr, Antenna Lab, Ohio State Univ, 62-65, asst prof elec eng, 64-65; asst prof eng, Case Inst Technol, 65-67; Nat Sci Found fel, Munich Tech Univ, 67-68; assoc prof elec eng, 68-78, PROF ELEC ENG, OHIO STATE UNIV, 78- *Mem:* Inst Elec & Electronics Engrs. *Res:* Electromagnetic theory; antennas; automatic control theory; radar; communications; adaptive antennas. *Mailing Add:* Dept of Elec Eng Ohio State Univ 2015 Neil Ave Columbus OH 43210

COMPTON, ROBERT NORMAN, b Metropolis, Ill, Nov 28, 38; m 61. ATOMIC PHYSICS, MOLECULAR PHYSICS. *Educ:* Berea Col, BA, 60; Univ Fla, MS, 62; Univ Tenn, PhD(physics), 66. *Prof Exp:* Consult, 63-64, PHYSICIST, HEALTH PHYSICS DIV, OAK RIDGE NAT LAB, 66- *Concurrent Pos:* Ford Found fel, Univ Tenn, 68, lectr, 69-; sr vis scientist, FOM Inst Atomic & Molecular Physics, Amsterdam, 78. *Mem:* Fel Am Phys Soc. *Res:* Laser multiphoton ionization of atoms and molecules; interaction of electrons with atoms and molecules. *Mailing Add:* Oak Ridge Nat Lab PO Box X Oak Ridge TN 37830

COMPTON, ROBERT ROSS, b Los Angeles, Calif, July 21, 22; m 48; c 5. GEOLOGY. *Educ:* Stanford Univ, BA, 43, PhD(geol), 49. *Prof Exp:* Geologist, P-1, US Geol Surv, 43-44; from instr to assoc prof, 47-61, PROF GEOL, STANFORD UNIV, 61- *Concurrent Pos:* Geologist, US Geol Surv, 51-52, 68-; NSF fel, 55-56; Guggenheim fel, 63-64. *Mem:* Geol Soc Am. *Res:* Igneous and metamorphic petrology and structure. *Mailing Add:* Stanford CA

COMPTON, THOMAS LEE, b Grafton, WVa, July 23, 42; m 65; c 2. BIOLOGY, ECOLOGY. *Educ:* Calif State Univ, San Jose, BA, 67; Univ Alaska, MS, 69; Univ Wyo, PhD(zool), 74. *Prof Exp:* Teaching asst biol, Univ Alaska, 67-69; instr zool, Pepperdine Univ, 69-70; teaching asst biol, Univ Wyo, 70-71; res assoc ecol, Wyo Game & Fish Comn, 71-74; chmn, Div Natural Sci, 76-81, PROF BIOL, LETOURNEAU COL, 74- *Concurrent Pos:* Res grants, Alaska Dept Agr, 68-69, Wyo Game & Fish Comn, 71-74 & Forage Unlimited Inc, 76-77; dir, Sci Camp Rockies, 77-; Danforth Assoc. *Mem:* Am Sci Affil; Sci Res Soc NAm; Nat Asn Biol Teachers; Nat Asn Sci Teachers. *Res:* Conservation and stewardship of natural resources. *Mailing Add:* Sci Camp the Rockies 2694 CR222 Durango CO 81301

COMPTON, WALTER DALE, b Chrisman, Ill, Jan 7, 29; m 51; c 3. PHYSICS. *Educ:* Wabash Col, BA, 49; Univ Okla, MS, 51; Univ Ill, PhD, 55. *Prof Exp:* Physicist, US Naval Ord Test Sta, Inyokern, 51-52; physicist, US Naval Res Lab, 55-61; prof physics, Univ Ill, Urbana, 61-70, dir coord sci lab, 65-70; dir chem & phys sci, 70-75, V PRES RES, FORD MOTOR CO, 75- *Concurrent Pos:* Fel, US Naval Ord Test Sta, 55-56; US Naval Res Lab award, 58; mem adv bd, Naval Weapons Ctr. *Mem:* Nat Acad Eng; Sigma Xi; Fel Am Phys Soc. *Res:* Solid state physics; radiation effects in solids; color centers in insulating crystals; luminescence; metal semiconductor junction. *Mailing Add:* Ford Motor Co Res Staff PO Box 1603 Dearborn MI 48121

COMPTON, WILLIAM A, b Richmond, Va, Aug 2, 27; m 55. GENETICS, STATISTICS. *Educ:* NC State Col, BS, 58, MS, 60; Univ Nebr, PhD(agron), 63. *Prof Exp:* Res asst genetics, NC State Col, 58-60; res asst, Univ Nebr, 60-62, consult statistician, 62-63; asst prof, NC State Univ, 63-65; asst prof agron, Univ Minn, 65-67; assoc prof, 67-75, PROF AGRON, UNIV NEBR, LINCOLN, 75- *Concurrent Pos:* Consult, Agrarian Univ, Peru, 63- *Mem:* Am Soc Agron; Crop Sci Soc Am. *Res:* Corn breeding; applied and basic quantitative genetics research with corn. *Mailing Add:* Dept of Agron Univ of Nebr Lincoln NE 68588

COMROE, JULIUS HIRAM, JR, b York, Pa, Mar 13, 11; m 36; c 1. PHYSIOLOGY. *Educ:* Univ Pa, AB, 31, MD, 34. *Hon Degrees:* MD, Karolinska Inst, Sweden, 68; DSc, Univ Chicago, 68 & Univ Pa, 78. *Prof Exp:* Instr pharmacol, Sch Med, Univ Pa, 36-40, assoc, 40-42, asst prof, 42-46, prof physiol & pharmacol, Grad Sch Med & clin physiologist, Hosp, 46-57; prof physiol, 57-78, dir, Cardiovascular Res Inst, 73-78, Morris Herzstein prof biol, 73-78, DIR, NAT PULMONARY FAC TRAINING CTR, UNIV CALIF, SAN FRANCISCO, 75-, EMER DIR, CARDIOVASC RES INST, 78-, EMER PROF PHYSIOL, 78- *Concurrent Pos:* Commonwealth Fund fel, Nat Inst Med Res, London, 39; chmn physiol sect, USPHS, 55-58; mem bd sci counsellors, Nat Heart Inst, 57-61; dir, Cardiovasc Res Int, 57-73; mem, Nat Adv Ment Health Coun, 58-62 & Nat Adv Heart Coun, 63-67; ed, Circulation Res, 66-70; mem, Nat Adv Heart & Lung Coun, 70-74; fel, Royal Col Physicians London, 71; consult ed, Circulation Res, 71-; ed, Annual Rev Physiol, 71-74; mem, President's Panel on Heart Dis, 72; adv comt to dir, NIH, 76-78; sci adv comt, Mass Gen Hosp, 75-79. *Honors & Awards:* Res Achievement Award, Am Heart Asn, 68; Carl J Wiggers Award, 74; Trudeau Medal, Am Lung Asn, 74; Gold Heart Award, Am Heart Asn, 75; Jessie Stevenson Kovalenko Medal, Nat Acad Sci, 76; Am Col Physicians Award, 77; Ray C Daggs Award, Am Physiol Soc, 77; Eugemo Morelli Int Award Pneumology, Accademia Del Lincei, Rome, 79. *Mem:* Nat Acad Sci; Am Physiol Soc (pres, 60-61); Am Acad Arts & Sci; Am Col Physicians; Am Soc Clin Invest. *Res:* Carotid and aortic bodies; autonomic drugs; regulation of respiration circulation; pulmonary function; neuromuscular transmission; history of biomedical discovery. *Mailing Add:* Cardiovasc Res Inst Univ of Calif San Francisco CA 94143

COMSTOCK, CRAIG, b Long Beach, Calif, June 11, 34; m 57; c 3. APPLIED MATHEMATICS. *Educ:* Cornell Univ, BEngPhys, 56; US Naval Postgrad Sch, MS, 61; Harvard Univ, PhD(appl math), 65. *Prof Exp:* Teaching fel appl math, Harvard Univ, 63-64; asst prof math, Pa State Univ, 64-68 & Univ Mich, 68-70; assoc prof, 70-73, PROF MATH, NAVAL POSTGRAD SCH, 73- *Concurrent Pos:* Consult, HRB-Singer, Inc, 65 & US Naval Ord Res Lab, 65-68. *Mem:* Math Asn Am; Soc Indust & Appl Math. *Res:* Asymptotic expansion of differential equations; wave propagation; plasmas in the geomagnetic field; finite element calculations in meteorology. *Mailing Add:* 3096 Sloat Rd Pebble Beach CA 93953

COMSTOCK, DALE ROBERT, b Frederic, Wis, Jan 18, 34; m 56; c 2. MATHEMATICS. *Educ:* Cent Wash State Col, BA, 55; Ore State Univ, MS, 62, PhD(algebra), 66. *Prof Exp:* Instr math, Columbia Basin Col, 56-57 & 59-60; teaching asst, Ore State Univ, 61-64; from asst prof to assoc prof, 64-70, PROF MATH & DEAN GRAD STUDIES, CENT WASH UNIV, 70- *Mem:* Math Asn Am; Am Math Soc; Soc Indust & Appl Math; Asn Comput Mach. *Res:* Algebra; computability. *Mailing Add:* Dept of Math Cent Wash Univ Ellensburg WA 98926

COMSTOCK, GEORGE WILLS, b Niagara Falls, NY, Jan 7, 15; m 39; c 3. EPIDEMIOLOGY. *Educ:* Antioch Col, BS, 37; Harvard Univ, MD, 41; Univ Mich, MPH, 51; Johns Hopkins Univ, DrPH, 56. *Prof Exp:* Dir, Muscogee County Tuberc Study, USPHS, 46-55; chief epidemiol studies, Tuberc Prog, 56-62; assoc prof, 62-65, PROF EPIDEMIOL, JOHNS HOPKINS UNIV, 65- *Concurrent Pos:* Consult tuberc prog, USPHS, 62-; dir, Training Ctr for Pub Health Res, Hagerstown, Md, 63-; ed-in-chief, Am J Epidemiol, 79- *Mem:* Am Pub Health Asn; Am Thoracic Soc; Am Epidemiol Soc; Soc Epidemiol Res. *Res:* Epidemiology of chronic diseases, especially tuberculosis and cardio-respiratory diseases. *Mailing Add:* Johns Hopkins Res Ctr Box 2067 Hagerstown MD 21740

COMSTOCK, GILBERT LEROY, forest products, see previous edition

COMSTOCK, JACK CHARLES, b Detroit, Mich, June 13, 43. PLANT PATHOLOGY. *Educ:* Mich State Univ, BS, 65, PhD(plant path), 71. *Prof Exp:* Res assoc corn path, Iowa State Univ, 71-74; asst pathologist, 74-75, ASSOC PATHOLOGIST, HAWAIIAN SUGAR PLANTERS ASN, 75- *Concurrent Pos:* Affil fac mem, Univ Hawaii, 75- *Mem:* Am Phytopath Soc; AAAS; Sigma Xi. *Res:* Sugarcane pathology; disease control, screening resistance. *Mailing Add:* Hawaiian Sugar Planters Asn PO Box 1057 Aiea HI 96701

COMSTOCK, VERNE EDWARD, b Kildeer, NDak, July 18, 19; m 41; c 6. PLANT BREEDING, PLANT GENETICS. *Educ:* State Col Wash, BS, 41, MS, 47; Univ Minn, PhD, 59. *Prof Exp:* Asst agronomist forage invest, Div Forage Crops & Dis, Bur Plant Indust, USDA, State Col Wash, 47-50, res agronomist flax breeding & invest, Southwestern Irrig Field Sta, Brawley, Calif, 50-53, flax qual invests, cereal crop sect, Crops Res Div, Agr Res Serv, Univ Minn, St Paul, 53-57, leader seedflax invests, Indust Crop Sect, 57-73; PROF AGRON & PLANT GENETICS, UNIV MINN, ST PAUL, 74- *Mem:* Am Soc Agron. *Res:* Range grass breeding; flax cultural studies under irrigation and quality investigations, flax breeding for disease resistance. *Mailing Add:* Dept of Agron Univ of Minn St Paul MN 55108

CONAN, ROBERT JAMES, JR, b Syracuse, NY, Oct 30, 24. PHYSICAL CHEMISTRY. *Educ:* Syracuse Univ, BS, 45, MS, 47; Fordham Univ, PhD(phys chem), 50. *Prof Exp:* Instr gen chem, Fordham Univ, 48; asst prof phys chem, 49-52, assoc prof, 53-56, PROF PHYS CHEM, LE MOYNE COL, NY, 57-, CHMN DEPT CHEM, 59-67 & 73- *Concurrent Pos:* Researcher, Stockholm, Sweden, 53 & Res Lab Phys Chem, Swiss Fed Inst Technol, 66-67. *Mem:* Am Chem Soc; Am Phys Soc. *Res:* Theory of liquids and solutions; surface phenomena; thermodynamics; education in chemistry. *Mailing Add:* Dept of Chem Le Moyne Col Syracuse NY 13214

CONANT, DALE HOLDREGE, b Casper, Wyo, July 5, 39. PHOTOGRAPHIC CHEMISTRY. *Educ:* Col Idaho, BS, 61; Ore State Univ, MS, 64; Ohio State Univ, PhD(phys chem), 69. *Prof Exp:* Engr, Kaiser Refractories, 63-65; sr chemist, Rochester, 69-74, res assoc, Photog Res Div, 74-75, develop engr, Plate Mfg Div, 75-79, SUPVR, LITHOPLATE PROD CONTROL, EASTMAN KODAK CO, 79- *Mem:* Am Chem Soc; Soc Photog Sci & Eng. *Res:* Interaction of chlorophyll and its derivatives with II-aromatic electron acceptor systems involving visible spectrum measurements, fluorescence quenching measurements and nuclear magnetic resonance measurements; research and development of photolithography. *Mailing Add:* 508 Canadian Parkway Fort Collins CO 80521

CONANT, FLOYD SANFORD, b Leroy, WVa, Nov 27, 14; m 38; c 2. POLYMER PHYSICS. *Educ:* Morris Harvey Col, BS, 34; WVa Univ, MS, 35. *Prof Exp:* Teacher high sch, 35-42; sr res scientist, Firestone Tire & Rubber Co, 42-75, res assoc, 75-80; MEM STAFF, STANDARDS TESTING LABS, 81- *Concurrent Pos:* Mem US deleg, Tech Comt 45, Int Stand Orgn, 75-79, convenor working group 10, 77-79. *Mem:* Am Chem Soc;

Am Soc Testing & Mat; Soc Automotive Engrs. *Res:* Low temperature properties of elastomers; vibration properties of pneumatic tires; coefficient of friction of rubber; tire dynamics. *Mailing Add:* 143 Gunarch Dr Akron OH 44319

CONANT, LOUIS COWLES, b Orford, NH, Sept 14, 02; m 30; c 2. GEOLOGY. *Educ:* Dartmouth Col, AB, 26; Cornell Univ, AM, 29, PhD(geol), 34. *Prof Exp:* Instr geol, Dartmouth Col, 26-27; asst, Cornell Univ, 27-28, instr, 28-29, 30-37; field geologist, NRhodesia, 29-30; asst geologist, Miss Geol Surv, 37-38, 40-42; supvr mineral surv, Works Progress Admin, 38-39; lectr, Smith Col, 39-40; geologist, US Geol Surv, 42-72. *Concurrent Pos:* Assoc prof, Univ Miss, 37-39, 40-42; geol map compiler, Agency Int Develop, Libya, 60-62. *Mem:* Fel AAAS; fel Geol Soc Am; Am Asn Petrol Geol. *Res:* Non-metallic economic geology; stratigraphy; Chattanooga shale; east Gulf Coastal Plain; fuels; geology of Libya. *Mailing Add:* 3070 Porter St NW Washington DC 20008

CONANT, ROBERT HENRY, b Rockland, Mass, Oct 5, 16; m 46; c 5. PHOTOGRAPHIC CHEMISTRY. *Educ:* Loyola Col, Md, BS, 37; Georgetown Univ, MS, 39, PhD(biochem), 42. *Prof Exp:* Instr chem, Georgetown Univ, 37-42; res chemist, Photo Repro Div, Gen Aniline & Film Corp, 45-47, sr res chemist & res group leader, 47-51, tech asst to film plant mgr, 51-54, sr opers supvr film emulsions dept, 54-56, sr emulsion specialist, 56-60, mgr film qual control dept, 60-63 & sensitometry dept, 63-64, res chemist, 64-67, qual control specialist gelatin, 67, prod qual specialist gelatin, 67-74, SUPVR EMULSION MFG, PHOTO-REPRO DIV, GAF CORP, 74- *Res:* Photographic emulsion; gelatin; tests for sugars; S-amino acids in proteins; cystine and methionine distribution in proteins of egg whites. *Mailing Add:* Emulsion Mfg 37-4 GAF Corp Charles St Binghamton NY 13902

CONANT, ROBERT M, b Binghamton, NY, Oct 19, 27; m 51; c 3. VIROLOGY, IMMUNOLOGY. *Educ:* Harpur Col, BA, 58; State Univ NY Buffalo, MA, 63, PhD(virol, immunol), 66. *Prof Exp:* Instr pub schs, NY, 59-60; from instr pediat to asst prof pediat & med microbiol, Col Med, Ohio State Univ, 65-70; scientist & adminr, Div Res Grants, NIH, 70-71, asst chief, Div Allied Health Manpower, Bur Health Manpower Educ, 71-73, chief off spec studies, 73-74, CHIEF MANPOWER UTILIZATION BR, BUR HEALTH MANPOWER, HEALTH RESOURCES ADMIN, DEPT HEALTH, EDUC & WELFARE, 74- *Concurrent Pos:* Mem bd vaccine develop, Rhinovirus Ref Ctr, Nat Inst Allergy & Infectious Dis, 65-70; NIH res grants, Children's Hosp Res Found & Res Found, Ohio State Univ, 66-67; regist, Registry Am Type Cult Collection, 67- *Mem:* AAAS; Am Soc Microbiol; NY Acad Sci. *Res:* Characterization of antigens distributed among enteroviruses by immunodiffusion methods; relationships betweeen variant strains of same enterovirus serotype by immunodiffusion; identification and classification of rhinoviruses; application of plaque and immunodiffusion techniques to the study of rhinoviruses. *Mailing Add:* Div of Assoc Health Professions Bur of Health Manpower Hyattsville MD 20782

CONANT, ROGER, b Mamaroneck, NY, May 6, 09; m 47, 79; c 2. HERPETOLOGY. *Hon Degrees:* ScD, Univ Colo, 71. *Prof Exp:* Cur reptiles, Toledo Zoo, Ohio, 29-33, educ dir, 31-33, cur, 33-35; cur reptiles, Philadelphia Zool Garden, 35-73, dir, 67-73; ADJ PROF BIOL, UNIV NMEX, 73- *Concurrent Pos:* Res assoc, Am Mus Natural Hist & Acad Natural Sci Philadelphia; consult, Am Philos Soc Proj for Adult Educ & Partic in Sci, 40-42 & Nat Res Coun, 59-62. *Mem:* Am Soc Ichthyol & Herpet (first vpres, 46, 56, secy, 58-60, pres, 62); Soc Systs Zool; Zool Soc London. *Res:* Distribution, natural history and speciation in reptiles and amphibians of the United States and Mexico. *Mailing Add:* Dept of Biol Univ of NMex Albuquerque NM 87131

CONANT, ROGER C, b Milwaukee, Wis, Apr 12, 38; m 65; c 1. ELECTRICAL ENGINEERING, CYBERNETICS. *Educ:* Purdue Univ, BS, 61; Univ Ill, Urbana, MS, 63, PhD(info transfer), 68. *Prof Exp:* Asst prof, 68-77, ASSOC PROF INFO ENG, UNIV ILL, CHICAGO CIRCLE, 77- *Mem:* AAAS; Am Soc Cybernet; Inst Elec & Electronics Engrs. *Res:* Information transfer in complex systems; technical aids for the handicapped. *Mailing Add:* Univ of Ill at Chicago Circle Box 4348 Chicago IL 60680

CONARD, GEORGE P(OWELL), b Brooklyn, NY, Sept 10, 19; m 46; c 3. PHYSICAL METALLURGY. *Educ:* Brown Univ, BS, 41; Stevens Inst Technol, MS, 48; Mass Inst Technol, ScD, 52. *Prof Exp:* Instr math, Stevens Inst Technol, 46-48; instr metall, Mass Inst Technol, 48-50, asst prof, 50-52; from asst prof to assoc prof, 52-60, asst dir magnetics proj, 52-56, dir, Magnetic Mat Lab, 56-76, chmn dept metall & mat sci, 69-80, PROF METALL, LEHIGH UNIV, 60- *Concurrent Pos:* Mem, Franklin Inst. *Mem:* AAAS; Am Soc Metals; Am Inst Mining, Metall & Petrol Engrs; Brit Inst Metals; Brit Iron & Steel Inst. *Res:* Deformation and annealing of metals; magnetics. *Mailing Add:* Dept of Metall & Mat Scis Lehigh Univ Bethlehem PA 18015

CONARD, GORDON JOSEPH, b Milwaukee, Wis, Sept 22, 39; div; c 3. BIOCHEMICAL PHARMACOLOGY, DRUG METABOLISM. *Educ:* Univ Wis-Madison, BS, 61, MS, 67, PhD(pharmacol), 69. *Prof Exp:* Instr, Sch Pharm, Univ Wis-Milwaukee, 68; res assoc biochem, Res Inst, Am Dent Asn, 68-72; sr biochem pharmacologist, 73-74, res specialist, 75-78, SR RES SPECIALIST, DRUG METAB, RIKER LAB, INC, 3M CO, 78- *Concurrent Pos:* Reviewer, J Pharmaceut Sci, 72-; asst prof, Col Pharm, Univ Minn, Minneapolis, 73- *Mem:* AAAS; Sigma Xi. *Res:* Metabolic disposition of new drug molecules in laboratory animals and in man with emphasis on relationships to pharmacologic and toxicologic activity. *Mailing Add:* Riker Lab Inc Bldg 270-3S 3M Ctr St Paul MN 55144

CONARD, ROBERT ALLEN, b Jacksonville, Fla, July 29, 13; m 48; c 4. MEDICAL RESEARCH. *Educ:* Univ SC, BS, 36, MD, 41. *Prof Exp:* Med officer, US Navy, 41-47, proj officer, Radiol Defense Lab, 47-50, with med res dist, 50-56; scientist & chief, Marshall Island Med Survs & sr scientist, Brookhaven Nat Lab, 56-79; RETIRED. *Concurrent Pos:* Prof path, State Univ NY Stony Brook. *Mem:* Am Soc Hemat; Tissue Cult Soc; Radiation Res Soc. *Res:* Radiation effects; medical surveys of Marshallese people exposed to radioactive fallout. *Mailing Add:* Brookhaven Nat Lab Upton NY 11973

CONAWAY, CHARLES WILLIAM, b Anniston, Ala, July 11, 43; m 73; c 2. INFORMATION SCIENCE. *Educ:* Jacksonville State Univ, AB, 64; Fla State Univ, MS, 65; Rutgers Univ, PhD(info sci), 74. *Prof Exp:* Head ref librn, Fla Atlantic Univ, 66-68; res fel, Rutgers Univ, 68-71; asst prof, Sch Info & Libr Studies, State Univ NY, Buffalo, 71-77; ASST PROF INFO SCI, SCH LIBR SCI, FLA STATE UNIV, 77- *Concurrent Pos:* Fulbright lectr, prog libr sci, Univ Iceland, 75-76; prin investr, index usability proj, State Univ NY, Buffalo, 75-76. *Mem:* Am Soc Info Sci; Special Libr Asn; Am Libr Asn & Res Roundtable; Asn Am Libr Schs. *Res:* Index usability; automatic and machine-aided indexing; on-line information retrieval systems; library systems analysis and automation; computerized bibliographic techniques; question negotiation and information gathering behavior; information science education; microcomputers in libraries. *Mailing Add:* Sch of Libr Sci Fla State Univ Tallahassee FL 32306

CONAWAY, HOWARD HERSCHEL, b Fairmont, WVa, Oct 2, 40; m 69; c 2. PHYSIOLOGY. *Educ:* Fairmont State Col, BS, 63; WVa Univ, MS, 67; Univ Mo-Columbia, PhD, 70. *Prof Exp:* NIH fel, Dept Pediat, Univ Mo-Columbia, 70-71; asst prof, 71-76, ASSOC PROF PHYSIOL & BIOPHYSICS, SCH MED, UNIV ARK, LITTLE ROCK, 76- *Mem:* AAAS; Endocrine Soc; Sigma Xi; Am Genetic Asn. *Res:* Endocrinology and metabolism; diabetes mellitus. *Mailing Add:* Dept Physiol & Biophysics Sch Med Univ Ark Little Rock AR 72205

CONCA, ROMEO JOHN, b New Haven, Conn, May 11, 26; m 46; c 2. ORGANIC CHEMISTRY. *Educ:* Yale Univ, BS, 49, PhD(org chem), 53. *Prof Exp:* Asst, Princeton Univ, 52-53; res chemist, G D Searle & Co, 53-55; res chemist, ITT Rayonier, Inc, 55-59, group leader, 59-62, sect leader, 62-64, res supvr, 64-78, mgr tech support, Olympic Res Div, 78-81. *Concurrent Pos:* Owner, Lost Mountain Winery, 81- *Mem:* Tech Asn Pulp & Paper Indust; Am Chem Soc. *Res:* Cellulose and wood chemistry; carbohydrates. *Mailing Add:* 730 Lost Mountain Rd Sequim WA 98382

CONCANNON, JOSEPH N, b New York, NY, Sept 25, 20; m 64; c 3. PARASITOLOGY, RADIOBIOLOGY. *Educ:* Univ Dayton, BS, 42; Ohio State Univ, MS, 51; St John's Univ, MS, 56, PhD(parasitol), 59. *Prof Exp:* Teacher high sch, 42-51; instr biol, Cath Univ PR, 52-54; asst prof, Univ Dayton, 59-62; asst prof, 62-64, actg chairperson, Dept Biol Sci, 74-77, ASSOC PROF BIOL, ST JOHN'S UNIV, NY, 64- *Concurrent Pos:* NSF res fel, Univ Rochester, 62. *Mem:* AAAS; Soc Protozool; Am Soc Parasitol; Nat Sci Teachers Asn. *Res:* Protozoan parasitology, especially the trichomonads; thyroid physiology and insect control. *Mailing Add:* Dept of Biol Sci St John's Univ Jamaica NY 11439

CONCIATORI, ANTHONY BERNARD, b New York, NY, Mar 4, 16; m 51; 2. ORGANIC CHEMISTRY. *Educ:* Fordham Univ, BSc, 38; Univ Cincinnati, PhD(chem), 49. *Prof Exp:* Res chemist, Interchem Res Labs, 39-44; sr res chemist, 49-60, res assoc, 60-68, sect head, 68-71, MGR, CELANESE CORP, 71- *Mem:* Am Chem Soc; Sigma Xi (pres, Sci Res Soc Am, 63-64). *Res:* Polymers; catalysis; coatings; fibers. *Mailing Add:* 27 Orchard St Chatham NJ 07928

CONCORDIA, CHARLES, b Schenectady, NY, June 20, 08; m 48. ENGINEERING. *Hon Degrees:* DSc, Union Col, 71. *Prof Exp:* Lab asst, Gen Elec Co, 26-31, engr, 31-36, appl engr, 36-51, mgr gen anal eng, 51-64, consult eng, 64-73; CONSULT, 73- *Concurrent Pos:* Mem, Int Conf Large Elec Systs, France; chmn, Int Comt Power Syst Planning & Oper. *Honors & Awards:* Coffin Award, Gen Elec Co, 42; Lamme Medal, Inst Elec & Electronics Engrs; Engr of Year Award, Schenectady Co, 63. *Mem:* Nat Acad Eng; fel Inst Elec & Electronics Engrs; fel Am Soc Mech Engrs; Nat Soc Prof Engrs; Asn Comput Mach (treas). *Res:* Air compressor design; governors; regulators; control systems; electric power system design, planning and operation; computing and electrical machinery; system dynamics. *Mailing Add:* Apt 402N 629 Alhambra Rd Venice FL 33595

CONCUS, PAUL, b Los Angeles, Calif, June 18, 33; m 59; c 2. APPLIED MATHEMATICS, NUMERICAL ANALYSIS. *Educ:* Calif Inst Technol, BS, 54; Harvard Univ, AM, 55, PhD(appl math), 59. *Prof Exp:* Appl mathematician, Int Bus Mach Corp, 59-60; mathematician, Lawrence Berkeley Lab, 60-80, PROF MATH, UNIV CALIF, BERKLEY, 78-, STAFF SCIENTIST, LAWRENCE BERKELY LAB, 80- *Concurrent Pos:* Lectr, Univ Calif, Berkeley, 63-65; consult, Lockheed Res Labs, 61-70 & Gen Elec, 73-77; sr vis fel, Sci Res Coun Gt Brit, 70-71. *Mem:* Soc Indust & Appl Math. *Res:* Capillary fluid mechanics; computation. *Mailing Add:* Lawrence Berkeley Lab Univ of Calif Berkeley CA 94720

CONDE, MARY ALICE FEAGIN, b Huntingdon, Pa, Jan 4, 47; m 70. MOLECULAR BIOLOGY. *Educ:* Otterbein Col, BS, 68; Duke Univ, PhD(zool), 74. *Prof Exp:* Instr biol, Univ Va, 74-75; res assoc biochem, Univ Fla, 75-78, plant path, 78-81; RES SCIENTIST PLANT MOLECULAR BIOL, UPJOHN CO, 81- *Mem:* Am Soc Cell Biol; Genetics Soc Am; Asn Women Sci; AAAS. *Res:* Analysis of higher plant mitochandrial and chloroplast genomes; identification of molecular mechanism of expression of cytoplasmic male sterility; regulation of interaction between nuclear and organelle genomes. *Mailing Add:* Exp Agr Sci 9602-18-2 Upjohn Co Kalamazoo MI 49001

CONDELL, WILLIAM JOHN, JR, b Melrose, Mass, Mar 29, 27; m 52; c 2. RESEARCH ADMINISTRATION, OPTICAL PHYSICS. *Educ:* Cath Univ Am, BChemE, 49, MS, 52, PhD(physics), 59. *Prof Exp:* Physicist, Naval Ord Lab, 51-52, Eng Res & Develop Lab, US Army, 52-58 & Lab Phys Sci, 58-66; physicist, 66-74, dir physics progs, 74-80, CHIEF SCIENTIST, LDR PHYSICS DIV, OFF NAVAL RES, 81- *Concurrent Pos:* Asst prof lectr, George Washington Univ, 57-66. *Mem:* Am Phys Soc; fel Optical Soc Am; Am Asn Physics Teachers. *Res:* Atomic spectroscopy; optics; lasers. *Mailing Add:* Physics Prog Off Code 421 Off of Naval Res Arlington VA 22217

CONDELL, YVONNE C, b Quitman, Ga, Aug 29, 31; m 52. HUMAN GENETICS. *Educ:* Fla Agr & Mech Col, BS, 52; Univ Conn, MA, 58, PhD(cellular biol), 65. *Prof Exp:* Teacher high sch, Fla, 55-57 & Minn, 58-60; instr biol, Fergus Falls Jr Col, 60-65; from asst prof to assoc prof, 65-80, PROF BIOL, MOORHEAD STATE UNIV, 80- *Concurrent Pos:* Lectr, Univ Conn, 63. *Mem:* AAAS; Soc Study Social Biol; Am Inst Biol Sci; Nat Asn Biol Teachers. *Res:* Cellular biology; biology education; science and society. *Mailing Add:* Dept of Biol Moorhead State Univ Moorhead MN 56560

CONDER, GEORGE ANTHONY, b Albuquerque, NMex, Oct 7, 50; m 52; c 2. CHEMOTHERAPY, IMMUNOPARASITOLOGY. *Educ:* Pomona Col, BA, 72; Univ NMex, MS, 75; Brigham Young Univ PhD(zool), 79. *Prof Exp:* Res & teaching asst, Univ NMex, 73-75 & Brigham Young Univ, 75-78; res assoc, Brigham Young Univ, NIH, 78-79; fel, Michigan State Univ, NIH, 79-81; MEM STAFF RES & DEVELOP, UPJOHN CO, 81- *Concurrent Pos:* Res grant, Argonne Nat Lab, 75. *Mem:* Am Soc Parasitologists; Soc Protozoologists; Wildlife Dis Asn; Am Soc Trop Med & Hyg. *Res:* Immunological reactions at the host-parasite interface; serodiagnosis of parasitic diseases; development of radiation-attenated vaccines against parasites; chemotherapy ofparasitic diseases. *Mailing Add:* Upjohn Co 9680-190-14 Kalamazoo MI 49001

CONDER, HAROLD LEE, b Salem, Ohio, Nov 26, 45; div; c 1. ORGANOMETALLIC CHEMISTRY. *Educ:* Youngstown Univ, BS, 67; Purdue Univ, PhD(inorg chem), 71. *Prof Exp:* Res asst chem, Tulane Univ, 71-73; ASSOC PROF CHEM, GROVE CITY COL, 73- *Concurrent Pos:* Vis asst prof, Purdue Univ, 81-82. *Mem:* Am Chem Soc. *Res:* Photochemical substitution reactions of transition metal phosphites and phosphines. *Mailing Add:* Grove City Col Grove City PA 16127

CONDIE, KENT CARL, b Salt Lake City, Utah, Nov 28, 36; m 63; c 1. PETROLOGY, GEOCHEMISTRY. *Educ:* Univ Utah, BS, 59, MA, 62; Univ Calif, San Diego, PhD(geochem), 65. *Prof Exp:* From asst prof to assoc prof geochem & petrol, Wash Univ, 64-70; assoc prof, 70-77, PROF GEOCHEM, NMEX INST MINING & TECHNOL, 77- *Mem:* Geol Soc Am; Geochem Soc; Am Geophys Union. *Res:* Trace element geochemistry; origin and growth of continents. *Mailing Add:* Dept of Geosci NMex Inst of Mining & Technol Socorro NM 87801

CONDIFF, DUANE W, chemical & nuclear engineering, see previous edition

CONDIKE, GEORGE FRANCIS, b Brockton, Mass, Dec 1, 16; m 41; c 2. INORGANIC CHEMISTRY. *Educ:* DePauw Univ, AB, 40; Cornell Univ, PhD(inorg chem), 43. *Prof Exp:* Fel, Mellon Inst Indust Res, 43-44; sr engr, Sylvania Elec Prod, Inc, 44; tech rep, Rohm and Haas Co, 44-47; assoc prof chem, 47-53, dean col, 54-56, PROF CHEM, FITCHBURG STATE COL, 56- *Concurrent Pos:* NSF grant, 64-66, mem, NSF Equip Comt, 68-69. *Mem:* Am Chem Soc. *Res:* Chelate compounds; donor-acceptor bonding. *Mailing Add:* Dept of Chem Fitchburg State Col Fitchburg MA 01420

CONDIT, PAUL BRAINARD, b Berkeley, Calif, Mar 12, 43; m 66; c 1. ORGANIC CHEMISTRY. *Educ:* Univ Calif, Riverside, BA, 65; Univ Mich, PhD(org chem), 70. *Prof Exp:* Res fel, Calif Inst Technol, 70-71; res chemist, Eastman Kodak Co, 71-76, lab head, 76-79; estimating supvr, Distrib Div, 79-80, SR SALES FORECASTER, PHOTOG DIV, EKCO, 80- *Mem:* AAAS; Am Chem Soc; Soc Photog Sci & Eng; Sigma Xi. *Res:* Stereochemistry and mechanism of organic reactions; organic chemistry of color photography. *Mailing Add:* 2711 Clover Pittsford NY 14534

CONDIT, PAUL CARR, b Cleveland, Ohio, Sept 19, 14; m 39; c 2. PETROLEUM CHEMISTRY. *Educ:* Yale Univ, BS, 36, PhD(org chem), 39. *Prof Exp:* Res chemist, Calif Res Corp, 39-46, sr res chemist, 46-52, sect supvr, 52-67; mgr polymer div, 67-69, sr res assoc, Patent Dept, Chevron Res Co, 69-77; RETIRED. *Mem:* Am Chem Soc. *Res:* Petrochemical research and development; polymers; patents. *Mailing Add:* 720 Butterfield Rd San Anselmo CA 94960

CONDIT, RALPH HOWELL, b Hollywood, Calif, May 12, 29; m 66; c 2. SOLID STATE CHEMISTRY. *Educ:* Princeton Univ, BA, 51, PhD(chem), 60. *Prof Exp:* Res adminr, Air Force Off Sci Res, 58-60; CHEMIST, LAWRENCE LIVERMORE LAB, UNIV CALIF, 60- *Concurrent Pos:* Consult, Air Force Off Sci Res; dir, Geos Corp, Calif. *Mem:* Am Chem Soc; Am Phys Soc; Am Inst Aeronaut & Astronaut; Am Inst Mining, Metall & Petrol Eng; Am Ceramic Soc. *Res:* Tracer techniques and diffusion in solids; hydrogen fuel economy; ceramics for turbines; laser isotope separation; materials problems in the fusion energy program; diffusion in minerals; plutonium. *Mailing Add:* 4602 Almond Circle Livermore CA 94550

CONDIT, RICHARD CARR, molecular biology, virology, see previous edition

CONDLIFFE, PETER GEORGE, b Christchurch, NZ, June 30, 22; nat US; m 42; c 3. BIOCHEMISTRY, RESEARCH ADMINISTRATION. *Educ:* Univ Calif, BA, 47, PhD(biochem), 52. *Prof Exp:* Asst biochem, Univ Calif, 50-52; res assoc, Med Col, Cornell Univ, 52-54; chemist, Nat Inst Arthritis & Metab Dis, 54-66, chief, Europ Off, Paris, 66-68, chief, Conf & Sem Prog Br, John E Fogerty Int Ctr Advan Study Health Sci, 68-73, res biochemist & hormone distrib officer, Lab Nutrit & Endocrinol, Nat Inst Arthritis, Metab & Digestive Dis, 73-75, distrib officer, Lab Nutrit & Endocrinol, Nat Inst Arthritis & Metab, 75-80, CHIEF, SCHOLARS IN RESIDENCE PROG BR, FOGARTY INT CTR, NIH, BETHESDA, 75- *Concurrent Pos:* Lectr, USDA Grad Sch, Washington, DC, 55-; fel, Nat Found Carlsberg Lab, Copenhagen, 59-60; vis res assoc comp physiol lab, Mus Natural Hist, Paris, 66-68. *Mem:* AAAS; Am Soc Biol Chemists; Endocrine Soc. *Res:* Biochemical endocrinology; pituitary biochemistry; chemistry of pituitary hormones; reproductive biology; social implications of biomedical research; ethical issues in biology and medicine; international aspects of research in biomedicine. *Mailing Add:* Scholars & Fels Prog Br Fogarty Int Ctr NIH Bethesda MD 20795

CONDO, ALBERT CARMAN, JR, b Hackensack, NJ, May 25, 24; m 47, 73; c 3. ENVIRONMENTAL SCIENCE ENGINEERING, MATERIALS SCIENCE ENGINEERING. *Educ:* Cornell Univ, BS, 49, MS, 51. *Prof Exp:* Instr anal chem, Cornell Univ, 49-51; from res chemist to prin chemist, Atlantic Richfield Co, 51-64, dir plastics develop, 64-69, mgr protective eng systs, 69-72, sr task mgr arctic civil eng, 72, supvr arctic-civil eng, Alyeska Pipeline Serv Co, 72-77, proj mgr com develop, 77-81, MGR NEW BUS DEVELOP, ARCO, 81- *Concurrent Pos:* From instr to asst prof, eve col, Drexel Univ, 54-72. *Mem:* Am Chem Soc; Soc Plastics Eng; Nat Asn Corrosion Eng; Sigma Xi; Soil Conserv Soc Am. *Res:* Petrochemicals; polymerization; plastics; coatings and corrosion control; protective environmental and geotechnical systems; insulated roads on permafrost; hydraulic and thermal erosion control; restoration; revegetation; arctic thermal regimes; oil spill cleanup. *Mailing Add:* 3424 Ivy Lane Newtown Square PA 19073

CONDO, GEORGE T, b East St Louis, Ill, May 14, 34; m 58; c 2. HIGH ENERGY PHYSICS. *Educ:* Univ Ill, BS, 56, MS, 57, PhD(physics), 62. *Prof Exp:* Res assoc physics, Univ Ill, 62-63; from asst prof to assoc prof physics, 63-76, PROF PHYSICS & ASTRON, UNIV TENN, 76- *Concurrent Pos:* Consult, Oak Ridge Nat Lab, 63- *Mem:* Am Phys Soc. *Res:* Elementary particles using nuclear research emulsions and bubble chamber technique. *Mailing Add:* Dept of Physics Univ of Tenn Knoxville TN 37916

CONDON, FRANCIS EDWARD, b Abington, Mass, Oct 12, 19; m 43; c 7. CHEMISTRY. *Educ:* Harvard Univ, AB, 41, AM, 43, PhD(org chem), 44. *Prof Exp:* Res chemist, Phillips Petrol Co, 44-52; from asst prof to assoc prof, 52-67, PROF CHEM, CITY COL NEW YORK, 67- *Concurrent Pos:* NSF fac fel, Univ Southern Calif, 64-65. *Res:* Hydrocarbon chemistry; structure-reactivity correlations; hydration and base strength; hydrazines; electrophilic aromatic substitution. *Mailing Add:* 471 Larch Ave Bogota NJ 07603

CONDON, JAMES BENTON, b Buffalo, NY, Aug 20, 40; c 1. PHYSICAL CHEMISTRY, SURFACE CHEMISTRY. *Educ:* State Univ NY Binghamton, AB, 62; Iowa State Univ, PhD(phys chem), 68. *Prof Exp:* DEVELOP CHEMIST, NUCLEAR DIV, UNION CARBIDE CO, 68- *Mem:* Am Chem Soc; AAAS; Sigma Xi; Am Electrochem Soc. *Res:* Catalysis; electrochemistry; corrosion; solid state chemistry; electrocrystallization; gas adsorption; solubility and diffusivity of gases in solids. *Mailing Add:* Nuclear Div Union Carbide Corp Oak Ridge TN 37830

CONDON, JAMES JUSTIN, b New Orleans, La, Apr 15, 45. ASTRONOMY. *Educ:* Cornell Univ, BS, 66, PhD(astron), 72. *Prof Exp:* Fel, Arecibo Observ, 72; res assoc, Nat Radio Astron Observ, 72-74; asst prof, 74-80, ASSOC PROF PHYS, VA POLYTECH INST & STATE UNIV, 80-, ASST SCIENTIST, NAT RADIO ASTRON OBSERV, 77- *Concurrent Pos:* Mem users' comt, Nat Radio Astron Observ, 75-; mem sci adv comt, Nat Astron & Ionosphere Ctr, 77-; fel Alfred P Sloan Found, 77- *Mem:* Am Astron Soc; Int Astron Union; Int Sci Radio Union. *Res:* Extragalactic radio astronomy; radio spectra, optical identifications, structure, variability and evolution of compact sources; radio sources in nearby galaxies; high-redshift 21 cm obsorption lines; low-frequency variable sources. *Mailing Add:* Dept of Physics Va Polytech Inst & State Univ Blacksburg VA 24060

CONDON, MICHAEL EDWARD, b Providence, RI, Jan 17, 45; m 68; c 2. ORGANIC CHEMISTRY. *Educ:* Providence Col, BS, 66; Yale Univ, PhD(org chem), 70. *Prof Exp:* Res staff molecular biophysicist chem, Yale Univ, 70-71, res staff chemist, 71-72; fel, Squibb Inst for Med Res, 72-73, res chemist, 73-77, sr res chemist, 77-81; RES ASSOC AGR CHEM GROUP, FMC CORP, 81- *Mem:* Am Chem Soc. *Res:* Design and synthesis of new pesticides. *Mailing Add:* FMC Corp Agr Chem Group Box 8 Princeton NJ 08540

CONDON, ROBERT EDWARD, b Albany, NY, Aug 13, 29; m 51; c 2. SURGERY, PHYSIOLOGY. *Educ:* Univ Rochester, AB, 51, MD, 57; Univ Wash, MS, 65; Am Bd Surg, dipl, 66. *Prof Exp:* Asst resident & intern, Univ Wash Hosps, Seattle, 57-63, chief resident surg, 63-65, res assoc, Sch Med, Univ Wash, 59-61, instr, 61-65; asst prof, Col Med, Baylor Univ, 65-67; from assoc prof to prof, Col Med, Univ Ill, Chicago, 67-71; prof surg & head dept, Col Med, Univ Iowa, 71-72; PROF SURG, MED COL WIS, 72-, CHMN, DEPT MED, 79- *Concurrent Pos:* Hon clin asst, Royal Free Hosp, London, 63-64; asst chief surg, Vet Admin Hosp, Houston, Tex, 65-67; attend surgeon, Univ Ill Hosp, 67-71; chief surg serv, Univ Iowa Hosp, 71-72 & Vet Admin Hosp, Wood, Wis, 72-80; dir surg, Milwaukee County Med Complex, 79-; chief of surg, Froedtert Mem Lutheran Hosp, 80- *Mem:* Am Col Surg; Soc Univ Surg; Am Surg Asn; Soc Surg Alimentary Tract; Soc Clin Surg. *Res:* Gastric and intestinal physiology; hernia. *Mailing Add:* 8700 W Wisconsin Ave Milwaukee WI 53226

CONDOULIS, WILLIAM V, immunology, developmental biology, see previous edition

CONDOURIS, GEORGE ANTHONY, b Passaic, NJ, Dec 9, 25; m 49; c 5. PHARMACOLOGY. *Educ:* Rutgers Univ, BS, 49; Yale Univ, MS, 53; Cornell Univ, PhD(pharmacol), 55. *Prof Exp:* Instr, Med Col, Cornell Univ, 56-57; vis investr, Rockefeller Inst, 57; from asst prof to assoc prof, 57-67, PROF PHARMACOL, COL MED & DENT NJ, 67-, CHMN DEPT, 72- *Concurrent Pos:* NSF fel, Med Col, Cornell Univ, 54-55; res fel, 55-56. *Mem:* AAAS; Am Soc Pharmacol & Exp Therapeut. *Res:* Pharmacology of the nervous system; biometrics. *Mailing Add:* NJ Med Sch Col of Med & Dent of NJ Newark NJ 07103

CONDRATE, ROBERT ADAM, b Worcester, Mass, Jan 19, 38; m 60; c 3. SOLID STATE CHEMISTRY. *Educ:* Worcester Polytech Inst, BS, 60; Ill Inst Technol, PhD(chem), 66. *Prof Exp:* NSF fel & res assoc chem, Univ Ariz, 66-67; asst prof, 67-71, assoc prof, 71-78, PROF SPECTROS, ALFRED UNIV, 78- *Concurrent Pos:* Finger Lakes grant-in-aid, 69; vis prof, Los Alamos Sci Lab, 72-73; Corning Glass Works Found grant-in-aid, 75-76;

Brockway Glass grant-in-aid, 76-77; ERDA Oil Shale grant, 76-77; Danforth Found Assoc, 76-; vis prof, GTE Sylvania, 80; US Bur Mines grant, 80. *Honors & Awards:* Award, Soc Appl Spectros, 64. *Mem:* AAAS; Am Chem Soc; Soc Appl Spectros; Am Phys Soc; Am Ceramic Soc. *Res:* Application of spectroscopy to elucidate the structure of molecules in solids. *Mailing Add:* Dept of Ceramic Sci Alfred Univ Alfred NY 14802

CONDRAY, BEN ROGERS, b Waco, Tex, July 4, 25; m 51; c 3. ORGANIC CHEMISTRY. *Educ:* Baylor Univ, BS, 48, PhD(org chem), 64; Purdue Univ, MS, 50. *Prof Exp:* From asst prof to assoc prof chem, ETex Baptist Col, 50-55; instr, Baylor Univ, 55-57; assoc prof, 58-65, PROF CHEM, E TEX BAPTIST COL, 65- *Mem:* AAAS; Am Chem Soc. *Res:* Synthesis of organosilicon compounds; separation and identification of natural products; organic-ozone chemistry and stabilities of organic ozonides; charge-transfer complexes; science education. *Mailing Add:* Dept Chem ETex Baptist Col Marshall TX 75670

CONE, CLARENCE DONALD, JR, b Savannah, Ga, Apr 17, 31; m 54; c 2. CELL BIOLOGY, ONCOLOGY. *Educ:* Ga Inst Technol, BChE, 54; Univ Va, MAeronE, 59; Med Col Va, PhD(biophys), 65. Chem engr, Buckeye Cellulose Corp, 54-55; res chemist, Herty Found Lab, 55-57; res aerodynamicist, Nat Adv Comt Aeronaut, 57-59; head hypersonic res, NASA, 59-61, head subsonic theory res, 61-64, res biophysicist, 64-65, head molecular biophys res, 65-72; dir molecular biol lab, Eastern Va Med Authority, 72-74; DIR CELLULAR & MOLECULAR BIOL LAB, VET ADMIN, 75- *Concurrent Pos:* Res assoc, Va Inst Marine Sci, 62-68 & Smithsonian Inst, 64-66; mem, Third Int Cong, Int Tech & Sci Orgn Soaring Flight, 63. *Honors & Awards:* Medal, Except Sci Achievement, NASA, 69. *Mem:* AAAS; Sigma Xi; Tissue Cult Asn; Biophys Soc; Am Soc Microbiol. *Res:* Molecular mechanisms of mitogenesis regulation; cytogenetic regulation; carcinogenesis mechanisms. *Mailing Add:* 104 Harbour Dr Yorktown VA 23690

CONE, CONRAD, b Wellington, NZ, Dec 3, 39; US citizen. ANALYTICAL CHEMISTRY, ORGANIC CHEMISTRY. *Educ:* Bristol Univ, BSc, 62, PhD(org chem), 66. *Prof Exp:* Fel, Mass Inst Technol, 65-68; fac assoc, Univ Tex, Austin, 68-70; asst prof, 70-73, res scientist org chem, 73-77; res chemist, Am Cyanamid Co, 78-79; SR RES CHEMIST, RES & DEVELOP, INTERNATIONAL FLAVORS & FRAGRANCES, 79- *Mem:* Am Chem Soc; Am Soc Mass Spectrometry; The Chem Soc. *Res:* Mass spectrometry of organic compounds; scientific data bases; laboratory computers. *Mailing Add:* Int Flavors & Fragrances Res & Develop 1515 Hwy 36 Union Beach CA 07735

CONE, DONALD R(OY), b Berkeley, Calif, Nov 3, 21; m 43; c 3. ELECTRONIC ENGINEERING. *Educ:* Univ Calif, Berkeley, BS, 43, MS, 51. *Prof Exp:* Engr res & develop, Lawrence Radiation Lab, Univ Calif, Berkeley, 46-52; tech dir, Chromatic TV Labs, 52-56; asst mgr, Litton Indust Elec Display Lab, 57-61; SR RES ENGR, SRI INT, MENLO PARK, 61- *Mem:* Inst Elec & Electronics Engrs; Sci Res Soc Am; Soc Info Display. *Res:* Electromechanical and electron optics; data processing and display. *Mailing Add:* 352 Churchill Ave Palo Alto CA 94301

CONE, EDWARD JACKSON, b Mobile, Ala, Sept 17, 42; m 63; c 2. DRUG METABOLISM. *Educ:* Mobile Col, BS, 67; Univ Ala, PhD(org chem), 71. *Prof Exp:* Lab instr chem, Mobile Col, 65-69; chem, Shell Oil Co, 69-71; instr chem, Univ Ala, 71; fel tobacco chem, Univ Ky, 71-72; CHEMIST, NAT INST DRUG ABUSE ADDICTION RES CTR, 72- *Concurrent Pos:* Asst prof, Sch Pharm, Univ Ky, 75-; consult, NIMH, 78. *Mem:* Int Soc Study Xenobiotics; Am Soc Pharmacol & Exp Therapeut; Am Chem Soc. *Res:* Studies on biotransformation of drugs of abuse in man and other animal species; concomitant development of analytical procedures useful for detection, isolation and quantification of drugs and their metabolites; mechanisms of action of drugs at molecular level. *Mailing Add:* NIDA Addiction Res Ctr PO Box 12390 Lexington KY 40583

CONE, MICHAEL MCKAY, b Washington, DC, Oct 14, 47; m 71. PHYSICAL ORGANIC CHEMISTRY, ORGANIC CHEMISTRY. *Educ:* Princeton Univ, AB, 69; Yale Univ, MPhil, 74, PhD(org chem), 76. *Prof Exp:* Postdoctoral assoc, Cornell Univ, 76-77; res chemist, 77-81, ASST DIV SUPT, E I DU PONT DE NEMOURS & CO INC, 81- *Mem:* Am Chem Soc; AAAS; Sigma Xi. *Res:* Organic chemistry: kinetics and mechanism; homogenous and heterogeneous catalysis; computer applications. *Mailing Add:* E I du Pont de Nemours & Co Inc PO Box 2000 LaPlace LA 70068

CONE, RICHARD ALLEN, b St Paul, Minn, May 23, 36. BIOPHYSICS. *Educ:* Mass Inst Technol, SB, 58; Univ Chicago, SM, 59, PhD(physics), 63. *Prof Exp:* Res assoc biophys, Univ Chicago, 63-64; from instr to asst prof biol, Harvard Univ, 64-69; assoc prof, 69-73, PROF BIOPHYS, JOHNS HOPKINS UNIV, 73- *Concurrent Pos:* USPHS fel, Univ Chicago, 64. *Honors & Awards:* Cole Award, Biophys Soc, 79. *Mem:* Biophys Soc; Soc Study Reprod. *Res:* Mechanism of visual excitation; membrane structure and function; sperm motility and sperm contraceptives. *Mailing Add:* Dept Biophys Johns Hopkins Univ Baltimore MD 21218

CONE, ROBERT EDWARD, b Brooklyn, NY, Aug 18, 43; m 66; c 2. IMMUNOLOGY. *Educ:* Brooklyn Col, BS, 64; Fla State Univ, MS, 67; Univ Mich, Ann Arbor, PhD(microbiol), 70. *Prof Exp:* Fel immunol, Walter & Eliza Hall Inst Med Res, Melbourne, Australia, 71-73; immunol & path mem, Basel Inst Immunol, Switz, 73-74; asst prof, 74-80, ASSOC PROF PATH & SURG, SCH MED, YALE UNIV, 80- *Concurrent Pos:* Damon Runyon Cancer Fund fel, 70; mem, UNESCO. *Mem:* Sigma Xi; AAAS; Am Asn Immunologists; Int Cell Res Orgn. *Res:* Structural and physiological properties of lymphocyte membranes; relationship of membrane structure to lymphocyte function. *Mailing Add:* Dept of Surg Yale Univ Sch of Med New Haven CT 06510

CONE, THOMAS E, JR, b Brooklyn, NY, Aug 15, 15; m 39; c 3. PEDIATRICS. *Educ:* Columbia Univ, BA, 36, MD, 39. *Prof Exp:* Chief pediat serv, US Naval Hosp, Philadelphia, Pa, 49-53; chief pediat serv, Nat Naval Med Ctr, Bethesda, Md, 53-63; chief med out-patient serv & asst dir adolescent unit, 63-73, chief med ambulatory serv & sr assoc med, 67-73, SR ASSOC CLIN GENETICS, CHILDREN'S HOSP MED CTR, 71- *Concurrent Pos:* Sr consult, Children's Hosp, Washington, DC, 53-63; consult, Nat Inst Neurol Dis & Blindness, 58-63; mem nat adv coun, Nat Inst Child Health & Human Develop, 63-64; assoc clin prof pediat, Harvard Med Sch, 63-67, clin prof, 67-; prof pediat, Southwest Med Sch, Univ Tex, Dallas; assoc ed, Pediatrics, 65-74. *Honors & Awards:* Officer, Order Naval Merit, Repub Brazil. *Mem:* AMA; fel Am Acad Pediat; Am Pediat Soc; NY Acad Sci; Am Asn Hist Med. *Res:* Physical growth and development of children; history of pediatrics; clinical pediatrics. *Mailing Add:* 300 Longwood Ave Boston MA 02115

CONE, WYATT WAYNE, b Plains, Mont, Mar 16, 34; m 56; c 3. ENTOMOLOGY. *Educ:* San Diego State Col, AB, 56; Wash State Univ, PhD(entom), 62. *Prof Exp:* From jr entomologist to assoc entomologist, 61-72, ENTOMOLOGIST, WASH STATE UNIV, 72- *Mem:* Entom Soc Am; Entom Soc Can. *Res:* Insecticide effect on predator-prey relationship in mite populations; biology and control of Brachyrhinus weevils on grapes; ecology of arthropods in native grasslands; biology and control of two-spotted spider mites, two-spotted spider mite sex attractant and pheromones. *Mailing Add:* Irrigated Agr Res & Exten Ctr Prosser WA 99350

CONEY, PETER JAMES, b Methewun, Mass. GEOLOGY. *Educ:* Cobly Col, BA, 51; Univ Maine, MS, 53; L'Ecole Nat Superierre Petrole, Paris, Eng, 55; Univ NMex, PhD(geol), 64. *Prof Exp:* Prof & chem geol, Middlebury Col, 64-75; PROF GEOL, UNIV ARIZ, 76- *Concurrent Pos:* Vis prof, Dept Geophysics, Stanford Univ, 70-71; Fulbright prof, Escuela Polytecnica Naz, Ecuador, 73; geologist, US Geol Surv, 75- *Res:* Regional tectonics of mountain systems, particularly the North American Cordillera, in the framework of plate tectonics. *Mailing Add:* Dept Geosci Univ Ariz Tucson AZ 85721

CONFALONE, PAT N, b Fountain Hill, Pa, Oct 6, 45; m 78; c 1. NATURAL PRODUCTS CHEMISTRY. *Educ:* Mass Inst Technol, BS, 67; Harvard Univ, MS, 68, PhD(org chem), 70. *Prof Exp:* Fel, Harvard Univ, 70-71; res fel, Hoffmann-La Roche, 71-81; adj prof, Rutgers Univ, 80; GROUP LEADER, E I DU PONT DE NEMOURS & CO, INC, 81- *Concurrent Pos:* Educ counr, Mass Inst Technol, 78- *Mem:* Am Chem Soc; Sigma Xi. *Res:* The total synthesis of natural products; synthesis of biologically active compounds for development as pharmaceuticals and agricultural chemicals; areas of interest include anti-cancer drugs, vitamins, central nervous system agents, and cardiovascular compounds. *Mailing Add:* Exp Sta Bldg 328 E I du Pont de Nemours & Co Inc Wilmington DE 19898

CONFER, ANTHONY WAYNE, b Hot Springs, Ark, July 29, 47; m 70; c 4. PATHOLOGY, IMMUNOLOGY. *Educ:* Okla State Univ, DVM, 72; Am Col Vet Pathologist, dipl, 77; Ohio State Univ, MS, 74; Univ Mo, Columbia, PhD(immunol), 78. *Prof Exp:* NIH trainee fel, Ohio State Univ, 72-74; pathologist, Armed Forces Inst Path, 74-76; Nat Cancer Inst fel, Univ Mo, 76-78; assoc prof vet path, La State Univ, 78-81; ASSOC PROF VET PATH, OKLA STATE UNIV, 81- *Mem:* Am Col Vet Path; Conf Res Workers Animal Dis; Am Vet Med Asn. *Res:* Activites in pathogenesis and immune respones, particularly cell-mediated, in infectious diseases of domestic animals; bovine pneumonic pasteurellosis. *Mailing Add:* Dept Vet Path Okla State Univ Stillwater OK 74078

CONFER, JOHN L, b Dayton, Ohio, Sept 15, 40. AQUATIC ECOLOGY, POPULATION ECOLOGY. *Educ:* Earlham Col, BA, 62; Wash State Univ, MS, 64; Univ Toronto, PhD(zool), 69. *Prof Exp:* Asst prof zool, Univ Fla, 69-70; asst prof, 70-80, ASSOC PROF, ITHACA COL, 80- *Res:* Phosphorus circulation in lakes; regulation of aquatic populations. *Mailing Add:* Dept of Biol Ithaca Col Ithaca NY 14850

CONGDON, CHARLES C, b Dunkirk, NY, Dec 13, 20; m 47; c 5. PATHOLOGY. *Educ:* Univ Mich, AB, 42, MD, 44, MS, 50. *Prof Exp:* Instr path, Univ Mich, 49-51; vis scientist, Nat Cancer Inst, NIH, 51-52, med officer path, 52-55; sr biologist, Biol Div, Oak Ridge Nat Lab, 55-73; part-time prof, Univ Tenn, Knoxville, 66-73, res prof & asst dir, 73-78, assoc dir, 78-81, PROF MED BIOL, UNIV TENN MEM RES CTR, 78- *Mem:* AAAS; Am Soc Exp Path; Am Asn Cancer Res; Am Asn Path & Bact; Soc Exp Biol & Med. *Res:* Biomedical research administration. *Mailing Add:* Univ of Tenn Mem Res Ctr 1924 Alcoa Hwy Knoxville TN 37920

CONGDON, JUSTIN DANIEL, b Kingston, Pa, Jan 5, 41; m 77. PHYSIOLOGICAL ECOLOGY, EVOLUTIONARY ECOLOGY. *Educ:* Calif State Polytech Univ, BS, 68, MS, 71; Ariz State Univ, PhD(zool), 77. *Prof Exp:* res scholar, Mus Zool, Univ Mich, 76-80; RES ASSOC, SAVANNAH RIVER ECOL LAB, 80- *Mem:* AAAS; Am Soc Naturalists; Am Soc Ichtyologists & Herpetologists; Herpetologists League; Sigma Xi. *Res:* Underlying physiological and ecological processes and adaptations which shape an animal's reproductive strategy; how organisms allocate energy to the compartments of reproduction, growth, storage and maintenance. *Mailing Add:* Savannah River Ecol Lab Drawer E Aiken SC 29801

CONGEL, FRANK JOSEPH, nuclear physics, see previous edition

CONGER, ALAN DOUGLAS, b Muskegon, Mich, Mar 23, 17; m 44; c 4. RADIOBIOLOGY, BIOPHYSICS. *Educ:* Harvard Univ, AB, 40, MA & PhD(biol), 47. *Prof Exp:* Sr res scientist biol, Oak Ridge Nat Lab, USAEC, 47-58; res prof radiobiol, Univ Fla, 58-65; PROF RADIOBIOL & HEAD DEPT, SCH MED, TEMPLE UNIV, 65- *Concurrent Pos:* Fulbright sr res scholar, Radiobiol Res Unit, Med Res Coun, London, Eng, 52-53; USAEC grant nuclear sci, Univ Fla, 58-65; Nat Cancer Inst fel radiobiol, Sch Med,

Temple Univ, 65-; sci proj officer, Oper Greenhouse Atomic Bomb Tests, Marshall Islands, 51-52; assoc ed, Radiation Res, 58-62, Radiation Bot, 61- & Mutation Res, 62-; consult biol, Oak Ridge & Brookhaven Nat Labs, USAEC, 58-; mem radiation study sect, NIH, 63-66; chmn panel low dose report, Nat Acad Sci-Nat Res Coun, 72-73, mem subcomt radiobiol, 72- *Mem:* Genetics Soc Am; Am Soc Nat; Radiation Res Soc (vpres, pres, 71-73). *Res:* Effects of radiation on cells; genetic effects of radiation. *Mailing Add:* Dept of Radiation Biol Temple Univ Sch of Med Philadelphia PA 19140

CONGER, BOB VERNON, b Greeley, Colo, July 2, 38; m 60; c 4. PLANT GENETICS. *Educ:* Colo State Univ, BS, 63; Wash State Univ, PhD(genetics), 67. *Prof Exp:* Asst prof genetics, Wash State Univ, 67-68; from asst prof to assoc prof, Univ Tenn-Dept Energy Comp Animal Res Lab & Dept Plant & Soil Sci, 68-78, PROF PLANT & SOIL SCI, UNIV TENN, KNOXVILLE, 78- *Concurrent Pos:* Ed, Crop Res Coun Rev in Plant Sci, 81- *Mem:* AAAS; Am Soc Agron; Am Genetic Asn; Tissue Cult Asn; Crop Sci Soc Am. *Res:* Mutagenesis and cell and tissue culture in higher plants; cytogenetics and breeding cool season forage grasses. *Mailing Add:* Dept of Plant & Soil Sci Univ of Tenn Knoxville TN 37996

CONGER, KYRIL BAILEY, b Berlin, Ger, Apr 11, 13; US citizen; m 46; c 4. SURGERY. *Educ:* Univ Mich, AB, 33, MD, 36; Am Bd Urol, dipl, 47. *Prof Exp:* Consult urol, US Army Mid Pac Area & Tripler Gen Hosp, Honolulu, 46; PROF UROL & HEAD DEPT, HOSP & MED SCH, TEMPLE UNIV, 47- *Concurrent Pos:* Consult, Vet Admin Hosp, Philadelphia & Mid-Atlantic Area, Vet Admin; attend urologist, St Christopher's Hosp for Children. *Mem:* Am Urol Asn; fel Am Col Surg. *Res:* Urological and prostatic surgery. *Mailing Add:* 3401 N Broad St Philadelphia PA 19148

CONGER, ROBERT PERRIGO, b Youngstown, Ohio, Dec 1, 22; m 48; c 2. PLASTICS CHEMISTRY. *Educ:* Cornell Univ, AB, 43, PhD(chem), 50. *Prof Exp:* Lab asst, Cornell Univ, 43-44, 46-50; instr chem, Col Med, Univ Tenn, 50-51; res chemist, Gen Labs, US Rubber Co, 51-61; mgr res, Congoleum Industs, Inc, 61-78, PRES, CONGER ASSOCS, CONSULTS, 78- *Mem:* AAAS; Am Chem Soc; Soc Plastics Eng. *Res:* Foamed plastics, especially polyvinyl chloride; chemical embossing; clear films of elastomers such as polyvinyl chloride and polyurethane; compounding and modification of various elastomers; water based inks for rotogravure and silk screen printing; special plastisol and water based inks. *Mailing Add:* 87 Oak Ave Park Ridge NJ 07656

CONGLETON, JAMES LEE, b Lexington, Ky, Dec 20, 42; c 2. PHYSIOLOGICAL ECOLOGY, FISHERIES. *Educ:* Univ Ky, BS, 64; Univ Calif, San Diego, PhD(marine biol), 70. *Prof Exp:* NIH fel, Univ Wash, 70-71; biologist aquaculture, Kramer, Chin & Mayo, Inc, 71-75; asst prof fisheries, Univ Wash, 75-80, spec unit asst, Coop Fishery Res Unit, 75-80; ASST LEADER, COOP FISHERY RES UNIT, UNIV IDAHO, 80- *Mem:* Am Fisheries Soc. *Res:* Fish ecology and fishery management. *Mailing Add:* Coop Fisheries Res Unit Dept Fisheries Resources Univ Wash Moscow ID 83843

CONIBEAR, SHIRLEY ANN, b Amboy, Ill, Aug 20, 46; m 75. OCCUPATIONAL MEDICINE, EPIDEMIOLOGY. *Educ:* Shimer Col, BA, 68; Univ Ill, MD, 73, MPH, 76. *Prof Exp:* Dir health hazard eval, Cook County Hosp, 77-79; VPRES, CARNOW, CONIBEAR & ASSOCS, LTD, 77-; DIR OCCUP MED RESIDENCY & ASST PROF, DEPT PREV MED & COMMUNITY HEALTH, MED SCH, UNIV ILL, 79- *Concurrent Pos:* Dir progs occup med, Great Lakes Educ Resource Ctr, Univ Ill, Chicago, 77-; epidemiologist, Argonne Nat Lab, 80-81. *Mem:* Am Col Prev Med; Am Pub Health Asn; AAAS; Am Occup Med Asn; Am Med Women's Asn. *Res:* Clinical epidemiologic studies on groups of workers exposed to toxic materials in the workplace; diagnosis and treatment of patients exposed to toxic materials in the workplace or environment. *Mailing Add:* Univ Ill Med Ctr Box 6998 Chicago IL 60680

CONIGLIARO, PETER JAMES, b Milwaukee, Wis, Jan 27, 42; m 65; c 3. ORGANIC CHEMISTRY, CHEMICAL INSTRUMENTATION. *Educ:* Marquette Univ, BS, 63, MS, 65; Ohio State Univ, PhD(org chem), 67. *Prof Exp:* Res chemist, 68-70, sr res chemist, 70-80, RES MGR, S C JOHNSON & SON, 80- *Mem:* Am Chem Soc. *Res:* Specialized organic analysis; analysis of chemical specialty consumer products. *Mailing Add:* 8731 W Glenwood Dr Glendale WI 53129

CONIGLIO, JOHN GIGLIO, b Tampa, Fla, July 21, 19; m 42; c 3. BIOCHEMISTRY. *Educ:* Furman Univ, BS, 40; Vanderbilt Univ, PhD(biochem), 49. *Prof Exp:* From instr to assoc prof, 51-63, PROF BIOCHEM, SCH MED, VANDERBILT UNIV, 63- *Concurrent Pos:* AEC fel biophys, Colo Med Ctr, 49-50; AEC fel biochem, Sch Med, Vanderbilt Univ, 50-51; assoc ed, Lipids, 69- *Honors & Awards:* Thomas Jefferson Award, Vanderbilt Univ, 78. *Mem:* AAAS; Am Inst Nutrit; Am Oil Chem Soc; Am Soc Biol Chem; Soc Exp Biol & Med. *Res:* Fat absorption and distribution; acetate utilization and fatty acid synthesis; effects of x-irradiation on fat absorption and on fatty acid synthesis; determination and metabolism of essential fatty acids; use of tracers in metabolism; interconversion of fatty acids; lipids in reproductive tissue. *Mailing Add:* Dept of Biochem Vanderbilt Med Sch Nashville TN 37232

CONINE, JAMES WILLIAM, b Newton, Iowa, May 13, 26; m 56; c 4. PHARMACEUTICAL CHEMISTRY. *Educ:* Univ Iowa, BS, 50, MS, 52, PhD(pharmaceut chem), 54. *Prof Exp:* Instr pharm, Univ Iowa, 52-54; PHARMACEUT CHEMIST, ELI LILLY & CO, 54- *Mem:* AAAS; Am Chem Soc; Am Pharmaceut Asn. *Res:* Stability of pharmaceutical products; product development of tablets and capsules. *Mailing Add:* Eli Lilly & Co 307 E McCarty St Indianapolis IN 46206

CONKIE, WILLIAM R, b Ayr, Scotland, Jan 10, 32; m 54; c 2. PHYSICS. *Educ:* Univ Toronto, BASc, 53; McGill Univ, MSc, 54; Univ Sask, PhD, 56. *Prof Exp:* Asst res officer physics, Atomic Energy Can, Ltd, 56-60; PROF PHYSICS, QUEEN'S UNIV, ONT, 60- *Mem:* Am Phys Soc; Can Asn Physicists. *Res:* Theoretical physics. *Mailing Add:* Dept of Physics Queen's Univ Kingston Can

CONKIN, JAMES E, b Glasgow, Ky, Oct 14, 24; m 51; c 4. GEOLOGY, PALEONTOLOGY. *Educ:* Univ Ky, BS, 50; Univ Kans, MS, 53; Univ Cincinnati, PhD(geol), 60. *Prof Exp:* Paleontologist, Union Producing Co Div, United Gas Corp, 53-56; instr geol, Univ Cincinnati, 56-57; from instr to asst prof natural sci, 57-63, assoc prof geol, 63-67, chmn dept, 63-76, PROF GEOL, UNIV LOUISVILLE, 67- *Concurrent Pos:* Fulbright res fel micropaleont, Tasmania, 64-65; mem, Paleont Res Inst. *Mem:* Paleont Soc; fel Geol Soc Am. *Res:* Paleozoic Foraminifera; paleozoic stratigraphy, the Mississippian system and Devonian bone beds. *Mailing Add:* Dept of Geol Univ of Louisville Louisville KY 40292

CONKIN, ROBERT A, b Green City, Mo, Dec 31, 20; m 46; c 1. ANALYTICAL CHEMISTRY, ORGANIC CHEMISTRY. *Educ:* Northeast Mo State Teachers Col, BS, 42, AB, 46. *Prof Exp:* Analyst, Ill, 46-47, lab supvr, 47-50, chief chemist, Ala, 50-53, res chemist, Mo, 53-62, res group leader, 62-72, regist mgr, 72-81, MGR INT REGIST, AGR PROD, MONSANTO CO, 81- *Mem:* Am Chem Soc. *Res:* Development and application of micro-analytical methods and techniques in the field of agricultural pesticide residues in or on farm produce and products; data review and petition preparation for submission to Environmental Protection Agency and other regulatory agencies worldwide. *Mailing Add:* Monsanto Co 800 N Lindbergh Blvd St Louis MO 63166

CONKLIN, DOUGLAS EDGAR, b Waukegan, Ill, June 4, 42; m 2. AQUACULTURE, NUTRITION. *Educ:* Colo State Univ, BS, 64, MS, 66; NY Univ, PhD(biol), 73. *Prof Exp:* Res asst marine nutrit, Haskins Labs, Yale Univ, 66-71; Nat Oceanic & Atmospheric Admin, Southwest Fisheries Ctr, La Jolla, Calif, 71-73; res nutritionist, 73-78, ASSOC DIR AQUACULT, UNIV CALIF, DAVIS, 78-, LECTR ANIMAL SCI, 80- *Concurrent Pos:* Chmn Nutrit Task Force, World Maricult Soc, 78. *Mem:* Sigma Xi; World Maricult Soc. *Res:* Crustacean nutrition of primarily the lobster, Homarus americanus and nutritional requirements of Moina macrocopa. *Mailing Add:* Bodega Marine Lab PO Box 247 Bodega Bay CA 94923

CONKLIN, DWIGHT BURR, b Dryden, NY, Dec 14, 15; m 48; c 6. CHEMISTRY, BIOLOGY. *Educ:* Syracuse Univ, BA, 40, AM, 42. *Prof Exp:* Teaching asst bot, Syracuse Univ, 42-43; res asst biol chem, Univ Iowa, 43-45; bacteriologist & chemist res, Wyandotte Chem, 45-56; SR CHEMIST RES, BETTIS ATOMIC POWER LAB, WESTINGHOUSE ELEC CORP, 56- *Mem:* Am Chem Soc. *Res:* Evaluation of chemical corrosion to materials related to atomic energy power plants and the production of high purity water. *Mailing Add:* 820 Vermont Ave Glassport PA 15045

CONKLIN, GLENN ERNEST, b Lyndon, Kans, June 2, 29; m 57; c 4. PHYSICS. *Educ:* Univ Wichita, BA, 51, MS, 53; Univ Kans, PhD(physics), 61. *Prof Exp:* Mem tech staff physics, Bell Tel Labs, 60-66; res scientist, Singer-Gen Precision, Inc, 66-70; RADIATION PHYSICIST, DIV COMPLIANCE, BUR RADIOL HEALTH, FOOD & DRUG ADMIN, 70- *Mem:* Asn Advan Med Inst. *Res:* Dielectric behavior of plastics at millimeter wavelengths; application of optically pumped nuclear magnetic resonance to communications; nonionizing radiation. *Mailing Add:* Bur of Radiol Health Food & Drug Admin 12721 Twinbrook Pkwy Rockville MD 20857

CONKLIN, JAMES BYRON, JR, b Charlotte, NC, July 29, 37; m 62; c 2. COMPUTING CENTER ADMINISTRATION, COMPUTER SCIENCE. *Educ:* Mass Inst Technol, SB, 59, SM, 61, ScD(solid state physics), 64. *Prof Exp:* Asst prof, Univ Fla, 64-71, assoc prof physics, 71-81, dir ctr instrnl & res comput activ, 75-81; DIR COMPUT FAC, SMITHSONIAN ASTROPHYS OBSERV, 81- *Concurrent Pos:* Assoc dir, Northeast Regional Data Ctr, State Univ Syst Fla, 73-74. *Mem:* AAAS; Am Comput Mach; Am Asn Physics Teachers; Am Phys Soc. *Res:* Computers as instructional tools; numerical mathematics; calculation of energy band structure and related electronic properties of semiconductors. *Mailing Add:* Smithsonian Astrophys Observ 60 Garden St Cambridge MA 02138

CONKLIN, JAMES L, anatomy, see previous edition

CONKLIN, JOHN DOUGLAS, b Middletown, NY, Mar 1, 33; m 59; c 2. BIOPHARMACEUTICS. *Educ:* Col Holy Cross, BSc, 56. *Prof Exp:* From jr res biochemist to res biochemist, 59-65, sr res, Drug Distrib Unit, Biol Res Div, 65-80, UNIT LEADER BIOCHEMIST, BIOPHARMACEUTICS UNIT, DRUG SAFETY DIV, NORWICH-EATON PHARMACEUTICALS, 80- *Mem:* Acad Pharmaceut Sci; Am Pharmaceut Asn. *Res:* The study of the bioavailability of drugs in man and animals by investigating drug absorption, distribution and excretion to optimize drug pharmacologic or therapeutic activity for clinical application. *Mailing Add:* Biopharmaceut Unit Drug Safety Div Norwich-Eaton Pharmaceuticals Norwich NY 13815

CONKLIN, R(OGER) N(ORTON), b Brooklyn, NY, Mar 18, 21; m 47; c 2. CHEMICAL ENGINEERING. *Educ:* Rensselaer Polytech Inst, BChE, 42, MChE, 47. *Prof Exp:* Chemist rubber technol, US Rubber Co, 42-45; instr chem & chem eng, Rensselaer Polytech Inst, 45-47; chemist, 47-55, tech rep, 55-61, tech sales rep, Switz, 61-64, tech rep, 64-71, tech coordr Int Rubber Technol, 71-80, SR TECH REP, E I DU PONT DE NEMOURS & CO, INC, 80- *Mem:* Am Chem Soc. *Res:* Sales development work in rubber field. *Mailing Add:* 3810 Valley Brook Dr Oakwood Hills 2 Hockessin DE 19707

CONKLIN, RICHARD LOUIS, b Rockford, Ill, Dec 9, 23; m 50; c 4. PHYSICAL OPTICS. *Educ:* Univ Ill, BS, 44, MS, 48; Univ Colo, PhD(solid state physics), 57. *Prof Exp:* Jr scientist, Los Alamos Lab, Univ Calif, 44-46; asst physics, Univ Ill, 46-49; asst prof, Huron Col, 49-53; instr, Univ Colo, 53-57; assoc prof, 57-58, PROF PHYSICS, HANOVER COL, 58- *Concurrent Pos:* Vis colleague, Univ Hawaii, 67-68. *Mem:* Am Asn Physics Teachers; Am Phys Soc. *Res:* Electron accelerators and their application to nuclear physics; luminescence of solids. *Mailing Add:* Dept of Physics Hanover Col Hanover IN 47243

CONLAN, JAMES, b San Francisco, Calif, Apr 15, 23; m 46. MATHEMATICS. *Educ:* Univ Calif, BA, 45; Univ Md, PhD(math), 58. *Prof Exp:* Mathematician, Aberdeen Proving Ground, 50-53 & Naval Ord Lab, 53-67; assoc prof math, Howard Univ, 67-68; PROF MATH, UNIV REGINA, 68- *Mem:* Am Math Soc. *Res:* Partial differential equations; fluid mechanics. *Mailing Add:* Dept of Math Univ of Regina Regina Can

CONLEE, ROBERT KEITH, b Los Angeles, Calif, July 28, 42; m 63; c 6. EXERCISE PHYSIOLOGY, EXERCISE SCIENCE. *Educ:* Brigham Young Univ, BS, 69, MS, 70; Univ Iowa, PhD(phys educ), 75. *Prof Exp:* Res fel, Sch Med, Washington Univ, 75-77; asst prof, 77-80, ASSOC PROF, PHYS EDUC, BRIGHAM YOUNG UNIV, 80- *Mem:* Am Col Sports Med; Am Alliance Health Educ Recreation. *Mailing Add:* Human Perf Res 118 Brigham Young Univ Provo UT 84602

CONLEY, BERNARD EDWARD, b Medina, NY, Jan 28, 19; m 45; c 4. PHARMACOLOGY, TOXICOLOGY. *Educ:* Duquesne Univ, BS, 42; Univ Chicago, SM, 51, PhD(pharmacol), 56. *Prof Exp:* Regional chief pharm serv, Vet Admin, Ohio, Mich & Ky, 46-48; admin assoc, AMA, 48-50, secy comt pesticides, 50-59, secy comt toxicol, 55-59, dir toxicol, 59-60; pharmacologist, US Pharmacopeia, 61-64; pharmacologist, Nat Inst Neurol Dis & Blindness, 64-66; chief commun studies prog, Off Pesticides, 66-67, chief air qual criteria, Nat Ctr Air Pollution Control, 67-69, dir grants & contracts rev br, 69-71, CHIEF DRUG UTILIZATION STUDIES, NAT CTR HEALTH SERV RES, USPHS, 71- *Concurrent Pos:* Tech ed, New & Nonofficial Remedies, 48-50; AMA rep, Food Protection Comt & Chem Comt, Nat Res Coun, 50-60; contrib ed, Am J Hosp Pharm, 50-60; mem comt adverse reactions drugs, US Food & Drug Admin, 56-60; sci consult, Nat Asn Practical Nurse Educ Serv, 62-80. *Mem:* AAAS; fel Am Pub Health Asn. *Res:* Biomedical and legal problems of hazardous substances; socio-economic aspects of drug utilization research. *Mailing Add:* Nat Ctr for Health Serv Res Health Resources Admin Bldg Hyattsville MD 20782

CONLEY, CARROLL LOCKARD, b Baltimore, Md, May 14, 15; m 43; c 2. MEDICINE. *Educ:* Johns Hopkins Univ, AB, 35; Columbia Univ, MD, 40. *Prof Exp:* Fel physiol, Univ Md, 36-37; intern & asst med, Presby Hosp, New York, 40-42; asst, 46-47, from instr to assoc prof, 47-56, prof med, 56-76, physician in charge hemat div, 47-80, distinguished serv prof med, 76, EMER PROF MED, SCH MED, JOHNS HOPKINS UNIV, 80- *Concurrent Pos:* Mem hematol study sect, NIH, 52-56, chmn, 62-65; mem comt on blood coagulation, Nat Res Coun, 54-59, mem comt blood related probs, 59-63, mem comt thrombosis & hemorrhage, 61-64, chmn, 62-64; secy anti-anemia preparations adv bd, US Pharmacopoeia, 54-59; hon assoc prof, Guys Hosp Med Sch, London, 57; consult, US Food & Drug Admin, 67-; mem NIH Arthritis & Metab Dis Prog Proj Comt, 67-71; mem, Comt to Rev Life Sci Prog of NASA, Nat Acad Sci, 70; mem sickle cell anemia adv comt, Dept Health, Educ & Welfare, 71-73; consult, US Army, US Vet Admin & USPHS. *Mem:* Am Soc Hemat (pres, 75-76); fel Royal Col Physicians (London); Am Soc Clin Invest; Soc Exp Biol & Med; fel Am Col Physicians. Res. Hematology; blood coagulation; hemoglobin. *Mailing Add:* Dept Med Johns Hopkins Hosp Baltimore MD 21205

CONLEY, CECIL, b Tomahawk, Ky, June 1, 22; m 64. BIOCHEMISTRY, AGRICULTURE. *Educ:* Univ Ky, BS, 48, MS, 50; NC State Col, PhD(biochem), 54. *Prof Exp:* Exten agent, Ky, 55-56; asst res scientist, Clemson Col, 56-63, statistician, Exp Sta, 60-62; chmn dept sci & math, Pembroke State Col, 63-68; prof chem & chmn div sci & math, Livingston Univ, 68-70; prof chem, 70-72, exec dean, 72-75, vpres, 75-78, PROVOST, PALM BEACH JR COL, 78- *Res:* Protein bound iodine; iron and copper requirements; irrigation. *Mailing Add:* 1041 S E Second St Belle Glade FL 33430

CONLEY, CHARLES CAMERON, b Royal Oak, Mich, Sept 26, 33; m 63; c 1. MATHEMATICS. *Educ:* Mass Inst Technol, PhD(math), 61. *Prof Exp:* Asst res scientist, Courant Inst Math Sci, NY Univ, 61-63, temp mem, 63; from asst prof to assoc prof, 63-68, PROF MATH, UNIV WIS-MADISON, 68- *Concurrent Pos:* Consult, NASA, 63-66; prof, Math Res Ctr, Univ Wis, 73-75. *Mem:* Am Math Soc. *Res:* Ordinary differential equations with emphasis on dynamical systems and topological dynamics. *Mailing Add:* Dept of Math Univ of Wis Madison WI 53706

CONLEY, FRANCIS RAYMOND, b Donora, Pa, Feb 11, 16; m 44; c 5. INORGANIC CHEMISTRY. *Educ:* St Bonaventure Univ, BS, 41. *Prof Exp:* Chemist, Ryder Scott Co, 41-43, lab foreman, 43, waterflood engr, 44-47, dir res, 47-51; res engr, Continental Oil Co, 51-55, res group leader, 55, supvr res chemist, 55-59, asst dir prod res, 59-65, dir prod res, 65-67, mgr prod res, 67-80; assoc gen mgr, Res & Develop Dept, Conoco Inc, 80-81; PETROL RECOVERY CONSULT, 81- *Mem:* Marine Technol Soc; Am Inst Mining, Metall & Petrol Engrs; Am Petrol Inst. *Res:* Petroleum secondary recovery; petrophysics reservoir mechanics; fluid flow in porous media; electric and radiation logging; coring; water flooding; production engineering and offshore technology; reservoir geology. *Mailing Add:* Res & Develop Dept Continental Oil Co PO Box 1267 Ponca City OK 74601

CONLEY, HARRY LEE, JR, b Somerset, Ky, June 8, 35; m 58; c 3. PHYSICAL CHEMISTRY. *Educ:* Univ Ky, BS, 57; Univ Calif, Berkeley, MS, 60; Univ Va, PhD(chem), 64. *Prof Exp:* Sr chemist, Res Ctr, Sprague Elec Co, 63-68; from asst prof to assoc prof, 68-77, PROF CHEM, MURRAY STATE UNIV, 77- *Mem:* AAAS; Am Chem Soc. *Res:* Kinetics; electrochemistry; organophosphates; thermodynamics. *Mailing Add:* Dept of Chem Murray State Univ Murray KY 42071

CONLEY, JACK MICHAEL, b Wichita, Kans, Aug 9, 43; m 75. ANALYTICAL CHEMISTRY. *Educ:* Colo Sch Mines, MEC, 69; Univ Ill, MS, 72, PhD(anal chem), 75. *Prof Exp:* Teaching asst chem, Univ Ill, 69-72, res asst, 72-74; res scientist chem, Res & Develop Div, Union Camp Corp, 74-80; MEM STAFF, AM CYANAMID, 80- *Mem:* AAAS; Am Chem Soc. *Res:* Applied research in analysis of products from pulp and paper industry. *Mailing Add:* Am Cyanamid PO Box 0400 Princeton NJ 08540

CONLEY, JAMES FRANKLIN, b Forest City, NC, Dec 28, 31; m 54; c 3. GEOLOGY. *Educ:* Berea Col, AB, 54; Ohio State Univ, MS, 56. *Prof Exp:* Geologist, NC Div Mineral Resources, 56-65; GEOLOGIST, VA DIV MINERAL RESOURCES, 65- *Mem:* Fel Geol Soc Am; Am Inst Mining, Metall & Petrol Engrs; Am Inst Prof Geologists. *Res:* Geologic mapping in central and southern Virginia Piedmont. *Mailing Add:* 1614 Trailridge Rd Charlottesville VA 22903

CONLEY, ROBERT T, b Summit, NJ, Dec 27, 31; m 55; c 3. ORGANIC CHEMISTRY, POLYMER CHEMISTRY. *Educ:* Seton Hall Univ, BS, 53; Princeton Univ, MA, 55, PhD(chem), 57. *Prof Exp:* Asst prof chem, Canisius Col, 56-61; from asst prof to prof, Seton Hall Univ, 61-67; chmn dept chem, Wright State Univ, 67-68, dean col sci & eng, 68-77, prof chem, 67-77, vpres planning & develop, 74-77; pres, Seton Hall Univ, 77-79; PRES, CMG MGT GROUP, 80- *Concurrent Pos:* Consult, Carborundum Co. *Mem:* AAAS; Am Chem Soc. *Res:* Thermal stability of polymers; molecular rearrangements; reaction mechanisms; synthesis of compounds of pharmacological activity; synthetic methods in alicyclic systems; infrared spectroscopy. *Mailing Add:* 162 Kline Blvd Berkeley Heights NJ 07922

CONLEY, VERONICA LUCEY, b Taunton, Mass, July 13, 19; m 45; c 4. PUBLIC HEALTH. *Educ:* Boston Univ, AB, 40; Yale Univ, MSN, 43; Univ Chicago, MA, 53, PhD(sci educ), 59. *Prof Exp:* Instr nursing, Ohio State Univ, 46-48; secy comt cosmetics, AMA, 48-60, dir dept nursing, 60-62; exec dir, Nat Asn Practical Nurse Educ & Serv, Inc, 62-65; chief allied health sect, Div Regional Med Progs, Pub Health Serv, 67-73, CHIEF, OFF OF COMT & REV ACTIVITIES, NAT CANCER INST, 73- *Concurrent Pos:* Ed monthly series, Today's Health Mag, 52-58; exec ed, J Practical Nursing, 62-80. *Mem:* AAAS; affil mem AMA. *Res:* Special problems of health education through mass media in field of biochemistry and physiology; medical aspects of the skin; nursing and administration. *Mailing Add:* 14706 Crossway Rd Rockville MD 20853

CONLEY, WELD E, b Naples, NY, Aug 22, 11; m 43; c 3. MECHANICAL ENGINEERING. *Educ:* Univ Rochester, BS, 33, MS, 34. *Prof Exp:* Chief engr, Thermal Eng Corp, 40-41; engr, Naval Ord Lab, 41-43, prin ord engr, 43-45; res engr, Rex Chainbelt Co, 45-53, chief develop engr, 53-55, mgr, Res & Develop Ctr, 55-61; tech dir, Votator Div, Chemetron Corp, 61-62, dir res, 62-63, mgr drying & sterilizing equip, 63-76; CONSULT ENGR, FOOD PROCESSING INDUST, 76- *Concurrent Pos:* Dir, Res & Develop Assocs, 54-62, vpres, 57-59, pres, 59-60, vchmn bd, 60-61, chmn bd, 61-62; tech consult, Food Processing Indust, 76- *Mem:* Inst Food Technologists; Nat Soc Prof Engrs; Am Soc Heating, Refrig & Airconditioning Engrs; Am Soc Mech Engrs. *Res:* Development of processes and equipment for food canning and dehydration; development of underwater ordnance. *Mailing Add:* 1804 Corona Ct Louisville KY 40222

CONLIN, BERNARD JOSEPH, b Columbus, Wis, Mar 15, 35; m 65; c 1. DAIRY SCIENCE, ANIMAL BREEDING. *Educ:* Univ Wis, BS, 57, MS, 63; Univ Minn, PhD(dairy sci), 66. *Prof Exp:* 4-H Club exten agent, Agr Exten Serv, Univ Wis, 57-58; prom dir, E Cent Breeders Coop, 58-60; res asst dairy sci, Univ Wis, 60-61, exten dairy specialist, 61-62, res asst dairy sci, 62; res asst dairy husb, 62-66, from asst prof to assoc prof, 66-71, exten dairyman, 66-78, PROF ANIMAL SCI, UNIV MINN, ST PAUL, 71-, PROG LEADER AGR, 78-, DIR COMPUT APPLICATIONS, 80- *Concurrent Pos:* Consult, US Agency Int Develop to Tunisia, 78. *Mem:* Am Dairy Sci Soc; Holstein-Friesian Asn Am. *Res:* Relative merits of inbred and non-inbred sires for use in artificial insemination and uniformity of their sire families. *Mailing Add:* Univ of Minn Haecker Hall St Paul MN 55101

CONLON, DANIEL R, b Brockton, Mass, Sept 20, 12; m 40; c 5. CHEMISTRY, INSTRUMENTATION. *Educ:* Union Col, BS, 35. *Prof Exp:* Res chemist phys chem, Atlantic Refining Co, 35-45; sr scientist, Rohm and Haas Co, 45-52, sr scientist instrumentation, 52-57; PRES, INSTRUMENTS FOR RES & INDUST, 57- *Mem:* Am Chem Soc; Instrument Soc Am. *Res:* Development of instruments to detect toxic gases, and for research and plant operations; design and manufacture of safety products for laboratory sciences and instruments for automatizing tedious laboratory tasks; design and manufacture of other devices that facilitate laboratory work in fields of chemistry and biochemistry. *Mailing Add:* 108 Franklin Ave Cheltenham PA 19012

CONLY, JOHN F, b Ridley Park, Pa, Sept 11, 33. ENGINEERING. *Educ:* Univ Pa, BS, 56, MS, 58; Columbia Univ, PhD(eng mech), 62. *Prof Exp:* Res asst eng mech, Columbia Univ, 60-62; from asst prof to assoc prof, 62-69, PROF AEROSPACE ENG, SAN DIEGO STATE COL, 69-, CHMN DEPT, 71- *Concurrent Pos:* Nat Sci Found res grant, 63- *Mem:* Am Inst Aeronaut & Astronaut; Am Soc Eng Educ. *Res:* Fluid and engineering mechanics. *Mailing Add:* Dept of Aerospace Eng & Eng Mech San Diego State Univ San Diego CA 92182

CONN, ARTHUR L(EONARD), b New York, NY, April 5, 13; m 37, 72; c 3. CHEMICAL ENGINEERING, SCIENCE & TECHNOLOGY. *Educ:* Mass Inst Technol, SB, 34, SM, 35. *Prof Exp:* Asst dir Boston Sta, Sch Chem Eng Practice, Mass Inst Technol, 35-36; asst to dir res, Blaw-Knox Co, Pittsburgh, 36; exp chemist, Alco Prods Div, Am Locomotive Co, NY, 36-39; chem engr, Standard Oil Co, Ind, 39-43, group leader in charge Manhattan Proj work, 43-45, sect leader, 45-50, dir pilot plant div, 50-55, dir process div, 55-59, supt tech serv, 59-60, dir process develop, Am Oil Co, 60-62, coordr processes eng & admin, 62-64, sr consult engr, 64-67, dir govt contracts, 67-78; PRES, ARTHUR L CONN & ASSOCS LTD, 78- *Concurrent Pos:* Consult, Off Coal Res, US Dept Interior, 69-75, Energy Res & Develop Admin & Dept Energy, 75-78; consult & chmn adv comt on coal res, City Col, City Univ New York, 72-; chmn panel refining of coal & shale liquids, Nat Acad Eng, 77-80. *Mem:* Fel AAAS; Am Chem Soc; fel Am Inst Chem Engrs (vpres, 69, pres, 70). *Res:* Petroleum process development; pilot plant operation; process design and economics; plant startup; fluid catalytic cracking, hydrocracking and synthetic fuels from oil shale and coal; ultraforming; process development in petroleum field; scale up of pilot plant results to commercial; science and technology of fossil fuels; pilot plant technology. *Mailing Add:* 1469 East Park Pl Chicago IL 60637

CONN, ERIC EDWARD, b Berthoud, Colo, Jan 6, 23; m 59; c 2. BIOCHEMISTRY. *Educ:* Univ Colo, AB, 44; Univ Chicago, PhD(biochem), 50. *Prof Exp:* Chemist, Manhattan Dist, 44-46; instr biochem, Univ Chicago, 50-52; plant nutrit & jr plant physiologist, Exp Sta, Univ Calif, Berkeley, 52-53, lectr & asst plant physiologist, 53-54, asst prof plant biochem & asst plant biochemist, 54-58; assoc prof & assoc biochemist, 58-63, head dept biochem & biophys, 63-66, PROF BIOCHEM, UNIV CALIF, DAVIS, 63- *Concurrent Pos:* NIH sr res fel, 60, mem, USPHS Fel Rev Panel for Biochem Nutrit, 63-66; Fulbright scholar, NZ, 65-66; ed, Arch Biochem & Biophys, 72-, Plant Physiol, 80 & Phytochem, 80- *Mem:* Am Soc Biol Chem; Am Soc Plant Physiol; Brit Biochem Soc; Phytochem Soc NAm. *Res:* Plant enzymes; intermediary metabolism of secondary plant products; cyanogenic glycosides. *Mailing Add:* Dept Biochem Univ Calif Davis CA 95616

CONN, HAROLD O, b Newark, NJ, Nov 16, 25; m 51. INTERNAL MEDICINE. *Educ:* Univ Mich, BS, 46, MD, 50; Am Bd Internal Med, dipl, cert gastroenterol. *Prof Exp:* Intern, Johns Hopkins Hosp, 50-51; asst resident physician, Grace New Haven Community Hosp, 51-52, chief resident physician, 55-56; from instr to assoc prof, 55-71, PROF INTERNAL MED, SCH MED, YALE UNIV, 71- *Concurrent Pos:* Browne res fel, Sch Med, Yale Univ, 52-53; dir med ed, Middlesex Mem Hosp, 56-57; clin investr, Vet Admin Hosp, West Haven, 57-60, actg chief med serv, 59-60, chief, Hepatic Res Lab, 60-; counr, Am Asn Study Liver Dis, 67-, vpres elect, 71, vpres, 72, pres, 73; vis prof, Sch Med, Wash Univ, 68-69; mem med sch coun, Yale Univ Sch Med, 70; assoc ed, Gastroenterology, 73-77; dir Am Gastroenterol Asn-NIH Workshop Diag Tech Hepatobiliary Dis, 78. *Honors & Awards:* William Beaumont Award Excellence in Clin Res, 74. *Mem:* Am Fedn Clin Res; Am Soc Clin Invest; Asn Am Physicians; Sydenham Soc (secy, 65-); Am Gastroenterol Asn. *Res:* Clinical management of liver disease; treatment of hepatic coma, esophageal varices and ammonia metabolism; abnormalities of protein metabolism. *Mailing Add:* Yale Univ Sch of Med 333 Cedar St New Haven CT 06510

CONN, JAMES FREDERICK, b Osborne, Kans, July 2, 24; m 48; c 2. CEREAL CHEMISTRY. *Educ:* Kans State Univ, BS, 48, MS, 49. *Prof Exp:* Wheat qual chemist, Int Multifoods Co, 49-57; sr res chemist, 57-66, res specialist, 66-78, SR RES SPECIALIST, CHEM LEAVENING CHEESE EMULSIFICATION RES, MONSANTO CO, 78- *Mem:* Am Asn Cereal Chemists; Inst Food Technologists; Sigma Xi. *Res:* Determining the functions of ortho-, pyro- and polyphosphates in chemical leavening, process cheese and processed meat with particular interest in the interactions with other ingredients and the rheological effects. *Mailing Add:* Monsanto Co 800 N Lindbergh Blvd St Louis MO 63166

CONN, JEROME W, b New York, NY, Sept 24, 07; m; c 2. MEDICINE. *Educ:* Univ Mich, MD, 32. *Hon Degrees:* DSc, Rutgers Univ, 64; Univ Turin, MD, 75. *Prof Exp:* From instr to prof internal med, 35-68, Louis Harry Newburgh Univ Prof med, 68-74, consult clin invest, Dept Internal Med, 74-76, EMER DISTINGUISHED UNIV PROF INTERNAL MED, MED SCH, UNIV MICH, ANN ARBOR, 74- *Concurrent Pos:* Distinguished physician, Vet Admin, 73-76. *Honors & Awards:* Mod Med Mag Award, 57; Bernard Medal, Univ Montreal, 57; Banting Medal, Am Diabetes Asn, 58 & Banting Mem Award, 63; Henry Russell Lectr Award, Univ Mich, 61; Wilson Medal, Am Clin & Climat Asn, 62; Gairdner Found Int Prize, 65; Phillips Mem Award, Am Col Physicians, 65; Howard Taylor Award, Am Therapeut Soc, 67; Ruth Gray Mem Medal, Evanston Hosp, 68; Stouffer Int Prize, 69; Gold Medal, Int Soc Progress Internal Med, 69; Heath Med Award & Medal, Univ Tex, Houston, 71; Award, Am Col Nutrit, 73. *Mem:* Nat Acad Sci; Nat Inst Med; Asn Am Physicians; Am Diabetes Asn (pres, 62-63, first vpres, 61, 2nd vpres, 60); hon fel Am Col Surgeons. *Res:* Human nutrition; normal metabolism; disorders of metabolism; endocrinology. *Mailing Add:* 2369 Gulf Shore Blvd N Naples FL 33940

CONN, P MICHAEL, b Oil City, Pa, May 12, 49. ENDOCRINOLOGY, CELL BIOLOGY. *Educ:* Univ Mich, BS & CEd, 71; NC State Univ, MS, 73; Baylor Col Med, PhD(cell biol), 76. *Prof Exp:* Fel endocrinol, NIH, 76-78; asst prof, 78-82, ASSOC PROF PHARMACOL, DUKE UNIV MED CTR, 82- *Concurrent Pos:* Sr fel aging, Ctr Study Aging & Human Develop, 78; res career develop award, NIH, 80. *Mem:* Endocrine Soc; Am Soc Cell Biol; Soc Study Reprod. *Res:* Mechanism of action of gonadotropin releasing hormone; mechanism of hormone action; molecular and cell biology of endocrine cells. *Mailing Add:* Dept Pharmacol Box 3813 Duke Univ Med Ctr Durham NC 27710

CONN, PAUL JOSEPH, b Kalispell, Mont, May 17, 40; m 61; c 3. PHYSICAL CHEMISTRY. *Educ:* Univ Calif, Davis, BS, 62; Univ Ore, MS, 64, PhD(phys chem), 66. *Prof Exp:* staff res chemist, 64-80, SR STAFF RES CHEMIST, SHELL DEVELOP CO, 80- *Concurrent Pos:* Exchange scientist, Koninklijke/Shell Lab, Amsterdam, 77-78. *Mem:* Am Chem Soc; Catalysis Soc. *Res:* Heterogeneous catalysis, preparation and characterization of catalysts, catalytic kinetics and mechanism. *Mailing Add:* 1414 Scenic Ridge Houston TX 77043

CONN, PAUL KOHLER, b Akron, Ohio, July 25, 29; m 54; c 3. MATERIALS SCIENCE. *Educ:* Kenyon Col, AB, 51; Kans State Univ, MS, 53, PhD(phys chem), 56. *Prof Exp:* Sr engr & prin engr, Aircraft Nuclear Propulsion Dept, Gen Elec Co, 55-61, supvr chem res, Nuclear Mat & Propulsion Oper, 61-64, unit mgr, Solid State Chem Res, 64-69; prin scientist & assoc dir advan mat res, 69-78, staff prin scientist, High Energy Lasers, 78-80, CHIEF ENGR MAT & CHEM, BELL AEROSPACE CO, TEXTRON INC, 80-, DIR, ENG LAB & TEST, 80- *Mem:* Am Chem Soc. *Res:* High temperature materials and coatings; solid state chemistry, including kinetics, diffusion, fission product transport processes; gas-solid reactions; hot atom chemistry; radiation effects in materials; viscoelastic composite materials; organic coatings. *Mailing Add:* 4682 W Park Dr Lewiston NY 14092

CONN, REX BOLAND, b Marengo, Iowa, Aug 3, 27; m 50; c 3. MEDICINE, CLINICAL PATHOLOGY. *Educ:* Iowa State Univ, BS, 49; Yale Univ, MD, 53; Oxford Univ, BSc, 55; Univ Minn, Minneapolis, MS, 60. *Prof Exp:* Instr lab med, Univ Minn, Minneapolis, 60; asst prof med, WVa Univ, 60-61, from asst prof to prof, 61-68; prof lab med & dir subdept lab med, Johns Hopkins Univ, 68-77; PROF PATH & LAB MED, EMORY UNIV & DIR CLIN LABS, EMORY UNIV HOSP, 77- *Concurrent Pos:* Mem path study sect, NIH, 68-72, mem path training comt, 72-73; mem comt chem path, Am Bd Path, 74-80; mem bd dirs, Am Soc Clin Path, 75-81. *Mem:* Fel Am Soc Clin Path; fel Col Am Path; Am Asn Pathologists; Am Fedn Clin Res; Acad Clin Lab Physicians & Scientists (pres, 72-73). *Res:* Creatine metabolism; methods in clinical chemistry. *Mailing Add:* Dept Path & Lab Med Emory Univ Sch Med Atlanta GA 30322

CONN, RICHARD LESLIE, b Watseka, Ill, Mar 14, 47; m 68; c 2. WEED SCIENCE, AGRONOMY. *Educ:* Univ Ill, BS, 69, MS, 70. *Prof Exp:* Regulatory specialist, 70-76, SR REGULATORY SPECIALIST PESTICIDE REGULATIONS, AGR DIV, CIBA-GEIGY CORP, 77- *Mem:* Weed Sci Soc Am. *Res:* Herbicides; evaluation of chemicals affecting food production. *Mailing Add:* Agr Div Ciba-Geigy Corp PO Box 11422 Greensboro NC 27409

CONN, ROBERT WILLIAM, b Brooklyn, NY, Dec 1, 42; m 73; c 2. PLASMA PHYSICS, NUCLEAR ENGINEERING. *Educ:* Pratt Inst, BS, 64; Calif Inst Technol, MS, 65, PhD(eng sci), 68. *Prof Exp:* Res assoc reactor physics, Brookhaven Nat Lab, 69-70; assoc prof, 72-75, PROF NUCLEAR ENG, UNIV WIS-MADISON, 75-, DIR FUSION RES PROG, 74- *Concurrent Pos:* NSF Fel, Euratom Community Ctr for Res, Ispra, Italy, 68-69; consult, Defense & Space Systs Div, TRW, Inc, 76-, McDonnell-Douglas Astronaut Co, 75- & Sandia Labs, 76-; Romnes fac fel, Univ Wis, 77. *Mem:* Am Nuclear Soc; Am Phys Soc. *Res:* Fusion reactor design and technology; plasma physics; neutron transport theory and methods for fusion and fission reactors; chemical physics, specifically molecular collision theory. *Mailing Add:* Dept of Nuclear Eng 1500 Johnson Dr Madison WI 53706

CONNALLY, GEORGE GORDON, geology, stratigraphy, see previous edition

CONNAMACHER, ROBERT HENLE, b Newark, NJ, Dec 20, 33; m 66; c 4. PHARMACOLOGY. *Educ:* Oberlin Col, AB, 55; NY Univ, MS, 59; George Washington Univ, PhD(pharmacol), 66. *Prof Exp:* From instr to asst prof, 67-73, ASSOC PROF PHARMACOL, SCH MED, UNIV PITTSBURGH, 73- *Concurrent Pos:* Fel molecular biol, Sch Med, Univ Pittsburgh, 66-67. *Mem:* Am Soc Microbiol; Biophys Soc; AAAS; NY Acad Sci; Fedn Am Sci. *Res:* Mechanism of action of antibiotics and biochemical mechanisms of adaptation, especially protein synthesis inhibitors, using tetracycline as the model drug. *Mailing Add:* Dept Pharmacol 627 Scaife Hall Univ Pittsburgh Sch Med Pittsburgh PA 15261

CONNAR, RICHARD GRIGSBY, b Zanesville, Ohio, Jan 11, 20; m 46; c 3. THORACIC SURGERY, CARDIOVASCULAR SURGERY. *Educ:* Duke Univ, AB, 41, MD, 44. *Prof Exp:* Intern & asst resident internal med, Duke Univ Hosp, 44-46, asst resident & resident surg, 48-53, from instr to asst prof, Sch Med, 50-55; CHMN DEPT SURG, TAMPA GEN HOSP, 55-68, 70-; prof surg, 68-74, CLIN PROF SURG, COL MED, UNIV SFLA, 74-, CHIEF SECT THORACIC & CARDIOVASC SURG, 74- *Concurrent Pos:* Chief thoracic surg sect, Vet Admin Hosp, 53-55; thoracic & cardiovasc surgeon, St Josephs Hosp, 55; consult, MacDill AFB Hosp; chmn, Duke Univ Nat Coun, 70-71; mem med adv comt, Col Med, Univ SFla, 70-; deleg, AMA, 71-, mem coun med educ, 74-; mem liaison comt grad med educ, 74- *Mem:* Am Col Surg; Am Asn Thoracic Surg; Soc Vascular Surg; Int Cardiovasc Soc; Am Col Chest Physicians. *Res:* Vascular and esophageal reconstruction; dermal transplants; veratrum derivatives and hypertension; cardiac surgery. *Mailing Add:* 3305 Jean Circle Tampa FL 33609

CONNELL, ALASTAIR MCCRAE, b Glasgow, Scotland, Dec 21, 29; div; c 5. GASTROENTEROLOGY. *Educ:* Univ Glasgow, BSc, 51, MB, ChB, 54, MD, 69; FRCP, 72; FACP, 73. *Prof Exp:* House physician, Stobhill Gen Hosp & house surgeon, Univ Dept Surg, Western Infirmary, Glasgow, 54-55; clin & res asst, Cent Middlesex Hosp, London, 57-60; mem sci staff, Med Res Coun Gastroenterol, Cent Middlesex Hosp & St Mark's Hosp London, 61-64; sr lectr clin sci, Queen's Univ, Belfast, 64-70; assoc dean, Col Med, Univ Cincinnati, 75-77, Mark Brown prof med & physiol & dir, Div Digestive Dis, 70-79; PROF INTERNAL MED & DEAN COL MED, MED CTR, UNIV NEBR, 79- *Concurrent Pos:* Consult physician, Northern Ireland Hosp Authority, Royal Victoria Hosp & SBelfast Hosp, Belfast, 64-70; attend physician, Cincinnati Gen Hosp, Ohio, 70-79; chief clinician, Div Digestive Dis, Med Ctr, Univ Cincinnati, 70-79; consult, Vet Admin Hosp, Cincinnati, 70-79 & Jewish Hosp, Cincinnati, 73-79. *Mem:* Brit Soc Gastroenterol; Am Gastroenterol Asn; Am Fedn Clin Res; Am Soc Digestive Endoscopy; Am Asn Study Liver Dis. *Res:* Motility of gastrointestinal tract; role of gastrointestinal hormones in control of motor activity; assessment of therapy of gastrointestinal disease; nutritional factors in pathogenesis of gastrointestinal disease. *Mailing Add:* Dean Col Med Univ Nebr Med Ctr Omaha NE 68105

CONNELL, CAROLYN JOANNE, b Indianapolis, Ind; c 2. ENDOCRINOLOGY, CELL BIOLOGY. *Educ:* Ind Univ, MS, 68, PhD(zool), 70. *Prof Exp:* Fel anat, Stanford Univ Med Sch, 70-71 & Temple Univ Med Sch, 71-72; staff res scientist cell biol, Stanford Res Inst, 72-75; asst res reproductive endocrinol, Univ Calif Med Sch, 75-78, asst prof, 78-79; ASSOC PROF ANAT, COLO STATE UNIV, 79- *Concurrent Pos:* Prin investr, NIH grant, 75-83. *Mem:* Am Soc Cell Biologists; Asn Women Sci; AAAS; Am Asn Anatomists; Am Soc Androl. *Res:* Role that peptide and steroid hormones play as provocateurs of differentiation of the interstitial and tubular cells of the testis as reflected by intramembranous and intercellular specializations; author or coauthor of numerous publications. *Mailing Add:* Dept Anat Col Vet Med & Biomed Sci Colo State Univ Fort Collins CO 80523

CONNELL, GEORGE EDWARD, b Saskatoon, Sask, June 20, 30; m 55; c 4. BIOCHEMISTRY. *Educ:* Univ Toronto, BA, 51, PhD(biochem), 55. *Prof Exp:* Nat Res Coun Can fel, 55-56; Nat Acad Sci-Nat Res Coun fel biochem, Sch Med, NY Univ, 56-57; from asst prof to assoc prof biochem, Univ Toronto, 57-65, prof & chmn dept, 65-70, assoc dean fac med, 72-74, vpres, 74-77; PRES, UNIV WESTERN ONT, 77- *Concurrent Pos:* Mem, Med Res Coun Can, 66-70; mem, Ont Coun Health, 78-; chmn, Coun Ont Univs, 81- *Mem:* Am Soc Human Genetics; Can Biochem Soc (pres, 73-74); fel Chem Inst Can; Royal Soc Can; Can Arthritis & Rheumatism Soc. *Res:* Protein chemistry; enzymology; immunochemistry; chemistry of human plasma proteins. *Mailing Add:* Univ Western Ont London ON N6A 5B8 Can

CONNELL, JAMES FREDERICK LOUIS, b Baltimore, Md, June 25, 20; m 43; c 1. GEOLOGY. *Educ:* La State Univ, BS, 49; Univ Okla, MS, 51, PhD, 55. *Prof Exp:* Mus preparator, Univ Okla, 49-51, instr geol, 51-53; asst prof, La Polytech Inst, 53-56; assoc prof, Univ Southern Miss, 56-57, State Univ NY, 57-58 & Univ Southwestern La, 58-62; acad marshall, 65-81, PROF GEOL, UNIV MONTEVALLO, 62- *Concurrent Pos:* Consult geologist, 62- *Mem:* AAAS; Paleont Res Inst; Am Inst Prof Geol; Am Asn Petrol Geol; Paleont Soc. *Res:* Appalachian and Gulf Coastal Plain stratigraphy and paleontology; Pennsylvanian flora of Alabama. *Mailing Add:* Drawer B Univ of Montevallo Montevallo AL 35115

CONNELL, JOSEPH H, b Gary, Ind, Oct 5, 23; m 54; c 4. POPULATION BIOLOGY. *Educ:* Univ Chicago, BS, 46; Univ Calif, MA, 53; Glasgow Univ, PhD(zool), 56. *Prof Exp:* Res assoc marine biol, Woods Hole Oceanog Inst, 55-56; prof zool, 56-80, PROF POP ECOL, UNIV CALIF, SANTA BARBARA, 80- *Concurrent Pos:* Guggenheim fel, 62-63, 71-72. *Honors & Awards:* Mercer Award, Ecol Soc Am, 63. *Mem:* AAAS; Am Soc Limnol & Oceanog; Brit Ecol Soc; Ecol Soc Am; Am Soc Naturalists. *Res:* Community ecology, especially succession and species diversity of tropical rain forests and coral reefs; population and community ecology of marine intertidal organisms, particularly predation, competition and spatial distribution. *Mailing Add:* Dept of Biol Sci Univ of Calif Santa Barbara CA 93106

CONNELL, LOUIS FRED, JR, b Honey Grove, Tex, June 25, 14; m 38; c 3. PHYSICS. *Educ:* Tex Col Arts & Indust, BA, 34; Univ Tex, MA, 36, PhD(physics), 48. *Prof Exp:* Teacher high schs, Tex, 34-37; from instr to asst prof physics, N Tex State Univ, 37-42; asst prof physics, Univ Tex, 47-51, mathematician, Mil Physics Lab, 48-51; prof, 51-75, dir dept, 51-69, EMER PROF PHYSICS, NORTH TEX STATE UNIV, 75- *Mem:* Am Asn Physics Teachers; Acoustical Soc Am; Am Phys Soc. *Res:* Electron diffraction; x-rays and crystal structure; electrical properties of semiconductors; acoustics and noise. *Mailing Add:* 924 Ridgecrest Circle Denton TX 76201

CONNELL, RICHARD ALLEN, b Lincoln, Nebr, Oct 31, 29; m 56; c 2. PHYSICS. *Educ:* Nebr Wesleyan Univ, BA, 51; Northwestern Univ, PhD, 57. *Prof Exp:* Asst gaseous discharges, Northwestern Univ, 51-54, low temperature solid state, 54-57; assoc physicist superconductivity, Res Lab, Int Bus Mach Corp, 57-59, proj physicist, 59-62, prof engr, 62-63; sr physicist, Midwest Res Lab, 62-67; sr physicist, 67-70, MGR MAT SCI GROUP, PITNEY-BOWES, INC, 70- *Mem:* Am Phys Soc; Sigma Xi. *Res:* Superconductivity; thin film physics; biophysics; photoconductivity; electrophotography. *Mailing Add:* Pitney-Bowes Inc Walnut & Pacific St Stamford CT 06903

CONNELL, ROSEMARY, b St Louis, Mo, Jan 31, 22. PHYSIOLOGY. *Educ:* Fontbonne Col, BS, 53; Univ Notre Dame, MS, 61, PhD(biol), 65. *Prof Exp:* Secondary teacher, St Joseph's Acad, 53-61 & Little Flower High Sch, 61-62; from instr to asst prof, 65-71, chmn dept biol, 66-72, assoc prof, 71-75, assoc prof life sci, 75-78, PROF LIFE SCI & CHMN DEPT, FONTBONNE COL, 78- *Concurrent Pos:* Assoc prof biol, Maryville Col, 74-75. *Mem:* Asn Midwest Col Biol Teachers; Inst Theol Encounter with Sci & Technol; Transplantation Soc; Exp Hemat Soc. *Res:* Radiation treatment and physiology; hematology. *Mailing Add:* 6800 Wydown St Louis MO 63105

CONNELL, WALTER FORD, b Kingston, Ont, Aug 24, 06; m 33; c 3. INTERNAL MEDICINE, CARDIOLOGY. *Educ:* Queen's Univ, Ont, MD & CM, 29; FRCP; FRCPS(C). *Hon Degrees:* LLD, Queen's Univ, Ont, 73. *Prof Exp:* Dir cardiol, Kingston Gen Hosp, 33-68; prof, 43-76, EMER PROF MED, QUEEN'S UNIV, ONT, 76- *Concurrent Pos:* Mem coun arteriosclerosis, Am Heart Asn. *Mem:* Am Heart Asn; Can Heart Asn. *Res:* Coronary heart disease. *Mailing Add:* 11 Arch St Kingston ON K7L 3N6 Can

CONNELL-TATUM, ELIZABETH BISHOP, b Springfield, Mass, Oct 17, 25; m 80; c 6. OBSTETRICS & GYNECOLOGY. *Educ:* Univ Pa, AB, 47, MD, 51; Am Bd Obstet & Gynec, dipl, 65. *Prof Exp:* Intern, Lankenau Hosp, Philadelphia, Pa, 51-52, resident path & anesthesia, 52-53; gen pract & anesthetist, Maine, 53-58; resident gynec, Grad Hosp, Univ Pa, 58-60; resident obstet, Mt Sinai Hosp, New York, 60-61; assoc prof obstet & gynec, NY Med Col, 62-69; assoc prof obstet & gynec, Col Physicians & Surgeons, Columbia Univ, 70-73, dir res & develop, Family Planning Serv, Int Inst Study Human Reproduction, 70-73; assoc dir health sci, Rockefeller Found, 73-78; assoc prof obstet & gynec, Northwestern Univ, 78-81; PROF GYNEC & OBSTET, EMORY UNIV, 81- *Concurrent Pos:* Am Cancer fel, Kings County Hosp, State Univ NY, 61-62; dir, Family Planning Ctr, NY Med Col-Metrop Hosp Med Ctr, 64-69; mem med adv bd, Planned Parenthood, New York, 64-; mem nat adv coun, Alan Guttmacher Inst, Planned Parenthood World Pop, 68-, chmn nat med comt, 74-; mem exec comt, Comt Med & Pub Health Asn Voluntary Sterilization, Inc; mem obstet & gynec adv comt, Food & Drug Admin, chmn over-the-counter rev panel; consult, Family Planning, New York Dept Health; family planning proj consult, Human Resources Admin; mem res adv comt, Agency Int Develop. *Mem:* Am Col Obstet & Gynec; Am Col Surg; Am Pub Health Asn; Am Fertil Soc; AMA. *Res:* Medicine; contraception. *Mailing Add:* Dept Gynec & Obstet Emory Univ Sch Med 69 Butler St Atlanta GA 30335

CONNELLY, CLARENCE MORLEY, b Jamestown, NY, Nov 4, 16; m 46; c 1. BIOPHYSICS. *Educ:* Cornell Univ, AB, 38; Univ Pa, PhD(biophys), 49. *Prof Exp:* Asst physics, Cornell Univ, 38-42; staff mem, Radiation Lab, Mass Inst Technol, 42-46; asst biophys, Univ Pa, 46-49; from instr to asst prof, Johns Hopkins Univ, 49-54; asst prof, 54-60, ASSOC PROF BIOPHYS, ROCKEFELLER UNIV, 60-, ASSOC DEAN GRAD STUDIES, 62- *Concurrent Pos:* Ed, J Gen Physiol, 61-64. *Mem:* Soc Gen Physiol; Am Phys Soc; Soc Neurosci; Biophys Soc. *Res:* Physiology of nerve and muscle. *Mailing Add:* Rockefeller Univ 66th St & York Ave New York NY 10021

CONNELLY, DONALD PATRICK, b Breckenridge, Minn, Oct 8, 42; m 67; c 3. LABORATORY MEDICINE, INFORMATION SCIENCES. *Educ:* NDak State Univ, BSEE, 64, MSEE, 65; Univ Minn, MD, 71, PhD(health info syst), 77. *Prof Exp:* Engr logic design, Int Bus Mach Corp, 65-66; engr med appln, Mayo Clin, 67; ASST PROF LAB MED & PATH & DIR LAB DATA DIV, UNIV MINN, 74- *Mem:* Acad Clin Lab Physicians & Scientists; Soc Comput Med; Sigma Xi. *Res:* Medical decision making; information sciences in medicine. *Mailing Add:* Box 70 May Bldg Univ of Minn Hosps Minneapolis MN 55455

CONNELLY, J(OSEPH) ALVIN, b Knoxville, Tenn, Nov 9, 42; m 64; c 4. ELECTRICAL ENGINEERING. *Educ:* Univ Tenn, BS, 64, MS, 65, PhD(elec eng), 68. *Prof Exp:* From asst prof to assoc prof, 68-79, PROF ELEC ENG, GA INST TECHNOL, 79- *Concurrent Pos:* Instr solid state circuits course, E Tenn State Univ, 69-75; consult, Harris Semiconductor, 72-75, Signetics, 77, Scientific Atlanta, 78 & Honeywell, 79-82. *Mem:* Inst Elec & Electronics Engrs; Sigma Xi; Am Asn Univ Professors. *Res:* Solid state device and circuit theory; nanosecond switching circuits; integrated circuits and applications; phase locked loop communication systems; switched capacitor circuits; low noise design. *Mailing Add:* Sch of Elec Eng Ga Inst Technol Atlanta GA 30332

CONNELLY, JOHN JOSEPH, JR, b Syracuse, NY, Apr 14, 25; m 47; c 3. EXPERIMENTAL SOLID STATE PHYSICS. *Educ:* Rensselaer Polytech Inst, BAeroE, 45; Univ Va, MS, 55, PhD(physics), 56. *Prof Exp:* Sci adv to chief aircraft nuclear propulsion off & mat technologist, US AEC, 56-60; prog officer energy conversion, Power Br, Off Naval Res, 60-64; assoc prof, 64-68, PROF PHYSICS, STATE UNIV NY COL FREDONIA, 68- *Concurrent Pos:* Mem comt elec eng systs, NASA. *Mem:* Assoc fel Am Inst Aeronaut & Astronaut; Am Phys Soc. *Res:* Very high speed ultra-centrifuges; high-temperature materials; advance type propulsion systems; direct energy conversion; crystal growth of halides, calcite and tellurates. *Mailing Add:* Dept of Physics State Univ of NY Col Fredonia NY 14063

CONNELLY, THOMAS GEORGE, b Oak Park, Ill, Sept 22, 45; m 66; c 2. ANATOMY, ZOOLOGY. *Educ:* Monmouth Col, Ill, AB, 66; Mich State Univ, PhD(zool), 70. *Prof Exp:* asst prof, 72-79, asst res scientist, 75-79, ASSOC PROF ANAT, MED SCH, UNIV MICH, ANN ARBOR, 79-, ASSOC RES SCIENTIST, CTR HUMAN GROWTH & DEVELOP, 79- *Concurrent Pos:* NIH res fel, Biol Div, Oak Ridge Nat Lab, 70-72. *Mem:* Am Asn Anat; Int Soc Develop Biol; Am Soc Zool; Soc Develop Biol. *Res:* Amphibian lens and limb regeneration; amphibian pituitary cytology. *Mailing Add:* Dept Anat Univ Mich Med Sch Ann Arbor MI 48109

CONNER, ALBERT Z, b Philadelphia, Pa, Dec 21, 21. ANALYTICAL CHEMISTRY. *Educ:* Drexel Inst Technol, BS, 47; Univ Del, MS, 52. *Prof Exp:* Chemist, Publicker Industs, 46-47; res chemist, Hercules Powder Co, 47-65, sr res chemist, 65-70, res scientist, 70-76, RES ASSOC, HERCULES INC, 70- *Mem:* Am Chem Soc; Am Inst Chemists. *Res:* Chromatography; organic analysis; analysis of rocket propellants. *Mailing Add:* 2118 Swinnen Dr Wilmington DE 19810

CONNER, BRENDA JEAN, b Savannah, Ga. BIOLOGY, MOLECULAR BIOLOGY. *Educ:* Emory Univ, BS, 67, MS, 69, PhD(molecular biol), 75. *Prof Exp:* Lab tech asst biol, Emory Univ, 67-70; NIH fel molecular biol, Univ Ga, 70-73; fel, 73-80, RES ASSOC CYTOGENETICS, CYTOLOGY & MOLECULAR BIOL, DEPT MED GENETICS, CITY OF HOPE MED CTR, 80- *Mem:* AAAS; Am Soc Cell Biol; Am Soc Human Genetics. *Res:* Molecular genetics; gene structure and function; prenatal diagnosis of hemoglobin disorders and other genetic diseases; autoimmune disease; systemic lupus erythematosus. *Mailing Add:* Dept of Med Genetics City of Hope Hosp Duarte CA 91010

CONNER, GEORGE WILLIAM, b Jackson, Miss, Nov 19, 35. INSECT & HUMAN GENETICS. *Educ:* Vanderbilt Univ, BA, 57; Emory Univ, MS, 59; Univ Ariz, PhD(zool), 65. *Prof Exp:* Instr biol, Univ Southwestern La, 59-61; asst prof zool, Univ SDak, 64-68; asst prof biol, NTex State Teachers Col, 68-72; fel human genetics, Univ Edinburgh, Scotland, 72-74; asst prof biol, Univ NB, 74-75; ASSOC PROF BIOL, LOYOLA COL, 75- *Concurrent Pos:* Fel, Muscular Dystrophy Asn Am, 73-74. *Mem:* Am Genetic Asn. *Res:* Genetics of complex loci in the hymenoptera; cytogenetics; human genetics. *Mailing Add:* Dept of Biol Loyola Col Baltimore MD 21210

CONNER, HOWARD EMMETT, b Madison, Wis, Sept 26, 30; m 54; c 3. MATHEMATICS. *Educ:* Univ Wis, BS, 56; Mass Inst Technol, PhD(math), 61. *Prof Exp:* Staff assoc math, Lincoln Lab, Mass Inst Technol, 57-61; mem staff, US Army Math Res Ctr, 61-62, from asst prof to assoc prof, 62-73, PROF MATH, UNIV WIS-MADISON, 73- *Concurrent Pos:* Vis assoc prof, Rockefeller Univ, 67-68. *Mem:* Am Math Soc. *Res:* Systematic study of the properties of the solutions of the integral-differential equations used in gas dynamics, plasma theory and kinetic theory. *Mailing Add:* Dept of Math Van Vleck Hall Univ of Wis Madison WI 53706

CONNER, JACK MICHAEL, b Jackson, Miss, Nov 2, 35. INORGANIC CHEMISTRY, PHYSICAL CHEMISTRY. *Educ:* Millsaps Col, BS, 56; Univ Wyo, PhD(chem), 66. *Prof Exp:* Chemist, Baxter Labs, Inc, Miss, 57-58; res chemist, Sch Med, Univ Miss, 58-59; res assoc inorg chem, Univ Kans, 66-67; asst prof chem, 67-75, ASSOC PROF CHEM, REGIS COL, 75- *Mem:* Am Inst Chem; Am Chem Soc. *Res:* Preparation and chemistry of transition-metal coordination compounds and oxides; aqueous solution equilibria. *Mailing Add:* Dept of Chem Regis Col Denver CO 80221

CONNER, JERRY POWER, b Sherman, Tex, Mar 20, 27; m 47; c 3. PHYSICS. *Educ:* Rice Inst, PhD(physics), 52. *Prof Exp:* MEM STAFF & PHYSICIST, LOS ALAMOS NAT LAB, 52- *Mem:* Am Phys Soc; Am Geophys Union; Am Astron Soc. *Res:* Space radiations. *Mailing Add:* 245 Rio Bravo Los Alamos NM 87544

CONNER, PIERRE EUCLIDE, JR, b Houston, Tex, June 27, 32; m 58; c 2. MATHEMATICS. *Educ:* Tulane Univ, BS, 52, MS, 53; Princeton Univ, PhD(math), 55. *Prof Exp:* Sloan fel, 60-64; vis mem, Inst Adv Study, 61-62; mem comt sci confs, Div Math, Nat Acad Sci, Nat Res Coun, 64-67; *Concurrent Pos:* Vis fel math, Inst Adv Study, 55-57; asst prof, Univ Mich, 57-58; from asst prof to prof, Univ Va, 48-71; NICHOLSON PROF MATH, LA STATE UNIV, 71- Concurrent. *Mem:* Am Math Soc; AAAS. *Res:* Applications of the methods of differential and algebraic topology to the study of transformation groups, especially periodic maps. *Mailing Add:* Dept Math La State Univ Baton Rouge LA 70803

CONNER, RAY M, bacteriology, deceased

CONNER, ROBERT LOUIS, b Wabash, Ind, Feb 3, 27; m 49; c 5. ZOOLOGY. *Educ:* Wash Univ, AB, 49; Ind Univ, PhD(zool), 54. *Prof Exp:* Res assoc, Ind Univ, 54; from asst prof to assoc prof, 54-66, actg chmn dept, 67 & 69-70, PROF BIOL, BRYN MAWR COL, 66- *Concurrent Pos:* Lalor fel, 55; USPHS fels, 61-62 & 68-69. *Mem:* AAAS; Soc Protozool (pres, 74-76); Brit Soc Gen Microbiol. *Res:* Biological chemistry; mode of action of steroids; nutritional requirements and physiology of protozoa; membrane chemistry; membrane biochemistry of protozoa. *Mailing Add:* Dept of Biol Bryn Mawr Col Bryn Mawr PA 19010

CONNER, ROBERT THOMAS, b Lisbon, NH, Oct 2, 10; m 40; c 1. BIOCHEMISTRY. *Educ:* Univ Vt, BS, 32; Columbia Univ, PhD(biochem), 36. *Prof Exp:* Asst chem, Columbia Univ, 32-36, instr, 36-39; chemist in chg div biochem, Cent Res Labs, Gen Foods Corp, 39-45; tech dir, William R Warner Co & actg dir Warner Inst Therapeut Res, New York, 45-46; vpres res & develop, Harrower Lab, Inc, 46-50, dir develop labs, 50-51; dir res & develop labs, Smith Kline & French Labs, 51-61 & Strasenburgh Labs, 61-63; dir labs, Max Factor & Co, 63-75; CONSULT, 75- *Mem:* Fel AAAS; Am Chem Soc; fel Am Inst Chemists; fel Soc Cosmetic Chemists; fel NY Acad Sci. *Res:* Organic, nutritional dnd medicinal chemistry; bacteriology. *Mailing Add:* 115 Vincent Rd Paoli PA 19301

CONNERNEY, JOHN E P, b Boston, Mass, Sept 25, 50. PLANETARY MAGNETOSPHERES. *Educ:* Cornell Univ, BS, 72, PhD(appl physics), 79. *Prof Exp:* Resident res assoc, Nat Res Coun & Nat Acad Sci, 79-80; SPACE SCIENTIST, LAB EXTRATERRESTRIAL PHYSICS, GODDARD SPACE FLIGHT CTR, NASA, 80- *Mem:* Am Geophys Union; AAAS; Planetary Soc. *Res:* Planetary and interplanetary magnetic fields and plasmas; interpretation of spacecraft observations (voyager, pioneer, magsat) in context of magnetospheric theory (earth, jupiter, saturn). *Mailing Add:* Lab Extraterrestrial Physics Code 695 Goddard Spaceflight Ctr Greenbelt MD 20771

CONNERS, GARY HAMILTON, b Rochester, NY, Feb 15, 36; m 59; c 4. APPLIED MECHANICS. *Educ:* St Lawrence Univ, BS, 57; Mich State Univ, PhD(appl mech), 63. *Prof Exp:* Physicist, Delco Appliance Div Gen Motors Corp, 57-59, sr physicist, 62-64; instr appl mech, Mich State Univ, 61-62; assoc lectr mech eng, Univ Rochester, 63-64, asst prof mech & aerospace sci, 64-67; res supvr, Apparatus Div, 67-70, supvr appl math res, Hawk-Eye Works, 70-75, prog mgr res & eng, 75-79, prog dir strategic planning, Kodak Off, 79-81, DIR RES & ENG, KODAK APPARATUS DIV, EASTMAN KODAK CO, 81- *Concurrent Pos:* Assoc prof mech & aerospace sci, Univ Rochester; chmn, Appl Math, Univ Col, Univ Rochester, 78-81. *Mem:* Am Phys Soc; Am Soc Mech Eng; Optical Soc Am; Sigma Xi. *Res:* Solid mechanics including elasticity, plasticity and thermal mechanics; optical manufacturing; optical systems design; optical and mechanical properties of continuous media; liquid crystals; solid mechanics and mechanics of structures. *Mailing Add:* Apparatus Div Eastman Kodak Co 901 Elmgrove Rd Rochester NY 14650

CONNETT, WILLIAM C, b Mexico City, Mex, Feb 22, 39; m 69. MATHEMATICAL ANALYSIS. *Educ:* Georgetown Univ, BS, 61; Univ Chicago, MS, 63, PhD(math), 69. *Prof Exp:* Asst prof, 69-77, ASSOC PROF MATH, UNIV MO-ST LOUIS, 77- *Mem:* Am Math Soc. *Res:* Multiple Fourier series; multiplier theory; singular integrals. *Mailing Add:* Dept of Math Univ of Mo St Louis MO 63121

CONNEY, ALLAN HOWARD, b Chicago, Ill, Mar 23, 30; m 54; c 2. BIOCHEMISTRY, PHARMACOLOGY. *Educ:* Univ Wis, BS, 52, MS, 54, PhD(oncol), 56. *Prof Exp:* Asst, Univ Wis, 52-56; pharmacologist, Nat Heart Inst, 57-60; head biochem pharmacol sect, Pharmacodynamics Div, Burroughs Wellcome & Co, 60-70; DIR DEPT BIOCHEM & DRUG METAB, HOFFMANN-LA ROCHE INC, 70- *Mem:* Am Soc Pharmacol & Exp Therapeut; Am Soc Biol Chem; Am Asn Cancer Res; Am Soc Toxicol; Acad Pharmaceut Sci. *Res:* Induced enzyme synthesis in mammals; metabolism of drugs, carcinogens, and steroid hormones; mechanism of drug action; ascorbic acid biosynthesis; carcinogenesis. *Mailing Add:* Dept of Biochem & Drug Metab Hoffmann-La Roche Inc Nutley NJ 07110

CONNICK, ROBERT ELWELL, b Eureka, Calif, July 29, 17; m 52; c 6. INORGANIC CHEMISTRY. *Educ:* Univ Calif, BS, 39, PhD(chem), 42. *Prof Exp:* Asst chem, 39-42, instr, 42-43, res, Manhattan Proj, 43-46, from asst prof to assoc prof chem, 45-52, chmn dept, 58-60, dean col chem, 60-65, vchancellor acad affairs, 65-67, vchancellor, 69-71, PROF CHEM, UNIV CALIF, BERKELEY, 52- *Concurrent Pos:* Guggenheim fels, 49 & 59. *Mem:* Nat Acad Sci; Am Chem Soc. *Res:* Radio chemistry; mechanisms of reactions; complex ions; aqueous solution chemistry of chromium and ruthenium; nuclear magnetic resonance studies of inorganic systems; sulfur chemistry. *Mailing Add:* Dept Chem Univ Calif Berkeley CA 94720

CONNOLLY, DENIS JOSEPH, b Detroit, Mich, Nov 8, 38; m 63; c 4. APPLIED PHYSICS, ELECTRONIC ENGINEERING. *Educ:* Univ Detroit, BEE, 61; Case Western Reserve Univ, MSEE, 66, PhD(elec eng & appl physics), 71. *Prof Exp:* res engr, 61-79, SECT HEAD, NASA LEWIS RES CTR, 79- *Mem:* Am Phys Soc; Inst Elec & Electronic Engrs; Am Vacuum Soc. *Res:* Solid State Electronics; microwave electronics. *Mailing Add:* NASA Lewis Res Ctr MS 54-5 21000 Brookpark Rd Cleveland OH 44135

CONNOLLY, JOHN E, b Omaha, Nebr, May 21, 23. SURGERY. *Educ:* Harvard Univ, AB, 45, MD, 48. *Prof Exp:* Giannini Found fel, Stanford Univ, 57, Markle scholar, 57-62, from instr to assoc prof surg, 57-65; PROF SURG & CHMN DEPT, UNIV CALIF, IRVINE, 65- *Concurrent Pos:* Chief consult, Vet Admin Hosp, Long Beach, 65-; chief surg, Med Ctr, Univ Calif, Irvine; staff mem, St Joseph's Hosp & Children's Hosp, Orange. *Mem:* Fel Am Col Surgeons; Am Surg Asn; Soc Univ Surgeons; Am Asn Thoracic Surg; Int Cardiovasc Soc. *Res:* Cardiovascular surgery. *Mailing Add:* Dept of Surg Univ of Calif Irvine CA 92717

CONNOLLY, JOHN FRANCIS, b Teaneck, NJ, Jan 22, 36; m 63; c 6. ORTHOPEDICS. *Educ:* St Peter's Col, NJ, BA, 57; NJ Col Med, MD, 61. *Prof Exp:* Asst prof orthop surg, Vanderbilt Univ, 68-73, asst prof biomed eng, 72-73; PROF ORTHOP SURG & REHAB, MED CTR, UNIV NEBR, OMAHA, 74- *Concurrent Pos:* Dir amputee clin & dir cerebral palsy clin, Med Ctr, Vanderbilt Univ, 68-73; chief orthop surg, Nashville Vet Admin Hosp, 68-73, Vet Admin Fund grant biomech fractures, 69-73, wear studies in arthritis, 76 & epiphyseal fractures, 77; chief orthop surg, Omaha Vet Admin Hosp, 74-; Vet Admin Fund grant elec osteogenesis, 80- *Mem:* Orthop Res Soc. *Res:* Pathophysiology and biomechanics of trauma and fracture healing, including nonunions and epiphyseal fractures; electrical stimulation of nonunions. *Mailing Add:* Dept Orthop Univ Nebr Med Ctr Omaha NE 68105

CONNOLLY, JOHN IRVING, JR, b Boston, Mass, June 23, 36. LOW TEMPERATURE PHYSICS, OPTICS. *Educ:* Mass Inst Technol, BS, 58; Univ Ill, Urbana, MS, 59, PhD(physics), 65; Northeastern Univ, MS, 71. *Prof Exp:* Fulbright lectr physics, Coun Sci Invests, 65-66; tech staff mem, Mitre Corp, 66-72; mem staff, 72-76, V PRES, SCI APPLNS, INC, 76- *Mem:* Am Phys Soc; Soc Indust & Appl Math; Inst Elec & Electronics Engrs. *Res:* Laser technology with emphasis on operational devices. *Mailing Add:* Sci Applns Inc 2361 Jefferson Davis Pkwy Arlington VA 22202

CONNOLLY, JOHN STEPHEN, b Butte, Mont, Nov 23, 36; m 63; c 3. PHYSICAL CHEMISTRY, PHOTOCHEMISTRY. *Educ:* Carroll Col, Mont, AB, 58; Univ Minn, MS, 60; Brandeis Univ, PhD(phys chem), 69. *Prof Exp:* Nuclear engr, Naval Reactors, USAEC, 60-61; res, US Naval Radiol Defense Lab, 61-63; fel photochem, C F Kettering Res Lab, 68-69, staff scientist, 69-72; vis res chemist chem lasers, Aerospace Res Labs, Wright-Patterson AFB, 72-73; sr NAS/NRS res assoc photochem, US Army Natick Labs, Mass, 73-74; res dir laser hazards, Life Sci Div, Technol Inc, San Antonio, 74-76; consult comput & software, San Antonio, 76-77; sr scientist, Biochem Conversion Br, 77-79, SR SCIENTIST & TASK LEADER PHOTOCHEM, PHOTOCONVERSION RES BR, SOLAR ENERGY RES INST, GOLDEN, COLO, 79- *Concurrent Pos:* Lectr chem, Wright State Univ, 71; consult, US Army Natick Labs, 74-77; adj assoc prof bioeng, Univ Tex Health Sci Ctr, San Antonio, 75-78; chmn, Third Int Conf Photochem Conversion & Storage of Solar Energy & Int Orgn Comt, 78-80. *Mem:* AAAS; Am Chem Soc; Am Soc Photobiol; Inter-Am Photochem Soc; Int Solar Energy Soc. *Res:* Applications of photochemistry to solar energy conversion and storage; photochemistry and photophysics of large molecules in condensed phase; interaction of laser radiation with molecules of biological interest; computerized data acquisition and analysis of kinetic and spectroscopic data. *Mailing Add:* Solar Energy Res Inst Photoconversion Res Br 1617 Cole Blvd Golden CO 80401

CONNOLLY, JOHN W, b Cincinnati, Ohio, Apr 4, 36; m 60; c 2. INORGANIC CHEMISTRY, BIOLOGICAL CHEMISTRY. *Educ:* Xavier Univ, Ohio, BS, 58; Purdue Univ, PhD(chem), 63. *Prof Exp:* Asst chem, Yale Univ, 62-64; asst prof chem, Marietta Col, 64-65; from asst prof to assoc prof, 65-77, PROF CHEM, UNIV MO-KANSAS CITY, 77- *Mem:* AAAS; Am Chem Soc. *Res:* Organometallic chemistry and enzyme model chemistry. *Mailing Add:* Dept of Chem Univ of Mo Kansas City MO 64110

CONNOLLY, JOHN WILLIAM DOMVILLE, b South Porcupine, Ont, July 18, 38; m 62, 77; c 2. THEORETICAL PHYSICS, SOLID STATE PHYSICS. *Educ:* Univ Toronto, BA, 60; Univ Fla, PhD(physics), 66. *Prof Exp:* Sr res assoc, Pratt & Whitney Aircraft Div, United Aircraft Corp, Conn, 67-70; assoc prof physics & mem staff, Quantum Theory Proj, Univ Fla, 70-76, prof, 76-78; assoc prog dir, Solid State Physics, 76-78, PROG DIR, CONDENSED MATTER THEORY, NSF, 78- *Concurrent Pos:* Res affil, Mass Inst Technol, 69. *Mem:* AAAS; fel Am Phys Soc. *Res:* Electronic structure of solids. *Mailing Add:* Div of Mat Res NSF Washington DC 20550

CONNOLLY, LEWIS TIMOTHY, b Indiana, Pa, Dec 21, 30; m 52; c 5. PHOTOGRAPHIC CHEMISTRY. *Educ:* Univ Rochester, BS, 63. *Prof Exp:* Res chemist, 63-67, sr research, 67-71, res assoc, 71-73, LAB HEAD PHOTOG CHEM, EASTMAN KODAK RES LABS, 73- *Mem:* Soc Photog Scientists & Engrs; Tech Asn Graphic Arts. *Res:* Photographic materials used in the graphic arts; processing of photographic materials. *Mailing Add:* 250 Rhea Crescent Rochester NY 14615

CONNOLLY, PHILIP LOUIS, b New Glasgow, NS, Can, Jan 9, 30; m 62. PHYSICS. *Educ:* St Francis Xavier, BA, 50; Catholic Univ, MSc, 52; Cornell Univ, PhD(physics), 59. *Prof Exp:* Res assoc physics, Cornell Univ, 59-60; asst physicist, 60-62 & assoc physicist, BROOKHAVEN NAT LAB, 62- *Concurrent Pos:* Ford Found vis scientist, Europ Orgn Nuclear Res, Switz, 64-65. *Mem:* Am Phys Soc. *Res:* High energy physics; bubble chambers; data processing. *Mailing Add:* Dept of Physics Bldg 510 Brookhaven Nat Lab Upton NY 11973

CONNOLLY, THOMAS WORTHINGTON, b Washington, DC, June 17, 23; m 49; c 4. NUCLEAR WEAPON EFFECTS ON ELECTRONICS. *Educ:* Ga Inst Technol, BChE, 49; Columbia Univ, MA, 53. *Prof Exp:* Mem, US Army Chem Corps, 49-65; RES ENGR & PROG MGR, KAMAN SCI CORP, 65- *Mem:* Am Defense Preparedness Asn. *Res:* Performs survivability analysis of military electronic systems for nuclear weapon environments, primarily electromagnetic pulse. *Mailing Add:* Kaman Sci Corp 1500 Garden of the Gods Rd Colorado Springs CO 80907

CONNOLLY, WALTER CURTIS, b Marysville, Ohio, May 1, 22; m 44; c 2. PHYSICS. *Educ:* Miami Univ, AB, 44; Univ Ill, MS, 46; Cath Univ Am, PhD, 54. *Prof Exp:* Asst physics, Univ Ill, 44-46; assoc prof, US Naval Acad, 46-55; sr scientist, Westinghouse Atomic Power, 55-56; assoc prof physics, Ala Polytech Inst, 56-58; sr physicist, Res Lab Eng Sci, Univ Va, 58-63; PROF PHYSICS, APPALACHIAN STATE UNIV, 63- *Mem:* Am Phys Soc; Am Asn Physics Teachers. *Res:* Energy sources; physics demonstration apparatus. *Mailing Add:* Dept of Physics Appalachian State Univ Boone NC 28608

CONNOR, DANIEL HENRY, b Aylmer, Ont, Mar 26, 28; US citizen; m 53; c 3. PATHOLOGY. *Educ:* Queen's Univ, MD, CM, 53. *Prof Exp:* From intern med to jr resident path, Emergency Hosp, Washington, DC, 53-55; from resident to chief resident path, Med Sch Hosp, George Washington Univ, 55-57; chief lab serv, Irwin Army Hosp, Ft Riley, Kans, 57-59; assoc pathologist, Liver & Pediat Br, Armed Forces Inst Path, 59-60, assoc pathologist, Skin & Gastrointestinal Br, 60-61; prin investr study path of endomyocardial fibrosis, WHO, 62-64; assoc pathologist, Infectious Dis Br, 64-67, chmn dept infectious & parasitic dis path, 74, CHIEF, INFECTIOUS DIS BR, ARMED FORCES INST PATH, 67-79, CHIEF, GEOG PATH DIV, 70-79. *Concurrent Pos:* Dir path, US Med Res & Develop Proj, Kampala, Uganda, 62-64; hon lectr path, Makerere Col Med Sch, Kampala, 62-64; adv African cardiopathies, WHO, 64; assoc mem, Comn Parasitic Dis, Armed Forces Epidemiol Bd, 69; consult med parasitol, Am Bd Path, 72, mem test comt med microbiol-med parasitol, 74-81; consult onchocerciasis, WHO, 72, mem sci adv panel, Onchocerciasis Control Prog, Volta River Basin, 74-79, consult, Spec Comt Parasitic Dis, 81-86. *Honors & Awards:* Official Commendations, Dept of Army, 64 & 71, Decoration for Meritorious Civilian Serv, 71. *Mem:* Int Acad Path; Am Asn Pathologists & Bacteriologists; Am Soc Exp Path; Col Am Pathologists; Am Soc Trop Med & Hyg. *Res:* Pathogenesis of tropical and exotic infectious diseases, especially those of tropical Africa, including onchocerciasis, Mycobacterium ulcerans infection, endomyocardial fibrosis, streptocerciasis and others. *Mailing Add:* Infectious & Parasitic Dis Path Armed Forces Inst of Path Washington DC 20306

CONNOR, DANIEL S, b Cleveland, Ohio, Feb 25, 38. SYNTHETIC ORGANIC CHEMISTRY, APPLIED CHEMISTRY. *Educ:* Brown Univ, ScB, 60; Yale Univ, PhD(chem), 65. *Prof Exp:* RES CHEMIST, MIAMI VALLEY LABS RES DIV, PROCTER & GAMBLE CO, 65- *Mem:* Am Chem Soc; Sigma Xi. *Res:* Analytical and polymer chemistry; immunochemistry. *Mailing Add:* PO Box 326 Ross OH 45061

CONNOR, DAVID THOMAS, b Batley, Eng, Nov 6, 39; m 67; c 2. ORGANIC CHEMISTRY. *Educ:* Univ Manchester, BSc, 62, MSc, 64, PhD(org chem), 65. *Prof Exp:* Res assoc org chem, Univ Chicago, 65-68; scientist, 69-74, sr scientist, 74-78, RES ASSOC, WARNER-LAMBERT RES INST, 78- *Mem:* Am Chem Soc. *Res:* Organic reaction mechanisms; synthetic methods for heterocyclic chemistry; natural product chemistry; antimicrobial agents; antiallergy and antisecretory agents. *Mailing Add:* Warner-Lambert/Parke Davis 2800 Plymouth Rd Ann Arbor MI 48106

CONNOR, DONALD W, b Chicago, Ill, Jan 2, 23; m 43; c 4. SOLID STATE PHYSICS. *Educ:* Univ Chicago, SB, 43, SM, 48, PhD, 60. *Prof Exp:* Jr physicist, Argonne Nat Lab, 46-49; elec engr, Univ Chicago, 49-50; assoc physicist, Brookhaven Nat Lab, 51; scientist, Chicago Midway Labs, 51-52; assoc physicist, 52-69, physicist, Solid State Div, 69-74, SR PHYSICIST, ENVIRON STATEMENT PROJ, ARGONNE NAT LAB, 74- *Mem:* AAAS; Inst Elec & Electronic Eng; Am Phys Soc; Am Nuclear Soc; Sigma Xi. *Res:* Nuclear moments; lattice vibrations; neutron scattering. *Mailing Add:* Environ Statement Proj Argonne Nat Lab 9700 S Cass Ave Argonne IL 60439

CONNOR, FRANK FIELD, b Chicago, Ill, June 15, 32; m 58; c 2. MATHEMATICS. *Educ:* Ill Inst Technol, BS, 54, MS, 56, PhD(math), 59. *Prof Exp:* Instr math, Ill Inst Technol, 58-60; res instr, La State Univ, 60-61, from asst prof to assoc prof, 61-70; chmn dept, 70-75, PROF MATH, N TEX STATE UNIV, 70- *Mem:* Am Math Soc; Math Asn Am. *Res:* Measure and integration; linear operators. *Mailing Add:* 1813 Stonegate Dr Denton TX 76201

CONNOR, JAMES D, b Colleton, SC, Nov 19, 26; m; c 3. PEDIATRICS, MICROBIOLOGY. *Educ:* Clemson Col, BS, 53; Med Col SC, MD, 53; Am Bd Pediat, dipl, 59. *Prof Exp:* Intern, Wayne County Gen Hosp, Eloise, Mich, 53-54; resident pediat, Children's Hosp, Mich, 54-55; instr, Sch Med, Wayne State Univ, 55-57; instr, Sch Med, Univ Miami, 57-59, clin asst prof, 59-60, from asst prof to assoc prof, 61-69; assoc prof, 70-74, PROF PEDIAT, UNIV CALIF, SAN DIEGO, 74- *Concurrent Pos:* Chief resident pediat, Children's Hosp, Mich, 55-57; med coordr, Variety Children's Hosp, Miami, 58-60, res assoc virol, Variety Children's Res Found, 60-; USPHS fel virol, 60-62; res asst prof microbiol, Univ Miami, 61-70. *Mem:* AAAS; AMA; Am Acad Pediat; Am Pub Health Asn; Infectious Dis Soc Am. *Res:* Virology and pharmacology of antivirals, therapeutics and bacterial infection; pertussis. *Mailing Add:* Dept Pediat M-009 La Jolla CA 92093

CONNOR, JAMES EDWARD, JR, b New Haven, Conn, Feb 14, 24; m 51; c 6. PHYSICAL ORGANIC CHEMISTRY. *Educ:* Harvard Univ, BA, 44, MS, 48, PhD(phys org chem), 49. *Prof Exp:* Sr res chemist, Atlantic Richfield Co, Glenolden, 49-54, supvr chemist, 54-60, asst mgr basic res div, 60-61, mgr chem res, 61-62, mgr res div, 62-71, mgr res & develop div, 62-71, mgr res & develop div, Res & Eng Dept, ARCO Chem Co Div, Glenolden, 71-79, vpres chem res & develop, 79-81, VPRES RES, ARCO CHEM CO, ATLANTIC RICHFIELD CO, NEWTOWN SQUARE, 81- *Mem:* Am Chem Soc. *Res:* Petroleum refining methods, especially hydrocarbon reactions and catalytic reactions; petrochemicals. *Mailing Add:* 1421 Hillside Rd Wynnewood PA 19096

CONNOR, JOHN D, b Coatesville, Pa, Jan 15, 33; m 63; c 2. PHARMACOLOGY. *Educ:* Philadelphia Col Pharm, BS, 60, MS, 62, PhD(pharmacol), 66. *Prof Exp:* Lab asst zool, Philadelphia Col Pharm, 60-62, lab asst pharmacol, 62-63; res assoc neuropharmacol, East Pa Psychiat Inst, 63-66; from asst prof to assoc prof, 69-75, PROF PHARMACOL, HERSHEY MED CTR, PA STATE UNIV, 75- *Concurrent Pos:* NIMH lab fel, 66-69; Borden Found Award. *Mem:* Am Soc Pharmacol & Exp Therapeut; Soc Neurosci; Sigma Xi. *Res:* Pharmacology and physiology of involuntary motor activity; temperature regulation; synaptic transmission in the central nervous system. *Mailing Add:* Dept of Pharmacol Hershey Med Ctr Pa State Univ Hershey PA 17033

CONNOR, JON JAMES, b Columbus, Ohio, Dec 12, 32; m 63. GEOLOGY. *Educ:* Ohio State Univ, BSc, 55; Univ Colo, PhD(geol), 63. *Prof Exp:* Geologist, 55-72, chief br regional geochem, 72-78, GEOLOGIST, US GEOL SURV, 78- *Concurrent Pos:* Liaison mem, US Nat Comt Geochem, Nat Acad Sci-Nat Res Coun, 72-75. *Mem:* Soc Environ Geochem & Health; Geol Soc Am; Int Asn Math Geol. *Res:* Geology of Colorado Plateau and Black Hills uranium deposits; groundwater investigations around Carlsbad, New Mexico; regional geochemistry of sedimentary rocks; environmental geochemistry and its relation to human and animal health; geochemistry of ore deposits in Belt Rocks, Montana. *Mailing Add:* US Geol Surv Denver Fed Ctr Lakewood CO 80225

CONNOR, JOSEPH GERARD, JR, b West Chester, Pa, Aug 15, 36; m 61; c 3. ENGINEERING PHYSICS, SCIENCE EDUCATION. *Educ:* Georgetown Univ, BS, 57; Pa State Univ, MS, 61, PhD(physics), 63. *Prof Exp:* RES PHYSICIST, NAVAL SURFACE WEAPONS CTR, WHITE OAK, 63- *Concurrent Pos:* Lectr, Montgomery Jr Col, 64-65, Trinity Col, DC, 65-72 & Montgomery Col, 81- *Mem:* AAAS; Am Asn Physics Teachers; Am Phys Soc. *Res:* Structural response; explosion effects in air and underwater. *Mailing Add:* 17805 Dominion Dr Sandy Spring MD 20860

CONNOR, LAWRENCE JOHN, b Kalamazoo, Mich, Aug 15, 45; m 68; c 2. EMTOMOLOGY, APICULTURE. *Educ:* Mich State Univ, BS, 67, MS, 69, PhD(entom), 72. *Prof Exp:* Asst prof entom, Ohio State Univ, 72-76; asst prof entom, Ohio Agr Res & Develop Ctr, 75-76; pres, Genetic Systs, Inc, 76-80; CONSULT & OWNER, BEEKEEPING EDUC SERV, 80- *Concurrent Pos:* Exten entomologist, Ohio Coop Exten Serv, 72-76. *Mem:* Sigma Xi; Bee Res Asn. *Res:* Honey bee breeding and genetics; crop pollination requirements and mechanisms. *Mailing Add:* PO Box 817 Cheshire CT 06410

CONNOR, RALPH (ALEXANDER), b Newton, Ill, July 12, 07; m 31; c 1. CHEMISTRY. *Educ:* Univ Ill, BS, 29; Univ Wis, PhD(org chem), 32. *Hon Degrees:* DSc, Phila Col Pharm, 54, Univ Pa, 59, Polytech Inst Brooklyn, 67; LLD, Lehigh Univ, 66. *Prof Exp:* Asst chem, Univ Wis, 29-31; instr org chem, Cornell Univ, 32-35; from asst prof to assoc prof, Univ Pa, 35-44; assoc dir res, Rohm and Haas Co & Resinous Prod & Chem Co, 45-48, vpres res, Rohm and Haas Co, 48-70, dir & mem exec comt, 49-73, chmn bd, 60-70, vpres & chmn exec comt, 70-73; RETIRED. *Concurrent Pos:* Res chemist, du Pont Co, 34; tech aide, sect chief & div chief, Nat Defense Res Comn, 41-46; mem div chem & chem tech, Nat Res Coun, 53-58; mem, Tech Adv Panel Biol & Chem Warfare, 54-60; chmn, US Nat Comt on Int Union Pure & Appl Chem; bd dirs, Ursinus Col, 71-80. *Honors & Awards:* Naval Ord Develop Award; Medal for Serv in Cause of Freedom (Brit); Medal for Merit; Gold Medal, Am Inst Chemists, 63, Chem Pioneer Award, 68; Chem Indust Medal, Soc Chem Indust, 65; Priestley Medal, Am Chem Soc, 67; Outstanding Civilian Serv Award, US Dept Army, 70; Achievement Award, Univ Ill, 71. *Mem:* Am Chem Soc; Am Inst Chemists; Soc Chem Indust. *Res:* Organic chemistry; catalysis; synthesis; explosives; mechanisms. *Mailing Add:* PO Box 1975 Sun City AZ 85372

CONNOR, ROBERT DICKSON, b Edinburgh, Scotland, May 15, 22; m 48; c 2. NUCLEAR PHYSICS. *Educ:* Univ Edinburgh, BSc, 42, PhD, 49. *Prof Exp:* From asst lectr to lectr physics, Univ Edinburgh, 48-57; from assoc prof to prof physics, 57-79, assoc dean arts & sci, 63-70, dean sci, 70-79, PROF FAC EDUC, UNIV MAN, 79- *Concurrent Pos:* Mem univ grants comn, Prov Man, 68- *Mem:* Can Asn Physicists; Sigma Xi; fel Brit Inst Physics. *Res:* Alpha, beta and gamma ray spectroscopy; history and philosophy of science. *Mailing Add:* Fac Educ Univ of Man Winnipeg MB R3T 2N2 Can

CONNOR, THOMAS BYRNE, b Baltimore, Md, Dec, 21, 21; m 57; c 2. MEDICINE. *Educ:* Loyola Col, Md, BA, 43; Univ Md, MD, 46. *Prof Exp:* Intern, Mercy Hosp, Baltimore, 46-47, resident, 49-51; from asst prof to assoc prof, 56-67, PROF MED, SCH MED, UNIV MD, BALTIMORE, 67-, DIR DIV ENDOCRINOL & METAB, 56-, DIR CLIN RES CTR, 62- *Concurrent Pos:* Fel endocrine & metab dis, Johns Hopkins Hosp, 51-56; asst physician outpatient dept, Diabetic Clin & Endocrine Clin, Johns Hopkins Hosp, 51-59; staff physician, Univ Md Hosp, 56-; consult med, Mercy Hosp, Baltimore, 60- & Baltimore Vet Admin Hosp, 65- *Mem:* AAAS; Endocrine Soc; Am Clin & Climat Asn; Am Soc Bone & Mineral Res; fel Am Col Physicians. *Res:* Clinical research in calcium and bone metabolism and parathyroid disorders; endocrinology and metabolism. *Mailing Add:* Dept of Med Sch of Med Univ of Md Baltimore MD 21201

CONNOR, WILLIAM ELLIOTT, b Pittsburgh, Pa, Sept 14, 21; m 46; c 5. INTERNAL MEDICINE. *Educ:* Univ Iowa, BA, 42, MD, 50; Am Bd Internal Med, dipl, 57; Am Bd Nutrit, dipl, 67. *Prof Exp:* Intern, USPHS Hosp, Calif, 50-51; asst med resident, San Joaquin Gen Hosp, 51-52; mem med staff, Enloe Hosp, 52-54; med resident, Vet Admin Hosp, Iowa, 54-56; from instr to prof internal med, Univ Iowa, 56-75, dir clin res ctr, 68-75;

PROF CARDIOL & METAB-NUTRIT, DIR, LIPID-ATHEROSCLEROSISLAB & ASSOC DIR, CLIN RES CTR, ORE HEALTH SCI UNIV, PORTLAND, 75- *Concurrent Pos:* Am Heart Asn res fel, Univ Iowa, 56-58; Am Col Physicians traveling fel, Oxford Univ, 60; vis prof, Med Cols & Basic Sci Med Inst, Karachi, Pakistan, 61; ed, J Lab & Clin Med, 70-73; mem & chmn, Coun Arteriosclerosis, Am Heart Asn; vis fel clin sci, Australian Nat Univ, Canberra, 70; chmn heart & lung prog, Proj Comn, Nat Heart & Lung Inst, NIH, 74-75; mem gen clin, Res Centers Comn, 76- *Mem:* AAAS; Am Inst Nutrit (pres, 78-79); Am Soc Clin Invest; Asn Am Physicians; Am Fedn Clin Res. *Res:* Atheriosclerosis; lipid metabolism; nutrition. *Mailing Add:* Dept Med L465 Ore Health Sci Univ 3181 SW Sam Jackson Park Rd Portland OR 97201

CONNOR, WILLIAM GORDEN, b El Paso, Tex, Nov 1, 36. MEDICAL PHYSICS. *Educ:* Tex Western Col, BSc, 62; Vanderbilt Univ, MSc, 64; Univ Calif, Los Angeles, PhD(med physics), 70. *Prof Exp:* Physicist, Michael Reese Hosp, Chicago, Ill, 64-66; asst prof radiol, Univ Wis-Madison, 70-72; asst prof, 72-76, ASSOC PROF RADIOL, UNIV ARIZ, 76- *Mem:* AAAS; Am Asn Physicists in Med; Health Physics Soc. *Res:* Application of ionizing radiations to the treatment of malignant diseases; cellular repair of damage due to ionizing radiations; use of hyperthermia as an adjunct to radiation therapy; high linear-energy transfer radiation therapy. *Mailing Add:* Dept of Radiol Univ of Ariz Med Ctr Tucson AZ 85721

CONNOR, WILLIAM KEITH, b Houston, Tex, Dec 19, 31; m 59; c 3. ACOUSTICS. *Educ:* Rice Inst, BA, 55; Southern Methodist Univ, MS, 61. *Prof Exp:* Engr trainee, Gen Motors Proving Ground, 55-56; proj engr, Electro-Mech Labs, White Sands Proving Ground, 57-58, Gen Motors Proving Ground, Noise & Vibration Lab, 58-59 & 61-62; consult acoust, Rudmose Assocs Inc, 62-63; consult acoust, 63-69, DIR ACOUST RES DEPT, TRACOR, INC, 69- *Concurrent Pos:* Sr lectr, Sch Archit, Univ Tex, Austin, 73- *Mem:* Inst Noise Control Eng; Sigma Xi; fel Acoust Soc Am; Audio Eng Soc. *Res:* Community noise, psychoacoustics; architectural acoustics; noise and vibration control; electroacoustics. *Mailing Add:* Tracor Inc 6500 Tracor Lane Austin TX 78721

CONNORS, DONALD R, b Saginaw, Mich, Oct 31, 28; m 50; c 3. NUCLEAR PHYSICS, LAW. *Educ:* Univ Notre Dame, BS 52, PhD(nuclear physics), 57; Duquesne Univ, JD, 68. *Prof Exp:* Sr engr exp physics, 56-60, mgr exp physics & anal, 60-65, mgr physics, reactor design & exp, 65-69, mgr reactor opers, 69-74, mgr light water breeder reactor proj design & opers, 74-77, MGR OPERS TRAINING, BETTIS ATOMIC POWER LAB, 77- *Concurrent Pos:* Chmn & mem Adv Safeguards Comt, Bettis Atomic Power Lab, 60- *Mem:* Am Nuclear Soc. *Res:* Nuclear reactor design and development; training of naval nuclear reactor operations personnel; reactor safety and environmental effects, public relations, legal aspects of reactor operation. *Mailing Add:* Bettis Atomic Power Lab PO Box 79 West Mifflin PA 15122

CONNORS, KENNETH A, b Torrington, Conn, Feb 19, 32. PHARMACEUTICS, ANALYTICAL CHEMISTRY. *Educ:* Univ Conn, BS, 54; Univ Wis, MS, 57, PhD(pharm), 59. *Prof Exp:* Res assoc phys-org chem, Ill Inst Technol, 59-60 & Northwestern Univ, 60-62; from asst prof to assoc prof pharmaceut anal, 62-70, asst dean grad studies, 68-72, PROF PHARMACEUT ANAL, UNIV WIS-MADISON, 70- *Concurrent Pos:* NIH fel, 60-62. *Honors & Awards:* Justin L Powers Award Res Achievement, 80. *Mem:* Fel AAAS; Am Chem Soc; Am Pharmaceut Asn. *Res:* Pharmaceutical analysis; mechanisms of organic reactions; molecular complexes especially of cyclodextrins. *Mailing Add:* Sch of Pharm Univ of Wis Madison WI 53706

CONNORS, NATALIE ANN, b St Louis, Mo. HISTOLOGY, HISTOCHEMISTRY. *Educ:* St Louis Univ, BS, 50, PhD(anat), 68; Univ Ill, Urbana-Champaign, MS, 52. *Prof Exp:* Technician, Monsanto Chem Co, Ill, 52-56; res assoc anat, 56-61, teaching asst, 61-68, instr, 68-70, ASST PROF ANAT, SCH MED, ST LOUIS UNIV, 70- *Mem:* Sigma Xi; Am Asn Univ Profs; AAAS. *Res:* Study of the autonomic nervous system using autoradiographic and horseradish peroxidase technics; teratogenic effects of chemical substances on the developing chick. *Mailing Add:* Dept of Anat St Louis Univ Sch of Med St Louis MO 63103

CONNORS, PHILIP IRVING, b Norfolk, Va, Oct 7, 37; m 59; c 3. ACADEMIC ADMINISTRATION, EXPERIMENTAL NUCLEAR PHYSICS. *Educ:* Univ Notre Dame, BS, 59; Pa State Univ, MS, 62, PhD(physics), 66. *Prof Exp:* Asst physics, Pa State Univ, 59-63; jr res assoc, Brookhaven Nat Lab, 63-65; res assoc, Dept Physics & Astron, Univ Md, 65-69, asst prof physics & dir col sci improv prog, 69-75; assoc prof & chmn, Div Environ & Natural Sci, Northern Va Community Col, Woodbridge Campus, 75-77; prof sci & acad dean, Cent New England Col, 77-80; PROF MARINE ENG, MASS MARITIME ACAD, 79- *Concurrent Pos:* Dir, Chesapeake Physics Asn, 69-75; Field Ctr Coordr, NSF Chautauqua Short Courses, 71-75; vis lectr comput sci, Worcester State Col, 81- & Math, Bridgewater State Col, 82- *Mem:* Fel AAAS; Am Phys Soc; Am Asn Physics Teachers; Nat Sci Teachers Asn. *Res:* Education and teacher training in physics on all levels; low energy nuclear experimental physics. *Mailing Add:* Mass Maritime Acad PO Box D Buzzards Bay MA 02532

CONNORS, ROBERT EDWARD, b Wellesley, Mass, Oct 1, 45. PHYSICAL CHEMISTRY, MOLECULAR SPECTROSCOPY. *Educ:* Univ Mass, BS, 67; Northeastern Univ, PhD(chem), 72. *Prof Exp:* Res assoc, Boston Univ, 72-76; asst prof, 76-81, L P Kinnicutt asst prof, 77-80, ASSOC PROF CHEM, WORCESTERR POLYTECH INST, 81- *Mem:* Am Chem Soc; AAAS. *Res:* Electronic spectroscopy and optical detection of magnetic resonance studies of organic and biological systems. *Mailing Add:* Dept of Chem Worcester Polytech Inst Worcester MA 01609

CONNORS, WILLIAM MATTHEW, b Canandaigua, NY, Sept 16, 21. BIOCHEMISTRY, INDUSTRIAL CHEMISTRY. *Educ:* St Bonaventure Col, BS, 42; Univ Southern Calif, MS, 47; James Martin Col, PhD, 71. *Hon Degrees:* LHD, James Martin Col, 69. *Prof Exp:* Chemist, Pillsbury Mills, 45; group leader, Nat Dairy Res Labs, Inc, 49-56; anal supvr, Gen Cigar Res & Develop Ctr, 56-73; MGR, CONNORS RES ASSOCS, 73- *Concurrent Pos:* Mem Manhattan Proj, 44-45. *Honors & Awards:* Meritorious Serv Award, Am Inst Chemists, 72. *Mem:* Fel AAAS; Am Chem Soc; fel Am Inst Chemists; NY Acad Sci; Am Soc Microbiol. *Res:* Biochemistry and analytical chemistry of tobacco products; commercial production of enzymes; nutrition of dairy products; energetics of ATPase; pharmacology and toxicology of uranium compounds; industrial engineering and chemical consulting; research and development. *Mailing Add:* PO Box 398 Bausman PA 17504

CONOLLY, JOHN R, b Sydney, Australia, July 23, 36; m 70. GEOLOGY, NATURAL RESOURCES. *Educ:* Univ Sydney, BSc, 58; Univ New South Wales, MSc, 60, PhD(geol), 63. *Prof Exp:* Sr demonstr geol, Univ New South Wales, 60-63; Ford Found fel, Lamont Geol Observ, NY, 63-65; vis prof, La State Univ, 65-66; Queen Elizabeth fel, Univ Sydney, 66-68; from assoc prof to prof, Univ SC, 69-72; explor geologist, B P Alaska Explor Inc, 72-74; Pres, Era NAm Inc, 75-78; MANAGING DIR, SYDNEY OIL CO LTD, 79- *Concurrent Pos:* Fulbright travel award, 63-66; consult, Scripps Inst Oceanog, 66; consult geologist, Univ Sydney, 68; consult, Oceanog Off, US Navy, 69-; consult, John R Conolly & Assocs Inc, 74-; adj assoc prof, Columbia Univ, 73-75; adj prof, City Col New York, 75 & C W Post Col, Long Island Univ, 75-76. *Honors & Awards:* Olle Prize, Royal Soc NSW, 67; Outstanding Paper Award, J Sedimentary Petrol, 74. *Mem:* Fel Geol Soc Am; Am Asn Petrol Geol; Geol Soc Australia; Australian Inst Mining & Metall; Petrol Explor Soc NY (vpres, 75-76, pres, 76-77). *Res:* Sedimentology of recent and ancient rocks; marine geology; petrology; glacial marine geology; origin of continental margins and geosyndines; exploration geology. *Mailing Add:* Sydney Oil Co Ltd 44 Marsret St Sydney Australia

CONOMOS, TASSO JOHN, b New Kensington, Pa, Sept 11, 38; m 69; c 3. OCEANOGRAPHY, GEOCHEMISTRY. *Educ:* San Jose State Univ, BS, 61, MS, 63; Univ Wash, PhD(oceanog), 68. *Prof Exp:* Tech asst geol, San Jose State Univ, 60-62; phys sci technician paleont & stratig, US Geol Surv, 62-63; res assoc oceanog, Univ Wash, 63-64 & 68-69, teaching assoc, 64-65; intern, Smithsonian Inst, 66-68; fel, 69-70, res oceanogr, 70-81, REGIONAL RES HYDROLOGIST, WATER RESOURCES DIV, US GEOL SURV, 81- *Mem:* AAAS; Soc Econ Paleontologists & Mineralogists; Am Soc Limnol & Oceanog; Estuarine Res Fedn. *Res:* Geochemistry and distribution of suspended particulate matter in river-ocean mixing systems; descriptive chemical oceanography of near-shore and in-shore waters; sedimentological geochemical studies of biogenic sediments; effects of man on estuarine processes. *Mailing Add:* Water Resources Div US Geol Surv 345 Middlefield Rd Menlo Park CA 94025

CONOMY, JOHN PAUL, b Cleveland, Ohio, July 31, 38; m 63; c 3. NEUROLOGY. *Educ:* John Carroll Univ, BS, 60; St Louis Univ, MD, 64. *Prof Exp:* Intern med, St Louis Univ Hosps, 64-65; resident neurol, Univ Hosps Cleveland, Case Western Reserve Univ, 65-68, fel neuropath, Cleveland Metrop Gen Hosp, 68; neurologist, US Air Force, 69 & 70; res fel neuroanat, Univ Pa, 70-71; asst prof med, Med Sch, Case Western Reserve Univ, 72-75, assoc prof med, 75-81; CHMN DEPT NEUROL, CLEVELAND CLIN FOUND, 75- *Concurrent Pos:* Career teaching fel award, Case Western Reserve Univ, 70; consult, Vet Admin Hosps, 72-; grants in aid, Vet Admin, 72 & 74, Mary B Lee Fund, 74, Mellon Fund & Reinberger Found, 76-81 & NIH, 78-81. *Mem:* Asn Res Nerv & Ment Dis; Soc Neurosci; fel Am Col Physicians; fel Am Acad Neurol; Asn Univ Profs Neurol. *Res:* Behavioral aspects of neurology, especially correlative studies of unit peripheral nerve and neuronal activity and behavior in animals and man; neurophysiologic action of central neurotransmitters; cerebrovascular disease. *Mailing Add:* Cleveland Clin Found 9500 Euclid Ave Cleveland OH 44106

CONOVER, CHARLES ALBERT, b Elizabeth, NJ, Apr 22, 34; m 57; c 1. ORNAMENTAL HORTICULTURE. *Educ:* Univ Fla, BSA, 62, MSA, 63; Univ Ga, PhD(plant sci), 70. *Prof Exp:* Asst ornamental horticulturist, Agr Exten Serv, 63-70, ORNAMENTAL HORTICULTURIST & CTR DIR, AGR RES CTR, UNIV FLA, 71- *Concurrent Pos:* Ornamental hort consult, United Brands Co, 69-74, Rainbird, 74-76 & Western Publ Co, 77- *Mem:* Int Soc Hort Sci; Am Soc Hort Sci. *Res:* Tropical ornamental plant nutrition; acclimatization of tropical ornamental plants for interior use; development of synthetic soil media; propagation of tropical ornamentals; commercial production of tropical ornamental foliage crops. *Mailing Add:* Agr Res Ctr Rt 3 Box 580 Apopka FL 32703

CONOVER, CLYDE S(TUART), b Springfield, Ill, June 25, 16; m 43; c 2. CIVIL ENGINEERING. *Educ:* Univ NMex, BS, 38. *Prof Exp:* Hydraul engr, Ground Water Invests, 38-48, asst dist engr, 48-51, dist engr, NMex, 51-57, asst chief, Ground Water Br, DC, 57-62, dist engr, Fla, 62-65, dist chief, Water Resources Div, 65-80, SR HYDROLOGIST, US GEOL SURV, 80- *Mem:* Am Geophys Union; Am Soc Civil Engrs; Am Water Works Asn; Am Water Resources Asn; Nat Water Well Asn (vpres, 64-65). *Res:* Ground water hydraulics, management and quantitative evaluation of resource. *Mailing Add:* Water Resources Div US Geol Surv 325 John Knox Rd Suite F-240 Tallahassee FL 32303

CONOVER, JAMES H, b Amsterdam, NY, Dec 22, 42; m 75; c 3. PHARMACOLOGY. *Educ:* Siena Col, BS, 65; NY Univ, MS, 67, PhD(biol), 69. *Prof Exp:* Asst pediat & human genetics, Mt Sinai Sch Med, City Univ New York, 69-70, instr, 70-71, assoc, 71-72, asst prof, 72-75; asst prof, Albert Einstein Sch Med, 75-77; asst prof, NY Univ Sch Med, 77-79; clin study analyst, 79-81, MGR CLIN RES ASSOC, LEDERLE LAB, AM CYANAMID CO, 81- *Concurrent Pos:* Career scientist award, Health Res Coun, New York City, 74; res scholar award, Nat Cystic Fibrosis Found, 76; prin investr grants, Nat Found March Dimes, 74-79, Health Res Coun, New

York City, 74-75, Nat Cystic Fibrosis Found, 76-79. *Mem:* Soc Pediat Res; Am Soc Human Genetics. *Res:* Tracking and analyzing clinical data for anti-cancer agents for the purpose of establishing new drugs to be used therapeutically. *Mailing Add:* 39-28 222nd St Bayside NY 11361

CONOVER, JOHN HOAGLAND, b McKeesport, Pa, Oct 26, 16; m 40; c 2. METEOROLOGY. *Prof Exp:* Weather observer, Blue Hill Meteorol Observ, Harvard Univ, 36-40, chief observer, 40-47, res asst & tech mgr, 47-52, meteorologist, 52-59, tech mgr, 52-57, actg dir, 57-58; METEOROLOGIST, AIR FORCE GEOPHYSICS LAB, 59-77; RES ASSOC, MT WASHINGTON OBSERV, 69- *Concurrent Pos:* Lab instr, Harvard Univ, 41-43; instr, US Weather Bur, 44; consult meteorologist, 47-56 & 77- *Mem:* Am Meteorol Soc. *Res:* Climatic change; microclimates in the arctic; cloud studies; satellite meteorology. *Mailing Add:* 15 Nobel Rd Dedham MA 02026

CONOVER, LLOYD HILLYARD, b Orange, NJ, June 13, 23; m 44; c 4. ORGANIC CHEMISTRY. *Educ:* Amherst Col, AB, 47; Univ Rochester, PhD(chem), 50. *Prof Exp:* Res chemist, Pfizer, Inc, 50-58, res supvr, 58-61, res mgr, 61-68, dir chem res-chemother, 68-71, res dir, Pfizer Ltd, Eng, 71-75, V PRES AGR PROD RES & DEVELOP, PFIZER, INC, 75- *Mem:* Am Chem Soc; Am Soc Microbiol; Soc Drug Res. *Res:* Synthesis of heterocycles; hydrogenolysis of oxygen functions; structure and synthesis of tetracycline antibiotics; synthesis of antiparasitic agents; drugs of microbiological origin; animal health agents. *Mailing Add:* Pfizer Cent Res Pfizer Ltd Sandwich Kent Britain

CONOVER, MICHAEL ROBERT, b Miami, Fla, Feb 16, 51; m 75. ANIMAL BEHAVIOR. *Educ:* Eckerd Col, BS, 73; Wash State Univ, MS, 75, MS, 78, PhD(zool), 78. *Prof Exp:* Asst prof animal behav, Ball State Univ, 78-79; ASST SCIENTIST, CONN AGR EXP STA, 79- *Concurrent Pos:* Nat Sci Found fel, Univ Calif, Irvine, 80-81. *Mem:* Wildlife Soc; Am Ornith Union; Cooper Ornith Soc; Sigma Xi; Animal Behav Soc. *Res:* Applied ethology; avian communication; behavioral ecology of wildlife species; wildlife damage control. *Mailing Add:* Dept Ecol & Climat Conn Agr Exp Sta Box 1106 New Haven CT 06504

CONOVER, ROBERT ARMINE, b Lima, Ill, Nov 5, 16; m 46; c 3. PLANT PATHOLOGY. *Educ:* Culver-Stockton Col, BS, 39; Univ Iowa, MS, 41; Univ Ill, PhD(plant path), 47. *Prof Exp:* Asst, Univ Iowa, 39-41; asst, Univ Ill, 41-42 & 46-47; from assoc plant pathologist to plant pathologist, Res & Educ Ctr, Univ Fla, Homestead, 47-62, plant pathologist & dir ctr, 62-75, PROF PLANT PATH, UNIV FLA, GAINESVILLE, 75- *Mem:* AAAS; Am Phytopath Soc; Am Inst Biol Sci; Am Soc Hort Sci. *Res:* Breeding for disease resistance. *Mailing Add:* Agr Res & Educ Ctr 18905 SW 280 St Homestead FL 33031

CONOVER, THOMAS ELLSWORTH, b Plainfield, NJ, Nov 20, 31; m 66; c 3. BIOCHEMISTRY. *Educ:* Oberlin Col, BA, 53; Univ Rochester, PhD(biochem), 59. *Prof Exp:* Res assoc, Johnson Found, Univ Pa, 62-64; asst mem, Inst Muscle Dis, 64-69; ASSOC PROF BIOL CHEM, HAHNEMANN MED COL, 70- *Concurrent Pos:* Nat Found fel, Wenner-Gren Inst, Univ Stockholm, 58-60; USPHS fel, Pub Health Res Inst, New York, 60-62; Muscular Dystrophy Asn fel, Inst Gen Path, Univ Padua, 69-70. *Mem:* Am Soc Biol Chem. *Res:* Oxidative phosphorylation; mitochondrial structure and function; respiration and phosphorylation in cell nuclei; metabolic significance of cellular structures. *Mailing Add:* Dept of Biol Chem Hahnemann Med Col & Hosp Philadelphia PA 19102

CONOVER, WILLIAM JAY, b Hays, Kans, Dec 6, 36; m 60; c 5. STATISTICS. *Educ:* Iowa State Univ, BS, 58; Cath Univ, MA, 62, PhD(math statist), 64. *Prof Exp:* Asst prof statist, Kans State Univ, 64-67, assoc prof statist & comput sci, 67-73; prof math & statist, 73-78, prof statist & coordr info systs & quant sci, 78-81, HORN PROF STATIST & ASSOC DEAN RES & GRAD PROGS, TEX TECH UNIV, 81- *Concurrent Pos:* Consult, Water Resources Div, US Geol Surv, 62-68; NSF res grant, 67-68 & 78; NIH career develop award, 69-73; prof, Univ Zurich, 70-71 & Univ Calif, Davis, 76-77; consult, Upjohn Co, 75, Schering, 75, Sandia Labs, 77- & Vick Co, 78-; vis staff mem, Los Alamos Sci Labs, 75- *Mem:* Inst Math Statist; Biomet Soc; Am Statist Asn. *Res:* Nonparametric statistics; stochastic models in hydrology and hydraulics. *Mailing Add:* Dept of Info Systs & Quant Sci Tex Tech Univ Lubbock TX 79406

CONOVER, WOODROW WILSON, b Terre Haute, Ind, July 30, 47; m 72. PHYSICAL BIOCHEMISTRY. *Educ:* Rose Hulman Polytech Inst, BS, 69; Ind Univ, Bloomington, PhD(chem), 73. *Prof Exp:* Fel biochem, Univ Chicago, 73-75; sr res assoc biochem & opers mgr, Stanford Magnetic Resonance Lab, Stanford Univ, 75-78; APPLN CHEMIST, NICOLET TECHNOL CORP, 78- *Mem:* Am Chem Soc. *Res:* Exploitation of nuclear magnetic resonance techniques in the study of fundamental biochemical mechanisms. *Mailing Add:* Nicolet Technol Corp 145 E Dana Mt View CA 94041

CONQUEST, LOVEDAY LOYCE, b Hilo, Hawaii, Jan 22, 48. STATISTICS. *Educ:* Pomona Col, BA, 70; Stanford Univ, MS, 72; Univ Wash, PhD(biostatist), 75. *Prof Exp:* Asst prof biostatist, Univ Hawaii, 75-76; from vis lectr to vis asst prof, Ctr Quant Sci, Col Fisheries, 76-77, vis asst prof, Dept Finance, Bus Econ & Quant Methods, Grad Sch Bus Admin, 77-78, ASST PROF STATIST, CTR QUANT SCI, COL FISHERIES, UNIV WASH, 78- *Concurrent Pos:* Statist consult, Tavolek, Inc, 76-80, Dept Surgery Diabetics Vascular Study, Univ Wash, 78-79, Bierly & Assocs, Waterway & Natural Resource Consults, 79-80, Oceanog Inst Wash, 79-81, JRB Assocs, Sci Applications, Inc, 81-, Municiplity Metrop Seattle, 81- *Mem:* Am Statist Asn; Biomet Soc; AAAS; Sigma Xi. *Res:* Statistical methods for analysis of water quality data, including water variables and ecological measures (species counts); ordered contingency tables and relationships to indicators of water quality. *Mailing Add:* Ctr Quant Sci HR-20 Univ Wash Seattle WA 98195

CONRAD, ALBERT G(ODFREY), b Norwalk, Ohio, May 19, 02; m 31; c 2. ELECTRICAL ENGINEERING. *Educ:* Ohio State Univ, BEE, 25, MS, 27; Yale Univ, EE, 31. *Prof Exp:* Prin high sch, Ohio, 21-22, instr, 22-24; asst instr elec eng, Ohio State Univ, 25-27 & Gen Elec Co, 27-28; from instr to assoc prof, Yale Univ, 28-44, prof & chmn dept, 44-62; prof elec eng & dean, Col Eng, 62-70, recalled, prof elec eng, 70-71, EMER PROF ELEC ENG & EMER DEAN COL ENG, UNIV CALIF, SANTA BARBARA, 70- *Concurrent Pos:* Assoc fel, Timothy Dwight Col; mem Eng Coun Prof Develop. *Mem:* Fel AAAS; Am Soc Eng Educ; fel Inst Elec & Electronics Engrs. *Res:* Induction motors; fatal electric shock; electro-physiology; engineering education; adjustable speed alternating current motors; constant torque and monocyclic motors. *Mailing Add:* Col Eng Univ Calif Santa Barbara CA 93106

CONRAD, BRUCE, b Ann Arbor, Mich, July 2, 43; m 64. TOPOLOGY. *Educ:* Harvey Mudd Col, BS, 64; Univ Calif, Berkeley, PhD(math), 69. *Prof Exp:* Asst prof, 69-74, ASSOC PROF MATH, TEMPLE UNIV, 74- *Mem:* AAAS; Am Math Soc; Math Asn Am. *Res:* Homology of groups; algebraic K-theory. *Mailing Add:* Dept of Math Temple Univ Philadelphia PA 19122

CONRAD, EDWARD EZRA, b Richmond, Calif, June 11, 27; m 51; c 3. SOLID STATE PHYSICS, RADIATION CHEMISTRY. *Educ:* Univ Calif, BA, 50; Univ Md, MS, 55, PhD(radiation chem), 70. *Prof Exp:* Physicist solid state, Nat Bur Standards, 51-52; physicist, Harry Diamond Labs, 52-70, chief nuclear radiation effects lab, 70-76, actg assoc dir, 75-76; asst dep dir, 76-79, DEP DIR, DEFENSE NUCLEAR ENERGY, 79- *Concurrent Pos:* Secy Army res & develop fel, 59; lectr, Univ Md, 70-; rep, US Nat Comt Int Electrotech Comn, 58- *Mem:* Fel Inst Elec & Electronics Engrs; Am Phys Soc. *Res:* Semiconductors; radiation effects; magnetics and dielectric measurements; radiation chemistry; pulse radiolysis. *Mailing Add:* 7500 Marbury Rd Bethesda MD 20014

CONRAD, EUGENE ANTHONY, b Clinton, Mass, Aug 15, 27; m 49; c 2. PHARMACOLOGY. *Educ:* Col of the Holy Cross, BS, 50; Univ NH, MS, 52; Vanderbilt Univ, PhD(pharmacol), 56. *Prof Exp:* Res bacteriologist, Charles Pfizer & Co, 52; asst pharmacol, Vanderbilt Univ, 55-56; instr physiol & pharmacol, Bowman Gray Sch Med, 56-58; res assoc pharmacol, Sterling-Winthrop Res Inst, 58-60, asst dir coord sect, 60-62, clin pharmacologist, 62-63; admin asst dept drugs, AMA, Ill, 63-65, dir drug doc sect, 64-66; dir res admin, Wampole Lab, 66-67, dir clin res, 67-70; ASSOC DIR MED, PURDUE FREDERICK CO, NORWALK, 70-, GOV LIAISON, 78- *Concurrent Pos:* Mem behav pharmacol comt, NIMH, 65-66. *Mem:* Am Soc Microbiol; AMA; Drug Info Asn; Soc Pharmacol & Exp Therapeut. *Res:* Drug research. *Mailing Add:* 99 West Lane Stamford CT 06905

CONRAD, FRANK H(EUSSY), b Seattle, Wash, July 9, 02; m 25; c 2. CHEMICAL ENGINEERING. *Educ:* Univ Wash, Seattle, BS, 23, PhD(chem eng), 34. *Prof Exp:* Chemist & mgr, Northwest Testing Labs, Seattle, 23-29; assoc chem eng, Univ Wash, Seattle, 31-32; anal chemist, Standard Oil Co of Calif, 34-36; from asst prof to prof chem eng, 36-69, EMER PROF CHEM ENG, UNIV MO-ROLLA, 69- *Concurrent Pos:* Consult, Monsanto Co, St Louis, Mo, 52, Gary Sheet & Tin Plant, US Steel Corp, Ind, 53 & US Naval Ord Test Sta, China Lake, Calif, 56-60. *Mem:* Am Chem Soc; Am Inst Chem Engrs; Am Soc Eng Educ. *Res:* Submerged combustion; equilibrium studies for sulfite pulp cooking liquors; grinding aids; heat transfer coefficients of liquids in cross flow; removal of dissolved organic materials from sewage plant effluents. *Mailing Add:* Sch of Eng Univ of Mo Rolla MO 65401

CONRAD, FRANKLIN, b Smithville, Ohio, Sept 27, 21; m 49; c 4. INDUSTRIAL CHEMISTRY. *Educ:* Col Wooster, BA, 43; Ohio State Univ, MS, 43, PhD(chem), 52. *Prof Exp:* Chemist, 52-55, supvr, 55-58, proj mgr chlorinated hydrocarbons, 58-60, supvr, 60-63, asst dir contract res, 63-66, DIR INDUST CHEM RES, ETHYL CORP, 66- *Mem:* Am Chem Soc. *Res:* Organometallics; metal hydrides; propellant chemicals; chlorinated hydrocarbons; all aspects of industrial chemicals research and development. *Mailing Add:* Ethyl Corp Baton Rouge Lab PO Box 341 Baton Rouge LA 70815

CONRAD, GARY WARREN, b Amsterdam, NY, Mar 24, 41. DEVELOPMENTAL BIOLOGY. *Educ:* Union Col, BS, 63; Yale Univ, MS, 65, PhD(biol), 68. *Prof Exp:* NIH fel polysaccharide biochem, Univ Chicago, 68-70; rom asst prof to assoc prof, 71-80, PROF DEVELOP BIOL, KANS STATE UNIV, 80- *Concurrent Pos:* vis prof, Mt Desert Island Biol Lab, 71-81. *Mem:* Am Soc Cell Biol; Int Soc Develop Biologists; Soc Develop Biol; AAAS. *Res:* Differentiation of connective tissue; fibroblasts; control of synthesis and polymerization of extracellular matrices, especially in the cornea; mechanisms of cytokinesis; mechanisms of cell movement, cell adhesion and cell shape change. *Mailing Add:* Div Biol Kans State Univ Manhattan KS 66506

CONRAD, HANS, b Konradstahl, Ger, Apr 19, 22; nat US; m 44; c 3. MATERIALS SCIENCE. *Educ:* Carnegie Inst Technol, BS, 43; Yale Univ, MEng, 51, DEng(metall eng), 56. *Prof Exp:* Res metallurgist, Aluminum Co Am, 43-45; chief chem engr, Napier Co, 45-46; dir res, R Wallace & Sons, 46-53; res metallurgist, Chase Brass & Copper Co, 53-55; supvry metallurgist, Res Labs, Westinghouse Elec Corp, 55-59; sr tech specialist, Atomics Int Div, NAm Aviation, Inc, 59-61; head physics dept, Aerospace Corp, 61-64; dir mat sci & eng div, Franklin Inst, 64-67; prof mat sci & chmn dept metall eng & mat sci, Univ, Ky, 67-81; PROF & HEAD, MAT ENG DEPT & DIR MINERALS & MAT RES PROGS, NC STATE UNIV, 81- *Mem:* Fel Am Soc Metals; Am Inst Mining, Metall & Petrol Engrs; Am Soc Testing & Mat; Am Ceramic Soc. *Res:* Mechanical properties; superconductivity; crystal growths and defects; casting, working, forming, fabrication and finishing of metals; alloy development. *Mailing Add:* Dept of Metall Eng & Mat Sci Anderson Hall Univ of Ky Lexington KY 40506

CONRAD, HARRY EDWARD, b Washington, DC, Jan 21, 29; m 52; c 2. BIOCHEMISTRY. *Educ:* La State Univ, BS, 49; Purdue Univ, MS, 52, PhD(biochem), 54. *Prof Exp:* Res chemist, Mead Johnson & Co, 54-58; res assoc, 58-60, from instr to assoc prof chem, 60-72, PROF BIOCHEM, UNIV ILL, URBANA-CHAMPAIGN, 72- *Mem:* Am Chem Soc; Am Soc Biol Chemists. *Res:* Chemistry and biochemistry of mucopolysaccharides; changes in metabolism of mucopolysaccharides and complex cell surface carbohydrates during embryonic development. *Mailing Add:* Dept Biochem Roger Adams Lab Univ Ill 1209 W California Urbana IL 61801

CONRAD, HARRY RUSSELL, b Burlington, Ky, Oct 3, 25; c 2. NUTRITION. *Educ:* Univ Ky, BSc, 48; Ohio State Univ, MSc, 49, PhD(dairy sci), 52. *Prof Exp:* From instr to prof, 52-64, PROF DAIRY SCI, OHIO AGR RES & DEVELOP CTR, 64- *Mem:* Am Dairy Sci Asn. *Res:* Rumen physiology; digestion; nitrogen metabolism and growth in cattle. *Mailing Add:* Dept of Dairy Sci Ohio Agr Res & Develop Ctr Wooster OH 44691

CONRAD, HERBERT M, b New York, NY, Feb 20, 27; m 51; c 3. BIOCHEMISTRY, NUTRITION. *Educ:* Cornell Univ, BS, 49; Univ Southern Calif, MS, 59, PhD(biochem), 65. *Prof Exp:* Chemist, Calif Grape Prod Corp, 50-52; chemist, Star-Kist Foods, Inc, 52-54; lab dir, Long Beach Water Dept, 54-59; proj engr, NAm Aviation, Inc, 62-67; dir biochem, RPC Corp, 67-71; PRES, ECOL SYSTS CORP, 71- *Concurrent Pos:* Consult munic water dist. *Mem:* Fel AAAS; Am Chem Soc; NY Acad Sci. *Res:* The effect of weightlessness upon physiological processes; mechanisms of plant hormones; biodegradation of hazardous materials. *Mailing Add:* Ecol Systs Corp 2200 Colorado Ave Santa Monica CA 90404

CONRAD, JOHN RUDOLPH, b San Antonio, Tex, Mar 21, 47; m 71. PLASMA PHYSICS. *Educ:* St Mary's Univ, Tex, BS, 68; Dartmouth Col, PhD(physics), 73. *Prof Exp:* Res assoc plasma physics, Inst Fluid Dynamics & Appl Math, Univ Md, 73-75; ASST PROF NUCLEAR ENG, UNIV WIS, MADISON, 75- *Mem:* Am Phys Soc; Sigma Xi. *Res:* Experimental research in the areas of beam-plasma interaction; plasma transport properties, ion source and neutral beam-technology. *Mailing Add:* Dept of Nuclear Eng Univ of Wis Madison WI 53706

CONRAD, JOHN TERRY, b New York, NY, Feb 13, 28; m 53; c 3. PHYSIOLOGY. *Educ:* NY Univ, AB, 51, MS, 55, PhD(muscle physiol), 61. *Prof Exp:* Res asst physiol, Wash Sq Col, NY Univ, 52-53; res asst radiobiol, Sloan-Kettering Inst, 53-54; res asst physiol, Sch Med, Yale Univ, 57-60, instr, 60-62; asst prof physiol, 62-67, ASSOC PROF PHYSIOL, BIOPHYS, OBSTET & GYNEC, SCH MED, UNIV WASH, 67-, CHMN PERINATAL BIOL, 75- *Mem:* AAAS; Biophys Soc; Am Physiol Soc; Am Asn Univ Prof; Perinatal Res Soc. *Res:* Uterine muscle physiology; muscular dystrophy; radiation induced skin changes; bioelectrical phenomena in muscle; reproductive tissue mechanics. *Mailing Add:* Dept of Obstet & Gynec Sch of Med Univ of Wash Seattle WA 98105

CONRAD, JOSEPH H, b Cass Co, Ind, Dec 6, 26; m 50; c 4. ANIMAL NUTRITION, BIOCHEMISTRY. *Educ:* Purdue Univ, BSA, 50, MS, 54, PhD(animal nutrit), 58. *Prof Exp:* From instr to prof animal sci, Purdue Univ, 53-71; PROF ANIMAL NUTRIT & COORDR TROP ANIMAL SCI PROGS, UNIV FLA, 71- *Concurrent Pos:* Animal nutritionist from Purdue Univ, Brazil Tech Asst Prog, Agr Univ Minas Gerais, USAID, 61-65; hon prof, 65. *Honors & Awards:* Distinguished Nutrit Award, Distillers Feed Res Coun, 64. *Mem:* AAAS; Am Soc Animal Sci; Latin Am Soc Animal Sci; Brazilian Soc Animal Sci. *Res:* Swine and cattle nutrition; amino acids; feed additives; livestock in small form systems; tropical forage utilization; phosphorus and trace element deficiencies under tropical conditions. *Mailing Add:* Dept of Animal Sci Univ of Fla Gainesville FL 32611

CONRAD, LESTER I, cosmetic chemistry, deceased

CONRAD, MALCOLM ALVIN, b Chicago, Ill, Apr 2, 27; m 53; c 2. MINERALOGY, CRYSTALLOGRAPHY. *Educ:* Mich Tech Univ, BS & MS, 52; Univ Mich, PhD(mineral), 60. *Prof Exp:* Geologist, Kennecott Copper Corp, 52-53; res assoc mineral, Univ Mich, 59-60; res engr, 60-62, res scientist, 62-66, chief exp mineral, 66-73, CHIEF RAW MAT, OWENS-ILL INC, 73- *Mem:* Mineral Soc Am; Geol Soc Am; Sigma Xi. *Res:* Industrial mineralogy; glass-ceramics; ceramic raw materials. *Mailing Add:* Owens-Ill Inc PO Box 1035 Toledo OH 43666

CONRAD, MARCEL E, b New York, NY, Aug 15, 28; m 48; c 5. INTERNAL MEDICINE, HEMATOLOGY. *Educ:* Georgetown Univ, BS, 49, MD, 53; Nat Bd Internal Med, dipl, 61. *Prof Exp:* Intern med, Med Corps, US Army, 53-54, resident internal med, 55-58, chief resident, 58-59, asst chief hemat, 58-60 & 61-65, chief hemat, Walter Reed Army Med Ctr, 65-74, dir div med, 69-71, dir clin invest serv, 71-74; PROF MED & DIR DIV HEMAT & ONCOL, UNIV ALA, BIRMINGHAM, 74- *Concurrent Pos:* From clin asst prof to clin assoc prof med, Sch Med, Georgetown Univ, 64-74. *Mem:* AAAS; fel Am Col Physicians; Am Soc Clin Invest; fel Int Soc Hemat; Asn Am Physicians. *Res:* Gastroenterology; iron metabolism; hemolytic disorders; intestinal transport; hepatitis; oncology. *Mailing Add:* Div of Hemat & Oncol Univ of Ala Birmingham AL 35294

CONRAD, MARGARET C, b Burlington, NC, Apr 4, 30; div; c 3. PHYSIOLOGY. *Educ:* Catawba Col, AB, 52; Univ NC, PhD(physiol), 55. *Prof Exp:* Asst physiol, Univ NC, 52-55; res asst path & oncol, Univ Kans Med Ctr, Kansas City, 55-56; from res asst to assoc prof physiol & pharmacol, Bowman Gray Sch Med, 59-63; from assoc prof to prof physiol, Med Univ SC, 63-73; PROF PHYSIOL, EASTERN VA MED SCH, 73- *Mem:* Am Physiol Soc; Am Heart Asn. *Res:* Physiology of peripheral vascular circulation. *Mailing Add:* Dept of Physiol Eastern Va Med Sch Norfolk VA 23507

CONRAD, MICHAEL, b New York, NY, Apr 30, 41. BIOPHYSICS, BIOMATHEMATICS. *Educ:* Harvard Univ, AB, 63; Stanford Univ, PhD(biophys), 69. *Prof Exp:* Fel biophys, Ctr Theoret Studies, Univ Miami, 69-70; fel math, Univ Calif, Berkeley, 72; asst prof, Inst Info Sci, Univ Tübingen, 72-74; assoc prof biol, City Col, 74-75; assoc prof comput & commun sci, Univ Mich, Ann Arbor, 75-79; PROF COMPUT SCI, WAYNE STATE UNIV, 79- *Concurrent Pos:* Res assoc, Inst Info Sci, Univ Tübingen, 74-76; adj prof biol sci, Wayne State Univ, 79- *Mem:* Biophys Soc; Soc Math Biol; Neth Soc Theoret Biol. *Res:* Computer modeling of biological systems; biophysics of information processing; brain models and intelligence; ecological and evolutionary problems; adaptability theory. *Mailing Add:* Dept Comput Sci Wayne State Univ Detroit MI 48202

CONRAD, PAUL, b Hempstead, NY, Oct 7, 21; m 43; c 1. MATHEMATICS. *Educ:* Univ Ill, PhD(math), 51. *Prof Exp:* From asst prof to prof math, Newcomb Col, Tulane Univ, 51-70; PROF MATH, UNIV KANS, 70- *Concurrent Pos:* NSF sr fel, Australian Nat Univ, 64-65; vis prof, Univ Paris, 67. *Honors & Awards:* Fulbright Lectr, Univ Ceylon, 56-57. *Mem:* Am Math Soc. *Res:* Ordered algebraic systems; group theory. *Mailing Add:* Dept of Math Univ of Kans Lawrence KS 66045

CONRAD, ROBERT DEAN, b El Reno, Okla, Sept 20, 23; m 47; c 3. LABORATORY ANIMAL MEDICINE. *Educ:* Univ Okla, BS, 49; Okla State Univ, MS & DVM, 53; Univ Calif, Davis, PhD(comp path), 70. *Prof Exp:* Asst prof vet microbiol, Wash State Univ, 53-59; pathologist, Heisdorf & Nelson Farms, Inc, 59-65; NIH fel epidemiol & prev med, Univ Calif, Davis, 65-67, specialist, Div Exp Animal Resources, Sch Vet Med, 67-71; assoc prof microbiol, Col Med & dir animal resource facilities, 71-76, VETERINARIAN & ASSOC PROF MED MICROBIOL, EPPLEY INST RES CANCER, UNIV NEBR, OMAHA, 76- *Concurrent Pos:* Dr Salsbury fel, 57-58. *Mem:* Am Vet Med Asn; Am Asn Avian Path; Am Soc Microbiol. *Res:* Bacterial and viral diseases of domestic and wild fowl. *Mailing Add:* Univ of Nebr Col of Med 42nd St & Dewey Ave Omaha NE 68105

CONRAD, WALTER EDMUND, b Forward, Pa, Nov 16, 20; m 49; c 2. ORGANIC CHEMISTRY. *Educ:* Wayne Univ, BS, 44, MS, 46; Univ Kans, PhD(org chem), 51. *Prof Exp:* Chemist, Armour Labs, 45-47; chemist, Sterling-Winthrop Res Inst, 47-48; res assoc, Med Sch, Tufts Univ, 51-53; instr chem, Univ Mass, 53-55; res chemist, Celanese Corp, 55-57, assoc prof & chmn dept, Ohio Northern Univ, 57-59; prof chem, Southeast Mass Univ, 59-77. *Mem:* Am Chem Soc. *Res:* Schmidt reaction; effect of ultraviolet irradiation on pyrimidines; catalytic debenzylation; lubricants; chemistry of phosphoranes. *Mailing Add:* 2409 Regal Dr Lutz FL 33549

CONRADI, JAN, solid state physics, see previous edition

CONRADI, MARK STEPHEN, b St Louis, Mo, Jan 25, 52. MAGNETIC RESONANCE. *Educ:* Wash Univ, BS, 73, PhD(physics), 77. *Prof Exp:* Res asst, Physics Dept, Washington Univ, 73-77; staff scientist & Wigner fel, Chem Div, Oak Ridge Nat Lab, 77-79; ASST PROF, PHYSICS DEPT, COL WILLIAM & MARY, 79- *Res:* Measurement of molecular motion in solids and liquids principally with nuclear magnetic relaxation; concentrating on glasses and disordered solids. *Mailing Add:* Dept Physics Col William & Mary Williamsburg VA 23185

CONRATH, BARNEY JAY, b Quincy, Ill, June 23, 35; m 62; c 3. DYNAMICS OF PLANETARY ATMOSPHERES, RADIATIVE TRANSFER. *Educ:* Culver-Stockton Col, BA, 57; Univ Iowa, MA, 59; Univ NH, PhD(physics), 66. *Prof Exp:* SPACE SCIENTIST, GODDARD SPACE FLIGHT CTR, NASA, 60- *Mem:* Am Geophys Union; Am Astron Soc. *Res:* Structure and dynamics of planetary atmospheres by means of remote sensing from spacecraft. *Mailing Add:* Code 6932 Goddard Space Flight Ctr Greenbelt MD 20771

CONREY, BERT L, b Glendale, Calif, Sept 9, 20; m 47. GEOLOGY. *Educ:* Univ Calif, Berkeley, AB, 47, MA, 48; Univ Southern Calif, PhD(geol), 59. *Prof Exp:* Field party chief petrol geol, Stanolind Oil & Gas Co, 48-50; div photogeologist, 50-51; from asst prof to assoc prof, 55-63, chmn dept, 60-64, PROF GEOL, CALIF STATE UNIV, LONG BEACH, 63- *Concurrent Pos:* NSF res grant, 63-64. *Mem:* Am Asn Petrol Geol; Geol Soc Am; Soc Econ Paleontologists & Mineralogists; Int Asn Sedimentol. *Res:* Marine geology and sedimentology. *Mailing Add:* Dept of Geol Calif State Univ Long Beach CA 90840

CONROW, KENNETH, b Philadelphia, Pa, Jan 22, 33; m 55; c 3. COMPUTER SCIENCE. *Educ:* Swarthmore Col, BA, 54; Univ Ill, PhD(org chem), 57. *Prof Exp:* From instr to asst prof chem, Univ Calif, Los Angeles, 57-61; from asst prof to assoc prof org chem, 61-71, asst dir, Comput Ctr, 74-76, ASSOC PROF COMPUT SCI, KANS STATE UNIV, 71-, ASSOC DIR, COMPUT CTR, 76-, MGR USER SERVS, 80- *Mem:* Am Chem Soc; Asn Comput Mach. *Res:* Programming language preprocessors; non-numeric programming. *Mailing Add:* Comput Ctr Kans State Univ Manhattan KS 66506

CONROY, CHARLES WILLIAM, b Neodesha, Kans, Dec 29, 27; m 49; c 5. PERIODONTICS, ORAL PATHOLOGY. *Educ:* Univ Kans, AB, 50; Univ Mo, DDS, 54, MSD, 57; Ohio State Univ, MSc, 58. *Prof Exp:* Asst prof med periodont, Univ Tex, 57-61; from asst prof to assoc prof, 61-70, PROF DENT, COL DENT, OHIO STATE UNIV, 70- *Concurrent Pos:* Consult, Procter & Gamble Co, 61- *Mem:* Int Asn Dent Res; Am Acad Periodont; Am Acad Dent Electrosurg (pres, 73-74). *Res:* Studies relating to the prevention of dental deposits on the teeth which cause periodontal disease. *Mailing Add:* Ohio State Univ Col of Dent 305 W 12th Ave Columbus OH 43210

CONROY, HAROLD, b Brooklyn, NY, Apr 1, 28; m 48; c 3. THEORETICAL CHEMISTRY. *Educ:* Mass Inst Technol, BS, 48; Harvard Univ, PhD(org chem), 50. *Prof Exp:* NIH fel, Harvard Univ, 50-51; instr chem, Columbia Univ, 51-52; sr chemist, Merck & Co, Inc, 52-55; asst prof chem, Brandeis

Univ, 55-58 & Yale Univ, 58-61; prof biol & chem, 67-72, sr fel, mellon inst, 61-, PROF CHEM, CARNEGIE-MELLON UNIV, 72- *Concurrent Pos:* NIH spec res fel, 70-71; vis prof, Mass Inst Technol, 70-71; exchange visitorship for Eastern Europe, Nat Acad Sci, 74. *Mem:* AAAS; Sigma Xi. *Res:* Mathematical properties of molecular wavejunctions and density matrices; quantum chemistry; structure of natural products; physical organic chemistry; organic reaction mechanisms. *Mailing Add:* Dept of Chem Carnegie-Mellon Univ 4400 Fifth Ave Pittsburgh PA 15213

CONROY, JAMES D, b Dayton, Ohio, Dec 15, 33; m 62; c 3. VETERINARY PATHOLOGY. *Educ:* Ohio State Univ, DVM, 60; Univ Ill, Urbana-Champaign, PhD(vet path), 68. *Prof Exp:* Fel clin res internal med, Animal Med Ctr, NY, 60-61, fel comp dermat, 61-62, staff vet, 62-64, sr resident vet path, 64; USPHS fel vet med sci, 64-68, from instr to asst prof vet path & hyg, 68-70, assoc prof vet path & hyg, Col Vet Med, Univ Ill, Urbana-Champaign, 70-77; PROF PARACLIN SCI, COL VET MED, MISS STATE UNIV, MISSISSIPPI STATE, 77- *Honors & Awards:* Clin Proficiency Award, Upjohn Co, Kalamazoo, Mich, 60. *Mem:* Am Vet Med Asn; Am Col Vet Path; Int Acad Path; Am Acad Vet Dermat (secy-treas, 64-68, vpres, 68-70, pres, 71-73); Am Col Vet Internal Med. *Res:* Development of cutaneous prenatal pigmentation; melanocytic tumors in domestic animals; cytopathology of infectious diseases; comparative dermatology; veterinary pathology. *Mailing Add:* Drawer V Col of Vet Med Mississippi State MS 39762

CONROY, JAMES STRICKLER, b Philadelphia, Pa, Aug 24, 31. FUEL CHEMISTRY. *Educ:* Univ Pa, AB, 53; Pa State Univ, MS, 56, PhD(fuel tech), 59. *Prof Exp:* Asst prof, 57-62, chmn dept sci, 73-78, ASSOC PROF CHEM, WIDENER COL, 62- *Mem:* Am Chem Soc; Am Inst Chem. *Res:* Condensed aromatic hydrocarbons; fuels and combustion; reaction mechanisms. *Mailing Add:* 1307 Maryland Ave Havertown PA 19083

CONROY, LAWRENCE EDWARD, b Providence, RI, Aug 29, 26; m 62; c 3. INORGANIC CHEMISTRY. *Educ:* Univ RI, BS, 49; Cornell Univ, MS, 52, PhD, 55. *Prof Exp:* Proj chemist phys chem, Colgate-Palmolive Co, 51-53; asst prof chem, Temple Univ, 55-59; asst prof, 59-63, ASSOC PROF INORG CHEM, UNIV MINN, MINNEAPOLIS, 63- *Concurrent Pos:* Consult, Minn Mining & Mfg Co, 62-65. *Mem:* AAAS; Am Chem Soc; Brit Chem Soc. *Res:* Solid state and high temperature inorganic chemistry; nonstoichiometric and metallic compounds; transport properties. *Mailing Add:* 1515 East River Rd Minneapolis MN 55414

CONS, JEAN MARIE ABELE, b Lancaster, Pa; m; c 2. DEVELOPMENTAL PHYSIOLOGY. *Educ:* Calif State Univ, San Francisco, BA, 60; Univ Calif, San Francisco, MS, 63, PhD(endocrinol), 72. *Prof Exp:* Lab technician develop anat, Univ Calif, San Francisco, 60-64, res anat, 64-68; consult, Med Sci Prog, Univ Calif, Berkeley, 72-73, fel, 72-74, asst res develop physiol, 74-75; asst prof, Col Notre Dame, Calif, 75-77; INSTR ANATOMY & PHYSIOL, COL SAN MATEO, 77- *Mem:* Soc Study Reproduction. *Res:* Developmental patterns of pituitary and plasma glycoproteins and the actions of these hormones during development. *Mailing Add:* Col San Mateo 1700 W Hillsdale Blvd San Mateo CA 94402

CONSELMAN, FRANK BUCKLEY, b New York, NY, Oct 1, 10; m 34; c 3. PETROLEUM GEOLOGY. *Educ:* NY Univ, BSc, 30, ScM, 31; Univ Mo, PhD(geol), 34. *Prof Exp:* Asst geol, NY Univ, 30-31; asst geol, Univ Mo, 31-32 & 33-34; geologist, Mo Geol Surv, 34-35; geologist, Gulf Oil Corp, 35-41; dist geologist, Great Lakes Carbon Corp, Tex, 45-46; dist mgr, Am Trading & Prod Corp, 47; prof geosci & dir, Int Ctr Arid & Semi-Arid Land Studies, Tex Tech Univ, 69-76; CONSULT GEOLOGIST, 47- *Concurrent Pos:* Vis lectr, Univ Tex, 57 & 68; ed, J Am Inst Prof Geologists, 63-65; mem US Nat Comn Geol, 69-73; mem, US Nat Comn for UNESCO, 76-79; trustee assoc, AAPG Found; dir gen geol & hydrol, Arid Lands Int, Inc; adj prof geosci, Tex Tech Univ, 78-; vpres & dir, Assoc Nuclear Consults Am, Inc, 79- *Honors & Awards:* Ben H Parker Medalist, Am Inst Prof Geologists, 67. *Mem:* Hon mem Am Asn Petrol Geologists (vpres, 60-61, pres, 68-69); Am Inst Mining, Metall & Petrol Engrs; Am Inst Prof Geol (pres, 74); Am Geol Inst (vpres, 74, pres, 75); fel Geol Soc Am. *Res:* Subsurface stratigraphy; oil and gas exploration; water supplies for arid lands; mineral resources; nuclear waste disposal. *Mailing Add:* 34 Lakeshore Dr Route 2 Slaton TX 79364

CONSIGLI, RICHARD ALBERT, b Brooklyn, NY, Mar 2, 31; m 60; c 3. VIROLOGY, CANCER. *Educ:* Brooklyn Col, BS, 54; Univ Kans, MA, 56, PhD(bact), 60. *Prof Exp:* Asst bact, Univ Kans, 54-59, instr, 59-60; USPHS fel virol, Univ Pa, 60-62; from asst prof to assoc prof bact, 62-69, PROF BACT, KANS STATE UNIV, 69-, SR SCIENTIST MID-AM CANCER CTR, UNIV MED CTR, 75- *Concurrent Pos:* Pa Plan scholar, 61-62; NIH res grants, 62-70; career develop award, USPHS, 67-; consult, NSF; assoc ed, Appl Microbiol. *Mem:* Am Soc Microbiol; Tissue Cult Asn; Soc Exp Biol & Med; NY Acad Sci; Am Acad Microbiol. *Res:* Investigation of the biochemical events during the animal virus infection of tissue culture cells; investigation of the host-parasite interrelationship during rickettsial infections; cancer research; biochemistry of tumor virus infection of cultured cells. *Mailing Add:* Subdiv Molecular Biol & Genetics Div Biol Kans State Univ Manhattan KS 66504

CONSROE, PAUL F, b Cortland, NY, Oct 18, 42; m 81. PHARMACOLOGY. *Educ:* Albany Col Pharm, BS, 66; Univ Tenn, Memphis, MS, 69, PhD(pharmacol), 71. *Prof Exp:* Assoc prof, 71-81, PROF PHARMACOL, COL PHARM, UNIV ARIZ, 81- *Concurrent Pos:* Nat Inst Drug Abuse grant, Univ Ariz, 72-; consult, Ariz Poison Control Inform Serv, 71- *Mem:* Soc Neurosci; Am Soc Pharmacol & Exp Therapeut. *Res:* Neuropsychopharmacological investigations of hallucinogens, marijuana and other psychotropic drugs. *Mailing Add:* Dept of Pharmacol & Toxicol Univ of Ariz Col of Pharm Tucson AZ 85721

CONSTABLE, JAMES HARRIS, b Dayton, Ohio, Mar 9, 42; m 68; c 2. SOLID STATE PHYSICS, LOW TEMPERATURE PHYSICS. *Educ:* Ohio State Univ, BSc, 66, MSc, 67, PhD(physics), 69. *Prof Exp:* Res assoc physics, Ohio State Univ, 69-72, vis asst prof, 72-74; asst prof, 74-79, ASSOC PROF PHYSICS, STATE UNIV NY BINGHAMTON, 79- *Mem:* Am Phys Soc. *Res:* Experimental studies of phonon processes, and the electrical, magnetic and thermal properties of the hydrogen solids. *Mailing Add:* SGSPE State Univ of NY Binghamton NY 13901

CONSTABLE, ROBERT L, b Detroit, Mich, Jan 20, 42; m 64; c 1. COMPUTER SCIENCE. *Educ:* Princeton Univ, AB, 64; Univ Wis, MA, 65, PhD(math), 68. *Prof Exp:* Instr comput sci, Univ Wis, 68; asst prof, 68-72, assoc prof, 72-78, PROF COMPUT SCI, CORNELL UNIV, 78- *Mem:* Asn Symbolic Logic; Asn Comput Mach; Soc Indust & Appl Math. *Res:* Theory of computation, especially program verification, computational complexity and constructive type theory. *Mailing Add:* Dept of Comput Sci Cornell Univ Ithaca NY 14853

CONSTANCE, LINCOLN, b Eugene, Ore, Feb 16, 09; m 36; c 1. BOTANY. *Educ:* Univ Calif, AM, 32, PhD(bot), 34. *Prof Exp:* Instr bot & cur herbarium, State Col Wash, 34-36, asst prof, 36-37; from asst prof to prof bot, 37-76, cur seed plant collections, 47-63, chmn dept bot, 54-55, dean col letters & sci, 55-62, vchancellor, 62-65, dir herbarium, 63-75, EMER PROF BOT, UNIV CALIF, BERKELEY, 76- *Concurrent Pos:* Vis lectr & acting dir, Gray Herbarium, Harvard Univ, 47-48; Guggenheim fel, 53-54. *Mem:* Bot Soc Am (pres, 70); Torrey Bot Club; Am Soc Plant Taxonomists (pres, 53); Soc Study Evolution; fel Am Acad Arts & Sci. *Res:* Systematic botany of Umbelliferae; cytotaxonomy of Hydrophyllaceae. *Mailing Add:* Dept of Botany Univ of Calif Berkeley CA 94720

CONSTANT, CLINTON, b Nelson, BC, Can, Mar 20, 12; US citizen. INORGANIC CHEMISTRY, CHEMICAL ENGINEERING. *Educ:* Univ Alta, BSc, 35. *Prof Exp:* Develop engr, Harshaw Chem Co, Ohio, 36-38, foreman & engr, Acid Plant, 38-43; plant supt, Nyotex Chem, Inc, Tex, 43-47, chief develop engr, 47-48; sr chem engr, Harshaw Chem Co, Ohio, 48-50; mgr eng, Ferro Chem Corp, 50-52; tech asst mfg dept, Plant Develop & Eng, Armour Agr Chem Co, Fla, 52-61, mgr, Fla Res Div, 61-63, proj mgr eng & design & mgr spec proj, Ga, 63-70; chem engr, Robert & Co Assoc, 70-79; chief engr, Almon Assoc Inc, 79-80; proj mgr, Eng Serv Assoc, Inc, 80-81; VPRES ENG, ACI INC, CALIF, 81- *Mem:* Fel AAAS; fel Am Inst Chem; fel Am Inst Chem Eng; assoc fel Am Inst Aeronaut & Astronaut; Water Pollution Control Fedn. *Res:* Chemical engineering design; phosphates; chemistry and production of anhydrous hydrofluoric acid; slide rule for complex chemical formulation; napalm and automated production. *Mailing Add:* PO Box 1217 Hesperia CA 92345

CONSTANT, FRANK WOODBRIDGE, b Minneapolis, Minn, June 1, 04; m 40; c 3. ENVIRONMENTAL PHYSICS. *Educ:* Princeton Univ, BS, 25; Yale Univ, PhD(physics), 28. *Prof Exp:* Nat res fel physics, Calif Inst Technol, 28-30; from instr to assoc prof, Duke Univ, 30-46; JARVIS PROF PHYSICS, TRINITY COL, CONN, 46- *Concurrent Pos:* Mem & off investr, Nat Defense Res Comt, Duke Univ, 42-46; instr, Dorr-Loomis Pre-Col Sci Ctr, 57, dir, 58 & 59. *Mem:* Fel Am Phys Soc; Am Asn Physics Teachers. *Res:* Ferromagnetism; theoretical physics; mechanics; electromagnetism; fundamental laws of physics and their environmental applications. *Mailing Add:* River Rd Essex CT 06426

CONSTANT, MARC DUNCAN, b Aledo, Ill, July 17, 41. ANALYTICAL CHEMISTRY. *Educ:* Monmouth Col, BA, 63; Southern Ill Univ, MA, 65; Kans State Univ, PhD(anal chem), 70. *Prof Exp:* Supvr anal chem, Am Maize Prod Co, 69-80; GROUP LEADER METHODS, MILLER BREWING CO, 80- *Mem:* Am Chem Soc; Am Soc Brewing Chem. *Res:* Applications of instrumental analysis to the food processing industries, including gas and liquid chromatography, infrared, and general applications of automated wet methods. *Mailing Add:* Miller Brewing Co 3939 W Highland Blvd Milwaukee WI 53201

CONSTANT, PAUL C, JR, b Kansas City, Mo, Sept 3, 22; m 49; c 4. ELECTRICAL ENGINEERING, MATHEMATICS. *Educ:* Univ Minn, BEE, 43; Univ Kansas City, MA, 56. *Prof Exp:* Asst instr elec eng, Univ Minn, 46-47; design engr, Ry Radiotel & Tel Co, Inc, 47-48; sr engr eng dept, 48-66, head electronics & elec eng sect & mgr tech utilization, 66-67, ASST DIR ENG, MIDWEST RES INST, 67- *Concurrent Pos:* Lectr, Univ Mo-Kansas City, 56-; mem, Sect Comt on RF radiation hazards, US Stand Inst, 60-, vchmn, 60-69 & Int Oceanog Found. *Mem:* Sigma Xi; Asn Comput Mach. *Res:* Mathematical and engineering analysis; design of electronic instrumentation and circuitry; electronic computers; bioengineering; system design; experimental design. *Mailing Add:* 1212 W 113th St Kansas City MO 64114

CONSTANTIN, JAMES MICHAEL, b Chicago, Ill, Sept 13, 22; m 48; c 3. LEATHER CHEMISTRY. *Educ:* Univ Notre Dame, BS, 43, PhD(org chem), 49. *Prof Exp:* Res chemist, Merck & Co, Inc, 49-53, sr res chemist, 53-54, purchasing engr, 54-55, purchasing res analyst, 55-57, prod develop specialist, 57-59, sr technologist, 59-63, mgr sales & mkt, 63-65; res assoc, Albert Trostel & Sons Co, 65-67; dir, 67-70, vpres, 70-81, SR VPRES RES & DEVELOP, PFISTER & VOGEL TANNING CO, 81- *Concurrent Pos:* Sci adv comt, Tanners Coun Am, 68-74. *Honors & Awards:* Alsop Award, Am Leather Chem Asn, 81. *Mem:* AAAS; Am Chem Soc; Am Leather Chem Asn (pres-elect, 78-80, pres, 80-); Soc Leather Technologists & Chemists Gt Brit. *Res:* Steroids and steroid total synthesis; medicinal chemicals; enzymatic processes in leather processing; purchasing research and value analysis; market development in leather chemicals; water pollution; tannery waste management. *Mailing Add:* Pfister & Vogel Tanning Co 1531 N Water St Milwaukee WI 53201

CONSTANTIN, MILTON J, plant breeding, botany, see previous edition

CONSTANTINE, ANTHONY BENEDICT, b Buffalo, NY, Jan 30, 16; m 43; c 4. PATHOLOGY. *Educ:* Univ Buffalo, BA, 38, MD, 43. *Prof Exp:* Asst anat, 39-41, instr path, 43-44, assoc, 46-56, CLIN ASST PROF PATH, SCH MED, STATE UNIV NY BUFFALO, 56- *Concurrent Pos:* Res fel, Buffalo Gen Hosp, 46-47, asst pathology, 47-51; pathologist, Vet Admin Hosp, NY, 47 & Buffalo Mercy Hosp, 47-; consult pathologist, Buffalo Vet Admin Hosp, 56-58. *Res:* Pathology of lymphoid diseases. *Mailing Add:* 51 Ruskin Rd East Aurora NY 14052

CONSTANTINE, DENNY G, b San Jose, Calif, May 5, 25; m 52; c 2. VETERINARY MEDICINE, EPIDEMIOLOGY. *Educ:* Univ Calif, Davis, BS, 53, DVM, 55; Univ Calif, Berkeley, MPH, 65. *Prof Exp:* Head wildlife ecol care prog, Arctic Health Res Ctr, Alaska, 50-51, chief wildlife rabies res, Communicable Dis Ctr, Ga, 55-56, chief rabies field unit, NMex, 56-58, chief southwest rabies invest sta, 58-66, chief naval biomed res lab, Ctr Dis Control Activities, USPHS, 66-76; PUB HEALTH VET, CALIF DEPT HEALTH SERV, 76- *Concurrent Pos:* Asst mammalogist, Los Angeles County Mus, 42-46; pvt res, 46-50; zool mus cur, Univ Calif, Davis, 51-55, mammalogist & lab technician, Sch Vet Med, 54-55; consult, Armed Forces Bat Bomb Proj, 43-44. *Mem:* Am Pub Health Asn; Am Vet Med Asn; Am Soc Mammal. *Res:* Public health, veterinary medicine; ecology, virology; physiology; mammalogy; wildlife diseases. *Mailing Add:* Calif Dept Health Serv Berkeley CA 94704

CONSTANTINE, GEORGE HARMON, JR, b San Francisco, Calif, Sept 30, 36; m 62; c 3. PHARMACY. *Educ:* Univ Utah, BS, 60, MS, 62, PhD(pharmacog), 66. *Prof Exp:* Asst chem, 62-63, asst pharm, 63-64, asst pharmacog, 64-66, asst prof, 66-71, assoc prof, 71-80, PROF PHARMACOG, ORE STATE UNIV, 80-, ASST DEAN & HEAD ADV PHARMACOL, 80- *Mem:* Am Pharmaceut Asn; Acad Pharmaceut Sci; Am Soc Pharmacog. *Res:* Natural products; steroid and triterpenoid constituents of higher plants; plant alkaloids; marine biomedicinals. *Mailing Add:* Dept of Pharmacog Ore State Univ Corvallis OR 97331

CONSTANTINE, HERBERT PATRICK, b Buffalo, NY, May 10, 29; m 54; c 2. PHYSIOLOGY, MEDICINE. *Educ:* Univ Buffalo, MD, 53. *Hon Degrees:* MA, Brown Univ, 67. *Prof Exp:* Nat Tuberc Asn fel, 57-59; Am Heart Asn res fel & instr med, Univ Rochester, 59-60; instr physiol, Univ Pa, 60-63; asst prof med, Boston Univ, 63-66; ASSOC PROF MED SCI, BROWN UNIV, 66- *Concurrent Pos:* NIMH grants, 64-68; consult, Vet Admin Hosp, Providence, RI, 66-; dir ambulatory care, RI Hosp, 70- *Mem:* Am Col Physicians; Am Fedn Clin Res; Am Thoracic Soc; Am Physiol Soc. *Res:* Respiratory physiology and mechanics; carbon dioxide reaction rates; laboratory automation; delivery of medical care. *Mailing Add:* Div of Biol & Med Brown Univ Providence RI 02912

CONSTANTINE, JAY WINFRED, b New York, NY, Feb 8, 26; m 52; c 2. PHYSIOLOGY. *Educ:* McGill Univ, BS, 51; Ohio State Univ, PhD(physiol), 59. *Prof Exp:* From asst to instr physiol, Ohio State Univ, 56-59; asst prof, NDak State Univ, 59-61; sr pharmacologist, 61-67, mgr gen pharmacol, 67-72, ASST DIR DEPT PHARMACOL, MED RES LABS, PFIZER, INC, 72- *Mem:* Am Soc Pharmacol & Exp Therapeut; Am Physiol Soc; Int Soc Hypertension. *Res:* Cardiovascular; platelet aggregation; general pharmacology. *Mailing Add:* Dept of Pharmacol Pfizer Inc Med Res Labs Groton CT 06340

CONSTANTINE-PATON, MARTHA, b New York City, NY, July 16, 47; m 71; c 2. DEVELOPMENTAL NEUROBIOLOGY. *Educ:* Jackson Col, Tufts Univ, BS, 69; Cornell Univ, PhD(neurobiol & behav), 76. *Prof Exp:* Fel electron micros, Sect Neurobiol, Behav & Appl Physics, Cornell Univ, 75-76; asst prof biol, 76-81, ASSOC PROF DEVELOP NEUROBIOL, PRINCETON UNIV, 81- *Concurrent Pos:* Prin investr res grants, Nat Eye Inst, 77-, NSF, 81-; participant, Cent Nervous Syst Workshop, Cold Spring Harbor, 78; vis assoc prof, Dept Neurobiol, Harvard Med Sch, 82-83; mem, Visual Sci Study Sect B, NIH, 82- *Mem:* AAAS; Soc Neurosci; Soc Cell Biol; Sigma Xi; Soc Develop Biol. *Res:* Cellular interactions involved in sterotyped axon growth and patterned synaptogenesis during the early development of vertebrate nervous system. *Mailing Add:* Biol Dept Guyot Hall Princeton Univ Princeton NJ 08544

CONSTANTINIDES, CHRISTOS T(HEODOROU), b Nicosia, Cyprus, Mar 22, 31; US citizen; m 62; c 2. ELECTRICAL ENGINEERING. *Educ:* Univ Manchester, BSc, 54, MSc, 55; Univ Kans, PhD(elec eng). *Prof Exp:* Res engr, Marconi's Wireless Tel Co Ltd, Eng, 55-58; asst prof elec eng, Univ Okla, 63-67; assoc prof, 67-75, PROF ELEC ENG, UNIV WYO, 75- *Mem:* Inst Elec & Electronics Engrs; Am Soc Eng Educ. *Res:* Non linear and optimum feedback control systems; distributed parameter systems. *Mailing Add:* Dept of Elec Eng Univ of Wyo Laramie WY 82071

CONSTANTINIDES, PARIS, b Smyrna, Asia Minor, Dec 21, 19; Can citizen; m 50; c 1. ANATOMY, ELECTRON MICROSCOPY. *Educ:* Univ Vienna, MD, 43; Univ Montreal, PhD(exp med), 53. *Prof Exp:* Asst exp med, Inst Exp Med, Univ Montreal, 47-50; from asst prof to prof anat, Med Sch, Univ BC, 50-64, hon prof path, 64-65, prof anat, 65-67, prof path, 67-77; PROF PATH, MED SCH, LA STATE UNIV, 77- *Concurrent Pos:* Vis prof, Wash Univ, 63-64; ed, J Atherosclerosis Res, 61; mem adv comt artificial heart, USPHS, 66; ed, Can J Physiol & Pharmacol, 69; consult, Nat Heart & Lung Inst. *Mem:* Soc Exp Biol & Med; Am Heart Asn; Am Asn Anatomists; Can Physiol Soc; Can Asn Anatomists. *Res:* Experimental pathology; aging degenerative diseases; endocrine. *Mailing Add:* Dept of Path Univ of BC Med Sch Vancouver Can

CONSTANTINIDES, SPIROS MINAS, b Thessaloniki, Greece, Nov 4, 32; m 59; c 2. FOOD SCIENCE, BIOCHEMISTRY. *Educ:* Univ Thessaloniki, BS, 57; Mich State Univ, MS, 63, PhD(food sci), 66. *Prof Exp:* Res assoc food technol, Univ Thessaloniki, 57-61; NIH fel biochem, Mich State Univ, 66-68; from asst prof to assoc prof, 68-74, PROF FOOD & NUTRIT SCI & BIOCHEM, UNIV RI, 74- *Concurrent Pos:* Vis prof, Cath Univ Valparaiso, Chile, 72 & Univ Campinas, Brazil, 75-76. *Mem:* Am Chem Soc; Inst Food Technologists; Am Soc Biol Chemists. *Res:* Structure and function of enzymes; multiple molecular forms and control mechanisms of enzymes; lysosomes and proteolytic enzymes in marine animals; biochemical aspects of preservation of marine foods; utilization of unconventional food resources; food and nutritional science for developing nations. *Mailing Add:* Dept of Food & Nutrit Sci 211 Quinn Hall Univ of RI Kingston RI 02881

CONSTANTOPOULOS, GEORGE, b Greece, Feb 21, 23; US citizen; m 54; c 1. BIOCHEMISTRY. *Educ:* Univ Athens, BSc, 48; Wayne State Univ, PhD(biochem), 62. *Prof Exp:* Clin chemist, Hotel Dieu Hosp, Windsor, Ont, 55-58; res assoc biochem, Wayne State Univ, 62-63; res biochemist, 66-78, SR RES BIOCHEMIST, NAT INST NEUROL COMMUN DIS & STROKE, 78- *Concurrent Pos:* Univ res fel chem, Harvard Univ, 63-66, NIH fel, 64-65. *Mem:* AAAS; Am Chem Soc; Am Soc Biol Chemists; Am Soc Neurochem; NY Acad Sci. *Res:* Pathogenesis of heritable neurological disorders; glycosaminoglycans; lipids; neurochemistry. *Mailing Add:* Nat Inst of Neurol Commun Dis & Stroke Bethesda MD 20205

CONSTANTZ, GEORGE DORAN, b Washington DC, Sept 29, 47; m 72. POPULATION ECOLOGY, ANIMAL BEHAVIOR. *Educ:* Univ Mo-St Louis, BA, 69; Ariz State Univ, MS, 72, PhD(zool), 76. *Prof Exp:* ASST CUR FISH BIOL, ACAD NATURAL SCI, 76- *Concurrent Pos:* Adj prof, Univ Pa, 77- *Mem:* Ecolog Soc Am; Soc Study Evolution; AAAS. *Res:* Population and behavioral ecology of fishes. *Mailing Add:* Acad Natural Sci 19th & the ParkWay Philadelphia PA 19103

CONSUL, PREM CHANDRA, b Meerut, India, Aug 10, 23; m 51; c 5. STATISTICS, MATHEMATICS. *Educ:* Agra Univ, BSc, 43, MSc, 46 & 47, PhD(math, statist), 57. *Prof Exp:* Lectr math, SD Col, Muzaffarnagar, India, 46-47; sr lectr, SM Col, Chandausi, 47-48; asst prof, NREC Col, Khurja, 48-50, assoc prof, 50-53, prof math & statist & head dept, 53-57; head dept statis & prin, MS Col, Saharanpur, 57-61; prof math & statist, Libya, Tripoli, 61-67; assoc prof, 67-71, PROF MATH & STATIST, UNIV CALGARY, 71- *Concurrent Pos:* Mem, Indian Statist Inst, 54-; convenor bd studies in statist, mem acad coun & fac sci, Agra Univ, 55-58, senate, 58-61, panel univ inspectros, 59-61. *Mem:* Int Statist Inst; Inst Math Statist; Am Statist Asn. *Res:* Probability distribution theory; statistical estimation and inference. *Mailing Add:* Dept of Math & Statist Univ of Calgary Calgary Can

CONTA, BART(HOLOMEW) J(OSEPH), b Rochester, NY, Mar 29, 14; m 37; c 3. MECHANICAL ENGINEERING. *Educ:* Univ Rochester, BS, 36; Cornell Univ, MS, 37. *Prof Exp:* Inst mech eng, Cornell Univ, 37-40; res engr, Texas Co, NY, 40-42; from instr to assoc prof heat-power eng, Cornell Univ, 42-47, in charge lab instr, Navy Steam Sch, 44-46; prof mech eng, Col Appl Sci, Syracuse Univ, 47-51; PROF MECH ENG, CORNELL UNIV, 51- *Concurrent Pos:* Ford Found vis prof, Univ Valle, Colombia, 64-65; Nat Sci Found sci fac fel, Univ Calif, Berkeley, 66-67. *Mem:* Soc Hist Technol; AAAS; Am Asn Univ Prof. *Res:* Thermodynamics; energy conversion; history of science and technology. *Mailing Add:* 220 Upson Hall Cornell Univ Ithaca NY 14853

CONTACOS, PETER GEORGE, medical parasitology, tropical medicine, see previous edition

CONTARIO, JOHN JOSEPH, b Detroit, Mich, Nov 23, 44; m 66; c 2. ANALYTICAL CHEMISTRY. *Educ:* Eastern Mich Univ, BS, 66; Iowa State Univ, MS, 68, PhD(anal chem), 71. *Prof Exp:* Group leader chem phys testing, Chem Div, Abbott Labs, 70-72, sr isotope analyst radiopharmaceuts, Diag Div, 72-73, group leader antibiotic & instrumental anal, Chem Div, 73-74, sect head anal serv & methods develop, Chem-Agr Prod Div, 74-80; SECT HEAD ANAL CHEM, MERRELL DOW PHARMACEUT, 80- *Mem:* Am Chem Soc; Sigma Xi; Am Soc Qual Control. *Res:* Analytical support and new test methods for pharmaceutical (new drug and dosage form) development. *Mailing Add:* Merrell Res Ctr 2110 E Galbraith Rd Cincinnati OH 45215

CONTE, FRANK PHILIP, b South Gate, Calif, Feb 2, 29; m 54; c 3. COMPARATIVE PHYSIOLOGY, CELL PHYSIOLOGY. *Educ:* Univ Calif, Berkeley, AB, 51, PhD(physiol, biochem), 61. *Prof Exp:* Asst physiol, Univ Calif, Berkeley, 51-52 & aero-med lab, Wright Air Develop Ctr, Ohio, 52-53; asst biol div, Oak Ridge Nat Lab, Tenn, 53-56; asst chem, Wash State Univ, 56-57; asst prof, Cent Ore Col, 57-59; asst radiation physiol, Donner Lab, Univ Calif, Berkeley, 59-60; from asst prof to assoc prof, 61-71, PROF ZOOL, ORE STATE UNIV, 71- *Concurrent Pos:* Sr fel, NIH, 68-69; vis prof, Dept Zool, Duke Univ, 68-69; prog dir regulatory biol, NSF, 72-73. *Mem:* AAAS; Am Soc Zoologists; Am Physiol Soc; Soc Gen Physiologists; Am Zool Soc. *Res:* Cellular regeneration in aquatic vertebrate; regulation of internal body fluids in aquatic vertebrates; biogenesis of cell membranes; exocrine glands in invertebrates. *Mailing Add:* Dept of Zool Ore State Univ Corvallis OR 97331

CONTE, JOHN SALVATORE, b Philadelphia, Pa, June 12, 32; m 60. ORGANIC CHEMISTRY. *Educ:* La Salle Col, AB, 54; La State Univ, MS, 56; Univ Pa, PhD(chem), 59. *Prof Exp:* Asst instr gen chem, La State Univ, 54-56; asst instr org chem, Univ Pa, 56-57; res group leader, Org Synthetic Sect, Scott Paper Co, 59-69; prod mgr, 69-80, DIV MKT MGR, QUAKER CHEM CO, 80- *Mem:* Am Chem Soc; The Chem Soc. *Res:* Kinetics and mechanism of organic reactions; mechanism of polymer reactions; resin synthesis and free radical polymerization; specialty chemicals for the pulp and paper industries. *Mailing Add:* 908 Pierce Rd Norristown PA 19403

CONTE, SAMUEL D, b Lackawanna, NY, June 5, 17; m 48; c 5. NUMERICAL ANALYSIS, SOFTWARE METRICS. *Educ:* Buffalo State Teachers Col, BS, 39; Univ Buffalo, MS, 43; Univ Mich, MA, 48, PhD(math), 50. *Prof Exp:* From instr to assoc prof math, Wayne Univ, 46-56; mgr math anal dept, Space Tech Labs, 56-61; mgr math dept, Aerospace Corp, 61-62; dir comput sci ctr, 62-66, head comput sci dept, 66-79, PROF COMPUT SCI, PURDUE UNIV, 79- *Mem:* Soc Indust & Appl Math; Am Math Soc; Math Asn Am; Asn Comput Mach. *Res:* Numerical analysis and computation; computer science education; software metrics and software engineering. *Mailing Add:* 3746 Capilano Dr West Lafayette IN 47906

CONTENTO, ISOBEL CORNEIL, b Wuwei, China, Sept 15, 40; US citizen; div. IMMUNOLOGY, NUTRITION. *Educ:* Univ Edinburgh, BSc, 62; Univ Calif, Berkeley, MA, 64, PhD(immunochem), 69. *Prof Exp:* Asst prof biol, Merritt Col, 64-65; fac fel, Johnston Col, Univ Redlands, 69-76; ASSOC PROF NUTRIT, TEACHERS COL, COLUMBIA UNIV, NY, 77- *Mem:* Soc Nutrit Educ; Nat Asn Res Sci Teaching. *Res:* Psycho-social determinants of eating behavior; developmental influences on nutrition and knowledge and behavior in children and adolescents; piagetian analysis of the roll of reasoning skills in consumer nutrition literacy. *Mailing Add:* Teachers Col Columbia Univ New York NY 10027

CONTI, JAMES J(OSEPH), b Coraopolis, Pa, Nov 2, 30; m 61; c 2. CHEMICAL ENGINEERING. *Educ:* Polytech Inst Brooklyn, BChE, 54, MChE, 56, DChE, 59. *Prof Exp:* Sr engr, Bettis Atomic Power Div, Westinghouse Elec Corp, 58-59; from asst prof to assoc prof, 59-64, head dept, 64-70, provost, 70-78, PROF CHEM ENG, POLYTECH INST BROOKLYN, 65-, VPRES EDUC DEVELOP, 78- *Concurrent Pos:* Vis chem engr, Brookhaven Nat Lab, 60 & Res Lab, Diamond Alkali Co, 61; consult, Mobil Oil Co, 62-64, Nat Inst Gen Med Sci, NIH, HEW, 68- *Mem:* AAAS; Am Inst Chem Engrs; Am Soc Eng Educ. *Res:* Transport phenomena, including effects of induced pulsations on heat and mass transfer; chemical reaction kinetics; optimal design of multistage operations; phase equilibrium thermodynamics. *Mailing Add:* Long Island Ctr Polytech Inst NY Rt 110 Farmingdale NY 11735

CONTI, PETER SELBY, b NY, Sept 5, 34; m 61; c 3. ASTROPHYSICS, ASTRONOMY. *Educ:* Rensselaer Polytech Inst, BS, 56; Univ Calif, Berkeley, PhD(astron), 63. *Prof Exp:* Fel & res assoc astron, Calif Inst Technol & Hale Observ, 63-66; asst prof astron & astronr, Univ Calif, Santa Cruz, 66-71; PROF ASTROPHYS, UNIV COLO, BOULDER, 71- *Concurrent Pos:* Fulbright vis prof, Univ Utrecht, Netherlands, 69-70; dir, Assoc Univ Res Astron Inc, 77-; chmn, Dept Astrophys, Planetary & Atmospheric Sci, 80- *Honors & Awards:* Gold Medal, Univ Liege, 75. *Mem:* Am Astron Soc; Int Astron Union; fel AAAS. *Res:* Spectroscopy of very hot and luminous stars; analysis of stellar winds. *Mailing Add:* Joint Inst Lab Astrophys Box 770 Univ of Colo Boulder CO 80329

CONTI, PIERRE ANDRE, b Williamsport, Pa, Dec 30, 34; m 60; c 2. LABORATORY ANIMAL MEDICINE. *Educ:* Pa State Univ, BS, 56; Univ Pa, VMD, 60; Am Col Lab Animal Med, dipl. *Prof Exp:* SR VET, MERCK, SHARP & DOHME, 63- *Mem:* Am Vet Med Asn; Am Asn Lab Animal Sci; Am Soc Lab Animal Practitioners; Am Col Lab Animal Med. *Res:* Laboratory animal medicine; colony management; primatology. *Mailing Add:* Merck Sharp & Dohme Res Labs West Point PA 19486

CONTI, RAUL J, b Cordoba, Argentina, Jan 15, 29; US citizen; m 52; c 4. AERONAUTICS, ASTRONAUTICS. *Educ:* Argentine Air Force Grad Sch, AeroE, 53; Stanford Univ, PhD(aeronaut, astronaut), 65. *Prof Exp:* Res engr, Aerotech Inst, Argentine Air Force, 53-55, head aerodyn dept, 55-56; res asst aerodyn, Princeton Univ, 57; res engr, Langley Res Ctr, NASA, 57-61 & Ames Res Ctr, 61-62; res asst fluid mech, Stanford Univ, 62-64; SR STAFF SCIENTIST FLUID MECH, LOCKHEED PALO ALTO RES LABS, 64- *Concurrent Pos:* Lectr appl math, Univ Santa Clara, 67- *Res:* Wind tunnel testing; shock tube and hypersonic shock tunnel work; aerodynamic heat transfer; transient heat conduction; high temperature gas dynamics; nonequilibrium gas dynamics; analytical methods. *Mailing Add:* Lockheed Palo Alto Res Lab Dept 52-33 3251 Hanover St Palo Alto CA 94304

CONTI, SAMUEL FRANCIS, microbiology, see previous edition

CONTINI, RENATO, b Rome, Italy, June 10, 04; US citizen; m 30. BIOMECHANICS. *Educ:* NY Univ, BS, 24. *Prof Exp:* Chief engr, Burnelli Aircraft Corp, 34-36; spec proj engr railway cars, Edward G Budd Mfg Co, 36-39; design engr aircraft, Glenn L Martin Co, 39-42; chief engr, Langley Aviation Corp, 42-44; vpres eng, Hub Indusrs, Inc, 44-46; sr res scientist eng, NY Univ, 46-70; sr develop engr, Dept Surg, Div Orthop, Univ Calif, Los Angeles, 70-81; CONSULT, 81- *Concurrent Pos:* Secy, Eng Col Res Coun, 54-59; consult comt prosthetic educ & info, Prosthetic Res Bd, Nat Res Coun, 59-62. *Mem:* Fel Am Soc Mech Engrs; fel Human Factors Soc (pres, 58-59); NY Acad Sci; assoc fel NY Acad Med. *Res:* Aircraft design; medical engineering; human factors. *Mailing Add:* 357 S Curson Ave Los Angeles CA 90036

CONTOGOURIS, ANDREAS P, b Athens, Greece, Oct 25, 31; m 57; c 2. THEORETICAL PHYSICS. *Educ:* Nat Tech Univ Athens, dipl elec eng, 54; Cornell Univ, PhD(physics), 61. *Prof Exp:* Res assoc thepret particle physics, Cornell Univ, 61-62; prof theoret physics, Democritus Nuclear Res Ctr, Greece, 62-64; res assoc theoret particle physics, Europ Orgn Nuclear Res, Geneva, Switz, 64-66; assoc lectr theoret physics, Univ Paris, Orsay, 66-68; ASSOC PROF THEORET PARTICLE PHYSICS, McGILL UNIV, 68- *Concurrent Pos:* Greek rep to gov coun, Europ Orgn Nuclear Res, 65-66; Nat Res Coun Can grantee, 68- *Mem:* Am Phys Soc. *Res:* THeoretical problems and phenomenological applications related to the interactions of elementary particles at high energies. *Mailing Add:* Dept of Physics McGill Univ Montreal Can

CONTOIS, DAVID ELY, b Battle Creek, Mich, Jan 18, 28; m 52; c 2. MICROBIOLOGY. *Educ:* Univ Calif, Los Angeles, BA, 50, PhD(microbiol), 57; Univ Hawaii, MS, 52. *Prof Exp:* Res microbiologist, Scripps Inst Oceanog, Univ Calif, 53-58; from asst prof to assoc prof, 58-68, asst dean, 64-69, PROF MICROBIOL, UNIV HAWAII, 68-, DEAN, 69- *Mem:* Am Soc Microbiologists; Brit Soc Gen Microbiol; AAAS. *Res:* Population dynamics; growth kinetics; marine microbiology; geomicrobiology; theory of steady-state microbial growth. *Mailing Add:* Dept Microbiol Univ Hawaii Honolulu HI 96822

CONTRACTOR, DINSHAW N, b Bangalore, India, Apr 23, 33; US citizen; m 58; c 5. HYDRAULIC MODELING, WATER QUALITY MODELING. *Educ:* Univ Baroda, BE, 57; State Univ Iowa, MS, 60; Univ Mich, Ann Arbor, PhD(civil eng), 63. *Prof Exp:* Res scientist, Hydronautics, Inc, Laurel, Md, 63-68; asst prof hydraulics, Va Polytech Inst & State Univ, 68-75, assoc prof, 75-81; PROF HYDRAULICS, WATER & ENERGY RES INST, UNIV GUAM, 80-81. *Mem:* Am Soc Civil Engrs; Am Soc Mech Engrs; Am Geophys Union. *Res:* Hydraulic modeling; optimization of hydraulic systems; simulation of groundwater systems; saltwater intrusion into aquifers; water quality modeling. *Mailing Add:* Dept Civil Eng & Eng Mech Univ Ariz Tucson AZ 85721

CONTRERA, JOSEPH FABIAN, b New York, NY, Nov 18, 38; m 62; c 1. VERTEBRATE PHYSIOLOGY, NEUROPHARMACOLOGY. *Educ:* NY Univ, BA, 60, MS, 61, PhD(endocrine physiol), 66. *Prof Exp:* Res asst neurochem, Sch Med, NY Univ, 60-62, res assoc physiol, Lab Exp Hemat, 63-66; asst prof, 67-70, assoc prof physiol, Univ Md, College Park, 70-77; neuropharmacologist, 77-81, SUPVRY NEUROPHARMACOLOGIST, BUR DRUGS, DEPT HEALTH & HUMAN SERV, FOOD & DRUG ADMIN, 81- *Concurrent Pos:* Lectr biol, Hunter Col, 63-64; post-doc trainee, Dept Pharmacol, Sch Med, Yale Univ, 66-67; vis instr, Dept Pharmacol & Exp Therapeut, Johns Hopkins Univ Sch Med, 75. *Mem:* AAAS; Soc Exp Biol & Med; Am Physiol Soc; Soc Neuro Sci. *Res:* Physiology and pharmacology of the autonomic and central nervous system; experimental hematology; endocrinology. *Mailing Add:* Bur of Drugs HFD-120 Health & Human Serv Food & Drug Admin Rockville MD 20857

CONTRERAS, THOMAS JOSE, b Morenci, Ariz, Mar 20, 45; m 65; c 2. BIOCHEMISTRY, PHYSIOLOGY. *Educ:* Northern Ariz Univ, BS, 67; Univ Utah, MS, 70. *Prof Exp:* Head spec chem clin serv, Long Beach Naval Hosp, 70; res chemist lipid chem, Naval Med Res Inst, 70-71; chief exp res div cryobiol, Naval Blood Res Lab, Boston, 71-76; RES BIOCHEMIST PHYSIOL, ARMED FORCES RADIOBIOLOGY RES INST, 76- *Concurrent Pos:* Consult, Naval Blood Res Lab, 76-, Ctr Blood Res 76- & Blood Bank, Naval Hosp, Bethesda, 77- *Mem:* AAAS; Am Asn Blood Banks. *Res:* Granulocyte isolation and preservation for postirradiation treatment: in vitro and in vivo evaluation. *Mailing Add:* Dept of Exp Hemat Armed Forces Radiobiol Res Inst Bethesda MD 20014

CONTROULIS, JOHN, b Chicago, Ill, Mar 31, 19; m 52; c 2. ORGANIC CHEMISTRY. *Educ:* Transylvania Col, AB, 40; Univ Cincinnati, MA, 41; Univ Mich, PhD(chem), 50. *Prof Exp:* Sr res chemist, 41-47, patent chemist, 49-50, asst dir prods develop, 50-62, mgr mkt res & develop, 62-71, supt capsule develop div, Parke Davis & Co, 71-78; MGR NEW PROD EVAL & PLANNING, WARNER-LAMBERT CO, 78- *Mem:* Am Chem Soc; AAAS; Sigma Xi. *Res:* Synthesis of organic chemicals for medicinal uses; organometallic compounds; nitrogen heterocyclic compounds; chloromycetin and intermediates. *Mailing Add:* 7 Indian Head Rd Morristown NJ 07960

CONTU, PAOLO, anatomy, neuroanatomy, see previous edition

CONVERSE, ALVIN O, b Ridley Park, Pa, Nov 6, 32; m 54; c 3. CHEMICAL ENGINEERING. *Educ:* Lehigh Univ, BS, 54; Univ Del, MChE, 58, PhD(chem eng), 61. *Prof Exp:* Tech serv engr, Sun Oil Co, 54-57; asst prof chem eng, Carnegie Inst Technol, 60-63; assoc prof, 63-69, PROF ENG, DARTMOUTH COL, 69- *Mem:* AAAS; Am Inst Chem Engrs. *Res:* Optimization theory and application; environmental resources and pollution. *Mailing Add:* Thayer Sch of Eng Dartmouth Col Hanover NH 03755

CONVERSE, JAMES CLARENCE, b Brainerd, Minn, Apr 2, 42; m 65; c 4. WASTE MANAGEMENT, AGRICULTURAL ENERGY. *Educ:* NDak State Univ, BS, 64, MS, 66; Univ Ill, PhD(agr eng), 70. *Prof Exp:* Asst prof, 70-75, assoc prof, 75-80, PROF AGR ENG, UNIV WIS-MADISON, 80- *Concurrent Pos:* Prin investr, Univ Wis-Madison, 70- *Mem:* Am Soc Agr Eng. *Res:* Domestic waste management with primary emphasis on mound development; methane production from animal and poultry manure; alcohol production from agricultural products. *Mailing Add:* 460 Henry Mall Madison WI 53706

CONVERSE, JIMMY G, b Scotts Bluff, Nebr, Aug 28, 38. CHEMICAL INSTRUMENTATION. *Educ:* San Diego State Col, BS, 63; Iowa State Univ, PhD(magnetic susceptibilities), 68. *Prof Exp:* Tool maker, Gen Dynamics-Convair, 57-61; sr res chemist, 68-76, PROCESS SPECIALIST, MONSANTO CO, 76- *Mem:* Am Chem Soc; Instrument Soc Am; Sigma Xi. *Res:* Molecular structure of molecules in the gaseous, liquid and solid state; electronic configuration; physical properties; instrumentation. *Mailing Add:* Monsanto Co T2D 800 N Lindbergh Blvd St Louis MO 63141

CONVERSE, JOHN MARQUIS, b San Francisco, Calif, Sept 29, 09. PLASTIC SURGERY, TRANSPLANTATION BIOLOGY. *Educ:* Univ Paris, MD, 35; Am Bd Plastic Surg, dipl, 51. *Prof Exp:* LAWRENCE D BELL PROF PLASTIC SURG, SCH MED & DIR INST RECONSTRUCTIVE PLASTIC SURG, MED CTR, NY UNIV, 57- *Concurrent Pos:* Chmn dept plastic surg, Manhattan Eye, Ear & Throat Hosp, 52-; dir plastic surg serv, Bellevue Hosp, 60- & NY Vet Admin Hosp, 62-; mem adv panel, Med & Dent Br, Off Naval Res, 64-; mem nat adv dent res coun, NIH, 65-; pres, Found Res Med & Biol; gov, Am Hosp Paris. *Mem:* Am Asn Plastic Surg; Am Soc Plastic & Reconstruct Surg; fel Am Col Surg; Am Cleft Palate Asn; Transplantation Soc (pres). *Res:* Vascularization of skin grafts; transplantation; burns research; clinical studies of congenital facial deformities, with emphasis on craniofacial malformations, hemifacial microsomia and second arch syndromes; reconstruction of the auricle. *Mailing Add:* Inst of Reconstructive Plastic Surg NY Univ Med Ctr New York NY 10016

CONVERSE, RICHARD HUGO, b Greenwich, Conn, Sept 18, 25; m 47; c 3. PHYTOPATHOLOGY. *Educ:* Univ Calif, BS, 47, MS, 48, PhD, 51. *Prof Exp:* Asst prof plant path, SDak State Col, 50-52; asst prof bot & plant path, Okla State Univ & asst plant pathologist & agent, USDA, 52-57; plant pathologist, Plant Indust Sta, USDA, 57-67; plant pathologist, USDA, 67-72, RES LEADER HORT CROPS, AGR RES SERV, USDA, 72-, PROF BOT, ORE STATE UNIV, 67- *Mem:* Am Soc Hort Sci; Am Phytopath Soc. *Res:* Small fruit diseases, particularly virus and viruslike diseases of Rubus, Fragaria, and Vaccinium. *Mailing Add:* Dept Bot & Plant Path Ore State Univ Corvallis OR 97331

CONVERTINO, VICTOR ANTHONY, b Troy, NY, Apr 26, 49; m 78. EXERCISE PHYSIOLOGY, ENVIRONMENTAL PHYSIOLOGY. *Educ:* San Jose State Univ, BA, 71, BS, 72; Univ Calif, Davis, MA, 74, PhD(philos), 81. *Prof Exp:* Teaching asst exercise physiol, Univ Calif, Davis, 72, 74, res asst, 74-76, res assoc, 77-78, supvr stress test, 78-79; res assoc exercise physiol, Sch Med, Stanford Univ, 79-81; ASST PROF, DEPT PHYS EDUC, UNIV ARIZ, 82- *Concurrent Pos:* Guest lectr, Dept Phys Educ, Univ Calif, Davis, 77-; test proctor, Calif Highway Patrol, Calif State Personnel Bd, 79; res assoc exercise physiol, NASA, 79; lectr, Dept Human Performance, San Jose State Univ, 81-, & Dept Aeronaut & Astronaut, Stanford Univ, 82- *Mem:* Am Col Sports Med; Aerospace Med Asn; AAAS; Am Physiol Soc. *Res:* Investigation into the effects of exercise training and bedrest deconditioning on chronic cardiovascular and fluid-electrolyte-endocrine adaptations; aerospace medicine; cardiac rehabilitation applications. *Mailing Add:* Dept Phys Ed Univ Ariz Tuscon AZ 85791

CONVERY, F RICHARD, b Olympia, Wash, June 12, 32; m 55; c 3. ORTHOPEDIC SURGERY. *Educ:* Univ Wash, BA, 54, MD, 58; Am Bd Orthop Surg, dipl, 69. *Prof Exp:* Resident, 61-66, from instr to assoc prof orthop surg, Sch Med, Univ Wash, 67-72; assoc prof & dir rehab, Div Orthop & Rehab, 72-77, PROF ORTHOP SURG, SCH MED, UNIV CALIF, SAN DIEGO, DIR REHAB, DIV ORTHOP & REHAB, SCH MED, 77- *Concurrent Pos:* Sr fel orthop surg, Sch Med, Univ Wash, 63-64; Southern Calif Arthritis Found clin fel, Ranchos Los Amigos Hosp, 66-67. *Honors & Awards:* Kappa Delta Award, Am Acad Orthop Surg, 73. *Mem:* Am Rheumatism Asn. *Res:* Degeneration and repair of articular cartilage as related to joint reconstruction; surgical management of rheumatoid arthritis. *Mailing Add:* Div Orthop & Rehab Univ Calif Sch Med San Diego CA 92103

CONVERY, ROBERT JAMES, b Philadelphia, Pa, Jan 17, 31; m 52; c 3. ORGANIC CHEMISTRY. *Educ:* St Joseph's Col, Philadelphia, BS, 52; Univ Notre Dame, MS, 56; Univ Pa, PhD(chem), 59. *Prof Exp:* Res chemist, Rohm and Haas Co, Pa, 54, Atlantic Refining Co, 55 & E I du Pont de Nemours & Co, 56-59; res chemist, Res & Develop Div, Sun Oil Co, 59-62 & Res Group, 62-63, asst sect chief, 63-64; from asst prof to assoc prof chem, 64-70, actg head dept, 64-66, assoc dean sci, 71-74, head dept, 66-71 & 74-78, PROF CHEM, COL STEUBENVILLE, 70-, DEAN FAC, 78- *Concurrent Pos:* Vis lectr, St Mary's Col, Ind, 54-55; instr, Evening Div, St Joseph's Col, Pa, 60-62. *Mem:* Sigma Xi. *Res:* Organic mechanisms and synthesis; free radicals. *Mailing Add:* Dept of Chem Col of Steubenville Steubenville OH 43952

CONVEY, EDWARD MICHAEL, b Hicksville, NY, Oct 12, 39; m 62; c 2. PHYSIOLOGY, ENDOCRINOLOGY. *Educ:* Mich State Univ, BS, 63, MS, 65; Rutgers Univ, PhD(physiol), 68. *Prof Exp:* From asst prof to assoc prof dairy physiol, 68-78, PROF PHYSIOL, MICH STATE UNIV, 78- *Mem:* Am Dairy Sci Asn; Am Soc Animal Sci; Endocrine Soc; AAAS; Soc Study Reproduction. *Res:* Lactational and reproduction physiology; anterior pituitary. *Mailing Add:* Dept Dairy Mich State Univ East Lansing MI 48823

CONWAY, ALVIN CHARLES, b Chicago, Ill, Jan 5, 22; m 48; c 2. PHARMACOLOGY. *Educ:* Univ Chicago, BS, 47, MS, 48. *Prof Exp:* Res asst anesthesiol & pharmacol, Univ Chicago, 47-48; res chemist, Swift & Co, 48-49; res pharmacologist, Irwin, Neisler & Co, 49-51; sr res pharmacologist, Lakeside Labs, 51-60, chief gen pharmacol sect, Colgate-Palmolive Co, 60-65; res specialist, 65-67, SR RES SPECIALIST, MINN MINING & MFG CO, 67- *Mem:* AAAS; NY Acad Sci; Am Chem Soc; Sigma Xi. *Res:* Behavioral screening; psychotropics. *Mailing Add:* Riker Labs Inc 218-2 Minn Mining & Mfg Co 3M Ctr St Paul MN 55101

CONWAY, BRIAN EVANS, b London, Eng, Jan 26, 27; m 54; c 1. PHYSICAL CHEMISTRY. *Educ:* Imp Col, London, BSc, 46, PhD & dipl, 49, DSc, 61. *Prof Exp:* Res assoc chem, Inst Cancer Res, London, 49-54; asst prof, Univ Pa, 54-56; from asst prof to assoc prof, 56-60, chmn dept, 66-69, PROF CHEM, UNIV OTTAWA, 60- *Concurrent Pos:* Consult tech ctr, Gen Motors; Commonwealth vis prof, Univs Southampton & Newcastle, 69-70. *Honors & Awards:* Novanda lectr award, Chem Inst Can, 64. *Mem:* The Chem Soc; Electrochem Soc; fel Brit Chem Soc; fel Royal Inst Chem; fel Royal Soc Can. *Res:* Electrochemistry; kinetics of electrode processes; adsorption at electrodes; isotopic effects in electrode reactions; polyelectrolytes; thermodynamics of polymer solutions. *Mailing Add:* Dept Chem Univ Ottawa 365 Nicholas St Ottawa ON K1N 6N5 Can

CONWAY, DWIGHT COLBUR, b Long Beach, Calif, Nov 14, 30; m 62; c 4. MASS SPECTROSCOPY. *Educ:* Univ Calif, BS, 52; Univ Chicago, PhD(chem), 56. *Prof Exp:* From instr to asst prof chem, Purdue Univ, 56-63; assoc prof, 63-67, PROF CHEM, TEX A&M UNIV, 67- *Mem:* Am Chem Soc; Am Phys Soc; Am Soc Mass Spectros; Sigma Xi. *Res:* Ion-molecule reactions; self consistent field-molecular orbit calculations; analysis of polymers by mass spectroscopy. *Mailing Add:* Dept Chem Tex A&M Univ College Station TX 77843

CONWAY, EDWARD DAIRE, III, b New Orleans, La, Feb 7, 37; m 61; c 2. MATHEMATICAL ANALYSIS. *Educ:* Loyola Univ, BS, 59; Ind Univ, MA, 63, PhD(math), 64. *Prof Exp:* Vis mem, Courant Inst Math Sci, NY Univ, 64-65; asst prof math, Univ Calif, San Diego, 65-67; from asst prof to assoc prof, 67-74, PROF MATH, TULANE UNIV, 74- *Mem:* Am Math Soc; Soc Indust & Appl Math; Math Asn Am; AAAS. *Res:* Nonlinear partial differential equations. *Mailing Add:* Dept of Math Tulane Univ New Orleans LA 70118

CONWAY, GENE FARRIS, b Cynthiana, Ky, Aug 24, 28; m 50; c 3. INTERNAL MEDICINE, CARDIOVASCULAR DISEASES. *Educ:* Univ Ky, BS, 49; Univ Cincinnati, MD, 52. *Prof Exp:* Intern med, Philadelphia Gen Hosp, 52-53; resident internal med, Louisville Gen Hosp, 53-54; chief med serv, US Air Force Hosp, Topeka, Kans, 54-56; from resident to chief resident internal med, Cincinnati Gen Hosp, 56-59, USPHS res fel cardiol, 59-61, from asst prof to assoc prof, 61-70, asst dir dept internal med, 73-75, PROF MED, COL MED, UNIV CINCINNATI, 70-, ASSOC DEAN RURAL HEALTH, 75- *Concurrent Pos:* Clin investr, Vet Admin Hosp, Cincinnati, 61-63, chief of cardiol, 63-, assoc chief of staff for res, 72-74; fel, Coun Clin Cardiol, Am Heart Asn, 69-; chief med serv, Vet Admin Hosp, Cincinnati, 72-75, prog adv cardiovasc res, Res Serv, Vet Admin, 74- *Mem:* Am Col Cardiol. *Res:* Chemistry of myocardial contractile proteins; myocardial biology; congestive heart failure; arrhythmias; ischemic heart disease. *Mailing Add:* MSB E152 Univ of Cincinnati Med Ctr Cincinnati OH 45267

CONWAY, H(ARRY) D(ONALD), b Chatham, Eng, Dec 3, 17; nat US; m; c 2. MECHANICS. *Educ:* Univ London, BSc, 42, PhD(mech), 45, DSc(mech), 49; Cambridge Univ, MA, 46, ScD, 70. *Prof Exp:* Eng apprentice, Dockyard, Eng, 34-38; stress analyst, Short Bros, 38-39; sci officer, Nat Phys Lab, 42-45; assoc prof, 47-48, PROF MECH, CORNELL UNIV, 48- *Concurrent Pos:* Guggenheim fel & vis prof, Imp Col, London, 53-54; Stone vis prof, Ohio State Univ, 58-59; Nat Sci Found sr fel, 61-62. *Honors & Awards:* Baden-Powell Prize, Royal Aeronaut Soc. *Mem:* Am Soc Mech Engrs. *Res:* Vibrations; elasticity; plates and shells. *Mailing Add:* Thurston Hall Cornell Univ Ithaca NY 14850

CONWAY, HERTSELL S, b Peoria, Ill, Sept 30, 14; m 40; c 2. INFORMATION SCIENCE, CHEMICAL LITERATURE. *Educ:* Univ Chicago, SB, 32, PhD(org chem), 37. *Prof Exp:* Asst, Emulsol Corp, Ill, 37-39; chemist, Food & Drug Admin, USDA, 39-41 & Lambert Pharmacal Co, Mo, 41-46; org chemist, US Govt Rubber Labs, 46-47; chemist, Standard Oil Co, Ind, 47-49, group leader, 49-55, sect leader, 55-60; res supvr, Am Oil Co, 60-65; sr info scientist, Standard Oil Co, Ind, 65-80; RETIRED. *Mem:* Am Chem Soc; Am Translators Asn. *Res:* Analysis of petroleum products and petrochemicals; indexing and searching; technical writing and editing. *Mailing Add:* Standard Oil Co Ind Munster IN 46321

CONWAY, JOHN BELL, b Madison, Wis, April 5, 36; m 61; c 2. WATER QUALITY. *Educ:* San Diego State Univ, BS, 64, MS, 67; Univ Minn, MPH, 70, PhD(environ biol), 73. *Prof Exp:* Marine technician, Scripps Inst Oceanog, Univ Calif, 58-59; pub health sanitarian, Div Sanit, San Diego County Health Dept, 64-65; pub health biologist, Dept Natural Resources, State Wis, 67-69; res asst pub health, Sch Pub Health, Univ Minn, 70-72; asst prof, Dept Biol Sci, Wright State Univ, Ohio, 72-76; assoc prof, Bacteriol & Pub Health, Wash State Univ, 76-81; PROF ENVIRON HEALTH, GRAD SCH PUB HEALTH, SAN DIEGO STATE UNIV, 81- *Concurrent Pos:* Adj asst prof, Sch Pub Health, Univ Minn, 74-76; lectr, Ctr Lake Superior Environ Studies, Univ Wis, 78; disaster consult, Greene Co Health Dept, Ohio, 74-75. *Mem:* Sigma Xi; Nat Environ Health Asn; Am Pub Health Asn. *Res:* Water quality research, emphasizing chemical, biological and bacteriological indicators of waste and potable water; investigations of the pollutants involved in diseases of man. *Mailing Add:* Grad Sch Pub Health San Diego State Univ San Diego CA 92182

CONWAY, JOHN BLIGH, b New Orleans, La, Sept 22, 39; m 64. MATHEMATICAL ANALYSIS. *Educ:* Loyola Univ, BS, 61; La State Univ, PhD(math), 65. *Prof Exp:* From asst prof to assoc prof, 65-77, PROF MATH, IND UNIV, BLOOMINGTON, 77- *Mem:* Am Math Soc; Math Asn Am. *Res:* Functional analysis. *Mailing Add:* Dept of Math Ind Univ Bloomington IN 47401

CONWAY, JOHN GEORGE, JR, b Pittsburgh, Pa, May 16, 22; m 47; c 7. ATOMIC SPECTROSCOPY. *Educ:* Univ Pittsburgh, BS, 44. *Prof Exp:* Chemist, Los Alamos Sci Lab, NMex, 44-46; asst physics, Univ Pittsburgh, 46; PHYSICIST, LAWRENCE BERKELEY LAB, UNIV CALIF, BERKELEY, 46- *Concurrent Pos:* Mem comt, Line Spectra of the Elements, Nat Acad Sci, 67; res assoc, Nat Ctr Sci Res, Orsay, France, 73-74; chmn comt line spectra of elements, Nat Res Coun, 74-75. *Honors & Awards:* William F Meggers Medal, Optical Soc Am, 80. *Mem:* Soc Appl Spectros; assoc Am Phys Soc; fel Optical Soc Am. *Res:* Spectroscopy; chemical analysis and absorption and emission of transuranium elements; the spectra of higher ionized atoms. *Mailing Add:* Lawrence Berkeley Lab Univ of Calif Berkeley CA 94720

CONWAY, JOHN RICHARD, b Cincinnati, Ohio, Feb 28, 43; m 69. ENTOMOLOGY, HUMAN ANATOMY. *Educ:* Ohio State Univ, BS, 65; Univ Colo, MA & PhD(biol), 75. *Prof Exp:* Asst prof, Marycrest Col, 76-78; ASST PROF HUMAN ANAT & PHYSIOL, ELMHURST COL, 78- *Mem:* Entomol Soc Am; AAAS. *Res:* Biology of the honey ant, Myrmecocystus mexicanus. *Mailing Add:* Dept of Biol Elmhurst Col Elmhurst IL 60126

CONWAY, JOSEPH C, b Wilkes-Barre, Pa, Mar 11, 39; m 65; c 3. ENGINEERING MECHANICS, EXPERIMENTAL STRESS ANALYSIS. *Educ:* Pa State Univ, BS, 61, MS, 63, PhD(eng mech), 68. *Prof Exp:* Proj engr, Ord Res Lab, 64-76, asst prof, 68-76, ASSOC PROF ENG MECH, PA STATE UNIV, 76- *Mem:* Am Soc Eng Educ; Am Soc Mech Engrs; Soc Exp Stress Anal. *Res:* Numerical analysis of crack propagation problems; shells and structures research utilizing numerical methods; experimental stress analysis of shells and structures. *Mailing Add:* Dept Eng Sci & Mech Col Eng Pa State Univ University Park PA 16802

CONWAY, KENNETH EDWARD, b Philadelphia, Pa, June 7, 43; m 68; c 3. PLANT PATHOLOGY, MYCOLOGY. *Educ:* State Univ NY Potsdam, BS, 66; State Univ NY Col of Forestry, Syracuse, MS, 68; Univ Fla, PhD(bot), 73. *Prof Exp:* Teacher biol & ecol, Alachua County Bd Pub Instr, 70-73; res asst, 73-75, asst res scientist plant path, Univ Fla, 75-78; ASST PROF PLANT PATH, OKLA STATE UNIV, 78- *Mem:* Mycol Soc Am; Am

Photopath Soc; Sigma Xi. *Res:* Etiology and control of diseases of horticultural crops (vegetables, fruits and ornamentals) and forest and shade trees; use of cercospora rodmanii as a biological control for water hyacinths. *Mailing Add:* Dept of Plant Path Okla State Univ Stillwater OK 74078

CONWAY, LYNN ANN, b Mt Vernon, NY, Jan 2, 38. COMPUTER SCIENCE, ELECTRICAL ENGINEERING. *Educ:* Columbia Univ, BS, 62, MSEE, 63. *Prof Exp:* Mem res staff comput archit, Int Bus Mach Corp, 64-69; sr staff engr, Memorex Corp, 69-73; mem res staff, Digital Syst Archit, 73-77, mgr, LSI Systs Area, 77-80, RES FEL & MGR VLSI SYST DESIGN AREA, XEROX PALO ALTO RES CTR, 80- *Concurrent Pos:* Consult, Syst Industs, 73-74; vis assoc prof elec eng & comput sci, Mass Inst Technol, 78-79. *Mem:* Inst Elec & Electronics Engrs; Asn Comput Mach; AAAS. *Res:* VLSI system architecture and design methodology; computer architecture; special purpose digital system architecture; digital image processing; artificial intelligence; knowledge engineering. *Mailing Add:* Xerox Palo Alto Res Ctr 3333 Coyote Hill Rd Palo Alto CA 94304

CONWAY, RICHARD WALTER, b Milwaukee, Wis, Dec 12, 31; m 53; c 3. OPERATIONS RESEARCH. *Educ:* Cornell Univ, BME, 54, PhD(opers res), 58. *Prof Exp:* Assoc prof indust eng & opers res, 58-65, PROF COMPUT SCI, CORNELL UNIV, 65- *Concurrent Pos:* Consult, Gen Elec Co, Int Bus Mach Corp, Western Elec Co & Rand Corp. *Mem:* Asn Comput Mach. *Res:* Production control; computer sciences. *Mailing Add:* Upson Hall Cornell Univ Ithaca NY 14850

CONWAY, THOMAS WILLIAM, b Aberdeen, SDak, June 6, 31; m 57; c 2. BIOCHEMISTRY. *Educ:* Col St Thomas, BS, 53; Univ Tex, MA, 55, PhD(biochem), 62. *Prof Exp:* Fel biochem, Rockefeller Inst, 62-64; res assoc, 64; from asst prof to assoc prof, 64-73, PROF BIOCHEM, UNIV IOWA, 73- *Concurrent Pos:* Vis prof, Univ Chile, 68; Am Cancer Soc scholar, London, 80-81. *Mem:* AAAS; Am Chem Soc; Am Soc Microbiol; Am Soc Biol Chem; hon mem Biol Soc Chile. *Res:* Mechanism and control of protein biosynthesis in phage-infected bacteria and interferon treated cells. *Mailing Add:* Dept of Biochem Univ of Iowa Iowa City IA 52242

CONWAY, WALTER DONALD, b Troy, NY, Feb 4, 31; m 58; c 4. SEPARATION METHODS, DRUG METABOLISM. *Educ:* Rensselaer Polytech Inst, BS, 52; Univ Rochester, PhD(org chem), 56. *Prof Exp:* Res chemist, Esso Res & Eng Co, 56-57, Nat Cancer Inst, US Dept Health, Educ & Welfare, 57-62 & Sterling-Winthrop Res Inst, 62-65; res assoc, Lab Chem Pharmacol, Nat Heart Inst, 65-67; asst prof, 67-71, assoc prof, 71-75, ASSOC PROF PHARMACEUT & MED CHEM, SCH PHARM, STATE UNIV NY BUFFALO, 75- *Concurrent Pos:* Mem US pharmacopeia comt rev, US Pharmacopeial Conv, 75- *Mem:* Am Chem Soc; Am Pharmaceut Asn; Acad Pharmaceut Sci; Am Soc Pharmacol & Exp Therapeut. *Res:* Analytical methodology; identification of drug metabolites; effect of species differences and route of administration on the metabolic fate of drugs. *Mailing Add:* Sch of Pharm State Univ of NY Amherst NY 14260

CONWAY, WILLIAM SCOTT, b Phillipsburg, Pa, Aug 12, 43; m 79; c 1. PHYTOPATHOLOGY. *Educ:* Pa State Univ, BS, 65; Univ NH, MS, 74, PhD(path), 76. *Prof Exp:* Asst prof hort, Delhi Agr & Tech Col, 76-79; RES PLANT PATHOLOGIST, BELTSVILLE AGR RES CTR, 79- *Mem:* Am Phytopath Soc. *Res:* Postharvest plant pathology; investigations into preventing loss due to pathogens of fruits in storage. *Mailing Add:* Hort Crops Qual Lab HSI ARS-USDA Agr Res Ctr Beltsville MD 20705

CONWELL, ESTHER MARLY, b New York, NY, May 23, 22; m 45; c 1. SOLID STATE PHYSICS. *Educ:* Brooklyn Col, BA, 42; Univ Rochester, MS, 45; Univ Chicago, PhD(physics), 48. *Prof Exp:* Instr physics, Brooklyn Col, 45-51; mem tech staff, Bell Tel Labs, 51-52; eng specialist, GTE Labs, 52-63, mgr physics dept, 63-72; prin scientist, 72-80, RES FEL, XEROX, 80- *Concurrent Pos:* Vis prof, Univ Paris, 62-63; Abbie Rockefeller Mauze prof, Mass Inst Technol, 72. *Honors & Awards:* Annual Award, Soc Women Eng, 60. *Mem:* Nat Acad Eng; fel Am Phys Soc; Inst Elec & Electronics Engrs; fel AAAS. *Res:* Quasi i-d conductors. *Mailing Add:* Xerox Xerox Square W114 Rochester NY 14644

CONYERS, EMERY SWINFORD, b Cynthiana, Ky, Aug 16, 39; m 64; c 2. SOIL SCIENCE. *Educ:* Univ Ky, BS, 61; Ohio State Univ, MS, 63, PhD(soil chem), 66, MBA, St Marys Col, 84. *Prof Exp:* Res asst soils, Ohio State Univ, 61-66, teaching assoc, 66; chemist, US Army Aviation Mat Labs, 66-68; res specialist, 68-74, proj mgr construct mat, 74-75, group leader membrane systs, 75-80, sales mgr, 80-81, MGR GOVT RELATIONS, DOW CHEM CO, 81- *Mem:* Am Soc Agron; Soil Sci Soc Am; Sigma Xi. *Res:* Fixation and release of potassium by soils and clays, metal ion-clay interactions, chemical control of soil erosion, land treatment of wastewater and membrane systems for water treatment. *Mailing Add:* Dow Chem Co PO Box 1706 Midland MI 48640

CONYNE, RICHARD FRANCIS, b Canandaigua, NY, June 26, 19; m 47; c 4. POLYMER CHEMISTRY, PLASICTS. *Educ:* Univ Rochester, AB, 41. *Prof Exp:* Chemist & group leader, Rohm & Haas Co, 41-56, head lab, 56-68, res supvr, 68-73, int plastics mgr, 73-76, res proj leader, 76-79; PLASTICS CONSULT, 79- *Mem:* Am Chem Soc; AAAS; Soc Plastics Eng. *Res:* Plastics; plasticizers; coatings; adhesives. *Mailing Add:* Wilkinson Rd Rushland PA 18956

CONZELMAN, GAYLORD MAURICE, JR, b Republic, Kans, Mar 30, 23; m 53; c 3. PHARMACOLOGY. *Educ:* Idaho State Col, BS, 49; George Washington Univ, PhD, 53. *Prof Exp:* Lilly Res Labs fel, Christ Hosp Inst Med Res, Cincinnati, Ohio, 53-55, res assoc, 55-63; res pharmacologist, 63-68, lectr, 68-69, asst prof, 69-74, assoc prof, 74-80, PROF PHARMACOL, DEPT PHYSIOL SCI, SCH VET MED, UNIV CALIF, DAVIS, 80- *Mem:* AAAS; Am Soc Pharmacol & Exp Therapeut; Am Asn Cancer Res; Soc Toxicol. *Res:* Cancer biology; biosynthesis of purines; chemotherapy; drug metabolism; carcinogenesis; drug induced nephropathy. *Mailing Add:* Dept of Physiol Sci Sch Vet Med Univ of Calif Davis CA 95616

CONZETT, HOMER EUGENE, b Dubuque, Iowa, Oct 16, 20; m 60; c 2. EXPERIMENTAL NUCLEAR PHYSICS. *Educ:* Univ Dubuque, BS, 42; Univ Calif, PhD(physics), 56. *Prof Exp:* Degaussing physicist, Bur Ord, Dept Navy, 42-44; res physicist, Radiation Lab, Univ Calif, 56-57; vis Fulbright lectr, Univ Tokyo, 57-58; res physicist, 58-64, dir 88-inch cyclotron, 64-71, SR RES PHYSICIST, LAWRENCE BERKELEY LAB, UNIV CALIF, 64- *Concurrent Pos:* Vis res physicist, Inst Nuclear Sci, Univ Grenoble, 66-67. *Mem:* Fel Am Phys Soc. *Res:* Nuclear reactions and scattering below 100 mev; spin-polarization phenomena in nuclear physics. *Mailing Add:* 318 Vassar Ave Kensington CA 94708

COOCH, FREDERICK GRAHAM, b Winnipeg, Man, May 4, 28; m 58; c 3. ECOLOGY, ORNITHOLOGY. *Educ:* Queen's Univ, Ont, BA, 51; Cornell Univ, MS, 53, PhD(wildlife mgt), 58. *Prof Exp:* Arctic ornithologist, Dept Environ, Can Wildlife Serv, 54-62, head biocide invests, 62-64, staff specialist, Migratory Birds Invests, head migratory bird pop sect, head Can banding off & migratory bird coordr, 64-79, SR SCIENTIST MIGRATORY BIRDS, CAN WILDLIFE SERV, 79- *Mem:* Fel AAAS; fel Arctic Inst NAm; Am Ornith Union; Wildlife Soc. *Res:* Wildlife ecology, especially Arctic; insecticides; vertebrate systematics. *Mailing Add:* 685 Echo Dr Ottawa ON K1S 1P2 Can

COODLEY, EUGENE LEON, b Los Angeles, Calif, Jan 14, 20; m 47; c 3. INTERNAL MEDICINE, CARDIOLOGY. *Educ:* Univ Calif, Berkeley, BA, 40; Univ Calif, San Francisco, MD, 43. *Prof Exp:* Consult cardiac dis & rehab, Calif Dept Rehab, 55-61; dir dept med, Lidcombe Hosp, Australia, 61-62; dir dept med, Kern County Hosp, 65-67; DIR DEPT MED, PHILADELPHIA GEN HOSP, 67-; PROF MED, HAHNEMANN MED COL, 67-, ASSOC CHMN DEPT, DIR DIV INTERNAL MED & DIR RESIDENCY TRAINING PROG, 74- *Concurrent Pos:* Guest lectr, Europ Cong Rheumatism, 59 & Int Cong Surg, 65; consult, Dept Rehab, Sydney, Australia, 61-62. *Mem:* Fel Am Col Physicians; Am Col Angiol; fel Am Col Cardiol; fel Am Col Gastroenterol. *Res:* Enzyme research, development of new enzyme procedures for diagnosis in medicine. *Mailing Add:* Dept of Med Hahnemann Med Col Philadelphia PA 19102

COOGAN, ALAN H, b Brooklyn, NY, Dec 19, 29. PALEONTOLOGY, GEOLOGY. *Educ:* Univ Calif, Berkeley, BA, 56, MA, 57; Univ Ill, PhD, 62; Univ Akron, JD, 77. *Prof Exp:* Instr geol, Cornell Col, 57-60; geologist, Humble Oil & Refining Co, 62-65; geologist, Esso Prod Res Co, 65-67; assoc dean res, 69-77, PROF GEOL, KENT STATE UNIV, 67- *Mem:* Am Asn Petrol Geologists; Am Paleont Soc; Soc Econ Paleontologists & Mineralogists; Am Bar Asn. *Res:* Paleontology and stratigraphy; carbonate petrology; environmental geology. *Mailing Add:* Dept of Geol Kent State Univ Kent OH 44242

COOGAN, CHARLES H(ENRY), JR, b Boston, Mass, Apr 2, 08; m 34; c 2. MECHANICAL ENGINEERING. *Educ:* Tufts Univ, BS, 30; Harvard Univ, MS, 31; Univ Pa, ME, 37. *Prof Exp:* Designer, Buerkel & Co, Inc, Mass, 30; instr mech eng, Univ Pa, 31-42; from asst prof to prof, 42-78, head dept, 47-68, EMER PROF MECH ENG, UNIV CONN, 78- *Concurrent Pos:* Consult, Elec Boat Div, Gen Dynamics, 55-68; secy, Conn State Bd Registr Prof Eng, 57-73; mem indust res adv comt, Gov of Conn, 61-65; mem, Res Comn, State of Conn, 65-73. *Mem:* Fel Am Soc Mech Engrs (vpres, 58-62); Am Soc Eng Educ; Nat Soc Prof Engrs. *Res:* Jet-type pumps; waste heat boilers; flow instruments; heat pump ground coil; heat transfer; two-phase flow. *Mailing Add:* RR 1 735 Storrs Rd Storrs CT 06268

COOGAN, PHILIP SHIELDS, b Peoria, Ill, Feb 13, 38; m 60; c 4. PATHOLOGY. *Educ:* St Louis Univ, MD, 62. *Prof Exp:* USPHS res trainee path, Presby-St Lukes Hosp, 62-64; instr path, Univ Ill, 64-68; Blake fel path, Presby-St Lukes Hosp, 69-72; asst prof path, Med Col, Rush Univ, 72-73, assoc prof, 73-74; assoc prof path, Northwestern Univ, 74-78; PROF & CHMN, DEPT PATH, COL MED, EAST TENN STATE UNIV, 78- *Concurrent Pos:* assoc attending pathologist & chmn, Tissue Comt, Presby-St Luke's Hosp, 72-74; dir, Res Path, Med Col, Rush Univ, 72-74, mem res & educ comt, 74; assoc attending pathologist & dir anat path, Northwestern Mem Hosp, 74-78, mem, Instnl Review Bd, 76-78. *Honors & Awards:* Hektoen Award, Chicago Path Soc, 69. *Mem:* Am Soc Pathologists & Bacteriologists; Int Acad Path; AMA; AAAS; Am Soc Exp Path. *Res:* Interaction of sex steroids as carcinogens with 2-Acetyl aminofluorene, a carcinogen capable of inducing carcinomas of the endometrium and urinary bladder in rabbits. *Mailing Add:* Dept Path Quillen-Dishner Col Med ETenn State Univ Pox 19540A Johnson City TN 37601

COOHILL, THOMAS PATRICK, b Brooklyn, NY, Aug 25, 41; m 62; c 3. BIOPHYSICS. *Educ:* Univ Toronto, BSc, 62; Univ Toledo, MSc, 64; Pa State Univ, PhD(biophys), 68. *Prof Exp:* Asst prof cell biol, Med Sch, Univ Pittsburgh, 68-72; res physicist, Vet Admin Hosp, Leech Farm, 68-72; assoc prof, 72-80, PROF BIOPHYS, WESTERN KY UNIV, 72- *Mem:* AAAS; Biophys Soc; Am Soc Photobiol. *Res:* Effects of ultraviolet light on fungi, on mammalian tissue culture cells, on human viruses and crustaceans; human tumor visuses; activation and development. *Mailing Add:* Biophys Prog Western Ky Univ Bowling Green KY 42101

COOIL, BRUCE JAMES, b Colfax, Wash, Aug 21, 14; m 44; c 2. PLANT PHYSIOLOGY. *Educ:* State Col Wash, BS, 36; Univ Hawaii, MS, 39; Univ Calif, PhD(plant physiol), 47. *Prof Exp:* Asst physiologist guayule res proj, Bur Plant Indust, Soils & Agr Eng, USDA, Calif, 42-45; asst plant physiologist, US Regional Salinity Lab, 45-47; assoc plant physiologist, 47-54, PROF BOT & PLANT PHYSIOLOGIST, AGR EXP STA, UNIV HAWAII, 54- *Mem:* Bot Soc Am; Am Soc Plant Physiol. *Res:* Translocation of organic materials in plants; mineral nutrition of plants; salt absorbtion and transport in plant roots. *Mailing Add:* Dept of Bot Univ Hawaii 3190 Maile Way Honolulu HI 96822

COOK, ADDISON GILBERT, b Caracas, Venezuela, Apr 1, 33; US citizen; m 56; c 3. ORGANIC CHEMISTRY. *Educ:* Wheaton Col, BS, 55; Univ Ill, PhD(org chem), 59. *Prof Exp:* Asst chem, Univ Ill, 55-56; fel, Cornell Univ, 59-60; from asst prof to assoc prof, 60-70, PROF CHEM & CHMN DEPT, VALPARAISO UNIV, 70- *Concurrent Pos:* Consult, Argonne Nat Labs, 62-73. *Mem:* Am Chem Soc. *Res:* Amines, heterocyclic compounds, bicyclic compounds, organophosphorus compounds and small ring compounds. *Mailing Add:* Dept of Chem Valparaiso Univ Valparaiso IN 46383

COOK, ALAN FREDERICK, b Harrow, Eng, July 15, 39; US citizen; m 64; c 2. CHEMISTRY. *Educ:* Univ Birmingham, BSc, 61; Univ London, PhD(chem), 64. *Prof Exp:* Fel, Syntex Corp, Calif, 64-66; CHEMIST, HOFFMANN-LA ROCHE INC, 66- *Mem:* Am Chem Soc. *Res:* Chemistry of nucleosides and nucleotides. *Mailing Add:* Hoffmann-La Roche Inc 340 Kingsland St Nutley NJ 07110

COOK, ALBERT MOORE, b Denver, Colo, June 24, 43; m 65; c 3. BIOMEDICAL ENGINEERING. *Educ:* Univ Colo, BS, 66; Univ Wyo, MS, 68, PhD(bioeng), 70. *Prof Exp:* PROF & DIR BIOMED ENGR, CALIF STATE UNIV, SACRAMENTO, 70-, CO-DIR ASSISTIVE DEVICE CTR, 77- *Concurrent Pos:* Consult, Sutter Hosp Med Res Found, Sacramento, 71-74 & Lawrence Livermore Lab, 74-79; fac res award, Calif State Univ, Sacramento, 75; prin investr, NSF, Instrnl Equip Prog, 76-78; co-prin investr, Oper Eng, commun enhancement grant; mem adv comt on res to aid handicapped, NSF. *Mem:* Inst Elec & Electronic Engrs; Am Soc Eng; Biomed Eng Soc; Asn Advan Med Instrumentation; Rehab Soc NAm. *Res:* Development and effective application of assistive devices for the disabled; development of systems for automation of clinical bacteriology; microprocessor applications in medicine and biology; non-oral communication system application and development. *Mailing Add:* Biomed Eng Prog 6000 Jay St Sacramento CA 95819

COOK, ALBERT WILLIAM, b Brooklyn, NY, July 23, 22; m 47; c 2. NEUROSURGERY. *Educ:* Dartmouth Col, AB, 44; Long Island Col Med, MD, 46; Am Bd Neurol Surg, dipl, 56. *Prof Exp:* Assoc prof surg & head div neurosurg, 59-71, chmn dept, 71-76, PROF NEUROSURG, STATE UNIV NY DOWNSTATE MED CTR, 71-; DIR DEPT NEUROSCI, LONG ISLAND COL HOSP, 77- *Concurrent Pos:* Consult regional hosps, Brooklyn, NY & Vet Admin Hosps, 59- *Mem:* AMA; Am Col Surgeons; Am Asn Neurol Surgeons; Soc Neurosci; Asn Res Nerv & Ment Dis. *Res:* Craniocerebral trauma; intracranial blood clots; cerebrovascular disease; surgical treatment of vascular anomalies; cerebral hemodynamics; respiratory and metabolic aspects of cerebral lesions; cerebral neoplasms; pain control; electrical stimulation of the spinal cord; multiple sclerosis. *Mailing Add:* 200 Hicks St Brooklyn NY 11201

COOK, ALLAN FAIRCHILD, II, b New York, NY, May 9, 22; m 59; c 3. ASTROPHYSICS. *Educ:* Princeton Univ, BSE, 47, AM, 50, PhD(astron), 52. *Prof Exp:* Asst astron, Princeton Univ, 48-49; instr astron & physics, Carleton Col, 50-51; asst, Col Observ, Harvard Univ, 51-57, res assoc, 57-59, res fel, 59-61, res assoc, 61-62, lectr, 61-74; physicist, 61-64, ASTROPHYSICIST, SMITHSONIAN ASTROPHYS OBSERV, 64- *Mem:* Am Astron Soc; fel Meteoritical Soc; fel Royal Astron Soc. *Res:* Asteroids; meteors; meteor spectra; planetary rings; planetary satellites. *Mailing Add:* Ctr Astrophys 60 Garden St Cambridge MA 02138

COOK, ALLYN AUSTIN, b Grandview, Ill, Feb 14, 27; m 48; c 2. PLANT PATHOLOGY. *Educ:* Univ Wis, PhD(plant path), 51. *Prof Exp:* Asst pathologist, SDak State Col, 52-54; agent pathologist, Spec Crops Sect, USDA, 54-56; from assoc plant pathologist to plant pathologist, Agr Exp Sta, 56-68, PROF PLANT PATH, UNIV FLA, 68- *Concurrent Pos:* Fulbright lectr, Ein Shams Univ, Cairo, 63-64; vis specialist, Univ Hawaii, 70-71; NSF fel, Brisbane, Australia, 79-80. *Mem:* Am Phytopath Soc; Am Hort Soc. *Res:* Developed bell peppers with multiple virus resistance; hypersensitive resistance to bacterial leafspot infection in pepper. *Mailing Add:* Dept Plant Path Univ Fla Gainesville FL 32601

COOK, ANCEL EUGENE, b Sadieville, Ky, Sept 15, 09; m 37; c 3. PHYSICAL OPTICS, MICROELECTRONICS. *Educ:* Georgetown Col, BA, 35; Univ Ky, MS, 48. *Prof Exp:* Teacher pub sch, Ky, 35-42; physicist, Indust Mgr Off, US Navy, La, 42-43; asst prof physics, Georgetown Col, 47-49; instr, Univ Ky, 49-51; physicist, Bur Ships, Navy Dept, 54-59; physicist, Off Naval Res, 59-74; RETIRED. *Concurrent Pos:* Sci secy laser res & explor develop panel, US Navy, 63-74, mem microelectronics panel, 66-74, coordr adv groups, industry & independent res & develop progs; US Navy mem, Dept Defense Adv Group Electron Devices; asst to US Navy mem, Armed Serv Res Specialist Comt; secy, Govt Microelectronics Applns Confs. *Mem:* Am Phys Soc; Am Soc Naval Eng; sr mem Inst Elec & Electronic Engrs. *Res:* Lasers and fluidic research and exploratory development; physical sciences. *Mailing Add:* 3021 Park Dr S E Washington DC 20020

COOK, BARNETT C, b Chicago, Ill, Nov 25, 23. PHYSICS. *Educ:* Northwestern Univ, BS, 46; Univ Chicago, PhD(physics), 56. *Prof Exp:* Physicist, Inst Nuclear Res, Univ Chicago, 52-56; asst prof physics, Univ Pa, 56-59; physicist, Midwest Univs Res Asn, 59-60; physicist, 60-61, asst prof physics, 61-75, ASSOC PHYSICIST, AMES LAB, IOWA STATE UNIV, 61-, ASSOC PROF PHYSICS, 74- *Mem:* AAAS; Am Phys Soc. *Res:* Photonuclear reactions; accelerator design. *Mailing Add:* Dept of Physics Iowa State Univ Ames IA 50011

COOK, BENJAMIN JACOB, b Upper Darby, Pa, Sept 26, 30; m 52; c 2. INSECT PHYSIOLOGY, BIOCHEMISTRY. *Educ:* Providence Col, AB, 58; Rutgers Univ, MS, 61, PhD(insect physiol), 63. *Prof Exp:* Asst prof biol, Col Holy Cross, 62-64; adj prof zool & asst prof entom, NDak State Univ & insect physiologist, Metab & Radiation Lab, USDA, 64-72; insect physiologist, Western Cotton Res Lab, USDA, Phoenix, Ariz, 72-76; INSECT PHYSIOLOGIST VET TOXICOL & ENTOM RES LAB, USDA, 76- *Mem:* Soc Gen Physiologists; Entom Soc Am. *Res:* Insect neurophysiology and neurochemistry; peripheral and central mechanisms of nerve impulse transmission; the isolation and pharmacodynamics of natural neurotransmitters and neurohormones. *Mailing Add:* PO Drawer GE College Station TX 77840

COOK, BILLY DEAN, b Oklahoma City, Okla, July 28, 35; div; c 2. PHYSICS. *Educ:* Okla State Univ, BS, 57; Mich State Univ, MS, 59, PhD(physics), 62. *Prof Exp:* Res instr, Mich State Univ, 62-63, asst prof res physics, 65-68; res assoc, 68-69, assoc prof, 69-76, PROF MECH & ELEC ENG, UNIV HOUSTON, 76- *Res:* Ultrasonic light diffraction; non-linear propagation of acoustical waves; optics and noise control; nondestructive testing. *Mailing Add:* Dept of Mech & Elec Eng Univ of Houston Houston TX 77004

COOK, CHARLES DAVENPORT, b Minneapolis, Minn, Nov 30, 19; m 45, 76; c 5. MEDICINE. *Educ:* Princeton Univ, AB, 41; Harvard Univ, MD, 44. *Prof Exp:* Asst prof pediat, Harvard Med Sch, 57-63, assoc clin prof, 63-64; prof pediat & chmn dept, Yale Univ, 64-75; PROF PEDIAT & CHMN DEPT, STATE UNIV NY DOWNSTATE MED CTR, 75- *Concurrent Pos:* Physician, Boston Children's Hosp, 58-64; chmn, Joint Coun Nat Pediat Socs, 70-73. *Mem:* Soc Pediat Res; Am Acad Pediat; Am Pediat Soc (secy-treas, 64-75); Am Physiol Soc. *Res:* Medical education; health care, delivery; quality assessment and assurance; ethics in medicine. *Mailing Add:* 450 Clarkson Ave Brooklyn NY 11203

COOK, CHARLES EMERSON, b New York, NY, Oct 27, 26; m 48; c 3. ELECTRICAL ENGINEERING. *Educ:* Harvard Univ, SB, 49; Polytech Inst Brooklyn, MEE, 54. *Prof Exp:* Engr, Melpar, Inc, 49-51; from engr to res engr, Sperry Gyroscope Co, 51-63, res sect head, 63-64, sr res sect head, 64-67, res dept head, Sperry Rand Res Ctr, 67-71; mem dept staff, 71-81, DIV STAFF CONSULT, COMMUN DIV, MITRE CORP, BEDFORD, 81- *Mem:* Fel Inst Elec & Electronics Engrs; Sigma Xi. *Res:* Radar system analysis and synthesis; research and development of signal processing techniques to improve the detection and resolution performance of radar and sonar systems; command and control communication systems analysis. *Mailing Add:* MITRE Corp PO Box 208 Bedford MA 01730

COOK, CHARLES F(OSTER), JR, b Peacock, Tex, Jan 23, 32; m 56; c 2. ELECTRON BEAM LITHOGRAPHY, MATERIALS SCIENCE. *Educ:* Tex Tech Univ, BS, 54; Rutgers Univ, MS, 76. *Prof Exp:* Phys scientist & electron microscopist, 56-60, RES PHYS SCIENTIST, US ARMY ELECTRONIC TECHNOL & DEVICES LAB, 60- *Honors & Awards:* Di Paul Siple Medallion & Award, US Army Sci Conf, 70. *Mem:* Electron Micros Soc Am; Microbeam Anal Soc. *Res:* Electron beam lithography research and development; materials science research, including semiconductors, thin films, ferroelectrics, ferromagnetics and solid state materials. *Mailing Add:* US Army Electronic Technol & Devices Lab DELET-ED Ft Monmouth NJ 07703

COOK, CHARLES FALK, b Jonesboro, Ark, Dec 21, 28; m 49; c 2. NUCLEAR PHYSICS, CHEMICAL PHYSICS. *Educ:* Tex Christian Univ, BA, 48, MA, 50; Rice Inst, PhD(physics), 53. *Prof Exp:* Fel physics, Rice Inst, 53-54; asst prof, Univ Fla, 54-55; sr nuclear eng, Convair Div, Gen Dynamics Corp, Ft Worth, Tex, 55-56, nuclear test lab engr, 56-58; nuclear physics sect mgr, 58-62, physics br mgr, 62-70, PHYSICS & ANAL BR MGR, RES DIV, PHILLIPS PETROL CO, DIR, 77- *Mem:* Am Phys Soc. *Res:* Nuclear reaction cross sections; electron spin resonance; molecular energy levels in hydrocarbon molecules using spectroscopic techniques; analytical chemistry; molecular structure. *Mailing Add:* Phillips Petrol Res & Develop Co 385 Frank Phillips Bldg Bartlesville OK 74004

COOK, CHARLES J, b West Point, Nebr, Oct 2, 23; m 45; c 2. ENERGY PLANNING, INDUSTRIAL PLANNING. *Educ:* Univ Nebr, BS, 48, MA, 50, PhD(physics), 53. *Prof Exp:* Res assoc, Univ Nebr, 53-54; physicist, SRI Int, 54-56, mgr, Molecular Physics Sect, 56-62, dir, Chem Physics Div, 62-69, exec dir phys sci, 69-76, vpres off res opers, 76-77, sr vpres res opers, 77-81; MGR INT PLANNING, BECHTEL GROUP, INC, 81- *Concurrent Pos:* Instr, San Jose City Col, 57-58 & Foothill Col, 59-62; sr res assoc, Queen's Univ, Belfast, 62-63; partic, Advan Mgt Prog, Harvard Grad Sch Bus, 68. *Mem:* Am Phys Soc; Am Asn Physics Teachers; Am Inst Aeronaut & Astronaut; Am Inst Physics; Am Defense Preparedness Asn. *Res:* Ionic and atomic impact phenomena; technology utilization and transfer; international planning. *Mailing Add:* Bechtel Group Inc 50 Beale St PO Box 3965 San Francisco CA 94119

COOK, CHARLES S, b Rochester, NY, Feb 19, 38; m 64; c 2. MECHANICAL ENGINEERING. *Educ:* Cornell Univ, BME, 60; Univ Rochester, MS, 64, PhD(mech & aerospace sci), 66. *Prof Exp:* Res engr pulsed plasma accelerator diag, 66-67, light detection & ranging systs, 67-71, magnetohydrodynamics power generation, 71-76, MGR MAGNETOHYDRODYNAMICS & COAL COMBUSTION COMPONENT DEVELOP, ENERGY SYSTS PROGS DEPT, GEN ELEC CO, 76- *Mem:* Sigma Xi. *Res:* Plasma diagnostics; atmospheric probing with light detection & ranging; mie scattering; optical transmissivity of smoke plumes; magnetohydrodynamics power generation; high temperature heat exchangers; coal combustion; open and closed magnetohydrodynamics cycle systems. *Mailing Add:* Gen Elec Space Sci Lab Rm L9515 Box 8555 Philadelphia PA 19101

COOK, CHARLES WAYNE, b Gove, Kans, Oct 28, 14; m 40; c 1. RANGE SCIENCE. *Educ:* Ft Hays Kans State Univ, BS, 40; Utah State Univ, MS, 42; Agr & Mech Univ, Tex, PhD, 50. *Prof Exp:* Range conservationist, Soil Conserv Serv, USDA, 42-43; res prof range mgt, Utah State Univ, 43-46, prof range sci, 46-67; PROF RANGE SCI & HEAD DEPT, COLO STATE UNIV, 67- *Honors & Awards:* Hoblitzelle Award, 53. *Mem:* AAAS; Am Inst Biol Sci; assoc Am Soc Animal Sci; assoc Soc Range Mgt; Soil Conserv Soc Am. *Res:* Range seeding and forage nutrition; bioecology of cactus on the central great plains; utilization of range plants and forage by herbivores; physiological responses of plants; energy flow in the range ecosystem. *Mailing Add:* Dept of Range Sci Colo State Univ Ft Collins CO 80521

COOK, CHARLES WILLIAM, b Yankton, SDak, Sept 27, 27; m 50; c 3. EXPERIMENTAL NUCLEAR PHYSICS. *Educ:* Univ SDak, AB, 51; Calif Inst Technol, MS, 54, PhD(physics), 57. *Prof Exp:* Sr res engr, Convair, 57-58, design specialist & head nuclear physics, 58-60; chief res ballistic missile defense, Inst Defense Anal, 60-61; adv res proj agency, Dept Defense, 61-62; res & develop specialist, NAm Aviation, Inc, Calif, 62-63, corp dir electronics, 63-67; independent consult, 67-71; asst dir, Dept Res & Eng, Dept Defense, 71-74; dep under secy, Air Force Space Systs, 74-79, DEP ASST SECY, AIR FORCE SPACE PLANS & POLICY, WASHINGTON, DC, 79- *Concurrent Pos:* Consult, Inst Defense Anal, 62-63 & McGraw-Hill Book Co, Inc, 62-80. *Mem:* Am Phys Soc; Am Inst Phys; Am Inst Aeronaut & Astronaut; Inst Elec & Electronics Engrs. *Res:* Energy generation and element synthesis reactions occurring in stellar interiors; electronics research and development. *Mailing Add:* 1180 Daleview Dr McLean VA 22102

COOK, CLARENCE EDGAR, b Jefferson City, Tenn, Apr 27, 36; m 57; c 3. BIOORGANIC CHEMISTRY. *Educ:* Carson-Newman Col, BS, 57; Univ NC, PhD(org chem), 61. *Prof Exp:* Am Chem Soc Petrol Res Fund fel, Cambridge Univ, 61-62; sr chemist, 62-68, group leader, 68-71, asst dir, Chem & Life Sci Div, 71-75, dir life sci, 75-80, DIR BIOORG CHEM, RES TRIANGLE INST, 75- *Concurrent Pos:* Vis scholar, Univ Liverpool, 79. *Mem:* AAAS; Am Chem Soc; Phytochem Soc NAm; fel NY Acad Sci; Am Soc Pharmacol & Exp Therapeut. *Res:* Drug metabolism; contraceptive drugs; synthesis of medicinal compounds; oxygen and nitrogen heterocycles; steroid chemistry; natural products; agricultural chemistry; immunoassay development. *Mailing Add:* Chem & Life Sci Group Res Triangle Inst PO Box 12194 Research Triangle Park NC 27709

COOK, CLARENCE HARLAN, b Winthrop, Iowa, Jan 16, 25; m 45; c 4. MATHEMATICS. *Educ:* Univ Iowa, BA, 48, MS, 50; Univ Colo, PhD(math), 62. *Prof Exp:* Asst prof math, Western State Col, Colo, 50-52; asst, Univ Tex, 52-53; engr, Convair, Tex, 53-54; sr mathematician, Martin Co, Md, 54-55, prin engr, Colo, 55-59, sragg engr opers res, 60-62; asst prof math, Univ Okla, 62-65; from asst prof to assoc prof, 65-76, PROF MATH, UNIV MD, COLLEGE PARK, 76- *Mem:* Am Math Soc; Math Soc Belg. *Res:* Functional analysis; topology. *Mailing Add:* Dept Math Univ Md College Park MD 20742

COOK, CLARENCE SHARP, b St Louis Crossing, Ind, Aug 18, 18; m 43; c 2. PHYSICS. *Educ:* DePauw Univ, AB, 40; Ind Univ, MA, 42, PhD(physics), 48. *Prof Exp:* Asst physics, Ind Univ, 40-42 & 46-48; asst prof, Wash Univ, St Louis, 48-53; head nuclear radiation br, US Naval Radiol Defense Lab, 53-59, head radiation effects br, 59-60, head nucleonics div, 60-61, physics consult to sci dir, 62-65, head radiation physics div, 65-69; lectr, Univ Santa Clara, 69-70; chmn dept, 70-72, PROF PHYSICS, UNIV TEX, EL PASO, 70-, CHMN DEPT, 80- *Concurrent Pos:* Mem bd exam scientists & engrs, US Civil Serv Comn, 55-58, chmn bd, 57-58, mem prof coun scientists & engrs, Calif-Nev area, 67-69; Fulbright res scholar, Aarhus Univ, 61-62. *Mem:* Am Phys Soc; Am Asn Physics Teachers; Am Geophys Union; Health Physics Soc. *Res:* Energy education; effects of ionizing radiations. *Mailing Add:* Box 204 Univ of Tex El Paso TX 79968

COOK, DAVID ALLAN, b Colby, Wis, Mar 11, 40; m 62; c 4. NUTRITIONAL BIOCHEMISTRY. *Educ:* Wis State Univ-River Falls, BS, 62; Iowa State Univ, PhD(animal nutrit), 67. *Prof Exp:* NIH res fel biochem, Univ Minn, St Paul, 67-68; sr investr, Dept Nutrit Res, 69-73, prin investr, 73-74, clin investr, Dept Clin Invest, 74-75, nutrit investr, 75-76, DIR, DEPT NUTRIT SCI, NUTRIT DIV, MEAD JOHNSON, 76- *Mem:* AAAS; Brit Nutrit Soc; Am Inst Nutrit; Sigma Xi; Nutrit Today Soc. *Res:* Ruminant fatty acid metabolism and absorption; oxalic acid formation from aromatic amino acids; infant nutrition; bile acid metabolism; atherosclerosis; mineral metabolism and bioavailability; clinical nutrition; gastroenterology. *Mailing Add:* Dept of Nutrit Res Mead Johnson Nutrit Div Evansville IN 47721

COOK, DAVID EDGAR, b Corpus Christi, Tex, Dec 13, 40; m 63; c 2. BIOCHEMISTRY. *Educ:* Southwest Tex State Col, BS, 62; Okla State Univ, MS, 65; Univ Tex, Austin, PhD(chem), 70. *Prof Exp:* From instr to asst prof chem, Northeastern State Col, Okla, 64-70; NIH res fel & res assoc biochem, Inst Enzyme Res, Univ Wis-Madison, 70-73; asst prof, 73-78, ASSOC PROF BIOCHEM, COL MED, UNIV NEBR MED CTR, OMAHA, 78- *Concurrent Pos:* NSF sci fac fel, Univ Tex, Austin, 68-69. *Mem:* Am Chem Soc; AAAS; Sigma Xi; Am Soc Biol Chem. *Res:* Biochemical pharmacology; metabolism. *Mailing Add:* Dept Biochem Univ Nebr Med Ctr Omaha NE 68105

COOK, DAVID EDWIN, b Houston, Tex, Dec 3, 35; m 58; c 2. TOPOLOGY. *Educ:* Univ Tex, BA, 58, MA, 60, PhD(math), 67. *Prof Exp:* Spec instr math, Univ Tex, 61-64, teaching assoc, 64-67; asst prof, 67-69, ASSOC PROF MATH, UNIV MISS, 69- *Mem:* Am Math Soc; Math Asn Am. *Res:* Point set topology. *Mailing Add:* Dept of Math Univ of Miss University MS 38677

COOK, DAVID GREENFIELD, b Birmingham, Eng, May 27, 41; Can citizen. INVERTEBRATE ZOOLOGY, SYSTEMATICS. *Educ:* Univ Liverpool, BSc, 64, PhD(zool), 67. *Prof Exp:* Fel systs, Marine Biol Lab, Woods Hole Mass, 67-69; fel zool, Nat Mus Natural Sci, Ottawa, Ont, Can, 69-71; benthic biologist, Great Lakes Biolimnol Lab Can Ctr Inland Waters, Burlington Ont, 73-75; ASST ED, SCI INFO & PUBL BR, FISHERIES & OCEANS CAN, 75- *Mem:* Freshwater Biol Asn. *Res:* Taxonomy, morphology and ecology of marine and freshwater microdrile oligochaetes; freshwater benthic ecology; scientific editing. *Mailing Add:* Sci Info & Publ Br Fisheries & Oceans Can Ottawa ON K1A 0E6 Can

COOK, DAVID MARSDEN, b Troy, NY, Apr 3, 38; m 65; c 2. THEORETICAL PHYSICS, INSTRUCTIONAL COMPUTING. *Educ:* Rensselaer Polytech Inst, BS, 59; Harvard Univ, AM, 60, PhD(physics), 65. *Prof Exp:* From asst prof to assoc prof, 65-79, PROF PHYSICS, LAWRENCE UNIV, 79- *Concurrent Pos:* NSF sci fac fel, Dartmouth Col, 71-72. *Mem:* Am Phys Soc; Am Asn Physics Teachers. *Res:* Plasma physics; applied mathematics; computers in physics education. *Mailing Add:* Dept of Physics Lawrence Univ Box 599 Appleton WI 54912

COOK, DAVID RUSSELL, b Hastings, Mich, Aug 9, 22; m 52; c 2. INVERTEBRATE ZOOLOGY, ENTOMOLOGY. *Educ:* Univ Mich, BS, 48, MA, 51, PhD, 52. *Prof Exp:* USDA entomologist, US Nat Mus, 52-53; from asst prof to assoc prof, 53-65, PROF BIOL, WAYNE STATE UNIV, 65- *Concurrent Pos:* Entomologist & malariologist, Int, Co-op Admin Malaria Control Prog, US Opers Mission to Liberia, 56-58; Fulbright res fel, India, 62-63; Fulbright lectr, Argentina, 75. *Res:* Acarina; Hydracarina. *Mailing Add:* Dept of Biol Wayne State Univ Detroit MI 48202

COOK, DAVID WILSON, b Wilkinson County, Miss, Nov 3, 39; m 61; c 2. MICROBIOLOGY. *Educ:* Miss State Univ, BS, 61, MS, 63, PhD(microbiol), 66. *Prof Exp:* HEAD MICROBIOL SECT, GULF COAST RES LAB, 66-, REGISTR, 71-, ASST DIR ADMIN & ACAD AFFAIRS, 72- *Concurrent Pos:* Assoc mem grad fac, Miss State Univ, 68-; asst prof biol, Univ Miss, 71- *Mem:* Am Soc Microbiol; Gulf Estuarine Soc; Sigma Xi. *Res:* Microbiology of the estuarine environment including pollution; nutrient turnover; diseases of fish and shellfish and spoilage of seafoods. *Mailing Add:* Gulf Coast Res Lab East Beach Ocean Springs MS 39564

COOK, DONALD BOWKER, b Easthampton, Mass, Jan 14, 17; m 43; c 6. PHYSICS. *Educ:* Princeton Univ, AB, 38; Columbia Univ, MA, 39, PhD(physics), 50. *Prof Exp:* Physicist, Manhattan Proj, Columbia Univ & Carbon & Carbide Chem Corp, NY, 42-44, sect leader, 44-45, group leader, 45-46, physicist, Div Govt Aid Res, Columbia Univ, 46-50; physicist, Nevis Cyclotron Lab, 47; res physicist, 50-57, SR RES PHYSICIST, E I DU PONT DE NEMOURS & CO, INC, 57- *Mem:* Am Phys Soc; Am Chem Soc; Sigma Xi. *Res:* Multilayer films; gas diffusion; cryogenics; structure of polyfibers. *Mailing Add:* RD 1 Box 126 Hockessin DE 19707

COOK, DONALD J, b Astoria, Ore, Feb 14, 20; m 44; c 2. MINERAL ENGINEERING. *Educ:* Univ Alaska, BS, 47, ME, 52; Pa State Univ, MS, 58, PhD(mineral beneficiation), 61. *Prof Exp:* Off engr, US Smelting, Refining & Mining Co, 47-50, mining engr, 54-57; assayer & engr, Alaska Div Mines & Minerals, 50-52; instr & asst, Univ Alaska, 52-54; asst mineral beneficiation, Pa State Univ, 57-59; from asst prof to assoc prof, 59-65, PROF MINERAL BENEFICIATION, UNIV ALASKA, 65- *Concurrent Pos:* NSF res grant, 60-64; vis prof, Cheng Kung Univ, Taiwan, 71; vpres, Bd Engrs & Archit Exam, State of Alaska. *Mem:* Am Inst Mining, Metall & Petrol Engrs; Nat Soc Prof Engrs. *Res:* Mineral beneficiation; magnetic susceptibility and dielectric constants of rocks and minerals. *Mailing Add:* Dept of Mineral Eng Univ of Alaska Fairbanks AK 99701

COOK, DONALD JACK, b Rock Island, Ill, Feb 12, 15; m 39; c 2. ORGANIC CHEMISTRY. *Educ:* Augustana Col, AB, 37; Univ Ill, MA, 38; Ind Univ, PhD(org chem), 44. *Prof Exp:* City chemist, Rock Island, Ill, 38-39; Am Container Corp, 39-40; instr chem, Augustana Col, 40-41; chemist, Texas Co, NY, 41-42; asst sci, Ind Univ, 42-44; res chemist, Lubri-Zol Corp, 44-45; from asst prof to prof, 45-80, head dept, 64-80, EMER PROF, DE PAUW UNIV, 80- *Concurrent Pos:* Assoc prof dir, Div Sci Personnel & Ed, NSF, 61-62. *Mem:* Am Chem Soc. *Res:* N-substituted carbostyrils; preparation and properties of substituted lepidones; SeO2 oxidations. *Mailing Add:* Dept of Chem DePauw Univ Greencastle IN 46135

COOK, DONALD LATIMER, b Arena, Wis, July 31, 16; m 43; c 2. PHARMACOLOGY. *Educ:* Univ Wis, BS, 38, PhD(pharmaceut chem), 43. *Prof Exp:* Instr pharmacol & physiol, Sch Pharm, Western Reserve Univ, 42-43; pharmacologist, G D Searle & Co, 46-70, head dept pharmacol, 70-74, ASSOC DIR DEPT BIOL RES, SEARLE LABS, G D SEARLE & CO, 74- *Mem:* Am Soc Pharmacol & Exp Therapeut; Soc Exp Biol & Med. *Res:* Phytochemical study of the leaves of Celastrus scandens Linne. *Mailing Add:* Res & Develop Div G D Searle & Co PO Box 5110 Chicago IL 60680

COOK, EARL FERGUSON, b Bellingham, Wash, May 24, 20; m 47, 69; c 3. RESOURCE GEOGRAPHY, VOLCANIC GEOLOGY. *Educ:* Univ Wash, Seattle, BS, 43, MS, 47, PhD(geol), 54. *Prof Exp:* Instr, Univ Wash, Seattle, 47-48; instr, Stanford Univ, 48; photogeologist, Geophoto Servs, 49-51; asst prof geol & geog & actg head, Univ Idaho, 51-52, assoc prof & head, 52-57, prof & dean, Col Mines, 57-65; exec secy, Div Earth Sci, Nat Acad Sci-Nat Res Coun, 64-66; prof geol & assoc dean, Col Geosci, 66-71, actg dean, Col Geosci, 68-69, prof geog & geol & dean, Col Geosci, 71-81, DISTINGUISHED PROF GEOG & GEOL & HARRIS PROF GEOSCI, TEX A&M UNIV, 81- *Concurrent Pos:* Dir, State Bur Mines & Geol, Idaho, 57-65; consult, Nat Acad Sci, 66-67, mem, Comt Alaska Earthquake, 67-73; mem US del, Orgn Econ Coop & Develop Adv Conf Tunnelling, 70. *Mem:* Geol Soc Am; Soc Econ Geologists; Am Inst Mining, Metall & Petrol Engrs; Asn Am Geog; Asn Am State Geol (pres, 63-64). *Res:* Environmental decision-making related to resource development and use; man and energy; resource geography; volcanic geology and structures related to volcanism. *Mailing Add:* Dept Geog Tex A&M Univ College Station TX 77843

COOK, EDWARD HOOPES, JR, b Harrisburg, Pa, May 21, 29; m 51; c 2. PHYSICAL CHEMISTRY, INORGANIC CHEMISTRY. *Educ:* Elizabethtown Col, BS, 50; Pa State Col, PhD(chem), 53. *Prof Exp:* SUPVR, HOOKER CHEM CORP, 63- *Mem:* Am Chem Soc; Electrochem Soc. *Res:* Electrochemical development; industrial electrolytic; theoretical electrochemistry; mechanism of corrosion processes. *Mailing Add:* 8424 Carol Ct Niagara Falls NY 14304

COOK, EDWIN FRANCIS, b San Francisco, Calif, Sept 11, 18; m 49; c 5. ENTOMOLOGY. *Educ:* Stanford Univ, AB, 43, AM, 44, PhD(biol sci), 48. *Prof Exp:* Actg instr gen biol, Stanford Univ, 46-48, actg asst prof entom, 48-49; PROF ENTOM, UNIV MINN, ST PAUL, 49- *Mem:* AAAS; Am Soc Syst Zool; Entom Soc Am. *Res:* Systematic entomology. *Mailing Add:* 1727 Lindig St St Paul MN 55113

COOK, ELIZABETH ANNE, b Colorado Springs, Colo, Sept 19, 26. MICROBIOLOGY. *Educ:* Univ Colo, BA, 48; Ind Univ, MA, 56, PhD(bact), 58. *Prof Exp:* Instr bact, Mankato State Col, 57-58; from instr to asst prof, 62-70, assoc prof bact, 70-80, PROF BIOL SCI, DOUGLASS COL, RUTGERS UNIV, 80- *Mem:* AAAS; Am Soc Microbiol. *Res:* Microbiological assays for vitamin B12 and folic acid; bacterial nutrition. *Mailing Add:* Dept Biol Sci Douglass Col Rutgers the State Univ New Brunswick NJ 08903

COOK, ELLSWORTH BARRETT, b Springfield, Mass, Jan 29, 16; m 41. PHARMACOLOGY. *Educ:* Springfield Col, BS, 38; Tufts Univ, PhD(med sci), 51. *Prof Exp:* Res assoc, Fatigue Labs, Harvard, 41-45; head visual screening & statist facil, Med Res Lab Submarine Base, Conn, 45-49; environ physiologist, Cold Injury Res Team, Korea, 51-52; consult biometrician, Army Med Res Lab, Ft Knox, Ky, 52; res pharmacologist, Nat Naval Med Res Inst, 52-57; head dept exp biol, Naval Med Field Res Lab, Camp Lejeune, NC, 57-61; exec officer, Am Soc Pharmacol & Exp Therapeut, 61-77; RETIRED. *Concurrent Pos:* Lectr, Med Sch, Howard Univ, 62-77. *Mem:* AAAS; Am Soc Pharmacol & Exp Therapeut; Biomet Soc; Psychomet Soc; Coun Biol Ed. *Res:* Acetylcholine analogues; standardization of bioassay techniques; biometrics and psychometrics. *Mailing Add:* 15500 Prince Frederick Way Silver Spring MD 20906

COOK, ELTON DAVIS, b Hale County, Tex, Apr 9, 04; m 29. AGRONOMY. *Educ:* Tex Tech Col, BS, 35; Kans State Col, MS, 48; Univ Nebr, PhD, 50. *Prof Exp:* Jr agronomist, Soil Conserv Serv, USDA, Tex, 35-36, asst soil conservationist, 36-44; supt agr res sta, Tex Res Found, 44-47; supt sub-sta, Tex Agr Sta, 49-51, agronomist, 52-69; chmn dept , 69-74; PROF AGR, LUBBOCK CHRISTIAN COL, 74- *Mem:* Am Soc Agron; Ecol Soc Am. *Res:* Use of green manure crops and commercial fertilizers in field crop production; root development; defoliation and mechanical harvesting of cotton. *Mailing Add:* Dept of Agr Lubbock Christian Col 5601 W 19th St Lubbock TX 79407

COOK, ELTON STRAUS, b Oberlin, Ohio, Dec 24, 09; m 35; c 2. MEDICINAL CHEMISTRY. *Educ:* Oberlin Col, AB, 30; Yale Univ, PhD(org chem), 33. *Prof Exp:* Asst chem, Yale Univ, 30-33, hon fel, 33-34; res chemist, Wm S Merrell Co, 34-37; asst dir res activities, 43-45, vpres, 55-70, PROF & HEAD DIV CHEM & BIOCHEM, ST THOMAS INST, 37-, DEAN, 46-, MEM CORP, 70- *Concurrent Pos:* Consult, War Prod Bd, 42; chmn & organizer Gibson Island Res Conf on Chem Growth promoters, AAAS, 42. *Honors & Awards:* Dipl Honor, Pan Am Cancer Cytol Cong, 57; Cert Award, Gordon Res Conf, 59; Am Chem Soc Award, 64. *Mem:* AAAS; Am Chem Soc; hon mem Am Inst Chem; Am Pharmaceut Asn; Am Asn Cancer Res. *Res:* Synthesis and pharmacology of local anesthetics and other drugs; cellular metabolism; cancer; mechanism of drug action approached through metabolism and enzymes; anti-infectious drugs. *Mailing Add:* St Thomas Inst 1842 Madison Rd Cincinnati OH 45206

COOK, ERNEST EWART, b Stratton St Margaret, Eng, Mar 23, 26; c 1. EXPLORATION GEOPHYSICS. *Educ:* Cambridge Univ, BA, 46, MA, 50. *Prof Exp:* Geophysicist, Cia Shell de Venezuela, 47-56, chief geophysicist, Pakistan Shell Oil Co, 56-57; chief geophysicist, Signal Oil & Gas Co, Venezuela, 57-60, geophysicist, Tex, 60-62, chief geophysicist, 62-65, asst mgr int explor, Calif, 65-68; vpres, Seismic Comput Corp, 68-71; pres, Invent Inc, 71-78; PRES, ZENITH EXPLOR CO, INC, 78- *Mem:* Am Asn Petrol Geologists; Soc Explor Geophys; Am Geophys Union; Geol Soc London; Europ Asn Explor Geophys. *Res:* Seismic refraction methods and interpretation techniques; application of seismic velocities to geologic interpretation. *Mailing Add:* Zenith Explor Co 908 Town & Country Blvd Houston TX 77024

COOK, EVERETT L, b Mounds, Okla, Sept 9, 27; m 48; c 4. AERONAUTICAL & STRUCTURAL ENGINEERING. *Educ:* Wichita State Univ, BS, 54, MS, 58; Okla State Univ, PhD(mech eng), 67. *Prof Exp:* Designer, Tech Training Aids, Inc, Okla, 50; instr, Spartan Col Aeronaut Eng, 51; stress analyst, Beech Aircraft Corp, Kans, 51-53; from instr to assoc prof aeronaut eng, Wichita State Univ, 53-67, dir digital comput, 64-67; assoc prof mech eng, Okla State Univ, 67-69; ASSOC PROF AERONAUT ENG, WICHITA STATE UNIV, 69- *Concurrent Pos:* Consult, Beech Aircraft Corp, 68-70 & Gates Learjet Corp, 75-; Nat Res Coun sr res assoc, NASA Marshall Space Flight Ctr, 74-75. *Mem:* Am Inst Aeronaut & Astronaut; Am Soc Eng Educ. *Res:* Discrete element methods of analysis and design of flight vehicle structures. *Mailing Add:* 2753 N Pershing Wichita KS 67220

COOK, EVIN LEE, b Waco, Tex, July 11, 18; m 41; c 1. PHYSICAL CHEMISTRY. *Educ:* Baylor Univ, AB, 39; Rice Inst, MA, 41; Univ Tex, PhD(phys chem), 49. *Prof Exp:* Res chemist petrol ref, Humble Oil & Refining Co, 41-43; res chemist petrol ref, Pan Am Ref Corp, 44-47; mgr oil recovey res, 49-79, SR PROD CONSULT, MOBIL RES & DEVELOP CORP, 80- *Mem:* Am Chem Soc; Am Inst Mining, Metall & Petrol Engrs; Sigma Xi. *Res:* Hydrous oxides; aviation gasoline research; unit processes; surface chemistry; fluid flow through porous media. *Mailing Add:* 6417 McCommas Dallas TX 75214

COOK, FRANKLAND SHAW, b Toronto, Nov 30, 21; m 45; c 3. BOTANY. *Educ:* Univ Toronto, BA, 50, PhD(bot), 56. *Prof Exp:* From asst prof to assoc prof, 52-69, PROF BOT, UNIV WESTERN ONT, 69- *Mem:* Can Bot Asn; Am Bryol & Lichenological Soc; Can Soc Plant Physiol. *Res:* Growth and physiology of pollen and spores; physiology of mosses; emzyme kinetics. *Mailing Add:* Dept Bot Univ of Western Ont London ON N6A 5B8 Can

COOK, FRED D, b Ottawa, Ont, Oct 30, 21; m 48; c 3. SOIL MICROBIOLOGY. *Educ:* Univ BC, BSA, 45, MSA, 47; Univ Edinburgh, PhD(microbiol), 60. *Prof Exp:* Res officer soil microbiol, Exp Farm, Swift Current, Sask, 50-57; officer soil microbiol, Microbiol Res Inst, Ottawa, 57-64; mem fac, 64-69, PROF SOIL SCI, UNIV ALTA, 69- *Mem:* Am Soc Microbiol; Can Soc Microbiol. *Res:* Petroleum microbiology; soil microbiology; microbial ecology. *Mailing Add:* Dept of Soil Sci Univ of Alta Edmonton AB T6G 2E8 Can

COOK, FREDERICK AHRENS, b Chicago, Ill, June 15, 50; m 75. SEISMOLOGY, TECTONICS. *Educ:* Univ Wyo, BS, 73, MS, 75; Cornell Univ, PhD(geophysics), 81. *Prof Exp:* Geophysicist, Continental Oil Co, 75-77; FEL, CORNELL UNIV, 80- *Mem:* Am Geophys Union; Geol Soc Am; Soc Explor Geophysicists; Am Asn Petrol Geologists. *Res:* Application of geophysical techniques to delineating the structure and evolution of the continental crust; computer modelling of seismic wave propagation. *Mailing Add:* Dept Geol Sci Cornell Univ Ithaca NY 14853

COOK, FREDERICK LEE, b Baltimore, Md, Mar 15, 40; m 62; c 2. MATHEMATICS. *Educ:* Ga Inst Technol, BS, 61, MS, 63, PhD(math), 67. *Prof Exp:* Res mathematician, George C Marshall Space Flight Ctr, NASA, 67-69; asst prof, 69-72, chmn, Dept Math, 72-74, asst to pres, 74-75, ASSOC PROF, UNIV ALA, HUNTSVILLE, 72-, CHMN DEPT MATH, 77- *Mem:* Am Math Soc; Soc Indust Appl Math; Math Asn Am. *Res:* Characterizations and applications of recursively generated Sturm-Liouville polynomial sequences; solutions of countably infinite systems of differential equations; determination of weight functions for given polynomial sequences; mathematical modeling in medicine and biology. *Mailing Add:* Dept of Math Univ of Ala Huntsville AL 35899

COOK, GEORGE EDWARD, b Memphis, Tenn, Apr 4, 38; m 65. ELECTRICAL ENGINEERING. *Educ:* Vanderbilt Univ, BE, 60, PhD(elec eng), 65; Univ Tenn, MS, 61. *Prof Exp:* Lab instr elec eng, Univ Tenn, 60-61; asst eng res, 61-62, asst elec eng, 62-63, from instr to assoc prof, 63-76, PROF ELEC ENG, VANDERBILT UNIV, 76- *Concurrent Pos:* Consult & dir elec design, Price-Bass Co, 63-64; consult, vpres & dir eng, Meerick Eng, Inc, 64-69; mem, Simulation Coun, 67; tech dir, Airtronics Indust Electronics Lab, 69- *Mem:* Inst Elec & Electronics Engrs; Am Welding Soc. *Res:* Control theory, especially adaptive control systems and statistical analysis; communication theory. *Mailing Add:* Elec Eng Prog Vanderbilt Univ Nashville TN 37240

COOK, GERALD, b Hazard, Ky, Oct 31, 37; m 62; c 2. ELECTRICAL ENGINEERING, AUTOMATIC CONTROL SYSTEMS. *Educ:* Va Polytech Inst, BS, 61; Mass Inst Technol, MS, 62, EE, 63, ScD(elec eng), 65. *Prof Exp:* Mem staff Apollo guid, Instrumentation Lab, Mass Inst Technol, 63-65; res engr automatic control, F J Seiler Res Lab, US Air Force Acad, 65-68; assoc prof elec eng, Univ Va, 68-73, prof, 73-81; PROF & CHMN, DEPT ELEC & BIOMED ENG, VANDERBILT UNIV, 81- *Concurrent Pos:* Res asst, Electronic Systs Lab, Mass Inst Technol, 64-65; lectr, Univ Colo, 66-68; consult, Kaman Corp, 66-68, Phillip Morris Tobacco Co & Melpar Corp, 69- & Babcock & Wilcox Corp, 71-; assoc ed, Trans on Indust Electronics & Control Instrumentation, 73- *Honors & Awards:* Off Aerospace Res Tech Achievement Award, 68; Outstanding Res Award, Southeastern Sect, Am Soc Eng Educ, 71. *Mem:* Inst Elec & Electronics Engrs (secy, 73-79); Indust Electronics & Control Instrumentation Soc (secy, 74-79). *Res:* Theory of optimization and suboptimal control; approximation techniques; trajectory optimation in pursuit-evasion tactics; numerical optimization and use of computer to achieve optimum design; biomedical engineering; eye movement behavior; industrial automation; computer control; robotics. *Mailing Add:* Dept Elec & Biomed Eng Vanderbilt Univ Nashville TN 37220

COOK, GLENN MELVIN, b Los Angeles, Calif, Sept 26, 35; m 60; c 2. PHYSICAL CHEMISTRY. *Educ:* Univ Calif, Berkeley, BS, 57; Univ Ill, PhD(phys chem), 61. *Prof Exp:* Res asst, Radiation Lab, Univ Calif, 57; teaching asst, Univ Ill, 57-60; from assoc res scientist to res scientist, Lockheed Missiles & Space Co, Calif, 61-66; mem tech staff, Sprague Elec Co, 66-70; sr electro chemist, Ledgemont Lab, Kennecott Copper Co, 70-73, sr process scientist, 73-77; MGR & GROUP LEADER ELECTROCHEM RES, ARGONNE NAT LAB, 77- *Mem:* AAAS; Am Chem Soc; Am Phys Soc; Electrochem Soc; Am Inst Mining, Metall & Petrol Engrs. *Res:* Visible, fluorescent and phosphorescent spectra; molecular and ionic interactions in non-aqueous electrolytes; aqueous and non-aqueous batteries; electroplating and corrosion; electrochemical processing; porous electrode; dilute solution hydrometallurgy. *Mailing Add:* 27 W Meadow Dr Naperville IL 60565

COOK, GORDON SMITH, b Newark, NY, Mar 5, 14; m 39; c 3. ORGANIC CHEMISTRY. *Educ:* Hope Col, AB, 37; Syracuse Univ, MS, 39. *Prof Exp:* Asst gen chem, Syracuse Univ, 37-39; control & develop chemist, Chambers Works, E I Du Pont De Nemours & Co, 40-49, tech rep org chem dept, Rubber Chem Div, 50-53, head div prod control & specifications, Elastomers Dept, 53-57, head foam-elastomers chem dept, 57-58, head prod control & specifications, 58-70, head tech develop div, 70-79; RETIRED. *Mem:* Am Chem Soc; Am Soc Qual Control. *Res:* Synthetic elastomers; cellulose chemistry. *Mailing Add:* 21 Briar Rd Wilmington DE 19803

COOK, HAROLD ANDREW, b Wheeling, WVa, July 10, 41; m 64; c 1. AGRICULTURAL MICROBIOLOGY. *Educ:* West Liberty State Col, BS, 64; WVa Univ, MS, 66, PhD(microbiol), 69. *Prof Exp:* From asst prof to assoc prof, 69-77, PROF BIOL, WEST LIBERTY STATE COL, 77- CHMN DEPT MED TECHNOL, 70- *Concurrent Pos:* Reviewer, Am Biol Teacher Today, 74-; adj course dir, Chautauqua-Type Short Course Prog, NSF, 75-76; consult, AAAS. *Mem:* Am Soc Microbiol. *Res:* Pollution; sanitary landfills; acid mine drainage; developing biology laboratory manual for non-science majors. *Mailing Add:* Dept of Biol West Liberty State Col West Liberty WV 26074

COOK, HARRY, endocrinology, physiology, see previous edition

COOK, HARRY E, III, b Fresno, Calif, June 11, 35; m 76; c 3. GEOLOGY. *Educ:* Univ Calif, Santa Barbara, BS, 61, Univ Calif, Berkeley, PhD(geol), 66. *Prof Exp:* Consult petrog, Hales Labs, Calif, 63-65; res geologist, Denver Res Ctr, Marathon Oil Co, 65-70; assoc prof, Univ Calif, Riverside, 70-74; RES GEOLOGIST, US GEOL SURV, 74- *Concurrent Pos:* Asst prof, San Francisco State Univ, 64-65. *Honors & Awards:* George C Matson Award, Am Asn Petrol Geologists, 72. *Mem:* AAAS; Geol Soc Am; Am Asn Petrol Geologists; Soc Econ Paleontologists & Mineralogists. *Res:* Petroleum geology of carbonates; marine geology; sedimentary carbonate bank and reef facies; continental slope and submarine fans; carbon and oxygen isotopes in carbonates; diagenesis; petroleum reservoirs; debris flows and turbidity currents; stratigraphy of Western Canada, Nevada and Equatorial Pacific. *Mailing Add:* US Geol Surv Oil & Gas Resources MS 99 345 Middlefield Rd Menlo Park CA 94025

COOK, HARRY EDGAR, b Americus, Ga, Feb 14, 39; m 61; c 2. MATERIALS SCIENCE. *Educ:* Case Inst Technol, BS, 60, MS, 62; Northwestern Univ, PhD(mat sci), 66. *Prof Exp:* Sr res scientist, Ford Motor Co, 67-69, sr engr, 69-70, prin engr chassis eng, 70-71, supvr, 71-72; from assoc prof metall & mech eng to prof, Univ Ill, Champaign-Urbana, 72-77; sr res scientist metall, 77-78, mgr mat eng, 78-79, mgr body component eng, 79-81, MGR METALL DEPT, FORD MOTOR CO, 81- *Honors & Awards:* Robert Lansing Hardy Medal, Am Inst Mining & Metall Engrs, 68; Teetor Award, Soc Automotive Engrs, 77. *Mem:* Am Soc Metals; Am Inst Mining & Metall Engrs; Soc Automotive Engrs. *Res:* Phase transformations; friction materials. *Mailing Add:* Ford Motor Co PO Box 2053 Dearborn MI 48121

COOK, HERBERT K(ENERSON), b South Berwick, Maine, Sept 23, 14; m 37; c 4. CHEMICAL ENGINEERING. *Educ:* Univ Maine, BS, 35. *Prof Exp:* Jr eng chem cent concrete lab, US Mil Acad, US Army Corps Engrs, 37-40, asst engr, 40-42, assoc engr, Mt Vernon, 42, engr & asst in charge lab concrete res, 42-46, asst chief concrete res div & civil engr, Waterways Exp Sta, Miss, 46-47, chief & civil engr, 47-54; asst dir res, Master Builders Div, Martin-Marietta Corp, 54-56, dir eng, 56-65, vpres res & eng, 56-78, vpres eng, 68-78; CONSULT ENGR CONCRETE, 78- *Concurrent Pos:* Mem bd dirs, Vacuum Concrete Corp Am, 63-65; mem comt durability of concrete, Hwy Res Bd, Nat Acad Sci-Nat Res Coun; mem US Comn on Large Dams. *Mem:* Fel Am Soc Testing & Mat; fel Am Concrete Inst. *Res:* Investigations of properties of concrete, concrete materials and construction methods; development of test methods; lean mass concrete for dams and cement replacement materials. *Mailing Add:* 2445 Derbyshire Rd Cleveland OH 44106

COOK, HOWARD, b Spartanburg, SC, June 13, 33; m 60; c 3. TOPOLOGY. *Educ:* Clemson Col, BS, 56; Univ Tex, PhD(math), 62. *Prof Exp:* Spec instr math, Univ Tex, 58-62; asst prof, Auburn Univ, 62-64, res asst prof, 64; asst prof, Univ NC, Chapel Hill, 64-66; assoc prof, 66-71, PROF MATH, UNIV HOUSTON, 71- *Concurrent Pos:* Vis prof pure math, Univ Tasmania, 72-73. *Res:* Point set theory. *Mailing Add:* Dept of Math Univ of Houston Houston TX 77004

COOK, JACK E, b Ind, Feb 3, 31; m 54; c 2. ORGANIC POLYMER CHEMISTRY. *Educ:* DePauw Univ, BA, 53; Northwestern Univ, PhD, 57. *Prof Exp:* Res chemist exploratory plastics, Phillips Petrol Co, 57-64; sr res chemist, 64-66, RES SPECIALIST NEW PROD DEVELOP, MINN MINING & MFG CO, 66- *Res:* Acrylics; electroplating; elastomers; polymer characterization; injection molding; surface topography; polymer synthesis; personal identification systems; retroreflective products; adhesion; security systems; document security. *Mailing Add:* 56 Michael St St Paul MN 55119

COOK, JAMES ARTHUR, b Ga, May 19, 20; m 54; c 5. PLANT NUTRITION, SOIL FERTILITY. *Educ:* Cornell Univ, PhD(pomol), 51. *Prof Exp:* From asst plant physiologist to assoc plant physiologist, USDA, 48-52; asst viticulturist, 53-58, assoc viticulturist & assoc prof viticulture, 58-64, chmn dept viticult & enol, 62-66, VITICULTURIST, EXP STA, UNIV CALIF, DAVIS, & PROF VITICULTURE, UNIV, 64- *Mem:* Am Soc Plant Physiol; Am Soc Hort Sci; Am Soc Enol & Viticulture. *Res:* Fertilizer requirements of dates, apples and grapes; foliage nutrient sprays; plant nutrition; mineral nutrition of grapevines; deficiencies as well as toxicities, as determined by visual symptoms, tissue analysis and field trial responses. *Mailing Add:* Dept Viticult & Enol Univ of Calif Davis CA 95616

COOK, JAMES DENNIS, b Tillsonburg, Ont, Can, July 7, 36; US citizen. HEMATOLOGY. *Educ:* Queen's Univ, Kingston, Ont, Can, MD, 60, CM, 60, MSc, 63. *Prof Exp:* Instr med, Sch Med, Univ Wash, 67-69, asst prof, 69-73, assoc prof, 73-75; PHILLIPS PROF MED & DIR, HEMAT DIV, UNIV KANS MED CTR, 75- *Concurrent Pos:* Mem, Int Nutrit Anemia Consult Group, 75-; mem, Panel Malnutrit, US-Japan Coop Med Sci Prog, 75-; prin investr, Control Iron Deficiency grant, US Agency Int Develop, 78-; chmn, Iron Panel, Int Comt Standardization Hemat, 80- *Mem:* fel Am Col Physicians; Am Soc Hemat; Am Fed Clin Res; Am Soc Clin Nutrit; Soc Exp Biol & Med. *Res:* Iron deficiency; iron absorption in humans; serum ferritin as a measure of iron status. *Mailing Add:* Div Hemat Univ Kans Med Ctr 39th & Rainbow Blvd Kansas City KS 66103

COOK, JAMES ELLSWORTH, b Eureka, Kans, Oct 20, 23; m 50; c 4. VETERINARY PATHOLOGY, COMPARATIVE PATHOLOGY. *Educ:* Okla State Univ, DVM, 51; Am Col Vet Path, dipl, 56; Kans State Univ, PhD(path), 70. *Prof Exp:* Asst prof path, Okla State Univ, 51-52; vet pathologist, Jensen Salsburys Labs, 52-53; resident comp path, Armed Forces Inst Path, 53-56, assoc pathologist, Aerospace Path Br, 56-57, pathologist, Vet Path Div, 65-69; chief vivarium br primate med, 6571st Aerospace Med Lab, Holloman AFB, NMex, 57-63; instr path, 69-70, actg head dept, 72-75, head dept path, 75-77, PROF PATH, KANS STATE UNIV, 70-, DIR ANIMAL RESOURCE FACILITY, COL VET MED, 74- *Mem:* Am Vet Med Asn; Am Soc Vet Clin Path. *Res:* Infectious and neoplastic diseases of primates and other laboratory animals; leptospirosis in domestic animals. *Mailing Add:* 301 N 15th St Manhattan KS 66502

COOK, JAMES H, JR, b Anderson, SC, Oct 28, 37; m; c 3. ELECTRICAL ENGINEERING. *Educ:* Ga Inst Technol, BEE, 61, MSEE, 70. *Prof Exp:* engr, Bendix Radio Div, Bendix Corp, 61-62, asst proj engr, 62-64; antenna engr, 64-66, sr engr, 64-68, mgr antenna & microwave prod, 68-72, prod line mgr telecommun prod, 73-75, prod line mgr antenna & microwave, 75-78, prin engr, 78-81, TECH DIR, TELECOMMUN GROUP, SCI-ATLANTA, INC, 80-82. *Mem:* Sr mem Inst Elec & Electronics Engrs; Asn Old Crows. *Res:* Communications systems analysis; electromagnetics; antenna design and analysis. *Mailing Add:* Sci-Atlanta Inc 3845 Pleasantdale Rd Atlanta GA 30340

COOK, JAMES MARION, b Franklin, Ky, Aug 16, 41; m 64; c 2. THEORETICAL PHYSICS, MATHEMATICAL ANALYSIS. *Educ:* Western Ky Univ, BS, 62; Vanderbilt Univ, PhD(physics), 67. *Prof Exp:* assoc prof, 66-77, PROF PHYSICS & CHEM, MID TENN STATE UNIV, 77- *Mem:* Am Asn Physics Teachers. *Res:* Differential equations. *Mailing Add:* Dept of Chem & Physics Mid Tenn State Univ Murfreesboro TN 37132

COOK, JAMES MINTON, b Bluefield, WVa, Aug 6, 45; c 2. NATURAL PRODUCTS CHEMISTRY, MEDICINAL CHEMISTRY. *Educ:* WVa Univ, BS, 67; Univ Mich, PhD(org chem), 71. *Prof Exp:* NIH fel natural prod, Univ BC, 72-73; asst prof, 73-79, ASSOC PROF CHEM, UNIV WIS-MILWAUKEE, 79- *Mem:* Am Chem Soc; The Chem Soc; Am Soc Pharmacog. *Res:* Synthesis of beta adrenergic antagonists for antihypertensive drug studies; Synthesis of B-carboline alkaloids and diazepam antagonists; construction of potential agents for treatment of Narcolepsey; synthesis of potential antimalarial agents; studies on the reactions of dicarbonyl compounds with dimethyl-3-ketoglutarate; general approach for the sythesis of polyquinanes; preparation of planar tetracordinate carbon atom. *Mailing Add:* Dept Chem Univ Wis Milwaukee WI 53201

COOK, JAMES RICHARD, b Maben, WVa, Nov 22, 29; m 59; c 2. CELL PHYSIOLOGY. *Educ:* Concord Col, BS, 50; WVa Univ, MS, 55; Univ Calif, Los Angeles, PhD(zool), 60. *Prof Exp:* NIH fel zool, Misaki Marine Biol Sta, Japan, 60-61; asst biophysicist, Lab Nuclear Med & Radiation Biol, Univ Calif, Los Angeles, 61-63; from asst prof to assoc prof zool, 63-74, PROF ZOOL & BOT, UNIV MAINE, ORONO, 74-, SAFETY OFFICER, RADIATION LAB, 81- *Concurrent Pos:* NIH res grant, 64-67, res career develop award, 68-78. *Mem:* Am Soc Cell Biol; Soc Protozool; Am Soc Plant Physiol. *Res:* Cell growth and division; adaptations of cells; chloroplast inheritance. *Mailing Add:* Murray Hall Univ of Maine Orono ME 04469

COOK, JAMES ROBERT, b Hamilton, Ont, Aug 21, 41; m 63; c 5. PHYSICS, ENGINEERING. *Educ:* McMaster Univ, BEng, 64, PhD(physics), 69. *Prof Exp:* Programmer refinery simulation, Shell Oil, Can, 62-63; programmer-customer engr info processing, IBM, Can, 63-64; SR STAFF ENGR, ARMCO STEEL CORP, 69- *Mem:* Inst Elec & Electronics Engrs. *Res:* Solid state physics; mechanical and electrical engineering; modelling and optimization; real-time control of metallurgical processing; thermal process simulation; sensor based computer control of processes. *Mailing Add:* Armco Res Curtiss St Middletown OH 45042

COOK, JOHN CALL, b Afton, Wyo, Apr 7, 18; m 49, 72; c 2. GEOPHYSICS. *Educ:* Univ Utah, BS, 42; Pa State Univ, MS, 47, PhD(geophys), 51. *Prof Exp:* Electronics res staff, Radiation Lab, Mass Inst Technol, 42-45; asst physics, Pa State Univ, 45-47, asst geophys, 47-49, res assoc, 49-51; sr physicist, Southwest Res Inst, 51-55, mgr geophys sect, 55-64; chief geophysicist, Geotech Corp, 64-66; PRIN GEOPHYSICIST, TELEDYNE GEOTECH CO, 66- *Concurrent Pos:* Instr math, Eve Div, San Antonio Col, 53-54; Int Geophys Year seismologist, Antarctica, Arctic Inst NAm, 57-58; asst prof physics, Trinity Univ, Tex, 58-59; assoc geophysicist, Scripps Inst Oceanog, 61; vis investr, Woods Hole Oceanog Inst Int Indian Ocean Exped, 64. *Mem:* Am Geophys Union; Soc Explor Geophys; Sigma Xi. *Res:* Detection and sensors; seismic, electromagnetic, infrared, magnetic, radioactivity and thermal; unorthodox prospecting methods; ground-probing radar; electronic circuits; properties of soils, ice and rock. *Mailing Add:* Teledyne Geotech Co 3401 Shiloh Rd Garland TX 75040

COOK, JOHN CAREY, b Ft Collins, Colo, Jan 13, 17; m 42; c 2. CIVIL ENGINEERING. *Educ:* Univ Idaho, BS, 47, CE, 66. *Prof Exp:* Testing engr, Idaho State Hwy Dept, 47-48, asst mat engr, 48-50; mat engr, Atomic Energy Comn, Idaho, 50-53; owner-pres, Wash Testing Lab, 53-64; mgr, Pittsburgh Testing Lab, Wash, 64-66; res engr, Hwy Res Sect, 66-69, actg head, 69-70, head, 70-82, PROF CIVIL ENG, WASH STATE UNIV, 77- *Concurrent Pos:* Mem, Hwy Res Bd, Nat Acad Sci-Nat Res Coun, 67-, mem comt mineral aggregates & comt nuclear principles & appln, 69. *Mem:* Am Soc Testing & Mat. *Res:* Construction materials engineering testing and research, highways, airports, dams and buildings; environmental impact of highways on urban areas; nuclear construction application. *Mailing Add:* Sloam 101 Wash State Univ Pullman WA 99164

COOK, JOHN P(HILIP), b Washington, DC, Aug 24, 24; m 52; c 8. CIVIL ENGINEERING. *Educ:* Catholic Univ, BCE, 51, BArchE, 52; Rensselaer Polytech Inst, MCE, 55, DEngSc, 63. *Prof Exp:* Bridge designer, McEnteer Assoc, WVa, 55-58; from instr to assoc prof civil eng, Rensselaer Polytech Inst, 58-67; assoc prof, 67-70, JACOB LICHTER PROF ENG CONSTRUCT, UNIV CINCINNATI, 70- *Concurrent Pos:* Mem, Sealants Comt, Highway Rds Bd, 63-68, 68-; consult, Thiokol Corp, NJ, 64-68, Watson-Bowman Assoc, NY, 70-74, South African Bur Standards, 72-, Japan Archit Waterproofing Res Asn, 73 & Procter & Gamble, Ohio, 73-; mem, Bldg Res Inst, 65-70; mem, Adhesives Comn, 68- *Mem:* Am Soc Civil Engrs; Am Soc Eng Educ; Soc Plastics Indust; Am Soc Testing & Mat. *Res:* Behavior of elastomeric joint sealants for buildings and highway pavements; behavior of bonded-aggregate composite beams using polyester adhesives; field performance of highway pavements; corrosion resistance of concrete; impact yielding sign supports; composite behavior of metal roof decks. *Mailing Add:* Dept of Civil Eng Univ of Cincinnati Cincinnati OH 45221

COOK, JOHN SAMUEL, b Wilmington, Del, Sept 7, 27; m 65. CELL PHYSIOLOGY. *Educ:* Princeton Univ, AB, 50, MA, 53, PhD(biol), 55. *Prof Exp:* US Pub Health fel, Bern Univ, 55-56; from instr to assoc prof physiol, Sch Med, NY Univ, 56-66; prof biol, Univ Tenn-Oak Ridge Grad Sch Biomed Sci, 67-70, assoc dir sch, 68-70; STAFF MEM BIOL DIV, OAK RIDGE NAT LAB, 70- *Concurrent Pos:* Mem, US Nat Comt Int Union Psychol Sci, 76-82; assoc ed, Am J Physiol, 81- *Mem:* Fel AAAS; Soc Gen Physiol (pres, 79-80); Biophys Soc; Am Physiol Soc. *Res:* Membrane physiology; effects of ultraviolet and visible radiations on living cells; biogenesis and turnover of cell membranes. *Mailing Add:* Biol Div Oak Ridge Nat Lab PO Box Y Oak Ridge TN 37830

COOK, JOSEPH MARION, b Oak Park, Ill, Feb 18, 24; m 56; c 3. MATHEMATICAL PHYSICS, SYSTEMS ANALYSIS. *Educ:* Univ Ill, BS, 47, MS, 48; Univ Chicago, PhD(math), 51. *Prof Exp:* Instr math, Johns Hopkins Univ, 51-52; NSF fel quantum mech, Harvard Univ, 52-53; assoc math, Argonne Nat Lab, 53-60; vis assoc prof, Univ Calif, Berkeley, 60-61; SR MATHEMATICIAN APPL MATH, ARGONNE NAT LAB, 61- *Mem:* Soc Indust & Appl Math; Am Math Soc. *Mailing Add:* Argonne Nat Lab Bldg 221 9700 S Cass Ave Argonne IL 60439

COOK, KELSEY DONALD, b Denver, Colo, Mar 16, 52. MASS SPECTROMETRY, SURFACTANT CHEMISTRY. *Educ:* Colo Col, BS, 74; Univ Wis-Madison, PhD(chem), 78. *Prof Exp:* Res fel, Univ Wis-Madison, 74-76, teaching asst, 75, res asst, 76-78; ASST PROF ANAL CHEM, UNIV ILL, URBANA-CHAMPAIGN, 78- *Mem:* Am Chem Soc; Am Soc Mass Spectrometry; Soc Appl Spectro; Sigma Xi. *Res:* Development of electrohydrodynamic ionization, mass spectrometry and characterization of polymer and related solutions by EHMS; spectroscopic and microscopic characterization of interactions in analytical applications of surfactants. *Mailing Add:* 44 Roger Adams Lab Univ Ill Box 49 1209 W Calif Urbana IL 61801

COOK, KENNETH EMERY, b Nebr, June 23, 28; m 52; c 3. ORGANIC CHEMISTRY. *Educ:* Hastings Col, BA, 53; Univ Nebr, MSc, 55, PhD(chem), 57. *Prof Exp:* From asst prof to assoc prof, 57-68, chmn dept, 62-74, PROF CHEM, ANDERSON COL, 68- *Mem:* Am Chem Soc; AAAS. *Res:* Synthetic organic chemistry; heterocyclic compounds. *Mailing Add:* 705 Maplewood Ave Anderson IN 46012

COOK, KENNETH LORIMER, b Middleton, NH, June 8, 15; m 46; c 3. GEOPHYSICS. *Educ:* Mass Inst Technol, BS, 39; Univ Chicago, PhD(geol & physics), 43. *Prof Exp:* Part-time instr phys sci, Univ Chicago, 41-43, geophysicist, US Bur Mines, Reno, Nev, 43-46; geophysicist, US Geol Surv, Nev, 46-49, Utah, 49-56; head dept, 52-68, dir univ seismog stas, 52-76, PROF GEOPHYS, UNIV UTAH, 52- *Mem:* AAAS; Am Inst Mining, Metall & Petrol Eng; Soc Explor Geophys; Geol Soc Am; Am Geophys Union. *Res:* Mass spectroscopy; magnetic, gravitational and electrical geophysical interpretation; relative abundance of isotopes of potassium in Pacific kelps and rocks; vertical magnetic intensity over veins; resitivity data over filled sinks; regional magnetic and gravity surveys; gravity and magnetics of Utah; crustal structure of earth; seismic recording of large blasts. *Mailing Add:* Dept of Geol & Geophys Univ of Utah Salt Lake City UT 84112

COOK, KENNETH MARLIN, b Braddock, Pa, Aug 5, 20; m 44; c 2. ZOOLOGY. *Educ:* Univ Pittsburgh, BS, 43, MS, 48, PhD(biol sci), 53. *Prof Exp:* Asst instr biol, Univ Pittsburgh, 46-50; res fel, Mellon Inst, 50-52; res assoc, Grad Sch Pub Health, Univ Pittsburgh, 52-54; from asst prof to assoc prof, 54-67, PROF BIOL, COE COL, 67-, HEAD DEPT, 76-, HEINS-JOHNSON PROF BIOL, 78- *Honors & Awards:* Co-winner of award, Indust Med Asn, 55. *Mem:* Am Soc Zool; Sigma Xi; AAAS; Aerospace Med Asn; Am Inst Biol Sci. *Res:* Retention of particule matter in the human lung; measurement of pulmonary functional capacity; effects of antithyroid drugs on reproduction; oxygen consumption of small mammals; effects of centrifugation on physiological factors. *Mailing Add:* 1225 29th St NE Cedar Rapids IA 52402

COOK, KENNETH R, b Oklahoma City, Okla, Jan 21, 31; m 59; c 2. ELECTRICAL ENGINEERING. *Educ:* Univ Okla, BS, 57; Mich State Univ, MS, 59; Univ NMex, ScD(elec eng), 62. *Prof Exp:* Res assoc electromagnetics, Univ NMex, 59-62; asst prof, Okla State Univ, 62-66; with Environ Sci Serv Admin Res Labs, 66-68; assoc prof, Colo State Univ, 68-70; chmn dept elec eng, 70-75, PROF ELEC ENG & ASSOC PROVOST, UNIV ARK, FAYETTEVILLE, 76- *Mem:* Inst Elec & Electronics Engrs; Am Soc Eng Educ. *Res:* Electromagnetics; remote sensing; electro-optics. *Mailing Add:* Admin 325 Univ of Ark Fayetteville AR 72701

COOK, LAWRENCE C, b July 5, 25; US citizen; m 47; c 4. ORGANIC CHEMISTRY. *Educ:* East Tenn State Univ, BS, 57. *Prof Exp:* Clin chemist, Mem Hosp, Johnson City, Tenn, 53-57; res org chemist, 57-67, develop chemist, 67-70, RES & DEVELOP MGR, R J REYNOLDS TOBACCO CO, 70- *Mem:* Am Chem Soc. *Res:* Clinical chemistry; isolation and identification of naturally occurring compounds. *Mailing Add:* Develop Ctr R J Reynolds Tobac Co Shorefair Dr Winston-Salem NC 27102

COOK, LEONARD, b Newark, NJ, June 27, 24; m 46; c 3. PHARMACOLOGY. *Educ:* Rutgers Univ, BA, 48; Yale Univ, PhD, 51. *Prof Exp:* Sr pharmacologist neuropharmacol, Smith, Kline & French Labs, 51-56, dir psychopharmacol res, 56-61, asst head pharmacol in charge res, 58-61, head psychopharmacol sect, 61-67, assoc dir pharmacol, 67-69; assoc dir pharmacol, 69-75, DIR PSYCHOTHERAPEUT RES, HOFFMANN-LA ROCHE INC, 69-, DIR PHARMACOL, 75- *Concurrent Pos:* Lectr, Woman's Med Col Pa, 59-; comt mem, Psychopharmacol Serv Ctr, NIH; Adj prof, Dept Psychiat, Med Sch, Rutgers Univ. *Honors & Awards:* AMA Sci Exhibit Awards, 54. *Mem:* Am Soc Pharmacol & Exp Therapeut; Biomet Soc; Am Psychol Asn (pres, Psychopharmacol Div, 73); fel Am Col Neuropsychopharmacol; fel Int Col Neuropsychopharmacol. *Res:* Neuropharmacology; central nervous system stimulants and depressants; drug potentiators; psycho-pharmacology; operant and classical conditioning techniques; neurobiochemistry; physiological conditioning; analgesics; gastrointestinal drugs; drugs affecting memory learning. *Mailing Add:* Hoffman-La Roche Inc Nutley NJ 07110

COOK, LEROY FRANKLIN, (JR), b Ashland, Ky, Dec 12, 31; m 57; c 3. PHYSICS. *Educ:* Univ Calif, Berkeley, AB, 53, MA, 57, PhD(physics), 59. *Prof Exp:* From instr to asst prof physics, Princeton Univ, 59-65; assoc prof, 65-68, actg head dept, 69-71, head dept physics & astron, 71-75, PROF PHYSICS, UNIV MASS, AMHERST, 68-, HEAD DEPT PHYSICS & ASTRON, 79- *Concurrent Pos:* Vis Fel, Clare Hall, Cambridge Univ, 71-72. *Mem:* Fel Am Phys Soc; Sigma Xi. *Res:* Dispersion relations; applications of gauge theories to weak, electromagnetic and strong interactions. *Mailing Add:* Dept Physics GRTWC Univ Mass Amherst MA 01002

COOK, LESLIE G(LADSTONE), b Paris, Ont, July 12, 14; m 40; c 3. RADIO CHEMISTRY, PHYSICAL METALLURGY. *Educ:* Univ Toronto, BA, 36; Univ Berlin, PhD(chem), 39. *Prof Exp:* Chemist, Aluminum Co of Can, 40-41; phys metallurgist, Aluminum Labs Ltd, 41-44; head chem br, Atomic Energy of Can, 44-53, dir chem & metall div, 53-56; proj analyst, Res Lab, Gen Elec Co, 56-59, mgr proj anal sect, 59-68, gen deleg policy & planning, Nat Res Coun Can, 68-69; mgr proj & prog planning, Corp Res Lab, ESSO Res & Eng, 69-77; PRES, L G COOK ASSOCS INC ENERGY CONSULTS, 77- *Mem:* Am Chem Soc; Am Nuclear Soc; Chem Inst Can. *Res:* Light alloy metallurgy; physical chemistry; research planning and management. *Mailing Add:* 98 Hobart Ave Summit NJ 07901

COOK, MARIE MILDRED, b Bridgeport, Conn, Nov 22, 39. ZOOLOGY, DEVELOPMENTAL BIOLOGY. *Educ:* Georgian Ct Col, AB, 64; Rutgers Univ, MS, 70, PhD(zool), 74. *Prof Exp:* Teacher, Camden Cath High Sch, 66-69; instr & asst, 64-66, asst prof, 66-69, PROF BIOL & CHMN DEPT, GEORGIAN CT COL, 80- *Mem:* Am Soc Zoologists; Am Inst Biol Sci; Nat Asn Biol Teachers; Nat Sci Teachers Asn. *Res:* Developmental patterns and mechanisms of expression of esterase isozymes in hybrid species of the teleost genus Brachydanio. *Mailing Add:* Georgian Ct Col Lakewood NJ 08701

COOK, MARY ROZELLA, b Ardmore, Okla, Sept 30, 36. PSYCHOPHYSIOLOGY, BEHAVIORAL MEDICINE. *Educ:* Univ Okla, BA, 61, PhD(biol psychol), 70. *Prof Exp:* Res assoc, Inst Pa Hosp, 70-74; sr psychophysiologist, 74-77, prin psychophysiologist, 77-78, SECT HEAD BIOBEHAV SCI, MIDWEST RES INST, 78- *Concurrent Pos:* Instr, Dept Psychiat, Univ Pa, 70-74; assoc ed, Biofeedback & Self-regulation, 78-; consult, Nat Cancer Inst, 80- *Mem:* Soc Psychophysiol Res; Sigma Xi; Biofeedback Soc Am. *Res:* Basic and applied studies in psychophysiology; effects of various stressors (environment, fatigue, work load, drugs) on human physiology and behavior; behavioral medicine including biofeedback. *Mailing Add:* Midwest Res Inst 425 Volker Blvd Kansas City MO 64110

COOK, MAURICE GAYLE, b Frankfort, Ky, Dec 26, 32; m 66; c 1. SOIL SCIENCE, AGRONOMY. *Educ:* Univ Ky, BS, 57, MS, 59; Va Polytech Inst & State Univ, PhD(agron), 61. *Prof Exp:* From asst prof to assoc prof, 61-70, PROF SOIL SCI, NC STATE UNIV, 70- *Concurrent Pos:* Vis prof agr chem & soils, Univ Agr Sci, Bangalore, India, 75-76. *Mem:* Soil Conserv Soc Am; Soil Sci Soc Am; Sigma Xi. *Res:* Soil mineralogy and its applications to soil genesis, morphology and classification; chemical and clay mineralogical interactions in soils. *Mailing Add:* Dept of Soil Sci NC State Univ Raleigh NC 27650

COOK, MELVIN ALONZO, b Swan Creek, Utah, Oct 10, 11; m 35; c 5. PHYSICAL CHEMISTRY, EXPLOSIVES. *Educ:* Univ Utah, BA, 33, MA, 34; Yale Univ, PhD(phys chem), 37. *Prof Exp:* Res chemist, E I duPont de Nemours & Co, Inc, 37-47; prof metall, Univ Utah, 47-70; pres, IRECO Chem, 62-72, chmn, 62-74; CHMN, COOK ASSOCS, INC, 73- *Honors & Awards:* E V Murphree Award, Am Chem Soc, 68; Nitro Nobel Medallian, Swedish Acad, Stockholm, 68; Chem Pioneer Award, Am Inst Chemists, 73. *Mem:* Am Chem Soc. *Res:* Commerical explosives, particularly slurry blasting agents; mechanism of detonation and rock blasting behavior. *Mailing Add:* Cook Assocs Inc 2026 Beneficial Life Tower Salt Lake City UT 84111

COOK, MICHAEL ARNOLD, b London, Eng, Dec 22, 44; m 68; c 3. PHARMACOLOGY, GASTROENTEROLOGY. *Educ:* Univ London, BSc, 67; Univ BC, PhD(physiol), 72. *Prof Exp:* Biochemist, Renal Unit, Royal Free Hosp, London, 67-68; Med Res Coun Can fel pharmacol, Univ Alta, 72-74; asst prof, 74-79, ASSOC PROF PHARMACOL, UNIV WESTERN ONT, 79- *Mem:* Can Physiol Soc; NY Acad Sci; Pharm Soc Can; Soc Neurosci. *Res:* Studies on the neural and hormonal control of gastrointestinal motor activity; pharmacology of the gastrointestinal polypeptide hormones. *Mailing Add:* Dept of Pharmacol Univ of Western Ont London ON N6A 5B8 Can

COOK, MICHAEL MILLER, b Pittsburgh, Pa, Oct 10, 45; m 67. ORGANIC CHEMISTRY, CHEMISTRY. *Educ:* Carnegie-Mellon Univ, BS, 67; Stanford Univ, PhD(org chem), 73. *Prof Exp:* Res chemist water treat, Calgon Corp, Merck & Co, Inc, 72-75; res chemist org chem purification, 75-76, GROUP LEADER APPL RES & TECH SERV, VENTRON CORP, THIOKOL CORP, 76- *Mem:* Am Chem Soc; Am Oil Chemists Soc; Soc Photog Scientists & Engrs. *Res:* Water soluble polymers for scale corrosion control; liquid and solid separation; dithionite bleaching of pulp, and clay leaching; borohydride chemistry-application to organic chemical purification, metal recovery. *Mailing Add:* Ventron Corp 12 Congress St Beverly MA 01915

COOK, NATHAN HENRY, b Ridgewood, NJ, Mar 17, 25; m 47; c 4. INSTRUMENTATION, COMPUTERS. *Educ:* Mass Inst Technol, SB, 50, SM, 51, ME, 54, ScD(mech eng), 55. *Prof Exp:* From asst prof to assoc prof, 53-65, PROF MECH ENG, MASS INST TECHNOL, 65- *Concurrent Pos:* Consult, 53- *Honors & Awards:* Blackall Award, Am Soc Mech Engrs; Educ Award, Soc Mfg Engrs. *Mem:* Fel Am Soc Mech Engrs; Soc Mfg Engrs; Int Inst Prod Eng Res. *Res:* Materials; materials processing; friction; lubrication and wear; bearings; computerized manufacturing systems; computerized biomedical data acquisition. *Mailing Add:* 450 Memorial Dr Cambridge MA 02172

COOK, NATHAN HOWARD, b Winston-Salem, NC, Apr 26, 39; m 61; c 2. CYTOLOGY, ZOOLOGY. *Educ:* NC Cent Univ, BS, 61, MA, 63; Okla State Univ, PhD(zool), 72. *Prof Exp:* Asst prof biol, Barber-Scotia Col, 62-68; teaching asst zool, Okla State Univ, 68-69; PROF BIOL, LINCOLN UNIV, 71-, HEAD DEPT, 74- *Concurrent Pos:* Proj dir, NSF Sci Equip Prog, 72-74 & Minority Biomed Support Prog Biol, NIH, Dept Health, Educ & Welfare, 72-; chmn, Mo Sickle Cell Anemia Adv Comt, 72- *Mem:* AAAS; Tissue Cult Asn; Sigma Xi. *Res:* In vitro effects of certain chemical carcinogens on the growth and chromosomes of mammalian cells. *Mailing Add:* Dept of Natural Sci & Math Lincoln Univ Jefferson City MO 65101

COOK, PAUL A C, chemical engineering, see previous edition

COOK, PAUL FABYAN, b Ware, Mass, Aug 2, 46; m 69; c 1. ENZYMOLOGY. *Educ:* Our Lady Lake Col, San Antonio, Tex, BA, 72; Univ Calif, Riverside, PhD(biochem), 76. *Prof Exp:* NIH fel biochem, Univ Wis, Madison, 76-80; asst prof biochem, La State Univ Med Ctr, 80-82; ASST PROF BIOCHEM, NTEX STATE UNIV, 82- *Concurrent Pos:* Reviewer, NIH Study Sect Res Grants, 81- *Mem:* Sigma Xi; AAAS; Am Chem Soc; Biophys Soc; Am Soc Biol Chemists. *Res:* Enzymology, specificlly mechanism of enzyme action which includes kinetic and chemical mechanism; extension of the kinetic theory as it applies to isotope effects in enzyme-catalyzeo reactions and determination of mechanism. *Mailing Add:* Dept Biochem NTex State Univ Denton TX 76203

COOK, PAUL LAVERNE, b Holland, Mich, Mar 2, 25; m 51; c 4. ORGANIC CHEMISTRY. *Educ:* Hope Col, BS, 50; Univ Ill, MS, 52, PhD, 54. *Prof Exp:* From instr to assoc prof, 54-64, PROF CHEM, ALBION COL, 65- *Mem:* Am Chem Soc; Sigma Xi. *Res:* Organic synthesis; products of pharmaceutical interest. *Mailing Add:* Dept of Chem Albion Col Albion MI 49224

COOK, PAUL PAKES, JR, b Topeka, Kans, Nov 25, 27; m 49; c 2. ECOLOGY, EVOLUTION. *Educ:* Univ Kans, AB, 51, MA, 52; Univ Calif, Berkeley, PhD(entom), 62. *Prof Exp:* Field rep insect control, Calif Spray-Chem Corp, 54-59; asst entom, Univ Calif, Berkeley, 61-62; asst prof, 62-68, ASSOC PROF BIOL, SEATTLE UNIV, 68- *Mem:* Animal Behavior Soc; Soc Syst Zool; Soc Study Evolution; Ecol Soc Am; Brit Ecol Soc. *Res:* Population biology, ecology and evolution; animal behavior. *Mailing Add:* Dept Biol Seattle Univ Seattle WA 98122

COOK, PHILIP W, b Underhill, Vt, Oct 6, 36. BOTANY. *Educ:* Univ Vt, BSc, 57, MSc, 59; Ind Univ, PhD(bot), 62. *Prof Exp:* NSF fel, 62-63; asst prof, 63-67, ASSOC PROF BOT, UNIV VT, 67- *Mem:* Bot Soc Am; Phycological Soc Am (pres, 71-72); Mycological Soc Am. *Res:* Fresh water algae; fungal parasites of algae. *Mailing Add:* Dept of Bot Univ of Vt Burlington VT 05401

COOK, PHILLIP DAN, b Clovis, NMex, Jan 2, 44; m 68; c 3. BIOCHEMISTRY. *Educ:* Eastern NMex Univ, BS, 67; Univ NMex, PhD(org chem), 73. *Prof Exp:* Scientist, Pharmaceut Res Div, 76-79, SR SCIENTIST CHEM, WARNER-LAMBERT/PARKE-DAVIS, 79- *Mem:* Am Chem Soc; Int Soc Heterocyclic Chem. *Res:* Design and synthesis of heterocycles, nucleosides and nucleotides as inhibitors of nucleic acid biosynthesis of tumor cells and viruses. *Mailing Add:* 2333 Georgetown Blvd Ann Arbor MI 48105

COOK, RAY LEWIS, b Okemos, Mich, Mar 10, 04; m 20; c 1. SOILS. *Educ:* Mich State Col, BS, 27, MS, 29; Univ Wis, PhD(soils), 34. *Prof Exp:* Asst soils, 27-29, res asst, 29-38, from asst prof to prof, 38-73, head dept soil sci, 53-69, EMER PROF SOILS, MICH STATE UNIV, 73-, PROF, INST INT AGR, 78- *Concurrent Pos:* Vis prof, Chung Hsing Univ, Taiwan, 69-70; consult, UN Develop Prog. *Mem:* fel Am Soc Agron; Soil Sci Soc Am; Int Soc Soil Sci; fel Soil Conserv Soc Am; hon mem Soil Sci Soc Taiwan. *Res:* Field experimental work, tillage nutrient levels; symptoms of nutritional disorders; soil and plant analyses. *Mailing Add:* 830 Newton Ave Lansing MI 48912

COOK, RICHARD ALFRED, b Portland, Maine, Aug 9, 42; div. HUMAN NUTRITION. *Educ:* Univ Maine, Orono, BS, 65, MS, 68, PhD(nutrit), 73. *Prof Exp:* Res asst nutritionist, 65-74, asst prof, 74-80, ASSOC PROF NUTRIT, SCH HUMAN DEVELOP, UNIV MAINE, 80- *Mem:* Am Dietetic Asn; Sigma Xi; Nutrit Today Soc. *Res:* Community nutrition; nutritional status assessment, monitoring, and surveillance; food consumption patterns. *Mailing Add:* 21 Merrill Hall Univ of Maine Orono ME 04469

COOK, RICHARD JAMES, b Alpena, Mich, Oct 20, 47; m 73. PHYSICAL ORGANIC CHEMISTRY. *Educ:* Univ Mich, BS, 69; Princeton Univ, MA, 71, PhD(chem), 73. *Prof Exp:* Res fel chem, Princeton Univ, 70-73; ASST PROF CHEM, KALAMAZOO COL, 73- *Concurrent Pos:* Res grant, Res Corp, 75-77. *Res:* Electronic effects upon the barriers to inversion of substituted imines. *Mailing Add:* Dept of Chem Kalamazoo Col Kalamazoo MI 49007

COOK, RICHARD KAUFMAN, b Chicago, Ill, June 30, 10; m 38; c 1. ACOUSTICS, PHYSICS. *Educ:* Univ Ill, BS, 31, MS, 32, PhD(physics), 35. *Prof Exp:* Asst physics, Univ Ill, 30-35; physicist, Nat Bur Standards, 35-42, chief sound sect, 42-66; chief geoacoustics group, Nat Oceanic & Atmospheric Admin, 66-71; spec asst acoust, Nat Bur Standards, 71-76; CONSULT PHYSICIST, 77- *Concurrent Pos:* Mem tech staff, Bell Tel Labs, 55-56; adj prof elec eng, Brooklyn Polytech Inst, 56; lectr mech eng, Cath Univ Am, 79 & 81. *Honors & Awards:* Wash Acad Eng Sci Award, 49; US Dept Com Except Serv Award, 64. *Mem:* Fel AAAS; fel Am Phys Soc; fel Acoust Soc Am (pres, 57-58); Am Geophys Union. *Res:* Solid state physics; applied mathematics; geophysics; physical acoustics; atmospheric sound propagation; acoustical measurements; mathematical acoustics. *Mailing Add:* 8517 Milford Ave Silver Spring MD 20910

COOK, RICHARD SHERRARD, b Philadelphia, Pa, Apr 11, 21. ORGANIC CHEMISTRY. *Educ:* Philadelphia Col Pharm, BS, 43; Temple Univ, MA, 56. *Prof Exp:* Control chemist, Barrett Div, Allied Chem & Dye Corp, 43-45; chemist, 47-56, GROUP LEADER CHEM, ROHM AND HAAS CO, 56- *Mem:* Am Chem Soc; fel Am Inst Chemists. *Res:* Synthesis of new organic agricultural pesticides, including herbicides, fungicides and insecticides. *Mailing Add:* 37 W Hillcrest Ave Havertown PA 19083

COOK, ROBERT CROSSLAND, b New Haven, Conn, June 5, 47; div; c 2. CHEMICAL PHYSICS, POLYMER PHYSICS. *Educ:* Lafayette Col, BS, 69; Yale Univ, MPh, 71, PhD(phys chem), 77. *Prof Exp:* asst prof chem, Lafayette Col, 73-81; RES SCIENTIST, LAWRENCE LIVERMORE NAT LAB, 81- *Mem:* Am Phys Soc; Am Chem Soc; Sigma Xi. *Res:* Solid and liquid state theory; phase transitions; polymer physics; statistical mechanics. *Mailing Add:* L-338 Lawrence Livermore Nat Lab Livermore CA 94550

COOK, ROBERT D(AVIS), b St Louis, Mo, Dec 20, 36; m 61. ENGINEERING MECHANICS. *Educ:* Univ Ill, BS, 58, MS, 60, PhD(appl mech), 63. *Prof Exp:* From asst prof to assoc prof, 63-74, PROF ENG MECH, UNIV WIS, MADISON, 74- *Concurrent Pos:* Consult. *Mem:* Am Soc Civil Engrs. *Res:* Solid body mechanics; numerical methods of stress analysis; structural mechanics. *Mailing Add:* Dept Eng Mech Univ Wis Madison WI 53706

COOK, ROBERT EDWARD, b Providence, RI, Sept 26, 46. POPULATION BIOLOGY, PLANT DEVELOPMENT. *Educ:* Harvard Univ, BA, 68; Yale Univ, PhD(biol), 73. *Prof Exp:* Instr biol, Yale Univ, 73-74; Cabot fel, 74-75, asst prof, 75-80, ASSOC PROF ECOL, DEPT BIOL, HARVARD UNIV, 80- *Concurrent Pos:* vis assoc prof, Cornell Univ, 81-82. *Res:* Plant population biology; plant development; history of ecology. *Mailing Add:* Dept of Biol Harvard Univ Cambridge MA 02138

COOK, ROBERT EDWARD, b Springhill, WVa, Aug 26, 27; m 50; c 2. GENETICS. *Educ:* WVa Univ, BS, 49, MS, 56; NC State Col, PhD(genetics), 58. *Prof Exp:* Instr poultry, WVa Univ, 54-56; asst prof, Univ Fla, 58-61; coordinator genetics, Agr Res Serv, USDA, 61-64; leader, Genetics Invests, 64-65; head dept poultry sci, Ohio State Univ, 65-69; HEAD DEPT POULTRY SCI, NC STATE UNIV, 69- *Mem:* Fel Poultry Sci Asn; World Poultry Sci Asn; Am Genetics Asn. *Res:* Basic genetics of the domestic fowl and systems of breeding for the improvement of poultry. *Mailing Add:* Dept of Poultry Sci NC State Univ PO Box 5307 Raleigh NC 27650

COOK, ROBERT JAMES, b Moorhead, Minn, Jan 14, 37; m 58; c 4. PLANT PATHOLOGY. *Educ:* NDak State Univ, BS, 58, MS, 61; Univ Calif, Berkeley, PhD(phytopath), 64. *Prof Exp:* NATO fel, Waite Inst, Australia, 64-65; asst, 65-68, PROJ LEADER, REGIONAL CEREAL DIS RES LAB, AGR RES SERV, USDA, WASH STATE UNIV, 68- *Concurrent Pos:* Guggenheim Mem Found fel, 73-74. *Honors & Awards:* Arthur Flemming Award, 75. *Mem:* Am Phytopath Soc; British Soc Plant Path; fel Am Phytopath Soc. *Res:* Biological control of soil born plant pathogens; water relations of soil microorganisms; cereal root rots. *Mailing Add:* SW 910 Mies Pullman WA 99163

COOK, ROBERT LEE, b Hollywood, Fla, Aug 30, 36; m 65; c 2. MOLECULAR SPECTROSCOPY. *Educ:* Univ Miami, BS, 58, MS, 60; Univ Notre Dame, PhD(phys chem), 63. *Prof Exp:* Res assoc microwave spectros, Duke Univ, 63-65, from instr to asst prof physics, 65-71; assoc prof physics, 71-74, PROF PHYSICS & CHEM, MISS STATE UNIV, 74- *Mem:* Am Phys Soc; Am Asn Physics Teachers; Am Chem Soc. *Res:* Microwave spectroscopy; centrifugal distortion effects in asymmetric rotors; determination of molecular force constants; molecular structure; hyperfine interactions; ring conformations; spectrochemical analysis; development of optical techniques to characterize the gas streams of coal burning power plants, (magnetohydrodynamics, coal gasification). *Mailing Add:* Dept Physics Miss State Univ Mississippi State MS 39762

COOK, ROBERT MEROLD, b Bethany, Ill, Aug 5, 30; m 49; c 5. ANIMAL NUTRITION, BIOCHEMISTRY. *Educ:* Univ Ill, BS, 57, MS, 61, PhD(dairy sci), 62. *Prof Exp:* Res asst dairy sci, Univ Ill, 57-62; asst prof, Univ Idaho, 62-66; from asst prof to assoc prof, 66-76, PROF ANIMAL SCI, MICH STATE UNIV, 76- *Mem:* Am Chem Soc; Am Dairy Sci Asn; Am Inst Nutrit. *Res:* Ruminant nutrition, control mechanisms regulating volatile fatty acid metabolism in ruminants; protein metabolism in rumen; xenobiotic metabolism in ruminants. *Mailing Add:* Dept Animal Sci Mich State Univ East Lansing MI 48823

COOK, ROBERT NEAL, b Marlette, Mich, Dec 10, 40; m 67; c 2. COMPUTER SCIENCE, APPLIED MATHEMATICS. *Educ:* Gen Motors Inst, BEE, 65; Univ Mich, MSE, 65; Univ Western Ont, MSc, 68, PhD(appl math), 76. *Prof Exp:* Sr engr, Gen Motors Corp, 59-68; res asst, Univ Western Ont, 68-71; asst prof comput sci, Frostburg State Col, 71-74 & Shippensburg State Col, 74-76; asst prof comput sci, Cent Mich Univ, 76-81; ASSOC PROF COMPUT SCI TECH, UNIV SOUTHERN COLO, 81- *Mem:* Asn Comput Mach; Simulation Coun Inc; Int Asn Math & Comput Simulation; Inst Elec & Electronics Engrs Comput Soc. *Mailing Add:* 42 S Brewer Dr Pueblo CO 81007

COOK, ROBERT PATTERSON, b Aug 30, 47. DISTRIBUTED PROGRAMMING, OPERATING SYSTEMS. *Educ:* Vanderbilt Univ, BS, 69, MS, 71, PhD(comput sci), 78. *Prof Exp:* Syst analyst, Vanderbilt Comput Ctr, 67-71; lectr, Univ Fla, 72-76; ASST PROF COMPUT SCI, UNIV WIS-MADISON, 78- *Concurrent Pos:* Consult, Rank Xerox, 71-72, Xerox Corp & Evergreen Assoc, 71-76, Nicolet Instruments, 80-82, Gen Dynamics, 81-82; prin investr grants, NSF, 78-79 & 81-82, Exp Comput Sci, 81- *Mem:* Asn Comput Mach; Inst Elec & Electronics Engrs. *Res:* Computer architecture. *Mailing Add:* Comput Sci Dept Univ Wis-Madison 1210 W Dayton St Madison WI 53706

COOK, ROBERT SEWELL, b Unity, Wis, Nov 25, 29; m 53; c 2. VERTEBRATE ECOLOGY. *Educ:* Univ Wis-Stevens Point, BS, 51; Univ Wis-Madison, MS, 58, PhD(vet sci), 66. *Prof Exp:* Res asst wildlife ecol, Univ Wis-Madison, 54-57; biologist, Wis Conserv Dept, 57-59; gen secy, Appleton YMCA, 59-61; biol instr high sch, Wis, 61-63; res asst vet sci, Univ Wis-Madison, 63-66; res participation grant, 66-69, asst prof physiol, 66-70, Alumni Res Found grant, 67-68, asst prof environ control, 70-71, assoc prof environ control, Univ Wis-Green Bay, 71-77; dep dir, US Fish & Wildlife Serv, 77-81; DEPT HEAD, FISHERY & WILDLIFE BIOL DEPT, COLO STATE UNIV, 81- *Concurrent Pos:* Mem, US Fish & Wildlife Serv Missions, India, 79, 80 & 82. *Mem:* AAAS; Wildlife Soc; Wildlife Dis Asn; Nature Conservancy Int Asn Fish & Wildlife Agencies. *Res:* Ecology of diseases in populations of wildlife that are transmissible to domestic animals and man; biological aspects of land-use planning; environmental impact analysis; communication and planning for fish and wildlife management. *Mailing Add:* Dep Dir Dept of Interior Washington DC 20240

COOK, ROBERT THOMAS, b Nebraska City, Nebr, Apr 27, 37; m 61; c 3. PATHOLOGY, BIOCHEMISTRY. *Educ:* Univ Kans, AB, 58, MD, 62, PhD(biochem), 67. *Prof Exp:* Assoc pathologist, Walter Reed Army Inst Res, 67-69; asst prof path, Inst Path, Case Western Reserve Univ, 69-76; ASSOC PROF PATH, UNIV IOWA, 77- *Mem:* Am Asn Pathologists; Am Chem Soc. *Res:* Cell control mechanisms in neoplasia. *Mailing Add:* Dept of Path Col of Med Univ Iowa Iowa City IA 52242

COOK, RONALD FRANK, b Buffalo, NY, July 22, 39; m 64; c 3. ANALYTICAL CHEMISTRY, RESEARCH ADMINISTRATION. *Educ:* Univ Buffalo, BA, 61. *Prof Exp:* From chemist to res chemist, 62-72, supvr, Residue Lab, Agr Chem Group, 72-81, MGR, RESIDUE CHEMISTRY, FMC CORP, 81- *Concurrent Pos:* Assoc referee, Asn Off Anal Chemists, 65-75. *Mem:* Am Chem Soc. *Res:* Development and application of analytical methods to the determination of pesticide content of formulations and the residue content of agricultural commodities; management of residue laboratory function; interaction with state and federal agencies relative to regulating compliance. *Mailing Add:* FMC Corp 100 Niagara St Middleport NY 14105

COOK, SHIRL ELDON, b Paris, Idaho, Mar 15, 18; m 44; c 1. CHEMISTRY. *Educ:* Brigham Young Univ, BS, 39; La State Univ, MS, 41. *Prof Exp:* Chemist, US Army, La, 41-42; chemist, La Ord Plant, 42-45; chemist, 45-76, SUPVR ANAL SERV, ETHYL CORP, 76- *Mem:* AAAS; Am Chem Soc. *Res:* Alkyl metal compounds; organometallics. *Mailing Add:* Ethyl Corp PO Box 341 Baton Rouge LA 70821

COOK, STANTON ARNOLD, b Oakland, Calif, Dec 10, 29; m 59; c 2. ECOLOGY, EVOLUTION. *Educ:* Harvard Univ, AB, 51; Univ Calif, Berkeley, PhD(bot), 61. *Prof Exp:* From asst prof to assoc prof, 60-80, PROF BIOL, UNIV ORE, 80- *Mem:* AAAS; Ecol Soc Am; Soc Study Evolution; Am Soc Naturalists. *Res:* Vascular plant population and genetic ecology; terrestrial ecosystem analysis. *Mailing Add:* 1832 Longview Eugene OR 94703

COOK, STUART D, b Boston, Mass, Oct 23, 36; m 60; c 3. NEUROLOGY, NEUROSCIENCES. *Educ:* Brandeis Univ, AB, 57; Univ Vt, MS, 59, MD, 62. *Prof Exp:* Intern med & surg, State Univ NY Upstate Med Ctr, 62-63; resident neurol, Albert Einstein Col Med, 65-68, instr, 68-69; asst prof, Col Physicians & Surgeons, Columbia Univ, 69-71; PROF MED, NJ MED SCH, COL MED & DENT NJ, 71-, PROF NEUROSCI & CHMN, 72- *Honors & Awards:* S Weir Mitchell Award, Am Acad Neurol, 69. *Mem:* Am Acad Neurol; Am Asn Neuropath; Am Fedn Clin Res; Harvey Soc; Reticuloendothelial Soc. *Res:* Neuroimmunology; demyelinating diseases. *Mailing Add:* NJ Med Sch 100 Bergen St Newark NJ 07103

COOK, THEODORE DAVIS, b Kentfield, Calif, Jan 23, 24; m 48; c 4. GEOLOGY. *Educ:* Univ Utah, BS, 48; Univ Calif, MA, 50. *Prof Exp:* SR STAFF GEOLOGIST, SHELL OIL CO, 50- *Mem:* Geol Soc Am. *Res:* Tertiary micropaleontology and stratigraphy; North and Central America stratigraphy. *Mailing Add:* Shell Oil Co Box 481 Houston TX 77001

COOK, THOMAS BRATTON, JR, b Rich Pond, Ky, Aug 28, 26; m 47; c 2. PHYSICS. *Educ:* Western Ky Univ, BS, 47; Vanderbilt Univ, MS, 49, PhD(physics), 51. *Prof Exp:* Mem staff, Weapons Effects Dept, Sandia Lab, 51-55, supvr, Vulnerability Studies Sect, 55-56, supvr nuclear burst studies div, 56-59, mgr nuclear burst dept, 59-62, dir nuclear burst physics & math res, 62-67, VPRES, SANDIA LABS, 67- *Mailing Add:* Sandia Labs Livermore CA 94550

COOK, THOMAS LEROY, b Phoenix, Ariz, Sept 15, 43; m 64; c 3. PHYSICS, FLUID DYNAMICS. *Educ:* Rice Univ, BA, 68, MA, 72, PhD(physics), 77. *Prof Exp:* STAFF MEMBER PHYSICS, LOS ALAMOS NAT LAB, 77- *Res:* Numerical fluid dynamics, expecially multiphase flow, high enthalpy pipe flow, protostellar collapse and shock propagation in geologic media. *Mailing Add:* PO Box 1663 Los Alamos Sci Lab Los Alamos NM 87545

COOK, THOMAS M, b Miami, Fla, Mar 12, 31; m 50; c 3. MICROBIOLOGY. *Educ:* Univ Md, BS, 55, MS, 57; Rutgers Univ, PhD(bact), 63. *Prof Exp:* Microbiologist, Merck Sharp & Dohme Res Labs, 57-61; assoc res biologist, Sterling-Winthrop Res Inst, 63-66; asst prof, 66-70, assoc prof, 70-77, PROF MICROBIOL, UNIV MD, COL PARK, 77- *Mem:* Am Soc Microbiol. *Res:* Microbial physiology and biochemistry; oxidative metabolism; fermentations; action of antimicrobial agents. *Mailing Add:* Dept of Microbiol Univ of Md College Park MD 20742

COOK, THURLOW ADREAN, b Utica, NY, June 2, 39; m 61. MATHEMATICS. *Educ:* Univ Rochester, BA, 61; State Univ NY Buffalo, MA, 65; Fla State Univ, PhD(math), 67. *Prof Exp:* asst prof, 67, ASSOC PROF MATH, UNIV MASS, AMHERST, 67- *Mem:* Am Math Soc; Math Asn Am. *Res:* Functional analysis; general theory of Schauder bases in locally convex topological vector spaces, particularly Schauder bases in Banach spaces; foundations of quantum mechanics. *Mailing Add:* Dept of Math Univ of Mass Amherst MA 01003

COOK, VICTOR, b Palenville, NY, July 13, 29; m 57; c 2. PHYSICS. *Educ:* Univ Calif, Berkeley, AB, 57, PhD(physics), 62. *Prof Exp:* Res physicist, Lawrence Radiation Lab, Univ Calif, 62-63; from asst prof to assoc prof, 63-77, PROF PHYSICS, UNIV WASH, 77- *Mem:* Am Phys Soc; Am Asn Physics Teachers; Fedn Am Sci. *Res:* Properties and interactions of elementary particles. *Mailing Add:* Dept of Physics Univ of Wash Seattle WA 98195

COOK, WARREN AYER, b Conway, Mass, July 22, 00; m 28; c 1. INDUSTRIAL HYGIENE. *Educ:* Dartmouth Col, AB, 23. *Prof Exp:* Head chem unit, Eng & Inspection Div, Travelers Ins Co, 25-28; chief indust hygienist, Bur Indust Hyg, State Dept Health, Conn, 28-37; dir div indust hyg

& eng res, Zurich-Am Ins Co, 37-53; res assoc & from assoc prof to prof, 53-71, EMER PROF INDUST HEALTH, INST INDUST HEALTH, UNIV MICH, 71- *Concurrent Pos:* Adj prof indust health, Univ NC, 71- *Honors & Awards:* Cummings Award, Am Indust Hyg Asn, 52; Meritorious Achievement Award, Am Conf Govt Indust Hygienists, 73; Bordon Found Award, Am Indust Hyg Asn, 79. *Mem:* Hon mem Am Indust Hyg Asn (pres, 40); hon mem Am Acad Occup Med; mem emer Am Soc Safety Eng; Am Pub Health Asn; Am Chem Soc. *Res:* Methods of determination of atmospheric contaminants; administrative phases of industrial hygiene; educational and training programs for occupational safety and health personnel. *Mailing Add:* 713 Emory Dr Chapel Hill NC 27514

COOK, WENDELL SHERWOOD, b Youngstown, Ohio, June 14, 16; m 47. ORGANIC CHEMISTRY. *Educ:* Miami Univ, Ohio, BA, 38; Mich Technol Univ, MS, 48. *Prof Exp:* Chemist, Mineral Aggregates, France Co Labs, 36-42; res scientist, Cent Res Labs, 42-46; instr org biochem & gen chem, Mich Col Mining & Technol, 47-51; RES SCIENTIST, CHEM & PHYS RES LABS, FIRESTONE TIRE & RUBBER CO, 50- *Mem:* Am Chem Soc. *Res:* Rubber chemistry; x-ray fluorescence of trace elements in polymers and vulcanizates; atomic absorption analysis of polymers and vulcanizates; use of ultraviolet, infrared, NMR and mass spectrometric analysis of rubber and rubber chemicals research; organic chemicals as accelerators and oxidation inhibitors in synthetic polymers and vulcanizates. *Mailing Add:* 812 S Canal St PO Box 4007 Canal Fulton OH 44614

COOK, WILLIAM BOYD, b Dallas, Tex, July 20, 18; m 42; c 1. ORGANIC CHEMISTRY. *Educ:* Univ Tex, AB, 40; Univ Colo, MS, 42; Univ Wyo, PhD(chem), 50. *Prof Exp:* Asst, Univ Colo, 40-42; chemist-analyst, Monsanto Chem Co, 42-43, res assoc, 43-47; from instr to asst prof chem, Univ Wyo, 47-53; assoc prof, Baylor Univ, 53-57; prof & head dept, Mont State Col, 57-65; vis prof, Stanford Univ, 65-67; dean col sci & arts, 67-68, PROF CHEM, COLO STATE UNIV, 67-, DEAN COL NATURAL SCI, 68- *Concurrent Pos:* Fund Adv Educ fel, 52-53; NSF grant, Cambridge Univ, 62-63; exec dir, Adv Coun Chem, 65-67, mem, 66-69; mem adv comt grants of Res Corp, 69-75; US rep comt teaching chem, Int Union Pure & Appl Chem, 77-; chmn bd publ, J Chem Educ, 75- *Honors & Awards:* Gold Medal, Am Chem Soc, 73. *Mem:* Fel AAAS; fel Am Inst Chemists; Am Chem Soc. *Res:* Isolation and structural studies of alkaloids; nitrogen heterocyclic compounds; science education curricula. *Mailing Add:* Col of Natural Sci Colo State Univ Ft Collins CO 80521

COOK, WILLIAM JOHN, b Des Moines, Iowa, Apr 12, 29; m 53; c 2. MECHANICAL ENGINEERING. *Educ:* Iowa State Univ, BS, 57, MS, 59, PhD(mech eng), 64. *Prof Exp:* From instr to assoc prof, 59-76, PROF MECH ENG, IOWA STATE UNIV, 76- *Mem:* Am Soc Eng; Am Soc Mech Engrs; Am Inst Aeronaut & Astronaut. *Res:* Thermodynamics; high speed fluid mechanics and heat transfer; instrumentation for heat transfer measurement. *Mailing Add:* Dept of Mech Eng Iowa State Univ Ames IA 50010

COOK, WILLIAM JOSEPH, Tuscaloosa, Ala, July 18, 49; m 69; c 2. SURGICAL PATHOLOGY, AUTOPSY PATHOLOGY. *Educ:* Univ Ala, BS, 71; Univ Ala, Birmingham, MD, 74, PhD(biochem), 76. *Prof Exp:* Resident path, NIH, 76-78; res assoc, 71-74, fel, 74-76, INVESTR, INST DENT RES, UNIV ALA, BIRMINGHAM, 78-, ASSOC SCIENTIST, COMPREHENSIVE CANCER CTR, 78-, ASST PROF PATH, 78- *Mem:* Am Crystallog Asn; Am Asn Pathologists; Int Acad Path; NY Acad Sci. *Res:* Structural studies of compounds of biological interest using x-ray crystallography; primarily proteins, but also small polypeptides and nucleic acid components. *Mailing Add:* 2517 Old Oak Lane Birmingham AL 35243

COOK, WILLIAM R, JR, b Boston, Mass, Nov 28, 27; m 50; c 4. SOLID STATE CHEMISTRY, MINERALOGY. *Educ:* Oberlin Col, BA, 49; Columbia Univ, MA, 50; Case Western Reserve Univ, PhD, 71. *Prof Exp:* Crystallographer, Brush Develop Co, 51-53; head crystallog sect, Electronic Res Div, Clevite Corp, Gould, Inc, 53-74; CONSULT, 74-; SECY, CLEVELAND CRYSTALS, INC, 73- *Concurrent Pos:* Mem, Int Conf for Thermal Anal. *Mem:* Am Crystallog Asn; Mineral Soc Am; Am Ceramic Soc; Am Chem Soc. *Res:* Ferroelectricity and piezoelectricity; nonlinear optical materials; mineral chemistry. *Mailing Add:* 684 Quilliams Rd Cleveland OH 44121

COOK, WILLIAM ROBERT, b Birmingham, UK, Dec 8, 30; m 65; c 3. VETERINARY MEDICINE. *Educ:* Royal Col Vet Surgeons, MRCVS, 52, FRCVS, 66; Univ Cambridge, PhD(vet sci), 76. *Prof Exp:* Practr vet med, Gen & Equine Pract, 52-59; house surgeon, Sch Vet Med, Univ Cambridge, 59-60; lectr surg, Royal Vet Col, Univ London, 60-65; sr lectr, Sch Vet Med, Univ Glasgow, 65-69; sci officer I equine res, Animal Health Trust, London, 69-77; prof equine med & surg, Sch Vet Med, Univ Ill, 77-80; MEM FAC, SCH VET MED, TUFTS UNIV, 80- *Concurrent Pos:* External examr MVSc degree, Univ Glasgow, 75-77; external examr vet surg, Sch Vet, Univ Bristol, 75-77. *Honors & Awards:* Sir Frederick Hobday Mem Prize, Brit Equine Vet Asn, 76; Steele-Bodger Mem Scholar, Brit Vet Asn, 77. *Mem:* Royal Soc Med; Brit Vet Asn; Brit Equine Vet Asn (vpres, 76, pres, 77); Am Vet Med Asn; Am Asn Equine Practr. *Res:* Clinical research into diseases of the ear, nose and throat in the horse; hereditary diseases of the horse. *Mailing Add:* Sch Vet Med Tufts Univ 200 Westborough Rd North Grafton MA 01536

COOKE, ANSON RICHARD, b Lawrence, Mass, Jan 12, 26; m 48; c 4. PLANT PHYSIOLOGY. *Educ:* Univ Mass, BS, 49, MS, 50; Univ Mich, PhD(bot), 53. *Prof Exp:* Asst bot, Univ Mich, 50-53; asst prof plant biochem, Univ Hawaii, 53-54; asst prof plant physiol, Okla State Univ, 55-56; res plant physiologist, E I du Pont de Nemours & Co, 56-63; dir biol res, Amchem Prod, Inc, 63-77; GROUP LEADER BIOL RES, UNION CARBIDE AGR PROD CO, 77- *Mem:* Am Chem Soc; Am Soc Plant Physiol; Weed Sci Soc Am; Plant Growth Regulator Soc Am. *Res:* Plant growth regulators; herbicides; flowering; stress physiology. *Mailing Add:* Union Carbide Agr Prod Co PO Box 12014 Res Triangle Park NC 27709

COOKE, CHARLES C, b Huntsville, Ohio, Sept 13, 16; m 44; c 4. PHYSICS, ENGINEERING. *Educ:* Ohio State Univ, BS, 38. *Prof Exp:* Lab asst physics, 39-41, jr engr, 43-45, sr proj engr glass forming, 45-56, res engr comput, 57-66, chief process anal, Control & Instrumentation, 66-73, CHIEF COMPUT TECHNOL, OWENS ILLINOIS INC, 73- *Concurrent Pos:* Vis prof, Physics Dept, Appalachian State Univ, 79-80. *Mem:* Instrument Soc Am; Asn Comput Mach; Sigma Xi. *Res:* Glass forming problems; glass manufacturing process control; technical computer applications. *Mailing Add:* Owens-Ill Inc Box 1035 NTC Toledo OH 43666

COOKE, CHARLES ROBERT, b Oak Hill, WVa, June 12, 29; m 51; c 4. MEDICINE. *Educ:* WVa Univ, AB, 50, BS, 52; Johns Hopkins Univ, MD, 54. *Prof Exp:* From instr to asst prof, 63-70, ASSOC PROF MED, SCH MED, JOHNS HOPKINS UNIV, 70- *Concurrent Pos:* Am Heart Asn fel, 59-60; USPHS fel, 60-61; asst chief med, Baltimore City Hosps, 63-67; consult, Vet Admin, 67- *Mem:* Fel Am Col Physicians; Am Fedn Clin Res; Am Soc Nephrology. *Res:* Renal physiology and electrolyte metabolism. *Mailing Add:* Dept Med Sch Med Johns Hopkins Univ Baltimore MD 21218

COOKE, DAVID WAYNE, b Hopkinsville, Ky, Mar 16, 47; m 68. SOLID STATE PHYSICS. *Educ:* Western Ky Univ, BS, 69, MS, 70; Univ Ala, PhD(physics), 77. *Prof Exp:* Med physicist, Med Ctr, WVa Univ, 71-72; fel, Univ Ala, 77; ASST PROF PHYSICS, MEMPHIS STATE UNIV, 78- *Concurrent Pos:* Grad coun res fel, Univ Ala, 76-77, Lockheed Aircraft fel, 77. *Honors & Awards:* Res Award, Sigma Xi, 80. *Mem:* Sigma Xi; Am Physi Soc; Health Phys Soc; AAAS; NY Acad Sci. *Res:* Low temperature solid state luminescence; thermoluminescent dosimetry; muon spin rotation. *Mailing Add:* Dept of Physics Memphis State Univ Memphis TN 38152

COOKE, DEAN WILLIAM, b Uniontown, Pa, Mar 12, 31; m 56; c 4. INORGANIC CHEMISTRY. *Educ:* Ohio State Univ, BS, 55, PhD(chem), 59. *Prof Exp:* From instr to assoc prof, 59-72, PROF CHEM, WESTERN MICH UNIV, 72- *Mem:* Am Chem Soc; Sigma Xi; Royal Soc Chem. *Res:* Coordination chemistry; stereochemistry; reactions of coordinated ligands; homogeneous catalysis; optical activity; mechanisms of substitution reactions. *Mailing Add:* Dept of Chem Western Mich Univ Kalamazoo MI 49008

COOKE, DERRY DOUGLAS, b Schenectady, NY, Jan 29, 37. PHYSICAL CHEMISTRY. *Educ:* Parsons Col, BS, 63; Clarkson Col Technol, PhD(phys chem), 69. *Prof Exp:* Fel phys chem, 68-73, RES ASST PROF CHEM, CLARKSON COL TECHNOL, 73- *Mem:* Am Chem Soc. *Res:* Aerosols; light scattering; submicron cylinders. *Mailing Add:* Fac of Arts & Sci Clarkson Col of Technol Potsdam NY 13676

COOKE, FRANCIS W, b Jersey City, NJ, Nov 3, 34; m 57; c 4. BIOMATERIALS, MATERIALS ENGINEERING. *Educ:* Univ Notre Dame, BS, 57; Rensselaer Polytech Inst, PhD(mat eng), 65. *Prof Exp:* Metallurgist, Oak Ridge Nat Lab, 57-61; res asst mat eng, Rensselaer Polytech Inst, 61-65; sr res metallurgist, Franklin Inst Res Labs, 65-66, mgr metall lab, 66-71, mgr bioeng lab, 69-71; assoc prof, 71-78, PROF MAT ENG & BIOENG, CLEMSON UNIV, 78-, HEAD DEPT INTERDISCIPLINARY STUDIES, 72- *Concurrent Pos:* NIH consult, 77-81. *Mem:* Soc Biomat (pres, 77-78). *Mailing Add:* Dept of Interdisciplinary Studies Clemson Univ Clemson SC 29631

COOKE, FRED, b Darlington, Eng, Oct 13, 36; m 63; c 2. GENETICS. *Educ:* Cambridge Univ, BA, 60, MA, 63, PhD(biol), 65. *Prof Exp:* Asst prof, 64-69, assoc prof biol, 69-78, PROF BIOL, QUEEN'S UNIV, ONT, 78- *Mem:* Genetics Soc Am; Genetics Soc Can; Am Ornithologists Union; Wilson Ornith Soc; Cooper Ornith Soc. *Res:* Population biology of a breeding colony of lesser snow geese using genetic, ecological, and behavioral approaches; population biology of the snow goose. *Mailing Add:* Dept of Biol Queen's Univ Kingston ON K7L 3N6 Can

COOKE, GEORGE DENNIS, b Ravenna, Ohio, June 29, 37; div; c 2. AQUATIC ECOLOGY, LAKE MANAGEMENT AND RESTORATION. *Educ:* Kent State Univ, BS, 59; Univ Iowa, MS, 63, PhD(zool), 65. *Prof Exp:* Asst biol, Kent State Univ, 60; asst zool & ecol, Univ Iowa, 60-65; USPHS fel ecol, Univ Ga, 65-67; asst prof, 67-71, assoc prof, 71-76, res assoc, Ctr Urban Regionalism & Environ Systs, 72-80, PROF, DEPT BIOL SCI, KENT STATE UNIV, 76- *Concurrent Pos:* Prin invest grants, US Environ Protection Agency, 70-79, mem staff, Corvallis Lab, 79, consult, Clean Lakes Prog, 79-81; consult, Polish govt, 77-78. *Mem:* Ecol Soc Am; Am Soc Limnol & Oceanog; Int Asn Theoret & Appl Limnol. *Res:* Eutrophication; lake restoration and mangement; experimental limnology. *Mailing Add:* Dept of Biol Sci Kent State Univ Kent OH 44242

COOKE, HELEN JOAN, b Greenfield, Mass, May 21, 43; c 2. INTESTINAL PHYSIOLOGY, INTESTINAL DEVELOPMENT. *Educ:* Univ Mass, BS, 65; Univ Calif, Los Angeles, MS, 67; Univ Sydney, Australia, PhD(physiol), 71. *Prof Exp:* Instr renal physiol, Sch Med, Univ Iowa, 71-73, asst prof, 73-76; asst prof renal & gastro-intestine, Univ Kans Med Ctr, 76-80; asst prof, 80-82, ASSOC PROF GASTRO-INTESTINE, SCH MED, UNIV NEV, 82- *Concurrent Pos:* Vis prof, Sch Med, Univ Nev, 79-80; res career develop award, Arthritis, Metab & digestive dis, NIH, 82. *Mem:* Am Fedn Clin Res; Am Physiol Soc; Am Women Sci; Am Gastroenterol Asn; Sigma Xi. *Res:* Development of intestinal transport processes; control of intestinal transport by nerves and hormones. *Mailing Add:* Dept Physiol Univ Nev Reno NV 89509

COOKE, HENRY CHARLES, b Poughkeepsie, NY, June 24, 13; m 39; c 2. MATHEMATICS. *Educ:* NC State Col, BS, 37, MS, 51. *Prof Exp:* Teacher high sch, NC, 37-40; from instr to asst prof, NC State Univ, 40-50, assoc prof math, 51-79, TV instr, 55-79; RETIRED. *Mem:* Sigma Xi. *Res:* Methods and techniques of audiovisual television presentation of instructional material. *Mailing Add:* Dept of Math NC State Univ Raleigh NC 27607

COOKE, HERBERT BASIL SUTTON, b Johannesburg, SAfrica, Oct 17, 15; m 43; c 2. GEOLOGY. *Educ:* Cambridge Univ, BA, 36, MA, 41; Univ Witwatersrand, MSc, 41, DSc(geol), 47. *Prof Exp:* Geologist, Cent Mining & Investment Co, Ltd, SAfrica, 36-38; lectr geol, Univ Witwatersrand, 38-47, sr lectr, 53-58, reader, 58-61; private consult, 47-52; assoc prof geol, Dalhousie Univ, 61-63, dean arts & sci, 63-68, prof geol, 63-81; CONSULT GEOL, 81- *Concurrent Pos:* Ed jour, SAfrican Asn Advan Sci, 45-57; Nuffield Found bursary, 55-56; Du Toit Mem Lectr, 57; vis res assoc, Univ Calif, Berkeley, 57-58; chmn, Bernard Price Inst Paleont Res, 58-61. *Mem:* Fel Geol Soc Am; fel Royal Soc SAfrica; SAfrica Archaeol Soc (pres, 51); SAfrican Geog Soc (pres, 46); SAfrican Asn Advan Sci (vpres, 60). *Res:* Later Cenozoic geology and fossil mammals, particularly African. *Mailing Add:* 2133 154th St White Rock BC V4A 4S5 Can

COOKE, HERMON RICHARD, JR, b Tonopah, Nev, Jan 3, 14; m 43; c 3. MINING GEOLOGY. *Educ:* Univ Nev, BA, 34, BS, 35; Harvard Univ, MA, 39, PhD(mining geol), 45. *Prof Exp:* Geologist, Black Mammoth Mining Co, Nev, 36; topog survr, US Nat Mus, Mo, 38; geologist, Original Sixteen to One Mine, Inc, Calif, 39-40; geologist, Am Metal Co, Ltd, Nev, 42; geologist, Basic Refractories, Inc, Nev, 42-43; geologist, US Geol Surv, Mont, 46; geologist, Chile Explor Co, 46-49; geologist, Patino Co, Bolivia & Volcan Mines, Peru, 49; consult geol, Graff & Kruger, Peru, 50; explor geol, Am Smelting & Refining Co, Peru, 51-54; consult, Martin Sykes & Assocs, Venezuela, 54-57; geologist, Cooke, Everett & Assocs, Nev, 58-68 & 70-74; chief geologist, Oper Hardrock, India, Parsons Corp, 68-70; MEM STAFF, GRÖNLANDS GEOLOGISKE UNDERSÖGELESE, DENMARK, 74- *Mem:* AAAS; Nat Soc Prof Engrs; Am Inst Mining, Metall & Petrol Engrs; Am Soc Photogram; Mineral Soc Am. *Res:* Mining exploration; applied geology. *Mailing Add:* Gronlands Geologiske Undersogelse Oster Voldgade 10 PK-1350 Copenhagen-K Denmark

COOKE, IAN MCLEAN, b Honolulu, Hawaii, Feb 6, 33; m 59; c 3. NEUROPHYSIOLOGY, COMPARATIVE PHYSIOLOGY. *Educ:* Harvard Univ, AB, 55, AM, 59, PhD(biol), 62. *Prof Exp:* Instr biol, Harvard Univ, 62; res assoc biophys, Univ Col London, 62-63; from instr to asst prof biol, Harvard Univ, 63-70; res assoc, Lab Cellular Neurophysiol, Nat Ctr Sci Res, Paris, 70-72; PROF ZOOL, UNIV HAWAII, MANOA, 72-, PROG DIR, BEKESY LAB NEUROBIOL, 75- *Mem:* Am Soc Zool; Soc Gen Physiol; Am Physiol Soc; Soc Neurosci. *Res:* Control and mechanisms of release of neurosecretory material; biophysics of patterned neuronal activity; cellular neurophysiology. *Mailing Add:* Bekesy Lab Neurobiol Univ of Hawaii-Manoa Honolulu HI 96822

COOKE, J DAVID, b Moncton, New Brunswick, Sept 23, 39; m 66; c 2. MOTOR CONTROL, NEUROPHYSIOLOGY. *Educ:* Mount Allison Univ, BSc, 60; Dalhousie Univ, MSc, 66, PhD(physiol), 70. *Prof Exp:* ASSOC PROF PHYSIOL, UNIV WESTERN ONT, 71- *Mem:* Can Physiol Soc; Soc Neurosci. *Res:* Control of arm movements in humans, including factors as limb mechanics, sensory information, reflex systems and central influences. *Mailing Add:* Dept Physiol Univ Western Ont London ON N6A 5B8 Can

COOKE, JAMES HORTON, b Ft Worth, Tex, Apr 26, 40. THEORETICAL PHYSICS. *Educ:* North Tex State Univ, BA, 62; Univ NC, PhD(physics), 67. *Prof Exp:* Fel physics, Univ Man, 66-68; asst prof, 68-74, ASSOC PROF PHYSICS, UNIV TEX, ARLINGTON, 74- *Res:* Investigation of various theories of relativistic interacting particles. *Mailing Add:* Dept of Physics Univ of Tex Arlington TX 76010

COOKE, JAMES LOUIS, b Canyon, Tex, Sept 20, 29; m 50; c 2. ELECTRICAL ENGINEERING. *Educ:* Tex Tech Col, BS, 51; Univ Tex, MS, 52; Northwestern Univ, PhD(elec eng), 60. *Prof Exp:* Elec eng, Southwestern Pub Serv Co, 52-53, 55-56; asst prof, 56-58, from assoc prof to prof, 60-71, dir grad studies, 78-80, REGENT'S PROF ELEC ENG, LAMAR UNIV, 71- *Concurrent Pos:* Consult, Gulf States Utilities Co, 56-58, 60-65, 71-, J&J Mfg Co, 60-71 & Texaco Res, 66-70. *Mem:* Inst Elec & Electronics Engrs. *Res:* Systems analysis and control; power systems engineering, protection and reliability; on-line and off-line computer applications in these areas. *Mailing Add:* Dept Elec Eng Lamar Univ Box 10029 Beaumont TX 77710

COOKE, JAMES ROBERT, b Mooresville, NC, Apr 14, 39; m 61; c 3. AGRICULTURAL ENGINEERING. *Educ:* NC State Univ, BS, 61, MS, 65, PhD(biol & agr eng), 66. *Prof Exp:* Asst prof, 66-71, ASSOC PROF AGR ENG, CORNELL UNIV, 71- *Mem:* Am Soc Agr Engrs. *Res:* Engineering properties of biological materials and systems; biological engineering analysis. *Mailing Add:* 228 Riley-Robb Hall Cornell Univ Ithaca NY 14850

COOKE, JOHN COOPER, b Lawrence, Mass, May 12, 39; m 63; c 1. MYCOLOGY. *Educ:* Univ Mass, BS, 61, MA, 63; Univ Ga, PhD(mycol), 67. *Prof Exp:* Teacher high sch, RI, 64; asst prof biol, Elizabethtown Col, 67-69; res assoc, 69-70, asst prof, 70-75, ASSOC PROF BIOL, UNIV CONN, 75- *Mem:* Mycol Soc Am; British Mycol Soc; Am Inst Biol Sci; Torrey Bot Club. *Res:* Morphology of fungi; ecology of soil fungi. *Mailing Add:* Dept of Biol Univ of Conn Avery Pt Groton CT 06340

COOKE, KENNETH LLOYD, b Kansas City, Mo, Aug 13, 25; m 50; c 3. APPLIED MATHEMATICS, BIOMATHEMATICS. *Educ:* Pomona Col, BA, 47; Stanford Univ, MS, 49, PhD(math), 52. *Prof Exp:* From instr to asst prof math, State Col Wash, 50-57; asst prof, 57-62, chmn dept, 61-71, PROF MATH, POMONA COL, 62- *Concurrent Pos:* Consult, Rand Corp, Calif, 56-65; assoc ed, J Math Anal & Appln, Utilitas Mathematica, 71- & J Computational & Appl Math, 74-81; researcher, Res Inst Adv Study, 63-64; NSF sci fac fel, Stanford Univ, 66-67; Fulbright res scholar, Univ Florence, 72; assoc, Ctr Study Dem Inst, 74-75; vis prof, Brown Univ, 78-79. *Mem:* Am Math Soc; Math Asn Am; Soc Indust & Appl Math; Soc Math Biol; Ital Math Union. *Res:* Ordinary, partial and functional differential equations; integral equations; difference equations; dynamic programming; mathematical models in the biological and social sciences. *Mailing Add:* Dept of Math Pomona Col Claremont CA 91711

COOKE, LLOYD MILLER, b La Salle, Ill, June 7, 16; m 57. CHEMISTRY. *Educ:* Univ Wis, BS, 37; McGill Univ, PhD(org chem), 41. *Prof Exp:* Lectr org chem, McGill Univ, 41-42; res chemist & sect leader, Corn Prod Refining Co, Ill, 42-46; group leader res, Food Prod Div, Union Carbide Corp, 46-49, mgr cellulose & casing res dept, 50-54, asst to mgr tech div, 54-59, asst dir res, 59-64, mgr mkt res, 64-67, mgr planning, 65-70, dir urban affairs, 70-73, corp dir univ rels, Union Carbide Corp, 73-76, dir community affairs, 76-78; sr consult pub affairs, 78-81; PRES, NACME, 81- *Concurrent Pos:* Trustee, Chicago Chem Libr Found; mem, Nat Sci Bd, 70-81; trustee, Carver Res Found, Tuskegee Inst, 71-78 & McCormick Theol Sem, Chicago, 73-79; consult, Off Technol Assessment, US Cong, 74-78. *Honors & Awards:* Proctor Prize in Sci, Sci Res Asn Am, 70; Honor Scroll Award, Am Inst Chemists, 70. *Mem:* NY Acad Sci; Am Inst Chem; Am Chem Soc. *Res:* Structure of lignin; starch modifications and derivatives; cellulose derivatives; viscose chemistry; carbohydrate and polymer chemistry; secondary mathematics and science education. *Mailing Add:* 1 Beaufort St White Plains NY 10607

COOKE, MANNING PATRICK, JR, b Suffolk, Va, July 24, 41; m 63; c 3. ORGANIC CHEMISTRY. *Educ:* Univ NC, AB, 63, MS, 66, PhD(chem), 67. *Prof Exp:* Fel org chem, Harvard Univ, 68-70 & Stanford Univ, 70-71; ASSOC PROF ORG CHEM, WASH STATE UNIV, 71- *Mem:* Am Chem Soc. *Res:* Synthesis and new synthetic methods in organic chemistry. *Mailing Add:* Dept of Chem Wash State Univ Pullman WA 99163

COOKE, NORMAN E(DWARD), b Vancouver, BC, Aug 30, 22; m 47, 77. CHEMICAL ENGINEERING. *Educ:* Univ BC, BASc, 45, MASc, 46; Mass Inst Technol, ScD(chem eng), 56. *Prof Exp:* Asst chem, Univ BC, 45-46; asst chemist, Pac Fisheries Exp Sta, Fisheries Res Bd, Can, 46-48, assoc chemist, 49-56; chem eng specialist, Eng Dept, Can Industs Ltd, 56-60, prin chem engr, 60-72, tech develop mgr, 72-74; CHIEF PROCESS ENGR, SURVEYER, NENNIGER & CHENEVERT INC, 74-, MGR TECH DEVELOP, 78- *Concurrent Pos:* Spec lectr, McGill Univ, 63-; assoc comt water pollution, Nat Res Coun Can, 65-67, assoc comt sci criteria environ qual, 70-; Can Dept Nat Health & Welfare Environ Health Comt, Pub Health Res Adv Comt, 67-71; mem adv comt, Can Ctr Inland Waters, 69-; chmn subcomt metals & certain other elements, 70-72; chmn expert panel, Lead in Can Environ & Sulphur in Can Environ, 72-74; chmn task force environ protection, Can Coun Resource & Environ Ministers' Conf on Man & Resources, 73; auxilary prof chem eng, McGill Univ, 76- *Honors & Awards:* Indust Wastes Medal, Water Pollution Control Fedn, 60. *Mem:* Fel Chem Inst Can; Can Soc Chem Eng (secy-treas, 64-67, vpres, 58 & 67-68, pres, 68-69); fel Am Inst Chem Engrs; assoc Oper Res Soc Am; Can Soc Mech Engrs. *Res:* Air pollution control; water pollution control; mass transfer; process design; coal conversion; solar energy. *Mailing Add:* SNC Inc Box 10 Complexe Desjardins Montreal PQ H5B 1C8 Can

COOKE, PETER HAYMAN, b Beverly, Mass, Feb 4, 43; c 2. CYTOLOGY. *Educ:* Springfield Col, BS, 64; Univ NH, PhD(zool), 67. *Prof Exp:* Res fel cell biol, Harvard Univ, 67-69; res fel muscle, Boston Biomed Res Inst, 69-71; asst prof physiol & cell biol, Univ Kans, 71-75; ASSOC PROF PHYSIOL, HEALTH CTR, UNIV CONN, 75- *Concurrent Pos:* Res fel, Muscular Dystrophy Asn Am, 69 & Am Heart Asn-Brit Heart Found, 74; vis res fel physics, The Open Univ, UK, 74-75; established investr, Am Heart Asn, 77-82. *Mem:* Am Soc Cell Biol; Sigma Xi. *Res:* Contractile mechanism of muscle. *Mailing Add:* Dept of Physiol Health Ctr Univ of Conn Farmington CT 06032

COOKE, ROBERT CLARK, b Duluth, Minn, April; m 63; c 2. OCEANOGRAPHY. *Educ:* Randolph-Macon Col, BSc, 63; Dalhousie Univ, PhD(oceanog), 71. *Prof Exp:* Phys chemist, Hercules, Inc, 64-66; asst prof, 71-77, ASSOC PROF OCEANOG, DALHOUSIE UNIV, 77- *Mem:* Am Geophys Union; Geochem Soc; Can Meteorol & Oceanog Soc. *Res:* Oceanic processes at high pressure; effect of ion-pairing on environmental chemistry; physical effects at small dimensions; diffusion; gas transfer; organic solubilization and the phase rule. *Mailing Add:* Dept Oceanog Dalhousie Univ Halifax NS B3H 4J1 Can

COOKE, ROBERT E, b Attleboro, Mass, Nov 13, 20; m 42; c 5. PEDIATRICS. *Educ:* Yale Univ, BS, 41, MD, 44. *Hon Degrees:* ScD, Univ Miami, 71. *Prof Exp:* Intern pediat, New Haven Hosp, 44-45, asst resident, 45-46; instr, Sch Med, Yale Univ, 50-51, from asst prof to assoc prof pediat & physiol, 51-56; Given Found prof pediat, Johns Hopkins Univ, 56-73, pediatrician-in-chief, Johns Hopkins Hosp, 56-73; prof pediat & vchancellor health sci, Univ Wis-Madison, 73-77; PRES, MED COL PA, 77- *Concurrent Pos:* NIH fel, 48-50; Markle scholar, 51-55; resident, Grace New Haven Hosps, 50-51; mem, President's Panel Ment Retardation, 61-62 & President's Comt Ment Retardation, 66-69; consult div hosps & med facil & mem comt areawide planning of facil ment retarded, USPHS, 63-65; mem, White House Adv Comt Ment Retardation, 63-65; mem res & demonstration panel, Off Educ, Dept Health, Educ & Welfare, 63-66; consult, Nat Found-March of Dimes, 68-70; mem, Nat Comn Protection Human Subjects of Biomed & Behav Res, Off Asst Secy Health, 74-76; mem, Health Manpower Training Assistance Rev Comt, Vet Admin, Washington, DC, 74-76; consult, Off Technol Assessment, Cong of US, 74-; mem, Nat Asn Retarded Children & Joseph P Kennedy Jr Mem Found; mem adv coun, Nat Inst Child Health & Human Develop; chmn steering comt, Oper Head Start, Off Econ Opportunity. *Honors & Awards:* Johnson Award, 54; St Coletta Award, Caritas Soc, 67; Kennedy Int Award, 68. *Mem:* AAAS; AMA; Am Asn Med Cols; Am Fedn Clin Res; Am Pub Health Asn. *Res:* Mental retardation; water and electrolyte physiology. *Mailing Add:* JP Kennedy Jr Found 1701 K St NW Ste 205 Washington DC 20006

COOKE, ROBERT SANDERSON, b Philadelphia, Pa, Nov 10, 44; m 74; c 2. ORGANIC CHEMISTRY, POLYMER CHEMISTRY. *Educ:* Wesleyan Univ, AB, 66; Calif Inst Technol, PhD(chem), 70. *Prof Exp:* Asst prof chem, Univ Ore, 70-75; RES CHEMIST, ALLIED CORP, 75- *Mem:* Am Chem Soc. *Res:* Kinetics and mechanistic studies related to organic processes and polymerization reactions. *Mailing Add:* Allied Corp PO Box 1021R-CRL Morristown NJ 07960

COOKE, ROGER, b Ann Arbor, Mich, Feb 22, 40. BIOPHYSICS. *Educ:* Mass Inst Technol, BS, 62; Univ Ill, MS, 64, PhD(physics), 68. *Prof Exp:* Res assoc, 70-71, asst prof, 71-80, ASSOC PROF BIOPHYS, UNIV CALIF, SAN FRANCISCO, 80- *Concurrent Pos:* USPHS fel, Univ Calif, San Francisco, 68-70; estab investr, Am Heart Asn, 71- *Mem:* Biophys Soc; Am Heart Asn. *Res:* Muscle biochemistry and biophysics; protein interactions; fluorescence; electron paramagnetic resonance; nuclear magnetic resonance; structure of intracellular water. *Mailing Add:* Dept Biochem & Biophys 841 HSW Univ Calif San Francisco CA 94143

COOKE, ROGER LEE, b Alton, Ill, July 31, 42; m 68; c 1. MATHEMATICS. *Educ:* Northwestern Univ, BA, 63; Princeton Univ, MA & PhD(math), 66. *Prof Exp:* Asst prof math, Vanderbilt Univ, 66-68; asst prof, 68-72, assoc prof, 72-77, PROF MATH, UNIV VT, 77- *Concurrent Pos:* NSF res grant, 69-71. *Mem:* Am Math Soc; Math Asn Am. *Res:* Trigonometric series in several variables. *Mailing Add:* Dept of Math Univ of Vt Burlington VT 05405

COOKE, RON CHARLES, b Chico, Calif, Dec 31, 47; c 1. SYNTHETIC ORGANIC CHEMISTRY, NATURAL PRODUCTS CHEMISTRY. *Educ:* Calif State Univ, Chico, BS, 70; Univ of the Pacific, MS, 73. *Prof Exp:* Chemist org chem, Calif State Univ, Chico, 70-71; instr pharmaceut sci, Univ of the Pacific, 73-75; lab dir plant tissue cult, Bailey's Nursery, Inc, 75-77; mem tech staff, Flow Labs, Inc, 77-81; INSTR CHEM, CALIF STATE UNIV, CHICO, 81- *Mem:* Am Soc Pharmacog; Electron Micros Soc; Tissue Cult Asn; AAAS. *Res:* Plant morphogenesis and asexual propagation of plants by tissue culture; production of drugs by plants in tissue culture. *Mailing Add:* Dept Chem Calif State Univ Chico CA 95926

COOKE, SAMUEL LEONARD, JR, b Atlanta, Ga, Nov 30, 31; m 54; c 3. ANALYTICAL CHEMISTRY, SCIENCE EDUCATION. *Educ:* Univ Richmond, BS, 52, MS, 54; Baylor Univ, PhD(phys chem), 57. *Prof Exp:* Res chemist, E I du Pont de Nemours & Co, 57-58; instrument designer, Intersci, Inc, 58-61, assoc prof chem, Ala Col, 61-63; from asst prof to assoc prof, 63-70, PROF CHEM, UNIV LOUISVILLE, 70- *Mem:* Am Chem Soc; Asn Comput Mach. *Res:* Instrumental methods of analysis; analytical chemistry; chemical application of computers. *Mailing Add:* Dept Chem Univ Louisville 2301 S Third St Louisville KY 40292

COOKE, STRATHMORE R(IDLEY) B(ARNOTT), b Wanganui, NZ, Jan 4, 07; nat US; m 33; c 1. METALLURGICAL ENGINEERING. *Educ:* Univ NZ, BSc, 27, BE, 28; Otago Univ, AOSM, 28; Mo Sch Mines, MS, 30; Univ Mo, PhD(metall), 33. *Prof Exp:* Res metallurgist, State Mining Exp Sta, Mo Sch Mines, 33-39, asst prof metall & ore dressing, 36-39; res prof mineral dressing, Mont Sch Mines, 39-46; prof geol & geophys, 46-74, head sch mines, 57-59, EMER PROF GEOL & GEOPHYS, UNIV MINN, MINNEAPOLIS, 74- *Concurrent Pos:* With US Bur Mines, 44. *Honors & Awards:* Richards Award, Am Inst Mining, Metall & Petrol Engrs, 79. *Mem:* Distinguished mem Am Inst Mining, Metall & Petrol Engrs; fel Mineral Soc Am; Brit Astron Asn. *Res:* Concentration of iron ores; colloidal phenomena in flotation; flotation of nonsulphide minerals; spectrochemical analysis of minerals, metallurgical analysis of archaeological materials. *Mailing Add:* 4408 Zenith Ave N Minneapolis MN 55422

COOKE, THEODORE FREDERIC, b Pittsfield, Mass, Jan 28, 13; m 40, 73; c 4. TEXTILE CHEMISTRY, POLYMER SCIENCE. *Educ:* Univ Mass, BS, 34; Yale Univ, PhD(phys chem), 37. *Prof Exp:* Res chemist, Standard Oil Develop Co, NJ, 37-40; res chemist, Org Chem Div, Am Cyanamid Co, 40-42, asst dir phys chem res, 45-48, asst dir appln res dept, 48-52, mgr textile resin lab, 52-54, asst to mgr textile resin dept, 54-58, mgr commercial develop, 58-60, dir chem res, 60-62, asst dir res & develop, 62-72, dir, Sci Serv Dept, Chem Res Div, 72-78; DIR, REGULATORY TECH INFO CTR, OFF COOP RES, TEXTILE RES INST, YALE UNIV, 78- *Concurrent Pos:* Consult, Southern Regional Res Labs, USDA, 54-60; chmn, Gordon Res Conf Textiles; chmn comt textile finishing, Nat Res Coun Adv Bd Qm Res & Develop; consult, 78- *Mem:* Am Chem Soc; fel Am Inst Chem; Asn Res Dirs. *Res:* Analytical chemistry; physical chemistry; cosmetic chemistry; polymer chemistry; cellulose and textile chemistry. *Mailing Add:* 287 Weed Ave Stamford CT 06902

COOKE, WILLIAM BRIDGE, b Foster, Ohio, July 16, 08; m 42. MYCOLOGY. *Educ:* Univ Cincinnati, BA, 37; Ore State Col, MS, 39; State Col Wash, PhD(bot), 50. *Prof Exp:* Mycologist, Trop Deterioration Res Lab, US Qm Corps, 45-46; res assoc, Dept Plant Path, State Col Wash, 50-51; mycologist, Bact Sect, Environ Health Ctr, US Pub Health Serv, 52-53, prin mycologist, Robert A Taft Sanit Eng Ctr, 53-56, sr mycologist, Microbiol Activities, Cincinnati Water Res Lab, Fed Water Pollution Control Admin, Dept Health, Educ & Welfare, 56-66; mycologist biol treatment activities, Advan Waste Treatment Prog, US Dept Interior, 66-69; res assoc dept bot, Miami Univ, 69-70; SR RES ASSOC, DEPT BIOL SCI, UNIV CINCINNATI, 70- *Honors & Awards:* Superior Service Award, Dept Health, Educ & Welfare, 59; Fed Water Pollution Control Admin Award, US Dept Interior. *Mem:* Fel AAAS; Mycol Soc Am; Soc Indust Microbiol; Am Soc Agron; Bot Soc Am. *Res:* Fungi of polluted water and sewage; taxonomy of Polyporaceae; flora and fungi of Mt Shasta and fungi of national parks; fungi of Ohio. *Mailing Add:* 1135 Wilshire Ct Cincinnati OH 45230

COOKE, WILLIAM DONALD, b Philadelphia, Pa, May 15, 18; m 46; c 6. ANALYTICAL CHEMISTRY. *Educ:* St Joseph's Col, Philadelphia, BS, 40; Univ Pa, MS & PhD, 49. *Prof Exp:* Chemist, Harshaw Chem Co, Pa, 40-42; Nat Res Coun fel, Princeton Univ, 49-51; from asst prof to assoc prof, 51-59, assoc dean col arts & sci, 62-64, dean grad sch, 64-69, PROF CHEM, CORNELL UNIV, 59-, VPRES RES, 69- *Concurrent Pos:* Pres, Asn Grad Schs, 70-71; mem bd trustees, Fordham Univ, 70- & Assoc Univs, Inc, 74-; mem, Nat Bd Grad Educ, 72-75. *Mem:* Am Chem Soc. *Res:* Electrochemical methods; absorption spectra; flame spectroscopy; nuclear magnetic resonance; gas chromatography. *Mailing Add:* Day Hall Cornell Univ Ithaca NY 14853

COOKE, WILLIAM JOSEPH, biochemical pharmacology, see previous edition

COOKE, WILLIAM PEYTON, JR, b Hobart, Okla, Jan 4, 34; m 61; c 3. MATHEMATICS, STATISTICS. *Educ:* West Tex State Univ, BS, 59; Tex Tech Col, MS, 61; Tex A&M Univ, PhD(statist), 68. *Prof Exp:* Instr math, Amarillo Col, 60-61; instr, Tex Tech Col, 61-62; from asst prof to assoc prof, WTex State Univ, 64-69; assoc prof, 69-77, PROF STATIST, UNIV WYO, 77- *Mem:* Math Asn Am; Am Statist Asn. *Res:* Mathematical programming; statistical reliability. *Mailing Add:* Dept of Statist Univ of Wyo Laramie WY 82071

COOK-IOANNIDIS, LESLIE PAMELA, b Kingston, Ont, Aug 23, 46; US citizen; m 72. APPLIED MATHEMATICS. *Educ:* Univ Rochester, BA, 67; Cornell Univ, MS, 69, PhD(appl math), 71. *Prof Exp:* NATO fel appl math, 71-72; instr & res assoc, Dept Theoret & Appl Mech & Dept Math, Cornell Univ, 72-73; adj asst prof, 73-75, asst prof, 75-80, ASSOC PROF, DEPT MATH, UNIV CALIF, LOS ANGELES, 80- *Mem:* Sigma Xi; Soc Indust & Appl Math; Soc Women Engrs; Am Acad Mech; Am Math Soc. *Res:* Transonic aerodynamics, biomathematics. *Mailing Add:* Dept Math Univ Calif Los Angeles CA 90024

COOKSEY, DONALD ERNEST, b Duncan, Okla, Dec 3, 15; m 40; c 1. ORAL SURGERY. *Educ:* Univ Southern Calif, DDS, 40; Georgetown Univ, MS, 54. *Prof Exp:* Chief oral surg sect, US Naval Dent Sch, US Dept Navy, 54-62, cmndg officer, US Naval Dent Clin, Yokosuka, Japan, 62-66, dist dent officer, Sixth Naval Dist, Charleston, SC, 66-67; ORAL SURGEON, 67-; PROF ORAL SURG, SCH DENT, UNIV SOUTHERN CALIF, 71- *Concurrent Pos:* Instr, Georgetown Univ, 53-54; spec lectr, Univ Pa, 55; lectr, Col Dent, Univ Calif, Los Angeles; consult, Nat Bd Dent Examrs & Coun Dent Educ, Am Dent Asn; past pres, Am Bd Oral Surg. *Mem:* Fel Am Col Dentists; Am Dent Asn; Am Soc Oral Surg. *Res:* Transplantation of freeze dried tissues to defects of the jaws. *Mailing Add:* Dept of Oral Surg Sch of Dent Univ of Southern Calif Los Angeles CA 90007

COOKSON, FRANCIS BERNARD, b Preston, Eng, Oct 30, 28; m 53; c 2. NEUROANATOMY, HISTOLOGY. *Educ:* Univ Manchester, BSc, 53, MB & ChB, 56; Royal Col Obstetricians & Gynaecologists, Eng, dipl obstet, 57. *Prof Exp:* Demonstr anat, Univ Manchester, 57-58; pvt pract med, Eng, 58-64; asst prof anat, Univ Sask, 64-66; assoc prof, 66-71, asst dean med, 74-80, PROF ANAT, UNIV ALTA, 71-, HON LECTR MED, 66-, DIR HEALTH SERV, 77-, ASSOC DEAN MED, 80- *Concurrent Pos:* Med Res Coun res grants, 65-69; Alta Heart Found res grant, 67-68. *Mem:* Fel Am Heart Asn; Anat Soc Gt Brit & Ireland; Can Med Asn; Brit Med Asn. *Res:* Histopathology; experimental atherosclerosis, etiology pathogenesis and preventions; hypertension incidence in university students; medical education. *Mailing Add:* 11119-30 Ave Edmonton AB T6J 3Y7 Can

COOKSON, JOHN T(HOMAS), JR, b East St Louis, Ill, July 7, 39; m 61; c 2. ENVIRONMENTAL ENGINEERING. *Educ:* Wash Univ, BS, 61, MS, 62; Calif Inst Technol, PhD(environ health eng), 66. *Prof Exp:* From asst prof to assoc prof civil eng, Univ Md, 65-75; PRES, JTC ENVIRON CONSULTS, INC, 75- *Concurrent Pos:* US Dept Interior grants, 66-75; dir environ health traineeships, USPHS, 68-71; environ adv, Proctor & Gamble Co, 73-74; tech reviewer & adv, Consumers' Union & Environ Defense Fund, 74-; mem comt safe drinking water, Nat Acad Sci-Nat Res Coun-Nat Acad Eng, 78-; environ consult, US Dept Labor. *Mem:* Am Soc Civil Engrs; Am Water Works Asn; Water Pollution Control Fedn. *Res:* Removal of viruses from water; adsorption of organics on activated carbon; theory of filtration; surface chemistry of activated carbon; biological processes; design of activated carbon adsorption beds; drinking water quality; toxic chemical control. *Mailing Add:* JTC Environ Consult 7979 Old Georgetown Rd Bethesda MD 20014

COOL, BINGHAM MERCUR, b Marion, Ill, Dec 21, 18; m 43; c 3. FORESTRY. *Educ:* La State Univ, BS, 40; Iowa State Univ, MS, 41; Mich State Univ, PhD(forestry), 57. *Prof Exp:* Asst, Iowa State Univ, 40-41; asst agr aide, Soil Conserv Serv, 41; asst forestry aide, Tenn Valley Authority, 42; asst county agent forestry, Ala Exten Serv, 45-47; timber mkt specialist, Miss Exten Serv, 47-48, state forest prods marketing specialist, 48-49; asst prof forestry, Ala Polytech Inst, 49-54, 56-58; asst, Mich State Univ, 54-56; assoc prof, 58-66, PROF FORESTRY, CLEMSON UNIV, 66- *Mem:* Soc Am Foresters. *Res:* Siviculture. *Mailing Add:* Dept of Forestry Clemson Univ Clemson SC 29631

COOL, RAYMOND DEAN, b Winchester, Va, Mar 14, 02. CHEMISTRY, CHEMICAL MICROSCOPY. *Educ:* Bridgewater Col, BS, 22; Univ Va, MS, 26, PhD(chem), 28. *Prof Exp:* Instr high sch, Va, 22-24; instr chem, Univ Nev, 28-29; instr, Univ Ore, 29-30; res assoc dept pharmacol, Sch Med, Univ Pa, 30-34; from instr to asst prof, Univ Akron, 34-41; asst prof, Univ Okla, 41-46; asst prof, WVa Univ, 46; prof, 46-72, EMER PROF CHEM, JAMES MADISON UNIV, 72- *Concurrent Pos:* Chemist, US Naval Ord Lab, 49-52 & 54-57. *Mem:* AAAS; Am Chem Soc; Am Microchem Soc; Sigma Xi. *Res:* Microanalytical methods for iodides and rarer elements; volumetric methods for nitrites; polymorphic transitions; distribution coefficients in gas-liquid systems; chemical microscopy; metallic complexes of diketones and picolines; analytical chemistry. *Mailing Add:* 405 E College St Bridgewater VA 22812

COOL, RODNEY LEE, b Platte, SDak, Mar 8, 20; m 49; c 4. PHYSICS. *Educ:* Univ SDak, BA, 42; Harvard Univ, MA, 47, PhD(physics), 49. *Prof Exp:* Res physicist, Brookhaven Nat Lab, 49-59, dep chmn high energy physics, 60-64, from asst dir to assoc dir, 64-70; PROF EXP HIGH ENERGY PHYSICS, ROCKEFELLER UNIV, 70- *Concurrent Pos:* Mem policy comt, Stanford Linear Acceleration Ctr, 62-67 & 76-; mem high energy panel, Assoc Univs Inc, 63-70; Walker Panel Comt on Sci & Pub Policy, Nat Acad Sci, 64; high energy physics adv panel, AEC, 67-70; chmn high energy adv comt, Brookhaven Nat Lab, 67-70; chmn physics adv comt, Nat Accelerator Lab, 67-70; mem adv panel physics, NSF, 70-73; sci assoc, European Ctr Nuclear Res, 73-; trustee, Univs Res Asn, 77-; mem rev comt, Argonne Univs Asn, 78-81; mem, High Energy Adv Comt, Brookhaven Nat Lab. *Mem:* Nat Acad Sci; fel Am Phys Soc. *Res:* Experimental high energy physics. *Mailing Add:* Rockefeller Univ New York NY 10021

COOL, TERRILL A, b Boulder, Colo, Aug 18, 36; m 59; c 3. APPLIED PHYSICS, CHEMICAL PHYSICS. *Educ:* Univ Calif, Los Angeles, BS, 61; Calif Inst Technol, MS, 62, PhD(eng), 65. *Prof Exp:* From asst prof to assoc prof thermal eng, 65-73, assoc prof appl physics, Sch Appl & Eng Physics, 73-75, PROF APPL PHYSICS, SCH APPL & ENG PHYSICS, CORNELL UNIV, 75- *Mem:* Fel Am Phys Soc. *Res:* Chemical lasers; molecular energy transfer. *Mailing Add:* Sch of Appl & Eng Physics 228 Clark Hall Cornell Univ Ithaca NY 14853

COOLBAUGH, RONALD CHARLES, b Missoula, Mont, Jan 21, 44; m 63; c 2. PLANT PHYSIOLOGY, PLANT BIOCHEMISTRY. *Educ:* Eastern Wash State Col, BA, 66; Ore State Univ, PhD(plant physiol), 70. *Prof Exp:* From asst prof to prof biol, Western Ore State Col, 70-80, dean arts & sci, 78-80; PROF & CHMN BOT, IOWA STATE UNIV, 80- *Concurrent Pos:* Res assoc, Univ Calif, Los Angeles, 75-76; grad fac, Ore State Univ, 76- *Mem:* Am Soc Plant Physiologists; Sigma Xi; Am Inst Biol Sci. *Res:* Biochemistry and physiology of plant growth substances; biosynthesis of Gibberellins. *Mailing Add:* Bot Dept Iowa State Univ Ames IA 50011

COOLER, FREDERICK WILLIAM, b Knoxville, Tenn, Dec 7, 30; m 52. FOOD TECHNOLOGY. *Educ:* Univ Tenn, BS, 52, MS, 58; Univ Md, PhD(food technol), 62. *Prof Exp:* Asst horticulturist, Univ Tenn, 56-58; asst food technol, Univ Md, 58-62; ASSOC PROF FOOD SCI & TECHNOL, VA POLYTECH INST & STATE UNIV, 62- *Mem:* Inst Food Technologists; Am Soc Hort Sci. *Res:* Rheological properties of foods; quality evaluation and control of foods; transportation, storage and quality maintenance of fruits and vegetables; food product development. *Mailing Add:* Dept of Food Sci & Technol Va Polytech Inst & State Univ Blacksburg VA 24061

COOLEY, ADRIAN B, JR, b Amelia, Tex, Sept 28, 28; m 48; c 3. PHYSICS, MATHEMATICS. *Educ:* Sam Houston State Univ, BS, 50, MA, 57; Univ Tex, Austin, PhD(sci educ), 70. *Prof Exp:* Teacher high sch, Tex, 50-56; asst prof physics, Sam Houston State Univ, 56-66; asst prof, Southwestern Univ, 66-67; teaching assoc educ, Univ Tex, Austin, 67-68; from asst prof to assoc prof, 68-72, PROF PHYSICS, SAM HOUSTON STATE UNIV, 72- *Mem:* Am Asn Physics Teachers; Nat Sci Teachers Asn. *Res:* Physical sciences. *Mailing Add:* Dept of Physics Sam Houston State Univ Huntsville TX 77340

COOLEY, ALBERT MARVIN, b Clarence, Mo, July 26, 08; m 39; c 2. CHEMICAL ENGINEERING. *Educ:* Mont State Col, BS, 30; Univ NDak, MS, 31. *Prof Exp:* Res chemist, C F Burgess Labs, Madison, 32-34; instr, 34-77, ASST PROF CHEM ENG, UNIV NDAK, 77- *Concurrent Pos:* Mem adv comt, US Bur Mines Coal Lab Western States. *Mem:* Am Chem Soc; Am Inst Mining, Metall & Petrol Engrs; Am Inst Chem Engrs; Am Soc Eng Educ; Inst Food Technol. *Res:* Lignite fuels; activated carbon; potatoes and agricultural wastes as commercial raw materials; industrial waste disposal. *Mailing Add:* 1106 University Ave Grand Forks ND 58201

COOLEY, DENTON ARTHUR, b Houston, Tex, Aug 22, 20; m 49; c 5. SURGERY. *Educ:* Univ Tex, BA, 41; Johns Hopkins Univ, MD, 44. *Prof Exp:* Resident surg, Johns Hopkins Hosp, 44-50; sr surg registr, Brompton Hosp Chest Dis, London, 50-51; from assoc prof to prof surg, Baylor Col Med, 51-69; SURGEON-IN-CHIEF, TEX HEART INST, 69-; PROF CLIN SURG, UNIV TEX MED SCH, HOUSTON, 75- *Concurrent Pos:* Consult surg serv, Tex Children's & St Lukes Episcopal Hosps, Houston, 63- *Mem:* AMA; Am Asn Thoracic Surg; Soc Vascular Surg; Am Col Surg; Soc Clin Surg. *Res:* Cardio-vascular surgery and diseases of the chest. *Mailing Add:* Tex Heart Inst 6621 Fannin St Houston TX 77025

COOLEY, DUANE STUART, b Batavia, NY, May 9, 23; m 49; c 2. METEOROLOGY. *Educ:* Mass Inst Technol, BS, 48, MS, 49, PhD(meteorol), 59. *Prof Exp:* Instr meteorol, Weather Sch, Chanute AFB, Dept Air Force, 49-51, meteorologist, Air Force Cambridge Res Ctr, 51-57, supvry atmospheric physicist, 57-60, supvry physicist, Electronic Systs Div, 496L Syst Proj Off, Air Force Syst Command, 60-61; sr res scientist, Travelers Res Ctr, Inc, 61-69; actg exec scientist, US Comt Global Atmospheric Res Prog, Nat Acad Sci, 69-70; CHIEF TECH PROCEDURES BR, NAT WEATHER SERV, NAT OCEANIC & ATMOSPHERIC ADMIN, 70- *Mem:* Fel Am Meteorol Soc; Am Geophys Union. *Res:* General atmospheric circulation; statistical and dynamical weather forecasting; atmospheric radiation; analysis and interpretation of meteorological satellite data. *Mailing Add:* 4503 Libbey Dr Fairfax VA 22032

COOLEY, IRWIN D, b Savannah, Ga, May 6, 22; m; c 1. MECHANICS, APPLIED MATHEMATICS. *Educ:* Duke Univ, BSCE, 51; Univ Fla, MSE, 58; Univ Tex, PhD(mech eng), 66. *Prof Exp:* Struct designer, Savannah Mach & Foundry Co, Ga, 51; asst engr, County of Ga Rwy, 51-52; asst to res engr, Robert Gair Co, Inc, 52-54; camera engr, RCA Serv Co, Patrick AFB, Fla, 54-56; instr eng mech, Univ Fla, 56-60 & 62; asst prof mech eng, Auburn Univ, 62-64 & 65, assoc prof, 66-68; prof math, Armstrong State Col, 68-69; ASSOC PROF MECH ENG, AUBURN UNIV, 69- *Res:* Elasticity; elastic stability; plate and shell theory; rigid body dynamics and vibrations. *Mailing Add:* Dept of Mech Eng Auburn Univ Auburn AL 36830

COOLEY, JAMES HOLLIS, b New York, NY, March 25, 30; m 55; c 2. ORGANIC CHEMISTRY. *Educ:* Middlebury Col, AB, 52, MS, 54; Univ Minn, PhD(org chem), 58. *Prof Exp:* Asst, Univ Minn, 54-57; from asst prof to assoc prof, 57-68, PROF CHEM, UNIV IDAHO, 68- *Concurrent Pos:* Res assoc, Columbia Univ, 63-66. *Mem:* Am Chem Soc. *Res:* Chemistry of the hydroxylamine compounds. *Mailing Add:* Dept of Chem Univ of Idaho Moscow ID 83843

COOLEY, JAMES WILLIAM, b New York, NY, Sept 18, 26; m 57; c 3. APPLIED MATHEMATICS. *Educ:* Manhattan Col, BA, 49; Columbia Univ, MA, 51, PhD(math), 61. *Prof Exp:* Programmer, Inst Advan Study, Princeton, 53-56; res asst math, Courant Inst, NY Univ, 56-62; RES STAFF MATH, IBM WATSON RES CTR, 62- *Concurrent Pos:* Prof comput sci, Royal Inst Technol, Sweden, 73-74. *Mem:* Fel Inst Elec & Electronics Engrs;

Sigma Xi. *Res:* Numerical methods; solution of partial and ordinary differential equations; digital signal processing; discrete Fourier methods; mathematical modeling of nerve membranes. *Mailing Add:* IBM Watson Res Ctr Box 218 Yorktown Heights NY 10598

COOLEY, NELSON REEDE, b Mobile, Ala, Nov 30, 20; m 51; c 2. PROTOZOOLOGY. *Educ:* Spring Hill Col, BS, 42; Univ Ala, MS, 47; Univ Ill, PhD(zool), 54. *Prof Exp:* From asst to instr biol, Univ Ala, 46-48; instr anat, Druid City Hosp, Ala, 47; asst zool, Univ Ill, 48-53; instr zool & physiol, Okla Agr & Mech Col, 53-54, asst prof zool, 54-56; fishery res biologist, US Fish & Wildlife Serv, 56-70; res biologist, Gulf Breeze Lab, 70-74, microbiologist, 74-76, RES MICROBIOLOGIST, US ENVIRON PROTECTION AGENCY, 76-, QUAL ASSURANCE OFFICER, 80- *Honors & Awards:* Bronze Medal, US Environ Protection Agency, 75 & 81. *Mem:* Soc Protozoologists. *Res:* Physiology of ciliate protozoa; blood protozoa of bats; biological control of oyster predators; estuarine faunal biology; pesticides vs ciliate protozoan population growth; pesticide bioaccumulation by ciliates. *Mailing Add:* US Environ Protection Agency Environ Res Lab Sabine Island Gulf Breeze FL 32561

COOLEY, RICHARD LEWIS, b Akron, Colo, Jan 11, 40; m 60; c 1 HYDROGEOLOGY, GEOMORPHOLOGY. HYDROLOGY, GEOMORPHOLOGY. *Educ:* Ariz State Univ, BS, 62; Pa State Univ, PhD(geol), 68. *Prof Exp:* Hydrologist, Hydrol Eng Ctr, US Corps Engrs, 68-70; res assoc, 70-72, assoc prof, Ctr Water Resources Res, 72-77, ADJ ASSOC PROF GEOL & GEOG, DESERT RES INST, UNIV NEV SYST, RENO, 77- *Concurrent Pos:* Inst Res Land & Water Resources scholar appointee, Pa State Univ, 68. *Mem:* Soc Econ Paleontologists & Mineralogists; Geol Soc Am; Am Geophys Union; AAAS. *Res:* Physics of water movement through porous media and its application in inferring the influence of geological conditions on ground water movement and recharge; analysis of ground water flow systems. *Mailing Add:* Ctr for Water Resources Res Desert Res Inst Univ of Nev Reno NV 89507

COOLEY, ROBERT LEE, b Birmingham, Ala, Feb 20, 27; m 52; c 4. MATHEMATICS. *Educ:* Univ Ala, BS, 48; Univ Va, LLB, 51; Purdue Univ, MS, 57, PhD(math), 64. *Prof Exp:* From asst to assoc prof math, 67-80, PROF MATH, WABASH COL, 80- *Concurrent Pos:* Lilley endowment fel, Cambridge, Eng. *Mem:* Am Bar Asn; Math Asn Am; Nat Coun Teachers Math. *Res:* Topological algebra. *Mailing Add:* Dept Math Wabash Col Crawfordsville IN 47933

COOLEY, ROBERT NELSON, b Woodlawn, Va, Mar 12, 11; m 48; c 3. RADIOLOGY. *Educ:* Univ Va, MD, 34. *Prof Exp:* From asst prof to assoc prof radiol, Med Sch, Johns Hopkins Univ, 48-53; PROF RADIOL & CHMN DEPT, UNIV TEX MED BR GALVESTON, 53- *Concurrent Pos:* Pres & trustee, Am Bd Radiol. *Honors & Awards:* Gold Medal, Am Col Radiol, 79. *Mem:* Am Col Radiol; Radiol Soc NAm; Am Roentgen Ray Soc; AMA; Asn Univ Radiol. *Res:* Radiological investigations in congenital and acquired heart disease. *Mailing Add:* Dept of Radiol Univ of Tex Med Br Galveston TX 77550

COOLEY, STONE DEAVOURS, b Laurel, Miss, Jan 13, 22; m 48; c 3. PHYSICAL CHEMISTRY. *Educ:* Univ Tex, BSChE, 49, PhD(chem), 53. *Prof Exp:* Res chemist, Celanese Corp Am, 53-55, group leader, 55-59, sect head, 59-62, asst to tech dir, Celanese Chem Co, 62-63, facil mgr Summit Res Lab, 64-68; asst dir res, Petro-Tex Chem Corp, 68-74, mgr tech serv, 74-77; MGR TECHNOL, DENKA CHEM CORP, 77- *Mem:* Am Chem Soc. *Res:* Hydrocarbon oxidation; synthetic rubber. *Mailing Add:* Denka Chem Corp 8701 Park Place Blvd Houston TX 77017

COOLEY, WILLIAM C, b Lakeland, Fla, Dec 19, 24; m 49; c 4. AEROSPACE TECHNOLOGY, MECHANICAL ENGINEERING. *Educ:* Mass Inst Technol, SB, 44, ScD(mech eng), 51; Calif Inst Technol, MS, 47. *Prof Exp:* Instr mech eng, Mass Inst Technol, 49-50; res engr, Atomic Energy Res Dept, NAm Aviation, Inc, 51-53; prin engr, Gen Elec Co, 53-55, supvr mech eng, 55-56, mgr systs anal, 56-58; asst prog engr, Rocketdyne Div, NAm Aviation, Inc, 58-59; chief adv tech, NASA Hq, 59-61; from vpres to pres, Exotech, Inc, 61-69; PRES, TERRASPACE INC, 69- *Concurrent Pos:* Consult, Oak Ridge Nat Lab, 50 & Gen Elec Co, 61-62. *Mem:* Am Inst Aeronaut & Astronaut; Am Soc Mech Engrs. *Res:* Radiation effects; advanced energy conversion; shock hydrodynamics; spacecraft sterilization; planetary quarantine; high pressure liquid jet technology. *Mailing Add:* 304 N Stonestreet Ave Rockville MD 20850

COOLEY, WILLIAM EDWARD, b St Louis, Mo, March 7, 30; m 52; c 4. DENTAL RESEARCH. *Educ:* Cent Col, Mo, AB, 51; Univ Ill, PhD(chem), 54. *Prof Exp:* Res chemist, 54-71, sect head, Prod Develop, 71-75, mgr, Regulatory Serv Toilet Goods Div, 75-81, MGR, SAFETY & REGULATORY SERV, HEALTH & PERSONAL CARE DIV, PROCTER & GAMBLE CO, 81- *Mem:* Am Chem Soc; Int Asn Dent Res; Am Asn Dent Res. *Res:* Chemistry of dental systems; fluorides; dentifrice abrasives; professional and regulatory affairs in oral health. *Mailing Add:* 531 Chisholm Trail Wyoming OH 45215

COOLEY, WILS LAHUGH, b Pittsburgh, Pa, Aug 23, 42; m 66; c 2. ELECTRICAL ENGINEERING. *Educ:* Carnegie-Mellon Univ, BS, 64, MS, 65, PhD(elec eng), 68. *Prof Exp:* Asst prof elec eng & biotech, Carnegie-Mellon Univ, 68-72; from asst prof to assoc prof, 72-80, PROF & ASST DEPT CHMN, WVA UNIV, 81- *Concurrent Pos:* Consult, Siltronics, Inc, 68-70; NIH grant thoracic imped- ance measurements, 69-70; Pa Sci & Eng Fund grant seeding med instrumentation indust in Western Pa, 69-71; res assoc, Univ Calif, 71; US Dept Interior-Bur Mines res grants, 74, 78, 79, 80 & 81; eng consult, Pa State Univ, 75-76, Bendix Corp, 76-77, several law firms & mining co, 79, 80 & 81. *Mem:* Inst Elec & Electronics Engrs; Am Soc Eng Educ; Sigma Xi; Nat Soc Prof Engrs. *Res:* Engineering education in problem solving; electrical safety in power systems; transient protection of grounded equipment; mine power systems. *Mailing Add:* Rte 3 Box 506 Morgantown WV 26505

COOLIDGE, ARDATH ANDERS, b Chicago, Ill, July 22, 19; m 49; c 5. NUTRITION. *Educ:* Earlham Col, AB, 41; Iowa State Col, PhD(nutrit), 46. *Prof Exp:* Teacher pub sch, Ill, 41-42; asst prof foods & nutrit, Western Reserve Univ, 46-47; asst prof, Berea Col, 47-49; home economist, Sensory Testing Food Res, Armour & Co, 58-62; lit scientist, Nutrit Res Div, Nat Dairy Coun, 62-66; from asst prof to assoc prof home econ, 66-80, PROF FOODS & NUTRIT, PURDUE UNIV, CALUMET CAMPUS, 80- *Mem:* Am Dietetic Asn; Am Home Econ Asn; Soc Nutrit Educ. *Res:* Biological utilization of ascorbic acid in apples. *Mailing Add:* Dept of Behav Sci Purdue Univ Calumet Campus Hammond IN 46323

COOLIDGE, EDWIN CHANNING, b Gambier, Ohio, Jan 30, 25; m 53; c 1. ANALYTICAL CHEMISTRY, ORGANIC CHEMISTRY. *Educ:* Kenyon Col, AB, 44; Johns Hopkins Univ, PhD(chem), 49. *Prof Exp:* Res org chemist, Procter & Gamble Co, 49-50 & 53-54; asst prof, Univ Utah, 51-52; res org chemist, Dugway Proving Ground, 52-53; asst prof chem, Hamilton Col, 54-58; asst prof, NMex Inst Mining & Technol, 58-61; assoc prof, 61-64, PROF CHEM, STETSON UNIV, 64- *Concurrent Pos:* Dir, Assoc Mid-Fla Cols Year Abroad Prog, 68, Freiburg, WGer, 69-70; consult, Tech Adv Serv for Attorneys, 75. *Mem:* Am Chem Soc; Royal Soc Chem; AAAS. *Res:* Organometallic chemistry; pyrrole and porphyrin synthesis; organophosphorus compounds; metal chelate stability and structure; ecological analysis. *Mailing Add:* Dept of Chem Stetson Univ De Land FL 32720

COOMBES, CHARLES ALLAN, b Nevada City, Calif, Feb 25, 34; m 56; c 3. PHYSICS. *Educ:* Univ Calif, AB, 55, PhD(physics), 60. *Prof Exp:* Asst prof physics, Idaho State Univ, 59-62 & San Jose State Col, 62-63; asst prof, 63-66, actg vdean fac arts & sci, 70-72, ASSOC PROF PHYSICS, UNIV CALGARY, 66-, ASST TO HEAD DEPT, 75- *Mem:* AAAS; Am Asn Physics Teachers; Am Physics Soc. *Res:* Dynamics of the lower atmosphere; foundations of quantum mechanics. *Mailing Add:* Dept of Physics Univ of Calgary Calgary AB T2N 1N4 Can

COOMBS, MARGERY CHALIFOUX, b Nashua, NH, Aug 12, 45; m 69; c 2. VERTEBRATE PALEONTOLOGY. *Educ:* Oberlin Col, BA, 67; Columbia Univ, MA, 68, PhD(biol sci), 73. *Prof Exp:* Asst prof, 73-80, ASSOC PROF ZOOL, UNIV MASS, AMHERST, 80- *Mem:* Soc Vert Paleont; Paleont Soc. *Res:* Chalicothere systematics and function; early Miocene biostratigraphy; clawed herbivores. *Mailing Add:* Dept of Zool Univ of Mass Amherst MA 01003

COOMBS, RENATE BANGERT, organic chemistry, see previous edition

COOMBS, ROBERT VICTOR, b Brighton, Eng, June 24, 37; m 63. ORGANIC CHEMISTRY. *Educ:* Univ London, BSc, 58, PhD(org chem), 61. *Prof Exp:* Fel, Univ Wis, 61-62 & 63-64; fel, Columbia Univ, 62-63; res chemist, Brit Drug Houses, Ltd, Eng, 64-66; fel, Synvar Res Inst, Calif, 66-67; sr scientist, Chem Dept, Sandoz-Warner, Inc, 67-71; group leader, 71-77, mem sr sci staff, 77-80, ASSOC SR SCI STAFF, SANDOZ, INC, 80- *Mem:* Am Chem Soc; Royal Soc Chem. *Res:* Synthetic organic and medicinal chemistry. *Mailing Add:* Chem Dept Sandoz Inc Rt 10 East Hanover NJ 07936

COOMBS, WILLIAM, JR, b Brooklyn, NY, Apr 30, 24; m 45; c 2. BIOMEDICAL ENGINEERING. *Educ:* Mass Inst Technol, BS, 47, MS, 48; Univ Rochester, MS, 56. *Prof Exp:* Res assoc biol, Mass Inst Technol, 47-48; develop engr, Eastman Kodak Co, 48-51; chief elec engr, Dept Physics, Univ Rochester, 51-59, head dept electronics res & develop, 59-63, dir electronics & biophys res & develop, 63-67, dir cent res labs, 67-68, gen mgr soflens contact lens, 68-71, VPRES SOFLENS CONTACT LENS DIV, BAUSCH & LOMB, INC, 71- *Concurrent Pos:* Consult, Xerox Corp & Taylor Instrument Co, 54-59; lectr univ sch, Univ Rochester, 55-60; indust rep, Ophthalmic Prosthetic Devices Subcomt, Food & Drug Admin, 76. *Mem:* Inst Elec & Electronics Eng. *Res:* Biomedical instruments and ophthalmic prosthetics. *Mailing Add:* Bausch & Lomb Inc 1400 N Goodman St Rochester NY 14602

COOMES, EDWARD ARTHUR, b Louisville, Ky, June 27, 09; m 40; c 5. PHYSICS. *Educ:* Univ Notre Dame, BS, 31, MS, 33; Mass Inst Technol, ScD(physics), 38. *Prof Exp:* From instr to assoc prof math & physics, 33-42, prof physics, 45-74, EMER PROF PHYSICS, UNIV NOTRE DAME, 74-; ADJ PROF PHYSICS, ST MARY'S COL, 76- *Concurrent Pos:* Mem staff radiation lab, Mass Inst Technol, 42-45; consult various industs & labs, 52-; lectr, Forever Learning Inst, 80- *Honors & Awards:* US Army-Navy Res Citation, 47. *Mem:* Fel Am Phys Soc; sr mem Inst Elec & Electronics Engrs. *Res:* Solid state electronics; oxide cathodes; surface physics and chemistry; thermionics; energy conversion. *Mailing Add:* 1546 Marigold Way South Bend IN 46617

COOMES, RICHARD MERRIL, b Provo, Utah, Oct 5, 39; m 63; c 2. ORGANIC CHEMISTRY, TOXICOLOGY. *Educ:* Utah State Univ, BS, 66, MS, 67; Colo State Univ, PhD(org chem), 69. *Prof Exp:* Fel chem, Ariz State Univ, 69-71; instr, Univ Va, 71-72; natural prod chemist, Gates Rubber Co, 72-73; group leader org res, 73-77, environ health coordr, 77-79, MGR ENVIRON HEALTH, TOSCO CORP, 79- *Mem:* Am Chem Soc; AAAS; Sigma Xi; Southwestern Asn Toxicologists; Am Col Toxicol. *Res:* Investigation of potential health effects of synthetic fuel processing, emphasizing toxicity, carcinogenicity, and chemistry of oil shale products and by-products; chemistry centers on polycyclic aromatic hydrocarbon analyses. *Mailing Add:* Tosco Corp 10100 Santa Monica Blvd Los Angeles CA 90067

COON, CARLOS WELDON, JR, b San Antonio, Tex, Dec 29, 38; m 60; c 2. MECHANICAL ENGINEERING. *Educ:* Tex Tech Univ, BS, 61, MS, 62; Univ Ariz, PhD(mech eng), 68. *Prof Exp:* Instr mech eng, Tex Tech Univ, 62-64; asst, Univ Ariz, 64- 68; from asst to assoc prof, Southern Methodist Univ, 68-73; sr res engr, Southwest Res Inst, 73-80; CONSULT ENGR, 81- *Mem:* Am Soc Mech Engrs. *Res:* High Temperature heat transfer; engine research; design of environmental control systems. *Mailing Add:* PO Box 327 Fredericksburg TX 78624

COON, CRAIG NELSON, b Big Springs, Tex, May 17, 44; m 62; c 1. NUTRITION, METABOLISM. *Educ:* Tex A&M Univ, BS, 66, MS, 70, PhD(biochem & nutrit), 73. *Prof Exp:* Asst prof nutrit & poultry sci, Univ Md, College Park, 73-75; from asst prof to assoc prof, 75-80, PROF ANIMAL SCI & NUTRIT, WASH STATE UNIV, 80- *Mem:* AAAS; Poultry Sci Asn. *Res:* Regulation of nitrogen metabolism; hormone-enzyme relationships as influenced by nutrition; amino acid availability and carbohydrate availability in feedstuffs. *Mailing Add:* Dept of Animal Sci Wash State Univ Pullman WA 99163

COON, DARRYL DOUGLAS, b Ticonderoga, NY, Apr 2, 41; m 67; c 1. SEMICONDUCTORS. *Educ:* Union Col, BS, 62; Princen Univ, MS, 65, PhD(physics), 67. *Prof Exp:* Res staff mem, Gen Elec Res & Develop Ctr, 60-64; res assoc, Univ Wash, 67-69, Univ Minn, 69-71; asst prof, 71-74, ASSOC PROF PHYSICS, UNIV PITTSBURGH, 74- *Mem:* Am Phys Soc; Inst Elec & Electronics Engrs. *Res:* Theoretical elementary particle physics; theoretical and experimental solid state physics; impurities in semiconductors; field ionization; low temperature physics; s-matrix theory and dual models. *Mailing Add:* Dept Physics & Astron Univ Pittsburgh Pittsburgh PA 15260

COON, JAMES HUNTINGTON, b Liberty, Mo, Nov 9, 14; m 55; c 3. SPACE PHYSICS. *Educ:* Ind Univ, AB, 37; Univ Chicago, PhD(physics), 42. *Prof Exp:* Res staff, Metall Lab, Univ Chicago, 42-43 & Los Alamos Sci Labs, 43-46; res assoc, Univ Wis, 47; res staff, 48-50, group leader, 50-77, CONSULT, LOS ALAMOS NAT LABS, 77- *Mem:* Fel AAAS; fel Am Phys Soc; Am Astron Soc. *Res:* Thermal neutron diffusion and capture; nuclear interactions between light particles; scattering of fast neutrons; space physics. *Mailing Add:* Los Alamos Nat Labs MS 436 Los Alamos NM 87545

COON, JULIUS MOSHER, b Liberty, Mo, Oct 29, 10; m 47; c 2. PHARMACOLOGY. *Educ:* Ind Univ, AB, 32; Univ Chicago, PhD(pharmacol), 38; Univ Ill, MD, 45. *Prof Exp:* Asst pharmacol, Univ Chicago, 35-39, instr, 39-45, pharmacologist, Toxicity Lab, 41-45; pharmacologist, US Food & Drug Admin, Washington, DC, 46; from asst prof to assoc prof pharmacol, Univ Chicago, 46-53, dir, Toxicity Lab, 48-51, dir, US Air Force Radiation Lab, 51-53; prof pharmacol & chmn dept, 53-76, EMER PROF PHARMACOL, THOMAS JEFFERSON UNIV, 76- *Concurrent Pos:* Mem pharmacol test comt, Nat Bd Med Exam, 54-57; mem food protection comt, Nat Acad Sci-Nat Res Coun, 54-72, mem comt radiation preservation of food, 69-74, chmn, 76-79; mem toxicol study sect, NIH, 58-62, chmn sect, 62-64; mem pharmacol adv comt, Walter Reed Army Inst Res, 66-70; mem adv comt protocols for safety eval, Food & Drug Admin, 66-70, mem panel rev of internal analgesic agents, 72-77; mem expert adv panel food additives, WHO, 66-76; chmn panel food safety, White House Conf Food, Nutrit & Health, 69; mem nominating comt gen comt revision, US Pharmacopoeia, 70; mem comt admissions, Nat Formulary, 70-75; mem subcomt interpretation of relevant human experience versus newly acquired exp data, Citizens' Comn Sci, Law & Food Supply, 73-75; mem expert panel on food safety & nutrit, Inst Food Technol, 74-; mem select comt on flavor evaluation criteria, Life Sci Res Off, Fedn Am Socs for Exp Biol, 75-76; mem, Expert Panel on Cosmetic Ingredient Rev, Cosmetic, Toiletry & Fragrance Asn, Inc, 77-; consult, Franklin Inst, Philadelphia, 78-; mem bd sci adv, Am Coun on Sci & Health, 80- *Mem:* Am Soc Pharmacol & Exp Therapeut (treas, 64-66); Soc Toxicol; Inst Food Technol; Soc Exp Biol & Med; fel NY Acad Sci. *Res:* Toxicology of insecticides; food toxicology; autonomic pharmacology. *Mailing Add:* Dept Pharmacol Thomas Jefferson Univ Philadelphia PA 19107

COON, LEWIS HULBERT, b Oklahoma City, Okla, Feb 26, 25; m 48; c 3. MATHEMATICS. *Educ:* Okla Agr & Mech Col, BS, 50; Ind Univ, MS, 51; Okla State Univ, MS, 58, EdD(math), 63. *Prof Exp:* Teacher Okla City Pub Schs, 50-57; asst prof math, Southwestern State Col, Okla, 58-61; staff asst, Okla State Univ, 62; asst prof educ res, Ohio State Univ, 63-65; PROF MATH, EASTERN ILL UNIV, 65- *Concurrent Pos:* Mem, NSF Col Conf, Carleton Col, 63. *Mem:* Math Asn Am; Am Math Asn; Nat Coun Teachers Math; Am Nat Metric Coun. *Res:* Hawthorne effect in mathematics education. *Mailing Add:* Dept of Math Eastern Ill Univ Charleston IL 61920

COON, MINOR J, b Englewood, Colo, July 29, 21; m 48; c 2. BIOCHEMISTRY, PHARMACOLOGY. *Educ:* Univ Colo, BA, 43; Univ Ill, PhD(biochem), 46. *Prof Exp:* Res asst, Univ Ill, Urbana, 46-47; from instr to assoc prof physiol chem, Univ Pa, 47-55; PROF BIOL CHEM, UNIV MICH, ANN ARBOR, 55-, CHMN DEPT, 70- *Concurrent Pos:* USPHS spec fel, NY Univ, 52-53; res fel, Swiss Fed Polytech Inst, Zurich, Switz, 61-62; NSF travel award, 69; mem biochem study sect, NIH, 63-66; mem res career award comt, Nat Inst Gen Med Sci, 66-70. *Honors & Awards:* Paul Lewis Award, Am Chem Soc, 59; William C Rose Award, Biochem Nutrit, 78; Bernard B Brodie Award, Drug Metab, 80. *Mem:* Am Chem Soc; Am Soc Biol Chem (secy, 81-83); Am Soc Pharmacol & Exp Therapeut; Am Soc Microbiol; Biophys Soc. *Res:* Enzyme reaction mechanisms; amino acid and lipid metabolism; cytochrome P-450; drug metabolism; detoxication. *Mailing Add:* Dept of Biol Chem Med Sch Univ of Mich Ann Arbor MI 48104

COON, ROBERT WILLIAM, b Billings, Mont, July 13, 20; m 47; c 3. PATHOLOGY. *Educ:* NDak Agr Col, BS, 42; Univ Rochester, MD, 44; Am Bd Path, dipl, 51. *Prof Exp:* Intern path, Stong Mem Hosp, 44-45; asst, Sch Med, Emory Univ, 45-46; lab officer, US Naval Hosp, RI, 46-47; fel path, Univ Rochester, 48-49; from assoc to assoc prof, Col Physicians & Surgeons, Columbia Univ, 49-55; prof path & chmn dept, Col Med, Univ Vt, 55-73, assoc dean div health sci, 68-73; asst chancellor, Univ Maine Bd of Trustees, 74-76; vchancellor health sci, WVa Bd Regents, Charlestown, WVa, 76; V PRES & DEAN, SCH MED, MARSHALL UNIV, 76- *Concurrent Pos:* Trustee, Am Bd Path, 60-72. *Mem:* Am Soc Clin Path (pres, 63-64); Am Soc Exp Path; Am Asn Pathologists & Bacteriologists; Col Am Pathologists; Int Acad Path. *Res:* Coagulation of blood. *Mailing Add:* Sch Med Marshall Univ Huntington WV 25701

COON, WILLIAM WARNER, b Saginaw, Mich, Aug 10, 25; m 49; c 3. SURGERY. *Educ:* Johns Hopkins Univ, MD, 49; Am Bd Surg, dipl, 57. *Prof Exp:* Dir blood bank, Univ Hosp, 56-64, from instr to assoc prof, 56-67, PROF SURG, UNIV MICH, ANN ARBOR, 67- *Concurrent Pos:* Attend surgeon, Ann Arbor Vet admin Hosp, 56-62, consult surgeon, 62- *Mem:* AAAS; Soc Univ Surg; Soc Exp Biol & Med. *Res:* Blood coagulation; thromboembolism; metabolism. *Mailing Add:* 1405 E Ann St Ann Arbor MI 48104

COONCE, HARRY B, b Independence, Mo, Mar 19, 38; m 65; c 2. MATHEMATICS. *Educ:* Iowa State Univ, BS, 59. Univ Del, PhD(math), 69. *Prof Exp:* Asst prof math, Wichita State Univ, 64-66, Del State Col, 66-67 & US Naval Acad, 67-69; from asst prof to assoc prof, 69-77, PROF MATH, MANKATO STATE COL, 77- *Concurrent Pos:* Consult, Boeing Co, Kans, 65-67. *Mem:* Am Math Soc; Math Asn Am. *Res:* Geometric function theory; univalent functions; functions with bounded boundary rotation; variational methods. *Mailing Add:* Dept of Math Mankato State Col Mankato MN 56001

COONEY, CHARLES LELAND, b Philadelphia, Pa, Nov 9, 44; m 78; c 2. BIOCHEMICAL ENGINEERING. *Educ:* Univ Pa, BS, 66; Mass Inst Technol, MS, 67, PhD(biochem eng), 70. *Prof Exp:* From instr to asst prof, 70-75, assoc prof, 75-81, PROF BIOCHEM ENG, MASS INST TECHNOL, 81- *Mem:* AAAS; Am Chem Soc; Am Inst Chem Engrs; Am Soc Microbiol; Inst Food Technol. *Res:* Fermentation technology; continuous microbial culture, production, isolation and application of enzymes; microbial protein production; engineering of microbial processes; biological processes for fuels and chemicals; microbiology of dental caries. *Mailing Add:* Dept of Nutrition & Food Sci Mass Inst of Technol Cambridge MA 02139

COONEY, DAVID OGDEN, b Boston, Mass, Dec 19, 39; m 66; c 2. CHEMICAL ENGINEERING. *Educ:* Yale Univ, BE, 61; Univ Wis, Madison, MS, 63, PhD(chem eng), 66. *Prof Exp:* Fel chem eng, Univ Wis, Madison, 66; res engr, Chevron Res Co, Calif, 66-69; from asst prof to prof chem eng, Clarkson Col Technol, 69-80; prog dir, NSF, 80-81; PROF CHEM ENG, UNIV WYO, 81- *Mem:* Am Inst Chem Engrs; Am Soc Eng Educ. *Res:* Mass transfer processes in general; biomedical applications of chemical engineering; fixed bed sorption theory. *Mailing Add:* Dept Chem Eng Univ Wyo Box 3295 Univ Sta Laramie WY 82071

COONEY, JOHN ANTHONY, b Jersey City, NJ, Oct 31, 22; m 50; c 3. ATMOSPHERIC PHYSICS. *Educ:* Fordham Univ, BS, 49, MS, 50; NY Univ, PhD(physics), 67. *Prof Exp:* Res engr syst eng, Vitro Labs, Pullman Corp, 50-54; res engr microwave eng, Sperry Corp, 55-60; res scientist plasma & atmospherics, RCA Labs, 60-70; assoc prof physics, 70-80, PROF PHYSICS & ATMOSPHERIC SCI, DREXEL UNIV, 80- *Res:* Laser radar probing of the atmosphere. *Mailing Add:* Dept Physics & Atmospheric Sci Drexel Univ Philadelphia PA 19104

COONEY, JOHN LEO, b Washington, DC, June 26, 28; m 56; c 1. PHYSICAL CHEMISTRY. *Educ:* Loyola Col, Md, BS, 52; Fordham Univ, MS, 54, PhD(phys chem), 57. *Prof Exp:* Lectr phys chem, Notre Dame Col, Staten Island, 54-55; SR PHYS CHEMIST, E I DU PONT DE NEMOURS & CO, INC, 57- *Mem:* Am Phys Soc; Am Chem Soc. *Res:* Physical properties of polymers; thermodynamics of irreversible processes; polymer morphology; vapor phase reactions. *Mailing Add:* Eng Dept E I du Pont de Nemours & Co Wilmington DE 19898

COONEY, JOSEPH JUDE, b Syracuse, NY, Jan 16, 34; m 57; c 4. MICROBIOLOGY. *Educ:* Le Moyne Col, NY, BS, 56; Syracuse Univ, MS, 58, PhD(microbiol), 61. *Prof Exp:* From asst prof to assoc prof bact, Loyola Univ, 61-65; from assoc prof to prof biol, Univ Dayton, 65-77; MEM STAFF CHESAPEAKE BIOL LABS, 77- *Concurrent Pos:* Res grants, NIH, 63-64 & La Div, Am Cancer Asn, 64-; sabbatical leave, dept biochem, Med Sch, Tufts Univ, 71; grants, Firestone Coated Fabrics Div, Monsanto Corp, US Dept Interior, Md Dept Natural Resources & Md sea grant. *Mem:* AAAS; Am Soc Microbiol; Soc Gen Microbiol; Soc Indust Microbiol; fel Am Acad Microbiol. *Res:* Microbial carotenoid pigments; metabolism of hydrocarbons; ecology and physiology of hydrocarbon-using organisms; oil pollution; microbiol interactions with heavy metals. *Mailing Add:* Chesapeake Biol Labs Univ Md Solomons MD 20688

COONEY, MARION KATHLEEN, b Mercedes, Tex, Feb 2, 20. MICROBIOLOGY. *Educ:* Col St Benedict, BS, 39; Univ Minn, Minneapolis, MS, 53, PhD(microbiol), 62; Am Bd Microbiol, dipl. *Prof Exp:* Med technologist, Fairview Hosp, Minn, 40-43; bacteriologist, Minn Dept Health, 43-46, bacteriologist & supvr sect virus & rickettsia, 46-53, bacteriologist, virologist & chief sect, 53-66; asst prof, 66-72, assoc prof, 72-78, PROF PATH, SCH PUB HEALTH & COMMUNITY MED, UNIV WASH, 78- *Mem:* AAAS; Am Soc Microbiol; Am Pub Health Asn; Am Asn Immunol; fel Am Acad Microbiol. *Res:* Cell culture, virology and immunology as related to the epidemiology of infectious disease; human rhinoviruses; rhinovirus infections; adeno-associated viruses; family studies of influenza. *Mailing Add:* Dept Pathobiol F262 Health Sci Univ Wash Sch Pub Hlth & Com Med Seattle WA 98195

COONEY, MIRIAM PATRICK, b South Bend, Ind, May 6, 25. MATHEMATICS. *Educ:* St Mary's Col, Ind, BS, 51; Univ Notre Dame, MS, 53; Univ Chicago, SM, 63, PhD(math), 69. *Prof Exp:* Assoc prof, 63-72, PROF MATH, ST MARY'S COL, IND, 72- *Concurrent Pos:* Vis lectr, St Patrick's Col, Marynooth, Ireland, 80. *Mem:* Am Math Soc; Math Asn Am; Nat Coun Teachers Math; Asn Women Math. *Res:* Algebra, especially finite groups; mathematical education on all levels. *Mailing Add:* Dept Math St Mary's Col Notre Dame IN 46556

COONS, FRED F(LEMING), b Woodland, Calif, Oct 14, 23; m 49; c 3. CHEMICAL ENGINEERING. *Educ:* Univ Calif, BSc, 44. *Prof Exp:* Asst chem, Univ Calif, 43-44; chem engr, Spreckels Sugar Co, 44-53, chief engr, 53-58; chief proj engr, Am Sugar Refining Co, NY, 58-60; chief engr, 60-76, vpres, 76-81, EXEC VPRES, SPRECKLES SUGAR DIV, AMSTAR CORP, 81- Mem: Am Chem Soc; Am Inst Chem Engrs. Res: Heat and heat transfer as connected with the sugar industry; filtration; settling; evaporation; diffusion; absorption; crystallization. Mailing Add: Spreckels Sugar Div 50 California St San Francisco CA 94111

COONS, LEWIS BENNION, b Salt Lake City, Utah, July 28, 38; m 60; c 4. ELECTRON MICROSCOPY, HISTOLOGY. Educ: Utah State Univ, BS, 64, MS, 66; NC State Univ, PhD, 70. Prof Exp: Fel electron micros, Molecular Toxicol Prog, NC State Univ, 70-73; head, Electron Micros Ctr, Miss State Univ, 73-76; head ctr, 76-80, DIR ELECTRON MICROS, MEMPHIS STATE UNIV, 80- Mem: AAAS; Electron Micros Soc Am. Res: Scanning and transmission electron microscopy of animal cell and organ systems. Mailing Add: Dept of Biol Electron Micros Ctr Memphis State Univ Memphis TN 38152

COOPE, JOHN ARTHUR ROBERT, b Liverpool, Eng, June 9, 31; Can citizen; m 54. MOLECULAR PHYSICS. Educ: Univ BC, BA, 50, MSc, 52; Univ Oxford, DPhil(theoret chem), 56. Prof Exp: Fel molecular physics, 56-57, lectr, 57-59, from instr to assoc prof, 59-73, PROF CHEM, UNIV BC, 73- Mem: Am Phys Soc. Res: Quantum theory; physics of atoms and small molecules; theoretical chemistry; solid state physics. Mailing Add: Dept of Chem Univ of BC Vancouver BC V6T 1W5 Can

COOPER, AARON DAVID, b Phildelphia, Pa, Nov 17, 28; m 56; c 2. ANALYTICAL CHEMISTRY. Educ: Temple Univ, BS, 50; Univ Wis, MS, 52, PhD(pharmaceut), 54. Prof Exp: Res scientist, Am Chem, Upjohn Co, 54-55; sr asst scientist, NIH, 55-57; res chemist, Atlas Powder Co, 57-61; head anal chem sect, 61-69, dir anal chem, 69-76, DIR QUAL ASSURANCE, VICK DIV RES & DEVELOP, RICHARDSON-VICKS, INC, 76- Concurrent Pos: Mem gen comn of revision US Pharmacopeia, 70-75. Mem: Am Chem Soc; Am Pharmaceut Asn. Res: Chromatography; pharmaceutical analyses; instrumental methods; quality control; biological analyses. Mailing Add: Vick Div Res & Develop Richardson-Vicks Inc Mt Vernon NY 10553

COOPER, ALFRED J(OSEPH), b New Orleans, La, Feb 2, 13; m 36; c 2. WATER RESOURCES. Educ: Tulane Univ, BE, 34; Univ Tenn, MSCE, 51. Prof Exp: Engr, R P Farnsworth, Inc, La, 34; draftsman, Tenn Valley Auth, 34-35, jr engr, 35-37, jr hydraul engr, 37-38, asst hydraul engr, 38-42, assoc hydraul engr, 42-46, hydraul engr, 46-52, head hydraul engr, 52-57, asst chief river control engr, 57-60, chief river control engr, 60-74; RETIRED. Concurrent Pos: Instr, Knoxville Adult Evening High Sch, 46-48; lectr, Univ Tenn, 48-49; consult, 78- Honors & Awards: La Eng Soc Prize, 34. Mem: Fel Am Soc Civil Engrs. Res: Correlation of rainfall and runoff; unit surface water runoff hydrographs; streamflow hydrology; analysis watershed hydrology; water control operations; river forecasting. Mailing Add: 3843 Kenilworth Dr SW Knoxville TN 37919

COOPER, ALFRED R, JR, b New York, NY, Jan 1, 24; m 48; c 5. CERAMICS. Educ: Alfred Univ, BS, 48; Mass Inst Technol, ScD(ceramics), 60. Prof Exp: Instr ceramics, Mass Inst Technol, 58-59, asst prof, 59-62, assoc prof, 62-65; assoc prof metall, 65-69, PROF CERAMICS, CASE WESTERN RESERVE UNIV, 69- Concurrent Pos: Vis prof, Univ Sheffield, 64-; consult, Am Optical Co, 58-71, Pittsburgh Plate Glass Co, 61-, Dow Corning, 63-71 & Gen Elec Co, 70-; chmn, Gordon Conf Ceramics, 69, v chmn, Gordon Conf Glass, 70. Honors & Awards: Raytheon Award, 66. Mem: Am Ceramic Soc; Brit Soc Glass Technol; Faraday Soc. Res: Diffusion in ceramic and glassy systems; multicomponent diffusion; process kinetics in ceramics; application of mathematical methods to ceramics; x-ray diffraction. Mailing Add: Dept of Metall & Mat Sci Case Western Reserve Univ Cleveland OH 44106

COOPER, ALFRED WILLIAM MADISON, b Dublin, Ireland, June 12, 32; US citizen; m 61; c 3. ATMOSPHERIC OPTICS, LASER PHYSICS. Educ: Trinity Col, Dublin, BA, 55, MA, 58; Queen's Univ, Northern Ireland, PhD(physics), 61. Prof Exp: Res asst physics, Queen's Univ, Belfast, 55-56, asst lectr, 56-57; asst prof, 57-64, assoc prof, 64-76, PROF PHYSICS, NAVAL POSTGRAD SCH, 76- Concurrent Pos: Mem tech staff, Aerospace Corp, 64. Mem: Optical Soc Am; Sigma Xi; Am Phys Soc; Asn Old Crows. Res: Gas discharge and laser physics; atmospheric propagation; electrooptic and infrared systems analysis. Mailing Add: Dept Physics Naval Postgrad Sch Monterey CA 93940

COOPER, ARTHUR JOSEPH L, b London, Eng, April 19, 46; m 72; c 2. NEUROLOGY, ENZYMOLOGY. Educ: London Univ, BSc, 67, MSc, 69; Cornell Univ Med Col, PhD(biochem), 74. Prof Exp: Asst prof biochem in neurol, 77-81, ASST PROF BIOCHEM, MED COL, CORNELL UNIV, 77-, ASSOC PROF DEPT NEUROL, 81- Concurrent Pos: Vis investr, Dept Neuro, Mem Sloan Kettering Cancer Ctr, 80- Mem: Am Chem Soc; Am Soc Biol Chemists. Res: Amonia, amino acid and keto acid metabolism in brain; study of enzymes and enzyme inhibitors; use of positron-emittins isotopes as tracers for brain biochemistry. Mailing Add: Dept Neurol Cornell Univ Med Col 1300 York Ave New York NY 10021

COOPER, ARTHUR WELLS, b Washington, DC, Aug 15, 31; m 53; c 2. ECOLOGY. Educ: Colgate Univ, BA, 53, MA, 55; Univ Mich, PhD(bot), 58. Prof Exp: Preceptor, Colgate Univ, 53-55, instr biol, 54-55; from asst prof to prof bot, NC State Univ, 58-71; dep dir, NC Dept Conserv & Develop 71, dir, 72-74; asst secy, NC Dept Natural & Econ Resources, 77-76; prof bot & forestry, 71-76, PROF FORESTRY, NC STATE UNIV, 76-, HEAD, DEPT FORESTRY, 79- Concurrent Pos: Bot ed, Ecol Monogr, 69-72. Honors & Awards: Conservation Award, Am Motors Corp, 73. Mem: AAAS; Bot Soc Am; Ecol Soc Am (vpres, 74, pres, 80). Res: Plant ecology; general plant sociology; microenvironments; resource management; forest productivity. Mailing Add: 719 Runnymede Rd Raleigh NC 27607

COOPER, BENJAMIN STUBBS, b Schenectady, NY, Apr 12, 41; m 62; c 4. NUCLEAR PHYSICS. Educ: Swarthmore Col, BA, 63; Univ Va, PhD(physics), 68. Prof Exp: Asst prof physics, Iowa State Univ, 67-73; cong sci fel, 73-74, MEM PROF STAFF, SENATE COMT ENERGY & NATURAL RESOURCES, 74- Mem: Am Phys Soc; AAAS. Res: Theoretical nuclear physics; science and public policy. Mailing Add: 3106 Dirksen Senate Off Bldg Washington DC 20510

COOPER, BERNARD A, b Plainfield, NJ, July 2, 28; Can citizen; m 55; c 3. HEMATOLOGY. Educ: McGill Univ, BSc, 49, MD, CM, 53; FRCPS(C), 58. Prof Exp: Demonstr med, 60-62, lectr, 62-63, asst prof, 63-65, assoc prof med & clin med, 65-70, prof exp med, 70-76, PROF MED & PHYSIOL, McGILL UNIV, 76-; DIR HEMAT DIV, ROYAL VICTORIA HOSP, 68- Concurrent Pos: Am Col Physicians res fel med, Harvard Univ, 56-57, Markle scholar med sci, 57-58; Med Res Coun Can career investr, 60-; asst physician, Royal Victoria Hosp, 63-68, physician, 69- Mem: Am Fedn Clin Res; Am Physiol Soc; Am Soc Clin Invest; fel Am Col Physicians; Can Soc Clin Invest. Res: Transport of vitamin B-twelve across the intestine and into other cells, and its interrelationship with folate in human metabolism. Mailing Add: Royal Victoria Hosp Montreal Can

COOPER, BERNARD RICHARD, b Everett, Mass, Apr 15, 36; m 62; c 3. SOLID STATE PHYSICS. Educ: Mass Inst Technol, BS, 57; Univ Calif, Berkeley, PhD(physics), 61. Prof Exp: Res assoc theoret physics, UK Atomic Energy Res Estab, Harwell, 62-63; res fel theoret solid state physics, Harvard Univ, 63-64; physicist, Gen Elec Res Lab, 64-68, Gen Elec Res & Develop Ctr, 68-74; CLAUDE WORTHINGTON BENEDUM PROF PHYSICS, W VA UNIV, 74- Mem: Fel Am Phys Soc. Res: Theory of magnetic properties of solids; physics of rare earth metals and compounds; theory of elecronic and optical properties of solids; theory of electronic properties of surface and interfaces. Mailing Add: Dept Physics WVa Univ Morgantown WV 26506

COOPER, BILLY HOWARD, b Tyler, Tex, Mar 15, 36; m 62; c 2. MEDICAL MYCOLOGY, MICROBIOLOGY. Educ: NTex State Univ, BA, 61, MA, 64; Tulane Univ, PhD(microbiol), 68. Prof Exp: NSF Univ Sci Develop Prog fac assoc microbiol, Univ Tex, Austin, 68-70; asst prof microbiol, Sch Med, Temple Univ, 70-75; DIR MYCOL, DEPT PATH, BAYLOR UNIV MED CTR, DALLAS, 75- Concurrent Pos: Adj prof biol, Southern Methodist Univ; clin asst prof health sci, Univ Tex Health Sci Ctr, Dallas; consult, Vet Admin Hosp, Dallas; asst prof microbiol, Baylor Dent Col. Mem: Am Soc Microbiol; Med Mycol Soc of the Americas; Int Soc Human & Animal Mycol. Res: Study of serological and biochemical activities of pathogenic dematiaceous fungi; host-parasite interactions in Candida albicans infections; morphogenetic control mechanisms in human pathogenic fungi. Mailing Add: Dept of Path Baylor Univ Med Ctr Dallas TX 75246

COOPER, CARL (MAJOR), b Pa, Aug 18, 19. CHEMICAL ENGINEERING. Educ: Univ Okla, BS, 36; Mass Inst Technol, ScD(chem eng), 49. Prof Exp: Chem engr, Dept Res & tech asst to vpres, Phillips Petrol Co, 36-42; proj engr & head process anal group, Vulcan Copper & Supply Co, 42-48; assoc prof, 48-52, PROF CHEM ENG, MICH STATE UNIV, 52- Concurrent Pos: Consult chem engr, 48-; mem, Develop Dept, Weyerhaeuser Timber Co, 51; tech dir, Vulcan-Cincinnati, 56. Mem: Am Chem Soc; Am Inst Chem Engrs; Am Soc Eng Educ. Res: Distillation; extraction; drying; heat transfer; hydrodynamics; thermodynamics; catalysis; corrosion; instrumentation; pulp and paper technology; petroleum technology; petrochemicals; industrial organic syntheses. Mailing Add: Dept Chem Eng Mich State Univ East Lansing MI 48823

COOPER, CARY WAYNE, b Camden, Maine, Sept 1, 39; m 62; c 2. BIOLOGY, PHARMACOLOGY. Educ: Bowdoin Col, AB, 61; Rice Univ, PhD(biol), 65. Prof Exp: From instr to assoc prof, 68-77, PROF PHARMACOL, SCH MED, UNIV NC, CHAPEL HILL, 77- Concurrent Pos: Nat Inst Dent Res fel pharmacol, Sch Dent Med, Harvard Univ, 65-66; Nat Inst Dent Res fel, Sch Med, Univ NC, Chapel Hill, 66-67, Nat Inst Arthritis & Metab Dis assoc fel, 67-69, career develop award, 72-76, res grant, 74-85; Merck Co Found grant fac develop, 69-70; Wellcome res travel grant, 80. Mem: Endocrine Soc; Am Soc Pharmacol & Exp Therapeut; AAAS; Soc Exp Biol Med; Am Physiol Soc. Res: Endocrine physiology and pharmacology, especially calcium and bone metabolism and GI hormones; hormonal control of calcium homeostasis and bone metabolism; parathyroid hormone and calcitonin; gastrin, CCK and somatostatin; radioimmunoassay; peptide hormones. Mailing Add: Dept Pharmacol Univ NC Sch Med Chapel Hill NC 27514

COOPER, CECIL, b Philadelphia, Pa, Dec 24, 22; m 46; c 2. BIOCHEMISTRY. Educ: George Washington Univ, BS, 49; Univ Pa, PhD(biochem), 54. Prof Exp: Instr physiol chem, Johns Hopkins Univ, 55-56; from asst prof to assoc prof biochem, 56-68, PROF BIOCHEM, CASE WESTERN RESERVE UNIV, 68- Mem: Am Soc Biol Chemists; Am Chem Soc; Brit Biochem Soc. Res: Oxidative phosphorylation; metal-nucleotide complexes; whole body lipid metabolism; effect of ethanol on liver. Mailing Add: Dept of Biochem Case Western Reserve Univ Cleveland OH 44106

COOPER, CHARLES BURLEIGH, b Parkesburg, Pa, Apr 18, 20; m 46; c 3. PHYSICS. Educ: Franklin & Marshall Col, BS, 41; Cornell Univ, MS, 43; Univ Md, PhD(physics), 51. Prof Exp: Asst physics, Cornell Univ, 41-44; tech supvr, Tenn Eastman Corp, Tenn, 44-46; instr physics, Univ Del, 46-49; asst physics, Univ Md, 49-51, asst prof, 51-52; vpres, Tagcraft Corp, Pa, 52-58; assoc prof, 58-65, PROF PHYSICS, UNIV DEL, 65-, ACTG CHMN DEPT, 80-82. Mem: Am Phys Soc; Am Asn Physics Teachers. Res: Mass spectroscopy; particle-solid interaction; surface physics; sputtering; high temperature specific heat measurements; optical properties; calutron. Mailing Add: Dept of Physics Univ of Del Newark DE 19711

COOPER, CHARLES DEWEY, b Whittier, NC, Jan 11, 24; m 46; c 3. PHYSICS. *Educ:* Berry Col, BS, 44; Duke Univ, AM, 48, PhD(physics), 50. *Prof Exp:* From asst prof to assoc prof, 50-61, dir arts & sci self study, 70-71, prof physics, 61-75, MEM STAFF PHYSICS & ASTRON, UNIV GA, 82- *Concurrent Pos:* Res fel, Harvard Univ, 54-55; consult, Oak Ridge Nat Lab, 66- *Mem:* AAAS; Am Phys Soc. *Res:* Visible and ultraviolet spectroscopy; atmospheric physics; electron and negative ion phyiscs; multiphoton ionization; third hamonic generation in rare gases. *Mailing Add:* 4235 Barnett Shoals Rd Athens GA 30605

COOPER, CHARLES F, b Kenosha, Wis, Sept 26, 24. ECOLOGY. *Educ:* Univ Minn, BS, 50; Univ Ariz, MS, 57; Duke Univ, PhD(bot), 58. *Prof Exp:* Forester, Bur Land Mgt, US Dept Interior, 50-55, forester, Watershed Prog, Ariz, 56; asst prof natural resources, Humboldt State Col, 58-60; ecologist, Agr Res Serv, USDA, Idaho, 60-64; lectr, Sch Natural Resources, Univ Mich, 64-65, from assoc prof to prof natural resources ecol, 65-71; PROF BIOL & DIR CTR REGIONAL ENVIRON STUDIES, SAN DIEGO STATE UNIV, 71- *Concurrent Pos:* Fulbright res fel, Australia, 62-63; hydrologist, USPHS, 64-65; prog dir, Ecosystem Studies, NSF, 69-71; mem US deleg, UNESCO, Man and the Biosphere, Intergovt Coord Coun, 71; chmn US deleg, US-Taiwan Coop Sci Prog Sem Forest Ecol, 72; mem exec comt, Inst Ecol, 77-81. *Mem:* Fel AAAS; Soc Am Foresters; Ecol Soc Am; Am Geophys Union. *Res:* Ecological implications of climate change; systems ecology; ecology and public policy. *Mailing Add:* Ctr for Regional Environ Studies San Diego State Univ San Diego CA 92182

COOPER, CLEE S, b Willow Creek, Mont, July 11, 22; m 47; c 2. AGRONOMY, PLANT PHYSIOLOGY. *Educ:* Mont State Col, BS, 48, MS, 50; Ore State Univ, PhD(agron), 64. *Prof Exp:* AGRONOMIST FORAGE CROPS, SCI & EDUC ADMIN, USDA, 51- *Mem:* Am Soc Agron. *Res:* Irrigated pasture establishment and management; forage crop physiology; pasture ecology. *Mailing Add:* 1714 Alder Ct Bozeman MT 59715

COOPER, DAVID B, b New York, NY, Jan 12, 33; m 60; c 2. ELECTRICAL ENGINEERING, APPLIED MATHEMATICS. *Educ:* Mass Inst Technol, BS, 54, MS, 57; Columbia Univ, PhD(appl math), 66. *Prof Exp:* Staff mem radar & detection systs, Sylvania Elec Prod, Inc, Calif, 57-59; sr res scientist & commun syst anal, Raytheon Co, Mass, 59-66; from asst prof to assoc prof, 66-78, PROF ELEC ENG, BROWN UNIV, 78- *Mem:* Asn Comput Mach; Inst Elec & Electronics Engrs. *Res:* Applied stochastic processes; computer vision; computer pattern recognition. *Mailing Add:* Div Eng Brown Univ Providence RI 02912

COOPER, DAVID GORDON, b Toronto, Ontario, Jan 9, 47. SURFACE ACTIVITY, OIL MICROBIOLOGY. *Educ:* Univ Toronto, BSc, 70, PhD(chem), 76. *Prof Exp:* Res assoc, Univ Western Ontario, 76-81, asst prof, 79-81; RES FEL ENG, McGILL UNIV, 81- *Mem:* Chem Inst Can; Can Soc Chem Eng; Am Soc Microbiol; Am Orchid Soc; Can Geog Soc. *Res:* Production, identification and application of surface active biological materials; enhanced oil recovery using microbial products; metal recovery using biomass absorption in dilute solutions; biopolymer research. *Mailing Add:* Dept Chem Eng McGill Univ 3480 University St Montreal PQ H3A 2A7 Can

COOPER, DAVID JOHN, organic chemistry, bio-organic chemistry, see previous edition

COOPER, DAVID YOUNG, b Henderson, NC, Aug 14, 24; m 55; c 2. MEDICINE. *Educ:* Univ Pa, MD, 48. *Prof Exp:* Intern, 48-49, asst instr pharmacol, 49-50, asst resident, 50, asst instr surg, 53-57, assoc, 57-59, from asst prof to assoc prof surg res, 59-68, PROF SURG RES, HOSP UNIV PA, 68- *Concurrent Pos:* Fel surg, Harrison Dept Surg Res, Univ Pa, 53-56, Kirby fel, 56-57, Finley fel, Col Surgeons, 57-60; estab investr, Am Heart Asn, 60- *Mem:* Am Physiol Soc; Endocrine Soc; Am Fedn Clin Res; Am Soc Biol Chem. *Res:* Adrenal physiology; relation of adrenal to hypertension; pulmonary physiology; oxygenases. *Mailing Add:* 1507 Ravdin Bldg 34th & Spruce St Philadelphia PA 19104

COOPER, DONALD RUSSELL, b Kalamazoo, Mich, Sept 8, 17; m 42; c 2. SURGERY. *Educ:* Univ Mich, AB, 39, MD, 42. *Prof Exp:* Intern, Univ Mich Hosp, 42-43, resident surg & instr, 46-50; assoc, 50-51, from asst prof to assoc prof, 51-59, PROF SURG, MED COL PA, 59- *Concurrent Pos:* Asst instr, Grad Sch Med, Univ Pa, 50-51, assoc, 51-52, from asst prof to assoc prof, 52-65; consult, US Navy Hosp, 55-77; chief surgeon, Philadelphia Gen Hosp, 56-65; consult surgeon, Vet Admin Hosp, 57- *Mem:* Am Col Surg; AMA; Pan-Pac Surg Soc; Int Soc Surg; Soc Surg Alimentary Tract. *Res:* Gastrointestinal surgery; surgical research in gastrointestinal and vascular fields. *Mailing Add:* Dept of Surg Med Col Pa 3300 Henry Ave Philadelphia PA 19129

COOPER, DOUGLAS ELHOFF, b New Boston, Ohio, May 21, 12; m 59. ORGANIC CHEMISTRY. *Educ:* Eastern Ky Univ, BS, 39; Univ Tenn, MS, 40; Purdue Univ, PhD(org chem), 43. *Prof Exp:* Asst chem, Univ Tenn, 39-40; asst, Purdue Univ, 40-41; res chemist, Bristol Labs, 43-52; res chemist, Res Labs, Ethyl Corp, Detroit, 52-66, res assoc, 66-69 & mkt anal, 69-74; res assoc toxicol support, Ethyl Corp, Baton Rouge, 74-77; CONSULT CHEMIST, OCCUP ENVIRON, 77- *Mem:* Health Physics Soc; Am Asn Consult Chemists & Chem Engrs; Am Indust Hyg Asn; Am Soc Safety Engrs; Am Chem Soc. *Res:* Organic synthesis; antimalarial synthesis; penicillin isolation, purification and production; dosage forms for penicillin; derivatives of 4-chloroquinoline; chemical aspects of internal combustion engine problems; radioisotopic tracer applications; steroids; chemical and engineering support of toxicology and medical activities. *Mailing Add:* 3065 Argonaut Sunset Whitney Ranch Rocklin CA 95677

COOPER, DUANE H(ERBERT), b Ill, Aug 21, 23; m 49; c 2. PHYSICS, ELECTRICAL ENGINEERING. *Educ:* Calif Inst Technol, BS, 50, PhD(physics), 55. *Prof Exp:* ASSOC PROF ELEC ENG & RES ASSOC PROF PHYSICS, COORD SCI LAB, UNIV ILL, URBANA-CHAMPAIGN, 54- *Concurrent Pos:* Consult, Consumers Union, NY, 63, Shure Brothers Inc, Ill, 64 & Nippon Columbia Co, Ltd, Japan, 71-76; proponent mem, Nation Quadraphonic Radio Comt, Electronic Industs Asn, 72-77. *Honors & Awards:* Emile Berliner Award, Audio Eng Soc, 68. *Mem:* Am Phys Soc; hon mem Audio Eng Soc (pres, 75-76); Acoust Soc Am; sr mem Inst Elec & Electronics Engrs. *Res:* Computer technology; information theory; signal analysis; acoustics. *Mailing Add:* 918 W Daniel St Champaign IL 61820

COOPER, EARL DANA, b Washington, DC, Apr 16, 26; m 49; c 2. ELECTRONICS, MANAGEMENT. *Educ:* George Washington Univ, BEE, 48; Nova Univ, DPA, 81. *Prof Exp:* Elec engr, Navy Bur Ships, 48-54, ord engr, Navy Bur Ord, 55-57, supvry guided missile design engr, 57-59; sr systs engr air-to-surface weapon systs, Bur Naval Weapons, 59-62, tech dir air launched weapons systs, 62-66, tech dir advan systs concepts, 66-71, tech dir advan systs, 71-76, dep prog mgr, Vertical Short Take-Off & Landing Aircraft Prog, 77-78, tech dir advan systs, 78-79, TECH DIR RES & TECHNOL, NAVAL AIR SYSTS COMMAND, 79- *Concurrent Pos:* Chmn, Naval Aviation Exec Inst, 74-75, mem exec bd, 75- *Honors & Awards:* Sr Exec Award, Secy Navy, 75; Meritorious Civilian Serv Award, Dept Navy, 76. *Mem:* Am Defense Preparedness Asn; Am Soc Pub Admin. *Res:* Aircraft and weapon system design; missile guidance; infrared detection; engineering administration; advanced aircraft systems and air launched weapons systems; executive development; public administration. *Mailing Add:* Res & Technol AIR-03A Naval Air Systs Command Washington DC 20361

COOPER, EDWIN LAVERN, b Utica, Mich, Aug 31, 19; m 41; c 2. FISH BIOLOGY. *Educ:* Univ Mich, BS, 40, MS, 47, PhD(zool), 49. *Prof Exp:* Res assoc, State Dept Conserv, Mich, 49-52; chief fishery biologist, Wis, 52-56; assoc prof zool, 56-62, PROF ZOOL, PA STATE UNIV, 62- *Mem:* AAAS; Am Inst Fishery Res Biologists (pres, 69-70); Am Fisheries Soc (pres, 71); Am Soc Ichthyologists & Herpetologists; Am Soc Limnol & Oceanog. *Res:* Ecology and zoogeography of fishes. *Mailing Add:* 315 Life Sci Bldg Pa State Univ University Park PA 16802

COOPER, EDWIN LOWELL, b Oakland, Tex, Dec 23, 36; m 69. IMMUNOLOGY, BIOLOGY. *Educ:* Tex Southern Univ, BS, 57; Atlanta Univ, MS, 59; Brown Univ, PhD(biol), 63. *Prof Exp:* From asst prof to assoc prof, 64-73, PROF ANAT, UNIV CALIF, LOS ANGELES, 73- *Concurrent Pos:* Nat Cancer Inst fel, Univ Calif, Los Angeles, 62-64; Guggenheim fel & hon Fulbright scholar, Bact Inst, Karolinska Inst, Sweden, 70-71; vis asst prof, Nat Polytech Inst, Mex, 66; mem, Pan Am Cong Anat; mem adv comt, Nat Res Coun, 72-73, mem comn human resources, 73-74; mem bd sci counr, Nat Inst Dent Res, 74-78; founder, Int J Develop & Comparative Immunol, 76; Eleanor Roosevelt fel, Int Union Against Cancer, Ludwig Inst Cancer Res, Lausane Switz, 77-78. *Mem:* Fel AAAS; Am Soc Zool; Am Asn Immunol; Soc Invert Path; Am Asn Anat. *Res:* Transplantation immunology; developmental and comparative immuno-biology. *Mailing Add:* Dept of Anat Univ of Calif Sch of Med Los Angeles CA 90024

COOPER, ELMER JAMES, b Milwaukee, Wis, Mar 31, 20; m 43; c 2. CEREAL CHEMISTRY. *Educ:* Marquette Univ, BS, 41, MS, 49. *Prof Exp:* Res chemist, Carnation Milk Co, 49-51 & Milwaukee County Hosp, 51; TECH MGR, CEREAL TECHNOL, UNIVERSAL FOODS CORP, 51- *Mem:* AAAS; Am Chem Soc; Am Asn Cereal Chemists; Am Soc Bakery Engrs. *Res:* Fermentation; baking; cereal technology. *Mailing Add:* 1633 N 57th St Milwaukee WI 53208

COOPER, EMERSON AMENHOTEP, b Panama, Jan 15, 24; US citizen; m 49; c 3. ORGANIC CHEMISTRY. *Educ:* Oakwood Col, BA, 49; Polytech Inst Brooklyn, MS, 54; Mich State Univ, PhD(org chem), 59. *Prof Exp:* Instr sci, Oakwood Acad, 48-50; chemist, Metric Chem Co, 50-51; from asst prof to assoc prof, 51-59, PROF CHEM, OAKWOOD COL, 59-, CHMN DEPT, 77- *Mem:* Am Chem Soc. *Res:* Cyanine dyes; synthesis of ninhydrin analogs. *Mailing Add:* Div of Math & Natural Sci Oakwood Col Huntsville AL 35806

COOPER, EUGENE PERRY, b Somerville, Mass, Aug 15, 15; m 42; c 4. PHYSICS. *Educ:* Mass Inst Technol, BS, 37; Univ Calif, PhD(theoret physics), 42. *Prof Exp:* Asst prof physics, Univ NC, 41-43; res physicist, Franklin Inst, Philadelphia, 43-45 & US Naval Ord Test Sta, Inyokern, Calif, 45-47; assoc prof physics, Univ Ore, 47-48; res physicist, US Naval Ord Test Sta, Calif, 48-51; assoc sci dir, US Naval Radiol Defense Lab, 52-60, sci dir, 60-70, consult to tech dir, Naval Undersea Ctr, 70-77; INDEPENDENT RES/EXPLOR DEVELOP DIR, NAVAL OCEAN SYSTS CTR, 77- *Concurrent Pos:* Instr math & theoret physics, Univ Exten, Univ Calif; consult physicist, Off Sci Res & Develop, 44. *Mem:* AAAS; fel Am Phys Soc. *Res:* Theoretical atomic and nuclear physics; interactions of matter and radiation; beta disintegration; nuclear isomerism; hydrodynamics; electromechanical instrument theory; radioactivity; nuclear weapon effects; physical and biological radiation effects. *Mailing Add:* Naval Ocean Systs Ctr San Diego CA 92152

COOPER, FRANKLIN SEANEY, b Robinson, Ill, Apr 29, 08; m 35; c 2. SPEECH, COMMUNICATION SCIENCE. *Educ:* Univ Ill, BS, 31; Mass Inst Technol, PhD(physics), 36. *Hon Degrees:* DSc, Yale Univ, 76. *Prof Exp:* Res engr, Gen Elec Res Labs, 36-39; assoc res dir, 39-55, pres & res dir, 55-75, ASSOC RES DIR, HASKINS LABS, 75- *Concurrent Pos:* Sci consult, Atomic Energy Comn Group, UN Secretariat, 46-47; consult, Off Secy of Defense, 49-50; mem vis comt, Modern Language Dept, Mass Inst Technol, 49-65; mem adv comt, Res Div, Col Eng, NY Univ, 49-65; adj prof phonetics, Columbia Univ, 55-65; mem bd dirs, Ctr Appl Linguistics, 68-74; chmn, Communicative Sci Interdisciplinary Cluster, President's Biomed Res Panel, 75; adj prof linguistics, Univ Conn, 69-; sr res assoc linguistics, Yale Univ, 70-76; mem, Nat Adv Neurol & Commun Dis Coun, NIH, 78-81. *Honors &*

Awards: President's Certificate of Merit, 48; Honors Asn, Am Speech & Hearing Asn, 66; Pioneer Award in Speech Communication, Inst Elec & Electronics Engrs, 72; Warren Medal, Soc Exp Psychol, 75; Silver Medal in Speech Communication, Acoust Soc Am, 75; Fletcher-Stevens Award, Brigham Young Univ, 77. *Mem:* AAAS; Am Phys Soc; fel Acoust Soc Am; fel Inst Elec & Electronics Engrs. *Res:* Perception and production of speech; voice communications systems; prosthetic aids for the blind. *Mailing Add:* Haskins Labs 270 Crown St New Haven CT 06510

COOPER, FREDERICK MICHAEL, b New York, NY, Apr 1, 44; m 72; c 2. ELEMENTARY PARTICLE PHYSICS. *Educ:* City Col New York, BS, 64; Harvard Univ, MA, 65, PhD(physics), 68. *Prof Exp:* Instr physics, Cornell Univ, 68-70; asst prof, Belfer Grad Sch Sci, Yeshiva Univ, 70-75; STAFF MEM PHYSICS, LOS ALAMOS NAT LAB, 75-, ACTG DEP GROUP LEADER, ELEM PART PHYSICS GROUP T-8, 81- *Concurrent Pos:* Frederick Cottrell Res Corp res grant, 71. *Mem:* Am Phys Soc. *Res:* Develop bound state perturbation theory and strong coupling perturbation theory and to understand the spectra of bound states in elementary particle physics. *Mailing Add:* Theory Div Los Alamos Nat Lab Los Alamos NM 87545

COOPER, GARRETT, b Watertown, Wis, July 24, 04; m 30; c 3. DERMATOLOGY. *Educ:* Univ Wis, BA, 32, MA, 33, MD, 35; Am Bd Dermat & Syphil, dipl. *Prof Exp:* Clin prof med & dermat, EMER CLIN PROF MED & DERMAT, MED SCH, UNIV WIS-MADISON, 77- *Concurrent Pos:* Chief consult derm, Madison Vet Admin Hosp; mem staff, Univ Hosps & Madison Gen Hosp; mem bd dirs, Health Planning Coun & Wis State Med Bd Health. *Mem:* Am Acad Dermat; AMA. *Res:* Histochemistry and lipoids of skin; histochemistry of psoriasis. *Mailing Add:* Univ Wis Med Sch Madison WI 53705

COOPER, GARY PETTUS, b York, Ala, Aug 30, 33; m 61; c 2. NEUROPHYSIOLOGY, NEUROTOXICOLOGY. *Educ:* Univ Ala, BA, 56; Tulane Univ, MS, 59, PhD(physiol), 63. *Prof Exp:* Res physiologist, US Naval Radiol Defense Lab, 63-66; asst prof, 66-72, assoc prof, 72-77, PROF ENVIRON HEALTH, COL MED, UNIV CINCINNATI, 77- *Mem:* AAAS; Am Physiol Soc; Soc Neurosci; Radiation Res Soc. *Res:* Synaptic transmission; heavy metal toxicology; effects of toxins on sensory systems. *Mailing Add:* Dept Environ Health Univ Cincinnati Col Med Cincinnati OH 45267

COOPER, GEOFFREY KENNETH, b Yonkers, NY, Oct 31, 49; m 73; c 2. ORGANIC CHEMISTRY, BIOLOGICAL CHEMISTRY. *Educ:* Univ Calif, Berkeley, BSc, 71; Univ Ore, Eugene, PhD(chem), 77. *Prof Exp:* Res fel alkaloid chem, Univ Calif, Berkeley, 77-78; RES CHEMIST, OLYMPIC RES DIV, ITT RAYONIER, INC, 79- *Mem:* Am Chem Soc; AAAS. *Res:* Natural products; chemical senses and neurochemistry; wood products chemistry; new regenerated cellulose process; preparation of pharmaceutical intermediates from pulping by-products; preparation of surfactants and dispersants from pulping by-products. *Mailing Add:* Olympic Res Div 409 E Harvard Ave Shelton WA 98584

COOPER, GEOFFREY MITCHELL, b Los Angeles, Calif, June 16, 48. MOLECULAR CARCINOGENESIS. *Educ:* Mass Inst Technol, BS, 69; Univ Miami, PhD(biochem), 73. *Prof Exp:* Fel virol, McArdle Lab Cancer Res, Univ Wis, 73-75; asst prof, 75-78, ASSOC PROF PATH, SIDNEY FARBER CANCER INST, HARVARD MED SCH, 78- *Mem:* Am Soc Microbiol; AAAS. *Res:* Molecular basis of oncogenic transformation; identification and characterization of cellular transforming genes activated in naturally occurring neoplasms. *Mailing Add:* Sidney Farber Cancer Inst 44 Binney St Boston MA 02115

COOPER, GEORGE EMERY, b Burley, Idaho, May 17, 16; m 41; c 4. AEROSPACE ENGINEERING, HUMAN FACTORS ENGINEERING. *Educ:* Univ Calif, BS, 40. *Prof Exp:* Eng test pilot, Ames Aeronaut Lab, Nat Adv Comt Aeronaut, 45-51, chief res pilot & asst chief flight, 51-57, chief flight opers br, Ames Res Ctr, NASA, 57-74, actg asst dir safety, NASA Hq, 69-70; consult, G E Cooper Assocs, 74-80; PRES, ERGODYNAMICS INC, 80- *Concurrent Pos:* Mem, NASA Res & Technol Subcomt on Aircraft Operating Probs. *Honors & Awards:* Arthur S Flemming Award, Nat Jr Chamber Com, 54; Octave Chanute Award, Inst Aerospace Sci, Am Inst Aeronaut & Astronaut, 54; Adm Luis de Florez Award, Flight Safety Found, 66; Richard Hansford Burroughs Award, 71. *Mem:* Fel Soc Exp Test Pilots; assoc fel Am Inst Aeronaut & Astronaut. *Res:* Flight and simulator research of advanced flight vehicles; handling qualities of aircraft and spacecraft; human factors; aviation safety; ergonomics; Cooper Harper Rating Scale. *Mailing Add:* 22701 Mt Eden Rd Saratoga CA 95070

COOPER, GEORGE EVERETT, b Tallahassee, Fla, June 29, 45; m 68; c 2. ANIMAL SCIENCE, AGRICULTURE. *Educ:* Fla A&M Univ, BS, 67; Tuskegee Inst, MS, 69; Univ Ill, Urbana, PhD(animal sci), 72. *Prof Exp:* Teaching asst animal nutrit, Tuskegee Inst, 67-69; fel, Univ Ill, Urbana, 69-72; asst prof, Tuskegee Inst, 72-76; animal nutritionist res & develop, Winrock Int Livestock Res & Training Ctr, Morrilton, Ark, 76-78; DEAN SCH APPL SCI, TUSKEGEE INST, 78- *Mem:* Am Soc Animal Sci. *Res:* Animal nutrition; international development; nutritive value of agricultural wastes. *Mailing Add:* Sch of Appl Sci Tuskegee Inst Tuskegee Institute AL 36088

COOPER, GEORGE R, b Connersville, Ind, Nov 29, 21; m 49; c 6. ELECTRICAL ENGINEERING. *Educ:* Purdue Univ, BS, 43, MS, 45, PhD(elec eng), 49. *Prof Exp:* From instr to assoc prof, 43-56, asst head grad study, 65-69, PROF ELEC ENG, PURDUE UNIV, 56- *Mem:* Fel Inst Elec & Electronics Engrs; Am Soc Eng Educ. *Res:* Communication theory; random processes; multiple-access communication systems; radar systems. *Mailing Add:* Sch of Elec Eng Purdue Univ Lafayette IN 47907

COOPER, GEORGE RAYMOND, b Denver, Colo, May 3, 16; m 43; c 1. PLANT ECOLOGY, PLANT PHYSIOLOGY. *Educ:* Univ Northern Colo, BS, 42; Iowa State Univ, MS, 48, PhD(plant ecol), 50. *Prof Exp:* Assoc prof, 50-59, PROF BOT, PLANT PHYSIOL & ECOL, UNIV MAINE, 59- *Mem:* AAAS; Am Soc Plant Physiol; Ecol Soc Am. *Res:* Remote sensing of the environment by aerial infrared photography; physiological changes in higher plants caused by fungicidal sprays. *Mailing Add:* Dept of Bot Deering Hall Univ of Maine Orono ME 04473

COOPER, GEORGE S, b Medicine Hat, Alta, Oct 18, 14; m 35; c 2. CROP SCIENCE, SOIL SCIENCE. *Educ:* Univ Alta, BSc, 49, MSc, 51; Univ Ill, PhD(crops, soils), Univ Ill, 53. *Prof Exp:* Mgr tech serv & develop, Cyanamind Can Ltd, 53-80; CONSULT PRESTICIDES, 80- *Concurrent Pos:* Exec mem, Can Comt Pesticide Use in Agr, 65-; mem, Can Assoc Comt Agr & Forestry Aviation, 65-; dir, Fourth Int Agr Aviation Cong, 69; chmn subcomt on pesticides & related compounds, Nat Res Coun Assoc Comt on Sci Criteria for Environ Qual, 72- *Mem:* Entom Soc Can; Can Agr Chem Asn (exec pres, 68-69 & 71); Agr Inst Can; Can Soc Agron (pres, 75-76); Can Soc Soil Sci. *Res:* Crop dessication; soil fertility; pesticide use patterns; pollution control measures for water and soils. *Mailing Add:* 2235 Denise Rd Mississauga ON L4X 1J2 Can

COOPER, GEORGE WALLACE, JR, reproductive biology, see previous edition

COOPER, GEORGE WILLIAM, b Mt Vernon, NY, Dec 16, 28; m 56; c 2. PHYSIOLOGY, HEMATOLOGY. *Educ:* NY Univ, AB, 49, PhD(physiol), 60; Columbia Univ, MA, 51. *Prof Exp:* Res asst radiobiol, Sloan-Kettering Inst, 57-59; USPHS fel physiol, Columbia Univ, 60-62; res assoc biol, NY Univ, 62-68; lectr, 62, from instr to asst prof, 62-72, ASSOC PROF BIOL, CITY COL NEW YORK, 73- *Honors & Awards:* Founders Day Award, NY Univ, 60. *Mem:* AAAS; Am Soc Hemat; Am Soc Physiol; Soc Exp Biol & Med; Harvey Soc. *Res:* Endocrine regulation of blood cell formation and release; effects of ionizing radiations on hematopoietic system and fetal development; action of hormones on enzyme systems; blood coagulation. *Mailing Add:* Dept Biol City Col New York New York NY 10031

COOPER, GERALD PAUL, b Alma, Mich, June 26, 10; m 35; c 3. FISH BIOLOGY. *Educ:* Mich State Norm Col, BS, 31; Univ Mich, AM, 32, PhD(fisheries), 38. *Prof Exp:* From instr to asst prof zool, Univ Maine, 36-44; from assoc fisheries biologist to fisheries biologist, Mich State Dept Conserv, 45-55, dir, 56-65, supvr fisheries res, Mich Dept Natural Resources, Inst Fisheries Res, 65-76; RETIRED. *Concurrent Pos:* Dir fish serv, Maine Dept Inland Fish & Game, 36-44; ichthyol ed, Copeia, 47-49, ed-in-chief, 50-55. *Mem:* AAAS; Am Fisheries Soc; Am Soc Ichthyol & Herpet; Am Soc Limnol & Oceanog; Wildlife Soc. *Res:* Lake and stream biological surveys; fish life histories; sport fish management. *Mailing Add:* 5430 W 32nd Mile Rd Romeo MI 48065

COOPER, GERALD RICE, b Scranton, SC, Nov 19, 14; m 46; c 3. PHYSICAL CHEMISTRY, MEDICINE. *Educ:* Duke Univ, AB, 36, AM, 38, PhD(phys chem), 39, MD, 50. *Prof Exp:* Res assoc, Med Sch, Duke Univ, 39-50; intern & resident, US Vet Admin Hosp, Atlanta, 50-52; chief phys chem lab, 52-54, chief hemat & biochem sect, 54-63, chief med lab sect, 63-70, chief clin chem & hemat br, 70-72, CHIEF, METAB BIOCHEM BR, CTR DIS CONTROL, USPHS, 72- *Concurrent Pos:* Fel, Med Sch, Duke Univ, 39-50. *Honors & Awards:* Hektoen Silver Medal, AMA, 54; Billings Silver Medal, 56; Commendation Medal, USPHS, 64; Am Asn Clin Chem Fisher Award, 75. *Mem:* AAAS; Am Asn Clin Chem; Am Soc Clin Path; Am Chem Soc; Soc Exp Biol & Med. *Res:* Electrophoresis; ultracentrifuge; diffusion; viscosity and electron microscopy of proteins and viruses; liver diseases and protein metabolism; lipids; standardization. *Mailing Add:* Metab Biochem Br Ctr for Dis Control Atlanta GA 30333

COOPER, GLENN ADAIR, JR, b Chicago, Ill, Aug 17, 31; m 56; c 3. WOOD SCIENCE & TECHNOLOGY. *Educ:* Iowa State Univ, BS, 53, MS, 59; Univ Minn, PhD, 70. *Prof Exp:* Prin wood scientist & proj leader, Forestry Sci Lab, Southern Ill Univ, Carbondale, 59-74; staff res forest prods technologist, 74-76, asst to dep chief, US Forest Serv, Washington, DC, 76-79, DEP DIR, PACIFIC NW FOREST & RANGE EXP STA, US FOREST SERV, PORTLAND, ORE, 79- *Mem:* Forest Prod Res Soc; Soc Am Foresters. *Res:* Wood-moisture relations; physical properties of wood; treatments and processes which alter wood properties; utilization of hardwoods; wood residues for energy. *Mailing Add:* 7985 SW Everett Ct Beaverton OR 97007

COOPER, GLENN DALE, b Hoxie, Ark, May 4, 19; m 49; c 2. ORGANIC CHEMISTRY. *Educ:* Ark State Col, BS, 40; Purdue Univ, PhD(chem), 49. *Prof Exp:* Res assoc, Northwestern Univ, 49-51; res assoc res lab, Gen Elec Co, 51-62; res prof chem, NMex State Univ, 62-67; SR SCIENTIST, CHEM DEVELOP OPER, GEN ELEC CO, 67- *Mem:* Am Chem Soc. *Res:* Organosilicon compounds; oxidative coupling; polymer blends. *Mailing Add:* The Crossway Elsmere NY 12144

COOPER, GUSTAV ARTHUR, b College Point, NY, Feb 9, 02; m 30; c 2. PALEOBIOLOGY. *Educ:* Colgate Univ, BS, 24, MS, 26, DSc(geol), 53; Yale Univ, PhD(geol), 29. *Prof Exp:* Asst, Peabody Mus, Yale Univ, 28-29, res assoc, 29-30; from asst cur to cur invert fossils, US Nat Mus, 30-56, head cur dept geol, 56-63, chmn dept paleobiol, 63-67, sr paleobiologist, 67-72, EMER PALEOBIOLOGIST, US NAT MUS, SMITHSONIAN INST, 72- *Honors & Awards:* Daniel Giraud Elliott Medal, Nat Acad Sci, 79; Raymond C Moore Medal, Soc Econ Paleontologists & Mineralogists, 81. *Mem:* Fel Geol Soc Am; Paleont Soc (pres, 56-57). *Res:* Stratigraphy; paleontology; stratigraphy of the Hamilton group of New York; invertebrate fossils; investigations on modern and fossil Brachiopoda. *Mailing Add:* US Nat Mus Smithsonian Inst Washington DC 20560

COOPER, HENRY FRANKLYN, JR, b Augusta, Ga, Nov 8, 36; m 58; c 3. NUCLEAR WEAPONS EFFECTS, STRATEGIC SYSTEMS ANALYSIS. *Educ:* Clemson Univ, BS, 58, MS, 60; NY Univ, PhD(mech eng), 64. *Prof Exp:* Instr eng mech, Clemson Univ, 58-60; mem tech staff, Eng Mech Dept, Bell Tel Labs, Inc, NY, 60-64; proj officer eng mech, Air Force Weapons Lab, 64-67, sci adv, 67-72; mem sr tech staff & prod mgr, 72-79, DEP STRATEGIC & SPACE SYSTS, OFF ASST SEC, AIR FORCE RES & DEVELOP, 79- *Concurrent Pos:* Mem var nat comts, Defense Sci Bd & Air Force Sci Adv Bd task forces. *Mem:* Am Soc Mech Engrs; AAAS; Am Soc Civil Engrs; Am Inst Aeronaut & Astronaut; NY Acad Sci. *Res:* Nuclear weapons effects; blast and shock phenomena; protective structures; wave propagation; structural dynamics; heat transfer; infrared transmission through the atmosphere; numerical methods; applied mathematics; operations research; technical management. *Mailing Add:* 7103 Holyrood Dr McLean VA 22101

COOPER, HERBERT ASEL, b Grand Junction, Colo, Feb 21, 38; m 63; c 2. EXPERIMENTAL PATHOLOGY, PEDIATRICS. *Educ:* Univ Kans, BA, 60, MD, 64. *Prof Exp:* Intern, Charles T Miller Hosp, St Paul, Minn, 64-65; resident pediat, Mayo Grad Sch Med, 65-67, assoc consult, Mayo Clin, 67, resident pediat hemat, Mayo Grad Sch Med, 69-71; fel exp path, 71-74, asst prof, 74-77, ASSOC PROF PATH & PEDIAT, SCH MED, UNIV NC, CHAPEL HILL, 77- *Concurrent Pos:* NIH res career develop award, 75; mem coun thrombosis, Am Heart Asn; vis res prof, Theodor Kocher Inst & adj prof hemat, Inselspital, Univ Bern, Switz, 77-78. *Mem:* Am Soc Hemat; Acad Clin Lab Physicians & Scientists; Am Soc Exp Pathologists; Int Soc Hemostasis & Thrombosis; Soc Pediat Res. *Res:* Hemostasis and thrombosis; the biochemistry of factor VIII and von Willebrand factor; interaction of platelets with von Willebrand and characterization of the platelet receptor for von Willebrand factor. *Mailing Add:* Dept of Path Preclin Educ Bldg 228-H Chapel Hill NC 27514

COOPER, HOWARD GORDON, b Joliet, Ill, Feb 16, 27; m 53; c 2. RESEARCH ADMINISTRATION, ELECTROOPTICS. *Educ:* Univ Ill, BS, 49, MS, 50, PhD(physics), 54. *Prof Exp:* Mem tech staff, Bell Tel Labs, Inc, 54-70; DIR RES, RECOGNITION EQUIP INC, 70- *Mem:* Am Phys Soc; Optical Soc Am; Inst Elec & Electronics Eng; Pattern Recognition Soc. *Res:* Technology forecasting; optical scanning; pattern recognition; image processing and information processing systems. *Mailing Add:* Recognition Equip Inc PO Box 222307 Dallas TX 75222

COOPER, IRVING S, b Atlantic City, NJ, July 15, 22; m 44; c 3. NEUROSURGERY. *Educ:* George Washington Univ, AB, 42, MD, 45; Univ Minn, MS & PhD, 51; Am Bd Psychiat & Neurol, dipl, 51; Am Bd Neurol Surg, dipl, 53. *Prof Exp:* Asst prof neurosurg, Postgrad Med Sch, NY Univ, 51-57, dir neuromuscular dis, 57-66, prof res surg, Bellevue Med Ctr, 57-66; RES PROF NEUROANAT, NY MED COL, 66-; HEAD CTR DIV PHYSIOLOGIC NEUROSURG, WESTCHESTER COUNTY MED CTR, 77- *Concurrent Pos:* Eliza Savage fel, Australia; assoc attend neurosurgeon, NY Univ Hosp, 51-66; assoc vis neurosurgeon & consult neurosurgeon, Inst Rehab, Bellevue Hosp, 51-; asst attend neurosurgeon, Hosp, Spec Surg & St Joseph's Hops, 51-; dir dept neurosurg, St Barnabas Hosp, 54-77; foreign acad corresp, Royal Acad Med, Madrid, 63. *Honors & Awards:* Hektoen Bronze Medal, AMA, 57 & 58, Cert of Merit, 61; Taylor Award, Am Therapeut Soc, 57; Award, St Barnabas Hosp, 59; Mod Med Award, 60; Alumni Award, George Washington Univ, 60, Merit Award, 67; Nat Cystic Fibrosis Found Award, 62; Merit Award, Chicago Nat Parkinson Found, 62; Outstanding Achievement Award, Univ Minn, 64; Merit Award, United Parkinson Found, 65; Henderson Lect Award, 67; Gold Medal, Worshipful Soc Apothecaries London, 67; Bronze Award, Am Cong Rehab Med, 67; Medal, Comenius Univ, 71. *Mem:* Am Asn Neurol Surg; AMA; Neurosurg Soc Am; Am Acad Neurol; fel Am Col Surg. *Res:* Neurosurgery in Parkinsonism; development of cryogenic surgery in humans. *Mailing Add:* Ctr for Physiologic Neurosurg Westchester County Med Ctr Valhalla NY 10595

COOPER, JACK LORING, b Steubenville, Ohio, Oct 26, 25; m 46; c 4. POLYMER CHEMISTRY. *Educ:* Univ Akron, BS, 50. *Prof Exp:* Res chemist, Gen Tire & Rubber Co, 50-56, group leader, Pilot Plant Opers, 56-62, sect head aqueous polymerization, 62-66, resident mgr res, Chem Pilot Plant, 66-68, MGR CHEM PILOT PLANT, 68- *Mem:* Am Chem Soc. *Res:* Rubber and polymer chemistry; pilot plant operations and administration; rubber and plastics development. *Mailing Add:* Chem Pilot Plant Gen Tire & Rubber Co Mogadore OH 44260

COOPER, JACK ROSS, b Ottawa, Can, July 26, 24; nat US; m 51; c 3. PHARMACOLOGY. *Educ:* Queen's Univ, Ont, BA, 48; George Washington Univ, MA, 52, PhD(biochem), 54. *Prof Exp:* Asst, NY Univ Res Serv, Goldwater Mem Hosp, 48-50; from instr to assoc prof, 56-71, PROF PHARMACOL, YALE UNIV, 71- *Concurrent Pos:* Fel, Pub Health Res Inst, NY, 54-56; Wellcome travel grant, Eng, 59; NIH spec fel & vis scientist, Maudsley Hosp, London, 65-66 & Nat Inst Med Res, 78. *Mem:* Am Soc Pharmacol & Exp Therapeut; Int Soc Neurochem; Am Soc Neurochem; Soc Neurosci. *Res:* Thiamine; acetylcholine; neurochemistry; neuropharmacology. *Mailing Add:* Dept Pharmacol Yale Univ Sch of Med New Haven CT 06510

COOPER, JAMES ALFRED, b Twin Falls, Idaho, Dec 20, 42. AVIAN ECOLOGY. *Educ:* Univ Washington, BS, 66; Univ Mass, Amherst, MS, 69, PhD(biol), 73. *Prof Exp:* asst prof, 72-79, ASSOC PROF WILDLIFE ECOL, UNIV MINN, 79- *Mem:* Am Ornithol Union; Wilson Ornithol Soc; The Wildlife Soc; Sigma Xi; AAAS. *Res:* Avian ecology, bioenergetics, incubation and nesting behavior, anatid reproduction and survival. *Mailing Add:* Dept of Entom Fisheries & Wildlife Univ of Minn St Paul MN 55108

COOPER, JAMES ERWIN, b Waxahachie, Tex, Aug 30, 33; m 54; c 2. ORGANIC GEOCHEMISTRY. *Educ:* NTex State Univ, BS, 54, MS, 55; Rice Univ, PhD(chem), 59. *Prof Exp:* Chemist, Core Labs, Inc, 55-56; sr res technologist, Field Res Labs, Socony Mobil Oil Co, Inc, 59-68, res assoc explor-prod res div, Mobil Res & Develop Corp, 68-73; adj prof, 74-80, ASSOC PROF GEOL, UNIV TEX, ARLINGTON, 80- *Concurrent Pos:* Lectr, Dallas Baptist Col, 69, 74-75. *Mem:* Geol Soc Am; assoc mem Am Asn Petrol Geologists; Am Chem Soc; Org Geochem Soc; Sigma Xi. *Res:* Organic reaction mechanisms; organic geochemistry and synthesis. *Mailing Add:* 2423 Bonnywood Lane Dallas TX 75233

COOPER, JAMES WILLIAM, b Buffalo, NY, Feb 7, 43; m 69; c 2. CHEMICAL INSTRUMENTATION, ORGANOMETALLIC CHEMISTRY. *Educ:* Oberlin Col, AB, 64; Ohio State Univ, MS, 67, PhD(chem), 69. *Prof Exp:* Instr chem, State Univ NY Buffalo, 69-70; Nmr appln programmer, Digital Equip Co, 70-71; anal appln mgr, Nicolet Instrument Corp, 71-74; asst prof chem, Tufts Univ, 74-80; VPRES SOFTWARE DEVELOP, BRUKER INSTRUMENTS, 80- *Mem:* Am Chem Soc. *Res:* Fourier transform Nmr; computers in chemistry; organometallic chemistry; non-benzenoid aromatic and pseudoaromatic systems. *Mailing Add:* Bruker Instruments Manning Park Billerica MA 01821

COOPER, JANE ELIZABETH, b Bethlehem, Pa, June 2, 37. GENETICS. *Educ:* Lindenwood Col, BA, 59; Univ Pa, PhD(zool), 65. *Prof Exp:* From instr to asst prof biol, Drexel Inst, 64-67; asst prof, 67-73, ASSOC PROF BIOL, PA STATE UNIV, 73- *Mem:* AAAS; Genetics Soc Am; Asn Adv Health Professions; Sigma Xi. *Res:* Swimming rates in Paramecium aurelia; control of protein system in Paramecium aurelia; host-endosymbiont interactions in Paramecium biaurelia; ethical issues in genetic counselling and genetic engineering. *Mailing Add:* Dept of Biol Pa State Univ Media PA 19063

COOPER, JOHN (HANWELL), b Tynemouth, Eng, Mar 15, 22; Can citizen; m 53; c 2. HUMAN PATHOLOGY, HISTOCHEMISTRY. *Educ:* Glasgow Univ, MB & ChB, 45; FRCPath, 69. *Prof Exp:* Registr path, Victoria Infirmary, Scotland, 49-56; assoc, Gen Hosp, St John's Nfld, 56-57; dir, Glace Bay Hosps, NS, 57-62; assoc, Path Inst, Dept Pub Health, Prov NS, 62-63, dir anat path, 63-65; assoc prof, 62-66, PROF PATH, DALHOUSIE UNIV, 66-; DEP HEAD, DEPT PATH, VICTORIA GEN HOSP, 75- *Concurrent Pos:* Med dir, Path Inst, Dept Pub Health, Prov NS, 65-74. *Mem:* AAAS; Histochem Soc; Int Acad Path; Can Med Asn; Can Asn Path. *Res:* Connective tissue histochemistry and pathology, especially elastic sheath-elastofibril system, amyloid, splenic follicular hyaline, actinic elastosis and protein histochemistry. *Mailing Add:* Dept of Path Victoria Gen Hosp Halifax NS B3H 2Y9 Can

COOPER, JOHN (JINX), b Norwich, Eng, Nov 30, 37; m 62; c 3. ATOMIC PHYSICS, PLASMA PHYSICS. *Educ:* Cambridge Univ, BA, 59, MA, 63; Imp Col, London, dipl, 61, PhD(physics), 62. *Prof Exp:* Asst lectr physics, Imp Col, London, 62-63, lectr, 63-65; from asst prof to assoc prof, 65-70, mem, 65-67, fel, Joint Inst Lab Astrophys, 67-80, PROF PHYSICS & ASTROPHYS, UNIV COLO, BOULDER, 70- *Concurrent Pos:* Consult, Atomic Energy Auth, UK, 63-65 & Radio Stands Lab, Nat Bur Stands, Colo, 68- *Mem:* Fel Am Inst Physics. *Res:* Experimental and theoretical interests in the radiation from hot gases of laboratory and astrophysical importance; line broadening, scattering of radiation and other aspects of plasma and laser spectroscopy. *Mailing Add:* Joint Inst for Lab Astrophys Univ of Colo Boulder CO 80302

COOPER, JOHN ALLEN DICKS, b El Paso, Tex, Dec 22, 18; m 44; c 4. BIOCHEMISTRY. *Educ:* NMex State Univ, BS, 39; Northwestern Univ, PhD(biochem), 43, MB, 50, MD, 51. *Hon Degrees:* Dr, Univ Brazil, 58; DSc, Northwestern Univ, 72, Duke Univ, 73, Med Col Ohio, 74, Med Col Wis, 78, NY Med Col, 81; DMedSc, Med Col Pa, 73. *Prof Exp:* From instr to prof biochem, Med Sch, Northwestern Univ, 43-69; PRES, ASN AM MED COLS, 69- *Concurrent Pos:* Consult, Vet Admin Res Hosp, Chicago, 54-69, dir radioisotope serv, 54-65; vis prof, Univ Brazil, 56 & Univ Buenos Aires, 58; mem comt licensure, US AEC, 56-68, mem adv comt educ & training, Div Biol & Med, 57-63; mem policy adv bd, Argonne Nat Lab, 57-63, chmn rev comt, Div Biol & Med Res & Radiol Physics, 58-62; mem med adv comt, PR Nuclear Ctr, 59-60; mem bd pub health adv, State of Ill, 62-69, mem, Ill Legis Comn on Atomic Energy, 63-69, mem bd higher educ, 64-69, mem, Gov Sci Adv Coun, 65-69, chmn, Sci Adv Coun of Ill, 67-69; ed, J Med Educ, 62-71; mem adv comt on investigational drugs, Food & Drug Admin, 63-65, consult to adminr, 65-70; mem coun, Assoc Midwest Univs, 63-68, vpres bd dirs, 64-65, pres, 65-66; mem med adv comt, W K Kellogg Found, 63-68, mem Latin Am adv comt, 64-68; treas admin comt, Pan Am Fedn Asns Med Schs, 63-76; mem adv comt on health sci, Eng & Biotechnol & Int Fel Rev Panel, NIH, 64, adv coun health res facil, 65-69, spec consult to dir, 68-70, consult to div physician & health professions educ, Bur Health Manpower Educ, 70-73; chmn extramural educ surv comt, Mayo Found, 65-66; vpres, Argonne Univs Asn, 65-68, mem bd trustees, 65-69; adv to adminr int health manpower, Agency Int Develop, 66-71; chmn adv comt on study of training progs in gen med sci, Nat Acad Sci-Nat Res Coun, 66-71, mem adv comt off sci personnel, 67-70; mem adv comt for instnl rels, NSF, 67-71; mem res strengthening group, Spec Prog Res & Training in Tropical Diseases, World Health Orgn, 77-80; mem spec med adv comt, Veterans Admin, 81- *Mem:* Nat Inst Med-Nat Acad Sci; hon mem Acad Med Inst Chile; Am Hosp Asn; Am Soc Biol Chem; Asn Am Med Cols. *Res:* Educational administration; radiobiology. *Mailing Add:* Asn Am Med Col One DuPont Circle Washington DC 20036

COOPER, JOHN C, JR, b Fullerton, Calif, Jan 16, 36; m 58; c 2. AUDIOLOGY. *Educ:* Auburn Univ, BS, 57; Wayne State Univ, MA, 65, PhD(audiol), 68. *Prof Exp:* Res asst audiol, Wayne State Univ, 65-67; asst prof, Vanderbilt Univ, 67-69; assoc prof, 69-80, PROF AUDIOL, MED SCH UNIV TEX, SAN ANTONIO, 80- *Concurrent Pos:* Assoc prof, Trinity Univ & Univ Tex, Austin, 70- *Mem:* Am Speech & Hearing Asn; Acad Rehab Audiol; Southern Audiol Soc; Am Auditory Soc. *Res:* Verbal learning in normal, hard of hearing and deaf children; discrimination of speech through hearing aids with lipreading and in noise; hearing screening; impedance audiometry; electronystagmography. *Mailing Add:* 123 Tall Oak San Antonio TX 78232

COOPER, JOHN NEALE, b San Antonio, Tex, May 25, 38; m 60, 78; c 2. PHYSICAL CHEMISTRY, INORGANIC CHEMISTRY. *Educ:* Calif Inst Technol, BS, 60; Univ Calif, Berkeley, PhD(chem), 64. *Prof Exp:* Lectr inorg chem, Makerere Univ Col, Uganda, 64-66; asst prof chem, Carleton Col, 66-67; asst prof, 67-74, ASSOC PROF CHEM, BUCKNELL UNIV, 74- *Concurrent Pos:* Vis asst prof, Univ Ill, Urbana, 71-72; fac res partic, Argonne Nat Lab, 75-76. *Mem:* Am Chem Soc. *Res:* Kinetics and mechanisms of inorganic reactions. *Mailing Add:* Dept of Chem Bucknell Univ Lewisburg PA 17837

COOPER, JOHN NIESSINK, b Kalamazoo, Mich, Feb 4, 14; m 36. PHYSICS. *Educ:* Kalamazoo Col, AB, 35; Cornell Univ, PhD(physics), 40. *Prof Exp:* Asst physics, Cornell Univ, 35-40; instr, Univ Southern Calif, 40-43; asst prof, Univ Okla, 43-46; from asst prof to prof, Ohio State Univ, 46-56; PROF PHYSICS, NAVAL POSTGRAD SCH, 56- *Concurrent Pos:* Res physicist, Radiation Lab, Univ Calif, 44-45; staff mem, Sandia Corp, 51-54; consult, Ramo-Woolridge Corp, 55-58, Space Tech Labs, 58-66 & Kaman Nuclear, 65. *Mem:* Fel Am Phys Soc; Am Asn Physics Teachers; sr mem Inst Elec & Electronics Engrs. *Res:* X-rays; nuclear spectroscopy; stopping of protons; superconductivity. *Mailing Add:* Dept of Physics Naval Postgrad Sch Monterey CA 93940

COOPER, JOHN RAYMOND, b Lafayette, Ala, Jan 2, 31; m 52; c 2. PHYSICS. *Educ:* Auburn Univ, BS, 52, PhD, 70; Ohio State Univ, MS, 55. *Prof Exp:* Sr physicist, Aircraft Nuclear Propulsion Dept, Gen Elec Co, 58-60; res physicist, Southern Res Inst, 60-65, sr physicist, 65-66; mem staff dept physics, 66-71, DIR NUCLEAR SCI CTR & ASST PROF PHYSICS, AUBURN UNIV, 71- *Mem:* Am Asn Physics Teachers. *Res:* Neutron scattering; scattering; neutron induced reactions; nuclear instrumentation; reactor physics; electrooptics. *Mailing Add:* Dept of Physics Auburn Univ Auburn AL 36830

COOPER, JOHN WESLEY, b Delta, Colo, Sept 7, 46; m 73. EXPERIMENTAL HIGH ENERGY PHYSICS. *Educ:* Univ Colo, Boulder, BA, 68; Univ Mich, Ann Arbor, MA, 69, PhD(physics), 75. *Prof Exp:* Res asst, Bubble Chamber Group, Univ Mich, 71-75; res assoc exp high energy physics, Univ Ill, 75-77, vis res asst prof, 77-80; ASST PROF PHYSICS, UNIV PA, 80- *Mem:* Sigma Xi; Am Phys Soc. *Res:* Experimental elementary particle research using the 30 inch bubble chamber hybrid spectrometer and the cyclotron magnet spectrometer. *Mailing Add:* High Energy Physics Group Dept Physics Univ Pa Philadelphia PA 19174

COOPER, JOSEPH E, b Philadelphia, Pa, May 14, 21; m 54; c 5. BIOCHEMISTRY, SANITARY ENGINEERING. *Educ:* Lincoln Univ, Pa, AB, 49. *Prof Exp:* Res chem pollution, City Philadelphia, 54-65, sanitary eng water resources, 65-66; res chem tobacco, 66-71, RES BIOCHEM HIDES & LEATHER, SEA SCI & EDUC ADMIN, USDA, 71-, PROJ LEADER TANNERY POLLUTION, 71- *Mem:* Prof Black Chemists & Chem Engrs; Am Leather Chemists Asn; Nat Tech Asn. *Res:* Determination of carcinogenic fractions in cigarette smoke; recovery of by-products from tannery and industrial wastes for conversion to marketable items; pilot plant design and scale-up to plant size industrial waste treatment. *Mailing Add:* Sea Sci & Educ Admin USDA 600 E Mermaid Lane Wyndmoor PA 19118

COOPER, KEITH EDWARD, b Frome, Eng, Aug 7, 22; m 46; c 2. PHYSIOLOGY. *Educ:* Univ London, MB, BS, 45, BSc, 48, MSc, 50; Oxford Univ, MA, 60, DSc(physiol), 70. *Prof Exp:* Resident, St Mary's Hosp, Univ London, 45-46, lectr physiol, 46-48; mem div human physiol, Med Res Coun Labs, Eng, 50-54; from founding mem to dir, Med Res Coun Body Temperature Res Unit, London & Oxford, 54-69; head div, 69-78, acad vpres, 78-80, PROF MED PHYSIOL, FAC MED, UNIV CALGARY, 69-, VPRES RES, 80- *Concurrent Pos:* Vis lectr, Vat Admin Hosp, Cincinnati, Ohio, 66; vis lectr clin invest, Yale Univ, 66; vis lectr biophys, Univ Western Ont & Rutgers Univ, 66; consult, Cowley Rd Hosp, Oxford, Eng, 66; examr, Oxford Univ, Univ WI & Queen's Univ, Belfast, 66; mem panel arctic med & climatic physiol, Can Defense Res Bd, 70-; mem bd dirs, Alberta Res Coun, 79- *Mem:* Brit Physiol Soc; Can Physiol Soc (vpres, 74, pres, 75-76); Am Physiol Soc; Brit Med Res Soc; Can Fedn Biol Sci (vchmn, 78-79, pres, 79-80). *Res:* Body temperature regulation; mechanism of fever. *Mailing Add:* Arts 105 Univ of Calgary Calgary AB T2N 1N4 Can

COOPER, KENNETH WILLARD, b Flushing, NY, Nov 29, 12; m 37; c 2. CYTOGENETICS, ENTOMOLOGY. *Educ:* Columbia Univ, AB, 34, AM, 35, PhD(cytol), 39. *Hon Degrees:* MA, Dartmouth Col, 62. *Prof Exp:* Asst zool, Columbia Univ, 34-37; instr, Univ Rochester, 38-39; from instr to assoc prof biol, Princeton Univ, 39-53; prof & chmn dept, Univ Rochester, 53-57; grad res prof, Univ Fla, 57-59; prof cytol, Dartmouth Med Sch, 59-62, cytol & genetics, 62-67; PROF BIOL, UNIV CALIF, RIVERSIDE, 67- *Concurrent Pos:* Guggenheim fel, Calif Inst Technol, 44, 45; vis lectr, Univ Colo, 50; mem vis comt, Brookhaven Nat Lab, 58-60, chmn vis comt, 60-61; mem gen training panel, NIH, 58-66, health res facilities, 66-69; mem FCP Coun, Smithsonian Inst, 72-76; consult, Energy Res & Develop Agency, 76-78. *Mem:* Fel AAAS; fel Am Acad Arts & Sci; fel Royal Entom Soc; Genetics Soc Am; Soc Study Evolution. *Res:* Experimental ecology; insect communication; biology and systematics of moss insects, beetles, wasps; fossil insects; chromosome structure and segregation; interchromosomal effects; non-gametic functions of gametes; mechanisms of mitosis and meiosis; evolution. *Mailing Add:* Dept of Biol Univ of Calif Riverside CA 92502

COOPER, LARRY RUSSELL, b Los Angeles, Calif, Sept 19, 34; m 65; c 5. ELECTRONICS, SOLID STATE PHYSICS. *Educ:* Univ Calif, Los Angeles, BS, 56; Ore State Univ, PhD(physics), 67. *Prof Exp:* Jr scientist physics, Edwards AFB, US Air Force, 56-57; res assoc, Ore State Univ, 63-67; Nat Acad Sci-Nat Res Coun res assoc, Cyclotron Lab, Naval Res Lab, 67-69; physicist, Nuclear Physics Br, 69-74, PHYSICIST, ELECTRONICS & SOLID STATE SCI PROG, OFF NAVAL RES, 74- *Mem:* Am Phys Soc. *Res:* Electronics and solid state sciences; physics of electron and electrooptic devices; solid state surfaces and interfaces; radiation effects in electronic materials; ion implantation; surface analysis techniques; solid state physics. *Mailing Add:* Elec & Solid State Sci Prog Off Naval Res Code 414 Arlington VA 22217

COOPER, LEON, operations research, computer science, deceased

COOPER, LEON N, b New York, NY, Feb 28, 30; m 69; c 2. THEORETICAL PHYSICS. *Educ:* Columbia Univ, AB, 51, AM, 53, PhD(physics), 54. *Hon Degrees:* DSc, Columbia Univ, 73, Univ Sussex, 73, Univ Ill, 74, Brown Univ, 74, Gustavus Adolphus Col, 75, Ohio State Univ, 76 & Univ Marie Curie, Paris, 77. *Prof Exp:* NSF fel, Inst Advan Study, 54-55; res assoc physics, Univ Ill, 55-57; asst prof, Ohio State Univ, 57-58; from assoc prof to prof physics, 58-66, Henry Ledyard Goddard univ prof, 66-74, THOMAS J WATSON, SR PROF SCI, BROWN UNIV, 74- *Concurrent Pos:* Vis prof, var univs & schs; consult, var govt agencies, indust & educ orgn; var pub lectr, int confs; Sloan Found res fel, 59-66; Guggenheim fel, 65-66. *Honors & Awards:* Comstock Prize, Nat Acad Sci, 68; Nobel Prize, 72; Descartes Medal, Acad Paris, Univ Rene Descartes, 77. *Mem:* Nat Acad Sci; fel Am Phys Soc; Am Acad Arts & Sci; Am Philos Soc; Fedn Am Scientists. *Res:* Nuclear, low temperature and elementary particle physics; field theory; superconductivity; many body problems. *Mailing Add:* Dept of Physics Brown Univ Providence RI 02912

COOPER, LOUIS ZUCKER, b Albany, Ga, Dec 25, 31; m 76; c 4. INFECTIOUS DISEASES, PEDIATRICS. *Educ:* Yale Univ, BS, 54, MD, 57. *Prof Exp:* USPHS fel, 61-63; instr med, Sch Med, Tufts Univ, 63-64; from instr to assoc prof pediat, Sch Med, NY Univ, 64-73; PROF PEDIAT, COL PHYSICIANS & SURGEONS, COLUMBIA UNIV, 73-; DIR PEDIAT SERV, ST LUKES-ROOSEVELT HOSP CTR, 73- *Concurrent Pos:* Career scientist, Health Res Coun, New York, 67-73; dir, Rubella Proj; consult, Bur Educ Handicapped, US Off Educ, 68-72; consult, President's Comt Ment Retardation, 70-; mem, NY State Comt Children, 70-74; mem & vchmn, Nat Adv Coun Develop Disabilities, HEW, 73-76. *Mem:* AAAS; fel Am Acad Pediat; Infectious Dis Soc Am; Am Pub Health Asn; Soc Pediat Res. *Res:* Rubella; handicapped children; viral immunology and vaccines; chemotherapy of infectious diseases. *Mailing Add:* Roosevelt Hosp Pediat Serv 428 W 59th St New York NY 10019

COOPER, MARGARET, b New York, NY. GEOLOGY. *Educ:* Hunter Col, AB, 35; Columbia Univ, AM, 37. *Prof Exp:* Res asst geol, Columbia Univ, 37-42; geographer geol, Army Map Serv, 42-43; geologist, Union Mines Develop Corp, 43-46 & AEC, 47-54; GEOLOGIST, US GEOL SURV, 54- *Mem:* Geol Soc Am; Mineral Soc Am; Soc Mining Engrs; AAAS; Geosci Info Soc. *Res:* Economic geology; commodity studies, especially uranium, titanium and precious metals; environmental geology; mineral leasing on federal lands. *Mailing Add:* US Geol Surv Nat Ctr MS954 Reston VA 22092

COOPER, MARGARET HARDESTY, b St Louis, Mo, June 7, 44. ANATOMY. *Educ:* Drury Col, AB, 66; St Louis Univ, MS, 69, PhD(anat), 71. *Prof Exp:* ASST prof anat, Sch Med, Wayne State Univ, 71-78; PROF OTOLARYNGOL & ANAT, ST LOUIS UNIV SCH MED, 78- *Mem:* Asn Res Otolaryngol; Am Asn Anat; Soc Neurosci; Cagal Club; Sigma Xi. *Res:* Neuroanatomy; light and electron microscopic studies of central nervous system nuclei; various aspects of otolaryngology including sugical procedures. *Mailing Add:* Dept of Anat 1402 S Grand St Louis MO 63104

COOPER, MARTIN, b Chicago, Ill, Dec 26, 28; m 55; c 2. ELECTRICAL ENGINEERING, COMMUNICATIONS. *Educ:* Ill Inst Technol, BS, 50, MS, 57. *Prof Exp:* Res engr data commun, Teletype Corp, 53-54; eng group leader commun, 54-58, eng mgr mobile commun, 58-65, prod mgr portable commun, 65-67, opers mgr, 67-69, vpres & dir portable opers, 69-72, vpres & gen mgr systs div, 72-78, V PRES & CORP DIR RES & DEVELOP, MOTOROLA, INC, 78- *Concurrent Pos:* Comt chmn, var tech comts, Electronics Industs Asn, 59-72; mem bd telecommun-comput appln, Nat Res Coun, 77-, mem comt telecommun policy, Inst Elec Engrs, 78-; mem Adv Bd, Univ Ill. *Mem:* Fel Inst Elec & Electronics Engrs (pres vehicular technol soc, 73 & 74). *Res:* Mobile and portable two-way radio communications; radio spectrum efficiency; quartz crystal material and resonator technology; data communication; management of technology. *Mailing Add:* Motorola Inc 1301 E Algonquin Rd Schaumburg IL 60196

COOPER, MARTIN DAVID, b Los Angeles, Calif, Sept 8, 45; m 69; c 3. PION NUCLEAR PHYSICS, WEAK INTERACTION PHYSICS. *Educ:* Calif Inst Technol, BS, 67; Univ Md, PhD(physics), 71. *Prof Exp:* NSF fel, Univ Md, 70-71; res assoc, Univ Washington, 71-74; res assoc, 74-75, STAFF SCIENTIST, LOS ALAMOS NAT LAB, 75- *Mem:* Am Phys Soc. *Res:* Investigation of nuclear properties with pions; measurement of nuclear radii; observations of pion double charge exchange; discovery of the isovector monopole mode in nuclei; development of high resolution pi spectrometer; best limits on neutrinoless muon decay. *Mailing Add:* Los Alamos Nat Lab MS 846 Group MP-4 Los Alamos NM 87545

COOPER, MARTIN JACOB, b Detroit, Mich, June 27, 39; m 65. TECHNICAL RESEARCH & DEVELOPMENT MANAGEMENT. *Educ:* Univ Mich, BSE, 61, MS, 63; Brandeis Univ, PhD(physics), 67. *Prof Exp:* Nat Res Coun res assoc, Nat Bur Standards, 66-68, res assoc statist physics, 68-72, prog analyst, 72-74; Presidential interchange exec, Corp Res & Develop, Gen Elec Co, 74-75; Physicist & adv, Energy Res & Develop Admin, 75-77; dir strategic planning & anal, NSF, 77-79; mgr strategic planning, Occidental Petrol Res, 79-82; PRIN CONSULT, MARTIN J COOPER & ASSOCS, 82- *Mem:* AAAS; Am Phys Soc; Am Chem Soc. *Res:* Many-body physics, phase transitions; science policy; research and development planning. *Mailing Add:* 10 Morning Dew Irvine CA 20006

COOPER, MARY WEIS, b St Louis Co, Mo, Aug 10, 42; m 68; c 2. OPERATIONS RESEARCH, APPLIED MATHEMATICS. *Educ:* Wash Univ, BA, 61, MS, 68, DSc(opers res), 70. *Prof Exp:* Analyst libr info retrieval, Monsanto Co, 59-61; sci programmer eng, McDonnell Automation Ctr, 62-64; res scientist, Advan Technol Ctr, 70-72; vis prof, 73, asst prof, 76-81, ASSOC PROF OPERS RES, SOUTHERN METHODIST UNIV, 81- *Concurrent Pos:* Consult, Degolyer-McNaughton Co, 70-71 & Advan Technol Ctr, 72-73. *Mem:* Opers Res Soc Am; Inst Mgt Sci; Am Women Sci; Sigma Xi. *Res:* Linear, non-linear and discrete programming. *Mailing Add:* Sch of Eng & Appl Sci Southern Methodist Univ Dallas TX 75275

COOPER, MAURICE ZEALOT, b Brooklyn, NY, Feb 19, 08; m 41; c 1. MEDICINE. *Educ:* Long Island Col Med, MD, 31. *Prof Exp:* Intern, Beth-el Hosp, Brooklyn, NY, 31-32; physician, Health Dept, 33-36; physician, Vet Admin, 36-40, chief outpatient & reception serv, Vet Admin Hosp, Togus, Maine, 40-42, chief med officer, Vet Admin Regional Off, RI, 42-46, chief outpatient serv, New Eng Br, 46-49, chief plans & policy develop, Med Serv, Washington, DC, 49-56, dir med criteria ed bd, 56-59, asst dir, Med Serv, 59-62, chief-of-staff, Vet Admin Hosp, Seattle, Wash, 62-68, dir, Vet Admin Hosp, Tex, 68-69, dir, Domiciliary, Los Angeles Ctr, 69-70, dir, Vet Admin Outpatient Clin, 70-77; RETIRED. *Mem:* AMA; Am Col Physicians. *Res:* Residuals and evaluations of medical diseases; hospital and medical system administration, effects of malnutrition and other hardships on the morality and morbidity of former United States prisoners of war and civilian internees of World War II. *Mailing Add:* 11854 Darlington Ave 49771 Los Angeles CA 90049

COOPER, MAX DALE, b Hazlehurst, Miss, Aug 31, 33; m 60; c 4. PEDIATRICS, IMMUNOLOGY. *Educ:* Tulane Univ, MD, 57; Am Bd Pediat, dipl, 62. *Prof Exp:* Intern med, Saginaw Gen Hosp, 57-58; resident, Sch Med, Tulane Univ, 58-60; house officer, Hosp Sick Children, London, Eng, 60, res asst neurophysiol, 61; instr pediat, Sch Med, Tulane Univ, 62-63; from instr to asst prof, Univ Minn, Minneapolis, 64-67; assoc prof microbiol, 67-73, PROF PEDIAT, SCH MED, UNIV ALA, BIRMINGHAM, 67-, PROF MICROBIOL, 73-, SR SCIENTIST, CANCER RES & TRAINING PROG, 71-, DIR, CELLULAR IMMUNOBIOL UNIT OF TUMOR INST, 76- *Concurrent Pos:* Fel pediat, Univ Calif, San Francisco, 61-62; Nat Tuberc Asn teaching traineeship award, Univ Minn, Minneapolis, 63-64; USPHS spec res fel, 64-66. *Honors & Awards:* Samuel J Melzer Award, Soc Exp Biol, 66. *Mem:* AAAS; Soc Pediat Res; Am Soc Exp Path; Am Asn Immunol; Am Soc Clin Invest. *Res:* Development and function of the lymphoid system; immunologic deficiency diseases; lymphoid malignancies. *Mailing Add:* Dept of Pediat Univ of Ala Med Ctr Birmingham AL 35294

COOPER, MILES ROBERT, b Elizabeth City, NC, Oct 21, 33; m 55; c 2. ONCOLOGY, HEMATOLOGY. *Educ:* Univ NC, Raleigh, BS, 55; Bowman Gray Sch Med, MD, 62. *Prof Exp:* From instr to assoc prof med, 67-75, PROF MED, BOWMAN GRAY SCH MED, 75- *Mem:* Am Col Physicians; Am Soc Hemat; Am Fedn Clin Res; Soc Clin Oncol. *Res:* Laboratory and clinical studies of the pathophysiology of leukocytes and platelets; evaluation of supportive therapies consisting of leukocyte and platelet transfusions and definitive therapy with various therapeutic programs in neoplastic disease. *Mailing Add:* Bowman Gray Sch of Med 300 S Hawthorne Rd Winston-Salem NC 27103

COOPER, MORRIS DAVIDSON, b Norton, Va, Oct 27, 43; m 67; c 2. MEDICAL MICROBIOLOGY, IMMUNOLOGY. *Educ:* King Col, BA, 65; Tenn Technol Univ, MS, 67; Univ Ga, PhD(microbiol), 71. *Prof Exp:* Prof biol, Bluefield Col, 67-69; res fel microbiol, Harvard Univ, 71-73; asst prof, 73-79, ASSOC PROF MED MICROBIOL, SCH MED, SOUTHERN ILL UNIV, 80- *Concurrent Pos:* NIH fel, Sch Pub Health, Harvard Univ, 71-73; consult microbiol, Univ Ore, 74-76; vis assoc prof, Dept Med, Vanderbilt Univ, 81-82. *Mem:* Am Soc Microbiol; NY Acad Sci; AAAS; Sigma Xi. *Res:* Immune response to microbial antigens particularly Neisseria gonorrhoease; purification of microbial antigens; immune response to enzymes. *Mailing Add:* Dept of Med Microbiol & Immunol Southern Ill Univ Springfield IL 62708

COOPER, MURRAY IRVING, entomology, deceased

COOPER, NORMAN JOHN, b Lurgan, Northern Ireland, Sept 18, 50; Brit citizen. SYNTHETIC INORGANIC & ORGANOMETTALIC CHEMISTRY. *Educ:* Balliol Col, Oxford Univ, BA, 73, DPhil, 76. *Prof Exp:* Res fel, 76-78, ASST PROF CHEM, HARVARD UNIV, 78- *Mem:* Am Chem Soc; Royal Soc Chem; NY Acad Sci. *Res:* Synthetic and mechanistic organotransition metal chemistry; catalytic applications of transtion metal complexes; organic chemistry of metal clusters. *Mailing Add:* Chem Dept Harvard Univ 12 Oxford St Cambridge MA 02138

COOPER, NORMAN S, b Brooklyn, NY, Dec 23, 20; m 45; c 1. RHEUMATOLOGIC PATHOLOGY, IMMUNOPATHOLOGY. *Educ:* Columbia Univ, AB, 40; Univ Rochester, MD, 43; Am Bd Path, dipl, 52. *Prof Exp:* Asst path, Med Col, Cornell Univ, 45-46; asst microbiol, 49-50, instr microbiol, 50-51, from instr to assoc prof path, 51-67, PROF PATH, SCH MED & MEM GRAD FAC ARTS & SCI, NY UNIV, 67-; CHIEF LAB SERV, NY VET ADMIN MED CTR, 67- *Concurrent Pos:* Hoskins fel, 51-53; Polachek Found med res fel, 54-59; intern, NY Hosp, 44 & 48-49, asst res, 44-45, res pathologist, 45-46; consult pathologist, Bellevue Hosp, 67-; attend pathologist, Univ Hosp, 67- *Mem:* Am Asn Pathologists; Am Soc Cell Biol; Am Rheumatism Asn; Am Asn Immunol; Int Acad Path. *Res:* Metabolic idiosyncrasies of murine plasmacy tower; pathology of rheumatic diseases. *Mailing Add:* Dept of Path NY Univ Sch of Med New York NY 10016

COOPER, PATRICIA J, b Greenville, Tex, Dec 9, 36; m 80; c 1. HUMAN BIOLOGY, DEVELOPMENTAL BIOLOGY. *Educ:* Univ Hawaii, BA, 60; Univ Calif, PhD(zool), 64. *Prof Exp:* USPHS fel develop biol, Med Sch, Univ Ore, 64-67, asst prof path, 67-69; mem fac, 69-71, res zoologist, 71-79, lectr, Dept Zool, 71-80, LECTR, HEALTH & MED SCI PROG, UNIV CALIF, BERKELEY, 79- *Mem:* AAAS; Asn Holistic Health; Soc Develop Biol; Soc Cell Biol. *Res:* Ultrastructure of early amphibian development; mechanics of morphogenetic movement; publications on women's health, medical problems of reproduction, life span developmental psychology in humans, and human sexual development. *Mailing Add:* 4 Maybeck Twin Dr Berkeley CA 94708

COOPER, PAUL DAVID, b Winnipeg, Man, May 10, 35; m 58; c 3. PHARMACOLOGY, ORGANIC CHEMISTRY. *Educ:* Univ Toronto, BSc, 58, MSc, 59; Univ Ottawa, PhD(chem), 62. *Prof Exp:* Res assoc chem, Banting Inst, Univ Toronto, 62-64; res dir pharmaceut, Penick Can Ltd, Ont, 64-65; res assoc, Pharmacol, Univ Toronto, 65-66, from asst prof to assoc prof, 66-70; ASSOC PROF PHARMACOL, FAC PHARM, UNIV MONTREAL, 70- *Concurrent Pos:* Lectr, Univ Toronto, 67-68; consult, Astra Pharmaceut Ltd, Ont, 67-69; vis scientist, Govt France, 68; fel, Int Cong Phatmacol, Switz, 69. *Mem:* Pharmacol Soc Can. *Res:* Structure-action relationships among cholinergic and adrenergic drugs, especially stereochemical and electronic aspects of molecules representing hallucinogenic drugs; receptor theory and the events leading from excitation to muscle contraction. *Mailing Add:* Dept Biochem Pharmacol Fac Pharm Univ Montreal Montreal PQ H3C 3J7 Can

COOPER, PAUL W, b New York, NY, Feb 25, 29. PATTERN RECOGNITION, STATISTICAL TESTING. *Educ:* Mass Inst Technol, BS, 50, MS, 51. *Prof Exp:* Mem tech staff, Bell Tel Labs, 53-56; sr engr, Appl Sci Div, Melpar, Inc, 58-60, staff consult, 60-62; eng specialist, Info Processing, Sylvania Electronic Syst, Gen Tel & Electronics Corp, 62-63, sr eng specialist, 63-66; INDEPENDENT CONSULT, 66- *Concurrent Pos:* Res asst, Stanford Univ, 56-58; lectr, Prof State-of-the-Arts Prog, Northeastern Univ, 70- *Mem:* Inst Elec & Electronics Engrs; Sigma Xi. *Res:* Adaptive systems; statistical pattern recognition; signal detection; information theory; communications systems; transistor circuitry and computers; pattern recognition applications; robotics; applied statistical techniques; design of experiments. *Mailing Add:* 2 Forest St Cambridge MA 02140

COOPER, PETER B(RUCE), b Manchester, Conn, Mar 30, 36; m 60; c 2. CIVIL & STRUCTURAL ENGINEERING. *Educ:* Lehigh Univ, BS, 57, MS, 60, PhD(civil eng), 65. *Prof Exp:* Engr, Elec Boat Div, Gen Dynamics Corp, Conn, 57-58; res asst indust testing, Lehigh Univ, 58-60, res instr civil eng, 60-65, res asst prof, 65-66; from asst prof to assoc prof, 66-76, PROF CIVIL ENG, KANS STATE UNIV, 76- *Mem:* Am Soc Civil Engrs; Nat Soc Prof Engrs; Am Soc Eng Educ. *Res:* Experimental and analytical research on the behavior and load-carrying capacity of steel structures, particularly welded plate girders. *Mailing Add:* Dept of Civil Eng Kans State Univ Manhattan KS 66506

COOPER, PHILIP HARLAN, b Charleston, WVa, Feb 20, 35; m 58; c 3. RADIATION BIOLOGY, RADIOLGOICAL PHYSICS. *Educ:* Vanderbilt Univ, BA, 59; Univ Rochester, MS, 60, PhD(radiation hemat), 66. *Prof Exp:* USAEC fel, Pac Northwest Labs, Battelle Mem Inst, 66-68; RES PHYSICIST, VET ADMIN HOSP, 68-, ASST CHIEF, 74-; RES INSTR EXP BIOL, COL MED, BAYLOR UNIV, 68- *Mem:* Am Asn Physicists in Med; Soc Nuclear Med. *Res:* Quantitative scintiscanning of isotopes used in nuclear medicine; hematopoietic cell proliferation following acute X-irradiation of dogs and chronic strontium-90 ingestion in swine. *Mailing Add:* Vet Admin Hosp 2002 Holcombe Blvd Houston TX 77211

COOPER, R(OBERT) S(HANKLIN), b Kansas City, Mo, Feb 8, 32; m 56; c 2. ELECTRICAL ENGINEERING. *Educ:* Univ Iowa, BSEE, 54; Ohio State Univ, MSEE, 58; Mass Inst Technol, ScD(elec eng), 63. *Prof Exp:* From instr to asst prof elec eng, Mass Inst Technol, 59-72; asst dir defense res & eng, Dept Defense, 72-75; dep dir, NASA/Goddard Space Flight Ctr, 75-76, dir, 76-80; MEM TECH STAFF, BELL TEL LABS, INC, 80- *Concurrent Pos:* Ford Found fel, 63-65; consult, Lincoln Labs, Mass Inst Technol, 64-66, mem staff, 66-70, group leader, 70-72; mem bd gov, Nat Space Club, 76-; mem bd adv, Electronic & Aerospace Systs Conf, 77- *Mem:* Am Inst Aeronaut & Astronaut; Am Astronaut Soc; Inst Elec & Electronics Engrs. *Res:* Plasma physics; magnetohydrodynamics; systems engineering; electrical network synthesis; laser physics and systems. *Mailing Add:* Bell Tel Labs Inc Indian Hill Naperville Rd Naperville IL 60540

COOPER, RALPH SHERMAN, b Newark, NJ, June 25, 31; m 56; c 2. THEORETICAL PHYSICS. *Educ:* Cooper Union, BChE, 53; Univ Ill, MS, 55, PhD(physics), 57. *Prof Exp:* Mem staff theoret physics, Los Alamos Sci Lab, Univ Calif, 57-65; chief scientist, Nuclear Lab, Donald W Douglas Labs, Douglas Aircraft Co, 65-69; staff mem, Los Alamos Sci Lab, Univ Calif, 69-70, alt group leader, 70-71, group leader 71-72, asst laser div leader, 72-75; dep dir, Radiation Physics Div, 75-80, DEP DIR, RES & DEVELOP DIV, PHYSICS INT CO, 81- *Concurrent Pos:* Consult, Inst Defense Anal, Washington, DC, 62-65; consult, Douglas Aircraft Co, Calif, 63- *Mem:* Am Phys Soc; Am Nuclear Soc; Sigma Xi. *Res:* Magnetic fusion, laser fusion and laser isotope enrichment; solid state physics; reactor physics; nuclear rocket propulsion; mission analysis; radiation effects; ion exchange column theory; integrated circuit fabrication. *Mailing Add:* Physics Int Co 2700 Merced St San Leandro CA 94577

COOPER, RAYMOND DAVID, b Kansas City, Kans, Dec 13, 27; m 54; c 3. ENERGY, ENVIRONMENT. *Educ:* Univ Ill, BS, 51; Iowa State Col, MS, 54; Mass Inst Technol, PhD, 67. *Prof Exp:* Asst physics, Ames Lab, AEC, 53-54; nuclear physicist, Pioneering Res Div, Quartermaster Res & Eng Ctr, 54-62; chief linear accelerator sect, US Army Natick Labs, 62-70; radiation physicist, USAEC, 70-74; physicist, US Energy Res & Develop Admin, 74-75; asst dir integrated assessment, 75-78; CONSULT, ENERGY & ENVIRON POLICY, 78-; RES PROF POLICY SCI, UNIV MD, BALTIMORE COUNTY, 79-81. *Concurrent Pos:* Lectr, Tufts Univ, 56-61. *Mem:* AAAS; Sigma Xi. *Res:* Physical mechanisms in radiation biology; dosimetry; accelerators; radiation interactions; energy and environmental systems analysis; risk analysis. *Mailing Add:* Energy & Environ Policy 12728 Middlevale Lane Wheaton MD 20906

COOPER, REGINALD RUDYARD, b Elkins, WVa, Jan 6, 32; m 54; c 4. ORTHOPEDIC SURGERY. *Educ:* Univ WVa, BA, 52, BS, 53; Med Col Va, MD, 55; Univ Iowa, MS, 60. *Prof Exp:* Resident surg, 56-57, resident orthop, 57-60, assoc, 62-65, from asst prof to assoc prof orthop surg, 65-71, PROF ORTHOP SURG, UNIV IOWA, 71-, CHMN DEPT ORTHOP, 73- *Concurrent Pos:* Res fel orthop surg & anat, Johns Hopkins Hosp, 64-65; Am, Brit & Can Orthop Asns exchange fel, 69. *Honors & Awards:* Outstanding Orthop Res Award, Kappa Delta, 71. *Mem:* AMA; fel Am Col Surg; Am Acad Orthop Surg; Orthop Res Soc; Am Asn Mil Surg. *Res:* Electron microscopy of bone and skeletal muscle as related to disuse atrophy and regeneration. *Mailing Add:* Dept of Orthop Surg Univ of Iowa Iowa City IA 52240

COOPER, RICHARD ARTHUR, marine biology, fisheries biology, see previous edition

COOPER, RICHARD GRANT, b New York, NY, Mar 8, 34. PHARMACOLOGY, PHYSIOLOGY. *Educ:* Univ Ky, BS, 56, MS, 60; Univ Tex, PhD(physiol), 64; Col Osteop Med & Surg, DO, 76. *Prof Exp:* From instr to asst prof physiol & agr chem, Univ Mo, 64-71, res assoc space sci res ctr, 65-71; assoc prof physiol, Col Osteop Med & Surg, 72-75; ASSOC PROF CLIN SCI, OKLA COL OSTEOP MED & 77- *Concurrent Pos:* Res assoc, Mo Regional Med Program, 67-68; mem coun thrombosis, Am Heart Asn. *Mem:* AAAS. *Res:* Mammalian physiology; blood coagulation and fibrinolysis; hemorrhagic diseases; hemodynamics; depressed metabolism. *Mailing Add:* 7424 E 53rd Pl Tulsa OK 74145

COOPER, RICHARD KENT, b Detroit, Mich, Apr 13, 37; m 57; c 2. ELECTROMAGNETICS, THEORETICAL PHYSICS. *Educ:* Calif Inst Technol, BS, 58, MS, 59; Univ Ariz, MS, 62, PhD(physics), 64. *Prof Exp:* Fulbright Scholar, Niels Bohr Inst, 64; prof physics & chmn dept, Calif State Univ, Hayward, 65-78; alt group leader, Storage Ring Technol Group, 76-82, GROUP LEADER, ACCELERATOR THEORY AND SIMULATION GROUP,LOS ALAMOS NAT LAB, 82- *Concurrent Pos:* Vis staff mem, Los Alamos Sci Lab, Univ Calif, 73-74, consult, 75-76; physicist, Lawrence Livermore Lab, Univ Calif, 74-75, consult, 75-76. *Mem:* Sigma Xi. *Res:* Electromagnetic phenomena in charged particle beams; accelerator theory. *Mailing Add:* 2137A 43rd St Los Alamos NM 87544

COOPER, RICHARD LEE, b Rensselear, Ind, Feb 28, 32; m 52; c 4. PLANT BREEDING, PLANT GENETICS. *Educ:* Purdue Univ, BS, 57; Mich State Univ, MS, 58, PhD(plant breeding & genetics), 62. *Prof Exp:* Res assoc soybean breeding & genetics, Dept Agron & Plant Genetics, Univ Minn, 61-67; assoc prof agron, Univ Ill, Urbana-Champaign, 69-73, res leader, US Regional Soybean Lab, 67-76, prof plant breeding, 77; RES LEADER, OHIO AGR RES & DEVELOP CTR, US DEPT AGR SOYBEAN INVEST, WOOSTER, 77-; PROF PLANT BREEDING, OHIO STATE UNIV, COLUMBUS, 77- *Honors & Awards:* Soybean Res Recognition Award, Am Soybean Asn, 81. *Mem:* Am Soc Agron; Crop Sci Soc Am. *Res:* Soybean breeding, genetics and cultural practices. *Mailing Add:* Ohio Agr Res & Develop Ctr Wooster OH 44691

COOPER, ROBERT ARTHUR, JR, b St Paul, Minn, Aug 27, 32; m 59; c 3. MEDICINE, ONCOLOGY. *Educ:* Univ Pa, AB, 54; Jefferson Med Col, MD, 58; Am Bd Path, cert path anat, 63. *Prof Exp:* From instr to prof path, Med Sch, Univ Ore, 62-69; from assoc prof to prof, 69-72, assoc dean curricular affairs, 69-73, head, Div Surg Path, 72-75, PROF ONCOL IN PATH & DIR, CANCER CTR, SCH MED, UNIV ROCHESTER, 74- *Concurrent Pos:* Am Cancer Soc fel, 60-61; teaching fel path, Harvard Med Sch, 62-63; Cancer Res Ctr grant, 75-; mem treatment comt, Breast Cancer Task Force, Nat Cancer Inst, 74-77, mem, Cancer Ctr Support Grant Rec Comt, 78-, chmn, 81-; mem jury, Albert & Mary Lasker Found Awards, 77; mem bd trustees, Janes P Williot Found, 81- *Mem:* Int Acad Path; AAAS; Am Soc Cancer Educ; Sigma Xi. *Res:* Experimental radiation pathology and toxicology; radiation carcinogenesis. *Mailing Add:* Cancer Ctr Univ of Rochester Box 704 Rochester NY 14642

COOPER, ROBERT CHAUNCEY, b San Francisco, Calif, July 4, 28; m 56; c 4. MICROBIOLOGY, PUBLIC HEALTH. *Educ:* Univ Calif, Berkeley, BS, 52; Mich State Univ, MS, 53, PhD(microbiol), 58. *Prof Exp:* from asst prof to assoc prof pub health, Sch Pub Health, 58-74, PROF, ENVIRON HEALTH SERV & DIR, SANIT ENG & ENVIRON HEALTH RES LAB, UNIV CALIF, BERKELEY, 80- *Mem:* AAAS; Am Soc Microbiol; Water Pollution Control Fedn; Int Asn Water Pollution Res. *Res:* Microbiological aspects of water quality; water quality and human health. *Mailing Add:* Sch Pub Health Univ Calif Berkeley CA 94720

COOPER, ROBERT MICHAEL, b Oakland, Calif, Oct 21, 39. PHARMACY. *Educ:* Univ Calif, San Francisco, PharmD. *Prof Exp:* Mem staff pharmaceut develop serv, Clin Ctr, NIH, 64-66; clin pharmacist, Long Beach Mem Hosp, Calif, 66; mem staff dose formulation unit, Cancer Chemother Serv Ctr, Nat Cancer Inst, 66-67; asst prof pharm, 67-71, actg chmn dept, 71-72, asst dean, 72-77, chmn, Dept Pharm, 78-82, ASSOC PROF PHARM, SCH PHARM, STATE UNIV NY BUFFALO, 71-, ASST DEAN, 81- *Mem:* Am Pharmaceut Asn; Am Soc Hosp Pharmacists. *Res:* Clinical pharmacy; sterile manufacturing. *Mailing Add:* Rm 373 Cooke Hall State Univ of NY Sch of Pharm Amherst NY 14260

COOPER, ROBERT WOODROW, b Scotia, Calif, Dec 9, 38; m 60, 75; c 5. PRIMATE BIOLOGY. *Educ:* Univ Calif, Davis, BS, 60, DVM, 62. *Prof Exp:* Assoc res biologist & dir primate res colony, Inst Comp Biol, Zool Soc San Diego, 62-71; wildlife biologist, Inst de Desarrollo de los Recursos Naturales Renovables, Repub Colombia, Smithsonian-Peace Corps Environ Prog, 71-73; ASSOC PROF ZOOL, SAN DIEGO STATE UNIV, 73- *Concurrent Pos:* Mem, Subcomt Primate Stand, Inst Lab Animal Resources, Div Biol & Agr, Nat Acad Sci-Nat Res Coun, 64-67. *Mem:* AAAS; Am Asn Lab Animal Sci; Int Primatological Soc; Am Soc Primatologists; Int Primate Protection League. *Res:* Comparative biology of small primate species, especially reproduction, social behavior, and stress imposed by conditions of captivity. *Mailing Add:* Dept of Zool San Diego State Univ San Diego CA 92182

COOPER, ROBIN D G, b Eastbourne, Eng, Sept 26, 38; m 70. ORGANIC CHEMISTRY. *Educ:* Univ London, BSc, 59, PhD(org chem), 62, DIC, 60; FRIC. *Prof Exp:* Glaxo res fel org chem, Imp Col, Univ London, 62-63; Nat Acad Sci vis res assoc, US Army Natick Labs, 63-65; sr res chemist, 65-70, res scientist, 70-75, RES ASSOC, ELI LILLY & CO, 75- *Mem:* Am Chem Soc; fel Royal Soc Chem. *Res:* Structural determination and synthesis of antibiotics, especially penicillin and cephalosporins; author of numerous publications. *Mailing Add:* 6740 Dover Rd Indianapolis IN 46220

COOPER, RONDA FERN, b Schenectady, NY, June 20, 43. MEDICAL MICROBIOLOGY. *Educ:* Okla State Univ, BS, 64; Kans State Univ, MS, 66, PhD(microbiol), 71. *Prof Exp:* Res assoc & instr path, Kans State Univ, 67-73; asst prof biol, Univ NMex, 73-74; asst prof microbiol, La State Univ, Baton Rouge, 74-77; asst prof, 78-80, ASSOC PROF MICROBIOL, NEW ENG COL OSTEOP MED, 80- *Concurrent Pos:* Lalor Found fel, 75- *Mem:* Am Soc Microbiol; Conf Pub Health Lab Dirs. *Res:* Interaction of microbial toxins with host tissues and other aspects of host-parasite relationships. *Mailing Add:* Dept Microbiol 11 Hills Beach Rd Biddeford ME 04005

COOPER, STEPHEN, b Brooklyn, NY, Aug 6, 37; m 60; c 2. MICROBIOLOGY, GENETICS. *Educ:* Union Col, NY, BA, 59; Rockefeller Inst, PhD(microbiol), 63. *Prof Exp:* NSF res fels, Univ Inst Microbiol, Copenhagen Univ, 63-64 & Med Res Coun Microbial Genetics Res Unit, Univ London, 64-65; res assoc biol chem, Med Sch, Tufts Univ, 65-66; asst res prof pediat, State Univ NY, Buffalo, 66-70, asst res prof biochem, 67-70, lectr biol, 69-70; assoc prof, 70-78, PROF MICROBIOL, SCH MED, UNIV MICH, 78- *Concurrent Pos:* Fogarty Int fel, Imp Cancer Res Fund, London, 76. *Mem:* AAAS; Am Soc Microbiol. *Res:* Biochemistry and genetics of viruses; protein synthesis; control of DNA replication and cell division in bacteria; microbial genetics; development of dictyostelium. *Mailing Add:* Dept of Microbiol Sch of Med Univ of Mich Ann Arbor MI 48109

COOPER, STEPHEN ALLEN, b Philadelphia, Pa, Apr 11, 46; m 71; c 2. ANALGESIOLOGY, ANXIETY AND PAIN CONTROL. *Educ:* Adelphi Univ, BS, 68; Univ Pa, DMD, 71; Georgetown Univ, PhD(pharmacol), 75. *Prof Exp:* Asst prof pharmacol, Georgetown Univ, 75-78; ASSOC DEAN RES, DENT SCH, UNIV MED & DENT, NJ, 78- *Concurrent Pos:* Vis prof, Georgetown Univ, 78-; consult, Hosp Ctr Orange, East Orange, NJ, 80- & United Hosps, Newark, 81- *Mem:* Am Soc Clin Pharmacol; Am Pain Soc; Am Asn Dent Res; NY Acad Sci. *Res:* Clinical evaluation of analgesic drugs; clinical evaluation of drugs used for intravenous sedation; new therapeutic approaches to treating peridontal diseases. *Mailing Add:* Dent Sch Univ Med & Dent 100 Bergen St Newark NJ 07103

COOPER, STUART L, b New York, NY, Aug 28, 41; m 65; c 2. BIOMATERIALS. *Educ:* Mass Inst Technol, BS, 63; Princeton Univ, MA, 65, PhD(chem eng), 67. *Prof Exp:* From asst prof to assoc prof, 67-74, PROF CHEM ENG, UNIV WIS-MADISON, 74- *Concurrent Pos:* Vis assoc prof, Univ Calif, Berkeley, 74; bd trustees, Argonne Univ Asn, 75-81; vis prof, Technion, Israel, 77. *Mem:* Am Chem Soc; fel Am Phys Soc; Am Inst Chem Engrs; Soc Plastic Engrs; Am Soc Artificial Internal Organs. *Res:* Structure-property relations of polymers including polyurethanes, ionomers and related block polymer systems; application of light and x-ray scattering, rheo-optical and thermal methods in polymer characterization; studies of protein and thrombus deposition on polymers used in biomedical applications. *Mailing Add:* Dept Chem Eng Univ Wis-Madison 1415 Johnson Dr Madison WI 53706

COOPER, TERENCE ALFRED, b Oxford, Eng, Feb 8, 41; m 66; c 2. POLYMER CHEMISTRY. *Educ:* Oxford Univ, BA, 62, BSc, 64, DPhil(phys org chem) & MA, 66; Drexel Univ, MBA, 73. *Prof Exp:* Res staff chemist, Sterling Chem Lab, Yale Univ, 66-68; res chemist, Elastomers Res Lab, 68-80, RES ASSOC, POLYMER PROD DEPT, EXP STA, E I DU PONT DE NEMOURS & CO, INC, 80- *Mem:* Am Chem Soc; The Chem Soc; Am Inst Chem Engrs. *Res:* Materials science and polymer engineering; colloid chemistry; adhesives, sealant and coating. *Mailing Add:* Polymer Prod Dept Exp Sta E I du Pont de Nemours & Co Inc Wilmington DE 19898

COOPER, THEODORE, b Trenton, NJ, Dec 28, 28; m 56; c 4. PHYSIOLOGY, PHARMACOLOGY. *Educ:* Georgetown Univ, BS, 49; St Louis Univ, MD, 54, PhD(physiol), 56. *Hon Degrees:* DSc, Col Osteopath Med & Surg, 76, Univ NMex & Univ Rochester, 79 & Sch Med, Georgetown Univ, 77 & 81; LHD, Loyola Univ Chicago, 79. *Prof Exp:* Intern, St Louis Univ Hosps, 54-55; sr asst surgeon, Nat Heart Inst, 56-58, asst res cardiovascular surg, 58-59, mem staff clin surg, 59-60; from asst prof to prof surg, St Louis Univ, 60-66, mem bd grad studies, 62-66; prof pharmacol & surg & chmn dept pharmacol, Sch Med, Univ NMex, 66-68; dir, Nat Heart & Lung Inst, 68-74; dep asst secy health, 74-75, asst secy health, HEW, 75-77; dean med col & provost med affairs, Cornell Univ, 77-80; EXEC VPRES, UPJOHN CO, 80- *Concurrent Pos:* mem pharmacol & exp therapeut study sect, USPHS, 64-67; sci adv bd, Leonard Wood Mem, Am Leprosy Found; bd dir, Nat Health Coun, Inc; expert adv panel cardiovasc dis, World Health Orgn; med & sci adv coun, Nat Hemophilia Found; vis fel, Woodrow Wilson Nat Fel Found; bd trustees, Milton Helpern Libr Legal Med; sci adv comt, Gen Motors Corp; tech bd, Milbank Mem Fund; med adv comt, White House Conf on aging, 81. *Honors & Awards:* Harvey W Wiley Medal, Food & Drug Admin, Pub Health Serv, Silver Springs, Md, 76; Tom A Spies Mem Award, Int Acad Preventive Med, 77; Albert Lasker Award, 78; Ellen Browning Scripps Medal, 80. *Mem:* Inst Med-Nat Acad Sci; Am Physiol Soc; Am Col Cardiol; Am Col Chest Physicians; Am Fedn Clin Res. *Res:* Experimental and clinical cardiovascular physiology and pharmacology. *Mailing Add:* Exec VPres UpJohn Co Kalamazoo MI 49001

COOPER, THOMAS D(AVID), b Dayton, Ohio, Apr 7, 32; m 53; c 3. PHYSICAL METALLURGY. *Educ:* Univ Cincinnati, MetE, 55; Ohio State Univ, MS, 64. *Prof Exp:* Metall engr, Westinghouse Elec Corp, 55-56; proj engr light metals, 56-59, proj engr high temperature metals, 59-60, tech mgr, 60-64, high strength metals, 64-66, chief, Processing & Nondestructive Testing Br, 66-72, chief, Nondestructive Testing & Mech Br, 72-73, chief, Aeronaut Systs Br, 73-77, CHIEF MAT INTEGRITY BR, US AIR FORCE MAT LAB, 77- *Mem:* Fel Am Soc Metals; assoc fel Am Inst Aeronaut & Astronaut; Am Inst Mining, Metall & Petrol Engrs; Sigma Xi; Am Soc Nondestructive Testing. *Res:* Promoting optimum applications of materials during development of aeronautical systems; operational organizations, including failure analysis, corrosion control, NDE, and materials property data generation. *Mailing Add:* Mats Lab Air Force Wright Aeronaut Labs/MLSA Wright-Patterson AFB OH 45433

COOPER, THOMAS EDWARD, b Lindsay, Calif, May 31, 43; m 68; c 1. MECHANICAL ENGINEERING, BIOENGINEERING. *Educ:* Univ Calif, Berkeley, BS, 66, MS, 67, PhD(mech eng), 70. *Prof Exp:* Actg asst prof mech eng, Univ Calif, Berkeley, 70; asst prof, 70-76, ASSOC PROF MECH ENG, NAVAL POSTGRAD SCH, 76- *Concurrent Pos:* Consult, Lawrence Radiation Lab, 70- *Res:* Thermal modeling of heat transfer processes occurring in tissue surrounding cryosurgical and radio-frequency probes; biological thermal property determinations. *Mailing Add:* Dept of Mech Eng Code 59Cg Naval Postgrad Sch Monterey CA 93940

COOPER, TOMMYE, b Bandana, Ky, May 17, 38; m 61; c 1. AGRICULTURE, STATISTICS. *Educ:* Murray State Univ, BS, 60; Univ Ky, MS, 62, PhD(dairy sci, statist), 66. *Prof Exp:* Anal statistician, 66-67, chief methods & opers unit, Comput Lab, 67-68, actg dir, Data Systs Appln Div, 68-70, dir, 70-73, DIR, FT COLLINS COMPUT CTR, US DEPT AGR, 73- *Mem:* Am Dairy Sci Asn; Am Soc Animal Sci; Am Asn Comput Mach. *Res:* Dairy cattle reproductive and genetic research using digital computer and statistical techniques to achieve these goals. *Mailing Add:* Ft Collins Comput Ctr 3825 E Mulberry St Ft Collins CO 80524

COOPER, W(ILLIAM) E(UGENE), b Erie, Pa, Jan 11, 24; m 46; c 5. PRESSURE VESSELS, NUCLEAR SYSTEMS. *Educ:* Ore State Col, BS, 47, MS, 48; Purdue Univ, PhD(eng mech), 51. *Prof Exp:* Instr eng mech, Purdue Univ, 48-52; consult engr, Knolls Atomic Power Lab, Gen Elec Co, 52-63; eng mgr, Lessells & Assocs, Inc, 63-68; sr vpres & tech dir, Teledyne Mat Res Co, 68-76; CONSULT ENGR, TELEDYNE ENG SERV, 76- *Concurrent Pos:* William M Murray lectr, Soc Exp Stress Anal, 77. *Honors & Awards:* B F Langer Nuclear Codes & Standards Award, Am Soc Mech Engrs, 78. *Mem:* Am Soc Mech Engrs; Soc Exp Stress Anal. *Res:* Structural analysis and evaluation; application of material properties to design; pressure vessel and pressure piping codes and standards. *Mailing Add:* Teledyne Eng Serv 130 Second Ave Waltham MA 02254

COOPER, WALTER, b Clairton, Pa, July 18, 28; m 53; c 2. PHYSICAL CHEMISTRY. *Educ:* Washington & Jefferson Col, BA, 50; Univ Rochester, PhD(phys chem), 57. *Prof Exp:* From res chemist to sr res chemist, 56-66, RES ASSOC, EASTMAN KODAK CO, 66- *Mem:* AAAS; Am Chem Soc; Am Phys Soc. *Res:* Gas-phase kinetics; photographic theory; solid state chemistry of silver halides; luminescence properties of dyes. *Mailing Add:* 68 Skyview Lane Rochester NY 14625

COOPER, WILLIAM ANDERSON, b Archer City, Tex, Feb 4, 27; m 52; c 4. ZOOLOGY, PHYSIOLOGY. *Educ:* NTex State Univ, BS, 48, MS, 50; Tex A&M Univ, PhD(zool), 57. *Prof Exp:* Instr natural sci, Paris Jr Col, 53-54; asst biol, Tex A&M Univ, 54-55, instr, 55-57; assoc prof, 57-65, PROF BIOL, WTEX STATE UNIV, 65- *Concurrent Pos:* Res assoc, Agr & Mech Res Found, NIH, 55-57; consult water qual control, Can River Munic Water Authority, Nat Parks Serv, Ecology Audits, Inc, Landlocked Fisheries, Inc & Tex Parks & Wildlife, 71-74. *Mem:* Am Micros Soc; Am Soc Zoologists; Sigma Xi. *Res:* Effects of vitamin deficiencies on embryo development in white rats; limnology; water quality and fisheries biology research. *Mailing Add:* Dept of Biol WTex State Univ Canyon TX 79016

COOPER, WILLIAM CECIL, b Salisbury, Md, Apr 6, 09; m 32; c 2. PLANT PHYSIOLOGY. *Educ:* Univ Md, BS, 29; Calif Inst Technol, MS, 36, PhD, 38. *Prof Exp:* Jr pomologist, Bur Plant Indust, 29-38, assoc plant physiologist, Subtrop Fruit Prod, 38-42, plant physiologist, Trop Tree Crops Propagation, Office For Agr Relations, 43-44, citrus rootstock invest, Bur Plant Indust, 44-54, sr plant physiologist, Hort Crops Br, 55-59, leader citrus invests, Plant Sci Res Div, 59-77, COLLABR, SCI & EDUC ADMIN-AGR RES, USDA, 77- *Mem:* Am Soc Plant Physiol; Am Soc Hort Sci. *Res:* Plant hormones and root and flower formation; salt tolerance; cold hardiness; citrus rootstocks and citrus pheonology; fruit abscission; ethylene physiology. *Mailing Add:* 443 Lakewood Dr Winter Park FL 32789

COOPER, WILLIAM CLARK, b Manila, Philippines, June 22, 12; m 37; c 4. MEDICINE. *Educ:* Univ Va, MD, 34; Harvard Univ, MPH, 58; Am Bd Internal Med, Am Bd Prev Med & Am Bd Indust Hyg, dipl. *Prof Exp:* Intern & asst resident, Univ Hosp, Cleveland, 34-37; instr bact, Sch Hyg & Pub Health, Johns Hopkins Univ, 40; from asst surgeon to surgeon, NIH, 41-51, chief & med dir occup health field hqs, 52-57, chief epidemiol serv, Occup Health Prog, Bur State Serv, 57-61, dep chief, 61-62, chief div occup health, USPHS, 62-63; res physician, Sch Pub Health, Univ Calif, Berkeley, 63-65, prof in residence occup health, 65-72; vpres, Equitable Environ Health, Inc, 73-77; CONSULT OCCUP HEALTH, 78- *Concurrent Pos:* Med consult, AEC, 64-72. *Mem:* Fel AAAS; fel Am Col Chest Physicians; fel Am Acad Occup Med; fel Am Acad Indust Hyg; Cosmos Club. *Res:* Nutrition; malaria; occupational health; epidemiology. *Mailing Add:* Suite 401 2150 Shattuck Ave Berkeley CA 94704

COOPER, WILLIAM E, b Orono, Maine, May 8, 38; m 60; c 1. ZOOLOGY. *Educ:* Mich State Univ, BS, 60; Univ Mich, MS, 62, PhD(zool), 64. *Prof Exp:* Asst prof zool, Univ Mass, 64-65; from asst prof to assoc prof, 65-72, PROF ZOOL, MICH STATE UNIV, 72- *Mem:* Ecol Soc Am; Am Soc Zoologists. *Res:* Population dynamics and regulation of fresh-water invertebrate populations. *Mailing Add:* Dept of Zool Mich State Univ Col Natural Sci East Lansing MI 48824

COOPER, WILLIAM EDWARD, b Akron, Ohio, Aug 26, 42; m 67; c 4. CRYOGENIC ENGINEERING, APPLIED SUPERCONDUCTIVITY. *Educ:* Oberlin Col, BA, 64; Harvard Univ, MA, 66, PhD(physics), 75. *Prof Exp:* Res assoc physics, Univ Mich, 71-73, Univ Pittsburgh, 75-79; PHYSICIST, FERMILAB, 79- *Mem:* Am Phys Soc. *Res:* Measurement of quench and field properties of superconducting magnets; helium liquification and refrigeration; experimental elementary particle physics. *Mailing Add:* Fermilab PO Box 500 Batavia IL 60510

COOPER, WILLIAM GREGORY, medical education, see previous edition

COOPER, WILLIAM S, b Winnipeg, Man, Nov 7, 35; m 64; c 3. INFORMATION SCIENCE. *Educ:* Principia Col, BSc, 56; Mass Inst Technol, MSc, 59; Univ Calif, Berkeley, PhD(logic & methodology), 64. *Prof Exp:* Alexander von Humboldt scholar, Univ Erlangen, 64-65; asst prof info sci, Univ Chicago, 66-70; actg assoc prof info sci & actg dir inst libr res, 70-71, assoc prof, 71-76, PROF INFO SCI, UNIV CALIF, BERKELEY, 76- *Concurrent Pos:* Miller prof, Miller Inst, Berkeley, Calif, 75-76; hon res fel, Univ Col, London, 77-78. *Mem:* AAAS; Asn Symbolic Logic; Am Soc Info Sci; Am Statist Asn; Asn Comput Mach. *Res:* Symbolic logic; descriptive linguistics; foundation of language; information storage and retrieval; theory of indexing; question and answering system; evolutionary theory. *Mailing Add:* Sch Library & Info Studies Univ Calif Berkeley CA 94720

COOPER, WILLIAM WAILES, b Salisbury, Md, June 24, 41; m 63; c 4. CHEMICAL ENGINEERING. *Educ:* Mass Inst Technol, SB, 63, SM, 64, ScD(chem eng), 67. *Prof Exp:* Res engr, 66-71, sr res engr, Cambridge, 71-73, mgr develop biomed prods, 73-75, mgr membrane mfg, 75-80, dir opers, 80-81, VPRES OPERS, ABCOR, INC, WILMINGTON, 81- *Mem:* Am Inst Chem Engrs; Am Chem Soc; Am Soc Artificial Internal Organs; Sigma Xi. *Res:* Biomedical engineering; membrane separation processes; plasma chemistry; ultrafiltration; reverse osmosis. *Mailing Add:* 11 Cedar Creek Rd Sudbury MA 01776

COOPER, WILSON WAYNE, b Checotah, Okla, July 28, 42; m 63; c 3. INDUSTRIAL CHEMISTRY, CHEMICAL ENGINEERING. *Educ:* Northeastern State Col, BS, 64; Univ Ark, Fayetteville, MS, 67, PhD(chem), 69. *Prof Exp:* Instr chem, Northwestern State Col, 66-67 & 69-70; res chem engr, 70-78, SR RES ENGR, PILOT PLANT CTR, US BORAX RES CORP, 78- *Mem:* Am Chem Soc. *Res:* Process development for both organic and inorganic systems and analytical techniques to support these studies. *Mailing Add:* US Borax Res Corp Pilot Plant Ctr Boron CA 93516

COOPER-DRIVER, GILLIAN AGNES, biology, chemistry, see previous edition

COOPERMAN, BARRY S, b New York, NY, Dec 11, 41; m 63; c 1. PHYSICAL ORGANIC CHEMISTRY, BIOCHEMISTRY. *Educ:* Columbia Univ, BA, 62; Harvard Univ, PhD(chem), 68. *Prof Exp:* NATO fel biochem, Pasteur Inst, 67-68; from asst prof to assoc prof, 68-77, PROF BIOORG CHEM, UNIV PA, 77- *Mem:* Am Soc Biol Chemists; Am Chem Soc. *Res:* Mechanism of phosphoryl transfer enxymes; photoaffinity labels for ribosome and adenylic acid receptor sites. *Mailing Add:* Dept of Chem 358 Chem Univ of Pa Philadelphia PA 19104

COOPERMAN, EDWARD LEE, b Sept 4, 36; US citizen; m 63; c 2. NUCLEAR PHYSICS. *Educ:* Lehigh Univ, BS, 58; Pa State Univ, PhD(physics), 63. *Prof Exp:* Asst prof physics, Ariz State Univ, 63-64; physicist, Los Alamos Sci Lab, 64; res physicist, Nat Res Ctr, Univ Strasbourg, 64-67; from asst prof to assoc prof, 67-74, actg chmn dept, 69-71, chmn dept, 74-78, PROF PHYSICS, CALIF STATE UNIV, FULLERTON, 74- *Res:* Fission process, especially U-235 and Cf-252; angular correlations and distributions of medium nuclei with the help of the Litherland method. *Mailing Add:* Dept of Physics Calif State Univ 800 N State College Blvd Fullerton CA 92631

COOPERMAN, JACK M, b New York, NY, Jan 13, 21; m 49; c 1. NUTRITIONAL BIOCHEMISTRY. *Educ:* City Col New York, BS, 41; Univ Wis, MS, 43, PhD(biochem), 45. *Prof Exp:* Sr res biochemist, Hoffman-La Roche Inc, 46-56; from asst prof to assoc prof, 57-71, PROF PEDIAT, NY MED COL, 71-, PROF COMMUNITY & PREV MED, 75-, DIR NUTRIT EDUC, 78- *Concurrent Pos:* Nat Found Infantile Paralysis fel, Univ Wis, 45-46; mem med adv bd, Cooley's Anemia & Res Found Children, Inc; staff mem, Off Sci Res & Develop; dir nutrit biochem, Touro Col, 76-81; vis prof, All India Inst Med Sci, New Delhi, 78. *Mem:* Fel AAAS; Am Chem Soc; Geront Soc; Soc Exp Biol & Med; fel NY Acad Sci. *Res:* Nutrition of hamster; nutrition of monkey; relation of nutrition of prevention of infectious diseases; microbiological vitamin assays; vitamins; unknown growth factors for animals and bacteria; enzymes; amino acids and anemias; vitamin B-twelve, folic acid and riboflavin metabolism; placental transfer; purine and pyrimidine metabolism and synthesis. *Mailing Add:* Dept Community & Prev Med NY Med Col Munger Pavillion Valhalla NY 10595

COOPERMAN, PHILIP, b US, Dec 3, 18; m 50; c 2. MATHEMATICS. *Educ:* City Col New York, 38; NY Univ, MS, 48, PhD(math), 51. *Prof Exp:* Teacher high sch, NY, 38-39; statist clerk, Dept Welfare, New York, 39-41; jr physicist, US Navy, 42-43; physicist, Fed Tel & Radio Corp, 43; physicist ultrasonics, Balco Labs, 46; asst physics, NY Univ, 48-49; physicist, Gaseous Electronics, Res Corp, 51-56; sr mathematician, Gulf Res & Develop Co, 56-58; asst prof math, Univ Pittsburgh, 58-61; assoc prof, 61-63, actg chmn dept, 63-64, PROF MATH, FAIRLEIGH DICKINSON UNIV, 63- *Concurrent Pos:* Dir res & develop, Res-Cottrell, Inc, 60, consult, 60-62; consult appl res labs, US Steel Corp; consult, Precipitair Pollution Control Work, 67- & Mikro Pul Corp, 78-80. *Mem:* Am Phys Soc; Am Math Soc; Air Pollution Control Asn; Math Asn Am. *Res:* Electricity; electronics; corona discharge id gases; calculus of variations; partial differential equations. *Mailing Add:* Dept of Math Fairleigh Dickinson Univ Rutherford NJ 07070

COOPERRIDER, DONALD ELMER, b Thornville, Ohio, Sept 21, 14; m 36. VETERINARY MEDICINE. *Educ:* Ohio State Univ, DVM, 36, MS, 42. *Prof Exp:* Jr veterinarian, USDA, 36-40; veterinarian, Civilian Conserv Corps, 40-41; asst vet parasitol, Ohio State Univ, 41-42; vet diagnostician, State Dept Agr, Ohio, 46; assoc veterinarian vet parasitol, Okla Agr & Mech Col, 46-48; assoc parasitologist, Univ Tenn, 48-49; assoc prof vet parasitol & path, Univ Ga, 49-54; chief diag labs, State Dept Agr, NC, 54-59; parasitologist, 59-68, chief, Bur Diag Labs, Fla Dept Agr, 68-76; VET CONSULT, 76- *Mem:* Am Vet Med Asn; US Animal Health Asn; Poultry Sci Asn; Am Asn Vet Parasitol (secy-treas, 61-69, pres, 71-73); Am Asn Vet Lab Diagnosticians (pres, 71-73). *Res:* Veterinary parasitology. *Mailing Add:* 1100 Diboe Lane SW Sanibel FL 33957

COOPERRIDER, NEIL KENNETH, b Oakland, Calif, Dec 18, 41; c 3. MECHANICAL ENGINEERING. *Educ:* Stanford Univ, BS, 63, MS, 64, PhD(mech eng), 68. *Prof Exp:* Systs engr, Mech Eng Lab, Gen Elec Res & Develop Ctr, 68-70; asst prof mach & struct, Rensselaer Polytech Inst, 70-73; assoc prof, 73-77, PROF MECH ENG, ARIZ STATE UNIV, 77- *Concurrent Pos:* Assoc dir Eng Design Lab, Rensselaer Polytech Inst, 70-73; consult, Rensselaer Res Corp, 70-74; partner, Acorn Assocs, 73-; mem comt ride qual, Transp Res Bd, 76-; guest scientist, German Res & Develop Ctr for Aeronaut & Astronaut, 78-79; res fel, Alexander von Humboldt Found, 78-79. *Mem:* Am Soc Mech Engrs. *Res:* System dynamics; control theory applications, transportation systems; vehicle dynamics; railway vehicles; design methods; problem solving techniques. *Mailing Add:* Dept of Mech Eng Ariz State Univ Tempe AZ 85281

COOPERRIDER, TOM SMITH, b Newark, Ohio, Apr 15, 27; m 53; c 2. PLANT TAXONOMY. *Educ:* Denison Univ, BA, 50; Univ Iowa, MS, 55, PhD(bot), 58. *Prof Exp:* Asst bot, Univ Iowa, 53-57; NSF fel, 57-58; from instr to asst prof biol sci, Kent State Univ, 58-62; asst prof bot, Univ Hawaii, 62-63; from asst prof to assoc prof, 63-69, PROF BIOL SCI, KENT STATE UNIV, 69-, CUR HERBARIUM, 66-, DIR BOT GARDENS & ARBORETUM, 72- *Concurrent Pos:* Consult, US Fish & Wildlife Serv, Dept Interior, 76- & Davey Tree Expert Co, 79- *Mem:* Bot Soc Am; Am Soc Plant Taxon; Int Asn Plant Taxon; AAAS. *Res:* Angiosperm taxonomy; floristics; interspecific hybridization; biosystematics. *Mailing Add:* Dept of Biol Sci Kent State Univ Kent OH 44242

COOPERSMITH, MICHAEL HENRY, b Brooklyn, NY, Aug 11, 36; m 59; c 3. THEORETICAL PHYSICS. *Educ:* Swarthmore Col, BA, 57; Cornell Univ, PhD(physics), 62. *Prof Exp:* NSF fel, Univ Paris, 61-62; res assoc physics, Univ Chicago, 62-64; asst prof, Case Inst Technol, 64-69; ASSOC PROF PHYSICS, UNIV VA, 69- *Res:* Statistical mechanics; phase transitions; homogeneity properties of thermodynamic systems; many-body theory; mobility of ions in helium; irreversible statistical mechanics. *Mailing Add:* Dept of Physics Univ of Va Charlottesville VA 22901

COOPERSTEIN, RAYMOND, b New York, NY, Nov 19, 24; m 52; c 3. INORGANIC CHEMISTRY. *Educ:* City Col New York, BS, 47; Syracuse Univ, MS, 49; Pa State Univ, PhD(inorg chem), 52. *Prof Exp:* Res assoc ceramics, Exp Sta, Sch Mineral Indust, Pa State Univ, 52-53; sr chemist inorg chem, Navy Ord Div, Eastman Kodak Co, 53-57; prin engr, Dept Aircraft Nuclear propulsion, Gen Elec Co, 57-59; sect chief, Beryllium Corp, 59-61; chemist refractory mat, Lawrence Radiation Lab, Univ Calif, Berkeley, 61-65; mgr new prod develop, Wood Ridge Chem Corp, 65; sr engr, Nuclear Reactor Dept, Gen Elec Co, 65-67; sr engr, Douglas United Nuclear, Inc, 67-72; mem staff, JRB Assocs, McLean, Va, 72-75; chem engr, US Nat Res Ctr, 75-80,; ENVIRON SPECIALIST, US DEPT ENERGY, 80- *Mem:* Am Chem Soc; Am Ceramic Soc; Am Soc Testing & Mat. *Res:* Coordination compounds; ferrites; photoconductors; nuclear ceramics; inorganic synthesis; silicate and molten salt chemistry; nuclear facility licensing; radioactive waste management. *Mailing Add:* 10935 Deborah Dr Potomac MD 20854

COOPERSTEIN, SHERWIN JEROME, b New York, NY, Sept 14, 23; m 47; c 2. ANATOMY, CELL PHYSIOLOGY. *Educ:* City Col New York, BS, 43; NY Univ, DDS, 48; Western Reserve Univ, PhD(anat), 51. *Prof Exp:* Instr biol, City Col New York, 43 & 46-48; instr anat, Western Reserve Univ, 48-49, sr instr, 51-52, from asst prof to assoc prof, 52-64, asst dean, 57-64; prof, Sch Dent Med, 64-65, PROF ANAT & HEAD DEPT, SCHS MED & DENT MED, UNIV CONN HEALTH CTR, 64-, HEAD DEPT, 65- *Concurrent Pos:* Res assoc physiol, Col Dent, NY Univ, 46-48; mem adv panel med student res, NSF, 60-61; mem anat sci training comt, Nat Inst Gen Med Sci, 66-70; mem spec study sect diabetes ctrs, Nat Inst Arthritis, Metab & Digestive Dis, 73-75; mem adv panel res personnel needs in basic biomed sci, Nat Acad Sci-Nat Res Coun, 76- *Mem:* AAAS; Am Diabetes Asn; Am Chem Soc; Am Asn Anat; Am Soc Biol Chem. *Res:* Metabolism of the islets of Langerhans; insulin secretion; mechanism of the diabetogenic action of alloxan. *Mailing Add:* Dept of Anat Univ of Conn Sch of Med Farmington CT 06032

COOPERSTOCK, FRED ISAAC, b Winnipeg, Man, Aug 20, 40; m 62; c 2. THEORETICAL PHYSICS. *Educ:* Univ Man, BSc, 62; Brown Univ, PhD(physics), 66. *Prof Exp:* Res scholar theoret physics, Dublin Inst Adv Studies, 66-67; from asst prof to assoc prof, 71-78, PROF PHYSICS, UNIV VICTORIA, 78- *Concurrent Pos:* Can-France sci exchange visitor, Inst Henri Poincare, Paris, 73-74 & 80-81. *Mem:* Am Phys Soc; Int Comt Gen Relativity & Gravitation. *Res:* General relativity; gravitational waves; relativistic astrophysics and cosmology; two-body problem; static and stationary solutions of Einstein-Maxwell equations. *Mailing Add:* Dept Physics Univ Victoria Victoria BC V8W 2Y2 Can

COOR, THOMAS, b Houston, Tex, Nov 21, 22; c 2. APPLIED PHYSICS, INSTRUMENTATION. *Educ:* Rice Univ, BA, 43; Princeton Univ, PhD(physics), 48. *Prof Exp:* Res physicist, Brookhaven Nat Lab, 50-53; sr res assoc plasma physics, Princeton Univ, 53-64; chief scientist & founder, Princeton Appl Res Corp, 62-80; PRES & FOUND, BIOTECH INT, INC, 81- *Concurrent Pos:* Sci secy, UN, 57-58. *Mem:* Am Phys Soc. *Res:* Instrumentation physics. *Mailing Add:* 60 Pheasant Hill Rd Princeton NJ 08540

COORTS, GERALD DUANE, b Emden, Ill, Feb 3, 32; m 57; c 3. FLORICULTURE, GREENHOUSE MANAGEMENT. *Educ:* Univ Mo, BS, 54, MS, 58; Univ Ill, PhD(hort), 64. *Prof Exp:* Asst prof hort, Univ RI, 64-68; assoc prof, 68-72, PROF PLANT & SOIL SCI, SOUTHERN ILL UNIV, CARBONDALE, 72-, CHMN DEPT, 73- *Concurrent Pos:* Floriculture mkt specialist, 59-61; consult horticulture therapy, 78- *Mem:* Am Hort Soc; Am Soc Hort Sci; Int Plant Propagators Soc; Am Inst Biol Sci; Am Soc Agron. *Res:* Plant growth regulators; growing ornamental plants in artificial media; grades and standards on cut roses; post-harvest physiology of roses; mineral nutrition of ornamental crops. *Mailing Add:* Dept of Plant & Soil Sci Southern Ill Univ Carbondale IL 62901

COOTE, DENIS RICHARD, Can citizen. SOIL DEGRADATION, AGRICULTURE. *Educ:* WScotland Agr Col, N Dip Agr Engr, 65; Cornell Univ, MS, 69, PhD(soils), 73. *Prof Exp:* Teacher agr eng, Jamaica Sch Agr, 65-66; engr soil & water conserv, Ministry Agr & Fisheries, Jamaica, 69-70; contract scientist agr & water qual, Great Lakes Studies, 73-77; PHYS SCIENTIST LAND & ENVIRON DEGRADATION, LAND RESOURCE RES INST, AGR CAN, 77- *Mem:* Can Soc Soil Sci; Can Soc Agr Eng; Soil Sci Soc Am; Int Soc Soil Sci. *Res:* Soil degradation and associated environmental impacts. *Mailing Add:* K W Neatby Bldg Land Resource Res Inst Agr Can Ottawa ON K1A 0C6 Can

COOTS, ALONZO FREEMAN, b Little Rock, Ark, May 6, 27; m 47. PHYSICAL CHEMISTRY. *Educ:* Vanderbilt Univ, BE, 49, PhD(chem), 54. *Prof Exp:* Instr phys chem, Fisk Univ, 52-53; res chemist, Anal Sta, Del, 56-58; ASSOC PROF CHEM, NC STATE UNIV, 58- *Mem:* Am Chem Soc. *Res:* Radioisotope principles and techniques; general and physical chemistry; radiochemistry. *Mailing Add:* Dept of Chem NC State Univ Raleigh NC 27607

COOTS, ROBERT HERMAN, b Kansas City, Mo, Feb 24, 28; m 57; c 1. BIOCHEMISTRY. *Educ:* Univ Mo, BS, 54; Univ Wis, MS, 56, PhD(biochem), 58. *Prof Exp:* Res biochemist, Procter & Gamble Co, 58-65, head physiol chem sect, 65-67, dent res sect, Miami Valley Labs, 67-69, dent & toxicol res sect, 69-70 & pharmacol & metab res sect, 70-71, ASSOC DIR RES & DEVELOP DEPT, MIAMI VALLEY LABS, PROCTER & GAMBLE CO, 71- *Mem:* Am Soc Biol Chem; Sigma Xi; Am Col Toxicol. *Res:* Intermediary metabolism; lipid metabolism; pharmacology and toxicology. *Mailing Add:* PO Box 39175 Cincinnati OH 45247

COOVER, HARRY WESLEY, JR, b Newark, Del, Mar 6, 19; m 41; c 3. ORGANOMETALLIC CHEMISTRY, POLYMER CHEMISTRY. *Educ:* Hobart Col, BS, 41; Cornell Univ, MS, 42, PhD, 44. *Prof Exp:* Res chemist, Eastman Kodak Co, 44-49; sr res chemist, Tenn Eastman Co, 49-54, res assoc, 54-63, div head polymers res div, 63-65, dir res, 65-73, vpres, 70-73, exec vpres, Tenn Eastman Co, 73-81, VPRES, EASTMAN KODAK CO, 81- *Honors & Awards:* Southern Chemist Award, Am Chem Soc, 60. *Mem:* Am Chem Soc; Textile Res Inst; Am Asn Textile Technologists; Indust Res Inst; NY Acad Sci. *Res:* Adhesives; insecticides; fungicides; high polymer chemistry; organophosphorus chemistry; synthetic fiber research. *Mailing Add:* PO Box 511 Tenn Eastman Co Kingsport TN 37662

COPE, CHARLES S(AMUEL), b Philadelphia, Pa, Mar 17, 28; m 70. CHEMICAL ENGINEERING. *Educ:* Cornell Univ, BChE, 49; Yale Univ, PhD(chem eng), 56. *Prof Exp:* RES ASSOC, POLYMER PROD DEPT, E I DU PONT DE NEMOURS & CO, 56- *Mem:* Am Inst Chem Engrs; Am Chem Soc; Sigma Xi. *Res:* Synthesis and behavior of fluorocarbon polymers. *Mailing Add:* Polymer Prod Dept E I du Pont de Nemours & Co Wilmington DE 19898

COPE, DAVID FRANKLIN, b Crumpler, WVa, June 28, 12; m 36; c 2. NUCLEAR SCIENCE, ENERGY CONVERSION. *Educ:* WVa Univ, AB, 33, MS, 34; Univ Va, PhD(physics), 52. *Prof Exp:* Instr phsyics, WVa Univ, 35-36; instr math, Agr & Mech Col, Texas, 37-38, physics, 46-47; asst prof, NMex Agr & Mech Col, 47-52; physicist, AEC, 52, chief res br, 53-56, dep dir, Res & Develop Div, Oak Ridge Opers, 56-59, dir, Reactor Div, 59-66, sr site rep reactor develop, 66-74, ENERGY CONSULT, OAK RIDGE NAT LAB, 74-; NUCLEAR ENERGY EXPERT & ENERGY EXPERT, ENERGY RES & DEVELOP OFF, OAK RIDGE 74- *Concurrent Pos:* US team leader, US-Mexico Study of Dual Purpose Nuclear Plants, 68-; chmn tech subcomt NSF Energy Fac Sifting Comn, 74-; spec assignment, Fed Energy Off, Washington, DC, 74; consult, Fed Energy Admin, 76; energy consult, 75- *Mem:* AAAS; Am Nuclear Soc; Am Phys Soc; Sigma Xi. *Res:* Magnetic properties of iron and nickel at high temperatures; analysis of rocket trajectories; nuclear science and technology; evaluation of nuclear energy centers; the nation's future energy requirement and assessmant of various options for meeting these needs; evaluative studies on ethical problems and nuclear energy. *Mailing Add:* 113 Orange Lane Oak Ridge TN 37830

COPE, FREEMAN, b Peekskill, NY, Aug 4, 30; wid. PHYSICAL BIOCHEMISTRY, PHYSIOLOGY. *Educ:* Harvard Col, AB, 51; Johns Hopkins Univ, MD, 55. *Prof Exp:* Intern, Church Home Hosp, Md, 55-56; proj officer physiol & aviation med, 57-59, BIOCHEMIST & PHYSIOLOGIST, BIOCHEM LAB, US NAVAL AIR DEVELOP CTR, 59- *Concurrent Pos:* Dir, Soc Math Biol, Assoc ed, Bull Math Biol & J Biol Physics. *Mem:* Am Chem Soc; Am Physiol Soc; Am Phys Soc; Biophys Soc; Soc Math Biol. *Res:* Applications of solid state physics to biochemistry and biology; sodium and potassium ion complexing in tissues by nuclear magnetic resonance; physics of human arterial system; aerospace medicine; biological superconductivity; biomagnetism; magnetic monopoles; mathematical biology. *Mailing Add:* Biochem Lab US Naval Air Develop Ctr Warminster PA 18974

COPE, JAMES FRANCIS, b Charleston, SC, Sept 10, 43; m 68; c 1. ORGANIC POLYMER CHEMISTRY, ORGANOMETALLIC CHEMISTRY. *Educ:* Hampden-Sydney Col, BS, 65; Clemson Univ, MS, 70, PhD(org chem), 71. *Prof Exp:* Res chemist textiles, West Point-Pepperell Inc, 71-72; RES CHEMIST SYNTHETIC FIBERS, PHILLIPS FIBERS CORP, DIV PHILLIPS PETROL CO, 72- *Mem:* Am Chem Soc; Royal Soc Chem. *Res:* Modification and development of synthetic fibers. *Mailing Add:* 201 Gilder Creek Dr Greenville SC 29607

COPE, JOHN THOMAS, JR, b Akron, Ohio, July 24, 21; m 45; c 3. SOIL FERTILITY. *Educ:* Auburn Univ, BS, 42, MS, 46; Cornell Univ, PhD(soil sci), 50. *Prof Exp:* Farm mgr, Fla, 46-47; assoc soil chemist, Nitrogen Res, 50-52, assoc agronomist in charge exp fields, 52-59, agronomist, 59-66, soil tester, 66-78, PROF AGRON & SOILS, AUBURN UNIV, 78- *Mem:* Am Soc Agron; Soil Sci Soc Am. *Res:* Soil fertility; nitrogen fertilization; soil organic matter; crop rotations; soil and crop management; soil test fertilizer recommendations and computer programs; soil test calibration; fertility index. *Mailing Add:* Dept of Agron Auburn Univ Auburn AL 36830

COPE, OLIVER, b Germantown, Pa, Aug 15, 02; m 32; c 2. SURGERY. *Educ:* Harvard Univ, AB, 23, MD, 28; Am Bd Surg, dipl. *Hon Degrees:* Dr, Univ Toulouse, 50. *Prof Exp:* Traveling fel, 33, from instr to asst prof, 34-38, from assoc prof to prof, 48-69, actg head dept, 68-69, EMER PROF SURG, MED SCH, HARVARD UNIV, 69- *Concurrent Pos:* From asst to assoc surgeon, Mass Gen Hosp, 34-46, vis surgeon, 46-69, actg chief surg serv, 68-69, mem bd consults, 69-, sr surgeon, 72-; investr, Off Sci Res & Develop, 42-45; mem subcomt burns, Nat Res Coun, 43-45; dir res under contract with Off Naval Res, 47-52; chief of staff, Boston Unit, Shriners Burn Inst, 64-69, emer chief of staff, 69- *Mem:* Inst of Med of Nat Acad Sci; fel Am Col Surgeons; Am Surg Asn (pres, 62-63); Int Soc Surg; AAAS. *Mailing Add:* Mass Gen Hosp 32 Fruit St Boston MA 02114

COPE, OLIVER BREWERN, b San Francisco, Calif, June 16, 16; m 42; c 2. FISHERY BIOLOGY. *Educ:* Stanford Univ, AB, 38, AM, 40, PhD(entomol), 42. *Prof Exp:* Agent, Bur Entomol & Plant Quarantine, US Dept Agr, Calif, 39; asst, Stanford Univ, 39-42; aquatic biologist, US Fish & Wildlife Serv, 46-50, chief cent valley invest, 50-52, chief Rocky Mt invests, 52-59, fish-pesticide res lab, 59-69, chief br fish husb res, US Bur Sport Fisheries & Wildlife, 69-71; phys scientist, Off of Water Resources Res, 71-74; consult-ed, 74-81. *Concurrent Pos:* Jr quarantine inspector, Calif State Dept Agr, 41. *Mem:* AAAS; Coun Biol Ed; Am Fisheries Soc; Wildlife Soc; Am Inst Fisheries Res Biol. *Res:* Insect morphology; fresh water fisheries; economic poisons and fish; fish husbandry. *Mailing Add:* 15 Adamswood Rd Asheville NC 28803

COPE, OSWALD JAMES, b Hanley, Eng, June 8, 34; div; c 2. POLYMER CHEMISTRY. *Educ:* Univ London, BSc, 55; Univ Alta, PhD(org chem), 62. *Prof Exp:* Asst lectr chem, Western Col, 56-57; chemist, Paint Res Labs, Can Indust Ltd, 57-58; asst chem, Univ Alta, 58-62; res assoc org chem, Purdue Univ, 62-63; chemist, Plastics Dept, Exp Sta, E I du Pont de Nemours & Co, Del, 63-69; sr chemist, Memorex Corp, Calif, 69-70; mgr, 70-74, VPRES RES & DEVELOP, XIDEX CORP, 74- *Mem:* Am Chem Soc; Soc Photog Sci & Eng. *Res:* Polymer synthesis and structure property relationships; non-silver imaging processes; vesicular and diazo film. *Mailing Add:* Xidex Corp 305 Soquel Way Sunnyvale CA 94086

COPE, VIRGIL W, b Storm Lake, Iowa, Feb 4, 43; m 65; c 2. INORGANIC CHEMISTRY. *Educ:* Iowa State Teachers Col, BA, 65; Univ Kans, PhD(inorg chem), 68. *Prof Exp:* Asst prof, 68-74, ASSOC PROF CHEM, UNIV MICH-FLINT, 74- *Concurrent Pos:* Vis prof chem, Boston Univ, 74-75; assoc prof, Washington Univ, 81-82. *Mem:* Am Chem Soc. *Res:* Mechanisms of reactions of coordination compounds, especially electron transfer reaction, photosubstitution and photo reduction; reactions of primary air pollutants with polycyclic aromatic hydrocarbons. *Mailing Add:* Dept of Chem Univ of Mich Flint MI 48503

COPE, WILL ALLEN, b Inverness, Ala, June 23, 22; m 50; c 1. GENETICS, PLANT BREEDING. *Educ:* Ala Polytech Inst, BS, 48, MS, 49; NC State Col, PhD(field crops), 56. *Prof Exp:* Asst prof field crops, 55-64, res assoc prof crop sci, 64-69, assoc prof crop sci & genetics, 69-71, PROF CROP SCI, NC STATE UNIV, 71-, PROF GENETICS, 76-, RES AGRONOMIST, SCI & EDUC ADMIN-AGR RES, USDA, 55- *Mem:* Am Soc Agron; Genetics Soc Am. *Res:* Breeding and genetics of Trifolium repens. *Mailing Add:* Dept of Crop Sci NC State Univ Raleigh NC 27607

COPELAND, ARTHUR HERBERT, JR, b Columbus, Tex, June 11, 26; m 47; c 3. MATHEMATICS. *Educ:* Univ Mich, BS, 49, MA, 50; Mass Inst Technol, PhD(math), 54. *Prof Exp:* Instr, Mass Inst Technol, 51-54; from instr to assoc prof math, Purdue Univ, 54-61; assoc prof, Northwestern Univ, 61-68; PROF MATH, UNIV NH, 68- *Mem:* Am Math Soc; Math Asn Am. *Res:* Algebraic topology; homotopy theory; Hopf and fibre spaces. *Mailing Add:* Dept of Math Univ of NH Durham NH 03824

COPELAND, BILLY JOE, b Mannsville, Okla, Nov 20, 36; m 63; c 2. ECOLOGY. *Educ:* Okla State Univ, BS, 59, MS, 61, PhD(zool), 63. *Prof Exp:* Asst limnol, Okla State Univ, 59-62; res scientist marine ecol, Inst Marine Sci, Univ Tex, 62-65, asst prof, Univ, 65-68, assoc prof, 68-70; assoc prof zool & bot & dir, Pamlico Marine Lab, 70-76, PROF ZOOL & BOT & DIR, NC SEA GRANT PROG, NC STATE UNIV, 76-, DIR MARINE SCI & ENG, 80- *Concurrent Pos:* Grants estuarine ecol & pollution control; consult, indust; chmn ecol comt, Univ Coun Water Resources. *Mem:* Am Soc Limnol & Oceanog; Ecol Soc Am; Water Pollution Control Fedn. *Res:* Estuarine ecology; effects of water resources development and pollution on fresh and saltwater ecology; systems analysis of estuarine ecosystems. *Mailing Add:* 1235 Burlington Labs NC State Univ Raleigh NC 27607

COPELAND, BRADLEY ELLSWORTH, b Wilkinsburg, Pa, Sept 8, 21; m 43; c 2. MEDICINE, CLINICAL PATHOLOGY. *Educ:* Dartmouth Col, AB, 43; Univ Pa, MD, 45. *Prof Exp:* Assoc path, New Eng Deaconess Hosp & New Eng Baptist Hosp, 50-59, clin pathologist, 59-72, chmn dept path, 72-75, chief, Div Clin Path, 75-79; CHIEF LAB SERV, VET ADMIN MED CTR, CINCINNATI, 79-; PROF PATH, MED SCH, UNIV CINCINNATI, 79- *Concurrent Pos:* Chmn comt world stands, World Asn Socs Anat & Clin Path, 60-; chmn subcomt documentation, Comt Path, Nat Acad Sci-Nat Res Coun, 69-71. *Mem:* Am Chem Soc; AMA; Am Soc Clin Path; Col Am Path. *Res:* Electrolytes; magnesium; hemoglobin; statistics and quality control; instrumentation. *Mailing Add:* Lab Serv Vet Admin Med Ctr 3200 Vine St Cincinnati OH 45220

COPELAND, CHARLES WESLEY, JR, b Hueytown, Ala, Oct 1, 32; m 57; c 2. STRATIGRAPHY, INVERTEBRATE PALEONTOLOGY. *Educ:* Birmingham-Southern Col, BS, 54; Univ NC, Chapel Hill, MS, 61. *Prof Exp:* Paleontologist & core libr supvr, 61-68, geol mapping supvr, 64-68, chief paleont & stratig div, 68-74, CHIEF GEOL DIV, GEOL SURV ALA, 74- *Mem:* Geol Soc Am; Sigma Xi; Brit Paleont Soc. *Res:* Subsurface stratigraphy, paleontology and structure; Pleistocene geology; coastal plain faults; solution collapse phenomena; ground water aquifer studies. *Mailing Add:* 203 32nd Place E Tuscaloosa AL 35405

COPELAND, DAVID ANTHONY, b Jasper, Ala, Dec 4, 42; m 67; C 2. CONSTRUCTION MANAGEMENT SYSTEMS, CHEMICAL PHYSICS. *Educ:* Univ Ala, BSChem, 65, MA, 66; La State Univ, PhD(chem physics), 70. *Prof Exp:* Res assoc inorg chem, La State Univ, 69-70; asst prof, 70-74, assoc prof inorg phys chem, Univ Tenn, Martin, 74-77; construc systs specialist, 77-80, sr construct systs specialist, 80-81; SUPVR CONSTRUCT SYSTS, ALA POWER CO, BIRMINGHAM, 81- *Mem:* Am Chem Soc; Sigma Xi. *Res:* Theoretical electronic structures of transition metal tetrahedral complexes and the theories of electrons in polar solvents; developing major construction project management data processing systems. *Mailing Add:* Ala Power Co Construct Dept PO Box 2641 Birmingham AL 35291

COPELAND, DONALD EUGENE, b Mendon, Ohio, Feb 6, 12; m 41; c 3. BIOLOGY. *Educ:* Univ Rochester, AB, 35; Amherst Col, MA, 37; Harvard Univ, PhD(zool), 41. *Prof Exp:* Instr biol, Univ NC, 41-42; from asst prof to assoc prof, Brown Univ, 46-54; prof assoc, Med Sci Div, Nat Res Coun, 53-55; exec secy, Div Res Grants, NIH, 56-59; prof zool, 59-70, prof biol, 70-77, EMER PROF BIOL, TULANE UNIV, 77- *Concurrent Pos:* mem physiol panel, Res & Develop Bd, US Dept Defense, 52-53; trustee, Marine Biol Lab, Woods Hole, 68-71, res investr, 77- *Mem:* Am Soc Zool; Am Asn Anat; Am Soc Cell Biol; Am Physiol Soc. *Res:* Electron microscopy of inorganic ion transport; fine structure of oxygen elevating tissue in fish eye and swim bladder; fine structure of teleost eye function. *Mailing Add:* Marine Biol Lab Woods Hole MA 02543

COPELAND, EDMUND SARGENT, b Lancaster, Pa, Mar 2, 36; m 65; c 2. BIOPHYSICAL CHEMISTRY, MAGNETIC RESONANCE. *Educ:* Cornell Univ, AB, 58; Univ Rochester, MS, 61, PhD(radiation biol), 64. *Prof Exp:* Fel biophys, Roswell Park Mem Inst, 64-65; USPHS fel biochem, Norsk Hydro's Inst Cancer Res, 65-67; chemist, Walter Reed Army Inst Res, 67-76; exec secy, Path B (AHR) Study Sect, 76-79, EXEC SECY, CHEM PATH STUDY SECT, DIV RES GRANTS, NIH, 79- *Concurrent Pos:* Vis scientist, Clin Neuropharmacol Br, Nat Inst Ment Health, NIH, 76- *Mem:* AAAS; Am Chem Soc; Am Soc Photobiol; Biophys Soc. *Res:* Mechanism of action of radioprotective drugs; chemical protection against phototoxicity; the opiate receptor, mechanism of action of antidepressants; science administration. *Mailing Add:* Westwood Bldg Rm 353 Nat Inst Health Bethesda MD 20014

COPELAND, FREDERICK CLEVELAND, b Brunswick, Maine, Oct 9, 12; m 39; c 3. BIOLOGY. *Educ:* Williams Col, AB, 35; Harvard Univ, AM, 37, PhD(biol), 40. *Prof Exp:* Asst biol, Harvard Univ, 37-40; instr, Trinity Col, Conn, 40-46, dir admis, 45-46; from asst prof to prof, 46-78, dean admis, 46-78, EMER PROF BIOL, WILLIAMS COL, 78-, EMER DEAN ADMIS, 78- *Concurrent Pos:* Trustee, Hotchkiss Sch, Lenox Sch, Educ Rec Bur & Trinity Sch, New York. *Honors & Awards:* Rogerson Cup Award, 69. *Mem:* Genetics Soc Am. *Res:* Cytogenetics; plant growth rates. *Mailing Add:* 1571 Oblong Rd Williamstown MA 01267

COPELAND, GARY EARL, b Maud, Okla, Aug 15, 40. CHEMICAL PHYSICS. *Educ:* Univ Okla, BS, 64, MS, 65, PhD(physics), 70. *Prof Exp:* Engr plasma physics, Tex Instruments, 64-65; instr physics, Univ Okla, 69-70; fel laser physics, Langley Res Ctr, NASA, 70-71; asst prof physics, 71-80, asst prof geophys sci, 76-80, ASSOC PROF PHYSICS & GEOPHYSICS, OLD DOMINION UNIV, 80- *Concurrent Pos:* Consult, Va State Air Pollution Control, 72- & Earth Resources Observ Bd, Goddard Space Flight Ctr, NASA, 74. *Mem:* Am Phys Soc; Am Chem Soc; Am Geophys Union; Air Pollution Control Asn; AAAS. *Res:* Chemical physics, laser physics, air pollution monitoring, atmospheric physics, environmental modelling. *Mailing Add:* Dept of Physics & Geophys Sci Old Dominion Univ Norfolk VA 23508

COPELAND, JAMES CLINTON, b Chicago, Ill, Nov 15, 37; m 60; c 5. MICROBIAL GENETICS, MOLECULAR GENETICS. *Educ:* Univ Ill, Urbana-Champaign, BS, 59; Univ Tenn, MS, 61; Rutgers Univ, PhD(microbiol), 65. *Prof Exp:* Am Cancer Soc fel molecular genetics, Albert Einstein Col Med, 65-67; from asst geneticist to assoc geneticist, Argonne Nat Lab, 67-72; assoc prof microbiol, Ohio State Univ, 72-77; dir res & develop, Moffett Tech Ctr, CPC Int, 77-81; PRES, ENZYME TECHNOL CORP, 81- *Concurrent Pos:* Vis lectr, Northern Ill Univ, 70-71; adj assoc prof, 71-72; NIH res career develop award, 72-77; ed Microbial Genetics Bull, 74-77. *Mem:* AAAS; Soc Ind Microbiol. *Res:* Structure and function of microbial chromosomes, especially their organization, regulation, replication, evolution, information storage and retrieval; genetic engineering; commercialization of biotechnology. *Mailing Add:* Enzyme Technol Corp 1725 S Indian Trail Naperville IL 60565

COPELAND, JAMES LEWIS, b Champaign, Ill, Apr 7, 31; m 55; c 2. PHYSICAL CHEMISTRY. *Educ:* Univ Ill, BS, 52; Ind Univ, PhD(phys chem), 62. *Prof Exp:* Res assoc & fel phys chem, Inst Atomic Res, Iowa State Univ, 61-62; from asst prof to assoc prof chem, 62-68, PROF CHEM, KANS STATE UNIV, 74-, ASSOC HEAD, DEPT CHEM, 81- *Concurrent Pos:* Grants, Bur of Gen Res, 63; Res Coord Coun, 64-65 & NSF, 65-74. *Mem:* Am Chem Soc; Am Phys Soc; Sigma Xi. *Res:* Physical chemistry of fused salt systems, including properties, electrochemistry, and theories of behavior; physical chemistry of high-temperature systems in general; high temperature reaction kinetics. *Mailing Add:* Dept Chem Kans State Univ Manhattan KS 66506

COPELAND, JOHN ALEXANDER, b Atlanta, Ga Feb 6, 41; m 60; c 2. SOLID STATE PHYSICS. *Educ:* Ga Inst Technol, BS, 62, MS, 63, PhD(physics), 65. *Prof Exp:* Res physicist, Ga Inst Technol, 65; MEM TECH STAFF BELL LABS, 65-, HEAD, REPEATER RES DEPT, 76- *Concurrent Pos:* Ed, Inst Elec & Electronics Engrs Transitions on Electron Devices, 71-73. *Honors & Awards:* Morris N Liebmann, Inst Elec & Electronics Engrs, 70. *Mem:* Inst Elec & Electronics Engrs; Am Phys Soc. *Res:* Solid state devices for lightwave communications and high-speed logic applications. *Mailing Add:* Lab R-241 Crawford Hill Holmdel NJ 07733

COPELAND, LAWRENCE O, crop science, see previous edition

COPELAND, MILES ALEXANDER, b Quebec City, Que, May 5, 34; m 62; c 1. ELECTRICAL ENGINEERING. *Educ:* Univ Man, BSc, 57; Univ Toronto, MASc, 62, PhD(elec eng), 65. *Prof Exp:* From asst prof to assoc prof, 65-77, PROF ELEC ENG, CARLETON UNIV, CAN, 77- *Concurrent Pos:* Consult, Northern Elec Co, Ont, 65. *Mem:* Inst Elec & Electronics Engrs. *Res:* Electrical engineering related to physics, especially solid state or device work; transducers; semi-conductors; solid state electronics. *Mailing Add:* Dept of Eng Carleton Univ Ottawa ON K1S 5B6 Can

COPELAND, MURRAY JOHN, b Toronto, Ont, Apr 23, 28; m 54; c 1. MICROPALEONTOLOGY, INVERTEBRATE PALEONTOLOGY. *Educ:* Univ Toronto, BA, 49, MA, 51; Univ Mich, PhD(geol), 55. *Prof Exp:* Field officer geol, 49-55, geologist, 55-65, RES SCIENTIST, GEOL SURV, CAN, 65- *Concurrent Pos:* Pres, Int Res Group, Paleozoic Ostracoda, Int Paleont Asn. *Mem:* Fel Geol Soc Am; Am Paleont Soc; Geol Asn Can. *Res:* Micropaleontology; Paleozoic and Mesozoic Ostracoda; Paleozoic and Mesozoic Arthropoda. *Mailing Add:* Geol Surv Can Bldg 601 Booth St Ottawa ON K2A 3J6 Can

COPELAND, MURRAY MARCUS, b McDonough, Ga, June 23, 02; m 31. SURGERY. *Educ:* Oglethorpe Univ, AB, 23; Johns Hopkins Univ, MD, 27; Am Bd Surg, dipl. *Hon Degrees:* DSc, Oglethorpe Univ, 53. *Prof Exp:* Intern, City Hosp, Baltimore, 27-28; resident surg, Union Mem Hosp, Baltimore, 33-37; instr, Univ Md, 37-44; instr, Johns Hopkins Hosp, 44-45; chief, Kennedy Vet Admin Hosp, Memphis, 46-47; prof & dir dept, 47-60, EMER PROF ONCOL, MED CTR, GEORGETOWN UNIV, 60-; prof surg, 68-81, vpres, Univ Cancer Found, 67-81, EMER PROF SURG, MED SCH & GRAD SCH BIOMED SCI, UNIV TEX, HOUSTON, 81-, EMER VPRES, UNIV CANCER FOUND, 81- *Concurrent Pos:* Fel, Mayo Clin, 29-30; fel, Mem Hosp, New York, 30-33; chmn cancer control comt, Nat Cancer Inst, 56-58, mem, Nat Adv Cancer Coun, 58-61 & 66-69, proj dir, Nat Large Bowel Cancer Proj, Div Cancer Res, Resources & Ctrs, Nat Cancer Inst, 71-81; chmn, USA comt, Int Union Against Cancer, 65-71. *Mem:* Am Cancer Soc (pres, 65); Am Radium Soc; Am Orthop Asn; Am Acad Orthop Surg; Am Col Surg. *Res:* Cancer control; neoplastic diseases; professional education. *Mailing Add:* Univ of Tex M D Anderson Hosp & Tumor Inst Houston TX 77030

COPELAND, NORMAN A(RLAND), b Mercer County, Ohio, Aug 16, 15; m 49; c 2. CHEMICAL ENGINEERING. *Educ:* Mass Inst Technol, SB, 36; Univ Del, MS, 48, PhD(chem eng), 49. *Prof Exp:* Develop engr, Eng Dept, E I du Pont de Nemours & Co, 37-45, design engr, 45-48, design proj mgr, 49-51, tech supt, Film Dept, 51-54, asst plant mgr, 54, plant mgr, 54-57, asst dir mfg, 57-59, res & develop, 59-62, dir, 62-63, asst gen mgr, 63-65, asst chief engr, Eng Dept, 65-70, chief engr, 70-73, sr vpres, 73-77; RETIRED. *Concurrent Pos:* Mem bd, E I du Pont de Nemours & Co. *Mem:* Nat Acad Eng; Am Chem Soc; Am Inst Chem Engrs. *Res:* Process development; engineering research. *Mailing Add:* 400 Beach Rd Tequesta FL 33458

COPELAND, RICHARD FRANKLIN, b Tyler, Tex, Oct 10, 38; m 68. PHYSICAL CHEMISTRY, ORGANOMETALLIC CHEMISTRY. *Educ:* Tex A&M Univ, BS, 61, MS, 63, PhD(chem), 65. *Prof Exp:* Robert A Welch fels, Tex A&M Univ, 65-66 & Univ Tex, Austin, 66-67; asst prof chem, Ball State Univ, 67-69 & Univ Mich, 69-71; assoc prof, 71-78, PROF CHEM, BETHUNE-COOKMAN COL, 78- *Concurrent Pos:* NSF grants, 68-69, 74- & NIH, 74- *Mem:* Am Chem Soc; Am Crystallog Asn. *Res:* Crystal and molecular structure of organometallic complexes; information science; educational uses of computers. *Mailing Add:* Dept of Chem Bethune-Cookman Col Daytona Beach FL 32015

COPELAND, THOMPSON PRESTON, b Ark, March 11, 21; m 50; c 2. ENTOMOLOGY. *Educ:* Ouachita Baptist Col, BS, 47; George Peabody Col, MA, 50; Univ Tenn, PhD, 62. *Prof Exp:* Instr biol, Ouachita Baptist Col, 47-49; asst prof, Union Univ, Tenn, 51-52; assoc prof, 54-64, chmn dept biol, 64-80, PROF BIOL, E TENN STATE UNIV, 64- *Concurrent Pos:* Danforth assoc, 64. *Mem:* AAAS; Am Entom Soc. *Res:* Taxonomy and ecology of Protura, Collembola and Zoraptera. *Mailing Add:* Dept of Biol E Tenn State Univ Johnson City TN 37601

COPELAND, WILLIAM D, b Colorado Springs, Colo, Mar 16, 34; m 57; c 3. PHYSICAL METALLURGY. *Educ:* Carleton Col, BA, 56; Univ Minn, PhD(metall), 66. *Prof Exp:* PROF METALL, COLO SCH MINES, 66-, DEAN GRAD SCH, 72- *Concurrent Pos:* Am Coun Educ admin fel, 70-71. *Mem:* Am Soc Metals; Metall Soc; Am Inst Mining, Metall & Petrol Engrs. *Res:* Transport processes in high temperature compounds; oxidation-corrosion mechanisms. *Mailing Add:* Grad Sch Colo Sch of Mines Golden CO 80401

COPELIN, EDWARD CASIMERE, b Philadelphia, Pa, Feb 16, 31; m 56; c 2. GEOCHEMISTRY. *Educ:* Pa State Univ, BS, 53; Purdue Univ, MS, 55, PhD(chem), 58. *Prof Exp:* RES CHEMIST, UNION OIL CO CALIF, 58- *Mem:* Am Chem Soc; Geochem Soc. *Res:* Petroleum geochemistry. *Mailing Add:* Union Oil Co Calif 376 S Valencia Ave Brea CA 92621

COPELIN, HARRY B, b Staten Island, NY, Aug 9, 18; m 43; c 3. ORGANIC CHEMISTRY. *Educ:* Cornell Univ, BS, 40, MS, 41. *Prof Exp:* Chemist, 41-58, tech assoc, 58-63, res assoc, 63-71, RES FEL, E I DU PONT DE NEMOURS & CO, INC, 71- *Res:* Organic chlorine compounds; coordination chemistry; catalysis; heterocyclic compounds; hydroformylation processes. *Mailing Add:* 2019 Longcome Dr Wilmington DE 19810

COPEMAN, ROBERT JAMES, b Regina, Sask, Can, Dec 18, 42; m 64; c 3. PHYTOBACTERIOLOGY. *Educ:* McGill Univ, BSc, 65; Wis Univ, PhD(plant path), 70. *Prof Exp:* asst prof, 69-78, ASSOC PROF PLANT SCI, PLANT SCI DEPT, UNIV BC, 78- *Mem:* Can Phytopath Soc (secy treas, 76-80; treas, 80-82); Am Phytopath Soc. *Res:* Identification and detection of phytopathogenic bacteria in epiphytological studies and crop certification programs. *Mailing Add:* Plant Sci Dept 248-2357 Main Mall Univ BC Vancouver BC V6T 2A2 Can

COPENHAVER, JOHN HARRISON, JR, b Ralston, Nebr, Dec 21, 22; m 46; c 5. BIOCHEMISTRY. *Educ:* Dartmouth Col, BA, 46; Univ Wis, MS, 49, PhD(zool), 50. *Prof Exp:* Nat Heart Inst fel enzyme res, Univ Wis, 50-51; asst prof pharmacol, Southwestern Med Sch, Univ Tex, 51-53; from asst prof to assoc prof zool, 53-60, PROF BIOL SCI, DARTMOUTH COL, 60- *Mem:* Am Soc Biol Chem. *Res:* Oxidative phosphorylation; enzyme chemistry of renal function; cell transport mechanisms. *Mailing Add:* Dept of Biol Sci Dartmouth Col Hanover NH 03755

COPENHAVER, THOMAS WESLEY, b Sioux City, Iowa, Oct 17, 45; m 78. BIOSTATISTICS. *Educ:* Univ Nebr, BS, 68; Univ Ark, MS, 70; Colo State Univ, PhD(statist), 76. *Prof Exp:* SUPVR PRECLIN STATIST, WYETH LABS, AM HOME PROD, 74- *Mem:* Biomet Soc; Am Statist Asn; Sigma Xi. *Res:* Statistical methods for analyzing dose-response curves. *Mailing Add:* Wyeth Labs PO Box 8299 Philadelphia PA 19101

COPENHAVER, WILFRED MONROE, b Westminster, Md, Dec 26, 98; m 27; c 2. ANATOMY. *Educ:* Western Md Col, AB, 21; Yale Univ, PhD(zool), 25. *Prof Exp:* Asst instr biol, Yale Univ, 21-24, asst instr anat, Sch Med, 24-25; from instr to asst prof, Univ Rochester, 25-28; from asst prof to prof, 28-67, chmn dept, 57-66, EMER PROF ANAT, COL PHYSICIANS & SURGEONS, COLUMBIA UNIV, 67-; PROF ANAT, SCH MED, UNIV MIAMI, 67- *Concurrent Pos:* Interim chmn dept anat, Sch Med, Univ Miami, 67-69. *Mem:* AAAS; Am Asn Anat; Am Soc Zool; Am Soc Exp Biol & Med; Soc Develop Biol. *Res:* Experimental embryology, especially of heart and blood; developmental anomalies; histology of heart conduction systems. *Mailing Add:* Dept Anat R-124 PO Box 016960 Miami FL 33101

COPES, FREDERICK ALBERT, b Tomahawk, Wis, Dec 25, 37; m 59; c 5. ECOLOGY, FISHERIES. *Educ:* Wis State Univ, Stevens Point, BS, 60; Univ NDak, MS, 65; Univ Wyo, PhD(zool), 70. *Prof Exp:* Teacher high sch, Wis, 60-63; from instr to assoc prof, 64-67, assoc prof biol & zool, 70-81, PROF BIOL, ZOOL & FISHERIES, UNIV WIS-STEVENS POINT, 78- *Concurrent Pos:* Secy, Wis Environ Pract Comn, 74-78. *Mem:* Am Fisheries Soc; Sigma Xi; NAm Native Fish Asn (vpres, 77-80). *Res:* Fishes of the Red River tributaries of North Dakota; ecology of the native fishes of east Wyoming; ecology of fishes; fishery production; vital statistics of the Lake Michigan Whitefish Fishery. *Mailing Add:* Dept of Biol Univ of Wis Stevens Point WI 54481

COPLAN, MICHAEL ALAN, b Cleveland, Ohio, Apr 26, 38. CHEMICAL PHYSICS, SPACE PHYSICS. *Educ:* Williams Col, BA, 60; Yale Univ, MS, 61, PhD(electrolytic conductance), 63. *Prof Exp:* NIH res fel electrochem, Univ Paris, 63-64, NATO fel, 64-65; res assoc, Univ Chicago, 65-67; res asst prof, 67-72, res assoc prof, 72-81, RES PROF INST PHYS SCI & TECHNOL, UNIV MD, 81- *Mem:* Am Phys Soc; Sigma Xi. *Res:* Chemical physics; atomic and molecular collisions; charged particle optics; space physics. *Mailing Add:* Inst Phys Sci & Technol Univ of Md College Park MD 20742

COPLAN, MYRON J, b Chicago, Ill, Jan 5, 22; m 52; c 5. MEMBRANE SYNTHESIS & OPERATIONS. *Educ:* Brooklyn Col, BA, 43. *Prof Exp:* Prod supt, Montrose Chem Co, 43-48; head chem eng, Inst Textile Technol, 48-51; sr res asst, Fabric Res Labs Inc, 51-61, dir, 61-65, vpres, 65-72; dir, 72-79, SR CORP SCIENTIST, ALBANY INT CO, 79- *Concurrent Pos:* Lectr, Northeastern Univ, 53-55; rev ed, Indust & Eng Chem, 65-68. *Mem:* Am Chem Soc; Am Inst Chem Engrs ; Fiber Soc; Textile Inst; NY Acad Sci. *Res:* Polymer physical and organic chemistry; fiber technologies; rheology of spinning; morphology and function of polymer systems; membrane structure, product and application in fluid separations such as reverse osmosis, dialysis, gas purification. *Mailing Add:* 47 Speen St Natick MA 01760

COPLEY, ALFRED LEWIN, b Ger, June 19, 10; nat US; wid; c 1. PHYSIOLOGY, EXPERIMENTAL MEDICINE. *Educ:* Univ Heidelberg, MD; Univ Basel, MD, 36. *Hon Degrees:* Dr Med, Univ Heidelberg, 72. *Prof Exp:* Asst med, Univ Basel, 36-37; intern, Trinity Lutheran Hosp, Mo, 39; res assoc, Hixon Lab Med Res, Univ Kans, 40-42; asst resident med, Goldwater Mem Hosp, New York, 42-43; head lab exp surg, Univ Va, 43-44, res assoc prev med & bact, 44-45; res assoc lab cellular physiol, NY Univ, 45-49, res fel hemat, Mt Sinai Hosp, 48-49; res assoc med & asst clin prof, NY Med Col, 49-52; sr researcher & head lab blood & vascular physiol, Res Labs, Int Children's Ctr, Paris, 52-55; sr researcher, Nat Inst Hyg & head res lab microcirculation, Nat Ctr Blood Transfusion, 55-57; dir exp res vascular dis, Med Res Labs, Charing Cross Hosp, London, 57-59; vis prof path, Royal Col Surgeons Eng, 59; assoc prof physiol, 60-61, head hemorrheol lab, 60-65, prof physiol, 62-64, res prof pharmacol, New York Med Col, 65-76, res prof med, 72-74; RES PROF LIFE SCI & BIOENG & DIR LAB BIORHEOL, POLYTECH INST NEW YORK, 74- *Concurrent Pos:* Celler fel, Univ Kans, 40; fel surg, Univ Va, 43-44; vis res assoc, Grad Sch Arts & Sci, NY Univ, 47-48; gen lectr, Int Rheol Cong, Neth, 48; dir, AEC Proj, 49-52; chief investr, Off Naval Res Proj, 50-52; mem med adv bd, Nat Blood Res Found, 54-; mem, Marine Biol Lab Corp, Woods Hole, 54-; gen lectr, Int Cong Blood Transfusion, Japan, 60; co-ed-in-chief & co-founder, Biorheol, 62-; co-ed, Rheologica Acta; assoc chief of staff res & educ, Vet Admin Hosp, East Orange, NJ, 65-67, chief hemorrhage & thrombosis res labs, 65-71; chmn sci organizing comt & conf chmn, Int Conf Hemorheol, Iceland, 66; adj res prof bioeng, NJ Inst Technol, 67-; invited lectr, Int Cong Rheol, Kyoto, Japan, 68, St Louis, France, 72; co-ed-in-chief & founder, Thrombosis Res, 72-; co-founder & adv, Acupuncture & Electrotherapeutic Res, 75-; co-ed-in-chief &

founder, Clin Hemorheology, 81- *Honors & Awards:* Poiseuille Gold Medal, Int Cong Biorheol, 72. *Mem:* Fel AAAS; Am Physiol Soc; Soc Study Blood; Int Soc Hemorheol (pres, 66-69); Int Soc Biorheol (pres, 69-72, past pres, 72-78). *Res:* Blood clotting; mechanisms of thrombosis, hemorrhage and hemostasis; blood vessel wall; surface rheology and adsorption of proteins; comparative hematology; blood platelets; physiology of the spleen; immunology; brain and liver metabolism; cholinesterase; radiobiology; biorheology of hair; experimental tuberculosis; microcirculation; hemorheology; survey and studies of snake venoms; biorheology. *Mailing Add:* Lab of Biorheol Polytech Inst of New York Brooklyn NY 11201

COPLEY, LAWRENCE GORDON, b Reading, Eng, July 17, 39. APPLIED PHYSICS. *Educ:* Univ Queensland, BMechEng, 60; Harvard Univ, SM, 62, PhD(appl physics), 65. *Prof Exp:* Mech engr, Queensland Railways, Australia, 60-61, res engr appl physics, 65-66; sr scientist, Cambridge Acoust Assocs, Inc, 66-70; INDEPENDENT CONSULT, 70- *Mem:* Acoust Soc Am; Inst Noise Control Eng. *Res:* Environmental acoustics and vibration. *Mailing Add:* 10 Bowers St Newton MA 02160

COPLIN, DAVID LOUIS, b Albuquerque, NMex, July 7, 45; m 68. PLANT PATHOLOGY. *Educ:* Univ Calif, Davis, BS, 67; Univ Wis, Madison, MS, 71, PhD(plant path & bact), 72. *Prof Exp:* Res assoc plant path, Univ Nebr, 72-74; asst prof, 74-80, ASSOC PROF PLANT PATH, OHIO AGR RES & DEVELOP CTR, OHIO STATE UNIV, 80- *Concurrent Pos:* Assoc ed, Phytopathology, 78-80 & Plant Dis, 81- *Mem:* Am Phytopath Soc; Am Soc Microbiol; AAAS; Sigma Xi. *Res:* Molecular genetics and physiology of plant pathogenic bacteria. *Mailing Add:* Dept Plant Path Ohio Agr Res & Develop Ctr Wooster OH 44691

COPP, ALBERT NILS, b Aurora, Ill, Feb 22, 37; m 60; c 1. CERAMICS ENGINEERING. *Educ:* Univ Mo Rolla, BS, 62; Pa State Univ, MS, 65, PhD(ceramic sci), 69. *Prof Exp:* Develop engr, Western Elec Co, 65-66; sr scientist, Basic Incorp, 69-74; DIR RES, C-E BASIC, DIV COMBUSTION ENG, INC, 74- *Mem:* Am Soc Testing & Mat; Am Ceramic Soc; Am Inst Mining, Metall & Petrol Engrs. *Res:* Development of granular and shaped basic refractories used by the metals refining industry; development and improvement of methods to extract and process refractory raw materials. *Mailing Add:* C-E Basic Res Ctr PO Box 392 Bettsville OH 44815

COPP, DOUGLAS HAROLD, b Toronto, Ont, Jan 16, 15; m 39; c 3. PHYSIOLOGY. *Educ:* Univ Toronto, BA, 36, MD, 39; Univ Calif, PhD(biochem), 43. *Hon Degrees:* LLD, Univ Toronto, 70, Queen's Univ, Ont, 60; DSc, Univ Ottawa, 73, Acadia Univ, NS, 75, Univ BC, 80; FRCP(C), 74. *Prof Exp:* Lectr biochem, Univ Calif, 42-43, from instr to asst prof physiol, 44-50; head dept, 50-80, PROF PHYSIOL, UNIV BC, 50- *Concurrent Pos:* Consult, Nat Res Coun, DC, 46-49; mem subcomt human applns, Adv Comt Isotope Distribution, US AEC, 49-50, mem, Adv Comt Clin Uses Radioisotopes, 52-; mem, Panel Radiation Protection, Defense Res Bd Can, 51-, chmn, 57-59; mem assoc comt dent res, Nat Res Coun Can, 53-59, chmn, 57-59, mem adv comt med res, 54-57; chmn, Gordon Res Conf Bones & Teeth, 57; mem sci secretariat, UN Int Conf Peaceful Uses Atomic Energy, 58; pres, Nat Cancer Inst Can, 68-70; Beaumont lectr, 70. *Honors & Awards:* Gairdner Found Award, 67; Nicolas Andry Award, Asn Bone & Joint Surgeons, 68; Officer, Order of Can, 71, Companion, 80; Jacobaeus Mem lectr, Gothenbourg, 71 & Helsinki, 80; Flavelle Medal, Royal Soc Can, 72; Steindler Award, Orthop Res Soc, 74; Gold Medal, Sci Coun BC, 80. *Mem:* Am Physiol Soc; Soc Exp Biol & Med; Endocrine Soc; Can Physiol Soc (pres, 63-64); Royal Soc Can. *Res:* Iron and bone metabolism; fission product metabolism; severe phosphorus deficiency; regulation of blood calcium; parathyroid function; calcitonin; bone blood flow; ultimobranchial function; corpuscles of stannius. *Mailing Add:* 4755 Belmont Ave Vancouver BC V6T 1A8 Can

COPPAGE, WILLIAM EUGENE, b Geary, Okla, Nov 24, 34; m 58; c 2. ALGEBRA. *Educ:* Tex A&M Univ, BA, 55, MS, 56; Ohio State Univ, PhD(math), 63. *Prof Exp:* Assoc prof math, Ind State Col, 63-64; asst prof, 64-67, coord dept math, 65-66, ASSOC PROF MATH, WRIGHT STATE UNIV, 67- *Concurrent Pos:* Consult, Inst Defense Anal, 63-69; consult, Aerospace Med Res Labs, 66- *Mem:* Am Math Soc; Math Asn Am. *Res:* Non-associative algebra and applications to geometry. *Mailing Add:* Dept of Math Wright State Univ Colonel Glenn Hwy Dayton OH 45431

COPPEL, CLAUDE PETER, b Zweibrucken, Ger, Aug 14, 32; nat US; m 60; c 2. PHYSICAL CHEMISTRY, PETROLEUM ENGINEERING. *Educ:* Univ Denver, BS, 54; Univ Calif, PhD(chem), 58. *Prof Exp:* Asst, Univ Calif, 54-55, asst radiation lab, 55-58; res scientist, Marathon Oil Res Ctr, Colo, 58-63; res chemist, Arthur D Little, Inc, Mass, 63-66; from res chemist to sr res chemist, 66-74, SR RES ASSOC, CHEVRON OIL FIELD RES CO, 74- *Mem:* AAAS; Am Chem Soc; Soc Petrol Engrs. *Res:* Colloidal and surface chemistry; high temperature physical measurements; fluid flow in porous media; well stimulation technology. *Mailing Add:* Chevron Oil Field Res Co PO Box 446 La Habra CA 90631

COPPEL, HARRY CHARLES, b Galt, Ont, Jan 2, 18; nat US; m 50; c 2. ENTOMOLOGY. *Educ:* Ont Agr Col, BSA, 43; Univ Wis, MSc, 46; NY State Col Forestry, Syracuse Univ, PhD(forest entom), 49. *Prof Exp:* Agr res officer, Entom Lab Sci Serv, Can Dept Agr, 43-57; from asst prof to assoc prof, 57-65, PROF ENTOM, UNIV WIS-MADISON, 65- *Mem:* Entom Soc Am; Entom Soc Can; Int Orgn Biol Control. *Res:* Biological control of forest insect pests. *Mailing Add:* Dept of Entom Univ of Wis Madison WI 53706

COPPENGER, CLAUDE JACKSON, b Beaumont, Tex, Oct 12, 27. PHYSIOLOGY. *Educ:* Stephen F Austin State Col, BS, 51; Tex A&M Univ, MS, 53, PhD(physiol), 64. *Prof Exp:* Asst physiol, Tex A&M Univ, 51-53, biochem, 54-55; instr, Pub Sch, Tex, 57-58; assoc prof zool, Amarillo Jr Col, 58-61; res assoc radiation biol, Tex A&M Univ, 61-63; from asst prof to assoc prof physiol, 63-74, chmn dept physiol & behav biol, 68-78, PROF BIOL, SAN FRANCISCO STATE UNIV, 74- *Mem:* AAAS; Am Zool Soc; Sigma Xi. *Res:* Mammalian physiology; physiological and behavioral sexual differentiation of mammals. *Mailing Add:* Dept of Biol San Francisco State Univ San Francisco CA 94132

COPPENS, ALAN BERCHARD, b Hollywood, Calif, June 26, 36; c 2. PHYSICS, ACOUSTICS. *Educ:* Cornell Univ, BEngPhys, 59; Brown Univ, MS, 62, PhD(physics), 65. *Prof Exp:* Asst prof, 64-69, ASSOC PROF PHYSICS, US NAVAL POST GRAD SCH, 69- *Mem:* Acoust Soc Am; fel Scientist's Inst Pub Info. *Res:* Finite-amplitude acoustic processes; properties of liquids; ocean acoustics. *Mailing Add:* 648 Sunset Dr Pacific Grove CA 93950

COPPENS, PHILIP, b Amersfoort, Holland, Oct 24, 30; m 56; c 3. CRYSTALLOGRAPHY, CHEMISTRY. *Educ:* Univ Amsterdam, Drs, 57, PhD(crystallog), 60. *Prof Exp:* Res asst, Weizmann Inst, 57-60, res assoc, 62-65; res assoc, Brookhaven Nat Lab, 60-62, scientist 65-68; assoc prof, 68-71, PROF CHEM, STATE UNIV NY BUFFALO, 71- *Concurrent Pos:* Vis prof, Fordham Univ, 66-67; res grants, NSF, Petrol Res Fund, AEC & NIH, 69; mem nat comt crystallog, Nat Res Coun-Nat Acad Sci, 72-75; adj prof, Univ Grenoble, 74-75; mem comn charge spin & momentum densities, Int Union Crystallog, 72-81, mem comn neutron diffraction, 75-78; mem comt facil, NSF, 79- *Mem:* AAAS; Am Crystallog Asn (pres, 78); Am Chem Soc. *Res:* Crystal structure determination; crystallographic computing; neutron diffraction; electron density determination by accurate diffraction methods; crystallography at liquid helium temperatures; crystallographic applications of synchrotron radiation. *Mailing Add:* 90 Scamridge Curve Williamsville NY 14221

COPPER, JOHN A(LAN), b Minneapolis, Minn, Sept 5, 34; m 57; c 2. GAS DYNAMICS. *Educ:* Univ Minn, BAE & BBA, 57; Univ Southern Calif, MS, 59; Calif Inst Technol, AE, 61. *Prof Exp:* Assoc develop engr, Coop Wind Tunnel, Calif Inst Technol, 57-59, develop engr, 59-60; mem tech staff, Nat Eng Sci Co, 60-61; res engr, Douglas Aircraft Co, Inc, 61-63, sect chief hypervelocity facil, 63-68, br chief, 68-76, CHIEF ENGR, McDONNELL DOUGLAS ASTRONAUT CO, McDONNELL DOUGLAS CORP, 76- *Mem:* Am Inst Aeronaut & Astronaut. *Res:* Missile flight mechanics. *Mailing Add:* McDonnell Douglas Astronaut Co 5301 Bolsa Huntington Beach CA 92647

COPPER, PAUL, b Surabaya, Indonesia, May 6, 40; Can citizen; m 67. PALEONTOLOGY. *Educ:* Univ Sask, BA, 60, MA, 62; Univ London, DIC & PhD(paleontol), 65. *Prof Exp:* Nat Res Coun fel paleontol, Queen's Univ, Ont, 65-67; asst prof geol, 67-70, assoc prof, 70-75, chmn dept, 74-77, PROF GEOL, LAURENTIAN UNIV, 75- . *Honors & Awards:* Huxley Prize, London, 68. *Res:* Brachiopod morphology, ecology and evolution, especially atrypida; evolution and paleoecology of early Paleozoic reef ecosystems. *Mailing Add:* Dept Geol Laurentian Univ Sudbury ON P3E 2C6 Can

COPPI, BRUNO, b Gonzaga, Italy, Nov 19, 35; m 63; c 3. PHYSICS. *Educ:* Milan Polytech Inst, Dr, 59. *Prof Exp:* Res leader & lectr, Milan Polytech Inst & Univ Milan, 60-61; mem plasma physics lab, Princeton Univ, 61-63; vis scientist, Princeton Univ, 62-63; asst prof & res asst physics, Univ Calif, San Diego, 64-67; mem, Inst Advan Study & Princeton Univ, 67-69; PROF PHYSICS, MASS INST TECHNOL, 69- *Concurrent Pos:* Ital Acad Sci grant, 62; Ital Acad Sci fel, 62, hon guest, 72; mem, Int Ctr Theoret Physics, Trieste, 66; consult, Princeton Univ & Am Sci & Eng, Cambridge, Mass, 69- & Naval Res Lab, Washington, DC; sci counr to bd dirs, Nat Comt Nuclear Energy Italy, 71; prof on leave, Advan Norm Sch, Pisa, 73; hon mem, Int Sch Plasma Physics, 75. *Honors & Awards:* Gold Medal, Milan Polytech Inst, 60; US Cert Contrib to Fusion Res, 77. *Mem:* Fel Am Acad Arts & Sci; fel Am Phys Soc; Ital Physics Soc. *Res:* Basic plasma physics; controlled thermonuclear fusion research; astrophysics; space physics; neutron transport theory; Alcator, Frascati Torus, and Ignitor experiments. *Mailing Add:* Dept of Physics Mass Inst of Technol Cambridge MA 02139

COPPIN, CHARLES ARTHUR, b Belton, Tex, July 18, 41; m 64; c 2. MATHEMATICAL ANALYSIS. *Educ:* Southwestern Univ, Tex, BS, 63; Univ Tex, Austin, MS, 65, PhD(math), 68. *Prof Exp:* Instr math, Univ Tex, Austin, 68; asst prof, 68-75, ASSOC PROF MATH, UNIV DALLAS, 75-, CHMN DEPT, 73- *Mem:* Am Math Soc; Math Asn Am. *Res:* Integration theory; primitive dispersion sets; relations on topological spaces. *Mailing Add:* Dept of Math Univ of Dallas Irving TX 75061

COPPINGER, RAYMOND PARKE, b Boston, Mass, Feb 7, 37; m 58; c 2. BIOLOGY, ECOLOGY. *Educ:* Boston Univ, AB, 59; Univ Mass, Amherst, MA, 64; Amherst Col via Univ Mass, PhD(biol), 68. *Prof Exp:* PROF BIOL, HAMPSHIRE COL, 69- *Concurrent Pos:* Res assoc, Dept Biol, Amherst Col, 68-70; mem sci adv bd, Behav Sci Found, Mass, 70- *Res:* Feeding behavior of birds exposed to novel food items; evolutionary and adaptive significance of acceptance or rejection of novelty; comparative biology and behavior of canids. *Mailing Add:* Sch of Natural Sci Hampshire Col Amherst MA 01002

COPPOC, GORDON LLOYD, b Larned, Kans, Nov 11, 39; m 62; c 2. PHARMACOLOGY, VETERINARY PHARMACOLOGY. *Educ:* Kans State Univ, BS, 61, DVM, 63; Harvard Univ PhD(pharmacol), 68. *Prof Exp:* Fel, Harvard Univ, 63-66; instr pharmacol, Sch Med, Univ NC, 66-67; res pharmacologist, US Air Force Sch Aerospace Med, 67-69; res fel, Ben May Lab Cancer Res, Univ Chicago, 69-71; asst prof, 71-73, assoc prof pharmacol, Sch Vet Sci & Med, 73-77, PROF VET PHARMACOL, SCH VET MED, PURDUE UNIV, 77-, HEAD, DEPT VET PHARMACOL & PHYSIOL, 79- *Mem:* AAAS; Am Vet Med Asn; Am Acad Vet Pharmacol & Therapeut; Asn Am Vet Med Col; Am Asn Vet Physiol & Pharmacol. *Res:* Biochemical pharmacology; pharmacokinetics; chemotherapy. *Mailing Add:* Sch of Vet Med Purdue Univ West Lafayette IN 47907

COPPOC, WILLIAM JOSEPH, b Cumberland, Iowa, July 14, 13; m 39; c 2. CHEMISTRY. *Educ:* Ottawa Univ, Kans, BSc, 35; Rice Inst Technol, MA, 37, PhD(chem), 39. *Hon Degrees:* DSc, Ottawa Univ, 55. *Prof Exp:* Chemist, Port Arthur, Tex, 39-44, asst to asst chief chemist, 44-47, 48-49, actg asst supvr, Grease Res, Beacon, NY, 47-48, asst dir, Res, 49-51, assoc dir, New York, 51-53, dir, 53-54, mgr res, Beacon, 54-57, res & develop, 57-60, sci planning & Info, 60-65, gen mgr res & tech dept, 65-68, vpres res & tech dept,

68-71, vpres environ protection, 71-78, CONSULT, TEXACO, INC, 78- *Concurrent Pos:* Mem, Gordon Res Conf Coun, 49-56, chmn, 55-56; mem environ studies bd, Nat Res Coun-Nat Acad Sci, 74-77; Woodrow Wilson vis fel, 81- *Mem:* AAAS; Am Chem Soc; fel Am Inst Chem; Soc Automotive Eng; Sigma Xi. *Res:* Coagulation of colloidal solutions; composition of hydrates; development of block type greases; ball and roller bearing greases; various industrial lubricants; soluble and non-soluble cutting oils; research administration; atmospheric chemistry. *Mailing Add:* 14 Lingwood Park Poughkeepsie NY 12601

COPPOCK, CARL EDWARD, b Dayton, Ohio, Dec 1, 32; m 59; c 3. ANIMAL NUTRITION. *Educ:* Ohio State Univ, BS, 54; Tex A&M Univ, MS, 55; Univ Md, PhD(dairy sci), 64. *Prof Exp:* Dairy husbandman, Agr Res Serv, USDA, 58-64; asst prof dairy cattle nutrit, Cornell Univ, 64-69, assoc prof animal sci, 69-77; PROF ANIMAL SCI, TEX A&M UNIV, 77- *Concurrent Pos:* Animal husbandman, Int Voluntary Serv, Laos, 56-58; vis prof, Purdue Univ, 70-71. *Mem:* Am Dairy Sci Asn; Am Soc Animal Sci; Am Inst Nutrit; Am Forage & Grassland Soc; Fedn Am Socs Exp Biol. *Res:* Energy metabolism of lactating cows; nonprotein nitrogen utilization by lactating cows; glucose availability to high producing cows; chloride-bicarbonate relationships in lactating cows. *Mailing Add:* Rm 218-B Kleberg Ctr Tex A&M Univ College Station TX 14850

COPPOCK, GLENN E(DGAR), b Cullman, Ala, May 18, 24; m 54; c 3. AGRICULTURAL ENGINEERING. *Educ:* Auburn Univ, BS, 49; Okla State Univ, MS, 55. *Prof Exp:* Res agr engr, tillage mach lab, 49-52, Okla State Univ, 53-56, cotton field sta, Calif, 56-57, RES AGR ENGR, USDA, FLA DEPT CITRUS, UNIV FLA, 57- *Mem:* Am Soc Agr Engrs. *Res:* Harvesting equipment and methods for peanuts, castor beans and citrus; mechanization of citrus harvest. *Mailing Add:* Univ of Fla Agr Res & Educ Ctr PO Box 1088 Lake Alfred FL 33850

COPPOCK, ROBERT WALTER, b Battle Creek, Mich, Aug 21, 42; m 65; c 3. TOXICOLOGY, PHARMACOLOGY. *Educ:* Andrews Univ, BSc, 65; Mich State Univ, DVM, 69; Am Bd Vet Toxicol, dipl, 78; Okla State Univ, MS, 81. *Prof Exp:* Clin vet pharmacologist, Parke, Davis & Co, 70-74; vet med, Inter Ridge Bet Clin, 75-77; vet toxicologist & pharmacologist, Dept Physiol Sci, Col Vet Med, Okla State Univ, 77-79; VET TOXICOLOGIST, UNIV ILL, URBANA, 80- *Mem:* Vet Med Asn BC; Am Vet Med Asn; Can Vet Med Asn. *Res:* Oil field toxicology; mycotoxins, grain fumigant. *Mailing Add:* Animal Poison Control Ctr Dept Vet Biosci Univ Ill Urbana IL 61801

COPPOLA, EDWARD DANTE, b Providence, RI, Dec 19, 30; m 56; c 4. SURGERY, MEDICAL EDUCATION. *Educ:* Amherst Col, AB, 51; Yale Univ, MD, 55; Am Bd Surg, dipl, 64. *Prof Exp:* Intern surg, Yale Univ Med Ctr, 55-56, asst resident, 56-61; from resident to chief resident, Hahnemann Med Col & Hosp, 61-63; from instr to sr instr, 63-66, from asst prof to assoc prof, 66-71; prof surg & chmn dept, Col Human Med, Mich State Univ, 71-77, chief surg, Univ Health Ctr, 71-77. *Concurrent Pos:* Clin fel, Am Cancer Soc, 61-63, advan clin fel, 63-66; attend surgeon, Hahnemann Med Col & Hosp, 63-71 & Philadelphia Vet Admin Hosp, 63-69; Markle scholar acad med, 66-71; asst attend physician, Philadelphia Gen Hosp, 63-67, attend physician, 67-71; attend staff, Edward W Sparrow Hosp, St Lawrence Hosp & Ingham Med Ctr, 71-; consult, Depts Surg, Wayne County Gen Hosp, Gratiot Community Hosp & Saginaw Vet Admin Hosp, 72- *Mem:* Fel Am Col Surgeons; Transplantation Soc; Am Asn Immunologists; Asn Acad Surg; Soc Exp Biol & Med. *Res:* Transplantation immunology. *Mailing Add:* Dept of Surg Col of Med Mich State Univ East Lansing MI 48824

COPPOLA, ELIA DOMENICO, b S Salvatore Telesino, Italy, Aug 2, 41; m 72; c 3. ANALYTICAL CHEMISTRY. *Educ:* Southern Conn State Col, BA, 67; Rensselaer Polytech Inst, PhD(anal chem), 72. *Prof Exp:* Chem technician, Upjohn Co, Conn, 64-67; res chemist anal chem, Conn Agr Exp Sta, 71-76; sr res chemist, 76-80, SUPVR ANAL, OCEAN SPRAY CRANBERRIES, MIDDLEBORO, 80- *Mem:* Am Chem Soc; Inst Food Technologists; Asn Official Anal Chemists. *Res:* The development of new analytical methods in food analysis; high-pressure liquid chromatography and thin-layer chromatography of food ingredients and contaminants; gas chromatography and high performance liquid chromatography of pesticide residues. *Mailing Add:* Ocean Spray Cranberries Bridge St Middleboro MA 02346

COPPOLA, JOHN ANTHONY, b Philadelphia, Pa, Jan 28, 38; div; c 2. ENDOCRINOLOGY, PHARMACOLOGY. *Educ:* La Salle Col, AB, 59; Hahnemann Med Col, MS, 61; Jefferson Med Col, PhD(pharmacol), 63. *Prof Exp:* Group leader endocrine pharmacol, Lederle Labs, Am Cyanamid Co, 63-72; dir med affairs, Schering Corp, 72-74; dir prof serv, Endo Labs, 74-78; dir sci mkt, Wm Douglas McAdams, 78-79; MED DIR, INTERCON BARMAK, 79- *Concurrent Pos:* Lederle fel, Univ Wis, 63-64. *Mem:* Endocrine Soc; Am Soc Pharmacol & Exp Therapeut; Soc Study Reproduction; Soc Study Fertil; Int Soc Res Reproduction. *Mailing Add:* Intercon Barmak 509 Madison Ave New York NY 10022

COPPOLA, PATRICK PAUL, b Buffalo, NY, June 30, 17; m 44; c 5. PHYSICAL CHEMISTRY, ELECTRONICS. *Educ:* Canisius Col, BS, 41, MS, 51. *Prof Exp:* Chemist, Anal Lab, Union Carbide & Carbon Corp, 41-42, chemist group leader, Metals Lab, 42-43, chemist, Res Lab, Manhattan Dist Contract, 43-46; res chemist, Philips Res Lab, 46-55; sr res engr, Radio Corp Am, 55-56; physicist & leader res group, Gen Elec Co, 56-60, mgr chem & phys electronics adv develop, 60-66, mgr mat develop, 66-68, mgr eng, Visual Commun Prod Dept, 68-72, mgr eng, Video Display Oper, 72-80; RETIRED. *Honors & Awards:* Award, US War Dept, 45. *Mem:* Am Chem Soc; NY Acad Sci; fel Am Inst Chem. *Res:* Electronic emission; vacuum physics; semiconductors; materials and processes; new business planning and organization. *Mailing Add:* 301 Fayette Dr Fayetteville NY 13066

COPPOLILLO, HENRY P, b Cervicati, Italy, July 27, 26; US citizen; m 62; c 3. PSYCHIATRY. *Educ:* Univ Rome, MD, 55. *Prof Exp:* Intern, Cook County Hosp, Ill, 55-56; res psychiat, Univ Chicago, 56-59; asst attend physician, Michael Reese Hosp, 59-61, pediat liaison psychiatrist, 61-65, assoc physician, 61-66, asst chief child psychiat, 63-65; asst prof, Med Sch, Univ Mich, 66-68, dir day care serv, Children's Psychiat Hosp, 66-68, assoc prof psychiat, Univ, 68-71, prof, 71, asst to chmn dept, 68-69, assoc chmn, 69-70, actg chmn, 70; prof psychiat & dir div child psychiat, Vanderbilt Univ, 71-76; PROF PSYCHIAT & DIR DIV CHILD PSYCHIAT, UNIV COLO MED CTR, 76- *Concurrent Pos:* Fel, Michael Reese Hosp, Chicago, 61-63; res asst psychiat, Northwestern Univ, 59-61, instr, 61-63; child psychiat consult, McLean County Health Clin, Ill, 59-66 & Med Sch, Univ Wis, 64; lectr, Col Lit, Sci & Arts, Univ Mich, 67; fac asst, Mich Psychoanal Inst, 69-70, lectr, 70-71. *Mem:* Fel Am Psychiat Asn; Am Acad Child Psychiat; fel Am Col Psychiat; Sigma Xi. *Res:* Child and adult psychiatry and psychoanalysis. *Mailing Add:* Div of Child Psychiat 4200 E Ninth Ave Denver CO 80262

COPPOLINO, ROBERT NUNZIO, applied mechanics, structural dynamics, see previous edition

COPSON, DAVID ARTHUR, b Boston, Mass, June 16, 18; m 60; c 7. BIOPHYSICS, MICROBIOLOGY. *Educ:* Univ Mass, BS, 40; Mass Inst Technol, PhD(tech), 53. *Prof Exp:* Group mgr res div, Raytheon Co, 53-58, consult microwave heating, 58-60; PROF BIOL, UNIV PR, MAYAGUEZ, 60- *Concurrent Pos:* Consult, IBM Corp, Whirlpool Corp, Sunbeam, FMC Corp & Am Can Co, 58-67. *Mem:* AAAS; Int Microwave Power Inst; Biophys Soc. *Res:* Microwave biophysics; athermic microwave effects; radiation and theoretical biology; information theory and biological communication; radiation hazards; automation of telecommunications analysis; electromagnetic spectrum characteristics, documentation and classification; integration of new technology in science education; informational bioelectromagnetics; microwave heating. *Mailing Add:* Box 3661 Mayaguez PR 00708

COPSON, HARRY ROLLASON, b Easthampton, Mass, July 8, 08; m 39, 74; c 3. CORROSION. *Educ:* Univ Mass, BS, 29; Yale Univ, PhD(phys chem), 32. *Prof Exp:* Res chemist, State Water Comn, Conn, 29-30; chief chemist, Apothecaries Hall Co, 33-34; res chemist, Int Nickel Co, 34-48, supvr corrosion sect, Res Lab, 48-62, chem res mgr, 62-72, res fel, 72-73; CONSULT, 73- *Honors & Awards:* Whitney Award, Nat Asn Corrosion Eng, 60; Dudley Medal, Am Soc Test & Mat, 46. *Mem:* Am Chem Soc; Electrochem Soc; Am Inst Chem Eng; Nat Asn Corrosion Eng. *Res:* Aqueous corrosion; high temperature dry corrosion; corrosion resisting alloys; coatings; electroplating; chemical engineering; nuclear engineering; electrochemistry; metallurgy. *Mailing Add:* 1 Deerfield Terrace Mahwah NJ 07430

COPULSKY, WILLIAM, b Zhitomir, Russia, Apr 4, 22; US citizen; m 48; c 3. INDUSTRIAL CHEMISTRY. *Educ:* NY Univ, BA, 42, PhD(econ), 57; City Col New York, MBA, 48. *Prof Exp:* Asst res dir, J J Beruner & Staff, 46-48; asst to pres, R S Aries & Assocs, 47-51; mgr com develop, 51-69, dir electronucleonics labs, 69-77, V PRES OPER SERV GROUP, W R GRACE & CO, 74- *Concurrent Pos:* Adj assoc prof, Baruch Col, 67-77. *Mem:* Am Chem Soc; Am Statist Asn; Am Mkt Asn. *Res:* Long range planning; forecasting of new technology; correlation techniques in forecasting; industrial chemical development. *Mailing Add:* W R Grace & Co 1114 Ave of the Americas New York NY 10036

CORAK, WILLIAM SYDNEY, b Philadelphia, Pa, Mar 10, 22; m 46; c 5. MATERIALS DEVELOPMENT, LOW TEMPERATURE PHYSICS. *Educ:* Univ Pa, BS, 43; Ohio State Univ, MS, 47; Univ Pittsburgh, PhD, 54. *Prof Exp:* Chem control engr, Davison Chem Corp, 43-44; res assoc, Johns Hopkins Univ, 44-45 & Ohio State Univ, 45-47; res engr, Westinghouse Res Labs, 47-55, mgr, Westinghouse Semi-Conductor Div, 55-64, MGR SOLID STATE TECHNOL, SCI & TECHNOL DEPT, SYSTS DEVELOP DIV, WESTINGHOUSE DEFENSE CTR, 64- *Mem:* Am Phys Soc; Inst Elec & Electronics Engrs. *Res:* Low temperature gas thermodynamics; low temperature techniques; superconductivity; low temperature specific heats; materials and process development; integrated circuit technology; solid state physics. *Mailing Add:* Advan Technol Div Westinghouse Defense Ctr B1521 Baltimore MD 21203

CORAN, AUBERT Y, b St Louis, Mo, Mar 24, 32; m 58; c 2. PHARMACY, ORGANIC CHEMISTRY. *Educ:* St Louis Col Pharm, BS, 53, MS, 55. *Prof Exp:* Instr chem, St Louis Col Pharm, 53-55; res chemist, Mo, 55-62, res group leader, WVa, 62-64, scientist, Mo, 64-70, sect mgr, Rubber Chem Res, Ohio, 70-75, DISTINGUISHED SCI FEL, MONSANTO CO, 75- *Concurrent Pos:* Ed, Rubber Chem & Technol J, 78- *Honors & Awards:* Thomas Midgley Award, Am Chem Soc, 80. *Mem:* Am Chem Soc; Sigma Xi. *Res:* Polymer and rubber science and technology; vulcanization kinetics and chemistry. *Mailing Add:* Monsanto Co Akron OH 44313

CORAOR, GEORGE ROBERT, b Jacksonville, Ill, May 10, 24; m 47; c 3. ORGANIC CHEMISTRY. *Educ:* Ill Col, AB, 47; Univ Ill, PhD(org chem), 50. *Prof Exp:* Res assoc org chem, Mass Inst Technol, 50-51; res chemist, 51-53, group leader, 53-55, sect head, 55-60, div head org chem, 60-76, SR CONSULT, E I DU PONT DE NEMOURS & CO, INC, 76- *Mem:* AAAS; Am Chem Soc. *Res:* Free radical reaction; coordination chemistry; photochemistry. *Mailing Add:* 29 Paxon Dr Penarth Wilmington DE 19803

CORBASCIO, ALDO NICOLA, b Castellana, Italy, Mar 21, 28; nat US; m 55; c 1. PHARMACOLOGY. *Educ:* Q Orazio Flacco, Bari, Italy, MA, 47; Univ Bari, MD, 53; Univ Pa, DSc(pharmacol), 58. *Prof Exp:* Intern, Med Clin, Univ Bari, 53-54; resident med, Univ Hosp, Univ Pa, 54-56, instr pharmacol, Sch Med, 56-59; asst res pharmacologist, Med Ctr, Univ Calif, San Francisco, 59-65; assoc prof, Sch Dent, Univ Pac, 63-67, prof pharmacol & chmn dept, 68-76; med dir, Rhone-Poulenc Inc, Birkerod, Denmark, 76-79;

NEUROPHARMACOLOGIST, NAPA STATE HOSP, IMOLA, CALIF, 79- *Concurrent Pos:* Lectr, Med Sch, Univ Ore; consult, Surgeon Gen, US Army Dept Anesthesiol, Med Sch, Stanford Univ. *Mem:* Am Soc Pharmacol & Exp Therapeut; Am Therapeut Soc. *Res:* Cardiovascular pharmacology. *Mailing Add:* 6451 Florio St Oakland CA 94618

CORBATO, CHARLES EDWARD, b Los Angeles, Calif, July 12, 32; m 57; c 3. GEOLOGY, GEOPHYSICS. *Educ:* Univ Calif, Los Angeles, BA, 54, PhD(geol), 60. *Prof Exp:* Instr geol, Univ Calif, Riverside, 59; from instr to asst prof, Univ Calif, Los Angeles, 59-66; assoc prof, 66-69, chmn, Dept Geol & Mineral, 72-80, PROF GEOL & MINERAL, OHIO STATE UNIV, 69- *Mem:* Geol Soc Am; Soc Explor Geophys; Am Geophys Union; Int Asn Math Geol; Am Inst Prof Geologists. *Res:* Exploration geophysics; structural geology; computer applications to geological problems. *Mailing Add:* Dept Geol & Mineral Ohio State Univ Columbus OH 43210

CORBATO, FERNANDO JOSE, b Oakland, Calif, July 1, 26; m 62, 75. PHYSICS, SOFTWARE SYSTEMS. *Educ:* Calif Inst Technol, BS, 50; Mass Inst Technol, PhD(physics), 56. *Prof Exp:* Res assoc, 56-59, asst dir prog res, Comput Ctr, 59-60, assoc dir, 60-63, dep dir, 63-66, group leader, Comput Systs Res Group, Lab Comput Sci, 63-72, co-head, Systs Res Div, 72-74, assoc head, Dept Comput Sci & Eng, 74-78, co-head, Automatic Prog Div, 72-74, assoc prof, 62-75, Cecil H Green prof, 78-80, PROF COMPUT SCI & ENG, MASS INST TECHNOL, 65-, DIR, COMPUT & TELECOMMUN RESOURCES, 80- *Concurrent Pos:* Mem comput sci & eng bd, Nat Acad Sci, 71-73. *Honors & Awards:* W W McDowall Award, Inst Elec & Electronics Eng, 66; Harry Goode Memorial Award, Am Fedn Info Processing Socs, 80. *Mem:* Nat Acad Eng; Asn Comput Mach; fel Inst Elec & Electronics Eng; fel Am Acad Arts & Sci; Am Phys Soc. *Res:* Computer operating systems; time-sharing systems; automatic programming and knowledge-based application systems. *Mailing Add:* Dept Comput Sci Mass Inst Technol 545 Technol Sq Rm 536 Cambridge MA 02139

CORBEELS, ROGER, b Kessel-Loo, Belgium, Apr 16, 36; m 62. FUEL SCIENCE, HIGH TEMPERATURE CHEMISTRY. *Educ:* Cath Univ Louvain, BS, 56, MS, 58, PhD(chem), 60. *Prof Exp:* Vis res assoc flame kinetics, Aerospace Res Labs, Wright-Patterson Air Force Base, Ohio, 62-64; sr chemist, 64-70, res chemist, 70-73, SR RES CHEMIST, TEXACO INC, 73- *Mem:* Am Chem Soc; Combustion Inst. *Res:* Kinetics of combustion reactions; coal chemistry. *Mailing Add:* Pine Ridge Dr Wappingers Falls NY 12590

CORBEN, HERBERT CHARLES, b Dorset, Eng, Apr 18, 14; US citizen; m 41, 57; c 3. THEORETICAL PHYSICS. *Educ:* Univ Melbourne, MA & MSc, 36; Cambridge Univ, PhD(theoret physics), 39. *Prof Exp:* Lectr math & physics, Univ Col Armidale, NSW, 41; dean, Trinity Col & lectr math & physics, Univ Melbourne, 42-44, sr lectr, 45-46; from assoc prof to prof physics, Carnegie Inst Technol, 46-56; mem tech staff, Ramo-Wooldridge Corp, 54-55, 56-57, assoc dir res lab, 57-61; dir quantum physics lab, TRW, Inc, 61-68, chief scientist, Phys Res Ctr, 66-68; prof physics, Cleveland State Univ, 68-72, dean faculties & grad studies, 68-70, vpres acad affairs, 70-72; chmn phys sci dept, 72-77, PROF PHYSICS, SCARBOROUGH COL, UNIV TORONTO, 72- *Concurrent Pos:* Rouse Ball res student, Trinity Col, Cambridge Univ, 36-39; Fulbright vis prof, Univs Genoa, Milan & Bologna, 51-53; consult, Ramo-Wooldridge Corp, 55-56; vis prof, Harvey Mudd Col, Claremont, Calif, 78-80. *Mem:* Fel Am Phys Soc. *Res:* Quantum theory; relativity theory; theory of nuclear forces; electromagnetic propagation; nuclear reactor theory; theory of elementary particles. *Mailing Add:* Phys Sci Group Scarborough Col Univ Toronto Toronto ON M1C 1A4 Can

CORBETT, GAIL RUSHFORD, b Rapid River, Mich, May 23, 36; m 59; c 2. PLANT ECOLOGY, TAXONOMIC BOTANY. *Educ:* Univ Mich, BA, 58, MS, 60, PhD(bot), 67. *Prof Exp:* Instr bot, W Va Univ, 63, res consult flora, 68-76, instr bot, 77; CONSULT FLORA, 77- *Concurrent Pos:* Consult eng firm, 80. *Mem:* Sigma Xi; Ecol Soc Am; Am Soc Plant Taxonomists; AAAS; Am Forestry Asn. *Res:* Phytosociological study of disturbed habitats. *Mailing Add:* 220 Atterbury Blvd Hudson OH 44236

CORBETT, JAMES MURRAY, b Welland, Ont, Can, Jan 29, 38; m 58; c 3. PHYSICS. *Educ:* Univ Toronto, BASc, 60; Univ Waterloo, MSc, 61, PhD(physics), 66. *Prof Exp:* Lectr, 62-66, asst prof, 66-74, ASSOC PROF PHYSICS, UNIV WATERLOO, 74- *Concurrent Pos:* Nat Res Coun Can res fel, Dept Metall, Oxford Univ, 67-68. *Mem:* Electron Micros Soc Am; Can Asn Physicists. *Res:* Nucleation, growth and structure of vacuum-deposited films; electron microscopy of thin crystals. *Mailing Add:* Dept of Physics Univ of Waterloo Waterloo ON N2L 3G1 Can

CORBETT, JAMES WILLIAM, b New York, NY, Aug 25, 28; m 54, 72; c 2. SOLID STATE PHYSICS. *Educ:* Univ Mo, BS, 51, MA, 52; Yale Univ, PhD(physics), 55; King Mem Col, DSc, 77. *Prof Exp:* Res assoc chem, Yale Univ, 55; res assoc, Gen Elec Res Lab, 55-68; chmn, Physics Dept, 69-70, prof physics, 68-81, DIR, INST STUDY DEFECTS IN SOLIDS, STATE UNIV NY, ALBANY, 74-, DISTINGUISHED SERV PROF, 81- *Concurrent Pos:* Adj prof, Rensselaer Polytech Inst, 64-68; chmn, Int Conf Radiation Effects in Semiconductors, 70 & Int Conf Radiation-Induced Voids in Metals, 71; exchange scholar, US-USSR Exchange Prog, Nat Acad Sci, 73; Guggenheim fel, 75; lectr oenology, State Univ NY Albany, 72-; vis prof, Am Univ Cairo, 73, Ecole Normale Superieure & Univ Paris VII, 76 & Tbilisi State Univ, 79. *Honors & Awards:* Ivane Javakishvili Medal, 77. *Mem:* Fel Am Phys Soc; Am Asn Physics Teachers; Inst Elec & Electronics Engrs; fel NY Acad Sci. *Res:* Point defects in semiconductors and metals; radiation damage; reaction kinetics; nucleation theory. *Mailing Add:* Dept of Physics State Univ of NY Albany NY 12222

CORBETT, JOHN DUDLEY, b Yakima, Wash, Mar 23, 26; m 48; c 3. INORGANIC CHEMISTRY. *Educ:* Univ Wash, BS, 48, PhD(chem), 52. *Prof Exp:* From assoc chemist to sr chemist, Ames Lab, US AEC, 52-63, div chief, 68-73; from asst prof to assoc prof chem, 52-63, chmn dept, 68-73, prog dir, Ames Lab, Dept Energy, 74-78, PROF CHEM, IOWA STATE UNIV, 63- *Concurrent Pos:* vis scientist, Max-Planck Inst fur Festkorperforschung, Stutlgart & Tech Univ Denmark, 79. *Mem:* Am Chem Soc. *Res:* Inorganic and physical chemistry; unfamiliar oxidation states; solid state chemistry. *Mailing Add:* Dept of Chem Iowa State Univ Ames IA 50011

CORBETT, JOHN FRANK, b Doncaster, Eng, May 8, 35; c 3. ORGANIC CHEMISTRY, COSMETIC CHEMISTRY. *Educ:* Royal Inst Chem, London, ARIC, 57; Univ Reading, PhD(org chem), 61. *Prof Exp:* Res scientist chem, Gillette Res Labs, Eng, 61-62, head dept org chem, 63-69; sr res scientist chem, Gillette Co, Chicago, 70-71; mgr special proj, Gillette Res Labs, Eng, 72; dir res chem, 72-74, VPRES RES, CLAIROL RES LAB, STAMFORD, CONN, 74- *Mem:* Fel Royal Inst Chem; The Chem Soc; Soc Cosmetic Chemists; Fel Soc Dyers & Colorists. *Res:* Synthesis and properties of dyestuffs, mechanism of oxidative dyeing processes. *Mailing Add:* Clairol Res Lab 2 Blachley Rd Stamford CT 06902

CORBETT, JULES JOHN, b Natrona, Pa, Apr 12, 19; m 50; c 3. MICROBIOLOGY. *Educ:* Univ Chicago, BS, 50; Ill Inst Technol, MS, 57. *Prof Exp:* Instr microbiol & chem, Sch Nursing & bacteriologist, Englewood Hosp, 50-54; dir labs, Beverly Med Arts Bldg, 54-55; from instr to assoc prof, 56-72, chmn biol dept, 74-78, PROF BIOL, ROOSEVELT UNIV, 72- *Concurrent Pos:* Bacteriologist, Borden Co, Ill, 55-64. *Mem:* AAAS; Am Soc Microbiol. *Res:* Immunology and pathogenicity of chromobacterium violaceum. *Mailing Add:* Dept of Biol Roosevelt Univ Chicago IL 60605

CORBETT, M KENNETH, b Port Lorne, NS, Sept 12, 27; m 50; c 3. PLANT PATHOLOGY. *Educ:* McGill Univ, BSc, 50; Cornell Univ, PhD(plant path), 54. *Prof Exp:* Asst plant path, Cornell Univ, 50-54; asst plant pathologist & asst prof, Univ Fla, 54-60, assoc virologist, Agr Exp Sta, 60-66; assoc prof, 66-69, PROF BOT, UNIV MD, 69- *Concurrent Pos:* Guggenheim fel, Netherlands, 64-65. *Mem:* Am Phytopath Soc. *Res:* Virology; biochemistry; plant physiology; plant breeding and pathology. *Mailing Add:* Dept of Bot Univ of Md Col of Agr College Park MD 20742

CORBETT, MICHAEL DENNIS, b Great Bend, Kans, Feb 23, 44; m 80; c 4. TOXICOLOGY. *Educ:* Univ Kans, BS, 66, PhD(med chem), 70. *Prof Exp:* Asst prof pharmacog, Univ Miss, 70-73, assoc prof, 73-74; sr chemist, Midwest Res Inst, 75-76; assoc prof marine chem, Univ Miami, 76-81, prof, 81; PROF FOOD SCI HUMAN NUTRIT, UNIV FLA, 81- *Concurrent Pos:* Res career develop award, Nat Inst Environ Health Sci, 78-83; adj prof biochem, Univ Fla, 81- *Mem:* Am Chem Soc; AAAS; Sigma Xi. *Res:* Bioorganic chemistry of agricultural and other industrial organic chemicals; metabolism of aromatic amine and nitro compounds, including microbial conversions and mineralization processes; biochemical activation of toxic materials. *Mailing Add:* Food Sci & Human Nutrit Dept Pesticide Res Lab Univ Fla Gainesville FL 33611

CORBETT, ROBERT B(ARNHART), b Akron, Ohio, May 15, 17; m 41, 55; c 3. METALLURGICAL ENGINEERING. *Educ:* Carnegie Inst Technol, BS, 39; Univ Pittsburgh, MS, 42, PhD(metall eng), 44. *Prof Exp:* Student engr, Jones & Laughlin Steel Corp, 39-40; instr ferrous & non-ferrous metall, Univ Pittsburgh, 40-42; metallurgist, US Bur Mines, 42-45; res metallurgist, Heppenstall Co, Pa, 45-51, dir res & asst to pres, 51-56, dir metall, Midvale-Heppenstall Co, 56-59, consult, 59-62; pres, Corbett Assocs, Inc, 64-69; tech dir, Roll Mfg Inst, 77-81; MGR RES & DEVELOP, MACKINTOSH-HEMPHILL DIV, GULF & WESTERN MFG CO, 81- *Concurrent Pos:* Vpres, Satec Corp, 52-64; Calsicat Corp, 58-64. *Mem:* Am Inst Mining, Metall & Petrol Engrs; Am Soc Testing & Mat; Am Soc Metals; Asn Iron & Steel Engrs; Am Steel & Foundry Asn. *Res:* Metallurgy; testing machines; design and consult. *Mailing Add:* 111 Meadow Lane Bakerstown PA 15007

CORBETT, ROBERT G, b Chicago, Ill, Mar 13, 35; m 59; c 1. ECONOMIC GEOLOGY, GEOCHEMISTRY. *Educ:* Univ Mich, BS, 58, MS, 59, PhD(geol), 64. *Prof Exp:* From asst prof to assoc prof geol, WVa Univ, 62-69, prin investr, Water Res Inst, 67-69; assoc prof, 69-75, PROF GEOL, UNIV AKRON, 75-, COORDR RES, 72- *Mem:* Mineral Soc Am; Geochem Soc; Nat Asn Geol Teachers; Geol Soc Am; Soc Res Adminr. *Res:* Formation of hydroxylapatite; geology and mineralogy of uranium deposits; chemical characteristics of natural waters; mineral deposits. *Mailing Add:* Dept of Geol Univ of Akron Akron OH 44304

CORBETT, THOMAS HUGHES, b Appelton, Wis, Oct 11, 38; m 61; c 2. CANCER CHEMOTHERAPY. *Educ:* Univ Wis, BS, 64, PhD(oncol), 70. *Prof Exp:* Technician cardiovasc, Sch Med, Univ Wis, 63; fel carcinogenesis, Oak Ridge Nat Lab, 70-72; HEAD SOLID TUMOR BIOL & TREAT DIV CANCER RES, SOUTHERN RES INST, 72- *Mem:* Am Asn Cancer Res. *Res:* Cancer chemotherapy of transplantable tumors in mice; chemical carcinogenesis. *Mailing Add:* Southern Res Inst 2000 Ninth Ave S Birmingham AL 35205

CORBIN, ALAN, b New York, NY, Sept 3, 34; m 59. NEUROENDOCRINOLOGY, REPRODUCTIVE PHYSIOLOGY. *Educ:* City Col New York, BS, 56; Univ Iowa, MS, 60, PhD(physiol), 61. *Prof Exp:* Instr anat, Albert Einstein Col Med, 61-63; instr, Inst Pharmacol, Milan, Italy, 63-64; sr investr endocrinol, Sci Div, Abbott Labs, 64-66; sr res scientist, Squibb Inst Med Res, 66-71; head endocrinol, 71-80, ASSOC DIR BIOL RES, WYETH LABS, 80- *Concurrent Pos:* Fel neuroanat, Albert Einstein Col Med, 61-63 & Inst Pharmacol, Milan, Italy, 63-64; NIH fel, 61-64; adj prof physiol, Rutgers Univ, New Brunswick; mem res grant review adv panel, NSF. *Mem:* Endocrine Soc; Int Soc Res Reproduction; Int Soc Neuroendocrinol; Am Physiol Soc. *Res:* Neuroendocrinology of mammalian reproduction; contraception; fertility regulation; general endocrinology; neuroanatomy; pharmacology of hypothalamic releasing factors; neuropharmacology. *Mailing Add:* Endocrinol Sect Wyeth Labs Box 8299 Philadelphia PA 19101

CORBIN, FREDERICK THOMAS, b Franklin, NC, Dec 2, 29; m 52; c 2. WEED SCIENCE, PLANT PHYSIOLOGY. *Educ:* Wake Forest Col, BS, 51; Univ NC, MEd, 56; NC State Univ, PhD(physiol, microbiol), 65. *Prof Exp:* Teacher high sch, NC, 53-56; instr chem & physics, Mars Hill Col, 56-60; asst prof physics, ECarolina Col, 60-62; res asst, 62-65, asst prof weed sci, 65-80, PROF CROP SCI, NC STATE UNIV, 80- *Concurrent Pos:* Agr Res Serv grant, 65-68. *Mem:* AAAS; Weed Sci Soc Am; Am Phys Soc. *Res:* Interactions between major classes of chemical pesticides; biotransformation of herbicides. *Mailing Add:* Dept Crop Sci N C State Univ Raleigh NC 27650

CORBIN, JACK DAVID, b Franklin, NC, Feb 8, 41; m 65; c 1. PHYSIOLOGY, BIOCHEMISTRY. *Educ:* Tenn Technol Univ, BS, 63; Vanderbilt Univ, PhD(physiol), 68. *Prof Exp:* ASSOC PROF PHYSIOL, VANDERBILT UNIV, 71- *Concurrent Pos:* NIH fel, Univ Calif, Davis, 68-70; Am Diabetes Asn fel, Univ Calif, Davis & Vanderbilt Univ, 70-71 & Vanderbilt Univ, 71-72; NIH res grant, 72, Diabetes Ctr grant, 74. *Mem:* AAAS; Am Soc Biol Chemists. *Res:* Molecular endocrinology; hormone regulation; cyclic nucleotide regulation; protein kinase. *Mailing Add:* Dept of Physiol Vanderbilt Univ Sch of Med Nashville TN 37232

CORBIN, JAMES EDWARD, b Providence, Ky, July 14, 21; m 50; c 4. ANIMAL NUTRITION. *Educ:* Univ Ky, BS, 43, MS, 47; Univ Ill, PhD(animal nutrit), 51. *Prof Exp:* Dir res, Nat Oats Co, 51-54; mgr special chows res, Ralston Purina Co, 54-59, mgr dog res, 59-67; dir pet care ctr, 67-73; PROF ANIMAL SCI, UNIV ILL, URBANA, 73- *Concurrent Pos:* Chmn dog nutrit subcomt, Nat Res Coun, 68-; chmn dog & cat standards, Inst Lab Animal Resources, Nat Acad Sci. *Mem:* Am Soc Animal Sci; Am Asn Lab Animal Sci (pres, 72-73); Am Inst Nutrit; Am Asn Lab Animal Sci; Brit Small Animal Vet Med Asn. *Res:* Nutrition of dogs and laboratory animals. *Mailing Add:* 160 Animal Sci Bldg Dept of Animal Sci Univ of Ill Urbana IL 61801

CORBIN, JAMES LEE, b Coshocton, Ohio, Oct 20, 35; m 60. ORGANIC CHEMISTRY. *Educ:* Bowling Green State Univ, BA, 57; Mich State Univ, PhD, 62. *Prof Exp:* Proj chemist, Am Oil Co, Ind, 62-63; INVESTR, KETTERING RES LAB, 63- *Mem:* Am Chem Soc; The Chem Soc. *Res:* Structure of natural products; synthesis; design and synthesis of novel ligand systems; metal complexes; siderophores. *Mailing Add:* Charles F Kettering Res Lab 150 E College St Yellow Springs OH 45387

CORBIN, KENDALL BROOKS, b Oak Park, Ill, Dec 31, 07; m 32; c 2. NEUROLOGY, MEDICAL ADMINISTRATION. *Educ:* Stanford Univ, AB, 31, MD, 35. *Prof Exp:* Instr anat, Stanford Univ, 34-38; from assoc prof to prof, Col Med, Univ Tenn, 38-46, chief div, 41-46, in charge neurol, 43-46; prof neuroanat, 46-54, prof neurol, 54-72, EMER PROF NEUROL, MAYO GRAD SCH, 72- *Concurrent Pos:* Nat Res Coun fel, Neurol Inst, Northwestern Univ, 37-38; assoc dir, Mayo Found, 50-54, pres staff, 68, chmn bd develop, 69-72; head sect neurol, Mayo Clin, 57-63, sr consult, 63-72, emer consult, Mayo Clin & Mayo Found, 72-; pres, Friends of Gardens, Mario Selby Bot Gardens, Fla, 75- *Mem:* Am Physiol Soc; Soc Exp Biol & Med; fel Am Neurol Asn; Am Asn Anat; fel Am Acad Neurol. *Res:* Neuroanatomy; neurophysiology; clinical neurology; medical administration. *Mailing Add:* 600 4th St SW Apt 304 Rochester MN 55901

CORBIN, KENDALL WALLACE, b Memphis, Tenn, Apr 5, 39; m 61, 81; c 2. EVOLUTIONARY BIOLOGY, POPULATION ECOLOGY. *Educ:* Carleton Col, BA, 61; Cornell Univ, PhD(vert biol), 65. *Prof Exp:* NIH res fel, 65-67; res assoc & lectr biol, Yale Univ, 67-70; asst prof ecol & behav biol, 70-73, ASSOC PROF ECOL & BEHAV BIOL, UNIV MINN, MINNEAPOLIS, 73-, CUR SYSTS, 70-, CHMN PROG EVOLUTIONARY & SYST BIOL, 74- *Mem:* AAAS; Soc Study Evolution; fel Am Ornith Union (secy, 77-81); Cooper Ornith Soc; Am Soc Naturalists. *Res:* Evolutionary relationships among bird species using comparative biochemical data on the structure of protein molecules; studies of protein polymorphisms and genetic structure of populations; gene flow and natural selection in animal populations. *Mailing Add:* Dept of Ecol & Behav Biol Univ of Minn Bell Mus Natural Hist Minneapolis MN 55455

CORBIN, MICHAEL H, US citizen. ENGINEERING. *Educ:* Univ Va, BS, 70; Mass Inst Technol, MS, 72. *Prof Exp:* Res asst, Mass Inst Technol, 70-72; engr, County of Fairfax, Va, 72-76; PROJ ENGR, WESTON, 76- *Mem:* Dipl Am Acad Environ Engrs; Sigma Xi. *Res:* Solid waste and hazardous waste management including disposal, collection, storage, transfer, shredding, and resource recovery; industrial waste disposal and sludge management disposal facility design and permiting. *Mailing Add:* Weston Weston Way West Chester PA 19380

CORBIN, THOMAS ELBERT, b Orange, NJ, Sept 6, 40; m 66; c 1. ASTRONOMY. *Educ:* Harvard Univ, AB, 62; Georgetown Univ, MA, 69; Univ Va, PhD(astron), 77. *Prof Exp:* ASTRONOMER, US NAVAL OBSERV, 64- *Mem:* Am Astron Soc; Int Astron Union; Sigma Xi. *Res:* Positional astronomy; fundamental astrometry; proper motion systems. *Mailing Add:* US Naval Observ Washington DC 20390

CORBITT, MAURICE R(AY), b St Matthews, SC, Jan 28, 31. CHEMICAL ENGINEERING. *Educ:* Clemson Univ, BS, 53. *Prof Exp:* Tech engr, viscose rayon, E I du Pont de Nemours & Co, Tenn, 53-54, cellulose sponges, 56-59; res assoc, 60-80, TECH GROUP LEADER, SONOCO PROD CO, 80- *Mem:* Am Soc Testing & Mat. *Res:* Viscose chemistry of rayon and cellulose sponges; engineering and physical testing of superior paper products for textile, paper, film, packaging and construction industries. *Mailing Add:* PO Box 1635 Hartsville SC 29550

CORBO, VINCENT JAMES, b Port Chester, NY, Apr 28, 43; m 65; c 2. PROCESS DEVELOPMENT. *Educ:* Manhattan Col, BChemE, 65; Princeton Univ, MA, 67, PhD(chem eng), 70. *Prof Exp:* Res engr, 69-74, sr res engr, 74-75, res supvr, 75-77, res mgr chem eng, 77, MGR, ENG SCI DIV, DEVELOP DEPT, HERCULES INC, 77- *Mem:* Am Chem Soc; Am Inst Chem Engrs. *Res:* Optimal control theory; computer applications; numerical analysis. *Mailing Add:* Hercules Res Ctr Wilmington DE 19899

CORBY, DONALD G, b Jamestown, NDak, Jan 13, 34; m 59; c 6. PEDIATRICS, HEMATOLOGY. *Educ:* Univ NDak, BSc, 57; Northwestern Univ, MD, 59; Am Bd Pediat, dipl, 65 & 74. *Prof Exp:* Intern, Evanston Hosp Asn, Ill, 59-60; resident pediat, Children's Mem Hosp, Chicago, 60-61; resident pediat, US Army, 61, chief pediat, 225th Sta Hosp, Europe, 61-63; resident pediat, Brooke Gen Hosp, Ft Sam Houston, Tex, 63-65, asst chief pediat, William Beaumont Gen Hosp, El Paso, 65-68, dir spec educ & clin res pediat, 70-71, CHIEF, DEPT CLIN INVEST, FITZSIMONS ARMY MED CTR, 71-; ASST CLIN PROF PEDIAT, SCH MED, UNIV COLO, DENVER, 70- *Concurrent Pos:* Fel pediat hemat, Univ Ill, 68-70; grad fac, Dept Micro, Sch Vet Med, Colo State Univ, Ft Collins. *Honors & Awards:* Cert of Achievement & Army Commendation Medal, William Beaumont Gen Hosp, 68. *Mem:* AAAS; fel Am Acad Pediat; Am Acad Clin Toxicol; Am Soc Hemat; Soc Pediat Res. *Res:* Toxicology; specifically prevention and treatment of accidental poisoning in childhood; coagulation physiology. *Mailing Add:* Clin Invest Serv Fitzsimons Army Med Ctr Denver CO 80240

CORCINO, JOSE JUAN, b Humacao, PR, May 22, 38; c 2. HEMATOLOGY, GASTROENTEROLOGY. *Educ:* Univ PR, BS, 58, MD, 62; Tulane Univ, MS, 64. *Prof Exp:* Fel hemat, Sch Med, Univ PR, 65-66; USPHS fel, Mt Sinai Sch Med, 68-70; trainee & instr gastroenterol, Sch Med, Univ Rochester, 70-72; DIR TROP MALABSORPTION UNIT, SCH MED, UNIV PR, 72-, DIR GEN CLIN RES CTR, 73- *Concurrent Pos:* NIH acad career award nutrit, Sch Med, Univ PR, 73- *Mem:* Am Soc Hemat; Am Soc Clin Nutrit; Am Fedn Clin Res; AAAS; Am Col Nutrit. *Res:* Nutritional anemias, especially megaloblastic anemias; vitamin B12 and folate metabolism; intestinal absorption and malabsorption; tropical sprue, etiology, pathogenism and therapy. *Mailing Add:* Gen Clin Res Ctr GPO Box 5067 San Juan PR 00936

CORCORAN, EUGENE FRANCIS, b Arthur, NDak, Nov 28, 16; m 40; c 2. OCEANOGRAPHY. *Educ:* NDak Agr Col, BS, 40; Univ Calif, PhD(oceanog), 58. *Prof Exp:* Instr math, San Diego State Col, 46-49; asst marine biochem, Scripps Inst, Univ Calif, 49-50, res biochemist, 52-57; from asst prof to assoc prof, 57-72, PROF BIOL & LIVING RESOURCES, DOROTHY H & LEWIS ROSENSTIEL SCH MARINE & ATMOSPHERIC SCI, UNIV MIAMI, 72- *Concurrent Pos:* Assoc prog dir facils & spec progs, NSF, 67-68. *Mem:* AAAS; Am Chem Soc; Geochem Soc; Am Soc Limnol & Oceanog; Marine Biol Asn UK. *Res:* Organic productivity of sea water; photosynthesis in marine plants; organic constituents and trace metals of sea water and marine sediments. *Mailing Add:* Sch of Marine & Atmospheric Sci Univ of Miami 4600 Rickenbacker Miami FL 33124

CORCORAN, JOHN W, b Dayton, Ohio, Sept 23, 24; m 49; c 2. PEDODONTICS. *Educ:* Miami Univ, BA, 48; Western Reserve Univ, DDS, 53; Am Bd Pedodontics, dipl, 62. *Prof Exp:* Intern, Univ Hosps, Cleveland, Ohio, 53-54, resident, 54-55; pvt pract pedodontics, 55-65; from asst prof to assoc prof pedodontics, Case Western Reserve Univ, 65-68; PROF PEDIAT DENT & CHMN DEPT, MED UNIV SC, 68-, STAFF MEM, DEPT DENT, UNIV HOSP, 69- *Concurrent Pos:* Supvr, Dent Fillings Clin, City Cleveland Babies & Children's Hosp, 58-65; assoc dent surgeon & dent surgeon, Univ Hosps, Cleveland, 65-68; dir dent serv, Coastal Habilitation Ctr, 68- *Mem:* Am Dent Asn; Am Acad Pedodontics; Am Soc Dent for Children. *Res:* Clinical research for the handicapped child. *Mailing Add:* Dept of Pediat Dent Med Univ of SC Charleston SC 29403

CORCORAN, JOHN WILLIAM, b Des Moines, Iowa, June 12, 27; m 48; c 2. BIOCHEMISTRY. *Educ:* Iowa State Univ, BS, 49; Western Reserve Univ, PhD, 55. *Prof Exp:* Instr biochem, Columbia Univ, 56-57; from asst prof to assoc prof, Western Reserve Univ, 57-68; PROF BIOCHEM & CHMN DEPT, MED SCH, NORTHWESTERN UNIV, CHICAGO, 68- *Concurrent Pos:* Vis fel, Columbia Univ, 55-56; Am Heart Asn res fel, 55-58; USPHS career develop award, 64-; estab investr, Am Heart Asn, 58-63; acad guest, Lab Org Chem, Swiss Fed Inst Technol, 64-65; pharmaceut consult, 68-; vis prof, Univ London, 78. *Mem:* AAAS; Am Soc Biol Chem; Am Soc Microbiol; Am Chem Soc. *Res:* Mechanisms of sensitivity and resistance to antibiotics; antibiotic chemistry; natural product chemistry; carbohydrate chemistry; biosynthesis of natural products; carbohydrate metabolism; actinomycete metabolism. *Mailing Add:* Dept of Biochem Northwestern Univ Med Sch Chicago IL 60611

CORCORAN, MARJORIE, b Dayton, Ohio, July 21, 50; m 72; c 1. PARTICLE PHYSICS. *Educ:* Univ Dayton, BS, 72; Ind Univ, PhD(physics), 77. *Prof Exp:* Res assoc physics, Univ Wis, 77-79; vis asst prof, 80-81, ASST PROF PHYSICS, RICE UNIV, 81- *Mem:* Am Phys Soc. *Res:* Hadronic reactions resulting in high transverse momentum secondary particles; such interactions are believed to arise from the hard scattering of the hadrons constituents; spin dependence of hadronic interactions. *Mailing Add:* T W Bonner Nuclear Labs Rice Univ PO Box 1892 Houston TX 77001

CORCORAN, MARY RITZEL, b Los Angeles, Calif, July 3, 28; m 57; c 2. GENETICS, PLANT PHYSIOLOGY. *Educ:* Univ Calif, Los Angeles, BA, 53, PhD(bot), 59. *Prof Exp:* Asst bot, Univ Calif, Los Angeles, 54-59, jr res botanist, 59-62; from asst prof to assoc prof, 62-71, PROF BIOL, CALIF STATE UNIV, NORTHRIDGE, 71- *Mem:* AAAS; Bot Soc Am; Am Soc Plant Physiol. *Res:* Plant growth hormones and inhibitors. *Mailing Add:* Dept of Biol Calif State Univ Northridge CA 91324

CORCORAN, VINCENT JOHN, b Chicago, Ill, Oct 7, 34; m 57; c 5. LASERS. *Educ:* Univ Notre Dame, BSEE, 57; Univ Ill, MSEE, 58; Univ Fla, PhD(elec eng), 68. *Prof Exp:* Staff mem infrared, Lab Appl Sci, Univ Chicago, 58-62; vpres lasers, Astromarine Prod Corp, 62-63; sr res scientist, Martin Marietta Aerospace, 63-73; RES STAFF MEM LASERS, INST DEFENSE ANAL, 73- *Mem:* Optical Soc Am; Inst Elec & Electronic Engrs. *Res:* Laser technology needed for technology base for future Department of Defense systems including blue-green laser, search radar, laser aided imaging, coherent receivers, optical phased arrays and atmospheric transmission properties in the far infrared region. *Mailing Add:* Inst for Defense Anal 400 Army-Navy Dr Arlington VA 22202

CORCORAN, WILLIAM H(ARRISON), b Los Angeles, Calif, Mar 11, 20; m 42; c 2. CHEMICAL ENGINEERING. *Educ:* Calif Inst Technol, BS, 41, MS, 42, PhD(chem eng), 48. *Prof Exp:* res supvr & develop engr, Off Sci Res & Develop contract, Calif Inst Technol, 42-46, Nat Res fel, 46-48; dir tech develop, Cutter Labs, 48-52; from assoc prof to prof chem eng, 52-79, exec officer chem eng, 67-79, INST PROF CHEM ENG, CALIF INST TECHNOL, 79- *Concurrent Pos:* Sci dir, Don Baxter, Inc, 57-59; Western Elec Fund award, 69-70; Phillips lectr, Okla State Univ, 71. *Honors & Awards:* Lamme Award, Am Soc Engr Educ, 79. *Mem:* Fel AAAS; fel Am Inst Chem; Am Chem Soc; fel Am Inst Chem Engrs; fel Inst Advan Eng. *Res:* Heat and mass tranfer in fluid systems; applied chemical kinetics; biochemical engineering; biomedical engineering. *Mailing Add:* Calif Inst Technol 1201 E California Blvd Pasadena CA 91125

CORCOS, ALAIN FRANCOIS, b Paris, France, June 7, 25; US citizen; m 50; c 2. GENETICS. *Educ:* Mich State Univ, BS, 51, MS, 52, PhD(plant breeding), 60. *Prof Exp:* Plant breeder, Grant Merrill Orchards, Inc, 58-60; assoc biol, Univ Calif, Santa Barbara, 61-63; instr, Ore Col Educ, 63-64; res assoc virol, Inst Cancer Res, Philadelphia, 64-65; from asst prof to assoc prof natural sci, 65-73, PROF NATURAL SCI, MICH STATE UNIV, 73- *Concurrent Pos:* Co-ed, Arabidopsis Inf Serv Newslett, 74- *Mem:* Genetics Soc Am; Am Genetic Asn; NY Acad Sci. *Res:* Genetics and molecular biology of Arabidopsis thaliana; history of biology and concepts; theories of aging. *Mailing Add:* 530 Marshall East Lansing MI 48823

CORCOS, GILLES M, b Paris, France, Sept 10, 26; US citizen; m; c 3. FLUID MECHANICS. *Educ:* Univ Mich, BS, 49, MS, 50, PhD(aero eng), 52. *Hon Degrees:* Doctorat d'Etat, Univ Grenoble, 80. *Prof Exp:* Fel fluid mech, Johns Hopkins Univ, 52-54; aerodyn engr, Douglas Aircraft Co, 54-58; from asst prof to assoc prof, 58-67, PROF AERONAUT SCI, UNIV CALIF, BERKELEY, 67- *Concurrent Pos:* Liaison scientist, Off Naval Res, London, Eng, 64-65; assoc forestry dept, Johns Hopkins Univ, 61- *Mem:* AAAS; Am Phys Soc. *Res:* Turbulent boundary layers; airfoil theory; aerodynamic noise; geophysical flows; blood flow; ocean currents; stratified flow turbulence; mantle convection; fluid dynamics of and transport in turbulent shear flows. *Mailing Add:* 506 Arlington Ave Berkeley CA 94707

CORDEA, JAMES NICHOLAS, b Akron, Ohio, July 15, 37; m 59; c 3. PHYSICAL METALLURGY. *Educ:* Case Inst Technol, BS, 59; Ohio State Univ, MS, 62, PhD(metall eng), 65. *Prof Exp:* Welding engr, Battelle Mem Inst, 59-62; res engr, 64-68, sr res metallurgist, 68-70, supvry res metallurgist, 70-77, SR STAFF METALLURGIST, ARMCO STEEL CORP, 77- *Concurrent Pos:* Chmn ship mat, fabrication & inspection adv group, Ship Res Comt, Nat Res Coun, 78-79. *Mem:* Am Soc Metals; Am Inst Mining, Metall & Petrol Engrs; Nat Asn Corrosion Engrs. *Res:* Welding processes; steel or ferrous metallurgy; basic science. *Mailing Add:* Res Ctr Armco Steel Corp Middletown OH 45042

CORDELL, BRUCE MONTEITH, b Shelby, Mich, Sept 10, 49; m 77. PLANETARY SCIENCE. *Educ:* Mich State Univ, BS, 71; Univ Calif, Los Angeles, MS, 73; Univ Ariz, PhD(planetary sci), 77. *Prof Exp:* Res fel planetary sci, Calif Inst Technol, 77-78; ASST PROF EARTH SCI, CENT CONN STATE COL, 78- *Mem:* Am Geophys Union; Am Astron Soc. *Res:* Origin and evolution of planets; planetary tectonics; atmosphersurface interactions; geophysics. *Mailing Add:* Dept of Physics Cent Conn State Col New Britain CT 06050

CORDELL, RICHARD WILLIAM, b Brooklyn, NY, Oct 4, 39; m 66. ANALYTICAL CHEMISTRY. *Educ:* Villanova Univ, BS, 61; Ohio Univ, PhD(anal chem), 66. *Prof Exp:* Asst prof, 65-69, ASSOC PROF CHEM, HEIDELBERG COL, 69- *Mem:* Am Chem Soc; Sigma Xi. *Res:* Platinum group metals; organic analytical reagents. *Mailing Add:* Dept of Chem Heidelberg Col Tiffin OH 44883

CORDELL, ROBERT JAMES, b Quincy, Ill, Jan 7, 17; m 42; c 3. PETROLEUM GEOLOGY. *Educ:* Univ Ill, BS, 39, MS, 40; Univ Mo, PhD(geol), 49. *Prof Exp:* Asst, Univ Ill, 39-40; asst instr geol, Univ Mo, 41-42, instr 46-47; instr Colgate Univ, 47-51; res geologist, Sun Oil Co, 51-53, dir res, Abilene Labs, 53-55, mgr geol res, 55-63, sr sect mgr basic res, 66-68 & paleontology, 68-70, res scientist, 70-75, sr res scientist, 75-76, sr prof scientist, 76-77; PRES, CORDELL REPORTS, INC, 77- *Concurrent Pos:* Mem US Potential Gas Comt, 75- *Mem:* Fel AAAS; Paleont Soc; Soc Econ Paleontologists & Mineralogists; Am Asn Petrol Geologists; fel Geol Soc Am. *Res:* Origin, migration and accumulation of oil and natural gas; determination of geological parameters-categories preferentially associated With petroleum; prediction of amount and distribution of undiscovered oil and gas. *Mailing Add:* Suite 727 13771 N Central Expressway Dallas TX 75243

CORDEN, MALCOLM ERNEST, b Portland, Ore, Nov 8, 27; m 48; c 6. PLANT PATHOLOGY. *Educ:* Ore State Univ, BS, 52, PhD(plant path), 55. *Prof Exp:* Asst plant pathologist, Crop Protection Inst, Conn Agr Exp Sta, 55-58; from asst prof to assoc prof, 58-66, PROF PLANT PATH, ORE STATE UNIV, 66- *Mem:* Am Phytopath Soc. *Res:* Physiology of parasitism in fungal diseases of plants and the mechanism of fungicidal action in wood. *Mailing Add:* Dept Bot & Plant Path Ore State Univ Corvallis OR 97331

CORDEN, PIERCE STEPHEN, b Chattanooga, Tenn, June 26, 41; m 75; c 2. PHYSICS. *Educ:* Georgetown Univ, BS, 63; Univ Pa, MS, 66, PhD(physics), 71. *Prof Exp:* PHYS SCI OFFICER WEAPONS TECHNOL & ARMS CONTROL, US ARMS CONTROL & DISARMAMENT AGENCY, WASHINGTON, DC, 71- *Concurrent Pos:* Res fel sci & soc, Tech Univ Trente, Netherlands, 77-78. *Mem:* Am Phys Soc; Arms Control Asn. *Res:* Science and technology for arms control and disarmament, especially verification of nuclear testing and aspects of environmental warfare. *Mailing Add:* US Arm Control & Disarmament Agency US Arm Control & Disarmament Washington DC 20451

CORDER, CLINTON NICHOLAS, b Oberlin, Kans, Aug 1, 41; m 61; c 5. PHARMACOLOGY, MEDICINE. *Educ:* Univ Kans, BS, 64; Marquette Univ, PhD(pharmacol), 68; Wash Univ, MD, 71. *Prof Exp:* Res asst pharmacol, Sch Med, Wash Univ, 71-72; asst prof pharmacol & med, Sch Med, Univ Pittsburgh, 72-78, assoc prof, 78-79; PROF & CHMN DEPT PHARMACOL & PROF MED, ORAL ROBERTS UNIV, TULSA, OK, 79- *Concurrent Pos:* Nat Inst Neurol Dis & Blindness fel, 68-69; Am Cancer Soc scholar, 69-71; NIH trainee clin pharm, Univ Pittsburgh, 72-74. *Mem:* Am Col Clin Pharmacol; Am Soc Pharmacol & Exp Therapeut; Am Pharmaceut Asn; Am Chem Soc; AMA. *Res:* Biochemical pharmacology, quantitative microbiochemical analysis, and drug biotransformation in clinical Pharmacology with emphasis on kidney, hepatic, and neoplastic tissues. *Mailing Add:* Dept Pharmacol Oral Roberts Univ Tulsa OK 74171

CORDERO, JULIO, b San Jose, Costa Rica, Jan 10, 23; US citizen; m 63; c 1. MAGNETOHYDRODYNAMICS, LASERS. *Educ:* Wayne State Univ, BS, 48; Univ Minn, MS, 51. *Prof Exp:* Meteorologist, Pan Am World Airways, 44; assoc scientist, Univ Minn, 51-53; scientist, Fluidyne Eng Corp, 53-55, proj engr, 55-60; sr scientist, Avco Res & Adv Develop Div, 60-64, sr staff scientist, 64-69; mem tech staff, Anal Serv, Inc, 69-75; mem res staff magnetohydrodynamics, 75-76, CHIEF ENGR, MAGNETOHYDRODYN RES FACIL, MASS INST TECHNOL, 76- *Mem:* Am Phys Soc; Am Astron Soc (secy, 69-70); Am Meteorol Soc; Am Inst Aeronaut & Astronaut; Sigma Xi. *Res:* Shock wave phenomena; supersonic and hypersonic aerodynamics; high temperature gas dynamics; radiation damage; plasma devices; rarefied gas flow; viscous and nonstationary flow; thermodynamics; ballistic and flight mechanics; impact phenomena; systems analysis; energy conversion; lasers. *Mailing Add:* 23 Mohawk St Danvers MA 01923

CORDERY, ROBERT ARTHUR, b London, Eng, Sept 25, 52. STATISTICAL PHYSICS, PHASE TRANSITIONS. *Educ:* Univ Toronto, BSc, 75, MSc, 76, PhD(physics), 80. *Prof Exp:* FEL PHYSICS, RUTGERS UNIV, 80- *Mem:* Am Phys Soc. *Mailing Add:* Dept Physics Rutgers Univ PO Box 849 Piscataway NJ 08854

CORDES, ARTHUR WALLACE, b Freeport, Ill, June 29, 34; m 56; c 4. INORGANIC CHEMISTRY. *Educ:* Northern Ill Univ, BS, 56; Univ Ill, MS, 58, PhD(inorg chem), 60. *Prof Exp:* From asst prof to assoc prof, 59-66, PROF INORG CHEM, UNIV ARK, FAYETTEVILLE, 66- *Mem:* Am Chem Soc; Am Crystallog Asn. *Res:* Inorganic chemistry of the elements phosphorus, nitrogen, sulfur and arsenic; crystal structure determinations. *Mailing Add:* Dept of Chem Univ of Ark Fayetteville AR 72701

CORDES, CARROLL LLOYD, b Eagle Pass, Tex, Nov 29, 38; m 71. COASTAL & ESTUARINE RESOURCES MANAGEMENT MODELS. *Educ:* Stephen F Austin State Univ, BS, 61; NC State Univ, MS, 65, PhD(zool), 71. *Prof Exp:* Res biologist virology, Baylor Univ, 61-63; res assoc, Univ Tex, 65-66; asst prof ecol, Univ Southwestern La, 69-76, assoc prof, 76-77; WILDLIFE ECOLOGIST RESOURCE ECOL, US DEPT INTERIOR, FISH & WILDLIFE SERV, 77- *Concurrent Pos:* Consult, Acadiana Planning & Evangeline Econ Develop Dist, 75-77; tech advr, St Tammany Parish Mosquito Abatement Dist, 77-79, dist comnr, 79-; res consult, La State Bd Regents, 78- *Mem:* Int Asn Impact Assessment; Ecol Soc Am; Wildlife Soc; Coastal Soc. *Res:* Development of a national environmental data base and management evaluation system for fish and wildlife resources in coastal ecosystems; development of information and technology transfer methods. *Mailing Add:* US Fish & Wildlife Serv NASA/Slidell Comput Complex Slidell LA 70548

CORDES, EUGENE H, b York, Nebr, Apr 7, 36; m 57; c 2. BIOCHEMISTRY, ORGANIC CHEMISTRY. *Educ:* Calif Inst Technol, BS, 58; Brandeis Univ, PhD(biochem), 62. *Prof Exp:* From instr to prof chem, Ind Univ, Bloomington, 62-78; chmn dept, 72-78; EXEC DIR BIOCHEM, MERCK, SHARP & DOHME RES LABS, 78- *Concurrent Pos:* Grants, NSF, 62-78 & NIH, 64-78. *Mem:* Am Chem Soc; Am Soc Biol Chem. *Res:* Mechanism of enzyme-catalyzed reactions; mechanism and catalysis of carbonyl addition reactions; lipoprotein chemistry. *Mailing Add:* Merck Sharp & Dohme Res Labs Rahway NJ 07065

CORDES, HERMAN FREDRICK, b Upland, Calif, May 30, 27. PHYSICAL CHEMISTRY. *Educ:* Pomona Col, BA, 50; Stanford Univ, PhD(chem), 54. *Prof Exp:* res chemist, Naval Weapons Ctr, 54-81; RETIRED. *Mem:* AAAS; Am Chem Soc; Sigma Xi. *Res:* Chemical kinetics; physical chemistry of propellant and explosive ingredients; mass spectrometry. *Mailing Add:* 1028 N Peg St Ridgecrest CA 93555

CORDES, JAMES MARTIN, radio astronomy, see previous edition

CORDES, WILLIAM CHARLES, b St Louis, Mo, Aug 17, 29; m 57; c 6. PLANT PHYSIOLOGY, CYTOCHEMISTRY. *Educ:* Univ Mo, BS, 55, MA, 57, PhD(plant physiol), 60. *Prof Exp:* From instr to asst prof biol, Creighton Univ, 60-65; actg chmn dept, 70-72, ASST PROF BIOL, LOYOLA UNIV CHICAGO, 65- *Mem:* AAAS; Bot Soc Am; Japanese Soc Plant Physiol. *Res:* Physiology of differentiation in plants; appearance of enzyme systems in time; plant wound enzymes. *Mailing Add:* Dept of Biol Loyola Univ Chicago IL 60611

CORDINER, JAMES B(EATTIE), JR, b Spokane, Wash, Nov 15, 15; m 47. CHEMICAL ENGINEERING. *Educ:* Univ Wash, Seattle, BS, 37, MS, 38, PhD(chem eng, chem), 41. *Prof Exp:* Chem engr, US Bur Mines, 46-50, asst supv engr, 51-52; tech report ed, cent res dept, Food Mach & Chem Corp, 53-54; sr chem engr, Kaiser Aluminum & Chem Corp, 55-57; from asst prof to assoc prof chem eng, 58-69, PROF CHEM ENG, LA STATE UNIV, 69- *Mem:* Am Soc Eng Educ; Am Chem Soc; Soc Am Mil Engrs; Am Inst Chem Engrs. *Res:* Coal gasification; combustion; physical properties of materials; unit operations; sugar technology; technical report editing; consulting. *Mailing Add:* Dept of Chem Eng La State Univ Baton Rouge LA 70803

CORDINGLY, RICHARD HENRY, b Denver, Colo, Aug 9, 31; m 56; c 2. PULP & PAPER TECHNOLOGY. *Educ:* Univ Colo, BS, 53; Inst Paper Chem, MS, 55, PhD(chem), 58. *Prof Exp:* Proj chemist papermaking, 58-60, asst tech dir, 61-62, res engr, 63-70, MGR RES & DEVELOP, WEYERHAEUSER CO, 71- *Mem:* Tech Asn Pulp & Paper Indust. *Res:* Wood pulping and bleaching; pulp refining; paper forming, pressing and drying; surface treating; paper product technology and new paper product development. *Mailing Add:* 7505 90th Ave SW Tacoma WA 98498

CORDON, MARTIN, b West New York, NJ, Aug 10, 28; m 53; c 3. ORGANIC CHEMISTRY. *Educ:* Rutgers Univ, BS, 50; Univ Calif, Los Angeles, PhD(chem), 55. *Prof Exp:* Sr res chemist, 55-70, res assoc, 70-79, SR RES ASSOC, COLGATE-PALMOLIVE CO, 79- *Mem:* Am Chem Soc. *Res:* Biochemistry of saliva; chemistry of hair; organic synthesis; cleaning and polishing agents for oral products. *Mailing Add:* 55 Grant Ave Highland Park NJ 08904

CORDOVA, VINCENT FRANK, b Philadelphia, Pa, Feb 24, 36; m 65; c 4. CRIMINALISTICS, TOXICOLOGY. *Educ:* Edison Col, BA, 77. *Prof Exp:* Biochemist toxicol, Med Examr Philadelphia, 57-65; police chemist criminalistics, Philadelphia Police Dept, 65-68, lab dir, 68-76; DIR CRIMINALISTICS, NAT MED SERV, 76- *Concurrent Pos:* Toxicol consult, Coroner's Off, Del County, Pa, 63-68; instr, Temple Community Col, 66-67, Lehigh Community Col, 69-73 & Breathalyzer Courses, Philadelphia Police Lab, 69-76; tech dir, Law Enforcement Assistance Admin grant, 72-73; forensic consult, Toxicon Ltd, 76- *Mem:* Am Chem Soc; fel Am Acad Forensic Sci; Soc Appl Spectros; Am Soc Testing & Mat. *Res:* Toxicology; criminalistics; environmental pollution analyses, gas chromatography, mass spectrometry, data systems. *Mailing Add:* Nat Med Serv Inc PO Box 433A Willow Grove PA 19090

CORDOVI, MARCEL A(VERY), b Sofia, Bulgaria, Nov 17, 15; nat US; m 41; c 1. METALLURGICAL ENGINEERING, CORROSION. *Educ:* Am Col, Bulgaria, Dipl, 35; Polytech Inst, Czech, IngC, 38; Polytech Inst Brooklyn, BME, 41, MME, 42, ME, 47, PE, 77. *Prof Exp:* Asst, Welding Res Coun, 43-44; supvr res & develop, Babcock & Wilcox Co, 44-49, staff engr, 49-53, mgr nuclear mat res & develop, 53-58; supvr power appln, 58-66, group leader, 66-68, mgr appln eng, 68-75, asst to pres, Inco US, Inc, 75-77, DIR SPEC PROJS, INCO LTD, 77-, VPRES, 80- *Concurrent Pos:* Adj prof, Polytech Inst Brooklyn, 50-70 & NY Univ, 58-60; consult, Brookhaven Nat Lab, 50-59, US del, Int Inst Welding, 50-60; lectr, City Col New York, 58-60. *Honors & Awards:* Award, Am Soc Metals, 57; merit award, Am Soc Testing & Mat, 67; award, Am Soc Mech Engrs, 68. *Mem:* Am Nuclear Soc; Am Soc Testing & Mat; Am Soc Metals; Am Soc Mech Engrs; Nat Asn Corrosion Engrs. *Res:* Metals sciences; solid state reactions; nuclear technology. *Mailing Add:* INCO Ltd One New York Plaza New York NY 10004

CORDS, CARL ERNEST, JR, b South Bend, Ind, Aug 24, 33; m 58; c 2. VIROLOGY, MEDICAL MICROBIOLOGY. *Educ:* Ariz State Univ, BS, 58; Univ Wash, PhD(microbiol), 64. *Prof Exp:* NIH fel, 64-65, from instr to asst prof microbiol, 65-72, ASSOC PROF MICROBIOL, SCH MED, UNIV NMEX, 72- *Mem:* AAAS; Soc Exp Biol & Med; Am Soc Microbiol; Tissue Cult Asn. *Res:* Genetics and mechanisms of replication of animal viruses and bacteriophage; tissue culture. *Mailing Add:* Dept of Microbiol Univ of NMex Sch of Med Albuquerque NM 87131

CORDS, DONALD PHILIP, b Evanston, Ill, Sept 18, 40; m 64; c 2. ORGANIC CHEMISTRY. *Educ:* Northwestern Univ, BA, 62; Ind Univ, PhD(org chem), 66. *Prof Exp:* Res chemist, 66-73, sr supvr, 73-79, tech serv supvr, 79-80, RES SUPVR, E I DU PONT DE NEMOURS & CO INC, 80- *Mem:* Am Chem Soc. *Res:* Applications of organometallics in organic synthesis; free radical rearrangement and elimination reactions; organic reaction mechanisms. *Mailing Add:* E I du Pont de Nemours & Co Specialty Chem & Prod Tech Div Wilmington DE 19898

CORDTS, RICHARD HENRY, JR, b Teaneck, NJ, May 1, 34; m 66; c 2. NUTRITION. *Educ:* Rutgers Univ, BS, 56, MS, 61, PhD(nutrit), 64. *Prof Exp:* Asst, Rutgers Univ, 61-64; dir nutrit res, Whitmoyer Labs, Inc, Rohm and Haas Co, 64-65, dir nutrit, 65-68; assoc dir res & develop, Nat Molasses Co, 68-70; nutritionist, 70-73, assoc mgr animal health tech serv, 73-75, mgr, 75-78, dir agr mkt res & planning, 79-80, DIR CHEM RES PLANNING & ADMIN, HOFFMANN-LAROCHE, 80- *Mem:* AAAS; Animal Nutrit Res Coun; NY Acad Sci; fel Am Inst Chemists; Am Mkt Asn. *Res:* Roughage utilization by ruminants; protein metabolism in monogastrics. *Mailing Add:* Chem Div Roche Park Nutley NJ 07110

CORDUNEANU, CONSTANTIN C, b Iasi, Romania, July 26, 28; m 49. STABILITY THEORY, PERIODIC FUNCTIONS. *Educ:* Univ Iasi, Romania, MS, 51, PhD(math), 56. *Prof Exp:* Instr math, Univ Iasi, Romania, 49-50, asst, 50-55, lectr, 55-62, assoc prof, 62-68, prof, 68-77; PROF MATH, UNIV TEX, ARLINGTON, 79- *Concurrent Pos:* Vis prof, Univ RI, 67-78 & Univ Tenn, Knoxville, 78-79; assoc ed, Nonlinear Anal, Oxford, 77-; ed, Libertas Math, Am Romanian Acad Arts & Sci, 81- *Honors & Awards:* State Dept Educ Prize, Romania, 63; Romanian Acad Sci Prize, 65. *Mem:* Am Math Soc; Soc Indust & Appl Math; Math Asn Am; Am Romanian Acad Arts & Sci. *Res:* Qualitative theory of various classes of differential, integral and related functional equations with main emphasis on stability and oscillations. *Mailing Add:* Dept Math Univ Tex Arlington TX 76019

CORDY, DONALD R, b Fall River, Wis, Feb 17, 13. VETERINARY PATHOLOGY. *Educ:* Univ Calif, Los Angeles, BA, 34; Iowa State Col, DVM, 37; Cornell Univ, MS, 38, PhD(vet path), 40. *Prof Exp:* Instr vet path, State Col Wash, 40-42, assoc prof, 46-50; from asst prof to assoc prof, 50-58, head dept, 58-69, PROF VET PATH, UNIV CALIF, DAVIS, 58- *Mem:* Am Col Vet Pathologists; Am Vet Med Asn; Am Asn Pathologists. *Res:* Pathology of communicable animal diseases; animal neuropathology. *Mailing Add:* Dept of Vet Path Univ of Calif Davis CA 95616

CORE, EARL LEMLEY, b Core, WVa, Jan 20, 02; m 25; c 4. BOTANY. *Educ:* WVa Univ, AB, 26, AM, 28; Columbia Univ, PhD(bot), 36. *Hon Degrees:* DSc, Waynesburg Col, 57; DSc, WVa Univ, 74. *Prof Exp:* From instr to assoc prof bot, 28-42, prof biol, 42-72, chmn dept bot, 48-66, cur herbarium, 66-72, EMER PROF BIOL, WVA UNIV, 72- *Concurrent Pos:* Botanist, Foreign Econ Admin, Colombia, 43-45; ed, Castanea, 36-70. *Mem:* AAAS; Am Soc Plant Taxonomists. *Res:* Taxonomy of vascular plants of eastern United States; American species of Scleria; flora of West Virginia. *Mailing Add:* Dept of Biol WVa Univ Morgantown WV 26506

CORE, HAROLD ADDISON, b Cassville, WVa, Nov 4, 20; m 43; c 2. FORESTRY. *Educ:* WVa Univ, BSF, 42; State Univ NY, MS, 49, PhD, 62. *Prof Exp:* From asst prof to assoc prof wood prod eng, State Univ NY Col Forestry, Syracuse, 46-66; PROF FORESTRY, COL AGR, UNIV TENN, KNOXVILLE, 66- *Mem:* Soc Am Foresters; Forest Prod Res Soc. *Res:* Wood and fiber anatomy; foreign woods. *Mailing Add:* Col of Agr Univ of Tenn Knoxville TN 37916

CORELL, ROBERT WALDEN, b Detroit, Mich, Nov 4, 34; m 56; c 3. MECHANICAL ENGINEERING, OCEAN ENGINEERING. *Educ:* Case Inst Technol, BSME, 56, PhD(mech eng), 64; Mass Inst Technol, MSME, 59. *Prof Exp:* Res engr, Gen Elec Corp, 55-57; instr mech eng, Univ NH, 57-58, asst prof, 59-60; res asst, Case Inst Technol, 60-64; assoc prof, 64-66, chmn dept, 64-72, PROF MECH ENG, UNIV NH, 66-, DIR SEA GRANT PROG & MARINE PROG, 75-, DIR, MARINE SYST ENG LAB, 77- *Concurrent Pos:* Eng assoc, Huggins Hosp, 58-60; instrumentation consult, Highland View Hosp, 61-64; res assoc, Scripps Inst Oceanog, Univ Calif, San Diego, 71-72; consult, Off Naval Res & var industs & bus. *Mem:* Am Soc Eng Educ; Marine Technol Soc; Inst Elec & Electronics Engrs; AAAS. *Res:* Design and research in medicine, biology, oceanography, ocean engineering, and arctic science and engineering. *Mailing Add:* Marine Prog Bldg Univ of NH Durham NH 03824

CORELLI, JOHN CHARLES, b Providence, RI, Aug 6, 30; m 59; c 1. MATERIALS SCIENCE ENGINEERING, SOLID STATE SCIENCE. *Educ:* Providence Col, BSc, 52; Brown Univ, MSc, 54; Purdue Univ, PhD(physics), 58. *Prof Exp:* Physicist, Knolls Atomic Power Lab, Gen Elec Co, 58-62; assoc prof, 62-65, PROF, DEPT NUCLEAR ENG & SCI, RENSSELAER POLYTECH INST, 65- *Concurrent Pos:* NIH fel, Univ Rochester, 71. *Mem:* Am Phys Soc; Am Nuclear Soc. *Res:* Radiation damage studies in silicone and ceramic materials; radiation alteration of polymer materials. *Mailing Add:* 33 Belle Ave Troy NY 12180

COREN, RICHARD L, b New York, NY, Sept 1, 32; m 55; c 3. PHYSICS, ELECTRICAL ENGINEERING. *Educ:* City Col New York, BS, 54; Polytech Inst Brooklyn, MS, 56, PhD(physics), 60. *Prof Exp:* Teaching fel physics, Polytech Inst Brooklyn, 54-56, res assoc, 56-60; res specialist magnetic films lab, Philco Corp, Pa, 60-64; prin physicist mat develop lab, Univac Div, Sperry Rand Corp, 64-65; from asst prof to assoc prof elec eng, 65-69, chmn fac coun, 69-71, PROF ELEC ENG & ELECTROPHYS, DREXEL UNIV, 69- *Concurrent Pos:* Adj instr, Cooper Union Col, 55-59; lectr, La Salle Col, 62-64; consult, Rockefeller Inst, 61-62; partner, C&M Assocs, Tech Consults, 67- *Mem:* AAAS; Inst Elec & Electronics Engrs; Am Phys Soc; Am Asn Physics Teachers; Am Soc Eng Educ. *Res:* Electrical, magnetic, and optical studies of magnetic films; physiology of reproduction. *Mailing Add:* Dept Elec Eng Drexel Univ Philadelphia PA 19104

CORET, IRVING ALLEN, b Salt Lake City, Utah, Apr 28, 20; m 46; c 1. PHARMACOLOGY. *Educ:* Emory Univ, AB, 40, MD, 43. *Prof Exp:* Intern, Piedmont Hosp, Ga, 44; instr pharmacol, Col Physicians & Surgeons, Columbia Univ, 47-48; from instr to assoc prof, 50-73, PROF PHARMACOL, SCH MED, ST LOUIS UNIV, 73- *Concurrent Pos:* Rockefeller fel, Col Physicians & Surgeons, Columbia Univ, 46-47; NIH fel, Univ Pa, 48-50. *Mem:* AAAS; Am Soc Pharmacol & Exp Therapeut. *Res:* Antibiotics; autonomic and cellular pharmacology. *Mailing Add:* Dept of Pharmacol Sch of Med St Louis Univ St Louis MO 63103

COREY, ALBERT EUGENE, b Gardner, Mass, July 4, 28; m 50; c 2. ORGANIC CHEMISTRY. *Educ:* Rensselaer Polytech, BS, 50. *Prof Exp:* Assoc chemist, Allied Chem & Dye Corp, 51-54; res chemist, Plymouth Cordage Co, 54-55; res specialist, Shawinigan Resins Corp, 55-69 & Plastics Prod & Resins Div, Monsanto Co, 69-73, SR RES SPECIALIST, MONSANTO PLASTICS & RESINS CO, 73- *Mem:* Am Chem Soc. *Res:* Glycerol; hydroxylation; non-electrolytic hydrogen peroxide; polymers; emulsion polymers; paper and surface coatings; textile applications; pressure sensitive adhesive applications. *Mailing Add:* 185 Mountainview Rd East Longmeadow MA 01028

COREY, ARTHUR THOMAS, b Anne Arundel County, Md, Apr 8, 19; m 43; c 2. AGRICULTURAL & GROUNDWATER ENGINEERING. *Educ:* Univ Md, BS, 47; Colo State Univ, MS, 49; Rutgers Univ, PhD(soil physics), 52. *Prof Exp:* Physicist, Gulf Res & Develop Co, Gulf Oil Corp, 52-56; res civil engr, 56-61, from assoc prof to prof & res agr engr, 58-77, EMER PROF AGR ENG, EXP STA, COLO STATE UNIV, 77- *Concurrent Pos:* Consult, petrol indust, 56-59; res grants, NSF, 58-59, 61-63, 65-67 & 68-71 & NIH, 62-64; prof hydraul eng from Colo State Univ to Seato Grad Sch Eng, Bangkok, USAID, 59-60; prof agr eng, Ore State Univ, 77-79; consult, 77. *Mem:* Am Soc Agr Engrs; Soil Sci Soc Am; Am Soc Civil Engrs. *Res:* Flow of immiscible fluid mixtures through porous media; irrigation and drainage engineering; water conservation. *Mailing Add:* 1620 S Whitcomb Ft Collins CO 80526

COREY, CLARK L(AWRENCE), b Mont, Sept 17, 21; m 44. METALLURGY, MATERIALS. *Educ:* Univ Mich, BS, 48, MS, 49, PhD, 51. *Prof Exp:* Res metallurgist, Babcock & Wilcox Co, 51-53; res engr, Univ Mich, 53-56; from assoc prof to PROF ENG, WAYNE STATE UNIV, 56- *Concurrent Pos:* Consult, Atomic Power Develop Asn, 57- *Mem:* Soc Metals; NY Acad Sci; Am Inst Mining, Metall & Petrol Engrs. *Res:* Physics of materials; x-ray crystallography; theory of alloying; theory of deformation. *Mailing Add:* Dept of Chem & Metall Eng Wayne State Univ Detroit MI 48202

COREY, ELIAS JAMES, b Methuen, Mass, July 12, 28; m 61; c 3. ORGANIC CHEMISTRY. *Educ:* Mass Inst Technol, BS, 48, PhD(chem), 51. *Hon Degrees:* DSc, Univ Chicago, 68, Hofstra Univ, 74 & Colby Col, 77. *Prof Exp:* Res chemist, A D Little Co, Inc, 48; from instr to prof chem, Univ Ill, 51-59; PROF CHEM, HARVARD UNIV, 59- *Concurrent Pos:* Consult, Chas Pfizer Co. *Honors & Awards:* Chem Award, Am Chem Soc, 60, Fritzsche Award, 68, Synthetic Chem & Harrison Howe Awards, 70, Linus Pauling Award, 73, Remsen Award, 74; Ciba Found Medal & Evans Award, Ohio State Univ, 72; Dickson Prize Sci, Carnegie Mellon Univ, 73; George Ledlie Prize Sci, Harvard Univ, 73; Arthur C Cope Award, 76; Nichols Medal, 77; Franklin Medal Sci, 78. *Mem:* Am Chem Soc. *Res:* Stereochemistry; structural, synthetic and theoretical organic chemistry. *Mailing Add:* Dept of Chem Harvard Univ Cambridge MA 02138

COREY, EUGENE R, b Oregon City, Ore, Nov 18, 35; m 62. INORGANIC CHEMISTRY, CRYSTALLOGRAPHY. *Educ:* Willamette Univ, BS, 58; Univ Wis, PhD(inorg chem), 63. *Prof Exp:* Instr chem, Univ Wis, 63-64; assoc prof, Univ Cincinnati, 64-69; assoc prof, 69-81, PROF CHEM, UNIV MO-ST LOUIS, 81- *Mem:* Am Chem Soc; Am Crystallog Asn; The Chem Soc; NY Acad Sci. *Res:* Chemical crystallography; single crystal structure determinations of organometallic compounds by the method of x-ray diffraction. *Mailing Add:* Dept Chem Univ Mo St Louis MO 63121

COREY, GILBERT, b Olathe, Colo, Feb 7, 23; m 49; c 3. AGRICULTURAL ENGINEERING. *Educ:* Colo State Univ, BS, 48, MS, 49, PhD(agr eng), 65. *Prof Exp:* Asst irrigationist, Univ Idaho, 49-54; irrig engr, Agr Res Serv, USDA, 54-55; irrig specialist & consult, Eduador Proj, Univ Idaho, 55-57, assoc prof agr eng, 57-72, chmn dept, 66-72, prof agr eng & agr engr, 72-77; WATER MGT SPECIALIST, OFF AGR, USDA, 76- *Mem:* Am Soc Agr Engrs; Am Soc Eng Educ; Nat Soc Prof Engrs. *Res:* Irrigation engineering, principally fundamentals governing the hydraulics of flow of water into, over and through a soil profile. *Mailing Add:* Off of Agr USDA 1521 Beulah Rd Vienna VA 22180

COREY, HAROLD SCOTT, b Bridgeport, Conn, May 14, 19; m 47; c 5. MECHANICAL ENGINEERING. *Educ:* Fitchburg State Col, BS, 47, EdM, 49. *Prof Exp:* Instr mach tool lab, Univ Mass, 48-49; instr graphics & descriptive geom, Syracuse Univ, 49-51; asst prof mech eng, 51-64, ASSOC PROF MECH ENG, WORCESTER POLYTECH INST, 64- *Mem:* Am Soc Eng Educ. *Res:* Design; materials processing. *Mailing Add:* Dept of Mech Eng Worcester Polytech Inst Worcester MA 01609

COREY, JOHN CHARLES, b Toronto, Ont, May 7, 38; US citizen; m 66; c 3. SOIL PHYSICS. *Educ:* Univ Toronto, BSA, 60; Univ Calif, MS, 62; Iowa State Univ, PhD(soil physics), 66. *Prof Exp:* Res physicist, 66-73, tech supvr, 73-78, RES SUPVR, SAVANNAH RIVER LAB, E I DU PONT DE NEMOURS & CO, INC, 78- *Mem:* Am Soc Agron; Int Soc Soil Sci. *Res:* Management of radioactive and industrial waste; ion transport; nuclear techniques for soil water movement studies. *Mailing Add:* 212 Lakeside Dr Aiken SC 29801

COREY, JOYCE YAGLA, b Waverly, Iowa, May 26, 38; m 62. INORGANIC CHEMISTRY. *Educ:* Univ NDak, BS, 60, MS, 61; Univ Wis, PhD(inorg chem), 64. *Prof Exp:* From instr to asst prof chem, Villa Madonna Col, 64-68; from asst prof to assoc prof chem, 68-79, PROF CHEM, UNIV MO-ST LOUIS, 80- *Concurrent Pos:* Vis prof chem, Univ Wis, 81. *Mem:* Am Chem Soc; Royal Soc Chem; Sigma Xi. *Res:* Synthetic organometallic chemistry of group IV, specifically analogs of antidepressants. *Mailing Add:* Dept of Chem Univ of Mo St Louis MO 63121

COREY, MARION WILLSON, b Jackson, Miss, Feb 11, 32; m 56; c 3. CIVIL & STRUCTURAL ENGINEERING. *Educ:* Auburn Univ, BS, 54; Miss State Univ, MS, 60; Ga Inst Technol, PhD(civil eng), 68. *Prof Exp:* From instr to asst prof civil eng, Miss State Univ, 58-61; instr civil technol, Southern Tech Inst, Ga Inst Technol, 61-63; assoc prof civil eng, 63-70, PROF CIVIL ENG, MISS STATE UNIV, 70- *Concurrent Pos:* Engr, Mitchell Eng Co, Miss, 62. *Mem:* Am Soc Civil Engrs; Am Soc Eng Educ. *Res:* Electronic computing; computer-aided design. *Mailing Add:* Dept of Civil Eng Miss State Univ Mississippi State MS 39762

COREY, PAUL FREDERICK, b Lakewood, NJ, Apr 9, 50; m 72. ORGANIC CHEMISTRY. *Educ:* Va Polytech Inst & State Univ, BS, 72; State Univ NY, Buffalo, PhD(medicinal chem), 77. *Prof Exp:* Res assoc pharm, Univ Wis, Madison, 77-79; SR RES SCIENTIST, MILES LABS, INC, ELKHART, IND, 79- *Mem:* Am Chem Soc. *Res:* Design and development of biologically active compounds as potential ethical pharmaceuticals, especially antieoplastic agents and prostaglandin analogs. *Mailing Add:* Miles Labs, Inc PO Box 40 Elkhart IN 46515

COREY, RICHARD BOARDMAN, b Wisconsin Rapids, Wis, Dec 25, 27. SOIL CHEMISTRY, SOIL FERTILITY. *Educ:* Univ Wis-Madison, BS, 49, MS, 51, PhD(soil chem), 53. *Prof Exp:* From asst prof to assoc prof soil sci, 54-65, PROF SOIL SCI, UNIV WIS-MADISON, 65- *Concurrent Pos:* Vis prof, Postgrad Col, Nat Sch Agr, Mex, 64; consult, US AID-Univ Wis Proj, Porto Alegre, Brazil, 65, prof, Univ Ife, Nigeria, 67-71, dean fac agr, 70-71; consult, US AID-Midwest Univ Consortium Int Activ Proj, Bogor, Indonesia, 72. *Mem:* AAAS; Am Soc Agron; Soil Sci Soc Am; Int Soc Soil Sci. *Res:* Reactions of phosphorus and potassium in soils; development of methods for determining available nutrients in soils; land application of waste materials; reactions of heavy metals in soils. *Mailing Add:* Dept Soil Sci Univ Wis Madison WI 53706

COREY, ROBERT ARDEN, b Wheeling, WVa, Aug 31, 20; m 44; c 3. ENTOMOLOGY. *Educ:* WVa Univ, BS, 47; Univ Calif, MS, 49. *Prof Exp:* Field aide forest insect div, Bur Entom & Plant Quar, USDA, 48; entomologist, Shell Develop Co, 49-81; RETIRED. *Mem:* Entom Soc Am. *Res:* Testing new compounds as potential insecticides. *Mailing Add:* 1906 Ralston Court Modesto CA 95350

COREY, ROLAND REECE, JR, microbiology, see previous edition

COREY, SHARON EVA, b Princeton, NJ, Sept 12, 45; m 70; c 2. PHARMACOLOGY, MORPHOLOGY. *Educ:* Grove City Col, BS, 67; WVa Univ, PhD(pharmacol), 71. *Prof Exp:* Fel cell biol, WVa Univ, 71-73, res assoc electron microscopy, 73-74; ASST PROF PHARMACOL, UNIV PITTSBURGH, 76- *Mem:* AAAS; Am Asn Col Pharm. *Res:* Autonomic pharmacology; morphology-pharmacology; effects of neurotoxins on the peripheral and central nervous systems, especially vinblastine and vincristine. *Mailing Add:* Dept of Pharmacol Univ of Pittsburgh Pittsburgh PA 15261

COREY, VICTOR BREWER, b Bynumville, Mo, Feb 9, 15; m 42; c 2. PHYSICS. *Educ:* Cent Col, Mo, AB, 37; Univ Iowa, MS, 39, PhD(physics), 42. *Prof Exp:* Asst physics, Univ Iowa, 37-42; res physicist, Sylvania Elec Prods, Inc, Pa & NY, 42-45; head electro-acoustics sect, Curtiss-Wright-Cornell Res Lab, 45-46; head electro-acoustics dept & actg head nuclear physics dept, Fredric Flader, Inc, 46-48, res coordr, 48-49; mgr eng physics div, 49-50, dir res, 50-51; exec engr, Electronics Div, Willys Motors, Inc, Toledo, 51-53; tech dir, Donner Sci Co, 53-59; pres, Palomar Sci Corp, Calif, 60-63; vpres & bd dir, United Control Corp, 63-67, gen mgr transducer div, 66, int vpres, 66-71, VPRES NEW BUS DEVELOP, SUNDSTRAND DATA CONTROL, INC, 71- *Mem:* AAAS; Am Phys Soc; Acoust Soc Am; Inst Elec & Electronics Engrs; Am Inst Aeronaut & Astronaut. *Res:* Simulators and analog computers; servomechanisms; telemetering; missile guidance, control components; trainers; servo accelerometers, electromechanical amplifiers, integrators; applied physics instrumentation; electronic test and measurement equipment; digital transducers; analog-digital converters; microelectronics; radio altimeters; ultrasonic acoustics; inertial sensors. *Mailing Add:* Sundstrand Data Control Inc Overlake Indust Park Redmond WA 98052

CORFIELD, PETER WILLIAM REGINALD, b Manchester, Eng, Sept 14, 37; m 63; c 2. INORGANIC CHEMISTRY, X-RAY CRYSTALLOGRAPHY. *Educ:* Univ Durham, BSc, 59, PhD(x-ray), 63. *Prof Exp:* Res assoc, Crystallog Lab, Univ Pittsburgh, 63-65; res instr chem, Northwestern Univ, 65-66, instr, 66-67; asst prof, Ohio State Univ, 67-73; assoc prof, 73-77, PROF CHEM, KING'S COL, 77- *Mem:* AAAS; Am Crystallog Asn; Am Chem Soc; Royal Soc Chem. *Res:* Crystal and molecular structure by x-ray methods; development of computer programs in crystallography. *Mailing Add:* Dept of Chem The Kings Col Briarcliff Manor NY 10510

CORFMAN, PHILIP ALBERT, b Berea, Ohio, July 19, 26; m 50; c 4. OBSTETRICS & GYNECOLOGY. *Educ:* Oberlin Col, BA, 50; Harvard Univ, MD, 54; Am Bd Obstet & Gynec, dipl. *Prof Exp:* Mem staff clin obstet & gynec, Rip Van Winkle Clin, Hudson, NY, 59-63; prog assoc population res, 65-67, asst to dir population res, 67-68, DIR CTR POPULATION RES, NAT INST CHILD HEALTH & HUMAN DEVELOP, 68- *Concurrent Pos:* Josiah Macy, Jr Found res fel cervical carcinogenesis & population res, Col Physicians & Surgeons, Columbia Univ, 63-65; adv, WHO. *Mem:* Am Col Obstet & Gynec. *Res:* Population research, including biological studies in animals and humans; research administration of this field. *Mailing Add:* Landow Bldg A721 Inst Child Health Human Develop Bethesda MD 20205

CORI, CARL FERDINAND, b Prague, Austria, Dec 5, 96; nat US; m 20; c 1. PHARMACOLOGY, BIOCHEMISTRY. *Educ:* Ger Univ, Prague, MD, 20. *Hon Degrees:* ScD, Western Reserve Univ & Yale Univ, 47, Boston Univ, 48, Cambridge Univ, 49, Gustavus Adolphus Col, 64, St Louis Univ & Brandeis Univ, 65, Wash Univ & Monash Univ, 66 & Univ Granada, 67; MD, Univ Trieste, 72. *Prof Exp:* Instr, 2nd Med Clin, Prague Univ, 19-20; asst, 1st Med Clin, Univ Vienna, 20-21; asst pharmacol, Graz Univ, 21; biochemist, State Inst Study Malignant Dis, NY, 22-31; prof pharmacol & biochem, Sch Med, Washington Univ, 31-66; DIR ENZYME RES LAB, MASS GEN HOSP, HARVARD MED SCH, 66- *Concurrent Pos:* Asst prof physiol, Univ Buffalo, 30-31; pres, Int Cong Biochem, Vienna, 58; vis prof biochem, Harvard Med Sch, 67- *Honors & Awards:* Nobel Prize, 47. *Mem:* Nat Acad Sci; AAAS; Am Philos Soc; Am Soc Biol Chem (pres, 50); Am Chem Soc. *Res:* Influence of ovariectomy on tumor incidence; fate of sugar in the animal body; intestinal absorption; action of epinephrin on metabolism; phosphate changes in muscle; isolation of glucose-1 phosphoric acid; enzymatic synthesis of glycogen; aerobic phosphorylation; isolation of crystalline enzymes; mechanism of action of insulin; regualtions; inborn errors of metabolism. *Mailing Add:* Enzyme Res Lab Mass Gen Hosp Boston MA 02114

CORIELL, KATHLEEN PATRICIA, b Cumberland, Md, Feb 19, 35; m 63. COMPUTER SCIENCES. *Educ:* Univ Md, BS, 59, MS, 66; Howard Univ, PhD(physics), 69. *Prof Exp:* Physicist, Nat Bur Standards, 59-63; asst prof physics, Hood Col, 69-70; instr, Montgomery Col, Md, 72; programmer analyst, Greenwich Data Systs, 73; mem tech staff, Comput Sci Corp, 74-76; COMPUT SYSTS ANALYST, FED GOVT, 76- *Mem:* Asn Comput Mach; Am Phys Soc. *Res:* Computer programming and analysis. *Mailing Add:* 15208 Spring Meadows Dr Germantown MD 20767

CORIELL, LEWIS L, b Sciotoville, Ohio, June 19, 11; m 36; c 3. BACTERIOLOGY. *Educ:* Univ Mont, BA, 34; Univ Kans, MA, 36, PhD(bact), 40, MD, 42. *Prof Exp:* Asst instr bot, Univ Mont, 34; from asst instr to instr bact, Univ Kans, 34-40; instr pediat, 46-49, assoc prof immunol pediat, 49-63, PROF PEDIAT, UNIV PA, 63-; DIR, INST MED RES, 55- *Concurrent Pos:* Nat Res sr fel virus dis, Inst Med Res, 47-49; med dir, Camden Munic Hosp for Contagious Dis, 49-61; pediatrist, Cooper Hosp, 49-; sr physician, Children's Hosp, 54-; consult, Philadelphia Naval Hosp, 56-66. *Mem:* AAAS; assoc AMA; assoc Am Soc Microbiol; assoc Asn Mil Surg US; assoc Soc Pediat Res. *Res:* Preservation of bacteria lymphilization; natural immunity and streptomycin therapy of tularemia; botulism; herpes simplex; herpes zoster; natural immunity of cats; poliomyelitis; antibiotics; tissue culture; cancer; pediatrics. *Mailing Add:* Inst for Med Res Copewood & Davis Sts Camden NJ 08103

CORIELL, SAM RAY, b Greenfield, Ohio, Dec 21, 35; m 63. PHYSICAL CHEMISTRY, PHYSICAL METALLURGY. *Educ:* Ohio State Univ, BSc, 56, PhD(phys chem), 61. *Prof Exp:* Phys chemist, Statist Physics Sect, 61-63, PHYS CHEMIST, METALL DIV, NAT BUR STANDARDS, 63- *Concurrent Pos:* Nat Res Coun-Nat Bur Standards res assoc, 61-63. *Mem:* AAAS; Am Chem Soc; Am Phys Soc; Am Inst Chemists; Metall Soc. *Res:* Crystal growth; solidification; heat flow and diffusion. *Mailing Add:* Nat Bur Standards Washington DC 20234

CORIGLIANO, HORACE JOHN, b Brooklyn, NY, Aug 1, 24; m 45; c 2. PHYSICAL METALLURGY, OPERATIONS RESEARCH. *Educ:* Polytech Inst Brooklyn, BMetE, 49, MMetE, 55; Columbia Univ, IE, 66. *Prof Exp:* Res & develop engr, Arma Div, Am Bosch Arma Corp, 48-51, tech asst to works mgr, 51-52, metall lab dir, 52-55, head qual eng, 55-59, asst mgr prod reliability, 59-64, mgr qual assurance, 64; dep dir mfg, Airborne Inst Lab Div, Cutler-Hammer, Inc, 64-70, dir mfg, 70-76, exec vpres, YIG Tek Corp, 76-78; MFG PROG MGR, EW SYSTS, RAYTHEON ELECTROMAGNETIC SYSTS DIV, GOLETA, 78-, MGR MFG TECH STAFF, 80- *Mem:* AAAS; Am Soc Metals; Am Soc Qual Control; Am Soc Testing & Mat; Asn Old Crows. *Res:* Special treatment of magnetic metals for obtaining optimum properties; effect of liquid metal on stainless steels; human factors; dimensional stability of materials; galvanic corrosion and protection of metals; operations research studies and reliability program formulation of inertial guidance components and systems. *Mailing Add:* 5110 Walnut Park Dr Santa Barbara CA 93111

CORINALDESI, ERNESTO, b Italy, Aug 20, 23. QUANTUM MECHANICS. *Educ:* Univ Rome, BS, 44; Univ Manchester, PhD(theoret physics), 51. *Prof Exp:* Asst, Univ Rome, 45-47; res fel, Nat Res Coun Can, 51-52; Higgins vis fel & instr, Palmer Phys Lab, Princeton Univ, 52-53; asst, Dublin Inst Adv Studies, 53-55; Imp Chem Industr res fel, Univ Glasgow, 55-57; lectr math, Univ Col North Staffordshire, 57-58; dir grad sch nuclear studies & in charge of theoret physics course, Nat Inst Nuclear Physics, Pisa, 59-61; mem, Inst Adv Study, 61-62; assoc vis prof, Univ Iowa, 62-63; vis prof, Univ Toronto, 63-64; vis prof, Boston Univ, 65; fel scientist, Westinghouse Res & Develop Ctr, Pa, 65-66; PROF PHYSICS, BOSTON UNIV, 66- *Concurrent Pos:* Prof ruolo, Univ Calabria, 76-77. *Mem:* Italian Phys Soc. *Res:* Quantum mechanics. *Mailing Add:* Dept of Physics 111 Cummington St Boston MA 02215

CORK, BRUCE, b Peck, Mich, Oct 21, 15; m 46; c 4. PARTICLE PHYSICS. *Educ:* Univ Mich, BS, 37; Polytech Inst New York, MS, 41; Univ Calif, Berkeley, PhD, 60. *Prof Exp:* Physicist, Tube Lab, Radio Corp Am, 37-40; physicist, Radiation Lab, Mass Inst Technol, 41-45 & Dept Physics, 46; physicist, Los Alamos Sci Lab, Univ Calif, 45-46 & Lawrence Radiation Lab, 46-68; assoc lab dir high energy physics, Argonne Nat Lab, 68-73; PHYSICIST, LAWRENCE BERKELEY LAB, UNIV CALIF, BERKELEY, 73- *Concurrent Pos:* Chmn Los Alamos Meson Physics Facil policy comt, Los Alamos Sci Lab, 73-75. *Mem:* Am Phys Soc. *Res:* Nuclear scattering; antiproton; antineutron; parity nonconservation; resonant states of nucleons; electron-positron annihilations. *Mailing Add:* Lawrence Berkeley Lab Univ of Calif Berkeley CA 94720

CORK, DOUGLAS J, b St Paul, Minn, May 5, 50; m 75; c 1. GAS BIOENGINEERING, AUTOTROPHIC BIOENGINEERING. *Educ:* Univ Ariz, BS, 72, MS, 74, PhD(agr biochem), 78. *Prof Exp:* Res group leader indust microbiol, Aquaterra Biochem, 78-79; asst prof biochem eng, Univ Miss, 79-80; ASST PROF BIOCHEM ENG, ILL INST TECHNOL, 80- *Concurrent Pos:* Consult, Nat Chemsearch Corp, 79, Nat Distillers Chem Corp, 80, Schaeffer & Roland Engrs, 80, Chicago Metrop Sanit Dist, 80, Genex Corp, 81-, WR Grace & Co, 81-, Inst Gas Technol, 81- *Mem:* Am Inst Chem Engrs; Am Chem Soc; Soc Indust Microbiol; Am Soc Microbiol. *Res:* Continuous gypsum sulfate reduction and sulfur production by biochemical and genetic engineering technology; process engineering of microbial systems of fuels and chemicals from waste gases and liquids. *Mailing Add:* Dept Biol Ill Inst Technol Chicago IL 60616

CORK, LINDA K COLLINS, b Texarkana, Tex, Dec 14, 36; div; c 2. VETERINARY PATHOLOGY. *Educ:* Tex A&M Univ, BS, 69, DVM, 70; Wash State Univ, PhD(exp path), 74; Am Col Vet Pathologists, dipl, 75. *Prof Exp:* Asst prof vet path, Univ Ga, 74-76; ASST PROF PATH, DIV COMP MED, SCH MED, JOHNS HOPKINS UNIV, 76- *Concurrent Pos:* NIH fel, Wash State Univ, 70-74; prin investr, inst res grant, Johns Hopkins Univ, 76-77 & Nat Mult Sclerosis Soc, 77; co-investr, Amyotrophic Lateral Sclerosis Soc, 77-80; mem ed bd, Vet Path, 77-; mem, Comt Animal Models & Genetic Stocks, Nat Res Coun, 78-; prin investr, Kroc Found, 78-80. *Mem:* Am Col Vet Pathologists; Am Asn Neuropathologist; Am Asn Path. *Res:* Comparative neuropathology; neurovirology; animal models of neurologic disease. *Mailing Add:* Dept of Path Johns Hopkins Hosp Baltimore MD 21205

CORKE, CHARLES THOMAS, b Stratford, Ont, Mar 19, 21; m 45; c 4. SOIL MICROBIOLOGY. *Educ:* Univ Western Ont, BSc, 50, MSc, 51; Rutgers Univ, PhD, 54. *Prof Exp:* From assoc prof to prof microbiol, Univ Guelph, 54-81; RETIRED. *Mem:* Agr Inst Can. *Res:* Pesticides degradation; microbial transformations of substituted anilines. *Mailing Add:* 20 Kitchener Guelph Can

CORKERN, WALTER HAROLD, b Washington Parish, La, Mar 28, 39; m 59; c 3. ORGANIC CHEMISTRY. *Educ:* La State Univ, BS, 61; Univ Ark, PhD(org chem), 66. *Prof Exp:* Res chemist, E I du Pont de Nemours & Co, Tex, 65-66; asst prof, 66-72, assoc prof, 72-77, PROF CHEM, SOUTHEASTERN LA UNIV, 77- *Mem:* AAAS. *Res:* Acid catalyzed ketone rearrangements; mechanistic studies; organic reaction mechanisms. *Mailing Add:* Dept of Chem Southeastern La Univ Hammond LA 70402

CORKIN, SUZANNE HAMMOND, b Hartford, Conn, May 18, 37; m 62; c 3. BEHAVIORAL NEUROBIOLOGY. *Educ:* Smith Col, BA, 59; McGill Univ, MSc, 61, PhD(psychol), 64. *Prof Exp:* Res & teaching asst neuropsychol, Dept Psychol, McGill Univ, 61-64; fel, Montreal Neuro Inst, 61-64; res assoc, Dept Psychol, 64-77, res assoc, Clin Res Ctr, 64-79, lectr neuropsychol, Dept Psychol, 77-79, prin res scientist, Dept Psychol, 79-81, SR INVESTR, CLIN RES CTR, MASS INST TECHNOL, 79-, ASSOC PROF, DEPT PSYCHOL, 81- *Concurrent Pos:* Consult psychol (neurosurg), Mass Gen Hosp, 75- *Mem:* Am Psychol Asn; AAAS; Soc Neurosci; Sigma Xi. *Res:* Brain-behavior relationships in man; somatosensory system; disorders of memory function; neuroplasticity. *Mailing Add:* Dept of Psychol E10-003A Mass Inst of Technol Cambridge MA 02139

CORKUM, KENNETH C, b Aurora, Ill, Aug 9, 30. PARASITOLOGY, INVERTEBRATE ZOOLOGY. *Educ:* Aurora Col BS, 58; La State Univ, MS, 60, PhD(zool), 63. *Prof Exp:* NIH fel parasitol, Sch Med, Tulane Univ, 63-65; from asst prof to assoc prof zool & physiol, 65-77, PROF ZOOL & PHYSIOL, LA STATE UNIV, BATON ROUGE, 77- *Mem:* Am Soc Parasitol; Am Micros Soc; Soc Syst Zool; Am Soc Zool. *Res:* Marine trematode taxonomy; cestode life cycles. *Mailing Add:* Dept of Zool & Physiol La State Univ Baton Rouge LA 70803

CORKUM, LYNDA DALE, freshwater biology, aquatic entomology, see previous edition

CORLESS, JOSEPH MICHAEL JAMES, b Orlando, Fla, July 28, 44; m 74; c 1. BIOPHYSICS, VISION. *Educ:* Georgetown Univ, BS, 66; Duke Univ, PhD(anat), 71, MD, 72. *Prof Exp:* Teaching asst bot & zool, Georgetown Univ, 65-66; instr micros anat, 68 & 69, teaching asst phys anthrop, 69, instr micros anat, 70, assoc anat, 72-73, asst prof, 74-80, ASSOC PROF ANAT & ASSOC OPHTHAL, MED CTR, DUKE UNIV, 80- *Concurrent Pos:* Fel, Med Res Coun Lab Molecular Biol, Cambridge, Eng, 73-74. *Mem:* Biophys Soc; Sigma Xi; Soc Photochem & Photobiol; NY Acad Sci. *Res:* Structure of visual photoreceptors; biomembrane structure. *Mailing Add:* Lab Biophys Cytol Dept Anat Box 3011 Duke Univ Med Ctr Durham NC 27710

CORLETT, MABEL ISOBEL, b Noranda, Que, Feb 7, 39. MINERALOGY. *Educ:* Queen's Univ, Ont, BSc, 60; Univ Chicago, SM, 62, PhD(mineral), 64. *Prof Exp:* Res asst mineral, Inst Crystallog & Petrog, Swiss Fed Inst Technol, 65-69; res assoc, 69-71, asst prof geol sci, 71-75, ASSOC PROF GEOL SCI, QUEEN'S UNIV, ONT, 75- *Mem:* Mineral Soc Am; Mineral Asn Can; Swiss Soc Mineral & Petrog. *Res:* Electron probe microanalysis; mineral chemistry. *Mailing Add:* Dept of Geol Sci Queen's Univ Kingston ON K7L 3N6 Can

CORLETT, MICHAEL PHILIP, b Toronto, Ont, Apr 28, 37. MYCOLOGY. *Educ:* Univ Toronto, BA, 59, MA, 62, PhD(mycol), 65. *Prof Exp:* RES MYCOLOGIST, BIOSYSTEMATICS RES INST, CAN DEPT AGR, 65- *Mem:* Mycol Soc Am; Can Bot Asn; Can Phytopath Soc. *Res:* Histology, morphology and development of fungi; taxonomy of the ascomycetes and fungi imperfecti. *Mailing Add:* Biosystematics Res Inst Agr Can Ottawa ON K1A 0C6 Can

CORLETT, RICHARD F, b Seattle, Wash, June 1, 28; m 50; c 3. NUCLEAR & CHEMICAL ENGINEERING. *Educ:* Univ Wash, BS, 52; Univ Idaho, MS, 61. *Prof Exp:* Engr, Hanford Labs, Gen Elec Co, 52-60, analyst reactor opers, 60-62, mgr reactor processing, 62-64; fast flu test facil proj engr, Pac Northwest Labs, Battelle Mem Inst, 64-66, mgr prog & anal, 65-66, res assoc, 67-69; exec engr, R W Beck & Assocs, 69-76; VPRES MATH SCI, NW INC. *Mem:* Am Inst Chem Engrs; Am Nuclear Soc. *Res:* Nuclear reactor design, construction, operations, siting and financing; environmental impact of power plants and industrial facilities. *Mailing Add:* Math Sci NW Inc 4215 94th NE Bellevue WA 98004

CORLEY, CALVIN, b West Columbia, SC, Feb 17, 27; m 51; c 2. ANALYTICAL CHEMISTRY. *Educ:* Allen Univ, BS, 50. *Prof Exp:* RES CHEMIST, ANAL CHEM LAB, USDA, 61- *Honors & Awards:* Super Serv Award, USDA, 64. *Mem:* Am Chem Soc; Asn Off Anal Chemists. *Res:* Development of analysis of insect control chemicals in agricultural products, soils and water. *Mailing Add:* 3209 St Lukes Lane Baltimore MD 21207

CORLEY, CHARLES CALHOUN, JR, b Charlotte, NC, June 30, 27; m 52; c 4. HEMATOLOGY, INTERNAL MEDICINE. *Educ:* Clemson Univ, BS, 53; Emory Univ, MD, 53. *Prof Exp:* From instr to assoc prof, 56-70, PROF HEMAT, EMORY UNIV, 70- *Concurrent Pos:* USPHS fel hemat, Emory Univ, 56-57. *Mem:* Am Col Physicians; Am Soc Hemat; Am Fed Clin Res; AMA. *Res:* Chemotherapy of hematologic malignancies. *Mailing Add:* Emory Univ Clin Sect Hemat 1365 Clifton Rd NE Atlanta GA 30322

CORLEY, GLYN JACKSON, b Carson, La, Jan 23, 16; m 39; c 5. MATHEMATICS. *Educ:* Northwestern State Univ, BA, 38; Columbia Univ, MA, 40; George Peabody Col, PhD(math), 59. *Prof Exp:* Instr math & physics, Springfield Col, 40; from instr to assoc prof math, Northwestern State Univ, 41-62; prof, ETex State Univ, 62-67, head dept, 66-67; prof math & head dept, La State Univ, Shreveport, 67-80; HEAD ACTUARY, WERNTZ & ASSOCS, 80- *Concurrent Pos:* Instr, Univ Tex, 46-47 & Vanderbuilt Univ, 54-55; mem Math Asn Am. *Res:* Analysis; statistics; actuarial mathematics. *Mailing Add:* 6117 Gaylyn Dr Shreveport LA 71105

CORLEY, JOHN BRYSON, b Calgary, Alta, Aug 29, 13; m 47; c 2. FAMILY MEDICINE. *Educ:* Univ Alta, BA, 36, MD, 42. *Prof Exp:* Sr partner, Chinook Med Clin, Calgary, 58-73; PROF FAMILY PRACT, MED UNIV SC, 73- *Concurrent Pos:* Prin investr, Nat Health Res Grant, Develop Grad Training Family Physicians, 66-69; vis prof dept community med, Univ Conn, 72; consult educ adv comt, Col Family Physicians Can, 73-; assoc ed self-assessment, Continuing Educ for Family Physician, 73-; mem clin prob solving skills comt, Nat Bd Med Examr, 74-75. *Mem:* Royal Col Med; fel Am Soc Clin Hypnosis; fel Can Col Family Physicians; Int Soc Res Med Educ; Am Educ Res Asn. *Res:* Development of prototype models of formative evaluation of post-graduate programs of specialty medical education. *Mailing Add:* Dept of Family Pract Med Univ of SC Charleston SC 29403

CORLEY, RONALD BRUCE, b Durham, NC, Oct 22, 48; m 80; c 1. CELLULAR IMMUNOLOGY, IMMUNOGENETICS. *Educ:* Duke Univ, BS, 70, PhD(microbiol), 75. *Prof Exp:* Mem scientist immunol, Basel Inst Immunol, Switzerland, 75-77; ASST PROF MICROBIOL & IMMUNOL, MED CTR, DUKE UNIV, 77- *Concurrent Pos:* Vis scientist, Basel Inst Immunol, Switzerland, 77, 79 & 80; mem fac, Comprehensive Cancer Ctr, Duke Univ, 78-; scholar award, Leukemia Soc Am, 79-84; prin investr res grants, Public Health Serv, 80-83, NIH, 80-85. *Mem:* Am Asn Immunologists; Am Asn Clin Histocompatibility Testing. *Res:* Intercellular communication among lymphocytes, in particular identifying the capacity of one class of T lymphocytes to regulate immune responses, and catalogue the types of hormones produced and used by these cells. *Mailing Add:* Div Immunol Box 3010 Med Ctr Duke Univ Durham NC 27710

CORLEY, TOM EDWARD, b Kellyton, Ala, Apr 25, 21; m 48; c 2. AGRICULTURAL ENGINEERING. *Educ:* Ala Polytech Inst, BS, 43, MS, 49. *Prof Exp:* Asst agr eng, 46-48, asst agr engr, 48-53, assoc, 53-63, prof, 63-66, ASST DIR AGR EXP STA, AUBURN UNIV, 66- *Mem:* Am Soc Agr Engrs; Sigma Xi. *Res:* Farm machinery development, design and testing. *Mailing Add:* Comer Hall Auburn Univ Auburn AL 36849

CORLEY, WILLIAM GENE, b Shelbyville, Ill, Dec 19, 35; m 59; c 3. STRUCTURAL ENGINEERING. *Educ:* Univ Ill, BS, 58, MS, 60, PhD(struct eng), 61. *Prof Exp:* Asst struct eng, Univ Ill, 59-61; develop engr, 64-66, mgr struct res sect, 66-74, dir, 74-78, DIV DIR, ENG DEVELOP DIV, RES & DEVELOP LABS, PORTLAND CEMENT ASN, SKOKIE, 78- *Honors & Awards:* Martin P Korn Award, Wason Medal for res, 70 & Bloem Award, 78, Am Concrete Inst; T Y Lin Award, Am Soc Civil Engrs. *Mem:* Am Concrete Inst; Am Soc Civil Engrs; Nat Soc Prof Engrs; Earthquake Eng Res Inst. *Res:* Structural research, especially structural concrete; structural concrete for earthquake resistant construction; uses of structural concrete in buildings and bridges. *Mailing Add:* 744 Glenayre Dr Glenview IL 60025

CORLISS, CHARLES HOWARD, b Medford, Mass, Oct 30, 19; m, 43; c 1. ATOMIC SPECTROSCOPY, LINE INTENSITY. *Educ:* Mass Inst Technol, BS, 41. *Prof Exp:* physicist, Nat Bur Standards, 42-81; PHYSICIST, FOREST HILLS LAB, 81- *Honors & Awards:* Silver Medal, US Dept Com, 63. *Mem:* AAAS; Optical Soc Am; Royal Astron Soc. *Res:* Description and analysis of atomic spectra; measurement of spectral intensity; transition probabilities; light sources; astronomical spectroscopy; compilation of energy levels. *Mailing Add:* Forest Hills Lab 2955 Albemarie St NW Washington DC 20008

CORLISS, CLARK EDWARD, b Coats, Kans, Nov 11, 19; m 50; c 3. ANATOMY. *Educ:* Univ Vt, BS, 42; Univ Mass, MS, 49; Brown Univ, PhD(biol), 52. *Prof Exp:* Asst prof microanat, Med Sch, Dalhousie Univ, 51-53; from instr to asst prof, Med Units, 53-63, ASSOC PROF ANAT, CTR HEALTH SCI, UNIV TENN, MEMPHIS, 63- *Mem:* Am Asn Anat; Soc Develop Biol. *Res:* Study of normal and abnormal development of the central nervous system in vertebrate embryos. *Mailing Add:* Dept of Anat Univ of Tenn Ctr for Health Sci Memphis TN 38163

CORLISS, EDITH LOU ROVNER, b Cleveland, Ohio, Sept 8, 20; m 43; c 2. PHYSICS. *Educ:* Mass Inst Technol, BS & MS, 41. *Prof Exp:* Jr physicist, Nat Bur Standards, 41-42 & US Weather Bur, 42-43; jr astronomer, US Naval Observ, 43-44; physicist, Nat Bur Standards, 44-80; MEM STAFF, FOREST HILLS LAB, 81- *Mem:* Am Phys Soc; Acoust Soc Am; Am Hort Soc; Inst Elec & Electronics Eng. *Res:* Analysis of transients; speech communication; physical problems in measurement of hearing. *Mailing Add:* Forest Hills Lab 2955 Albemarie St NW Washington DC 20008

CORLISS, GLENN ARTHUR, food science, see previous edition

CORLISS, JOHN BURT, b Pasadena, Calif, Apr 16, 36; m 61; c 3. ORIGIN OF LIFE, SUBMARINE HOT SPRINGS. *Educ:* Ariz State, BS, 58; Scripps Inst Oceanog, PhD(oceanog), 70. *Prof Exp:* ASSOC PROF OCEANOG, ORE STATE UNIV, 70- *Concurrent Pos:* Vis prof, Yale Univ, 71-72. *Mem:* Am Geophys Union. *Res:* Submarine hydrothermal systems: chemistry, geology and biology; descriptive structures and the origin of life on earth; submarine hydrothermal ore deposits. *Mailing Add:* Sch Oceanog Ore State Univ Corvallis OR 97331

CORLISS, JOHN FRANKLIN, soil science, see previous edition

CORLISS, JOHN OZRO, b Coats, Kans, Feb 23, 22; m 68; c 5. PROTOZOOLOGY. *Educ:* Univ Chicago, BS, 44; Univ Vt, AB, 47; NY Univ, PhD(biol), 51. *Prof Exp:* US Atomic Energy Comn res fel biol sci, Col France, 51-52; instr zool, Yale Univ, 52-54; from asst prof to prof, 54-64, head dept biol sci, Univ Ill, 64-69; dir syst biol, NSF, 69-70; PROF ZOOL & HEAD DEPT, UNIV MD, COLLEGE PARK, 70- *Concurrent Pos:* Vis prof, Univs London & Exeter, 60-62; ed J, Am Micros Soc, 66-80; chmn US Nat comt, Int Union Biol Sci, 71-73; mem & comnr, Int Comn Zool Nomenclature, 72-; mem, Corp of Marine Biol Lab, Woods Hole, Mass, 74-; ed, J Protozool, 80-; vis hon prof, East China Normal Univ, Shanghai, Repub China, 80; vis res prof, Univ Geneva, Switzerland, 80. *Mem:* Soc Protozool (secy, 58-61, pres, 64-65); Am Syst Zool (pres, 71-72); Soc Syst Zool (pres, 69-70); Am Micros Soc (pres, 65-66); Coun Biol Eds. *Res:* Comparative morphology, systematics, evolution, and phylogeny of ciliate protozoa; anatomy of the infraciliature; morphogenesis; nomenclature; international collection of ciliate type-specimens. *Mailing Add:* Dept Zool Univ Md College Park MD 20742

CORLISS, LESTER MYRON, b NJ, Mar 29, 19; m 41; c 2. SOLID STATE PHYSICS. *Educ:* City Col New York, BS, 40; Harvard Univ, MA, 48, PhD(chem phys), 51. *Prof Exp:* Chemist, Manhattan Proj, 43-46; SR CHEMIST, BROOKHAVEN NAT LAB, 49- *Concurrent Pos:* NSF sr fel, Univ Grenoble, 59-60; mem comn neutron diffraction, Int Union Crystallog, 66-75, chmn 69-75. *Mem:* Fel Am Phys Soc. *Res:* Neutron diffraction; magnetism; phase transformations; critical phenomena. *Mailing Add:* Brookhaven Nat Lab Upton NY 11973

CORMACK, ALLAN MACLEOD, b Johannesburg, SAfrica, Feb 23, 24; m 50; c 3. NUCLEAR PHYSICS, COMPUTED TOMOGRAPHY. *Educ:* Univ Cape Town, BSc, 44, MSc, 45. *Hon Degrees:* DSc, Tufts Univ, 80. *Prof Exp:* From jr lectr to lectr, Univ Cape Town, 46-56; res fel, Harvard Univ, 56-57; From asst prof to prof, 57-80, UNIV PROF PHYSICS, TUFTS UNIV, 80- *Concurrent Pos:* Assoc ed, J Computed Tomography, 77- *Honors & Awards:* Nobel Prize in Med, 79. *Mem:* SAfrican Inst Physics; Fel Am Phys Soc; Fel Am Acad Arts & Sci; hon mem Swedish Radiol Soc. *Res:* Mathematics. *Mailing Add:* Physics Dept Tufts Univ Medford MA 02155

CORMACK, DOUGLAS VILLY, biophysics, see previous edition

CORMACK, GEORGE DOUGLAS, b Killam, Alta, Sept 11, 33; m 59; c 3. COMMUNICATIONS ENGINEERING. *Educ:* Univ BC, BASc, 55, MSc, 60, PhD(physics), 62. *Prof Exp:* Instrumentation engr, Comput Devices Can, Ltd, 57-59; NATO overseas fel, 62-64; from asst prof to assoc prof, Carleton Univ, 64-76; systs consult, Dept Commun, Govt Can, 76-80; vpres eng, Can Cable TV Asn, 80-82; PROF ELEC ENG, UNIV ALBERTA, 82- *Concurrent Pos:* Consult, Nat Res Coun Can, 64-65, Comput Devices Can, Ltd, 65-68 & Northern Elec Co, 66-76; sr mem, Bell Tel Labs, 70-71. *Mem:* Inst Elec & Electronics Engrs. *Res:* Computer techniques; electromagnetics; communication systems; CATV; demographics; economics of rural communications. *Mailing Add:* Dept Elec Eng Univ Alberta Edmonton AB T5L 2W4 Can

CORMACK, JAMES FREDERICK, b Portland, Ore, Mar 13, 27; m 52; c 5. ENVIRONMENTAL CHEMISTRY. *Educ:* Reed Col, BA, 48; Ore State Col, PhD(biochem), 53. *Prof Exp:* Asst, Ore State Col, 48-49; res chemist, 53-59, SUPVR WATER PROGS, CROWN-ZELLERBACH, 59- *Mem:* AAAS; Am Chem Soc; Tech Asn Pulp & Paper Indust. *Res:* Industrial fermentations; stream improvement; waste treatment; industrial slimicides; continuous analysis. *Mailing Add:* Environ Serv Div Crown-Zellerbach Camas WA 98607

CORMACK, MELVILLE WALLACE, b Rossburn, Man, July 29, 08; m 33; c 2. PLANT PATHOLOGY. *Educ:* Univ Man, BSA, 30; Univ Alta, MSc, 31; Univ Minn, PhD(plant path), 37. *Prof Exp:* Plant dis investr, Dom Lab Plant Path, 28-31, asst plant pathologist, 31-47, head plant path sect, Sci Serv Lab, 48-57; dir, Can Agr Res Sta, 57-69; dir, Plant Breeding Sta, Njoro, Kenya, 69-73; RETIRED. *Mem:* Am Phytopath Soc; fel Royal Soc Can; Agr Inst Can. *Res:* Diseases of forage crop legumes and grasses; low temperature fungi; wheat improvement. *Mailing Add:* RR 1 Sechelt BC V0N 3A0 Can

CORMACK, ROBERT GEORGE HALL, b Cedar Rapids, Iowa, Feb 2, 04; m 39; c 2. BOTANY. *Educ:* Univ Toronto, BA, 29, MA, 31, PhD(biol), 34. *Prof Exp:* Demonstr bot, Univ Toronto, 29-36; lectr, 36-45, from asst prof to prof, 45-69, EMER PROF BOT, UNIV ALTA, 69- *Concurrent Pos:* Bot consult, Northwest Proj Study Group, MacKenzie Valley, NWT, Can, 70-71. *Mem:* Can Inst Forestry; Royal Soc Can. *Res:* Developmental anatomy; forest and wildlife conservation. *Mailing Add:* 9835-113th St Apt 1106 Edmonton AB T5K 1N4 Can

CORMAN, EMMETT GARY, b Kansas City, Kans, Aug 2, 30; m 57; c 4. THEORETICAL PHYSICS, NUCLEAR PHYSICS. *Educ:* Univ Kans, BS, 52, MS, 54, PhD(physics), 60. *Prof Exp:* Assoc physicist, Vitro Corp Am, 52-53; physicist, Los Alamos Sci Lab, 54-56; RES PHYSICIST, LAWRENCE RADIATION LAB, UNIV CALIF, LIVERMORE, 60- *Res:* Optical model analysis of high energy nucleons; Monte Carlo photon-matter interactions; physics of nuclear weapons; numerical solutions on high speed computers; physics of plasma-magnetic field interactions; multi-group and Monte Carlo ion transport. *Mailing Add:* Theoret Div Bldg 113 L-71 Lawrence Livermore Lab PO Box 808 Livermore CA 94550

CORMELL, LAIRD RENNY, b Youngstown, Ohio, Aug 25, 48; m 76; c 2. ELEMENTARY PARTICLE PHYSICS. *Educ:* Univ Okla, BS, 70; Univ Ill, MS, 71, PhD(physics), 75. *Prof Exp:* Res investr, 75-77, ASST PROF PHYSICS, UNIV PA, 77- *Concurrent Pos:* Fel, Alfred P Sloan Found, NY, 81- *Mem:* Am Phys Soc. *Res:* High energy physics studying high transverse momentum processes in hadronic interactions and in photoproduction; photoproduction of massive particles. *Mailing Add:* 30 W 120 Wildwood Ct Warrenville IL 60555

CORMIA, ROBERT L, b Ilion, NY, June 9, 35; m 55; c 3. PASSIVE SOLAR TECHNOLOGY, MECHANICAL ENGINEERING. *Educ:* Union Col, Schenectady, BS, 66. *Prof Exp:* Tech specialist phys chem, Gen Elec Res & Develop Ctr, 56-66, physicist vacuum & thin films, 66-70; mgr vacuum prod eng source develop, Airco-Temescal Corp, Berkeley, 70-78; DIR DEVELOP, APPL RES & VACUUM THIN FILMS, SOUTHWALL CORP, PALO ALTO, 78- *Res:* Kinetics of crystallization from glassy phases; plasma enhanced physical vapor deposition processes; nucleation and growth of vacuum deposited coatings; state of art production scales; thin film coating apparatus from research prototypes. *Mailing Add:* 1131 Shenandoah Dr Sunnyvale CA 94087

CORMIER, ALAN DENNIS, b Lynn, Mass, Feb 16, 45; m 68; c 2. ANALYTICAL CHEMISTRY, PHYSICAL CHEMISTRY. *Educ:* Northeastern Univ, BA, 68; Univ NH, PhD(spectros), 72. *Prof Exp:* Fel spectros, Marquette Univ, 72-74; instr phys chem, Boston Univ, 74-76; PROF LEADER ELECTROANAL CHEM, INSTRUMENTATION LAB INC, 76- *Concurrent Pos:* NDEA res fel, Univ NH, 69-72; consult/sci programmer, US Forest Serv, 70-74. *Mem:* Am Chem Soc; Sigma Xi. *Res:* Sensors, techniques and instrumental fluidic design for quantitative analytical determinations in biological fluids; potentiometric and polargraphic electrodes and selected spectrophotometric methods. *Mailing Add:* 36 Charles St Newbury Port MA 01950

CORMIER, BRUNO M, b Laurierville, Que, Nov 14, 19; m. PSYCHIATRY. *Educ:* Univ Montreal, BA, 42, MD, 47; McGill Univ, dipl psychiat, 52. *Prof Exp:* From asst prof to assoc prof psychiat, 53-67, dir criminal res, 67-74, lectr psychiat, 63-74, assoc prof psychiat, 74-78, PROF FORENSIC PSYCHIAT, McGILL UNIV, 78- *Concurrent Pos:* Clin asst psychiat, Royal Victoria Hosp, Montreal, 53-55, assoc psychiatrist, 56-63; 55-70; consult, NY State Correctional Serv, 66-72. *Mem:* Am Psychiat Asn; Can Psychiat Asn; Can Corrections Asn; Can Psychoanal Soc. *Res:* Clinical criminology; psychopathology of deprivation of liberty; persistent criminality. *Mailing Add:* Clin in Forensic Psychiat 509 Pine Ave W Montreal PQ H2W 1S4 Can

CORMIER, MILTON JOSEPH, b DeRidder, La, Nov 29, 26; m 51; c 3. BIOCHEMISTRY. *Educ:* Southwestern La Inst, BS, 48; Univ Tex, MA, 51; Univ Tenn, PhD(microbiol), 56. *Prof Exp:* Assoc biochemist, Biol Div, Oak Ridge Nat Lab, 56-58; from asst prof to prof bioluminescence, 58-66, RES PROF BIOLUMINESCENCE, UNIV GA, 66- *Mem:* Am Chem Soc; Am Soc Microbiol; Am Soc Biol Chem. *Res:* Mechanisms of bioluminescent reactions. *Mailing Add:* Dept of Biochem Univ of Ga Athens GA 30602

CORMIER, RANDAL, b Truro, NS, Mar 9, 30; m 55; c 6. GEOLOGY. *Educ:* St Francis Xavier Univ, Can. BSc, 51; Mass Inst Technol, PhD(geol), 56. *Prof Exp:* Assoc prof, 57-74, PROF GEOL, ST FRANCIS XAVIER UNIV, 74- *Mem:* Can Geol Soc; Can Inst Min & Metall. *Res:* Geochronology; geochemical prospecting. *Mailing Add:* Dept of Geol St Francis Xavier Univ Antigonish Can

CORMIER, ROMAE JOSEPH, b New York, NY, May 17, 28; m 54; c 4. MATHEMATICS. *Educ:* Univ Chattanooga, BS, 51; Univ Tenn, MA, 56; Univ Mo, MA, 63. *Prof Exp:* Mathematician ballistics, Vitro Corp Am, 55; ASST PROF MATH, NORTHERN ILL UNIV, 56- *Concurrent Pos:* Consult, Gen Elec Co, 65 & NAm Mineral Explor, 69-; Solutions ed, J Recreational Math, 77- *Mem:* Am Math Soc; Int Tensor Soc. *Res:* Steiner symmetrization; differential equations; combinatorics. *Mailing Add:* Dept of Math Northern Ill Univ De Kalb IL 60115

CORMIER, THOMAS MICHAEL, b Waltham, Mass, Nov 15, 47. NUCLEAR STRUCTURE, NUCLEAR REACTIONS. *Educ:* Mass Inst Technol, SB, 71, PhD(physics), 74. *Prof Exp:* Res assoc, Mass Inst Technol, 74-75, State Univ NY, Stony Brook, 75-77; vis scientist, Max Planck Inst Nuclear Physics, Heidelberg, 77-78; PROF, UNIV ROCHESTER, 78- *Concurrent Pos:* Fel, Alfred P Sloan Found, 81-83. *Mem:* Am Phys Soc; AAAS. *Mailing Add:* Dept Physics & Astron Univ Rochester Rochester NY 14627

CORN, HERMAN, b Philadelphia, Pa, Oct 7, 21; c 3. PERIODONTOLOGY. *Educ:* Temple Univ, DDS, 44; Am Bd Periodont, dipl, 63. *Prof Exp:* Instr periodont, Grad Sch Med, 58-63, assoc, Sch Dent Med & Grad Sch Med, 63-65, asst prof, Sch Dent Med, 65-68, assoc prof, 68-74, PROF PERIODONT, SCH DENT MED, UNIV PA, 74- *Concurrent Pos:* Oral surgeon, Lower Bucks County Hosp, 54-; lectr, Dent Schs, Wash Univ & Univ Ky, 68, Temple Univ & Case Western Reserve Univ, 69 & Boston Univ, 69-; lectr post grad educ, Sch Dent Med, Univ Pa; clin assoc prof & dir prev dent, Med Col Pa, 74- *Mem:* Fel Am Col Dentists; Am Dent Asn; Am Acad Periodont; Am Soc Prev Dent (pres, 73-74). *Res:* Clinical periodontics; periodontal therapy; mucogingival surgery. *Mailing Add:* 1310 Frosty Hollow Rd Levittown PA 19056

CORN, JOHN W(ILLIAM), b Dallas, Tex, Oct 20, 20; m 44; c 2. CHEMICAL ENGINEERING. *Educ:* Univ Colo, BS, 45, MS, 47. *Prof Exp:* Jr res engr, eng exp sta, Univ Colo, 45-47; eng tech sect, Res & Develop Lab, E I du Pont de Nemours & Co, 47-51, tech supvr, 51-52, tech asst supt, 52-58, supvr, 58-60, sr res engr, 60-70, staff engr, Tech Dept, Sabine River Works, 70-80; CONSULT CHEM ENG & ENVIRON ENG, 80- *Mem:* Am Inst Chem Engrs; Am Chem Soc. *Res:* Production of organic chemicals and plastics. *Mailing Add:* 204 Crestwood Dr Fredericksburg TX 78624

CORN, MORTON, b New York, NY, Oct 18, 33; m 55; c 2. SANITARY ENGINEERING. *Educ:* Cooper Union, BChE, 55; Harvard Univ, MS, 56, PhD(sanit eng), 61. *Prof Exp:* Asst sanit engr, R A Taft Sanit Eng Ctr, Ohio, 56-58; res assoc, Sch Pub Health, Harvard Univ, 60-61; from asst prof to assoc prof environ health, Grad Sch Pub Health, Univ Pittsburgh, 62-67, prof indust health & air eng & prof chem eng, 67-79; PROF & DIV DIR, ENVIRON HEALTH ENG, JOHNS HOPKINS UNIV, 80- *Concurrent Pos:* NSF fel, Sch Hyg, Univ London, 61-62; consult, Health Physics Div, Oak Ridge Nat Lab, 63-, Div Biol & Med, US Atomic Energy Comn, 63-, Los Alamos Sci Lab, 65- & Nat Acad Sci-Nat Res Coun Comt Biol Effects Air Pollution, 70-; consult nat air pollution control admin, USPHS, 63-, chmn air pollution res grants adv comt, 69-71; US rep to panel of experts on aerosols, Int Atomic Energy Agency, Vienna, 67; mem, Air Pollution Adv Comt, Allegheny County, Pa; adv ed, Atmospheric Environment, Environ Letters, J Air Pollution Control Asn, Ann Occcup Hyg (London); asst secy labor, Occup Safety & Health Act, 75-77; mem, panel experts occup health, WHO, 75-, sci adv bd, US Environ Protection Agency, 78-81, nat adv comt health & vital statist, Dept Health & Human Serv, 79- & comt on risk assessment, Nat Acad Sci, 81- *Mem:* AAAS; Am Chem Soc; Am Indust Hyg Asn; Am Inst Chem Engrs; Air Pollution Control Asn. *Res:* Aerosol physics; air pollution, particularly engineering control and analytical assessment; industrial hygiene and ventilation. *Mailing Add:* Grad Sch Pub Health Univ of Pittsburgh Pittsburgh PA 15213

CORNACCHIO, JOSEPH V(INCENT), b New York, NY, Dec 27, 34; m 60; c 2. COMPUTER SCIENCE, ENGINEERING. *Educ:* Pa State Univ, BS, 56; Syracuse Univ, MS, 59, PhD(elec eng), 62. *Prof Exp:* Instr elec eng, Syracuse Univ, 59-62; mem staff, Int Bus Mach Corp, 62-69; assoc prof advan technol, 69-72, prof, Sch Advan Technol, 72-77, chmn, Dept Comput Sci, 77-78, PROF, DEPT COMPUT SCI, STATE UNIV NY BINGHAMTON, 77- *Mem:* Asn Comput Mach; Inst Elec & Electronics Engrs. *Res:* Software complexity measures; computer-assisted decision systems. *Mailing Add:* Dept of Comput Sci State Univ NY Binghamton NY 13901

CORNATZER, WILLIAM EUGENE, b Mocksville, NC, Sept 28, 18; m 46; c 2. BIOCHEMISTRY. *Educ:* Wake Forest Col, BS, 39; Bowman Gray Sch Med, MD, 51; Univ NC, MS, 41, PhD(biochem), 44; Am Bd Clin Chem, dipl. *Prof Exp:* Asst zool, Wake Forest Col, 37-38, asst phys chem, 38-39; asst biol chem, Univ NC, 39-41; asst prof biochem, Bowman Gray Sch Med, 46-51; Chester Fritz distinguished prof, 73-80, PROF BIOCHEM & HEAD DEPT, SCH MED, UNIV NDAK, 51-, DIR, IRELAND RES LAB, 53- *Concurrent Pos:* NSF travel award, Int Cong Biochem, Paris, 52, Tokyo, 67; USAEC travel award, Int Cancer Cong, London, 58; Int Union Physiol Sci travel award, Int Cong Pharmacol, Stockholm, 61; Am Inst Nutrit travel award, Int Cong Nutrit, Prague, 69 & Mexico City, 72; consult med div, Oak Ridge Inst Nuclear Studies, 51-; mem, Am Bd Clin Chem; mem biochem test comt, Nat Bd Med Exam. *Honors & Awards:* Billing Award, AMA, 51. *Mem:* AAAS; Am Chem Soc; Am Soc Biol Chem; Am Fedn Clin Res; Soc Exp Biol & Med. *Res:* Properties of proteins; quinine metabolism and absorption; antimalarial testing; phospholipid metabolism; liver function tests and disease; radiation of effects and toxicity of isotopes; lipotropic agents. *Mailing Add:* Dept of Biochem Univ of NDak Med SCh Grand Forks ND 58201

CORNBLATH, MARVIN, b St Louis, Mo, June 18, 25; m 48; c 3. PEDIATRICS, BIOCHEMISTRY. *Educ:* Wash Univ, MD, 47. *Prof Exp:* Asst pediat, Wash Univ, 49-50; from instr to asst prof, Johns Hopkins Univ, 53-59; from asst prof to assoc prof, Northwestern Univ, 59-61; from assoc prof to prof, Univ Ill, 61-68; chmn dept pediat, 68-78, PROF PEDIAT, SCH MED, UNIV MD, BALTIMORE, 68- *Concurrent Pos:* USPHS fel biochem, Wash Univ, 50-51; res assoc, Sinai Hosp, Md, 53-59; asst chmn div pediat, Michael Reese Hosp, Ill, 59-61; spec asst to sci dir & actg br chief, perinatal & pediat med, Nat Inst Child Health & Human Develop, NIH, Bethesda, 78-82. *Mem:* Soc Pediat Res; Am Soc Biol Chemists; Am Physiol Soc; Brit Biochem Soc; Am Pediat Soc. *Res:* Physiological and biochemical maturation of newborn and premature infants; carbohydrate metabolism and enzymology. *Mailing Add:* 3809 St Paul St Baltimore MD 21201

CORNEIL, ERNEST RAY, b Nov 11, 32; m 56; c 4. SYSTEMS & CONTROL ENGINEERING. *Educ:* Queen's Univ, Ont, BSc, 55; Univ London, PhD & DIC, 60. *Prof Exp:* Lectr, 58-61, asst prof, 61-64, dir, Comput Ctr, 64-65, assoc prof, 64-70, head dept, 78-81, PROF MECH ENG, QUEEN'S UNIV, ONT, 70- *Concurrent Pos:* Consult info systs & comput appln; eng consult, Transport Can, 75-76. *Mem:* Am Soc Mech Engrs; Am Soc Heating, Refrig & Air-Conditioning Engrs. *Res:* Control systems using nonlinear feedback and adaptive systems; heat pump design and application; North American railway electrification. *Mailing Add:* Dept of Mech Eng Queen's Univ Kingston ON K7L 3N6 Can

CORNEIL, PAUL HAMPTON, physical chemistry, see previous edition

CORNELIUS, ARCHIE J(UNIOR), b Westmoreland, Kans, Oct 16, 31; m 53; c 4. MECHANICAL ENGINEERING. *Educ:* Kans State Univ, BS, 58; Okla State Univ, MS, 63, PhD(mech eng), 65. *Prof Exp:* Res engr, Jersey Prod Res Co, Okla, 58-64; RES ENGR, PHILLIPS PETROL CO, 65- *Mem:* Am Inst Mining, Metall & Petrol Engrs. *Res:* Petroleum recovery by thermal methods; heat transfer to supercritical fluids; improved oil recovery methods. *Mailing Add:* Phillips Petrol Co 335 FPB Bartlesville OK 74004

CORNELIUS, CHARLES EDWARD, b Walnut Park, Calif, Dec 19, 27; m 48; c 4. PHYSIOLOGY. *Educ:* Univ Calif, BS, 49 & 51, DVM, 53, PhD(comp path), 58. *Prof Exp:* Lectr clin path, Univ Calif, Davis, 54-58, from asst prof to assoc prof, 58-66, assoc dean, 62-64; prof physiol & dean col vet med, Kans State Univ, 66-71; dean, Col Vet Med, Univ Fla, 71-81, prof path, 74-81, chmn, Dept Vet Sci, 76-78; DIR, CALIF PRIMATE RES CTR, UNIV CALIF, DAVIS, 81- *Concurrent Pos:* Mem res grants study sect gen med, NIH, 65-69, Nat Adv Comt health res facilities, 69-71; chmn, Comt Animal Health, Nat Acad Sci, 72-73; mem, Biomed Res Develop grant panel, NIH, 79-81. *Mem:* Am Physiol Soc; Soc Exp Biol & Med; Am Gastroenterol Asn; Am Vet Med Asn; Am Asn Liver Dis. *Res:* Hepatic physiology; bile pigment and anion transport; comparative hepatic dysfunction. *Mailing Add:* Calif Primate Res Ctr Univ Calif Davis CA 95618

CORNELIUS, E(DWARD) B(ERNARD), b Laredo, Tex, Nov 6, 18; m 46; c 2. CHEMICAL ENGINEERING. *Educ:* Princeton Univ, BS, 40, BChE, 41. *Prof Exp:* Jr develop engr, Houdry Process & Chem Co Div, Air Prod & Chem, Inc, 41-46, asst res chemist, 46-50, proj dir, 50-57, sect chief, 57-70, sr res chemist & admin asst, 71-74; sr res chemist, Matthey Bishop Inc, 74-78; sr res chemist, 78-80, SR RES GROUP LEADER, ASHLAND PETROL CO DIV, ASHLAND OIL CO, 80- *Concurrent Pos:* Mem Int Cong Catalysis, 56- *Mem:* Am Chem Soc; Am Inst Chem Engrs; Clay Minerals Soc; Nat Catalysis Soc; Sigma Xi. *Res:* Preparation, characterization and performance of hydrocarbon conversion catalysts useful in petroleum and chemical industry. *Mailing Add:* Ashland Petrol Co Res Dept PO Box 391 Ashland KY 41101

CORNELIUS, LARRY MAX, b Washington, Ind, Apr 30, 43; m 65; c 1. VETERINARY MEDICINE. *Educ:* Purdue Univ, DVM, 67; Univ Mo-Columbia, PhD(clin path), 71. *Prof Exp:* Intern, Angell Mem Animal Hosp, Boston, Mass, 67-68; res assoc vet med, Univ Mo-Columbia, 68-74; mem fac, 74-80, ASSOC PROF ANIMAL MED, UNIV GA, 80- *Concurrent Pos:* Speaker, Technicon Int Cong, Chicago, 69; Nat Inst Arthritis & Metab Dis fel, 69-72. *Mem:* Am Vet Med Asn; Comp Gastroenterol Soc. *Res:* Fluid and electrolyte balance in veterinary medicine. *Mailing Add:* Dept Animal Med Univ of Ga Athens GA 30601

CORNELIUS, RICHARD DEAN, b Chicago, Ill, Sept 18, 47; m 70; c 3. INORGANIC CHEMISTRY, BIOINORGANIC CHEMISTRY. *Educ:* Carleton Col, BA, 69; Univ Iowa, PhD(inorg chem), 74. *Prof Exp:* Res assoc biochem, Univ Wis-Madison, 74-77; ASST PROF CHEM, WICHITA STATE UNIV, 77- *Mem:* Am Chem Soc; Sigma Xi. *Res:* Coordination chemistry; solution kinetics; science education. *Mailing Add:* Dept of Chem Wichita State Univ Wichita KS 67208

CORNELIUS, STEVEN GREGORY, b Alton, Ill, Mar 17, 51; m 72; c 2. SYSTEMS ANALYSIS & MODELING. *Educ:* Univ Ill, Urbana, BS, 72, PhD(animal sci & nutrit), 76. *Prof Exp:* Res chemist, US Meat Animal Res Ctr, 76-78; ASST PROF NUTRIT & ANIMAL SWINE, DEPT ANIMAL SCI, UNIV MINN, 78- *Mem:* Am Soc Animal Sci; Animal Nutrit Res Coun; Biomet Soc. *Res:* Factors influencing the digestion and absorption of nutrients by the pig; application of systems analysis techniques to animal agriculture problems; swine growth and the influence of environment on growth; general swine nutrition. *Mailing Add:* 131 Peters Hall 1404 Gortner Ave St Paul MN 55108

CORNELIUSSEN, ROGER DUWAYNE, b Fargo, NDak, Aug 1, 31; m 54; c 4. POLYMER MORPHOLOGY, FAILURE MECHANISMS. *Educ:* Concordia Col, Moorhead, Minn, BA, 53; Univ Chicago, MS, 60, PhD(phys chem), 62. *Prof Exp:* Chemist, Am Oil Co, 58-60; asst prof chem, Luther Col, 61-64; chemist polymer chem, Res Traingle Inst, 64-67; sr chemist, NStar Res Inst, 67-68; pres polymer physics, Res Serv, Inc, 69-70; assoc prof, 70-80, PROF MAT ENG, DREXEL UNIV, 80- *Concurrent Pos:* Dir, Drexel Polymer Prog, 71-, Ctr Insulation Technol, 80-; vis prof, For Motor Co & Bell Telephone Labs, Columbus, Ohio, 79; lectr, Soc plastic Engrs, 79- *Mem:* Am Chem Soc; Soc Plastics Engrs; Am Soc Testing Mat; Am Soc Eng Educ. *Res:* Polymer morphology; structure properly relationships; mechanical properties; failure analysis. *Mailing Add:* Drexel Univ Philadelphia PA 19104

CORNELL, ALAN, b Fall River, Mass, May 4, 29; m 52; c 3. FOOD SCIENCE. *Educ:* Univ Mass, BS, 51; Mass Inst Technol, PhD(food sci), 60. *Prof Exp:* Res chemist, Res Ctr, Philip Morris, Inc, 60-65, sr scientist, 65-67; mgr food sci div, Cent Labs, Ralston Purina Co, 67-69; asst vpres res & develop, 69-73, VPRES RES & PROD DEVELOP, CONSOL CIGAR CORP, 73- *Mem:* Am Chem Soc; Inst Food Technol; NY Acad Sci. *Res:* Subjective effects on constituents in tobacco and resultant smoke; subjective evaluation; product development of consumer products; research management; tobacco and smoke chemistry; quality control; product safety and health. *Mailing Add:* Consol Cigar Corp One Gulf & Western Plaza New York NY 10023

CORNELL, C(ARL) ALLIN, b Mobridge, SDak, Sept 19, 38; m 59; c 3. STRUCTURAL ENGINEERING. *Educ:* Stanford Univ, AB, 60, MS, 61, PhD(struct eng), 64. *Prof Exp:* Actg asst prof struct eng, Stanford Univ, 63-64; from asst prof to assoc prof civil eng, 64-76, PROF CIVIL ENG, MASS INST TECHNOL, 76- *Concurrent Pos:* Ford Found eng fel, 64-66; vis prof, Univ Calif, Berkeley, 70-71. *Mem:* Nat Acad Eng; Inst Math Statist; Seismol Soc Am; Am Concrete Inst; Am Soc Civil Engrs. *Res:* Application of probability theory and statistics in civil and structural engineering. *Mailing Add:* Dept of Civil Eng Mass Inst of Technol Cambridge MA 02139

CORNELL, CREIGHTON N, b Rolfe, Iowa, Mar 20, 33; m 58; c 2. PHYSIOLOGY, BIOCHEMISTRY. *Educ:* Univ Mo, BS, 54, DVM, 62, MS, 69. *Prof Exp:* Instr agr chem & vet physiol, 62-63, instr agr chem, 63-65, ASST PROF AGR CHEM, UNIV MO-COLUMBIA, 65- *Res:* Biochemistry and physiology of the intoxication occurring in cattle feeding on toxic fescue grass pastures or hay, causing gangrene and sloughing of the distal portions of the extremities. *Mailing Add:* 105 Schweitzer Hall Univ of Mo Columbia MO 65201

CORNELL, DAVID, b Elmira, NY, Aug 19, 25; m 48; c 4. CHEMICAL ENGINEERING. *Educ:* Univ Mich, BSChE, 47, MSChE, 49, PhD(chem eng), 52. *Prof Exp:* Asst res & develop labs, Blaw-Knox Div, Blaw-Knox Co, 48-50; asst prof chem eng, Univ Tex, 52-55; res engr, Monsanto Chem Co, 55-58; assoc prof petrol eng, Okla State Univ, 58-61; PROF CHEM ENG, MISS STATE UNIV, 61- *Concurrent Pos:* Res engr, Tex Petrol Res Comt, Univ Tex, 52-53. *Mem:* Am Inst Chem Engrs; Am Chem Soc; Am Soc Petrol Engrs; Am Soc Eng Educ. *Res:* Unsteady state flow of natural gas in natural gas reservoirs; flow through porous media. *Mailing Add:* 208 Windsor Rd Starkville MS 39759

CORNELL, DAVID ALLAN, b St Paul, Minn, Dec 29, 37; m 62; c 2. PHYSICS. *Educ:* Principia Col, BS, 59; Univ Calif, Berkeley, PhD(physics), 64. *Prof Exp:* From instr to assoc prof, 64-78, prof, 78-80, ASSOC PROF PHYSICS, PRINCIPIA COL, 80- *Mem:* Am Asn Physics Teachers. *Res:* Nuclear magnetic resonance phenomena in metals and alloys; hydrogen diffusion in metallic crystals. *Mailing Add:* Dept of Physics Principia Col Elsah IL 62028

CORNELL, HOWARD VERNON, b Berwyn, Ill, Apr 13, 47; m 71. BIOGEOGRAPHY, ECOLOGY. *Educ:* Tufts Univ, BS, 69; Cornell Univ, PhD(ecol), 75. *Prof Exp:* asst prof, 75-81, ASSOC PROF BIOL SCI, UNIV DEL, 81- *Mem:* AAAS; Ecol Soc Am; Am Soc Naturalists. *Res:* Ecology of host plant-herbivore systems. *Mailing Add:* Sch of Life & Health Sci Univ of Del Newark DE 19711

CORNELL, JAMES MORRIS, b Bismarck, NDak, Sept 8, 37; m 57; c 2. ANIMAL BEHAVIOR. *Educ:* Univ Wash, BS, 60, MS, 62, PhD(psychol), 63. *Prof Exp:* Asst prof psychol, Mont State Col, 63-64; asst prof, 64-68, ASSOC PROF PSYCHOL, UNIV WATERLOO, 68- *Concurrent Pos:* Nat Res Coun Can res grants, 64- *Mem:* AAAS; Am Psychol Asn; Animal Behavior Soc. *Res:* Conidtioning in animals; imprinting; memory. *Mailing Add:* 28 Furness Dr Kitchener ON N2M 1S7 Can

CORNELL, JAMES S, b Harrisburg, Pa, Apr 9, 47. BIOLOGICAL CHEMISTRY, ENDOCRINOLOGY. *Educ:* Mich State Univ, BS, 69; Univ Calif, Los Angeles, PhD(biol chem), 73. *Prof Exp:* Fel, Univ Calif, Los Angeles, 73; res assoc, 73-75, ASST PROF BIOCHEM & ASST DIR LAB CLIN BIOCHEM, MED COL, CORNELL UNIV, 75- *Mem:* Endocrine Soc; Am Chem Soc; AAAS; NY Acad Sci. *Res:* Reproductive biochemistry-the protein chemistry of the placenta; factors influencing the induction of labour. *Mailing Add:* Dept of Biochem Cornell Univ Med Col New York NY 10021

CORNELL, JOHN ANDREW, b Westerly, RI, Apr 29, 41; m 63; c 2. APPLIED STATISTICS. *Educ:* Univ Fla, BSEd, 62, MStat, 66; Va Polytech Inst, PhD(statist), 69. *Prof Exp:* Appl statistician, Tenn Eastman Co, 65-66; asst prof statist, Univ Fla, 68-72; lectr statist, Birkbeck Col, Univ London, 72-73; assoc prof, 73-78, PROF STATIST, UNIV FLA, 78- *Concurrent Pos:* Statist consult, Tenn Eastman Co, 65-66 & Agr Exp Sta, Univ Fla, 68-72. *Mem:* Am Statist Asn; Inst Math Statist. *Res:* Design and analysis of statistical experiments in agricultural, social, physical and biological sciences, design and analysis of experiments with mixtures. *Mailing Add:* Dept of Statist 219 Rolfs Hall Univ of Fla Gainesville FL 32601

CORNELL, NEAL WILLIAM, b Savannah, Ga, July 29, 37; m 67. BIOCHEMISTRY. *Educ:* Univ Redlands, BS, 60; Univ Calif, Los Angeles, PhD(biochem), 64. *Prof Exp:* Res fel biol chem, Harvard Med Sch, 63-66; from asst prof to assoc prof chem, Pomona Col, 66-72; Med Res Coun investr, Oxford Univ, 72-74; RES CHEMIST, LAB METAB, NAT INST ALCOHOL ABUSE & ALCOHOLISM, 74- *Concurrent Pos:* Investr, Marine Biol Lab, Woods Hole, 70, 71 & 72, mem corp, 71- *Mem:* Brit Biochem Soc; Am Soc Biol Chem; Am Inst Nutrit. *Res:* Metabolic control; cell biology; enzyme rates in living cells; membrane transport; comparative biochemistry of regulatory enzymes. *Mailing Add:* NIAAA Lab of Metab 12501 Washington Ave Rockville MD 20852

CORNELL, RICHARD GARTH, b Cleveland, Ohio, Nov 18, 30; m 61; c 3. BIOSTATISTICS. *Educ:* Univ Rochester, AB, 52; Va Polytech Inst, MS, 54, PhD(statist), 56. *Prof Exp:* Asst, Va Polytech Inst, 52-54, Oak Ridge Inst Nuclear Studies fel, 55-56; statistician, Commun Dis Ctr, USPHS, Ga, 56-58, chief lab & field sta, Statist Unit, 58-60; from assoc prof to prof statist, Fla State Univ, 60-71; PROF BIOSTATIST & CHMN DEPT, UNIV MICH, ANN ARBOR, 71- *Mem:* Fel Am Statist Asn; Biomet Soc; Am Sci Affil. *Res:* Biometry. *Mailing Add:* Dept Biostatist Univ Mich Ann Arbor MI 48109

CORNELL, ROBERT JOSEPH, b Westerly, RI, Oct 1, 40; m 67; c 2. POLYMER CHEMISTRY. *Educ:* Clarkson Col Technol, BS, 62, MS, 64; Worcester Polytech Inst, PhD(org chem), 67. *Prof Exp:* Res chemist polymer chem, 67-70, res scientist, Polymer Res Group, 70-73, sr group leader paracril res, 73-77, res & develop mgr spec chem, Chem Div, 78-81, RES & DEVELOP MGR CHEM, CHEM DIV, UNIROYAL INC, 81- *Mem:* Am Chem Soc; Sigma Xi. *Res:* Plastic additives; petroleum additives, chemical blowing agents and rubber chemicals. *Mailing Add:* Uniroyal Inc Chem Div Elm St Naugatuck CT 06770

CORNELL, SAMUEL DOUGLAS, b Buffalo, NY, Apr 16, 15; m 39, 69; c 4. SCIENCE ADMINISTRATION, ACADEMIC ADMINISTRATION. *Educ:* Yale Univ, BA, 35, PhD(physics), 38. *Prof Exp:* Develop physicist, Eastman Kodak Co, NY, 38-42; sci warfare adv, Res & Develop Bd, Washington, DC, 46-52; exec officer, Nat Acad Sci-Nat Res Coun, 52-65; pres, Mackinac Col, 65-70; consult sci admin, Nat Acad Sci, 70-72, asst to the pres, 72-81; RETIRED. *Mem:* AAAS; Am Phys Soc. *Res:* Molecular spectroscopy; design of motion picture equipment. *Mailing Add:* Nat Acad Sci 2101 Constitution Ave NW Washington DC 20418

CORNELL, STEPHEN WATSON, b Chicago, Ill, May 21, 42; m 69; c 2. POLYMER ENGINEERING, CHEMICAL ENGINEERING. *Educ:* Rensselaer Polytech Inst, BChE, 64; Case Western Reserve Univ, MS, 66, PhD(polymer sci), 69. *Prof Exp:* Proj scientist res & develop, Chem & Plastics Div, Union Carbide Corp, 68-74; mgr mat res, Corp Res & Develop Div, Continental Can Co, 74-76; mgr mat & prod develop, Continental Plastics Indust, 76-79, DIR SPEC PROJ, CONTINENTAL PACKAGING CO, CONTINENTAL GROUP, INC, 80- *Mem:* Am Chem Soc; Am Phys Soc; AAAS; Soc Plastics Engrs. *Res:* New product development; new packaging development; food packaging development; polymer-filler interactions; surface modification; degradable polyolefin compositions. *Mailing Add:* 66 High Point Rd West Port CT 06880

CORNELL, W(ARREN) A(LVAN), b Attleboro, Mass, July 2, 21; m 43; c 4. COMMUNICATIONS NETWORKS. *Educ:* Rensselaer Polytech Inst, BEE, 42. *Prof Exp:* Dir digital commun syst eng, 66-67, dir data commun eng, 67-70, dir opers res, 70-81, DIR NETWORK ANAL, BELL LABS, 81- *Mem:* Inst Elec & Electronics Engrs; Asn Comput Mach; Opers Res Soc Am. *Res:* Electronic telephone switching; digital computers; military surveillance; communication systems; operations research. *Mailing Add:* 18 Crest Dr Little Silver NJ 07739

CORNELL, WILLIAM CROWNINSHIELD, b Attleboro, Mass, May 5, 41; m 69; c 2. MICROPALEONTOLOGY, PALYNOLOGY. *Educ:* Univ RI, BS, 65, MS, 67; Univ Calif, Los Angeles, PhD(geol), 72. *Prof Exp:* Asst prof, 71-75, ASSOC PROF GEOL, UNIV TEX, EL PASO, 75- *Concurrent Pos:* Actg chmn dept geol sci, Univ Tex, El Paso, 75-77 & 78-79, asst dean, Col Sci, 81- *Mem:* Soc Econ Paleontologists & Mineralogists; AAAS; Am Asn Stratig Palynologists; Sigma Xi; NAm Micropaleontological Soc. *Res:* Mesozoic and Cenozoic siliceous; organic walled phytoplankton. *Mailing Add:* Dept of Geol Sci Univ of Tex El Paso TX 79968

CORNELY, PAUL BERTAU, b French West Indies, Mar 9, 06; nat US; m 34; c 1. PUBLIC HEALTH. *Educ:* Univ Mich, AB, 28, MD, 31, DrPH, 34; Am Bd Prev Med, dipl. *Hon Degrees:* DSc, Univ Mich, 68; DPS, Univ of the Pac, 73. *Prof Exp:* Asst prof, 34-35, assoc prof, 35-47, dir health serv, 37-47, head dept community health pract, 55-70, prof, 47-73, EMER PROF PREV MED & PUB HEALTH, COL MED, HOWARD UNIV, 73-; MEM STAFF, HEALTH SERVS EVAL SYST SCI, INC, 73- *Concurrent Pos:* Med dir, Freedmen's Hosp, 47-58; consult, Nat Urban League, 44-47 & Am Health Educ African Develop, US AID; pres, Community Group Health Found, 68-; mem, President's Comn Population Growth & Am Future, 70-72. *Mem:* Fel Am Pub Health Asn (pres, 69-70); fel Am Col Prev Med; hon fel Am Col Hosp Adminr. *Res:* Medical education; distribution and supply of professional personnel; Negro health problems; student health program; health motivation among low income families. *Mailing Add:* 1338 Geranium St NW Washington DC 20012

CORNER, GEORGE WASHINGTON, anatomy, deceased

CORNER, JAMES OLIVER, b Toronto, Ont, July 19, 17; nat US; m 45; c 3. ORGANIC POLYMER CHEMISTRY. *Educ:* Dartmouth Col, AB, 39; Univ Ill, AM, 40, PhD(org chem), 42. *Prof Exp:* Chemist, Exp Sta, 42-52, res supvr, Exp Sta, 52-57, sr supvr, 57-61, res mgr, 61, res mgr, Textile Res Lab, 62-63, lab dir, Dacron Res Lab, 63-64, actg tech supt, Kinston Plant, 64-65, res dir, Dacron Tech Div, 65-68, Nylon Tech Div, 68-69 & Indust Fibers Div, 70-71, tech mgr, Nylon Tech Div, 71-76, lab dir, Textile Res Lab, 77-78, MGR MKT RES DIV, MKT COMMUN DEPT, E I DU PONT DE NEMOURS & CO, INC, 78- *Mem:* Am Chem Soc. *Res:* Synthetic organic chemistry; polymer chemistry; textile fibers. *Mailing Add:* Mkt Commun Dept E I du Pont de Nemours & Co Inc Wilmington DE 19898

CORNER, THOMAS RICHARD, b Waterloo, NY, Jan 6, 40; m 61; c 3. MICROBIOLOGY. *Educ:* Cornell Univ, BS, 62, MS, 64; Univ Rochester, PhD(microbiol), 68. *Prof Exp:* NIH fel, 68-70, ASST PROF MICROBIOL, MICH STATE UNIV, 70- *Concurrent Pos:* Res biologist, Lab Molecular Biol, Nat Inst Neurol Dis & Stroke, NIH, 77-78. *Mem:* Am Soc Microbiol; Soc Gen Microbiol; Int Soc Biorheology. *Res:* Structure and function of bacterial membranes and cell walls; action of organochlorine compounds and other ecotoxicants on bacteria; biomechanical and biorheological properties of cells; bacterial spore heat resistance mechanisms. *Mailing Add:* Dept of Microbiol Mich State Univ East Lansing MI 48824

CORNESKY, ROBERT ANDREW, health sciences, see previous edition

CORNET, BRUCE, paleopalynology, geology, see previous edition

CORNET, I(SRAEL) I(SAAC), b New York, NY, Dec 13, 12; m 40; c 2. MECHANICAL ENGINEERING. *Educ:* Univ Calif, Los Angeles, AB, 33; Univ Calif, PhD(soil sci), 42. *Prof Exp:* Reader & lab asst chem, Univ Calif, Los Angeles, 32-33; analyst & technician, agron div, col agr, Univ Calif, 34-36; jr soil surveyor, soil conserv serv, USDA, Ore, 38-40 & 41-42; asst civil engr, US War Dept, 42; res engr, Off Sci Res & Develop & Nat Defense Res Comt projs, Calif, 42-43, instr eng, sci & mgt war training, 43; sr metal engr, Permanente Metals Corp, Calif, 43-46; engr, Nat Adv Comt Aeronaut proj, 46, from asst prof to assoc prof, 46-57, prof, 57-78, EMER PROF MECH ENG, UNIV CALIF, BERKELEY, 78- *Concurrent Pos:* Guggenheim fel, 56-57; res prof, Miller Inst Basic Res Sci, 60-61. *Mem:* AAAS; Am Chem Soc; Am Inst Mining, Metall & Petrol Engrs; Am Soc Eng Educ; Nat Asn Corrosion Engrs. *Res:* Corrosion science and engineering; metal failure. *Mailing Add:* Dept of Mech Eng Univ of Calif Berkeley CA 94720

CORNETET, WENDELL HILLIS, JR, b Huntington, WVa, Oct 20, 23; m 67; c 2. ELECTRICAL ENGINEERING. *Educ:* WVa Univ, BSEE, 48, MSEE, 51; Ohio State Univ, PhD(elec eng), 58. *Prof Exp:* Instr electronics, WVa Univ, 48-51; res assoc, 51-56, from instr to assoc prof, 56-66, PROF ELECTRONICS, OHIO STATE UNIV, 66- *Concurrent Pos:* Consult, Indust Nucleonics Corp, 62-68 & Energystics Inc, 77-78; trustee, Nat Electronics Conf, 69-71. *Mem:* Sigma Xi; Inst Elec & Electronics Engrs. *Res:* Electron devices; microwave electronics. *Mailing Add:* Dept of Elec Eng 2015 Neil Ave Columbus OH 43210

CORNETT, JAMES BRYCE, b Orange, Calif, Apr 30, 45; m 78. MOLECULAR BIOLOGY, CHEMOTHERAPY. *Educ:* Univ Calif, Riverside, BA, 67, Univ Calif, Davis, MS, 69; Univ Ariz, PhD(molecular biol), 73. *Prof Exp:* Res asst prof microbiol, Sch Med, Temple Univ, 77-78; sr res biologist chemother, 78-81, GROUP LEADER, STERLING-WINTHROP RES INST, 81- *Concurrent Pos:* NIH fel, 75-77. *Mem:* Am Soc Microbiol. *Res:* Development of antimicrobial agents for clinical use. *Mailing Add:* Dept of Microbiol Sterling-Winthrop Res Inst Rensselaer NY 12144

CORNETT, RICHARD ORIN, b Driftwood, Okla, Nov 14, 13; m 43; c 3. PHYSICS, COMMUNICATIONS SCIENCE. *Educ:* Okla Baptist Univ, BS, 34; Okla Univ, MS, 37; Univ Tex, PhD(physics), 40. *Hon Degrees:* DSc, Hardin Simmons Univ, 54; LittD, Jacksonville Univ, 64; LLD, Belknap Col, 67. *Prof Exp:* From instr to assoc prof physics, Okla Baptist Univ, 35-41; asst supvr physics, eng, sci & mgt defense training prog, Pa State Univ, 41-42; lectr electronics, Harvard Univ, 42-45; prof physics & asst to the pres, Okla Baptist Univ, 45-46, head dept physics & vpres, 46-47, exec vpres, 47-51; exec secy educ comn, Southern Baptist Convention & ed, Southern Baptist Educr, 51-58; specialist col & univ orgn, Off Educ, Dept Health, Educ & Welfare, Washington, DC, 59, exec asst to dir div higher educ, 60-61, actg asst comnr & dir div, 61-63, dir div educ admin, 64-65; vpres, 65-75, RES PROF & DIR CUED SPEECH PROGS, GALLAUDET COL, 75-, CHMN, CTR STUDIES IN LANGUAGE & COMMUN, 81- *Concurrent Pos:* Originator of Cued Speech, new method of commun for deaf, 66; consult, Am Optometric Asn, 68- *Res:* Acoustics; theory of hearing; diplacusis; communication for the hearing impaired; development of electronic lipreading aid for the deaf; design of hearing aids for improved auditory processing. *Mailing Add:* 8702 Royal Ridge Lane Laurel MD 20811

CORNETTE, JAMES L, b Bowling Green, Ky, May 8, 35; m 62; c 2. MATHEMATICS. *Educ:* WTex State Col, BS, 55; Univ Tex, MA, 59, PhD(math), 62. *Prof Exp:* From asst prof to assoc prof, 62-70, PROF MATH, IOWA STATE UNIV, 70- *Concurrent Pos:* Fulbright lectr, Nat Univ Malaysia, 73-74. *Mem:* Am Math Soc; Math Asn Am; Soc Indust & Appl Math. *Res:* Biomathematics; point set topology; mathematical models in population genetics. *Mailing Add:* Dept of Math Iowa State Univ Ames IA 50011

CORNFELD, DAVID, b Philadelphia, Pa, Apr 5, 26; m 56; c 3. PEDIATRICS. *Educ:* Univ Pa, MD, 48, MSc, 66. *Prof Exp:* Asst instr, 51-52, assoc, 54-57, from asst prof to assoc prof, 57-72, actg chmn pediat, 72-80, PROF PEDIAT, SCH MED, UNIV PA, 72-, ASSOC CHMN DEPT, 80- *Concurrent Pos:* Asst chief univ serv, Philadelphia Gen Hosp, 55-68; dir pediat clin, Hosp Univ Pa, 56-62; dir outpatient dept & sr physician, Children's Hosp Philadelphia, 62-, co-dir nephrology serv, 63- *Mem:* Am Acad Pediat; Am Pediat Soc. *Res:* Nephrology; patient care. *Mailing Add:* 1120 Woodbine Ave Narberth PA 19072

CORNFORTH, CLARENCE MICHAEL, b Kansas City, Mo, Aug 9, 40; m 78; c 3. OPERATIONS RESEARCH. *Educ:* US Naval Acad, BS, 62; Iowa State Univ, PhD(physics), 69. *Prof Exp:* US Navy, 62-, weapons officer, 62-74, oper res analyst eng, Naval Ship Weapons Eng Sta, 74-77, opers res analyst eng, 77-80, REP TO COMDR, THIRD FLEET, CTR NAVAL ANAL, 80- *Concurrent Pos:* Sci analyst surface warfare to dep chief naval opers, 77-80. *Mem:* AAAS; US Naval Inst; Am Phys Soc. *Res:* Naval operations research. *Mailing Add:* Com Third Fleet N701 Pearl Harbor HI 96860

CORNGOLD, NOEL ROBERT DAVID, b New York, NY, Jan 20, 29; m 52; c 2. REACTOR PHYSICS, STATISTICAL MECHANICS. *Educ:* Columbia Univ, AB, 49; Harvard Univ, AM, 50, PhD(physics), 54. *Prof Exp:* Asst phys sci, Harvard Univ, 50-51; res assoc, Brookhaven Nat Labs, 51-54, from assoc physicist to physicist, 54-66; PROF APPL SCI, DIV ENG & APPL SCI, CALIF INST TECHNOL, 66- *Concurrent Pos:* Consult, Los Alamos Sci Lab, 67-73 & Brookhaven Nat Lab, 74- *Mem:* Fel Am Nuclear Soc; Am Phys Soc. *Res:* Theory of neutron scattering and transport; reactor physics; statistical physics. *Mailing Add:* 549 San Marino Ave San Marino CA 91108

CORNHILL, JOHN FREDRICK, b Chatham, Ont, July 21, 49; m 72; c 2. CARDIOVASCULAR PHYSIOLOGY, EXPERIMENTAL PATHOLOGY. *Educ:* Univ Western Ont, BSc, 72; Univ Oxford, PhD(eng), 76. *Prof Exp:* Lectr biophysics, Univ Western Ont, 75-76; ASST PROF SURG, OHIO STATE UNIV, 76- *Concurrent Pos:* Ont scholar, Univ Western Ont, 68; overseas sci scholar, Royal Comn Exhib 1851, London, Eng, 72-75. *Honors & Awards:* Edward Chapman Res Prize, Magdalen Col, Univ Oxford, 77. *Mem:* Am Physiol Soc; Can Physiol Soc; Biophys Soc; Can Cardiovasc Soc; Am Soc Artifical Internal Organs. *Res:* Arterial wall mass transport and atherosclerosis; cardiovascular hemodynamics and its relationship to atherosclerosis; dynamics of prosthetic heart valves; coronary hemodynamics; environmental factor and heart disease and cancer. *Mailing Add:* Cardiovasc Res Lab 2005 Wiseman Hall 400 W 12th Ave Columbus OH 43210

CORNICK, JOHN WALTER, b St Johns, Nfld, June 23, 35; m 60; c 2. MICROBIOLOGY, BIOLOGY. *Educ:* Univ Toronto, BSA, 61, MSA, 63. *Prof Exp:* Asst scientist microbiol, Fisheries Res Bd Can, 63-65; BIOLOGIST MICROBIOL, CAN DEPT FISHERIES, 67- *Res:* Diagnosis and epidemiology of fish diseases; disease and natural defense mechanism in Crustaceans. *Mailing Add:* Fish Health Unit Maritimes Region PO Box 550 Halifax Can

CORNIE, JAMES ALLEN, b Buhl, Idaho, Mar 7, 37; m 58; c 2. PHYSICAL METALLURGY. *Educ:* Univ Idaho, BS, 60 & 61; Rensselaer Polytech Inst, MS, 65; Univ Pittsburgh, PhD(metall eng), 71. *Prof Exp:* Engr casting, Kennecott Copper Co, 61-63; engr phys metall, Pratt & Whitney Aircraft, 63-65; sr engr alloy develop, Astronuclear Lab, Westinghouse Elec Co, 65-70, sr scientist phys metall, Res Lab, 70-77; MGR METAL MATRIX MAT, SPECIALTY MAT DIV, AVCO CORP, 77- *Concurrent Pos:* Westinghouse fel, Univ Pittsburgh, 69-70; NSF fel, 77-78. *Mem:* Metall Soc; Am Inst Mining, Metall & Petrol Engrs; Am Soc Metals. *Res:* Interfaces in composites; composites technology; metal matrix composites; scanning electron microscopy; transmission electron microscopy; x-ray diffraction; Auger spectroscopy; phase relationships; reaction kinetics. *Mailing Add:* Avco Corp Specialty Mat Div 2 Industrial Ave Lowell MA 01851

CORNILSEN, BAHNE CARL, b Savanna, Ill, Apr 3, 45; m 77. SOLID STATE CHEMISTRY, CERAMIC SCIENCE. *Educ:* Ill Inst Technol, BS, 68; Marquette Univ, MS, 71; NY State Col Ceramics, PhD(ceramics), 75. *Prof Exp:* Res chemist, Globe-Union Inc, 68-69; fel, Ore Grad Ctr Study & Res, 75-77; ASST PROF CHEM, MICH TECHNOL UNIV, 77- *Concurrent Pos:* Co-investr, NSF grant, 77-81. *Mem:* Am Chem Soc; Am Ceramic Soc; Soc Appl Spectros; Sigma Xi. *Res:* Preparation and structure of solid state compounds, including the point defect structure of nonstoichiometric materials; laser Raman vibrational spectroscopy, used to study the structure of solids, nonstoichiometry, and solid state phase transitions; interfacial structure. *Mailing Add:* Dept of Chem & Chem Eng Mich Technol Univ Houghton MI 49931

CORNING, GERALD, aerospace engineering, design engineering, deceased

CORNING, MARY ELIZABETH, b Norwich, Conn, Oct 19, 25. INTERNATIONAL BIOMEDICAL COMMUNICATIONS, PHYSICAL CHEMISTRY. *Educ:* Conn Col, BA, 47; Mt Holyoke Col, MA, 49. *Prof Exp:* Asst chemist, Mt Holyoke Col, 47-49; chemist, Nat Bur Standards, 49-58; spec asst to sci adv, US Dept State, 58-60; proj dir, Ed & Int Activities Planning Group, NSF, 60-61, spec asst to head, Off Int Sci Activities, 61-62, assoc prom dir, 62-64; chief, Publ & Trans Div, 64-66, spec asst to dep dir, 66-67, spec asst to dir, 67-72, ASST DIR INT PROGS, NAT LIBR MED, DEPT HEALTH & HUMAN SERV, 72- *Concurrent Pos:* Mem chem panel, US Civil Serv Bd Examr, 53-60, tech ed & writer panel, 55-60; US Nat Liaison Officer to Orgn Econ Coop & Develop, 62; mem, US Nat Comt, Int Comn Optics, 61-67, Int Fedn Doc, 64-65 & Int Coun Sci Union Abstr Bd, 73-; mem bd dirs & exec comt, Gorgas Mem Inst Trop & Prev Med, Inc, 72-, secy, 74-; consult on biomed commun to nat & int bodies. *Honors & Awards:* Silver Medal for Superior Serv, Dept Health, Educ & welfare, 71. *Mem:* AAAS; Med Libr Asn; Am Chem Soc; fel Optical Soc Am. *Res:* Far ultraviolet absorption spectra of organic compounds; color and chemical constitution; spectrophotometry; organization of science; science information and documentation; development of national and regional biomedical communication programs. *Mailing Add:* Nat Libr of Med 8600 Rockville Pike Bethesda MD 20014

CORNISH, HERBERT HARRY, b Fremont, Ohio, Sept 22, 16; m 43; c 4. TOXICOLOGY. *Educ:* Bowling Green State Univ, BS, 39; Univ Mich, MS, 52, PhD(biol chem), 56. *Prof Exp:* Clin chemist, 46-50; instr biol chem, 54-59, from asst prof to assoc prof indust health, 59-67, PROF ENVIRON &

INDUST HEALTH, UNIV MICH, ANN ARBOR, 67-, DIR TOXICOL PROG, 68- *Mem:* Am Chem Soc; Soc Toxicol; Am Indust Hyg Asn. *Res:* Metabolism of caffeine, chlorinated aromatics and aromatic nitro compounds; potentiation of toxicity and organic solvents; toxicity of combustion products of plastics. *Mailing Add:* Sch of Pub Health Univ of Mich Ann Arbor MI 48104

CORNMAN, IVOR, b Cleveland, Ohio, May 22, 14; m 47. ZOOLOGY. *Educ:* Oberlin Col, AB, 36; NY Univ, MS, 39; Univ Mich, PhD, 49. *Prof Exp:* Asst zool, Univ Mich, 41-42; fel cytol, Sloan-Kettering Inst, 46-49; asst prof anat, Med Sch, George Washington Univ, 49-55; head dept cellular physiol, Hazleton Labs, Va, 55-59, asst dir res, 59-64; independent biol consult, 64-68; vpres, Environ Develop, Inc, 68-69; BIOL CONSULT, 69- *Concurrent Pos:* Mem corp, Marine Biol Lab, Woods Hole, 47-; guest, Univ West Indies, 64-78. *Mem:* Am Soc Zool. *Res:* Cancer chemotherapy; carcinogenesis; experimental alteration of cell division in normal and malignant plant and animal cells; marine biology; biological systems adapted to development of new drugs. *Mailing Add:* 10-A Orchard St Woods Hole MA 02543

CORNS, WILLIAM GEORGE, b Taber, Alta, Oct 27, 16; m 43; c 2. PLANT SCIENCE, WEED SCIENCE. *Educ:* Univ Alta, BSc, 42, MSc, 44; Univ Toronto, PhD (plant physiol & ecol), 46. *Prof Exp:* Teacher pub & high sch, 33-38; asst plant biochem, 41-44, asst prof plant sci, 46-50, assoc prof crop ecol, 50-56, head dept, 61-71, PROF PLANT SCI, UNIV ALTA, 56- *Mem:* Agr Inst Can. *Res:* Crop ecology; reforestation. *Mailing Add:* Dept of Plant Sci Univ of Alta Edmonton AB T6G 2E1 Can

CORNSWEET, TOM NORMAN, b Cleveland, Ohio, Apr 29, 29. VISION, OPHTHALMIC INSTRUMENTATION. *Educ:* Cornell Univ, AB, 51; Brown Univ, MSc, 53, PhD(exp psychol), 55. *Prof Exp:* From instr to asst prof psychol, Yale Univ, 55-59; from asst prof to prof, Univ Calif, Berkeley, 59-65; staff scientist biomed res, Stanford Res Inst, 65-71; chief scientist, Acuity Systs, Inc, Va, 71-73; assoc prof ophthal, Baylor Col Med, 74-76; PROF PSYCHOL, UNIV CALIF, IRVINE, 76- *Concurrent Pos:* NIH grants, Yale Univ, Univ Calif, Berkeley & Stanford Res Inst, 56-71; NASA grants, Stanford Res Inst, 66-71; Retina Res Found grant, Baylor Col Med, 74- *Mem:* AAAS; fel Optical Soc Am; Asn Res Vision & Ophthal. *Res:* Glaucoma; oculomotor system; ophthalmic instrumentation; visual aids for visually handicapped. *Mailing Add:* 23652 Calle Hogar Mission Viejo CA 92691

CORNWALL, JOHN MICHAEL, b Denver, Colo, Aug 19, 34; m 65. THEORETICAL PHYSICS. *Educ:* Harvard Univ, AB, 56; Univ Denver, MS, 59; Univ Calif, Berkeley, PhD(physics), 62. *Prof Exp:* NSF fel physics, Calif Inst Technol, 62-63; mem, Inst Adv Study, 63-65; from asst prof to assoc prof, 65-74, PROF PHYSICS, UNIV CALIF, LOS ANGELES, 74- *Concurrent Pos:* Consult, Aerospace Corp, El Segundo, 62-; Alfred P Sloan Found fel, 67-69; consult, NASA, 75-; mem adv bd, Nat Inst Theoret Physics, 79-, chmn bd, 81-82. *Mem:* Am Phys Soc; Am Geophys Union. *Res:* Theoretical elementary particle and high energy physics; emphasis on quantum chromodynamics; theoretical space and plasma physics; Van Allen belt studies. *Mailing Add:* Dept of Physics Univ of Calif Los Angeles CA 90024

CORNWELL, CHARLES DANIEL, b Williamsport, Pa, Dec 27, 24; m 51. MOLECULAR SPECTROSCOPY, MOLECULAR PHYSICS. *Educ:* Cornell Univ, AB, 47; Harvard Univ, MS, 49, PhD(chem physics), 51. *Prof Exp:* Res assoc chem, Univ Iowa, 50-52; from instr to assoc prof, 52-62, PROF CHEM, UNIV WIS-MADISON, 62- *Mem:* AAAS; Am Phys Soc; Am Chem Soc. *Res:* Nuclear magnetic resonance, nuclear quadrupole resonance and microwave molecular rotational spectra; relationship of spectroscopic parameters to molecular structure and chemical binding; spin relaxation in gases. *Mailing Add:* Dept of Chem Univ of Wis Madison WI 53706

CORNWELL, DAVID GEORGE, b San Rafael, Calif, Oct 8, 27; m 59; c 2. BIOCHEMISTRY. *Educ:* Col of Wooster, BA, 50; Ohio State Univ, MA, 52; Stanford Univ, PhD(chem), 55. *Prof Exp:* Asst physiol chem, Ohio State Univ, 50-52; asst chem, Stanford Univ, 52-53; fel, Nat Res Coun, Harvard Univ, 54-56; from asst prof to assoc prof, 56-63, PROF PHYSIOL CHEM, OHIO STATE UNIV, 63-, CHMN DEPT, 65- *Concurrent Pos:* Mem nutrit study sect, NIH, 66-70, nutrit sci training comt, 70-73. *Honors & Awards:* Hon Mention, Int Cong Hematol, 56. *Mem:* Am Chem Soc; Biophys Soc; Am Soc Biol Chem; Am Inst Nutrit; Am Oil Chem Soc. *Res:* Chemistry and metabolism of lipids, lipoproteins, fat soluble vitamins and membranes. *Mailing Add:* Dept of Physiol Chem Ohio State Univ 333 W 10th Ave Columbus OH 43210

CORNWELL, GEORGE WILLIAM, b Benton Harbor, Mich, Dec 4, 29; m 52. WILDLIFE ECOLOGY, ENVIRONMENTAL SCIENCES. *Educ:* Mich State Univ, BS, 55; Univ Utah, MScE, 59; Univ Mich, PhD(wildlife path), 66. *Prof Exp:* Conserv aide, Mich Dept Conserv, 53-55; wildlife biol aide, US Fish & Wildlife Serv, 56; teacher high schs, Mich, 56-59; sta pathologist, Delta Waterfowl Res Sta, Man, Can, 60-62; asst prof wildlife biol & ornith, Va Polytech Inst & State Univ, 63-67; assoc prof wildlife ecol, Sch Forestry, Univ Fla, 67-73; PRES, ECOIMPACT, INC, 73-; PRES, BIOMASS ENERGY SYSTS, INC, 80- *Honors & Awards:* Conserv Award, Gov of Fla, 70. *Mem:* Wildlife Soc; Ecol Soc Am; Nat Assoc Environ Professionals; AAAS; Am Inst Planners. *Res:* Wetland ecology; waterfowl biology; resource management and conservation; regional planning; natural systems restoration; environmental impact assessment; ecological planning. *Mailing Add:* EcoImpact Inc 417 SE 2nd St Gainesville FL 32601

CORNWELL, JOHN CALHOUN, b Chester, SC, Dec 21, 44. EQUINE PHYSIOLOGY. *Educ:* Clemson Univ, BS, 70; La State Univ, MS, 72, PhD(animal sci), 76. *Prof Exp:* Grad asst instr equine reproductive physiol, Animal Sci Dept, La State Univ, 70-76, instr, Sch Vet Med, 76-78; ASST PROF HORSE SCI, ANIMAL SCI DEPT, NC STATE UNIV, 78- *Mem:* Am Soc Animal Sci; Am Asn Vet Anatomists; Sigma Xi. *Res:* Hormone levels in periparturient mares and newborn foals; induction of estrus in mares and control of ovalation; seasonal variation in stallion semen; freezing stallion semen; puberty in the colt. *Mailing Add:* Dept Animal Sci NC State Univ PO Box 5127 Raleigh NC 27650

CORNWELL, LARRY WILMER, b Quincy, Ill, July 29, 41; m 63; c 4. OPERATIONS RESEARCH, COMPUTER SCIENCE. *Educ:* Culver-Stockton Col, BA, 63; Southern Ill Univ, MS, 65; Univ Mo, Rolla, PhD(math), 72. *Prof Exp:* Teacher math, Murphysboro High Sch, 64-65; instr, Forest Park Community Col, 65-66; asst prof, Culver-Stockton Col, 66-69; prof math, Western Ill Univ, 71-80; ASSOC PROF, BRADLEY UNIV, 80- *Concurrent Pos:* Resident assoc, Argonne Nat Lab, 76-77, consult, 77-78. *Mem:* Opers Res Soc Am; Inst Mgt Sci; Asn Comput Mach. *Res:* Nonlinear programming; nonlinear least squares; unconstrained and constrained optimization; generation of the distribution of the product of two normal random variables; heuristic programming; mathematical modeling; applications of mathematics. *Mailing Add:* Bus Mgt & Admin Bradley Univ Peoria IL 61625

CORNYN, JOHN JOSEPH, b Pittsburgh, Pa, Dec 20, 44. COMPUTER SCIENCE, UNDERWATER ACOUSTICS. *Educ:* Carnegie-Mellon Univ, BS, 67, MS, 69; Univ Md, MS, 74. *Prof Exp:* Physicist underwater acoust, Naval Res Lab, 68-72, physicist signal processing, 72-76; physicist underwater acoust, Naval Ocean Res & Develop Activ, 76-81; COMPUT CONSULT & PRES, THIRD WAVE DATA SYSTS, INC, 81- *Mem:* Asn Comput Mach; Inst Elec & Electronics Engrs Comput Soc; Independent Comput Consult Asn. *Mailing Add:* Third Wave Data Systs Inc PO Box 270531 Tampa FL 33618

CORONITI, FERDINAND VINCENT, b Boston, Mass, June 14, 43; m 69; c 2. SPACE PHYSICS, PLASMA PHYSICS. *Educ:* Harvard Univ, BA, 65; Univ Calif, Berkeley, PhD(physics), 69. *Prof Exp:* Res asst physics, Univ Calif, Berkeley, 65-69; asst res physicist, 69-70, from asst prof to assoc prof physics & space physics, 70-78, PROF PHYSICS & ASTRON, UNIV CALIF, LOS ANGELES, 78- *Concurrent Pos:* Consult, TRW Syst, 69- & Los Alamos Sci Lab, 73- *Mem:* Am Geophys Union; Int Union Radio Sci; Am Astron Soc. *Res:* Magnetospheric dynamics; Jupiter radiation belts and magnetospheric structure; magnetic field reconnection; nonlinear plasma theory; plasma astrophysics. *Mailing Add:* Dept Physics Univ Calif Los Angeles CA 90024

COROTIS, ROSS BARRY, b Woodbury, NJ, Jan 15, 45. CIVIL ENGINEERING. *Educ:* Mass Inst Technol, SB, 67, SM, 68, PhD(civil eng), 71. *Prof Exp:* Asst prof civil eng, Northwestern Univ, 71-74, assoc prof, 75-79, prof, 79-81; PROF CIVIL ENG, JOHNS HOPKINS UNIV, 81- *Concurrent Pos:* Live loads chmn, Bldg Code Comt, Am Nat Standards Inst, 78- *Mem:* Am Concrete Inst, Am Soc Civil Engrs. *Res:* Structural safety; earthquake engineering; wind energy. *Mailing Add:* Dept of Civil Eng Johns Hopkins Univ Baltimore MD 21218

CORPE, WILLIAM ALBERT, b Walworth, Wis, Jan 11, 24; m 49; c 2. MICROBIAL ATTACHMENT TO SURFACES. *Educ:* Univ Wis, Madison, BS, 48, MS, 50; Pa State Univ, PhD(microbiol), 56. *Prof Exp:* Teaching asst bacteriol, Univ Wis, 48-49, res asst, 49-50; asst prof, Western Ky State Col, 50-53; res asst microbiol, Pa State Univ, 53-56; asst prof, Dept Biol, Columbia Univ & Barnard Col, NY, 56-60; assoc prof, 60-67, PROF BIOL SCI, COLUMBIA UNIV, 67- *Concurrent Pos:* Res fel, Microbiol Dept, US Pub Health Serv, Univ New South Whales, Australia, 63-64; res collabr, Brookhaven Nat Lab, 65-71. *Mem:* Am Soc Microbiol; Can Soc Microbiol; NY Acad Sci; Soc Indust Microbiol; AAAS. *Res:* Bacterial physiology and ecology; cyanide metabolism; hydrolytic enzyme secretion; exopolymer production; mechanisms of attachment to and colonization of solid surfaces by microbial species. *Mailing Add:* 49 Alpine Dr Closter NJ 07624

CORRADINO, ROBERT ANTHONY, b Lancaster, Pa, Aug 6, 38; m 63; c 1. CELL PHYSIOLOGY, ENDOCRINOLOGY. *Educ:* Millersville State Col, BS, 60; Purdue Univ, MS, 62; Cornell Univ, PhD(physiol), 66. *Prof Exp:* Res assoc, Wyeth Labs, Inc, Radnor, Pa, 62-64; res assoc, 66-72, sr res assoc, 72-80, ASSOC PROF, DEPT PHYSIOL, CORNELL UNIV, 80- *Concurrent Pos:* Prin investr res grants, Nat Inst Arthritis, Metab & Digestive Dis & NIH, 71-; Res Career Develop Award, NIH, 75-80; grant reviewer, NIH, NSF, & USDA, 76- *Mem:* Am Physiol Soc; Am Inst Nutrit; Soc Exp Biol & Med; Tissue Cult Asn; Sigma Xi. *Res:* Hormone mechanisms at the cellular and molecular levels with specific emphasis on the mode of action of cholecalciferol (vitamin D3). *Mailing Add:* Dept Physiol 720 VRT NY State Col Vet Med Cornell Univ Ithaca NY 14853

CORREIA, JOHN ARTHUR, b Brookline, Mass, June 8, 45; m 67; c 1. MEDICAL PHYSICS. *Educ:* Lowell Technol Inst, BS, 67, PhD(nuclear physics), 73. *Prof Exp:* Res fel physics, 72-74, asst physicist, 74-79, ASSOC PHYSICIST, MASS GEN HOSP, 79- *Concurrent Pos:* Res fel, Sch Med, Harvard Univ, 72-74, res assoc, 74-79, asst prof radiol, 79- *Mem:* Am Phys Soc; Am Nuclear Soc; Am Asn Physicists Med; Soc Nuclear Med. *Res:* Application of computers to nuclear medicine; development of instrumentation and computational schemes for the measurement of cerebral blood flow and for three dimensional reconstruction using radioisotopes; cyclotrons in medicine; positron imaging; x-ray charge transfer image processing. *Mailing Add:* 306 Salem St Wakefield MA 01880

CORRIERE, JOSEPH N, JR, b Easton, Pa, Apr 3, 37; m 60; c 4. UROLOGY. *Educ:* Univ Pa, BA, 59; Seton Hall Col Med, MD, 63. *Prof Exp:* Resident urol, Hosp Univ Pa, 64-69; asst prof, Univ Pa, 71-74; PROF UROL & DIR DIV, UNIV TEX MED SCH HOUSTON, 74- *Concurrent Pos:* USPHS res trainee urol, Univ Pa, 67-68. *Mem:* Asn Acad Surg; Soc Univ Surg; Acad Pediat; Am Col Surg; Am Urol Asn. *Res:* Urinary tract infection and the use of isotopes in the urinary tract. *Mailing Add:* Univ Tex Med Sch 6431 Fannin St Houston TX 77030

CORRIGAN, JAMES JOHN, JR, b Pittsburgh, Pa, Aug 28, 35; m 60; c 2. HEMATOLOGY, PEDIATRICS. *Educ:* Juniata Col, BS, 57; Univ Pittsburgh, MD, 61. *Prof Exp:* Intern med, Univ Colo, 61-62, resident pediat, 62-64; assoc, Sch Med, Emory Univ, 66-67, asst prof, 67-70; assoc prof, 71-74, PROF PEDIAT, COL MED, UNIV ARIZ, 74-; DIR, MOUNTAIN

STATES HEMOPHILIA CTR, 76- *Concurrent Pos:* Fel pediat hemat, Col Med, Univ Ill, 64-66; NIH res grants, 67-; Ga Heart Inc res grant, 68-70. *Honors & Awards:* Ross Award, Pediat Res, 75. *Mem:* Am Soc Pediat; fel Am Acad Pediat; Am Soc Hemat; Soc Pediat Res; Int Soc Thrombosis & Haemostasis. *Res:* Disorders of blood coagulation mechanisms, particularly those conditions associated with disseminated intravascular coagulation and hyperfibrinolysis. *Mailing Add:* Dept of Pediat Univ of Ariz Col of Med Tucson AZ 85724

CORRIGAN, JOHN JOSEPH, b Chicago, Ill, Jan 17, 29; m 54; c 4. BIOCHEMISTRY. *Educ:* Carleton Col, AB, 50; Univ Ill, MS, 57, PhD(entom), 59. *Prof Exp:* Physiologist, Baxter Labs, 50-52; asst entom, Ill Natural Hist Surv, 52-53; res fel biochem, Sch Med, Tufts Univ, 59-62, sr instr, 62-63, asst prof, 63-70; assoc prof life sci & biochem, 70-75, PROF LIFE SCI & ADJ PROF BIOCHEM, IND STATE UNIV, 75-, ASSOC DEAN COL ARTS & SCI, 70- *Mem:* AAAS; Am Chem Soc; Entom Soc Am. *Res:* Metabolism of amino acids and proteins in insects; biochemistry of insect metamorphosis; silk fibroin biosynthesis in lepidoptera; biochemical basis of insecticide action; stereospecific metabolism of amino acids; biochemistry of development. *Mailing Add:* Dept of Life Sci Ind State Univ Terre Haute IN 47809

CORRIGAN, JOHN RAYMOND, b Fargo, NDak, Apr 28, 19; wid; c 4. ORGANIC CHEMISTRY. *Educ:* Univ Portland, BS, 40; Univ Notre Dame, MS, 42, PhD(chem), 49. *Prof Exp:* Asst, Univ Notre Dame, 41-43; res assoc, Frederick Stearns & Co, 43-47; res fel, Sterling-Winthrop Res Inst, 47-49, res assoc, 49-51; res assoc, Sharp & Dohme, 51-55; sr chemist, Mead Johnson & Co, 55-57, group leader, 57-59, from asst dir to dir dept, 59-68, dir process eng, 68-78; OWNER, HOUCK'S PROCESS STRIPPING CTR, 78- *Mem:* AAAS; Am Chem Soc; Am Inst Chemists; Am Inst Chem Engrs. *Res:* Synthetic organic medicinals. *Mailing Add:* Rt 5 Fontainbleau 2 Newburgh IN 47630

CORRIGAN, THOMAS E(DWARD), b Cleveland, Ohio, Mar 1, 18; m 44; c 4. CHEMICAL ENGINEERING. *Educ:* Cleveland State Univ, Fenn Col, BS, 41; Univ Mich, MS, 42; Univ Wis, PhD(chem eng), 49. *Prof Exp:* Pilot plant engr, Allied Chem & Dye Corp, 42-43; plant res engr, Wyandotte Chems Corp, 43-45; asst chem, Univ Wis, 45-47; asst prof chem eng, Univ WVa, 48-51; process design engr, Vulcan-Cincinnati Eng Co, 51-53; sr res engr, Olin Mathieson Chem Corp, 53, mgr eng planning, 53-54, mgr develop, 54-59; assoc prof chem eng, Ohio State Univ, 59-66; MEM STAFF FINANCIAL PLANNING & ANAL, MOBIL CHEM CO, 66- *Mem:* Am Chem Soc; Am Inst Chem Engrs; Sigma Xi. *Res:* Chemical engineering kinetics; chemical engineering thermodynamics; process development; technical economics. *Mailing Add:* 8 Nagle Dr Somerville NJ 08876

CORRIPIO, ARMANDO BENITO, b Mantua, Cuba, Mar 6, 41; US citizen; m 62; c 4. CHEMICAL ENGINEERING, AUTOMATIC CONTROL SYSTEMS. *Educ:* La State Univ, Baton Rouge, BSc, 63, MS, 67, PhD(chem eng), 70. *Prof Exp:* Control systs engr, Dow Chem Co, La, 63-68; from instr to assoc prof, 68-81, PROF CHEM ENG, LA STATE UNIV, BATON ROUGE, 81- *Concurrent Pos:* Consult, Dow Chem Co, 68-69 & La Div, 74-; investr, Proj Themis, Off Sci Res, US Air Force, 69-; distinguished fac fel, La State Univ Found, 74; vis engr, Mass Inst Technol, 78-79. *Mem:* Am Inst Chem Engrs; Instrument Soc Am; Soc Comput Simulation. *Res:* Mathematical modeling and dynamic simulation of chemical processes; automatic control systems design, especially application of digital computers to process control; practical application of modern control theory to the control of non-linear systems; computer-aided process design. *Mailing Add:* Dept of Chem Eng La State Univ Baton Rouge LA 70803

CORRIVEAU, ARMAND GERARD, b Sept 26, 45; Can citizen. GENETICS, FOREST SCIENCE. *Educ:* Laval Univ, Baccalaureat, 69; NC State Univ, PhD(genetics), 74. *Prof Exp:* Res officer sylvicult, 69-70, res officer tree improvement, 70-71, RES SCIENTIST GENETICS, CAN FORESTRY SERV, 74- *Mem:* Can Tree Improvement Asn; Genetics Soc Can. *Res:* Genetics and improvement of forest tree species. *Mailing Add:* 1800 route du Vallon CP 3800 Ste Foy PQ G1V 4C7 Can

CORROW, CARLTON JACOB, b Barton, Vt, June 3, 44; m 71; c 2. METALLURGY, MECHANICAL ENGINEERING. *Educ:* Northeastern Univ, BS, 67; Mass Inst Technol, MS, 69, PhD(mech eng), 71. *Prof Exp:* Res asst mat res, Mass Inst Technol, 67-71; res engr, 71-74, RES SPECIALIST METALL, CORP RES CTR, UNIROYAL INC, 74- *Mem:* Am Soc Metals; Sigma Xi. *Res:* Deformation, fracture, fatigue and corrosion of metals; scanning electron microscope fractography and rolling contact fatigue. *Mailing Add:* Corp Res Ctr Uniroyal Inc Middlebury CT 06749

CORRSIN, STANLEY, b Philadelphia, Pa, Apr 3, 20; m 45; c 2. FLUID MECHANICS. *Educ:* Univ Pa, BS, 40; Calif Inst Technol, MS & AE, 42, PhD(aeronaut), 47. *Hon Degrees:* Dr, Univ Lyon I, 74. *Prof Exp:* Asst, Calif Inst Technol, 40-45, instr aeronaut, 45-47; from asst prof to assoc prof, 51-55, prof mech eng & chmn dept, 55-60, prof mech, 60-79, PROF CHEM ENG & BIOMED ENG, JOHNS HOPKINS UNIV, 79- *Honors & Awards:* Sigma Xi paper award, 61; LaPorte lectr, Am Phys Soc, 79. *Mem:* Nat Acad Eng; fel Am Acad Arts & Sci; fel Am Phys Soc; Am Inst Aeronaut & Astronaut; fel Am Soc Mech Engrs. *Res:* Turbulent flow and its effects; random processes; biomedical fluid mechanics. *Mailing Add:* Dept Chem Eng Johns Hopkins Univ Baltimore MD 21218

CORRUCCINI, LINTON REID, b Corvallis, Ore, Jan 1, 44; m 72. LOW TEMPERATURE PHYSICS. *Educ:* Swarthmore Col, BA, 66; Cornell Univ, PhD(physics), 72. *Prof Exp:* NSF fel physics, Cornell Univ, 67-71; mem tech staff, Aerospace Corp, 71-73; asst prof, 73-78, ASSOC PROF PHYSICS, UNIV CALIF, DAVIS, 78- *Mem:* Am Phys Soc. *Res:* Liquid helium three-helium four solutions; superfluid helium 3; nuclear magnetic resonance. *Mailing Add:* Dept Physics Univ Calif Davis CA 95616

CORRUCCINI, ROBERT SPENCER, b Tokoma Park, Md, May 21, 49. ODONTOLOGY, ANTHROPOLOGICAL EPIDEMIOLOGY. *Educ:* Colo Univ, BA, 71; Univ Calif, Berkeley, PhD(anthrop), 75. *Prof Exp:* Res assoc, Smithsonian Inst, 76-78; asst prof, 78-82, ASSOC PROF ANTHROP, SOUTHERN ILL UNIV, 82- *Concurrent Pos:* NATO fel, Univ Florence, Italy, 80-81. *Mem:* Am Asn Physical Anthropologists; Soc Syst Zool. *Res:* Dental anthropology; hominid evolution; cross-cultural approaches to epidemiology; quantitative methods; morphometrics; relative growth in primate structures. *Mailing Add:* Dept Anthrop Southern Ill Univ Carbondale IL 62901

CORRY, ANDREW F, b Lynn, Mass, 1922. ELECTRICAL ENGINEERING. *Educ:* Mass Inst Technol, BS, 44. *Prof Exp:* Mem staff, 47-75, vpres elec opers & eng, 75-80, VPRES & CORP RES OFFICER, BOSTON EDISON CO, 80- *Mem:* Nat Acad Eng; fel Inst Elec & Electronics Engrs. *Res:* Research and development of electric transmission technology. *Mailing Add:* Boston Edison Co 800 Boylston St Boston MA 02199

CORRY, THOMAS M, b Pittsburgh, Pa, June 9, 26; m 51; c 4. ELECTRICAL ENGINEERING. *Educ:* Carnegie Inst Technol, BS, 51. *Prof Exp:* Develop engr radar, A B Dumont Labs, 51-52; proj engr control systs, Femco, Inc, 52-54; supvr engr, Westinghouse Res Labs, 54-63 & Defense Res Labs, Gen Motors Corp, 63-75; PRES, ENERGY SCI CORP, 76- *Mem:* Inst Elec & Electronics Engrs. *Res:* Aircraft electrical systems; supervisory control systems; semiconductor power switching circuits; thermoelectric generators; high energy physics; experimental machines. *Mailing Add:* Energy Sci Corp PO Box 152 Goleta CA 93017

CORSARO, ROBERT DOMINIC, b Elizabeth, NJ, Nov 5, 44; m 67; c 2. PHYSICAL CHEMISTRY, ACOUSTICS. *Educ:* Lebanon Valley Col, BS, 66; Univ Md, PhD(chem), 71. *Prof Exp:* RES CHEMIST ACOUST, NAVAL RES LAB, 70- *Mem:* Am Chem Soc; Am Phys Soc; Acoust Soc Am; Sigma Xi. *Res:* Acoustic propagation in materials; acoustic techniques in material science; fast reaction kinetics; underwater sound and parametric sonar. *Mailing Add:* Code 5135 Naval Res Lab Washington DC 20375

CORSE, JOSEPH WALTERS, b Denver, Colo, Sept 7, 13; m 36; c 4. PHYTOCHEMISTRY. *Educ:* Univ Calif, Los Angeles, BA, 36; Univ Ill, PhD(org chem), 40. *Prof Exp:* Asst, Univ Ill, 37-39; res chemist, Eli Lilly Co, 40-46; asst, Calif Inst Technol, 46-47; res assoc, Univ Calif, Los Angeles, 47-48; CHEMIST, WESTERN REGIONAL RES LAB, AGR RES SERV, US DEPT AGR, 48- *Mem:* Am Chem Soc; Phytochem Soc NAm. *Res:* Synthetic drugs; biosynthesis of penicillin; enzyme reactions and synthesis of metabolites; chemical interactions in plant growth. *Mailing Add:* Western Regional Res Lab US Dept of Agr Agr Res Serv Albany CA 94706

CORSINI, A, b Hamilton, Ont, Apr 28, 34; m 61; c 1. ANALYTICAL CHEMISTRY. *Educ:* McMaster Univ, BSc, 56, PhD(anal chem), 61. *Prof Exp:* Atomic Energy Comn fel chelate chem, Univ Ariz, 61-63; from asst prof to assoc prof anal & inorg chem, 63-72, PROF CHEM, McMASTER UNIV, 72- *Concurrent Pos:* Nat Res Coun Can grant, 63- *Honors & Awards:* Louis Gordon Mem Award, Pergamon Press, 73. *Mem:* Chem Inst Can. *Res:* Instrumental analysis; chemistry of metal chelates, heteropolytungstates, metalloporphyrins and analytical applications. *Mailing Add:* Dept of Chem McMaster Univ Hamilton ON L8S 4M1 Can

CORSINI, DENNIS LEE, b Los Angeles, Calif, Nov 8, 42; m 63; c 3. AGRICULTURAL BIOCHEMISTRY. *Educ:* Univ Calif, Los Angeles, BA, 65; Univ Idaho, PhD(agr biochem), 71. *Prof Exp:* Fel plant path, Univ Calif, Riverside, 71-72; res assoc plant sci, 73-76, RES PATHOLOGIST, SCI & EDUC ADMIN, USDA, UNIV IDAHO, 76- *Mem:* Potato Asn Am; Am Phytopathological Soc; Am Chem Soc. *Res:* Develop new potato cultivars with multiple disease resistance. *Mailing Add:* Univ of Idaho Res & Exten Ctr Aberdeen ID 83210

CORSON, DALE RAYMOND, b Pittsburg, Kans, Apr 5, 14; m 38; c 4. NUCLEAR PHYSICS. *Educ:* Col Emporia, AB, 34; Univ Kans, AM, 35; Univ Calif, PhD(physics), 38. *Hon Degrees:* LHD, Emporia Col, 70; LLD, Columbia Univ, 72 & Hamilton Col, 73; DSc, Univ Rochester, 75 & Elmira Col, 77. *Prof Exp:* Asst, Univ Calif, 36-38, res fel, 38-39, instr physics, 39-40; from asst prof to assoc prof, Univ Mo, 40-45; staff mem, Los Alamos Sci Lab, 45-46; from asst prof to prof physics, 46-63, chmn dept, 56-59, dean, Col Eng, 59-63, provost, 63-69, pres, 69-77, chancellor, 77-79, EMER PRES, CORNELL UNIV, 79- *Concurrent Pos:* Mem staff, Radiation Lab, Mass Inst Technol, 41-43; radar consult, US Army Air Force, 43-45. *Mem:* Nat Acad Eng; fel Am Acad Arts & Sci; Am Phys Soc. *Res:* Cosmic rays; nuclear physics; engineering. *Mailing Add:* 300 Day Hall Cornell Univ Ithaca NY 14853

CORSON, GEORGE EDWIN, JR, b Sebastopol, Calif, Aug 2, 40; div; c 2. PLANT MORPHOGENESIS. *Educ:* Univ of the Pac, MS, 64; Univ Calif, Davis, PhD(bot), 68. *Prof Exp:* NSF trainee, Univ Calif, Davis, 66-68; PROF, CALIF STATE UNIV, CHICO, 68- *Mem:* Bot Soc Am; Int Soc Plant Morphol. *Res:* Cell division rates of the root apical cell and its derivatives in Equisetum hyemale; callus and protoplast formation and differentiation in Equisetum hyemale. *Mailing Add:* Dept of Biol Sci Calif State Univ Chico CA 95929

CORSON, HARRY HERBERT, b Nashville, Tenn, Feb 2, 31; m 53; c 2. MATHEMATICS. *Educ:* Vanderbilt Univ, AB, 52; Duke Univ, MA, 54, PhD(math), 57. *Prof Exp:* Res instr math, Tulane Univ, 56-58; res asst prof, 58-62, assoc prof, 62-65, PROF MATH, UNIV WASH, 65- *Concurrent Pos:* Fel, Off Naval Res, 58-59. *Mem:* Am Math Soc. *Res:* Topology; linear spaces. *Mailing Add:* Dept of Math Univ of Wash Seattle WA 98105

CORSON, SAMUEL ABRAHAM, b Odessa, Russia, Dec 31, 09; nat US; m 47; c 3. PHYSIOLOGY, PHARMACOLOGY. *Educ:* NY Univ, BS, 30; Univ Pa, MS, 31; Univ Tex, PhD, 42. *Prof Exp:* Asst physiol, Sch Med, Univ Pa, 32-35; res assoc cell physiol, NY Univ, 35-37; instr physiol, Div Gen Educ, NY, 37-39; consult physiologist, New York, 38-40; instr zool & physiol, Univ Tex, 40-42; asst prof physiol, Sch Med, Univ Okla, 42-43; instr pharmacol, Sch Med, Georgetown Univ, 43-44; from instr to asst prof physiol, Med Col, Univ Minn, 44-47, instr sci Russian & coordr contemp Russian, Exten Div, 45-47; assoc prof, Col Med, Howard Univ, 47-50; chief dept physiol, Toledo Hosp Inst Med Res, 50-51; prof pharmacol & head dept, Kirksville Col Osteop & Surg, 51-54; assoc prof pharmacol & physiol, Sch Med, Univ Ark, 54-59; res assoc hist med, Sch Med, Yale Univ, 59-60; assoc prof psychiat, 60-67, prof psychiat, Col Med, 67-80, prof biophys, Col Biol Sci, 69-80, dir lab, Cerebrovisceral Physiol, 60-80, EMER PROF BIOPHYS, COL MED, OHIO STATE UNIV, 80- *Concurrent Pos:* Consult, hosp staff, Univ Ark, 58-59; ed in chief, Int J Psychobiol, 70-73; mem consult roster, Behav Med Br, Div Heart & Vascular Dis, Nat Heart, Lung & Blood Inst, NIH, 79-; Book rev ed, Pavlovian J Biol Sci, 81- *Honors & Awards:* Anokhin Mem Medal, P K Anokhin Inst, USSR Acad Sci, 79. *Mem:* Fel AAAS; Am Physiol Soc; fel Am Col Cardiol; Am Psychosom Soc; Sigma Xi. *Res:* Cerebrovisceral and renal physiology; psychopharmacology; cybernetics and systems approach in psychophysiology; individual differences in reactions to psychologic stress; Pavlovian and operant conditioned reflexes; interaction of pharmacologic and psychosocial factors in the control of aggression and hyperkinesis; minimal brain dysfunction; paradoxical effects of amphetamines; psychobiologic integrative mechanisms; physiologic basis of psychosomatic medicine; pet-facilitated therapy; psychiatry, psychobiology and psychology in the USSR and East Eurropean countries; comparative studies on Pavlovian and Freudian Contributions to psychiatry; gerontology; stress coping mechanisms. *Mailing Add:* Dept Psychiat Upham Hall Ohio State Univ Col of Med Columbus OH 43210

CORSTVET, RICHARD E, b Big Bend, Wis, Oct 12, 28; m 54; c 3. VETERINARY MICROBIOLOGY, VETERINARY PATHOLOGY. *Educ:* Univ Wis, BS, 51, MS, 55; Univ Calif, Davis, PhD(comp path), 65. *Prof Exp:* Lab technician avian med, Sch Vet Med, Univ Calif, Davis, 55-59, pub health, 59-65; asst res microbiologist, 65; from asst prof to assoc prof microbiol, 65-72, actg head dept, 77-80, PROF MICROBIOL & PUB HEALTH, COL VET MED, OKLA STATE UNIV, 72- *Mem:* Poultry Sci Asn; US Animal Health Asn; NY Acad Sci; Am Asn Avian Path. *Res:* Infection and immunity in Newcastle disease; relationship of various disease syndromes to the wholesomeness of market poultry; carrier states in animals; multiple infections in animals. *Mailing Add:* Col of Vet Med Okla State Univ Stillwater OK 74074

CORT, WINIFRED MITCHELL, b Cleveland, Ohio; m 47; c 2. MICROBIAL BIOCHEMISTRY. *Educ:* Univ Ill, BS, 41, MS, 43, PhD(bact, biochem), 46. *Prof Exp:* Res microbiologist, Commercial Solvents Corp, 43-45; res asst biochem, Univ Ill, 45; res biochemist, Chas Pfizer & Co, 45-47; res microbiologist, Nat Dairy Res Labs, Inc, 51-54; sect leader, Res & Develop Div, 54-58, sect leader enzymes, Evans Res & Develop Corp, 58-64; group leader, Res & Develop, Beechnut Life Savers, 64-65; sr biochemist, 65-73, group leader, 73-81, ASSOC DIR PROD DEVELOP, HOFFMANN-LA ROCHE INC, 81- *Concurrent Pos:* Lectr, Adelphi Univ, 59-62; consult, Evans Res & Develop Corp, 61-62 & Food & Drug Res, Inc, 62; NY distinguished food scientist award, 73-74. *Honors & Awards:* Co-author Bond Award, Am Oil Chem Soc, 74. *Mem:* Am Soc Microbiol; Am Chem Soc; Am Pharmacol Asn; AAAS; Inst Food Technol. *Res:* Mechanism of action of antioxidants; DeV. test systs for antioxidants and antibiotics, vitamin stabilization; chemical and microbiological fermentation. *Mailing Add:* 120 Francisco Ave Little Falls NJ 07424

CORTELYOU, W(ILLIAM) HARLAN, b New Jersey, Feb 5, 06; m 33; c 1. ELECTRICAL ENGINEERING. *Educ:* Rutgers Univ, BS, 27. *Prof Exp:* Tech staff, Bell Tel Labs, 27-32; test engr elec motors, Diehl Mfg Co, 36-37; test engr elec wires & cables, Gen Cable Corp, 39-46, res engr, 46-56, res supvr, 56-71; CONSULT, PHELPS DODGE CABLE & WIRE CO, 71- *Concurrent Pos:* Mem conf elec insulation, Nat Res Coun, 51-59. *Mem:* Inst Elec & Electronics Engrs; Am Soc Testing & Mat. *Res:* Components, methods and problems of manufacture of high voltage power cables. *Mailing Add:* 335 Ward Ave South Amboy NJ 08879

CORTH, RICHARD, b New York, NY, Apr 14, 25; m 44; c 3. PHYSICAL CHEMISTRY, ANALYTICAL CHEMISTRY. *Educ:* Brooklyn Col, BS, 48; Polytech Inst Brooklyn, PhD(radiation chem), 63. *Prof Exp:* Res engr, 55-56, sr res scientist, 56-78, FEL RES SCIENTIST, WESTINGHOUSE ELEC CORP, 73- *Mem:* AAAS; Am Soc Photobiol; Am Inst Biol Sci; Am Chem Soc. *Res:* Visual perception; photobiology; radiochemistry; radiation chemistry; solid state diffusion; gas-metal reactions; gas chromatography; activation analysis. *Mailing Add:* Dept 8006 Lamp Div Westinghouse Elec Corp Bloomfield NJ 07003

CORTNER, JEAN A, b Nashville, Tenn, Nov 10, 30; m; c 3. BIOCHEMICAL GENETICS. *Educ:* Vanderbilt Univ, BA, 52, MD, 55. *Prof Exp:* Guest investr human genetics & asst physician, Rockefeller Inst, 62-63; chief dept pediat, Roswell Park Mem Inst, 63-67; prof pediat & chmn dept, State Univ NY, Buffalo, 67-74, physician-in-chief, Children's Hosp, 67-74, PHYSICIAN-IN-CHIEF, CHILDREN'S HOSP PHILADELPHIA, 74-, PROF & CHMN DEPT, SCH MED, UNIV PA, 74- *Concurrent Pos:* NIH vis fel dept pediat & biochem, Babies Hosp & Columbia Univ, 61-63; NIH fel, Galton Lab Human Genetics, Univ London, 72-73. *Mem:* AAAS; Am Soc Human Genetics; Am Fedn Clin Res; Soc Pediat Res; Am Acad Pediat. *Res:* Human genetics; pediatrics. *Mailing Add:* Dept of Pediat Children's Hosp 34th St & Civic Ctr Blvd Philadelphia PA 19104

CORTRIGHT, EDGAR MAUICE, b Hastings, Pa, July 29, 23; m 45; c 2. AERONAUTICAL ENGINEERING. *Educ:* Rensselaer Polytech Inst, BS, 47, MS, 49. *Hon Degrees:* DEng, Rensselaer Polytech Inst, 75; DSc, George Washington Univ, 73. *Prof Exp:* Aeronaut res scientist aerodyn, Lewis Flight Propulsion Ctr, NASA, Cleveland, 48-58; chief advan tech progs, NASA, Washington, 58-60, asst dir lunar and planetary progs, 60-61, dep assoc adminr, Off Space sci & Appln, 61-67 & Off Manned Space Flight, 67-68; dir, Langley Res Ctr, Va, 68-75; vpres tech dir, Owens-Ill, Inc, Toledo, 75-78; PRES, LOCKHEED CALIF CO, 79- *Concurrent Pos:* Organizer, Tiros & Nimbus Progs, 58-60, Ranger, Mariner & Surveyor progs, 60-61 & Viking, 68-75. *Honors & Awards:* NASA medals, 66, 67 & 77; Space Flight award, Am Astronaut Soc, 71. *Mem:* Fel Am Astronaut Soc; Am Inst Aerospace & Astronaut (pres, 76); AAAS; Nat Acad Eng; Sigma Xi. *Mailing Add:* Lockheed Calif Co PO Box 551 Burbank CA 91520

CORTY, CLAUDE, b Bochum, Ger, May 16, 24; nat US; m 48; c 2. CHEMICAL ENGINEERING. *Educ:* Mass Inst Technol, BS, 44; Univ Mich, MS, 48, PhD(chem eng), 51. *Prof Exp:* Chemist, Atlas Powder Co, 46-47; res engr, 51-57, res supvr, Indust & Biochem Dept, 57-81, RES MGR, BIOCHEM DEPT, E I DU PONT DE NEMOURS & CO, INC, 81- *Mem:* Am Chem Soc; Am Inst Chem Engrs. *Res:* Heat transfer; agricultural formulations. *Mailing Add:* 1511 Emory Rd Green Acres Wilmington DE 19803

CORUM, JAMES FREDERIC, b Natick, Mass, Aug 15, 43; m 70; c 3. ELECTRICAL ENGINEERING. *Educ:* Univ Lowell, BS, 65; Ohio State Univ, MSc, 67, PhD(elec eng), 74. *Prof Exp:* Electronic engr antennas, Nat Security Agency, 65-66; res asst radio astron, Ohio State Univ, 67-70; prof math & physics, Ohio Inst Technol, 70-74; asst prof elec eng, WVa Univ, 74-79; pres, Radiation Dynamics Inc, 79-80; PRES, CPG COMMUN, INC, 80-; ASSOC PROF ELEC ENG, WVA UNIV, 81- *Concurrent Pos:* Consult, AM/FM Radio Stations, Satellite Television Earth Stations & US Govt Agencies. *Mem:* Inst Elec & Electronics Engrs; Am Soc Physics Teachers; Sigma Xi; AAAS; Am Soc Eng Educ. *Res:* Relativistic electrodynamics; differential geometry; general relativity; antennas and practical radiating systems; communications; wave propagation; satellite communications; electronic location finder. *Mailing Add:* Dept Elec Eng WVa Univ Morgantown WV 26506

CORWIN, H(AROLD) E(ARL), b New York, NY, Feb 8, 19; m 49; c 3. CHEMICAL ENGINEERING. *Educ:* City Col New York, BChE, 40; Syracuse Univ, MChE, 51, PhD(chem eng), 52; Univ Conn, MBA, 72. *Prof Exp:* Prin engr, draftsman & jr naval architect, Philadelphia Navy Yard, 42-44; designer & chem engr, Solvay Process Div, Allied Chem Co, 46-49; prin chem engr, Battelle Mem Inst, 51-53; proj coordr & lectr chem eng, Syracuse Univ, 54-56; dir process & qual control, Molded-Packaging Div, 56-63, asst dir res, 63-69, VPRES & TECH DIR, FIBER PROD DIV, DIAMOND INT CORP, 69- *Mem:* Am Chem Soc; Am Soc Qual Control; Am Inst Chem Engrs; Tech Asn Pulp & Paper Indust. *Res:* Pulp and paper; packaging; deinking; resinous cements; color; process development and instrumentation; quality control. *Mailing Add:* Diamond Int Corp 733 Third Ave New York NY 10017

CORWIN, HARRY O, b Los Angeles, Calif, Apr 30, 38; m 61; c 1. GENETICS. *Educ:* Univ Calif, Santa Barbara, BA, 61; Univ Calif, Los Angeles, MA, 62, PhD(zool), 66. *Prof Exp:* Teaching asst biol, embryol, anat & genetics, Univ Calif, Los Angeles, 62-66; asst prof genetics, 66-71, assoc prof biol, 71-80, PROF BIOL, UNIV PITTSBURGH, 80- *Mem:* AAAS. *Res:* Genetic analysis of mutagens effect on Drosophila melanogaster. *Mailing Add:* Dept of Biol Sci Univ of Pittsburgh Pittsburgh PA 15260

CORWIN, JAMES FAY, b Blanchester, Ohio, Oct 31, 07; m 31; c 1. CHEMISTRY. *Educ:* Ohio Univ, BA, 32, MA, 34; Ohio State Univ, PhD(chem), 44. *Prof Exp:* Teacher high sch, Ohio, 34-35; res chemist, Wheeling Steel Corp, WVa, 35-37; teacher high sch, Ohio, 37-40; asst anal chem, Ohio State Univ, 40-41; from instr to prof gen & anal chem & metall, 41-73, chmn dept chem, 48-61, chmn phys sci area, 64-70, EMER PROF GEN & ANAL CHEM & METALL, ANTIOCH COL, 73- *Concurrent Pos:* Res dir & asst to pres, Vernay Labs, Inc, Ohio, 44-74, mem bd dirs, 74-77, consult, 74-; dir teachers progs, NSF, 57-73, dir hydrothermal res, 54-70; vis res prof, Inst Marine Sci, Univ Miami, 60-68, adj prof, 67-72; consult, US AID, India, 65. *Mem:* Fel AAAS; Am Chem Soc; Soc Plastics Engrs. *Res:* Quantitative analytical chemistry; physical organic chemistry; conductometric titrations with organic reagents; quartz crystal growth; reactions in water solutions in the super-critical state; oceanography and environmental studies; consulting in industrial and academic science services. *Mailing Add:* 528 Palo Verde Dr Hawthorne at Leesburg Leesburg FL 32748

CORWIN, JEFFREY TODD, b Riverhead, NY, Oct 15, 51. NEUROBIOLOGY, SENSORY PHYSIOLOGY. *Educ:* Cornell Univ, BS, 73; Univ Hawaii, MS, 75; Univ Calif, San Diego, PHD(neurosci), 80. *Prof Exp:* Vis fel neurophysiol, Plymouth Lab, Marine Biol Asn UK, Plymouth, Eng, 80-81; ASST PROF ZOOL, UNIV HAWAII, 81- *Concurrent Pos:* Mem, Bekesy Lab Neurobiol & Pac Biomed Res Ctr, Univ Hawaii, 81- *Mem:* Soc Neurosci; Am Physiol Soc; Am Soc Zoologists; Asn Res Otlaryngol; Am Soc Ichthyologists & Herpetologists. *Res:* Comparative neurophysiology and neuroanatomy, especially growth and regeneration in sensory systems; sensory biology of sharks, rays, and other fishes; comparative studies of sound detection by vertebrates. *Mailing Add:* Dept Zool 2538 The Mall Univ Hawaii Honolulu HI 96822

CORWIN, LAURENCE MARTIN, b Rochester, NY, Aug 26, 29; m 52; c 3. BIOCHEMISTRY. *Educ:* Univ Chicago, PhB, 48; Syracuse Univ, BA, 50; Wayne State Univ, PhD(biochem), 56. *Prof Exp:* Res fel biol, Calif Inst Technol, 57-58; biochemist, NIH, 58-61; biochemist, Walter Reed Army Inst Res, 61-67; assoc prof, 67-73, PROF MICROBIOL & NUTRIT SCI, SCH MED, BOSTON UNIV, 73- *Mem:* Am Soc Biol Chemists; Am Inst Nutrit; Am Soc Microbiol. *Res:* Biochemical function of vitamin E; biochemical genetics in microorganisms; effect of vitamin E in immunology and cancer. *Mailing Add:* Dept of Microbiol Boston Univ Sch of Med Boston MA 02118

CORWIN, LAWRENCE JAY, b E Orange, NJ, Jan 20, 43; m 78. MATHEMATICAL ANALYSIS. *Educ:* Harvard Univ, BA, 64, AM, 65, PhD(math), 68. *Prof Exp:* C L E Moore Instr, Mass Inst Technol, 68-70; vis mem, Courant Inst Math Sci, NY Univ, 70-71; asst prof, Yale Univ, 71-75; assoc prof, 75-80, PROF MATH, RUTGERS UNIV, NEW BRUNSWICK, 80- *Concurrent Pos:* Sloan Found fel, 72-74; mem Inst Advance Sci Stud, 74, 78. *Mem:* Am Math Soc; Math Asn Am. *Res:* Harmonic analysis on nilpotent lie groups; representations of p-adic groups. *Mailing Add:* Dept of Math Rutgers Univ New Brunswick NJ 08903

CORWIN, THOMAS LEWIS, b Newburgh, NY, Oct 9, 47; m 71; c 1. MATHEMATICAL STATISTICS. *Educ:* Villanova Univ, BS, 69; Princeton Univ, MS, 71, PhD(statist), 73. *Prof Exp:* Sr assoc statist, 73-80, VPRES, DANIEL H WAGNER ASSOC, 80- *Mem:* Inst Math Statist; Am Statist Asn; Soc Appl & Indust Math. *Res:* Development of analytical tools to perform real-time, operational analysis of naval search problems; developing Bayesian information processing techniques for use in search problems. *Mailing Add:* Daniel H Wagner Assoc Station Square One Paoli PA 19301

CORY, JOSEPH G, b Tampa, Fla, Jan 27, 37; m 63; c 1. BIOCHEMISTRY. *Educ:* Univ Tampa, BS, 58; Fla State Univ, PhD(chem), 63. *Prof Exp:* Fel chem, Fla State Univ, 63; fel biochem, Albert Einstein Med Ctr, 63-64; asst mem, 64-65; asst prof, Fla State Univ, 65-69; assoc prof biochem, 69-73, prof med microbiol, Col Med, 73-74, PROF BIOCHEM & CHMN DEPT, COL MED, UNIV S FLA, 74- *Mem:* Am Chem Soc; Am Soc Biol Chem; Am Asn Cancer Res; Soc Exp Biol & Med. *Res:* Enzymology of nucleotide interconversions and nucleic acid synthesis; cancer biochemistry. *Mailing Add:* Dept of Biochem Univ of SFla Col of Med Tampa FL 33620

CORY, MICHAEL, b New York, NY, Dec 5, 41; m 66; c 2. MEDICINAL CHEMISTRY. *Educ:* San Jose State Col, BS, 64; Univ Calif, Santa Barbara, PhD(org chem), 71. *Prof Exp:* Chemist org chem, Stanford Res Inst, 64-68 & 71-77; RES SCIENTIST ORG CHEM, WELLCOME RES LABS, BURROUGHS WELLCOME CO, 77- *Mem:* Am Chem Soc. *Res:* Drug design; enzyme inhibitor design; interaction of drugs with macromolecules. *Mailing Add:* Wellcome Res Labs Research Triangle Park CA 27709

CORY, ROBERT MACKENZIE, b Washington, DC, Feb 22, 43; m 66; c 1. SYNTHETIC ORGANIC CHEMISTRY. *Educ:* Harvey Mudd Col, BS, 65; Univ Wis, PhD(org chem), 71. *Prof Exp:* Fel, Univ Colo, 71-72 & Rice Univ, 72-73; asst prof chem, Ohio Univ, 73-74; asst prof, 74-81, ASSOC PROF CHEM, UNIV WESTERN ONT, 81- *Mem:* Am Chem Soc; The Chem Soc; Chem Inst Can. *Res:* Bicycloannulation reactions, carbon atom equivalents, diazo compounds, nitro-olefins and vinyl sulfones, terpenes, alkaloids, steroids, antibiotics, prostaglandins, strained polycyclic systems, spiroconjugated and homoaromatic systems; computer-assisted design. *Mailing Add:* Dept of Chem Univ of Western Ont London Can

CORY, WILLIAM EUGENE, b Dallas, Tex, Apr 5, 27; m 47; c 2. ELECTRICAL ENGINEERING. *Educ:* Tex A&M Univ, BS, 50; Univ Calif, Los Angeles, MS, 59. *Prof Exp:* Elec engr, US Air Force Security Serv, 50-51 & 52-57; electronic systs engr, Lockheed Aircraft Corp, 57-59, aircraft develop engr, 59; sr res engr, 59-61, mgr commun, 61-65, dir, electronic systs res dept, 65-72, V PRES, ELECTRONIC SYSTS & GEOSCI DIV, SOUTHWEST RES INST, 72- *Mem:* Fel Inst Elec & Electionics Engrs; Sigma Xi. *Res:* Electromagnetic compatibility, interference and propagation; signal detection, recognition, extraction, processing, storage and retrieval; communications, navigation and identification systems engineering applied to defense, urban and ocean problems; research and development management. *Mailing Add:* Electronic Systs Res Dept PO Drawer 28510 San Antonio TX 78284

CORYELL, MARGARET E, b Great Falls, Mont, Jan 25, 13; m 41; c 3. BIOLOGICAL CHEMISTRY. *Educ:* Univ Colo, AB, 35; Univ Mich, MA, 37, PhD, 41. *Prof Exp:* Asst, Childrens Fund of Mich, 40-48; instr cell biol, 56-76, ASST RES PROF, CELL & MOLECULAR BIOL, MED COL GA, 76- *Res:* Biochemical defects in mentally retarded children. *Mailing Add:* Dept of Biochem Med Col of Ga Augusta GA 30902

COSBY, LYNWOOD ANTHONY, b Richmond, Va, June 11, 28; m 51; c 7. ELECTRONICS. *Educ:* Univ Richmond, BS, 49; Va Polytech Inst, MS, 51. *Prof Exp:* Instr physics, Va Mil Inst, 50-51; from physicist to br head advan tech, 51-71, HEAD, DIV ELECTRONIC WARFARE, US NAVAL RES LAB, 71-, CHMN, NAVAL ELECTRONIC WARFARE ADV GROUP, 73- *Concurrent Pos:* mem threat environ steering comt, Airborne Warning & Control Syst, 75- *Honors & Awards:* US Navy Distinguished Civilian Serv Award, 58; Am Soc Naval Engrs Gold Medal Award, 68; Dept of Defense Distinguished Civilian Serv Award, 74. *Mem:* Fel Inst Elec & Electronic Engrs; Sigma Xi; Am Soc Naval Engrs; Asn Old Crows (pres, 81-). *Res:* Administrative and technical leadership for advancement of technology and systems for all Navy electronic warfare applications; development of circuits, electron devices, antennas and the design of special research development technical and engineering facilities. *Mailing Add:* US Naval Res Lab Code 5700 Washington DC 20375

COSBY, RICHARD SHERIDAN, b New York, NY, July 6, 13; m 48. MEDICINE. *Educ:* Harvard Univ, AB, 34, MD, 38; Am Bd Internal Med, dipl, 48; Am Bd Cardiovasc Dis, dipl, 41. *Prof Exp:* Fel physiol, Sch Med, Western Reserve Univ, 39; resident cardiol, Mass Gen Hosp, 40-41; instr med, Harvard Med Sch, 42; assoc clin prof, 54-67, CLIN PROF MED, SCH MED, UNIV SOUTHERN CALIF, 67-; DIR, FOUND CARDIOVASC RES, 66- *Concurrent Pos:* Consult, Good Samaritan Hosp & Huntington Mem Hosp, Pasadena; consult ed, Med Electronics & Data. *Mem:* AMA; Am Heart Asn; fel Am Col Physicians; fel Am Col Chest Physicians; fel Am Col Cardiol. *Res:* Electrocardiography; cardiopulmonary. *Mailing Add:* 1245 Wilshire Blvd Suite 611 Los Angeles CA 90017

COSCARELLI, WALDIMERO, b Brooklyn, NY, Nov 5, 26; m 48; c 3. MICROBIOLOGY, BIOCHEMISTRY. *Educ:* Wagner Col, BS, 56; Rutgers Univ, PhD(microbiol), 61. *Prof Exp:* Bacteriologist, Chase Chem Co, NJ, 56; microbiologist, Schering Corp, 56-58; mem tech staff microbiol deterioration, Bell Tel Labs, Inc, 61-68; sr scientist, 68-69, mgr microbiol, Div Cent Res, Shulton, Inc, 69-73, mgr, Clin Res Serv, 73-76, assoc dir prod safety and govt regulatory affairs, 76-77, dir prod & regulatory affairs, consumer prod div, Shulton Inc, 77-79, DIR PROD & RES DIV, AM CYANAMID CO, 79- *Mem:* Am Soc Microbiol; Soc Cosmetic Chemists; NY Acad Sci. *Res:* Effects of microorganisms on plastics, including bacteria and fungi; isolation of organisms to study their metabolic requirements from plastics; transformations of steroid compound by microorganisms. *Mailing Add:* Am Cyanamid Co 697 Route 46 Clifton NJ 07015

COSCIA, ANTHONY THOMAS, b New York, NY, Nov 1, 28; m 51; c 4. POLYMER CHEMISTRY, ENVIRONMENTAL SCIENCES. *Educ:* Fordham Col, BS, 50; NY Univ, PhD(chem), 56. *Prof Exp:* Asst, NY Univ, 50-52; res chemist, Fleischmann Labs, 52-55; res chemist, 55-60, group leader org chem, 60-65, group leader polymer res, 65-66, mgr org & polymer res, Indust Chem Div, 66-71, mgr flocculants, Indust Chem & Plastics Div, 71-72, mgr polymer res, Chem Res Div, 72-80, CONSULT TECHNOL, INDUST PROD RES, 80- *Mem:* Am Chem Soc. *Res:* Polysaccharide isolation and identification; synthesis of nitrogen heterocycles; studies of alkylation reactions; synthesis and polymerization of new monomers; water soluble polymers; resins and coatings for paper; new product research on flocculants, water treating chemicals, mining and enhanced oil recovery polymers. *Mailing Add:* Chem Res Div Am Cyanamid Co 1937 W Main St Stamford CT 06904

COSCIA, CARMINE JAMES, b New York, NY, July 26, 35; m 56; c 3. BIOCHEMISTRY. *Educ:* Manhattan Col, BS, 57; Fordham Univ, MS, 60, PhD(org chem), 62. *Prof Exp:* NATO res fel org chem, Swiss Fed Inst Technol, 62-63, USPHS fel, 63-64; res fel biochem, Univ Pittsburgh, 64-65; from asst prof to assoc prof, 65-73, PROF BIOCHEM, SCH MED, ST LOUIS UNIV, 73- *Mem:* Am Soc Biol Chemists. *Res:* Secondary metabolism in plants and animals. *Mailing Add:* Dept of Biochem St Louis Univ Sch of Med St Louis MO 63104

COSENS, KENNETH W, b Fairgrove, Mich, June 22, 15; m 36; c 4. SANITARY ENGINEERING. *Educ:* Mich State Univ, BS, 38, MS, 46, CE, 48. *Prof Exp:* Asst city engr, Pontiac, Mich, 38-41; from instr to asst prof civil eng, Mich State Univ, 41-47; aircraft struct engr, Fisher Body Div, Gen Motors Corp, 44-45, struct engr, Olds- mobile Div, 45; asst prof civil eng, Univ Tex, 47-49; assoc prof civil & sanit eng, Ohio State Univ, 49-70, acting chmn dept, 53-55; sanit engr, 70-74, head pub works div, 78-80, PARTNER, ALDEN E STILSON & ASSOC, 74-; CITY PLANTS COORDR, DIV WATER, COLUMBUS, OH, 81- *Concurrent Pos:* Consult, 43-64; Dipl, Am Sanit Eng Intersoc Bd, 56. *Honors & Awards:* George W Fuller Award, Am Water Works Asn, 80. *Mem:* Fel Am Soc Civil Engrs; Nat Soc Prof Engrs; Am Water Works Asn; Water Pollution Control Fedn. *Res:* Water quality, especially taste and odor studies; waste water quality including aerobic and anaerobic disposal methods for small installations; garbage disposal with household grinders; lime recovery from water softening sludge. *Mailing Add:* 2620 Chester Rd Columbus OH 43221

COSGAREA, ANDREW, JR, b Highland Park, Mich, Aug 8, 34; m 58; c 3. METALLURGICAL & CHEMICAL ENGINEERING. *Educ:* Univ Mich, BSChE, 55, MSNucE, 56, PhD(chem, metall eng), 59. *Prof Exp:* Res asst liquid metals, Res Inst, Univ Mich, 56-59; from asst prof to assoc prof eng, Univ Okla, 59-65, dir nuclear reactor lab, 60-64; assoc chem engr & group leader, Chem Eng Div, Argonne Nat Lab, 65-66; sect chief, Avco Systs Div, 66-68, proj mgr, 68-69; prin consult scientist, 69-72; DIR, RES & DEVELOP, FRANKLIN MINT CORP, 72- *Concurrent Pos:* NSF & Mil Serv res grants, 60-72; mem bd dirs & pres, Int Precious Metals Inst, 76- *Mem:* AAAS; Am Inst Metall Engrs; Audio Eng Soc. *Res:* Physical and chemical properties of precious metals; thermal and chemical response of systems; thermodynamics; energetics. *Mailing Add:* Franklin Mint Corp Franklin Center PA 19091

COSGRIFF, JOHN W, JR, b Denver, Colo, Nov 10, 31; m 57; c 2. VERTEBRATE PALEONTOLOGY. *Educ:* Univ Ariz, BA, 53; Univ Calif, Berkeley, MA, 60, PhD(paleont), 63. *Prof Exp:* Sr res fel paleont, Univ Tasmania, 64-67; PROF BIOL, WAYNE STATE UNIV, 67- *Concurrent Pos:* Res assoc geol, Univ Tasmania, 75- *Mem:* AAAS; Soc Vert Paleont; Paleont Soc. *Res:* Mesozoic vertebrate faunas of Australia, Antarctica, Africa and North America. *Mailing Add:* Dept of Biol Col of Lib Arts Wayne State Univ Detroit MI 48202

COSGROVE, CLIFFORD JAMES, b Torrington, Conn, Jan 31, 27; m 52; c 3. DAIRY SCIENCE, FOOD SCIENCE. *Educ:* Univ Conn, BS, 51; Southern Conn State Col, BS, 53; Univ RI, MS, 57. *Prof Exp:* Assoc prof animal sci, 53-76, PROF FOOD SCI & TECHNOL, NUTRIT & DIETETICS, UNIV RI, 76- *Concurrent Pos:* Expert dairy technol, Food & Agr Orgn of UN, 76-77; Chile & Bolivia, 78-79. *Res:* Food technology, especially dairy products and their substitution by imitations or synthetics. *Mailing Add:* Dept Food & Nutrit 201 Quinn Hall Univ RI Kingston RI 02881

COSGROVE, GERALD EDWARD, b Dubuque, Iowa, July 13, 20; m 43; c 7. PATHOLOGY. *Educ:* Univ Notre Dame, BS, 45; Univ Mich, MD, 44; Am Bd Path, dipl, 50. *Prof Exp:* Hosp pathologist, Klamath Falls, Ore, 50-52; hosp pathologist, Rapid City, SDak, 52-55; hosp pathologist, Gorgas Hosp, Ancon, CZ, 55-57; biologist, Biol Div, Oak Ridge Nat Lab, 57-77; PATHOLOGIST, ZOOL SOC SAN DIEGO, 77- *Mem:* Radiation Res Soc; Am Soc Exp Path; Am Soc Parasitol; Am Soc Ichthyologists & Herpetologists; Wildlife Dis Asn. *Res:* Comparative pathology; parasitology; delayed effects of radiation. *Mailing Add:* Zool Soc San Diego PO Box 551 San Diego CA 92112

COSGROVE, JAMES FRANCIS, b Bridgeport, Conn, Aug 3, 29; m 53; c 8. MATERIALS SCIENCE, ANALYTICAL CHEMISTRY. *Educ:* Col of Holy Cross, BS, 51, MS, 52. *Prof Exp:* Res asst chem, Col of Holy Cross, 51-52; res chemist, Sylvania Elec Prod, NY, 52-60; sect head radiochem, 60-68, mgr mat anal, 68-72, res mgr mat eval, 72-78, DIR PRECISION MAT TECHNOL LAB, GEN TEL & ELECTRONICS LABS, INC, 78- *Mem:* Am Chem Soc; AAAS; Sigma Xi. *Res:* Development and application of trace methods of analysis; development and engineering in luminescent materials, ceramics, refractory and hard metals, precious metals; development of process monitoring techniques. *Mailing Add:* Gen Tel & Electronics Labs Inc 40 Sylvan Rd Waltham MA 02154

COSGROVE, STANLEY LEONARD, b Dorset, Eng, Mar 10, 26; US citizen; m 51; c 5. ORGANIC CHEMISTRY, ENGINEERING. *Educ:* Oxford Univ, BA, 48, BSc, 49, DPhil(org chem), 50. *Prof Exp:* Fel org chem, Univ Chicago, 50-51; res technician petrol chem, Shell Oil Co, 51-55; asst div chief org chem, Battelle Mem Inst, 55-61; res mgr appl phys, Columbia Broadcasting Syst, 61-62; asst dean eng, 76-79, ASSOC PROF CHEM ENG, UNIV CINCINNATI, 62-, ASSOC DEAN ENG, 79- *Concurrent Pos:* Vis prof, McGill Univ, 69-70; consult, Nuclear Eng Co, 73-76. *Mem:* Am Chem Soc; Am Soc Eng Educ. *Res:* Applied organic chemistry; polymer chemistry; radioactive waste and toxic waste immobilization. *Mailing Add:* Dept of Chem & Nuclear Eng Univ of Cincinnati Cincinnati OH 45221

COSGROVE, WILLIAM BURNHAM, b New York, NY, June 11, 20; m 49; c 2. PHYSIOLOGY. *Educ:* Cornell Univ, AB, 41; NY Univ, MS, 47, PhD(zool), 49. *Prof Exp:* Assoc zool, Univ Iowa, 49-51, from asst prof to assoc prof, 51-57; from assoc prof to prof, 57-69, head dept, 64-72, ALUMNI FOUND PROF ZOOL, UNIV GA, 69- *Honors & Awards:* Michael Award, 67. *Mem:* AAAS; Am Soc Cell Biol; Am Soc Zool; Soc Protozool (pres, 70-71). *Res:* Comparative physiology of respiratory pigments; cell biology of trypanosomatids; physiology of protozoa; membrane transport. *Mailing Add:* Dept of Zool Univ of Ga Athens GA 30602

COSMIDES, GEORGE JAMES, b Pittsburgh, Pa, July 23, 26; m 48; c 1. TOXICOLOGY, ENVIRONMENTAL CHEMICALS. *Educ:* Univ Pittsburgh, BS, 52; Purdue Univ, MS, 54, PhD(pharmacol), 56. *Prof Exp:* Pharmacist, Pittsburgh, 52; pharmacist, Purdue Univ, 52-54; sr scientist, Smith, Kline & French Labs, 56-57; asst prof pharmacol, Univ RI, 57-59; sr res pharmacologist, Psychopharmacol Serv Ctr, NIMH, 59-63, prog adminr, Pharmacol & Behav Sci Training Prog, Nat Inst Gen Med Sci, 63-64, exec secy pharmacol-toxicol prog comt, 64-74, prog dir pharmacol-toxicol prog & mem pharmacol res assoc training comt, NIH, 64-74, DEP DIR TOXICOL INFO PROG & DEP ASSOC DIR SPECIALIZED INFO SERV, NAT LIBR MED, NIH, 74- *Concurrent Pos:* Consult, Sci Criminal Invest, RI, 57-59; mem reference panel, Am Hosp Formulary Serv, 63-76; adj prof pharmacol, Univ Pittsburgh, 63-; mem comt probs of drug safety, Nat Acad Sci-Nat Res Coun, 64-69 & US Nat Comt for CODATA, Numerical Data Adv Bd, 77-; consult pharmacol & toxicol, WHO, 65 ; consult biomed commun for radio & TV, NIH, 70-, Surgeon Gen, USPHS, 71-, mem rev panel disposal lethal chem. *Honors & Awards:* Vavro Mem Award & Bristol Award, 51-52; Distinguished Scientist Award Pharmaceut Sci, AAAS, 71. *Mem:* AAAS; Am Soc Info Sci; Am Soc Pharmacol & Exp Therapeut; Environ Mutagen Soc; Soc Toxicol. *Res:* Psychopharmacology; effects of drugs on human behavior; drug metabolism; environmental chemicals; environmental toxicology; toxicology information systems; computer-based data retrieval systems; drug use, misuse and abuse; drug safety and efficacy; rational pharmacotherapy. *Mailing Add:* 639 Crocus Dr Rockville MD 20850

COSPER, DAVID RUSSELL, b Ypsilanti, Mich, Oct 3, 42; m 65; c 3. ORGANIC CHEMISTRY, POLYMER CHEMISTRY. *Educ:* Purdue Univ, BS, 64; Univ Wis, Madison, PhD(chem), 69. *Prof Exp:* Chemist, 69-73, group leader, 73-80, RES SCIENTIST, NALCO CHEM CO, 80- *Mem:* Am Chem Soc; Sigma Xi. *Res:* Synthesis of organic compounds and polymers for water treatment applications; design of chemical additives for pulp and paper manufacturing. *Mailing Add:* 6824 Valley View Dr Downers Grove IL 60515

COSPER, SAMMIE WAYNE, b Greggton, Tex, Oct 8, 33; m 54; c 3. NUCLEAR PHYSICS. *Educ:* Univ of Southwestern La, BS, 60; Purdue Univ, PhD(nuclear physics), 65. *Prof Exp:* Res appointee nuclear chem, Lawrence Radiation Lab, Univ Calif, 65-67; assoc prof, 67-70, head dept, 67-72, prof physics, 70-72, dean, Col Liberal Arts, 72-74, ACAD V PRES, UNIV SOUTHWESTERN LA, 74- *Mem:* Am Asn Physics Teachers; Am Phys Soc. *Res:* Low-energy charged particle nuclear reactions and scattering; charged particle identification techniques; charged particles from spontaneous fission; nuclear physics; instrumentation. *Mailing Add:* Univ of Southwestern La PO Box 41810 Lafayette LA 70504

COSS, RONALD ALLEN, b Long Beach, Calif, Apr 24, 47. CELL BIOLOGY, RADIATION BIOLOGY. *Educ:* Univ Calif, Riverside, BA, 69; Univ Colo, PhD(biol), 74. *Prof Exp:* NIH teaching & res asst, Dept Molecular, Cellular & Develop Biol, Univ Colo, Boulder, 69-74; NIH fel cell biol, Rockefeller Univ, 74-76; fel, Dept Radiol & Radiation Biol, Colo State Univ, 76-81, asst prof, Dept Radiol & Radiation Biol, 81-82; ASST PROF, DEPT RADIATION THERAPY & NUCLEAR MEDICINE, THOMAS JEFFERSON UNIV HOSP, 82- *Mem:* Am Soc Cell Biol; Radiation Res Soc; AAAS; Sigma Xi. *Res:* Mechanisms of mitosis and cytokinesis; cell cycle related changes in the cytoskeleton and plasma membrane; mechanisms of action of hyperthermia and radiosensitization by hyperthermia; cell cycle phase specific proteins. *Mailing Add:* Dept of Radiol & Radiation Biol Colo State Univ Ft Collins CO 80523

COSSAIRT, JACK DONALD, b Indianapolis, Ind, Oct 11, 48; m 73; c 2. ENVIRONMENTAL HEALTH, ELEMENTARY PARTICLE PHYSICS. *Educ:* Ind Cent Col, BA, 70; Ind Univ, Bloomington, MS, 72, PhD(physics), 75. *Prof Exp:* Res assoc, Cyclotron Inst, Tex A&M Univ, 75-78; ASSOC SCIENTIST, FERMI NAT ACCELERATOR LAB, 78- *Mem:* Am Phys Soc; Health Physics Soc. *Res:* Mass measurements of nuclei far from stability using charged particle transfer reactions: nuclear structure inalpha particle pickup reactions and polaritation measurements; accelerator shielding for hadrons and muons. *Mailing Add:* Fermi Nat Accelerator Lab PO Box 500 Batavia IL 60510

COSSINS, EDWIN ALBERT, b Romford, Eng, Feb 28, 37; m 62; c 2. PLANT PHYSIOLOGY, BIOCHEMISTRY. *Educ:* Univ London, BSc, 58, PhD(plant biochem), 61, DSc(plant biochem), 81. *Prof Exp:* Res assoc biol sci, Purdue Univ, 61-62; from asst prof to assoc prof, 62-69, actg head dept, 65-66, coordr, Introd Biol Prog, 74-77, PROF BOT, UNIV ALTA, 69- *Concurrent Pos:* Vis prof, Univ Geneva, Switz, 72-73. *Honors & Awards:* Centennial Medal, Govt Can, 67. *Mem:* Am Soc Plant Physiol; Can Soc Plant Physiol (pres, 76-77); Brit Biochem Soc; fel Royal Soc Can. *Res:* Pteroylglutamates in plants; amino acid biosynthesis; biochemistry of germinating tissues; intermediary metabolism of plant tissues. *Mailing Add:* Dept of Bot Univ of Alta Edmonton AB T6G 2E9 Can

COST, J(OE) L(EWIS), b Sidney, Ohio, Feb 26, 20; m 43; c 1. CHEMICAL ENGINEERING. *Educ:* Ohio State Univ, BChE, 43; Univ Del, MS, 49. *Prof Exp:* Process engr chem eng, Elliott Co, 44-49; chief process engr low temperature eng, Stacey Bros, 49-53; chief process eng, Air Prods, Inc, 53-57, mgr eng, 57-64, tech dir, Air Prod, Ltd, London, Eng, 64-67, mgr process develop, 67-69, mgr eng chem, 69-76, assoc dir eng, 76-80, TECH ADV CHEM, AIR PROD & CHEM, 80- *Mem:* Am Chem Soc; Am Inst Chem Engrs. *Res:* Engineering of complete low temperature liquefaction and separation facilities; air separation, helium recovery, hydrogen purification and methane; hydrogen and helium liquefaction plants; engineering of company owned chemical plants. *Mailing Add:* 2625 Liberty St Allentown PA 18104

COST, JAMES R(ICHARD), physical metallurgy, see previous edition

COST, THOMAS LEE, b Birmingham, Ala, Dec 24, 37; m 59; c 2. AEROSPACE ENGINEERING, STRUCTURAL ENGINEERING. *Educ:* Univ Ala, BS, 60, PhD(eng mech), 69; Univ Ill, MS, 62. *Prof Exp:* Res engr, Boeing Co, Wash, 61-62; head appl mech team, Rohm & Haas Co, 62-69; PROF AEROSPACE ENG, UNIV ALA, 69- *Concurrent Pos:* Consult, Army Res Off, 70-, Hercules Inc, 70-, US Army Missile Res & Develop Command, 70- & Olin Co, 77-; pres, Athena Eng Co, 73- *Mem:* Am Inst Aeronaut & Astronaut; Am Acad Mech; Am Soc Eng Educ; Am Soc Civil Eng; Am Soc Mech Eng. *Res:* Structural analysis; finite element methods; viscoelasticity; thermal stress; dynamic structural response. *Mailing Add:* Dept of Aerospace Eng Univ of Ala Tuscaloosa AL 35486

COSTA, DANIEL LOUIS, b Fall River, Mass, Apr 29, 48; m 75; c 4. TOXICOLOGY, OCCUPATIONAL HEALTH. *Educ:* Providence Col, BS, 70; Rutgers Univ, MS, 73; Harvard Univ, MS, 73, ScD(physiol), 77. *Prof Exp:* Res assoc toxicol, 77-79, asst scientist, 79-80, ASSOC SCIENTIST, ASSOC UNIVS INC, 80-; INSTR PHYSIOL, STATE UNIV NY STONY BROOK, 79- *Concurrent Pos:* Consult occup health, 76- *Mem:* AAAS; Am Thoracic Soc; NY Acad Sci; Sigma Xi. *Res:* Development of animal models of lung disease; assessment of physiological and chemical interaction of gaseous and particulate substances on the lungs of animals. *Mailing Add:* Dept of Med Bldg 490 Brookhaven Nat Lab Upton NY 11973

COSTA, DANIEL PAUL, b Van Nuys, Calif, Jan 23, 52. ZOOLOGY. *Educ:* Univ Calif, Los Angeles, BA, 74, Santa Cruz, PhD(biol), 78. *Prof Exp:* PHYSIOLOGIST, SCRIPPS INST OCEANOG, 78- *Mem:* AAAS; Ecol Soc Am; Am Soc Mammalogists. *Res:* Physiological ecological of marine mammals and birds with an emphasis on material and energy flux; water balance and reproductive energetics of marine mammals. *Mailing Add:* Scripps Inst Oceanog Univ Calif San Diego CA 92093

COSTA, ERMINIO, b Cagliari, Italy, Mar 9, 24; US citizen; m 50; c 3. PHARMACOLOGY. *Educ:* Univ Cagliari, Sardinia, MD, 47. *Prof Exp:* Asst prof, Univ Cagliari, Sardinia, 47-54, assoc prof pharmacol, 54-55; Fulbright res fel, Dept Physiol & Pharmacol, Chicago Med Sch, 55; med res assoc, Galesburg State Res Hosp, 56-61; vis scientist, Nat Heart Inst, 60-61, head sect clin pharmacol, Lab Chem Pharmacol, 61-65; assoc prof pharmacol, Col Physicians & Surgeons, Columbia Univ, 65-68; CHIEF LAB PRECLIN PHARMACOL, NIMH, 68- *Honors & Awards:* Bennett Found Award, 60. *Mem:* Fel AAAS; Am Soc Pharmacol & Exp Therapeut; Am Acad Neurol; fel Am Col Neuropsychopharmacol; Am Physiol Soc. *Res:* Antirheumatic drugs; anticoagulants; curari; cholinesterase inhibitors; chemotherapy of cancer; chemotherapy of tuberculosis; glucagon; effect of drugs and physiological control of the turnover rate of neuronal catecholamines, indolealkylamines, acetylcholine and cyclic adenosine monophosphate; mechanism of habituation to amphetamines and morphine. *Mailing Add:* Lab of Preclin Pharmacol St Elizabeth's Hosp Washington DC 20032

COSTA, JOHN EMIL, b Ithaca, NY, Aug 14, 47; m 73. GEOMORPHOLOGY, ENVIRONMENTAL GEOLOGY. *Educ:* State Univ NY Col Oneonta, BS, 69; Johns Hopkins Univ, PhD(geog & environ eng), 73. *Prof Exp:* Instr geog, Towson State Col, 71-72; geologist, Md Geol Surv, 70-73; asst prof geog, 73-78, ASSOC PROF GEOG, UNIV DENVER, 78-; HYDROLOGIST, US GEOL SURV, 74 & 78- *Mem:* Geol Soc Am; Am Geophys Union; Asn Eng Geol. *Res:* Fluvial processes; geomorphic responses to extreme events. *Mailing Add:* Dept of Geog Univ of Denver Denver CO 80208

COSTA, LORENZO F, b Genova, Italy, Feb 10, 31; m 66; c 4. ELECTRONIC SPECTROSCOPY, SPECTRO-ENGINEERING. *Educ:* Birmingham-Southern Col, BS, 61; State Univ NY Buffalo, MS, 68. *Prof Exp:* Cancer scientist, Roswell Park Mem Inst, 61-67; res chemist, 67-74, sr res chemist, 74-77, RES ASSOC, EASTMAN KODAK CO, 77- *Mem:* Soc Appl Spectros; Am Chem Soc; Soc Photog Scientists & Engrs; Am Optical Soc. *Res:* Photophysics; absolute luminescence methodology; optical spectroscopy; spectrophotometry of optically turbid media; photosensitivity mechanisms; molecular electronics; electromagnetic photosensing devices. *Mailing Add:* 67 Merchants Rd Rochester NY 14609

COSTA, MAX, b Cagliari, Italy, Jan 10, 52; US citizen; m 74. PHARMACOLOGY, BIOCHEMISTRY. *Educ:* Georgetown Univ, BS, 74; Univ Ariz, PhD(pharmacol), 76. *Prof Exp:* Res asst met health, NIMH, 70-72; res asst cancer, Nat Cancer Inst, 72-74; res asst, Dept Pharmacol, Univ Ariz, 74-76, res assoc, Dept Radiation Oncol, 76; asst prof, Sch Med, Univ Conn, 77-79; ASST PROF, DEPT MED PHARMACOL & TOXICOL, TEX A&M UNIV, 79- *Concurrent Pos:* Nat Cancer Inst & NIH fels, 77; lectr, Advan Study Inst, NATO, 77; consult, Amax Inc, 78-79. *Mem:* AAAS; Am Soc Pharmacol & Exp Therapeut; Am Soc Biol Chemists; Am Soc Cell Biol. *Res:* Metal carcinogenesis in tissue culture; regulation of ornithine decarboxylase by asparagine and cAMP; differences in enzyme regulation in normal and neoplastic cells. *Mailing Add:* Dept of Pharmacol & Toxicol Tex A&M Univ Col of Med College Station TX 77843

COSTA, RAYMOND LINCOLN, JR, b Baltimore, Md, Feb 12, 48; m 69; c 2. PHYSICAL ANTHROPOLOGY, ANATOMY. *Educ:* Univ Calif, Berkeley, BS, 69; Univ Pa, PhD(anthrop), 77. *Prof Exp:* Instr anthrop, Pa State Univ, 75-76 & Univ Pa, 76; anthropologist, Smithsonian Inst, 77-78; ASST PROF ORAL ANAT, COL DENT, UNIV ILL MED CTR, 78- *Mem:* Am Asn Phys Anthropologists; Am Anthrop Asn; PaleoPaleopathol Asn; AAAS. *Res:* Comparative paleopathology of dental and oral diseases in dried skeletal material derived from archeological sites; Hominid and pre-Hominid paleontology. *Mailing Add:* Dept of Oral Anat Univ of Ill Med Ctr Chicago IL 60612

COSTAIN, JOHN KENDALL, b Boston, Mass, Nov 18, 29; m 56; c 3. GEOPHYSICS. *Educ:* Boston Univ, BA, 51; Univ Utah, PhD(geol), 60. *Prof Exp:* Geophysicist, Socony Vacuum Oil Co Venezuela, 51-54; asst prof physics, San Jose State Col, 59-60; from asst prof to assoc prof geophys, Univ Utah, 60-67; assoc prof, 67-69, PROF GEOPHYS, VA POLYTECH INST & STATE UNIV, 69- *Concurrent Pos:* NSF grants, 64-; Dept Energy contracts, 75- *Mem:* Am Geophys Union; Am Asn Petrol Geol; Geol Soc Am; Soc Explor Geophys. *Res:* Exploration seismology; terrestrial heat flow; geothermal energy. *Mailing Add:* Dept of Geol Sci Va Polytech Inst & State Univ Blacksburg VA 24060

COSTAIN, ROBERT ANTHONY, nutrition, see previous edition

COSTANTINO, MARC SHAW, b Oakland, Calif, Nov 8, 45; m 66; c 3. HIGH PRESSURE PHYSICS, GEOPHYSICS. *Educ:* Rensselaer Polytech Inst, BS, 67; Princeton Univ, PhD(solid state physics), 72. *Prof Exp:* Physicist, US Mil Acad, West Point, 71-74; PHYSICIST GEOPHYS, LAWRENCE LIVERMORE LAB, 74- *Mem:* Am Phys Soc. *Res:* High pressure thermodynamics; physics of geological materials. *Mailing Add:* 959 Venus Way Livermore CA 94550

COSTANTINO, ROBERT FRANCIS, b Everett, Mass, Mar 21, 41; m 63; c 5. POPULATION BIOLOGY. *Educ:* Univ NH, BS, 63; Purdue Univ, MS, 65, PhD(genetics), 67. *Prof Exp:* Asst prof genetics, Pa State Univ, 67-72; PROF ZOOL, UNIV RI, 72- *Mem:* Genetics Soc Am; AAAS; Sigma Xi. *Res:* Population genetics of tribolium; genetics of competing species. *Mailing Add:* Dept of Zool Univ of RI Kingston RI 02881

COSTANZA, ALBERT JAMES, b Pittsburgh, Pa, Dec 3, 17; m 43; c 3. POLYMER CHEMISTRY, RUBBER CHEMISTRY. *Educ:* Univ Pittsburgh, BS, 40; Univ Akron, MS, 50. *Prof Exp:* Jr chemist, US Govt, 40-43; proj chemist, Govt Synthetic Rubber Lab, Univ Akron, 46-50; sr res chemist, 50-71, sect head specialty rubbers, 71-74, RES SCIENTIST, GOODYEAR TIRE & RUBBER CO, 74- *Mem:* Am Chem Soc. *Res:* Synthetic latices and polymers; emulsion and emulsifier free polymerizations; liquid polymers; functional and group polymers; reactive copolymers; specialty rubbers. *Mailing Add:* Res Div Goodyear Tire & Rubber Co Akron OH 44316

COSTANZA, ROBERT, b Pittsburgh, Pa, Sept 14, 50. ENERGY ANALYSIS, ECOLOGICAL ECONOMICS. *Educ:* Univ Fla, BA, 73, MA, 74, PhD(syst ecol), 79. *Prof Exp:* Grad res asst, Dept Archit, Univ Fla, 74; res assoc, Ctr Wetlands, Univ Fla, 74-75, grad res asst, 75-79; energy analyst, Fla Gov Energy Off, 79; res asst, 79-81, ASST PROF, CTR WETLAND RESOURCES, LA STATE UNIV, 81- *Concurrent Pos:* Consult, US Environ Protection Agency, 80- *Mem:* AAAS; Ecol Soc Am; Am Soc Naturalists; Am Inst Biol Sci. *Res:* Research in systems ecology, resource management and energy analysis with special emphasis on modeling human environment interactions; estimation of environmental costs of coastal wetland modifications, net energy analysis of geopressured energy sources, and integrated analysis of the coastal zone. *Mailing Add:* Coastal Ecol Lab Ctr Wetland Resources La State Univ Baton Rouge LA 70803

COSTANZO, JAMES NOEL, b Yonkers, NY, Dec 26, 45; m 68; c 1. PHYSICAL CHEMISTRY, ANALYTICAL CHEMISTRY. *Educ:* St Lawrence Univ, BS, 67; Fairleigh Dickinson Univ, MS, 70; Rutgers Univ, PhD(phys chem), 76. *Prof Exp:* Chemist clin pharmacol, Hoffmann-LaRoche Inc, 68-70; teacher chem, Ursuline Sch, 73-74; sr chemist food, Pepsico Inc, 74-81; DIR BUR, GOOD HOUSEKEEPING INST, 81- *Mem:* Am Chem Soc; Inst Food Technologists; Food & Drug Law Inst; Soc Cosmetic Chemists. *Res:* Chemical kinetics; thermodynamics; protein binding studies. *Mailing Add:* 208 Claflin Blvd Franklin Square NY 11010

COSTEA, NICOLAS V, b Bucharest, Romania, Nov 10, 27; US citizen. IMMUNOHEMATOLOGY. *Educ:* Univ Paris, MD, 56. *Prof Exp:* Instr med, Sch Med, Tufts Univ, 59-63; Lederle fac award, 63-66; from asst prof to prof med, Sch Med, Univ Ill, Chicago Circle, 70-72; chief hemat-oncol div, Univ Calif, Los Angeles-San Fernando Valley Prog, 72; PROF MED, SCH MED, UNIV CALIF, LOS ANGELES, 72-, COORDR, HEMAT-ONCOL PROG, 72- *Concurrent Pos:* Dir hemat, Cook County Hosp, 70-72; NIH grants. *Mem:* Am Soc Hemat; Am Fedn Clin Res; Am Asn Immunologists; Am Rheumatism Asn. *Res:* Hematology. *Mailing Add:* Hemat Dept Vet Admin Sepulveda Hosp Los Angeles CA 91343

COSTELLO, CATHERINE E, b Medford, Mass, May 11, 43. MASS SPECTROMETRY, ORGANIC BIOCHEMISTRY. *Educ:* Emmanuel Col, AB, 64; Georgetown Univ, MS, 67, PhD(org chem), 70. *Prof Exp:* Chemist, Div Food Chem, US Food & Drug Admin, Dept Health Educ & Welfare, 66-67 & USDA, 69; res assoc mass spectrometry, 70-79, PRIN RES SCIENTIST, MASS INST TECHNOL, 79- *Concurrent Pos:* Assoc dir, Mass Spectrometry Facil, Northeastern Univ, 76-, lectr, 80- *Mem:* Am Chem Soc; Am Soc Mass Spectrometry; AAAS; Asn Women Sci. *Res:* Applications of advanced methods of organic chemical analysis, particularly mass spectrometry to biomedical problems including metabolic disorders, drug metabolism and toxicology. *Mailing Add:* Rm 56-029 Mass Inst of Technol Cambridge MA 02139

COSTELLO, CHRISTOPHER HOLLET, b St John's, Nfld, Jan 19, 13; nat US; m 46; c 5. PHARMACOLOGY. *Educ:* Mass Col Pharm, BS, 36, MS, 41, PhD(chem & pharmacol), 50. *Prof Exp:* Pharmacist, Mass Gen Hosp, 35-36; chief chemist, Pinkham Co, 38-41; instr chem, Mass Col Pharm, 46-49; vpres & sci dir, Columbus Pharmacol Co, 49-60; dir res, Pharmaceut Labs, Colgate-Palmolive Co, 60-62, dir res biol prod, 62-69, assoc dir corp res, 69-75, adminr regulatory affairs, 76-79; consult, 78-81; RETIRED. *Concurrent Pos:* Drug indust liaison, Rev Panel Oral Cavity Drugs, Food & Drug Admin, 74-80; consult, Proprietary Asn, 70. *Mem:* Fel AAAS; Am Chem Soc; Am Pharm Asn; fel Am Inst Chemists; Soc Clin Pharmacol & Therapeut. *Res:* Pharmaceutical and cosmetic chemistry; chemistry and pharmacology of botanical drugs; isolated estrone from licorice; sustained release medication; antilipemic agents; proprietary drugs; dermatological, dental and hair products. *Mailing Add:* Lower Rd Putnam Sta NY 12861

COSTELLO, DAVID FRANCIS, b Nebr, Sept 1, 04; m 29; c 3. ENVIRONMENTAL BIOLOGY. *Educ:* Nebr State Teachers Col, AB, 25; Univ Chicago, MS, 26, PhD(plant ecol), 34. *Prof Exp:* Instr bot, Marquette Univ, 26-32; forest ecologist, Rocky Mountain Forest & Range Exp Sta, US Forest Serv, 34-37; chief div range res, 37-53, chief div range res, Pac NW Forest & Range Exp Sta, 53-61, chief div range, wildlife habitat & recreation res, 61-65; WRITER NATURAL SCI BOOKS, 65-; CONSULT ENVIRON BIOL, 71- *Concurrent Pos:* Spec lectr, Colo State Univ, 42-53; guest prof, State Col Wash, 57; guest speaker, Univ Col NWales, 62; mem range comt, Western Agr Res Coun, 55-64. *Honors & Awards:* Citation for Outstanding Achievement & Serv, Am Soc Range Mgt, 70. *Mem:* Fel AAAS; Ecol Soc Am; Sigma Xi; Am Inst Biol Sci. *Res:* Plant ecology; environmental relations of plants and animals; social background of outdoor recreationists; psychology of recreation. *Mailing Add:* 4965 Hogan Dr Ft Collins CO 80525

COSTELLO, DONALD F, b New York, NY, Mar 12, 34; m 61; c 7. STATISTICS, COMPUTER SCIENCE. *Educ:* Manhattan Col, BS, 54; Univ Notre Dame, MS, 59. *Prof Exp:* Instr math, Univ Alaska, 56-57 & La Salle Col, 59-60; teaching asst, Univ Nebr, 60-63; asst prof & dir comput ctr, Wis State Univ, 63-64; res assoc, Univ Wis, 64-65; asst dir comput ctr, 65-70, assoc prof comput sci, 70-76, dir comput ctr, 72-76, LECTR MGT, UNIV NEBR, 76-, DIR ACAD COMPUT, UNIV COMPUT NETWORK, 76- *Concurrent Pos:* Asst prof, Colo State Univ, 65-68; proj dir, Mo Valley Planning Info Ctr; pres, Costello & Assocs, Mgt Consults. *Mem:* Asn Comput Mach; Inst Math Statist. *Res:* Analytic techniques useful in managing information systems environments. *Mailing Add:* Comput Network 220 Regents Hall Univ of Nebr Lincoln NE 68583

COSTELLO, ERNEST F, JR, b Fall River, Mass, June 9, 23; m 48; c 4. PHYSICS. *Educ:* Boston Univ, AB, 49; Lehigh Univ, MS, 51, PhD(physics), 59. *Prof Exp:* Asst physics, Lehigh Univ, 49-52, instr, 52-59; assoc prof, 59-67, chmn dept, 68-69, dir div lib arts & sci, 69-74, asst dir, 63-69, dean sci & eng, 74-77, PROF PHYSICS, MERRIMACK COL, 67-, HEALTH PROF ADV, 77- *Concurrent Pos:* Sr engr physics, Raytheon Co, 62- *Mem:* Am Phys Soc; Am Asn Physics Teachers. *Res:* Magnet thin films; magnetic powders; thin film circuits. *Mailing Add:* Dept of Physics Merrimack Col North Andover MA 01845

COSTELLO, FREDERICK ALEXANDER, mechanical & aerospace engineering, see previous edition

COSTELLO, LESLIE CARL, cell physiology, endocrinology, see previous edition

COSTELLO, RICHARD GRAY, b New York, NY, Apr 16, 38; m 59; c 3. COMPUTER HARDWARE, CONTROL SYSTEMS DESIGN. *Educ:* Cooper Union, BS, 59; NY Univ, MS, 60; Univ Wis, PhD(manual control), 66. *Prof Exp:* Engr, Autonetics Div, N Am Aviation, 60-61; assoc engr, Cornell Aeronaut Labs, 66-67; assoc prof, 67-80, chmn elec eng curric group, 77-81, PROF ELEC ENG, COOPER UNION, 80- *Concurrent Pos:* Consult, US Consumer Prod Safety Comn, 76; consult for lawyers & inventors, New York. *Honors & Awards:* Rossi Prize res writing, 69. *Res:* Control theory; man-machine systems; guidance and manual control of vehicular systems; micro computers in bioengineering and system control; medical electronics. *Mailing Add:* Dept of Elec Eng Cooper Square New York NY 10003

COSTELLO, WALTER JAMES, b San Antonio, Tex, Nov 5, 45; div; c 1. NEUROBIOLOGY. *Educ:* Trinity Univ, BA, 66, MS, 69; Boston Univ, PhD(neurobiol), 78. *Prof Exp:* Res asst physiol, Trinity Col, 66-69; teaching fel biol, Boston Univ, 72-74; res asst neurobiol, Marine Prog-Woods Hole, Boston Univ, 74-77; fel neurogenetics, Yale Univ, 77-81; ASST PROF BIOMED SCI, OHIO UNIV, 81- *Concurrent Pos:* Fel, NIH, 78 & Muscular Dystrophy Asn Am, 78-; researcher, Bermuda Biol Sta, 78 & Marine Biol Lab, Woods Hole, 79, 80 & 81. *Mem:* Am Soc Zoologists; AAAS; Soc Neurosci; Am Inst Biol Sci; NY Acad Sci. *Res:* Development of neuromuscular systems; neurogenetics; neurobiological approaches to behavior. *Mailing Add:* Dept Zool Col Osteop Med Ohio Univ Athens OH 45701

COSTELLO, WILLIAM JAMES, b Cavalier, NDak, Aug 2, 32; m 58; c 2. ANIMAL SCIENCE, MEAT SCIENCE. *Educ:* NDak State Univ, BS, 54; Okla State Univ, MS, 60, PhD(meat sci), 63. *Prof Exp:* Res nutritionist, Res Lab, John Morrell & Co, 62-65; asst prof, 65-75, ASSOC PROF ANIMAL SCI, SDAK STATE UNIV, 75- *Mem:* Am Meat Sci Asn; Am Soc Animal Sci; Inst Food Technol. *Res:* Quality studies of beef and pork; quantity aspects of beef, pork and lamb carcasses; fast freezing and packaging beef; tranquilizers associated with beef cattle marketing. *Mailing Add:* Dept of Animal Sci S Dak State Univ Brookings SD 57006

COSTER, JOSEPH CONSTANT, b Diekirch, Luxembourg; US citizen. PHYSICS. *Educ:* Mass Inst Technol, SB, 57; Univ Calif, Berkeley, PhD(physics), 67. *Prof Exp:* PROF PHYSICS, WESTERN ILL UNIV, 67- *Mem:* Am Asn Physics Teachers. *Res:* S-matrix theory. *Mailing Add:* Dept of Physics Western Ill Univ Macomb IL 61455

COSTERTON, J WILLIAM F, b Vernon, BC, July 21, 34; m 55; c 4. MICROBIOLOGY. *Educ:* Univ BC, BA, 55, MA, 56; Univ Western Ont, PhD(microbiol), 60. *Prof Exp:* Prof biol, Baring Union Christian Col, Punjab, India, 60-62, dean sci, 63-64; fel bot, Cambridge Univ, 65; prof assoc microbiol, McGill Univ, 66-67, asst prof, 68-70; assoc prof, 70-75, PROF MICROBIOL, UNIV CALGARY, 75- *Mem:* Can Soc Microbiol; Am Soc Microbiol. *Res:* Architecture of bacterial cell walls, including extracellular carbohydrate coats, especially as it relates to physiological processes, to the presence of periplasmic enzymes and to adhesion to inert or cellular surfaces. *Mailing Add:* Dept of Biol Univ of Calgary Calgary AB T2N 1N4 Can

COSTES, NICHOLAS CONSTANTINE, b Athens, Greece, Sept 20, 26; US citizen; m 58; c 3. GEOTECHNICAL ENGINEERING, RESEARCH ADMINISTRATION. *Educ:* Darmouth Col, NH, AB, 50; Darmouth Col-Thayer Sch Eng, MSCE, 51 & NC State Univ, 55; Harvard Univ, AM & ME, 61; NC State Univ, PhD(eng), 65. *Prof Exp:* Teaching fel soil mech, Dept Civil Eng, NC State Univ, 51-53; mat engr geotech eng, NC State Highway & Public Works Co, 53-56; contract scientist snow & ice mech, US Snow Ice & Permafrost Res Estab, 56-59; res civil eng, US Cold Regions Res & Eng Lab, 59-62; instr & Ford Found fel soil mech & viscoelasticity, Dept Civil Eng, NC State Univ, 62-64; SR STAFF SCIENTIST SPACE SCI LAB, GEORGE C MARSHALL SPACE FLIGHT CTR, NASA, 65- *Concurrent Pos:* mem numerous ad hoc comt & tech mgt teams, NASA, 65-; team leader, Apollo 11 Soil Mech Invest Sci Team, 67-70; co-investr, Lunar Geol Exp, Apollo Missions 12 & 13, 69-71, Apollo Soil Mech Exp, Apollo Mission 14-17, 71-74; lectr, Dept Eng Mech, Univ Ala, Huntsville, 72-; invited lectr, Acad Inst, Govt Agencies & Pvt Orgns. *Honors & Awards:* Norman Medal, Am Soc Civil Engrs, 72; Martin Schilling Award, Am Inst Aeronaut & Astronaut, 79. *Mem:* Sigma Xi; AAAS; Am Geophys Union; fel Am Soc Civil Engrs; Am Inst Aeronaut & Astronaut. *Res:* Soil mechanics and geotechnical engineering; mechanical behavior of snow and ice as engineering materials; spacelab experiment definition on soil behavior; author or coauthor of 50 publications. *Mailing Add:* 4216 Huntington Rd SE Huntsville AL 35802

COSTICH, EMMETT RAND, b Rochester, NY, July 15, 21; m 45; c 6. ORAL SURGERY. *Educ:* Univ Pa, DDS, 45; Univ Rochester, MS, 49, PhD(path), 54; Colgate Univ, BA, 56. *Prof Exp:* Instr dent surg, Sch Med & Dent, Univ Rochester, 47-55; asst prof dent, Sch Dent, Univ Mich, 55-58, assoc prof, 58-62; chmn dept oral surg, 62-69, assoc dean col dent, 69-72, asst for extramural educ prog coord to vpres for med ctr, 72-78, PROF ORAL SURG, COL DENT, UNIV KY, 62-, PROF MAXILLOFACIAL SURG, 80- *Concurrent Pos:* Res assoc & supvr periodont & oral path, Eastman Dent Dispensary, 49-55; consult, US Vet Hosp, Lexington, Ky, 62- & NIMH Hosp, 63-73. *Mem:* Am Dent Asn; Int Asn Dent Res. *Res:* Transplantation; bone physiology. *Mailing Add:* Rm D510 Col Dent Univ Ky Lexington KY 40536

COSTILL, DAVID LEE, b Feb 7, 36; US citizen; m 60; c 2. HUMAN PHYSIOLOGY. *Educ:* Ohio Univ, BSEd, 59; Miami Univ, MA, 61; Ohio State Univ, PhD(physiol), 65. *Prof Exp:* Instr physiol, Ohio State Univ, 63-64; asst prof, State Univ NY Cortland, 64-66; PROF PHYS ED & BIOL, HUMAN PERFORMANCE LAB, BALL STATE UNIV, 66- *Concurrent Pos:* Vis fac, Desert Res Inst, 68; hon lectr, Univ Sulford, Eng, 72; res assoc, Gymnastik-och idrottshogskolan, Stockholm, 72-73. *Honors & Awards:* McClintock Award, Ball State Univ Found, 72. *Mem:* Am Physiol Soc; Am Soc Zoologists. *Res:* Alterations in skeletal muscle water and electrolytes following prolonged exercise and dehydration in man; glycolytic-oxidative enzyme and fiber composition in human skeletal muscle. *Mailing Add:* Human Performance Lab Ball State Univ Muncie IN 47306

COSTILOW, RALPH NORMAN, b Oxford, WVa, Oct 23, 22; c 2. MICROBIOLOGY. *Educ:* WVa Univ, BS, 48; NC State Col, MS, 50; Mich State Col, PhD(bact), 53. *Prof Exp:* Instr bact, NC State Col, 49-51; from asst prof to assoc prof, 53-60, PROF MICROBIOL & PUB HEALTH, MICH STATE UNIV, 60- *Concurrent Pos:* NIH spec fel biochem, Univ Calif, Berkeley, 64-65. *Mem:* AAAS; Am Soc Microbiol; Am Soc Biol Chemists. *Res:* Microbial physiology; amino acid metabolism; industrial and foods microbiology. *Mailing Add:* Dept of Microbiol & Pub Health Mich State Univ East Lansing MI 48824

COSTIN, ANATOL, b Bucharest, Rumania, Aug 26, 26; m 55; c 2. NEUROSCIENCES. *Educ:* Inst Med & Pharm, Bucharest, 52; Rumanian Acad Sci, PhD(physiol, physiopath), 56. *Prof Exp:* Asst prof physiol, Inst Med & Pharm, Bucharest, 49-57; sr res fel, Inst Physiol, Rumanian Acad Sci, 56-61; sr lectr pharmacol, Hadassah Med Sch, Hebrew Univ, Israel, 61-70; res assoc, 70-72, ASSOC PROF ANAT, UNIV CALIF, LOS ANGELES, 72- *Concurrent Pos:* Res asst anat, Univ Calif, Los Angeles, 67-68. *Mem:* Am Physiol Soc; Soc Neurosci; Am Asn Anatomists; Royal Soc Med; Fedn Am Socs Exp Biol. *Res:* Neurophysiology; neurochemistry. *Mailing Add:* Brain Res Inst Univ of Calif Los Angeles CA 90024

COSTLOW, JOHN DEFOREST, b Brookville, Pa, Jan 28, 27; m 52; c 2. MARINE INVERTEBRATE ZOOLOGY. *Educ:* Western Md Col, BS, 50; Duke Univ, PhD(zool), 55. *Prof Exp:* Asst biol, Western Md Col, 50; asst zool, 50-51, 53-54, marine zool, Off Naval Res, 51-53, res assoc, NSF contracts, 54-59, from asst prof to assoc prof, 59-68, PROF ZOOL, DUKE UNIV, 68-, DIR MARINE LAB, 68- *Mem:* Am Soc Limnol & Oceanog; Am Soc Zool; Brit Marine Biol Asn. *Res:* Organogenesis; larval development; molting, growth and physiology of Cirripedia; larval development of Crustacea in relation to environmental factors; endocrine mechanisms in larvae of marine Crustacea. *Mailing Add:* Marine Lab Duke Univ Beaufort NC 28516

COSTLOW, MARK ENOCH, b Bridgeport, Conn, June 14, 42; m 65; c 1. ENDOCRINOLOGY, ONCOLOGY. *Educ:* Univ Conn, BA, 65; Univ Kans, PhD(microbiol), 72. *Prof Exp:* Fel, Temple Med Sch, 71-72; fel, Med Sch, Univ Tex, 72-76; asst mem, 76-82, ASSOC MEM, ST JUDE CHILDREN'S RES HOSP, 82- *Concurrent Pos:* Adj asst prof biochem, Ctr Health Sci, Univ Tenn, 77- *Mem:* Tissue Culture Asn; Soc Cell Biol; Sigma Xi; Endocrine Soc. *Res:* Hormone receptor regulation in mammary carcinoma; mechanism of prolactin action; growth and differentiation in mammary glands; glucocorticord receptors in childhood leukemia. *Mailing Add:* Dept Biochem St Jude Children's Res Hosp 332 N Lauderdale Memphis TN 38101

COSTLOW, RICHARD DALE, b Johnstown, Pa, July 19, 25; m 45; c 4. MICROBIOLOGY, BIOCHEMISTRY. *Educ:* Pa State Univ, BS, 49, MS, 52, PhD(bact), 54. *Prof Exp:* Res microbiologist, US Army Biolabs, Ft Detrick, 54-69, chief virus & rickettsia div, 69-71; dir cancer chemother dept, Microbiol Assocs, Inc, 71-75; CHIEF PROG DIR CANCER PREVENTION BR, DIV CANCER CONTROL & REHABILITATION, NAT CANCER INST, 75- *Mem:* Am Soc Microbiol; AAAS; NIH, Sigma Xi; NY Acad Sci. *Res:* Bacterial physiology; enzymology; microbiological chemistry; virology; research administration. *Mailing Add:* Detection Diag & Pretreat NIH Bethesda MD 20014

COSTOFF, ALLEN, b Milwaukee, Wis, Sept 26, 35. ZOOLOGY, ENDOCRINOLOGY. *Educ:* Marquette Univ, BS, 57, MS, 59; Univ Wis-Madison, PhD(zool, biochem), 69. *Prof Exp:* Res technician life sci, Marquette Univ, 59-60; head biol res, Aldrich Chem Co, 60-61; teaching asst zool, Univ Wis-Madison, 61-63, NIH-NSF res asst, 63-65, NIH-Ford Found trainee, 65-69, trainee reproductive physiol, 69-70; instr, 70-73, asst prof endocrinol, 73-77, ASSOC PROF ENDOCRINOL, MED COL GA, 77- *Mem:* AAAS; Endocrine Soc; Am Asn Anatomists; Am Soc Cell Biol; Sigma Xi. *Res:* Ultrastructure of anterior pituitary gland; fractionation and bioassay of pituitary secretory granules; hypothalamo-pituitary-ovarian axis in aging; morphometry of gonadotropes and mammotropes in rat adenohypophyses; experimentally produced and natural occurring tumors in rats; control of gonadotropins. *Mailing Add:* Dept of Endocrinol Med Col of Ga Augusta GA 30902

COSTON, TULLOS OSWELL, b Dixie, La, Sept 17, 05; m 30; c 3. OPHTHALMOLOGY. *Educ:* Univ Tex, AB, 26; Johns Hopkins Univ, MD, 30; Am Bd Ophthal, dipl, 39. *Prof Exp:* Intern med, Johns Hopkins Hosp, 30-31, resident ophthal, 31-35, mem fac, Sch Med, Johns Hopkins Univ, 35-36; clin prof, 54-70, PROF OPHTHAL, HEALTH SCI CTR, UNIV OKLA, 70-, CHMN DEPT, 62-, SR CONSULT, MCGEE EYE INST, 80- *Mem:* Am Soc Prev Blindness; Am Ophthal Soc; Am Acad Ophthal & Otolaryngol; Int Eye Found. *Mailing Add:* 608 Stanton L Young Blvd Oklahoma City OK 73104

COSTRELL, LOUIS, b Bangor, Maine, June 26, 15; m 42; c 3. NUCLEAR PHYSICS, NUCLEAR SCIENCE. *Educ:* Univ Maine, BS, 39; Univ Md, MS, 49. *Prof Exp:* Elec designer, Westinghouse Elec Corp, Pa, 40-41; elec engr, Bur Ships, US Dept Navy, 41-46; PHYSICIST, NAT BUR STANDARDS, 46- *Concurrent Pos:* Chmn comt N42 on nuclear instrumentation, Am Nat Standards Inst, 62-; tech adv to US Nat Comt of Int Electrotech Comn, 62- *Honors & Awards:* Outstanding Achievement Award, US Dept Com, 63, Gold Medal Award, 67; Standards Citation, Inst Elec & Electronics Engrs, 73, Harry Diamond Mem Award, 75. *Mem:* Am Phys Soc; fel Inst Elec & Electronics Engrs. *Res:* Nucleonic instrumentation; electronics. *Mailing Add:* Nat Bur of Standards Washington DC 20234

COSULICH, DONNA BERNICE, b Albuquerque, NMex, Dec 2, 18. DRUG METABOLISM. *Educ:* Univ Ariz, BS, 39, MS, 40; Stanford Univ, PhD(org chem), 43. *Prof Exp:* Res chemist, Calco Chem Div, 43-55, RES CHEMIST, LEDERLE LABS, AM CYANAMID CO, 55- *Honors & Awards:* Sr Res Award, Am Cyanamid Co, Geneva, 58; Iota Sigma Pi Res Award, 54. *Mem:* Am Chem Soc. *Res:* Identification of drug metabolites by mass spectrometry; crystal and molecular structures of pharmaceutical compounds by x-ray crystallographic analysis; pteroylglutamic acid and related compounds; proof of structure work by degradation of hemicellulose, echinocystaic acid and antibiotics; pharmaceutical chemistry; synthetic organic chemistry. *Mailing Add:* Lederle Labs Am Cyanamid Co Pearl River NY 10965

COSWAY, HARRY F(RANCIS), b Toledo, Ohio, Jan 24, 32; m 64; c 4. CHEMICAL ENGINEERING. *Educ:* Univ Toledo, BS, 53; Northwestern Univ, MS, 54; Univ Mich, PhD(chem eng), 58. *Prof Exp:* Res scientist, Cent Res Div, Stamford Res Lab, Am Cyanamid Co, 58-62 & Plastics & Resins Div, 62-66; sr chem engr, Polaroid Corp, 66-74; SR RES ENGR, FORMICA CORP, 75- *Mem:* Am Inst Chem Engrs. *Res:* Low temperature vapor-liquid equilibria; distillation and heat transfer; chemical kinetics; rheology; non-Newtonian fluid flow; fluid metering and dispensing systems. *Mailing Add:* Formica Inc 10155 Reading Rd Cincinnati OH 45241

COTA, HAROLD MAURICE, b San Diego, Calif, Apr 16, 36; m 59; c 3. ENVIRONMENTAL & CHEMICAL ENGINEERING. *Educ:* Univ Calif, Berkeley, BS, 59; Northwestern Univ, MS, 61; Univ Okla, PhD(chem eng), 66. *Prof Exp:* Res engr, Lockheed Missiles & Space Co, Calif, 60-62; res asst chem eng, Univ Okla, 62-65; assoc prof enivron eng, 66-73, PROF ENVIRON ENG, CALIF POLYTECH STATE UNIV, SAN LUIS

OBISPO, 73- *Concurrent Pos:* Mem, Cent Coast Region, Calif State Water Qual Control Bd, 70-, chmn, 76-77; consult noise & air pollution control, 77- *Mem:* Air Pollution Control Asn; Am Inst Chem Engrs; Am Indust Hygiene Asn. *Res:* Solid-gas interactions in the atmosphere; heterogeneous catalysis; electrochemistry; thermodynamics; noise control. *Mailing Add:* Dept Environ Eng Calif Polytech State Univ San Luis Obispo CA 93407

COTABISH, HARRY N(ELSON), b Lakewood, Ohio, Apr 20, 16; m 42; c 4. CHEMICAL ENGINEERING, PHYSICAL CHEMISTRY. *Educ:* Case Inst Technol, BS, 38, MS, 39. *Prof Exp:* Chemist, Parker Appliance Co, 38; res dept, Mine Safety Appliances Co, 39-42, res chemist, 42-50, sr chemist & group supvr, 50-53, prin chemist & supvr, 53-57, chief chemist, Tech Prod Div, 57-61, mgr develop & eng, safety prod group, 61-67, assoc dir, Res & Eng Div, 67-81; RETIRED. *Mem:* Am Chem Soc; Am Inst Chem Engrs; Am Indust Hyg Asn. *Res:* Catalytic removal of combustibles in air; handling and mixing of gases; design of cryogenic equipment; development of chemical analysis instrumentation and protective equipment for use in toxic environments. *Mailing Add:* 3007 Sturbridge Ct Allison Park PA 15101

COTANCH, PATRICIA HOLLERAN, b Pittsburgh, Pa, Aug 26, 45; m 71; c 1. NURSING. *Educ:* Univ Pittsburgh, BSN, 69, Med, 74, PhD(higher educ & nursing), 79. *Prof Exp:* Staff nurse, Braddock Hosp, 66-68; instr, Montefiore Hosp, 69-74 & Univ Pittsburgh, 75-76; asst prof, 78, ASSOC PROF NURSING, DUKE UNIV, 79- *Concurrent Pos:* Res proj assoc, Sch Nursing, Duke Univ, 76-79; fac mem, Duke Univ Comprehensive Cancer Ctr, 77-, res consult, 79-; prin investr, Behav Med Sect, Nat Cancer Inst, 80- *Mem:* Soc Behav Med; Oncol Nurses Soc. *Res:* Clinical application of behavioral medicine techniques for symptom management for cancer patients receiving chemotherapy. *Mailing Add:* Sch Nursing Duke Univ Durham NC 27710

COTANCH, STEPHEN ROBERT, b Quincy, Ill, May 7, 47. THEORETICAL NUCLEAR PHYSICS. *Educ:* Ind Univ, BS, 69; Fla State Univ, PhD(theoret physics), 73. *Prof Exp:* Res assoc physics, Univ Pittsburgh, 73-76; asst prof, 76-81, ASSOC PROF PHYSICS, NC STATE UNIV, 81- *Concurrent Pos:* Prin investr, Dept Energy grant; consult, Triangle Univ Nuclear Lab, NC. *Mem:* Am Phys Soc. *Res:* Direct nuclear reaction studies at low and medium energies; investigation of nuclear and meson-nucleus photonuclear processes. *Mailing Add:* Dept Physics NC State Univ Raleigh NC 27650

COTA-ROBLES, EUGENE H, b Nogales, Ariz, July 13, 26; m 57; c 3. MICROBIOLOGY, CYTOLOGY. *Educ:* Univ Ariz, BS, 50; Univ Calif, MA, 54, PhD(microbiol), 56. *Prof Exp:* Instr bact, Univ Calif, Riverside, 56-58, from asst prof to prof microbiol, 58-70, asst dean col letters & sci, 68-69, spec asst to chancellor, 69-70; prof & head dept, Pa State Univ, 70-73; vchancellor acad admin, 73-75, acad vchancellor & dir affirmative action, 75-80, PROF BIOL, UNIV CALIF, SANTA CRUZ, 73- *Concurrent Pos:* USPHS fel, Sabbatsberg Hosp, Stockholm, Sweden, 57-58; fel, Biochem Inst, Univ Uppsala, 63-64; consult, Mex-Am & Puerto Rican predoctoral fel selection comt, Ford Found, 69-71. *Mem:* AAAS; Am Soc Microbiol; Electron Micros Soc Am. *Res:* Biochemical organization of microbial cells; chemical structure of microbial membranes; membrane morphogenesis in lipid containing bacteriophages. *Mailing Add:* 192 Cent Serv Univ of Calif Santa Cruz CA 95064

COTE, LOUIS J, b Detroit, Mich, July 18, 21; m 48; c 4. MATHEMATICAL STATISTICS. *Educ:* Univ Mich, AB, 43, AM, 47; Columbia Univ, PhD(math statist), 54. *Prof Exp:* Asst prof math & statist, Purdue Univ, 54-56; asst prof math, Syracuse Univ, 56-59; ASSOC PROF MATH & STATIST, PURDUE UNIV, 59- *Concurrent Pos:* Consult, Midwest Appl Sci Corp, 61- *Mem:* Am Math Soc; Inst Math Statist; Am Statist Soc; Math Asn Am. *Res:* Sums of random variables; statistical estimation. *Mailing Add:* Dept of Statist Purdue Univ West Lafayette IN 47907

COTE, LUCIEN JOSEPH, b Angers, Que, Jan 4, 28; m 60; c 1. BIOCHEMISTRY, NEUROLOGY. *Educ:* Univ Vt, BS, 51, MD, 54. *Prof Exp:* Physician, Buffalo Gen Hosp, NY, 54-56; resident neurol, Neurol Inst, New York, 58-61; NIH fel, NY State Psychiat Inst, 61-68, asst prof, 68-70, ASSOC PROF NEUROL, MED CTR, COLUMBIA UNIV, 70-, ASSOC PROF REHAB MED, 80- *Mem:* AAAS. *Res:* Clinical neurochemistry. *Mailing Add:* Dept of Neurol Columbia Univ Med Ctr New York NY 10032

COTE, PHILIP NORMAN, b Norwich, Conn, Oct 1, 42; m 67; c 3. ORGANIC CHEMISTRY, DYSTUFF CHEMISTRY. *Educ:* Univ Conn, BA, 64; Univ RI, PhD(chem), 70. *Prof Exp:* Spec instr chem, Univ RI, 70-71; chemist res & develop, Toms River Chem Corp, 72-76; res chemist, 76-78, GROUP LEADER, DISPERSE DYES, SODYECO DIV, MARTIN MARIETTA CHEMS, 78- *Concurrent Pos:* Res assoc, Univ RI, 71-72. *Mem:* Am Chem Soc; Am Asn Textile Chemists & Colorists; Sigma Xi. *Res:* Electronic effects in free radical rearrangement reactions; synthesis of textile dyestuffs and related intermediates. *Mailing Add:* Martin Marietta Chem Sodyeco Div PO Box 33429 Charlotte NC 28233

COTE, RAYMOND-HENRI, immunochemistry, biophysical chemistry, see previous edition

COTE, ROGER ALBERT, b Manchester, NH, Aug 28, 28; m 52; c 5. PATHOLOGY. *Educ:* Assumption Col, Mass, BA, 50; Univ Montreal, MD, 55; Marquette Univ, MS, 64; FRCP(C). *Prof Exp:* Chief immunohemat sect, Vet Admin Hosp, Milwaukee, Wis, 60-61, asst chief lab serv, 61-62, actg chief, 62-63, chief anat path, 63-64, chief lab serv, Boston, 64-69, chief, Boston Area Reference Lab Syst, 67-69; chmn dept, 69-77, PROF PATH, MED SCH, UNIV SHERBROOKE, 69- *Concurrent Pos:* Asst prof, Sch Med, Marquette Univ, 62-64; instr, Sch Med, Harvard Univ, 64-69; asst prof, Sch Med, Tufts Univ, 64-68, assoc prof, 68-69, lectr, Sch Dent Med, 67-69; co-dir, Lab Comput Proj, Boston Vet Admin Hosp, 67-69; mem path & lab med res eval comt, Vet Admin Cent Off, Washington, DC, 67-69; ed-in-chief, Systematized Nomenclature of Med; Can rep sci adv bd, Institut de Recherch

d'Informatique et d'Automatique. *Mem:* Int Acad Path; Am Soc Clin Path; fel Col Am Path; Am Fedn Clin Res; Am Thoracic Soc. *Res:* Pulmonary pathology, emphysema; clinical pathology, methodology; medical nomenclature; computer technology; laboratory medicine. *Mailing Add:* Dept Path Fac Med Univ of Sherbrooke Sherbrooke Can

COTE, WILFRED ARTHUR, JR, b Willimantic, Conn, May 27, 24; m 47; c 5. ELECTRON MICROSCOPY, WOOD SCIENCE. *Educ:* Univ Maine, BS, 49; Duke Univ, MF, 50; State Univ NY Col Forestry, Syracuse, PhD(wood prod eng), 58. *Prof Exp:* Instr wood technol, 50-58, from asst prof to assoc prof wood prod eng, 58-65, dean, Sch Environ & Resource Eng, 76-80, PROF WOOD PROD ENG, STATE UNIV NY COL ENVIRON SCI & FORESTRY, 65-, DIR N C BROWN CTR ULTRASTRUCTURE STUDIES, 70-, DIR, RENEWABLE MAT INST, 80- *Concurrent Pos:* Fulbright res fel, Univ Munich, 59-60; Walker-Ames vis prof, Univ Wash, 66; vis prof, Tech Univ Denmark, 72; guest scholar, Japan Soc Promotion Sci Sponsorship, Kyoto Univ, 78. *Mem:* Electron Micros Soc Am; Soc Wood Sci & Technol; fel Int Acad Wood Sci; Int Asn Wood Anat (secy, 70-76). *Res:* Ultrastructure of the cells of wood as revealed by light and electron microscopy; interaction of wood ultrastructure with adhesives, coatings and processing chemicals. *Mailing Add:* 207 Brookford Rd Syracuse NY 13224

COTELLESSA, ROBERT F(RANCIS), b Passaic, NJ, June 7, 23; m 48; c 3. ELECTRICAL ENGINEERING. *Educ:* Stevens Inst Technol, ME, 44, MS, 49; Columbia Univ, PhD(physics), 62. *Prof Exp:* Instr math, Stevens Inst Technol, 46-48; intermediate engr, Allen B DuMont Labs, Inc, 49-51; tech coordr elec eng, Sch Eng & Sci, NY Univ, 51-55, from asst prof to assoc prof, 55-62, prof elec eng & dir lab electrosci res, 62-68; prof elec eng & chmn dept, Sch Eng, Clarkson Col Technol, 68-80; PROVOST & PROF ELEC ENG & COMPUT SCI, STEVENS INST TECHNOL, 80- *Concurrent Pos:* Consult, Radio Corp Am, 56, US Naval Appl Sci Lab, 63-69, Naval Ship Res & Develop Lab, 69- & Sprague Elec Co, 64-65. *Mem:* Fel AAAS; Electrochem Soc; Am Soc Eng Educ; Am Phys Soc; fel Inst Elec & Electronics Engrs. *Res:* Solid state electronics; low temperature physics; physics of thin films. *Mailing Add:* Dept of Elec Eng Clarkson Col of Technol Potsdam NY 13706

COTERA, AUGUSTUS S, JR, b Houston, Tex, Jan 2, 31; m 55; c 2. GEOLOGY. *Educ:* Univ Tex, BS, 52, MA, 56, PhD(geol), 62. *Prof Exp:* Res geologist, Tex Pac Coal & Oil Co, 52 & 54; explor geologist, Carter Oil Co, 56-57; from asst prof to assoc prof geol, Allegheny Col, 61-67; assoc prof, 67-70, vpres acad affairs, 80, asst to pres, 81, PROF GEOL, NORTHERN ARIZ UNIV, 70-, CHMN DEPT, 68-, CHMN FAC, 79- *Concurrent Pos:* NSF res grant, 64-68; NSF cause grant, 79-82. *Mem:* Geol Soc Am; Soc Econ Paleont & Mineral. *Res:* Sedimentary petrology, paleogeography and environments of deposition during the Mississippian, Pennsylvanian and Cretaceous Periods; eolian deposition on Navajo Reservation; field mapping in Sonora, Mexico. *Mailing Add:* Off Pres Northern Ariz Univ Flagstaff AZ 86011

COTHERN, CHARLES RICHARD, b Indianapolis, Ind, Sept 6, 37; m 76; c 2. ENVIRONMENTAL PHYSICS. *Educ:* Miami Univ, BA, 59; Yale Univ, MS, 60; Univ Man, PhD(physics), 65. *Prof Exp:* Lectr physics, Univ Man, 61-65; asst prof, 65-70, assoc prof physics, Univ Dayton, 70-78; PHYSICIST, ENVIRON PROTECTION AGENCY, 78- *Mem:* Am Asn Physics Teachers; Am Phys Soc; AAAS; Inst Environ Sci; Sigma Xi (pres, 75-76). *Res:* Health physics; low energy nuclear spectroscopy; environmental physics-heavy metals in air, water and sludge; surface physics-photoelectron and Auger spectroscopies. *Mailing Add:* 1705 N Stafford St Arlington VA 22207

COTHRAN, WARREN RODERIC, insect ecology, see previous edition

COTMAN, CARL WAYNE, b Cleveland, Ohio, Apr 5, 40; m ; c 4. BIOCHEMISTRY, CELL BIOLOGY. *Educ:* Wooster Col, BA, 62; Wesleyan Univ, MA, 64; Ind Univ, PhD(biochem), 68. *Prof Exp:* From asst prof to assoc prof, 68-74, PROF PSYCHOBIOL, UNIV CALIF, IRVINE, 74-, PROF NEUROCHEM & MOLECULAR PSYCHOL, 80- *Concurrent Pos:* Mem, Neurol Bd Study Sect, NIH, 72-77; prin investr, Nat Inst Neurol & Commun Dis & Stroke, 75, NIMH, 75 & Nat Inst Aging, 77; res sci grant, Nat Inst Drug Abuse, 76. *Mem:* AAAS; Am Soc Neurochem; Soc Neurosci; Am Soc Cell Biol. *Res:* Chemistry of the nervous system; formation and long-term modification of synaptic connections in the central nervous system; recovery after brain damage. *Mailing Add:* Dept of Psychobiol Univ of Calif Irvine CA 92717

COTRAN, RAMZI S, b Haifa, Palestine, Dec 7, 32; m 56; c 4. MEDICINE, PATHOLOGY. *Educ:* Am Univ Beirut, BA, 52, MD, 56; Am Bd Path, dipl. *Prof Exp:* From intern to chief resident path, Mallory Inst, Boston, 56-59; from instr to assoc prof, 60-72, FRANK B MALLORY PROF PATH, HARVARD MED SCH, 72-; PATHOLOGIST-IN-CHIEF, BRIGHAM & WOMEN'S HOSP, 74- *Concurrent Pos:* Fel, Mem Ctr Cancer & Allied Dis, NY, 59-60; vis res fel, Sloan-Kettering Inst Cancer Res, 59-60; assoc dir, Mallory Inst Path, 69-74; mem coun circ & renal sect, Am Heart Asn. *Mem:* Am Asn Path & Bact; Am Soc Nephrol; Am Soc Cell Biologists; Int Acad Path; Am Soc Exp Path. *Res:* Pathology and pathogenesis of renal disease; electron microscopy; pathogenesis of inflammation; endothelial injury. *Mailing Add:* Brigham & Women's Hosp 75 Francis St Boston MA 02115

COTRUFO, COSIMO (GUS), b New York, NY, May 7, 24; m 56; c 5. PLANT PHYSIOLOGY. *Educ:* Univ Mo, BS, 52, MS, 53, PhD(bot), 58. *Prof Exp:* Asst prof hort, NDak State Univ, 57-61; RES PLANT PHYSIOLOGIST, SOUTHEASTERN FOREST EXP STA, US FOREST SERV, 61- *Mem:* Am Soc Hort Sci; Am Hort Soc; Am Soc Plant Physiol. *Res:* Physiology of forest trees; hardwoods. *Mailing Add:* Southeastern Forest Exp Sta US Forest Serv PO Box 12254 Research Triangle Park NC 27709

COTRUVO, JOSEPH ALFRED, b Toledo, Ohio, Aug 3, 42. ORGANIC CHEMISTRY. *Educ:* Toledo Univ, BS, 63; Ohio State Univ, PhD(chem), 68. *Prof Exp:* Chemist, Chemsampco, Inc, 70-73; tech policy analyst, US Environ Protection Agency, 73-75, SCI ADV, WATER SUPPLY OFF, US ENVIRON PROTECTION AGENCY, 75-, DIR, CRITERIA & STANDARDS DIV, OFF DRINKING WATER, 76- *Concurrent Pos:* Prof lectr, Prince Georges Community Col, 74-75; adj prof, Dept Chem, George Washington Univ, 81; dir drinking water pilot proj, Comt Challenges Mod Soc, NATO, 77-81. *Mem:* Am Chem Soc; Am Water Works Asn. *Res:* Synthesis and application of insect sex attractants; heterocyclic chemistry; diazo compounds and electronic properties of carbenes; chemical products of chlorine and ozone disinfection of drinking water and waste water. *Mailing Add:* 5015 46th St NW Washington DC 20016

COTSONAS, NICHOLAS JOHN, JR, b Boston, Mass, Jan 28, 19; m 70; c 3. MEDICINE. *Educ:* Harvard Col, AB, 40; Georgetown Univ, MD, 43. *Prof Exp:* Rotating intern, Gallinger Munic Hosp, Washington, DC, 44; res clin dir, Tuberc Div, 46-47, asst med res, Med Div, 47-48, chief med res, 48-49, chief med officer, 51-53; from instr to prof, 49-70, PROF MED & DEAN, PEORIA SCH MED, UNIV ILL COL MED, 70- *Concurrent Pos:* Chief med serv, Res & Educ Hosp, Univ Ill Med Ctr, 68-70; fel coun clin cardiol, Am Heart Asn. *Mem:* AMA; fel Am Col Cardiol; Am Fedn Clin Res. *Res:* Internal medicine; cardiology; medical education. *Mailing Add:* Peoria Sch of Med Univ of Ill Col of Med Peoria IL 61606

COTT, JERRY MASON, b San Antonio, Tex, Oct 16, 46; m 73; c 3. PSYCHOPHARMACOLOGY, NEUROPHARMACOLOGY. *Educ:* Cent State Univ, BS, 69; Univ NC, Chapel Hill, PhD(pharmacol), 75. *Prof Exp:* Lectr pharmacol, Univ Ibadan, 76-78; res scientist psychopharmacol, Astra Lakemedel Ab, 78-80; REV PHARMACOLOGIST, NEUROPHARMACOL DIV, FOOD & DRUG ADMIN, ROCKVILLE, MD, 80- *Concurrent Pos:* Guest worker, Psychobiol Sect, NIMH, Bethesda, Md, 81- *Mem:* Soc Neurosci; Brit Brain Res Asn; Europ Brain & Behav Soc; AAAS; WAfrican Soc Pharmacol. *Res:* Role of brain monoamines and peptides in the mediation of behaviors which may be correlated with human mental disease and movement disorders; mechanism of action of neuroleptics, antidepressants and anxiolytics. *Mailing Add:* Neuropharmacol Div Food & Drug Admin 5600 Fishers Lane Rockville MD 20857

COTTAM, GENE LARRY, b Coffeyville, Kans, Nov 3, 40; m 63; c 3. BIOCHEMISTRY. *Educ:* Univ Kans, BA, 62; Univ Mich, MS, 63 & 65, PhD(biochem), 67. *Prof Exp:* USPHS trainee biochem, Univ Tex & Vet Admin Hosp, Dallas, 67-68; ASSOC PROF BIOCHEM, UNIV TEX HEALTH SCI CTR DALLAS, 68- *Mem:* Am Biochem Soc; Am Chem Soc. *Res:* Elucidation of mechanism of chemical reactions catalyzed by enzymes; active sites; metabolic control. *Mailing Add:* Dept of Biochem Univ of Tex Health Sci Ctr Dallas TX 75235

COTTAM, GRANT, b Sandy, Utah, Aug 26, 18; m 42; c 5. ECOLOGY, ACADEMIC ADMINISTRATION. *Educ:* Univ Utah, BA, 39; Univ Wis, PhD(bot), 48. *Prof Exp:* Teacher high sch, Utah, 39-40; asst prof bot, Univ Hawaii, 48-49; from asst prof to assoc prof, 49-60, chmn dept, 70-73, chmn instrnl prog, Inst Environ Studies, 74-78, PROF BOT, UNIV WISMADISON, 60-, CHMN DEPT, 79- *Concurrent Pos:* Guggenheim fel, 54-55. *Mem:* AAAS; Ecol Soc Am; Brit Ecol Soc; Inst Ecol. *Res:* Methods of phytosociology; forest phytosociology; interdisciplinary environmental research. *Mailing Add:* Dept of Bot Birge Hall Univ of Wis Madison WI 53706

COTTELL, PHILIP L, b Ladysmith, BC, June 21, 41; m 65; c 2. FOREST HARVESTING, ERGONOMICS. *Educ:* Univ BC, BSF, 66, MF, 67; Yale Univ, PhD(forestry), 72. *Prof Exp:* Assoc res forester, Pulp & Paper Res Inst Can, Montreal, 67-79, res forester, Vancouver, 72-74; res dir, Forest Eng Res Inst Can, 75-77; assoc prof, Fac Forestry, Univ BC, 77-80; DIR WOOD HARVESTING RES, MACMILLAN BLOEDEL LTD, 80- *Concurrent Pos:* Adj assoc prof, Fac Forestry, Univ BC, 80- *Mem:* Can Inst Forestry. *Res:* Analysis of factors influencing productivity and economics of forest harvesting operations, particulary man-machine interactions. *Mailing Add:* 3971 W 33 Ave Vancouver BC V6N 2H7 Can

COTTEN, GEORGE RICHARD, b Warsaw, Poland, Mar 21, 29; US citizen; m 57; c 3. POLYMER CHEMISTRY, PHYSICAL CHEMISTRY. *Educ:* Univ London, BS, 52, PhD(chem), 56. *Prof Exp:* Nat Res Coun Can fel, 56-57; res chemist, Visking Co Div, Union Carbide Corp, 58-60 & Fibers Div, Am Cyanamid Co, 60-63; group leader carbon black res dept, 63-69, res assoc, Res & Develop Div, 69-72, SR RES ASSOC, RES & DEVELOP DIV, CABOT CORP, 72- *Mem:* Am Chem Soc; assoc Brit Inst Rubber Indust. *Res:* Reaction kinetics; characterization and viscoelastic properties of polymers; rubber reinforcement; statistics; polymer characterization. *Mailing Add:* Res & Develop Div Cabot Corp Concord Rd Billerica MA 01821

COTTER, DAVID JAMES, b Glens Falls, NY, July 24, 32; m 53; c 3. PLANT ECOLOGY. *Educ:* Univ Ala, BS, 52, AB, 53, MS, 55; Emory Univ, PhD(biol), 58. *Prof Exp:* Res assoc, Atomic Energy Comn, Emory Univ, 57-58; from asst prof to assoc prof biol, Ala Col, 58-66; PROF BIOL, & CHMN DEPT, GA COL MILLEDGEVILLE, 66- *Concurrent Pos:* Res assoc, Atomic Energy Comn, Emory Univ, 63; consult, Bd Educ & dir, NSF Summer Insts, 63 & 64, Talladega, Shelby & Montgomery Counties, 64 & 65; NSF Undergrad Res Participation, 67, 70, 71, 73, 74, & 75; fel, Inst Radiation Ecol, Savannah River Plant, 65-67; staff biologist, Comn Undergrad Educ Biol Sci, Am Inst Biol Sci; consult, Outdoor Educ Inst, Ga Col, 69- *Mem:* Ecol Soc Am. *Res:* Radiation biology; effects of environmental stress on plant communities. *Mailing Add:* 1652 Pine Valley Rd Milledgeville GA 31061

COTTER, DONALD JAMES, b Providence, RI, Jan 13, 30; m 52; c 3. HORTICULTURE, PLANT PHYSIOLOGY. *Educ:* Univ RI, BS, 52; Cornell Univ, MS, 54, PhD(veg crops), 56. *Prof Exp:* From asst prof to assoc prof hort, Univ Ky, 56-69; PROF HORT, N MEX STATE UNIV, 69- *Mem:* Am Soc Hort Sci; Sigma Xi; Int Soc Hort Sci. *Res:* Physiological and environmental studies on vegetable plants; media for crop culture; water use on urban landscapes. *Mailing Add:* Dept of Hort N Mex State Univ Las Cruces NM 88003

COTTER, DOUGLAS ADRIAN, b Brockport, NY, Aug 15, 43; m 65; c 2. COMPUTER ENGINEERING, ELECTRICAL ENGINEERING. *Educ:* Duke Univ, BSEE, 65; NC State Univ, ME, 67, PhD(elec eng), 70. *Prof Exp:* Elec engr design, Elec Res Lab, 66-70, sr res engr, Biomed Tech Ctr, 70-72, mgr comput syst res & develop, 73-76, mgr instrument develop, Sullivan Sci Park, 76-78, mgr bus develop, Corning Med, 78-80, MGR, MED/SCI RES & DEVELOP PORTFOLIO, CORNING GLASS WORKS, 80- *Concurrent Pos:* Adj asst prof elec eng, NC State Univ, 73-76. *Mem:* Sr mem Inst Elec & Electronics Engrs; Sigma Xi. *Res:* Automatic design systems for digital computers; pattern recognition in medical applications; biomedical instrumentation. *Mailing Add:* Corning Glass Works Medfield Indust Park Medfield MA 02052

COTTER, EDWARD, b Everett, Mass, May 30, 36. SEDIMENTOLOGY. *Educ:* Tufts Univ, BS, 58; Princeton Univ, MA, 61, PhD(geol), 63. *Prof Exp:* Res geologist, Jersey Prod Res Co, Okla, 62-64; asst prof geol, Tufts Univ, 64-65; asst prof, 65-76, ASSOC PROF GEOL, BUCKNELL UNIV, 76- *Mem:* Geol Soc Am; Soc Econ Paleont & Mineral; Int Asn Sedimentol. *Res:* Sedimentary petrology of carbonate and clastic rocks. *Mailing Add:* Dept of Geol & Geog Bucknell Univ Lewisburg PA 17837

COTTER, EDWARD F, b Baltimore, Md, Feb 15, 10; m 45; c 1. INTERNAL MEDICINE. *Educ:* Univ Md, MD, 35. *Prof Exp:* Asst med, 39-40, instr path, 40-42, asst neurol, 40-47, instr, 47-48, asst prof med, 47-53, assoc neurol, 48-58, assoc prof med, 53-77, EMER ASSOC PROF MED, SCH MED, UNIV MD, BALTIMORE CITY, 77- *Concurrent Pos:* Hitchcock fel neurosurg, Sch Med, Univ Md, 40-42; pvt pract, 46-63 & 69-; consult, Vet Admin, 50; dir demyelinating dis clin, Univ Md Hosp, 54-63; chief dept med, Md Gen Hosp, 52-63, dir educ, Dept Med, 63-69. *Mem:* AMA; Am Col Physicians. *Res:* Clinical medicine. *Mailing Add:* 1900 E Northern Pkwy Baltimore MD 21239

COTTER, MARTHA ANN, b Granite City, Ill, Mar 18, 43; m 75. STATISTICAL MECHANICS, LIQUID CRYSTAL THEORY. *Educ:* Southern Ill Univ, Ba, 64; Georgetown Univ, PhD(chem), 69. *Prof Exp:* Assoc chem, Cornell Univ, 69-70, assoc chem physics, Bell Telephone Labs, 70-72; asst prof, 72-78, ASSOC PROF CHEM, RUTGERS UNIV, 78- *Concurrent Pos:* Res fel, Alfred P Sloan Found, 74-78; vis scientist, Bell Telephone Labs, Murray Hill, 75-76. *Res:* Equilibrium statistical mechanics; molecular theory of liquid crystalline and micellar phases; theory of liquids and liquid mixtures. *Mailing Add:* Dept Chem Rutgers Univ New Brunswick NJ 08903

COTTER, MAURICE JOSEPH, b New York, NY, Apr 20, 33. PHYSICS. *Educ:* Fordham Univ, AB, 54, MS, 59, PhD(physics), 62. *Prof Exp:* Mathematician, US Navy Bur Ships, Washington, DC, 54-55; jr res assoc, Brookhaven Nat Lab, 60-62; asst prof, 62-71, assoc prof, 71-79, PROF PHYSICS, QUEENS COL, NY, 79- *Concurrent Pos:* Res assoc, Chem Dept, Brookhaven Nat Lab, 69-; guest scientist, Dept Physics, State Univ NY Stony Brook, 75-76. *Mem:* Am Phys Soc; Sigma Xi. *Res:* Nuclear reactor physics; neutron spectroscopy; application of neutron activation analysis techniques to oil paintings. *Mailing Add:* Dept of Physics Queens Col Flushing NY 11367

COTTER, RICHARD, b Brooklyn, NY, Dec 29, 43; m 69; c 2. BIOCHEMISTRY, CELL PHYSIOLOGY. *Educ:* St Johns Univ, BS, 67, PhD(cell physiol), 74; Adelphi Univ, MS, 69. *Prof Exp:* Biologist virol, State Dept Health, NY, 67; biol res asst biochem & pharmacol, US Army Res Inst Environ Med, 69-71; asst prof, New York Med Col, 76-77; MGR BIOCHEM NUTRIT SECT, PHARMACOL DEPT, BAXTER TRAVENOL LABS, 77- *Concurrent Pos:* Fel, NY Med Col, 74-76. *Mem:* AAAS; Soc Complex Carbohydrates; Am Soc Parenteral & Enteral Nutrit; Am Physiol Soc. *Res:* Biochemistry and nutrition; protein, carbohydrate, lipid and vitamin metabolism; isolation, characterization and physiological role of biological receptors; biochemical aspects of pharmacology and toxicology; development of new assay techniques. *Mailing Add:* Pharmacol Dept 6301 Lincoln Ave Morton Grove IL 60053

COTTER, ROBERT JAMES, b Washington, DC, July 15, 43; c 1. ANALYTICAL CHEMISTRY. *Educ:* Col of Holy Cross, BS, 65; Johns Hopkins Univ, MS, 71, PhD(phys chem), 72. *Prof Exp:* Instr chem, Towson State Col, 72-74; asst prof anal chem, Gettysburg Col, 74-78; MGR MASS SPECTROS, NSF REGIONAL CTR & RES ASSOC PHARMACOL, SCH MED, JOHNS HOPKINS UNIV, 78- *Concurrent Pos:* NASA fel, 65-68, fel, Witco Chem Corp, 68-69; Petrol Res Fund grant, 78; NSF grant, 78, 81. *Mem:* Am Soc Mass Spectrometry; Am Chem Soc. *Res:* Mass spectroscopy; instrumentation and computer design applied to analytical chemistry; ionization methods for nonvolatile, high molecular weight biological compounds. *Mailing Add:* Dept Pharmacol 725 N Wolfe St Baltimore MD 21205

COTTER, ROBERT JAMES, b New Bedford, Mass, Apr 15, 30; m 59; c 3. POLYMER CHEMISTRY, COMPOSITES. *Educ:* Brown Univ, ScB, 51; Mass Inst Technol, PhD(org chem), 54. *Prof Exp:* Chemist, Res Dept, Bakelite Div, 54-56, group leader, Res & Develop Dept, Plastics Div, 56-61, sr group leader, Chem & Plastics Opers Div, 61-71, res assoc, 71-75, CORP RES FEL, UNION CARBIDE CORP, 75- *Mem:* AAAS; Am Chem Soc; Sigma Xi. *Res:* Product and process development; polystyrenes; engineering plastics; polymer additives; organic chemicals; pollution control polymers; exploratory research and development; composite fabrication processes; emerging technologies. *Mailing Add:* Chem & Plastics Union Carbide Corp PO Box 670 Bound Brook NJ 08805

COTTER, SUSAN M, b Evanston, Ill, June 26, 43. VETERINARY MEDICINE. *Educ:* Univ Ill, BS, 64, DVM, 66; Am Col Vet Internal Med, dipl, 76. *Prof Exp:* mem staff internal med, Angell Mem Animal Hosp, 66-81; res assoc oncol, Sch Pub Helath, 75-80, LECTR CANCER BIOL, HARVARD UNIV, 80-; ASSOC PROF MED, TUFTS UNIV SCH VET MED, 81- *Concurrent Pos:* Adj asst prof vet med, Univ Pa, 71- *Honors & Awards:* Woman Vet of Year, Women's Vet Med Asn, 78. *Mem:* Am Vet Med Asn; Vet Cancer Soc; Int Soc Res Leukemia & Related Dis. *Res:* Comparative oncology and hematology, primarily as it concerns feline leukemia virus; studies concerning epidemiology, immunology, and treatment of feline leukemia. *Mailing Add:* 22 Chestnut Place Brookline MA 02146

COTTER, WILLIAM BRYAN, JR, b Hartford, Conn, May 8, 26; m 48; c 6. GENETICS, ANATOMY. *Educ:* Wesleyan Univ, BA, 49, MA, 51; Yale Univ, PhD(zool), 56. *Prof Exp:* Asst prof biol, Col Charleston, 55-56; asst prof, Wesleyan Univ, 56-57; asst prof biol, Col Charleston, 57-59; teaching fel anat, Med Col SC, 59-60; from asst prof to assoc prof, 60-74, actg chmn dept, 63-64, PROF ANAT, MED CTR, UNIV KY, 74- *Mem:* AAAS; Am Soc Human Genetics; Soc Study Evolution; Genetics Soc Am; Am Asn Anat. *Res:* Physiological genetics and evolution; effects of genes on behavior. *Mailing Add:* Dept of Anat Univ of Ky Med Ctr Lexington KY 40506

COTTINGHAM, JAMES GARRY, b Salt Lake City, Utah, June 7, 27; m 46; c 2. ACCELERATOR ENGINEERING, SOLAR ENERGY. *Educ:* Univ Ill, BS, 49. *Prof Exp:* Assoc physicist accelerator develop, Brookhaven Nat Lab, 59- 49-58; sr engr radar, RCA Corp, 58-59; elec engr accelerator develop, 59-76, SR ENGR SOLAR & ACCELERATOR ENG, BROOKHAVEN NAT LAB, 76- *Mem:* Int Solar Energy Soc. *Res:* Development of proton accelerators such as Cosmotron, AGS and ISABELLE; solar heat pump, cooling and heliostat systems. *Mailing Add:* 10 Cedar Ctr Upton NY 11935

COTTLE, MERVA KATHRYN WARREN, b Calgary, Alta, Oct 8, 28; m 50; c 3. PHYSIOLOGY, PHARMACOLOGY. *Educ:* Univ BC, BA, 49, MA, 51; Univ Wash, PhD(physiol), 56. *Prof Exp:* Lectr physiol, Univ Alta, 56-67; Wellcome res fel, Inst Physiol, Agr Res Coun, Cambridge, Eng, 67-68; res assoc & lectr pharmacol, Univ Alta, 69-76, sessional lectr, 76-77, asst prof pharm, 78-81. *Mem:* Can Physiol Soc. *Res:* Histological studies of central nervous system and peripheral nervous system, including afferent and efferent innervation of the heart; fetal maternal physiology. *Mailing Add:* SM R1 Dent Pharm Bldg Univ Alta Edmonton AB T6G 2N8 Can

COTTLE, RICHARD W, b Chicago, Ill, June 29, 34; m 59; c 2. MATHEMATICS, OPERATIONS RESEARCH. *Educ:* Harvard Univ, AB, 57, AM, 58; Univ Calif, Berkeley, PhD(math), 64. *Prof Exp:* Instr math, Middlesex Sch, Mass, 58-60; mem tech staff, Bell Tel Labs, Inc, NJ, 64-66; assoc prof opers res, 69-73, PROF OPERS RES, STANFORD UNIV, 73- *Honors & Awards:* US Sr Scientist Award, Alexander von Humboldt Found. *Mem:* Am Math Soc; Math Asn Am; Inst Mgt Sci; Math Prog Soc; Soc Indust & Appl Math. *Res:* Mathematical programming. *Mailing Add:* Dept of Opers Res Stanford Univ Stanford CA 94305

COTTLE, WALTER HENRY, b Edmonton, June 9, 21; m 50; c 3. PHYSIOLOGY. *Educ:* Univ BC, BA, 49, MA, 51; Univ Wash, Seattle, PhD, 56. *Prof Exp:* Asst prof, 56-60, assoc prof physiol, 60-76, PROF PHYS EDUC, UNIV ALTA, 76- *Mem:* Can Physiol Soc; Can Asn Sport Sci; Am Physiol Soc. *Res:* Thermoregulatory responses to environmental temperature and exercise. *Mailing Add:* Dept of Phys Educ Univ of Alta Edmonton AB T6G 2E1 Can

COTTOM, MELVIN C(LYDE), b Coffeyville, Kans, Oct 11, 24; m 68. ELECTRICAL ENGINEERING. *Educ:* Univ Kans, BSEE, 45, MS, 48. *Prof Exp:* Instr elec eng, Univ Kans, 45-50; elec design engr, Black & Veatch, Consult Engr, Mo, 50-55; ASST PROF ELEC ENG, KANS STATE UNIV, 55- *Mem:* Sr mem Inst Elec & Electronics Engrs. *Res:* Electrical noise generated at the sliding contact; a study of random noise generated at slip ring-carbon brush contacts. *Mailing Add:* Dept of Elec Eng Kans State Univ Manhattan KS 66502

COTTON, FRANK ALBERT, b Philadelphia, Pa, Apr 9, 30; m 59; c 2. CHEMISTRY. *Educ:* Temple Univ, AB, 51; Harvard Univ, PhD(chem), 55. *Hon Degrees:* DSc, Temple Univ, 63; Dr rer nat, Bielefeld Univ, 79; DSc, Columbia Univ, 80; DSc, Northwestern Univ, 81; DSc, Univ de Bordeaux, 81. *Prof Exp:* From instr to prof chem, Mass Inst Technol, 55-69; Dreyfus prof, 69-71, Robert A Welch prof, 72-73, ROBERT A WELCH DISTINGUISHED PROF CHEM, TEX A&M UNIV, 73- *Concurrent Pos:* Guggenheim fel, 56; Alfred P Sloan Found fel, 61-65; vis prof, Nat Univ Buenos Aires, 65, Univ Strasbourg, 75; F P Dwyer Mem lectr & Medallist, Univ New South Wales, 66; lectr, Var US & Foreign Univs, 62-78. *Honors & Awards:* Am Chem Soc Award, 62; Baekeland Medal, 63; William Lloyd Evans Award, Ohio State Univ, 73; Am Chem Soc Award for Distinguished Serv in the Advan of Inorg Chem, 74; Nichols Medal & Harrison Howe Award, Am Chem Soc, 75, Edgar Fahs Smith Award & Linus Pauling Medal, 76, Southwest Regional Award, 77; John G Kirkwood Medal, Yale Univ, 78; Will & Gibbs Medal, Am Chem Soc, 80. *Mem:* Nat Acad Sci; hon mem NY Acad Sci; Am Acad Arts & Sci; Am Chem Soc; hon mem Royal Soc Chem; Am Soc Biol Chemists. *Res:* Application of valence theory and physical and preparative studies to elucidate molecular structures and bonding in inorganic compounds; molecular structure of enzymes and proteins. *Mailing Add:* Dept Chem Tex A&M Univ College Station TX 77843

COTTON, FRANK ETHRIDGE, JR, b Corinth, Miss, Aug 14, 23; m 78; c 3. INDUSTRIAL ENGINEERING, ENGINEERING ECONOMICS. *Educ:* Miss State Univ, BS, 46 & 47; Univ Pittsburgh, MLitt, 51, PhD(econ), 62. *Prof Exp:* Indust engr, Westinghouse Elec Corp, Pa, 47-51; sr engr-economist, int hqs, Gulf Oil Corp, 51-58; dir eng exten serv, 58-68, assoc prof indust eng, 59-62, PROF & HEAD DEPT INDUST ENG, MISS STATE UNIV, 62- *Concurrent Pos:* Consult, indust, NASA & res orgns, 58-; rep dir & bd dirs, Engrs Coun Prof Develop, 73- *Mem:* Fel Am Inst Indust Engrs (vpres, 67-69, pres, 70-71); Am Soc Eng Educ. *Res:* Management systems and controls; economic analysis; technical and management planning. *Mailing Add:* PO Box U Mississippi State MS 39762

COTTON, JOHN EDWARD, b Minneapolis, Minn, Dec 21, 24; m 51; c 7. PHYSICAL CHEMISTRY. *Educ:* San Francisco State Col, AB, 53; Univ Ore, MS, 55, PhD(phys chem), 59. *Prof Exp:* Asst, Univ Ore, 54-57; PHYS CHEMIST, BOEING CO, 59- *Mem:* AAAS; Am Chem Soc. *Res:* Transport properties of gases; polarography; gas chromatography; mass spectroscopy. *Mailing Add:* 2512 102nd Ave NE Bellevue WA 98004

COTTON, ROBERT HENRY, b Newton, Mass, Nov 17, 14; m 48; c 3. FOOD SCIENCE, NUTRITION. *Educ:* Bowdoin Col, BS, 37; Mass Inst Technol, SM, 39; Pa State Univ, PhD(plant nutrit), 44. *Prof Exp:* Chemist, Gen Elec Co, Mass, 39-40; asst plant nutrit, Pa State Univ, 40-43, instr & asst prof human nutrit res, 43-45; dir, Plymouth, Fla Div, Nat Res Corp, 45-47; prof & supvry chemist, Citrus Exp Sta, Univ Fla, 47-48; dir res, Holly Sugar Corp, 48-53; dir res, Huron Milling Co, 54-58; dir res, ITT Continental Baking Co, Inc, Int Tel & Tel Corp, 58-65, vpres, 65-79, chief scientist, Food Group, 74-79; PRES, CONSULFOOD, INC, 81- *Concurrent Pos:* Mem indust adv comt, Sugar Res Found, 48-53 & sci adv comt, Am Inst Baking, 58-; chmn tech liaison comt, Am Bakers Asn-US Dept Agr, 59-77; mem vis comt, Dept Nutrit & Food Sci, Mass Inst Technol, 65-69; mem panel V-3, White House Conf Food, Nutrit & Health, 69; chmn comt cereals & gen prod adv bd mil personnel supplies, Nat Res Coun-Nat Acad Sci, 69-, adv comt nutrit guidelines for foods, 70; dir gen, Found Chile, Santiago, Chile, 75-78; consult nutrit, New Prod Develop & Mgt, 79- *Honors & Awards:* C M Frey Award, Am Asn Cereal Chem, 78; Babcock-Hart Award, Inst Food Technol & Nutrit Found, 79. *Mem:* Fel AAAS; Am Chem Soc; Inst Food Technol; Asn Res Dir (pres, 64-65); Am Asn Cereal Chem (pres, 65-66). *Res:* Plant nutrition; food technology; analytical chemistry; new technics to increase storage life of orange juice powder; cattle nutrition; sugar beet technology; by-product development; application food science to combat malnutrition; cereal science. *Mailing Add:* 570 Hammock Ct Marco FL 33937

COTTON, THERESE MARIE, b Peru, Ill. RAMAN SPECTROSCOPY, ELECTROCHEMISTRY. *Educ:* Bradley Univ, AB, 61; Northwestern Univ, Ill, PhD(chem), 76. *Prof Exp:* Res asst, Northern Regional Lab, USDA, 61-63; res asst, Argonne Nat Lab, 66-71; fel, Northwestern Univ, 76-81; ASST PROF ANAL CHEM, ILL INST TECHNOL, 81- *Concurrent Pos:* Vis asst prof, Northwestern Univ, 81- *Mem:* Am Chem Soc; Am Soc Photobiol; Biophys Soc; Electrochem Soc; Asn Women Sci. *Res:* Electroanalytical methods for the study of electron transfer reactions in biomolecules, especially photosynthetic preparations; application of surface enhanced Raman spectroscopy to proteins adsorbed at electrodes and as a sensitive analytical method for detecting low concentrations of chromophoric species. *Mailing Add:* Dept Chem Ill Inst Technol 3255 S Dearborn St Chicago IL 60616

COTTON, WILLIAM REUBEN, b Little Falls, NY, Oct 27, 40; m; c 2. ATMOSPHERIC SCIENCE, CLOUD PHYSICS. *Educ:* State Univ NY Albany, BS, 64, MS, 66; Pa State Univ, PhD(meteorol), 70. *Prof Exp:* Res asst cloud physics, Atmospheric Sci Res Ctr, State Univ NY, 64-66 & Pa State Univ, 66-70; res meteorologist, Exp Meteorol Lab, Nat Oceanic & Atmospheric Admin, 70-74; asst prof, 75-78, assoc prof, 78-80, PROF ATMOSPHERIC SCI, COLO STATE UNIV, 80- *Mem:* Am Meteorol Soc; Sigma Xi. *Res:* Numerical modeling and observational analysis of the physics and dynamics of cumulus clouds and convective mesoscale systems; modification of convective systems. *Mailing Add:* Dept of Atmospheric Sci Colo State Univ Ft Collins CO 80523

COTTON, WILLIAM ROBERT, b Miami, Fla, Nov 29, 31; m 74; c 4. MICROSCOPIC ANATOMY, ORAL MICROANATOMY. *Educ:* Univ Md, DDS, 55; Northwestern Univ, MS, 63; Roosevelt Univ, MA, 73; George Washington Univ, EdS, 80. *Prof Exp:* Asst dent officer, Naval Training Ctr, Bainbridge, Md & Camp Lejeune, NC, Naval Med Res Inst, 55-57 & Mobilization Team, Miami, Fla, 57-58, asst dent officer & clin supvr, Dent Detachment, Marine Corps Sch, Quantico, Va, 58-59, postgrad officer, Naval Dent Sch, Bethesda, Md, 59-60, asst dent officer, USS F D Roosevelt (CVA-42), Mayport, Fla, 60-61, head exp path div, Dent Res Dept, Naval Med Res Inst, Nat Naval Med Ctr, 63-67, dent officer, USS Fulton (AS-11), New London, Conn, 67-69, chief histopath div, Naval Dent Res Inst, Great Lakes, Ill, 69-76, exec officer, 72-73, dep cmndg officer, 73-76, chmn, Dent Sci Dept, 76-79, dir, Casualty Care Res Prog Ctr, 79-81; ASSOC PROF & DIR RES, DEPT OPER DENT, TEMPLE UNIV, 81- *Concurrent Pos:* Mem sect, Working Group Five, Comn on Mat, Instruments, Equipment & Therapeut, Int Dent Fedn, 74-, consult, Intercomn Group Uniform Definition of Dent Terms, 77-; mem adv comt, Dent Lab Technol Prog, Sch Tech Careers, Southern Ill Univ, Carbondale, 75-; ed rev, Scanning Electron Micros, 75-; lectr microbiol, Nat Naval Dent Ctr, 76-81; res assoc, Nat Res Coun, 77-81; ed rev, J Dent Res, 76- *Mem:* NY Acad Sci; Soc Exp Biol & Med; Am Dent Asn; Int Asn Dent Res; Am Asn Dent Res. *Res:* Biological and toxicity testing of dental materials in animals and human clinical trials; bone resorption research introduced osteopetrotic (tl) rat which has deficient bone resorption; dental caries research. *Mailing Add:* Oper Dent Dept Temple Univ Sch Dent 3223 N Broad St Philadelphia PA 19140

COTTON, WYATT DANIEL, b Mexia, Tex, Feb 2, 43; m 68; c 3. ORGANIC CHEMISTRY, FOOD PRODUCT DEVELOPMENT. *Educ:* Calif State Univ, Los Angeles, BS, 69; Univ Calif, Los Angeles, PhD(org chem), 74. *Prof Exp:* res chemist phys & synthetic org chem, 74-77, TECH BRAND MGR, FOOD PROD DEVELOP, PROCTER & GAMBLE CO, 77- *Mem:* Am Chem Soc. *Res:* Amino acid synthesis; sultone chemistry; synthetic sweeteners; fats and oil chemistry; food science. *Mailing Add:* Procter & Gamble Co 6071 Center Hill Rd Cincinnati OH 45239

COTTONY, HERMAN VLADIMIR, b Nizhni-Novgorod, Russia, Mar 27, 09; nat US; m 40; c 2. ELECTRICAL ENGINEERING. *Educ:* Cooper Union, BS, 32, EE, 46; Columbia Univ, MS, 33. *Prof Exp:* Res engr, Sonotone Corp, 35-37; physicist, Nat Bur Standards, 37-41, electronic engr & chief antenna res sect, 46-65; prog leader antennas, Environ Sci Serv Admin, 65-70; consult, Off Telecommun, Inst Telecommun Sci, 70-73; CONSULT ENGR, 73- *Concurrent Pos:* Mem, Comns A and B, US Nat Comt, Int Union Radio Sci; ed, Trans Antennas & Propagation, 62-65. *Mem:* Fel Inst Elec & Electronics Engrs; Am Phys Soc; AAAS. *Res:* Antennas; measurement of electromagnetic fields; radio wave propagation; antenna data processing; radar; systems engineering. *Mailing Add:* 5204 Wilson Lane Bethesda MD 20814

COTTRELL, IAN WILLIAM, b York, Eng, June 18, 43; m 69. CARBOHYDRATE CHEMISTRY. *Educ:* Univ Edinburgh, BSc, 65, PhD(polysaccharide chem), 68. *Prof Exp:* Fel carbohydrate chem, Trent Univ, 68-70; res chem guar gum, Stein Hall & Co, Celanese Corp, 70-72; sr res chemist, Kelco Co, Merck, Inc, 72-73, sect head, 73-75; asst res dir, Kelco Div, 76-79, DIR, BASIC RES & DEVELOP, MERCK & CO, INC, 79- *Mem:* Am Chem Soc; AAAS; Brit Biophys Soc. *Res:* Preparation of industrially useful polymers with special emphasis on polysaccharides. *Mailing Add:* 713 San Mario Dr Solana Beach CA 92075

COTTRELL, ROGER LESLIE ANDERTON, b Birmingham, Eng, Jan 20, 40; m 67; c 2. HIGH ENERGY PHYSICS, COMPUTING. *Educ:* Manchester Univ, Eng, BSc, 62, PhD(nuclear physics), 67. *Prof Exp:* Asst lectr physics, Manchester Univ, Eng, 65-66, res asst nuclear physics, 66-67; STAFF MEM, STANFORD LINEAR ACCELERATOR CTR, STANFORD UNIV, 67- *Concurrent Pos:* Vis scientist, Europ Orgn Nuclear Res, Switz, 72-73; mem software working group, Nuclear Instrumentation Module-Computer-Aided Measurement & Control, AEC, 72-74; vis scientist, IBM UK Kingdom Labs, Ltd, Hursley, 79-80. *Mem:* Brit Comput Soc. *Mailing Add:* Stanford Linear Accelerator Ctr PO Box 4349 Stanford CA 94305

COTTRELL, THOMAS S, b Chicago, Ill, Feb 2, 34; m 59; c 3. PATHOLOGY. *Educ:* Brown Univ, AB, 55; Columbia Univ, MD, 65. *Prof Exp:* Fel path, Columbia Univ-Presby Hosp, 65-68, instr, Columbia Univ, 68-69; assoc prof path, New York Med Col, 68-79; ASSOC PROF PATH & ASSOC DEAN, SCH MED, STATE UNIV NY STONY BROOK, 79- *Concurrent Pos:* Asst vis pathologist, Metrop Hosp, NY, 68-; Markle scholar acad med, 69-74; assoc attend physician, West County Med Ctr Hosp, 78-79. *Mem:* Fel NY Acad Med; NY Acad Sci; AAAS. *Res:* Ultrastructural correlation of normal and abnormal cardio-respiratory physiology. *Mailing Add:* Sch Med State Univ NY Stony Brook NY 11794

COTTRELL, WILLIAM BARBER, b Brooklyn, NY, Apr 17, 24; m 44; c 5. NUCLEAR ENGINEERING. *Educ:* Alfred Univ, BA, 43. *Prof Exp:* Res engr calutrons, Tenn Eastman Corp, 44-46; res engr guided missiles, Glenn L Martin Co, Md, 46-47; SR DEVELOP ENGR, UNION CARBIDE NUCLEAR, TENN, 47- *Concurrent Pos:* Mem First Utility Dist Knox County, 56-65, pres, 65-77; dir, Nuclear Opers Anal Ctr. *Mem:* Fel Am Nuclear Soc. *Res:* Nuclear power reactor safety; fission product behavior; containment; core cooling. *Mailing Add:* 10433 Grovedale Dr Knoxville TN 37922

COTTS, ARTHUR C(LEMENT), b Kansas City, Mo, July 27, 22; m 51; c 2. ELECTRICAL ENGINEERING. *Educ:* Kans State Univ, BS, 49, MS, 50. *Prof Exp:* Sr instr radio & TV, Cent Radio & TV Sch, Mo, 46; asst appl mech, Kans State Univ, 49, asst elec eng, 49-50; engr, Eng Mech Div, Midwest Res Inst, 50-51; engr, Appl Physics Lab, Johns Hopkins Univ, 51-55; res engr & head analog comput appln group, Midwest Res Inst, 55-57; proj supvr, Polaris Submarine Navig, Appl Physics Lab, 57-71, MEM PRIN PROF STAFF, APPL PHYSICS LAB & PROG SUPVR, POLARIS SUBMARINE PATROL ANAL, JOHNS HOPKINS UNIV, 71- *Concurrent Pos:* Lectr, Cath Univ Am, 51-53. *Mem:* AAAS; Sigma Xi; sr mem Inst Elec & Electronics Engrs. *Res:* Operation of reflex klystron oscillators; control systems; inertial navigation; system analysis and evaluation. *Mailing Add:* Appl Physics Lab Johns Hopkins Univ Baltimore MD 21205

COTTS, DAVID BRYAN, b Washington, DC, July 26, 54; m 80. POLYMER PHYSICS, LIGHT SCATTERING. *Educ:* Eckerd Col, BS, 75; Carnegie-Mellon Univ, PhD(chem), 79. *Prof Exp:* Polymer chemist, SRI Int, 79- *Mem:* AAAS; Am Chem Soc. *Res:* Polymer physical chemistry, molecular characterization, morphology, rheology; conducting polymers; application of light scattering techniques to the study of solids and liquids. *Mailing Add:* SRI Int 333 Ravenswood Ave Menlo Park CA 94025

COTTS, PATRICIA METZGER, b New York, NY, Sept 14, 53; m 79. LIGHT-SCATTERING, HIGH TEMPERATURE POLYMERS. *Educ:* Col William & Mary, BS, 75; Carnegie-Mellon Univ, PhD(chem), 79. *Prof Exp:* Fel, 80-81, RES STAFF MEM, IBM RES LAB, 81- *Mem:* Am Chem Soc; Am Phys Soc. *Res:* Structure/property relations in polymers with emphasis on new high performance polymers and characterization of these with light scattering techniques. *Mailing Add:* IBM Res Lab K42-282 5600 Cottle Rd San Jose CA 91593

COTTS, ROBERT MILO, b Green Bay, Wis, Aug 22, 27; m 50; c 4. NUCLEAR MAGNETIC RESONANCE. *Educ:* Univ Wis, BS, 50; Univ Calif, PhD(physics), 54. *Prof Exp:* Instr physics, Stanford Univ, 54-57; from asst prof to assoc prof, 57-67, PROF PHYSICS, CORNELL UNIV, 67- *Concurrent Pos:* Physicist, Nat Bur Standards, 63-64; vis prof physics, Univ BC, 70-71 & Univ Warwick, UK, 78. *Mem:* Am Phys Soc; Am Asn Physics Teachers. *Res:* Solid state physics. *Mailing Add:* Clark Hall Cornell Univ Ithaca NY 14853

COTTY, VAL FRANCIS, b New York, NY, July 11, 26; m 51; c 3. PHARMACOLOGY, TOXICOLOGY. *Educ:* St John's Col, BS, 48, MSc, 50; NY Univ, PhD(biol), 55. *Prof Exp:* From instr to asst prof biol, St John's Col, 50-55; staff mem, Boyce Thompson Inst, 55-57; head dept biochem, 57-70, DIR BIOL RES, BRISTOL-MYERS CO, 70- *Concurrent Pos:* Res assoc, Sch Med, NY Univ, 61-65. *Mem:* NY Acad Sci; Am Chem Soc; Am Soc Microbiol; Int Asn Dent Res; Soc Toxicol. *Res:* Pharmacology and toxicology of drugs. *Mailing Add:* 236 Avon Rd Westfield NJ 07090

COTY, UGO A, b Boston, Mass, June 28, 24; m 46; c 4. AERODYNAMICS. *Educ:* Ind Inst Technol, BS, 49; Univ Mich, BSE, 50, MSE, 51. *Prof Exp:* Res assoc electronic comput air defense systs, Univ Mich, 51-53; res engr missiles, Calif Div, Lockheed Aircraft Corp, 53-55, asst proj engr, X-17, Missile Systs Div, 55-57, mgr polaris missile, 57-59, div mgr design support systs, 59-61; asst to plant mgr, Azusa Plant, Aerojet Gen Corp, 61-63, div mgr aerospace vehicles, 63-64, mgr mfg aerospace prods, 64-65, asst works mgr, 65; sr res & develop engr, Aircraft & Rotary Wing, 65-67, DEPT ENGR RES & DEVELOP, LOCKHEED-CALIF CO, LOCKHEED AIRCRAFT CORP, 67- *Concurrent Pos:* Mem, US Naval Inst. *Mem:* Assoc fel Am Inst Aeronaut & Astronaut; Am Helicopter Soc. *Res:* Research and development planning; long range planning; helicopter dynamics and control; hydraulics system contaminants; automatic reduction of wind tunnel data in real time. *Mailing Add:* 6831 N Calder Dr Glendora CA 91740

COTY, VERNON FRANK, b St Paul, Minn, Sept 18, 22; m 48; c 6. MICROBIOLOGY. *Educ:* St Thomas Col, BS, 48; Marquette Univ, MS, 50; Purdue Univ, PhD(bact), 54. *Prof Exp:* Teaching asst biol, Marquette Univ, 48-50; teaching asst bact, Purdue Univ, 51-52, res fel, 50-51, 52-53; sr res technologist, Socony Mobil Oil Co, 53-68, RES ASSOC, MOBIL OIL RES & DEVELOP CORP, 68- *Mem:* Am Soc Microbiol; Sigma Xi. *Res:* Physiological studies of streptomyces griseus; microbiology related to petroleum industry; environmental pollution control. *Mailing Add:* Mobil Oil Res & Develop Corp Billingsport Rd Paulsboro NJ 08066

COTY, WILLIAM ALLEN, b Los Angeles, Calif, Apr 10, 48; m 65; c 3. BIOCHEMISTRY, ENDOCRINOLOGY. *Educ:* Calif Inst Technol, BS, 69; Sch Med, Johns Hopkins Univ, PhD(biochem), 74. *Prof Exp:* Fel biochem endocrinol, Col Med, Baylor Univ, 74-76; ASST PROF BIOCHEM, SCH MED, UNIV CALIF, LOS ANGELES, 77- *Concurrent Pos:* Fel, Nat Inst Arthritis, Metab & Digestive Dis, 74-76. *Mem:* Am Soc Biol Chemists; Endocrine Soc. *Res:* Mechanism of steroid hormone action; mechanism and regulation of calcium transport. *Mailing Add:* Dept of Biol Chem Sch of Med Univ of Calif Los Angeles CA 90024

COUCH, EARL J, b Grand Prairie, Tex, Nov 12, 24; m 69. CHEMICAL ENGINEERING. *Educ:* Univ Tex, BS, 50, MS, 52, PhD(chem eng), 56. *Prof Exp:* RES ASSOC, MOBIL RES & DEVELOP CORP, 56- *Mem:* Am Inst Chem Engrs; Sigma Xi; Am Inst Mining, Metall & Petrol Engrs. *Res:* Oil recovery methods, especially in situ combustion and other thermal recovery processes; reservoir simulation; reservoir engineering. *Mailing Add:* Mobil Res & Develop Corp PO Box 900 Dallas TX 75221

COUCH, HOUSTON BROWN, b Estill Springs, Tenn, July 1, 24; m 45; c 3. PLANT PATHOLOGY. *Educ:* Tenn Polytech Inst, BS, 50; Univ Calif, PhD(plant path), 54. *Prof Exp:* From asst prof to assoc prof plant path, Pa State Univ, 54-65; head dept, 65-80, PROF PLANT PHYSIOL & PATH, VA POLYTECH INST & STATE UNIV, 65- *Mem:* Am Phytopath Soc; Am Agron Soc; Soil Sci Soc Am; Crop Sci Soc Am. *Res:* Diseases of turfgrasses and forage crops; physiology of parasitism; role of physical environment in plant disease development. *Mailing Add:* Dept of Plant Physiol & Path Va Polytech Inst & State Univ Blacksburg VA 24061

COUCH, JACK GARY, b Pocatello, Idaho, Apr 5, 36; m 55; c 5. NUCLEAR PHYSICS. *Educ:* Utah State Univ, BS, 58; Vanderbilt Univ, MS, 59; Tex A&M Univ, PhD(physics), 66. *Prof Exp:* Chmn dept phys sci, Church Col Hawaii, 59-61; asst prof physics, Wash State Univ, 66-67; assoc prof, 67-80, chmn dept, 67-74, PROF PHYSICS, SOUTHERN ORE STATE COL, 80- *Mem:* Am Asn Physics Teachers; Am Phys Soc. *Res:* Neutron transfer between heavy ions; neutron scattering by metal hydride systems; bose condensate in liquid helium; molecular infrared spectroscopy; physics education. *Mailing Add:* Dept of Physics Southern Ore State Col Ashland OR 97520

COUCH, JAMES RUSSELL, b Grandview, Tex, June 10, 09; m 34; c 4 BIOCHEMISTRY, NUTRITION. BIOCHEMISTRY, NUTRITION. *Educ:* Agr & Mech Col Tex, BS, 31, MS, 34; Univ Wis, PhD(biochem), 48. *Prof Exp:* From asst poultry husbandman to poultry husbandman, Exp Sta, Univ Tex, 31-41; prof, 48-74, EMER PROF BIOCHEM & POULTRY SCI, TEX A&M UNIV, 74- *Honors & Awards:* Am Feed Mfrs Award, Poultry Sci Asn, 51. *Mem:* AAAS; fel Poultry Sci Asn; Am Inst Nutrit; Fedn Am Socs Exp Biol; Am Soc Biol Chem. *Res:* Poultry nutrition; embryology; physiology; nutritional significance and metabolic functions of vitamins and trace elements in the domestic fowl; vitamin B12; folic acid; antibiotics; unidentified growth factors; trace elements; proteins and amino acids; fats and fatty acids. *Mailing Add:* Dept of Poultry Sci Tex A&M Univ College Station TX 77841

COUCH, JAMES RUSSELL, JR, b Bryan, Tex, Oct 25, 39; m 64; c 1. NEUROLOGY, NEUROPHARMACOLOGY. *Educ:* Tex A&M Univ, BS, 61; Baylor Col Med, MD, 65, PhD(physiol), 66. *Prof Exp:* Nat Heart Inst fel, Baylor Col Med, 65-66; NIH staff fel, Lab Neuropharmacol, NIMH, 67-69; Nat Inst Neurol Dis & Stroke spec trainee, Washington Univ, 69-72; asst prof, 72-76, assoc prof neurol, Univ Kans Med Ctr, 76-79; PROF & CHIEF, DIV NEUROL, SOUTHERN ILL UNIV SCH MED, SPRINGFIELD, ILL, 79- *Concurrent Pos:* Consult, Kansas City Vet Admin Hosp & Kansas City Gen Hosp, Kans; attending staff, Mem Med Ctr, St John's Hosp, Springfield, Ill & Lincoln Develop Ctr, Lincoln, Ill, 79- *Mem:* Fel Am Acad Neurol; Soc Neurosci; Am Geriatrics Soc. *Res:* Neuropharmacology and neurotransmitters; movement disorders; headache; stroke. *Mailing Add:* Sch Med Southern Ill Univ PO Box 3926 Springfield IL 62708

COUCH, JOHN ALEXANDER, b Washington, DC, Feb 12, 38; m 63; c 2. PATHOBIOLOGY, PROTOZOOLOGY. *Educ:* Univ Ala, BS, 61; Fla State Univ, MS, 64, PhD(morphogenesis, cell biol), 71. *Prof Exp:* Teaching asst zool, Fla State Univ, 61-64; parasitologist, Biol Lab, Nat Marine Fisheries Serv, Nat Oceanic & Atmospheric Admin, 64-71; PATHOBIOLOGIST, BIOL LAB, ENVIRON PROTECTION AGENCY, 71- *Concurrent Pos:* US Dept Interior training assignment, Fla State Univ, 67-68; scientist-aquanaut, Tektite II, 70; fac assoc, Univ WFla, 75- *Mem:* Sigma Xi; Gulf Estuarine Res Soc; Soc Invert Path; Soc Protozoologists. *Res:* Evolution of commensal-host relationships of marine protozoa; aquatic animal pathology; interaction of pollutants and natural disease; neoplasia; experimental carcinogenesis. *Mailing Add:* Biol Lab US Environ Protect Agency Sabine Island Gulf Breeze FL 32561

COUCH, JOHN NATHANIEL, b Prince Edward Co, Va, Oct 12, 96; m 27; c 2. BOTANY. *Educ:* Univ NC, AB, 19, AM, 22, PhD(bot), 24. *Hon Degrees:* ScD, Catawba Col, 46, Duke Univ, 65 & Univ NC, 72. *Prof Exp:* Teacher high schs, NC, 19-21; instr, 17-18, 22-25, from asst prof to prof, 25-45, Kenan prof, 45-68, chmn dept, 44-60, EMER KENAN PROF BOT, UNIV NC, CHAPEL HILL, 68- *Concurrent Pos:* Nat Res fel, Sta Exp Evolution, Carnegie Inst, 25-26 & Mo Bot Garden, 26-27; vis assoc prof, Johns Hopkins Univ, 33, vis prof, 34, 35; vis researcher, Exp Sta, NC State Col, 43; mem adv panel syst biol, NSF, 55-58. *Honors & Awards:* Walker Grand Prize, Boston Soc Natural Hist, 38; Jefferson Medal, NC Acad, 37; Cert of Merit, Mycol Soc Am, 56. *Mem:* Nat Acad Sci; AAAS (vpres, 62); Am Soc Nat; Bot Soc Am; Mycol Soc Am (secy-treas, 39-41, vpres, 42, pres, 43). *Res:* Culture, sexuality and ciliary structure of water fungi; fungi parasitic in mosquito larvae, symbiosis between fungi and scale insects; Actinomy cetales. *Mailing Add:* Carol Woods Chapel Hill NC 27514

COUCH, LEON WORTHINGTON, II, b Durham, NC, July 6, 41; m 64; c 3. ELECTRICAL ENGINEERING. *Educ:* Duke Univ, BS, 63; Univ Fla, ME, 64, PhD(elec eng), 68. *Prof Exp:* Asst elec eng, 63-68, asst prof, 68-74, ASSOC PROF ELEC ENG, UNIV FLA, 74- *Mem:* Sr mem Inst Elec & Electronics Engrs; Am Soc Eng Educ. *Res:* Performance of radar and communication systems and subsystems in the presence of noise; modulation systems; realistic systems, analog and digital. *Mailing Add:* Dept of Elec Eng Univ of Fla Gainesville FL 32611

COUCH, MARGARET WHELAND, b Chicago, Ill, Aug 27, 41; m 64; c 3. ORGANIC CHEMISTRY. *Educ:* Duke Univ, BS, 63; Univ Fla, MS, 66, PhD(org chem), 69. *Prof Exp:* res asst, Dept Radiol, 69-70, ASST RES PROF, DEPT RADIATION CHEM, UNIV FLA, 71-; RES CHEMIST, VET ADMIN HOSP, GAINESVILLE, 71- *Mem:* Am Chem Soc; Sigma Xi; Am Soc Mass Spectrometry. *Res:* Identification by means of mass spectrometry-gas chromatography of aromatic acids and amines present in biological fluids of patients with neurological disorders; radiopharmaceuticals for aromatic amines in mammals, occurance and metabolism of adrenal scanning. *Mailing Add:* 3524 NW 51st Ave Gainesville FL 32605

COUCH, RICHARD W, b Dayton, Ohio, June 9, 31; m 62; c 2. GEOPHYSICS, SEISMOLOGY. *Educ:* Mich State Univ, BS, 58; Ore State Univ, MS, 63, PhD(geophys), 69. *Prof Exp:* Electronics engr, Gen Dynamics/ Electronics, NY, 58-60, mem res staff, 60-62; res asst marine geophys, 63-65, res fel geophys, 65-66, from instr to asst prof, 66-73, ASSOC PROF GEOPHYS, SCH OCEANOG, ORE STATE UNIV, 73- *Mem:* Soc Exploration Geophys; Seismol Soc Am. *Res:* Structure and tectonics of continental margins of the Eastern Pacific Ocean; geophysical exploration for geothermal resources; earthquake seismology and geological hazards. *Mailing Add:* Sch of Oceanog Ore State Univ Corvallis OR 97331

COUCH, RICHARD WESLEY, b Pryor, Okla, Mar 30, 37; m 60; c 2. PLANT PHYSIOLOGY. *Educ:* Okla State Univ, BS, 59; Univ Tenn, MS, 61; Auburn Univ, PhD(bot biochem), 66. *Prof Exp:* Asst county agent, Exten Serv, Univ Tenn, 61-63; prof biol, Athens Col, 65-73, chmn dept, 66-73; assoc prof, 73-77, PROF BIOL, ORAL ROBERTS UNIV, 77- *Concurrent Pos:* Consult, US Corps Engrs, contract, 68- *Mem:* Nat Sci Teachers Asn. *Res:* Herbicidal plant physiology; aquatic biology; aquatic weed control; aquatic plants of Oklahoma. *Mailing Add:* Dept of Natural Sci Oral Roberts Univ Tulsa OK 74102

COUCH, ROBERT BARNARD, b Guntersville, Ala, Sept 25, 30; m 55; c 4. INTERNAL MEDICINE, INFECTIOUS DISEASES. *Educ:* Vanderbilt Univ, BA, 52, MD, 56. *Prof Exp:* From intern to chief resident, Vanderbilt Univ Hosp, 56-61; clin assoc surg, Nat Cancer Inst, 57-59, sr investr, Lab Clin Invest, Nat Inst Allergy & Infectious Dis, 61-65, head clin virol, 65-66; assoc prof, 66-71, PROF MICROBIOL & MED, BAYLOR COL MED, 71-, PROF IMMUNOL, 76- *Mem:* Am Fedn Clin Res; Soc Exp Biol & Med; Am Soc Microbiol. *Res:* Clinical and general virology; immunology. *Mailing Add:* Dept of Microbiol Baylor Col of Med Houston TX 77030

COUCH, TERRY LEE, b Middletown, Pa, Jan 8, 44; m 65; c 2. ENTOMOLOGY. *Educ:* Franklin & Marshall Col, AB, 65; Pa State Univ, MS, 68, PhD(entom), 70. *Prof Exp:* Res entomologist, 70-75, group leader entom res, Chem & Agr Prod Div, 75-76, ASSOC RES FEL, SCI LADDER, ABBOTT LABS, 76- *Mem:* Entom Soc Am; Am Inst Biol Sci; Sigma Xi; Soc Invert Path. *Res:* Discovery and development of microbial insecticides and narrow spectrum and chemical insecticides. *Mailing Add:* Abbott Labs D-912 Bldg T-9 14th St & Sheridan Rd North Chicago IL 60064

COUCHELL, GUS PERRY, b Henderson, NC, Apr 14, 39; m 68. NUCLEAR PHYSICS. *Educ:* NC State Univ, BS, 61, MS, 63; Columbia Univ, PhD(physics), 68. *Prof Exp:* Asst prof physics & appl physics, 68-73, assoc prof, 73-79, PROF PHYSICS, UNIV LOWELL, 79- *Res:* Isobaric analog states; nuclear spectroscopy; fast neutron scattering; nuclear resonance fluorescence; energy spectra of delayed neutrons following neutron-induced fission. *Mailing Add:* 10 Cathy Rd Chelmsford MA 01824

COUCHMAN, JAMES C, b Cincinnati, Ohio, Aug 28, 29; m 48; c 3. PHYSICS. *Educ:* Cent Col, Iowa, BA, 53; Vanderbilt Univ, MA, 55; Tex Christian Univ, PhD(math physics), 65. *Prof Exp:* Radiation safety area rep, Argonne Nat Lab, 55-56; nuclear engr, Convair, Tex, 56-58; sr nuclear engr, Gen Dynamics/Ft Worth, 58-61, 63-65; sci specialist, Edgerton, Germeshausen & Grier, Calif, 65-67; PROJ NUCLEAR PHYSICIST, GEN DYNAMICS CORP, 67- *Mem:* Health Physics Soc; Am Nuclear Soc. *Res:* Nuclear weapons effects research; aerospace nuclear safeguards; health physics; use of digital computer techniques in studying nuclear reactor, criticality; evaluation of potential environmental hazards associated with the uses of nuclear energy. *Mailing Add:* 8112 Rush St Ft Worth TX 76116

COUCOUVANIS, DIMITRI N, b Athens, Greece, Nov 20, 40; US citizen; m 63; c 2. INORGANIC CHEMISTRY, CRYSTALLOGRAPHY. *Educ:* Allegheny Col, BS, 63; Case Inst Technol, PhD(chem), 67. *Prof Exp:* Res assoc, Case Inst Technol, 67 & Columbia Univ, 67-68; assoc prof, 68-75, PROF CHEM, UNIV IOWA, 75- *Mem:* Am Chem Soc. *Res:* Synthesis and structure of polynuclear coordination complexes and their use as models for metal containing enzymes. *Mailing Add:* Dept of Chem Univ of Iowa Iowa City IA 52240

COUDRON, THOMAS A, b Marshall, Minn, 1951. ANALYTICAL BIOCHEMISTRY, INSECT BIOCHEMISTRY. *Educ:* St John's Univ, BS, 73; NDak State Univ, PhD(biochem), 78. *Prof Exp:* Res assoc biochem, Univ Chicago, 78-80; PROJ LEADER BIOCHEM, BIOL CONTROL INSECTS, USDA, 80- *Mem:* AAAS; Sigma Xi. *Res:* Hormonal control of insect development; effects of natural products on insects and nutritional requirements of insects from a biochemical perspective for studies. *Mailing Add:* Biol Control Insect Res Lab USDA Agr Res Serv PO Box A Columbia MO 65205

COUEY, H MELVIN, b Shedd, Ore, May 22, 26; m 55; c 2. PLANT PHYSIOLOGY. *Educ:* Ore State Col, BS, 51, MS, 54; Iowa State Col, PhD(plant physiol), 56. *Prof Exp:* From assoc plant physiologist to plant physiologist, Sci & Educ Admin-Agr Res, Fresno, Calif, 56-63, sr plant physiologist, 63-68, invests leader, Northwest Fruit Invests, Wenatchee, Wash, 68-73, location leader prod, harvesting & handling tree fruits, Mkt Qual Div, 73-77, RES LEADER, COMMODITY TREAT, HANDLING & TRANSP UNIT, AGR RES SERV, USDA, HAWAII, 77-; RES LEADER, COMMODITY TREAT, HANDLING & TRANSP UNIT, AGR RES SERV, USDA, HAWAII, 77- *Mem:* AAAS; Am Soc Hort Sci; Am Soc Plant Physiol; Am Phytopath Soc. *Res:* Post-harvest physiology of fruits; fruit storage and storage disorders; physiology of fungus spores. *Mailing Add:* Agr Res Serv USDA Box 917 Hilo HI 98801

COUGER, J DANIEL, b Olney, Tex, Oct 20, 29; m 51; c 4. COMPUTER SCIENCE. *Educ:* Phillips Univ, BA, 51; Univ Mo-Kansas City, MA, 58; Univ Colo, DBA(mgt sci), 64. *Prof Exp:* Indust engr, Nat Gypsum Co, 53-54; supvr, Indust Eng Dept, Hallmark Cards, Inc, 54-58; sect chief, Comput Dept, Martin-Marietta, Inc, 58-65; PROF MGT SCI, UNIV COLO, COLORADO SPRINGS, 65-, PROF COMPUTER SCI, 80- *Concurrent Pos:* Consult, Int Bus Mach Corp & Dow Chem Corp. *Honors & Awards:* Distinguished Serv Award, Asn Systs Mgt. *Mem:* Asn Comput Mach; Opers Res Soc Am; Soc Mgt Info Systs; Asn Systs Mgt. *Res:* Use of computer for application of management sciences; design of computer-based management information systems. *Mailing Add:* Sch of Bus Univ of Colo Cragmor Rd Colorado Springs CO 80907

COUGHANOWR, D(ONALD) R(AY), b Brazil, Ind, Mar 11, 28; m 55; c 3. CHEMICAL ENGINEERING. *Educ:* Rose Polytech Inst, BS, 49; Univ Pa, MS, 51; Univ Ill, PhD(chem eng), 56. *Prof Exp:* Chem engr, Standard Oil Co, Ind, 51-53; from asst prof to prof chem eng, Purdue Univ, 56-67; PROF CHEM ENG & HEAD DEPT, DREXEL UNIV, 67- *Concurrent Pos:* Mem staff, Case Inst Technol, 63-64 & Electronic Assocs, Inc, 64. *Mem:* Instrument Soc Am; Am Soc Eng Educ; Am Inst Chem Engrs. *Res:* Process dynamics and control; analog computation; mass transfer; aerosols. *Mailing Add:* Dept of Chem Eng Drexel Univ Philadelphia PA 19104

COUGHENOUR, MICHAEL B, b Oak Park, Ill, Sept 22, 52. ECOLOGY. *Educ:* Univ Ill, BS, 73, MS, 74; Colo State Univ, PhD(ecol), 78. *Prof Exp:* RES ASSOC ECOL, DEPT BIOL, SYRACUSE UNIV, 78- *Concurrent Pos:* NSF fel, 78-80. *Mem:* Ecol Soc Am; Am Soc Naturalists; AAAS; Sigma Xi. *Res:* Grassland ecology; systems ecology; nutrient cycling; grazing systems; plant-animal interactions; decomposition ecology; production ecology; applied ecology; ruminant ecology. *Mailing Add:* Biol Res Lab Syracuse Univ 130 College Pl Syracuse NY 13210

COUGHLIN, JAMES ROBERT, b Albany, NY, Sept 8, 46; m 69; c 3. TOXICOLOGY, FOOD SAFETY. *Educ:* Siena Col, NY, BS, 68; Univ Calif, Davis, MS, 74, PhD(agr & environ chem), 79. *Prof Exp:* Food safety scientist, Armour Res Ctr, 79-81; MGR TOXICOL AFFAIRS, GEN FOODS CORP, 81- *Concurrent Pos:* Fel trainee, Dept Environ Toxicol, Univ Calif, Davis, 79. *Mem:* AAAS; Inst Food Technologists; Am Chem Soc; Coun Agr Sci & Technol. *Res:* Safety assessment and toxicological evaluation of components in the food supply and environment particularly affecting human health. *Mailing Add:* Gen Foods Corp 250 North St White Plains NY 10625

COUGHLIN, RAYMOND FRANCIS, b Chicago, Ill, Oct 6, 43; m 70; c 2. ALGEBRA. *Educ:* Lewis Col, BA, 65; Loyola Univ Chicago, MA, 67; Ill Inst Technol, PhD(math), 69. *Prof Exp:* From instr to asst prof math, Loyola Univ, Chicago, 67-70; asst prof, 70-77, ASSOC PROF MATH, TEMPLE UNIV, 77- *Mem:* Am Math Soc; Math Asn Am. *Res:* Non-associative algebras satisfying the associo-symmetric identity and non-associative rings satisfying the m-associative ring identity. *Mailing Add:* Dept of Math Temple Univ Philadelphia PA 19122

COUGHLIN, ROBERT WILLIAM, b Brooklyn, NY, June 18, 34; m 60; c 2. CHEMICAL ENGINEERING, APPLIED CHEMISTRY. *Educ:* Fordham Univ, BS, 56; Cornell Univ, PhD(chem eng), 61. *Prof Exp:* Fulbright fel, Univ Heidelberg, 60-61; chem engr, Esso Res & Eng Co, NJ, 61-64; sr scientist, Isotopes Inc, 64, mgr eng sci & data processing, 64-65; from assoc prof to prof chem eng, Lehigh Univ, 65-78, assoc dir ctr marine & environ sci, 68-78; PROF & HEAD DEPT CHEM ENG, UNIV CONN, STORRS, 77- *Concurrent Pos:* Adj asst prof, NY Univ, 62-64; vis lectr, Stevens Inst Technol, 64-65; prof & dir inst environ studies & grad prog environ eng & sci, Drexel Univ, 71; prin investr various res grants & contracts from govt agencies, found & indust corp, consult to various indust corp, univs & govt agencies. *Honors & Awards:* Robinson Award, Lehigh Univ, 67. *Mem:* Am Chem Soc; Am Inst Chem Engrs; Catalysis Soc. *Res:* Catalysis; kinetics; surface chemistry; fuel technology and petroleum engineering; chemical reactor engineering; electrochemistry; applied biochemistry. *Mailing Add:* Dept of Chem Eng U-139 Univ of Conn Storrs CT 06268

COUILLARD, PIERRE, b Montmagny, Que, Mar 19, 28; m 55; c 3. CELL PHYSIOLOGY. *Educ:* Laval Univ, BA, 47, BSc, 51; Univ Pa, PhD(zool), 55. *Prof Exp:* Fel, Belgium, 55-56; from asst prof to assoc prof, 56-70, head dept, 63-67, PROF BIOL, UNIV MONTREAL, 70- *Mem:* AAAS; Soc Protozool; Fr Asn Physiol; Can Soc Cell Biol. *Res:* Physiology of amoeba. *Mailing Add:* 631 Davaar Outremont Can

COULL, BRUCE CHARLES, b New York, NY, Sept 16, 42; m 67. ECOLOGY, BIOLOGICAL OCEANOGRAPHY. *Educ:* Moravian Col, BS, 64; Lehigh Univ, MS, 66, PhD(biol), 68. *Prof Exp:* Res asst biol, Lehigh Univ, 64-68; NSF award biol oceanog, Marine Lab, Duke Univ, 68-70; asst prof zool, Clark Univ, 70-73; assoc prof biol & marine sci, 73-78, PROF BIOL & MARINE SCI, UNIV SC, 78- *Concurrent Pos:* Prin investr, NSF grant, 72-83; ed, Psammonalia, 73-75; Fulbright res scholar, Victoria Univ, NZ, 81. *Mem:* Am Micros Soc; Ecol Soc Am; Soc Syst Zool; Sigma Xi; Int Asn Meiobenthologists (chmn, 73-75). *Res:* Meiobenthic ecology; harpacticoid copepod systematics; benthic metabolism; population dynamics; zoogeography. *Mailing Add:* Baruch Inst Mar Biol & Coast Res Univ of SC Columbia SC 29208

COULMAN, G(EORGE) A(LBERT), b Detroit, Mich, June 29, 30; m 56; c 2. CHEMICAL ENGINEERING. *Educ:* Case Inst Technol, BS, 52, PhD(chem eng), 62; Univ Mich, MS, 58. *Prof Exp:* Develop engr, pilot plant, Dow Corning Corp, 54-57; mgr develop, Am Metal Prod, 58-60; asst prof chem eng, Univ Waterloo, 61-64; from asst prof to prof chem eng & eng res, Mich State Univ, 64-76; PROF CHEM ENG & CHMN DEPT, CLEVELAND STATE UNIV, 76- *Concurrent Pos:* Nat Res Coun res grant, 62-64; NSF grants, 65-, numerous govt & indust res grants. *Mem:* Am Inst Chem Engrs; Am Chem Soc. *Res:* Systems engineering applied to chemical processing, particularly the analysis and modeling of process systems for use in system design methods; dynamic characteristics of chemical processes and use in improved operation and control. *Mailing Add:* Dept of Chem Eng Rm SH-106 1960 E 24th St Cleveland OH 44115

COULOMBE, HARRY N, b Long Beach, Calif, Oct 7, 39; m 75; c 1. VERTEBRATE BIOLOGY, ENVIRONMENTAL MANAGEMENT. *Educ:* Univ Calif, Los Angeles, 62, MA, 65, PhD(zool), 68. *Prof Exp:* Asst prof zoophysiol, Inst Arctic Biol, Univ Alaska, 68-69; asst prof ecol, San Diego State Col, 69-74, dir bur ecol & mem exec comt, Ctr Regional Environ Studies, 70-74, proj mgr, 74-75; oil shale res mgr, Western Energy & Land Use Team, 75-77, leader, Nat Habitat Assessment Group, 77-79, ASST TEAM LEADER, WESTERN ENERGY & LAND USE TEAM, US FISH & WILDLIFE SERV, 79- . *Concurrent Pos:* Anal & modeling coordr, Tundra Biome, Anal of Ecosyst Sect, US Int Biol Prog, 68-; chmn ad hoc comt rabies control, County of San Diego, 70-; mem, Oil Shale Environ Adv Panel, Dept Interior, 76-78. *Mem:* AAAS; Ecol Soc Am; Am Soc Mammal; Cooper Ornith Soc; Wildlife Soc. *Res:* Project development and management in regional environmental planning; ecosystem modeling and simulation; predator population ecology; ecology of cetaceans; adaptive physiology of vertebrates. *Mailing Add:* 2625 Reedwing Rd US Fish & Wildlife Serv Ft Collins CO 80526

COULOMBE, LOUIS JOSEPH, b Lac-St-Jean, Que, Dec 16, 20; m 47; c 7. AGRICULTURE. *Educ:* Laval Univ, BA, 43, BSA, 47; McGill Univ, MSc, 49, PhD, 56. *Prof Exp:* Res scientist, Can Dept Agr, 48-61; mem tech dept & sales, Niagara Brand Chem Co, 61-64; RES SCIENTIST, CAN DEPT AGR, 64- *Mem:* Can Phytopath Soc. *Res:* Creation of apple cultivars resistant to scab, mildew and fire blight; ecological aspect of fruit pesticides; new programs for scab and mildew control. *Mailing Add:* 1415 DuVallon Beloeil PQ J3G 3Y4 Can

COULOMBRE, ALFRED JOSEPH, b Boston, Mass, Aug 15, 22. EMBRYOLOGY. *Educ:* Catholic Univ, BS, 47, MS, 49; Johns Hopkins Univ, PhD(embryol), 53. *Prof Exp:* Instr biol, Wabash Col, 48; from instr to asst prof anat, Sch Med, Yale Univ, 53-61; head, Sect Exp Embryol, Nat Inst Neurol Dis & Blindness, 61-67, chief lab neuroanat sci, 62-67; assoc dir intramural res, Nat Inst Child Health & Human Develop, 67-68; head sect exp embryol, 68-81, HEAD SECT EXP BIOL, NAT EYE INST, 81- *Concurrent Pos:* Mem develop biol panel, NSF, 58-62; training comt mem, Nat Inst Child Health & Human Develop, 62-67; asst ed, J Exp Zool, 63-66, 69-73; comnr & vpres, Sci Manpower Comn, 63-68; asst ed, Develop Biol, 64-68; mem panel develop biol, Subcomt Life Sci, Nat Acad Sci-Nat Res Coun, 66-67; mem, Sr Exec Serv, 79- *Honors & Awards:* Jonas Friedenwald Award, 69. *Mem:* Asn Res Ophthal; Soc Develop Biol (treas, 65-68); Int Soc Develop Biol. *Res:* Morphogenesis and developmental physiology of the vertebrate eye. *Mailing Add:* 5604 Madison St Bethesda MD 20817

COULSON, DALE ROBERT, b Monessen, Pa, Oct 26, 38; m 67; c 2. ORGANIC CHEMISTRY, ORGANOMETALLIC CHEMISTRY. *Educ:* Carnegie Inst Technol, BS, 60; Columbia Univ, MA, 61, PhD(chem), 64. *Prof Exp:* NSF fel photochem, Univ Chicago, 64-65, NIH fel, 65-66; res chemist, 66-74, RES SUPVR, E I DU PONT DE NEMOURS & CO, INC, 74- *Mem:* Am Chem Soc. *Res:* Homogeneous catalysis; organometallic synthesis. *Mailing Add:* 2314 Empire Dr Wilmington DE 19810

COULSON, JACK RICHARD, b Manhattan, Kans, Jan 31, 31; m 64; c 2. ENTOMOLOGY. *Educ:* Iowa State Univ, BS, 52. *Prof Exp:* Biologist, Insect Identification & Parasite Introd Res Br, Washington, DC, 56-61, biologist, Plant Indust Sta, Md, 61-63, entomologist, 63-64, entomologist, Introduced Beneficial Insects Lab, NJ, 64-65 & Europ Parasite Lab, Paris, France, 65-67, asst to br chief taxon & biol control, Plant Indust Sta, Beltsville, Md, 67-72, CHIEF, BENEFICIAL INSECT INTROD LAB, INSECT IDENTIFICATION & BENEFICIAL INSECT INTROD INST, AGR RES SERV, USDA, BELTSVILLE, MD, 72- *Mem:* Entom Soc Am; Int Orgn Biol Control. *Res:* Taxonomic entomology, especially bibliographic; biological control of insect pests. *Mailing Add:* Beltsville Agr Res Ctr E Bldg 417 USDA Agr Res Serv Beltsville MD 20705

COULSON, KINSELL LEROY, b Hatfield, Mo, Oct 7, 16; m 47. METEOROLOGY, ATMOSPHERIC PHYSICS. *Educ:* Northwest Mo State Col, BS, 42; Univ Calif, Los Angeles, MA, 52, PhD(meteorol), 59. *Prof Exp:* Meteorologist, Univ Chicago, 42-43 & US Naval Ord Test Sta, Calif, 49-51; res meteorologist, Univ Calif, Los Angeles, 51-59 & Stanford Res Inst, 59-60; mgr geophys, Space Sci Lab, Gen Elec Co, 60-65; prof agr eng, Univ Calif, Davis, 65-66, prof meteorol, 67-79; DIR, MAUNA LOA OBSERV, HILO, HAWAII, 79- *Concurrent Pos:* USSR exchange fel, Nat Acad Sci, 72 & 80; consult, Lawrence Livermore Lab, 74- *Mem:* AAAS; Am Meteorol Soc; Am Geophys Union; Solar Energy Soc; Sigma Xi. *Res:* Atmospheric radiation, especially solar radiation regime; molecular and aerosol scattering of radiation in planetary atmospheres; reflection from planetary surfaces; planetary albedo; space environment. *Mailing Add:* Mauna Loa Observ Federal Bldg Rm 202 Hilo HI 96720

COULSON, LARRY VERNON, b LaFollette, Tenn, Oct 15, 43; m 66; c 3. PARTICLE PHYSICS, RADIATION PHYSICS. *Educ:* Kans State Univ, BS, 65; Univ Va, PhD(physics), 70. *Prof Exp:* Fel particle physics, Rice Univ, 70-72; staff physicist, 72-76, SR RADIATION SAFETY OFFICER, FERMI NAT ACCELERATOR LAB, 76-, ASST HEAD, SAFETY SECT, 78- *Res:* Radiation related problems and dosimetry of accelerator produced radiation; isotope production cross sections at high energies. *Mailing Add:* Fermi Nat Accelerator Lab PO Box 500 Batavia IL 60510

COULSON, PATRICIA BUNKER, b Kankakee, Ill, Apr 27, 42; m 65; c 2. REPRODUCTIVE ENDOCRINOLOGY, CELL PHYSIOLOGY. *Educ:* Univ Ill, BS, 64, MS, 65, PhD(reproductive endocrinol), 70. *Prof Exp:* Lab asst reproductive endocrinol, Univ Ill, 65-66; res reproduction, 70-72, asst prof endocrinol, Univ Tenn, Knoxville, 72-77, asst res prof, Mem Res Ctr, 77-78; assoc prof physiol, Col Med, East Tenn State Univ, Johnson City, 78-81; ASSOC PROF OBSTET GYNEC & ASSOC PROF MED BIOL, UNIV TENN CTR HEALTH SCI, KNOXVILLE, TENN, 81- *Mem:* AAAS; Sigma Xi; Soc Study Reproduction; Am Tissue Cult Asn; Fedn Am Soc Exp Biol. *Res:* Hormone action; endocrine control of the female reproductive tract emphasizing modulation of receptors for estrogen, progesterone and the gonadotropic hormones in the uterus, vagina, pituitary, hypothalamus, ovary and mammary cells; hormonal control of cancer cells; clinical assays for reproductive hormones. *Mailing Add:* Dept Med Biol & Obstet Gynec Mem Res Ctr Univ Tenn 1927 Alcoa Hwy Knoxville TN 37920

COULSON, ROBERT N, b Dallas, Tex, Mar 1, 43. INSECT ECOLOGY, FOREST ENTOMOLOGY. *Educ:* Furman Univ, BS, 65; Univ Ga, MS, 67, PhD(entom), 69. *Prof Exp:* Prin entomologist pest control sect, Tex Forest Serv, 69-73; from asst prof to assoc prof, 73-79, PROF ENTOM, TEX A&M UNIV, 79- *Concurrent Pos:* Res assoc entom, Univ Ga, 67-70. *Mem:* Entom Soc Am; Entom Soc Can; Ecol Soc Am. *Res:* Forest insect community and population ecology in relation to pest management. *Mailing Add:* Dept Entom Tex A&M Univ College Station TX 77840

COULSON, ROLAND ARMSTRONG, b Rolla, Kans, Dec 20, 15; m 44; c 2. BIOCHEMISTRY. *Educ:* Univ Wichita, BA, 37; La State Univ, MS, 39; Univ London, PhD(biochem), 44. *Prof Exp:* From instr to assoc prof, 44-53, PROF BIOCHEM, SCH MED, LA STATE UNIV, NEW ORLEANS, 53- *Mem:* Soc Exp Biol & Med; Am Soc Biol Chem; Am Asn Clin Chem; Am Phys Soc; Am Inst Nutrit. *Res:* Nutrition; biochemical studies on Alligator mississippiensis; theory of metabolic rate and anaerobic glycolysis; protein digestion, absorption, and amino acid metabolism. *Mailing Add:* Dept of Biochem La State Univ Sch of Med New Orleans LA 70112

COULSON, WALTER F, b Harrogate, Eng, Dec 17, 26; nat US; c 5. PATHOLOGY. *Educ:* Univ Edinburgh, MB, ChB, 49, BSc, 54, MD, 67; FRCPath, 72. *Prof Exp:* Resident med, Royal Infirmary, Edinburgh, Scotland, 49-50; registr path, Western Gen Hosp, 54-55; lectr, Univ Edinburgh, 55-60; asst prof, Univ Utah, 60-64, assoc prof, 64-68; assoc prof, 68-70, PROF PATH, CTR HEALTH SCI, SCH MED, UNIV CALIF, LOS ANGELES, 70-, VCHMN DEPT, 71- *Concurrent Pos:* Brown res fel, Yale Univ, 57-58; consult, Salt Lake Gen Hosp, 60-68; chief lab serv, Vet Admin Hosp, 62-68; res assoc, Univ Col, Univ London, 66-67; head div surg path, Univ Calif, Los Angeles, 68-; consult, Dept Path, Radiation Effects Res Found, Japan, 80-81; vis sr lectr, Dept Path, Ninewells Hosp & Med Sch, Scotland, 81. *Mem:* Am Asn Pathologists; Path Soc Gt Brit & Ireland; Int Acad Path; Am Inst Nutrit; Am Soc Clin Path. *Res:* Morphology and biochemistry of connective tissue, including bone, particularly mechanical properties and the changes induced by copper deficiency. *Mailing Add:* Dept of Path Ctr for Health Sci Univ of Calif Los Angeles CA 90024

COULTER, BYRON LEONARD, b Phenix City, Ala, Aug 16, 41; m 62; c 1. THEORETICAL PHYSICS, SOLAR ENERGY. *Educ:* Univ Ala, BS, 62, PhD(physics), 66. *Prof Exp:* From asst prof to assoc prof, 66-77, PROF PHYSICS, E CAROLINA UNIV, 77- *Mem:* Am Phys Soc; Am Asn Physics Teachers; Int Solar Energy Soc; Sigma Xi. *Res:* Computer simulation of physics problems; available work from solar radiation; computer simulations. *Mailing Add:* Dept Physics E Carolina Univ Greenville NC 27834

COULTER, CHARLES L, b Akron, Ohio, Jan 10, 33; m 55; c 3. STRUCTURAL CHEMISTRY, BIOPHYSICAL CHEMISTRY. *Educ:* Miami Univ, AB, 54, MA, 56; Univ Calif, Los Angeles, PhD(phys chem), 60. *Prof Exp:* USPHS fel, Med Res Coun Unit for Molecular Biol, Cambridge, Eng, 60-62; fel, Lab Molecular Biol, NIH, 62-64, prog dir anal biochem, Div Res Facil & Resources, 65-66; from asst prof to assoc prof anat, Univ Chicago, 66-76; HEAD BIOL STRUCT SECT, DIV RES RESOURCES, NIH, 76- *Mem:* AAAS; Am Crystallog Asn. *Res:* Protein crystallography; crystal structures of biologically important compounds; structural biochemistry. *Mailing Add:* Biotechnol Resources Prog Div of Res Resources NIH Bethesda MD 20205

COULTER, CLAUDE ALTON, b Phenix City, Ala, Mar 30, 36; m 60; c 2. RADIATION PHYSICS, QUANTUM OPTICS. *Educ:* Samford Univ, BA, 56; Univ Ala, MS, 59; Harvard Univ, MA, 63, PhD(physics), 64. *Prof Exp:* Asst prof physics, Univ Ala, 63-66; from asst prof to assoc prof, Clark Univ, 66-71; from assoc prof to prof physics, Univ Ala, Tuscaloosa, 71-77; STAFF MEM, LOS ALAMOS NAT LAB, 82- *Concurrent Pos:* Consult, Phys Sci Directorate, US Army Missile Command, Redstone Arsenal, Ala, 63-; vis staff mem, Los Alamos Sci Lab, 74-81. *Mem:* Am Phys Soc. *Res:* Radiation damage in metals; quantum optics. *Mailing Add:* Q U MS 541 Los Alamos Nat Lab University AL 35486

COULTER, DWIGHT BERNARD, b Iowa City, Iowa, Jan 8, 35; m 61; c 2. VETERINARY PHYSIOLOGY. *Educ:* Iowa State Univ, DVM, 60, MS, 65, PhD(physiol), 69. *Prof Exp:* From instr to assoc prof physiol, Col Vet Med, Iowa State Univ, 62-72; assoc prof, 72-79, PROF PHYSIOL, COL VET MED, UNIV GA, 79- *Concurrent Pos:* Adj prof, Col Vet Med, Miss State Univ, 79-80. *Mem:* Am Vet Med Asn; Am Physiol Soc; Conf Res Workers Animal Dis. *Res:* Comparative electrocardiography; comparative neurophysiology. *Mailing Add:* Dept Physiol Univ Ga Col Vet Med Athens GA 30602

COULTER, ELIZABETH JACKSON, b Baltimore, Md, Nov 2, 19; m 51; c 1. BIOSTATISTICS, HEALTH ECONOMICS. *Educ:* Swarthmore Col, Pa, AB, 41; Radcliffe Col, AM, 46, PhD(econ), 48. *Prof Exp:* Asst dir health study, Bur Labor Statist, San Juan, PR, 46; res asst, Milbank Mem Fund, New York, 48-51; economist, Off Defense Prod, Washington, DC, 51-52; res analyst, Children's Bur, US Dept Health, Educ & Welfare, 52-53; statistician, Ohio Dept Health, Columbus, 54-55, chief statistician, 55-65; assoc prof, 65-72, PROF BIOSTATIST, SCH PUB HEALTH, UNIV NC, CHAPEL HILL, 72-, ASSOC DEAN UNDERGRAD STUDIES, 76- *Concurrent Pos:* Lectr, Ohio State Univ, Columbus, 54-55, clin asst prof prev med, 63-65; asst clin prof biostatist, Sch Pub Health, Univ Pittsburgh, Pa, 58-62; assoc prof econ, Univ NC, Chapel Hill, 65-78; adj assoc prof hosp admin, Duke Univ, 72-79. *Mem:* fel Am Pub Health Asn; Am Econ Asn; Am Statist Asn; Am Acad Polit & Social Sci; AAAS. *Res:* Socio-economic factors in natality, mortality and utilization of health services; quantitative approaches in health planning and evaluation; application of cost-benefit and cost-effectiveness techniques in the health field. *Mailing Add:* 1825 N Lake Shore Dr Chapel Hill NC 27514

COULTER, GLENN HARTMAN, b Orangeville, Ont, Jan 28, 47; m 70; c 2. REPRODUCTIVE PHYSIOLOGY, ANIMAL SCIENCE. *Educ:* Univ Guelph, BSc, 69; Cornell Univ, PhD(reproductive physiol), 73. *Prof Exp:* Res specialist reproductive physiol, Cornell Univ, 72-73, res assoc, 73-74; RES SCIENTIST REPRODUCTIVE PHYSIOL, LETHBRIDGE RES STA, AGR CAN, 74- *Mem:* Am Soc Animal Sci; Soc Stud Fertility; Am Dairy Sci Asn; Can Soc Cell Biol. *Res:* Reproductive physiology of the male with emphasis on the testicular development; general breeding soundness and management factors effecting reproduction in young beef bulls. *Mailing Add:* Res Sta Agr Can Lethbridge AB T1J 4B1 Can

COULTER, HERBERT DAVID, JR, b Enid, Okla, Dec 31, 39; m 64; c 2. ANATOMY. *Educ:* Westminster Col, Mo, BA, 61; Univ Tenn, PhD(anat), 68. *Prof Exp:* Instr, 68-70, ASST PROF ANAT, SCH MED, UNIV MINN, MINNEAPOLIS, 70- *Mem:* AAAS; Am Soc Cell Biol; Electron Micros Soc Am; Soc Neurosci; Am Asn Anatomists. *Res:* Immunocytochemistry; neurocytology. *Mailing Add:* Dept of Anat Univ of Minn Sch of Med Minneapolis MN 55455

COULTER, JOE DAN, b Victoria, Tex, July 25, 44; m 67; c 2. NEUROPHYSIOLOGY, NEUROANATOMY. *Educ:* Univ Okla, BA, 66, PhD(psychiat & behav sci), 71. *Prof Exp:* NIH fel, Marine Biomed Inst, Univ Tex Med Br Galveston, 71-73; Found fund res psychiat fel, Inst Physiol, Univ Pisa, 73-74 & Univ Edinburgh, 74-75; asst prof, 75-77, ASSOC PROF PHYSIOL, BIOPHYS, PSYCHIAT & BEHAV SCI, MARINE BIOMED INST, UNIV TEX MED BR GALVESTON, 77- *Concurrent Pos:* Assoc dir, Sensor Physiol & Perception Prog, NSF, 80-81; mem, Neurol B Study Sect, NIH, 81- *Mem:* AAAS; Am Asn Anatomists; Am Physiol Soc; Soc Neurosci. *Res:* Monoaminergic and peptidergic transmitters; neural basis of perception; neuroanatomy; motor control; states of consciousness and sleep. *Mailing Add:* Marine Biomed Inst Univ of Tex Med Br Galveston TX 77550

COULTER, LLEWELLYN LEGRANDE, b Rochester, Mich, Jan 29, 21; m 42; c 5. WEED SCIENCE, WILDLIFE MANAGEMENT. *Educ:* Mich State Univ, BS, 47, MS, 48. *Prof Exp:* Field res specialist herbicides, Dow Chem Co, 46-53, proj leader, Bioprod Dept, 53-59, proj leader & sect supvr, 59-64, mgr, Dow Int Bioprod Bus Develop, 64-66, mgr bioprod, Europ Area, Dow Chem Int, 66-71, inter-area tech mgr agr prod, 71-81; RETIRED. *Mem:* Soc Am Foresters. *Res:* Woody plant control with herbicides; industrial vegetation control; wildlife management; weed control in crops. *Mailing Add:* 5109 Foxcroft Midland MI 48640

COULTER, LOWELL VERNON, b Marion, Ohio, July 3, 13; m 37; c 2. PHYSICAL CHEMISTRY, SOLID STATE CHEMISTRY. *Educ:* Heidelberg Col, BS, 35; Colo Col, AM, 37; Univ Calif, Berkeley, PhD(chem), 40. *Prof Exp:* Instr chem, Colo Col, 35-37; asst, Univ Calif, 37-40; instr, Univ Idaho, 40-42; instr, Boston Univ, 42-44, from asst prof to assoc prof chem, 46-55, prof, 55-79, chmn dept, 61-72; RETIRED. *Concurrent Pos:* Group leader, Manhattan Proj, Monsanto Chem Co, Ohio, 44-45. *Mem:* Fel AAAS; Am Chem Soc; Am Phys Soc; Sigma Xi. *Res:* Application of the third law of thermodynamics; low temperature calorimetry; solution calorimetry; properties of liquid ammonia solutions of metals; thermodynamic properties of clathrates. *Mailing Add:* 14 Foxhill St Westwood MA 02090

COULTER, MALCOLM WILFORD, b Suffield, Conn, Dec 30, 20; m 48; c 5. WILDLIFE ECOLOGY. *Educ:* Univ Conn, BS, 42; Univ Maine, MS, 48; Syracuse Univ, PhD, 66. *Prof Exp:* Proj leader furbearers, Vt State Fish & Game Serv, 48-49; instr wildlife resources & asst leader res unit, 49-52, from asst prof to assoc prof, 52-62, PROF WILDLIFE RESOURCES, UNIV MAINE, ORONO, 62-, ASSOC DIR SCH FOREST RESOURCES, 68- *Mem:* AAAS; Wildlife Soc; Am Soc Mammal. *Res:* Ecology and behavior of furbearing animals; waterfowl breeding biology, ecology, behavior and population dynamics; marsh ecology and management. *Mailing Add:* Sch of Forest Resources Univ of Maine Orono ME 04469

COULTER, MURRAY WHITFIELD, b El Dorado, Ark, May 2, 32; m 59; c 2. PLANT PHYSIOLOGY, GENETICS. *Educ:* Emory Univ, BA, 54; Univ Ariz, MS, 56; Univ Calif, Los Angeles, PhD(plant sci), 63. *Prof Exp:* Teaching fel bot, Univ Ariz, 55-56; asst, Univ Calif, Los Angeles, 56-58, teaching & res assoc, 58-59; asst prof biol, Calif State Univ, Northridge, 59-62; res botanist, Inst Geophys & Planetary Physics & fel bot & plant biochem, Univ Calif, Los Angeles, 62-64; asst prof, 64-67, ASSOC PROF BIOL SCI, TEX TECH UNIV, 67- *Concurrent Pos:* Calif Res Found grant, 58-59; consult, NAm Aviation, Inc, 62-63. *Mem:* Fel AAAS; Genetics Soc Am; Am Soc Plant Physiol; Bot Soc Am; Am Inst Biol Sci. *Res:* Physiological genetics; Gibberellin studies with microorganisms and genetic mutants of maize; photoperiod and endogenous rhythms as related to biological clocks; environmental control of plant growth and development; hormones and plant growth regulators; biochemistry. *Mailing Add:* Dept of Biol Sci Tex Tech Univ Lubbock TX 79409

COULTER, NEAL STANLEY, b Columbus, Ga, May 3, 44; m 66; c 2. COMPUTER SCIENCE, INFORMATION SCIENCE. *Educ:* Univ Ala, BS, 65, MA, 66; Ga Inst Technol, MS, 72, PhD(info & comput sci), 74. *Prof Exp:* Assoc res engr appl math, Boeing Co, Ala, 66-67; asst prof math & comput sci, Columbus Col, 67-75; assoc prof & dir comput systs, 75-81, ASSOC PROF COMPUT & INFO SYSTS, FLA ATLANTIC UNIV, 81- *Concurrent Pos:* Fac assoc, IBM, 81. *Mem:* Asn Comput Mach; Inst Elec & Electronics Engrs; Comput Soc. *Res:* Application of semantic information measures based on logical probability in the simulation of inductive and deductive processes; cognitive processes and computer programming. *Mailing Add:* Dept of Comput Systs Fla Atlantic Univ Boca Raton FL 33431

COULTER, NORMAN ARTHUR, JR, b Atlanta, Ga, Jan 9, 20; m 51; c 1. PHYSIOLOGY, BIOPHYSICS. *Educ:* Va Polytech Inst, BS, 41; Harvard Univ, MD, 50. *Prof Exp:* Instr math, Va Polytech Inst, 46; Nat Res Coun fel, Johns Hopkins Univ, 50-52; asst prof physiol, Ohio State Univ, 52-55, from asst prof to assoc prof physiol & biophys, 55-65; assoc prof, 65-67, sci dir, A F Fortune Biomed Comput Ctr, 70-78, PROF BIOENG & BIOMATH, UNIV NC, CHAPEL HILL, 67-, CHMN BIOMED ENG & MATH CURRICULUM, 69- *Concurrent Pos:* Consult, NIH. *Mem:* Am Soc Cybernet; Biophys Soc; Am Physiol Soc; Biomed Eng Soc; Inst Elec & Electronics Engrs. *Res:* Hemodynamics; teleogenic system theory; biological cybernetics; biomathematics; biomedical computing. *Mailing Add:* Dept of Surg Univ NC 152 Macnider 202 H Chapel Hill NC 27514

COULTER, PHILIP W, b Phenix City, Ala, Apr 19, 38; m 60; c 2. THEORETICAL NUCLEAR PHYSICS. *Educ:* Univ Ala, BS, 59, MS, 61; Stanford Univ, PhD(physics), 65. *Prof Exp:* Res assoc physics, Univ Mich, 65-67; asst res physicist, Univ Calif, Irvine, 67-68, asst prof physics, 67-71; assoc prof, 71-76, PROF PHYSICS, UNIV ALA, 76- *Mem:* Am Phys Soc; Sigma Xi. *Res:* Atomic and molecular collisions and interactions. *Mailing Add:* Dept of Physics & Astron Univ of Ala University AL 35486

COULTER, RICHARD LINCOLN, b Pittsburgh, Pa, Feb 12, 45; m 74. ATMOSPHERIC PHYSICS. *Educ:* Kalamazoo Col, BA, 67; Rutgers Univ, MS, 69; Pa State Univ, PhD(meteorol), 76. *Prof Exp:* Sr proj assoc meteorol, Pa State Univ, 76-77; asst meteorologist, 77-81, METEOROLOGIST, ARGONNE NAT LAB, 81- *Concurrent Pos:* Consult. *Mem:* Sigma Xi; Am Meteorol Soc. *Res:* Remote sensing of the atmosphere; acoustic sounding in the atmosphere; micrometeorology. *Mailing Add:* Atmospheric Physics Sect Argonne Nat Lab Argonne IL 60439

COULTER, SAMUEL TODD, b Weiser, Idaho, Sept 15, 03; m 28; c 3. DAIRY MANUFACTURING. *Educ:* Ore State Col, BS, 25; Univ Minn, MS, 30, PhD(dairy husb), 33. *Prof Exp:* Asst, Dairy Div, Univ Minn, 25-28; mgr, State Exp Creamery, Minn, 28-30; from instr to prof dairy husb, 30-72, head dept dairy indust, 59-66 & dept food sci & indust, 66-72, EMER PROF FOOD SCI & NUTRIT, UNIV MINN, ST PAUL, 72- *Concurrent Pos:* Sect chmn, Int Dairy Cong, Australia, 70. *Honors & Awards:* Borden Award. *Mem:* Fel AAAS; Inst Food Technol; Am Dairy Sci Asn (vpres, 62-63, pres, 63-64). *Res:* Quality and deterioration of dry milk products; design of spray driers; manufacture of foreign type cheeses; food dehydration; processes for cheese manufacture. *Mailing Add:* Dept of Food Sci & Indust Univ of Minn St Paul MN 55108

COULTHARD, THOMAS LIONEL, b Abernethy, Sask, July 17, 09; m 34; c 1. AGRICULTURAL & SANITARY ENGINEERING. *Educ:* Univ Sask, BE, 35; Univ Calif, MSc, 51; Univ Delft, dipl sanit eng, 70. *Prof Exp:* Refinery chemist, Consumers Co-op Refineries, Sask, 35-37; sales mgr, Brackman-Kerr Milling Co, 38-42; refinery chemist, Standard Oil Co of BC, Ltd, 42-47; from asst prof to prof agr eng, 47-75, chmn dept, 54-69, EMER PROF AGR ENG & MECH, UNIV BC, 75- *Concurrent Pos:* Can Govt External Aid Dept rep, prog agr eng & head dept, dean fac agr & mem univ coun, Univ Ghana, 62-63; tech officer, Food & Agr Orgn, UN, East Pakistan, 65. *Mem:* Soc Automotive

Engrs; Am Soc Agr Engrs. *Res:* Problems relating to drainage, irrigation water management, water quality, sanitary engineering, processing of animal manures, sludges from municipal treatment plants. *Mailing Add:* 4433 W Sixth Ave Vancouver BC V6R 1V2 Can

COUNCE, SHEILA JEAN, b Hayes Center, Nebr, Mar 18, 27; m 60. GENETICS, EMBRYOLOGY. *Educ:* Univ Colo, BA, 48, MA, 50; Univ Edinburgh, PhD(genetics), 54. *Prof Exp:* Lab asst biol, embryol & genetics, Univ Colo, 48-50, instr, 50; demonstr gentics, Univ Edinburgh, 51; lab assoc, Jackson Mem Lab, 54-55; Macauley fel, Univ Edinburgh, 55-56; NSF fel, Zurich, Switz, 56-57; from res asst to res assoc biol, Yale Univ, 57-65; assoc anat, 67-68, res assoc zool, 65-78, from asst prof to assoc prof, 69-78, PROF ANAT, SCH MED, DUKE UNIV, 78- *Mem:* Fel AAAS; Soc Develop Biol; Am Soc Zool; Am Soc Naturalists; Genetics Soc Am. *Res:* Developmental genetics; experimental embryology, especially with insects. *Mailing Add:* Dept of Anat Box 3011 Duke Univ Med Ctr Durham NC 27710

COUNCIL, MARION EARL, b Palmetto, Fla, May 20, 29; m 53; c 3. ELECTRICAL ENGINEERING. *Educ:* Univ Fla, BSEE, 57; La State Univ, MSEE, 60; Okla State Univ, PhD(eng), 65. *Prof Exp:* Transmission & distrib engr, Gulf State Utilities Co, 57-60; instr elec eng, La State Univ, 60-62 & Okla State Univ, 62-65; prof, La State Univ, 65-73; Dir, Sch Elec Eng & Comput Sci, 78-80, OKLA GAS & ELEC PROF ENG, UNIV OKLA, 73- *Concurrent Pos:* Ed-in-chief, Elec Power Systs J, 77-; prin investr, elec distrib syst proj, US Dept Energy & mandatory lighting stand proj, Okla Dept Energy, 78-79; head, Dept Electronics & Instruments, Barbay Engrs, Inc, 80-81. *Honors & Awards:* Halliburton Teaching Excellence Award; Western Elec Award for Excellence in Teaching. *Mem:* Inst Elec & Electronics Engrs; Am Soc Eng Educ. *Res:* Electric power systems, specifically distribution and planning; energy conservation; electrical components. *Mailing Add:* Sch Elec Eng & Comput Sci 202 W Boyd Rm 219 Norman OK 73019

COUNCILL, RICHARD J, b Greenville, SC, May 26, 23; m 49; c 5. PETROGRAPHY, SEDIMENTOLOGY. *Educ:* Univ NC, BS, 48, MS, 56. *Prof Exp:* Geologist, US Geol Surv, 48-51; econ geologist, NC Dept Conserv & Develop, 52-55; indust geologist, Atlantic Coast Line RR, 55-60, gen indust geologist, 60-67; gen indust geologist, Seaboard Coast Line RR, 67-73, MGR INDUST DEVELOP & CHIEF GEOLOGIST, SEABOARD COAST LINE RR & LOUISVILLE & NASHVILLE RR, 73-; DIR, INT RESOURCES DEVELOP CORP, 68- *Mem:* Am Inst Prof Geol; Am Inst Mining & Metall Eng; Geol Soc Am. *Res:* Resources development. *Mailing Add:* 3126 Bridlewood Lane Jacksonville FL 32217

COUNSELL, RAYMOND ERNEST, b Vancouver, BC, Aug 20, 30; US citizen; c 3. MEDICINAL CHEMISTRY, PHARMACOLOGY. *Educ:* Univ BC, BSP, 53; Univ Minn, PhD(pharmaceut & org chem), 57. *Prof Exp:* Lectr, Univ BC, 53-54; sr res chemist, G D Searle & Co, 57-64; assoc prof, 64-69, PROF MED CHEM, UNIV MICH, ANN ARBOR, 69-, PROF PHARMACOL, 72- *Concurrent Pos:* Res assoc, Am Cancer Soc, 64-71; mem med chem study sect A, NIH, 68-72; E Roosevelt Inst fel cancer res, Univ Milan & Univ Uppsala, 72-73; mem prog comt pharmacol & toxicol, Nat Inst Gen Med Sci; consult, Nat Inst Child Health & Develop, G D Searle & Co & Los Alamos Sci Labs; sect ed, Ann Reports in Med Chem. Assoc Award, Am. *Honors & Awards:* Czerniak Prize, Ahavat Zion Found, Israel, 74; T O Soine Mem Award, 81. *Mem:* Fel AAAS; Am Chem Soc; Am Soc Pharmacol & Exp Therapeut; fel Acad Pharmaceut Sci; Soc Nuclear Med. *Res:* Synthesis and molecular mode of action of chemical regulators of biological processes, especially adrenal hormone biogenesis; radiopharmaceuticals for diagnosis and treatment of cancer. *Mailing Add:* Dept of Pharmacol Univ of Mich Med Sch Ann Arbor MI 48109

COUNSELMAN, C J, b West Palm Beach, Fla, July 4, 25; m 49; c 4. ENTOMOLOGY, ICHTHYOLOGY. *Educ:* Auburn Univ, BS, 52, MS, 53. *Prof Exp:* Prod mgr, Big Springs Minnow Farm, 53-55; proj leader, Biol Surv Unit, State of Fla, 55-57; entom & plant path, Vero Beach Labs, Inc, 57-63; asst dir, 63-67, dir, Agr Chem Res, 67-70, MGR VERO BEACH STA, CIBA-GEIGY AGR DIV, CIBA AGROCHEM CO, 70- *Mem:* Entom Soc Am; Am Phytopath Soc; Soc Nematol; Am Inst Biol Sci: NY Acad Sci. *Res:* Research, development and registration of chemicals for agricultural purposes. *Mailing Add:* PO Box 1090 Vero Beach FL 32960

COUNSELMAN, CHARLES CLAUDE, III, b Baltimore, Md, Apr 27, 43; m 66. GEODESY, PLANETARY SCIENCES. *Educ:* Mass Inst Technol, BSEE, 64, MSEE, 65, PhD(instrumentation), 69. *Prof Exp:* Asst prof, 69-74, ASSOC PROF PLANETARY SCI, MASS INST TECHNOL, 74- *Mem:* Int Astron Union; Int Sci Radio Union; Am Geophys Union; Am Astron Soc; Inst Elec & Electronics Eng. *Res:* Long baseline radio interferometry applications to astronomy, geodesy, geophysics, solar system dynamics and testing general relativity. *Mailing Add:* Dept Earth & Planetary Sci Mass Inst Technol Cambridge MA 02139

COUNTER, FREDERICK T, JR, b Lowell, Mass, Dec 16, 34; m 63. VIROLOGY. *Educ:* Mass Col Pharm, BS, 56, MS, 58; Univ Mass, PhD(microbiol), 63. *Prof Exp:* Sr bacteriologist, 63-68, mgr biol develop, 68-69, HEAD IMMUNIZATION BIOL RES & DEVELOP, ELI LILLY & CO, 69- *Mem:* AAAS; Am Soc Microbiol; NY Acad Sci. *Res:* Biological research and development in bacterial and virus vaccines. *Mailing Add:* Eli Lilly & Co W National Rd Greenfield IN 46140

COUNTRYMAN, DAVID WAYNE, b Ottumwa, Iowa, May 21, 43; m 65; c 2. FOREST MANAGEMENT. *Educ:* Iowa State Univ, BS, 66, MF, 68; Univ Mich, PhD(forest mgt & planning), 73. *Prof Exp:* Actg exten forester, Iowa State Univ Exten Serv, USDA, 67-68, forester, Poplar Bluff Ranger Dist, Forest Serv, 68-70, Region 9 Off, 70-73 & Washington, DC Off, 73-74; assoc prof, 75-80, PROF FOREST MGT, IOWA STATE UNIV, 80- *Mem:* Soc Am Foresters; AAAS. *Res:* Forest administration and planning systems and processes; policy analysis and land use planning. *Mailing Add:* 251 Bessey Hall Iowa State Univ Ames IA 50011

COUNTRYMAN, JAMES JOSEPH, algebra, see previous edition

COUNTS, JON MILTON, b Richlands, Va, July 31, 37. PUBLIC HEALTH ADMINSTRATION. *Educ:* Univ Ariz, BS, 59; Tulane Univ, MPH, 63; Univ NC, DrPH(lab pract), 66. *Prof Exp:* Bacteriologist pub health, 60-62, asst dir, 66-73, dir lab licensure, 70-75, actg chief, 73-75, CHIEF BUR EPIDEMIOL & LAB HEALTH, SERV, STATE LAB, ARIZ DEPT HEALTH SERV, 75- *Concurrent Pos:* Chmn comt lab mgt, Nat Commun Dis Ctr Task Force, 71-73; qual assurance coordr, Adv Comt, Region IX, Environ Protection Agency, 74- *Mem:* Am Pub Health Asn; Am Soc Microbiologists; Conf State & Prov Pub Health Lab Dirs. *Res:* Laboratory management; development of clinical laboratories in quality assurance; disease control, immunization and epidemiology. *Mailing Add:* 1520 W Adams Phoenix AZ 85007

COUNTS, WAYNE BOYD, b Prosperity, SC, Oct 27, 36; m 62; c 1. ORGANIC CHEMISTRY. *Educ:* Furman Univ, BS, 58; Univ NC, PhD(org chem), 64. *Prof Exp:* Staff fel, Nat Cancer Inst, 63-66; prof chem, Lincoln Mem Univ, 66-69, head dept, 68-69; assoc prof, 69-73, PROF CHEM, GA SOUTHWESTERN COL, 73-, COORDR DEPT, 80- *Mem:* Am Chem Soc. *Res:* Organic synthesis; heterocyclic chemistry. *Mailing Add:* Dept of Chem Ga Southwestern Col Americus GA 31709

COUPER, JAMES R(ILEY), b St Louis, Mo, Dec 10, 25; m 53; c 2. CHEMICAL ENGINEERING. *Educ:* Washington Univ, St Louis, BS, 49, MS, 50, DSc(chem eng), 57. *Prof Exp:* Res chemist, Presstite Eng Co, Mo, 50; res engr, Mo Portland Cement Co, 50-51; eng trainee, Monsanto Chem Co, 52-53, chem engr, 53-56, sr engr, 56-58, prod supvr, 58-59; assoc prof chem eng, 59-65, acting head dept, 68-69, admin asst res coordr, 65-68, head dept chem eng, 69-79, PROF CHEM ENG, UNIV ARK, FAYETTEVILLE, 65- *Mem:* Fel Am Inst Chem; Am Inst Chem Engrs; Am Chem Soc; Am Soc Eng Educ; Am Asn Cost Engrs. *Res:* Heat transfer and thermal properties of two-phase systems; rheology of complex materials; fluidization; plant design and economics. *Mailing Add:* Dept of Chem Eng Univ of Ark Fayetteville AR 72701

COUPERUS, MOLLEURUS, b Essen, Ger, Jan 27, 06; nat US; m 39; c 4. DERMATOLOGY. *Educ:* Andrews Univ, BA, 27; Loma Linda Univ, MD, 34. *Prof Exp:* Prof dermat & syphilol, 47-80, chmn dept dermat, 64-77, PROF PHYS ANTHROP, LOMA LINDA UNIV, 75- *Mem:* Am Acad Dermat; Soc Invest Dermat. *Res:* Tumors of the skin; physical anthropology. *Mailing Add:* PO Box 6 Angwin CA 94508

COUPET, JOSEPH, b Port-Au-Prince, Haiti, Sept 7, 37; US citizen; m 63; c 2. BIOCHEMICAL PHARMACOLOGY. *Educ:* Ny Univ, BS, 62, MS, 69, PhD(biochem pharmacol), 72. *Prof Exp:* Res asst, Hillside Psychiat Hosp, 62-64; res assoc, Med Ctr, NY Univ, 64-73; SR RES SCIENTIST, BIOCHEM PHARMACOL, LEDERLE LABS, 73- *Concurrent Pos:* Instr, NY Univ Med Ctr, 72-73. *Mem:* Am Chem Soc; AAAS. *Res:* Cyclic nucleotide system; kinetics of receptor binding pertaining to the mechanism of action of antipsychotic and anxiolytic agents. *Mailing Add:* 28 Haller Crescent Spring Valley NY 10977

COUPLAND, ROBERT THOMAS, b Winnipeg, Man, Jan 24, 20; m 45; c 1. GRASSLAND ECOLOGY, SYSTEMS ECOLOGY. *Educ:* Univ Man, BSA, 46; Univ Nebr, PhD(bot), 49. *Prof Exp:* Student asst range studies, Dom Dept Agr, Sask, 41-46; officer in chg, Dom Forest Serv, Man, 46; asst bot, Univ Nebr, 46-47; from asst prof to assoc prof, 48-57, PROF PLANT ECOL, UNIV SASK, 57-, HEAD DEPT, 48- *Concurrent Pos:* Dir Matador Proj, Int Ctr Grasslands Studies, Int Biol Prog, 67-77, chmn int coord comt grasslands & mem productivity terrestrial sect comt. *Honors & Awards:* Can Centennial Medal. *Mem:* Fel AAAS; Am Inst Biol Sci; Brit Ecol Soc; Int Asn Ecol; Ecol Soc Am. *Res:* Nutrient balance and energy flow in cropland and natural grassland ecosystems; classification of grasslands; autecology of native plants, weeds and crop plants; studies of succession resulting from grazing and land abandonment. *Mailing Add:* Dept Plant Ecol Univ Sask Saskatoon SK S7H 0W0 Can

COURANT, ERNEST DAVID, b Goettingen, Ger, Mar 26, 20; nat US; m 44; c 2. THEORETICAL PHYSICS. *Educ:* Swarthmore Col, BA, 40; Univ Rochester, MS, 42, PhD(physics), 43. *Prof Exp:* Asst physics, Univ Rochester, 40-43; sci officer, Nat Res Coun Can, 43-46; res assoc theoret physics, Cornell Univ, 46-48; consult, 47-48, from assoc physicist to physicist, 48-60, SR PHYSICIST, BROOKHAVEN NAT LAB, 60- *Concurrent Pos:* Vis asst prof, Princeton Univ, 50-51; Fulbright res grant, Cambridge Univ, 56; consult, Gen Atomic Div, Gen Dynamics Corp, 58; vis prof, Yale Univ, 61-62, Brookhaven prof, 62-67; prof, State Univ NY Stony Brook, 67-; vis physicist, Nat Accelerator Lab, 68-69; vis scientist, Europ Orgn Nuclear Res, 74. *Honors & Awards:* Plegel Prize, NY Acad Sci, 79. *Mem:* Nat Acad Sci; fel AAAS; Am Phys Soc; NY Acad Sci. *Res:* Theory of solids; chain reactors, particle accelerators and nuclear reactions. *Mailing Add:* Brookhaven Nat Lab Upton NY 11973

COURANT, HANS WOLFGANG JULIUS, b Ger, Oct 30, 24; nat US; div; c 3. HIGH ENERGY PHYSICS. *Educ:* Mass Inst Technol, BS, 49, PhD(physics), 54. *Prof Exp:* Asst, Mass Inst Technol, 49-54, res assoc physics, 54; Fulbright grant, Polytech Sch, Paris, 54-55; asst res physicist, Univ Calif, 55-56; from instr to asst prof, Yale Univ, 56-61; Ford Found fel, 61-62; NSF sr fel, Europ Orgn Nuclear Res, Geneva, 62-63; assoc prof, 63-68, PROF PHYSICS, UNIV MINN, MINNEAPOLIS, 68- *Concurrent Pos:* Vis assoc physicist, Brookhaven Nat Lab, 56-57, 58, 59-, guest physicist, 57, 58-; physicist, Radiation Lab, Univ Calif, 57; consult, Argonne Nat Lab, 64-70; vis prof, Univ Heidelberg, 69-70. *Mem:* Am Phys Soc. *Res:* Experimental high energy physics; cosmic rays. *Mailing Add:* Sch of Physics Univ of Minn Minneapolis MN 55455

COURCHENE, WILLIAM LEON, b Springfield, Mass, Nov 15, 26; m 48; c 3. PHYSICAL CHEMISTRY. *Educ:* Univ Mass, BS, 48; Cornell Univ, PhD(chem), 52. *Prof Exp:* Asst, Cornell Univ, 48-52; res chemist, 52-67, sect head, 67-74, ASSOC DIR, PROCTER & GAMBLE, 74- *Mem:* Am Chem Soc; AAAS; Sigma Xi. *Res:* Infrared and mass spectroscopy; solution thermodynamics; proteins. *Mailing Add:* 8678 Elmtree Ave Cincinnati OH 45231

COURCHESNE, ERIC, b Berkeley, Calif, Apr 3, 49; m 70; c 1. NEUROPSYCHOLOGY, NEUROPHYSIOLOGY. *Educ:* Univ Calif, Berkeley, BA, 70; Univ Calif, San Diego, PhD(neurosci), 75. *Prof Exp:* Res neuroscientist, Sch Med, Univ Calif, San Diego, 75; scholar psychiat, Sch Med, Stanford Univ, 76-77, res assoc psychol, 77-78; ASST PROF NEUROSCI, SCH MED, UNIV CALIF, SAN DIEGO, 78- *Res:* Relationships between the maturation of the central nervous system and the development of cognitive, attentional and memory abilities in normal and neurologically impaired individuals. *Mailing Add:* 5535 Beaumont Ave La Jolla CA 92037

COURI, DANIEL, b Streator, Ill, Oct 4, 30; m 59; c 4. TOXICOLOGY, BIOCHEMICAL PHARMACOLOGY. *Educ:* Queens Col, BS, 54; New York Univ, MS, 58; State Univ NY, Brooklyn, PHD(pharmacol), 65. *Prof Exp:* PROF PHARMACOL, DEPT PHARMACOL, OHIO STATE UNIV, 65-, DIR, DIV TOXICOL, 67- *Mem:* Am Soc Pharmacol & Exp Therapeut; Am Indust Hygiene Asn; Am Acad Forensic Sci; Am Conf Govt Indust Hygienists; Soc Toxicol. *Res:* Mechanism of action of chemical agents on living systems resulting in beneficial or deleterious effects, especially the enzymatic and molecular aspects. *Mailing Add:* Dept Pharm Ohio State Univ 333 W 10th Ave Columbus OH 43210

COURNAND, ANDRE FREDERIC, b Paris, France, Sept 24, 95; nat US; m 24; c 3. MEDICINE. *Educ:* Univ Paris, BA, 13, PCN, 14, MD, 30; Univ Nancy, DHC, 69. *Hon Degrees:* DUniv, Univ Strasbourg, 57, Univ Lyon, 58, Free Univ Brussels, 59, Univ Pisa, 60; DSc, Univ Birmingham, 61, Gustavus Adolphus Col, 63, Columbia Univ, 65. *Prof Exp:* From instr to assoc, 34-42, from asst prof to prof, 42-64, EMER PROF MED, COL PHYSICIANS & SURGEONS, COLUMBIA UNIV, 64- *Honors & Awards:* Nobel Prize Med & Physiol, 56; Retzius Silver Medal, Swedish Soc Internal Med, 46; Lasker Award, Am Pub Health Asn, 49; Phillips Award, Am Col Physicians, 52; Gold Medal, Royal Acad Med, Brussels, 56; Jiminez Diaz Award, Madrid, 70. *Mem:* Nat Acad Sci; Am Physiol Soc; Asn Thoracic Surg; Am Thoracic Soc; hon fel Royal Soc Med. *Res:* Applied physiology of respiration and circulation. *Mailing Add:* 1361 Madison Ave New York NY 10010

COURSEN, BRADNER WOOD, b Roselle Park, NJ, Feb 10, 29; m 54; c 3. CELLULAR AGING. *Educ:* Drew Univ, BA, 52; Univ Md, MS, 57, PhD(fungus physiol), 59. *Prof Exp:* Jr chemist, Res Dept, Am Can Co, 52-55; instr biol & plant physiol, Lawrence Univ, 59-61, from asst prof to assoc prof biol, 61-68; assoc prof, 68-69, PROF BIOL, COL WILLIAM & MARY, 69- *Concurrent Pos:* Pres, Wis State Bd Exam in Basic Sci, 65-69. *Mem:* Bot Soc Am. *Res:* Mechanism of action of antibiotics; fungus physiology and metabolism; biology and biochemistry of cellular aging. *Mailing Add:* Dept of Biol Col of William & Mary Williamsburg VA 23185

COURSEN, DAVID LINN, b Newark, NJ, May 7, 23; m 45; c 4. ROCK MECHANICS. *Educ:* Columbia Univ, BA, 43; Cornell Univ, PhD(chem), 51. *Prof Exp:* Res chemist, 50-58, sr res chemist, 58-59, tech assoc, 59-61, res assoc, 61-66, prod mgr, 66-67, res & develop mgr, 67-70, RES FEL, E I DU PONT DE NEMOURS & CO, INC, 70- *Concurrent Pos:* Assoc, Woods Hole Oceanog Inst. *Mem:* Am Chem Soc; Int Soc Rock Mech; Soc Explor Geophysicists; Sigma Xi. *Res:* Crystal structure; x-ray diffraction; explosives; radiography; underwater acoustics; mining and quarrying oil and gas well stimulation; working of mineral deposits in place. *Mailing Add:* 6850 Tippetts Dr Mercersburg PA 17236

COURSEY, BERT MARCEL, b Birmingham, Ala, Mar 27, 42; m 65; c 3. RADIO CHEMISTRY, NUCLEAR MEDICINE. *Educ:* Univ Ga, BS Chem, 65, PhD(phys chem), 70. *Prof Exp:* Rubber chemist mfg, SEastern Rubber Mfg Co, 64-67; teaching asst, Chem Dept, Undergrad Lab, Univ Ga, 67-68; with Army off nuclear power, US Army Engr Reactors Group, 69-71; RES CHEMIST RADIOACTIVITY, US NAT BUR STANDARDS, 72- *Concurrent Pos:* Ed, Int J Appl Radiation & Isotopes, 77- *Mem:* Am Chem Soc; Am Nuclear Soc; AAAs; Am Soc Testing & Mat. *Res:* Methods for the accurate measurement of radioisotopes. *Mailing Add:* Radioactivity Group Rm C114 Bldg 245 Nat Bur Standards Washington DC 20234

COURT, ANITA, b Chicago, Ill, Aug 15, 30. REACTOR PHYSICS, PHYSICAL INORGANIC CHEMISTRY. *Educ:* Ill Inst Technol, BS, 52; Mich State Univ, PhD(chem), 56. *Prof Exp:* Asst chemist, M W Kellogg Co Div, Pullman, Inc, 56-59; chemist, Brookhaven Nat Lab, 59-70; scientist, 70-75, prin engr, 75-76, ADV ENGR, ADVAN REACTORS DIV, WESTINGHOUSE ELEC CORP, 76- *Mem:* Am Chem Soc; Am Nuclear Soc. *Res:* Shielding, safety analysis, core mechanics testing. *Mailing Add:* Advan Reactor Div Westinghouse Elec Corp Madison PA 15663

COURT, ARNOLD, b Seattle, Wash, June 20, 14; m 41; c 3. CLIMATOLOGY. *Educ:* Univ Okla, BA, 34, Univ Wash, Seattle, MS, 49; Univ Calif, Berkeley, PhD(geog), 56. *Prof Exp:* Meteorologist, US Weather Bur, 38-43; climatologist & head climat unit, Res & Develop Br, Off Qm Gen, US Dept Army, 46-51; res meteorologist, Statist Lab, Univ Calif, Berkeley, 52-54, lectr meteorol & climat, 56-57 & 58; meteorologist, Pac Southwest Forest & Range Exp Sta, US Forest Serv, 56-60; chief appl climat br, Geophys Res Directorate, Air Force Cambridge Res Labs, 60-62; res scientist, Lockheed-Calif Co, 62-64; chmn dept geog, 70-72, PROF CLIMAT, CALIF STATE UNIV, NORTHRIDGE, 62- *Concurrent Pos:* Chief meteorologist, US Antarctic Serv, Little Am, 40-41; consult, Lockheed-Calif Co, 64-78. *Mem:* AAAS; Am Geophys Union; Asn Am Geog; Am Meteorol Soc; fel Am Statist Asn. *Res:* History and principles of climatic diagrams; statistical analysis of climate; cloud seeding evaluation; wind energy computations. *Mailing Add:* 17168 Septo St Northridge CA 91325

COURT, WILLIAM ARTHUR, b Canmore, Alta, Feb 14, 43; m 66; c 2. ORGANIC CHEMISTRY, ANALYTICAL CHEMISTRY. *Educ:* Carleton Univ, BSc, 65, MSc, 68; Univ NB, PhD(chem), 70. *Prof Exp:* RES SCIENTIST, AGR CAN RES STA, 73- *Mem:* Am Chem Soc; Chem Inst Can. *Res:* Synthesis and structural elucidation of compounds of biological interest; chemical and biological studies of tobacco; analytical methodology of plant constituents of biological interest. *Mailing Add:* Agr Can Chem Lab Res Sta Delhi ON N4B 2W9 Can

COURTENAY, WALTER ROWE, JR, b Neenah, Wis, Nov 6, 33; m 60; c 2. MARINE BIOLOGY, ICHTHYOLOGY. *Educ:* Vanderbilt Univ, BA, 56; Univ Miami, Fla, MS, 60, PhD(marine biol), 65. *Prof Exp:* Temp instr zool, Duke Univ, 63-64, vis asst prof, 64-65; asst prof biol, Boston Univ, 65-67; assoc ichthyol, Mus Comp Zool, Harvard Univ, 65-68; from asst prof to assoc prof, 67-72, PROF ZOOL, FLA ATLANTIC UNIV, 72- *Concurrent Pos:* NSF res grants, 65-69. *Mem:* Am Soc Ichthyol & Herpet; Am Fisheries Soc; Soc Syst Zool. *Res:* Systematics, functional morphology and ecology of marine fishes, especially within the families of Ophidiidae, Brotulidae, Serranidae, Pomadasyidae and related groups; sonic mechanisms in fishes; introduced exotic fishes. *Mailing Add:* Dept of Biol Sci Fla Atlantic Univ Boca Raton FL 33431

COURTER, R(OBERT) W(AYNE), b Denver, Colo, June 12, 35; m 56; c 3. FLUID MECHANICS, AERODYNAMICS. *Educ:* Univ Tex, BS, 57, MS, 58, PhD(aerospace eng), 65. *Prof Exp:* Assoc engr, McDonnell Aircraft Corp, Mo, 58-60; instr aerospace eng, Univ Tex, 60-64; asst prof mech eng, Univ Wyo, 64-68; ASSOC PROF MECH ENG, LA STATE UNIV, BATON ROUGE, 68-, ASST TO DEAN, 80- *Concurrent Pos:* Am Soc Eng Educ-Ford Found resident eng, Gen Dynamics Corp, Tex, 69-70. *Mem:* Am Inst Aeronaut & Astronaut; Am Soc Eng Educ. *Res:* Hypervelocity impact; rarefied gas dynamics; subsonic aerodynamics; flight mechanics; vehicle design. *Mailing Add:* Dept of Mech Eng La State Univ Baton Rouge LA 70803

COURTNEY, GLADYS (ATKINS), b Erwin, Tenn, June 10, 30; m 67; c 2. MAMMALIAN PHYSIOLOGY, ENDOCRINOLOGY. *Educ:* La Col, BS, 56; La State Univ, MS, 58; Univ Ill Med Ctr, USPHS fel, 63-64, PhD(physiol), 64. *Prof Exp:* Gen duty nurse, Baptist Hosp, La, 52-56; teaching asst zool, La State Univ, 56-58; teaching asst physiol, Univ Ill, Urbana, 58-60; teaching asst & asst instr, Univ Ill Med Ctr, 60-65; asst prof biol, Malone Col, 65-68; assoc prof nursing & physiol, Univ Ill Med Ctr, 69-71, proj dir nurse scientist prog, Col Nursing, 69-76, prof nursing & physiol & head dept gen nursing, 71-76; dean, Sch Nursing, Univ Mo-Columbia, 76-80; DEAN, COL NURSING, MICH STATE UNIV, 81- *Res:* Relationship of adrenal cortex to ovarian function; prolongation of pseudopregnancy in hamsters; adrenal cortical function during environmental stress. *Mailing Add:* Col Nursing Mich State Univ East Lansing MI 48824

COURTNEY, KATHERINE DIANE, pharmacology, see previous edition

COURTNEY, KENNETH OLIVER, b St Paul, Minn, Nov 13, 06; m 41; c 3. MEDICAL RESEARCH. *Educ:* Ore State Col, BS, 29; McGill Univ, MD, 35; London Sch Trop Med, DMT & H, 48; Am Bd Prev Med, dipl, 49. *Prof Exp:* Technician, Mediter Fruitfly Campaign, USDA, 29-30; instr bact, San Diego State Col, 30-31, assoc prof, 32-33; intern, Gorgas Hosp, Panama CZ, 35-36, resident, 36-37, med officer, outpatient clins & leper colony, 37-39, health officer, Panama City, 39-40, asst chief health officer, 41-51, yellow fever campaign coordr for Armed Forces, Panama Canal & Repub of Panama, 49-50; zone rep, Pan-Am Serv Bur & WHO, Brazil, 51-58; mem staff, Dept Clin Invest, Parke, Davis & Co, 58-67, assoc dir clin therapeut, 67-69; INDEPENDENT CONSULT TROP MED, 69- *Mem:* AMA; Am Pub Health Asn; Am Soc Trop Med & Hyg; Royal Soc Trop Med & Hyg; Brazilian Soc Hyg & Pub Health. *Res:* Tropical diseases; malaria; yellow fever; leprosy; gastroenteritis; public health administration. *Mailing Add:* 12338 Filera Rd San Diego CA 92128

COURTNEY, KENNETH RANDALL, b Snohomish, Wash, Dec 24, 44; m 66; c 3. PHYSIOLOGY, PHARMACOLOGY. *Educ:* Wash State Univ, BS, 67; Univ Wash, MS, 68, PhD(physiol biophysics), 74. *Prof Exp:* Instr math, Centralia Col, 69-71; fel neurobiol, Univ Colo, 74-75; res assoc epilepsy, Med Ctr, Stanford Univ, 75-76 & res assoc membrane physiol, 76-77; cardiovasc pharmacologist, Stanford Res Inst, 76-78; sr res assoc physiol & pharmacol, 78-81, INVESTR PHYSIOL, PALO ALTO MED FOUND, 81- *Concurrent Pos:* NIH fel, 67-68 & 71-74; prin investr, Heart, Lung & Blood Inst grant, NIH, 77-; prin investr, NIH grant, 79- *Mem:* Soc Neurosci; Biophys Soc. *Res:* Factors determining stability of excitable tissues, including electrophysical characterization of anesthetic and anticonvulsant actions; antiarrythmic drug actions and drug development; cardiac automaticity and its autonomic control. *Mailing Add:* Palo Alto Med Res Found 860 Bryant St Palo Alto CA 94301

COURTNEY, RICHARD JAMES, b Greenville, Pa, July 2, 41; m 66; c 2. VIROLOGY. *Educ:* Grove City Col, BS, 63; Syracuse Univ, MS, 66, PhD(microbiol), 68. *Prof Exp:* NIH fel, Baylor Col Med, 68-70, from asst prof to assoc prof virol, 70-78; assoc prof, 78-81, PROF MICROBIOL, UNIV TENN, KNOXVILLE, 81- *Mem:* Am Soc Microbiol; Sigma Xi. *Res:* The biochemical and immunological characterization of the proteins and glycoproteins of herpes simplex viruses and to identify their functional role in virus-infected and transformed cells. *Mailing Add:* Dept of Microbiol Univ of Tenn Knoxville TN 37996

COURTNEY, THOMAS HUGH, b Dallas, Tex, Sept 26, 38; m 60; c 4. PHYSICAL METALLURGY, MATERIALS SCIENCE. *Educ:* Mass Inst Technol, SB, 60, ScD(phys metall), 64; Cornell Univ, MS, 62. *Prof Exp:* Res metallurgist, Res Ctr, Babcock & Wilcox Co, Ohio, 64-66; res assoc phys metall, Mass Inst Technol, 66-68; from asst prof to prof mech eng, Univ Tex, Austin, 68-75; PROF METALL ENG, MICH TECHNOL UNIV, 75- *Concurrent Pos:* Guest scientist, Powder Metall Labs, Max Planck Inst Metals Res, Stuttgart, WGer. *Honors & Awards:* Adams Memorial Membership, Am Welding Soc, 73. *Mem:* Am Soc Metals; Am Inst Mining, Metall & Petrol Engrs; Am Soc Metals. *Res:* Fiber composite materials; mechanical behavior; powder metallurgy; stability of microstructure. *Mailing Add:* Dept of Metall Eng Mich Technol Univ Houghton MI 49931

COURTNEY, WELBY GILLETTE, b Hamilton, Ohio, Sept 17, 25. PHYSICAL CHEMISTRY. *Educ:* Oberlin Col, BA, 49; Iowa State Col, PhD(phys chem), 51. *Prof Exp:* Fel, Inst Atomic Res, Iowa, 51-52; sr chemist, Chem Construct Corp, NY, 52-55; res chemist, Freeport Sulphur Co, La, 55-56; sr scientist, Exp, Inc, 56-62; sect supvr heterogeneous combustion, Thiokol Chem Corp, 62-65, actg mgr physics dept, 65-68; SUPVRY RES CHEMIST, US BUR MINES, 68- *Concurrent Pos:* Consult phase transformation, Switz, 58. *Res:* Kinetics and thermodynamics of phase transformation; coupled kinetics-gas dynamics; reduction of respirable and float dust in coal and noncoal mines. *Mailing Add:* US Bur of Mines Pittsburgh Res Ctr PO Box 18070 Pittsburgh PA 15236

COURTNEY-PRATT, JEOFRY STUART, b Hobart, Australia, Jan 31, 20; m 57. PHYSICS, ENGINEERING. *Educ:* Univ Tasmania, BE, 42; Cambridge Univ, PhD, 49; ScD, 58. *Prof Exp:* From asst res officer to res officer, Lubricants & Bearings Div, Coun Sci & Indust Res, Australia, 41-44; res officer ballistic instrumentation, Brit Admiralty, Eng, 44-45; asst dir res, Depts Phys Chem & Physics, Cambridge Univ, 52-57; head, Dept Mech & Optics, 58-69, HEAD APPL PHYSICS DEPT, BELL TEL LABS, 69- *Concurrent Pos:* Consult, Tube Investments, Ltd, 53-55; Gen Elec Co, 55, Bell Tel Labs, 56-58 & Brit Ministry Supply; lectr, US, 52 & German Phys Soc, 55. *Honors & Awards:* Stewart Prize, 46; Civic Medal, High Speed Photog Cong, Paris, 54; Boys Prize, 54; Gold Medal, Photog Soc Vienna, 61; Dupont Gold Medal, Soc Motion Picture & TV Eng, 61; Progress Medal, 69; Alan Gordon Mem Award, Soc Photo-Optical Instrument Engrs, 74. *Mem:* Hon mem Soc Motion Picture & TV Eng; fel Optical Soc Am; fel Royal Photog Soc Gt Brit; Brit Inst Mech Eng; Brit Inst Physics. *Res:* Applied physics; instrumentation; high speed photography; optics; ballistics; physics of contact of solids friction; adhesion; electrical contacts; optical measurements on satellites; acoustics; electro-optics; recording systems. *Mailing Add:* Wigwam Rd Locust NJ 07760

COURTRIGHT, JAMES BEN, b El Dorado, Kans, Dec 7, 41; m 67; c 2. BIOCHEMICAL GENETICS, BIOCHEMISTRY. *Educ:* Yale Univ, AB, 63; Johns Hopkins Univ, PhD(genetics), 67. *Prof Exp:* Sci asst, Max Planck Inst Biol, 67-69; fac assoc, Univ Tex, Austin, 69-70; asst prof, 70-75, ASSOC PROF BIOL, MARQUETTE UNIV, 75- *Concurrent Pos:* Am Cancer Soc fel, 68-69; NSF grant, 69-70; Am Heart A Asn grant, 71-73; Am Cancer Soc grant, 71-76; NASA grant, 78-80; NIH grant, 79-82, 80-83. *Mem:* Am Genetic Asn; AAAS; Am Soc Microbiol; Genetics Soc Am. *Res:* Genetic control and regulation of membrane assembly in higher organisms; molecular mechanisms involved in mitochondrial membrane formation; Tissue specific gene expression in drosophila. *Mailing Add:* Dept of Biol Marquette Univ Milwaukee WI 53233

COURVILLE, JACQUES, b Montreal, PQ, Mar 17, 35; m 58; c 2. NEUROANATOMY. *Educ:* Univ Montreal, BA, 54, MD, 60, MSc, 62; Univ Oslo, Dr Med, 68. *Prof Exp:* Asst prof neurol & neurosurg, McGill Univ, 66-70; assoc prof, 70-76, PROF NEUROANAT, UNIV MONTREAL, 76-, HEAD DEPT NEUROSCI, 80- *Concurrent Pos:* Can Med Res Coun scholar, 67; mem res group neurol sci, Univ Montreal, 72. *Mem:* Am Asn Anatomists; Can Asn Anatomists; Soc Neurosci. *Res:* Experimental neuroanatomy with silver impregnation methods and injections of labelled amino acids; electron microscopy; red nucleus, facial nucleus, intracerebellar nuclei, cerebellar cortex, thalamic nuclei, inferior olive and pontine nuclei. *Mailing Add:* Dept of Physiol Univ of Montreal CP 6128 Montreal PQ H3C 3J7 Can

COURY, ARTHUR JOSEPH, b Coaldale, Pa, Dec 5, 40; m 67; c 2. ORGANIC CHEMISTRY, POLYMER CHEMISTRY. *Educ:* Univ Del, BS, 62; Univ Minn, PhD(org chem), 65. *Prof Exp:* SR RES CHEMIST II, GEN MILLS CHEM, INC, 65- *Mem:* Am Chem Soc. *Res:* Synthesis of monomers and polymers. *Mailing Add:* 2225 Hillside Ave St Paul MN 55108

COUSER, RAYMOND DOWELL, b Oklahoma City, Okla, Mar 11, 31; m 54; c 2. ENTOMOLOGY, INVERTEBRATE ZOOLOGY. *Educ:* Northeastern State Col, BSEd, 56; Univ Okla, MS, 59, PhD(zool), 67. *Prof Exp:* Instr biol, Baker Univ, 58-61; assoc prof zool, 65-75, PROF BIOL, ARK TECH UNIV, 75- *Res:* Insect physiology; cold tolerance. *Mailing Add:* Dept of Biol Ark Polytech Col Russellville AR 72801

COUSIN, MARIBETH ANN, b Beloit, Wis, Jan 26, 49. FOOD MICROBIOLOGY, DAIRY SCIENCE. *Educ:* Univ Wis, BS, 71, MS, 72, PhD(food sci), 76. *Prof Exp:* Res asst food microbiol, Univ Wis, 71-76; mgr dairy res & develop, Great Atlantic & Pac Tea Co, 77-78; ASST PROF FOOD MICROBIOL, PURDUE UNIV, 78- *Honors & Awards:* Richard M Hoyt Mem Award, Nat Milk Producers Fedn, Am Dairy Sci Asn, 77. *Mem:* Am Dairy Sci Asn; Inst Food Technologists; Soc Indust Microbiol; Nutrit Today Soc; Coun Agr Sci & Technol. *Res:* Psychrotrophs in milk and dairy products and their relation to keeping quality and various biochemical alterations in the milk products; chemical detection of mold in food products. *Mailing Add:* Dept of Animal Sci Purdue Univ West Lafayette IN 47907

COUSINEAU, GILLES H, b Montreal, Que, Sept 19, 32; m 59; c 2. MOLECULAR BIOLOGY, BIOCHEMISTRY. *Educ:* Col Ste-Marie de Montreal, BA, 54; Univ Montreal, BS, 58; NY Univ, MS, 61; Brown Univ, PhD(biochem), 64. *Prof Exp:* Res asst biol, Haskins Labs, 58-61; teaching fel, Brown Univ, 61-65; asst prof molecular biol, 65-71, ASSOC PROF BIOL SCI, UNIV MONTREAL, 71- *Concurrent Pos:* Res asst, Marine Biol Lab, Woods Hole, 58-63; independent investr, 66-; fel biol, Zool Sta, Naples, Italy, 64-65; grants, Nat Res Coun Can, 65-69, Montreal, 65-69; Damon Runyon Mem Fund, 66-68; Childs Mem Fund, 66-67; Donner Can Found, 66-67; Soc Sigma Xi, 66-67 & Defense Res Bd Can, 67-69. *Mem:* Electron Micros Soc Am; Can Soc Cell Biol; Am Soc Cell Biol; NY Acad Sci; Int Soc Develop Biol. *Res:* Synthesis of macromolecules in developing sea urchin eggs; cell division and differentiation. *Mailing Add:* Lab of Molecular Biol Univ of Montreal Montreal PQ H3C 3J7 Can

COUSINS, ROBERT JOHN, b New York, NY, Apr 5, 41; m 69; c 3. NUTRITIONAL BIOCHEMISTRY. *Educ:* Univ Vt, BA, 63; Univ Conn, MS, 65, PhD(exp nutrit), 68. *Prof Exp:* Res assoc biochem, Univ Wis, 68-69, NIH fel, 69-70; asst prof, Rutgers Univ, 71-74, assoc prof nutrit, 74-77, prof nutrit biochem, 77-79, distinguished prof, 79-82; BOSTON FAMILY PROF HUMAN NUTRIT, UNIV FLA, 82- *Honors & Awards:* Mead Johnson Award, Am Inst Nutrit. *Mem:* Am Chem Soc; Am Inst Nutrit; Am Soc Biol Chem; Soc Exp Biol Med; Soc Toxicol. *Res:* Function of metals in mammalian systems, emphasizing nutrition and disease; regulatory aspects of zinc, copper and cadmium metabolism; control of metalloprotein biosynthesis and degradation; mineral nutrition, mineral absorption and transport; deficiency diseases and toxicology. *Mailing Add:* Dept Food Sci Human Nutrit Univ Fla Gainesville FL 32611

COUSMINER, HAROLD L, micropaleontology, geology, see previous edition

COUTANT, CHARLES COE, b Jamestown, NY, Aug 2, 38; m 62; c 2. AQUATIC ECOLOGY, ZOOLOGY. *Educ:* Lehigh Univ, BA, 60, MS, 62, PhD(biol), 65. *Prof Exp:* Res scientist, Pac Northwest Div, Battelle Mem Inst, 65-70; prog mgr aquatic ecol, 70-78, SR RES ECOLOGIST, OAK RIDGE NAT LAB, 79- *Concurrent Pos:* Mem Comt Water Qual Criteria, Nat Acad Sci, 71-72; consult, Nat Comn Water Qual, 73-74; mem adv coun, Elec Power Res Inst, 73-80; adj assoc prof, Univ Tenn, Knoxville, 74- *Honors & Awards:* Darbaker Prize, Pa Acad Sci, 64; Battelle Excellence in Sci & Technol Award & Dir Award, Battelle Mem Inst, 68. *Mem:* AAAS; Sigma Xi; Am Fisheries Soc; Ecol Soc Am; Am Inst Fishery Res Biologists. *Res:* Effects of human alterations, particularly power plant cooling, on aquatic systems, including thermal effects, fish behavior, predator-prey relationships, population and community dynamics; energy-environment policy analysis; transport and fate modeling of chemicals in the environment. *Mailing Add:* Environ Sci Div Oak Ridge Nat Lab Oak Ridge TN 37830

COUTCHIE, PAMELA ANN, b San Mateo, Calif. INVERTEBRATE PHYSIOLOGY. *Educ:* Univ Calif, Santa Barbara, BA, 71; Univ Calif, Davis, PhD(zool), 77. *Prof Exp:* Res fel, Zool Dept, Univ Toronto, 77-80; ASST PROF, BIOL DEPT, SIENA COL, 80- *Concurrent Pos:* Res assoc, Zool Dept, Univ Toronto, 81. *Mem:* Am Soc Zoologists; Sigma Xi; AAAS. *Res:* Problem of water balance in invertebrates with a particular emphasis on desert arthropods; the mechanism of water vapor absorption and the physiological control of hemolymph osmolarity in larvae of tenebrionid beetles. *Mailing Add:* Biol Dept Siena Col Loudonville NY 12211

COUTINHO, CLAUDE BERNARD, b Bombay, India, Aug 19, 31; m 57; c 5. BIOCHEMISTRY, EXPERIMENTAL MEDICINE. *Educ:* Univ Bombay, BS, 52; Univ Bristol, dipl, 53; Univ Belfast, BM, 55; Inst Divi Thomae, PhD(exp med, biochem), 63; Rutgers Univ, NJ, MS, 75. *Prof Exp:* Res microbiologist, Inst Laryngol & Otol, London, 55-57; asst chief chemother & microbiol, Aspro-Nicholas Pharmaceut Co, Ltd, Eng, 57-58; dept chief, 58-60; res scientist, Warner-Lambert Res Inst, 63-65; sr res assoc, Arthur D Little, Inc, 65-67; from res group chief to sr res group chief, Hoffman-La Roche, 67-75, sr clin pharmacologist, 75-78; assoc dir clin pharmacol, USV Pharmaceut Corp, 78-80; SR DIR, DEPT CLIN PHARMACOL, IVES LABS DIV, AM HOME PROD, 80- *Mem:* AAAS; Am Soc Microbiol; Am Soc Pharmacol & Exp Therapeut; Am Soc Toxicol; NY Acad Sci. *Res:* Mechanism of pharmacological and toxicological drug action as related to biochemical changes and drug metabolism; pharmacokinetics; pharmacodynamics; tissue immunity; cancer; cellular metabolism; clinical pharmacology of therapeutic agents; pharmaceuticals and general chemotherapy. *Mailing Add:* Dept Clin Pharmacol, Ives Labs Div Am Home Prod New York NY 10017

COUTINHO, JOHN, US citizen; m 42; c 2. ENGINEERING. *Educ:* NY Univ, MAeroE, 41; Berlin Tech Univ, DrIng, 70. *Prof Exp:* Engr, Grumman Aerospace Corp, 39-72; GEN ENGR, US ARMY MAT SYSTS ANAL ACTIV, 72- *Concurrent Pos:* Adj prof aircraft design, Polytech Inst NY, 51-60. *Honors & Awards:* Laskowitz Gold Medal, NY Acad Sci, 64; Brumbaugh Award, Am Soc Qual Control, 72; Outstanding Serv Award, US Naval Air Systs Command, 72. *Mem:* Fel Am Soc Mech Engrs; fel Am Soc Qual Control; fel NY Acad Sci. *Res:* Reliability and maintainability for aircraft and space systems; stress analysis; structural design; control systems design. *Mailing Add:* 602 Westgate Rd Aberdeen MD 21005

COUTO, WALTER, b Montevideo, Uruguay, Jan 29, 32; m 62; c 2. SOIL SCIENCE, AGRONOMY. *Educ:* Univ of Repub, Uruguay, Ing Agr, 61; Postgrad Col, Mex, MC, 71; Cornell Univ, PhD(soils), 76. *Prof Exp:* Adv soil fertility, Agromax SA, 62-63; res assoc, Ctr Invest Agr Alberto Boerger, La Estanzuela, 64-73; asst prof trop soils, NC State Univ, 76-77; SR SCIENTIST SOILS & PASTURE DEVELOP, CTR INT AGR TROP, CALI, COLOMBIA, 77- *Mem:* Am Soc Agron; Soil Sci Soc Am; Int Soc Soil Sci. *Res:* Soil fertility and soil chemistry in relation to major soil classification systems; soil fertility restrains for pasture development in the tropics. *Mailing Add:* Inst Interam de Ciencias Agr QI 5 Com Loc Bl D SHIS Brasilia DF Brazil

COUTTS, JOHN WALLACE, b Neepawa, Man, Feb 2, 23; nat US; m 59; c 1. PHYSICAL CHEMISTRY. *Educ:* Univ Man, BSc, 45, MSc, 47; Purdue Univ, PhD(chem), 50. *Prof Exp:* Asst, Purdue Univ, 46-48; asst prof chem, Mt Union Col, 50-55; assoc prof, 55-62, PROF CHEM, LAKE FOREST COL, 62-, CHMN DEPT, 61- *Concurrent Pos:* Fulbright lectr, Univ Peshawar, Pakistan, 58-59; NSF fac fel, Univ Calif, Berkeley, 67-68; vis prof, 68; vis prof, Rensselaer Polytech Inst, 74-75. *Mem:* AAAS; Am Chem Soc; Sigma Xi. *Res:* Molecular structure. *Mailing Add:* 106 E Sheridan Rd Lake Bluff IL 60044

COUTTS, RONALD THOMSON, b Glasgow, Scotland, June 19, 31; m 57; c 3. ORGANIC CHEMISTRY, MEDICINAL CHEMISTRY. *Educ:* Univ Glasgow, BSc, 55, PhD(pharmaceut chem), 60, DSc(med chem & drug metals), 76. *Prof Exp:* Asst lectr pharmaceut chem, Royal Col Sci & Technol, Univ Glasgow, 56-59; lectr, Sunderland Tech Col, Eng, 59-63; from asst prof to assoc prof, Univ Sask, 63-66; assoc prof, 66-69, PROF PHARMACEUT CHEM, UNIV ALTA, 69- *Concurrent Pos:* Asst sci ed, Can J Pharmaceut Sci, Can Pharmaceut Asn, 66-69, sci ed, 69-72; fel, Chem Inst Can, 71; vis res prof, Dept Pharm, Chelsea Col, Univ London, Eng, 72-73; fel, Royal Inst Chem, 75. *Mem:* Chem Inst Can; Brit Pharmaceut Soc; fel Royal Inst Chem; Royal Soc Chem; fel Royal Soc Can. *Res:* Synthesis, pharmacology, toxicology and metabolism of physiologically-active amines and analogs; mass spectrometry of medicinal compounds and metabolites; neurochemistry. *Mailing Add:* Fac Pharm Univ Alta Edmonton AB T6G 2N8 Can

COUTTS, STEPHEN MAITLAND, b Bronxville, NY, Feb 16, 41; m 66; c 3. BIOCHEMISTRY, IMMUNOLOGY. *Educ:* Calif State Univ, San Diego, BS, 62; Harvard Univ, PhD(biochem), 67. *Prof Exp:* Fel biophys chem res, NATO, Gesellschaft Molekulare Biol Forschung, Braunschweig, WGer, 67-68, scientist, 68-72; fel & lectr biochem res, Princeton Univ, 72-76; sr biochemist, Biochem Immunol Res, USV Pharmaceut Corp, Tuckahoe, NY, 76-78, sr res scientist, 78-81; RES FEL, BIOCHEM IMMUNOL RES, REVLON HEALTH CARE GROUP, TUCKAHOE, NY, 81- *Concurrent Pos:* NIH fel biochem, Princeton Univ, 72-74, Nat Cancer Inst fel, 74-75. *Mem:* Am Chem Soc. *Res:* Development and utilization of in-vitro models to detect anti-asthma and anti-allergy drugs; the mechanism of action of transfer RNA in protein biosynthesis. *Mailing Add:* Revlon Health Care Group Res & Develop Scarsdale Rd Tuckahoe NY 10707

COUTURE, ROGER, b Hull, PQ, May 7, 30; m 58; c 6. INTERNAL MEDICINE, NEPHROLOGY. *Educ:* Univ Ottawa, BA & BSc, 52; McGill Univ, MD, 57; FRCP(C), 64. *Prof Exp:* Lectr, 65-70, asst prof, 70-73, ASSOC PROF MED, FAC MED, UNIV OTTAWA, 73- *Mem:* Can Med Asn; Royal Col Physicians & Surgeons Can; Can Soc Nephrology. *Res:*Hemodialysis and renal transplantation. *Mailing Add:* Dept Med Ottawa Gen Hosp Ottawa ON K1H 8L6 Can

COUVILLION, JOHN LEE, b Jackson, Miss, Oct 20, 41; m 63; c 2. ORGANIC CHEMISTRY. *Educ:* La State Univ, New Orleans, BS, 63, Baton Rouge, MS, 65, PhD(chem), 67. *Prof Exp:* Teaching asst org chem, La State Univ, Baton Rouge, 63-65; res chemist, Tech Ctr, Celanese Chem Co, 67-72; res chemist, Food & Drug Admin, Washington, DC, 72-74; assoc prof chem, 74-79, PROF CHEM & DIR DEVELOP, LA STATE UNIV, EUNICE, 79- *Concurrent Pos:* Ed, Proc La Acad Sci, 76. *Mem:* Am Chem Soc. *Res:* Organic chemical synthesis; heterogeneous catalysis; toxicology; biochemical toxicology. *Mailing Add:* 110 S Tanglewood Dr Eunice LA 70535

COVA, DARIO R, b Benld, Ill, Feb 7, 28; m 53; c 3. CHEMICAL ENGINEERING. *Educ:* Univ Ill, BS, 51, MS, 53, PhD, 55. *Prof Exp:* Res engr, 54-63, ENG FEL, MONSANTO CO, ST LOUIS, 67- *Concurrent Pos:* Lectr, Washington Univ, 57-58. *Mem:* Am Inst Chem Engrs; Sigma Xi. *Res:* Distillation; interphase mass transfer; mixing; process development. *Mailing Add:* 418 N Taylor Kirkwood MO 63122

COVALT-DUNNING, DOROTHY, b Washington, DC, Jan 1, 37; m 60. ANIMAL PHYSIOLOGY, ANIMAL BEHAVIOR. *Educ:* Mt Holyoke Col, MA, 60; Tufts Univ, PhD(biol), 66. *Prof Exp:* Asst zool, Yale Univ, 60-61; asst biol, Harvard Univ, 61-62; fel, Max-Planck Inst Behav Physiol, 67; temporary instr zool, Duke Univ, 68-69; asst prof, 69-74, ASSOC PROF BIOL, WVA UNIV, 74- *Mem:* AAAS; Am Soc Zool; Am Soc Mammal. *Res:* Sensory physiology and behavior of bats; prey-predator interactions between bats and moths; hibernation and social behavior in bats; auditory neurophysiology and behavior in insects. *Mailing Add:* Dept of Biol WVa Univ Morgantown WV 26506

COVAN, JACK PHILLIP, b Cleveland, Ohio, Aug 20, 12; m 39; c 2. INDUSTRIAL ENGINEERING. *Educ:* Ohio State Univ, BSME & BSIE, 35; Univ Ill, MS, 42. *Prof Exp:* Draftsman, Jeffry Mfg Co, Ohio, 35-36; indust engr, Am Steel Wire Co, 36-37; instr mech eng, Univ Ill, 37-43; prod engr, Murphy Chair Co, Ky, 43-44; prod mgr, SPO Inc, Ohio, 44-46; assoc prof indust eng, Tex A&M Univ, 46-54; plant mgr, Orton Ceramic Found, Ohio, 54-55; prof indust eng, 55-74, EMER PROF INDUST ENG, TEX A&M UNIV, 74- *Concurrent Pos:* On loan to USAID prog, E Pakistan Univ Eng & Technol, 61-63. *Mem:* Am Inst Indust Engrs; Am Soc Eng Educ; Am Soc Tool & Mfg Engrs. *Res:* Tool design; manufacturing engineering; statistical quality control. *Mailing Add:* Dept of Indust Eng Tex A&M Univ College Station TX 77843

COVAULT, DONALD O, b Ft Wayne, Ind, Apr 19, 26; m 51; c 4. CIVIL ENGINEERING, TRAFFIC ENGINEERING. *Educ:* Purdue Univ, BSCE, 48, MSCE, 50, PhD, 59. *Prof Exp:* Instr civil eng, Purdue Univ, 48-50, res engr, 55-58; instr, Univ Colo, 50-51; hwy engr, Wis Hwy Dept, 51-55; PROF CIVIL ENG, GA INST TECHNOL, 58- *Concurrent Pos:* Consult, Ind State Hwy Dept, 57, Dept Traffic & Transp, Metrop Dade County, Fla, 59 & Ga State Hwy Dept, 59. *Mem:* Am Soc Civil Engrs; Inst Transp Engrs; Am Rd & Transp Builders Asn. *Res:* Highway engineering; traffic and planning of transportation facilities. *Mailing Add:* Sch Civil Eng 225 North Ave NW Atlanta GA 30332

COVEL, MITCHEL DALE, b Oakland, Calif, July 10, 17; m 71. MEDICINE. *Educ:* Univ Calif, AB, 39, MD, 42. *Prof Exp:* Assoc clin prof med, Loma Linda Univ, 51-60; asst clin prof, Ctr Health Sci, 60-65, assoc clin prof, 65-73, dep dir regional med progs, 67-73, CLIN PROF MED, MED CTR, UNIV CALIF, LOS ANGELES, 65-, DEP DIR REGIONAL MED PROGS, INST CHRONIC DIS & REHAB, 68-, ASSOC DEAN CLIN AFFAIRS, SCH MED, 79- *Concurrent Pos:* Chief outpatient serv, Los Angeles County Hosp, 49-52; mem staff, Hosp Good Samaritan, 51-; fel coun clin cardiol, Am Heart Asn. *Mem:* Am Heart Asn; fel Am Col Physicians; fel Am Col Cardiol; fel NY Acad Sci; Am Heart Asn. *Mailing Add:* 9730 Wilshire Blvd Beverly Hills CA 90212

COVELL, CHARLES VANORDEN, JR, b Washington, DC, Dec 10, 35; m 58; c 3. ENTOMOLOGY. *Educ:* Univ NC, BA, 58; Va Polytech Inst, MS, 62, PhD(entom), 65. *Prof Exp:* Teacher, Norfolk Acad Sch Boys, 58-60; asst entom, Va Polytech Inst, 60-64; from instr to assoc prof, 64-74, PROF BIOL, UNIV LOUISVILLE, 74- *Concurrent Pos:* Consult, Health Dept, Louisville-Jefferson County, Ky, 65- *Mem:* Entom Soc Am; Am Entom Soc; Lepidop Soc; Am Mosquito Control Asn. *Res:* Taxonomy, distribution, ecology and life history of lepidopterous insects, especially the moth family Geometridae; faunistics of Kentucky insects, especially lepidoptera and mosquitoes. *Mailing Add:* Dept of Biol Univ of Louisville Louisville KY 40292

COVELL, DAVID GENE, b Toledo, Ohio, Oct 3, 49. BIOENGINEERING. *Educ:* Univ Mich, BSE, 71, MSE, 75, PhD(bioeng), 79. *Prof Exp:* Mich heart fel, Dept Physiol, Univ Mich, 79-80; STAFF FEL MATH BIOL, LAB THEORET BIOL, NIH, 80- *Mem:* Inst Elec & Electronics Engrs; AAAS; Biomed Eng Soc. *Res:* Mathematical characterization of biological functions; mathematical models used to more efficiently analyze experimental results and design further testing as well as designing methods to better control biological processes. *Mailing Add:* Rm 4B56 Bldg 10 NIH Bethesda MD 20205

COVELL, JAMES WACHOB, b San Francisco, Calif, Aug 13, 36; div; c 2. CARDIOVASCULAR PHYSIOLOGY, BIOMEDICAL ENGINEERING. *Educ:* Carleton Col, BA, 58; Univ Chicago, MD, 62. *Prof Exp:* Intern surg, Univ Chicago Hosps & Clin, 62-63, resident, 63-64; res assoc cardiol, Nat Heart & Lung Inst, 64-66, sr investr, 66-68; from asst prof to assoc prof, 68-76, PROF MED, SCH MED, UNIV CALIF, SAN DIEGO, 76- *Concurrent Pos:* USPHS fel, 63-64, career develop award, 70-75. *Mem:* Am Fedn Clin Res; Am Heart Asn; Am Physiol Soc; Fedn Am Soc Exp Biol; Cardiac Muscle Soc. *Res:* Factors influencing cardiac performance in the normal and diseased heart; mechanics of muscle contraction; on-line data analysis and control of hemodynamic parameters. *Mailing Add:* Dept of Med M-013 Univ of Calif San Diego La Jolla CA 92093

COVENEY, RAYMOND MARTIN, JR, b Marlboro, Mass, Oct 15, 42; m 65; c 3. GEOLOGY. *Educ:* Tufts Univ, BS, 64; Univ Mich, MS, 68, PhD(geol), 71. *Prof Exp:* Mine geologist, Dickey Explor Co, 69-71; asst prof, 71-77, ASSOC PROF GEOL, UNIV MO, KANSAS CITY, 77- *Mem:* Geol Soc Am; Mineral Soc Am; Sigma Xi. *Res:* Geology and mineralogy of ore deposits; fluid inclusion research; determinative mineralogy with emphasis on x-ray and optical techniques. *Mailing Add:* Dept Geosci Univ Mo Kansas City MO 64110

COVENTRY, MARK BINGHAM, b Duluth, Minn, Mar 30, 13; m 37; c 3. ORTHOPEDIC SURGERY. *Educ:* Univ Mich, MD, 37; Univ Minn, MS, 42. *Prof Exp:* PROF ORTHOP SURG, MAYO MED SCH, 58-; CONSULT, SECT ORTHOP SURG, MAYO CLIN, 42- *Concurrent Pos:* Head dept orthop, Mayo Clin, 68-74. *Mem:* Am Acad Orthop Surg; Clin Orthop Soc; Am Orthop Asn; Am Col Surg; hon fel Brit Orthop Asn. *Mailing Add:* Mayo Clin 200 First St SW Rochester MN 55901

COVER, HERBERT LEE, b Elkton, Va, Dec 28, 21; m 45; c 1. PHYSICAL CHEMISTRY. *Educ:* Univ Va, BS, 45, MS, 46, PhD(chem), 49. *Prof Exp:* From instr to prof qual & quant anal, 49-74, PROF CHEM, MARY WASHINGTON COL, 74- *Res:* Catalytic oxidation of carbon monoxide; catalytic hydration of ethylene; analytical chemistry and electronics. *Mailing Add:* Dept of Chem Mary Washington Col Fredericksburg VA 22401

COVER, MORRIS SEIFERT, b Harrisburg, Pa, July 25, 16; m 38; c 2. VETERINARY PATHOLOGY. *Educ:* Univ Pa, VMD, 38; Kans State Col, MS, 43; Univ Ill, PhD, 52. *Prof Exp:* Asst poultry pathologist, Univ NH, 38-40; assoc prof anat & physiol, Kans State Col, 40-46; asst prof anat & histol, Univ Ill, 47-52; assoc prof poultry path, Univ Del, 52-59, prof & head dept, 59-67, dir agr exp sta, 62-67; mgr vet serv & vet labs, 67-73, DIR VET SERV & REGULATORY DEPT, RALSTON PURINA CO, 73- *Concurrent Pos:* Inspector, Sheffield Farms, Pa, 46. *Mem:* Am Vet Med Asn. *Res:* Pathology; anatomy; histology; embryology; cytology; veterinary surgery; mycotoxicosis. *Mailing Add:* Vet Serv & Regulatory Dept Ralston Purina Co Checkerboard Sq St Louis MO 63188

COVER, RICHARD EDWARD, b Youngsville, Pa, Nov 7, 26; m 48; c 3. ANALYTICAL CHEMISTRY. *Educ:* Pa State Univ, BS, 47; Polytech Inst Brooklyn, MS, 60, PhD(anal chem), 62. *Prof Exp:* Chemist, US Steel Corp, 48-50 & Fairchild Camera & Instrument Co, 50-57; sr chemist, Socony Mobil Oil Co, 57-64; PROF ANAL CHEM, ST JOHN'S UNIV, NY, 64- *Concurrent Pos:* Mem, Simulation Coun, 65- *Mem:* Am Chem Soc; Soc Indust & Appl Math. *Res:* Electroanalytical chemistry; gas chromatography; chemical kinetics; computer applications to chemistry; applied mathematics. *Mailing Add:* Dept of Chem St John's Univ Grad Sch Jamaica NY 11439

COVER, THOMAS MERRILL, b Pasadena, Calif, Aug 7, 38; m 68. INFORMATION THEORY, STATISTICS. *Educ:* Mass Inst Technol, BS, 60; Stanford Univ, MS, 61, PhD(elec eng), 64. *Prof Exp:* prof elec eng, 64-67, assoc prof statist, 70-72, ASSOC PROF ELEC ENG, STANFORD UNIV, 68-, PROF STATIST, 72- *Concurrent Pos:* Consult, Rand Corp, 60-64, FMC Corp, 67-68, Stanford Res Inst, 63-65, Sylvania Elec Prod, Inc, 68-72 & SRI, 76-; assoc ed, Inst Elec & Electronics Engrs Trans on Info Theory, 71- *Mem:* Fel Inst Elec & Electronics Engrs; Soc Indust & Appl Math; Am Math Soc; fel Inst Math Statist. *Res:* Applied statistics; pattern recognition and learning. *Mailing Add:* Dept of Elec Eng Stanford Univ Stanford CA 94305

COVERT, EUGENE EDZARDS, b Rapid City, SDak, Feb 6, 26; m 46; c 4. AERONAUTICAL ENGINEERING, UNSTEADY FLUID MECHANICS. *Educ:* Univ Minn, BS, 46, MS, 48; Mass Inst Technol, ScD, 58. *Prof Exp:* PROF AERODYN, MASS INST TECHNOL, 63- *Concurrent Pos:* Consult, Hercules Inc, 63- & Sverdrup Technol Inc, 76-; chief scientist, USAF, 71-72; consult & dir, Megatech Inc, 71-; vchmn, Sci Adv Bd, USAF, 77-; mem, Gas Turbine Technol Adv Comt, NASA, 79; dir, Gas Turbine Lab,

Mass Inst Technol, 79-; chmn, Power & Energetics Panel, NATO, 80- *Mem:* Nat Acad Eng; fel Am Inst Aeronaut & Astronaut; fel Royal Astron Soc; Sigma Xi. *Res:* Unsteady aerodynamics of boundary layers, both in unseparating and separating state. *Mailing Add:* Rm 31-264 Mass Inst Technol Cambridge MA 02139

COVERT, ROGER A(LLEN), b Muncie, Ind, May 9, 29; m; c 2. METALLURGY, CORROSION. *Educ:* Purdue Univ, BS, 51; Mass Inst Technol, SM, 54, ScD(metall), 57. *Prof Exp:* Asst, Mass Inst Technol, 56-57; serv engr, E I du Pont de Nemours & Co, 57-58; proj supvr & asst tech dir, Alloyd Electronics Corp, 58-62; res consult, Avesta Jernwerks, Sweden, 62-63; sr metallurgist, 63-67, corrosion engr, 67-68, in charge corrosion eng, Prod Develop, 67-70, sect mgr corrosion eng, Prod Res & Develop, Int Nickel Co, NY, 70-72, proj mgr mkt develop, 72-75, asst mgr distribr sales mkt, Int Nickel Co, Europe, London, UK, 75-77, mgr plating sales mkt, 77-80, gen sales mgr, 80-81, GEN SALES MGR PLATING & CHEM IND, INT NICKEL CO, NY, 81- *Mem:* AAAS; Electrochem Soc; Am Inst Mining, Metall & Petrol Engrs; Nat Asn Corrosion Engrs; Electroplating Soc. *Res:* Corrosion of metals; physical metallurgy; theoretical electrochemistry; electroplating. *Mailing Add:* 94 Deepdale Dr Middletown NJ 07748

COVEY, DOUGLAS FLOYD, b Baltimore, Md, May 25, 45; m 72; c 1. ENDOCRINOLOGY, STEROID HORMONES. *Educ:* Loyola Col, BS, 67; Johns Hopkins Univ, MA, 69, PhD(chem), 73. *Prof Exp:* Fel res, Johns Hopkins Univ, 73-74, pharmacol, 74-77; ASST PROF PHARMACOL, SCH MED, WASHINGTON UNIV, 77- *Concurrent Pos:* NIH res career develop award, 82- *Mem:* Am Chem Soc. *Res:* Design and evaluation of inhibitors of steroid biosynthesis, enzymology and endocrinology of steroid hormones; application of computer graphics to the delineation of the binding sites of biological macromolecules for pharmacological agents. *Mailing Add:* Dept Pharmacol Sch Med Washington Univ 660 S Euclid Ave St Louis MO 63110

COVEY, RONALD PERRIN, JR, b Jamestown, NY, Aug 19, 29; m 52; c 3. PLANT PATHOLOGY. *Educ:* Univ Minn, BS, 56, MS, 59, PhD(plant path), 62. *Prof Exp:* Asst plant pathologist, 62-73, ASSOC PLANT PATHOLOGIST, TREE FRUIT RES CTR, UNIV WASH, 73- *Mem:* Am Phytopath Soc. *Res:* Bacterial and fungal disease of tree fruits; phytophthora cactorum. *Mailing Add:* Tree Fruit Res Ctr Univ of Wash 1100 N Western Ave Wenatchee WA 98801

COVEY, RUPERT ALDEN, b Manchester, NH, July 24, 29; m 56; c 3. ORGANIC CHEMISTRY. *Educ:* Middlebury Col, AB, 51; Univ NH, MS, 53; Univ Mich, PhD(pharmaceut chem), 58. *Prof Exp:* Sr res chemist agr chem, Naugatuck Chem Div, US Rubber Co, 57-67; sr res chemist, 67-70, res scientist, 70-79, sr res scientist, 79-81, RES ASSOC, UNIROYAL CHEM DIV, UNIROYAL, INC, 81- *Mem:* Am Chem Soc. *Res:* Crop protection chemicals; synthesis of organic compounds as pesticides; organic sulfite esters; heterocyclic compounds. *Mailing Add:* Uniroyal Chem Div Uniroyal Inc Naugatuck CT 06770

COVEY, WILLIAM DANNY, b Sacramento, Calif, June 10, 40. PHYSICAL INORGANIC CHEMISTRY, CHEMICAL KINETICS. *Educ:* Univ Calif, Berkeley, BS, 67; Sacramento State Col, MS, 70; Univ Ill, Champaign-Urbana, PhD(phys inorg chem), 73. *Prof Exp:* Asst chemist qual control, Pac Gas & Elec Co, Calif, 62-65; chem tech, Consortium Electrochem Indust, Munich, Ger, 65-67; res assoc bio-inorg kinetics, Ohio State Univ, 72-74 & Occidental Col, 74-76; sr chemist anal chem serv, Avery Int, 77; asst prof chem, Occidental Col, 76-80; ASST PROF CHEM, L A PIERCE COL, 80- *Concurrent Pos:* Sigma Xi grant-in-aid, 75. *Mem:* Am Chem Soc; AAAS; Sigma Xi. *Mailing Add:* Dept of Chem Occidental Col Los Angeles CA 90041

COVEY, WINTON GUY, JR, b Glen Daniel, WVa, Feb 3, 29; m 52; c 2. MICROMETEOROLOGY. *Educ:* Johns Hopkins Univ, AB, 49; Tex A&M Univ, MS, 59, PhD(soil physics), 65. *Prof Exp:* Micrometeorologist, Tex A&M Univ, 55-59; soil physicist, Tex Agr Exp Sta, 59-60; res soil scientist, Agr Res Serv, USDA, 60-65; assoc prof meteorol, Cornell Univ, 65-68; assoc prof, 68-74, PROF NATURAL SCI, CONCORD COL, 74- *Mailing Add:* Dept of Phys Sci Concord Col Athens WV 24712

COVINO, BENJAMIN GENE, b Lawrence, Mass, Sept 12, 30; m 53; c 2. PHYSIOLOGY. *Educ:* Col of the Holy Cross, AB, 51; Boston Col, MS, 53; Boston Univ, PhD(physiol), 55; State Univ NY Buffalo, MD, 61. *Prof Exp:* Res scientist, Arctic Aeromed Lab, 55-57; asst prof pharmacol, Sch Med, Tufts Univ, 57-59; asst prof physiol, Sch Med, State Univ NY Buffalo, 59-63; med dir, Astra Pharmaceut Prod, Inc, 63-77, vpres res & develop, 67-77, vpres & dir res, Astra Res Lab, 77-79; PROF ANESTHESIOL, MED SCH, UNIV MASS, WORCESTER, 75-; CHMN, DEPT ANESTHESIOL, BRIGHAM & WOMEN'S HOSP, 79-; PROF ANESTHESIOL, HARVARD MED SCH, 79- *Concurrent Pos:* Lectr, Harvard Med Sch, 78-; clin assoc anesthesiol, Mass Gen Hosp; consult physiologist & clin pharmacologist, St Vincent's Hosp, Worcester. *Mem:* Am Physiol Soc; Am Fedn Clin Res; Int Col Angiol; Am Col Clin Pharmacol & Chemother. *Res:* Cardiovascular physiology and pharmacology of local anesthetics; physiology of temperature regulation. *Mailing Add:* Brigham & Women's Hosp 25 Francis St Boston MA 02115

COWAN, ALAN, b Selkirk, Scotland, July 6, 42; m 68; c 2. PSYCHOPHARMACOLOGY. *Educ:* Univ Glasgow, BSc, 64, Univ Strathclyde, PhD(pharmacol), 68. *Prof Exp:* Sect leader, Reckitt & Colman, Eng, 68-76; ASST PROF, MED SCH, TEMPLE UNIV, 77- *Mem:* Am Soc Pharmacol & Exp Therapeut; Int Soc Psychoneuroendocrinol; Pharmaceut Soc Gt Brit. *Res:* Psychopharmacology of opioids and behaviorally active peptides; pharmacology of substance abuse; thermopharmacology. *Mailing Add:* Dept Pharmacol Sch Med Temple Univ Philadelphia PA 19140

COWAN, ANDREW M(ERLE), b Dallas, Tex, Aug 11, 29; m 52; c 3. AGRICULTURAL ENGINEERING, ENGINEERING MECHANICS. *Educ:* Purdue Univ, BSAE, 51; Iowa State Univ, MSAE, 55, PhD(agr eng), 67. *Prof Exp:* Res engr, US Army Biol Labs, 57-63, chief detection systs, 63-64, asst sci dir, 64-67, chief spec opers div, 67-70; from assoc prof to prof agr eng, Univ Md, College Park, 70-75; staff scientist, Indust Use Agr Prods, 75-79, chief, Postharvest Sci & Tech, 79-81, ACTING ASSOC DIR, NORTHERN REGIONAL RES CTR, AGR RES SERV, USDA, 81- *Mem:* Am Soc Agr Engrs; Nat Soc Prof Engrs; Am Inst Chem Engrs. *Res:* Pre-treatment and compaction of grass silage; design and development of biological research facilities; development of biological warfare detection instrumentation and systems; processing of agricultural materials; industrial use of agricultural materials such as starch, hides, leather, oils and fats. *Mailing Add:* 5666 Vantage Point Rd Columbia MD 21044

COWAN, ARCHIBALD B, b Ambia, Ind, July 14, 15; m 42; c 3. WILDLIFE DISEASES, WILDLIFE MANAGEMENT. *Educ:* Univ Mich, BSF, 40, PhD(wildlife mgt), 54. *Prof Exp:* Res leader pheasant res proj, State Natural Hist Surv, Ill, 46-49; wildlife res biologist, Patuxent Res Refuge, 54-56; asst prof wildlife mgt, Univ Mich, Ann Arbor, 56-62, assoc prof, 62-80; RETIRED. *Mem:* Wildlife Soc; Wildlife Dis Asn (treas, 58-63, vpres, 65-67, pres, 67-69); Am Inst Biol Sci. *Res:* Parasites and diseases of wildlife. *Mailing Add:* 1341 Wines Dr Ann Arbor MI 48103

COWAN, CARL E, b Muskogee, Okla, Aug 2, 39; m 61; c 2. PHYSICS. *Educ:* Bates Col, BS, 61. *Prof Exp:* Physicist electrophotography, 61-66, from res physicist to sr res physicist, 66-79, RES ASSOC ELECTROPHOTOGRAPHY, EASTMAN KODAK CO, 79- *Res:* Exploratory electrophotographic systems. *Mailing Add:* B-82 Kodak Park Rochester NY 14650

COWAN, DANIEL FRANCIS, b Mineola, NY, Aug 7, 34; m 60; c 3. PATHOLOGY. *Educ:* Antioch Col, BA, 56; McGill Univ, MDCM, 60. *Prof Exp:* NIH spec fel comp path, 66-67; from asst prof to asscc prof path, Mich State Univ, 67-73; chmn dept path, Eastern Va Med Sch, 73-77; PROF PATH, UNIV TEX MED SCH HOUSTON, 77- *Mem:* NY Acad Sci; AMA; fel Col Am Pathologist; fel Am Soc Clin Pathologist; Wildlife Dis Asn. *Res:* Research in anatomic pathology; comparative pathology; diseases of marine mammals. *Mailing Add:* Dept of Path Univ of Tex Med Sch PO Box 20708 77025

COWAN, DAVID J, b San Antonio, Tex, Aug 5, 36; m 65. PHYSICS. *Educ:* Univ Tex, BS, 58, MA, 60, PhD(physics), 65. *Prof Exp:* Assoc physicist, Int Bus Mach Corp, 60-61; NIH traineeship, 64-65; asst prof, 65-74, chmn dept, 74-80, ASSOC PROF PHYSICS, GETTSBURG COL, 74- *Mem:* Am Phys Soc; Am Asn Physics Teachers. *Res:* Investigation of biological ultrastructure by x-ray diffraction. *Mailing Add:* Dept of Physics Gettysburg Col Gettysburg PA 17325

COWAN, DAVID LAWRENCE, b Havre, Mont, Oct 18, 36; m 60. SOLID STATE PHYSICS. *Educ:* Univ Wis, BS, 56, MS, 58, PhD(physics), 64. *Prof Exp:* Res engr, NAm Aviation, Inc, Calif, 58-60; res assoc physics, Cornell Univ, 64-67; mem tech staff, Sandia Corp, NMex, 67-68; asst prof, 68-74, ASSOC PROF PHYSICS, UNIV MO-COLUMBIA, 74- *Mem:* Am Phys Soc. *Res:* Ferromagnetic properties of metals; electron spin resonance; nuclear magnetic resonance; optical properties of solids. *Mailing Add:* Dept of Physics Univ of Mo Columbia MO 65201

COWAN, DAVID PRIME, b Aurora, Ill. BIOLOGY. *Educ:* Univ Mich, BS, 70, PhD(zool), 78. *Prof Exp:* ASST PROF BIOL, WESTERN MICH UNIV, 79- *Res:* Evolution and ecology of insect life histories and behavior. *Mailing Add:* Dept Biol Western Mich Univ Kalamazoo MI 49008

COWAN, DONALD D, b Toronto, Ont, Mar 11, 38; m; c 3. COMPUTER SCIENCE. *Educ:* Univ Toronto, BASc, 60; Univ Waterloo, MSc, 61, PhD(appl math), 65. *Prof Exp:* Fel math, 60-62, lectr, 61-65, asst prof, 65-67, chmn, Dept Appl Anal & Comput Sci, Fac Math, 66-72, assoc prof, 67-75, assoc dean grad studies, Fac Math, 74-78, PROF MATH, DEPT COMPUT SCI, UNIV WATERLOO, 75- *Concurrent Pos:* Nat Res Coun grant, 75-79; Defence Res Bd grant, 68-74. *Mem:* Asn Comput Mach; Inst Elec & Electronics Engrs; Soc Indust & Appl Math; Can Info Processing Soc. *Res:* Computer systems and communications. *Mailing Add:* Dept of Comput Sci Fac Math Univ of Waterloo Waterloo ON N2L 3G1 Can

COWAN, DWAINE O, b Fresno, Calif, Nov 25, 35; m 63. ORGANIC CHEMISTRY. *Educ:* Fresno State Col, BS, 58; Stanford Univ, PhD(org chem), 62. *Prof Exp:* Res fel chem, Calif Inst Technol, 62-63; from asst prof to assoc prof, 63-72, PROF CHEM, JOHNS HOPKINS UNIV, 72- *Concurrent Pos:* Sloan res fel, 68-70; Guggenheim fel, Phys Chem Inst, Univ Basel, 70-71. *Mem:* Am Chem Soc; Brit Chem Soc. *Res:* Physical organic chemistry; mixed valence organometallic compounds, electron transfer reactions, organic solid state chemistry, synthesis and study of organic metals, organic photochemistry; a charge transfer salt from tetrathiafulvalene and tetracyanoquinodimethane. *Mailing Add:* Dept of Chem Johns Hopkins Univ Baltimore MD 21218

COWAN, EUGENE WOODVILLE, b Ree Heights, SDak, Sept 30, 20; m 56; c 2. PHYSICS. *Educ:* Univ Mo, BS, 41; Mass Inst Technol, SM, 43; Calif Inst Technol, PhD(physics), 48. *Prof Exp:* Instr elec commun, Mass Inst Technol, 43-44, staff mem, Radiation Lab, 44-45; res fel, 48-50, from asst prof to assoc prof, 50-61, PROF PHYSICS, CALIF INST TECHNOL, 61- *Mem:* Am Phys Soc. *Res:* Radar; electrical circuits; electrical measurements; cosmic rays. *Mailing Add:* Dept of Physics Calif Inst of Technol Pasadena CA 91125

COWAN, F BRIAN M, b Chatham, Ont, Apr 15, 38; m 62; c 2. ZOOLOGY, PHYSIOLOGY. *Educ:* Queen's Univ, BA, 62; Univ Toronto, MA & dipl electron micros, 65, PhD(zool), 70. *Prof Exp:* Instr zool, 69-70, asst prof, 70-77, ASSOC PROF BIOL, UNIV NB, 77- *Mem:* AAAS; Am Soc Zoologists;

Int Soc Stereology; Can Soc Zoologists. *Res:* Activation of salt secreting epithelia during times of osmotic stress using euryhaline reptilian species as test system and studying ultrastrucure, stereology, histochemistry and biochemistry; electrical events in cardiac cycle in animals with apparent physiological alterations in plasma ion concentrations; effect of pesticides on blood cell structure. *Mailing Add:* Dept of Biol Univ of NB Fredericton NB E3B 5A3 Can

COWAN, FREDERICK FLETCHER, JR, b Washington, DC, Jan 17, 33; m 60; c 1. PHARMACOLOGY. *Educ:* George Washington Univ, BS, 55; Georgetown Univ, PhD(pharmacol), 59. *Prof Exp:* Pharmacist, Bretler Pharm, 55-56; instr pharmacol, Schs Med & Dent, Georgetown Univ, 60-62, asst prof, 62-66; assoc prof, 66-73, PROF PHARMACOL & CHMN DEPT, DENT SCH, UNIV ORE, 73- *Concurrent Pos:* Fel, Nat Heart Inst, 59; prin co-investr, USPHS res grants, 61- & prin investr, 64-; prin investr, NSF res grant, 62. *Mem:* AAAS; Am Pharmaceut Asn; Am Soc Pharmacol & Exp Therapeut. *Res:* Pharmacology of the autonomic ganglia and the peripheral sympathetic nervous system; tachyphylaxis of sympathomimetic amines; pharmacology of carotid body chemoreceptors. *Mailing Add:* Health Sci Ctr Sch of Dent Univ of Ore Portland OR 97201

COWAN, FREDERICK PIERCE, b Bar Harbor, Maine, July 3, 06; m 34. HEALTH PHYSICS. *Educ:* Bowdoin Col, AB, 28; Harvard Univ, AM, 31, PhD(physics), 35. *Prof Exp:* Instr physics, Bowdoin Col, 28-29; asst, Harvard Univ, 29-34, instr, 34-35; from instr to asst prof, Rensselaer Polytech Inst, 35-43; res assoc, Radio Res Lab, Harvard Univ, 43-45; res assoc, Eng Div, Chrysler Corp, Detroit, 45-47; head health physics div, Brookhaven Nat Lab, 47-71; MEM ATOMIC SAFETY & LICENSING BD, NUCLEAR REGULATORY COMN, 72- *Concurrent Pos:* Asst, Radcliffe Col, 34-35; chmn, Am Bd Health Physics, 63-64; mem comt 3, Int Comn Radiation Protection, 65-73; mem, Int Comn Radiation Units & Measurements, 65-73; mem, Nat Coun Radiation Protection, 67-73, bd dirs, 69-73; mem adv comt radiobiol aspects of supersonic transport, Fed Aviation Admin, 67-74. *Mem:* AAAS; Am Phys Soc; Radiation Res Soc; Health Physics Soc (pres elect, 56-57, pres, 57-58). *Res:* Thermal measurements on electron tubes; electronic temperature control; radiation dosimetry. *Mailing Add:* 6152 N Verde Trail Apt B-125 Boca Raton FL 33494

COWAN, GARRY IAN MCTAGGART, b Victoria, BC, July 9, 40; m 62; c 2. SYSTEMATICS. *Educ:* Univ BC, BSc, 63, MSc, 66, PhD(zool), 68. *Prof Exp:* Asst prof, 68-71, ASSOC PROF BIOL, MEM UNIV NFLD, 71- *Concurrent Pos:* Nat Res Coun Can res grant in aid, 68-; res scientist, Marine Sci Res Lab, 70- *Mem:* Am Soc Ichthyol & Herpet; Soc Study Evolution; Soc Syst Zool. *Res:* Systematics of marine organisms based on their morphological and biochemical characteristics. *Mailing Add:* Marine Sci Res Lab Mem Univ of Nfld St John's NF A1C 5S7 Can

COWAN, GEORGE A, b Worcester, Mass, Feb 15, 20; m 46. RADIOCHEMISTRY. *Educ:* Worcester Polytech Inst, BS, 41; Carnegie Inst Technol, DSc(chem), 50. *Prof Exp:* Res scientist, Metall Lab, Univ Chicago, 42-45; res scientist, 45-46, assoc div leader, Test Div, 56-70, div leader chem, 71-79, assoc dir, 79-81, MEM STAFF RADIOCHEM, LOS ALAMOS NAT LAB, UNIV CALIF, 49-, GROUP LEADER, 55-, SR FEL, 81- *Honors & Awards:* E O Lawrence Award, 65. *Mem:* Fel AAAS; Am Chem Soc; fel Am Phys Soc; Am Nuclear Soc. *Res:* Radiochemical diagnostics; nuclear reactions; solar neutrino physics. *Mailing Add:* PO Box 1663 Los Alamos NM 87545

COWAN, IAN MCTAGGART, b Edinburgh, Scotland, June 25, 10; m 36; c 2. MAMMALOGY, WILDLIFE ECOLOGY. *Educ:* Univ BC, BA, 32; Univ Calif, PhD(vert zool), 35. *Hon Degrees:* LLD, Univ Alta, 71; DEnviron Sci, Univ Waterloo, 75; DSc, Univ BC, 77; LLD, Simon Fraser Univ, 81. *Prof Exp:* Insect pest investr, Dom Govt, Can, 29; field asst, Nat Mus Can, 30-31; asst biologist, BC Prov Mus, 35-38, asst dir, 38-40; from asst prof to prof zool, 40-75, head dept, 53-64, dean fac grad studies, 64-75, EMER PROF ZOOL, UNIV BC, 75- *Concurrent Pos:* Carnegie traveling fel, Am Mus & US Nat Mus, 37; Nuffield fel, 52; Am Inst Biol Sci foreign vis lectr, 63; Erskine fel, Univ Canterbury, 69; mem, Environ Protection Bd, 69-75; chmn, Acad Bd BC, 69-75; mem, Can Environ Adv Coun, 72-75, chmn, 75-79; chmn, Can Comt Whales & Whaling, 77- & Acad Coun Prov BC, 78-; chancellor, Univ Victoria, 79- *Honors & Awards:* Order of Can, 72; Leopold Medal & Arthur Einarsen Award, Wildlife Soc, 70; Fry Medal, Can Soc Zool, 76. *Mem:* Am Ornith Union; Wildlife Soc (pres, 49); Am Soc Mammalogists; Soc Syst Zool; fel Royal Soc Can. *Res:* Ecology and environmental physiology of native ungulates; problems of insularity in vertebrates; vertebrate distribution and speciation in Canada; behavior of carnivorous mammals. *Mailing Add:* 3919 Woodhaven Terr Victoria BC V8N 1S7 Can

COWAN, JACK DAVID, b Leeds, Eng, Aug 24, 33; m 58; c 2. APPLIED MATHEMATICS, BIOMATHEMATICS. *Educ:* Univ Edinburgh, BSc, 55; Mass Inst Technol, SM, 60; Imp Col, dipl elec eng, 59, Univ London, PhD(elec eng), 67. *Prof Exp:* Res engr & mathematician, Instrument & Fire Control Sect, Ferranti Ltd, Scotland, 55-58; staff mem neurophysiol group, Res Lab Electronics, Mass Inst Technol, 60-62; acad vis math biol, Imp Col, 62-67; chmn dept & prof theoret biol, 67-73, PROF BIOPHYS & THEORET BIOL, UNIV CHICAGO, 73- *Concurrent Pos:* Res assoc & consult, Northeastern Univ & US Air Force Cambridge Res Lab, 60; vis prof, Univ Naples, 65; guest worker, Nat Phys Lab, Eng, 66-67; mem, NIH comn training grants in epidemiol & biomet, 69-73; chmn adv coun, Lab Cybernet, Nat Res Coun, Italy, 69-73; mem vis comt, Dept Psychol, Mass Inst Technol, 72-75; mem, Am Math Soc comt math in life sci, 70-77; mem comn on communication & control, Int Union Pure & Appl Biophys, 75-78. *Mem:* AAAS; Am Math Soc; Am Phys Soc; Soc Am Neurosci. *Res:* Theory of nervous activity; theoretical biology; vision research; applied mathematics. *Mailing Add:* Dept Biophys & Theoret Biol Univ of Chicago 920 E 58th St Chicago IL 60637

COWAN, JAMES W, b Beaver Falls, Pa, Aug 23, 30; m 60. NUTRITION, BIOCHEMISTRY. *Educ:* Pa State Univ, BS, 55, MS, 59, PhD(biochem), 61. *Prof Exp:* Assoc prof food tech & nutrit, 61-73, assoc dean sch agr sci, 70-73, prof nutrit & dean sch agr sci, Am Univ Beirut, 73-77; DIR INT PROGS & STUDIES OFF, NAT ASN STATE UNIVS & LAND GRANT COLS, 77- *Mem:* AAAS; Am Nutrit Soc; Am Soc Clin Nutrit. *Res:* Iodine metabolism; iron utilization. *Mailing Add:* Nat Asn State Univs & Land Grant Cols 1 Du Pont Circle Washington DC 20036

COWAN, JOHN ARTHUR, b Winnipeg, Man, July 8, 21; m 46; c 4. FLUID PHYSICS. *Educ:* Univ Man, BSc, 43; Univ Toronto, MA, 47, PhD(physics), 50. *Prof Exp:* Lectr, Dept Math, Univ Man, 46; sci officer, Can Defense Res Bd, 50-57; chmn dept, 57-68, PROF PHYSICS, UNIV WATERLOO, 57- *Mem:* Can Acoustical Asn; Can Asn Physicists. *Res:* Speech communication; experimental studies of transport properties of liquids. *Mailing Add:* 237 Erb St E Waterloo ON N2J 1M9 Can

COWAN, JOHN C, b Danville, Ill, Oct 25, 11; m 38; c 2. ORGANIC CHEMISTRY. *Educ:* Univ Ill, AB, 34, PhD(chem), 38. *Prof Exp:* Asst, Univ Ill, 35-38, du Pont fel, 38-39; instr, DePauw Univ, 39-40; assoc chemist, Northern Regional Res Lab, Agr Res Serv, USDA, 40-41, from chemist to head oil & protein sect, Agr Res Serv, 53-57, chief oilseed crops lab, 57-73; CONSULT, 73- *Concurrent Pos:* Mem, Soybean Res Coun, 45-73; adj prof chem, Bradley Univ, 73-; mem adv panel, Soybean Utilization Res. *Honors & Awards:* Superior Serv Award, USDA, 48, Superior Serv Team Awards, 52, 63; A E Bailey Medal, Am Oil Chem Soc, 61; Meritorious Serv Award, Am Soybean Asn, 70; Chevreul Medal, French Asn for Study of Oil Substances, 75. *Mem:* Am Chem Soc; Am Oil Chem Soc (pres, 68-69); Inst Food Technol; Am Asn Cereal Chemists. *Res:* Condensation and vinyl polymers; edible oil spreads; flavor stability of soybean oil; metal-inactivation agents; cyclic fatty acids; aldehydic esters; amino acid derivatives; uses for soybeans, linseed oil, and soybean protein products. *Mailing Add:* 225 Olin Hall Bradley Univ Peoria IL 61625

COWAN, JOHN D, JR, b Willshire, Ohio, Sept 7, 18; m 40; c 2. ELECTRICAL ENGINEERING, MECHANICAL ENGINEERING. *Educ:* Ohio State Univ, BSME, 47, MSEE, 55. *Prof Exp:* Shop-lab coordr, 48-55, from instr to assoc prof elec eng, 50-64, consult, dept aviation psychol, 48-54, PROF ELEC ENG, OHIO STATE UNIV, 64- *Concurrent Pos:* Consult, NAm Aviation Co, 57-74 & Ohio State Fire Marshals Arson Crime Lab, 78-; mem, Nat Comt Elec Eng Films, 62-68. *Mem:* Sr mem Inst Elec & Electronics Engrs. *Res:* Electromechanical systems; circuit theory. *Mailing Add:* Dept of Elec Eng 2015 Neil Ave Columbus OH 43210

COWAN, KEITH MORRIS, b Salt Lake City, Utah, Sept 7, 21; m 44; c 3. IMMUNOCHEMISTRY. *Educ:* Southern Calif Univ, AB, 48, MS, 50; Johns Hopkins Univ, ScD(immunochem), 55. *Prof Exp:* Res assoc, Johns Hopkins Univ, 52-55; dir biol control, Cutter Labs, Calif, 55-56; investr for Howard Hughes Med Inst & res assoc, Dept Microbiol, Yale Univ, 56-58; microbiologist, Sci & Educ Admin-Agr Res, USDA, 58-81. *Mem:* Am Asn Immunol; Am Col Vet Microbiol; AAAS. *Res:* Immunochemical characterization of antibodies and virus antigens pertaining primarily to foot-and-mouth disease. *Mailing Add:* 12234A Rancho Bernardo Rd San Diego CA 92128

COWAN, MAYNARD, JR, b Independence, Mo, Dec 15, 25; m 45; c 3. PHYSICS. *Educ:* William Jewel Col, BA, 48; Univ NMex, MS, 51. *Prof Exp:* Mem staff, Weapons Effects Studies, 51-60, div supvr, Magneto Physics Res Div, 60-69, mgr, Shock Simulation Dept, 69-75, mgr, Simulation Res Dept, 75-80, MGR, ADVAN ENERGY CONVERSION SYSTS DEPT, SANDIA LABS, 80- *Res:* Technical management; pulsed power engineering; plasma physics; nuclear burst effects. *Mailing Add:* Sandia Labs PO Box 5800 Albuquerque NM 87185

COWAN, RAYMOND, b Marion, Ind, Nov 14, 14; m 40; c 2. PHYSICS. *Educ:* Butler Univ, BS, 54, MS, 55. *Prof Exp:* From asst prof to assoc prof, 55-67, chmn, Sci Div, 60-79, PROF PHYSICS, FRANKLIN COL, 67-, CHMN DEPT, 57- *Mem:* Am Asn Physics Teachers. *Res:* Electronics. *Mailing Add:* Dept of Physics Franklin Col Franklin IN 46131

COWAN, RICHARD SUMNER, b Crawfordsville, Ind, Jan 23, 21; m 41; c 3. PLANT TAXONOMY. *Educ:* Wabash Col, AB, 42; Univ Hawaii, MS, 48; Columbia Univ, PhD, 52. *Prof Exp:* Tech asst, NY Bot Garden, 48-52, asst cur, 52-57; assoc cur, Smithsonian Inst, 57-62, asst dir, Nat Mus Natural Hist, 62-65, dir, 65-73, SR BOTANIST, DEPT BOT, SMITHSONIAN INST, NAT MUS NATURAL HIST, 73- *Concurrent Pos:* NSF fel, 52-53. *Mem:* AAAS; Am Inst Biol Sci; Am Soc Plant Taxon; Asn Trop Biol; Bot Soc Am. *Res:* Phanerogamic taxonomy; Leguminosae of northern South America; Rutaceae of Guayana Highland; flora of Venezuela; botanical bibliography. *Mailing Add:* 4409 Tonquil Pl Smithsonian Inst Beltsville MD 20705

COWAN, ROBERT DUANE, b Lincoln, Nebr, Nov 24, 19; m 44; c 4. ATOMIC PHYSICS. *Educ:* Friends Univ, AB, 42; Johns Hopkins Univ, PhD(physics), 46. *Prof Exp:* Jr instr physics, Johns Hopkins Univ, 43-46, lab asst, 44-46; Nat Res fel, Univ Chicago, 46-47, res assoc spectros, 47-48; prof physics & head dept, Friends Univ, 48-51; PHYSICIST, LOS ALAMOS NAT LAB, 51- *Concurrent Pos:* Fulbright lectr, Peru, 58-59; vis prof, Purdue Univ, 71; consult, Culham Lab, Eng, 77. *Mem:* Fel Am Phys Soc; fel Optical Soc Am. *Res:* Visible and ultraviolet spectroscopy; selfabsorption of spectral lines; equations of state at extreme pressures and temperatures; theoretical atomic spectroscopy. *Mailing Add:* Los Alamos Nat Lab Los Alamos NM 87545

COWAN, ROBERT LEE, b Beaver County, Pa, Nov 20, 20; m 45; c 5. ANIMAL NUTRITION. *Educ:* Pa State Col, BS, 43, MS, 49, PhD, 52. *Prof Exp:* Chemist food processing, Gen Foods, Inc, 43-44; asst agr biol chem, 46-48, from instr to assoc prof, 48-65, PROF ANIMAL NUTRIT, PA STATE UNIV, 65- *Concurrent Pos:* Fulbright res scholar, Massey Col, NZ, 56-57.

Mem: Am Soc Animal Sci; NY Acad Sci; Am Inst Nutrit; Wildlife Soc. *Res:* Nutritive values of forages; preservation of grass silage; nutrition of deer and mink. *Mailing Add:* Dept of Animal Sci 305 Animal Industs Bldg Pa State Univ University Park PA 16802

COWAN, RUSSELL (WALTER), b Oakland, Calif, Feb 26, 12; m 48. APPLIED MATHEMATICS. *Educ:* Univ Calif, AB, 32, MA, 33, PhD(math), 35. *Prof Exp:* Instr math & astron, Col of St Scholastica, 35-38; from instr to asst prof math, Univ Ala, 38-47; assoc prof, Univ Fla, 47-66; PROF MATH, LAMAR UNIV, 66- *Mem:* Am Math Soc; Math Asn Am. *Res:* Analysis; differential equations; difference equations; solution of a linear difference equation of the second order with quadratic coefficients; differential equations, special functions and gamma functions. *Mailing Add:* Dept Math Lamar Univ Beaumont TX 77710

COWAN, W MAXWELL, b Johannesburg, SAfrica, Sept 27, 31; m 56; c 3. NEUROANATOMY. *Educ:* Univ Witwatersrand, BSc, 52; Oxford Univ, DPhil(neuroanat), 56, BM & BCh, 58. *Hon Degrees:* MA, Oxford Univ, 58. *Prof Exp:* Asst anat, Univ Witwatersrand, 51-53; dept demonstr, Oxford Univ, 53-58, lectr, 59-66, tutor, Pembroke Col, 56-66; assoc prof, Univ Wis-Madison, 66-68; prof & head dept, Sch Med, Wash Univ, 68-80; RES PROF & DIR, DEVELOP NEUROBIOL LAB, SALK INST, 80- *Concurrent Pos:* Fel, Pembroke Col, 56-66, lectr, Balliol Col, 62-66; vis assoc prof, Wash Univ, 64-65; managing ed, J Comp Neurol, 69-80; ed, Ann Rev Neurosci & J Neurosci, 80-; fel Salk Inst; mem, Asn Neurosci Res Prog. *Mem:* Inst Med-Nat Acad Sci; fel AAAS; Anat Soc Gt Brit & Ireland; fel Royal Micros Soc; Soc Neurosci (pres, 77-78). *Res:* Neuroembryology, especially the structure and development of the mammalian forebrain and the avian visual system. *Mailing Add:* Salk Inst Biol Studies PO Box 85800 San Diego CA 92138

COWAN, WILLIAM ALLEN, b Pittsfield, Mass, Oct 4, 20; m 46. ANIMAL BREEDING. *Educ:* Mass State Col, BS, 42; Univ Minn, MS, 48, PhD(animal breeding, dairy prod), 52. *Prof Exp:* Asst farm mgr, Grafton State Hosp, Mass, 42-43; instr & farm supt, RI State Col, 43-45; asst & assoc prof animal husb, Univ Mass, 46-52; head dept, 52-74, PROF ANIMAL INDUSTS, UNIV CONN, 52-, HEAD DEPT, 80- *Mem:* Am Soc Animal Sci; Am Dairy Sci Asn; Am Genetic Asn. *Res:* Animal production; dairy herd and livestock management. *Mailing Add:* Dept of Animal Industs Univ of Conn Storrs CT 06268

COWARD, DAVID HAND, b Buffalo, NY, Nov 16, 34; m 60; c 3. HIGH ENERGY PHYSICS. *Educ:* Cornell Univ, BEng, 57; Stanford Univ, MS, 58, PhD(physics), 63. *Prof Exp:* EXP PHYSICIST, STANFORD LINEAR ACCELERATOR CTR, STANFORD UNIV, 63- *Concurrent Pos:* Sci assoc, Europ Ctr Nuclear Res, Geneva, 76-77. *Mem:* Am Phys Soc. *Res:* High energy physics involving electron-positron and electron-proton colliding beams, and electron and photon beams on stationary targets. *Mailing Add:* Stanford Linear Accelerator Ctr PO Box 4349 Stanford CA 94305

COWARD, JAMES KENDERDINE, b Buffalo, NY, Oct 13, 38; m 75; c 1. BIO-ORGANIC CHEMISTRY, MEDICINAL CHEMISTRY. *Educ:* Middlebury Col, AB, 60; Duke Univ, MA, 64; State Univ NY Buffalo, PhD(med chem), 67. *Prof Exp:* NIH fel, Univ Calif, Santa Barbara, 66-68; asst prof, Sch Med, Yale Univ, 69-74, assoc prof, 75-79; ASSOC PROF CHEM, RENSSELAER POLYTECH INST, NY, 79- *Concurrent Pos:* Vis prof, Salk Inst Biol Sci, 77-78; mem exp therapeut study sect, NIH, 79- *Mem:* Am Chem Soc; Royal Soc Chem; Am Soc Biol Chem; AAAS. *Res:* Investigation of the mechanism of enzyme-catalyzed reactions as a basis for the design and synthesis of new mechanism-based enzyme inhibitors. *Mailing Add:* Dept Chem Rensselaer Polytech Inst Troy NY 12181

COWARD, JOE EDWIN, b Searcy, Ark, Mar 27, 38; m 59; c 2. VIROLOGY, MICROBIOLOGY. *Educ:* State Col Ark, BSE, 59; Univ Ark, Fayetteville, MS, 62; Univ Miss, PhD(microbiol), 68. *Prof Exp:* Res assoc, Col Physicians & Surgeons, Columbia Univ, 68-70, asst prof microbiol, 70-75; assoc prof microbiol, 75-80, ASSOC PROF MICROBIOL & IMMUNOL, SCH MED, LA STATE UNIV MED CTR, NEW ORLEANS, 80- *Mem:* Am Soc Microbiol. *Res:* Viral replication as studied by electron microscopy; development of the slow viruses and their relationship to human disease. *Mailing Add:* Dept of Microbiol Sch of Med La State Univ Med Ctr New Orleans LA 70112

COWARD, NATHAN A, b Belton, SC, Jan 7, 27; m 53; c 4. PHYSICAL CHEMISTRY. *Educ:* The Citadel, BS, 50; Univ Rochester, PhD(phys chem), 54. *Prof Exp:* Res chemist, F H Levey Co Div, Columbian Carbon Co, 54-57 & Am Viscose Corp, 57-59; from instr to assoc prof, 59-69, actg chmn dept, 64-65, 68-69, PROF CHEM, UNIV WIS-SUPERIOR, 69- *Concurrent Pos:* Vis prof, Univ Wis-Madison, 67-68. *Mem:* Am Chem Soc; Sigma Xi. *Res:* Fluorescence; photochemistry; printing inks; analytical methods and instrumentation; liquid phase weak complexes of lanthanide ions; trace metals in fuels and natural waters. *Mailing Add:* Dept of Chem Univ of Wis Superior WI 54880

COWARD, STUART JESS, b New York, NY, June 7, 36; m 65. DEVELOPMENTAL BIOLOGY. *Educ:* Univ Miami, Fla, BS, 58; Univ Iowa, MS, 61; Univ Calif, Davis, PhD(zool), 64. *Prof Exp:* Res assoc, State Univ NY Buffalo, 64-65; asst prof, 65-69, ASSOC PROF ZOOL, UNIV GA, 69- *Concurrent Pos:* NIH fel, 64-65; NIH spec fel, Harvard Univ Med Sch, 70-71. *Mem:* AAAS; Soc Develop Biol; Am Soc Cell Biol. *Res:* Regeneration in planaria; biochemical aspects of amphibian development. *Mailing Add:* Dept of Zool Univ of Ga Athens GA 30602

COWBURN, DAVID, b Sale, Cheshire, Eng, July 13, 45; m 77; c 1. PHYSICAL BIOCHEMISTRY, BIOPHYSICS. *Educ:* Univ Manchester, Eng, BSc Hons, 65; Long Univ, PhD(biophys), 70. *Hon Degrees:* DSc, Univ London, 81. *Prof Exp:* Res assoc, Columbia Univ Col Physicians & Surgeons, 70-73; asst prof, 73-78, ASSOC PROF, ROCKEFELLER UNIV, 78- *Concurrent Pos:* Fel, Res Training Prog, Dept Psychiat, Columbia Univ Col Physicians & Surgeons, 71-73. *Mem:* Am Soc Biol Chemists; NY Acad Sci; Am Chem Soc. *Res:* Structure-function relationships in biological chemistry; intracellular communication by hormones, neurotransmitters and trophic factors; nuclear magnetic resonance. *Mailing Add:* Rockefeller Univ Box 299 1230 York Ave New York NY 10021

COWDEN, RONALD REED, b Memphis, Tenn, July 9, 31; m 56. CYTOLOGY, EMBRYOLOGY. *Educ:* La State Univ, Baton Rouge, BS, 53; Univ Vienna, DrPhil(zool), 56. *Prof Exp:* USPHS fel biol, Oak Ridge Nat Lab, 56-57; asst prof biol, Johns Hopkins Univ, 57-60; asst mem cell biol, Inst Muscle Dis, 60-61; asst prof path, Col Med, Univ Fla, 61-66, USPHS career develop award, 62-66; assoc prof anat, La State Univ Med Ctr, New Orleans, 66-68; prof biol sci & chmn dept, Univ Denver, 68-71; prof anat & chmn dept, Albany Med Col, 72-75; assoc dean basic sci, 75-80, PROF BIOPHYS & CHMN DEPT, COL MED, EAST TENN STATE UNIV, 80- *Mem:* Am Soc Cell Biologists; Soc Develop Biol; Am Asn Anatomists; Am Zool Soc; Royal Micros Soc. *Res:* Quantitative cytochemistry; cytochemistry of oogenesis and development; comparative hematology and immunity. *Mailing Add:* Col Med East Tenn State Univ Johnson City TN 37614

COWDREY, ERIC JOHN, b Ste Agathe des Monts, Que, Sept 15, 45; m 75. HEALTH PHYSICS, PHYSICS. *Educ:* Concordia Univ, BSc, 67, MSc, 70. *Prof Exp:* Res scientist textiles, Bobtex Corp, 70-71; res physicist paper, Pulmac Instruments Ltd, 72-74; res physicist explosives res, Can Industs Ltd, 74-78; health physicist nuclear res, 78-80, HEAD, RADIATION & INDUST SAFETY BR, ATOMIC ENERGY CAN LTD, MANITOBA, 80- *Mem:* Health Physics Soc; Can Radiation Protection Asn. *Res:* Dosimetry of ionizing radiations; radiation and industrial safety. *Mailing Add:* Whiteshell Nuclear Res Estab Atomic Energy of Can Pinawa MB R0E 1L0 Can

COWELL, BRUCE CRAIG, b Buffalo, NY, Oct 20, 37; m 65; c 2. LIMNOLOGY. *Educ:* Bowling Green State Univ, BA, 58, MA, 59; Cornell Univ, PhD(limnol ecol), 63. *Prof Exp:* Fishery res biologist limnol, NCent Reservoir Invest, US Fish & Wildlife Serv, 63-67; asst prof zool, 67-75, ASSOC PROF BIOL, UNIV S FLA, 75- *Mem:* Am Inst Fishery Res Biologists; Am Soc Limnol & Oceanog; Ecol Soc Am; Int Soc Limnol; NAm Benthological Soc. *Res:* Production and population dynamics of plankton and benthic invertebrate communities; lake management and restoration. *Mailing Add:* Dept of Biol Univ of SFla Tampa FL 33620

COWELL, JAMES LEO, b Wilkes-Barre, Pa, May 4, 44; m 69; c 1. BACTERIAL INFECTIONS & PATHOGENESIS, VACCINES. *Educ:* King's Col, Pa, BS, 66; St John's Univ, NY, MS, 68; Univ Ill, Urbana, PhD(microbiol), 72. *Prof Exp:* Res asst biochem, Cornell Univ, 72-74; res asst microbiol, Sch Med, NY Univ, 74-78; RES MICROBIOLOGIST, DIV BACT PROD, BUR BIOLOGICS, FOOD & DRUG ADMIN, 78- *Concurrent Pos:* NIH fel, 72. *Mem:* Am Soc Microbiol; Sigma Xi; Am Inst Biol Sci; NY Acad Sci. *Res:* Physiology, biochemistry and pathogenicity of Bordetella pertussis. *Mailing Add:* Div Bact Prod Bur of Biologics 8800 Rockville Pike Bethesda MD 20205

COWELL, WAYNE RUSSELL, b Wakefield, Kans, June 27, 26; m 53; c 3. APPLIED MATHEMATICS. *Educ:* Kans State Univ, BS, 48, MS, 50; Univ Wis, PhD(math), 54. *Prof Exp:* Asst math, Kans State Univ, 48-50 & Univ Wis, 50-54; asst prof, Mont State Univ, 54-59; mem tech staff, Bell Tel Labs, 59-61; assoc mathematician, 61-72, COMPUTER SCIENTIST, ARGONNE NAT LAB, 72- *Concurrent Pos:* Asst to pres, Argonne Univs Asn, 68-71. *Mem:* Asn Comput Mach; Soc Indust & Appl Math. *Res:* Mathematical software. *Mailing Add:* Appl Math Div Argonne Nat Lab Argonne IL 60439

COWEN, CARL CLANDIUS, JR, b Madison, Ind, Nov 15, 45; m 70; c 1. OPERATOR THEORY, COMPLEX ANALYSIS. *Educ:* Ind Univ, Bloomington, AB, 67, AM, 71; Univ Calif, Berkeley, PhD(math), 76. *Prof Exp:* Vis lectr math, Univ Ill, Urbana, 76-78; ASST PROF MATH, PURDUE UNIV, 78- *Mem:* Am Math Soc; Math Asn Am. *Res:* Cammutants of analytic toeplitz operators and composition operators on water. *Mailing Add:* Dept Math Purdue Univ West Lafayette IN 47907

COWEN, DAVID, b New York, NY, July 29, 07. NEUROPATHOLOGY. *Educ:* Columbia Col, AB, 28; Columbia Univ, MD, 32. *Prof Exp:* Asst pathologist, Neurol Inst, NY, 37-46; instr neurol, 37-39, from instr neuropath to assoc prof, 39-63, prof, 63-76, EMER NEUROPATH, COL PHYSICIANS & SURGEONS, COLUMBIA UNIV, 76-, SPEC LECTR, 77- *Concurrent Pos:* From asst attend neuropathologist to attend neuropathologist, Columbia-Presby Med Ctr, 45-73, consult neuropathologist, 73-; consult neuropathologist, Vet Admin Hosp, East Orange, NJ, 53- & Lenox Hill Hosp, NY; ed, J Neuropath & Exp Neurol. *Honors & Awards:* Neuropath Contributions Award, Am Asn Neuropath, 79. *Mem:* Am Asn Neuropath; Am Neurol Asn; Harvey Soc; Am Soc Exp Path; NY Acad Med. *Res:* Infections of the nervous system; neurological diseases of prenatal origin. *Mailing Add:* Columbia Univ Div Neuropath Col Physicians & Surgeons New York NY 10032

COWEN, JERRY ARNOLD, b Toledo, Ohio, July 17, 24; m 46; c 5. PHYSICS. *Educ:* Harvard Col, BS, 48; Mich State Col, MS, 50, PhD, 54. *Prof Exp:* Asst physics, Mich State Col, 49-53; asst prof, Colo Agr & Mech Col, 53-55; from asst prof to assoc prof, 55-69, PROF PHYSICS, COL NATURAL SCI, MICH STATE UNIV, 69- *Concurrent Pos:* NSF fel, Saclay Nuclear Res Ctr, France, 64-65; res physicist, Nat Bur Standards, 55 & Lockheed Res Lab, 60-61. *Mem:* Am Phys Soc; Am Asn Physics Teachers. *Res:* Microwave resonance. *Mailing Add:* Dept of Physics Mich State Univ East Lansing MI 48824

COWEN, RICHARD, b Workington, Eng, Jan 24, 40. PALEONTOLOGY. *Educ:* Cambridge Univ, BA, 62, PhD(geol), 66. *Prof Exp:* Res asst geol, Cambridge Univ, 65-67; from asst prof to assoc prof, 67-79, chmn dept, 76-79, PROF GEOL, UNIV CALIF, DAVIS, 79- *Mem:* Paleontol Soc; Brit Palaeontol Asn; AAAS. *Res:* Anatomical and functional studies in living and fossil invertebrates, especially brachiopods, their implications for evolution and paleobiogeography. *Mailing Add:* Dept Geol Univ Calif Davis CA 95616

COWEN, WILLIAM FRANK, b Oshkosh, Wis, Aug 20, 45; m 67; c 3. WATER CHEMISTRY. *Educ:* Univ Wis, Madison, BS, 67, MS, 69, PhD(water chem), 74. *Prof Exp:* Res chemist environ chem, US Army Bioeng Res & Develop Lab, Environ Protection Div, 73-78; SR ANAL CHEMIST & TECH SUPVR, MARCUS HOOK LAB, CATALYTIC INC, 78- *Mem:* Am Chem Soc; Water Pollution Control Fedn. *Res:* Methods for analysis of trace organic compounds in water supplies and in wastewaters. *Mailing Add:* 141 S Brentwood Dr Mt Laurel NJ 08054

COWETT, EVERETT R, b Ashland, Maine, Mar 6, 35; m 60; c 5. AGRONOMY, PLANT PHYSIOLOGY. *Educ:* Univ Maine, BS, 57, MS, 58; Rutgers Univ, PhD(farm crops), 61. *Prof Exp:* Asst prof agron, Univ NH, 61-63; rep field res plant protection, Geigy Chem Corp, 63-65, herbicide specialist, 65-67, field res mgr plant protection, 67-70, mgr plant sci res, Ciba-Geigy Ltd, Ardsley, 70-73, DIR TECH SERVS, AGR DIV, CIBA-GEIGY CORP, 73- *Mem:* Am Soc Agron; Weed Sci Soc Am; Entom Soc Am. *Res:* Plant physiology; forage crop management; weed control; insect and disease control; plant growth regulators. *Mailing Add:* Ciba-Geigy Corp PO Box 11422 Greensboro NC 27409

COWGER, MARILYN L, b Douglas, Nebr, June 7, 31. PEDIATRICS, BIOCHEMISTRY. *Educ:* Univ Omaha, BA, 53; Univ Nebr, MD, 56; Am Bd Pediat, dipl, 62. *Prof Exp:* Intern med, Bryan Mem Hosp, Lincoln, Nebr, 56-57; fel pediat, Mayo Clin, Minn, 57-60; from asst to assoc prof pediat, Sch Med, Univ Wash, 60-70; assoc prof, 70-76, PROF PEDIAT, ALBANY MED COL, 76- *Concurrent Pos:* NIH trainee, 60-63, career develop award, 65-74; Am Heart Asn advan res fel, 63-65; res assoc prof chem, State Univ NY Albany, 70-76, vis prof, 76- *Mem:* Am Acad Pediat; Soc Pediat Res. *Res:* Mechanism of bilirubin toxicity; electron transport inhibitors; clinical and biochemical studies of the porphyrias; mechanism of mental retardation in inborn errors of metabolism. *Mailing Add:* Dept of Pediat Albany Med Col Albany NY 12208

COWGILL, JAMES JOSEPH, physical chemistry, deceased

COWGILL, ROBERT WARREN, b Topeka, Kans, Jan 31, 20; m 44; c 2. BIOCHEMISTRY. *Educ:* Univ Kans, BA, 41; Rensselaer Polytech Inst, MS, 42; Johns Hopkins Univ, PhD(biochem), 50. *Prof Exp:* Res chemist, Hercules Powder Co, 42-45; instr biochem, Wash Univ, 50-52; instr, Univ Calif, 53-56; asst prof, Univ Colo, 56-62; prof, 62-80, EMER PROF BIOCHEM, BOWMAN GRAY SCH MED, 80- *Mem:* Am Soc Biol Chemists; Am Chem Soc. *Res:* Mechanism of enzyme action; protein structure. *Mailing Add:* 320 Palm Warbler Rd Kiawah Island SC 29455

COWGILL, URSULA MOSER, b Bern, Switz, Nov 9, 27; US citizen; m 54. GEOCHEMISTRY. *Educ:* Hunter Col, AB, 48; Kans State Univ, MS, 52; Iowa State Univ, PhD(soil chem), 56. *Prof Exp:* Mem staff, Lincoln Lab, Mass Inst Technol, 57-58 & Doherty Charitable Found Inc, Guatemala, 58-60; res assoc ecol & anthrop geochem, Yale Univ, 60-68; prof biol sci, Univ Pittsburgh, 68-81, prof anthrop, 72-81; ENVIRON SCIENTIST, DOW CHEM CO, 81- *Concurrent Pos:* Mem sci adv bd, US Environ Protection Agency, 76- *Mem:* Am Soc Naturalists; Mineral Soc Am; Clay Minerals Soc; Int Asn Theoret & Appl Limnol; Soc Environ Geochem & Health. *Res:* Ecological and anthropological geochemistry; primitive agriculture; phosphate mineralogy; history of lake basins; exotic demography; prosimian behavior. *Mailing Add:* Environ Sci Res Dow Chem Co Bldg 1702 Midland MI 48640

COWHERD, CHATTEN, JR, b Kansas City, Mo, May 16, 39; m 61; c 4. AIR POLLUTION. *Educ:* Rockhurst Col, BS, 60; Johns Hopkins Univ, PhD(chem eng), 64. *Prof Exp:* From asst prof to assoc prof eng sci, Rockhurst Col, 64-69; sr engr, 70-74, prin engr, 74-76, SECT HEAD, MIDWEST RES INST, 76- *Mem:* Air Pollution Control Asn; Sigma Xi. *Res:* Convective heat and mass transfer; aerosol sizing and flux measurement; air pollution source and ambient sampling; kinetics and mechanisms of atmospheric dust generation by wind erosion or materials handling; cost-effectiveness evaluation of pollution control. *Mailing Add:* Midwest Res Inst 425 Volker Blvd Kansas City MO 64110

COWIE, ALEXANDER, b Glasgow, Scotland, Sept 28, 01; US citizen; m 41. MECHANICAL ENGINEERING. *Educ:* Univ Wis, BS, 31; Univ Mich, MSE, 32. *Prof Exp:* Res engr, Westinghouse Elec Corp, 32-33; instr mech eng, Univ Minn, 33-37 & Armour Inst, Ill Inst Technol, 38-42; anal engr, Foote Bros Gear & Mach Corp, 42-47; prof mech eng, 48-67, EMER PROF MECH ENG, ILL INST TECHNOL, 67- *Concurrent Pos:* Indust consult, 48-; tech writer, Encycl Britannica, 67-72; vis lectr, Univ Ill, Chicago Circle Campus, 71-81; consult, Argonne Nat Lab, 76-78. *Mem:* Fel Am Soc Mech Engrs. *Res:* Gearing and stress analysis. *Mailing Add:* 1440 N Lake Shore Dr Chicago IL 60610

COWIE, LENNOX LAUCHLAN, b Jedburgh, Scotland, Oct 18, 50. ASTROPHYSICS, ASTRONOMY. *Educ:* Edinburgh Univ, BSc, 69; Harvard Univ, PhD(theoret physics), 76. *Prof Exp:* Res assoc, Princeton Univ, 76-78, res staff mem astrophysics, 78-81, res astronomer & assoc prof, 79-81; ASSOC PROF PHYSICS, MASS INST TECHNOL, 80- *Mem:* Fel Royal Astron Soc; Am Astron Soc; Am Phys Soc; Int Astron Soc. *Res:* Gas dynamics of the interstellar and intergalactic medium. *Mailing Add:* Physics Dept Mass Inst Technol Cambridge MA 02139

COWIE, MARTIN, b Aberdeen, Scotland, Feb 27, 47; Can citizen; m 69; c 2. INORGANIC CHEMISTRY, X-RAY CRYSTALLOGRAPHY. *Educ:* McMaster Univ, BSc, 69; Univ Alta, PhD(x-ray crystallog), 74. *Prof Exp:* ASST PROF CHEM, UNIV ALTA, 76- *Concurrent Pos:* NATO fel, Northwestern Univ, 74-76. *Mem:* Chem Inst Can; Am Chem Soc; Am Crystallog Asn. *Res:* Coordination of small molecules to transition metals; chemistry of binuclear diphosphine-bridged, metal complexes; low temperature x-ray diffraction. *Mailing Add:* Dept of Chem Univ Alta Edmonton AB T6G 2G2 Can

COWIN, STEPHEN CORTEEN, b Elmira, NY, Oct 26, 34; m 56; c 2. APPLIED MECHANICS, BIOMEDICAL ENGINEERING. *Educ:* Johns Hopkins Univ, BS, 56, MS, 58; Pa State Univ, PhD(eng mech), 62. *Prof Exp:* Asst dynamics, Johns Hopkins Univ, 56-58; struct engr, Aircraft Armaments, Inc, Md, 58, sr struct engr, 58-59; from instr to asst prof mech, Pa State Univ, 59-63; from asst prof to prof mech eng, 63-77, PROF MECH, DEPT BIOMED ENG, TULANE UNIV, 77- *Concurrent Pos:* Instr, Loyola Col, Md, 58-59; sr vis fel, Res Coun Gt Brit, 74; prof-in-charge, Tulane Univ-Newcomb Jr Yr Abroad Prog, Gt Brit, 74-75; chmn, Master Sci Appl Math Prog & Eng Curriculum Prog, 75-79; adj prof orthopaedics, Sch Med, Tulane Univ, 78- *Mem:* Soc Rheol; Soc Natural Philos; Soc Eng Sci; Math Asn Am; Sigma Xi. *Res:* Continuum mechanics, rheology, mechanics of granular media, continuum theories representing the microstructure of materials; theory of constitutive relations; biomechanics. *Mailing Add:* Sch of Eng Tulane Univ New Orleans LA 70118

COWLES, EDWARD J, b Careywood, Idaho, July 15, 18; m 48; c 2. CHEMISTRY. *Educ:* Univ Wash, Seattle, BS, 40, PhD(chem), 53. *Prof Exp:* Jr chemist, Western Regional Res Lab, Bur Agr & Indust Chem, USDA, 41-42; shift chemist, Rayonier, Inc, 46; instr chem & Ger, Grays Harbor Col, 46-47; chemist, Philippine Fishery Prog, 47-48; assoc prof chem, Whitworth Col, 52-54; from asst prof to assoc prof, 54-69, PROF CHEM, UNIV MINN, DULUTH, 69- *Concurrent Pos:* Consult, Hilding Res Fund, US Dept Health, Educ & Welfare, 62-72. *Mem:* AAAS; Am Chem Soc; Sigma Xi. *Res:* Electrophilic substitution reactions of azulene; identification of the pigments of maize; determination of ammonia; spectra of azulene and related compounds; solubility of inorganic compounds; empirical applications of the computer to chemical problems. *Mailing Add:* Dept of Chem Univ of Minn Duluth MN 55812

COWLES, HAROLD ANDREWS, b Flandreau, SDak, Apr 12, 24; m 53; c 3. ECONOMIC & INDUSTRIAL ENGINEERING. *Educ:* Iowa State Univ, BS, 49, MS, 53, PhD(eng valuation), 57. *Prof Exp:* From instr gen eng to assoc prof indust eng, 49-61, PROF INDUST ENG, IOWA STATE UNIV, 61- *Mem:* Am Inst Indust Engrs; Opers Res Soc Am; Am Soc Eng Educ. *Res:* Industrial property depreciation, mortality and valuation; engineering economy; operations research-cost effectiveness studies. *Mailing Add:* Dept of Indust Eng Iowa State Univ Ames IA 50011

COWLES, JOE RICHARD, b Edmonson County, Ky, Oct 29, 41; m 65; c 2. PLANT PHYSIOLOGY. *Educ:* Western Ky Univ, BS, 63; Univ Ky, MS, 65; Ore State Univ, PhD(plant physiol), 68. *Prof Exp:* Res assoc plant physiol, Purdue Univ, 68-69, Univ Ga, 69-70; asst prof, 70-76, ASSOC PROF BIOL, UNIV HOUSTON, 76-, CHMN BIOL, 81- *Concurrent Pos:* Prin investr, 73- *Mem:* Am Soc Plant Physiol; AAAS; Sigma Xi. *Res:* Physiological and biochemical parameters associated with the establishment of symbiosis in leguminous plants, developmental changes associated with the regulation of aromatic biosynthesis in plants, and biomass conversion. *Mailing Add:* Dept of Biol Univ of Houston Houston TX 77004

COWLES, JOHN RICHARD, b Berkeley, Calif, Aug 26, 45; m 69; c 2. AUTOMATED THEOREM PROVING. *Educ:* Univ Wyo, BA, 68; Univ Nebr, MA, 70; Pa State Univ, PhD(math), 75. *Prof Exp:* Grad asst math, Univ Nebr, 68-71 & Pa State Univ, 71-75; mem staff, Dept Math, Inst Advan Study, 75-76 & 78; lectr, Univ Va, 76-78; ASST PROF, UNIV WYO, 78- *Mem:* Am Math Soc; Asn Comput Mach; Asn Symbolic Logic; Math Asn Am. *Res:* Number theory and mathematical logic; automated theorem provers; theory of computation, program correctness and synthesis; number theory; mathematical logic. *Mailing Add:* Dept Comput Sci Univ Wyo Laramie WY 82071

COWLES, WILLIAM WARREN, b New York, NY, Feb 22, 34; m 56; c 3. ELECTRICAL & ELECTRONIC ENGINEERING. *Educ:* Princeton Univ, BSE, 55; Yale Univ, MEng, 57, DEng(elec eng), 63. *Prof Exp:* Instr elec eng, Yale Univ, 57-63; asst prof, Moore Sch Elec Eng, Univ Pa, 63-70; mem tech staff, Res & Develop Lab, SCM Corp, 70-73, prin electronics engr, 73-75, sr mem tech staff, 75-80; SR STAFF ENGR, PERKIN-ELMER CORP, 80- *Concurrent Pos:* Consult, Hamilton-Standard Div, United Aircraft Corp, 56-57 & McNeal Electronics Conn, 57-63; mem tech staff, Bell Tel Labs, Inc, summers 54 & 64; engr, Proj Matterhorn, Princeton Univ, 56-59; NSF grant, Yale Univ, 61 & 62; proj supvr, Moore Sch Elec Eng, Univ Pa, 63-70. *Mem:* Inst Elec & Electronics Engrs; Am Soc Eng Educ; Soc Info Display. *Res:* Image and word processing; microprocessors; video displays; impact and non-impact printers; incremental motion systems; stepping motor design. *Mailing Add:* 10 Musket Lane West Redding CT 06896

COWLEY, ALAN H, b Manchester, Eng, Jan 29, 34; m 76; c 4. INORGANIC CHEMISTRY. *Educ:* Univ Manchester, BS, 55, MS, 56, PhD(chem), 58. *Prof Exp:* Fel chem, Univ Fla, 58-60; tech officer, Billingham Div, Imp Chem Industs Gt Brit, 60-62; from asst prof to assoc prof, 62-70, PROF CHEM, UNIV TEX, AUSTIN, 70- *Concurrent Pos:* Welch res grant, 64-; NIH res grant, 64-67; NSF grant, 69-; res panel, Army Res Off, 79. *Honors & Awards:* Jeremy I Musher lectr, Hebrew Univ, Jerusalem, Israel, 79; Main-Group Elem Chem Award, Royal Soc Chem, 80. *Mem:* Am Chem Soc; Royal Soc Chemists. *Res:* Chemistry of non-metals; inorganic free radicals; nuclear magnetic resonance; photoelectron spectroscopy. *Mailing Add:* Dept Chem Univ Tex Austin TX 78712

COWLEY, ALLEN WILSON, JR, b Harrisburg, Pa, Jan 21, 40; m 65. PHYSIOLOGY, CARDIOVASCULAR PHYSIOLOGY. *Educ:* Trinity Col, BA, 61; Hahnemann Med Col, MS, 65, PhD(physiol & biophys), 68. *Prof Exp:* NIH grant, Med Ctr, Univ Miss, 68-69, from instr to assoc prof, 68-74, prof physiol & biophys, 74-80, dir grad studies, 78-80; CHMN PHYSIOL, MED COL WIS, 80- *Concurrent Pos:* NIH res grant hypertension res, 71-85; Am Heart Asn estab investr, 73-78; mem adv bd, Coun High Blood Pressure Res, Am Heart Asn; mem, Study Sect, NIH, 80-83. *Mem:* Int Soc Hypertension; AAAS; Am Physiol Soc; Am Heart Asn. *Res:* Quantitative analysis of interacting neural and hormonal control systems in the overall regulation of arterial blood pressure. *Mailing Add:* Dept Physiol Med Col Wis PO Box 26509 Milwaukee WI 53226

COWLEY, ANNE PYNE, b Boston, Mass, Feb 25, 38; m 60; c 2. ASTRONOMY. *Educ:* Wellesley Col, BA, 59; Univ Mich, MA, 61, PhD(astron), 63. *Prof Exp:* Res assoc astron, Yerkes Observ, Univ Chicago, 63-68; res assoc astron, 68-73, assoc res scientist, 73-77, RES SCIENTIST, UNIV MICH, ANN ARBOR, 77- *Concurrent Pos:* Guest worker, Dom Astrophys Observ, 74-75 & 77-78. *Mem:* Am Astron Soc; Int Astron Union. *Res:* Stellar spectroscopy; x-ray sources. *Mailing Add:* Dept of Astron Physics-Astron Bldg Univ of Mich Ann Arbor MI 48109

COWLEY, CHARLES RAMSAY, b Aguana, Guam, Sept 13, 34; US citizen; m 60; c 2. ASTRONOMY. *Educ:* Univ Va, BA, 55, MA, 58; Univ Mich, PhD(astron), 63. *Prof Exp:* From instr to asst prof astron, Univ Chicago, 63-67; from asst prof to assoc prof, 67-77, PROF ASTRON, UNIV MICH, 77- *Mem:* Am Astron Soc; Royal Astron Soc; Int Astron Union. *Res:* Stellar atmospheres. *Mailing Add:* Dept of Astron Univ of Mich Ann Arbor MI 48109

COWLEY, GERALD TAYLOR, b Barron, Wis, Aug 1, 31; m 57; c 4. MYCOLOGY. *Educ:* Univ Wis, BS, 53, MS, 57, PhD(bot), 62. *Prof Exp:* Teacher high sch, Wis, 55-56; asst prof biol, 62-67, asst dean col arts & sci, 69-72, asst vprovost, Div Lib & Cult Disciplines, 72-73, ASSOC PROF BIOL, UNIV SC, 67-, ASST HEAD DEPT, 73- *Mem:* Mycol Soc Am. *Res:* Ecology and physiology of soil and litter microfungi. *Mailing Add:* 70 Beacon Hill Rd Columbia SC 29210

COWLEY, JOHN MAXWELL, b Peterborough, S Australia, Feb 18, 23; m 51; c 2. PHYSICS, MATERIALS SCIENCE. *Educ:* Univ Adelaide, BSc, 42, MSc, 45, DSc(phys), 57; Mass Inst Technol, PhD(phys), 49. *Prof Exp:* Res officer, Commonwealth Sci & Indust Res Orgn, Australia, 47-62; prof phys, Univ Melbourne, Australia, 63-70; GALVIN PROF PHYSICS, ARIZ STATE UNIV, 70- *Concurrent Pos:* Res assoc, Mass Inst Technol, 62-63; mem Comn Electron Diffraction, Int Univ Crystallog, 57-63, mem exec comt, 63-69; Int Union Crystallog rep, Solid State Comn, Int Union Pure & Appl Physics, 69-78; mem US Nat Comt Crystallog, 73-78; co-ed, Acta Crystallog, 71-80. *Honors & Awards:* B E Warren Award, Am Crystallog Asn, 76; Res Medal, Royal Soc Victoria, 62. *Mem:* Electron Micros Soc Am; Am Crystallog Asn; fel Inst Physics, London; fel Australian Inst Physics; fel Australian Acad Sci. *Res:* Electron diffraction and electron microscopy; diffraction and imaging theory; disorder and imperfections in crystals. *Mailing Add:* Dept of Physics Ariz State Univ Tempe AZ 85281

COWLEY, THOMAS GLADMAN, b Clifton Springs, NY, Aug 20, 38; m 77; c 2. ANALYTICAL CHEMISTRY, SPECTROCHEMISTRY. *Educ:* Rochester Inst Technol, BS, 61; Iowa State Univ, PhD(anal chem), 66. *Prof Exp:* Assoc, AEC Ames Lab, 66-67; SR RES SCIENTIST, CONTINENTAL OIL CO, 67- *Mem:* Am Chem Soc; Soc Appl Spectros. *Res:* Chemical and physical behavior of spectroscopic sources and their uses in analytical chemistry; development of flame emission spectroscopy as an analytical tool; application of spectrochemistry to environmental sciences; analysis of petroleum and petroleum products; physical and chemical analysis of plastics. *Mailing Add:* 2316 El Camino Ponca City OK 74601

COWLING, ELLIS BREVIER, b Waukegan, Ill, Dec 11, 32; m 56; c 2. FOREST PATHOLOGY, BIOCHEMISTRY. *Educ:* State Univ NY Col Forestry, Syracuse, BS, 54, MS, 56; Univ Wis, PhD(plant path & biochem), 59; Univ Uppsala, FilDr(physiol bot), 70. *Prof Exp:* Chemist wood properties res, Dow Chem Co, 55-56; wood pathologist, Forest Prod Lab, USDA, 56-59; asst prof forest path, Sch Forestry, Yale Univ, 60-68; assoc prof, 65-69, prof plant path, forestry & wood & paper sci, 68-78, ASSOC DEAN RES, SCH FOREST RESOURCES & ASST DIR, NC AGR RES SERV, NC STATE UNIV, 78- *Concurrent Pos:* USPHS fel, Royal Pharmaceut Inst Stockholm, Sweden, 59-60; vis prof, Inst Physiol Bot, Univ Uppsala, Sweden, 70-71; assoc ed, Ann Rev Phytopath, Ann Revs, Inc, Palo Alto, Calif, 71- *Honors & Awards:* Res Award, Sigma Xi, 68; O Max Gardner Award, 81. *Mem:* Nat Acad Sci; AAAS; fel Int Acad Wood Sci; fel Am Phytopath Soc. *Res:* Forest and wood products pathology; physiology of trees and of tree diseases; enzymatic degradation of plant cell walls; acid precipitation and its ecological effects. *Mailing Add:* Sch Forest Resources NC State Univ PO Box 5488 Raleigh NC 27650

COWLING, PETER WARNING, mechanical engineering, see previous edition

COWLING, VINCENT FREDERICK, b St Louis, Mo, Dec 15, 18; m 44; c 1. MATHEMATICS. *Educ:* Rice Inst, BA, 41, MA, 43, PhD(math), 44. *Prof Exp:* Instr math, Ohio State Univ, 45-46; asst prof, Lehigh Univ, 46-49; from assoc prof to prof, Univ Ky, 49-61; prof, Rutgers Univ, 61-67; dean, Col Sci & Math, 72-80, PROF MATH, STATE UNIV NY, ALBANY, 66- *Concurrent Pos:* Ford Found fel, Yale Univ, 52-53. *Mem:* Am Math Soc; Math Asn Am. *Res:* Complex variable theory; applications of functional analysis. *Mailing Add:* Dept of Math State Univ of NY Albany NY 12222

COWLISHAW, JOHN DAVID, b Grand Rapids, Mich, Sept 10, 38; div; c 3. BIOPHYSICS. *Educ:* Univ Mich, BS, 60, MS, 61; Pa State Univ, PhD(biophys), 68. *Prof Exp:* Asst engr, Air Arm Div, Westinghouse Elec Corp, 61-63; instr physics, Westminster Col, Pa, 63-65; asst prof, 68-74, ASSOC PROF BIOL SCI, OAKLAND UNIV, 74- *Mem:* AAAS; Biophys Soc. *Res:* Theory of information and energy-processing by biological systems; viruses of bacteria and algae. *Mailing Add:* Dept of Biol Sci Oakland Univ Rochester MN 48063

COWMAN, RICHARD AMMON, b Brainerd, Minn, Apr 24, 38; m 65; c 1. MICROBIOLOGY, BIOCHEMISTRY. *Educ:* Univ Minn, BS, 61; NC State Univ, MS, 63, PhD(food sci), 66. *Prof Exp:* Instr food microbiol, NC State Univ, 66-67, asst prof, 67-70; asst prof microbiol & biochem, Inst Oral Biol, Univ Miami, 70-74; RES MICROBIOLOGIST, US VET ADMIN HOSP, 70-, RES ASSOC PROF MICROBIOL, UNIV MIAMI, 77- *Mem:* Am Chem Soc; Am Soc Microbiol; Soc Cryobiol; NY Acad Sci. *Res:* Freeze-damage of microorganisms; nutritional aspects of microorganisms involved in dental caries. *Mailing Add:* Vet Admin Hosp Dent Res Unit 151 1201 NW 16th St Miami FL 33125

COWPER, GEORGE, b Newcastle-upon-Tyne, Eng, Sept 6, 21; Can citizen; m 51; c 3. PHYSICS. *Educ:* Durham Univ, BSc, 43. *Prof Exp:* Sci officer, Telecommun Res Estab, Eng, 43-48; from jr res officer to assoc res officer, 48-58, sr res officer & head radiation dosimetry br, 58-67, HEAD HEALTH PHYSICS BR, ATOMIC ENERGY CAN, LTD, 67- *Concurrent Pos:* Chmn subcomt electronic mat res, Defence Res Bd Can, 57-63, mem, 63-65, mem panel radiation protection & treatment, 58-66; chmn panel adequate stand personnel dosimetry, Int Atomic Energy Agency, 63-64; WHO vis prof, Bhabha Atomic Res Ctr, Bombay, India, 71; news ed, Health Physics, Health Phys Soc, 71-75; health physics adv comt, Oak Ridge Nat Lab, 71-75; assoc comt environ quality, Nat Res Coun Can, 75- *Mem:* Health Phys Soc; Can Radiation Protection Soc; Int Comn Radiation Units & Measurements; Int Radiation Protection Asn (vpres, 80-). *Res:* Instrumentation for health physics; radiation dosimetry; detection of ionizing radiation as applied to nuclear chemistry and geophysical prospecting. *Mailing Add:* Health Physics Br Atomic Energy Can Ltd Chalk River ON K0J 1J0 Can

COWPER, GEORGE RICHARD, b Galt, Ont, June 9, 30. APPLIED MATHEMATICS. *Educ:* Queen's Univ, BSc, 52, MSc, 54; Brown Univ, PhD(appl math), 59. *Prof Exp:* RES OFFICER APPL MECH, NAT AERONAUT ESTAB, NAT RES COUN CAN, 59- *Mem:* Am Soc Mech Engrs. *Res:* Finite element method; theory of elasticity. *Mailing Add:* Nat Res Coun Can Ottawa ON K1A 0R6 Can

COWPERTHWAITE, MICHAEL, b Keswick, Eng, June 18, 32; m 56; c 4. CHEMISTRY, THERMODYNAMICS. *Educ:* Manchester Univ, Eng, BSc, 54, MSc, 56, PhD(chem), 58. *Prof Exp:* Fel chem, Cornell Univ, 58-61; sr sci officer detonation, Explosives Res & Develop Estab, 61-64; SR CHEM PHYSICIST DETONATION, SRI INT, 64- *Mem:* Combustion Inst. *Res:* Shock wave physics and chemistry; detonation; thermodynamics. *Mailing Add:* SRI Int 333 Ravenswood Ave Menlo Park CA 94025

COWSAR, DONALD ROY, b Baton Rouge, La, Dec 12, 42; m 66; c 3. BIOMATERIALS, POLYMER CHEMISTRY. *Educ:* La State Univ, BS, 64; Rice Univ, PhD(org chem), 69. *Prof Exp:* Res chemist, 68-70, sr chemist, 70-73, head biomat sect, 74-77, head, Biosysts Div, 77-80, ASSOC DIR, APPL SCI DEPT, SOUTHERN RES INST, 80- *Concurrent Pos:* Consult, NIH, 73- *Mem:* Am Chem Soc. *Res:* New biomaterials and biomedical devices including controlled-release drug-delivery systems, microcapsules, liposomes, polymeric drugs, polymeric pesticides, biodegradable implants, hemoperfusion devices, prosthetic polymers, and hydrogels; in vivo evaluation of materials and devices. *Mailing Add:* Southern Res Inst PO Box 3307-A Birmingham AL 35255

COWSER, KENNETH EMERY, b Chicago, Ill, Apr 12, 26; m 47; c 3. HEALTH PHYSICS, ENVIRONMENTAL ENGINEERING. *Educ:* Univ Ill, Champaign-Urbana, BS, 47; Univ Tenn, Knoxville, MS, 59; Oak Ridge Sch Reactor Technol, grad, 63. *Prof Exp:* Eng aide, Ill Dept Hwys, 46; dist engr, Ill Dept Pub Health, 47-51, actg regional engr, 51-53; engr leader res & develop, Oak Ridge Nat Lab, 53-67, sect chief res & develop, Radioactive Waste Disposal Sect, Health Physics Div, 67-71, asst to assoc dir biomed & environ sci, 71-75; asst to asst adminr environ & safety, Energy Res & Develop Admin, 75-77; sect chief med physics & internal dose sect, Health Physics Div, 77, coordr, 77-80, MGR, LIFE SCI SYNTHETIC FUELS PROG, OAK RIDGE NAT LAB, 80- *Concurrent Pos:* Mem subcomt radioactive waste disposal, Am Standards Asn, 60-69; mem panel, Internal AEC, 67-70 & 73-77; mem subcomt radioactive waste mgt, Am Nat Standards, 69-71; mem sci comt, task group krypton-85 & sci comt radiation nuclear power generation, Nat Coun Radiation Protection & Measurements; vis lectr health physics prog, Vanderbilt Univ. *Mem:* Health Physics Soc; Sigma Xi; AAAS. *Res:* Waste management; siting and operating nuclear and fossil energy facilities; plant and environmental monitoring and testing; environmental and health assessments. *Mailing Add:* 937 W Outer Dr Oak Ridge TN 37830

COX, AARON J, b Topeka, Kans, Apr 6, 41; m 70. PHYSICS. *Educ:* Univ NMex, BS, 63, MS, 65; Univ Ariz, PhD(physics), 70. *Prof Exp:* Res asst physics, Univ Ariz, 67-70; assoc prof, 70-80, PROF PHYSICS, UNIV REDLANDS, 80- *Concurrent Pos:* Res physicist chem, Univ Calif, Riverside, 76- *Mem:* Optical Soc Am; Sigma Xi. *Res:* Quantum optics and laser spectroscopy; picosecond laser spectroscopy; dye laser. *Mailing Add:* Dept of Physics 1200 E Colton Ave Redlands CA 92373

COX, ALLAN CLAYTON, nutrition, physiology, see previous edition

COX, ALLAN VERNE, b Santa Ana, Calif, Dec 17, 26. GEOPHYSICS. *Educ:* Univ Calif, BA & MA, 57, PhD, 59. *Prof Exp:* Geol field asst, US Geol Surv, 50-51, 54; asst geol, Univ Calif, 56-57; geophysicist, US Geol Surv, 57-68; CECIL & IDA GREEN PROF GEOPHYS, STANFORD UNIV, 68-, DEAN SCH EARTH SCI, 79- *Honors & Awards:* John A Fleming Medal, Am Geophys Union; Vetlesen Prize, 71; Day Medal, Geol Soc Am, 75. *Mem:* Nat Acad Sci; Am Geophys Union (pres, 78-80); Geol Soc Am; Am Acad Arts & Sci; Soc Explor Geophys. *Res:* Pleistocene geology; paleomagnetism; geomagnetism; tectonics; geomorphology; history of earth's magnetic field determined from paleomagnetism of rocks. *Mailing Add:* Dept Geophys Stanford Univ Stanford CA 94305

COX, ALVIN JOSEPH, JR, b Manila, PR, Mar 6, 07; m 46; c 3. PATHOLOGY. *Educ:* Stanford Univ, AB, 27, MD, 31. *Prof Exp:* From asst to prof path, 31-64, PROF DERMAT, SCH MED, STANFORD UNIV, 64-, EMER PROF PATH, 80- *Concurrent Pos:* Fel Harvard Univ, 57-58; exchange asst, Path Inst, Freiburg, 35-36; consult pathologist, Western Utilization Res Br, USDA, 37; consult pathologist, San Francisco Hosp, 41-59. *Mem:* Fel AMA; Am Asn Path & Bact; Soc Exp Biol & Med; Soc Invest Dermat; Am Soc Dermatopath. Res Coccidioidal infection; pathology of stomach; arteriosclerosis; experimental tumor production; dermatopathology. *Mailing Add:* Rm R166 Stanford Univ Sch of Med Stanford CA 94305

COX, ANDREW CHADWICK, b Hattiesburg, Miss, July 20, 36; m 61; c 2. BIOCHEMISTRY, BIOPHYSICS. *Educ:* Univ Tex, BS, 59; Univ Houston, MS, 63; Duke Univ, PhD(biochem), 67. *Prof Exp:* Fel, Am Cancer Soc, 66-68; asst prof biochem, 69-72, ASSOC PROF BIOCHEM, SCH MED, UNIV OKLA, 72- *Mem:* Am Chem Soc. *Res:* Elucidation of lipid-protein interactions and their relations to mechanisms and structures, particularly plasma alpha-lipoprotein, prothrombin and cellular membranes. *Mailing Add:* Dept of Biochem Univ of Okla Health Sci Ctr Oklahoma City OK 73190

COX, ARTHUR NELSON, b Van Nuys, Calif, Oct 12, 27; m 73; c 5. ASTROPHYSICS, HYDRODYNAMICS. *Educ:* Calif Inst Technol, BA, 48; Ind Univ, AM, 52, PhD(astron), 53. *Hon Degrees:* DSc, Ind Univ, 73. *Prof Exp:* Staff mem physics, 48-49, staff mem field testing, 53-57, group leader, 57-74, STAFF MEM THEORET DIV, LOS ALAMOS SCI LAB, 75- *Concurrent Pos:* Vis prof, Univ Calif, Los Angeles, 66; NATO sr fel sci, Univ Liege, Belgium, 68, Fulbright res scholar, 68-69; NSF prog dir, 73-74. *Mem:* AAAS; Am Astron Soc; Int Astron Union; Sigma Xi. *Res:* Calculations of stellar stability and pulsation; compilation of equations of state and opacities for astrophysics; studies of stellar atmosphere, interior structure and stellar evolution; hydrodynamical problems in astrophysics; total solar eclipses. *Mailing Add:* PO Box 1663 Los Alamos Sci Lab Los Alamos NM 87545

COX, B(RIAN), b Liverpool, Eng, Aug 4, 31; m 55; c 2. MATERIALS SCIENCE. *Educ:* Cambridge Univ, BA, 52, MA & PhD(chem), 55. *Prof Exp:* Sect leader reactor chem, Atomic Energy Res Estab, Harwell, 55-63, leader, Corrosion Group, 63-67, HEAD MAT SCI BR, ATOMIC ENERGY CAN, LTD, 67- *Honors & Awards:* A B Campbell Award, Nat Asn Corrosion Engrs, 61; Zirconium Award, W J Kroll Inst, Colo Sch Mines, 76. *Res:* Oxidation, corrosion, stress corrosion cracking and deformation of zirconium alloys; effects of irradiation on these and the basic physical processes involved, especially diffusion, charge transport, point defect production and agglomeration. *Mailing Add:* Atomic Energy Can Ltd Chalk River ON K0J 1J0 Can

COX, BEVERLEY LENORE, b Huntington, Pa, Jan 11, 29. ZOOLOGY, PHYSIOLOGY. *Educ:* Pa State Univ, BS, 51, MS, 53; Univ Okla, PhD(invert physiol), 60. *Prof Exp:* Instr physiol, Univ Okla, 59-60; res assoc & NIH fel, Univ Ore, 60-61; from asst prof to assoc prof, 61-70, PROF BIOL, CENT STATE UNIV, OKLA, 70- *Concurrent Pos:* NIH fel cardiovasc physiol, Sch Med, Univ Okla, 63-, vis assoc prof, 67, 68, 69 & 74, NSF fel isotope & nuclear reactor technol 63, 64, 65. *Mem:* AAAS; Am Soc Zool. *Res:* Physiology of insect tarsal chemoreception; gull food-finding behavior; recorded gull calls as repellants and attractants; endocrinology of mammalian salivary glands, molting in arachnids and electrolyte balance in lower vertebrates; bat blood studies. *Mailing Add:* 9701 N Bryant Britton OK 73131

COX, BRADLEY BURTON, b Danville, Ky, Oct 29, 41; div; c 1. ELEMENTARY PARTICLE PHYSICS. *Educ:* Duke Univ, PhD(physics), 67. *Prof Exp:* Res assoc high energy physics, Johns Hopkins Univ, 67, consult, 67-69, asst prof high energy physics, 69-73; group leader, Proton Lab, 73-74, assoc head, 74-76, head Proton Lab, 76-77, head superconducting magnet group, Proton Dept, 77-78, proj leader & design physicist, High Intensity Lab, 78-79, HEAD, RES SERV DEPT-FERMILAB, FERMI NAT ACCELERATOR LAB, 81- *Concurrent Pos:* Mem high energy discussion group, Brookhaven Nat Lab, 69-72; consult, Nuclear Effects Lab, 69-70; mem high energy physics rev comt, Lawrence Berkeley Lab, 77-; mem sci adv comt, Fermi Nat Accelerator Lab, 77-78, sci spokesman for Fermilab exp & res group leader, Fermilab Physics Dept. *Mem:* AAAS; Am Phys Soc. *Res:* Electromagnetic, weak and strong interactions of elementary particles; low energy fusion reactions and identical target-projectile heavy ion nuclear reactions; direct photon production in hodronic interactions; Drell Yen production of lepton pores in antiproton interactions. *Mailing Add:* Fermi Nat Accelerator Lab PO Box 500 Batavia IL 60510

COX, BRIAN MARTYN, b Sutton, Eng, Nov 3, 39; m 64; c 3. NEUROSCIENCE, DRUG ADDICTION. *Educ:* Coun Nat Acad Awards, London, UK, Dipl Technol, 62; Univ London, PhD(pharmacol), 65. *Prof Exp:* Lectr pharmacol, Chelsea Col, Univ London, 65-74; res assoc, Med Sch, Stanford Univ, 73-75; assoc dir, Addiction Res Found, Palo Alto, Calif, 75-81; PROF PHARMACOL, UNIFORMED SERV UNIV HEALTH SCI, 81- *Concurrent Pos:* Lectr & consult assoc prof, Dept Pharmacol, Med Sch, Stanford Univ, 75-78; mem, Exec Comt, Int Narcotics Res Conf, 81-; res scientist award, US Public Health Serv, Nat Inst Drug Abuse, 78-81. *Mem:* Brit Pharmacol Soc; Am Soc Pharmacol & Exp Therapeut; Soc Neurosci. *Res:* Structure, properties and functions of endogeneons opioid peptides and other related neuropeptides; mechanisms associated with the development of drug tolerance and dependence; pharmacology of drugs of abuse. *Mailing Add:* Dept Pharmacol Uniformed Serv Univ Health Sci 4301 Jones Bridge Rd Bethesda MD 20814

COX, CATHLEEN RUTH, b Vallejo, Calif, Oct 20, 48. REPRODUCTIVE BEHAVIOR, SOCIOBIOLOGY. *Educ:* Univ Calif, San Diego, BA, 70; Stanford Univ, PhD(psychol), 76. *Prof Exp:* Fel animal behav, Am Mus Natural Hist, 76-78; res assoc psychol, Barnard Col, Columbia Univ, 78-79; FEL BIOL, UNIV CALIF, LOS ANGELES, 79-; ASST PROF PSYCHOL, CALIF STATE UNIV, NORTHRIDGE, 80- *Concurrent Pos:* Vis prof psychol, Scripps Co, 79; res assoc biol, City Col, City Univ NY, 76-78; instr, Stanford Univ, 75; res assoc ornith, Los Angeles Mus Natural Hist, 79-; lectr biol, Univ Calif, Los Angeles, 80-; dir res, Los Angeles Zoo, 81- *Mem:* Animal Behav Soc; Am Ornith Union; Asn Women Sci; Am Asn Zool Parks & Aquaria; Am Primatological Soc. *Res:* Animal social behavior, specifically aggressive, sexual and reproductive; reproductive success of endangered species housed in zoos. *Mailing Add:* Los Angeles Zoo 5333 Zoo Dr Los Angeles CA 90027

COX, CHARLES DONALD, b Danville, Ill, Sept 10, 18; m 42; c 2. MEDICAL MICROBIOLOGY. *Educ:* Univ Ill, BS, 40, MS, 41, PhD(bact), 47. *Prof Exp:* Asst bact, Univ Ill, 40-42, 46-47; asst prof, Med Col Va, 47-49; assoc prof, Pa State Col, 49-51; prof microbiol & pub health & head dept, Sch Med, Univ SDak, 51-60; head microbiol br, Off Naval Res, Washington, DC, 60-62; head dept, 62-72, PROF MICROBIOL, UNIV MASS, AMHERST, 62- *Concurrent Pos:* Mem ed bd, J Bact, 57-70; mem adv panel environ biol, NASA, 65-72; mem comt naval med res, Nat Res Coun, 66-73; mem exobiol panel, Space Sci Bd, Nat Acad Sci, 74-77. *Mem:* AAAS; Am Soc Microbiol; Am Acad Microbiol; Soc Exp Biol & Med; NY Acad Sci. *Res:* Medical bacteriology and immunology; physiology and virulence of spirochetes. *Mailing Add:* Dept of Microbiol Univ of Mass Amherst MA 01002

COX, CHARLES PHILIP, b Eng, Dec 15, 19; m 62. STATISTICS, BIOMETRICS. *Educ:* Oxford Univ, BA, 40, MA, 47. *Prof Exp:* Head sect 4a, Army Oper Res Group, Eng, 45-46; head statist, Nat Inst Res Dairying, 48-61; PROF STATIST, IOWA STATE UNIV, 61- *Concurrent Pos:* Ministry of Agr res scholar, Exp Sta, Rothamsted, 47-48. *Mem:* Am Statist Asn; Biomet Soc; Royal Statist Soc. *Res:* Design and analysis of experiments; biological assay; biomathematics. *Mailing Add:* Statist Lab Iowa State Univ Ames IA 50011

COX, CHARLES SHIPLEY, b Hawaii, Sept 11, 22; m 51; c 5. OCEANOGRAPHY. *Educ:* Calif Inst Technol, BS, 44; Univ Calif, PhD, 54. *Prof Exp:* Asst oceanogr, 54-60, assoc prof, 60-66, chmn ocean res div, 73-76, PROF OCEANOG, SCRIPPS INST OCEANOG, UNIV CALIF, SAN DIEGO, 66- *Concurrent Pos:* NSF fel, 57; Fulbright res fel, 57-58; vis prof, Mass Inst Technol, 69-70. *Mem:* Fel Am Geophys Union; Royal Astron Soc. *Res:* Physical oceanography; geophysics relating to oceanic microstructure and magnetism. *Mailing Add:* Scripps Inst of Oceanog Univ of Calif at San Diego La Jolla CA 92093

COX, CLAIR EDWARD, II, b Lawrence Co, Ill, Sept 2, 33; m 58; c 4. SURGERY, UROLOGY. *Educ:* Univ Mich, MD, 58; Am Bd Urol, dipl, 66. *Prof Exp:* Intern med, Med Ctr, Univ Colo, 58-59, resident surg, 59-60; resident urol, Med Ctr, Univ Calif, San Francisco, 60-63; from instr to prof, Bowman Gray Sch Med, 63-73; CHMN DEPT UROL, COL MED, UNIV TENN, MEMPHIS, 73- *Concurrent Pos:* Nat Cancer Inst res grant, 69- *Mem:* Am Urol Asn; Am Col Surg; Am Asn Genitourinary Surg; Infectious Dis Soc Am; Soc Univ Urol. *Res:* Epidemiology of urinary tract infection; urological cancer. *Mailing Add:* Dept of Urol Univ of Tenn Col of Med Memphis TN 38163

COX, CYRUS W(ILLIAM), b West Terre Haute, Ind, Apr 20, 24; m 46; c 4. ELECTRICAL ENGINEERING. *Educ:* Rose Polytech Inst, BS, 49; Purdue Univ, MS, 51. *Prof Exp:* Elec engr, US Bur Reclamation, 49-50; from instr to assoc prof, 51-64, PROF ELEC ENG, S DAK SCH MINES & TECHNOL, 64- *Concurrent Pos:* Consult, Argonne Nat Lab, 65- & Detroit Edison Co, 78-79. *Mem:* Am Soc Eng Educ; Nat Soc Prof Engrs; Inst Elec & Electronics Engrs. *Res:* Undergraduate electric circuits and systems; nondestructive testing of nuclear fuels; energy efficiency in rotating machines; models for voltage and steam control in generating systems; real-time rating of power system components. *Mailing Add:* Dept of Elec Eng S Dak Sch of Mines & Technol Rapid City SD 57701

COX, DAVID BUCHTEL, b Denver, Colo, Jan 25, 27; m 53; c 2. RHEOLOGY, ORGANIC CHEMISTRY. *Educ:* DePauw Univ, AB, 48; Stanford Univ, MS, 50; Univ NMex, PhD(org chem), 53. *Prof Exp:* From technologist to sr technologist, Socony Mobil Oil Co, Inc, 53-58, res assoc, 58-67; sr res chemist, Battelle Mem Inst, 67-69, assoc chief lubrication mech div, 69-70; chief chemist, 70-73, tech dir, 73-76, V PRES TECH OPERS, CHEM-TREND, INC, 76- *Mem:* Am Chem Soc; Soc Rheol. *Res:* Rheology of lubricants, fuels and other petroleum products; polymer solutions; colloid chemistry of lubricants; mold release agents for urethane foams; die-casting lubricants; fire-resistant hydraulic fluids. *Mailing Add:* 1620 Sheridan Dr Ann Arbor MI 48104

COX, DAVID ERNEST, b Rochford, Eng, Dec 12, 34; m 57; c 4. CRYSTALLOGRAPHY, SOLID STATE CHEMISTRY. *Educ:* Univ London, BSc, 55, PhD(inorg chem), 59. *Prof Exp:* Tech officer ceramics, Steatite & Porcelain Prod Div, Imp Chem Industs, Ltd, 58-59; from chemist to sr chemist, Res Labs, Westinghouse Elec Corp, 59-63; assoc physicist, 63-66, PHYSICIST, BROOKHAVEN NAT LAB, 66- *Concurrent Pos:* Asst ed, J Physics & Chem of Solids, 69; mem neutron diffraction comn, Int Union Crystallog, 72-81, chmn comn, 78-81; assoc ed, J Physics & Chem Solids, 76-; ed, J Physics & Chem Solids, 81- *Mem:* Fel Am Phys Soc; Am Chem Soc; Am Asn Crystal Growth; Am Crystallog Asn. *Res:* Neutron and x-ray diffraction; magnetic and crystal structures; synthesis and characterization of inorganic materials; crystal growth; magnetic measurements. *Mailing Add:* Physics Dept Brookhaven Nat Lab Upton NY 11973

COX, DAVID FRAME, b New York, NY, Feb 19, 31; m 54; c 1. STATISTICS. *Educ:* Cornell Univ, BS, 53; NC State Col, MS, 57; Iowa State Univ, PhD(animal breeding, genetics), 59. *Prof Exp:* Assoc prof animal sci, 59-66, PROF STATIST, IOWA STATE UNIV, 66- *Mem:* Biomet Soc; Am Soc Animal Sci. *Res:* Design and analysis of experiments; genetic statistics. *Mailing Add:* Dept Statist Iowa State Univ Ames IA 50011

COX, DAVID JACKSON, b New York, NY, Dec 22, 34; m 58; c 3. PHYSICAL BIOCHEMISTRY. *Educ:* Wesleyan Univ, BA, 56; Univ Pa, PhD(biochem), 60. *Prof Exp:* Instr biochem, Univ Wash, Seattle, 60-63; from asst prof to assoc prof chem, Univ Tex, Austin, 63-73; PROF BIOCHEM & HEAD DEPT, KANS STATE UNIV, 73- *Concurrent Pos:* Investr, Howard Hughes Med Inst, 60-63; NSF fel & vis prof, Univ Va, 70-71. *Mem:* AAAS; Am Chem Soc; Am Soc Biol Chem; NY Acad Sci. *Res:* Physical chemistry of macromolecules; protein chemistry. *Mailing Add:* Dept of Biochem Kans State Univ Manhattan KS 66506

COX, DENNIS DEAN, b Denver, Colo, Apr 7, 50; m 70; c 1. NONPARAMETRIC REGRESSION, TIME SERIES ANALYSIS. *Educ:* Univ Colo, Boulder, BA, 72; Univ Denver, MS, 76; Univ Wash, PhD(math), 80. *Prof Exp:* Develop engr, Honeywell Marine Syst Ctr, 77-80; ASST PROF STATIST, UNIV WIS, 80- *Mem:* Inst Math Statist; Math Asn Am; Am Math Soc; Am Statist Asn; Royal Statist Soc. *Res:* Statistical inference for curve estimation and time series; probability theory on abstract spaces; approximation theory; differential operators. *Mailing Add:* Dept Statist Univ Wis 1210 W Dayton St Madison WI 53706

COX, DENNIS HENRY, b St Paul, Minn, Aug 12, 25; m 50; c 1. ANIMAL NUTRITION. *Educ:* Univ Minn, BS, 50, MS, 53; Univ Fla, PhD(animal nutrit), 55. *Prof Exp:* Assoc toxicologist, Ga Coastal Plain Exp Sta, 55-62; asst prof, Univ Iowa, 62-63 & Coker Col, 63-64; asst prof foods & nutrit, Pa State Univ, 64-68, assoc prof nutrit, 68-71; RES CHEMIST, DEPT HEALTH, EDUC & WELFARE, 71- *Mem:* Am Chem Soc; Am Inst Nutrit; Sigma Xi. *Res:* Various aspects of animal and human nutrition, especially trace and macro minerals and their various interrelationships; trace element methodology. *Mailing Add:* Bldg 31 Chamblee Ctr Dis Control Atlanta GA 30333

COX, DENNIS PURVER, b Seattle, Wash, Sept 12, 29; wid; c 4. ECONOMIC GEOLOGY. *Educ:* Stanford Univ, BS, 51, MS, 54, PhD(geol), 56. *Prof Exp:* Geologist mineral deposits explor, Anaconda Co, 56-59; vis prof geol, Univ Bahia, Brazil, 59-61; geologist mil geol, 61-65, geologist mineral resources, 65-72, mgr mineral resource specialist prog, 76-78, COPPER RESOURCES SPECIALIST, US GEOL SURV, 72-82. *Concurrent Pos:* Staff consult, Off Technol Assessment, US Cong. *Mem:* Geol Soc Am; Soc Econ Geol. *Res:* Geology of porphyry copper deposits; mineral resource modeling and resource estimation. *Mailing Add:* US Geol Surv MS 41 345 Middlefield Rd Menlo Park CA 94025

COX, DIANE WILSON, b Belleville, Ont, May 18, 37; m 61; c 3. HUMAN GENETICS. *Educ:* Univ Western Ont, BSc, 59; Univ Toronto, MA, 61; McGill Univ, PhD(genetics), 68. *Prof Exp:* Res asst genetics, McGill Univ, 63-64; fel, Hosp for Sick Children, 67-70, investr, 71-77; asst prof, Depts Pediat & Med Genetics, 75-77, ASSOC PROF, DEPTS PEDIAT, MED GENETICS, MED BIOPHYS & INST MED SCI, UNIV TORONTO, 77- *Concurrent Pos:* Fel, Can Col Med Genetics, 76- *Mem:* Genetics Soc Can; Am Soc Human Genetics. *Res:* Human serum protein polymorphisms; alpha-1-antitrypsin; population studies; proteases and protease inhibitors: role in disease, production and gene mapping by cells in culture; apolipoprotein disorders. *Mailing Add:* Pediat Dept & Res Inst 555 University Ave Toronto ON M5G 1X8 Can

COX, DOAK CAREY, b Wailuku, Maui, Hawaii, Jan 16, 17; m 41; c 5. ENVIRONMENTAL MANAGEMENT, ENVIRONMENTAL GEOLOGY. *Educ:* Univ Hawaii, BS, 38; Harvard Univ, AM, 41, PhD, 65. *Prof Exp:* Geologist, US Geol Surv, 41-46; geophysicist, Exp Sta, Hawaiian Sugar Planters Asn, 46-60; geophysicist, Inst Geophys, 60-64, dir, Water Resources Res Ctr, 64-70, PROF GEOL, UNIV HAWAII, 60-, DIR ENVIRON CTR, 70- *Concurrent Pos:* Consult, Pac Islands, 46-64; hydrologist, Arno Exped, Pac Sci Bd, 50; secy, Tsunami Comt Int Union Geod & Geophys, 60-67; Tsunami adv, Hawaii State Civil Defense Div, 60-66; chmn oceanog panel, Comt on Alaska Earthquake, Nat Acad Sci-Nat Res Coun, 64-73; Hawaii State Water Comn, 78. *Mem:* Fel AAAS; fel Geol Soc Am; Seismol Soc Am; Am Geophys Union; Ecol Soc Am. *Res:* Hawaii and Pacific geology and hydrology; tsunamis. *Mailing Add:* Environ Ctr Univ Hawaii 2550 Campus Rd Honolulu HI 96822

COX, DONALD CLYDE, b Lincoln, Nebr, Nov 22, 37; m 61; c 2. ELECTRICAL ENGINEERING, RADIO PHYSICS. *Educ:* Univ Nebr, Lincoln, BS, 59, MS, 60; Stanford Univ, PhD(elec eng), 68. *Prof Exp:* Res asst elec eng, Stanford Univ, 63-66, res assoc radio propagation, Stanford Electronics Labs, 67-68; mem tech staff, Radio Transmission Res Dept, 68-73, SUPVR, SATELLITE SYSTS RES DEPT, BELL LABS, 73- *Concurrent Pos:* Mem Comns B, C & F, US Nat Comt, Int Union Radio Sci, 69- *Mem:* fel Inst Elec & Electronics Engrs; Sigma Xi. *Res:* Radio propagation; communications systems; satellite systems; electronics; atmospheric physics; radio measurement techniques. *Mailing Add:* Bell Labs HOH R-127 Holmdel NJ 07733

COX, DONALD CODY, b Peoria, Ill, Mar 31, 36; m 63; c 2. VIROLOGY, MOLECULAR BIOLOGY. *Educ:* Northwestern Univ, BA, 58; Univ Mich, PhD(epidemiol sci), 65. *Prof Exp:* From asst prof to assoc prof microbiol, Univ Okla, 65-72, assoc prof bot & microbiol, 72-78; PROF & CHAIRPERSON DEPT MICROBIOL, MIAMI UNIV, 78- *Mem:* AAAS; Sigma Xi; Am Soc Microbiol. *Res:* Studies concerning biochemical alterations occurring in virus-infected cells. *Mailing Add:* Dept Microbiol Miami Univ Oxford OH 45050

COX, DONALD DAVID, b Maben, WVa, Aug 2, 26; m 46; c 3. PLANT SCIENCE. *Educ:* Marshall Univ, AB, 49, MA, 50; Syracuse Univ, PhD(plant sci), 58. *Prof Exp:* Teacher pub sch, WVa, 49-50; prof biol, Marshall Univ, 50-62; consult biol sci curric study, Univ Colo, Boulder, 62-63; actg chmn dept, 74-76, PROF BIOL, STATE UNIV NY COL OSWEGO, 63-, DIR, RICE CREEK BIOL FIELD STA, 81- *Concurrent Pos:* Chmn dept biol, Marshall Univ, 57-62; res botanist, Corps Engrs, US Army, Miss Waterways Exp Sta, 62; staff biologist, Comn Undergrad Educ Biol Sci, NSF, 70-71. *Mem:* Ecol Soc Am; Sigma Xi. *Res:* Post glacial forests in New York State as determined by the method of pollen analysis. *Mailing Add:* Dept of Biol State Univ of NY Col Oswego NY 13126

COX, DUDLEY, b Brooklyn, NY, Mar 3, 29; m 55; c 2. MICROBIOLOGY, CELL PHYSIOLOGY. *Educ:* Howard Univ, BS, 56; Long Island Univ, MS, 58; NY Univ, PhD(microbiol), 66. *Prof Exp:* RES ASSOC MICROBIOL, HASKINS LABS, 58-; PROF BIOL, PACE UNIV, 66- *Mem:* AAAS; Soc Protozool. *Res:* Nutrition and metabolic activity of microorganisms; conversion of cellulosic wastes to useful products; methanogenesis. *Mailing Add:* Pace Univ Pace Plaza New York NY 10038

COX, EDMOND RUDOLPH, JR, b Pascagoula, Miss, Nov 15, 32; m 59; c 1. PHYCOLOGY, MICROBIOLOGY. *Educ:* Univ Ala, BS, 57, MS, 60, PhD(bot), 67. *Prof Exp:* From instr to assoc prof biol, Middle Tenn State Univ, 61-68; chmn dept, 68-77, PROF BIOL, TENN WESLEYAN COL, 68- *Mem:* Phycol Soc Am; Int Phycol Soc. *Res:* Soil algae. *Mailing Add:* Dept of Biol Tenn Wesleyan Col Athens TN 37303

COX, EDWARD CHARLES, b Alberni, Can, June 28, 37; US citizen; m 60; c 3. GENETICS. *Educ:* Univ BC, BSc, 59; Univ Pa, PhD(biochem), 64. *Prof Exp:* Instr biochem, Univ Pa, 61-62; fel genetics, Stanford Univ, 64-67; asst prof biol & biochem, 67-72, assoc prof biol & assoc dean of col, 72-77, PROF BIOL & CHMN DEPT, PRINCETON UNIV, 77- *Mem:* Genetics Soc Am. *Res:* The genetic control of mutation rates; developmental genetics of the cellular slime molds. *Mailing Add:* Dept of Biol Princeton Univ Princeton NJ 08540

COX, EDWIN, III, b Richmond, Va, Oct 31, 31; m; c 4. CHEMICAL ENGINEERING, PHYSICAL CHEMISTRY. *Educ:* Va Mil Inst, BS, 53; Univ Va, MChE, 60. *Prof Exp:* Asst instr chem, Univ Va, 57-59; assoc, Cox & Gillespie, 59-60, partner & chem engr, 60-66; CHEM ENGR, EDWIN COX ASSOCS, 66- *Concurrent Pos:* Secy-treas, Commonwealth Lab, Inc, 59-67, pres, 67-; mem personal staff, Gov of Va, 60-68 & 72- *Mem:* Fel Am Inst Chem; Nat Soc Prof Engrs; Am Chem Soc; Am Soc Metals; Am Soc Testing & Mat. *Res:* Surface chemistry; phosphate rock; phosphorus production; phosphoric acid production; fertilizers; material science; catalysis; air and water pollution and abatement. *Mailing Add:* Edwin Cox Assocs 2209 E Broad St Richmond VA 23223

COX, ELENOR R, b Georgetown, Tex. PHYCOLOGY. *Educ:* Rice Univ, BA, 52; Univ Tex, Austin, MS, 61, PhD(bot), 66. *Prof Exp:* From asst prof to assoc prof, 67-81, PROF BIOL, TEX A&M UNIV, 81- *Mem:* Phycol Soc Am (secy, 75-78, vpres & pres-elect, 79, pres, 80). *Res:* Phylogeny of the photosynthetic dinoflagellates. *Mailing Add:* Dept Biol Tex A&M Univ College Station TX 77840

COX, EUGENE FLOYD, organic chemistry, plant physiology, see previous edition

COX, FRANK EDMOND, b Dorset, Ohio, Aug 4, 24; m 45; c 2. ENGINEERING. *Educ:* Purdue Univ, BSME, 49; Ariz State Univ, MSE, 64. *Prof Exp:* Mem, US Air Force, 42-72; lectr, 72-73, assoc prof & chmn, aeronaut, 73-79, assoc prof technol, 79-80, PROF TECHNOL, ARIZ STATE UNIV, 80-, DIR, 79- *Mem:* Am Soc Eng Educ; Nat Asn Indust Technol; Soc Eng Technol. *Mailing Add:* 2041 E Laguna Dr Tempe AZ 85282

COX, FRED WARD, JR, b Atlanta, Ga, Dec 10, 14; m 39; c 3. INDUSTRIAL CHEMISTRY, RESEARCH ADMINISTRATION. *Educ:* Ga Inst Technol, BS, 36; Univ Wis, PhD(org chem), 39. *Prof Exp:* Res chemist, Rohm and Haas Co, Philadelphia, 38; res chemist, Goodyear Tire & Rubber Co, Akron, 39-42, group leader, 42-45; group leader, Southern Res Inst, 45-49, head appl chem div, 46-49; asst dir, Eng Exp Sta, Ga Inst Technol, 49-53; chief chemist, Deering Milliken Res Trust, 53-56; mgr, Atlas Res & Develop Lab, 56-79, DIR RES & DEVELOP, ATLAS POWDER CO, TYLER CORP, 79- *Concurrent Pos:* Mem, Tamaqua Area Sch Bd, 63-73, pres, 70-73; mem, Schuylkill County Bd Educ, 65-73 & Schuylkill County Area Voc Schs Oper Bd. *Mem:* Am Chem Soc; Am Soc Testing & Mat; Franklin Inst; Soc Rheol. *Res:* High polymer technology; organic process development; textiles; explosives; research administration; explosive slurries and emulsions; blasting initiators. *Mailing Add:* Rd No 2 Box 95 Tamaqua PA 18252

COX, FREDERICK EUGENE, b Quincy, Mass, Nov 4, 38; m 67; c 2. PEDIATRICS, INFECTIOUS DISEASES. *Educ:* Boston Univ, BA, 60; Boston Univ, MD, 64. *Prof Exp:* Surg intern, Univ Hosp, Boston, 64-65; gen med officer, US Coast Guard Acad Hosp, USPHS, New London, Conn, 65-67; resident path, Boston City Hosp, Mass, 67-68; resident pediat, St Elizabeth's Hosp, Brighton, Mass, 68-69 & Boston Floating Hosp, 69-70; fel pediat infectious dis, Cleveland Metrop Gen Hosp, Ohio, 70-72; fel, St Jude Children's Res Hosp, Memphis, Tenn, 72-74, res assoc infectious dis serv, 74-77; ASST PROF PEDIAT & CHIEF INFECTIOUS DIS DIV, MED COL GA, 77- *Mem:* Fel Am Acad Pediat; Sigma Xi. *Res:* Bacterial and fungal adherence. *Mailing Add:* Dept Pediat Med Col Ga Augusta GA 30901

COX, FREDERICK RUSSELL, b Sutherland, Nebr, Mar 11, 32; m 59; c 2. SOIL SCIENCE. *Educ:* Univ Nebr, BS, 53, MS, 58; NC State Univ, PhD(soils), 61. *Prof Exp:* Assoc prof, 61-76, PROF SOIL SCI, NC STATE UNIV, 76- *Mem:* Am Soc Agron; Soil Sci Soc Am. *Res:* Soil fertility; micronutrient research. *Mailing Add:* Dept of Soil Sci NC State Univ Raleigh NC 27607

COX, GENE SPRACHER, b Norton, Va, Mar 21, 21; m 46; c 2. FOREST SOILS. *Educ:* Duke Univ, BS, 47, MF, 48, PhD(forestry), 53. *Prof Exp:* Asst prof forestry, Stephen F Austin State Univ, 51-53; from asst prof to assoc prof, Univ Mont, 53-60; assoc prof, 60-63, PROF FORESTRY, UNIV MO, COLUMBIA, 63- *Mem:* Am Soc Agron; Soil Sci Soc Am; Soc Am Foresters; Ecol Soc Am. *Res:* Forest ecology. *Mailing Add:* Sch of Forestry, Fish & Wildlife Univ of Mo Columbia MO 65201

COX, GEORGE ELTON, b Ayden, NC, July 22, 31; m 56; c 2. EXPERIMENTAL & TOXICOLOGIC PATHOLOGY. *Educ:* Univ NC, BA, 51, MS, 54; Univ Ill, MD, 56. *Prof Exp:* Intern path, Presby Hosp, Chicago, 56-57; resident, Presby-St Luke's Hosp, Chicago, 57-60; dir exp path, Evanston Hosp, 61-62; res assoc biol chem, Col Med, Univ Ill, 62-64; res assoc & asst prof path, Med Units, Univ Tenn, 64-65; res assoc, May Inst Med Res, Cincinnati, 65-69; asst prof path, Col Med, Univ Cincinnati, 66-69; pathologist, Food & Drug Res Labs, Inc, 69-81; RES ASSOC & SR PATHOLOGIST, MOBIL OIL CORP, PRINCETON, NJ, 81- *Mem:* Am Asn Pathologists. *Res:* Experimental study of etiology of atherosclerosis; spontaneous neoplasia in laboratory animals; histopathologic effects of industrial chemicals. *Mailing Add:* Toxicol Div Mobil Corp PO Box 1029 Princeton NJ 08540

COX, GEORGE STANLEY, b Roswell, NMex, Jan 26, 46; m 67; c 2. BIOCHEMISTRY, MOLECULAR BIOLOGY. *Educ:* NMex State Univ, BS, 68; Univ Iowa, PhD(biochem), 73. *Prof Exp:* Fel, Roche Inst Molecular Biol, 72-74; staff fel, Lab Molecular Biol, Nat Inst Arthritis, Metab & Digestive Dis, NIH, 74-76; ASST PROF BIOCHEM & BIOPHYS, IOWA STATE UNIV, 76- *Mem:* Am Soc Microbiol; Sigma Xi. *Res:* Regulation of gene expression in eukaryotes including transcription, translation, and nuclear-cytoplasmic transport of macromolecules; molecular oncology. *Mailing Add:* Dept of Biochem & Biophys Iowa State Univ Ames IA 50011

COX, GEORGE W, b Williamson, WVa, Feb 10, 35; m 57; c 2. ECOLOGY, ORNITHOLOGY. *Educ:* Ohio Wesleyan Univ, AB, 56; Univ Ill, MS, 58, PhD(zool), 60. *Prof Exp:* Asst prof biol, Univ Alaska, 60-61 & Calif Western Univ, 61-62; from asst prof to assoc prof, 62-69, PROF BIOL, SAN DIEGO STATE UNIV, 69- *Mem:* AAAS; Ecol Soc Am; Am Ornith Union; Wilson Ornith Soc. *Res:* Physiological ecology of birds; evolution and speciation in birds; ecology of chaparral communities; agricultural and conservation ecology. *Mailing Add:* Dept of Biol San Diego State Univ San Diego CA 92182

COX, GERALDINE ANNE VANG, b Philadelphia, Pa, Jan 10, 44; m 65. ENVIRONMENTAL SCIENCE, BIOLOGY. *Educ:* Drexel Univ, BS, 66, MS, 67, PhD(environ sci), 70. *Prof Exp:* Tech coordr environ progs, Raytheon Co, 70-76; White House fel, spec asst to secy, US Dept Labor, 76-77; environ scientist biol, Am Petrol Inst, 77-79; VPRES & TECH DIR, CHEM MFG ASN, 79- *Concurrent Pos:* Mem Environ Measurement Panel Nat Bur Standards, Nat Acad Sci, 77-80; lectr, Sch Nursing, Univ Pa; lab suprvr, Sanitary Landfill Proj & instr, Sanitary Microbiol Lab, Drexel Univ; food technologist, Keebler Biscuit Co, C Schmidt & Sons. *Mem:* Am Soc Testing Mat; Water Pollution Control Fedn; Soc Petrol Indust Biologists; Fedn Orgn Professional Women; Soc Environ Toxicol & Chem. *Res:* Oil pollution; marine pollution; fresh water pollution; ecological damage assessment; environmental health. *Mailing Add:* 2501 M St NW Washington DC 20037

COX, GORDON F N, b Montreal, Que, Nov 25, 48; US citizen; m 69. ARCTIC OFFSHORE ENGINEERING, SEA ICE PHYSICS. *Educ:* McGill Univ, Montreal, BSc Hons, 70; Dartmouth Col, MA, 73, PhD(glaciol), 74. *Prof Exp:* Sr res engr, Amoco Prod Co, 74-78; arctic mgr consult, Oceanog Serv, Inc, 78-80; GEOPHYSICIST ARCTIC RES, COLD REGIONS RES & ENG LAB, 80- *Concurrent Pos:* Mem, Nat Acad Sci Sea Ice Mech Panel, 80-81 & Glaciol Panel, 80-83; consult, Oceanog Serv, Inc, 80- *Mem:* Int Glaciol Soc; Am Geophys Union; Arctic Inst NAm. *Res:* Mechanical properties of multi-year sea ice considering ice salinity, structure, temperature, strain-rate, and confining pressure; ice stress sensor to measure ice loads on arctic offshore structures. *Mailing Add:* US Cold Regions Res & Eng Lab 72 Lyme Rd Hanover NH 03755

COX, H C, b Melrose, NMex, May 18, 27; m 54; c 2. ENTOMOLOGY. *Educ:* Univ NMex, BS, 50; Iowa State Univ, MS, 52, PhD(entom), 55. *Hon Degrees:* LLD, NMex State Univ, 81. *Prof Exp:* Asst, Iowa State Univ, 50-53. *Concurrent Pos:* Fel, Princeton Univ, 66-67. *Mem:* Entom Soc Am; Am Asn Prof Entomologists. *Res:* Animal and veterinary sciences; agricultural engineering; soil and water conservation; plant and entomological sciences; market quality; agricultural product transportation and storage; agricultural products utilization and industrial processing research; human nutrition. *Mailing Add:* 1333 Broadway-Suite 400 Oakland CA 94612

COX, HAROLD A(NDERSEN), JR, chemical engineering, see previous edition

COX, HENRY MIOT, b Stephens Co, Ga, 07; m 35; c 1. MATHEMATICS, PSYCHOMETRICS. *Educ:* Emory Univ, BS, 28; Duke Univ, AM, 31. *Prof Exp:* Instr math & asst exam, Univ Syst Ga, 30-39; from asst dir to dir, 39-73, EMER DIR, BUR INSTR RES & EXAM SERV, UNIV NEBR, LINCOLN, 73- *Concurrent Pos:* Exec dir, Ann High Sch Math Exam, Math Asn Am, Soc Actuaries, Mu Alpha Theta & Nat Coun Teachers Math, 70-76. *Mem:* AAAS; Math Asn Am; Psychomet Soc; Nat Coun Measurement in Educ. *Res:* Measurement; instructional research; student guidance. *Mailing Add:* 1145 N 44th St Lincoln NE 68503

COX, HERALD REA, b Rosedale, Ind, Feb 28, 07; m 32; c 3. VIROLOGY. *Educ:* Ind State Col, AB, 28; Johns Hopkins Univ, ScD(filterable viruses), 31. *Hon Degrees:* ScD, Univ Mont, 42, Ind State Univ, 64 & Roswell Park Mem Inst, 72. *Prof Exp:* Instr immunol, Johns Hopkins Univ, 31-32; asst path & bact, Rockefeller Inst Med Res, 32-36; assoc bacteriologist, USPHS, 36-40, prin bacteriologist, 40-42; from assoc dir to dir viral res, Lederle Labs, 42-68; dir cancer res, Viral Oncol Sect, Roswell Park Mem Inst, 68-72; RETIRED. *Honors & Awards:* Theobald Smith Award, 41; Typhus Comn Medal, Secy of War, 46; Ricketts Award, Univ Chicago, 51. *Mem:* AAAS; hon mem Am Soc Microbiol (vpres, Am Soc Bact, 59-60, pres, 60-61); Am Soc Immunologists; Am Soc Trop Med & Hyg; Am Pub Health Asn. *Res:* Neurotropic viral diseases; rickettsial diseases; viral infections of man and animal; living trivalent polio vaccine; living virus vaccines, human and veterinary; causative organism. *Mailing Add:* PO Box 937 Hamilton MT 59840

COX, HERBERT WALTON, b Clarkton, NC, Mar 15, 18; m 45. MALARIOLOGY. *Educ:* Univ NC, AB, 41, MPH, 48, PhD(parasitol), 52. *Prof Exp:* Instr prev med, Bowman Gray Sch Med, 48-49; instr bact, Med Col, Cornell Univ, 52-54; from instr to asst prof microbiol, State Univ NY Downstate Med Ctr, 54-64; asst prof path & hyg, Col Vet Med, Univ Ill, 64-66; assoc prof microbiol & pub health, 66-74, PROF MICROBIOL & PUB HEALTH, MICH STATE UNIV, 75- *Mem:* Am Soc Trop Med & Hyg; Am Soc Parasitol; Royal Soc Trop Med & Hyg; Soc Protozool; NY Acad Sci. *Res:* Immunopathology of malaria and infectious anemias. *Mailing Add:* Dept of Microbiol & Pub Health Mich State Univ East Lansing MI 48823

COX, HIDEN TOY, b Greenville, SC, Mar 3, 17; m 43; c 1. PLANT MORPHOLOGY, PLANT ANATOMY. *Educ:* Furman Univ, BS, 36, BA, 37; Univ NC, MA, 39, PhD(bot), 47. *Prof Exp:* Asst prof biol, Howard Col, 41-46; assoc prof bot, Agnes Scott Col, 46-49; from assoc prof to prof, Va Polytech Inst, 49-55; dep exec dir, Am Inst Biol Sci, 53-54, exec dir, 55-63; coordr res, 63-67, dean sch letters & sci, 67-71, PROF BIOL, CALIF STATE UNIV, LONG BEACH, 71- *Concurrent Pos:* Asst adminr pub affairs, NASA, 61-62; Beattie lectr, 64; mem, Calif Curric Comn, 65-66, 67-69; chmn, Calif Sci Adv Comt, 66-67. *Honors & Awards:* Distinguished Serv Citation, NASA, 62. *Mem:* Fel AAAS; Sigma Xi; Asn Advan Biomed Educ. *Res:* Comparative wood anatomy; plant embryology. *Mailing Add:* Dept of Biol Calif State Univ 1250 Bellflower Long Beach CA 90840

COX, HOLLACE LAWTON, JR, b Oak Park, Ill, Nov 17, 35; m 59. MEDICAL PHYSICS, CHEMICAL PHYSICS. *Educ:* Univ Rochester, AB, 59; Ind Univ, Bloomington, PhD(chem physics), 67. *Prof Exp:* Mem tech staff, Tex Instruments, Inc, 67-69; Robert A Welch res fel, Baylor Univ, 70-73; Robert A Welch res fel path, Univ Tex Syst Cancer Ctr, M D Anderson Hosp & Tumor Inst Houston, 73-75, res fel physics, 75-76; instr, Mallinckrodt Inst Radiol, Washington Univ Sch Med, 76-77; asst prof, Dept Radiation Oncol, Univ Kans Med Ctr, 77-80; ASSOC PROF, TEHRAPEUT RADIOL DEPT, SCH MED, UNIV LOUISVILLE, 80- *Mem:* Am Asn Physicists in Med; Sigma Xi; Am Phys Soc; Optical Soc Am. *Res:* X-ray spectroscopy; x-ray and electron scattering; laser spectroscopy; interaction of laser radiation with cells and molecules of biological interest; stopping power of alpha particles. *Mailing Add:* Therapeut Radiol Dept Sch Med Univ Louisville Louisville KY 40292

COX, J E, b Waco, Tex, Aug 29, 35. MECHANICAL ENGINEERING. *Educ:* Southern Methodist Univ, BS, 58, MS, 60; Okla State Univ, PhD(eng), 63. *Prof Exp:* Engr, Astronaut Div, Chance Vought Corp, 56-59; instr, Okla State Univ, 61-63; prof mech eng, Univ Houston, 63-81; WASH REP, AM SOC HEATING, REFRIG & AIR CONDITIONING ENGRS, 81- *Concurrent Pos:* Am Soc Mech Engrs cong fel with Sci & Technol Comt, US House Rep, 75. *Mem:* Fel Am Soc Mech Engrs; Am Soc Heating Refrig & Air Conditioning Engrs. *Res:* Heat transfer; fluid mechanics; thermodynamics. *Mailing Add:* PO Box 57104 Washington DC 20037

COX, JAMES ALLAN, b Chisholm, Minn, Sept 19, 41; m 65; c 2. ANALYTICAL CHEMISTRY, ELECTROCHEMISTRY. *Educ:* Univ Minn, BS, 63; Univ Ill, PhD(chem), 67. *Prof Exp:* Lectr chem, Univ Wis, 67-69; asst prof, 69-74, ASSOC PROF CHEM, SOUTHERN ILL UNIV, CARBONDALE, 74- *Mem:* Am Chem Soc; Soc Appl Spectroscopists; Sigma Xi. *Res:* Trace methods for anions; ion exchange membrane applications to trace analysis, rates and mechanisms of heterogeneous electron transfer reactions. *Mailing Add:* Dept of Chem Neckers Bldg Southern Ill Univ Carbondale IL 62901

COX, JAMES LEE, b Wayne Co, Ind, Oct 5, 38; m 71. ANIMAL NUTRITION. *Educ:* Purdue Univ, BS, 61; Univ Ill, MS, 63, PhD(animal nutrit), 67. *Prof Exp:* Sr res physiologist, 67-71, animal sci data analyst, 71-74, RES FEL, MERCK SHARP & DOHME RES LABS, 74- *Mem:* AAAS; Am Soc Animal Sci; Poultry Sci Asn; Sigma Xi; World Poultry Sci Asn. *Res:* Design and analysis of animal experiments; environmental effects on pregnant animals; mineral nutrition and physiological functions; influence of drugs on growth of animals. *Mailing Add:* Merck Sharp & Dohme Res Labs Rahway NJ 07065

COX, JAMES LESTER, JR, b Reidsville, NC, Nov 12, 42; m 63; c 2. PLASMA PHYSICS. *Educ:* NC State Univ, BS, 63, MS, 65, PhD(physics), 69. *Prof Exp:* Asst prof, 69-75, ASSOC PROF PHYSICS, OLD DOMINION UNIV, 75- *Mem:* AAAS; Am Phys Soc. *Res:* Relativistic electron beams. *Mailing Add:* 905 Bentley Health Common Virginia Beach VA 23452

COX, JAMES REED, JR, b Nashville, Tenn, Mar 25, 32. ORGANIC CHEMISTRY. *Educ:* Vanderbilt Univ, BA, 54, MA, 55; Harvard Univ, PhD(chem), 59. *Prof Exp:* NSF fel chem, Univ Munich, 58-59; from asst prof to assoc prof, Ga Inst Technol, 59-66; ASSOC PROF CHEM, UNIV HOUSTON, 66- *Mem:* Am Chem Soc. *Res:* Structure-reactivity relationships; mechanisms of reaction of organic and bio-organic chemical systems. *Mailing Add:* Dept of Chem Univ of Houston Houston TX 77004

COX, JEROME R(OCKHOLD), JR, b Washington, DC, May 24, 25; m 51; c 3. ELECTRICAL ENGINEERING. *Educ:* Mass Inst Technol, BS, 47, MS, 49, ScD(elec eng), 54. *Prof Exp:* Asst, Acoust Lab, Mass Inst Technol, 48-52; acoust engr, Liberty Mutual Life Ins Co, 52-55; from asst prof to assoc prof, 55-61, dir, Biomed Comput Lab, 64-75, PROF ELEC ENG, WASHINGTON UNIV, 61-, CHMN COMPUT LABS, 67-, CHMN & PROF, DEPT COMPUT SCI, 75- *Concurrent Pos:* Res assoc, Cent Inst Deaf, 55-61; co-chmn, Comput Cardiol Int Conf, 74- *Mem:* Inst Med of Nat Acad Sci; fel Acoust Soc Am; fel Inst Elec & Electronics Engrs; Asn Comput Mach; Biomed Eng Soc. *Res:* Computer design; biomedical engineering; statistical communication theory; acoustics. *Mailing Add:* Dept Comput Sci Box 1045 Washington Univ St Louis MO 63130

COX, JOHN DAVID, b San Juan, Puerto Rico, Oct 5, 54; US citizen; m 80. LASER DEVELOPMENT, NUCLEAR EXCITED PLASMAS. *Educ:* Univ Fla, BS, 78, ME, 79, PhD(eng physics), 82. *Prof Exp:* RES ENGR, RTS LABS, INC, 81- *Concurrent Pos:* Res scientist, nuclear eng dept, Univ Fla, 80- *Res:* Basic research on nuclear and solar pumped lasers; synthetic fuels and combustion modifiers. *Mailing Add:* RTS Labs 2603 NW 74th Pl Gainesville FL 32606

COX, JOHN E(DWARD), b Danville, Ill, Mar 28, 23; m 56; c 2. CERAMIC ENGINEERING. *Educ:* Univ Ill, BS, 50, MS, 51, PhD(eng), 53; Univ Hartford, BS, 68. *Prof Exp:* Res engr, NJ Zinc Co, 53-54; res fel, Mellon Inst, 54-60; dir res & develop, O Hommell Co, 60-62; sr res scientist, United Aircraft Corp, 62-68; dir res, Ceramic Dept, R T Vanderbilt Co, 68-73; midwest mgr, O Hommel Co, 73-75, mat mgr, 75-78; mgr coatings, Alpha Metals, 78-81; SPEC PROJ MGR, O HOMMEL CO, 81- *Mem:* Am Ceramic Soc; Am Soc Testing & Mat. *Res:* Porcelain enamel, glass and related ceramic materials; metal fibers. *Mailing Add:* Unit 415 1500 Cochran Rd Pittsburgh PA 15243

COX, JOHN JAY, JR, b Pa, Apr 1, 29; m 53; c 2. METALLURGY. *Educ:* Carnegie Inst Technol, MS & ScD, 53. *Prof Exp:* Res supvr mat tech, Eng Dept, 53-64, res supvr chlorine prod sect, 64-66, develop mgr electronic prod, 66-70, mgr electronic packaging, 70-74, tech mgr, 74-78, prod mkt mgr, 78-81, DIR SALES, PHOTO PROD DEPT, E I DU PONT DE NEMOURS & CO, INC, 81- *Mem:* Sigma Xi; Am Inst Mining, Metall & Petrol Engrs; Int Soc Hybrid Microelectronics. *Res:* Physical metallurgy; phase equilibria; precipitation from solids; x-ray diffractions; alloy development; electron microscopy; structure of crystalline polymers; thick film electronic materials. *Mailing Add:* 506 Rothbury Rd Wilmington DE 19803

COX, JOHN LAYTON, b Pendleton, Ore, Dec 30, 43; m 66; c 2. INORGANIC CHEMISTRY, PHYSICAL CHEMISTRY. *Educ:* Eastern Ore State Col, BS, 66; Univ Wyo, PhD(chem), 71. *Prof Exp:* Res scientist coal gasification, Natural Resources Res Inst, Univ Wyo, 71-72, dept mineral eng, 72-73; sr res engr fossil fuels, Battelle Northwest Labs, Battelle Mem Inst, 74-78; MGT BASIC RES, GAS RES INST, 78- *Mem:* Am Chem Soc; Sigma Xi. *Res:* Synthetic fuels from fossil fuels; kinetics and catalysis. *Mailing Add:* Gas Res Inst 8600 West Bryn Mawr Chicago IL 60631

COX, JOHN PAUL, b Ft Myers, Fla, Nov 4, 26. THEORETICAL ASTROPHYSICS. *Educ:* Ind Univ, AB, 49, MS, 50, PhD(theoret astrophys), 54. *Prof Exp:* Asst, Ind Univ, 49-54; from instr to asst prof astron, Cornell Univ, 54-62; vis scientist, Courant Inst Math Sci, NY Univ, 62-63; vis fel, Joint Inst Lab Astrophys, 63, assoc prof, 63-65, PROF ASTROPHYS, UNIV COLO, BOULDER, 65- *Concurrent Pos:* Cotterell res grant, 56; consult, Smithsonian Astrophys Observ, Cambridge, Mass, 57, 59 & 60; asst engr, Pratt & Whitney Aircraft Corp, Conn, 58; consult, Los Alamos Sci Lab, 60-; vis prof math, Monash Univ, Melbourne, 72; res lectr, Coun Res & Creative Work, Univ Colo, 80. *Mem:* Int Astron Union; Sigma Xi; Am Astron Soc; Am Phys Soc; NY Acad Sci. *Res:* Theory of stellar variability; stellar interiors and evolution. *Mailing Add:* Joint Inst for Lab Astrophys Univ of Colo Boulder CO 80309

COX, JOHN THOMAS, b Johnstown, Pa. PHYSICS, MATERIALS SCIENCE. *Educ:* Col William & Mary, BS, 50; Duke Univ, PhD(physics), 54. *Prof Exp:* Res physicist thin films, Eng & Develop Lab, 54-65 & Night Vision Lab, 65-71, supvr res physics uncooled thermal imaging, 71-80, STAFF SCIENTIST, NIGHT VISION & ELECTRO-OPTICS LAB, DEPT ARMY, 80- *Mem:* Optical Soc Am. *Res:* Properties and applications of optical thin films from the far ultraviolet to the far infrared; uncooled thermal imaging materials. *Mailing Add:* Night Vision & Electro-Optics Lab US Army ERADCOM Ft Belvoir VA 22060

COX, JOHN WILLIAM, b St Louis, Mo, Aug 31, 28; m 50; c 1. MEDICAL EDUCATION, CARDIOLOGY. *Educ:* St Louis Univ, MD, 51, PhD(physiol), 53; Am Bd Internal Med, dipl. *Prof Exp:* Chief res, Labs, Vet Admin Hosp, St Louis, 53-54; US Navy, 54-, chief cardiopulmonary lab, Dept Internal Med, US Naval Hosp, San Diego, 54-56, resident internal med, 56-59, staff supvr, Dept Internal Med, US Naval Hosp, San Diego, 59-61, chief med & dir clin serv, US Naval Hosp, Subic Bay, Philippines, 61-63, head cardio-respiratory dis br, US Naval Hosp, Philadelphia, 63-65, chief med & dir res, 65-69, head training & clin serv br, 69-72, dir med educ & training, Navy Dept, 72-77, cmndg officer, Naval Health Sci Educ & Training Command, 75-77, asst chief, Bur Med & Surg, 77-78, CMNDG OFFICER, NAVAL REGIONAL MED CTR, SAN DIEGO, 78- OFFICER, NAVAL HEALTH SCI EDUC & TRAINING COMMAND, 75- *Concurrent Pos:* Assoc prof med, Jefferson Med Col, 64-72; Navy deleg, House Deleg Am Med Asn, 72-84. *Honors & Awards:* Borden Award Med Res, 51. *Mem:* Fel Am Col Physicians; Am Col Chest Physicians; Am Col Cardiol (treas, 74-79); Am Heart Asn; Asn Mil Surg US. *Res:* Clinical investigations; cardiopulmonary physiology. *Mailing Add:* Surg Gen US Navy Washington DC 20372

COX, JOSEPH ROBERT, b Lafayette, Ind, Mar 15, 34; m 56; c 3. PHYSICS. *Educ:* Harvard Univ, BA, 56; Ind Univ, MS, 57, PhD(physics), 62. *Prof Exp:* Asst prof physics, Univ Miami, 62-64; from asst prof to assoc prof, 64-76, PROF PHYSICS, FLA ATLANTIC UNIV, 76- *Concurrent Pos:* Res assoc, Yale Univ, 67-68. *Mem:* Am Phys Soc. *Res:* Scattering theory. *Mailing Add:* Dept of Physics Fla Atlantic Univ Boca Raton FL 33431

COX, JULIUS GRADY, b Ayden, NC, Dec 6, 26; m 46; c 2. INDUSTRIAL ENGINEERING, OPERATIONS RESEARCH. *Educ:* Auburn Univ, BS, 48, MS, 50; Purdue Univ, PhD(indust eng), 64. *Prof Exp:* Instr math, Auburn Univ, 49-51; chief statistician, weapons sect, air proving ground ctr, Eglin AFB, Fla, 51-53, opers analyst, 55-56; head comput, math serv, Vitro Corp, 56-58; assoc prof mech eng, 58-62, head, Dept Indust Eng, 63-66, from asst dean eng to assoc dean eng, 66-68, dean eng, 69-72 & 79-80, PROF INDUST ENG, AUBURN UNIV, 71-, EXEC VPRES, 80- *Concurrent Pos:* Consult,

Battelle Mem Inst, 77- *Honors & Awards:* Civil Serv Award, 59. *Mem:* Am Soc Eng Educ; Am Inst Indust Engrs; Opers Res Soc Am. *Res:* Application of techniques of mathematics, engineering and computer science to problems in military operations; applied decision theory; applied statistics. *Mailing Add:* Samford Hall Auburn Univ Auburn AL 36830

COX, KENNETH EDWARD, b Tientsin, China, May 5, 36; m 69; c 3. CHEMICAL ENGINEERING. *Educ:* Univ London, BSc, 56; Univ BC, MASc, 59; Mont State Univ, PhD(chem eng), 62. *Prof Exp:* Res engr, Dow Chem Co, 62-65; from asst prof to prof chem eng, Univ NMex, 65-77; PROJ MGR HYDROGEN, LOS ALAMOS NAT LAB, 77- *Concurrent Pos:* Ed-in-chief, Hydrogen, Its Technol & Implications, 76-79; mem thermochem hydrogen rev panel, US Dept Energy, 78- *Mem:* Am Inst Chem Engrs; Am Chem Soc; Sigma Xi. *Res:* Thermochemical production of hydrogen from water; solar energy; fusion energy; techno-economic evaluation; applied thermodynamics. *Mailing Add:* CMB-3 MS 348 Los Almos Sci Lab Los Alamos NM 87545

COX, LAWRENCE EDWARD, b Salina, Kans, May 4, 44; div; c 2. SPECTROCHEMISTRY. *Educ:* Kans State Univ, BS, 66; Ind Univ, PhD(chem), 70. *Prof Exp:* Fel chem, Univ Ga, 70-72; STAFF MEM CHEM, LOS ALAMOS NAT LAB, 72- *Mem:* Am Chem Soc. *Res:* surface analysis utilizing x-ray photoelectron and auger spectroscopies. *Mailing Add:* 85 Joya Loop Los Alamos NM 87544

COX, LIONEL AUDLEY, b Winnipeg, Man, Sept 18, 16; m 42; c 3. ORGANIC CHEMISTRY, PHYSICAL CHEMISTRY. *Educ:* Univ BC, BA, 41, MA, 43; McGill Univ, PhD(chem), 46, PEng, 75. *Prof Exp:* Teacher sci, Univ Sch, Victoria, BC, 35-40; chief chemist & consult, Sidney Roofing & Paper Co, BC, 41-44; res chemist, Am Viscose Corp, Pa, 46-51, sr res chemist, 51-53; vpres & dir res, Johnson & Johnson, Ltd, Can, 53-61, vpres & dir res & eng, Personal Prod Co, div Johnson & Johnson, NJ, 61-65; dir res, MacMillan Bloedel Ltd, 65-73, dir technol assessment, 73-77; CONSULT, LIONEL A COX, INC, 77- *Concurrent Pos:* Lectr, Univ BC, 43-44; mem Sci Coun Can; mem bd dir, Educ Inst BC; mem, Nat Res Coun Can. *Mem:* Fel AAAS; Can Pulp & Paper Asn; The Chem Soc; Can Res Mgt Asn; Am Chem Soc. *Res:* Natural and man-made fibers; wood products; pulp and paper; pollution control technology; research and development management; management and administration of research and development engineering; improving interactions between academics, government and industry. *Mailing Add:* Lionel A Cox Inc 4185 Yuculta Cres Vancouver Can

COX, MARTHA, b Chappaqua, NY, Oct 23, 08. PHYSICS. *Educ:* Cornell Univ, AB, 29; Bryn Mawr Col, AM, 36, PhD(physics), 42. *Prof Exp:* Asst to res physicist, Taylor Instrument Co, 29-30; lectr physics, Huguenot Univ Col, SAfrica, 31-33; demonstr, Bryn Mawr Col, 34-36; teacher, Shipley Sch, 36-38; instr, Bryn Mawr Col, 39-43; asst prof, Newcomb Col, Tulane Univ, 43-44; res physicist, Lukas Harold Corp, Ind, 44-45; physicist, US Naval Avionics Facil, 45-46, from actg head to head physics div, 46-58, tech consult, Appl Res Dept, 58-73, mgr mat lab & consult div, 73-75; RETIRED. *Mem:* Am Phys Soc; Sigma Xi. *Res:* Design of avionics equipment; guidance and control; mathematical and numerical analysis. *Mailing Add:* Apt 1106 8140 Township Line Rd Indianapolis IN 46260

COX, MARY E, b Detroit, Mich, Nov 11, 37; m 61; c 1. OPTICS. *Educ:* Albion Col, BA, 59; Univ Mich, MA, 61. *Prof Exp:* Lectr physics, Univ NDak, 62-66; lectr physics, 66-71, asst prof, 71-76, assoc dean, 80-81, ASSOC PROF PHYSICS, UNIV MICH, FLINT, 76-, ACTG DEAN, COL ARTS & SCI, 81- *Concurrent Pos:* Prin investr, Off Naval Res, 69-72 & NIH, 75-77; consult, Off Naval Res, 69-74, Alza Corp, 74-79 & Univ Basel, 79-81; fac develop grant, NSF, 77-78. *Mem:* Am Asn Physics Teachers; Optical Soc Am; Soc Photo-Optical Instrumentation Engrs. *Res:* Application of coherent optics to biomedical problems; devices for optical engineering. *Mailing Add:* Dept Physics & Astron Univ Mich Flint MI 48503

COX, MILTON D, b Indianapolis, Ind, Jan 13, 39; m 66; c 3. FACULTY DEVELOPMENT, MATHEMATICS EDUCATION. *Educ:* DePauw Univ, BA, 61; Ind Univ, MA, 64, PhD(quasi-finite fields), 66. *Prof Exp:* From asst prof to ASSOC PROF MATH, MIAMI UNIV, 66- *Concurrent Pos:* dir, Lilly post doctoral teaching awards prog, 81-82, admin fels prog, Miami Univ, 81-82. *Mem:* Am Math Soc; Math Asn Am. *Res:* Class field theory; quasi-finite fields. *Mailing Add:* Dept Math & Statist Miami Univ Oxford OH 45056

COX, NEIL D, b Lawton, Okla, Aug 6, 32; m 65; c 5. CHEMICAL ENGINEERING, APPLIED STATISTICS. *Educ:* Univ Tex, BSChE, 55; Univ Wis, MSChE, 60, PhD(chem eng), 62. *Prof Exp:* Prod foreman soap mfg, Procter & Gamble Co, 55-56; prof chem eng, Univ Ariz, 62-73; ENG SPECIALIST, EG&G IDAHO, INC, 74- *Concurrent Pos:* Ford Found grant eng, 65-66. *Mem:* Am Inst Chem Engrs; Am Nuclear Soc. *Res:* Data analysis; reliability of processes; energy conservation; nuclear waste processing. *Mailing Add:* 1199 S Holmes Ave Idaho Falls ID 83401

COX, NELSON ANTHONY, b New Orleans, La, Jan 6, 43; m 63; c 3. MICROBIOLOGY. *Educ:* La State Univ, Baton Rouge, BS, 66, MS, 68, PhD(poultry sci), 71. *Prof Exp:* Microbiol consult, Supreme Sugar Refinery, La, 69-70; MICROBIOLOGIST, RICHARD B RUSSELL AGR RES CTR, AGR RES SERV, USDA, 71- *Honors & Awards:* Ralston Purina Res Award, Southern Asn Agr Scientists, 72; Poultry & Egg Inst Am Award, 77. *Mem:* Am Soc Microbiologists; Inst Food Technologists; Poultry Sci Asn; Soc Appl Bact; World's Poultry Sci Asn. *Res:* Destruction of salmonellae on poultry carcasses; development of improved sampling and cultural methods for detection of salmonellae in poultry; microbiological evaluation of immersion versus air chilling of broilers. *Mailing Add:* Food Protect & Process Res Unit Russell Res Ctr Athens GA 30613

COX, PARKER GRAHAM, b Grosse Pointe Farms, Mich, June 3, 13; m 46; c 3. ENGINEERING. *Educ:* Univ Mich, BSE, 34, MSE, 36. *Prof Exp:* Engr, Zenith Carburetor Div, Bendix Aviation Corp, 36-43, priorities mgr, 40-45, termination mgr, 44-46; owner & engr, Multiple Prod Co, 46-47; engr, Genco Elec Co, 47-48; physicist, Bausch & Lomb Optical Co, 48-56; proj engr, Mishawaka Div, Bendix Corp, 56-58, chief engr, 58-67, mem doc staff, Launch Support Div, 67-74; ENG/TECH WRITER, PLANNING RES CORP, 74- *Concurrent Pos:* Mem, Nat Aerospace Stand Comt, 62-67. *Mem:* Aerospace Industs Asn Am. *Res:* Fluid filtration and lubrication of pneumatic equipment. *Mailing Add:* 2755 Las Palmas Titusville FL 32780

COX, PAUL REED, JR, b Birmingham, Ala, Nov 25, 28; m 52; c 2. PHYSICAL CHEMISTRY, TEXTILE ENGINEERING. *Educ:* Auburn Univ, BS, 54. *Prof Exp:* Res chemist synthetic fibers, Chemstrand Corp, 54-61; explor res group leader, Chemstrand Res Ctr, Inc, 61-67; tech adv, Rohm & Haas Co, 67-69; SR RES CHEMIST SYNTHETIC FIBERS, HERCULES, INC, 69- *Mem:* Am Chem Soc. *Res:* Modification and improvement of polyolefin fibers including fiber formation, texturing and chemical modification; new and novel techniques and equipment for producing new and novel textured fiber, non-woven and fibrous materials. *Mailing Add:* 5192 W Shore Dr Conyers GA 30208

COX, PRENTISS GWENDOLYN, b New Augusta, Miss, June 9, 32; m 53; c 4. DEVELOPMENTAL BIOLOGY. *Educ:* Southern Miss Univ, BS, 57; Univ Miss, MS, 61; Case Western Reserve Univ, PhD(regeneration), 68. *Prof Exp:* Instr sci, Clark Memo Col, 57-64; NIH res fel, Case Western Reserve Univ, 68-69; assoc prof, 69-77; PROF BIOL, MISS COL, 77-, HEAD DEPT, 81- *Concurrent Pos:* Vis prof microbiol, Univ Miss Sch Med, 78- *Mem:* AAAS; Sigma Xi; Am Inst Biol Sci; Am Soc Zool; Soc Develop Biol. *Res:* Vertebrate regeneration, especially lizard tail regeneration and in vitro culture of myogeneic cells from the regenerating tail; iron metabolism in muscle cultures. *Mailing Add:* Dept of Biol Sci Miss Col Clinton MS 39058

COX, RAY, b Donalsonville, Ga, Dec 2, 43; m 65; c 2. BIOCHEMISTRY. *Educ:* Berry Col, BS, 65; Auburn Univ, MS, 67, PhD(biochem), 70. *Prof Exp:* CLIN ASST PROF BIOCHEM, UT ADMIN HOSP & UNIV TENN, 72- *Concurrent Pos:* Fel, Fels Res Inst, Sch Med, Temple Univ, 71-72. *Mem:* Am Asn Cancer Res. *Res:* Biochemistry of chemical carcinogenesis. *Mailing Add:* Dept of Biochem 800 Madison Ave Memphis TN 38163

COX, RAYMOND H, b Meadville, Pa, Mar 26, 36. MATHEMATICS. *Educ:* Allegheny Col, BS, 58; Univ NC, MA, 61, PhD(math), 63. *Prof Exp:* Asst prof, 63-69, ASSOC PROF MATH, UNIV KY, 69- *Mem:* Am Math Soc. *Res:* Hilbert space theory; linear space theory. *Mailing Add:* Dept of Math Univ of Ky Lexington KY 40506

COX, RAYMOND H, JR, psychopharmacology, see previous edition

COX, RICHARD HARVEY, b Oakland, Ky, May 21, 43; m 67. NUCLEAR MAGNETIC RESONANCE, ORGANIC CHEMISTRY. *Educ:* Univ Western Ky, BS, 63; Univ Ky, PhD(org chem), 66. *Prof Exp:* Res chemist, Northern Regional Lab, USDA, summer 63; res fel chem, Mellon Inst, 67; from asst prof to assoc prof chem, Univ Ga, 68-78; res chemist, Nat Inst Environ Health Sci, 78-81; SR SCIENTIST, PHILIP MORRIS USA RES CTR, 81- *Mem:* Am Chem Soc; The Chem Soc. *Res:* Applications of nuclear magnetic resonance in chemistry; conformational analysis; theoretical aspects of nuclear magnetic resonance spectroscopy. *Mailing Add:* Philip Morris USA Res Ctr PO Box 26583 Richmond VA 23261

COX, RICHARD HORTON, b Paia, Hawaii, Oct 10, 20; m; c 6. CIVIL ENGINEERING. *Educ:* Calif Inst Technol, BS, 42, MS, 46. *Prof Exp:* Range supvr, Calif Inst Technol, 42-46; civil engr, McBryde Sugar Co, Inc, Hawaii, 46-56; mgr real estate div, 56-71, vpres properties group, 71-74, V PRES ENG, ALEXANDER & BALDWIN INC, 74- *Mem:* Am Soc Civil Engrs; assoc Am Geophys Union. *Res:* Irrigation. *Mailing Add:* 1951 Kakela Dr Honolulu HI 96822

COX, ROBERT HAROLD, b Philadelphia, Pa, Sept 10, 37; m 62; c 2. PHYSIOLOGY, BIOENGINEERING. *Educ:* Drexel Inst Technol, BS, 61, MS, 62; Univ Pa, PhD(biomed eng), 67. *Prof Exp:* Assoc physiol, 67-69, asst prof, 69-72, ASSOC PROF PHYSIOL, UNIV PA, 72-, ASSOC PROF BIOMECH, 73-, ASSOC DIR BOCKUS RES INST, 70- *Concurrent Pos:* Nat Heart & Lung Inst grant, Bockus Res Inst, Univ Pa, 75-78. *Mem:* Inst Elec & Electronic Engrs; AAAS; Sigma Xi; Am Physiol Soc. *Res:* Vascular smooth muscle mechanics; arterial wall physiology; hypertension; carotid sinus reflex. *Mailing Add:* Univ of Pa Bockus Res Inst 19th & Lombard Sts Philadelphia PA 19146

COX, RODY POWELL, b New Brighton, Pa, June 24, 26; m 53; c 3. MEDICAL GENETICS. *Educ:* Univ Pa, MD, 52. *Prof Exp:* Asst clin instr med, Univ Mich, 53-54; instr, Univ Pa, 54-56, assoc, 56-68, asst prof med & res med, 58-60; res assoc genetics, Glasgow Univ, 60-61; from asst prof to assoc prof med, NY Univ, 61-71, assoc prof pharmacol, 70-71, prof med & pharmacol, 71-79; PROF MED, VCHMN & CHIEF MED SERV, VET ADMIN MED CTR, CASE WESTERN UNIV, 79- *Concurrent Pos:* Fel, Arthritis & Rheumatism Found, 57-59; USPHS res fel, 60-61; career scientist, Health Res Coun, New York, 61-; dir summer res inst, Will Rogers Hosp, 62-66; dir coun, Asn Career Scientists, 66-68; dir med scientist training prog, NY Univ, 67-; mem metab study sect, NIH, 70-73, chmn genetics study sect, 78-81; mem panel clin sci, Nat Res Coun, 76-, dir, Div Human Genetics, NY Univ, 73-79. *Mem:* Am Soc Clin Invest; Am Soc Human Genetics; Asn Am Physicians; Am Col Physicians; Harvey Soc. *Res:* Biochemical genetics; somatic cell genetics; mammalian cell regulatory mechanism; mechanisms of hormone action; pharmacology; tissue culture. *Mailing Add:* Case Western Reserve Univ VA Med Ctr 10701 East Blvd Cleveland OH 44106

COX, STEPHEN KENT, b Galesburg, Ill, Sept 2, 40; m 61; c 3. ATMOSPHERIC PHYSICS. *Educ:* Knox Col, Ill, BA, 62; Univ Wis, Madison, MS, 64, PhD(meteorol), 67. *Prof Exp:* Res meteorologist, Atmospheric Physics & Chem Lab, Environ Sci Serv Admin, 64-66; scientist, Space Sci & Eng Ctr, Univ Wis, 66-69; from asst prof to assoc prof, 69-76, PROF ATMOSPHERIC SCI, COLO STATE UNIV, 72- *Concurrent Pos:* Scientist, Dept Meteorol, Univ Wis, 67-69; prin investr, Environ Sci Serv Admin grant, Univ Wis, 68-69 & Colo State Univ, 69-70; NSF grant, Colo State Univ, 69-; chmn flight facil adv panel, Nat Ctr Atmospheric Res, 70-73; Global Atmospheric Res Prog-Atlantic Trop Exp Radiation Subprog scientist, 74-, mem, Nat Acad Sci Global Atmospheric Res Prog-Atlantic Trop Exp adv panel & Nat Acad Sci Monsoon Exp Adv Panel, 74-; US Global Atmospheric Res Prog-Atlantic Trop Exp Radiation Subprog coordr, 75- *Mem:* Am Meteorol Soc. *Res:* Atmospheric heat budget; radiation parameterization for numerical models; meteorological field experiments; radiative transfer. *Mailing Add:* Dept Atmospheric Sci Colo State Univ Ft Collins CO 80521

COX, WILLIAM EDWARD, b Pulaski, Va, Feb 18, 44; m 65; c 1. WATER RESOURCES MANAGEMENT. *Educ:* Va Polytech Inst & State Univ, BS, 66, MS, 68, PhD(civil eng), 76. *Prof Exp:* Asst prof, Civil Eng Tech, Va Commonwealth Univ, 68-72; res assoc, Water Resources Res, 72-77, asst prof, 77-81, ASSOC PROF, CIVIL ENG DEPT, VA POLYTECH INST & STATE UNIV, 81- *Concurrent Pos:* Consult, GKY & Assocs, Inc, 81; lectr, Ferrum Col, 81; prin investr res grants, Off Water Res & Technol, 75-; mem, UN Educ Sci & Cultural Org Working Group Importance Water Resources Socio-Econ Develop, 80- *Mem:* Am Soc Civil Engrs; Am Water Resources Asn; Sigma Xi. *Res:* Water resources planning and management, with emphasis on public policy and institutional arrangements related to conflict resolution. *Mailing Add:* Civil Eng Dept Va Polytech Inst & State Univ Blacksburg VA 24061

COX, WILLIAM LESTER, b Youngstown, Ohio, Sept 18, 24; m 47, 67; c 9. PHYSICAL CHEMISTRY, ORGANIC CHEMISTRY. *Educ:* Muskingum Col, BS, 48; Case Western Reserve Univ, MS, 50, PhD(org chem), 53. *Prof Exp:* Instr chem, Case Western Reserve Univ, 52-54; res chemist, Universal Oil Prod Co, 54-59, res coordr, 59-62, asst dir chem prod res, 62-64; res scientist, 64-66, mgr rubber chem res, 66-75, mgr sci liaison, 73-75, MGR ORG CHEM RES, GOODYEAR TIRE & RUBBER CO, 75- *Mem:* Am Chem Soc; Am Mgt Asn; AAAS. *Res:* Rubber chemistry; organic synthesis; polymer degradation. *Mailing Add:* Goodyear Tire & Rubber Co Res Div 142 Goodyear Blvd Akron OH 44316

COXETER, HAROLD SCOTT MACDONALD, b London, Eng, Feb 9, 07; m 36; c 2. MATHEMATICS. *Educ:* Cambridge Univ, BA, 29, PhD(geom), 31. *Hon Degrees:* LLD, Univ Alta, 57, Univ Trent, 73, Univ Toronto, 79; DMath, Waterloo Univ, 69; DSc, Acadia Univ, 71. *Prof Exp:* Fel, Trinity Col, Cambridge Univ, 31-35; from asst prof to assoc prof, 36-48, PROF MATH, UNIV TORONTO, 48- *Concurrent Pos:* Rockefeller Found fel, Princeton Univ, 32-33, Procter fel, 34-35; vis prof, Univ Notre Dame, 47, Columbia Univ, 49, Dartmouth Col, 64, Fla Atlantic Univ, 65, Univ Amsterdam, 66, Univ Edinburgh, 67, Univ E Anglia, 68, Australian Nat Univ, 69, Univ Sussex, 72 & Univ Warwick, 76, Calif Inst Technol, 77 & Univ Bologna, 78; ed in chief, Can J Math, 49-58; pres, Int Cong Mathematicians, 74. *Honors &. Honors & Awards:* Tory Medal, 49. *Mem:* Am Math Soc; Math Asn Am; fel Royal Soc; fel Royal Soc Can; for mem Royal Netherlands Acad Arts & Sci. *Res:* Regular and semi-regular polytopes; abstract groups; non-Euclidean geometry; configurations. *Mailing Add:* 67 Roxborough Dr Toronto ON M4W 1X2 Can

COY, DAVID HOWARD, b Manchester, Eng, Sept 15, 44; m 66; c 1. ENDOCRINOLOGY. *Educ:* Univ Manchester, BSc, 66, PhD(chem), 69. *Prof Exp:* Res assoc chem, Univ Toledo, 69-70; teaching assoc biochem, Med Col Ohio, 70-72; asst prof, 72-76, ASSOC PROF MED, SCH MED, TULANE UNIV, 76- *Concurrent Pos:* Res assoc, Vet Admin Hosp, New Orleans, 72-; assoc ed, Peptides. *Mem:* Endocrine Soc; Am Asn Advan Sci; Am Chem Soc; NY Acad Sci. *Res:* Chemistry and biological properties of neuro-gastrointestinal peptide hormones and their analogs. *Mailing Add:* Dept of Med Tulane Univ Sch of Med New Orleans LA 70112

COY, RICHARD EUGENE, b New Kensington, Pa, Oct 28, 25; m 57; c 2. DENTISTRY. *Educ:* Univ Pittsburgh, BS, 49, DDS, 51, MS, 59. *Prof Exp:* Assoc prof prosthodontics, Univ Pittsburgh, 60-70; PROF PROSTHODONTICS, SCH DENT MED, SOUTHERN ILL UNIV, EDWARDSVILLE, 70-, ASST DEAN CLIN AFFAIRS, 75- *Concurrent Pos:* Consult, Vet Admin Hosps, 63-; assoc prof, Med Ctr, St Louis Univ, 71-; chmn continuing educ, Am Asn Dent Schs, 74, chmn prosthodont, 76. *Mem:* Fel Am Col Dentists; fel Am Col Prosthodontists; Int Asn Dent Res; Int Asn Dento-Facial Abnormalities; Am Equilibration Soc (secy, 68-). *Res:* Study of craniofacial abnormalities; study of pain in temporomandibular dysfunction syndrome. *Mailing Add:* Sch Dent Med Southern Ill Univ Edwardsville IL 62025

COYE, ROBERT DUDLEY, b Los Angeles, Calif, Dec 17, 24; m 46; c 3. ANATOMIC PATHOLOGY. *Educ:* Williams Col, BA, 48; Univ Rochester, MD, 52. *Prof Exp:* Resident path, Univ Rochester, 52-55; from asst prof to prof, Univ Wis-Madison, 55-72; DEAN SCH MED, WAYNE STATE UNIV, 72-, PROF PATH, 80- *Res:* Pathology of kidney. *Mailing Add:* 540 E Canfield Ave Detroit MI 48202

COYER, PHILIP EXTON, b Harrisburg, Pa, May 20, 48; m 77. PHYSIOLOGY, NEUROPHYSIOLOGY. *Educ:* Franklin & Marshall Col, AB, 70; Col William & Mary, MA, 72; Univ Mass, Amherst, PhD(zool), 77. *Prof Exp:* Teaching asst biol, Col William & Mary, 70-71; teaching assoc dept zool, Univ Mass, 72-76; res asst zool & neurophysiol, Univ Mass, 76-77; res assoc, 77-81, RES ASST PROF NEUROL, MED CTR, UNIV ALA, 81- *Concurrent Pos:* NIH traineeship neurophysiol & cerebral metab dept neurol, Univ Ala, 78- *Mem:* Soc Neurosci; Sigma Xi; Am Soc Zoologists; Int Soc Oxygen Transp Tissue; Am Physiol Soc. *Res:* Neurophysiology; neuronal basis underlying rhythmic respiratory patterns; single cell analysis of oxygen effects on neural functioning; oxygen transport in the nervous system; cerebral metabolism. *Mailing Add:* Dept Neurol & Neurosci Univ Ala Med Ctr University Station AL 35294

COYIER, DUANE L, b Aurora, Ill, Mar 14, 26; m 47; c 3. HORTICULTURE. *Educ:* Univ Wis, BS, 50, PhD(plant path), 61. *Prof Exp:* Plant pathologist, Tree Fruit Dis Invests, 61-73, PLANT PATHOLOGIST, FUNGUS & BACT DIS TREE FRUITS, FOLIAR DIS ORNAMENTAL PLANTS, SCI EDUC ADMIN-FED RES, USDA, 73- *Mem:* Am Phytopath Soc; Sigma Xi; Coun Agr Sci & Technol; Int Plant Propagators Soc. *Res:* Erysiphacae which attack ornamental plants with emphasis on rose powdery mildew. *Mailing Add:* 3220 Northwest McKinley Dr Corvallis OR 97330

COYKENDALL, ALAN LITTLEFIELD, b Hartford, Conn, Jan 11, 37; m 59; c 1. ORAL MICROBIOLOGY. *Educ:* Bates Col, BS, 59; Tufts Univ, DMD, 63; George Washington Univ, MS, 70. *Prof Exp:* Fel microbiol, US Naval Dent Res Inst, 64-65, microbiologist, US Naval Med Res Inst, 67-71, microbiologist, US Naval Dent Res Inst, 71-72; res assoc dent, 72-75, clin investr, Vet Admin Hosp, Newington, 75-78; ASST PROF MICROBIOL, UNIV CONN SCH DENT MED, 78- *Mem:* AAAS; Int Asn Dent Res; Am Soc Microbiol. *Res:* Tooth replantation; taxonomy of oral bacteria; retention of sugar in the mouth; nucleic acids of cariogenic streptococci; guanine-cytosine content and homologies. *Mailing Add:* Dept of Oral Diagnosis Univ Conn Sch of Dent Med Farmington CT 06032

COYLE, BERNARD ANDREW, b Pukekohe, NZ, May 2, 34; m 60; c 5. INORGANIC CHEMISTRY, CRYSTALLOGRAPHY. *Educ:* Univ NZ, BSc, 55, MSc, 56; Northwestern Univ, PhD(inorg chem), 69. *Prof Exp:* Instr chem, City Col San Francisco, 60-66; asst prof, NCent Col, Ill, 69-71; prof chem, City Col San Francisco, 71-80; DEAN ACAD AFFAIRS, PALMER COL WEST, 80- *Concurrent Pos:* Guest scientist, Argonne Nat Lab, 67-73; vis chemist, Brookhaven Nat Lab, 70-71; lectr chem, Univ of San Francisco, 74-77 & San Francisco State Univ, 74- *Mem:* Am Chem Soc; Nat Coun Resource Develop; Asn Educ Data Systs. *Res:* Computers in chemical education; educational administration. *Mailing Add:* Palmer Col West 1095 Dunford Way Sunnyvale CA 94087

COYLE, CATHERINE LOUISE, b New York, NY, May 16, 52. BIOINORGANIC CHEMISTRY, CATALYSIS. *Educ:* Hunter Col, City Univ New York, BS, 74; Calif Inst Technol, PhD(chem), 77. *Prof Exp:* Fel chem, Stanford Univ, 77-79; res chemist, 79-80, SR CHEMIST, EXXON RES & ENGR, 80- *Concurrent Pos:* Res award, Sigma Xi, 77; adj asst prof, Hunter Col, City Univ New York, 81- *Mem:* Am Chem Soc; AAAS; Am Inst Chemists. *Res:* Bioinorganic chemistry with specific emphasis on the kinetics of metalloprotein reactions; preparation and charcterization of transition metal-sulfur synthetic analogs of the active sties in proteins and catalysts. *Mailing Add:* Exxon Res & Eng Box 45 Linden NJ 07036

COYLE, FREDERICK ALEXANDER, b Port Jefferson, NY, May 31, 42; div; c 2. SYSTEMATICS, BEHAVIOR. *Educ:* Col Wooster, BA, 64; Harvard Univ, MA, 66, PhD(biol), 70. *Prof Exp:* ASSOC PROF BIOL, WESTERN CAROLINA UNIV, 69- *Concurrent Pos:* Res assoc, Entomol Dept, Am Mus Natural Hist. *Mem:* Am Arachnol Soc; Brit Arachnol Soc. *Res:* Systematics, behavior and ecology of spiders, especially Mygalomorph spiders. *Mailing Add:* Dept Biol Western Carolina Univ Cullowhee NC 28723

COYLE, GEORGE J, JR, b Philadelphia, Pa, Apr 2, 51. X-RAY PHOTOELECTRON SPECTROSCOPY, SURFACE SCIENCE. *Educ:* Univ Md, BS, 72, PhD(chem), 81. *Prof Exp:* Teaching asst, chem, Univ Md, 76-78, res asst, 78-81; SURFACE SCIENTIST CHEM, IBM CORP, ENDICOTT, NY, 81-; CONSULT RES CHEMIST, US AIR FORCE WRIGHT AERONAUT LABS, WRIGHT PATTERSON-AFB, OHIO, 79- *Mem:* Am Vacuum Soc; Am Chem Soc; Soc Appl Spectros; Sigma Xi. *Res:* X-ray photoelectron spectroscopy of inorganic and organic surfaces; chemical alteration of these sufaces by low energy ion bombardment and the mechanism by which these changes occur. *Mailing Add:* IBM Corp 1701 N St Endicott NY 13760

COYLE, HARRY MICHAEL, b Johnstown, Pa, Jan 7, 27; m 55; c 4. CIVIL ENGINEERING. *Educ:* US Mil Acad, BS, 50; Mass Inst Technol, MS, 56; Univ Tex, PhD(civil eng), 65. *Prof Exp:* Instr civil eng & res engr, Univ Tex, 62-65; asst prof civil eng & res engr, 65-68, assoc prof, 68-72, PROF CIVIL ENG, TEX A&M UNIV, 72-, HEAD GEOENG GROUP & GEOTECH DIV, 73- *Concurrent Pos:* Consult, Exxon, Shell & McClelland Eng. *Mem:* Nat Soc Prof Engrs; Am Soc Civil Engrs; Am Soc Testing & Mat. *Res:* Soil-structure interaction; soil mechanics and foundation engineering; pile-soil interaction. *Mailing Add:* Dept of Civil Eng Tex A&M Univ College Station TX 77843

COYLE, MARIE BRIDGET, b Chicago, Ill, May 13, 35. MEDICAL MICROBIOLOGY, MICROBIAL GENETICS. *Educ:* St Louis Univ, MS, 63; Kans State Univ, PhD(genetics), 65. *Prof Exp:* Instr sci, Columbus Hosp Sch Nursing, Chicago, 57-59; fel microbiol, Univ Chicago, 64-67, res assoc molecular genetics, 67-70; instr microbiol, Med Ctr, Univ Ill, Chicago Circle, 70-71; fel microbiol, Temple Univ, 71-73; ASST PROF MICROBIOL, SCH MED, UNIV WASH, 73- *Mem:* Am Soc Microbiol; Sigma Xi; Am Asn Univ Prof; Acad Clin Lab Physicians & Scientists. *Res:* Mitotic recombination in Neurospora crassa; DNA repair mechanisms in mammalian cells after treatment with alkylating agents; genetics of bacterial virulence; antibiotic resistance and susceptibility testing. *Mailing Add:* Dept of Microbiol Univ of Wash Sch of Med Seattle WA 98195

COYLE, PETER, b Hanover, NH, Mar 4, 39; m 67. NEUROANATOMY, NEUROPHYSIOLOGY. *Educ:* Univ Vt, BA, 62; Univ Mich, MS, 64, PhD(anat), 67. *Prof Exp:* From instr to asst prof, 67-76, ASSOC PROF ANAT, MED SCH, UNIV MICH, ANN ARBOR, 77- *Concurrent Pos:* Rackham fac res grant, Med Sch, Univ Mich, Ann Arbor, 68-70, USPHS

grants, 70-74 & 81-84; Mich Heart Asn grant, 77-78 & 79-81; Univ Mich Phoenix Proj grant, 77-78. *Mem:* AAAS; Am Asn Anatomists; Neurosci Soc; Sigma Xi; assoc Am Acad Neurol. *Res:* Experimental and descriptive studies of the cerebrovasculature of normotensive and genetically stroke-prone rats; signal properties of the hippocampal theta rhythm. *Mailing Add:* Dept Anat Univ of Mich Med Sch Ann Arbor MI 48104

COYLE, THOMAS DAVIDSON, b Glen Cove, NY, Sept 25, 31; m 54. INORGANIC CHEMISTRY, MATERIALS SCIENCE. *Educ:* Univ Rochester, BS, 52; Harvard Univ, AM, 59, PhD(chem), 61. *Prof Exp:* NATO fel, 61-62; chemist, 62-64, chief inorg chem sect, 64-78, CHIEF CHEM STABILITY & CORROSION DIV, NAT BUR STANDARDS, 78- *Mem:* AAAS; Am Chem Soc; Royal Soc Chem. *Res:* Inorganic and organometallic chemistry; boron chemistry; nuclear magnetic resonance and applications to inorganic chemistry; coordination chemistry of main group elements; inorganic halides; stability of inorganic materials. *Mailing Add:* Chem Stability & Corrosion Div Nat Bur of Standards Washington DC 20234

COYNE, DERMOT P, b Dublin, Ireland, July 4, 29; US citizen; m 57; c 6. PLANT BREEDING. *Educ:* Univ Col, Dublin, BAgrSc, 53, MAgrSc, 54; Cornell Univ, PhD(plant develop), 58. *Prof Exp:* Asst mgr agr develop, Campbell Soups, Ltd, Eng, 58-60; asst prof, 61-68, PROF HORTICULTURE, UNIV NEBR, LINCOLN, 68- *Concurrent Pos:* Chmn tech adv comt, Int Ctr Trop Agr, Cali, Colombia, 74-79; vpres elect, Res Div, Am Soc Hort Sci, 78. *Honors & Awards:* Nat Canner's Asn Award, 67; Asgrow Award, 74; Campbell Award, 75; Bean Improv Coop Meritorious Award, 75; Marion W Meadows Award, Am Soc Hort Sci, 76. *Mem:* Fel Am Soc Hort Sci; Am Genetic Asn; Bean Improv Coop. *Res:* Germplasm identification; breeding and genetics of tolerance to bacterial root rot and white mold pathogens in beans; genetics and breeding investigation in the following areas in beans, interspecific hybridization, photoperiodism, adaptation, physiological and morpho genetical components of yields and seed quality; breeding improved types of winter squash. *Mailing Add:* Dept of Hort Univ of Nebr Lincoln NE 68583

COYNE, DONALD GERALD, b Hutchinson, Kans, Oct 28, 36; m 59; c 2. HIGH ENERGY PHYSICS. *Educ:* Univ Kans, BS, 58; Calif Inst Technol, PhD(physics), 67. *Prof Exp:* Teaching asst physics, Calif Inst Technol, 58-59, res asst, 59-66; fel, Lawrence Radiation Lab, 66-70; asst prof, 70-76, res physicist, 76-80, SR RES PHYSICIST, PRINCETON UNIV, 81- *Concurrent Pos:* Mem positron-electron proj policy comt, Stanford Univ/Univ Calif, 75-78; chmn, Stanford Linear Accelerator Ctr/Lawrence Berkeley Lab Orgn, 78-79. *Mem:* Am Phys Soc. *Res:* Experimental high energy particle physics; apparatus and analysis for experiments using electron/positron colliding beam machines. *Mailing Add:* Joseph Henry Lab of Physics Princeton Univ Princeton NJ 08540

COYNE, GEORGE VINCENT, b Baltimore, Md, Jan 19, 33. ASTRONOMY. *Educ:* Fordham Univ, AB, 57, PhilosL, 58; Georgetown Univ, PhD(astron), 62. *Prof Exp:* Res assoc astron & investr NASA grant, Res Inst Natural Sci, Woodstock Col, 63-70; asst prof, 70-76, assoc dir observ, 77-78, SR RES FEL, LUNAR & PLANETARY LAB & LECTR, DEPT ASTRON, UNIV ARIZONA, 76-, ACTG DIR & HEAD OBSERV, 79-; DIR, VATICAN OBSERV, 78- *Concurrent Pos:* Asst astronr, Vatican Observ, Italy, 70- *Mem:* Int Astron Union; Am Astron Soc; Astron Soc Pacific; Am Phys Soc; Optical Soc Am. *Res:* Evolution in young stellar associations; polarimetry; interstellar material; stars with extended atmospheres. *Mailing Add:* Lunar & Planetary Lab Univ of Ariz Tucson AZ 85721

COYNE, MARY FRANCES D, b Lynn, Mass, Jan 17, 38; m 61; c 2. ENDOCRINOLOGY. *Educ:* Emmanuel Col, Mass, AB, 59; Wellesley Col, MA, 61; Univ Va, PhD(physiol), 64. *Prof Exp:* Instr physiol, Sch Med, Univ Va, 66-67, asst prof, 67-68; asst prof physiol, La State Univ Med Ctr, New Orleans, 68-70; asst prof, 70-74, chmn dept, 75-78, assoc prof, 74-80, PROF BIOL SCI, WELLESLEY COL, 80- *Concurrent Pos:* USPHS fel, 64-66, res grant, 67-72, res corp grant, 80-82; vis lectr pharmacol, Harvard Med Sch, 78-79. *Mem:* Endocrine Soc; AAAS; Sigma Xi; NY Acad Sci. *Res:* Pituitary and adrenal gland interrelationships particularly mechanisms regulating adrenal response to corticotropin. *Mailing Add:* Dept of Biol Sci Wellesley Col Wellesley MA 02181

COYNE, PATRICK IVAN, b Wichita, Kans, Feb 26, 44; m 64; c 2. PHYSIOLOGICAL ECOLOGY. *Educ:* Kans State Univ, BS, 66; Utah State Univ, PhD(range sci), 70. *Prof Exp:* Plant physiologist arctic tundra, US Army Cold Regions Res & Eng Lab, 70-72; asst prof forest tree physiol, Forest Soil Lab, Univ Alaska, 73-74; PLANT PHYSIOLOGIST AIR POLLUTION EFFECTS ON PLANTS, LAWRENCE LIVERMORE LAB, UNIV CALIF, 75- *Concurrent Pos:* Consult, US Army Cold Regions & Eng Lab, 73-74. *Mem:* AAAS; Soc Range Mgt; Am Soc Agron; Crop Sci Soc Am; Soil Sci Soc Am. *Res:* Effects of interactions of gaseous air pollutants with other environmental stresses on plant physiology and plant community ecology. *Mailing Add:* Lawrence Livermore Lab Univ of Calif PO Box 5507 Livermore CA 94550

COYNER, EUGENE CASPER, b Conover, NC, Dec 25, 18; m 43; c 3. CHEMISTRY. *Educ:* Univ Ill, BS, 40; Univ Minn, PhD(org chem), 44. *Prof Exp:* From asst to instr chem, Univ Minn, 40-44; res chemist, chem dept, E I du Pont de Nemours & Co, 44-46; asst prof chem, Univ Tenn, 46-48; group leader, res dept, Mallinckrodt Chem Works, 49-54; res supvr, E I Du Pont de Nemours & Co, 55, tech assoc, Freon Prod Div, 66-69, sr bus analyst, Org Chem Dept, 69-79, sr indust economist, 79-80; CONSULT CHEM ECON, SRI INT, 81- *Mem:* AAAS; Am Chem Soc. *Res:* General organic chemistry; fluoro-organic compounds; product development. *Mailing Add:* 453 Alberto Way D242 Los Gatos CA 95030

COZAD, GEORGE CARMON, b Corning, Kans, Mar 5, 27; m 51; c 4. MEDICAL MYCOLOGY, IMMUNOLOGY. *Educ:* Univ Kans, AB, 50; Univ Okla, MS, 54; Duke Univ, PhD(microbiol), 57; Am Bd Med Microbiol, dipl. *Prof Exp:* From res assoc med mycol to assoc prof microbiol, 57-70, PROF MICROBIOL, UNIV OKLA, 70- *Concurrent Pos:* La State Univ trainee, Costa Rica & Colombia, 69. *Mem:* Am Soc Microbiol; Mycol Soc Am; Int Soc Human & Animal Mycol; Am Thoracic Soc; Am Soc Trop Med & Hyg. *Res:* Pathogenic mechanisms of systemic fungal agents; immunology of systemic fungus diseases; effects of fungus infection on basic immune mechanisms of host. *Mailing Add:* Dept of Microbiol Univ of Okla Norman OK 73019

COZZARELLI, FRANCIS A(NTHONY), b Jersey City, NJ, Apr 8, 33; m 58; c 6. CREEP MECHANICS, LITHOSPHERE FLEXURE. *Educ:* Stevens Inst Technol, BS, 55, MS, 58; Polytech Inst Brooklyn, PhD(appl mech), 64. *Prof Exp:* Stress analyst, Gibbs & Cox, Inc, NY, 55-57; from instr to asst prof eng sci, Pratt Inst, 57-62; from asst prof to assoc prof, 62-71, PROF ENG SCI, STATE UNIV NY BUFFALO, 71- *Concurrent Pos:* Vis prof, Technol, Univ Delft, 68-69 & Politechico di Milano, 76; NSF Sci Fac Award, 68-69; vis scientist, Euratom, Ispra, Italy, 77; Fulbright Res Award, 76-77. *Mem:* Am Soc Mech Engrs; Soc Eng Sci; Am Acad Mech. *Res:* Creep in plates and shells; compressibility effects; temperature effects; random parameters in creep; inelastic wave propagation; irradiation induced creep; creep rupture; effect of geothermal gradients on lithospheric flexure. *Mailing Add:* 393 Starin Ave Buffalo NY 14216

COZZARELLI, NICHOLAS ROBERT, b Jersey City, NJ, Mar 26, 38; m 67. BIOCHEMISTRY. *Educ:* Princeton Univ, AB, 60; Harvard Univ, PhD(biochem), 66. *Prof Exp:* NSF fel biochem, Stanford Univ, 66-68; from asst prof to assoc prof, Univ Chicago, 68-77, prof biochem, 77-82; PROF, DEPT MOLECULAR BIOL, UNIV CALIF, BERKELEY, 82- *Res:* Synthesis of DNA in vitro; mechanism of DNA transposition. *Mailing Add:* Depts Biochem Biophys & Theoret Biol Univ of Chicago Chicago IL 60637

COZZENS, ROBERT F, b Alexandria, Va, Sept 6, 41. PHYSICAL CHEMISTRY. *Educ:* Univ Va, BS, 63, PhD(chem), 66. *Prof Exp:* Nat Res Coun-Nat Acad Sci fel, US Naval Res Lab, 66-67; PROF CHEM, GEORGE MASON UNIV, 67- *Concurrent Pos:* Consult, chem div, US Naval Res Lab, 67-; chmn, Gordon Res Conf. *Mem:* AAAS; Am Chem Soc; Sigma Xi; Inter-Am Photochem Soc. *Res:* Photochemistry and energy transfer processes, especially polymer intramolecular energy transfer and polymer photoconductors. *Mailing Add:* Dept of Chem George Mason Univ Fairfax VA 22030

CRABB, NORMAN T, b Kent, Ohio, Feb 17, 33; m 54; c 3. ANALYTICAL CHEMISTRY, POLYMER PROPERTIES. *Educ:* Kent State Univ, BS, 55; Ohio State Univ, MS, 58, PhD(anal chem), 61. *Prof Exp:* Anal res chemist, Union Carbide Chemicals & Plastics, 61-69; anal group leader, Int Paper Co, 69-72; lab mgr res serv, Owen-Corning Fiberglas Corp, 72-76; lab sect mgr polymer properties, 76-80, MGR, NORTHERN PETROCHEM CO, 80- *Mem:* Am Chem Soc; Am Inst Chemists; Sigma Xi. *Res:* Separation and measurement of trace components in industrial products; study of the relationship between product properties and product performance. *Mailing Add:* 104 Red Bud Ln Morris IL 60450

CRABBE, PIERRE, b Brussels, Belgium, Dec 29, 28; m 56; c 3. CHEMISTRY. *Educ:* Inst Meurice-Chimie, Belgium, dipl, 52; Univ Paris, doctorate, 54; Univ Strasbourg, PhD(org chem), 67. *Prof Exp:* Asst prof org chem, Univ Ibero-Am, Mex, 62-73; prof, Univ Med Sci, Grenoble, France, 73-79; CHMN & PROF CHEM, UNIV MO, COLUMBIA, 79- *Concurrent Pos:* Res dir, Syntex, SAm, 64-73; assoc prof org chem, Univ Nacional Autonoma, Mex, 68-75; consult, Unilever Res, 74-76; Wellcome Lab, 76-78; UNESCO, 75-, World Health Orgn, 75-; secy-gen, Int Orgn Chem Sci Develop, 81- *Honors & Awards:* Nat Award, Acad Sci, Mex, 68. *Mem:* Am Chem Soc; Mex Acad Sci; NY Acad Sci; Royal Chem Soc; Belgian Chem Soc. *Res:* Organic chemistry, structure determination, and synthesis of molecules of potential biological interest; application of physical methods in organic chemistry; steroid hormones; prostaglandins. *Mailing Add:* 7 E Burnam Rd Columbia MO 65201

CRABILL, EDWARD VAUGHN, b Winamac, Ind, May 30, 30. ANATOMY. *Educ:* DePauw Univ, BA, 52; NY Univ, PhD(anat), 57. *Prof Exp:* From instr to assoc prof anat, Albany Med Col, 56-77; PROF ANAT, UNIV PITTSBURGH, 77- *Mem:* Sigma Xi. *Res:* Pituitary cytology; hair growth; skin physiology. *Mailing Add:* Dept of Anat & Histol Univ Pittsburgh Sch Dent Med Pittsburgh PA 15261

CRABLE, GEORGE FRANCIS, b New Castle, Pa, June 10, 22; m 45; c 3. PHYSICS. *Educ:* Geneva Col, BS, 43; Univ Mich, MS, 47; Duke Univ, PhD(physics), 51. *Prof Exp:* Asst, Carnegie Inst Technol, 43-44; chemist, Koppers Co, 44-45; physicist, Gulf Res & Develop Co, Pa, 51-61; chmn dept physics, Geneva Col, 61-63; physicist, 63-70, SR RES PHYSICIST, DOW CHEM CO, 70- *Mem:* Am Phys Soc; Am Chem Soc; NY Acad Sci; Sigma Xi. *Res:* Microwave; mass and infrared spectroscopy; nuclear magnetic resonance; x-ray photoelectron spectroscopy. *Mailing Add:* 1007 Trinity Ct Midland MI 48640

CRABTREE, DAVID MELVIN, b Upper Lake, Calif, Aug 29, 45; m 72; c 3. MARINE BIOLOGY, INVERTEBRATE ZOOLOGY. *Educ:* Pac Union Col, BS, 68, MA, 70; Loma Linda Univ, PhD(biol), 75. *Prof Exp:* CHMN DEPT BIOL, ANTILLIAN COL, 75- *Honors & Awards:* Aquanaut Cert, Nat Oceanic & Atmospheric Admin. *Mem:* AAAS. *Res:* Invertebrate growth lines, ecological and paleoecological applications; effects of environmental conditions on coral growth. *Mailing Add:* Dept Biol Antillian Col Box 118 Mayaguez PR 00708

CRABTREE, DOUGLAS EVERETT, b Boston, Mass, June 14, 38; m 59; c 3. MATHEMATICS. *Educ:* Bowdoin Col, BA, 60; Harvard Univ, MA, 61; Univ NC, PhD(amth), 65. *Prof Exp:* Fel math, Univ NC, 61-64; asst prof, Univ Mass, 64-66; asst prof, Amherst Col, 66-72; INSTR MATH, PHILLIPS ACAD, MASS, 72- *Mem:* Am Math Soc; Math Asn Am. *Res:* Theory of matrices; theory of rings. *Mailing Add:* Dept of Math Phillips Acad Andover MA 01810

CRABTREE, GARVIN (DUDLEY), b Eugene, Ore, Nov 29, 29; M 65; c 2. HORTICULTURE, WEED SCIENCE. *Educ:* Ore State Univ, BS, 51; Cornell Univ, MS, 55, PhD, 58. *Prof Exp:* From asst prof & asst horticulturist to assoc prof, 58-80, PROF HORT, ORE STATE UNIV, 80- *Concurrent Pos:* Res assoc, Mich State Univ, 75-76. *Mem:* Weed Sci Soc Am; Am Soc Hort Sci. *Res:* Weed control in horticultural crops and application of plant growth regulators. *Mailing Add:* Dept of Hort Ore State Univ Corvallis OR 97331

CRABTREE, GEORGE WILLIAM, b Little Rock, Ark, Nov 28, 44; m 67. SOLID STATE PHYSICS. *Educ:* Northwestern Univ, BS, 67; Univ Wash, MS, 68; Univ Ill, Chicago Circle, PhD(physics), 74. *Prof Exp:* asst scientist, 74-79, ASSOC SCIENTIST SOLID STATE PHYSICS, ARGONNE NAT LAB, 79- *Concurrent Pos:* Vis prof, Univ Ore, 77. *Mem:* Am Physics Soc; AAAS. *Res:* Metals physics. *Mailing Add:* Solid State Sci Div Argonne Nat Lab Argonne IL 60439

CRABTREE, GERALD WINSTON, b Manchester, Eng, June 29, 41; Can citizen; m 65; c 2. BIOCHEMISTRY, PHARMACOLOGY. *Educ:* Univ Guelph, BSA, 63, MS, 65; Univ Alta, PhD(purine metab), 70. *Prof Exp:* Res assoc purine metab, 70-72, instr, 72-74, asst prof purine metab, 74-76, asst prof biochem pharmacol, 76-80, ASSOC PROF MED SCI, BROWN UNIV, 80- *Mem:* AAAS; Can Biochem Soc. *Res:* Purine nucleotide metabolism in intact mammalian cells; effects of purine analogues on normal purine metabolic pathways; metabolism of purine analogues; purine metabolism of schistosomes. *Mailing Add:* Div Biol & Med Sci Brown Univ Providence RI 02912

CRABTREE, JAMES BRUCE, b Wichita, Kans, Dec 11, 18. MATHEMATICS. *Educ:* Univ Kans, AB, 41, MA, 42; Harvard Univ, PhD(math), 50. *Prof Exp:* Instr math, Univ Chicago, 47-48; from asst prof to assoc prof, Univ NH, 50-56; ASSOC PROF MATH, STEVENS INST TECHNOL, 56- *Mem:* Am Math Soc. *Res:* Functional analysis; analytic functions on algebras. *Mailing Add:* Dept of Math Stevens Inst of Technol Hoboken NJ 07030

CRABTREE, KOBY TAKAYASHI, b Tokyo, Japan, Apr 29, 34; US citizen; m 58; c 2. MICROBIOLOGY, CIVIL ENGINEERING. *Educ:* Ohio Wesleyan Univ, BA, 58; Univ Wis, MS, 63, PhD(bact, civil eng), 65. *Prof Exp:* Fel civil eng, Univ Wis, 65-66; from asst prof to assoc prof bact, 66-73, PROF BACT, UNIV WIS, MARATHON CAMPUS, 73-; CHMN DEPT BIOL SCI, UNIV WIS CTR SYST, 75- *Concurrent Pos:* USDA Off Solid Wastes grant, 66-68; consult, Dept Mineral Res, Mich Technol Univ, 67-69; Wis State Dept Natural Resources grants, 67-70; consult, Zimpro, Wis, 67-, Nekoosa Papers, 76-, Mosinee Paper Corp, 80- & Hopewell Regional Water Works Treatment Facil, Va, 80- *Mem:* AAAS; Am Soc Microbiol; Am Chem Soc. *Res:* Microbial ecology; water and solid waste pollution; methane fermentation; ecology of hyphomicrobia. *Mailing Add:* Dept of Bact Sci Hall Univ of Wis Wausau WI 54401

CRABTREE, ROSS EDWARD, b Arkansas City, Kans, Mar 20, 32; m 54; c 2. DRUG METABOLISM, RADIOIMMUNOASSAYS. *Educ:* Southwestern State Col, Okla, BS, 54; Purdue Univ, MS, 56, PhD, 57. *Prof Exp:* Sr phys chemist, 57-63, sr anal res chemist, 63-70, RES SCIENTIST, LILLY CLIN, ELI LILLY & CO, 70- *Mem:* Am Asn Clin Chemists; Health Phys Soc. *Res:* Use of radioisotopes in diagnostic tests and in metabolism studies. *Mailing Add:* 5344 Daniel Dr Indianapolis IN 46226

CRACRAFT, JOEL LESTER, b Wichita, Kans, July 31, 42. VERTEBRATE MORPHOLOGY, BIOSYSTEMATICS. *Educ:* Univ Okla, BS, 64; La State Univ, MS, 66; Columbia Univ, PhD(biol), 69. *Prof Exp:* Res fel, Am Mus Natural Hist, 69-70; asst prof, 70-76, ASSOC PROF ANAT, UNIV ILL MED CTR, 77- *Mem:* Am Soc Naturalists; Soc Study Evolution; Soc Syst Zool; Am Soc Zoologists; Am Ornithologists Union. *Res:* Functional morphology of birds; multivariate morphometric analysis of size and shape; avian evolution; systematic theory; vertebrate biogeography. *Mailing Add:* Dept of Anat Univ of Ill Med Ctr Chicago IL 60680

CRADDOCK, (JOHN) CAMPBELL, b Chicago, Ill, Apr 3, 30; m 53; c 3. STRUCTURAL GEOLOGY, TECTONICS. *Educ:* DePauw Univ, BA, 51; Columbia Univ, MA, 53, PhD(geol), 54. *Prof Exp:* Asst geol, Columbia Univ, 53-54; geologist, Shell Oil Co, 54-56; from asst prof to assoc prof geol, Univ Minn, Minneapolis, 56-67; PROF GEOL, UNIV WIS, MADISON, 67-, CHMN DEPT, 77- *Concurrent Pos:* Dir, Antarctic Res Expeds, 59-69, Alaskan Expeds, 68-81, Spitsbergen Expeds, 77-81; geologist, Minn Geol Surv, 59, 64; vis scientist, NZ Geol Surv, 62-63, co-chief scientist, Leg 35, Deep Sea Drilling Proj; consult, Corps Engrs, US Army, NStar Res Inst & US State Dept; US mem & chmn, Working Group on Geol & Int Union Geol Sci del, Sci Comt on Antarctic Res; mem comm tectonics, Int Union Geol Sci; mem, Comn Geol Map of World. *Honors & Awards:* US Antarctic Serv Medal, 68; Bellingshausen-Lazarev Medal, Soviet Acad Sci, 70. *Mem:* AAAS; fel Geol Soc Am; Am Asn Petrol Geol; Am Geophys Union; Seismol Soc Am. *Res:* Overthrusts; folds; transcurrent faults; Antarctic, Spitsbergen and Alaskan geology; gravity; precambrian geology. *Mailing Add:* Dept of Geol & Geophys Univ of Wis Madison WI 53706

CRADDOCK, ELYSSE MARGARET, b Sydney, Australia, Sept 7, 44; m 73; c 1. EVOLUTIONARY BIOLOGY, CYTOGENETICS. *Educ:* Univ Sydney, BSc, 65, PhD(cytoevolution), 71. *Prof Exp:* Fel evolution, Univ Hawaii, 71-72 & Yale Univ, 72; res fel pop biol, Australian Nat Univ, 73; RES SCIENTIST, DEPT BIOL, NY UNIV, 74- *Mem:* Genetics Soc Am; Soc

Study Evolution; AAAS; NY Acad Sci. *Res:* Chromosomal and genetic aspects of the speciation process, in particular, chromosome rearrangements, evolutionary changes in the satellite DNA sequences and the role of regulatory genes in evolution. *Mailing Add:* Dept of Biol 952 Brown Bldg NY Univ New York NY 10003

CRADDOCK, GARNET ROY, b Chatham, Va, May 7, 26; m 49; c 2. AGRONOMY. *Educ:* Va Polytech Inst, BS, 52; Univ Wis, PhD(soils), 55. *Prof Exp:* From asst prof to assoc prof, 55-67, PROF AGRON, CLEMSON UNIV, 67-, HEAD DEPT AGRON & SOILS, 72- *Concurrent Pos:* Asst soil scientist, Exp Sta, Clemson Univ, 55-57, assoc soil scientist, 57-66. *Mem:* Am Soc Agron; Soil Sci Soc Am; Soil Conserv Soc Am. *Res:* Potassium and its relationship to soil mineralogy; pediological investigations relative to southeastern soils. *Mailing Add:* Dept of Agron & Soils Col of Agr Sci Clemson Univ Clemson SC 29631

CRADDOCK, JOHN HARVEY, b Memphis, Tenn, May 30, 36; m 67; c 2. PRODUCT & ENVIRONMENTAL SAFETY, POLYCHLORINATED BIPHENYLS. *Educ:* Memphis State Univ, BS, 58; Vanderbilt Univ, PhD(inorg chem), 61. *Prof Exp:* Res chem, M W Kellogg Co Div, Pullman, Inc, 61-65; res specialist, Cent Res Dept, 65-68, res group leader, 68-73, supvr com develop, Polymers & Petrochem Co, 73-74, mgr com develop, Indust Chem Co, 74-78, mgr prod & environ safety, 78-81, DIR, INDUST CHEM CO, MONSANTO CO, 81- *Concurrent Pos:* Res assoc, Princeton Univ, 64; mem, Comt on Disposal of Hazardous Indust Wastes, Nat Res Coun, Nat Acad Sci, 81-82. *Mem:* Am Chem Soc; Royal Soc Chem; Am Inst Chem. *Res:* Homogeneous catalysis; petrochemical reactions and processes; coordination chemistry; chemical food preservatives and antimicrobials; polychlorinated biphenyls, health and environmental effects and disposal. *Mailing Add:* Monsanto Co 800 N Lindbergh Blvd St Louis MO 63166

CRADDOCK, MICHAEL KEVIN, b Portsmouth, Eng, Apr 15, 36; m 70. NUCLEAR PHYSICS, PARTICLE PHYSICS. *Educ:* Oxford Univ, MA, 61, DPhil(nuclear physics), 64. *Prof Exp:* Sci officer nuclear physics, Rutherford High Energy Lab, Nat Inst Res Nuclear Sci, Chilton, Eng, 61-64; from asst prof to assoc prof, 64-77, PROF PHYSICS, UNIV BC, 77- *Concurrent Pos:* Group leader beam dynamics, Triumf, BC, 68-81, div head, Accelerator Res, 81- *Mem:* Brit Inst Physics & Phys Soc (fel Phys Soc); Can Asn Physicists; Am Phys Soc. *Res:* Medium energy proton scattering; polarized ion sources; cyclotrons. *Mailing Add:* Dept of Physics Univ of BC Vancouver BC V6T 2A6 Can

CRADDUCK, TREVOR DAVID, b London, Eng; m 59; c 3. MEDICAL PHYSICS. *Educ:* Bristol Univ, Eng, BSc, 58; Univ Sask, MSc, 63, Dr Phil (physics), 66. *Prof Exp:* Apprentice elec eng, Gen Elec Co, Coventry, Eng, 58-60; res fel, Nat Cancer Inst Can, 61-65; physicist & tech dir nuclear med, Manitoba Cancer Found, Winnipeg, 65-67; consult physicist, Foothills Hosp, Calgary, Alta, 67-70; physicist, Toronto Gen Hosp, 70-76; PHYSICIST, VICTORIA HOSP, LONDON, ONT, 77- *Concurrent Pos:* Assoc prof, Fac Med, Univ Calgary, 68-70; asst prof, Fac Med, Univ Toronto, 73-76; asst prof, Fac Med, Univ Western Ont, 77- *Mem:* Soc Nuclear Med (secy, 74-77); Am Asn Physicists Med; Can Col Physicists Med. *Res:* Physics in nuclear medicine; scintillation cameras; computers applied to nuclear medicine and radiology. *Mailing Add:* Dept Nuclear Med Victoria Hosp London ON N6A 4G5 Can

CRAFT, GEORGE ARTHUR, b Youngstown, Ohio, Nov 16, 16; m 46; c 1. MATHEMATICS. *Educ:* Miami Univ, BS, 39; Ind Univ, MA, 50; Ohio State Univ, PhD(math), 57. *Prof Exp:* Instr math, Mont State Univ, 50-53 & Ohio State Univ, 57-58; asst prof, Denison Univ, 58-61; asst prof, 61-63, ASSOC PROF MATH, HARPUR COL, STATE UNIV NY BINGHAMTON, 63- *Mem:* Am Math Soc. *Res:* Continuous transformations in Euclidean n-space; group spaces and topological vector spaces. *Mailing Add:* Dept of Math Harpur Col State Univ of NY Binghamton NY 13901

CRAFT, HAROLD DUMONT, JR, b Newark, NJ, May 28, 38; m 62; c 2. RADIO ASTRONOMY, RADIOPHYSICS. *Educ:* Cornell Univ, BEE, 61; NY Univ, MEE, 63; Cornell Univ, PhD(radio astron), 70. *Prof Exp:* Staff mem tech commun syst, Bell Tel Lab, 61-65; mem tech radio propagation, COMSAT Lab, 69-71; tech coordr astron, Nat Astron & Ionosphere Ctr, Cornell Univ, 71-73; dir opers, Arecibo Observ, 73-81, ACTG DIR, NAT ASTRON & IONOSPHERE CTR, CORNELL UNIV, 81- *Mem:* AAAS; Int Union Radio Sci; Inst Elec & Electronics Engrs; Am Astron Soc; Am Geophys Union. *Res:* Pulsar physics and radio emission mechanisms; radio propagation studies particularly with respect to atmospheric and ionospheric effects. *Mailing Add:* Arecibo Observ PO Box 995 Arecibo PR 00612

CRAFT, THOMAS FISHER, b Macon, Ga, 1924; m 48; c 1. ENVIRONMENTAL SCIENCES, NUCLEAR SCIENCE. *Educ:* Mercer Univ, AB, 45; Emory Univ, MA, 47; Ga Inst Technol, MS, 65, PhD(nuclear eng), 69. *Prof Exp:* Instr chem, Mercer Univ, 45-46; tech salesman chem, Dow Chem Co, 49-62; SR RES SCIENTIST ENVIRON & NUCLEAR SCI, GA INST TECHNOL, 62- *Mem:* Water Pollution Control Asn; Soc Environ Geochem & Health; Am Water Works Asn; Am Nuclear Soc; AAAS. *Res:* Radiation processing of industrial wastewater; fixation and mobilization of radionuclides in soil; water and wastewater treatment processes; neutron activation analysis; trace elements in water and elsewhere; radioactive tracer techniques; irradiation of items for nuclear environmental qualification testing. *Mailing Add:* Georgia Inst Tech 225 North Ave NW Atlanta GA 30332

CRAFT, THOMAS JACOB, SR, b Monticello, Ky, Dec 27, 24; m 48; c 2. CELL BIOLOGY, DEVELOPMENTAL BIOLOGY. *Educ:* Cent State Univ, BS, 48; Kent State Univ, MA, 50; Ohio State Univ, PhD(develop biol), 63. *Prof Exp:* Lab asst biol, Cent State Col, Ohio, 47-48; asst lab instr vert anat, Kent State Univ, 49-50; from instr to assoc prof, Biol, Cent State Univ, 50-67, dir, 64-65, prof biol, 67-79; DIR, DIV NATURE SCI & MATH, FLA MEM COL, MIAMI, 81-, DIR ENERGY PROG, 80- *Concurrent Pos:*

Consult, NSF, US AID, India, 67-69; Eli Lilly grant; mem, Nat Adv Res Resources Coun, NIH; adv, Ohio Health Manpower Linkage Syst Proj, Ohio Dept Health; mem exec comt, Ohio Acad Sci; adj prof anat, Sch Med, Wright State Univ, 73-79. *Mem:* Fel AAAS; NY Acad Sci; Am Inst Biol Sci; Sigma Xi. *Res:* Experimental morphology and embryology; pigment cell biology; swimming in common brown bats; melanogenesis and the homograft reaction; effect of atmospheric pollutants; energy utilization among the low income segment of society. *Mailing Add:* 5579 NW 194th Circle Terr Miami FL 33055

CRAFT, WILLARD LEAHMAN, JR, b Benton Harbor, Mich, Nov 1, 38; m 61. CHEMISTRY. *Educ:* Univ Mich, BS, 61; Univ Wash, PhD(chem), 66. *Prof Exp:* Great Lakes Cols Asn Kettering intern, Col Wooster, 66-67; asst prof, 67-74, assoc prof, 74-80, PROF CHEM, ADRIAN COL, 80- *Mem:* Am Chem Soc; Am Phys Soc. *Res:* Lambda phase transitions in solids and helix coil transitions in biologically interesting polymers. *Mailing Add:* Dept of Chem Adrian Col Adrian MI 49221

CRAFTON, PAUL A(RTHUR), b New York, NY, June 11, 23; m 53; c 1. ENGINEERING. *Educ:* City Col New York, BME, 44; Univ Md, MS, 50, PhD, 56. *Prof Exp:* Res engr, Naval Res Lab, 44-46, sect head, 46-56; assoc prof mech eng, 56-60, PROF ENG & APPL SCI, GEORGE WASHINGTON UNIV, 60- *Concurrent Pos:* Lectr civil eng, Univ Md, 54-55; lectr mech eng, George Washington Univ, 54-56; consult, 56- *Mem:* AAAS; Sigma Xi; Am Geophys Union; Am Inst Aeronaut & Astronaut; Inst Elec & Electronics Engrs. *Res:* Automatic control; systems analysis; engineering administration. *Mailing Add:* Sch of Eng & Appl Sci George Washington Univ Washington DC 20052

CRAFTS, ROGER CONANT, b Lewiston, Maine, Jan 26, 11; m 38; c 2. ANATOMY. *Educ:* Bates Col, BS, 33; Columbia Univ, PhD(anat), 41. *Prof Exp:* Instr, Col Physicians & Surgeons, Columbia Univ, 39-40; from instr to assoc prof anat, Sch Med, Boston Univ, 43-50; prof anat & chmn dept, 50-79, Francis Brunning prof, 79-81, EMER FRANCIS BRUNNING PROF ANAT, COL MED, UNIV CINCINNATI, 81- *Concurrent Pos:* Instr, Boston City Hosp, 42-49; consult, Div Fels, NIH, 60-63. *Mem:* Fel AAAS; Am Asn Anatomists; Asn Am Med Cols. *Res:* Endocrinology; reproduction; pituitary gland; endocrines and hemopoiesis. *Mailing Add:* Dept Anat Univ Cincinnati Col Med Cincinnati OH 45267

CRAGG, HOYT J, b Rabun Co, Ga, Dec 12, 19; m 42; c 2. ORGANIC CHEMISTRY. *Educ:* Berry Col, BS, 41; Emory Univ, MS, 42. *Prof Exp:* Chemist, Chem Warfare Serv, 42-43 & Tenn Eastman, AEC, 43-47; CHEMIST, ETHYL CORP, 47- *Mem:* AAAS; fel Am Inst Chem; Am Chem Soc. *Res:* Chlorination; hydrochlorination; organometallics; separation and purification. *Mailing Add:* 6045 Hibiscus Dr Baton Rouge LA 70808

CRAGGS, ROBERT F, b South Charleston, Ohio, June 9, 37. TOPOLOGY. *Educ:* Ohio Univ, Athens, AB, 59; Univ Wis-Madison, MS, 60, PhD(math), 66. *Prof Exp:* Instr math, Ohio Univ, Athens, 61-63; fel math, Inst Adv Study, Princeton, 66-68; asst prof, 68-74, ASSOC PROF MATH, UNIV ILL, URBANA, 74- *Concurrent Pos:* Sabbatical vis, Sci Inst, Univ Iceland, 74-75. *Res:* Topology of 3-and 4-manifolds; Heegaard theory; Poincare conjecture. *Mailing Add:* Dept of Math Univ of Ill Urbana IL 61801

CRAGLE, RAYMOND GEORGE, b Orangeville, Pa, Feb 28, 26; m 50; c 3. ANIMAL PHYSIOLOGY, NUTRITION. *Educ:* NC State Col, BS, 51, MS, 54; Univ Ill, PhD(dairy sci), 57. *Prof Exp:* From asst prof to prof physiol & nutrit, Agr Res Lab, AEC, Univ Tenn, 57-68; vis prof, Lab Genetics, Univ Wis, Madison, 68-69; prof dairy sci & head dept, Va Polytech Inst & State Univ, 70-78; DIR, AGR EXP STA, UNIV ILL, 78- *Mem:* Am Dairy Sci Asn; Am Soc Animal Sci; Am Inst Nutrit; fel AAAS. *Res:* Physiology and nutrition of the dairy cow; metabolism of fission products; mineral metabolism; gastrointestinal absorption and secretion of mineral elements; chimerism in large animals; tissue transplantation in cattle. *Mailing Add:* Agr Exp Sta Univ Ill 1301 W Gregory Dr Blacksburg VA 24061

CRAGOE, EDWARD JETHRO, JR, b Tulsa, Okla, July 16, 17; c 3. MEDICINAL CHEMISTRY, ORGANIC CHEMISTRY. *Educ:* Baker Univ, BA, 39; Univ Nebr-Lincoln, MA, 41, PhD(org chem), 44. *Prof Exp:* Res assoc, Sharp and Dohme, Inc, 44-56; instr chem, Pa State Col, 47-48; res assoc, 56-60, from asst dir to dir, 60-74, sr dir med chem, 75-79, DISTINGUISHED SR SCIENTIST, MERCK SHARP & DOHME RES LAB, MERCK & CO, INC, 79- *Mem:* Am Chem Soc; Sigma Xi; fel NY Acad Sci; fel Am Inst Chemists; Soc Chem Indust. *Res:* Synthetic drugs; chemotherapy; antidiabetic agents; antihypertensive agents; mental health drugs; gastrointestinal drugs; organic synthesis; heterocyclic compounds; agents for renal lithiasis; antiallergy drugs; antiasthmatic agents; hypolemic drugs; antiatherosclerosis drugs; antiallergy agents; ophthalmic drugs and drugs for brain injury. *Mailing Add:* Dept of Med Chem Merck Sharp & Dohme Res Lab West Point PA 19486

CRAGWALL, J(OSEPH) S(AMUEL), JR, b Richmond, Va, Aug 3, 19; m 41; c 1. HYDROLOGY, CIVIL ENGINEERING. *Educ:* Univ Va, BCE, 40. *Prof Exp:* Engr, Solvay Process Co, 40-41; hydraul engr, US Geol Surv, 41-58, dist engr, Tenn, 58-62, dist chief, 62-67; staff asst planning, Water Resources Prog, US Dept Interior, 67-68; asst chief hydrol for opers, Water Resources Div, US Geol Surv, 68-73, asst dir progs, 73-74, chief hydrologist, 74-79, assoc dir, 79-80; CONSULT HYDROLOGIST, 80- *Concurrent Pos:* Chmn, US Nat Comt Sci Hydrol, 75-79. *Honors & Awards:* Distinguished Serv Award, Dept Interior, 76. *Mem:* Am Soc Civil Engrs; Am Geophys Union; Nat Soc Prof Engrs; Am Water Resources Asn. *Res:* Hydrology and hydraulics of surface streams; measurement of open-channel flow; floods and low flow water resource appraisal. *Mailing Add:* US Geol Surv Nat Ctr Mail Stop 409 Reston VA 22092

CRAIB, JAMES F(REDERICK), b Buffalo, NY, June 25, 13; m 45; c 2. ELECTRONICS. *Educ:* Rensselaer Polytech Inst, EE, 36. *Prof Exp:* Mem staff res & develop electronics, Stromberg-Carlson, 36-40; gen mgr, Technifinish Labs, 40-41; gen mgr develop mil electronics, Hazeltine Corp, 41-45; gen mgr electronic develop, Kryptar Corp, 46-48; eng consult, Airborne Instruments Lab Div, Cutler-Hammer Inc, 48-66, res scientist, 66-72, head, Cent Res Div, 72-75; RETIRED. *Mem:* Inst Elec & Electronics Engrs. *Res:* Electronic circuitry; radar. *Mailing Add:* RD 1 Rome PA 18837

CRAIG, ALAN DANIEL, b Hempstead, NY, Feb 11, 35; m 60; c 4. INDUSTRIAL CHEMISTRY, POLYMER CHEMISTRY. *Educ:* Hofstra Univ, BA, 56; Univ Pa, PhD(inorg chem), 61. *Prof Exp:* Asst instr chem, Univ Pa, 56-59; res chemist res ctr, Hercules Inc, 61-66, mgr high energy res div, 67-70, sr venture analyst, New Enterprise Dept, 70-74; vpres, Adria Labs, Inc, 74-78; MGR PROD DEVELOP, HERCULES, INC, 78- *Mem:* Am Chem Soc; Sigma Xi. *Res:* Nitrogen-fluorine chemistry; silicon and other light metal hydride chemistry; pharmaceutical development; polymer fabrication and modification. *Mailing Add:* Res Ctr Hercules Inc Wilmington DE 19899

CRAIG, ALBERT BURCHFIELD, JR, b Sewickley, Pa, April 19, 24; m 47; c 4. PHYSIOLOGY, MEDICINE. *Educ:* Cornell Univ, MD, 48. *Prof Exp:* Intern, Dept Med, 48-49, asst resident, 50-51, instr, 53-55, instr physiol & med, 55-59, from asst prof to assoc prof physiol, 59-72, PROF PHYSIOL, SCH MED & DENT, UNIV ROCHESTER, 72- *Concurrent Pos:* Fel med, Sch Med & Dent, Univ Rochester, 49-50, USPHS res fel, 53-55; estab investr, Am Heart Asn, 61-66. *Mem:* Am Col Sports Med; Am Physiol Soc. *Res:* Man in water; respiration. *Mailing Add:* Dept of Physiol Univ of Rochester Sch of Med & Dent Rochester NY 14642

CRAIG, ALBERT MORRIE, b San Francisco, Calif, Oct 13, 43. BIOPHYSICS. *Educ:* Ore State Univ, BS, 65, PhD(biochem, biophys), 70. *Prof Exp:* Am Cancer Inst res assoc, Ore State Univ, 70-73; NIH res assoc, Univ Ore, 73-75; asst prof biophys, 75-80, ASST PROF VET MED, ORE STATE UNIV, 80- *Mem:* Biochem-Biophys Soc; Sigma Xi; AAAS. *Mailing Add:* Sch of Vet Med Ore State Univ Corvallis OR 97331

CRAIG, ARNOLD CHARLES, b Johnstown, NY, Sept 5, 33; m 59; c 3. PHYSICAL ORGANIC CHEMISTRY. *Educ:* Syracuse Univ, BA, 54; Cornell Univ, PhD(org chem), 59. *Prof Exp:* Res chemist, Eastman Kodak Co, 59-65; from asst prof to assoc prof, 65-75, PROF CHEM, MONT STATE UNIV, 75- *Mem:* Am Chem Soc. *Res:* Synthesis of natural products and heterocycles; color and constitution relation of sensitizing dyes; effect of environment on radiative transitions. *Mailing Add:* Dept of Chem Mont State Univ Bozeman MT 59717

CRAIG, BOBBY GLENN, b Littlefield, Tex, Sept 21, 28; m 55; c 2. PHYSICS, INSTRUMENTATION. *Educ:* Univ Calif, Riverside, BA, 57. *Prof Exp:* Engr electronics, Motorola Res Lab, 57; staff mem detonation physics, 57-77, asst M-Div leader, Diverse Projs, 77-80, PROG MGR, ENERGETIC MATS & DIRECTED ENERGY, LOS ALAMOS NAT LAB, 80- *Concurrent Pos:* Consult, US Navy Strategic Systs Proj Off, 76-80 & Air Force Weapons Lab, 78-79; mem, Joint Army Navy NASA Air Force Interagency Propulsion Comt. *Mem:* Combustion Inst; Am Inst Aeronaut & Astronaut. *Res:* Detonation and shock wave phenomena in explosives, propellants, and inerts; nuclear and chemical explosive weapons; high speed optical, radiographic, and transducer instrumentation; blasting and blasting agents; safety; directed energy weapons, lasers and particle beams. *Mailing Add:* Los Alamos Sci Lab NSP/DST MS245 PO Box 1663 Los Alamos NM 87545

CRAIG, BRUCE GORDON, b London, Ont, Mar 30, 22; m 48; c 2. GLACIAL GEOLOGY. *Educ:* Univ Western Ont, BSc, 49; Univ Mich, MS, 50, PhD, 56. *Prof Exp:* Geologist, Div Quaternary Res & Geomorphol, 49-70, ASST DIR, TERRAIN SCI DIV, GEOL SURV CAN, 71- *Mem:* Geol Asn Can. *Res:* Pleistocene geology, especially of Arctic Canada. *Mailing Add:* 1125 Sherman Dr Ottawa ON K2C 2M3 Can

CRAIG, BURTON MACKAY, b Vermilion, Alta, May 29, 18; m 45; c 2. AGRICULTURAL BIOCHEMISTRY. *Educ:* Univ Sask, BScA, 44, MSc, 46; Univ Minn, PhD, 50. *Prof Exp:* Lab asst, 41-44, asst, 44-46, from asst res officer to prin res officer, 50-69, assoc dir, 69-70, DIR FATS & OILS LAB, PRAIRIE REGIONAL LAB, UNIV SASK, 70- *Honors & Awards:* Canola Award, 81. *Mem:* Am Oil Chem Soc; Chem Inst Can. *Res:* Nutrition of fats; biosynthesis of fatty acids; fatty acid composition of oils and fats; gas liquid chromatography in fats and oils. *Mailing Add:* Prairie Regional Lab Nat Res Coun Saskatoon Can

CRAIG, CHARLES ROBERT, b Buckhannon, WVa, Jan 24, 36; m 60; c 1. PHARMACOLOGY. *Educ:* Univ Wis, PhD(pharmacol), 64. *Prof Exp:* Sr investr neuropharmacol, G D Searle & Co, 64-66; from asst prof to assoc prof pharmacol, 66-75, PROF PHARMACOL, MED CTR, W VA UNIV, 75- *Mem:* Am Soc Pharmacol & Exp Therapeut; Am Soc Neurochem; Sigma Xi; Soc Neurosci; Can Col Neuropsychopharmacol. *Res:* Pharmacological changes in the chronically epileptic rat. *Mailing Add:* Dept Pharmacol WVa Univ Med Ctr Morgantown WV 26506

CRAIG, DEXTER HILDRETH, b Pontiac, Mich, Feb 12, 24; m 49; c 2. GEOLOGY. *Educ:* Univ Mich, BS, 50; Univ Tex, MA, 52. *Prof Exp:* From asst geologist to geologist, Tex, 52-61, from geologist to sr geologist, Colo, 61-77, SR RES GEOLOGIST, DENVER RES CTR, MARATHON OIL CO, COLO, 77- *Mem:* AAAS; Am Asn Petrol Geol; Soc Econ Paleont & Mineral; Am Inst Mining, Metall & Petrol Eng; Sigma Xi. *Res:* Geology of petroleum deposits; stratigraphy and sedimentology of carbonate rocks. *Mailing Add:* Marathon Oil Co PO Box 269 Littleton CO 80160

CRAIG, DONALD LAIRD, b Kentville, NS, Dec 18, 23; m 48; c 4. HORTICULTURE. *Educ:* McGill Univ, BSc, 47; Univ NH, MSc, 55, PhD(plant breeding), 59. *Prof Exp:* AGR RES SCIENTIST, RES STA, CAN DEPT AGR, 47-, HEAD, BERRY CROPS SECT, 68- *Mem:* Am Soc Hort Sci; Can Soc Hort Sci. *Res:* Culture and breeding of berry crops. *Mailing Add:* Res Sta Can Dept of Agr Kentville NS B4N 1J5 Can

CRAIG, DONALD SPENCE, b Ridgetown, Ont, Aug 13, 23; m 52; c 3. NUCLEAR PHYSICS. *Educ:* Queen's Univ, Ont, BSc, 45; Univ Wis, PhD(physics), 52. *Prof Exp:* Jr res physicist, Nat Res Coun Can, 45-47; asst res physicist, 52-57, assoc res officer, 57-67, SR RES OFFICER, ATOMIC ENERGY LTD, CAN, 67- *Mem:* Am Nuclear Soc; Can Asn Physicists. *Res:* Reactor physics. *Mailing Add:* 18 Cabot Pl Deep River ON K0J 1P0 Can

CRAIG, DOUGLAS ABERCROMBIE M, b Nelson, NZ, Oct 24, 39; m 62; c 2. INSECT MORPHOLOGY, INVERTEBRATE LIMNOLOGY. *Educ:* Univ Canterbury, BSc, 62, PhD(zool), 66. *Prof Exp:* Asst lectr zool, Univ Canterbury, 62-66; session lectr, 66-67, lectr, 67-68, asst prof, 68-74, assoc prof entom, 74-79, PROF ENTOM, UNIV ALTA, 79- *Mem:* Entom Soc Can; Entom Soc Can; Microbiol Soc Can; AAAS. *Res:* Phylogeny of nematocera; filter-feeding of larval simuliidae; larval sensory organs; hydrodynamics of filter-feeding; extensive collecting of simuliidae in South Pacific; taxonomy of Pacific simuliidae. *Mailing Add:* Dept of Entom Univ of Alta Edmonton AB T6G 2E8 Can

CRAIG, DOUGLAS KENNETH, air pollution, radiobiology, see previous edition

CRAIG, EDWARD J(OSEPH), b Springfield, Mass, July 17, 24; m 47; c 5. ELECTRICAL ENGINEERING. *Educ:* Union Col, NY, BS, 48; Mass Inst Technol, ScD(elec eng), 54. *Prof Exp:* Instr math, Union Col, NY, 48-49; asst elec eng, Mass Inst Technol, 49-51, instr, 51-53; asst prof commun, Northeastern Univ, 53-55, assoc prof elec eng, 55-56; from assoc prof to prof, 56-77, PROF ELEC ENG & COMPUT SCI & CO-CHMN DEPT, UNION COL, NY, 77- *Concurrent Pos:* Consult, Tube Dept, Adv Tech Lab, Gen Elec Co, 56-70. *Mem:* Am Soc Eng Educ; Inst Elec & Electronics Engrs. *Res:* Electromagnetic field theory; microwave tubes; system theory; digital computers. *Mailing Add:* Div Eng & Appl Sci Union Col Schenectady NY 12308

CRAIG, FRANK RANKIN, b Mt Holly, NC, Apr 6, 21; m 47; c 1. VETERINARY MEDICINE. *Educ:* NC State Univ, BS, 46, MS, 52; Univ Ga, DVM, 56. *Prof Exp:* Assoc poultry pathologist, NC State Univ, 48-52, from exten poultry pathologist & assoc prof to prof poultry sci, 56-70; DIR HEALTH & HEALTH SERV, A W PERDUE & SONS, INC, 70- *Mem:* Am Vet Med Asn; Poultry Sci Asn; Am Asn Avian Pathologists. *Res:* Microbiology, hematology and pathology of fowl. *Mailing Add:* A W Perdue & Sons Inc Salisbury MD 21801

CRAIG, GEORGE BLACK, physical metallurgy, see previous edition

CRAIG, GEORGE BROWNLEE, JR, b Chicago, Ill, July 8, 30; m 54; c 4. ENTOMOLOGY. *Educ:* Ind Univ, BA, 51; Univ Ill, MS, 52, PhD(entom), 56. *Prof Exp:* Asst, Dept Entom, Univ Ill, 51-53; from asst prof to prof biol, 57-74, CLARK DISTINGUISHED PROF BIOL, UNIV NOTRE DAME, 74- *Concurrent Pos:* WHO travel fel, 60, consult, 63; entomologist, Prev Med Unit, Md, 54 & Chem Corps Med Labs, Army Chem Ctr, 54-57; dir, N D Vector Biol Lab, 60- & WHO Int Ref Ctr for Aedes, 66-; res dir, Int Ctr Insect Physiol & Ecol, Nairobi, Kenya, 70-77; NIH study sect trop med, 69-74. *Mem:* Fel AAAS; Entom Soc Am; Am Soc Trop Med & Hyg; Genetics Soc Am; fel Am Acad Arts & Sci. *Res:* Culicidae; genetics, systematics bionomics and physiology of Aedes; systematics of aedine eggs; evolutionary mechanisms; zoogeography; Arctic insects; vector genetics. *Mailing Add:* Dept Biol Univ Notre Dame Notre Dame IN 46556

CRAIG, HARMON, b New York, NY, Mar 15, 26; m 47; c 3. GEOCHEMISTRY, OCEANOGRAPHY. *Educ:* Univ Chicago, PhD(geol), 51. *Prof Exp:* Res assoc geochem, Inst Nuclear Studies, Univ Chicago, 51-55; assoc prof geochem, 59-64, RES GEOCHEMIST, SCRIPPS INST OCEANOG, UNIV CALIF, 55-, PROF GEOCHEM, 64- *Concurrent Pos:* Guggenheim fel, Univ Pisa, 62-63; mem oceanog expeds, Monsoon, 61, Zephyrus, 63 & Carrousel, 64. *Mem:* Am Geophys Union. *Res:* Isotopic geochemistry; geothermal areas; thermodynamics; physical oceanography; atmospheric chemistry; origin and history of ocean and atmosphere; Lake Tanganyika studies; Ethiopian Rift Valley. *Mailing Add:* Scripps Inst Oceanog Univ of Calif San Diego La Jolla CA 92093

CRAIG, JAMES CLIFFORD, JR, b Connellsville, Pa, Aug 10, 36; m 61; c 3. FOOD ENGINEERING, OPTIMIZATION & SIMULATION. *Educ:* Johns Hopkins Univ, BES, 58. *Prof Exp:* Chem engr, 59-74, res leader, 74-81, CHIEF, ENG SCI LAB, EASTERN REGIONAL RES CTR, AGR RES SERV, US DEPT AGR, 81- *Mem:* Am Inst Chem Engrs; Inst Food Technologists; AAAS. *Res:* Food and agricultural products; process studies; engineering science phenomena; optimization and simulation. *Mailing Add:* 600 E Mermaid Lane Eastern Regional Res Ctr US Dept Agr Philadelphia PA 19118

CRAIG, JAMES I, b Philadelphia, Pa, Feb 13, 42; m 65; c 3. SOLID MECHANICS, SOLAR ENERGY. *Educ:* Mass Inst Technol, BS, 64; Stanford Univ, MS, 66, PhD(aeronaut, astronaut), 69. *Prof Exp:* Asst prof, 68-74, assoc prof, 75-80, PROF AEROSPACE ENG, GA INST TECHNOL, 81- *Mem:* Am Inst Aeronaut & Astronaut; Instrument Soc Am. *Res:* Experimental mechanics; aerospace structures; experimental stress analysis; building structural dynamics; low-medium temperature solar energy; systems design and simulation. *Mailing Add:* Dept Aerospace Eng Ga Inst Technol Atlanta GA 30332

CRAIG, JAMES MORRISON, b Drayton, NDak, June 21, 16; m 39; c 2. MICROBIOLOGY. *Educ:* San Jose State Col, AB, 38; Stanford Univ, MA, 48; Ore State Univ, PhD(microbiol), 68. *Prof Exp:* Chemist, B Cribari & Sons, 39-40; chemist & bacteriologist, Eng-Skell Co, 40-42; chief chemist & bacteriologist, Goldfield Consol Mines, 42-45; chief chemist & asst supt, L De-Martini Co, 45-48; instr zool & biol, 48-51, asst prof bact, 51-57, assoc prof, 57-68, PROF MICROBIOL, SAN JOSE STATE UNIV, 68- *Concurrent Pos:* NSF grant, Ore State Univ, 58 & Univ PR, 63; AEC grant,

Univ Wash; NIH spec grant, Ore State Univ, 64. *Mem:* AAAS; Am Inst Biol Sci; Am Soc Microbiol; Soc Indust Microbiol; Nat Sci Teachers Asn. *Res:* General bacteriology; aquatic, sanitary and industrial microbiology. *Mailing Add:* 2201 Gundersen Dr San Jose CA 95125

CRAIG, JAMES PORTER, JR, b Mobile, Ala, Oct 4, 26; m 50; c 2. PHYSICAL CHEMISTRY. *Educ:* La State Univ, BS, 48, MS, 50, PhD(chem), 53. *Prof Exp:* Chemist, Bound Brook Labs, Am Cyanamid Co, 50-51; finish chemist, Nylon plant, Chemstrand Corp, 53-54, res chemist, 54-60, group leader phys chem, Res Ctr, NC, 60-70, group leader phys chem, 70-76, SUPVR ACRILAN DEVELOP, TECH CTR, MONSANTO TEXTILE DIV, 76- *Mem:* AAAS; Am Chem Soc. *Res:* Colloid and surface chemistry of polymers; polymer physical chemistry. *Mailing Add:* Tech Ctr Monsanto Textile Div Decatur AL 35601

CRAIG, JAMES ROLAND, b Philadelphia, Pa, Feb 16, 40; m 62; c 2. GEOCHEMISTRY. *Educ:* Univ Pa, BA, 62; Lehigh Univ, MS, 64, PhD(geol), 66. *Prof Exp:* Fel, Carnegie Inst, 65-67; asst prof geochem, Tex Tech Univ, 67-70; ASST PROF GEOCHEM & PROF GEOL, VA POLYTECH INST & STATE UNIV, 70- *Mem:* Mineral Soc Am; Soc Econ Geologists; Mineral Asn Can. *Res:* Phase relations of ore minerals; ore deposits; thermochemistry and phase equilibria of ore minerals; evaporite minerals. *Mailing Add:* Dept Geol Sci Va Polytech Inst & State Univ Blacksburg VA 24061

CRAIG, JAMES VERNE, b Bonner Springs, Kans, Feb 7, 24; m 48; c 3. GENETICS. *Educ:* Univ Ill, BS, 48, MS, 49; Univ Wis, PhD(genetics), 52. *Prof Exp:* First asst animal sci, Univ Ill, 52-54, asst prof, 54-55; assoc prof poultry husb, 55-60, PROF ANIMAL SCI, KANS STATE UNIV, 60- *Concurrent Pos:* NIH spec res fel, Poultry Res Ctr, Scotland, 61-62. *Honors & Awards:* Poultry Sci Res Award, 61. *Mem:* AAAS; Poultry Sci Asn; Animal Behav Soc. *Res:* Animal behavior; population genetics. *Mailing Add:* Dept of Animal Sci Kans State Univ Manhattan KS 66506

CRAIG, JAMES WILLIAM, b West Liberty, Ohio, Jan 23, 21; m; c 8. MEDICINE. *Educ:* Case Western Reserve Univ, BS, 43, MD, 45. *Prof Exp:* From instr to assoc prof med, Sch Med, Case Western Reserve Univ, 52-72; PROF MED & ASSOC DEAN SCH MED, UNIV VA, 72- *Mem:* Soc Exp Biol & Med; Am Fedn Clin Res; Am Diabetes Asn; Am Inst Nutrit. *Res:* Internal medicine; clinical research in intermediary metabolism, particularly carbohydrate metabolism and diabetes mellitus. *Mailing Add:* Sch of Med Univ of Va Charlottesville VA 22908

CRAIG, JOHN CLAYTON, JR, b West Point, Miss, Aug 29, 42; m 63; c 2. ORGANIC CHEMISTRY, BIOCHEMISTRY. *Educ:* David Lipscomb Col, BA, 64; Vanderbilt Univ, PhD(org chem), 68. *Prof Exp:* Res assoc org chem, Ohio State Univ, 68-69; asst prof chem, David Lipscomb Col, 69-73; asst dir phys sci, Res Inst Pharm Sci, 73-76; assoc prof chem, Western Ky Univ, 76-79; dir, Hazardous Mat Training Inst, State Tenn, 79-80; DIR, TECH SERV, RESOURCE RECYCLING TECHNOLOGIES, NASHVILLE, TENN, 80- *Mem:* Am Chem Soc; AAAS; Sigma Xi. *Res:* Isolation and characterization of natural product with pharmacological potential. *Mailing Add:* Resource Recycling Technologies 2003 Gallatin Rd Madison TN 37115

CRAIG, JOHN CYMERMAN, b Berlin, Ger, Jan 23, 20; m 45; c 2. ORGANIC CHEMISTRY. *Educ:* Univ London, BSc, 42, PhD(org chem), 45; Univ Sydney, DSc, 61. *Prof Exp:* Res chemist, Boots Pure Drug Co, Eng, 45-47; lectr org chem, Univ London, 47-48; from lectr to sr lectr, Univ Sydney, 48-60; from vchmn to chmn dept, 63-70, PROF CHEM & PHARMACEUT CHEM, UNIV CALIF, SAN FRANCISCO, 60- *Concurrent Pos:* Nuffield Found Dom traveling fel, Dyson Perrins Lab, Oxford Univ, 56-57; vis scientist, Lab Chem Natural Prod, NIH, 59; mem panel, psychopharmacol chem NIMH, 63-68 & mem Preclin psychopharmacol res rev comt, NIMH, 68-72; mem panel, Polycyclic Org Matter, Nat Acad Sci, 70-72 & Vapor-Phase Org Pollutants, 72-75; fac res lectr, Acad Senate, Univ Calif, San Francisco, 74-75. *Honors & Awards:* Res Achievement Award, Am Pharmaceut Asn Res Found, 67. *Mem:* Am Chem Soc; The Chem Soc; Swiss Chem Soc; fel Acad Pharmaceut Sci. *Res:* Biomedical mass spectrometry; deuterium labeling in clinical research; acetylene chemistry and biosynthesis; mechanisms of biological reactions; chemistry of sulfur compounds. *Mailing Add:* Dept of Pharmaceut Chem Univ of Calif San Francisco CA 94143

CRAIG, JOHN HORACE, b Macon, Ga, Dec 25, 42; m 68. ORGANIC CHEMISTRY. *Educ:* George Washington Univ, BS, 64; Georgetown Univ, PhD(org chem), 69. *Prof Exp:* NIH Fel chem, Univ Ill, Urbana-Champaign, 69-70, res assoc org chem, 70-71; asst prof, 71-75, ASSOC PROF ORG CHEM, CALIF STATE COL, SAN BERNARDINO, 75- *Mem:* Am Chem Soc. *Res:* Reaction mechanisms; strained sigma and pi bonds; bridged small and medium ring compounds; aliphatic nitrogen heterocycles; conformational analysis; stereo-chemistry; molecular rearrangements; physiologically active compounds. *Mailing Add:* Dept Chem Calif State Col San Bernardino CA 92407

CRAIG, JOHN MERRILL, b Pasadena, Calif, Oct 14, 13; m 49; c 3. PATHOLOGY. *Educ:* Univ Calif, AB, 36, MA, 38; Harvard Univ, MD, 41. *Prof Exp:* Asst prof path, Children's Hosp, Harvard Med Sch, 55-59; prof, Sch Med, Univ Pittsburgh, 59-60; clin prof, 60-70, PROF PATH, HARVARD MED SCH, 70-; pathologist-in-chief, Boston Hosp Women, 60-79; RESIDENT PSYCHIAT, MT HOLYOKE COL, 70- *Concurrent Pos:* Res assoc, Children's Cancer Res Found, 50-59; pathologist, Children's Hosp, 59-60; dir labs, E S Magee Hosp, 59-60; mem path study sect, USPHS, 59-64; assoc ed, Am J Path, 64-70. *Mem:* Am Soc Exp Path; Am Asn Path & Bact; Soc Pediat Res; Int Acad Path; Am Psychiat Asn. *Res:* Experimental and morphological pediatric, gynecologic and obstetric pathology. *Mailing Add:* 41 Sargent-Beechwood Brookline MA 02146

CRAIG, JOHN PHILIP, b West Liberty, Ohio, Nov 29, 23. MICROBIOLOGY, INFECTIOUS DISEASES. *Educ:* Western Reserve Univ, MD, 47; Harvard Univ, MPH, 53. *Prof Exp:* Epidemiologist, 406th Med Gen Lab, Tokyo, Japan, 51-52; fel virol, Div Med & Pub Health, Rockefeller Found, 53-54; from asst prof to assoc prof, 54-72, PROF MICROBIOL & IMMUNOL, STATE UNIV NY DOWNSTATE MED CTR, 72- *Concurrent Pos:* NIH spec res fel, Lister Inst Prev Med, London, Eng, 58-59 & Pakistan-SEATO Cholera Res Lab, Dacca, EPakistan, 64; Nat Inst Allergy & Infectious Dis res grants, 60-; mem, NIH Cholera Adv Comt, 70-73; mem cholera panel, US-Japan Coop Med Sci Prog, 70-, chmn, 72-77; chmn steering comt bact enteric infections, Diarrheal Dis Control Prog, WHO, 79-; mem, Bact & Mycol Study Sect, Nat Inst Allergy & Infectious Dis, NIH, 80-; vis prof bact, Osaka Univ, Japan, 79-80. *Mem:* Infectious Dis Soc Am; Am Asn Immunologists; Am Soc Trop Med & Hyg; fel Am Pub Health Asn; Am Acad Microbiol. *Res:* Pathogenesis and epidemiology of infectious diseases; bacterial toxins; cholera and other enteric diseases. *Mailing Add:* Dept of Microbiol & Immunol State Univ NY Downstate Med Ctr Brooklyn NY 11203

CRAIG, KENNETH ALEXANDER, b Keosauqua, Iowa, Apr 4, 08; m 39, 63. ANALYTICAL CHEMISTRY. *Educ:* Iowa Wesleyan Col, BS, 30; Pa State Col, MS & PhD(anal chem), 34. *Prof Exp:* Asst, Iowa Wesleyan Col, 28-30 & Pa State Col, 30-34, instr chem, exten serv, 34-36; asst prof, Lawrence Col, 36-39; res chemist, Kimberly Clark Corp, 39-44, coordr for plastics, 44-48, res chemist in charge pulp res, 48-50, supt pulp paper & newsprint lab, 50-58, chief paper & newsprint dept, 58-63, mgr paper dept, 63-65, sr res assoc, 65-73; CONSULT, PULP & PAPER INDUSTS, 73- *Concurrent Pos:* Instr continuing educ courses, Kimberly Clark Corp, Inst Paper Chem. *Mem:* Am Chem Soc; Am Tech Asn Pulp & Paper Indust. *Res:* Starch modification; paper machine efficiency; secondary fiber utilization; groundwood pulp bleaching; groundwood pitch control. *Mailing Add:* 329 Ninth St Neenah WI 54956

CRAIG, LAWRENCE CAREY, b Plainview, Tex, May 14, 18; m 41; c 3. STRATIGRAPHY, ECONOMIC GEOLOGY. *Educ:* Swarthmore Col, AB, 39; Columbia Univ, MA, 41, PhD(geol). 49. *Prof Exp:* Geologist, Tenn, 42-43, Calif & Nev, 43-45, Colo, 45-61, chief paleotectonic map sect, 61-74, dep chief br oil & gas resources, 74, geologist, 74-78, prog mgr, Nat Uranium Resource Eval, Br Uranium & Thorium Resources, 78-81, GEOLOGIST, US GEOL SURV, 81- *Mem:* AAAS; Geol Soc Am; Am Asn Petrol Geol; Soc Econ Paleont & Mineral. *Res:* Frontier uranium studies in Uinta and Piceance Basins of Colorado and Utah; Middle Ordovician stratigraphy of New York and Pennsylvania; Mesozoic stratigraphy of the Colorado Plateau; manganese deposits of eastern Tennessee; lead-zinc deposits of California and Nevada; paleotectonic maps of United States. *Mailing Add:* 1801 Balsam Denver CO 80215

CRAIG, LOUIS ELWOOD, b Clifton Hill, Mo, Dec 10, 21; m 43; c 4. ORGANIC CHEMISTRY. *Educ:* Cent Col, Mo, BA, 43; Univ Rochester, PhD(org chem), 48. *Prof Exp:* Chemist, Am Cyanamid Co, Conn, 43-46 & Gen Aniline & Film Corp, 48-54; supv res chemist, Grand River Chem Div, Deere & Co, 54-56, dir res, 56-58, dir res & tech serv, John Deere Chem Co, 58-65; mgr mkt res & develop, Kerr-McGee Chem Corp, 65-68, mgr mfg, 68-69, vpres mfg, 69-70, vpres info ser, 70-72, vpres, Chem Mfg Div, 72-77, dir energy info div, Kerr-McGee Chem Corp, 77-79, DIR INFO DIV, KERR-MCGEE CORP, 79- *Mem:* AAAS; Am Chem Soc; Am Mgt Asn. *Res:* Polymerization; pharmaceuticals; heterocyclics; inorganic chemicals; fertilizers; marketing; manufacturing. *Mailing Add:* Kerr-McGee Corp Kerr-McGee Ctr Oklahoma City OK 73125

CRAIG, NESSLY COILE, b Honolulu, Hawaii, Nov 20, 42; m 68. CELL BIOLOGY. *Educ:* Reed Col, BA, 63; Univ Pa, PhD(biol), 67. *Prof Exp:* Fel molecular biol, Inst Cancer Res, 67-70; asst prof, 70-75, ASSOC PROF BIOL SCI, UNIV MD, BALTIMORE COUNTY, 75- *Concurrent Pos:* USPHS fel, NIH, 68-70. *Mem:* AAAS; Am Soc Cell Biol; Soc Develop Biol. *Res:* Control of protein synthesis; synthesis and function of nucleic acids; control of growth and development in higher organisms. *Mailing Add:* Div of Biol Sci Univ of Md Baltimore County Baltimore MD 21228

CRAIG, NORMAN CASTLEMAN, b Washington, DC, Nov 12, 31; m 55; c 3. PHYSICAL CHEMISTRY. *Educ:* Oberlin Col, BA, 53; Harvard Univ, MA, 55, PhD(chem), 57. *Prof Exp:* From asst prof to assoc prof, 57-65, assoc dean, 67-68, chmn dept, 73-74 & 75-80, PROF CHEM, OBERLIN COL, 65- *Concurrent Pos:* Hon fel chem, Univ Minn, 63-64; NSF sci fac fel, Univ Calif, Berkeley, 70-71; vis prof chem, Princeton Univ, 74-75; vis prof, NIH, 78-79. *Mem:* AAAS; Am Chem Soc; Sigma Xi. *Res:* Infrared and Raman spectroscopy; normal coordinate analysis; laser applications. *Mailing Add:* Dept Chem Oberlin Col Oberlin OH 44074

CRAIG, PAUL PALMER, b Reading, Pa, July 29, 33; div; c 2. PHYSICS, SCIENCE. *Educ:* Haverford Col, BS, 54; Calif Inst Technol, PhD(physics), 59. *Prof Exp:* Mem staff cryogenics, Los Alamos Sci Lab, 58-62; assoc physicist, Brookhaven Nat Lab, 62-66, group leader, 62-72, physicist, 66-72; PROF PHYSICS, UNIV CALIF, DAVIS, 77- *Concurrent Pos:* Guggenheim Found fel, 65-66; assoc prof, State Univ NY Stony Brook, 67-71; mem bd trustees, Environ Defense Fund, 67-71; mem staff, NSF, 71-74, dep dir & actg dir, Off Energy Res & Develop Policy, 74-75; dir, Energy & Resources Coun, Univ Calif, 75-78; scientist, Lawrence Berkely Lab, Univ Calif, 77-81. *Mem:* Fel Am Phys Soc. *Res:* Energy policy; alternative energy strategies; energy conservation; cryogenics. *Mailing Add:* 2425 Elendil Lane Davis CA 95616

CRAIG, PETER C, b Flushing, NY, Jan 28, 45. FISH BIOLOGY, ECOLOGY. *Educ:* Stanford Univ, BA, 67; Univ Calif, Santa Barbara, MA, 69, PhD(biol), 73. *Prof Exp:* Sr biologist fish, Aquatic Environ Ltd, 73-77; SR BIOLOGIST FISH, LGL LTD ENVIRON RES ASN, 77- *Res:* Ecology of fishes in Alaska, western Canada and Beaufort Sea. *Mailing Add:* LGL Ltd Suite 333 2453 Beacon Ave Sidney BC V8L 1X7 Can

CRAIG, PETER HARRY, b Pittsburgh, Pa, Dec 25, 29; m 54; c 3. PATHOLOGY. *Educ:* Pa State Univ, BS, 52; Univ Pa, VMD, 55, MS, 58. *Prof Exp:* Instr vet path, Univ Pa, 55-58; mem staff, Armed Forces Inst Path, 58-59 & 60-61; mem staff, Aviation Med Acceleration Lab, 59-60; asst prof vet path, Univ Pa, 61-65; a assoc prof path, State Univ NY Vet Col, Cornell Univ, 65-73; MGR PATH & TOXICOL, MOBIL OIL CORP, 78- *Mem:* Am Vet Med Asn; NY Acad Sci; Am Col Vet Path. *Res:* Experimental pathology, transplantation, cancer, radiation; laboratory animal, aviation, and veterinary pathology; toxicology. *Mailing Add:* 7 Mallard Pl Pennington NJ 08534

CRAIG, RAYMOND ALLEN, b Mansfield, Ohio, Apr 19, 20; m 48; c 3. CHEMISTRY. *Educ:* Muskingum Col, BS, 43; Ohio State Univ, MS & PhD(phys & org chem), 48. *Prof Exp:* Chemist, Am Petrol Inst, Ohio, 43-44; asst chem, Ohio State Univ, 44-47; res chemist nylon res lab, 48-51, res supvr, 52-54, dacron res lab, 54-57, sr res supvr, 57-59, res mgr, 59-63, textile res lab, Del, 63-66, dir, Benger Lab, Va, 66-68, tech dir, Du Pont Int, SA, Switz, 68-74, TECH MGR, E I DU PONT DE NEMOURS & CO, INC, 74- *Mem:* Am Chem Soc. *Res:* High polymer chemistry and polymer chemistry; synthetic fibers. *Mailing Add:* 512 Kerfoot Farm Rd Woodbrook Wilmington DE 19803

CRAIG, RAYMOND S, b DeLand, Fla, Jan 11, 17; m 50; c 2. PHYSICAL CHEMISTRY. *Educ:* Stetson Univ, BS, 39; Univ Pittsburgh, PhD(chem), 44. *Prof Exp:* Res assoc, Allegany Ballistics Lab, 44-46; sr res fel, 46-49, from asst res prof to assoc res prof, 49-59, PROF CHEM, UNIV PITTSBURGH, 59- *Mem:* Am Chem Soc. *Res:* Magnetic and thermal properties of metals and intermetallic compounds; low temperature calorimetry. *Mailing Add:* Dept of Chem Univ of Pittsburgh Pittsburgh PA 15260

CRAIG, RICHARD, b Carnegie, Pa, July 14, 37; m 61; c 3. PLANT GENETICS, PLANT BREEDING. *Educ:* Pa State Univ, BS, 59, MS, 60, PhD(genetics & breeding), 63. *Prof Exp:* Asst hort, 59-61 & comput sci, 61-62, instr plant breeding & asst prof, 63-71, ASSOC PROF PLANT BREEDING, PA STATE UNIV, 71-, ASSOC PROF HORT EXTEN, 77- *Honors & Awards:* Spec Recommendation Hort Achievement, 64. *Mem:* Am Soc Hort Sci. *Res:* Genetics, cytology and breeding of floricultural plants, including geraniums, zinnias, and holly. *Mailing Add:* Dept of Hort 106 Tyson Bldg Pa State Univ University Park PA 16802

CRAIG, RICHARD ANDERSON, theoretical physics, solid state physics, see previous edition

CRAIG, RICHARD ANSEL, b Abington, Mass, Mar 23, 22; m 44; c 5. METEOROLOGY. *Educ:* Harvard Univ, AB, 42; Mass Inst Technol, SM, 44, ScD(meteorol), 48. *Prof Exp:* Asst astron, Harvard Observ, 40-42; asst, Mass Inst Technol, 44, res assoc meteorol, 47; fel, Harvard Observ, 48-51; meteorologist, Air Force Cambridge Res Ctr, 51-58; PROF METEOROL, FLA STATE UNIV, 58- *Concurrent Pos:* Mem staff, Oceanog Inst, Woods Hole, 46. *Mem:* Fel Am Meteorol Soc; Am Geophys Union. *Res:* Spherical harmonics applied to atmosphere; atmospheric ozone; stratospheric meteorology. *Mailing Add:* Dept of Meteorol Fla State Univ Tallahassee FL 32306

CRAIG, ROBERT BRUCE, b Washington, DC, Apr 22, 44; m 66; c 2. ANIMAL ECOLOGY. *Educ:* Univ Calif, Davis, BS, 70, MS, 72, PhD(ecol), 74. *Prof Exp:* Res assoc zool, Univ Calif, Davis; res staff mem ecol, Environ Sci Div, Oak Ridge Nat Lab, 74-78, prog mgr ecol, 78-81; DEPT MGR, HENNINGSON, DURHAM & RICHARDSON, 81- *Mem:* Ecol Soc Am; Am Ornithologists Union; Am Nuclear Soc. *Res:* Predation theory and predatory behavior of insectivorous birds; environmental impact analysis and environmental effects of developing energy technologies. *Mailing Add:* Bldg 1505 Environ Sci Div Oak Ridge Nat Lab Box X Oak Ridge TN 37830

CRAIG, ROBERT GEORGE, b Charlevoix, Mich, Sept 8, 23; m 45; c 3. DENTAL RESEARCH. *Educ:* Univ Mich, BS, 44, MS, 51, PhD(chem), 55. *Prof Exp:* Chemist, anal res, Linde Air Prods, 44-50 & friction & lubrication, Tex Co, 54-55; assoc res chemist high polymers, Eng Res Inst, 55-57, from asst prof to assoc prof, 57-65, PROF DENT, UNIV MICH, 65-, CHMN DEPT DENT MAT, 69- *Honors & Awards:* Thomas Young Award, 69; Wilmer Souder Award in Dent Mat, Dent Mat Group, Int Asn Dent Res, 75; Clemson Award, Soc Biomat, 78. *Mem:* Am Chem Soc; Am Asn Dent Schs; Int Asn Dent Res; Soc Biomat. *Res:* Colloid and surface chemistry; polymer chemistry; dental materials; bio-engineering; friction and wear; stress analysis. *Mailing Add:* 1503 Wells St Ann Arbor MI 48104

CRAIG, ROY PHILLIP, b Durango, Colo, May 10, 24. ENVIRONMENTAL MANAGEMENT, SCIENCE WRITING. *Educ:* Univ Colo, BA, 48; Calif Inst Technol, MS, 50; Iowa State Col, PhD(chem), 52. *Prof Exp:* Asst, Iowa State Col, 49-52; prof chemist, Dow Chem Co, 52-56, group leader, 56-60; lectr phys chem, Univ Colo, 61-65, assoc prof phys chem & coordr phys sci, div integrated studies, 65-68; vis prof, Univ Hawaii, 69 & Colo Col, 79; TECH & EDUC CONSULT & SCI WRITER, 69-; pres, 74-81, DIR, FOUR CORNERS ENVIRON RES INST, 74- *Mem:* AAAS. *Res:* Impact of science on society; relation between science and the humanities; physical sciences for nonscience majors; solution adsorption; environmental management; solar energy utilization. *Mailing Add:* La Boca Ranch Box 711 Ignacio CO 81137

CRAIG, STANLEY HAROLD, b New York, NY, Oct 24, 09. RADIOLOGY. *Educ:* NY Univ, BS, 30; Univ Basel, MD, 35. *Prof Exp:* Resident radiol, Beth Israel Hosp, NY, 35-38; PROF RADIOL, NEW YORK MED COL, 48- *Concurrent Pos:* Consult radiol, Med Dept, NY Times, 48- *Mem:* Radiol Soc NAm; Int Skeletal Soc; AMA; fel Am Col Gastroenterol; fel Am Col Radiol. *Mailing Add:* 1 Manor Ln Lawrence NY 11559

CRAIG, SUSAN WALKER, b New York, NY; m 68. IMMUNOBIOLOGY. *Educ:* Univ Pa, BA, 67; Johns Hopkins Univ, PhD(biol), 73. *Prof Exp:* Fel molecular pharmacol, Dept Pharmacol, 73-75, ASST PROF PHYSIOL CHEM, SCH MED, JOHNS HOPKINS UNIV, 75- *Concurrent Pos:* Fel, Jane Coffin Childs Mem Fund Med Res, 73-75. *Res:* Cell surface control of lymphocyte physiology. *Mailing Add:* Sch of Med Johns Hopkins Univ Dept Physiol Chem 725 N Wolfe St Baltimore MD 21205

CRAIG, THEODORE WARREN, b San Francisco, Calif, May 21, 40; m 67; c 2. FOOD SCIENCE. *Educ:* Univ Calif, Berkeley, BS, 62, MBA, 75; Mass Inst Technol, PhD(org chem), 66. *Prof Exp:* Sr res chemist, Cent Res Labs, Gen Mills, Inc, Minn, 65-68; proj leader, Foremost Res Ctr, 68-71, group leader, 71-73, tech mgr, Food Prod Div, 73-74, mgr prod/process develop, 74-76, DIR RES & DEVELOP, FOREMOST FOODS CO, 76- *Mem:* Inst Food Technol; Am Dairy Sci Asn. *Res:* Food and protein chemistry; cereal and dairy by-products technology; food product development. *Mailing Add:* Foremost Res & Develop Ctr Foremost Foods Co 6363 Clark Ave Dublin CA 94566

CRAIG, WILFRED STUART, b New Hartford, Mo, Aug 11, 16; m 44; c 3. ENTOMOLOGY. *Educ:* Univ Mo, BS & AB, 47; Iowa State Col, PhD(entom), 53. *Prof Exp:* Asst state entomologist, Mo, 47-49; asst entomologist, Iowa State Col, 49-53, asst state entomologist, Iowa State Univ, 53-60, state entomologist, Univ & entomologist, Exp Sta, 60-65; EXTEN ENTOMOLOGIST, UNIV MO, COLUMBIA, 65- *Mem:* Entom Soc Am. *Res:* Biology and control of nursery insects; taxonomy of Anthicidae and other Coleoptera. *Mailing Add:* 2313 Braemore Rd Columbia MO 65201

CRAIG, WILLIAM F, agronomy, plant genetics, see previous edition

CRAIG, WILLIAM WARREN, b Kansas City, Mo, Apr 1, 35; m 61; c 4. GEOLOGY. *Educ:* Univ Mo, Columbia, BA, 57, MA, 61; Univ Tex, Austin, PhD(geol), 68. *Prof Exp:* Assoc prof geol, Northeastern Mo State Col, 65-68; asst prof, 68-71, assoc prof, 71-77, PROF EARTH SCI, UNIV NEW ORLEANS, 77- *Mem:* Geol Soc Am; Soc Econ Paleont & Mineral. *Res:* Cretaceous nonmarine Ostracodes; midcontinent Ordovician and Silurian stratigraphy and conodont biostratigraphy. *Mailing Add:* Dept of Earth Sci Univ of New Orleans Lakefront New Orleans LA 70148

CRAIG, WINSTON JOHN, b Melbourne, Australia, Sept 21, 47; m 71; c 1. NUTRITIONAL BIOCHEMISTRY, LIPID BIOCHEMISTRY. *Educ:* Univ Newcastle, Australia, BSc Hons, 68; Univ Queensland, Australia, PhD(organ chem), 71; Loma Linda Univ, MPH, 75. *Prof Exp:* Fel marine chem, Australian Nat Univ, 71-72; res assoc insect chem, Col Environ Sci & Forestry, State Univ NY, 72, res assoc marine chem, sci & forestry, Univ Okla, 72-73; res asst nutrit, Loma Linda Univ, 74; instr sci, Kingsway Col, Can, 74-76; asst prof sci, chem & health, Adventist Col, WAfrica, 76-79; ASST PROF NUTRIT, SCH HEALTH, LOMA LINDA UNIV, 79- *Concurrent Pos:* Consult, Med Ctr, Loma Linda Univ, 81- & coordr, Grad Nutrit Prog, 81-; lectr, Cent Am Master Sci Pub Health Prog, 79-; guest lectr, Col Osteop Med, Pomona, Calif, 82- *Mem:* Am Dietetic Asn. *Res:* Effect of dietary factors (dietary fiber, type of fat, trace minerals and caffeine) upon a persons health and nutritional well-being; advantages of a vegetarian diet; nutritional status of refugees in orange county, California. *Mailing Add:* 222 Harruby Dr Calimesa CA 92320

CRAIGE, ERNEST, b El Paso, Tex, 1918; m 46; c 4. MEDICINE. *Educ:* Univ NC, BA, 39; Harvard Univ, MD, 43. *Prof Exp:* From intern to resident med, Mass Gen Hosp, 43-48, resident cardiol, 49-50, asst med, 50-52; from asst prof to assoc prof, 52-62, PROF MED, SCH MED, UNIV NC, CHAPEL HILL, 62- *Concurrent Pos:* Clin & res fel med, Mass Gen Hosp, 49-50; fel med, Harvard Med Sch, 49-50; chief cardiol, NC Mem Hosp, 52-78. *Mem:* Asn Univ Cardiologists; Am Heart Asn; fel Am Col Physicians; fel Am Col Cardiol; Am Clin & Climat Asn. *Res:* Echo-phono-cardiography and other non-invasive methods of studying cardiac function. *Mailing Add:* 338 Clin Sci Bldg 229H Univ of NC Sch of Med Chapel Hill NC 27514

CRAIGHEAD, JOHN EDWARD, b Pittsburgh, Pa, Aug 14, 30; m 57; c 2. PATHOLOGY, VIROLOGY. *Educ:* Univ Utah, BS, 52, MD, 56. *Prof Exp:* Intern med, Barnes Hosp, St Louis, Mo, 56-57; jr asst resident, Peter Bent Brigham Hosp, 60-61, sr asst resident, 61-62, chief resident path, 62-63, assoc, 63-68; PROF PATH, COL MED, UNIV VT, 68-, CHMN DEPT, 74- *Concurrent Pos:* Teaching fel, Harvard Med Sch, 61-63; assoc, 63-66, asst prof, 66-68; assoc mem comn viral infections, Armed Forces Epidemiol Bd, 66; mem infectious dis adv comt, Nat Inst Allergy & Infectious Dis, 71-75. *Mem:* Am Soc Exp path; Am Asn Path & Bact; Int Acad Path; Soc Exp Biol & Med; Am Soc Clin Path. *Res:* Biology, pathogenesis and pathology of virus disease in man and animals; diabetes; pulmonary disease. *Mailing Add:* Dept Path Col Med Univ Vt Burlington VT 05401

CRAIGHEAD, JOHN J, b Washington, DC, Aug 14, 16; m 44; c 3. ECOLOGY. *Educ:* Pa State Col, BA, 39; Univ Mich, MS, 40, PhD, 50. *Prof Exp:* Biologist, NY Zool Soc, 47-49; dir survival training for armed forces, US Dept Defense, 50-52; wildlife biologist & leader Mont Coop Wildlife Res Unit, Bur Sport Fisheries & Wildlife, 52-77; PROF ZOOL & FORESTRY, UNIV MONT, 52- *Concurrent Pos:* Grants, Wildlife Mgt Inst, leader wildlife ecol of grizzly bear & radiotracking grizzly bears; AEC, radiotracking & telemetering systs large western mammals; NASA, satellite tracking large mammals & habitat mapping; Bur Sport Fisheries & Wildlife, surv peregrine eyries & studies ecol grizzly bear; US Forest Serv & Mont Fish & Game Dept, eval grizzly bear habitat. *Honors & Awards:* Bur Sport Fisheries & Wildlife Superior Performance Award, 65; Citation for Organizing & Admin Navy's Land Survival Training Prog, Secy Defense; Arthur S Einarsen Award, Wildlife Soc, 77; Am Motors Conserv Award, 78; John Oliver LaGorce Gold Medal, Nat Geol Soc, 79. *Mem:* Wildlife Soc (vpres, 62-63); AAAS; Wilderness Alliance. *Res:* Raptor predation; waterfowl; population dynamics. *Mailing Add:* 5125 Orchard Lane Missoula MT 59801

CRAIGMILES, JULIAN PRYOR, b Thomasville, Ga, Jan 17, 21; m 48; c 3. AGRONOMY. *Educ:* Univ Ga, BSA, 42, MSA, 48; Cornell Univ, PhD, 52. *Prof Exp:* Asst, Coker Pedigreed Seed Co, SC, 41; asst agronomist, Ga Crop Improv Asn, 46-48; agronomist, Ga Exp Sta, 48-64; PROF & RESIDENT DIR, AGR RES & EXTEN CTR, TEX A&M UNIV, 64- *Concurrent Pos:* Res award, Ga Plant Food Educ Soc, 59- *Honors & Awards:* Outstanding Researcher, Sears Roebuck & Co, 58. *Mem:* Am Soc Agron; Weed Sci Soc Am; Am Genetic Asn; Crop Sci Soc Am. *Res:* Soybean breeding; rice and forage management; seed production of rice, soybeans and forages; developed cytoplasmic sterile sudan grass, which led to development and release of hybrid sudan grass; developement of varieties of grasses and soybeans; management of rice, soybeans, forages and other crops. *Mailing Add:* Tex A&M Agr Res & Exten Ctr Rte 7 Box 999 Beaumont TX 77706

CRAIK, DONALD WILLIAM, b Man, Can, Aug 26, 31; m 53; c 3. MECHANICAL ENGINEERING. *Educ:* Univ Man, BSc, 56; Univ Minn, MSc, 61. *Prof Exp:* Lectr metall & heat transfer, Univ Man, 57-58, asst prof, 58-64; dir res, Man Res Coun, 64-67; minister minerals & natural resources, Man Govt, 68-69, minister educ, 68-69; pres & gen mgr, Interdisciplinery Systs Ltd, 69-76; CONSULT ENGR, 76- *Concurrent Pos:* Nat Res Coun & Defense Res Bd grants; mem, Man Legis Assembly, 66-81. *Mem:* Am Soc Metals; Eng Inst Can. *Res:* Heat transfer, especially infrared radiometry; solar radiometry; low grade energy collection. *Mailing Add:* 3 River Lane Winnipeg MB R2M 3Y8 Can

CRAIK, EVA LEE, b Gatesville, Tex, Aug 12, 19; m 41; c 4. BIOLOGY, SCIENCE EDUCATION. *Educ:* Tex Women's Univ, BS, 40; Hardin-Simmons Univ, MEd, 60; NTex State Univ, EdD(biol), 66. *Prof Exp:* Teacher, Ranger High Sch & Jr Col, Tex, 40-43, pub sch, Kans, 43-44 & pub schs, Tex, 59-62; from instr to assoc prof, 62-73, PROF BIOL, HARDIN-SIMMONS UNIV, 73-, COORDR SCI EDUC, 67- *Mem:* Nat Sci Teachers Asn; Nat Asn Biol Teachers. *Res:* Relative effectiveness of inductive-deductive and deductive-descriptive methods of teaching college zoology. *Mailing Add:* 1802 N 11th Abilene TX 79603

CRAIN, CULLEN MALONE, b Goodnight, Tex, Sept 10, 20; m 43; c 2. ELECTRONICS. *Educ:* Univ Tex, BS, 42, MS, 47, PhD(elec eng), 52. *Prof Exp:* Engr, Philco Corp, Philadelphia, 42-43; instr elec eng, Univ Tex, 43-44; proj engr, Off Res & Inventions, US Dept Navy, Washington, DC, 45-46; asst prof elec eng & elec engr, Res Lab, Univ Tex, 46-52, assoc prof, 52-57; group leader, Electronic Dept, 57-68, dep dept head, Eng Sci Dept, 68-76, ASSOC DEPT HEAD, ENG & APPL SCI DEPT, RAND CORP, 76- *Concurrent Pos:* Chmn, US Comn F, Internation Union Radio Sci, 63-66; mem frequency mgt adv coun, Off Telecommun Policy, Exec Off of the President, 65- *Mem:* Nat Acad Eng; fel Inst Elec & Electronics Engrs. *Res:* Propagation of radio waves; radio communication systems; radio physics. *Mailing Add:* Eng & Appl Sci Dept Rand Corp 1700 Main St Santa Monica CA 90406

CRAIN, DONALD LEE, b St Joseph, Mo, Apr 20, 33; m 53; c 3. ORGANIC CHEMISTRY. *Educ:* William Jewell Col, AB, 54; Purdue Univ, PhD(org chem), 58. *Prof Exp:* Res chemist, Res & Develop, 58-78, group leader, 62-65, sect suprv, 65-68, br mgr, 68-76, budget mgr chem group, 76-77, dir plastics & anal, 77-81, MGR, POLYMERS & MAT DIV, RES & DEVELOP, PHILLIPS PETROL CO, 81- *Mem:* Am Chem Soc; Soc Plastics Engrs. *Res:* Petrochemicals; polymers, composites and advanced materials. *Mailing Add:* 254 RB-7 Phillips Petrol Co Bartlesville OK 74004

CRAIN, JAMES LARRY, zoology, see previous edition

CRAIN, RICHARD CULLEN, b Portsmouth, Va, Feb 8, 51; m 72; c 2. LIPIDOLOGY. *Educ:* Dartmouth Col, BA, 73; Univ Rochester, PhD(biochem), 78. *Prof Exp:* Fel biochem, Cornell Univ, 78-80; ASST PROF, UNIV CONN, 80- *Mem:* Am Chem Soc; Sigma Xi. *Res:* Structure and function of biological membranes; phospholipid transfer proteins and their role in regulation of membrane phospholipid composition; membrane abnormalities of neoplastic cells. *Mailing Add:* Biol Sci Group U-125 Univ Conn Storrs CT 06268

CRAIN, RICHARD WILLSON, JR, b Denver, Colo, July 2, 31; m 55; c 6. MECHANICAL ENGINEERING. *Educ:* Univ Wash, BS, 53, MS, 55; Univ Mich, PhD(mech eng), 65. *Prof Exp:* Assoc prof, 65-74, PROF MECH ENG, WASH STATE UNIV, 74-, CHMN DEPT, 76- *Mem:* AAAS; Am Soc Mech Engrs; Am Soc Eng Educ; Sigma Xi. *Res:* Evaluation of thermodynamic properties, especially at cryogenic temperatures; equations of state for gases; thermal pollution of water bodies; applied thermodynamics; thermal power systems; waste heat utilization. *Mailing Add:* Dept of Mech Eng Wash State Univ Pullman WA 99164

CRAIN, STANLEY M, b New York, NY, Feb 5, 23; m 46; c 2. NEUROPHYSIOLOGY, DEVELOPMENTAL NEUROBIOLOGY. *Educ:* Brooklyn Col, AB, 43; Columbia Univ, PhD(biophys), 54. *Prof Exp:* Group leader radiol res, Health Physics Div, Argonne Nat Lab, 45-47; res electrophysiologist, Dept Neurol, Columbia Univ, 50-57; res cell physiologist & sect head nerve tissue cult lab, Abbott Labs, Ill, 57-61; asst prof anat, Dept Neurol, Col Physicians & Surgeons, Columbia Univ, 61-65; from assoc prof to prof physiol, 65-74, PROF NEUROSCI & PHYSIOL, ALBERT EINSTEIN COL MED, 69- *Concurrent Pos:* Grass res fel, Marine Biol Lab, Woods Hole, Mass, 57; NIH res career develop fel, 61-65; Kennedy scholar, Rose F Kennedy Ctr Ment Retardation & Human Develop, 65-75; assoc ed, J Neurobiol, 70-, Develop Neurosci, 78- & Develop Brain Res, 81-; chmn med adv bd, Dysautonomia Found, 77-79 & 81-82. *Honors & Awards:* Lucy Moses Prize Neurol Award, Col Physicians & Surgeons, Columbia Univ, 66; Dysautonomia Found Annual Award, 78. *Mem:* Am Physiol Soc; Am Asn Anatomists; Am Soc Cell Biologists; Soc Neurosci; Biophys Soc. *Res:* Electrophysiologic and cytologic research on tissue cultures of mammalian brain, spinal cord and neuromuscular systems, especially during development of synaptic and other organotypic relations after isolation of fetal neural tissues in vitro. *Mailing Add:* Albert Einstein Col of Med 1300 Morris Park Ave Bronx NY 10461

CRAIN, WILLIAM RATHBONE, JR, b Cuero, Tex, Nov 30, 44. MOLECULAR BIOLOGY. *Educ:* Univ Tex, Austin, BA, 67; Univ Houston, MS, 69; Grad Sch Biomed Sci, Univ Tex, PhD(molecular biol), 74. *Prof Exp:* Fel molecular biol, Calif Inst Technol, 74-76; STAFF SCIENTIST MOLECULAR BIOL, WORCESTER FOUND EXP BIOL, 76- *Mem:* AAAS; Am Soc Cell Biol. *Res:* Control of gene expression; organization, function and evolution of genetic information. *Mailing Add:* Worcester Found for Exp Biol Shrewsbury MA 01545

CRAINE, ELLIOTT MAURICE, b Burlington, Iowa, Oct 5, 24; m 50; c 2. ANALYTICAL BIOCHEMISTRY. *Educ:* Univ Ill, AB, 49, BS, 51, PhD(biochem), 52. *Prof Exp:* Chemist, Agr Res Serv, USDA, 54-58; res chemist, Upjohn Co, 58-63; res biochemist, Hess & Clark Div, Rhodia, Inc, 63-65, head biochem, 65-80; MGR, METAB & ANAL CHEM, WIL RES LABS, 80- *Mem:* AAAS; Am Chem Soc. *Res:* Chemistry of seed proteins; isolation of antibiotics; drug metabolism; biochemistry of ruminants; metabolism of foreign compounds in animals, plants and soil; drugs and pesticides; analytical biochemistry; isolation of natural chemicals. *Mailing Add:* 827 Ridge Rd Ashland OH 44805

CRAINE, LLOYD BERNARD, b St Paul, Minn, July 8, 21; m 45; c 4. ELECTRICAL ENGINEERING. *Educ:* Ore State Col, BS, 47, MS, 50, EE, 53. *Prof Exp:* Instr elec eng, Ore State Col, 48-50; asst prof, Univ Idaho, 50-56; assoc prof, 56-64, PROF ELEC ENG, WASH STATE UNIV, 64- *Concurrent Pos:* Prog dir aeronomy, NSF, 65-66; Cong fel, Inst Elec & Electronic Engrs, 74-75; prof dir, Wash Energy Exten Serv, 77-78. *Mem:* Inst Elec & Electronics Engrs; Am Soc Eng Educ; Am Geophys Union; AAAS. *Res:* Electromagnetic wave propagation; transmission line radio noise problems; upper atmosphere physics; electrical measurements; energy technology and behavior modification. *Mailing Add:* Dept of Elec Eng Wash State Univ Pullman WA 99164

CRAKER, LYLE E, b Reedsburg, Wis, Feb 3, 41; m 63; c 3. PLANT PHYSIOLOGY. *Educ:* Univ Wis, Madison, BS, 63; Univ Minn, St Paul, PhD(agron), 67. *Prof Exp:* From asst prof to assoc prof, 69-75, actg assoc dean, Grad Sch, 78-80, PROF PLANT PHYSIOL, UNIV MASS, 75- *Mem:* Am Soc Plant Physiol; Am Soc Agron; Crop Sci Soc Am. *Res:* Utilization of lights and plant hormones for regulated crop production and storage. *Mailing Add:* Dept of Plant & Soil Sci Univ of Mass Amherst MA 01002

CRALL, JAMES MONROE, b Monongahela, Pa, July 13, 14; m 43; c 2. PLANT BREEDING, PLANT PATHOLOGY. *Educ:* Purdue Univ, BS, 39; Univ Mo, AM, 41, PhD(plant path), 48. *Prof Exp:* Tomato blight agent, Exp Sta, Purdue Univ & Bur Plant Indust, USDA, 38-39; asst bot, Univ Mo, 39-42, jr plant pathologist, Exp Sta, 46-48; res asst prof plant path, Iowa State Univ & assoc path, USDA, 48-52, dir, Agr Res Ctr, Leesburg, Agr Exp Sta, Inst Food & Agr Sci, USDA, Univ Fla, 52-77, PROF PLANT PATH, UNIV FLA, 52- *Mem:* AAAS; Am Soc Hort Sci; Am Phytopath Soc; Mycol Soc Am; Coun Agr Sci & Technol. *Res:* Diseases of watermelon and grape; watermelon breeding. *Mailing Add:* Agr Res Ctr Univ of Fla PO Box 388 Leesburg FL 32748

CRALLEY, JOHN CLEMENT, b Carmi, Ill, Oct 16, 32; m 63; c 3. HUMAN ANATOMY, PHYSIOLOGY. *Educ:* Univ Ill, BS, 56, MS, 60, PhD(zool), 65. *Prof Exp:* Asst prof zool, 63-76, ASSOC PROF ANAT, ILL STATE UNIV, 76- *Mem:* AAAS. *Res:* Fish physiology and acclimation; blood vascular systems; functional anatomy of the human foot. *Mailing Add:* Dept of Biol Ill State Univ Normal IL 61761

CRAM, DONALD JAMES, b Chester, Vt, Apr 22, 19; m 69. ORGANIC CHEMISTRY. *Educ:* Rollins Col, BS, 41; Univ Nebr, MS, 42; Harvard Univ, PhD(org chem), 47. *Prof Exp:* Res chemist, Merck & Co, NJ, 42-45; instr org chem & Am Chem Soc fel mold metabolites, 47-48, from asst prof to assoc prof chem, 48-56, PROF CHEM, UNIV CALIF, LOS ANGELES, 56- *Concurrent Pos:* Guggenheim fel, 54-55. *Honors & Awards:* Herbert Newby McCoy Award; Soc Chem Mfg Asn Award; Award Creative Work Synthetic Org Chem, Am Chem Soc, 65, Arthur C Cope Award, 74; Calif Scientist of Year, Calif Mus Sci & Indust, 74. *Mem:* Nat Acad Sci; Am Chem Soc; Swiss Chem Soc; Am Acad Arts & Sci. *Res:* Stereochemistry, especially of carbanions and substitutions at sulfur; macro ring chemistry; synthetic multiheteromacrocycles that model enzyme systems in complexation and catalysis; highly structured molecular complexes; host-guest chemistry. *Mailing Add:* Dept Chem Univ Calif Los Angeles CA 90024

CRAM, LEIGHTON SCOTT, b Emporia, Kans, Oct 21, 42; m 65. BIOPHYSICS. *Educ:* Kans State Teachers Col, BA, 64; Vanderbilt Univ, MS, 66; Pa State Univ, PhD(biophys), 69. *Prof Exp:* Fel, 69-71, STAFF MEM BIOPHYS, BIOMED RES GROUP, LOS ALAMOS NAT LAB, 71- *Concurrent Pos:* Consult, Particle Technol Inc, 72-75 & Coulter Electronics, 75- *Mem:* AAAS; Biophys Soc; Soc Anal Cytol. *Res:* Photon emission from thin films bombarded by electrons and DNA conformation in bacterial viruses; development and application of high speed methods of obtaining data on cellular properties and intracellular components, and cytogenetics of tumorigenic cells. *Mailing Add:* Biomed Res Group H-10 Los Alamos Nat Lab Los Alamos NM 87544

CRAM, SHELDON LEWIS, b Maxbass, NDak, Nov 21, 19; m 43; c 5. PHYSICS. *Educ:* NDak State Teacher's Col, BA, 40; Ore State Col, BS, 41; Colo State Univ, AM, 50. *Prof Exp:* Prof physics, NDak State Teacher's Col, 46-49; prof physics, Westmar Col, 50-75; PROF PHYSICS, IOWA CENT COMMUNITY COL, 75- *Mem:* AAAS; Am Asn Physics Teachers; Am Inst Physics. *Res:* Science education; electronics. *Mailing Add:* Dept of Physics Iowa Cent Community Col Ft Dodge IA 50501

CRAM, STUART PROUD, b Emporia, Kans, Apr 23, 39; m 62; c 2. ANALYTICAL CHEMISTRY. *Educ:* Kans State Teachers Col, BA, 61; Univ Wis, MS, 63; Univ Ill, PhD(chem), 66. *Prof Exp:* Asst prof chem, Univ Fla, 66-74; MGR GAS CHROMATOGRAPHY, VARIAN AEROGRAPH,

74- *Mem:* Am Chem Soc; Soc Appl Spectros. *Res:* Analytical chemistry, including gas chromatography, neutron activation analysis, and the development of analytical instrumentation and methodology. *Mailing Add:* Varian Aerograph 2700 Mitchell Dr Walnut Creek CA 94598

CRAM, WILLIAM THOMAS, b South Burnaby, BC, Oct 20, 27; m 51; c 2. ENTOMOLOGY. *Educ:* Univ BC, BSA, 50; Ore State Univ, MS, 55, PhD(entom), 64. *Prof Exp:* SCIENTIST, RES STA, CAN DEPT AGR, 50- *Mem:* Entom Soc Am; Entom Soc Can. *Res:* Ecology of root weevils as pests of berry crops; nutrition, host selection and fecundity of root weevils, especially Otiorhynchus sulcatus; pests of berry crops. *Mailing Add:* 2526 Edgar Crescent Vancouver BC V6L 2G5 Can

CRAMBLETT, HENRY G, b Scio, Ohio, Feb 8, 29; m 60; c 2. PEDIATRICS, VIROLOGY. *Educ:* Mt Union Col, BS, 50; Univ Cincinnati, MD, 53; Am Bd Pediat, dipl; Am Bd Med Microbiol, dipl. *Prof Exp:* Intern med, Harvard Med Serv, Boston City Hosp, 53-54; resident pediat, Children's Hosp, Cincinnati, Ohio, 54-55; res assoc, Clin Ctr, NIH, 55-57; resident & instr pediat, Univ Iowa, 57-58, asst prof, 58-60; dir virol lab, Bowman Gray Sch Med, 60-64, assoc prof pediat, 60-63, prof, 63-64; chmn dept med microbiol, 66-73, dean col med, 73-80, actg vpres med affairs, 74-80, PROF PEDIAT, OHIO STATE UNIV, 64-, PROF MED MICROBIOL, 66-, VPRES HEALTH SCI, 80- *Concurrent Pos:* Leukemia chemother grant, 58-60; career develop award, 62; Carey & Hofheimer scholastic awards, Univ Cincinnati; dir res & div microbiol, Children's Hosp, Columbus, 64-66, exec dir, Res Found, 66-73. *Mem:* Soc Pediat Res; Soc Exp Biol & Med; Am Acad Pediat; Infectious Dis Soc Am; fel Am Acad Microbiol. *Res:* Pediatric virology; infectious diseases; antibiotic research and immunology of the newborn and infant. *Mailing Add:* Off Health Sci Ohio State Univ 370 W Ninth Ave Columbus OH 43210

CRAMER, ARCHIE BARRETT, b Winnipeg, Man, Oct 23, 09; m 35; c 2. FOOD CHEMISTRY. *Educ:* Univ Man, BSc, 34, MSc, 35; McGill Univ, PhD(wood chem), 39. *Prof Exp:* Asst, Carnegie Inst Technol, 39-41; res chemist, Miner Labs, 41-46; chief chemist, 46-63, VPRES RES & TECH DIR, F & F LABS, 63- *Honors & Awards:* Stroud Jordan Award, 63. *Mem:* AAAS; Am Chem Soc; Am Inst Chem; Am Asn Candy Technol; Nat Confectioners Asn US. *Res:* Wood and lignin chemistry; chemistry and preparation of lecithin; general carbohydrate chemistry; general chemistry of candy and food manufacture; preparation of certain oils and derivatives from lignin; preparation of glycerine derivatives; carbohydrate food flavor. *Mailing Add:* F & F Labs Inc 3501 W 48th Pl Chicago IL 60632

CRAMER, CALVIN O, b Prairie du Sac, Wis, May 18, 26; m 52; c 2. AGRICULTURAL & CIVIL ENGINEERING. *Educ:* Univ Wis-Madison, BS(agr) & BS(civil eng), 52, MS, 54, PhD(civil eng), 67. *Prof Exp:* From instr to asst prof agr eng, Univ Wis-Madison, 54-64; res engr, US Forest Prod Lab, 64-66; assoc prof agr eng, 67-71, PROF AGR ENG, UNIV WIS-MADISON, 72- *Mem:* Am Soc Agr Engrs; Am Soc Civil Engrs. *Res:* Dairy cattle and swine housing; timber design; farm waste disposal. *Mailing Add:* Dept of Agr Eng Univ of Wis Madison WI 53706

CRAMER, CARL FREDERICK, b Raton, NMex, June 7, 22; m 49; c 2. PHYSIOLOGY. *Educ:* Univ NMex, BS, 44, MS, 47; Univ Calif, PhD(physiol), 53. *Prof Exp:* Res assoc physiol, Med Sch, Tulane Univ, 54; ASSOC PROF PHYSIOL, UNIV BC, 55- *Mem:* Am Physiol Soc; Am Inst Nutrit; Can Physiol Soc. *Res:* Bone and gastrointestinal mineral physiology; turnover of radioactive tracers and removal of fission products. *Mailing Add:* Dept of Physiol Univ of BC Vancouver BC V6T 1W5 Can

CRAMER, DAVID ALAN, b Ann Arbor, Mich, Aug 7, 25; m 45; c 3. ANIMAL NUTRITION. *Educ:* Colo State Univ, BS, 49, MS, 55; Ore State Univ, PhD(animal nutrit & biochem), 60. *Prof Exp:* Res chemist, Arapahoe Chem, Inc, 55-56; asst prof animal nutrit & vet sci, Calif State Polytech Col, 56-58; from asst prof to assoc prof biochem of animal prods, 60-68, prof, 68-80, PROF ANIMAL SCI, COLO STATE UNIV, 80- *Concurrent Pos:* Fulbright scholar, Dept Sci & Indust Res, NZ, 65-66. *Mem:* Am Soc Animal Sci; Am Meat Sci Asn; Am Oil Chem Soc; Inst Food Technol; Am Dairy Sci Asn. *Res:* Lipid metabolism in domestic animals, especially in the ruminant; meat flavor analysis; rumen metabolism. *Mailing Add:* Dept of Animal Sci Colo State Univ Ft Collins CO 80523

CRAMER, EVA BROWN, b New York, NY, June 6, 44; m 68; c 2. CELL BIOLOGY, IMMMUNOLOGY. *Educ:* Cornell Univ, BS, 65; Jefferson Med Col, MS, 67, PhD(anat), 69. *Prof Exp:* asst prof, 73-80, ASSOC PROF ANAT, STATE UNIV NY DOWNSTATE MED CTR, 80- *Concurrent Pos:* NIH fel, Col Physicians & Surgeons, Columbia Univ, 69-70; NH Heart Asn fel, Univ NH, 72-73. *Honors & Awards:* Charles W Labell Prize, Jefferson Med Col. *Mem:* Am Asn Anatomists; Am Soc Cell Biol; NY Acad Sci. *Res:* leucocyte chemotaxis, drapedesis; immunology. *Mailing Add:* Dept of Anat 450 Clarkson Ave Brooklyn NY 11203

CRAMER, GISELA TÜRCK, b Rohrbach, Ger, Mar 13, 34; m 67; c 3. BIOLOGICAL CHEMISTRY. *Educ:* Univ Frankfort, Dr phil nat(pharmaceut chem), 66. *Prof Exp:* Fel, Dept Pharmacol, Col Med, Univ Fla, 73; lab asst, Sch Med Sci, Univ Nev, Reno, 74-75, res asst, 75-81; MEM FAC, SCH MED, MERCER UNIV, GA, 81- *Concurrent Pos:* Anna Fuller Fund fel, Sch Med, Yale Univ, 66-67 & Col Med, Univ Fla, 67-68. *Res:* Cellular mechanisms of antitumor drugs; photodynamic action of dyes. *Mailing Add:* Sch Med Mercer Univ Macon GA 31027

CRAMER, HARRISON EMERY, b Johnstown, Pa, May 27, 19; m 42; c 4. AIR POLLUTION, METEOROLOGY. *Educ:* Amherst Col, AB, 41; Mass Inst Technol, SM, 43, ScD(meteorol), 48. *Prof Exp:* Instr meteorol, Mass Inst Technol, 42-44; meteorologist, Am Export Air Lines, 44; res assoc, Mass Inst Technol, 46-48, res meteorologist, 48-65; sr staff scientist, GCA Technol Div, 65-66, dir environ sci lab, 67-72, vpres, 69-72; PRES, H E CRAMER CO, INC, 72- *Mem:* Fel AAAS; NY Acad Sci; fel Am Meteorol Soc; Am Geophys Union; Royal Meteorol Soc. *Res:* Development and implemantation of mathematical models for air pollution and toxic hazard applications, meteorological instrumentation and air pollution data systems; quantitative assessment of air pollution and toxic hazard problems; analysis of air pollution and meteorological measurements. *Mailing Add:* H E Cramer Co Inc PO Box 8049 Salt Lake City UT 84108

CRAMER, HOWARD ROSS, b Chicago, Ill, Sept 17, 25; m 50. STRATIGRAPHY, INVERTEBRATE PALEONTOLOGY. *Educ:* Univ Ill, BS, 49, MS, 50; Northwestern Univ, PhD(geol), 54. *Prof Exp:* From instr to asst prof geol, Franklin & Marshall Col, 53-58; from asst prof to assoc prof, 58-79, PROF GEOL, EMORY UNIV, 79- *Mem:* Geol Soc Am; Am Asn Petrol Geol; Paleont Soc; Nat Asn Geol Teachers. *Res:* Bibliography; geology and history; petroleum and stratigraphy of Georgia. *Mailing Add:* Dept of Geol Emory Univ Atlanta GA 30322

CRAMER, JAMES D, b Canton, Ohio, Aug 4, 37; m 57; c 2. NUCLEAR PHYSICS. *Educ:* Calif State Univ, BS, 60; Univ Ore, MS, 62; Univ NMex, PhD(physics), 69. *Prof Exp:* Staff mem, Los Alamos Sci Lab, 62-70; staff scientist, Sci Applns Inc, 70-75, vpres, 75-78, dir, 72-80, sr vpres, 78-80; PRES, SCIENCE & ENG ASSOCS INC, 80- *Concurrent Pos:* Consult, Los Alamos Sci Lab, 70-72. *Mem:* Am Phys Soc; Inst Elec & Electronics Engrs. *Res:* Physics of gases and nuclear physics. *Mailing Add:* Sci & Eng Assocs Inc PO Box 3722 Albuquerque NM 87190

CRAMER, JANE HARRIS, b Chicago, Ill, Dec 1, 42; m 66; c 2. MOLECULAR BIOLOGY. *Educ:* Carleton Col, BA, 64; Northwestern Univ, PhD(microbiol), 70. *Prof Exp:* Fel, Univ Wis-Madison, 70-74, asst scientist, 74-77, assoc scientist molecular biol, 77-82; RES SCIENTIST, AGRIGENETICS CORP, 81- *Mem:* AAAS; Am Soc Microbiol; Genetics Soc Am; Sigma Xi; Asn Women in Sci. *Res:* Structure and organization of ribosomal RNA cistrons in yeast, their arrangement on different chromosomes and their replication during the cell cycle; structure, organization and replication of repetitive DNA in yeast; construction of cloning vectors and expression of foreign genes in yeast; development of vector systems for higher plants. *Mailing Add:* Agrigenetics Res Park 5649 E Buckeye Rd Madison WI 53716

CRAMER, JOHN ALLEN, b June 25, 43; US citizen; m 71; c 1. PHYSICS. *Educ:* Wheaton Col, Ill, BS, 65; Ohio Univ, MS, 68; Tex A&M Univ, PhD(physics), 75. *Prof Exp:* Instr physics, Wheaton Col, Ill, 68-71; asst prof physics, King's Col, NY, 76-80; ASST PROF PHYSICS, OGLETHORP UNIV, GA, 80- *Mem:* Am Phys Soc; AAAS; Am Sci Affil. *Res:* Magnetic effects in gases and solids. *Mailing Add:* Dept of Physics Oglethorpe Univ Atlanta GA 30319

CRAMER, JOHN GLEASON, b Houston, Tex, Oct 24, 34; m 61; c 3. NUCLEAR PHYSICS. *Educ:* Rice Univ, BA, 57, MA, 59, PhD(physics), 61. *Prof Exp:* Res assoc nuclear physics, Ind Univ, 61-63, asst prof physics, 63-64; from asst prof to assoc prof, 64-73, PROF PHYSICS, UNIV WASH, 73- *Mem:* AAAS; fel Am Phys Soc. *Res:* Heavy ion reactions and scattering; reactions with polarized particles; nuclear reactions and reaction mechanisms through measurements of reaction cross sections and angular correlations; applications of computers to nuclear research; nuclear astrophysics and gamma ray astronomy. *Mailing Add:* Nuclear Physics Lab GL-10 Univ of Wash Seattle WA 98195

CRAMER, JOHN WESLEY, b Freeport, Ill, Oct 15, 28; m 67; c 3. BIOCHEMISTRY. *Educ:* Beloit Col, BS, 50; Univ Wis, MS, 52, PhD(biochem), 55. *Prof Exp:* Instr oncol, Univ Wis, 59; instr pharmacol, Sch Med, Yale Univ, 59-61, asst prof, 61-67; assoc prof, Sch Med, Univ Fla, 67-73; prof pharmacol, Sch Med Sci, Univ Nev, Reno, 74-81; PROF PHARMACOL, SCH MED, MERCER UNIV, 81- *Concurrent Pos:* Fel biochem, Univ Wis, 55-57, fel oncol, 57-59; NIH & Am Cancer Soc grants. *Mem:* AAAS; Am Soc Pharmacol & Exp Therapeut; Am Asn Cancer Res; Am Soc Microbiol; Tissue Cult Asn. *Res:* Nutrition; vitamin D; cancer aromatic hydrocarbons; cell and viral nucleic acid synthesis and inhibition; antimetabolites. *Mailing Add:* Sch Med Mercer Univ Macon GA 31207

CRAMER, JOSEPH BENJAMIN, b Rochester, NY, Aug 24, 14; m 46; c 2. PSYCHIATRY, PSYCHOANALYSIS. *Educ:* Univ Rochester, BA, 36; NY Med Col, MD, 41; Inst Psychoanal, Chicago, cert psychoanal, 55. *Prof Exp:* Scottish Rite res fel schizophrenia, Sch Med, NY Univ, 47-49; assoc prof child psychiat, Univ Pittsburgh, 51-55; assoc prof & dir child psychiat, 55-68, PROF PSYCHIAT & PEDIAT, ALBERT EINSTEIN COL MED, 68- *Concurrent Pos:* Dir, Pittsburgh Guid Ctr, 51-53; consult, Scranton Guid Ctr, Pa, 55-57, Jewish Child Care Asn NY, 55-65 & Wiltwyck Sch, 73-74; mem steering comt, Conf Training in Child Psychiat, 63; mem, Conf Psychiat & Med Educ, 67. *Mem:* Am Acad Child Psychiat; Am Psychoanal Asn; Am Psychiat Asn; Am Orthopsychiat Asn. *Res:* Childhood schizophrenia; psychotherapy; medical education. *Mailing Add:* Dept of Psychiat Albert Einstein Col of Med New York NY 10461

CRAMER, KENNETH R(OBERT), b Dayton, Ohio, Mar 12, 27; m 50; c 1. AEROSPACE ENGINEERING. *Educ:* Univ Dayton, BME, 51; Ohio State Univ, MS, 56. *Prof Exp:* Aerospace res engr, Thermomech Res Lab, 51-72, AEROSPACE ENGR, FLIGHT DYNAMICS LAB, WRIGHT-PATTERSON AFB, 72- *Res:* Plasma theory; magnetofluid dynamics theory; heat transfer theory; boundary layer theory; two phase flow theory and experiment, electric arc heater theory and experiment; numerical aerodynamics. *Mailing Add:* 5596 Hugh Dr Dayton OH 45459

CRAMER, MICHAEL BROWN, b Dayton, Ohio, July 4, 38; m 62; c 3. CLINICAL RESEARCH. *Educ:* Purdue Univ, BS, 61, MS, 63, PhD(pharmacol), 65. *Prof Exp:* Prin investr, Armed Forces Radiobiol Res Inst, Defense Atomic Support Agency, US Army, 65-67; res pharmacologist, Procter & Gamble Co, 67-70; asst prof pharmcol, Col Pharm, Univ Houston, 70-75, assoc prof, 75-80; asst dir res support, Merrell Nat Lab, Richardson-Merrell Inc, 80-81, SR CLIN RES SCIENTIST, MERRELL-DOW

PHARMACEUTS, DOW CHEM CO, 81- *Concurrent Pos:* Zool instr, Montgomery Jr Col, 66-67; lectr pharm, Tex Tripartate Comt Continuing Educ, 73-80, Adv Course Pharmacol, Food & Drug Admin, Univ Houston, 74-79; fac adv, Poison Prevention Prog, Univ Houston, 72-80. *Mem:* AAAS. *Res:* New drug development: preparation of clinical research protocols, monitoring, evaluation of data and preparation of sponsor's summaries; evaluation and interpretation of clinical and preclinical data in preparation of investigator's brochures, investigation of new drugs and new drug application. *Mailing Add:* 2110 E Galbraith Rd Merrell-Dow Pharmaceuts Cincinnati OH 45215

CRAMER, ONEIDA MORNINGSTAR, neuroendocrinology, see previous edition

CRAMER, RICHARD (DAVID), b Mifflin, Pa, Aug 12, 13; m 37; c 4. ORGANOMETALLIC CHEMISTRY. *Educ:* Juniata Col, BS, 35; Harvard Univ, MA, 36, PhD(chem), 40. *Prof Exp:* Asst prof org chem, Carnegie Inst Technol, 40-41; res chemist, E I Du Pont De Nemours & Co, Inc, 41-78. *Honors & Awards:* Del Sect Awards, Am Chem Soc, 65, 67. *Mem:* Am Chem Soc. *Res:* Synthesis of organics from radioactive carbon; chemistry of organic fluorine compounds; polymer synthesis; modified polyethylenes and synthesis of fluorine containing monomers; radioactive lactic acid in biological studies; chemistry of triphenylfuryl ketones; organo-transition metal chemistry. *Mailing Add:* RD 1 Box 221 Landenberg PA 19350

CRAMER, RICHARD DAVID, III, b Wilmington, Del, Feb 26, 42; m 79; c 1. MEDICINAL CHEMISTRY, PHYSICAL ORGANIC CHEMISTRY. *Educ:* Harvard Univ, AB, 63; Mass Inst Technol, PhD(org chem), 67. *Prof Exp:* Scientist org chem, Polaroid Corp, 67-69; res fel, Harvard Univ, 69-71; sr scientist technol assessment, 71-74, SR INVESTR RES CHEM, SMITH KLINE & FRENCH LABS, 74-, ASST DIR RES CHEM, 80- *Mem:* AAAS; Am Chem Soc. Can. *Res:* Quantitative structure/activity relationships, molecular modelling, and other applications of computer science to organic chemistry. *Mailing Add:* Smith Kline & French Labs 1500 Spring Garden St Philadelphia PA 19101

CRAMER, ROGER EARL, b Findlay, Ohio, Sept 14, 43; m 67; c 2. INORGANIC CHEMISTRY. *Educ:* Bowling Green State Univ, BS, 65; Univ Ill, MS, 67, PhD(inorg chem), 69. *Prof Exp:* Asst prof, 69-73, assoc prof, 73-80, PROF & CHMN CHEM, UNIV HAWAII, 80- *Concurrent Pos:* Vis prof, Northwestern Univ, 78. *Mem:* Am Chem Soc. *Res:* Nuclear magnetic resonance of paramagnetic molecules; coordination chemistry; metal-ion complexes in medicine; organouranium chemistry. *Mailing Add:* Dept of Chem 2524 The Mall Univ of Hawaii Honolulu HI 96822

CRAMER, WILLIAM ANTHONY, b New York, NY, June 11, 38; m 64; c 4. BIOPHYSICS. *Educ:* Mass Inst Technol, BS, 59; Univ Chicago, MS, 60, PhD(biophys), 65. *Prof Exp:* NSF fel photosynthesis, Univ Calif, San Diego, 65-67, res assoc, 67-68; from asst prof to assoc prof, 68-78, PROF BIOL SCI, PURDUE UNIV, 78- *Concurrent Pos:* Nat Inst Gen Med Sci res career develop award, 70-75; Europ Molecular Biol Org sr fel, 74-75; mem molecular biol panel, NSF, 78-80. *Mem:* Am Soc Biol Chem; Biophys Soc. *Res:* Photosynthetic electron transport and energy coupling; bioenergetics; mechanism of action of colicin. *Mailing Add:* Dept of Biol Sci Purdue Univ West Lafayette IN 47907

CRAMER, WILLIAM HERBERT, b Chambersburg, Pa, Dec 4, 21. PHYSICAL CHEMISTRY. *Educ:* Pa State Univ, BS, 42, PhD(phys chem), 50. *Prof Exp:* Supvr, Control Lab, Photo Prod Dept, E I du Pont de Nemours & Co, 43-44; asst phys chem, Pa State Univ, 46-49; fel, Mellon Inst, 50-51; res assoc, Forrestal Res Ctr, 51-53; asst prof, Univ Fla, 53-62; asst prog dir chem, 62-63, assoc prog dir phys chem, 64-68, prog dir quantum chem, 68-80, PROG DIR CHEM PHYSICS, NSF, 80- *Mem:* AAAS; Am Chem Soc; Am Phys Soc. *Res:* Atomic and molecular structure and properties; positive ion scattering; gaseous electrical discharges. *Mailing Add:* Chem Div NSF Washington DC 20550

CRAMER, WILLIAM SMITH, b Frederick, Md, Aug 25, 14; m 47; c 2. PHYSICS. *Educ:* Ursinus Col, BS, 37; Brown Univ, MS, 38, PhD(physics), 48. *Prof Exp:* Asst math, Univ Md, 38-39; teacher math & sci, Pikeville Col, 39-40; physicist, US Naval Ord Lab, 42-56 & Off Naval Res, 56-66, physicist, Naval Ship Res & Develop Ctr, Washington, DC, 66-76; PHYSICIST, MAR ASSOCS, INC, ROCKVILLE, 76- Acoust Soc Am (vpres, 75-76). *Res:* Acoustic properties of plastics; underwater and physical acoustics. *Mailing Add:* 11512 Colt Terr Silver Spring MD 20902

CRAMPTON, DAVID, b Eng, Jan 27, 42; Can citizen; m 64; c 2. ASTRONOMY. *Educ:* Univ Toronto, BSc, 63, MA, 64, PhD(astron), 67. *Prof Exp:* RES SCIENTIST ASTRON, DOMINION ASTROPHYS OBSERV, 67- *Res:* Galactic structure, spectroscopic observations of x-ray binaries. *Mailing Add:* 813-100 Hinchey Ave Ottawa K1Y 4L9 Can

CRAMPTON, JAMES MYLAN, b Mitchell, SDak, Nov 26, 23; m 50; c 6. PHARMACOLOGY. *Educ:* Creighton Univ, BS, 50; Univ Fla, MS, 51, PhD(pharmacol), 53. *Prof Exp:* Asst prof pharmacol, Xavier Univ, 53-58; asst prof biol sci, Sch Pharm, 58 & 67, prof, 67-70, dir dept biol sci, 58-71, dir clin studies, 71-74, assoc dean sch pharm, 75-78, PROF BIOPHARM, SCH PHARM & PROF PHYSIOL & PHARMACOL, SCH MED, CREIGHTON UNIV, 70- *Mem:* Am Pharmaceut Asn. *Res:* Castrix toxicity; salicyclamide. *Mailing Add:* Sch of Pharm Creighton Univ Omaha NE 68102

CRAMPTON, STUART J B, b New York, NY, Nov 3, 36; m 61; c 3. ATOMIC PHYSICS. *Educ:* Williams Col, BA, 58; Oxford Univ, BA, 60; Harvard Univ, PhD(physics), 64. *Prof Exp:* From asst prof to assoc prof, 65-75, PROF PHYSICS, WILLIAMS COL, 75- *Concurrent Pos:* NSF fel, Harvard Univ, 64-65; Alfred P Sloan Found res fel, 67-69; NATO sr fel, 75. *Mem:* Fel Am Phys Soc; Am Asn Physics Teachers. *Res:* Atom-atom interactions, particularly electron spin exchange collisions and atom-surface interactions at low temperatures. *Mailing Add:* Dept Physics Williams Col Williamstown MA 01267

CRAMPTON, THEODORE HENRY MILLER, b Patchogue, NY, Apr 4, 26; m 55. MATHEMATICS, RADIOBIOLOGY. *Educ:* Hamilton Col, AB, 49; Ind Univ, MA, 54, PhD(math), 55. *Prof Exp:* Instr math, Mt Holyoke Col, 55-57, asst prof, 57-58; instr nuclear weapons, US Army Engr Sch, Va, 58-61; mathematician, Armed Forces Radiobiol Res Inst, Nat Naval Med Ctr, Md, 61-64; instr math, US Mil Acad, 64-66, asst prof, 66-69; chief weapons effects sect, Joint Strategic Target Planning Staff,, 69-72; systs analyst, Int Security Affairs, Energy Res & Develop Admin, 72-77; sr res fel & chief climate proj, res directorate, Nat Defense Univ, 77-81; DIR, OPERS PLANS & POLICY, DEFENSE NUCLEAR AGENCY, 81- *Mem:* AAAS; Math Asn Am; Sigma Xi. *Res:* Class field theory; radiation transport theory; radiation dosimetry; international affairs analysis and climatic change; radiation shielding. *Mailing Add:* Crampton 6 Lakeside Overlook Rockville MD 20850

CRAMTON, THOMAS JAMES, b Chadron, Nebr, Oct 23, 38; m 60; c 2. MATHEMATICS. *Educ:* Harvard Univ, AB, 60; Clark Univ, AM, 62; Dartmouth Col, PhD(math), 70. *Prof Exp:* Instr math, US Naval Nuclear Power Sch, Md, 62-66, dir off dept, 63-66; asst prof math, Purdue Univ, Ft Wayne, 69-76; ASSOC ACTUARY, LOUIS BEHR ORGN, INC, 77- *Res:* Inverse eigenvalue problems in dimension 2 or higher. *Mailing Add:* Suite 445 401 N Michigan Ave Chicago IL 60611

CRANCH, EDMUND TITUS, b Brooklyn, NY, Nov 15, 22; m 46; c 3. MECHANICS. *Educ:* Cornell Univ, BME, 45, PhD(mech), 52. *Prof Exp:* Mem tech staff appl mech, Bell Tel Labs, 47-48; from asst prof to prof mech & mat, 51-62, head dept, 56-62, assoc dean eng, 67-77, PROF MECH, CORNELL UNIV, 62-, DEAN COL ENG, 77- *Concurrent Pos:* Consult, Lincoln Lab, Mass Inst Technol, 51-53, Cornell Aeronaut Lab, 55-61, Aerojet-Gen Corp, Calif, 57, Bausch & Lomb Corp, NY, 61, Int Bus Mach Corp, 63- & Battelle Mem Inst, 63-; NSF fac fel, Stanford Univ, 58-59, sr fel, Swiss Fed Inst Technol, 64-65. *Mem:* Am Soc Mech Engrs; Am Soc Testing & Mat; Soc Exp Stress Anal; Am Soc Eng Educ. *Res:* Dynamics; vibration theory; elasticity; applied mathematics; materials; shells. *Mailing Add:* Carpenter Hall Cornell Univ Ithaca NY 14850

CRANDALL, ARTHUR JARED, b Syracuse, NY, Mar 14, 39; m 64; c 3. PHYSICS. *Educ:* St Lawrence Univ, BS, 61; Mich State Univ, MS, 64, PhD(physics), 67. *Prof Exp:* Asst prof, 67-74, ASSOC PROF PHYSICS, BOWLING GREEN STATE UNIV, 74- *Mem:* Acoust Soc Am. *Res:* Physics teaching; ultrasonics; diffraction effects and interaction of light with sound. *Mailing Add:* Dept of Physics Bowling Green State Univ Bowling Green OH 43403

CRANDALL, DANA IRVING, b New York, NY, Sept 4, 15; m 42; c 3. BIOCHEMISTRY. *Educ:* Columbia Univ, AB, 36; Univ Pa, PhD(biochem), 45. *Prof Exp:* From instr to asst prof physiol chem, Univ Pa, 46-50; assoc prof, 50-62, prof, 62-80, EMER PROF BIOL CHEM, UNIV CINCINNATI, 80- *Mem:* Am Soc Biol Chemists. *Res:* Metabolism of tyrosine in mammalian tissues; properties and mechanism of action of homogentisate dioxygenase; role of oxygenases in mammalian metabolism. *Mailing Add:* 1231 Halpin Cincinnati OH 45208

CRANDALL, DAVID HUGH, b Chicago, Ill, July 9, 42; m 76; c 3. ATOMIC PHYSICS, ELECTRON PHYSICS. *Educ:* Sioux Falls Col, BS, 64; Univ Nebr-Lincoln, MS, 67, PhD(physics), 70. *Prof Exp:* Vis asst prof physics, Univ Mo-Rolla, 70-71; res assoc, Joint Inst Lab Astrophys, Nat Bur Standards & Univ Colo, Boulder, 71-74; res physicist, 74-79, MGR ATOMIC & PLASMA PHYSICS RES GROUP, OAK RIDGE NAT LAB, 79- *Mem:* Am Phys Soc; Sigma Xi. *Res:* Atomic collisions between ions and atoms or electrons using ion beams of a few keV energy, important processes of charge exchange, impact excitation and ionization. *Mailing Add:* Physics Div Bldg 6003 Box X Oak Ridge Nat Lab Oak Ridge TN 37830

CRANDALL, DAVID L, b Creston, Iowa, Sept 1, 52; m 82. CARDIOVASCULAR PHYSIOLOGY, ENDOCRINOLOGY. *Educ:* Tulane Univ, BS, 74; Iowa State Univ, MS, 77, PhD(physiol), 79. *Prof Exp:* NIH fel endocrinol, Sch Med, Emory Univ, 79-81; SR RES PHARMACOLOGIST, CARDIOVASC BIOL, LEDERLE LABS, AM CYANAMID, 81- *Mem:* Sigma Xi; NY Acad Sci; AAAS. *Res:* Prevention of myocardial infarction and the relationship of obesity and cardiovascular disease. *Mailing Add:* 56-242 Lederle Labs Am Cyanamid Co Pearl River NY 10965

CRANDALL, EDWARD D, b Brooklyn, NY, Aug 10, 38; m 63; c 2. PULMONARY PHYSIOLOGY. *Educ:* Cooper Union, BChE, 60; Northwestern Univ, MS, 62, PhD(chem eng), 64; Univ Pa, MD, 72. *Prof Exp:* From asst prof to assoc prof chem eng, Univ Notre Dame, 64-68; lectr, Dept Physiol, Univ Pa, 68-74, asst prof physiol, med & bioeng, 74-79; ASSOC PROF MED, UNIV CALIF, LOS ANGELES, 79- *Concurrent Pos:* USPHS spec fel, 68-70; med internship & residency, Hosp, Univ Pa, 72-74, pulmonary fel, Hosp, 74-78. *Honors & Awards:* Res Career Develop Award, NIH, 75. *Mem:* Am Col Physicians; Am Thoracic Soc; Am Soc Clin Invest; Am Physiol Soc; Am Inst Chem Eng. *Res:* Lung epithelial transport; pulmonary physiology and disease; pulmonary gas exchange; cell membrane structure and function. *Mailing Add:* Dept Med Univ Calif Los Angeles CA 90024

CRANDALL, ELBERT WILLIAMS, b Normal, Ill, Nov 4, 20; m 51; c 4. ORGANIC CHEMISTRY. *Educ:* Ill State Norm Univ, BEd, 42; Univ Mo, MA, 48, PhD(org chem), 50. *Prof Exp:* Prof chem, Ky Wesleyan Col, 50-51; res & develop, US Rubber Co, 51-52; PROF CHEM, PITTSBURG STATE UNIV, 52- *Mem:* Am Chem Soc. *Res:* Nitric acid oxidations; near infrared spectra of polymers; organic compounds in natural waters; conversion of waste cellulose to ethanol. *Mailing Add:* Dept of Chem Pittsburg State Univ Pittsburg KS 66762

CRANDALL, JACK KENNETH, b Fillmore, Calif, June 8, 37; m 60; c 1. ORGANIC CHEMISTRY. *Educ:* Univ Calif, Berkeley, BS, 60; Cornell Univ, PhD(org chem), 63. *Prof Exp:* NIH fel, 64; from instr to assoc prof, 64-72, PROF CHEM, IND UNIV, BLOOMINGTON, 72- *Concurrent Pos:* Alfred P Sloan res fel, 68-70; John Simon Guggenheim fel, 70-71. *Mem:* Am Chem Soc; The Chem Soc. *Res:* Synthetic organic chemistry; small ring compounds; epoxides; allenes; organometallic chemistry; C-13 nuclear magnetic resonance. *Mailing Add:* Dept of Chem Ind Univ Bloomington IN 47401

CRANDALL, JOHN LOU, b Hart, Mich, Sept 18, 20; m 43; c 1. CHEMISTRY. *Educ:* Mass Inst Technol, BS, 42, PhD(phys chem), 48. *Prof Exp:* Res chemist, Chem Dept, 48-52, res mgr exp phys, Savannah River Lab, 53-67, from asst dir advan oper planning to dir advan oper planning, Atomic Energy Div, 67-75, dir environ sci sect, 75-78, dir adv planning, 78-80, PROG MGR, SAVANNAH RIVER LAB, E I DU PONT DE NEMOURS & CO, INC, 80- *Mem:* Am Chem Soc; fel Am Nuclear Soc. *Res:* High polymers; photochemistry; reactor physics; operations analysis; environmental management; nuclear waste management. *Mailing Add:* Savannah River Lab E I du Pont de Nemours & Co Inc Aiken SC 29808

CRANDALL, JOHN R, b Seattle, Wash, Aug 19, 14; m 48. PETROLEUM RESERVOIR ENGINEERING. *Educ:* Carnegie Inst Technol, BS, 35. *Prof Exp:* Labor oil drilling & prod, Humble Oil & Refining Co, 37-38, eng assignments from jr petrol engr to sr supv engr, 39-58, petrol econ engr on loan to Standard Oil NJ, 58-59, div staff engr, 59-61, staff coordr petrol econ & diversification studies, 61-63, res assoc, Prod Res Div, 63-64; res coordr, Esso Prod Res Co, 64-66; planning adv, Coal & Shale Oil Dept, Humble Oil & Refining Co, 66-69 & Carter Oil Co, 69-76; MANAGING TRUSTEE, RODERIC CRANDALL TRUST, 71-; PRES, CRANDALL & ASSOCS, INC, 79- *Concurrent Pos:* On loan, Non-hydrocarbon Mineral Activ, Standard Oil Co, NJ, 70-71. *Mem:* Soc Petrol Engrs. *Mailing Add:* Crandall & Assocs Inc 721 Ourlane Circle Houston TX 77024

CRANDALL, LEE W(ALTER), b Hartford, Wis, July 26, 13; m 38; c 1. CIVIL & STRUCTURAL ENGINEERING. *Educ:* Univ Wis, BS, 36, MS, 37; Stanford Univ, PhD(civil eng), 52. *Prof Exp:* Instr civil eng, Univ Colo, 37-38, asst prof, 43-46, assoc prof, 47-48; asst struct engr, Bur Reclamation, 39-42; from assoc prof to prof civil eng, 48-77, prof, 77-80, EMER PROF CIVIL & ENVIRON ENG & MEM GRAD FAC, UNIV WIS-MADISON, 80- *Concurrent Pos:* Fulbright res scholar, Finland, 53-54; consult, Food & Agr Orgn, UN Rome, at the Forest Prod Res Inst, Philippines, 61-62. *Mem:* Am Soc Civil Engrs; Am Soc Eng Educ; Nat Soc Prof Engrs; Forest Prod Res Soc; Am Forestry Asn. *Res:* Economic selection; design of timber and steel structures; distress or failed structures; timber allowable loads; reports and expert witness testimony in courts of 12 states on unusual, distressed or failed structures, products or components for attorneys, casualty insurers, fabricators or owners. *Mailing Add:* 2228 Eng Bldg Univ of Wis Madison WI 53706

CRANDALL, MICHAEL GRAIN, b Baton Rouge, La, Nov 29, 40; m 62; c 3. MATHEMATICS. *Educ:* Univ Calif, Berkeley, BS, 62, MA, 64, PhD(math), 65. *Prof Exp:* Instr math, Univ Calif, Berkeley, 65-66; asst prof math, Stanford Univ, 66-69; from asst prof to prof, Univ Calif, Los Angeles, 69-74; PROF MATH, MATH RES CTR, UNIV WIS-MADISON, 74- *Concurrent Pos:* Vis prof math, Math Res Ctr, Univ Wis-Madison, 71-72; assoc ed, J Nonlinear Anal, 76- *Mem:* Am Math Soc; Soc Indust Appl Math. *Res:* Nonlinear differential equations in both abstract and concrete cases; the abstract setting involves nonlinear evolution governed by accretive operators; concrete problems are nonlinear elliptic, parabolic and hyperbolic equations. *Mailing Add:* Math Res Ctr Univ Wis 610 Walnut St Madison WI 53706

CRANDALL, PAUL HERBERT, b Essex, Vt, Feb 15, 23; m 51; c 4. MEDICINE. *Educ:* Univ Vt, BS, 43, MD, 47; Am Bd Neurol Surg, dipl, 56. *Prof Exp:* Asst chief neurosurg serv, Wadsworth Vet Admin Hosp, Calif, 54-56; from instr to assoc prof surg & neurosurg, 54-72, PROF NEUROSURG & NEUROL, SCH MED, UNIV CALIF, LOS ANGELES, 72- *Concurrent Pos:* Consult, Vet Admin Hosp & Wadsworth Gen Hosp, Calif. *Mem:* AMA; Am Asn Neurol Surg; NY Acad Sci; fel Am Col Surg. *Res:* Stereotaxic surgery; depth electrode studies in epilepsy; radioisotopic brain scanning. *Mailing Add:* Dept of Surg Univ of Calif Med Sch Los Angeles CA 90024

CRANDALL, PERRY CLARENCE, b Chillicothe, Mo, May 9, 15; m 41; c 4. HORTICULTURE. *Educ:* Iowa State Univ, BS, 40, PhD(hort, plant physiol), 51; Ohio State Univ, MS, 41. *Prof Exp:* Supt, Bluffs Exp Fruit Farm, Iowa State Univ, 46-51; asst prof, 51-58, supt & horticulturist, 58-80, EMER SUPT & HORTICULTURIST, SOUTHWESTERN WASH RES UNIT, WASH STATE UNIV, 80- *Mem:* Am Soc Hort Sci; Am Pomol Soc; Int Soc Hort Sci. *Res:* Small fruits; tree fruits, and vegetables physiology and culture. *Mailing Add:* Southwestern Wash Res Unit 1918 NE 78th St Vancouver WA 98665

CRANDALL, PHILIP GLEN, b Manhattan, Kans, Nov 4, 48; m 69; c 1. FOOD SCIENCE, HORTICULTURE. *Educ:* Kans State Univ, BS, 70; Purdue Univ, MS, 72, PhD(food sci), 75. *Prof Exp:* asst prof, 75-80, ASSOC PROF CITRUS RES, INST FOOD & AGR SCI, AGR RES & EDUC CTR, UNIV FLA, LAKE ALFRED, 80-, FOOD SCIENTIST, 75- *Mem:* Inst Food Technologists; Int Soc Citricult. *Res:* Citrus specialty products; waste monitoring instrumentation. *Mailing Add:* Inst Food & Agr Sci Univ Fla PO Box 1088 Lake Alfred FL 33850

CRANDALL, RICHARD B, b Greencastle, Ind, Sept 8, 28; m 58. PARASITOLOGY, IMMUNOLOGY. *Educ:* DePauw Univ, AB, 49; Univ Mass, MA, 53, Purdue Univ, PhD(zool), 59. *Prof Exp:* NIH trainee, Sch Pub Health, Univ NC, 59-60; instr med microbiol, 60-64, from asst prof to assoc prof, 65-73, PROF PARASITOL, COL MED, UNIV FLA, 74- *Mem:* Am Soc Parasitol; Am Soc Trop Med & Hyg; Am Asn Immunol. *Res:* Immunology of parasitic infections; medical parasitology and microbiology. *Mailing Add:* Dept of Immunol & Med Microbiol Univ of Fla Col of Med Gainesville FL 32601

CRANDALL, WALTER ELLIS, b Norwich, Conn, Dec 18, 16; m 44; c 2. NUCLEAR PHYSICS. *Educ:* Worcester Polytech Inst, BS, 40; Univ Calif, PhD(physics), 52. *Prof Exp:* Physicist, US Naval Ord Lab, 41-42; physicist, Radiation Lab, Univ Calif, 48-52 & 54-62; physicist, Calif Res & Develop Co, 53; mgr, Sci & Technol Dept, Northrop Corp, 62-70, vpres & mgr, Northrop Corp Labs, 70-75, CHIEF SCIENTIST, NORTHROP RES AND TECHNOL CTR, 75- *Concurrent Pos:* Consult, Boeing Airplane Co. *Mem:* Am Phys Soc. *Res:* High energy nuclear physics; neutral meson; nuclear radii; nuclear weapons; magnetics; electrooptics; biophysics. *Mailing Add:* 21930 Carbon Mesa Rd Malibu CA 90265

CRANDALL, WILLIAM B, b Andover, NY, Feb 24, 21; m 42; c 3. CERAMICS, MATERIALS SCIENCE. *Educ:* Alfred Univ, BS, 42, MS, 44. *Prof Exp:* Res assoc, Off Naval Res proj, Alfred Univ, 46-50, proj dir, 50-57; assoc prof ceramic eng, State Univ NY Col Ceramics, 57-63; consult mat res, Wireless Div, Matsushita Elec Co, Japan, 63; asst dir res, Pfaudler Co, Pfaudler-Permutit Corp, NY, 63, dir res, 63-64, vpres mat res, Pfaudler Co, Sybron Corp, NY, 65-70; dir ceramics res, IIT Res Inst, 70-74; DIR, ALFRED UNIV RES FOUND, 74- *Concurrent Pos:* Co-founder, Materiadyne Corp, NY, 60-63; mem, Mat Adv Bd, Nat Acad Sci, 60-63; mem adv ceramic dept, Univ Ill, Urbana-Champaign, 69- *Mem:* Fel Am Ceramic Soc; Nat Inst Ceramic Engrs; Int Plansee Soc Powder Metall. *Res:* Ceramic materials, such as glass, crystalline oxides, carbides, cermets, coatings and composites. *Mailing Add:* Alfred Univ Res Found Alfred NY 14802

CRANDALL-STOTLER, BARBARA JEAN, b Jamestown, NY, Mar 4, 42; m 69. BOTANY. *Educ:* Keuka Col, BA, 64; Univ Cincinnati, MS, 66, PhD(bot), 68. *Prof Exp:* Fel bot, Univ Tex, Austin, 68-69; asst prof, 70-76, ASSOC PROF BOT, SOUTHERN ILL UNIV, 76- *Honors & Awards:* Diamond Award, NSF & Am Bot Soc, 75. *Mem:* Am Bryol & Lichenol Soc; Bot Soc Am; Brit Bryol Soc; Int Asn Bryologists; Sigma Xi. *Res:* Morphogenesis and developmental anatomy of the mosses, liverworts, and hornworts. *Mailing Add:* Dept of Bot Southern Ill Univ Carbondale IL 62901

CRANDELL, CLIFTON E, US citizen. DENTISTRY. *Educ:* ECarolina Col, BS, 49; Med Col Va, DDS, 53; Univ Pa, MS, 61; Duke Univ, MEd, 61. *Prof Exp:* Pvt pract, Southport, NC, 53-55; PROF ORAL DIAG & TREATMENT, SCH DENT, UNIV NC, CHAPEL HILL, 55- *Mem:* Am Dent Asn; Am Acad Dent Radiol (pres, 69-70). *Res:* Dental radiology; oral diagnosis; half-value layer relation to film quality; radiation protection; computers in dental education; linear programming. *Mailing Add:* Univ of NC Sch of Dent Chapel Hill NC 27514

CRANDELL, DWIGHT RAYMOND, b Galesburg, Ill, Jan 25, 23; m 43; c 3. GEOLOGY. *Educ:* Knox Col, BA, 46; Yale Univ, MS, 48, PhD(geol), 51. *Prof Exp:* Field asst, 47, GEOLOGIST, US GEOL SURV, 48- *Concurrent Pos:* Asst, Yale Univ, 48-51. *Honors & Awards:* Kirk Bryan Award, Geol Soc Am, 72. *Mem:* Fel Geol Soc Am. *Res:* Stratigraphy of unconsolidated deposits; glacial geology; volcanic mudflows; volcanic hazards in Western United States. *Mailing Add:* Eng Geol Br US Geol Surv Fed Ctr Denver CO 80225

CRANDELL, GEORGE FRANK, b Astoria, Ore, Dec 5, 32; m 56; c 5. BIOLOGICAL OCEANOGRAPHY. *Educ:* Ore State Univ, BS, 60, MS, 63, PhD(oceanog), 66. *Prof Exp:* From asst prof to assoc prof, 66-75, PROF OCEANOG, HUMBOLDT STATE UNIV, 75- *Mem:* Am Soc Limnol & Oceanog. *Res:* Zooplankton and benthic ecology. *Mailing Add:* Dept of Oceanog Humboldt State Univ Arcata CA 95521

CRANDELL, MERRELL EDWARD, b Clearfield, Pa, Mar 19, 38; m 60; c 2. PHYSICS. *Educ:* Hobart Col, BS, 59; Syracuse Univ, MS, 61, PhD(physics), 67. *Prof Exp:* Asst physics, Syracuse Univ, 59-63; instr physics, Le Moyne Col, NY, 63-67; asst prof, 67-70, ASSOC PROF PHYSICS, MUSKINGUM COL, 70- *Concurrent Pos:* Vis res fel, Kammerlingh Onnes Lab, State Univ Leiden, 74-75. *Mem:* Am Phys Soc; Am Asn Physics Teachers. *Res:* Optical and transport properties of metals and alloys. *Mailing Add:* Dept of Physics Muskingum Col New Concord OH 43762

CRANDELL, ROBERT ALLEN, b Three Rivers, Mich, July 30, 24; m 50; c 4. VETERINARY VIROLOGY. *Educ:* Mich State Col, BS, 47, DVM, 49; Univ Calif, MPH, 55; Am Bd Vet Pub Health, dipl; Am Col Vet Microbiologists, dipl. *Prof Exp:* Practitioner vet med, 49-51; base vet, Vet Corps, US Air Force, Selfridge AFB, Mich, 51-52, asst chief animal farm, Ft Detrick, Md, 52-54, lab officer, Naval Biol Lab, 54-56, asst chief virol br, Armed Forces Inst Path, 56-60, chief virol br, US Air Force Epidemiol Lab, Lackland AFB, Tex, 60-67, res epidemiologist, Pan Am Foot-and-Mouth Dis Ctr, Brazil, 67-69, chief biosci div, US Air Force Sch Aerospace Med, 69-70, chief epidemiol div, 70-71; SR MICROBIOLOGIST, COL VET MED, VET DIAG MED, UNIV ILL, URBANA, 71-, PROF, DEPT PATH & HYG, 75- *Concurrent Pos:* Mem, Animal Resources Adv Comt, NIH, 75-79; actg dir, Lab Vet Diag Med, Col Vet Med, Univ Ill, 76-78, dir, 78-81; diag microbiol, Tex Vet Med Diag Lab, 81- *Mem:* Am Vet Med Asn; Am Soc Microbiol; US Animal Health Asn; Am Asn Vet Lab Daiagnosticians; Confederate Res Workers Animal Dis. *Res:* Isolation and charcaterization of new respiratory viruses of the domestic feline and bovine species; virologic studies and control of zoonoses and diseases of laboratory animals; basic studies with rabies virus; diagnostic virology; research administration. *Mailing Add:* Tex Vet Med Diag Lab College Station TX 77841

CRANDELL, WALTER BAIN, b New York, NY, July 26, 11; m 35; c 4. SURGERY, METABOLISM. *Educ:* Dartmouth Col, AB, 34; NY Univ, MD, 37. *Prof Exp:* Intern, Mary Hitchcock Mem Hosp, 37-38; clin asst chest surg, Hitchcock Clin, Hanover, NH, 39; asst resident surg, Mass Gen Hosp, Boston, 39-41; from asst resident to resident chest surg, Bellevue Hosp, New York, 41-42, asst vis consult surg & chest surg, 46-47; attend thoracic surg, Vet Admin Hosp, Bronx, NY, 47; chief surg serv, Vet Admin Hosp, White River Jct, 47-79; prof surg, Dartmouth Med Sch, 75-79; RETIRED. *Concurrent Pos:* Instr anat, Dartmouth Med Sch, 39; from asst clin prof to assoc clin prof surg, Dartmouth Med Sch, 47-68, clin prof surg, 68-75; adj surgeon, Lenox Hill Hosp, New York, 47; instr anat & oper surg, Postgrad Sch, NY Univ, 46, instr anat, Col Med, 46-47; consult surg, Mary Hitchcock Hosp, Hanover, NH, 70-79. *Mem:* Am Col Surg; Am Asn Thoracic Surg. *Res:* Metabolic disorders in surgical patients; especially disorders of acid-base and osmolality; pulmonary and renal insufficiency. *Mailing Add:* Vet Admin Ctr Surg Serv N Hartland Rd White River Junction VT 05001

CRANDLEMERE, ROBERT WAYNE, b South Weymouth, Mass, Mar 5, 47; m 66; c 2. APPLIED CHEMISTRY, FORENSIC SCIENCE. *Educ:* Suffolk Univ, BS, 70, MS, 75; Am Inst Chemists, cert, 76. *Prof Exp:* Assoc res scientist, Factory Mutual Res Corp, 67-70; chemist, NE Indust Chem Corp, 72-73; CHIEF CHEMIST & VPRES, BRIGGS ENG & TESTING CO, INC, 73- *Concurrent Pos:* Mem, Chem Week Adv Bd, 76. *Mem:* Am Chem Soc; Am Inst Chemists; AAAS; Nat Fire Protection Asn. *Res:* Investigation of weathering and other effects on bituminous materials used in roofing and development of test procedures in analysis of cement concrete. *Mailing Add:* Briggs Eng & Testing Co Inc 164 Washington St Norwell MA 02061

CRANE, ANATOLE, b New Brunswick, NJ, Feb 23, 33; m 56; c 2. MICROBIOLOGY. *Educ:* Univ Ill, BS, 54, MS, 56; Univ Ind, PhD(bact), 60. *Prof Exp:* Proj leader microbiol, 59-68, MGR MICROBIOL, QUAKER OATS CO, 68- *Mem:* Am Soc Microbiol; Am Asn Cereal Chemists; Inst Food Technologists. *Res:* Food microbiology and preservation. *Mailing Add:* Quaker Oats Co 121 S Wilke Rd Arlington Heights IL 60005

CRANE, AUGUST REYNOLDS, b Brooklyn, NY, Dec 16, 08; m 35. MEDICINE, PATHOLOGY. *Educ:* Hamilton Col, AB, 29; Cornell Univ, MD, 33. *Prof Exp:* Asst prof path, Jefferson Med Col, 47-57; prof, 57-75, EMER PROF PATH, SCH MED, UNIV PA, 75- *Concurrent Pos:* Consult, USPHS, 44-46 & US Army Med Corps, 47-73; dir, Ayer Clin Lab, Pa Hosp, 46-74, consult, 74-; sr mem, Inst Cancer Res, Philadelphia, 75-; trustee, Hamilton Col. *Mem:* Fel Am Soc Clin Path; Am Asn Path & Bact; AMA; fel Col Am Path; fel Am Col Physicians. *Res:* Cancer research; teaching. *Mailing Add:* Inst Cancer Res Foxchase Philadelphia PA 19111

CRANE, CHARLES RUSSELL, b Mangum, Okla, Jan 19, 28; m 54; c 4. BIOCHEMISTRY, TOXICOLOGY. *Educ:* Univ Okla, BS, 51, MS, 52; Fla State Univ, PhD(biochem), 56. *Prof Exp:* Asst prof biochem, Okla State Univ, 56-61; CHIEF BIOCHEM RES, CIVIL AEROMED INST, FED AVIATION ADMIN, DEPT TRANSP, 61- *Mem:* AAAS; Am Chem Soc. *Res:* Aviation toxicology; drug metabolism; pesticides; enzymology; composition and inhalation toxicology of combustion/pyrolysis products. *Mailing Add:* Civil Aeromed Inst AAC-114 PO Box 25082 Oklahoma City OK 73125

CRANE, EDWARD MASTIN, b Brattleboro, Vt, Mar 23, 20; m 44; c 3. COMPUTER GRAPHICS, PHOTOGRAPHIC SCIENCE. *Educ:* Dartmouth Col, AB, 42; Harvard Univ, AM, 43, PhD(chem), 49. *Prof Exp:* Res chemist, 49-56, res assoc, Eastman Kodak Co, 57-82; RETIRED. *Res:* Photographic sharpness, graininess, modulation transfer function; computer software development; computer graphics system development. *Mailing Add:* Eastman Kodak Res Labs 1999 Lake Ave Rochester NY 14650

CRANE, FREDERICK LORING, b Mass, Dec 3, 25; m 50; c 4. BIOCHEMISTRY. *Educ:* Univ Mich, BS, 50, MS, 51, PhD(bot), 53. *Prof Exp:* Trainee, Inst Enzyme Res, Univ Wis, 53-57, asst prof, 57-59; asst prof chem, Univ Tex, 59-60; assoc prof, 60-62, PROF BIOL, PURDUE UNIV, WEST LAFAYETTE, 62- *Concurrent Pos:* Newcombe fel, Univ Mich, 52-53; NSF sr fel, Univ Stockholm, 63-64; NIH career investr, 64; Fulbright vis fel, Australian Nat Univ, 71-72 & 79-80. *Honors & Awards:* Eli Lilly Award, Am Chem Soc, 64. *Mem:* Am Soc Plant Physiol; Am Soc Biol Chem; Am Chem Soc; Am Soc Cell Biol; Am Inst Biol Sci. *Res:* Vitamin biosynthesis in plants; fatty acid metabolism; biological oxidations and energy coupling; coenzyme Q and plastoquinones; ultrastructure of subcellular particles; hormone control of cell function. *Mailing Add:* Dept of Biol Sci Purdue Univ West Lafayette IN 47907

CRANE, GEORGE THOMAS, b Nephi, Utah, Nov 6, 28; m 54; c 4. MICROBIOLOGY, VIROLOGY. *Educ:* Utah State Univ, BS, 58; Colo State Univ, 62-63; Brigham Young Univ, MSc, 69. *Prof Exp:* Microbiologist, Dis Ecol Sect, USPHS, Colo, 58-66; MICROBIOLOGIST, ENVIRON & ECOL BR, DUGWAY, 66- *Mem:* Am Soc Trop Med & Hyg; Am Mosquito Control Asn. *Res:* Arbovirus and rickettsial surveillance of the fauna of North America. *Mailing Add:* 698 N Nelson Tooele UT 84074

CRANE, GRANT, organic chemistry, deceased

CRANE, HEWITT DAVID, b Jersey City, NJ, Apr 27, 27; m 54; c 3. ELECTRICAL ENGINEERING. *Educ:* Columbia Univ, BS, 47; Stanford Univ, PhD(elec eng), 60. *Prof Exp:* Engr, Western Union Tel Co, 48-49; eng maintenance, Int Bus Mach Corp, 50-52; engr, Inst Advan Study, 52-55 & Radio Corp of Am, Princeton Univ, 55-56; STAFF SCIENTIST, SRI INT, 56- *Concurrent Pos:* VChmn, Nat Joint Comput Conf, 62. *Honors & Awards:* Inst Elec & Electronics Engrs Award, 62; NASA Award for sci achievement, 70; Indust Res IR-100 Awards, 74 & 76. *Mem:* Fel Inst Elec & Electronics Engrs. *Res:* Digital device systems; neurophysiological and sensory devices and phenomena. *Mailing Add:* SRI Int 333 Ravenswood Ave Menlo Park CA 94025

CRANE, HORACE RICHARD, b Turlock, Calif, Nov 4, 07; m 34; c 2. PHYSICS. *Educ:* Calif Inst Technol, BS, 30, PhD(physics), 34. *Prof Exp:* Res fel physics, Calif Inst Technol, 34-35; instr & res physicist, 35-38, from asst prof to prof, 38-78, chmn dept, 65-72, EMER PROF PHYSICS, UNIV MICH, ANN ARBOR, 78- *Concurrent Pos:* Res assoc, Mass Inst Technol, 40 & dept terrestrial magnetism, Carnegie Inst Technol, 41; dir proximity fuze proj, Univ Mich, 42-45; pres, Midwestern Univs Res Asn, 57-60; mem policy adv bd, Argonne Nat Lab, 57-67; mem, Comn Col Physics, 62-70, vpres,

68-70; mem standing comt controlled thermonuclear res, Atomic Energy Comn, 69-72; chmn bd gov, Am Inst Physics, 71-75; mem, Comn Human Resources, 77-80; mem, Coun Int Exchange Scholars, 77-80. *Honors & Awards:* Davisson-Germer Prize, Am Phys Soc, 68. *Mem:* Nat Acad Sci; fel AAAS; fel Am Phys Soc; Am Asn Physics Teachers (pres), 65); fel Am Acad Arts & Sci. *Res:* Nuclear physics; high energy accelerators; g-factor of electron; physics teaching methods; geomagnetism. *Mailing Add:* 830 Avon Rd Ann Arbor MI 48104

CRANE, JOSEPH LELAND, b Wilmot, NH, Jan 9, 35. MYCOLOGY. *Educ:* Univ Maine, BS, 61; Univ Del, MS, 64; Univ Md, PhD(mycol), 67. *Prof Exp:* From asst mycologist to assoc mycologist, 67-79, MYCOLOGIST, ILL NATURAL HIST SURV, 79-; ASSOC PROF BOT & PLANT PATH, UNIV ILL, 76- *Mem:* Bot Soc Am; Mycol Soc Am; Am Inst Biol Sci; Brit Mycol Soc; Soc Mycol France. *Res:* Aquatic hyphomycetes; marine fungi; taxonomy of fungi imperfecti. *Mailing Add:* 218 Natural Resources Annex Ill Natural Hist Surv Urbana IL 61801

CRANE, JULES M, JR, b New York, NY, Sept 5, 28; m 55; c 4. ICHTHYOLOGY, MARINE BIOLOGY. *Educ:* NY Univ, AB, 54; Calif State Col Los Angeles, MA, 63. *Prof Exp:* Chmn, Dept Biol, 64-70 & 74-78, PROF BIOL, CERRITOS COL, 62-, . *Concurrent Pos:* Lectr, Calif State Col Long Beach, 65-73. *Mem:* AAAS; Am Soc Ichthyologists & Herpetologists; Marine Biol Soc UK. *Res:* Behavioral and biochemical aspects of bioluminescence in fishes; evolution of deep sea fishes; marine ecology. *Mailing Add:* Dept of Biol Cerritos Col 11110 E Alondra Blvd Norwalk CA 90650

CRANE, JULIAN COBURN, b Morgantown, WVa, Mar 7, 18; m 42. POMOLOGY. *Educ:* Univ Md, BS, 39, PhD(hort), 42. *Prof Exp:* Asst, Univ Md, 39-42, asst horticulturist, 42; assoc agronomist, Off for Agr Rels, USDA, 43-45, horticulturist, 46; from asst prof to assoc prof, 46-58, PROF POMOL, COL AGR, UNIV CALIF, DAVIS, 58- *Concurrent Pos:* NSF fel, 57. *Mem:* AAAS; Am Soc Plant Physiol; fel Am Soc Hort Sci; Am Inst Biol Sci. *Res:* Plant physiology; hormones in fruit set, growth and maturation; fig and pistachio culture. *Mailing Add:* Dept of Pomol Univ of Calif Davis CA 95616

CRANE, LANGDON TEACHOUT, JR, b Detroit, Mich, Feb 23, 30; m; c 4. SOLID STATE PHYSICS, RESEARCH ADMINISTRATION. *Educ:* Amherst Col, BA, 52; Univ Md, PhD(physics), 60. *Prof Exp:* Res physicist, Sci Lab, Ford Motor Co, 59-63; from asst prog dir to assoc prog dir, Physics Sect, NSF, 63-68, prog dir atomic & molecular physics, 68-69; res prof & dir inst fluid dynamics & appl math, Univ Md, 69-74; SPECIALIST SCI & TECHNOL & HEAD MGT & POLICY SCI SECT, SCI POLICY RES DIV, CONG RES SERV, LIBR CONG, WASHINGTON, DC, 74- *Concurrent Pos:* Mem comt atomic & molecular physics, Nat Acad Sci-Nat Res Coun, 71-73; prof, Inst Fluid Dynamics & Appl Math, Univ Md, 74-76. *Mem:* Fel AAAS; fel Am Phys Soc; Sigma Xi. *Res:* Low temperature, atomic, molecular and plasma physics; areas of superconductivity; low temperature specific heats and magnetic properties of metals and alloys; nuclear magnetic resonance; analysis of national policies and legislation affecting or employing science and technology and effectiveness of federally sponsored research programs; technology transfer and innovation. *Mailing Add:* 4008 Rosemary St Chevy Chase MD 20015

CRANE, LAURA JANE, b Middletown, Ohio, Nov 2, 41; m 72. TECHNICAL MANAGEMENT. *Educ:* Carnegie-Mellon Univ, BS, 63; Harvard Univ, MA, 64; Rutgers Univ, PhD(biochem), 73. *Prof Exp:* Asst scientist clin biochem, Warner-Lambert Pharmaceut Co, 67-68; assoc scientist polymer chem, W R Grace, Inc, 68-69; from fel to res assoc biochem, Roche Inst Molecular Biol, Hoffmann-La Roche Inc, 72-75; scientist clin biochem, Warner-Lambert Co, 75-78, sr scientist & group leader clin coagulation & haemat, 78-79; mgr lab prod res & develop, 79-80, ASST DIR LAB PROD RES & DEVELOP, J T BAKER CHEM CO, 80- *Mem:* AAAS; NY Acad Sci; Am Chem Soc. *Res:* Development of bonded phases on silica gel for high performance liquid chromatography and other applications. *Mailing Add:* 70 W Valley Brook Rd Long Valley NJ 07853

CRANE, LEO STANLEY, b Cincinnati, Ohio, Sept 7, 15; m 76; c 2. ENGINEERING, INDUSTRIAL ENGINEERING. *Educ:* George Washington Univ, BSE, 38. *Prof Exp:* Mem staff, 37-48, engr of tests, 48-56, mech res engr, 56-59, vpres eng & res, 65-70, exec vpres opers, 70-76, chief admin officer, 76-77, PRES, SOUTHERN RWY CO, 76-, CHIEF EXEC OFFICER & DIR, 77- *Concurrent Pos:* Dir, Am Security & Trust Co; mem exec comt, Nat Res Coun-Transp Res Bd. *Honors & Awards:* Res Recognition Award, Progressive Railroading, 67; Outstanding Achievement in Mgt Award, Am Inst Indust Engrs, 76. *Mem:* Fel Am Soc Testing & Mat (pres); Soc Automotive Engrs; Am Rwy Eng Asn; Am Soc Traffic & Transp. *Res:* Application of modern and creative engineering concepts to more productive railroad equipment and operations. *Mailing Add:* PO Box 1808 Washington DC 20013

CRANE, PATRICK CONRAD, b Salt Lake City, Utah, Mar 17, 48. RADIO ASTRONOMY, PHYSICS. *Educ:* Mass Inst Technol, SB, 70, PhD(physics), 77. *Prof Exp:* res assoc astron, 76-79, SCI ASSOC II, NAT RADIO ASTRON OBSERV, 79- *Mem:* Am Astron Soc; Am Phys Soc; Am Asn Physics Teachers; Int Union Radio Sci. *Res:* Galaxies; galactic nuclei; radio interferometry and aperture synthesis; extragalactic radio sources. *Mailing Add:* Nat Radio Astron Observ PO Box 0 Socorro NM 87801

CRANE, PAUL LEVI, b Clayton, NMex, Oct 17, 25; m 51; c 3. PLANT BREEDING, AGRONOMY. *Educ:* NMex State Col, BS, 50; Iowa State Col, MS, 51; Purdue Univ, PhD, 56. *Prof Exp:* Asst agronomist, 51-60, assoc prof, 60-71, PROF AGRON, PURDUE UNIV, 71- *Res:* Genetics and breeding of maize. *Mailing Add:* Dept of Agron Purdue Univ West Lafayette IN 47907

CRANE, PHILLIPE, b New Haven, Conn, July 18, 43; m 65; c 3. ASTROPHYSICS, PHYSICS. *Educ:* Yale Univ, BS, 65, MS, 66, PhD(physics), 69. *Prof Exp:* Res physicist, Yale Univ, 69-70; from instr to asst prof physics, Princeton Univ, 70-75; ASTRONOMER & PHYSICIST, EUROP SOUTHERN OBSERV, 75-, HEAD, IMAGE PROCESSING, 81- *Concurrent Pos:* US Mem ESA Faint Object Camera Instrument Sci Team, NASA & Syst Gen Corp, 78-83. *Mem:* Am Phys Soc; Am Astron Soc. *Res:* Extragalactic astronomy; radio sources, galaxies; instrument development related to research interests. *Mailing Add:* Karl-Schwarzschild-Strasse 2 D-8046 Garching Bei Munchen West Germany

CRANE, ROBERT KELLOGG, b Palmyra, NJ, Dec 20, 19; m 41; c 2. BIOLOGICAL CHEMISTRY, PHYSIOLOGY. *Educ:* Wash Col, BS, 42; Harvard Univ, PhD(biol chem), 50. *Prof Exp:* Res assoc, Reynolds Exp Lab, Atlas Powder Co, 42-43; instr chem, Northeast Mo State Teachers Col, 43-44; asst biochemist, Mass Gen Hosp, 49-50; from instr to assoc prof biol chem, Sch Med, Washington Univ, 50-61; prof biochem & head dept, Chicago Med Sch, 61-66; PROF PHYSIOL & CHMN DEPT, COL MED & DENT NJ, RUTGERS MED SCH, PISCATAWAY, 66- *Mem:* Am Physiol Soc; Am Soc Cell Biologists; Biophys Soc; Am Chem Soc; Am Soc Biol Chemists. *Res:* Intermediary metabolism; transport of carbohydrates. *Mailing Add:* Col Med & Dent NJ Dept Physiol Rutgers Med Sch Piscataway NJ 08854

CRANE, ROBERT KENDALL, b Worcester, Mass, Dec 9, 35; m 57; c 4. RADIOPHYSICS, METEOROLOGY. *Educ:* Worcester Polytech Inst, BS, 57, MS, 59, PhD(elec eng), 70. *Prof Exp:* Mem tech staff, Mitre Corp, 59-64; mem tech staff, Lincoln Lab, Mass Inst Technol, 64-76; dep div mgr, Environ Res & Technol Inc, 76-81; RES PROF ENG, THAYER SCH ENG, DARTMOUTH COL, 81- *Concurrent Pos:* Chmn, US Comn F, Int Sci Radio Union, 67-; mem, InterUnion Comn Radio Meteorol, 78-81; mem US study groups 5 & 6, Int Radio Consultative Comt, 68-; asst ed, Trans Antennas & Propagation, Inst Elec & Electronic Engrs, 72-74. *Mem:* Fel Inst Elec & Electronics Engrs; Am Meteorol Soc; Am Geophys Union; Royal Meteorol Soc; Sigma Xi. *Res:* Applied meteorology; radar meteorology; radio propagation. *Mailing Add:* Thayer Sch Eng Dartmouth Col Hanover NH 03755

CRANE, ROGER L, b Monroe, Iowa, June 27, 33; m 59; c 1. MATHEMATICS. *Educ:* Iowa State Univ, BS, 56, MS, 61, PhD(math), 62. *Prof Exp:* Engr, Univac Remington-Rand Corp, Minn, 56-59; instr math, Iowa State Univ, 62-63; mem tech staff, Radio Corp Am Labs, 63-69, MEM TECH STAFF, RCA CORP, 69- *Mem:* Soc Indust & Appl Math; Inst Elec & Electronics Eng; Asn Comput Mach. *Res:* Numerical analysis and scientific applications of digital computers. *Mailing Add:* RCA Corp Princeton NJ 08540

CRANE, SARA W, b Tallahassee, Fla, Nov 24, 51; m 70. PHYSICS. *Educ:* Univ Ill at Chicago Circle, BS, 76, MS, 78, PhD(physics), 82. *Prof Exp:* RES PHYSICIST, AMOCO RES CTR, STANDARD OIL CO, 81- *Mem:* Am Phys Soc; Inst Elec & Electronics Engrs; AAAS. *Res:* Magnetic properties of alloys; materials development primarily concerned with ceramics. *Mailing Add:* #810 5110 S Kenwood Chicago IL 60615

CRANE, SHELDON CYR, b Long Beach, Calif, Dec 22, 18; m 56; c 1. ANALYTICAL INSTRUMENTATION, ENVIRONMENTAL SCIENCES. *Educ:* Calif Inst Technol, BS, 40; Univ Calif, Los Angeles, PhD(phys biol sci), 49. *Prof Exp:* Res fel chem, Calif Inst Technol, 49-55; proj engr, Gyro Div, Giannini Controls Corp, 56-59; specialist engr inertial navig, Monterey Eng Lab, Dalmo Victor Corp, 59-60; res opers engr, Combat Develop Exp Ctr, Stanford Res Inst, 60-61; partner, Del Monte Tech Assocs, 61-62; opers res analyst, Combat Develop Exp Ctr, Stanford Res Inst, Ft Ord, 62-63, US Army Concept Team, Viet Nam, 63-64, combat develop exp ctr, 64, sr res engr marine tech, Systs Sci Dept, 64-65, bioengr med res, Life Sci, 65-72; sr res assoc, Haile Sellassie I Univ, Addis Ababa, Ethiopia, 72-74; head, Monitoring Div, Guam Environ Protection Agency, 74-76; head, Anal Lab, Environ Health & Safety, 76-79, RES ASSOC CHEM, UNIV HAWAII, 79- *Mem:* Am Chem Soc; AAAS; Sigma Xi. *Res:* Studies of respiratory function and effects of artificially induced emphysema in rats and monkeys; development of pilot manufacturing facility for concentrating the molluscicidal principle in the soap berry Endod for schistosomiasis control; instrumentation for air pollution monitoring; noise pollution studies; chemical analysis for air and water pollution; analog and digital systems in chemical instrumentation; gas chromatography. *Mailing Add:* 6616 Kii Pl Honolulu HI 96825

CRANEFIELD, PAUL FREDERIC, b Madison, Wis, Apr 28, 25. PHYSIOLOGY. *Educ:* Univ Wis, PhB, 46, PhD(physiol), 51; Albert Einstein Col Med, MD, 64. *Prof Exp:* From instr to to assoc prof, Dept Physiol, State Univ NY Downstate Med Ctr, 53-62; exec secy, Comt Pub & Med Info & ed bull, NY Acad Med, 63-66; assoc prof physiol, 66-75; PROF PHYSIOL, ROCKEFELLER UNIV, 75-; ED, J GEN PHYSIOL, 66- *Concurrent Pos:* Rockefeller Found-Nat Res Coun fel, Dept Biophys, Johns Hopkins Univ, 51-53; sr res fel, Dept Psychiat, Albert Einstein Col Med, 60-64; assoc prof pharm, Col Physicians & Surgeons, Columbia Univ, 64-66, adj assoc prof, 66-75, adj prof, 75- *Honors & Awards:* Schumann Prize, 56. *Mem:* Am Physiol Soc; Biophys Soc; Soc Gen Physiologists; Am Asn Hist Med; fel Int Acad Hist Med. *Res:* Electrophysiology of single cardiac cells; electrophysiological basis of cardiac arrhythmias; antiarrhythmic drugs; history of 19th century physiology and mental retardation. *Mailing Add:* Rockefeller Univ New York NY 10021

CRANFORD, JACK ALLEN, b San Francisco, Calif, Dec 23, 39. MAMMALIAN ECOLOGY, PHYSIOLOGICAL ECOLOGY. *Educ:* San Francisco State Col, BA, 67, MA, 70; Univ Utah, PhD(ecol), 77. *Prof Exp:* Res asst ecol, Dr J G Hall, N Rim, Grand Canyon, Ariz, 70; park naturalist park ecol, Mt Rainier Nat Park, Longmire, Wash, 71-72; instr biol, Hartnell Col, Salinas, Calif, 73; ASST PROF ZOOL & CUR MAMMALS, VA POLYTECH INST & STATE UNIV, 77- *Concurrent Pos:* Acad fac, Corresp Study Sch, Univ Utah, 74-; prin investr, Va Polytech Inst & State Univ res grants, 78-81, Dept Interior res grant, 80-83. *Honors & Awards:* A Brazier Howell Award, Am Soc Mammalogists, 76. *Mem:* Am Soc Mammalogists; Am Soc Zoologist; Am Soc Naturalists; Am Ecol Soc; Am Inst Biol Sci. *Res:* Ecology, behavior and physiology of mammals; with special emphasis on field ecology, circadian rhythms, cirannual rhythms and physiological regulation of hibernation in small mammals. *Mailing Add:* Dept of Biol Va Polytech Inst & State Univ Blacksburg VA 24061

CRANFORD, JERRY L, b Heber Springs, Ark, Mar 12, 42; m 67. NEUROPSYCHOLOGY, PSYCHOPHYSIOLOGY. *Educ:* Wichita State Univ, BA, 64; Vanderbilt Univ, PhD(exp psychol), 68. *Prof Exp:* USPHS trainee, Med Ctr, Duke Univ, 68-70; res assoc neuropsychol, Ind Univ, Bloomington, 70-73, asst prof physiol psychol, 72-73; asst prof auditory psychophysiol, Baylor Col Med, 73-78; ASST PROF AUDITORY PSYCHOPHYSIOL, UNIV TEX MED BR, 78- *Mem:* Soc Neurosci; Int Brain Res Orgn. *Res:* Neuroanatomical and neurophysiological substrates of auditory nervous system function. *Mailing Add:* Otolaryngol Dept Univ of Tex Med Br Galveston TX 77550

CRANFORD, ROBERT HENRY, b Columbia, Tenn, Sept 10, 35; m 60; c 3. MATHEMATICS. *Educ:* Mid Tenn State Col, BS, 57; La State Univ, MS, 59, PhD(algebra), 64. *Prof Exp:* Asst prof math, NTex State Univ, 64-73; assoc prof, 73-76, PROF MATH, TEX EASTERN UNIV, 76-, CHMN DEPT MATH & COMPUT SCI, 80- *Mem:* Math Asn Am; Nat Coun Teachers Math. *Res:* Ideal theory in commutative rings with unity. *Mailing Add:* Dept of Math Tex Eastern Univ Tyler TX 75701

CRANFORD, WILLIAM B(RETT), b Chatham, Ont, Dec 20, 20; m 50; c 2. CHEMICAL ENGINEERING. *Educ:* Univ Toronto, BASc, 42, MASc, 47. *Prof Exp:* Res engr, Indust Cellulose Res Ltd, 47-60, chemist in charge chem eng & new prod lab, 60-63, mgr, Process Develop Div, Int Cellulose Res, Ltd, 63-70; V PRES & SECY, CIP RES LTD, 70- *Mem:* Sr mem Can Tech Asn Pulp & Paper Indust; sr mem Can Pulp & Paper Asn. *Res:* Cellulose and related substances and its application to industrial processes involving either pulping and bleaching of pulp and paper or the recovery of by-products. *Mailing Add:* CIP Res Ltd 179 Main St W Hawkesbury Can

CRANG, RICHARD EARL, b Clinton, Ill, Dec 2, 36; m 58; c 2. PLANT CYTOLOGY, ELECTRON MICROSCOPY. *Educ:* Eastern Ill Univ, BS, 58; Univ SDak, MA, 62; Univ Iowa, PhD(bot), 65. *Prof Exp:* Teacher high sch, Ill, 58-61; asst prof biol, Wittenberg Univ, 65-69; assoc prof biol, 69-74, PROF BIOL SCI, BOWLING GREEN STATE UNIV, 74- *Concurrent Pos:* Mem educ comt, Electron Microscopy Soc Am, 72-; adj prof anat, Med Col Ohio, 74- *Mem:* AAAS; Am Soc Cell Biol; Bot Soc Am; Electron Micros Soc Am; Sigma Xi. *Res:* Plant ultrastructure, particularly fine structure of fungal cells as effected by environmental mercury; analyses with transmission and scanning electron microscopy and x-ray microanalysis. *Mailing Add:* Dept of Biol Sci Bowling Green State Univ Bowling Green OH 43403

CRANMER, MORRIS F, pharmacology, biochemistry, see previous edition

CRANNELL, CAROL JO ARGUS, b Columbus, Ohio, Nov 15, 38; m 61; c 3. ASTROPHYSICS. *Educ:* Miami Univ, Ohio, BA, 60; Stanford Univ, PhD(physics), 67. *Prof Exp:* Fel exp nuclear physics, Cath Univ, 67-70; res assoc high energy cosmic ray physics, Fed City Col & Goddard Space Flight Ctr, NASA, 70-73; res scientist, Imp Col, Univ London, 73-74; vis scientist, Mass Inst Technol, 74; ASTROPHYSICIST, GODDARD SPACE FLIGHT CTR, NASA, 74- *Concurrent Pos:* Asst prof, Howard Univ, 68-69. *Mem:* Am Phys Soc. *Res:* Solar physics. *Mailing Add:* Code 684 NASA Goddard Space Flight Ctr Greenbelt MD 20771

CRANNELL, HALL L, b Berkeley, Calif, Feb 23, 36; m 61; c 3. NUCLEAR PHYSICS. *Educ:* Miami Univ, BA, 56, MA, 58; Stanford Univ, PhD(physics), 64. *Prof Exp:* Res assoc high energy physics, Stanford Univ, 64-67; assoc prof, 67-72, chmn dept, 78-80, PROF PHYSICS, CATH UNIV AM, 72- . *Concurrent Pos:* Vis sr scientist & vis prof, Westfield Col, Univ London, 73-74; vis prof, Mass Inst Technol, 74. *Mem:* AAAS; fel Am Phys Soc; Am Asn Phys Teachers; Am Asn Univ Prof. *Res:* Electron scattering at medium energies; astrophysics; nuclear instrumentation. *Mailing Add:* 10000 Branch View Ct Silver Spring MD 20903

CRANO, JOHN CARL, b Akron, Ohio, Nov 16, 35; m 58; c 3. ORGANIC CHEMISTRY. *Educ:* Univ Notre Dame, BS, 57; Case Inst Technol, MS, 59, PhD(org chem), 62. *Prof Exp:* Sr res chemist, Chem Div, Pittsburgh Plate Glass Co, 61-63, res supvr, 63-65, res assoc, 65-78, SR RES ASSOC, CHEM DIV, PPG INDUSTS, INC, 78- *Mem:* AAAS; Am Chem Soc. *Res:* Mechanism of halocarbon pyrolyses; fluorine chemistry; heterogeneous catalysis; halogen exchange reactions; polymerization; bromine chemistry. *Mailing Add:* PPG Industs Inc PO Box 31 Barberton OH 44203

CRANSTON, FREDERICK PITKIN, JR, b Denver, Colo, Aug 28, 22; m 46; c 4. PHYSICS. *Educ:* Colgate Univ, BA, 43; Stanford Univ, MS, 50, PhD(physics), 59. *Prof Exp:* Asst physics, Stanford Univ, 47-53; mem staff nuclear physics, Los Alamos Sci Lab, 53-62; assoc prof, 62-66, PROF PHYSICS, HUMBOLDT STATE UNIV, 66- *Concurrent Pos:* Consult, Lawrence Livermore Lab, Univ Calif, 64-70. *Mem:* Am Phys Soc; Am Asn Physics Teachers; Fedn Am Scientists. *Res:* Nuclear spectroscopy; radiation hazards; nuclear weapons effects; x-ray fluorescence; forensic physics. *Mailing Add:* Dept of Physics Humboldt State Univ Arcata CA 95521

CRAPO, HENRY HOWLAND, b Detroit, Mich, Aug 12, 32; m 62; c 3. MATHEMATICS. *Educ:* Univ Mich, AB, 54; Mass Inst Technol, PhD(math), 64. *Prof Exp:* Prof math, Univ Waterloo, 65-77; prof math, Mem Univ Nfld, 77-81; RESEARCHER, APPL MATH, UNIV MONTREAL, 81- *Concurrent Pos:* Mem coun, Can Math Cong, 75-79; mem, Ctr Math Res, Montreal, mem, Res Group Struct Topology; vis prof archit, Univ Montreal, 78-81. *Mem:* Am Math Soc; Math Asn Am; NY Acad Sci. *Res:* Combinatorial geometry; abstract linear dependence; lattices and ordered sets; applications of projective and combinatorial geometry to architecture and structural engineering. *Mailing Add:* Res Group on Struct Topology Univ of Montreal CP 6128 Montreal PQ H3C 3J7 Can

CRAPPER, DONALD RAYMOND, b Windsor, Ont, Can, Oct 4, 32; m 58; c 2. NEUROPHYSIOLOGY, NEUROLOGY. *Educ:* Univ Toronto, MD, 57; FRCP(C), 66. *Prof Exp:* HC Storrs fel ment retardation, Neuropath, Letchworth Village, NY, 58-60; fel neurophysiol, State Univ NY, Buffalo, 60-63; PROF PHYSIOL & ASSOC PROF MED, UNIV TORONTO, 66- *Concurrent Pos:* Staff neurologist, Toronto Gen Hosp, 66-; consult neurologist, Clark Inst Psychiat, 76- *Mem:* Can Neurol Soc; Soc Neurosci. *Res:* Trace metals and brain aging; chromatin structure and brain aging; neurophysiology of dementia. *Mailing Add:* Dept of Physiol Univ of Toronto Toronto ON M5S 1A1 Can

CRAPUCHETTES, PAUL W(YTHE), b San Francisco, Calif, Feb 12, 17; m 41; c 7. ANALYTICAL ENGINEERING. *Educ:* Univ Calif, BS, 40. *Prof Exp:* Test engr, Gen Elec Co, NY, 41, design engr, 42-43, 44-45; proj engr, Electronic Res Assocs, Calif, 46; DIR ENG, VACUUM TUBE DIV, LITTON INDUSTS, 46-, VPRES, 64-, TECH DIR, 76- *Concurrent Pos:* Mem bd dirs, Dirks Electronics, 69; mem bd trustees, Fuller Theol Sem, 69- *Mem:* Fel Inst Elec & Electronics Engrs. *Res:* Gaseous conductors; ultra-high frequency devices, particularly magnetron design; thyratron counter and multiple collector for counters; H-2 thyrathron for radar pulsing. *Mailing Add:* Box 13 Goodyear Rd Benicia CA 94510

CRARY, ALBERT PADDOCK, b Pierrepont, NY, July 25, 11; m 68; c 1. GEOPHYSICS. *Educ:* St Lawrence Univ, BS, 31; Lehigh Univ, MS, 33. *Hon Degrees:* PhD, St Lawrence Univ, 59. *Prof Exp:* Explor geophysicist, Independent Explor Co, 35-41; proj scientist, Woods Hole Oceanog Inst, 41-42; explor geophysicist, United Geophys Co, 42-46; proj scientist, US Air Force Cambridge Res Ctr, 46-60; chief scientist, Off Antarctic Prog, NSF, 60-67, dep dir, 67-69, dir, Div Environ Sci, 69-75 & dir, Div Earth Sci, 76; RES ASSOC, HAVERFORD COL, 79-82. *Concurrent Pos:* Dep chief scientist, US Nat Comt, Int Geophys Year, Antarctic Prog, Nat Acad Sci, 56-58. *Honors & Awards:* Vega Medal, Swedish Soc Anthrop & Geog; Cullum Medal, Am Geog Soc, 59; Patrons Medal, Royal Geog Soc, 63. *Mem:* AAAS; Am Geophys Union; Am Geog Soc. *Res:* Seismic exploration for oil; atmospheric acoustic studies; geophysical work in Arctic Ocean Basin and Antarctica. *Mailing Add:* 8301 Beech Tree Rd Bethesda MD 20817

CRARY, JAMES WALTER, b Lexington, Ky, June 21, 30; m 54; c 2. ORGANIC CHEMISTRY. *Educ:* Univ Ky, BS, 52; Emory Univ, PhD(chem), 55. *Prof Exp:* RES CHEMIST, EXP STA, E I DU PONT DE NEMOURS & CO, 55- *Res:* Polymer chemistry, particularly elastomers. *Mailing Add:* 3017 Ridgevale Rd Wilmington DE 19808

CRARY, SELDEN BRONSON, b Schenectady, NY, May 10, 49; m 75. PHYSICS. *Educ:* Brown Univ, ScB, 71; Univ Wash, MS, 73, PhD(physics), 78. *Prof Exp:* ASST PROF PHYSICS, AMHERST COL, 78- *Concurrent Pos:* Vis asst prof physics, Univ Mass, Amherst, 81- *Mem:* Am Phys Soc; Am Asn Physics Teachers; AAAS. *Res:* Properties of helium films. *Mailing Add:* Dept of Physics Amherst Col Amherst MA 01002

CRASEMANN, BERND, b Hamburg, Ger, Jan 23, 22; nat; m 52. ATOMIC PHYSICS. *Educ:* Univ Calif, Los Angeles, AB, 48; Univ Calif, Berkeley, PhD(physics), 53. *Prof Exp:* From asst prof to assoc prof, 53-63, PROF PHYSICS, UNIV ORE, 63-, HEAD DEPT, 76- *Concurrent Pos:* Consult, Lawrence Radiation Lab, Berkeley, 54-68; guest assoc physicist, Brookhaven Nat Lab, 61-62; vis prof, physics dept, Univ Calif, Berkeley, 68-69; chmn ad hoc panel on accelerator-related atomic physics res, Comt Atomic & Molecular Physics, Nat Acad Sci-Nat Res Coun, 74-, vchmn, Comt, 78-; vis scientist, Ames Res Ctr, NASA, 75-76; vis prof, Univ Paris VI & Lab Curie, 77; mem proposal rev panel, Stanford Synchrotron Radiation Lab, 78-; mem physics, subcomt, adv comt for review of atomic, molecular & plasma physics, NSF, 81; chmn organizing comt, Int Conf on X-ray & Atomic Inner-Shell Physics, 82. *Mem:* Fel Am Phys Soc; Am Asn Physics Teachers; AAAS. *Res:* Atomic inner-shell processes; transition probabilities; interface of atomic and nuclear physics. *Mailing Add:* Dept of Physics Univ of Ore Eugene OR 97403

CRASS, MAURICE FREDERICK, III, b Akron, Ohio, Nov 15, 34; m 60; c 3. PHYSIOLOGY, BIOCHEMISTRY. *Educ:* Univ Md, BS, 57, MS, 59; Vanderbilt Univ, PhD(physiol), 65. *Prof Exp:* Instr physiol, Sch Med, Vanderbilt Univ, 65-66; asst prof med & physiol, Col Med, Univ Fla, 69-70; from asst prof to assoc prof biochem & med, Col Med, Univ Nebr, 70-73; assoc prof, 73-81, PROF PHYSIOL, SCH MED, TEX TECH UNIV, 81- *Concurrent Pos:* Res fel, Tenn Heart Asn, 65-66; res fel med, Col Med, Univ Fla, 66-69. *Mem:* AAAS; Am Physiol Soc; Soc Exp Biol & Med. *Res:* Cardiovascular physiology and biochemistry; carbohydrate and lipid metabolism; hormonal regulation of metabolism; vascular smooth muscle function. *Mailing Add:* Dept of Physiol Tex Tech Univ Sch of Med Lubbock TX 79430

CRAST, LEONARD BRUCE, JR, b Adams, NY, June 1, 36; m 55; c 4. ORGANIC CHEMISTRY, MEDICINAL CHEMISTRY. *Educ:* Syracuse Univ, AB, 58. *Prof Exp:* Jr chemist, 58-65, SR RES SCIENTIST CHEM, BRISTOL LABS, INC, 65- *Mem:* Am Chem Soc. *Res:* Semi-synthetic penicillins and cephalosporins, most notably cephapirin and cefadroxil. *Mailing Add:* 108 Deborah Ln North Syracuse NY 13212

CRASWELL, KEITH J, b Kent, Wash, Dec 17, 36; m 58; c 2. MATHEMATICS. *Educ:* Univ Wash, BS, 59, MSc, 61, PhD(math), 63. *Prof Exp:* Actg instr math, Univ Wash, 62-63; staff mem, Statist Res Div, Sandia Corp, 63-65; asst prof math & statist, Colo State Univ, 65-67; assoc prof, 67-80, PROF MATH, WESTERN WASH STATE UNIV, 80- *Mem:* Inst Math Statist; Am Math Soc; Math Asn Am. *Res:* Stochastic processes. *Mailing Add:* Dept of Math & Comput Sci Western Wash State Univ Bellingham WA 98225

CRATER, HORACE WILLIAM, b Washington, DC, May 26, 42; m 63; c 2. PARTICLE PHYSICS, QUANTUM MECHANICS. *Educ:* Col William & Mary, BS, 64; Yale Univ, MS, 65, MPhil & PhD(physics), 68. *Prof Exp:* Vis mem, Inst Advan Study, 68-70; asst prof physics, Vanderbilt Univ, 70-75; mem staff, 75-80, ASST PROF PHYSICS, SPACE INST, UNIV TENN, 80- *Mem:* Am Phys Soc. *Res:* Theoretical particle physics, current algebra; meson-meson scattering; phenomenological quantum field theory; non-perturbative techniques in quantum field theory; Pade approximants; two body relativistic quantum mechanic and quark models. *Mailing Add:* Dept of Physics Univ of Tenn Space Inst Tullahoma TN 37388

CRATIN, PAUL DAVID, b Moline, Ill, Feb 26, 29; m 57; c 5. PHYSICAL CHEMISTRY. *Educ:* Spring Hill Col, BS, 51; St Louis Univ, MS, 54; Tex A&M Univ, PhD(thermodyn), 62. *Prof Exp:* Anal chemist, Chemstrand Corp, 55-58; instr chem, Ga Inst Technol, 58-59 & Tex A&M Univ, 59-62; res chemist, Jersey Prod Res Co, 62-64; assoc prof, Spring Hill Col, 64-67; res assoc, St Regis Paper Co, 67-68; assoc prof, Univ Miami, 68-70; chmn dept chem, 71-73, PROF CHEM, CENT MICH UNIV, 71- *Mem:* Am Chem Soc. *Res:* Excess thermodynamic properties of binary liquid solutions; application of thermodynamics to surface and interfacial phenomena; kinetics and mechanisms of homogeneous chemical reactions; hyperbaric processes as related to oceanography. *Mailing Add:* Dept Chem Cent Mich Univ Mt Pleasant MI 48859

CRATTY, LELAND EARL, JR, b Oregon, Ill, June 3, 30; m 56; c 3. PHYSICAL CHEMISTRY, SURFACE CHEMISTRY. *Educ:* Beloit Col, BS, 52; Brown Univ, PhD(chem), 57. *Prof Exp:* Res chemist, Linde Co, 56-58; from asst prof to assoc prof, 58-73, PROF CHEM, HAMILTON COL, 73- *Concurrent Pos:* Vis fel, Mellon Inst, 64-65; chemist, Ames Lab, US Atomic Energy Comn, 69-70. *Mem:* AAAS; Am Chem Soc. *Res:* Ultra high vacuum techniques; adsorption state in clean surfaces; surface chemistry and catalysis, particularly at metal and alloy surfaces; rates of adsorption at very low pressures. *Mailing Add:* Dept of Chem Hamilton Col Clinton NY 13323

CRAVEN, BRYAN MAXWELL, b Wellington, NZ, Feb 12, 32; m 56; c 1. STRUCTURAL CHEMISTRY. *Educ:* Univ Auckland, BSc, 53, MSc, 54, PhD(chem), 58. *Prof Exp:* Jr lectr, Univ Auckland, 56; res assoc & instr, 57-59, from asst res prof to assoc prof, 59-71, chmn dept crystallog, 74-77, PROF CHEM CRYSTALLOG, UNIV PITTSBURGH, 71- *Concurrent Pos:* Rothmans sr fel, Univ Sydney, 62-64. *Res:* Crystal structure determination of drugs and biomolecules, including lipids, serum albumin. *Mailing Add:* Dept of Crystallog Univ of Pittsburgh Pittsburgh PA 15260

CRAVEN, CHARLES WALLER, b Hastings, Okla, Jan 5, 20; m 43; c 2. CHEMISTRY, BIOCHEMISTRY. *Educ:* Okla Agr & Mech Col, BS, 47, MS, 49; Ohio State Univ, PhD(biochem), 53. *Prof Exp:* Chief biochem br, Air Force Armament Ctr, US Air Force, Eglin Air Force Base, Fla, 53-55, dir biosci, Air Force Off Sci Res, Washington, DC, 55-57, dept dir adv studies, Pasadena, Calif, 57-59, chief, Tech Div, Regional Off, Air Force Res & Develop Command, Hollywood, 59-60, dept chief bioastronaut, Space Systs Div, Los Angeles, 60-62, manned military vehicle directorate, 62-63, dir, Manned Environ Systs Directorate, 63-65, dept dir space prog, 65-67; planetary quarantine mgr, Voyager Proj, Jet Propulsion Lab, Calif Inst Technol, 67-69, mem tech staff long range planning & exec asst to dir, 69-73, mgr planetary quarantine proj off, 73-77, CONSULT, CALIF INST TECHNOL, 77- *Mem:* AAAS; Sigma Xi. *Mailing Add:* 4535 Alveo Rd La Canada CA 91011

CRAVEN, CLAUDE JACKSON, b Concord, NC, Jan 13, 08. PHYSICS. *Educ:* Univ NC, AB, 31, MA, 33, PhD(physics), 35. *Prof Exp:* Asst prof physics & math, Delta State Teachers Col, 35-36; assoc prof physics, Furman Univ, 36-39; asst prof physics & math, Emory Univ, 39-42; scientist, Columbia Univ, 42-45; physicist, Carbide & Carbon Chem Corp, NY & Tenn, 45-46; physicist, Fiber Res Lab, 46-52, from assoc physicist agr exp sta to prof univ, 52-77, EMER PROF, UNIV TENN, 77- *Concurrent Pos:* Consult, Oak Ridge Nat Lab, 46-; prin scientist, Oak Ridge Inst Nuclear Studies, 60-66. *Mem:* AAAS; Am Phys Soc. *Res:* Infrared spectroscopy; gaseous diffusion through porous media; physical properties of fibers. *Mailing Add:* 3605 Montlake Dr Knoxville TN 37920

CRAVEN, JAMES MILTON, polymer chemistry, see previous edition

CRAVEN, JOHN P(INNA), b Brooklyn, NY, Oct 30, 24; m 51; c 2. ENGINEERING PHYSICS. *Educ:* Cornell Univ, BS, 46; Calif Inst Technol, MS, 47; Univ Iowa, PhD, 51; George Washington Univ, JurDr, 58. *Prof Exp:* Assoc hydraul, Univ Iowa, 49-51; phys sci adminr, David Taylor Model Basin, 51-59; chief scientist, Special Proj Off, US Naval Bur Weapons, 59-70; dean marine progs, 70-80, PROF OCEAN ENG, UNIV HAWAII, 70-, CHMN BD, NATURAL ENERGY LAB HAWAII, 80- *Concurrent Pos:* Vis prof, Dept Naval Archit & Marine Eng, Mass Inst Technol, 69-70; marine affairs coordr, State of Hawaii, 70-; dir, Law of Sea Inst, 77- *Honors & Awards:* Distinguished Civilian Serv Award, US Dept Defense; Meritorious Civilian Serv Award, US Navy. *Mem:* Nat Acad Eng; Am Soc Mech Engrs; Am Phys Soc; Soc Naval Archit & Marine Engrs. *Res:* Ocean engineering and development. *Mailing Add:* Off of Dean Marine Progs Univ Hawaii 2540 Dole St Honolulu HI 96822

CRAVEN, ROBERT LEE, organic chemistry, see previous edition

CRAVENS, THOMAS EDWARD, b Honolulu, Hawaii, Oct 14, 48; m 75; c 1. PLANETARY ATMOSPHERES, IONOSPHERIC PHYSICS. *Educ:* State Univ NY Stony Brook, BS, 70; Harvard Univ, PhD(astron), 75. *Prof Exp:* Fel atmospheric physics, Univ Colo, 74-76 & Univ Fla, 76-77; asst res scientist, 77-81, ASSOC RES SCIENTIST SPACE PHYSICS, UNIV MICH, 81-, MEM FAC ELEC COMPUT ENG, 80- *Mem:* Am Geophys Union; AAAS. *Res:* Atmospheric and space physics, particularly upper atmospheres and ionospheres of Venus, Mars, and Jupiter, and the terrestrial ionosphere-magnetosphere coupling. *Mailing Add:* Space Physics Res Lab Univ Mich 2455 Hayward Ann Arbor MI 48109

CRAVENS, WILLIAM WINDSOR, b Daviess Co, Ky, Oct 24, 14; m 39; c 5. NUTRITION, RESEARCH ADMINISTRATION. *Educ:* Univ Ky, BS, 35; Iowa State Col, MS, 37; Univ Wis, PhD(biochem), 40. *Prof Exp:* Asst animal chem & nutrit, Iowa State Col, 35-37; from asst to instr poultry, Univ Wis, 37-41, from asst prof to prof poultry husb, 41-53; dir feed res, Cent Soya Co, 53-68, vpres res, 68-78; RETIRED. *Honors & Awards:* Am Feed Mfrs Award, 50. *Mem:* Am Chem Soc; Poultry Sci Asn; Soc Exp Biol & Med; Am Soc Animal Sci; Am Inst Nutrit. *Res:* Nutrition of livestock and poultry; animal production; feed formulation; soybean processing; food technology. *Mailing Add:* 11112 Carriage Pl Ft Wayne IN 46825

CRAVER, CLARA DIDDLE (SMITH), b Portsmouth, Ohio, Dec 3, 24; m 46, 70; c 4. SPECTROCHEMISTRY, PETROLEUM CHEMISTRY. *Educ:* Ohio State Univ, BSc, 45. *Hon Degrees:* DSc, Fisk Univ, 74. *Prof Exp:* Tech man spectros, Esso Res Labs, 45-48; res engr, Battelle Mem Inst, 49-55, group leader, 55-57, consult, 57-58; SPECTROS CONSULT & OWNER CHEMIR LABS, 58- *Concurrent Pos:* Carbide & carbon chem award, Am Chem Soc, 55-56; ed, Coblentz Soc Spectral Data, 56-; instr chem, Ohio State Univ, 57-58; guest lectr, Infrared Inst, Fisk Univ, 59-69 & Fisk Infrared Inst, Sao Paulo, Brazil, 65 & fac mem, 65; guest lectr, Infrared Inst, Univ Minn, 61-62, 64-65 & 67-68 & Canisius Col, 61; consult, Nat Stand Ref Data Prog, 65-; consult, US Coast Guard, 75. *Honors & Awards:* A K Doolittle Award, Union Carbide & Am Chem Soc, 56. *Mem:* Am Chem Soc; Optical Soc Am; Coblentz Soc; Soc Appl Spectros; Am Soc Test & Mat. *Res:* Application of chemical spectroscopy to research and analysis in polymers, coatings, marine environment, air pollution, petroleum products, asphalts, paper and cellulose chemistry; standard data compilations and computer retrieval of spectroscopic data; absorption spectroscopy; applications of infrared spectroscopy; polymer science; forensic science. *Mailing Add:* 761 W Kirkham Ave Glendale MO 63122

CRAVER, JOHN KENNETH, b Jonesboro, Ill, May 1, 15; m 39, 70; c 4. CHEMISTRY, TECHNOLOGICAL FORECASTING. *Educ:* Southern Ill Univ, BEd, 37; Syracuse Univ, MS, 38. *Prof Exp:* Res chemist, Monsanto Co, 38-46, coordr plasticizers, 46-51, develop mgr resin mat & functional fluids, 51-54; develop dir, Gen Mills, Inc, 55-56; develop mgr, Res & Eng Div, 56-61, res assoc org div, 61-67, sr res assoc, Cent Res Dept, 67-70, mgr, 70-79, PRES, FUTURESEARCH & MGT CONSULT, MONSANTO CO, 79- *Concurrent Pos:* Chmn, Gordon Res Conf, 66. *Mem:* Fel AAAS; Am Chem Soc (chmn, Chem Mkt & Econ Div, 75); Commercial Chem Develop Asn. *Res:* Long range planning; decision analysis; paper and polymer chemistry; applied research; commercial development. *Mailing Add:* 761 W Kirkham Glendale MO 63122

CRAVIOTO, HUMBERTO, b Pachuca, Mex, Oct 4, 24. NEUROPATHOLOGY, NEUROLOGY. *Educ:* Sci & Lit Inst, Mex, BS, 45; Nat Univ Mex, MD, 52; State Univ NY, MD, 64. *Prof Exp:* Jr & sr resident path, Univ Vt, 52-54; resident neurol, Bellevue Med Ctr, NY Univ, 54-56, instr neurol & neuropath, 56-58, asst prof neuropath, 58-64; assoc prof path & neurol, Sch Med, Univ Southern Calif, 64-68; assoc prof, 68-77, PROF NEUROPATH, SCH MED, NY UNIV, 77- *Concurrent Pos:* Alexander von Humboldt Soc res fel electron micros, Berlin, 61-62. *Mem:* Am Acad Neurol; Am Asn Neuropath (asst secy-treas, 61-64); Histochem Soc; NY Acad Sci; AAAS. *Res:* Electron microscopy; brain tumor immunology. *Mailing Add:* NY Univ Sch of Med 550 First Ave New York NY 10016

CRAVITZ, LEO, b Chelsea, Mass, Nov 26, 18; m 44; c 3. BACTERIOLOGY, IMMUNOLOGY. *Educ:* Boston Univ, BS, 41; Mass Inst Technol, DrPH, 44. *Prof Exp:* Fel pub health lab methods, Mass Inst Technol, 42-44; MED MICROBIOLOGIST, ROCHESTER GEN HOSP, 46-, HOSP EPIDEMIOLOGIST, 68- *Concurrent Pos:* Res assoc, Boston Health Dept, 42-44; instr, Wilson Sch, Mass, 43-44; consult, Pennwalt Pharmaceut Labs, Pennwalt Corp, 50-, Castle Co, Sybron Corp, 58-, Park-Ridge Hosp, Rochester, 63- & Myers Community Hosp, Sodus, NY, 67- *Mem:* Soc Hosp Epidemiol Am; Sigma Xi; Am Soc Microbiol. *Res:* Pertussis immunization; immunology of glanders and meliodosis; clostridium perfringens food poisoning; laboratory diagnosis of rheumatic diseases; immunologic factors in allergic disease; antibiotic synergism; sterilization with chemical agents; surgical antisepsis and hospital infection. *Mailing Add:* Rochester Gen Hosp 1425 Portland Ave Rochester NY 14621

CRAWFORD, BRYCE (LOW), JR, b New Orleans, La, Nov 27, 14; m 40; c 3. PHYSICAL CHEMISTRY, MOLECULAR SPECTROSCOPY. *Educ:* Stanford Univ, AB, 34, AM, 35, PhD(chem), 37. *Prof Exp:* Asst chem, Stanford Univ, 33-35; Nat Res Found fel, Harvard Univ, 37-39; instr chem, Yale Univ, 39-40; from asst prof to assoc prof, 40-46, chmn dept, 55-60, dean grad sch, 60-72, mem grad record exam bd, 68-72, PROF PHYS CHEM, UNIV MINN, MINNEAPOLIS, 46- *Concurrent Pos:* Guggenheim Found fel, Calif Inst Technol & Oxford Univ, 50-51; Fulbright fel, Oxford Univ, 51; chmn, Coun Grad Schs US, 62-63; mem bd dirs, North Star Res Found, Midwest Res Inst, 63-; Fulbright prof, Univ Tokyo, 66; mem adv comt, Off Sci Personnel, Nat Res Coun, 67-71, mem gov bd, 75-78; ed, J Phys Chem, 70-80. *Honors & Awards:* Presidential Cert Merit; Minn Award, Am Chem Soc, 68; Pittsburgh Spectros Award, 77; Ellis Lippincott Award, 78; Priestley Medal, 82. *Mem:* Nat Acad Sci (secy, 79-); Am Chem Soc; Asn Grad Schs (pres, 70); Optical Soc Am; Am Acad Arts & Sci. *Res:* Molecular spectra; statistical thermodynamics; kinetics; molecular dynamics. *Mailing Add:* Dept Chem 13 Smith Hall Univ Minn Minneapolis MN 55455

CRAWFORD, CLIFFORD SMEED, b Beirut, Lebanon, July 30, 32; US citizen; m 58; c 3. DESERT INVERTEBRATES. *Educ:* Whitman Col, BA, 54; Wash State Univ, MS, 58, PhD(entom), 61. *Prof Exp:* Instr biol, Portland State Col, 61-64; from asst prof to assoc prof, 64-73, chmn dept, 75-78, PROF BIOL, UNIV NMEX, 73- *Mem:* AAAS; Entom Soc Am; Ecol Soc Am; Int Asn Ecol. *Res:* Ecology and physiology of arid-land invertebrates. *Mailing Add:* Dept of Biol Univ of NMex Albuquerque NM 87131

CRAWFORD, CRAYTON MCCANTS, b Greenville, SC, Sept 20, 26; m 55; c 3. PHYSICAL CHEMISTRY. *Educ:* Clemson Col, BS, 49; Univ NC, PhD(phys chem), 57. *Prof Exp:* Mem staff, Los Alamos Sci Lab, 55-59; asst prof, 59, ASSOC PROF PHYS CHEM, MISS STATE UNIV, 59- *Concurrent Pos:* Ed, J Miss Acad Sci, 68-76. *Mem:* Am Chem Soc; Sigma Xi. *Res:* Precision absorptiometry; thermodynamics; photochemical kinetics. *Mailing Add:* Dept of Chem Miss State Univ Drawer CH Mississippi State MS 39762

CRAWFORD, DANIEL JOHN, b Columbus Junction, Iowa, May 27, 42; m 61; c 2. PLANT TAXONOMY. *Educ:* Univ Iowa, BA, 64, MS, 66, PhD(bot), 69. *Prof Exp:* from asst prof to assoc prof bot, Univ Wyo, 69-77; PROF BOT, OHIO STATE UNIV, 77- *Mem:* Bot Soc Am; Int Asn Plant Taxon; Am Soc Plant Taxon. *Res:* Systematics and evolution of flowering plants; use of flavonoid compounds and allozymes in elucidating plant relationships. *Mailing Add:* Dept Bot Ohio State Univ Columbus OH 43210

CRAWFORD, DAVID LEE, b Hays, Kans, Nov 30, 35; m 57; c 2. FOOD SCIENCE, FOOD BIOCHEMISTRY. *Educ:* Ore State Col, BS, 58, Ore State Univ, MS, 61, PhD(food sci), 66. *Prof Exp:* Chemist I, 58-60, from asst to asst prof food sci, 64-70, assoc prof food sci & technol, 70-76, PROF FOOD SCI & TECHNOL, ORE STATE UNIV, 76-, PROG DIR SEAFOODS LAB, 66- *Concurrent Pos:* Grants, Sea Grant Prog, Bur Com Fisheries, 66- & Ore Dept Fish & Wildlife, 66- *Mem:* Inst Food Technologists. *Res:* Basic and applied research of food science, especially investigation of basic chemistry of biological systems as related to food preservation, quality and physiological response. *Mailing Add:* Seafoods Lab Ore State Univ 250 36th St Astoria OR 97103

CRAWFORD, DAVID LIVINGSTONE, b Tarentum, Pa, Mar 2, 31; m 63; c 3. ASTRONOMY. *Educ:* Univ Chicago, PhD(astron), 58. *Prof Exp:* Asst, Yerkes Observ, Univ Chicago, 53-57; asst prof physics & astron, Vanderbilt Univ, 58-60; assoc dir, 70-74, ASTRONR, KITT PEAK NAT OBSERV, 60- *Mem:* Am Astron Soc; Astron Soc Pac; Int Astron Union. *Res:* Galactic structure; stellar photometry; observational instruments and techniques; light pollution and control. *Mailing Add:* Kitt Peak Nat Observ Box 26732 Tucson AZ 85726

CRAWFORD, DONALD LEE, b Santa Ana, Tex, Sept 28, 47; m 70; c 1. MICROBIOLOGY. *Educ:* Oklahoma City Univ, BA, 70; Univ Wis, MS, 72, PhD(bact), 73. *Prof Exp:* Asst prof biol, George Mason Univ, 73-76; asst prof, 76-80, ASSOC PROF BACT BIOCHEM, UNIV IDAHO, 80- *Mem:* Am Soc Microbiol; Sigma Xi. *Res:* Microbial physiology with emphasis on metabolism of organic matter by bacteria and on the bioconversion of biomass to useful products. *Mailing Add:* Dept of Bact Biochem Univ of Idaho Moscow ID 83843

CRAWFORD, DONALD R(OBERT), fluid mechanics, see previous edition

CRAWFORD, DONALD W, b St Louis, Mo, Mar 9, 28; m 57; c 3. CARDIOVASCULAR DISEASES. *Educ:* Washington Univ, BA, 50, MD, 54. *Prof Exp:* Intern, Grady Mem Hosp, Emory Univ, 54-55; resident med, Med Ctr, Stanford Univ, 58-60; NIH trainee clin cardiol, Univ Calif, San Francisco, 60-62, fel cardiopulmonary physiol, Cardiovasc Res Inst, 62-63; chief cardiol sect & cardiopulmonary lab, Long Beach Vet Admin Hosp, 63-66; asst clin prof med, Col Med, Univ Calif, 65-66; asst prof, 66-70, assoc prof, 70-80, PROF MED, SCH MED, UNIV SOUTHERN CALIF, 80- *Concurrent Pos:* Fel coun clin cardiol & coun arteriosclerosis, Am Heart Asn. *Honors & Awards:* Long Beach Vet Admin Hosp Award, 65. *Mem:* Am Fedn Clin Res; fel Am Col Cardiol. *Res:* Atherosclerosis and clinical physiology. *Mailing Add:* Dept of Med Univ of Southern Calif Med Ctr Los Angeles CA 90033

CRAWFORD, DUANE AUSTIN, b Oblong, Ill, Feb 28, 29; m 52; c 2. PETROLEUM ENGINEERING. *Educ:* Mo Sch Mines, BS, 52; Pa State Univ, MSc, 59. *Prof Exp:* Jr petrol engr, Marathon Oil Co, 50, 54-55, assoc petrol engr, 55-56; res assoc, Pa State Univ, 56-58; ASSOC PROF PETROL ENG, TEX TECH UNIV, 58- *Concurrent Pos:* Reservoir engr, Pan Am Petrol Corp, 62, 66 & 73-78 & Humble Oil & Ref Co, 69. *Mem:* Soc Petrol Engrs. *Res:* Reservoir mechanics and fluid flow problems of petroleum reservoirs and ground water hydrology; sweep efficiencies and playa lake ground water recharge. *Mailing Add:* Petrol Eng Dept PO Box 4099 Tech Sta Lubbock TX 79409

CRAWFORD, EUGENE CARSON, JR, b Mt Gilead, NC, Nov 13, 31; m 55; c 2. PHYSIOLOGY, ZOOLOGY. *Educ:* ECarolina Col, AB, 57; Duke Univ, MA, 60, PhD(physiol), 65. *Prof Exp:* From asst prof to assoc prof, 65-75, PROF ZOOL, PHYSIOL & BIOPHYS, UNIV KY, 75- *Concurrent Pos:* NIH fel zool, Duke Univ, 65; NSF res grants, 68-77; res fel, Max Planck Inst Exp Med, 73. *Mem:* AAAS; Am Soc Zool; Am Physiol Soc. *Res:* Comparative physiology; temperature regulation; respiration metabolism. *Mailing Add:* Sch of Biol Sci Univ of Ky Lexington KY 40506

CRAWFORD, FRANK STEVENS, JR, b Scranton, Pa, Oct 25, 23; m 62. PHYSICS. *Educ:* Univ Calif, AB, 48, PhD(physics), 53. *Prof Exp:* Res assoc, Radiation Lab, 53-58, from asst prof to assoc prof, 58-65, PROF PHYSICS, UNIV CALIF, BERKELEY, 65- *Mem:* Am Phys Soc; Am Asn Physics Teachers. *Res:* Experimental nuclear physics. *Mailing Add:* 2826 Garber St Berkeley CA 94705

CRAWFORD, FREDERICK WILLIAM, b Birmingham, Eng, July 28, 31; m 63; c 2. PLASMA PHYSICS. *Educ:* Univ London, BSc, 52 & 54, MSc, 58; Univ Liverpool, PhD, 55, dipl ed, 56, DEng, 65. *Hon Degrees:* DSc, Univ London, 75. *Prof Exp:* Res trainee, J Lucas Ltd, Birmingham, Eng, 48-52; scientist, Mining Res Estab, Nat Coal Bd, Isleworth, 56-57; sr lectr elec eng, Col Advan Technol, Birmingham, 58-59; res assoc, microwave lab, Stanford Univ, 59-61; vis scientist, Fr Atomic Energy Comn, Saclay, 61-62; res physicist, Microwave Lab, Stanford Univ, 62-64, adj prof, 64-67, assoc prof, 67-69, prof elec eng & chmn, Inst Plasma Res, 69-80; VCHANCELLOR,

ASTON UNIV, 80- *Concurrent Pos:* Consult, Compagnie Francaise Thomson-Houston, Paris, 61-62; chmn comn H, Int Sci Radio Union, 78-81. *Mem:* Fel Brit Inst Math & Appl Math; fel Inst Elec & Electronics Engrs; fel Am Phys Soc; fel Brit Inst Elec Engrs; fel Brit Inst Physics. *Res:* Plasma wave propagation phenomena. *Mailing Add:* VChancellor's Off Univ Aston Birmingham B4 7ET UK

CRAWFORD, GEORGE WILLIAM, b Statesville, NC, Oct 21, 06; m 34. PHYSICS. *Educ:* Davidson Col, BS, 29; Univ NC, MS, 49; Ohio State Univ, PhD, 59. *Prof Exp:* Teacher, pub schs, NC, 29-40; instr physics, NC State Col, 46-50; asst prof, Davidson Col, 51-60; from assoc prof to prof, 60-73, EMER PROF PHYSICS, COL WILLIAM & MARY, 73- *Mem:* AAAS; Am Asn Physics Teachers; Optical Soc Am. *Mailing Add:* 205 John Wythe Pl Williamsburg VA 23185

CRAWFORD, GEORGE WOLF, b San Antonio, Tex, May 7, 22; m 46; c 3. ENVIRONMENTAL PHYSICS, NUCLEAR PHYSICS. *Educ:* Univ Tex, BS, 47, MA, 49, PhD(physics), 51. *Prof Exp:* Res physicist, Optical Res Lab, Univ Tex, 49-51; assoc prof physics, Clemson Col, 51-55; asst dir, Tex Petrol Res Comt & asst prof petrol eng, Univ Tex, 55-59; nuclear physicist & chief physics br, Sch Aerospace Med, Brooks AFB, 59-63; PROF PHYSICS, SOUTHERN METHODIST UNIV, 63-, CHMN DEPT, 75- *Concurrent Pos:* Res physicist, Deering Millikin Res Trust, 52-54 & Grad Res Ctr Southwest, 63-64. *Mem:* Am & Int Solar Energy Socs; Am Phys Soc; Am Asn Physics Teachers; Sigma Xi. *Res:* Solar and wind energy storage and conversion. *Mailing Add:* Dept of Physics Southern Methodist Univ Dallas TX 75275

CRAWFORD, GERALD JAMES BROWNING, b St John's, Nfld, Can, Oct 2, 26; m 59; c 3. EXPERIMENTAL PHYSICS. *Educ:* Dalhousie Univ, MSc, 51; McGill Univ, PhD(exp physics), 54. *Hon Degrees:* BSc, Univ King's Col, 49. *Prof Exp:* Res assoc, McGill Univ, 54-55; res physicist, McGraw Edison Co, 55-61; sect head, Schlumberger Well Serv, 61-72; dept mgr, Addressograph Multigraph Corp, 72-75; dir res, Birdwell Div, Seismograph Serv Corp, 75-79; STAFF SCIENTIST, RES CTR, AMOCO PROD CO, 79- *Mem:* Can Asn Physicists; Acoust Soc Am; Soc Info Display. *Res:* Nuclear magnetic resonance and acoustics applied to study of porous oil bearing formations; electrographics and facsimile systems; modern oil and gas well logging technology. *Mailing Add:* 6737 S 73rd E Ave Tulsa OK 74133

CRAWFORD, HEWLETTE SPENCER, JR, b Syracuse, NY, June 4, 31; m 52; c 4. WILDLIFE ECOLOGY, FOREST ECOLOGY. *Educ:* Univ Mich, BS, 54, MS, 57; Univ Mo, Columbia, PhD(ecol, forest wildlife), 67. *Prof Exp:* Asst wildlife mgt, Univ Mich, 53-54 & 56-57; res forester, Southern Exp Sta, 57-64, proj leader, Cent States Exp Sta, 64-68, prin wildlife ecologist & proj leader wildlife habitat res, Southeastern Forest Exp Sta, 68-74, prin ecologist, Northeastern Forest Exp Sta, 74-75, PRIN RES WILDLIFE ECOLOGIST, NORTHEASTERN FOREST EXP STA, FOREST SERV, USDA, 75- *Concurrent Pos:* Mem grad fac, Col Life Sci & Agr, Univ Maine, 75- *Mem:* Wildlife Soc; Soc Am Foresters. *Res:* Wildlife habitat research, especially as influenced by forest management practices. *Mailing Add:* USDA Bldg Univ of Maine Orono ME 04469

CRAWFORD, IRVING POPE, b Cleveland, Ohio, Nov 20, 30; m 55; c 2. MICROBIAL GENETICS. *Educ:* Stanford Univ, AB, 51, MD, 55. *Prof Exp:* Med officer, virus diag sect, Walter Reed Army Inst Res, 55-57; res assoc biol sci, Stanford Univ, 58-59; assoc prof microbiol, sch med, Western Reserve Univ, 59-65; mem dept microbiol, Scripps Clin & Res Found, 65-77; PROF MICROBIOL & CHMN DEPT, UNIV IOWA, 78- *Concurrent Pos:* Fel, Nat Found Infantile Paralysis, 58-59; sr fel, USPHS, 59, career develop award, 61-65. *Honors & Awards:* Borden Res Award, 54. *Mem:* AAAS; Am Soc Microbiol; Genetics Soc Am; Am Soc Biol Chemists. *Res:* Genetics of microorganisms; human genetics. *Mailing Add:* Dept of Microbiol Univ of Iowa Iowa City IA 52242

CRAWFORD, ISAAC LYLE, b Houston, Tex, Aug 22, 42; m 63; c 2. NEUROBIOLOGY. *Educ:* Univ Tex, Austin, BA, 64; Pa State Univ, PhD(pharmacol), 74. *Prof Exp:* Physical scientist chem, US Dept Interior, 65-67; physiologist, NIMH, 67-70; res asst pharmacol, Pa State Univ, 70-74; inst, Pa State Col Med, 74-75; ASST PROF NEUROL & PHARMACOL, UNIV TEX SOUTHWESTERN MED SCH, 75-; PHARMACOLOGIST NEUROPHARMACOLOGY, VET ADMIN MED CTR, DALLAS, 75- *Concurrent Pos:* Grad fel, Med Sch, Georgetown Univ, 68-70; fac lectr, Baylor Univ Med Ctr Dallas, 76; consult, Tex Dept Mental Health & Mental Retardation, 77; lectr, Tex A&M Univ, 77; vis scientist, NIMH, Washington, 78; consult, Working Conf on Circulation, Neurobiol & Behav, NIH, 81. *Mem:* Am Physiol Soc; Neurosci Soc; Epilepsy Asn Am; NY Acad Sci; Am Chem Soc. *Res:* Mechanism of drug action on neurons in limbic brain sites are studied using neurochemical and neurophysiologic approaches; epileptic seizure disorders, and the relationship of the central nervous system to hypertension. *Mailing Add:* Dept Neurol/Pharmacol Southwestern Med Sch Univ Tex Dallas TX 75235

CRAWFORD, JAMES DALTON, b Clyde, Tex, Aug 2, 19; m 43; c 1. ORGANIC CHEMISTRY. *Educ:* Hardin-Simmons Univ, BA, 52, MA, 53. *Prof Exp:* Chemist, Cardinal Chem Inc, 53-54, dir res, 54-60; TECH DIR, CONTINENTAL PROD TEX, 60- *Mem:* AAAS; Am Chem Soc; Nat Asn Corrosion Engrs. *Res:* Oil field chemicals for prevention of corrosion in production of petroleum; water treatment; demulsifiers; surfactants. *Mailing Add:* Continental Prod Hydrochem 100 Indust Ave PO Box 3627 Odessa TX 79760

CRAWFORD, JAMES GORDON, b Alma, Mich, Sept 12, 29; m 53; c 3. MICROBIOLOGY, BIOCHEMISTRY. *Educ:* Alma Col, BS, 51; Univ Mich, MS, 53, PhD(bact), 55. *Prof Exp:* Sr asst scientist, Div Biol Standards, NIH, 55-58; head biol control labs, 58-61, proj dir infectious hepatitis res, 62-65, dir biol develop, 63-68, DIR FERMENTATION DEVELOP, PFIZER, INC, 68- *Concurrent Pos:* Vis prof, Ind State Col, 63- *Mem:* Am Soc Microbiol; NY Acad Sci; Fedn Am Scientist. *Res:* Etiology and prophylaxis of infectious hepatitis; development of human and veterinary vaccines. *Mailing Add:* Fermentation Devel Dept Pfizer Inc Terre Haute IN 47808

CRAWFORD, JAMES HOMER, JR, b Union, SC, May 19, 22; m 44; c 1. SOLID STATE PHYSICS. *Educ:* Wofford Col, AB, 43; Univ NC, PhD(chem), 49. *Hon Degrees:* DSc, Wofford Col, 68. *Prof Exp:* Instr chem, Univ NC, 48-49; res physicist solid state physics, Oak Ridge Nat Lab, 49-52, assoc dir solid state div, 52-67; chmn dept physics & astron, 67-77, PROF PHYSICS, ASTRON, UNIV NC, CHAPEL HILL, 67- *Mem:* Sigma Xi; Am Phys Soc. *Res:* Properties of semiconductors; radiation effects in solids; electronic and optical processes in ionic crystals. *Mailing Add:* Dept of Physics Univ of NC Chapel Hill NC 27514

CRAWFORD, JAMES JOSEPH L, b June 23, 31; US citizen; m 51; c 6. MICROBIOLOGY. *Educ:* Univ Mo, BA, 53, MA, 54; Univ NC, PhD(microbiol), 62. *Prof Exp:* Asst instr microbiol, Sch Med, Univ Mo, 53-54; teaching asst, Med Sch, Univ Minn, 54-56; from res asst to res assoc, Sch Med, 57-60, instr oral microbiol, Sch Dent, 60-65, trainee, Dept Bact, Sch Med, 62-63, from asst prof to assoc prof oral microbiol, Sch Dent, 65-74, assoc prof endodontics & lectr bacteriol, 74-80, PROF ENDODONTICS, RES & BACTERIOL, SCH MED, UNIV NC, CHAPEL HILL, 80- *Concurrent Pos:* Consult, Microbiol Labs, NC Mem Hosp, 59-; prin investr, USPHS, 65-68; mem, Am Asn Dent Schs; consult, Womack Army Hosp, Ft Bragg, 67-77; coordr infection control, Dent Clin, Univ NC, 73- *Mem:* Am Soc Microbiol; Am Asn Endodontics. *Res:* Mechanisms of host resistance; clinical and oral microbiology. *Mailing Add:* Dept of Endodontics Sch of Dent Univ of NC Chapel Hill NC 27514

CRAWFORD, JAMES WELDON, b Napoleon, Ohio, Oct 27, 27; m 55; c 1. PSYCHIATRY, EXPERIMENTAL PSYCHOLOGY. *Educ:* Oberlin Col, AB, 50; Univ Chicago, MD, 54, PhD, 61. *Prof Exp:* Clin instr psychiat, Chicago Med Sch, 62-63, clin assoc, 63-65, clin asst prof, 65-69, clin assoc prof & assoc dir undergrad educ, Dept Psychiat & Behav Sci, 69-70; CHMN & ORGANIZER OF DEPT PSYCHIAT, RAVENSWOOD HOSP MED CTR, 70- *Concurrent Pos:* Nat Inst Neurol Dis & Blindness res grants, 55-59; staff psychiatrist, Field Clin, Chicago, Ill, 62-65, partner, 65-78; assoc staff, Mt Sinai Hosp, 66-; courtesy staff, Louis A Weiss Mem Hosp, 71-; attend staff, Fox River Hosp, 71-74; clin assoc prof, Dept Psychiat, Abraham Lincoln Sch Med, Univ Ill, 71-; vpres, 78-80, pres, J W Crawford Asn, Inc, 80- *Mem:* AAAS; fel Am Psychiat Asn; Asn Am Med Cols; Am Med Asn; Am Asn Univ Profs. *Res:* Changes in attitudes of medical students during psychiatric training differences between individual and couples or family therapy; visual behavior and thyroid function in cats; various organic therapies in psychiatry; empathy in psychotherapy; administration in psychiatry; work stress psychiatry in business and industry. *Mailing Add:* 2418 Lincoln St Evanston IL 60201

CRAWFORD, JAMES WORTHINGTON, b Newport, RI, Feb 25, 44; m 65; c 1. ORGANIC CHEMISTRY, PHOTOCHEMISTRY. *Educ:* The Citadel, BS, 65; Univ SC, PhD(org photochem), 69. *Prof Exp:* From staff scientist to sr engr, Off Prod Div, IBM Corp, 69-79; PROG MGR, MEAD OFF SYSTS, 79- *Mem:* Am Chem Soc. *Res:* Development of organic photoconducting polymers and small molecule photoconductors for use in electrophotography; development of ink jet technology and ink jet printing machines. *Mailing Add:* Mead Off Systs 1307 Glenville Dr Richardson TX 75081

CRAWFORD, JEAN VEGHTE, b Buffalo, NY, Mar 13, 19. ORGANIC CHEMISTRY. *Educ:* Mt Holyoke Col, AB, 40; Oberlin Col, AM, 42; Univ Ill, PhD(chem), 50. *Prof Exp:* Instr chem, Mt Holyoke Col, 42-45; chemist, Eastman Kodak Co, 45-47; adj prof chem, Randolph-Macon Woman's Col, 50-51; from asst prof to prof, 51-74, CHARLES FITCH ROBERTS PROF CHEM, WELLESLEY COL, 74- *Mem:* Am Chem Soc. *Res:* Heterocyclic nitrogen compounds; mechanism of organic reactions. *Mailing Add:* Dept of Chem Wellesley Col Wellesley MA 02181

CRAWFORD, JOHN ARTHUR, b Fort Dodge, Iowa, July 24, 46; m 67. ANIMAL HABITAT RELATIONSHIPS. *Educ:* Creighton Univ, BS, 68; Univ Nebr, Omaha, MS, 71; Tex Tech Univ, PhD(range & wildlife mgt), 74. *Prof Exp:* Teaching asst biol, Univ Nebr, Omaha, 69-71; res asst wildlife, Tex Tech Univ, 71-74; asst prof, 79, ASSOC PROF WILDLIFE, ORE STATE UNIV, 79- *Mem:* Wildlife Soc; Am Ornithologists Union. *Res:* The habitat requirements of upland gamebirds and determination of animal habitat relationships. *Mailing Add:* Dept Fisheries Wildlife Ore State Univ Corvallis OR 97331

CRAWFORD, JOHN CLARK, b Liberty, Tex, Sept 27, 35; m 55; c 2. PHYSICS. *Educ:* Phillips Univ, BA, 57; Kans State Univ, MS, 59, PhD(physics), 62. *Prof Exp:* Mem staff physics, 62-67, div supvr solid state electronics res, 67-71, mgr, Electron Tube Develop Dept, 71-77, DIR, COMPONENTS & STANDARDS SYSTS, SANDIA NAT LAB, 77- *Mem:* Sr mem Inst Elec & Electronics Engrs. *Res:* X-ray diffraction as applied to ferroelectric whiskers; pulsed high magnetic fields; thin films semiconductors; piezoelectric devices; neutron sources; technical management. *Mailing Add:* Sandia Nat Labs Orgn 2500 Albuquerque NM 87185

CRAWFORD, JOHN DOUGLAS, b Boston, Mass, Apr 16, 20; m 49; c 3. ENDOCRINOLOGY, METABOLISM. *Educ:* Harvard Med Sch, MD, 44. *Prof Exp:* From asst prof to assoc prof, 54-79, PROF PEDIAT, HARVARD MED SCH, 79- *Concurrent Pos:* Chief pediat, Burns Inst, Boston Unit, Shriners Hosps Crippled Children; chief, Endocrine-Metab Unit, Children's Serv, Mass Gen Hosp, Boston. *Mem:* Am Pediat Soc; Soc Pediat Res; Am Soc Clin Invest; Endocrine Soc. *Res:* Clinical endocrinology; renal physiology. *Mailing Add:* Children's Serv Mass Gen Hosp Boston MA 02114

CRAWFORD, JOHN S, b Toronto, Ont, Dec 5, 21; m 44; c 3. INTERNAL MEDICINE, REHABILITATION MEDICINE. *Educ:* Univ Toronto, MD, 44; FRCP(C), 52. *Prof Exp:* J J McKenzie fel path, Banting Inst, Univ Toronto, 48-49, McLaughlin traveling fel med, Fac Med, 53-54, clin teacher med & rehab med, 54-60, assoc rehab med, 60-63, assoc med, 60-64, asst prof rehab med, 63-68, asst prof med, 64-68, assoc prof med & rehab med, 68-75, prof med, Fac Med, 68-80, PROF REHAB MED & CHMN DEPT, UNIV

TORONTO, 73-, PROF OPHTHAL, 80-; DIR REHAB MED, TORONTO WESTERN HOSP, 54- Concurrent Pos: Mem med adv bd, Rehab Found Disabled, 61-; med dir, Hillcrest Hosp, 64-75; chmn med adv bd, Toronto Rehab Ctr, 66-; mem div rehab, Coun Health, Prov Ont, 69- Mem: Can Asn Phys Med & Rehab (pres, 65). Res: Electrodiagnosis; electromyegraphy. Mailing Add: Dept of Rehab Med Toronto Western Hosp Toronto ON M5S 1A1 Can

CRAWFORD, LESTER M, b Demopolis, Ala, Mar 13, 38; m 63; c 2. ANTIBIOTIC TOXICOLOGY. Educ: Auburn Univ, DVM, 63; Univ Ga, PhD(pharmacol), 69. Prof Exp: Asst dean, Col Vet Med, Univ Ga, 68-70, assoc dean, 70-75; Pharmacologist, Bur Vet Med, Food & Drug Admin, 75-76; assoc prof pharmacol, Col Vet Med, Univ Ga, 76-78; dir, Bur Vet Med, Food & Drug Admin, 78-80; HEAD PHARMACOL, DEPT PHYSIOL-PHARMACOL, COL VET MED, UNIV GA, 81- Honors & Awards: A M Mills Award, Univ Ga, 79. Mem: AAAS; NY Acad Sci; Sigma Xi; Am Vet Med Asn; Am Col Vet Pharmacol & Ther. Res: Biotic toxicology; veterinary medical history; veterinary educational methodology. Mailing Add: Col Vet Med Univ Ga Athens GA 30602

CRAWFORD, LLOYD W(ILLIAM), b Prince Albert, Sask, Nov 20, 28; m 57; c 2. CHEMICAL ENGINEERING. Educ: Univ Sask, BSc, 50, MSc, 51; Univ Cincinnati, PhD(chem eng), 61. Prof Exp: Res assoc chem eng, Univ Sask, 52-56; res engr, Film Dept, Yerkes Res & Develop Lab, E I du Pont de Nemours & Co, NY, 61-64; assoc prof mech eng, Tenn Polytech Inst, 64-67; assoc prof chem eng, 67-76, PROF MECH ENG, SPACE INST, UNIV TENN, 76- Mem: Am Inst Chem Engrs; Am Chem Soc. Res: Heat transfer and thermodynamics; mass transfer and fluid flow. Mailing Add: Dept of Chem & Metall Eng Univ of Tenn Space Inst Tullahoma TN 37388

CRAWFORD, MARIA LUISA BUSE, b Beverly, Mass, July 18, 39; m 63. PETROLOGY, MINERALOGY. Educ: Bryn Mawr Col, BA, 60; Univ Calif, Berkeley, PhD(geol), 65. Prof Exp: from asst prof to assoc prof, 65-79, PROF GEOL, BRYN MAWR COL, 79-, CHMN DEPT, 76- Mem: Geol Soc Am; Mineral Soc Am; Am Geophys Union; Am Women in Sci; Mineral Asn Can. Res: Petrology, mineralogy and geochemistry of metamorphic and igneous rocks; fluid inclusion studies; structure and tectonics of metamorphic terranes. Mailing Add: Dept Geol Bryn Mawr Col Bryn Mawr PA 19010

CRAWFORD, MARTIN, b Lake City, Tenn, Mar 10, 34; m 68; c 2. MECHANICAL ENGINEERING. Educ: Univ Tenn, BS, 54, MS, 58; Ga Inst Technol, PhD(mech eng), 63. Prof Exp: Instr mech eng, Univ Tenn, 55-56; asst prof, Va Polytech Inst, 56-58; instr Ga Inst Technol, 58-59, asst prof, 59-62; assoc prof, Va Polytech Inst, 62-68; assoc prof, 68-70, PROF MECH ENG, UNIV ALA, BIRMINGHAM, 70- Mem: AAAS; Am Soc Eng Educ; Am Soc Mech Engrs; Air Pollution Control Asn. Res: Heat transfer; thermodynamics; fluid mechanics; air pollution control theory. Mailing Add: Sch Eng Univ Ala Univ Sta Birmingham AL 35294

CRAWFORD, MORRIS LEE JACKSON, b Ellijay, Ga, Jan 20, 33; m 60; c 1. PHYSIOLOGICAL PSYCHOLOGY. Educ: Univ Ga, BS, 59, MS, 60, PhD(psychol), 62. Prof Exp: Asst prof res & psychol, Univ Ga, 62-63; Nat Inst Neurol Dis & Blindness fel, 63-64; instr res, Sch Med, Univ Miss, 65; asst prof psychol, Col Med, Baylor Univ, 66-70; ASSOC PROF NEURAL SCI, UNIV TEX HEALTH CTR HOUSTON, 70- Res: Behavioral science; central nervous system control of behavior; visual system encoding. Mailing Add: 1911 Swift Blvd Houston TX 77030

CRAWFORD, NICHOLAS CHARLES, b Dayton, Ohio, June 2, 42; m 69; c 1. HYDROGEOLOGY, CLIMATOLOGY. Educ: Tenn Technol Univ, BS, 65; E Tenn State Univ, MS, 67; Clark Univ, PhD(geog), 78. Prof Exp: Instr geog, Austin Peay State Univ, 67-68; from instr to asst prof geog, Peabody Col, 68-76; asst prof, Vanderbilt Univ, 72-76; ASST PROF GEOG & GEOL, WESTERN KY UNIV, 76- Mem: Asn Am Geographers; Nat Speleol Soc. Res: Hydrogeology, Karst hydrology, speleology, climatology. Mailing Add: Dept of Geog & Geol Western Ky Univ Bowling Green KY 42101

CRAWFORD, NORMAN HOLMES, b Stettler, Alta, July 30, 35; US citizen; m 64; c 2. HYDROLOGY, HYDRAULICS. Educ: Univ Alta, BSc, 58; Stanford Univ, MS, 59, PhD(hydraul, hydrol), 62. Prof Exp: Res asst hydraul, Stanford Univ, 60-62, asst prof, 62-68; dir, 68-76, PRES, HYDROCOMP INT, 76- Concurrent Pos: consult, United Nations & Govt India; lectr, Univ Padua, Univ New SWales. Mem: Am Geophys Union. Res: Digital computer simulation of river systems. Mailing Add: 2386 Branner Dr Menlo Park CA 94025

CRAWFORD, OAKLEY H, b Bridgeton, NJ, Sept 29, 38; m 63; c 2. PARTICLE-SOLID INTERACTIONS. Educ: Carson-Newman Col, BS, 59; Univ Ill, PhD(phys chem), 66. Prof Exp: Sr res fel appl math, Queen's Univ, Belfast, 66-67; asst prof chem, Pa State Univ, 67-74; assoc prof chem, Barnard Col, Columbia Univ, 74-76; STAFF SCIENTIST, CHEM DIV, OAK RIDGE NAT LAB, 76- Mem: AAAS; Am Phys Soc; Am Chem Soc. Res: Reaction dynamics in crossed molecular beams; atomic and molecular scattering; calculation of chemical reaction rates from first principles; particle-solid interactions; molecular scattering and intramolecule forces; stopping power of swift ions; channeling; atomic physics of channeled ions. Mailing Add: Chem Div Oak Ridge Nat Lab Oak Ridge TN 37830

CRAWFORD, PAUL B(ERLOWITZ), b Stamford, Tex, July 28, 21; m 48; c 3. PETROLEUM ENGINEERING. Educ: Tex Tech Col, BS, 43; Univ Tex, MS, 46, PhD(chem eng), 49. Prof Exp: Res engr, Am Cyanamid & Chem Corp, 43-44; instr, Univ Tex, 46-47; res engr, Magnolia Petrol Co, 47-52; ASST DIR TEX PETROL RES COMT, TEX A&M UNIV, 52-, PROF COMN, PETROL ENG, 62- Concurrent Pos: Chmn long range planning comt, Sul Ross Sch; pres libr bd, Carnegie Libr; mem bd, United Fund; mem, Interstate Oil Compact Comn, chmn libr comt, vchmn res comt; mem, Water-for-Tex Comt. Mem: Am Inst Mining, Metall & Petrol Engrs. Res: Petroleum production; underground combustion; formation fracturing; catalytic cracking of gas-oils; heat transfer; natural gas; thermal oil recovery; nuclear bomb applications. Mailing Add: Tex Petrol Res Comn Tex A&M Univ College Station TX 77840

CRAWFORD, PAUL VINCENT, b Concord, NH, Jan 9, 33; m 65; c 2. PHYSICAL GEOGRAPHY, CARTOGRAPHY. Educ: Univ Okla, BA, 56, MA, 58; Univ Kans, PhD(geog), 69. Prof Exp: Instr geog, RI Col, 60-65; asst prof, 69-71, assoc prof, 71-76, PROF GEOG, BOWLING GREEN STATE UNIV, 76- Mem: Am Geog Soc; Asn Am Geog; Am Cong Surv & Mapping; Sigma Xi. Res: Cartographic perception; three dimensional mapping; interrelationships of soil genesis and geomorphic processes. Mailing Add: Dept of Geog Bowling Green State Univ Bowling Green OH 43403

CRAWFORD, RAYMOND BERTRAM, b Chipman, NB, Jan 10, 20; US citizen; m 49; c 2. MEDICINE. Educ: Andrews Univ, BA, 45; Loma Linda Univ, MD, 49. Prof Exp: Resident internal med, White Mem Hosp, Calif, 49-52; asst prof med, 54-62, dir cardiac diag lab, 62-69, ASSOC PROF MED, LOMA LINDA UNIV, 62- Concurrent Pos: Nat Heart Inst fel, 60-61. Mem: Am Col Cardiol; Am Col Physicians. Res: Cardiovascular dynamics. Mailing Add: Loma Linda Univ Sch of Med Loma Linda CA 92354

CRAWFORD, RAYMOND MAXWELL, JR, b Charleston, SC, July 28, 33; m 51; c 5. NUCLEAR & CHEMICAL ENGINEERING. Educ: Wayne State Univ, BSc, 58, MSc, 60; Univ Calif, Los Angeles, PhD(nuclear eng), 69. Prof Exp: Instr chem eng, Wayne State Univ, 60-63; asst prof eng, San Fernando Valley State Col, 63-66; mem tech staff reactor safety, Atomics Int, 69-71; assoc nuclear engr, Argonne Nat Lab, 71-74; asst head, Nuclear Safeguards & Assoc, Sargent & Lundy, 74-81; VPRES, SCI APPL INC, 81- Concurrent Pos: Consult, Atomic Power Develop Assoc, Inc, 62-63. Honors & Awards: Analog Comput Educ Users Group Achievement Award, 65. Mem: AAAS; Am Inst Chem Engrs; Am Chem Soc; Am Nuclear Soc; Nat Soc Prof Engrs. Res: Reactor safety analysis of light-water reactors and liquid-metal fastbreeder reactors; mathematical studies of control and stability of lumped-parameter and distributed-parameter systems; chemical catalysis on solid surfaces; high-vacuum technology. Mailing Add: 1005 E Kennebec Lane Naperville IL 60540

CRAWFORD, RICHARD BRADWAY, b Kalamazoo, Mich, Feb 16, 33; m 54; c 4. BIOCHEMISTRY. Educ: Kalamazoo Col, AB, 54; Univ Rochester, PhD(biochem), 59. Prof Exp: Fel biochem, Univ Rochester, 59; instr microbiol, Sch Dent, Univ Pa, 59-60, assoc, 60-61, from asst prof to assoc prof microbiol, 61-67, instr biochem, Sch Med, 59-61, assoc, 61-67; assoc prof, 67-74, PROF BIOL, TRINITY COL, CONN, 74-, CHMN DEPT, 78- Concurrent Pos: Sr investr, Mt Desert Island Biol Lab, Salisbury Cove, Maine, 62-, mem corp, 62-, asst dir, 66-, trustee, 65-71 & 76-80. Mem: AAAS; Am Soc Zoologists; Sigma Xi. Res: Role of lipids in bioenergetics; biochemistry of fertilization and embryogenesis; xenobiotic effects on development; comparative enzymology. Mailing Add: Dept of Biol Trinity Col Hartford CT 06106

CRAWFORD, RICHARD DWIGHT, b Kirksville, Mo, Nov 16, 47; m 66; c 1. WILDLIFE ECOLOGY. Educ: Northeast Mo State Univ, BS, 68, MS, 69; Iowa State Univ, PhD(wildlife biol), 75. Prof Exp: Sec sch teacher math-biol, Adair County RII Sch Dist, 68-69; instr wildlife biol, Iowa State Univ, 73-75; asst prof, 75-80, ASSOC PROF WILDLIFE ECOL, UNIV NDAK, 80-, CHMN DEPT BIOL, 81- Concurrent Pos: Assoc ed, J Wildlife Mgt, 80- Mem: Sigma Xi; Wildlife Soc; Am Ornithologists Union; Wilson Ornith Soc; Cooper Ornith Soc. Res: Population ecology; habitat management and conservation of waterfowl; upland game and nongame birds. Mailing Add: Dept Biol Univ NDak Grand Forks ND 58201

CRAWFORD, RICHARD H, b St Paul, Minn, Mar 21, 23; m 44; c 3. MECHANICAL ENGINEERING, MECHANICAL DESIGN. Educ: Univ Minn, BS, 45; Univ Colo, MS, 51. Prof Exp: Stress analyst design, Ryan Aeronaut Co, 44-45; plastics engr design & develop, Erie Resistor, 45; staff mem, Proj Lincoln, Mass Inst Technol, 54-56; plastics researcher, Eastman Kodak Co, 56-59; chief engr res & develop, Ball Bros Res Corp, 59-62; prof 47-78, EMER PROF MECH DESIGN & ECON EVAL, UNIV COLO, 78-; ENG CONSULT, PONDEROSA ASSOCS, LTD, 74- Concurrent Pos: Consult, var firms, univs, and govt bureaus. Honors & Awards: Merit Award, Soc Mfg Engrs. Mem: Am Soc Mech Engrs; Soc Plastics Engrs (vpres & pres), Nat Soc Prof Engrs; Am Soc Eng Educ; Soc Mfg Engrs (vpres & pres). Res: Engineering design; failure analysis; product review and evaluation. Mailing Add: Ponderosa Assocs Ltd 800 Jefferson Ave Louisville CO 80027

CRAWFORD, RICHARD WHITTIER, b Modesto, Calif, Aug 18, 36; m 60; c 2. MASS SPECTROSCOPY, COMPUTER AUTOMATION OF INSTRUMENTS. Educ: San Jose State Univ, BS, 58. Prof Exp: CHEMIST, LAWRENCE LIVERMORE NAT LAB, 58- Mem: Am Soc Mass Spectros; Am Chem Soc. Res: Principal developer of capillary column GC/MS/FT-IR. Mailing Add: Lawrence Livermore Nat Lab PO Box 808 L-310 Livermore CA 94550

CRAWFORD, ROBERT FIELD, b Martinez, Calif, Feb 18, 30; m 55; c 2. AGRONOMY, SOIL SCIENCE. Educ: Calif State Polytech Col, BS, 56; Cornell Univ, MS, 58, PhD(agron), 60. Prof Exp: Lab asst, Union Oil Co, 52; agr res scientist, US Borax Res Corp, 60-64; mgr agr res & develop dept, 64-67; assoc prof chem & dean col, 67-80, VPRES, BUS & FINANCIAL AFFAIRS, BIOLA COL, 80- Mem: Am Soc Agron; Weed Sci Soc Am. Res: Crop production and physiology; plant-animal relations; chemistry. Mailing Add: Biola Col La Mirada CA 90638

CRAWFORD, ROBERT JAMES, b Edmonton, Alta, July 8, 29; m 56; c 4. ORGANIC CHEMISTRY. Educ: Univ Alta, BSc, 52, MSc, 54; Univ Ill, PhD, 56. Prof Exp: From asst prof to assoc prof, 56-67, PROF CHEM, UNIV ALTA, 67-, CHMN DEPT, 79- Mem: Am Chem Soc; Chem Inst Can; The Chem Soc. Res: Reaction mechanisms; azo and diazo chemistry; racemization of cycloalkanes and epoxides. Mailing Add: Dept of Chem Univ of Alta Edmonton AB T6G 2E8 Can

CRAWFORD, RONALD LYLE, b Santa Ana, Tex, Sept 28, 47; m 67; c 1. MICROBIOLOGY, ECOLOGY. *Educ:* Okla City Univ, BA, 70; Univ Wis, MS, 72, PhD(bact), 73. *Prof Exp:* Assoc, Univ Minn, St Paul, 73-74; res scientist, Div Labs & Res, NY State Health Dept, 74-75; asst prof, 75-79, ASSOC PROF MICROBIOL, FRESHWATER BIOL INST, UNIV MINN, TWIN CITIES, 79- *Mem:* Sigma Xi; Am Soc Microbiol. *Res:* Degradation of aromatic compounds in natural environments; microbial ecology; lignin biodegradation; biological oxidations. *Mailing Add:* Freshwater Biol Inst PO Box 100 Navarre MN 55392

CRAWFORD, ROY DOUGLAS, b Vancouver, BC, June 6, 33. POULTRY GENETICS. *Educ:* Univ Sask, BSA, 55; Cornell Univ, MS, 57; Univ Mass, PhD(poultry genetics), 63. *Prof Exp:* Poultry geneticist, Res Br, Can Dept Agr, Ottawa, 57-58, Charlottetown, 58-63 & Kentville, 63-64; from asst prof to assoc prof, 64-74, PROF POULTRY GENETICS, UNIV SASK, 74- *Mem:* Poultry Sci Asn; Am Genetic Asn; Agr Inst Can; World Poultry Sci Asn. *Res:* Physiological and behavioral genetics of domestic fowl; effects of environment and management on domestic fowl. *Mailing Add:* Dept of Animal & Poultry Sci Univ of Sask Saskatoon SK S7H 0W0 Can

CRAWFORD, ROY KENT, b Wilmington, NC, Oct 21, 41. MATERIALS SCIENCE, FLUID PHYSICS. *Educ:* Kans State Univ, BS, 63; Princeton Univ, PhD(physics), 68. *Prof Exp:* Sloan fel, Princeton Univ, 68-69, res assoc mat sci, 69-70, mem res staff & lectr, 70-71; asst prof physics, Univ Ill, Urbana, 71-75; res assoc, 75-77, ASST PHYSICIST, ARGONNE NAT LAB, 77- *Mem:* Am Phys Soc. *Res:* Neutron scattering instrumentation; neutron scattering studies of phase transition and surface adsorbed molecules. *Mailing Add:* Solid State Sci Div Argonne Nat Lab Argonne IL 60439

CRAWFORD, STANLEY EVERETT, b Dallas, Tex, Nov 9, 24; m 48; c 3. PEDIATRICS, MEDICAL ADMINISTRATION. *Educ:* Univ Tex, BA, 45, MD, 48; Am Bd Pediat, dipl, 54. *Prof Exp:* Intern, Univ Chicago Clins & Albert Merritt Billings Hosp, 48-49; resident, Univ Tex, Galveston, 50-51; resident Univ Minn Hosps, 52-53; pvt pract, Children's Clin, Jackson, Tenn, 54-61; assoc prof pediat, LeBonheur Children's Hosp, Col Med, Univ Tenn, 63-68; prof pediat & chmn dept, Univ Tex Med Ctr, San Antonio, 68-73, dean, 73-80; DEAN & VPRES MED AFFAIRS, UNIV SOUTH ALA, 80- *Concurrent Pos:* Off examr, Am Bd Pediat, 67-, mem residency rev comt, 70; mem exec comt, Children's Hosp Found, San Antonio, 68, bd dirs, 68-; pediatrician-in-chief, Bexar County Hosp Dist Teaching Hosps, 68-73; civilian regional consult, Wilford Hall, US Air Force Hosp, 69-; mem adv comt, Foster Grandparent Proj, 70. *Mem:* AMA; fel Am Acad Pediat; Asn Med Schs. *Res:* Clinical pediatrics. *Mailing Add:* Dean's Off Univ Ala Col Med Mobile AL 36688

CRAWFORD, SUSAN N, b Vancouver, BC, May 11, 27; m 56; c 1. INFORMATION SCIENCE. *Educ:* Univ BC, BA, 48; Univ Toronto, BLS, 50; Univ Chicago, MA, 56, PhD(info sci), 70. *Prof Exp:* Res assoc, Am Med Asn, 56-59, dir info sci, 60-81; PROF & DIR, MED LIBR, WASHINGTON UNIV, ST LOUIS, 81- *Concurrent Pos:* Prin investr, Nat Libr Med-NIH grant, 68-73; chmn, Comn Surv & Statist, Med Libr Asn, 67-75; assoc prof, Columbia Univ, 71-75; mem bd regents, US Nat Libr Med, 71-75; mem panel, Universal Guid Contribr Sci Publ, 78-79; co-prin investr, Third Surv Health Sci in US, 78-80. *Honors & Awards:* Cert Achievement, USPHS, 75; Eliot Prize, Med Libr Asn, 76. *Mem:* Sigma Xi; AAAS; Am Soc Info Sci; Med Libr Asn; Am Libr Asn; Spec Libr Asn. *Res:* Social organization of scientists in communication; statistical survey of health sciences libraries in the United States. *Mailing Add:* 2418 Lincoln St Evanston IL 60201

CRAWFORD, THOMAS CHARLES, b Muskegon, Mich, July 31, 45; m 72. ORGANIC CHEMISTRY. *Educ:* Kalamazoo Col, BA, 67; Univ Calif, Los Angeles, MS, 69, PhD(chem), 74. *Prof Exp:* RESEARCHER SYNTHETIC ORG CHEM, PFIZER, INC, 74- *Mem:* Am Chem Soc; The Chem Soc; Sigma Xi. *Res:* Synthesis of biologically important molecules, development of new synthetic methods and utilization of organometallics in synthesis. *Mailing Add:* Cent Res Pfizer Inc Groton CT 06340

CRAWFORD, THOMAS H, b Oct 22, 31; US citizen; m 54; c 2. INORGANIC CHEMISTRY. *Educ:* Univ Louisville, BS, 58, PhD(phys chem), 61. *Prof Exp:* From asst prof to assoc prof, 61-70, chmn dept, 71-75, actg dean, Col Arts & Sci, 73-74, fac assoc, Off of Pres, 75-77, asst exec vpres admin, 77-79, PROF CHEM, UNIV LOUISVILLE, 70-, ASSOC VPRES ACAD AFFAIRS, 79- *Concurrent Pos:* Vis assoc prof, Calif Inst Technol, 68-69. *Mem:* AAAS; Am Chem Soc. *Res:* Preparation and characterization of transition metal coordination compounds and the study of molecular complexes of antimony trichloride and organic substrates. *Mailing Add:* Off of Pres Univ Louisville Louisville KY 40208

CRAWFORD, THOMAS MICHAEL, b Cleveland, Ohio, Aug 13, 28; m 51; c 3. FOOD TECHNOLOGY. *Educ:* Ohio State Univ, BA, 50, MSc, 54, PhD(food tech), 57. *Prof Exp:* Technician, Cleveland Clin Found, 50; chemist, Walter Reed Army Med Serv Grad Sch, 53; asst, Ohio Agr Exp Sta, 54-57; food technologist, Res & Develop Div, Nat Dairy Prod Corp, 57-62; sect chief res & develop ctr, Pet Milk Co, Ill, 62-66, group mgr, 66-68; tech mgr, 68-71, sr scientist, Food Technol Group, Res & Develop, Pillsbury Co, Minneapolis, 71-75; mgr res & develop dept, 75-77, ASST DIR RES & DEVELOP & QUAL CONTROL, CENT LABS, STOKELY-VAN CAMP, INC, 77- *Mem:* Inst Food Technol; Am Soc Hort Sci; Am Asn Cereal Chem. *Res:* Product development and quality control of canned, frozen, refrigerated and shelf stable fruits, vegetables, meats, cereals and fabricated single and multicomponent food products. *Mailing Add:* 4013 Rolling Springs Dr Carmel IN 46032

CRAWFORD, TODD V, b Los Angeles, Calif, Aug 9, 31; m 59; c 3. METEOROLOGY. *Educ:* Calif Polytech State Col, BS, 53; Univ Calif, Los Angeles, MA, 58, PhD(meteorol), 65. *Prof Exp:* Res asst numerical meteorol, Univ Calif, Los Angeles, 57-58, asst agr engr & lectr, Davis, 58-65, physicist, Lawrence Livermore Lab, 65-72; RES MGR, SAVANNAH RIVER LAB, E I DU PONT DE NEMOURS & CO, 72- *Mem:* Am Meteorol Soc; Am Soc Agr Eng; Am Geophys Union; Royal Meteorol Soc. *Res:* Energy balance, turbulent properties of the lower atmosphere and atmospheric diffusion from small scale to continental scale; managing a multi disciplined environmental research group. *Mailing Add:* Savannah River Lab E I du Pont de Nemours & Co Aiken SC 29801

CRAWFORD, VAN HALE, b Philadelphia, Pa, Aug 10, 46; m 76; c 2. INORGANIC CHEMISTRY. *Educ:* Denison Univ, BS, 68; Univ NC, PhD(inorg chem), 76. *Prof Exp:* Vis asst prof chem, State Univ NY Col, Oswego, 75-77; ASST PROF CHEM, MERCER UNIV, 77- *Mem:* Am Chem Soc; Sigma Xi; AAAS. *Res:* Electronic and magnetic properties of condensed transition metal complexes. *Mailing Add:* Dept Chem Mercer Univ Macon GA 31207

CRAWFORD, VERNON, b Amherst, NS, Feb 13, 19; nat US; m 43; c 2. PHYSICS. *Educ:* Mt Allison Univ, BA, 39; Dalhousie Univ, MSc, 44; Univ Va, PhD(physics), 49. *Prof Exp:* Lectr physics, Dalhousie Univ, 44-47; assoc prof, 49-56, dir physics, 64-68, vpres acad affairs, 68-80, PROF PHYSICS, GA INST TECHNOL, 56-, CHANCELLOR, CHIEF ADMIN OFFICER, UNIV SYSTEM & CHIEF EXEC OFFICER BD REGENTS, 80- *Res:* Optics; electromagnetics. *Mailing Add:* Ga Inst of Technol Atlanta GA 30332

CRAWFORD, WILLIAM ARTHUR, b Norman, Okla, Mar 25, 35; m 63. GEOCHEMISTRY. *Educ:* Kans State Univ, BS, 57; Univ Kans, MS, 60; Univ Calif, Berkeley, PhD(geol, geochem), 65. *Prof Exp:* Teaching asst geol, Univ Kans, 59-60; instr geol, Univ Calif, Berkeley, 65; from asst prof to assoc prof, 65-81, PROF GEOL, BRYN MAWR COL, 81- *Mem:* Mineral Soc Am; Nat Asn Geol Teachers; fel Geol Soc Am; Geochem Soc. *Res:* High pressure-high temperature experimental petrology; chemical analysis of rocks and minerals; studying field relations and mapping of igneous and metamorphic rock bodies. *Mailing Add:* Dept of Geol Bryn Mawr Col Bryn Mawr PA 19010

CRAWFORD, WILLIAM HOWARD, JR, b Montclair, NJ, Apr 14, 37; m 58; c 2. PATHOLOGY, ORAL PATHOLOGY. *Educ:* Univ Southern Calif, BA, 58, DDS, 62, MS, 64. *Prof Exp:* Asst prof, 66-68, asst dean, 69-71, assoc dean acad affairs, 71-77, interim dean sch dent, 72-75, ASSOC PROF PATH & ORAL PATH, SCH DENT, UNIV SOUTHERN CALIF, 68-, DEAN SCH DENT, 77- *Concurrent Pos:* Nat Inst Dent Res res fel, 62-64. *Mem:* AAAS; fel Am Acad Oral Path; fel Int Col Dent; fel Am Col Dent; Am Asn Dent Schs. *Res:* Detailed histology and pathogenesis of keratinizing cysts of the oral cavity. *Mailing Add:* Sch of Dent Univ of Southern Calif Los Angeles CA 90007

CRAWFORD, WILLIAM STANLEY HAYES, b St John, NB, Apr 17, 18; m 43; c 2. MATHEMATICS. *Educ:* Mt Allison Univ, BA, 39; Univ Minn, MA, 42, PhD(math), 50. *Hon Degrees:* DSc, Univ Nebr, 79. *Prof Exp:* Instr math, Univ Minn, 42-43; from asst prof to prof & head dept, 43-73, dean sci, 56-62, dean fac, 62-65, vpres, 62-69, pres, 75-80, OBED EDMUND SMITH PROF MATH, MT ALLISON UNIV, 46- *Concurrent Pos:* Mem, NB Higher Educ Comn, 67-74. *Mem:* AAAS; Am Math Soc; Math Asn Am; Can Math Soc (vpres, 67-69). *Res:* Analysis; integration in function space; history of mathematics. *Mailing Add:* Mt Allison Univ Sackville NB E0A 3C0 Can

CRAWLEY, GERARD MARCUS, b Airdrie, Scotland, Apr 10, 38; m 61; c 4. NUCLEAR PHYSICS. *Educ:* Univ Melbourne, BSc, 59, MSc, 61; Princeton Univ, PhD(physics), 65. *Prof Exp:* Res assoc, Cyclotron Lab, Mich State Univ, 65-66; Queen Elizabeth fel, Dept Nuclear Physics, Australian Nat Univ, 66-68; from asst prof to assoc prof, 68-74, PROF PHYSICS, MICH STATE UNIV, 74- *Concurrent Pos:* Fulbright scholar & Ford Int fel, 61; vis fel, Australian Nat Univ, 74-75; prog officer nuclear physics, NSF, 75- *Mem:* Am Phys Soc. *Res:* Nuclear reactions, particularly inelastic scattering and multinuclear transfer reactions. *Mailing Add:* Cyclotron Lab Mich State Univ East Lansing MI 48823

CRAWLEY, JACQUELINE N, b Philadelphia, Pa, June 14, 50. NEUROCHEMISTRY, ANIMAL BEHAVIOR. *Educ:* Univ Pa, BA, 71; Univ Md, MS, 73, PhD(zool), 76. *Prof Exp:* Instr biol, Univ Md, 72-76; res fel psychopharmacol, Sch Med, Yale Univ, 76-79; STAFF FEL, CLIN PSYCHOBIOL BR, NIMH, 79- *Concurrent Pos:* Lectr, Undergrad Sem Prog, Yale Univ, 78-79. *Mem:* Soc Neurosci; Animal Behav Soc. *Res:* Neurochemical substrates of behavior; clinically-oriented basic research in neuropsychopharmacology. *Mailing Add:* Neurobiol Prog Cardiol Life Sci De Pont Glenolden Labs Glenolden PA 19036

CRAWLEY, JAMES WINSTON, JR, b Louisville, Ky, Mar 17, 47; m 67; c 2. MATHEMATICS, COMPUTER SCIENCE. *Educ:* Carson-Newman Col, BS, 68; Univ Tenn, Knoxville, PhD(math), 76. *Prof Exp:* asst prof, 76-80, ASSOC PROF MATH & COMPUT SCI, SHIPPENSBURG STATE COL, 80- *Concurrent Pos:* Consult, Info Systs Design & Implementation. *Mem:* Am Math Soc; Math Asn Am; Asn Educ Date Systs. *Mailing Add:* Dept of Math & Comput Sci Shippensburg State Col Shippensburg PA 17257

CRAWLEY, LANTZ STEPHEN, b Martinsburg, WVa, Oct 18, 44; m 73; c 1. CHEMISTY. *Educ:* Am Univ, BS, 67; Univ Pittsburgh, PhD(chem), 70. *Prof Exp:* Fel chem, Harvard Univ, 70-71; sr res chemist & group leader med res, 72-77, mgr admin consumer prod, 77-78, sect mgr, 78-79, prod mgr, 79-80, bus mgr indust prod, 80-81, DIR RES CONSUMER PROD, AM CYANAMID CO, 81- *Mem:* Am Chem Soc; Soc Heterocyclic Chem; Soc Cosmetic Chemists. *Res:* Development of new consumer products in the household, toiletries and fragrance areas. *Mailing Add:* Consumer Res Ctr Cons Prod Res Div Am Cyanamid Co 697 Rt 46 Clifton NJ 07015

CRAWSHAW, LARRY INGRAM, b Los Angeles, Calif, Nov 5, 42; m 68; c 1. COMPARATIVE PHYSIOLOGY. *Educ:* Univ Calif, Los Angeles, BA, 64; Univ Calif, Santa Barbara, PhD(physiol psychol), 70. *Prof Exp:* Res asst psychol, Univ Calif, Los Angeles, 63-64; res & teaching asst, Univ Calif, Santa

Barbara, 68-70, NSF res assoc, 68-70; NSF res assoc physiol, Scripps Inst Oceanog, Univ Calif, San Diego, 70-71, NIMH fel, 71-72; asst fel, John B Pierce Found, 72-76; asst prof, Sch Med, Yale Univ, 73-76; assoc prof biol, Portland State Univ, 76-78; asst prof rehab med & pharmacol, Col Physicians & Surgeons, Columbia Univ, 78-81; ASSOC PROF, DEPT BIOL, PORTLAND STATE UNIV, 81- *Mailing Add:* Portland State Univ Dept Biol PO Box 751 Portland OR 97207

CRAWSHAW, RALPH SHELTON, b Brooklyn, NY, July 3, 21; m 48; c 2. PSYCHIATRY. *Educ:* Middlebury Col, AB, 43; NY Univ Col Med, MD, 47. *Prof Exp:* Pvt pract, Washington, DC, 54; staff psychiatrist, C F Menninger Mem Hosp, Topeka, Kans, 54-57; asst chief, Vet Admin Ment Hyg Clin, Topeka, Kans, 57-60; PVT PRACT, PORTLAND, ORE, 60- *Concurrent Pos:* Staff psychiatrist, Community Child Guid Clin, Portland, Ore, 60-63; clin dir, Tualatin Valley Guid Clin, Beaverton, Ore, 61-67; Holladay Park Hosp, Portland, Ore, 61-; lectr child psychiat, Univ Ore Med Sch, 61-63; lectr, Sch Social Work, Portland State Univ, 64-67; consult, Dept Health, Educ & Welfare, 64- & Albina Child Develop Ctr, Ore, 65-75; mem, Gov Adv Comt Ment Health, 66-72; pres, Benjamin Rush Found, 68-; assoc clin prof psychiat, Univ Ore Med Sch, 76; Gov Adv Comt Med Care to Indigent, 76- *Mem:* Nat Acad Sci Inst Med; AMA; fel Am Psychiat Asn; Nat Med Asn; Am Psychol Asn. *Mailing Add:* 2525 NW Lovejoy Portland OR 97210

CRAYTHORNE, N W BRIAN, b Belfast, Northern Ireland, Jan 1, 31; m 57, 81; c 2. ANESTHESIOLOGY. *Educ:* Queen's Univ, Belfast, MB, BCh, 54; Am Bd Anesthesiol, dipl, 63. *Prof Exp:* Asst instr anesthesiol, Univ Pa, 57-58, instr, 58-59; clin asst, Royal Victoria Hosp, 59-60; consult anesthetist, Queen Mary Vet Hosp, 60-61; prof anesthesiol & chmn dept, WVa Univ Med Ctr, 61-70; prof anaesthesia & chmn dept, Univ Cincinnati Med Ctr, 70-74; PROF ANESTHESIOL & CHMN DEPT, SCH MED, UNIV MIAMI, 75- *Concurrent Pos:* Demonstr anesthesiol, McGill Univ, 60-61; anesthetist-in-chief, Cincinnati Gen Hosp, 70-75. *Mem:* Am Soc Anesthesiologists; Int Anesthesia Res Soc; Am Med Asn; Fel Am Col Anesthesiologists; fac fel Royal Col Surg Ireland. *Mailing Add:* Dept of Anesthesiol Sch of Med Univ of Miami PO Box 016370 Miami FL 33101

CRAYTON, PHILIP HASTINGS, b Seneca Falls, NY, Jan 22, 28; m 51; c 2. INORGANIC CHEMISTRY. *Educ:* Alfred Univ, BA, 49; Univ Buffalo, MA, 51, PhD(chem), 56. *Prof Exp:* Res chemist, Metals Res Labs, Union Carbide Metals Co, 52-59, sect leader, 59-61; sr res chemist res & develop div, Carborundum Co, 61-63; from asst prof to assoc prof, 63-74, head div eng & sci, 74-77, PROF CHEM & NY STATE COL CERAMICS, ALFRED UNIV, 74- *Concurrent Pos:* Consult, Carborundum Co, 63-66; res assoc, Max Planck Inst Metall Res, Stuttgart, 70 & 78. *Mem:* Am Ceramic Soc. *Res:* Synthesis and properties of the transition metal carbides, borides and nitrides; description and mechanism of ceramic hot pressing; chemistry of process metallurgy; synthesis of oxides, carbides, nitrides and borides. *Mailing Add:* Div of Eng & Sci NY State Col Ceramic Alfred Univ Alfred NY 14802

CREAGAN, ROBERT JOSEPH, b Rockford, Ill, Aug 24, 19; m 48; c 4. APPLIED PHYSICS. *Educ:* Ill Inst Technol, BS, 42; Yale Univ, MS, 43, PhD(physics), 49. *Prof Exp:* Physicist, Argonne Nat Lab, 46-47; physicist, Atomic Power Div, Westinghouse Elec Co, 49-57; dir nuclear prog, Bendix Aviation Corp, 57-60; eng mgr, Atomic Power Div, 60-69, proj mgr liquid metal fast breeder reactor, Adv Reactor Div, 69-75, dir technol assessment, 75-78, CONSULT SCIENTIST, WESTINGHOUSE ELEC CO, 78- *Mem:* Nat Acad Eng; fel Am Nuclear Soc; Am Phys Soc. *Res:* Nuclear power reactors; instrumentation; energy. *Mailing Add:* 2305 Haymaker Rd Monroeville PA 15146

CREAGER, CHARLES BICKNELL, b Bicknell, Ind, Oct 5, 24; m 51; c 3. NUCLEAR PHYSICS. *Educ:* Western Reserve Univ, BS, 51, MS, 53; Ind Univ, PhD, 59. *Prof Exp:* From asst prof to assoc prof physics, Kans Wesleyan Univ, 53-69, prof physics & fac dir res & grants, 69-71; PROF PHYSICS & CHMN DIV PHYS SCI, EMPORIA STATE UNIV 71- *Concurrent Pos:* Res assoc, Ind Univ, 56-59. *Mem:* AAAS; Am Phys Soc; Am Asn Physics Teachers. *Res:* Beta-gamma ray spectroscopy. *Mailing Add:* Div Phys Sci Emporia State Univ Emporia KS 66801

CREAGER, JOAN GUYNN, b Austin, Ind, Dec 8, 32; m 52; c 4. EMBRYOLOGY. *Educ:* Trinity Univ, Tex, BS, 55, MS, 58; George Washington Univ, PhD(zool), 64. *Prof Exp:* Part-time res analyst, Bionetics Res Labs, Va, 63-67; res assoc, off sci personnel, Nat Acad Sci, Washington, DC, 67-69; assoc prof biol, Northern Va Community Col, Alexandra Campus, 69-72 & 74-80; PROF SCI, MARYMOUNT COL VA, ARLINGTON, 80- *Concurrent Pos:* Staff biologist, Comn Undergrad Educ Biol Sci, 69; consult, AAAS, 70-; ed, Am Biol Teacher, 74-80. *Res:* Personnel research, especially two-year college biologists; curriculum development in undergraduate education in biology. *Mailing Add:* 1101 N Potomac St Arlington VA 22205

CREAGER, JOE SCOTT, b Vernon, Tex, Aug 30, 29; m 51; c 2. GEOLOGICAL OCEANOGRAPHY. *Educ:* Colo Col, BS, 51; Agr & Mech Col Tex, MS, 53, PhD(oceanog), 58. *Prof Exp:* Asst geol & eng oceanog, Agr & Mech Col Tex, 51-52; phys sci asst, US Army Beach Erosion Bd, 53-55; from asst prof to assoc prof geol oceanog, 58-66, PROF GEOL OCEANOG & ASSOC DEAN COL ARTS & SCI, UNIV WASH, 66- *Concurrent Pos:* Asst geol & eng oceanog, Agr & Mech Col, Tex, 55-58; prog dir oceanog, NSF, 65-66; chmn, Joides Planning Comt, 70-72 & 76-78; co-ed, Quaternary Res, 70-79. *Mem:* Fel AAAS; fel Geol Soc Am; Soc Econ Paleont & Mineral; Am Asn Quaternary Res; Am Geophys Union; Int Asn Sedimentol. *Res:* Submarine geology relating to continental shelves, slopes and shorelines; sedimentation and micropaleontology; bottom sediment transport. *Mailing Add:* Sch Oceanog WB-10 Univ of Wash Seattle WA 98195

CREAGH, LINDA TRUITT, b Denton, Tex, May 25, 41; m 61; c 2. PHYSICAL ORGANIC CHEMISTRY. *Educ:* NTex State Univ, BS, 62, MS, 63, PhD(chem), 67. *Prof Exp:* Res technician org synthesis, NTex State Univ, 58-63, teaching fel, 62-66; mem tech staff, cent res & eng, Tex Instruments

Inc, 66-68; asst prof chem, Tex Woman's Univ, 68-69; mem staff res & develop, Tex Instruments Inc, 69-73; sr scientist, 73-75, MGR, XEROX INC, 75- *Mem:* AAAS; Am Inst Chemists; Am Chem Soc; Sigma Xi. *Res:* Laser development and applications; photochemistry; liquid crystals chemistry, characterization for displays; development and evaluation of materials for marking technologies. *Mailing Add:* Rte 1 Argyle TX 76226

CREAMER, ROBERT M, b Baltimore, Md, Nov 17, 17; m 46; c 2. ANALYTICAL CHEMISTRY, PHYSICAL ORGANIC CHEMISTRY. *Educ:* Univ Md, BS, 38, PhD(inorg chem), 52. *Prof Exp:* Chemist, Celanese Corp Am, 38-45; res chemist, US Bur Mines, 51-54; res assoc, USDA, 54-60; from res chemist to sr res chemist, 60-68, SR SCIENTIST, PHILIP MORRIS RES CTR, 68- *Concurrent Pos:* Vis sr fel, City Univ, London, Eng, 73-74. *Mem:* Am Chem Soc; Am Inst Chem. *Res:* Electroplating; fertilizers and insecticides; razor blade lubricants; tobacco and smoke chemistry; aerosol science. *Mailing Add:* Philip Morris Res Ctr Box 26583 Richmond VA 23261

CREAN, JOSEPH GAYLORD, b Chicago, Ill, Oct 6, 19; m 41; c 2. PLANT PHYSIOLOGY, PLANT BIOCHEMISTRY. *Educ:* Chicago Teachers Col, BEd, 42; De Paul Univ, MS, 49; Univ Chicago, PhD(bot), 66. *Prof Exp:* Teacher, Northwestern Mil Acad, 45-48; teacher pub schs, Ill, 48-56, Wilson Br, Chicago Jr Col Syst, 56-62 & Loop Br, 62-66; PROF BIOL, NORTHEASTERN ILL UNIV, 66- *Mem:* AAAS; Am Inst Biol Sci; Bot Soc Am; Phycol Soc Am. *Res:* Systematics, biochemical genetics and elucidation of synthetic pathways of enzymes and pigments; general physiological study of the Lemnaceae; research in water relations and translocation. *Mailing Add:* Dept of Biol Northeastern Ill Univ Chicago IL 60625

CREAN, PATRICK J, organic chemistry, see previous edition

CREANGE, JOHN ELLYSON, endocrinology, see previous edition

CREASEY, SAVILL CYRUS, b Portland, Ore, July 17, 17; m 43; c 2. GEOLOGY. *Educ:* Univ Calif, Los Angeles, AB, 39, AM, 41, PhD(geol), 49. *Prof Exp:* GEOLOGIST, US GEOL SURV, 41- *Honors & Awards:* Meritorious Serv Award, US Geol Surv, 71. *Mem:* Geol Soc Am; Soc Econ Geol. *Res:* Geology of base metal deposits, especially porphyry coppers; structural geology; petrology of igneous and metamorphic rocks. *Mailing Add:* US Geol Surv 345 Middlefield Rd Menlo Park CA 94025

CREASEY, WILLIAM ALFRED, b London, Eng, May 12, 33; US citizen; m 57; c 1. BIOCHEMISTRY, PHARMACOLOGY. *Educ:* Oxford Univ, BA, 55, MA & DPhil(radiobiol), 59. *Prof Exp:* Asst tutor org chem, St Catherine's Col, Oxford Univ, 58-59; from res asst to assoc prof pharmacol, Yale Univ, 68-76; PROF PHARMACOL & PED, SCH MED, UNIV PA, 76- *Concurrent Pos:* USPHS fel, Yale Univ, 59-61; mem cancer clin invest rev comt, Nat Cancer Inst, 72-76; mem working cadre, Nat Bladder Cancer Proj, 74-77; mem develop therapeut comt, Nat Cancer Inst, 77-80. *Mem:* AAAS; fel The Chem Soc; Am Soc Pharmacol & Exp Therapeut; Am Soc Biol Chem; Am Asn Cancer Res. *Res:* Biochemical effects of ionizing radiations; influence of dietary pyrimidines on pyrimidine and lipid metabolism; enzymatic studies with agents that influence nucleotide metabolism; metabolic studies with antineoplastic and antimitotic agents; studies with plant derivatives; clinical pharmacology. *Mailing Add:* Dept of Pharmacol G3 Sch of Med Univ of Pa Philadelphia PA 19104

CREASIA, DONALD ANTHONY, b Milford, Mass, Mar 28, 37; m 63; c 2. RESPIRATORY TOXICOLOGY, IMMUNOTOXICOLOGY. *Educ:* Univ Vt, BA, 61; Harvard Univ, MS, 67; Univ Tenn, PhD(immunotoxicol), 71. *Prof Exp:* Biochemist, Mason Res Inst, 61-63; chemist, Sch Med, Harvard Univ, 63-65, res assoc, 67-70; toxicologist, Biol Div, Oak Ridge Nat Lab, 70-77; PROG HEAD, IN VIVO CARCINOGENESIS PROG, FREDERICK CANCER RES FACIL, NAT CANCER INST, 77- *Concurrent Pos:* Prin investr, Oak Ridge Nat Lab, Nat Cancer Inst, 70-77, Frederick Cancer Res Facil, 77-, lectr, 81-; student adv, Hood Col, 79-; consult, Enviro-Control, Inc, 79. *Mem:* Sigma Xi; AAAS; Air Pollution Control Asn; Nat Asn Environ Professionals; Am Col Toxicol. *Res:* Respiratory toxicology of inhaled atmospheric pollutants; physiological parameters studied include: respiratory deposition and clearance of inhaled particles; respiratory immunology; respiratory cancer and metastastic foci in the lungs; pulmonary function; respiratory physiology. *Mailing Add:* NCI-Frederick Cancer Res Facil Bldg 539 PO Box B Frederick MD 21701

CREASY, LEROY L, b White Plains, NY, Feb 21, 38; m 60; c 2. PLANT PHYSIOLOGY. *Educ:* Cornell Univ, BS, 60, MS, 61; Univ Calif, Davis, PhD(plant physiol), 64. *Prof Exp:* NSF fel, Low Temperature Res Sta, Cambridge Univ, Eng, 64-65; asst prof, 65-69, assoc prof, 69-78, PROF POMOL, CORNELL UNIV, 78- *Mem:* Phytochem Soc NAm; Am Soc Hort Sci. *Res:* Physiology and biochemistry of secondary plant products derived from phenylalanine. *Mailing Add:* Dept of Pomol 117 Plant Sci Bldg Cornell Univ Ithaca NY 14853

CREAVEN, PATRICK JOSEPH, b London, Eng, Jan 31, 33; m 63; c 4. CLINICAL PHARMACOLOGY. *Educ:* Univ London, MB, BS, 56, PhD(biochem), 64. *Prof Exp:* Asst lectr biochem, St Mary's Hosp Med Sch, Univ London, 63-64, lectr, 64-66; chief biochem sect, Tex Res Inst Ment Sci, 66-69; chief oncol pharmacol, Med Oncol Br, Nat Cancer Inst, Vet Admin Hosp, 69-75; assoc chief cancer res clinician, Dept Exp Therapeut & Dept Med A, 75-79, CHIEF CANCER RES CLINICIAN, DEPT CLIN PHARMACOL & THERAPEUT, ROSWELL PARK MEM INST, 79- *Concurrent Pos:* Asst prof, Col Med, Baylor Univ, 66-69; asst prof, Grad Sch Biomed Sci, Univ Tex, 67-69, assoc prof, 69; assoc res prof, Grad Sch, State Univ NY Buffalo, 75- *Mem:* Fel Royal Soc Health; fel Am Col Clin Pharmacol; Am Soc Pharmacol & Exp Therapeut; NY Acad Sci; Acad Pharm Sci. *Res:* Clinical pharmacology, pharmacokinetics, metabolism and biochemical pharmacology of anti-cancer agents; initial clinical testing of anticancer agents; induction of drug metabolizing enzymes. *Mailing Add:* Roswell Park Mem Inst 666 Elm St Buffalo NY 14263

CREBBIN, KENNETH CLIVE, b Nelson, BC, June 5, 24; US citizen; m 55; c 3. ACCELERATOR PHYSICS. *Educ:* Univ Calif, Berkeley, AB, 49, MA, 51. *Prof Exp:* PHYSICIST PARTICLE ACCELERATORS, LAWRENCE BERKELEY LAB, UNIV CALIF, 51- *Mem:* Am Phys Soc. *Res:* Particle dynamics, beam diagnostics and control in particle accelerators, Bevatron/Bevalac. *Mailing Add:* Lawrence Berkeley Lab 1 Cyclotron Rd Berkeley CA 94720

CRECELIUS, ROBERT LEE, b Volin, SDak, Dec 8, 22; m 45; c 4. CHEMISTRY. *Educ:* Mont State Col, BSChem E, 47, MS, 49; Univ Wyo, PhD(chem), 54. *Prof Exp:* Chem engr, US Bur Mines, 49-52, 53-54; SR STAFF RES CHEMIST, SHELL DEVELOP CO, 54- *Res:* Catalytic polyforming of shale oil; para-Claisen rearrangement; high pressure hydrogenation of shale oil; oil reaction processes; hydrotreating; hydrocracking; catalytic cracking; catalysis; catalyst formulation and development. *Mailing Add:* 12527 Blackstone Ct Houston TX 77077

CRECELY, ROGER WILLIAM, b Rochester, NY, Jan 12, 42; m 67. ANALYTICAL CHEMISTRY. *Educ:* Univ Rochester, BS, 64; Emory Univ, PhD(chem), 69. *Prof Exp:* LAB DIR, BRANDYWINE RES LAB, INC, 70- *Mem:* Am Chem Soc; Coblentz Soc. *Res:* Proton and carbon nuclear magnetic resonance studies; high pressure liquid chromatography; infrared spectroscopic analysis of polymers. *Mailing Add:* 21 Cornwall Dr Newark DE 19711

CREDE, ROBERT H, b Chicago, Ill, Aug 11, 15; m 47; c 3. INTERNAL MEDICINE. *Educ:* Univ Calif, Berkeley, AB, 37; Univ Calif, San Francisco, MD, 41. *Prof Exp:* Commonwealth fel med & instr med, Col Med, Univ Cincinnati, 47-49; from asst prof to assoc prof, 49-60, asst dean sch med, 56-60, PROF MED, SCH MED, UNIV CALIF, SAN FRANCISCO, 60-, CHMN DIV AMBULATORY & COMMUNITY MED, 67-, ASSOC DEAN ACAD AFFAIRS & PROF MED, DEPT FAMILY & COMMUNITY MED, 80- *Mem:* Am Psychosom Soc; Am Fedn Clin Res; AMA; Asn Teachers Prev Med; Am Col Prev Med. *Res:* Psychosomatic medicine; delivery of health services; community medicine. *Mailing Add:* Div Ambulatory & Community Med Univ of Calif Med Ctr San Francisco CA 94143

CREDO, ROBERT BRUCE, biochemistry, chemistry, see previous edition

CREE, ALLAN, b Congress, Ariz, July 10, 10; m 37; c 2. PETROLEUM GEOLOGY. *Educ:* Northern Ariz Univ, AB, 33; Ohio Univ, Athens, MA, 35; Univ Colo, PhD(geol), 48. *Prof Exp:* Tech asst, Lowell Observ, 28-33; teacher high sch, Ariz, 35-36; supv critic phys sci & math, Ohio Univ, Athens, 36-41; asst geol, Univ Colo, 41-43; geologist, Shell Oil Co, Inc, Wyo, 43-46; asst prof geol, Univ Nev, 46-48; geologist, Cities Serv Oil Co, 48-50, dist geologist, 50-53, actg div geologist, 53-54, chief geologist, Cities Serv Petrol, Inc, 54-59, Cities Serv Co, 59-63 & Int Cities Serv Oil Co, 63-67, mgr explor, Int Div, Cities Serv Oil Co, 67-70, explor coordr, Cities Serv Int, 70-72; PETROL CONSULT, ULSTER PETROLS LTD, 72-, MEM BD DIRS, 74- *Concurrent Pos:* Dir OSEC Petrol AG, Munich, 72-73; mem bd dirs, OSEC Inc, Oklahoma City, 74-78. *Mem:* Am Asn Petrol Geol; Asn Prof Geol Scientists; fel Explorers Club. *Res:* Subsurface geology; structural and stratigraphic geology and photogeologic mapping; petrographic and petrologic study of igneous rocks; metasomatism and replacement phenomena resulting in igneous rocks; exploration for petroleum on concessions in the Middle East, Europe, Africa, South America, Indonesia, Canada, Australia, Southeast Asia and India. *Mailing Add:* Box 3945 West Sedona AZ 86340

CREECH, HENRY BRYANT, audiology, speech pathology, see previous edition

CREECH, HUGH JOHN, b Exeter, Ont, June 27, 10; nat US; m 37; c 2. IMMUNOCHEMISTRY, CANCER. *Educ:* Univ Western Ont, BA, 33, MA, 35; Univ Toronto, PhD(biochem), 38. *Prof Exp:* Asst chem, Harvard Univ, 38-41; from asst prof to assoc prof, Univ Md, 41-45; immunochemist, Lankenau Hosp Res Inst, 45-47; chmn admin comt, Inst Cancer Res, 47-54, head dept chemother & immunochem, 47-57, chmn div chemother, 57-70, SR MEM, INST CANCER RES, 49- *Concurrent Pos:* Lectr, Bryn Mawr Col, 45-47; mem US comt, Int Union Against Cancer, 57-60 & 80- *Mem:* Sigma Xi; Am Asn Cancer Res (secy-treas, 52-77, vpres, 77-78, pres, 78-79). *Res:* Synthetic organic chemistry; chemotherapy and immunology of polysaccharides and protein complexes in cancer research; chemoantigens; carcinogenesis; alkylating agents; antimalarials; fluorescent antibodies; frameshift mutagens. *Mailing Add:* Inst for Cancer Res Fox Chase Cancer Ctr Philadelphia PA 19111

CREECH, RICHARD HEARNE, b Boston, Mass, Apr 6, 40; m 63; c 2. CLINICAL INVESTIGATION, MEDICAL ONCOLOGY. *Educ:* Johns Hopkins Univ, AB, 61; Univ Pa, MD, 65. *Prof Exp:* Intern resident internal med, Hosp Univ Pa, 65-67; clin assoc med oncol, Nat Cancer Inst, 67-70; fel immunol & hemat, Hosp Univ Pa, 70-71; chief med oncol, Pa Gen Hosp, Univ Pa Serv, 71-72; ASSOC PHYSICIAN MED ONCOL, AM ONCOL HOSP, THE FOX CHASE CANCER CTR, 72-, DIR, OUT-PATIENT DEPT, 75-, DIR MED ADMIN, 80- *Concurrent Pos:* Assoc in med, Univ Pa, 71-73, asst prof clin med, 73-79, adj asst prof med, 79-; prin investr, Eastern Coop Oncol Group, Am Oncol Hosp, 72-; consult, Mercer Med Ctr & Germantown Hosp, 79-; chmn, Mid-Atlantic Regional Coop Oncol Group, 81- *Mem:* Am Soc Clin Oncol; Am Asn Cancer Res; AMA. *Res:* Clinical investigation of maximally effective, but minimally toxic, chemotherapy regimens for the treatment of breast cancer; clarification of the roles of chemotherapy and radiotherapy in the management of small cell carcinoma of the lung. *Mailing Add:* Am Oncol Hosp The Fox Chase Cancer Ctr Philadelphia PA 19111

CREECH, ROY G, b Center, Tex, Jan 24, 35; m 57; c 3. GENETICS, PLANT BREEDING. *Educ:* Stephen F Austin State Univ, BS, 56; Purdue Univ, MS, 58, PhD(genetics), 60. *Prof Exp:* Asst genetics, Purdue Univ, 56-60; from asst prof to prof plant genetics, Pa State Univ, 60-72; PROF AGRON & HEAD DEPT, MISS STATE UNIV, 72- *Concurrent Pos:* Am Soc Agron rep, Am Inst Biol Sci-Campbell Award Comt, 63-72, NE-66 Regional Proj Comt, 63-; vis prof, Univ Ill, 69-70; secy, S-9 Tech Comt Germplasm Resources & New Crops, 73-; chmn, Southern Region Task Force New Crops, 74-; mem meterol study, Panel Agr Res Inst, 74-, chmn, 76-77. *Mem:* Genetics Soc Am; Crop Sci Soc Am (pres, 79); fel Am Soc Agron; Am Soc Hort Sci; Nat Sweet Corn Breeders Asn (pres, 73). *Res:* Genetic regulation of metabolic pathways in plants, especially carbohydrate metabolism in maize. *Mailing Add:* Dept of Agron PO Box 5248 Miss State Univ Mississippi State MS 39762

CREED, DAVID, b Colchester, Eng, Sept 22, 43; m 72; c 1. PHOTOCHEMISTRY. *Educ:* Univ Manchester, BS, 65, MS, 66, PhD(chem), 68. *Prof Exp:* Res assoc biol, Southwest Ctr, Advan Studies, 68-69; res assoc biol, Univ Tex, Dallas, 69-71; SRC res fel, Royal Inst, Univ London, 71-72; temp lectr, Univ Warwick, 72-73; Robert A Welch Found fel, Univ Tex, Dallas, 73-77; asst prof, 77-81, ASSOC PROF CHEM, UNIV SOUTHERN MISS, 81- *Mem:* Inter-Am Photochem Soc; Soc Photobiol; The Chem Soc; Am Chem Soc. *Res:* Reaction mechanisms in organic photochemistry; the molecular basis of some biological effects of ultraviolet light; photochemical aspects of solar energy conversion. *Mailing Add:* Box 9222 Univ Southern Miss Hattiesburg MS 39406

CREEK, JEFFERSON LOUIS, b Oak Ridge, Tenn, Jan 7, 45; m 68; c 2. PHYSICAL CHEMISTRY, ANALYTICAL CHEMISTRY. *Educ:* Mid Tenn State Univ, BS, 67; Southern Ill Univ, MS, 70, PhD(phys chem) 76. *Prof Exp:* Fel phys chem, Univ Calif, Los Angeles, 75-77; RES CHEM PHYS CHEM, CHEVRON OIL FIELD RES CO, 77- *Mem:* Am Chem Soc; Sigma Xi; Soc Petrol Engrs of Am Inst Mining Engrs. *Res:* Solution thermodynamics and phase behavior of reservoir fluid systems. *Mailing Add:* Chevron Oil Field Res Co PO Box 446 La Habra CA 90631

CREEK, ROBERT OMER, b Harrisburg, Ill, June 30, 28; m 58; c 2. ENDOCRINOLOGY. *Educ:* Univ Ill, BS, 50; Southern Ill Univ, MS, 55; Univ Ind, PhD(zool), 60. *Prof Exp:* NIH fel, Sloan-Kettering Inst, NY, 60-61; trainee endocrinol, Univ Wis, 61-64; from asst prof to assoc prof physiol, 64-72, PROF PHYSIOL, SCH MED, CREIGHTON UNIV, 72- *Mem:* Endocrine Soc. *Res:* Mechanisms of hormone action; effect of thyroid stimulating hormone on the thyroid. *Mailing Add:* Dept of Physiol Sch of Med Creighton Univ Omaha NE 68178

CREEL, DONNELL JOSEPH, b Kansas City, Mo, June 17, 42. NEUROPSYCHOLOGY. *Educ:* Univ Mo, Kansas City, BA, 64, MA, 66; Univ Utah, PhD(neuropsychol), 69. *Prof Exp:* Res assoc, Vet Admin Hosp, Kansas City, 69-71; asst prof psychol, Univ Mo-Kansas City, 71; chief psychol res, Vet Admin Hosp, Phoenix, 71-76; res neuropsychologist, 76-79, RES PSYCHOLOGIST & CAREER SCIENTIST, VET ADMIN HOSP, SALT LAKE CITY, 79- *Concurrent Pos:* Adj assoc prof, Ariz State Univ, 71-76 & Univ Utah, 76- *Mem:* Soc Neurosci; Sigma Xi; Int Pigmentation Cell Soc. *Res:* Functional anatomy of sensory systems; inherited anomalies of sensory systems specifically those correlated with genes controlling pigmentation, albinism; the scalp-recorded evoked potential, and ERG as diagnostic tools. *Mailing Add:* Neuropsychol Res Vet Admin Hosp Salt Lake City UT 84148

CREEL, GORDON C, b Daisetta, Tex, Oct 14, 26; m 49; c 3. GENETICS. *Educ:* Howard Payne Col, BA, 49; Univ Tex, MA, 58; Mont State Univ, PhD(genetics), 64. *Prof Exp:* Teacher high sch, 50-57; asst prof biol, Wayland Baptist Col, 58-62; NSF res grant, 62-63; prof biol & chmn div, Howard Payne Col, 64-65; PROF BIOL, ANGELO STATE UNIV, 65- *Mem:* AAAS; Am Genetic Asn. *Res:* Genetics of vertebrates. *Mailing Add:* Dept of Biol Angelo State Univ ASU Sta Box 10890 San Angelo TX 76909

CREELY, ROBERT SCOTT, b Kentfield, Calif, Aug 29, 26; m 52; c 4. PETROLEUM EXPLORATION. *Educ:* Univ Calif, Berkeley, BS, 50, PhD(geol), 55. *Prof Exp:* Geologist, Wm Ross Cabeen & Assoc, Colo, 55-60; from instr to assoc prof geol, Colo State Univ, 60-68, chmn dept, 65-68; chmn dept, 68-76, PROF GEOL, SAN JOSE STATE UNIV, 68- *Mem:* AAAS; Geol Soc Am; Nat Asn Geol Teachers. *Res:* Structural geology; petrology. *Mailing Add:* Dept of Geol San Jose State Univ San Jose CA 95192

CREESE, IAN N, b Bristol, Eng, Apr 4, 49; m 72. PSYCHOPHARMACOLOGY, NEUROCHEMISTRY. *Educ:* Univ Cambridge, Eng, BA, 70, MA, 72, PhD(psychol), 73. *Prof Exp:* Fel pharmacol, Sch Med, Johns Hopkins Univ, 73-76, res assoc, 76-78; asst prof, 78-80, ASSOC PROF NEUROSCI, SCH MED, UNIV CALIF, SAN DIEGO, 80- *Concurrent Pos:* Alfred P Sloan Found fel, 78-80; NIMH study sect preclin psychopharm, 78-82; Smith-Kline vis prof, Australia, 79. *Mem:* Soc Neurosci; Am Soc Neurochem; Am Soc Pharmacol & Exp Therapeut. *Res:* Mechanisms of CNS drug action; neurotransmitter and drug receptors; receptor changes in psychiatric and neurological diseases. *Mailing Add:* Dept of Neurosci M008 Univ Calif San Diego La Jolla CA 92093

CREESE, THOMAS MORTON, b New York, NY, June 19, 34. MATHEMATICS. *Educ:* Mass Inst Technol, BS, 56; Univ Calif, Berkeley, MA, 63, PhD(math), 64. *Prof Exp:* Res mathematician, Univ Calif, Berkeley, 64; ASST PROF MATH, UNIV KANS, 64- *Concurrent Pos:* Lectr, Univ Oslo, 67-68. *Mem:* Am Math Soc; Math Asn Am. *Res:* Complex and functional analysis; several complex variables. *Mailing Add:* Dept of Math Univ of Kans Lawrence KS 66045

CREGER, CLARENCE R, b Carona, Kans, June 8, 34. BIOCHEMISTRY. *Educ:* Kans State Univ, BS, 56, MS, 57; Tex A&M Univ, PhD(biochem, nutrit), 61. *Prof Exp:* Res asst, Kans State Univ, 56-57 & Tex A&M Univ, 58-61; res assoc, Allied Mills Inc, 61-62; from asst prof to prof poultry sci, biochem & nutrit, 62-77, PROF BIOCHEM & BIOPHYS, TEX A&M UNIV,

77- *Mem:* Am Chem Soc; Am Inst Chem; Poultry Sci Asn. *Res:* Metabolism of various radio elements; intermediary metabolism in biosynthetic mechanism. *Mailing Add:* Dept Biochem & Biophys Tex A&M Univ College Station TX 77843

CREGER, PAUL LEROY, b Cresco, Iowa, Oct 26, 30; m 60; c 3. ORGANIC CHEMISTRY. *Educ:* Univ Ill, BS, 52; Univ Nebr, MS, 55, PhD(chem), 57; Univ Mich, MBA, 76. *Prof Exp:* From assoc res chemist to res chemist, 58-71, SR RES CHEMIST, PARKE, DAVIS & CO, 71- *Concurrent Pos:* Fel, Columbia Univ, 57-58. *Honors & Awards:* Indust Res Award, Am Chem Soc, 71. *Mem:* Am Chem Soc. *Res:* Syntheses and reactions of simple nitrogenous heterocycles; qualitative structure; spectral relationships; reaction mechanisms; medicinal chemistry. *Mailing Add:* Warner-Lambert/Parke-Davis 2800 Plymouth Rd Ann Arbor MI 48105

CREIGHTON, CHARLIE SCATTERGOOD, b Orlando, Fla, Aug 23, 26; m 52; c 3. ENTOMOLOGY. *Educ:* Clemson Univ, BS, 50. *Prof Exp:* Biol aide tobacco insect invests, Entom Res Serv, 52-56, entomologist, 56-61, ENTOMOLOGIST, VEG INSECT INVESTS, USDA, 61- *Mem:* Entom Soc Am. *Res:* Biology and control of insects affecting tobacco; investigation of the biology, ecology and control of insects affecting vegetable crops in the South. *Mailing Add:* Veg Insect Invests 2875 Savannah Hwy Charleston SC 29407

CREIGHTON, DONALD JOHN, b Stockton, Calif, Jan 25, 46; m 69; c 2. ENZYMOLOGY, PROTEIN CHEMISTRY. *Educ:* Calif State Univ, Fresno, BS, 68; Univ Calif, Los Angeles, PhD(biochem), 72. *Prof Exp:* Fel biochem, Inst Cancer Res, Philadelphia, 72-75; asst prof, 75-80, ASSOC PROF CHEM, UNIV MD, 80- *Concurrent Pos:* Prin investr, Am Cancer Soc & NIH, 79- *Mem:* Am Chem Soc; Sigma Xi. *Res:* Mechanism of action of sulfhydryl proteases as well as on the mechanism of action of glutathione-dependent enzymes. *Mailing Add:* Chem Dept Univ Md Baltimore County 5401 Wilkens Ave Baltimore MD 21228

CREIGHTON, DONALD L, b Hays, Kans, Jan 3, 32; m 53; c 1. MECHANICAL ENGINEERING, MATERIALS SCIENCE. *Educ:* Univ Kans, BSME, 54, MSME, 61; Univ Ariz, PhD(mech eng), 64. *Prof Exp:* Res & develop engr, Aeronaut Div, Minneapolis-Honeywell Regulator Co, 57-58; test engr, Rocketdyne Div, NAm Aviation, Inc, 58-59; instr mech eng, Univ Kans, 59-61; res assoc mat & vacuum, Univ Ariz, 63-64; asst prof mech eng, 64-68, assoc prof, 68-78, PROF MECH & AEROSPACE ENG, UNIV MO-COLUMBIA, 78- *Mem:* Am Soc Metals; Am Soc Testing & Mat; Am Soc Eng Educ; Am Soc Biomat; Am Welding Soc. *Res:* Materials; cryogenics; failure analysis; fatigue of materials; heat transfer; biomaterials; fracture mechanics; design; systems design. *Mailing Add:* Dept of Mech & Aerospace Eng Univ of Mo Columbia MO 65211

CREIGHTON, HARRIET BALDWIN, b Delavan, Ill, June 27, 09. BOTANY. *Educ:* Wellesley Col, AB, 29; Cornell Univ, PhD(bot), 33. *Prof Exp:* Asst bot, Cornell Univ, 29-32, instr cytol & microtechnique, 32-34; asst prof bot, Conn Col, 34-40; from assoc prof to prof, 40-74, EMER PROF BOT, WELLESLEY COL, 74- *Concurrent Pos:* Fulbright lectr, Australia, 52-53 & Peru, 59-60. *Mem:* Fel AAAS (secy, 60-63, vpres, 64); Genetics Soc Am; Am Soc Naturalists; Soc Develop Biol; Bot Soc Am (secy, 50-54, vpres, 55, pres, 56). *Res:* Cell physiology; plant growth hormones; plant morphogenesis. *Mailing Add:* Dept of Biol Sci Wellesley Col Wellesley MA 02181

CREIGHTON, JOHN THOMAS, entomology, deceased

CREIGHTON, PHILLIP DAVID, b Irwin, Pa, June 18, 45. ORNITHOLOGY, BEHAVIORAL ECOLOGY. *Educ:* Tarkio Col, Mo, BA, 66; Colo State Univ, MS, 70, PhD(zool), 74. *Prof Exp:* Jr biologist, Midwest Res Inst, 66-68; asst prof, 73-76, ASSOC PROF BIOL, TOWSON STATE UNIV, 76- *Concurrent Pos:* Assoc res consult, Ecol Consult, Inc, 70-73; co-dir, Inst Animal Behav, Towson State Univ, 79- *Mem:* Am Ornith Union; Wilson Ornith Soc; Cooper Ornith Soc; Sigma Xi; Am Soc Zoologists. *Res:* Community inter-relationships as demonstrated by variations of resource utilization; niche segregation and behavioral time budgets; emphasis is placed on behavioral ecology; nestling energetics and parental behavior of birds. *Mailing Add:* Dept Biol Sci Towson State Univ Towson MD 21204

CREIGHTON, STEPHEN MARK, b Sask, Aug 2, 20; m 46; c 1. ORGANIC CHEMISTRY, PHYSICAL CHEMISTRY. *Educ:* Queen's Univ, Ont, BA, 48, MA, 49; Yale Univ, PhD(org chem), 54. *Prof Exp:* Chemist, Can Packers Ltd, 49-51; chemist, Hooker Chem Corp, 53-56, res assoc polyolefins, 56-59, res supvr polymers, 59-63; HEAD PROD RES & DEVELOP, RES COUN ALTA, 63- *Concurrent Pos:* Lectr & adv, Niagara Univ, 57-58. *Mem:* Am Chem Soc; fel Chem Inst Can. *Res:* Steroids; fat and fatty acids; chlorinated hydrocarbons; pesticides; light stability and fire-retardance of plastics; polyurethane foams; polyolefins; polythers; polyesters; expoxies; sugar and sugar cane; building products. *Mailing Add:* Alta Res Coun 11315 87th Ave Edmonton AB T6G 2C2 Can

CREIGHTON, THOMAS EDWIN, b St Louis, Mo, Apr 20, 40; m 63; c 3. MOLECULAR BIOLOGY. *Educ:* Calif Inst Technol, BS, 62; Stanford Univ, PhD(biol), 66. *Prof Exp:* Air Force Off Sci Res-Nat Acad Sci res fel, Med Res Coun Lab Molecular Biol, Cambridge Univ, 66-67; asst prof biol, Yale Univ, 67-69; SR SCIENTIST, MED RES COUN LAB MOLECULAR BIOL, CAMBRIDGE, 69- *Concurrent Pos:* Vis scientist, Weizmann Inst, Israel, 76. *Res:* Protein structure, folding, and chemistry. *Mailing Add:* Med Res Coun Lab Molecular Biol Hills Rd Cambridge England

CREININ, HOWARD LEE, b Chicago, Ill, Sept 5, 42; m 63; c 2. FOOD SCIENCE. *Educ:* Univ Ill, Urbana, BS, 63, PhD(food sci), 71. *Prof Exp:* Prod develop chemist food sci, Res & Develop Div, Lever Brothers Co, NJ, 70-74; prod develop scientist food sci, Marschall Div, Miles Labs, 74-77; sr proj leader protein chemist, Ross Labs, Columbus, 77-82; SUPVR PROD UTILIZATION, KROGER CO, CINCINNATI, 82- *Mailing Add:* Kroger Co 1212 State Ave Cincinnati OH 45204

CRELIN, EDMUND SLOCUM, b Red Bank, NJ, Apr 26, 23; m 48; c 4. HUMAN ANATOMY, HUMAN DEVELOPMENT. *Educ:* Cent Col, Iowa, BA, 47; Yale Univ, PhD(anat), 51. *Hon Degrees:* DSc, Cent Col, Iowa, 69. *Prof Exp:* From instr to assoc prof human anat, 51-68, PROF ANAT, SCH MED, YALE UNIV, 68-; CHMN HUMAN GROWTH & DEVELOP STUDY UNIT, YALE-NEW HAVEN MED CTR, 72- *Concurrent Pos:* Consult, Ciba-Geigy Pharmaceut Co Inc, 61-; assoc ed, Anat Record, 68-74. *Honors & Awards:* Award, Sch Med, Yale Univ, 61; Kappa Delta Res Award, Am Acad Orthop Surgeons, 76. *Mem:* AAAS; AMA; Sigma Xi; Am Asn Anatomists. *Res:* Structure and physiology of connective tissues; developmental biology; anthropology. *Mailing Add:* Dept of Surg Yale Univ Sch of Med New Haven CT 06510

CRELLING, JOHN CRAWFORD, b Philadelphia, Pa, June 13, 41; m 67; c 2. COAL PETROLOGY, COAL GEOLOGY. *Educ:* Univ Del, BA, 64; Pa State Univ, MS, 67, PhD(geol), 73. *Prof Exp:* Res geologist, Bethlehem Steel Corp, 72-77; asst prof, 77-81, ASSOC PROF GEOL, SOUTHERN ILL UNIV, CARBONDALE, 81- *Concurrent Pos:* Sr vis res fel, Univ Newcastle-Upon-Tyne, Eng, 81. *Mem:* Geol Soc Am; Am Inst Mining, Metall & Petrol Engrs; AAAS; Am Soc Photogram. *Res:* Basic and applied coal petrology including fluorescence microscopy and fluorescence spectral analysis of coal minerology, petrology of Rocky Mountain coals, properties of pseudonitrinite and resinite, automated petrographic analysis, weathered coal and carbonization. *Mailing Add:* Dept Geol Southern Ill Univ Carbondale IL 62901

CREMENS, WALTER SAMUEL, b Tampa, Fla, Aug 14, 26; m 50; c 2. PHYSICAL METALLURGY, MATERIAL SCIENCE. *Educ:* Mass Inst Technol, BS, 49, MS, 54, ScD, 57, Ga State Univ, MBA, 74. *Prof Exp:* Engr, Schnectady Works Lab & Res Lab, Gen Elec Co, 49-50, Thomson Lab, 50-53; res asst metall, Mass Inst Technol, 53-57; civilian tech liaison off, Hq, US Air Forces, Europe, 57-60; res metallurgist, 60-62, head powder metall sect, Mat & Struct Div, Lewis Res Ctr, NASA, 62-67; staff scientist & mgr graphite composites task force, 67-70, mat scientist adv struct dept, 70-81, PRIN STRUCT & MAT SCIENTIST, ADV RES ORGN, LOCKHEED-GA CO, 81- *Mem:* Am Soc Metals; Soc Aerospace Mat & Process Engrs; Am Inst Aeronaut & Astronaut. *Res:* Fiber composites; powder metallurgy; fracture mechanics; high temperature alloys; research management; composite materials. *Mailing Add:* Dept 72-11 Zone 403 Lockheed-Ga Co Marietta GA 30063

CREMER, NATALIE E, b Minot, NDak, Sept 13, 19. IMMUNOLOGY, VIROLOGY. *Educ:* Univ Minn, BS, 44, MS, 56, PhD, 60. *Prof Exp:* RES SPECIALIST IMMUNOL, STATE OF CALIF DEPT HEALTH SERV, 62- *Concurrent Pos:* NIH res fel immunochem, Calif Inst Technol, 60-62; lectr, Sch Pub Health, Univ Calif, 71-; consult, Immunologic Devices Panel, Food & Drug Admin, 78- *Mem:* AAAS; Am Soc Microbiol; Am Asn Immunologists; NY Acad Sci; Soc Exp Biol & Med. *Res:* Immunology of viruses and viral infection; latent viral infections; chronic degenerative disease. *Mailing Add:* Viral & Rickettsial Dis Lab State of Calif Dept Health Serv Berkeley CA 97404

CREMER, SHELDON E, b Parkersburg, WVa, Oct 24, 35; m 65; c 2. ORGANIC CHEMISTRY. *Educ:* Carnegie Inst Technol, BS, 57; Univ Rochester, PhD(org chem), 61. *Prof Exp:* Asst prof chem, Ill Inst Technol, 63-69; assoc prof, 69-74, PROF CHEM, MARQUETTE UNIV, 74- *Concurrent Pos:* Fels, Ohio State Univ, 61-62 & Univ Ill, 62-63; sr res associateship, Nat Res Coun, Wright-Patterson Air Force Base, Dayton, Ohio, 74-75. *Mem:* Fel Am Inst Chem; Brit Chem Soc; Am Chem Soc. *Res:* Organic photochemistry; organo-phosphorus chemistry; organosilicon and organoarsenic chemistry; organic synthesis. *Mailing Add:* Dept of Chem Marquette Univ 535 N 14th St Milwaukee WI 53233

CREMERS, CLIFFORD J, b Minneapolis, Minn, Mar 27, 33; m 54; c 5. MECHANICAL ENGINEERING. *Educ:* Univ Minn, BS, 57, MS, 61, PhD(mech eng), 64. *Prof Exp:* Res fel mech eng, Univ Minn, 59-61, instr, 61-64; asst prof, Ga Inst Technol, 64-66; assoc prof, 66-71, PROF MECH ENG, UNIV KY, 71-, CHMN DEPT, 75- *Concurrent Pos:* Lectr, Gen Elec A Course, 65-66; NSF grants, 66, 69, 75 & 81; NASA res grant, 68-74; consult, UNESCO, 76- *Mem:* AAAS; fel Am Soc Mech Engrs; Am Inst Aeronaut & Astronaut; Am Inst Eng Educ; Sigma Xi. *Res:* Turbulent flow in non-circular ducts; solar energy utilization; plasma heat transfer; biological heat transfer; heat transfer in frost; direct energy conversion; lunar thermophysical properties and heat transfer. *Mailing Add:* Dept Mech Eng Univ Ky Lexington KY 40506

CRENSHAW, DAVID BROOKS, b Columbia, Mo, May 15, 45; m 66; c 2. ANIMAL BREEDING. *Educ:* Univ Mo-Columbia, BS, 68, MS, 69, PhD(animal husb & cytogenetics), 72. *Prof Exp:* Asst prof, 72-75, ASSOC PROF ANIMAL SCI, TEX A&I UNIV, 75-, ASSOC PROF, COL AGR, 80- *Mem:* Am Soc Animal Sci. *Res:* Genetics of fertility in Texas Longhorn cattle; cytogenetics of early embryonic mortality in beef cattle; hormonal manipulation of postpartum estrus in range beef cattle. *Mailing Add:* Col of Agr Box 156 Tex A&I Univ Kingsville TX 78363

CRENSHAW, JACK WESTCOTT, computer sciences, see previous edition

CRENSHAW, JOHN WALDEN, JR, b Atlanta, Ga, May 17, 23; m 46; c 2. POPULATION GENETICS. *Educ:* Emory Univ, AB, 48; Univ Ga, MS, 51; Univ Fla, PhD(zool), 55. *Prof Exp:* Instr zool, Univ Mo, 55-56; asst prof biol, Antioch Col, 56-60; asst prof zool, Southern Ill Univ, 60-62; assoc prof zool, Univ Md, 62-65 & prof, 65-67; prof zool, Univ RI, 67-72; dir, 72-81, PROF SCH BIOL, GA INST TECHNOL, ATLANTA, 72- *Concurrent Pos:* Am Philos Soc res grant, 57-58; NSF res grants, 58-64 & sci fac fel, Univ Calif, Berkeley, 59-60; USPHS res grants, 62-67 & res contracts, 68-70 & 75-78; consult, NSF Int Sci Activities, 63-67, Biol Sci Curriculum Study, 60-68 & US AID, Latin Am, 69. *Mem:* Fel AAAS; Am Soc Nat; Genetics Soc Am; Am Genetic Asn; Am Inst Biol Sci. *Res:* Ascertainment of and effects on fitness of mutagen induced polygenic mutations in mice and fish; origin and maintenance of polygenic variation. *Mailing Add:* Sch of Biol Ga Inst Technol Atlanta GA 30332

CRENSHAW, MILES AUBREY, b Earlysville, Va, Mar 22, 32; div; c 3. COMPARATIVE PHYSIOLOGY. *Educ:* Univ Va, BA, 59; Duke Univ, MA, 62, PhD(zool), 64. *Prof Exp:* Asst physiol, Med Sch, Univ Va, 54-59; asst zool, Duke Univ, 60, instr, 64; instr physiol, Sch Dent Med, Harvard Univ & staff assoc histol, Forsyth Dent Ctr, 64-67; asst prof dent sci, 67-71, assoc prof oral biol, Dent Res Ctr, 71-79, adj assoc prof zool, 73-79, assoc prof marine sci, 76-79, PROF PEDONTICS & MARINE SCI, SCH DENT, UNIV NC CHAPEL HILL, 79- *Mem:* AAAS; Am Dent Asn; Am Soc Zoologists; Am Soc Zoologists; Int Asn Dent Res. *Res:* Comparative biology of mineralizing tissues. *Mailing Add:* Dent Res Ctr Univ NC Chapel Hill NC 27514

CRENSHAW, RONNIE RAY, b Earlington, Ky, Dec 24, 36; m 59; c 2. MEDICINAL CHEMISTRY. *Educ:* Vanderbilt Univ, BA, 58, PhD(org chem), 63. *Prof Exp:* Assoc chemist, Mead Johnson Labs, Ind, 58-59; sr chemist, 63-77, asst dir med chem, 77-80, ASSOC DIR MED CHEM, BRISTOL LABS, 80-, PROJ DIR, GASTROINTESTINAL AREA, 80- *Mem:* Am Chem Soc. *Res:* Synthetic organic chemistry; organic sulfur chemistry; pharmaceuticals. *Mailing Add:* 107 Charing Rd DeWitt NY 13214

CRENTZ, WILLIAM LUTHER, b Baltimore, Md, May 1, 10; m 57. CHEMISTRY. *Educ:* Univ Md, BS, 32, MS, 33. *Prof Exp:* Statistician, Smokeless Coal Code Authority, Washington, DC, 34-35; researcher, US Procurement Div, 35-37; econ analyst, Coal Div, US Dept Interior, 37-43; coal technologist, US Bur Mines, 43-52, chem engr, 52-60, asst to chief, Div Bituminous Coal, 60-63, from asst dir to dir coal res, 63-70, asst dir energy, 70-73; consult, Off Secy, US Dept Interior, 74-75; consult, Energy Res Develop Admin, 75-77, CONSULT, DEPT ENERGY, 75- *Honors & Awards:* Chevalier de l'Ordre de la Couronune, Belg, 59; Distinguished Serv Award & Gold Medal, US Dept Interior, 68. *Mem:* Am Inst Mining, Metall & Petrol Eng. *Res:* Coal preparation and utilization; petroleum and natural gas research; shale oil research; production and conservation of helium. *Mailing Add:* 3850 Tunlaw Rd NW Washington DC 20007

CREPEA, SEYMOUR B, b New York, NY, Oct 25, 18; m 53; c 2. MEDICINE, ALLERGY. *Educ:* Tulane Univ, BS, 39, MD, 42; Columbia Univ, DMedSc, 48. *Prof Exp:* Assoc prof med & head dept allergy, Sch Med, Univ Wis, 49-60; resident med dir & resident physician, Dept Res Eng, Sahuaro Sch Asthmatic Children, Univ Ariz, 60-70; ASSOC MED DIR, SYNTEX LABS, INC, 70- *Concurrent Pos:* Consult, Vet Admin Hosp. *Mem:* AMA; Trudeau Soc; fel Am Acad Allergy; fel Am Col Physicians. *Res:* Immunology. *Mailing Add:* Syntex Labs Inc 3401 Hillview Ave Palo Alto CA 94304

CREPEAU, RICHARD HANES, biophysics, see previous edition

CREPET, WILLIAM LOUIS, b New York, NY, Aug 10, 46; m 72. PALEOBOTANY, EVOLUTIONARY BIOLOGY. *Educ:* State Univ NY Binghamton, BA, 69; Yale Univ, MPh, 71, PhD(biol), 73. *Prof Exp:* Lectr bot, Ind Univ, 73-75; asst prof, 75-79, ASSOC PROF BIOL, UNIV CONN, 79- *Mem:* Am Inst Biol Sci; AAAS; Bot Soc Am; Int Asn Angiosperm Paleobot; Explorers Club. *Res:* Evolution of the angiosperms with emphasis on the evolution of floral structure and the evolution of pollination mechanisms and pollen; cycadophyte evolution. *Mailing Add:* Dept Biol Sci Univ Conn U-42 Storrs CT 06268

CRERAR, DAVID ALEXANDER, b Toronto, Ont, July 23, 45; m 72. GEOCHEMISTRY. *Educ:* Univ Toronto, BSc, 67, MSc, 69; Pa State Univ, PhD(geochem), 74. *Prof Exp:* asst prof, 74-80, ASSOC PROF GEOCHEM, PRINCETON UNIV, 80- *Mem:* Geochem Soc; Soc Econ Geologists. *Res:* Hydrothermal geochemistry; processes of ore deposition; chemistry of natural water; environmental geochemistry; thermodynamics. *Mailing Add:* Guyot Hall Princeton Univ Princeton NJ 08540

CRESCITELLI, FREDERICK, b Providence, RI, June 23, 09; m 41; c 3. VISUAL PHYSIOLOGY. *Educ:* Brown Univ, PhB, 30, MS, 32, PhD(physiol), 34. *Hon Degrees:* MD, Univ Linkoping, Sweden, 75. *Prof Exp:* Keen fel, Brown Univ, 34-35; instr, Colby Jr Col, 35-36; res assoc zool, Univ Iowa, 36-40; instr, Univ Wash, 40-42; actg asst prof, Stanford Univ, 42-43; vis asst prof, Univ Southern Calif, 43-44; physiologist, Chem Warfare Serv, US Army, Edgewood Arsenal, Md, 44-46; Mellon fel, Johns Hopkins Hosp, 46; assoc prof zool, 46-51, prof, 51-76, EMER PROF CELL BIOL, UNIV CALIF, LOS ANGELES, 76- *Concurrent Pos:* Nat Res Coun fel, 35-36; vis prof, Univ Cologne, 66-67; ed, Vision Res; mem adv bd, J Comparable Physiol; mem adv bd, Nat Eye Inst, 74-75. *Mem:* Am Physiol Soc; Soc Gen Physiol; fel Optical Soc Am. *Res:* Neurophysiology; effects of drugs; visual physiology; aviation physiology; physiology and biochemistry of retina. *Mailing Add:* Dept of Biol Univ of Calif Los Angeles CA 90024

CRESPI, HENRY LEWIS, b Joliet, Ill, Mar 18, 26; m 55; c 6. PHYSICAL CHEMISTRY. *Educ:* Univ Ill, BS, 52, PhD(chem), 55. *Prof Exp:* Asst chemist, 55-59, assoc chemist, 59-76, ASST DIR CHEM DIV, ARGONNE NAT LAB, 76- *Concurrent Pos:* Vis lectr, St Procopius Col, 57-62. *Mem:* Am Chem Soc. *Res:* Biological effects of deuterium, with special reference to algae and other microorganisms; chemistry of proteins. *Mailing Add:* Argonne Nat Lab 9700 Cass Ave Argonne IL 60439

CRESPO, JORGE H, b Santiago, Chile, May 19, 44; m 71; c 2. MEDICAL EDUCATION. *Educ:* San Simon Univ, Cochabamba, Bolivia, MD, 70. *Prof Exp:* Res assoc indust toxicol, Dept Environ Med, Med Col Wis, 72-73; ASST PROF MED, DEPT LATERAL MED, WRIGHT STATE UNIV, DAYTON, OHIO, 78-; ASSOC DIR, LATERAL MED RESIDENCY PROG, KETTERING MED CTR, OHIO, 78- *Mem:* Am Col Physicians; AMA. *Res:* Rapid diagnostic methods in infectious diseases. *Mailing Add:* Kettering Med Ctr 3535 Southern Blvd Kettering OH 45429

CRESS, CHARLES EDWIN, b Rowan Co, NC, Aug 17, 34; m 57. STATISTICS, QUANTITATIVE GENETICS. *Educ:* NC State Univ, BS, 56, MS, 61; Iowa State Univ, PhD(statist), 65. *Prof Exp:* Asst prof statist, Rutgers Univ, 65-66; from asst prof to assoc prof, 66-75, PROF CROP & SOIL SCI, MICH STATE UNIV, 75- *Mem:* Biomet Soc; Am Statist Asn; Am Soc Agron. *Res:* Methods of statistical data analysis. *Mailing Add:* Dept of Crop & Soil Sci Mich State Univ East Lansing MI 48824

CRESS, DANIEL HUGG, b Canon City, Colo, Sept 13, 44; m 66; c 2. SENSOR ANALYST. *Educ:* Univ Southern Colo, BS, 67; Tex Tech Univ, MS, 71; PhD(physics), 74. *Prof Exp:* Physicist, Waterways Exp Sta, 73-79, engr, Transp Test Ctr, 79-81, PHYSICIST, WATERWAYS EXP STA, US ARMY, 81- *Concurrent Pos:* Prin investr, various grants, 78-81; secy, Res Study Group II, NATO, 79-80. *Mem:* Sigma Xi; Am Inst Physics. *Res:* Mechanical and electromagnetic wave propagation; response of transducers and detectors to wave phenomenon with emphasis on the effect of geophysical phenomena on the observed waveforms. *Mailing Add:* US Army Waterways Exp Sta PO Box 631 Vicksburg MS 39180

CRESS, DONALD CHAUNCEY, entomology, see previous edition

CRESSEY, ROGER F, b Stoughton, Mass, June 9, 30. PARASITOLOGY. *Educ:* Boston Univ, AB, 56, AM, 58, PhD(biol), 65. *Prof Exp:* Instr biol, Boston Univ, 64-65; CUR CRUSTACEA, SMITHSONIAN INST, 65- *Concurrent Pos:* Res assoc, Mote Marine Lab, Fla; adj lectr biol sci, George Washington Univ; ed, Biol Soc Wash; adj prof, Dunbarton Col, 74; panel mem, Food & Agr Orgn, UN, 74- *Mem:* Am Soc Ichthyologists & Herpetologists; Am Soc Zool; Soc Syst Zool (secy). *Res:* Taxonomy, evolution and systematics of copepods parasitic on fishes; taxonomy of synodontid fishes. *Mailing Add:* Dept Invert Zool Smithsonian Inst Washington DC 20560

CRESSMAN, GEORGE PARMLEY, b West Chester, Pa, Oct 7, 19; m 75; c 4. METEOROLOGY. *Educ:* Univ Chicago, PhD(meteorol), 49. *Prof Exp:* Asst meteorol, Univ Chicago, 45-49; consult, Air Weather Serv, 49-54; dir, Joint Numerical Weather Prediction Unit, 54-58; Nat Meteorol Serv, US Weather Bur, 58-65; Environ Sci Serv Admin, 65-70, dir, Nat Oceanic & Atmospheric Agency, 70-79, RES METEOROLOGIST, NAT WEATHER SERV, 79- *Honors & Awards:* Losey Award, Am Inst Astronaut & Aeronaut, 67; Appl Meteorol Award, Am Meteorol Soc, 72 & Cleveland Abbe Award, 75; Int Meteorol Orgn Prize, 78. *Mem:* Am Meteorol Soc (pres, 78); Am Geophys Union. *Res:* Synoptic meteorology; atmospheric dynamics. *Mailing Add:* 11 Old Stage Ct Rockville MD 20852

CRESSMAN, WILLIAM ARTHUR, b Philadelphia, Pa, Feb 1, 41; m 63; c 2. PHARMACOLOGY. *Educ:* Philadelphia Col Pharm, BSc, 63, MSc, 65, PhD(biopharmaceut), 67. *Prof Exp:* Group leader, 67-73, sr proj coordr, 73-76, dir new prod, 76-77, exec dir new prod & int mkt develop, 77-81, VPRES NEW PROD PLANNING, WYETH INT LTD, MCNEIL LABS, INC, 81- *Mem:* Am Pharmaceut Asn; Acad Pharmaceut Sci; Am Chem Soc; Am Soc Pharmacol & Exp Therapeut; Am Soc Clin Pharmacol. *Res:* Physical pharmacy; drug dosage form design and evaluation; drug metabolism and kinetics; bioavailability and new drug development. *Mailing Add:* Int Mkt Develop McNeil Pharmaceut Spring House PA 19477

CRESWELL, MICHAEL WILLIAM, b Gloucester, Eng, Apr 26, 37; m 63; c 2. ELECTRONICS. *Educ:* Univ London, BSc, 58; Pa State Univ, MS, 61, PhD(physics), 65; Univ Pittsburgh, MBA, 75. *Prof Exp:* Sr engr, 65-80, MGR, POWER DEVICES LAB, WESTINGHOUSE RES & DEVELOP CTR, 80- *Mem:* Am Phys Soc; Inst Elec & Electronics Engrs. *Res:* Nuclear physics, including observation and analysis of reactions with photographic emulsions; semiconductors, including influence of mechanical stress on electrical properties of semiconductor materials; computer process control in power semiconductor device manufacture; effects of nuclear radiation on silicon devices. *Mailing Add:* 691 Presque Isle Dr Pittsburgh PA 15239

CRESWELL, PETER, b Mexborough, Eng, Mar 6, 45; m 69; c 1. IMMUNOLOGY. *Educ:* Univ Newcastle Upon Tyne, BSc, 66, MSc, 67; London Univ, PhD(biochem & immunol), 71. *Prof Exp:* Res assoc biochem & molecular biol, Harvard Univ, 71-73; assoc, 73-74, asst prof, 74-78, ASSOC PROF IMMUNOL, MED CTR, DUKE UNIV, 78- *Mem:* Am Asn Immunol. *Res:* Structure and function of products of the human major histocompatibility complex; lymphocyte surface markers; lymphocyte activation and function; somatic cell hybridization; genetics of human lymphocyte antigens; cell surface lectins. *Mailing Add:* Bos 3010 Div Immunol Med Ctr Duke Univ Durham NC 27710

CRETIN, SHAN, b New Orleans, La, Dec, 5, 46; m 76; c 3. OPERATIONS RESEARCH. *Educ:* Mass Inst Technol, SB, 68, PhD(opers res), 75; Yale Univ, MPH, 70. *Prof Exp:* Res assoc public health, Dept Epidemiol & Pub Health, Yale Univ, 70-71; asst prof, biostatist, Harvard Sch Pub Health, 74-76; asst prof, 76-81, ASSOC PROF, HEALTH SCI, SCH PUB HEALTH, UNIV CALIF, LOS ANGELES, 81- *Concurrent Pos:* Consult, Rand Corp, 76-, Nat Ctr Health Serv Res, 80-; assoc ed, Mgt Sci & Eval Rev, 81-; vis assoc prof, Mass Inst Technol & Harvard Med Sch, 82. *Mem:* Opers Res Soc Am; Am Pub Health Asn. *Res:* Applications of operations research to the evaluation of health services. *Mailing Add:* 402 15th St Santa Monica CA 90402

CREUTZ, CARL EUGENE, b Pittsburgh, Pa, Oct 15, 47. BIOCHEMISTRY, BIOPHYSICS. *Educ:* Stanford Univ, BS, 69; Univ Wis-Madison, MS, 70; Johns Hopkins Univ, PhD(biophys), 76. *Prof Exp:* STAFF FEL RES, NAT INST HEALTH, 76- *Mem:* Soc Neurosci; Biophys Soc. *Res:* Structure and function of cytoplasm. *Mailing Add:* Nat Inst Health Nat Inst Arthritis Metabolism & Digestive Diseases Bldg 10 Rm 9N250 Bethesda MD 20205

CREUTZ, CAROL (ANN), b Washington, DC, Oct 20, 44; m 65; c 1. INORGANIC CHEMISTRY. *Educ:* Univ Calif, Los Angeles, BS, 66; Stanford Univ, PhD(chem), 70. *Prof Exp:* Asst prof chem, Georgetown Univ, 70-72; res assoc, 72-75, assoc chemist, 75-77, CHEMIST, BROOKHAVEN NAT LAB, 77- *Mem:* Am Chem Soc. *Res:* Synthesis and properties of unusual transition metal complexes; dynamics of inorganic reactions in solution. *Mailing Add:* Dept of Chem Brookhaven Nat Lab Upton NY 11973

CREUTZ, EDWARD (CHESTER), b Beaver Dam, Wis, Jan 23, 13; m 37; c 3. NUCLEAR PHYSICS. *Educ:* Univ Wis, BS, 36, PhD(physics), 39. *Prof Exp:* Res assoc, Princeton Univ, 38-39, instr physics, 40-41; physicist, Nat Defense Res Coun, 41-42, metall lab, Univ Chicago, 42-44 & Manhattan Proj, Univ Calif, Los Alamos, 44-45; assoc prof physics, Carnegie Inst Technol, 46-49, prof physics, head dept & dir nuclear res ctr, 49-55; dir res, Gen Atomic Div, Gen Dynamics Corp, 55-59, vpres res & develop, 59-67; vpres res, Gulf Gen Atomic, Inc, 67-70; asst dir res, 70-75, asst dir math & phys sci & eng, NSF, Washington, DC, 75-77; DIR BERNICE P BISHOP MUS, 77- *Concurrent Pos:* Consult, Manhattan Proj, 46, Oak Ridge Nat Lab, 46-58, Lawrence Radiation Lab, Univ Calif, 46, 56 & NSF, 50-; mem coun exec bd, Argonne Nat Lab, 46-51; appointments comt, Am Inst Physics, 55-58, vis scientists prog comt, 58-, col physics comt, 59, adv comt corp assocs, 64 & dir-at-large bd gov, 65-; scientist-at-large, Proj Sherwood Div Res, US AEC, 55-56; dir, John Jay Hopkins Lab Pure & Appl Sci, 55-67; mem adv coun & seawater conversion tech adv comt, Water Resources Ctr, Univ Calif, 58-; adv panel gen sci, US Dept Defense, 59-63; adv comt to off sci personnel, Nat Res Coun, 60-; res adv comt electrophys, NASA, 64-; mem comt sr reviewers, Energy Res & Develop Admin, 73-, fusion power coord comt, 74- *Mem:* Nat Acad Sci; fel Am Phys Soc; fel Am Nuclear Soc; NY Acad Sci; Am Soc Eng Educ. *Res:* Proton-proton and proton-lithium scattering; artificial radioactivity; metallurgy of uranium and beryllium; deuteron-neutron reactions; neutron absorption in uranium; synchrocyclotron design; meson reactions; nuclear reactors; thermonuclear reactions; gas flow in porous media. *Mailing Add:* Off of the Dir PO Box 19000A Honolulu HI 96818

CREUTZ, MICHAEL JOHN, b Los Alamos, NMex, Nov 24, 44; m 66; c 1. THEORETICAL PHYSICS. *Educ:* Calif Inst Technol, BS, 66; Stanford Univ, MS, 68, PhD(physics), 70. *Prof Exp:* Res assoc, Stanford Linear Accelerator Ctr, 70; fel physics, Univ Md, 70-72; asst physicist, 72-74, assoc physicist, 74-76, PHYSICIST, BROOKHAVEN NAT LAB, 76- *Mem:* Am Phys Soc. *Res:* Theoretical applications of quantum field theory to elementary particle physics. *Mailing Add:* Dept of Physics Brookhaven Nat Lab Upton NY 11973

CREVASSE, GARY A, b Cedar Key, Fla, Oct 16, 34; m 59. FOOD SCIENCE. *Educ:* Univ Fla, BS, 61, MS, 63; Mich State Univ, PhD(food sci), 67. *Prof Exp:* Asst prof food sci, Univ Ariz, 67-68; DIR RES COLLAGEN SAUSAGE CASINGS, BRECHTEEN CO DIV, HYGRADE FOOD PROD CORP, 68- *Mem:* Inst Food Technol. *Res:* Meat science, specifically collagen and its application to meat industry as a packaging medium; proteolytic enzyme effects on acid soluble collagen and isolation of the resulting components. *Mailing Add:* Brechteen Co 50750 E Russell Schmidt Mt Clemens MI 48043

CREVELING, CYRUS ROBBINS, b Washington, DC, May 30, 30; m 54; c 2. BIOCHEMISTRY, PHARMACOLOGY. *Educ:* George Washington Univ, BS, 53, MS, 55, PhD(pharmacol), 62. *Prof Exp:* Chemist, Naval Ord Res Lab, Washington, DC, 52-53; asst biochem, George Washington Univ, 54-55; chemist, Hunter Mem Labs, DC, 56-58; biochemist, Nat Heart Inst, 58-62; from asst to assoc biochem, Sch Med, Harvard Univ, 62-64; PHARMACOLOGIST, NAT INST ARTHRITIS, METAB & DIGESTIVE & KIDNEY DIS, 64- *Concurrent Pos:* Mem staff, Pharmacol Study Sect, Dis Res Grants, NIH, 66-70; assoc, Med Sch, Howard Univ, 70-; chmn, Int Conf Transmethylation, 78-81; chmn, Sato Mem Award Committee, 79-; mem, task force on environ cancer & heart & lung dis, Environ Protection Agency, 79- *Honors & Awards:* Distinguished Scientist Award, Soc Exp Biol Med, 80. *Mem:* AAAS; Am Soc Pharmacol & Exp Therapeut; Am Chem Soc; fel Am Int Chemists; Soc Neurosci. *Res:* Biosynthesis and metabolism of biogenic amines; drug metabolism; central nervous system pharmacology; cyclic adenosine monophosphate. *Mailing Add:* Sect Pharmacodynamics Nat Inst Arth Metab & Dig Dis Bethesda MD 20014

CREVIER, WILLIAM FRANCIS, b Los Angeles, Calif, Oct 29, 41; m 65; c 2. PLASMA PHYSICS, ELECTRODYNAMICS. *Educ:* Univ Santa Clara, BS, 63; Univ Southern Calif, MS, 65; Univ Md, PhD(physics), 70. *Prof Exp:* Res engr, Fairchild Semiconductor, 65-66; physicist, Gen Elec Co, 70-71; PHYSICIST, MISSION RES CORP, 71- *Res:* Effects of electromagnetic fields produced by nuclear explosions interacting with the atmosphere or directly with a particular system such as a satellite. *Mailing Add:* Mission Res Corp Drawer 719 Santa Barbara CA 93102

CREW, JOHN EDWIN, b Chicago, Ill, July 10, 30; m 58; c 4. NUCLEAR PHYSICS. *Educ:* Univ Chicago, BS, 52, MS, 53; Univ Ill, PhD(physics), 57. *Prof Exp:* Physicist, X-ray Sect, Radiation Physics Lab, Nat Bur Standards, 57-59; res asst prof physics, Univ Ill, 59-61; assoc prof, Millikin Univ, 61-63; assoc prof, 63-69, PROF PHYSICS, ILL STATE UNIV, 69- *Mem:* Am Phys Soc; Am Asn Physics Teachers. *Res:* High energy nuclear physics; penetration of matter by fast electrons. *Mailing Add:* Dept of Physics Ill State Univ Normal IL 61761

CREW, MALCOLM CHARLES, b Columbus, Ohio, May 11, 27; m 52; c 3. DRUG METABOLISM. *Educ:* Ohio Wesleyan Univ, BA, 48; Columbia Univ, MA, 50, PhD(chem), 54. *Prof Exp:* Asst chem, Columbia Univ, 49-51; pharmaceut res chemist, Wallace & Tiernan, Inc, 52-56; sr proj leader, Fleischmann Labs, Stand Brands, Inc, Conn, 56-65; scientist, Biochem Dept, Warner-Lambert Res Inst, 65-68, sr scientist, 68-71, sr res assoc, Dept Drug Metab, 71-77; CHIEF, BIOCHEM SECT, RES & DEVELOP, NORWICH-EATON PHARMACEUT, 77- *Mem:* Am Chem Soc; The Chem Soc; Am Soc Pharmacol & Exp Therapeut. *Res:* Pharmaceuticals; foods; flavor; analytical instrumentation. *Mailing Add:* Norwich Eaton Pharmaceut PO Box 191 Norwich NY 13815

CREWE, ALBERT VICTOR, b Bradford, Eng, Feb 18, 27; m 49; c 4. PHYSICS. *Educ:* Univ Liverpool, BSc, 47, PhD(cosmic rays), 50. *Prof Exp:* Lectr physics, Univ Liverpool, 50-55; res assoc, 55-56, from asst prof to assoc prof, 56-63, PROF PHYSICS, UNIV CHICAGO, 63-, DEAN, PHYS SCI DIV, 71-, WILLIAM E WRATHER DISTINGUISHED SERV PROF PHYSICS & BIOPHYSICS, 77-; MEM STAFF, ENRICO FERMI INST, 67- *Concurrent Pos:* Dir, Argonne Nat Lab, 61-67, dir particle accelerator div, 58-61; tech dir cyclotron, Univ Chicago, 56-58; William E Raether distinguished professorship, 77. *Honors & Awards:* Michelson Medal, Franklin Inst, 77. *Mem:* Am Phys Soc; Am Nuclear Soc; Electron Micros Soc Am. *Res:* High energy physics; electron microscopes. *Mailing Add:* Enrico Fermi Inst 5630 Ellis Ave Chicago IL 60637

CREWS, ANITA L, b Memphis, Tenn, Jan 9, 52. STRATIGRAPHY. *Educ:* Univ Tex, Austin, BA, 73; Univ Houston, MS, 75; Univ Calif, Los Angeles, PHD(geol), 80. *Prof Exp:* Res geologist, Union Oil Co of Calif, 75-76; ASST PROF SEDIMENTOLOGY & STRATIG, UNIV MINN, 80- *Mem:* Soc Econ Paleontologists & Mineralogists; Am Asn Petrol Geologists; Geol Soc Am; Int Asn Sedimentologists. *Mailing Add:* Dept Geol & Geophys Univ Minn Minneaplis MN 55455

CREWS, DAVID PAFFORD, b Jacksonville, Fla, Apr 18, 47. PSYCHOBIOLOGY, BEHAVIORAL ENDOCRINOLOGY. *Educ:* Univ Md, Col Park, 69; Rutgers Univ, PhD(psychobiol), 73. *Prof Exp:* Trainee psychobiol, Inst Animal Behav, Rutgers Univ, 69-73; res assoc zool, Univ Calif, Berkeley, 73-75; assoc herpet, Mus Comp Zool, Harvard Univ, 75-76, lectr biol, 76-77, from asst prof to assoc prof biol & physchol, 77-82; PROF ZOOL, UNIV TEXAS, AUSTIN, 82- *Concurrent Pos:* Sloan fel basic neurosci, 78-80. *Honors & Awards:* Res Scientist Develop Award, 77. *Mem:* Endocrine Soc; Soc Neurosci; Soc Study Reproduction; Animal Behav Soc; Am Soc Zoologists. *Res:* Effects of external stimuli, both physical and social, on hormone secretion, and the consequent effects of these endocrine secretions on the animal's reproductive behavior and physiology. *Mailing Add:* Dept Zool Univ Texas Austin TX 78712

CREWS, FULTON T, b Raleigh, NC, July 2, 50; m 74; c 1. NEUROPHARMACOLOGY, IMMUNOPHARMACOLOGY. *Educ:* Syracuse Univ, BS, 71; Univ Mich, PhD(pharmacol), 78. *Prof Exp:* Res technician, Endo Pharmaceut, 71-73; staff fel, Nat Inst Mental Health, 78-81; ASST PROF PHARMACOL, MED SCH, UNIV FLA, 81- *Mem:* Neurosci Soc; NY Acad Sci; AAAS; Int Soc Neurochem. *Res:* Hormone, neurotransmitter and prostaglandin receptors; receptor stimulated changes in phospholipid metabolism and membrane fluidity; antidepressants and other psychoactive drugs and their actions on central nervous sytem receptors and membranes. *Mailing Add:* Box J-267 Dept Pharmacol & Exp Therapeut Med Sch Univ Fla Gainsville FL 32610

CREWS, LOWELL THOMAS, b University City, Mo, Oct 16, 15; m 43; c 2. PETROLEUM CHEMISTRY. *Educ:* Southern Ill Univ, BEd, 37; Okla Agr & Mech Col, MS, 39. *Prof Exp:* Asst chem, Okla Agr & Mech Col, 37-39; res chemist, Armour & Co, 43-48; group leader, Toni Co, 48-51; res chemist, Standard Oil Co Ind, 51-52, group leader, 52-61; group leader, Am Oil Co, 62-63, proj mgr, Am Oil Co, 64-77; CONSULT, 77- *Mem:* Am Chem Soc; Tech Asn Pulp & Paper Indust; Am Soc Testing & Mat. *Res:* Petroleum waxes; asphalts. *Mailing Add:* 17851 Gladville Ave Homewood IL 60430

CREWS, PHILLIP O, b Urbana, Ill, Aug 15, 43; m 67. ORGANIC CHEMISTRY. *Educ:* Univ Calif, Los Angeles, BS, 66; Univ Calif, Santa Barbara, PhD(org chem), 69. *Prof Exp:* From asst to assoc chem, Univ Calif, Santa Barbara, 66-68; NSF fel, Princeton Univ, 69-70; asst prof, 70-77, ASSOC PROF CHEM, UNIV CALIF, SANTA CRUZ, 77- *Mem:* Am Chem Soc; Royal Soc Chem. *Res:* Application of nuclear magnetic resonance to problems of organic structure and stereochemistry; marine natural products chemistry; synthesis and study of organometalloids. *Mailing Add:* Thimann Labs Univ of Calif Santa Cruz CA 95060

CREWS, ROBERT WAYNE, b Pendleton, Ore, Feb 11, 19; m 45; c 4. PHYSICS. *Educ:* Ore State Univ, BS, 47, MA, 48, PhD(physics), 52. *Prof Exp:* Sr res physicist eng, Stanford Res Inst, 52-64; mem fac, Col San Mateo, 64-65; MEM STAFF, CHABOT COL, 65- *Mem:* Am Asn Physics Teachers. *Res:* Charged particle interactions; electron devices. *Mailing Add:* Dept of Math & Sci Chabot Col 25555 Hesperian Blvd Hayward CA 94545

CRIBBEN, LARRY DEAN, b Jackson, Ohio, July 3, 40; m 72. PLANT ECOLOGY. *Educ:* Rio Grande Col, BS, 62; Univ Okla, MNS, 68; Ohio Univ, PhD(bot), 72. *Prof Exp:* ASST PROF BIOL, MONTCLAIR STATE COL, 72- *Mem:* Sigma Xi. *Res:* The effects of acid mine drainage on river bottom plant communities. *Mailing Add:* Dept of Biol Montclair State Col Upper Montclair NJ 07043

CRIBBINS, PAUL DAY, b Jacksonville, Fla, June 24, 27; m 51; c 3. CIVIL ENGINEERING. *Educ:* US Merchant Marine Acad, BS, 48; Univ Ala, BS, 52; Purdue Univ, MS, 57, PhD(civil eng), 59. *Prof Exp:* Cost engr, E I du Pont de Nemours & Co, 52; instr civil eng, Purdue Univ, 52-53 & 55-59; from asst prof to assoc prof, 59-67, PROF CIVIL ENG, NC STATE UNIV, 67- *Concurrent Pos:* Mem adv panel, Nat Coop Res Prog, US Merchant Marine, 45-49; mem hwy engr econ comn, Hwy Res Bd, Nat Acad Sci-Nat Res Coun, 61-; consult transp projs, Venezuelan Ministry Pub Works & World Bank, 62- *Mem:* Am Soc Civil Engrs; Am Soc Eng Educ; Soc Naval Archit & Marine Engrs; Inst Transp Eng; Nat Soc Prof Engrs. *Res:* Transportation research related to traffic flow, economic impact and highway design; feasibility and design of inland waterways. *Mailing Add:* Dept of Civil Eng NC State Univ Raleigh NC 27607

CRIBBS, RICHARD MADISON, genetics, see previous edition

CRICCHI, JAMES RONALD, b Glen Ridge, NJ, Jan 22, 35; m 59; c 4. SEMICONDUCTOR TECHNOLOGY. *Educ:* John Hopkins Univ, BS, 60. *Prof Exp:* From assoc engr to fel engr, 59-74, ADV ENGR, ADVAN TECHNOL DIV, WESTINGHOUSE ELEC CORP, 74- *Concurrent Pos:* Guest ed, Inst Elec & Electronics Engrs, 76-78. *Mem:* Inst Elec & Electronics Engrs. *Res:* Metal-nitride-oxide silicon tunneling theories; understanding of nonvolatile semiconductor memory endurance phenomena; invention of new memory device structures; metal-nitride-oxide silicon integrated circuit memory arays; complementary metal-oxide-semiconductor very-large-scale integration technology. *Mailing Add:* Advan Technol Div MS 3127 Box 1521 Westinghouse Elec Corp Baltimore MD 21203

CRICHTON, DAVID, b Central Falls, RI, Mar 7, 31. ANALYTICAL CHEMISTRY. *Educ:* Hope Col, AB, 52; Purdue Univ, MS, 55; Univ Iowa, PhD(spectrophotom), 62. *Prof Exp:* From instr to assoc prof, 55-71, PROF CHEM, CENT COL, IOWA, 71- *Mem:* Am Chem Soc. *Res:* Spectrophotometry; stability constants. *Mailing Add:* Dept of Chem Cent Col Pella IA 50219

CRICK, REX EDWARD, Cunningham, Kans, Dec 21, 43. BIOGEOCHEMISTRY. *Educ:* Univ Kans, BA, 73, MSc, 76; Univ Rochester, Phd(geol), 78. *Prof Exp:* Vis asst prof paleont, Dept Geol, Univ Mich, 78-79; ASST PROF GEOL, UNIV TEX, ARLINGTON, 79- *Mem:* Am Asn Petrol Geologists; Geol Soc Am; Int Paleont Asn; Paleont Asn London; Paleont Soc Am. *Res:* Systematics, paleobiology, and paleobiogeography of Phanerozoic ammonoid and nautiloid cephalopods. *Mailing Add:* Dept Geol UTA Box 19049 Univ Tex Arlington TX 76019

CRICKMAY, COLIN HAYTER, b Vancouver, BC, Apr 6, 99; m 27; c 5. GEOLOGY. *Educ:* Univ BC, BA, 22; Stanford Univ, PhD(geol), 25. *Prof Exp:* Asst prof geol, Univ Calif, Los Angeles, 26-31 & Univ Ill, 31-33; consult, 33-45; geologist, Imperial Oil Ltd, 45-69; RETIRED. *Mem:* Hon mem Can Soc Petrol Geologists. *Res:* Paleontology and geologic history; geomorphology and surface processes. *Mailing Add:* 525 Salem Ave Calgary AB T3C 2K7 Can

CRICO, AURELIO MARC, b Milan Italy, Dec 4, 24; French citizen; m 54. CHEMICAL ENGINEERING. *Educ:* Univ Milan, ScD(chem eng), 48. *Prof Exp:* Process engr develop, Chem Div, Pechiney, Paris, 49-57; group leader comput appl 57-60; mgr process anal comput control, TRW Comput Co, Paris, 60-64; sr process engr, Corpus Christi, Tex, 64-71; supvr optimization plant opers, Lake Charles, La, SR PROJ ENGR DEVELOP, PPG INDUSTS, INC, CORPUS CHRISTI, TEX, 78- *Mem:* Am Inst Chem Engrs. *Res:* Phase equilibrium; catalysis and reactor design; computer application to chemical engineering science. *Mailing Add:* PPG Industs Inc PO Box 4026 Corpus Christi TX 78408

CRIDDLE, RICHARD S, b Logan, Utah, Sept 20, 36. BIOCHEMISTRY. *Educ:* Utah State Univ, BS, 58; Univ Wis, MS, 60, PhD(biochem), 62. *Prof Exp:* Asst prof biophys, 62-73, PROF BIOPHYS & BIOCHEM & BIOPHYSICIST EXP STA, UNIV CALIF, DAVIS, 73- *Res:* Protein structure and protein-protein interactions in relation to enzyme activity; biosynthesis of organelles. *Mailing Add:* Dept of Biochem Univ of Calif Davis CA 95616

CRIDER, FRETWELL GOER, b Centerville, Ala, June 8, 23; m 47; c 4. PHYSICAL CHEMISTRY. *Educ:* Univ NC, BS, 45, PhD(phys chem), 53. *Prof Exp:* Instr chem, Armstrong Col, Ga, 47-48; asst, Univ NC, 48-52 & Off Naval Res, 52-53; sr res technologist, Field Res Labs, Socony Mobil Oil Co, Inc, 53-64; chmn dept chem & physics, Armstrong State Col, 64-72; dean, Gordon Jr Col, 72-73; DEAN ADMIN, MID GA COL, 73-, PROF CHEM, 77- *Concurrent Pos:* Exec dir, Armstrong Res Inst, 66-72. *Mem:* Am Chem Soc; Combustion Inst; fel Am Inst Chemists. *Res:* Kinetics of photochemical decomposition; combustion kinetics; oxidation of carbon and hydrocarbons; diffusion flames; mechanics and chemistry of geological formations; corrosion; pollution chemistry; water analysis. *Mailing Add:* Dean Admin Mid Ga Col Cochran GA 31014

CRIDLAND, ARTHUR A, b London, Eng, Mar 29, 36; m 56; c 2. PALEOBOTANY, BRYOLOGY. *Educ:* Univ Reading, BSc, 57; Univ Kans, PhD(bot), 61. *Prof Exp:* Res assoc, Inst Polar Studies, Ohio State Univ, 61-62; asst prof bot & biol sci, 62-66, ASSOC PROF BOT, WASH STATE UNIV, 66- *Mem:* Bot Soc Am; Bryol & Lichenol Soc; Geol Soc Am; Brit Bryol Soc; Int Orgn Paleobot. *Mailing Add:* Dept of Bot Wash State Univ Pullman WA 99163

CRIGLER, JOHN F, JR, b Charlotte, NC, Sept 11, 19; m 44; c 4. PEDIATRICS. *Educ:* Duke Univ, AB, 39; Johns Hopkins Univ, MD, 43. *Prof Exp:* Intern med, Mass Mem Hosp, 43-44; intern pediat, Johns Hopkins Hosp, 46-47, asst resident, 47-48, physician-in-chg outpatient dept, 48-49, resident, 49-50; instr pediat, 55-56, assoc, 56-62, asst prof, 62-68, ASSOC PROF PEDIAT, HARVARD MED SCH, CHILDREN'S HOSP, BOSTON, 68- *Concurrent Pos:* Fel pediat endocrinol, Johns Hopkins Hosp, 50-51; Nat Found fel biol, Mass Inst Technol, 51-55; instr, Sch Med, Johns Hopkins Univ, 48-50; assoc physician, Children's Hosp Med Ctr, 56-61, physician, 61-62, sr assoc med, 62-, dir gen clin res ctr for children, 64-76, chief endocrine div, Dept Med, 66- *Mem:* Am Acad Pediat; Endocrine Soc; Soc Pediat Res; Am Pediat Soc; Am Fedn Clin Res. *Res:* Pediatric endocrinology and metabolism; biological effects of pituitary hormones in human beings; steroid hormone metabolism. *Mailing Add:* 300 Longwood Ave Boston MA 02115

CRIGLER, JOSEPH CARTER, food science, see previous edition

CRILEY, BRUCE, b Chicago, Ill, Apr 13, 39; m 67; c 2. EXPERIMENTAL EMBRYOLOGY. *Educ:* Univ Ill, BS, 60, MS, 62, PhD(zool), 67. *Prof Exp:* Instr embryol, Univ Ill, 65-66; asst prof, Univ Colo, 66-70, assoc prof embryol & chmn organismic biol div, 70-71; prof, 73-80, GEORGE C & ELLA BEACH LEWIS PROF BIOL, ILL WESLEYAN UNIV, 80-, CHMN DEPT, 71- *Mem:* AAAS; Am Zool Soc. *Res:* Neuroembryology; vertebrate morphogenesis. *Mailing Add:* Dept Biol Ill Wesleyan Univ Bloomington IL 61701

CRILL, PAT, plant breeding, plant pathology, see previous edition

CRIM, JOE WILLIAM, b Wichita Falls, Tex, Nov 19, 45; m 75. ENDOCRINOLOGY, COMPARATIVE ENDOCRINOLOGY. *Educ:* Univ Calif, Berkeley, AB, 68, MA, 72, PhD(zool), 74. *Prof Exp:* Teaching asst dept zool, Univ Calif, Berkeley, 70-71; res sci cancer res, Am Med Ctr Denver, Spivak, Colo, 74-75; res assoc zool, Univ Wash, 75-78; ASST PROF DEPT ZOOL, UNIV GA, 78- *Concurrent Pos:* Res fel Pub Health Serv, Nat Inst Arthritis, Metab & Digestive Dis, Univ Wash, 75-77. *Mem:* Am Soc Zool; Sigma Xi. *Res:* Function and evolution of the vertebrate hypothalamopituitary complex; neurobiology of hypophysiotropic and other peptides; comparative endocrinology of prolactin; endocrinology of fishes. *Mailing Add:* Dept of Zool Univ Ga Athens GA 30602

CRIM, STERLING CROMWELL, b Corsicana, Tex, Jan 5, 27; m 54; c 2. MATHEMATICS. *Educ:* Baylor Univ, BS, 50; NTex Univ, MEd, 52; George Peabody Col, MA, 58; Univ Tex, Austin, PhD(math), 68. *Prof Exp:* Teacher high sch, Tex, 51-53 & jr high sch, 53-57; teacher math, WGa Col, 58-59; spec instr, Univ Tex, Austin, 59-64; PROF MATH, LAMAR UNIV, 64- *Mem:* Math Asn Am. *Res:* Integral transforms. *Mailing Add:* Dept of Math Lamar Univ Beaumont TX 77710

CRIMINALE, WILLIAM OLIVER, JR, b Mobile, Ala, Nov 29, 33; m 62; c 2. PHYSICAL OCEANOGRAPHY, APPLIED MATHEMATICS. *Educ:* Univ Ala, BS, 55; Johns Hopkins Univ, PhD(aeronaut), 60. *Prof Exp:* Asst fluid mech & appl math, Johns Hopkins Univ, 56-60; asst prof, Dept Aerospace & Mech Sci, Princeton Univ, 62-68; assoc prof oceanog & geophys, 69-73, PROF OCEANOG & GEOPHYS, UNIV WASH, 73-, PROF APPL MATH & CHMN GROUP, 76- *Concurrent Pos:* NATO fel, Inst Appl Math, Ger, 60-61; sr vis, Cambridge Univ, 61-; consult, Aerospace Corp, Calif, 63, 65; guest prof, Can Armament Res & Develop Estab, Que, 65; guest prof, Inst Mech Statist of Turbulence, France, 67-68; consult adv group aeronaut res & develop, NATO, 67-68; Nat Acad Sci exchange scientist, USSR, 69; consult, Boeing Sci Res Labs, 69-70, Math Sci Northwest Inc, 70-73 & Appl Physics Lab, 73; sr res award, Alexander von Humboldt Found, Ger, 73-74; guest prof, Royal Inst Technol, Stockholm & Inst Oceanog, Gothenburg, 73-74. *Mem:* AAAS; Am Geophys Union; Am Asn Univ Prof; Am Phys Soc; Soc Indust & Appl Math. *Res:* Non-linear mechanics; geophysical fluid dynamics, especially stability and turbulence. *Mailing Add:* Dept of Oceanog & Geophys Prog WB-10 Univ of Wash Seattle WA 98195

CRIMMINS, TIMOTHY FRANCIS, b Hempstead, NY, Oct 14, 39; m 66. ORGANIC CHEMISTRY. *Educ:* St Johns Univ, NY, BS, 61; Purdue Univ, MS, 63, PhD(org chem), 65. *Prof Exp:* Res assoc of Dr C R Hauser & dir res, Duke Univ, 65-66; assoc prof, 66-76, PROF CHEM, UNIV WIS, OSHKOSH, 76- *Mem:* Am Chem Soc. *Res:* Organosodium metalation reactions employing tetramethylenediamine activated pentasodium. *Mailing Add:* Dept Chem Univ Wis Oshkosh WI 54901

CRIPPEN, GORDON MARVIN, b Cheyenne, Wyo, Apr 2, 45; m 70; c 1. BIOPHYSICAL CHEMISTRY, THEORETICAL CHEMISTRY. *Educ:* Univ Wash, BS, 67; Cornell Univ, PhD(biophys chem), 72. *Prof Exp:* Res chemist phys chem, Cardiovasc Res Inst, Univ Calif, San Francisco, 72-73; instr chem & physics, Bur Schs, Hamburg, Ger, 73-75; asst prof phys chem, Sch Pharm, Univ Calif, San Francisco, 75-80; ASST PROF PHYS CHEM, DEPT CHEM, TEX A&M UNIV, COLLEGE STATION, 80- *Mem:* Am Chem Soc. *Res:* Theoretical studies on the conformation of proteins, calculation of binding of ligands to proteins and related subjects. *Mailing Add:* Dept Chem Tex A&M Univ College Station TX 77843

CRIPPEN, RAYMOND CHARLES, b Brooklyn, NY, Mar 1, 17; m 41; c 2. ANALYTICAL CHEMISTRY, BIOCHEMISTRY. *Educ:* Iowa State Univ, BS, 39; Johns Hopkins Univ, MS, 48; St Thomas Inst Advan Studies, PhD(anal chem), 70. *Prof Exp:* Group leader chem coatings, E I du Pont de Nemours & Co Inc, 40-45; res & develop mgr indust chem, Penniman & Browne, Baltimore, Md, 48-49; dir indust consult, Crippen Labs, Div Foster D Snell Inc, Baltimore, Md, 49-61; group leader chromatog, Res Ctr, Atlas Chem Indust, Wilmington, 61-66; sect head anal res & develop, Stauffer Chem Co, Adrian, Mich, 66-68; group leader anal methods develop, Richardson-Merrell Corp, Cincinnati, Ohio, 68-70; instr chem & geol, Northern Ky Univ, Highland Heights, 70-75; DIR CONSULT CHEM, CRIPPEN LABS, INC, 75- *Mem:* Am Chem Soc; Soc Appl Spectros; Am Soc Testing & Mat. *Res:* Development of analytical methods for styrene in rubber polymers; isolation and identification of physiological active peptides in yeast extract. *Mailing Add:* 4027 New Castle Ave New Castle DE 19720

CRIPPS, DEREK J, b London, Eng, Sept 17, 28; m 63; c 4. DERMATOLOGY, PHOTOBIOLOGY. *Educ:* Univ London, MB & BS, 53, MD, 65; Univ Mich, MS, 61; Am Bd Dermat, dipl, 69. *Prof Exp:* Intern med, London Hosps, 53-54; resident dermat, Med Ctr, Univ Mich, 59-62; sr registr, Inst Dermat, Eng, 62-65; asst prof med, 65-68, assoc prof dermat, 68-72, PROF DERMAT & CHMN DEPT, MED CTR, UNIV WIS-MADISON, 72- *Concurrent Pos:* NIH grant, 66-; mem, Study Comt, NIH, 69- *Mem:* Brit Dermat Asn; Am Acad Dermat; Am Fedn Clin Res; Soc Invest Dermat; fel Am Col Physicians. *Res:* Investigation of persons sensitive to sunlight and diseases of prophyrin metabolism. *Mailing Add:* Med Ctr Univ Wis 600 Highland Ave Madison WI 53792

CRIPPS, HARRY NORMAN, b Webster, NY, May 14, 25; m 48; c 4. ORGANIC CHEMISTRY. *Educ:* Ga Inst Technol, BS, 46; Univ Rochester, BS, 48; Univ Ill, PhD(chem), 51. *Prof Exp:* Chemist, Eastman Kodak Co, 48; CHEMIST, CENT RES & Develop Dept, E I DU PONT DE NEMOURS & CO, 51- *Mem:* Sigma Xi. *Res:* Organic synthesis; polymers. *Mailing Add:* E I du Pont de Nemours & Co E328/205 Wilmington DE 19898

CRISCUOLO, DOMINIC, b New Haven, Conn, June 14, 08; m 46; c 2. BIOCHEMISTRY. *Educ:* Univ Pittsburgh, BS, 32; Trinity Univ, MS, 53. *Prof Exp:* Biochemist, Food Res Labs, 39-41, Sch Aviation Med, Randolph Field, 46-58 & Surg Res Lab, Lackland AFB Hosp, 58-68; chemist, Regional Environ Lab, Kelly AFB, 68-73; ADMINR, ST ANTHONY'S SPEC EDUC SCH, 73- *Mem:* Fel AAAS; Am Chem Soc; fel Am Inst Chemists; NY Acad Sci; Sigma Xi. *Res:* Enzymes; hematology; blood volumes; acclimatization to adverse environments; anesthesiology. *Mailing Add:* 321 Concord Ave San Antonio TX 78201

CRISLER, JOSEPH PRESLEY, b Hedley, Tex, Sept 12, 22; m 60; c 4. MICROCHEMISTRY. *Educ:* WTex State Univ, BS, 42, MA, 47; Univ Colo, PhD(chem micros), 62; Drexel Inst Technol, dipl elec micros, 63. *Prof Exp:* Head dept chem, Buena Vista Col, 47-54; instr inorg chem, Univ Colo, 54-55; asst prof anal chem, Tex Col Arts & Industs, 55-56; instr, Colo Sch Mines, 56-59; chemist micros, Univ Colo, 59-62; res chemist, US Naval Ord Sta, 62-69; CHIEF CHEM BR, DEPT HUMAN RESOURCES, GOVT DC, 69- *Mem:* Am Chem Soc; fel Royal Micros Soc. *Res:* Micro methods for the determination of trace elements, erythrocyte protoporphyrin and drugs of abuse in body fluids; chemical microscopy. *Mailing Add:* PO Box 251 Clinton MD 20735

CRISLEY, FRANCIS DANIEL, b Braddock, Pa, Aug 19, 26; m 60; c 3. MICROBIOLOGY, BACTERIOLOGY. *Educ:* Univ Pittsburgh, BS, 50, MS, 52, PhD(microbiol), 59. *Prof Exp:* Asst bact, Univ Pittsburgh, 50-52; instr, Miami Univ, 52-54 & Univ Pittsburgh, 54-58, res assoc microbiol, Dept Biol Sci, 59-61; microbiologist, Robert A Taft Sanit Eng Ctr, Ohio, 61-67; chmn dept biol, 67-75, PROF BIOL, NORTHEASTERN UNIV, 67- *Concurrent Pos:* Vis scientist, Natick Army Res & Develop Command, Natick, Mass, 78. *Mem:* Am Soc Microbiol; Soc Indust Microbiol. *Res:* Bacterial physiology; microbial ecology; public health microbiology; microbial toxins; food and industrial microbiology. *Mailing Add:* Dept Biol 360 Huntington Ave Northeastern Univ Boston MA 02115

CRISMON, JEFFERSON MARTINEAU, b Philadelphia, Pa, Feb 4, 08; m 37; c 2. PHYSIOLOGY. *Educ:* Stanford Univ, AB, 31, MD, 38. *Prof Exp:* Asst physiol, 32-33, asst pharmacol, 36-37, from instr to emer physiol, 37-73, from actg exec to exec dept, 49-63, EMER PROF PHYSIOL, STANFORD UNIV, 73- *Concurrent Pos:* Hon fel, Yale Univ, 40-41; Guggenheim fel, 57-58; consult, Off Naval Res, 50-51 & Surgeon-Gen, US Army, 52-53, 58-70. *Mem:* AAAS; Am Physiol Soc; Microcirculatory Soc. *Res:* Cardiac actions of vasoconstrictor amines; isolated tissue metabolism; metabolism of water and electrolytes; effects of low body temperature on mammals; effects of regional ischemia; frostbite; control capillary blood-flow; human skin blood flow. *Mailing Add:* 1805 Guinda St Palo Alto CA 94303

CRISONA, NANCY JANE, b New York, NY, Oct 3, 46. BACTERIAL GENETICS, CELL BIOLOGY. *Educ:* Univ Calif, Berkeley, BA, 68, PhD(molecular biol), 78. *Prof Exp:* Fel cell biol, Sch Med, Johns Hopkins Univ, 78-79; fel zool, Univ Calif, 79-80; MEM STAFF, INT PLANT RES INST, 80- *Concurrent Pos:* Muscular Dystrophy Asn fel, 78-80. *Mem:* Sigma Xi. *Res:* Mechanism of bacterial conjugation; cell movement and recognition during development; mechanism of cell motility. *Mailing Add:* Int Plant Res Inst 853 Industrial Rd San Carlos CA 94070

CRISP, CARL EUGENE, b Buhl, Idaho, Aug 1, 31; m 55. BIOCHEMISTRY, PLANT PHYSIOLOGY. *Educ:* Univ Idaho, BS, 55, MS, 59; Univ Calif, Davis, PhD(plant physiol), 65. *Prof Exp:* Jr flight test engr, Lockheed Missile Systs Div, 55; teaching asst plant physiol, Univ Calif, Davis, 59-64; plant physiologist, Insecticide Eval Proj, US Forest Serv, 67-81; SR RES BIOCHEMIST RES & DEVELOP, CHEVRON CHEM CO, RICHMOND, CALIF, 81- *Mem:* AAAS; Am Chem Soc; Am Inst Biol Sci; Am Soc Plant Physiol; Sigma Xi. *Res:* Investigations into the anatomy and chemical composition of plant surfaces, the biopolymer cutin, the design of systemic insecticides, the mechanisms of phloem transport in plants and biotechnology research and development. *Mailing Add:* Chevron Chem Co 940 Hensley St Richmond CA 94804

CRISP, EDWARD LEE, petroleum geology, geochemistry, see previous edition

CRISP, MICHAEL DENNIS, b Elmhurst, Ill, Apr 27, 42; m 65. QUANTUM OPTICS, LASERS. *Educ:* Bradley Univ, AB, 64; Washington Univ, MS, 66, PhD(physics), 68. *Prof Exp:* Res assoc physics, Columbia Univ, 68-70; scientist, Owens-Ill Inc, 70-72; sr scientist, Toledo, 72-77; legis asst for energy, off of US Sen Howard H Baker, Jr, 77-78; prof staff mem, Sen Comt on Com, Sci & Transp, 78-80; DIR, FED GOVT TECH LIAISON, OWENS-ILL, INC, WASHINGTON, DC, 80- *Concurrent Pos:* Res assoc, Argonne Nat Lab, 65; instr physics, Univ Toledo, 72; Cong sci & eng fel, AAAS/Optical Soc Am, 76. *Mem:* Am Phys Soc; Optical Soc Am; Inst Elec & Electronics Engrs; Soc Info Display; AAAS. *Res:* Interaction of coherent light with matter, including laser physics, nonlinear optics, coherent pulse propagation and coherent spectroscopy; neoclassical radiation theory; laser-induced damage and gas-discharge display devices. *Mailing Add:* 9113 Fairview Dr Silver Spring MD 20910

CRISP, ROBERT M, JR, b Ft Smith, Ark, Aug 20, 40; m 64; c 3. INDUSTRIAL ENGINEERING. *Educ:* Univ Ark, BSIE, 63, MSIE, 64; Univ Tex, PhD(mech eng), 67. *Prof Exp:* Assoc systs engr, Int Bus Mach Corp, 64-65; assoc prof, 67-73, PROF INDUST ENG, UNIV ARK, 73- *Mem:* Am Inst Indust Engrs. *Res:* Applications and theory of nonserial dynamic programming; application of operations research to production problems; energy systems analysis. *Mailing Add:* Dept of Indust Eng Univ of Ark Fayetteville AR 72701

CRISP, THOMAS MITCHELL, JR, b San Antonio, Tex, Sept 29, 39; m 65; c 2. ANATOMY, ENDOCRINOLOGY. *Educ:* Univ St Thomas, Houston, BA, 61; Rice Univ, MA, 64; Rice Univ, PhD(anat), 66. *Prof Exp:* Res asst endocrinol, Dent Br, Univ Tex, 60-61; teaching asst biol, Rice Univ, 61-63; from instr to asst prof, 66-72, ASSOC PROF ANAT, SCH MED & DENT, GEORGETOWN UNIV, 72- *Concurrent Pos:* NIH teaching fel anat, Med Br, Univ Tex, 63-66; consult, Army Oral Biol Prog, 66-70 & Navy Dent Sch, Bethesda Naval Hosp, 67-69; hon res fel, Dept Clin Endocrinol, Women's Hosp, Univ Birmingham, 74-75; spec res fel, Rockefeller Found, 74-75. *Mem:* AAAS; Am Soc Zoologists; Am Asn Anatomists; Soc Study Reprod; Endocrine Soc. *Res:* Electron microscopy of mammalian corpora lutea; ovarian tissue culture. *Mailing Add:* Dept Anat Georgetown Univ Washington DC 20007

CRISPELL, KENNETH RAYMOND, b Ithaca, NY, Oct 30, 16; m 42; c 6. MEDICINE. *Educ:* Philadelphia Col Pharm & Sci, BS, 38; Univ Mich, MD, 43; Am Bd Internal Med, dipl, 50. *Prof Exp:* From instr to assoc prof internal med, Univ Va, 49-58; prof med & dir dept, NY Med Col, 58-60; asst dean, Sch Med, 62, actg dean, 62-64, dean, 64-71, vpres health sci, 71-76, PROF MED & LAW, UNIV VA, 76- *Concurrent Pos:* Fel internal med, Ochsner Clin, La, 47-48; fel biophys, Tulane Univ, 48-49; Commonwealth fel, Univ Va, 49-51; physician, Univ Hosp, Va, 49-58 & 60. *Mem:* Endocrine Soc; Am Soc Clin Invest; Am Thyroid Asn; AMA; fel Am Col Physicians. *Res:* Endocrinology. *Mailing Add:* Med Ctr Box 423 Univ of Va Charlottesville VA 22901

CRISPEN, RAY GLENN, b Franklin, Pa, June 26, 28; m 56; c 2. MICROBIOLOGY. *Educ:* Allegheny Col, BA, 50; Univ Pittsburgh, MS, 55; Northwestern Univ, MS, 66, PhD, 66. *Prof Exp:* Sr chemist micros, Res Div, Goodyear Tire & Rubber Co, 55-61; prof staff microbiol, Northwestern Univ, 61-67; DIR, INST TUBERCULOSIS RES, UNIV ILL, 67-, ASST PROF MICROBIOL, 69- *Concurrent Pos:* Chmn IRB, Ill Cancer Ctr, 76- *Mem:* Am Soc Microbiol; Am Soc Prev Oncol; Reticuloendothelial Soc; Soc Cryobiol. *Res:* Cellular immunology as developed through vaccines; immunotherapy of cancer; immunological means of preventing cancer. *Mailing Add:* 904 W Adams St Chicago IL 60607

CRISPENS, CHARLES GANGLOFF, JR, b Bellevue, Pa, Aug 3, 30; m 53; c 1. ONCOLOGY. *Educ:* Pa State Univ, BS, 53; Ohio State Univ, MS, 55; Wash State Univ, PhD(zool), 59. *Prof Exp:* Fel, Jackson Lab, Bar Harbor, Maine, 59-60; from instr to assoc prof anat, Sch Med, Univ Md, 60-68; fac med, Univ Sherbrooke, 68-69; PROF BIOL, UNIV ALA, BIRMINGHAM, 69- *Concurrent Pos:* Mem bd dirs, Southeastern Cancer Res Asn, 72- *Honors & Awards:* Lederle Med Fac Award, 64. *Mem:* Am Asn Lab Animal Sci; Am Asn Anat; NY Acad Sci; Am Asn Cancer Res; Sigma Xi. *Res:* Chemically and virus-induced neoplasms in chickens; serum enzymes and diagnosis of cancer; lactate dehydrogenase virus and murine tumorigenesis; reticulum cell neoplasms of mice. *Mailing Add:* Dept of Biol Univ of Ala Univ Sta Birmingham AL 35294

CRISS, CECIL M, b Wheeling, WVa, Apr 22, 34; m 58; c 2. PHYSICAL CHEMISTRY. *Educ:* Kenyon Col, AB, 56; Purdue Univ, PhD(phys chem), 61. *Prof Exp:* Asst prof chem, Univ Vt, 61-65; from asst prof to assoc prof, 65-76, PROF CHEM, UNIV MIAMI, 76- *Honors & Awards:* Florida Award, Am Chem Soc, 77. *Mem:* AAAS; Am Chem Soc; The Chem Soc. *Res:* Thermodynamic properties of aqueous ionic solutions at higher temperatures; ionic heat capacities; ionic entropies, ionic volumes and oxidation-reduction potentials in nonaqueous solutions. *Mailing Add:* Dept of Chem Univ of Miami Coral Gables FL 33124

CRISS, DARRELL E, b Terre Haute, Ind, Aug 25, 21; m 43; c 7. ELECTRICAL ENGINEERING, COMPUTER SCIENCE. *Educ:* Rose Polytech Inst, BS, 43; Univ Ill, MS, 50, PhD(elec eng), 59. *Prof Exp:* From instr to assoc prof elec eng, 46-59, head dept, 61-65, assoc dean fac, 65-67, dean, 67-70, dir inst res, 70-75 & Computer Ctr, 62-75, PROF ELEC ENG, ROSE-HULMAN INST TECHNOL, 59-, HEAD COMPUTER SCI, 75- *Concurrent Pos:* Consult, Ind State Bd Regist for Engrs, 51-75, Nat Sch Aeronaut, 63- & Western Paper & Mfg Co, 64; consult elec eng, Peabody Coal Co, 76-77; consult comput sci, NSF, 77- *Mem:* Inst Elec & Electronics Engrs; Am Soc Eng Educ; Asn Comput Mach. *Res:* Control systems; nonlinear analysis; advanced computer logic; system simulation; computer education. *Mailing Add:* RR 25 Box 66 Terre Haute IN 47802

CRISS, ROBERT EVERETT, b Akron, Ohio, Aug 1, 51; m 81. STABLE ISOTOPE GEOCHEMISTRY. *Educ:* Case Western Reserve Univ, BS, 73; Calif Inst Technol, MS, 74, PhD(geochem), 81. *Prof Exp:* GEOLOGIST, UNITED STATES GEOL SURV, 80- *Mem:* Am Geophys Union; Geol Soc Am. *Res:* Stable isotope geochemistry of modern and ancient gesthermal systems, emphasizing the relationships of fluid flew geometry to geologic structures and ore deposits; petrographic effects of hydrothermal alternation including modification of magnetic properties. *Mailing Add:* US Geol Surv MS 18 345 Middlefield Rd Menlo Park CA 94025

CRISS, THOMAS BENJAMIN, b Clarksburg, WVa, June 30, 49; m 80. THEORETICAL PHYSICS, IMAGE PROCESSING. *Educ:* WVa Univ, BS, 71; Univ Tex, Austin, PhD(physics), 75. *Prof Exp:* PHYSICIST SUBMARINE NAVIG, JOHNS HOPKINS APPL PHYSICS LAB, 76-, PHYSICIST BIOMED IMAGE PROCESSING, 81- *Res:* Relativity; astrophysics; image processing. *Mailing Add:* Johns Hopkins Physics Lab Johns Hopkins Rd Laurel MD 20810

CRISS, WAYNE ELDON, b Washington, Iowa, Mar 7, 40. CANCER, ENDOCRINOLOGY. *Educ:* William Penn Col, BS, 62; Univ Fla, MS, 64, PhD(biochem), 68. *Prof Exp:* Asst prof obstet & gynec, Med Sch, Univ Fla, 70-75, biochem, 74-75; DIR CANCER RES, COMPREHENSIVE CANCER CTR, HOWARD UNIV, 75-, ASSOC PROF BIOCHEM & ONCOL, 80- *Concurrent Pos:* Am Cancer Soc fel, Fels Inst, Temple Univ, 68-70; Nat Cancer Inst res career develop award, 74-79; consult, NSF, NIH,

Cancer Res, Biochimica Biophysica Acta & Infection & Immunity. *Mem:* Endocrine Soc; Am Asn Univ Profs; Nat Tissue Cult Asn; Am Asn Cancer Res; Am Soc Biol Chemists. *Res:* Cancer metabolism, modified regulatory control mechanisms in cancer tissues. *Mailing Add:* Comprehensive Cancer Ctr Howard Univ Washington DC 20060

CRISSMAN, JACK KENNETH, JR, b Bellefonte, Pa, Jan 25, 44; m 66; c 2. CELLULAR & MOLECULAR BIOLOGY. *Educ:* Juniata Col, BS, 65; WVa Univ, PhD(biol), 72. *Prof Exp:* Instr biol, WVa Univ, 68-72, res assoc biochem, 72-73; asst prof biol, Wabash Col, 73-79; RES BIOCHEMIST, SUPELCO INC, 79- *Concurrent Pos:* Res fel, Am Cancer Soc, 71-72; res assoc, WVa Univ, 72-73; Grass Found res fel, 76-; film & book reviewer, AAAS, 77-; NSF prog reviewer, Div Sci Educ Develop & Res, 78- *Mem:* AAAS; Am Inst Biol Sci; Sigma Xi; Soc Study Reprod; Am Oil Chemists Soc. *Res:* Reproductive physiology-function and biochemistry of the mammalian cryptoorchid testis. *Mailing Add:* Supelco Inc Supelco Park Bellefonte PA 16823

CRISSMAN, JOHN MATTHEWS, b Evanston, Ill, Oct 21, 35; m 68. POLYMER SCIENCE. *Educ:* Pa State Univ, PhD(physics), 63. *Prof Exp:* PHYSICIST, NAT BUR STANDARDS, 63- *Concurrent Pos:* Nat Acad Sci-Nat Res Coun physicist, Nat Bur Standards, 63-65. *Mem:* Am Phys Soc. *Res:* Mechanical and other bulk properties of polymeric materials. *Mailing Add:* Rm B 354 Polymers Bldg Nat Bur of Standards Gaithersburg MD 20013

CRISSMAN, JUDITH ANNE, b Clarion, Pa, July 11, 42. INORGANIC CHEMISTRY. *Educ:* Thiel Col, BA, 64; Univ NC, Chapel Hill, PhD(inorg chem), 70. *Prof Exp:* From asst prof to assoc prof chem, 68-80, PROF CHEM, MARY WASHINGTON COL, 80- *Mem:* Am Chem Soc. *Res:* Schiff base complexes of transition metals. *Mailing Add:* Dept of Chem Mary Washington Col Fredericksburg VA 22401

CRIST, BUCKLEY, JR, b Plainfield, NJ, Jan 12, 41; m 66; c 2. POLYMER SCIENCE. *Educ:* Williams Col, BA, 62; Duke Univ, PhD(chem), 66. *Prof Exp:* Phys chemist, Camille Dreyfus Lab, Res Triangle Inst, 66-73; asst prof, 73-79, ASSOC PROF MAT SCI & ENG & CHEM ENG, NORTHWESTERN UNIV, EVANSTON, 79- *Mem:* Am Chem Soc; Am Phys Soc. *Res:* Morphology and mechanical properties of semicrystalline polymers; scattering of light and x-rays by polymer solids; molecular motion and relaxation effects. *Mailing Add:* Dept of Mat Sci & Eng Northwestern Univ Evanston IL 60201

CRIST, DELANSON ROSS, b New York, NY, July 16, 40; m 62; c 3. PHYSICAL ORGANIC CHEMISTRY. *Educ:* Swarthmore Col, AB, 62; Mass Inst Technol, PhD(organic chem), 67. *Concurrent Pos:* NSF fel, 67-68; asst prof org chem, 68-72, ASSOC PROF ORG CHEM, GEORGETOWN UNIV, 72- *Mem:* AAAS; Am Chem Soc. *Res:* Mechanisms of organic reactions of synthetic or biological importance; investigations concerning the stability and reactions of species containing positive-charged nitrogen atoms. *Mailing Add:* Dept Chem Georgetown Univ Washington DC 20007

CRIST, JOHN BENJAMIN, b Washington, DC, Jan 16, 41; m 63; c 3. WOOD SCIENCE & TECHNOLOGY, FORESTRY. *Educ:* Va Polytech Inst & State Univ, BS, 67, PhD(wood sci), 72. *Prof Exp:* Forest prod technologist, Duluth, Minn, 71-76, forest prod technologist wood sci, NCent Forest Exp Sta, 76-80, FIELD REP RESOURCE USE, FOREST SERV, USDA, 80- *Concurrent Pos:* Adj asst prof, Dept Forest Prod, Col Forestry, Univ Minn, 74-80; adj assoc prof, 80- *Mem:* Forest Prod Res Soc; Soc Wood Sci & Technol; Tech Asn Pulp & Paper Indust. *Res:* Anatomy and physical properties of woody materials grown under short rotation; intensive culture, and the properties of various wood products made from the above raw materials. *Mailing Add:* Forestry Sci Lab 180 Canfield St Morgantown WV 26505

CRISTOFALO, VINCENT JOSEPH, b Philadelphia, Pa, Mar, 19, 33; m 64; c 6. PHYSIOLOGY, BIOCHEMISTRY. *Educ:* St Joseph's Col, BS, 55; Temple Univ, MA, 58; Univ Del, PhD, 62. *Prof Exp:* Asst instr gen biol, Temple Univ, 57-58; res asst, Univ Del, 58-60, NSF fel, 60-61; USPHS fel, Temple Univ, 61-62; mem, Wistar, Inst Anat & Biol, 63-69; from asst prof to assoc prof biochem, 67-74, PROF BIOCHEM, DIV ANIMAL BIOL, SCH VET MED, UNIV PA, 74-; MEM, WISTAR INST ANAT & BIOL, 76- *Concurrent Pos:* Res asst, Oak Ridge Nat Lab, 59; instr, Dept Chem, Temple Univ, 62-72, res assoc, 63; assoc mem, Wistar Inst Anat & Biol, 69-76; reviewer, NIH, Molecular Biol Study Sect, 74-75 & Molecular Cytol Study Sect, 75-79. *Mem:* AAAS; Tissue Culture Asn; Am Cell Biol Geront Soc; Soc Exp Biol & Med. *Res:* Effects of oxygen and radiation on development; intermediary metabolism; neoplastic tissues; tissue culture cells; aging in cell and tissue culture. *Mailing Add:* Wistar Inst of Anat & Biol 36th St & Spruce Philadelphia PA 19104

CRISTOL, STANLEY JEROME, b Chicago, Ill, June 14, 16; m 57; c 2. CHEMISTRY. *Educ:* Northwestern Univ, BS, 37; Univ Calif, Los Angeles, MA, 39, PhD(org chem), 43. *Prof Exp:* Asst chem, Univ Calif, Los Angeles, 37-38; res chemist, Stand Oil Co, Calif, 38-41; from asst to instr chem, Univ Calif, Los Angeles, 41-43; res fel, Univ Ill, 43-44; res chemist, USDA, Md, 44-46; from asst prof to assoc prof chem, 46-55, chmn dept, 60-62, fac res lectr, 60, prof, 55-79, DISTINGUISHED PROF, UNIV COLO, BOULDER, 79- *Concurrent Pos:* Guggenheim fel, 55-56 & 81-82; assoc ed, Chem Rev, 57-59; vis prof, Stanford Univ, 60 & Univ Geneva, Switz, 75; mem, NSF Adv Comt, 57-63, 69-72 & NIH Adv Comt, 68-72. *Honors & Awards:* Stearns Award, 71; James Flack Norris Award, Am Chem Soc, 72. *Mem:* Nat Acad Sci; AAAS; Am Chem Soc; The Chem Soc. *Res:* Organic chemistry; mechanisms of organic reactions; photochemistry. *Mailing Add:* Dept Chem Univ of Colo Boulder CO 80302

CRISWELL, BENNIE SUE, b Huntsville, Tex, Nov 17, 42; m 64; c 2. IMMUNOLOGY, INFECTIOUS DISEASES. *Educ:* NTex State Univ, BS, 64; Registry Med Technol, cert, 64; Baylor Col Med, MS, 68, PhD(immunol), 69. *Prof Exp:* Instr, 72-74, ASST PROF MICROBIOL, BAYLOR COL MED, 74- *Concurrent Pos:* NASA fel, Manned Spacecraft Ctr, Houston, 69-72; vis scientist, NASA Johnson Space Ctr, 72- *Res:* Early detection of viral respiratory illness. *Mailing Add:* Microbiol Dept Baylor Col Med 1200 Moursund Ave Houston TX 77030

CRISWELL, DAVID RUSSELL, b Ft Worth, Tex, July 17, 41; c 2. SPACE PHYSICS, PSYCHOLOGY. *Educ:* N Tex State Univ, BS, 63, MS, 64; Rice Univ, Phd(space physics), 68. *Prof Exp:* Prof staff eng, TRW Syst, Houston Opers, 68-70; staff scientist res admin, Lunar & Planetary Inst, 71-80; VIS RES PHYSICIST, CALIF SPACE INST, UNIV CALIF, SAN DIEGO, 80- *Concurrent Pos:* Exec dir, Lunar & Planetary Rev Panel, 71-78; prin investr, NASA grant, 74-77, mem staff, NASA Ames Res Ctr, Space Indust, 75, Sci Asn Inc, 76, prin investr, NASA grant, 77-78. *Res:* Space industrialization; plasma physics as applied to moon solar wind interactions; physical descriptions of psychology; seismology; management and cybernetics. *Mailing Add:* A-030 Calif Space Inst Univ Calif San Diego La Jolla CA 92093

CRITCHFIELD, CHARLES LOUIS, b Shreve, Ohio, June 7, 10; m 35; c 4. MATHEMATICAL PHYSICS. *Educ:* George Washington Univ, BS, 34, MA, 36, PhD(physics), 39. *Prof Exp:* Instr, Univ Rochester, 39-40 & Harvard Univ, 41-42; physicist, Geophys Lab, 42-43 & Monsanto Chem Co, 46-47; assoc prof physics, George Washington Univ, 46; from assoc prof to prof, Univ Minn, 47-55; dir sci res, Convair Div, Gen Dynamics, 55-60; vpres res, Telecomput Corp, 60-61; physicist, Los Alamos Sci Lab, 43-46, assoc diV & group leader nuclear physics, 61-67; RETIRED. *Concurrent Pos:* Mem planetology subcomt, NASA, 64-69. *Mem:* Fel Am Phys Soc. *Res:* Scalar potentials in the Dirac equation for nuclear and particle physics. *Mailing Add:* 391 El Conejo Los Alamos NM 87544

CRITCHFIELD, WILLIAM BURKE, b Minneapolis, Minn, Nov 21, 23. FOREST GENETICS. *Educ:* Univ Calif, BS, 49, PhD(bot), 56. *Prof Exp:* Forest geneticist, Cabot Found, Harvard Univ, 56-59; GENETICIST, PAC SOUTHWEST FOREST & RANGE EXP STA, US FOREST SERV, 59- *Mem:* Bot Soc Am. *Res:* Geographic variation and evolution in forest trees; leaf variation and shoot development in trees. *Mailing Add:* Pac Southwest Forest & Range Exp Sta PO Box 245 Berkeley CA 94701

CRITCHLOW, BURTIS VAUGHN, b Hotchkiss, Colo, Mar 5, 27; m 48; c 4. ANATOMY. *Educ:* Occidental Col, BA, 51; Univ Calif, Los Angeles, PhD(neuroendocrinol), 57. *Prof Exp:* From instr to prof anat, Baylor Col Med, 57-72; PROF ANAT & CHMN DEPT, ORE HEALTH SCI UNIV, 72- *Concurrent Pos:* Sr res fel, 59-64; USPHS res career develop award, 64-69; mem, Reprod Biol Study Sect, NIH, 69-73, consult. *Mem:* Am Asn Anatomists; Endocrine Soc; Int Soc Res Reprod; Am Physiol Soc; Int Brain Res Orgn. *Res:* Brain and endocrine interrelations; neural control of pituitary functions. *Mailing Add:* Med Sch Dept of Anat Ore Health Sci Univ Portland OR 97201

CRITCHLOW, D(ALE), b Harrisville, Pa, Jan 6, 32; m 55; c 2. ELECTRICAL ENGINEERING. *Educ:* Grove City Col, BS, 53; Carnegie Inst Technol, MS, 54, PhD(elec eng), 56. *Prof Exp:* Engr magnetic amplifiers develop, Magnetics, Inc, 52-53; proj engr magnetic devices res, Carnegie Inst Technol, 53-56, assoc prof elec eng, 56-58; staff engr, 58-59, adv engr, 59-64, res staff mem, Yorktown Heights, 64-80, SR ENGR, RES CTR, IBM CORP, HOPEWELL JCT, 80- *Concurrent Pos:* Consult, Magnetic Amplifiers Inc, 56- & Johnstone Foundry, 54- *Mem:* Inst Elec & Electronics Engrs; Sigma Xi. *Res:* Logic circuit work. *Mailing Add:* Rte 202 Lincolndale NY 10540

CRITES, JOHN L, b Wilmington, Ohio, July 10, 23; m 46; c 2. ZOOLOGY. *Educ:* Univ Idaho, BS, 49, MSc, 51; Ohio State Univ, PhD(zool), 56. *Prof Exp:* Asst zool, Univ Idaho, 49-51; asst, 51-54, asst instr, 54-55, from instr to assoc prof, 55-67, assoc dir, Stone Lab, 62-81, chmn, Dept Zool, 81, PROF ZOOL, OHIO STATE UNIV, 67- *Concurrent Pos:* Consult, US AID, Sci Inst, India, 63- *Mem:* Am Soc Parasitol; Wildlife Dis Asn; Int Soc Nematol. *Res:* Nematode parasites of animals; nematode parasites of plants; free-living nematodes, both marine and fresh water. *Mailing Add:* Ohio State Univ Dept of Zool 1735 Neil Ave Columbus OH 43210

CRITOPH, E(UGENE), b Vancouver, BC, March 29, 29; m 52; c 4. ENGINEERING PHYSICS. *Educ:* Univ BC, BASc, 51, MASc, 57. *Prof Exp:* Sr res off, 53-68, head, Reactor Physics Br, 68-75, dir, Fuels & Mat Div, 75-76, dir, Advan Projs & Reactor Physics Div, 76-78, VPRES & GEN MGR, ATOMIC ENERGY CAN LTD, 79- *Concurrent Pos:* Chmn Europ Am Comt Reactor Physics, 68-69. *Mem:* Am Nuclear Soc; Can Asn Physicists. *Res:* Reactor physics; power reactor design and the physics of heavy water-uranium lattices. *Mailing Add:* 4 Darwin Crescent Deep River ON K0J 1P0 Can

CRITS, GEORGE J(OHN), b Norristown, Pa, Feb 11, 22; m 48; c 2. CHEMICAL ENGINEERING. *Educ:* Pa State Univ, BS, 43; Columbia Univ, MS, 50. *Prof Exp:* With Kellex Corp, 43-45; with Harshaw Chem Co, 45; with Barrett Div, Allied Chem & Dye Corp, 45-46; design & chem engr, Los Alamos Sci Labs, 46-47; chem engr, Welding Engr, 48-49; physicist & chem engr, J Razek Labs, 49; mgr chem res, 50-67, tech consult, 67-68, TECH DIR, COCHRANE DIV, CRANE CO, 68- *Concurrent Pos:* Mem, Franklin Inst. *Mem:* Am Chem Soc; Am Soc Testing & Mat; Nat Asn Corrosion Engrs. *Res:* Water and waste treatment research; ion exchange technology in equipment manufacturing and operation for industry. *Mailing Add:* Cochrane Div Crane Co Third Ave King of Prussia PA 19406

CRITTENDEN, ALDEN LA RUE, b Wichita, Kans, Nov 27, 20; m 58. CHEMISTRY. *Educ:* Univ Ill, BS, 42, PhD(chem), 47. *Prof Exp:* From instr to asst prof, 47-60, ASSOC PROF CHEM, UNIV WASH, 60- *Mem:* Am Chem Soc. *Res:* Polarography. *Mailing Add:* Dept of Chem Univ of Wash Seattle WA 98195

CRITTENDEN, LYMAN BUTLER, b New Haven, Conn, May 27, 26; m 59; c 2. GENETICS. *Educ:* Calif Polytech Inst, BS, 51; Purdue Univ, MS, 55, PhD, 58. *Prof Exp:* Geneticist, Nedlar Farms, 51-53; instr genetics, Purdue Univ, 55-57; geneticist, Creighton Bros, 57-58 & Nat Cancer Inst, 58-61; geneticist, Regional Poultry Res Lab, 61-67 & Animal Physiol & Genetics Inst, Beltsville, Md, 67-75, RES GENETICIST, REGIONAL POULTRY RES LAB, MICH, USDA, 75- *Mem:* AAAS; Poultry Sci Asn; Genetics Soc Am. *Res:* Quantitative genetics; genetics of disease resistance; virology. *Mailing Add:* Regional Poultry Res Lab 3606 E Mt Hope Rd East Lansing MI 48823

CRITTENDEN, MAX DERMONT, JR, b Seattle, Wash, May 12, 17; m 42; c 4. ENVIRONMENTAL GEOLOGY. *Educ:* San Jose State Col, BA, 39; Univ Calif, PhD, 49. *Prof Exp:* Asst geol, Univ Calif, 40-42; geologist, 42-65, chief southwestern br, 65-70, RES GEOLOGIST, US GEOL SURV, 65- *Concurrent Pos:* Vis prof, Univ Calif, Santa Cruz, 69; chmn, Geothermal Environ Adv Panel, 74-79. *Mem:* Fel Geol Soc Am. *Res:* Geology of manganese deposits especially origin and occurence in the Western states; geologic history of Wasatch Mountains, Utah, especially Pre-Cambrian rocks and Laramide structural history; isostatic recovery of Lake Bonneville, Utah and viscosity of earth. *Mailing Add:* US Geol Surv MS-75 345 Middlefield Rd Menlo Park CA 94025

CRITTENDEN, RAY RYLAND, b Galesburg, Mich, Mar 19, 31; m 62; c 3. PHYSICS. *Educ:* Willamette Univ, BA, 54; Univ Wis, MS, 56, PhD(physics), 60. *Prof Exp:* Assoc scientist, Brookhaven Nat Lab, 60-63; from asst prof to assoc prof, 63-74, PROF PHYSICS, COL ARTS & SCI, GRAD SCH, IND UNIV, BLOOMINGTON, 74- *Mem:* Am Phys Soc. *Res:* High energy nuclear physics. *Mailing Add:* Dept of Physics Ind Univ Bloomington IN 47405

CRITTENDEN, REBECCA SLOVER, b Lake City, Tenn, July 10, 36; m 66. ALGEBRA. *Educ:* Georgetown Col, BS, 58; Univ NC, Chapel Hill, MA, 62, PhD(math), 63. *Prof Exp:* Asst prof math, Georgetown Col, 63-64, Va Polytech, 64-66 & Vanderbilt Univ, 66-67; asst prof, 67-70, ASSOC PROF MATH, VA POLYTECH INST & STATE UNIV, 70- *Concurrent Pos:* Woodrow Wilson fel. *Mem:* Am Math Soc; Math Asn Am. *Res:* Ring theory. *Mailing Add:* Dept of Math Va Polytech Inst & State Univ Blacksburg VA 24061

CRITTENDEN, RICHARD JAMES, b Milwaukee, Wis, Feb 28, 30; m 53; c 3. MATHEMATICS. *Educ:* Williams Col, AB, 52; Oxford Univ, BA, 54; Mass Inst Technol, PhD(math), 60. *Prof Exp:* Asst prof math, Northwestern Univ, 60-64; assoc ed, Math Rev, 64-68, exec ed, 68-71; chmn dept, 71-74, PROF MATH, COL GEN STUDIES, UNIV ALA, BIRMINGHAM, 71- *Mem:* Am Math Soc. *Res:* Differential geometry; Riemannian geometry; G-structures. *Mailing Add:* Dept of Math Col Gen Studies Univ of Ala Birmingham AL 35294

CRITZ, JERRY B, b Boonville, Mo, Apr 9, 34; m 55; c 2. PHYSIOLOGY. *Educ:* Univ Mo, BS, 56, MA, 58, PhD(physiol), 61. *Prof Exp:* From asst prof to assoc prof physiol, Univ SDak, 61-67; assoc prof, Univ Western Ont, assoc prof physiol, Ctr Med Educ, Sch Med, Ind Univ, 73-75; prof physiol, Sch Med, Southern Ill Univ, Carbondale, 75-77; HEALTH SCIENTIST ADMINR, NAT HEART LUNG & BLOOD INST, CARDIAC FUNCTION BR, 77- *Mem:* AAAS; Soc Exp Biol Med. *Res:* Cardiovascular effects of exercise and training. *Mailing Add:* Nat Heart Lung & Blood Inst 7550 Wisconsin Ave Bethesda MD 20014

CRIVELLO, JAMES V, b Grand Rapids, Mich, July 30, 40. ORGANIC CHEMISTRY. *Educ:* Aquinas Col, BS, 62; Univ Notre Dame, PhD(org chem), 66. *Prof Exp:* RES CHEMIST, RES & DEVELOP CTR, GEN ELEC CO, 66- *Mem:* Am Chem Soc. *Res:* Polymer science; thermally stable polymers; synthesis and characterization; oxidation and nitration chemistry; organic photochemistry, photoinitiated cationic polymerizations. *Mailing Add:* Gen Elec Res & Develop Ctr Bldg K-1 PO Box 8 Schenectady NY 12301

CROASDALE, HANNAH THOMPSON, b Daylesford, Pa, Nov 18, 05. BOTANY. *Educ:* Univ Pa, BS, 28, MS, 31, PhD(bot), 35. *Prof Exp:* Mem staff, Biol Abstracts, 28-32; prepateur bot, Univ Pa, 32-33; res asst, 35-46, assoc zool, 46-59, from asst prof to prof biol, 59-71, EMER PROF BIOL, DARTMOUTH COL, 71- *Mem:* Am Phycol Soc; Am Micros Soc; Sigma Xi; Brit Phycol Soc; Phycol Soc India. *Res:* Systematics of freshwater algae; arctic and tropical desmids; desmid flora of North America; desmid flora of New Zealand. *Mailing Add:* Dept of Biol Dartmouth Col Hanover NH 03755

CROAT, JOHN JOSEPH, b St Marys, Iowa, May 23, 43. PHYSICAL METALLURGY, SOLID STATE PHYSICS. *Educ:* Simpson Col, BA, 65; Iowa State Univ, MS, 69, PhD(metall), 72. *Prof Exp:* Jr metallurgist, Ames Lab, AEC, 65-69; res asst, Iowa State Univ, 69-72; sr res scientist, 72-80, STAFF SCIENTIST, GEN MOTORS RES LABS, 80- *Honors & Awards:* McCuen Award, Gen Motors Res Labs, 77. *Mem:* Am Soc Metals; Am Phys Soc. *Res:* Magnetic and magnetoelastic properties of rare earth transition metal alloys. *Mailing Add:* 4666 Barcroft Way Sterling Heights MI 48077

CROAT, THOMAS BERNARD, b St Mary's, Iowa, May 23, 38; m 65; c 2. BOTANY. *Educ:* Simpson Col, BA, 62; Univ Kans, MA, 66, PhD(bot), 67. *Prof Exp:* High sch teacher biol, Virgin Islands Govt- Knoxville, Iowa Pub Sch, 62-64; asst res botanist, 67-71; cur phanerograms, 74-77, P A SCHULZE CUR BOT, MO BOT GARDEN, 77- *Concurrent Pos:* Vis fel, Smithsonian Trop Res Inst, 68-71; cur, Summit Herbarium & Libr, 70-71; fac assoc biol, Wash Univ, 70-; mem, NSF Adv Comt Resources in Syst Bot, 72-; mem, Comn Orgn for Flora Neotropica, 75-; adj prof, biol, Univ Mo, 74- *Mem:* Am Soc Plant Taxonomists; Inst Soc Plant Taxonomists; Asn Trop Biol; Bot Soc Am; Am Inst Biol Sci. *Res:* Systematic and evolutionary studies of the Araceae and Sapindaceae; floristics of the neotropics; phenological behavior of tropical floras. *Mailing Add:* Mo Bot Garden 2315 Tower Grove Ave St Louis MO 63110

CROBER, DONALD CURTIS, b Morrisburg, Ont, July 20, 39; m 64; c 2. ANIMAL GENETICS, ANIMAL PHYSIOLOGY. *Educ:* McGill Univ, BSc, 61, MSc, 64; Univ BC, PhD(animal genetics), 71. *Prof Exp:* Biometrician, Can Wildlife Serv, Ottawa, 69-71; ASSOC PROF ANIMAL SCI, NS AGR COL, 71- *Concurrent Pos:* Vis sr lectr dept animal sci, Makerere Univ, Kampala, Uganda, 72 & dept animal prod, Univ Sci & Technol, Kumasi, Ghana, 73-74. *Mem:* Poultry Sci Asn; Genetics Soc Can. *Res:* Poultry breeding and physiology; poultry management. *Mailing Add:* NS Agr Col Truro NS B2N 5E3 Can

CROCE, CARLO MARIA, b Milan, Italy, Dec 17, 77; nat US; c 1. MOLECULAR GENETICS. *Educ:* Univ Rome, MD, 69. *Prof Exp:* Assoc scientist, 70-71, res assoc, 71-74, assoc mem, 74-76, prof, 76-80, ASSOC DIR & INST PROF, WISTAR INST ANAT & BIOL, 80- *Concurrent Pos:* Vis scientist, Carnegie Inst, 78-79; mem, Mammalian Genetics Study Sect, NIH, Behtesda, 79-83. *Res:* Study of the organization of the human genome; regulation of gene expression during mammalian embryogenesis; differentiation in vitro. *Mailing Add:* Wistar Inst Anat & Biol 36th St at Spruce Philadelphia PA 19104

CROCE, LOUIS J, b New York, NY, Sept 17, 21; m 48; c 2. PHYSICAL CHEMISTRY, ORGANIC CHEMISTRY. *Educ:* St John's Univ, NY, BS, 48; NY Univ, PhD(phys org chem), 52. *Prof Exp:* Group leader org res, Evans Res & Develop Co, 51-52; res chemist, Socony-Mobile Oil Co, Inc, 52-55; res chemist, 55-58, group leader, 58-60, res supvr, 60-61, res mgr, 61-66, assoc dir res, 66-74, DIR RES, PETRO-TEX CHEM CORP, 74- *Mem:* AAAS; Am Chem Soc. *Res:* Petrochemicals, including monomer synthesis, catalytic dehydrogenation, dehydrocyclization, ammoxidation; reactions of olefins and dienes; polyolefins; petroleum research in hydrocracking, hydrocarbon separations, alkylation. *Mailing Add:* 135 Driftwood Dr Seabrook TX 77586

CROCKER, ALLEN CARROL, b Boston, Mass, Dec 25, 25; m 53; c 3. PEDIATRICS. *Educ:* Mass Inst Technol, 42-44; Harvard Univ, MD, 48. *Prof Exp:* Lab house officer, 48-49; jr asst resident med, 49-51; from asst physician to assoc physician, 56-62, res assoc path, 56-58, assoc med, 62-66, SR ASSOC MED, CHILDREN'S HOSP MED CTR, 66- *Concurrent Pos:* Fel path, Children's Hosp Med Ctr, 53-56; res assoc path, Harvard Med Sch, 56-60, res assoc pediat, 60-66, asst clin prof, 66-69, assoc prof pediat, 69-, tutor med sci, 64- *Res:* Clinical investigation; pediatric metabolic diseases; biochemistry of the lipids; mental retardation. *Mailing Add:* Children's Hosp Med Ctr 300 Longwood Ave Boston MA 02115

CROCKER, BURTON B(LAIR), b Atlanta, Ga, Jan 1, 20; m 54; c 2. CHEMICAL ENGINEERING, GAS-SOLIDS PROCESSING. *Educ:* Ga Sch Technol, BS, 41; Mass Inst Technol, SM, 47. *Prof Exp:* Jr eng aide, Dept Chem Eng, Tenn Valley Authority, 39-41; jr chem engr, Phosphate Div, Monsanto Chem Co, 45-46, chem engr, Phosphate Div, 47-50, sr engr, 50-52, resident engr, Res Dept, 52-53, asst chief chem eng, Eng Dept, Inorg Chem Div, 53-59, technologist, 59-66, advan technologist, Phosphorus Dept, 66-69, sr eng fel corp eng, 70-81, DISTINGUISHED ENG FEL, CORP ENG DEPT, MONSANTO CO, 81- *Mem:* Fel Am Inst Chem Engrs; Air Pollution Control Asn (vpres, 72-75). *Res:* Combustion of fuels; refractory design; phosphorus, phosphate salt process and equipment design; design of air pollution control equipment; air pollution studies, including effects on vegetation; meteorology; process systems; fluidization. *Mailing Add:* 811 Mary Meadows St Louis MO 63135

CROCKER, DENTON WINSLOW, b Salem, Mass, May 1, 19; m 46; c 4. INVERTEBRATE ZOOLOGY. *Educ:* Northeastern Univ, BA, 42; Cornell Univ, MA, 48, PhD(zool), 52. *Prof Exp:* Instr biol, Amherst Col, 51-53; from instr to assoc prof, Colby Col, 53-60; chmn dept, 60-77, PROF BIOL, SKIDMORE COL, 60- *Mem:* AAAS; Am Inst Biol Sci; Am Soc Zoologists; Sigma Xi. *Res:* Systematics and physiological ecology of crayfishes. *Mailing Add:* Dept of Biol Skidmore Col Saratoga Springs NY 12866

CROCKER, DIANE WINSTON, b Cambridge, Mass, Nov 23, 26; m 49, 74; c 3. PATHOLOGY, DATA PROCESSING. *Educ:* Wellesley Col, BA, 46; Brown Univ, MS, 48; Boston Univ, MD, 52. *Prof Exp:* Asst path, Univ Southern Calif, 55-56; asst, Col Physicians & Surgeons, Columbia Univ, 57-58; instr, Harvard Med Sch, 58-65, assoc, 65-68, asst clin prof, 68-69; from asst prof to prof path & chief dept, Health Sci Ctr Hosp, Temple Univ, 69-73; CHIEF ANAT PATH DATA PROCESSING, LOS ANGELES COUNTY-UNIV SOUTHERN CALIF MED CTR & PROF PATH, UNIV SOUTHERN CALIF, 73- *Concurrent Pos:* Los Angeles County Heart Asn res grant, Los Angeles Children's Hosp, 55-56; Am Cancer Soc fel, Francis Delafield Hosp, New York, 56-57 & Presby Hosp, 58; surg pathologist & chief cytol, Peter Bent Brigham Hosp, Boston, 58-70, attend & consult, 70-71; attend, Vet Admin Hosp, West Roxbury, Mass, 60-70. *Mem:* AAAS; fel Royal Soc Med; Am Soc Nephrology; Int Acad Path; Int Soc Nephrology. *Res:* Renal disease and hypertension. *Mailing Add:* UT Med Ctr 858 Madison Ave Memphis TN 38163

CROCKER, IAIN HAY, b Hamilton, Ont, July 28, 28; m 55; c 3. ANALYTICAL CHEMISTRY. *Educ:* McMaster Univ, BSc, 50. *Prof Exp:* Anal chemist, NAm Cyanamid Co, 50-52; chemist, NRX Reactor Opers, 52-53, Chem Process Develop, 53-55 & Develop Chem, 55-62, assoc res officer, 62-72, sect head, Mass Spectrometry & Fuel Anal, 72-79, BR HEAD, GEN CHEMISTRY, CHALK RIVER NUCLEAR LABS, ATOMIC ENERGY, CAN, LTD, 79- *Mem:* Chem Inst Can; Am Soc Mass Spectrometry; Can Nuclear Soc. *Res:* Mass spectrometry-spark source and thermionic; nuclear fuel analyses; burnup; trace analyses; environmental analyses. *Mailing Add:* Chalk River Nuclear Labs Atomic Energy of Can Ltd Chalk River ON K0J 1J0 Can

CROCKER, THOMAS TIMOTHY, b Barranquilla, Colombia, May 9, 20; div; c 4. INFECTIOUS DISEASES, VIROLOGY. *Educ:* Univ Calif, AB, 42, MD, 44. *Prof Exp:* Asst med, Hosp & Sch Med, Univ Calif, 45-46; asst med, Grace-New Haven Community Hosp, 48-49; from asst prof to prof med, Univ

Calif, San Francisco, 50-71; PROF MED & CHMN DEPT COMMUN & ENVIRON MED, UNIV CALIF, IRVINE, 71- *Concurrent Pos:* Nat Res Coun fel virol, Sch Med, Yale Univ, 49-50; Markle Found scholar, 50-55; Guggenheim fel, Clare Col, Cambridge Univ, 57-58; res assoc, Cancer Res Inst, Univ Calif, San Francisco, 57-71; consult, Calif State Dept Pub Health, Nat Cancer Inst, & Biol Div, Oak Ridge Nat Lab; mem extramural grants adv comt, Air Pollution Control Off, Environ Protection Agency, Agency; mem sci adv comn, Calif Air Resources Bd & Southern Calif Air Qual Mgt Dist; co-chmn panel on polycyclic org matter, Environ Protection Agency. *Mem:* AAAS; Am Asn Cancer Res; Am Soc Cell Biol; Am Thoracic Soc; Am Pub Health Asn. *Res:* Cellular physiology of mammalian respiratory epithelia and tumors; environmental toxicology including chemical carcinogenesis with correlation between rodent and primate susceptibility to epithelial metaplasia and transformation; health effects of air pollutants. *Mailing Add:* Col Med Univ Calif Irvine CA 92717

CROCKET, DAVID SCOTT, b Cranford, NJ, Mar 6, 31; m 53; c 5. INORGANIC CHEMISTRY. *Educ:* Colby Col, AB, 52; Univ NH, MS, 54, PhD(inorg chem), 60. *Prof Exp:* Trainee, Owens-Corning Fiberglass, 53-54; asst prof inorg chem, 59-65, asst dean acad affairs, 65-67, assoc dean col, 67-68, dean spec progs, 68-73, assoc provost, 73-80, ASSOC PROF CHEM, LAFAYETTE COL, 65-, DIR RES, 80- *Concurrent Pos:* Dir, Univ City Sci Ctr, 72-80. *Mem:* Am Chem Soc. *Res:* Study of complex fluorides, particularly in the solid state by means of x-ray diffraction; infrared spectro-photometry; application of scanning electron microscopy to geochemical problems. *Mailing Add:* 206 Olin Hall Lafayette Col Easton PA 18042

CROCKET, JAMES HARVIE, b Fredericton, NB, June 27, 32; m 58; c 2. GEOCHEMISTRY, GEOLOGY. *Educ:* Univ NB, BSc, 55; Oxford Univ, BSc, 57; Mass Inst Technol, PhD(geochem), 61. *Prof Exp:* From asst prof to assoc prof, 61-74, PROF GEOL, MCMASTER UNIV, 74- *Mem:* Geochem Soc; Am Geophys Union. *Res:* Neutron activation studies of the geochemistry of precious metals in basic rocks; genesis of ore deposits; geochronology. *Mailing Add:* Dept of Geol McMaster Univ Hamilton ON L8S 4L8 Can

CROCKETT, ALLEN BRUCE, b Ft Worth, Tex, June 8, 44. TERRESTRIAL ECOLOGY, ORNITHOLOGY. *Educ:* Univ Okla, BS, 67; Univ Colo, PhD(ecol), 75. *Prof Exp:* Lectr, Univ Colo Boulder, 74-75; ecologist & geologist, Environ Consult, 75-77; ECOLOGIST & GEOLOGIST, CDM ENVIRON CONSULT, 77- *Mem:* Ecol Soc; Am Ornith Union; Cooper Ornith Soc; Wilson Ornith Soc; Geol Soc Am. *Res:* Avian behavioral ecology and zoogeography; woodpeckers; habitat utilization; restoration of wildlife habitat following surface mining; sedimentary stratigraphy. *Mailing Add:* 11455 W 48th Ave Wheatridge CO 80033

CROCKETT, EARL DAVID, electrical engineering, computer science, see previous edition

CROCKETT, JERRY J, b Chickasha, Okla, May 25, 28; m 51; c 3. PLANT ECOLOGY. *Educ:* Northwestern State Col, Okla, BS, 51; Ft Hays Kans State Col, MS, 60; Univ Okla, PhD(bot), 62. *Prof Exp:* Teacher high school, Tex, 51-52; develop & res chemist, Continental Oil Co, Okla, 52-55; corrosion engr, Tech Serv Dept, Petrolite Corp, 55-59; asst bot & plant ecol, Ft Hays Kans State Col, 59-60; asst & instr bot, Univ Okla, 60-62; from asst prof to assoc prof, Okla State Univ, 62-67; prof & assoc dean col letters & sci, Univ Idaho, 67-68; prof bot & dir arts & sci exten, 68-77, PROF ECOL, DEPT BOT, OKLA STATE UNIV, 77- *Mem:* Ecol Soc Am; Am Soc Range Mgt; Grassland Res Found (secy, 62-64); Sigma Xi. *Res:* Mechanisms of secondary plant succession; productivity of grasslands; strip-mine reclamation; terrestrial pollution. *Mailing Add:* Dept Bot Okla State Univ Stillwater OK 74074

CROCKETT, JOE RICHARD, animal genetics, see previous edition

CROFFORD, OSCAR BLEDSOE, b Chickasha, Okla, Mar 29, 30; m 57; c 3. MEDICAL RESEARCH, INTERNAL MEDICINE. *Educ:* Vanderbilt Univ, AB, 52, MD, 55. *Prof Exp:* Intern med, Hosp, Vanderbilt Univ, 55-56, asst resident, 56-57; USPHS res fel clin physiol, Univ, 59-62, resident med, Hosp, 62-63; USPHS fel clin biochem, Univ Geneva, 63-65; from asst prof to assoc prof, 65-74, PROF MED, SCH MED, VANDERBILT UNIV, 74-, ASSOC PROF PHYSIOL, 70- *Concurrent Pos:* Investr, Howard Hughes Med Inst, 65-71; mem, Metab Study Sect, NIH, 70-74; chmn, 72-74; Addison B Scoville, Jr Chair Diabetes & Metab, Sch Med, Vanderbilt Univ, 73-, div head diabetes & metab, Dept Med, 73-, dir, Diabetes-Endocrinol Ctr, 73-78; chmn, Nat Comn Diabetes, 75-76; dir, Diabetes Res & Training Ctr, 78- *Honors & Awards:* Lilly Award, Am Diabetes Asn, 70, Charles H Best Award, 76; Humanitarian Award, Juv Diabetes Found, 76. *Mem:* Am Diabetes Asn (pres, 81); Am Physiol Soc; Endocrine Soc; Am Soc Clin Invest; Asn Am Physicians. *Res:* Hormone control of metabolism in adipocytes; mechanism of action of insulin; sugar transport; pathophysiology and treatment of Diabetes Mellitus; pathophysiology and treatment of obesity. *Mailing Add:* A-5119 Med Ctr Sch Med Vanderbilt Univ Nashville TN 37232

CROFT, ALFRED RUSSELL, b Ogden, Utah, July 29, 96; m 21; c 4. ECOLOGY. *Educ:* Utah State Univ, BS, 20, MS, 25. *Hon Degrees:* DHL, Weber State Col, 79. *Prof Exp:* Teacher high sch, Utah, 20-24 & Weber Col, 26-34; forest ecologist, Intermountain Forest & Range Exp Sta, US Forest Serv, 34-50; forest hydrologist, Nat Forest Admin, 50-62; consult forest hydrologist, 62-64; prof, Univ Ariz, 64-67; CONSULT HYDROLOGIST, 68- *Honors & Awards:* Super Serv Award, USDA, 57; Distinguished Serv Award, Ariz Water Resources Comt, 66. *Mem:* Soc Am Foresters; hon mem Soil Conserv Soc Am; Am Geophys Union. *Res:* Forest hydrology; consumptive use of water; erosion control. *Mailing Add:* 3921 S 895 E Ogden UT 84403

CROFT, BARBARA YODER, b Port Chester, NY, Aug 11, 40; m 77. NUCLEAR MEDICINE, PHYSICAL CHEMISTRY. *Educ:* Swarthmore Col, BA, 62; Johns Hopkins Univ, MA, 64, PhD(phys chem), 67. *Prof Exp:* Sr scientist, Johnston Labs, 67-68; programmer, Comput Sci Ctr, 68, instr, Sch Med, 69-71, ASST PROF RADIOL, SCH MED, UNIV VA, 72- *Concurrent Pos:* Res partic, Med Div, Oak Ridge Assoc Univs, Inc, 72. *Mem:* Soc Nuclear Med; Am Chem Soc; Am Phys Soc. *Res:* Computers in nuclear medicine; xenon ventilation and perfusion studies. *Mailing Add:* Dept Radiol Univ Va Sch Med Charlottesville VA 22908

CROFT, CHARLES CLAYTON, b Washington, DC, June 16, 14; m 44; c 2. MICROBIOLOGY, PUBLIC HEALTH. *Educ:* Univ Md, BS, 36, MS, 37; Johns Hopkins Univ, ScD(bact), 49; Am Bd Microbiol, dipl. *Prof Exp:* Lab technician, Md State Health Dept, 37; sr bacteriologist, State Lab, 38-43; asst chief labs, Ohio Dept Health, 49-61, chief div labs, 61-81; RETIRED. *Concurrent Pos:* Consult, WHO, 60; chmn, Intersoc Comt Lab Serv Related to Health, 61-64. *Mem:* Am Soc Microbiol; fel Am Pub Health Asn; fel Am Acad Microbiol. *Res:* Public health laboratory administration; virology; syphilis serology; enteric bacteriology; hemolytic antibody. *Mailing Add:* 149 Leland Ave Columbus OH 43214

CROFT, GEORGE THOMAS, b Washington, DC, Sept 29, 26; m 48; c 3. PHYSICS. *Educ:* Western Md Col, BS, 48; Univ Pa, PhD(physics), 53. *Prof Exp:* Physicist, Sound Div, Naval Res Lab, 47-48; physicist, Frankford Arsenal, 49-50; res physicist, Edison Lab, McGraw Edison, Inc, 53-58; supvr appl res, Pitney-Bowes Inc, 58-61, mgr, Appl Res Lab, 61-68, dir corp res & develop, Addressograph Multigraph Corp, 71, vpres, dir res & develop, 72, vpres corp res & develop, Ohio, 75-76; vpres res & develop, Optical Prod Div, Am Optical Corp, 76-80; CONSULT, 80- *Concurrent Pos:* Mem dean's adv coun, Eng Sch, Univ Mass, 81- *Mem:* Am Phys Soc; Inst Elec & Electronics Engrs; Electrochem Soc; Am Mgt Asn; Am Inst Physics. *Res:* Low temperature physics; semiconductors; mechanisms of electrochemical reactions; mathematical analysis; graphics communication systems; medical instruments; automated systems design. *Mailing Add:* RFD1 Fiskdale MA 01518

CROFT, PAUL DOUGLAS, b Ft Erie, Ont, Oct 16, 37; US citizen; m 61; c 3. NUCLEAR CHEMISTRY. *Educ:* Univ Western Ont, BSc, 59; Univ Calif, Berkeley, PhD(chem), 64. *Prof Exp:* Res assoc & instr chem, State Univ NY Stony Brook, 64-66, lectr chem & dir chem labs, 66-72; dean for admin, Univ Mich, Flint, 72-75; EXEC OFFICER CHEM, UNIV CALIF, SAN DIEGO, 75- *Concurrent Pos:* Res collab, Brookhaven Nat Labs, 64-66. *Mem:* AAAS; Am Chem Soc; Chem Inst Can. *Mailing Add:* Univ of Calif at San Diego B-032 La Jolla CA 92093

CROFT, THOMAS A(RTHUR), b Denver, Colo, Feb 15, 31; m 64; c 3. ELECTRICAL ENGINEERING. *Educ:* Dartmouth Col, BA, 53, MS, 54; Stanford Univ, PhD(elec eng), 64. *Prof Exp:* Elec engr, Convair/Astronaut, Gen Dynamics Corp, 57-59; adj prof, Radiosci Lab, Stanford Univ, 59-75; STAFF SCIENTIST, SRI INT, 75- *Concurrent Pos:* Consult, Stanford Res Inst, 65-75, Appl Tech Inc, 65-75, Barry Res Corp, 68-75 & NAS, 71; assoc ed, Radio Sci, US Nat Comt-Int Sci Radio Union Comn III. *Mem:* Am Geophys Union; AAAS Div Planetary Sci; Inst Elec & Electronics Engrs; Soc Motion Picture & TV Engrs; Inst Union Radio Sci. *Res:* Ionospheric physics; simulation of the performance of radar systems by means of digital-computer wave propagation analysis and synthesis; solar wind density and planetary atmospheric structure measurement by radio propagation to spacecraft. *Mailing Add:* SRI Int Bldg G-204 Menlo Park CA 94025

CROFT, THOMAS STONE, b Marfa, Tex, May 9, 38; m. ORGANIC CHEMISTRY. *Educ:* Univ Fla, BS, 61; Univ Colo, PhD(org chem), 65. *Prof Exp:* Sr chemist, 66-71, res specialist, 71-77, PROD DEVELOP SPECIALIST, 3M CO, 77- *Mem:* Am Chem Soc. *Res:* Organic fluorine chemistry; heterocycles, chemical specialty formulations, including emulsions, polishes, abrasion resistant and fire retardant coatings; polymeric coatings and surfaces. *Mailing Add:* Automotive Trades Div 3M Ctr Bldg 251-2E St Paul MN 55144

CROFT, WALTER LAWRENCE, b Longview, Miss, June 28, 35; m 68; c 1. PHYSICS. *Educ:* Miss State Univ, BS, 57; Vanderbilt Univ, PhD(physics), 64. *Prof Exp:* From asst prof to assoc prof, 62-71, PROF PHYSICS, MISS STATE UNIV, 71- *Mem:* Int Solar Energy Soc; Am Asn Physics Teachers. *Res:* Nuclear spectroscopy; solar energy; microwave spectroscopy. *Mailing Add:* Mississippi State MS

CROFT, WILLIAM JOSEPH, b New York, NY, Nov 29, 26; m 49; c 2. CRYSTALLOGRAPHY. *Educ:* Columbia Univ, BS, 50, MA, 52, PhD(mineral, crystallog), 54. *Prof Exp:* Asst mineral, Columbia Univ, 52-54; instr, Hofstra Col, 54-55; staff mem crystallog, Lincoln Lab, Mass Inst Technol, 55-57; sr staff mem, Radio Corp Am, 57-61; staff mem, Sperry Rand Res Ctr, 61-69; RES CHEMIST, ARMY MAT & MECH RES CTR, 69- *Concurrent Pos:* Vis prof, Brown Univ, 70-72 & 80-82. *Mem:* AAAS; fel Mineral Soc Am; Am Crystallog Asn; Mineral Soc Gt Brit & Ireland. *Res:* X-ray crystallographic studies of oxides; high and low temperature phase transformations; lattice distortion and crystallite size in multiple oxides. *Mailing Add:* Army Mat & Mech Res Ctr Watertown MA 02172

CROFTS, GEOFFREY, b Winnipeg, Man, May 12, 24; m 49; c 3. ACTUARIAL MATHEMATICS. *Educ:* Univ Man, BCom, 46. *Prof Exp:* Assoc prof actuarial math, Univ Man, 49-55 & Occidental Col, 55-59; actuarial training dir, Occidental Life Ins Co Calif, 59-64; DEAN & DIR, GRAD SCH ACTUARIAL SCI, NORTHEASTERN UNIV, 64- *Mem:* Fel Soc Actuaries; Casualty Actuarial Soc. *Res:* Actuarial science. *Mailing Add:* Grad Sch of Actuarial Sci Northeastern Univ Boston MA 02115

CROKE, EDWARD JOHN, b Oak Park, Ill, Nov 13, 35; m 65; c 2. COMPUTER APPLICATIONS, TECHNICAL MANAGEMENT. *Educ:* Univ Ill, BS, 57; Princeton Univ, MS, 60; Nogoya Univ, DEng, 77; Univ Chicago, MBA, 81. *Prof Exp:* Res asst aerospace eng, James Forrestal Res Ctr, Princeton Univ, 58-60; tech proj officer aerospace tech, US Air Force, 60-63; res engr nuclear reactor devices, Reactor Eng Div, 63-66, energy engr, Advanced Concepts Group, 66-67, sect mgr natural resources & environ studies, Environ Natrual Res Sect, 67-69, dep dir, Ctr Environ Studies, 69-71, DIV DIR, ENERGY, ENVIRON & NATURAL RESOURCES, ENERGY & ENVIRON SYSTS DIV, ARGONNE NAT LAB, 71- *Concurrent Pos:* Adj prof, Dept Energy Eng, Univ Ill, 77-; mem tech adv comt, Gas Res Inst, 80-; consult, Ill Dept Energy & Natural Resources, 81- *Mem:* Sigma Xi. *Res:* Technical and economic assessment of energy supply, conservation technologies, environmental control technologies, and polices; micro and mainframe computer data base management, mathematical modeling and systems analysis. *Mailing Add:* 815 Forest Ave River Forest IL 60305

CROKER, ROBERT ARTHUR, b New York, NY, Sept 4, 32; m 72; c 2. ECOLOGY. *Educ:* Adelphi Col, AB, 58; Univ Miami, MS, 60; Emory Univ, PhD(biol), 66. *Prof Exp:* Asst fisheries, Univ Miami, 58-59; marine biologist, Bur Sport Fisheries & Wildlife, US Dept Interior, 60-62 & Bur Commercial Fisheries, 62-64; res asst marine benthic communities, Marine Inst, Univ Ga, 64; asst prof, 66-71, assoc prof, 71-81, PROF ZOOL, UNIV NH, 81- *Concurrent Pos:* Res asst Oyster Lab, Rutgers Univ, 60; panel mem, Nat Res Coun, 73-77. *Mem:* Fel AAAS; Am Acad Arts & Sci; Ecol Soc Am; Marine Biol Asn UK. *Res:* Ecology of Gammaridean Amphipods; marine sand communities; littoral and estuarine ecology; soil zoology; history of ecology. *Mailing Add:* Dept Zool Spaulding Bldg Univ NH Durham NH 03824

CROLEY, THOMAS EDGAR, b Gladewater, Tex, Apr 30, 40; m 64; c 2. ANATOMY, MICROBIOLOGY. *Educ:* ETex State Univ, BS, 63, MS, 64; Southwestern Univ, cytotechnol degree, 66; Baylor Univ, PhD(anat), 71. *Prof Exp:* Adj prof, NTex State Univ, 71-72; asst prof anat, La State Univ Med Ctr, 72-77; ASST PROF ANAT, TEX COL OSTEOP MED, 77- *Concurrent Pos:* NASA-Manned Spacecraft Ctr fel, 71-72. *Mem:* Am Soc Clin Path; Int Asn Dent Res. *Res:* Calcified tissue research, particularly developing teeth; hormone relationship to epithelial development; placenta morphology. *Mailing Add:* Dept of Anat Camp Bowie at Montgomery Ft Worth TX 76107

CROLL, IAN MURRAY, b Regina, Sask, Dec 7, 29; m 55; c 2. PHYSICAL CHEMISTRY. *Educ:* Univ Man, BSc, 50, MSc, 58; Univ Calif, Los Angeles, PhD(chem), 58. *Prof Exp:* Chemist, Defence Res Bd Can, 51-52; chemist fed systs div, Int Bus Mach Corp, NY, 58-61, mem res staff, Watson Res Ctr, 61-63, mgr chem res, 63-67, mgr mem & storage res, 67-72, dir technol, 72-73, MGR MAT TECHNOL, IBM CORP, 73- *Mem:* Am Chem Soc; Inst Elec & Electronics Eng; Electrochem Soc. *Res:* Thermodynamics; solution chemistry; electrochemistry; electrodeposition; structure and magnetic properties of metal films. *Mailing Add:* IBM Corp Monterey & Cottle Rds San Jose CA 95123

CROLL, NEIL ARGO, parasitology, behavioral physiology, deceased

CROMARTIE, THOMAS HOUSTON, b Raleigh, NC, Aug 9, 46. BIOCHEMISTRY. *Educ:* Duke Univ, BS, 68; Mass Inst Technol, PhD(chem), 73. *Prof Exp:* Res assoc, Mass Inst Technol, 73-75; asst prof chem, Univ Va, 75-81; SUPVR, STAUFFER CHEM CO, 81- *Mem:* Am Chem Soc; Sigma Xi; AAAS. *Res:* Reaction mechanisms of enzymes, especially flavoenzymes and isomerases; rational design of herbicides and insecticides; heavy atom and hydrogen kinetic isotope effects. *Mailing Add:* Stauffer Chem Co 1200 S 47th St Richmond CA 94804

CROMARTIE, WILLIAM JAMES, b Garland, NC, May 19, 13; m 45; c 5. MICROBIOLOGY, INFECTIOUS DISEASES. *Educ:* Emory Univ, MD, 37; Am Bd Path, dipl, 48, Am Bd Internal Med, dipl, 51. *Prof Exp:* Intern, Grady Hosp, Emory Univ, 37-38; asst resident path, Vanderbilt Univ Hosp, 38-39, instr, Sch Med, 39-41; asst resident med, Bowman-Gray Sch Med, 42; dir res lab & asst chief med serv, Vet Admin Hosp, 46-49; assoc prof med & bact, Med Sch, Univ Minn, 49-51; assoc prof, 51-59, PROF MED & BACT, SCH MED, UNIV NC, CHAPEL HILL, 59-, ASSOC DEAN CLIN SCI, 69- *Concurrent Pos:* Instr, Med Col, Southwestern Univ, 47-49; mem, Adv Panel Microbiol, Off Naval Res, 50-55, Bact Test Comt, Nat Bd Med Examrs, 61-69; chief staff, NC Mem Hosp, 69-74; mem, Infectious Dis Adv Comt, Nat Inst Allergy & Infectious Dis, 71-75. *Mem:* Am Acad Microbiol; fel Am Col Physicians; Am Asn Path & Bact; Am Soc Exp Path; Am Soc Microbiol. *Res:* Pathogenesis of rheumatoid arthritis and rheumatic fever. *Mailing Add:* Univ of NC Sch of Med Chapel Hill NC 27514

CROMARTIE, WILLIAM JAMES, JR, b Dallas, Tex, Oct 14, 47. ECOLOGY, NATURAL HISTORY. *Educ:* St Johns Col, AB, 69; Cornell Univ, PhD(ecol), 74. *Prof Exp:* asst 74-80, ASSOC PROF ENVIRON STUDIES, STOCKTON STATE COL, 80-, DIR, CTR ENVIRON RES, 79- *Mem:* AAAS; Ecol Soc Am; Entom Soc Am; Brit Ecol Soc. *Res:* Biogeography and evolution of plant-arthropod associations; coastal plain biogeography, especially pine barrens and pocosins; insects associated with pines; endangered and threatened plants and animals. *Mailing Add:* Dept of Environ Studies Stockton State Col Pomona NJ 08240

CROMER, ALAN H, b Chicago, Ill, Aug 15, 35; wid. SCIENCE WRITING, PHYSICS. *Educ:* Univ Wis, BS, 54; Cornell Univ, PHD(theoret physics), 60. *Prof Exp:* Res fel physics, Harvard Univ, 59-61; from asst prof to assoc prof, 61-70, PROF PHYSICS, NORTHEASTERN UNIV, 70- *Concurrent Pos:* Pres, Edutech, Inc, Newton, 80- *Mem:* AAAS; Am Phys Soc; Am Asn Physics Teachers. *Res:* Physics for the life sciences; theoretical mechanics; physics in science and industry; educational software. *Mailing Add:* Dept of Physics Northeastern Univ Boston MA 02115

CROMER, DON TIFFANY, b South Bend, Ind, July 27, 23; m 45; c 5. X-RAY CRYSTALLOGRAPHY. *Educ:* Univ Wis, BS, 47, PhD(chem), 51. *Prof Exp:* Chemist, Nat Lead Co, 50-52; MEM STAFF, LOS ALAMOS NAT LAB, 52- *Concurrent Pos:* Vis scientist, Puerto Rico Nuclear Ctr, 65, Ctr Nat Sci Res, Grenoble, France, 72-73; prog mgr, Div Mat Sci, Dept Energy, 80-82. *Honors & Awards:* E O Lawrence Award, Atomic Energy Comn, 69. *Mem:* Am Chem Soc; Am Crystallog Asn. *Res:* X-ray crystallography. *Mailing Add:* MS 730 Los Alamos Nat Lab Los Alamos NM 87545

CROMER, JERRY HALTIWANGER, b Anderson, SC, Apr 4, 35; m 62. DEVELOPMENTAL BIOLOGY, PHYSIOLOGY. *Educ:* Wofford Col, BS, 57; Univ SC, MS, 65; Vanderbilt Univ, PhD(develop biol), 68. *Prof Exp:* Asst prof, 68-74, ASSOC PROF BIOL, CONVERSE COL, 74- *Concurrent Pos:* Fac res grant, 68-69. *Mem:* AAAS; Am Soc Zool; NY Acad Sci. *Res:* Quantitative analysis of impulse transmission in the aortic depressor nerve of rabbits; development of hepatic xanthine dehydrogenase in hatching chick embryos; histochemistry; enzyme development; developmental genetics and physiology. *Mailing Add:* Dept of Biol Converse Col Spartanburg SC 29301

CROMER, JOHN A, b Logansport, Ind, Nov 29, 38; m 58; c 4. PHYSIOLOGY. *Educ:* Taylor Univ, BA, 62; Ball State Univ, MS, 68; Univ NDak, PhD(physiol), 72. *Prof Exp:* Asst prof biol, Pasadena Col, 71-73; chmn dept biol, Point Loma Col, 73-74; asst dean & health prof adv, Duke Univ, 76-78; asst dean student affairs, Oral Roberts Univ, 78, asst dean med educ, 78-80; VPRES ACAD AFFAIRS & DEAN, ILL COL OPTOM, 80- *Concurrent Pos:* Partic, Human Genetics & Societal Probs, NSF Chautauqua Course, 72-73. *Mem:* Sigma Xi; AAAS; Undersea Med Soc. *Res:* Central nervous system during exposure to hyperbaric environments; described high pressure nervous syndrome from sterotaxically implanted electrodes in the basal ganglia to provide evidence of the origin of EEg changes. *Mailing Add:* 3241 S Mich Ill Col Optom Chicago IL 60616

CROMPTON, ALFRED W, b Durban, SAfrica, Feb 21, 27; m 54; c 3. VERTEBRATE PALEONTOLOGY. *Educ:* Univ Stellenbosch, BSc, 47, MSc, 49, PhD(zool), 51; Cambridge Univ, PhD(paleont), 53. *Prof Exp:* Cur fossil vertebrates, Nat Mus, Bloemfontein, SAfrica, 54-56; dir, SAfrican Mus, Cape Town, 56-64; dir, Peabody Mus Natural Hist & prof biol & geol, Yale Univ, 64-70; DIR, MUS COMP ZOOL, HARVARD UNIV, 70- *Concurrent Pos:* Lectr, Univ Cape Town, 58-64. *Mem:* Fel Zool Soc London; SAfrican Asn Adv Sci; fel Am Acad Arts & Sci; Soc Vertebrate Paleont; Am Soc Zool. *Res:* Evolution of mammals and dinosaurs; functional anatomy. *Mailing Add:* Mus of Comp Zool Harvard Univ Cambridge MA 02138

CROMPTON, CHARLES EDWARD, b St George Island, Alaska, Oct 8, 22; m 45; c 2. PHYSICAL CHEMISTRY. *Educ:* Univ Calif, Berkeley, BS, 43; Univ Tenn, PhD(chem), 49. *Prof Exp:* Res chemist, Manhattan Proj, Berkeley, Calif & Oak Ridge, Tenn, 43-46; tech reviewer, Isotopes Div, USAEC, 49-51; dep dir, 53-56; dir radioactivity div, US Testing Co, 51-53; assoc tech dir, Nat Lead Co Ohio, 56-60; dir nuclear chem, Martin-Nuclear Div, Martin Marietta Corp, 60-62; tech dir pigments div, Chem Group, Glidden Co, 62-63, dir res, Consol Inorg Res, 63-66; dir res inorg div, Chemetron Corp, 66-74, dir develop, Chem Group, 74-77, dir res & develop, Chem Prod Div, 77-80; PRES, CPI CONSULTS, INC, 80- *Concurrent Pos:* Consult, USAEC, 51-52 & Am Med Asn, 54-55; mem sci adv bd, New Eng Nuclear Corp, 56-; consult, Martin Co, Md, 62-63; mem comt on depleted uranium, Nat Mat Adv Bd, 70-71. *Mem:* Fel Am Inst Chem; Am Chem Soc; Asn Res Dirs; Com Develop Asn; Sigma Xi. *Res:* Nuclear chemistry; homogeneous and heterogeneous catalysis; kinetics surface chemistry of inorganic solids, metals and ceramics; catalytic hydrogenation; physical chemistry and metallurgy of uranium and plutonium; pigments; fire retardants; plastic additives; phosgene and phosgene derivatives. *Mailing Add:* CPI Consults, Inc 602 Bayard Ave Rehoboth Beach DE 19971

CROMROY, HARVEY LEONARD, b Lawrence, Mass, Jan 5, 30; m 57, 70; c 4. RADIOBIOLOGY, ENTOMOLOGY. *Educ:* Northeastern Univ, BSc, 51; NC State Col, PhD(entom), 58. *Prof Exp:* Entomologist, NC State Bd Health, 56-57; assoc prof entom & biophys, Col Agr, Univ PR, 57-60; res scientist, Oak Ridge Nat Lab, 60-61; sci adminr radiol health, USPHS, 61-64; assoc prof nuclear sci, 64-70, PROF ENTOM & NEMATOL, UNIV FLA, 70- *Concurrent Pos:* Adv mem on agr, Southern Interstate Nuclear Bd, 73-; guest prof, Inst Appl Zool, Univ Bonn, WGer, 78. *Mem:* Health Physics Soc; Enom Soc Am; Am Acarological Soc. *Res:* Taxonomy of plant feeding mites; uses of isotopes in entomology. *Mailing Add:* Newell 214 Univ Fla Gainesville FL 32611

CROMWELL, GARY LEON, b Salina, Kans, Oct 6, 38; m 60; c 3. ANIMAL NUTRITION. *Educ:* Kans State Univ, BS, 60; Purdue Univ, MS, 65, PhD(animal nutrit), 67. *Prof Exp:* Teacher high sch, Kans, 60-64; res asst animal nutrit, Purdue Univ, 64-67; from asst prof to assoc prof, 67-76, PROF ANIMAL SCI, UNIV KY, 76- *Mem:* Am Soc Animal Sci. *Res:* Swine nutrition. *Mailing Add:* Dept of Animal Sci Univ of Ky Lexington KY 40506

CROMWELL, LESLIE, b Manchester, Eng, Apr 2, 24; m 56; c 3. BIOMEDICAL ENGINEERING. *Educ:* Univ Manchester, BScTech, 43, MScTech, 61; Univ Calif, Los Angeles, MS, 51, PhD, 67. *Prof Exp:* Res engr, Salford Elec Instruments, 43-44; design engr, Aircraft Elec Div, English Elec Co, 44-46; chief engr elec eng, B Cromwell & Co, Ltd, Eng, 46-48; lectr eng, Univ Calif, Los Angeles, 48-53; from asst prof to assoc prof, 53-57, head dept, 55-64, PROF ENG, CALIF STATE UNIV, LOS ANGELES, 57-, CHMN DEPT INTERDISCIPLINARY ENG, 68-, DEAN SCH ENG, 77- *Concurrent Pos:* Consult, Ed Develop Prog, Univ Calif, Los Angeles, 62- *Mem:* Inst Elec & Electronics Engrs; Am Soc Eng Educ. *Res:* Aircraft electrical equipment design; industrial electronics; electric power equipment; electric machinery; control systems; biomedical instrumentation. *Mailing Add:* Sch of Eng Calif State Univ Los Angeles CA 90032

CROMWELL, NORMAN HENRY, b Terre Haute, Ind, Nov 22, 13; m 55; c 2. ORGANIC CHEMISTRY, CHEMOTHERAPY. *Educ:* Rose Hulman Inst, BS, 35; Univ Minn, PhD(org chem), 39. *Prof Exp:* Asst chem, Univ Minn, 35-39; from instr to prof org chem, 39-60, mem res coun, 47-49, mem grad coun, 51-60, Howard S Wilson prof chem, 60-70, chmn dept, 64-70, vpres grad studies & res, Univ Nebr Syst, 72-73, REGENTS PROF CHEM, UNIV NEBR-LINCOLN, 73-, INTERIM DIR, EPPLEY INST CANCER RES, MED CTR, 79- *Concurrent Pos:* Consult, Parke, Davis & Co, 44-45, Smith Kline & French, Pa, 46-49, USPHS, 53-, Philip Morris, Inc & Nat Cancer Inst, 54-65; Fulbright scholar & Guggenheim fel, 50 & 58; hon res assoc, Univ Col, Univ London, 50-51, 58-59 & Calif Inst Technol, 58; guest, Mass Inst Technol, 67; pres, Int Heterocyclic Chem Cong, 69, plenary lectr, 75; asst ed, Int J Heterocyclic Chem, 73-; exchange scientist, India, 77. *Mem:* Am Chem Soc; The Chem Soc; Sigma Xi; Int Soc Heterocyclic Chem. *Res:* Reaction mechanisms; aziridines and azetidines; amino ketones; beta chloro amines; benzacridines; synthetic and physical organic chemistry; small-ring compounds; heterocyclics of biological interest in carcinogenesis and carcinostasis; pyrrols; activated allylsystems. *Mailing Add:* 837 Hamilton Hall Univ Nebr Lincoln NE 68588

CRONAN, CHRISTOPHER SHAW, plant ecology, biogeochemistry, see previous edition

CRONAN, JOHN EMERSON, JR, b Long Beach, Calif, Dec 2, 42; m 73; c 2. BIOCHEMISTRY, MOLECULAR BIOLOGY. *Educ:* San Fernando Valley State Col, BA, 65; Univ Calif, Irvine, PhD(molecular biol), 68. *Prof Exp:* Instr biol chem, Sch Med, Washington Univ, 68-70; from asst prof to assoc prof molecular biophys & biochem, Yale Univ, 74-78; PROF MICROBIOL, UNIV ILL, 78- *Concurrent Pos:* NIH fel, Sch Med, Washington Univ, 68-70; NIH res grant & NSF res grant, Yale Univ, & Univ Ill, 71- NIH career development award, 72-77; mem, Metab Biol Panel, NSF, 75-76; mem physiol chem study comt, Am Heart Asn, 81- *Mem:* Am Soc Microbiol; Am Soc Biol Chemists. *Res:* Microbial lipid metabolism and chemistry; biogenesis of biological membranes; bacteriophage infection physiology; biochemical genetics. *Mailing Add:* Dept of Microbiol Univ of Ill Urbana IL 61801

CRONAUER, DONALD (CHARLES), b Sewickley, Pa, Nov 4, 36; m 62; c 3. CHEMICAL ENGINEERING. *Educ:* Carnegie Inst, Technol, BS, 58, MS, 59, PhD(chem eng), 62. *Prof Exp:* Proj chem engr, Res & Develop Dept, Amoco Chem Corp, 61-66; sr chem engr, Born Warner Develop Div, Marbon Chem, 66-67, res assoc, 67-70; res engr, 70-73, sr res engr, 73-76, STAFF ENGR, GULF RES & DEVELOP CO, 76- *Mem:* Am Chem Soc; Am Inst Chem Engrs; Sigma Xi. *Res:* Process development with emphasis on kinetics and catalysis; mechanism of coal hydrogenation and liquefaction including catalysis and hydrogen transfer; fundamentals of conversion of shale and heavy fuels. *Mailing Add:* 525 Edgehill Dr Gibsonia PA 15044

CRONE, ANTHONY JOSEPH, b Boston, Mass, Jan 3, 47; m 74. EARTHQUAKE HAZARD ASSESSMENT. *Educ:* Clark Univ, BA, 69; Univ Colo, PhD(geol), 75. *Prof Exp:* Proj geologist oil & gas explor, Bond Explor Co, Inc, 74-76; consult, 76-78; GEOLOGIST, US GEOL SURV, 78- *Mem:* Geol Soc Am; Soc Econ Paleontologists & Mineralogists. *Res:* Assessment of earthquake hazards in the midcontinent and northern Rocky Mountains; utilizing geologic and geophysical information to investigate causes and to determine the size and frequency of major earthquakes in the areas. *Mailing Add:* MS 966 US Geol Surv Box 25046 Denver Fed Ctr Denver CO 80225

CRONE, LAWRENCE JOHN, b Orangeville, Ill, May 18, 35. PLANT PATHOLOGY. *Educ:* Carthage Col, AB, 56; Rutgers Univ, PhD(plant path), 62. *Prof Exp:* Asst prof, 62-67, ASSOC PROF BIOL, UNIV WISWHITEWATER, 67- *Res:* Diseases of trees and ornamental plants. *Mailing Add:* Dept of Biol Univ of Wis Whitewater WI 53190

CRONEMEYER, DONALD CHARLES, b Chanute, Kans, Nov 10, 25; m 53; c 5. PHYSICS. *Educ:* Mass Inst Technol, ScD(physics), 51. *Prof Exp:* Res physicist, Gen Elec Co, 51-57 & Bendix Aviation Res Lab, Mich, 57-67; RES PHYSICIST, T J WATSON RES CTR, IBM CORP, 68- *Concurrent Pos:* Instr physics, Wayne State Univ, 58- *Mem:* Creation Res Soc; Electrochem Soc; Am Phys Soc; Inst Elec & Electronic Engrs. *Res:* Electrical and otpical properties of semi-conductors; lasers; magnetic properties of materials; properties of superconductors. *Mailing Add:* 211 Barnes St Ossining NY 10562

CRONENBERG, AUGUST WILLIAM, b Teaneck, NJ, Apr 22, 44. ENGINEERING SCIENCE. *Educ:* Newark Col Eng, BS, 66; Northwestern Univ, MS, 69, PhD(eng sci), 71. *Prof Exp:* Assoc engr eng sci, Argonne Nat Lab, 71-74; asst prof chem & nuclear eng, Univ NMex, 74-77; sr scientist mat eng, EG&G Idaho, Inc, 77-79; CONSULT ENG SCI & ANAL, 79- *Concurrent Pos:* NSF fel, Argonne Nat Lab, 72-73. *Mem:* Am Nuclear Soc; Am Inst Chem Engrs; Am Soc Mech Engrs. *Res:* Material science; boiling heat transfer; nuclear fuel behavior; nuclear reactor safety; thermophysical properties. *Mailing Add:* 836 Clairview Lane Idaho Falls ID 83402

CRONENBERGER, JO HELEN, b LaGrange, Tex, Mar 17, 39. IMMUNOLOGY, BIOCHEMISTRY. *Educ:* Univ Tex, Austin, BA(microbiol) & BS(med technol), 62; Univ Houston, PhD(biophysics), 72. *Prof Exp:* Spec chemist clin chem, Methodist Hosp, Houston, 61-64; dir med technol, Bentaub Hosp, Baylor Col Med, 64-65, res assoc immunol, 65-68; Max-Planck Inst fel, 72-74; res fel, Ger Res Soc, 74-75; ASST PROF LIFE SCI, UNIV TEX, SAN ANTONIO, 75-, DIR MED TECHNOL, 75- & ADJ ASST PROF PATH, UNIV TEX HEALTH SCI CTR, 76- *Honors & Awards:* Hematol Merit Award, Am Soc Med Technol, 63. *Mem:* NY Acad Sci; Am Soc Cell Biology; Am Soc Microbiol; Am Chem Soc; Sigma Xi. *Res:* Biosynthesis of immunoglobulins; liposomal carriers in manipulation of the immune system; in vitro-ribosomal level study of translational events; posttranslational modification of amino acids; glycosylation; controls of kinetics of translation. *Mailing Add:* Div Allied Health & Life Sci Univ of Tex San Antonio TX 78285

CRONENWETT, WILLIAM TREADWELL, b Texarkana, Tex, Jan 3, 32; div; c 2. ELECTRICAL ENGINEERING. *Educ:* Tex Col Arts & Indust, BS, 54; Univ Tex, MS, 60, PhD, 66. *Prof Exp:* Res engr, Elec Eng Res Lab, Univ Tex, 55-59; res engr, Electro-Mech Co, Tex, 60-62; Welch Found fel physics, Univ Tex, 64-66; res fel, Chem Dept, Univ Leicester, 66-68; asst prof, 68-75, ASSOC PROF, DEPT ELEC ENG & COMPUT SCI, UNIV OKLA, 75-, ELEC & ELECTRONIC DESIGN CONSULT, 69- *Mem:* Inst Elec & Electronics Engrs; Am Meteorol Soc; Soc Automotive Engrs. *Res:* Electric field theory; electronic conduction processes; electronic instrument design; medical instrument design. *Mailing Add:* Dept Elec Eng & Comput Sci Univ Okla 202 W Boyd St Norman OK 73019

CRONHEIM, GEORG ERICH, b Berlin, Ger, Jan 15, 06; nat US; m 32. PHARMACOLOGY. *Educ:* Univ Berlin, PhD(phys chem), 30. *Prof Exp:* Asst & instr, Inst Phys Chem, Univ Berlin, 30-32; head, Biochem Lab, Inst Phys Agron & res chemist, Inst Exp Med, Leningrad, 32-36; res chemist, Phys Inst, Univ Stockholm, 37-39; res chemist, NY State Res Inst, 40; chief chemist, G F Harvey Co, NY, 41-45; res dir, S E Massengill Co, 46-52; dir biol sci, 52-67, tech liaison exec, 67-73, CONSULT, RIKER LABS, INC, 73- *Mem:* AAAS; Am Soc Clin Pharmacol; Am Soc Pharmacol; NY Acad Sci. *Res:* Biochemistry; pharmacology. *Mailing Add:* Riker Labs Inc 19901 Nordhoff St Northridge CA 91324

CRONHOLM, LOIS S, b St Louis, Mo, Aug 15, 30; div; c 2. MICROBIOLOGY. *Educ:* Univ Louisville, BA, 62, PhD(bot), 67. *Prof Exp:* Nat Inst Health fel, Dept microbiol, 66-79, from asst prof to assoc prof, 72-79, PROF MICROBIOL, UNIV LOUISVILLE, 79-, RES ASSOC, WATER RESOURCES LAB, 73-, ASSOC, DEPT MICROBIOL, SCH MED, 75-, DEAN, COL ARTS & SCI, 79- *Concurrent Pos:* Assoc dean, Col Arts & Sci, Univ Louisville, 77-78, actg dean, 78-79. *Mem:* Am Soc Microbiol; AAAS; Am Water Resources Asn. *Res:* Bacterial endotoxins; histoplasma capsulatum and bird roosts; viruses in water and waste water; bacterial aerosols from waste water. *Mailing Add:* Dean's Off Col Arts & Sci Univ Louisville Louisville KY 40208

CRONIN, JAMES LAWRENCE, JR, b St Louis, Mo, Mar 14, 19; m. APPLIED MECHANICS, CIVIL ENGINEERING. *Educ:* Washington Univ, St Louis, BS, 41, MS, 49, DSc(appl mech), 57. *Prof Exp:* Res engr, Res Found, Washington Univ, St Louis, 46-49, instr, 46-51; from asst prof to assoc prof eng, St Louis Univ, 51-61, prof civil eng, 61-68, prof elec eng, 68-71; chief elec sect, 72-77, CHIEF STRUCT SECT, US ARMY CORPS ENGRS, ST LOUIS DIST, 77- *Concurrent Pos:* Alvey Conveyor Mfg Co, 46-; indust consult, Emerson Elec Co, 53-68; vis prof mgt sci, Southern Ill Univ, Edwardsville, 72- *Mem:* Soc Am Military Engrs. *Res:* Theoretical mechanics. *Mailing Add:* Structural Sect ED-DA US Army Corp Engrs 210 Tucker Blvd N St Louis MO 63101

CRONIN, JAMES WATSON, b Chicago, Ill, Sept 29, 21; m 54; c 2. NUCLEAR PHYSICS. *Educ:* Southern Methodist Univ, BS, 51; Univ Chicago, MS, 53, PhD(physics), 55. *Prof Exp:* Asst physicist, Brookhaven Nat Lab, 55-58; from asst prof to prof, Princeton Univ, 58-71, PROF PHYSICS, UNIV CHICAGO, 71- *Concurrent Pos:* Physicist, Nat Accelerator, Ill, 70-71; mem panel elem particle physics, Div Phys Sci, Nat Acad Sci. *Mem:* Nat Acad Sci; Am Phys Soc. *Res:* Elementary particles; experiments on pion-proton total cross sections; hyperon decay asymmetries; development of improved detection techniques. *Mailing Add:* Dept of Physics Univ of Chicago Chicago IL 60637

CRONIN, JANE SMILEY, b New York, NY, July 17, 22; div; c 4. BIOMATHEMATICS. *Educ:* Univ Mich, PhD(math), 49. *Prof Exp:* Mathematician, US Air Force Cambridge Res Ctr, 51-54; instr, Wheaton Col, 54-55; mathematician, Am Optical Co, 56; from asst prof to prof math, Polytech Inst Brooklyn, 57-65, PROF MATH, RUTGERS UNIV, 65- *Mem:* Soc Indust & Appl Math; Am Math Soc. *Res:* Topological degree; functional analysis; ordinary differential equations; applications of analysis in medicine and biology. *Mailing Add:* 110 Valentine St Highland Park NJ 08904

CRONIN, JOHN READ, b Marietta, Ohio, Mar 5, 37; m 63; c 3. BIOCHEMISTRY. *Educ:* Col Wooster, BA, 59; Univ Colo, PhD(biochem), 64. *Prof Exp:* Res assoc biochem, Sch Med, Yale Univ, 64-66; from asst prof to assoc prof, 66-78, PROF, DEPT CHEM, ARIZ STATE UNIV, 78- *Concurrent Pos:* NIH fel, 64-65; temp staff mem org geochem, Carnegie Inst Wash, 74-75. *Mem:* AAAS; Am Chem Soc; Am Soc Biol Chem; Meteoritical Soc; Sigma Xi. *Res:* Organic chemistry of carbonaceous meteorites; chemical evolution; protein chemistry; analytical biochemistry. *Mailing Add:* Dept of Chem Ariz State Univ Tempe AZ 85287

CRONIN, LEWIS EUGENE, b Aberdeen, Md, May 11, 17; m 45; c 3. MARINE ECOLOGY, ZOOLOGY. *Educ:* Western Md Col, AB, 38; Univ Md, MS, 42, PhD(zool), 46. *Hon Degrees:* DSc, Western Md Col, 66. *Prof Exp:* Teacher high sch, Md, 38-40; biologist, State Dept Res & Educ, Md, 43-50; dir marine lab & assoc prof biol sci, Univ Del, 50-55; dir & biologist, Dept Res & Educ, 55-61; dir, Natural Resources Inst & Chesapeake Biol Lab, 61-75, assoc dir res, Ctr Environ & Estuarine Studies, 75-77, PROF, UNIV MD, 61-, DIR, CHESAPEAKE RES CONSORTIUM, 77- *Concurrent Pos:* Consult coastal ecol off chief engr, CEngr, US Army; consult pesticides, USDA & Environ Protection Agency & Mem Md Water Pollution Comn, 55-63; mem, Md Bd Nat Resources, 55-69, Chesapeake Res Coun, chmn, 66-67, Md Comn Pesticides, chmn, 67-69 & Md Comn Environ Educ, 70-; mem, Interstate Comn Potomac River Basin, 63-, Secys Comn Pesticides & Relationship Environ Health, Dept Health, Educ & Welfare, 69, Adv Comt Water Resources Sci Info Ctr, Dept Interior, 69-73 & Panel Oceanog & Marine Res, Comn Space Prog Earth Observation, Adv to Dept Interior, Nat Acad Sci; mem, Nat Marine Fish Adv Comn, Dept Com, 71-73; mem, Law of the Sea Adv Comn, US State Dept, 73-; mem, Mid-Atlantic Fisheries Mgt Coun, 76-77. *Honors & Awards:* Award, Oyster Inst NAm, Isaac Walton League & Chesapeake Bay Seafood Indust Asn; Am Motors consult Award, 71. *Mem:* AAAS; Am Soc Zool; Am Inst Fishery Res Biol; Am Fisheries Soc;

Nat Shell Fisheries Asn (pres, 60); Estuarine Res Fedn (pres, 71-73). *Res:* Fisheries and pollution; resource management; environmental education; estuarine ecology and biology; research administration. *Mailing Add:* Chesapeake Res Consortium 1419 Forest Dr Suite 207 Annapolis MD 21613

CRONIN, MICHAEL JOHN, b Los Angeles, Calif, Nov 19, 49; m 79. NEUROENDOCRINOLOGY. *Educ:* Loyola-Marymount Univ, Los Angeles, BS, 71; Univ Southern Calif, PhD(physiol), 76. *Prof Exp:* Fel neuroendocrinol, Univ Calif, San Francisco, 76-79; ASST PROF PHYSIOL, SCH MED, UNIV VA, 79- *Mem:* Endocrine Soc; Soc Neurosci; Am Physiol Soc; Int Soc Neuroendocrinol. *Res:* Study of hormones released by the brain to elucidate the subsequent mechanisms by which the anterior pituitary responds to these hormones in mammals and cell culture systems. *Mailing Add:* Dept Physiol Box 449 Sch Med Univ Va Charlottesville VA 22908

CRONIN, MICHAEL THOMAS IGNATIUS, b Glasgow, Scotland, Feb 1, 24; nat US; m 50; c 9. PATHOLOGY. *Educ:* Vet Col Ireland, MRCVS, 45; Univ Dublin, MSc, 46, PhD(path, bact), 48; Georgetown Univ, MD, 65. *Prof Exp:* Res officer, Equine Res Sta, Eng, 50-52; dir, Regional Diag Lab, Va, 52-53; bacteriologist, Dept Animal Path, Univ Ky, 53-55; assoc pathologist, Penrose Res Lab & asst prof vet path, Univ Pa, 55-57; head dept path & toxicol, Schering Corp, 57-61; pathologist, Woodard Res Corp, 61-65; intern, Grace-New Haven Community Hosp, Med Ctr, Yale Univ, 65-66; asst resident, Yale Univ-New Haven Hosp, 66-67 & Vet Admin Hosp, 67-68; PATHOLOGIST, MEM HOSP, MERIDEN, 68-72, 74- *Concurrent Pos:* Consult pathologist, Woodard Res Corp, 65-71; pathologist, Masonic Home & Hosp, Wallingford, 68-70, 72-; consult ed, Am Scientist, 71-; assoc pathologist, Hosp of St Raphael, 72-76. *Mem:* Am Asn Path; Am Col Vet Path; Int Acad Path; Am Med Asn. *Mailing Add:* 67 Edgehill Rd New Haven CT 06511

CRONIN, ROBERT FRANCIS PATRICK, b London, Eng, Sept 1, 26; Can citizen; m 54; c 3. PHYSIOLOGY. *Educ:* McGill Univ, MD & CM, 53, MSc, 60; FRCP(C). *Prof Exp:* Lectr med, 59-64, asst prof med & physiol, 64-68, assoc prof med & assoc dean med fac, 68-72, dean, Med Fac, 72-77, PROF MED, MCGILL UNIV, 72- *Concurrent Pos:* Can Life Ins res fel, 59-62; consult cardiol, Can Dept Vet Affairs, 61-70; res assoc, Can Heart Found, 62-66. *Mem:* Fel Am Col Physicians; Can Soc Clin Invest; Can Physiol Soc; Am Physiol Soc. *Res:* Exercise physiology; physiology of the coronary circulation; myocardial metabolism. *Mailing Add:* Montreal Gen Hosp 1650 Cedar Ave Montreal PQ H3G 1A4 Can

CRONIN, THOMAS MARK, b Bronx, NY, July 20, 50; m 79. EARTH SCIENCES, PALEONTOLOGY. *Educ:* Colgate Univ, BA 72; Harvard Univ, MA, 74, PhD(geol), 77. *Prof Exp:* Res assoc, 77-78, GEOLOGIST, US GEOL SURV, 78- *Mem:* Paleont Soc Am; Sigma Xi; AAAS; Am Quaternary Asn; Soc Econ Paleontol Minerals. *Res:* Cenozoic ostracode and foraminifer biostratigraphy, paleoecology and taxonomy; quaternary paleooceanography and paleoclimatology. *Mailing Add:* Nat Ctr MS 971 US Geol Surv Reston VA 22092

CRONIN, THOMAS WELLS, b Baltimore, Md, May 19, 45; m 74; c 1. CRUSTACEAN VISUAL PHYSIOLOGY. *Educ:* Dickinson Col, BS, 67; Duke Univ, MA, 69, PhD(zool), 79. *Prof Exp:* Vol biol, US Peace Corp, 69-73; staff res biologist, 79-81, FEL BIOL, YALE UNIV, 81- *Mem:* AAAS; Am Soc Zoologists. *Res:* Visual and physiological adaptation of invertebrates, especially crustaceans and their larvae, to marine and other aquatic environments; eye structure; visual physiology; phototaxis; endogenous rhythms. *Mailing Add:* Dept Biol Yale Univ PO Box 6666 New Haven CT 06511

CRONIN, TIMOTHY H, b Boston, Mass, June 4, 39; m 63; c 2. ORGANIC CHEMISTRY. *Educ:* Boston Col, BS, 60; Mass Inst Technol, PhD(org chem), 64. *Prof Exp:* Res chemist, Chas Pfizer & Co, Inc, 65-70, proj leader, 70-71, mgr, 71-75, dir med chem, Infectious Dis, 75-81, DIR RES, AGR PROD RES & DEVELOP, PFIZER, INC, 81- *Mem:* Am Chem Soc. *Res:* Intramolecular Diels-Alder reactions; synthetic organic chemistry. *Mailing Add:* Pfizer Inc Eastern Point Rd Groton CT 06340

CRONK, ALFRED E(DWARD), b Hudson, Wis, July 1, 15; m 40; c 4. AERONAUTICAL ENGINEERING. *Educ:* Col St Thomas, BS, 37; Univ Minn, MS, 46. *Prof Exp:* From instr to assoc prof aeronaut eng, Univ Minn, 43-56; prof & head dept, 56-78, EMER PROF AERONAUT ENG, TEX A&M UNIV, 78- *Concurrent Pos:* Consult, Flui-Dyne Eng Corp, Gen Mills, Inc, Minneapolis Honeywell Regulator Co & Minn Mining & Mfg Co. *Mem:* Assoc fel Am Inst Aeronaut & Astronaut; Am Soc Eng Educ. *Res:* Stability and control of aircraft; experimental aerodynamics. *Mailing Add:* 727 N Rosemary Bryan TX 77801

CRONK, CASPAR, b West Newton, Mass, Apr 21, 35; m 60; c 3. EXPLORATION GEOPHYSICS, GEOLOGY. *Educ:* Harvard Univ, AB, 57; Ohio State Univ, PhD(geol), 68. *Prof Exp:* Glaciologist Antarctic res, Arctic Inst NAm, 57-59; res geophysicist explor processing & interpreting, Gulf Res & Develop Co, Gulf Oil Corp, 67-69, geophysicist, Gulf Oil Korea, 69-72, Houston Tech Serv Ctr, 72-73; asst prof geol geophys, Western Mich Univ, 73-78; SR GEOPHYSICIST, PHILLIPS PETROL CO, EUROPE/AFRICA, 78- *Mem:* AAAS; Soc Explor Geologists; Int Glaciol Soc; Am Geophys Union. *Res:* Gravity anomalies related to reef structures; gravity studies for gravel and ground water location and to delineate muck deposits; seismic studies for engineering; plate tectonics of the Indonesia area. *Mailing Add:* Phillips Petrol Co Europe/Africa Portland House Stag Pl London England

CRONK, CHRISTINE ELIZABETH, b Detroit, Mich, Oct 25, 44; m 68. PHYSICAL GROWTH. *Educ:* Western Mich Univ, BA, 66, MA, 75; Harvard Univ, MS, 77, ScD, 80. *Prof Exp:* Anthropologist, Children's Hosp Med Ctr, 72-80; RES ASSOC, FELS RES INST, 80- *Mem:* Human Biol Coun; Am Asn Phys Anthrop; Am Pub Health Asn. *Res:* Description and control of growth; natural history of body fatness; effects of malnutrition on fetal and postnatal growth; ultrasound measurement of fetal growth. *Mailing Add:* Fels Res Inst 800 Livermore St Yellow Springs OH 45387

CRONK, GARY ARNOLD, b Syracuse, NY, July 15, 14; m 39; c 3. PHARMACOLOGY. *Educ:* Syracuse Univ, BA, 36, MD, 39. *Prof Exp:* Assoc prof health & prev med, State Univ NY Upstate Med Ctr, 46-60; assoc med dir, Wallace Labs, Carter Prod, 60-61; dir clin res, 62-65, DIR RES PHARMACEUT, ORTHO PHARMACEUT CORP, 65-, VPRES, 66- *Mem:* Fel Am Col Physicians; AMA; Am Col Pharmacol & Chemother; NY Acad Sci. *Res:* Drug metabolism; clinical chemotherapy. *Mailing Add:* Ortho Pharmaceut Corp Raritan NJ 08869

CRONK, TED CLIFFORD, b Ridgway, Pa, May 25, 46. FOOD SCIENCE. *Educ:* Pa State Univ, BS, 68, MS, 71; Cornell Univ, PhD(food sci), 75. *Prof Exp:* Asst prof food & nutrit, Univ Ga, 74-75; sr scientist, 75-80, RES MGR, FROZEN FOODS DIV, PILLSBURY CO, 80- *Mem:* Mycol Soc Am; Inst Food Technologist. *Mailing Add:* Pillsbury Co 311 Second St SE Minneapolis MN 55414

CRONKHITE, LEONARD WOOLSEY, JR, b Newton, Mass, May 4, 19; c 4. MEDICINE. *Educ:* Bowdoin Col, BS, 41; Harvard Med Sch, MD, 50. *Hon Degrees:* LLD, Northeastern Univ, 70; LHD, Curry Col, 77; LLD, Bowdoin Col, 79. *Prof Exp:* Pres, Children's Hosp Med Ctr, 61-77; PRES, MED COL WIS, 77- *Concurrent Pos:* Trustee, Bowdoin Col, 73- *Mem:* Nat Inst Med-Nat Acad Sci; Asn Am Med Cols; Soc Med Adminr (pres, 70-71). *Mailing Add:* Med Col of Wis 8701 Watertown Plank Rd Milwaukee WI 53226

CRONKITE, DONALD LEE, b Denver, Colo, Dec 10, 44; m 68; c 2. CELL BIOLOGY, GENETICS. *Educ:* Ind Univ, AB, 66, PhD(zool), 72. *Prof Exp:* Asst prof, Univ Redlands, 72-78; asst prof, 78-81, PROF BIOL, HOPE COL, 81- *Concurrent Pos:* Exchange of Persons fel, Japan Soc Prom Sci, Tohoku Univ, 76. *Mem:* Genetics Soc Am; Am Soc Cell Biol. *Res:* Genetics of membrane function in paramecium; mechanism of mating in paramecium; cellular water regulation; ciliate-algal symbiosis. *Mailing Add:* Dept of Biol Hope Col Holland MI 49423

CRONKITE, EUGENE PITCHER, b Los Angeles, Calif, Dec 11, 14; m 40; c 1. MEDICINE. *Educ:* Stanford Univ, AB, 36, MD, 41. *Hon Degrees:* DSc, Univ Long Island, 62. *Prof Exp:* Intern, Stanford Univ Hosp, 40-41, asst resident, 41-42; hematologist, Naval Med Res Inst, 46-54; physician & chmn med dept, 67-79, HEMATOLOGIST, MED RES CTR, BROOKHAVEN NAT LAB, 54- *Concurrent Pos:* Mem, Naval Studies Bd, Nat Acad Sci; prof med & dean, Brookhaven Clin Campus, State Univ NY Stony Brook; hematologist, Atomic Bomb Tests, 46, 51-54. *Honors & Awards:* Wellcome Prize, 48; Alfred Benzon Prize, Govt Denmark; Ludwig Heilmeyer Gold Medal, Govt WGer, 74; Semmelweis Medal, Govt Hungary, 75. *Mem:* Am Asn Physicians; Am Soc Hemat; Soc Exp Biol & Med; Am Physiol Soc; Am Soc Clin Invest. *Res:* Control of hemopoiesis in health and disease. *Mailing Add:* Med Res Ctr Brookhaven Nat Lab Upton NY 11973

CRONKRIGHT, WALTER ALLYN, JR, b East Orange, NJ, July 23, 31; m 54; c 3. POLLUTION CHEMISTRY, ANALYTICAL CHEMISTRY. *Educ:* Rutgers Univ, BS, 52; Drexel Inst Technol, MS, 60; Polytech Inst Brooklyn, PhD(anal chem), 68. *Prof Exp:* Anal chemist, M W Kellogg Co, Lab, Pullman Inc, 59-61, res chemist, 61-65, supvr, 65-68, sect head, Pullman-Kellogg Div, Pullman Inc, 68-71, MGR ANAL SERVS, PULLMAN-KELLOGG DIV, PULLMAN INC, 71- *Mem:* Am Chem Soc; Am Soc Test & Mat; Sigma Xi. *Res:* Development of improved processes for removal of SO2 from waste gases; standardization of analytical methods for atmospheric pollutants. *Mailing Add:* Pullman-Kellogg Res & Develop Ctr Industrial Park Ten Houston TX 77084

CRONQUIST, ARTHUR JOHN, b San Jose, Calif, Mar 19, 19; m 40; c 2. SYSTEMATIC BOTANY. *Educ:* Utah State Col, BS, 38, MS, 40; Univ Minn, PhD(bot), 44. *Prof Exp:* Tech asst, NY Bot Garden, 43-44, asst cur, 44-46; asst prof bot, Univ Ga, 46-48; asst prof, State Col Wash, 48-51; assoc cur, 52-57, cur, 57-65, sr cur, 65-71, dir bot, 71-74, SR SCIENTIST, NEW YORK BOT GARDEN, 74- *Concurrent Pos:* Tech consult, Econ Co-op Admin, Brussels, 51-52; adj prof, Columbia Univ, 64- & Lehman Col, City Univ New York, 69-; ed, Bot Rev, 69- *Mem:* Am Soc Plant Taxon (pres, 62); Bot Soc Am (pres, 73); Asn Trop Biol; Ecol Soc Am; Torrey Bot Club (pres, 76). *Res:* Taxonomy of American species of Compositae; flora of temperate North America; systems of angiosperms; general system of plants. *Mailing Add:* New York Bot Garden Bronx NY 10458

CRONSHAW, JAMES, b Oswaldtwistle, Eng, Mar 11, 33; m 56; c 1. CELL BIOLOGY, PLANT PHYSIOLOGY. *Educ:* Univ Leeds, BSc, 54, PhD(bot), 57, DSc, 73. *Prof Exp:* Res officer, Commonwealth Sci & Indust Res Orgn, Australia, 57-62; asst prof biol, Yale Univ, 62-65; assoc prof, 65-70, PROF BIOL, UNIV CALIF, SANTA BARBARA, 70- *Mem:* Fel AAAS; Bot Soc Am; Electron Micros Soc Am; Am Soc Cell Biol; fel Royal Micros Soc. *Res:* Electron microscopy of phloem and xylem cells; structure and function of the avian adrenal gland; effects of petroleum on marine birds; endocrinology. *Mailing Add:* Dept Biol Sci Univ Calif Santa Barbara CA 93106

CRONSON, HARRY MARVIN, b Providence, RI, May 31, 37; m 62; c 2. ELECTRICAL ENGINEERING. *Educ:* Brown Univ, ScB, 59, ScM, 61, PhD(elec eng), 63. *Prof Exp:* Corinna Borden Keen fel from Brown Univ, Oxford Univ, 63-64; asst prof electrophys, Grad Ctr, Polytech Inst Brooklyn, 64-66; staff scientist, Avco Space Systs Div, 66-67, sr staff scientist, 67-68; sr scientist, Ikor, Inc, 68-71; MEM TECH STAFF, SPERRY RES CTR, 71- *Concurrent Pos:* NSF res grant, 65-66. *Mem:* Inst Elec & Electronics Engrs. *Res:* Microwave and millimeter wave metrology; subnanosecond pulse technology. *Mailing Add:* Sperry Res Ctr 100 North Rd Sudbury MA 01776

CRONVICH, JAMES A(NTHONY), b New Orleans, La, Oct 26, 14; m 51; c 5. ELECTRICAL ENGINEERING. *Educ:* Tulane Univ, BE, 35, MS, 37; Mass Inst Technol, SM(elec eng), 38. *Prof Exp:* Instr elec eng, Tulane Univ, 38-41; from asst to assoc elec engr, Panama Canal, 41-42; from asst prof to assoc prof elec eng, 42-49, assoc prof biophysics, Dept Med, 46-49, PROF ELEC ENG & BIOMED ENG, TULANE UNIV, 49-, HEAD DEPT ELEC

ENG, 56- *Concurrent Pos:* Asst ed, Am Heart J, 78- *Mem:* Fel Inst Elec & Electronics Engrs; Am Soc Eng Educ. *Res:* Bioengineering in cardiovascular studies; electrical measurements. *Mailing Add:* 101 Colonial Club Dr Harahan LA 70118

CRONVICH, LESTER LOUIS, b New Orleans, La, Aug 21, 16; m 45; c 1. AERODYNAMICS, FLUID MECHANICS. *Educ:* Tulane Univ, BEng, 36, MS, 38; Univ Wis, PhD(appl math), 42. *Prof Exp:* Instr math, Northwestern Univ, 41-42; stress analyst aircraft struct, McDonnell Aircraft Corp, 42-45; asst proj supvr aerodyn, 51-55, proj supvr, 55-57, asst group supvr, 57-58, MATHEMATICIAN, APPL PHYSICS LAB, JOHNS HOPKINS UNIV, 45-, GROUP SUPVR, 58-, ASST DIV SUPVR AERONAUT, 74-. *Concurrent Pos:* Mem, Navy Aeroballistics Comt, 58-, Am Inst Aeronaut & Astronaut Tech Comt on Atmospheric Flight Mech, 67-70, Publ Comt, 71-74 & NASA Res & Technol Adv Coun Comt on Aerodyn & Configurations, 77. *Mem:* Am Inst Aeronaut & Astronaut. *Res:* Stability and control in aerodynamics. *Mailing Add:* Appl Physics Lab Johns Hopkins Rd Laurel MD 20810

CRONYN, MARSHALL WILLIAM, b Oakland, Calif, June 22, 19; m 42; c 3. ORGANIC CHEMISTRY. *Educ:* Reed Col, BA, 40; Univ Mich, PhD(org chem), 44. *Prof Exp:* Res assoc comt med res, Univ Mich, 44-46; lectr & Am Chem Soc fel, Univ Calif, 46-48, from instr to asst prof org chem, 48-52; from asst prof to assoc prof, 52-60, chmn dept, 66-73, PROF ORG CHEM, REED COL, 60- *Concurrent Pos:* NIH res fel, Cambridge Univ, 60-61; consult, USPHS, 61-66. *Mem:* AAAS; Am Chem Soc. *Res:* Organic sulfur chemistry; lignin; chemotherapy. *Mailing Add:* Dept of Chem Reed Col Portland OR 97202

CROOK, JAMES RICHARD, b Ft Worth, Tex, Dec 20, 35; m 69. INFECTIOUS DISEASE, EPIDEMIOLOGY. *Educ:* Univ Utah, BS, 58, MS, 59, PhD(parasitol & infectious dis), 64; Univ Med Sci, Bangkok, DTM & Sch Trop Med, UK, DSc, 67; Am Bd Path, dipl, 50; Med Res Prog, Manila, P.I., dipl epidemiol. *Prof Exp:* Crew chief, Glen Canyon Ecol Res, Utah, 58; res path res asst tumor res, 60-61, NSF grant & res asst parasitol, 61-64; res parasitologist, Walter Reed Inst Res, 64-65; chief med zool div, Med Res Lab, SEATO & vis prof Fac Trop Med, Univ Med Sci, Bangkok, 65-67; mem staff, Linfield Col, 67-69, prof biol, 70-75; lectr microbiol & immunol, Univ Ore Med Sch, 73-75; dir, Off of Allied Health Sci, Navajo Health Authority, Navajo Nation, 75; PROF MED SCI & CHMN DEPT, INFECTIOUS DIS & PATH, WASH, ALASKA, MONT & IDAHO MED EDUC PROG, UNIV ALASKA, 76- *Concurrent Pos:* Consult, Upper Mekong River Med Eval Bd, WHO & Org Am States. *Mem:* AAAS; Am Soc Parasitol; Int Col Trop Med; Royal Soc Trop Med & Hyg; Am Soc Trop Med & Hyg. *Res:* Endoparasite life cycles and natural ecology and pathology. *Mailing Add:* WAMI Med Educ Prog Univ of Alaska Fairbanks AK 99701

CROOK, JAMES WASHINGTON, b Baltimore, Md, July 23, 20; m 46; c 5. PHARMACOLOGY. *Educ:* Loyola Col, BA, 43; Univ Md, BS, 49. *Prof Exp:* Aircraft assemblyman, Glenn L Martin Co, 46; technician med biol, 50, RES PHARMACOLOGIST, EDGEWOOD ARSENAL, 51- *Res:* Chemical warfare; vapor toxicology; respiration; pharmacology of toxic agents; prophylaxis and treatment of casualties; research and development on new drugs and protective devices; air pollution. *Mailing Add:* 6005 Eastern Parkway Baltimore MD 21206

CROOK, JOSEPH RAYMOND, b Reno, Nev, Oct 16, 36; m 58; c 2. INORGANIC CHEMISTRY. *Educ:* Univ Nev, BS, 58; Ill Inst Technol, PhD(chem), 63. *Prof Exp:* NSF fel, Univ Colo, 63-64; asst prof inorg chem, San Jose State Col, 64-66; from asst to assoc prof chem, Cleveland State Univ, 66-70; ASSOC PROF CHEM, WESTERN WASH STATE UNIV, 70- *Mem:* Am Chem Soc. *Res:* Synthetic and mechanistic chemistry of transition elements. *Mailing Add:* Dept of Chem Western Wash State Univ Bellingham WA 98225

CROOK, PHILIP GEORGE, b Washington, DC, Oct 21, 25. MICROBIOLOGY. *Educ:* Univ Md, BS, 49; Univ NMex, MS, 51; Pa State Univ, PhD(bact), 55. *Prof Exp:* Asst instr bact, Pa State Univ, 53-55; assoc prof biol, Hope Col, 55-69, chmn dept, 62-69; CHAS A DANA PROF BIOL, COLGATE UNIV, 69- *Concurrent Pos:* NSF grant, Am Cancer Soc grant & Nat Cancer Inst grant, Hope Col, 58-60. *Mem:* AAAS; Am Soc Parasitol; Am Soc Microbiol; Soc Protozool. *Res:* Intermediate metabolism of carbohydrates in bacteria and protozoa; axenic culture of protozoa; biochemical action of hormones. *Mailing Add:* Dept of Biol Colgate Univ Hamilton NY 13346

CROOKE, PHILIP SCHUYLER, b Summit, NJ, Mar 10, 44; m 68. APPLIED MATHEMATICS. *Educ:* Stevens Inst Technol, BS, 66; Cornell Univ, PhD(applied math), 70. *Prof Exp:* Asst prof, 70-76, ASSOC PROF MATH, VANDERBILT UNIV, 76- *Mem:* Soc Indust & Appl Math. *Res:* Partial differential equations; isoperimetric inequalities; dusty gas equations; mathematically modelling of fermentation processes. *Mailing Add:* Box 6205 Sta B Vanderbilt Univ Nashville TN 37235

CROOKER, NANCY USS, b Chicago, Ill, Apr 1, 44. SPACE PHYSICS. *Educ:* Knox Col, Ill, AB, 66; Univ Calif, Los Angeles, MS, 68, PhD(meteorol), 72. *Prof Exp:* Engr scientist atmospheric sci, McDonnell Douglas Astronaut Co, 69; res assoc space physics, Cornell Univ, 73 & Mass Inst Technol, 73-75; assst res meteorologist, 75-80, RES ASSOC SPACE PHYSICS, UNIV CALIF, LOS ANGELES, 80- *Concurrent Pos:* Consult, Physics Dept, Boston Univ, 75- *Mem:* Am Geophys Union. *Res:* The coupling of the solar wind and the earth's magnetosphere. *Mailing Add:* Dept of Atmospheric Sci Univ of Calif Los Angeles CA 90024

CROOKER, PETER PEIRCE, b Westerly, RI, Apr 4, 37; m 67; c 2. OPTICAL PHYSICS. *Educ:* Ore State Univ, BS, 59; Naval Postgrad Sch, PhD(physics), 67. *Prof Exp:* Proj officer, David Taylor Model Basin, 59-60; instr physics, Naval Postgrad Sch, 60-67; fel, Lincoln Lab, Mass Inst Technol, 68-70; asst prof physics, Calif State Polytech Col, 70; asst prof, 70-76, ASSOC PROF PHYSICS, UNIV HAWAII, 76- *Mem:* Am Phys Soc. *Res:* Electron paramagnetic resonance; acoustic paramagnetic resonance; raman spectroscopy; Rayleigh and Brillouin spectroscopy in liquid crystals; structures and phase transitions of liquid crystals. *Mailing Add:* Dept of Physics & Astron Univ of Hawaii Honolulu HI 96822

CROOKS, GEORGE CHAPMAN, b North Brookfield, Mass, Jan 21, 05; m 34; c 2. PHYSIOLOGICAL CHEMISTRY. *Educ:* Amherst Col, AB, 28; Mass State Col, PhD(biochem), 37. *Prof Exp:* Asst chem, Mass State Col, 28-30; instr, 30-35, 36-39; asst prof, 39-40, 46-48; assoc prof, 48-50, 52-69, PROF CHEM, UNIV VT, 69- *Concurrent Pos:* Consult, Univ Vt, 71- *Mem:* Am Chem Soc. *Res:* Blood proteins; chemical and nutritive studies on fish muscle; carotene studies in blood, milk and plant materials. *Mailing Add:* Cook Phys Sci Hall Univ Vt Burlington VT 05405

CROOKS, MICHAEL JOHN CHAMBERLAIN, b Victoria, BC, Oct 25, 30; m 59; c 3. LOW TEMPERATURE PHYSICS. *Educ:* Reed Col, BA, 53; Univ BC, MA, 57; Yale Univ, PhD(physics), 63. *Prof Exp:* Res assoc physics, Duke Univ, 62-63; asst prof, 63-72, ASSOC PROF PHYSICS, UNIV BC, 72- *Concurrent Pos:* Sr vis res fel, Univ of Sussex, Eng, 71-72 & 80-81. *Mem:* Am Phys Soc; Am Asn Physics Teachers; Can Asn Physicists. *Res:* Properties of liquid and solid states of helium-three and helium-four; critical phenomena in super fluid helium. *Mailing Add:* Dept of Physics Univ of BC Vancouver BC V6T 1W5 Can

CROOKSHANK, HERMAN ROBERT, b Linneus, Mo, June 7, 16; m 45. CLINICAL CHEMISTRY. *Educ:* Northeast Mo State Teachers Col, BS, 38; Univ Iowa, MS, 40, PhD(biochem), 42. *Prof Exp:* Asst biochem, Univ Iowa, 38-42; instr, Med Col, Univ Ala, 46-49; asst secy, Am Inst Biol Sci, Washington, DC, 49; animal nutritionist, Animal Husb Res Div, USDA, 49-70, res chemist, Sci & Educ Admin, 70-79; RETIRED. *Concurrent Pos:* Assoc prof animal husb, Tex Technol Col, 54-59; asst exec secy, Div Biol & Agr, Nat Res Coun, 49-; dipl, Am Bd Nutrit & Am Bd Clin Chem. *Mem:* Am Chem Soc; fel Am Inst Chem; Am Soc Animal Sci. *Res:* Grass tetany and urinary caluli; pesticide residues in livestock; physiological and biochemical interactions of mineral in livestock. *Mailing Add:* 3812 Plainsman Lane Bryan TX 77801

CROOKSTON, J(AMES) A(DAMSON), b Benld, Ill, Dec 8, 19; m 42; c 2. CERAMIC ENGINEERING. *Educ:* Mo Sch Mines, BS, 42, MS, 47; Univ Ill, PhD, 49. *Prof Exp:* Ceramic res engr, A C Spark Plug Div, 42-44; ceramic res engr, Harbison-Walker Refractories Co, 49-51, lab mgr, 51-54, asst to dir res, 54-55; from mgr new prod develop to res dir, A P Green Fire Brick Co, 55-61; DIR RES, A P GREEN REFRACTORIES CO, 61-, V PRES RES, 66- *Mem:* Am Ceramic Soc; Nat Inst Ceramic Engrs; Sigma Xi. *Res:* Refractories; clay; base exchange phenomena. *Mailing Add:* 2 Country Club Mexico MO 65265

CROOKSTON, JOHN HAMILL, b Fernie, BC, July 30, 22; m 57; c 2. HEMATOLOGY. *Educ:* Univ Toronto, MD, 47, BSc, 48; Cambridge Univ, PhD(biol), 54; FRCP(C), 68. *Prof Exp:* PROF MED & PATH, FAC MED, UNIV TORONTO, 68-; HEMATOLOGIST-IN-CHIEF, TORONTO GEN HOSP, 70- *Mem:* Am Soc Hemat; Int Soc Blood Transfusion. *Res:* Clinical and laboratory hematology, especially hereditary and acquired hemolytic anemias. *Mailing Add:* Dept Hematol Toronto Gen Hosp Toronto ON M5S 1L7 Can

CROOKSTON, MARIE CUTBUSH, b Dean, Victoria, Australia, Aug 15, 20; m 57; c 2. IMMUNOHEMATOLOGY. *Educ:* Univ Melbourne, BSc, 40. *Prof Exp:* Head lab clin path, St Andrew's Hosp, 41-46; res scientist, Blood Transfusion Res Unit, Med Res Coun, Eng, 47-57; res assoc immunohemat, 64-78, ASSOC PROF PATH, UNIV TORONTO, 78- *Concurrent Pos:* Nuffield grant, India, 52. *Mem:* Am Soc Human Genetics; Can Soc Immunol; Brit Soc Immunol; Int Soc Blood Transfusion. *Res:* Hemolytic disease of the newborn; Duffy blood group system; survival of red cells after low temperature storage; effect of incompatible antibodies on red cell survival; blood-group chimeras; blood-group antigens in plasma; specificity and behavior of auto-antibodies. *Mailing Add:* Dept Path Univ Toronto Toronto Gen Hosp Toronto ON M5G 1L7 Can

CROOKSTON, REID B, b Pittsburgh, Pa, Mar 21, 39; m 66; c 2. CHEMICAL & PETROLEUM ENGINEERING. *Educ:* Univ Pittsburgh, BS, 61; Carnegie-Mellon Univ, MS, 63, PhD(chem eng), 66. *Prof Exp:* Res engr, 66-68, sr res engr, 68-73, dir enhanced recovery processes, 73-81, TECH CONSULT, GULF SCI & TECHNOL CO, 81- *Concurrent Pos:* Instr, Univ Pittsburgh, 77-80. *Mem:* Soc Petrol Engrs; Sigma Xi. *Res:* Chemical reactor engineering; mathematical modeling; optimization; process development; reservoir simulation; enhanced oil recovery processes. *Mailing Add:* Gulf Sci & Develop Co PO Drawer 2038 Pittsburgh PA 15230

CROOM, FREDERICK HAILEY, b Lumberton, NC, Aug 6, 41; m 63; c 2. MATHEMATICS. *Educ:* Univ NC, BS, 63, PhD(math), 67. *Prof Exp:* Asst prof math, Univ Ky, 67-71; from asst prof to assoc prof, 71-81, PROF MATH, UNIV OF THE SOUTH, 81- *Concurrent Pos:* Vis scholar, Vanderbilt Univ, 81. *Mem:* Am Math Soc; Math Asn Am; Sigma Xi. *Res:* Algebraic topology; point set topology. *Mailing Add:* Dept of Math Univ of the South Sewanee TN 37375

CROOM, HENRIETTA BROWN, b Burlington, NC, Sept 23, 40; m 63; c 2. BIOCHEMISTRY. *Educ:* Univ NC, AB, 62, PhD(biochem), 68. *Prof Exp:* Res assoc anat, Univ Ky, 69-70; asst prof, 72-81, ASSOC PROF BIOL, UNIV OF THE SOUTH, 81- *Concurrent Pos:* Vis prof, Dept Microbiol, La State Univ, 77-78; vis scholar, Dept Molecular Biol, Vanderbilt Univ, 81-82. *Mem:* Sigma Xi. *Res:* The effects of low-frequency electromagnetic fields on the mitotic cycle of Physarum polycephalum; interaction between guanine nucleotides and tubulin from bovine brain. *Mailing Add:* Box 1247 SPO Univ of the South Sewanee TN 37375

CROOM, HERMAN LEE, b Wilmington, NC, Nov 21, 09; m 35; c 1. SCIENCE ADMINISTRATION, METEOROLOGY. *Educ:* NY Univ, BS, 50; Am Univ, MA, 55. *Prof Exp:* Meteorologist, US Weather Bur, 36-53; res adminr phys sci, US Govt, 53-70; consult, 70-74; RETIRED. *Honors & Awards:* Sustained Outstanding Performance Award, US Govt, 59, Merit Award, 70. *Mem:* Am Meteorol Soc. *Res:* Physical sciences; synoptic meteorology and weather forecasting; upper air and space physica. *Mailing Add:* 1996 NW Fork Rd Stuart FL 33494

CROPP, FREDERICK WILLIAM, III, b Wheeling, WVa, Dec 9, 32; m 55. GEOLOGY, PALYNOLOGY. *Educ:* Col Wooster, BA, 54; Univ Ill, MS, 56, PhD(geol), 58. *Prof Exp:* Asst, Univ Ill, 54-58, from instr to asst prof geol, 58-64; assoc prof & assoc dean, 64-68, dean & vpres acad affairs, 68-77, PROF GEOL, COL WOOSTER, 68- *Concurrent Pos:* Ellis L Phillips Found intern acad admin, 62-63. *Mem:* Geol Soc Am; Soc Econ Paleontologists & Mineralogists; Nat Asn Geol Teachers; Am Asn Petrol Geol. *Res:* Use of Pennsylvania spores for stratigraphic purposes; geology of Ohio State Parks. *Mailing Add:* Dept of Geol Col of Wooster Wooster OH 44691

CROPP, GERD J A, b Delmenhorst, WGer, July 2, 30; US citizen; m 57; c 3. PHYSIOLOGY, PEDIATRICS. *Educ:* Univ Western Ont, MD, 58, PhD(biophys), 65. *Prof Exp:* From asst prof to assoc prof, Sch Med, Univ Colo, 65-72, assoc clin prof pediat, Sch Med, 72-76; PROF PEDIAT, STATE UNIV NY BUFFALO & DIR, CHILDREN'S LUNG & CYSTIC FIBROSIS CTR, CHILDREN'S HOSP, BUFFALO, 76- *Concurrent Pos:* Dir, Dept Clin Physiol, Nat Asthma Ctr, Denver, Colo, 72-76. *Mem:* Soc Pediat Res; Am Physiol Soc. *Res:* Pathophysiology of anemia; control of respiration; exercise; pathophysiology of asthma; pathophysiology of cystic fibrosis; pulmonary disease. *Mailing Add:* Children's Lung Ctr Children's Hosp 219 Bryant St Buffalo NY 14222

CROPPER, WALTER V, b Xenia, Ohio, July 31, 17; m 41, 55; c 5. INSTRUMENTATION, RESEARCH ADMINISTRATION. *Educ:* Ky Wesleyan Col, BS, 38; Univ Ky, MS, 40. *Prof Exp:* Materials engr, State Hwy Dept, Ky, 38-39; res engr, Servel, Inc, 40-42; chemist, Stand Oil Co, Ind, 42-46, group leader, 46-52, asst chief chemist, 52-53, chief chemist, 54-60; gen mgr, Precision Sci Develop Co, 60-65, vpres, 65-69; consult, 69-70; SPEC ASST TO PRES, AM SOC TESTING & MAT, 70-; PRES, CABELL GROUP, 79- *Mem:* Instrument Soc Am; Am Soc Testing & Mat; Am Chem Soc. *Res:* Catalyzed photochemical reactions; corrosion in saline systems; petroleum technology; quality sensitive processing monitors; instrument development; energy conservation; solar heating and cooling; biomass conversion processes; analysis of new technological developments regarding impact on productivity, foreign competition, and international trade; strategic planning for medium-sized firms concerning product innovation, quality control, and government regulation. *Mailing Add:* Am Soc Test & Mat 1916 Race St Philadelphia PA 19103

CROPPER, WENDELL PARKER, b Gary, Ind, June 22, 51. ECOLOGY. *Educ:* Cornell Col, Iowa, BA, 73; Emory Univ, Georgia, MS, 77, PhD(biol), 80. *Prof Exp:* Res asst, Emory Univ, 74-77, teaching asst, 77-80, asst prof biol & environ sci, 81; RES ASSOC, SCH FOREST RESOURCES & CONSERV, UNIV FLA, 81- *Mem:* Ecol Soc Am; Asn Southeastern Biologists; AAAS; Am Inst Biol Sci. *Res:* Lead uptake and translocation in an urban tree species; carbon cycling below ground in managed forest ecosystems and on a computer model of carbon cyclying in forests; analysis of the stability of ecosystem models of nutrient cycling. *Mailing Add:* Sch Forest Resources & Conserv Univ Fla Gainesville FL 32611

CROSBIE, EDWIN ALEXANDER, b Washington, Pa, July 23, 21; m 46; c 2. PHYSICS. *Educ:* Washington & Jefferson Col, BA, 42, MA, 48; Univ Pittsburgh, PhD(physics), 51. *Prof Exp:* ASSOC PHYSICIST, ARGONNE NAT LAB, 52- *Mem:* Am Phys Soc. *Res:* Theoretical nuclear physics; high energy particle physics, particle accelerators; field theory. *Mailing Add:* Argonne Nat Lab 360 9700 S Cass Ave Argonne IL 60439

CROSBY, ALAN HUBERT, b Columbia, Pa, Oct 17, 22; m 53; c 3. ORGANIC CHEMISTRY. *Educ:* Ursinus Col, BS, 43; Univ Va, MS, 50, PhD, 51. *Prof Exp:* From asst prof to prof chem, Northwestern State Col La, 50-69, head dept phys sci, 57-69; PROF CHEM, DEPT CHEM & PHYSICS, LOCK HAVEN STATE COL, 69- *Mem:* Am Chem Soc. *Res:* Chemistry of quinones. *Mailing Add:* Dept of Chem & Physics Lock Haven State Col Lock Haven PA 17745

CROSBY, DAVID S, b St George, Utah, June 4, 38; m 62; c 1. APPLIED STATISTICS, MATHEMATICAL STATISTICS. *Educ:* Am Univ, BA, 62; Univ Ariz, MA, 64, PhD(math), 66. *Prof Exp:* Mathematician, Harry Diamond Labs, 62-64; asst prof math & statist, 66-75, chmn dept, 75-77, PROF MATH, STATIST & COMPUT SCI, AM UNIV, 75- *Concurrent Pos:* Statist consult, Nat Environ Satellite Ctr, 68- *Mem:* Math Asn Am; Inst Math Statist; Am Statist Asn. *Res:* Multidimensional probability distributions; statistical problems of inversion techniques. *Mailing Add:* Dept of Math & Statist Am Univ Massachusetts & Nebraska Ave Washington DC 20016

CROSBY, DONALD GIBSON, b Portland, Ore, Sept 11, 28; m 53; c 2. ENVIRONMENTAL CHEMISTRY, PESTICIDE CHEMISTRY. *Educ:* Pomona Col, BA, 50; Calif Inst Technol, PhD(chem), 54. *Prof Exp:* Chemist, Union Carbide Chem Co, 54-55, group leader biol chem, 56-61; assoc toxicologist, Exp Sta, 61-62, toxicologist & lectr food sci & technol, 62-69, chmn, Agr Toxicol & Residue Res Lab, 62-66 & Regional Res Proj W-45, 68-70, PROF ENVIRON TOXICOL, UNIV CALIF, DAVIS, 69-, TOXICOLOGIST, EXP STA, 63- *Concurrent Pos:* mem comn pesticide chem, Inst Union Pure Appl Chem, 74-; mem mat hazard adv comt, Environ Protection Agency, 75-79; assoc ed, J Agr Food Chem, 79- *Mem:* Fel AAAS; fel Am Chem Soc; Oceanic Soc. *Res:* Chemistry of natural products; nutritional and food chemistry; pesticide chemistry and metabolism; chemical ecology; environmental chemistry; marine environment toxicology. *Mailing Add:* Dept of Environ Toxicol Univ of Calif Davis CA 95616

CROSBY, EMORY SPEAR, b Georgetown, SC, Jan 17, 28; m 53; c 2. FOREST PATHOLOGY, PLANT PHYSIOLOGY. *Educ:* Western Ky Univ, BS, 60, MA, 61; Clemson Univ, PhD(plant path), 65. *Prof Exp:* Assoc prof biol, Armstrong State Col, 66-68; assoc prof, 68-80, PROF BIOL, THE CITADEL, 80- *Res:* Fungus morphology and physiology. *Mailing Add:* Dept of Biol The Citadel Charleston SC 29409

CROSBY, GARY WAYNE, b Vidor, Tex, June 13, 31; m 56; c 4. STRUCTURAL GEOLOGY, GEOPHYSICS. *Educ:* Brigham Young Univ, BS, 58, MS, 59; Columbia Univ, PhD(struct geol, geophys), 63. *Prof Exp:* Res geophysicist, Atlantic Richfield Co, 62-65; asst prof struct geol & geophys, ETex State Univ, 65-66; prof geophys, Univ Mont, 66-74; MGR GEOPHYS BR, PHILLIPS PETROL CO, 74- *Mem:* Geol Soc Am; Am Geophys Union; Am Asn Petrol Geol; Soc Explor Geophys. *Res:* Gravity and magnetic interpretation; exploration seismology; mechanical principles of rock deformation. *Mailing Add:* Phillips Petrol Co 71-C PRC Bartlesville OK 74004

CROSBY, GAYLE MARCELLA, b Battle Creek, Mich. DEVELOPMENTAL BIOLOGY. *Educ:* Albion Col, BA, 55; Univ Mich, MS, 57; Brandeis Univ, PhD(develop biol), 67. *Prof Exp:* Asst prof biol, St Mary's Col, 69-73; res asst anat, Univ Wis, 73-75; ASST PROF ANAT, HOWARD UNIV, 75- *Mem:* Soc Develop Biol. *Res:* Determination and analysis of the morphogenetic factors responsible for normal development of the vertebrate limb. *Mailing Add:* 4614 Nottingham Dr Chevy Chase MD 20015

CROSBY, GLENN ARTHUR, b Hempfield Township, Pa, July 30, 28; m 50; c 3. PHYSICAL CHEMISTRY. *Educ:* Waynesburg Col, BS, 50; Univ Wash, PhD(phys chem), 54. *Prof Exp:* Res assoc chem, Fla State Univ, 55-57, vis asst prof physics, 57; from asst prof to assoc prof chem, Univ NMex, 57-67; PROF CHEM & CHEM PHYSICS, WASH STATE UNIV, 67-, CHMN CHEM PHYSICS PROG, 77- *Concurrent Pos:* Fulbright lectr, Univ Tübingen, WGer, 64; vis prof physics, Univ Canterbury, Christchurch, NZ, 74; consult, Indust & Govt Agencies; vis prof phys chem, Univ Hohenheim, WGer, 78-79; mem, Res Corp Cottrell Progs Adv Bd, 81- *Mem:* Fel AAAS; Am Chem Soc (chmn, Div Chem Educ, 82); Am Phys Soc. *Res:* Perturbations of ions and molecules by chemical environments; luminescence of transition-metal and rare-earth complexes; optical, magnetic and electrical properties of complexes and solids with extended interactions; design of electro-optical materials. *Mailing Add:* Dept of Chem Wash State Univ Pullman WA 99164

CROSBY, GUY ALEXANDER, b Beverly, Mass, June 10, 42; m 66; c 2. SYNTHETIC ORGANIC CHEMISTRY. *Educ:* Univ NH, ScB, 64; Brown Univ, PhD(chem), 69. *Prof Exp:* Fel chem, Stanford Univ, 69-70; res scientist, Alza Corp, 70-72; dir chem synthesis, Dynapol Corp, 72-80; DIR ORGANIC CHEM, FMC CORP AGR CHEM GROUP, 80- *Concurrent Pos:* Prin scientist, Nat Inst Dent Res Contract, 76-79; consult asst prof, Stanford Univ, 75-78. *Mem:* Am Chem Soc; The Chem Soc; AAAS. *Res:* Chemistry of taste; new synthetic sweeteners; polymeric reagents; natural products; food chemistry; agricultural chemistry. *Mailing Add:* FMC Corp-Agr Chem Group Box 8 Princeton NJ 08540

CROSBY, LON OWEN, b Webster City, Iowa, Aug 6, 45; m 67; c 2. NUTRITION, NUTRITIONAL BIOCHEMISTRY. *Educ:* Iowa State Univ, BS, 67; Purdue Univ, PhD(nutrit), 71. *Prof Exp:* Res assoc biochem nutrit, Cornell Univ, 71-73; head monogastric nutrit, Syntex Corp, 73-75; sr prog scientist nutrit, Enviro Control, Inc, 75-79; RES ASST PROF NUTRIT & EXEC DIR, CLIN NUTRIT CTR, UNIV PA, 79- *Concurrent Pos:* Asst ed, Nutrit & Cancer: An Int J; consult, Philadelphia Vet Admin Med Ctr; adminr, Nutrit Support Serv, Univ Pa Hosp, 79- *Mem:* Am Col Nutrit; Am Soc Parenteral & Enteral Nutrit; Am Chem Soc; AAAS; Inst Food Technologists. *Res:* Interrelationship between diet, nutrition and cancer, including nutritional and biochemical interactions and the use of nutrition in disease prevention and treatment. *Mailing Add:* 13814 Drake Dr Rockville MD 20853

CROSBY, ROBERT H(OWELL), JR, b Picayune, Miss, Oct 5, 20; m 44; c 4. CHEMICAL ENGINEERING. *Educ:* Mass Inst Technol, BS, 42. *Prof Exp:* Chemist, 39-41, chem engr, 45-46, plant mgr & vpres, 46-52, pres, 52-80, CHIEF EXEC OFFICER, CROSBY CHEM, INC, 80- *Mem:* Am Inst Chem Engrs; Am Chem Soc. *Res:* Tall oil distillation for high grade fatty acids and rosin acids; resins and paper sizes. *Mailing Add:* Crosby Chem Inc Box 32 De Ridder LA 70634

CROSBY, WARREN MELVILLE, b Topeka, Kans, Mar 19, 31; m 54; c 1. OBSTETRICS & GYNECOLOGY. *Educ:* Washburn Univ, Topeka, BS, 53; Univ Kans, MD, 57; Am Bd Obstet & Gynec, dipl, 65. *Prof Exp:* Intern, St Luke's Hosp, Kansas City, Mo, 57-58; resident obstet & gynec, Univ Calif, San Francisco, 58-62; from instr to assoc prof, 62-70, PROF OBSTET & GYNEC & VCHMN DEPT, UNIV OKLA, 70- *Mem:* AMA; fel Am Asn Obstet & Gynec; Soc Gynec Invest; fel Am Col Obstet & Gynec; Cent Asn Obstet & Gynec. *Res:* Erythroblastosis Fetalis; intrauterine fetal transfusion; studies of impact and decompression in pregnant women and animals; fetal malnutrition. *Mailing Add:* Dept of Gynec & Obstet Univ of Okla Oklahoma City OK 73104

CROSBY, WILLIAM HOLMES, JR, b Wheeling, WVa, Dec 1, 14; m 40, 59; c 7. HEMATOLOGY. *Educ:* Univ Pa, AB, 36, MD, 40. *Prof Exp:* Intern, Walter Reed Gen Hosp, US Army, 40-41, instr, Off Cand Sch, Med Field Serv, 41-43, 45-46, regimental surgeon, 85th Infantry Div, Italy, 43-45, resident internal med, Brooke Gen Hosp, 46-48, res fel hematol, Pratt Diagnostic Hosp, 49-50, med specialist, Queen Alexandria Mil Hosp, London, 50-51, chief dept hematol, Walter Reed Army Inst Res, 51-65; chief hemat, dir blood res & sr physician, NEng Med Ctr Hosps & prof med, Sch Med, Tufts Univ, 65-72; head, Div Hemat & Oncol & dir, L C Jacobson Blood Ctr, Scripps Clin & Res Found, 72-79; CHIEF, DEPT HEMAT, WALTER REED ARMY INST RES, 79-; PROF MED, UNIFORMED SERV UNIV,

81- *Concurrent Pos:* Dir surg res team, Korea, 52-53; chief hematol serv, Walter Reed Gen Hosp, 53-65; cancer chemother prog, 60-65, dir div med, 59-65; spec lectr hemat, Dept Med, George Washington Univ, 53-65; consult, Surgeon Gen, US Army, Vet Admin Hosp, La Jolla, El Centro Hosp & San Diego Naval Hosp; mem med adv comt, Blood Res Found; mem hematol test comt, Am Bd Internal Med, 70-76; mem res advy comt, Nat Hemophilia Found, 71-; adj prof med, Univ Calif, San Diego, 72-; clin prof med, George Washington Univ, 80- *Honors & Awards:* Order of Carlos J Finlay, Cuba, 55; Stitt Award, 64; McCollum Award, 70. *Mem:* Am Soc Clin Invest; fel Am Col Physicians; Am Soc Hematol; Asn Am Physicians; Asn Mil Surgeons. *Hematol. Res:* Clinical hematology; iron metabolism; marrow; spleen. *Mailing Add:* Walter Reed Army Inst Res Washington DC 20012

CROSEN, ROBERT GLENN, b Maitland, Mo, Mar 12, 00; m 25; c 3. ANALYTICAL CHEMISTRY, SCIENCE EDUCATION. *Educ:* Tarkio Col, BS, 23; Univ SDak, AM, 25; Columbia Univ, PhD(chem), 33. *Prof Exp:* Instr chem, Univ SDak, 23-28; asst instr, Exten Div, Columbia Univ, 28-29; from instr to assoc prof, Lafayette Col, 31-46, dean col, 41-46, dean fac, 46-57; prof chem & chmn dept, Abadan Inst Technol, Iran, 57-62; prof, 62-70, chmn dept, 63-70, EMER PROF CHEM, STERLING COL, 70- *Mem:* Am Chem Soc; Sigma Xi. *Res:* Saponification of oils, fats and waxes; quantitative spectrographic analysis by emission and absorption. *Mailing Add:* Box 24 RD 2 Sterling KS 67579

CROSIER, (HAROLD) E(DGAR), chemical engineering, see previous edition

CROSLEY, DAVID RISDON, b Webster City, Iowa, Mar 4, 41; m 63; c 1. PHYSICAL CHEMISTRY, ATOMIC AND MOLECULAR PHYSICS. *Educ:* Iowa State Univ, BS, 62; Columbia Univ, MA, 63, PhD(phys chem), 66. *Prof Exp:* Res assoc physics, Joint Inst Lab Astrophys, 66-68; asst prof phys chem, Univ Wis-Madison, 68-75; proj leader, Ballistic Res Labs, Aberdeen Proving Ground, Md, 75-79; prog mgr, 79-80, SR CHEM PHYSICIST, MOLECULAR PHYSICS LAB, SRI INT, MENLO PARK, CALIF, 79- *Concurrent Pos:* Joint Inst Lab Astrophys fel, 66-68. *Mem:* Am Phys Soc; AAAS; Combustion Inst. *Res:* Spectroscopy and chemical dynamics, reaction and energy transfer, of small state-selected molecules; laser-based combustion diagnostics. *Mailing Add:* Molecular Physics Lab SRI Int Menlo Park CA 94025

CROSNO, C(HARLES) DONALD, b Mt Vernon, Ill, Dec 27, 06; m 34; c 3. ELECTRICAL ENGINEERING. *Educ:* Univ NMex, BS, 28; Iowa State Col, MS, 29, PhD(elec eng), 33. *Prof Exp:* Instr math & eng, Amarillo Jr Col, 36-37, head dept, 37-38; prof eng & head dept, Ark State Col, 38-41 & NMex Sch Mines, 41-47; prof elec eng, 47-76, EMER PROF ELEC & COMPUT ENG, NMEX STATE UNIV, 76- *Mem:* Am Soc Eng Educ. *Res:* Rocket research; effect of preparation conditions of the properties of copper oxide rectifiers. *Mailing Add:* Dept of Elec & Comput Eng NMex State Univ Las Cruces NM 88003

CROSS, ALEXANDER DENNIS, b Leicester, Eng, Mar 29, 32. ORGANIC CHEMISTRY. *Educ:* Univ Nottingham, BSc, 52, PhD(org chem), 55; FRIC. *Hon Degrees:* DSc, Univ Nottingham, 66. *Prof Exp:* Fulbright travel scholar & fel, Univ Rochester, 55-57; sr fel & res asst, Dept Sci & Indust Res, Imp Col, London, 57-58; from asst lectr to lectr, 58-60; sr chemist, Syntex SAm, 61-62, asst dir chem res, 62-64, from assoc dir to dir, Syntex Inst Steroid Chem, 64-67, vpres, Syntex Res, 66-67, vpres, Com Rels, 67-70 & Chem Group 67-72, pres, Syntex Sci Systs, 70-74, pres, Int Pharm Div, 74-78, sr vpres, Corp Econ & Strategic Planning, Syntex Corp, 78-79, EXEC VPRES, ZOECON CORP, 79- *Concurrent Pos:* Vis lectr, Stanford Univ, 67. *Mem:* Am Chem Soc; The Chem Soc. *Res:* Elucidation of structure and synthesis of natural products; synthesis of biologically active steroids; applications of spectroscopic methods to problems in stereochemistry and structure. *Mailing Add:* Zoecon Corp 3401 Hillview Ave Palo Alto CA 94304

CROSS, CHARLES KENNETH, b Toronto, Ont, June 25, 27; m 54; c 2. ANALYTICAL CHEMISTRY. *Educ:* Univ Toronto, BA, 52, MA, 53. *Prof Exp:* RES CHEMIST, CAN PACKERS INC, 53- *Mem:* Chem Inst Can. *Res:* Trace contaminants in food, particularly nitrosamines in cured meats; analytical chemistry in the field of fats and oils. *Mailing Add:* Can Packers Inc 2211 St Clair Ave W Toronto ON M6N 1K5 Can

CROSS, CHESTER ELLSWORTH, b Boston, Mass, May 5, 13; m 41; c 3. BOTANY. *Educ:* Mass State Col, BS, 35, MS, 37; Harvard Univ, PhD(paleobot), 40. *Prof Exp:* Res specialist, Mass State Col, 37-41; from asst prof to assoc prof, 41-51; res prof in chg, 52-56, HEAD, CRANBERRY EXP STA, UNIV MASS, 56- *Concurrent Pos:* Assoc, Northeastern States Weed Control Conf, 47 & 48. *Mem:* Bot Soc Am. *Res:* Weed control and weather in cranberry culture. *Mailing Add:* Cranberry Exp Sta Rt 1 Box 7 East Wareham MA 02538

CROSS, CLARK IRWIN, b Olds, Alta, Sept 20, 13; US citizen; m 46; c 2. PHYSICAL GEOGRAPHY. *Educ:* Univ Wash, MS, 47, PhD(geog), 51. *Prof Exp:* Instr geog, Southern Methodist Univ, 46-47; from instr to prof, 49-80, chmn dept geog & phys sci, 78-80, EMER PROF GEOG & PHYS SCI, UNIV FLA, 80- *Concurrent Pos:* State climatologist Fla. *Mem:* Soc Am Foresters; Asn Am Geog. *Res:* Geography of USSR; air photo interpretation. *Mailing Add:* Dept of Geog 3141 GPA Univ of Fla Gainesville FL 32611

CROSS, DAVID RALSTON, b Lawrence, Mass, Mar 16, 28; m 58; c 3. SOLAR ELECTROCHEMISTRY, APPLIED SOLAR ENERGY. *Educ:* Wesleyan Univ, AB, 49, MA, 51; Syracuse Univ, PhD(phys & org chem), 60. *Prof Exp:* Sr res chemist, Res Labs, Eastman Kodak Co, NY, 57-64; from asst prof to assoc prof phys chem, 64-74, PROF CHEM, WESTERN MD COL, 74- *Concurrent Pos:* NSF res grant, 68-; vis prof, Case Western Reserve Univ, 70-71; Gas Res Inst grant, Am Soc Electronics Engrs, 81- *Mem:* Solar Energy Soc; Electrochem Soc. *Res:* Chromatography; chemiluminescence; photochemistry; chemical and electrode kinetics; electrochemistry; solvated electrons; photochemistry of phytochrome. *Mailing Add:* Dept of Chem Western Md Col Westminster MD 21157

CROSS, EARLE ALBRIGHT, JR, b Memphis, Tenn, Nov 23, 25; m 48; c 4. INSECT TAXONOMY, INSECT ECOLOGY. *Educ:* Utah State Univ, BS, 51; Univ Kans, MA, 55, PhD(entom), 62. *Prof Exp:* Instr entom, Purdue Univ, 57-58; vis instr, Univ Kans, 58-59, NIH res assoc, 59-60; from asst prof to prof biol sci, Northwestern State Col La, 60-70; assoc prof biol, 70-73, PROF BIOL, UNIV ALA, 73- *Concurrent Pos:* NIH res grant, 64-67; US Forest Serv coop res matching grant, 66-67 & 75-76; NSF teaching grant, 72 & res grant, 72-74; Ala Sch Mines energy develop grant, 78-81. *Mem:* Cent States Entom Soc; Entom Soc Am; Ecol Soc Am; Am Coun Reclamation Res. *Res:* Systematics and ecology of insects and acarines; systematics and ecology of mite family Pyemotidae; ecological energetics; strip mine succession. *Mailing Add:* Dept of Biol Univ of Ala Tuscaloosa AL 35486

CROSS, EDWARD F, b Brooklyn, NY, Nov 16, 08; m 35; c 2. MECHANICAL & CIVIL ENGINEERING. *Educ:* Stevens Inst Technol, MechE, 29; Columbia Univ, MA, 38. *Hon Degrees:* DEng, Walla Walla Col, 74. *Prof Exp:* Pub utility engr, Columbia Eng & Mgt Corp, 29-32; construct engr, Godfrey M Weinstein Construct Co, 32-33; mach design engr, Multi-Needle Eng Corp, 33-35; teacher, High Schs, NY, 35-37, 38-41, NJ, 37-38 & Manhattan Sch Aviation Trades, NY, 41-47; from asst prof to assoc prof, 47-58, head dept, 47-74, prof mech & civil eng, 58-79, EMER DEAN ENG, WALLA WALLA COL, 79- *Concurrent Pos:* Consult engr, Walla Walla Col, 47- & City of College Place, 52-66. *Mem:* Nat Soc Prof Engrs; Am Soc Eng Educ. *Res:* Thermodynamics; engineering mechanics; structural analysis and design; fluid mechanics; mechanical and electrical design of buildings. *Mailing Add:* PO Box 247 College Place WA 99324

CROSS, ERNEST JAMES, JR, b Loganton, Pa, Aug 3, 30; m 52; c 6. AERODYNAMICS, FLIGHT MECHANICS. *Educ:* Pa State Univ, BS, 59; Univ Tex, Austin, MA, 65, PhD(aerospace eng), 68. *Prof Exp:* Aeronaut engr, Aircraft Lab, Wright-Patterson AFB, 59-62, res engr gas dynamics, Hypersonic Res Lab, Aerospace Res Lab, 64-69, chief, VISTUL Technol Div, Air Force Flight Dynamics Lab, 70-71 & Prototpe Div, 71-73; prof & dir, Aerospace Eng Dept, Raspet Flight Res Lab, Miss State Univ, 73-79; PROF & HEAD, AEROSPACE ENG DEPT, TEX A&M UNIV, 79- *Concurrent Pos:* Mem, Int Tripartite Tech Coord Panel, VISTUL, 71-72, USAF/NASA VISTUL Transp Technol Ad Hoc Working Group, 72-73, Flight Dynamics Adv Panel, Air Force Flight Dynamics Lab, 75; US rep, US/Fed Repub Ger, res & develop prog, VISTUL Corp & proj officer, US/France Mutual Weapons Develop Data Exchange Agreement, VISTUL Technol, 71-73. *Mem:* Am Inst Aeronaut & Astronaut; Am Soc Eng Educ; Sigma Xi. *Res:* Experimental investigation of the aerodynamics and performance of subsonic aircraft and ground vehicles including automobiles, trucks and rail systems; facilities utilization including wind tunnel and full-scale flight test. *Mailing Add:* Aerospace Eng Dept Tex A&M Univ College Station TX 77843

CROSS, FRANK BERNARD, b Kansas City, Mo, Sept 17, 25; m 54; c 3. ZOOLOGY. *Educ:* Okla Agr & Mech Col, BS, 47, MS, 49, PhD(zool), 51. *Prof Exp:* Instr biol, 51-53, asst prof zool, 53-59, assoc prof & assoc dir, State Biol Surv, 59-67, PROF SYSTS & ECOL & DIR STATE BIOL SURV, 67-, CUR FISHES, MUS NATURAL HIST, 67- *Mem:* AAAS; Am Fisheries Soc; Am Soc Ichthyologists & Herpetologists; Wildlife Soc. *Res:* Ichthyology and fishery biology. *Mailing Add:* Dyche Hall Univ of Kans Lawrence KS 66045

CROSS, GEORGE ELLIOT, b Auburndale, NS, Apr 17, 28; m 52; c 6. PURE MATHEMATICS. *Educ:* Dalhousie Univ, BA, 52, MA, 54; Univ BC, PhD(math), 58. *Prof Exp:* From instr to asst prof math, Victoria Col, BC, 56-59; from asst prof to assoc prof, Univ Western Ont, 59-63; assoc prof, 63-65, dean grad studies, 67-72, PROF MATH, UNIV WATERLOO, 65-, CHMN DEPT PURE MATH, 78- *Mem:* Can Math Cong; Am Math Soc. *Res:* General theories of integration and summability of series as they relate to problems in Fourier analysis. *Mailing Add:* Dept of Pure Math Univ of Waterloo Waterloo ON N2L 3G1 Can

CROSS, GERALD HOWARD, b Marshall, Minn, Nov 15, 33; m 55; c 3. WILDLIFE MANAGEMENT. *Educ:* Univ Minn, Duluth, BA, 55; Ohio State Univ, MA, 64; NDak State Univ, PhD(zool), 73. *Prof Exp:* Exten specialist wildlife, 73-76, DEPT HEAD FISHERIES & WILDLIFE, VA POLYTECH INST & STATE UNIV, 76- *Mem:* Wildlife Soc; Am Fisheries Soc. *Res:* Wildlife land use interrelationships. *Mailing Add:* Dept Fisheries & Wildlife Sci Va Polytech Inst & State Univ Blacksburg VA 24061

CROSS, HAROLD DICK, b Wellington, Kans, Apr 2, 30; m 47; c 4. MEDICINE. *Educ:* Colby Col, BA, 53; Yale Univ, MD, 57. *Prof Exp:* CLIN ASSOC PROF MED & FAMILY PRACT, COL MED, UNIV VT, 71- *Concurrent Pos:* Internship, Eastern Maine Med Ctr, 57-58; attend med staff mem, 58-; pract physician, 58-; co-dir prob oriented med info serv, Augusta Gen Hosp, 69-70. *Mem:* Inst of Med of Nat Acad Sci; AMA. *Res:* Delivery of health care; ambulatory. *Mailing Add:* Promis Clin Main Rd Hampden Highlands ME 04445

CROSS, HIRAM RUSSELL, food science, animal science, see previous edition

CROSS, HOWARD C(LINTON), b Washington, DC, June 4, 04; m 30; c 2. METALLURGY. *Educ:* George Washington Univ, BS, 27. *Prof Exp:* Asst metallurgist, Bur Standards, 21-29; asst tech coord dir, Battelle Mem Inst, 29-69; RETIRED. *Concurrent Pos:* Consult, 69- *Honors & Awards:* Award Merit, Soc Testing & Mat, 64. *Mem:* Am Soc Metals; Am Soc Testing & Mat. *Res:* Metals for high temperature service, steam power plants, oil industry and gas turbines; jet engines. *Mailing Add:* 10450 Sutters Gold Lane Sun City AZ 85351

CROSS, JOHN HENRY, medical parasitology, see previous edition

CROSS, JOHN MILTON, b Little Falls, NJ, Jan 2, 15; m 45; c 4. PHARMACEUTICAL CHEMISTRY. *Educ:* Rutgers Univ, BS, 36; Univ Md, MS, 39, PhD(pharm), 43. *Prof Exp:* Res chemist, Merck & Co, Inc, NJ, 42-46; asst prof pharm, 46-49, assoc prof chem, 49-52, PROF PHARMACEUT CHEM & CHMN DEPT, COL PHARM, RUTGERS UNIV, 52- *Mem:* Am Pharmaceut Asn; Am Chem Soc. *Res:* Preparation of iodine compounds for roentgenology; fats and oils; analysis of foods and drugs; synthesis of fungicides; photo-decomposition of foods and drugs. *Mailing Add:* Col of Pharm Rutgers Univ Busch Campus New Brunswick NJ 08903

CROSS, JOHN PARSON, b Bloomington, Ill, Mar 23, 50; m 74; c 1. ORGANIC CHEMISTRY. *Educ:* Mass Inst Technol, SB, 72, PhD(org chem), 76. *Prof Exp:* Res chemist, Milliken Res Corp, 76-78; develop chemist, Milliken Chem, Div Milliken & Co, 78-80; sr res chemist, 80-81, GROUP LEADER, NEW BUS DEVELOP, SPECIALTIES TECHNOL DIV, EXXON CHEM CO, 82- *Mem:* Am Chem Soc; Soc Mining Engrs. *Res:* Specialty chemicals and process development. *Mailing Add:* Exxon Chem 8230 Stedman St Houston TX 77029

CROSS, JOHN WILLIAM, b Memphis, Tenn, Feb 9, 47; m 73; c 2. PLANT BIOCHEMISTRY, PLANT CYTOLOGY. *Educ:* Vanderbilt Univ, BA, 69; Calif Inst Technol, PhD(cell biol & genetics), 76. *Prof Exp:* Carnegie fel, Dept Plant Biol, Carnegie Inst of Wash, 75-78; staff scientist biochem, 78-81, SR RES SCIENTIST, PLANT GENETICS GROUP, PFIZER CENT RES, 81- *Mem:* AAAS; Am Soc Plant Physiologists; Am Chem Soc. *Res:* Regulation of protein synthesis and of organelle development; mechanism of action of plant hormones; function and organization of cellular organelles; developmental biochemistry of plants. *Mailing Add:* Plant Genetics Group Pfizer Cent Res Groton CT 06340

CROSS, JON BYRON, b New York, NY, July 16, 37; div; c 3. CHEMICAL PHYSICS, PHYSICAL CHEMISTRY. *Educ:* Univ Colo, BS, 60; Univ Ill, PhD(chem physics), 67. *Prof Exp:* MEM STAFF, LOS ALAMOS NAT LAB, UNIV CALIF, 66- *Concurrent Pos:* Adj prof chem, Univ NMex, 78- *Mem:* Am Phys Soc; Am Chem Soc. *Res:* Dynamics of chemical reactions; measurement of reactive scattering differential cross sections and product translational energy distributions using crossed molecular beam apparatus and mass spectrometer detector; photoionization of large organic molecules; photodissociation dynamics; gas-surface interactions using molecular beam techniques. *Mailing Add:* Los Alamos Nat Lab CNC-2 MS 732 Los Alamos NM 87544

CROSS, LEE ALAN, b Flint, Mich, Sept 23, 34; m; c 3. LASERS. *Educ:* Univ Mich, BS, 57, MS, 58, PhD(physics), 66. *Prof Exp:* Consult lasers, Laser Systs Ctr, Lear-Seigler Inc, 66-67; prof physics, Western Ill Univ, 67-78; RES PHYSICIST & ASSOC PROF IMPACT PHYSICS, RES INST, UNIV DAYTON, 78- *Concurrent Pos:* Fel, Dept Chem, Univ Mich, 66-67; consult, Avionics Div, Lear-Seigler Inc, 67-68; vis scholar, Dept Chem, Univ Mich, 78- *Mem:* Am Phys Soc; Inst Electronics & Elec Engrs. *Res:* Pulsed and CW metal vapor lasers; laser Q-switching; molecular spectroscopy; impact physics. *Mailing Add:* Res Inst Univ Dayton 300 College Park Dayton OH 45469

CROSS, LESLIE ERIC, b Leeds, Eng, Aug 14, 23; m 50; c 6. PHYSICS. *Educ:* Univ Leeds, BSc, 48, PhD(physics), 52. *Prof Exp:* Exp off electronics, Brit Admiralty, 43-46; asst lectr physics, Univ Leeds, 49-51; Imp Chem Indust fel, 51-54; sr res assoc, Brit Elec Res Assoc, 54-61; sr res assoc, 61-63, assoc prof physics, 63-68, PROF ELEC ENG, PA STATE UNIV, 68-, ASSOC DIR MAT RES LAB, 69- *Mem:* Fel Am Ceramic Soc; Phys Soc Japan; fel Am Inst Phys. *Res:* Material science; ferroelectric and antiferroelectric properties of titanates and niobates; thermodynamics of ferroelectricity; high permittivity materials; dielectric measuring techniques; dielectric properties of glass systems. *Mailing Add:* Mat Res Lab Rm 251-A Eng Sci Bldg Pa State Univ University Park PA 16802

CROSS, RALPH DONALD, b Quincy, Ill, Dec 31, 31; m 55; c 4. CLIMATOLOGY, WATER RESOURCES GEOGRAPHY. *Educ:* Eastern Mich Univ, AB, 60; Univ Okla, MA, 61; Mich State Univ, PhD(geog), 68. *Prof Exp:* Instr geog, Southeast Mo State Col, 61-63; asst prof, Okla State Univ, 66-68 & Boston Univ, 68-71; assoc prof, 71-79, PROF GEOG, UNIV SOUTHERN MISS, 79- *Concurrent Pos:* Boston Univ Grad Sch grant soil moisture, Payne County, Okla, 68-70; Univ Southern Miss grant, Miss State Atlas, 72-74; res consult, Miss Marina Resources Coun, 75, Miss Water Resources Inst, 75-76, US Fish & Wildlife Serv, 79-81 & Miss Dept Natural Resources, 81-82. *Mem:* Am Water Resources Asn; Soil Conserv Soc Am; Asn Am Geog; Am Meteorol Soc. *Res:* Hydroclimatology; water resources; a regional interest in the Union of Soviet Socialist Republics; air quality analysis. *Mailing Add:* Southern Sta Box 352 Univ of Southern Miss Hattiesburg MS 39401

CROSS, RALPH HERBERT, III, b Oakland, Calif, Aug 17, 38; m 59; c 2. COASTAL ENGINEERING & OCEANOGRAPHY. *Educ:* Univ Calif, Berkeley, BS, 61, MS, 62, PhD(civil eng), 66. *Prof Exp:* Jr civil eng, Univ Calif, Berkeley, 61-66; asst prof civil eng, Mass Inst Technol, 66-71; asst vpres, Alpine Geophys Assoc, 71-74; ASST VPRES & SR COASTAL ENGR, WOODWARD-CLYDE CONSULTS, 74- *Mem:* Am Geophys Union; Marine Technol Soc; Am Soc Civil Engrs. *Res:* Water waves; coastal structures; nearshore oceanography; coastal site surveys. *Mailing Add:* Woodward-Clyde Consults 5120 Butler Pike Plymouth Meeting PA 19462

CROSS, RICHARD JAMES, b New York, NY, Mar 31, 15; m 39; c 5. INTERNAL MEDICINE, COMMUNITY HEALTH. *Educ:* Yale Univ, BA, 37; Columbia Univ, MD, 41, ScD(med), 49. *Prof Exp:* From instr to asst prof med, Columbia Univ, 47-59; asst dean, 57-59; assoc dean, Univ Pittsburgh, 59-63; assoc prof, Sch Med, Temple Univ, 63-64; adminr, Asn Am Med Cols, 64-65; prof med & assoc dean, 65-70, PROF COMMUNITY MED & CHMN DEPT, COL MED & DENT NJ-RUTGERS MED SCH, PISCATAWAY,

NJ, 70- *Concurrent Pos:* Dean, Fac Med, Univ Ghana, 63-64. *Res:* Treatment of thrombo-embolic disease; aerobic phosphorylation; renal tubular transport in rabbit kidney slices; medical school administration. *Mailing Add:* Col of Med & Dent of NJ-Rutgers Med Sch PO Box 101 Piscataway NJ 08854

CROSS, RICHARD LESTER, b Hoboken, NJ, Aug 26, 43; m 71; c 1. BIOCHEMISTRY, BIOENERGETICS. *Educ:* Hartwick Col, BA, 66; Yale Univ, PhD(chem), 70. *Prof Exp:* Asst prof, 73-78, ASSOC PROF BIOCHEM, STATE UNIV NY UPSTATE MED CTR, 78- *Concurrent Pos:* Jane Coffin Childs Fund fel, Univ Calif, Los Angeles, 70-73; mem res comt, NY State Am Heart Asn, 78-81; ad hoc mem, Mat Biol Panel, NSF, 81; vis prof biochem, Public Health Inst, New York, 81-82. *Mem:* Sigma Xi; Fedn Am Scientists; Am Soc Biol Chem; Biophys Soc. *Res:* Energy-transducing membrane systems; mechanism of Adenosine Triphosphate synthesis by oxidative phosphorylation and photophosphorylation. *Mailing Add:* Dept Biochem State Univ NY Upstate Med Ctr Syracuse NY 13210

CROSS, ROBERT EDWARD, b Toledo, Ohio, July 24, 42; m 67; c 3. CLINICAL BIOCHEMISTRY. *Educ:* Univ Toledo, BS, 65, MS, 67; Univ Fla, PhD(org chem), 71. *Prof Exp:* DIR, CLIN CHEM LABS, NC MEM HOSP, 81-, DIR, TOXICOL & CLIN PHARMACOL LAB, 78-; ASSOC PROF, DEPT PATH, MED & CLIN PHARMACOL, UNIV NC SCH MED, 79- *Mem:* Nat Acad Clin Biochem; Am Asn Clin Chem; Acad Clin Lab Physicians & Scientists; AAAS; NY Acad Sci. *Res:* Development of improved instrumentation and methodology in clinical chemistry; interpretation of laboratory tests; clinical enzymology; toxicology and clinical pharmacology. *Mailing Add:* Clin Chem Labs 1071 Patient Support Tower NC Mem Hosp Chapel Hill NC 27514

CROSS, ROBERT FRANKLIN, b Columbus, Ohio, May 6, 24; m 46; c 4. VETERINARY PATHOLOGY. *Educ:* Ohio State Univ, DVM, 48; Purdue Univ, PhD(vet path), 61. *Prof Exp:* Instr vet path, Ohio State Univ, 48-50; vet pathologist, Territory of Hawaii, 50-58; from instr to assoc prof, Purdue Univ, 58-66; VET PATHOLOGIST, OHIO AGR RES & DEVELOP CTR, 66- *Concurrent Pos:* Lectr, Univ Hawaii, 55-58. *Mem:* Am Vet Med Asn; Am Col Vet Path; Conf Res Workers Animal Dis; Am Soc Vet Clin Path. *Res:* Veterinary clinical pathology. *Mailing Add:* Dept Vet Sci Ohio Agr Res & Develop Ctr Wooster OH 44691

CROSS, RONALD ALLAN, b Chicago, Ill, Sept 19, 31. MICROBIAL GENETICS. *Educ:* Univ Calif, Los Angeles, AB, 54, MA, 62, PhD(genetics), 65. *Prof Exp:* Res assoc microbial genetics, 65-67, vis asst prof microbiol, 67-70, ASST PROF MICROBIOL & CURRICULUM COORD, SCH MED, UNIV SOUTHERN CALIF, 70- *Concurrent Pos:* NIH fel, 65-67. *Mem:* AAAS; Genetics Soc Am; Am Soc Microbiol. *Res:* Mutagenesis in microorganisms; mechanisms of gene action and control in bacteriophage lambda; genetics of the genus Neisseria and neisseriaphage. *Mailing Add:* Dept of Microbiol Sch Med Univ of Southern Calif Los Angeles CA 90033

CROSS, STEPHEN P, b Los Angeles, Calif, Apr 10, 38; m 59; c 4. MAMMALOGY, WILDLIFE BIOLOGY. *Educ:* Calif State Polytech Col, BS, 60; Univ Ariz, MS, 62, PhD(zool), 69. *Prof Exp:* From instr to asst prof biol, 69-77, PROF BIOL, SOUTHERN ORE STATE COL, 78- *Concurrent Pos:* Consult, Bur Reclamation, 73-74, Park Serv, 76-77 & US Forest Serv, 77-78; wildlife biologist, Bur Land Mgt, 80-81. *Mem:* Am Soc Ichthyologists & Herpetologists; Am Soc Mammal; Northwest Sci Asn. *Res:* Vertebrate utilization of special and unique habitats; behavioral ecology of small mammals, including bats, especially as related to mans manipulation of habitats. *Mailing Add:* Dept of Biol Southern Ore State Col Ashland OR 97520

CROSS, TIMOTHY AUREAL, b Pittsburgh, Pa, Jan 22, 46; m 70; c 1. SEDIMENTOLOGY, TECTONICS. *Educ:* Oberlin Col, BA, 67; Univ Mich, Ann Arbor, MS, 69; Univ Southern Calif, PhD(geol), 76. *Prof Exp:* Explor geologist, Texaco, Inc, 69-72; asst prof sedimentology & tectonics, Univ NDak, Grand Forks, 75-78; assoc prof, Purdue Univ, 78-79; RES GEOLOGIST, EXXON PROD RES CO, HOUSTON, 79- *Mem:* Am Asn Petrol Geologists; Soc Econ Paleontologists & Mineralogists; Geol Soc Am; Int Asn Sedimentologists. *Res:* History of igneous activity, western United States with relation to plate tectonics; Mississippian bioherms; Carbonate sedimentology, Williston Basin; coal geology and sedimentology; foreland basin sedimentation and tectonics; Calcareous algae. *Mailing Add:* EXXON Prod Res Co PO Box 2189 Houston TX 77001

CROSS, VIRGINIA ROSE, b Portland, Ore, May 15, 50; m 74; c 1. SURFACE CHEMISTRY, CATALYSIS. *Educ:* Ore State Univ, BS, 72; Mass Inst Technol, PhD(phys chem), 76. *Prof Exp:* Res chemist phys chem, Celanese Plastics Co, 76-79 & Am Hoechst Co, 79-80; RES CHEMIST, EXXON CHEM CO, 80- *Mem:* Am Chem Soc; Sigma Xi. *Res:* Catalysis of petroleum products. *Mailing Add:* Exxon Chem PO Box 4900 Baytown TX 77520

CROSS, WILLIAM GUNN, nuclear physics, see previous edition

CROSS, WILLIAM HENLEY, b Baker Co, Ga, Dec 10, 28; m 52; c 5. ENTOMOLOGY, ECOLOGY. *Educ:* Fla State Univ, BS, 49, MS, 51; Univ Ga, PhD(zool), 56. *Prof Exp:* Asst, Fla State Univ, 49-51 & Univ Ga, 51-55; ENTOMOLOGIST, AGR RES SERV, USDA, 57-; ADJ PROF ZOOL, MISS STATE UNIV, 63- *Mem:* Entom Soc Am; Ecol Soc Am. *Res:* Taxonomy and ecology in insect orders, especially Odonata, Orthoptera and Coleoptera; behavior and population ecology, especially insects. *Mailing Add:* Boll Weevil Res Lab PO Box 5367 Mississippi State MS 39762

CROSSAN, DONALD FRANKLIN, b Wilmington, Del, Apr 8, 26; m 48; c 3. PLANT PATHOLOGY. *Educ:* Univ Del, BS, 50; NC State Col, MS, 52, PhD(plant path), 54. *Prof Exp:* Res asst veg dis, NC State Col, 50-54; assoc prof, 54-66, asst dean col agr sci & asst dir agr exp sta, 66-69, assoc dean col agr sci, 69-76, assoc dir, Del Agr Exp Sta, 69-79, PROF PLANT SCI, COL

AGR SCI, UNIV DEL, 66-, DEAN, 76-, DIR, DEL AGR EXP STA, 79-, VPRES, UNIV RES, 72- *Mem:* AAAS; Am Phytopath Soc. *Res:* Vegetable plant diseases; disease resistance; fungus physiology. *Mailing Add:* Col of Agr Univ of Del Newark DE 19711

CROSSER, ORRIN KINGSBERY, b Akron, Ohio, Mar 2, 29; m 56; c 2. CHEMICAL ENGINEERING. *Educ:* Univ Mo, BS, 50, MS, 51; Rice Univ, PhD(chem eng), 55. *Prof Exp:* Instr chem eng, Univ Mo, 51-52; from asst prof to prof, Univ Okla, 55-66, actg dir dept, 65-66; PROF CHEM ENG, UNIV MO-ROLLA, 66- *Concurrent Pos:* Fulbright travel grant, 61-62. *Mem:* Am Inst Chem Engrs; Am Chem Soc; Nat Soc Prof Engrs; Am Soc Eng Educ. *Res:* Mass and heat transport phenomena; chemical kinetic technology. *Mailing Add:* Dept of Chem Eng Univ of Mo Rolla MO 65401

CROSSFIELD, A SCOTT, b Berkeley, Calif, Oct 2, 21; m 43; c 6. AERONAUTICAL ENGINEERING. *Educ:* Univ Wash, BS, 49, MS, 50. *Prof Exp:* Prod expediter, Boeing Airplane Co, 41-42; design specialist, Seeger Aircraft Specialties, 46-49; aeronaut res pilot, Nat Adv Comt for Aero High Speed Flight Sta, Calif, 50-55; eng test pilot & design specialist, N Am Aviation, Inc, 55-60, div dir test & qual assurance, Space & Info Systs Div, 60-66, tech dir res & develop, Space Div, 66-67; div vpres flight res & develop, Eastern Air Lines, 67-73; sr vpres, Hawker Siddeley Aviation, Inc, 74-75; TECH CONSULT, HOUSE REP COMT SCI & TECHNOL, 77- *Concurrent Pos:* Wind tunnel operator, Aeronaut Lab, Univ Wash, 46-50; aeronaut consult, 75-77. *Honors & Awards:* Lawrence Sperry Award, 54; Octave Chanute Award, 56; Award, Air Force Asn, 59, Schilling Award, 61; Inst Aeronaut Sci Award, Inst Aeronaut & Astronaut, 59, Rocket Soc Award, 60; Kincheloe Award, Soc Exp Test Pilots, 60, Ray E Tenhoff Award, 78; Award, Flying Physicians, 61; Harmon Trophy, 61; Collier Trophy, 61; Montgomery Award, Nat Soc Aerospace Profs, 62; Kittyhawk Mem Award, 69. *Mem:* Fel Inst Aeronaut & Astronaut; fel Soc Exp Test Pilots; hon fel Aerospace Med Asn. *Res:* Wind tunnel experiments and flight test of high speed research aircraft. *Mailing Add:* 12100 Thoroughbred Rd Herndon VA 22070

CROSSLEY, DAVID JOHN, b Salisbury, Eng, May 10, 44. GEOPHYSICS. *Educ:* Univ Newcastle-upon-Tyne, BSc, 66; Univ BC, MSc, 69, PhD(geophys), 73. *Prof Exp:* Res scientist, ICI Fibers Div, 66-67; fel, 73-74, res assoc physics, Mem Univ Nfld, 74-76; ASST PROF APPL GEOPHYSICS, McGILL UNIV, 76- *Mem:* Can Asn Physicists; Am Geophys Union. *Res:* Solid earth and planetary geophysics, especially dynamics of the earth's core and free oscillation theory; theory; inversion of geophysical data in areas of pure and applied geophysics. *Mailing Add:* Dept of Mining & Metall Eng McGill Univ 3480 Univ St Montreal Can

CROSSLEY, DERYEE ASHTON, JR, b Kingsville, Tex, Nov 6, 27; m 50, 61; c 1. RADIATION ECOLOGY. *Educ:* Tex Technol Col, BA, 49, MS, 51; Univ Kans, PhD(entom), 57. *Prof Exp:* Instr biol, Tex Technol Col, 49-51; asst, Univ Kans, 51-56; biologist, Oak Ridge Nat Lab, 56-67; PROF ENTOM, UNIV GA, 67- *Mem:* Ecol Soc Am; Entom Soc Am; Am Soc Naturalists. *Res:* Radioisotope movement in food chains; mineral cycling in ecosystems; role of soil arthropods in ecosystems; taxonomy of soil mites. *Mailing Add:* Dept of Entom Univ of Ga Athens GA 30602

CROSSLEY, F(RANCIS) R(ENDEL) ERSKINE, b Derby, Eng, July 21, 15; nat US; m 41; c 2. MECHANICAL ENGINEERING, MECHANICS. *Educ:* Cambridge Univ, Eng, BA, 37, MA, 41; Yale Univ, DEng, 49. *Prof Exp:* Asst, Gen Motors Res Corp, 37-38; designer, Ford Motor Co, 39-42; instr mech drawing, Univ Detroit, 42-44, asst prof mech eng, 44-54; assoc prof, Yale Univ, 54-65; vis prof, Inst Sci & Technol, Univ Manchester, 64-; prof mech eng, Ga Inst Technol, 65-68; prof mech & aerospace eng, 69-78, prof civil eng, 78-80, EMER PROF, UNIV MASS, AMHERST, 80- *Concurrent Pos:* Guest lectr, Tech Univ Braunschweig, 59; ed, Proc Int Conf Teachers Mechanisms, 61; organizer, Int Conf Mechanisms, Yale Univ, 61; Fulbright sr lectr, Munich & Aachen Tech Univs, 62-63; mem, Verein Deutscher Ingenieure, 62-78; invited lectr tour, seven German tech univs, 64; ed-in-chief, J Mechanisms, 66-71; mem bd dirs, Int Asn Exchange Students Tech Experience; chmn, Tenth Am Soc Mech Engrs Mechanisms Conf, 68; pres, US Coun Theory Mach & Mechanisms, Inc, 68-70; first vpres, Int Fedn Theory Mach & Mechanisms, 69-75, chmn, Publ Comn & chmn, Nominations Comt, 75-79; exec ed, int jour Mechanism & Mach Theory, 71-; vis researcher, Tech Univ Warsaw, Poland, 75; vis prof, Rhein-Westphal Tech Hochschule Aachen, 75-76; Fulbright lectr, Bucharest, Rumania, 76; guest lectr, Acad Sci, USSR, Inst Mach Studies, 76; hon chmn, Fifth World Cong Theory Mach & Mechanisms, Montreal, 79; staff scientist, Conn State Legis, Off Legis Res, Hartford, 81- *Honors & Awards:* von Humboldt Sr Scientist Award, Fed Repub Ger, 75; Mechanisms Award, Am Soc Mech Engrs, 76; Centennial Medal, Am Soc Mech Engrs, 80. *Mem:* Fel Am Soc Mech Engrs; Am Soc Eng Educ; Sigma Xi. *Res:* Nonlinear vibration; dynamics and vibration of machines; kinematics and mechanisms; forest harvesting methodology. *Mailing Add:* 282 Pine Orchard Rd Branford CT 06405

CROSSLEY, FRANK ALPHONSO, b Chicago, Ill, Feb 19, 25; m 50; c 1. TITANIUM SCIENCE, TITANIUM TECHNOLOGY. *Educ:* Ill Inst Technol, BS, 45, MS, 47, PhD(metall eng), 50. *Prof Exp:* Instr metall, Ill Inst Technol, 47-49; prof & dept head foundry eng, Tenn State Univ, Nashville, 50-52; sr scientist, Res Inst, Ill Inst Technol, 52-66; sr mem res lab, 66-74, dept mgr, 74-79, CONSULT ENGR, LOCKHEED MISSILES & SPACE CO, 79- *Mem:* Fel Am Soc Metals; Metall Soc; Am Inst Aeronaut & Astronaut; Soc Advan Mat & Process Eng; Sigma Xi. *Res:* Titanium science and technology including: phase relationships, heat treatment, mechanical properties and alloy development; stress-corrosion of metal alloys; grain refinement of metals. *Mailing Add:* Lockheed Missiles & Space Co Orgn 81-04 Bldg 154 PO Box 504 Sunnyvale CA 94086

CROSSLEY, ROBERT WILLIAM, mechanical engineering, see previous edition

CROSSMAN, EDWIN JOHN, b Niagara Falls, Ont, Sept 21, 29; m 52; c 2. ICHTHYOLOGY. *Educ:* Queen's Univ, Can, BA, 52; Univ Toronto, MA, 54; Univ BC, PhD, 57. *Prof Exp:* Fishery biologist, Biol Sta, Queen's Univ, Can, 50; biologist, Toronto Anglers & Hunters Conserv Proj, 51-54; fishery biologist, BC Game Comn, 54-57; asst cur, Dept Fishes, 57-64, assoc cur, Dept Ichthyol & Herpet, 64-68, cur, 68-74, CUR-IN-CHG, DEPT ICHTHYOL & HERPET, ROYAL ONT MUS, 74-; PROF ZOOL, UNIV TORONTO, 68- *Mem:* Am Fisheries Soc Am; Soc Ichthyologists & Herpetologists; Soc Syst Zool; Am Inst Fishery Res Biol; Can Soc Zool. *Res:* Biology, distributions and systematics of freshwater fishes, particularly esocoid fishes. *Mailing Add:* Dept Zool Royal Ont Mus St George Campus Toronto ON M5S 2C6 Can

CROSSMON, GERMAIN CHARLES, b Prattsburg, NY, May 9, 05; m 31. MICROSCOPY. *Educ:* Alfred Univ, BS, 28. *Prof Exp:* Teacher high sch, NJ, 29-31; bacteriologist, Sch Med & Dent, Univ Rochester, 35-42; biol & chem microscopist & indust hyg chemist, Bausch & Lomb, Inc, 42-74; CONSULT INDUST HYG & MICROS, 74- *Mem:* AAAS; Am Indust Hyg Asn; Am Chem Soc; Am Micros Soc; Am soc Microbiol. *Res:* Biological and chemical microscopy; industrial hygiene chemistry. *Mailing Add:* 23 Esternay Lane Pittsford NY 14534

CROSSNER, KENNETH ALAN, b New York, NY, Oct 10, 46; m 72; c 1. POPULATION ECOLOGY, MAMMALOGY. *Educ:* City Col New York, BS, 69, MA, 72; Rutgers Univ, PhD(ecol), 76. *Prof Exp:* Asst prof biol, Univ Col, Rutgers Univ, 76-77; ASST PROF BIOL, SETON HALL UNIV, 77- *Concurrent Pos:* Co-adj asst prof, Univ Col, Rutgers Univ, 77- *Mem:* Am Soc Mammalogists; Ecol Soc Am; Wildlife Soc; Mammal Soc; Am Inst Biol Sci. *Res:* Mammal population ecology and their responses to urbanization and other environmental perturbations; distribution of mammals in suburbia; ecological needs of mammal populations in urban reservations. *Mailing Add:* Dept of Biol Seton Hall Univ South Orange NJ 07079

CROSSON, ROBERT SCOTT, b Fairbanks, Alaska, Oct 19, 38; m 59; c 2. GEOPHYSICS, SEISMOLOGY. *Educ:* Univ Wash, BS, 61; Univ Utah, MS, 63; Stanford Univ, PhD(geophys), 66. *Prof Exp:* From asst prof to assoc prof, 66-78, PROF GEOPHYS & GEOL, UNIV WASH, 78- *Mem:* Seismol Soc Am; Soc Explor Geophys; Am Geophys Union. *Res:* Physical properties and structure of earth's crust and upper mantle; characteristics and distribution of earthquakes and their tectonic implications; elastic characteristics of rocks; seismology of volcanic regions. *Mailing Add:* Geophys Prog Univ Wash Seattle WA 98105

CROSSWHITE, CAROL D, b Perth Amboy, NJ, Aug 1, 40; m 61; c 3. DESERT ECOLOGY, ENTOMOLOGY. *Educ:* Univ Calif, Riverside, BS, 61; Univ Wis, Madison, MS, 64, PhD(entom), 68. *Prof Exp:* Instr entom, Univ Wis, Madison, 68-70; CUR ZOOL, DESERT BIOL STA, BOYCE THOMPSON SOUTHWESTERN ARBORETUM, UNIV ARIZ, 71- *Mem:* Ecol Soc Am; Soc Syst Zool. *Res:* Classification and ecology of Hymenoptera; pollination ecology; desert biology. *Mailing Add:* Univ Ariz Desert Biol Sta PO Box AB Boyce Thompson Southwestern Arboretum Superior AZ 85273

CROSSWHITE, F JOE, b Springfield, Mo, Oct 13, 29; m 49; c 3. MATHEMATICS EDUCATION. *Educ:* Univ Mo, BSEd, 53, MEd, 58; Ohio State Univ, PhD(math educ), 64. *Prof Exp:* Teacher math, Salem High Sch, Mo, 53-57; instr, Keokuk Community Col, Iowa, 57-61; from instr to assoc prof, 62-70, PROF MATH EDUC, OHIO STATE UNIV, 70- *Concurrent Pos:* US Off Educ fel, Stanford Univ, 68-69; prog mgr, NSF, 75-76. *Mem:* Nat Coun Teachers Math; Math Asn Am; Am Educ Res Asn. *Res:* Teaching and learning of mathematics at the precollege level including the education of teachers for this level. *Mailing Add:* 283 Arps Hall Ohio State Univ Columbus OH 43210

CROSSWHITE, FRANK SAMUEL, b Atchison, Kans, Sept 23, 40; m 61; c 3. BOTANY, BIOGEOGRAPHY. *Educ:* Ariz State Univ, BS, 62; Univ Wis, Madison, MS, 65, PhD, 71. *Prof Exp:* Res asst bot, Univ Wis, Madison, 69-70; asst prof, Univ Wis Ctr, Waukesha, 70-71; CUR BOT, BOYCE THOMPSON SOUTHWESTERN ARBORETUM, UNIV ARIZ, 71- *Mem:* Am Soc Plant Taxon; Int Asn Plant Taxon; Bot Soc Am. *Res:* Classification of Scrophulariaceae; pollination ecology; history of botany; geography of North American communities. *Mailing Add:* Univ of Ariz PO Box AB Boyce Thompson Southwestern Arboretum Superior AZ 85273

CROSSWHITE, HENRY MILTON, JR, b Riverdale, Md, March 26, 19; m 44; c 3. PHYSICS. *Educ:* Western Md Col, AB, 40; Johns Hopkins Univ, PhD(physics), 46. *Prof Exp:* Asst, Nat Res Coun war contract, Johns Hopkins Univ, 42-46, instr physics, 46-47, asst prof, 47-50, res assoc, 50-58, res scientist, 58-63, prin res scientist, 63-65, adj prof, 65-75; SR CHEMIST, CHEM DIV, ARGONNE NAT LAB, 75- *Mem:* Am Phys Soc. *Res:* Visible and ultraviolet spectroscopy. *Mailing Add:* 918 Hickory Ln Darien IL 60439

CROSTHWAITE, JOHN LESLIE, b Winnipeg, Man, Dec 22, 40; m 65; c 2. MECHANICAL ENGINEERING. *Educ:* Univ Man, BSc, 62; Univ Birmingham, MSc, 64. *Prof Exp:* Lectr thermodyn, Univ Man, 65-66; ASSOC RES OFFICER NUCLEAR FUEL DEVELOP & WASTE MGT, ATOMIC ENERGY CAN LTD, 66- *Mem:* Chem Inst Can. *Res:* Nuclear fuel development; heat transfer and thermodynamics in relation to nuclear energy development; nuclear waste management studies. *Mailing Add:* Whiteshell Nuclear Res Estab Atomic Energy of Can Ltd Pinawa MB R0E 1L0 Can

CROTEAU, RODNEY, b Springfield, Mass, Dec 6, 45; m 67; c 2. BIOCHEMISTRY. *Educ:* Univ Mass, Amherst, BS, 67, PhD(food sci), 70. *Prof Exp:* NIH res assoc biochem, Ore State Univ, 70-72; res assoc, 73-75, asst agr chemist, 75-78, assoc agr chemist, 78-80, ASSOC PROF DEPT CHEM, WASH STATE UNIV, 80- *Mem:* Am Chem Soc; Am Soc Plant Physiologists; Phytochem Soc NAm; Inst Food Technologists; Am Soc Biol Chemists. *Res:* Biosynthesis and catabolism of terpenoids. *Mailing Add:* Dept of Agr Chem Wash State Univ Pullman WA 99163

CROTHERS, DONALD M, b Fatehgarh, India, Jan 28, 37; US citizen; m 60; c 2. BIOPHYSICAL CHEMISTRY. *Educ:* Yale Univ, BS, 58; Cambridge Univ, BA, 60; Univ Calif, San Diego, PhD(chem), 63. *Prof Exp:* NSF fel, 63-64; from asst prof to assoc prof, 64-71, chmn, Dept Chem, 75-81, PROF CHEM & MOLECULAR BIOPHYS, YALE UNIV, 71- *Concurrent Pos:* Guggenheim fel, 78-79; sr scientist award, von Humboldt Found, 81. *Mem:* Am Soc Biol Chemists; Biophys Soc. *Res:* Physical chemistry of biological macromolecules. *Mailing Add:* Dept of Chem Yale Univ New Haven CT 06520

CROTOGINO, REINHOLD HERMANN, b Teplitz, Czechoslovakia, Aug 2, 42; m; c 2. PULP & PAPER TECHNOLOGY. *Educ:* Univ BC, BASc, 66; McGill Univ, PhD(chem eng), 71. *Prof Exp:* Res engr, Voith Gesellschaft Mit Beschraenkter Haftung, 71-76; SCIENTIST & SECT HEAD, PULP & PAPER RES INST CAN, 76- *Concurrent Pos:* Auxiliary prof chem eng, McGill Univ, 76- *Honors & Awards:* H I Weldon Medal, Can Pulp & Paper Asn, 80. *Mem:* Can Pulp & Paper Asn. *Res:* Physical processes used in the manufacture of pulp and paper; fundamentals of calendering and drying of paper, pulp washing, and bonding of air formed paper webs; developing new calendering and pulp washing techniques. *Mailing Add:* Pulp & Paper Res Inst Can 570 St John's Blvd Pointe Claire PQ T19R 3J9 Can

CROTTY, WILLIAM JOSEPH, b NJ, Sept 25, 22; m 46; c 4. PLANT MORPHOGENESIS. *Educ:* City Col New York, BS, 48; Rutgers Univ, PhD(bot), 52. *Prof Exp:* Teaching fel bot, Rutgers Univ, 49-52; from asst prof to assoc prof, 52-73, chmn dept, 52-73, dir undergrad studies, 73-77, PROF BIOL, WASH SQ COL, NY UNIV, 73- *Mem:* Torrey Bot Club; Bot Soc Am; Am Soc Cell Biol. *Res:* Plant development. *Mailing Add:* Dept of Biol Wash Sq Col NY Univ New York NY 10003

CROUCH, BILLY G, b Port Lavaca, Tex, May 14, 30. CLINICAL PHARMACOLOGY, RADIATION BIOLOGY. *Educ:* Baylor Univ, BS, 54, MS, 55; Univ Tenn, PhD(clin physiol), 58. *Prof Exp:* Instr biol, Baylor Univ, 54-55; asst clin physiol, Col Med, Univ Tenn, 55-58, lectr, 56-58; radiation biologist, US Naval Radiol Defense Lab, Calif, 60-63; clin res pharmacologist, Sterling-Winthrop Res Inst, 63-64, sr clin pharmacologist, 64-65; dir med commun, Winthrop Labs, 65-68; dir drug regulatory affairs, Sterling Drug, Inc, 68-76; exec vpres, 77-78, PRES & CHIEF EXEC OFFICER, SANOFI RES CO, INC, 78- *Concurrent Pos:* Nat Acad Sci-Nat Res Coun Donner fel, Radiobiol Sect, Nat Defense Res Coun, Neth, 58-59; Nat Heart Inst res fel, 59-60; vis lectr, Fac Med, State Univ Leiden, 59-60; vpres & mem bd dir, Choay Labs, Inc, 77-; mem nat comn clin use interferon, French Ministry Health, 80-81; mem bd dir, Girpi, Paris, 80-82; dir med affairs, Sanofi, SAm, Paris, 80-82; mem bd gov, Am Hosp Paris, 81-; vpres, Sanofi Pharmaceuticals, Inc, 81- *Mem:* Am Physiol Soc; Am Fedn Clin Res; Radiation Res Soc; Royal Soc Med; Neth Soc Radiobiol. *Res:* Clinical physiology; bone marrow transplantation in irradiation sickness; clinical evaluation of new drug substances. *Mailing Add:* Sanofi Res Co Inc 9 W 57th St New York NY 10019

CROUCH, GLENN LEROY, b Los Angeles, Calif, Jan 14, 29; m 52; c 4. WILDLIFE ECOLOGY, FORESTRY. *Educ:* Univ Idaho, BS, 59; Colo State Univ, MS, 61; Ore State Univ, PhD(range mgt), 64. *Prof Exp:* Range scientist, 64-76, RES WILDLIFE BIOLOGIST, US FOREST SERV, 76- *Mem:* Wildlife Soc; Soc Range Mgt; Soc Am Foresters. *Res:* Forest wildlife relationships; protection of forest regeneration from animals. *Mailing Add:* 240 W Prospect Ft Collins CO 80526

CROUCH, JAMES ENSIGN, b Urbana, Ill, Jan 28, 08; m 31; c 2. ORNITHOLOGY, ANATOMY. *Educ:* Cornell Univ, MS, 31; Univ Southern Calif, PhD(vert zool), 39. *Prof Exp:* Mem, Dept Zool, 32-42, prof, 42-73, chmn, Div Life Sci, 62-69, EMER PROF ZOOL, SAN DIEGO STATE UNIV, 73- *Mem:* AAAS; assoc Am Ornithologists Union; assoc Cooper Ornith Soc. *Res:* Bird behavior; life history of Phainopepla nitens lepida. *Mailing Add:* 10430 Russell Rd La Mesa CA 92041

CROUCH, MADGE LOUISE, b Winston-Salem, NC, Sept 21, 19. PUBLIC HEALTH ADMINISTRATION. *Educ:* Methodist Hosp Sch Nursing, Brooklyn, dipl, 41; Columbia Univ, BS, 47; George Washington Univ, MA, 61. *Prof Exp:* Instr basic nursing & microbiol, Methodist Sch Nursing, Brooklyn, 41-43; nat nursing dir, Am Nat Res Cross, 48-65; asst to chief blood bank prod lab, Div Biol Standards, NIH, 65-71; dir blood bank prod br, Div Blood & Blood Prod, 72-77, DEP DIR DIV BIOL EVAL, BUR BIOL FOOD & DRUG ADMIN, 77- *Concurrent Pos:* Mem comt plasma & plasma substitutes, Div Med Sci, Nat Acad Sci, 69-70; mem secy task force nat blood policy, Dept of Health, Educ & Welfare, 72-74. *Mem:* Int Soc Blood Transfusion. *Res:* Development of improved blood banking procedures for prolonged storage of red blood cells; greater efficacy of components; training of personnel; techniques and equipment. *Mailing Add:* Bur of Biol 8800 Rockville Pike Bethesda MD 20014

CROUCH, MARSHALL FOX, b St Louis, Mo, Nov 22, 20; m 49; c 4. PHYSICS. *Educ:* Univ Mich, BS, 41; Univ Wash, PhD(physics), 50. *Prof Exp:* Res assoc, Nat Defense Res Comt, Univ Mich, 41-42; mem staff, Radiation Lab, Mass Inst Technol, 42-43 & Los Alamos Lab, 43; PROF PHYSICS, CASE WESTERN RESERVE UNIV, 50- *Concurrent Pos:* Fulbright res prof, Univ Tokyo, 56-57; dep sci attache, Am Embassy, Tokyo, 59-61. *Mem:* Am Phys Soc. *Res:* Nuetrino physics; cosmic rays. *Mailing Add:* Dept of Physics Case Western Reserve Univ Cleveland OH 44106

CROUCH, MARTHA LOUISE, b East Lasing, Mich, Sept 15, 51. DEVELOPMENTAL BIOLOGY. *Educ:* Ore State Univ, BS, 74, Yale Univ, MPh, 78, PhD(biol), 79. *Prof Exp:* ASST PROF PLANT SCI, BIOL DEPT, IND UNIV, 79- *Concurrent Pos:* Res assoc biol dept, Univ Calif, Los Angeles, 80-81. *Mem:* Soc Develop Biol; Am Soc Plant Physiol; Botanical Soc Am. *Res:* Developmental biology of higher plants; switch from embryonic growth to germination in embryos of Brassica napus by studying the regulation of storage protein synthesis. *Mailing Add:* Dept Biol Ind Univ Bloomington IN 47405

CROUCH, NORMAN ALBERT, b Monroe, Wis, June 7, 40; m 63; c 3. VIROLOGY. *Educ:* Univ Wis, BS, 62, MS, 66, PhD(med microbiol), 69. *Prof Exp:* Fel, Col Med, Baylor Univ, 69-70 & Pa State Univ, 70-72; asst prof microbiol, Univ Iowa, 72-78; ASST PROF MICROBIOL, UNIV ILL, 78- *Mem:* Am Soc Microbiol. *Res:* Noncytocidal virus-induced alterations which affect the behavior and function of cells in the infected animal host. *Mailing Add:* Dept of Biomed Sci Col of Med Univ Ill Rockford IL 61101

CROUCH, ROBERT WHEELER, b Detroit, Mich, Feb 27, 21; m 48. MICROPALEONTOLOGY, PALEOECOLOGY. *Educ:* Univ Southern Calif, BS, 47, MS, 48. *Prof Exp:* Paleontologist foraminifera, Richfield Oil Corp, 48-51; chief paleontologist, John W Mecom-Oil Independent, 53-65; sr paleontologist, 65-73, CONSULT PALEONTOLOGIST FORAMINIFERA, AMOCO PROD CO, STANDARD OIL, IND, 73- *Mem:* Am Asn Petrol Geologists; fel Geol Soc Am; Sigma Xi. *Res:* World wide plancktonic foraminiferal research. *Mailing Add:* 633 Ramona Ave Space 96 Los Osos CA 93402

CROUCH, ROGER KEITH, b Jamestown, Tenn, Sept 12, 40; c 3. SOLID STATE PHYSICS. *Educ:* Tenn Technol Univ, BS, 62; Va Polytech Inst & State Univ, MS, 68, PhD(physics), 71. *Prof Exp:* PHYSICIST SEMICONDUCTORS, LANGLEY RES CTR, NASA, 62- FLOYD THOMPSON FEL, 79- *Concurrent Pos:* Vis scientist, Mass Inst Technol, 79-80. *Mem:* Am Phys Soc; Am Asn Crystal Growth. *Res:* Materials processing in space; semiconductor crystal growth; infrared detectors and arrays; electrical and optical properties of impurities in semiconductors. *Mailing Add:* Mail Stop 473 NASA Langley Res Ctr Hampton VA 23665

CROUCH, STANLEY ROSS, b Turlock, Calif, Sept 23, 40. ANALYTICAL CHEMISTRY. *Educ:* Stanford Univ, MS, 63; Univ Ill, PhD(chem), 67. *Prof Exp:* Instr chem, Univ Ill, 67, vis asst prof, 67-68; asst prof, 68-74, assoc prof, 74-77, PROF CHEM, MICH STATE UNIV, 77- *Mem:* AAAS; Am Chem Soc; Optical Soc Am; Soc Appl Spectros. *Res:* Kinetics and mechanisms of analytical reactions; fast reaction kinetics; chemical instrumentation; analytical spectroscopy. *Mailing Add:* Dept of Chem Mich State Univ East Lansing MI 48824

CROUNSE, NATHAN NORMAN, b Omaha, Nebr, May 25, 17; m 39; c 3. ORGANIC CHEMISTRY. *Educ:* Iowa State Col, BS, 38; Univ Iowa, PhD(chem), 42. *Prof Exp:* Chemist, C M Bundy Co, 42-43; sr chemist org res, Hilton-Davis Chem Co, 43-47 & Inst Med Res, Christ Hosp, 47-51; assoc dir res, Hilton-Davis Chem Co, 51-62, dir chem res, 62-75, sr scientist, 75-80; CONSULT, 80- *Mem:* Am Chem Soc. *Res:* pigments, fluorescent compounds; colorless duplicating papers; structure studies in dyes and drug metabolism; germicides; aliphatic synthesis; dyes. *Mailing Add:* 302 Club Circle Myrtle Beach SC 29577

CROUNSE, ROBERT GRIFFITH, b Albany, NY, Mar 23, 31; m 55; c 2. DERMATOLOGY, BIOCHEMISTRY. *Educ:* Yale Univ, BS, 52, MD, 55; Am Bd Dermat, dipl, 63. *Prof Exp:* Intern, Grace-New Haven Hosp, Conn, 55-56; clin assoc, Nat Cancer Inst, 57-58; res asst prof, Sch Med, Univ Miami, 61, from asst prof to assoc prof, 63-64; assoc prof & chmn, sub-dept, Sch Med, Johns Hopkins Univ, 64-67; prof dermat & biochem & res dir, Med Col Ga, 67-73, assoc dean, Sch Med, & dir, Off Instrnl Systs, 71-73; prof dermat, 73-75, assoc dean, 73-80, chmn, Dept Med Allied Health Prof, 78-80, PROF EXPLOR SURG, DEPT SURG, EAST CAROLINA, UNIV GREENVILLE, NC, 80- *Concurrent Pos:* Fel dermat, Sch Med, Yale Univ, 56-57; Nat Cancer Inst spec res fel biochem, Sch Med, Univ Miami, 61-62; Nat Inst Arthritis & Metab Dis res career develop award, 62-64. *Mem:* Am Chem Soc; AMA; Soc Invest Dermat; Am Fedn Clin Res. *Res:* Biochemistry of epidermal keratinization; protein chemistry of epidermal structures; skin physiology and pharmacology. *Mailing Add:* Dept of Dermat Univ of NC Sch of Med Chapel Hill NC 27514

CROUSE, DALE MCCLISH, b Los Angeles, Calif, Aug 27, 41; m 66. ORGANIC CHEMISTRY. *Educ:* Stanford Univ, BS, 64; Ore State Univ, MS, 67; Univ Del, PhD(org chem), 78. *Prof Exp:* Res chemist, Res & Develop, 69-78, mfg asst, 78-79, SR SUPR, RES & DEVELOP, E I DU PONT DE NEMOURS & CO, INC, 80- *Mem:* Am Chem Soc. *Res:* Dialkyl carbene chemistry; Wittig reaction; organophosphorus; nuclear magnetic resonance spectroscopy; fluorocarbons; aromatic intermediates; specialty chemicals. *Mailing Add:* 3301 Market E I du Pont de Nemours & Co Inc Wilmington DE 19898

CROUSE, DAVID AUSTIN, b Canton, Ill, Aug 29, 44; m 68; c 2. HEMATOLOGY, DEVELOPMENTAL IMMUNOLOGY. *Educ:* Western Ill Univ, BS, 66, MS, 68; Univ Iowa, PhD(radiobiol), 74. *Prof Exp:* NDEA IV fel radiobiol, Univ Iowa, 71-74; app, Argonne Nat Lab, 75-76; MEM FAC, DEPT ANAT, UNIV NEBR MED CTR, OMAHA, 76- *Mem:* Radiation Res Soc; Am Asn Immunol; Int Soc Exp Hematol; Soc Cell Kinetics. *Res:* Role of the thymus in T-cell differentiation; regulation of thehematopoietic stem cell compartment; radiation and drug effects on hematopoietic and lymphoid cells; microenviromental interactions between stem cell and stromal cell populations in the lymphohematopoietic system. *Mailing Add:* Dept of Anat 42nd & Dewey Ave Omaha NE 68105

CROUSE, DAVID J, JR, b Johnstown, Pa, Jan 16, 20; m 54; c 2. CHEMICAL ENGINEERING. *Educ:* Pa State Univ, BS, 42. *Prof Exp:* Chem engr, Elec Storage Battery Co, 42-46 & Jaunty Fabric Corp, 47-48; ASST SECT CHIEF ATOMIC ENERGY RES, OAK RIDGE NAT LAB, 48- *Honors & Awards:* Indust Res-100 Award, 80. *Mem:* Am Nuclear Soc; Am Chem Soc. *Res:* Recovery of metals from ores by solvent extraction techniques; processing of atomic reactor fuels. *Mailing Add:* 249 Iroquois Rd Oak Ridge TN 37830

CROUSE, GAIL, b Connellsville, Pa, May 10, 23; m 51; c 3. ANATOMY. *Educ:* Heidelberg Col, BS, 50; Univ Mich, AM, 52, PhD(zool), 56. *Prof Exp:* From instr to asst prof anat, Hahnemann Med Col, 55-61; asst prof, 61-67, ASSOC PROF ANAT, SCH MED, TEMPLE UNIV, 67- *Mem:* Am Asn

Anatomists. Res: Experimental mammalian tissue transplantation, especially differentiation of embryonic tissue after transplantation to the brain; reactivity to prostheses in animals; transplantation site; progressive development of the autonomic nervous system in human fetuses. *Mailing Add:* Dept Anat Temple Univ Sch of Med Philadelphia PA 19140

CROUT, JOHN RICHARD, b Portland, Ore, Dec 30, 29; m 54; c 3. CLINICAL PHARMACOLOGY, PUBLIC HEALTH ADMINISTRATION. *Educ:* Oberlin Col, AB, 51; Northwestern Univ, MD, 55, MS, 56; Am Bd Internal Med, dipl, 62. *Prof Exp:* Intern, Passavant Mem Hosp, Chicago, Ill, 55-56; asst resident med, Vet Admin Res Hosp, Chicago, 56-57; clin assoc, Nat Heart Inst, 57-60; asst resident, NY Univ-Bellevue Hosp Med Ctr, 60-61; instr pharmacol, Harvard Med Sch, 61-63; from asst prof to assoc prof pharmacol & internal med, Univ Tex Southwestern Med Sch, 63-70; prof pharmacol & med, Col Human Med, Mich State Univ, 70-71; dep dir, Bur Drugs, 71-72, dir, off Sci Eval, 72-73, DIR, BUR DRUGS, FOOD & DRUG ADMIN, 73- *Concurrent Pos:* Res fel pharmacol, Harvard Med Sch, 61-62; USPHS fel, 61-63, Burroughs-Wellcome scholar clin pharmacol, 65-70; mem, Coun High Blood Pressure Res, Am Heart Asn, Anesthesiol Training Grant Comt, Nat Inst Gen Med Sci, 66-68, Pharmacol, Toxicol Prog Comt, 69-71, Comt Myocardial Info Study Ctrs, NIH, 67 & Ad Hoc Sci Adv Comt, Food & Drug Admin, 70-71; field ed, J Am Soc Pharmacol & Exp Therapeut, 68-71. *Mem:* Am Fedn Clin Res; Am Soc Pharmacol & Exp Therapeut; Am Soc Clin Pharmacol & Therapeut; Am Soc Clin Invest; fel Am Col Physicians. *Res:* Catecholamine metabolism; pheochromocytoma; cardiovascular pharmacology; hypertension; clinical pharmacology; drug regulation policy. *Mailing Add:* HFD-1 Food & Drug Admin 5600 Fishers Lane Rockville MD 20857

CROUTHAMEL, CARL EUGENE, b Lansdale, Pa, Dec 25, 20; m 44; c 3. INORGANIC CHEMISTRY. *Educ:* Eastern Nazarene Col, BS, 42; Boston Univ, MA, 43; Iowa State Col, PhD(chem), 50. *Prof Exp:* Inorg chem res, Manhattan Proj, 43-44; res assoc, Inst Atomic Res, Iowa State Col, 46-50; sr chemist, Argonne Lab, 50-66, 67-73; SR ENGR, EXXON NUCLEAR CORP, 73- *Mem:* AAAS; NY Acad Sci; Am Chem Soc; Sigma Xi; Am Nuclear Soc. *Res:* Inorganic chemistry of transuranium elements; rare earths; fused salt-liquid metals chemistry; development of high temperature fast breeder reactor fuel and materials; fuel performance of LWR reactor fuel. *Mailing Add:* 71 Park St Richland WA 99352

CROUTHAMEL, WILLIAM GUY, b Sellersville, Pa, Feb 11, 42; m 66; c 4. PHARMACY, PHARMACEUTICS. *Educ:* Philadelphia Col Pharm & Sci, BS, 65, MS, 67; Univ Ky, PhD(pharmaceut), 70. *Prof Exp:* From asst prof to assoc prof pharmaceut, WVa Univ, 70-75; assoc prof pharm, Univ Md, Baltimore City, 75-78; group chief, 78-80, SECT HEAD, BIOPHARMACEUT, HOFFMANN-LA ROCHE, 80- *Mem:* Am Pharmaceut Asn; Sigma Xi. *Res:* Effect of factors such as pH and intestinal blood flow on the kinetics of gastrointestinal drug absorption; effect of disease states on drug kinetics; dosage form effects on the absorption of drugs. *Mailing Add:* Dept Biochem & Drug Metab Hoffmann-La Roche Inc Nutley NJ 07110

CROVELLO, THEODORE JOHN, b Brooklyn, NY, Nov 20, 40; m 62; c 2. SYSTEMATICS, BIOCOMPUTING. *Educ:* State Univ NY Col Forestry, Syracuse, BS, 62; Univ Calif, Berkeley, PhD(bot), 66. *Prof Exp:* Res assoc bot & entom, Univ Kans, 66-67; from asst prof to assoc prof biol, 66-75, PROF BIOL, UNIV NOTRE DAME, 75-, CUR HERBARIUM, 66- *Concurrent Pos:* Chmn, Int Register Comput Proj Systs, 74-; mem adv bd, Plant Systs & Evolution, Int J, 74-; mem proposal rev panel, Res Sci Educ Prog, NSF, 81. *Mem:* Fel Am Soc Naturalists; Bot Soc Am; Soc Syst Zool; Am Soc Plant Taxon; Soc Study Evolution. *Res:* Computerized information retrieval of herbarium and floristic data; plant geography; Indiana biological survey; systematics and evolutionary strategies of the mustard family; computers in biological teaching. *Mailing Add:* Dept of Biol Univ of Notre Dame Notre Dame IN 46556

CROVETTI, ALDO JOSEPH, b Lake Forest, Ill, Apr 2, 30; m 59. ORGANIC CHEMISTRY. *Educ:* Lake Forest Col, BA, 51; Univ Ill, MS, 52, PhD(org chem), 55. *Prof Exp:* Res chemist, 55-65, group leader, 65-67, res org chemist, 67-70, sect head & dept mgr, Agr Prod Res & Develop, Agr & Indust Prod Res & Develop, 70-75, mgr agr chem res & develop, 75-78, MGR AGR CHEM FIELD RES & DEVELOP, ABBOTT LABS, 78- *Mem:* Am Chem Soc; Sigma Xi; Am Soc Hort Sci; Plant Growth Regulator Soc Am; Int Soc Heterocyclic Chem. *Res:* Synthesis in the fields of heterocyclic compounds, mainly nitrogen; agricultural chemistry and biological research, including field research. *Mailing Add:* D-986 Abbott Labs 14th & Sheridan Rd North Chicago IL 60064

CROW, ALONZO BIGLER, b Warren, Pa, Aug 27, 10; m 35; c 1. FOREST ECOLOGY. *Educ:* NC State Col, BS, 34; Yale Univ, MF, 41. *Prof Exp:* Jr forester, US Forest Serv, Mo, 34-35 & Pa, 35-40; asst agr aide & jr soil conservationist, Soil Conserv Serv, USDA, Md, 41-42, asst soil conservationist, 42-45; from asst to regional consult, Am Forestry Asn, Washington, DC, 45-46; from asst prof to prof, 46-76, EMER PROF FORESTRY, LA STATE UNIV, BATON ROUGE, 76- *Mem:* Soc Am Foresters. *Res:* Forest ecology; southern pines; geographic seed sources loblolly pine; forest fire control and use. *Mailing Add:* 1957 Cherrydale Ave Baton Rouge LA 70808

CROW, EDWIN LEE, b Clinton, Mo, Apr 26, 39; m 62. ORGANIC CHEMISTRY. *Educ:* Univ Mo, PhD(chem), 66. *Prof Exp:* Chemist, Electrochem Dept, Del, 65-68, develop chemist, Tex, 68-70, res supvr, Wilmington, Del, 70-74, tech supt, 74-78, prod supt, Gibbstown, NJ & Memphis, Tenn, 78-80, ENVIRON MGR, E I DU PONT DE NEMOURS & CO, WILMINGTON, DEL, 80- *Mem:* Am Chem Soc. *Res:* Catalytic reactions; organometallic chemistry; chemistry of carbenes; chemistry of olefins. *Mailing Add:* 2604 W 17th St Wilmington DE 19806

CROW, EDWIN LOUIS, b Cadiz Twp, Wis, Sept 15, 16; m 42; c 2. STATISTICS, MATHEMATICS. *Educ:* Beloit Col, BS, 37; Univ Wis, PhM, 38, PhD(math), 41. *Prof Exp:* Instr math, Case Sch Appl Sci, 41-42; mathematician res & develop div, Bur Ord, US Navy Dept, 42-46; mathematician, US Naval Ord Test Sta, 46-54, head statist br, 50-54; consult statist, Boulder Labs, Nat Bur Stand, 54-65, Environ Sci Serv Admin, 65-70 & Off Telecommun, US Dept Com, 70-73; STATISTICIAN, INST TELECOMMUN SCI, US DEPT COM, 74-, NAT CTR ATMOSPHERIC RES, 75- *Concurrent Pos:* Instr exten div, Univ Calif, Los Angeles, 47-54 & Metrop State Col, 74; Govt Employees Training Act trainee, London, 61-62; adj prof appl math, Univ Colo, 63-81. *Honors & Awards:* Bronze Medal, US Dept Com, 70. *Mem:* Fel AAAS; Soc Indust & Appl Math; Inst Math Statist; fel Am Statist Asn; Royal Statist Soc. *Res:* Expansion problems associated with ordinary differential equations; mathematical statistics with applications in ordnance, radio propagation, radio standards, communication systems and weather modification. *Mailing Add:* 605 20th St Boulder CO 80302

CROW, FRANK WARREN, b Madison, Wis, Feb 10, 51; m 78. ANALYTICAL CHEMISTRY, MASS SPECTROMETRY. *Educ:* Univ Wis-Stevens Point, BS, 73; Univ Va, PhD(chem), 78. *Prof Exp:* Res scientist anal chem, Columbus Labs, Battelle Mem Inst, 78-79; ASST DIR, DEPT CHEM, MIDWEST CTR MASS SPECTROMETRY, UNIV NEBR, 79- *Mem:* Am Chem Soc; Am Soc Mass Spectrometry. *Res:* Gas chromatography; computer applications; negative ion chemical ionization mass spectrometry; chemical derivatization; mass spectrometry; fast atom bombardment. *Mailing Add:* Midwest Ctr Mass Spectrometry Rm 8 Hamilton Hall Chem Dept Univ Nebr Lincoln NE 68588

CROW, FRANKLIN ROMIG, b Liverpool, Pa, Dec 28, 17; m 42; c 3. AGRICULTURAL ENGINEERING. *Educ:* Pa State Univ, BS, 40; Okla State Univ, MS, 52. *Prof Exp:* Agr engr, US Soil Conserv Serv, 40-43, 46-49; from instr to assoc prof agr eng, 49-77, PROF AGR ENG, OKLA STATE UNIV, 77- *Mem:* Am Soc Agr Engrs; Am Geophys Union. *Res:* Use of monomolecular films to reduce evaporation from water supply reservoirs. *Mailing Add:* Dept of Agr Eng Okla State Univ Stillwater OK 74074

CROW, GARRETT EUGENE, b Phoenix, Ariz, Dec 11, 42; m 72; c 3. SYSTEMATIC BOTANY, AQUATIC PLANTS. *Educ:* Taylor Univ, AB, 65; Mich State Univ, MS, 68, PhD(bot), 74. *Prof Exp:* Instr, Mich State Univ, 73-74, fel syst bot & man & biosphere, 74-75; asst prof, 75-81, ASSOC PROF SYST BOT & CUR, HERBARIUM, UNIV NH, 81- *Concurrent Pos:* US-USSR scientific exchange, 81. *Mem:* Int Asn Plant Taxonomists; Am Soc Plant Taxonomists; Sigma Xi; Bot Soc Am; Am Inst Biol Sci. *Res:* Plant systematics, particularly Caryophyllaceae Sagina; scanning electron microscope studies in seed morphology in Caryophyllaceae, floristics, ecology and phytogeography of arctic, subantarctic, alpine plants, bogs, aquatic plants; flora and endangered species of plants of New Hampshire. *Mailing Add:* Dept of Bot & Plant Path Univ of NH Durham NH 03824

CROW, JAMES FRANKLIN, b Phoenixville, Pa, Jan 18, 16; m 41; c 3. GENETICS. *Educ:* Friends Univ, AB, 37; Univ Tex, PhD(genetics), 41. *Prof Exp:* Tutor zool, Univ Tex, 37-40; from instr zool to asst prof zool & prev med, Med Sch, Dartmouth Col, 41-48; from asst prof to prof zool & genetics, 48-58, actg dean, Med Sch, 63-65, chmn, Dept Genetics & Med Genetics, 65-70, PROF MED GENETICS, UNIV WIS-MADISON, 58- *Mem:* Nat Acad Sci; Genetics Soc Am (pres, 60); Am Soc Human Genetics (pres, 63); AAAS; Soc Study Evolution. *Res:* Genetics of Drosophila; population genetics. *Mailing Add:* Dept Genetics Univ Wis Madison WI 53706

CROW, JOHN H, b San Pedro, Calif, Nov 18, 42; m 66. PLANT ECOLOGY. *Educ:* Whittier Col, BA, 64; Wash State Univ, PhD(bot), 68. *Prof Exp:* Asst prof bot, 68-71, chmn dept, 72-78, ASSOC PROF BOT, RUTGERS UNIV, 71- *Concurrent Pos:* Ecol consult, State of Wash, 68-69, US Dept Interior, 74- & State of NJ Dept Pub Advocate, 75 & State Alaska Dept Fish & Game, 76-; mem panel productivity, Nat Wetlands Tech Coun, 78-79; solid waste coordr & dir, Dept Environ, Warrey Co, NJ, 81. *Honors & Awards:* A G Tausley Award, 81. *Mem:* AAAS; Am Inst Biol; Ecol Soc Am; Sigma Xi. *Res:* Ecological investigations of the salt marshes of Pacific Coastal Alaska; food habits of marsh, estuarine and marine organisms; secondary productivity; Atriplex salt balance physiological research; wetland vegetation of New Jersey; upland forest composition and environmental studies; salt marsh pollution; solid waste and resource recovery. *Mailing Add:* Dept of Bot Rutgers Univ Newark NJ 07102

CROW, TERRY TOM, b Sapulpa, Okla, Sept 16, 31; m 54; c 3. ELECTROMAGNETISM. *Educ:* Miss State Univ, BS, 53; Vanderbilt Univ, MA, 57, PhD(physics), 60. *Prof Exp:* Asst prof physics, Miss State Univ, 60-62; physicist, Lawrence Radiation Lab, Univ Calif, 62-64; assoc prof, 64-67, PROF PHYSICS, MISS STATE UNIV, 67-, DEPT HEAD, 79- *Mem:* Inst Elec & Electronics Engrs; Am Phys Soc. *Res:* Electromagnetic theory. *Mailing Add:* Dept of Physics Miss State Univ Mississippi State MS 39762

CROW, THOMAS RALPH, forest ecology, see previous edition

CROW, WESLEY BLANKE, metallurgical engineering, see previous edition

CROWDER, ADELE A, plant ecology, see previous edition

CROWDER, GENE AUTREY, b Wichita Falls, Tex, Oct 25, 36; m 65; c 2. PHYSICAL CHEMISTRY. *Educ:* Cent State Col, Okla, BS, 58; Univ Fla, MS, 61; Okla State Univ, PhD(phys chem), 64. *Prof Exp:* Asst res chemist, Petrol Chems, Inc & Cities Serv-Continental Oil Co, 58-59; from asst prof to assoc prof, 64-68, PROF CHEM, W TEX STATE UNIV, 68-, HEAD DEPT, 70- *Mem:* Am Chem Soc; Soc Appl Spectros; Coblentz Soc; Sigma Xi. *Res:* Molecular spectroscopy; vibrational assignments and normal coordinate calculations; rotational isomerism. *Mailing Add:* Dept Chem W Tex State Univ Canyon TX 79015

CROWDER, LARRY A, b Mattoon, Ill, Mar 12, 42; m 64; c 2. INSECT PHYSIOLOGY, TOXICOLOGY. *Educ:* Eastern Ill Univ, BS, 64; Purdue Univ, MS, 66, PhD(entom), 70. *Prof Exp:* assoc prof, 69-80, PROF INSECT PHYSIOL, UNIV ARIZ, 80- *Mem:* AAAS; Entom Soc Am; Am Chem Soc; Am Registry Prof Entomologists; Sigma Xi. *Res:* Significance of 5-hydroxytryptamine in insects; mode of action of cyclodiene insecticides; regulation of insect diapause; insect resistance. *Mailing Add:* Dept Entom Univ Ariz Tucson AZ 85721

CROWDER, LOY VAN, plant breeding, see previous edition

CROWE, ARLENE JOYCE, b Wakaw, Sask, Can, Oct 8, 31. BIOCHEMISTRY. *Educ:* Univ Alta, BSc, 50; McGill Univ, MSc, 56, PhD(biochem), 62. *Prof Exp:* Res asst liver dis, Hammersmith Hosp, Postgrad Sch, London, 56-57; chief technologist biochem, Montreal Children's Hosp, Que, 57-59; BIOCHEMIST, HOTEL DIEU HOSP, 62- *Concurrent Pos:* Lectr, Queen's Univ, Ont, 62-; ed, Can Soc Clin Chem Newslett. *Honors & Awards:* Ames Award, Can Soc Clin Chem, 78. *Mem:* Can Soc Clin Chem; Am Asn Clin Chem; NY Acad Sci. *Mailing Add:* Dept Biochem Hotel Dieu Hosp Kingston ON K7L 3H6 Can

CROWE, CAMERON MACMILLAN, b Montreal, Que, Oct 6, 31; m 69. CHEMICAL ENGINEERING. *Educ:* McGill Univ, BEng, 53; Cambridge Univ, PhD(chem eng), 57. *Prof Exp:* Sr develop engr, Du Pont of Can, 57-59; from asst prof to assoc prof, 59-70, chmn dept, 71-74, PROF CHEM ENG, McMASTER UNIV, 70- *Concurrent Pos:* C D Howe Mem fel, Rice Univ, 67-68; assoc ed, Can J Chem Eng, 75-81. *Mem:* Am Inst Chem Engrs; fel Chem Inst Can. *Res:* Design, optimization and simulation of reactors and chemical systems; applications of mathematics and numerical methods. *Mailing Add:* Dept Chem Eng McMaster Univ Hamilton ON L8S 4L7 Can

CROWE, CHRISTOPHER, b London, Eng, Dec 4, 28; m 52; c 3. GEOPHYSICS. *Educ:* Western Ont Univ, BSc, 52, PhD(physics), 56. *Prof Exp:* Teacher pub schs, Ont, 46-47; physics demonstr, Western Ont Univ, 52-55; 1851 Exhib Overseas scholar, Dept Geod & Geophys, Cambridge Univ, 56-58; asst prof geophys, Pa State Univ, 58-63; staff geophysicist, Tex Instruments, Inc, 64-66; scientist, 66-69; sr geophysicist, Sun Oil Co, 69-70, res scientist, 70-77; STAFF RES SCIENTIST, RES CTR, AMOCO PROD CO, 77- *Concurrent Pos:* Consult, Earth Sci Curric Proj, Am Geol Inst, 63-65. *Mem:* AAAS; Brit Inst Physics; Am Geophys Union; Soc Explor Geophys; Can Asn Physicists. *Res:* Heat flow; geophysical exploration; physical properties of materials; seismic absorption and dispersion; direct hydrocarbon detection. *Mailing Add:* Res Ctr 4502 E 41st St PO Box 591 Tulsa OK 74102

CROWE, DAVID BURNS, b New Brighton, Pa, Oct 6, 30; m 56; c 2. ZOOLOGY. *Educ:* Washington & Jefferson Col, BA, 52; Univ Mich, MS, 57; Univ Louisville, PhD(biol), 64. *Prof Exp:* Instr biol, State Univ NY, 58-61; PROF BIOL, UNIV WIS-EAU CLAIRE, 64- *Mem:* Am Soc Ichthyologists & Herpetologists. *Res:* Orientation of social piscine groups with emphasis on integrative role of the sense organs. *Mailing Add:* Dept of Biol Univ of Wis Eau Claire WI 54701

CROWE, DONALD WARREN, b Lincoln, Nebr, Oct 28, 27; m 53; c 3. MATHEMATICS. *Educ:* Univ Nebr, BS, 49, MA, 51; Univ Mich, PhD(math), 59. *Prof Exp:* Instr math, Univ BC, 55-57; lectr, Univ Toronto, 57-59 & Univ Col, Ibadan, 59-62; from asst prof to assoc prof, 62-68, PROF MATH, UNIV WIS, MADISON, 68- *Concurrent Pos:* Vis distinguished prof, Calif State Univ, Chico, 78 & 81. *Mem:* Math Asn Am. *Res:* Geometry, especially combinatorial problems and applications to archeology. *Mailing Add:* Dept Math Univ Wis Madison WI 53706

CROWE, GEORGE JOSEPH, b Brooklyn, NY, Oct 1, 21; m 52; c 11. SOLID STATE PHYSICS. *Educ:* Manhattan Col, BS, 43; Columbia Univ, MA, 47; Carnegie Inst Technol, MS, 61, PhD(physics), 66. *Prof Exp:* Instr physics, Manhattan Col, 46-48; assoc prof, Seton Hill Col, 48-64; proj physicist, Carnegie Inst Technol, 64-65, instr physics, 65; assoc prof, 65-74, chmn dept, 68-77, PROF PHYSICS, MANHATTAN COL, 74- *Mem:* AAAS; Am Phys Soc; Am Asn Physics Teachers. *Res:* Point defects in alkali halides; electron irradiated cadmium sulfide x-ray spectroscopy. *Mailing Add:* Dept of Physics Manhattan Col Riverdale NY 10471

CROWE, JOHN H, b Columbia, SC, Apr 12, 43. COMPARATIVE PHYSIOLOGY. *Educ:* Wake Forest Univ, BS, 65, MA, 67; Univ Calif, Riverside, PhD(biol), 70. *Prof Exp:* From asst prof to assoc prof, 70-79, PROF ZOOL, UNIV CALIF, DAVIS, 79- *Concurrent Pos:* Consult, Review Panelist, NSF, 75-78; chmn, Div Comp Physiol & Biochem, Am Soc Zoologist, 80-81. *Mem:* Sigma Xi; Am Soc Zoologists; fel AAAS; Am Micros Soc; Biophys Soc Am. *Res:* Physiology of the induction of cryptobiotic states; intracellular water; water and membrane structure; cryobiology. *Mailing Add:* Dept Zool Univ Calif Davis CA 95616

CROWE, KENNETH MORSE, b Boston, Mass, Oct 6, 26; m 63; c 3. PHYSICS. *Educ:* Brown Univ, BS, 48, PhD(physics), 53. *Prof Exp:* Physicist, Radiation Lab, Univ Calif, 49-51; res assoc, High-Energy Physics Lab, Stanford Univ, 51-56; from asst prof to assoc prof, 58-69, PROF PHYSICS, UNIV CALIF, BERKELEY, 69-, PHYSICIST, LAWRENCE RADIATION LAB, 56- *Mem:* Am Phys Soc. *Res:* High-energy particle physics. *Mailing Add:* Dept of Physics Univ of Calif Berkeley CA 94720

CROWELL, ALBERT DARY, b Dover, NH, Feb 12, 25; m 47; c 3. SURFACE PHYSICS. *Educ:* Brown Univ, BEE, 46, PhD(physics), 50; Harvard Univ, MS, 47. *Prof Exp:* From instr to asst prof, Amherst Col, 50-55; from asst prof to assoc prof, 55-61, chmn dept, 61-75, PROF PHYSICS, UNIV VT, 61- *Concurrent Pos:* Vis prof, Bristol Univ, 68 & Univ Southampton, UK, 76. *Mem:* AAAS; Am Asn Physics Teachers; Am Phys Soc; Am Vacuum Soc. *Res:* Adsorption of gases. *Mailing Add:* Dept of Physics Univ of Vt Burlington VT 05401

CROWELL, CLARENCE ROBERT, b Sweetsburg, Que, July 29, 28. ELECTRICAL ENGINEERING, MATERIALS SCIENCE. *Educ:* McGill Univ, BA, 49, MSc, 51, PhD(physics), 55. *Prof Exp:* Jr res officer elec eng, Radio & Elec Eng Div, Nat Res Coun Can, 54-55; asst prof physics, McGill Univ, 55-60; mem tech staff semiconductor device res & develop, Bell Labs, 60-66; PROF ELEC ENG & MAT SCI, UNIV SOUTHERN CALIF, 66- *Concurrent Pos:* Consult, Chem Physics Dept, Hughes Res Lab, 69-; Humboldt fel, 74. *Mem:* Am Vacuum Soc; fel Inst Elec & Electronics Engrs; Sigma Xi. *Res:* Semiconductor device and interface physics; charge storage and charge transport in metal-semiconductor systems. *Mailing Add:* Dept Mat Sci University Park Los Angeles CA 90007

CROWELL, EDWIN PATRICK, b Elizabeth, NJ, Feb 27, 34; m 58; c 6. CHEMISTRY. *Educ:* Seton Hall Univ, BS, 56; Univ Richmond, MS, 62. *Prof Exp:* Control anal chemist, Ethylene Oxide Unit, Gen Aniline & Film Corp, 56-58; assoc chemist, Anal Res, Phillip Morris, Inc, 58-62; res chemist, Agr Div, Am Cyanamid Co, 62-63; res scientist, 63-70, group leader, 70-74, sect leader, 74-81, ASST LAB DIR, RES & DEVELOP DIV, UNION CAMP CORP, 81- *Mem:* Am Chem Soc; Tech Asn Pulp & Paper Indust; Am Indust Hyg Asn. *Res:* Development of instrumental and chemical analytical procedures in support of research program in paper pulp and chemical byproducts; tobacco and agricultural chemicals. *Mailing Add:* Res Div Union Camp Corp Box 412 Princeton NJ 08540

CROWELL, HAMBLIN HOWES, b Portland, Ore, Aug 23, 13; m 39; c 1. ENTOMOLOGY. *Educ:* Ore State Col, BS, 35, MS, 37; Ohio State Univ, PhD(entom), 40. *Prof Exp:* Asst biol surv, Ore State Col, 35-37 & zool & entom, Ohio State Univ, 37-40; sanit inspector, Health Dept, CZ, 40-44; asst entomologist, Exp Sta, 46-51; assoc prof, 51-66, actg head entom dept, 58-59, prof, 66-77, EMER PROF ENTOM, ORE STATE UNIV, 77- *Mem:* AAAS; Entom Soc Am. *Res:* Economic entomology and malacology. *Mailing Add:* Dept of Entom Ore State Univ Corvallis OR 97331

CROWELL, JACK WESLEY, physiology, biophysics, see previous edition

CROWELL, JOHN CHAMBERS, b State College, Pa, May 12, 17; m 46; c 1. GEOLOGY. *Educ:* Univ Tex, BS, 39; Univ Calif, Los Angeles, MA, 46, PhD(geol), 47. *Hon Degrees:* DSc, Cath Univ Louvain, 66. *Prof Exp:* Asst geologist, Shell Oil Co, Inc, 41-43; from instr to prof geol, Univ Calif, Los Angeles, 47-67, chmn dept, 57-60, 63-67; PROF GEOL, UNIV CALIF, SANTA BARBARA, 67- *Concurrent Pos:* Guggenheim Found fel, 53-54; Fulbright res prof, Austria, 53-54; NSF sr res fel, Scotland, 60-61; distinguished lectr, Am Asn Petrol Geologists; nat lectr, Sigma Xi, 80-82. *Honors & Awards:* Chrestien Mica Gondwanaland Medal, Mining, Geol & Metall Inst India, 72. *Mem:* Geol Soc Am; Am Asn Petrol Geol; Am Geophys Union; Soc Econ Paleont & Mineral; Sigma Xi. *Res:* Structural and general geology; tectonics; paleoclimatology of ancient ice ages. *Mailing Add:* Dept of Geol Univ of Calif Santa Barbara CA 93106

CROWELL, JOHN MARSHALL, b Mobile, Ala, June 30, 42. BIOMEDICAL INSTRUMENTATION, ENVIRONMENTAL INSTRUMENTATION. *Educ:* Ga Inst Technol, BS, 64; Johns Hopkins Univ, PhD(physics), 73. *Prof Exp:* PHYSICIST, LOS ALAMOS SCI LAB, UNIV CALIF, 73- *Mem:* Am Phys Soc; Inst Elec & Electronic Engrs; Asn Comput Mach. *Res:* Intelligent instrumentation; nuclear instrumentation. *Mailing Add:* H-4/MS 493 Measurements & Instrumentation Los Alamos Sci Lab PO Box 1663 Los Alamos NM 87545

CROWELL, JULIAN, b Shelbyville, Tenn, Jan 24, 34; m 58; c 3. MATHEMATICS. *Educ:* Univ Tenn, BS, 56; Vanderbilt Univ, MS, 59, PhD(physics), 66. *Prof Exp:* Lectr physics, Gordon Col, Rawalpindi, Pakistan, 58-61; asst prof physics, Roanoke Col, 65-67; assoc prof physics & math, St Andrews Presby Col, 67-69; assoc prof math, Bosphorus Univ, Istanbul, Turkey, 69-78, chmn dept, 71-76; PROF MATH & PHYSICS, INST NAT D'ELECTRICITE ET D'ELECTRONIQUE, BOUMERDES, ALGERIA, 78- *Concurrent Pos:* Consult- 66-70. *Mem:* Math Asn Am; Nat Coun Teachers Math. *Res:* Positron annihilation in metals; collective phenomena in metals. *Mailing Add:* INELEC Boumerdes Algeria

CROWELL, KENNETH L, b Glen Ridge, NJ, July 19, 33; m 62; c 1. VERTEBRATE ECOLOGY, ZOOGEOGRAPHY. *Educ:* Yale Univ, BS, 55; Univ Pa, PhD(zool), 61. *Prof Exp:* Instr zool, Duke Univ, 61-62; mem fac biol, Marlboro Col, 62-66; fel zool, Calgary Univ, 66-67, instr, 67; asst prof, 67-74, ASSOC PROF BIOL, ST LAWRENCE UNIV, 74- *Concurrent Pos:* Chapman Mem Fund grant, Am Mus Natural Hist, 59-60, 66; Jessup Fund grant, Acad Natural Sci Philadelphia, 61; Res Soc grant, Soc Sigma Xi, 62; NSF grants, 62-72; dir, Planned Parenthood Northern NY, 69-71; trustee, Adirondack Conservancy Comt, 75- *Mem:* Fel AAAS; Ecol Soc Am; Am Ornith Union; Am Soc Mammal. *Res:* Population dynamics and niche segregation through studies of competition and habitat selection in mammals of islands of Gulf of Maine and birds of Bermuda and West Indies, habitat islands in northern New York, rare species in Adirondack region. *Mailing Add:* Dept of Biol St Lawrence Univ Canton NY 13617

CROWELL, MERTON HOWARD, b Corry, Pa, June 5, 32. ELECTRO-OPTICS. *Educ:* Pa State Univ, BS, 56; New York Univ, MS, 60; Polytech Inst Brooklyn, PhD(electro-phys), 70. *Prof Exp:* Group supvr electron devices, Bell Tel Labs, 56-69; dir device res, 69-74, MGR, ELECTRO-OPTICAL LAB, PHILIPS LABS, 76- *Mem:* Fel Inst Elec & Electronics Engrs. *Res:* Simulation of electro-optics; author or coauthor of over 50 publications. *Mailing Add:* Syst Planning Corp 1500 Wilson Blvd Arlington VA 22209

CROWELL, RICHARD HENRY, b Northeast, Pa, Apr 6, 28; m 55; c 2. MATHEMATICS. *Educ:* Harvard Univ, AB, 49; Princeton Univ, MA, 53, PhD(math), 55. *Hon Degrees:* MA, Dartmouth Col, 67. *Prof Exp:* Asst anal res group, Forrestal Res Ctr, Princeton Univ, 55-57; lectr, Mass Inst Technol, 57-58; from asst prof to assoc prof, 58-67, chmn dept, 73-79, PROF MATH, DARTMOUTH COL, 67- *Mem:* Am Math Soc; Math Asn Am. *Res:* Topology, knot theory and algebraic topology. *Mailing Add:* Dept Math Dartmouth Col Hanover NH 03755

CROWELL, RICHARD LANE, b Springfield, Mo, Sept 27, 30; m 53; c 4. VIROLOGY. *Educ:* Univ Buffalo, BA, 52; Univ Minn, MS, 54, PhD(microbiol), 58; Am Bd Med Microbiol dipl. *Prof Exp:* Nat Cancer Inst trainee & instr microbiol, Univ Minn, 58-60; from asst prof to assoc prof, 60-71, PROF MICROBIOL, HAHNEMANN MED COL, 71-, CHMN DEPT MICROBIOL & IMMUNOL, 79- *Concurrent Pos:* Nat Inst Allergy & Infectious Dis res career develop award, 62-72; consult, Virus-Tissue Resources Br, Nat Cancer Inst, 66-68; vis res scientist, Univ Uppsala, 69-70; consult, Smith Kline Corp, 75-77 & Lehn & Fink Prod, Inc, 76-80. *Mem:* Sigma Xi; Am Soc Microbiol; AAAS; Am Asn Immunologists; fel Am Acad Microbiol. *Res:* Human enteroviruses in mammalian cell cultures, with emphasis on enzyme levels, chronic infection, viral interference, cell susceptibility, characterization of viral receptors of cells and viral proteins; relationship between cellular differentiation and factors controlling virus susceptibility as studied in tissue culture systems; role of coxsackieviruses in heart disease and diabetes. *Mailing Add:* Dept of Microbiol & Immunol 230 N Broad St Philadelphia PA 19102

CROWELL, ROBERT MERRILL, b Sandusky, Ohio, May 29, 21; m 46; c 3. ZOOLOGY, ENTOMOLOGY. *Educ:* Bowling Green State Univ, AB, 45, MA, 47; Ohio State Univ, PhD(zool), 57. *Prof Exp:* Asst biol, Bowling Green State Univ, 45-47; instr, Kent State Univ, 47-48; asst zool, Duke Univ, 48-51; instr biol, Col Wooster, 51-55; from asst prof to assoc prof, 56-67, PROF BIOL, ST LAWRENCE UNIV, 67- *Concurrent Pos:* NSF res grants, 61-63 & 69-71; trainee, Ohio State Univ, 67-68; vis scholar, Univ Amsterdam, 76; guest investr, Freshwater Biol Asn, 77. *Mem:* Entom Soc Am; Am Soc Parasitol; Entom Soc Can. *Res:* Systematics; developmental cycles; host-parasite relationships of the Hydracarina. *Mailing Add:* Dept of Biol St Lawrence Univ Canton NY 13617

CROWELL, (PRINCE) SEARS, (JR), b Natick, Mass, May 2, 09; m 38; c 3. DEVELOPMENTAL BIOLOGY, INVERTEBRATE ZOOLOGY. *Educ:* Bowdoin Col, AB, 30; Harvard Univ, AM, 31, PhD(biol), 35. *Prof Exp:* Instr, Brooklyn Col, 35-36; from instr to assoc prof zool, Miami Univ, Ohio, 36-48; from asst prof to prof, 48-79, EMER PROF ZOOL, IND UNIV, BLOOMINGTON, 79- *Concurrent Pos:* Mem corp, Marine Biol Lab, Woods Hole, trustee, 58-66, 67-75, mem exec comt trustees, 63-66, 67-70 & secy bd trustees, 72-75; managing ed, Am Zoologist, Am Soc Zoologists, 61-65. *Mem:* AAAS; Am Soc Zoologists; Soc Develop Biol; Int Soc Develop Biol. *Res:* Morphogenesis and natural history of hydroids; regeneration in worms. *Mailing Add:* Dept of Biol Indiana Univ Bloomington IN 47401

CROWELL, THOMAS IRVING, b Glen Ridge, NJ, July 9, 21; m 50; c 2. PHYSICAL ORGANIC CHEMISTRY. *Educ:* Harvard Univ, BS, 43; Columbia Univ, AM, 47, PhD(chem), 48. *Prof Exp:* Asst, Manhattan Proj, 43-45; asst chem, Columbia Univ, 45-46; instr math, Bard Col, 46-47; from asst prof to assoc prof, 48-61, chmn dept, 57-62, PROF CHEM, UNIV VA, 61- *Mem:* Am Chem Soc; Sigma Xi. *Res:* Organic reaction kinetics; fused salts. *Mailing Add:* Dept of Chem Univ of Va Charlottesville VA 22901

CROWELL, WAYNE ALLEN, b Sterling, Colo, Nov 25, 40; m 63; c 2. VETERINARY PATHOLOGY, VETERINARY MEDICINE. *Educ:* Colo State Univ, BS, 63, DVM, 64; Univ Ga, PhD, 73. *Prof Exp:* Post vet, US Army, 66-68; res vet animal sci, Com Solvents Corp, 68-70; res assoc to asst prof path, Univ Ga, 70-74; assoc prof path, La State Univ, 74-76; ASSOC PROF PATH, UNIV GA, 76- *Honors & Awards:* Nat Award of Excellence, Am Vet Med Asn, 78. *Mem:* Am Vet Med Asn; Am Col Vet Path; Int Acad Path; Soc. Vet Urol; Am Asn Vet Med Col. *Res:* Renal disease of animals, amyliodosis, pathology of parasitic diseases in animals, educational methods. *Mailing Add:* Dept of Vet Path Univ of Ga Athens GA 30602

CROWELL, WILFRED J, b Can, Jan 23, 18; US citizen; m 53; c 3. PHARMACEUTICAL CHEMISTRY. *Educ:* Univ Sask, BA, 48; Univ Ill, MS, 52; Univ Calif, PhD(pharmaceut chem), 58. *Prof Exp:* Asst prof, 57-61, ASSOC PROF PHARM, UNIV SOUTHERN CALIF, 61- *Res:* Factors influencing absorption of medicaments from suppository and suspension dosage forms. *Mailing Add:* Sch of Pharm Univ of Southern Calif Los Angeles CA 90007

CROWL, GEORGE HENRY, b Wooster, Ohio, Apr 10, 10; m 35; c 3. GLACIAL GEOLOGY, GEOMORPHOLOGY. *Educ:* Col Wooster, BA, 32; Harvard Univ, MA, 34; Princeton Univ, PhD, 50. *Prof Exp:* Topographer, US Engrs, Ohio, 34-35; jr geologist, Gulf Oil Corp, Arabia & Venezuela, 35-37; geologist, Shell Oil Co, Ill, 38-39; instr geol, Rutgers Univ, 39-41 & Vanderbilt Univ, 42-43; asst prof, Hamilton Col, 43-44; geologist, Carter Oil Co, Wyo, 44-46; asst prof geol, Pa State Col, 46-47; from asst prof to prof, 47-75, head dept, 47-62, EMER PROF GEOL, OHIO WESLEYAN UNIV, 75- *Concurrent Pos:* Vis prof, US State Dept, Univ Rangoon, 52-54; with expeds, Greenland, 63-65 & US Educ Found, India, 66; exped glacial geol, Del Valley, Pa, 68-72. *Mem:* Geol Soc Am; Nat Asn Geol Teachers. *Res:* Geomorphology; structural geology; glacial geology of Greenland; erosion surfaces of Adirondacks; glacial geology of Northern Pennsylvania. *Mailing Add:* Dept of Geol Ohio Wesleyan Univ Delaware OH 43015

CROWL, ROBERT HAROLD, b Wellsville, Ohio, Apr 17, 25; m 47; c 3. ANIMAL GENETICS. *Educ:* Harvard Univ, SB, 49; Miami Univ, MS, 50; Ohio State Univ, PhD, 64. *Prof Exp:* Instr zool, Miami Univ, 50-51; sales rep pharmaceut, Bowman Bros Drug Co, 51-54, Winthrop Labs, 54-59 & Columbus Pharmacal Co, 59-60; teaching asst zool, Ohio State Univ, 60-64; from asst prof to assoc prof biol, 64-71, PROF BIOL, PFEIFFER COL, 71- *Mem:* NY Acad Sci; AAAS. *Res:* Pysiological genetics. *Mailing Add:* Dept of Biol Pfeiffer Col Misenheimer NC 28109

CROWLE, ALFRED JOHN, b Mexico, DF, Mex, Apr 15, 30; US citizen; m 54; c 2. IMMUNOLOGY, MICROBIOLOGY. *Educ:* San Jose State Univ, AB, 51; Stanford Univ, PhD(microbiol), 54. *Prof Exp:* Researcher, Webb-Waring Lung Inst, 56-59, from instr to assoc prof, Sch Med, 56-74, PROF MICROBIOL, SCH MED, UNIV COLO MED CTR, DENVER, 74-, HEAD DIV IMMUNOL, WEBB-WARING LUNG INST, 59- *Concurrent Pos:* Nat Tuberc Asn med res fel, Stanford Univ, 53-55, Nat Acad Sci-Nat Res Coun fel, 55-56; NY Tuberc & Health Asn fel, Sch Med, Univ Colo Med Ctr, Denver, 59-61. *Mem:* Reticuloendothelial Soc; Am Asn Immunol; Am Soc Microbiol; Soc Exp Biol & Med; Am Col Allergists. *Res:* Immunochemistry, immunodiffusion and applications of immunodiffusion techniques; delayed hypersensitivity, its induction and control; specific acquired immunity and tuberculoimmunity. *Mailing Add:* Webb-Waring Inst Div Immunol Univ Colo Med Ctr Box 122 Denver CO 80262

CROWLEY, JAMES PATRICK, b Birmingham, Eng, Oct 15, 43; US citizen; m 68; c 1. HEMATOLOGY & INFLAMMATION. *Educ:* Providence Col, AB, 65; Georgetown Univ, Washington, MD, 69. *Hon Degrees:* MA, Brown Univ, 82. *Prof Exp:* Clin asst med, Harvard Med Sch, 69-72; res med officer, Blood Res, US Navy, 72-75; asst prof, 76-81, ASSOC PROF MED, BROWN UNIV, PROVIDENCE, 81- *Concurrent Pos:* Consult, Armed Forces Radio Biol Res Inst, 74-75, Naval Blood Res Lab, Boston, 75-; adj asst prof med, Sch Med, Boston Univ, 80-; vis prof, Va Commonwealth Med Sch, 80. *Mem:* Am Fedn Clin Res; Soc Exp Biol & Med; Am Soc Hemat; Am Soc Microbiol; NY Acad Sci. *Res:* Plasma factors that modulate and facilitate the interaction of phagocytic cells with tumor cells and with bacteria. *Mailing Add:* Div Clin Hemat RI Hosp 593 Eddy St Providence RI 02902

CROWLEY, JOHN JAMES, b San Diego, Calif, Feb 20, 46; m 69; c 3. BIOSTATISTICS. *Educ:* Pomona Col, BA, 68; Univ Wash, MS, 70, PhD(biomath), 73. *Prof Exp:* Fel biostatist, Stanford Univ, 73-74; asst prof statist & human oncol, Univ Wis-Madison, 74-79, assoc prof, 79-81; ASSOC PROF BIOSTATIST, UNIV WASH, 81- *Concurrent Pos:* Assoc mem, Fred Hutchinson Cancer Res Ctr, 81- *Mem:* Am Statist Asn; Biometric Soc; Inst Math Statist; AAAS. *Res:* Methods for analyzing censored survival data; biostatistical methods in cancer research. *Mailing Add:* Dept of Statist Univ of Wis 1210 W Dayton St Madison WI 53706

CROWLEY, JOSEPH MICHAEL, b Philadelphia, Pa, Sept 9, 40; m 63; c 5. ELECTRICAL ENGINEERING, FLUID MECHANICS. *Educ:* Mass Inst Technol, BS, 62, MS, 63, PhD(elec eng), 65. *Prof Exp:* Guest scientist, Max Planck Inst, Gottingen, 65-66; asst prof, 66-71, assoc prof, 71-79, PROF ELEC ENG, UNIV ILL, URBANA, 79- *Concurrent Pos:* NATO fel, 65-66; consult, Xerox Corp, 68-; pres, Joseph M Crowley, Inc, 81- *Mem:* Am Phys Soc; Inst Elec & Electronics Engrs; Electrostatic Soc Am; Soc Info Display. *Res:* Feedback control of wave motion in fluids and plasmas; electrohydrodynamics of jets and drops; instabilities in viscous two-phase flows; electrical effects in biological systems; electrostatics; ink jet printers; computer output devices. *Mailing Add:* Dept of Elec Eng Univ of Ill Urbana IL 61801

CROWLEY, LAWRENCE GRANDJEAN, b Newark, NJ, July 2, 19; m 45; c 3. SURGERY. *Educ:* Yale Univ, BA, 41, MD, 44. *Prof Exp:* From instr to asst prof surg, Sch Med, Yale Univ, 51-53; attend, Southern Calif Permanente Med Group, 53-55; clin asst prof, Sch Med, Univ Southern Calif, 55-64; from assoc prof to prof, Sch Med, Stanford Univ, 64-74, assoc dean, 72-74; prof surg & dean, Sch Med, Univ Wis-Madison, 74-77; dep dean, Sch Med, 77-80, PROF SURG, SCH MED, STANFORD UNIV, 77-, ACTG VPRES MED AFFAIRS & ACTG DEAN, SCH MED, 80-, MED DIR HOSP, 77- *Concurrent Pos:* Am Cancer Soc clin fel, Med Ctr, Yale Univ, 49-51; mem, Bd Dirs, Casa Colina Rehab Hosp, Pomona, Calif, 59-74, pres, 63-66; mem spec grants comt, Calif Div, Am Cancer Soc, 67-70; mem, Cancer Categorical Comt, Calif Regional Med Prog, 68-71; mem, Cancer Adv Coun, State Calif, 70-74. *Honors & Awards:* Cert Merit, Conn Div, Am Cancer Soc, 53. *Mem:* Am Col Surgeons. *Res:* Endocrine relationships with mammary carcinoma. *Mailing Add:* Off of the Dean Med Sch Stanford Univ Stanford CA 94305

CROWLEY, LEONARD VINCENT, b Binghamton, NY, Jan 12, 26; m 51; c 5. MEDICINE, PATHOLOGY. *Educ:* Univ Vt, MD, 49; Ohio State Univ, MSc, 56. *Prof Exp:* Instr path, Col Physicians & Surgeons, Columbia Univ, 52-54; instr, Med Sch, Ohio State Univ, 54-56; from asst prof to assoc prof, Col Med, Univ Vt, 56-60; ASST PROF PATH, MED COL, UNIV MINN, MINNEAPOLIS, 62- *Mem:* AMA; Am Fedn Clin Res; Am Soc Exp Path. *Res:* Immunohematology; clinical chemistry. *Mailing Add:* 5337 Kellogg Ave Minneapolis MN 55424

CROWLEY, MICHAEL SUMMERS, b Chicago, Ill, Dec 24, 28; m 50; c 2. CERAMICS ENGINEERING, MATERIALS SCIENCE. *Educ:* Iowa State Univ, BS, 53; Pa State Univ, PhD(geochem), 59. *Prof Exp:* Res engr mat, Standard Oil Co, Ind, 53-55; Am Petrol Inst fel geochem, Pa State Univ, 55-58; sr res engr, 58-80, RES ASSOC, MAT RES & SERV DIV, STANDARD OIL CO IND, 80- *Concurrent Pos:* Consult, US Dept Energy, 75- & Argonne Nat Labs, 78; co-chmn, Metals Prop Coun Task Force on Mat for Coal Gasification, 72-77. *Mem:* Fel Am Ceramic Soc; Nat Inst Ceramics Engrs; Sigma Xi. *Res:* Non-metallic materials of construction such as refractories, insulation, fire proofing, coatings and plastics. *Mailing Add:* Amoco Res Ctr Box 400 Naperville IL 60540

CROWLEY, PATRICK ARTHUR, b Titusville, Pa, June 6, 41; m 64; c 1. NUCLEAR PHYSICS, FLUID PHYSICS. *Educ:* Carnegie Inst Technol, BS, 63; Univ Pittsburgh, PhD(physics), 68. *Prof Exp:* Staff physicist, Columbia Res Corp, 68-70; physicist, US Army Foreign Sci & Technol Ctr, 70-78; PROJ OFFICER, DEFENSE NUCLEAR AGENCY, 78- *Mem:* Am Phys Soc; Am Inst Physics; Am Geophys Union. *Res:* Nuclear structures and reactions; ionospheric physics; radiation effects; atmospheric phenomena. *Mailing Add:* 2200 Sanibel Dr Reston VA 22091

CROWLEY, PHILIP HANEY, b Ft Worth, Tex, Dec 8, 46; m 72; c 1. ECOLOGY, MATHEMATICAL BIOLOGY. *Educ:* Rice Univ, BA, 69, MS, 72; Mich State Univ, PhD(zool), 75. *Prof Exp:* Res assoc, Dept Elec Eng & Systs Sci, Mich State Univ, 75-76; ASST PROF ECOL, THOMAS HUNT MORGAN SCH BIOL SCI, UNIV KY, 76- *Mem:* Ecol Soc Am; Am Soc Limnol & Oceanogr; Int Soc Theoret & Appl Limnol. *Res:* Predator-prey interactions; population regulation and ecosystem stability; population and community ecology of Odonata and Cladocera; mathematical modeling of biological systems. *Mailing Add:* Thomas Hunt Morgan Sch Biol Sci Univ of Ky Lexington KY 40506

CROWLEY, THOMAS HENRY, b Bowling Green, Ohio, June 7, 24; m 47; c 14. COMPUTER SCIENCE. *Educ:* Ohio State Univ, BEE, 48, MA, 50, PhD(math), 54. *Prof Exp:* Res assoc antenna lab, Ohio State Univ, 48-54; mem tech staff, Bell Tel Labs, Inc, 54-64, head comput res dept, 64-65, dir comput sci res ctr, 65-68, exec dir safeguard design div, 68-75, exec dir, Bus Systs & Technol Div, 75-79, EXEC DIR, COMPUT TECHNOL & DESIGN, BELL LABS, 79- *Mem:* Inst Elec & Electronics Eng. *Res:* Computers; switching and control. *Mailing Add:* Bell Labs 600 Mountain Ave Murray Hill NJ 07974

CROWLEY, WILLIAM PATRICK, geology, see previous edition

CROWLEY, WILLIAM ROBERT, b Bristol, Conn, May 20, 48. NEUROPHARMACOLOGY, NEUROENDOCRINOLOGY. *Educ:* Univ Conn, BA, 70; Villanova Univ, MS, 72; Rutgers Univ, PhD(psychobiol), 76. *Prof Exp:* ASST PROF PHARMACOL, CTR HEALTH SCI, UNIV TENN, 78- *Concurrent Pos:* NIMH fel, 76-78. *Mem:* Soc Neurosci; Int Soc Psychoneuroendocrinol; AAAS. *Res:* Neurochemical mechanisms in control of reproductive processes. *Mailing Add:* Dept of Pharmacol Ctr for Health Sci Memphis TN 38163

CROWNFIELD, FREDERIC RUDOLPH, JR, b Boston, Mass, Feb 25, 27; m 56, 71; c 2. PLASMA PHYSICS. *Educ:* Harvard Univ, AB, 48; Lehigh Univ, MS, 49, PhD(physics), 53. *Prof Exp:* Asst physics, Lehigh Univ, 48-50; instr, Univ Akron, 51-53 & NC State Col, 53-56; from asst prof to assoc prof, 56-68, PROF PHYSICS, COL WILLIAM & MARY, 68- *Concurrent Pos:* Consult, Guilford Tel Co, 50-56; vis prof appl math, Univ St Andrews, Scotland, 76-77. *Mem:* Am Phys Soc; Am Asn Physics Teachers; Inst Elec & Electronic Engrs; Nuclear & Plasma Physics Soc. *Res:* Ionized gases; quantum theory; field theory; plasma kinetic theory; stability and wave properties of spatially non-uniform plasmas. *Mailing Add:* Dept of Physics Col of William & Mary Williamsburg VA 23185

CROWNOVER, RICHARD MCCRANIE, b Quincy, Fla, Oct 11, 36; m 58; c 3. MATHEMATICAL ANALYSIS. *Educ:* Ga Inst Technol, BS, 58, MS, 60; La State Univ, PhD(math), 64. *Prof Exp:* Instr math, Ga Inst Technol, 59-61 & La State Univ, 63-64; asst prof, 64-72, ASSOC PROF MATH, UNIV MO-COLUMBIA, 72- *Mem:* Am Math Soc; Math Asn Am; Sigma Xi; Soc Indust & Appl Math. *Res:* Spaces and algebras of functions and operators. *Mailing Add:* Dept of Math Univ of Mo Columbia MO 65211

CROWSON, CHARLES NEVILLE, b Ottawa, Ont, Sept 21, 19; m 51; c 2. PATHOLOGY. *Educ:* Queen's Univ, Ont, BA, 41, MA, 43; McGill Univ, MD, 49; Univ Edinburgh, PhD(path), 54; FRCPS(C). *Prof Exp:* Biochemist, Nat Res Coun, Can, 42-43; lectr path, Queen's Univ, Ont, 54-55; dir labs, Deer Lodge Hosp, 55-60; DIR LABS, MISERICORDIA GEN HOSP, 60- *Concurrent Pos:* Asst prof, Univ Man, 55-67; dir, Cent Med Lab, 59-; consult pathologist aviation crash path, Can Armed Forces, 55- & traumatics, Can Forces Med Coun, 71- *Mem:* Am Soc Clin Path; Am Asn Path & Bact; Can Asn Pathologists; Int Acad Path. *Res:* Hepato-renal syndrome and renal pathology; pathogenesis of nephrotoxic chemical lesions. *Mailing Add:* Misericordia Gen Hosp 99 Cornish Winnipeg MB R3C 1A2 Can

CROWSON, HENRY L, b Okeechobee, Fla, Apr 16, 27; m 51; c 3. MATHEMATICS. *Educ:* Univ Fla, BChE, 53, MS, 55, PhD(math), 59. *Prof Exp:* Instr math, Univ Fla, 58-59. asst prof, 59-60; staff mathematician, 60-65, ADV MATHEMATICIAN, IBM CORP, 65- *Mem:* Am Math Soc; Math Asn Am; Soc Indust & Appl Math. *Res:* Classical mathematical analysis, especially ordinary differential equations; signal analysis. *Mailing Add:* IBM Corp 10215 Fernwood Rd Bethesda MD 20021

CROWTHER, C RICHARD, b Waterloo, Iowa, July 16, 24; m 49; c 3. FORESTRY. *Educ:* Iowa State Col, BS, 47, MS, 56; Univ Mich, PhD, 71. *Prof Exp:* Forester, Cent States Exp Sta, US Forest Serv, 47; assoc ed, Naval Stores Rev, 47-48; ed, Lake Mills Graphic, Iowa, 48-53; from instr to assoc prof, 56-72, PROF FORESTRY, MICH TECHNOL UNIV, 72- *Concurrent Pos:* Alumni Found res grant; McIntire-Stennis grants, 72 & 80; Nat Park Serv grant, 80. *Mem:* Soc Am Foresters. *Res:* Forest recreation. *Mailing Add:* Dept of Forestry Mich Technol Univ Houghton MI 49931

CROXALL, WILLARD (JOSEPH), b Aberdeen, Wash, Nov 11, 10; m 32; c 5. CHEMISTRY. *Educ:* Univ Notre Dame, BS, 32, MS, 33, PhD(org chem), 35. *Prof Exp:* Garyin fel, Univ Notre Dame, 35; res chemist, Gen Chem Co, NY, 35-36; res chemist, Rohm & Haas Co, 36-46, res chemist & lab head hydrocarbon explor, 46-48, res chemist & lab head insecticides, 48-50, from asst dir res to dir res, Sumner Chem Co, Inc, 50-56, mem bd dirs, 53-36, gen mgr, 56-59, asst to mgr & coordr res & develop, Miles Chem Co, 59-62, dir, 62-64, vpres, 64-69, vpres & sr sci officer, Process Indust Group, 69-72; RETIRED. *Mem:* Am Chem Soc. *Res:* Emulsion polymerization; synthetic monomers; acetylene chemistry; organic insecticides and fungicides; organic chemical development. *Mailing Add:* 2806 Pleasant Plain Ave Elkhart IN 46514

CROXDALE, JUDITH GEROW, b Oakland, Calif, Aug 27, 41; div; c 1. BOTANY. *Educ:* Univ Calif, Berkeley, AB, 71, PhD(bot), 75. *Prof Exp:* Asst prof bot, Va Polytech Inst & State Univ, 75-79; ASST PROF BOT, UNIV WIS-MADISON, 79- *Mem:* Bot Soc Am; Am Soc Plant Physiologists; Sigma Xi. *Res:* Structural and functional aspects of vegetative plant development; quantitative histochemistry. *Mailing Add:* Dept Botany Univ Wisconsin Madison WI 53706

CROXTON, FRANK CUTSHAW, b Washington, DC, June 26, 07; m 30; c 2. CHEMISTRY, RESEARCH ADMINISTRATION. *Educ:* Ohio State Univ, AB, 27, AM, 28, PhD(phys chem), 30. *Hon Degrees:* DSc, Denison Univ, 65. *Prof Exp:* Res chemist, Standard Oil Co of Ind, 30-39; res chemist, Battelle Mem Inst, 39-42, res asst suprvr to supvr, 42-47, asst dir, 47-53, tech dir, 53-64, asst dir, 64-72; CONSULT, 72- *Concurrent Pos:* Mem bd trustees, Denison Univ Res Found, 52-75 & Children's Hosp Res Found, 66-75. *Mem:* Brit Inst Chem Engrs; Am Chem Soc; Am Inst Chem Eng; Com Develop Asn; Sigma Xi (pres, 71-72). *Res:* Petroleum technology; lubrication oil refining; lubricant additive; structure of aluminum carbide. *Mailing Add:* 1921 Collingswood Rd Columbus OH 43221

CROY, LAVOY I, b Pauls Valley, Okla, Dec 4, 30; m 54; c 5. CROP PHYSIOLOGY, PLANT BIOCHEMISTRY. *Educ:* Okla State Univ, BS, 55, MS, 59; Univ Ill, Urbana, PhD(crop physiol), 67. *Prof Exp:* From instr to assoc prof, 55-78, PROF AGRON, OKLA STATE UNIV, 78- *Concurrent Pos:* Asst to head dept agron, Univ Ill, Urbana-Champaign, 64-66; assoc ed, Am Soc Agron, 77-81. *Mem:* AAAS; Am Soc Agron; Crop Sci Soc Am; Am Soc Plant Physiol. *Res:* Protein production in cereal grains; physiology of nitrate reduction in wheat; genetics of physiology and morphology of wheat. *Mailing Add:* Dept Agron Okla State Univ Stillwater OK 74078

CROZAZ, GHISLAINE M, b Brussels, Belg, Aug 31, 39; m 78. GEOCHEMISTRY. *Educ:* Univ Brussels, BSc, 61, PhD(nuclear geochem), 67. *Prof Exp:* Res assoc, Univ Brussels, 67-71; vis assoc geochem, Calif Inst Technol, 72; asst prof earth & planetary sci, 73-76, ASSOC PROF EARTH & PLANETARY SCI, WASHINGTON UNIV, 76- *Concurrent Pos:* Res assoc, Wash Univ, 69-73. *Mem:* Meteoritical Soc; Am Geophys Union. *Mailing Add:* Dept of Earth & Planetary Sci Washington Univ St Louis MO 63130

CROZIER, EDGAR DARYL, b Montreal, Que, Apr 9, 39; m 64; c 2. METAL PHYSICS, SEMICONDUCTORS. *Educ:* Univ Toronto, BSc, 61; Queen's Univ, Ont, PhD(phys chem), 65. *Prof Exp:* Nat Res Coun Can overseas fel, 65-67; asst prof, 67-74, ASSOC PROF PHYSICS, SIMON FRASER UNIV, 74- *Mem:* Can Asn Physicists. *Res:* Fluid and electronic properties of liquid metals and liquid semiconductors being investigated by linear and non-linear optical measurements, ultrasonics, extended x-ray absorption fine structure technique. *Mailing Add:* Dept of Physics Simon Fraser Univ Burnaby BC V5A 1S6 Can

CRUCE, WILLIAM L R, b Galveston, Tex, Oct 2, 42. NEUROBIOLOGY, MOTOR SYSTEMS. *Educ:* Univ Chicago, BS, 64; Rockefeller Univ, PhD(physiol), 71. *Prof Exp:* Fel neuroanat, Univ Nijmegen, Netherlands, 71-72 & Univ Wis-Madison, 72-74; asst prof anat, Howard Univ, Washington, DC, 74-77; ASSOC PROF NEUROBIOL, NORTHEAST OHIO UNIVS COL MED, 77-; ASSOC PROF BIOL, GRAD SCH, KENT STATE UNIV, 77- *Concurrent Pos:* Vis investr neurobiol, Armed Forces Radiobiol Res Inst, Bethesda, 75-77; ad hoc mem, Neurol B Grants Rev, NIH, 80. *Mem:* Neurosci Soc; Am Asn Anatomists; Am Physiol Soc; Asn Comput Mach. *Res:* Evolution of the brain; motor systems; spinal cord; brainstem; neuroanatomy; neurophysiology; neuronal response to injury. *Mailing Add:* Neurobiol Dept Northeast Ohio Univs Col Med Rootstown OH 44272

CRUDDACE, RAYMOND GIBSON, b Richmond, Eng, June 3, 36; US citizen. XRAY ASTRONOMY. *Educ:* Imp Col, Univ London, BSc, 58; Linacre Col, Oxford Univ, DPhil(physics), 68; Univ Calif, Berkeley, MA, 73. *Prof Exp:* Sci officer, Rocket Propulsion Estab, UK Ministry Aviation, 59-62; asst prof mech eng, Sacramento State Col, 65-66; physicist, Nuclear Rocket Opers, Aerojet-Gen Corp, 66-69; res physicist, Space Sci Lab, Univ Calif, Berkeley, 71-74; ASTROPHYSICIST, SPACE SCI DIV, NAVAL RES LAB, 74- *Mem:* Am Astron Soc; Brit Interplanetary Soc. *Mailing Add:* Code 7129.5 Space Sci Div Naval Res Lab Washington DC 20375

CRUDEN, ROBERT WILLIAM, b Cleveland, Ohio, Mar 18, 36; m 67; c 2. ECOLOGY, EVOLUTION. *Educ:* Hiram Col, BA, 58; Ohio State Univ, MSc, 60; Univ Calif, Berkeley, PhD(bot), 67. *Prof Exp:* From asst prof to assoc prof, 67-78, PROF BOT, UNIV IOWA, 78- *Mem:* Ecol Soc Am; Brit Ecol Soc; Am Soc Plant Taxonomists; Am Bot Soc; Soc Study Evolution. *Res:* Breeding systems, pollination biology, other animal-plant interactions and other life history parameters of plants and their evolution; systematics. *Mailing Add:* Dept of Bot Univ of Iowa Iowa City IA 52242

CRUICE, WILLIAM JAMES, b New York, NY, Aug 22, 37; m 65; c 1. PHYSICAL CHEMISTRY, CHEMICAL ENGINEERING. *Educ:* St John's Univ, BS, 60, BA, 61, MS, 64. *Prof Exp:* From chemist to sr chemist aerospace, Reaction Motors Div, Thiokol Corp, 63-69; asst vpres res eng, US Banknote Corp, 69-70; V PRES & GEN MGR CHEM & ENG, HAZARDS RES CORP, 69- *Mem:* Am Inst Chem Engrs; Am Soc Testing & Mat; Am Chem Soc; Nat Fire Protection Asn; Combustion Inst. *Res:* Fire and explosion hazards of chemicals and chemical processes. *Mailing Add:* 15 Valley Rd Denville NJ 07834

CRUICKSHANK, ALEXANDER MIDDLETON, b Marlboro, NH, Dec 13, 19; m 45; c 2. INORGANIC CHEMISTRY, ANALYTICAL CHEMISTRY. *Educ:* RI State Col, BS, 43, MS, 45; Univ Mass, PhD(chem), 54. *Prof Exp:* Asst chem, RI State Col, 43-45, instr, 45-48; instr, Univ Mass, 48-53; from asst prof to assoc prof, 53-69, PROF CHEM, UNIV RI, 69- *Concurrent Pos:* Instr, Holyoke Jr Col, 50-53; asst to dir, Gordon Res Confs, AAAS, 47-68, dir, 68- *Mem:* Am Chem Soc; Am Asn Textile Chem & Colorists. *Res:* Polarography; metal complexes of amino and hydroxyl acids; alkyd resins; textiles. *Mailing Add:* Dept of Chem Univ of RI Kingston RI 02881

CRUICKSHANK, BRUCE, b Edinburgh, Scotland, May 27, 20; m 43; c 2. ANATOMIC PATHOLOGY, CYTOLOGY. *Educ:* Univ Edinburgh, MB & ChB, 43, PhD(rheumatic dis), 52, MD, 58; FRCPS(G), 65; Royal Col Path, fel, 68; FRCPS(C), 69. *Prof Exp:* Lectr path, Univ Edinburgh, 52-56; sr lectr, Glasgow Univ, 56-59 & 60-63; assoc dir, Mallory Inst Path, 59-60; prof &

head dept, Univ Col Rhodesia & Nyasaland, 64-68; PROF PATH, UNIV TORONTO & HEAD DEPT, SUNNYBROOK HOSP, 68- *Concurrent Pos:* Vis prof, Boston Univ & vis lectr, Harvard Univ & Tufts Univ, 59-60; 60; hon consult pathologist, Glasgow Royal Infirmary, 60-63; mem, Panel, Can Tumor Ref Ctr, 68- *Mem:* Am Asn Path & Bact; Int Acad Path; Path Soc Gt Brit & Ireland; Brit Soc Immunol; Heberden Soc. *Res:* Histopathology and pathogenesis of rheumatic diseases; immunofluorescence of tissue antigens. *Mailing Add:* Dept Path Sunnybrook Hosp Univ Toronto Toronto ON M5S 2R8 Can

CRUICKSHANK, MICHAEL JAMES, b Glasgow, Scotland, July 9, 29. MARINE MINING, DEEP SEABED MINING. *Educ:* Camborne Sch Mines, ACSM, 53; Colo Sch Mines, MSc, 62; Univ Wis, Madison, PhD(oecanog & limnol), 78. *Prof Exp:* Dist engr, Anglo-Greek Magnesite Co, Ltd, 53-55; min mgr, Muirshiel Barytes Co, Ltd, 56-61; res geologist, Scripps Inst Oceanog, 63-64; asst prof mining, Univ Alaska, 64-65; res specialist, Lockheed Missiles & Space Co, Ltd, 65-66; res supvr, US Bur Mines, 66-69; res coordr, Marine Mineral Technol Ctr, Nat Oceanic & Atmospheric Admin, 69-73; MARINE MINING ENGR, US GEOL SURV, 73- *Concurrent Pos:* Ed-in-chief, Draft Environ Statement Deep Sea Mining, 73-74; Sloan fel, Grad Sch Bus, Stanford Univ, 75-76; mem, Group Experts Sci Aspects Marine Pollution, UN, 77; chmn, Task Force Outer Continental Shelf Mining Policy, US Dept Interior, 78; consult, Offshore Exploration, UN, Thailand, 79-80; vis prof, Henry Krumb Sch Mines, Columbia Univ, 81-83. *Mem:* Soc Mining Engrs; Marine Technol Soc; World Dredging Asn. *Res:* International development of mineral resources and technology in marine and coastal areas. *Mailing Add:* Henry Krumb Sch Mines Columbia Univ New York NY 10027

CRUICKSHANK, P A, b Bremerton, Wash, Oct 11, 29; m 53; c 3. PESTICIDE CHEMISTRY. *Educ:* Univ Wash, BSc, 51; Mass Inst Technol, PhD(org chem), 55. *Prof Exp:* Chemist, E I du Pont de Nemours Co, 55-58; group leader peptides, Res Inst Med & Chem, 58-63; interdisciplinary scientist, 63-66, RES MGR, AGR CHEM GROUP, FMC CORP, 66- *Mem:* Am Chem Soc. *Res:* Synthesis of peptides and steroids; chromatographic methods of analysis; insect hormones; insecticides; nematicides; quantitative structure activity relationships. *Mailing Add:* 211 Dodds Lane Princeton NJ 08540

CRUIKSHANK, DALE PAUL, b Des Moines, Iowa, Aug 10, 39; m 64, 75; c 3. PLANETARY PHYSICS, GEOSCIENCE. *Educ:* Iowa State Univ, BS, 61; Univ Ariz, MS, 65 & PhD(planetary geol), 68. *Prof Exp:* Res asst, Lunar & Planetary Lab, Univ Ariz, 61-68, res assoc, 69-70; From asst astronr to assoc astronr, 70-79, ASTRONR, INST ASTRON, UNIV HAWAII, 79- *Concurrent Pos:* Mem, Canada-France-Hawaii Telescope Corp, 80-; assoc ed, Icarus, Int J of Solar Syst, 82- *Mem:* Int Astron Union; Am Astron Soc; Am Geophys Union. *Res:* Physics and geology of the planets and their satellites, asteroids, and the comets as determined largely through astronomical techniques of spectroscopy and photometry; detection and study of atmospheres. *Mailing Add:* Inst Astron 2680 Woodlawn Dr Honolulu HI 96822

CRUIKSHANK, DONALD BURGOYNE, JR, b Boise, Idaho, Aug 2, 39; m 65; c 1. ACOUSTICS. *Educ:* Kalamazoo Col, BA, 64; Univ Rochester, MS, 66, PhD(acoustics), 70. *Prof Exp:* Asst prof physics, Cornell Col, 69-71; from asst prof to assoc prof, 71-80, PROF PHYSICS, ANDERSON COL, 80- *Mem:* Acoust Soc Am; Am Asn Physics Teachers. *Res:* Finite-amplitude acoustic resonance oscillations in closed, rigid-walled tubes. *Mailing Add:* Dept of Physics Anderson Col Anderson IN 46011

CRUISE, DONALD RICHARD, b Los Angeles, Calif, Feb 17, 34; m 65; c 2. APPLIED MATHEMATICS. *Educ:* Fresno State Col, AB, 56. *Prof Exp:* MATHEMATICIAN, NAVAL WEAPONS CTR, CHINA LAKE, 56- *Mem:* Sigma Xi. *Res:* Mathematical models for chemical equilibrium; far fields of cylindrical lasers; digital tuning. *Mailing Add:* RR 1 2051 S Inyo St Ridgecrest CA 93555

CRUISE, JAMES E, b Port Dover, Ont, June 26, 25. PLANT TAXONOMY. *Educ:* Univ Toronto, BA, 50; Cornell Univ, MS, 51, PhD, 54. *Prof Exp:* Lab instr, Cornell Univ, 51-56; from asst prof to prof biol, Trenton State Col, 56-63; assoc prof, Univ Toronto, 63-69, prof biol & cur, 69-75; DIR, ROYAL ONT MUS, 75- *Mem:* Am Soc Plant Taxon; Can Bot Asn; Int Soc Plant Taxon. *Res:* Taxonomy of vascular plants; flora of Ontario. *Mailing Add:* 100 Queen's Park Toronto ON M5S 2C6 Can

CRUM, EDWARD HIBBERT, b South Charleston, WVa, Sept 21, 40; m 63; c 2. BIOCHEMICAL ENGINEERING. *Educ:* WVa Inst Technol, BS, 62; Mo Sch Mines, MS, 64; Univ Mo-Rolla, PhD(chem eng), 67. *Prof Exp:* From asst prof to assoc prof, 66-77, PROF CHEM ENG, WVA INST TECHNOL, 77-, CHMN DEPT, 80- *Concurrent Pos:* res fel, NASA; NSF fel, Union Carbide Corp. *Mem:* Am Chem Soc; Am Inst Chem Engrs; Instrument Soc Am. *Res:* Thiobacillus thiooxidans cell walls; air and waste water treatment; technological forecasting. *Mailing Add:* PO Box 117 Charlton Heights WV 25040

CRUM, FLOYD M(AXILAS), b Baton Rouge, La, Apr 28, 22; m 43; c 5. ELECTRICAL ENGINEERING. *Educ:* La State Univ, BS, 47, MS, 51. *Prof Exp:* Assoc prof elec eng, La State Univ, 47-55; PROF ELEC ENG, LAMAR UNIV, 55- *Concurrent Pos:* Design engr, Stone & Webster Consult Engrs, 47; electronic scientist, Naval Res Lab, 51-53, 55 & 61-69 & Boeing Aircraft, 54; consult, Sun Oil Geophys Lab, 55-61; Naval res electronic consult engr, 62-76. *Mem:* Am Soc Eng Educ; sr mem Inst Elec & Electronic Engrs; sr mem Instrument Soc Am. *Res:* Solid state electronics; network synthesis; information theory. *Mailing Add:* Dept of Elec Eng Lamar Univ PO Box 10029 Beaumont TX 77710

CRUM, GLEN F(RANCIS), b Humboldt, Ill, June 13, 25; m 49; c 2. CHEMICAL ENGINEERING. *Educ:* Univ Ill, BS, 48, MS, 58, PhD(chem eng), 61. *Prof Exp:* Res engr, Gen Elec Co, 48-52; res assoc, Upjohn Co, 52-56; res specialist, Monsanto Co, 60-67; res & develop engr, 67-76, RES ASSOC, EL PASO PROD CO, 76- *Mem:* Am Chem Soc; Am Inst Chem Engrs. *Res:* Distillations; chemical reactions; catalysis. *Mailing Add:* 2101 Grayson Odessa TX 79761

CRUM, HOWARD ALVIN, b Mishawaka, Ind, July 14, 22; m 60; c 2. BRYOLOGY. *Educ:* Western Mich Col, BS, 47; Univ Mich, MS, 49, PhD(bot), 51. *Prof Exp:* Instr, Western Mich Col, 46-47; teaching fel, Univ Mich, 48-49; res biol & actg asst prof, Stanford Univ, 51-53; asst prof, Univ Louisville, 53-54; biologist, Nat Mus Can, 54-65; PROF BOT & CUR BRYOPHYTES & LICHENS, UNIV MICH, 65- *Concurrent Pos:* Ed, Am Bryological & Lichenological Soc, 53-62, assoc ed, 62-77; assoc ed, Brit Bryological Soc, 72-77; pres, Mich Bot Club, 73-74, assoc ed, 75, ed, 77- *Honors & Awards:* Henry Allen Gleason Award, 81. *Mem:* Fel Amn Bryological & Lichenological Soc (pres, 62-63); Brit Bryological Soc. *Res:* Taxonomy of bryophytes; mosses; monographic studies in the genus Sphagnum; lecanora esculata (desert manna) and its potential use by grazing animals. *Mailing Add:* Herbarium 2002 N Univ Bldg Univ of Mich Ann Arbor MI 48109

CRUM, JAMES DAVIDSON, b Ironton, Ohio, July 29, 30; m 56; c 2. ORGANIC CHEMISTRY. *Educ:* Ohio State Univ, BSc, 52, PhD(org chem), 58; Marshall Univ, MSc, 53. *Prof Exp:* Asst, Marshall Col, 52-53; from asst to asst instr, Ohio State Univ, 53-57; NIH res fel, Harvard Univ, 58-59; from instr to asst prof chem, Case Western Reserve Univ, 59-66; assoc prof, 66-69, chmn dept, 70-72, PROF CHEM, CALIF STATE COL, SAN BERNARDINO, 69-, DEAN, SCH NATURAL SCI, 72- *Concurrent Pos:* Consult, Nat Sci Found-US Agency Int Develop, 65-68. *Mem:* Fel AAAS; fel Am Inst Chem; Am Chem Soc; fel India Inst Chem; Royal Soc Chem. *Res:* Natural products; carbohydrates and steroids; reaction mechanisms; synthesis. *Mailing Add:* Sch of Natural Sci Calif State Col San Bernardino CA 92407

CRUM, JOHN KISTLER, b Brownsville, Tex, July 28, 36. INORGANIC CHEMISTRY, SCIENCE ADMINISTRATION. *Educ:* Univ Tex, BSChE, 60, PhD(chem), 64; Harvard Univ, Advan Mgt Prog dipl, 75. *Prof Exp:* From asst ed to assoc ed anal chem, 64-68, managing ed publ, 68-70, group mgr jour, 70-71, dir books & jour div, 71-75, treas & chief financial officer, 75-80, DEP EXEC DIR & CHIEF OPERATING OFFICER, AM CHEM SOC, 81- *Concurrent Pos:* Consult, Joint Comt Atomic & Molecular Phys Data. *Mem:* Am Chem Soc; Royal Soc Chem; Coun Eng & Sci Soc Execs. *Res:* Chemistry of reactions in liquid ammonia; design of scientific publications; chemical literature; information retrieval. *Mailing Add:* Am Chem Soc 1155 16th St NW Washington DC 20036

CRUM, LAWRENCE ARTHUR, b Caldwell, Ohio, Oct 25, 41; m 63; c 3. ACOUSTICS. *Educ:* Ohio Univ, BS, 63, MS, 65, PhD(physics), 67. *Prof Exp:* Res fel, Harvard Univ, 67-68; asst prof, 68-72, ASSOC PROF PHYSICS, US NAVAL ACAD, 72- *Concurrent Pos:* Consult, Planning Syst Inc, 72- & Naval Ord Sta, 73-; pres, Acad Assoc, Inc, 75-; sr vis scientist, Univ Col, Cardiff, Wales, 76-77; assoc prof physics, Univ Miss, 77-78, prof, 78- *Mem:* Acoust Soc Am; Am Asn Physics Teachers; fel Acoust Soc Am. *Res:* Acoustic cavitation and effects of sound fields on bubbles; instability development in human erythrocytes. *Mailing Add:* Dept Physics Univ Mississippi University MS 38677

CRUM, RALPH G, b Youngstown, Ohio, July 22, 30; m 59; c 3. APPLIED MECHANICS, CIVIL ENGINEERING. *Educ:* Carnegie Inst Technol, BS, 53, MS, 54, PhD, 56. *Prof Exp:* Asst civil eng, Carnegie Inst Technol, 56-61; sr research engr, Ford Motor Co, 61-62; prin scientist, NAm Aviation, 62-70; assoc prof, 70-75, PROF CIVIL ENG, YOUNGSTOWN STATE UNIV, 75- *Concurrent Pos:* Ford Found fel, 60; mat & mech consult, 61-68; environ consult, 69-70; NASA fel, 71-73; assoc, Verna Eng, Inc, 78- *Mem:* Am Soc Civil Engrs; Am Soc Test & Mat; Soc Exp Stress Anal; Am Soc Eng Educ. *Res:* Materials, mechanics, environmental engineering. *Mailing Add:* Eng Technol Youngstown State Univ Youngstown OH 44503

CRUMB, EDGAR ALVIN, b Cape Charles, Va, July 5, 16; m 69. SCIENCE ADMINISTRATION. *Educ:* Industrial Col Armed Forces, dipl, 55; George Washington Univ, BA, 59, MBA, 61. *Prof Exp:* Chief eng div, Res & Develop Div, Off of Chief Chem Warfare Serv, US Army, 39-44, chief engr, 47-48, dep chief, Chem Corps, 48-49; Civilian dep, 49-53, exec dir, Army Chem Ctr, 53-58, exec dir tech progs, 58-61; tech dir, Chem-Biol-Radiol Agency, 62-66; dir, US Army Munitions Command Opers Res Group, 66-73; dir, US Army Chem Lab, 73-77; CHIEF RES, CHEM SYSTS LAB, US ARMY, ABERDEAN PROVING GROUND, MD, 77- *Mem:* Am Chem Soc; AAAS; Am Soc Mech Engrs; Am Ord Soc. *Res:* Systems laboratory, chemistry, toxicology, physics and mathematics programs; technical management of major research development engineering and operations research programs for the army. *Mailing Add:* 600 Banyan Ct Edgewood MD 21040

CRUMB, GLENN HOWARD, b Burlingame, Kans, Dec 21, 27; m 50; c 4. ACADEMIC ADMINISTRATION. *Educ:* Kans State Teachers Col, BS, 51, MS, 56; Univ Nebr, PhD(sci educ), 64. *Prof Exp:* Teacher high schs, Kans, 51-56; instr phys sci, Kans State Teachers Col, 56-59; physics, Univ Nebr High Sch, 59-63; assoc prof phys sci, Kans State Teachers Col, 63-65, prof, 65-71, head dept, 64-71, dir res & grants ctr, 69-71; PROF EDUC & DIR GRANT & CONTRACT SERVS, WESTERN KY UNIV, 71- *Concurrent Pos:* Shell Oil Co Merit fac fel, 69. *Mem:* Am Asn Physics Teachers; Nat Sci Teachers Asn; Nat Coun Univ Res Adminrs. *Res:* Atomic and nuclear physics; optics; science teaching strategies; reasoning in science. *Mailing Add:* Dir Grant & Contract Servs Western Ky Univ Bowling Green KY 42101

CRUMB, STEPHEN FRANKLIN, b Greenville, Tex, Jan 18, 20; m 50; c 2. ELECTRICAL ENGINEERING. *Educ:* Univ Tex, BS, 43, MS, 47; Calif Inst Technol, PhD(elec eng, physics), 55. *Prof Exp:* Test engr, Gen Elec Co, 43-44; jr engr, Magnolia Pipe Line Co, 47-48; instr elec eng, Univ Tex, 48-50; sr aerophys engr, Gen Dynamics Corp/Ft Worth, 54-55, group engr, 55-59, asst proj engr, 59-61; PROF ELEC ENG, UNIV TEX, ARLINGTON, 61- *Concurrent Pos:* Grad lectr, Southern Methodist Univ, 54-57; sr engr specialist, LTV Aerospace, 67. *Mem:* Inst Elec & Electronics Engrs; Nat Soc Prof Engrs; Am Soc Eng Educ. *Res:* Vibrations analysis; navigation and guidance systems; network theory; information transmission. *Mailing Add:* Dept of Elec Eng Univ of Tex Arlington TX 76019

CRUME, ENYEART CHARLES, JR, b Dayton, Ohio, Nov 14, 31; c 3. PLASMA PHYSICS, NUCLEAR ENGINEERING. *Educ:* Wabash Col, AB, 53; Wesleyan Univ, MA, 55; Univ Tenn, PhD(physics), 72. *Prof Exp:* Asst proj engr exp nuclear eng, CANEL Proj, Pratt & Whitney Aircraft, United Aircraft Corp, 56-64; physicist nuclear criticality safety, Y-12 Plant, Nuclear Div, 64-72, THEORETICAL PHYSICIST PLASMA PHYSICS, FUSION ENERGY DIV, NUCLEAR DIV OAK RIDGE NAT LAB, UNION CARBIDE CORP, 72- *Mem:* Am Phys Soc. *Res:* Theory and numerical simulation of transport processes in fusion energy related plasmas, especially transport of plasma impurities and its consequences. *Mailing Add:* Fusion Energy Div Union Carbide Corp PO Box Y Oak Ridge TN 37830

CRUMMETT, WARREN B, b Moyers, WVa, Apr 4, 22; m 48; c 2. ANALYTICAL CHEMISTRY. *Educ:* Bridgewater Col, BA, 43; Ohio State Univ, PhD(chem), 51. *Prof Exp:* Control chemist, Solvay Process Co, 43-46; anal chemist, 51-55, group leader, 55-61, asst dir anal labs, 61-71, ANAL SCIENTIST, DOW CHEM CO, 71- *Concurrent Pos:* Mem adv bd, Anal Chem, 74-76; mem environ measurements adv comt, Sci Adv Bd, Environ Protection Agency, 76-78, consult, Sci Adv Bd, US Air Force, 81. *Honors & Awards:* H H Dow Medal, 80. *Mem:* AAAS; Am Inst Chem; Am Chem Soc; NY Acad Sci; Sigma Xi. *Res:* Ion exchange; platinum metals; ultraviolet and near infrared spectrophotometry; purity of organic compounds; liquid chromatography; analytical systems; environmental analysis; measurements near the limit of detection. *Mailing Add:* 808 Crescent Dr Midland MI 48640

CRUMMY, ANDREW B, b Newark, NJ, Jan 30, 30; m 58; c 3. RADIOLOGY. *Educ:* Bowdoin Col, AB, 51; Boston Univ, MD, 55. *Prof Exp:* Intern, Univ Wis Hosps, 55-56, resident radiol, 58-61; asst prof, Univ Colo, 63-64; from asst prof to assoc prof, 64-70, PROF RADIOL, UNIV WIS-MADISON, 70- *Concurrent Pos:* Fel radiol, Mt Auburn Hosp, Cambridge, Mass, 61-62; fel cardiovasc radiol, Yale Univ, 62-63. *Mem:* Fel Am Col Angiol; fel Am Col Radiol; fel Am Heart Asn; AMA. *Res:* Diagnostic radiology; cardiovascular radiology. *Mailing Add:* Dept of Radiol 203 Bradley Univ Hosps 1300 University Ave Madison WI 53706

CRUMMY, PRESSLEY LEE, b Glade Mills, Pa, Oct 1, 06; m 34. HISTOLOGY, HUMAN ANATOMY. *Educ:* Grove City Col, BS, 29; Univ Pittsburgh, MS, 32, PhD(zool), 34. *Prof Exp:* Teacher rural sch, Pa, 25-26, high sch, 29-30; asst biol, Grove City Col, 27-29 & zool, Univ Pittsburgh, 30-34; head dept sci, High Sch, Pa, 34-35; from instr to asst prof biol, Juniata Col, 35-47, prof, 47-49, from actg registr to registr, 42-49; assoc prof, 49-60, prof, 60-77, EMER PROF ANAT, KIRKSVILLE COL OSTEOP MED, 77- *Mem:* Fel AAAS. *Res:* Histology; gross human anatomy; morphological anomalies; biological effects of x-rays. *Mailing Add:* 910 E Harrison St Kirksville MO 63501

CRUMP, JESSE FRANKLIN, b Pine Bluff, Ark, July 20, 27; m 59. BIOMEDICAL ENGINEERING, INTERNAL MEDICINE. *Educ:* Univ Nebr, BSEE, 50, MD, 56. *Prof Exp:* Intern, Methodist Hosp, Brooklyn, 56-57, asst resident, 57-58; resident internal med, Long Island Col Hosp, 61-62; from asst prof to assoc prof elec eng, 62-68, ASSOC PROF BIOENG, POLYTECH INST NEW YORK, 68- *Concurrent Pos:* NIH res fel psychosom med, State Univ NY, 58-59 & cardiol, Long Island Col Hosp, Brooklyn, 59-61; consult, Dept Psychol, Princeton Univ, 57-62; Biomed Eng Rehab Dept, Montefiore Hosp, New York, 65-77; vis res physiologist, Princeton Univ, 62-75; assoc attend, Long Island Col Hosp, 62-; prin investr, USPHS grant, 66-68. *Mem:* AAAS; NY Acad Sci; Asn Advan Med Instrumentation; Inst Elec & Electronics Engrs. *Res:* Auditory, cardiology and cardiovascular physiology; biomedical instrumentation. *Mailing Add:* Dept of Bioeng Polytech Inst of NY Brooklyn NY 11201

CRUMP, JOHN C, III, b Richmond, Va, Feb 21, 40. SOLID STATE PHYSICS. *Educ:* Hampden-Sydney Col, BS, 60; Univ Va, MS, 62, PhD(physics), 64. *Prof Exp:* Res assoc physics, Univ Va, 64-66; res physicist, Oak Ridge Nat Lab, 66-69; RES SCIENTIST, PHILIP MORRIS INC, 69- *Mem:* Am Phys Soc; Electron Micros Soc Am; Sigma Xi. *Res:* Dislocation phenomena and irradiation effects in solid materials; aerosol and thermokinetic physics. *Mailing Add:* Philip Morris Inc Res Ctr Po Box 3 D Richmond VA 23206

CRUMP, JOHN WILLIAM, b Santa Rosa, Calif, Jan 18, 32; m 55; c 4. ORGANIC CHEMISTRY. *Educ:* Univ Calif, BA, 53; Univ Ill, PhD(org chem), 57. *Prof Exp:* Res chemist, Dow Chem Co, 57-62; from asst prof to assoc prof, 62-69, PROF CHEM, ALBION COL, 69-, CHAIRPERSON DEPT, 69- *Concurrent Pos:* NSF sci fac fel, Univ Leiden, Neth, 70-71; on leave, Lucknow Christian Col, India, 77-78. *Mem:* Am Chem Soc. *Res:* Organic reaction mechanisms and their application to synthetic control. *Mailing Add:* Dept of Chem Albion Col Albion MI 49224

CRUMP, KENNY SHERMAN, b Haynesville, La, Oct 13, 39; m 61; c 3. MATHEMATICS, STATISTICS. *Educ:* La Tech Univ, BS, 61; Univ Denver, MA, 63; Mont State Univ, PhD(math), 68. *Prof Exp:* Instr, Mont State Univ, 63-66; assoc prof math, La Tech Univ, 66-78, prof math & statist, 78-81; PRES, SCI RES SYSTS, INC, 81- *Concurrent Pos:* Res assoc, State Univ NY Buffalo, 67-68; vis scientist, Nat Inst Environ Health Sci, 74-75. *Mem:* Am Statist Asn; Biometric Soc; Inst Math Statist; Soc Epidemiol Res; AAAS. *Res:* Applications of statistics and stochastic processes to problems related to biology and health. *Mailing Add:* Sci Res Systs, Inc 1201 Gaines St Ruston LA 71270

CRUMP, MALCOLM HART, b Culpeper, Va, Aug 10, 26; m 52; c 3. GASTROENTEROLOGY. *Educ:* Va Polytech Inst, BS, 51; Univ Ga, DVM, 58; Univ Wis, MS, 61, PhD(physiol), 65. *Prof Exp:* Res assoc physiol, Univ Wis, 60-65; asst prof, 64-66, ASSOC PROF PHYSIOL, IOWA STATE UNIV, 66- *Mem:* Am Vet Med Asn; assoc Am Physiol Soc. *Res:* Pharmacological action of mycotoxins; drug metabolism; comparative gastroenterology; control mechanisms in the large intestine. *Mailing Add:* Dept of Physiol Iowa State Univ Col of Vet Med Ames IA 50010

CRUMP, MARTHA LYNN, b Madison, Wis, Aug 23, 46. ECOLOGY, BIOLOGY. *Educ:* Univ Kans, BA, 68, MA, 71, PhD(ecol & systs), 74. *Prof Exp:* Fel, City Univ New York, 74-76; asst prof ecol, 76-80, ASSOC PROF ZOOL, UNIV FLA, 80- *Concurrent Pos:* NSF res grant, 75-76 & 78-79; res assoc, Am Mus Natural Hist, 76-; affil asst cur herpetol, Fla State Mus, 78- *Mem:* AAAS; Brit Ecol Soc; Soc Study Amphibians & Reptiles; Soc Study Evolution; Ecol Soc Am. *Res:* Population and community ecology of amphibians; life history strategies of tropical amphibians; energetics and behavior of amphibian reproduction. *Mailing Add:* Dept of Zool Univ of Fla Gainesville FL 32611

CRUMP, STUART FAULKNER, b Boston, Mass, Feb 20, 21; m 44; c 4. PHYSICS, RESEARCH ADMINISTRATION. *Educ:* Brown Univ, BA, 43. *Prof Exp:* Physicist, David W Taylor Model Basin, 43-45, 56-59, naval architect, 45-49, 52-56, hydraul engr, 49-52, phys sci administr, 59-60; physicist, Navy Bur Ships, 60-61; physicist, David W Taylor Naval Ship Res & Develop Ctr, 61-62, phys sci adminstr, 62-67, contract res adminstr, 67-79; SR CONSULT, VECTOR RES CO & DESIGNERS & PLANNERS INC, 79- *Concurrent Pos:* Consult, 61-62. *Honors & Awards:* Super Accomplishment Award, US Navy, 52 & 60. *Mem:* Am Soc Naval Engrs; Marine Technol Soc. *Res:* Hydromechanics of naval architecture; underwater acoustics; cavitation research; engineering physics; contract research administration; ship silencing. *Mailing Add:* David W Taylor Naval Ship Res & Develop Ctr Code 1505 Bethesda MD 20084

CRUMPACKER, DAVID WILSON, b Enid, Okla, Mar 29, 29; m 55; c 4. GENETICS, AGRONOMY. *Educ:* Okla Agr & Mech Col, BS, 51; Univ Calif, Davis, PhD(genetics), 59. *Prof Exp:* Asst agron, Univ Calif, Davis, 55-59; assoc prof, Colo State Univ, 59-70; chmn dept, 77-80, PROF ENVIRON, POP & ORGANISMIC BIOL, UNIV COLO, BOULDER, 70- *Concurrent Pos:* USPHS spec fel, Rockefeller Univ, 65-66. *Mem:* Am Soc Agron; Crop Sci Soc Am; fel Am Soc Naturalists; Genetics Soc Am. *Res:* Evolution and population genetics of maize and Drosophila; biometrical genetics of wheat; maize breeding. *Mailing Add:* Dept of Biol Univ of Colo Boulder CO 80309

CRUMPLER, THOMAS BIGELOW, b Louisa, Ky, July 20, 09; m 35; c 2. ANALYTICAL CHEMISTRY. *Educ:* Va Polytech Inst, BS, 31, MS, 32; Univ Va, PhD(chem), 36. *Prof Exp:* Res, Univ Va, 36-37; from instr to assoc prof, 37-43, head dept, 42-62, prof, 43-74, EMER PROF CHEM, TULANE UNIV, 74- *Concurrent Pos:* Ford fac fel, 51-52. *Mem:* Fel Am Inst Chem; Am Chem Soc. *Res:* Photoelectric colorimetry and polarimetry; colorimetric reagents; paper chromatography. *Mailing Add:* PO Box 831 Highlands NC 28741

CRUMPTON, CARL F, b Ogden, Kans, Nov 14, 24; wid; c 5. ENGINEERING GEOLOGY, GOECHEMISTRY. *Educ:* Kans State Univ, BS, 49, MS, 51. *Prof Exp:* Geologist eng, State Hwy Comn Kans, 51-54, res geologist, 54-65; chief phys res, 65-70; ASST ENGR PLANNING & DEVELOP RES, DEVELOP & IMPLEMENTATION SECT, KANS DEPT TRANSP, 70- *Concurrent Pos:* Lectr geol, Washburn Univ, Topeka, 67-72; adj asst prof, 72-74; chmn concrete performance-chem aspects comt, Transp Res Bd, 70-76 & concrete sect, 76-82, mem corrosion comt, 70-; mem adv panel influence of repair on durability of bridge decks, Nat Coop Hwy Res Prog, 74-78, polymers in concrete, 72- & bridge deck durability, 77-79. *Mem:* Clay Minerals Soc; Nat Geog Soc; Int Platform Asn. *Res:* Concrete performance; engineering geology; clay and carbonate mineralogy; geochemistry; biodeterioration; corrosion; bridges and bridge decks; reflectorized highway paint stripes; safety; highway and bridge maintenance; epoxy injection; engineering properties of loess. *Mailing Add:* Res & Mat Lab 2300 Van Buren Topeka KS 66611

CRUMRINE, ANN LOUISE, synthetic organic chemistry, see previous edition

CRUMRINE, DAVID SHAFER, b Memphis, Tenn, Aug, 12, 44; m 67; c 2. PHYSICAL ORGANIC CHEMISTRY. *Educ:* Ashland Col, AB, 66; Univ Wis-Madison, PhD(org chem), 71. *Prof Exp:* Fel org chem, Mass Inst Technol & Ga Inst Technol, 71-72; asst prof, 72-76, ASSOC PROF ORG PHYS CHEM, LOYOLA UNIV, CHICAGO, 76- *Concurrent Pos:* Vis foreign scientist, Inst Molecular Sci, Okazaki, Japan, 80 & Dyson Perrins Lab, Oxford Univ, 81. *Mem:* Am Chem Soc; Sigma Xi. *Res:* Carbene and carbenoid reactions; mechanistic and exploratory organic photochemistry; synthesis of novel systems; NMR spectroscopy. *Mailing Add:* Dept of Chem Loyola Univ Chicago IL 60626

CRUSBERG, THEODORE CLIFFORD, b Meriden, Conn, Feb 23, 41; m 66; c 3. BIOCHEMISTRY. *Educ:* Univ Conn, BA, 63; Yale Univ, MS, 64; Clark Univ, PhD(chem), 68. *Prof Exp:* NIH trainee biochem, Sch Med, Tufts Univ, 68-69; ASSOC PROF LIFE SCI, WORCESTER POLYTECH INST, 69- *Mem:* AAAS; Sigma Xi. *Res:* Cell surface characteristics determined by scanning electron microscope and biochemical methods; erythrocyte membrane proteins and erythrocyte morphology and function. *Mailing Add:* Dept of Life Sci Worcester Polytech Inst Worcester MA 01609

CRUSE, CARL MAX, b St Charles, Va, Aug 4, 36; m 58; c 2. CHEMICAL ENGINEERING. *Educ:* Univ Tenn, BS, 59. *Prof Exp:* Res chem engr, Monsanto Chem Co, 59-61; process develop engr, Holston Defense Corp, Eastman Kodak Co, 61-63; res engr, 63-69, process specialist, 69-71, mfg supvr, 71-77, prin engr, 77-79, MFG SUPT, MONSANTO CO, 79- *Mem:* Am Inst Chem Engrs. *Res:* Kinetic studies of the pyrolysis of hydrocarbon mixtures; low-pressure carbonylation of alcohols using noble metal catalysts. *Mailing Add:* Monsanto Co PO Box 1311 Texas City TX 77590

CRUSE, JULIUS MAJOR, JR, b New Albany, Miss, Feb 15, 37. IMMUNOLOGY, PATHOLOGY. *Educ:* Univ Miss, BA, 58, BS, 59; Graz Univ, MS, 60; Univ Tenn, MD, 64, PhD(immunol & path), 66. *Prof Exp:* Prof biol & res prof immunol, Grad Sch, 67-74, asst prof microbiol, Sch Med, 68-74, ASSOC PROF MICROBIOL, PROF PATH & DIR GRAD STUDIES PATH, SCH MED, UNIV MISS, 74- *Concurrent Pos:* USPHS fel path, Inst Path, Tenn Med Units, 64-67; lectr, Col Med, Univ Tenn, 67- *Honors & Awards:* Physician's Recognition Award in Continuing Med Educ, AMA, 69 & 75. *Mem:* Fel AAAS; Am Asn Path & Bact; Am Soc Exp Path; Am Chem Soc; Am Soc Microbiol. *Res:* Immunopathology; tumor immunology; histocompatability antigens; cellular and humoral immune responses to tissue allografts; immunological enhancement. *Mailing Add:* Dept of Path Univ of Miss Med Ctr Jackson MI 39216

CRUSE, ROBERT RIDGELY, b Tucson, Ariz, Aug 20, 20; m 47; c 1. APPLIED CHEMISTRY. *Educ:* Antioch Col, BS, 42. *Prof Exp:* Res engr, Battelle Mem Inst, 42-47; anal chemist, US Bur Mines, Ariz, 53-55, extractive metallurgist, 55; assoc indust chemist, Southwest Res Inst, 55-61; res chemist, Nitrogen Div, Allied Chem Corp, 61-68; RES CHEMIST, AGR PROD TECHNOL RES, USDA, 68- *Concurrent Pos:* Instr org chem, Trinity Univ, 56-57; assoc, Southwest Agr Inst, Tex, 59-60. *Mem:* Fel AAAS; fel Am Inst Chem; Am Chem Soc; Sigma Xi. *Res:* Chemurgy; organic synthesis; pharmaceuticals; fuels; insecticides; fertilizers; foods. *Mailing Add:* 1106 W Third St Weslaco TX 78596

CRUSE, THOMAS ALLEN, b Anderson, Ind, Sept 7, 41; m 63; c 2. ENGINEERING PROGRAM MANAGEMENT, STRUCTURES TECHNOLOGY. *Educ:* Stanford Univ, BS, 63, MS, 64; Univ Wash, PhD(eng mech), 67. *Prof Exp:* Assoc res engr, Airplane Div, Boeing Co, Wash, 64-65; assoc prof mech eng, Carnegie-Mellon Univ, 67-73; DEVELOP ENGR, PRATT & WHITNEY/COM PROD, UNITED TECHNOL CORP, 73- *Mem:* Am Soc Mech Engrs; Am Soc Testing Mats; Am Inst Aeronaut & Astronaut. *Res:* Investigation of numerical solutions in three dimensional elastostatics utilizing the direct potential method and integral equations; examination of two dimensional elastodynamics; fracture mechanics of surface cracks; fatigue of gas turbine engine components. *Mailing Add:* Pratt & Whitney/Com Prod 400 Main St MS Eb35-3 East Hartford CT 06108

CRUSER, STEPHEN ALAN, b Greensburg, Ind, Dec 12, 42; m 67; c 2. ANALYTICAL CHEMISTRY, PHYSICAL CHEMISTRY. *Educ:* Ind Univ, Bloomington, BS, 64; Univ Tex, Austin, PhD(chem), 68. *Prof Exp:* Chemist, 68-69, sr chemist, 70-72, res chemist, 72-77, sr res chemist, 78-81, ASST SUPVR, TEXACO INC, BELLAIRE, 81- *Mem:* Nat Asn Corrosion Engrs. *Res:* Electroanalytical chemistry; corrosion control; inhibitor mechanisms. *Mailing Add:* 12042 Corona Lane Houston TX 77072

CRUTCHER, HAROLD L, b Cheraw, Colo, Nov 18, 13; m 43; c 2. METEOROLOGY, CHEMISTRY. *Educ:* Southeastern State Col, BA, 33, BS, 34; NY Univ, MS, 51, PhD(meteorol), 60. *Prof Exp:* Teacher pub schs, Okla, 35-39; from jr observer to sr observer, 39-42, meteorologist, 42-45, forecaster, 45-47, meteorologist, Opers Div, 47-50, Climat & Hydrol Serv Div, 51-52, Climat Serv Div, 52-53 & Nat Climatic Ctr, 53-63, RES METEOROLOGIST, NAT CLIMATIC CTR, NAT OCEANIC & ATMOSPHERIC ADMIN, 63- *Concurrent Pos:* Mem opers anal standby unit, Univ NC, 59-69. *Honors & Awards:* Silver Award, US Dept Com, 62, Gold Medal, 71. *Mem:* Am Meteorol Soc; Am Geophys Union; Am Soc Qual Control; Am Statist Asn; fel Am Inst Chem. *Res:* Upper air climatology; stochastic and dynamic models. *Mailing Add:* 35 Westall Ave Asheville NC 28804

CRUTCHER, KEITH A, b Ft Lauderdale, Fla, May 29, 53; m 72; c 3. NEUROBIOLOGY, COMPARATIVE NEUROANATOMY. *Educ:* Pt Loma Col, BA, 74; Ohio State Univ, PhD(anat), 77. *Prof Exp:* Fel neurobiol, Med Ctr, Duke Univ, 77-80; ASST PROF ANAT, UNIV UTAH, 80- *Mem:* AAAS; Am Asn Anatomists; Soc Neurosci. *Res:* Neuronal plasticity with particular emphasis on transmitter-specific rearrangement which may underly the recovery of function following injury to the central nervous system. *Mailing Add:* Dept Anat Sch Med Univ Utah Salt Lake City UT 84132

CRUTCHER, RICHARD METCALF, b Lexington, Ky, April 18, 45; m 72; c 2. INTERSTELLAR MEDIUM. *Educ:* Univ Ky, BS, 67; Univ Calif, Los Angeles, MA, 69, PhD(astron), 72. *Prof Exp:* Res fel, Calif Inst Technol, 72-74; asst prof, 74-78, ASSOC PROF ASTRON, UNIV ILL, 78- *Concurrent Pos:* Res assoc, Radio Astron Lab, Univ Calif, Berkeley, 80-81. *Mem:* Am Astron Soc; Int Astron Union; Union Radio Sci Int. *Res:* Physics and chemistry of the interstellar medium by observations at ultraviolet, visual, infrared and radio wavelengths. *Mailing Add:* 341 Astron Bldg Univ Ill Urbana IL 61801

CRUTCHFIELD, CHARLIE, b Norwood, Pa, Dec 29, 28; m 62; c 2. ANALYTICAL CHEMISTRY, INORGANIC CHEMISTRY. *Educ:* Univ Pa, BA, 50, MS, 53, PhD(chem), 60. *Prof Exp:* Anal chemist, Dalare Assocs, Pa, 50-55; instr gen & anal chem, Flint Jr Col, 59-61; electrochemist, Stanford Res Inst, 61-66, anal chemist, 66-69; TECH DIR, TRUESDAIL LABS, INC, 69- *Mem:* Am Chem Soc. *Res:* Complex compounds. *Mailing Add:* Truesdail Labs Inc 4101 N Figuerosa Los Angeles CA 90065

CRUTCHFIELD, FLOY LOVE, b Branch, La, Dec 22, 22; m 43; c 2. ENDOCRINOLOGY. *Educ:* La Col, BS, 43; Med Col Pa, MS, 69, PhD(anat), 72. *Prof Exp:* RES ASSOC ENDOCRINOL, VET ADMIN HOSP & MED COL PA, 72-, RES ASST PROF MED, 75- *Concurrent Pos:* Instr histol neuroanat, Med Col Pa, 72-73. *Mem:* Am Soc Zoologists; Soc Develop Biol. *Res:* Investigating the metabolism of thyroxine in the adrenergic nervous system. *Mailing Add:* Dept of Med Med Col of Pa 3300 Henry Ave Philadelphia PA 19129

CRUTCHFIELD, MARVIN MACK, b Oxford, NC, Sept 15, 34; m 56; c 2. PHYSICAL CHEMISTRY, DETERGENT CHEMICALS. *Educ:* Duke Univ, BS, 56; Brown Univ, PhD(phys chem), 60. *Prof Exp:* Sr res chemist, 60-63, res specialist, 63-65, scientist, 65-70, SCI FEL, MONSANTO CO, 70- *Mem:* AAAS; Am Chem Soc; Sigma Xi; Am Oil Chemist Soc. *Res:* Peroxoanions; nuclear magnetic resonance; metal ion complexing; chemistry of phosphorus compounds; surface active agents; detergents; builders; polyelectrolytes; biodegradation; molecular structure-physical property relationships; calcium ion equilibria. *Mailing Add:* Monsanto Co 800 N Lindbergh Blvd St Louis MO 63166

CRUTHERS, LARRY RANDALL, b Kenosha, Wis, Mar 15, 45; m 67; c 2. VETERINARY PARASITOLOGY. *Educ:* Univ Wis, Stevens Point, BS, 67; Kans State Univ, MS, 71, PhD(parasitol), 73. *Prof Exp:* Instr biol, Kans State Univ, 70-73; res investr, E R Squibb & Sons, 74-77, sr res investr parasitol, 77-80; sr res parasitologist, 80-82, RES ASSOC, DIAMOND SHAMROCK CORP, 82- *Mem:* Am Asn Vet Parasitologists; Conf Res Workers Animal Dis; Mem: Am Soc Parasitol; Sigma Xi. *Res:* Chemotherapy of helminth and protozoan parasites of economic and companion animals. *Mailing Add:* Animal Health Res Diamond Shamrock Corp PO Box 348 Painesville OH 44077

CRUZ, ALEXANDER, b New York, NY, July 12, 41; m 63; c 2. ECOLOGY, VERTEBRATE ZOOLOGY. *Educ:* City Univ New York, BS, 64; Univ Fla, PhD(ecol & zool), 73. *Prof Exp:* Microbiologist, New York Dept Health, Bur Labs, 64-68; asst prof, 73-80, ASSOC PROF BIOL, ENVIRON, POP & ORG, UNIV COLO, BOULDER, 80- *Concurrent Pos:* Consult, Biol & Health Sci Educ Opportunities Prog, Univ Colo, 73- & Ecol Analysts Inc, 74-; fac res initiation fel, Univ Colo, 74. *Mem:* Ecol Soc Am; Am Ornithologists Union; Wilson Ornith Soc; Sigma Xi. *Res:* Ecology and behavior of vertebrates with a special interest in avian ecology and behavior, ornithology, community analysis, tropical and insular biology. *Mailing Add:* Dept of Environ Pop & Univ of Colo Boulder CO 80309

CRUZ, ANATOLIO BENEDICTO, JR, b Marikina, Philippines, June 20, 33; US citizen; m 55; c 4. SURGERY, SURGICAL ONCOLOGY. *Educ:* Univ Philippines, AA, 52, MD, 57; Univ Minn, MS, 63. *Prof Exp:* Instr surg, Univ Minn, Minneapolis, 64 & Univ E Med Ctr, Quezon City, Philippines, 64-65; researcher cardiovasc surg, Univ Alta, 65-66; from asst prof to assoc prof surg, 66-74, PROF SURG & ANAT, UNIV TEX HEALTH SCI CTR, 74- *Concurrent Pos:* Co-prin investr, Nat Surg Adj Breast Proj, NIH grant, 66-; consult gen surg, US Air Force Med Ctr, San Antonio; consult thoracic surg, San Antonio State Chest Hosp, 67-; dir tumor clin & chief, head & neck, soft tissue tumor, surg oncol & burn serv, Bexar County Teaching Hosps, 69-; mem serv & rehab comt, Am Cancer Soc, Bexar County Unit, 72-; staff physician gen surg, Audie L Murphy Mem Vet Hosp, 73-; prin investr, Southwest Oncol Group, NIH grant, 76-; mem bd dirs, STex Health Educ Ctr, 78- *Mem:* Am Soc Clin Oncol; Am Soc Prev Oncol; Soc Surg Oncol Inc. *Res:* Development of combination modalities in the treatment of cancer in addition to activities related to understanding the problems in cancer in general. *Mailing Add:* 7703 Floyd Curl Dr San Antonio TX 78284

CRUZ, CARLOS, b Aguadilla, PR, Dec 24, 40; US citizen; m 71; c 3. ENTOMOLOGY. *Educ:* Univ PR, Mayagüez, BSA, 63; Rutgers Univ, MS, 68, PhD(entom), 72. *Prof Exp:* Agr agt, Agr Exten Serv, 63-65; res asst sugar cane, Agr Exp Sta, PR, 65-66; res asst entom, Rutgers Univ, 66-68 & Agr Exp Sta, PR, 68-69; asst entomologist, 72-76, ASSOC ENTOMOLOGIST, AGR EXP STA, UNIV PR, 76- *Mem:* Entom Soc Am; PR Soc Agr Sci; Sigma Xi; Caribbean Food Crop Soc; Soc Entomol PR. *Res:* Insect pest management on legumes and vegetables; study of all measures of insect control, particularly the use of resistant varieties, parasites, predators and selective insecticides. *Mailing Add:* Agr Exp Sta Univ of PR Isabela Substa Box 506 Isabela PR 00662

CRUZ, JOSE B(EJAR), JR, b Bacolod City, Philippines, Sept 17, 32; US citizen; m 53; c 5. CONTROL SYSTEMS, SYSTEMS ENGINEERING. *Educ:* Univ Philippines, BSEE, 53; Mass Inst Technol, SM, 56; Univ Ill, PhD, 59. *Prof Exp:* Instr elec eng, Univ Philippines, 53-54; asst res lab electronics, Mass Inst Technol, 54-56; from instr to assoc prof elec eng, 56-65, assoc mem, Ctr Advan Studies, 67-68, PROF ELEC ENG, UNIV ILL, URBANA, 65- *Concurrent Pos:* Vis assoc prof, Univ Calif, Berkeley, 64-65; ed, Inst Elec & Electronics Engrs Trans Automatic Control, 71-73; vis prof, Mass Inst Technol & Harvard Univ, 73; pres, Dynamic Systs, 78-; assoc ed, J Franklin Inst, 78- & J Optimization Theory & Applns, 81-; ed, Advances in Large Scale Systs, 82- *Honors & Awards:* Curtis W McGraw Res Award, Am Soc Eng Educ, 72. *Mem:* Nat Acad Eng; fel Inst Elec & Electronics Engrs; Nat Soc Prof Engrs. *Res:* Control of systems containing uncertainties; strategies for systems with multiple decision makers; sensitivity analysis of dynamic systems. *Mailing Add:* 2014 Silver Court W Urbana IL 61801

CRUZ, MAMERTO MANAHAN, JR, b Manila, Philippines, July 15, 18; US citizen; m 50; c 2. CHEMISTRY. *Educ:* Univ Philippines, BS, 39; Mass Inst Technol, SM, 41; State Univ NY Col Forestry, Syracuse, PhD(chem), 54. *Prof Exp:* Chemist, Am Viscose Corp, Pa, 42-47; lectr chem processes, Mapua Inst Technol, Philippines, 48; chem engr, Philippines Mission to Japan, 48, tech investr, 48-49; sr res chemist, Am Viscose Corp, Pa, 53-55; sect chief colloid chem, Olin Mathieson Chem Corp, Conn, 55-57; group leader pulp & bleaching, Ketchikan Res, Am Viscose Corp, 57-59, paper fibers, Com Develop Dept, 59-60, head avicel pilot opers, Corp Res Dept, 61-62, avicel plant mgr, 62, sect leader prod develop, 63, & spec prod, Am Viscose Div, 63, sr scientist new prod explor res, 63-64 & chem div, 64-66, mgr probing res & mgr new polymer prod, Cent Res Dept, 66-70, mgr prod & res develop, Avicon, Inc, FMC Corp, 71-79; PRES & TECH DIR, MORCA, INC, 79- *Mem:* Fel AAAS; Am Chem Soc; NY Acad Sci; Am Inst Chemists; Am Leather Chemists Asn. *Res:* Textile engineering; pulping and bleaching of wood pulps; rayon fiber and cellophane film technology; cellulose reactions; cellulose derivatives; synthetic polymeric coatings; wet strength paper and non-wovens; wood chemistry; collagen based medical products; microcrystalline cellulose. *Mailing Add:* Box 334Y RR 1 Pennington NJ 08534

CRUZAN, JOHN, b Bridgeton, NJ, Jan 6, 42; m 64; c 2. ECOLOGY. *Educ:* King's Col, BA, 65; Univ Colo, PhD(zool), 68. *Prof Exp:* From asst prof to assoc prof, 68-79, PROF BIOL, GENEVA COL, 79- *Mem:* Am Soc Mammal; Am Sci Affiliation; Ecol Soc Am; Am Inst Biol Sci. *Res:* Ecology, behavior and geography of mammals and other vertebrates; Soil community structure. *Mailing Add:* Dept of Biol Geneva Col Beaver Falls PA 15010

CRYBERG, RICHARD LEE, b Los Angeles, Calif, Nov 2, 41; m 63; c 2. ORGANIC CHEMISTRY. *Educ:* Iowa State Univ, BS, 63; Ohio State Univ, PhD(org chem), 69. *Prof Exp:* Chief chemist, G F Smith Chem Co, 63-68; sr res chemist, 69-74, group leader chem, 74-76, group leader polymers, 76-77, GROUP LEADER ANAL, T R EVANS RES CTR, DIAMOND SHAMROCK CORP, 77- *Mem:* Am Chem Soc. *Res:* Spectroscopy, x-ray and microscopy. *Mailing Add:* T R Evans Res Ctr Box 348 Painesville OH 44077

CRYER, COLIN WALKER, b Leeds, Eng, Aug 28, 35; m 68; c 1. COMPUTER SCIENCE. *Educ:* Univ Pretoria, BS, 54, MS, 58; Cambridge Univ, PhD(comput sci), 62. *Prof Exp:* Asst res officer, Nat Phys Lab, SAfrica, 55-58; res officer, Nat Res Inst Math Sci SAfrica, 62-63; res fel comput sci, Calif Inst Technol, 63-65; mem res staff, Math Res Ctr, 65-66, from asst prof to assoc prof, 66-77, PROF COMPUT SCI, UNIV WIS-MADISON, 77- *Mem:* Am Math Soc; Asn Comput Mach. *Res:* Numerical solution of integral and partial differential equations. *Mailing Add:* Dept of Comput Sci Univ of Wis Madison WI 53706

CRYER, JONATHAN D, b Toledo, Ohio, Feb 10, 39; m 61; c 3. STATISTICS. *Educ:* DePauw Univ, BA, 61; Univ NC, PhD(statist), 66. *Prof Exp:* Statistician, Res Triangle Inst, 63-66; asst prof, 66-70, ASSOC PROF STATIST, UNIV IOWA, 70-, STATISTICIAN. *Concurrent Pos:* Consult, Amana Refrig, Inc, 74- & Am Col Testing, 77- *Mem:* Inst Math Statist; Am Statist Asn. *Res:* Stochastic processes and mathematical statistics. *Mailing Add:* Dept of Statist Univ of Iowa Iowa City IA 52242

CRYER, PHILIP EUGENE, b ElPaso, Ill, Jan 5, 40; m 63; c 2. ENDOCRINOLOGY, METABOLISM. *Educ:* Northwestern Univ, BA, 62, MD, 65. *Prof Exp:* Resident, Barnes Hosp, St Louis, 65-67; fel metab, 67-68, instr med, 71-72, asst prof, 72-77, assoc prof, 77-81, PROF MED, SCH MED, WASHINGTON UNIV, 81- *Concurrent Pos:* Resident med, Barnes Hosp, St Louis, 68-69; dir, Clin Res Ctr, Sch Med, Washington Univ, 78- *Mem:* Am Fedn Clin Res; Am Diabetes Asn; Endocrine Soc; Cent Soc Clin Res; Am Soc Clin Invest. *Res:* The sympathoadrenal system in human metabolic physiology and pathophysiology. *Mailing Add:* Sch Med Metab Div Washington Univ 660 S Euclid St Louis MO 63110

CRYNES, BILLY LEE, b Worthington, Ind, Mar 16, 38; m 57; c 3. CHEMICAL ENGINEERING. *Educ:* Rose Polytech Inst, BS, 63; Purdue Univ, MA, 66, PhD(chem eng), 68. *Prof Exp:* Technician, Lab, Commercial Solvents Corp, 61-63; design engr, Pilot Plant, E I du Pont de Nemours & Co, 63-64; from asst prof to assoc prof, 67-73, PROF CHEM ENG, OKLA STATE UNIV, 73-, HEAD DEPT, 78- *Mem:* Am Chem Soc; Am Inst Chem Engrs; Am Soc Eng Educ. *Res:* Pyrolysis of hydrocarbons; hydrodesulfurization catalysts; synthetic crudes from coal; reactor engineering. *Mailing Add:* Sch of Chem Eng Okla State Univ Stillwater OK 74074

CRYSTAL, GEORGE JEFFREY, b Newark, NJ, Apr 5, 48. CARDIOVASCULAR PHYSIOLOGY, CORONARY PHYSIOLOGY. *Educ:* Rutgers Univ, New Brunswick, NJ, AB, 70, MS, 74, PhD(physiol), 77. *Prof Exp:* Teaching asst physiol, Rutgers Med Sch, Piscataway, NJ, 74-77; fel physiol, 77-79, ASST PROF PHYSIOL, UNIV TEX HEALTH SCI CTR, DALLAS, 79- *Concurrent Pos:* Mem, Am Heart Asn. *Mem:* Am Physiol Soc. *Res:* Reflex control of the cardiovascular system; metabolic regulation of coronary blood flow. *Mailing Add:* Cardiovascular Res Lab PO Box 225999 Dallas TX 75265

CRYSTAL, MAXWELL MELVIN, b New York, NY, Oct 9, 24; m 49; c 1. MEDICAL & VETERINARY ENTOMOLOGY. *Educ:* Brooklyn Col, AB, 47; Ohio State Univ, MSc, 48; Univ Calif, PhD(parasitol), 56. *Prof Exp:* Asst helminth & med entom, Univ Calif, 51-55; asst prof biol, NY Teachers Col, New Paltz, 56-57; instr parasitol, Albert Einstein Col Med, 57-58; Nat Cancer Inst res grant, 58-59; asst med physics, Montefiore Hosp, 59-60; res entomologist, Screwworm Res Lab, Agr Res Serv, 61-77, res entomologist, Biol Eval Chem Lab, Agr Environ Qual Inst, 77-79, Insect Reproduction Lab, 79-81, RES ENTOMOLOGIST, LIVESTOCK INSECTS LAB, AGR RES SERV, USDA, 81- *Mem:* AAAS; Sigma Xi; Inst Biol Sci; Entom Soc Am; Am Registry Prof Entomologists. *Res:* Insect chemosterilants: evaluation procedures, reliability of technique, structure, activity relationships, effects on reproduction; screwworm fly biology: mating, longevity, irradiation, flight mill studies, new strain development. *Mailing Add:* Livestock Insects Lab Agr Res Serv USDA Bldg 476 BARC-East Beltsville MD 20705

CRYSTAL, RONALD GEORGE, b Newark, NJ, Apr 23, 41; m 65; c 2. INTERNAL MEDICINE, BIOCHEMISTRY. *Educ:* Tufts Univ, BA, 62; Univ Pa, MS, 63, MD, 68. *Prof Exp:* Intern internal med, Mass Gen Hosp, Boston, 68-69, resident, 69-70; res assoc molecular hemat, 70-72, head pulmonary biochem sect, 72-75, CHIEF PULMONARY BR, NAT HEART,

LUNG & BLOOD INST, 75- *Concurrent Pos:* Clin fel, Harvard Univ, 69-70 & Univ Calif, San Francisco, 73; adj prof genetics, George Washington Univ, 75- *Mem:* Am Soc Biol Chemists; Am Soc Clin Invest; Am Thoracic Soc; Am Fed Clin Res. *Res:* Lung structure and function in health and disease; connective tissue biochemistry; inflammation and immune processes in lung. *Mailing Add:* Nat Heart Lung & Blood Inst 6D06 Bldg 10 NIH Bethesda MD 20205

CSAKY, TIHAMER ZOLTAN, b Hungary, Aug 12, 15; nat US; m 53; c 2. PHYSIOLOGY, PHARMACOLOGY. *Educ:* Univ Budapest, MD, 39. *Prof Exp:* Asst prof physiol, Univ Budapest, 40-45; res adj, Hungarian Biol Res Inst, 46-47; res assoc, Duke Univ, 49-51; from asst prof to assoc prof pharmacol, Sch Med, Univ NC, 51-61; prof pharmacol, Sch Med, Univ Ky, Lexington, 61-79, chmn dept, 61-76; PROF PHARMACOL, SCH MED, UNIV MO, COLUMBIA, 79- *Concurrent Pos:* Res fel, Biochem Inst, Helsinki, 47-48; res fel, Microbiol Inst, Uppsala, 48-49; vis prof & USPHS spec fel, Univ Milan, 68-69; A V Humboldt sr award, Univ Bochum & Saar Univ, Hamburg, Ger. *Mem:* Int Soc Biochem Pharmacol; Soc Exp Biol & Med; Am Soc Pharmacol & Exp Therapeut; Am Physiol Soc; Soc Gen Physiol. *Res:* Biological transport. *Mailing Add:* Dept Pharmacol Univ Mo Sch Med Columbia MO 65212

CSALLANY, AGNES SAARI, b Budapest, Hungary, Apr 20, 32; US citizen; m 54. ORGANIC CHEMISTRY. *Educ:* Budapest Tech Univ, BS, MS, 55, ScD(lipid chem), 70. *Prof Exp:* Head qual control lab, Duna Canning Co, Budapest, 55-56; from res asst to res assoc animal sci, Univ Ill, Urbana, 57-65, res asst prof, 65-69, res asst prof food sci, 69-71; assoc prof food chem, 72-80, PROF FOOD SCI & NUTRIT, UNIV MINN, ST PAUL, 80- *Concurrent Pos:* Deleg, Int Nutrit Cong, 60, 69 & 75 & Int Biochem Cong, 64; Am Inst Nutrit travel grants, 69 & 75. *Mem:* Am Chem Soc; Am Inst Nutrit; Sigma Xi. *Res:* Basic research in the field of vitamin E; determination of chemical structures; air and water pollution; effect of nitrate, nitrogen dioxide and ozone on rats and mice. *Mailing Add:* Dept of Food Sci & Nutrit Univ of Minn St Paul MN 55108

CSANADY, GABRIEL TIBOR, b Budapest, Hungary, Dec 10, 25; m 45, 69; c 4. PHYSICAL OCEANOGRAPHY, FLUID MECHANICS. *Educ:* Munich Tech Univ, Dipl Ing, 48; Univ New South Wales, PhD(mech eng), 58. *Prof Exp:* Engr, Brown, Boveri Co, Ger, 48-49, Elec Comn New South Wales, Australia, 49-52 & Elec Comn Victoria, 52-54; lectr mech eng, Univ New South Wales, 54-61; assoc prof, Univ Windsor, 61-63; prof, Univ Waterloo, 63-73, chmn dept, 63-67; SR SCIENTIST, WOODS HOLE OCEANOG INST, 73- *Concurrent Pos:* Sr res fel aerodyn, Col Aeronaut Eng, 60-61; vis prof, Univ Wis, 69. *Honors & Awards:* President's Prize, Can Meteorol Soc, 70; Ed Award, Am Meteorol Soc, 75; Chandler-Misener Award, Int Asn Great Lakes Res, 77. *Mem:* Am Meteorol Soc; Am Soc Mech Engrs; Am Geophys Union; Royal Meteorol Soc; Can Meteorol Soc. *Res:* Dynamics of shallow seas; continental shelves; coastal ocean; upper ocean dynamics; air-sea interaction; effluent disposal. *Mailing Add:* Woods Hole Oceanog Inst Woods Hole MA 02543

CSAPILLA, JOSEPH, b Budapest, Hungary, Feb 26, 34; US citizen. ORGANIC CHEMISTRY, TEXTILE CHEMISTRY. *Educ:* Univ Basel, PhD(org chem), 61. *Prof Exp:* USPHS fel reaction mechanism, Univ Mich, 61-63; res chemist, 63-70, SR RES CHEMIST, AM CYANAMID CO, 70- *Res:* Synthetic, physical-organic and photochemistry; acrylic fibers. *Mailing Add:* Res Labs Am Cyanamid Co Stamford CT 06904

CSAPO, ARPAD ISTVAN, physiology, deceased

CSAVINSZKY, PETER JOHN, b Budapest, Hungary, July 10, 31; US citizen; m 76. THEORETICAL SOLID STATE PHYSICS. *Educ:* Tech Univ Budapest, diplom ing chem, 54; Univ Ottawa, PhD(theoret physics), 59. *Prof Exp:* Mem tech staff, Semiconductor Div, Hughes Aircraft Co, 59-60; sr physicist, Electronics Div, Gen Dynamics Corp, 60-62; mem tech staff, Tex Instruments Inc, 62-65 & TRW Systems Inc, 65-70; assoc prof, 70-75, PROF PHYSICS, UNIV MAINE, ORONO, 75- *Mem:* Fel Am Phys Soc; Am Asn Univ Prof; AAAS; NY Acad Sci; Sigma Xi. *Res:* Quantum theoretical studies of charge transport in solids; the structure of impurities and defects in solids. *Mailing Add:* Dept Physics Univ Maine Orono ME 04469

CSEJKA, DAVID ANDREW, b Passaic, NJ, June 9, 35; m 65; c 5. PHYSICAL CHEMISTRY, ANALYTICAL CHEMISTRY. *Educ:* Fordham Univ, BS, 56; Iowa State Univ, PhD(phys chem), 61. *Prof Exp:* Sr res chemist, 61-74, res assoc, 74-76, group leader, 76-80, MGR CHEM SECT, OLIN CORP, 80- *Mem:* Sigma Xi; Am Chem Soc; NY Acad Sci. *Res:* Chemical and physical properties of aqueous and non-aqueous solutions; electroanalytical chemistry, polarography, coulometry, voltammetry. *Mailing Add:* Olin Corp 275 Winchester Ave New Haven CT 06511

CSEJTEY, BELA, JR, b Budapest, Hungary, Jan 26, 34; US citizen; m 67; c 1. STRUCTURAL GEOLOGY, PETROLOGY. *Educ:* Princeton Univ, PhD(geol), 63. *Prof Exp:* Res asst geophys, Dept Geol, Princeton Univ, 63; geologist petrol, Richfield Oil Corp, 63-66; GEOLOGIST, US GEOL SURV, 66- *Concurrent Pos:* Exchange scientist, Geochem Res Lab, Hungarian Acad Sci, 73. *Honors & Awards:* Antarctic Serv Medal, US Cong, 64. *Mem:* Fel Geol Soc Am; AAAS; Sigma Xi; Am Polar Soc. *Res:* Study of plutonic rocks and structural features of southern Alaska in order to decipher the plate-tectonic evolution of the region. *Mailing Add:* US Geol Surv MS 17 345 Middlefield Rd Menlo Park CA 94025

CSENDES, ERNEST, b Satu-Mare, Rumania, Mar 2, 26; nat US; m 53; c 2. ORGANIC CHEMISTRY. *Educ:* Col Hungary, BA, 44; Univ Heidelberg, BS, 48, MS & PhD, 51. *Prof Exp:* Asst, Univ Heidelberg, 51; res assoc biochem, Tulane Univ, 52; fel, Harvard Univ, 52-53; res chemist, Org Chem Dept, E I du Pont de Nemours & Co, Del, 53-56, res chemist, Elastomer Chem Dept, 56-61; dir res, Armour & Co, 61-62, dir res & develop, Agr Chem Div, 62-63; vpres corp develop, Occidental Petrol Corp, 63-64, exec vpres res eng & develop & mem exec comt, 64-68, exec vpres, Occidental Res Eng Corp, 63-68, dir, Occidental Res & Eng, Ltd, UK, 64-68; PRES & CHIEF EXEC, TEX REPUB INDUSTS, 68- *Concurrent Pos:* Pres & chief exec, TRI Ltd, Bermuda, 71-, chmn & dir, TRI Int Ltd, Bermuda, 71-, managing dir, TRI Holdings SA, Luxembourg, 71- & TRI Capital NV, Neth, 71- *Mem:* Fel AAAS; fel Am Inst Chemists; Am Chem Soc; Am Defense Preparedness Asn; Am Inst Aeronaut & Astronaut. *Res:* International projects related to energy resources and agriculture; international finance related to leasing; banking, trusts, insurance; administration of research, engineering and industrial development. *Mailing Add:* 1601 Casale Rd Pacific Palisades CA 90272

CSENDES, ZOLTAN JOSEPH, b Feffernitz, Austria, May 16, 46; Can citizen. NUMERICAL ANALYSIS, ELECTRICAL ENGINEERING. *Educ:* Univ Mich, BSE, 68; McGill Univ, MEng, 70, PhD(elec eng), 73. *Prof Exp:* Prof assoc, Dept Elec Eng, McGill Univ, 72-74; engr, Gen Elec Co, 74-77; pres, Csendes Assoc, Inc, 77-78; ENGR ELECTROMAGNETICS, CORP RES & DEVELOP, GEN ELEC CO, 78- *Mem:* Inst Elec & Electronics Engrs; Int Asn Math & Comput in Simulation; Sigma Xi. *Res:* Numerical methods for partial differential equations; finite element methods; matrix theory; generalized inverses; electromagnetic field theory; electric machine modeling; modeling of microwave circuits. *Mailing Add:* Corp Res & Develop Bldg 37-373 PO Box 43 Schenectady NY 12301

CSERMELY, THOMAS J(OHN), b Szombathely, Hungary, June 25, 31; US citizen; m 61; c 1. COMPUTER ENGINEERING, BIOMEDICAL ENGINEERING. *Educ:* Tech Univ Budapest, Dipl, 53; Syracuse Univ, PhD(physics-sci teaching), 68. *Prof Exp:* Instr, Tech Univ Budapest, Inst Theoret Physics, 53-56; res engr, Res & Develop Div, Carrier Corp, NY, 57-67; res assoc biophys, Syracuse Univ, 67-68; asst prof physiol & biophys, State Univ NY Upstate Med Ctr, 68-76; asst prof physics dept, Le Moyne Col, 76-77; asst prof, 77-80, ASSOC PROF ELEC & COMPUT ENG, SYRACUSE UNIV, 80- *Concurrent Pos:* Consult, Design Bur for Power Stas, Budapest, 56. *Honors & Awards:* Wolverine Diamond Key Award, Soc Heat, Refrig & Air-Conditioning Engrs, 65. *Mem:* AAAS; Am Phys Soc; Am Asn Physics Teachers; Inst Elec & Electronics Engrs; Biophys Soc. *Res:* Systems analysis and dynamics; mathematical modeling and computer simulation of systems; neural networks; medical computation and data systems. *Mailing Add:* Dept Elec & Comput Eng 111 Link Hall Syracuse Univ Syracuse NY 13210

CSERNA, EUGENE GEORGE, b Budapest, Hungary, Jan 2, 20; nat US; m 50; c 3. STRUCTURAL GEOLOGY. *Educ:* Univ Budapest, Dr Polit Sci, 43; Columbia Univ, MA, 50, PhD(geol), 56. *Prof Exp:* Asst geol, Columbia Univ, 50-51; geologist & explorer, Gulf Oil Corp, 51-54; instr geol, Hunter Col, 55; field geologist, US Geol Surv, 55-57; asst prof, Idaho State Col, 57-59; PROF GEOL, CALIF STATE UNIV, FRESNO, 59- *Concurrent Pos:* NSF fac fel, Swiss Fed Inst Technol, 66-67; Nat Acad Sci exchange fel, Hungary & Romania, 74; exchange deleg, Nat Acad Sci, Czech, 79. *Mem:* Asn Petrol Geologists; Sigma Xi; Geol Soc Am. *Res:* structure and stratigraphy of Fra Cristobal Area, New Mexico, Poison Spider, Oil Mountain, Pine Mountain in Wyoming; revision of portions of the New Tectonic Map of the United States. *Mailing Add:* Dept of Geol Calif State Univ Fresno CA 93740

CSERR, HELEN F, b Boston, Mass, June 23, 37; m 62; c 1. PHYSIOLOGY. *Educ:* Middlebury Col, BA, 59; Harvard Univ, PhD(physiol), 65. *Prof Exp:* Instr neurol, Harvard Med Sch, 68-70; lectr, 70-71, asst prof, 71-76, ASSOC PROF MED SCI, BROWN UNIV, 76- *Concurrent Pos:* United Cerebral Palsy Res & Educ Found fel physiol, Harvard Med Sch, 65-68; Nat Inst Neurol Dis & Stroke career develop award, 73-78; trustee, Mt Desert Island Biol Lab, 71-77, mem, Exec Comt, 75-77; mem, Physiol Study Sect, NIH, 75-79. *Mem:* AAAS; Soc Gen Physiol; Royal Soc Med; Am Physiol Soc. *Res:* Physiology of cerebrospinal fluid. *Mailing Add:* Div of Biol & Med Brown Univ Providence RI 02912

CSICSERY, SIGMUND MARIA, b Budapest, Hungary, Feb 3, 29; US citizen; m 56. SURFACE CHEMISTRY, PETROLEUM CHEMISTRY. *Educ:* Budapest Tech Univ, MS, 51; Northwestern Univ, PhD(org chem), 61. *Prof Exp:* Res chemist, Res & Eng Div, Monsanto Chem Co, Ohio, 57-59 & Calif Res Corp, 61-66; sr res chemist, 66-70, SR RES ASSOC, CHEVRON RES CO, 70- *Concurrent Pos:* Exten instr, Univ Calif, Berkeley, 65-; dir, Calif Catalysis Soc, 76-80. *Mem:* Am Chem Soc. *Res:* Catalysis and chemistry of petroleum hydrocarbons; structure, activation, and preparation of acidic and metal-containing heterogeneous catalysts; application of molecular sieves as catalysts. *Mailing Add:* Chevron Res Co PO Box 1627 Richmond CA 94802

CSONKA, PAUL L, b Aug 10, 38; US citizen. ELEMENTARY PARTICLE PHYSICS. *Educ:* Johns Hopkins Univ, PhD(theoret physics), 63. *Prof Exp:* Res assoc, Johns Hopkins Univ, 63-64; fel theoret physics, Lawrence Radiation Lab, Univ Calif, 64-66; NSF fel, Europ Org Nuclear Res Labs, 66-67; from asst prof to assoc prof, 68-76, res assoc, Inst Theoret Sci, 68-77, PROF THEORET PHYSICS, UNIV ORE, 76-, DIR, INST THEORET SCI, 77- *Concurrent Pos:* Alfred P Sloan fel, 70-72. *Mem:* Am Phys Soc. *Res:* Particle beams; invariance principles; causality; lasers. *Mailing Add:* Inst of Theoret Sci Univ of Ore Eugene OR 97403

CSORGO, MIKLOS, b Egerfarmos, Hungary, Mar 12, 32; Can citizen; m 57; c 1. MATHEMATICS. *Educ:* Sch Econ, Budapest, BA, 55; McGill Univ, MA, 61, PhD(math), 63. *Prof Exp:* Lectr statist, Sch Econ, Budapest, 55-56; instr math, Princeton Univ, 63-65; from asst prof to assoc prof, McGill Univ, 65-72; PROF MATH, CARLETON UNIV, 72- *Concurrent Pos:* Vis prof, Math Inst, Univ Vienna, 69-70. *Mem:* Can Math Soc; Am Math Soc; Inst Math Statist; Statist Soc Can. *Res:* Probability theory; mathematical statistics. *Mailing Add:* Dept Math Carleton Univ Colonel By Dr Ottawa ON K1S 5B6 Can

CUADRA, CARLOS A(LBERT), b San Francisco, Calif, Dec 21, 25; m 47; c 3. INFORMATION SCIENCE, ONLINE INFORMATION SYSTEMS. *Educ:* Univ Calif, AB, 49, PhD(psychol), 53. *Prof Exp:* Psychol res supvr, Vet Admin Hosp, Downey, Ill, 53-56; training specialist air defense, Syst Develop Div, Rand Corp, 56-57; head personnel planning & training group, Syst Develop Corp, 57-59, proj team, Air Force 466L Syst, 59-60, proj team, Intel Systs Br, 60-62, develop staff, Spec Develop Dept, 63-64, tech asst to head technol directorate, 65-66, head info systs technol staff, 66-67, mgr, Libr & Doc Systs Dept, 68-71, mgr, Educ & Libr Systs Dept, 71-74, gen mgr, SDC Search Serv, 74-78; FOUNDER & PRES, CUADRA ASSOC, INC, 78- *Concurrent Pos:* Ed, Ann Rev Info Sci & Technol, 64-75; consult, Comt Sci & Tech Commun, Nat Acad Sci, 68-69; mem, Nat Comn Libr & Info Sci, 71-; adj prof, Grad Sch Libr & Info Sci, Univ Calif, Los Angeles, 79-80. *Honors & Awards:* Award of Merit, Am Soc Info Sci, 68; Miles Conrad Award, Nat Fedn Abstr & Indexing Serv, 80. *Mem:* Sigma Xi; Am Soc Info Sci; Spec Libr Asn. *Res:* Behavioral aspects of professional communication; research methodology; use of technology in libraries; state-of-the-art reviews in information science; on-line database systems and services from scientific, technical and financial standpoint; professional communications; library and information science, including evaluation of current and prospective research. *Mailing Add:* 13213 Warren Ave Mar Vista CA 90066

CUANY, ROBIN LOUIS, b Glasgow, Scotland, Oct 17, 26; US citizen; m 51; c 6. PLANT GENETICS. *Educ:* Cambridge Univ, BA, 47, MA, 51; Iowa State Univ, PhD(crop breeding, genetics), 58. *Prof Exp:* Cytogeneticist cotton breeding sect, Empire Cotton Growing Corp & Sudan Govt, 48-53; asst dept agron, Iowa State Univ, 54-56; res assoc biol dept, Brookhaven Nat Lab, 56-58, asst geneticist, 58-59; geneticist nuclear energy prog, Inter-Am Inst Agr Sci, 59-62; asst prof bot, Univ Iowa, 62-68; asst prof agron, crops, 68-75, ASSOC PROF AGRON, CROPS, COLO STATE UNIV, 75- *Concurrent Pos:* Chmn, High Altitude Reveg Comt, 74-82. *Mem:* Am Soc Agron; Am Genetic Asn; Soc Range Mgt. *Res:* Genetics and breeding of maize; grasses for forage and revegetation; photoperiodism and climatic adaptation; genecology; use of marker genes in detecting outcrossing and somatic mutation; cytogenetics; forage and range feed supply for cattle in the Gambia. *Mailing Add:* Dept of Agron Colo State Univ Ft Collins CO 80523

CUATRECASAS, PEDRO, b Madrid, Spain, Sept 27, 36; US citizen; m 59; c 4. BIOCHEMISTRY, MEDICINE. *Educ:* Washington Univ, AB, 58, MD, 62. *Prof Exp:* Intern & resident internal med, Johns Hopkins Univ Hosp, 62-64; clin assoc clin endocrinol, Nat Inst Arthritis & Metab Dis, 64-66, med officer, Lab Chem Biol, 68-70; assoc prof med & pharmacol, Burroughs Wellcome prof clin pharmacol & dir div, 70-72, prof pharmacol & assoc prof med, Sch Med, Johns Hopkins Univ, 72-75; VPRES RES, DEVELOP & MED, WELLCOME RES LABS & DIR, BURROUGHS WELLCOME CO, 75- *Concurrent Pos:* USPHS spec fel, NIH Lab Chem Biol, 67-68; prof lectr biochem, George Washington Univ, 67-70; mem, Adv Comt Personnel for Res, Am Cancer Soc, 73-75; dir, Burroughs Wellcome Fund, 75-; adj prof, Dept Med & Depts Pharmacol & Physiol, Duke Univ, 75-; adj prof, Dept Med & Dept Pharmacol, Univ NC, 75-; ed, J Solid-Phase Biochem; mem, Adv Comt Cancer Res Prog, Univ NC; distinguished lectr med sci, Dept Med, Mayo Clin, 79; pharmacy alumni lectr, Univ Toronto, 81. *Honors & Awards:* John Jacob Abel Prize Pharmacol, 72; Lilly Award, Am Diabetes Asn, 75; Laude Prize, Pharmaceut World, 74 & 75; Beerman lectr & Beerman Award, Soc Investigative Dermat, 81; Ernest Cotlove Mem lectr, Acad Clin Lab Physicians & Scientists, 81; Edward E Smissman lectr, Univ Kans, 81. *Mem:* Am Chem Soc; Sigma Xi; Am Soc Biol Chemists; Am Soc Pharmacol & Exp Therapeut; Am Soc Clin Invest. *Res:* Cell membranes; protein and glycolipid chemistry; mechanism of action of hormones; membrane receptors; cell growth; affinity chromatography; pharmacology. *Mailing Add:* Wellcome Res Labs Burroughs Wellcome 3030 Cornwallis Rd Research Triangle Park NC 27709

CUBBAGE, HENRY D, b Washington, DC, Apr 3, 20; m 42; c 6. ELECTRONIC ENGINEERING, PHYSICS. *Educ:* St John's Col, Md, BA, 41; Univ Md, EE, 48. *Prof Exp:* Jr physicist, Nat Bur Standards, 42-43; electronic engr, 46-48, admin asst, 49-51, sci staff asst, 51-54, electronic scientist, 54-56, sect head mobile commun, 56-69, head syst sect, Radio Div, 69-80, CONSULT, US NAVAL RES LAB, 80- *Concurrent Pos:* Mem ad hoc comt, Joint Meteorol Satellite Adv Comt, 62-63. *Mem:* Inst Elec & Electronics Engrs; Sigma Xi. *Res:* Electronic navigation; balloon and satellite electronics for the collection of global meteorological data; radio communication techniques to enable submerged submarines to receive and transmit electromagnetic signals; oblique ionospheric sounders; special communications systems. *Mailing Add:* 8113 Murray Hill Dr SE Oxon Hill MD 20021

CUBBERLEY, ADRIAN H, b Westfield, NJ, Feb 1, 18; m 41; c 2. TECHNOLOGY ASSESSMENT, RESEARCH ADMINISTRATION. *Educ:* Columbia Univ, AB, 39. *Prof Exp:* Res chemist, Norda Essential Oil & Chem Co, 39-42; res chemist, Barrett Div, Allied Chem Corp, 42-54, admin asst res & develop, 54-58 & plastics div, 58-62, proj mgr com develop, 62-65, dep sci dir, Allied Chem SA, Belg, 66-69, sr technico-econ planner, Allied Chem Corp, NJ, 69-70; res planner, Corp Res Ctr, 70-74, mgr res intel, Corp Res & Develop Div, 74-77, mgr sci & tech studies, 77-79, mgr indust health & prod safety, 79-80, mgr health serv, 80-81, MGR SPEC STUDIES, SCI & TECH, INT PAPER CO, TUXEDOPARK, NY, 81- *Mem:* Am Chem Soc; fel Am Inst Chem; Tech Asn Pulp & Paper Indust; Com Develop Asn. *Res:* Research management, strategy and planning; technical liaison; commercial development; technology assessment. *Mailing Add:* Sands Point Rd Washingtonville NY 10992

CUBBERLEY, VIRGINIA, b Trenton, NJ, Apr 30, 46; m 69; c 2. TOXICOLOGY. *Educ:* Fairleigh Dickinson Univ, BS, 68; Rutgers Univ, MS, 75; NY Univ, PhD(biol), 80. *Prof Exp:* Asst Pharmacologist, Carter Wallace Inc, 68-71; asst biochemist, Hoffmann La Roche, 72-74; assoc res scientist, Dept Environ Med, NY Univ, 75-78; ASST PROF, PACE UNIV, NEW YORK, 79-; RES BIOLOGIST, AM CYANAMID CO, 81- *Concurrent Pos:* Consult, Am Cyanamid Co, 80-81. *Mem:* Am Women Sci; Am Soc Cell Biol. *Res:* Data collection and evaluation. *Mailing Add:* 60 Pleasant Ave Upper Saddle River NJ 07458

CUBICCIOTTI, DANIEL DAVID, JR, b Philadelphia, Pa, June 28, 21; m 48; c 3. HIGH TEMPERATURE CHEMISTRY, PHYSICAL INORGANIC CHEMISTRY. *Educ:* Univ Calif, BS, 42, PhD(chem), 46. *Prof Exp:* Asst chem, Manhattan Proj, Univ Calif, 44-46; instr, NY Univ, 46-47 & Univ Calif, 47-48; res asst prof, Ill Inst Technol, 48-51; res chemist, Atomic Energy Res Lab, NAm Aviation, Inc, 51-55; res chemist, Stanford Res Inst, 55-63, sci fel, 63-72; tech specialist, Nuclear Energy Div, Gen Elec Co, 72-74; sr scientist, SRI Int, 74-80; PROJ MGR, NUCLEAR DIV, ELEC POWER RES INST, 80- *Concurrent Pos:* Mem, Nat Res Coun-Nat Acad Sci Comt High Temperature Sci & Technol, 67-74, chmn, 71-74; US rep, Int Union Pure & Appl Chem Comn High Temperatures & Refractories, 70-74; div ed jour, Electrochem Soc, 75- *Mem:* Am Chem Soc; Electrochem Soc; Am Inst Mining, Metall & Petrol Engrs; Am Nuclear Soc. *Res:* Reactions of metals with molten salts and with gases at high temperatures; evaporation of materials; chemistry of nuclear reactor fuels; thermodynamics of inorganic systems; corrosion by high temperature water. *Mailing Add:* Elec Power Res Inst PO Box 10412 Palo Alto CA 94303

CUBITT, JOHN MALCOLM, geology, statistical analysis, see previous edition

CUCCI, CESARE ELEUTERIO, b Italy, Dec 22, 25; US citizen; m 49, 66; c 3. MEDICINE. *Educ:* Univ Perugia, MD, 49; Univ Rome, dipl cardiol, 53; Am Bd Pediat, dipl, 58, cert cardiol, 63. *Prof Exp:* Assoc prof, 60-76, PROF CLIN PEDIAT, NY UNIV, 76-; CHIEF CHILDREN'S CARDIAC SERV, LENOX HILL HOSP, 63- *Concurrent Pos:* Vis pediatrician, Bellevue Hosp, New York, 65-; consult pediat cardiol, Booth Mem Hosp, 60- & Flushing Hosp & Methodist Hosp, 63- *Mem:* AAAS; fel Am Col Physicians; Am Acad Pediat; Am Col Chest Physicians; Am Col Cardiol. *Res:* Cardio-pulmonary physiology; pediatric cardiology. *Mailing Add:* 45 E 62nd St New York NY 10021

CUCULO, JOHN ANTHONY, b Providence, RI, June 23, 24; m 46; c 3. POLYMER CHEMISTRY, MATERIALS SCIENCE. *Educ:* Brown Univ, ScB, 46; Duke Univ, PhD(chem), 50. *Prof Exp:* Res chemist, Polychem Dept, E I du Pont de Nemours & Co, Inc, 50-60, sr res chemist, Textiles Fibers Dept, 60-68; res asst, 68-69, assoc prof, 69-75, PROF FIBER SCI, NC STATE UNIV, 75- *Concurrent Pos:* Consult various indust firms, 72-; prin investr, NSF grant, 75- *Mem:* Am Chem Soc; Nat Asn Advan Sci; Sigma Xi; Fiber Soc. *Res:* Fiber and polymer science, specifically stress-induced crystallinity and the solubility and modification of cellulose. *Mailing Add:* Sch of Textiles PO Box 5666 Raleigh NC 27650

CUDABACK, DAVID DILL, b Napa, Calif, Jan 18, 29; m 53; c 1. RADIO & INFRARED ASTRONOMY, TELESCOPE DEVELOPMENT. *Educ:* Univ Calif, Berkeley, BA, 51, PhD(astron), 62. *Prof Exp:* Physicist, Lawrence Radiation Lab, Univ Calif, 50-57; astronr, Radio Astron Inst, Stanford Univ, 58-62. *Concurrent Pos:* Physicist, Los Alamos Sci Lab, 53-54. *Mem:* AAAS; Am Astron Soc; Int Astron Union; Int Sci Radio Union. *Res:* Radio and infrared studies of interstellar material and star formation; instrumentation for same; high altitude observatory development for same. *Mailing Add:* Dept of Astron Univ of Calif Berkeley CA 94720

CUDDY, LEE JOSEPH, b Philadelphia, Pa, Nov 28, 29; m 53; c 1. METALLURGY. *Educ:* Drexel Inst, BS, 52; Columbia Univ, MS, 58, DEngSc(metall), 61. *Prof Exp:* Res metallurgist, Battelle Mem Inst, 52-56; res metallurgist, 61-70, sr scientist, 70-76, ASSOC RES CONSULT, US STEEL CORP RES CTR, 76- *Mem:* Am Inst Mining, Metall & Petrol Engrs; Metall Soc. *Res:* Lattice defects and their effects on diffusional processes in solids; high temperature plastic deformation; internal nitriding; thermomechanical treatment of steels; deformation structures. *Mailing Add:* Res Lab US Steel Corp Monroeville PA 15146

CUDE, JOE E, b Austin, Tex, Feb 23, 39; m 68. TOPOLOGY, ALGEBRA. *Educ:* Southwest Tex State Univ, BS, 60; Univ Tex, MA, 62, PhD(math), 66. *Prof Exp:* Asst prof math, Wash State Univ, 66-69; assoc prof & chmn dept, Dallas Baptist Col, 69-72; PROF MATH & HEAD DEPT, TARLETON STATE COL, 72- *Mem:* Am Math Soc; Math Asn Am. *Res:* Topological rings. *Mailing Add:* Dept of Math Tarleton State Col Stephenville TX 76402

CUDE, WILLIS AUGUSTUS, JR, b Luling, Tex, Jan 2, 22; m 44; c 4. INORGANIC CHEMISTRY, CRYSTALLOGRAPHY. *Educ:* Univ Tex, Austin, BS, 42, PhD(chem), 68; Ohio State Univ, MS, 53. *Prof Exp:* Meteorologist, US Army Air Corps, US, 43-44 & Okinawa, 45-49; instr meteorol, Chanute Air Force Base, Ill, 49-51; sci liaison nuclear sci, Los Alamos Sci Labs, 53-56; res scientist, Aeronaut Res Labs, Wright Patterson AFB, Ohio, 56-59; from instr to assoc prof chem, US Air Force Acad, 59-63; asst prof, 63-66, ASSOC PROF CHEM, SOUTHWEST TEX STATE UNIV, 67- *Concurrent Pos:* Partic, NSF Col Teacher Res Prog, Univ Ark, Fayetteville, 68-69. *Mem:* Am Crystallog Asn; Am Chem Soc. *Res:* Coordination compounds; structure of mu-bridged complexes. *Mailing Add:* Dept of Chem Southwest Tex State Univ San Marcos TX 78666

CUDERMAN, JERRY FERDINAND, b Crosby, Minn, Aug 1, 35; m 61; c 2. EXPERIMENTAL ATOMIC PHYSICS. *Educ:* Univ Minn, BME, 58; Ore State Univ, PhD(physics), 66. *Prof Exp:* Exp engr, United Aircraft Corp, 58-59; STAFF MEM, SANDIA LAB, 65- *Mem:* Am Phys Soc. *Res:* Atomic physics; fast alkali metal atom interactions with other atomic species and surfaces; laser plasma physics; x-ray spectroscopy; arc physics; propellant technology development for increasing natural gas production. *Mailing Add:* 4300 Andrew Dr NE Albuquerque NM 87109

CUDKOWICZ, GUSTAVO, b Zurich, Switz, July 27, 27; m 57; c 3. IMMUNOBIOLOGY, TUMOR IMMUNOLOGY. *Educ:* Univ Milan, MD, 52, cert med radiol, 55. *Prof Exp:* Asst prof exp path, Inst Gen Path, Univ Milan, 52-53, 54-55; vis fel biochem, Univ Uppsala, 53-54; asst prof path, Nat Cancer Inst, Milan, Italy, 56-59; vis investr, Biol Div, Oak Ridge Nat Lab, 60, biologist, 61-65; assoc cancer res scientist, Roswell Park Mem Inst, 65-67,

prin cancer res scientist, 67-69; actg chmn dept path, 73-74, PROF PATH & MICROBIOL, STATE UNIV NY BUFFALO, 69- *Concurrent Pos:* Int Atomic Energy Agency, Austria fel, 60. *Honors & Awards:* Marie T Bonazinga Award, Reticuloendothelial Soc, 80. *Mem:* Am Asn Path; AAAS; Int Soc Exp Hemat; Reticuloendothelial Soc; Soc Exp Biol Med. *Res:* Natural resistance systems against normal and neoplastic cells; immunogenetics of hemopoietic grafts; regulatory and effector mechanisms in cell-mediated immunity. *Mailing Add:* 232 Farber Hall State Univ of NY Buffalo NY 14214

CUDWORTH, KYLE MCCABE, b Minneapolis, Minn, June 7, 47. ASTRONOMY. *Educ:* Univ Minn, BPhys, 69; Univ Calif, Santa Cruz, PhD(astron), 74. *Prof Exp:* Asst prof, 74-81, ASSOC PROF ASTRON, YERKES OBSERV, UNIV CHICAGO, 81- *Concurrent Pos:* Alfred P Sloan Found fel, 80-82. *Mem:* Am Astron Soc; Am Sci Affil; Astron Soc Pacific. *Res:* Measuring proper motions and parallaxes of stars; star clusters and planetary nebulae; stellar photometry. *Mailing Add:* Yerkes Observ Williams Bay WI 53191

CUE, BERKELEY WENDELL, JR, b Arlington, Mass, June 10, 47. ORGANIC CHEMISTRY, MEDICINAL CHEMISTRY. *Educ:* Univ Mass, Boston, BA, 69; Univ Ala, PhD(org chem), 74. *Prof Exp:* Fel org chem, Ohio State Univ, 73-74 & Univ Minn, 74-75; RES & DEVELOP SCIENTIST AGR PROD, PFIZER INC, 75- *Mem:* Am Chem Soc. *Res:* Heterocyclic chemistry; medicinal chemistry; total synthesis of natural products. *Mailing Add:* Pfizer Inc-Cent Res Eastern Point Rd Groton CT 06340

CUE, NELSON, b Cavite City, Philippines, Aug 10, 41; US citizen; m; c 2. EXPERIMENTAL PHYSICS. *Educ:* Feati Univ, Philippines, BS, 61; Univ Wash, PhD, 67. *Prof Exp:* Res assoc, Univ Wash, 67 & State Univ NY Stony Brook, 67-70; asst prof, 70-76, ASSOC PROF PHYSICS, STATE UNIV NY ALBANY, 76- *Concurrent Pos:* Vis prof physics, Univ Lyon I, 78-79; co-dir, NATO Advan Study Inst, State Univ NY, Albany, 78; lectr, Int Winter Sch Nuclear Physics, Beijing, 80; NATO & Heineman sr scientist fel, 79-80. *Mem:* Am Phys Soc; Am Asn Physics Teachers. *Res:* Interactions of relativistic electrons with solids; atomic collisions in solids; breakup of fast molecular ions; ion implantation. *Mailing Add:* Dept of Physics State Univ of NY Albany NY 12222

CUELLAR, ORLANDO, b San Antonio, Tex, Sept 6, 34; m 59; c 3. EVOLUTIONARY BIOLOGY, HERPETOLOGY. *Educ:* Univ Tex, Austin, BA, 64; Tex Tech Univ, MS, 65; Univ Colo, Boulder, PhD(biol), 69. *Prof Exp:* Res asst, Univ Tex, 61-63; teaching asst, Tex Tech Univ, 64-65; res asst, Univ Colo, 65-67; NIH fel, Univ Mich, 69-72; ASSOC PROF BIOL, UNIV UTAH, 72- *Concurrent Pos:* Panelist, Nat Res Coun NSF grad fels, 75-76 & NSF nat needs res grants, 77-; prin investr, NIH Gen Med Sci grant, 73-76. *Mem:* Am Soc Zool; AAAS; Am Asn Ichthyologists & Herpetologists; Am Soc Naturalists; Asn Study Animal Behav. *Res:* Ecology; evolution and cytogenetics of parthenogenetic animals; behavior and population biology of lizards. *Mailing Add:* Dept Biol Univ Utah Salt Lake City UT 84112

CUETO, CIPRIANO, JR, b Tampa, Fla, July 15, 23; m 41; c 3. PHARMACOLOGY, TOXICOLOGY. *Educ:* Univ Tampa, BS, 49; Emory Univ, MS, 57, PhD(pharmacol), 64. *Prof Exp:* Chemist, Bur Agr & Indust Chem, USDA, Fla, 50-51, chemist, Bur Entom & Plant Quarantine, Ga, 51-53; chemist, Tech Develop Labs, Dept Health, Educ & Welfare, USPHS, Ga, 53-58, chemist, Phoenix Field Sta, Ariz, 58-59, chemist, Toxicol Sect, Commun Dis Ctr, 59-66, supvry res pharmacologist & chief pharmacol sect, Fla, 66-69; chief staff officer, Human Safety Eval of Pesticides, USDA & Environ Protection Agency, Washington, DC, 69-71; chief chronic studies div, Nat Ctr Toxicol Res, Ark, 71-74; pharmacologist-toxicologist, Nat Cancer Inst, 74-78, chief, Toxicol Br, 78-79; assoc dir, Dept Toxicol, Litton Bionetics, 80; SR SCI ADVR, CLEMENT ASSOCS, VA, 81- *Mem:* Am Chem Soc; Fed Am Soc Exp Biol; Soc Toxicol; Am Col Toxicol. *Res:* Toxicology of pesticides; adrenocortical inhibitions and its effects on the response of the cardiovascular system to catecholamines; chemical carcinogen bioassay and research; data evaluation and risk analysis. *Mailing Add:* 205 Nelson St Rockville MD 20850

CUFF, DAVID J, b Edmonton, Alta, May 11, 33; m 61; c 1. CARTOGRAPHY, ENERGY RESOURCES. *Educ:* Univ Alta, BSc, 54; Pa State Univ, MSc, 68, PhD(geog), 72. *Prof Exp:* Geologist, Texaco Explor Co, Calgary, 54-56, Gallup, Buckland & Farney Co, 56-63 & Can Indust Gas Corp, 63-64; asst prof, 68-78, ASSOC PROF GEOG, TEMPLE UNIV, 78- *Mem:* Am Congress Surveying & Mapping. *Res:* The role of color in map design; applications of three-dimensional maps (statistical surfaces). *Mailing Add:* Dept of Geog Temple Univ 1822 Park Ave Philadelphia PA 19122

CUFFEY, ROGER JAMES, b Indianapolis, Ind, May 2, 39; m 64; c 2. INVERTEBRATE PALEONTOLOGY. *Educ:* Ind Univ, Bloomington, BA, 61, MA, 65, PhD(paleont), 66. *Prof Exp:* from asst prof to assoc prof, 67-80, PROF PALEONT, PA STATE UNIV, UNIVERSITY PARK, 80- *Mem:* AAAS; Paleont Soc; Soc Vert Paleont; Geol Soc Am; Soc Econ Paleont & Mineral. *Res:* Taxonomy, morphology, evolution and paleoecology of fossil and living bryozoans; role of bryozoans in fossil and living reefs. *Mailing Add:* Dept Geosci Pa State Univ University Park PA 16802

CUFFIN, BENJAMIN NEIL, b McKeesport, Pa, Apr 21, 41. ELECTROCARDIOGRAPHY, MAGNETOCARDIOGRAPHY. *Educ:* Pa State Univ, BS, 63, MS, 65, PhD(elec eng), 74. *Prof Exp:* Antenna engr, Radio Corp Am, 65-66; instr elec eng, Pa State Univ, 69-74; STAFF SCIENTIST, MASS INST TECHNOL, 74- *Concurrent Pos:* Nat Heart, Lung & Blood Inst fel, 76-78; prin investr, NIH grant, 79-81. *Res:* Computer modeling and simulation of forward and inverse problem of electrocardiography, magnetocardiography, electroencephalography and magnetoencephalography. *Mailing Add:* Magnet Lab Bldg NW-14 Mass Inst Technol Cambridge MA 02139

CUGELL, DAVID WOLF, b New Haven, Conn, Sept 19, 23. PULMONARY DISEASES. *Educ:* Yale Univ, BS, 45; LI Col Med, MD, 47. *Prof Exp:* Asst med, Albany Med Col, 49-50; assoc, 55-57, from asst prof to assoc prof, 57-69, BAZLEY PROF MED, SCH MED, NORTHWESTERN UNIV, 69- *Concurrent Pos:* Res fel, Harvard Med Sch, 50-51, 53-55, Am Heart Asn fel, 53-55; USPHS res career develop award, 62-68; dir pulmonary labs, Northwestern Univ; attend physician, Vet Admin Res Hosp, Cook County Hosp, Northwestern Mem Hosp; mem pulmonary dis subspeciality bd, Am Bd Internal Med, 66-72. *Mem:* Am Col Physicians; Am Thoracic Soc; Am Col Chest Physicians; Am Fedn Clin Res. *Res:* Cardiopulmonary disease. *Mailing Add:* Northwestern Univ Med Sch Chicago IL 60611

CUJEC, BIBIJANA DOBOVISEK, b Ljubljana, Yugoslavia, Dec 25, 26; Can citizen; m 56; c 4. NUCLEAR PHYSICS. *Educ:* Univ Ljubljana, MSc, 51, PhD(physics), 59. *Prof Exp:* Res asst physics, Inst J Stefan, Ljubljana, 50-55, res officer, 55-61; res assoc, Univ Pittsburgh, 61-63 & Univ Alta, 63-64; from asst prof to assoc prof, 64-70, PROF PHYSICS, LAVAL UNIV, 70- *Concurrent Pos:* Vis assoc, Calif Inst Technol, 71-72 & 78-79. *Mem:* Am Phys Soc; Can Asn Physicists. *Res:* Nuclear structure; nuclear reactions and scattering. *Mailing Add:* Dept Physics Laval Univ Quebec PQ G1K 7P4 Can

CUKIER, ROBERT ISAAC, b New York, NY, Oct 10, 44. THEORETICAL CHEMISTRY. *Educ:* Harpur Col, BA, 65; Princeton Univ, MS, 67, PhD(chem), 69. *Prof Exp:* NATO fel, Lorentz Inst Theoret Physics, 69-71; res chemist, Univ Calif, San Diego, 71-72; from asst prof to assoc prof chem, 72-80, PROF CHEM, MICH STATE UNIV, 80- *Mem:* Am Phys Soc. *Res:* Applications of nonequilibrium statistical mechanics to physical chemistry problems. *Mailing Add:* Dept of Chem Mich State Univ East Lansing MI 48824

CUKOR, GEORGE, b Szolnok, Hungary, Mar 16, 46; US citizen; m 69; c 2. MICROBIOLOGY, VIROLOGY. *Educ:* Brooklyn Col, BA, 68; Rutgers Univ, PhD(microbiol), 73. *Prof Exp:* Fel, Sch Med, Boston Univ, 73-76; from instr to asst prof, 76-80, ASSOC PROF MICROBIOL, MED SCH, UNIV MASS, 80- *Concurrent Pos:* Nat Cancer Inst fel, 74-76; instr, Northeastern Univ, 74-75 & Anna Maria Col, 78- *Mem:* Am Soc Microbiol; Am Asn Immunologists; AAAS. *Res:* Viral gastroenteritis; diagnostic virology; microbial toxins. *Mailing Add:* Div of Infectious Dis Univ of Mass Med Sch Worcester MA 01605

CUKOR, PETER, b Szolnok, Hungary, Aug 29, 36; US citizen; m 64; c 3. ANALYTICAL CHEMISTRY, POLYMER CHEMISTRY. *Educ:* City Col New York, BChEng, 61; St John's Univ, NY, MS, 63, PhD(phys & anal chem), 66. *Prof Exp:* Res technologist anal chem, Customer Serv Dept, Mobil Oil Co, 64-66, eng specialist anal chem & metal-org, 67-69, head absorption spectros & chromatog sect, 69-78, head, Org Anal & Org Mat Sect, 78-79, TECH MGR, ADVAN TECHNOL LAB, GEN TEL & ELECTRONICS RES LABS, INC, 79- *Mem:* Am Chem Soc; NY Acad Sci. *Res:* Sorption and emission spectroscopy; thermal analysis; gas and liquid chromatography; conducting polymers; radioimmunoassay; photopolymers; photoresist technology; metalloenzymes; membrane transport. *Mailing Add:* Gen Tel & Electronics Res Labs 40 Sylvan Rd Waltham MA 02154

CULBERSON, CHARLES HENRY, b Philadelphia, Pa, March 16, 43; m 79; c 1. OCEANOGRAPHY. *Educ:* Univ Wash, BS, 65; Ore State Univ, MS, 68, PhD(oceanog), 72. *Prof Exp:* Res assoc oceanog, Sch Oceanog, Ore State Univ, 72-75; res assoc chem, Dept Chem, Univ Fla, 75-77; ASST PROF OCEANOG, COL MARINE STUDIES, UNIV DEL, 77- *Res:* Physical chemistry of seawater, especially the acid-base system and carbonate chemistry; chemistry of estuaries. *Mailing Add:* Col Marine Studies Univ Del Newark DE 19711

CULBERSON, CHICITA FRANCES, b Philadelphia, Pa, Nov 1, 31; m 53. ORGANIC CHEMISTRY. *Educ:* Univ Cincinnati, BS, 53; Univ Wis, MS, 54; Duke Univ, PhD(chem), 59. *Prof Exp:* Res assoc org chem, 59-61, sr res assoc bot, 61-81, lectr, 71-81, ADJ PROF, DUKE UNIV, 81- *Mem:* AAAS; Am Chem Soc. *Res:* Secondary products of lichen-forming fungi. *Mailing Add:* Dept Bot Duke Univ Durham NC 27706

CULBERSON, JAMES LEE, b Pana, Ill, Sept 18, 41; m 62; c 3. ANATOMY. *Educ:* Ill Wesleyan Univ, AB, 63; Tulane Univ, PhD(anat), 68. *Prof Exp:* Instr anat, Tulane Univ, 67-68; from instr to asst prof, 68-72, ASSOC PROF ANAT, MED CTR, WVA UNIV, 72- *Concurrent Pos:* Vis sr lectr, Univ Otago, Dunedin, NZ, 78. *Res:* Comparative neuroanatomy and neurophysiology. *Mailing Add:* Dept Anat WVa Univ Med Ctr Morgantown WV 26506

CULBERSON, ORAN L(OUIS), b Houston, Tex, May 2, 21; m 49; c 3. CHEMICAL ENGINEERING. *Educ:* Agr & Mech Col, Tex, BS, 43; Univ Tex, MS, 48, PhD(chem eng), 50. *Prof Exp:* Chem engr, Gulf Res & Develop Co, 50-53; chem engr, Celanese Petrochem Res Lab, Celanese Corp Am, 53-57, mgr data processing syst, Celanese Chem Div, Tex, 57-61, mgr math serv dept, NC, 61-65; assoc prof chem eng, 65-69, PROF CHEM ENG, UNIV TENN, KNOXVILLE, 69- *Res:* Solubilities in liquid phase for systems water-methane and water-ethane at temperatures to 340 degrees Fahrenheit and pressures to 10,000 pounds per square inch; economic, design and operations research. *Mailing Add:* Col of Eng Univ of Tenn Knoxville TN 37916

CULBERSON, WILLIAM LOUIS, b Indianapolis, Ind, Apr 5, 29; m 53. BOTANY. *Educ:* Univ Cincinnati, BS, 51; Sorbonne, France, dipl, 52; Univ Wis, PhD(bot), 54. *Prof Exp:* From instr to assoc prof, 55-70, PROF BOT, DUKE UNIV, 70- *Concurrent Pos:* Grants, NSF & Lalor Found, 57-79; ed, Bryologist, Am Bryol & Lichenological Soc, 62-70; ed, Brittonia, Am Soc Plant Taxon, 75; ed, Syst Bot, Am Soc Plant Taxonomy, 76-77; vis prof res, Mus Nat d'Hist Naturelle, Paris, 80. *Mem:* Bot Soc Am; Am Soc Plant Taxon; Am Bryol & Lichenological Soc; Mycol Soc Am. *Res:* Taxonomy, ecology, morphology and natural-product chemistry of lichens. *Mailing Add:* Dept of Bot Duke Univ Durham NC 27706

CULBERT, JOHN ROBERT, b Rossville, Ill, Dec 18, 14; m 45; c 2. FLORICULTURE. *Educ:* Univ Ill, BS, 37; Ohio State Univ, MS, 39. *Prof Exp:* Instr floricult, Pa State Col, 39-43 & 45-46; from asst prof to assoc prof, 46-65, PROF FLORICULT, UNIV ILL, URBANA-CHAMPAIGN, 65- *Concurrent Pos:* Consult, Framptons Nurseries, Eng, 59-60. *Honors & Awards:* Res award, Soc Am Florists, 56. *Mem:* Am Soc Hort Sci. *Res:* Breeding of chrysanthemums. *Mailing Add:* 100 Floricult Bldg Univ of Ill Urbana IL 61801

CULBERTSON, BILLY MURIEL, b Hillside, Ky, Aug 23, 29; m 49; c 3. ORGANIC CHEMISTRY, PHYSICAL CHEMISTRY. *Educ:* Augustana Col, Ill, BA, 59; Univ Iowa, MS, 62, PhD(org chem), 63. *Prof Exp:* Sr res chemist, Archer Daniels Midland Co, Minn, 62-67; sr res chemist, 67-69, RES ASSOC, ASHLAND CHEM CO, 69- *Concurrent Pos:* Ed, Minn Chemist. *Mem:* Am Chem Soc (chmn, Polymer Div, 78); Mfg Chemists Asn; The Chem Soc; Sigma Xi. *Res:* Organic syntheses, monomer syntheses and polymerization studies; polymerization mechanisms and kinetics studies; cyclopolymerization studies; synthesis of plastics for space applications; synthesis and physical studies of polymers having high thermal stability; amine acylimide monomers and polymers. *Mailing Add:* Ashland Chem Co PO Box 2219 Columbus OH 43216

CULBERTSON, CLYDE GRAY, b Vevay, Ind, July 27, 06; m 31. PATHOLOGY. *Educ:* Ind Univ, BS, 28, MD, 31. *Prof Exp:* From instr to asst prof path, Sch Med, Ind Univ, 31-42, prof clin path & chmn dept, 43-63; from asst dir to dir biol div, 46-63, res adv, 63-70, Lilly res consult, Lilly Res Labs, 70-71; prof path, Sch Med, Ind Univ, Indianapolis, 63-77; consult, Eli Lilly & Co, 71-73; EMER CLIN PROF ANAT PATH, SCH MED, IND UNIV, INDIANAPOLIS, 77- *Concurrent Pos:* Dir lab, Sch Med, Ind Univ, 31-46, dir labs, State Bd Health, Ind, 33-46. *Mem:* AMA; Am Asn Immunologists; Soc Protozoologists; Tissue Cult Asn; Am Soc Clin Path (secy-treas, 49-58, vpres, 59-68, pres, 70). *Res:* Clinical pathology; medical microbiology and parasitology. *Mailing Add:* Lilly Lab for Clin Res Wishard Mem Hosp Indianapolis IN 46202

CULBERTSON, DON M(AX), hydraulic engineering, deceased

CULBERTSON, EDWIN CHARLES, b Charleroi, Pa, Jan 5, 50; m 71; c 2. POLYMER CHEMISTRY. *Educ:* Washington & Jefferson Col, BA, 72; Univ SC, PhD(inorg chem), 76. *Prof Exp:* Chemist, Celanese Plastics Co, 77-79; tech chemist, Mobay Chem Co, 79-80; RES CHEMIST, AM HOECHST CORP, 80- *Res:* Development of new coatings for polyester pentaerythritol film which are used in the reprographics and microfilm areas. *Mailing Add:* 107 Saratoga Dr Greer SC 29651

CULBERTSON, GEORGE EDWARD, b Cranes Nest, Va, Oct 23, 37; m 59; c 3. MATHEMATICS. *Educ:* Va Polytech Inst, BS, 59, MS, 62, PhD(math), 70. *Prof Exp:* Engr, Radford Army Ammunition Plant, Hercules, Inc, Va, 62-63, sr engr, 63-64, asst area supvr, 64; asst prof math, US Naval Acad, 64-70; assoc prof, 70-71, REGISTR & ASST DEAN, CLINCH VALLEY COL, UNIV VA, 71-, PROF MATH, 75- *Concurrent Pos:* Pres, Systech Corp, Md, 69-70. *Mem:* Math Asn Am. *Res:* A basic variable study of the propellant used in the Minuteman Missile; geometry of paths of particles traveling in force fields under certain constraints; an extension of Halphen's Theorem. *Mailing Add:* Dept of Math Clinch Valley Col Univ of Va Wise VA 24293

CULBERTSON, TOWNLEY PAYNE, b Durant, Okla, May 13, 29; m 69; c 1. CHEMISTRY. *Educ:* Univ Okla, BS, 51, MS, 52; Univ Iowa, PhD(org chem), 58. *Prof Exp:* Fel org chem, Univ Ill, 58-59; assoc res chemist, Warner-Lambert/Parke, 60-65; res chemist, David Pharmaceut, 65-70; SR RES CHEMIST, RES DIV, WARNER-LAMBERT CO, 70- *Mem:* Am Chem Soc. *Res:* Synthetic modifications of steroids; antiviral compounds; aminoglycoside antibiotics; diquins as antifungal agents; cephalosporins; nalidic acid type compounds as antibacterial agents. *Mailing Add:* 2800 Plymouth Rd Ann Arbor MI 48105

CULBERTSON, WILLIAM RICHARDSON, b Coeburn, Va, May 16, 16; m 50; c 2. MEDICINE. *Educ:* Transylvania Col, AB, 37; Vanderbilt Univ, MD, 41; Am Bd Surg, dipl, 55. *Prof Exp:* Intern, St Joseph's Hosp, Lexington, Ky, 41-42; asst resident surg, Cincinnati Gen Hosp, 46-53; from asst prof to assoc prof, 57-70, PROF SURG, UNIV CINCINNATI, 70- *Mem:* Fel Am Col Surg; Am Surg Asn; Soc Surg Alimentary Tract; AMA. *Res:* Bacteriology of surgical infections; hemorrhage shock; shock due to sepsis. *Mailing Add:* Dept of Surg Univ of Cincinnati Med Ctr Cincinnati OH 45267

CULGAN, JOHN M(CDONALD), b Pittsburgh, Pa, Sept 13, 22; m 47; c 4. CHEMICAL ENGINEERING. *Educ:* Ga Inst Technol, BChE, 49, PhD(chem eng), 52. *Prof Exp:* Tech engr, Carbide & Carbon Chem Corp, 49; sr engr, 52-62, SR RES ENGR, E I DU PONT DE NEMOURS & CO, INC, WILMINGTON, 62- *Mem:* Am Inst Chem Engrs. *Res:* Conveying of granular solids in gaseous media; unit operations, especially related to production of synthetic fibers; long range planning. *Mailing Add:* RR 2 Box 45C Lafayette Pl Chadds Ford PA 19317

CULICK, FRED E(LLSWORTH) C(LOW), b US, Oct 25, 33; m 60; c 2. AERONAUTICAL ENGINEERING. *Educ:* Mass Inst Technol, SB & SM, 57, PhD(aero eng), 61. *Prof Exp:* Res fel, 61-63, from asst prof to assoc prof, 63-71, PROF APPL PHYSICS & JET PROPULSION, CALIF INST TECHNOL, 71- *Honors & Awards:* Pendray Aerospace Lit Award, 80. *Mem:* Am Phys Soc; Am Inst Aeronaut & Astronaut. *Res:* Fluid mechanics; heat transfer; combustion and propulsion; thermodynamics; plasma physics; kinetic theory; molecular gas lasers; applied aerodynamics and flight mechanics. *Mailing Add:* 1375 E Hull Lane Altadena CA 91001

CULKOWSKI, WALTER MARTIN, b Cleveland, Ohio, Sept 26, 28; m 53. METEOROLOGY. *Educ:* Western Reserve Univ, BS, 50. *Prof Exp:* Engr, Nat Tool Co, 51-52; RES METEOROLOGIST, ENVIRON SCI SERV ADMIN, 56- *Mem:* AAAS; Am Meteorol Soc; Prof Photogr Asn. *Res:*

Problems and instrumentation in the fields of atmospheric transport, diffusion and depletion of material, especially associated with nuclear industry, considering various environments and source geometries; problems in atmospheric optics and laser applications; numerical modeling techniques for various scales of atmospheric pollution. *Mailing Add:* Dept of Energy Box E Oak Ridge TN 37830

CULL, NEVILLE, b Victoria, BC, Can, July 24, 20; nat US; m 44; c 3. INORGANIC CHEMISTRY. *Educ:* Tulane Univ, BS, 47, MS, 48, PhD(chem), 50. *Prof Exp:* Asst prof, Inst Sci & Technol, Univ Ark, 50-51; govt res, Ordark, 50-51; RES ASSOC, EXXON RES & DEVELOP LABS, EXXON CO, 51- *Mem:* Am Chem Soc. *Res:* Petrochemicals; catalyst research petroleum processes; development of catalysts and processes for NOx and SOx abatement. *Mailing Add:* Rolling Acres Dr Baker LA 70714

CULLEN, ABBEY BOYD, JR, b Oxford, Miss, Dec 25, 15; m 43; c 1. APPLIED PHYSICS. *Educ:* Univ Miss, BA, 37, MS, 42; Univ Va, PhD(physics), 47. *Prof Exp:* Technician develop physiol res apparatus, Sch Med, Univ Miss, 37-40; engr & physicist, Naval Res Lab, 42-45; assoc prof, 47-70, chmn dept physics & astron, 57-80, PROF PHYSICS, UNIV MISS, 70-, DIR RADIATION RES, 80- *Mem:* Am Phys Soc. *Res:* Microwave electron accelerator; electronic instruments. *Mailing Add:* 108 Physics Bldg Univ of Miss University MS 38677

CULLEN, BRUCE F, b Iowa City, Iowa, May 6, 40; m 60; c 3. ANESTHESIOLOGY. *Educ:* Stanford Univ, BS, 62; Univ Calif, Los Angeles, MD, 66. *Prof Exp:* Staff anesthesiologist, NIH, 70-72; asst prof, 72-75, from asst prof to assoc prof, anesthesiol, Univ Wash, 72-76; PROF ANESTHESIOL & CHMN DEPT, UNIV CALIF, IRVINE, 76- *Mem:* Am Soc Anesthesiologists; Int Anesthesia Res Soc; Asn Univ Anesthetists; Soc Neuroanesthesia & Neurol Intensive Care. *Res:* Immunologic and cellular effects of anesthesia. *Mailing Add:* Irvine Med Ctr 101 City Dr S Univ of Calif Orange CA 92668

CULLEN, CHARLES G, b Elmira, NY, Nov 6, 32; m 54; c 2. MATHEMATICS. *Educ:* State Univ NY Albany, BA, 54; Univ NH, MA, 56; Case Inst Technol, PhD(math), 62. *Prof Exp:* Instr math, Worcester Polytech Inst, 56-59 & Case Inst Technol, 59-61; asst prof, 62-66, ASSOC PROF MATH, UNIV PITTSBURGH, 66- *Mem:* Soc Indust & Appl Math; Math Asn Am. *Res:* Linear algebra; matrix analysis; functions of matrices and matrix algebras; numerical analysis. *Mailing Add:* Dept of Math Univ of Pittsburgh Pittsburgh PA 15260

CULLEN, DANIEL EDWARD, b Oak Park, Ill, Feb 16, 42; m 63; c 2. OPERATIONS RESEARCH. *Educ:* Stanford Univ, BS, 63; Univ Ill, MS, 64; Wash Univ, ScD(appl math), 67. *Prof Exp:* Mem tech staff appl math, Bell Tel Labs, 67-68; V PRES MGT & TECH STUDIES, MATHEMATICA, 68- *Mem:* Am Math Soc; Soc Indust & Appl Math; Opers Res Soc Am; Inst Mgt Sci; Financial Mgt Asn. *Res:* Development of analytic and scientific methods for the solution of business and government problems. *Mailing Add:* 980 Stuart Rd Princeton NJ 08540

CULLEN, DERMOTT EDWARD, b Brooklyn, NY, Nov 22, 39; m 65; c 1. NUCLEAR PHYSICS, COMPUTER SCIENCE. *Educ:* US Merchant Marine Acad, BS, 61; Columbia Univ, MS, 64, PhD(nuclear eng), 68. *Prof Exp:* Asst prof elec eng, US Merchant Marine Acad, 63-64; nuclear consult, Nat Lead Co, 66-67; from asst scientist to scientist, Nat Neutron Cross Sect Ctr, Brookhaven Nat Lab, 67-72; physicist, Lawrence Livermore Lab, 72-79; PHYSICIST, INT ATOMIC ENERGY AGENCY, 79- *Concurrent Pos:* Nuclear consult, 61-71, Lawrence Radiation Lab, 67-71. *Mem:* Am Nuclear Soc; Sigma Xi. *Res:* Neutron transport theory, theory and application to high speed computers; organization of nuclear data files; interactive graphics. *Mailing Add:* Lawrence Livermore Lab PO Box 808 Livermore CA 94550

CULLEN, GLENN WHERRY, b Nashville, Tenn, June 27, 31; m 56. SOLID STATE CHEMISTRY, MATERIALS CHARACTERIZATION. *Educ:* Univ Cincinnati, BS, 53; Univ Ill, MS, 54, PhD(chem), 56. *Prof Exp:* HEAD MAT APPL SYNTHESIS GROUP, DAVID SARNOFF LABS, RCA CORP, 58- *Concurrent Pos:* Assoc ed, J Crystal Growth, 74-; div ed jour, Electrochem Soc, 75-; mem, Air Force Sci & Technol Adv Group, 80; mem comt high purity silicon, Nat Mat Adv Bd, 80; chmn, Electronic Div, The Electrochem Soc, 77-79; chmn, Gordon Conf Crystal Growth, 80. *Mem:* Am Asn Crystal Growth; Am Chem Soc; Electrochem Soc. *Res:* Semiconductor materials chemistry; homoepitaxial and heteroepitaxial thin film silicon growth; bulk silicon growth and characterization; superconductor materials chemistry, rare-earth metals chemistry; silicon growth and characterization. *Mailing Add:* David Sarnoff Labs RCA Corp Princeton NJ 08540

CULLEN, HELEN FRANCES, b Boston, Mass, Jan 4, 19. MATHEMATICS. *Educ:* Radcliffe Col, AB, 40; Univ Mich, AM, 44, PhD(math), 50. *Prof Exp:* From asst prof to assoc prof, 49-71, PROF MATH, UNIV MASS, AMHERST, 71- *Mem:* Am Math Soc; Math Asn Am; Sigma Xi; Am Phys Soc. *Res:* Topology; relativity. *Mailing Add:* Dept Math GRC Towers Univ Mass Amherst MA 01003

CULLEN, JAMES ROBERT, b Brooklyn, NY, Jan 28, 36; m; c 1. SOLID STATE PHYSICS. *Educ:* St John's Univ, NY, BS, 58; Univ Md, PhD(physics), 65. *Prof Exp:* Physicist, US Army Night Vision Lab, Ft Belvoir, Va, 65-66; PHYSICIST, US NAVAL ORD LAB, 66- *Concurrent Pos:* Lectr, George Washington Univ, 66; vis asst prof, Dept Physics, Univ Wis-Milwaukee, 68-69. *Mem:* Am Phys Soc. *Res:* Superconductivity, fluctuation phenomena, theory of ultrasonic waves in superconductors; semiconductors, interactions between impurities; magnetism, theory of electron-electron interactions and their effects on susceptibility and neutron scattering experiments; Hall effect in rare-earth metals; metal-insulator transition in transition metal-oxides, especially in magnetite. *Mailing Add:* US Naval Surface Weapons Ctr Code R45 Silver Spring MD 20910

CULLEN, JOHN KNOX, b Denver, Colo, Jan 2, 36; m 57; c 2. PHYSIOLOGY, ELECTRICAL ENGINEERING. *Educ:* Univ Md, BS, 60, MS, 69; La State Med Ctr, New Orleans, PhD, 75. *Prof Exp:* Engr, NIH, 60-62, res engr, Psychopharmacol Res Ctr, 62-64; res engr, Neurocommun Lab, Sch Med, Johns Hopkins Univ, 64-68; ASSOC PROF, KRESGE HEARING LAB, LA STATE UNIV MED CTR, NEW ORLEANS, 68- *Mem:* AAAS; Acoust Soc Am; Asn Res Otolaryngol. *Res:* Biomedical research; speech, hearing physiology; animal communications. *Mailing Add:* Bldg 164 La State Univ Med Ctr New Orleans LA 70119

CULLEN, MICHAEL JOSEPH, b Cleveland, Ohio, July 27, 45; m 68; c 2. NEUROANATOMY, NEUROCYTOLOGY. *Educ:* Case Western Reserve Univ, AB, 67, PhD(anat), 75. *Prof Exp:* Staff fel, Lab Neuropath & Neuroanat Sci, Nat Inst Neurol & Commun Disorders & Stroke, 75-78; ASST PROF ANAT, SCH MED, UNIV SOUTHERN CALIF, 78- *Mem:* Am Asn Anatomists; Soc Neurosci; Am Soc Cell Biol. *Res:* Cellular mechanisms of myelin formation and maintenance; neuron-glial cell interactions; mechanisms of neuron connectivity and plasticity. *Mailing Add:* Dept of Anat 2025 Zonal Ave Los Angeles CA 90033

CULLEN, SUSAN ELIZABETH, b New York, NY, Jan 12, 44; m 74; c 2. IMMUNOCHEMISTRY, IMMUNOGENETICS. *Educ:* Col Mt St Vincent, NY, BS, 65; Albert Einstein Col Med, NY, PhD(microbiol & immunol), 71. *Prof Exp:* Res assoc, Basel Inst Immunol, Switz, 71-72; res assoc, Albert Einstein Col Med, NY, 72-74; vis fel, Immunol Br, Div Cancer Biol& Diag, Nat Cancer Inst, NIH, 74-76; asst prof, 76-80, ASSOC PROF MICROBIOL & IMMUNOL, SCH MED, WASHINGTON UNIV, ST LOUIS, 80- *Concurrent Pos:* Career develop award, NIH, 77-82; mem, Allergy & Immunol Study Sect, NIH, 80-84; prin investr, Am Cancer Soc, 76-81, NIH, 76-; assoc ed & sect head, J Immunol, 78-; adv ed, Molecular Immunol, 82- *Mem:* Am Asn Immunologists. *Res:* Biochemical approach correlating between structure and function of lymphoid and myeloid cell surface molecules involved in the regulation of immune responsiveness. *Mailing Add:* Sch Med Box 8093 Washington Univ 660 S Euclid St Louis MO 63110

CULLEN, THEODORE JOHN, b St Louis, Mo, Dec 19, 28; m 47; c 4. MATHEMATICS. *Educ:* DePaul Univ, BS, 55, MS, 56. *Prof Exp:* Asst math, Univ Ill, 56-57; asst prof, Ariz State Col, 57-59 & Los Angeles State Col, 59-68; assoc prof, 68-77, PROF MATH, CALIF STATE POLYTECH UNIV, POMONA, 77- *Concurrent Pos:* Engr, Jet Propulsion Lab, Pasadena, 62- *Mem:* Math Asn Am. *Res:* Abstract algebra; hilbert and banach spaces; set theory and point set toplogy; functional analysis; numerical analysis; computers. *Mailing Add:* Dept of Math Calif State Polytech Univ Pomona CA 91768

CULLEN, WILLIAM CHARLES, b Buffalo, NY, Nov 6, 19; m 52; c 3. ORGANIC CHEMISTRY. *Educ:* Canisius Col, BS, 48. *Prof Exp:* Chemist, Bldg Res Div, Nat Appl Tech, 48-67, sect chief, 67-73, dep chief struct, mat & safety div, 73-78, dep dir, Off Eng Standards, Nat Eng Lab, Nat Bur Standards, 78-81; CONSULT, 81- *Concurrent Pos:* US Dept Com sci fel, 65-66. *Honors & Awards:* Dept of Com Silver Medal Award, 68; J A Piper Award, Nat Roofing Contractors Asn, 74; Edward Bennett Rosa Award, Nat Bur Standards, 75; Walter C Voss Award, Am Soc Testing & Mat, 78; Gold Medal Award, Dept Com, 80. *Mem:* Hon mem Am Soc Testing & Mat. *Res:* Mechanisms of chemical degradation and physical deterioration of organic roofing materials; methods to determine engineering properties of roof systems; durability and performance of building materials; application and impact of engineering standards. *Mailing Add:* 11718 Tifton Dr Potomac MD 20854

CULLEN, WILLIAM ROBERT, b Dunedin, NZ, May 4, 33; m 56; c 3. INORGANIC CHEMISTRY. *Educ:* Univ Otago, NZ, BSc, 55, MSc, 57; Cambridge Univ, PhD(chem), 59. *Prof Exp:* From instr to assoc prof, 58-69, PROF CHEM, UNIV BC, 69- *Concurrent Pos:* Nat Res Coun Can fel, 66-67. *Mem:* Am Chem Soc; Chem Inst Can. *Res:* Organometallic chemistry of the main group elements, especially fluorocarbon derivatives; coordination chemistry of arsines and phosphines; conformational problems in coordination chemistry; bioinorganic chemistry; asymmetric catalysis; biological transformations of inorganic and organometallic compounds; analytical environmental chemistry. *Mailing Add:* Dept Chem Univ BC Vancouver Can

CULLER, DONALD MERRILL, b Hicksville, Ohio, Nov 17, 29; m 50; c 3. ELECTRONIC ENGINEERING, SYSTEMS DESIGN. *Educ:* Carnegie Inst Technol, BS, 51; Univ Calif, MS, 53. *Prof Exp:* Dynamics engr, Gen Dynamics/Convair, 51-53; proj engr, Farnsworth Electronic Co, Div Int Tel & Tel Corp, 53-54, mgr, Systs Anal & Design Sect, 54-55, assoc head adv develop, 55-57, head, 57-58, assoc lab dir space electronics, ITT Fed Labs Div, 58-61, lab dir, 61-63, dir, Astrionics Ctr, 63-66; lab mgr, 66-71, adv systs mgr, 71-75, BUS AREA MGR, TRW DEFENSE SYSTS GROUP, 75- *Concurrent Pos:* Secy, Nat Telemetry Conf, 56. *Mem:* Sr mem Inst Elec & Electronics Engrs; assoc fel Am Inst Aeronaut & Astronaut. *Res:* Missile and space systems analysis and design; guidance and control systems; satellite communication systems; optical and RF tracking equipment; computer and information systems; laser systems; systems sciences. *Mailing Add:* TRW Inc 1 Space Park B1/1673 Redondo Beach CA 90278

CULLER, F(LOYD) L(EROY), JR, b Washington, DC, Jan 5, 23; m 46; c 1. ENERGY, ELECTRICAL ENERGY. *Educ:* John Hopkins Univ, BS, 43. *Prof Exp:* Design engr, Eastman Kodak Co, 43-44; develop engr, Tenn Eastman Co, 44-47; sr design engr, Radio-Chem Plant Design, Oak Ridge Nat Lab, Monsanto Chem Co, 47-48; dir chem tech div, Nuclear Div, Union Carbide Corp, 48-64, asst lab dir, 64-70, assoc dir, Oak Ridge Nat Lab, 63-71, dep dir, 71-77; PRES, ELEC POWER RES INST, 78- *Concurrent Pos:* Mem sci adv comt, Int Atomic Energy Agency, 74- *Honors & Awards:* E O Lawrence Award, 65; Atoms for Peace Award, 69; Robert E Wilson Award, Am Inst Chem Engrs, 72; Am Nuclear Soc Spec Award, 77. *Mem:* Nat Acad Eng; fel Am Inst Chem; fel Am Nuclear Soc; fel Am Inst Chem Engrs; Am

Chem Soc. Res: Nuclear energy, research and development; fuel reprocessing, reactor technology; economics; radioactive waste disposal and treatment; fuel cycle; radiochemical plant design, construction and operation; laboratory-scale chemical research and development; solvent extraction; electric energy, fossil, solar, wind, geothermal conservation, storage, energy policy, economics. Mailing Add: 1385 Corinne Lane Menlo Park CA 94025

CULLER, VAUGHN EDGAR, physics, see previous edition

CULLERS, ROBERT LEE, b North Manchester, Ind, May 19, 37; m 70; c 2. GEOCHEMISTRY. Educ: Ind Univ, Bloomington, BS, 59, MA, 62; Univ Wis-Madison, PhD(geochem), 71. Prof Exp: Teacher math, Vevay Town Schs, Ind, 60-61; teacher math-chem, Goshen City Schs, 61-63; teacher chem, Park Ridge, Ill, 64-67; res asst, Univ Wis-Madison, 67-69, NSF fel geochem, 69-71; from asst prof to assoc prof geochem, 71-81, PROF GEOCHEM & PETROLOGY, KANS STATE UNIV, 81- Mem: Geochem Soc Am; Am Chem Soc; Geol Soc Am. Res: Trace element geochemistry; experimental igneous and metamorphic trace element partitioning; neutron activation analysis of igneous, metamorphic and sedimentary rocks. Mailing Add: Dept Geol Kans State Univ Manhattan KS 66506

CULLEY, BENJAMIN HAYS, b Hollywood, Calif, Oct 16, 13. MATHEMATICS. Educ: Univ Southern Calif, AB, 34, MS, 36, EdD, 49. Prof Exp: Teacher high sch, Calif, 36-43; from instr to asst prof math, 43-59, assoc prof, 60-66, dean men, 44-69, assoc dean students, 69-76, dean students, 76-80, PROF MATH, OCCIDENTAL COL, 66- Res: Statistics in physical and social sciences. Mailing Add: Dept of Math Occidental Col Los Angeles CA 90041

CULLEY, DUDLEY DEAN, JR, b Jackson, Miss, May 14, 37. ZOOLOGY. Educ: Millsaps Col, BS, 59; Univ Miss, MEd, 61; Miss State Univ, MS, 64, PhD(zool), 68. Prof Exp: Teacher, Univ High Sch, Miss, 59-61; teacher-counsr pub schs, 61-63; asst prof fisheries, pollution biol & aquatic ecol, 68-74, assoc prof, 74-80, PROF FORESTRY & WILDLIFE MGT, LA STATE UNIV, BATON ROUGE, 80- Mem: Am Fisheries Soc; Am Chem Soc; Ecol Soc Am; Wildlife Soc. Res: Pesticide effects on wildlife; productivity in lakes; pollution surveys; waterfowl restoration; aquatic plant studies; development of laboratory amphibians. Mailing Add: Dept of Forestry & Wildlife Mgt La State Univ Baton Rouge LA 70803

CULLEY, WILLIAM JAMES, b Peoria, Ill, Nov 13, 28; m 59; c 4. BIOCHEMISTRY. Educ: Bradley Univ, BS, 53; Purdue Univ, MS, 57, PhD(biochem), 59. Prof Exp: DIR MENT RETARDATION RES LAB, MUSCATATUCK STATE HOSP, 59- Mem: AAAS; Am Chem Soc; Am Asn Ment Deficiency; Fedn Am Soc Exp Biol. Res: Biochemical aspects of mental retardation; neurochemistry; nutrition. Mailing Add: Ment Retardation Res Lab Muscatatuck State Hosp Butlerville IN 47223

CULLIMORE, DENIS ROY, b Oxford, Eng, Apr 7, 36; m 62. MICROBIAL ECOLOGY, BACTERIOLOGY. Educ: Univ Nottingham, BSc, 59, PhD(agr microbiol), 62. Prof Exp: Lectr microbiol, Univ Surrey, 62-68; from asst prof to assoc prof, 68-74, PROF MICROBIOL, UNIV REGINA, 74-; DIR, REGINA WATER RES INST, 75- Mem: Can Soc Microbiol; Brit Soc Appl Bact; Am Soc Microbiol; fel Royal Soc Arts. Res: Bioassay systems using algae; effects of herbicides on soil and water microflora; simplified classification of bacteria; novel uses of microorganisms; control of iron bacteria in wells. Mailing Add: Dept of Biol Univ of Regina Regina SK S4S 3N1 Can

CULLINAN, HARRY T(HOMAS), JR, b New York, NY, May 27, 38; m 64; c 3. CHEMICAL ENGINEERING. Educ: Univ Detroit, BChE, 61; Carnegie Inst Technol, MS, 63, PhD(chem eng), 65. Prof Exp: Res engr, Westinghouse Res Labs, 63-64; from asst prof to prof chem eng, State Univ NY Buffalo, 64-76, chmn dept, 69-76; ACAD DEAN, INST PAPER CHEM, 76-, VPRES ACAD AFFAIRS, 77- Mem: Am Inst Chem Engrs; Tech Asn Pulp & Paper Indust. Res: Multicomponent diffusion; thermodynamic properties of multicomponent mixtures; pulp and paper process engineering. Mailing Add: Inst Paper Chem 1043 E South River St Appleton WI 54912

CULLINANE, THOMAS PAUL, b Brockton, Mass, Dec 24, 42; m 67; c 1. ENGINEERING. Educ: Boston Univ, BS, 66; Northeastern Univ, MSIE, 68; Va Polytech Inst & State Univ, PhD(eng), 72. Prof Exp: Instr eng, Northeastern Univ, 68-69; asst prof, Va Polytech & State Univ, 71-72, Univ Ala, Huntsville, 72-73 & Univ Notre Dame, 74-78; assoc prof, Univ Mass, 78-79, Univ Notre Dame, 79-81; ASSOC PROF ENG, NORTHEASTERN UNIV, 81- Concurrent Pos: Mem bd dir, Gainsboro Elec Mfg Co, 71-73. Mem: Am Inst Indust Engrs; Col Indust Coun Mat Handling Educ; Inst Mgt Sci; Soc Mfg Engrs; Am Soc Eng Educ. Res: Application of operations research methodologies for the optimization of production systems and economic decision making. Mailing Add: 77 Woodland Ave Brockton MA 02401

CULLIS, PIETER RUTTER, b Barnard Castle, Eng, May 12, 46; Can citizen. BIOCHEMISTRY. Educ: Univ BC, BSc, 67, PhD(physics), 72. Prof Exp: Fel biochem, Univ Oxford, 73-76 & State Univ Utrecht, 77; ASST PROF BIOCHEM, UNIV BC, 78- Concurrent Pos: Scholar, Med Res Coun, Can, 78- Res: Application of nuclear magnetic resonance techniques to biological systems; polymorphic phase behavior of lipids in relation to membrane function. Mailing Add: Dept of Biochem Univ of BC Vancouver Can

CULLISON, ARTHUR EDISON, b Lawrence Co, Ill, Oct 30, 14; m 39; c 3. ANIMAL NUTRITION. Educ: Univ Ill, BS, 36, MS, 37, PhD(animal husb), 48. Prof Exp: Asst animal husb, Univ Ill, 36-39; asst prof, Miss State Col, 39-43; prof, Ala Polytech Inst, 46-48; head dept animal husb, Univ Ga, prof 58-78. Mem: Fel AAAS; Am Soc Animal Sci. Res: Ruminant nutrition; silage preservation; by-products for livestock feeding; recycling animal wastes. Mailing Add: Dept of Animal & Dairy Sci Univ of Ga Athens GA 30601

CULLISON, WILLIAM LESTER, b Baltimore, Md, Aug 26, 31; m 53; c 1. ENGINEERING, BUSINESS. Educ: US Merchant Marine Acad, BS, 53; LaSalle Exten Univ, LLB, 68; Fla Atlantic Univ, MBA, 75. Prof Exp: Engr officer, Am Trading & Prod Co, 56-57; coordr petrol res, Am Petrol Inst, 57-61, asst dir sci & technol, 61-67 & Air & Water Conserv, 68; dir tech opers pulp & paper res, 68-75, TREAS & DEP EXEC DIR, TECH ASN PULP & PAPER INDUST, 75- Concurrent Pos: Mem decimalized inch comt, Am Standards Asn, 60-64, calibration of instruments comt, 61-64 & dimensional metrol comt, 61-63; mem pulp & paper comt, US Standards Inst, 69; pres, Collab Testing Servs, Inc, 77- Mem: Am Soc Mech Engrs; Soc Res Adminr; Tech Asn Pulp & Paper Indust; Am Soc Asn Execs. Res: Administration of chemical, geologic, medical and engineering research projects; liaison between scientists and management. Mailing Add: Tech Asn of Pulp & Paper Indust One Dunwoody Park Atlanta GA 30338

CULLITY, B(ERNARD) D(ENNIS), physical metallurgy, deceased

CULLO, LEONARD A(NTHONY), b New York, NY, Apr 29, 26; m 55; c 4. CHEMICAL ENGINEERING. Educ: Cath Univ Am, BChE, 48; Johns Hopkins Univ, MChE, 49; Rensselaer Polytech Inst, PhD(chem eng), 52. Prof Exp: Teaching asst eng, Rensselaer Polytech Inst, 49-51; chem engr, Am Cyanamid Co, 52-56, group leader catalyst develop, 56-61; TECH DIR CATALYST DEVELOP, HARSHAW CHEM CO, 61- Mem: AAAS; Am Chem Soc; Am Inst Chem Engrs; Am Inst Chem. Res: Catalyst research and development; process development; petrochemical processes; agricultural chemical process development; reaction kinetics; fluidized bed reactors; catalysis. Mailing Add: 32760 Woodsdale Lane Solon OH 44139

CULLUM, JANE KEHOE, b Norfolk, Va, Sept 17, 38; m 59; c 2. APPLIED MATHEMATICS. Educ: Va Polytech Inst, BS, 60, MS, 62; Univ Calif, Berkeley, PhD(appl math), 66. Prof Exp: Tech asst to dir res, 75, RES STAFF MEM MATH SCI, IBM CORP, 66-, MGR NUMERICAL METHODS & APPL ANAL, MATH SCI DEPT, T J WATSON RES CTR, 79- Concurrent Pos: Mem adv panel elec sci & anal sect engr div, NSF, 75-76. Mem: Soc Indust & Appl Math (secy, 72-76, vpres, 80-81); Math Asn Am; Inst Elec & Electronic Engrs. Res: Design, analysis and development of algorithms for solving various kinds of scientific and engineering problems, especially problems involving large eigenvalue computations, optimization and/or data analysis. Mailing Add: T J Watson Res Ctr IBM Corp Yorktown Heights NY 10598

CULLUM, MALFORD EUGENE, b Guymon, Okla, Apr 14, 51. RETINOIDS CHEMISTRY. Educ: Okla Panhandle State Univ, BS, 73; Univ Okla, MS, 77, PhD(biochem), 79. Prof Exp: Sr technician, Okla Med Res Found, 77-78; res assoc biochem, Iowa State Univ, 79-81; RES ASSOC FOOD SCI & HUMAN NUTRIT, MICH STATE UNIV, 81- Mem: NY Acad Sci; Sigma Xi. Res: Function of vitamin A at the molecular level; control of cell proliferation by nutrients. Mailing Add: Dept Food Sci & Human Nutrit 229 Food Sci Bldg East Lansing MI 48824

CULLUMBINE, HARRY, b Eng, Dec 29, 12; m 59; c 1. PHARMACOLOGY. Educ: Univ Sheffield, BSc, 33, MSc, 34, MB & ChB, 37, MD, 45. Prof Exp: Prof & head dept physiol & pharmacol, Univ Ceylon, 47-51; chief med officer res, Chem Defense Exp Estab, Eng, 52-56; prof & head dept pharmacol, Univ Toronto, 56-58; pres, Air Shields, Inc, 58-67; vpres & corp med dir, 67-77, CONSULT, NARCO SCI INDUST, 77- Mem: Asn Advan Med Instrumentation; Am Soc Pharmacol & Exp Therapeut; Brit Pharmacol Soc; Brit Physiol Soc. Res: Anticholinergic; anticholinesterase agents; toxicology; atmospheric pollution; physiology of respiratory mechanisms. Mailing Add: NARCO Sci Indust Ft Wash Industrial Park Ft Washington PA 19034

CULNAN, ROBERT NEVILLE, b Riverside, Calif, July 10, 15; m 41; c 3. METEOROLOGY. Educ: Univ Calif, AB, 37; NY Univ, MS, 41. Prof Exp: Meteorologist, US Weather Bur, 39-40; instr, NY Univ, 40-42, asst prof & exec secy, Dept Meteorol, 43-46; meteorologist, US Weather Bur, 46-52, exec officer, Off Meteorol Res, 62-65, liaison officer, 65-71, dep dir off progs, 71-76, sr prog develop scientist, Environ Res Labs, Nat Oceanic & Atmospheric Admin, 76-80; RETIRED. Concurrent Pos: Treas, Boulder County Hospice, 80- Mem: Am Meteorol Soc. Res: Administration of research. Mailing Add: 910 McIntire Boulder CO 80303

CULO, DAVID ALBERT, b Sunbury, Pa, Oct 19, 19; m 43. MEDICINE. Educ: Bucknell Univ, BS, 41; Jefferson Med Col, MD, 44; Am Bd Urol, dipl. Prof Exp: Intern, Geiginger Mem Hosp, 44-45; resident urol, 45-46; resident, Watts Hosp, 48-50; asst, 50-51; from instr to assoc prof, 51-61, PROF UROL, HOSP & COL MED, UNIV IOWA, 61-, CHMN DEPT, 70- Mem: AMA; fel Am Col Surgeons; Am Urol Asn; Am Asn Genito-Urinary Surgeons; Am Clin Soc Genito-Urinary Surg. Res: Clinical use of radioactive gold in treatment of carcinoma of the prostate gland. Mailing Add: Dept of Urol Univ of Iowa Col of Med Iowa City IA 52240

CULP, ARCHIE W, b St Joseph, Mo, Jan 20, 31; m 57; c 3. MECHANICAL & NUCLEAR ENGINEERING. Educ: Mo Sch Mines, BS, 52, MS, 54; Univ Mo-Columbia, PhD, 70. Prof Exp: Nuclear engr, Gen Dynamics/Convair, Tex, 55-56; nuclear engr, Astra, Inc, Conn, 56-58, dir nuclear eng, 58-61; asst prof mech eng, 61-64, ASSOC PROF MECH ENG, UNIV MO-ROLLA, 64- Concurrent Pos: NSF fac fel, 67-68. Mem: Am Nuclear Soc; Am Soc Eng Educ. Res: Design of nuclear reactors; principles of nuclear engineering. Mailing Add: Dept Mech Eng Univ Mo Rolla MO 65401

CULP, FREDERICK LYNN, b Duquesne, Pa, May 12, 27; m 53; c 2. PHYSICS. Educ: Carnegie Inst Technol, BS, 49, MS, 60; Vanderbilt Univ, PhD, 66. Prof Exp: Asst, US Steel Res Lab, 50-51; electronics engr, Pratt & Whitney Air Craft Corp, 52-54; res physicist, Stand Piezo Co, Pa, 54-55 & Westinghouse Lab, 55-56; asst elec & magnetism, Carnegie Inst Technol, 57-59, asst shaped charges & hyperballistics, 57-59; from asst prof to assoc prof, 59-64, PROF PHYSICS & CHMN DEPT, TENN TECHNOL UNIV, 64-

Mem: AAAS; Am Asn Physics Teachers; Am Phys Soc. Res: Physics of fluids; electronic instrumentation; piezoelectricity; photoconductivity; shaped charges and hyperballistics; exploding wires; relaxation times in gases. Mailing Add: Dept of Physics Tenn Technol Univ Cookeville TN 38501

CULP, LLOYD ANTHONY, b Elkhart, Ind, Dec 23, 42; m 65; c 2. VIROLOGY, CELL BIOLOGY. Educ: Case Inst Technol, BS, 64; Mass Inst Technol, PhD(biochem), 69. Prof Exp: Fel virol, Harvard Med Sch & Mass Gen Hosp, 69-71; asst prof, 72-77, ASSOC PROF MICROBIOL, SCH MED, CASE WESTERN RESERVE UNIV, 77- Concurrent Pos: Mem, NIH Cellular Physiol Study Sect, 78-; vis scientist, Univ Calif, San Diego, 78-79. Mem: AAAS; Am Soc Microbiol; Sigma Xi; Am Soc Cell Biol; NY Acad Sci. Res: Study of the molecular mechanism of substrate adhesion of normal growth-controlled mammalian cells and possible alteration after transformation to a malignant state by oncogenic viruses; study of neuronal cell adhesion to extracellular matrices and requirements for growth cone extension. Mailing Add: Dept Microbiol Sch Med Case Western Reserve Univ Cleveland OH 44106

CULP, NEIL J, b Reading, Pa, Feb 12, 30; m 52; c 6. METALLURGY. Educ: Lehigh Univ, BS, 52. Prof Exp: Res metallurgist, 52-55, supvr tool & alloy steels, 55-57, supvry metallurgist, 57-59, asst mgr res, 59-60, mgr res labs, 60-69, dir res, 69-71, asst vpres res & develop, 71-75, ASST V PRES CORP DEVELOP & PLANNING, CARPENTER TECHNOL CORP, 75- Mem: Am Soc Metals; Am Soc Test & Mat; Indust Res Inst. Res: Tool steels for abrasion resistance and exceptional toughness; tool steels for cutting tools and dies. Mailing Add: Carpenter Technol Corp PO Box 662 Reading PA 19603

CULP, ROBERT D(UDLEY), b McAlester, Okla, Feb 28, 38; m 60; c 2. CELESTIAL MECHANICS, ASTRONAUTICS. Educ: Univ Okla, BS, 60; Univ Colo, Boulder, MS, 63, PhD(aerospace eng), 66. Prof Exp: Engr, Martin Co, Colo, 60-62; res assoc orbital mech, 66-68, asst prof, 68-74, assoc prof, 74-80, PROF AEROSPACE ENG SCI, UNIV COLO, BOULDER, 80- Mem: Assoc fel Am Inst Aeronaut & Astronaut; fel Am Astronaut Soc; Am Soc Eng Educ. Res: Orbital mechanics; optimal transfer; optimization techniques; mathematical modeling of sonic boom; atmospheric entry and maneuvering of orbital vehicles; optimal control of trajectories. Mailing Add: Dept Aerospace Eng Sci Univ Colo Boulder CO 80302

CULVAHOUSE, JACK WAYNE, b Mt Park, Okla, Sept 15, 29; m 52; c 3. MAGNETISM. Educ: Univ Okla, BS, 51, AM, 54; Harvard Univ, PhD(physics), 58. Prof Exp: Physicist, Gen Elec Co, 51-53; asst prof physics, Univ Okla, 57-58; from asst prof to assoc prof, 58-64, PROF PHYSICS, UNIV KANS, 64- Concurrent Pos: Consult, Hycon Eastern Inc, 58-59; Guggenheim fel, 68-69. Mem: Fel Am Phys Soc. Res: Low temperature physics; magnetic resonance; solid state physics. Mailing Add: Dept Physics & Astron Univ Kans Lawrence KS 66045

CULVER, CHARLES GEORGE, b Bethlehem, Pa, Dec 4, 37; m 64; c 1. CIVIL & STRUCTURAL ENGINEERING. Educ: Lehigh Univ, BS, 59, MS, 61, PhD(civil eng), 65. Prof Exp: Engr, Sandia Corp, 61; instr, Lehigh Univ, 61-63; proj engr, US Navy Marine Eng Lab, 63-66; from asst prof to assoc prof civil eng, Carnegie-Mellon Univ, 66-72; res mgr, 72-80, DEP DIR, CTR BLDG TECHNOL, NAT BUR STANDARDS, 80- Concurrent Pos: Commerce sci fel, Exec Off of President-Off Mgt & Budget, 78- Honors & Awards: Civil Eng Res Prize, Am Soc Civil Engrs, 73; Silver Medal, Dept Commerce, 77. Mem: Am Soc Civil Engrs; Am Arbit Asn; Sigma Xi. Res: Structural vibrations; structural stability; earthquake engineering; building research; fire research. Mailing Add: Ctr for Bldg Technol Nat Bur of Standards Washington DC 20234

CULVER, DAVID ALAN, b Oak Ridge, Tenn, Feb 14, 45; m 67; c 2. AQUATIC ECOLOGY, ZOOLOGY. Educ: Cornell Univ, AB, 67; Univ Wash, MS, 69, PhD(zool), 73. Prof Exp: Asst prof biol, Queen's Univ, Ont, 73-75; asst prof, 75-81, ASSOC PROF ZOOL, OHIO STATE UNIV, COLUMBUS, 81- Concurrent Pos: Res grant, Nat Res Coun Can, 73-75; Environ Can, 74-75; Off Water Resources Technol, US Dept Interior, 76-82; US Environ Protection Agency, 77-78 & Sea Grant, US Dept Com, 80-82. Mem: Am Soc Limnol & Oceanog; Ecol Soc Am; Int Asn Theoret & Appl Limnol; AAAS; Sigma Xi. Res: Plankton ecology: primary and secondary productivity, cyclomorphosis, eutrophication; meromictic lakes: plankton, chemical cycles, sedimentary history, stratification; power plant impacts on plankton; limnology of Laurentian Great Lakes; aquaculture of larval fishes. Mailing Add: Dept of Zool 1735 Neil Ave Columbus OH 43210

CULVER, DAVID CLAIR, b Waverly, Iowa, Sept 23, 44; m 68. ECOLOGY. Educ: Grinnell Col, BA, 66; Yale Univ, PhD(biol), 70. Prof Exp: Fel pop biol, Univ Chicago, 70-71; from asst prof to prof biol, 71-81, PROF & CHMN ECOL & EVOLUTIONARY BIOL, NORTHWESTERN UNIV, EVANSTON, 81- Concurrent Pos: Vis assoc prof human ecol, Harvard Sch Pub Health, 75. Mem: Nat Speleol Soc; Ecol Soc Am. Res: Cave biology; control of species diversity; theoretical ecology. Mailing Add: Dept of Biol Sci Northwestern Univ Evanston IL 60201

CULVER, JAMES F, b Macon, Ga, June 10, 21; m 47. OPHTHALMOLOGY. Educ: Univ Ga, MD, 45; Am Bd Ophthal, dipl, 53. Prof Exp: Clin asst, Med Sch, Northwestern Univ, 52; pvt pract, 53-59; chief, Ophthal Br, US Air Force Sch Aerospace Med, 59-66, asst dir res & develop, Aerospace Med Div, Brooks AFB, Tex, 66-69, CHIEF MED RES GROUP, OFF SURGEON GEN, US AIR FORCE, 69- Concurrent Pos: Fel ophthal, Wesley Mem & Passavant Mem Hosps, Chicago, 51-52; mem, Consult Group & Med Debriefing Team, Projs Mercury & Gemini, 61-, Exec Coun, Armed Forces-Nat Res Coun Comt Vision, 62- & Vision Comt, Adv Group Aerospace Res & Develop, Aerospace Med Panel, NATO, 64- Honors & Awards: Tuttle Award, Aerospace Med Asn, 66. Mem: AMA; Aerospace Med Asn; Am Acad Ophthal & Otolaryngol. Res: Medicine and surgery; aerospace medicine and ophthalmology. Mailing Add: Command Surgeon Hq Pac Air Forces Hickam AFB HI 96818

CULVER, RICHARD S, b Berkeley, Calif, July 26, 37; m 62; c 4. MATERIALS SCIENCE. Educ: Vanderbilt Univ, BE, 59; Stanford Univ, MSc, 60; Cambridge Univ, PhD(mech of mat), 64. Prof Exp: Asst prof mech & actg dir mining res lab, Colo Sch Mines, 64-68; lectr mech eng, Ahmadu Bello Univ, Nigeria, 68-70; res assoc explosives appln, Univ Calgary, 70-72; dean students, 74-79, assoc prof, 72-79, PROF BASIC ENG, COLO SCH MINES, 79- Concurrent Pos: Consult, Union Carbide Nuclear Co, Tenn, 61-63. Mem: Am Soc Mech Engrs; Am Soc Eng Educ; Nat Asn Student Personnel Adminrs; Sigma Xi. Res: Explosive metal forming; dynamics of impact; dynamic behavior of materials; engineering education. Mailing Add: Colo Sch Mines Golden CO 80401

CULVER, ROGER BRUCE, b Brigham City, Utah, Sept 6, 40; m 65; c 3. ASTRONOMY. Educ: Univ Calif, Riverside, BA, 62; Ohio State Univ, MSc, 66, PhD(astron), 71. Prof Exp: Instr astron & math, 66-70; PROF ASTRON, COLO STATE UNIV, 70- Concurrent Pos: Mem user's comt, Kitt Peak Nat Observ, 74-76. Mem: Am Astron Int Astron Union; Astron Soc Pac. Res: Physical properties of cool stars having unusual chemical compositions. Mailing Add: Dept of Physics Colo State Univ Ft Collins CO 80523

CULVER, WILLIAM HOWARD, b Eau Claire, Wis, Feb 17, 27; m 59; c 3. PHYSICS. Educ: Mass Inst Technol, BS, 50; Univ Calif, Los Angeles, MS, 54, PhD, 61. Prof Exp: Res asst, Mass Inst Technol, 50-52 & Scripps Inst Oceanog, Univ Calif, 52-54; physicist, Rand Corp, 55-61 & Inst Defense Anal, 61-66; mgr, Quantum Electronics Dept, IBM Corp, 66-72; corp laser strategist, 67-69; PRES, OPTELECOM INC, GAITHERSBURG, MD, 72- Concurrent Pos: Mem, Spec Group Optical Masers, Dept Defense, 62-66; mem interdept comt atmospheric sci, Dept Com, 64-65; mem, Nat Acad Sci adv comt to Nat Bur Standards Cent Radio Propagation Lab, 65; mem, NASA Res & Technol Adv Comt on Commun & Tracking, 67-69. Mem: Optical Soc Am; Am Phys Soc; Inst Elec & Electronics Engrs. Res: Quantum electronics; optical and microwave spectroscopy; applications of lasers to communication systems. Mailing Add: Optelecom Inc 15940 Shady Rd Gaithersburg MD 20760

CUMBERBATCH, ELLIS, b Eng, Apr 19, 34; m 57; c 4. APPLIED MATHEMATICS. Educ: Univ Manchester, BSc, 55, PhD(appl math), 58. Prof Exp: Res fel appl mech, Calif Inst Technol, 58-60; res assoc, Courant Inst Math Sci, NY Univ, 60-61; lectr, Univ Leeds, 61-64; from asst prof to prof math, Purdue Univ, West Lafayette, 64-81; PROF MATH, CLAREMONT GRAD SCH, 81- Res: Fluid dynamics; mathematics. Mailing Add: Dept of Math Claremont Grad Sch Claremont CA 91711

CUMBERLAND, WILLIAM GLEN, b Can, Feb 7, 48. SAMPLING THEORY, DEMOGRAPHY. Educ: McGill Univ, BSc, 68; Johns Hopkins Univ, MA, 72, PhD(statist), 75. Prof Exp: Fel pop dynamics, Johns Hopkins Univ, 75-76; ASST PROF BIOSTATIST, UNIV CALIF, LOS ANGELES, 76- Mem: Am Statist Asn; Biometric Soc; Int Math Statist. Res: Variance estimation in finite population sampling; stochastic models for population growth. Mailing Add: Div Biostatist Univ Calif Sch Pub Health Los Angeles CA 90024

CUMBIE, BILLY GLENN, b Dickens, Tex, Mar 21, 30; m 51; c 3. BOTANY. Educ: Tex Tech Col, BS, 51, MS, 52; Univ Tex, PhD(bot), 60. Prof Exp: Spec instr bot, Univ Tex, 57-58; from instr to asst prof, Tex Tech Col, 58-61; asst prof bot, 61-77, PROF BIOL SCI, UNIV MO-COLUMBIA, 77- Mem: Bot Soc Am; Int Asn Wood Anat. Res: Development of the vascular cambium and xylem in dicotyledons. Mailing Add: Div of Biol Sci Univ of Mo Columbia MO 65201

CUMMEROW, ROBERT LEGGETT, b Toledo, Ohio, Jan 7, 15; m 48; c 2. PHYSICS. Educ: Univ Toledo, BE, 38; Univ Pittsburgh, MS, 40, PhD(physics), 47. Prof Exp: Asst physics, Univ Pittsburgh, 38-42; spec res assoc underwater sound lab, Harvard Univ, 42-45; mem staff, US Navy Underwater Sound Lab, Conn, 45-46; res assoc, Knolls Atomic Power Lab, Gen Elec Co, 48-55; group leader solid state physics, Nat Carbon Res Labs, 55-63; group leader, Union Carbide Res Inst, 63-70, SR SCIENTIST, TARRYTOWN TECH CTR, UNION CARBIDE CORP, 70- Mem: Am Phys Soc. Res: Elastic and damping constants of metals and alloys; underwater sound detection equipment; paramagnetic resonance absorption in salts of the iron group; radiation-induced property changes in semiconductors and metals; photo-effects in semiconductors; plastic behavior of semiconductors and refractory materials; superconductivity. Mailing Add: Tarrytown Tech Ctr Union Carbide Corp Tarrytown NY 10591

CUMMIN, ALFRED SAMUEL, b London, Eng, Sept 5, 24; nat US; m 45; c 1. PHYSICAL CHEMISTRY. Educ: Polytech Inst Brooklyn, BS, 43, PhD, 46; Univ Buffalo, MBA, 59. Prof Exp: Res chemist, Substitute Alloy Mats Lab, Manhattan Proj, Columbia Univ, 43-44; plant supvr & head res, Metal & Plastic Processing Co, 46-51; res chemist gen chem div, Allied Chem & Dye Corp, 51-53; sr chemist, Congoleum Nairn, 53-54; prof math & sci, US Merchant Marine Acad, 54; capacitor div, Gen Elec Co, 54-56, supvr dielectric adv develop, 54-56; mgr indust prof res dept, Spencer Kellog & Sons, Inc, 56-59; mgr plastics div, Trancoa Chem Corp, 59-62; assoc dir, Prod Develop & Serv Labs, Chem Div, Merck & Co, Inc, NJ, 62-69; dir prod develop, Chem Div, Borden Co, 69-72; tech dir, Borden Chem Div, Borden Inc, NY, 72-73, corp tech dir, 73-78, vpres prod safety & qual, 78-80, VPRES SCI & TECHNOL, BORDEN INC, 81- Concurrent Pos: Instr, Polytech Inst Brooklyn, 46-47; asst prof, Adelphi Col, 52-54; adj prof mgt, Mgt Inst, NY Univ, 68- Honors & Awards: Roon Cert Award, Fedn Socs Paint Technol, 65. Mem: Am Chem Soc; Inst Food Technol; Fedn Coatings Technol; Am Soc Tes Mat; Nutrit Found. Res: Polymers; electrochemistry; food packaging; colloid chemistry; preservatives; agricultural chemicals; dielectrics and insulating materials; paints; adhesives; surgical adhesives; nutrition; industrial hygiene; occupational health. Mailing Add: Borden Inc 960 Kingsmill Pkwy Columbus OH 43229

CUMMING, BRUCE GORDON, b London, Eng, Oct 12, 25; Can citizen; m 69. PLANT PHYSIOLOGY. *Educ:* Univ Reading, BS, 52; McGill Univ, PhD(plant physiol, agron), 56. *Prof Exp:* Res off, Plant Res Inst, Can Dept Agr, 57-65; prof bot, Western Ont Univ, 65-71; chmn dept, 71-74, PROF BIOL, UNIV NB, 71- *Concurrent Pos:* Del gen assembly, Int Union Biol Sci, 70 & 73. *Mem:* Can Soc Plant Physiol (pres, 69-70). *Res:* Physiology; photobiology; photoperiodism; endogenous rhythms and phytochrome, particularly in germination and flowering; tissue culture and morphogenesis. *Mailing Add:* Dept of Biol Univ of NB Fredericton NB E3B 5A3 Can

CUMMING, GEORGE LESLIE, b Saskatoon, Saskatchewan, Feb 11, 30; m 54; c 3. GEOCHRONOLOGY, SEISMOLOGY. *Educ:* Univ Saskatchewan, BA, 51, MA, 53; Univ Toronto, PhD(geophysics), 55. *Prof Exp:* Geophysicist, Gulf Oil Co, 55-59; PROF GEOPHYSICS, UNIV ALTA, 59-, DIR, INST EARTH & PLANETARY PHYSICS, 81- *Mem:* Am Geophys Union; Soc Explor Geophysicists; Geol Soc Can; Can Geophys Union. *Res:* Geochronology with emphasis on lead isotope variations; crustal seismic exploration using reflection and refraction. *Mailing Add:* Dept Physics Univ Alta Edmonton AB T6G 2J1 Can

CUMMING, JAMES, b Jamaica, NY, June 6, 28; m 53; c 3. NUCLEAR CHEMISTRY. *Educ:* Yale Univ, BS, 49; Columbia Univ, MA, 51, PhD(nuclear chem), 54. *Prof Exp:* Res assoc, 54-55, from assoc chemist to chemist, 55-69, SR CHEMIST, BROOKHAVEN NAT LAB, 69- *Mem:* Am Phys Soc; Am Chem Soc; Sigma Xi. *Res:* Nuclear reactions induced by energetic light-ions and heavy-ions; nuclear decay schemes. *Mailing Add:* Chem Dept Brookhaven Nat Lab Upton NY 11973

CUMMING, LESLIE MERRILL, b Joggins, NS, Nov 5, 25; m 58; c 3. GEOLOGY. *Educ:* Univ NB, BSc, 48, MSc, 51; Univ Wis, PhD(geol), 55. *Prof Exp:* Asst to prov geologist, NB Dept Mines, 44-46; field asst, 47-49, tech officer, 49-54, geologist, 55-67, RES SCIENTIST, GEOL SURV CAN, 67- *Mem:* Am Paleont Soc; fel Geol Asn Can; fel Royal Can Geog Soc; Brit Palaeontolograph Soc; Can Inst Mining & Metall. *Res:* Regional Paleozoic geology of the Appalachians; regional geology of the Hudson Bay lowlands and Arctic Canada; Paleozoic faunas; graptolite morphology. *Mailing Add:* Geol Surv of Can 601 Booth St Ottawa ON K1A 0E8 Can

CUMMING, WILLIAM ALBON, b Detroit, Mich, July 16, 26; Can citizen; m 47; c 2. RADIO PHYSICS, ELECTRICAL ENGINEERING. *Educ:* Queen's Univ, Ont, BSc, 47. *Prof Exp:* Res officer, 47-65, head, Antenna Eng Sect, 65-78, dir, Radio & Elec Eng Div, 68-78, asst vpres labs, 71-74, VPRES LABS, NAT RES COUN CAN, 74-, SR VPRES, 78-, EXEC VPRES, 81- *Mem:* Sr mem Inst Elec & Electronics Engrs; Eng Inst Can. *Res:* Antenna development and general research in the fields of electromagnetics and radio physics. *Mailing Add:* Nat Res Coun of Can Ottawa ON K1A 0R6 Can

CUMMINGS, DAVID, b New York, NY, Feb 11, 32. GEOLOGY, GEOPHYSICS. *Educ:* City Col New York, BS, 57; Univ Tenn, MS, 59; Mich State Univ, PhD(geol), 62. *Prof Exp:* Mineralogist & petrologist, Electrotech Res Lab, US Bur Mines, 59; geologist, US Geol Surv, 62-68; PROF GEOL, OCCIDENTAL COL, 68- *Concurrent Pos:* Consult, US Geol Surv, 68-75; independent consult, 70-; pres, Ryland-Cummings, Inc, 79- *Mem:* Am Geophys Union; Asn Eng Geologists; Geol Soc Am; Int Asn Eng Geologists; Am Asn Petrol Geologists. *Res:* Theoretical and applied mechanics used to solve structural geologic problems, engineering geologic problems; applied geophysics. *Mailing Add:* Dept of Geol Occidental Col Los Angeles CA 90041

CUMMINGS, DENNIS PAUL, b Yonkers, NY, Apr 19, 40. MICROBIOLOGY. *Educ:* Manhattan Col, BS, 61; St John's Univ, NY, MS, 63, PhD(microbiol), 68. *Prof Exp:* Asst microbiol, St John's Univ, NY, 62-63; res microbiologist, 68-72, sr res scientist, 72-78, SUPVR MICROBIOL DEVELOP LAB, MILES LABS, INC, 78- *Mem:* Am Soc Microbiol; Soc Indust Microbiol. *Res:* Medical microbiology; antifungal and antibacterial agents; analytical microbiology; microbiological aspects of pharmaceutical development. *Mailing Add:* Dome Labs Div of Miles Labs Inc 400 Morgan Lane West Haven CT 06516

CUMMINGS, DONALD JOSEPH, b Staten Island, NY, Mar 4, 30; m 58; c 3. BIOPHYSICS. *Educ:* George Washington Univ, BS, 55; Univ Chicago, MS, 57, PhD(biophys), 59. *Prof Exp:* Biophysicist, NIH, 53-55; USPHS fel, Copenhagen Univ, 59-60; res physicist, Nat Inst Neurol Dis & Blindness, 60-64; from asst prof to assoc prof, 64-71, PROF MICROBIOL, MED SCH, UNIV COLO, DENVER, 71- *Concurrent Pos:* Josiah Macy Jr fac scholar, 77-78. *Res:* Effect of canavanine on head morphogenesis in T-even bacteriophages of Entamba coli; replication and function of mitochondria from Paramecium and Podospora; biochemistry and morphology of aging in Paramecium and Podospora. *Mailing Add:* Dept Microbiol Univ Colo Med Sch Denver CO 80220

CUMMINGS, EDMUND GEORGE, b Albany, NY, Aug 2, 28; m 55; c 2. PHYSIOLOGY. *Educ:* Union Col, BS, 50; NC State Col, MS, 53, PhD(ecol), 55. *Prof Exp:* Asst zool, NC State Col, 51-55, instr, Exten Sch, 54; instr, Duke Univ, 55-56; physiologist & chief respiratory sect, 56-78, physiologist, chem systs lab, 78-80, CHIEF, CHEM-PHYSIOL TOXICOL, CHEM SYSTS LAB, RES DIV, EDGEWOOD ARSENAL, 80- *Concurrent Pos:* Asst prof, Harford Col, 59-62, assoc prof, 67-69; asst prof, Univ Md Exten Sch, 64- *Mem:* AAAS; Am Soc Zool; Am Physiol Soc. *Res:* Culture of slime molds; food habits of game birds; osmoregulation in fish; respiratory and exercise physiology; thermoregulation and anticholinergics; environment and skin penetration; evaluation of respiratory protective devices; toxicity of anticholinesterases. *Mailing Add:* Chem Systs Lab Res Div Aberdeen Proving Ground MD 21010

CUMMINGS, FRANK EDSON, b Berkeley, Calif, Feb 19, 40; m 67; c 2. PHYSICAL CHEMISTRY. *Educ:* Harvey Mudd Col, BS, 62; Harvard Univ, PhD(chem), 72. *Prof Exp:* From instr to assoc prof, 67-81, PROF CHEM, ATLANTA UNIV, 81-, CHMN DEPT, 79- *Concurrent Pos:* Chief investr, NIH grant, 72-76 & NSF grant, 76-77; proj dir, Dept Energy grant, 78-81. *Mem:* Am Phys Soc. *Res:* High resolution studies of diatomic molecules, electronic states and long range forces between atoms. *Mailing Add:* Dept of Chem Atlanta Univ Atlanta GA 30314

CUMMINGS, FREDERICK W, b New Orleans, La, Nov 21, 31. THEORETICAL PHYSICS, MATHEMATICS. *Educ:* La State Univ, BS, 55; Stanford Univ, PhD(physics), 60. *Prof Exp:* Res scientist theoret physics, Aeronutronic Div, Philco Corp, Calif, 60-63; from asst prof to assoc prof, 63-74, PROF PHYSICS, UNIV CALIF, RIVERSIDE, 74- *Concurrent Pos:* Consult, Aeronutronic Div, Philco Corp, 64-66; ed, Coop Phenomena. *Mem:* AAAS; Am Phys Soc; Am Sci Teachers Asn. *Res:* Coherence in radiation; solid state; many particles. *Mailing Add:* Dept of Physics Univ of Calif Riverside CA 92507

CUMMINGS, GEORGE AUGUST, b Cortland, Ind, Dec 17, 27; m 53; c 3. SOIL SCIENCE. *Educ:* Purdue Univ, BS, 51, MS, 57, PhD(agron), 61. *Prof Exp:* Teacher high sch, Ind, 51-58; from asst prof to assoc prof, 61-78, prof soil fertil, 78-80, PROF BIOL SCI, NC STATE UNIV, 80- *Mem:* Am Soc Hort Sci; Am Soc Agron; Soil Sci Soc Am. *Res:* Determination of effects of plant nutrition upon biochemical constituents of plants; influence of nutrition upon yield and quality of fruits; influence of animal waste upon soil plant systems; runoff and ground water. *Mailing Add:* Dept of Soil Sci NC State Univ Raleigh NC 27607

CUMMINGS, GEORGE H(ERBERT), b Cape May, NJ, Dec 28, 13; m 39; c 4. CHEMICAL ENGINEERING. *Educ:* Pa State Univ, BS, 35, PhD(chem eng), 41; Mass Inst Technol, SM, 36. *Prof Exp:* Asst chem, Pa State Univ, 36-39, instr chem eng, 39-41; chem engr, Houston Plant, Rohm and Haas Co, 41-51, chief chem engr, 51-76; RETIRED. *Mem:* Am Chem Soc; Am Inst Chem Engrs. *Res:* Solvent extraction; distillation; petroleum refining; chemical engineering process design. *Mailing Add:* 5108 Doe Valley Lane Austin TX 78759

CUMMINGS, JOHN ALBERT, b Evanston, Ill, May 3, 31; m 51; c 2. RADIOBIOLOGY. *Educ:* Wis State Univ-Whitewater, BS, 53; Univ Wis, MS, 59; Univ Northern Colo, EdD, 66. *Prof Exp:* Teacher high sch, Wis, 53-61; PROF BIOL, UNIV WIS-WHITEWATER, 61- *Concurrent Pos:* Dir, NSF Inserv Inst Molecular Biol, 64-65 & 68-69, dir, NSF Inst Environ Sci, 71-72; AEC grant, Nuclear Sci Instrumentation for Radiation Biol Lab, Univ Wis-Whitewater, 64-65; acad dir, Univ Wis Syst, Pigeon Lake Field Sta, 76- *Mem:* Nat Asn Biol Teachers; Am Inst Biol Sci. *Res:* Concentration of various radioisotopes in Orconectes virilis in various intermolt stages; radioisotope accumulation by radioautographic methods in crustaceans and reptiles; crayfish population of Wisconsin. *Mailing Add:* 1264 Satinwood Lane Whitewater WI 53190

CUMMINGS, JOHN FRANCIS, b Newark, NJ, Sept 3, 36; m 61; c 5. VETERINARY ANATOMY, COMPARATIVE NEUROLOGY. *Educ:* Cornell Univ, BS, 58, DVM, 62, MS, 63, PhD(vet anat), 66. *Prof Exp:* Asst vet anat, 63-65, asst prof anat, 67-71, assoc prof anat, 71-77, PROF ANAT, NY STATE COL VET MED, CORNELL UNIV, 77- *Concurrent Pos:* Consult, Div Neuropsychiat, Walter Reed Army Inst Res, 75- *Res:* Neuroanatomy and neuropathology. *Mailing Add:* Dept of Anat NY State Col of Vet Med Cornell Univ Ithaca NY 14853

CUMMINGS, JOHN JOSEPH, b Camden, NJ, Dec 18, 08; m 32. ELECTRONICS. *Prof Exp:* Electronics engr, Barker & Williamson, 47; radio & electronics engr, Naval Security Sta, Washington, DC, 47-57; dir lab, Frankford Arsenal Philadelphia, 57-58, chief div eng support, Res & Develop Group, 58-64, dir qual assurance, 64-72; RETIRED. *Mem:* Inst Elec & Electronics Engrs; Sigma Xi; Nat Soc Prof Engrs. *Res:* Radiowave propagation; military fire control; testing of materials; management. *Mailing Add:* 280 Middle Holland Rd Apt 806 Holland PA 18966

CUMMINGS, JOHN PATRICK, b Westfield, Mass, June 28, 33; c 6. ECOLOGY, PHYSICAL CHEMISTRY. *Educ:* St Michael's Col, BS(philos) & BS(chem), 55; Univ Tex, Austin, PhD(chem), 69; Univ Toledo, JD, 73, MS, 77. *Prof Exp:* Instr, Univ Tex, 63-66; dist mgr, ITT Hamilton Mgt Corp, 62-68; sr chemist, Owens-Ill Inc, 68-70, ecologist, 71-76, prod safety mgr, 76-78, legal coun, 78-79, MGR LEGIS COMPLIANCE, OWENS-ILL INC, 79- *Concurrent Pos:* Consult, Environ Protection Agency, Glass Packaging Inst, Nat Ctr Resource Recovery, 71-76. *Mem:* Sigma Xi; Royal Soc Chem; Am Ceramic Soc; Am Chem Soc; Am Crystallog Asn. *Res:* Ecology, physical chemistry, international law, resource recovery and legislative aspects. *Mailing Add:* One Segate Ctr PO Box 1035 Toledo OH 43666

CUMMINGS, JOHN RHODES, b Detroit, Mich, Feb 4, 26; m 53; c 2. PHARMACOLOGY. *Educ:* Kalamazoo Col, BA, 50; Wayne State Univ, MS, 52, PhD(pharmacol), 54. *Prof Exp:* Asst prof pharmacol, Med Sch, Tufts Univ, 54-57; group leader cardiovasc pharmacol, Lederle Labs Div, Am Cyanamid Co, 57-69, head dept cardiovasc-renal pharmacol, 69-73; DIR DEPT PHARMACOL, AYERST RES LABS DIV, AM HOME PROD CORP, 73- *Mem:* Am Soc Pharmacol & Exp Therapeut; Soc Exp Biol & Med; Am Heart Asn; Am Chem Soc. *Res:* Cardiovascular pharmacology, particularly in the fields of arrhythmia, hypertension and diuretic research. *Mailing Add:* Dept of Pharmacol Ayerst Labs Montreal Can

CUMMINGS, JON CLARK, b Saranac Lake, NY, Apr 30, 30; div; c 3. GEOLOGY. *Educ:* Stanford Univ, BS, 52, MS, 56, PhD(geol), 60. *Prof Exp:* Asst prof geol, Ore State Univ, 58-64; assoc prof, 64-71, chmn, Dept Geol Sci, 69-76, PROF GEOL, CALIF STATE UNIV, HAYWARD, 71-, CHMN, DEPT GEOL SCI, 79- *Concurrent Pos:* Geologist, WAE, US Geol Surv, 67-71 & Portola Valley & Woodside, Calif, 71- *Mem:* Geol Soc Am; Am Asn Petrol Geol; Soc Econ Paleont & Mineral. *Res:* Stratigraphy; sedimentation; California coast range geology; environmental geology. *Mailing Add:* Dept Geol Sci Calif State Univ Hayward CA 94542

CUMMINGS, KENNETH ROSS, animal nutrition, see previous edition

CUMMINGS, LARRY JEAN, b Chicago, Ill, Oct 1, 37; m 63; c 2. ALGEBRA. *Educ:* Roosevelt Univ, BS, 61; DePaul Univ, MS, 63; Univ BC, PhD(math), 67. *Prof Exp:* Teaching asst math, Univ BC, 63-67; ASST PROF MATH, UNIV WATERLOO, 67- *Res:* Multilinear algebra; generalized matrix functions and matrix inequalities. *Mailing Add:* 109 Allen W Waterloo N2L 1E6 Can

CUMMINGS, MARTIN MARC, b Camden, NJ, Sept 7, 20; m 42; c 3. MEDICINE. *Educ:* Bucknell Univ, BS, 41; Duke Univ, MD, 44. *Hon Degrees:* DSc, Bucknell Univ, 68; ScD, Univ Nebr, Emory Univ & Georgetown Univ, 71; MD, Karolinska Inst, Sweden, 72; hon Dr, Acad Med, Lodz, Poland, 77. *Prof Exp:* Med intern, Boston Marine Hosp, USPHS, 44, asst resident med, 45, med officer, Tuberc Div, 46-47, dir, Tuberc Eval Lab, Commun Dis Ctr, 47-49; dir, Tuberc Res Lab, Vet Admin Hosp, Atlanta, Ga, 49-53; dir res serv, US Vet Admin, 53-59; prof microbiol & chief dept, Univ Okla, 59-61; chief off int res, NIH, 61-63, assoc dir res grant, 63; DIR, NAT LIBR MED, USPHS, 64- *Concurrent Pos:* Asst prof & assoc prof, Sch Med, Emory Univ, 51-53; prof lectr, Sch Med, George Washington Univ, 53-54. *Mem:* Nat Inst Med-Nat Acad Sci; Am Soc Clin Invest; Am Clin & Climat Asn; Am Acad Microbiol; Asn Am Med Cols. *Res:* Laboratory diagnosis of tuberculosis and experimental methods; epidemiology of sarcoidosis; library and information science. *Mailing Add:* Nat Libr of Med 8600 Rockville Pike Bethesda MD 20209

CUMMINGS, MICHAEL R, b Chicago, Ill, July 7, 41; m 66; c 2. DEVELOPMENTAL GENETICS. *Educ:* St Mary's Col, Minn, BA, 63; Northwestern Univ, MS, 65, PhD(biol), 68. *Prof Exp:* Instr genetics, Northwestern Univ, 68-69; asst prof genetics, 69-72, ASSOC PROF BIOL SCI, UNIV ILL, CHICAGO CIRCLE, 72- *Concurrent Pos:* res assoc prof, Inst Study Develop Disabilities, Univ Ill, Chicago, 78-; Assoc prof, Ctr Genetics, Univ Ill Med Ctr, Chicago, 79- *Mem:* Soc Develop Biol; Am Soc Cell Biol; Gen Soc Am; Am Soc Human Genetics. *Res:* Regulation of gene expression; developmental genetics. *Mailing Add:* Dept of Biol Sci Univ of Ill Chicago Cir Chicago IL 60680

CUMMINGS, NANCY BOUCOT, b Philadelphia, Pa, Feb 21, 27; m 59; c 3. NEPHROLOGY, INTERNAL MEDICINE. *Educ:* Oberlin Col, BA, 47; Univ Pa, MD, 51. *Prof Exp:* Rotating intern, Pa Hosp, 51-52; resident internal med, Univ Pa Hosp, 52-54; res & clin asst med, Royal Hosp St Bartholomew, London, 54-55; res & clin asst med, Manchester Royal Infirmary, Eng, 55; asst med, Peter Bent Brigham Hosp, 55-58; guest worker, Nat Inst Arthritis '& Metab Dis, 59-62; res med officer, Walter Reed Army Inst Res, 62-66; res med officer, Div Exp Med, Naval Med Res Inst & consult nephrol, Dept Med, Naval Hosp, Md, 66-72; prog officer, 72-73, spec asst to dir renal & urol dir, 73-74, actg assoc dir renal & urol dis, 74-76, ASSOC DIR KIDNEY, UROL & HEMAT DIS, NAT INST ARTHRITIS, DIABETES, DIGESTIVE & KIDNEY DIS, NIH, 76- *Concurrent Pos:* Res fel med, Harvard Med Sch, 55-58, res fel biol chem, 58-59; Am Heart Asn fel, 55-57, advan res fel, 57-62; Nat Found res fel, Royal Hosp St Bartholomew & Manchester Royal Infirmary, 54-55; mem, Res Comt, Washington Heart Asn, 69-78, chmn res comt, Am Heart Asn, Nat Capitol Area, 76-78. & med adv bd, Washington Chap, Nat Kidney Found, 69-; from clin instr med to clin asst prof, Georgetown Univ, 60-81, clin assoc prof, 81-; co-chmn, Adv Comt Epidemiol & Statist Kidney Dis, Nat Kidney Found, mem, Sci Adv Bd & trustee at large; consult, Coord Comt Coun Urol; mem, Res Comt, Am Urol Asn. *Mem:* AAAS; Am Soc Hemat; Am Soc Nephrology; Am Soc Artificial Internal Organs; Am Fedn Clin Res. *Res:* Epidemiology and statistics of renal disease; biochemistry of uremia; renal physiology and pathophysiology. *Mailing Add:* 2811 35th St NW Washington DC 20007

CUMMINGS, NORMAN ALLEN, b New York, NY, Mar 26, 35; m 60; c 2. INTERNAL MEDICINE. *Educ:* NY Univ, AB, 55; State Univ NY, MD, 59; Am Bd Internal Med, dipl, 72. *Prof Exp:* Intern med, Jewish Hosp, Brooklyn, 59-60, resident, 61; resident med, Med Sch, Univ Mich, 61-62; res assoc protein chem, Nat Cancer Inst, 64-66; asst prof internal med, Col Med, Baylor Univ, 66-67; med officer & head connective tissue dis prog, Oral Med & Surg Br, Nat Inst Dent Res, 67-74; assoc prof, 74-78, PROF MED, SCH MED, UNIV LOUISVILLE, 78-, CHIEF CLIN IMMUNOL & CONNECTIVE TISSUE DIS DIV & DIR ARTHRITIS CTR, SCH MED, UNIV LOUISVILLE, 74- *Concurrent Pos:* Vis fel rheumatic dis, NY Univ-Bellevue Hosp Med Ctr, 62; USPHS physician trainee grant rheumatic dis, 62-64; fel biophys & arthritis, Med Sch, Univ Mich, 62-64; Kayser Found sci grant, 66-67; asst attend physician, Ben Taub Gen Hosp & Vet Admin Hosp, Houston, 66-67; attend physician, Louisville Gen Hosp; consult, Louisville Vet Admin Hosp, Jewish Hosp & Nat Inst Dent Res, NIH, 67-74; consult, Norton's Children's Hosp & Louisville Baptist Hosp. *Honors & Awards:* Res Award, Jewish Hosp Brooklyn, 61. *Mem:* Am Rheumatism Asn. *Res:* Protein-mucopolysaccharide interactions; metallo-proteins of serum; joint pH; protein solubility and conformation; cryoprecipitation of cryoglobulins; oral-mucosal manifestations of connective tissue diseases; immunochemistry and cellular immunology in rheumatic diseases. *Mailing Add:* Col Med PO Box 35260 Louisville KY 40292

CUMMINGS, RALPH WALDO, JR, b Ithaca, NY, July 20, 38; m 61; c 2. AGRICULTURAL ECONOMICS. *Educ:* Univ NC, AB, 60; Univ Mich, PhD(econ), 65. *Prof Exp:* Asst prof econ, Univ Ill, 65-70; consult, Bur Near East & S Asia, AID, 70; adv agr econ, Harvard Adv Group & Nat Develop Planning Agency Indonesia, 70-72; agr economist, 72-76, prog officer, Int Agr Develop Serv, 76-80, AGR ECONOMIST, ROCKEFELLER FOUND, 80- *Concurrent Pos:* Asst dir, Midwestern Univs Consortium Int Activ, 66-67; chief agr econ div, Off Agr Develop, AID, India, 67-69. *Mem:* Am Agr Econ Asn. *Res:* General problems of agricultural development, particularly improving standards of living in rural areas. *Mailing Add:* Rockefeller Found 1133 Ave of the Americas New York NY 10036

CUMMINGS, SUE CAROL, b Dayton, Ohio, Apr 24, 41; m 76. INORGANIC CHEMISTRY, BIOINORGANIC CHEMISTRY. *Educ:* Northwestern Univ, BA, 63; Ohio State Univ, MSc, 65, PhD(inorg chem), 68. *Prof Exp:* Vis res assoc inorg chem, Aerospace Res Labs, Wright-Patterson AFB, 68-69; from asst prof to assoc prof, 69-77, PROF CHEM, WRIGHT STATE UNIV, 77- *Concurrent Pos:* Petrol Res Fund grant, 69-72; Cottrell res grant, 73; Nat Heart & Lung Inst res grant, 73-81; vis scientist, C F Kettering Res Labs, Ohio, 81-82. *Mem:* AAAS; Am Chem Soc. *Res:* Coordination chemistry; synthesis, characterization, stereochemistry and reactions of metal complexes containing multidentate, macrocyclic or cage-type ligands; synthetic oxygen carriers; study of metal complexes as models for biologically important molecules. *Mailing Add:* Dept Chem Wright State Univ Dayton OH 45435

CUMMINGS, THOMAS FULTON, b Taxila, India, Oct 25, 25; US citizen; m 48; c 4. PHYSICAL CHEMISTRY, ANALYTICAL CHEMISTRY. *Educ:* Mass Inst Technol, BSc, 47; Case Inst Technol, MSc, 52, PhD(chem), 55. *Prof Exp:* Chem engr, Res Ctr, B F Goodrich Co, 48-49; asst chem, Case Inst Technol, 49-52; instr, Westminster Col, 52-55; from asst prof to assoc prof, 55-67, PROF CHEM, BRADLEY UNIV, 67- *Concurrent Pos:* Vis prof chem, Anal Inst, Univ Vienna, 66-67 & Univ Birmingham, Eng, 73-74 & 80-81. *Mem:* Am Chem Soc; Am Sci Affiliation; Soc Appl Spectros. *Res:* Kinetics; instrumental analysis; water and air pollution analysis, government support. *Mailing Add:* Dept of Chem Bradley Univ Peoria IL 61625

CUMMINGS, WILLIAM CHARLES, b Boston, Mass, Apr 6, 32; m 55; c 2. UNDERWATER ACOUSTICS, MARINE BIOLOGY. *Educ:* Bates Col, BS, 54; Univ Miami, MS, 60, PhD(marine sci), 68. *Prof Exp:* Biol oceanogr, Univ RI, 58-60; instr bioacoustics, Univ Miami, 60-65; oceanogr, Naval Ocean Systs Ctr, 65-70, head, Underwater Bioacoustics Br, 70-77; chief scientist, SDak Nat Hist Mus, 77-79; DIR, OCEANOGRAPHICS CONSULT, 79- *Concurrent Pos:* Consult, 63-; prof writer & ed, 68- *Mem:* Acoust Soc Am; Oceanic Soc; Am Cetacean Soc; Sigma Xi. *Res:* Underwater acoustics; bioacoustics; research methodology; environmental science; mammalogy and polar research. *Mailing Add:* 5948 Eaton Ct San Diego CA 92122

CUMMINGS-SAXTON, JAMES, b Pittsburgh, Pa, Dec 5, 36; m 59; c 3. CHEMICAL ENGINEERING. *Educ:* Johns Hopkins Univ, BES, 59; Univ Calif, Berkeley, PhD(chem eng), 66. *Prof Exp:* Mem tech staff systs eng, Bellcomm, Inc, 64-66, supvr systs eng, 66-71; sr res staff, Int Res & Technol Corp, 71-74, vpres, 74-76, sr vpres & mem bd trustees, 76-79; DEP TECH DIR, INT ENERGY DEVELOP PROGS, ARGONNE NAT LAB, 79- *Concurrent Pos:* lectr chem eng, Catholic Univ Am, 74 & Ill Inst Technol, 79; mem, Nat Acad Sci Panel, Socioecon Impacts Comt, Alternatives for Reduction Chlorofluoro Carbon Emmissions, 79. *Mem:* AAAS; fel Am Inst Chemists; Am Inst Chem Engrs (secy, 77-78). *Res:* Application of analytic techniques to environmental, energy and social problems; chemical engineering process modeling; environmental and ecological systems analysis. *Mailing Add:* 5547 S Harper Ave Reston VA 60637

CUMMINS, ALVIN J, b Wheeling, WVa, Apr 26, 19; m 47; c 3. INTERNAL MEDICINE, GASTROENTEROLOGY. *Educ:* Georgetown Univ, BS, 41; Johns Hopkins Univ, MD, 44. *Prof Exp:* Asst instr med, Med Sch, Univ Pa, 51-52, instr, 52-53, assoc, 53-54, from asst prof to assoc prof, 57-63, prof med & chief sect gastroenterol, 63-71, CLIN PROF MED, MED COL, UNIV TENN, 71- *Concurrent Pos:* Fel med, Cornell Med Ctr, 50-51; hon consult, Blytheville AFB, Ark, 61; chmn, Gastroenterol Res Group, 61-62; consult, Vet Admin Hosp, Memphis, 62-71; pvt pract gastroenterol. *Mem:* AMA; Am Col Physicians; Am Gastroenterol Asn; Am Fedn Clin Res; Sigma Xi. *Res:* Clinical and investigative gastroenterology; intestinal absorption; intestinal blood flow; pharmacology of gastrointestinal tract. *Mailing Add:* 1324 Peabody Memphis TN 38104

CUMMINS, CECIL STRATFORD, b Monkstown, Ireland, Nov 20, 18; m 59; c 2. MICROBIOLOGY. *Educ:* Univ Dublin, BA, 41, MB, BCh, BAO, 43, ScD, 64. *Prof Exp:* House physician, Sir Patrick Dun's Hosp, Dublin, Ireland, 43; asst to prof bact, Trinity Col, Dublin, 44; lectr bact, London Hosp Med Col, London, 48-64, reader, 64-67; PROF MICROBIOL, ANAEROBE LAB, DIV BASIC SCI, COL AGR, VA POLYTECH INST & STATE UNIV, 67- *Mem:* Am Soc Microbiol; Brit Soc Gen Microbiol; Path Soc Gt Brit. *Res:* Chemical morphology; taxonomy. *Mailing Add:* Anaerobe Lab Div Basic Sci Va Polytech Inst & State Univ Blacksburg VA 24061

CUMMINS, DAVID GRAY, b Cookeville, Tenn, June 29, 36; m 59; c 3. AGRONOMY. *Educ:* Tenn Polytech Inst, BS, 57; Univ Tenn, MS, 59; Univ Ga, PhD(agron), 62. *Prof Exp:* Soil scientist, US Forest Serv, Ky, 62-63; from asst prof to assoc prof, 63-76, PROF DEPT AGRON, GA EXP STA, UNIV GA, 76- *Concurrent Pos:* Assoc planning dir, USAID grant, Peanut Collaborative Res Support Prog, Univ Ga, 80-82. *Mem:* Am Soc Agron; Crop Sci Soc Am; Am Peanut Res Educ Soc. *Res:* Determining more efficient practices for production of corn and sorghum for grain and silage. *Mailing Add:* Dept of Agron Exp Sta Univ of Ga Experiment GA 30212

CUMMINS, EARL WESLEY, b Woodbine, Ky, Dec 12, 23; m 50; c 3. ORGANIC CHEMISTRY. *Educ:* Detroit Inst Technol, BSc, 43; Wayne Univ, PhD(chem), 51. *Prof Exp:* Res chemist, R P Scherer Co, 45-47; res chemist, 51-80, RES ASSOC, E I DU PONT DE NEMOURS & CO, INC, 80- *Mem:* Am Chem Soc. *Res:* Herbicides; insecticides; nutrionac chemicals. *Mailing Add:* E I du Pont de Nemours & Co Inc 1007 Market St Wilmington DE 19803

CUMMINS, ERNIE LEE, b Warrenton, Ore, July 13, 21; m 43; c 1. SCIENCE EDUCATION. *Educ:* Ore State Univ, BS, 43, MS, 52, EdD(sci educ), 60. *Prof Exp:* Chemist, Scott Paper Co, 47-48 & Evans Prod Co, 49-50; teacher gen sci, Jr High Sch, Ore, 51-53 & High Sch, 53-57; asst prof phys sci & sci educ, Ore Col Educ, 57-61, assoc prof phys sci, 61-66, prof phys sci & sci educ, 66-80, PROF PHYS SCI & SCI EDUC, WESTERN ORE STATE

COL, 80- Concurrent Pos: Dir in-serv insts, NSF, 62-69. Mem: Fel AAAS; Nat Asn Res Sci Teaching; Am Asn Physics Teachers; Nat Sci Teachers Asn. Res: Physics; general science. Mailing Add: Dept Sci Western Ore State Col Monmouth OR 97361

CUMMINS, HERMAN Z, b Rochester, NY, Apr 23, 33; m 63. QUANTUM OPTICS, SOLID STATE PHYSICS. Educ: Ohio State Univ, BS & MS, 56; Columbia Univ, PhD(physics), 63. Prof Exp: Res physicist, Radiation Lab, Columbia Univ, 62-64; from asst prof to prof physics, Johns Hopkins Univ, 64-71; prof, NY Univ, 71-73; DISTINGUISHED PROF PHYSICS, CITY COL NEW YORK, 73- Mem: Fel Am Phys Soc. Res: Phase transitions in liquids and crystals, ferroelectrics and light scattering spectroscopy; critical phenomena. Mailing Add: Dept of Physics City Col of New York New York NY 10031

CUMMINS, JACK D, b Shreveport, La, Dec 28, 39; m 60; c 2. INORGANIC CHEMISTRY. Educ: Western State Col Colo, BA, 61; Univ MNex, MS, 66, PhD(inorg chem), 67. Prof Exp: Asst prof, 66-74, PROF CHEM, METROP STATE COL, 74-, CHMN DEPT, 71- Concurrent Pos: Res grant, Educ Media Inst, Univ Colo, 67-68; fel, Univ Mo, St Louis, 69-70. Mem: Am Chem Soc. Res: Study of bonding by characterization and preparation of boron hydrides and boronium cations; x-ray crystallography of amalgams. Mailing Add: Dept of Chem Metrop State Col Denver CO 80204

CUMMINS, JAMES NELSON, b Dix, Ill, Jan 22, 25; m 48; c 5. POMOLOGY, PLANT MORPHOGENESIS. Educ: Univ Ill, BS, 48; Southern Ill Univ, MS, 60, PhD(bot), 65; Univ Wis, MS, 61. Prof Exp: Exec secy, Ill Fruit Coun, 48-50; self employed orchardist, 53-55; instr, Anna-Jonesboro High Sch, Ill, 55-57 & Mt Vernon High Sch & Mt Vernon Community Col, 57-60; asst prof sci educ, Southern Ill Univ, 61-67; ASSOC PROF POMOL, NY STATE AGR EXP STA, CORNELL UNIV, 67- Honors & Awards: Shepard Award, Am Pomol Soc, 80. Mem: Am Soc Hort Sci; Am Pomol Soc; Int Soc Hort Sci. Res: Breeding, testing and development of rootstocks for deciduous fruit trees; rhizogenesis in stem tissues of woody plants; virus diseases of deciduous fruit trees. Mailing Add: Hedrick Hall New York State Agr Exp Sta Geneva NY 14456

CUMMINS, JOSEPH E, b Whitefish, Mont, Feb 5, 33; m 62; c 1. GENETICS, CELL BIOLOGY. Educ: Washington State Univ, BS, 55; Univ Wis, PhD(bot), 62. Prof Exp: NIH res fel zool, Univ Edinburgh, 62-64; cancer res, McArdle Lab, Univ Wis, 64-66; asst prof biol sci, Rutgers Univ, 66-67; asst prof zool, Univ Wash, 67-72; asst prof, 72-76, ASSOC PROF PLANT SCI, UNIV WESTERN ONT, 72- Concurrent Pos: Fel, Karolinska Inst, Stockholm, Sweden, 69. Mem: Am 76- Cell Biol; Brit Biochem Soc; Genetics Soc Am; Environ Mutagens Soc; Can Genetics Soc. Res: Cell cycle; morphogenesis; environmental mutagenesis. Mailing Add: Dept of Plant Sci Univ of Western Ont London Can

CUMMINS, KENNETH BURDETTE, b New Washington, Ohio, July 27, 11. MATHEMATICS. Educ: Ohio Wesleyan Univ, AB, 33; Bowling Green State Univ, MA, 39; Ohio State Univ, PhD(math educ), 58. Prof Exp: Teacher pub schs, Ohio, 33-40, 41-55, 56-57; from asst prof to prof math, 57-81, chmn dept, 64-65, EMER PROF MATH, KENT STATE UNIV, 81- Honors & Awards: G O Higley Award, Ohio Wesleyan Univ, 33. Mem: Am Math Asn. Res: Methodology in the teaching of collegiate and high school mathematics; an experiential approach to mathematics education. Mailing Add: 421 S Center St New Washington OH 44854

CUMMINS, KENNETH WILLIAM, b Chicago, Ill, Mar 28, 33; div; c 2. LIMNOLOGY. Educ: Lawrence Col, BA, 55; Univ Mich, MS, 57, PhD(zool), 61. Prof Exp: Instr zool, Univ Mich, 60-61; asst prof biol sci, Northwestern Univ, 61-62 & biol, Univ Pittsburgh, 62-68; prof biol, Kellogg Biol Lab, Mich State Univ, 68-78; PROF FISHERIES & WILDLIFE, ORE STATE UNIV, 78- Concurrent Pos: Prin investr, USPHS res grant, 63-, AEC res grant, 66- & NSF res grants, 70-; chmn water ecosysts, Inst Ecol, 73-; aquatics ed, Ecol Soc Am, 74- Mem: Ecol Soc Am; Am Soc Limnol & Oceanog; Brit Freshwater Biol Asn; Int Asn Theoret & Appl Limnol. Res: Structure and function of stream ecosystems. Mailing Add: Dept Fisheries & Wildlife Ore State Univ Corvallis OR 97331

CUMMINS, LARRY BILL, b Uvalde, Tex, Nov 18, 41; m 62; c 1. VETERINARY MEDICINE. Educ: Tex A&M Univ, BS, 70, DVM, 71. Prof Exp: Resident vet, Yerkes Regional Primate Res Ctr, 71-73; vet, Atlanta Zool Garden & Emory Univ, 73-74; ASSOC FOUND VET, SOUTHWEST FOUND RES & EDUC, 74- Concurrent Pos: Vet consult, Atlanta Zool Garden, 74- & San Antonio Zool Garden, 75- Mem: Am Vet Med Asn; Am Asn Lab Animal Sci; Am Asn Zoo Vets; Am Asn Primatologists; Am Soc Lab Animal Practitioners. Res: Infectious diseases of nonhuman primates; clinical medicine of zoologic animals. Mailing Add: Southwest Found for Res & Educ 8848 W Commerce at Loop 410 San Antonio TX 78284

CUMMINS, RICHARD L, b Sullivan, Ill, Aug 1, 29; m 60; c 3. ELECTRICAL ENGINEERING. Educ: Univ Ill, BS, 53, MS, 59, PhD(elec eng), 62. Prof Exp: Jr elec engr, Res Lab, Cook Elec Co, 54-55; sr elec engr, 55-58; asst, Digital Comput Lab, Univ Ill, 58-62, res assoc, 62-63; asst prof, 63-80, ASSOC PROF ELECTRONIC ENG, OKLA STATE UNIV, 80- Mem: Inst Elec & Electronics Engrs. Res: Graph theory; network topology and synthesis; digital computer applications; minicomputers. Mailing Add: 910 Lakeridge Dr Stillwater OK 74074

CUMMINS, RICHARD WILLIAMSON, b Allen, Mich, May 10, 20; m 43; c 2. SYNTHETIC ORGANIC CHEMISTRY. Educ: Univ Mich, BS, 42; Polytech Inst Brooklyn, MS, 46, PhD(chem), 53. Prof Exp: Res chemist, Westvaco Mineral Prod Div, Food Mach & Chem Corp, 42-64, sr res chemist, RES ASSOC, 78-; FMC Corp, 64-68, res assoc, 68-73, sr res assoc, 73-78, RES ASSOC, FMC CORP, 78-, INTERNAL CONSULT, 81- Mem: Am Chem Soc. Res: Organic synthesis reaction mechanisms; organic phosphorus compounds; triazine chemistry; detergent builders; flame retardants functional fluids. Mailing Add: FMC Corp PO Box 8 Princeton NJ 08540

CUMMINS, STEWART EDWARD, b Elkhart, Ind, July 7, 32; m 56; c 4. ELECTRONIC ENGINEERING, MATERIALS SCIENCE. Educ: Purdue Univ, BSEE, 56, MSEE, 57. Prof Exp: Proj engr, US Air Force Electronic Technol Lab, 57-61, proj engr electronic mat, 61-67, sr res scientist ferroelec, 67-72, sr res scientist memory technol, 72-74, TECH PROG MGR MAGNETIC BUBBLE MEMORY, US AIR FORCE AVIONICS LAB, 74- Honors & Awards: Eng Achievement Award, Dayton Eng Joint Coun, 66; Res Award, Res Soc Am, 67; Burka Award, Air Force Avionics Lab, 72. Mem: Inst Elec & Electronics Engrs; Sigma Xi. Res: Memory devices including ferroelectric and related materials; applied physics; optical devices. Mailing Add: Air Force Avionics Lab/DHE-2 Wright-Patterson AFB OH 45433

CUMMINS, W(ILLIAM) RAYMOND, b Hamilton, Ont, May 9, 44; m 67; c 2. STRESS PHYSIOLOGY, ARCTIC BIOLOGY. Educ: McMaster Univ, BSc, 67; Mich State Univ, PhD(bot & biochem), 72. Prof Exp: Res fel biophys, Stanford Univ, 71-73; asst prof biol, York Univ, Toronto, 73-74; asst prof, 74-79, ASSOC PROF BOT, ERINDALE COL, UNIV TORONTO, 79- Concurrent Pos: Res fel plant physiol, Plant Res Lab, Atomic Energy Comn; consult, Sci Adv Bd, Govt Northwest Territories, 81-82; chmn, Arctic Working Group, Univ Toronto, 81- Mem: Can Soc Plant Physiologists; Am Soc Plant Physiologists; Can Asn Univ Teachers. Res: Responses to cold and drought stress particularly in arctic plants; determine mechanism of thermal acclimation using biophysical techniques; assess limits to agricultural production in arctic and subarctic Canada. Mailing Add: Erindale Col Univ Toronto Rm 3042 Mississauga ON L5L 1C6 Can

CUMMISKEY, CHARLES, b St Louis, Mo, Feb 12, 24. INORGANIC CHEMISTRY. Educ: Dayton Univ, BS, 43; Northwestern Univ, MS, 52; Univ Notre Dame, PhD(chem), 56. Prof Exp: Teacher sec schs, 43-52; assoc, Univ Notre Dame, 53-55; from instr to assoc prof chem, 55-65, head dept, 57-66, vpres & dean faculties, 66-75, PROF CHEM, ST MARY'S UNIV, TEX, 65-, HEAD DEPT, 78- Concurrent Pos: Am Chem Soc vis scientist to sec schs, 62-66; Piper Found prof, 79. Mem: Am Chem Soc; Sigma Xi. Res: Chemical effects of radioactive decay; ion exchange methodology, especially as applied to inorganic analytical separations and complex ions. Mailing Add: Dept of Chem St Mary's Univ San Antonio TX 78284

CUNDALL, DAVID LANGDON, b Altringham, Cheshire, Eng, July 21, 45; Can citizen; m 69; c 1. VERTEBRATE MORPHOLOGY, SYSTEMATICS. Educ: McGill Univ, BSc, 67; Univ Ark, MS, 70, PhD(zool), 74. Prof Exp: Asst prof biol, Va Commonwealth Univ, 74-75; asst prof, 75-80, ASSOC PROF BIOL, LEHIGH UNIV, 80- Mem: AAAS; Am Soc Zool; Am Soc Ichthyologists & Herpetologists; Animal Behav Soc; Soc Syst Zool. Res: Feeding mechanics in squamate reptiles; systematics of snakes; patterns of growth in the snake skull; habitat selection and resource partitioning in snakes. Mailing Add: Dept Biol Lehigh Univ Bethlehem PA 18015

CUNDIFF, JOHN SKELTON, agricultural engineering, see previous edition

CUNDIFF, LARRY VERL, b Abilene, Kans, Dec 9, 39; m 60; c 3. ANIMAL BREEDING, POPULATION GENETICS. Educ: Kans State Univ, BS, 61; Okla State Univ, MS, 64, PhD(animal breeding), 66. Prof Exp: Asst prof animal sci, Univ Ky, 65-67; REGIONAL COORDR & GENETICIST, US MEAT ANIMAL RES CTR, NCENT REGION, AGR RES SERV, USDA, 67-, RES LEADER GENETICS & BREEDING, 76- Concurrent Pos: Prof animal sci, Univ Nebr, Lincoln, 67- Mem: Am Soc Animal Sci. Res: Beef cattle breeding. Mailing Add: US Meat Animal Res Ctr PO Box 166 Clay Center NE 68933

CUNDIFF, MILFORD FIELDS, b Baker, Ore, Dec 7, 36; m 80; c 2. VERTEBRATE PHYSIOLOGY, ECOLOGY. Educ: Univ Colo, BS, 60, PhD(zool), 66. Prof Exp: Teaching assoc biol, Univ Colo, 61-62; from instr to assoc prof, Austin Col, 64-70; ASSOC PROF BIOL & COORDR BIOL SCI, UNIV COLO, BOULDER, 70- Mem: AAAS; Am Inst Biol Sci. Res: Altitude physiology of blood; nuclear activation analysis of trace metals in biological systems. Mailing Add: Ctr Interdisciplinary Studies Univ Colo Box 331 Boulder CO 80309

CUNDIFF, ROBERT HALL, b Winchester, Ky, Apr 10, 22; m 44; c 2. RESEARCH ADMINISTRATION, ANALYTICAL CHEMISTRY. Educ: Univ Ky, BS, 48, MS, 49. Prof Exp: Res chemist, Com Solvents Corp, Ind, 49-52; res chemist, 52-66, head anal serv sect & blends & filter develop sect, 66-70, mgr tobacco prod develop div, 70-76, dir, Tobacco Develop Dept, 76-78, DIR, BLENDS & PROCESSES, R J REYNOLDS TOBACCO CO, 78- Honors & Awards: Philip Morris Award, 67. Mem: Am Chem Soc. Res: Tobacco products development, including chewing and smoking tobacco, cigarettes and filter technology; tobacco processing, blending and flavoring; analytical chemistry of tobacco, tobacco additives and tobacco smoke; development administration. Mailing Add: R J Reynolds Tobacco Co Winston-Salem NC 27102

CUNDY, KENNETH RAYMOND, b Spearfish, SDak, Dec 22, 29; m 57. MEDICAL MICROBIOLOGY, CLINICAL MICROBIOLOGY. Educ: Stanford Univ, BA, 50; Univ Wash, MS, 53; Univ Calif, Davis, PhD(comp path), 65; Am Bd Med Microbiol, dipl, 69. Prof Exp: Res microbiologist, Univ Calif, Berkeley, 57-60; bacteriologist, Gerber Prod Co, Calif, 60-61; res microbiologist, Univ Calif, Davis, 61-65; from instr to assoc prof, 67-71, assoc prof microbiol & immunol, 71-77, PROF MICROBIOL & IMMUNOL, SCH MED, TEMPLE UNIV, 77-, DIR CLIN MICROBIOL LABS, UNIV HOSP & HEALTH SCI CTR, 70- Concurrent Pos: Fel microbiol, Sch Med, Temple Univ, 65-67 & Nat Cystic Fibrosis Res Found, 68-69; assoc dir microbiol, Lab, St Christopher's Hosp Children, 67-68; dir diag microbiol, 68-70. Mem: Fel Am Acad Microbiol; Sigma Xi; AAAS; Am Soc Microbiol; NY Acad Sci. Res: Mechanisms of pathogenicity as related to microorganisms, particularly with reference to Pseudomonas and anaerobes; infectious diseases and their laboratory diagnosis. Mailing Add: Dept of Microbiol & Immunol Temple Univ Sch of Med Philadelphia PA 19140

CUNHA, TONY JOSEPH, b Los Banos, Calif, Aug 22, 16; m 41; c 3. ANIMAL HUSBANDRY, NUTRITION. *Educ:* Utah State Agr Col, BS, 40, MS, 41; Univ Wis, PhD(animal nutrit), 44. *Prof Exp:* From instr to assoc prof animal husb, State Col Wash, 44-48; prof animal sci & head dept, Univ Fla, 48-75; dean, Sch Agr, 75-80, EMER DEAN, CALIF POLYTECH UNIV, 80-, UNIV CONSULT AGR, 80- *Concurrent Pos:* Am Soc Animal Sci res award, 68-; chmn swine nutrient requirements comt, Nat Res Coun, 65-75, chmn animal nutrit comt, 72-76; mem, White House Conf on Food, Nutrit & Health, 69; consult, Univ Tenn-AEC, Oak Ridge & USDA Meat Animal Res Ctr, Nebr. *Mem:* AAAS; Am Soc Animal Sci (vpres, 61, pres, 62); Soc Exp Biol & Med; Am Inst Nutrit. *Res:* Nutrition and feeding of swine, beef, cattle, sheep, horses and small animals. *Mailing Add:* Dean Sch of Agr Calif Polytech Univ Pomona CA 91769

CUNIA, TIBERIUS, b Edessa, Greece, Jan 10, 26; US citizen; m 57; c 4. STATISTICS. *Educ:* McGill Univ, MSc, 57. *Prof Exp:* Forester mensuration, Can Int Paper Co, 51-52, forest opers, 52-54, comput appln, 54-58, forest statistician, 58-68; prof forest mensuration & statist, 68-70, PROF STATIST & OPERS RES, STATE UNIV NY COL FORESTRY, SYRACUSE 70- *Mem:* Am Statist Asn; Biomet Soc; Can Inst Forestry; Soc Am Foresters. *Res:* Forest mensuration and biomass inventory; applications of the statistical methodology, operations research methods and computers to forestry problems; experimental designs in pulp and paper. *Mailing Add:* State Univ NY Col Environ & Forestry Syracuse NY 13210

CUNICO, ROBERT FREDERICK, b Detroit, Mich, Feb 25, 41; m 66. ORGANIC CHEMISTRY. *Educ:* Univ Detroit, BS, 62; Purdue Univ, PhD(organosilicon chem), 66. *Prof Exp:* Res assoc with Dr Melvin S Newman, Ohio State Univ, 66-68; from asst prof to assoc prof, 68-81, PROF CHEM, NORTHERN ILL UNIV, 81- *Mem:* Am Chem Soc. *Res:* Organosilicon chemistry; synthetic methods in organic chemistry. *Mailing Add:* Dept of Chem Northern Ill Univ De Kalb IL 60115

CUNKLE, CHARLES HENRY, b Ft Smith, Ark, May 28, 15; m 49; c 2. MATHEMATICS. *Educ:* Ind Univ, AB, 38; La State Univ, MA, 41; Univ Mo, PhD(math), 55. *Prof Exp:* Instr math, Agr & Mech Col, Univ Tex, 41-42; adv, US Mil Govt, Ger, 47-49; instr math, La State Univ, 49-51 & Univ Mo, 51-55; asst prof, Univ Idaho, 55-56; sr res engr, Convair, Calif, 56-57; asst prof math, Colo State Univ, 57-58; res mathematician, Aeronaut Lab, Cornell Univ, 58-59; assoc prof math, Utah State Univ, 59-63; prof & chmn dept, Clarkson Col Technol, 63-65; prof, Kans State Univ, 65-67; chmn dept, 67-71, prof math, 71-80, EMER PROF, SLIPPERY ROCK STATE COL, 80- *Concurrent Pos:* Mathematician, Ballistics Res Labs, 58. *Mem:* Am Math Soc; Math Asn Am. *Res:* Topology; Boolean algebras. *Mailing Add:* Dept of Math Slippery Rock State Col Slippery Rock PA 16057

CUNLIFFE, HARRY R, veterinary immunology, animal virology, deceased

CUNNEA, WILLIAM M, b Chicago, Ill, Oct 31, 27; m 71. MATHEMATICS, ALGEBRA. *Educ:* Univ Chicago, PhB, 46, MS, 56; Univ Calif, Berkeley, PhD(math), 62. *Prof Exp:* Asst prof, 61-66, ASSOC PROF MATH, WASH STATE UNIV, 66- *Concurrent Pos:* Vis scholar, Univ Victoria, 68-69. *Mem:* AAAS; Math Asn Am; Am Math Soc. *Res:* Ideal and valuation theory; algebraic geometry; lattice theory; history of mathematics. *Mailing Add:* Dept Math Wash State Univ Pullman WA 99164

CUNNIFF, PATRICIA A, b Washington, DC, Dec 6, 38; m 60; c 4. PHYSICAL CHEMISTRY. *Educ:* Dunbarton Col Holy Cross, BA, 59; Univ Md, College Park, MS, 62, PhD(phys chem), 72. *Prof Exp:* Ed asst, Anal Chem, Am Chem Soc, 61-62; from asst prof to assoc prof, 72-79, PROF CHEM, PRINCE GEORGE'S COMMUNITY COL, 79-, PRES, FAC ORGN, 81- *Mem:* AAAS; Am Chem Soc; Sigma Xi. *Res:* Academic education in chemistry; instrumental analysis; energy education. *Mailing Add:* Prince George's Community Col Largo MD 20870

CUNNIFF, PATRICK F, b New York, NY, Oct 25, 33; m 60; c 4. ENGINEERING MECHANICS. *Educ:* Manhattan Col, BCE, 55; Va Polytech Inst, MS, 57, PhD(eng mech), 62. *Prof Exp:* Res engr, Mech Div, US Naval Res Lab, 60-63; from asst prof to assoc prof, 63-69, PROF MECH ENG, UNIV MD, 69-, CHMN DEPT, 75- *Mem:* Am Soc Mech Engrs; Am Soc Eng Educ. *Res:* Structural response to shock and vibration excitations; nonlinear vibrations; acoustics and noise pollution problems. *Mailing Add:* Dept of Mech Eng Univ of Md College Park MD 20742

CUNNING, JOE DAVID, b Mt Ayr, Iowa, May 31, 36; m 63; c 2. CHEMICAL ENGINEERING. *Educ:* Iowa State Univ, BS, 58, MS, 62, PhD(chem eng), 65. *Prof Exp:* Engr, E I du Pont de Nemours & Co, SC, 58-60, res engr, Va, 65-67, supvr res & develop, 67-70, sr supvr, 70-73, supt, 73-78, MFG MGR, E I DU PONT DE NEMOURS & CO, WILMINGTON, 78- *Mem:* Am Inst Chem Engrs; Am Chem Soc. *Res:* Textile fiber research and development; polymerization processes; product development; heat transfer on fiber processing; reaction kinetics; distillation; nylon and polyester fiber development. *Mailing Add:* E I du Pont de Nemours & Co Nemours Bldg Wilmington DE 19898

CUNNINGHAM, ALICE JEANNE, b Walnut Ridge, Ark, Sept 23, 37. ELECTROCHEMISTRY, POLAROGRAPHY. *Educ:* Univ Ark, BA, 59; Emory Univ, PhD(chem), 66. *Prof Exp:* Chemist, Layne Res, Tenn, 59; instr chem, Brenau Acad, 59-61 & Atlanta Pub Schs, 61-62; vis asst prof, Agnes Scott Col, 66-67; res assoc, Univ Tex, 67-68; from asst prof to assoc prof, 72-80, PROF CHEM, AGNES SCOTT COL, 80-, CHMN DEPT, 78- *Mem:* AAAS; Am Chem Soc (secy, Div Anal Chem, 78-); Sigma Xi; Electrochem Soc. *Res:* Electrochemistry of pyridine nucleotides, ribonuclease, indophenols and ferredoxin; mechanisms of biological oxidation-reduction reactions; free radical intermediates in electro-organic chemistry. *Mailing Add:* Dept of Chem Agnes Scott Col Decatur GA 30030

CUNNINGHAM, BRUCE ARTHUR, b Winnebago, Ill, Jan 18, 40; m 65; c 2. BIOCHEMISTRY. *Educ:* Univ Dubuque, BS, 62; Yale Univ, PhD(biochem), 66. *Prof Exp:* NSF fel biochem, 66-68, asst prof, 68-71, assoc prof biochem, 71-78, PROF MOLECULAR & CELL BIOL, ROCKEFELLER UNIV, 78- *Honors & Awards:* Career Scientist, Irma T Hirschl Trust, 75. *Mem:* AAAS; Am Chem Soc; Am Asn Immunologists; Am Soc Biol Chemists; Harvey Soc. *Res:* Structure and function of cell-surface proteins; structure of antibodies; primary structure of proteins. *Mailing Add:* Dept of Molecular & Cell Biol Rockefeller Univ New York NY 10021

CUNNINGHAM, BRYCE A, b Brainerd, Minn, June 21, 32; m 56; c 4. BIOCHEMISTRY. *Educ:* Univ Minn, BA, 55, BS, 58, PhD(biochem), 63. *Prof Exp:* Asst prof, 63-72, ASSOC PROF BIOCHEM, KANS STATE UNIV, 72- *Mem:* AAAS; Am Chem Soc. *Res:* Enzyme chemistry; peroxidases. *Mailing Add:* Dept of Biochem Kans State Univ Manhattan KS 66502

CUNNINGHAM, CHARLES EVERETT, b Washburn, Maine, Dec 21, 24; m 45; c 3. PLANT GENETICS, AGRONOMY. *Educ:* Univ Maine, BS, 48, MS, 52; Univ Wis, PhD(genetics), 62. *Prof Exp:* Asst agronomist, Univ Maine, 49-55, asst prof agron, 55-57; plant geneticist, Red Dot Foods, Inc, Wis, 57-61; dir vegetable res, 79, GENETICIST, CAMPBELL SOUP CO, 62-, VPRES PIONEER RES, 76- *Mem:* hon mem Potato Asn Am (secy, 63-65, vpres, 66, pres, 68). *Res:* Nutrition and culture of the potato; development of new potato varieties for processing. *Mailing Add:* Campbell Inst Res & Technol Campbell Pl Camden NJ 08101

CUNNINGHAM, CHARLES HENRY, b Washington, DC, Apr 12, 13; m 40; c 4. VETERINARY MICROBIOLOGY. *Educ:* Univ Md, BS, 34; Iowa State Univ, MS, 37, DVM, 38; Mich State Univ, PhD, 53; Am Bd Med Microbiol, dipl; Am Col Vet Microbiol, dipl. *Prof Exp:* Asst prof & vet inspector, Univ Md, 38-42; assoc prof poultry husb, Univ RI, 42-45; assoc prof microbiol & pub health, 45-54, prof, 54-78, EMER PROF MICROBIOL & PUB HEALTH, MICH STATE UNIV, 78- *Concurrent Pos:* Consult vet microbiol, Univ Tenn Int Agr Prog; consult, vet virology, Food Agr Org, 78; mem, Food Agr Orgn Prog, WHO, 71-78. *Mem:* Fel AAAS; Am Asn Avian Path; NY Acad Sci; Am Soc Microbiol; Am Vet Med Asn. *Res:* Virology; veterinary virology; animal diseases. *Mailing Add:* 612 Snyder Rd East Lansing MI 48823

CUNNINGHAM, CLARENCE MARION, b Cooper, Tex, July 24, 20; m 51; c 4. PHYSICAL CHEMISTRY. *Educ:* Agr & Mech Col Tex, BS, 42; Univ Calif, MS, 48; Ohio State Univ, PhD(chem), 54. *Prof Exp:* Instr chem, Calif State Polytech Col, 48-49; cryogenic engr, AEC Proj, 52; consult, Herrick L Johnston, Inc, 53; ASSOC PROF CHEM, OKLA STATE UNIV, 54- *Mem:* AAAS; Am Chem Soc; Am Phys Soc; Am Asn Univ Prof. *Res:* Theoretical and experimental investigation of physical absorption of gases on solid surfaces at low temperatures; thermodynamic properties of nonaqueous solutions. *Mailing Add:* Dept Chem Okla State Univ Stillwater OK 74074

CUNNINGHAM, DAVID A, b Toronto, Ont, Mar 18, 37; m 61; c 3. PHYSIOLOGY. *Educ:* Univ Western Ont, BA, 60; Univ Alta, MSc, 63; Univ Mich, PhD(phys educ, physiol), 66. *Prof Exp:* Res assoc epidemiol, Univ Mich, 66-69; assoc prof, 69-80, PROF PHYSIOL & PHYS EDUC, UNIV WESTERN ONT, 80- *Concurrent Pos:* Res assoc, Dept Nat Health & Welfare, Can, 69-72. *Mem:* Am Physiol Soc; Can Physiol Soc; Can Asn Sports Sci. *Res:* Physiology of exercise with special interest in the relationship of heart disease and physical activity. *Mailing Add:* Dept of Physiol Univ of Western Ont London ON N6A 3K7 Can

CUNNINGHAM, DAVID KENNETH, b Victoria, BC, Feb 28, 20; m 49. AGRICULTURAL BIOCHEMISTRY. *Educ:* Univ BC, BA, 41; Univ Minn, PhD(biochem), 53. *Prof Exp:* Chemist, Defense Industs, 41-43 & Grain Res Lab, 45-58; tech mgr refrig res & develop, 58-64, res assoc methods & develop, 64-68, RES ASSOC CORP RES, PILLSBURY CO, 69- *Mem:* Am Chem Soc; Am Asn Cereal Chem; NY Acad Sci. *Res:* Cereal and analytical chemistry; flour quality and improving agents; physical properties of doughs; chemistry of leavening agents. *Mailing Add:* 4830 Grand Ave S Minneapolis MN 55409

CUNNINGHAM, DENNIS DEAN, b Des Moines, Iowa, Aug 16, 39. CELL BIOLOGY, BIOCHEMISTRY. *Educ:* State Univ Iowa, BA, 61; Univ Chicago, PhD(biochem), 67. *Prof Exp:* From asst prof to assoc prof, 70-78, PROF MED MICROBIOL, COL MED, UNIV CALIF, IRVINE, 78- *Concurrent Pos:* NSF res fel, Princeton Univ, 67-70; USPHS res grant, 71. *Res:* Control of cell division in cultured fibroblasts. *Mailing Add:* Dept of Med Microbiol Univ of Calif Col of Med Irvine CA 92717

CUNNINGHAM, DONALD EUGENE, b Providence, RI, May 18, 30; m 57; c 2. PHYSICS. *Educ:* Brown Univ, AB, 51; Case Univ, MA, 54, PhD(physics), 59. *Prof Exp:* Instr physics, Case Univ, 53-57; plasma physics group leader, Thompson Ramo Wooldridge, Inc, 57-59; dir vis scientist progs, Am Inst Physics, 59-62; asst prof physics & asst dir inst sci & math, Adelphi Univ, 62-63; assoc prof physics & dir progs space related sci, 63-66; prof physics & dean res, Miami Univ, 66-70; spec asst to dir, NSF, Washington, DC, 70-74; sr res scientist, Res Inst, 74-77, DIR, CTR PUB ISSUES, UNIV DENVER, 77- *Concurrent Pos:* Res engr, Westinghouse Elec Co, 54; consult, Thompson Ramo Wooldridge, Inc, 59-61, Mayer & Sklar, Inc, 61 & Am Inst Physics, 62-; lectr, Manhattan Col, 61-62; dir, NSF High Sch Teacher Inst, 62; chmn vis scientist prog high schs, NY, 63-66; prin investr, NASA Grant, 63-67. *Mem:* Am Phys Soc; Am Asn Physics Teachers; fel AAAS. *Res:* Atomic collision processes; optical pumping techniques; plasma and low temperature physics; magnetism; impacts of resource development on a regional bases. *Mailing Add:* 6660 S Piney Creek Circle Denver CO 80210

CUNNINGHAM, DOROTHY J, b Jersey City, NJ, Nov 7, 27. PHYSIOLOGY. *Educ:* Caldwell Col Women, BA, 49; Cath Univ, MS, 51; Yale Univ, PhD(physiol), 66. *Prof Exp:* Res asst physiol, Sch Med, Univ Pa, 57-58; asst prof biol sci, Montclair State Col, 58-62; fel epidemiol & pub health & environ physiol, Sch Med, Yale Univ, 66-67, lectr, 67-69, asst prof, 69-70, asst fel, John B Pierce Found Lab, 66-70; assoc prof, Sch Health Sci, 70-74, PROF PHYSIOL, SCH HEALTH SCI, HUNTER COL, 75- *Concurrent Pos:* Lectr dept community med, Div Environ Med, Mt Sinae Sch Med, 71-; adj prof environ med, Inst Environ Med, New York Univ Med Ctr, 81- *Mem:* AAAS; Am Physiol Soc; fel NY Acad Sci; assoc fel NY Acad Med; Harvey Soc. *Res:* Temperature regulation; environmental physiology. *Mailing Add:* City Univ New York 440 E 26 St New York NY 10010

CUNNINGHAM, EARLENE BROWN, b Cleveland, Ohio, Aug 27, 30. BIOCHEMISTRY, ORGANIC CHEMISTRY. *Educ:* Univ Ill, BS, 49; Univ Calif, Los Angeles, MS, 51; Univ Southern Calif, PhD(org chem), 54. *Prof Exp:* Asst clin path, Sch Med, Ind Univ, 54-56, res assoc med, 56-59; from asst prof to assoc prof, Col Med, Howard Univ, 59-64; res physiologist, Univ Calif, Berkeley, 66-68; res assoc chem, Univ SC, 68-69, asst prof, 69-70, lectr, 70-71; assoc prof biochem, Med Univ SC, 71-78; ASSOC PROF BIOCHEM, NJ MED SCH, 78- *Honors & Awards:* Lederle Med Fac Award, 61-64. *Mem:* Am Chem Soc. *Res:* Mechanisms by which biological membranes perform their vital or maintenance functions; emphasis upon regulatory processes involving membrane proteins or membrane phospholipids with Ca 2plus and calmodulin or with cyclic adenosine monophosphate and the protein kinase regulatory protein. *Mailing Add:* CMDNJ Dept Biochem NJ Med Sch Newark NJ 07103

CUNNINGHAM, ELLEN M, b Chicago, Ill, June 20, 40. MATHEMATICAL LOGIC. *Educ:* St Mary of the Woods Col, BA, 63; Cath Univ Am, MA, 70; Univ Md, PhD(math), 74. *Prof Exp:* Asst prof, 74-80, ASSOC PROF MATH, ST MARY OF THE WOODS COL, 80- *Mem:* Math Asn Am; Am Math Soc; Nat Coun Teachers Math; Soc Indust & Appl Math; Peace Sci Soc. *Res:* Chain models and infinite-quantifier languages. *Mailing Add:* St Mary of the Woods Col St Mary of the Woods IN 47876

CUNNINGHAM, FAY LAVERE, b Lansing, Mich, July 26, 22; m 48; c 2. CHEMICAL ENGINEERING. *Educ:* Mich State Univ, BS, 48. *Prof Exp:* Mech engr, Manhattan Dist, Mass Inst Technol, 44-46; chem engr, 48-58, res sect head, 58-70, res mgr, Fermentation Pilot Plant, 70-72, RES MGR, CHEM ENG DEVELOP, UPJOHN CO, 72- *Concurrent Pos:* Radiation monitor-opers crossroads, Atomic Energy Comn, 46. *Mem:* AAAS; Am Chem Soc; Am Inst Chem Engrs. *Res:* Chemical and fermentation process development; scale up of organic reactions; separation and purification operations. *Mailing Add:* 4323 Sunset Dr Kalamazoo MI 49008

CUNNINGHAM, FLOYD MITCHELL, b Estherville, Iowa, Nov 13, 31; m 54; c 5. ENGINEERING MECHANICS, AGRICULTURAL ENGINEERING. *Educ:* Iowa State Univ, BS, 53, MS, 57, PhD(agr eng, eng mech), 60. *Prof Exp:* From asst prof to assoc prof agr eng, Va Polytech Inst, 60-66; asst prof eng mech, 66-68, ASSOC PROF ENG MECH, UNIV MO-ROLLA, 68- *Mem:* Am Soc Agr Engrs. *Res:* Design relationships for fertilizer distributors; mechanical aids to apple harvesting; vibration of shells. *Mailing Add:* Dept of Eng Mech Univ of Mo Rolla MO 65401

CUNNINGHAM, FRANCES, b New York, NY. CELL BIOLOGY. *Educ:* Manhattanville Col, BA, 30; Villanova Col, MS, 50; Cath Univ Am, PhD, 56. *Prof Exp:* Teacher, Convents Sacred Heart, 32-52; prof, 52-74, EMER PROF BIOL, NEWTON COL SACRED HEART, 74-; RESEARCHER CYTOL, CLIN FOUND-BROOKS HOSP, 72- *Mem:* Am Soc Cell Biol; Am Soc Cytol. *Res:* Exfoliative cytology; hematology; environmental cytology. *Mailing Add:* Convent of the Sacred Heart 785 Centre St Newton MA 02158

CUNNINGHAM, FRANKLIN E, b Huntington, WVa, Mar 2, 27; m 51; c 5. FOOD SCIENCE, BIOCHEMISTRY. *Educ:* Kans State Univ, BS, 57; Univ Mo, MS, 59, PhD(poultry prod), 63. *Prof Exp:* Res chemist biochem, Western Regional Res Lab, USDA, 63-69; assoc prof, 69-80, PROF ANIMAL SCI, KANS STATE UNIV, 80- *Mem:* Poultry Sci Asn; Inst Food Technol. *Res:* Constituents of poultry and eggs; new and improved food items or processes. *Mailing Add:* Dept Animal Sci Call Hall Kans State Univ Manhattan KS 66502

CUNNINGHAM, FREDERIC, JR, b Cooperstown, NY, Sept 6, 21; m 47; c 3. MATHEMATICS. *Educ:* Harvard Univ, BS, 43, MA, 47, PhD(math), 53. *Prof Exp:* Teaching fel math, Harvard Univ, 47-50; from instr to asst prof, Univ NH, 51-56; lectr, Bryn Mawr Col, 56-57; asst prof, Wesleyan Univ, 57-59; assoc prof, 59-69, PROF MATH, BRYN MAWR COL, 69- *Mem:* AAAS; Am Math Soc; Math Asn Am; Math Soc France. *Res:* L-structure and related structures on Banach spaces. *Mailing Add:* Dept of Math Bryn Mawr Col Bryn Mawr PA 19010

CUNNINGHAM, FREDERICK WILLIAM, b Stamford, Conn, Mar 23, 02; m 41; c 3. PHYSICS. *Educ:* Mass Inst Technol, SB, 24, ScD(physics), 36. *Prof Exp:* Asst physics, Mass Inst Technol, 25-26, res assoc, 26-28; develop engr, Arma Eng Co, Inc, 34-38; develop engr, Arma Corp, 36-44, sr develop engr in chg servomech, 44-48, gen consult, 48-60; PRES, CUNNINGHAM INDUSTS, INC, 53- *Honors & Awards:* Naval Ord Develop Award, 45. *Mem:* Am Phys Soc; Optical Soc Am. *Res:* Automatic spectrophotometers; servomechanisms; illumination for dark adaptation; high intensity searchlights; electrical computers; alternating current potentiometers; non-circular gears; color reproduction. *Mailing Add:* 56 Hubbard Ave Stamford CT 06905

CUNNINGHAM, GEORGE J, b Belfast, N Ireland, Sept 7, 06; m 57. MEDICINE, PATHOLOGY. *Educ:* Univ London, MBBS, 33, MD, 37; FRCP, 63. *Prof Exp:* Sr asst pathologist, Royal Sussex County Hosp, Brighton, 36-42; sr lectr path, St Bartholomew's Hosp, Univ London, 46-55, prof, Royal Col Surgeons, Eng, 55-68; prof, 68-79, chmn, Dept Acad Path, 73-79, EMER PROF PATH, MED COL VA, VA COMMONWEALTH UNIV, 79- *Concurrent Pos:* Med Res Coun traveling fel, 51; vis prof path, State Univ NY Downstate Med Ctr, 62, Cairo Univ, 63 & Univ Ala, Birmingham, 67; mem, Ministry Health Comt Radiation & Cancer Ther, 58-66 & Brit Govt Safety-in-Drugs Comt, 65-68. *Honors & Awards:* Mem mil div, Order of Brit Empire, 45. *Mem:* Int Acad Path (pres, 66-); fel NY Acad Sci; Brit Asn Clin Path (pres, 65-66); Path Soc Gt Brit & Ireland. *Res:* General pathology, especially cellular damage; cancer research, especially cancer of liver and lung. *Mailing Add:* 300 W Franklin Richmond VA 23220

CUNNINGHAM, GEORGE LEWIS, JR, b New Orleans, La, Nov 20, 23; m 53; c 2. PHYSICAL CHEMISTRY. *Educ:* Tulane Univ, BE, 44; Univ Calif, Berkeley, MS, 47, PhD(phys chem), 50. *Prof Exp:* Asst prof chem, La State Univ, 50-53; from assoc prof to prof, Southwest State Col, Okla, 53-61; assoc prof, 61-66, PROF CHEM, EASTERN ILL UNIV, 66- *Mem:* AAAS; Am Chem Soc. *Res:* Microwave spectra; molecular structure; digital computer applications to chemistry. *Mailing Add:* Dept of Chem Eastern Ill Univ Charleston IL 61920

CUNNINGHAM, GLENN N, b Spring City, Tenn, Sept 13, 40; m 62; c 2. BIOCHEMISTRY, NUTRITION. *Educ:* Univ Tenn, Knoxville, BS, 61; NC State Univ, MS, 64, PhD(nutrit, biochem), 66. *Prof Exp:* Fel biochem, Clayton Found Biochem Inst, Univ Tex, Austin, 66-68; asst prof chem, Northeast La State Col, 68-69; from asst prof to assoc prof, 69-78, PROF CHEM, UNIV CENT FLA, 78- *Mem:* AAAS; Am Chem Soc; Am Inst Biol Sci. *Res:* Biochemical regulation; eucaryotic developmental biochemistry. *Mailing Add:* Dept of Chem Univ Cent Fla Orlando FL 32816

CUNNINGHAM, GORDON ROWE, b Oswego, Kans, May 11, 22; m 46; c 3. FORESTRY. *Educ:* Mich State Univ, BS, 48, PhD(forest econ), 66; Pa State Univ, MS, 50. *Prof Exp:* Asst exten forester, Univ Ill, 49-54; from asst prof to assoc prof forestry & exten forester, Cornell Univ, 54-61; asst prof, 63-66, exten forester, 63-80, assoc prof forestry, 66-80, PROF FORESTRY, UNIV WIS-MADISON, 80- *Mem:* Soc Am Foresters. *Res:* Management of small woodlands. *Mailing Add:* Dept of Forestry Univ of Wis Madison WI 53706

CUNNINGHAM, HARRY N, JR, b Imperial, Pa, Mar 7, 35; m 57; c 2. VERTEBRATE ECOLOGY, TERRESTRIAL MICROCOMMUNITIES. *Educ:* Univ Pittsburgh, BS, 55, MS, 60, PhD(ecol), 66. *Prof Exp:* Instr biol, Mt Union Col, 59-61; asst prof, Thiel Col, 63-67, chmn dept, 65-67; asst prof, 67-71, ASSOC PROF BIOL, BEHREND COL, PA STATE UNIV, 71- *Concurrent Pos:* NSF instnl grant, Pa State Univ, 67-; consult, Aquatic Ecol Assocs, 73- *Mem:* Ecol Soc Am; Am Soc Mammal; Am Inst Biol Sci. *Res:* Energy relationships of small mammal populations; aspects of ecology of short-tailed shrew, Blarina brevicauda; lipid changes in small mammals, heavy metals in terrestrial microcommunities. *Mailing Add:* Dept of Biol Behrend Col of Pa State Univ Erie PA 16563

CUNNINGHAM, HOWARD CHARLES, b Philadelphia, Pa, Aug 22, 42. ORGANIC CHEMISTRY. *Educ:* Univ Pa, BS, 64, PhD(org chem), 69. *Prof Exp:* Sr develop chemist, Res Ctr, Lever Bros Co, NJ, 69-71; tech serv rep, Chem Div, Pfizer, Inc, 71-74; mkt res analyst, 74-76, MGR REGULATORY COMPLIANCE, WITCO CHEM CORP, 76- *Mem:* Am Chem Soc. *Res:* Organic synthesis-pharmaceuticals; preparation and evaluation of new actives in detergent formulations; organic specialty chemicals; managing and directing compliance with federal, state and local regulations affecting the chemical industry. *Mailing Add:* 323 W Champlost Ave Philadelphia PA 19120

CUNNINGHAM, HUGH MEREDITH, b Brandon, Man, Dec 28, 27; m 50; c 4. FOOD CHEMISTRY. *Educ:* Univ Man, BSA, 49, MSc, 50; Cornell Univ, PhD(animal nutrit), 53. *Prof Exp:* Res scientist, Can Dept Agr, 53-70; head food additives & contaminants, Food Div, Food & Drug Directorate, 70-79, HEAD TASK FORCE, REASSESSMENT CHEM SAFETY, DEPT NAT HEALTH & WELFARE, 79- *Concurrent Pos:* Res scientist, Inst Animal Physiol, Cambridge, Eng, 67-68. *Mem:* Am Soc Animal Sci; Nutrit Soc Can; Agr Inst Can; Prof Inst Pub Serv Can; Can Soc Animal Prod. *Res:* Lipid biochemistry; physiology; nutrition. *Mailing Add:* Food Div Food & Drug Dir Dept of Nat Health & Welfare Ottawa ON K1A 0L2 Can

CUNNINGHAM, JAMES GORDON, b Pittsburgh, Pa, Dec 13, 40; c 3. NEUROPHYSIOLOGY, NEUROLOGY. *Educ:* Purdue Univ, DVM, 64; Univ Calif, Davis, PhD(physiol), 71. *Prof Exp:* Lectr physiol, Univ Ibadan, 64-66; ASSOC PROF PHYSIOL & NEUROL, MICH STATE UNIV, 72- *Concurrent Pos:* Consult, Peace Corps & Agency for Int Develop. *Mem:* AAAS; Am Vet Neurol Asn; Am Soc Vet Physiol & Pharmacol. *Res:* Neurophysiologic basis of seizures; animal models for epilepsy. *Mailing Add:* Dept of Physiol Mich State Univ East Lansing MI 48824

CUNNINGHAM, JOHN (ROBERT), b Regina, Sask, Jan 5, 27; m 51; c 5. MEDICAL PHYSICS. *Educ:* Univ Sask, BEng, 50, MSc, 51; Univ Toronto, PhD(physics), 55. *Prof Exp:* Physicist, Grain Res Lab, 51-53 & Can Defense Res Bd, 55-58; PHYSICIST, ONT CANCER INST, TORONTO, 58- *Concurrent Pos:* Tech adv to Govt of Ceylon, Int Atomic Energy Agency, 64-65; assoc prof, Physics in Med Biol, 80- *Mem:* Can Asn Physicists; Brit Hosp Physicists Asn; Am Asn Physicists in Med; Can Col Phys Med. *Res:* Scattering absorption and measurement of x-rays, gamma rays; application to medical physics and radiobiology; computer applications in radiotherapy. *Mailing Add:* 6 Marshfield Ct Don Mills ON M3C 2E3 Can

CUNNINGHAM, JOHN CASTEL, b Aberdeen, Scotland, Jan 28, 42; m 68, 81; c 2. INSECT PATHOLOGY. *Educ:* Glasgow Univ, BSc, 64; Oxford Univ, DPhil(insect virol), 67. *Prof Exp:* RES SCIENTIST, FOREST PEST MGT INST, 67- *Mem:* Soc Invert Path; Entom Soc Can. *Res:* Various aspects of insect virology, including use of viruses in forest insect control; safety testing and registration of viruses, formulation and application technology. *Mailing Add:* Forest Pest Mgt Inst Can Forestry Serv PO Box 490 Sault Ste Marie ON P6A 5M7 Can

CUNNINGHAM, JOHN E, b Malone, NY, Apr 18, 31; m 59; c 4. GEOLOGY. *Educ:* Dartmouth Col, AB, 53; Univ Ariz, PhD(geol), 65. *Prof Exp:* Asst geologist, Bear Creek Mining Co, 56, 57 & 68; asst prof geol & anthrop, Eastern NMex Univ, 62-63; geologist, Minerals Br, Superior Oil Co, 63; from asst prof to assoc prof, 64-79, PROF GEOL & ANTHROP, WESTERN NMEX UNIV, 79- *Concurrent Pos:* Consult, Ariz Bur Mines, 79, Amax, 80 & DeKalb, 81. *Mem:* Geol Soc Am. *Res:* Economic and structural geology; geologic map of Circle Mesa Quadrangle, New Mexico. *Mailing Add:* Dept of Phys Sci Western NMex Univ Silver City NM 88061

CUNNINGHAM, JOHN EDWARD, b Chicago, Ill, Mar 18, 20; m 44; c 5. MATERIALS SCIENCE, NUCLEAR MATERIALS TECHNOLOGY. *Educ:* Univ Ill, BS, 44; Univ Tenn, MS, 50. *Prof Exp:* Develop engr aircraft-auto engine components, Thompson Prod, Inc, 44; spec eng detachment construct, Corps Engrs, US Army, 44-46; assoc metallurgist, Clinton Labs, 46-48; supvr reactor technol, Fabrication Lab, 48-55; asst dir, 55-68, ASSOC DIR, METALS & CERAMICS DIV, OAK RIDGE NAT LAB, 68- *Concurrent Pos:* Mem & chmn adv bd, Dept Ceramic Eng, Univ Ill, 73-76; assoc ed, Nuclear Eng Mat Handbook, Am Nuclear Soc & Am Soc Metals, 77- *Honors & Awards:* Cert of Merit, Am Nuclear Soc, 65. *Mem:* Fel Am Nuclear Soc; fel Am Soc Metals; Am Soc Mech Engrs. *Res:* Materials science and engineering related to energy production from nuclear, fossil, solar and geothermal sources; energy transmission, use and conservation; total materials cycle from production of raw materials to use and eventual disposal; metallurgy and physical metallurgical engineering. *Mailing Add:* Oak Ridge Nat Lab PO Box X Oak Ridge TN 37830

CUNNINGHAM, JOHN L, b Tifton, Ga, Sept 2, 35; m 58; c 2. MYCOLOGY, PLANT PATHOLOGY. *Educ:* Bowling Green State Univ, BS, 57; Univ Wis, PhD(plant path), 61. *Prof Exp:* Instr bot, Univ Toledo, 61-62, asst prof, 62-65; res mycologist, Crops Protection Res Br, USDA, 65-69; sr mycologist, Am Type Cult Collection, 70-73; from asst prof to assoc prof biol & chmn, Northwestern Col, 73-77, chmn art & sci div, 73-77; head, Dept Sci, 77-80, PROF BIOL, MARANATHA COL, 77- *Concurrent Pos:* NSF lectr, 62-63, res grant, 63-65; assoc cur fungi, Smithsonian Inst, 66-69; partic, Bredin-Archbold-Smithsonian Biol Surv of Dominica, BWI, 66; mem adv sci comt, Life Sci B, Coun Int Exchange Scholars, 73-76. *Mem:* Am Phytopath Soc; Mycol Soc Am. *Res:* Rusts and other parasitic fungi; taxonomy and evolution of fungi; microfossils. *Mailing Add:* Maranatha Col Box 438 Watertown WI 53094

CUNNINGHAM, LEON WILLIAM, b Columbus, Ga, June 9, 27; m 48; c 3. BIOCHEMISTRY. *Educ:* Auburn Univ, BS, 47; Univ Ill, MS, 49, PhD(biochem), 51. *Prof Exp:* From asst prof to assoc prof, 53-65, assoc dean, 67-72, PROF BIOCHEM, SCH MED, VANDERBILT UNIV, 65-, CHMN DEPT, 72- *Concurrent Pos:* Fel, Dept Biochem, Univ Wash, 51-53; USPHS spec fel, Netherlands Nat Defense Orgn, 61-62; vis staff, Nat Inst Med Res, Mill Hill, London, Eng, 78; vis prof, Dept Physiol Chem, Univ Utrecht, Netherlands, 80. *Mem:* AAAS; NY Acad Sci; Am Chem Soc; Am Soc Biol Chemists. *Res:* Protein structure and function; glycoproteins; enzyme mechanisms; collagens. *Mailing Add:* Dept of Biochem Vanderbilt Univ Sch of Med Nashville TN 37232

CUNNINGHAM, MARY ELIZABETH, b Newark, NJ, Apr 21, 31. FLUID DYNAMICS. *Educ:* Mt Holyoke Col, AB, 53; Univ Ill, MS, 55; Univ Ore, PhD(physics), 64; Univ Conn, MD, 82. *Prof Exp:* Sr physicist, Lawrence Livermore Lab, 64-78. *Concurrent Pos:* Reviewer, Am J Physics, Am Phys Soc, 75- *Mem:* Am Phys Soc; NY Acad Sci; AAAS; Am Med Asn; Sigma Xi. *Res:* High temperatures fluid dynamics, 1, 2, and 3 dimensional computer codes for work in this field. *Mailing Add:* Box 503 Univ Conn Health Ctr Farmington CT 06032

CUNNINGHAM, MICHAEL PAUL, b St John, NB, Mar 5, 43; m 66; c 1. PHOTOCHEMISTRY, PHOTOGRAPHIC CHEMISTRY. *Educ:* St Francis Xavier Univ, BSc, 64; McGill Univ, MSc, 69, PhD(chem), 71. *Prof Exp:* Indust fel, Bristol Meyers Corp, 70-71; CHEMIST, EASTMAN KODAK CO RES LABS, 71- *Res:* Organic photochemistry; chemistry of light-sensitive polymers; photo-imaging processes; photographic sensitizing dyes and dye forming processes. *Mailing Add:* 180 Parklands Dr Rochester NY 14616

CUNNINGHAM, NEWLIN BUCHANAN, b Boone's Path, Va, July 15, 17; m 47; c 4. INDUSTRIAL CHEMISTRY, FIBERS INTERMEDIATES. *Educ:* Emory & Henry Col, BS, 38; WVa Univ, MS, 63. *Prof Exp:* Chemist, 38-43, asst chief chemist, 43-70, sr chemist, 70-80, STAFF CHEMIST, BELLE WORKS, E I DU PONT DE NEMOURS & CO, INC, 80- *Mem:* AAAS; Am Chem Soc. *Res:* Analytical chemistry; waste treatment. *Mailing Add:* 1531 Bedford Rd Charleston WV 25314

CUNNINGHAM, PAUL THOMAS, b Newton, Iowa, Oct 16, 36; m 61; c 3. PHYSICAL CHEMISTRY. *Educ:* Univ Idaho, BS, 58; San Diego State Col, MS, 65; Univ Calif, Berkeley, PhD(phys chem), 68. *Prof Exp:* Mem staff, 68-75, group leader, environ chem, 75-76, head anal & environ sect, 77-81, MGR ANAL CHEM LAB, CHEM ENG DIV, ARGONNE NAT LAB, 77- *Mem:* Optical Soc Am; Am Chem Soc; AAAS. *Res:* Atmospheric chemistry; chemical analysis of airborne particulates; sulfur emission control chemistry; molecular spectroscopy; chemical kinetics of reactions related to environmental pollution; analytical chemistry. *Mailing Add:* Chem Eng Div Argonne Nat Lab Argonne IL 60439

CUNNINGHAM, PETER JOHN, animal breeding, see previous edition

CUNNINGHAM, RICHARD G(REENLAW), b Olney, Ill, Sept 23, 21; m 44; c 3. MECHANICAL ENGINEERING, RESEARCH ADMINISTRATION. *Educ:* Northwestern Univ, BS, 43, MS, 47, PhD, 50. *Prof Exp:* Res engr, Res & Develop Labs, Pure Oil Co, 50-51; proj engr, Dept of Eng Res, Pa State Univ, 51-52, assoc prof eng res, 52-54; res group leader, Wood River Res Labs, Shell Oil Co, 54-56, res group leader, 56-60, sr res engr, Mfg Res Dept, 60-61; head dept, 62-71, chmn univ fac senate, 67-68, PROF MECH ENG, PA STATE UNIV, 61-, VPRES RES & GRAD STUDIES, 71-, SPEC ASST TO PRES FOR COMPUT & INFO SYSTS, 81- *Concurrent Pos:* Vpres for educ, Am Soc Mech Engrs, 73-75. *Honors & Awards:* L P Moody Award, Am Soc Mech Engrs, 74. *Mem:* Fel AAAS; Am Soc Mech Engrs; Am Soc Eng Educ. *Res:* Fluid mechanics; jet pumps; cavitation; two-phase flow. *Mailing Add:* 207 Old Main Bldg Pa State Univ University Park PA 16802

CUNNINGHAM, ROBERT ASHLEY, b Lovington, NMex, May 24, 23; m 48; c 6. MECHANICAL ENGINEERING. *Educ:* Rice Inst, BS, 49, MS, 55. *Prof Exp:* Proj engr design, 50-52, asst develop engr, 53-58, res engr, Drilling Res, 59-70, dir prog res, 70-78, DIR, ADVANCED TECHNOL PROJS & DIV LIAISON, HUGHES TOOL CO, 78- *Mem:* Am Inst Mining, Metall & Petrol Engrs; Soc Petrol Engrs; Am Petrol Inst. *Res:* Lubrication; drilling research; physical properties of solids; theory of fracture of brittle materials; resistance of brittle materials to impact; theory of plasticity; new product development and improvement. *Mailing Add:* Hughes Tool Co PO Box 2539 Houston TX 77001

CUNNINGHAM, ROBERT ELWIN, b Parkersburg, WVa, Mar 16, 29; m 54; c 2. POLYMER CHEMISTRY. *Educ:* WVa Univ, BS, 51, PhD(chem), 55. *Prof Exp:* Instr WVa Univ, 54; sr res chemist, 55-75, RES SCIENTIST, GOODYEAR TIRE & RUBBER CO, 75- *Mem:* Am Chem Soc. *Res:* Stereospecific polymerizations of olefins and diolefins; anionic polymerizations initiated by lithium alkyls; preparation and properties of block polymers using anionic techniques. *Mailing Add:* 342 Kenilworth Dr Akron OH 44313

CUNNINGHAM, ROBERT GAIL, b Manton, Mich, July 2, 28; m 47; c 2. SURFACE PHYSICS, SOLID STATE PHYSICS. *Educ:* Mich State Univ, BS, 50, PhD(physics), 57. *Prof Exp:* Res physicist, Eastman Kodak Res Labs, 57-69, sr engr, Eastman Kodak Eng Div, 69-77, SR TECHNOLOGIST, TECHNOL DIV, EASTMAN KODAK, 77- *Res:* Static electrification of photographic materials. *Mailing Add:* Bldg 23 Eastman Kodak Co Kodak Park Rochester NY 14650

CUNNINGHAM, ROBERT LESTER, b Fullerton, Nebr, July 6, 29; m; c 4. SOIL GENESIS & MORPHOLOGY. *Educ:* Univ Nebr, BS, 59, MS, 61; Wash State Univ, PhD(soil genesis & morphol), 64. *Prof Exp:* Res asst soil genesis, Wash State Univ, 60-64; asst prof soil technol, 64-68; assoc prof, 68-74, PROF SOIL GENESIS & MORPHOL, PA STATE UNIV, 74- *Mem:* Soc Conserv Soc Am; Soil Sci Soc Am. *Res:* Movement of soil materials; arrangement of genetic soil parts; relationships of soils to the ecosystem of which they are a part; characteristics, interpretations and use of Pennsylvania soils; micromorphology examination of certain soil features; application of remote sensing techniques in differentiating soils in the field. *Mailing Add:* 311 Tyson Bldg Pa State Univ University Park PA 16802

CUNNINGHAM, ROBERT M, b Boston, Mass, July 1, 19; m 45; c 3. METEOROLOGY. *Educ:* Mass Inst Technol, SB, 42, ScD(meteorol), 52. *Prof Exp:* Instr meteorol instruments, Mass Inst Technol, 42-43, asst meteorol, 43-46, res assoc, 46-52; proj scientist, 52-61, br chief, 61-74, SR SCIENTIST METEOROL, AIR FORCE GEOPHYSICS LAB, 74- *Concurrent Pos:* Mem, Nat Adv Comt Aeronaut Subcomt Icing, 52-57; mem, Weather Modification Panel, World Meteorol Orgn, 66- *Mem:* Am Meteorol Soc; Am Geophys Union; Royal Meteorol Soc. *Res:* Physics of the atmosphere; cloud physics; particle size; water content; cloud dynamics; airborne meteorological instrumentation; weather erosion effects on high speed flight. *Mailing Add:* Meteorol Div L G Hanscom AFB Bedford MA 01731

CUNNINGHAM, ROBERT STEPHEN, b Springfield, Mo, June 28, 42; m 64. MATHEMATICS, COMPUTER SCIENCE. *Educ:* Drury Col, BA, 64; Univ Ore, MA, 66, PhD(math), 69. *Prof Exp:* Asst prof math, Univ Kans, 69-74; ASSOC PROF MATH & COMPUT SCI, BIRMINGHAM-SOUTHERN COL, 74- *Mem:* Asn Comput Mach. *Res:* Noncommutative ring theory; coding theory. *Mailing Add:* Dept Comput Sci Birmingham-Southern Col Birmingham AL 35204

CUNNINGHAM, ROY THOMAS, entomology, see previous edition

CUNNINGHAM, THOMAS B, b Washington, DC, May 8, 46; m 68; c 2. AEROSPACE ENGINEERING, AUTOMATIC CONTROL SYSTEMS. *Educ:* Univ Nebr, BS, 69; Purdue Univ, MS, 72, PhD(eng), 73. *Prof Exp:* RES ENGR AUTOMATIC CONTROL, HONEYWELL INC, 73- *Concurrent Pos:* Adj prof, Univ Minn, 78- *Mem:* Sigma Xi; Am Inst Aeronaut & Astronaut; Inst Elec & Electronics Engrs. *Res:* Applications of modern control and estimation theory to aerospace and industrial problems. *Mailing Add:* 1598 21st Ave NW New Brighton MN 55112

CUNNINGHAM, VIRGIL DWAYNE, b Artesian, SDak, Nov 29, 30; m 56; c 1. ENTOMOLOGY, PLANT PATHOLOGY. *Educ:* NDak State Univ, BS, 58, MS, 60; Iowa State Univ, PhD(entom), 63. *Prof Exp:* Entomologist, 63-69, supvr entom, 69-70, dept head entom, 70-74, develop mgr animal health, 74-78, DIR DEVELOP, BIOL SCI RES CTR, SHELL DEVELOP CO, 78- *Mem:* Entom Soc Am; Sigma Xi. *Res:* Agricultural chemicals; insecticides, herbicides and plant growth regulators. *Mailing Add:* 2708 Deerfield Pl Modesto CA 95355

CUNNINGHAM, W(ALTER) J(ACK), b Comanche, Tex, Aug 21, 17; m 44; c 2. ELECTRICAL ENGINEERING. *Educ:* Univ Tex, AB, 37, AM, 38; Harvard Univ, ScM, 39, PhD(eng sci), 47. *Prof Exp:* Tutor physics, Univ Tex, 35-38; instr physics & commun eng, Harvard Univ, 39-45; from asst prof to prof elec eng, 46-63, assoc chmn, Dept Eng & Appl Sci, 69-72, prof eng & appl sci, 63-81, PROF ELEC ENG, YALE UNIV, 81- *Concurrent Pos:* Fel, Trumbull Col, 48-; assoc ed, J Franklin Inst, 62-75. *Mem:* Inst Elec & Electronics Engrs; Acoust Soc Am; Am Soc Eng Educ. *Res:* Systems theory; nonlinear analysis; applied mathematics. *Mailing Add:* Becton Ctr Yale Univ New Haven CT 06520

CUNNINGHAM, WILLIAM A(ARON), b Comanche, Tex, May 22, 04; m 30; c 4. CHEMICAL ENGINEERING. *Educ:* Univ Tex, BS, 27, MS, 29, PhD(chem eng), 41. *Prof Exp:* Process engr, Tex Pac Coal & Oil Co, Tex, 29-30; chem engr, Freeport Sulphur Co, 30-31; chemist, Univ Lands, San Angelo, 32-36; chief engr, Tex Potash Corp, 36-39; res technologist, Bur Indust Chem, 39-41, from asst prof to prof, 41-71, EMER PROF CHEM ENG, UNIV TEX, AUSTIN, 71- *Honors & Awards:* Founders Award, Am Inst Chem Engrs, 70. *Mem:* Am Chem Soc; Am Inst Chem Engrs. *Mailing Add:* Dept of Chem Engr Univ of Tex Austin TX 78712

CUNNINHAM-RUNDLES, CHARLOTTE, b Ann Arbor, Mich, July 12, 43. IMMUNOLOGY, IMMUNOCHEMISTRY. *Educ:* Duke Univ, BS, 65; Columbia Univ, MD, 69; New York Univ, PhD(immunol), 74. *Prof Exp:* Intern med, New York Univ, 69-70, resident, 70-72, asst scientist, 72-74; assoc immunol, Sloan Kettering Inst, 74-76; ASST PROF IMMUNOL & BIOCHEM, CORNELL GRAD SCH ARTS & SCI, 76- *Concurrent Pos:* Attending physician, Dept Med, Med Ctr, New York Univ, 72- & Mem Hosp, 74-; senate exec comt mem, Mem Sloan Kettering Cancer Ctr, 77- prin investr, Immunodeficiency Prog, 82. *Mem:* Fel Am Col Physicians; Am Asn Immunologists; Am Fedn Clin Res. *Res:* Secretory immune system; immuno deficiency diseases of man; immune complexes; network theory of immunity in man. *Mailing Add:* 1275 York Ave New York NY 10021

CUNNOLD, DEREK M, meteorology, see previous edition

CUNNY, ROBERT WILLIAM, b Chicago, Ill, July 22, 24; m 60; c 2. SOIL MECHANICS, EARTH DAM DESIGN. *Educ:* Purdue Univ, BS, 46, MS, 48. *Prof Exp:* Engr, US Army Engr Waterways Exp Sta, 48-50 & Portland Cement Asn, 52-54; engr soils div, US Army Engr Waterways Exp Sta, 54-74, dir, Soil Mech Info Anal Ctr, Geotech Lab, 74-80; CONSULT, 80- *Concurrent Pos:* Mem comt properties soil & rock, Dept Soils, Geol & Found, Hwy Res Bd, Nat Acad Sci-Nat Res Coun, 64- *Mem:* Am Soc Civil Engrs; Nat Soc Prof Engrs; Soc Am Mil Engrs. *Res:* Performance education of completed earth structures; collection, analysis, evaluation and dissemination of geotechnical information as related to stability of foundations, earth and rockfill dams and navigation and flood control structures; develop computerized data base of geotechnical information. *Mailing Add:* 12 Signal Hill Lane Vicksburg MS 39180

CUNOV, CARL HENRY, b Detroit, Mich, Feb 19, 18; m 42; c 3. MEDICINAL CHEMISTRY, ORGANIC CHEMISTRY. *Educ:* Wayne State Univ, BS, 41, PhD(chem), 51. *Prof Exp:* Chief chemist drug mfg, Jamieson Pharmacal, 39-46 & McKay-Davis, 46-47; asst plant tech dir drug mfg, Smith, Kline & French Labs, 50-54, plant tech dir, 54-58, process dept mgr, 58-60, mfr proj dir, 60-61; assoc prof chem, Cent Mo State Col, 62-65; assoc prof Keuka Col, 65-66; prof & head dept, 66-68; CHEM RES SUPVR, PENNWALT CORP, 68- *Concurrent Pos:* Consult, 61- *Mem:* AAAS; Am Chem Soc; Am Pharmaceut Asn; Pharmaceut Mfrs Asn. *Res:* Mills-Nixon effect; cyclobutane derivatives; medicinal chemistry; analytical methods. *Mailing Add:* Pharmaceut Div Pennwalt Corp 755 Jefferson Rd Rochester NY 14623

CUPERY, KENNETH N, b Wilmington, Del, May 27, 37; div; c 2. OPTICS. *Educ:* Oberlin Col, BA, 59; Johns Hopkins Univ, MA, 64. *Prof Exp:* Develop engr, 65-66, sr develop engr, 66-69, sr res physicist, 69-72, SUPVR OPTICS RES, KODAK APPARATUS DIV, RES LAB, 72- *Mem:* Optical Soc Am. *Res:* Modulation transfer function and relation to subjective quality of optical images; MTF based optical test systems; micrographic system development. *Mailing Add:* 400 Westminster Rd Rochester NY 14607

CUPERY, WILLIS ELI, b Wilmington, Del, July 1, 32; m 55; c 3. PESTICIDE CHEMISTRY. *Educ:* Oberlin Col, AB, 54; Univ Ill, PhD(org chem), 58. *Prof Exp:* Res chemist, 58-66, SR RES CHEMIST, E I DU PONT DE NEMOURS & CO, INC, 66- *Mem:* Am Chem Soc. *Res:* Pesticide formulation development. *Mailing Add:* 13 Crestfield Rd Wilmington DE 19810

CUPIT, CHARLES R(ICHARD), b New Orleans, La, Sept 8, 30; m 58; c 2. CHEMICAL ENGINEERING. *Educ:* Miss State Univ, BS, 54; Univ Ill, MS, 56, PhD(chem eng), 58. *Prof Exp:* Res engr, Mobil Oil Co, 54; asst chem eng, Univ Ill, 54-55, instr, 57-58; res engr, Shell Oil Co, 58-65; sr engr, Lockheed Electronics Corp, 65-68; sect head, TRW Systs Group, 68-69; chem eng consult, 69-70; sr scientist chem div, 70-77, ENGR GROUP LEADER, CHEM DIV, RES & DEVELOP, VULCAN MAT CO, 77- *Mem:* Am Inst Chem Engrs. *Res:* Process design and development of chemical plants; chemical plant economic studies; design pilot plant and commercial plant process schemes and equipment; manage pilot plant projects. *Mailing Add:* Chem Div Res & Develop Vulcan Mat Co PO Box 12283 Wichita KS 67277

CUPP, CALVIN R, b Toronto, Ont, June 7, 24; m 49; c 4. METALLURGY. *Educ:* Univ Toronto, BASc, 50, MASc, 51, PhD(metall), 53. *Prof Exp:* Res metallurgist, Int Nickel Co Can, 53-56; spec assignment, Atomic Energy of Can, Ltd, 57-61; supvr metal physics & metallog, 61-74; res mgr phys/anal group, 74-78, RES MGR CHEM DEPT, INT NICKEL CO, INC, 78- *Mem:* Fel Am Soc Metals; Am Nuclear Soc; Am Soc Testing & Mat; Am Phys Soc. *Res:* Physical metallurgy; gases in metals; plastic deformation; radiation effects in metals; electron microscopy; electron probe microanalysis; radioisotopes as tracers; electrodeposition; batteries; polymeric materials. *Mailing Add:* Paul D Merica Res Lab Int Nickel Co Inc Sterling Forest Suffern NY 10901

CUPP, EDDIE WAYNE, b Highsplint, Ky, Apr 17, 41; m 64; c 1. ENTOMOLOGY, PARASITOLOGY. *Educ:* Murray State Univ, BA, 64; Univ Ill, Urbana, PhD(entom), 69. *Prof Exp:* Res fel, Sch Pub Health & Trop Med, Tulane Univ, 69-70; res biologist, Gulf South Res Inst, La, 70-71; asst prof biol, Univ Southern Miss, 71-74; asst prof, 74-78, ASSOC PROF ENTOM, CORNELL UNIV, 78- *Concurrent Pos:* Adj asst prof, Sch Pub Health & Trop Med, Tulane Univ, 70-71. *Mem:* Entom Soc Am; Am Soc Trop Med & Hyg; Am Mosquito Control Asn; Royal Soc Trop Med & Hyg. *Res:* Bionomics of medically important Diptera; ecology of arboviral diseases; dynamics of transmission of filariae. *Mailing Add:* 26 James St Box 415 Okyden NY 13053

CUPP, PAUL VERNON, JR, b Corbin, Ky, Oct 18, 42; m 69. PHYSIOLOGICAL ECOLOGY, HERPETOLOGY. *Educ:* Eastern Ky Univ, BS, 65, MS, 70; Clemson Univ, PhD(zool), 74. *Prof Exp:* Asst prof biol, Ga Southern Col, 73-74; asst prof, 74-80, ASSOC PROF BIOL, EASTERN KY UNIV, 80- *Mem:* Sigma Xi; Am Soc Zoologists; Am Inst Biol Sci; Ecol Soc Am; Soc Study Amphibians & Reptiles. *Res:* Thermal tolerance and acclimation and physiological responses to temperature in amphibians and reptiles; aggressive and courtship behavior of amphibians. *Mailing Add:* Dept Biol Sci Eastern Ky Univ Richmond KY 40475

CUPPAGE, FRANCIS EDWARD, b Cleveland, Ohio, Aug 17, 32; m 56; c 3. PATHOLOGY. *Educ:* Case Western Univ, BS, 54; Ohio State Univ, MS, 59, MD, 59. *Prof Exp:* Rotating intern med, Univ Hosps, Cleveland, 59-60, resident path, 60-63; instr, Case Western Reserve Univ, 64-65; asst prof, Ohio State Univ, 65-67; from asst prof to assoc prof, 67-73, PROF PATH, UNIV KANS MED CTR, KANSAS CITY, 73- *Concurrent Pos:* NIH fel path, Case Western Univ, 63-64. *Mem:* Int Soc Nephrol; Am Asn Path & Bact; Int Acad Path; Am Soc Exp Path. *Res:* Kidney response of nephron to injury and repair. *Mailing Add:* Dept of Path Univ of Kans Med Ctr Kansas City KS 66103

CUPPER, ROBERT ALTON, b Tyrone, Pa, Jan 7, 18; m 41; c 4. ORGANIC CHEMISTRY, PETROLEUM CHEMISTRY. *Educ:* Juniata Col, BS, 40. *Prof Exp:* Chemist chem petrol prods, United Ref Co, 41-46; indust fel org chem, Mellon Inst, 46-59; group leader, Chem & Plastic Div, Union Carbide Corp, 60-69; res scientist, Res & Develop Dept, 69-80; CONSULT, FUELS, LUBRICANTS & SYNTHETIC LUBRICANTS, 80- *Mem:* AAAS; Am Chem Soc; Soc Automotive Eng; Am Soc Lubrication Eng; NY Acad Sci. *Res:* Fuels and lubricants; additives and chemical inter-synthetic lubricants; synthesis and formulation; agricultural chemicals; pesticide intermediates and formulants. *Mailing Add:* Rt 1 Box 169A Liberty PA 16930

CUPPLES, BARRETT L(EMOYNE), b Osceola Mills, Pa, Nov 18, 41; m 63; c 3. CHEMICAL ENGINEERING. *Educ:* Pa State Univ, BS, 63, MS, 65, PhD(chem eng), 69. *Prof Exp:* Res engr, Gulf Sci & Technol Co, 68-74, proj engr, 74-78, staff engr, 78-80; DEVELOP MGR, GULF OIL CHEM CO, 81- *Mem:* Am Chem Soc; Sigma Xi; Am Soc Lubrication Engrs; Soc Auto Engrs. *Res:* Development of chemical processes such as the oligomerization of olefins for use as synthetic functional fluids. *Mailing Add:* 4819 Shore Hills Rd Kingwood TX 77339

CUPPS, PERRY THOMAS, b Granby, Mo, June 18, 16; m 44; c 4. ANIMAL PHYSIOLOGY. *Educ:* Univ Mo, BS, 39; Cornell Univ, PhD(animal physiol), 43. *Prof Exp:* Asst, Cornell Univ, 39-43; from asst prof to assoc prof, 46-59, PROF ANIMAL HUSB, UNIV CALIF, DAVIS, 59- *Concurrent Pos:* NSF fel, 61-62. *Res:* Endocrinology; thyrotrophic hormone assays; normal change of reproductive tract during estrous cycle; joint lesions in horses; estrous cycle in cattle; adrenal physiology; embryo transfer. *Mailing Add:* Dept of Animal Sci Univ of Calif Davis CA 95616

CURATOLO, WILLIAM JOHN, biophysics, see previous edition

CURCIO, JOSEPH VINCENT, chemical engineering, see previous edition

CURD, MILTON RAYBURN, b Tulsa, Okla, July 18, 28; m 52; c 4. ZOOLOGY. *Educ:* Okla State Univ, BS, 50, MS, 51, PhD(zool), 66. *Prof Exp:* asst prof, 64-68, ASSOC PROF ZOOL, OKLA STATE UNIV, 68- *Mem:* Am Soc Ichthyol & Herpet. *Res:* Anatomy and taxonomy of freshwater fishes; structure and phylogeny of sense organs, especially the eye. *Mailing Add:* Sch of Biol Sci Okla State Univ Stillwater OK 74074

CURETON, GLEN LEE, b Santa Cruz, Calif, Mar 29, 38; m 64; c 1. PHARMACEUTICS. *Educ:* Univ Calif, San Francisco, PharmD, 62; Harvard Univ, MBA, 64. *Prof Exp:* Asst dir life sci res, Stanford Res Inst, 64-65; indust economist, 65-66, health economist, 66-67; dir new prod develop, Chattem Drug & Chem Co, 67-68, dir res & new prod develop, 68-72; dir res & develop, Barnes-Hind Pharmaceuticals, Inc, 72-76; COM DEVELOP MGR, CUTTER LABS, INC, 72- *Mem:* AAAS; Am Chem Soc; Am Pharmaceut Asn; Am Acad Dermat; Asn Res in Vision & Ophthalmol. *Res:* Antacids, antiperspirants and other chemicals, including high purity aluminas; development of pharmaceuticals; ophthalmologic contact lens solutions; dermatologicals; technoeconomic analyses of life sciences research, pharmaceutical industry and cosmetics. *Mailing Add:* 714 Raymundo Ave Los Altos CA 94022

CURETON, THOMAS (KIRK), JR, b Fernandina, Fla, Aug 4, 01; m; c 3. APPLIED PHYSIOLOGY. *Educ:* Yale Univ, BS, 25; Int YMCA Col, BPE, 29, MPE, 30; Columbia Univ, AM, 36, PhD(educ res), 39. *Hon Degrees:* DSc, Univ Ottawa, 68, Univ Southern Ill, 69. *Prof Exp:* Phys dir & teacher biol & gen sci, Suffield Sch, Conn, 25-29; prof appl physics & animal mech, Springfield Col, 29-41; dir res nat sci & phys educ, 35-42; from assoc prof to prof, 42-74, EMER PROF PHYS EDUC, UNIV ILL, URBANA-CHAMPAIGN, 74-, EMER DIR PHYS FITNESS INST, 70- *Concurrent Pos:* Supvr res, Col Phys Educ, Univ Ill, Urbana-Champaign, 42-74. *Honors & Awards:* Robert-Gulick Award, Phys Educ Soc, 45; Am Col Sports Med Award, 68; Am Dent Asn Citation, 68; Gulick Medal, Am Asn Health, Phys Educ & Recreation, 75; Hetherington Award, Am Acad Phys Educ, 76; Pres Award, Coun Phys Fitness & Sports, 78. *Mem:* Am Physiol Soc; fel Soc Res Child Develop; fel Am Pub Health Asn; fel Am Asn Health, Phys Educ & Recreation; NY Acad Sci. *Res:* Body mechanics; anthropometry; physical fitness; physiology of exercise; aquatics; athletics; gymnastics; sport medicine; physical education. *Mailing Add:* Col of Phys Educ Univ of Ill Urbana IL 61820

CURIE-COHEN, MARTIN MICHAEL, b Indianapolis, Ind, July 23, 51; c 1. POPULATION GENETICS, INBREEDING. *Educ:* Ind Univ, Bloomington, BA & MA, 73; Univ Wis-Madison, PhD(genetics), 77. *Prof Exp:* Res asst, 73-77, trainee genetics, 77-80, ASST SCIENTIST, UNIV WIS-MADISON, 80-, ASST SCIENTIST, WIS REGIONAL PRIMATE RES CTR, 80- *Mem:* Genetics Soc Am. *Res:* Population genetics, particularly of immunologic markers; inbreeding; linkage disequilibrium and correlations between genes and disease. *Mailing Add:* Lab of Genetics Univ of Wis Madison WI 53706

CURJEL, CASPAR ROBERT, b Switz, Nov 21, 31; m 55; c 2. MATHEMATICS. *Educ:* Swiss Fed Inst Technol, dipl, 54, DrScMath, 60. *Prof Exp:* From instr to asst prof, Cornell Univ, 60-64; vis assoc prof, 64-65, assoc prof, 65-69, PROF MATH, UNIV WASH, 69- *Concurrent Pos:* Mem, Inst Advan Study, 63-64. *Res:* Algebraic topology; algebra. *Mailing Add:* Dept of Math Univ of Wash Seattle WA 98195

CURL, ELROY ARVEL, b Marmaduke, Ark, Dec 1, 21. PLANT PATHOLOGY. *Educ:* La Polytech Inst, BS, 49; Univ Ark, MS, 50; Univ Ill, PhD(plant path), 54. *Prof Exp:* Spec res asst plant path, State Natural Hist Surv, Ill, 50-54, asst plant pathologist, 54; asst plant pathologist, 54-57, assoc prof, 57-67, PROF BOT & MICROBIOL, AUBURN UNIV, 67- *Mem:* Am Phytopath Soc; Mycol Soc Am. *Res:* Soil microbiology; soil fungus ecology; soil microbe-pesticide interactions; biological control; root diseases of plants. *Mailing Add:* Dept of Bot & Microbiol Auburn Univ Auburn AL 36830

CURL, HERBERT (CHARLES), JR, b New York, NY, Feb 26, 28; m 73; c 2. BIOLOGICAL OCEANOGRAPHY. *Educ:* Wagner Col, BS, 50; Ohio State Univ, MS, 51; Fla State Univ, PhD(biol oceanog), 56. *Prof Exp:* Asst, Oceanog Inst, 54-56; res assoc, Woods Hole Oceanog Inst, 56-61; from assoc prof to prof oceanog, Ore State Univ, 61-74; fisheries oceanog coordr, Nat Marine Fisheries Serv, 74-75; ecologist, Environ Res Labs, Boulder, Colo, 75-77, SUPVRY OCEANOGRAPHER, PAC MARINE ENVIRON LAB, NAT OCEANIC & ATMOSPHERIC ADMIN, 77- *Concurrent Pos:* Fulbright grant, Colombia, SAm, 71. *Mem:* Fel AAAS; Ecol Soc Am; Am Soc Naturalists; Am Soc Limnol & Oceanog(secy, 64-66); Int Asn Limnol. *Res:* Physiological ecology of marine organisms; ecosystem computer simulation; biogeochemistry. *Mailing Add:* RF 28 Pac Marine Environ Lab Bldg 32 7600 Sand Point Way NE Seattle WA 98115

CURL, RANE L(OCKE), b New York, NY, July 5, 29; m 54, 63; c 2. CHEMICAL ENGINEERING. *Educ:* Mass Inst Tech, SB, 51, ScD(chem eng), 55. *Prof Exp:* Asst chem eng, Mass Inst Technol, 54-55; chem engr, Shell Develop Co, 55-61; hon res asst statist & tutor chem eng, Univ Col, London, 61-62; res assoc phys tech, Eindhoven Tech, 62-64; assoc prof chem eng, 64-68, PROF CHEM ENG, UNIV MICH, ANN ARBOR, 68- *Concurrent Pos:* Instr eng exten, Univ Calif, 58-59; consult, Orgn Control Serv, 74-; adv, Space Processing Payload Adv Subcomt, 76-77; adj secy, Int Union Speleol, 81-; chmn, Eighth Int Cong Speleol, 81. *Mem:* AAAS; Am Chem Soc; Am Inst Chem Engrs; hon mem Nat Speleol Soc (pres, 70-74); Int Asn Hydrogeologists. *Res:* Automatic process control; high temperature chemistry; fluid dynamics and mass transfer; chemical reactors; stochastic process and computer applications; geomorphologic process; dispersion dynamics; thermochemical hydrogen production; speleology. *Mailing Add:* Dept Chem Eng Univ Mich Ann Arbor MI 48109

CURL, ROBERT FLOYD, JR, b Alice, Tex, Aug 23, 33; m 55; c 2. PHYSICAL CHEMISTRY. *Educ:* Rice Inst, BA, 54; Univ Calif, PhD, 57. *Prof Exp:* Res fel, Harvard Univ, 57-58; from asst prof to assoc prof, 58-67, PROF CHEM, RICE UNIV, 67- *Concurrent Pos:* NATO fel, Oxford Univ, 64-65; vis res officer, Nat Res Coun Can, 72-73; vis prof, Inst Molecular Sci, Okazaki, Japan, 77. *Honors & Awards:* Clayton Prize, Inst Mech Eng, 58. *Mem:* Am Chem Soc. *Res:* Microwave and laser spectroscopy. *Mailing Add:* Dept of Chem Rice Univ Houston TX 77001

CURLEE, NEIL J(AMES), JR, b Schenectady, NY, July 14, 30; m 52; c 6. MECHANICAL & NUCLEAR ENGINEERING. *Educ:* Mass Inst Technol, SB, 52; Carnegie Inst Technol, MS, 55; Univ Pittsburgh, PhD(mech eng), 61. *Prof Exp:* Scientist, Bettis Atomic Power Lab, 55-62, sr scientist, 62-67, supvr thermal & hydraul anal, 67-72, mgr thermal & hydraul lab, 72-76, ADV ENGR, NUCLEAR STEAM GENERATION DIV, WESTINGHOUSE ELEC CORP, 76- *Concurrent Pos:* Instr, Eve Sch, Carnegie Inst Technol, 62. *Mem:* Am Soc Mech Engrs. *Res:* Nuclear reactor dynamics and control; magnetohydrodynamics; transient convective heat transfer. *Mailing Add:* Nuclear Steam Generation Div PO Box 855 Pittsburgh PA 15230

CURLESS, WILLIAM TOOLE, b Quincy, Ill, Mar 11, 28; div; c 3. ENVIRONMENTAL SCIENCES, PESTICIDE CHEMISTRY. *Educ:* Univ Ill, BS, 49; Univ Kans, MS, 56. *Prof Exp:* Anal chemist, Victor Chem Works, 49-51, inorg res chemist, 51-53; res chemist, Columbia-Southern Chem Corp, 55-61; res chemist, Spencer Chem Co, 62-66; sr res chemist, Gulf Oil Corp, 66-80; SR RES SCIENTIST, FARMLAND INDUSTS, 80- *Mem:* Am Chem Soc. *Res:* Nonaqueous solvents; condensed phosphates; phase diagrams; fertilizer technology; pesticide environmental studies in soil; pesticide residue analytical method development. *Mailing Add:* 102441 Woodson Dr Overland Pk KS 66207

CURLEY, JAMES EDWARD, b Winchester, Mass, Apr 10, 44; m 66; c 2. ANALYTICAL CHEMISTRY. *Educ:* Univ Mass, Amherst, BS, 66, MS, 68, PhD(chem), 70. *Prof Exp:* Staff chemist, Med Res Lab, 70-73, sr res scientist, Pfizer Cent Res, 73-75, sect supvr, Pfizer Qual Control, 75-80, PROJ LEADER, PFIZER CTR RES, 80- *Mem:* Am Chem Soc; Sigma Xi. *Res:* Analytical methodology for penicillin products; analysis of pharmaceuticals by high pressure liquid chromatography; computer aided analytical chemistry. *Mailing Add:* Pfizer Inc Groton CT 06340

CURLIN, GEORGE TAMS, b Mayfield, Ky, Sept 13, 39; m 62; c 2. EPIDEMIOLOGY, INFECTIOUS DISEASE. *Educ:* Centre Col Ky, BA, 61; Vanderbilt Univ, MD, 65; Johns Hopkins Univ, MPH, 73. *Prof Exp:* Intern int med, Univ Ky Hosp, 65-66; epidemic intel serv officer, Ctr Dis Control, USPHS, 66-68; fel int med, Johns Hopkins Hosp, 68-69; med epidemiologist cholera, Cholera Res Lab, Dacca, Bangladesh, 69-71; resident int med, Johns Hopkins Hosp, 71-72; head epidemiol div, Cholera Res Lab, 73-77; CHIEF EPIDEMIOL & BIOMET BR, NAT INST ALLERGY & INFECTIOUS DIS, NIH, 77- *Concurrent Pos:* Interim dir, Cholera Res Lab, 73-74. *Mem:* AAAS; Am Pub Health Asn. *Res:* Epidemiology of enteric disease; field trials of vaccines; assessment of interventions for the control of infectious enteric disease; antitoxin immunity in cholera and other enterotoxigenic diarrheal diseases. *Mailing Add:* Nat Inst of Allergy 9000 Rockville Pike Bethesda MD 20014

CURLIN, LEMUEL CALVERT, b Waxahachie, Tex, Feb 1, 13; m 40; c 3. PHARMACEUTICAL CHEMISTRY. *Educ:* Trinity Univ, Tex, BS, 34; Univ Chicago, MS, 36, PhD(biochem), 40. *Prof Exp:* Chemist, Ideal Lab, Univ Tex, 35-36; lab asst, Univ Chicago, 37-40, Armour & Co fel, 40; asst dir develop lab, Armour & Co, 40-41, res chemist, 41-43; secy, 64-69, chief chemist, L Perrigo Co, 43-78, exec vpres, 69-78; RETIRED. *Concurrent Pos:* Consult drug & cosmetic indust, 78- *Res:* Separation plasma proteins; synthetic thyroid; organic synthesis. *Mailing Add:* 422 Lake Dr RR 6 Allegan MI 49010

CURME, HENRY GARRETT, b Niagara Falls, NY, Dec 31, 23; m 48; c 3. PHYSICAL CHEMISTRY. *Educ:* Northwestern Univ, BS, 45, MS, 47; Univ Calif, PhD(chem), 50. *Prof Exp:* Chemist, Manhattan Proj, Tenn Eastman Co, 44-46; asst, Northwestern Univ, 46-47 & Univ Calif, 47-50; res chemist & res assoc, 50-65, lab head, 65-70, SR LAB HEAD, EASTMAN KODAK CO, 70- *Mem:* Am Chem Soc; Am Asn Clin Chem. *Res:* Interactions between proteins and small molecules; photochemistry; polymer solutions; bulk properties and morphology of hydrophilic polymers; polymer networks; adsorption of polymers; surface properties of polymers; development of analytical techniques for clinical chemistry. *Mailing Add:* Res Lab Kodak Park Works Eastman Kodak Co Rochester NY 14650

CURME, JOHN HENRY, plant genetics, see previous edition

CURNEN, EDWARD CHARLES, JR, b Yonkers, NY, Jan 5, 09; m 42, 68; c 7. PEDIATRICS, MICROBIOLOGY. *Educ:* Yale Univ, AB, 31; Harvard Univ, MD, 35. *Prof Exp:* Res bacteriologist, Children's Hosp, Boston, Mass, 35-36, med intern, 36-38, med resident, 38-39; asst, Rockefeller Inst, NY, 39-46; from asst prof prev med to assoc prof prev med & pediat, Sch Med, Yale Univ, 46-52; prof pediat & chmn dept, Univ NC, 52-60; chmn dept, 60-70, Carpentier prof, 60-74, EMER CARPENTIER PROF PEDIAT, COL PHYSICIANS & SURGEONS, COLUMBIA UNIV, 74-, SPEC LECTR, 74- *Concurrent Pos:* Harvard Med Sch fel, Thorndike Mem Lab, Boston City Hosp, 38; asst, Harvard Med Sch, 38-39; asst resident physician, Rockefeller Inst Hosp, 39-46, mem, US Naval Res Unit, 41-46; res worker, Off Sci Res, 41-46; asst physician, New Haven Community Hosp, Conn, 46-48, assoc pediatrician, 48-52; chief pediat serv, NC Mem Hosp, 52-60, chief staff, 59-60; consult pediatrician, US Army Hosp, Ft Bragg, NC & NC State Bd Health, 52-60; dir pediat serv, Babies Hosp, Columbia Presby Med Ctr, 60-70, attend pediatrician, 60-74, consult, 74-; Schick lectr, Mt Sinai Hosp, New York, 62; consult pediatrician, St Albans Naval Hosp, NY, 63-73 & St Luke's Hosp, New York, 66-80; attend pediatrician, Harlem Hosp, 74-78; assoc, Comn Influenza, US Armed Forces Epidemiol Bd, 47-69; mem, Planning Comt Studies Cardiovasc Effects Oriental Influenza, Nat Heart Inst & Influenza Res Comt, NIH, 57, Bd Sci counr, Div Biol Stand, 59-63, Infectious Dis & Trop Med Training Grant Comt, Nat Int Allergy & Infectious Dis, 60-63; chmn, Allergy & Infectious Dis Panel & mem, Rev Panel, Health Res Coun New York, 62-68, mem, Exec Comt, 68-72. *Honors & Awards:* Presidential Award, Int Poliomyelitis Cong, 58. *Mem:* Fel AAAS; Am Acad Pediat; Am Pediat Soc (vpres, 69); fel NY Acad Sci. *Res:* Infectious diseases; bacteriology and virology; hemagglutination phenomena. *Mailing Add:* Columbia Presby Med Ctr 630 W 168th St New York NY 10032

CURNEN, MARY G MCCREA, b Belgium; m 55, 68; c 7. EPIDEMIOLOGY, PEDIATRICS. *Educ:* Cath Univ Louvain, MD, 48; Inst Trop Med, Belg, DTM, 49; Columbia Univ, DrPH(epidemiol), 73. *Prof Exp:* Intern pediat, Cath Univ Louvain Hosp, 47-48; resident, Bellevue Med Ctr, Col Med, NY Univ, 52-53; instr prev med, Sch Med, Yale Univ, 53-54, instr prev med, 53-56, instr prev med & pediat, 54-56, clin physician child health and pub schs, New Haven City Health Dept, 59-64; res assoc pediat, Yale Univ, 64-66, res assoc med, Yale Univ Virol Lab, Vet Admin Hosp, West Haven & Yale Univ, 67-69; res assoc epidemiol, 73-74, asst prof, 74-77, ASSOC PROF EPIDEMIOL, SCH PUB HEALTH, COLUMBIA UNIV, 77- ASSOC MED & PEDIAT, YALE-NEW HAVEN HOSP, 68- *Concurrent Pos:* Clin res fel pediat, Sch Med, Yale Univ, 49-52 & 53-54; exec dir & pediatrician in chg, New Haven Live Poliomyelitis Vaccine Trial, 60. *Mem:* Am Pub Health Asn; Harvey Soc; Soc Epidemiol Res; hon mem Peruvian Pediat Soc; Sigma Xi. *Res:* Cancer epidemiology; virology. *Mailing Add:* Fac of Med Dept of Epidemiol Columbia Univ Sch Pub Health New York NY 10032

CURNOW, RICHARD DENNIS, b Omaha, Nebr, Dec 8, 43; m 68; c 2. WILDLIFE BIOLOGY, TERRESTRIAL ECOLOGY. *Educ:* Colo State Univ, BS, 66, MS, 68, PhD(wildlife biol), 70. *Prof Exp:* Res assoc, Dept Fish & Wildlife Biol, Colo State Univ, 70-71; asst leader res, Ohio Coop Wildlife Res Unit, 71-74, staff specialist, Div Coop Res, 74-75, actg chief, 75-76, asst dir, Denver Widlife Res Ctr, 77-78, actg dir res, 78-79, ASST DIR, DENVER WILDLIFE RES CTR, US FISH & WILDLIFE SERV, 79- *Concurrent Pos:* Adj asst prof, Dept Zool, Ohio State Univ, 71-74. *Mem:* Wildlife Soc; Sigma Xi; Audubon Soc. *Res:* Ecological relationships of land use and development and natural resource management to fish and wildlife populations; fate and effects of radionuclides and environmental contaminants in ecological systems. *Mailing Add:* Fed Ctr Bldg 16 US Fish & Widlife Serv Denver CO 80225

CURNUTT, JERRY LEE, b Elwood, Ind, Nov 15, 42; m 63; c 1. PHYSICAL CHEMISTRY. *Educ:* Franklin Col, BA, 64; Univ Nebr, MS, 66, PhD(chem), 68. *Prof Exp:* NASA res traineeship, 66-68; res chemist, Thermal Res Lab, 68-78, RES SPECIALIST, DOW CHEM CO, 78- *Mem:* Am Chem Soc. *Res:* Thermodynamic properties of electrolytes; use of gas adsorption techniques to characterize pore structures in solid materials. *Mailing Add:* 2800 Mt Vernon Dr Midland MI 48640

CURNUTTE, BASIL, JR, b Portsmouth, Ohio, Mar 1, 23; m 45; c 2. PHYSICS. *Educ:* US Naval Acad, BS, 45; Ohio State Univ, PhD(physics), 53. *Prof Exp:* Res assoc physics, Ohio State Univ, 53-54; from asst prof to assoc prof, 54-64, PROF PHYSICS, KANS STATE UNIV, 64- *Mem:* AAAS; fel Am Phys Soc; Am Asn Physics Teachers; fel Optical Soc Am. *Res:* Chemical physics; molecular spectra and structure; atomic spectroscopy. *Mailing Add:* Dept of Physics Kans State Univ Manhattan KS 66504

CUROTT, DAVID RICHARD, b Passaic, NJ, June 3, 37; m 78; c 1. PHYSICS, ASTROPHYSICS. *Educ:* Stevens Inst Technol, BSc, 59; Princeton Univ, MA, 62, PhD(physics), 65. *Prof Exp:* Res assoc astrophys, Princeton Univ, 65-66, instr physics, 66-67; asst prof, Wesleyan Univ, 67-75; assoc prof, 75-81, PROF PHYSICS & DIR, PLANETARIUM, UNIV NORTHALA, 81- *Mem:* Am Asn Physics Teachers; Am Phys Soc; Am Astron Soc. *Res:* Relativity; experimental and observational cosmology and astrophysics; astronomical electronic instrumentation. *Mailing Add:* Box 5050 Univ North Ala Florence AL 35630

CURPHEY, THOMAS JOHN, b New York, NY, Oct 7, 34; m 59; c 2. ORGANIC CHEMISTRY. *Educ:* Harvard Univ, BA, 56, PhD(chem), 60. *Prof Exp:* Res assoc chem, Univ Wis, 60-62; instr, Yale Univ, 62-64; from asst prof to prof chem, St Louis Univ, 64-75; sr res assoc path, 75-80, RES ASSOC PROF PATH, DARTMOUTH MED SCH, 80-; ADJ PROF CHEM, DARTMOUTH COL, 75- *Mem:* Am Chem Soc; Royal Soc Chem. *Res:* Synthetic organic chemistry; chemical carcinogenesis; chemical and biochemical reaction mechanisms; natural products chemistry. *Mailing Add:* Dept of Path Dartmouth Med Sch Hanover NH 03755

CURRAH, JACK ELLWOOD, b Toronto, Ont, Sept 12, 20; m 44; c 3. ANALYTICAL CHEMISTRY. *Educ:* Univ Toronto, BA, 41, MA, 42, PhD(anal & inorg chem), 44. *Prof Exp:* Asst chem, Univ Toronto, 41-43; res chemist, Atomic Energy Proj, Nat Res Coun Can, 44-46; res chemist, Cent Res Lab, Can Industs, Ltd, 46-51, res group leader, 51-56, sect leader, Res Dept, Textile Fibers Div, 56-57 & Process & Prod Res Sect, Tech Dept, 57-62, res sect mgr, Tech Dept, 62-65; tech mgr, Millhaven Fibres Ltd, 65-67; res & tech mgr plastics group, Can Industs Ltd, McMasterville, 67-70, res leader, Cent Res Lab, 70-73, sr res chemist, Chem Res Lab, 73-80; RES SCIENTIST, CHEM RES LAB, CIL INC, MISSISSAUGA, ONT, 80- *Mem:* Chem Inst Can; Can Soc Chem Eng; Am Soc Mass Spectrometry. *Res:* Synthetic textile fibers; polyester fibers; mass spectrometry. *Mailing Add:* 1092 Gloucester Dr Burlington ON L7P 2W5 Can

CURRAN, DAVID JAMES, b Kitchener, Ont, Sept 19, 32; US citizen; m 57; c 6. ANALYTICAL CHEMISTRY. *Educ:* Univ Mass, BS, 53; Boston Col, MS, 58; Univ Ill, PhD(polarography), 61. *Prof Exp:* Asst prof anal chem, Seton Hall Univ, 61-63; asst prof, 63-69, assoc prof, 69-78, PROF ANAL CHEM, UNIV MASS, AMHERST, 78- *Concurrent Pos:* Consult, Tar Foxboro Co. *Mem:* Am Chem Soc; Electrochem Soc. *Res:* Electroanalytical chemistry; solid electrodes in potentiometry, coulometry, amperometry and voltammetry-polarography; chemical instrumentation; pressure transducers in chemical analysis. *Mailing Add:* 28 Valleyview Circle Amherst MA 01002

CURRAN, DENNIS PATRICK, b Easton, Pa, June 10, 53; m 79. CHEMISTRY. *Educ:* Boston Col, BS, 75; Univ Rochester, PhD(chem), 79. *Prof Exp:* NIH fel chem, Dept Chem, Univ Wis, 79-81; ASST PROF CHEM, DEPT CHEM, UNIV PITTSBURGH, 81- *Concurrent Pos:* Dreyfus award, 81-86. *Mem:* Am Chem Soc. *Res:* Total synthesis of natural products and development of new synthetic methodology. *Mailing Add:* Dept Chem Univ Pittsburgh Pittsburgh PA 15260

CURRAN, DONALD ROBERT, b Aurora, Ill, Mar 10, 32; m 59. PHYSICS. *Educ:* Iowa State Univ, BS, 53; Wash State Univ, MS, 56, PhD(physics), 60. *Prof Exp:* Physicist, Stanford Res Inst, 56-62; res physicist, Norweg Defense Res Estab, 62-67; physicist, Ernst Mach Inst, WGer, 67-70; PHYSICIST, SRI INT, 70- *Res:* Shock wave and high pressure physics; fluid dynamics; mechanical behavior of solids; fracture mechanics. *Mailing Add:* Redwood City CA

CURRAN, HAROLD ALLEN, b Washington, DC, Dec 2, 40; m 63; c 2. PALEONTOLOGY, PALEOECOLOGY. *Educ:* Washington & Lee Univ, BS, 62; Univ NC, MS, 65, PhD(geol), 68. *Prof Exp:* Asst dept geol, Univ NC, 63-68; asst prof dept earth, space & graphic sci, US Mil Acad, 68-70; from asst prof to assoc prof, 70-81, PROF GEOL, SMITH COL, 81- *Mem:* Geol Soc Am; Soc Econ Paleont & Mineral; AAAS. *Res:* Upper Cretaceous and Cenozoic Foraminifera; trace fossils; Atlantic Coastal Plain stratigraphy; problems in paleoecology and marine geology. *Mailing Add:* Dept Geol Clark Sci Ctr Smith Col Northampton MA 01063

CURRAN, HENRY M, b Calgary, Can, Feb 12, 18; nat US. MECHANICAL ENGINEERING, ENERGY CONVERSION SYSTEMS. *Educ:* Univ BC, BASc, 42; Univ Tex, MS, 52, PhD(mech eng), 55. *Prof Exp:* Engr res & develop, Elliott Co, 46-48; from instr to prof eng, St Edwards Univ, 49-65; assoc prof mech eng, Cath Univ Am, 65-72; dir eng, 72-75, SR PRIN ENGR, HITTMAN ASSOCS, INC, COLUMBIA, 75- *Mem:* Am Soc Mech Engrs; Am Soc Heating, Refrigerating & Air Conditioning Engrs; Nat Soc Prof Engrs; Int Solar Energy Soc. *Res:* Saline water conversion; gas turbines; rankine engines; refrigeration systems; solar energy. *Mailing Add:* Hittman Assocs Inc 9190 Red Branch Rd Columbia MD 21045

CURRAN, JOHN FRANKLIN, b Los Angeles, Calif, Feb 13, 17; wid; c 4. PETROLEUM & ENGINEERING GEOLOGY. *Educ:* Stanford Univ, BA, 41, MA, 43. *Prof Exp:* Geologist, Gen Petrol Corp, Calif, 46-52; geologist, Honolulu Oil Corp, 52-59, dist geologist, 59; CONSULT GEOLOGIST, 59- *Concurrent Pos:* Vpres & dir, Seven Cities Oil Co, San Mateo, 67-72; mem, Calif State Bd Registr Geol, 69-76. *Mem:* Fel AAAS; Am Asn Petrol Geologists; fel Geol Soc Am; Soc Petrol Engrs; Am Inst Prof Geologists. *Mailing Add:* 1010 Mission Canyon Rd Santa Barbara CA 93105

CURRAN, JOHN PHINEAS, b New Brunswick, NJ, Sept 21, 28; m 53; c 4. PEDIATRICS, MEDICAL GENETICS. *Educ:* Rutgers Univ, BS, 51; New York Med Col, MD, 55. *Prof Exp:* Intern, Mountainside Hosp, Montclair, NJ, 55-56; resident, Children's Hosp, Philadelphia, 59-60, resident, US Naval Hosp, Philadelphia, 59-61; assoc prof pediat, New York Med Col, 63-66; pediatrician in chief, Margaret Hague Maternity Hosp, 66-75; assoc prof pediat, 74-76. PROF GEN & ORAL PATH, NJ DENT SCH, 71-, PROF PEDIAT, NJ MED SCH, 76-; MED DIR, CHILDREN'S SPECIALIZED HOSP, MOUNTAINSIDE-WESTFIELD, NJ, 75- *Concurrent Pos:* Consult pediat, Pollack Hosp, Jersey City, 69-; dir pediat, Jersey City Med Ctr, 66-75; clin assoc prof, NJ Med Sch, 73-74. *Mem:* AAAS; fel Am Acad Pediat; Am Soc Human Genetics; Am Col Clin Pharmacol. *Res:* Malformation syndromes; genetics. *Mailing Add:* Children's Spec Hosp New Providence Rd Westfield-Mountainside NJ 07091

CURRAN, JOHN S, b Camden, NJ, Sept 11, 40; m; c 2. PEDIATRICS. *Educ:* Rutgers Univ, AB, 62; Univ Pa, MD, 66. *Prof Exp:* Med intern, Univ Pa Hosp, 66-67; pediat resident, Children's Hosp of Philadelphia, 67-69; chief newborn serv, US Air Force Hosp, Wiesbaden, Ger, 69-72; ASSOC PROF PEDIAT, CHIEF NEONATAL SECT & DIR REGIONAL NEWBORN INTENSIVE CARE CTR, COL MED, UNIV S FLA, TAMPA, 72- *Mem:* Fel Am Acad Pediat. *Res:* Interactions of shope papilloma virus and rabbit skin cells in vitro; retinopathy of prematurity; evaluation of incidence, natural history and resolution by fundus photography and intravenous flourescein angiography. *Mailing Add:* Dept of Pediat Univ of S Fla Col Med Tampa FL 33609

CURRAN, ROBERT JAMES, b Cheyenne, Wyo, Dec 4, 42; m 67; c 2. ATMOSPHERIC RADIATION, SATELLITE REMOTE SENSING. *Educ:* Creighton Univ, BS, 64; Univ Ariz, MS, 70, PhD(physics), 71. *Prof Exp:* RES SCIENTIST ATMOSPHERIC PHYSICS, LAB ATMOSPHERIC SCI, GODDARD SPACE FLIGHT CTR, NASA, 71-, SR SCIENTIST, 77- *Concurrent Pos:* Prin investr, Cloud Radiation Exp, NASA, 79-82, Earth Radiation Budget Exp Team, 80-86; invited mem, Comt Radiation Energetics, Am Meteorol Soc, 78-84; proj scientist, Earth Radiation Budget Exp, NASA, 79-86; assoc ed, J Appl Meteorol, 82- *Mem:* AAAS; Am Geophys Union; Am Meterol Soc. *Res:* Understanding radiation properties of the earth's atmosphere and the atmospheres of other planets; emphasis placed on understanding the role of clouds in planetary atmospheres. *Mailing Add:* Lab Atmospheric Sci Code 915 Goddard Space Flight Ctr NASA Greenbelt MD 20771

CURRAN, ROBERT KYRAN, b Kingston, Pa, Aug 8, 31; m 55; c 4. PHYSICS. *Educ:* Univ Scranton, BS, 53; Univ Pittsburgh, PhD(physics), 59; New York Univ, MBA, 76. *Prof Exp:* Physicist, Westinghouse Elec Corp, 59-62 & Air Prod & Chem Inc, Pa, 62-64; PHYSICIST, BELL LABS, INC, 64- *Mem:* Am Phys Soc; Sigma Xi. *Res:* Atomic collisions; mass spectrometry; vacuum technique; optics; semiconductor technology; digital systems. *Mailing Add:* 64 Winding Way Stirling NJ 07980

CURRAN, ROBERT M, b Cohoes, NY, May 23, 21; m 44; c 3. METALLURGICAL ENGINEERING. *Educ:* Rensselaer Polytech Inst, BSMetE, 42, MSMetE, 47. *Prof Exp:* Electronics officer, US Navy, 43-46; res assoc welding, Rensselaer Polytech Inst, 46-48; supvr welding develop, Works Lab, 48-56, MGR TURBINE MAT ENG, GEN ELEC CO, SCHENECTADY, 56- *Concurrent Pos:* Chmn, Tech Adv Comt, Metal Properties Coun. *Mem:* Fel Am Soc Metals; fel Am Soc Mech Engrs; Am Soc Testing & Mat. *Res:* Mechanical behavior of metals; steels for large steam turbine construction; toughness and high temperature properties; stress corrosion cracking-erosion. *Mailing Add:* 330 Columbia St Cohoes NY 12047

CURRAN, WILLIAM VINCENT, b Easton, Pa, Nov 30, 29; m 52; c 5. ORGANIC CHEMISTRY. *Educ:* Lafayette Col, BS, 52; Col Holy Cross, MS, 53; NY Univ, PhD, 68. *Prof Exp:* Res worker org chem, Columbia Univ, 54-56; res chemist, Lederle Labs, Am Cyanamid Co, 56-65; asst prof chem, Fairleigh Dickinson Univ, 65-67; res chemist, 68-69, SR RES CHEMIST, AM CYANAMID CO, 69- *Mem:* Am Chem Soc. *Mailing Add:* Am Cyanamid Co Lederle Labs Div Pearl River NY 10965

CURRARINO, GUIDO, b Levanto, Italy, Dec 17, 20. MEDICINE. *Educ:* Univ Genoa, MD, 45. *Prof Exp:* Asst prof radiol & pediat, Med Sch, Univ Cincinnati, 56-60; assoc prof, Med Sch, Cornell Univ, 61-64; PROF RADIOL & PEDIAT, UNIV TEX HEALTH SCI CTR, DALLAS, 65- *Res:* Pediatric radiology. *Mailing Add:* Univ Tex Health Sci Ctr 4550 Crooked Lane Dallas TX 75229

CURRAY, JOSEPH ROSS, b Cedar Rapids, Iowa, Jan 19, 27; m 49; c 3. MARINE GEOLOGY. *Educ:* Calif Inst Technol, BS, 49; Pa State Univ, MS, 51; Univ Calif, PhD(oceanog), 59. *Prof Exp:* Asst & instr geol & mineral, Pa State Univ, 49-51; res geologist, Res Lab, Carter Oil Co, 51-53; asst marine geol & res staff, 53-67, assoc prof oceanog, 67-70, chmn grad dept, 73-75, chmn geol res div, 76-78, PROF OCEANOG & RES GEOLOGIST, SCRIPPS INST OCEANOG, UNIV CALIF, 70- *Concurrent Pos:* Dir, Nertron, Inc, 58-; ed, Marine Geol, 63-66; trustee, Found Ocean Res, 71- *Honors & Awards:* Shepard Medal, Soc Econ Paleontologists & Mineralogists, 70. *Mem:* AAAS; fel Geol Soc Am; Am Asn Petrol Geologists; Soc Econ Paleontologists & Mineralogists; fel Am Geophys Union. *Res:* Sediments; structures; history of continental margin. *Mailing Add:* Scripps Inst of Oceanog A-015 La Jolla CA 92093

CURRELL, DOUGLAS LEO, b Tulsa, Okla, Feb 5, 27. ORGANIC CHEMISTRY. *Educ:* Univ Colo, BA, 50, MA, 54; Univ Ark, PhD(chem), 56. *Prof Exp:* Res fel chem, Calif Inst Technol, 56-57; from asst prof to assoc prof, 57-65, chmn dept, 65-68, PROF CHEM, CALIF STATE UNIV, LOS ANGELES, 65- *Concurrent Pos:* Vis prof, Univ Rome, 68-69, 70-71 & 78-79. *Mem:* Am Chem Soc; Sigma Xi. *Res:* Mechanisms of organic reactions; hemoglobin chemistry. *Mailing Add:* Dept of Chem Calif State Univ Los Angeles CA 90032

CURREN, THOMAS, b St John's, Nfld, Aug 2, 39; m 62; c 2. PLANT PATHOLOGY. *Educ:* Mem Univ, BSc, 61; Univ Toronto, MA, 63, PhD(plant path), 66. *Prof Exp:* Res scientist, Res Sta, Can Dept Agr, 66-69; lectr biol, Carleton Univ, 69-70; HERBICIDE EVAL OFF, PLANT PROD DIV, CONTROL PROD SECT, AGR CAN, 70- *Res:* Physiology of parasitism of storage diseases of carrot and squash, especially the role of pectic enzymes in disease process; herbicides. *Mailing Add:* Plant Prod Div Control Prod Sect Agr Can Ottawa ON K1A 0C6 Can

CURRENT, DAVID HARLAN, b Connerville, Ind, July 26, 41; m 66; c 2. EXPERIMENTAL SOLID STATE PHYSICS, NUCLEAR MAGNETIC RESONANCE. *Educ:* Carleton Col, BA, 63; Northwestern Univ, MS, 66; Mich State Univ, PhD(physics), 71. *Prof Exp:* From instr to assoc prof, 66-79, PROF PHYSICS, CENT MICH UNIV, 79- *Mem:* Am Phys Soc; Am Asn Physics Teachers; Am Asn Univ Prof; Int Soc Magnetic Resonance; Sigma Xi. *Res:* Experimental chlorine nuclear quadrupole resonance in insulators, including temperature dependence and phase transitions; optical relaxation in solids and vapors; laser spectroscopy. *Mailing Add:* Dept Physics Cent Mich Univ Mt Pleasant MI 48859

CURRENT, JERRY H, b Anderson, Ind, Mar 2, 35; m 61; c 3. PROCESS CONTROL, PROCESS MONITORING. *Educ:* Ind Univ, BS, 57; Univ Wash, PhD(phys chem), 61. *Prof Exp:* NSF fel, Univ Calif, Berkeley, 62-64; asst prof chem, Univ Mich, 64-70; res chemist, 70-80, SECT DIR, GULF RES & DEVELOP CO, 80- *Mem:* Am Chem Soc; Inst Soc am. *Res:* Gas phase kinetics; x-ray photoelectron spectroscopy; process control. *Mailing Add:* Gulf Res & Develop Co PO Drawer 2038 Pittsburgh PA 15230

CURRENT, MICHAEL IRA, b Washington, DC, Dec 14, 45; m 74. SURFACE PHYSICS, ION IMPLANTATION. *Educ:* Rensselaer Polytech Inst, BS, 67, MS, 73, PhD(physics), 74. *Prof Exp:* Fel, Mat Div, Rensselaer Polytech Inst, 74-76; fel mat sci, Cornell Univ, 76-80; MEM TECH STAFF, PHILIPS RES LAB, SIGNETICS CORP, 80- *Mem:* Am Asn Physics Teachers; Am Vacuum Soc; Electrochem Soc; Mat Res Soc. *Res:* Development of ion implantation for fabrication of very large scale integration bipolar and metal-oxide-silicon integrated circuit devices; use of surface sensitive processes to study chemistry of catalytic oxidation of sulfur oxides on smoke stack particles and vanadium oxide surfaces. *Mailing Add:* Philips Res Lab Sunnyvale Signetics Corp 811 E Arques Ave Sunnyvale CA 94086

CURRENT, STEVEN P, b Downers Grove, Ill, May 20, 50; m 73. CATALYSIS. *Educ:* Univ Chicago, BS, 72; Stanford Univ, PhD(org chem), 75. *Prof Exp:* Res assoc, Case Western Reserve Univ, 75-76; res assoc, Mass Inst Technol, 76-77; RES CHEMIST, CHEVRON RES CO, 77- *Mem:* Am Chem Soc. *Res:* Organic and organometallic chemistry; homogeneous and heterogeneous catalysis, especially of small molecules including carbon monoxide, hydrogen, methanol and olefins; new routes to petrochemicals and polymers. *Mailing Add:* Chem Res Dept Chevron Res Co 576 Standard Ave Richmond CA 94802

CURRENT, WILLIAM L, b Durango, Colo, July 23, 49; m 71; c 1. PROTOZOOLOGY, PARASITOLOGY. *Educ:* NMex State Univ, BS, 72; Eatern Wash State Col, MS, 74; Univ Nebr-Lincoln, PhD(life sci), 77. *Prof Exp:* asst prof 77-80, ASSOC PROF ZOOL, AUBURN UNIV, 80- *Honors & Awards:* Chester A Herrick Award, Ann Midwest Conf Parasitologists, 76. *Mem:* Am Soc Parasitologists; Soc Protozoologists. *Res:* Electron microscopy; host-parasite relationships of myxosporidans, trypanosomatids and sporozoans; cell-to-cell interactions and cellular interactions at the species-to-species interface. *Mailing Add:* Dept Zool-Entom Auburn Univ Auburn AL 36830

CURRERI, P WILLIAM, b Milwaukee, Wis, Sept 2, 36; m 75; c 3. SURGERY. *Educ:* Swarthmore Col, AB, 58; Univ Pa, MD, 62. *Prof Exp:* Asst prof, Univ Pa Hosp, 63-66, instr surg, 67-68; chief clin div, US Army Inst Surg Res, Brooke Army Med Ctr, Ft Sam Houston, 68-71; asst prof, Southwest Med Sch, Univ Tex, 71-74; assoc prof, Sch Med, Univ Wash, 74-77; Johnson & Johnson prof surg, Med Ctr, Cornell Univ, New York, 77-81; PROF & CHMN, DEPT SURG, UNIV SC, MOBILE, 81- *Concurrent Pos:* Fel, Harrison Dept Surg Res, 63-68 & Am Cancer Soc, 67-68; clin instr, Med Sch, Univ Tex, 68-71; NIH res career develop award, 72-77. *Mem:* Soc Univ Surgeons; Am Burn Asn; Asn for Acad Sug; Am Asn for Surg of Trauma; Am Col Surgeons. *Res:* Metabolism and nutrition in burns and trauma; hematological alterations after trauma; pulmonary dysfunction following trauma. *Mailing Add:* Cornell Med Ctr 525 E 68th St Rm F-758 New York NY 10021

CURRIE, BALFOUR WATSON, physics, deceased

CURRIE, BRUCE LAMONTE, b Pasadena, Calif, Mar 1, 45; m 65; c 3. MEDICINAL CHEMISTRY, ORGANIC CHEMISTRY. *Educ:* Ariz State Univ, BS, 66; Univ Utah, PhD(org chem), 70. *Prof Exp:* Robert A Welch fel, Inst Biomed Res, Univ Tex, Austin, 69-72, res assoc biochem & endocrinol, 72-74; asst prof, 74-81, ASSOC PROF MEDICINAL CHEM, COL PHARM, UNIV ILL MED CTR, 81- *Concurrent Pos:* guest scientist, Argonne Nat Lab, 80- *Mem:* Int Soc Heterocyclic Chem; Am Chem Soc. *Res:* Design and synthesis of small peptide hormone agonists and antagonists; peptide sequence and structure determination; anticancer nucleoside analogs; conformationally restricted peptides; peptide anti-sickling agents. *Mailing Add:* Dept Medicinal Chem Col Pharm PO Box 6998 Univ of Ill Med Ctr Chicago IL 60680

CURRIE, CHARLES H, US citizen. ELECTRICAL ENGINEERING. *Educ:* Ga Inst Technol, BEE, 52, MSEE, 56. *Prof Exp:* Electrician, City Tallahassee, Fla, 41-42; from radar technician to electronics officer, US Air Force, 43-49; electrician, Harrison Wright Construct Co, 49; res asst, Eng Exp Sta, Ga Inst Technol, 50-52, res engr, 52-54, asst proj dir, 54-56; chief electronics engr, 56-59, dir & vpres mfg div, 59-63, vpres & mgr prod develop, 64-67, prin engr & mgr advan develop group, 67-75, PRIN ENGR MICROWAVE INSTRUMENTATION STAFF, SCI-ATLANTA, INC, 75- *Mem:* Assoc mem Inst Elec & Electronics Engrs; assoc mem Sigma Xi. *Res:* Radar systems design; analog and digital instrumentation systems; receiving systems; signal sources; electronic circuits; antenna test instrumentation; servo mechanisms; reliability; human engineering; CATV systems; security systems; microwave links; packaging techniques. *Mailing Add:* Sci-Atlanta Inc 3845 Pleasantdale Rd Atlanta GA 30340

CURRIE, GUSTAVUS NOEL, II, pharmacology, endocrinology, see previous edition

CURRIE, IAIN GEORGE, b Glasgow, Scotland, Mar 11, 36; m 58; c 2. MECHANICAL ENGINEERING. *Educ:* Univ Strathclyde, BSc, 60; Univ BC, MASc, 62; Calif Inst Technol, PhD(appl mech), 66. *Prof Exp:* Asst prof, 66-69, assoc prof, 69-81, PROF MECH ENG, UNIV TORONTO, 81- *Mem:* Am Soc Mech Engrs; Am Inst Aeronaut & Astronaut; Can Soc Mech Engrs. *Res:* Analytical and experimental fluid mechanics with and without heat transfer. *Mailing Add:* Dept of Mech Eng Univ of Toronto Toronto ON M5S 2R8 Can

CURRIE, JAMES A(LFRED), b Philadelphia, Pa, Jan 8, 42; m 63; c 3. MATERIALS & POLYMER SCIENCE. *Educ:* Villanova Univ, BME, 64; Northwestern Univ, PhD(mat sci), 68. *Prof Exp:* Asst prof, 68-74, ASSOC PROF MECH ENG, VILLANOVA UNIV, 74- *Mailing Add:* Dept of Mech Eng Villanova Univ Villanova PA 19085

CURRIE, JAMES ORR, JR, b Canton, Ohio, July 28, 43; m 69; c 1. ORGANIC CHEMISTRY. *Educ:* Ohio State Univ, BS, 65; Univ Wash, PhD(org chem), 70. *Prof Exp:* Asst prof org chem, Univ Nev, Reno, 70-71; assoc org synthesis, Utah State Univ, 71-72; asst prof chem, 72-78, chmn dept, 76-80, ASSOC PROF CHEM, PAC UNIV, 78- *Mem:* Sigma Xi (pres, 76-); Am Chem Soc. *Res:* Synthesis and study of alkyldiazonium salts in virtually aprotic media; synthesis of optically active heterocycles; synthesis of nonbenzenoid aromatic systems. *Mailing Add:* Dept of Chem Pac Univ Forest Grove OR 97116

CURRIE, JOHN BICKELL, b Guelph Township, Ont, May 29, 22; m 48; c 2. GEOLOGY. *Educ:* McMaster Univ, BA, 46; Univ Toronto, MA, 47, PhD, 50. *Prof Exp:* Res geologist & sect head, Geol & Geochem Div, Gulf Res & Develop Co, 50-59; assoc prof, 59-64, PROF GEOL SCI, UNIV TORONTO, 64- *Mem:* Geol Soc Am; Am Asn Petrol Geol; Am Geophys Union. *Res:* Structural geology; mechanical development of geological structures; regional tectonics; petroleum geology. *Mailing Add:* Dept of Geol Univ of Toronto Toronto ON M5S 1A1 Can

CURRIE, JULIA RUTH, b Freeport, Tex, Dec 13, 44; m 71; c 3. NEUROSCIENCES. *Educ:* Radcliffe Col, AB, 67; Washington Univ, PhD(neurobiol), 74. *Prof Exp:* Res asst neurobiol, Harvard Med Sch, 67-69; res assoc physiol, Med Col, Cornell Univ, 74-76, NIH fel, 75-76; NIH trainee & sr staff assoc anat & opthalmol, 76-78, res assoc anat, 78-80, ASST PROF ANAT, COL PHYSICIANS & SURGEONS, COLUMBIA UNIV, 80- *Mem:* Am Soc Cell Biol; AAAS; Soc Neurosci; Asn Res Vision & Opthalmol; Am Asn Anatomists. *Res:* Experimental neuroembryology in general; membrane cell biology, in particular, using cyto chemical, autoradiographic, and ultrastructural techniques; vertebrate visual system; nerve regeneration; axondl transport. *Mailing Add:* Col Physicians & Surgeons Columbia Univ 630 W 168th St New York NY 10032

CURRIE, LLOYD ARTHUR, b Portland, Ore, Mar 14, 30; m 59; c 4. PHYSICAL CHEMISTRY, RADIOCHEMISTRY. *Educ:* Mass Inst Technol, BS, 52; Univ Chicago, PhD(phys chem), 55. *Prof Exp:* Asst prof chem, Pa State Univ, 55-62; NUCLEAR CHEMIST, NAT BUR STANDARDS, 62- *Concurrent Pos:* Lectr, Am Univ, 62-66; mem, Int Comn on Radiation Units & Measurements Task Group, 65-; vis prof, Inst Nuclear Sci, Univ Ghent & phys inst, Univ Bern, 70-71. *Honors & Awards:* Silver Medal, Dept Com, 80. *Mem:* Fel Am Inst Chemists; Am Chem Soc; AAAS; Am Geophys Union. *Res:* Nuclear reactions; electromagnetic isotope-separation of reaction products; low-level and environmental radioactivity; statistical aspects of nuclear decay and data analysis; application of nuclear methods to trace analysis and physical chemistry. *Mailing Add:* 215 Rolling Rd Gaithersburg MD 20760

CURRIE, NICHOLAS CHARLES, b Warner Robins, Ga, Apr 7, 45. ELECTROMAGNETIC SCATTERING, RADAR SYSTEMS. *Educ:* Ga Inst Technol, BS, 67, MS, 73. *Prof Exp:* Asst res phys, 67-73, res engr II, 73-77, SR RES ENGR & CHIEF RADAR EXP, ENG EXP STA, GA INST TECHNOL, 79- *Concurrent Pos:* Lectr, Continuing Educ Dept, Ga Inst Technol, 76-; consult, McGraw Hill Co, 79-80 & Battelle Columbus Labs, 80-81. *Mem:* Sr mem Inst Elec & Electronics Engrs; Sigma Xi. *Res:* Radar scattering, millimeter wave systems and computer controlled tracking systems. *Mailing Add:* Eng Exp Sta RAIL/RED Ga Inst Technol Atlanta GA 30332

CURRIE, PHILIP JOHN, b Toronto, Ont, Mar 13, 49; m 71; c 3. VERTEBRATE PALEONTOLOGY. *Educ:* Univ Toronto, BSc, 72; McGill Univ, MSc, 75, PhD(biol), 81. *Prof Exp:* Mus curator palaeont, Provincial Mus Alberta, 76-81; mus curator, Paleont Mus & Res Inst, 81-82; ASST DIR RES, TYRRELL MUS PALAEONT, 82- *Concurrent Pos:* Secy, Alberta Palaeont Adv Comt, 77-; Treas, Palaeont Can, 81- *Mem:* Soc Vertebrate Paleont; Paleont Soc; Sigma Xi; Can Soc Petrol Geologists; Am Soc Zoologists. *Res:* Fossil reptiles including Permian Sphenacoronts from Europe and United States; permian eosuchians from Africa and Madagascar; cretaceous dinosaurs from Canada and their footprints. *Mailing Add:* Palaeont Mus & Res Inst 12845 102 Ave Edmonton AL T5N 0M6 Can

CURRIE, R(OBERT) M(ARION), b Connersville, Ind, Mar 15, 24; m 46; c 2. CHEMICAL ENGINEERING. *Educ:* Purdue Univ, BS, 45, PhD(chem eng), 50. *Prof Exp:* Res engr, Yerkes Res Lab, NY, 50-54, Mylar Polyester Film Plant, Ohio, 54-58 & Res & Develop Lab, 58-60, process develop supvr, SC, 60-67, econ anal supvr, Film Dept, Wilmington, 67-70, sr res engr, 70-78, RES ASSOC, CIRCLEVILLE RES LAB, E I DU PONT DE NEMOURS & CO, INC, 78- *Res:* Polymerization; polymer processing; film handling. *Mailing Add:* 1200 Cambridge Pl Circleville OH 43113

CURRIE, ROBERT GUINN, b Dermott, Tex, Dec 31, 35; div. GEOPHYSICS. *Educ:* Univ Calif, Berkeley, BA, 60, MA, 62; Univ Calif, Los Angeles, PhD(geophys), 65. *Prof Exp:* Nat Acad Sci fel space physics, Ames Res Ctr, NASA, 65-67; sr engr appl math, Varian Assoc, 68-70; chief scientist geophys, SAfrican Coun Sci Indust Res, 71-76; SR RES GEOPHYSICIST DATA PROCESSING, ATLANTIC RICHFIELD CO, 77- *Mem:* Fel Royal Astron Soc; Soc Explor Geophys. *Res:* Geomagnetism; seismology; climatology; earth rotation; paleomagnetism; space physics; time series analysis. *Mailing Add:* 300 Main Street Roscoe TX 79545

CURRIE, THOMAS ESWIN, b Bolton, Eng, Feb 16, 26; US citizen; m 58; c 3. CERAMICS ENGINEERING, MATERIALS SCIENCE. *Educ:* Leeds Univ, BSc, 51, PhD(ceramics), 54. *Prof Exp:* Res assoc ceramics, Pa State Univ, 54-57; ceramics engr, US Naval Boiler & Turbine Lab, 57 & Foote Mineral Co, 57-60; RES ASSOC MAT SCI, GEN ELEC CO, 60- *Mem:* Fel Am Ceramic Soc; Soc Plastics Engrs; Appliance Engrs Soc. *Res:* Materials characterization; microwave properties of plastic materials, structure of glasses and vitreous enamels. *Mailing Add:* Gen Elec Co AP35-1101 Appliance Park Louisville KY 40225

CURRIE, WILLIAM DEEMS, b Wallace, NC, Sept 4, 35; m 61; c 2. BIOCHEMISTRY. *Educ:* Davidson Col, BS, 57; Univ NC, MS, 62, PhD(biochem), 64. *Prof Exp:* Res asst biochem, Univ NC, 60-62; appointee, Biol & Med Res Group, Los Alamos Sci Lab, Univ Calif, 64-66; asst prof biol, East Carolina Univ, 66-67; asst prof radiobiol, 67-73, ASSOC PROF RADIOBIOL, MED CTR, DUKE UNIV, 73- *Mem:* AAAS; Am Chem Soc; Biophys Soc. *Res:* Control of energy metabolism; nuclear metabolism; effects of hyperbaric oxygen; oxidative phosphorylation; metabolism of cancer cells; seizure activity and energy metabolism. *Mailing Add:* Box 3224 Duke Univ Med Ctr Durham NC 27706

CURRIER, HERBERT BASHFORD, b Richwood, Ohio, Oct 16, 11; m 34; c 2. PLANT PHYSIOLOGY. *Educ:* Ohio State Univ, BS, 32; Utah State Col, MS, 38; Univ Calif, PhD(plant physiol), 43. *Prof Exp:* Asst, Utah State Col, 37-38; asst col agr, Univ Calif, 38-39, assoc bot, 39-42; res chemist, Basic Veg Prod Co, 43-46; asst prof bot & asst botanist, 46-52, assoc prof bot & assoc botanist, 52-58, prof, 58-77, EMER PROF BOT, UNIV CALIF, DAVIS, 77- BOTANIST, EXP STA, 58- *Concurrent Pos:* Guggenheim fel, 54-55 & 61-62; guest prof, Univ Gottingen, 74. *Mem:* Am Soc Plant Physiol; Bot Soc Am; Scand Soc Plant Physiol; Japanese Soc Plant Physiol. *Res:* Cellular physiology; phloem translocation; plant water relations; toxicity; structural-functional studies of the phloem tissue of higher plants. *Mailing Add:* Dept of Bot Univ of Calif Davis CA 95616

CURRIER, RICHARD A, US citizen. ENGINEERING. *Educ:* Mich Col Mining & Technol, BS, 63; Northeastern Univ, MS, 68. *Prof Exp:* Engr, US Army, Corps Engrs, 63-66; supt pub works, Town of Milford, 66-68; design engr, Rollins, King & McKone, Inc, 68-69, Anderson Nichols and Co, Inc, 69-71; VPRES, WESTON, 71- *Res:* Project supervision; cost control; client and regulatory agency liaison; water pollution control; facility plans; water supply and distribution; subsurface disposal of solid and liquid wastes. *Mailing Add:* Weston Weston Way West Chester PA 19380

CURRIER, ROBERT DAVID, b Grand Rapids, Mich, Feb 19, 25; m 51; c 2. NEUROLOGY. *Educ:* Univ Mich, AB, 48, MD, 52, MS, 55. *Prof Exp:* From asst prof to assoc prof neurol, Univ Mich, 57-61; assoc prof, 61-69, PROF MED, MED CTR, UNIV MISS, 69-, CHIEF DIV NEUROL, 61-, CHMN DEPT NEUROL, 77- *Concurrent Pos:* Consult, Wayne County Gen Hosp & Ann Arbor Vet Admin Hosp, Mich, 59-61 & Jackson Vet Admin Hosp, Miss, 61- *Mem:* Fel Am Acad Neurol. *Res:* Clinical, academic and research neurology. *Mailing Add:* Dept of Neurol Univ of Miss Med Ctr Jackson MS 39216

CURRIER, THOMAS CURTIS, b Sturgis, Mich, Feb 13, 47; m 72. MOLECULAR BIOLOGY, GENETICS. *Educ:* Ind Univ, BS, 70; Univ Wash, MS, 72, PhD(microbiol), 76. *Prof Exp:* Res assoc genetics of cyanobacteria, Dept Energy, Mich State Univ, 76-78; ASST PROF PHYTOPATH BACTERIA, KANS STATE UNIV, 79- *Mem:* Am Soc Microbiologists. *Res:* Genetics and molecular biology of cyanobacteria; the molecular biology of crown gall tumor induction by Agrobacterium tumefaciens and host-parasite interactions of phytopathogenic bacteria. *Mailing Add:* Dept of Plant Path Kans State Univ Manhattan KS 66507

CURRIER, VERNON ARTHUR, b Sheboygan, Wis, Dec 13, 25; m 48; c 4. PETROLEUM CHEMISTRY. *Educ:* Univ Wis, BS, 50. *Prof Exp:* From chemist to sr res chemist, 50-62, res specialist tech serv, 62-63, sr proj chemist, 63-65, sect supvr tech serv, 65-71, MGR TECH SERV, JEFFERSON CHEM CO, INC, 71- *Mem:* Am Chem Soc; Soc Plastics Indust. *Res:* Petrochemical research in ethylene and propylene based chemicals. *Mailing Add:* PO Box 4128 North Austin Sta Austin TX 78765

CURRIER, WILLIAM WESLEY, b Seattle, Wash, Sept 18, 47; m 69; c 1. PLANT BIOCHEMISTRY. *Educ:* Univ Wash, BS, 69; Purdue Univ, PhD(biochem), 74. *Prof Exp:* Fel plant path, Mont State Univ, 74-77; ASST PROF MICROBIOL & BIOCHEM, UNIV VT, 77- *Mem:* AAAS; Am Soc for Microbiol; Sigma Xi; Am Soc Plant Physiologists. *Res:* Biochemical recognition; plant disease resistance; biological nitrogen fixation; bacterial chemotaxis; plant amino acid transport; pesticide drift. *Mailing Add:* Dept Microbiol & Biochem 115 Hills Bldg Burlington VT 05405

CURRO, JOHN GILLETTE, b Detroit, Mich, Oct 5, 42; m 67; c 2. POLYMER PHYSICS. *Educ:* Univ Detroit, BChE, 65; Calif Inst Technol, PhD(mat sci), 69. *Prof Exp:* Res assoc theoret physics, Inst Appl Math & Fluid Dynamics, Univ Md, College Park, 69-70; staff mem, 70-75, DIV SUPVR POLYMER PHYSICS, SANDIA LABS, 75- *Mem:* Am Phys Soc; Am Inst Chem Engrs. *Res:* Conformation of polymer chains and its relationship to physical properties; viscoelasticity of polymers undergoing chemical reaction. *Mailing Add:* Div 5813 Sandia Labs Albuquerque NM 87115

CURRY, BILL PERRY, b Hopkinsville, Ky, Mar 14, 37; wid; c 2. THEORETICAL & APPLIED PHYSICS. *Educ:* Vanderbilt Univ, AB, 59; Univ Tenn, MS, 65. *Prof Exp:* Res engr gas kinetics, plasmas & magnetohydrodyn phenomena, ARO Inc, Tenn, 60-66; sr physicist high temperature gas physics & nuclear weapons technol, Physics Int Corp, Calif, 66-68; sr physicist scattering phenomena, nuclear weapons technol & chem lasers, Lawrence Livermore Lab, Univ Calif, 68-73; res scientist & prog mgr magnetohydrodyn develop, STD Res Corp, Calif, 73-76; physicist electromagnetics & laser diag, ARO Inc, Sverdrup Corp, 76-80; PHYSICIST, ARVIN/CALSPAN FIELD SERV, INC, 80- *Concurrent Pos:* Lectr math, Calif State Col, Hayward, 68-70. *Mem:* Am Phys Soc; AAAS. *Res:* Theoretical and computational applied physics related to quantum kinetic phenomena; fluid and plasma dynamics; magnetohydrodynamic devices; nuclear weapons technology; chemical laser technology; electromagnetic wave propagation and scattering. *Mailing Add:* Lakeview Dr Rte 1 Decherd TN 37324

CURRY, DONALD LAWRENCE, b Bridgeport, Conn, Mar 26, 36; m 69; c 3. MEDICAL PHYSIOLOGY. *Educ:* Sacramento State Col, AB, 63; Univ Calif, San Francisco, PhD(physiol), 67. *Prof Exp:* Asst res physiologist, Med Ctr, Univ Calif, San Francisco, 67-69, lectr, 68-69; asst prof, 69-75, ASSOC PROF PHYSIOL SCI, SCH VET MED, UNIV CALIF, DAVIS, 75- *Concurrent Pos:* NIH-Am Diabetes Asn res grants, 74- *Mem:* Am Physiol Soc; Endocrine Soc. *Res:* Study of factors which control insulin secretion by the perfused pancreas. *Mailing Add:* Dept of Physiol Sci Univ Calif Sch of Vet Med Davis CA 95616

CURRY, FRANCIS J, b San Francisco, Calif, July 19, 11; m 48; c 8. INTERNAL MEDICINE. *Educ:* San Francisco Univ, BSc, 36; Stanford Univ, MD, 46; Univ Calif, MPH, 64. *Prof Exp:* Asst med bact, Stanford Univ, 41-42, asst path, 42-43; chief tuberc & pulmonary dis sect, Army Specialized Treatment Ctr, Ft Carson, Colo, 53-54, chief tuberc sect, Army & Air Force Specialized Treatment Ctr & coordr clin res, Fitzsimons Army Hosp, Denver, 54-56; chief tuberc control div, 56-60, asst dir pub health, 60-70, DIR PUB HEALTH, HOSPS & MENT HEALTH, SAN FRANCISCO HEALTH DEPT, 70-76. *Concurrent Pos:* Dir chest clin, San Francisco Gen Hosp, 56-76; prof med, Univ Calif, 58-, lectr, Sch Pub Health, 60-, prof ambulatory & community med, Sch Med, 66-; assoc prof, Stanford Univ, 62; USPHS clin res grant, 62-76; consult, Nat Jewish Hosp, Denver, Colo, 64-; consult, Tuberc Commun Dis Div & mem, Adv Comt Tuberc Control, USPHS, Ga, 65-; consult, Nat Commun Dis Ctr. *Mem:* Fel Am Col Chest Physicians; fel Am Col Prev Med; Am Thoracic Soc; fel Am Col Physicians; fel Am Trauma Soc. *Res:* Pulmonary fungus diseases, particularly histoplasmosis and coccidioidomycosis; atypical mycobacteria infections of man; social and behavioral problems of staff and patients and their effect upon each other and upon the maintenance of treatment by patients; tuberculin skin testing on large population groups. *Mailing Add:* Univ of Calif 217 Kensington Way San Francisco CA 94127

CURRY, GEORGE MONTGOMERY, b Halifax, NS, Nov 7, 26; nat US; m 50; c 2. PLANT PHYSIOLOGY. *Educ:* Acadia Univ, BA, 46; Yale Univ, MS, 47; Harvard Univ, AM, 54, PhD, 58. *Prof Exp:* Teacher pub sch, Mass, 47-52; from instr to assoc prof biol, Tufts Univ, 58-70; head dept, 70-76, PROF BIOL, ACADIA UNIV, 70- *Mem:* AAAS; Am Soc Plant Physiol. *Res:* Effects of light on unicellular and multicellular plants. *Mailing Add:* Dept of Biol Acadia Univ Wolfville NS B0P 1X0 Can

CURRY, GEORGE RICHARD, b Detroit, Mich, June 4, 32; m 67; c 2. ELECTRICAL ENGINEERING, SYSTEMS ANALYSIS. *Educ:* Univ Mich, BS(elec eng) & BS(math), 55; Mass Inst Technol, SM, 59. *Prof Exp:* Staff engr, Lincoln Lab, Mass Inst Technol, 58-64 & Raytheon Co, 64-66; DIR SCI, TECHNOL OPERS & ASSOC DIR, SANTA BARBARA DIV, GEN RES CORP, FLOW GEN, INC, 66- *Mem:* Inst Elec & Electronics Engrs. *Res:* Design and analysis of military systems; radar systems; ballistic missile defense; satellite and space systems; tactical warfare technology; avionics; communications; strategic defense. *Mailing Add:* Gen Res Corp PO Box 6770 Santa Barbara CA 93111

CURRY, HIRAM BENJAMIN, b Midville, Ga, Sept 19, 27; m 51; c 4. NEUROLOGY. *Educ:* Col Charleston, BS, 47; Med Col SC, MD, 50. *Prof Exp:* Gen practr, 51-57; intern internal med, Vet Admin Hosp, Lake City, Fla, 58; assoc, 63-64, from asst prof to assoc prof, 64-77, PROF NEUROL, MED UNIV SC, 77- PROF FAMILY PRACT & CHMN SECT, 70- *Concurrent Pos:* Nat Inst Neurol Dis & Blindness spec fel, 60-63; prin investr, USPHS grant, 63-70, co-prin investr, 67-69; chief neurol serv, Vet Admin Hosp, Charleston, SC, 66-68; pres prof staff & mem exec comt, Med Univ Hosp, Charleston, SC, 70-; med dir outpatient clins, dir family pract residency prog & mem behav sci comt, Med Univ SC, 70-; coordr, SC Statewide Family Pract Residency Syst, 73-78. *Mem:* Am Acad Neurol; Asn Res Nerv & Ment Dis; Am Aacd Gen Pract. *Res:* Cerebral circulation; cerebral vascular disease; epidemiology of vascular disease; health care delivery; medical education. *Mailing Add:* Dept of Family Pract Med Univ of SC Charleston SC 29401

CURRY, HOWARD MILLARD, b Haverhill, Mass, Mar 8, 24; m 80; c 2. ORGANIC CHEMISTRY. *Educ:* Northeastern Univ, BS, 45; Boston Univ, AM, 47, PhD(org chem), 50. *Prof Exp:* Instr chem, Bates Col, 49-50; assoc prof, 51-60, PROF CHEM, WITTENBERG UNIV, 60-, CHMN DEPT, 74- *Concurrent Pos:* Consult, C F Kettering Found, 57- *Mem:* Am Chem Soc. *Res:* Nitrogen organics. *Mailing Add:* 1511 N Plum St Apt D Springfield OH 45504

CURRY, JAMES EUGENE, b Rome, Ga, Oct 15, 26; m 49; c 4. CHEMICAL ENGINEERING, MATERIALS SCIENCE. *Educ:* Ga Inst Technol, BS, 50, MS, 51; Univ Ala, PhD(chem eng), 72. *Prof Exp:* Chem engr, Southern Res Inst, 15-53 & Herty Found Lab, 54-55; area supvr prod, Diamond Alkali Co, 55-57; mat specialist, Army Ballistic Missile Agency, 57-60; CHIEF, NONMETALLIC MAT DIV AEROSPACE, MARSHALL SPACE FLIGHT CTR, NASA, 60- *Honors & Awards:* Except Serv Medal, NASA, 75. *Res:* Polymer science. *Mailing Add:* 1201 Nolan Blvd Madison AL 35758

CURRY, JAMES KENNETH, b Amarillo, Tex, Nov 30, 20; m 45; c 3. GEOLOGY. *Educ:* Tex Tech Univ, BS, 42; Univ Calif, Los Angeles, cert meteorol. *Prof Exp:* Geologist, Panhandle Eastern Pipeline Co, 46-48, asst dist geologist, 48-52, dist geologist, 52-54, div geologist, 54-55, mgr geol, 55-64, mgr, Geol Div, 64-69, mgr explor, 69-73, mgr, Rocky Mountain Region, 75-81; CONSULT GEOLOGIST, 81- *Mem:* Am Asn Petrol Geologists; Am Inst Mining, Metall & Petrol Engrs; Am Inst Prof Geologists. *Res:* Exploratory geology in search of oil and gas. *Mailing Add:* 5687 S Geneva St Englewood CO 80111

CURRY, JOHN D, b Xenia, Ohio, Nov 16, 38; m 60; c 2. INORGANIC CHEMISTRY. *Educ:* Wilmington Col, Ohio, BA, 60; Ohio State Univ, PhD(inorg chem), 64. *Prof Exp:* William Ramsay Mem & NATO fels, Oxford Univ, 64-65; RES CHEMIST, WINTON HILL TECH CTR, PROCTER & GAMBLE CO, CINCINNATI, 65- *Mem:* Am Chem Soc; The Chem Soc; Sigma Xi. *Res:* Homogeneous catalysis; reactions of coordinated ligands; phosphorus chemistry; surfactants. *Mailing Add:* 709 Marcia Dr Oxford OH 45056

CURRY, JOHN JOSEPH, III, b Brooklyn, NY, Nov 1, 40; m 66; c 2. NEUROENDOCRINOLOGY. *Educ:* State Univ NY Col Plattsburgh, BS, 62; Adelphi Univ, MS, 64; Univ Calif, Berkeley, PhD(physiol), 69. *Prof Exp:* From instr to asst prof physiol, Sch Med, Boston Univ, 68-73; asst prof, 73-77, ASSOC PROF PHYSIOL, OHIO STATE UNIV, 77- *Mem:* Am Physiol Soc; Endocrine Soc; Soc Neurosci; Am Asn Univ Professors. *Res:* Central nervous system regulation of reproductive behavior and gonadotrophin secretion; sensory and hormonal factors controlling ovulation; mechanisms of hypertensive disease of pregnancy (pre-eclampsia). *Mailing Add:* Dept of Physiol Ohio State Univ 1645 Neil Ave Columbus OH 43210

CURRY, MARY GRACE, b New Orleans, La, June 16, 47. LIMNOLOGY, ECOLOGY. *Educ:* Univ New Orleans, BS, 69, MS, 71; La State Univ, Baton Rouge, PhD(bot), 73. *Prof Exp:* Vis asst prof bot, La State Univ, Baton Rouge, 74; environ scientist life sci, VTN Louisiana, Inc, 74-79; ENVIRON IMPACT OFFICER, JEFFERSON PARISH, LOUISIANA, 79- *Concurrent Pos:* Pvt environ consult. *Mem:* Ecol Soc Am; Bot Soc Am; Am Inst Biol Sci; Coastal Soc; Sigma Xi. *Res:* Taxonomy, ecology and distribution of freshwater leeches; vascular plant taxonomy. *Mailing Add:* 3404 Tolmas Dr Metairie LA 70002

CURRY, MICHAEL JOSEPH, b Brooklyn, NY, Aug 15, 20; m 58; c 4. PLASTICS, CHEMISTRY. *Educ:* St John's Col, NY, BS, 41; Univ Wis-Madison, PhD(org chem), 48. *Prof Exp:* Chemist chem warfare, US Naval Res Lab, 42-45; asst prof org chem, Col St Thomas, 48-50; develop chemist, Calco Div, Am Cyanamid Co, 50-51; prod develop engr, Celanese Corp, 51-54, tech serv mgr, 54-59, lab mgr, 60-61, plastics develop dir, 61-67; assoc, Heidrick & Struggles, 67-71; PRES, MICHAEL J CURRY ASSOCS, INC, 71- *Mem:* Am Chem Soc; Asn Consult Chemists & Chem Engrs. *Res:* Plastics research; chemical marketing; laboratory administration; technical personnel administration. *Mailing Add:* 941 St Marks Ave Westfield NJ 07090

CURRY, R(OBERT) BRUCE, b Iowa City, Iowa, Sept 24, 29; m 56; c 2. AGRICULTURAL ENGINEERING. *Educ:* Kans State Univ, BS, 51; Colo State Univ, MS, 55; Univ Mo, PhD, 60. *Prof Exp:* Design engr bur reclamation, US Dept Interior, 51-52; asst, Colo State Univ, 54-55; instr agr eng, Univ Mo, 55-60; from asst prof to assoc prof, 60-68, PROF AGR ENG, OHIO AGR RES & DEVELOP CTR & OHIO STATE UNIV, 68- *Concurrent Pos:* Vis fel, Clare Hall, Cambridge Univ, 67-68. *Mem:* Fel AAAS; Am Soc Agr Engrs; Am Soc Eng Educ; Soc Comput Simulation; Am Soc Agron. *Res:* Biological modeling and simulation; dynamics of soil-water relationships in plant growth; mathematical modeling and dynamic simulation of plant growth systems; controlled environment for food production. *Mailing Add:* Dept of Agr Eng Ohio Agr Res & Develop Ctr Wooster OH 44691

CURRY, RENWICK EUGENE, JR, b Portchester, NY, Dec 13, 37; m 62; c 3. STOCHASTIC SYSTEMS, AVIATION PSYCHOLOGY. *Educ:* Middlebury Col, AB, 59; Mass Inst Technol, BS & MS, 62, EAA, 63, PhD(estimation & control), 68. *Prof Exp:* Asst prof elec eng, Cornell Univ, 68-69; asst prof aeronaut & astronaut, Mass Inst Technol, 69-76; RES SCIENTIST, NAT AERONAUT & SPACE ADMIN, 76- *Mem:* Inst Elec & Electronics Engrs. *Res:* Human detection of failures; monitoring and control of unreliable systems. *Mailing Add:* NASA Ames Res Ctr Moffett Field CA 94035

CURRY, ROBERT RODNEY, geomorphology, ecology, see previous edition

CURRY, THOMAS F(ORTSON), b Thomasville, Ga, Nov 22, 26; m 49; c 6. ELECTRONICS, COMMUNICATIONS. *Educ:* Ga Inst Technol, BEE, 49; Pa State Univ, MS, 54; Carnegie Inst Technol, PhD(elec eng), 59. *Prof Exp:* Teaching asst, Pa State Univ, 49-51; mem tech staff, Bell Tel Labs, NJ, 57-58; dir, Electronics Res Lab, Syracuse Univ Res Corp, NY, 58-64; chmn bd & consult, Microwave/Systs, Inc, 64-65; mgr, Appl Electronics & chief engr, Melpar Div, Am Standard, Inc, 65-70; tech adv to pres, E-Systs, Inc, 70-74; vpres, Microwave Systs, Inc, 74-75; dir, Signal Intelligence Systs, Off Asst Secy Defense, Intel, Dept Defense, 76-77, sr staff specialist, Tactical Reconnaissance, Off Under Secy Defense, Res & Eng, 77-80, ASSOC DEP ASST, OFF SECY NAVY, DEPT DEFENSE, 80- *Concurrent Pos:* Consult, Dept Defense, Indust & Eng Joint Coun, 60-76. *Mem:* Sigma Xi; fel Inst Elec

& Electronics Engrs. *Res:* Sequential decision theory applied to signal detection/estimation; adaptive Bayesian sequential observer for signal recognition, classification, and sorting; computer controlled electronic warfare and SIGINT systems design and analysis. *Mailing Add:* 2403 Beekay Ct Vienna VA 22180

CURRY, THOMAS HARVEY, b Sullivan Co, Ind, Oct 7, 21; m 45; c 3. ORGANIC CHEMISTRY, CHEMICAL ENGINEERING. *Educ:* Purdue Univ, BChE, 42; Ohio State Univ, PhD(org chem), 53. *Prof Exp:* Tech supvr, Holston Ord Works, Tenn Eastman Corp, 43-45; instr chem, Antioch Col, 50-52; from asst prof to assoc prof, Univ Ohio, Athens, 53-61, chmn dept chem eng, 56-61; dean, Col Technol, Univ Maine, 61-67; dir resident res associateships, Nat Acad Sci, 67-69, dir associateships, Comn Human Resources, 69-74, exec secy, Bd Fel & Associateships, 74-77, dir fel, 74-78, RETIRED. *Concurrent Pos:* NSF sci fac fel, 57-60. *Res:* Chemistry of pyrroles and porphyrins. *Mailing Add:* 409 S Orlando Cocoa Beach FL 32931

CURRY, WARREN H(ENRY), b Rochester, NY, Jan 13, 24; m 47; c 4. AERONAUTICAL ENGINEERING. *Educ:* Univ Mich, BSE(aeronaut eng) & BSE(math), 45, MS, 46, AeE, 52. *Prof Exp:* Engr, Gen Elec Co, NY, 46-48; res assoc exp aerodyn, Univ Mich, 48-51; staff mem, 51-56, supvr eng aerodyn div, 56-65, supvr exp aerodyn div, 65-72, STAFF MEM, SANDIA CORP, 73- *Mem:* Assoc fel Am Inst Aeronaut & Astronaut. *Res:* Aeronautical engineering and aerodynamics associated with the development of ballistic vehicles, rocket systems and experimental facilities. *Mailing Add:* 3409 Stardust Ct NE Albuquerque NM 87110

CURRY, WILLIAM HIRST, III, b San Antonio, Tex, Feb 3, 32; m 54; c 4. GEOLOGY. *Educ:* Cornell Univ, BA, 54; Princeton Univ, PhD(geol), 59. *Prof Exp:* Geologist, Marathon Oil Co, 59-65; PRES, CURRY OIL CO, 66- *Concurrent Pos:* Consult geologist, 65- *Mem:* Sigma Xi; Am Asn Petrol Geologists. *Res:* Search for more effective oil and gas exploration tools and combinations of concepts and tools. *Mailing Add:* PO Box 3001 Casper WY 82602

CURTICE, JAY STEPHEN, b Dallas, Tex, Jan 19, 28; m 57; c 2. PHYSICAL ORGANIC CHEMISTRY. *Educ:* Southern Methodist Univ, BS, 48; Iowa State Univ, PhD(chem), 54. *Prof Exp:* Res chemist, Sinclair Res, Inc, 54-62; assoc prof, 62-68, PROF CHEM, ROOSEVELT UNIV, 68- *Mem:* AAAS; Am Chem Soc. *Res:* Mechanisms of free radical reactions; organometallics. *Mailing Add:* 3135 Priscilla Ave Highland Park IL 60035

CURTICE, WALTER R, b Rochester, NY, Sept 14, 35; m 58; c 3. ELECTRICAL ENGINEERING. *Educ:* Cornell Univ, BEE, 58, MS, 60, PhD(elec eng), 62. *Prof Exp:* Sr res & develop engr, Raytheon Co, Mass, 62-67; vis asst prof elec eng, Univ Mich, 67-69, assoc prof, 69-72; MEM TECH STAFF, RCA LABS, 73- *Mem:* Inst Elec & Electronics Engrs. *Res:* Microwave electronics; solid state devices; linear beam microwave tubes. *Mailing Add:* RCA Lab PO Box 800 Princeton NJ 08540

CURTIN, CHARLES BYRON, b Cohoes, NY, Aug 2, 17; m 45; c 2. BIOLOGY. *Educ:* George Washington Univ, BS, 45; Catholic Univ, MS, 47; Univ Pittsburgh, PhD, 56. *Prof Exp:* Asst, Catholic Univ, 46-47; prof biol, Mt St Mary's Col, Md, 47-57; staff ed life sci, McGraw-Hill Encycl Sci & Technol, 57-62; ASSOC PROF BIOL, CREIGHTON UNIV, 62- *Concurrent Pos:* Asst, Univ Pittsburgh, 52-53; consult ed, McGraw-Hill, 71. *Mem:* Am Soc Syst Zool; Ecol Soc Am; Sigma Xi; Am Micros Soc. *Res:* Taxonomy and ecology of Tardigrada; parasitology; microtechnique. *Mailing Add:* 6218 Florence Blvd Omaha NE 68110

CURTIN, DAVID YARROW, b Philadelphia, Pa, Aug 22, 20; m 50; c 4. ORGANIC CHEMISTRY. *Educ:* Swarthmore Col, AB, 43; Univ Ill, PhD(chem), 45. *Prof Exp:* Rockefeller Inst grant, Harvard Univ, 45-46; from instr to asst prof chem, Columbia Univ, 46-51; from asst prof to assoc prof, 51-54, PROF CHEM, UNIV ILL, URBANA, 54- *Mem:* Nat Acad Sci; fel Royal Soc Chem; Swiss Chem Soc; Am Crystallog Asn; Am Chem Soc. *Res:* Reaction mechanisms and exploratory synthetic organic chemistry; solid state organic chemistry. *Mailing Add:* Dept of Chem Univ of Ill Urbana IL 61801

CURTIN, GERALD F, JR, b Ossining, NY, May 22, 22; m 47; c 4. CHEMICAL ENGINEERING. *Educ:* Yale Univ, BE, 42. *Prof Exp:* Engr, Ammonia Dept, Exp Sta, 43-49, res supvr, Polychem Dept, 49-52, asst tech supt, Mfg Div, Tex, 52-53, tech supt, WVa, 53-54, gen supt, Polychem Dept, Tech Sect, 54, asst mgr, 54-58, prod mgr, Res & Develop Div, 58-64, mgr, Res Fluorocarbon Div, 64-70, tech mgr nylon intermediates, 70-81, GEN MGR, PETROCHEM DEPT, E I DU PONT DE NEMOURS & CO, INC, 81- *Res:* Nylon and vinyl polymers. *Mailing Add:* E I DuPont de Nemours & Co Inc PO Box 123 Mendanhall PA 19357

CURTIN, LEO VINCENT, b Christian Co, Ill, Mar 2, 23; m 81; c 2. ANIMAL NUTRITION. *Educ:* Univ Ill, BS, 47, MS, 48; Cornell Univ, PhD(nutrit), 52. *Prof Exp:* Animal nutritionist, Buckeye Cotton Oil Co, 48-50, head prod res dept, 52-55; asst dir feed res & nutrit, Cent Soya Co, Ind, 55-66; dir res & develop, 66-69, vpres, Nat Molasses Co, 69-75, SR VPRES, NAMOLCO, INC, 75- *Mem:* Am Soc Animal Sci; Poultry Sci Asn; Am Dairy Sci Asn. *Res:* Nutritional requirements of farm animals; soybean processing; feed manufacturing. *Mailing Add:* NAMOLCO Willow Grove PA 19090

CURTIN, RICHARD BRENDAN, b New York, NY, Mar 29, 40. ELECTRICAL ENGINEERING, COMPUTER SCIENCES. *Educ:* Manhattan Col, BEE, 61; Yale Univ, MEE, 62; Trinity Univ, MBA, 67. *Prof Exp:* Res engr guidance & navig, NAm Aviation, 62; proj engr tempest eng, US Air Force Security Serv, 62-65; sr res engr electronics res, Southwest Res Inst, 65-67; mgr electromagnetic interference prod electronic filters, Sanders Assoc, 67-68; DIR DATA SYSTS DEPT, SOUTHWEST RES INST, 68- *Res:* Research and development in advanced digital systems utilizing minicomputer, microprocessor and fiber-optic technology; data communications; electronic warfare; imitative communications deception; automatic test equipment, robotics and automation. *Mailing Add:* Southwest Res Inst PO Drawer 28510 San Antonio TX 78284

CURTIN, TERRENCE M, b Spencer, SDak, June 9, 26; m 53; c 4. VETERINARY MEDICINE, PHYSIOLOGY. *Educ:* Univ Minn, BS & DVM, 54; Purdue Univ, MS, 63, PhD(vet physiol), 64. *Prof Exp:* Pvt vet practice, SDak, 54-58; exten vet, Purdue Univ, 58-61, NIH fel, 61-64 & grant, 61-65, asst prof vet physiol, 64-66; prof vet physiol & dir continuing educ, Univ Mo-Columbia, 66-68, prof & chmn dept vet physiol & pharmacol, Sch Vet Med, 68-73; head dept, 73-80, PROF VET SCI, NC STATE UNIV, 73-, DEAN SCH, 80- *Concurrent Pos:* USDA res grant, 65-66. *Mem:* AAAS; Am Vet Med Asn; US Animal Health Asn; Am Phys Soc; NY Acad Sci. *Res:* Esophagogastric ulcers of swine; mycotoxin induced hepatitis. *Mailing Add:* Dept of Vet Sci NC State Univ Raleigh NC 27650

CURTIN, THOMAS J, b New York, NY; c 4. ENTOMOLOGY, RESEARCH ADMINISTRATION. *Educ:* Manhattan Col, BS, 40; Univ Fla, MS, 51; Univ Md, College Park, PhD(entom), 59. *Prof Exp:* Consult drugs, Sandoz Pharmaceut, 46-51; consult entom, Strategic Air Command, USAF, 54-59, sect chief entom, USAF Epidemial Lab, Turkey, 59-62, br chief, Tex, 62-68; assoc dir life sci res, Ohio State Univ Res Ctr, 68-73; dir, Off Res & Sponsored Progs Serv, Wayne State Univ, 73-78, adj prof biol, 76-80; DIR RES, TEX WOMAN'S UNIV, 80- *Concurrent Pos:* Consult, US Army, 50-51; adv, UN Korean Relief Admin, 52-53 & Turkist Govt, 61-62; del, Int Cong Entom, USAF, 60; Dept Air Force del, US Dept Defense Pesticide Bd, 62-68. *Mem:* AAAS; Am Inst Biol Sci; Entom Soc Am; Am Mosquito Control Asn. *Res:* Physiology of insect reproductive systems; insect susceptibility to pesticides; plant hormonal activity. *Mailing Add:* Off of Res & Grants Admin Tex Woman's Univ Denton TX 76204

CURTIS, BRIAN ALBERT, b New York, NY, Nov 25, 36; m 60; c 1. PHYSIOLOGY. *Educ:* Univ Rochester, BA, 58; Rockefeller Inst, PhD(physiol), 63. *Prof Exp:* Guest investr, Physiol Lab, Cambridge Univ, 60-61; from instr to assoc prof physiol, Sch Med & Sch Dent, Tufts Univ, 65-74, asst dean educ planning, 70-73; asst dean undergrad med educ, 74-79, ASSOC PROF PHYSIOL, PEORIA SCH MED, UNIV ILL, 74- *Mem:* Soc Gen Physiol (secy, 67-69); Biophys Soc; Am Physiol Soc; Fed Am Soc Exp Biol. *Res:* Muscle physiology. *Mailing Add:* Dept of Physiol Peoria Sch Med Peoria IL 61656

CURTIS, BRUCE FRANKLIN, b Denver, Colo, Dec 16, 18; m 58. GEOLOGY, HYDROLOGY. *Educ:* Oberlin Col, AB, 41; Univ Colo, MA, 42; Harvard Univ, PhD(geol), 49. *Prof Exp:* field asst, US Geol Surv, 42; geologist to regional geologist, Continental Oil Co, 49-57; assoc prof, 57-61, chmn dept, 61-68, PROF GEOL, UNIV COLO, BOULDER, 61- *Concurrent Pos:* consult geol, 57- *Mem:* Fel Geol Soc Am; Am Asn Petrol Geologists; Nat Water Well Asn. *Res:* Subsurface fluids; hydrology; petroleum. *Mailing Add:* 375 Harvard Lane Boulder CO 80303

CURTIS, BYRD COLLINS, b Roosevelt, Okla, Feb 25, 26; m 45; c 6. PLANT BREEDING, PLANT GENETICS. *Educ:* Okla State Univ, BS, 50, PhD(plant breeding, plant genetics), 59; Kans State Univ, MS, 51. *Prof Exp:* Vet instr agr pub sch, Okla, 52-53; from asst prof to assoc prof agron, Okla State Univ, 53-62; prof, Colo State Univ, 63-67; mgr wheat res, Cargill, Inc, 67-79, mgr hybrid small grains breeding, 75-81; DIR WHEAT PROG, INT MAIZE & WHEAT IMPROV CTR, INT AGR RES INST, MEXICO, 81- *Mem:* Am Soc Agron. *Res:* Wheat breeding; research management. *Mailing Add:* Cent Int de Mejoramiento de Maiz y Trigo Airport Dist Off-6-641 Delg Cuauhtemoc 06600 Mexico DF Mexico

CURTIS, CASSIUS W, b Indianapolis, Ind, Mar 9, 06; m 42; c 3. PHYSICS. *Educ:* Williams Col, AB, 28; Hamilton Col, MA, 30; Princeton Univ, PhD(physics), 36. *Prof Exp:* Instr physics, Hamilton Col, 28-30; asst prof, Western Reserve Univ, 36-42; mem Nat Defense Res Comt, 42-46; from assoc prof to prof, 46-74, EMER PROF PHYSICS, LEHIGH UNIV, 74- *Concurrent Pos:* Consult, Frankford Arsenal, US Army, 46-66. *Mem:* Fel Am Phys Soc; Am Asn Physics Teachers. *Res:* Spectroscopy, ballistics and armor plate; solid state physics; dynamic behavior of metals. *Mailing Add:* Dept of Physics Lehigh Univ Bethlehem PA 18015

CURTIS, CHARLES ELLIOTT, b Bentonville, Ark, Mar 16, 37; m 60; c 3. ENTOMOLOGY. *Educ:* Univ Tex, BA, 59; Univ Ark, MS, 62; Purdue Univ, PhD(entom), 66. *Prof Exp:* Inspector, Food & Drug Admin, Dept Health, Educ & Welfare, 59-60; res asst, Univ Ark, 60-62 & Purdue Univ, 62-66; res entomologist, Sci & Educ Admin, Agr Res, 66-81, RES ENTOMOLOGIST, AGR RES SERV, USDA, 81- *Mem:* Entom Soc Am. *Res:* Pest management of insects in tree nuts and dried fruits with emphasis on area-wide suppression of insect populations in almond orchards using non-insecticidal approaches; orchard sanitation, early harvest and other cultural controls; using sex phenomones for mating disruption. *Mailing Add:* Agr Res Serv USDA 5578 Air Terminal Dr Fresno CA 93727

CURTIS, CHARLES R, b Ault, Colo, Oct 6, 38; m 66; c 2. PLANT PATHOLOGY, ENVIRONMENTAL SCIENCES. *Educ:* Colo State Univ, BS, 61, MS, 63, PhD(bot sci), 65. *Prof Exp:* Assigned to NASA Ames Res Ctr, 66-67; from asst prof to prof plant path, Univ Md, 67-77; prof & chairperson, Dept Plant Sci, 78-81, SPEC ASST PRES & PROVOST, UNIV DEL, 80- *Concurrent Pos:* Vis prof, Univ Tex, 75; rep, Title XII, Int Strengthening Grant, Univ Del, 80- *Mem:* Am Phytopath Soc; Am Soc Plant Physiol; Am Bot Soc. *Res:* Host-parasite relationships; physiology of disease; environmental pollution. *Mailing Add:* 3 The Horseshoe Covered Bridge Farms Newark DE 19711

CURTIS, CHARLES WHITTLESEY, b Providence, RI, Oct 13, 26; m 50; c 3. MATHEMATICS. *Educ:* Bowdoin Col, BA, 47; Yale Univ, MA, 48, PhD(math), 51. *Prof Exp:* Asst instr math, Yale Univ, 49-51; from instr to prof, Univ Wis, 51-63; PROF MATH, UNIV ORE, 63- *Concurrent Pos:* Nat Res Coun fel, 54-55; NSF sr fel, 63-64. *Mem:* Am Math Soc; Math Asn Am; London Math Soc. *Res:* Representation theory. *Mailing Add:* Dept Math Univ Ore Eugene OR 97403

CURTIS, CYRIL DEAN, b Albion, Ill, Sept 18, 20; m 48; c 2. PHYSICS. *Educ:* McKendree Col, BS, 43; Univ Ill, MS, 47, PhD(physics), 51. *Prof Exp:* Asst, McKendree Col, 41-43 & Univ Ill, 46-50; assoc physicist, Argonne Nat Lab, 51-53; asst prof physics, Vanderbilt Univ, 53-59; scientist, Midwest Univs Res Asn, 59-67; PHYSICIST, FERMI NAT ACCELERATOR LAB, 67- *Mem:* Am Phys Soc; Sigma Xi; AAAS. *Res:* Experimental nuclear reactions with charged particles and neutrons; electronic instrumentation; reactor physics; bremsstrahlung production; ion sources and accelerator physics. *Mailing Add:* 230 Woodland Hills Rd Batavia IL 60510

CURTIS, DAVID WILLIAM, b Kalamazoo, Mich, Oct 2, 24; m 55; c 4. APPLIED PHYSICS. *Educ:* Western Mich Univ, BS, 48; Iowa State Univ, PhD(physics), 55. *Prof Exp:* Asst, Ames Lab, AEC, 49-55; sr develop engr, Goodyear Aerospace Corp, 55-57, head theoret group, Aerophys Dept, 57-63, head physics group, Res & Develop Sect, Electronics Eng Div, 63-66; mem tech staff, Advan Develop Oper, Aeronaut Div, Philco-Ford Corp, 66-71; TECH CONSULT RES & DEVELOP, ARIZ ENG DIV, GOODYEAR AEROSPACE CORP, 71- *Mem:* Am Phys Soc. *Res:* Engineering analysis; information theory; probability theory in physics and engineering; synthetic array radar; microwave halography; physical optics; data processing systems. *Mailing Add:* Goodyear Aeorspace Corp Litchfield Blvd Litchfield Park AZ 85340

CURTIS, DWAYNE H, b Caldwell, Idaho, May 9, 30; m 54; c 4. PHYSIOLOGY. *Educ:* Idaho State Col, BS, 53; Univ Utah, MA, 60, PhD(exp biol), 63. *Prof Exp:* From asst prof to assoc prof, 63-73, PROF BIOL SCI, CALIF STATE UNIV, CHICO, 73- *Concurrent Pos:* Pulmonary function testing technician & consult, N T Enloe Mem Hosp, 69-72. *Res:* Effect of chemical crosslinking agents on the mechanical properties of rat-tail tendon; taxonomy of Myxomycetes in the states of California, Idaho and Oregon; pulmonary physiology function testing. *Mailing Add:* Dept of Biol Calif State Univ Chico CA 95926

CURTIS, EARL CLIFTON, JR, b Vt, Oct 15, 32; m 61; c 2. LASERS, SPECTROSCOPY. *Educ:* Univ Vt, BS, 54; Univ Minn, PhD(phys chem), 59. *Prof Exp:* MEM TECH STAFF, ROCKETDYNE DIV, ROCKWELL INT CORP, 60- *Mem:* Am Phys Soc. *Res:* Molecular vibrations; infrared spectroscopy; lasers; diagnostic measurements of and performance analysis of high energy chemical lasers; infrared spectra of simple molecules. *Mailing Add:* 2424 Tuna Gyn Topanga CA 90290

CURTIS, FREDERICK AUGUSTUS, JR, b Washington, DC, Nov 19, 22; m 46; c 2. AERONAUTICS, MECHANICS. *Educ:* Haverford Col, BS, 44; Worcester Polytech Inst, BS, 48; Calif Inst Technol, MS, 49. *Prof Exp:* Aerodynamicist, Convair, 49, aerodyn engr, 49-50, aerophys engr, 50-52, sr aerophys engr, 52-53, sr & proj aerophys engr, 53-55, aerosysts group engr, Gen Dynamics, Ft Worth, 55-60, chief stability & flight controls, 60-63, mgr stability, guid & control, 63-69, DIR ENG PROJ OFF, CONVAIR AEROSPACE DIV, GEN DYNAMICS, 69- *Concurrent Pos:* Consult subcomt aircraft flight dynamics, Off Advan Res & Technol, NASA, 67-; vpres & F-16 dep prog dir, Plans, Controls, Finances & Contracts, Fort Worth Div, Gen Dynamics, 78- *Mem:* Am Inst Aeronaut & Astronaut; Aerospace Indust Asn Am; Nat Mgt Asn. *Res:* Aerodynamic stability and control; flying qualities; navigation and attack systems functional operation and systems integration; analog computational and servo system design and operations; program management. *Mailing Add:* Convair Aerospace Div Gen Dynamics PO Box 748 Ft Worth TX 76116

CURTIS, GARY LYNN, b Belleville, Ill, Jan 21, 44; m 70. BIOCHEMISTRY, IMMUNOLOGY. *Educ:* Nebr Wesleyan Univ, BA, 66; Univ Nebr, PhD(biochem), 71. *Prof Exp:* Instr biochem, 73-76, asst prof & res asst prof, 76-81, ASSOC PROF BIOCHEM & RES ASSOC PROF OBSTET & GYNEC, MED CTR, UNIV NEBR, 81- *Concurrent Pos:* USPHS trainee, Eppley Cancer Inst, Univ Nebr, 72-75, oncologist, 73-75. *Res:* Chemical carcinogenesis; tumor immunology; reproductive biology. *Mailing Add:* Dept Biochem Univ Nebr Med Ctr Omaha NE 68105

CURTIS, GEORGE CLIFTON, b St Petersburg, Fla, Dec 10, 26; m 55; c 3. PSYCHIATRY, PSYCHOSOMATIC MEDICINE. *Educ:* Lambuth Col, BA, 50; Vanderbilt Univ, MD, 53; McGill Univ, MSc, 59. *Prof Exp:* Demonstr psychiat, McGill Univ, 57-59; assoc, Univ Pa, 59-60, from asst prof to assoc prof, 60-72; PROF PSYCHIAT, UNIV MICH, ANN ARBOR, 72-, RES SCIENTIST, 73-, DIR, ANXIETY DISORDERS PROG, 79- *Concurrent Pos:* USPHS res fel psychiat, McGill Univ, 58-59; NIMH career investr, Univ Pa, 61-66; clin asst psychiat, Royal Victoria Hosp, Montreal, Que, 57-59; med res scientist, Eastern Pa Psychiat Inst, 59-72; consult clin res, Mercy Douglass Hosp, Philadelphia, Pa, 60-62; assoc mem, Albert Einstein Med Ctr, 62-68; actg dir clin res, Philadelphia Gen Hosp, 68-72. *Mem:* Am Psychiat Asn; Am Psychosom Soc; AAAS. *Res:* Psychiatry; phobids and anxiety disorders; psychobiology; psychotherapy. *Mailing Add:* Neuropsychiat Inst Univ of Mich Ann Arbor MI 48104

CURTIS, GEORGE WILLIAM, b Brussels, Belg, Mar 9, 25; US citizen; m 51; c 4. ASTROPHYSICS, SOLAR PHYSICS. *Educ:* Univ Colo, BS, 49, MS, 52, PhD(astrophys), 63. *Prof Exp:* Physicist, Nat Bur Standards, 52-55; Fulbright fel, Inst Astrophys, Paris, 55-56; observer in charge, High Altitude Observ, 56-59, fel solar physics, Joint Inst Lab Astrophys, 63-64; res scientist, Sacramento Peak Observ, Air Force Cambridge Res Labs, 64-67; res scientist, 67-73, DEP DIR HIGH ALTITUDE OBSERV, NAT CTR ATMOSPHERIC RES, 73- *Concurrent Pos:* Sci coordr & exped leader, Solar Eclipse Exped, Nat Ctr Atmospheric Res, 71-73. *Mem:* Am Astron Soc; Royal Astron Soc; Am Inst Physics. *Res:* Low temperature properties of metal and insulating materials; design and development of low temperature instrumentation; acquisition, reduction and analysis of solar observational data on the corona, chromosphere and photosphere, especially spectral data. *Mailing Add:* 937 15th St Boulder CO 80302

CURTIS, HERBERT JOHN, b Oak Park, Ill, Aug 18, 18; m 50; c 2. MATHEMATICS. *Educ:* Yale Univ, BA, 39; Ill Inst Technol, MS, 48, PhD(math), 54. *Prof Exp:* Instr math, Ill Inst Technol, 48-54; from asst prof to assoc prof, 54-65, from actg head to head div, 60-64, PROF MATH, UNIV ILL, CHICAGO CIRCLE, 65-, EXEC SECY DEPT, 64- *Mem:* Am Math Soc; Math Asn Am. *Mailing Add:* Dept of Math Univ of Ill at Chicago Circle Chicago IL 60680

CURTIS, HUNTINGTON W(OODMAN), b US, Jan 31, 21; m 48; c 3. ENGINEERING SCIENCE. *Educ:* Col William & Mary, BS, 42; Univ NH, MS, 48; Univ Iowa, PhD(elec eng), 50. *Prof Exp:* Asst prof elec eng, Univ Va, 50-51, US Mil Acad, 51-53 & Thayer Sch Eng, Dartmouth Col, 53-59; mem syst anal dept, Int Bus Mach Corp, 59-60, mem commun systs ctr, 61-62, mgr tech requirements, Hqs, 62-63, tech adv to vpres res & eng, 63-64, dir, Govt Tech Liaison, Corp Tech & Eng, 64-66, dir sci & technol info, Corp Eng Prog & Technol Staff, 66-71, dir integrated circuit adv technol staff, 71-76, sr tech generalist, IBM Corp, 76-78, sr tech generalist, 76-80, SR SYST ARCHITECT, IBM CORP, 80- *Concurrent Pos:* Consult, Mt Wash Meteorol Observ, 55-59, trustee, 57-; mem ionosphere physics adv panel, US Nat Comt Int Geophys Year, 57-59. *Mem:* Sr mem Inst Elec & Electronics Engrs; Eng Med & Biol Soc; Asn Advan Med Instramentation; Sigma Xi. *Res:* Applied science management. *Mailing Add:* IBM Corp Biomed Systs 110 S Bedford Rd Mt Kisco NY 10549

CURTIS, JAMES O(WEN), b Lincoln, Nebr, Apr 27, 23; m 46; c 5. AGRICULTURAL ENGINEERING. *Educ:* Univ Ill, BS, 47, MS, 48; Purdue Univ, PhD(agr eng), 62. *Prof Exp:* From instr to assoc prof, 48-70, PROF AGR ENG, UNIV ILL, URBANA-CHAMPAIGN, 70- *Concurrent Pos:* Nat Sci Found fel, 59-60. *Mem:* Am Soc Agr Engrs; Am Soc Eng Educ. *Res:* Analysis and design of timber structures; experimental stress analysis of wooden structural members and frames; strengths of pole anchorage systems. *Mailing Add:* Dept of Agr Eng Univ of Ill Urbana IL 61801

CURTIS, JERRY LEON, biochemistry, see previous edition

CURTIS, JOHN RUSSELL, b Bessemer City, NC, Nov 7, 34; m 58, 77; c 3. PSYCHIATRY. *Educ:* Univ NC, AB, 56, MD, 60. *Prof Exp:* Clin instr psychiat, Sch Med, Univ Ky, 64-66, consult psychiatrist, Student Health Serv, 64-55, dir psychiat sect, 66-68, asst prof psychiat, 66-68; assoc prof psychiat, Dept Psychol, Ga, 68-74, CHIEF PSYCHIATRIST & DIR, UNIV HEALTH SERV, UNIV GA, 68-; ASSOC PROF PSYCHIAT, MED COL GA, 68- *Concurrent Pos:* Staff psychiatrist, Clin Res Ctr, NIMH, 64-65, chief ment addiction serv, 65-66; consult psychiatrist, Berea Col, 66-69, Clin Ctr Addiction Res, Ky, 67-69 & Stephens County Pub Health Dept, Ga, 69-; chmn, Gov Adv Coun Mental Health & Mental Retardation, Ga. *Mem:* Fel Am Psychiat Asn; Am Col Health Asn (pres, 78-79). *Res:* College health with emphasis on college mental health; health care delivery systems; community health and mental health. *Mailing Add:* Off of the Dir Univ Health Serv Univ of Ga Athens GA 30602

CURTIS, JOSEPH C, b Manchester, NH, Feb 14, 30; m 59; c 4. CELL BIOLOGY, BIOPHYSICS. *Educ:* Cornell Univ, BA, 51; Brown Univ, PhD(biol), 60. *Prof Exp:* Res assoc biol, Brown Univ, 60-63; from asst prof to prof biol, 63-70, PROF ZOOL, CLARK UNIV, 70- *Concurrent Pos:* USPHS fel, 60-62. *Mem:* Am Soc Zoologists; Am Soc Cell Biol; Electron Microscopy Soc Am. *Res:* Biological effects of ultrasound; cytology; cytochemistry; cell fine structure and biochemistry of steroid-producing tissues; experimental pathology. *Mailing Add:* Dept of Biol Clark Univ Worcester MA 01610

CURTIS, KENT KRUEGER, b Charles City, Iowa, Jan 24, 27; m 71; c 5. COMPUTER SCIENCE. *Educ:* Yale Univ, BS, 48; Dartmouth Col, MS, 50. *Prof Exp:* Mathematician, Lawrence Radiation Lab, Univ Calif, Berkeley, 53-57, head math & comput, 57-67; HEAD, COMPUT SCI SECT, NSF, 67- *Concurrent Pos:* Asst br chief appl math, US Atomic Energy Comn, 63-64; sr lectr, Dept Elec Eng & Comput Sci, Univ Calif, Berkeley, 64-67; consult, High Energy Physics Adv Panel, 65-67; consult, Lawrence Livermore Lab, 67-78, Los Alamos Nat Lab, 72-80, Nat Swedish Bd Tech Develop, 80-; sr res scientist, Courant Inst Math Sci, NY Univ, 72-73. *Mem:* Asn Computing Machinery; AAAS. *Res:* Acoustics; meson field theory; computer operating systems; computer graphics; programming languages; research administration in all areas of computer science and computer engineering. *Mailing Add:* Div Math & Comput Sci NSF Washington DC 20550

CURTIS, LAWRENCE ANDREW, b Hartford, Conn, Apr 14, 42. INVERTEBRATE ZOOLOGY, ESTUARINE ECOLOGY. *Educ:* Nasson Col, BA, 65; Univ NH, MS, 67; Univ Del, PhD(biol sci), 73. *Prof Exp:* Lectr bot & zool, Fairleigh Dickinson Univ, 67-68; instr, 72-73, ASST PROF BIOL SCI, UNIV DEL, 73- *Mem:* AAAS; Am Soc Zool; Estuarine Res Fedn. *Res:* Adaptations and strategies that enable estuarine and marine invertebrates to be successful in intertidal environments, especially the estuarine neogastropod, Ilyanassa Obsoleta. *Mailing Add:* Sch Life & Health Sci Univ Del Newark DE 19711

CURTIS, LORENZO JAN, b St Johns, Mich, Nov 4, 35; div. ATOMIC PHYSICS. *Educ:* Univ Toledo, BS, 58; Univ Mich, MS, 61, PhD(high energy physics), 63. *Prof Exp:* Asst prof physics, 63-68, assoc prof physics & astron, 68-72, assoc prof, 72-80, PROF PHYSICS, UNIV TOLEDO, 80- *Concurrent Pos:* NSF res grant, 64-65, fel, Latin Am Sch Physics, Mexico City, 65; vis scientist, Woods Hole Oceanog Inst, 67 & Nobel Inst, Sweden, 70-75; Docent physics, Univ Lund, Sweden, 76-79; Dept Energy res grant, 80- *Mem:* Am Phys Soc; Optical Soc Am; Europ Phys Soc. *Res:* Atomic and ionic spectra; transition probabilities; collision processes, utilizing beam-foil and pulsed electron beam methods. *Mailing Add:* Dept of Physics Univ of Toledo Toledo OH 43606

CURTIS, MORTON LANDERS, b Tex, Nov 11, 21; m 44; c 2. MATHEMATICS. *Educ:* Tex Col Arts & Indust, BS, 43; Univ Mich, PhD(math), 51. *Prof Exp:* Instr math, Northwestern Univ, 50-51; mem, Inst Adv Study, 51-53; asst prof math, Northwestern Univ, 53-56; prof, Univ Ga, 56-59 & Fla State Univ, 59-64; chmn dept, 64-69, W L MOODY JR PROF MATH, RICE UNIV, 67- *Concurrent Pos:* NSF fel, Cauis Col, Cambidge, 59-60. *Mem:* Am Math Soc. *Res:* Topology. *Mailing Add:* Dept of Math Rice Univ Houston TX 77001

CURTIS, MYRON DAVID, b Mt Vernon, Ind, Oct 17, 38; m 66; c 2. INORGANIC CHEMISTRY, ORGANOMETALLIC CHEMISTRY. *Educ:* Wabash Col, AB, 60; Northwestern Univ, PhD, 65. *Prof Exp:* Res chemist, Hooker Chem Corp, 64-66; instr chem, Northwestern Univ, 66-67; from asst prof to assoc prof, 67-77, PROF CHEM, UNIV MICH, ANN ARBOR, 77- *Concurrent Pos:* Petrol Res Fund grant, 67-69; fac res fel, Univ Mich, 69; Am Metals Climax Found grant, 75-76; NSF grants, 77-79 & 80-83; Off Naval Res grants, 77-80 & 81-84; Petrol Res Fund grant, 77-80 & 81-82. *Mem:* Am Chem Soc. *Res:* Nature of bonding in organometallic compounds; synthesis and structure of organometallic and inorganic systems related to catalysis; structural studies in homogeneous catalysis, molybdenum compounds and silicones. *Mailing Add:* Dept Chem 4019 Chem Bldg Univ of Mich Ann Arbor MI 48104

CURTIS, ORLIE LINDSEY, JR, b Hutchinson, Kans, Feb 27, 34; m 55; c 2. SOLID STATE PHYSICS. *Educ:* Union Col, Nebr, BA, 54; Purdue Univ, MS, 56; Univ Tenn, PhD, 61; Univ Southern Calif, JD, 77. *Prof Exp:* Chief semiconductors, Oak Ridge Nat Lab, 56-63; chief, Solid State Physics, Ventura Div, Northrop Corp, 63-67, asst dir, Solid State Electronics Lab, 67-68, dir, Solid State Electronics Lab, 68-77; PARTNER, KROLOFF, BELCHER, SMART, PERRY & CHRISSOPHERSON, 77- *Concurrent Pos:* Vis lectr, Univ Calif, Berkeley, 70-71. *Mem:* Fel Am Phys Soc; fel Inst Elec & Electronics Eng. *Res:* Radiation effects on materials, devices, circuits and systems; electronic properties of solids; device physics. *Mailing Add:* Kroloff Belcher Smart et al 1044 N El Dorado Stockton CA 95201

CURTIS, OTIS FREEMAN, JR, b Ithaca, NY, Jan 28, 15; m 39; c 2. HORTICULTURE, PLANT PHYSIOLOGY. *Educ:* Oberlin Col, AB, 36; Cornell Univ, PhD(plant physiol), 40. *Prof Exp:* Asst bot, Cornell Univ, 36-40; instr floricult & jr plant physiologist, Univ Calif, Los Angeles, 40-43; assoc plant physiologist, Bur Plant Indust, USDA, Calif, 43-45, assoc plant physiologist, Indio, 45-46; asst prof, 46-52, assoc prof, 52-80, EMER PROF POMOL, NY AGR EXP STA, CORNELL UNIV, 80- *Mem:* Weed Sci Soc Am; Am Soc Hort Sci. *Res:* Chemical weed control; apple fruit set and growth; fruit crop response to pesticides; rubber. *Mailing Add:* 5 Hillcrest Ave Geneva NY 14456

CURTIS, PAUL ROBINSON, b Hanumakonda, S India, Aug 14, 31; US citizen; m 61; c 2. MICROBIOLOGY. *Educ:* Col Wooster, BA, 52; Ohio State Univ, MS, 57, PhD(bact), 61. *Prof Exp:* Asst, Ohio State Univ, 55-60; from asst prof to assoc prof biol, Am Univ, 60-70; PROF BIOL, DIV SCI & MATH, EISENHOWER COL, 70- *Mem:* AAAS; Am Soc Microbiol; Sigma Xi; Am Inst Biol Sci. *Res:* Bacteriophages; bacterial and viral genetics; environmental and food microbiology. *Mailing Add:* Div of Sci & Math Eisenhower Col Seneca Falls NY 13148

CURTIS, PHILIP CHADSEY, JR, b Providence, RI, Mar 6, 28; m 50; c 5. MATHEMATICS. *Educ:* Brown Univ, AB, 50; Yale Univ, MA, 52, PhD(math), 55. *Prof Exp:* From instr to assoc prof, 55-67, chmn dept, 71-75, PROF MATH, UNIV CALIF, LOS ANGELES, 67- *Concurrent Pos:* Fulbright travel fel, Aarhus Univ, 69-70; consult, Space Tech Labs, TRW Inc, 56-; vis prof, Univ Copenhagen, 75-76. *Mem:* Am Math Soc; Math Asn Am. *Res:* Functional analysis; Banach algebras; harmonic analysis. *Mailing Add:* Dept of Math Univ of Calif Los Angeles CA 90024

CURTIS, RALPH WENDELL, b Cuba City, Wis, Oct 20, 36; m 57; c 3. METALLURGICAL CHEMISTRY. *Educ:* Univ Wis-Platteville, BS, 58; Iowa State Univ, PhD(metall), 62. *Prof Exp:* AEC fel metall, Iowa State Univ, 62-63; teacher chem, 63-69, head dept chem, 69-77, ASST V CHANCELLOR, UNIV WIS-PLATTEVILLE, 77- *Mailing Add:* Dept of Chem Univ of Wis Platteville WI 53818

CURTIS, ROBERT ARTHUR, b Weymouth, Mass, July 15, 54. PHARMACOLOGY. *Educ:* Mass Col Pharm, BS, 77; Univ Mo-Kansas City, PhD(clin pharm), 78. *Prof Exp:* Resident clin pharm, Truman Med Ctr, Mo, 78-79; ASST PROF PHARM PRACTICE, UNIV ILL MED CTR, 79-, COORDR, RESIDENCY PROG PHARM, UNIV HOSP, 80- *Mem:* Am Soc Hosp Pharmacists; Am Asn Col Pharm; Am Col Clin Pharm. *Res:* Clinical pharmacology trials in the emergency medicine enviroment. *Mailing Add:* Med Ctr Univ Ill Chicago IL 60612

CURTIS, ROBERT ORIN, b Portland, Maine, Oct 27, 27; m 52; c 2. FOREST MENSURATION. *Educ:* Yale Univ, BS, 50, MF, 51; Univ Wash, PhD(forestry), 65. *Prof Exp:* Forester, Northeastern Forest Exp Sta, 51-54, res forester, 54-62, PRIN MENSURATIONIST, PAC NORTHWEST FOREST & RANGE EXP STA, US FOREST SERV, 65- *Mem:* Soc Am Foresters. *Res:* Mensuration research in forest yield studies, site-growth relationships and related measurement problems. *Mailing Add:* Pac Northwest Forest & Range Exp Sta Forestry Sci Lab 3625 93rd Ave SW Olympia WA 98502

CURTIS, ROBERT W, b Phalanx Sta, Ohio, May 18, 20; m 45; c 2. MECHANICAL ENGINEERING, THERMODYNAMICS. *Educ:* Case Inst Technol, BS, 41. *Prof Exp:* Expeditor, Tube Div, Babcock & Wilcox, 42, test engr, Refractories Lab, 42-43, engr, Field Test Crew, 46-47, test engr, Res Ctr, 47-54, res engr, 54-60, sect chief fluid mech, 60-67, mgr facilities, 67-75, mgr, Design & Develop Lab, Res & Develop Div, 75-81; RETIRED. *Mem:* Am Soc Mech Engrs. *Res:* Fluid mechanics; combustion; heat transfer. *Mailing Add:* 345 E Beech Alliance OH 44601

CURTIS, ROBIN LIVINGSTONE, b Bellingham, Wash, Jan, 16, 26; m 50, 60; c 1. NEUROANATOMY, PHYSIOLOGICAL PSYCHOLOGY. *Educ:* Wesleyan Univ, BA, 48, MA, 50; Brown Univ, PhD(exp psychol), 54. *Prof Exp:* Chem analyst, E I du Pont de Nemours & Co, NY, 46-47; psychiat aide, Middletown State Hosp, Conn, 47-48; asst biol, Wesleyan Univ, 49-50; spec asst, Brown Univ, 52, asst psychol, 52-53; from instr to assoc prof, NJ Col Med & Dent, 56-67; ASSOC PROF ANAT, MED COL WIS, 67- *Concurrent Pos:* USPHS fel, 53-55; Nat Multiple Sclerosis Soc fel anat, Col Med, NY Univ, 55-56. *Mem:* AAAS; Am Psychol Asn; Tissue Cult Asn; Am Asn Anat; Am Genetic Asn. *Res:* Genetics, behavior and neuroanatomy of hereditary neuromuscular abnormalities in rodents; comparative neurology and animal behavior; plasticity in the rodent central nervous system; motor unit function. *Mailing Add:* Dept Anat Med Col Wis PO Box 26509 Milwaukee WI 53226

CURTIS, STANLEY BARTLETT, b Evanston, Ill, Feb 16, 32; div; c 3. RADIATION BIOPHYSICS. *Educ:* Carleton Col, BA, 54; Univ Wash, PhD(physics), 62. *Prof Exp:* Res scientist, Biophys Res Div, Lockheed-Calif Co, 62-63; res specialist, Space Physics Group, Boeing Co, 63-66; biophysicist, Donner Lab, 66-78, SR STAFF BIOPHYSICIST, DIV BIOL MED, LAWRENCE BERKELEY LAB, UNIV CALIF, BERKELEY, 78- *Concurrent Pos:* Mem radiation biol panel, NASA, 60; Eleanor Roosevelt fel, 70-71; physics counr, Coun Radiation Res Soc, 72-75; chmn, Int Comn Radiation Units & Measurements, 76-79; sr int Fogarty fel, 81-82. *Mem:* Am Phys Soc; Radiation Res Soc; Fed Am Scientists; AAAS. *Res:* Biological effects of ionizing radiation in space; high linear energy transfer effects on biological systems; tumor cell kinetics. *Mailing Add:* 800 Spruce Berkeley CA 94707

CURTIS, STANLEY EVAN, animal science, environmental physiology, see previous edition

CURTIS, SUSAN JULIA, b Tuskegee, Ala, Jan 30, 45. MEMBRANE BIOCHEMISTRY. *Educ:* Radcliffe Col, Cambridge, Mass, AB, 66; Univ Chicago, MS, 69, PhD(biochem), 73. *Prof Exp:* Fel, Cornell Univ, 73-75; fel, Harvard Univ, 75-78; ASST PROF BIOCHEM, COL MED, HOWARD UNIV, 78- *Concurrent Pos:* Adj asst prof oncol, Howard Univ Cancer Ctr, 81- *Mem:* Sigma Xi; Am Soc Microbiol; Am Chem Soc; AAAS. *Res:* Biochemistry of the structure and function of cell membranes; function of the penicillin-binding proteins of the cell wall of E coli in cell wall synthesis; the role of these proteins in the mechanism of action of penicillin. *Mailing Add:* Dept Biochem Col Med Howard Univ Washington DC 20059

CURTIS, THOMAS EDWIN, b Miami, Okla, Oct 2, 27; m 46; c 4. PSYCHIATRY. *Educ:* Duke Univ, MD, 50; Univ NC-Duke Univ Training Prog, cand, 60. *Prof Exp:* Intern, St John's Hosp, Okla, 50-51; resident psychiat, Fairfield State Hosp, Conn, 52; resident, Dorthea Dix State Hosp, NC, 52-54; from instr to assoc prof, 54-69, PROF PSYCHIAT, SCH MED, UNIC NC, CHAPEL HILL, 69-, CHMN DEPT, 73- *Concurrent Pos:* Resident, NC Mem Hosp, 54-55. *Mem:* AMA; fel Am Psychiat Asn; Am Asn Med Cols. *Res:* Experimental teaching; group analytic psychotherapy; family study and treatment; clinical research in psychotherapy; psychiatric nursing, teaching and administration. *Mailing Add:* Dept Psychiat Sch Med Univ NC Chapel Hill NC 27514

CURTIS, THOMAS HASBROOK, b Detroit, Mich, July 26, 41; m 79; c 2. TELECOMMUNICATION SYSTEMS, SATELLITE COMMUNICATION. *Educ:* Kenyon Col, BA, 63; Yale Univ, MS, 65, PhD(physics), 68. *Prof Exp:* Res physicist, Lawrence Radiation Lab, Univ Calif, 68-70; mem tech staff, 70-80, SUPVR, ECHO CONTROL GROUP, BELL LABS, 80- *Concurrent Pos:* Consult, Lycoming Div, Avco Corp, Conn, 67 & Automation Res Mechanisms, Inc, Calif, 68-69. *Mem:* Inst Elec & Electronics Engrs; AAAS; Am Phys Soc; NY Acad Sci. *Res:* Digital processing for satellite communication; physics of speech and hearing; digital processing of acoustic signals; applications of computers to system control; nuclear physics. *Mailing Add:* Bell Labs 2E-326 Holmdel NJ 07733

CURTIS, VERONICA ANNE, b Reading, Eng, Oct 8, 48; US citizen. NATURAL PRODUCT SYNTHESIS. *Educ:* Univ Ill, Chicago, BA, 71, MS, 73, PhD(chem), 80. *Prof Exp:* Lectr chem, Univ Wis, Whitewater, 77-78; fel, 79-80, ASST PROF CHEM, LOYOLA UNIV, CHICAGO, 80- *Res:* Development of new general methods of deamination and investigations into organic reaction mechansims to improve synthetic methods. *Mailing Add:* Dept Chem 6525 N Sheridan Rd Loyola Univ Chicago IL 60626

CURTIS, WESLEY E, b Westfield, NY, Aug 25, 18; m 49; c 2. ENGINEERING, COMPUTER SCIENCE. *Educ:* Alfred Univ, BS, 40. *Prof Exp:* Anal chemist, Atlas Feldspar Corp, 40-42; res assoc, Ansbacher-Siegle Corp, 42, Alfred Univ, 42-44 & Underwater Explosives Res Lab, Woods Hole Oceanog Inst, 44-47; physicist, Ballistic Res Labs, Aberdeen Proving Ground, 47-56; sr opers analyst, Tech Opers, Inc, 56-67; sr res analyst, 67-80, DIR SPEC PROJ, HANCOCK/DIKEWOOD SERV, INC, 80- *Mem:* Oper Res Soc Am; AAAS. *Res:* Cost Effectiveness analysis; computer system science; nuclear weapon phenomenology. *Mailing Add:* Dikewood Corp Hancock Dikewood Serv Inc Albuquerque NM 87106

CURTISS, CHARLES FRANCIS, b Chicago, Ill, Apr 4, 21; m 46; c 3. THEORETICAL CHEMISTRY. *Educ:* Univ Wis, BS, 42, PhD(chem), 48. *Prof Exp:* Chemist, Geophys Lab, Carnegie Inst, 42-45; assoc, Allegany Ballistics Lab, George Washington Univ, 45; proj assoc, 48-49, from asst prof to assoc prof, 49-60, PROF CHEM, UNIV WIS-MADISON, 60- *Mem:* AAAS; Am Chem Soc; Am Phys Soc. *Res:* Statistical mechanics; kinetic theory of gases. *Mailing Add:* 1101 Univ Ave Univ Wis Madison WI 53706

CURTISS, HOWARD C(ROSBY), JR, b Chicago, Ill, Mar 17, 30; m 56; c 2. AERONAUTICAL ENGINEERING. *Educ:* Rensselaer Polytech Inst, BAeroE, 52; Princeton Univ, MSE, 57, PhD(aerodyn), 65. *Prof Exp:* Res staff mem aerospace & mech sci, 57-65, lectr, 63-65, from asst prof to assoc prof, 65-71, PROF MECH & AEROSPACE ENG, PRINCETON UNIV, 71- *Concurrent Pos:* Vis lectr, Stevens Inst Technol, 60-61. *Mem:* Am Inst Aeronaut & Astronaut; Am Helicopter Soc. *Res:* Aerodynamics, stability and control of helicopters and vertical take off and landing aircraft, experimental and theoretical. *Mailing Add:* Dept of Aerospace & Mech Sci Princeton Univ Forrestal Campus Princeton NJ 08540

CURTISS, LARRY ALAN, b Madison, Wis, Sept 16, 47; m 78; c 1. HYDROGEN BONDING, MOLECULAR INTERACTIONS. *Educ:* Univ Wis, BS, 69; Carnegie-Mellon Univ, MS, 71, PhD(chem), 73. *Prof Exp:* Fel, Batelle Mem Inst, 73-76; ASST CHEMIST, ARGONNE NAT LAB, 76- *Res:* Quantum mechanical and experimental studies of molecular interations in the gas phase including hydrogen bonded and lonic complexes; reaction pathways in homogeneous catalysis reactions. *Mailing Add:* Chem Eng Div Argonne Nat Lab Argonne IL 60439

CURTISS, ROY, III, b New York, NY, May 27, 34; c 6. MICROBIAL GENETICS, MOLECULAR GENETICS. *Educ:* Cornell Univ, BS, 56; Univ Chicago, PhD(microbiol), 62. *Prof Exp:* Jr technical specialist, Biol Div, Brookhaven Nat Lab, 56-58; biologist, Oak Ridge Nat Lab, 63-72, group leader microbial genetics & radiation microbiol group, Biol Div, 69-72; prof microbiol, Univ Tenn-Oak Ridge Grad Sch Biomed Sci, 69-72, assoc dir, 70-71, interim dir, 71-72; prof, 72-78, CHARLES H MCCAULEY PROF MICROBIOL, UNIV ALA, BIRMINGHAM, 78-, VCHMN, DEPT MICROBIOL, 81-, SR SCIENTIST, INST DENT RES & COMPREHENSIVE CANCER CTR, 72-, DIR MOLECULAR CELL BIOL GRAD TRAINING PROG, 73-, DIR & SR SCIENTIST, CYCSTIC FIBROSIS RES CTR, 81- *Concurrent Pos:* Lectr microbiol, Univ Tenn, 65-72 & Oak Ridge Grad Sch Biomed Sci, 67-69; vis prof, Venezuelan Inst Sci Res, 69, Univ PR, 72 & Cath Univ Chile, 73; lectr, Am Found Microbiol, 69-70, 79-80 & 81-82; ed, J Bact, 70-; mem, NIH Recombinant DNA Molecule Prog Adv Comt, 74-77; mem, NSF Genetic Biol Study Sect, 75-78; dir, Nat Inst Gen Med Sci Predoctoral & Postdoctoral Training Grants, 75-; mem, NIH Genetic Basis Dis Rev Comt, 80-, chmn, 81- *Honors & Awards:* P R Edwards Award, Am Acad Microbiol, 77. *Mem:* Fel Am Acad Microbiol; hon mem Microbiol Asn Chile; Am Soc Microbiol; Genetics Soc Am; Brit Soc Gen Microbiol. *Res:* Genetic and biochemcial mechanisms for bacterial pathogenicity; bacterial genetics and molecular biology. *Mailing Add:* Dept of Microbiol Box 11 SDB Univ of Ala Birmingham AL 35294

CURTRIGHT, THOMAS LYNN, b Moberly, Mo, Aug 21, 48; m 68; c 3. SUPERSYMMETRY, QUANTUM FIELD THEORY. *Educ:* Univ Mo, BS & MS, 70; Calif Inst Technol, PhD(theoret physics), 77. *Prof Exp:* Res assoc, Univ Calif, Irvine, 76-78; McCormick fel, Enrico Fermi Inst, Univ Chicago, 78-80; ASSOC PROF, DEPT PHYSICS, UNIV FLA, 80- *Mem:* Am Phys Soc. *Res:* The use of symmetries in physical theories, with emphasis on the interplay between quantum mechanics and symmetries in relatistic field theories. *Mailing Add:* Dept Physics Univ Fla Gainesville FL 32611

CURTZ, THADDEUS BANKSON, b New York, NY, Mar 16, 22; m 42; c 4. COMPUTER SCIENCE. *Educ:* Baldwin-Wallace Col, BA, 48; Yale Univ, MA, 49, PhD, 60. *Prof Exp:* Res assoc & proj mgr, Willow Run Labs, Univ Mich, 51-58, head comput dept, 58-61; dir comput ctr, Conductron Corp, 61-67; vpres, KMS Industs, Inc, 67-68; vis prof comput sci, 69-70, assoc prof, 70-72, chmn dept, 70-78, PROF COMPUT SCI, UNIV KY, 72- *Mem:* Am Math Soc. *Res:* Data processing; differential equations; computation. *Mailing Add:* Dept of Comput Sci Univ of Ky Lexington KY 40506

CURWEN, DAVID, b Ridgewood, NJ, May 25, 35; m 57; c 2. HORTICULTURE, FOOD TECHNOLOGY. *Educ:* Univ Vt, BS, 57; Pa State Univ, MS, 60, PhD(hort), 64. *Prof Exp:* Asst prof & area hort agent veg exten & res, 63-71, assoc prof, 71-80, PROF AGR EXTEN & HORT & AREA EXTEN HORTICULTURIST, UNIV WIS-MADISON, 80- *Mem:* Am Soc Hort Sci; Am Inst Biol Sci. *Mailing Add:* Dept of Hort Univ of Wis Madison WI 53706

CUSACHS, LOUIS CHOPIN, b Orange, NJ, Sept 9, 33; m 80; c 3. COMPUTER SCIENCE, QUANTUM CHEMISTRY. *Educ:* US Naval Acad, BS, 56; Univ Paris, dipl, 61; Northwestern Univ, PhD, 61. *Prof Exp:* Du Pont teaching asst, Northwestern Univ, 58-59; Fulbright exchange prof, Univ Valencia, 61-62; from asst prof to assoc prof phys chem, Tulane Univ, 62-72; prof comput sci, Loyola Univ, La, 72-77; RES SPECIALIST, EXXON PROD RES CO, 77- *Concurrent Pos:* Lectr, Fulbright Prog, Nat Univ Buenos Aires & Univ La Plata, Arg, 74. *Mem:* Am Chem Soc; Inst Elec & Electronics Eng; Am Phys Soc; Int Soc Quantum Biol (vpres, 73-75, pres, 75-77). *Res:* Scientific computation; electronic structure of molecules; theoretical chemistry and computer modeling; geochemistry. *Mailing Add:* 1107 Jocelyn Houston TX 77023

CUSANO, DOMINIC A, b Schenectady, NY, May 20, 24; m 45; c 3. SOLID STATE LUMINESCENCE. *Educ:* Union Col, BS, 49, MS, 53; Rensselaer Polytech Inst, PhD(solid state physics), 59. *Prof Exp:* PHYSICIST RES & DEVELOP, GEN ELEC CORP, 49- *Mem:* Am Phys Soc; Electrochem Soc; Sigma Xi. *Res:* Solid state x-ray detectors; solar photovoltaic energy conversion; thin film luminescense; photoemission incandescent and fluorescent lamp studies; semiconductor hybrid and packaging techniques; current-voltage diagram processing; wide band gap semiconductors. *Mailing Add:* 2017 Morrow Ave Schenectady NY 12309

CUSANOVICH, MICHAEL A, b Los Angeles, Calif, Mar 2, 42; m 63; c 2. BIOCHEMISTRY. *Educ:* Univ of the Pac, BS, 63; Univ Calif, San Diego, PhD(chem), 67. *Prof Exp:* NIH fel biochem, Univ Calif, San Diego, 67-68 & Cornell Univ, 68-69; asst prof, 69-74, assoc prof chem, 74-78, assoc prof biochem, 78-79, PROF BIOCHEM & CHEM, UNIV ARIZ, 79- *Concurrent Pos:* NIH Career Develop Award, 75. *Mem:* Am Chem Soc; Biophys Soc; Am Soc Biol Chem; NY Acad Sci; Am Soc Photobiol. *Res:* Mechanism of electron transfer as catalyzed by cytochromes and coupled energy conservation; mechanism of action of the visual pigment rhodopsin; myosin ATPase. *Mailing Add:* Dept of Biochem Univ of Ariz Tucson AZ 85721

CUSCURIDA, MICHAEL, b Waco, Tex, Nov 16, 26. ORGANIC CHEMISTRY. *Educ:* Tex Agr & Mech Col, BS, 48; Baylor Univ, MS, 51, PhD, 55. *Prof Exp:* Assoc res chemist, Midwest Res Inst, 55-57; sr res chemist, 57-65, proj chemist, 65-69, SR PROJ CHEMIST, JEFFERSON CHEM CO, INC, 69- *Mem:* Am Chem Soc. *Res:* Organic chemistry; polyurethane chemistry; polymers of alkylene oxides; inorganic chemistry; chemistry of metal hydrides; high energy fuels based on boron compounds. *Mailing Add:* Texaco Chem Co Box 15730 Austin TX 78761

CUSHEN, WALTER EDWARD, b Hagerstown, Md, Mar 21, 25; m 49; c 2. OPERATIONS RESEARCH, GOVERNMENT POLICY ANALYSIS. *Educ:* Western Md Col, BA, 48, ScD, 66; Univ Edinburgh, PhD(metaphys), 51. *Prof Exp:* Mathematician, Ballistic Res Labs, 48 & 51-52; sr programmer, Remington Rand, Inc, 52; chmn res group, Opers Res Off, 52-61; assoc prof opers res, Case Inst Technol, 61-63; staff mem, Inst Defense Anal, 63-64; chief, Tech Anal Div, Nat Bur Standards, 64-74; actg asst dir, Off Energy Systs, FPC, 74-75; vpres & dir, Mathtech Washington, Mathematica, Inc, 75-81; CONSULT, 81- *Concurrent Pos:* Consult, FAA, 63-64; mem, Md Water Sci Adv Bd, 68-76, Gov Sci Adv Coun, 67-73 & Bd Trustees, Western Md Col, 71-75. *Mem:* Fel AAAS; Opers Res Soc Am (pres, 70-71); Inst Mgt Sci; Am Acad Polit & Soc Sci. *Res:* Leading policy analysis on US civilian and military problems; economic modeling of programs to improve agricultural productivity in Egypt. *Mailing Add:* 6910 Maple Ave Chevy Chase MD 20815

CUSHING, COLBERT ELLIS, JR, b Ft Collins, Colo, Jan 9, 31; m 59; c 3. FRESH WATER ECOLOGY. *Educ:* Colo State Univ, BSc, 52, MSc, 56; Univ Sask, PhD(biol), 61. *Prof Exp:* Fishery biologist, Mont Fish & Game Dept, 56-58; biol scientist, Hanford Labs, Gen Elec Co, 61-65; res scientist, 65-67, SR RES SCIENTIST, PAC NORTHWEST LAB, BATTELLE MEM INST, 67- *Concurrent Pos:* Lectr, Joint Ctr Grad Studies, Wash State Univ, 79-; consult, Nat Acad Sci FREIR Comt, 80. *Mem:* Am Soc Limnol & Oceanog; Ecol Soc Am; Am Fisheries Soc; Int Asn Theoret & Appl Limnol; NAm Benthol Soc. *Res:* Stream ecology; radioecological and nutrient cycling studies of aquatic ecosystems; primary productivity. *Mailing Add:* Ecol Sci Dept Pac Northwest Lab Battelle Mem Inst Richland WA 99352

CUSHING, EDWARD JOHN, b St Louis, Mo, Nov 15, 33; m 55; c 5. ECOLOGY. *Educ:* Wash Univ, AB, 54; Univ Minn, PhD(geol), 63. *Prof Exp:* Res fel geol, Sch Earth Sci, Univ Minn, Minneapolis, 63-64, asst prof, 64-66, from asst prof to prof bot, 66-74; PROF ECOL & BEHAV BIOL, UNIV MINN, MINNEAPOLIS, 75- *Concurrent Pos:* NATO fel, Univ NWales, Bangor, 66-67. *Mem:* AAAS; Geol Soc Am; Ecol Soc Am; Bot Soc Am; Brit Ecol Soc. *Res:* Quaternary pollen analysis and paleoecology; plant ecology; glacial geology. *Mailing Add:* Dept of Ecol & Behav Biol Univ of Minn Minneapolis MN 55455

CUSHING, JAMES THOMAS, theoretical physics, see previous edition

CUSHING, JIM MICHAEL, b North Platte, Nebr, Mar 20, 42. APPLIED MATHEMATICS. *Educ:* Univ Colo, BA, 64; Univ Md, PhD(math), 68. *Prof Exp:* Asst prof, 68-74, ASSOC PROF MATH, UNIV ARIZ, 74- *Concurrent Pos:* IBM fel, 71-72; Alexander von Humboldt fel, 77-78. *Mem:* Am Math Soc; Math Asn Am; Soc Indust & Appl Math. *Res:* Qualitative theory of integral, differential and integrodifferential equations and applications; population dynamics; mathematical ecology. *Mailing Add:* Dept Math Bldg 89 Univ of Ariz Tucson AZ 85721

CUSHING, JOHN (ELDRIDGE), JR, b San Francisco, Calif, Aug 25, 16; m 41; c 2. BIOLOGY. *Educ:* Univ Calif, AB, 38; Calif Inst Technol, PhD(genetics & immunol), 43. *Prof Exp:* Asst immunochem, Calif Inst Technol, 43-45; instr biol, Johns Hopkins Univ, 45-48; from asst prof to prof biol, 48-69, prof, 69-80, EMER PROF IMMUNOL, UNIV CALIF, SANTA BARBARA, 80- *Concurrent Pos:* Guggenheim fel, 58-59. *Mem:* Am Asn Immunologists; Am Soc Naturalists. *Res:* Comparative immunology; evolution studies; blood groups of marine animals; immune reactions of invertebrates. *Mailing Add:* Dept of Biol Sci Univ of Calif Santa Barbara CA 93106

CUSHING, KENNETH MAYHEW, b Charlotte, NC, Aug 16, 47. LIGHT SCATTERING PHYSICS, POLLUTION CONTROL RESEARCH. *Educ:* Southwestern Univ, Memphis, BS, 69; Univ Fla, MS, 72. *Prof Exp:* Assoc, 72-75, res, 75-78, head, Aerosol Physics Sect, 78-80, SR PHYSICIST, SOUTHERN RES INST, 80- *Mem:* Air Pollution Control Asn. *Res:* Operating behavior of fabric filters and wet and dry scrubber; particle sizing measurement techniques including interial, optical, electrical and diffusional methods. *Mailing Add:* Southern Res Inst PO Box 3307-A Birmingham AL 35255

CUSHING, MERCHANT LEROY, b Haverhill, Mass, Jan 31, 10; m 39; c 4. CARBOHYDRATE CHEMISTRY. *Educ:* Univ NH, BS, 31, MS, 33; Columbia Univ, PhD(Org chem), 41. *Prof Exp:* Res chemist, Stein, Hall & Co, NY, 37-42, chief chemist, Starch Explor Lab, 46-48, dir, NY Labs, 48-50, chief chemist, Paper Lab, 52-55; head paper lab, A E Staley Mfg Co, Ill, 55-62; mgr paper res, Fiber Prods Res Ctr, Inc, 62-65; group leader, Paper Appln, CIBA Corp, NJ, 65-69; group leader paper res & develop, Am Maize Prods Co, 69-74; res assoc, Bergstrom Paper Co, 74-78; CONSULT PAPER TECHNOL, 78- *Mem:* Tech Asn Pulp & Paper Indust. *Res:* Carbohydrate chemistry oriented to new industrial products; modifications of natural raw materials for use in papermaking; wet end additives for improving interfiber bonding and filler retention; enzyme conversion of starches; deinking recycled waste papers; new product development; cold corrugating adhesive; high performance vegetable glue remoistenable adhesives. *Mailing Add:* 365 Cleveland St Menosha WI 54952

CUSHING, ROBERT LEAVITT, b Ord, Nebr, Apr 12, 14; m 38; c 3. AGRONOMY. *Educ:* Univ Nebr, BSc, 36, MSc, 38. *Hon Degrees:* DSc, Univ Hawaii, 62. *Prof Exp:* Asst agronomist, Nebr Agr Exp Sta, 38-42 & USDA, 42-43; from asst prof to assoc prof plant breeding, Cornell Univ, 43-47; agronomist, Hawaiian Pineapple Co, 47-49; from assoc prof to prof plant breeding, Cornell Univ, 49-51; asst dir, Pineapple Res Inst Hawaii, 51-52, dir, 52-63, pres, 58-63; dir, Exp Sta, 63-79, VPRES & SECY, HAWAIIAN SUGAR PLANTERS ASN, 66- *Concurrent Pos:* Mem bd regents, Univ Hawaii, 67, chmn, 68; consult, Int Agr Develop Serv & World Bank, 79- *Mem:* AAAS; Am Soc Agron; Am Genetic Asn; Inst Food Technol. *Res:* Plant breeding; plant genetics. *Mailing Add:* 2325 Armstrong St Honolulu HI 96822

CUSHING, VINCENT JEROME, applied physics, see previous edition

CUSHLEY, ROBERT JOHN, b Edmonton, Alta, July 12, 36; m 65; c 2. SPECTROSCOPY, PHYSICAL BIOCHEMISTRY. *Educ:* Univ Alta, BSc, 57, MSc, 59, PhD(org chem), 65. *Prof Exp:* Res assoc chem, Sloan-Kettering Inst Cancer Res, 65-68; asst prof, Med Sch, Yale Univ, 68-73, assoc prof, 73-74; assoc prof, 74-79, PROF CHEM, SIMON FRASER UNIV, 79- *Concurrent Pos:* Lectr, Sloan-Kettering Div, Cornell Univ, 67-68. *Mem:* Am Chem Soc; Chem Inst Can; Int Soc Magnetic Resonance; Can Biochem Soc; Can Fed Biol Soc. *Res:* Fourier transform spectroscopy; nuclear magnetic resonance studies of compounds of biological significance; membrane biochemistry; Lipoprotein biophysics. *Mailing Add:* Dept Chem Simon Fraser Univ Burnaby Can

CUSHMAN, DAVID WAYNE, b Indianapolis, Ind, Nov 15, 39; m 64; c 2. BIOCHEMICAL PHARMACOLOGY. *Educ:* Wabash Col, AB, 61; Univ Ill, Urbana, PhD(biochem), 66. *Prof Exp:* Sr res scientist, 66-70, sr res investr, 70-74, res fel, 74-78, SR RES FEL, SQUIBB INST MED RES, 78- *Honors & Awards:* Alfred Burger Award, Am Chem Soc, 82. *Mem:* AAAS; Am Chem Soc; Am Soc Pharmacol & Exp Therapeut; Am Soc Biol Chemists. *Res:* Bacterial hydroxylases and related electron transport systems; non-heme iron proteins; enzymology and pharmacology of vasoactive polypeptides, prostaglandins and enkaphalins. *Mailing Add:* Squibb Inst for Med Res Princeton NJ 08540

CUSHMAN, JOHN HOWARD, b Ames, Iowa, Jan 19, 51; m 74. SOIL PHYSICS, APPLIED MATHEMATICS. *Educ:* Iowa State Univ, BS, 75, MS, 76, PhD(mat & agron), 78. *Prof Exp:* ASST PROF SOIL PHYSICS, DEPT AGRON, PURDUE UNIV, 78- *Mem:* Am Math Soc; Soc Indust & Appl Math; Am Geophys Union; Am Soc Agron; Sigma Xi. *Res:* Numerical and analytical modeling of groundwater and soluble transport; stochastic soil physics; theoretical averaging procedures. *Mailing Add:* Dept Agron Life Sci Bldg Purdue Univ West Lafayette IN 47907

CUSHMAN, MARK, b Fresno, Calif, Aug 20, 45. ORGANIC CHEMISTRY, MEDICINAL CHEMISTRY. *Educ:* Univ Calif, San Francisco, Pharm D, 69, PhD(med chem), 73. *Prof Exp:* NIH fel chem, Mass Inst Technol, 73-75; asst prof, 75-80, ASSOC PROF MED CHEM, PURDUE UNIV, 80- *Mem:* Am Chem Soc. *Res:* New synthetic methods; organic reaction mechanisms; natural products synthesis; structure-activity relationships in pharmacology and the isolation and structure elucidation of natural products. *Mailing Add:* Dept of Med Chem & Pharmacog Purdue Univ West Lafayette IN 47907

CUSHMAN, PAUL, JR, b New York, NY, Feb 4, 30; m 59; c 2. ENDOCRINOLOGY, DRUG ABUSE. *Educ:* Yale Univ, BA, 51; Columbia Univ, MD, 55. *Prof Exp:* Instr med, Columbia Univ, 62-68, assoc, 68-69, asst clin prof, 69-71; NY Heart Asn sr investr, 71-72, asst prof med, 71-77; ASSOC PROF MED, PHYCIAT & PHARMACOL, MED COL WIS, 77- *Concurrent Pos:* NIH res fel endocrinol, Univ Rochester, 59-61, St Luke's Hosp, 62-64 & 67-75; consult, Vet Admin Hosp, Batavia, NY, 60-62; from assoc dir to dir endocrinol, St Luke's Hosp, 62-73; assoc attend physician, 65-77, dir clin pharmacol, 73-77; consult, De Paul Rehab Hosp, 77-; lectr, alcohol & drug abuse, 79. *Mem:* AAAS; Endocrine Soc; Am Fedn Clin Res; Am Physiol Soc; fel Am Col Physicians. *Res:* Narcotics, alcohol and marijuana. *Mailing Add:* De Paul Rehab Hosp Milwaukee WI 53221

CUSHMAN, ROBERT VITTUM, b Middlebury, Vt, Dec 14, 16; m 42; c 3. HYDROGEOLOGY. *Educ:* Middlebury Col, AB, 39; Northwestern Univ, MS, 41. *Prof Exp:* Recorder, US Geol Surv, Alaska, 41; mining geologist, Slide Mines, Inc, Colo, 41-42; mineral economist, US Bur Mines, 42-45; geologist, Water Resources Div, US Geol Surv, 46-47, Conn, 47-61, Ky, 61-71, assoc dist chief, 67-71, dist chief, 71-75; CONSULT GROUND WATER, GEOL & HYDROLOGY, 75- *Mem:* Geol Soc Am; Am Geophys Union. *Mailing Add:* 20 Court St Middlebury VT 05753

CUSHMAN, SAMUEL WRIGHT, b Bryn Mawr, Pa, Oct 2, 41; m 64; c 3. CELL PHYSIOLOGY, BIOCHEMISTRY. *Educ:* Bowdoin Col, AB, 63; Rockefeller Univ, PhD(physiol chem), 69. *Prof Exp:* Res asst, Inst Clin Biochem, Sch Med, Univ Geneva, 69-71; res asst prof med, Dartmouth Med Sch, 71-73, asst prof med & adj asst prof biochem, 73-80; ASSOC CHIEF, CELLULAR METAB & OBESITY SECT, NAT INST ALLERGY, DIGESTIVE DIS, KIDNEYS, NIH, 76- *Concurrent Pos:* Am Cancer Soc fel, Inst Clin Biochem, Geneva, Switz, 69-71; Am Diabetes Asn career develop award, Dartmouth Med Sch, 72-74. *Mem:* Am Diabetes Asn; Am Soc Cellular Biol; Am Fedn Clin Res; Europ Asn Study Diabetes; Endocrine Soc. *Res:* Adipose tissue and cell structure and function; obesity; mechanism of hormone action, especially insulin and epinephrine; diabetes mellitus. *Mailing Add:* Cellular Metab & Obesity Sect Nat Inst Allergy Digestive Dis Kidney/NIH Bethesda MD 20205

CUSICK, THOMAS WILLIAM, b Joliet, Ill, Sept 18, 43; m 65; c 2. NUMBER THEORY, COMBINATORICS. *Educ:* Univ Ill, Urbana, BS, 64; Cambridge Univ, PhD(math), 67. *Prof Exp:* From asst prof to assoc prof, 68-77, PROF MATH, STATE UNIV NY, BUFFALO, 77- *Mem:* Am Math Soc. *Res:* Diophantine approximation. *Mailing Add:* Dept of Math State Univ of NY Buffalo Buffalo NY 14214

CUSSLER, EDWARD L, chemical engineering, see previous edition

CUSSON, RONALD YVON, b Drummondville, Que, July 3, 38; US citizen. THEORETICAL NUCLEAR PHYSICS. *Educ:* Univ Montreal, BSc, 60; Calif Inst Technol, PhD(physics, math), 65. *Prof Exp:* Res fel physics, Calif Inst Technol, 65-66; Alexander von Humboldt fel, Inst Theoret Physics, Univ Heidelberg, 66-67; physicist, Chalk River Nuclear Lab, Atomic Energy Can Ltd, 67-70; assoc prof, 70-78, PROF PHYSICS, DUKE UNIV, 78- *Concurrent Pos:* Consult, Oak Ridge Nat Lab, 71- & Lawrence Livermore Lab, 71- *Honors & Awards:* Alexander von Humboldt Sr Scientist Award, 78. *Mem:* Am Phys Soc. *Res:* Group theory of nuclear collective motion; parastatistics and its applications; nuclear structure calculations. *Mailing Add:* Dept Physics Duke Univ Durham NC 27706

CUSTARD, HERMAN CECIL, b Cleburne, Tex, Aug 19, 29; m 55; c 3. PHYSICAL CHEMISTRY. *Educ:* Baylor Univ, BS, 57, PhD(chem), 62. *Prof Exp:* RES ASSOC & ACTIV LEADER, FIELD RES LAB, MOBIL RES & DEVELOP CORP, 62- *Mem:* Am Chem Soc; Electrochem Soc. *Res:* Dipole moments; electrochemistry of membrane systems; physical chemistry of electrolytic solutions. *Mailing Add:* 4016 S Better Dr Dallas TX 75229

CUSTER, HUBERT MINTER, b Johnstown, Pa, Sept 19, 22; m 51; c 1. PHYSICS. *Educ:* Carnegie Inst Technol, BSEE, 43; Franklin & Marshall Col, MS, 59. *Prof Exp:* Asst prof, 52-61, ASSOC PROF PHYSICS, ELIZABETHTOWN COL, 61- *Concurrent Pos:* Asst prof physics, Johnstown Col, 61-63, assoc prof, 63- *Mem:* Inst Elec & Electronics Engrs; Am Asn Physics Teachers. *Res:* Trapping levels in zinc sulfide. *Mailing Add:* Dept of Physics Elizabethtown Col Elizabethtown PA 17022

CUSTER, MICHAEL, b Lowell, Mass, Oct 29, 10. CHEMISTRY. *Educ:* St Anselm's Col, AB, 35; Cath Univ Am, MS, 44. *Prof Exp:* CHMN DEPT CHEM, ST ANSELM'S COL, 48- *Mem:* Am Chem Soc. *Mailing Add:* Dept of Chem St Anselm's Col Manchester NH 03102

CUSTER, RICHARD PHILIP, b Munhall, Pa, July 14, 03; m 39, 74; c 2. ONCOLOGY. *Educ:* Jefferson Med Col, MD, 28. *Prof Exp:* From asst instr to prof, 29-70, EMER PROF PATH, SCH MED, UNIV PA, 70-; SR MEM, INST CANCER RES, FOX CHASE, 69- *Concurrent Pos:* Fel, Path Anat Inst, Innsbruck, 30 & 32; chief path, Philadelphia Gen Hosp, 31-38 & consult, 38-; dir labs, Presby Hosp, Philadelphia, 38-59, chmn chief hemat & chemother, 59-68; trustee, Am Bd Path, 44-52, life trustee, 61; consult, Children's Heart Hosp, Philadelphia, 46-, Armed Forces Inst Path, 46-56 & US Naval Hospital, Philadelphia, 47-70. *Honors & Awards:* Gerhard Gold Medalist, Philadelphia Path Soc, 55. *Mem:* AAAS; AMA; Am Asn Path & Bact. *Res:* Hematology, particularly etiology, interrelationships and treatment of the lymphomas and leukemias; basic cancer research. *Mailing Add:* Inst for Cancer Res Fox Chase Philadelphia PA 19111

CUSUMANO, JAMES A, b Elizabeth, NJ, Apr 14, 42; m 64; c 1. CATALYSIS. *Educ:* Rutgers Univ, BA, 64, PhD(chem physics), 68. *Prof Exp:* Res chemist heterogeneous catalysis, Esso Res & Eng Co, 67-74; PRES, CATALYTICA ASSOC, INC, 74- *Honors & Awards:* Colloid & Surface Chem Award, Continental Oil Co, 64. *Mem:* Am Chem Soc; Catalysis Soc; Am Phys Soc. *Res:* Catalysis, chemistry and physics of small metal particle systems; infrared spectroscopic studies of adsorbed species; chemical kinetics of catalytic reactions; theory and measurement of surface thermal transients. *Mailing Add:* Catalytica Assoc Inc Suite 7E 3255 Scott Blvd Santa Clara CA 95051

CUTCHINS, ERNEST CHARLES, b Newsoms, Va, Aug 19, 22. BACTERIOLOGY, VIROLOGY. *Educ:* Va Polytech Inst, BS, 43; Univ Md, MS, 51, PhD(bact), 55; Am Bd Med Microbiol, dipl. *Prof Exp:* Bacteriologist, Walter Reed Army Inst Res, 55-56 & NIH, 56-59; res assoc, Chas Pfizer & Co, Inc, 60-61; ASSOC PROF VIROL, DEPT BIOL, CATH UNIV AM, 61-, CHMN DEPT, 78- *Mem:* Am Asn Immunologists; Am Soc Microbiol. *Res:* Viral inactivation; virus-host interaction; immunology and serology of viruses. *Mailing Add:* Dept of Biol Cath Univ of Am Washington DC 20017

CUTCHINS, MALCOLM ARMSTRONG, b Franklin, Va, Mar 27, 35; m 54; c 3. AEROSPACE ENGINEERING, ENGINEERING MECHANICS. *Educ:* Va Polytech Inst, BS, 56, MS, 64, PhD(eng mech), 67. *Prof Exp:* Assoc aircraft engr, Lockheed-Ga Co, Ga, 56-61, jr mech engr, 61-62, sr mech engr, 62; instr undergrad mech, Va Polytech Inst, 62-66; assoc prof, 66-79, PROF AEROSPACE ENG, AUBURN UNIV, 79- *Concurrent Pos:* NSF analog/hybrid grant; aerial seeding investr, US Forestry Serv, 67-72; systs eng study, NASA at Marshall Space Flight Ctr, 69-70; consult, Combustion Eng, 73; prin investr, Eglin AFB, Aeroservoelastic Studies, 76-79. *Honors & Awards:* IR-100 Award, Indust Res, 73. *Mem:* Assoc fel Am Inst Aeronaut & Astronaut; Am Soc Eng Educ; Nat Soc Prof Engrs; Am Acad Mech; Sigma Xi. *Res:* Structural response and system design as related to dynamics and vibrations; more effective teaching of advanced engineering concepts; aeroelasticity, analog hybrid and digital simulation of systems. *Mailing Add:* Dept of Aerospace Eng Auburn Univ Auburn AL 36849

CUTCLIFFE, JACK ALEXANDER, b Quincy, Mass, Aug 10, 29; Can citizen; m 54; c 6. OLERICULTURE. *Educ:* McGill Univ, BSc, 52, MSc, 54. *Prof Exp:* Exten hort crops, Ont Dept Agr, 54-62; RES OLERICULT, AGR CAN RES BR, 62-, SECT HEAD HORT, AGR CAN RES STA, 70- *Mem:* Agr Inst Can; Can Soc Hort Sci; Am Soc Hort Sci; Int Soc Hort Sci. *Res:* Conduct research on macro- and micro-nutrient requirements and on management practices to improve efficiency of production of broccoli, cauliflower, brussel sprouts, rutabagas and peas. *Mailing Add:* Agr Can Res Sta PO Box 1210 Charlottetown Can

CUTFORTH, HOWARD GLEN, b Topeka, Kans, May 6, 20; m 44; c 3. CHEMISTRY, AEROSPACE SCIENCES. *Educ:* Univ Wichita, BA, 42; Northwestern Univ, PhD(phys chem), 48. *Prof Exp:* Res chemist, Rohm & Haas Co, 47-48 & Phillips Petrol Co, 48-59; sect chief, 59-71, BR MGR, CHEM SYSTS DIV, UNITED TECHNOL CORP, 71- *Mem:* Am Chem Soc. *Res:* Magnetic study of free radicals; chemistry of rare earths; colloid problems in crude oil production; magnetic susceptibility of substituted hexaryl ethanes and related compounds; direct tailoring of standard and development of new solid, composite, rocket fuels; production processing; solid fueled rocket motors. *Mailing Add:* 7011 Vie Valverde San Jose CA 95135

CUTHILL, ELIZABETH, b Southington, Conn, Oct 16, 23; m 50; c 1. MATHEMATICS. *Educ:* Univ Buffalo, BA, 44; Brown Univ, MA, 46; Univ Minn, PhD, 51. *Prof Exp:* Chemist, Res & Develop Labs, Socony Vacuum Oil Co, 44-45; asst math, Univ Minn, 46-48 & Conn Col, 48-49; instr, Purdue Univ, 50-52 & Univ Md, 52-53; MATHEMATICIAN, COMPUT, LOGISTICS & MATH DEPT, DAVID W TAYLOR NAVAL SHIP RES & DEVELOP CTR, 53- *Concurrent Pos:* Prof lectr, Am Univ, 67-70. *Mem:* Fel AAAS; Am Math Soc; Soc Indust & Appl Math; Math Asn Am; Asn Comput Mach; Sigma Xi. *Res:* Development of mathematical methods and digital computer programs for solution of problems arising in areas relating to ship research including nuclear reactor design; structural mechanics; hydrodynamics. *Mailing Add:* David W Taylor Naval Ship Ctr Washington DC 20084

CUTHILL, JOHN R(OBERT), b Buffalo, NY, Dec 19, 18; m 50; c 1. PHYSICAL METALLURGY. *Educ:* Purdue Univ, BS, 48, PhD(metall), 52. *Prof Exp:* Phys metallurgist, 52-57, RES METALLURGIST, NAT BUR STANDARDS, 57- *Mem:* Am Phys Soc; Am Soc Metals; Am Inst Mining, Metall & Petrol Engrs. *Res:* Soft x-ray spectroscopy; electronic structure of metals as related to phase transformations and alloying; electronprobe analysis to determine composition and structure of microconstituents; kinetic data. *Mailing Add:* 12700 River Rd Potomac MD 20854

CUTHRELL, ROBERT EUGENE, b Houston, Tex, Nov 6, 33; m 54; c 4. SURFACE CHEMISTRY, SURFACE PHYSICS. *Educ:* Univ Tex, Austin, BA, 54, BS, 61, PhD(inorg chem), 64. *Prof Exp:* STAFF MEM CHEM, SANDIA LABS, 63-68 & 69- *Concurrent Pos:* Res scientist, Air Force Weapons Lab, Kirtland AFB, 70-76; staff develop eng, 76-; counr & treas, NMex Inst Chemists, 74-78. *Mem:* Fel Chem Soc London; fel Am Inst Chemists; Sigma Xi; Am Chem Soc. *Res:* Ultrahigh vacuum study of the chemistry, physics and mechanics of the surface and the near-surface region of solids; applied research in metal-metal bonding, design of electrical contacts, arc theory, hydrogen embrittlement, friction and wear, and atmospheric pollution. *Mailing Add:* Sandia Labs PO Box 5834 Albuquerque NM 87115

CUTKOMP, LAURENCE KREMER, b Wapello, Iowa, Jan 24, 16; m 39; c 4. INSECT TOXICOLOGY, ECONOMIC ENTOMOLOGY. *Educ:* Iowa Wesleyan Col, BA, 36; Cornell Univ, PhD(econ entom), 42. *Prof Exp:* Asst entom, Cornell Univ, 42-43; fel zool, Univ Pa, 43-45; res assoc entom, Univ Minn, 45-46; assoc entomologist, TVA, 46-47; from asst prof to assoc prof, 47-60, PROF ENTOM, UNIV MINN, ST PAUL, 60- *Concurrent Pos:* Consult, Eli Lilly & Co, 59-64 & Onamia Corp, 63-64; entomologist, Int Atomic Energy Agency, Vienna, 65-67 & consult entom & insect biochem, India, 74. *Mem:* AAAS; Entom Soc Am; Sigma Xi. *Res:* Insecticidal action; toxicity of insecticides; insect rhythms as related to insecticide effectiveness. *Mailing Add:* Dept of Entom, Fisheries & Wildlife Univ of Minn 1980 Folwell Ave St Paul MN 55108

CUTKOSKY, RICHARD EDWIN, b Minneapolis, Minn, July 29, 28; m 52; c 2. THEORETICAL HIGH ENERGY PHYSICS. *Educ:* Carnegie Inst Technol, BS & MS, 50, PhD(physics), 53. *Prof Exp:* Res physicist, Carnegie Inst Technol, 53-54; NSF fel, Inst Theoret Physics, Denmark, 54-55; from asst prof to prof physics, 55-78, BUHL PROF THEORET PHYSICS, CARNEGIE-MELLON UNIV, 63- *Concurrent Pos:* Sloan Found res fel, 56-61; NSF res fel, Nordic Inst Theoret Atomic Physics, Denmark, 61-62. *Mem:* AAAS; Am Phys Soc. *Res:* Field theory; high energy physics. *Mailing Add:* Dept of Physics Carnegie-Mellon Univ Pittsburgh PA 15213

CUTLER, CASSIUS CHAPIN, b Springfield, Mass, Dec 16, 14; m 41; c 3. PHYSICS. *Educ:* Worcester Polytech Inst, 37. *Prof Exp:* Dir electronic & comput systs res, Bell Tel Labs, 37-78; EMER PROF APPL PHYSICS, STANFORD UNIV, 79- *Concurrent Pos:* Ed, Spectrum, 66-68. *Honors & Awards:* Edison Medal, Inst Elec & Electronic Engrs, 81. *Mem:* Nat Acad Sci; Nat Acad Eng; fel Inst Elec & Electronics Engrs; fel AAAS. *Res:* Radio transmitter design; design of radar antennas; microwave electron tube research; satellite communication; digital coding. *Mailing Add:* Hansen Lab Stanford Univ Stanford CA 94305

CUTLER, DOYLE O, b Corpus Christi, Tex, Jan 20, 36; m 60; c 2. MATHEMATICS. *Educ:* Tex Christian Univ, BA, 59, MA, 61; NMex State Univ, PhD(math), 64. *Prof Exp:* Asst prof math, Tex Christian Univ, 64-65; asst prof, 65-71, ASSOC PROF MATH, UNIV CALIF, DAVIS, 71- *Mem:* Am Math Soc; Math Asn Am. *Res:* Infinite Abelian groups; algebra. *Mailing Add:* Dept of Math Univ of Calif Davis CA 95616

CUTLER, E(LLIOTT) C(ARR), JR, b Boston, Mass, June 15, 20; m 46; c 2. ELECTRICAL ENGINEERING. *Educ:* US Mil Acad, BS, 42; Ga Inst Technol, MS, 54, PhD, 60. *Prof Exp:* USA, 42-77, instr elec, US Mil Acad, 45-48, from assoc prof to prof, 55-77, head dept, 61-77; RETIRED. *Mem:* Inst Elec & Electronics Engrs. *Res:* Network theory. *Mailing Add:* RR2 Box 68 Jackson Ave New Windsor NY 12550

CUTLER, EDWARD BAYLER, b Plymouth, Mich, May 28, 35; m 61; c 2. MARINE BIOLOGY. *Educ:* Wayne State Univ, BS, 61; Univ Mich, MS, 62; Univ RI, PhD(zool), 67. *Prof Exp:* Asst prof biol, Lynchburg Col, 62-64; oceanog trainee, Coop Oceanog Prog, Marine Lab, Duke Univ, 66-67; asst prof, 67-71, assoc prof, 71-77, PROF BIOL, UTICA COL, 77- *Mem:* AAAS; Am Soc Zoologists; Soc Syst Zool; Am Soc Limnol & Oceanog; Marine Biol Asn UK. *Res:* Systematics; zoogeography; ecology; evolution of benthic marine invertebrates, particularly the Sipuncula and Pogonophora. *Mailing Add:* Dept of Biol Utica Col Utica NY 13502

CUTLER, FRANK ALLEN, JR, b Pana, Ill, Nov 14, 20; m 46; c 3. CHEMISTRY, RESEARCH ADMINISTRATION. *Educ:* Univ Ill, BS, 42; Univ Minn, PhD(org chem), 48. *Prof Exp:* Jr chemist synthetic rubber res, B F Goodrich Co, 44-46; sr chemist develop res, 48-59, tech adv to patent dept, 59-61, coordr compound eval, 61-65, mgr res compounds, 65-77, MGR SYSTS & DATA HANDLING, MERCK & CO, INC, 77- *Mem:* Am Chem Soc. *Res:* Quinones; cortical steroids; pharmaceuticals; information retrieval; substructure searching by computer. *Mailing Add:* 41 Faulkner Dr Westfield NJ 07090

CUTLER, HORACE GARNETT, b London, Eng, Nov 21, 32; US citizen; m 55; c 7. PLANT PHYSIOLOGY, PLANT NEMATOLOGY. *Educ:* Univ Md, BS, 64, MS, 66, PhD(plant path & nematol), 67. *Prof Exp:* Res asst plant physiol, Boyce Thompson Inst Plant Res, 54-59; plant physiologist, Cent Agr Res Sta, WI, 59-62; asst bot, Univ Md, 63-67; plant physiologist, Ga Costal Plain Exp Sta, 67-80, PLANT PHYSIOLOGIST & RES LEADER, PLANT PHYSIOL UNIT, RICHARD B RUSSELL RES CTR, AGR RES SERV, USDA, 80- *Honors & Awards:* Carroll E Cox Scholarship Award, 66. *Mem:* NY Acad Sci; Japanese Soc Plant Physiol; Sigma Xi; Am Chem Soc; Am Soc Plant Growth Regulators. *Res:* Herbicides; defoliants; growth substances from sugarcane; nematodes and micro-organisms; growth inhibitors from tobacco; mode of action and biochemistry of auxins and other regulators; biologically active natural products from microorganisms, identification and isolation; biologically active natural products. *Mailing Add:* Richard B Russell Res Ctr USDA PO Box 5677 Athens GA 30613

CUTLER, HUGH CARSON, b Milwaukee, Wis, Sept 8, 12; m 40; c 1. BOTANY. *Educ:* Univ Wis, BA, 35, MA, 36; Univ Wash, PhD(bot), 39. *Prof Exp:* Fel, Univ Wash, 29-40; res assoc, Harvard Univ, 40-43; field technician, Rubber Develop Corp, Brazil, 43-45; res assoc, Harvard Univ, 46-47; cur econ bot, Chicago Natural Hist Mus, 47-52; cur econ bot, Mus Useful Plants, 53-54, from asst dir to exec dir, 54-64, cur useful plants, Mo Bot Garden, 64-77; CONSULT ETHNOBOT & ECON BOT, 77- *Concurrent Pos:* Guggenheim fel, 42-43 & 46-47; assoc prof bot, Wash Univ, 53-72, adj prof anthrop & biol, 72-77. *Res:* Useful cultivated plants of the New World and their wild relatives; evolution of maize and cucurbits; ethnobotany; economic botany. *Mailing Add:* 2300 Tice Creek 2 Walnut Creek CA 94595

CUTLER, JANICE ZEMANEK, b Chicago, Ill, May 3, 42; m 73; c 2. ALGEBRA. *Educ:* Univ Wis-Madison, BS, 64; Univ Ill, Urbana-Champaign, MA, 65, PhD(math), 70. *Prof Exp:* Instr math, Univ Ill, Urbana-Champaign, 70; asst prof math, La State Univ, Baton Rouge, 70-76. *Mem:* Am Math Soc; Math Asn Am. *Res:* Integral representation theory. *Mailing Add:* 1020 Augusta Wausau WI 54401

CUTLER, JEFFREY ALAN, b Cambridge, Mass, June 30, 42; m 66; c 2. EPIDEMIOLOGY, PREVENTIVE MEDICINE. *Educ:* Wesleyan Univ, Conn, BA, 64; Univ Ky, MD, 68; Harvard Univ, MPH, 71. *Prof Exp:* Intern and resident internal med, Med Ctr, Univ Vt, 68-70; resident health serv admin prev med, Harvard Sch Pub Health, 70-71, resident & fel health serv res, Ctr Community Health & Med Care, 71-72; med officer prev med, Sch Health Care Sci, US Air Force, 72-74; asst prof, Med Col Wis, 74-79; med officer epidemiol, Nat Inst Arthritis, Metab & Digestive Dis, 77-80, med officer, Nat Ctr Health Care Tech, 80-81; MED OFFICER, NAT HEART, LUNG & BLOOD INST, 81- *Concurrent Pos:* Fel, Ctr Community Health & Med Care, 71-72; med adv, Health Dept, West Allis, 76-77; clin asst prof, Dept Prev Med, Uniformed Serv Sch Med, 78-; consult subcomt health maintenance systs, Armed Forces Epidemiol Bd, 77- *Mem:* Am Col Prev Med; Am Pub Health Asn; Asn Teachers of Prev Med; Soc Epidemiol Res. *Res:* Epidemiology and etiology of glomerulonephritis; epidemiologic data applied to health policy; renal disease. *Mailing Add:* Nat Heart Lung & Blood Inst NIH Rm 216 Fed Bldg Bethesda MD 20205

CUTLER, JIMMY EDWARD, b Los Angeles, Calif, Nov 28, 44; m 65; c 2. MICROBIOLOGY. *Educ:* Calif State Univ, Long Beach, BS, 67, MS, 69; Sch Med, Tulane Univ, PhD(microbiol), 72. *Prof Exp:* NIH fel microbiol, Rocky Mountain Lab, Nat Inst Allergy & Infectious Disease, 73-74; asst prof, 74-80, ASSOC PROF MICROBIOL, MONT STATE UNIV, 80- *Mem:* Am Soc Microbiol. *Res:* Host parasite relationships; host innate and acquired immune responses; parasite virulence factors. *Mailing Add:* Dept of Microbiol Mont State Univ Bozeman MT 59715

CUTLER, JOHN CHARLES, b Cleveland, Ohio, June 29, 15; m 42. PUBLIC HEALTH. *Educ:* Western Reserve Univ, BA, 37, MD, 41; Johns Hopkins Univ, MPH, 51; Am Bd Prev Med, dipl, 51. *Prof Exp:* Mem staff, Venereal Dis Res Lab, USPHS, 43-46 & Pan-Am Sanit Bur, 46-48; head, Venereal Dis Demonstration Team, WHO, Southeast Asia, 48-50; head, Bur State Serv, USPHS, 50-58; asst dir, Nat Inst Allergy & Infectious Dis, 58-59; dist health officer, Allegheny County Health Dept, Pa, 59-60; dep dir, Pan-Am Sanit Bur, 60-67; PROF INT HEALTH, GRAD SCH PUBLIC HEALTH, UNIV PITTSBURGH, 67- *Concurrent Pos:* Mem, Int Comt & mem, Bd Dirs, Asn Voluntary Sterilization, 71-, pres, 77-; mem, Bd Dirs, Family Planning Coun, Western Pa & Med Adv Comt, Planned Parenthood Ctr, Pittsburgh; dir, WHO Collab Ctr for Ref & Res in Prophylactic Methods for Control of Sexually Transmitted Dis, 77- *Mem:* Fel Am Pub Health Asn; Am Venereal Dis Asn; Asn Vol Sterilization. *Res:* Combined contraceptive venereal disease prophylactic preparation. *Mailing Add:* Pop Prog Grad Sch Pub Health Univ Pittsburgh Pittsburgh PA 15261

CUTLER, LEONARD SAMUEL, b Los Angeles, Calif, Jan 10, 28; m 54; c 4. PHYSICS, MATHEMATICS. *Educ:* Stanford Univ, BS, 58, MS, 60, PhD(physics), 66. *Prof Exp:* Chief engr, Gertsch Prod Inc, 49-55, vpres, 55-57; res engr, 57-62, eng sect leader, 62-64, dir res, 64-67, mgr, Frequency & Time Div, 67-69, dir, Phys Res Lab, 69-81, DIR, PHYS SCI LAB, HEWLETT-PACKARD CO, 81- *Concurrent Pos:* Mem adv panel, Nat Bur Standards under Nat Acad Sci contract, 68- *Mem:* Fel Inst Elec & Electronics Engrs; AAAS. *Res:* Frequency measuring devices; quartz and atomic frequency standards; noise theory; frequency stability theory; quantum electronics; atomic beam work; lasers; precision alternating current transformers; magnetic bubble memories; disc memories. *Mailing Add:* Phys Res Lab Hewlett-Packard Co 3500 Deer Creek Rd Palo Alto CA 94304

CUTLER, LESLIE STUART, b New Brunswick, NJ, Jan 20, 43; m 66; c 2. DEVELOPMENTAL BIOLOGY, PATHOBIOLOGY. *Educ:* Washington Univ, DDS, 68; State Univ NY Buffalo, PhD(path), 73. *Prof Exp:* Fel path, Sch Med, State Univ NY Buffalo, 68-73; from asst prof to assoc prof, 73-81, PROF & CHMN ORAL DIAG, SCH DENT MED, HEALTH CTR, UNIV CONN, 81- *Mem:* AAAS; Am Soc Cell Biol; Soc Develop Biol; Histochem Soc; Int Asn Dent Res. *Res:* Epithelial-mesenchymal interactions; adenylate cyclase and other enzymes in cyclic nucleotide metabolism; biochemical and electron microscopic cytochemical studies-salivary glands-developmental aspects of neoplasia. *Mailing Add:* Dept of Oral Diag Sch of Dent Med Univ of Conn Health Ctr Farmington CT 06032

CUTLER, LOUISE MARIE, b Troy, NY, Oct 1, 21. CHEMISTRY. *Educ:* Good Counsel Col, BS, 43; Fordham Univ, MS, 52; Columbia Univ, PhD(chem), 62. *Prof Exp:* Instr chem, Good Counsel Acad, 43-44; from instr to assoc prof, 45-62, PROF CHEM, COL WHITE PLAINS, 62- *Concurrent Pos:* Trustee, Good Counsel Col, 63-; NSF grant, NY Univ, 65. *Mem:* AAAS; Am Chem Soc. *Res:* Chelation equilibria and kinetics; study of complexing agents by gas chromatography procedures; history and philosophy of science. *Mailing Add:* Dept of Chem Pace Univ White Plains NY 10603

CUTLER, MELVIN, b Beaumont, Tex, Dec 18, 23; m 50; c 2. SOLID STATE PHYSICS. *Educ:* City Col New York, BS, 43; Columbia Univ, AM, 47, PhD(chem), 51. *Prof Exp:* Mem tech staff, Hughes Aircraft Co, 51-58; mem staff, John Jay Hopkins Lab Pure & Appl Sci, Gen Atomic Div, Gen Dynamics Corp, 58-63; assoc prof, 63-69, PROF PHYSICS, ORE STATE UNIV, 69- *Mem:* Am Phys Soc. *Res:* Electronic properties of disordered systems. *Mailing Add:* 835 Merrie Dr Corvallis OR 97330

CUTLER, MELVIN M, b Philadelphia, Pa, Oct 6, 47. DESIGN VERIFICATION, COMPUTER ARCHITECTURE. *Educ:* Cornell Univ, BS, 69; Univ Calif, Los Angeles, MS, 73, PhD(comput sci), 80. *Prof Exp:* Mem tech staff, Addv Comput Systs Dept, Data Systs Div, Hughes Aircraft Co, 69-75, staff engr, Advan Progs Orgn, 75-80, sr staff engr, Micro Electronics Eng Dept, Strategic Systs Div, 80-81; RES SCIENTIST, INFO SCI RES OFF, AEROSPACE CORP, 81- *Concurrent Pos:* Guest ed, J Digital Systs, 81-83. *Mem:* Asn Comput Mach. *Res:* Developing and applying techniques by which complex computer designs, hardware and software, can be described formally, verified against similar formal specifications and synthesized. *Mailing Add:* 4801 La Villa Marina Marina del Rey CA 90291

CUTLER, PAUL, b Philadelphia, Pa, Mar 27, 20; m 47; c 2. INTERNAL MEDICINE. *Educ:* Univ Pa, BA, 40; Jefferson Med Col, MD, 44. *Prof Exp:* Pvt pract, 50-65; team capt, Care-Medico, Afghanistan, 65-67; prof med & physiol, 68-74, ASSOC DEAN CLIN AFFAIRS, UNIV TEX HEALTH SCI CTR SAN ANTONIO, 71- *Mem:* Fel Am Col Physicians. *Mailing Add:* Univ Tex Health Sci Ctr 7703 Floyd Curl Dr San Antonio TX 78284

CUTLER, RICHARD GAIL, b Lovell, Wyo, Aug 6, 35; m 62; c 3. CELL BIOLOGY. *Educ:* Long Beach State Col, BS, 61; Univ Houston, MS & PhD(biophys), 66. *Prof Exp:* Fel geront, Brookhaven Nat Lab, 66-69; asst prof biol, Univ Tex, Dallas, 69-76; RES CHEMIST, GERONTOL RES CTR, NAT INST AGING, BALTIMORE, 76- *Honors & Awards:* Karl August Forster Award, 76. *Mem:* AAAS; Geront Soc; Biophys Soc. *Res:* Comparative biochemistry of mammalian aging and life-maintenance processes; physical-chemical accumulation of damage in the genetic apparatus with age; age-dependent alteration of gene expression; level of repair and protective processes as a function of age and innate aging rate in different mammalian species. *Mailing Add:* Gerontol Res Ctr Nat Inst on Aging Baltimore City Hosps Baltimore MD 21224

CUTLER, ROBERT W P, b New York, NY, Aug 3, 33; m 61; c 3. NEUROLOGY, NEUROCHEMISTRY. *Educ:* Tufts Univ, MD, 57. *Prof Exp:* Assoc neurol, Med Sch, Harvard Univ, 64-68; assoc prof neurol, Univ Chicago, 68-76; PROF NEUROL, DEPT NEUROL, STANFORD UNIV HOSP, CALIF, 76-, ACAD CONSULT, 80- *Concurrent Pos:* Asst, Children's Hosp Med Ctr, Boston, Mass, 64-68; prin investr, USPHS grant, 69. *Mem:* AAAS; Am Soc Neurochem; Am Acad Neurol; Asn Res Nerv & Ment Dis. *Res:* Physiology of cerebrospinal fluid and bloodbrain barrier mechanisms. *Mailing Add:* Dept of Neurol Stanford Univ Hosp Stanford CA 94305

CUTLER, ROGER T, b Washington, DC, June 28, 46. GEOPHYSICS. *Educ:* Univ Chicago, BA, 69; Univ Ill, MS, 73, PhD(physics), 75. *Prof Exp:* Res fel high energy physics, Univ Ill, 73-75; fel high energy physics, Argonne Nat Lab, 75-77; res geophysicist, 77-79, SECT DIR GEOPHYSICS, GULF RES & DEVELOP, 79- *Mem:* Soc Explor Geophysicists; Am Phys Soc. *Res:* Applications of inversion theory to geophysics and geology; rock properties research. *Mailing Add:* Gulf Res & Develop Ctr Bldg 1 PO Drawer 2038 Pittsburg PA 15230

CUTLER, ROYAL ANZLY, JR, b Spokane, Wash, March 10, 18; m 43; c 3. ORGANIC CHEMISTRY. *Educ:* Whitman Col, AB, 41; Rensselaer Polytech Inst, MS, 42, PhD(org chem), 47. *Prof Exp:* Lab asst chem, Whitman Col, 40-41; asst, Rensselaer Polytech Inst, 41-42, instr chem, 43-44; jr res chemist, Winthrop Chem Co, 44-47, sr res chemist, 47-60, sr res chemist & tech liaison, 60-66, asst dir prod develop, 66-77, qual assurance adminr good mfg pract, 77-81, SR QUAL ASSURANCE ADMINR GOOD MFG PRACT, STERLING-WINTHROP RES INST, 81- *Mem:* Am Chem Soc. *Res:* Product development; pharmaceutical chemicals; pharmaceutical dosage forms; antimicrobials and chemical specialties. *Mailing Add:* 36 Euclid Ave Delmar NY 12054

CUTLER, SIDNEY JOSHUA, b Russia, Apr 13, 17; nat US; m 47; c 3. MEDICAL STATISTICS, EPIDEMIOLOGY. *Educ:* City Col New York, BS, 38; Columbia Univ, MA, 41; Univ Pittsburgh, ScD, 61. *Prof Exp:* Statistician, United Serv for New Am, 39-42; sr statistician, City Dept Health, New York, 46-47; med res statistician, Sch Aviation Med, 47-48; anal statistician, Nat Cancer Inst, 48-75; epidemiologist, Sch Med, Wayne State Univ & Mich Cancer Found, 75-76; BIOSTATISTICIAN, SCH MED, GEORGETOWN UNIV, 76- *Mem:* Fel Am Statist Asn; Soc Epidemiol Res. *Res:* Epidemiology of cancer. *Mailing Add:* 3610 Spruell Dr Silver Spring MD 20902

CUTLER, VERNE CLIFTON, b Brookings, SDak, Jan 2, 26; m 48; c 5. ENGINEERING MECHANICS, CIVIL ENGINEERING. *Educ:* Kans State Univ, BS, 50, MS, 51; Univ Wis, PhD(eng mech), 60. *Prof Exp:* Instr civil eng, Kans State Univ, 50-51; from instr to assoc prof, 51-66, chmn dept, 63-74, PROF ENG MECH, UNIV WIS-MILWAUKEE, 66- *Concurrent Pos:* Res consult, A O Smith Corp, 58-60. *Mem:* Am Soc Eng Educ. *Res:* Reinforced plastics; structural analysis properties of structural concrete; experimental stress analysis. *Mailing Add:* Dept of Mech Univ of Wis Milwaukee WI 53211

CUTLER, WARREN GALE, b Avon, Ill, Jan 31, 22; m 49; c 4. FLUID PHYSICS. *Educ:* Monmouth Col, BA, 47; Pa State Univ, MS, 53, PhD(physics), 55. *Prof Exp:* Instr physics & math, Monmouth Col, 47-51; asst physics, Pa State Univ, 51-53; assoc prof, Mankato State Col, 55-57, head dept, 56-57; assoc res physicist, 57-59, mgr mech eng res, 59-60, res dir, 60-68, DIR CORP RES, WHIRLPOOL CORP RES LABS, 68- *Concurrent Pos:* Sr exec course, Sloan Sch Mgt, Mass Inst Technol, 66. *Mem:* Am Phys Soc; Am Chem Soc; Am Oil Chemists Soc; Sigma Xi. *Res:* Physics of high pressure; physical properties of liquid; surface properties of solutions containing surface-active agents. *Mailing Add:* 218 Crofton Circle St Joseph MI 49085

CUTLER, WILLIAM HERBERT, b Swissvale, Pa, Apr 27, 36; m 57; c 2. ENERGY SYSTEMS. *Educ:* Cornell Univ, BS, 58; Stanford Univ, MS, 60, PhD(physics), 65. *Prof Exp:* Scientist physics, 58-65, res engr & specialist spacecraft systs, 65-76, DESIGN SPECIALIST OCEAN ENERGY, LOCKHEED MISSILES & SPACE CO, 76- *Res:* System design of ocean thermal energy conversion powerplants. *Mailing Add:* 4114 Park Blvd Palo Alto CA 94306

CUTLER, WINNIFRED BERG, b Philadelphia, Pa, Oct 13, 44; m 62; c 2. BEHAVIORAL ENDOCRINOLOGY. *Educ:* Ursinus Col, BS, 73; Univ Pa, PhD(biol), 79. *Prof Exp:* Fel, Dept Physiol, Sch Med, Stanford Univ, 79-80; AFFILIATED SCIENTIST, MONELL CHEM SENSES CTR, 81-; ASST PROF BIOL, BEAVER COL, 81- *Concurrent Pos:* Adj researcher, Dept Obstet & Gynec, Sch Med, Univ Pa, 80- *Mem:* Int Soc Psychoneuroendocrinology; Am Fertil Soc; Sigma Xi; Human Biol Coun. *Res:* Menopause; human pheromones, sexual behavioral and menstrual cycle pattern; reproductive physiology and behavior. *Mailing Add:* Beaver Col Glenside PA 19038

CUTLIP, MICHAEL B, b Portsmouth, Ohio, Sept 21, 41; m 66; c 1. CHEMICAL ENGINEERING. *Educ:* Ohio State Univ, BChE & MS, 64; Univ Colo, Boulder, PhD(chem eng), 68. *Prof Exp:* Res assoc chem eng, Univ Colo, 67-68; from asst prof to assoc prof 68-81, PROF CHEM ENG, UNIV CONN, 81- *Mem:* Am Inst Chem Engrs; Am Chem Soc; Catalysis Soc; Am Soc Eng Educ. *Res:* Chemical reaction engineering; catalysis; air pollution control. *Mailing Add:* Dept of Chem Eng Univ of Conn Storrs CT 06268

CUTLIP, RANDALL CURRY, b Hillsboro, WVa, Sept 30, 34; m 57; c 10. VETERINARY PATHOLOGY. *Educ:* Ohio State Univ, DVM, 61; Iowa State Univ, MS, 65, PhD(vet path), 71. *Prof Exp:* RES VET PATH, NAT ANIMAL DIS CTR, USDA, 61- *Mem:* Am Col Vet Pathologists; Am Vet Med Asn; Conf Res Workers in Animal Dis; Am Asn Sheep & Goat Practr. *Res:* Respiratory diseases of sheep-identify individual disease entities, establish their etiologies and evaluate their pathogenesis with emphasis on chronic diseases of the sheep lung. *Mailing Add:* Nat Animal Dis Ctr PO Box 70 Sci & Educ Admin USDA Ames IA 50010

CUTLIP, WILLIAM FREDERICK, b Lincoln, Ill, Oct 20, 36; m 57; c 3. MATHEMATICS, COMPUTER SCIENCE. *Educ:* Eastern Ill Univ, BSEd, 58; Univ Ill, MA, 61; Mich State Univ, PhD(math), 68. *Prof Exp:* Pub sch prin & teacher, Ill, 55-56, teacher, 58-60; from instr to asst prof math, Northern Mich Univ, 61-64; asst prof, 68-70, assoc prof math, 70-79, PROF & DEPT CHMN, CENT WASH UNIV, 79- *Mem:* Asn Comput Mach; Math Asn Am; Nat Coun Teachers of Math. *Res:* Decomposition and synthesis of finite automata. *Mailing Add:* Dept of Math Cent Wash Univ Ellensburg WA 98926

CUTNELL, JOHN DANIEL, b Pittsburgh, Pa, Aug 30, 40; m 68. PHYSICAL CHEMISTRY. *Educ:* Lehigh Univ, AB, 62; Univ Wis-Madison, PhD(phys chem), 67. *Prof Exp:* Monsanto Chem Co fel, 67-68; asst prof, 68-76, ASSOC PROF PHYSICS, SOUTHERN ILL UNIV, CARBONDALE, 76- *Mem:* Am Phys Soc. *Res:* Fourier transform nuclear magnetic resonance; applications to chemical and biophysical problems. *Mailing Add:* Dept of Physics Southern Ill Univ Carbondale IL 62901

CUTRESS, CHARLES ERNEST, b Calgary, Can, Mar 8, 21; nat US; m 46. INVERTEBRATE ZOOLOGY. *Educ:* Ore State Col, BS, 48, MS, 49. *Prof Exp:* USPHS fel, Univ Hawaii, 53-55; assoc cur, Div Marine Invert, US Nat Mus, Smithsonian Inst, 56-65; assoc prof marine biol, 65-70, PROF MARINE SCI, UNIV PR, MAYAGUEZ, 70- *Mem:* AAAS; Soc Syst Zool; Am Inst Biol Sci; Am Soc Zoologists. *Res:* Systematics; biology; behavior; marine invertebrates, particularly coelenterates. *Mailing Add:* Dept of Marine Sci Univ of PR Mayaguez PR 00708

CUTRIGHT, DUANE EDWIN, b Bliss, Idaho, Oct 1, 26; m 44; c 2. PATHOLOGY. *Educ:* St Louis Univ, DDS, 56; Georgetown Univ, PhD(nucleic acids), 65. *Prof Exp:* Resident, 65-66, chief div oral path, 70-74, CHIEF, US ARMY INST DENT RES, 74- ASST PROF PATH & ASSOC PROF CLIN PATH, MED SCH, GEORGETOWN UNIV, 66- *Mem:* Am Dent Asn; Am Acad Oral Path; Asn Mil Surg US. *Res:* Uses for tissue adhesives; turnover rates of oral epithelium; nucleic acid reutilization and fate in oral epithelium; geriatric oral diseases; microcirculation; cyanocrylates; cryobiology; biodegradable sutures and bone plates; tissue levels in mercury exposure; long tern subcutaneous drug administration; implants; tendon gliding devices. *Mailing Add:* Georgetown Univ Med Sch Washington DC 20057

CUTRONA, LOUIS J, b Buffalo, NY, Mar 11, 15; m 38; c 2. ELECTRICAL ENGINEERING. *Educ:* Cornell Univ, BA, 36, Univ Ill, MA, 38, PhD(physics), 40. *Prof Exp:* Instr physics, Duluth Jr Col, 40-42; mem tech staff radar, Bell Tel Labs, 43-45; mem tech staff commun, Fed Tel Commun Lab, 45-47; mem tech staff radar, Sperry Gyroscope Co, 47-49; div head, Willow Run Labs, Mich, 49-56; physicist radar dept, Space Tech Lab, 56-57; prof elec eng, Univ Mich, 57-59, head radar lab, 59-61, prof elec eng, 61-76; vpres appl res div, Conductron Corp, 61-76; RES PHYSICIST, VISIBILITY LAB, UNIV CALIF, SAN DIEGO, 76- *Concurrent Pos:* Physicist, York Safe & Lock Co, 42-43; consult, Wright Air Develop Ctr, US Air Force. *Mem:* Am Phys Soc; Inst Elec & Electronics Engrs. *Res:* Radar, communication and information theory. *Mailing Add:* Visibility Lab Univ of Calif of San Diego La Jolla CA 92093

CUTSHALL, NORMAN HOLLIS, b Glens Falls, NY, Mar 21, 38; m 61; c 2. CHEMICAL OCEANOGRAPHY. *Educ:* Ore State Univ, BS, 61, MS, 63, PhD(oceanog), 67. *Prof Exp:* Instr oceanog, Ore State Univ, 65-66; chemist, Oak Ridge Nat Lab, 67-68; marine scientist, AEC, 68-69; res assoc oceanog, Ore State Univ, 69-75; mem res staff, 75-80, PROG MGR, LOW-LEVEL WASTE PROG, OAK RIDGE NAT LAB, 80- *Mem:* AAAS; Am Chem Soc; Am Soc Limnol & Oceanog; Ecol Soc Am; Am Geophys Union. *Res:* Environmental radioactivity; geochemistry; economic geology. *Mailing Add:* Bldg 3504 Oak Ridge Nat Lab Oak Ridge TN 37830

CUTSHALL, THEODORE WAYNE, b Lafayette, Ind, Mar 22, 28; m 52; c 2. ORGANIC CHEMISTRY. *Educ:* Purdue Univ, BS, 49; Northwestern Univ, MS, 59, PhD(org chem), 64. *Prof Exp:* Res engr, Am Can Co, 49-50 & 53-58; from asst prof to assoc prof chem, Purdue Univ, Indianapolis, 61-66; ASSOC PROF CHEM, IND UNIV-PURDUE UNIV, INDIANAPOLIS, 66- *Concurrent Pos:* Vis lectr, Franklin Col, 62-63 & Butler Univ, 65-66. *Mem:* Am Chem Soc. *Res:* Synthesis of heteroaromatic systems; reaction mechanisms; stereochemistry. *Mailing Add:* Dept of Chem Ind Univ-Purdue Univ Indianapolis IN 46205

CUTT, ROGER ALAN, b Rochester, NY, Aug 4, 36; m 59; c 2. PHYSIOLOGICAL PSYCHOLOGY, AUDIOLOGY. *Educ:* Franklin & Marshall Col, BA, 57; Univ Del, MA, 59, PhD(physiol psychol), 62. *Prof Exp:* Res assoc, Otol Res Lab, Presby-Univ Pa Med Ctr, 62-65, dir res, 65-70; med serv specialist, Social & Rehab Serv, Dept Health, Educ & Welfare, Philadelphia, 70-73; COMNR MED PROGS, PA DEPT PUB WELFARE, HARRISBURG, 73- *Concurrent Pos:* NIH & John A Hartford Found res grants, 63-70; instr, Dept Otolaryngol, Sch Med, Univ Pa, 62-65, assoc, 65-70, asst prof, 70-73; asst prof community med, Med Col Pa, 73- *Mem:* AAAS. *Res:* Basic and medical research in auditory and vestibular physiology, including behavioral hearing tests on animals, temporal bone histology, electrophysiology, electron microscopy and electronystagmography. *Mailing Add:* 5280 Strathmore Dr Mechanicsburg PA 17055

CUTTER, LOIS JOTTER, b Weaverville, Calif, Mar 11, 14; m 42; c 2. SYSTEMATIC BOTANY, PLANT MORPHOLOGY. *Educ:* Univ Mich, BA, 35, MS, 36, PhD, 43. *Prof Exp:* Res asst plant breeding, Parke, Davis & Co, Mich, 49-50; lectr biol, 63-65, ASST PROF BIOL, UNIV NC, GREENSBORO, 65- *Mem:* Sigma Xi. *Mailing Add:* Dept Biol Univ NC Greensboro NC 27412

CUTTS, CHARLES E(UGENE), b Sioux Falls, SDak, May 15, 14; m 46; c 2. STRUCTURAL ENGINEERING. *Educ:* Univ Minn, BCE, 36, MSCE, 39, PhD(civil eng, mech), 49. *Prof Exp:* Instrument man, Chicago, Milwaukee, St Paul & Pac RR Co, 36-38; asst civil eng, Univ Minn, 38-39; from instr to asst prof, Robert Col, Turkey, 39-43; instr math & mech, Univ Minn, 46-47, from instr to asst prof civil eng, 47-50; assoc res engr & assoc prof civil eng, Univ Fla, 50-53; engr res admin, NSF, 53-56; chmn dept eng, 56-69, PROF CIVIL ENG, MICH STATE UNIV, 56- *Concurrent Pos:* Mem panel sci equip, NSF, 67-70; univ rep, Hwy Res Bd, 68-79; chmn, Engrs Coun Prof Develop, Region V, 73-74. *Mem:* Am Soc Civil Engrs; Am Concrete Inst; Am Soc Eng Educ (vpres, 70-72); Nat Soc Prof Engrs. *Res:* Prestressed concrete; fatigue of materials; numerical methods of analysis; model analysis. *Mailing Add:* 4599 Ottawa Dr Okemos MI 48864

CUTTS, DAVID, b Providence, RI, Dec 12, 40; c 2. EXPERIMENTAL PARTICLE PHYSICS. *Educ:* Harvard Univ, AB, 62; Univ Calif, Berkeley, PhD(physics), 68. *Prof Exp:* Res assoc physics, State Univ NY Stony Brook, 68-71 & Rutherford High Energy Lab, Eng, 71-73; asst prof, 73-79, ASSOC PROF PHYSICS, BROWN UNIV, 79- *Concurrent Pos:* Vis scientist, Rutherford Lab, Eng, 80-81. *Mem:* Am Phys Soc. *Res:* Experimental studies of particle interactions and decays using electronic techniques. *Mailing Add:* Dept of Physics Brown Univ Providence RI 02912

CUTTS, JAMES ALFRED JOHN, b Liverpool, Eng, Sept 29, 43; m 67; c 2. DIGITAL IMAGE PROCESSING. *Educ:* Cambridge Univ, BA, 65; Calif Inst Technol, MS, 67, PhD(planetary sci), 71. *Prof Exp:* Assoc engr, Jet Propulsion Lab, 67-69, image processing analyst, 69-71; res fel, Calif Inst Technol, 71-72; sr scientist, Jet Propulsion Lab, 72-73, mem tech staff, 73-74; dept mgr, 76-80, SR SCIENTIST, PLANETARY SCI INST, SCI APPLN INC, 75-, DIV MGR, 80- *Mem:* Am Geophys Union; AAAS; Am Astron Soc; Soc Photo-optical & Instrumentation Engrs. *Res:* Analysis of remote sensing data; digital image analysis and pattern recognition. *Mailing Add:* Sci Appln Inc 283 S Lake Suite 218 Pasadena CA 91101

CUTTS, JAMES HARRY, b Barnsley, Eng, June 12, 26; Can citizen; m; c 2. HISTOLOGY, HEMATOLOGY. *Educ:* Univ Sask, BA, 48; Dalhousie Univ, MSc, 56; Univ Western Ont, PhD(med res), 58. *Prof Exp:* Chief technician hemat, Gray Nuns Hosp, Regina, Sask, 48-50; technician & head dept, St Paul's Hosp, Vancouver, BC, 50-53; prof hematologist, NS Dept Pub Health, 53-56; from asst prof to assoc prof anat, Univ Western Ont, 60-68; assoc prof, 68-73, chmn dept, 72-73, PROF ANAT, SCH MED, UNIV MO-COLUMBIA, 73- *Concurrent Pos:* Nat Cancer Inst Can fel med res, Univ Western Ont, 56-68, Ross Mem fel, 58-60; lectr, Dalhousie Univ, 53-56; adv fac, Belknap Col, 64- *Honors & Awards:* SAMA Golden Apple Award, 72. *Mem:* Am Asn Cancer Res; NY Acad Sci; Am Asn Anatomists; Am Soc Zoologists; Can Asn Anatomists. *Res:* Oncology; postnatal development of the opossum; comparative hematology. *Mailing Add:* Dept of Anat Sch of Med Univ of Mo Columbia MO 65201

CUTTS, ROBERT IRVING, b Chicago, Ill, Jan 16, 15; m 48; c 2. PSYCHIATRY. *Educ:* Lewis Inst Technol, BS, 36; Univ Ill, MD, 40. *Prof Exp:* Clin asst internal med, Res & Educ Hosp, Univ Ill, 46-47; staff psychiatrist, Vet Admin Hosp, Ill, 49-53 chief continued treatment serv, 53-57; chief serv, Vet Admin Hosp, Tucson, Ariz, 57-59; pvt practr, 59-66; dir, Southern Ariz Ment Health Ctr, 66-68; chief psychiat serv, Vet Admin Hosp, 68-72; ASST PROF PSYCHIAT, MED COL, UNIV ARIZ, 72- *Concurrent Pos:* Clin asst psychiat, Med Sch, Northwestern Univ, 53-55; consult, Southern Ariz Med Health Ctr & Vet Admin Hosp; adj assoc prof, Med Col, Univ Ariz. *Mem:* Fel AAAS; AMA; fel Am Psychiat Asn. *Res:* Outpatient psychiatry. *Mailing Add:* Ariz Med Ctr Tucson AZ 85724

CVANCARA, ALAN MILTON, b Ross, NDak, Mar 7, 33; m 59; c 2. PALEOBIOLOGY. *Educ:* Univ NDak, BS, 55, MS, 57; Univ Mich, PhD(geol), 65. *Prof Exp:* From asst prof to assoc prof, 63-72, PROF GEOL, UNIV N DAK, 72- *Mem:* Am Paleont Soc; Sigma Xi; Am Malacol Union. *Res:* Upper Cretaceous and Lower Tertiary stratigraphy and mollusks in north-central United States; Quaternary freshwater and terrestrial mollusks. *Mailing Add:* Dept of Geol Univ of NDak Grand Forks ND 58202

CVANCARA, VICTOR ALAN, b Ross, NDak, Aug 29, 37; m 58; c 4. PHYSIOLOGY. *Educ:* Minot State Col, BS, 59; Univ SDak, MS, 64, PhD(physiol), 68. *Prof Exp:* Sci instr, Seyyida Maatuka Col, Zanzibar, EAfrica, 61-63; teaching asst, Univ SDak, 64-66, res assoc physiol, 67-69; fel, Ore State Univ, 69-71; asst prof, Beloit Col, 71-72; assoc prof physiol, 72-80, ASSOC PROF BIOL, UNIV WIS-EAU CLAIRE, 80- *Mem:* Am Soc Zoologists; Sigma Xi; Am Fisheries Soc. *Res:* Temperature adaptation, protein synthesis and enzyme induction in teleost fishes. *Mailing Add:* Dept of Biol Univ of Wis Eau Claire WI 54701

CVETANOVIC, RATIMIR J, b Belgrade, Yugoslavia, May 19, 13; Can citizen; m 55; c 3. PHYSICAL CHEMISTRY. *Educ:* Univ Edinburgh, BSc, 36; Univ Belgrade, BASc, 42; Univ Toronto, MA, 50, PhD(chem), 51. *Prof Exp:* With lead-zinc flotation plant, Trepca Mines, Ltd, 37-38; with agr res div, Ministry Agr, Yugoslavia, 38-42; supt, Coop Veg Oil Factory, 42-45; asst lectr phys chem, Univ Belgrade, 45-47; fel, 51-52, res officer, 52-59, head, Kinetics, Photochem & Catalysis Sect, 55-78, PRIN RES OFFICER, DIV CHEM, NAT RES COUN CAN, 59- *Concurrent Pos:* Vis prof, Cornell Univ, 63, Univ Calif, Davis, 64 & Univ Calif, Irvine, 78-79; overseas fel, Churchhill Col, Cambridge, 67; vis scientist, Off Environ Measurements, Nat Bur Standards, Washington, DC, 80-82. *Honors & Awards:* Catalysis Award, Chem Inst Can, 77; Chem Inst Can Medal, 78. *Mem:* Fel Royal Soc Can. *Res:* Chemical kinetics; photochemistry; heterogeneous catalysis. *Mailing Add:* Off Environ Measurements Nat Bur Standards Washington DC 20234

CVIJANOVICH, GEORGE, b Maradik, Yugoslavia, Oct 29, 21; nat US; m 50. PHYSICS. *Educ:* Univ Vienna, BA, 43; Columbia Univ, MA, 56; Univ Bern, PhD(physics), 61. *Prof Exp:* Asst, Nat Ctr Sci Res, France, 47-51; head res & develop, Comet A G Bern, Switz, 51-52; asst, Radiation Lab, Columbia Univ, 52-54; asst prof physics, Upsala Col, 54-57; res asst, Lamont Geol Observ, Columbia Univ, 57-64; privat docent theoret physics, Phys Inst, Univ Bern, 64-67; prof, 67-73, chmn dept, 67-79, WAHLSTROM FOUND PROF PHYSICS, UPSALA COL, 73- *Concurrent Pos:* Chief scientist, Proj Ice Skate, Drift Sta Alpha, Arctic, 58. *Mem:* Am Asn Physics Teachers; AAAS; NY Acad Sci. *Res:* Geophysics; magnetohydrodynamics; nuclear physics as applied to earth science; physics of elementary particles. *Mailing Add:* 30 Cumberland Rd Glen Rock NJ 07452

CWALINA, GUSTAV EDWARD, b Baltimore, Md, Feb 6, 09; m 43; c 2. MEDICINAL CHEMISTRY. *Educ:* Univ Md, BS, 31, MS, 33, PhD(pharmaceut chem), 37. *Prof Exp:* Asst chem, Univ Md, 31-37; from asst prof to assoc prof, Creighton Univ, 37-42; from asst prof to prof, 46-75, EMER PROF PHARMACEUT SCI, COL PHARM, PURDUE UNIV, 75-, ASSOC DEAN, 63- *Mem:* Am Chem Soc; Am Pharmaceut Asn. *Res:* Phytochemical investigation of Ipomea pes-caprae; plant analysis. *Mailing Add:* 1634 Northwestern Ave West Lafayette IN 47906

CYBRIWSKY, ALEX, b Pidsosniw, Ukraine, Mar 26, 14; US citizen; m 45; c 4. PHYSICS. *Educ:* Univ Vienna, PhD(physics), 45. *Prof Exp:* Asst physics, Univ Vienna, 43-46; chief chemist, Archer Chem Co, Ky, 50-51; sect head, Reynolds Metals Co, 51-58, proj dir, 58-60; res physicist, Gen Elec Co, 60-62; RES PHYSICIST, ALLIS-CHALMERS MFG CO, 62- *Mem:* Am Phys Soc; Am Soc Metals. *Res:* Nuclear and cosmic rays studies by nuclear photographic emulsions; recovery, finishing and alloying of aluminum; alumina catalyst; thermoelectric and galvano-thermomagnetic phenomena; energy conversion. *Mailing Add:* Allis-Chalmers Mfg Co PO Box 512 Milwaukee WI 53201

CYGAN, NORBERT EVERETT, b Chicago, Ill, June 5, 30; m 57; c 2. GEOLOGY, PALEONTOLOGY. *Educ:* Univ Ill, PhD(geol), 62. *Prof Exp:* Instr geol, Ohio Wesleyan Univ, 56-59; asst, Univ Ill, 59-62; div stratigrapher, 62-71, MINERALS STAFF GEOLOGIST, CHEVRON OIL CO, 71- *Concurrent Pos:* Lectr, Univ Houston. *Mem:* Am Asn Petrol Geol; fel Geol Soc Am. *Res:* Cambrian and Ordovician conodonts; tertiary micro fauna; stratigraphy; uranium geology; paleoecology. *Mailing Add:* Standard Oil Co PO Box 599 Denver CO 80201

CYMERMAN, ALLEN, b New York, NY, Feb 4, 42; m 66; c 1. PHYSIOLOGY, BIOCHEMISTRY. *Educ:* Rutgers Univ, BA, 63; Jefferson Med Col, MS, 66, PhD(physiol), 68. *Prof Exp:* Res technician clin endocrinol, Temple Univ Hosp & Med Sch, 63-64; sr investr biochem & pharmacol, 68-70, SR INVEST ALTITUDE RES DIV, US ARMY RES INST ENVIRON MED, 70- *Mem:* Am Physiol Soc; Am Col Sports Med. *Res:* Effects of environmental extreme on normal and drug altered physiological and biochemical mechanisms. *Mailing Add:* Altitude Res Div US Army Inst of Environ Med Natick MA 01760

CYNADER, MAX SIGMUND, b Berlin, WGer, Feb 24, 47; Can citizen. NEUROPHYSIOLOGY, VISION. *Educ:* McGill Univ, BSc, 67; Mass Inst Technol, PhD(neurosci), 72. *Prof Exp:* Asst prof psychol, 73-77, assoc prof, 77-81, ASSOC PROF PHYSIOL, DALHOUSIE UNIV MED SCH, 79-, PROF PSYCHOL, 81- *Concurrent Pos:* E W R Steacie fel, Nat Sci & Eng Res Coun Can, 79-81; vis prof physiol, Univ Calif, San Francisco, 81. *Mem:* Soc Neurosci; Asn Res Vision & Ophthal; Can Physiol Soc; Int Strabismological Soc. *Res:* Study of newal mechanisms underlying the organization of neocortex and its development, using the visual system as a model system for understanding the function of the brain. *Mailing Add:* Dept Psychol Dalhousie Univ Halifax NS B3H 4J1 Can

CYNKIN, MORRIS ABRAHAM, b Brooklyn, NY, Nov 23, 30; m; c 2. BIOCHEMISTRY, MICROBIOLOGY. *Educ:* City Col New York, BS, 52; Cornell Univ, PhD(bact), 57. *Prof Exp:* Vis scientist, NIH, 58-60; from asst prof to assoc prof, 60-71, PROF BIOCHEM, SCH MED, TUFTS UNIV, 71-, PROF PHARMACOL, 80- *Concurrent Pos:* Vis fel biochem, Cornell Univ, 56-58; USPHS fel, 56-58; Arthritis & Rheumatism Soc fel, 58-59; Am Cancer Soc fel, 59-60; USPHS res career develop award, 61-71. *Mem:* Am Soc Microbiol; Am Chem Soc; Am Soc Biol Chem. *Res:* Carbohydrate metabolism; structure and biosynthesis of bacterial and mammalian polysaccharides and glycoproteins. *Mailing Add:* Dept of Biochem & Pharmacol Tufts Univ Med Sch Boston MA 02111

CYPESS, RAYMOND HAROLD, b Brooklyn, NY, June 27, 40; c 2. PARASITOLOGY. *Educ:* Brooklyn Col, BS, 61; Univ Ill, BVS, 65, DVM, 67; Univ NC, Chapel Hill, PhD(parasitol), 71. *Prof Exp:* Res asst parasitol, Univ Ill, Urbana, 63-67; fel parasitol, Univ NC, Chapel Hill, 67-69, NIH spec fel, 69-70; asst prof parasitol & epidemiol, Grad Sch Pub Health, Univ Pittsburgh, 70-74, assoc prof, 74-76; PROF MICROBIOL & DIR DIAG LAB, CORNELL UNIV, 77-, CHMN PREV MED, 78-; PROF, STATE UNIV NY, UPSTATE MED CTR, SYRACUSE, 78- *Concurrent Pos:* Adj prof, Grad Sch Pub Health, Univ Pittsburgh, 77-; fel, Fogarty Int, 75 & NIH, Nat Inst Allergy & Infectious Dis, 75-79. *Mem:* Am Soc Parasitol; Am Epidemiol Soc; Am Soc Trop Med & Hyg. *Res:* Immunoparasitology and infectious diseases; epidemiology; comparative medicine. *Mailing Add:* Diag Lab Box 786 NY State Col Vet Med Cornell Univ Ithaca NY 14850

CYPHERS, ROBERT E(LLSWORTH), JR, b East Orange, NJ, Sept 28, 15; m 39; c 2. CIVIL ENGINEERING. *Educ:* Newark Col Eng, BS, 38. *Prof Exp:* Jr hydraul engr, State Water Policy Comn, NJ, 39-41; engr hydraul, Data Div, Tenn Valley Authority, 41-42; prin hydraul engr, Div Water Policy & Supply, 46-51, supv engr, 53-59, CHIEF BUR WATER RESOURCES, STATE DEPT ENVIRON PROTECTION, NJ, 59- *Mem:* Am Soc Civil Engrs; Am Geophys Union. *Res:* Hydrology; hydraulics. *Mailing Add:* 135 King George Rd Pennington NJ 08534

CYPLESS, RAYMOND HAROLD, b Brooklyn, NY, July 27, 40; m 64; c 2. PARASITOLOGY, PREVENTIVE MEDICINE. *Educ:* Brooklyn Col, BS, 61; Univ Ill, Urbana, BVS, 65, DVM, 67; Univ NC, Chapel Hill, PhD(parasitol), 71. *Prof Exp:* Res asst parasitol, Univ Ill, Urbana, 65-67; fel, Sch Pub Health, Univ NC, 67-69, NIH fel, 69-70; from asst prof parasitol & epidemiol to assoc prof, Univ Pittsburgh, 70-76; PROF MICROBIOL & DIR DIAG LAB, NY STATE COL VET MED, CORNELL UNIV, 77-, CHMN DEPT PREV MED, 78- *Concurrent Pos:* Consult pediat & infectious dis, Sch Med, Univ Pittsburgh, 71-77, lectr, 73-; Fogerty Int fel, Univ Pittsburgh, 75; Nat Inst Allergy & Infectious Dis career develop award, 75; mem trop med & parasitol study sect, NIH, 77-; adj prof, Grad Sch Pub Health, Univ Pittsburgh, 77-; adj prof prev med, Upstate Med Sch, Syracuse, 78-; dir clin microbiol lab, Gannett Clin, Cornell Univ, 78- *Mem:* Sigma Xi; Am Soc Parasitologists; Am Soc Trop Med & Hyg; Teachers Vet Med Asn; Am Vet Med Asn. *Res:* Immunoparasitology of gastrointestinal helminthiasis; parasitic zoonoses, their epidemiology and diagnosis. *Mailing Add:* Dept of Prev Med Cornell Univ Ithaca NY 14853

CYR, GILMAN NORMAN, b Van Buren, Maine, Feb 14, 23; m 45; c 6. PHARMACY. *Educ:* Mass Col Pharm, BS, 43, MS, 47; Purdue Univ, PhD(pharm), 49. *Prof Exp:* Asst pharm, Mass Col Pharm, 46, asst prof, 48-52; head, Dept Pharm Res, 52-66, asst dir pharmaceut res, 66-70, dir pharmaceut res & develop, 70-79, DIR RES PLANNING & COORD, SQUIBB INST MED RES, 79- *Mem:* AAAS; Am Pharmaceut Asn. *Res:* Pharmaceutical formulations, especially oral and dermatological products. *Mailing Add:* Squibb Inst Med Res Pharmaceut Res & Develop Dept New Brunswick NJ 08903

CYR, WILBUR HOWARD, b New Haven, Vt, Mar 16, 43. RADIATION GENETICS, RISK ANALYSIS. *Educ:* Univ Vt, BA, 65; Pa State Univ, MS, 66, PhD(biophys), 72. *Prof Exp:* Res biophys, Armed Force Inst Path, 70-74; RES RADIATION GENETICS, DIV BIOL EFFECTS, BUR RADIOL HEALTH, FOOD & DRUG ADMIN, DEPT HEALTH, EDUC & WELFARE, 74- *Mem:* Biophys Soc; Sigma Xi; Radiation Res Soc. *Res:* Electron microscopic studies of radiation induced chromosomal aberrations. *Mailing Add:* 517 3rd St NE Washington DC 20002

CYWINSKI, NORBERT FRANCIS, b Brown Co, Wis, Aug 24, 29; m 61; c 1. ORGANIC CHEMISTRY. *Educ:* Univ Wis, BS, 54; Northwestern Univ, PhD(org chem), 62. *Prof Exp:* Res chemist, Phillips Petrol Co, 59-65, sr res chemist, 65-77, STAFF RES CHEMIST, EL PASO PROD CO, 77- *Mem:*

Am Chem Soc. *Res:* Bicyclic systems; cyclization and dehydrocyclization reactions; free radical reactions; diolefin synthesis; hydrocarbon oxidation; petrochemicals; nylon intermediates. *Mailing Add:* 4251 Candy Lane Odessa TX 79762

CZAMANSKE, GERALD KENT, b Chicago, Ill, Jan 17, 34; m 57; c 2. GEOCHEMISTRY. *Educ:* Univ Chicago, BA, 53, BS, 55; Stanford Univ, PhD(geol), 61. *Prof Exp:* NSF fel, Univ Oslo, 60-61; res assoc geochem, Mass Inst Technol, 61-62; asst prof geol, Univ Wash, 62-65; GEOLOGIST, US GEOL SURV, 65- *Concurrent Pos:* Assoc ed, Am Mineral, 80- *Mem:* Mineral Soc Am; Geochem Soc; Soc Econ Geologists; Mineral Asn Can. *Res:* Inorganic geochemistry; sulfide mineralogy and phase relationships; use of mafic silicate chemistry to elucidate problems in igneous petrology; chemistry of hydrothermal ore metal transport and deposition. *Mailing Add:* 750 W Greenwich Pl Palo Alto CA 94303

CZANDERNA, ALVIN WARREN, b LaPorte, Ind, May 27, 30; m 53; c 3. SURFACE SCIENCE, MATERIALS CHEMISTRY. *Educ:* Purdue Univ, BS, 51, PhD(phys chem), 57. *Prof Exp:* Jr res metallurgist, Aluminum Co Am, Pa, 53; sr res physicist, Parma Res Lab, Union Carbide Corp, 57-63, res scientist, Chem Div, 63-65; mem inst Clarkson Col Technol, 65-68, mem inst colloid & surface sci, 65-78, assoc dir inst colloid & surface sci, 68-74, coun mem, Inst Colloid & Surface Sci, 66-77, prof physics, Col, 68-78; sr scientist, 78-79, GROUP MGR, SOLAR ENERGY RES INST, GOLDEN, 79- *Concurrent Pos:* Consult, Los Alamos Nat Lab, 68-77, Owens-Ill Inc, 69-70, Lawrence Livermore Lab, 77, Babcock & Wilcox, 77 & Exxon, 81; vis scientist, Fritz-Haber-Inst, Max Planck Soc, Berlin, Ger, 71-72; adj prof chem, Univ Denver, 79-, adj prof physics, 80- *Mem:* Am Chem Soc; Am Vacuum Soc; Catalysis Soc; Sigma Xi. *Res:* Solar materials science; surface science; surface analysis; desorption; chemisorption; reactions at interfaces; properties of thin films; catalysis; oxidation; applications of vacuum ultramicrogravimetry and surface analytical techniques. *Mailing Add:* 2619 S Zephyr Ct PO Box 27209 Lakewood CO 80227

CZAPSKI, ULRICH HANS, b Munich, Ger, July 15, 25; m 54. METEOROLOGY, GEOPHYSICS. *Educ:* Univ Hamburg, PhD(meteorol), 53. *Prof Exp:* Guest staff mem, Int Inst Meteorol, Stockholm, 52; staff mem geophys instruments, Askania-Werke, AG, Berlin, Ger, 53-55; geophysicist, Seismos GmbH, Hannover, 55-61; UN tech expert meteorol & geophys, Mission to Pakistan, World Meteorol Orgn, UN Tech Assistance Admin, 61-62; lectr meteorol, Imp Col, Univ London, 62-64; ASSOC PROF ATMOSPHERIC SCI, STATE UNIV NY ALBANY, 64- *Mem:* Am Meteorol Soc; Am Geophys Union. *Res:* Res: Cooling towers; dispersion of air pollutants; thermal waste use and dispersion; solar energy; transfer and convection; hydrometeorology. *Mailing Add:* Dept of Atmospheric Sci State Univ of NY Albany NY 12222

CZARNECKI, CAROLINE MARY ANNE, b Detroit, Mich, Aug 3, 29. VETERINARY ANATOMY. *Educ:* Bemidji State Col, BS, 50; State Col Iowa, MA, 60; Univ Minn, Minneapolis, PhD(anat), 67. *Prof Exp:* Instr high schs, 50-62; teaching asst anat, 62-67, instr, 67, from asst prof to assoc prof, 67-76, PROF VET ANAT, UNIV MINN, ST PAUL, 76- *Mem:* AAAS; Am Asn Vet Anat; World Asn Vet Anat; Am Asn Anatomists; Conf Res Workers Animal Dis. *Res:* Histochemistry of glycogen; Purkinje system of heart; roundheart disease in turkeys; glycogen storage diseases; ultrastructure of avian heart. *Mailing Add:* Dept of Vet Biol Univ of Minn St Paul MN 55108

CZARNETZKY, EDWARD JOHN, agriculture, deceased

CZARNY, MICHAEL RICHARD, b New Britain, Conn, Jan 26, 50; m 78. ORGANIC CHEMISTRY. *Educ:* Providence Col, BS, 72; Dartmouth Col, PhD(chem), 77. *Prof Exp:* NIH fel, Cornell Univ, 77-78; RES CHEMIST ORG & MED CHEM, STERLING-WINTHROP RES INST, 78- *Mem:* Am Chem Soc; Sigma Xi. *Res:* Natural products; steroids; synthetic methods. *Mailing Add:* Sterling-Winthrop Res Inst Rensselaer NY 12144

CZECH, MICHAEL PAUL, b Pawtucket, RI, June 24, 45; m 69; c 1. BIOCHEMISTRY. *Educ:* Brown Univ, BA, 67, PhD(biochem), 72; Duke Univ, MA, 69. *Prof Exp:* Fel biochem, Duke Univ, 72-74; from asst prof to prof physiol chem, Div Biol & Med Sci, Brown Univ, 74-81; PROF & CHMN, DEPT BIOCHEM, MED CTR, UNIV MASS, 81- *Honors & Awards:* Res & Develop Award, Am Diabetes Asn, 74, Elliot P Joslin Award, 75. *Mem:* Endocrine Soc; Am Diabetes Asn; Am Soc Biol Chemists. *Res:* Biochemistry of the modulation of hexose transport activity by insulin and other agents in plasma membranes from isolated fat cells. *Mailing Add:* Dept Biochem Univ Mass Worcester MA 01605

CZEISLER, CHARLES ANDREW, b Chicago, Ill, Nov 7, 52. CIRCADIAN PHYSIOLOGY. *Educ:* Harvard Univ, AB, 74; Stanford Univ, PhD(neuro & bio behav sci), 78; Stanford Med Sch, MD, 81. *Prof Exp:* Proj dir res, Lab Human Chronophysiol, Montefiore Hosp & Med Ctr, Ablert Einstein Col Med, 76-81; JOSIAH T MACY SR FEL HEALTH POLICY, DIV HEALTH POLICY RES & EDUC, HARVARD UNIV, 81- *Concurrent Pos:* Adj instr biol sci, Grad Sch Arts & Sci, Fordham Univ, 78; guest ed, Sleep, 79-80; lectr, Stanford Univ, 79; res assoc, Dept Physiol & Biophysics, Harvard Med Sch, 79-80; appointee, Sleep Schedules, 80-; mem, Task Force Health & Behav, Res Agenda, Inst Med, Nat Acad Sci, 81-82; partic, Consensus Develop Workshop Insomnia & Sleep Disorders, NIH, 81. *Mem:* AAAS; Int Soc Chronobiol; Asn Psychophysiol Study Sleep; Soc Neurosci; Am Physiol Soc. *Res:* The physiology of the human carcadian timing system; neuroendocrine control of hormonal secretory patterns; sleep physiology and pathology; applications of circadian physiology to shift work schedule design and occupational health policy. *Mailing Add:* Div Health Policy Res & Educ Harvard Univ 79 Boylston St Cambridge MA 02138

CZEISLER, JEFFREY LANCE, b New York, NY, July 20, 42; m 73. PHYSICAL CHEMISTRY. *Educ:* Harpur Col, BA, 64; State Univ NY Binghamton, MA, 66; Case Western Reserve Univ, PhD(chem), 70. *Prof Exp:* Fel sch med, Johns Hopkins Univ, 70-71, NIH fel, 72, fel, 72-73; Fulbright-Hays sr fel & vis prof biochem, Univ Cayetano Heredia, Peru, 73; instr physiol chem sch med, Johns Hopkins Univ, 74; res investr phys chem, 75-79, HEAD, PHYS PHARM LABS, G D SEARLE & CO, 80- *Concurrent Pos:* Adj asst prof pharmacol, Chicago Med Sch, 78- *Mem:* Am Chem Soc; Am Pharm Asn; NY Acad Sci. *Res:* Molecular associations of biological importance; uses of nuclear magnetic resonance in biochemistry and biophysics; physiochemical properties of pharmaceutical materials. *Mailing Add:* Searle Labs G D Searle & Co Box 5110 Chicago IL 60680

CZEPIEL, THOMAS P, b Deep River, Conn, May 2, 32; m 55; c 3. PAPER CHEMISTRY. *Educ:* Wesleyan Univ, BA, 54; Inst Paper Chem, Lawrence Univ, MS, 56, PhD(chem), 59. *Prof Exp:* Res group leader, 59-61, mgr tech servs paper mill, Maine, 61-64, tech dir, Detroit, Mich, 64-68 & Pa, 68-72, paper mill supt, Chester, Pa, 72-75, dir venture mfg, Philadelphia, 76-78, PLANT MGR, SCOTT PAPER CO, WASH, 79- *Mem:* Am Chem Soc; Tech Asn Pulp & Paper Indust. *Res:* Influence of metal traces on color stability of cellulose; preparation and utilization of synthetic fibers for papermaking; pulp and paper technology. *Mailing Add:* Scott Paper Co PO Box 925 Everett WA 98206

CZEPYHA, CHESTER GEORGE REINHOLD, b New Brunswick, NJ, Sept 14, 27; m 50; c 5. ATMOSPHERIC PHYSICS, SYSTEMS DEVELOPMENT. *Educ:* Lehigh Univ, BSEE, 50; Air Force Inst Technol, MSEE, 56. *Prof Exp:* Navigator, US Air Force, 50-56, proj officer, Missile Develop, Air Force Missile Test Ctr, 56-60, electronics engr, Air Force Cambridge Res Labs, 62-69, master navigator, Southeast Asia, 69-70, wing chief of plans, Repub of Philippines, 71, chief eng systs prog off, Electronic Systs Div, Hanscom AFB, US Air Force, 71-73; dir metrol, Directorate Metrol, 73, vcomdr, Aerospace Guid & Metrol Ctr, 73-76, VCOMDR, GEOPHYS LAB, 76-79. *Concurrent Pos:* US Air Force, 50-79. *Mem:* Am Geophys Union; Sigma Xi. *Res:* Sterics as a means of severe weather identification; development of high altitude balloon systems for upper air research. *Mailing Add:* 2 Majestic Lane South Merrimack NH 03054

CZERLINSKI, GEORGE HEINRICH, b Cuxhaven, Ger, Dec 31, 24; US citizen; c 2. BIOPHYSICS, BIOCHEMISTRY. *Educ:* Univ Hamburg, BA, 52; Northwestern Univ, MS, 55; Univ Gottingen, PhD(phys chem), 58. *Prof Exp:* Res assoc biophys, Univ Pa, 60-64, asst prof, 64-67; ASSOC PROF BIOCHEM, NORTHWESTERN UNIV, CHICAGO, 67- *Concurrent Pos:* E R Johns Found fel, Univ Pa, 58-60; vis asst prof biochem, Cornell Univ, 66-67. *Mem:* AAAS; AAAS; Biophys Soc; Am Soc Biol Chemists; Sigma Xi. *Res:* Instrumentation, theory and application of chemical relaxation for the investigation of the mechanism of enzyme function; rapid kinetics of enzyme reactions; allosteric behavior; temperature-jump method; production and coating of submicron-sized particles; magnetomechanic and magnetocaloric application of microspheres in biology. *Mailing Add:* Dept of Biochem Northwestern Univ Chicago IL 60611

CZERNIAKIEWICZ, ANASTASIA JUANA, b Buenos Aires, Arg, July 23, 43. MATHEMATICS. *Educ:* Univ Buenos Aires, Lic, 66; NY Univ, PhD(math), 70. *Prof Exp:* J F Ritts asst prof math, Columbia Univ, 71-74; asst prof math, Queens Col, City Univ New York, 74-77; MEM RES STAFF, DATA GEN CO, 78- *Mem:* Am Math Soc. *Res:* Theory of graphs; problems involving coloring of graphs, including ramsey type questions, groups of graphs and chromatic numbers. *Mailing Add:* 2900 Alabama Durham NC 27705

CZERNOBILSKY, BERNARD, b Konigsberg, Ger, Jan 1, 28; US citizen; m 54; c 3. PATHOLOGY. *Educ:* Univ Lausanne, MD, 53. *Prof Exp:* Intern, Jewish Hosp Asn, Cincinnati, Ohio, 53-54, asst resident path, 54-55; asst resident, Israel Beth Hosp, Boston, 57-58, resident, 58-59; chief resident, Mallory Inst, Boston City Hosp, 59-60; assoc pathologist, Women's Med Col Pa, 60-61, from asst prof to assoc prof, 61-65; asst prof surg path, Lab Path Anat, Hosp Univ Pa, 65-69, assoc prof path, 69-70; CHIEF DEPT PATH, KAPLAN HOSP, ISRAEL, 70-; assoc prof, 71-81, PROF PATH, HEBREW UNIV, JERUSALEM, 81- *Concurrent Pos:* Teaching fel path, Harvard Med Sch, 58-59; instr, Sch Med, Tufts Univ, 59-60. *Mem:* NY Acad Sci; Am Asn Pathologists & Bacteriologists; Int Acad Path; Int Soc Gynec Pathologists; Fedn Am Soc Exp Biol. *Res:* Spleen; pancreas; kidneys; breast; cardiovascular system; tissue culture; bilirubin metabolism; gynecologic pathology; ovarian tumors. *Mailing Add:* Dept of Path Kaplan Hosp Rehovot Israel

CZEROPSKI, ROBERT S(TEPHEN), b Chicago, Ill, Nov 15, 23; m 47; c 3. CHEMICAL ENGINEERING. *Educ:* Ill Inst Tech, BS, 47. *Prof Exp:* Mgr prod develop, 56-59, dir appl res printing inks, 59-61, asst vpres, Res & Develop, 62-66, asst plant mgr, 66-67, plant mgr, 67-72; TECH DIR, MARISOL INC, 72- *Mem:* Am Chem Soc. *Res:* Patents; recovery and recycling of industrial wastes. *Mailing Add:* 1167 Tanglewood Lane Scotch Plains NJ 07076

CZERWINSKI, ANTHONY WILLIAM, b St Louis, Mo, Feb 10, 34; m 64; c 3. NEPHROLOGY, PHARMACOLOGY. *Educ:* St Louis Univ, BS, 55, MD, 59. *Prof Exp:* Fel clin nephrology, Vet Admin Hosp, Boston, Mass, 63-64; fel metab, Univ NC, 64-66; from asst prof to assoc prof, 69-77, PROF MED, HEALTH SCI CTR, UNIV OKLA, 77- *Concurrent Pos:* Assoc chief renal sect & chief clin nephrology, Univ Okla Health Sci Ctr & Oklahoma City Vet Admin Hosp, 75- *Mem:* Sigma Xi; Am Soc Nephrology; Am Col Physicians; Int Soc Nephrology; Am Soc Pharmacol & Exp Therapeut. *Mailing Add:* Univ of Okla Health Sci Ctr PO Box 26901 Oklahoma City OK 73190

CZERWINSKI, EDMUND WILLIAM, b Mojave, Calif, Jan 7, 40; m 61; c 2. PROTEIN CRYSTALLOGRAPHY. *Educ:* Univ Calif, Berkeley, AB, 62; Ind Univ, PhD(biochem), 71. *Prof Exp:* Res zoologist, Univ Calif, Berkeley, 62-64; biochemist, Eli Lilly & Co, Ind, 64-68; grad student biochem, Med Sch, Ind Univ, 68-71; res asst prof biochem, Med Sch, Washington Univ, Mo, 72-78; ASST PROF BIOCHEM, UNIV TEX MED BR, GALVESTON, 78- *Mem:* Am Crystallog Asn; Am Chem Soc; AAAS; Sigma Xi. *Res:* Crystallographic structure determination of proteins and other molecules of biological importance; structure/function relationships of proteins. *Mailing Add:* Div Biochem Univ Tex Med Br Galveston TX 77550

CZIKK, A(LFRED) M(ICHAEL), chemical engineering, see previous edition

CZOP, JOYCE K, b Chestnut Hill, Pa, Apr 26, 45. CELL BIOLOGY, IMMUNOCHEMISTRY. *Educ:* Pa State Univ, BS, 67; Univ Wis, MS, 70, PhD(bacteriol & biochem), 72. *Prof Exp:* Fel immunol, Med Col Ohio, 72-74; trainee, Sch Med, NY Univ, 74-76; RES FEL MED, HARVARD MED SCH, ROBERT B BRIGHAM HOSP, 76- *Concurrent Pos:* NIH training grant, Harvard Med Sch, 76-77; Arthritis Found fel, 77- *Mem:* Sigma Xi; AAAS. *Res:* Opsonin-independent phagocytosis of activators of the human alternative complement pathway by human monocytes through a recognition unit distinct from the Fc receptors. *Mailing Add:* Harvard Med Sch at 250 Longwood Ave Boston MA 02115

CZUBA, LEONARD J, b East Chicago, Ind, Feb 28, 37; m 60; c 3. MEDICINAL CHEMISTRY. *Educ:* Ind Univ, AB, 61; Univ Minn, PhD(org chem), 67. *Prof Exp:* Chemist, Sinclair Res, Inc, 61-63; NIH fel org chem, Mass Inst Technol, 67-68; res chemist, 68-72, proj leader, 72-77, mgr, 77-81, ASST DIR CENT RES, PFIZER, INC, 81- *Mem:* Am Chem Soc; NY Acad Sci. *Res:* Synthetic organic chemistry. *Mailing Add:* Cent Res Pfizer Inc Groton CT 06340

CZUBA, MARGARET, b Hohenfels, Ger, Dec 7, 47; Can citizen. PLANT PHYSIOLOGY. *Educ:* Univ Toronto, BSc, 69, MSc, 72; Univ Guelph, PhD(environ physiol, 78. *Prof Exp:* Res asst environ physiol, Univ Guelph, 72-77; RES ASSOC ECOTOXICOL, NAT RES COUN, CAN, 77- *Mem:* Int Soc Soil Sci; Can Soc Plant Physiol; Am Soc Plant Physiol; Am Soc Agron; Can Bot Asn. *Res:* Interaction of persistant metals with one another or other factors, pollutants or nutrient elements, as they affect plant function metabolically, toxicologically, or mutagenetically in ecosystem. *Mailing Add:* Nat Res Coun Can 100 Sussex Dr Ottawa Can

CZUCHLEWSKI, STEPHEN JOHN, b New York, NY, Apr 17, 44. LASER PHYSICS, LASER-INITIATED PLASMA PHYSICS. *Educ:* Manhattan Col, BS, 65; Yale Univ, MS, 66, PhD(physics), 73. *Prof Exp:* Res asst, Yale Univ, 65-73; res assoc, Kans State Univ, 73-74; MEM STAFF, LOS ALAMOS NAT LAB, UNIV CALIF, 75- *Mem:* Am Phys Soc; Inst Elec & Electronic Engrs; Am Inst Aeronaut & Astronaut. *Res:* High-power short-pulse carbon dioxide lasers for fusion applications; multiphoton absorption in polyatomic molecules; nonlinear optical effects. *Mailing Add:* Los Alamos Nat Lab MS 545 Los Alamos NM 87545

CZUHA, MICHAEL, JR, b Peninsula, Ohio, July 20, 22; m 51. PHYSICAL CHEMISTRY, ENGINEERING. *Educ:* Kent State Univ, BS, 44. *Prof Exp:* Res chemist polymer chem, Govt Labs, Univ Akron, 46-53, Arnold O Beckman, Inc, 53-56 & Consolidated Electrodynamics Corp, 56-59; sr res chemist, Res Ctr, Bell & Howell, 59-70; sr engr instruments, E I Du Pont de Nemours & Co, Inc, 70-80; CONSULT, MOISTURE ANALYSIS, 80- *Mem:* Sr mem Am Chem Soc; sr mem Instrument Soc Am. *Res:* Chemistry and physics of high polymers; instrumental analysis and physical testing; research and development of analytical laboratory and process instruments; applications of electron spectrometers. *Mailing Add:* 6510 Wheeler Ave LaVerne CA 91750

CZYZAK, STANLEY JOACHIM, b Cleveland, Ohio, Aug 21, 16; m 42; c 4. PHYSICS. *Educ:* Fenn Col, BS(chem eng), 35, BS(civil eng), 36; John Carroll Univ, MS, 39; Univ Cincinnati, DSc(physics), 48. *Prof Exp:* Res metallurgist, Aluminum Co of Am, 36; chief metallurgist, Master Metals, Inc, 36-38; res engr, Una Welding, Inc, 38-40; assoc res physicist, Argonne Nat Lab, 48-49; res physicist, Battelle Mem Inst, 49-50; asst prof physics, Univ Detroit, 50-51; chief basic physics sect, Aeronaut Res Lab, Wright Air Develop Ctr, Wright-Patterson AFB, 51-54; from assoc prof to prof physics, Univ Detroit, 54-61; dir gen physics lab, Aerospace Res Labs, 61-66, PROF ASTRON, OHIO STATE UNIV, 66- *Mem:* Am Astron Soc; Royal Astron Soc. *Res:* Atomic structure calculations; transition probabilities; collision cross-sections; gaseous nebulae and interstellar medium. *Mailing Add:* Dept Astron Ohio State Univ Columbus OH 43210

CZYZEWSKI, HARRY, b Chicago, Ill, Feb 13, 18; m 43; c 3. PHYSICAL METALLURGY. *Educ:* Univ Ill, BS, 41, MS, 49. *Prof Exp:* Res lab engr, Caterpillar Tractor Co, Ill, 41-46; asst prof metall eng, Univ Ill, 47-51; PRES & TECH DIR, MEI-CHARLTON, INC, 46- *Concurrent Pos:* Instr, Bradley Polytech, 42-46; mem, Dept Planning & Develop, Sci, Eng & New Technol Comt, 60-67; mem, State Bd Health, Radiation Adv Comt, 60-72; past pres, State Bd Eng Examiners, 61-73; treas, Consult Engrs Coun US, 62-64; gen chmn, Pac Northwest Metals & Mining Conf, 63; rep, Gov's Manpower Coord Comt, 68-71; mem, State Adv Coun Ore, Inst Technol, 71-79; rep from Nat Coun Eng Examiners to bd dirs, Engrs Coun Prof Develop, 72-74; mem adv panel D10-10, Trans Res Bd, Nat Coop Hwy Res Prog, 73-76; mem, Ad Hoc Comt on Eval of Ore Dept Environ Qual Lab Appl Res Div, 76; pres-elec, Am Coun Independent Labs, Inc, 77-78, pres, 79-81. *Honors & Awards:* Award, Am Inst Mining, Metall & Petrol Engrs, 42; Eng Excellence Awards, Am Consult Engrs Coun, 70 & 77; Engr of the Year Award, Prof Engrs Ore, 72; Distinguished Serv Award, Nat Coun Eng Examiners, 74. *Mem:* Fel Am Inst Chem; Am Soc Metals; Am Inst Mining, Metall & Petrol Engrs; Sigma Xi. *Res:* Physics, wear and strength of metals; ferrous and non-ferrous physical metallurgy in machinery and industrial equipment field. *Mailing Add:* 2233 SW Canyon Rd Portland OR 97201

D

DAAMS, HERMAN, b Apeldoorn, Netherlands, May 8, 17; Can citizen; m 51; c 1. PHYSICS. *Educ:* Delft Univ Technol, Engr, 49. *Prof Exp:* Asst x-ray diffraction, Delft Univ Technol, 49-52; patent exam gen physics, Patent Off, The Hague, Holland, 52-54; sci officer instrumentation, Delft Univ Technol, 54-57; RES OFFICER FREQUENCY STANDARDS, PHYSICS DIV, NAT RES COUN CAN, 57- *Mem:* Inst Elec & Electronics Engrs; Can Asn Physicists; Netherlands Phys Soc. *Res:* X-ray diffraction, small angle scattering; instrumentation; atomic frequency standards. *Mailing Add:* Physics Div Nat Res Coun Ottawa ON K1A 0R6 Can

DAANE, ADRIAN HILL, b Stillwater, Okla, June 19, 19; m 44; c 3. INORGANIC CHEMISTRY. *Educ:* Univ Fla, BS, 41; Iowa State Col, PhD(chem), 50. *Prof Exp:* Asst phys chem, Off Sci Res & Develop & Manhattan Proj, Iowa State Col, 42-43, group leader, 43-46, from assoc chemist to sr chemist, AEC, 50-63; from asst prof to prof chem, Iowa State Univ, 50-72; prof chem and head dept, Kans State Univ, 63-72; dean, Col Arts & Sci, 72-79, PROF CHEM, UNIV MO-ROLLA, 72-, DEAN GRAD STUDY, 79- *Mem:* Am Chem Soc; Am Inst Mining, Metall & Petrol Engrs. *Res:* High temperature chemistry; chemistry of rare earth metals; vapor pressures of metals; chemical education. *Mailing Add:* Grad Col Univ Mo Rolla MO 65401

DAANE, ROBERT A, b Oostburg, Wis, June 18, 21; m 45; c 1. ENGINEERING MECHANICS, MECHANICAL ENGINEERING. *Educ:* Univ Wis, BSME, 43, PhD(eng mech), 59; Purdue Univ, MS, 49. *Prof Exp:* Engr eng div, Chrysler Corp, 43-46; instr eng mech, Purdue Univ, 46-50; assoc engr, Argonne Nat Lab, 50-54; sr engr, Nuclear Develop Assoc, 54-55; res engr, Beloit Corp, 55-59; assoc prof nuclear eng, Stanford Univ, 59-61; area res dir heat transfer, Beloit Corp, 61-67, dir res, 67-69, vpres res, 69-77; dir res, 77-80, RES CONSULT, TEC SYSTS INC, 80- *Concurrent Pos:* Consult, Atomic Power Develop Assocs, 58-62 & Beloit Corp, 59-61. *Mem:* Am Soc Mech Engrs; Tech Asn Pulp & Paper Indust. *Res:* Stress analysis; nuclear reactor dynamics and safety; heat transfer; numerical analysis and computer simulation of engineering problems; paper drying; industrial research management; development of press drying process. *Mailing Add:* Tec Systs Inc PO Box 30 DePere WI 54115

DABBAH, ROGER, b Alexandria, Egypt, Dec 23, 37; US citizen; m 64; c 2. MICROBIOLOGY, BIOCHEMISTRY. *Educ:* Univ Minn, Minneapolis, BA, 61; Univ Minn, St Paul, MS, 65; Univ Md, College Park, PhD, 70; Univ Dayton, MBA, 76. *Prof Exp:* Technician, Gen Mills, Inc, 59-61; res asst dairy microbiol, Univ Minn, 61-65; res microbiologist, Agr Res Serv, USDA, 65-71; mgr microbiol, Div Qual Assurance, 71-74; mgr biol & info sci, Tech Serv Admin & Res & Develop, Ross Labs-Abbott Labs, 74-76, mgr, Res & Develop Admin, 76-77; assoc dir, 77-81, DIR CORP MICROBIOL RES & DEVELOP, TRAVENOL LABS INC, 81- *Mem:* Am Pub Health Asn; Asn MBA Execs; Am Soc Microbiologists; Inst Food Technologists; Parenterol Drug Asn. *Res:* Inhibition of growth of Salmonella by citrus oils; protein from microorganisms; sterilization systems; food processing, liquid and medical devices and pharmaceutical products; sterilization by radiation, steam, ethylene oxide; research and development administration with zero-based budgeting systems and program planning. *Mailing Add:* 955 Auburn Ave Highland Park IL 60035

DABBERDT, WALTER F, b New York, NY, Oct 12, 42; m 67; c 2. AIR POLLUTION. *Educ:* State Univ NY, BS, 64; Univ Wis, MS, 66, PhD(meteorol), 69. *Prof Exp:* Res asst meteorol, Univ Wis, Madison, 64-69; Nat Acad Sci-Nat Res Coun vis scientist, US Army Natick Labs, 69-70; ASSOC DIR, ATMOSPHERIC SCI LAB, SRI INT, 70- *Concurrent Pos:* Mem comt highways & air qual, Transp Res Bd, Nat Res Coun, 75-81; res fel, Alexander von Humboldt Found, Fed Repub Ger. *Mem:* Air Pollution Control Asn; Am Meteorol Soc. *Res:* Air pollution; momentum and heat transport in the planetary boundary layer; surface heat budget; urban diffusion modeling; optical propagation in the atmosphere. *Mailing Add:* Atmospheric Sci Lab SRI Int Menlo Park CA 94025

DABBS, DONALD HENRY, b Forestburg, Alta, Sept 12, 21; m 43; c 3. HORTICULTURE. *Educ:* Univ Alta, BSc, 50, MSc, 52. *Prof Exp:* Horticulturist, Exp Farm, Can Dept Agr, 52-61; asst prof, 61-70, assoc prof, 70-78, PROF HORT, UNIV SASK, 78- *Mem:* Potato Asn Am; Am Soc Hort Sci; Can Soc Hort Sci; Int Soc Hort Sci; Agr Inst Can. *Res:* Vegetable crops, especially nutrition, moisture stress studies; weed control. *Mailing Add:* 2017 Sommerfeld Ave Saskatoon Can

DABBS, JOHN WILSON THOMAS, b Nashville, Tenn, Dec 11, 21; m 45; c 3. NUCLEAR PHYSICS, CRYOGENICS. *Educ:* Univ Tenn, BS, 44, PhD(physics), 55. *Prof Exp:* Asst physics, Metall Lab, Univ Chicago, 44-45; jr physicist, Appl Physics Lab, Johns Hopkins Univ, 45; PHYSICIST, OAK RIDGE NAT LAB, 46- *Mem:* Fel Am Phys Soc; Sigma Xi; Nat Soc Prof Engrs. *Res:* Nuclear polarization; neutron time-of-flight studies; nuclear fission; mechanical engineering. *Mailing Add:* Oak Ridge Nat Lab Box X Oak Ridge TN 37830

DABICH, DANICA, b Detroit, Mich, Aug 6, 30. BIOCHEMISTRY. *Educ:* Univ Mich, BSc, 52; Ohio State Univ, MSc, 55; Univ Ill, PhD(biochem), 60. *Prof Exp:* Anal chemist, Phillips Petrol Co, Okla, 52-53; asst biochem, Edsel B Ford Ford Inst Med Res, Mich, 55-56; res assoc, 61-63, from instr to asst prof, 63-70, ASSOC PROF MED, WAYNE STATE UNIV, 70- *Concurrent Pos:* NIH fel, Univ Freiburg, 60-61. *Mem:* AAAS; Am Chem Soc; Sigma Xi; Am Soc Biol Chemists. *Res:* Biochemistry of development. *Mailing Add:* Dept of Biochem Wayne State Univ Col of Med Detroit MI 48201

DABORA, ELI K, b Baghdad, Iraq, Sept 24, 28; US citizen; m 57; c 4. GAS DYNAMICS. *Educ:* Mass Inst Technol, SB, 51, SM, 52; Univ Mich, PhD(mech eng), 63. *Prof Exp:* Instr mech eng, Northeastern Univ, 52-53; anal engr, Power Generators Inc, 53-55; res engr, Sci Lab, Ford Motor Co, 55-56; res assoc heat transfer, Univ Mich, 57-61, assoc res engr combustion, 61-64, res engr detonations, 64-68; ASSOC PROF MECH & AEROSPACE ENG, UNIV CONN, 68- *Concurrent Pos:* Consult, Feltman Res Lab, Picatinny Arsenal, 70- *Mem:* Assoc fel Am Inst Aeronaut & Astronaut; Combustion Inst. *Res:* Combustion; heat transfer as related to the design of regenerative heat exchangers; detonation phenomena; standing detonation wave and detonation-boundary interactions; detonations in heterogeneous systems; two-phase phenomena. *Mailing Add:* Dept of Mech Eng U-139 Univ of Conn Storrs CT 06268

DABRAMO, LOUIS RALPH, b Waterbury, Conn, Nov 6, 49; m 72; c 1. AQUACULTURE. *Educ:* Assumption Col, Mass, BA, 71; Yale Univ, MS, 75, PhD(ecol & evolutionary biol), 79. *Prof Exp:* RES NUTRITIONIST ANIMAL SCI AQUACULTURE, BODEGA MARINE LAB, UNIV CALIF, 79- *Mem:* Am Soc Limnol & Oceanog; World Mariculture Soc; Ecol Soc Am; AAAS. *Res:* Physiological and population ecology of marine and freshwater invertebrates, particularly crustacea, with emphasis on nutritional factors; physiological and nutritional studies of species of aquaculture potential. *Mailing Add:* Bodega Marine Lab Univ Calif PO Box 247 Bodega Bay CA 94923

DABROWIAK, JAMES CHESTER, b South Bend, Ind, Apr 11, 42; m 66, 80; c 4. CHEMISTRY. *Educ:* Purdue Univ, BS, 65; Western Mich Univ, Kalamazoo, MS, 67, PhD(chem), 70. *Prof Exp:* Fel, Ohio State Univ, 70-72; asst prof, 72-78, ASSOC PROF CHEM, SYRACUSE UNIV, 78- *Mem:* Am Chem Soc; Biophys Soc. *Res:* Metal-drug interactions; drug-DNA interaction, synthesis of metal containing antibiotics. *Mailing Add:* Dept Chem Syracuse Univ Syracuse NY 13210

DACEY, GEORGE CLEMENT, b Chicago, Ill, Jan 23, 21; m 54; c 3. RESEARCH ADMINISTRATION, SOLID STATE PHYSICS. *Educ:* Univ Ill, BS, 42; Calif Inst Technol, PhD(physics), 51. *Prof Exp:* Res engr, Westinghouse Res Labs, 42-45; mem tech staff & res physicist, Bell Tel Labs, Inc, 51-58, asst dir solid state electronic res, 58-60, dir, 60-61; vpres res, Sandia Corp, 61-63; exec dir tel & power div, Bel Tel Labs, 63-68, vpres customer equip develop, 68-70, vpres transmission systs, 70-79, vpres opers systs & network planning, 79-81; PRES, SANDIA NAT LABS, 81- *Honors & Awards:* Elec Eng Asn Distinguished Alumnus Award, Univ Ill, 71. *Mem:* Nat Acad Eng; fel Am Phys Soc; fel Inst Elec & Electronics Engrs. *Res:* Semiconductors and transistors; semiconductor devices; microwave electronics. *Mailing Add:* Sandia Nat Labs PO Box 5800 Albuquerque NM 87185

DACEY, JOHN ROBERT, b Manchester, Eng, Apr 28, 14; Can citizen; m 40; c 3. PHYSICAL CHEMISTRY. *Educ:* Dalhousie Univ, BSc, 36, MSc, 38; McGill Univ, PhD(phys chem), 40. *Prof Exp:* Res asst, Nat Res Coun Can, 40; supt, Defense Res Chem Labs, 47-49, dean sci, 63-67, prof chem, 49-77, prin, 67-80, EMER PROF, ROYAL MIL COL, 80- *Honors & Awards:* Mem, Order Brit Empire. *Mem:* Am Chem Soc; Chem Inst Can; Sigma Xi. *Res:* Chemical warfare, smoke and flame warfare; surface chemistry, adsorption of gases on charcoal; chemical kinetics, photochemistry of fluorine compounds. *Mailing Add:* Dept of Chem Royal Mil Col Kingston ON K7L 2W3 Can

DACEY, JOHN W H, b Kingston, Ont, Mar 26, 52; m 78. PHYSIOLOGICAL ECOLOGY. *Educ:* Dalhousie Univ, BSc, 73; Mich State Univ, PhD(zool), 79. *Prof Exp:* Scholar, 79-80, ASST SCIENTIST, WOODS HOLE OCEANOG INST, 80- *Honors & Awards:* Murray F Buell Award, Ecol Soc Am, 79. *Mem:* Ecol Soc Am; Bot Soc Am; AAAS. *Res:* Plant-air gas exchange; gas transport in plants; soil gases; atmospheric emissions. *Mailing Add:* Woods Hole Oceanog Inst Woods Hole MA 02543

DACHEUX, RAMON F, II, b York, Pa, July 30, 47; m 69; c 2. ELECTROPHYSIOLOGY, NEUROBIOLOGY. *Educ:* Lycoming Col, BA, 69; State Univ NY, Buffalo, MA, 71, PhD(physiol), 78. *Prof Exp:* Res assoc visual, Neurosensory Lab, State Univ NY, Buffalo, 71-72, res assoc retinal, Neurobiol Div, 73-77; res fel, 77-80, instr, 80-81, ASST PROF ANAT, HARVARD MED SCH, 81- *Mem:* Asn Res Vis & Ophthalmol; AAAS; Am Asn Anatomists. *Res:* Intracellular microelectrode recording techniques and intracellular staining methods to investigate the physiology of individually identified neurons of a mammalian (rabbit) retina; examination of the connectivity and synptology of the identified cells to understand cell communication within the retina. *Mailing Add:* Dept Anat Harvard Med Sch 25 Shattuck St Boston MA 02115

DACHILLE, FRANK, b New York, NY, Sept 15, 17; m 42; c 3. GEOCHEMISTRY. *Educ:* City Col New York, BChE, 39; Pa State Univ, PhD(geochem), 59. *Prof Exp:* Mem staff res & develop resin lab, US Indust Chems, 39-41, plant construct & chem supvr, 41-43, asst plant mgr, Pensacola Div, 43-55; asst, 55-59, res assoc geochem, 59-62, from asst prof to assoc prof, 63-75, PROF GEOCHEM, PA STATE UNIV, 75- *Concurrent Pos:* Consult, Div Undergrad Studies, Pa State Univ, 74- *Mem:* Am Chem Soc; Geochem Soc; Meteoritic Soc; Am Geophysics Union; Mineral Soc Am. *Res:* Application of x-ray methods to study of shock deformation of crystals; parameters and processes in formation of ancient and modern sediments; planetary atmospheres; crystal chemistry at high pressures; geological scope of meteorite and cometary collisions with earth. *Mailing Add:* Deike Bldg Pa State Univ University Park PA 16802

DACHTLER, SALLY LOUISE, genetics, see previous edition

DACK, SIMON, b New York, NY, April 19, 08; m 49; c 2. MEDICINE. *Educ:* City Col New York, BS, 28; NY Med Col, MD, 32. *Prof Exp:* Asst, Cardiographic Lab, 34-35, sr clin asst, Cardiac Clin, 35-41; adj physician cardiol, 45-58, chief, Cardiac Clin, 49-55, chief, Div Cardiol, 72-74, CHIEF PRENATAL CARDIAC CLIN, MT SINAI HOSP, 53-; EMER CLIN PROF, MT SINAI SCH MED, 77- *Concurrent Pos:* Res fel, Cardiographic Lab, Mt Sinai Hosp, 34-35; lectr, Columbia Univ, 35-; mem, Congenital Cardiac Group, Mt Sinai Hosp, 45-, assoc physician, 58-70, attend physician, 70-; from asst attend physician to assoc attend physician, Flower Fifth Ave Hosp, 55-66, attend physician, 66-; assoc vis physician, Metrop Hosp, 55-61, vis physician, 61-; assoc attend physician, Bird S Coler Mem Hosp, 55-; asst clin prof, NY Med Col, 55-59, assoc clin prof, 59-; ed in chief, Am J Cardiol, 58-; assoc clin prof, Mt Sinai Sch Med, 66-67, assoc prof, 67-70, clin prof, 70-77, chief cardiol, Hosp, 72-74. *Mem:* Am Heart Asn; Am Fedn Clin Res; fel Am Col Physicians; fel Am Col Chest Physicians; Am Col Cardiol (pres, 56-57). *Mailing Add:* 1111 Park Ave New York NY 10028

DACRE, JACK CRAVEN, b Auckland, NZ; US citizen; m 50; c 3. TOXICOLOGY, BIOCHEMISTRY. *Educ:* Univ NZ, BSc, 43, MSc, 46; Univ London, PhD(biochem), 50. *Prof Exp:* Biochemist microbiol, Dairy Res Inst, NZ, 51-54; sr biochemist, Toxicol Res Unit, NZ Med Res Coun, Univ Otago Med Sch, 54-61, toxicologist, Path Res Unit, 61-67, head toxicol, Toxicol Res Unit, 68-70; assoc prof environ med, Sch Med, Tulane Univ, 70-74; RES TOXICOLOGIST ENVIRON TOXICOL, US ARMY MED BIOENG RES & DEVELOP LAB, FT DETRICK, MD, 74- *Concurrent Pos:* NZ Med Res Coun proj grant, Med Sch, Univ Otago, NZ, 61-67; vis res biochemist, St Mary's Hosp Med Sch, London, 61-62; vis prof, San Francisco Med Ctr & Sch Pub Health, Univ Calif, Berkeley, 67-68; vis toxicologist, Nat Commun Dis Ctr, Atlanta, 68; mem, Expert Comt & consult, Expert Adv Panel Food Additives & Pesticide Residues, WHO, Geneva, 67-83; mem, Task Force & consult, US Army Med Res & Develop Command, 73. *Honors & Awards:* I C I Silver Medal & Prize, NZ Inst Chem for Imp Chem Indust, 73. *Mem:* Fel NZ Inst Chem; The Chem Soc; Brit Biochem Soc; Soc Toxicol. *Res:* Toxicological, biochemical and metabolic fate studies of food additives, food colors, pesticides and environmental chemicals especially munitions products, chemical agents, fungal metabolites and trace metals. *Mailing Add:* US Army Med Bioeng Res & Dev Lab Environ Protection Res Div Ft Detrick MD 21701

DA CUNHA, ANTONIO BRITO, b Sao Paulo, Brazil, June 17, 25; m 49; c 2. POPULATION GENETICS, CYTOGENETICS. *Educ:* Univ Sao Paulo, PhD, 48. *Prof Exp:* Asst, 45-48, privat docent, 48-55, from asst prof to assoc prof, 55-73, actg head dept, 64-66 & 68-70, head dept, 70-73, PROF BIOL, UNIV SAO PAULO, 73-, DIR INST BIOL SCI, 73-, V PRES, 78- *Concurrent Pos:* Rockefeller Found fels, 49 & 61; vis prof, Univ Tex, Austin, 71. *Mem:* Soc Study Evolution (vpres, 62 & 71); Am Soc Naturalists; Genetics Soc Am; Brazilian Soc Genetics; Brazilian Acad Sci. *Res:* Evolutionary processes; differentiation; chromosomal effects of pathogenic agents; symbiosis; philosophy of science, biology. *Mailing Add:* Rua Itapicuru 777 apt 21 05006 - Sao Paulo SP Brazil

D'ADAMO, AMEDEO FILIBERTO, JR, b Brooklyn, NY, Apr 15, 29; m 62; c 4. MOLECULAR BIOLOGY, NEUROBIOLOGY. *Educ:* Rutgers Univ, BSc, 50, PhD(chem), 55. *Prof Exp:* Res assoc, Am Cyanamid Co, 53-55, Columbia Univ, 55-56 & Ortho Res Found, 56-58; asst prof biochem, Albert Einstein Col Med, 58-61; asst prof, NJ Col Med, 61-63; assoc prof, Albert Einstein Col Med, 63-68; PROF BIOL, YORK COL, CITY UNIV NEW YORK, 68- *Concurrent Pos:* Adj prof chem, Manhattanville Col, 75. *Mem:* Am Inst Chem; Am Soc Neurochem; AAAS; Am Chem Soc; Sigma Xi. *Res:* Metabolic pathways; control of metabolism; lipogenesis and myelia synthesis; synaptosomal metabolism; effects of hormones on metabolism of the central nervous system. *Mailing Add:* Dept of Biol York Col City Univ of New York Jamaica NY 11451

DADE, PHILIP EUGENE, b Hutchinson, Kans, Feb 2, 29; m 56; c 3. AGRONOMY. *Educ:* Kans State Col, BS, 51, MS, 52; State Col Wash, PhD(forage crop prod), 59. *Prof Exp:* Res agronomist, Agr Res Serv, USDA, 57-67; res agronomist, 67-74, mgr seed res & prod, 74-79, PROG DIR, SEED RES & PROD, O M SCOTT & SONS, 79- *Mem:* Sigma Xi; Am Soc Agron; Crop Sci Soc Am. *Res:* Pasture and forage crop management; forage and turf grass seed production. *Mailing Add:* 3505 Begonia Dr Salem OR 97304

DADSWELL, MICHAEL JOHN, b Dafoe, Sask, July 12, 44; m 68; c 2. FISH ECOLOGY, ZOOGEOGRAPHY. *Educ:* Carleton Univ, Ottawa, BSc, 67, PhD(zoogeog), 73. *Prof Exp:* Res scientist, Huntsman Marine Lab, 73-78; RES SCIENTIST, DEPT FISHERIES & OCEANS, BIOL STA, 78- *Concurrent Pos:* Mem, Shortnose Sturgeon US Nat Marine Fisheries Serv Recovery Team, 76-81; lectr, Acadia Univ, Wolfville, NS, 81. *Mem:* Am Fisheries Soc; Can Zool Soc; Soc Systs Zool; Crustacean Soc; Am Soc Limnol & Oceanog. *Res:* Migration and ocean ecology of American shad (Alosa sapadissima); biology of shortnose sturgeon (Acipenser breoiroshrum); zoogeography and taxonomy of crustaceans. *Mailing Add:* Dept Fisheries & Oceans Biol Sta St Andrews NB E0G 2X0 Can

DAEHLER, MARK, b Cedar Rapids, Iowa, Mar 21, 34. PHYSICS. *Educ:* Coe Col, BA, 55; Univ Wis, MA, 57, PhD(physics), 66. *Prof Exp:* Fel, Los Alamos Sci Lab, Univ Calif, 66-68; staff physicist, Inst Plasmaphysik, Munich, Ger, 68-71; RES PHYSICIST, US NAVAL RES LAB, 71- *Mem:* Optical Soc Am; Am Phys Soc; Am Astron Soc; Inst Elec & Electronic Engrs. *Res:* High resolution interferometric optical spectroscopy; solar and plasma spectroscopy; zodiacal light spectroscopy; infrared rocket photometry; cryogenically-cooled spectroscopic instrumentation; astrophysics of infrared-emitting objects. *Mailing Add:* Code 4139.3 US Naval Res Lab Washington DC 20375

DAEHLER, MAX, JR, b Cedar Rapids, Iowa, Mar 21, 34. PHYSICS. *Educ:* Coe Col, BA, 55; Univ Wis, MA, 57, PhD, 62. *Prof Exp:* Sr engr res, Autonetics Div, NAm Aviation, Inc, 62-68; sr scientist, Exsar Corp, 68-71; sr res engr, Quantic Industs, 71-79; RES SPECIALIST, LOCKHEED MISSILES & SPACE CO, 79- *Res:* Electron spin resonance; star-tracking devices; electro-optical sensors; infrared target simulation. *Mailing Add:* 2309 Monserat Ave Belmont CA 94002

DAEHNICK, WILFRIED W, b Berlin, Ger, Dec 30, 28; US citizen; m 60; c 3. EXPERIMENTAL NUCLEAR PHYSICS. *Educ:* Munich Tech Univ, BS, 51; Univ Hamburg, MA, 55, Wash Univ, PhD(physics), 58. *Prof Exp:* Res assoc nuclear physics, Wash Univ, 58-59; res assoc, Princeton Univ, 59-60, instr, 60-62; from asst prof to assoc prof, 62-69, chmn, Comput Ctr Exec Comt, 77-80, dir, Sarah Mellon Scaife Nuclear Physics Lab, 78-79, PROF NUCLEAR PHYSICS, UNIV PITTSBURGH, 69-, CHMN, UNIV SENATE BUDGET POLICIES COMT, 81- *Concurrent Pos:* Vis prof, Max Planck Inst, Heidelberg, 73-74; mem, Adv Comt Physics, NSF, 76-79. *Mem:* Fel Am Phys Soc; Am Asn Univ Prof. *Res:* Nuclear structure and nuclear reactions induced by light and heavy ions; nuclear instrumentation; consulting. *Mailing Add:* Dept of Physics Univ of Pittsburgh Pittsburgh PA 15260

DAELLENBACH, CHARLES BYRON, b Minneapolis, Minn, Nov 16, 39; m 62; c 3. EXTRACTIVE & PHYSICAL METALLURGY. *Educ:* Univ Wis, BS, 62, MS, 63. *Prof Exp:* Extractive metallurgist, Twin City Metall Res Ctr, US Bur Mines, US Dept Interior, 63-64, res extractive metallurgist, 64-66, res metallurgist, 66-67, res metallurgist, Iron Range Demonstration Plant, Keewatin, Minn, 67-69, res metallurgist, Twin Cities Metall Res Ctr, Minn, 69-75, SUPVRY METALLURGIST, ALBANY METALL RES CTR, US BUR MINES, ORE, 75- *Honors & Awards:* 1974 Young Engr of the Year Award, Am Inst Mining, Metall & Petrol Engrs, Minn Sect, 75. *Mem:* Am Chem Soc; Am Inst Mining, Metall & Petrol Engrs. *Res:* Extractive metallurgy and mineral beneficiation; physical and foundry metallurgy. *Mailing Add:* Albany Metall Res Ctr US Bur of Mines PO Box 70 Albany OR 97321

DAESCHNER, CHARLES WILLIAM, JR, b Houston, Tex, Dec 24, 20; m 48; c 3. PEDIATRICS. *Educ:* Rice Inst, BA, 42; Univ Tex, MD, 45. *Prof Exp:* Intern, Hermann Hosp, Houston, Tex, 45-46; jr resident, St Louis Children's Hosp, 48-49, asst resident, 49-50; sr resident, Boston Children's Hosp, 50-51; from instr to assoc prof pediat, Med Col, Baylor Univ, 51-60; PROF PEDIAT & CHMN DEPT, UNIV TEX MED BR, 60- *Mem:* Acad Pediat; Soc Pediat Res. *Res:* Metabolic and renal diseases in children. *Mailing Add:* Dept of Pediat Univ of Tex Med Br Galveston TX 77551

DAESSLE, CLAUDE, b France, Mar 29, 29; Can citizen; m 64; c 1. ORGANIC CHEMISTRY. *Educ:* Swiss Fed Inst Technol EthETH-Zurich, ChE, 54, DrScPhys, 57. *Prof Exp:* Res chemist, Monsanto Can Ltd, 57-60; OWNER, ORG MICROANAL, 60- *Res:* General organic synthesis, especially natural products. *Mailing Add:* 305 Morrison Ave Montreal PQ H3R 1K8 Can

DAFERMOS, CONSTANTINE M, b Athens, Greece, May 26, 41; m 64. APPLIED MATHEMATICS. *Educ:* Athens Tech Univ, dipl civil eng, 64; Johns Hopkins Univ, PhD(mech), 67. *Prof Exp:* Fel theoret mech, Johns Hopkins Univ, 67-68; asst prof, Cornell Univ, 68-71; assoc prof, 71-76, PROF APPL MATH, BROWN UNIV, 76- *Mem:* Soc Natural Philos (treas, 75-77); Am Math Soc. *Res:* Stability theory in continuum mechanics; partial differential equations; dynamical systems; hyperbolic conservation laws. *Mailing Add:* Div of Appl Math Brown Univ Providence RI 02912

DAFERMOS, STELLA, b Athens, Greece, Apr 14, 40; US citizen; m 64; c 2. TRANSPORTATION SCIENCE. *Educ:* Athens Nat Tech Univ, dipl, 64; Johns Hopkins Univ, PhD(oper res), 68. *Prof Exp:* Instr oper res, Cornell Univ, 68-69; asst prof, 69-71; asst prof appl math, 72-78, assoc prof, 78-82, PROF APPL MATH, BROWN UNIV, 82- *Mem:* Opers Res Soc Am. *Res:* Mathematical programming; equilibrium programming; networks and large scale systems applications to transportation and communication networks. *Mailing Add:* Div Appl Math Brown Univ Providence RI 02912

DAFFORN, GEOFFREY ALAN, b Kingman, Kans, Feb 4, 44; m 73. BIO-ORGANIC CHEMISTRY. *Educ:* Harvard Univ, BA, 66; Univ Calif, Berkeley, PhD(chem), 70. *Prof Exp:* Fel biochem, Univ Calif, Berkeley, 70-73; asst prof, Univ Tex, Austin, 73-74; asst prof, 74-79, ASSOC PROF CHEM, BOWLING GREEN STATE UNIV, 79- *Concurrent Pos:* NIH fel, 70-72; adj prof pharmacol, Med Col Ohio, 76- *Mem:* Am Chem Soc. *Res:* Transition state analogs and the mechanism of acetylcholinesterase and other esterases; synthetic catalysts with enzyme-like properties. *Mailing Add:* Dept Chem Bowling Green Univ Bowling Green OH 43403

DAFNY, NACHUM, b Tel-Aviv, Israel, Mar 5, 34; m 69; c 3. NEUROPHYSIOLOGY, NEUROENDOCRINOLOGY. *Educ:* Hebrew Univ, BSc, 62, MSc, 65, PhD(neurophysiol), 68. *Prof Exp:* Lectr neurosci, Hadassah Med Sch, Hebrew Univ, Israel, 68-69; fel, Calif Inst Technol & Univ Calif, Los Angeles, mem staff, Col Physicians & Surgeons, Columbia Univ, 70-72; asst prof neurosci, 72-74, assoc prof, 74-77, PROF NEUROBIOL & ANAT, UNIV TEX MED SCH, HOUSTON & GRAD SCH BIOMED SCI, UNIV HOUSTON, 77- *Concurrent Pos:* NSF fel, Calif Inst Technol, 69-70; Ford Found fel Brain Res & Anat, Univ Calif, Los Angeles, 70; NIH spec fel neurol, Col Physicians & Surgeons, Columbia Univ, 71-72; sr fac fel, Fogarty Int, 80-81. *Mem:* Israeli EEG & Clin Neurophysiol Soc; Israeli Pharmacol & Physiol Soc; Soc Neurosci; Soc Exp Biol & Med; Am Physiol Soc. *Res:* Neuroendocrinology; neuropharmacology; neurobiology. *Mailing Add:* 6118 Yarwell Houston TX 77035

DAGA, RAMAN LALL, b Purulia, India, Jan 5, 44; US citizen; m 72; c 2. METALLURGY, MECHANICS. *Educ:* Bihar Inst Technol, BS, 66; NMex Inst Mining & Technol, MS, 68; Case Western Reserve Univ, PhD(metall), 70. *Prof Exp:* Tech leader & res scientist refractory metal res & develop, Gen Elec Co, 70-78; eng specialist, Chem & Metal Div, 79-82, ENG MGR METALS RES, GTE PROD CORP, TOWANDA, PA, 82- *Mem:* Am Soc Metals; Am Soc Mfg Engrs. *Res:* Physical and mechanical metallurgy; structure property relationship; deformation mechanisms; applied metal processing; processing and properties of refractory metals. *Mailing Add:* 27 Oak Hill RD2 Sayre PA 18840

DAGANZO, CARLOS FRANCISCO, b Barcelona, Spain, May 15, 48; m 70; c 3. TRANSPORTATION ENGINEERING, OPERATIONS RESEARCH. *Educ:* Univ Madrid, dipl civil eng, 72; Univ Mich, MSE, 73, PhD(civil eng), 75. *Prof Exp:* Asst prof transp, Mass Inst Technol, 75-76; asst prof, 76-80, ASSOC PROF TRANSP ENG, UNIV CALIF, BERKELEY, 80- *Concurrent Pos:* Assoc ed, Transp Sci, 76-; prin investr, NSF res grants, 77-; consult, Gen Motors, 77-; assoc ed, Transp Res, Series B, Methodological, 78- *Mem:* Transp Res Bd; Inst Transp Engrs; Opers Res Soc Am. *Res:* Theoretical modelling of transportation processes and systems, and development of the necessary analytical tools; mathematical programming, statistical inference, and applied probability and mathematical methods. *Mailing Add:* Dept Civil Eng Univ Calif Berkeley CA 94720

DAGE, RICHARD CYRUS, b Kalamazoo, Mich. PHARMACOLOGY. *Educ:* Ferris State Col, BS, 60; Marquette Univ, PhD(pharmacol), 67. *Prof Exp:* Pharmacologist cardiovasc pharmacol, Lakeside Labs, Div Colgate Palmolive Co, 67-75; sr res pharmacologist cardiovasc pharmacol, Merrell Nat Labs Div Richardson-Merrell Inc, 75-81; SR RES PHARMACOLOGIST CARDIOVASC PHARMACOL, MERRELL RES CTR, MERRELL DOW PHARMACEUT INC, 81- *Concurrent Pos:* From clin instr to clin asst prof pharmacol, Med Col Wis, 67-75. *Mem:* Am Soc Pharmacol Exp Therapeutics. *Res:* Cardiovascular pharmacology; mechanism of hypertension; antihypertensive drugs; cardiotonic drugs; mechanism of action of cardiotonic drugs; autonomic pharmacology. *Mailing Add:* Merrell Res Ctr 2110 E Galbraith Rd Cincinnati OH 45215

DAGG, ANNE INNIS, b Toronto, Ont, Jan 25, 33; m 57; c 3. MAMMALOGY. *Educ:* Univ Toronto, BA, 55, MA, 56; Univ Waterloo, PhD(mammal), 67. *Prof Exp:* Asst prof zool, Univ Guelph, 68-72; res asst prof biol, Univ Waterloo, 72-76; FREE LANCE WRITER & RESEARCHER, 76- *Mem:* Am Soc Mammalogists; Can Soc Environ Biologists; Writers Union Can. *Res:* Behavior ecology of giraffe and camel; analysis of movements and gaits of birds and mammals; relationship of wildlife and man in Canada, especially in cities; sexual differences in behavior of mammals. *Mailing Add:* 81 Albert St Waterloo ON N2L 3G1 Can

DAGG, CHARLES PATRICK, b Nebr, July 21, 23. REPRODUCTIVE BIOLOGY. *Educ:* George Washington Univ, BS, 48; Univ Calif, Los Angeles, PhD(zool), 53. *Prof Exp:* Asst cancer, Univ Calif, Los Angeles, 52-53; USPHS res fel embryol & cancer, Sloan-Kettering Inst, 54-55, asst, 55-56; vis asst prof biol, Brown Univ, 56-58; from assoc staff scientist to staff scientist, Jackson Lab, 58-67; chmn dept biol, Univ Ala, Birmingham, 67-74, PROF DENT & PROF BIOL, UNIV ALA, BIRMINGHAM & PROF BIOL, TUSCALOOSA, 67- *Mem:* Am Soc Zoologists; Am Asn Anatomists; Genetics Soc Am; Soc Develop Biol; Teratology Soc (secy-treas, 62-66). *Res:* Embryology; reproductive physiology. *Mailing Add:* 1752 Shades Crest Rd Birmingham AL 35216

DAGG, IAN RALPH, b Winnipeg, Man, Mar 20, 28; m 57; c 3. MICROWAVE PHYSICS. *Educ:* Univ Man, BSc, 49; Pa State Col, MS, 50; Univ Toronto, PhD(physics), 53. *Prof Exp:* Lectr physics, Univ Toronto, 53-54; Nat Res Coun Can fel, Oxford Univ, 54-55; asst res officer appl physics, nat Res Coun Can, 55-59; assoc prof, 59-69, PROF PHYSICS, UNIV WATERLOO, 69- *Concurrent Pos:* Nat Res Coun Can res grants, 60- *Mem:* Can Asn Physicists. *Res:* Infrared and Raman spectroscopy; electric field induced and pressure induced absorption in infrared and microwave regions; acoustics, microphone standards and noise control. *Mailing Add:* Dept Physics Univ Waterloo Waterloo ON N2L 3G1 Can

DAGG, MICHAEL JOHN, biological oceanography, see previous edition

DAGGERHART, JAMES ALVIN, JR, b Shelby, NC, Dec 6, 42; m 63; c 2. GAS DYNAMICS. *Educ:* NC State Univ, BS, 64, PhD(mech eng), 69. *Prof Exp:* Res assoc rarefied gas dynamics, 66-69, ASST PROF MECH & AEROSPACE ENG, NC STATE UNIV, 69- *Concurrent Pos:* NASA res grant, 69-71. *Mem:* Am Inst Aeronaut & Astronaut; Am Vacuum Soc. *Res:* Rarefied gas dynamics; cryoentrainment mechanism for vacuum pump application; high altitude simulation; performance of ionization type vacuum gauges in various environments. *Mailing Add:* Dept of Mech & Aerospace Eng NC State Univ Raleigh NC 27607

DAGGY, RICHARD HENRY, b St Paul, Minn, Aug 23, 14. ENTOMOLOGY, PUBLIC HEALTH. *Educ:* Univ Minn, BS, 34, MS, 38, PhD(entom), 41; Harvard Univ, MPH, 52, DrPH(trop pub health), 58. *Prof Exp:* Instr high sch, Minn, 34; asst, Univ Minn, 35-39; instr biol, Bemidji State Col, 39-41; asst entomologist, Bur Entom & Plant Quarantine, USDA, Fla, 42; assoc entomologist, Commun Dis Ctr, USPHS, 45; asst prof entom, Univ Minn, 45-47; from med entomologist to med dir, Arabian Am Oil Co, Saudi Arabia, 47-64; assoc dean int prog, 64-73, actg dean sch pub health, 71-72, LECTR TROP PUB HEALTH, HARVARD UNIV, 64- *Concurrent Pos:* Vis lectr, Sch Pub Health, Harvard Univ, 54-64; hon consult, US Air Force, Europe, 57. *Mem:* AAAS; Am Entom Soc; Am Soc Trop Med & Hyg; fel Am Pub Health Asn; Royal Soc Trop Med & Hyg. *Res:* Biology and ecology of anophelines; malaria control; tropical public health. *Mailing Add:* Sch of Pub Health Harvard Univ Boston MA 02115

DAGGY, TOM, b Mooresville, Ind, July 16, 15; m 39; c 2. BIOLOGY. *Educ:* Earlham Col, BA, 37; Northwestern Univ, MS, 39, PhD(zool), 46. *Prof Exp:* Asst zool, Northwestern Univ, 37-42; instr biol, Maine Twp Jr Col, Ill, 39-42 & Univ Toledo, 42-43; tutor, Olivet Col, 43-47; assoc prof, 47-55, PROF BIOL, DAVIDSON COL, 55- *Concurrent Pos:* Biol illusr, 38-43. *Mem:* AAAS; Ecol Soc Am; Am Soc Study Evolution; Soc Syst Zool. *Res:* Ecology and taxonomy of insects; immature stages of Coleoptera. *Mailing Add:* Dept of Biol Davidson Col Davidson NC 28036

DAGIRMANJIAN, ROSE, b Whitinsville, Mass, July 4, 30. PHARMACOLOGY, TOXICOLOGY. *Educ:* Clark Univ, AB, 52; Univ Rochester, MS, 54, PhD(pharmacol), 60. *Prof Exp:* Res assoc pharmacol, Univ Rochester, 52-60; asst prof pharmacol, Col Med, Ohio State Univ, 63-69; assoc prof, 69-75, PROF PHARMACOL, SCH MED, UNIV LOUISVILLE, 75- *Concurrent Pos:* Riker Int fel, Eng, 60-62; consult, USPHS & NIH, 72- & Food & Drug Admin, 75-80; mem toxicol adv bd, Consumer Prod Safety Comn, 79-82; panel mem, Nat Acad Sci, 80-81. *Mem:* Am Soc Pharmacol & Exp Therapeut; Soc Toxicol; Soc Exp Biol & Med; Soc Neurosci. *Res:* Pharmacology of tetrahydracannabinols; effects of drugs and magnesium on the biogenic amines in the central nervous system; neuropharmacology of heavy metals. *Mailing Add:* Dept Pharmacol/Toxicol Univ of Louisville Health Sci Ctr Louisville KY 40292

DAGLEY, STANLEY, b Burton, UK, Apr 1, 16; m 39; c 4. BIOCHEMISTRY. *Educ:* Oxford Univ, MA & BSc, 38; Univ London, MSc, 48, DSc(biochem), 55. *Prof Exp:* Lectr biochem, Univ Leeds, 47-52, reader, 52-62, prof, 62-66; prof biochem, 66-80, REGENTS PROF BIOCHEM, UNIV MINN, 80- *Concurrent Pos:* Vis prof biochem, Univ Ill, Urbana, 63-64; mem, Comt Agr & Environ, Nat Res Coun, 71-74 & Comt Educ Affairs, Soc Biol Chemists, 74-76; co-ed, Biochem Educ, 74-; mem educ comt, Int Union Biochem, 75- *Mem:* Am Soc Biol Chemists; Am Soc Microbiol; Biochem Soc; Soc Gen Microbiol; Am Chem Soc. *Res:* Enzymatic reactions used by micro-organisms to degrade natural products and man-made compounds, especially those containing the benzene nucleus. *Mailing Add:* Dept of Biochem Col of Biol Sci Univ of Minn St Paul MN 55108

D'AGOSTINO, ANTHONY N, pathology, neuropathology, see previous edition

D'AGOSTINO, RALPH B, b Somerville, Mass, Aug 16, 40; m 65; c 2. MATHEMATICAL STATISTICS, EXPERIMENTAL STATISTICS. *Educ:* Boston Univ, AB, 62, AM, 64; Harvard Univ, PhD(statist), 68. *Prof Exp:* Lectr, 64-68, asst prof, 68-71, assoc prof, 71-77, assoc dean, Grad Sch, 76-78, PROF MATH, BOSTON UNIV, 77- *Concurrent Pos:* Statist consult, United Brands, 68-76, Walden Res Corp, 73-, Lakey Clin Found, 73-, US Food & Drug Admin, 75- & Boston City Hosp, 75-; ed, Emergency Health Serv Quart, 81- *Mem:* Am Soc Qual Control; Inst Math Statist; Am Statist Asn; Sigma Xi. *Res:* Statistics. *Mailing Add:* Dept of Math Boston Univ Boston MA 02215

D'AGROSA, LOUIS SALVATORE, b Brooklyn, NY, Oct 23, 29; m 54; c 5. MEDICAL PHYSIOLOGY. *Educ:* City Col New York, BS, 52; St Louis Univ, PhD(physiol), 62. *Prof Exp:* Pharmacol res asst, Nepera Chem Co, 54-56; sect head, Grove Labs, 56-58; from instr to asst prof prof, 62-71, ASSOC PROF PHYSIOL, ST LOUIS UNIV, 71- *Mem:* AAAS; Am Physiol Soc; Microcirc Soc; Electron Micros Soc Am; Sigma Xi. *Res:* Ultrastructure and electrophysiology of the heart. *Mailing Add:* Dept of Physiol St Louis Univ 1402 S Grand Blvd St Louis MO 63104

D'AGUANNO, WILLIAM, physiology, pharmacology, deceased

DAGUE, RICHARD R(AY), b Little Sioux, Iowa, Feb 20, 31; m 52; c 4. ENVIRONMENTAL ENGINEERING, CIVIL ENGINEERING. *Educ:* Iowa State Univ, BS, 59, MS, 60; Univ Kans, PhD(environ health eng), 67. *Prof Exp:* Surv party chief, Smith Eng Co, Iowa, 53-55; design eng, B H Backlund & Assoc, Nebr, 60-61; instr sanit eng, Iowa State Univ, 61-62; owner engr, Dague Eng Co, Iowa, 62-64; asst prof sanit eng, Kans State Univ, 66-67; from asst prof to assoc prof, Univ Iowa, 67-72; sr environ consult, Henningson, Durham & Richardson, 72-75; PROF ENG & CHMN DEPT, UNIV IOWA, 75- *Mem:* Am Soc Civil Engrs; Water Pollution Control Fedn; Am Water Works Asn; Asn Environ Eng Prof. *Res:* Water quality control, especially chemical and biological water and wastewater treatment. *Mailing Add:* Col of Eng Univ of Iowa Iowa City IA 52242

DAHILL, ROBERT T, JR, b Perth Amboy, NJ, Jan 15, 37; m 63; c 1. ORGANIC CHEMISTRY. *Educ:* Tufts Univ, BS, 59; Worcester Polytech Inst, MS, 61; Stevens Inst Technol, PhD(org chem), 64. *Prof Exp:* group leader, 64-75, asst dir, 75-80, DIR PROD MGT, GIVAUDAN CORP, CLIFTON, 80- *Mem:* Am Chem Soc; Royal Soc Chem; fel Am Inst Chemists; Sigma Xi. *Res:* Synthetic organic chemistry, especially compound of interest to flavor and fragrance industry. *Mailing Add:* 8 Sweetbriar Lane Holmdel NJ 07733

DAHIYA, RAGHUNATH S, b Halalpur, Punjab, India, Oct 4, 31; m 55; c 2. FOOD MICROBIOLOGY. *Educ:* Govt Agr Col, Ludhiana, India, BSc, 51, MSc, 53; State Col, PhD(food sci), 62. *Prof Exp:* Agr inspector, Punjab State Agr Dept, India, 53-56; lectr dairy sci & dairy mgr, Govt Agr Col, Ludhiana, 56-58; res assoc food microbiol, NC State Univ, 62-65, asst prof, 65-71; CHIEF MICROBIOLOGIST, NC DEPT AGR, 71- *Mem:* Am Soc Microbiol; Inst Food Technologists; Asn Food & Drug Officials; Int Asn Milk, Food & Environ Sanitarians. *Res:* Microbiological surveillance of foods, drugs and cosmetics for safety; development of faster and more accurate methods of identification of food borne pathogens. *Mailing Add:* Food & Drug Protection Div NC Dept Agr Raleigh NC 27611

DAHIYA, RAJBIR SINGH, b Rattangarh, India, Dec 3, 40; m 66; c 2. MATHEMATICS. *Educ:* Birla Sci Col, Pilani, India, BSc 60, MSc, 62; Birla Inst CSci & Technol, PhD(math), 67. *Prof Exp:* From asst lectr to lectr math, Birla Inst Technol & Sci, Pilani, India, 62-68; from asst prof to assoc prof, 68-78, PROF MATH, IOWA STATE UNIV, 78- *Mem:* Am Math Soc. *Res:* Integral transforms; special functions and delay differential equations; special functions and use of these various transforms and special funtion for computation techniques in analysis. *Mailing Add:* Dept Math Iowa State Univ Ames IA 50010

DAHL, ADRIAN HILMAN, b Mott, NDak, Dec 6, 19; m 42; c 2. BIOPHYSICS. *Educ:* St Olaf Col, BA, 41; Univ Rochester, PhD(biophys), 53. *Prof Exp:* Jr res physicist, Eastman Kodak Co, NY, 41-43, Tenn Eastman Corp, 43, sr physicist, 43-46; physicist AEC, 46-47; asst chief radiation, Instrument Br, Wash Div Prod, 47, chief, 47-49; chief instrumentation sect, Atomic Energy Proj, Sch Med, Univ Rochester, 50-59; prin scientist, Oak Ridge Inst Nuclear Studies, 59-61; prof phys & radiation biol & dir radiol health training prog, Colo State Univ, 61-69; chief astrogeophys, Space Sci Dept, Martin Marietta Corp, 69-71; CHIEF ENVIRON SCI BR, US ENERGY RES & DEVELOP ADMIN, 71- *Concurrent Pos:* Consult radiation instrumentation, Armed Forces Spec Weapons Proj, 48-52, Fed Civil Defense, 56; Fulbright lectr health physics, Arg, 59-; Int AEC expert radioisotope technol, Indonesia, 61; coordr, Nat Environ Res Center, Idaho Nuclear Eng Lab, 75- *Mem:* Assoc Am Phys Soc; assoc Am Asn Physics Teachers; Inst Elec & Electronics Eng; Health Phys Soc. *Res:* Nuclear radiation effects on photographic emulsions; industrial radiography; photographic dosimetry; circuit design of radiation detection; instruments and components; space physics; planetary geology and atmospheric science; seismology. *Mailing Add:* 348 Kumberly Ln White Rock NM 87544

DAHL, ALTON, b Clifton, Tex, Jan 8, 37; m 59. PHYSICAL CHEMISTRY. *Educ:* Tex Lutheran Col, BA, 59; Univ Mich, MS, 61, PhD(chem), 63. *Prof Exp:* Instr chem, Univ Mich, 63-64; chemist, 64-68, SR RES CHEMIST, EXP STA, E I DU PONT DE NEMOURS & CO, INC, 68- *Mem:* Am Chem Soc; Soc Appl Spectros; Sigma Xi. *Res:* Infrared and Raman spectroscopy; polymerization; polymer development. *Mailing Add:* 2117 Meadow Lane Arden Wilmington DE 19810

DAHL, ANTHONY ORVILLE, b Minneapolis, Minn, Apr 18, 10. BOTANY. *Educ:* Univ Minn, BS, 32, MS, 33, PhD(bot), 38. *Prof Exp:* Asst bot, Univ Minn, 32-38; instr biol, Harvard Univ, 38-41, fac instr, 41-44, tutor, 38-44; from assoc prof to prof bot, Univ Minn, 44-67, chmn dept, 47-57; prof, 67-80, EMER PROF, MORRIS ARBORETUM, UNIV PA, 80-, DIR, 67- *Concurrent Pos:* Res assoc, Karolinska Inst, Sweden, 50-51 & Denmarks Geol Undersgelse, 57-58; res investr, Univ Pa, 64-66. NSF award, 57-64; NIH award, 61-62; NASA award, 63- *Mem:* Int Comt Palynol, 54-56. *Mem:* AAAS; NY Acad Sci; Am Bot Soc; Am Soc Naturalists; Int Soc Cell Biol. *Res:* Cytology; pollen morphology; atmospheric pollen; cytotaxonomy; electron microscopy. *Mailing Add:* Morris Arboretum Univ of Pa 9414 Meadowbrook Ave Chestnut Hill Philadelphia PA 19104

DAHL, ARTHUR LYON, b Palo Alto, Calif, Aug 13, 42; m 75; c 2. MARINE ECOLOGY, PHYCOLOGY. *Educ:* Stanford Univ, AB, 64; Univ Calif, Santa Barbara, PhD(biol), 69. *Prof Exp:* Vis res assoc bot, Smithsonian Inst, 69-70, assoc cur algae, 70-74; REGIONAL ECOL ADV, SOUTH PAC COMN, 74-, COORDR, REGIONAL ENVIRON PROG, 80- . *Concurrent Pos:* Res assoc, Smithsonian Inst, 74- *Mem:* Int Soc Reef Studies; Ecol Soc Am; Int Phycol Soc; Phycol Soc Am; Pac Sci Asn. *Res:* Development and experimental ecology of benthic marine algae; tropical reef ecosystems and algal communities of coral reefs; environmental management of tropical island systems. *Mailing Add:* South Pac Comn BPD-5 Noumea Cedex New Caledonia

DAHL, ARTHUR RICHARD, b Des Moines, Iowa, Nov 25, 30; m 52; c 4. GEOLOGY, CIVIL ENGINEERING. *Educ:* Iowa State Univ, BS, 54, MS, 58; Iowa State Univ, PhD(geol, eng), 61. *Prof Exp:* Assoc civil eng, Iowa State Univ, 57-61; geologist, Humble Oil & Refining Co, 61-64; geol engr, Esso Prod Res Co, 64-66; sr geologist, 66-67, supv geologist, 67-70, DIST GEOLOGIST, EXXON CO, USA, 70-, MGR METALS EXPLOR, 80- *Concurrent Pos:* Off Naval Res grant, 58-60. *Mem:* Geol Soc Am; Am Asn Petrol Geologists; Am Inst Mining, Metall & Petrol Engrs; Am Geol Inst. *Res:* Geology and engineering of unconsolidated earth materials; exploration and exploitation of base metals and nuclear fuel. *Mailing Add:* Exxon Minerals Co

DAHL, BILLIE EUGENE, b Cement, Okla, Oct 24, 29; m 53; c 3. RANGE MANAGEMENT, ANIMAL HUSBANDRY. *Educ:* Okla State Univ, BS, 51; Utah State Univ, MS, 53; Idaho Univ, PhD(range mgt, soils), 66. *Prof Exp:* Range conservationist, Bur Land Mgt, Wyo, 53, range mgr, 54-56; asst range conservationist, Agr Exp Sta, Colo State Univ, 56-66, assoc range conservationist, Eastern Colo Range Sta, 66-67, assoc prof range mgt 67; assoc prof, 67-73, PROF RANGE MGT, TEX TECH UNIV, 73- *Concurrent Pos:* Res asst, Range & Forestry Exp Sta, Univ Idaho, 62-64. *Mem:* Soc Range Mgt. *Res:* Grazing management; systems of grazing; legume adaptation studies; range nutrition, improvement, ecology and economics; sand dune stabilization and management. *Mailing Add:* Dept of Range & Wildlife Mgt Tex Tech Univ Lubbock TX 79409

DAHL, ELMER VERNON, b Colby, Kans, Apr 17, 21; m 44; c 5. PATHOLOGY, EPIDEMIOLOGY. *Educ:* Univ Southern Calif, BS, 43, MD, 52; Univ Minn, MS, 58. *Prof Exp:* Intern, Walter Reed Army Hosp, US Air Force, 52-53; chief path br, US Air Force Sch Aerospace Med, 59-61, comdr epidemiol lab, Lackland AFB, 61-68, comdr epidemiol flight, Manila, Philippines, 68-69; res assoc prof, Univ Tex Med Br, 69-75, prof path, 75-76; PROF PATH, SCH MED, TEX TECH UNIV, 76- *Concurrent Pos:* Fel path, Sch Med, Duke Univ, 53-54, Mayo Found fel, 54-59; consult, US Air Force Sch Aerospace Med, 61-69, surgeon gen, 61-65, Aeromed Res Lab, Holloman AFB, 64-69. *Mem:* Fel Am Col Path; Int Acad Path. *Res:* Infectious diseases; experimental pathology. *Mailing Add:* 5760 Kingsfield Ave El Paso TX 79912

DAHL, HARRY MARTIN, b Yonkers, NY, June 23, 26; m 54; c 3. PETROLEUM GEOLOGY, EXPLORATION GEOLOGY. *Educ:* Hunter Col, AB, 50; Columbia Univ, AM, 51, PhD(geol), 54. *Prof Exp:* Geologist, US AEC, Colo, 54-55, area geologist, 55-56, res geologist, 56-57; res geologist, 57-73, proj leader, 69-72, sr res geologist, 73-77, RES ASSOC, TEXACO INC, 77- *Concurrent Pos:* Chmn, Coord Comt, Am Petrol Inst Res Proj, 55 & 64-66. *Mem:* Mineral Soc Am; Geol Soc Am; Sigma Xi; Am Asn Petrol Geologists. *Res:* Petroleum exploration and recovery techniques in the fields of other energy resources. *Mailing Add:* Texaco Inc PO Box 425 Bellaire TX 77401

DAHL, HARVEY A, b Waldheim, Sask, Feb 19, 26; US citizen. PHYSICS. *Educ:* Stanford Univ, BS, 51, PhD(physics), 63. *Prof Exp:* From res asst to res assoc, High Energy Physics Lab, Stanford Univ, 56-64; ASST PROF PHYSICS, NAVAL POSTGRAD SCH, 64- *Mem:* Am Phys Soc; Am Asn Physics Teachers. *Res:* High energy nuclear physics, especially electromagnetically induced disintegrations of nuclei; electron scattering at high energies. *Mailing Add:* Naval Postgrad Sch Dept Physics 660 Fernwood St Monterey CA 93940

DAHL, KLAUS JOACHIM, b Berlin, Ger, July 27, 36; Can citizen; m 63; c 2. ORGANIC CHEMISTRY, POLYMER CHEMISTRY. *Educ:* State Sch Eng, Berlin, Ing(HTL), 59; McGill Univ, BSc, 63, PhD(org chem), 66. *Prof Exp:* Fel org chem, Univ Munich, 66-67; DIR CHEM RES POLYMERS, RAYCHEM CORP, 67- *Mem:* Am Chem Soc; Ger Chem Soc. *Res:* Synthesis of high temperature resistant polymers; radiation chemistry of polymers; antioxidant and adhesives synthesis. *Mailing Add:* Raychem Corp 300 Constitution Dr Menlo Park CA 94025

DAHL, LAWRENCE FREDERICK, b Chicago, Ill, June 2, 29; m 56; c 3. PHYSICAL INORGANIC CHEMISTRY. *Educ:* Univ Louisville, BS, 51; Iowa State Col, PhD(phys chem), 56. *Prof Exp:* AEC fel, Ames Lab, Iowa State Col, 57; from instr to prof, 57-78, R E RUNDLE, PROF CHEM, UNIV WIS-MADISON, 78- *Concurrent Pos:* Alfred P Sloan fel, 63-65; Guggenheim fel, 70-71. *Honors & Awards:* Award in Inorganic Chem, Am Chem Soc-Tex Instruments, 74; NY Acad Sci fel, 75. *Mem:* AAAS; Am Crystallog Asn; Am Chem Soc; Am Phys Soc; Royal Soc Chem. *Res:* Synthesis, structure and bonding of inorganic compounds, and organometallic complexes, especially metal clusters; preparation and stereochemical characterization of new, unusual transition metal cluster systems as models for metal catalysis and chemisorption on transition metal surfaces; experimental and theoretical studies of influence of valence electrons upon molecular geometries of metal clusters. *Mailing Add:* Dept of Chem Univ of Wis Madison WI 53706

DAHL, NANCY ANN, b Colby, Kans, July 18, 32; m 52; c 2. NEUROBIOLOGY. *Educ:* Univ Kans, AB, 56, PhD(physiol), 62. *Prof Exp:* Asst instr physiol, Univ Kans, 62-63; res assoc neuropsychiat unit, Med Res Coun Labs, Carshalton, Eng, 63-64; asst prof human develop, 64-66, asst prof, 66-70, ASSOC PROF PHYSIOL, UNIV KANS, 70- *Mem:* Am Physiol Soc; Am Soc Cell Biol; Soc Neurosci; Am Soc Neurochem; Brit Biochem Soc. *Res:* Neurobiology; energy flow in the nervous system; mechanisms of ischemic nerve damage; perception of mirror images. *Mailing Add:* Dept of Physiol & Cell Biol Univ of Kans Lawrence KS 66045

DAHL, NORMAN C(HRISTIAN), b Seattle, Wash, May 21, 18; m 43; c 2. MECHANICAL ENGINEERING, APPLIED MECHANICS. *Educ:* Univ Wash, BS, 41; Mass Inst Technol, ScD(mech eng), 52. *Hon Degrees:* ScD, Indian Inst Technol, Kanpur, 68. *Prof Exp:* Field serv consult, Off Sci Res & Develop, 44-45; from asst prof to prof mech eng, Mass Inst Technol, 48-68; dep rep India, Ford Found, 68-71; prog adv, 71-73; consult to pres & provost, Mass Inst Technol, 74-77; spec asst to pres, Am Acad Arts & Sci, 77-79; CONSULT, 79- *Concurrent Pos:* Fulbright lectr, Cambridge Univ, 50-51; prog leader, Kanpur Indo-Am Prog, Indian Inst Technol, 62-64. *Mem:* Am Soc Mech Engrs. *Res:* Stress analysis; educational development; technological development. *Mailing Add:* 40 Fern St Lexington MA 02173

DAHL, ORIN I, b Chicago, Ill, July 21, 35. EXPERIMENTAL HIGH ENERGY PHYSICS. *Educ:* Univ Ill, Urbana, BS, 57; Univ Calif, Berkeley, PhD(physics), 62. *Prof Exp:* PHYSICIST, LAWRENCE BERKELEY LAB, UNIV CALIF, 62- *Mem:* Am Phys Soc. *Res:* Study of strong and weak interactions of elementary particles using high speed digital computer techniques. *Mailing Add:* Lawrence Berkeley Lab Univ of Calif Berkeley CA 94720

DAHL, PER FRIDTJOF, b Washington, DC, Aug 1, 32; m 66; c 2. NUCLEAR PHYSICS. *Educ:* Univ Wis, BS, 56, MS, 57, PhD(nuclear physics), 60. *Prof Exp:* Res assoc nuclear physics, Univ Wis, 60; Ford Found res grant, Inst Theoret Physics, Univ Copenhagen, 60-62; proj scientist, Air Force Weapons Lab, 62-63; asst physicist, 63-65, assoc physicst, 65-71, PHYSICIST, BROOKHAVEN NAT LAB, 71- *Mem:* AAAS; Am Phys Soc. *Res:* Applied superconductivity; high energy accelerator design; history of physics. *Mailing Add:* Accelerator Dept Brookhaven Nat Lab Upton NY 11973

DAHL, PETER STEFFEN, b Port-of-Spain, Trinidad, Nov 17, 48; US citizen; m 73. METAMORPHIC PETROLOGY, GEOCHEMISTRY. *Educ:* Ind Univ, BA, 69, MA & PhD(geol), 77. *Prof Exp:* Anal chemist, O A Labs, Inc, 70-71; electronics technician, US Navy, 71-73; electroplating engr, Delco Electronics, 73-74; asst prof, 77-82, ASSOC PROF GEOCHEM, KENT STATE UNIV, 82- *Concurrent Pos:* Grants, Cottrell Res Corp & Kent State Univ Res Coun, 78-79; NSF grant, 80-82. *Mem:* Mineral Soc Am; Mineral Asn Can; Am Geophys Union; Sigma Xi. *Res:* Mineral-pair geothermometry of metamorphic rocks; oxygen isotope geochemistry of metamorphic iron-formations; Precambrian geology of the western United States; petrology of arbicular granites from South Victoria Land, Antarctica. *Mailing Add:* Dept of Geol Kent State Univ Kent OH 44242

DAHL, ROY DENNIS, b New Britain, Conn, July 5, 39; div; c 2. NEUROBIOLOGY, BIOPHYSICS. *Educ:* Cent Conn State Col, BS, 64; Univ Del, PhD(physiol psychol), 73. *Prof Exp:* Instr biol, Temple Univ, 73-74; res scientist neurobiol, Inst Neurobiol, Nuclear Res Ctr, Julich, WGer, 74-76; asst prof physiol, Sch Med, State Univ NY Buffalo, 76-78; asst prof biol, C W Post Ctr, Greenvale, NY, 78-81; RES ASSOC, ROCKEFELLER UNIV, NY, 81- *Honors & Awards:* Award, Am Philos Soc, 73; Award, Nat Acad Sci, 74; Individual NRSA Award, Nat Eye Inst, 76-78. *Mem:* Soc Neurosci; Asn Res in Vision & Opthal. *Res:* Photoreceptor physiology, especially photopigment kinetics and mechanisms of adaptation. *Mailing Add:* Dept Neurophysiol Rockefeller Univ New York NY 10021

DAHLBERG, ALBERT A, b Chicago, Ill, Nov 20, 08; m 34; c 3. DENTAL ANTHROPOLOGY. *Educ:* Loyola Univ, Ill, BS & DDS, 32. *Prof Exp:* Resident & instr dent surg, Univ Chicago, 32-36; attend dent surgeon, Chicago Mem Hosp, 37-53; assoc prof anthrop, 49-67, actg dir clin, 67-69, res assoc phys anthrop, 49-80, prof & res assoc, Dept Anthrop, 67-80, EMER ASSOC RES PROF DENT & EMER ASSOC RES PROF ANTHROP & EMER PROF COMT EVOLUTIONARY BIOL, UNIV CHICAGO, 80- *Concurrent Pos:* Res assoc, Chicago Natural Hist Mus. *Mem:* Fel AAAS; Am Dent Asn; Am Asn Phys Anthrop; Am Anthrop Asn; fel Am Col Dent. *Res:* Genetics and morphology of the human dentition. *Mailing Add:* Walter G Zoller Mem Dent Clin Univ of Chicago Chicago IL 60637

DAHLBERG, ALBERT EDWARD, b Chicago, Ill, Sept 19, 38; m 63; c 3. BIOCHEMISTRY. *Educ:* Haverford Col, BS, 60; Univ Chicago, MD, 65, PhD, 68. *Prof Exp:* Staff assoc biochem, Nat Cancer Inst, 67-70; from asst prof to assoc prof, 72-82, PROF, DIV BIOL & MED, BROWN UNIV, 82- *Concurrent Pos:* Am Cancer Soc fel, Dept Molecular Biol, Aarhus Univ, 70-72. *Mem:* Am Soc Biol Chemists. *Res:* Ribosome structure and function. *Mailing Add:* Div Biol & Med Brown Univ Providence RI 02912

DAHLBERG, DUANE ARLEN, b Parshall, NDak, July 15, 31; m 57; c 3. PHYSICS, ENVIRONMENTAL SCIENCES. *Educ:* Mich Technol Univ, BS, 53, MS, 54; Luther Theol Sem, BD, 60; Mont State Univ, PhD(physics), 67. *Prof Exp:* Res asst neutron physics, Argonne Nat Lab, 53-54; instr, 60-64, asst prof, 67-68, ASSOC PROF PHYSICS, CONCORDIA COL, MOORHEAD, MINN, 68-, ACTG DIR, TRI COL ENVIRON STUDIES CTR, 78- *Mem:* Am Asn Physics Teachers; Optical Soc Am; Inst Environ Sci. *Res:* Neutron cross sections; optical excitation cross sections. *Mailing Add:* Dept of Physics Concordia Col Moorhead MN 56560

DAHLBERG, EARL DAN, b Fort Worth, Tex, Aug 17, 48. PHYSICS. *Educ:* Univ Tex, Arlington, BS, 70, MA, 72; Univ Calif, Los Angeles, MS, 74, PhD(physics), 78. *Prof Exp:* Res assoc, 78-80, ASST PROF PHYSICS, UNIV MINN, 80- *Concurrent Pos:* Res fel, Alfred P Sloan Found, 81. *Mem:* Am Phys Soc; AAAS. *Res:* Effects of disorder on the transport properties of materials and the study of disordered and/or dilute magnetic systems. *Mailing Add:* Sch Physics & Astron Univ Minn 116 Church St SE Minneapolis MN 55455

DAHLBERG, JAMES ERIC, b Chicago, Ill, May 30, 40; m 63. BIOCHEMISTRY, MOLECULAR BIOLOGY. *Educ:* Haverford Col, BA, 62; Univ Chicago, PhD(biochem), 66. *Prof Exp:* Res assoc, Med Res Coun Lab Molecular Biol, Cambridge, Eng, 66-68; res assoc, Lab Biophys, Univ Geneva, 68-69; from asst prof to assoc prof, 69-74, PROF PHYSIOL CHEM, MED SCH, UNIV WIS-MADISON, 74- *Concurrent Pos:* US Air Force Off Sci Res fel, 66-67; Am Cancer Soc fel, 67-69. *Honors & Awards:* Eli Lilly Award Biol Chem, Am Chem Soc, 74. *Mem:* AAAS; Am Micros Soc; Am Soc Biol Chemists. *Res:* Structure and function of ribosomal and messenger RNA; RNA tumor virus structure and function; sequence of genetic punctuation; DNA synthesis initiation. *Mailing Add:* Dept of Physiol Chem 671 Med Sci Bldg Univ Wis Madison WI 53706

DAHLBERG, MICHAEL D, b Syracuse, NY, May 11, 40. ZOOLOGY. *Educ:* Cornell Univ, BS, 62; Tulane Univ, PhD(zool), 66. *Prof Exp:* Asst prof zool, Univ Ga, 66-74; MEM STAFF, C W RICE DIV, NUS CORP, 74- *Mem:* Am Soc Ichthyologists & Herpetologists; Am Fisheries Soc; Am Ichthyology; systematics and ecology of fish. *Mailing Add:* C W Rice Div NUS Corp Manor Oak II 1910 Cochran Rd Pittsburgh PA 15220

DAHLBERG, MICHAEL LEE, b Miami, Fla, Jan 19, 39; m 58; c 2. FISHERIES, BIOMETRICS. *Educ:* Ore State Univ, BS, 62, MS, 63; Univ Wash, PhD(fisheries), 68. *Prof Exp:* Res assoc fisheries, Fisheries Res Inst, Univ Wash, 63-68; asst prof, Va Polytech Inst, 68-70; supvry fisheries res biologist, 70-77, SUPVRY MATH STATISTICIAN, NAT MARINE FISHERIES SERV, 77- *Concurrent Pos:* Consult, US Bur Sport Fisheries & Wildlife, 68-69 & Sport Fishing Inst, Washington, DC, 68-70; adv, Int N Pac Fisheries Comn, N Pac Fishery Mgt Coun & US Dept State. *Mem:* AAAS; Am Inst Fishery Res Biol; Am Fisheries Soc; Am Statist Asn. *Res:* Population dynamics of freshwater and marine fish, including the application of digital computers to solving fishery research problems through data processing and systems simulation; limnology. *Mailing Add:* Auke Bay Fisheries Lab Nat Marine Fisheries Serv Auke Bay AK 99821

DAHLBERG, RICHARD CRAIG, b Astoria, Ore, July 23, 29; m 56; c 3. ENGINEERING MANAGEMENT, NUCLEAR ENGINEERING. *Educ:* Univ Ore, BS, 51; Univ Mich, MS, 54; Rensselaer Polytech Inst, PhD, 64. *Prof Exp:* Prod supvr, Hanford Works, Gen Elec Co, 51-53, mgr reactor physics, Knolls Atomic Power Lab, 54-64, reactor physicist, Gen Atomic Div, Gen Dynamics Co, 64-67, mgr HT&R reactor physics, 67-69; mgr nuclear anal & reactor physics dept, Gulf Energy & Environ Systs, Gulf Oil Corp, 72-; dir, Fuel Eng Div, 75-80, DIR, GEN ENG DIV, GEN ATOMIC CO, 80- *Mem:* Fel Am Nuclear Soc; Sigma Xi; AAAS. *Res:* Reactor physics; nuclear engineering; reactor design. *Mailing Add:* 7733 Esterel Dr La Jolla CA 92037

DAHLBERG, SUSAN CLARDY, b Washington, DC, Dec 8, 47. SURFACE CHEMISTRY. *Educ:* Brown Univ, BS, 69; Cornell Univ, MS, 71, PhD(chem), 74. *Prof Exp:* MEM TECH STAFF, BELL LABS, 74- *Mem:* Am Vacuum Soc; Am Chem Soc. *Res:* Surface chemistry of semiconductors, monitored by such techniques as photovoltage spectroscopy and modulated plasma etching. *Mailing Add:* Rm 1A-334 Bell Labs 600 Mountain Ave Murray Hill NJ 07974

DAHLE, LELAND KENNETH, b Marietta, Minn, June 19, 26; m 58; c 2. CEREAL CHEMISTRY. *Educ:* St Olaf, BA, 50; Purdue Univ, MS, 53; Univ Minn, PhD(physiol chem), 61. *Prof Exp:* Instr chem, Ausburg Col, 52-56; res cereal chemist, Flour Mills, Peavey Co, 61-69; sr res scientist, 69-72, DIV HEAD CEREAL SCI, CAMPBELL SOUP CO, 72- *Mem:* Am Chem Soc; Am Asn Cereal Chemists; Inst Food Technologists. *Res:* Lipid oxidation;

autoxidation phenomena; thiobarbituric acid reaction assay; oxidative stability of pigments; functional effects of flour protein sulfhydryl groups on dough rheology and behavior; functional properties of protein and starch in bread systems; interactions of protein and starch. *Mailing Add:* Campbell Soup Co Campbell Place Camden NJ 08101

DAHLEN, FRANCIS ANTHONY, JR, b American Falls, Idaho, Dec 5, 42; m 67. GEOPHYSICS. *Educ:* Calif Inst Technol, BS, 64; Univ Calif, San Diego, MS, 67, PhD(geophys), 69. *Prof Exp:* NSF fel geod & geophys, Cambridge Univ, 70-71; Alfred P Sloan Found fel, 71-73, asst prof, 71-75, assoc prof, 75-80, PROF GEOPHYS, PRINCETON UNIV, 80- *Mem:* Am Geophys Union; Seismol Soc Am. *Res:* Theoretical seismology; free oscillations of the earth; rotation of the earth; lateral heterogeneity of the earth; seismic source mechanism. *Mailing Add:* Dept of Geol & Geophys Sci Princeton Univ Princeton NJ 08540

DAHLEN, R(OLF) J(OHN), b Wilmington, Del, Mar 18, 37; m 65; c 1. MECHANICAL ENGINEERING. *Educ:* Univ Del, BME, 58; Purdue Univ, MSME, 59, PhD(mech eng), 62. *Prof Exp:* Res engr, 62-67, tech rep, 67-73, consult, 73-75, sr prod specialist, 75-77, tech consult, 77-81, SR TECH SPECIALIST POLYMER PROD, E I DU PONT DE NEMOURS & CO, 81- *Res:* Heat and mass transfer; process development for plastics and plastic products. *Mailing Add:* Tech Serv Lab Chestnut Run Wilmington DE 19898

DAHLEN, ROGER W, b Iola, Wis, Sept 7, 35; m 62; c 3. MEDICAL PHYSIOLOGY, SCIENCE ADMINISTRATION. *Educ:* Luther Col, Iowa, BA, 56; Univ Iowa, MS, 58, PhD(physiol), 60. *Prof Exp:* Instr physiol, Sch Med, Boston Univ, 60-62; asst prof, NJ Col Med & Dent, 62-68; health scientist adminr, Training Grants & Awards Br, Nat Heart Inst, 68-71, CHIEF, DIV BIOMED INFO SUPPORT, NAT LIBR MED, NAT INSTS HEALTH, 71- *Concurrent Pos:* Mem bd trustees, Upsala Col, 64-68. *Res:* Cardiac electrophysiology; effects of hypothermia. *Mailing Add:* 306 Carr Ave Nat Insts of Health Rockville MD 20850

DAHLER, JOHN S, b Wichita, Kans, May 7, 30; m 54. PHYSICAL CHEMISTRY. *Educ:* Univ Wichita, BS, 51, MS, 52; Univ Wis, PhD(theoret chem), 55. *Prof Exp:* NSF fel, Univ Amsterdam, 55-56; task scientist, Aeronaut Res Lab, Wright Air Develop Ctr, 56-58; from asst prof to assoc prof chem eng, 59-63, PROF CHEM ENG & CHEM, UNIV MINN, MINNEAPOLIS, 63- *Concurrent Pos:* Sloan fel, 64-; NSF sr fel, 65-66; vis prof, Chem Lab III, H C Orsted Inst, Univ Copenhagen, 73. *Mem:* Am Phys Soc; Soc Natural Philos; Am Fedn Scientists. *Res:* Theoretical physical chemistry; equilibrium statistical mechanics; theory of fluid transport phenomena; electronic and atomic collision processes. *Mailing Add:* Depts of Chem Eng & Chem Univ of Minn Minneapolis MN 55455

DAHLGARD, MURIEL GENEVIEVE, b West Haven, Conn, July 5, 20. ORGANIC CHEMISTRY. *Educ:* Univ Conn, BS, 46, MS, 49; Univ Kans, PhD(org chem), 56. *Prof Exp:* Asst, Univ Conn, 46-48; asst res chemist, Nopco Chem Co, NJ, 48-53; asst, Univ Kans, 53-56; asst res prof cancer res lab, Univ Fla, 56-61; asst prof, 61-64, ASSOC PROF CHEM, RANDOLPH-MACON WOMAN'S COL, 64-, CHMN DEPT, 75- *Mem:* AAAS; Am Chem Soc. *Res:* Aliphatic diamines; diaryl ethrers; carbohydrates; carcinogenic derivatives of fluorene and biphenyl; antimetabolites. *Mailing Add:* Dept of Chem Randolph-Macon Woman's Col Lynchburg VA 24503

DAHLGREN, GEORGE, b Chicago, Ill, Apr 12, 29; m 51; c 3. PHYSICAL CHEMISTRY. *Educ:* Ill Wesleyan Univ, BS, 51; Univ Wyo, MS, 56, PhD(chem), 58. *Prof Exp:* Res assoc chem, Cornell Univ, 58-59; from asst prof to assoc prof, Univ Alaska, 59-66, head dept, 64-66; prof, Univ Cincinnati, 66-75, asst head dept, 66-71, head dept, 71-75; dean, Col Arts & Sci, Univ Mo-Kansas City, 75-78; VPRES, FRANKLIN INST, 78- *Mem:* Am Chem Soc; fel AAAS. *Res:* Kinetics and thermodynamics. *Mailing Add:* Franklin Inst Philadelphia PA 19103

DAHLGREN, RICHARD MARC, b Riverside, Calif, Sept 20, 52. INORGANIC & PHYSICAL CHEMISTRY. *Educ:* Univ Calif, Riverside, BS, 73; Univ Calif, Los Angeles, PhD(chem), 78. *Prof Exp:* STAFF RES CHEMIST, MIAMI VALLEY LABS, PROCTER & GAMBLE CO, 78- *Mem:* Am Chem Soc. *Res:* Physical chemistry of the excited state, particular emphasis in the areas of photocatalysis and energy-conversion processes. *Mailing Add:* 34 Applewood Dr Fairfield OH 45014

DAHLGREN, ROBERT BERNARD, b Walnut Grove, Minn, Jan 27, 29; m 51; c 6. WILDLIFE RESEARCH. *Educ:* SDak State Univ, BS, 50, PhD, 72; Utah State Univ, MS, 55. *Prof Exp:* Small game biologist, SDak Dept of Game, Fish & Parks, 52-61, leader small game & furbearer res proj, 61-65, asst chief, Game Div, 65-67; asst leader, SDak Coop Wildlife Res Unit, 67-73, LEADER, IOWA COOP WILDLIFE RES UNIT, FISH & WILDLIFE SERV, US DEPT INTERIOR, 73- *Mem:* Wildlife Soc. *Res:* Population ecology and dynamics of wildlife populations; pesticide effects on game birds. *Mailing Add:* Iowa Coop Wildlife Res Unit Iowa State Univ Ames IA 50011

DAHLGREN, ROBERT R, b Lincoln, Nebr, May 17, 35; m 57; c 2. VETERINARY PATHOLOGY. *Educ:* Okla State Univ, DVM, 63, MS, 66. *Prof Exp:* Instr path, Okla State Univ, 63-66; pathologist, Ralston Purina Co, 66-68; assoc prof path, Univ Nebr, 68-69; PATHOLOGIST, RALSTON PURINA CO, 69- *Concurrent Pos:* Consult comp path, Sch Med, Washington Univ, 67- *Mem:* NY Acad Sci; Am Vet Med Asn. *Res:* Comparative neuropathology and immunology. *Mailing Add:* 9200 Cherry Brook Lane St Louis MO 63126

DAHLIN, DAVID CARL, b Beresford, SDak, Sept 3, 17; m 41; c 3. PATHOLOGY. *Educ:* Univ SDak, BS, 38; Univ Chicago, MD, 40; Univ Minn, MS, 48. *Prof Exp:* Intern & resident path, Ancker Hosp, St Paul, 41 & 42; asst prof, 53-61, PROF PATH, MAYO MED SCH, UNIV MINN, 61-; CHMN DEPT SURG PATH, 70-; CONSULT SURG PATH, MAYO CLIN, 48- *Mem:* Am Soc Clin Path; Am Asn Pathologists & Bacteriologists; AMA; Am Cancer Soc. *Res:* Bone tumors. *Mailing Add:* Dept of Path Mayo Med Sch Univ of Minn Rochester MN 55902

DAHLKE, WALTER EMIL, b Berlin, Ger, Aug 24, 10; m 40. PHYSICS, ELECTRICAL ENGINEERING. *Educ:* Univ Berlin, Dr phil(physics), 36; Univ Jena, Dr habil(physics), 39. *Prof Exp:* Head microwave lab, Ger Aviation Res Estab, 40-45; head appl res group & adv develop, tube & semiconductor div & inst res, Telefunken AG, Ger, 49-65; NSF vis prof, 64-65, PROF ELEC ENG, LEHIGH UNIV, 65- *Concurrent Pos:* Lectr, Univ Heidelberg, 55-56 & Stuttgart Tech, 56-59; lectr, Karlsruhe Tech, 60-65, hon prof, 61. *Mem:* Fel Inst Elec & Electronics Engrs; Ger Phys Soc; Ger Telecommun Asn. *Res:* Electronic devices; electrical noise. *Mailing Add:* Dept of Elec Eng Lehigh Univ Bethlehem PA 18015

DAHLMAN, DOUGLAS LEE, b Bertha, Minn, Sept 29, 40; m 60; c 3. INSECT PHYSIOLOGY. *Educ:* St Cloud State Col, BS, 61; Iowa State Univ, MS, 63, PhD(entom), 65. *Prof Exp:* Res assoc entom, Iowa State Univ, 65; asst prof, 65-71, ASSOC PROF ENTOM, UNIV KY, 71-, ASSOC PROF TOXICOL, GRAD CTR, 79- *Mem:* AAAS; Entom Soc Am. *Res:* Insect parasite-host interactions; physiological and biochemical interactions between insects and naturally occurring substances; insect growth, development and aging. *Mailing Add:* Dept Entom Univ Ky Lexington KY 40506

DAHLQUIST, FREDERICK WILLIS, b Chicago, Ill, June 15, 43; m 63; c 2. BIOPHYSICAL CHEMISTRY. *Educ:* Wabash Col, BA, 64; Calif Inst Technol, PhD(chem), 69. *Prof Exp:* Miller fel biochem, Univ Calif, Berkeley, 69-71; from asst prof to assoc prof, 71-81, PROF CHEM, UNIV ORE, 81- *Concurrent Pos:* Alfred P Sloan Found fel, 75-77. *Honors & Awards:* Fac Res Award, American Cancer Soc, 81. *Res:* Nuclear magnetic resonance studies of biological systems; enzyme mechanisms; mechanism of chemotaxis in bacteria. *Mailing Add:* Dept of Chem Univ of Ore Eugene OR 97403

DAHLQUIST, WILBUR LYNN, b DeQuincy, La, Sept 2, 42; m 61; c 2. SOLID STATE PHYSICS. *Educ:* McNeese State Col, BS, 63; La State Univ, PhD(physics), 67. *Prof Exp:* From asst prof to assoc prof, 67-75, PROF PHYSICS & HEAD DEPT, MCNEESE STATE UNIV, 75- *Mem:* Am Phys Soc. *Res:* Transport properties of electrons in metals at low temperatures utilizing resonance techniques. *Mailing Add:* Dept of Physics McNeese State Univ Lake Charles LA 70609

DAHLSTEN, DONALD L, b Clay Center, Nebr, Dec 8, 33; m 57; c 4. FOREST ENTOMOLOGY. *Educ:* Univ Calif, Davis, BS, 56; Univ Calif, Berkeley, MS, 60, PhD(entom), 63. *Prof Exp:* Lab technician forest entom, Univ Calif, Berkeley, 59-62; asst prof zool, Calif State Col, Los Angeles, 62-63; asst entomologist, 63-65, lectr, 65-68, from asst prof to assoc prof, 68-74, PROF ENTOM, UNIV CALIF, BERKELEY, 74- *Mem:* AAAS; Am Inst Biol Sci; Ecol Soc Am; Soc Am Foresters; Entom Soc Am. *Res:* Biological control; population dynamics of forest insects, especially parasites and predators of bark beetles; neodiprion sawflies and the Douglas fir tussock moth; evaluation of insectivorous birds in the forest and their role in natural control of forest pests. *Mailing Add:* Div Biol Control Univ Calif Berkeley CA 94720

DAHLSTROM, BERTIL PHILIP, JR, b Elizabeth, NJ, Aug 22, 31; m 52; c 3. PHYSICAL CHEMISTRY. *Educ:* Upsala Col, BS, 53; Univ Wis, MS, 55; Temple Univ, MBA, 58. *Prof Exp:* Teach asst chem, Univ Wis, 53-55; res chemist, Rohm & Haas, 55-57, teach asst spec prod, 57-60, staff asst, Prod Control Dept, 60-61, asst mgr spec prod dept, 61-63, mgr, 63-68; gen mgr indust div, vpres & mem, Bd Dirs, Sartomer Resins, Inc, 68-70; owner, Dahlstrom Assocs, Inc, 68-70; develop mgr, Ionac Chem Co, 73-81; PRES, TREAS & DIR, CHEM INSTRUMENTS CORP, 71-; MGR, MGT INFO SYSTS, SYBRON CORP, 81- *Concurrent Pos:* Instr, Temple Univ, 59-61. *Mem:* Am Chem Soc. *Res:* High pressure reactions; stereospecific polymerization; physical properties of high polymers; sales management. *Mailing Add:* Chem Instruments Corp PO Box 399 Woodbury NJ 08096

DAHLSTROM, DONALD A(LBERT), b Minneapolis, Minn Jan 16, 20; m 42; c 5. CHEMICAL ENGINEERING. *Educ:* Univ Minn, BS, 42; Northwestern Univ, PhD(chem eng), 49. *Prof Exp:* Petrol & chem engr, Int Petrol Co, Peru, 42-45; from instr to assoc prof chem eng, Northwestern Univ, 46-56; dir res & develop, Eimco Corp, 53-60, vpres & dir, 60-69, vpres & dir, Eimco Envirotech, 69-74; VPRES RES & DEVELOP, PROCESS MACH GROUP, ENVIROTECH CORP, 71-, DIR, 74- *Concurrent Pos:* Adj prof, Univ Utah, 72- & Utah State Univ, 77- *Honors & Awards:* Raymond Award, 52 & Richards Award, 76, Am Inst Mining, Metall & Petrol Engrs; Founders Award, 72 & Environ Award, 77, Am Inst Chem Engrs. *Mem:* Nat Acad Eng; Water Pollution Control Fedn; Am Chem Soc; Am Inst Mining, Metall & Petrol Engrs (vpres, 76); Am Inst Chem Engrs. *Res:* Liquid cyclones; filtration; classification; flow of fluids; sedimentation; colloids; centrifugal forces in hydraulic fields; water; waste; sewage treatment; industrial processing; industrial and municipal waste treatment; liquid-solids separation; hydraulics; fine particle technology. *Mailing Add:* Envirotech Corp PO Box 300 Salt Lake City UT 84110

DAHLSTROM, ROBERT V, biochemistry, see previous edition

DAHM, ARNOLD J, b Oskaloosa, Iowa, Sept 12, 32; m 68; c 2. PHYSICS. *Educ:* Cent Col Iowa, BA, 58; Univ Minn, Minneapolis, MS, 60, PhD(physics), 65. *Prof Exp:* Fel physics, Univ Pa, 66-68; asst prof, 68-73, assoc prof, 73-80, PROF PHYSICS, CASE WESTERN RESERVE UNIV, 80- *Concurrent Pos:* Fulbright Hays fel, 76-77. *Mem:* Am Phys Soc; Am Asn Univ Professors. *Res:* Liquid and solid helium, superconductors and two dimensional systems. *Mailing Add:* Dept of Physics Case Western Reserve Univ Cleveland OH 44106

DAHM, CORNELIUS GEORGE, b St Louis, Mo, Oct 23, 08; m 35; c 3. SEISMOLOGY. *Educ:* St Louis Univ, AB, 30, MS, 32, PhD(seismol), 34. *Prof Exp:* Instr, St Louis Univ, 34-36; party chief, Root Petrol Co, 36-38; supvr, Magnolia Petrol Co, 38-53; chief geophysicist, Hunt Oil Co, 53-73; CHIEF GEOPHYSICIST, INT FIV, TEX PAC OIL CO, 74- *Mem:* Am Geophys Union; Soc Explor Geophys. *Res:* Seismology and seismic prospecting. *Mailing Add:* 11219 Shelterwood Dallas TX 75229

DAHM, DONALD B, b Fargo, NDak, Aug 15, 38; m 60; c 3. PHYSICAL CHEMISTRY. *Educ:* NDak State Univ, BS, 59; SDak State Univ, MS, 61; Ohio State Univ, PhD(phys chem), 66. *Prof Exp:* Asst phys chem, Ohio State Univ, 61-62; sr res engr, Martin Co, 63; asst phys chem, Ohio State Univ, 64-66; res chemist, Res Ctr, Babcock & Wilcox Co, 66-68; res specialist, Dayton Lab, Monsanto Res Corp, 68-71; mem staff, Sinvalco Litho Prod, 71-72; tech dir, Mazer Corp, 72; TECH MGR, DAP, INC, DIV SCHERING-PLOUGH CORP, 73-; VPRES RES & DEVELOP, ILL BRONZE PAINT CO, 78- *Mem:* Am Chem Soc. *Res:* Chemical kinetics, fast reactions in gas and liquid phases and in shock tube; combustion kinetics; printing inks, chemicals; paints, coatings, caulks, sealants. *Mailing Add:* Ill Bronze Paint Co 300 E Main St Lake Zurich IL 60047

DAHM, DONALD J, b Mahaska Co, Iowa, Oct 26, 41; m 64; c 3. RESIN PRODUCTS. *Educ:* Cent Col, Iowa, BA, 63; Iowa State Univ, PhD(phys chem), 68. *Prof Exp:* Sr res chemist, Cent Res Dept, 68-74, group leader struct chem, 74-76, spec asst to vpres technol, 76-77, mgr, Environ Anal Sci Ctr, 77-81, MGR, RESINS TECHNOL MKT SUPPORT, MONSANTO, CO, 81- *Mem:* Am Chem Soc. *Mailing Add:* Monsanto Co 190 Grochmal Ave Indian Orchard MA 01051

DAHM, DOUGLAS BARRETT, b Buffalo, NY, Apr 12, 28; m 58; c 3. SYSTEMS MANAGEMENT, TECHNICAL MANAGEMENT. *Educ:* Northwestern Univ, BS, 50; State Univ NY Buffalo, MS, 64. *Prof Exp:* Exec training engr, Caterpillar Tractor Co, 47-51; assoc engr, Cornell Aeronaut Lab, Inc, 56-58, res engr, 58-62, prin engr, 62-67, staff scientist, 67-70, dept head, Environ Systs, 70-76, vpres info sci serv group, 77-80, VPRES PLANS & PROGS, ADVAN TECHNOL CTR, CALSPAN CORP, 80- *Mem:* Nat Security Indust Asn; Armed Forces Commun & Electronics Asn. *Res:* Multi-disciplinary programs in environment and military science; remote sensing; aircraft avionics systems, especially methods to improve the survivability of military aircraft; intelligence information systems; instructional systems design. *Mailing Add:* Calspan Corp Info Sci Serv PO Box 400 Buffalo NY 14225

DAHM, KARL HEINZ, b Duisburg, Ger, Jan 20, 35; m 68; c 4. BIOCHEMISTRY. *Educ:* Univ Gottingen, Diplom-Chemiker, 61, Dr rer nat, 64. *Prof Exp:* Sci asst org chem inst, Univ Gottingen, 62-66; proj assoc zool, Univ Wis-Madison, 66-68; assoc prof biol, 68-76, assoc prof chem, 71-76, PROF CHEM & BIOL, TEX A&M UNIV, 76- *Mem:* Am Chem Soc; Soc Ger Chemists. *Res:* Chemistry of natural products; biochemistry of insect development; insect hormones and pheromones. *Mailing Add:* Inst of Develop Biol Tex A&M Univ College Station TX 77843

DAHM, PAUL ADOLPH, b Minneapolis, Minn, Nov 15, 17; m 41; c 4. ENTOMOLOGY, BIOCHEMISTRY. *Educ:* Univ Ill, AB, 40, MA, 41, PhD(entom), 47. *Prof Exp:* From asst prof to prof entom, Kans State Univ, 47-53; prof entom, 53-80, CHARLES F CURTISS DISTINGUISHED PROF AGR, IOWA STATE UNIV, 80-, CHMN DEPT, 75- *Mem:* Entom Soc Am; Sigma Xi. *Res:* Insecticide toxicology and biochemistry; economic entomology. *Mailing Add:* Dept of Entom 407 Sci II Iowa State Univ Ames IA 50011

DAHMEN, JEROME J, b Johnston, Wash, Nov 22, 19; m 47; c 5. GENETICS, REPRODUCTIVE PHYSIOLOGY. *Educ:* Univ Idaho, BS, 47; Ore State Univ, MS, 52, PhD(genetics), 66. *Prof Exp:* County agent, Exten Serv, 47-55; animal husbandman, 55-58, res prof animal sci, Caldwell Br & supt, Agr Exp Sta, 58-74, PROF ANIMAL SCI & ANIMAL SCIENTIST, DEPT ANIMAL SCI, UNIV IDAHO, 74- *Mem:* Am Soc Animal Sci. *Res:* Management; physiology; breeding, sheep, wool and meat. *Mailing Add:* Dept of Animal Sci Univ of Idaho Moscow ID 83843

DAHMS, ARTHUR STEPHEN, JR, b Mankato, Minn, Sept 12, 43; m 66; c 2. BIOCHEMISTRY. *Educ:* Col St Thomas, BS, 65; Mich State Univ, PhD(biochem), 69. *Prof Exp:* NSF & AEC fels chem, Univ Calif, Los Angeles, 69-71, lectr, 71-72; from asst prof to assoc prof, 72-79, PROF CHEM, SAN DIEGO STATE UNIV, 79- *Concurrent Pos:* Alexander von Humboldt Found fel, Univ Munich, 79-80. *Mem:* AAAS; Am Chem Soc; Am Soc Biol Chem; Am Soc Microbiol. *Res:* Bioenergetics; structure and function of biological membranes; membrane transport; oxidative phosphorylation; enzymology of carbohydrate biodegration. *Mailing Add:* Dept Chem San Diego State Univ San Diego CA 92182

DAHMS, THOMAS EDWARD, b Springfield, Mass, May 14, 42; m 64; c 2. PHYSIOLOGY. *Educ:* Col of Wooster, BA, 64; Univ Calif, Santa Barbara, PhD(physiol), 70. *Prof Exp:* Asst res physiologist, Inst Environ Stress, Univ Calif, Santa Barbara, 70-74; ASST RES PROF PHYSIOL, MED SCH, ST LOUIS UNIV, 74- *Mem:* Am Physiol Soc; NY Acad Sci. *Res:* Influence of environmental factors on cardiovascular and respiratory systems. *Mailing Add:* Dept of Physiol St Louis Univ Med Sch St Louis MO 63103

DAHMUS, MICHAEL E, b Waterloo, Iowa, Feb 20, 41; m. BIOCHEMISTRY. *Educ:* Iowa State Univ, BS, 63; Calif Inst Technol, PhD(biochem), 68. *Prof Exp:* Fel, Calif Inst Technol, 68-69; asst prof, 69-76, ASSOC PROF BIOCHEM, UNIV CALIF, DAVIS, 76- *Mem:* Am Soc Biol Chemists. *Res:* Biochemical aspects of gene regulation in higher organisms. *Mailing Add:* Dept of Biochem & Biophys Univ of Calif Davis CA 95616

DAHN, CONARD CURTIS, b Utica, NY, Oct 10, 39; m 62; c 2. ASTRONOMY. *Educ:* Wesleyan Univ, BA, 61; Case Inst Technol, PhD(astron), 67. *Prof Exp:* Astron, Naval Observ, Washington, DC, 67-70, ASTRONR, NAVAL OBSERV, FLAGSTAFF STA, 70- *Mem:* AAAS; Am Astron Soc; Sigma Xi. *Res:* Astrometry; trigonometric parallax measurements of nearby stars; interstellar matter; studies of the light scattering and/or extinction properties of interstellar dust particles. *Mailing Add:* Naval Observ Flagstaff Sta PO Box 1149 Flagstaff AZ 86001

DAHNEKE, BARTON EUGENE, b San Jose, Calif, Apr 4, 39; m 61; c 7. ENVIRONMENTAL SCIENCES, PARTICLE PHYSICS. *Educ:* Brigham Young Univ, BS, 63; Univ Minn, MS, 65, PhD(mech eng), 67. *Prof Exp:* NIH res fel, Calif Inst Technol, 67-69; res scientist, Inst Aerobiol, 69-72; asst prof biophys, 72-78, assoc prof biophys & chem eng, 78-81, SR SCIENTIST, CHEM ENG DEPT, UNIV ROCHESTER, 81-; SR DESIGN ENGR, EASTMAN KODAK CO, ROCHESTER, 81- *Mem:* Am Inst Chem Engrs. *Res:* Measurement of airborne particulates; diffusion theory and practice; kinetic theory of particles. *Mailing Add:* Dept Chem Eng Univ of Rochester Rochester NY 14627

DAI, PETER K, civil engineering, see previous edition

DAIBER, FRANKLIN CARL, b Middletown, NY, Oct 19, 19; m 53; c 2. MARINE BIOLOGY, TIDAL MARSH ECOLOGY. *Educ:* Alfred Univ, AB, 41; Mich State Col, MS, 47; Ohio State Univ, PhD(hydrobiol), 50. *Prof Exp:* Grad asst zool, Mich State Col, 41-42, 46-47; asst prof biol, Alfred Univ, 49-52; from asst prof to assoc prof, 52-68, PROF MARINE STUDIES, UNIV DEL, 69- *Concurrent Pos:* Mem, Biol Comt, Atlantic States Marine Fisheries Comn, 59-71; mem licensing bd panel, Nuclear Regulatory Comn, 72-78. *Mem:* Sigma Xi; Am Soc Ichthyologist & Herpetologists; Ecol Soc Am; Am Fisheries Soc. *Res:* General ecology and utilization of tidal marshes. *Mailing Add:* Col of Marine Studies Univ of Del Newark DE 19711

DAICOFF, GEORGE RONALD, b Granite City, Ill, Nov 10, 30; m 72; c 2. SURGERY. *Educ:* Ind Univ, AB, 53, MD, 56. *Prof Exp:* Extern, Sunnyside Sanitorium, Indianapolis, 54-56; intern, Univ Chicago, 56-57, from jr asst resident to sr asst resident surg, 57-59, instr & sr resident, 61-62, chief resident gen surg & instr, 62, instr thoracic and cardiovasc surg, 63; from asst prof to assoc prof, 63-70, prof thoracic & cardiovasc surg & chief div, Col Med, Univ Fla, 70-77; CHIEF CARDIAC SURG, ALL CHILDREN'S HOSP, ST PETERSBURG, 77- *Concurrent Pos:* Schweppe Found res fel, 63-66; fel cardiovasc surg, Mayo Clin, 66; vis colleague, Royal Postgrad Med Sch, Univ London, 65. *Mem:* Am Col Surg; Am Asn Thoracic Surg; Am Col Cardiol; Int Soc Cardiol; Soc Thoracic Surgeons. *Res:* Cardiovascular surgery. *Mailing Add:* 747 Sixth Ave S St Petersburg FL 33701

DAIGH, JOHN D(AVID), b Parsons, Kans, Jan 14, 30; m 51; c 3. ENGINEERING, MATHEMATICS. *Educ:* US Mil Acad, BS, 51; Univ Ill, MS, 57, PhD(civil eng), 57. *Prof Exp:* From instr to assoc prof mech, US Mil Acad, 61-71; INSTR ENG, EASTFIELD COL, 71-, CHMN DIV MATH & ENG, 73- *Mem:* Am Soc Civil Engrs; Nat Soc Prof Engrs; NY Acad Sci; Am Inst Aeronaut & Astronaut; Math Asn Am. *Res:* Structural dynamics; civil and structural engineering; engineering mechanics; fluid mechanics. *Mailing Add:* Div Math & Eng Eastfield Col 3737 Motley Dr Mesquite TX 75150

DAIGLE, DONALD J, b St Louis, Mo, Mar 1, 39; m 63; c 2. CHEMISTRY. *Educ:* Tulane Univ, BS, 61, PhD, 65; Univ Southern Miss, MS, 63. *Prof Exp:* RES CHEMIST, SOUTHERN REGIONAL RES CTR, US DEPT AGR, 65- *Honors & Awards:* USDA Superior Serv Award, 73. *Mem:* Am Chem Soc; Am Asn Textile Chemists & Colorists; Sigma Xi. *Res:* Phosphites, phosponates and their respective acids; phosphines, diphosphines and their oxides; polymers containing phosphorus for use in textiles. *Mailing Add:* South Regional Res Ctr US Dept of Agr PO Box 19687 New Orleans LA 70119

DAIGLE, JOSEPHINE SIRAGUSA, b Brooklyn, NY, Nov 16, 26; m 65; c 1. PHARMACEUTICS. *Educ:* Columbia Univ Pharm, NY, BS, 47, MS, 49; Univ Fla, Gainesville, PhD(pharm), 55. *Prof Exp:* Asst & assoc prof pharmaceut chem, Howard Col, Birmingham, Ala, 49-52; instr chem & pharm, Univ Fla, Gainesville, 52-54; asst prof pharm, Loyola Univ, New Orleans, 55-64 & Univ Tenn, Memphis, 64-66; assoc prof, 72-77, PROF PHARMACEUT, XAVIER UNIV LA, NEW ORLEANS, 77- *Mem:* Am Pharmaceut Asn; Am Asn Col Pharm. *Res:* Emulsifiers; suspending agents; equipment testing for making polyphasic preparations; pharmaceuticals; stability of these preparations. *Mailing Add:* Col of Pharm Xavier Univ 7325 Palmetto St New Orleans LA 70125

DAIGNEAULT, AUBERT, b Montreal, Que, Mar 6, 32; m 61; c 1. MATHEMATICAL LOGIC. *Educ:* Univ Montreal, BSc, 54, MSc, 56; Princeton Univ, PhD(math), 59. *Prof Exp:* Lectr math, Royal Mil Col, Can, 58-59; asst prof, Univ Ottawa, 59-60 & Univ Montreal, 60-63; vis asst prof, Univ Calif, Berkeley, 63-64; assoc prof, 64-70, PROF MATH, UNIV MONTREAL, 70- *Concurrent Pos:* Nat Res Coun Can fel, 64-65. *Mem:* Am Math Soc; Math Asn Am; Asn Symbolic Logic; Can Math Cong; Math Soc France. *Res:* Algebriac logic. *Mailing Add:* Dept of Math Univ of Montreal PO Box 6128 Montreal PQ H3C 3J7 Can

DAIGNEAULT, ERNEST ALBERT, b Holyoke, Mass, Aug 16, 28; m 54; c 4. PHARMACOLOGY. *Educ:* Mass Col Pharm W, BS, 52; Univ Mo-Kansas City, MS, 54, PhD(pharmacol), 57. *Prof Exp:* Asst instr pharm, Univ Kansas City, 53-54; from instr to asst prof pharmacol, Univ Tenn, 57-60; from asst prof to assoc prof, 62-69, prof pharmacol, La State Univ Med Ctr, 69-77; PROF & CHMN DEPT PHARMACOL, E TENN STATE UNIV, 77- *Concurrent Pos:* NIH spec fel, 69-70; consult, Vet Admin Hosp, 78- *Mem:* AAAS; Soc Neurosci; Soc Pharmacol & Exp Therapeut; Soc Nuclear Med; Acoustical Soc Am. *Res:* Cardiovascular and autonomic nervous system; aspects of tachyphylaxis with sympathomimetic amines; clinical pharmacology; auditory pharmacology. *Mailing Add:* Dept of Pharmacol Col Med E Tenn State Univ Johnson City TN 37601

DAIL, CLARENCE WILDING, b Ger, July 7, 07; US citizen; m 31; c 2. PHYSICAL MEDICINE & REHABILITATION. *Educ:* Pac Union Col, AB, 30; Loma Linda Univ, MD, 35. *Prof Exp:* From instr to assoc prof orthop surg & rehab-phys med, 35-59, PROF ORTHOP SURG & REHAB-PHYS MED, SCH MED, LOMA LINDA UNIV, 59- *Concurrent Pos:* Mem staff, Hosps. *Mem:* AMA; Am Cong Rehab Med; Am Acad Phys Med & Rehab; Am Asn Electromyog & Electrodiag. *Res:* Glossopharyngeal breathing; physiology of muscle breathing patterns and swallowing in muscle weakness. *Mailing Add:* Dept of Phys Med & Rehab Sch of Med Loma Linda Univ Loma Linda CA 92354

DAILEY, BENJAMIN PETER, b San Marcos, Tex, Sept 1, 19; m 45; c 3. CHEMISTRY. *Educ:* Southwest Tex State Teachers Col, BA, 38; Univ Tex, MA, 40, PhD(chem), 42. *Prof Exp:* Res assoc, Explosives Res Lab, Pa, 42-45; fel, Harvard Univ, 46-47; from instr to assoc prof, 47-56, chmn dept, 68-70, PROF CHEM, COLUMBIA UNIV, 56- *Concurrent Pos:* NSF sr fel, 63-64; Guggenheim fel, 71-72. *Mem:* Am Chem Soc; fel Am Phys Soc; fel Am Acad Arts & Sci. *Res:* Thermodynamic properties; molecular structure; microwave spectra; nuclear magnetic resonance. *Mailing Add:* Rm 868 Chandler Lab Columbia Univ New York NY 10027

DAILEY, C(HARLES) L(EE), b Reedley, Calif, Nov 12, 17; m 49; c 6. AERONAUTICS. *Educ:* Calif Inst Technol, BS, 41, MS, 42, PhD, 54. *Prof Exp:* Mem staff, Douglas Aircraft Co, 42-45; chief, Aeronaut Res Eng Ctr, Univ Southern Calif, 45-47; dir, Aeronaut Dept, Wiancko Eng Co, 57-60, chief plasma propulsion proj, 60; CHIEF PLASMA PROPULSION PROJ, TRW SYSTS, REDONDO BEACH, 60- *Res:* Plasma propulsion; supersonic diffuser instability; airplane aerodynamics. *Mailing Add:* 953 Granvia Altamira Palos Verdes Estates CA 90274

DAILEY, CHARLES E(LMER), III, b Pittsburgh, Pa, Feb 14, 26; m 54; c 3. CHEMICAL ENGINEERING. *Educ:* Carnegie Inst Tech, BS, 50, MS, 52, PhD(chem eng), 55. *Prof Exp:* Chem engr org chem dept, Plant Tech Sect, Chambers Works, 54-60, res engr, Jackson Lab, 60-62, sr res engr, 62-64, group supvr org chem dept, Chambers Works, 64-72, chief supvr, 72-77, CHIEF SUPVR, CD&P DEPT, CHAMBERS WORKS, E I DU PONT DE NEMOURS & CO, 78- *Mem:* Am Inst Chem Engrs; Am Chem Soc. *Res:* Simultaneous heat, mass and momentum transfer; economic evaluation; long-range planning; market analyses; process simulation and hazards; physical properties; organic diisocyanates; organometallic compounds; fluorocarbons; air and water pollution abatement. *Mailing Add:* 13 Wayne Dr Wilmington DE 19809

DAILEY, FRANK ALLEN, b South Haven, Mich, Dec 8, 46; m 76; c 1. ALLERGY. *Educ:* Mich State Univ, BS, 69; Univ Calif, Davis, PhD(biochem), 77. *Prof Exp:* Asst prof biochem, Univ Nev, Reno, 78-79; res assoc, agron dept, Washington State Univ, 79-80; res biochemist, 80-82, SR RES BIOCHEMIST, HOLLISTER-STIER, WASH, 82- *Res:* Photosynthesis; lignin degradation; nitrate reduction; immunology; allergy. *Mailing Add:* Hollister-Stier PO Box 3145 Spokane WA 99220

DAILEY, GEORGE, b Lexington, Ky, Feb 17, 38; m 70; c 2. APPLIED MECHANICS, MECHANICAL ENGINEERING. *Educ:* Univ Louisville, BME, 61; Kans State Univ, MS, 62, PhD(appl mech), 66. *Prof Exp:* SR ENGR APPL MECH, JOHNS HOPKINS UNIV, 66- *Res:* Dynamic and static finite element analysis of structures and other analytic methods in solid and fluid mechanics. *Mailing Add:* Appl Physics Lab Johns Hopkins Rd Laurel MD 20707

DAILEY, HARRY A, b Santa Cruz, Calif, Feb 21, 50. HEME BIOSYNTHESIS, MEMBRANE PROTEINS. *Educ:* Univ Calif, Los Angeles, BA, 72, PhD(microbiol), 76. *Prof Exp:* Fel, Dept Biochem, Univ Conn Health Ctr, 76-80; ASST PROF MICROBIOL, UNIV GA, 80- *Mem:* Am Soc Microbiol; AAAS. *Res:* Terminal, membrane bound enzymes of the heme biosynthetic pathway and iron metabolism; purification, characterization and reconstitution of the enzymes into defined liposomes. *Mailing Add:* Dept Microbiol Univ Ga Athens GA 30602

DAILEY, JOHN WILLIAM, b Keyser, WVa, Feb 10, 43; m 73. PHARMACOLOGY. *Educ:* Univ Md, BS, 66; Univ Va, PhD(pharmacol), 71. *Prof Exp:* Fel, Karolinska Inst, 70-72; res assoc, Cleveland Clin Found, 72-73; asst prof, Med Sch, George Washington Univ, 73-76; asst prof, 76-78, ASSOC PROF PHARMACOL, MED CTR, LA STATE UNIV, SHREVEPORT, 78- *Mem:* Am Neurosci; Am Heart Asn; Am Soc Pharmacol & Exp Therapeut. *Res:* Adrenergic nervous system pharmacology in relation to disease states and mechanisms of drug action. *Mailing Add:* Dept of Pharmacol La State Univ Med Ctr Shreveport LA 71130

DAILEY, JOSEPH PATRICK, b Penfield, Ill, Nov 14, 22; m 51; c 5. ORGANIC CHEMISTRY. *Educ:* Univ Ill, BS, 44; Univ Notre Dame, PhD(chem), 50. *Prof Exp:* Chemist, Cent Res Labs, Gen Aniline & Film Corp, 44-46; res chemist, Res Dept, Armour Labs, 49-53, head org chem dept, Armour Pharmaceut Co, 53-59, dir res, 59-67, dir res & develop, 67-71, vpres res & develop, 71-80; SR SCI COORDR, REVLON HEALTH CARE GROUP, 80- *Mem:* AAAS; Am Heart Asn; Am Chem Soc; assoc Royal Soc Med. *Res:* Pharmaceutical organic chemistry; chemotherapy; intravenous fat emulsions, quinolines; ethyleneimines; vinyl ethers; hypothalamic research; lipid metabolism; enzymes; hormones; blood components. *Mailing Add:* 7 Juneberry Lane Ridgefield CT 06877

DAILEY, PAUL WILLIAM, JR, b Ft Wayne, Ind, Sept 29, 37; m 59; c 3. METEOROLOGY. *Educ:* Ball State Univ, BS, 59; Purdue Univ, MS, 68. *Prof Exp:* Agr forecaster, Indianapolis, Ind, 66-68, state climatologist, State College, Pa, 68-71, lead forecaster, Des Moines, Iowa, 71-73, meteorologist-in-chg, Cincinnati, Ohio, 73-75, lead forecaster, Des Moines, 75-78, DEP METEOROLOGIST-IN-CHG, NAT WEATHER SERV, NAT OCEANIC & ATMOSPHERIC ADMIN, CLEVELAND, 78- *Concurrent Pos:* Adj asst prof, Dept Meteorol, Pa State Univ, 69-71. *Mem:* Am Meteorol Soc; Nat Weather Asn. *Res:* Climatology. *Mailing Add:* Nat Weather Serv Forecast Off Hopkins Airport Cleveland OH 44135

DAILEY, ROBERT ARTHUR, b Charles Town, WVa, May 20, 45; m 71. REPRODUCTIVE PHYSIOLOGY, ENDOCRINOLOGY. *Educ:* WVa Univ, BS, 67; Univ Wis-Madison, MS, 69, PhD(reproductive physiol), 73. *Prof Exp:* Specialist food inspection, US Army, 69-71; res fel neuroendocrinol, Emory Univ, 73-75, instr, 75-77, asst prof, 77-80, ASSOC PROF REPRODUCTIVE PHYSIOL, WVA UNIV, 80- *Concurrent Pos:* Fel, Emory Univ, 73-77. *Mem:* Soc Study Reproductive Biol; Am Soc Animal Scientists; Endocrine Soc. *Res:* Neuroendocrine regulation of gonadotropic hormone secretion in mammals; factors associated with the control of ovarian follicular growth, maturation and atresia in domestic animals. *Mailing Add:* Div of Animal & Vet Sci WVa Univ Morgantown WV 26506

DAILEY, ROBERT ENGLE, b Martinsburg, WVa, Oct 3, 23; m 49; c 3. BIOCHEMISTRY, PHARMACOLOGY. *Educ:* George Washington Univ, BS, 48, MS, 49. *Prof Exp:* Pharmacologist, Smith Kline & French Labs, 49-51; biochemist, Vet Admin Ctr, WVa, 51-66; RES CHEMIST, FOOD & DRUG ADMIN, 66- *Mem:* AAAS; Am Chem Soc. *Res:* Metabolism of pesticides; nitrosamine formation from food additives; toxicology and metabolism of mycotoxins; animal derived food safety; toxicology and metabolism of food additives. *Mailing Add:* Food & Drug Admin Div of Toxicol Metab Br Washington DC 20204

DAILEY, FAY KENOYER, b Indianapolis, Ind, Feb 17, 11; m 37. BOTANY. *Educ:* Butler Univ, BA, 35, MS, 52. *Prof Exp:* Lab technician, Eli Lilly & Co, Ind, 35-37, Abbott Labs, Ill, 39 & Wm S Merrell Co, Ohio, 40-41; lubrication chemist, Indianapolis Propellor Div, Curtiss-Wright Corp, NY, 45; lectr bot, 47-49, instr immunol & microbiol, 57-58, lectr microbiol, 62-63, MEM HERBARIUM STAFF, BUTLER UNIV, 49- *Mem:* Am Inst Biol Sci; Bot Soc Am; Phycol Soc Am; Int Phycol Soc; Sigma Xi. *Res:* Charophyta. *Mailing Add:* 5884 Compton St Indianapolis IN 46220

DAILY, JAMES W(ALLACE), b Columbia, Mo, Mar 19, 13; m 38; c 2. FLUID MECHANICS, HYDRAULIC ENGINEERING. *Educ:* Stanford Univ, AB, 35; Calif Inst Technol, MS, 37, PhD(mech eng), 45. *Prof Exp:* Test engr, Byron Jackson Co, Calif, 35; asst, Calif Inst Technol, 36-37, mgr, Hydraul Mach Lab, 37-40, instr mech eng, 40-46, hydraul engr, Off Sci Res & Develop Proj, 41-46; asst prof hydraul, Mass Inst Technol, 46-49, assoc prof, 49-55, prof, Hydrodynamics Lab, 55-64; prof eng mech & chmn dept, 64-70, prof, 70-80, EMER PROF FLUID MECH & HYDRAUL, UNIV MICH, 80- *Concurrent Pos:* Vis prof, Delft Technol Univ, 71; vis scientist, E D F Res & Testing Ctr, Paris, 71. *Honors & Awards:* Naval Ord Develop Award, 45. *Mem:* Am Soc Mech Engrs; Am Soc Civil Engrs; Int Asn Hydraul Res (pres, 67-71); hon mem Japan Soc Civil Engrs. *Res:* General fluid mechanics; hydraulic machinery; pumps and turbines; hydrodynamics of submerged bodies, cavitation; non-Newtonian fluid mechanics. *Mailing Add:* Dept of Eng Mech 201 W Eng Bldg Ann Arbor MI 48104

DAILY, JOHN W, b Pasadena, Calif, Mar 22, 43; m 67; c 1. MECHANICAL ENGINEERING, APPLIED PHYSICS. *Educ:* Univ Mich, BSME, 68, MSME, 69; Stanford Univ, PhD(mech eng), 75. *Prof Exp:* Res asst comput design, Civil Eng Comput Lab, Mass Inst Technol, 60-62; sport car mech, Competetion Asn, Cambridge, Mass, 63-65; res asst air pollution, Automotive Lab, Univ Mich, 66-69; heat transfer analyst rocket design, Aerojet Liquid Rocket Co, 70-71; res asst, Dept Mech Eng, Stanford Univ, 71-75; asst prof, 75-81, ASSOC PROF MECH ENG, UNIV CALIF, BERKELEY, 81- *Concurrent Pos:* Investr, Dept of Energy grant, 75-; prin investr, NASA grant, 75-, USAF Off of Sci Res grant, 76- & NSF grant, 77- *Mem:* Am Inst Aeronaut & Astronaut; Am Soc Mech Engrs; Combustion Inst; Optical Soc Am. *Res:* Combustion fluid mechanics; heat transfer; laser spectroscopy. *Mailing Add:* Dept of Mech Eng Univ of Calif Berkeley CA 94720

DAILY, OTIS PATRICK, molecular biology, microbiology, see previous edition

DAILY, WILLIAM ALLEN, b Indianapolis, Ind, Nov 10, 12; m 37. MICROBIOLOGY. *Educ:* Butler Univ, BS, 36; Northwestern Univ, MS, 38. *Prof Exp:* Lab asst, Northwestern Univ, 36-38; lab asst, Univ Cincinnati, 40-41; asst sr microbiologist, Eli Lilly & Co, 41-77; RETIRED. *Concurrent Pos:* Mem staff, Herbarium, Butler Univ, 42- *Mem:* AAAS; Sigma Xi; Soc Phycol Am (secy, 58, secy-treas, 59, pres, 63); Bot Soc Am; Int Asn Plant Taxon. *Res:* Isolation and development of new antibiotics; preservation of microorganisms; taxonomy of the coccoid Myxophyceae; phytoplankton of Indiana. *Mailing Add:* 5884 Compton St Indianapolis IN 46220

DAIN, JEREMY GEORGE, b New York, NY, July 1, 41; m 74. ORGANIC CHEMISTRY, DRUG METABOLISM. *Educ:* Lowell Technol Inst, BS, 64, MS, 67; Duquesne Univ, PhD(chem), 70. *Prof Exp:* Fel, Univ Pittsburgh, 70-72; SR SCIENTIST, SANDOZ PHARMACEUT, 72-, GROUP LEADER BIOTRANSFORMATION, 80- *Mem:* Am Chem Soc; AAAS; Drug Metab Group. *Res:* Isolation, characterization, identification quantitation and synthesis of drug metabolites; synthesis of labeled compounds; methods of quantitation; in vitro metabolism of xenobiotics. *Mailing Add:* Drug Metab Sandoz Pharmaceut Rte 10 East Hanover NJ 07936

DAIN, JOEL A, b New York, NY, Oct 26, 31; m 56; c 3. BIOCHEMISTRY. *Educ:* Univ Ill, BS, 53; Cornell Univ, PhD(biochem), 56. *Prof Exp:* Res fel, Col Physicians & Surgeons, Columbia Univ, 56-57, res fel & assoc biochem, 57-59; res assoc biochem glycoproteins, Boston Dispensary & Med Sch, Tufts Univ, 59-62; from asst prof to assoc prof, 62-73, PROF BIOCHEM, UNIV RI, 73- *Concurrent Pos:* NIH grant, 64-82. *Mem:* AAAS; Am Chem Soc; Am Soc Microbiol; Am Soc Biol Chemists; Am Soc Neurochem. *Res:* Mechanisms of action of nervous tissue glycolipid metabolic enzymes; nonenzymatic protein glycosulation. *Mailing Add:* Dept of Biochem & Biophysics Univ of RI Kingston RI 02881

DAINELLO, FRANK JOSEPH, plant science, agriculture, see previous edition

DAINTY, ANTON MICHAEL, b Cambridge, Eng, Dec 26, 42. SEISMOLOGY. *Educ:* Univ Edinburgh, BSc, 63; Dalhousie Univ, PhD(physics), 67. *Prof Exp:* Fel physics, Univ Toronto, 67-69; lectr, 69-71; res assoc earth & planetary sci, Mass Inst Technol, 71-77; ASSOC PROF, SCH GEOPHYS SCI, GA INST TECHNOL, 77- *Mem:* AAAS; Am Geophys Union; Seismol Soc Am; Geol Soc Am; Sigma Xi. *Res:* Lunar seismology; seismicity and central structure of South Eastern United States; filtering of seismograms. *Mailing Add:* Sch Geophys Sci 225 North Ave Atlanta GA 30332

DAINTY, JACK, b Mexborough, Eng, May 7, 19. PLANT PHYSIOLOGY. *Educ:* Cambridge Univ, BA, 40, MA, 43; Univ Edinburgh, DSc(plant physiol), 58. *Prof Exp:* Res scientist, Cambridge Univ, 40-46; res scientist, Atomic Energy Can, Ltd, 46-49; lectr physics, Univ Edinburgh, 49-52, sr lectr biophys, 52-58, reader, 58-63; prof biol, Univ EAnglia, 63-69; prof bot, Univ Calif, Los Angeles, 69-71; prof, 71-77, UNIV PROF BOT, UNIV TORONTO, 77- *Mem:* Can Soc Plant Physiologists; Am Soc Plant Physiologists; Brit Ecol Soc; Brit Soc Exp Biol; Royal Soc Edinburgh. *Res:* Transport of ions and water across the membranes of plant cells. *Mailing Add:* Dept of Bot Univ of Toronto Toronto ON M5S 1A1 Can

DAIRIKI, NED TSUNEO, b Sacramento, Calif, Dec 16, 36; m 61; c 1. PHYSICS, COMPUTER SCIENCE. *Educ:* Reed Col, BA, 60; Univ Calif, Berkeley, PhD(physics), 68. *Prof Exp:* Res assoc physics, Lawrence Berkeley Lab, 68, STAFF PHYSICIST, LAWRENCE LIVERMORE LAB, UNIV CALIF, 69- *Mem:* Am Phys Soc; AAAS. *Res:* Particle physics; computer language software systems; numerical techniques. *Mailing Add:* Univ of Calif PO Box 808 Livermore CA 94550

DAIRIKI, SETSUO, b Penryn, Calif, Feb 11, 22; m 45; c 3. ELECTRICAL ENGINEERING. *Educ:* Stanford Univ, AB, 42; Univ Nebr, MS, 45; Harvard Univ, MA, 47. *Prof Exp:* Instr physics, Univ Nebr, 43-45; engr, Lab for Electronics, Inc, Mass, 48-51; engr, Raytheon Mfg Co, 51-53, sr engr, 54-60; mem staff commun, Lincoln Lab, Mass Inst Technol, 53-54; SR RES ENGR, SRI INT, 60- *Mem:* Sigma Xi; Inst Elec & Electronics Engrs. *Res:* Electromagnetic theory and applications; communication theory and application. *Mailing Add:* 625 Hale Palo Alto CA 94301

DAIRMAN, WALLACE, biochemistry, pharmacology, see previous edition

DAISEY, JOAN M, b New York, NY, Oct 4, 41; m 63; c 1. ATMOSPHERIC CHEMISTRY, ENVIRONMENTAL HEALTH. *Educ:* Georgian Court Col, BA, 62; Seton Hall Univ, PhD(phys chem), 70. *Prof Exp:* Chemist, Carter-Wallace Inc, 63-64 & Wallace & Tiernan Inc, 64-66; asst prof chem, Mt St Mary Col, 70-75; asst res scientist, 76-77, assoc res scientist, 77-78, res scientist atmospheric chem, 78-79, PROF ENVIRON MED, MED CTR, NY UNIV, 79- *Mem:* Am Chem Soc; NY Acad Sci; Air Pollution Control Asn; Am Conf Gov Indust Hygienist; Sigma Xi. *Res:* Nature, origin and fate of organic compounds in the ambient atmosphere and the implications for human health. *Mailing Add:* Med Ctr NY Univ 550 First Ave New York NY 10016

DAITCH, P(AUL) B(ERNARD), b Boston, Mass, May 19, 25. NUCLEAR ENGINEERING & SCIENCE. *Educ:* Yale Univ, BS, 45; Brown Univ, MS, 47; Univ Rochester, PhD, 52. *Prof Exp:* Instr, Yale Univ, 52-55; asst prof, Univ Nebr, 55-56; sr physicist, Nuclear Div, Combustion Eng, Inc, 56-60; PROF NUCLEAR ENG & SCI, RENSSELAER POLYTECH INST, 60-, PROF BIOMED ENG, 76- *Concurrent Pos:* Consult, Nuclear Div, Alco Prod Inc, 61-62, Acad Press, Inc, 63-64 & Gen Elec Co, 64- *Mem:* Am Phys Soc; Am Nuclear Soc. *Res:* Low energy nuclear physics; analysis of nuclear reactors; transport theory; asymptotic and transient analysis of pulsed neutron systems. *Mailing Add:* Dept of Biomed Eng Rensselaer Polytech Inst Troy NY 12181

DAJANI, ESAM ZAFER, b Jaffa, Palestine, May 30, 40; m 64; c 3. PHARMACOLOGY, TOXICOLOGY. *Educ:* Univ Mo-Kansas City, BS, 63; Auburn Univ, MS, 66; Purdue Univ, PhD(pharmacol, toxicol), 68. *Prof Exp:* Sr pharmacologist, Rohm & Haas Res Labs, 68-72; sr res investr, 72-74, group leader gastrointestinal pharmacol, 75-79, sect head, 79-80, ASST DIR, GASTROENTEROL CLIN BR, G D SEARLE & CO, 80- *Mem:* Am Soc Pharmacol; NY Acad Sci; Am Pharmaceut Asn; Am Col Gastroenterol; Soc Exp Biol & Med. *Res:* Gastrointestinal, autonomic and central nervous system pharmacology. *Mailing Add:* Res & Develop Div PO Box 5110 Chicago IL 60680

DAJANI, JARIR SUBHI, b Jerusalem, Palestine, Apr 5, 40; m 65; c 3. CIVIL ENGINEERING. *Educ:* Am Univ Beirut, BEng, 61; Stanford Univ, MSc, 66; Northwestern Univ, PhD(civil eng), 71. *Prof Exp:* Resident engr, Assoc Consult Engrs, 61-65; community planner, De Leuw, Cather & Co, Chicago, 68-71; assoc prof civil eng, Duke Univ, 71-76; ASSOC PROF CIVIL ENG, STANFORD UNIV, 76- *Concurrent Pos:* Vpres, Pub Systs Assoc Inc, 73-77; consult, US AID, 78- *Mem:* Am Soc Civil Engrs; Am Planning Asn; Transp Res Bd; Am Soc Pub Admin; Opers Res Soc Am. *Res:* Methods for planning for and forecasting the impacts of infrastructure facilities on land-use and community development; transportation and land-use planning techniques. *Mailing Add:* Dept of Civil Eng Stanford Univ Stanford CA 94305

DAKIN, JAMES THOMAS, b Pittsburgh, Pa, May 23, 45; m 69; c 2. PHYSICS, ENGINEERING. *Educ:* Harvard Univ, BS, 67; Princeton Univ, MS, 69, & PhD(physics), 71. *Prof Exp:* Instr physics, Princeton Univ, 71; res assoc physics, Stanford Linear Accelerator Ctr, 71-74; asst prof physics, Univ Mass, Amherst, 74-75; res staff physics, 75-78, LIAISON SCIENTIST, CORP RES & DEVELOP, GEN ELEC, 78- *Mem:* Am Phys Soc; AAAS. *Res:* Elementary particle physics, experiments and phenomenology of electromagnetic interactions; fluid mechanics, heat transfer, two-phase flow. *Mailing Add:* Gen Elec Co Corp Res & Develop PO Box 8 Schenectady NY 12301

DAKIN, MATT EITEL, b Skene, Miss, Dec 11, 36; m 57; c 2. ENTOMOLOGY. *Educ:* Delta State Col, BS, 58; Auburn Univ, MS, 60, PhD(entom), 64. *Prof Exp:* Instr biol, Univ Southwestern La, 60-61 & 63-64; asst prof zool, Auburn Univ, 64; from asst prof to assoc prof, 64-71, PROF BIOL, UNIV SOUTHWESTERN LA, 71- *Mem:* Entom Soc Am; Pan-Am Acridological Soc; Am Entom Soc. *Res:* Taxonomy of the Orthoptera of the United States. *Mailing Add:* Box 41435 Univ Southwestern La Lafayette LA 70504

DAKIN, THOMAS WENDELL, b Minneapolis, Minn, May 5, 15; m 42; c 2. PHYSICAL CHEMISTRY. *Educ:* Univ Minn, AB, 35; Mich State Univ, MS, 38; Harvard Univ, AM, 39, PhD(phys chem), 41. *Prof Exp:* Asst phys chem, Mich State Univ, 35-38; group leader, Insulation Dept, 46-50, mgr physics, Insulation Sect, 50-68, mgr elec performance insulation mat, 68-77, consult scientist, 77-79, CONSULT, WESTINGHOUSE RES LABS, 80- *Concurrent Pos:* Elec insulation div ed, Electrochem Technol; chmn, Nat Res Coun Conf on Elec Insulations, 57; US rep insulating mat, Int Conf Large Elec Systs. *Mem:* Nat Acad Eng; Am Phys Soc; fel Inst Elec & Electronics Eng; Am Chem Soc. *Res:* Electrochemistry; viscosity of ionic solutions; dielectrics; microwave; high frequency measurements; high polymers; electrical insulation. *Mailing Add:* 3138 Oak St Murrysville PA 15668

DAKSHINAMURTI, KRISHNAMURTI, b Vellore, India, May 20, 28; m 61; c 2. BIOCHEMISTRY, NUTRITION. *Educ:* Univ Madras, BSc, 46; Univ Rajasthan, India, MSc, 52, PhD(biochem), 57; FRIC. *Prof Exp:* Lectr chem, Christian Med Col, India, 52-56; sr lectr biochem, 56-58; res assoc animal nutrit, Univ Ill, 58-62; res assoc nutrit, Mass Inst Technol, 62-63; assoc dir res, St Joseph Hosp, Lancaster, Pa, 63-65; assoc prof, 65-73, PROF BIOCHEM, UNIV MAN, 73- *Concurrent Pos:* Assoc ed, Can J Biochem, 71-75; vis prof, Rockefeller Univ, NY, 74-75. *Honors & Awards:* Borden Award, Nutrit Soc Can, 73. *Mem:* Am Inst Nutrit; Brit Biochem Soc; Am Soc Biol Chem; Am Soc Neurochem. *Res:* Metabolic functions of biotin and pyridoxine; development of the central nervous system; regulation of protein synthesis. *Mailing Add:* Dept of Biochem Univ of Man Winnipeg MB R3E 0W3 Can

DAKSS, MARK LUDMER, b New York, NY, Mar 1, 40. PHYSICAL OPTICS. *Educ:* Cooper Union, BEE, 60; Columbia Univ, AM, 62, PhD(physics), 66. *Prof Exp:* Mem res staff, T J Watson Res Ctr, IBM Corp, 66-71; MEM TECH STAFF, GEN TEL & ELECTRONICS LABS, 71- *Mem:* Optical Soc Am; Inst Elec & Electronics Engrs. *Res:* Fiber-optical communications; optical guided waves; solid state physics and lasers; acoustic surface waves. *Mailing Add:* Gen Tel & Electronics Labs Inc 40 Sylvan Rd Waltham MA 02254

DALAL, FRAM RUSTOM, b Madras, India, Jan 24, 35; m 61; c 1. CLINICAL CHEMISTRY, BIOCHEMISTRY. *Educ:* Univ Bombay, BS, 54 & 56, PhD(biochem), 61. *Prof Exp:* Coun Sci & Indust Res fel, Univ Bombay, 60-61; chief technologist, D & P Prod, Ltd, India, 61-64; res assoc microbial biochem, Sch Med, Univ Pa, 64-67; assoc prof microbiol, Dept Chem Technol, Univ Bombay, 67-69; assoc chief biochem, Dept Labs, Albert Einstein Med Ctr, Philadelphia, 69-78; DIR CLIN BIOCHEM, TEMPLE UNIV HOSP, 78- 69- *Mem:* Am Asn Clin Chemists. *Res:* Diagnostic applications of enzymes in blood and tissues; improvements in automation of enzyme assays; unusual paraproteins in myeloma. *Mailing Add:* Clin Labs Temple Univ Hosp 3401 N Broad St Philadelphia PA 19140

DALAL, HARISH MANEKLAL, b Bombay, India, Sept 4, 43; m 69; c 1. MATERIALS SCIENCE, QUALITY ASSURANCE. *Educ:* Indian Inst Technol, BTech, 65; Mass Inst Technol, ScD(mat sci), 70. *Prof Exp:* Res asst powder metall, Mass Inst Technol, 65-70, fel, 70-71; mat scientist tribology, SKF Industs, Inc, 72-78; mgr res & develop, KSM Fastening Syst, Moorestown NJ, 78-80; MGR MAT PROCESS & EVAL, ADVAN ENERGY PROD DIV, GEN ELEC CO, VALLEY FORGE, PA, 80- *Mem:* Am Soc Metals; Am Soc Lubrication Engrs; Am Soc Mech Engrs; Am Ceramic Soc. *Res:* Structure, property relationships in materials, developing processes to generate desired structures in materials and developing/adapting quality assurance techniques to assure consistent product quality. *Mailing Add:* 914 Florence Lane Audubon PA 19407

DALAL, NAR S, b Panjab, India, May 11, 41; Can citizen; m 66; c 2. PHYSICAL CHEMISTRY, CHEMICAL PHYSICS. *Educ:* Panjab Univ, BSc, 62, MSc, 63; Univ BC, PhD(chem), 71. *Prof Exp:* Killam fel, Univ BC, 71-74; vis scientist & World Trade fel, IBM Res Lab, 74-75; Nat Res Coun res assoc, 76-78; ASST PROF PHYS CHEM, W VA UNIV, 78- *Mem:* Am Chem Soc; Chem Inst Can. *Res:* High resolution Endor spectroscopy as applied to structural phase transitions in molecular crystals and coal related problems. *Mailing Add:* Dept Chem WVa Univ Morgantown WV 26506

DALAL, SIDDHARTHA RAMANLAL, b Ahmedabad, India, Oct 1, 48. STATISTICS. *Educ:* Univ Bombay, BSc, 69; Univ Rochester, MBA, 73, MA & PhD(statist), 75. *Prof Exp:* Asst prof appl & math statist, Rutgers Univ, New Brunswick, NJ, 74-80; MEM TECH STAFF, BELL LABS, MURRAY HILL, NJ, 80- *Mem:* Inst Math Statist; Am Statist Asn. *Res:* Development of robust procedures with finite sample optimality, robust estimation of location, of linear regression; topics in Bayes Nonparametric Decision theory, inequality theory, ranking and selection. *Mailing Add:* Bell Labs Murray Hill NJ 07974

DALAL, VIKRAM, b Bombay, India, Feb 4, 44; US citizen. SEMICONDUCTOR PHYSICS, ENGINEERING. *Educ:* Univ Bombay, BS, 64; Princeton Univ, PhD(elec eng), 69, MPA, 75. *Prof Exp:* Res asst physics, Princeton Univ, 66-69; res scientist, RCA Labs, 69-74; mgr physics, Univ Del, 76-81; PRES, RES & DEVELOP, CHRONAR CORP, 81- *Mem:* Inst Elec & Electronic Engrs; AAAS. *Res:* Semiconductor physics; solar energy; energy and environment; economic growth and environmental policy. *Mailing Add:* Chronar Corp 330 Baker Basin Rd Trenton NJ 08638

D'ALARCAO, HUGO T, b Lisbon, Port, Feb 15, 37; m 56; c 3. ALGEBRA, ARTIFICIAL INTELLIGENCE. *Educ:* Univ Nebr, Lincoln, BA, 59, MA, 61; Pa State Univ, PhD(math), 66. *Prof Exp:* Instr math, Univ Nebr, 61-62; instr, Univ Mass, 62-63; asst prof, State Univ NY Stony Brook, 66-71; assoc prof, 71-78, PROF MATH, BRIDGEWATER STATE COL, 78- *Concurrent Pos:* Vis res prof, Univ Chile, 69. *Mem:* Am Math Soc; Asn Comput Mach; NY Acad Sci; Port Math Soc. *Res:* Algebraic theory of semigroups; universal algebra; mathematical neurology. *Mailing Add:* Dept Math Bridgewater State Col Bridgewater MA 02324

DALBEC, PAUL EUCLIDE, b New Bedford, Mass, June 26, 35; m 63; c 1. SOLID STATE PHYSICS. *Educ:* Univ Notre Dame, MS, 59; Georgetown Univ, PhD(physics), 66. *Prof Exp:* Physicist, Phys Sci Lab, Melpar, Inc, Va, 59-60; head, Thin Films Dept, Appl Phys Lab, Gen Instrument Corp, NJ, 60-61; assoc prof, 71-78, PROF PHYSICS, YOUNGSTOWN STATE UNIV, 78- *Concurrent Pos:* Fac improv leave, Inst Recherche sur les Interfaces Solides, Namur, Belg, 78-79. *Mem:* Am Phys Soc; Am Asn Physics Teachers; Am Vacuum Soc; Am Soc Testing & Mat. *Res:* Photoelectric properties of solids; electronic properties of semiconductor and metallic thin films; vacuum ultraviolet spectroscopy; techniques for preparing thin films including epitaxial growth and sputtering; electron spectroscopy. *Mailing Add:* Dept Physics & Astron Youngstown State Univ Youngstown OH 44555

DALBY, FREDERICK WILLIAM, b Edmonton, Alta, May 5, 28; m 52; c 2. PHYSICS. *Educ:* Univ Alta, BSc, 50; Univ BC, MA, 62; Ohio State Univ, PhD(physics), 55. *Prof Exp:* Res physicist, Radiation Physics Lab, E I du Pont de Nemours & Co, 57-61; assoc prof, 61-66, PROF PHYSICS, UNIV BC, 66- *Res:* Molecular spectroscopy; chemical physics. *Mailing Add:* Dept of Physics Univ of BC Vancouver BC V6T 1W5 Can

DALBY, PETER LENN, b Flint, Mich, Feb 26, 43; m 67; c 2. VERTEBRATE BIOLOGY. *Educ:* Mich State Univ, BS, 65, MS, 68, PhD(zool), 74. *Prof Exp:* Curatorial technician, Mammal Div, Mich State Univ, 70-73; vis asst prof dept zool, Ohio State Univ, 73; asst prof & cur mammals, Dept Biol, Va Polytech Inst & State Univ, 73-75; vis asst prof dept biol, Univ Va, 75-76; ASST PROF DEPT BIOL, CLARION STATE COL, 76- *Concurrent Pos:* Nat Park Serv fel, 75-77; fel Western Pa Conservancy, 78- *Mem:* Am Soc Mammalogists; Ecol Soc Am; Wildlife Soc; Sigma Xi; Animal Behav Soc. *Res:* Ecology of South American grassland rodents; evolution, ecology, and behavior of eastern North American rodents; effects of strip-mining on vertebrate populations; fire ecology. *Mailing Add:* Dept of Biol Clarion State Col Clarion PA 16214

DALBY, THOMAS GREEN, b Minneapolis, Minn, Sept 1, 26; m 50; c 3. ELECTRICAL ENGINEERING. *Educ:* Univ Minn, BS, 48, MS, 51. *Prof Exp:* Res engr, 51-58, group engr commun & electromagnetic res & develop, 58-62, sect head command & control res & develop, 62-64, tech mgr, Voyager Spacecraft Systs, 65-66, tech mgr, Adv Surface Missile Syst, 67-69, ENG MGR, BOEING CO, 69- *Concurrent Pos:* Prog chmn, Region Inst Radio Eng, 62. *Mem:* AAAS; Inst Elec & Electronics Engrs. *Res:* Antennas and microwave circuitry; communications. *Mailing Add:* Boeing Co PO Box 3999 Seattle WA 98124

DAL CANTO, MAURO CARLO, b Soriano, Italy, Jan 1, 44; US citizen; m 68; c 2. NEUROPATHOLOGY, ELECTRON MICROSCOPY. *Educ:* Sci Lyceum, Livorno, Italy, dipl, 61; Sch Med, Univ Pisa, MD, 67. *Prof Exp:* Asst instr neuropath, Albert Einstein Col Med, 73-74; assoc path, 74-75, asst prof, 75-77, assoc prof, 77-81, dir neuropath, Childrens Mem Hosp, 79-81, DIR NEUROPATH & PROF PATH & NEUROL, SCH MED, NORTHWESTERN UNIV, 81- *Concurrent Pos:* Consult, Evanston Hsop, 74-; reviewer, J Neuropath & Exp Neurol, J Histochem & Cytochem, J Neuroradiol, & Kroc Found, 74- *Mem:* Am Asn Neuropathologists; AAAS; NY Acad Sci. *Res:* Multiple sclerosis; ultrastructural, immunohistochemical and immunopathological studies of several experimental models of myelin degeneration produced either by auto-sensitization to myelin proteins or by infection with different viruses. *Mailing Add:* Dept Path Med Sch Northwestern Univ 303 E Chicago Ave Chicago IL 60611

DALE, ALVIN C, b Nashville, Tenn, Aug 12, 19; m 47; c 4. AGRICULTURAL & CIVIL ENGINEERING. *Educ:* Univ Tenn, BS, 41; Iowa State Univ, MS, 42, PhD(agr & civil eng), 50; Univ Chicago, cert, 44. *Prof Exp:* Jr civil engr, US Engrs Off, Ill, 42-43, asst civil engr, 46; from instr to asst prof agr eng, Iowa State Univ, 46-49; from asst prof to assoc prof, 49-56, PROF AGR ENG, PURDUE UNIV, 56- *Honors & Awards:* Award, Metal Bldg Mfrs Asn, 62. *Mem:* Am Soc Agr Engrs; Am Soc Eng Educ; Nat Soc Prof Engrs. *Res:* Environmental control and structural areas of farm structures; farm waste handling and disposal. *Mailing Add:* Dept of Agr Eng Purdue Univ West Lafayette IN 47907

DALE, BRIAN, b Goole, Eng, June 19, 30; m 55; c 3. ELECTRONICS, PHYSICS. *Educ:* Univ London, BSc, 51, PhD(physics), 54. *Prof Exp:* Res scientist, Res Labs, Gen Elec Co, Eng, 54-59; mgr device physics, Transitron Elec Corp, Mass, 59-62; chief engr, Sylvania Elec, Mass, 62-69; dir, Electronic Comp Lab, 69-78, dir consumer electronics, 78-81, DIR, ADV COMP LAB, GTE LABS, 81- *Concurrent Pos:* Vis assoc prof, Tufts Univ, 77. *Mem:* Sr mem Inst Elec & Electronics Engrs; Soc Info Display. *Res:* Very large scale integrated circuits; semiconductor processing technology and device physics; home computers. *Mailing Add:* GTE Labs 40 Sylvan Rd Waltham MA 02154

DALE, DOUGLAS KEITH, b Ottawa, Ont, Oct 10, 24; m 51; c 5. MATHEMATICAL STATISTICS. *Educ:* Queen's Univ, Ont, BA, 47, Hons, 49; Univ NC, MS, 58. *Prof Exp:* Lectr math, Queen's Univ, Ont, 46-49; asst to math adv, Dominion Bur Statist, 49-51, chief sampling & anal, 51-60; chief statist div, Nat Energy Bd, 60-62; from asst prof to assoc prof, 62-65, chmn dept, 63-67, PROF MATH, CARLETON UNIV, ONT, 65- *Concurrent Pos:* Lectr, Carleton Univ, Can, 49-52 & 53-60; consult, Can Advert Res Found, 63-64 & Bur Broadcast Measurement, 63- *Mem:* Am Statist Soc; Soc; fel Royal Statist Soc. *Res:* Sampling theory; distribution theory; probability theory. *Mailing Add:* Dept of Math Carleton Univ Ottawa ON K1S 5B6 Can

DALE, EDWARD EVERETT, JR, b Norman, Okla, Aug 18, 20; m 42; c 2. PLANT ECOLOGY. *Educ:* Univ Okla, BA, 42, MS, 47; Univ Nebr, PhD, 51. *Prof Exp:* Asst bot, Ind Univ, 46-47 & Univ Nebr, 47-50; asst prof biol, Baylor Univ, 51-52 & Tex Christian Univ, 52-57; from asst prof to assoc prof, 57-68, prof bact & chmn dept bot & bact, 75-78, PROF BOT, UNIV ARK, FAYETTEVILLE, 68- *Mem:* Bot Soc Am; Ecol Soc Am; Am Soc Range Mgt. *Res:* Grassland ecology; vegetation of Arkansas. *Mailing Add:* Dept of Bot & Bact Univ of Ark Fayetteville AR 72701

DALE, EDWIN, b Louisville, Ky, Oct 17, 33; m 56; c 3. ENDOCRINOLOGY. *Educ:* Eastern Ky State Col, BS, 54; Univ Ky, MS, 56; Univ Iowa, PhD(zool), 60. *Prof Exp:* Res assoc endocrinol, Univ Iowa, 60-61; trainee steroid biochem, Worcester Found Exp Biol, 61-62; from instr anat to asst prof obstet & gynec, Col Med, Univ Ky, 62-66, asst prof zool, 66-68; asst prof, 68-72, ASSOC PROF OBSTET & GYNEC, SCH MED, EMORY UNIV, 72- *Mem:* AAAS. *Res:* Steroid biochemistry; distribution, metabolism and functions of steroids; chemical evaluation of the high-risk obstetric patient; menstrual dysfunction in athletes; correlation of various parameters of evaluation of the fetus; health related aspects of female athletes including nutrition, physical fitness, personality profiles and cardiovascular assessment. *Mailing Add:* Dept of Gynec & Obstet Sch of Med Emory Univ Atlanta GA 30303

DALE, ERNEST BROCK, b Jackson Co, Okla, Dec 15, 18; m 46; c 3. PHYSICS. *Educ:* Univ Okla, BS, 40, MS, 44; Ohio State Univ, PhD(physics), 53. *Prof Exp:* Engr infrared anal, Phillips Petrol Co, 44-47; res assoc infrared detecting systs, Ohio State Univ, 49-50; proj leader semiconductors, Battelle Mem Inst, 52-57; assoc prof, 57-67, PROF PHYSICS, KANS STATE UNIV, 67- *Res:* Channeling and Rutherford scattering; musical acoustics; solid state physics; thin films. *Mailing Add:* Dept of Physics Kans State Univ Manhattan KS 66506

DALE, GEORGE LESLIE, b Glendale, Calif, July 14, 48; m 68. METABOLISM. *Educ:* Univ Calif, Riverside, BS, 70, Los Angeles, PhD(biochem), 75. *Prof Exp:* Fel biochem genetics, City Hope Med Ctr, 75-77, res scientist, 77-79; ASST MEM BIOCHEM, SCRIPPS CLIN & RES FOUND, 79- *Mem:* Am Soc Human Genetics. *Res:* Molecular aspects of human genetic disorders including treatment of lipid storage disease; drug delivery systems; red cell metabolism. *Mailing Add:* Dept Clin Res Scripps Clin & Res Found 10666 N Torrey Pines Rd La Jolla CA 92037

DALE, GLENN H(ILBURN), b Mountain Park, Okla, Aug 25, 23; m 47; c 3. CHEMICAL ENGINEERING. *Educ:* Univ Okla, BS, 44. *Prof Exp:* Chem engr, 44-47, group leader pilot plant, 47-49, process design engr, 50-51, pilot plant supvr, 52-57, sect mgr separations, 58-60, br mgr separations processes, 60-71, staff engr petrol processes, 71-74, staff engr, Refining & Separations Br, 74-80, STAFF ENGR, ALT ENERGY BR, PHILLIPS PETROL CO, 81- *Mem:* Am Inst Chem Engrs; Am Chem Soc. *Res:* Equipment and process development in the separations field; distillation; adsorption; liquid-liquid extraction; crystallation; filtration; centrifugation; catalytic cracking of heavy oils. *Mailing Add:* 2900 Staats Dr Bartlesville OK 74003

DALE, HOMER ELDON, b Minneapolis, Minn, June 11, 22; m 47; c 4. VETERINARY PHYSIOLOGY. *Educ:* Iowa State Col, DVM, 44, MS, 49; Univ Mo, PhD(physiol), 53. *Prof Exp:* Instr vet physiol, Iowa State Col, 47-49; asst prof, Agr & Mech Col Tex, 49-50; instr vet sci, Univ Wis, 50-51; instr vet physiol, 51-53, assoc prof, 53-56, PROF VET PHYSIOL & PHARMACOL, UNIV MO-COLUMBIA, 56- *Mem:* AAAS; Am Vet Med Asn; Am Physiol Soc. *Res:* Environmental physiology, endocrinology; immunology. *Mailing Add:* Dept Vet Physiol Univ Mo Columbia MO 65201

DALE, HUGH MONRO, b Toronto, Ont, Nov 24, 19; m 45; c 2. AQUATIC ECOLOGY. *Educ:* Univ Toronto, BA, 48, MA, 50, PhD, 56. *Prof Exp:* Sr chem master, St Andrew's Col, 50-52; lectr bot, Univ Toronto, 53-56, asst prof, 56-57; assoc prof, 57-68, PROF BOT, UNIV GUELPH, ONT, 68- *Concurrent Pos:* Res fel, Univ Calif, Davis, 66; mem gov bd, Biol Coun Can, 68-71. *Mem:* Ecol Soc Am; Am Inst Biol Sci; Can Bot Asn (pres, 69-70); Humanities Asn Can. *Res:* Experimental ecology of aquatic macrophytes; including distribution patterns and effects on environments. *Mailing Add:* Dept of Bot & Genetics Univ of Guelph Guelph ON N1G 2W1 Can

DALE, J(AMES) D(OUGLAS), b Edmonton, Alta, Dec 5, 39; m 63; c 1. MECHANICAL ENGINEERING, COMBUSTION. *Educ:* Univ Alta, BS, 61, MS, 63; Univ Wash, PhD(mech eng), 69. *Prof Exp:* Sessional lectr mech eng, Univ Alta, 63-64; asst res off, Res Coun Alta, 64-65; asst prof, 69-72, ASSOC PROF MECH ENG, UNIV ALTA, 72- *Mem:* Can Soc Mech Engrs; assoc mem Am Soc Mech Engrs; Soc Automotive Engrs; Combustion Inst. *Res:* Natural convection heat transfer to non-Newtonian fluids; air pollution from combustion sources; laser and plasma jet ignition for SI engines. *Mailing Add:* Dept of Mech Eng Univ of Alta Edmonton AB T6G 2E1 Can

DALE, JACK KYLE, b Manhattan, Kans, Apr 6, 21; m 47; c 3. PHARMACEUTICAL CHEMISTRY. *Educ:* Univ Fla, BS, 43, MS, 44, PhD(pharm), 47. *Prof Exp:* Asst pharmacy & chem, Univ Fla, 43-46; sr scientist, Upjohn Co, 47-61, head vet res & develop sect, 61-66; vpres & tech dir, Kapco Inc, 66-72; VPRES QUAL CONTROL, CARTER GLAGAU DIV, REVCO DRUG STORES, INC, GLENDALE, 72- *Mem:* AAAS; sr mem Am Chem Soc; Am Pharmaceut Asn; Acad Pharmaceut Sci; Parenteral Drug Asn. *Res:* Zinc salt hydrolysis; isotonic, adjusted, buffered and preserved collyria; alkaloidal extraction; pharmacy of adrenal cortical hormones; penicillin, neomycin, erythromycin pharmacy; veterinary pharmacy; drug incompatibilities; antacids; drug stability. *Mailing Add:* 8601 N 16th Ave Phoenix AZ 85021

DALE, JAMES LOWELL, b Olney, Ill, Dec 1, 22; m 46; c 1. PLANT PATHOLOGY. *Educ:* Eastern Ill State Col, BS, 52; Univ Ill, MS, 53, PhD(plant path), 56. *Prof Exp:* Asst plant path, Univ Ill, 52-56; exten plant pathologist, Col Agr, 56-57, from asst prof to assoc prof, 57-65, PROF PLANT PATH, UNIV ARK, FAYETTEVILLE, 65- *Mem:* Am Phytopath Soc; Am Inst Biol Sci. *Res:* Corn and turf diseases; plant mycoplasma diseases. *Mailing Add:* Dept Plant Path Univ Ark Fayetteville AR 72701

DALE, JOHN IRVIN, III, b Knoxville, Tenn, May 14, 35; m 62, 81; c 1. ORGANIC CHEMISTRY. *Educ:* Carson-Newman Col, BS, 56; Univ NC, MA, 59; Univ Va, PhD(org chem), 63. *Prof Exp:* From chemist to sr chemist, Res Labs, 62-67, SR CHEMIST, ORG CHEM DIV, TENN EASTMAN CO, 67- *Mem:* Am Chem Soc; Am Inst Chem Engrs. *Res:* Synthetic organic chemistry; heterocylic and aromatic compounds; textile dyes and intermediates. *Mailing Add:* Rte 6 Jonesboro TN 37659

DALE, WESLEY JOHN, b Milwaukee, Wis, Aug 8, 21; m 49; c 1. ORGANIC CHEMISTRY. *Educ:* Univ Ill, BS, 43; Univ Minn, PhD(chem), 49. *Prof Exp:* Asst, Univ Minn, 43, res chemist, Govt Synthetic Rubber Res Prog, 43-46; from asst prof to prof chem, Univ Mo-Columbia, 49-66, asst to dean, Col Arts & Sci, 54-55, chmn dept chem, 61-64; univ res adminr, 69-72, actg provost & dean fac, 71, dean sch grad studies, 66-72, actg chancellor, 76-77, PROF CHEM, UNIV MO-KANSAS CITY, 66-, PROVOST, 72- *Concurrent Pos:* Staff assoc, Sci Facilities Eval Group, Div Instl Prog, NSF, 64, sr staff assoc, Sci Develop Eval Group, 64-66; mem, Bd Dirs, Sci Pioneers, 67 & Inst Community Studies, Kansas City, Mo, 70-73; trustee, Mid-Continent Regional Educational Lab, 72-73; mem, Adv Comt, US Army Command & Gen Staff Col, Ft Leavenworth, Kans, 73. *Mem:* AAAS; Am Chem Soc; Sigma Xi. *Res:* Chemistry and spectra of vinylaromatic systems; boronic acids; cyclopropanes; carbenes. *Mailing Add:* 5600 State Line Shawnee Mission KS 66208

DALE, WILLIAM ANDREW, b Nashville, Tenn, Mar 13, 20; m 44; c 4. SURGERY. *Educ:* Davidson Col, AB, 41; Vanderbilt Univ, MD, 44; Am Bd Surg, dipl; Am Bd Thoracic Surg, dipl. *Prof Exp:* Intern surg, Strong Mem Hosp, 44-45, asst resident, 45-46, 48-49, chief resident surgeon, 50; instr surg, Univ Rochester, 50-53, instr physiol, 53-54, instr surg anat, 53-55, asst prof physiol, 54-57, surg, 54-58, dir surg exp lab, 53-58; clin asst prof surg, 58; PROF CLIN SURG, VANDERBILT UNIV, 58- *Concurrent Pos:* Vol fel physiol, Univ Rochester, 51-53; asst surgeon, Strong Mem Hosp, 51-58; attend surgeon, Genessee Hosp, 52-58; asst prof surg, Med Col Ala, 52; mem attend surg staff, Vanderbilt Univ Hosp, St Thomas Hosp & Mid-State Baptist Hosp. *Mem:* Fel Am Col Surg; AMA; Soc Univ Surg; Soc Vascular Surg; Int Cardiovasc Soc. *Mailing Add:* 520 Mid-State Med Ctr Nashville TN 37203

DALE, WILLIAM CRISPIN, b Long Branch, NJ, Sept 13, 42. POLYMER MECHANICS. *Educ:* Yale Univ, BS, 66; Cas Inst Technol, MS, 70; Case-Western Reserve Univ, PhD(macromolecular sci), 74. *Prof Exp:* Sr res engr, Monsanto Textiles Co, 74-78, TECHNOL SPECIALIST, MONSANTO PLASTICS & RESINS CO, 78- *Mem:* Am Phys Soc; Am Chem Soc; AAAS. *Res:* Mechanical properties of polymers; deformation and fracture morphology; orientation and anisotropy; processing; composites; structural biological polymers. *Mailing Add:* Monsanto Plastics & Resins Co 730 Worcester St Indian Orchard MA 01151

D'ALECY, LOUIS GEORGE, b Staten Island, NY, Nov 21, 41; m 64; c 3. PHYSIOLOGY. *Educ:* NJ Col Med & Dent, DMD, 66; Sch Med, Univ Pa, PhD(physiol), 71. *Prof Exp:* Res asst anat, NJ Col Med & Dent, 62-64; vis scientist physiol, Sch Med, Univ Wash, 69-71, from instr to asst prof physiol, 71-73; asst prof, 73-77, ASSOC PROF PHYSIOL, SCH MED, UNIV MICH, 73- *Concurrent Pos:* NIH fel, 66-71 & spec fel, 71; estab investr, Am Heart Asn, 75-80. *Honors & Awards:* Excellence Award, Am Acad Oral Roentgenol, 66; Irving S Wright Award, Stroke Coun, Am Heart Asn, 72. *Mem:* AAAS; Am Heart Asn; Am Physiol Soc. *Res:* Biological sciences; cardiovascular physiology; control of blood flow to the brain, demonstrating that autonomic nerves, when activated directly or reflexly, produce major brain blood flow changes. *Mailing Add:* Sch Med Dept of Physiol Univ of Mich 7622 Med Sci II Ann Arbor MI 48109

DALEHITE, THOMAS H, b Memphis, Tenn, Sept 14, 18; m 42; c 3. AERONAUTICAL ENGINEERING, PHYSICS. *Educ:* Miss State Univ, BS, 39. *Prof Exp:* Gen engr, Air Proving Ground Command, 51-58, tech dir, 58-60, dir plans & progs, Off Secy Air Force, Supreme Hq Allied Powers Europe Tech Ctr, Netherlands, 60-62, sci adv foreign technol, Air Force Systs Command, 62-63, dep eng, Off Secy Air Force, 63-66, chief scientist, Air Proving Ground Ctr, 66-68 & Armament Develop & Test Ctr, 68-74; RETIRED. *Concurrent Pos:* Consult to US Defense Rep, NAtlantic Alliance, 60-62, Systs Res Lab, Dayton, 74-77 & Lockheed Missile & Spacecraft, Sunnyvale, 74-78; mem, Coun Air Force Scientist, 62-63, group environ panel, Aeronaut Coord Bd, NASA-Dept Defense, 63-66, tech mgt coun, Air Force Systs Command, 66- & Small Arms Adv Comt, Adv Res Projs Agency, Dept Defense, 68- *Honors & Awards:* Exceptional Serv Decorations, Secy Air Force, 62, 65 & 68. *Mem:* Am Ord Asn; Am Inst Aeronaut & Astronaut. *Res:* Non-nuclear munitions, guided missiles systems and high performance aircraft exploratory, advanced and engineering development; global range instrumentation; electromagnetic warfare. *Mailing Add:* 47 Longwood Dr Shalimar FL 32579

DALES, SAMUEL, b Warsaw, Poland, Aug 31, 27; Can citizen; m 52; c 2. VIROLOGY, CELL BIOLOGY. *Educ:* Univ BC, BA, 51, MA, 53; Univ Toronto, PhD(zool, biochem), 57. *Prof Exp:* Nat Cancer Inst Can res fel cell biol, Univ Toronto, 57-60; res assoc cytol & cell biol, Rockefeller Inst, 60-61, asst prof virol & cytol, 61-66; from res assoc prof to res prof microbiol, Post Grad Med Sch, NY Univ & mem, Pub Health res Inst City of NY, 66-76; PROF BACTERIOL & IMMUNOL & CHMN, UNIV WESTERN ONT, LONDON, 76- *Concurrent Pos:* Ed, J Cell Biol, 72- *Mem:* Harvey Soc; Am Soc Cell Biol; Electron Micros Soc Am. *Res:* Cell virus interactions and the early events in the process of infection; cell fine structure and function; cell physiology. *Mailing Add:* Dept of Bacteriol & Immunol Univ of Western Ont London ON N6A 5B8 Can

D'ALESANDRO, PHILIP ANTHONY, b Bound Brook, NJ, Apr 2, 1927; m 61. PARASITOLOGY, IMMUNOLOGY. *Educ:* Rutgers Univ, BSc, 52, MSc, 54; Univ Chicago, PhD(microbiol), 58. *Prof Exp:* Res assoc parasitol, Univ Chicago, 58-59; guest investr, Rockefeller Univ, 59-61, from asst prof to assoc prof, 61-75; ASSOC PROF PARASITOL, COLUMBIA UNIV, 75-, ACTG HEAD DIV TROP MED, 77- *Concurrent Pos:* USPHS res fel, 59-61 & res grant, 72-; asst ed, J Protozool, 64-65, ed, 80-; adj prof, Rockefeller Univ, 75-; mem, Trop Med & Parasitol Study Sect, NIH, 76-80, chmn, 77-80. *Mem:* Fel AAAS; Am Soc Parasitol; Soc Protozool; Am Soc Trop Med & Hyg; Sigma Xi. *Res:* Parasitic hemoflagellates; immunological, biochemical and nutritional aspects of the host-parasite relationship. *Mailing Add:* Sch of Pub Health Columbia Univ 630 W 168th St New York NY 10032

D'ALESSANDRO-BACIGALUPO, ANTONIO, b Buenos Aires, Arg, Apr 6, 26; m 59; c 2. PARASITOLOGY, TROPICAL MEDICINE. *Educ:* Univ Buenos Aires, MD, 51; Tulane Univ, MPH&TM, 57, PhD, 61. *Prof Exp:* Asst parasitol, Med Sch, Univ Buenos Aires, 45-51, chief resident, 52-55, asst prof, 56-61; from asst prof to assoc prof, 61-80, PROF TROP MED, TULANE UNIV, 80- *Concurrent Pos:* Dazian Found Med res fel, 57-59; univ fel trop med & pub health, Tulane Univ, 57-61; liaison officer for Tulane Univ, Int Ctr Med Res & Training, Cali, Colombia, 61-63, asst dir, 63-65, assoc dir, 75-76, chief mission & gen coordr progs, 76-; vis prof, Univ Valle, Colombia, 61- *Mem:* Am Soc Trop Med & Hyg; Royal Soc Trop Med & Hyg; Am Soc Parasitol; Arg Soc Parasitol; Colombian Soc Parasitol & Trop Med. *Res:* Parasitology, especially American trypanosomiasis and echinococcosis. *Mailing Add:* Dept Trop Med Tulane Univ New Orleans LA 70112

DALEY, DANIEL H, b Elmira, NY, Mar 9, 20; c 4. THERMODYNAMICS, AERODYNAMICS. *Educ:* Purdue Univ, BS, 42; Mass Inst Technol, SMAE, 46. *Prof Exp:* US AIR FORCE, 42-49, 51-, assoc prof & actg head mech eng, US Air Force Inst Technol, 52-55, atomic test support group, Eniwetok, 55-56, 483rd Troop Carrier Wing, Japan, 56-58, chief aerodyn sect, B-70 Proj Off, Wright Patterson Air Force Base, 58-61; assoc prof aeronaut, US Air Force Acad, 61-64, prof & head dept, 64-65; head, Dept Mech Eng, Pakistan Air Force Col Aeronaut Eng, 65-67; PROF AERONAUT & HEAD DEPT, US AIR FORCE ACAD, 67- *Mem:* Am Inst Aeronaut & Astronaut; Japan Soc Aeronaut & Space Sci. *Res:* Airplane performance; stability and control; thermodynamics; gas dynamics; aerospace propulsion. *Mailing Add:* Dept of Aeronaut US Air Force Acad CO 80840

DALEY, DARRYL LEE, b Detroit, Mich, Sept 28, 50. NEUROBIOLOGY. *Educ:* Wayne State Univ, BS, 72, MS, 75; Univ Ill, PhD(biol), 78. *Prof Exp:* RES ASSOC FEL, SECT NEUROBIOL & BEHAV, CORNELL UNIV, 78- *Mem:* AAAS; Soc Neurosci. *Res:* Neurophysiological mechanisms underlying simple behaviors at the level of single identifiable neurons. *Mailing Add:* Sect Neurobiol & Behav Cornell Univ Ithaca NY 14853

DALEY, HENRY OWEN, JR, b Quincy, Mass, June 18, 36; m 61; c 3. PHYSICAL CHEMISTRY. *Educ:* Mass State Col Bridgewater, BS, 58; Boston Col, PhD(chem), 64. *Prof Exp:* Res chemist, Am Cyanamid Co, 63-64; asst prof phys chem, 64-67, assoc prof, 67-71, PROF CHEM, BRIDGEWATER STATE COL, 71- *Mem:* Am Chem Soc; Electrochem Soc. *Res:* Determination of trace metals in an ecosystem. *Mailing Add:* 115 Robinswood Rd South Weymouth MA 02190

DALEY, LAURENCE STEPHEN, b Liverpool, Eng, Sept 21, 36; US citizen; m 70; c 3. PLANT PHYSIOLOGY, BIOCHEMISTRY. *Educ:* Univ Fla, BSA, 64, MSA, 65; Univ Calif, Davis, PhD(plant physiol & biochem), 75. *Prof Exp:* Fel, Univ Ga, 75-77 & Boyce Thompson Inst, 77-78; asst prof, 78-79, ASSOC PROF BIOL SCI, EAST TEX STATE UNIV, 81- *Concurrent Pos:* Vis prof, Mont State Univ, 81. *Mem:* Am Soc Plant Physiologists; AAAS; NY Acad Sci. *Res:* Phosynthesis, carbon fixation; plant cell wall enzymes and their role in plant resistance to fungal attack; horticultural crops, chemistry and physiology of dormancy; cultural practice in CAM plants; value of reiteration in teaching botanical sciences; tropical crop biochemistry. *Mailing Add:* Biol Dept East Tex State Univ Commerce TX 75428

DALGARNO, ALEXANDER, b London, Eng, Jan 5, 28; m 57; c 4. THEORETICAL PHYSICS, ASTROPHYSICS. *Educ:* Univ Col, Univ London, BSc, 47, PhD(physics), 51. *Hon Degrees:* AM, Harvard Univ, 67; DSc, Queen's Univ, Belfast, 80. *Prof Exp:* Prof math, Queen's Univ, Belfast, 51-67; actg dir, Harvard Col Observ, 71-72, prof astron, 67-77, chmn dept, 71-76, PHILLIPS PROF ASTRON, HARVARD UNIV, 67- *Concurrent Pos:* Mem, Smithsonian Astrophys Observ, 67- *Honors & Awards:* Int Acad Quantum Molecular Sci Prize, 67; Hodgkins Medal, Smithsonian Inst, 77; Davisson-Germer Award, Am Phys Soc, 80. *Mem:* Fel Am Acad Arts & Sci; Am Geophys Union; Am Astron Soc; fel Brit Inst Physics & Phys Soc; fel Royal Soc. *Res:* Theoretical atomic and molecular physics; planetary atmospheres; quantum chemistry; astrophysics. *Mailing Add:* Harvard Col Observ Cambridge MA 02138

DALGLEISH, ARTHUR E, b Wilmington, Calif, Aug 14, 20; m 43; c 2. ANATOMY. *Educ:* La Sierra Col, BA, 45; Loma Linda Univ, MS, 60; Stanford Univ, PhD(anat), 64. *Prof Exp:* Instr, 64-65, asst prof, 65-75, ASSOC PROF ANAT, SCH MED, LOMA LINDA UNIV, 75- *Res:* Development of the limbs of the mouse. *Mailing Add:* Dept Anat Sch Med Loma Linda Univ Loma Linda CA 92350

DALGLEISH, ROBERT CAMPBELL, b Paisley, Scotland, Mar 31, 40; US citizen; m 62; c 3. SYSTEMATIC ENTOMOLOGY. *Educ:* San Diego State Col, BS, 62; Cornell Univ, PhD(entom), 67. *Prof Exp:* DIR, EDMUND NILES HUYCK PRESERVE, INC, 66- *Concurrent Pos:* Asst prof biol, Union Col, NY, 69-74; secy-treas, Orgn of Inland Biol Field Stas, 69-73, ed Newslett, 77-79; mem bd gov, Am Inst Biol Sci, 73-79. *Mem:* AAAS; Royal Entom Soc London; Entom Soc Can; Am Entom Soc; Ecol Soc Am. *Res:* Taxonomy and biology of biting lice. *Mailing Add:* E N Huyck Preserve Inc PO Box 87 Rensselaerville NY 12147

DALIA, FRANK J, b New Orleans, La, Nov 10, 28; m 51; c 4. STRUCTURAL ENGINEERING. *Educ:* Tulane Univ, BS, 49, MS, 52, PhD(econs), 64. *Prof Exp:* Civil engr, F C Gandolfo & Assocs, 49-52; assoc prof, 60-68, PROF CIVIL ENG, TULANE UNIV, 68-; CONSULT ENGR, 55- *Mem:* Am Soc Civil Engrs; Nat Soc Prof Engrs. *Res:* Prestressed concrete; engineering economics. *Mailing Add:* Dept of Civil Eng Tulane Univ New Orleans LA 70118

DALINS, ILMARS, b Aizviki, Latvia, Apr 10, 27; US citizen; c 2. SURFACE PHYSICS, SEISMOLOGY. *Educ:* Tex Lutheran Col, BA, 52; Univ Tex, Austin, MA, 53; Univ Cincinnati, PhD(appl sci), 56. *Prof Exp:* Sr electronics scientist dielec mat, Antenna & Radome Group, NAm Aviation Inc, 56; elec propulsion & surface sci, Appl Res, Flight Propulsion Lab, Gen Elec Co,

56-58; sr staff scientist elec propulsion & surface physics, Appl Res, Astronaut Div, Gen Dynamics Corp, 58-60; PHYSICIST SURFACE SCI & SEISMOL, SPACE SCI LAB, MARSHALL SPACE FLIGHT CTR, NASA, 60- *Mem:* Am Inst Physics; Sigma Xi; Inst Electronics & Elec Engrs. *Res:* Surface science of semiconductors (infra-red detector materials) and metals, including molten state (surface science of liquids) for material processing in space applications, solar energy conversion and microelectronics; acoustic-seismic resonance effects produced by rockets (space shuttle) and other atmospheric noise sources. *Mailing Add:* Space Sci Lab Code ES 71 Marshall Space Flight Ctr NASA Huntsville AL 35812

D'ALISA, ROSE M, b Savona, Italy, Mar 14, 48; US citizen. IMMUNOLOGY, CELL BIOLOGY. *Educ:* Lehman Col, AB, 69; Columbia Univ, MS, 74, PhD(microbiol), 75. *Prof Exp:* Fac fel virol, Rockefeller Univ, 75-78; res assoc immunol, Columbia Univ, 78-81; SR RES SCIENTIST, REVLON HEALTH CARE GROUP, 81- *Mem:* Sigma Xi; NY Acad Sci. *Res:* Cellular biology and physiology; immunochemistry; virology. *Mailing Add:* 2430 Lurting Ave Bronx NY 10469

DALLA, RONALD HAROLD, b Silverton, Colo, Mar 7, 42; m 62; c 3. ALGEBRA. *Educ:* Ft Lewis Col, BA, 64; Univ Wyo, MS, 66, PhD(math), 71; Wash State Univ, MEd, 76. *Prof Exp:* Instr, Colo State Univ, 66-67 & Univ Wyo, 67-70; asst prof, 70-74, assoc prof, 74-78, PROF MATH, EASTERN WASH UNIV, 78-, CHMN, DEPT MATH & COMPUT SCI, 78- *Mem:* Am Math Soc; Math Asn Am; Nat Coun Teachers Math. *Res:* Counting the number of solutions of matric equations over finite fields; finding a canonical form for orthogonal similarity of matrices over finite fields. *Mailing Add:* Dept of Math Eastern Wash Univ Cheney WA 99004

DALLA BETTA, RALPH A, b Craig, Colo, Mar 7, 45. SURFACE CHEMISTRY. *Educ:* Colo Col, BS, 67; Stanford Univ, PhD(phys chem), 72. *Prof Exp:* Res scientist, Sci Res Staff, Ford Motor Co, 71-75; VPRES, CATALYTICA ASSOCS, 76-; RES ASSOC, DEPT CHEM ENG, STANFORD UNIV, 76- *Mem:* Am Chem Soc; NAm Catalysis Soc. *Res:* Catalysis and surface chemistry; catalytic automotive pollution control; adsorption on and infrared spectroscopy of supported metals and zeolites; kinetics of methane synthesis and catalyst deactivation and poisoning; process development and catalyst testing. *Mailing Add:* Catalytica Assocs 3255 Scott Blvd 7-E Santa Clara CA 95051

DALLAIRE, LOUIS, b Montreal, Que, Apr 10, 35; m 61; c 4. MEDICINE, MEDICAL GENETICS. *Educ:* Univ Montreal, BA, 54; Laval Univ, MD, 60; McGill Univ, PhD(genetics), 64. *Prof Exp:* Sci dir & dir med genetics lab, Children's Serv, Douglas Hosp, Montreal, 64-70; DIR CLIN MED GENETICS, STE JUSTINE HOSP, 70- *Concurrent Pos:* Assoc scientist, Royal Victoria Hosp, Montreal, 69; consult med genetics, Lakeshore Gen Hosp, Montreal. *Mem:* Am Soc Human Genetics; Soc Pediat Res; Can Soc Clin Invest; Can Pediat Soc; Genetics Soc Can. *Res:* Role of chromosomal aberrations in familial multiple malformations; relationship between autoimmunity and chromosomal non-disjunction; study on the influence of maternal amino acid levels on the amino acid content of amniotic fluid; prenatal diagnosis of genetic diseases; research on the mode of inheritance of multiple malformation syndromes; neural tube defects. *Mailing Add:* Clin Med Genetics Ste Justine Hosp Montreal PQ H3T 1C5 Can

DALLA LANA, I(VO) G(IOVANNI), b Trail, BC, July 5, 26; m 56; c 5. CHEMICAL ENGINEERING. *Educ:* Univ BC, BASc, 48; Univ Alta, MSc, 53; Univ Minn, PhD(chem eng), 58. *Prof Exp:* Develop engr, Consol Mining & Smelting Co, 48-51; instr, 52-53, from asst prof to assoc prof, 58-68, PROF CHEM ENG, UNIV ALBERTA, 68- *Mem:* Am Inst Chem Engrs; fel Chem Inst Can. *Res:* Kinetics and heterogeneous catalysis; applications of IR spectroscopy; surface chemistry; chemical economics and design. *Mailing Add:* Dept of Chem & Petrol Eng Univ of Alta Edmonton AB T6G 2E1 Can

DALLAM, RICHARD DUNCAN, b Kansas City, Mo, Dec 12, 25; m 51; c 2. BIOCHEMISTRY. *Educ:* Univ Mo, AB, 48, MA, 50, PhD(biochem), 52. *Prof Exp:* Res assoc biochem, Univ Mo, 52-53; from instr to assoc prof, 53-68, PROF BIOCHEM, SCH MED, UNIV LOUISVILLE, 68- *Concurrent Pos:* Estab investr, Am Heart Asn, 60-65. *Mem:* Am Soc Biol Chem; Biophys Soc. *Res:* Oxidation phosphorylation; chemical fraction of mammalian spermatozoa and cellular particulates; cytochemistry of mitochondria; lipoproteins related to enzyme systems; vitamin K; metabolism of dietary sulfates; acetate metabolism. *Mailing Add:* Dept of Biochem Sch of Med Univ of Louisville Louisville KY 40201

DALLDORF, FREDERIC GILBERT, b New York, NY, Mar 12, 32; m 56; c 3. PATHOLOGY. *Educ:* Bowdoin Col, BA, 54; Cornell Univ, MD, 58; Am Bd Path, cert anat & clin path, 65. *Prof Exp:* Intern, path, New York Hosp, 58-59, resident, 59-60; resident, NC Mem Hosp, Chapel Hill, 60-63; projs coordr, Path Div, US Army Biol Labs, Ft Detrick, Md, 63-65; from asst prof to assoc prof, 65-73, PROF PATH, SCH MED, UNIV NC, CHAPEL HILL, 73-, COURSE DIR GEN PATH, 65- *Concurrent Pos:* NIH grant, 60-63; med dir blood bank, NC Mem Hosp, 65-66 & autopsy serv, 66- *Mem:* Am Soc Path. *Res:* Mechanisms of disease; natural history of rheumatic heart disease; endocrinologic aspects of arteriosclerotic vascular disease in man; mechanisms of shock and death in bacterial septicemias; capillary permeability and bacterial toxins. *Mailing Add:* Dept Path Univ NC Chapel Hill NC 27514

DALLDORF, GILBERT, pathology, deceased

DALLEY, ARTHUR FREDERICK, II, b Rupert, Idaho, Jan 28, 48; m 69; c 2. GROSS ANATOMY, MORPHOLOGY. *Educ:* Univ Utah, BS, 70, PhD(anat), 75. *Prof Exp:* ASST PROF ANAT, SCH MED, CREIGHTON UNIV, 74- *Mem:* Am Soc Zoologists; Amm Inst Biol Sci; Am Asn Univ Professors. *Res:* Comparative morphology; micro-anatomy; ultrastructure and morphogenesis of vascular and microcirculatory systems, emphasizing venous plexuses sinusoidal structures, arteriovenous anastomoses and lymphaticovenous communications. *Mailing Add:* Dept of Anat Sch of Med Creighton Univ Omaha NE 68178

DALLEY, JOSEPH W(INTHROP), b Aberdeen, Idaho, Aug 12, 18; m 43; c 5. ENGINEERING MECHANICS, AERONAUTICAL ENGINEERING. *Educ:* Univ Tex, BS, 47, MS, 51, PhD(eng mech), 59. *Prof Exp:* Stress analyst, McDonnell Aircraft Corp, 47-48; instr mech eng, Univ Tex, Austin, 48-49, instr eng mech, 49-51, asst prof aeronaut eng, 51-59; prof & head, Dept Aeronaut Eng, Univ Wichita, 59-60; prof eng mech & head dept, 60-70, prof aerospace & eng mech, 70-73, ASSOC DEAN, COL ENG, UNIV TEX, ARLINGTON, 73- *Concurrent Pos:* Res engr, Defense Res Lab, Univ Tex, Austin, 48-59; consult, Boeing Aircraft Co, 59-60 & LTV Vought Aeronaut, 60-77. *Mem:* Am Inst Aeronaut & Astronaut; fel Soc Exp Stress Anal (pres, 75-76); Am Soc Eng Educ; Sigma Xi; Nat Soc Prof Engrs. *Res:* Experimental mechanics; aircraft structures; structural dynamics; aeroelasticity. *Mailing Add:* Off of Dean of Eng Eng Bldg 204 Univ of Tex Arlington TX 76019

D'ALLI, SEBASTIAN J(OHN), b Messina, Italy, July 7, 21; US citizen; m 41; c 3. AEROSPACE ENGINEERING & TECHNOLOGY. *Educ:* Polytech Inst Brooklyn, BAeE, 50; Brevard Col, MS, 61. *Prof Exp:* Test engr rocket propulsion, NAm Aviation, Inc, 51-52; field rep, Northrop Aeronaut Inst, 52-54; supvr interceptor missile launching, Boeing Co, 54-59; sect chief re-entry vehicles, Avco-Res & Advan Develop Div, 59-62; staff scientist missile opers, Chrysler Corp, 63-68; prog-proj rep, Space Div, NAm Rockwell Corp, 68-70; prof engr scientist, 70-71; county engr, 71-76, exec dir civil defense & dir resource recovery, 76-80, EXEC DIR CIVIL DEFENSE, SARASOTA COUNTY, FLA, 80- *Concurrent Pos:* Vpres & consult, Tanner Thomson Corp, 59-63; instr Brevard Eng Col, 58-67, chmn dept space technol, 61-67. *Res:* Liquid propellant and variable thrust rocket propulsion systems; low emission combustion engineering and liquid cooled beryllium mirrors for reflecting high energy laser beams. *Mailing Add:* 2405 Ixora Ave Sarasota FL 33580

DALLMAN, PETER R, b Berlin, Ger, Nov 19, 29; US citizen; m 59; c 3. PEDIATRICS, HEMATOLOGY. *Educ:* Dartmouth Col, BA, 51; Harvard Med Sch, MD, 54. *Prof Exp:* From instr to asst prof pediat, Stanford Univ, 63-68; asst prof, 68-70, assoc prof, 70-76, PROF PEDIAT, SCH MED, UNIV CALIF, SAN FRANCISCO, 76- *Concurrent Pos:* NIH award, 66-; res biochem, Wenner-Gren Inst, Stockholm, 67-68. *Mem:* AAAS; Am Pediat Soc; Soc Pediat Res; Am Acad Pediat. *Res:* Nutritional anemias; iron metabolism. *Mailing Add:* Dept of Pediat Sch of Med Univ of Calif San Francisco CA 94143

DALLMEYER, R DAVID, b St Louis, Mo, Feb 8, 44; m 75. GEOCHRONOLOGY. *Educ:* Long Island Univ, BS, 67; State Univ NY, Stony Brook, MS, 69, PhD(geol), 72. *Prof Exp:* Asst prof geol, 72-76, MEM FAC, UNIV GA, 76- *Mem:* Geol Soc Am; Am Geophys Union. *Res:* Thermal and deformational evolution of metamorphic terranes; emphasis on chronologic development of orogenic events and their interactions. *Mailing Add:* Dept of Geol Univ of Ga Athens GA 30602

DALLON, DALE SHERMAN, b Boulder City, Nev, Aug 28, 34; m 57; c 4. PRODUCT DEVELOPMENT, MANUFACTORING MANAGEMENT. *Educ:* Univ Utah, BS, 57, PhD(chem eng), 67. *Prof Exp:* Sr res chemist photographic sci, Color Photog Div, 67-69, lab head color physics & eng, 69-73, supvr personnel develop, Admin Div, 73-76, PHOTO CHEM DIV, KODAK RES LAB, 76- *Mailing Add:* 73 Pine Valley Dr Rochester NY 14626

DALLOS, ANDRAS, b Szeged, Hungary, Apr 25, 21; m 47; c 2. ELECTRONIC PHYSICS. *Educ:* Univ Budapest, PhD(electron multiplier), 48; Hungarian Acad Sci, Cand Tech Sci, 62, Dr Tech Sci, 67. *Prof Exp:* Scientist electron tubes, Tungsram Res Lab, Budapest, Hungary, 45-50; dept head electron & vacuum devices, Res Inst Telecommun, Budapest, 51-68; sci adv, Tungsram Res Lab, Budapest, 68-70; SR RES & DEVELOP PHYSICIST, RAYTHEON CO, 73- *Concurrent Pos:* Vis scientist, Univ Ill, Urbana, 64-65; chief tech adv, UNESCO, Univ Islamabad, Pakistan, 70-73. *Honors & Awards:* Kossuth Prize, Hungarian Govt, 55. *Mem:* Sr mem Inst Elec & Electronics Engrs; Soc Info Display. *Res:* Electrochromism in solids as a passive electro-optical transducer for matrix addressed flat panel displays; high current density cathodes for displays; electron beam litography. *Mailing Add:* Raytheon Co 465 Centre Quincy MA 02169

DALLOS, PETER JOHN, b Budapest, Hungary, Nov 26, 34; US citizen; m 77; c 1. NEUROBIOLOGY, BIOPHYSICS. *Educ:* Ill Inst Technol, BS, 58; Northwestern Univ, MS, 59, PhD(elec eng), 62. *Prof Exp:* Asst res engr, Am Mach & Foundry Co, 59, consult engr, Mech Res Div, 59-60; from asst prof to assoc prof audiol, 62-69, PROF AUDIOL & ELEC ENG & OTOLARYNGOL, NORTHWESTERN UNIV, EVANSTON, 69-, PROF & CHMN, DEPT NEUROBIOL & PHYSIOL, 81- *Concurrent Pos:* Mem comt hearing bioacoust & biomech, Nat Res Coun-Nat Acad Sci, 67-; mem commun dis res training comt, Nat Inst Neurol Dis & Stroke, 69-73; vis scientist, Karolinska Inst, Stockholm, Sweden, 77-78; assoc ed, Hearing Res, 77-79; Guggenheim fel, 77. *Honors & Awards:* 12th Ann Beltone Award Hearing Res. *Mem:* AAAS; fel Acoust Soc Am; Int Soc Audiol; fel Inst Elec & Electronics Engrs; Soc Neurosci. *Res:* Biophysics and physiology of hearing; physiological acoustics; biomedical engineering. *Mailing Add:* Auditory Res Lab Northwestern Univ Evanston IL 60201

DALLY, EDGAR B, b Akron, Ohio, Mar 7, 31; m 54; c 4. RESEARCH INSTRUMENTATION, CATHODES. *Educ:* Miami Univ, BA, 53, MA, 55; Stanford Univ, PhD(high energy physics), 61. *Prof Exp:* Res assoc high energy physics, Hansen Labs, Stanford Univ, 60-61; instr, Physics Inst, Univ Zurich, 61-63; res worker, Inst Nuclear Res, Univ Strasbourg, 63-66; res physicist high energy physics, Hansen Labs, Stanford Univ, 66-68; staff mem, Stanford Linear Accelerator Ctr, 68-70; assoc prof physics, Naval Postgrad Sch, 70-76; mgr accelerator eng, asst mgr res & eng & sr scientist, Radiation Div, Varian Assocs, 76-78, sr scientist & prog mgr labs & process eng, Tube Div, 78-81; MGR DEVELOP, SIEMENS MED LABS, 81- *Concurrent Pos:* Assoc prof, Univ Calif, Los Angeles, 70-71, partic high energy physics exp with Am group, Russian accelerator, Serpukhov, 70-71; mem staff, Fermilab, 74-76. *Mem:* AAAS; Am Phys Soc; NY Acad Sci; Sigma Xi. *Res:* Nuclear and nucleon charge distributions; elementary particle physics. *Mailing Add:* Siemens Med Labs 2404 N Main St Walnut Creek CA 94596

DALLY, JAMES WILLIAM, b Sardis, Ohio, Aug 2, 29; m 55; c 1. MECHANICAL ENGINEERING, MECHANICS. *Educ:* Carnegie Inst Tech, BS, 51, MS, 53; Ill Inst Tech, PhD(mech), 58. *Prof Exp:* Engr in training, Mesta Mach Co, 51-53; assoc res engr, Armour Res Found, 53-55, res engr, 55-57, sr res engr, 58; asst prof mech, Cornell Univ, 58-61; asst dir res, IIT Res Inst, 61-64; prof mech, Ill Inst Technol, 64-71; prof mech eng, Univ Md, College Park, 71-79; DEAN ENG, UNIV RI, 79. *Concurrent Pos:* Adv, NSF, 78-80. *Honors & Awards:* Frocht Award, Soc Exp Stress Anal, 76; William Murray Lectureship Award, Soc Exp Stress Anal, 79. *Mem:* Fel Soc Exp Stress Anal (pres, 71); fel Am Soc Mech Engrs; Am Soc Eng Educ. *Res:* Experimental stress analysis; photoelasticity; fatigue and fracture. *Mailing Add:* Dept Eng Univ RI Kingston RI 02881

DALLY, JESSE LEROY, b Fayette Co, Pa, Sept 3, 23; m 50; c 2. GEOLOGY. *Educ:* WVa Univ, BS, 47; Columbia Univ, MA, 49, PhD(geol), 56. *Prof Exp:* Instr geol, WVa Univ, 49-56; chief paleontologist, Esso Stand, Inc, Turkey, 56-57, supvr cent lab, 57-58; staff geologist, Pan-Am Petrol Corp, Standard Oil Co, Ind, 58-68; vpres, Desanna Corp, 68-78; OWNER, JESSE L DALLY & ASSOC, 78- *Concurrent Pos:* Coop geologist, WVa Geol Surv, 53-56. *Mem:* Geol Soc Am; Soc Econ Paleontologists & Mineralogists; Am Asn Petrol Geologists. *Res:* Stratigraphy; sedimentology; paleontology; basin analysis. *Mailing Add:* 2508 Sinclair Ave Midland TX 79701

DALMAN, G(ISLI) CONRAD, b Winnipeg, Man, Apr 7, 17; US citizen; m 41; c 4. ELECTRICAL ENGINEERING, MICROWAVE ELECTRONICS. *Educ:* City Col New York, BEE, 40; Polytech Inst Brooklyn, MEE, 47, DEE, 49. *Prof Exp:* Lectr elec eng, City Col New York, 52-54; adj prof, Polytech Inst Brooklyn, 53-56; mfg engr electronic tubes, RCA, 40-45; mem tech staff, Bell Tel Labs, 45-47; sect head microwave tubes, Sperry Gyroscope Co, 47-56; dir, Sch Elec Eng, 75-80, PROF ELEC ENG, CORNELL UNIV, 56- *Concurrent Pos:* Consult, Electronic Tube Div, Westinghouse Elec Corp, 56-62, Aeronaut Lab, Cornell Univ, 56-57 & TRW, 80-81; consult & founder, Cayuga Assoc Inc. *Honors & Awards:* Cert Distinction, Polytech Inst Brooklyn, 57. *Mem:* Fel AAAS; fel Inst Elec & Electronics Engrs; Sigma Xi. *Res:* Electron devices; solid state microwave and millimeter wave devices; electrical noise problems; microwave subsystems; electrical engineering education; physical electronics. *Mailing Add:* 506 Hanshaw Rd Ithaca NY 14850

DALMAN, GARY, b Grandville, Mich, Oct 1, 36; m 58; c 3. ORGANIC CHEMISTRY. *Educ:* Hope Col, BA, 58; Okla State Univ, PhD(reactions of mercaptans), 63. *Prof Exp:* Res chemist, 62-67, proj leader, Benzene Res Lab, 67-69, group leader, Org Chem Prod Res Dept, 69-70, res mgr, 70-73, res mgr, Western Div Res Labs, 73-79, LAB DIR, WESTERN DIV RES & DEVELOP, DOW CHEM CO, 79- *Mem:* Am Chem Soc. *Mailing Add:* Dow Chem Co PO Box 1398 Pittsburg CA 94565

DALMASSO, AGUSTIN PASCUAL, b Cordoba, Arg, Apr 15, 33; m 60; c 3. MEDICINE, IMMUNOLOGY. *Educ:* Univ Cordoba, MD, 58, DrMedS, 63. *Prof Exp:* Instr physiol, Univ Cordoba, 58-60; head sect immunol, Inst Med Res, Univ Buenos Aires, 66-70; assoc prof, 70-74, PROF LAB MED & PATH, MED SCH, UNIV MINN, MINNEAPOLIS, 74- *Concurrent Pos:* Res fel, Univ Minn, 60-63; res fel immunol, Scripps Clin & Res Found, 63-66; mem staff, Vet Admin Hosp, Minneapolis, 70- *Mem:* Am Asn Immunol; Am Soc Exp Path. *Res:* Role of the thymus in immunology; chemistry and biology of the complement system and of cell membranes. *Mailing Add:* Vet Admin Hosp Minneapolis MN 55417

DALMAT, HERBERT THEODORE, b New York, NY, June 5, 19; m 47; c 2. PUBLIC HEALTH ADMINISTRATION. *Educ:* City Col New York, BS, 39; Iowa State Univ, MS, 41; George Washington Univ, PhD, 57. *Prof Exp:* High sch teacher, NY, 38-39; aide, Exp Sta, Iowa State Univ, 40-41; instr med entom & parasitol, Cornell Univ, 42-43; scientist, Lab Trop Dis, NIH, 47-58, scientist, Lab Trop Virol, 58-60, res grants coodr, Nat Inst Neurol Dis & Blindness, 60-62, asst chief, Latin Am Off, Rio de Janeiro, Brazil, 62-65, chief res & training grants br, Div Air Pollution, USPHS, 65-67, chief off res grants, Nat Ctr Air Pollution Control, 67-68, spec asst to comnr, Nat Air Pollution Control Admin, US Dept Health, Educ & Welfare, 68; dep chief health & population div, Latin Am Bur, AID, US Dept State, 69-71, div health, 71-72; asst dir deids, Div Int Health Prog, Am Pub Health Asn, 72-80; INDEPENDENT CONSULT INT HEALTH, 80- *Concurrent Pos:* Med entomologist & chief co-op onchoceriasis proj, Pan-Am Sanit Bur-USPHS, Guatemala, Cent Am, 47-53; trustee, Thomas Say Found, 58-63. *Mem:* AAAS; Int Health Soc US; Entom Soc Am; Am Soc Parasitol; Am Soc Trop Med & Hyg. *Res:* Arthropod transmission of parasitic and virus disease; virus tumors; onchocerciasis; international health and research, especially Latin America; research administration; population; family planning. *Mailing Add:* 3900 Watson Pl NW Washington DC 20016

DALPE, YOLANDE, b Waterloo, Que, Dec 19, 48. MYCOLOGY, MYCORRHIZAS. *Educ:* Montreal Univ, BSc, 72, MSc, 75; Univ Paul Sabatier, Toulouse, France, DSc, 81. *Prof Exp:* MYCOLOGIST & TAXONOMIST, BIOSYST RES INST AGR CAN, 81- *Mem:* Can Bot Asn; Asn Can Fr Pour L'avan Des Sci. *Res:* The physiology of some species of the genus Ceratocystis, their nutrition, vitamin deficiency and lipid physiology; mycorrhizas; mainly endomycorrhizas, their collection, their production in vitro and identification. *Mailing Add:* Biosyst Res Inst Saunders Bldg Exp Farm Ottawa ON K1A 0C6 Can

DALQUEST, WALTER WOELBERG, b Seattle, Wash, Sept 11, 17; m 40; c 1. VERTEBRATE ZOOLOGY. *Educ:* Univ Wash, BS, 40, MS, 41; Univ La, PhD(zool), 51. *Prof Exp:* Res assoc mammals, Mus Natural Hist, Kans, 45-49; fel zool, Univ La, 49-51, asst biochem, 51-52; PROF BIOL, MIDWESTERN UNIV, 52-; AQUATIC BIOLOGIST, STATE GAME & FISH COMN, TEX, 53- *Mem:* Am Soc Mammalogists; Soc Syst Zool. *Res:* Mammals and fishes. *Mailing Add:* Dept of Biol Midwestern Univ Wichita Falls TX 76308

DALRYMPLE, DAVID LAWRENCE, b Fredericktown, Ohio, Oct 26, 40. SCIENTIFIC COMPUTER APPLICATIONS. *Educ:* Col Wooster, AB, 62; Univ Vt, PhD(org chem), 66. *Prof Exp:* NSF fel, Harvard Univ, 66-67, res fel, 67-68; asst prof chem, Univ Del, 68-74, nuclear magnetic resonance spectroscopist, 75-76; MEM STAFF SOFTWARE DEVELOP, NICOLET MAGNETICS, 76- *Mem:* AAAS; Am Chem Soc; Sigma Xi. *Res:* Nuclear magnetic resonance spectroscopy; applications of computers in chemistry. *Mailing Add:* 1180 Reed Ave Apt 9 Sunnyvale CA 94086

DALRYMPLE, DESMOND GRANT, b May 6, 38; Can citizen; m 65; c 1. MECHANICAL ENGINEERING, NUCLEAR ENGINEERING. *Educ:* Univ Man, BSc, 60; Univ Sask, MSc, 62; Univ Manchester, PhD(appl mech), 67. *Prof Exp:* Mem staff, Appl Res & Develop, 62-76, mgr, Mech Equip Develop, 76-79, mem staff, Nondestructive Testing, 79-80, DIR, SPEC PROJ DIV, ATOMIC ENERGY CAN LTD, 80-; develop engr eng res, 67-76, BR HEAD MECH ENG DEVELOP, ATOMIC ENERGY OF CAN RES CO, 76- *Mem:* Can Nuclear Soc; Can Soc Nondestructive Testing. *Res:* Out-reactor components; recycle fuel manufacture; equipment development. *Mailing Add:* Chalk River Nuclear Labs Atomic Energy Can Res Co Chalk River ON K0J 1J0 Can

DALRYMPLE, GARY BRENT, b Alhambra, Calif, May 9, 37; m 59; c 3. GEOLOGY. *Educ:* Occidental Col, AB, 59; Univ Calif, Berkeley, PhD(geol), 63. *Prof Exp:* Geologist, Br Theoret Geophys, 63-70, geologist, Br Isotope Geol, 70-81, ASST CHIEF GEOLOGIST, WESTERN REGION, US GEOL SURV, 81- *Concurrent Pos:* Prin investr, Apollo Lunar Samples. *Mem:* Fel Am Geophys Union; fel Geol Soc Am. *Res:* Isotope geology; potassium-argon dating of young volcanic rocks; geochronology of secular variation and of reversals of the earth's magnetic field; thermoluminescence of geologic materials; origin of Pacific Ocean seamounts; origin of Hawaiian Islands. *Mailing Add:* Br of Isotope Geol US Geol Surv 345 Middlefield Rd Menlo Park CA 94025

DALRYMPLE, GLENN VOGT, b Little Rock, Ark, Dec 28, 34; m 55; c 2. MEDICINE, RADIOBIOLOGY. *Educ:* Univ Ark, BS, 56, MD, 58. *Prof Exp:* Resident radiol, Med Ctr, Univ Ark, 59; asst, Med Ctr, Univ Colo, 61-62, resident, 62, instr, 62-63; asst prof, Sch Med, Univ Ark, Little Rock, 65-68, assoc prof, Med Ctr, 68-71, head div nuclear med & radiation biol, 69-73, prof radiol, Depts Radiol, Biomet, Physiol & Biophys, Med Ctr, 71-76, chmn dept radiol, 73-76, prof med physics, 74-76; MEM STAFF RADIOL CONSULT, 76- *Mem:* Am Col Radiol; Soc Nuclear Med; Radiation Res Soc; Radiol Soc NAm; AMA. *Res:* Aspects of radiobiology dealing with the effects of radiation on mammalian cells in culture; effects of radiation on the fetus; mathematical biology and use of computing machinery in biomedical research; clinical radiology and nuclear medicine. *Mailing Add:* Radiol Consult 1100 Med Towers Little Rock AR 72205

DALRYMPLE, JOEL MCKEITH, b Salt Lake City, Utah, June 18, 39; m 66; c 2. VIROLOGY. *Educ:* Univ Utah, BS, 62, MS, 64, PhD(microbiol), 68. *Prof Exp:* Teaching asst microbiol, Univ Utah, 62-68, res assoc virol, 64-68; res virol, Walter Reed Army Inst Res, 68-73, investr med res virol, 73-80; CHIEF, DEPT VIRAL BIOL, VIROL DIV, US ARMY MED RES INST INFECTIOUS DIS, 80- *Concurrent Pos:* Mem, Am Comt Arthropod-borne Viruses, 68-, subcomt interrelationships among catalogued arboviruses, 72- & subcomt appl molecular arbovirol, 75- *Mem:* Am Soc Microbiol; Soc Gen Microbiol; Am Soc Trop Med & Hyg; AAAS; Sigma Xi. *Res:* Biochemical and biophysical investigations of molecular biology of Togavirus antigens and their immunological interactions; ecological and epidemiological investigations of medically important arthropod transmitted viruses. *Mailing Add:* Dept Viral Biol Virol Div US Army Med Res Inst Infectious Dis Frederick MD 21701

DALRYMPLE, ROBERT ANTHONY, b Camp Rucker, Ala, May 30, 45; m 68; c 1. COASTAL ENGINEERING, MARINE SCIENCES. *Educ:* Dartmouth Col, AB, 67; Univ Hawaii, MS, 68; Univ Fla, PhD(coastal & civil eng), 73. *Prof Exp:* Asst eng, Coastal Eng Lab, Univ Fla, 68-71, res assoc, 71-73; asst prof, 73-77, ASSOC PROF CIVIL ENG, UNIV DEL, 77-, COL MARINE STUDIES, 74, INST APPL MATH, 78-, ASST DEAN, COL ENG, 79- *Concurrent Pos:* Consult, Argonne Nat Lab, 77-, dir, Coastal & Offshore Lab, 77- *Mem:* Am Soc Civil Engrs; Am Geophys Union; Sigma Xi. *Res:* Nearshore hydrodynamics and sediment transport on beaches; wave forces on structures. *Mailing Add:* Dept Civil Eng Univ Del Newark DE 19711

DALRYMPLE, ROBERT WALKER, geology, sedimentology, see previous edition

DALRYMPLE, RONALD HOWELL, b Elizabeth, NJ, Nov 16, 43; m 74; c 1. MEAT SCIENCE, MUSCLE BIOLOGY. *Educ:* Del Valley Col, BS, 65; Va Polytech Inst & State Univ, MS, 69; Univ Wis, PhD(animal sci), 72. *Prof Exp:* Vis res scientist meat sci, Fed Inst for Meat Res, Fed Ministry for Nutrit, Agr & Forestry, Ger, 72-74; res scientist, Animal Sci, Agr Div, 74-78, mgr, Animal Prod Develop, Far East Region, 78-81, PRIN SCIENTIST, NUTRIT & PHYSIOL, AM CYANAMID CO, 81- *Mem:* Am Meat Sci Asn; Am Soc Animal Sci; Inst Food Technol; Nutrit Today Soc; Sigma Xi. *Res:* Control of muscle growth and lipid deposition in meat producing animals. *Mailing Add:* Agr Div Am Cyanamid Co PO Box 400 Princeton NJ 08540

DALRYMPLE, STEPHEN HARRIS, b Austin, Tex, Dec 2, 32; m 52; c 4. COMPUTER SCIENCES. *Educ:* Univ Tex, BA, 54, MA, 59. *Prof Exp:* Staff mem nuclear, Los Alamos Sci Lab, 54-60; supvr numerical anal, Autonetics Div, NAm Aviation, 60-65; tech mgr, Planning Res Corp, 65-67; supvr syst anal, Autonetics Div, Rockwell Int, 67-69; dir serv bur, Cent Comput Corp, 69-70; BR MGR COMPUT SCI, McDONNELL DOUGLAS ASTRONAUT CO, 70- *Concurrent Pos:* Fel, AEC, 58. *Mem:* Asn Comput Mach; Inst Elec & Electronics Engrs. *Res:* Computer architecture, microprogramming and emulation; software and firmware tools to aid development of emulations; multiple emulations and operating systems; emulation of unusual architectures. *Mailing Add:* 1332 Arloura Way Tustin CA 92680

DALSKE, HOWARD FREDERICK, pharmacology, see previous edition

DALTERIO, SUSAN LINDA, b Worcester, Mass, July 19, 49. REPRODUCTIVE BIOLOGY, ENDOCRINE PHARMACOLOGY. *Educ:* Boston Univ, BA, 71; Assumption Col, Mass, MA, 76; Tufts Univ, PhD(physiol psychol), 78. *Prof Exp:* Res asst, Worcester Found Exp Biol, 72-78; fel, 78-79, RES ASST PROF, UNIV TEX HEALTH SCI CTR, 79- *Mem:* Soc Study Reproduction. *Res:* Elucidation of the effects of marihuana on the development and/or function of the male reproductive system in mice; studies also involving the role of gonadal steroids in male sexual behavior and the feedback mechanisms controlling the hypothalmic pituitary testicular axis. *Mailing Add:* Dept Obstet & Gynecol Univ Tex Health Sci Ctr San Antonio TX 78284

DALTON, ALBERT JOSEPH, b New London, Conn, Nov 9, 05; m 30; c 3. BIOLOGY. *Educ:* Wesleyan Univ, BS, 27; Harvard Univ, AM, 29, PhD(embryol), 34. *Prof Exp:* Asst biol, Wesleyan Univ, 26-28; tutor, City Col New York, 29-32; asst biol, Harvard Univ, 32-33; instr histol & embryol, Sch Med, Case Western Reserve Univ, 34-38; lectr anat, McGill Univ, 38-41; res fel, 41-42, cytologist, 42-46, prin cytologist, 46-64, chief lab viral carcinogenesis, 64-67, chief viral biol br, 67-70, coordr ultrastruct studies, 70-75, EMER SCIENTIST, NAT CANCER INST, 75- *Mem:* Soc Exp Biol & Med; Am Asn Anat; Am Asn Cancer Res; Am Soc Exp Path; Electron Micros Soc Am. *Res:* Virology; cytogenesis; cytopathology of neoplasia; chemical cytology; electron microscopy. *Mailing Add:* 11916 Reynolds Ave Potomac MD 20854

DALTON, AUGUSTINE IVANHOE, JR, b Richmond, Va, Nov 17, 42; m 65; c 2. PHYSICAL ORGANIC CHEMISTRY, CATALYSIS INDUSTRIAL GASES. *Educ:* Va Mil Inst, BS, 65; Univ SC, PhD(org chem), 72. *Prof Exp:* Res asst new prod develop, Am Brands, 65-66; mem staff chem, US Army Chem Corps, 66-68; Robert A Welch fel, Rich Univ, 72-73; sr res chemist, 73-81, PRIN RES CHEMIST, AIR PROD & CHEM INC, 81- *Mem:* Am Chem Soc; Org Reactions Catalysis Soc; Mat Res Soc; Sigma Xi. *Res:* Catalytic processes; free radical processes; oxidations; peroxide reactions; industrial gases. *Mailing Add:* Air Prod & Chem PO Box 538 Allentown PA 18105

DALTON, CHARLES CHESTER, physics, see previous edition

DALTON, COLIN, b Hull, Eng, July 19, 36; m 62; c 2. BIOCHEMICAL PHARMACOLOGY. *Educ:* Univ Hull, BSc, 60; State Univ NY Buffalo, PhD(biochem pharmacol), 65. *Prof Exp:* Sr biochemist, 65-70, res group chief biochem pharmacol, 70-76, RES PLANNING MGR, HOFFMANN-LA ROCHE INC, 76- *Concurrent Pos:* Fel coun on arteriosclerosis, Am Heart Asn, 70. *Mem:* AAAS; Am Soc Pharmacol & Exp Therapeut; Am Heart Asn. *Res:* Mechanism of action of anti-hyperlipidemic and anti-thrombotic drugs; regulation of prostaglandin biosynthesis in different tissues; factors controlling adipose tissue lipolysis; automation of analytical biochemistry procedures. *Mailing Add:* Res Div Hoffmann-La Roche Inc Nutley NJ 07110

DALTON, DAVID ROBERT, b Chicago, Ill, Nov 16, 36; m 58. ORGANIC CHEMISTRY. *Educ:* Northwestern Univ, BA, 57; Univ Calif, Los Angeles, PhD(org chem), 62. *Prof Exp:* Res chemist, Dayton Labs, Monsanto Res Corp, 62-63; instr chem & fel, Ohio State Univ, 64-65; from asst prof to assoc prof, 65-73, PROF CHEM, TEMPLE UNIV, 73- *Concurrent Pos:* NIH fels, 62- *Mem:* AAAS; Am Chem Soc; Royal Soc Chem. *Res:* Isolation, identification and synthesis of natural products; reaction mechanisms. *Mailing Add:* 143 Gulph Hills Rd Radnor PA 19087

DALTON, G(EORGE) RONALD, b Detroit, Mich, Sept 28, 32; m 58; c 3. NUCLEAR ENGINEERING. *Educ:* Univ Mich, BS, 54, PhD(nuclear eng), 60. *Prof Exp:* From asst prof to assoc prof, 60-68, actg chmn, Dept Nuclear Eng Sci, 68-69, PROF NUCLEAR ENG, UNIV FLA, 68- *Concurrent Pos:* Ford Found eng resident, Atomic Power Div, Westinghouse Elec Corp, 65-66. *Mem:* Am Soc Eng Educ; Am Nuclear Soc. *Res:* Nuclear systems and numerical analysis; digital computer graphics; neutron transport theory; theory of radiation detection. *Mailing Add:* Dept Nuclear Eng Sci Univ Fla Gainesville FL 32601

DALTON, HARRY P, b Holyoke, Mass, Sept 16, 29; m 53; c 8. BIOCHEMISTRY, MICROBIOLOGY. *Educ:* Am Int Col, AB, 52; Univ Mass, MS, 56, PhD(microbiol, biochem), 62. *Prof Exp:* Asst prof biochem, Hampden Col Pharm, 59-62; chief microbiologist & teaching supvr, Holyoke Hosp, Mass, 56-62 & Montefiore Hosp, 62-66; assoc prof clin path, 66-76, PROF CLIN PATH & MICROBIOL, MED COL VA, 76- *Concurrent Pos:* Res grants, 63-71; asst prof, Med Col Va & Dent Sch, Univ Pittsburgh, 65-66. *Mem:* AAAS; Am Soc Microbiol; Am Soc Med Technol; Am Burn Soc; NY Acad Sci. *Res:* Medical microbiology; mycoplasma; bacterial L-forms; diagnostics systems for rapid identification. *Mailing Add:* Dept of Path Med Col of Va Richmond VA 23298

DALTON, HOWARD CLARK, b Brooklyn, NY, Aug 7, 15; m 48. EMBRYOLOGY, GENETICS. *Educ:* Wesleyan Univ, AB, 36, AM, 37; Stanford Univ, PhD(biol), 40. *Prof Exp:* Instr zool, Univ Rochester, 40-41; instr, biol, Brown Univ, 46-47; asst prof, Bates Col, 47-48; fel, Genetics Dept, Carnegie Inst, 48-50; from asst prof to assoc prof, 50-61, prof & chmn dept, Univ Col, 61-67; prof, 67-75, EMER PROF BIOL, PA STATE UNIV, 75- *Mem:* Am Soc Zool; Am Soc Develop Biol (treas, 59-62); Am Asn Anat; Am Soc Naturalists (Secy, 65-68); Int Soc Develop Biol. *Res:* Development of pigment patterns, genetic control of pigment development. *Mailing Add:* RR 1 Box 293-E4 Kapaa HI 96746

DALTON, JACK L, b Hominy, Okla, July 20, 31; m 53; c 3. BIOCHEMISTRY, ORGANIC CHEMISTRY. *Educ:* Chadron State Col, BS, 53; Kans State Univ, MS, 58. *Prof Exp:* Instr chem, Boise Jr Col, 58-64; assoc prof, 64-70, actg chmn dept, 68-70, PROF CHEM & CHMN DEPT, BOISE STATE UNIV, 71- *Mem:* AAAS. *Res:* Plant waxes; isolation of natural products. *Mailing Add:* Dept Chem Boise State Univ 1910 University Dr Boise ID 83725

DALTON, JAMES CHRISTOPHER, b Corning, NY, Dec 1, 43; m 71; c 1. ORGANIC CHEMISTRY, PHOTOCHEMISTRY. *Educ:* Calif Inst Technol, BS, 65; Columbia Univ, PhD(chem), 70. *Prof Exp:* Asst prof chem, Univ Rochester, 70-77; ASSOC PROF CHEM, BOWLING GREEN STATE UNIV, 77- *Mem:* Am Chem Soc; Royal Soc Chem. *Res:* Organic photochemistry; fluorescence and phosphorescence properties of organic compounds. *Mailing Add:* Dept of Chem Bowling Green State Univ Bowling Green OH 43403

DALTON, JOHN CHARLES, b Clintwood, Va, Apr 11, 31; m 64; c 2. ZOOLOGY, PHYSIOLOGY. *Educ:* Univ Va, BA, 51; Harvard Univ, AM, 52, PhD(biol), 55. *Prof Exp:* From instr to assoc prof biol, Univ Buffalo, 57-62; exec secy, Metab Study Sect, Div Res Grants, NIH, 62-65; asst cheif for rev, Res Grants Rev Br, 65-70, chief prog planning staff, Off Prog Planning & Eval, Bur Health Manpower Educ, 70-72, spec asst to assoc dir, Regional Opers, Bur Health Manpower Educ, 72-73, spec asst to assoc adminr, Opers & Mgt, Health Resources Admin, 74-75, chief planning & eval, Off Prog Develop, Bur Health Manpower, Health Resources Admin, 75-76, dep assoc dir, Prog Activ, Nat Inst Gen Med Sci, 76-78, DIR EXTRAMURAL ACTIV PROG, NAT INST NEUROL & COMMUN DISORDERS & STROKE, NIH, 78- *Res:* Comparative physiology; neurophysiology. *Mailing Add:* Extramural Activ Prog Disorders & Stroke Fed Bldg Rm 1016 Bethesda MD 20014

DALTON, LARRY RAYMOND, b Belpre, Ohio, Apr 25, 43; m 66. CHEMICAL PHYSICS. *Educ:* Mich State Univ, BS, 65, MS, 66; Harvard Univ, AM, 71, PhD(chem), 72. *Prof Exp:* From asst prof to assoc prof chem, Vanderbilt Univ, 71-77; from assoc prof to prof chem, State Univ NY Stony Brook, 77-82; PROF CHEM, CARNEGIE-MELLON UNIV, 82- *Concurrent Pos:* Distinguished consult natural sci, Spring Arbor Col, 71-; consult, Varian Assocs, 71-74, Bruker Physik, 76-77 & IBM, 77-; fel, Alfred P Sloan Found, 74-77; NIH res career develop award, 76-81; res prof biochem, Med Sch, Vanderbilt Univ, 77- *Honors & Awards:* Teacher-Scholar Award, Camille & Henry Dreyfus Found, 75. *Mem:* Am Chem Soc. *Res:* Development of new spectroscopic techniques and application to biomedical research, to the investigation of the dynamics of classical liquids and to the study of solid state organic materials, particularly conducting prolymers. *Mailing Add:* Dept of Chem State Univ NY Stony Brook NY 11794

DALTON, LONNIE GENE, b Carter, Okla, July 20, 34; m 60; c 3. GENETICS, AGRONOMY. *Educ:* Okla State Univ, BS, 56, MS, 57; NC State Univ, PhD(genetics), 65. *Prof Exp:* Asst plant breeding, Okla State Univ, 57; asst genetics, NC State Univ, 65; plant breeder, 65-67, DIR RES, PIONEER SORGHUM CO, 67- *Mem:* Am Soc Agron. *Res:* Accumulation of knowledge, perfection of skills and development of material that leads to a major advance in commercial sorghum hybrids. *Mailing Add:* 301 Kirchwood Dr Plainview TX 79072

DALTON, PATRICK DALY, b Salt Lake City, Utah, Oct 11, 22; m 48; c 3. ECOLOGY, BOTANY. *Educ:* Ariz State Univ, BS, 49; Utah State Univ, MS, 51; Univ Ariz, PhD(plant ecol), 61. *Prof Exp:* Range mgr, Soil Conserv Serv, USDA, Utah, 51-52; range mgr, Bur Land Mgt, US Dept Interior, 52-53; instr, Liahona High Sch, Tonga, 53-55; asst prof agr, biol & phys sci, Church Col Hawaii, 55-58; res assoc range res, Univ Ariz, 58-61; asst prof range mgt, Univ Nev, Reno, 61-62; dir range & forest res, UN Korean Upland Proj, 62-63; pres, Latter-day Saint Mission, Tonga, 63-66; PROF BOT, BRIGHAM YOUNG UNIV, HAWAII CAMPUS LAIE, 66- *Mem:* AAAS; Am Inst Biol Sci; Ecol Soc Am; Bot Soc Am; Am Soc Range Mgt. *Res:* Ecology of Southwestern ranges and Pacific Island. *Mailing Add:* Dept Biol Sci Brigham Young Univ Hawaii Box 46 Laie HI 96762

DALTON, PHILIP BENJAMIN, b New York, NY, July 21, 23; m 44; c 2. ORGANIC CHEMISTRY. *Educ:* Univ Ill, BA, 44; Columbia Univ, MS, 47. *Prof Exp:* Org chemist, Sun Chem Corp, 47-50; tech engr, Colgate-Palmolive Co, 50-54; develop engr, Com Develop Dept, GAF Corp, 54-55, sales engr, Acetylene Chem Dept, 55-58, mgr, 58-61, mkt mgr, 61-63, dir com develop, 63-64, vpres develop, 64-67, vpres photo & repro div, 67, exec vpres, 67-77, pres & chief operating officer, 77-79; PRES, DALTON ASSOCS, 79- *Mem:* Am Chem Soc; Soc Chem Indust; Com Develop Asn; Am Inst Chem. *Res:* Reppe chemistry; reactions of acetylene and aldehydes under high pressure. *Mailing Add:* 263 Cliffside Dr Torrington CT 06790

DALTON, RICHARD LEE, b Wentzville, Mo, Aug 24, 27; m 46; c 5. INORGANIC CHEMISTRY. *Educ:* Cent Col, Mo, AB, 48; Univ Ill, MS, 49, PhD(chem), 51. *Prof Exp:* Res chemist, Indust & Biochem Dept, 51-54, res supvr, 54-65, develop & serv rep, 65-66, prod mgr, 66-68, asst sales mgr, 68-70, asst regional sales mgr, 70-72, com develop mgr, 72-76, vpres mkt, Endo Labs, Inc, 76-80, DIR, PHARMACEUT ADMIN & PLANNING, E I DU PONT DE NEMOURS & CO, INC, 81- *Mem:* Sci Res Soc Am. *Res:* Inorganic complex compounds; inorganic colloids; analytical and agricultural chemistry. *Mailing Add:* E I Du Pont de Nemours & Co 1007 Market St Wilmington DE 19898

DALTON, ROBERT HENNAH, chemistry, deceased

DALTON, ROGER WAYNE, b Sweatman, Miss, Jan 1, 36; m 58; c 3. ANALYTICAL CHEMISTRY, PHYSICAL CHEMISTRY. *Educ:* Delta State Univ, BS, 58; Univ Miss, MS, 60. *Prof Exp:* Lab asst chem, Univ Miss, 58-59; qual control engr rockets, 60-63, develop chemist pyrotechnics, 63-65, res chemist, Allegany Ballistics Lab, 65-67, sr process engr, 67-76, SR TECH ENGR PROPELLANTS, HERCULES, INC, 76-; SCIENTIST, 76- *Concurrent Pos:* Gas chromatographic consult, Hercules, Inc, 67-, liquid chromatographic & anal consult, 74-; comt mem, Joint Army-Navy-Air Force Propellant Characterization Working Group, 69- *Res:* Analytical techniques and process applications pertaining to propellants and explosives; chromatographic techniques. *Mailing Add:* Hercules Inc Radford Army Ammunition Plant Radford VA 24141

DALVEN, RICHARD, b Brooklyn, NY, Sept 3, 31; m 55. SOLID STATE PHYSICS. *Educ:* Columbia Univ, AB, 53, AM, 54; Mass Inst Technol, PhD(chem physics), 58. *Prof Exp:* Mem res staff, Raytheon Corp, 58-62; mem res staff, RCA Labs, 62-71; RES ASSOC & LECTR, DEPT PHYS, UNIV CALIF, BERKELEY, 69-70 & 71- *Mem:* Am Phys Soc. *Res:* Electronic structure of solids, particularly semiconductors with small energy gaps; studies of the electronic structure of the lead salt semiconductors; applications of solid state physics. *Mailing Add:* Dept of Physics Univ of Calif Berkeley CA 94720

DALY, BARTHOLOMEW JOSEPH, b Brooklyn, NY, Jan 3, 29; m 59; c 5. FLUID DYNAMICS. *Educ:* Univ Wyo, BA, 50; Ariz State Univ, MA, 60. *Prof Exp:* Seismologist, Petty Geophys Eng Co, 51-55; geophysicist, Southern Geophys Co, 55-57; party chief, Bible Geophys Co, 57-59; PROJ LEADER NUMERICAL FLUID DYNAMICS, LOS ALAMOS NAT LAB, UNIV CALIF, 60- *Res:* Numerical techniques for calculating compressible and incompressible fluid dynamics. *Mailing Add:* 533 Todd Loop Los Alamos NM 87544

DALY, COLIN HENRY, b Glasgow, Scotland, Aug 22, 40. BIOENGINEERING. *Educ:* Univ Glasgow, BSc Hons, 63; Univ Strathclyde, PhD(bioeng), 66. *Prof Exp:* From asst prof to assoc prof, 67-78, PROF MECH ENG, UNIV WASH, 78- *Concurrent Pos:* Res fel, Ctr for Bioeng, Univ Wash, 66-67; affil, Ctr for Res in Oral Biol, Univ Wash, 70-75. *Mem:* Am Soc Mech Engrs; Inst Mech Eng. *Res:* Biomechanics of the skin and other soft tissues; biomechanics of the oral mucosa and the periodontium. *Mailing Add:* Dept of Mech Eng FU-10 Univ of Wash Seattle WA 98195

DALY, DANIEL FRANCIS, JR, b Brooklyn, NY, Sept 19, 39. ELECTRONICS, SOLID STATE PHYSICS. *Educ:* St Bonaventure Univ, BS, 61; Columbia Univ, MA, 63, PhD(physics), 66. *Prof Exp:* Res asst solid state physics, Columbia Radiation Lab, Columbia Univ, 63-65; res asst, Purdue Univ, 65-66, res assoc, 66-68; MEM TECH STAFF, BELL LABS, 68- *Mem:* Am Phys Soc; Am Asn Physics Teachers. *Res:* Electron paramagnetic resonance; radiation damage in semiconductors; ion implantation; color centers in alkali halides; semiconductor electronics; integrated circuits. *Mailing Add:* Bell Labs Bldg 2 600 Mountain Ave Murray Hill NJ 07974

DALY, DAVID DEROUEN, b St Louis, Mo, Oct 17, 19; m 46; c 4. NEUROLOGY. *Educ:* Stanford Univ, BA, 40; Univ Minn, BS, 42, BM, 44, MD, 45, PhD(neurol), 51; Am Bd Psychiat & Neurol, dipl, 51. *Prof Exp:* Resident neurol, Univ Minn, 45-46, asst, 47-48, instr, 48-49, asst neurol & electroencephalog, Mayo Clin, 49-51, from asst prof to assoc prof neurol, Mayo Found, 56-61; chmn div neurol, Barrow Neurol Inst, Ariz, 61-66; prof, 66-70, SCOTTISH RITE PROF NEUROL, UNIV TEX HEALTH SCI CTR DALLAS, 70-; PROF COMMUN DISORDERS, UNIV TEX, DALLAS, 73- *Mem:* Am Neurol Asn; fel Am Acad Neurol; Soc Clin Neurol (pres, 62); Int League Against Epilepsy (pres, 73-77). *Res:* Electroencephalography; epilepsy; narcolepsy. *Mailing Add:* Dept of Neurol Univ of Tex Health Sci Ctr Dallas TX 75235

DALY, FREDERICK THOMAS, b Kansas City, Mo, Apr 25, 13. MATHEMATICS. *Educ:* St Louis Univ, BS, 35, MS, 38. *Prof Exp:* Instr math, Creighton Prep Sch, 38-41; lectr, St Louis Univ, 41-45; instr, Marquette Univ, 49-50; asst prof, Gonzaga Univ, 52-53; head dept math, 53-80, from assoc prof to prof, 59-80, EMER PROF MATH, REGIS COL, COLO, 80- *Mem:* Am Math Soc; Math Asn Am. *Res:* Number theory; nonlinear differential equations. *Mailing Add:* Dept Math Regis Col 3539 W 50th Parkway Denver CO 80221

DALY, HOWELL VANN, b Dallas, Tex, Oct 30, 33; m 53; c 1. ENTOMOLOGY. *Educ:* Southern Methodist Univ, BS, 53; Univ Kans, MA, 55, PhD(entom), 60. *Prof Exp:* Instr zool, La State Univ, 59-60; from asst prof to assoc prof, 60-71, PROF ENTOM, UNIV CALIF, BERKELEY, 71- *Concurrent Pos:* Res grants, NIH, 62-67 & NSF, 68-75. *Mem:* AAAS; Soc Study Evolution; Soc Syst Zool; fel Royal Entom Soc London; Entomol Soc Am. *Res:* Systematic and evolutionary biology; biosystematics of Apoidea; comparative morphology of Hymenoptera. *Mailing Add:* Div of Entom Univ of Calif Berkeley CA 94720

DALY, JAMES C(AFFREY), b Hartford, Conn, June 10, 38; m 62; c 5. ELECTRICAL ENGINEERING. *Educ:* Univ Conn, BS, 60; Rensselaer Polytech Inst, MEE, 62, PhD(elec eng), 67. *Prof Exp:* Instr elec eng, Rensselaer Polytech Inst, 62-66; mem tech staff, Bell Tel Labs, 66-69; asst prof elec eng, 69-73, ASSOC PROF ELEC ENG, UNIV RI, 73- *Mem:* Inst Elec & Electronics Engrs; Optical Soc Am. *Res:* Optical beam waveguides; electromagnetic wave interactions with solid state plasmas; solar optics; industrial instrumentation. *Mailing Add:* Dept of Elec Eng Univ of RI Kingston RI 02881

DALY, JAMES EDWARD, b Compton, Calif, Mar 18, 48; m 69; c 1. MATHEMATICAL ANALYSIS. *Educ:* Humboldt State Univ, AB, 70; NMex State Univ, PhD(math), 74. *Prof Exp:* Fel math, NMex State Univ, 74-75; vis asst prof math, Univ Ore, 75-76; INSTR DEPT MATH, COL OF THE REDWOODS, 76- *Mem:* Am Math Soc; Math Asn Am. *Res:* Harmonic analysis; local field singular integrals and multipliers. *Mailing Add:* Dept of Math Col of the Redwoods Eureka CA 95501

DALY, JAMES JOSEPH, b Detroit, Mich, Sept 6, 35; m 65; c 3. MEDICAL PARASITOLOGY. *Educ:* Wayne State Univ, BS, 61, MS, 64; La State Univ, New Orleans, PhD(parasitol), 68. *Prof Exp:* Asst prof microbiol, Univ Ark Med Ctr, 68-74, ASSOC PROF MICROBIOL, UNIV ARK MED SCI CAMPUS, 75- *Concurrent Pos:* Fel trop med, Int Ctr Med Res & Training, 71- vis assoc prof, Rockefeller Univ, New York, 77-78. *Mem:* Am Soc Parasitologists; Soc Protozoologists; Wildlife Dis Asn. *Res:* Parasite physiology and biochemistry; protozoology; carbohydrate metabolism of trichomonads; hematozoa of cold-blooded vertebrates; biology of land planaria; sparganosis; C-type viruses of invertebrates and cold-blooded vertebrates. *Mailing Add:* Dept of Microbiol & Immunol Univ of Ark Med Sci Campus Little Rock AR 72201

DALY, JAMES WILLIAM, b Chicago, Ill, Jan 5, 31; m 53; c 3. OBSTETRICS & GYNECOLOGY, ONCOLOGY. *Educ:* Univ Santa Clara, 48-51; Loyola Univ Chicago, MD, 55; Am Bd Obstet & Gynec, dipl, 66 & 76. *Prof Exp:* Intern, St Mary's Hosp, Gary, Ind, 56; mem staff obstet & gynec, US Air Force Hosp, Lockbourne AFB, 57-59, chief prof serv, 58-59; resident obstet & gynec, US Air Force Hosp, San Antonio, Tex, 59-62, chief gynec serv & training officers residency prog, 63-68; assoc prof, 68-77, PROF OBSTET & GYNEC & DIR TUMOR DIV, UNIV FLA, 77- CHIEF GYNEC SERV, 70-; DIR TUMOR CLIN & REGISTRY, SHAND'S TEACHING HOSP & CLINS, 70- *Concurrent Pos:* Fel gynec oncol, Univ Tex M D Anderson Hosp & Tumor Inst, 62-63. *Mem:* AMA; Am Radium Soc; fel Am Col Obstet & Gynec; Soc Gynec Oncol. *Res:* Clinical research in cancer of the female genitalia. *Mailing Add:* Dept of Obstet & Gynec Col of Med Univ of Fla Gainesville FL 32611

DALY, JOHN F, b Jersey City, NJ, June 10, 12; m 41; c 1. OTOLARYNGOLOGY. *Educ:* Fordham Univ, AB, 33; Long Island Col Med, MD, 37. *Prof Exp:* Dir dept otolaryngol, Bellevue Hosp, 47-80, dir otolaryngol, Univ Hosp, 49-80, PROF OTOLARYNGOL & CHMN DEPT SCH MED, NY UNIV, 49- *Concurrent Pos:* Dir Bellevue Hearing & Speech Ctr; consult aural surgeon, NY Eye & Ear Infirmary, 49-; consult, Hackensack Hosp, NJ, 53-, Vet Admin Hosp, Manhattan, NY, Bergen Pines County Hosp, NJ, & Holy Name Hosp, Teaneck, 54-, St Albans Naval Hosp, NY & Phelps Mem Hosp Asn, Tarrytown, 55-; Brookhaven Mem Hosp Asn, Patchogue, 56-, St Joseph's Hosp, Stamford, Conn, 58-, Greenwich Hosp Asn, Conn & Nyack Hosp, NY, 59-, Elizabeth A Horton Mem Hosp, Middletown, 63-, Columbus Hosp, NY, Stamford Hosp, Conn, Speech Rehab Inst, NY & Goldwater Mem Hosp, NY; mem bd dirs, Am Bd Otolaryngol; chmn tech adv comt hearing & speech, Dept Health, New York; mem proj comt, Nat Inst Neurol Dis & Blindness, 64-70; chmn sci rev comt, Deafness Res Found, 64-70, mem, 70-; mem, Am Coun Otolaryngol. *Mem:* AAAS; fel Am Col Surg; Am Laryngol, Rhinol & Otol Soc; fel Am Laryngol Asn; fel Am Acad Ophthal & Otolaryngol (vpres, 68-69). *Res:* Audiology; otology; laryngology. *Mailing Add:* Postgrad Med Sch NY Univ New York NY 10016

DALY, JOHN FRANCIS, b Kansas City, Mo, Dec 27, 16. ALGEBRA. *Educ:* St Louis Univ, AB, 40, MS, 43. *Prof Exp:* Teacher pvt sch, 43-45; from asst prof to assoc prof, 53-70, PROF MATH, ST LOUIS UNIV, 70- *Mem:* Am Math Soc; Am Soc Eng Educ; Math Asn Am; Sigma Xi. *Res:* Modern abstract algebra; topology; algebraic topology; history of mathematics. *Mailing Add:* Col Arts & Sci St Louis Univ 221 N Grand Ave St Louis MO 63103

DALY, JOHN JOSEPH, JR, b St Paul, Minn, Aug 7, 26; m 50; c 3. ORGANIC CHEMISTRY. *Educ:* Col St Thomas, BS, 50; Univ Md, PhD, 54. *Prof Exp:* Res chemist, 54-61, develop specialist, 62-68, tech assoc, 68-69, mgr tech & mkt develop, 69-75, tech mgr aerosol, 75-78, TECH MGR SOLVENTS & DEVELOP, FREON PROD DIV, E I DU PONT DE NEMOURS CO, INC, 78- *Mem:* Am Chem Soc; Chem Specialties Mfrs Asn. *Res:* Organic intermediates; dyes; textile chemicals; synthetic lubricants and additives; fluorine chemistry and fluorocarbon development; pyrolysis of esters. *Mailing Add:* 4658 Dartmoor Dr Liftwood Estates Wilmington DE 19803

DALY, JOHN MATTHEW, b Lexington, Ky, Aug 1, 25; m 53; c 5. INORGANIC CHEMISTRY. *Educ:* Xavier Univ, Ohio, BS, 50, MS, 51; Univ Notre Dame, PhD(chem), 58. *Prof Exp:* Res & develop, Kaiser-Frazer Corp, 51-52; chemist, E I du Pont de Nemours & Co, Inc, 52-53; from asst prof to assoc prof, 53-64, PROF CHEM, BELLARMINE COL, 64-, CHMN DEPT, 59- *Mem:* AAAS; Am Chem Soc. *Res:* Stability of chelates compounds; effect of metal ions on organic reaction mechanisms; pk values or organic acids and bases; benzyne intermediates. *Mailing Add:* Dept of Chem Bellarmine Col Louisville KY 40205

DALY, JOHN WILLIAM, b Portland, Ore, June 8, 33. NEUROCHEMISTRY, NATURAL PRODUCTS CHEMISTRY. *Educ:* Ore State Col, BS, 54, MA, 56; Stanford Univ, PhD(org chem), 58. *Prof Exp:* Res biochemist, Nat Inst Arthritis & Metab Dis, 60-69, CHIEF, LAB BIOORG CHEM, NAT INST ARTHRITIS, METAB & DIGESTIVE DIS, NIH, 69- *Honors & Awards:* Super Serv Award, Dept Health, Educ & Welfare, 72; Hillebrand Prize, Am Chem Soc, 77. *Mem:* AAAS; Am Chem Soc; Int Soc Neurochemists; Am Soc Pharmacol & Exp Therapeut. *Res:* Natural products and structure elucidation; biochemistry and pharmacology biogenic amines; cyclic nucleotides and other neuroactive compounds; metabolic transformations. *Mailing Add:* Lab Bioorg Chem Bldg 4 Nat Inst Arthritis Metab & Digest Dis NIH Bethesda MD 20014

DALY, JOSEPH MICHAEL, b Hoboken, NJ, Apr 9, 22; m 51; c 2. PLANT BIOCHEMISTRY, PLANT PHYSIOLOGY. *Educ:* RI State Col, BS, 44; Univ Minn, MS, 47, PhD(plant physiol), 52. *Prof Exp:* From asst to instr plant path, Univ Minn, 44-50, res fel bot, 50-51; MacMillan res fel, 51-52; asst prof biol, Univ Notre Dame, 52-55; from asst prof to assoc prof bot, 55-63, assoc plant pathologist, Exp Sta, 57-63, prof bot & biochem, Univ, 63-66, C Petrus Peterson prof biochem & nutrit, 66-76, MEM FAC LIFE SCI, UNIV NEBR, LINCOLN, 76- *Mem:* AAAS; Am Phytopath Soc; Am Soc Plant Physiol. *Res:* Biochemistry of disease resistance and microorganisms; biochemistry and physiology of plant diseases. *Mailing Add:* Dept of Biochem & Nutrit Univ of Nebr Lincoln NE 68588

DALY, KEVIN RICHARD, b San Francisco, Calif, May 31, 31; m 62; c 3. GENETICS. *Educ:* Univ Calif, Davis, BS, 53; Cornell Univ, PhD(genetics), 58. *Prof Exp:* Asst genetics, Cornell Univ, 54-56; USPHS res fel, 58-60; asst prof, 60-64, ASSOC PROF BIOL, CALIF STATE UNIV, NORTHRIDGE, 64- *Concurrent Pos:* NIH spec res fel, 70-71. *Mem:* Soc Study Evolution; Genetics Soc Am. *Res:* Quantitative genetics. *Mailing Add:* Dept of Biol Calif State Univ Northridge CA 91330

DALY, MARIE MAYNARD, b New York NY, Apr 16, 21; m 61. BIOCHEMISTRY. *Educ:* Queens Col, NY, BS, 42; NY Univ, MS, 43; Columbia Univ, PhD(chem), 47. *Prof Exp:* Tutor, Queens Col, NY, 43-44; instr, Howard Univ, 47-48; asst, Rockefeller Inst, 51-55; assoc, Columbia Univ Res Serv, Goldwater Mem Hosp, 55-59; asst prof biochem, 60-71, ASSOC PROF BIOCHEM & MED, ALBERT EINSTEIN COL MED, 71- *Concurrent Pos:* Am Cancer Soc fel, Rockefeller Inst, 48-51; estab investr, Am Heart Asn, 58-63; career scientist, Health Res Coun, City of New York, 62-72; fel coun arteriosclerosis, Am Heart Asn. *Mem:* Fel AAAS; Am Chem Soc; fel NY Acad Sci; Am Soc Biol Chem. *Res:* Lipids; arterial smooth muscle. *Mailing Add:* Dept Biochem Albert Einstein Col Med Yeshiva Univ 1300 Morris Park Ave Bronx NY 10461

DALY, PATRICK JOSEPH, b Mullingar, Ireland, Feb 2, 33; m 62; c 3. NUCLEAR CHEMISTRY. *Educ:* Nat Univ Ireland, BSc, 56, MSc, 59; Oxford Univ, DPhil(nuclear chem), 63. *Prof Exp:* From instr to assoc prof, 63-76, PROF CHEM, PURDUE UNIV, WEST LAFAYETTE UNIV, 70- *Mem:* Am Phys Soc. *Res:* Nuclear reactions and spectroscopy. *Mailing Add:* Dept of Chem Purdue Univ West Lafayette IN 47907

DALY, PATRICK WILLIAM, b Toronto, On, May 22, 47; m 68. MAGNETOSPHERIC PHYSICS. *Educ:* Bishop's Univ, BSc, 68; Univ BC, PhD(physics), 73. *Prof Exp:* Fel low temperature, Clarendon Lab, Oxford Univ, Eng, 73-75; res assoc magnetosphere, Nat Res Coun Can, 75-78; MPG STIPENDIAT MAGNETOSPHERE, MAC PLANCK INST AERONOMY, GER, 78- *Mem:* Am Geophys Union. *Res:* Particles and fields in the magnetosphere, especially in auroras and dayside magnetopause; solar wind particles and fields. *Mailing Add:* Max Planck Inst Aeronomy D-3411 Katlenburg Lindau 3 Germany, Federal Republic of

DALY, ROBERT E, b Cambridge, Mass, Mar 1, 37; m 66. ANALYTICAL CHEMISTRY. *Educ:* Mass Col Pharm, BS, 61, MS, 63; Purdue Univ, PhD(med anal chem), 68. *Prof Exp:* From scientist to sr scientist, 67-73, sr res assoc, 73-75, ASSOC DIR, WARNER-LAMBERT RES INST, 75- *Mem:* Am Chem Soc. *Res:* Application of electroanalytic and/or spectroscopic methods to analysis of specific medicaments in complex pharmaceutical formulations. *Mailing Add:* 283 Washington Valley Rd Randolph NJ 07869

DALY, ROBERT FRANCIS, b Chicago, Ill, Oct 23, 32; m 71; c 4. TELECOMMUNICATIONS SCIENCES, COMPUTER SCIENCE. *Educ:* Univ Ill, BS, 56; Univ Southern Calif, MS, 58; Stanford Univ, PhD(elec eng), 66. *Prof Exp:* Res engr telecommun, Stanford Res Inst, 59-65, sr res engr, 65-68, dir telecommun, Commun Technol Lab, 68-70, dir telecommun dept, 70-72 & telecommun sci ctr, 72-75; spec asst to dir technol assessment, 75-80, RES & DEVELOP PROG MGR, OFF TECHNOL ASSESSMENT, US CONG, 80- *Concurrent Pos:* Mem, Comn C, US Nat Comt, URSI, 76-; consult, Comt Telecommun Policy, Inst of Elec & Electronic Engrs, 78- *Mem:* Inst Elec & Electronic Engrs; Info Theory Group; Commun Soc; Syst, Man & Cybernetics Soc. *Res:* Telecommunications; computers; technology assessment; information sciences; telecommunications policy; information policy. *Mailing Add:* Off Technol Assessment US Cong 600 Pennsylvania Ave SE Washington DC 20510

DALY, ROBERT WARD, b Watertown, NY, Oct 1, 32; m 58; c 5. PSYCHIATRY, PSYCHOANALYSIS. *Educ:* St Lawrence Univ, BS, 57; State Univ NY Upstate Med Ctr, MD, 57. *Prof Exp:* Rotating intern clin med, Albert Einstein Med Ctr, 57-58; resident psychiat, State Univ NY Upstate Med Ctr, 58-60, chief resident, 60-61; from instr to assoc prof, 63-75, PROF PSYCHIAT, STATE UNIV NY UPSTATE MED CTR, 75- *Concurrent Pos:* Pvt pract psychiat, 63-69 & 70-; supv psychiatrist, Syracuse Psychiat Hosp, 63-66; dir adult psychiat clin, State Univ Hosp, Syracuse, 66-; vis prof med admin, Cornell Univ, 67-; vis scholar philos, Dept Hist & Philos Sci, Cambridge Univ & NY State fel, Dept Ment Hyg, 69-70; consult, Peace Corps, Bd Consults, Psychoanal Rev & Nat Libr; fel, Nat Endowment for Humanities, 74-75; co-dir, Syracuse Consortium Cult Found Med, 78-79, exec dir, 79-; examr, Am Bd Psychiat & Neurol, 80- *Mem:* Fel Am Psychiat Asn; Int Soc Comp Study Civilizations; Soc Health & Human Values. *Res:* Theoretical presupposition of psychiatry, psychoanalysis and medicine; case studies using the object relations theory of personality; historical, social-cultural and economic determinates of contemporary psychiatric institutions. *Mailing Add:* Dept Psychiatry State Univ Hosp 750 E Adams St Syracuse NY 13210

DALY, WALTER J, b Michigan City, Ind, Jan 12, 30; m 53; c 2. INTERNAL MEDICINE. *Educ:* Ind Univ, AB, 51, MD, 55; Am Bd Internal Med, dipl pulmonary dis. *Prof Exp:* Instr physiol, 55, from instr to assoc prof med, 62-68; PROF MED, IND UNIV, INDIANAPOLIS, 68-, CHMN DEPT, 70-, DIR, REGENSTRIEF INST, 80- *Concurrent Pos:* USPHS fel med, Ind Univ, Indianapolis, 60-62. *Mem:* Fel Am Col Physicians; fel Am Col Cardiol; Asn Am Physicians; Am Soc Clin Invest; Am Clin & Climat Asn. *Res:* Pulmonary and cardiopulmonary physiology. *Mailing Add:* Dept of Med Ind Univ Med Ctr Indianapolis IN 46200

DALY, WILLIAM HOWARD, b San Francisco, Calif, Jan 22, 39; m 60; c 2. ORGANIC CHEMISTRY, POLYMER CHEMISTRY. *Educ:* Baldwin-Wallace Col, BSc, 60; Polytech Inst Brooklyn, PhD(org chem), 64. *Prof Exp:* Fel polymer synthesis, Univ Mainz, 64-66; asst prof, 66-71, assoc prof, 71-78, PROF ORG POLYMER CHEM, LA STATE UNIV, 78- *Mem:* Am Chem Soc; The Chem Soc. *Res:* Modification of condensation polymers; catalysis of cellulose modification; purification of microbial proteins; reactivity of polymeric substrates; enzyme immobilization; preparation of polymer reagents. *Mailing Add:* Dept of Chem La State Univ Baton Rouge LA 70803

DALZELL, ROBERT CLINTON, b Pittsburgh, Pa, Aug 31, 19; m 44; c 3. MEDICAL MICROBIOLOGY. *Educ:* Univ Pittsburgh, BS, 41; Pa State Univ, MS, 56, PhD(microbiol), 57; Am Bd Microbiol, dipl. *Prof Exp:* Chief clin lab, Army Hosp, Edgewood, Md, 45-48; sci adminr biol prod, Biol Opers,

US Army, 57-58; chief biol br, Chem Corps Sch, 58-59, tech adv, Orientation Course, Chem, Biol & Radiol Weapons, 59-62; asst prof microbiol, Morehead State Col, 62-63; asst lab mgr, Melpar, Inc, 63-64; res scientist, Travelers Res Ctr, Inc, 64-65; assoc prof, 65-67, PROF BIOL, KY WESLEYAN COL, 67- *Mem:* Am Acad Microbiol; Am Soc Microbiol. *Res:* Ultrasonic and sonic sound fields; serological studies of plant virus disease; life and medical sciences; immunology; serology. *Mailing Add:* 3844 Bowlands Ct Owensboro KY 42301

DALZELL, WILLIAM HOWARD, b Chatham, NY, Sept 6, 36; m 67; c 2. CHEMICAL ENGINEERING. *Educ:* Mass Inst Technol, BS, 58, SM, 60, ScD, 65. *Prof Exp:* Ford Found res fel, Mass Inst Technol, 65-67, asst prof chem eng, 65-68, 69-70; res group leader, 70-72, SR DEPT MGR, POLAROID CORP, 72- *Concurrent Pos:* Vis lectr, Imp Col, Univ London, 68-69. *Mem:* Am Chem Soc; Am Inst Chem Engrs. *Res:* Combustion; heat transfer; radiative heat transfer; light scattering; quality control; photographic films. *Mailing Add:* 300 Old Ocean St Marshfield MA 02050

DALZIEL, IAN WILLIAM DRUMMOND, b Glasgow, Scotland, Nov 26, 37; m 60. STRUCTURAL GEOLOGY. *Educ:* Univ Edinburgh, BSc, 59, PhD(geol), 63. *Prof Exp:* Asst lectr geol, Univ Edinburgh, 59-63; vis lectr, Univ Wis, 63-64, asst prof, 64-66; assoc prof, 66-74, PROF GEOL, COLUMBIA UNIV, 74-, MEM STAFF, LAMONT-DOHERTY GEOL OBSERV, 68- *Concurrent Pos:* Co-leader exped Somerset Island, Arctic Can, 64-65; consult, Que Cartier Mining Co, 65-; leader expeds, S Shetland Islands, S Omchez Islands, Antarctic Peninsula & Tierra del Fuego, 69-; mem deep sea drilling proj, Joint Oceanog Insts Deep Earth Sampling Antarctic Adv Panel, 71- *Mem:* AAAS; fel Geol Soc Am; fel Geol Soc London; Am Geophys Union. *Res:* Relations of deformation and metamorphism in orogenic belts; development of mountain belts; fault mechanics; stress history of folded rocks; reconstruction of Gondwanaland; development of island arc systems. *Mailing Add:* Lamont-Doherty Geol Observ Columbia Univ Palisades NY 10964

DAM, CECIL FREDERICK, b Kalamazoo, Mich, June 30, 23; m 50; c 2 PHYSICS. PHYSICS. *Educ:* Kalamazoo Col, BA, 48; Cornell Univ, MS, 53; Ohio State Univ, PhD(physics), 56. *Prof Exp:* Asst prof physics & math, Hamline Univ, 57-58; from asst prof to assoc prof, 58-62, PROF PHYSICS, CORNELL COL, 63-, CHMN, DEPT PHYSICS, 80- *Concurrent Pos:* Resident res assoc, Argonne Nat Lab, 65-66. *Mem:* Am Asn Physics Teachers; Optical Soc Am; Am Hist Sci Soc; Am Meteorol Soc; Soc Hist Technol. *Res:* Atmospheric electricity. *Mailing Add:* Dept of Physics Cornell Col Mt Vernon IA 52314

DAM, RICHARD, b Kalamazoo, Mich, Sept 17, 29; m 59; c 1. BIOCHEMISTRY, NUTRITION. *Educ:* Kalamazoo Col, BA, 51; Cornell Univ, MS, 56, PhD(animal nutrit), 59. *Prof Exp:* Asst biochemist, 58-60, asst prof biochem, 60-76, mem fac life sci, 76-80, ASST PROF LIFE SCI, UNIV NEBR, LINCOLN, 80- *Mem:* AAAS; Am Chem Soc; Am Inst Nutrit; Am Soc Microbiol. *Res:* Isolation and characterization proteins; protein complexes and interactions; nutritional utilization proteins. *Mailing Add:* Dept of Biochem & Nutrit Univ of Nebr Lincoln NE 68588

DAM, RUDY JOHAN, b Semarang, Indonesia, Nov 30, 49; US citizen; m 78; c 2. PHYSICAL CHEMISTRY, ENVIRONMENTAL ENGINEERING. *Educ:* Calif Inst Technol, BS, 72; Univ Ore, PhD(chem), 76. *Prof Exp:* RES PHYSICIST INSTRUMENT RES & DEVELOP, ENG PHYSICS LAB, E I DU PONT DE NEMOURS & CO, 77- *Res:* Environmental instrument development; industrial toxicology; molecular genetics instrumentation. *Mailing Add:* Eng Physics Lab E357/209 E I du Pont de Nemours & Co Wilmington DE 19898

DAMADIAN, RAYMOND, b New York, NY, Mar 16, 36; m 60; c 3. BIOCHEMISTRY, BIOPHYSICS. *Educ:* Univ Wis, BS, 56; Albert Einstein Col Med, MD, 60. *Prof Exp:* Sr investr, US Air Force Sch Aerospace Med, 65-67; asst prof, 67-71, assoc prof biophys, 71-80, ASSOC PROF MED, STATE UNIV NY DOWNSTATE MED CTR, 80- *Concurrent Pos:* Univ res fel biophys, Harvard Univ, 63-65; Health Res Coun of City of New York, res grant, 67-69, career investr, 67-72. *Mem:* Am Chem Soc; Biophys Soc; Am Soc Microbiol. *Res:* Biophysical chemistry of alkali cation accumulation in living cells; physical chemistry of the submolecular structure of cells; nuclear magnetic resonance techniques for cancer detection. *Mailing Add:* Dept of Med & Biophys Kings County Hosp Ctr Brooklyn NY 11203

DAMAN, ERNEST L, b Hannover, Ger, Mar 14, 23; US citizen; m 45; c 3. MECHANICAL ENGINEERING. *Educ:* Polytech Inst Brooklyn, BME, 43. *Prof Exp:* Develop engr, 46-49, proj engr, 49-53, res engr, 53-55, dept dir res, 55-59, dir res, 59-74, vpres res, 74-81, SR VPRES, FOSTER WHEELER CORP, 81-, CHMN BD, FOSTER WHEELER DEVELOP CORP, 77- *Concurrent Pos:* Mem exec comt, Pressure Vessel Res Comt, Welding Res Coun, 63-, vchmn, 81-; mem, Nat Res Coun & Coal Indust Adv Comt, DOE, 78-80; dir, Metals Properties Coun, 81- *Mem:* Fel Am Soc Mech Engrs; Am Nuclear Soc; Air Pollution Control Asn; Mat Properties Coun; fel Inst Energy. *Res:* Heat transfer; fluid flow as applied to power generation equipment; metallurgy and structural analysis as applied to power generation; combustion. *Mailing Add:* Foster Wheeler Corp 110 S Orange Ave Livingston NJ 07039

DAMAN, HARLAN RICHARD, b New York, NY, Nov 1, 41. MEDICINE, ASTHMATIC DISORDERS. *Educ:* Harvard Col, AB, 63; Albert Einstein Col Med, MD, 67. *Prof Exp:* Intern & resident pediat, Yale Univ-Yale New Haven Hosp, 67; fel allergy-immunol, Univ Colo Med Ctr, 71-73; MEM TEACHING STAFF PEDIAT, ALBERT EINSTEIN COL MED, 74-; MEM TEACHING STAFF MED, MT SINAI SCH MED, 75- *Concurrent Pos:* Consult pediat allergy, Lawrence Hosp, Bronxville, 77- *Mem:* Fel Am Acad Allergy; fel Am Acad Pediat; fel Am Col Allergists; fel Am Col Chest Physicians; NY Acad Sci. *Mailing Add:* 769 Kimball Ave Yonkers NY 10704

DAMANN, KENNETH EUGENE, JR, b Chicago, Ill, Apr 27, 44; m 68; c 2. PLANT PATHOLOGY. *Educ:* Eastern Ill Univ, BSE, 66; Univ Ark, MS, 69; Mich State Univ, PhD(bot, plant path), 74. *Prof Exp:* Asst prof, 74-78, ASSOC PROF DEPT PLANT PATH, LA STATE UNIV, BATON ROUGE, 78- *Mem:* Am Phytopath Soc; Am Soc Plant Physiologists. *Res:* Etiology of the ratoon stunting disease of sugarcane; physiology of plant disease. *Mailing Add:* Dept of Plant Path & Crop Physiol La State Univ Baton Rouge LA 70803

DAMASK, ARTHUR CONSTANTINE, b Woodstown, NJ, July 28, 24. BIOPHYSICS. *Educ:* Muhlenberg Col, BS, 49; Iowa State Univ, MS, 54, PhD(physics), 64. *Prof Exp:* Physicist, Frankford Arsenal, 53-65; PROF PHYSICS, QUEENS COL, NY, 65- *Concurrent Pos:* Guest scientist, Brookhaven Nat Lab; mem solid state sci panel, Nat Res Coun, 64-74; consult, Lawrence Livermore Lab, 73-; ed, J Semiconductors & Insulators, 73-78, J Phys Chem Solids, 74-; chmn, Comn Army Procurement, Nat Acad Sci, 75-76; mem nat mat adv bd, Nat Res Coun, 76-79; vis prof, New York Univ Ctr Sci & Technol Policy, 79- *Mem:* Fel Am Phys Soc. *Res:* Metals physics radiation effects; defects in solids; organic crystals; medical physics, biophysics. *Mailing Add:* 29 Brewster Lane Bellport NY 11713

DAMASKUS, CHARLES WILLIAM, b Ill, Oct 28, 24; m 49; c 3. BIOCHEMISTRY, ZOOLOGY. *Educ:* Valparaiso Univ, BA, 49. *Prof Exp:* Res chemist, Baxter Labs, 49-51; sr scientist, Armour Pharmaceut Co, 51-63; clin res scientist, Arnar Stone Labs, Am Hosp Supply Corp, 63-66; PRES, ALPAR LABS, INC, 66- *Mem:* Am Chem Soc; AAAS. *Res:* Pharmaceutical clinical research; pharmaceutical product development; layer lyophilized products; pet product development; layering process for pharmaceuticals; use of Alpha Chymotrypsin in Zonulysis; medicinal uses of Chymotrypsin and trypsin; development of clinical uses of pituitary hormones. *Mailing Add:* 132 S Kensington La Grange IL 60525

DAMASSA, AL JOHN, b Lucca, Italy, Oct 16, 29; US citizen; m 51; c 3. COMPARATIVE PATHOLOGY, ENTOMOLOGY. *Educ:* Calif State Univ, Chico, AB, 56; Univ Calif, Davis, MS, 63, PhD(comp path), 77. *Prof Exp:* RES ASSOC AVIAN MED & ANIMAL MYCOPLASMOSIS, SCH VET MED, UNIV CALIF, DAVIS, 56- *Res:* Avian spirochetosis; vectors and the disease process; avian and animal mycoplasmosis. *Mailing Add:* Dept of Epidemiol & Prev Med Univ of Calif Sch of Vet Med Davis CA 95616

DAMASSA, DAVID ALLEN, b Bayshore, NY, Sept 17, 50; m 74; c 1. ENDOCRINOLOGY, NEUROENDOCRINOLOGY. *Educ:* Stanford Univ, BS, 72, PhD(physiol), 77. *Prof Exp:* Fel, Dept Anat, Brain Res Inst, Univ Calif, Los Angeles, 77-79; ASST PROF ANAT, MED SCH, TUFTS UNIV, 79- *Concurrent Pos:* Prin investr, NIH, 80- *Mem:* Endocrine Soc; Am Asn Anatomists; Soc Neurosci; Soc Study Reproduction. *Res:* investigation of the neuroendocrine control of reproduction, specifically the effects of steriods on pituitary hormone secretion, reproductive behavior and the ontogeny of brain-pituitary gonadal interactions. *Mailing Add:* Dept Anat & Cellular Biol Med Sch Tufts Univ 136 Harrison Ave Boston MA 02111

D'AMATO, CONSTANCE JOAN, b Shrub Oak, NY, Jan 5, 33. NEUROBIOLOGY, NEUROPATHOLOGY. *Educ:* Tufts Univ, BS, 55. *Prof Exp:* Sr res asst neurobiol, New Eng Deaconness Hosp & Harvard Med Sch, 55-62; res assoc neurobiol & neuropathol, Med Ctr, 62-72, ASST PROF NEUROBIOL, DEPT PATH, UNIV MICH, 72- *Concurrent Pos:* Counr premed students, Univ Mich, 71-; mem, Neurol & Behav Sci Curric, Univ Mich, 80- *Mem:* Soc Neurosci; Am Acad Neurol; Teratology Soc; Asn Am Med Col; Behav Teratology Soc. *Res:* Experimental effects of radiation, trauma, and drugs on developing brain and behavior. *Mailing Add:* Dept of Path Univ of Mich Med Ctr Ann Arbor MI 48109

D'AMATO, DONALD PAUL, b New York, NY, Sept 12, 43. PHYSICS. *Educ:* Ohio Wesleyan Univ, BA, 64; Ohio State Univ, MSc, 70, PhD(nuclear physics), 72. *Prof Exp:* Fel, Ohio State Univ, 72-73; ASST PROF SURG-PHYSICS, UNIV CONN HEALTH CTR, 73- *Mem:* Am Phys Soc. *Res:* Development of instrumentation and techniques for clinical eye research. *Mailing Add:* Dept Surg PO Box G Univ of Conn Health Ctr Farmington CT 06032

D'AMATO, HENRY EDWARD, b Shrewsbury, Mass, Oct 3, 28; m 53; c 4. PHARMACOLOGY. *Educ:* Col of Holy Cross, AB, 49; Boston Univ, MA, 51, PhD(physiol), 54. *Prof Exp:* From instr to asst prof pharmacol, Tufts Univ, 54-59; pharmacologist, Astra Biol Labs, 59-67, ASSOC SCI DIR, ASTRA PHARMACEUT PROD, INC, 67- *Concurrent Pos:* Lederle med fac award, 56-59. *Res:* Experimental hypothermia; cardiovascular physiology and pharmacology; antispasmodic, antihistaminic and antiarrhythmic drugs; iron metabolism. *Mailing Add:* Astra Pharmaceut Prod Inc 7 Neponset St Worcester MA 01606

D'AMATO, RICHARD JOHN, b Springfield, Mass, Sept 24, 40; m 61; c 2. PHYSICAL CHEMISTRY. *Educ:* Am Int Col, BA, 62; Univ Ill, Champaign-Urbana, MS, 65, PhD(phys chem), 71. *Prof Exp:* Res chemist polymer phys chem, Monsanto Co, 65-67; sci specialist, Scott Graphics, Inc, 70-75, sr group leader phys chem, 75-76, mgr prod develop, 76-78; DIR, IMAGING & CUSTOM RES & DEVELOP, JAMES RIVER GRAPHICS, 78- *Mem:* Am Chem Soc; Soc Photog Scientists & Engrs. *Res:* High temperature gas phase reaction kinetics; polymer physical chemistry; physical chemical aspects of adhesion; chemistry and physics of organic photo conductors. *Mailing Add:* 19 Chapel Hill Dr South Hadley MA 01075

DAMBACH, GEORGE ERNEST, b Dayton, Ohio, June 10, 42; m 64; c 2. ELECTROPHYSIOLOGY. *Educ:* Ohio State Univ, BS, 64, PhD(pharmacol), 68. *Prof Exp:* Res fel cardiol, Philadelphia Gen Hosp, 68-69; fel pharmacol, Univ Pa, 69-71, scholar, 71-74; ASSOC PROF PHARMACOL, WAYNE STATE UNIV, 74-, DIR GRAD PROG & ASST DEAN CURRICULAR AFFAIRS, 80- *Mem:* Biophys Soc. *Res:* Cellular electrogenesis; mechanisms of normal and abnormal biological electrical activity; pharmacological modulation of electrogenesis. *Mailing Add:* Sch Med Wayne State Univ 540 E Canfield Ave Detroit MI 48202

DAMBERGER, HEINZ HEINRICH, b Komotau, Czech, Dec 15, 33; m 63; c 4. GEOLOGY. *Educ:* Univ Mainz, Vordiplom, 56; Clausthal Tech Univ, dipl geol, 60, Dr rer nat(geol), 66. *Prof Exp:* Geologist, Saarbergwerke AG, WGer, 60-68; from assoc geologist to geologist, Ill State Geol Surv, 68-76; chief geologist, Explor & Bergbau GMBH, Washington, Pa, 76-77; assoc prof geol, Univ Pittsburgh, 78; GEOLOGIST & HEAD COAL SECTION, ILL STATE GEOL SURV, 78- *Concurrent Pos:* Lectr geol & mineral, Sch Mining Eng, Saarbrücken, 61-68. *Mem:* Geol Soc Am; Am Soc Test & Mat; Ger Geol Soc; Ger Geol Asn; Int Comn Coal Petrog. *Res:* Coal geology, including coal quality, coalification, coal mining geology and coal petrography; classification of coal; microstructure of coal; study of geological parameters that control roof stability or roof failure in underground coal mines; coal reserve evaluation. *Mailing Add:* Ill State Geol Surv Urbana IL 61801

DAMBORG, MARK J(OHANNES), b Ft Dodge, Iowa, Dec 6, 39; m 69. ELECTRICAL ENGINEERING. *Educ:* Iowa State Univ, BS, 62; Univ Mich, MSE, 63, PhD(comput, info & control eng), 69. *Prof Exp:* Asst res engr, Systs Eng Lab, Univ Mich, 65-66, 67-69; asst prof, 69-74, ASSOC PROF ELEC ENG, UNIV WASH, 74- *Concurrent Pos:* Syst control engr, Elec Energy Systs Div, US Dept Energy, 77-78. *Mem:* AAAS; Inst Elec & Electronics Engrs; Am Nuclear Soc. *Res:* Stability of nonlinear systems; large-scale system simulation and modeling of electrical energy generation and distribution systems. *Mailing Add:* Dept of Elec Eng Univ of Wash Seattle WA 98195

D'AMBROSIO, STEVEN M, b Philadelphia, Pa, May 7, 49; m 81. TOXICOLOGY, GENETICS. *Educ:* St Joseph's Univ, BS, 71; Tex A&M Univ, PhD(bio-org chem), 75. *Prof Exp:* Res assoc molecular biol, Brookhaven Nat Lab, 75-77; asst prof, 77-82, ASSOC PROF PHARMACOL & RADIOL, OHIO STATE UNIV, 82- *Concurrent Pos:* Consult health effects, US Environ Protection Agency, 80; prin investr, US Environ Protection Agency & NIH, 78, Nat Inst Environ Health Sci, 81. *Mem:* Am Soc Pharmacol & Exp Therpeut; AAAS; Am Soc Photochem; NY Acad Sci. *Res:* Determining the molecular mechanisms of cancer, mutation and aging, including genetic toxicology, human health effects, means of prevention as well as reversing toxic effects. *Mailing Add:* Dept Pharmacol Ohio State Univ 333 W 10th Ave Columbus OH 43210

D'AMBROSIO, UBIRATAN, b Sao Paulo, Brazil, Dec 8, 32; m 58; c 2. MATHEMATICS, EDUCATION. *Educ:* Univ Sao Paulo, BSc, 54, PhD(math), 63. *Prof Exp:* Regente math, Fac Philos, Univ Sao Paulo, 60-64; res assoc, Brown Univ, 64-65; asst prof, State Univ NY Buffalo, 65-66; assoc prof, Univ RI, 66-68; assoc prof & dir grad studies, State Univ NY Buffalo, 68-74; PROF, INST MATH, UNIV CAMPINAS, BRAZIL, 74- *Concurrent Pos:* Ida Beam vis prof, Univ Iowa, 80-81; head, Unit Improv Educ Systs, Orgn Am States, 80-81; pres, InterAm Comt Math Educ, 79-83; vpres, Int Comn Math Instr, 79-83. *Mem:* Math Union Italy; Math Soc France; London Math Soc; Am Math Soc; AAAS. *Res:* Existence and regularity problems in the calculus of variations; systems with memory; social history of mathematics; metrically based curriculum development. *Mailing Add:* Inst of Math Univ of Campinas CP 1170 (13100) Sao Paulo Brazil

DAME, CHARLES, b Providence, RI, July 18, 29; m 68; c 2. HORTICULTURE, FOOD SCIENCE. *Educ:* Univ RI, BS, 51; Univ Calif, MS, 55. *Prof Exp:* Assoc food sci, Univ Calif, 55-57; res chemist, Standard Fruit & Steamship Co, 57-60; group leader, Gen Foods Corp, 60-68; dir res & qual control, Nat Sugar Refining Co, 68-72; VPRES RES & DEVELOP, STANGE CO, 72- *Mem:* Inst Food Technol; Sigma Xi. *Res:* Food science with special interest in spices and their extractives; natural and artificial flavors; artificial colors. *Mailing Add:* 1121 West St Naperville IL 60540

DAME, DAVID ALLAN, b Greenfield, Mass, Oct 4, 31; m 52; c 2. ENTOMOLOGY. *Educ:* Dartmouth Col, AB, 54; Univ Mass, PhD(entom), 61. *Prof Exp:* RES ENTOMOLOGIST, INSECTS AFFECTING MAN & ANIMALS LAB, AGR RES SERV, USDA, 61- *Concurrent Pos:* Mem, Expert Comt Parasitic Dis, WHO & Expert Comt Trypanosomsasis, Foreign Agr Orgn; prof entom, Univ Fla. *Mem:* AAAS; Entom Soc Am; Am Mosquito Control Asn. *Res:* Control of insects of medical importance involving insect behavior, ecology, chemosterilization, radiosterilization, juvenile hormones, biological agents and insecticides. *Mailing Add:* Insects Res Lab PO Box 14565 Gainesville FL 32604

DAME, RICHARD EDWARD, b Lewisburg, Pa, May 31, 37; m 61. ENGINEERING, MATHEMATICS. *Educ:* George Washington Univ, BCE, 60, MSE, 63; Cath Univ Am, PhD(eng, math), 72. *Prof Exp:* Civil engr, Fed Aviation Agency, 59-62; sr engr, Dept Defense, DIA, 62-63 & Fairchild Hiller, 64-65; proj engr, Booz Allen Appl Res, 65-66; proj engr, 66-70, DIR ENG, MEGA ENG, 70- *Concurrent Pos:* Dept Energy grant, 77-79; asst prof, Cath Univ Am, 78- *Honors & Awards:* Patent Award, NASA, 74. *Mem:* Am Inst Aeronaut & Astronaut; Am Asn Small Res Co; Consult Engrs Coun. *Res:* Solid mechanics; variational methods; solar energy systems; energy economics. *Mailing Add:* 10701 Harper Ave Silver Spring MD 20901

DAMERAU, FREDERICK JACOB, b Parma, Ohio, Dec 25, 31; m 54; c 2. INFORMATION SCIENCE, NATURAL LANGUAGE PROCESSING. *Educ:* Cornell Univ, BA, 53; Yale Univ, MA, 57, PhD(ling), 66. *Prof Exp:* Programmer, Fed Systs Div, 57-61, res staff info sci, 61-68, RES STAFF COMPUTATIONAL LING, RES DIV, IBM CORP, 68- *Concurrent Pos:* Assoc ed, Asn Comput Ling, 74-78; adj fac, Pace Univ, 81- *Mem:* AAAS; Asn Comput Ling; Asn Comput Mach; Ling Soc Am. *Res:* Computer understanding of natural language directed particularly toward data base enquiry. *Mailing Add:* Thomas J Watson Res Ctr PO Box 218 Yorktown Heights NY 10598

DAMEROW, RICHARD AASEN, b Thief River Falls, Minn, Sept 4, 36; m 57; c 2. PHYSICS. *Educ:* Univ Minn, BS, 58, MS, 60, PhD(mass spectros), 63. *Prof Exp:* Mem staff, Sandia Labs, 63-71, div supvr, 71-78, sci adv, US Dept Energy/Mil Appl, 78-79, DIV SUPVR, SANDIA LABS, 79- *Mem:* Am Phys Soc; Am Asn Physics Teachers. *Res:* Mass spectroscopy, precision atomic masses; high magnetic fields; nuclear weapon effects. *Mailing Add:* 2924 Espanola N E Albuquerque NM 87110

DAMEWOOD, GLENN, US citizen. APPLIED PHYSICS. *Educ:* Tex Col Mines, BS, 49. *Prof Exp:* Chief instrumentation, US Army Field Forces Bd No 4, Ft Bliss, Tex, 50-51; asst chief, White Sands Proving Grounds, 51-52; sr engr, El Paso Natural Gas Co, 53-55; proj leader, Dept Physics, Spec Projs Lab, 55-56, mgr indust appln sect, 57-59, dept dir, 59-72, tech vpres & dir, 72, V PRES APPL PHYSICS DIV, SOUTHWEST RES INST, 74- *Res:* Acoustics, analog computer design and nondestructive testing, including radiography; eddy current and magnetic techniques; fluid dynamics, instrumentation and machine design. *Mailing Add:* Appl Physics Div Southwest Res Inst PO Drawer 28510 6220 Culebra Rd San Antonio TX 78284

DAMIAN, RAYMOND T, b Philadelphia, Pa, Aug 11, 34; m 57; c 3. PARASITOLOGY, IMMUNOLOGY. *Educ:* Univ Akron, BS, 56; Fla State Univ, MS, 58, PhD(parasitol), 62. *Prof Exp:* Res assoc parasitol, Fla State Univ, 62-63; asst prof biol, Emory Univ, 63-67; immunologist, Southwest Found Res & Educ, 67-69, assoc found scientist, Dept Immunol, 69-73; assoc prof, 73-77, PROF ZOOL, UNIV GA, 77- *Concurrent Pos:* Adj assoc prof microbiol, Univ Tex Med Sch, San Antonio, 72-73. *Honors & Awards:* Henry Baldwin Ward Medal, Am Soc Parasitol, 74. *Mem:* Royal Soc Trop Med & Hyg; Am Asn Immunol; NY Acad Sci; Am Soc Parasitol; Am Soc Trop Med & Hyg. *Res:* Immunological parasitology; schistosomiasis; immunology of nonhuman primates. *Mailing Add:* Dept of Zool Univ of Ga Athens GA 30602

DAMJANOV, IVAN, b Subotica, Yugoslavia, Mar 31, 41; m 64; c 3. PATHOLOGY. *Educ:* Univ Zagreb, MD, 64, MSc, 66, PhD(path), 71. *Prof Exp:* Asst prof path, Sch Med, Univ Zagreb, 71-73; from asst prof to assoc prof path, Sch Med, Univ Conn, Farmington, 73-77; assoc prof, 77-80, PROF PATH, HAHNEMANN MED COL & HOSP, PHILADELPHIA, 80- *Res:* Developmental aspects of neoplasia. *Mailing Add:* Hahnemann Med Col 230 N Broad St Philadelphia PA 19102

DAMKAER, DAVID MARTIN, b Portland, Ore, Oct 11, 38. ZOOPLANKTON, COPEPODA. *Educ:* Univ Wash, Seattle, BS, 60, MS, 64; George Washington Univ, PhD(zool), 73. *Prof Exp:* Marine biologist zool plankton, Smithsonian Inst, 65-71; fisheries biologist, Nat Marine Fisheries Serv, 71-73, oceanographer biol oceanog, Environ Res Labs, 73-79, FISHERIES BIOLOGIST, NAT OCEANIC & ATMOSPHERIC ADMIN, 79- *Concurrent Pos:* Affil assoc prof oceanog, Sch Oceanog, Univ Wash, 74- *Mem:* Sigma Xi; Crustacean Soc; Challenger Soc; Marine Biol Asn UK. *Res:* Systematics and ecology of free-living marine Copepoda; history of the study of Copepoda; effects of environmental pollution, especially of enhanced solar ultraviolet radiation; fisheries enhancement and management (salmonids). *Mailing Add:* Dept Oceanog WB-10 Univ Wash Seattle WA 98195

DAMLE, SURESH B, b Bombay, India, Aug 4, 35; US citizen; m 60; c 1. ORGANIC CHEMISTRY, BIOCHEMISTRY. *Educ:* Univ Bombay, BSc Hons, 58, MSc, 60; Rutgers Univ, New Brunswick, PhD(org chem, biochem), 64. *Prof Exp:* Anal chemist, Shell Refineries, Bombay, India, 54-60; res fel cancer chemother, Med Sch, Univ Pa, 64-65; res chemist, M&T Chem Inc, Rahway, NJ, 65-69 & Am Cyanamid Co, Bound Brook, 69-70; instr biochem, Rutgers Med Sch, 70-73; sr scientist, Indust Chem Div, NL Industs, Hightstown, NJ, 74, sect leader org chem, 75; RES ASSOC ORG CHEM, CHEM PROD DIV, PPG IND, INC, 76- *Mem:* Sigma Xi; The Chem Soc; Am Chem Soc; fel Am Inst Chemists. *Res:* Organic and organometallic chemistry synthesis and mechanisms; cancer chemotherapy; enzyme mechanisms; flame retardants; stabilizers; antioxidants and other plastic additives; Grighard chemistry; organotin, organolead and organosilicon chemistry; bicyclic chemistry. *Mailing Add:* Spec Prod Div PPG Ind Inc PO Box 66251 AMF-O'Hare Chicago IL 60666

DAMM, CHARLES CONRAD, b New York, NY, Nov 20, 24; m 49; c 2. PLASMA PHYSICS. *Educ:* Rensselaer Polytech, BEE, 45; NY Univ, PhD(physics), 52. *Prof Exp:* Physicist, Picatinny Arsenal, NJ, 51-54; physicist, Brookhaven Nat Lab, NY, 54-56; PHYSICIST, LAWRENCE LIVERMORE LAB, UNIV CALIF, 56- *Mem:* Fel Am Phys Soc. *Res:* Cosmic ray interactions; precision atomic mass measurements; plasma physics as related to controlled fusion research. *Mailing Add:* Lawrence Livermore Lab Univ Calif Livermore CA 94550

DAMMAN, ANTONI WILLEM HERMANUS, b Utrecht, Netherlands, Apr 21, 32; US citizen; m 56; c 2. PLANT ECOLOGY. *Educ:* Univ Wageningen, BSc, 53, MSc, 56; Univ Mich, PhD, 67. *Prof Exp:* Res officer, Res Br, Nfld Dist, Can Dept Forestry, 56-65, res scientist & head tree biol & land classification sect, 65-67; assoc prof, 67-78, PROF PLANT ECOL, UNIV CONN, 78- *Concurrent Pos:* Mem, Nat Adv Comt Forest Land, Can, 64-67 & Subcomt Conserv Terrestial Ecosysts, Can Int Biol Prog, 66-67; Univ Conn Res Found grant, 67-70; NSF grant, 69-71. *Mem:* AAAS; Ecol Soc Am; Can Bot Asn; Can Inst Forestry; Can Soc Soil Sci. *Res:* Vegetation survey and ecological land classification; soil vegetation relationships; plant geography of Eastern North America; floristic composition, biogeochemistry and development of Sphagnum bogs. *Mailing Add:* Biol Sci Group Life Sci Bldg U-42 Univ of Conn Storrs CT 06268

DAMMANN, JOHN FRANCIS, b Chicago, Ill, Feb 21, 17; m 41; c 4. SURGERY. *Educ:* Harvard Univ, AB, 41; Univ Cincinnati, MD, 43. *Prof Exp:* Intern, Evanston Hosp, Ill, 44; researcher & chief resident, Children's Mem Hosp, Chicago, 44-46; asst prof pediat, Univ Calif, Los Angeles, 50-55; assoc prof surg cardiol, Univ Hosp, 55-60, assoc prof surg cardiol & pediat, Med Ctr, 60-61, prof, 61-68, PROF PEDIAT & BIOMED ENG, MED CTR, UNIV VA, 68-, NIH CAREER RES PROF, 62- *Concurrent Pos:* Fel pediat cardiol, Children's Mem Hosp, Chicago, 48; sr fel, Johns Hopkins Hosp, 49-50; consult, Vet Admin. *Mem:* AAAS; AMA; Am Col Cardiol; Soc Pediat Res. *Res:* Critical care medicine; pediatric cardiology; postoperative care and monitoring. *Mailing Add:* Div of Pediat Cardiol Res Univ of Va Med Ctr Charlottesville VA 22904

DAMMIN, GUSTAVE JOHN, b New York, NY, Sept 17, 11; m 41; c 3. MEDICINE, PATHOLOGY. *Educ:* Cornell Univ, AB, 34, MD, 38; Univ Havana, cert, 37; Am Bd Path, dipl. *Prof Exp:* Intern med, Johns Hopkins Hosp, 39, asst resident, Peter Bent Brigham Hosp, 40; instr path, Col Physicians & Surgeons, Columbia Univ, 41; from asst prof med & path to prof path & chmn dept, Wash Univ, 46-52; prof, 53-62, Friedman prof, 62-78, EMER PROF PATH, HARVARD MED SCH, 78- *Concurrent Pos:* Niles lectr, Cornell Univ; Held lectr, Beth Israel Hosp, New York; pathologist-in-chief, Barnes Hosp, St Louis, Mo, 51-52 & Peter Bent Brigham Hosp, 52-74; consult path, West Roxbury Vet Admin Hosp, 54-75, actg chief lab serv, 76-77, assoc chief, 78-, actg chief, consult path, 81-; consult, Surgeon Gen, US Dept Army, Far East, 56, 64, 66, Europe, 59, 63, 68, 70 & Surgeon Gen, USPHS; lab consult, Off Civil & Defense Mobilization, 50-60; mem comn enteric infections, Armed Forces Epidemiol Bd, 51- & comn parasitic dis, 54-, dir comn parasitic dis, 59-60, pres bd, 60-73; mem trop med & parasitol study sect, NIH, 59-62, mem cholera adv comt, 65-, mem, Int Ctr Comt, 72; mem panel, Inst Defense Anal, 61-62; mem sci adv bd, Armed Forces Inst Path, 61-71; mem subcomt geog path, Nat Res Coun, 62-65; mem heart spec proj comt, Nat Heart Inst, 63-; chmn Geneva expert comt enteric infections, WHO, 63-; mem sci adv comt, New Eng Regional Primate Res Ctr; mem bd dirs, Gorgas Mem Inst, 67-; mem, Leonard Wood Mem Adv Med Bd, 69-; mem ad hoc comt, Div Med Sci, Nat Acad Sci, 70; mem kidney adv comt, Joint Comn Accreditation Hosps, 72-74; mem US deleg, US-Japan Coop Med Sci Prof, Dept State, 72-74; lectr trop pub health, Harvard Sch Pub Health, 78- *Honors & Awards:* Walter Reed Medallion, 71; Award Meritorious Serv, Armed Forces Inst Path, 72; Medal Distinguished Pub Serv, Dept Defense, 73. *Mem:* Asn Am Physicians; Am Asn Path; Am Soc Clin Invest; Am Soc Exp Path; Am Soc Trop Med & Hyg. *Res:* Pathogenesis of diffuse vascular diseases; epidemiology of intestinal infections; kidney and other organ transplantation; babesiosis. *Mailing Add:* Dept Path Harvard Med Sch Boston MA 02115

DAMODARAN, KALYANI MUNIRATNAM, b Gudiyattam, India, June 9, 38; m 70; c 1. ORGANIC & MEDICINAL CHEMISTRY. *Educ:* Univ Madras, BS, 59, MS, 61; Indian Inst Sci, Bangalore, PhD(org chem), 70. *Prof Exp:* Teaching asst chem, Loyola Col, Madras, India, 61-62; sr res fel org chem, Indian Inst Sci, Bangalore, 67-69, sr res asst, 69-71; res fel, Temple Univ, 71-72 & Univ Pittsburgh, 72-73; res assoc, Temple Univ, 74-76; res scientist, 76-79, ASSOC SCIENTIST, SOUTHWEST FOUND RES & EDUC, 79- *Mem:* Am Chem Soc. *Res:* Synthetic organic chemistry of natural products and medicinally significant substances. *Mailing Add:* Dept Org & Biol Chem PO Box 28147 San Antonio TX 78284

DAMON, DWIGHT HILLS, b Northampton, Mass, Feb 2, 31; m 55; c 2. PHYSICS. *Educ:* Amherst Col, AB, 53; Purdue Univ, MS, 55, PhD(physics), 61. *Prof Exp:* Res physicist, Westinghouse Res Labs, 61-70; assoc prof, 70-74, PROF PHYSICS, UNIV CONN, 74- *Concurrent Pos:* Mem gov bd, Int Thermal Conductivity Conf, 75- *Mem:* Am Phys Soc; AAAS. *Res:* Solid state physics, principally in magnetic and transport properties, electrical and thermal conduction, and galvanomagnetic phenomena. *Mailing Add:* Dept of Physics Univ of Conn U-46 Storrs CT 06268

DAMON, EDWARD GEORGE, b Richland, NMex, Feb 21, 27; m 46; c 3. ENVIRONMENTAL BIOLOGY, INHALATION TOXICOLOGY. *Educ:* Eastern NMex Univ, BS, 50; Okla State Univ, MS, 57; Univ NMex, PhD(biol sci), 65. *Prof Exp:* Teacher high sch, NMex, 51-56; instr res cytogenetics, Okla State Univ, 57-58, res assoc, 60-61; sci instr, Jimma Agr Tech Sch Ethiopia, 58-60; head sci dept, High Sch, NMex, 61-62; res biologist, 62-65, ASSOC SCIENTIST, INHALATION TOXICOL RES INST, LOVELACE BIOMED ENVIRON RES INST, 65- *Mem:* AAAS; Bot Soc Am; assoc mem Am Physiol Soc. *Res:* Blast biology; physiological effects of air blast; pulmonary physiology; cultivated sorghums of Ethiopia; radiobiology and inhalation toxicology. *Mailing Add:* Inhalation Toxicol Res Inst Lovelace Biomed Environ Res Inst PO Box 5890 Albuquerque NM 87185

DAMON, EDWARD K(ENNAN), b Concord, Mass, Jan 3, 28; m 50; c 2. ELECTRICAL ENGINEERING. *Educ:* Bowdoin Col, BSc, 49; Ohio State Univ, MS, 54. *Prof Exp:* Res assoc elec eng, Antenna Lab, 50-58, asst supvr, 58-64, assoc supvr, 64-67, tech dir, Lasers & Optical Propagation, 67-75, ASSOC PROF ELEC ENG, OHIO STATE UNIV, 71- *Concurrent Pos:* Dir & treas, Ladar Systs, Inc, 64-70; consult, Data Corp, 64-67, Battelle Mem Inst, 70-73 & IIT Res Inst, 81- *Mem:* Sr mem Inst Elec & Electronics Engrs; Am Phys Soc; Optical Soc Am. *Res:* Electrical physics; microwave circuits and antennas; optical masers; nonlinear optical interactions; atmospheric spectroscopy. *Mailing Add:* 2193 Farleigh Rd Columbus OH 43221

DAMON, JAMES NORMAN, b Baltimore, Md, Aug 31, 45; m 71; c 1. DIFFERENTIAL TOPOLOGY. *Educ:* Dartmouth Col, BA, 67; Oxford Univ, dipl adv math, 69; Harvard Univ, PhD(math), 72. *Prof Exp:* Asst prof math, Tufts Univ, 72-73; Fulbright lectr, Univ Tecnica del Estado, Chile, 73-74; asst prof, Queens Col, 74-76; asst prof, 76-80, ASSOC PROF MATH, UNIV NC, CHAPEL HILL, 80- *Concurrent Pos:* Sr Fulbright-Hayes scholar, 73-74; Res Found, City Univ New York grant, 75-76; NSF res grant, 75-76; sr vis fel, Univ Liverpool, 79-80. *Mem:* Am Math Soc. *Res:* Singularities of smooth mappings and their applications to differential topology, differential equations; smooth and topological stability; topological structure of singularities; stratification techniques; relation to equisingularity problems in algebraic geometry. *Mailing Add:* 360 Phillips Hall 039A Univ of NC Chapel Hill NC 27514

DAMON, PAUL EDWARD, b Brooklawn, NJ, Mar 12, 21; m 47; c 2. GEOCHRONOLOGY, GEOCHEMISTRY. *Educ:* Bucknell Univ, BS, 43; Univ Mo, MS, 49; Columbia Univ, PhD, 57. *Hon Degrees:* DSc, Bucknell Univ, 78. *Prof Exp:* Asst prof physics, Univ Ark, 49-54; res assoc geol, Lamont Geol Observ, Columbia Univ, 54-57; assoc prof, 57-60, PROF GEOL & GEOCHRONOL, UNIV ARIZ, 61- *Concurrent Pos:* Consult, Isotopes, Inc, 56-57. *Mem:* Fel Geol Soc Am; fel AAAS; Geochem Soc; Am Geophys Union. *Res:* Geochronology, geochemistry and tectonics of ore deposits and volcanic rocks within the North American Cordillera; relationships between radiocarbon, solar activity, geomagnetism and climate; geochemistry of toxic industrial pollutants. *Mailing Add:* 2321 E Hawthorne St Tucson AZ 85719

DAMON, RICHARD WINSLOW, b Concord, Mass, May 14, 23; m 46; c 3. SOLID STATE PHYSICS. *Educ:* Harvard Univ, BS, 44, MA, 47, PhD(physics), 52. *Prof Exp:* Asst appl physics, Harvard Univ, 50-51; develop engr, Raytheon Mfg Co, 48-49; res assoc, Res Labs, Gen Elec Co, 51-60; dept head microwave device develop, Microwave Assocs, 60-62; mem staff, 63, dept head explor studies, Solid State Sci, 64-67, assoc mgr solid state sci lab, 67-70, DIR, APPL PHYSICS LAB, RES CTR, SPERRY CORP, 70- *Concurrent Pos:* Vis lectr, Harvard Univ, 61-62; mem, Adv Subcomt Electrophys, NASA, 66-71, chmn, 69-71, mem, Adv Group Electronic Mat, 67-71, Adv Comt Basic Res, 69-71; lectr, Nat Electronics Conf, 68; mem, Adv Panel Electromagnetics Div, Nat Bur Standards, Nat Res Coun, 69-74, chmn, 71-73; Nat Microwave Lectr, Inst Elec & Electronics Engrs, 69; mem, US Comn I, Fr-Int Sci Radio Union, 70-; mem, Nat Bur Standards Electronic Study Group, 72-74; consult mem, Adv Group Electron Devices, Working Group A, Off Dir Defense Res & Eng, 73-; mem bd dirs & dir Div IV, Inst Elec & Electronics Engrs, 77-78. *Mem:* AAAS; fel Am Phys Soc; fel Inst Elec & Electronics Engrs (pres, 81). *Res:* Microwave and optical properties of solids; magnetic resonance; magnetic materials and devices; optics and optical devices; displays; electron beam lithography; research management. *Mailing Add:* 1623 Main St Concord MA 01742

DAMON, ROBERT A(RTHUR), b Weston, Ore, July, 21, 32; m 57; c 3. CHEMICAL ENGINEERING. *Educ:* Mont State Col, BS, 55, MS, 59, PhD(chem eng), 61. *Prof Exp:* Eng aide, US Bur Reclamation, 52-53; asst engr, Shell Oil Co, 54; asst instr math, 56-58; asst prof chem eng, Univ Ariz, 59-63; RES ASSOC, CENT RES DIV, CROWN ZELLERBACH CORP, 63- *Concurrent Pos:* Res fel, 55-58. *Mem:* Am Inst Chem Engrs; Am Chem Soc; Sigma Xi; Asn Energy Engrs; Tech Asn Pulp & Paper Indust. *Res:* Exploratory and process research in pulp, paper and wood-chemicals; reaction kinetics; polymer fiber processes; energy processes. *Mailing Add:* Cent Res Div Crown Zellerbach Corp Camas WA 98607

D'AMORE, MICHAEL BRIAN, b Providence, RI, June 7, 45; m 71; c 4. CATALYSIS, ORGANIC CHEMISTRY. *Educ:* Providence Col, BS, 67; Calif Inst Technol, PhD(org chem), 72. *Prof Exp:* Res chemist, 73-77, SR RES CHEMIST CATALYSIS, E I DU PONT DE NEMOURS & CO INC, 77- *Mem:* Am Chem Soc; Am Soc Testing & Mat; Catalysis Soc. *Res:* Homogeneous and heterogeneous catalysis; reaction mechanisms of industrial importance. *Mailing Add:* Petrochem Dept Exp Sta E I du Pont de Nemours & Co Inc Wilmington DE 19898

DAMOS, DIANE LYNN, b Waukegan, Ill, May 29, 49; m 71. HUMAN FACTORS ENGINEERING, AVIATION PSYCHOLOGY. *Educ:* Univ Ill, BS, 70, MA, 73, PhD(psychol), 77. *Prof Exp:* Mem tech staff human factors, Bell Tel Labs, 72-73; asst prof indust eng, State Univ NY Buffalo, 77-81; ASST PROF PSYCHOL, ARIZ STATE UNIV, 81- *Concurrent Pos:* Consult, Calspan, 77- & Naval Aerospace Med Res Lab, New Orleans, 77- *Mem:* Human Factors Soc; Am Psychol Asn; Asn Aviation Psychologists; Ergonomics. *Res:* Multiple task performance, timesharing, human information processing, pilot selection and training. *Mailing Add:* Dept Psychol Ariz State Univ Tempe AZ 85201

DAMOUR, PAUL LAWRENCE, b Concord, NH, Jan 26, 37; m; c 4. PHYSICAL CHEMISTRY. *Educ:* St Anselm's Col, BA, 58; Cath Univ Am, PhD(chem), 63. *Prof Exp:* From instr to asst prof, 62-68, ASSOC PROF CHEM, ST ANSELM'S COL, 68- *Mem:* Am Chem Soc. *Res:* Photochemical reduction of coordinated complexes; electrokinetic properties of membrane electrodes. *Mailing Add:* Dept of Chem St Anselm's Col Manchester NH 03102

DAMOUTH, DAVID EARL, b Flint, Mich, Jan 27, 37; m 60; c 2. ELECTRONIC PRINTERS, OFFICE AUTOMATION. *Educ:* Univ Mich, BSE(eng physics) & BSE(eng math), 59, MS, 60, PhD(physics), 63. *Prof Exp:* Teaching fel physics, Univ Mich, 59-61; res scientist, NY, 63-67, sr scientist, Advan Eng Div, 67-68, mgr recording processes area, Info Systs Div, 68-71, prin scientist & mgr pattern recognition br, Palo Alto Res Ctr, 71-74, LAB MGR, WEBSTER RES CTR, XEROX CORP, NY, 74- *Res:* Office automation; electronic circuits and systems; electronic imaging systems; pattern recognition. *Mailing Add:* Xerox Corp Bldg 114 Webster Res Ctr Rochester NY 14644

DAMPIER, FREDERICK WALTER, b Winnipeg, Man, Oct 1, 41; US citizen. PHYSICAL CHEMISTRY, ELECTROCHEMISTRY. *Educ:* Univ Man, BSc, 62; Rensselaer Polytech Inst, MS, 64, PhD(phys chem), 68. *Prof Exp:* Fel phys chem, Univ Calif, Berkeley, 68-70; sr scientist electrochem, Technol Ctr, ESB Inc, 70-75 & EIC Corp, 75-78; MEM TECH STAFF ELECTROCHEM, POWER SOURCES CTR, GTE LABS, 78- *Mem:* Am Chem Soc; Electrochem Soc; Sigma Xi. *Res:* Non-aqueous electrochemistry, molten salts, preparation and characterization of permselective membranes, primary and secondary lithium batteries. *Mailing Add:* GTE Labs Inc 40 Sylvan Rd Waltham MA 02154

DAMRON, BOBBY LEON, b Ocala, Fla, Nov 6, 41; m 68. POULTRY NUTRITION. *Educ:* Univ Fla, BSA, 63, MSA, 64, PhD(animal sci), 68. *Prof Exp:* Res assoc, 66-68, asst prof, 68-74, ASSOC PROF POULTRY SCI, UNIV FLA, 74-, ASSOC NUTRITIONIST, 77- *Mem:* Poultry Sci Asn; Sigma Xi; Soc Exp Biol & Med. *Res:* Mineral interrelationships and requirements of chicks, broilers and laying hens; amino acid and energy requirements of laying hens; evaluation of various feed additives and nutrient sources. *Mailing Add:* Dept of Poultry Sci Univ of Fla Gainesville FL 32611

DAMSTEEGT, VERNON DALE, b Waupun, Wis, Oct 19, 36; m 62; c 2. PLANT PATHOLOGY. *Educ:* Cent Col, Iowa, BA, 58; Wash State Univ, PhD(plant path), 62. *Prof Exp:* Asst plant path, Wash State Univ, 58-62; res plant pathologist, Crops Div, US Army Biol Labs, 62-71; PLANT PATHOLOGIST, SCI & EDUC ADMIN, AGR RES SERV, USDA, 71- *Mem:* Am Phytopath Soc. *Res:* Inheritance of resistance and pathogenicity; interaction of host and pathogen; epidemiology of virus diseases; modes of transmission and other general factors affecting disease severity. *Mailing Add:* USDA Sci & Educ Admin Agr Res Serv Dis Res Lab Box 1209 Frederick MD 21701

DAMUSIS, ADOLFAS, b Toscica, Russia, June 16, 08; nat US; m 37; c 4. CHEMISTRY. *Educ:* Univ Vytautas the Great, Lithuania, Chem Eng, 34; Berlin-Charllot Tech Hochschule, Ger, BS & MS, 38, PhD(chem), 40. *Prof Exp:* Asst chem tech, Univ Vytautas the Great, Lithuania, 34-39, assoc prof tech silicates, fac eng, 40-43, dean, 42-43; consult, Lithuanian Dept Bldg Mat, 39-42; mem staff, E I du Pont de Nemours & Co, 47-49 & Sherwin-Williams Co, 49-57; res assoc, Wyandotte Chems Corp, 57-71; BASF Wyandotte Corp, 71-73; RES PROF, POLYMER INST, UNIV DETROIT, 73- *Concurrent Pos:* Consult, sealant companies, 73- *Mem:* Am Chem Soc; Soc Rheol. *Res:* Silicates; portland cements; adhesives; alumina-iron oxide ratio and shrinkage of portland cements; extender pigments; treatment of carbon blacks; silicate vehicles; amines as curing agents of epoxy-resins; urethane coatings and sealants; polymer research; polymer chemistry in the areas of urethane, epoxies and acrylics. *Mailing Add:* Polymer Inst Univ of Detroit 4001 Nichols Rd Detroit MI 48221

DAN, TERUKI CLARK, b Tokyo, Japan, Jan 19, 38; US citizen; m 65; c 2. BIOCHEMISTRY, PSYCHOLOGY. *Educ:* Col Wooster, BA, 66; Ill Inst Technol, MS, 70, PhD(psychol), 73. *Prof Exp:* RES FEL PHYSIOL PSYCHOL & BIOCHEM, NORTHWEST INST MED RES, 69- *Concurrent Pos:* Biochemist, Northwest Hosp, Chicago, 73-; lectr, Ind Univ Northwest, 74-; clin instr, Med Lab Tech Prog, Triton Col, 74- *Mem:* AAAS; Am Psychol Asn. *Res:* Intraocular fluids; biological transparency; operant conditioning. *Mailing Add:* NW Inst Med Res 5656 W Addison St Chicago IL 60634

DANA, M TERRY, b Oklahoma City, Okla, Nov 17, 43. ATMOSPHERIC PHYSICS, METEOROLOGY. *Educ:* Univ Wash, BS, 65; Ariz State Univ, MS, 67. *Prof Exp:* SR RES SCIENTIST ATMOSPHERIC SCI, PAC NORTHWEST DIV, BATTELLE MEM INST, 67- *Mem:* Am Meteorol Soc; Am Geophys Union; Fed Am Scientist; Union Concerned Scientists. *Res:* Precipitation chemistry; precipitation scavenging. *Mailing Add:* Box 999 Richland WA 99352

DANA, MALCOLM NIVEN, b Pomfret, Vt, Dec 8, 22; m 46; c 2. HORTICULTURE. *Educ:* Univ Vt, BS, 48; Iowa State Col, MS, 49, PhD(hort), 52. *Prof Exp:* From asst prof to assoc prof, 52-67, chmn dept, 73-78, PROF HORT, UNIV WIS-MADISON, 67- *Mem:* Am Soc Hort Sci; Weed Sci Soc Am; Am Pomol Soc. *Res:* Weed control in cranberries; cultural studies on strawberries. *Mailing Add:* Dept Hort Univ Wis Madison WI 53706

DANA, ROBERT CLARK, b Cedar Falls, Iowa, Feb 19, 44; m 67; c 2. ORGANIC CHEMISTRY. *Educ:* Austin Col, BA, 66; Univ Tex, Austin, PhD(org chem), 71; Ohio State Univ, MA, 79. *Prof Exp:* Doc analyst, 71-75, ASST MGR ORG CHEM, CHEMICAL ABSTR SERV, 75- *Mem:* Am Chem Soc. *Mailing Add:* Chem Abstr Serv PO Box 3012 Columbus OH 43210

DANA, ROBERT WATSON, b Oklahoma City, Okla; m 67; c 2. REMOTE SENSING, OPTICAL PHYSICS. *Educ:* Univ Wash, BS, 63, MS, 69. *Prof Exp:* Physicist, Pac Southwest Forest & Range Exp Sta, Calif, 69-76, PHYSICIST REMOTE SENSING, ROCKY MOUNTAIN FOREST & RANGE EXP STA, FOREST SERV, USDA, 76- *Honors & Awards:* Group Superior Serv Award, USDA, 71. *Mem:* Am Soc Photogram; Coun Optical Radiation Measurements. *Res:* Remote sensing of forest and range resources; radiometry photometry; image processing; microdensitometry; atmospheric radiative transfer. *Mailing Add:* US Forest Serv 240 W Prospect Ft Collins CO 80526

DANA, STEPHEN WINCHESTER, b Kelleys' Island, Ohio, Apr 10, 20. GEOLOGY. *Educ:* Oberlin Col, AB, 40; Univ Southern Calif, MS, 42; Calif Inst Technol, PhD(geophysics), 44. *Prof Exp:* Vis lectr, Whittier Col, 41-42; computer, Seismic Surv Div, Shell Oil Co, Los Angeles, 44-45; assoc prof, 45-58 & 49-53, PROF GEOL, UNIV REDLANDS, 53- *Concurrent Pos:* Geologist, US Geol Surv, 48-49, consult, 49-, consult ground water br, 52-; res geophysicist, United Geophys Soc, Inc, 49-53; consult, Standard Oil Co, Calif & San Bernardino Valley Munic Water District, 52-; consult geologist, South Calif Edison Co, 57- *Mem:* Fel Geol Soc Am; Am Geophys Union; Soc Explor Geophys; Am Asn Petrol Geologists; Seismol Soc Am. *Res:* Seismology; core analysis; petroleum engineering; sedimentation; refinement of field techniques of eletrical, gravitational and magnetic prospecting; structural geology. *Mailing Add:* Dept of Geol Univ of Redlands Redlands CA 92373

DANARD, MAURICE BEVERLEY, meteorology, see previous edition

DANBERG, JAMES E(DWARD), b New Haven, Conn, Oct 13, 27; m 53; c 5. AERONAUTICAL ENGINEERING. *Educ:* Cath Univ, BAE, 49, MAE, 52, DE, 64. *Prof Exp:* Aeronaut engr, Field Eval Div, US Naval Ord Lab, 51-55, aeronaut res engr, Spec Prob Br, Aerophys Div, 55-56, hypersonics group, 56-60, chief, 60-62; prog mgr, Fluid Physics Br, Res Div, Off Adv Res & Technol, Hqs, NASA, 62-67; assoc prof, 67-74, assoc dean, Col Eng, 70-74, PROF MECH & AEROSPACE ENG, UNIV DEL, 74- *Concurrent Pos:* Lectr, George Washington Univ, 60; mem heat transfer panel, Comt Aeroballistics, Bur Naval Weapons, 61; exec secy, Res Adv Comt Fluid Mech, NASA, 63-67. *Mem:* Am Inst Aeronaut & Astronaut. *Res:* Hypersonic aerodynamics; viscous flow and aerodynamic heating; heat transfer and skin friction characteristics of turbulent boundary layer including the effects of mass transfer at hypersonic speeds. *Mailing Add:* Col Eng Univ Del Newark DE 19711

DANBY, GORDON THOMPSON, b Can, Nov 8, 29; m 62; c 2. PHYSICS. *Educ:* Carleton Univ, Can, BSc, 52; McGill Univ, PhD(physics), 56. *Prof Exp:* MEM STAFF, BROOKHAVEN NAT LAB, 57- *Mem:* Am Phys Soc. *Res:* Accelerator development; apparatus for high energy physics, especially magnets and beam transport; experiments with neutrinos; magnetic levitation and applications to high speed vehicles. *Mailing Add:* Brookhaven Nat Lab Bldg 911 Upton NY 11973

DANBY, JOHN MICHAEL ANTHONY, b London, Eng, Aug 5, 29; m 58; c 2. CELESTIAL MECHANICS. *Educ:* Oxford Univ, BA, 50, MA, 54; Univ Manchester, PhD(astron), 53. *Prof Exp:* Asst prof astron, Univ Minn, 57-61; asst prof, Yale Univ, 61-67; PROF MATH & PHYSICS, NC STATE UNIV, 67- *Concurrent Pos:* Consult, Honeywell, Inc, 58-; consult, Air Force Chart & Info Ctr; pres, Celestial Mech Inst, 75-, mem ed comt, Celestial Mech, 73- *Mem:* Am Astron Soc; Int Astron Union; fel Royal Astron Soc. *Res:* Celestial mechanics; stellar dynamics; properties of dynamical systems. *Mailing Add:* Dept of Math NC State Univ Raleigh NC 27607

DANCE, ELDRED LEROY, b Blackfoot, Idaho, Dec 22, 17; m 46; c 3. CHEMISTRY. *Educ:* Univ Calif, BS, 43. *Prof Exp:* Res & develop chemist & chem engr, 43-63, sr res chem engr, 63-66, ASSOC SCIENTIST, DOW CHEM CO, PITTSBURG, 66- *Mem:* Am Inst Chem Engrs. *Res:* Process evaluation and development including unit operations of reactor design; distillation; refrigeration; process control; heat and mass transfer; fluid mixing; production of plastics and polymers; hollow fiber technology. *Mailing Add:* 37 Hornet Ct PO Box 1398 Pittsburg CA 94565

DANCHIK, RICHARD S, b Pittsburgh, Pa, Mar 21, 43. ANALYTICAL CHEMISTRY, INDUSTRIAL HYGIENE CHEMISTRY. *Educ:* Duquesne Univ, BS, 65; Wayne State Univ, PhD(anal chem), 68. *Prof Exp:* Res scientist, 68-74, sr scientist, 74-79, MGR ENVIRON HEALTH, ALCOA LABS, ALUMINUM CO, AM, 79- *Mem:* Am Chem Soc; Sigma Xi; Am Soc Testing & Mat; Am Indust Hyg Asn. *Res:* Indirect spectrophotometric and atomic absorption spectrometric methods of analysis; electroanalytical methods of analysis; investigation and application of selective ion electrodes; ultraviolet and visible absorption spectrometry; development of automated process control systems; environmental chemistry; industrial hygiene chemistry. *Mailing Add:* Alcoa Labs Aluminum Co Am Alcoa Center PA 15069

DANCIK, BRUCE PAUL, b Chicago, Ill, Dec 27, 43; Can citizen; m 72. POPULATION GENETICS, GENECOLOGY. *Educ:* Univ Mich, BS, 65, MF, 67, PhD(forest genetics), 72. *Prof Exp:* Asst prof bot, Saginaw Valley Col, Mich, 72-73; asst prof, 73-77, ASSOC PROF FOREST GENETICS, UNIV ALTA, 77- *Concurrent Pos:* Assoc ed, Forestry Chronicle, 76-; chmn, Forestry Panel, Environ Coun Alta, 77-81; ed, Can J Forest Res, 81- *Mem:* AAAS; Genetics Soc Am; Genetics Soc Can; Soc Study Evolution; Sigma Xi. *Res:* Genic (allozyme) variation, molecular genetics, population structure, ecological differentiation, evolution, and mating system dynamics of woody plant species, especially those of western North America. *Mailing Add:* Dept Forest Sci Univ Alta Edmonton AB T6G 2G6 Can

DANCIS, JOSEPH, b New York, NY, Mar 19, 16; m 48; c 2. MEDICINE, BIOCHEMISTRY. *Educ:* Columbia Col, BA, 34; St Louis Univ, MD, 38. *Prof Exp:* Palmer sr investr, 54-56; PROF PEDIAT, COL MED, NY UNIV, 63-, CHMN DEPT, 74- *Concurrent Pos:* Nat Res Found res fel, 51-53; Markle scholar, 56-61; res career investr, NIH, 61- *Honors & Awards:* Borden Award, 71. *Mem:* Am Acad Pediat; Soc Pediat Res; Am Pediat Soc; NY Acad Sci; Harvey Soc. *Res:* Placental physiology; metabolic errors. *Mailing Add:* NY Univ Med Ctr New York NY 10016

DANCY, TERENCE E(RNEST), b Coulsdon, Surrey, Eng, Mar 5, 25; nat US; m 47; c 2. METALLURGY. *Educ:* Univ London, BSc, 45, PhD(fuel tech) & DIC, 48. *Prof Exp:* Sr sci officer, Iron Making Div, Brit Iron & Steel Res Asn, 47-53; metall liaison officer, Brit Embassy, Washington, DC, 53-54; prin sci officer commercial develop, Brit Iron & Steel Res Asn, 54-56; res supvr, Jones & Laughlin Steel Corp, 56-61, asst dir res, 61-64, asst to vpres eng & plant, 64-66, mgr process eng, 66-71; vpres eng & develop, 71-79, SR VPRES ENG & DEVELOP, SIDBEC/DOSCO, 79- , VPRES TECHNOL, SIDBEC & SIDBEC/DOSCO & BD DIRS, SIDBEC/NORMINES, 76- *Concurrent Pos:* UK deleg, Orgn European Econ Co-op, France, 50-52, consult, European Productivity Agency, 54; UK rep, Comite Int du Bas Fourneau, Belgium, 50-53. *Honors & Awards:* Hunt Award, Am Inst Mining, Metall & Petrol Engrs, 60; Kelly First Award, Asn Iron & Steel Engrs, 64; Medal, Am Iron & Steel Inst, 65 & 81; Howe Mem lectr, Am Inst Mining, Metall & Petrol Engrs, 76. *Mem:* Fel Am Soc Metals; Am Inst Mining, Metall & Petrol Engrs; Asn Iron & Steel Engrs; Am Iron & Steel Inst; Can Inst Mining & Metall. *Res:* Extractive metallurgy and steel processing research; blast furnace; steel refining and primary processing; engineering development, iron ore pelletizing, direct reduction, electric furnace operation. *Mailing Add:* Sidbec/Dosco 507 Place D'Armes Montreal PQ H2Y 2W8 Can

DANDAPANI, RAMASWAMI, b Nagpur, India, Feb 26, 46; m 77; c 2. COMPUTER SCIENCE. *Educ:* Univ Nagpur, BSc, 64; Indian Inst Sci, BE, 67; Univ Iowa, MS, 69, PhD(comput sci), 74. *Prof Exp:* Teaching & res asst elec eng, Univ Iowa, 68-71, res asst comput sci, 71-74; asst prof, 74-79, ASSOC PROF COMPUT SCI, YOUNGSTOWN STATE UNIV, 79- *Mem:* Inst Elec & Electronic Engrs; Sigma Xi. *Res:* Combinational logic circuits; fault detection in logic circuits; testable design of logic circuits. *Mailing Add:* Dept of Math & Comput Sci Youngstown State Univ Youngstown OH 44555

DANDEKAR, BALKRISHNA S, b Khed-Ratnagiri, India, Sept 13, 33; m 59; c 2. GEOPHYSICS, AERONOMY. *Educ:* Univ Poona, BSc, 53, MSc, 55; Gujarat Univ, PhD(physics), 62. *Prof Exp:* Lectr physics, Khalsa Col, India, 55; jr res asst, Phys Res Lab, Ahmedabad, 58-61; prof & head dept, Maharashtra Educ Soc Col, Poona, 61-62; res physicist, Wentworth Inst, 62-65; sr res assoc aeronomy, Northeastern Univ, 65-68; RES PHYSICIST, AIR FORCE GEOPHYSICS LAB, 68- *Mem:* Am Geophys Union. *Res:* Optical emissions from the upper atmosphere; polar atmospheric processes; ionospheric physics. *Mailing Add:* Air Force Cambridge Res Lab LIB Hanscom AFB Bedford MA 01730

DANDLIKER, WALTER BEACH, b Greensburg, Pa, Jan 24, 18; m 67; c 3. IMMUNOCHEMISTRY. *Educ:* Rollins Col, BS, 40; Calif Inst Technol, PhD(bio-org chem), 45. *Prof Exp:* Asst, Cutter Labs, Calif, 42-44; asst, Calif Inst Technol, 44-45, fel chem, 45-46; fel chem, Univ Calif, 46-47, instr, 47-48; NIH fel, Harvard Med Sch, 48-50, res assoc, 50-51; from asst prof to assoc prof biochem, Univ Washington, Seattle, 51-58; from assoc prof to prof, Univ Miami, Fla, 58-63; MEM, SCRIPPS CLIN & RES FOUND, 63- *Mem:* Am Chem Soc; Am Soc Biol Chemists; Am Soc Immunologists. *Res:* Biophysical chemistry; immunochemistry; fluorescence polarization. *Mailing Add:* Dept of Biochem Scripps Clinic & Res Found La Jolla CA 92037

DANDONA, ANIL K, petroleum engineering, see previous edition

DANDY, JAMES WILLIAM TREVOR, b Preston, Eng, July 18, 29; m 59; c 4. ZOOLOGY, PHYSIOLOGY. *Educ:* Univ Natal, BSc, 53, MSc, 55; Univ Toronto, PhD(zool), 67. *Prof Exp:* Lectr zool, Univ Col Fort Hare, 56-59; asst prof, 65-74, ASSOC PROF ZOOL, UNIV MAN, 74- *Concurrent Pos:* Nat Res Coun Can operating grant, 65-; Fisheries Res Bd Can res grant, 66- *Mem:* AAAS; Marine Biol Asn UK; Brit Soc Exp Biol; Can Soc Zoologists. *Res:* Environmental physiology. *Mailing Add:* Dept of Zool Univ of Man Winnipeg MB R3B 2E9 Can

DANE, BENJAMIN, b Boston, Mass, Nov 22, 33; m 57; c 2. ANIMAL BEHAVIOR, PHYSIOLOGY. *Educ:* Harvard Univ, AB, 56; Cornell Univ, PhD(zool), 61. *Prof Exp:* Asst biol, Cornell Univ, 59-60; res assoc physiol, Med Ctr, NY Univ, 61-62, instr, 62-63; actg asst prof animal behav, Stanford Univ, 63-66; asst prof, 66-69, ASSOC PROF BIOL, TUFTS UNIV, 69- *Concurrent Pos:* Consult, Santa Rite Tech, Inc, Calif, 64-66. *Mem:* AAAS; Am Soc Zoologists; Animal Behav Soc; Cooper Ornith Soc; Am Ornithologists Union. *Mailing Add:* Dept of Biol Tufts Univ Medford MA 02155

DANE, CHARLES WARREN, b Washington, DC, Sept 21, 34; m 57; c 2. ECOLOGY, AVIAN PHYSIOLOGY. *Educ:* Cornell Univ, BS, 56, MS, 57; Purdue Univ, PhD(vert ecol), 65. *Prof Exp:* Res biologist avian physiol, Northern Prairie Wildlife Res Ctr, 64-76, MIGRATORY BIRD RES SPECIALIST, DIV WILDLIFE RES, US FISH & WILDLIFE SERV, 76- *Mem:* Wildlife Soc; Cooper Ornith Soc. *Res:* Influence of environmental factors on waterfowl reproductive physiology. *Mailing Add:* Div of Wildlife Res Dept of Interior Washington DC 20240

DANEHY, JAMES PHILIP, b Ft Wayne, Ind, Apr 27, 12; m 34; c 3. ORGANIC CHEMISTRY. *Educ:* Univ Notre Dame, BS, 33, MS, 34, PhD(org chem), 36. *Prof Exp:* Res chemist, Gen Chem Co, New York, 36-38; res chemist, Harris-Seybold-Potter Co, Cleveland, 38-42; group leader, Corn Prods Refining Co, Argo, Ill, 42-48; keratin group leader, Toni Co, 48-51; asst prof liberal educ, Univ Notre Dame, 51-55, from assoc prof to prof chem, 55-77; SR CONSULT, BERNARD WOLNAK & ASSOCS, CHICAGO, 78- *Concurrent Pos:* Fulbright lectr, Univ Col, Cork, 61-62. *Mem:* Am Chem Soc. *Res:* Chemistry of vegetable proteins; zein; keratin; organic sulfur chemistry; mechanisms of reactions of organic divalent sulfur compounds. *Mailing Add:* 1839 Churchill Dr South Bend IN 46617

DANEN, WAYNE C, b Green Bay, Wis, Dec 24, 41; m 64; c 4. ORGANIC CHEMISTRY. *Educ:* St Norbert Col, BA, 64; Iowa State Univ, PhD(org chem), 67. *Prof Exp:* Asst prof, 67-71, assoc prof, 72-77, PROF CHEM, KANS STATE UNIV, 78- *Concurrent Pos:* Petrol Res Fund grant, 67-69, 71-75 & 75-78. Res Corp grant, 73-75; NSF grant, 78-81; sabbital leave, Los Alamos Nat Lab, 77-78. *Mem:* Am Chem Soc. *Res:* Organic free radical chemistry; electron spin resonance studies of stable and transient free radicals; laser induced organic reactions; laser diagnostics. *Mailing Add:* Dept Chem Kans State Univ Manhattan KS 66506

DANEO-MOORE, LOLITA, b Nimes, France, Feb 18, 29; US citizen; m 50; c 4. MICROBIOLOGY. *Educ:* Univ Pa, BA, 60, MS, 63; Rutgers Univ, PhD(microbiol), 65. *Prof Exp:* Assoc ed cancer chemother, Triple I, 60-65; from instr to assoc prof, 66-78, PROF MICROBIOL, SCH MED, TEMPLE UNIV, 78- *Concurrent Pos:* Fels, Arthritis Found, Temple Univ, 65-67, Am Cancer Soc, 67-69 & Res Corp, 72- *Mem:* Am Soc Microbiol. *Res:* Regulatory mechanisms; ribosomes; cell membranes; cell growth and division; ageing; mode of action of antibiotics. *Mailing Add:* Temple Univ Sch Med 3400 N Broad St Philadelphia PA 19140

DANES, ZDENKO FRANKENBERGER, b Prague, Czech, Aug 25, 20; nat US; m 45; c 2. GEOPHYSICS. *Educ:* Charles Univ, Prague, BS, 46, PhD(math), 48, PhD(physics), 49. *Prof Exp:* Asst, State Geophys Inst, Czech, 46-47; asst prof, Physics Inst, Charles Univ, Prague, 48-50; geophys interpreter, Gulf Res & Develop Co, Pa, 53-59; res engr, Boeing Airplane Co, 59-62; PROF PHYSICS, UNIV PUGET SOUND, 62- *Concurrent Pos:* Vis prof, Univ Minn, 62; consult various oil & aerospace industs; vis prof, Univ of Technol, Vienna, Austria, 74-75; pres, Danes Res Assocs, 78- *Mem:* Am Geophys Union; Soc Explor Geophys. *Res:* Gravity; geomagnetism; radiation; constitution of earth; lunar physics; electromagnetic theory. *Mailing Add:* Dept of Physics Univ of Puget Sound Tacoma WA 98416

DANESE, ARTHUR E, b Mt Morris, NY, May 11, 22. MATHEMATICS. *Educ:* Univ Rochester, AB, 47, PhD, 56; Harvard Univ, AM, 49. *Prof Exp:* Instr math, Univ Rochester, 48-54; asst prof, Univ Tenn, 55; mathematician, Eastman Kodak Co, 55-58; asst prof math, Union Univ, NY, 58-64; assoc prof, State Univ NY Buffalo, 64-67; PROF MATH, STATE UNIV NY COL FREDONIA, 67- *Mem:* Am Math Soc; Math Asn Am. *Res:* Operational calculus; mathematical analysis; orthogonal polynomials; special functions; inequalities; classical analysis. *Mailing Add:* Dept of Math State Univ of NY Col Fredonia NY 14063

DANFORTH, DAVID NEWTON, b Evanston, Ill, Aug 25, 12; m 38; c 1. OBSTETRICS & GYNECOLOGY. *Educ:* Northwestern Univ, BS, 34, MS, 36, PhD(physiol), 38, MD, 39. *Prof Exp:* Asst physiol, Med Sch, Northwestern Univ, 35-38; intern, NY Post-Grad Med Sch & Hosp, Columbia Univ, 38-39; from asst resident to resident obstet & gynec, Sloane Hosp Women, 39-44; clin asst, 46-47, from asst prof to assoc prof, 47-59, chmn dept, 65-72, prof, 59-80, EMER PROF OBSTET & GYNEC, MED SCH, NORTHWESTERN UNIV, 80- *Concurrent Pos:* Chief dept obstet &

gynec, Evanston Hosp, 47-65 & Chicago Wesley Mem Hosp, 65-71; dir, Am Bd Obstet & Gynec, 66-73. *Mem:* AAAS; Am Gynec Soc (vpres, 73, pres, 74); AMA; Am Col Obstet & Gynec (1st vpres, 69); Am Col Surg. *Res:* Anatomy and physiology of cervix; gynecological pathology. *Mailing Add:* 2530 Ridge Ave Evanston IL 60201

DANFORTH, JOSEPH DAVIS, b Danville, Ill, Mar 7, 12; m 40; c 4. PHYSICAL CHEMISTRY. *Educ:* Wabash Col, AB, 34; Purdue Univ, PhD(phys chem), 38. *Prof Exp:* Res chemist, Universal Oil Prod Co, 38-47; assoc prof, 47-54, PROF CHEM, GRINNELL COL, 54- *Concurrent Pos:* Consult, NCent Asn Sec Schs & Cols, 73- *Mem:* AAAS; Am Chem Soc. *Res:* Thermal analysis, catalysis; mechanisms and kinetics of solid state decompositions. *Mailing Add:* Dept of Chem Grinnell Col Grinnell IA 50112

DANFORTH, RAYMOND HEWES, b Mineola, NY, Nov 24, 44; m 67; c 2. CHEMISTRY. *Educ:* Bates Col, BS, 66; Princeton Univ, PhD(org chem), 71. *Prof Exp:* Res chemist, Nat Patent Develop Corp, 71-73; asst tech dir pulp chem, Berlin-Gorham Div, Brown Co, 73-80; DIR ENVIRON & TECH SERV, JAMES RIVER CORP, 80- *Mem:* Am Chem Soc; Tech Asn Pulp & Paper Indust. *Res:* environmental and technical activities in a kraft pulp mill; purified cellulose and cellulose derivatives. *Mailing Add:* Star Rte 44 Gorham NH 03581

DANFORTH, WILLIAM (FRANK), b Washington, DC, Jan 12, 28. FRESH WATER ECOLOGY. *Educ:* Univ Iowa, AB, 48; Columbia Univ, AM, 49; Univ Calif, Los Angeles, PhD(zool), 52. *Prof Exp:* From asst prof to assoc prof, 52-63, PROF BIOL, ILL INST TECHNOL, 63- *Mem:* AAAS; Am Soc Zool; Soc Protozool; Phycol Soc Am; Am Soc Limnol & Oceanog. *Res:* Ecology and physiology of planktonic algae. *Mailing Add:* Dept of Biol Ill Inst of Technol Chicago IL 60616

DANFORTH, WILLIAM H, b St Louis, Mo, Apr 10, 26; m 50; c 4. MEDICINE. *Educ:* Princeton Univ, AB, 47; Harvard Med Sch, MD, 51. *Hon Degrees:* Numerous from US Cols & Univs, 71-81. *Prof Exp:* Intern, Barnes Hosp, St Louis, 51-52, from asst resident to resident, 54-57; asst resident, Children's Hosp, St Louis, 55-56; from instr to assoc prof med, 57-67, vchancellor med affairs & pres sch med & assoc hosps, 65-71, CHANCELLOR, WASH UNIV, 71-, PROF INTERNAL MED, SCH MED, 67- *Concurrent Pos:* Univ fel cardiol, Wash Univ, 57-58, NIH fel biochem, 61-63; physician, Vet Admin Hosp, St Louis, 58-61; attend physician, Barnes Hosp, 58-; mem exec comt, St Louis Br, Nat Asn Advan Colored People, 78-; pres, Independent Cols & Univs Mo, 79-; mem comt, Asn Am Univs/Nat Asn State Univs & Land Grant Cols Joint Health Policy, 78-, chmn, 78-81. *Mem:* Inst Med-Nat Acad Sci; Cent Soc Clin Res; Am Soc Clin Invest. *Mailing Add:* Wash Univ St Louis MO 63130

DANG, PETER HUNG-CHEN, b Kwangsi, China, Sept 7, 18; US citizen; m 47; c 4. PHARMACOLOGY, BIOCHEMISTRY. *Educ:* Nat Cent Univ, Nanking, China, BS, 44; Mont State Univ, MS, 59; Univ Chicago, PhD(pharmacol), 64. *Prof Exp:* Instr, Paisha Col, China, 44-45; asst biochemist, biochem & dis, Vet Res Lab, Mont, 56-58; res asst, Univ Chicago, 58-63, res assoc, 63-64; res assoc animal nutrit, drug & dis, Cornell Univ, 64-67; head pharmacol, Food & Drug Res Labs, 67-71, mgr, 72-73; DIR PHARMACOL, DIAGNOSTIC DATA INC, 73- *Mem:* Am Chem Soc; AAAS; NY Acad Sci. *Res:* Enzymological, immunological, biochemical and physiological effect on chemicals; drug toxicity and pharmokinetic, nutrition and disease; studies on laxative, antispasmotic agents; antiinflammatory agents for arthritis and degenerative diseases. *Mailing Add:* 877 San Ardo Way Mountain View CA 94043

DANG, VI DUONG, US citizen; m 71; c 2. CHEMICAL ENGINEERING, CHEMISTRY. *Educ:* Nat Taiwan Univ, BS, 66; Clarkson Col Technol, MS, 68, PhD(chem eng), 71. *Prof Exp:* Environ engr environ med, NY Univ Med Ctr, 71-72 & Johns Hopkins Univ, 72-73; chem engr electrochem eng, P R Mallory, Inc, 73-74; chem engr chem & nuclear eng, Brookhaven Nat Lab, 74-80; ASSOC PROF, CATHOLIC UNIV AM, 80- *Concurrent Pos:* Res assoc, Calif Inst Technol, 72. *Mem:* Am Inst Mem: Am Inst Chem Engrs; Am Chem Soc; Am Nuclear Soc; AAS; NY Acad Sci. *Res:* Fundamental research in heat and mass transfer with or without chemical reactions; nuclear fusion with particular application to chemical processing; coal conversion; electrochemical engineering. *Mailing Add:* 6304 Phyllis Lane Bethesda MD 20817

D'ANGELO, HENRY, b New York, NY, Dec 20, 32; m 62; c 4. ELECTRICAL ENGINEERING. *Educ:* City Univ New York, BEE, 55; Kans State Univ, MS, 57, Univ Wis, PhD(elec eng), 64. *Prof Exp:* Instr elec eng, Kans State Univ, 55-57; engr navig systs, Sperry Gyroscope Co div, Sperry-Rand Co, 57-60; asst prof elec eng, Univ Denver, 60-62 & 64-66, assoc prof, 66-68, prof, 68-69; prof & head dept, Mich Technol Univ, 69-73; prof math sci, Dept Math, Memphis State Univ, 73-79; PROF MFG ENG & ASSOC DEAN ENG, COL ENG, BOSTON UNIV, 79- *Concurrent Pos:* NSF res grant, 65-67; NASA res grant, 66-67; vis prof dept math, Morehouse Col, 68-69. *Honors & Awards:* Am Soc Eng Educ Award, 73. *Res:* Operations research; learning-adaptive control systems; linear and nonlinear time-varying systems; systems modeling and simulation; microcomputer structures. *Mailing Add:* Boston Univ Boston MA 20015

D'ANGELO, JOHN PHILIP, b Philadelphia, Pa, Mar 5, 51. MATHEMATICS. *Educ:* Univ Pa, BA, 72; Princeton Univ, PhD(math), 76. *Prof Exp:* Moore instr math, Mass Inst Technol, 76-78; ASST PROF MATH, UNIV ILL, URBANA, 78- *Mem:* Am Math Soc. *Res:* Several complex variables, partial differential equations. *Mailing Add:* Dept of Math Univ of Ill Urbana IL 61801

D'ANGELO, NICOLA, b Ripatransone, Italy, Jan 8, 31; US citizen; m 63. PLASMA PHYSICS. *Educ:* Univ Rome, DSc, 53, specialization degree, 55. *Prof Exp:* Res asst physics, Univ Rome, 53-54 & 1st Superior Sanita, 54-56; res assoc, Argonne Nat Lab, 56-59; res physicist, Princeton Univ, 59-66;

leader plasma group, Danish Atomic Energy Comn, Riso, 66-68; head diag group, Europ Space Res Inst, 68-70, dir, 70-72; mem staff, Danish Space Res Inst, 72-76; PROF DEPT PHYSICS & ASTRON, UNIV IOWA, 76- *Mem:* Am Geophys Union. *Res:* Cosmic rays; neutron, nuclear plasma and space physics. *Mailing Add:* Dept Physics & Astron Univ Iowa Iowa City IA 52242

D'ANGIO, GIULIO J, b New York, NY, May 2, 22; m 55; c 2. RADIOTHERAPY. *Educ:* Columbia Univ, AB, 43; Harvard Univ, MD, 45; FRCR, 81. *Prof Exp:* Intern, Children's Hosp, Boston, Mass, 45-46; resident path, Vet Admin Hosp, West Roxbury, Mass, 48-49; resident radiol, Boston City Hosp, Mass, 49-53; asst, Harvard Med Sch, 53-56, instr, 56-62, clin assoc, 62-64; prof radiol & dir div radiation ther, Univ Minn Hosps, 64-68; div chief, Sloan-Kettering Inst Cancer Res, 68-76; chmn, Dept Radiation Ther, Mem Hosp, 68-76; PROF RADIATION THER & PEDIAT ONCOL, SCH MED, UNIV PA, 76-; DIR CHILDREN'S CANCER RES CTR, CHILDREN'S HOSP PHILADELPHIA, 76- 68- *Concurrent Pos:* Fel path, Babies Hosp, NY, 48; asst, Boston City Hosp, 53-55, asst physician, 55-64; asst, Children's Hosp, Boston, 56-59, assoc radiologist, 59-62, radiotherapist, 63-64; res assoc Children's Cancer Res Found, 56-59, radiotherapist, 59-64; asst radiologist, Mass Gen Hosp, Boston, 61-62, consult, 62-64; assoc res radiologist, Donner Lab, Univ Calif, Berkeley, 62-63, consult, Donner Lab & Lawrence Radiation Lab, 64-76; consult, Hennepin County Gen Hosp, 66-68; vis radiation therapist, James Ewing Hosp, 68-; attend radiation therapist, Mem Hosp, 68-76; attend radiologist, NY Hosp, prof radiol, Med Col, Cornell Univ, 68-76; chmn, Nat Wilms' Tumor study. *Honors & Awards:* Heath Mem Award, Am Cancer Soc, 78; M D Anderson Tumor & Cancer Inst Award, 79. *Mem:* AAAS; Royal Soc Med; Am Asn Cancer Res; Am Col Radiol; Am Radium Soc. *Res:* Clinical radiotherapy; combined chemotherapy and radiotherapy; mechanisms of cancer growth; late radiation effects. *Mailing Add:* Children's Hosp of Philadelphia Philadelphia PA 19104

DANGLE, RICHARD L, b New Castle, Pa, July 24, 30; m 56; c 2. NUCLEAR PHYSICS. *Educ:* Westminster Col, Pa, BS, 58; Univ Wis, MS, 60, PhD(physics), 63. *Prof Exp:* Fel physics, Univ Sao Paulo, 63-64; instr, Univ Wis, 64-65; from asst prof to assoc prof, Univ Ga, 65-74, asst dean, Col Arts & Sci, 68-74; PROF PHYSICS & DEAN SCH ARTS & SCI, W GA COL, 74- *Mem:* AAAS; Am Phys Soc. *Res:* Low energy nuclear physics, primarily in charged particle spectroscopy. *Mailing Add:* 116 Brandywine Tr Carrollton GA 30117

DANHEISER, RICK LANE, b New York, NY, Oct 12, 51. ORGANIC CHEMISTRY. *Educ:* Columbia Col, BA, 72; Harvard Univ, MA, 75, PhD(chem), 78. *Prof Exp:* ASST PROF CHEM, MASS INST TECHNOL, 78- *Concurrent Pos:* fel, Alfred E Sloan Found. *Mem:* Am Chem Soc; Chem Soc Brit. *Res:* Development of new synthetic methods and their application in the total synthesis of biologically significant natural products. *Mailing Add:* Dept of Chem Mass Inst of Technol Cambridge MA 02139

DANHOF, IVAN EDWARD, b Grand Haven, Mich, June 24, 28; m 50; c 4. PHYSIOLOGY. *Educ:* NTex State Col, BA & MA, 49; Univ Ill, PhD(physiol), 53; Univ Tex, MD, 62. *Prof Exp:* Teacher pub sch, 49-50; asst, Univ Ill, 50-53, instr physiol, 53; res assoc, 53-54, from instr to assoc prof, 54-75, PROF PHYSIOL, UNIV TEX HEALTH SCI CTR DALLAS, 75- *Concurrent Pos:* Dir med educ, Methodist Hosp Dallas, 69; Fulbright lectr, Med Fac, Nangrahar Univ, Afghanistan, 69-70. *Mem:* AAAS; assoc Soc Exp Biol & Med; Am Physiol Soc. *Res:* Motility and hormonal regulation of gastrointestinal tract; nutrition related to gastrointestinal function. *Mailing Add:* Univ Tex Southwestern Med Sch Dallas TX 75235

DANIEL, ALFRED, b Nimes, France, Nov 21, 42; French & Can Citizen; m 75. ORGANIC CHEMISTRY. *Educ:* Univ Montpellier, DSc, 70; Univ Alta, MBA, 77. *Prof Exp:* Teaching asst, Univ Montpellier, 66-70; fell, Univ Alta, 70-71; res chemist, Clin-Midy, 71-75; V PRES OPERS, CHEMBIOMED LTD, 77- *Mem:* Soc Chimique de France; Asn Nat Docteur Sci. *Res:* Management of a chemical research and development intensified company. *Mailing Add:* Chembiomed Ltd Univ of Alta Edmonton Can

DANIEL, CHARLES DWELLE, JR, b San Antonio, Tex, Oct 30, 25; m 46; c 2. PHYSICS, ELECTRONICS. *Educ:* US Mil Acad, BS, 46; Tulane Univ, MS, 61, PhD(physics), 68. *Prof Exp:* Dir missiles & space develop, HQ, Dept of Army, 70-71; comdr gen artillery opers, I Corps Group Artillery, US Army, Korea, 71-72; dir Army res, Basic Res, HQ, Dept of Army, 72-74; dep commandant, Educ Admin, Nat War Col, 74-75; spec asst, Res & Develop Orgn, HQ, US Army Mat Develop & Readiness Command, 74-77; COMDR GEN, ELECTRONICS RES & DEVELOP ACQUISITION, US ARMY ELECTRONICS RES & DEVELOP COMMAND, 77- *Res:* Nuclear physics; solid state physics. *Mailing Add:* HQ US Army Electronics Res 2800 Powder Mill Rd Adelphi MD 20703

DANIEL, CHARLES PACK, b Greenville, SC, July 26, 25; m 48; c 2. BIOLOGY. *Educ:* Furman Univ, BS, 48; Univ NC, Chapel Hill, MA, 55; Emory Univ, MS, 65. *Prof Exp:* Teacher pub sch, Va, 49-52; instr biol, High Point Col, 55-58; res assoc radiation ecol, Emory Univ, 60-62; asst prof biol, Furman Univ, 62-67; asst prof radiation ecol, Emory Univ, 67; ASSOC PROF BIOL, GA COL, 67- *Mem:* Ecol Soc Am; Am Inst Biol Sci; Sigma Xi. *Res:* Effects of ionizing radiation on old-field succession; population changes; dominance related to environment; physiological changes in photoperiod and germination. *Mailing Add:* Dept of Biol Ga Col Milledgeville GA 31061

DANIEL, CHARLES WALLER, b Annapolis, Md, June 16, 33; m 61; c 3. BIOLOGY. *Educ:* Univ NMex, AB, 54; Univ Hawaii, MS, 60; Univ Calif, Berkeley, PhD(zool), 65. *Prof Exp:* From asst prof to assoc prof, 65-77, PROF BIOL, UNIV CALIF, SANTA CRUZ, 77- *Res:* Normal and neoplastic biology of mammary tissues; differentiation in vitro; cellular aging. *Mailing Add:* Dept Biol Univ Calif Santa Cruz CA 95064

DANIEL, DANIEL S, b Basrah, Iraq, July 1, 34; m 65; c 3. PHYSICAL CHEMISTRY, ORGANIC CHEMISTRY. *Educ:* Univ London, BSc, 55, PhD(chem), 59. *Prof Exp:* Res chemist, Carnegie Inst Technol, 60-63; sr res chemist, 64-69, RES ASSOC, RES LAB, EASTMAN KODAK CO, 69- *Concurrent Pos:* Adj fac, Rochester Inst Technol. *Mem:* Am Chem Soc; Royal Soc Chem; Sigma Xi; AAAS; Am Asn Clin Chemists. *Res:* Clinical chemistry; synthetic organic chemistry; biochemistry; electrode phenomena. *Mailing Add:* Res Lab Eastman Kodak Co Rochester NY 14650

DANIEL, DONALD CLIFTON, b Atlanta, Ga, May 21, 42; m 76; c 1. MISSILE AERODYNAMICS, APPLIED MATHEMATICS. *Educ:* Univ Fla, BASE, 64, MSE, 65, PhD(aerospace eng), 73. *Prof Exp:* Res engr astrodyn, Boeing Co, 65-68; res assoc flight mech, Univ Fla, 71-72; AEROSPACE ENGR FLIGHT MECH & AERODYN, US AIR FORCE ARMAMENT LAB, 72- *Concurrent Pos:* Res asst, Univ Fla, 64-65, NSF trainee, 68-71, adj asst prof, 77- *Honors & Awards:* Tech Achievement Award Basic Res, US Air Force Systs Command, 78. *Mem:* Assoc fel Am Inst Aeronaut & Astronaut; Inst Elec & Electronic Engrs. *Res:* Missile aerodynamics with emphasis on high angle of attack vortex phenomena and hypersonic flow about lifting bodies. *Mailing Add:* US Air Force Armament Lab AFATL/DLB Eglin AFB FL 32542

DANIEL, EDWIN EMBREY, b Chattanooga, Tenn, Sept 23, 25; m 48, 73; c 3. PHARMACOLOGY. *Educ:* Johns Hopkins Univ, BA, 47, MA, 49; Univ Utah, PhD(pharmacol), 52. *Prof Exp:* Lab instr biol, anat & physiol, Johns Hopkins Univ, 47-49; asst pharmacol, Univ Utah, 49-52; from asst prof to assoc prof, Univ BC, 52-61; prof pharmacol, Univ Alta, 61-72, head dept, 61-72; PROF NEUROSCI, McMASTER UNIV, 76- *Mem:* AAAS; Am Soc Pharmacol & Exp Therapeut; Pharmacol Soc Can; Can Physiol Soc. *Res:* Nature of control of activity of smooth and cardiac muscle, especially membrane phenomena and cations. *Mailing Add:* Dept of Neurosci McMaster Univ Hamilton Can

DANIEL, HAL J, b Memphis, Tenn, Nov 10, 42. NEUROANATOMY, CRANIO-FACIAL ANATOMY. *Educ:* Univ Tenn, BS, 64, MA, 67; Univ Southern Miss, PhD(speech/hearing sci), 69. *Prof Exp:* PROF SPEECH & HEARING SCI, EAST CAROLINA UNIV, 69- *Concurrent Pos:* Adj prof anat, East Carolina Univ, 73-78, anthrop, 81-; vis scholar, Univ Wash, 80-81. *Mem:* Am Acad Advan Sci; Am Asn Phys Anthropologists; Sigma Xi; Am Speech & Hearing Asn. *Res:* Evolution of human communication from an anatomical and physiological point of view; evolution of the auditory system. *Mailing Add:* Sch Allied Health East Carolina Univ Greenville NC 27834

DANIEL, ISAAC M, b Salonica, Greece, Oct 7, 33; US citizen. EXPERIMENTAL MECHANICS, MATERIALS SCIENCE. *Educ:* Ill Inst Tech, BS, 57, MS, 59, PhD(civil eng), 64. *Prof Exp:* Asst res engr stress anal, 59-60, from assoc res engr to sr res engr, 60-66, mgr, 66-80, SCI ADV, IIT RES INST, 75- *Concurrent Pos:* Lectr, Soc Exp Stress Anal; mem comt on characterization of org matrix composites, Nat Mat Adv Bd-Nat Res Coun, 78-80. *Honors & Awards:* Award, Am Soc Civil Engrs, Ill Sect, 57. *Mem:* Am Soc Civil Engrs; fel Soc Exp Stress Anal; Am Soc Testing & Mat; Am Acad Mech. *Res:* Photoelasticity; moire analysis; wave propagation; viscoelasticity; experimental stress analysis; composite materials; strain gages; fracture mechanics; high-rate testing; nondestructive evaluation; test methods; impact. *Mailing Add:* IIT Res Inst 10 W 35th St Chicago IL 60616

DANIEL, JACK LELAND, b Spokane, Wash, Dec 15, 24; m 49; c 3. ELECTRON MICROSCOPY, MATERIALS SCIENCE. *Educ:* Univ Wash, Seattle, BS, 45, MS, 48; Ore State Univ, PhD(anal chem), 60. *Prof Exp:* Appl res chemist, Hanford Labs, Gen Elec Co, 48-49, sr chemist, 51-57, specialist, Tech Personnel Placement, 57-59, sr chemist, 59-60, sr scientist, 60-64; res assoc, ceramics, Electron Micros, 65-76, STAFF SCIENTIST, MICROSTRUCTURAL ANAL, ELECTRON MICROS, PAC NORTHWEST LABS, BATTELLE MEM INST, 76- *Concurrent Pos:* Specialist US team first US-Japan info exchange meeting oxide & carbide fuels, AEC, 63; vis chief res scientist, Mitsubishi Atomic Power Indust, Tokyo, 65-66. *Mem:* AAAS; NY Acad Sci; Am Soc Test & Mat; Electron Micros Soc Am; Int Stereol Soc. *Res:* Dynamic and scanning electron microscopy, especially of ceramics, high temperature materials and radioactive specimens; materials research; techniques of instrumental analysis, especially x-ray, quantitative metallography and nuclear ceramic fuels; stereology and quantitative image analysis. *Mailing Add:* Pacific Northwest Labs Battelle Mem Inst Battelle Blvd Richland WA 99352

DANIEL, JAMES WILSON, b Indianapolis, Ind, Sept 16, 40; m 62; c 2. NUMERICAL ANALYSIS, COMPUTER SCIENCES. *Educ:* Wabash Col, BA, 62; Stanford Univ, MA, 63, PhD(math), 65. *Prof Exp:* Res mathematician comput, IBM Corp, 65; res assoc math, Off Naval Res, 66; from asst prof to assoc prof comput sci, Univ Wis, 67-70; assoc prof, 70-74, PROF COMPUT SCI & MATH, UNIV TEX, 74-, CHMM, MATH DEPT, 77- *Concurrent Pos:* Vis mem, Math Res Ctr, Univ Wis, 66-70; vis staff mem, Los Alamos Sci Lab, 70- *Mem:* Am Math Soc; Soc Indust & Appl Math. *Res:* Efficient and accurate numerical methods for approximate solution of differential equations and optimization problems. *Mailing Add:* Dept Math Univ Tex Austin TX 78712

DANIEL, JOHN HARRISON, b Darlington, SC, Sept, 6, 15; m 42; c 2. PHYSICS. *Educ:* The Citadel, BS, 35; Univ Ky, MS, 37; Mass Inst Technol, ScD(physics), 40. *Prof Exp:* Asst, Univ Ky, 35-37; res fel, Nat Cancer Inst, USPHS, 40-41; asst physicist, Div Indust Hygiene, 41-42; res physicist, Firestone Res Lab, Ohio, 46-48; sr physicist, Lab Phys Biol, NIH, 48-53; physicist, Evans Signal Lab, 53-56; analyst, Inst for Defense Anal, 56-80; RETIRED. *Concurrent Pos:* Fel ctr advan eng stud, Mass Inst Technol, 69-70. *Mem:* AAAS; Inst Elec & Electronics Engrs; Am Phys Soc. *Res:* Weapons systems evaluation; missile and air defense; electron theory and surface phenomena of metals; detection of nuclear radiation; electron microscopy; dielectric measurements. *Mailing Add:* 5502 Cromwell Dr Bethesda MD 20816

DANIEL, JOHN SAGAR, b Banstead, Eng, May 31, 42; Can citizen; m 66; c 3. METALLURGY, EDUCATIONAL TECHNOLOGY. *Educ:* Oxford Univ, BA, 64, MA, 69; Univ Paris, France, DSc(metall), 69. *Prof Exp:* From asst prof to assoc prof metall, Ecole Polytech, Univ Montreal, 69-73; dir studies, Tele-Universite, Univ Quebec, 73-77; vpres, Athabasca Univ, Alta, 78-80; VRECTOR ACAD, CONCORDIA UNIV, 80- *Honors & Awards:* Distinguished Young Mem Award, Am Soc Metals, 73. *Mem:* Int Coun Correspondence Educ. *Res:* Communications; educational technology; educational administration; open learning; distance learning. *Mailing Add:* Concordia Univ 1455 de Maisonneauve W Montreal PQ H3G 1M8 Can

DANIEL, JON CAMERON, b Salem, Ore, Oct 17, 42. DEVELOPMENTAL BIOLOGY, CELL BIOLOGY. *Educ:* Calif State Univ, Northridge, BS, 65, MS, 67; State Univ NY Buffalo, PhD(develop biol), 71. *Prof Exp:* Asst prof anat, Northwestern Univ, Chicago, 73-78; ASSOC PROF HISTOL, COL DENT, UNIV ILL, CHICAGO, 78- *Concurrent Pos:* USPHS fel, Univ Pa, 71-73. *Mem:* Soc Develop Biol; Am Soc Cell Biol; Tissue Culture Asn. *Res:* Molecular mechanisms involved in the maintenance of the differentiated state in cell culture of chick embryo chondrocytes. *Mailing Add:* Dept Histol Col Dent PO Box 6996 Chicago IL 60680

DANIEL, JOSEPH CAR, JR, b Murphysboro, Ill, Aug 21, 27; m 51; c 6. DEVELOPMENTAL BIOLOGY, REPRODUCTIVE PHYSIOLOGY. *Educ:* St Louis Univ, BS, 49; Univ Mich, MS, 50; Univ Colo, PhD, 56. *Prof Exp:* Lab instr biol, Univ Denver, 50-51; from instr to assoc prof, Adams State Col, 52-60; sr res fel biophys, Med Ctr, Univ Colo, Boulder, 60-62, from asst prof to assoc prof, 62-66, Inst Develop Biol, 66-68 & dept molecular, cellular & develop biol, 68-71; prof & head dept zool, 71-78, PROF ZOOL, UNIV TENN, KNOXVILLE, 79- *Concurrent Pos:* Guest lectr, Univ Colo, 58; assoc dir, Oak Ridge Pop Res Inst, 72-75, consult biol div, Oak Ridge Nat Lab, 73-; Fulbright prof, Univ Nairobi, Kenya, 79-80. *Mem:* Fel AAAS; Am Soc Zool; Soc Study Develop Biol; Am Soc Cell Biol; Soc Study Reproduction. *Res:* Mammalian embryology and reproductive physiology. *Mailing Add:* 5505 Crestwood Dr Knoxville TN 37914

DANIEL, KENNETH JOHN, b Chicago, Ill, Feb 1, 50; m 76; c 1. COMPUTER MODELING PROCESSES. *Educ:* Purdue Univ, BS, 72, MS, 73, PhD(eng), 76. *Prof Exp:* RES ENGR ENERGY CONVERSION, GEN ELEC CO, 76- *Mem:* Am Soc Mech Engrs. *Res:* Determination of performance and economic advantages of advanced power plant designs. *Mailing Add:* Corp Res & Develop Gen Elec Co PO Box 43 5-345 Schenectady NY 12345

DANIEL, KENNETH WAYNE, b Dallas, Tex, June 12, 44; m 80; c 1. SIGNAL PROCESSING. *Educ:* Ga Inst Technol, BEE, 67, MSEE, 68; George Washington Univ, BEng, 78. *Prof Exp:* Proj engr, US Naval Security Group Command HQ, 69-70, Nat Security Agency, Ft Meade, MD, 70-72; sr engr, Tetra Tech, Inc, 72-76; engr scientist, Melpar Div, E-Systems, Inc, 76-80; TECH DIR, RADAR & OPTICS DIV, ENVIRON RES INST MICH, 80- *Mem:* Inst Elec & Electronics Engrs. *Res:* Systems analysis and development of reconnaissance and remote sensing systems; synthetic aperture radar; applications of communications theory and digital signal processing. *Mailing Add:* 3514 N Quebec St Arlington VA 22207

DANIEL, LEONARD RUPERT, b Seattle, Wash, May 13, 26; m 49; c 2. COMPUTER SCIENCES. *Educ:* Ga Inst Technol, BChE, 46, PhD(chem eng), 52. *Prof Exp:* Asst prof math, Ga Inst Technol, 46-52; prof chem, Corpus Christi Univ, 52-55, chmn sci & eng div, 53-55; prof chem, Howard Payne Col, 55-63, chmn sci & math div, 58-63; chmn div sci & math, WGa Col, 63-69; dean, 69-70, PROF CHEM & DIR COMPUT SERV, CLAYTON JR COL, 70- *Mem:* Asn Comput Mach. *Mailing Add:* Clayton Jr Col Morrow GA 30260

DANIEL, LOUISE JANE, b Philadelphia, Pa, Oct 28, 12. BIOCHEMISTRY. *Educ:* Univ Pa, BS, 35; Pa State Col, MS, 36; Cornell Univ, PhD(nutrit), 45. *Prof Exp:* Prof chem & physics, Penn Hall Jr Col, 36-42; res assoc, 45-48, from asst prof to prof, 48-73, EMER PROF BIOCHEM, CORNELL UNIV, 73- *Mem:* Am Soc Biol Chemists; Am Inst Nutrit; NY Acad Sci; Soc Exp Biol & Med; Am Chem Soc. *Res:* Functions of folic acid and vitamin B12 in intermediary metabolism; trace mineral interrelationships. *Mailing Add:* 210 Highgate Rd Ithaca NY 14850

DANIEL, MICHAEL ROGER, b Harrogate, Eng, Feb 26, 37; US citizen; m 60; c 3. CRYOGENICS, MAGNETISM. *Educ:* Univ Leeds, BSc, 59, PhD(physics), 62. *Prof Exp:* Res assoc physics, Northwestern Univ, 62-64; asst prof, Univ Birmingham, 64-65; res fel, Univ Essex, 65-68; sr scientist, 68-80, FEL SCIENTIST PHYSICS, WESTINGHOUSE ELEC CORP, 80- *Mem:* Am Phys Soc. *Res:* New superconductors in practical conductor form for magnet application and Josephson junctions as microwave sources; surface acoustic waves on piezoelectoic crystals for signal processing applications; magnetostatic wave devices using magnetic films for microwave applications. *Mailing Add:* Westinghouse Elec Corp Res & Develop 1310 Beulah Rd Pittsburgh PA 15235

DANIEL, O'DELL G, b Paris, Ark, Aug 15, 20; m 44; c 3. ANIMAL HUSBANDRY. *Educ:* Univ Md, BS, 49; Okla State Univ, MS, 51, PhD(animal husb), 57. *Prof Exp:* Assoc prof animal husb, Panhandle Agr & Mech Col, 51-56, head div agr, 57-58; PROF & HEAD EXTEN ANIMAL SCI DEPT, UNIV GA, 58- *Mailing Add:* Exten Animal Sci Dept Univ of Ga Agr Exten Athens GA 30602

DANIEL, PAUL MASON, b Philadelphia, Pa, July 12, 24; m 48; c 4. ZOOLOGY. *Educ:* Univ Cincinnati, BS, 49; Miami Univ, Ohio, MS, 54; Ohio State Univ, PhD(zool), 65. *Prof Exp:* Asst biol, Western Col, 49-50; prof sci, Cuttington Col, Liberia, 50-54; teacher pub schs, Ohio, 54-59; from instr to asst prof, 59-70, ASSOC PROF ZOOL, MIAMI UNIV, 70- *Mem:* Am Soc Ichthyologists & Herpetologists; Nat Asn Biol Teachers; Soc Study Amphibians & Reptiles. *Res:* Ecology of benthic organisms; herpetology; biological science instruction in public schools; Ohio vertebrate distribution. *Mailing Add:* Dept of Zool Miami Univ Oxford OH 45056

DANIEL, PETER FRANCIS, b Caterham, Eng, April 8, 45; m 74; c 2. COMPLEX CARBOHYDRATES. *Educ:* Christ Church, Oxford Univ, BA, 68; MA, 72; DPhil, 72. *Prof Exp:* Res assoc res & teaching, Dept Nutrit & Food Sci, Mass Inst Technol, 72-75; res fel biochem & neurol, Mass Gen Hosp, Boston, 75-76; sr res fel, 75-76, res assoc, 76-78, ASST BIOCHEMIST, EUNICE KENNEDY SHRIVER CTR, MASS, 78- *Mem:* Biochem Soc UK; Soc Complex Carbohydrates. *Res:* The biochemical and clinical basis of mannosidosis; comparison of human and bovine mannosidosis; glycoprotein storage diseases in general; methodology development for separation and analysis of oligosaccharide by high pressure liquid chromatography; the chemical basis for cell recognition during neurogenesis; galactosemia. *Mailing Add:* Eunice Kennedy Shriver Ctr Biochem Div 200 Trapelo Rd Waltham MA 02254

DANIEL, ROBERT EUGENE, b Birmingham, Ala, Jan 22, 38. ANALYTICAL CHEMISTRY. *Educ:* Samford Univ, AB, 60; Univ Ala, MS, 63, PhD(anal chem), 66. *Prof Exp:* Res asst chem, US Army Missile Command, Redstone Arsenal, 64; asst prof, Ala Col, 65-66; asst prof, Samford Univ, 66-71; ANAL RES CHEMIST, US PIPE & FOUNDRY CO, 71- *Mem:* AAAS; Am Chem Soc. *Res:* Structure and chemical characteristics of phenol complexes of tantalum, niobium, tungsten and molybdenum; kinetic aspects of the complex-forming reaction. *Mailing Add:* US Pipe & Foundry Co 3300 First Ave N Birmingham AL 35203

DANIEL, RONALD SCOTT, b Spencer, Iowa, Oct 10, 36; m 74; c 2. ELECTRON MICROSCOPY. *Educ:* San Jose State Col, BS, 60, MA, 63; Univ Minn, Minneapolis, PhD(entom), 68. *Prof Exp:* Teacher, high sch, Calif, 61-64; res asst entom, Univ Minn, 65-66, res fel, 66-68; PROF BIOL SCI, CALIF STATE POLYTECH UNIV, KELLOGG-VOORHIS, 68-, DIR, ELECTRON MICROSCOPE CTR, 71- *Concurrent Pos:* Bd dirs, Sex Info & Educ Coun, US. *Mem:* AAAS; Am Inst Biol Sci; Electron Microscopy Soc Am; Sigma Xi. *Res:* Biological electron microscopy. *Mailing Add:* Dept of Biol Sci 3801 W Temple Ave Pomona CA 91768

DANIEL, SAM MORDOCHAI, b Veria, Greece, Mar 25, 41; US citizen; m 65; c 1. COMPUTER MODELING, COMPUTER EMULATION. *Educ:* Univ Ill, BS, 64, MS, 65, PhD(elec eng), 71. *Prof Exp:* Engr microwaves, Harris Corp, 65-67; sr engr anal, Magnavox Co, 67-73; MEM TECH STAFF SYSTS ANAL & DESIGN, MOTOROLA INC, 73- *Concurrent Pos:* Instr Russian, Fla Inst Technol, 66. *Mem:* Inst Elec & Electronics Engrs; Soc Photo-Optical Instrumentation Engrs. *Res:* Adaptive radar signal processing; definition of credible system math models; comparative performance of candidate algorithms via computer simulation; validation of an architectural implementation via precise computer evaluation. *Mailing Add:* 921 E Driftwood Dr Tempe AZ 85283

DANIEL, THOMAS BRUCE, b Kansas City, Mo, Sept 7, 26; m 54; c 2. SOLID STATE PHYSICS. *Educ:* Univ Kans, BS, 50, MS, 54, PhD(physics), 59. *Prof Exp:* Asst, Radiation Biophys Proj, AEC, Kans, 51-53, instr physics, 53-56; assoc physicist, Midwest Res Inst, 58-60; sr physicist, 60-62; assoc prof, 62-64; PROF PHYSICS, PITTSBURG STATE UNIV, 64-, CHMN DEPT, 62- *Mem:* Am Asn Physics Teachers. *Mailing Add:* Dept of Physics Pittsburg State Univ Pittsburg KS 66762

DANIEL, THOMAS MALLON, b Minneapolis, Minn, Oct 27, 28; m 53; c 4. IMMUNOCHEMISTRY, PULMONARY DISEASES. *Educ:* Yale Univ, BS, 51; Harvard Univ, MD, 55. *Prof Exp:* Resident med, Univ Hosps, 55-59; captain, US Army Med Corps, 59-61; fel microbiol, 61-63, instr med, 63-65, sr instr, 65-66, asst prof, 66-69, assoc prof, 69-77, PROF MED, CASE WESTERN RESERVE UNIV, 77- *Concurrent Pos:* Physician, Univ Hosp, 77-; consult, Vet Admin Hosp, 72-, Int Child Care Tuberculosis Control Prog, 74-; scholar, John & Mary Markle Found, 67. *Mem:* Cent Soc Clin Res; Am Thoracic Soc; Infectious Dis Soc Am; Am Fed Clin Res. *Res:* Immunologic responses to mycobacterial antigens; purification and immunochemistry of mycobacterial antigens; tuberculosis epidemiology and control in developing nations. *Mailing Add:* Dept Med Univ Hosp Cleveland OH 44106

DANIEL, VICTOR WAYNE, b Baltimore, Md, July 21, 43. MATHEMATICS. *Educ:* Univ NC, Chapel Hill, BS, 65; Univ Va, PhD(math), 70. *Prof Exp:* Asst prof, Univ Wyo, 70-72; ASSOC PROF & CHMN DEPT MATH & COMPUT SCI, SC STATE COL, 73- *Mem:* Am Math Soc; Math Asn Am. *Res:* Study of certain convolution and integral operators on Lebesque spaces of the half-line; determining their invariant subspaces and when they are Volterra, unicellular or similar to the integration operator. *Mailing Add:* Dept of Math & Comput Sci SC State Col Box 2038 Orangeburg SC 29117

DANIEL, WILLIAM A, JR, b Thomaston, Ga, May 13, 14. PEDIATRICS. *Educ:* Northwestern Univ, BS, 36, MD, 40. *Prof Exp:* Intern, Charity Hosp, New Orleans, 39-40; resident pediat, Children's Hosp, Dallas, 40-41 & Children's Mem Hosp, Chicago, 41-42; pvt pract, Ala, 42-66; PROF PEDIAT, SCH MED, UNIV ALA, 66-, DIR ADOLESCENT UNIT, 66- *Concurrent Pos:* Proj dir, Children & Youth Proj 622, 66-; contrib ed, J Pediat; mem staff, Children's Hosp, Birmingham. *Mem:* Am Pediat Soc; Am Acad Pediat; Soc Adolescent Med. *Mailing Add:* Adolescent Unit Univ of Ala Sch of Med Birmingham AL 35294

DANIEL, WILLIAM HUGH, b Ark, Dec 31, 19; m 44; c 2. AGRONOMY. *Educ:* Ouachita Col, BA, 41; Univ Ark, BSA, 46; Mich State Univ, MS, 48, PhD(agron, turf mgt), 50. *Prof Exp:* PROF TURF MGT, PURDUE UNIV, 50- *Concurrent Pos:* Secy, Midwest Regional Turf Found, Purdue Univ. *Honors & Awards:* Agron Serv Award, Am Soc Agron, 73. *Mem:* Fel Am Soc Agron; Weed Sci Soc Am. *Res:* Turfgrass management; soil science; crop ecology. *Mailing Add:* Dept Agron Purdue Univ West Lafayette IN 47907

DANIEL, WILLIAM L, b Wyandotte, Mich, Sept 20, 42; m 64. HUMAN GENETICS, BIOCHEMICAL GENETICS. *Educ:* Mich State Univ, BS, 64, PhD(zool), 67. *Prof Exp:* From asst prof to assoc prof genetics, Ill State Univ, Normal, 67-72; asst prof, 72-77, ASSOC PROF GENETICS, SCH BASIC MED SCI & DEPT GENETICS & DEVELOP, UNIV ILL, URBANA, 77- *Mem:* AAAS; Am Soc Human Genetics; Genetics Soc Am; Am Genetics Asn; NY Acad Sci. *Res:* Genetic control of enzyme realization, specifically of developmental, quantitative and qualitative murine arylsulfatase variation. *Mailing Add:* Dept Genetics & Develop 515 Morrill Hall Univ of Ill Urbana IL 61801

DANIELEY, EARL, b Alamance Co, NC, July 28, 24; m 48; c 3. ORGANIC CHEMISTRY. *Educ:* Elon Col, AB, 46; Univ NC, MA, 49, PhD(org chem), 54. *Prof Exp:* From instr to assoc prof chem, 46-50, dean col, 53-56, pres, 57-73, PROF CHEM, ELON COL, 52- *Concurrent Pos:* Fel, Johns Hopkins Univ, 56-57; lectr chem, Univ NC, 52. *Honors & Awards:* Award, Elon Col, 58. *Mem:* Am Chem Soc. *Res:* Cyclobutane compounds; porphyrins in petroleum. *Mailing Add:* PO Box 245 Elon College NC 27244

DANIELL, ELLEN, b New Haven, Conn, July 14. 47. MOLECULAR BIOLOGY. *Educ:* Swarthmore Col, AB, 69; Univ Calif, San Diego, PhD(chem), 73. *Prof Exp:* Fel tumor virol, Cold Spring Harbor Lab, 73-75; ASST PROF MOLECULAR BIOL, UNIV CALIF, BERKELEY, 76- *Concurrent Pos:* Fel, Helen Hay Whitney Found, 74-75. *Mem:* Sigma Xi. *Mailing Add:* Dept of Molecular Biol Univ of Calif Berkeley CA 94720

DANIELL, HERMAN BURCH, b Cadwell, Ga, May 25, 29; m 57; c 3. PHARMACOLOGY. *Educ:* Univ Ga, BS, 51, MS, 64; Med Col SC, PhD(pharmacol), 66. *Prof Exp:* Instr pharm, Univ Ga, 62-63; assoc pharmacol, 67-68, asst prof, 68-70, assoc prof, 70-78, PROF PHARMACOL, MED UNIV SC, 78- *Mem:* Am Soc Pharmacol & Exp Therapeut; Sigma Xi. *Res:* Cardiovascular diseases. *Mailing Add:* Dept of Pharmacol Med Univ of SC 171 Ashley Ave Charleston SC 29401

DANIELL, JEFF WALTER, b Cadwell, Ga, June 29, 24; m 53; c 2. HORTICULTURE. *Educ:* Univ Ga, BS, 48; Clemson Col, MS, 62; Va Polytech Inst, PhD(plant physiol), 66. *Prof Exp:* Teacher agr, Dodge County Bd Educ, Eastman, Ga, 48-54; assoc county agent, Coop Exten Serv, Univ Ga, 54-62; asst prof, 66-78, ASSOC HORTICULTURIST FRUIT & NUT CROPS, GA AGR EXP STA, 78- *Mem:* Sigma Xi; Am Soc Plant Physiologists; Am Soc Hort Sci. *Res:* Physiological problems in peaches and pecans, irrigation, chemical thinning of peaches and chemical weed control. *Mailing Add:* Ga Sta Dept of Hort Experiment GA 30212

DANIELLI, JAMES F, b Wembley, Eng, Nov 13, 11; m 37; c 2. BIOLOGY. *Educ:* Univ Col, London, BSc, 31, PhD(chem), 33, DSc(cell biol), 38; Cambridge Univ, PhD(biochem & physiol), 42. *Hon Degrees:* ScD, Univ Ghent, 53. *Prof Exp:* Physiologist, Marine Biol Asn, 45-46; reader cell biol, Royal Cancer Hosp, Univ London, 46-49, prof & chmn dept zool, Kings Col, 49-62; prof med chem & biochem pharmacol & chmn dept, State Univ NY Buffalo, 62-65, dir ctr theoret biol, 65-71, provost fac natural sci & math, 67-69; prof, 74-78, EMER PROF LIFE SCI, WORCESTER POLYTECH INST, 78-; DIR, DANIELLI ASSOCS, 78- *Concurrent Pos:* Ed, Int Rev Cytol, 50-, J Theoret Biol, 60-, Progress Surface & Membrane Sci, 62-80 & J Social & Biol Structures, 62- *Honors & Awards:* Landsteiner Award, Am Asn Blood Banks, 81. *Mem:* Am Soc Cell Biol; fel Royal Soc; Brit Soc Exp Biol (secy, 48-58); Brit Biochem Soc; Int Soc Cell Biol (secy, 47-57). *Res:* Cell biology; surface science; theoretical biology; physiology; cell synthesis. *Mailing Add:* Danielli Assocs Inc 185 Highland St Worcester MA 01609

DANIELS, ALMA U(RIAH), b Salt Lake City, Utah, Mar 18, 39; m 61; c 3. BIOMATERIALS, ORTHOPEDIC BIOMECHANICS. *Educ:* Univ Utah, BS, 61, PhD(metall), 66. *Prof Exp:* Res asst metall, Univ Utah, 61-65; res chemist indust & biochem dept, Exp Sta, E I du Pont de Nemours & Co, Inc, 65-69, sr res chemist, 69, develop & serv rep, 69-70; res engr, Metcut Res Assoc, Inc, Ohio, 70; sr mat engr, Univ Utah Res Inst, 71-73, head mat sect, 74-77, assoc dir eng dept, 77-78, dir eng dept, UBTL Div, 78-79, DIR ORTHOP BIOENG LAB, DIV ORTHOP SURG, UNIV UTAH SCH MED, 79- *Concurrent Pos:* From adj asst prof to adj assoc prof, Dept Mat Sci & Eng, Univ Utah, 72-, adj asst prof, Dept Surgery, 76-79, res assoc prof, Dept Bioeng, 79- *Mem:* Soc Biomat; Orthopedic Res Soc; Am Soc Testing & Mat. *Res:* Orthopedic implant design and development biomaterials-properties, effects on tissue; surgical and medical devices-test methods, failure analysis; refractory and wear resistant materials and cutting tools-properties, fabrication processes, testing. *Mailing Add:* 1226 Logan Ave Salt Lake City UT 84105

DANIELS, ARUNA C, b Nagpur, India, Jan 4, 40. NEUROPATHOLOGY. *Educ:* Panjab Univ, India, ISc, 56, MB & BS, 61. *Prof Exp:* Resident path, Univ Chicago, 65-67; from instr to asst prof, 69-74; fel neuropath & electron micros, Northwestern Univ & Vet Admin Hosp, Hines, Ill, 67-69; assoc prof neurol, Sch Med, 74-76; assoc prof neurol & neuropath, 77-80, PROF NEUROL & PATH, CHICAGO MED SCH, 80-; STAFF NEUROPATHOLOGIST, VET ADMIN MED CTR, NORTH CHICAGO, 77-; CONSULT & ASSOC PROF, CHICAGO OSTEOP COL & HOSP, 78- *Concurrent Pos:* House physician internal med, Irwin Hosp, New Delhi, India, 62; demonstr path, Christian Med Col, Ludhiana, India, 62, house physician internal med, 63; asst dir autopsy serv, Dept Path, Univ Chicago, 70-72, assoc dir neuropath, 70-74. *Mem:* Am Asn Neuropathologists; Int Acad Path; jr mem Am Acad Neurol; Sigma Xi. *Res:* Clincial neuropathology and electron microscopy; chromatolysis and axonal reaction in spinal cord motor neurons. *Mailing Add:* 5550 Blackstone Chicago IL 60637

DANIELS, BARBARA ANN, b San Francisco, Calif, Sept 10, 51. MYCORRHIZAL FUNGI, SOIL MICROBIOLOGY. *Educ:* Ohio Wesleyan Univ, BA, 73; Wash State Univ, MS, 75; Ore State Univ, PhD(plant path), 78. *Prof Exp:* Fel, Univ Calif, Riverside, 78-80; ASST PROF PLANT PATH, KANS STATE UNIV, 80- *Concurrent Pos:* Consult, Lehigh Univ,

82-83. *Mem:* Am Phytopath Soc; Sigma Xi. *Res:* Ecology of vesicular-arbuscular mycorrhizal fungi and their potential for commercialization; use of these fungi to retard drought stress or to stimulate plant growth in infertile soils. *Mailing Add:* Dept Plant Path Kans State Univ Manhattan KS 66506

DANIELS, CAROLE ANGELA, materials science, see previous edition

DANIELS, EDWARD WILLIAM, b Tracy, Minn, Jan 19, 17; m 43; c 4. CELL BIOLOGY, ECOLOGY. *Educ:* Cornell Col, BA, 41; Univ Ill, MS, 47, PhD(zool, physiol), 50. *Prof Exp:* Teacher high sch, 41-43; mem staff, Univ Ill, 46-50; from instr to asst prof physiol, Univ Chicago, 50-54; mem, Toxicol Labs & US Air Force Radiation Lab, 50-54; biologist, Div Biol & Med Res, 54-71, biologist, Environ Impact Studies Div, 71-81, group leader, 78-81, PROJ LEADER AQUATIC ECOL, ENVIRON IMPACT STUDIES DIV, ARGONNE NAT LAB, 81- *Mem:* Fel AAAS; Soc Protozool; Am Inst Biol Sci; Electon Micros Soc Am; Int Asn Gt Lakes Res. *Res:* Recovery of cells from potentially lethal radiation damage; transplantation tolerance; origin and fate of subcellular components studied in part with electron microscopy and micrurgy; analyses of environmental impacts of power generation systems. *Mailing Add:* 626 S Wright St Naperville IL 60540

DANIELS, FARRINGTON, JR, b Worcester, Mass, Sept 29, 18; m 51; c 3. PHYSIOLOGY. *Educ:* Univ Wis, BA, 40, MA, 42; Harvard Univ, MD, 43, MPH, 52. *Prof Exp:* Intern med, New York Hosp, 44, asst resident, 47-49; head physiol unit, Qm Climatic Res Lab, Mass, 50-53; chief stress physiol br, Environ Protection Div, Qm Res & Develop Ctr, 53-55; asst prof dermat, Med Sch, Univ Ore, 55-61; assoc prof, Univ Ill, 61-62; assoc prof med, 62-69, head, Dermat Div, 62-81, PROF MED, MED COL, CORNELL UNIV, 69-, PROF PUB HEALTH, 72-, PROF PATH, GRAD SCH MED SCI, 77- *Concurrent Pos:* Res fel med, Med Sch, Cornell Univ, 47-49; res fel nutrit, Sch Pub Health, Harvard Univ, 49-50; Army rep physiol panel, Comt Med Sci, Res & Develop Bd, 51-53; mem photobiol comt, Nat Acad Sci. *Mem:* AAAS; Am Dermat Asn; Am Acad Dermat; Soc Invest Dermat; Human Factors Soc. *Res:* Medicine; spinal cord concussion; environmental physiology; human adaptation to heat, cold and ultraviolet radiation; military load-carrying; effects of footwear and clothing on skin; histochemistry of skin; environmental factors in human skin color and skin cancer. *Mailing Add:* Dermat Div Med Col Cornell Univ New York NY 10021

DANIELS, GILBERT S, botany, see previous edition

DANIELS, JAMES MAURICE, b Leeds, Eng, Aug 26, 24; m 65; c 2. SOLID STATE PHYSICS, MAGNETISM. *Educ:* Jesus Col, Oxford Univ, BA, 45, MA, 49, DPhil(physics), 52. *Prof Exp:* Asst exp officer, Radar Res & Develop Estab, Ministry Supply, 44-46; tech officer physics, Imp Chem Industs, Ltd, 46-47; Imp Chem Industs res fel low temperature physics, Clarendon Lab, Oxford Univ, 52-53; from asst prof to prof physics, Univ BC, 53-61; chmn dept, 69-73, PROF PHYSICS, UNIV TORONTO, 61- *Concurrent Pos:* Consult, Pa State Univ, 58; UNESCO expert exp physics, Univ Buenos Aires, 58-59; vis prof Balseiro Inst Physics, Arg, 60-61; secy-treas & trustee, Inst Particle Physics, 70-73; vis prof, Low Temperature Lab, Helsinki Univ Technol, 76; vis prof physics dept, Columbia Univ, 78; Guggenheim fel. *Mem:* Fel Royal Soc Can; Brit Inst Physics & Phys Soc; Arg Physics Asn; Can Asn Physicists; fel Royal Soc Arts. *Res:* Adiabatic demagnetisation; spatial orientation of atomic nuclei; magnetic resonance and relaxation; Mossbauer spectroscopy. *Mailing Add:* Dept of Physics Univ of Toronto Toronto ON M5S 1A1 Can

DANIELS, JEFFREY IRWIN, b San Mateo, Calif, Dec 26, 51; m 82. RISK ASSESSMENT. *Educ:* Calif State Univ, Northridge, MS, 78; Univ Calif, Los Angeles, BA, 74, DEnv, 81. *Prof Exp:* SR SCIENTIST, ENVIRON SCI DIV, LAWRENCE LIVERMORE NAT LAB, 79- *Concurrent Pos:* Ed, Environ Sci & Eng Soc Newsletter, 79- *Mem:* AAAS; Soc Risk Anal; Sigma Xi; Environ Sci & Eng Soc. *Res:* Environmental, health, and safety analysis and risk assessment of energy technologies and waste disposal procedures. *Mailing Add:* Environ Sci Div L-453 Lawrence Livermore Nat Lab PO Box 5507 Livermore CA 94550

DANIELS, JESS DONALD, b Sugar Land, Tex, Oct 20, 34; m 56; c 3. FOREST GENETICS, PLANT BREEDING. *Educ:* Mont State Univ, BS, 57; Univ Idaho, MF, 65, PhD(forest genetics), 69. *Prof Exp:* Forester, US Forest Serv, USDA, 57-63; instr forestry, Col Forestry, Wildlife & Range Sci, Univ Idaho, 65-66; FOREST GENETICIST, WESTERN FORESTRY RES CTR, WEYERHAEUSER CO, 68- *Concurrent Pos:* Co-chmn, Working Party on Progeny Testing, Int Union Forestry Res Orgn, 78- *Mem:* Soc Am Foresters. *Res:* Tree improvement, variation inheritance of characteristics related to growth, yield and quality of wood; breeding for yield improvement; technology of seed production and orchard management. *Mailing Add:* Weyerhaeuser Forestry Res Ctr PO Box 420 Centralia WA 98531

DANIELS, JOHN HARTLEY, b Regina, Sask, July 18, 31; m 56; c 3. STRUCTURAL ENGINEERING. *Educ:* Univ Alta, BSc, 55; Univ Ill, MS, 59; Lehigh Univ, PhD(civil eng), 67. *Prof Exp:* Resident engr, Dept Hwys, Alta, Can, 55-56, design engr, 56-58; chief struct engr, Assoc Eng Serv, Ltd, 59-64; res asst, 64-67, from asst prof to assoc prof, 67-76, PROF CIVIL ENG, LEHIGH UNIV, 76- *Concurrent Pos:* Mem, Transp Res Bd. *Mem:* Am Soc Civil Engrs; Int Asn Bridge & Struct Eng. *Res:* Plastic design and analysis of multi-story frames; plasticity; composite steel-concrete structures; optimization techniques; fatigue and fracture of welded steel structures. *Mailing Add:* Fritz Lab No 13 Lehigh Univ Bethlehem PA 18015

DANIELS, JOHN MAYNARD, b Binghamton, NY, Aug 17, 35; m 58; c 3. WATER CHEMISTRY. *Educ:* Trinity Col, BS, 57; Brandeis Univ, PhD(chem), 65. *Prof Exp:* Phys chemist, Nat Bur Standards, 64-66; asst prof chem, Union Col, NY, 66-72; PRES, CAPITOL DIST WATER TREAT, INC, 71- *Concurrent Pos:* MKT DIR, ENCOTECH INC, 78- *Mem:* Am Chem Soc; Am Water Works Asn. *Mailing Add:* 1718 Eastern Parkway Schenectady NY 12309

DANIELS, MALCOLM, b Wingate, Eng, Jan 27, 30; m 64. PHYSICAL CHEMISTRY. *Educ:* Univ Durham, BSc, 51, PhD(chem), 55. *Prof Exp:* Asst radiation chem & photochem, King's Col, Newcastle, 54-57; resident res assoc, Argonne Nat Lab, 57-60; lectr chem, Univ West Indies, 60-62; assoc prof radiation chem & photochem, Univ PR, 62-65; head radiation prog, PR Nuclear Ctr, 62-65; assoc prof dept chem, 65-73, PROF DEPT CHEM, ORE STATE UNIV, 73- *Mem:* Radiation Res Soc; Royal Soc Chem; Faraday Soc. *Res:* Radiation chemistry, photochemistry and spectroscopy; aqueous solutions of oxyanions; free radicals; transient species; radiation biophysics; transformations of nucleic acids and constituents; photogalvanic effect; artificial photosynthesis. *Mailing Add:* Radiation Ctr Ore State Univ Corvallis OR 97331

DANIELS, MATHEW PAUL, b New York, NY, Feb 7, 44; m 68; c 2. NEUROBIOLOGY, CELL BIOLOGY. *Educ:* Queens Col, NY, BA, 64; Univ Chicago, PhD(biol), 70. *Prof Exp:* Nat Inst Neurol Dis & Stroke res fel neurobiol, Albert Einstein Col Med, Yeshiva Univ, 70-71; guest worker, 71-73, staff fel, 73-77, RES BIOLOGIST NEUROBIOL, BIOCHEM GENETICS LAB, NAT HEART LUNG & BLOOD INST, NIH, 77- *Concurrent Pos:* Am Cancer Soc res fel, 71-73. *Mem:* Am Soc Cell Biol; Soc Neurosci. *Res:* Development and function of synapses; morphological distribution of neurotransmitter receptors; neurotransmitter storage and secretion. *Mailing Add:* Lab of Biochem Genetics NIH Bethesda MD 20014

DANIELS, PETER JOHN LOVELL, b Stockport, Eng, June 7, 34. ORGANIC BIOCHEMISTRY. *Educ:* Univ Manchester, BSc, 56, MSc, 57; Univ London, PhD(chem), 60. *Prof Exp:* Fel, Royal Inst Tech, Sweden, 60-61; AP Sloane res assoc, Johns Hopkins Univ, 61-62; res medicinal chemist, 62-73, assoc dir anti-infectives, 73-80, DIR CHEM RES, SCHERING CORP, 80- *Mem:* Am Chem Soc; Royal Soc Chem. *Res:* Antibiotics; synthetic medicinals; microbial biochemistry. *Mailing Add:* Chem Res Schering Corp Bloomfield NJ 07003

DANIELS, RALPH, b New York, NY, May 2, 21; m 44; c 3. ORGANIC CHEMISTRY. *Educ:* Brooklyn Col, AB, 44; Harvard Univ, AM, 49, PhD, 50. *Prof Exp:* Res chemist, Givaudan-Delawanna Res Inst, 44-46; fel nonaromatic steroids, Univ Wis, 50-51; instr chem, Purdue Univ, 51-52; from asst prof to prof, Col Pharm, Univ Ill Med Ctr, 52-77, asst dean grad col, 70-72, actg dean grad col, 75-77; ASSOC DEAN, GRAD COL, DIR, OFF RES ADMIN & PROF PHARM, UNIV OKLA HEALTH SCI CTR, 77- *Concurrent Pos:* Vis scientist, Univ London, 61-62. *Mem:* Am Chem Soc; Am Asn Col Pharmacol; AAAS; Nat Coun Univ Res Admin. *Res:* Synthesis of pharmacologically active compounds; natural products; heterocyclic chemistry; radiation protective compounds; reaction mechanisms; spectra or organic compounds. *Mailing Add:* Univ Okla Health Sci Ctr PO Box 26901 Oklahoma City OK 73190

DANIELS, RAYMOND BRYANT, b Adair, Iowa, Feb 15, 25; m 45; c 2. SOIL GENESIS, GEOMORPHOLOGY. *Educ:* Iowa State Col, BS, 50, MS, 55, PhD(soil genesis), 57. *Prof Exp:* Res soil scientist, Soil Conserv Serv, USDA, NC, 57-68; from assoc prof to prof soil sci, NC State Univ, 68-77; dir soil surv invests, Soil Conserv Serv, USDA, 77-80; PROF, SOIL SCI DEPT, NC STATE UNIV, 81- *Mem:* Mem: Soil Conserv Soc Am; Geol Soc Am; Am Quaternary Asn. *Res:* Soil genesis and stratigraphic geomorphic interrelations. *Mailing Add:* NC State Univ PO Box 5907 Raleigh NC 27650

DANIELS, RAYMOND D(EWITT), b Cleveland, Ohio, Feb 14, 28; m 52; c 1. PHYSICAL METALLURGY, CORROSION. *Educ:* Case Inst Technol, BS, 50, MS, 53, PhD(phys metall), 58. *Prof Exp:* Physicist, Nat Bur Stand, 50-51; asst physics, Case Inst Technol, 51-54; res engr, Linde Co, 54-55; asst & spec lectr metall, Case Inst Technol, 55-58; from asst prof to assoc prof metall eng, 58-64, chmn sch, 62-63, dir sch chem eng & mat sci, 63-65, 69-70, assoc dean eng for res & grad study, 65-68, dir off res admin, 73-78, PROF METALL ENG, UNIV OKLA, 64-, EXEC DIR, RES INST, 71- *Concurrent Pos:* Dupont res grant, 58; consult, US Air Force, 58-59, Autoclave Engrs, 59-62 & Avco Corp, 63-66; NSF sci fac fel, Univ Neuchatel, 68-69; mem, Nat Res Coun Comt, 75-78. *Mem:* Am Soc Metals; Am Inst Mining, Metall & Petrol Engrs; Nat Asn Corrosion Engrs; Am Soc Eng Educ. *Res:* Physical metallurgy; mechanical properties of metals; embrittlement phenomena; corrosion-fatigue; administration of research. *Mailing Add:* Rm 23 Sch Chem Eng & Mat Sci Univ Okla 202 W Boyd Norman OK 73019

DANIELS, REBECCA JO, b Ames, Iowa, Feb 21. CLINICAL NUTRITION, MEDICAL PHYSIOLOGY. *Educ:* Univ NMex, BS, 75; Univ Calif, San Diego, PhD(physiol & pharmacol), 80. *Prof Exp:* NIH staff fel, Phoenix Clin Res Sect, NIH, 80-82; ASST PROF BIOL & CHEM, ST EDWARDS UNIV, AUSTIN, 82- *Res:* Energy balance; thermo genesis; obesity and diabetes; specifically, alteration in thermic responses to norepinephrine; food and exercise during different nutritional states; lipoprotein metabolism; nuclear medicine. *Mailing Add:* 3320 W Belmont Ave Phoenix AZ 85021

DANIELS, ROBERT (SANFORD), b Indianapolis, Ind, Aug 12, 27; m 50; c 4. MEDICINE, PSYCHIATRY. *Educ:* Univ Cincinnati, BS, 48, MD, 51. *Prof Exp:* Asst prof psychiat, Univ Chicago, 57-63, assoc prof & actg chmn dept, 63-68, prof psychiat & social med, assoc dean social & community med & dir ctr health admin studies, 68-71; prof psychiat & dir dept, 71-75, interim dean col med, 72-75, DEAN COL MED, UNIV CINCINNATI, 75- *Concurrent Pos:* Consult, Cook County Hosp, 58-68, Ill State Psychiat Inst, 59-68 & Thresholds, 63-67; chief of staff, Cincinnati Gen Hosp & Holmes Hosp, 72- *Res:* Medical education; group psychotherapy; clinical psychiatric research, medical care organization and financing. *Mailing Add:* Univ of Cincinnati Col of Med Cincinnati OH 45221

DANIELS, ROBERT ARTIE, b St Charles, Mo, Feb 14, 49; m 77; c 1. FISHERIES BIOLOGY, AQUATIC ECOLOGY. *Educ:* Univ Calif, Los Angeles, BA, 71; Univ Calif, Davis, MS, 77, PhD(ecology), 79. *Prof Exp:* Researcher, Univ Calif, 80-81; SR SCIENTIST, BIOL SURV, NY STATE MUS, 81- *Mem:* AAAS; Am Fisheries Soc; Am Soc Ichthyologists &

Herpetologists; Ecol Soc Am; Am Soc Naturalists. *Res:* Life histories of fishes and aquatic macroinvertebrates and mechanisms of coexistence among sympatric species. *Mailing Add:* CEC Rm 3132 NY State Mus Albany NY 12230

DANIELS, STACY LEROY, b Frankfort, Mich, Aug 29, 37; m 64; c 1. ENVIRONMENTAL SCIENCE & ENGINEERING. *Educ:* Univ Mich, Ann Arbor, BSE, 60, MSE, 61 & 63, PhD(chem eng), 67. *Prof Exp:* Res engr, Chem Dept Res Lab, 66-69, develop engr, Environ Control Syst Tech Serv & Develop, 69-72, sr res engr, 72-74, res specialist, Functional Prod & Systs Dept, 74-76, RES SPECIALIST, ENVIRON SCI RES LAB, DOW CHEM USA, 76- *Concurrent Pos:* Mem res biol lab, US Bur Com Fisheries, 61-65; adj assoc prof, Dept Chem Eng, Univ Mich, 71-81. *Mem:* Am Inst Chem Engrs; Am Water Works Asn; Int Asn Water Pollution Res; Nat Solid Waste Mgt Asn; Sigma Xi. *Res:* Solids/liquid separations (coagulation, flocculation); coordinating information on the assessment of environmental impacts of chemical products; consulting on waste treatment and disposal technologies and other environmental problems; interfacing with Federal and State governments on water, waste-water and solid hazardous waste management regulations; author of 110 publications. *Mailing Add:* Environ Sci Res Lab Dow Chem USA Bldg 1702 Midland MI 48640

DANIELS, WILEY EDGAR, organic chemistry, see previous edition

DANIELS, WILLIAM BURTON, b Buffalo, NY, Dec 21, 30; m 58. EXPERIMENTAL SOLID STATE PHYSICS. *Educ:* Univ Buffalo, BS, 52; Case Western Reserve Univ, MS, 55, PhD, 57. *Prof Exp:* Instr physics, Case Western Reserve Univ, 57-58, asst prof, 58-59; res scientist, Res Labs, Nat Carbon Co, 59-61; from asst prof to prof solid state sci, Princeton Univ, 61-72; UNIDEL PROF PHYSICS, UNIV DEL, 72-, CHMN DEPT, 77- *Concurrent Pos:* Res collabr, Brookhaven Nat Lab; Guggenheim Mem Found fel, 76-77; Alexander von Humboldt sr award, 81-82. *Mem:* Fel Am Phys Soc. *Res:* Solid state and lattice dynamics at high pressure; solidified rare gases and molecular solids; liquid and plastic crystals; Raman and neutron scattering. *Mailing Add:* Dept of Physics Univ of Del Newark DE 19711

DANIELS, WILLIAM FOWLER, SR, b New Bern, NC, Feb 22, 20; m 47; c 3. BIOCHEMISTRY, BIOENGINEERING. *Educ:* La State Univ, BSChE, 42; Univ Fla, MS, 50; Univ Ky, PhD(bact physiol), 57. *Prof Exp:* Consult engr & chemist bldg mat, H C Nutting Co, 47-48; asst indust & eng exp sta, Univ Fla, 49; res bacteriologist water bact, Environ Health Ctr, USPHS, 50-51; asst bact, Univ Ky, 52; res chemist, Hwy Res Lab, State Dept Hwy, Ky, 53-55, head chem test, 56; prin investr biochem eng, Pilot Plants Div, Ft Detrick, 56-58 & Process Res Div, 58-70; biologist consult, Appl Sci Div, US Adv Mat Concepts Agency, Va, 70-74; phys sci adminr, US Army Mat Develop & Readiness Command, 74-76; GEN ENGR, US ARMY MED RES & DEVELOP COMMAND, 76- *Concurrent Pos:* Consult, 59- *Mem:* Soc Am Microbiologists; Am Chem Soc; Am Inst Chemists; Sigma Xi. *Res:* Paper electrophoresis of carbohydrate compounds; constitution and characterization of asphalt; organic synthesis via microbial oxidation; sterile filtrations; submerged tissue and continuous bacterial fermentation. *Mailing Add:* 7819 Spout Spring Rd Frederick MD 21701

DANIELS, WILLIAM LAWRENCE, b Burlington, Wis, Sept 22, 47; m 69; c 4. EXERCISE PHYSIOLOGY. *Educ:* Ill Benedictine Col, BS, 69; Wayne State Univ, MS, 71, PhD(physiol), 74. *Prof Exp:* Physiologist, Clin Invest Serv, Army Med Ctr, Denver, 75-77; PHYSIOLOGIST, EXERCISE PHYSIOL DIV, US ARMY RES INST ENVIRON MED, 77- *Mem:* Am Col Sports Med; AAAS. *Res:* Aerobic fitness of males and females; lactic acid production during exercise and its correlation with ventilatory parameters; exercise and its use to reduce coronary risk factors. *Mailing Add:* US Army Res Inst Environ Med Natick MA 01760

DANIELS, WILLIAM RICHARD, b Dayton, Iowa, Apr 16, 31; m 51; c 4. RADIOCHEMISTRY. *Educ:* Iowa State Univ, BS, 53; Washington Univ, MA, 55; Univ NMex, PhD(radiochem), 65. *Prof Exp:* Mem staff radiochem, 57-80, ASSOC GROUP LEADER RADIOCHEM, LOS ALAMOS NAT LAB, 80- *Mem:* fel Am Inst Chemists. *Res:* Short-lived fission products; nuclear spectroscopy; nuclear waste disposal. *Mailing Add:* 40 La Cueva Los Alamos NM 87544

DANIELS, WILLIAM WARD, b Norfolk, Va, Apr, 13, 26; m 48; c 6. PHYSICAL CHEMISTRY, RESEARCH ADMINISTRATION. *Educ:* La State Univ, BS, 49, MS, 50, PhD(phys chem), 54. *Prof Exp:* Res chem, Dacron Res Lab, 53-58, res supvr, 58-62, sr supvr, Chattanooga Tech Lab, 62-64, res mgr, Carothers Res Lab, 64-67, tech supt, Seaford Tech Lab, 67-69, LAB DIR, DACRON RES LAB, E I DU PONT DE NEMOURS & CO, INC, 69- *Mem:* Am Chem Soc. *Res:* Infrared and raman spectroscopy; fiber structure-property relationships. *Mailing Add:* E I du Pont de Nemours & Co Inc Dacron Res Lab PO Box 800 Kinston NC 28501

DANIELSON, DAVID MURRAY, b Aurora, Nebr, Feb 24, 29; m 53; c 3. ANIMAL NUTRITION. *Educ:* Univ Nebr, BS, 52, MS, 58; Utah State Univ, PhD(animal prod), 64. *Prof Exp:* PROF ANIMAL NUTRIT, UNIV NEBR, NORTH PLATTE, 58- *Mem:* Am Soc Animal Sci. *Res:* Carbohydrates for baby pig diets; limited feeding of growing-finishing swine diets; source and quality of nitrogen and energy for swine gestation diets; automation in rearing baby pigs; feeding corn, millet, wheat, grain sorghum alone or in combination to finishing swine. *Mailing Add:* North Platte Sta Rte 4 Box 46A Univ of Nebr North Platte NE 69101

DANIELSON, DONALD ALFRED, applied mathematics, applied mechanics, see previous edition

DANIELSON, GEORGE EDWARD, JR, b Bozeman, Mont, May 10, 39; m 63; c 4. SPACE INSTRUMENTATION. *Educ:* Principia Col, BS, 61; Univ Ill, Urbana, MS, 63; Univ Rochester, MS, 67. *Prof Exp:* Physicist, United Aircraft Res Lab, 63-65; group supvr, Jet Propulsion Lab, Photo Sci Group,

71-74, asst sect mgr, space photog sect, 74-75, from staff asst to dir, 74-77, dep sect mgr, 77-78; MEM PROF STAFF & SR SCIENTIST, CALIF INST TECHNOL, 78- *Concurrent Pos:* Co-investr, Mariner Venus Mercury Imaging Sci Team, 70-75, Voyager Imaging Sci Team, 74-, Galileo Near Infrared Imaging Spectrometer, 77- & Space Telescope Wide Field/Planetary Camera IDT, 78-; consult, Giotta Halley multicolour camera, 81-; mem staff, Palomar Observ, 81- *Mem:* Am Astron Soc. *Res:* Space photography instrument development; ground based astronomical instrumentation. *Mailing Add:* Div Geol Planetary Sci Calif Inst Technol MS 170-25 Pasadena CA 91125

DANIELSON, GORDON CHARLES, b Dover, Idaho, Oct 28, 12; m 39; c 4. SOLID STATE PHYSICS. *Educ:* Univ BC, BA, 33, MA, 35; Purdue Univ, PhD(physics), 40. *Prof Exp:* Res physicist, US Rubber Co, Detroit, 40-41; asst prof physics, Univ Idaho, 41-42; staff mem, Radiation Lab, Mass Inst Technol, 42-46; tech staff mem, Bell Tel Labs, 46-48; from assoc prof to prof, 48-64, DISTINGUISHED PROF PHYSICS, COL SCI & HUMANITIES, IOWA STATE UNIV, 64- *Concurrent Pos:* Sr physicist & Guggenheim fel, Inst Atomic Res, Cambridge Univ, 58-59; chmn comt thermoelec conversion, Off Naval Res, 58; mem metall & solid state rev comt, Argonne Nat Lab, 60-63, chmn, 62-63; vis scientist, Am Inst Physics, 60-72; consult, NSF, 63-66; mem solid state sci panel, Nat Res Coun, 63-74; univ adv, Tex Instruments, Inc, 64-68. *Mem:* Fel Am Phys Soc. *Res:* Solid state physics; electrical conductivities and Hall coefficients of metals and semiconductors; thermal conductivity and thermal diffusivity of metals; diffusion coefficients and specific heats of metals; optical properties of counting diamonds; physical properties of sodium tungsten bronze; ferro-electric crystals; radar beacons; x-ray diffraction of liquids, Fourier analysis. *Mailing Add:* Dept of Physics Iowa State Univ Ames IA 50011

DANIELSON, GORDON KENNETH, b Burlington, Iowa, Dec 5, 31; m 61; c 7. CARDIOVASCULAR SURGERY. *Educ:* Univ Pa, BA, 53, MD, 56; Am Bd Surg & Am Bd Thoracic Surg, dipl, 63. *Prof Exp:* Asst instr surg, Univ Pa, 57-61, instr, Sch Med, 61-62, assoc, 62-65, asst prof, 65; assoc prof, Col Med, Univ Ky, 65-67; from asst prof to assoc prof, Mayo Grad Sch Med, 67-73, assoc prof, Mayo Med Sch, 73-75, PROF SURG, MAYO MED SCH, 75-, CONSULT CARDIOVASCULAR SURG, MAYO CLIN, 67- *Concurrent Pos:* Univ fel, Harrison Dept Surg Res, Univ Pa, 57-62, fel phys med & rehab, 59-60, Am Cancer Soc fel, 60-61, fel diag & treatment of cancer, 61-62; Markle scholar, 62-67; vis fel, Stockholm, Sweden, 63-64; gen & thoracic surgeon, Hosp Univ Pa, 62-65, asst chief, Surg Div I, 62-65; asst attend physician, Dept Surg & Surg Specialities, Philadelphia Gen Hosp, 64-65; attend physician, Vet Admin Hosp, Philadelphia, 64-65; assoc surg & chief cardiac surg, Univ Hosp, Lexington, Ky, 66-67; consult, Vet Admin Hosp, Lexington, Ky, 66-67, USPHS Hosp, 66-67 & St Mary's Hosp, Rochester, Minn, 67-; mem cent adv comt, coun cardiovasc surg, Am Heart Asn; ed, Cardiovascular Surg, Harper & Row Pubs. *Mem:* Fel Am Col Surg; Soc Univ Surg; Am Heart Asn; fel Am Col Cardiol; fel Am Col Chest Physicians. *Res:* Cardiac physiology; cardiac and vascular surgery. *Mailing Add:* Surg Sect Mayo Clin Rochester MN 55901

DANIELSON, LEE ROBERT, b Summit, NJ, June 19, 46; m 79. SURFACE PHYSICS. *Educ:* Iowa State Univ, BS, 68; Univ Wash, MS, 69; Wash State Univ, PhD(physics), 77. *Prof Exp:* Res assoc, Ore Grad Ctr, 76-78; sr engr physics, 79-80, RES PHYSICIST, THERMO ELECTRON CORP, 80- *Mem:* Am Asn Physics Teachers; Am Vacuum Soc. *Res:* Electronic, structural and chemical properties of surfaces, especially refractory metals; ultra-high vacuum physics and thermionic conversion. *Mailing Add:* Thermo Electron Corp PO Box 459 Waltham MA 02254

DANIELSON, LORAN LEROY, b Havelock, Nebr, July 2, 13; m 33. PLANT PHYSIOLOGY. *Educ:* Univ Iowa, AB, 38, MS, 40, PhD(plant physiol), 41. *Prof Exp:* Chemist & plant physiologist, Delmonte Corp, Ill, 41-44; asst prof bot, Mont State Col, 45; res asst & prof bot, Iowa State Col, 45; plant physiologist, Va Truck Exp Sta, 45-57; ADJ PROF BIOL, UNIV NC, CHARLOTTE, 77- *Concurrent Pos:* Invest leader, Weed Control, Hort crops, 57-72; ed, Weed Sci, 77-80. *Mem:* Am Chem Soc; Am Soc Plant Physiologists; fel Weed Sci Soc Am; Sigma Xi. *Res:* Physiology of vegetable crops; weed control in horticultural crops. *Mailing Add:* 4500 Creemore Dr Charlotte NC 28213

DANIELSON, NEIL DAVID, b Ames, Iowa, July 25, 50. ANALYTICAL CHEMISTRY. *Educ:* Iowa State Univ, BS, 72; Univ Nebr, MS, 74; Univ Ga, PhD(anal chem), 78. *Prof Exp:* ASST PROF CHEM, MIAMI UNIV, 78- *Mem:* Am Chem Soc; Sigma Xi. *Res:* Gas chromatography; high performance liquid chromatography; fluorescence. *Mailing Add:* Hughes Labs Miami Univ Oxford OH 45056

DANIELSON, PAUL STEPHEN, b Passaic, NJ, May 14, 47; m 69; c 2. INORGANIC CHEMISTRY, GLASS CHEMISTRY. *Educ:* Franklin & Marshall Col, AB, 69; Univ Conn, PhD(inorg chem), 74. *Prof Exp:* Res assoc glass mat sci, Vitreous State Labs, Cath Univ Am, 74-76; sr chemist glass chem, Tech Staffs Div, 76-79, SR RES CHEMIST GLASS CHEM, RES & DEVELOP DIV, CORNING GLASS WORKS, 79- *Mem:* Am Ceramic Soc; Am Chem Soc. *Res:* Glass chemistry research; transition metals in glasses; solid state inorganic chemistry. *Mailing Add:* Sullivan Park Corning Glass Works Corning NY 14830

DANIELSON, ROBERT ELDON, b Brush, Colo, Jan 14, 22; m 49; c 2. SOIL PHYSICS. *Educ:* Colo State Univ, BS, 48; Cornell Univ, MS, 49; Univ Ill, PhD(soil physics), 55. *Prof Exp:* Instr soils, 49-52, from asst prof to assoc prof soil physics, 55-64, PROF SOIL PHYSICS, COLO STATE UNIV, 64- *Mem:* Fel Am Soc Agron; fel Soil Sci Soc Am; Int Soc Soil Sci. *Res:* Soil physical properties; influence on the growth of plants; irrigation; soil aeration and structure. *Mailing Add:* Dept of Agron Colo State Univ Ft Collins CO 80521

DANIELS-SEVERS, ANNE ELIZABETH, b San Francisco, Calif, June 13, 40; m 70; c 5. PHARMACOLOGY. *Educ:* San Francisco Col Women, BA, 57; Univ Calif, San Francisco, MS, 65; Univ Pittsburgh, PhD(pharmacol), 68. *Prof Exp:* Asst prof pharmacol, Sch Med, Hershey Med Ctr, Pa State Univ, Hershey, 70-73. *Concurrent Pos:* Nat Acad Sci resident res fel pharmacol, NASA Ames Res Ctr, Moffett Field, Calif, 68-70; consult, Proj Biosattelite, Univ Calif, Los Angeles, 71; mem coun basic res, Am Heart Asn, 71- *Mem:* Am Soc Pharmacol & Exp Therapeut; Am Fedn Clin Res. *Res:* Centrally mediated effects of angiotensin including cardiovascular, adrenal and salt-water balance activity; effects of stress on the pituitary-adrenal system; child growth and development. *Mailing Add:* 1011 Grubb Rd Palmyra PA 17078

DANIHER, FRANCIS ANDREWS, b Pittsburgh, Pa, Dec 4, 39; m 63; c 4. ORGANIC CHEMISTRY. *Educ:* Duquesne Univ, BS, 61; Wayne State Univ, PhD(chem), 64. *Prof Exp:* Res chemist indust chem, Ash-Stevens Inc, 64-66 & Exxon Res & Eng, 66-67; sect head, CPC Int Inc, 67-74; mgr res, Mich Chem Corp, 74-77; DIR RES INDUST CHEM, VELSICOL CHEM CORP, 77- *Mem:* Am Chem Soc; AAAS. *Res:* Halogenated organic synthesis; heterocycles; flame retardants; polymer additives; mechanism of action of flame retardants and other additives. *Mailing Add:* Velsicol Chem Corp 1975 Green Rd Ann Arbor MI 48105

DANIS, PETER GODFREY, b Ottawa, Ont, Apr 12, 09; nat US; m 31; c 10. PEDIATRICS. *Educ:* St Louis Univ, BS, 29, MD, 31, MS, 35. *Prof Exp:* From asst instr to sr instr pediat, 35-47, assoc prof, 48-50, prof, 71-79, EMER PROF PEDIAT & EMER CHMN DEPT, ST LOUIS UNIV HOSP, 79- *Concurrent Pos:* Chmn dept pediat, Univ Hosps, St Louis, 47-56; chief of staff, Cardinal Glennon Mem Hosp for Children, 56-58; mem, Nat Adv Comt United Cerebral Palsy Asn & pediatrician med adv bd spec educ, St Louis County Pub Schs. *Mem:* Am Acad Pediat; AMA; fel Am Acad Cerebral Palsy; assoc Am Acad Neurol; Soc Res Child Develop. *Res:* Neurology; cerebral palsy; convulsive disorders. *Mailing Add:* 2821 Ballas Rd St Louis MO 63131

DANISHEFSKY, ISIDORE, b Poland, Apr 3, 23; US citizen; m 51; c 2. BIOCHEMISTRY, ORGANIC CHEMISTRY. *Educ:* Yeshiva Univ, BA, 44; NY Univ, MSc, 47, PhD(chem), 51. *Prof Exp:* Res assoc chem, Polytech Inst Brooklyn, 51-52; res assoc biochem, Col Physicians & Surgeons, Columbia Univ, 52-55; from asst prof to assoc prof, 55-66, PROF BIOCHEM, NEW YORK MED COL, 66-, CHMN DEPT, 77- *Honors & Awards:* Bernard Revel Mem Award, Yeshiva Univ, 61; Honor Achievement Award, Am Col Angiology, 63. *Mem:* AAAS; Am Soc Biol Chem; Soc Complex Carbohydrates (treas, 72-74); Am Chem Soc; Am Asn Cancer Res. *Res:* Blood coagulation and anticoagulants; mucopolysaccharide structure and metabolism; nucleotide sugars; carcinogenesis. *Mailing Add:* Dept of Biochem New York Med Col Valhalla NY 10595

DANK, MILTON, b Philadelphia, Pa, Sept 12, 20; m 54; c 2. SOLID STATE PHYSICS, MATHEMATICS. *Educ:* Univ Pa, BA, 47, PhD(physics), 53. *Prof Exp:* Asst instr physics, Univ Pa, 47-53; res physicist, Owens-Ill Glass Co, 53-56; res physicist, Burroughs Corp, 56; consult physicist, Missile & Space Div, Gen Elec Co, 56-60, mgr superpressure studies, Space Sci Lab, 60-68, consult physicist laser effects, 68-71; CONSULT SOLID STATE PHYSICS, NDA, INC, 71- *Mem:* Am Phys Soc; Am Inst Aeronaut & Astronaut. *Res:* Effect of dynamic high pressures on solids; shock wave phenomena in solids; equations of state of solids at megabar pressures; hypervelocity particle impact effects; laser effects on solids; laser containment for thermonuclear fusion power. *Mailing Add:* NDA, Inc 1022 Serpentine Wyncote PA 19095

DANKE, RICHARD JOHN, b New London, Wis, Sept 21, 37; m 62; c 3. ANIMAL NUTRITION. *Educ:* Wis State Col, River Falls, BS, 59; Okla State Univ, Stillwater, MS, 62, PhD(animal nutrit), 65. *Prof Exp:* Proj supvr develop animal nutrit, Monsanto Co, 65-68, res specialist animal nutrit, 68-69, tech specialist comput technol, 69-71; ruminant nutritionist animal nutrit, Farmers Union Grain Terminal Asn, 71-74, res & formulation coordr, 74-75; ruminant res nutritionist, Conagra, Inc, 75-77; vpres & gen mgr, Int Nutrit, Inc, 77-81; MGR, FEED INGREDIENT MKT, ALLIED CHEM CORP, 81- *Mem:* Am Soc Animal Sci; Am Dairy Sci Asn; Poultry Sci Asn; Sigma Xi; AAAS. *Res:* Improving the nutrient availability of feedstuffs for domestic animals; improving the productive efficiency of domestic animals. *Mailing Add:* 16625 Gold Omaha NE 68130

DANKEL, THADDEUS GEORGE, JR, b Waycross, Ga, Nov 18, 42; m 71. MATHEMATICAL PHYSICS, OCEANOGRAPHY. *Educ:* Duke Univ, BS, 64; Princeton Univ, MA, 66, PhD(math), 69. *Prof Exp:* Asst prof math, Duke Univ, 68-71; assoc prof, 71-77, PROF MATH, UNIV NC, WILMINGTON, 77- *Concurrent Pos:* NSF fel, 64; fel, Woodrow Wilson Found, 64, Southern Regional Adv Panel, 71-; vis assoc prof math, Univ NC, Chapel Hill, 77. *Honors & Awards:* Poteat Award, NC Acad Sci, 74. *Mem:* Am Math Soc; Math Asn Am; Soc Indust & Appl Math. *Res:* Mathematical problems arising from quantum physics, especially the relations between the theory of stochastic processes and quantum theories; geophysical fluid mechanics; coastal engineering. *Mailing Add:* Dept Math Sci Univ NC PO Box 3725 Wilmington NC 28406

DANKS, HUGH VICTOR, b Farnham, Eng, Sept 16, 43; m 71; c 3. ENTOMOLOGY. *Educ:* Univ London, BSc & ARCS, 65, PhD(entom) & DIC, 68. *Prof Exp:* Fel overwintering of Chironomidae, Entom Res Inst, Agr Can, 68-70, res asst arctic Chironomidae, 71; res asst arctic Culicidae, Dept Biol, Univ Waterloo, 71-72; res assoc biol of Tachinidae, Dept Entom, NC State Univ, 72-74; asst prof biol ecol & entom, Dept Biol Sci, Brock Univ, 74-77; entomologist-in-chg, Biol Surv Proj, Entom Soc Can, 77-80; DIR, BIOL SURV CAN TERRESTRIAL ARTHROPODS, NAT MUS NATURAL SCI, 80- *Honors & Awards:* Hewitt Award, Entom Soc Can, 80. *Mem:* Fel Royal Entom Soc London; Entom Soc Can. *Res:* Modes of seasonal adaptation in insects; seasonality in aquatic insects, especially Chironomidae; ecology of Chironomidae; arctic insects. *Mailing Add:* 1031 Wiseman Cres 3 Ottawa ON K1V 8J3 Can

DANLY, DONALD ERNEST, b Washington, DC, June 14, 29; m 53; c 3. CHEMICAL ENGINEERING. *Educ:* Cornell Univ, BChE, 52; Univ Fla, PhD(chem eng), 58. *Prof Exp:* Chem engr, Textile Intermediates Res & Develop, 58-60, sr chem engr, 60-62, proj leader, 62-63, supvr, 63-65, sect head, 65-71, mgr, 71-76, DIR, FIBER INTERMEDIATES TECHNOL, MONSANTO CHEM INTERMEDIATES CO, 76- *Mem:* Am Inst Chem Engrs; Am Chem Soc; Sigma Xi; AAAS. *Res:* Research and development studies on new and improved chemical processes for manufacture of intermediates used in production of synthetic fibers. *Mailing Add:* 4810 Manolete Dr Pensacola FL 32504

DANN, JOHN ROBERT, b Minneapolis, Minn, Sept 6, 21; m 43; c 3. ADHESION THEORY. *Educ:* Univ SDak, BA, 43; Univ Colo, PhD(chem), 52. *Prof Exp:* Chemist, State Chem Lab, SDak, 41-43; chemist, Eastman Kodak Co, 43-44, group leader, 46-48, res chemist, Res Labs, 52-58, res assoc, 58-72, sr res assoc, 72-81; RETIRED. *Mem:* Am Chem Soc. *Res:* High polymers; Diels-Alder reaction; chemistry of gelatin; heterocyclic chemistry; theory of adhesion. *Mailing Add:* 371 Olympic View Lane Friday Harbor WA 98250

DANN, RAYMOND EUGENE, b Binghamton, NY, Nov 15, 43; m 66; c 4. PHARMACOLOGY, BIOCHEMISTRY. *Educ:* Cornell Univ, BS, 65; Ohio State Univ, MS, 68, PhD(pharmacol), 70. *Prof Exp:* Res assoc environ health, Univ Cincinnati, 71-72; asst prof molecular & quantum biol, Univ Tenn, 72-73; sr biochemist, 73-76, sr regulatory affairs specialist, 76-80, MGR, REGULATORY AFFAIRS, NORWICH-EATON PHARMACEUT DIV, MORTON-NORWICH PROD INC, 80- *Mem:* Am Chem Soc; Drug Info Asn; Regulatory Affairs Prof Soc. *Res:* Drug development. *Mailing Add:* Norwich-Eaton Pharmaceut Div PO Box 191 Norwich NY 13815

DANNA, KATHLEEN JANET, b Beaumont, Tex, Aug 21, 45; m 76. VIROLOGY, MOLECULAR BIOLOGY. *Educ:* NMex Inst Mining & Technol, BS, 67; Johns Hopkins Univ, PhD(microbiol), 72. *Prof Exp:* Res fel, Lab Molecular Biol, Rijksuniversiteit-Gent, Belgium, 72-73; res fel, Dept Biol, Mass Inst Technol, 73-75; ASST PROF MOLECULAR, CELLULAR & DEVELOP BIOL, UNIV COLO, 75- *Concurrent Pos:* NIH res grant, 75-78. *Honors & Awards:* Wilson S Stone Mem Award Basic Biomed Res, M D Anderson Hosp, Univ Tex, 73. *Mem:* Am Soc Microbiol; Am Women Sci. *Res:* Transcriptional control of Simian virus 40 gene expression; Simian virus 40 early proteins with possible roles in transforming cultured cells and in oncogenesis. *Mailing Add:* Dept MCD Biol Univ Colo Campus Box 347 Boulder CO 80309

DANNENBERG, ARTHUR MILTON, JR, b Philadelphia, Pa, Oct 17, 23; m 48; c 3. PATHOLOGY, IMMUNOLOGY. *Educ:* Swarthmore Col, AB, 44; Harvard Univ, MD, 47; Univ Pa, MA, 51, PhD(microbiol), 52; Am Bd Microbiol, dipl. *Prof Exp:* Intern, Albert Einstein Med Ctr, 47-48; res resident, Children's Hosp of Philadelphia, Univ Pa, 48-49, asst prof exp path, Henry Phipps Inst, 56-64, asst prof microbiol, Sch Med & Grad Sch Arts & Sci, Univ Pa, 58-64; assoc prof radiol sci, 64-73, assoc prof path, Sch Med, 64-78, PROF ENVIRON HEALTH SCI & EPIDEMIOL, SCH HYG & PUB HEALTH, JOHN HOPKINS UNIV, 73-, PROF PATH, SCH MED, 78- *Concurrent Pos:* Nat Tuberc Asn fel exp path, Henry Phipps Inst, Univ Pa, 50-52; Nat Res Coun fel biochem, Univ Utah, 52-54; assoc ed, Am Rev Respiratory Dis, 79- *Mem:* Am Asn Path; Am Asn Immunol; Histochem Soc; Soc Exp Biol & Med; Am Thoracic Soc. *Res:* Enzymes in pathogenesis of acute and chronic inflammation; tuberculosis; macrophages; allergic, infectious and environmental diseases. *Mailing Add:* Dept Environ Health Sci Johns Hopkins Univ Sch Hyg Baltimore MD 21205

DANNENBERG, E(LI) M, b Bridgeport, Conn, Oct 10, 17; m 44; c 3. CARBON & CARBON BLACK, RUBBER FILLERS. *Educ:* Mass Inst Technol, SB, 39, SM, 40. *Hon Degrees:* DSc, Univ Louis Pasteur, Strasbourg, France, 73. *Prof Exp:* Res assoc, Div Indust Coop, Mass Inst Technol, 40-43; res chemist, Labs, Am Cyanamid Co, Conn, 43-44; res chemist, Sprague Elec Co, Mass, 44-45; mgr rubber lab, Godfrey L Cabot, Inc, 45-50, assoc dir res, 50-57, dir res, Cabot Corp, 57-63, dir res & develop, 63-68, vpres & sci dir, Performance Chem Group, 68-74, dir, Chem Res Prog, 74-76, corp res fel, 74-76; sr res scientist, 77-78, CONSULT, GA INST TECHNOL, 78- *Concurrent Pos:* Mem adv panel, Chemtech, 75- *Mem:* Am Chem Soc; fel Plastics & Rubber Inst; fel Am Inst Chem Engrs; AAAS; Am Inst Chem Eng. *Res:* Surface chemistry of fine pigments; mechanism of rubber reinforcement; carbon black and carbon products; silica; silicates; clays; fillers; rubber plastics; research administration. *Mailing Add:* 566 Troon Way Mashpee MA 02649

DANNENBERG, JOSEPH, b New York, NY. PHYSICAL ORGANIC CHEMISTRY, THEORETICAL CHEMISTRY. *Educ:* Columbia Col, AB, 62; Calif Inst Technol, PhD(chem), 67. *Prof Exp:* USPHS fel theoret chem, Centre du Mecanique Ondulatoire Appliquee, Paris, 66-67; res assoc phys org chem, Columbia Univ, 67-68; asst prof, 68-72, assoc prof, 72-77, PROF CHEM, HUNTER COL, 77- *Concurrent Pos:* Vis prof, Univ Paris, 74-75. *Mem:* Am Chem Soc; Am Phys Soc; The Chem Soc; Europ Acad Sci Arts & Letters. *Res:* Theoretical energy surfaces for organic reactions; structures of intermediates; mechanisms of substitution and elimination reactions; mechanisms of diazere decomposition. *Mailing Add:* Dept of Chem Hunter Col 695 Park Ave New York NY 10021

DANNENBERG, KONRAD K, b Weissenfels, Ger, Aug 5, 12; US citizen; m 44; c 1. ASTRONAUTICS, ENGINEERING. *Educ:* Hanover Tech Univ, MS, 38. *Prof Exp:* Asst combustion eng, Hanover Tech Univ, 38-39; engr, VDO, Univ Frankfurt, 39-40 & Rocket Test Sta, Peenemuende, 41-45; engr, US Army, Ft Bliss, Tex, 45-50, engr develop opers, Redstone Arsenal, Ala, 50-55, dir, Jupiter prog, Army Ballistic Missile Agency, 55-60, Marshall Space Flight Ctr, NASA, 60-70, dep dir missions & payload planning prog develop, 70-73; assoc prof, Univ Tenn Space Inst, Tullohoma, Tenn, 73-78; CONSULT, ALA SPACE & ROCKET CTR, 78- *Mem:* Am Inst Aeronaut & Astronaut; Hermann Oberth Soc; World Future Soc; L-5 Soc; Int Asn

Educr World Peace. *Res:* Combustion engineering; rocket engine development; space vehicle design, test, check-out and launching; space station design and experiments. *Mailing Add:* 5130 Panorama Dr SE Huntsville AL 35801

DANNENBURG, WARREN NATHANIEL, b Tulsa, Okla, Jan 9, 26; m 49; c 3. BIOCHEMICAL PHARMACOLOGY. *Educ:* Va Polytech Inst, BS, 48; Agr & Mech Col, Tex, MS, 55, PhD(biochem, nutrit), 57. *Prof Exp:* Res microbiologist, S E Massengill Co, 48-53; res biochemist, R J Reynolds Tobacco Co, 57-60; res asst prof biochem, Bowman Gray Sch Med, 60-65; GROUP MANAGER MOLECULAR BIOCHEM, A H ROBINS CO, 65- *Concurrent Pos:* NIH career develop award, 64-65. *Mem:* Am Chem Soc; Am Inst Nutrit; Am Oil Chemists Soc; Soc Exp Biol & Med. *Res:* Therapeutic use and mechanism of action of drugs that affect lipid and carbohydrate metabolism in the intact animal as well as their investigation at the cellular and enzyme levels. *Mailing Add:* A H Robins Co Res Dept 1211 Sherwood Ave Richmond VA 23220

DANNER, DEAN JAY, b Milwaukee, Wis, Sept 26, 41; m 68; c 2. BIOCHEMISTRY, MEDICAL GENETICS. *Educ:* Lakeland Col, BS, 63; Univ NDak, MS, 65, PhD(biochem), 68. *Prof Exp:* Instr biochem, Med Units, Univ Tenn, Memphis, 67-70; asst prof, Northwestern State Univ, La, 70-73; ASSOC PROF PEDIAT, MED SCH, EMORY UNIV, 73-, ASST PROF BIOCHEM, 78- *Concurrent Pos:* Am Cancer Soc fel, St Jude Children's Res Hosp, Memphis, Tenn, 67-70. *Mem:* AAAS; Am Soc Biol Chemists; Am Chem Soc; Am Soc Human Genetics; Soc Inherited Metab Disorders. *Res:* Multienzyme complexes; membrane structure and function; vitamin responsive genetic abnormalities. *Mailing Add:* Div Med Genetics Sch Med Emory Univ Atlanta GA 30322

DANNER, JEAN, b Baltimore, Md. BIOCHEMISTRY. *Educ:* Univ Md, BS, 59; Brandeis Univ, PhD(biochem), 64. *Prof Exp:* Fel, Dept Biochem, Brandeis Univ, 64-65; biochemist, Dept Life Sci, Univ Calif, Riverside, 65-66, chemist, Dept Chem, 68-70; asst res biologist, Dept Develop & Cell Biol, UNIV CALIF, IRVINE, Univ Calif, Irvine, 72-76; assoc dept biochem & molecular biol, Univ Fla, Gainesville, 76-78; CHEMIST, NAT INST OCCUPATIONAL SAFETY & HEALTH-ALOSH, MORGANTOWN, 78- *Mem:* Am Chem Soc; AAAS; NY Acad Sci. *Res:* Glutathione; quantitative affinity chromatography; model membranes; mixed function osidasases. *Mailing Add:* Nat Inst of Occupational Safety & 944 Chestnut Ridge Rd Morgantown WV 26505

DANNER, RONALD PAUL, b New Holland, Pa, Aug 29, 39; m 60; c 2. THERMODYNAMICS, ADSORPTION. *Educ:* Lehigh Univ, BS, 61, MS, 63, PhD(chem eng), 66. *Prof Exp:* Sr chemist, Eastman Kodak Labs, 65-67; from asst prof to assoc prof chem eng, 67-78, PROF CHEM ENG, PA STATE UNIV, UNIVERSITY PARK, 78- *Concurrent Pos:* Fac fel, US Gen Accounting Off, 74-75. *Mem:* Am Inst Chem Engrs; Sigma Xi; Am Soc Eng Educ. *Res:* Physical adsorption of gaseous mixtures; physical and thermodynamic properties of chemicals; theory of corresponding states. *Mailing Add:* 169 Fairlawn Ave State College PA 16801

DANNER, WILBERT ROOSEVELT, b Seattle, Wash, Feb 28, 24. GEOLOGY. *Educ:* Univ Wash, BSc, 46, MSc, 49, PhD(geol), 57. *Prof Exp:* Asst, Univ Wash, 46-50; instr, Everett Jr Col, 50 & Col of Wooster, 50-54; from instr to assoc prof, 54-67, asst dean fac, 74-79, PROF GEOL, UNIV BC, 67- *Concurrent Pos:* Consult, Permanente Cement Co, 48, Northwest Portland Cement Co, 49-57, Riverside Cement Co, 56 & BC Dept Mines, Geol Surv Can. *Mem:* Geol Soc Am; Soc Econ Paleontologists & Mineralogists; Mineral Soc Am; Am Asn Petrol Geologists; Mineral Asn Can. *Res:* General geology; stratigraphy and regional geology; limestone. *Mailing Add:* Dept Geol Univ BC Vancouver BC V6T 1W5 Can

D'ANNESSA, A(NTHONY) T(HOMAS), b Youngstown, Ohio, July 10, 33; m 57; c 2. METALLURGY. *Educ:* Ohio State Univ, BWE, 58, MSc, 60. *Prof Exp:* Res engr, Columbus Div, N Am Aviation, Inc, 55-59 & Eng Exp Sta, Ohio State Univ, 59-61; sr scientist, Lockheed-Palo Alto Lab Div, Lockheed Aircraft Corp, 61-65, res scientist, Lockheed-Ga Res Lab Div, 65-72; MEM TECH STAFF, BELL TEL LABS, 72- *Concurrent Pos:* Consult, 64-; tech adv, consult & mem bd dirs, Weldwire, Inc, Ga, 70-73. *Honors & Awards:* Award, Am Welding Soc, 71. *Mem:* Am Soc Metals; Am Welding Soc. *Res:* Metallurgical engineering; metallurgy, mechanical behavior and solidification mechanics of weldments; development of advanced welding processes and nondestructive testing techniques. *Mailing Add:* 3743 Fox Hills Dr SE Marietta GA 30067

DANNHAUSER, WALTER, b Munich, Ger, June 2, 30; nat US; m 53; c 3. PHYSICAL CHEMISTRY. *Educ:* Rutgers Univ, BSc, 51; Brown Univ, PhD(chem), 54. *Prof Exp:* Res chemist, E I du Pont de Nemours & Co, Inc, 54-56; proj assoc chem, Univ Wis, 56-57; asst prof, Univ Buffalo, 57-62; ASSOC PROF CHEM, STATE UNIV NY BUFFALO, 62- *Mem:* AAAS; Am Chem Soc. *Res:* Polymer physical chemistry; dielectrics. *Mailing Add:* Dept of Chem Acheson Hall State Univ of NY Buffalo NY 14214

DANNIES, PRISCILLA SHAW, b Englewood, NJ, May 3, 45; m 67. ENDOCRINOLOGY, BIOCHEMISTRY. *Educ:* Smith Col, AB, 67; Brandeis Univ, PhD(biochem), 71. *Prof Exp:* Res fel pharmacol, Sch Dent Med & Med Sch, Harvard Univ, 71-74, instr, 74-76; asst prof, 76-80, PROF PHARMACOL, SCH MED, YALE UNIV, 81- *Concurrent Pos:* Arthrities Found res fel, 71-74; res career develop award, 80-85. *Mem:* Endocrinol Soc. *Res:* Control of synthesis and secretion of pituitary hormones by hypothalamic releasing factors and steroid hormones. *Mailing Add:* Dept Pharmacol Yale Univ New Haven CT 06510

DANNLEY, RALPH LAWRENCE, b Chicago, Ill, June 25, 14; m 50; c 3. ORGANIC CHEMISTRY. *Educ:* Univ Denver, BS, 36; Univ Chicago, PhD(org chem), 43. *Prof Exp:* Res chemist, Nat Defense Res Comt, Univ Chicago, 41-42, instr chem, 42-43; dir oil res, Devoe & Raynolds, Inc, 43-45; from asst prof to assoc prof, 45-64, PROF CHEM, CASE WESTERN RESERVE UNIV, 64- *Mem:* Am Chem Soc. *Res:* Mechanism of polymerization; free radical chemistry; peroxides of elements other than carbon; heterocyclic phosphorus compounds; organic fluorine derivatives; aromatic arylsulfonoxylation. *Mailing Add:* Dept of Chem Case Western Reserve Univ Cleveland OH 44106

DANOS, MICHAEL, b Riga, Latvia, Jan 10, 22; nat US; m 49; c 3. NUCLEAR PHYSICS. *Educ:* Tech Univ, Ger, MS, 48; Univ Heidelberg, PhD(physics), 50. *Prof Exp:* Jr asst weak current inst, Tech Univ, Dresden, Ger, 44; asst theoret physics inst, Tech Univ, Hannover, 48-49; asst, Univ Heidelberg, 49-50, asst physics inst, 51; res assoc radiation lab, Columbia Univ, 52-54; PHYSICIST, NAT BUR STANDARDS, 54- *Concurrent Pos:* Guggenheim fel, 59; Sir Thomas Lyle res fel, 70; Alexander V Humboldt sr fel, 74; vis prof var Am & Europ univs. *Mem:* AAAS; Am Phys Soc; Fedn Am Scientists. *Res:* Theoretical nuclear and high energy physics; microwave physics. *Mailing Add:* Nat Bur Standards Washington DC 20234

DANOWSKI, THADDEUS STANLEY, b Wallington, NJ, Sept 6, 14; m 49; c 1. MEDICINE. *Educ:* Yale Univ, BA, 36, MD, 40. *Prof Exp:* Asst med, Sch Med, Yale Univ, 40-43, from instr to asst prof, 43-47; prof, 47-73, CLIN PROF MED, SCH MED, UNIV PITTSBURGH, 73-; DIR MED, SHADYSIDE HOSP, 73- *Concurrent Pos:* Guggenheim fel, 53; intern, New Haven Hosp, 40-41, asst resident, 41-43; sr staff physician, Presby Children's & Women's Hosps, 47-, Elizabeth Steel Magee Hosp, 49- & Shadyside Hosp, 58-; consult, Vet Admin Hosp, 47-; spec consult, NIH, 57-61, 62-; chief med & head endocrine metab unit, Magee-Womens Hosp, 69-73. *Honors & Awards:* Achievement Award, Polish Med Alliance, 64; Banting Mem Award, 64; Sword of Hope, Pa Div, Am Cancer Soc, 66; Nat Bronze Medal, Am Cancer Soc, 68; Alfred Jurzykowski Award, 69. *Mem:* Am Soc Clin Invest; Am Physiol Soc; fel Am Col Physicians; fel AMA; Am Diabetes Asn (pres elect, 64, pres, 65). *Res:* Clinical investigation; fluid and electrolytes; diseases of the thyroid gland. *Mailing Add:* Shadyside Hosp 5230 Centre Ave Pittsburgh PA 15232

DANSBY, DORIS, b New Albany, Miss, Apr 22, 18. HEMATOLOGY. *Educ:* Univ Miss, BA, 40; Univ Tenn, Cert Med Technol, 41. *Prof Exp:* Med technologist serol & bact, Baptist Hosp Lab, Tenn, 41-45; res assoc mycol res, Lederle Labs, Am Cyanamid Co, NY, 45-54; pharmacologist hematol, 54-63, SR SCIENTIST, MEAD JOHNSON RES CTR, 63- *Mem:* Am Soc Microbiol; Am Soc Med Technol; NY Acad Sci. *Res:* Microbiology; antibiotics; mycology in relation to microorganisms producing antibiotics; hematologic aspects of the toxicology of potential therapeutic agents. *Mailing Add:* 1100 Erie Evansville IN 47715

DANSEREAU, PIERRE, b Montreal, Que, Can, Oct 5, 11; m 35. ECOLOGY, ENVIRONMENTAL SCIENCES. *Educ:* Univ Montreal, BA, 31; Univ Geneva, DSc(plant taxon), 39. *Hon Degrees:* LLD, Univ Sask, 59; DSc, Univ NB, 59, Univ Strasbourg, 70, Univ Sherbrooke & Sir George Williams Univ, 71, Guelph Univ & Univ Western Ont, 73, Mem Univ Nfld, 74, McGill Univ, 76 & Univ Ottawa, 77; DEnvSc, Univ Waterloo, 72. *Prof Exp:* Botanist, Montreal Bot Garden, 39-40, asst dir tech serv, 40-42; dir, Prov Biogeog Serv, 43-50; instr bot, Univ Montreal, 40-45, asst prof, 45-50; from asst prof to assoc prof, Univ Mich, 50-55; chmn dept bot & dean fac sci, Univ Montreal, 55-61; asst dir bot, NY Bot Garden, 61-66, head dept ecol, 61-68; prof ecol & urban studies, Univ Montreal, 68-71; prof & dir sci, Ctr Ecol Res Montreal, 71-72; prof ecol, Ctr Environ Sci Res, 72-76, hon prof, 76-80, EMER PROF ECOL, UNIV QUEBEC, MONTREAL, 80- *Concurrent Pos:* Grants, Nat Res Coun, 40, 41, 44, 45-47, 48, 56-57, 59 & 60, Huyck Preserve, 44, Brazilian Res Coun & Nat Geog Coun, 45 & 46, Am Philos Soc, 48, NSF, 54-55 & 62-65; lectr, Macdonald Col, McGill Univ, 42-44; vis prof, Univ Brazil, 46, Univ Paris, 58, Univ NZ, 61, Univ PR, 63 & Univ Lisbon, 77; Off Can del, Pac Sci Cong, 49, del, 53 & 61; del, Int Bot Cong, 54, 1st vpres, 59; hon counr, Adv Coun Sci Res, Madrid, 60; hon mem, Acad Sci Toulouse, 60; vchmn, Can Comn Int Biol Prog, 69-77; proj dir, Nat Res Coun Ecol Study New Montreal Int Airport Zone, 70-73; vchmn, Can Environ Adv Coun, 72-75; pres, First Int Film Festival Human Environ, 73; observr, UN Env Prog, Nairobi, Kenya, 74; adv environ, Kairouan, Tunisia, Can AID, 74; mem, Econ Comn Latin Am, Mex, 77. *Honors & Awards:* Pariseau Medal, French-Can Asn Advan Sci, 65; Distinguished Serv Award, NY Bot Garden, 69; Companion Order of Can, Govt Can, 69; Massey Medal, Royal Can Geog Soc, 73; Molson Prize, Can Coun, 75. *Mem:* Ecol Soc Am; World Soc Ekistics; Asn Am Geogrs; fel Royal Soc Can; Can Geog Soc. *Res:* Taxonomy and evolution of Cistus, Potentilla, Viola and Acer; comparative structure and dynamics of vegetation in tropical to arctic climates; interdisciplinary research on land use; urban ecology. *Mailing Add:* Univ of Quebec CP 888 Montreal PQ H3C 3P8 Can

DANTI, AUGUST GABRIEL, b New Eagle, Pa, Jan 26, 23; m 50; c 1. PHARMACY, CHEMISTRY. *Educ:* Univ Pittsburgh, BS, 50, MS, 52; Ohio State Univ, PhD(pharm), 55. *Prof Exp:* Instr pharm, Univ Pittsburgh, 52-53; asst prof, Wayne State Univ, 56-59; assoc prof, 59-64, head dept allied health sci, 68-71, PROF SCH PHARM, NORTHEAST LA UNIV, 64- *Honors & Awards:* Pres Award, Squibb & Sons, Inc, 69 & McKesson-Robbins & Co, 69; A H Robins Bowl Hygeia, 70; Serv Recognition Award, Arthritis Found, 79; William P O'Brien Clin Pharm Award, 81. *Mem:* AAAS; Am Col Apothecaries; Am Asn Col Pharm; Acad Pharmaceut Sci; Am Pharmaceut Asn. *Res:* The release of medicaments from various pharmaceutical dosage forms. *Mailing Add:* Sch Pharm Col Pharm & Health Sci Northeast La Univ Monroe LA 71209

DANTIN, ELVIN J, SR, b Golden Meadow, La, Jan 13, 27; m 47; c 5. CIVIL ENGINEERING, WATER RESOURCES. *Educ:* La State Univ, BS, 49, MS, 52; Stanford Univ, PhD(struct), 60. *Prof Exp:* Instr civil eng, 49-52, from asst prof to assoc prof, 52-62, PROF CIVIL ENG & DIR DIV ENG RES, LA STATE UNIV, BATON ROUGE, 62- *Concurrent Pos:* Consult, E E Evans, Consult Engr, La, 54-58, Humble Oil & Refining Co, Tex, 57 & La Dept Pub Works, 61; dir, La Water Resources Res Inst, 70- *Mem:* Am Concrete Inst. *Res:* Structural engineering; reinforced concrete; structures. *Mailing Add:* Div of Eng Res La State Univ Baton Rouge LA 70803

D'ANTONIO, CARMINE R, physical metallurgy, see previous edition

D'ANTONIO, PETER, b Brooklyn, NY, Nov 10, 41; m 66; c 1. STRUCTURAL CHEMISTRY. *Educ:* St John's Univ, BS, 63; Polytech Inst Brooklyn, PhD(phys chem), 67. *Prof Exp:* RES CHEMIST, US NAVAL RES LAB, 67- *Mem:* Am Chem Soc; Sigma Xi; Am Crystallog Asn. *Res:* Molecular structure determinations of substances in the vapor phase and structural analysis of semiconductor thin films using electron diffraction techniques. *Mailing Add:* 12003 Wimbleton Upper Marlboro MD 20870

DANTZIG, GEORGE BERNARD, b Portland, Ore, Nov 8, 14; m 36; c 3. MATHEMATICAL STATISTICS. *Educ:* Univ Md, AB, 36; Univ Mich, MA, 37; Univ Calif, Berkeley, PhD(math), 46. *Hon Degrees:* DSc, Israel Inst Technol, 73; Dr, Univ Linkoping, Sweden, 75, Univ Md, 76 & Yale Univ, 78. *Prof Exp:* Jr statistician, US Bur Labor Statist, 37-39; statistician, Air Force, 41-45, chief mathematician, Air Force Hq Comptroller, 45-52; res mathematician, Rand Corp, 52-60; prof eng sci & chmn oper res ctr, Univ Calif, Berkeley, 60-66; PROF OPER RES & COMP SCI, STANFORD UNIV, 66- *Concurrent Pos:* Mem fac, Univ Calif, Los Angeles, 54-60. *Honors & Awards:* Except Meritorious Serv Medal, War Dept, 44; Nat Medal Sci, 75; Von Neumann Theory Prize, Opers Res Soc & Mat Sci Soc, 75; Appl Math & Numerical Anal Prize, Nat Acad Sci, 76. *Mem:* Nat Acad Sci; fel Am Acad Arts & Sci; assoc Am Math Soc; fel Oper Res Soc; fel Inst Mgt Sci (pres, 66). *Res:* Existence of similar regions in theory of mathematical statistics; operations research; mathematical theory of optimization in large scale interrelated systems. *Mailing Add:* Dept of Opers Res Stanford Univ Stanford CA 94305

DANTZLER, HERMAN LEE, JR, b Walterboro, SC, Nov 19, 45; m 69; c 2. PHYSICAL OCEANOGRAPHY. *Educ:* US Naval Acad, BS, 68; Johns Hopkins Univ, MA, 73, PhD(phys oceanog), 75. *Prof Exp:* Fac oceanog & meteorol, US Naval Acad, 74-78; prog mgr upper ocean variability, US Naval Oceanog Off, 78-80; OCEAN/ATMOSPHERIC SCI RES POLICY & PROG DEVELOP & SPEC ASST TO CHIEF OF NAVAL RES ON OCEAN SCI, OFF NAVAL RES, WASHINGTON, DC, 80- *Concurrent Pos:* Prin investr, Upper Ocean Variability Study, Off Naval Res, 75-78; guest investr, Woods Hole Oceanog Inst, 75; mem, Density Comt, US Polymode Orgn, Mass Inst Technol, 75-77. *Mem:* Am Meteorol Soc. *Res:* Upper ocean variability. *Mailing Add:* 7225 Dockside Lane Columbia MD 21045

DANTZLER, WILLIAM HOYT, b Mt Holly, NJ, Aug 25, 35; m 59; c 2. PHYSIOLOGY. *Educ:* Princeton Univ, AB, 57; Columbia Univ, MD, 61; Duke Univ, PhD(zool), 64. *Prof Exp:* Intern med, Univ Wash Hosp, 61-62; asst prof pharmacol, Col Physicians & Surgeons, Columbia Univ, 64-68; assoc prof, 68-74, PROF PHYSIOL, COL MED, UNIV ARIZ, 74- *Mem:* AAAS; Am Soc Nephrology; Int Soc Nephrology; Am Soc Zool; Am Physiol Soc. *Res:* Comparative renal physiology; excretion of end products of nitrogen metabolism; control of excretion of ions and water in vertebrates. *Mailing Add:* Dept of Physiol Univ of Ariz Col of Med Tucson AZ 85724

DANYLUK, STEVEN, b Dec 25, 45; m 64; c 2. MATERIALS SCIENCE. *Educ:* Univ Del, BS, 69; Cornell Univ, PhD(mat sci & eng), 74. *Prof Exp:* Mem staff, Tex Instruments, Inc, 73-74; asst metallurgist, Mat Sci Div, Argonne Nat Lab, 74-79; ASSOC PROF MAT SCI & ENG, UNIV ILL, CHICAGO, 79- *Concurrent Pos:* Sr engr, Jet Propulsion Lab, Calif Inst Technol, 80; resident assoc, Argonne Nat Lab, 80-; consult, Inst Gas Technol, 80- *Mem:* Am Soc Metals; Nat Soc Corrosion Engrs; Am Inst Metal Engrs. *Res:* Effects of microstructure on mechanical properties of stainless steel; abrasion and wear of photovoltaic materials. *Mailing Add:* Mat Eng Dept Univ Ill PO Box 4348 Chicago IL 60680

DANZER, LAURENCE ALFRED, b Chicago, Ill, July 27, 37; m 65; c 1. CLINICAL CHEMISTRY, PHYSICAL CHEMISTRY. *Educ:* Valparaiso Univ, BA, 59; Univ Ky, MS, 63, PhD(chem), 69. *Prof Exp:* Res chemist, Pulmonary Div, Dept Med, Univ Ky, 62-67, chief chemist clin res ctr, 67-69; asst prof path, Univ Kans Med Ctr, 69-77; CLIN CHEMIST, MERCY HOSP, DES MOINES, 77- *Concurrent Pos:* Consult, Vet Admin Hosp, Kansas City, Mo, 74- *Mem:* Am Chem Soc; Am Asn Clin Chemists. *Res:* Protein chemistry; structure in non aqueous solvents; tissue enzyme levels; radioimmunoassay of hormones. *Mailing Add:* Dept of Path Mercy Hosp Sixth & University Des Moines IA 50314

DANZIG, MORRIS JUDA, b Staten Island, NY, July 31, 25; m 55; c 2. ORGANIC CHEMISTRY, INORGANIC CHEMISTRY. *Educ:* Univ Miami, BS, 49, MS, 51; Tulane Univ, PhD(org chem), 53. *Prof Exp:* Du Pont fel org chem, Univ Minn, 53-54; supvry chemist, North Regional Res Lab, USDA, 54-56; from sr org chemist to head org res, Lord Mfg Co, 56-60; from sr org chemist to sect leader, Am Viscose Corp, 60-64; mgr adv develop chem & plastics, Gen Tire & Rubber Co, 64-68; dir, Corn Prod Corp, 68-70, dir, 70-74, VPRES RES & DEVELOP, CPC NORTH AM, 74- *Concurrent Pos:* Mem bd dirs, Acme Resin Corp. *Mem:* Am Chem Soc; Am Inst Chem. *Res:* Industrial product and process research and development. *Mailing Add:* CPC North Am Moffett Tech Ctr Box 345 Argo IL 60501

DANZIGER, LAWRENCE, b New York, NY, July 17, 32; m 60; c 2. STATISTICS. *Educ:* City Col New York, BA, 53, MA, 54; NY Univ, PhD(indust eng), 71. *Prof Exp:* Statistician, 56-57, assoc statistician, 57-58, staff statistician, 58-62, mgr statist anal, 62-68, mgr appl statist res, 68-71, SR STATISTICIAN, IBM CORP, 71- *Concurrent Pos:* Adj prof, Union Col, NY, 67- *Mem:* Am Statist Asn. *Res:* Application of statistical theory to computer software analysis and modelling; industrial reliability and quality control. *Mailing Add:* 3 Spur Way Poughkeepsie NY 12603

DAO, FU TAK, b Shanghai, China, Nov 22, 43; US citizen; m 72. PARTICLE PHYSICS. *Educ:* Mass Inst Technol, BA, 66, MS, 67, PhD(particle physics), 70. *Prof Exp:* Fel high energy physics res, Mass Inst Technol, 70-71; res assoc, Fermi Nat Accelerator Lab, 71-74; res assoc & instr, Tufts Univ, 74-76, asst prof physics, 76-79; MEM TECH STAFF, BELL LABS, MURRAY HILL, NJ, 79- *Mem:* Am Phys Soc; Sigma Xi. *Res:* Research in nature of interaction among elementary particles at high energy, and various experimental techniques used in particle physics research. *Mailing Add:* Bus Anal Syst Ctr Bell Labs Murray Hill NJ 07974

DAO, THOMAS LING YUAN, b Soochow, China, Apr 27, 21; nat US; m 54; c 4. MEDICINE. *Educ:* Soochow Univ, BS, 40; St Johns Univ, China, MS, 42, MD, 45. *Prof Exp:* From instr to asst prof surg, Sch Med, Univ Chicago, 51-57; asst prof surg, RES PROF PHYSIOL & ASSOC PROF SURG, SCH MED, STATE UNIV NY BUFFALO, 66-, CHIEF DEPT BREAST SURG, ROSWELL PARK MEM INST, 57-; PROF BIOL, NIAGARA UNIV, 67- *Concurrent Pos:* Sr fel surg, Wash Univ, 49-51. *Mem:* AAAS; Am Col Surg; Endocrine Soc; Am Asn Cancer Res; NY Acad Sci. *Res:* Physiology; endocrine physiology; endocrine aspect of neoplastic disease; chemical carcinogenesis; experimental pathology. *Mailing Add:* Roswell Park Mem Inst 666 Elm St Buffalo NY 14263

DAO, TRONG TICH, m 56; c 3. COMPUTER ENGINEERING. *Educ:* Univ Paris, BS, 52; Nat Sch Advan Telecommun, Paris, EE, 55; Stanford Univ, MS, 65; Grenoble Univ, DSc, 78. *Prof Exp:* Mem res staff, Ampex Corp, Redwood City, 67-73; sr scientist, Signetics Corp, Sunnyvale, 73-80; ENG MGR, MICROPROCESSOR DIV, FAIRCHILD CAMERA & INSTRUMENT, 80- *Mem:* Inst Elec & Electronics Engrs. *Res:* Logic systems; integrated circuits. *Mailing Add:* 22446 Linda Ann Ct Cupertino CA 95014

DAOUD, ASSAAD S, b Zebdani, Syria, Oct 21, 23; US citizen; m 57; c 3. PATHOLOGY. *Educ:* Univ Paris, MD, 51. *Prof Exp:* Intern, St Memmie Hosp, Chalons sur Marne, France, 50-51; intern path, Springfield Hosp, Mass, 52, resident, 52-54; instr path & bact, 54-56, from asst prof to assoc prof path, 56-67, PROF PATH, ALBANY MED COL, 67-; CHIEF LAB SERV, VET ADMIN HOSP, 61- *Concurrent Pos:* Mem coun arteriosclerosis & coun epidemiol, Am Heart Asn. *Mem:* AMA; Int Acad Path. *Res:* Arteriosclerosis. *Mailing Add:* Lab Serv Vet Admin Hosp Albany NY 12208

DAOUD, GEORGES, b Lattakiat, Syria, Mar 27, 27; US citizen; m 54; c 3. CARDIOLOGY. *Educ:* St Joseph Univ, Beirut, MD, 57; Am Bd Internal Med, dipl, 68; Am Bd Cardiovasc Dis, 72. *Prof Exp:* Asst med, 61-67, clin assoc prof med, 67-75, CLIN PROF MED, UNIV CINCINNATI, 75-, CLIN ASSOC PROF PEDIAT, 67-; INSTR & CLINICIAN, DEPT INTERNAL MED & DIR CARDIAC LAB, GOOD SAMARITAN HOSP, 66- *Concurrent Pos:* Fel coun clin cardiol & coun thrombosis, Am Heart Asn. *Mem:* Am Fedn Clin Res; fel Am Col Chest Physicians; Am Heart Asn; fel Am Col Cardiol; Int Cardiovasc Soc. *Res:* Cardiac hemodynamics; phonocardiography; clinical cardiology. *Mailing Add:* 2328 Auburn Ave Cincinnati OH 45219

D'AOUST, ANDRE LUCIEN, b Montreal, Que, Nov 23, 40; m 66; c 2. PLANT PHYSIOLOGY, PLANT BIOCHEMISTRY. *Educ:* Univ Montreal, BSc, 63; Queen's Univ, Ont, MSc, 67, PhD(plant physiol), 70. *Prof Exp:* RES SCIENTIST TREE BIOL, LAURENTIAN FOREST RES CTR, LAND FOREST & WILDLIFE SERV CAN, 69- *Concurrent Pos:* Nat Res Coun Can fel, 70. *Mem:* AAAS; Am Soc Plant Physiologists; Can Soc Plant Physiologists; French-Can Asn Advan Sci. *Res:* Tree biology; tree physiology with special emphasis on genetic superiority. *Mailing Add:* Laurentian Forest Res Ctr CP 3800 Ste-Foy ON G1V 4C7 Can

D'AOUST, BRIAN GILBERT, b Powell River, BC, Mar 7, 38; m 59; c 3. CELL & HYPERBARIC PHYSIOLOGY. *Educ:* Queen's Univ, Ont, BSc, 61; Univ Calif, San Diego, PhD(marine biol), 67. *Prof Exp:* Nat Res Coun-Nat Acad Sci res fel physiol, Naval Med Res Inst, Nat Naval Med Ctr, Md, 67-69; asst res physiologist, Univ Calif Naval Biol Lab, Oakland, 70; investr, 70-73, sr investr hyperbaric res & diving physiol, 73-78, DIR HYPERBARIC PHYSIOL, VIRGINIA MASON RES CTR, 78- *Concurrent Pos:* Scientist, Seatransit Exped & Bering Sea Exped, 68; NIH res career develop award, 72-77; asst prof, Univ Wash, 73- *Mem:* AAAS; Am Soc Limnol & Oceanog; Undersea Med Soc; Am Physiol Soc. *Res:* Catabolic processes in oxygen-adapted tissue and physiological studies of gas secretion in teleost swim bladder; natural, evolutionary and dynamic physiological adaptations to high gas and hydrostatic pressure; physiological adjustments to diving; the etiology of decompression sickness; use of isobaric techniques to evaluate critical conditions for decompression sickness. *Mailing Add:* Virginia Mason Res Ctr 1000 Seneca St Seattle WA 98101

DAOUST, DONALD ROGER, b Worcester, Mass, Aug 13, 35; m 59; c 3. MICROBIOLOGY. *Educ:* Univ Conn, BA, 57; Univ Mass, MS, 59, PhD(phage), 62. *Prof Exp:* Sr res microbiologist, Merck Sharp & Dohme Res Labs, 62-70, res fel, 70-72, mgr biol qual control, 72-75; dir qual control, Armour Pharmaceut Co, 75-76; vpres, Qual Assurance & Regulatory Compliance, Armour Pharmaceut Co, Phoenix, 76-78; V PRES, QUAL CONTROL, CARTER-WALLACE, INC, 78- *Mem:* AAAS; Am Soc Microbiol; Parenteral Drug Asn; Proprietary Asn. *Res:* Microbial production of natural substances. *Mailing Add:* Carter-Wallace Inc Cranbury NJ 08512

DAOUST, HUBERT, b Montreal, Que, Apr 13, 28; m 52; c 4. PHYSICAL CHEMISTRY. *Educ:* Univ Montreal, BSc, 50, MSc, 51, PhD(chem), 54. *Prof Exp:* Res assoc, Baker Lab, Cornell Univ, 53-54; asst prof, 54-74, PROF CHEM, UNIV MONTREAL, 74- *Mem:* Am Chem Soc; Chem Inst Can. *Res:* Thermodynamics of high polymer solutions including polyelectrolytes and polypeptides; microcalorimetry; osmometry; viscosimetry; ultracentrifugation. *Mailing Add:* Dept of Chem Univ of Montreal Montreal PQ H3C 3J7 Can

D'AOUST, MAURICE, plant physiology, see previous edition

DAOUST, RICHARD ALAN, b Fitchburg, Mass, Jan 26, 48; m 71; c 2. INSECT PATHOLGOY, MICROBIOLOGY. *Educ:* Univ Mass, BS, 70, MS, 74, PhD(environ microbiol), 78. *Prof Exp:* Res entomologist insect path, Ministry Agr, Botswana, Peace Corps Proj, 70-72; fel insect path, 78-81, RES ASSOC, BOYCE THOMPSON INST PLANT RES, CORNELL UNIV, 81-; RES SCIENTIST, CENTRO NACIONAL DE PESQUISA, 81- *Mem:* Am Soc Microbiol; Entomol Soc Am; Soc Invertebrate Path; Sigma Xi. *Res:* Basic and applied research in insect pathology and medical entomology; mode of action and efficacy of microbial agents in the control of agricultural and medical pests; control of mosquitoes with entomopathogenic fungi; microbial control of principal insect pests of cowpeas. *Mailing Add:* Ctr Nat Pesquisa Arroz Feijao Caixa Postal 179 Goiania 74000 Brazil

DAOUST, ROGER, b Valleyfield, Que, Oct 13, 24; m 50; c 2. HISTOPATHOLOGY, CANCER. *Educ:* Univ Montreal, BSc, 47, MSc, 50; McGill Univ, PhD(anat), 53. *Prof Exp:* Res assoc, Montreal Cancer Inst, Notre-Dame Hosp, 50-60, dir res labs, 67-74, res assoc prof med, Univ, 60-67, Nat Cancer Inst Can res assoc, Montreal Cancer Inst, 60-75, PROF ANAT, UNIV MONTREAL, 67-, GEN DIR, MONTREAL CANCER INST, 74- *Concurrent Pos:* Damon Runyon Mem Fund Cancer Res fel, 52-55; Brit Empire Cancer Campaign exchange fel, London, 55-56; Nat Cancer Inst Can fel, Copenhagen, 56-57. *Mem:* AAAS; Histochem Soc; Am Asn Cancer Res; NY Acad Sci. *Res:* Cytology; histochemistry; nucleic acids metabolism in normal and neoplastic tissues. *Mailing Add:* Off Dir Montreal Cancer Inst Notre Dame Hosp 1560 Sherbrooke Montreal PQ H2L 4M1 Can

DAPKUS, DAVID CONRAD, b Oct 23, 44; US citizen; m 65. GENETICS. *Educ:* Univ Minn, BS, 68, MS, 69, PhD(zool), 75. *Prof Exp:* Assoc, 75-79, ASST PROF BIOL, WINONA STATE UNIV, 79- *Mailing Add:* Dept Biol Winona State Univ Winona MN 55987

DAPPEN, GLEN MARSHALL, b Guernsey, Iowa, Nov 18, 35; m 76; c 6. ORGANIC CHEMISTRY. *Educ:* Wis State Col, Superior, BS, 57; Iowa State Univ, PhD(org chem), 62. *Prof Exp:* From res chemist to sr res chemist, 61-69, RES ASSOC, EASTMAN KODAK CO, 70- *Mem:* Am Asn Clin Chemists. *Res:* Polymer and photographic chemistry; clinical chemistry. *Mailing Add:* Eastman Kodak Co Res Lab 343 State St Rochester NY 14650

DAPPLES, EDWARD CHARLES, b Chicago, Ill, Dec 13, 06; m 31; c 2. GEOLOGY. *Educ:* Northwestern Univ, BS, 28, MS, 34; Harvard Univ, MA, 35; Univ Wis, PhD(geol), 38. *Prof Exp:* Geologist, Zeigler Coal Co, 28; geologist, Truax-Traer Coal Co, 28-32, mine supt, 31-32; from instr to prof, 36-74, EMER PROF GEOL, NORTHWESTERN UNIV, EVANSTON, 74- *Concurrent Pos:* Asst geologist, State Geol Surv, Ill, 39; consult geologist, Sinclair Oil Co, 45-50 & Pure Oil Co, 51; sr vis scientist, Univ Lausanne, 60-61; prof, Univ Geneva, 70. *Mem:* AAAS; fel Geol Soc Am; fel Soc Econ Geologists; Soc Econ Paleontologists & Mineralogists (pres, 70); hon mem Am Inst Mining, Metall & Petrol Engrs. *Res:* Petrography and deposition of sedimentary rocks. *Mailing Add:* 13035 98th Dr Sun City AZ 85351

D'APPOLONIA, BERT LUIGI, b Capreol, Ont, Nov 6, 39. CEREAL CHEMISTRY. *Educ:* Laurentian Univ, BA, 62; NDak State Univ, MS, 66, PhD(cereal chem), 68. *Prof Exp:* Asst prof, 68-72, assoc prof, 72-78, PROF CEREAL CHEM, NDAK STATE UNIV, 78- *Mem:* Am Chem Soc; Am Asn Cereal Chemists (secy, 81); Inst Food Technologists. *Res:* Quality evaluation of hard red spring wheat; investigation of carbohydrates, including starch, pentosans and simple sugars of wheat products; carbohydrates of cereals; starches, pentosans, polysaccharides; bread baking research. *Mailing Add:* Cereal Chem & Technol NDak State Univ Fargo ND 58102

DAPSON, RICHARD W, b Flushing, NY, Sept 5, 41; m 62; c 2. ANATOMY, ECOLOGY. *Educ:* Cornell Univ, BS, 63, PhD(vert zool), 66. *Prof Exp:* From asst prof to assoc prof, 66-74, chmn dept, 74-77, PROF BIOL, UNIV MICH-FLINT, 74-, DAVID M FRENCH DISTINGUISHED PROF, 81- *Concurrent Pos:* Fac res assoc, Savannah River Ecol Lab, Univ Ga, 72-73; adj prof, Wayne State Univ, 81- *Mem:* NY Acad Sci; Am Soc Mammal; Am Soc Zool; Nat Soc Histotechnol. *Res:* Age determination; mechanisms of staining with ionic dyes; rate of ageing in wild vertabrate populations; biostastics. *Mailing Add:* Dept Biol Univ Mich Flint MI 48503

DARAVINGAS, GEORGE VASILIOS, b Thessaloniki, Greece, Apr 22, 34; m 68. FOOD SCIENCE, BIOCHEMISTRY. *Educ:* Univ Thessaloniki, 58; Ore State Univ, MS, 63, PhD(food sci), 65. *Prof Exp:* Qual control chemist, Agr Corp Polygyros, Greece, 57-58; chemist, Geigy, Greece, 60-61; res asst, Ore Agr Exp Sta, 61-65; proj leader food res & develop, Hunt Wesson Foods, Div of Norton Simon, 65-68; mgr food sci & qual assurance dept, Glidden Durkee, Div of SCM Corp, 68-73; dir, 73-76, DIR RES & DEVELOP, GEN MILLS, INC, 76-; lectr, Univ Calif, Riverside & Irvine, 67-68. *Concurrent Pos:* Instr, Euclides Univ Prep Inst, Greece, 60-61; lectr, Univ Calif, Riverside & Irvine, 67-68. *Mem:* Am Chem Soc; Inst Food Technol. *Res:* Research and development effort including basic food research, exploratory food research, product development, engineering and process development; quality assurance in food processing plants. *Mailing Add:* JFB Tech Ctr 9000 Plymouth Ave N Minneapolis MN 55427

DARBY, DAVID G, b Oak Park, Ill, Sept 10, 32; m 57; c 2. INVERTEBRATE PALEONTOLOGY. *Educ:* Univ Mich, BS, 59, MS, 61, PhD(paleont), 64. *Prof Exp:* Scientist, US Antarctic Res Prog, 60-61; NSF assoc investr, 62-64; geologist, Mobil Oil Corp, Peru, 64-68; grad sch res grant, 69-71, ASSOC PROF GEOL, UNIV MINN, DULUTH, 68- *Mem:* Fel AAAS; Geol Soc Am; Soc Econ Paleontologists & Mineralogists, Paleont Soc. *Res:* Ecology and taxonomy of recent and fossil Ostracoda; Precambrian algal remains; habitat of early vertebrates. *Mailing Add:* Dept of Geol Univ of Minn Duluth MN 55812

DARBY, DENNIS ARNOLD, b Pittsburgh, Pa, Oct 31, 44; m 72. SEDIMENTARY PETROLOGY. *Educ:* Univ Pittsburgh, BS, 66, MS, 68; Univ Wis-Madison, PhD(geol), 71. *Prof Exp:* Asst prof geol, Hunter Col, 71-74; adj asst prof oceanog & asst prof geol, 74-78, chmn dept, 78-81, ASSOC PROF OCEANOG, INST OCEANOG & ASSOC PROF GEOL & GEOPHYS SCI, OLD DOMINION UNIV, 78- *Concurrent Pos:* Lectr geol, NY Univ, 73. *Mem:* Sigma Xi; Soc Econ Paleontologists & Mineralogists; Am Geophys Union; Geol Soc Am; Nat Asn Geol Teachers. *Res:* Cation exchange capacity of sediments and the mobilization of trace metals in estuaries; arctic geology and paleoclimatology; coastal plain sedimentation and stratigraphy. *Mailing Add:* Dept of Geophys Sci Old Dominion Univ Norfolk VA 23508

DARBY, EDSEL KENNETH, b Montreal, Que, Apr 23, 24; m 47; c 4. GEOPHYSICS. *Educ:* Univ Sask, MS, 48; Univ BC, PhD(physics), 52. *Prof Exp:* GEOPHYSICIST, GULF RES & DEVELOP CO, 52- *Mem:* Soc Explor Geophys; Europ Asn Geophys. *Mailing Add:* 7923 Union Ave Pittsburgh PA 15218

DARBY, ELEANOR MURIEL KAPP, b Easton, Pa, Feb 4, 05; m 28. MEDICAL RESEARCH ADMINISTRATION. *Educ:* Columbia Univ, AB, 25, PhD(biochem), 42; Univ Pa, MSc, 27. *Prof Exp:* Asst biol, Washington Sq Col, NY Univ, 26-28; asst entomologist, Entom Lab, USDA, 28-31; technician, Dept Med, Col Physicians & Surgeons, Columbia Univ, 32-41, asst dermat, 41-43, instr chem, Dept Nursing & res assoc, Dept Orthop Surg, 46-48; exec secy cardiovasc study sect, Div Res Grants, NIH, 48-58, head confs & publ sect, Grants & Training Br, Nat Heart Inst, 58-62, mem spec projs br, Extramural Progs, 62-69, exec secy therapeut eval comt, Clin Appln Prog, Nat Heart & Lung Inst, 69-73, grants adminr, 69-75. *Concurrent Pos:* Asst, Sch Nursing, NY Hosp, 32-33; fel coun epidemiol, Am Heart Asn. *Mem:* Am Heart Asn; Int Soc Cardiol. *Res:* Salt balance in vertebrate blood; insect physiology, especially fruit flies; blood sedimentation; urinary porphyrins; salicylate metabolism; collagen behavior; spectroscopic analysis; immunochemistry; cardiovascular and cerebrovascular research; cooperative projects; research administration. *Mailing Add:* Rte 5 Box 309 Mt Airy MD 21771

DARBY, JOHN FEASTER, b Chester, SC, Oct 22, 16; m 41; c 2. PLANT PATHOLOGY. *Educ:* Univ Fla, BSA, 48, MSA, 49; Univ Wis, PhD(plant path), 51. *Prof Exp:* Asst plant pathologist, Indian River Field Lab, 51-54, assoc plant pathologist, Inst Food & Agr Sci, 54-64, plant pathologist, 64-66, PROF PLANT PATH & DIR AGR RES & EDUC CTR, INST FOOD & AGR SCI, UNIV FLA, 66- *Mem:* Am Phytopath Soc. *Res:* Diseases of vegetable crops. *Mailing Add:* Agr Res & Educ Ctr PO Box 909 Sanford FL 32771

DARBY, JOSEPH B(RANCH), JR, b Petersburg, Va, Dec 12, 25; m 51; c 4. MATERIALS SCIENCE, NUCLEAR MATERIALS. *Educ:* Col William & Mary, BS, 48; Va Polytech Inst & State Univ, BS, 51; Univ Ill, MS, 55, PhD(metall), 58. *Prof Exp:* Chemist, Allied Dye & Chem Corp, 48-49; metallurgist, Nat Carbon Div, Union Carbide & Carbon Corp, 51-53; phys metallurgist, 58-73, group leader, Mat Sci Div, 66-73, asst div dir, 73-74, ASSOC DIR, FUSION POWER PROG, ARGONNE NAT LAB, 74- *Concurrent Pos:* Sci res coun sr fel, Dept Phys Metall & Sci of Mat, Univ Birmingham, 70-71; co-ed, J Nuclear Mat, 74- *Mem:* Fel Am Soc Metals; Am Inst Mining, Metall & Petrol Engrs; AAAS. *Res:* Electronic structure of metals and alloys; alloy chemistry; thermodynamic properties of alloys; defects in solids; nuclear materials, glasses. *Mailing Add:* Mat Sci Div Bldg 212 Argonne Nat Lab Argonne IL 60439

DARBY, JOSEPH RAYMOND, b Boonville, Mo, Aug 6, 11; m 46; c 6. ORGANIC CHEMISTRY, POLYMER SCIENCE. *Educ:* St Louis Univ, BS, 33. *Prof Exp:* Control chemist, Monsanto Co, 33-35, res chemist, 35-46, res group leader, 46-63, res mgr, 63-76; PRES, DARBY CONSULT INC, 77- *Mem:* Soc Plastics Engrs; Am Chem Soc; hon mem Soc Testing Mat; Res Soc Am. *Res:* Plasticization, stabilization and modification of all polymers, with particular emphasis on polyvinyl chloride. *Mailing Add:* 335 Papin Webster Grove MO 63119

DARBY, NICHOLAS, b Bristol, Eng, Dec 19, 46; Can citizen; m 74. SYNTHETIC ORGANIC CHEMISTRY. *Educ:* Queen's Univ, Ont, BSc, 68; Univ Alta, PhD(chem), 72. *Prof Exp:* Res chemist prof, Raylo Chem Ltd, 76-79; RES LEADER, DOW CHEM CAN, LTD, 79- *Mem:* Chem Inst Can; Am Chem Soc. *Res:* Synthesis and production process development for agricultural chemicals, pharmaceuticals and petrochemicals. *Mailing Add:* Dow Chem Can Ltd PO Box 759 Fort Saskatchewan AB T8L 2P4 Can

DARBY, RALPH LEWIS, b Youngstown, Ohio, Nov 13, 18; m 42; c 2. INFORMATION SCIENCE, CHEMICAL ENGINEERING. *Educ:* Ohio State Univ, BChE, 42; Univ Chicago, cert meteorol, 43. *Prof Exp:* Res engr chem, Commonwealth Eng Co, Ohio, 46-47; res engr, Graphic Arts Res Div, Battelle Columbus Labs, 47-51, prin chem engr, Info Res Div, 52-63, group dir, Dept Info Res & Econ, 63-65, div chief, 65-70, chief proj mgr, Dept Social & Mgt Sci, Battelle Mem Inst, 70-75, assoc sect mgr, Security Anal & Assessment Sect, 75-81; RETIRED. *Mem:* Am Chem Soc; Am Soc Info Sci; fel Am Inst Chemists. *Res:* Scientific communication; design of information storage and retrieval systems; information center operations and management national security technology assessment. *Mailing Add:* 3112 Leeds Rd Upper Arlington OH 43221

DARBY, ROBERT ALBERT, b Birmingham, Ala, May 6, 30; m 52; c 4. ORGANIC CHEMISTRY. *Educ:* Birmingham-Southern Col, BS, 51; Univ Va, MS, 53, PhD(chem), 57. *Prof Exp:* Res chemist, Exp Sta, 57-63, sr res chemist, Washington Works, 63-66, sr res supvr, Exp Sta, 66-69, res mgr, polyolefins div, Plastics Dept, 69-70, Lab dir, Plastics Dept, Res & Develop Div, 70-72, plant mgr, Plastics Dept, Washington Works, Parkersburg, WVa, 72-74, gen mkt mgr, Plastics Dept, Com Resins Div, 74-76, dir res & develop, Feedstocks Div, 76-78, dir Chem Dyes & Pigments Dept, Res & Develop Div, 78-80, DIR, CHEM & PIGMENTS DEPT, DEPT PLANS DIV, E I DU PONT DE NEMOURS & CO, INC, WILMINGTON, 80- *Mem:* Am Chem Soc; Soc Chem Indust; Sigma Xi. *Res:* Conjugation and unsaturation in 1, 2-diaroylcyclopropanes; fluorocarbon chemistry; fluorocarbon polymers synthesis and properties; nylon and acrylic polymer processes. *Mailing Add:* Chem Dyes & Pigments Dept E I du Pont de Nemours & Co Inc Wilmington DE 19898

DARBY, RONALD, b La Veta, Colo, Sept 12, 32; m 61; c 2. FLUID DYNAMICS, RHEOLOGY. *Educ:* Rice Univ, BA & BS, 55, PhD(chem eng), 62. *Prof Exp:* NSF fel chem eng, Cambridge Univ, 61-62; sr scientist electrochem, Ling-Temco-Vought Res Ctr, 63-65; from asst prof to assoc prof chem eng, 65-69, PROF CHEM ENG, TEX A&M UNIV, 69- *Mem:* Am Inst Chem Engrs; Nat Asn Corrosion Engrs; Soc Rheol. *Res:* Applied electrochemistry and corrosion; heat transfer; viscoelastic fluids; polymers; porous fuel cell electrodes; nucleate boiling; two phase fluid flow; non-Newtonian flow; process dynamics; rate processes. *Mailing Add:* Dept of Chem Eng Tex A&M Univ College Station TX 77843

DARBY, WILLIAM JEFFERSON, b Little Rock, Ark, Nov 6, 13; m 35; c 3. BIOCHEMISTRY, NUTRITION. *Educ:* Univ Ark, BS, 36, MD, 37; Univ Mich, MS, 41, PhD(biochem), 42. *Hon Degrees:* ScD, Univ Mich, 66, Utah State Univ, 73. *Prof Exp:* Asst physiol chem, Sch Med, Univ Ark, 30-37, instr, 37-39; asst res prof pub health nutrit, Sch Pub Health, Univ NC & dir med nutrit, State Bd Health, NC, 43-44; from asst prof biochem & med to assoc prof biochem, 44-48, prof biochem & nutrit & dir, Div Nutrit, 48-79, head, Dept Biochem, 49-71, prof nutrit, 64-79, prof med in nutrit, 65-79, EMER PROF BIOCHEM, SCH MED, VANDERBILT UNIV, 79-; PRES, THE NUTRIT FOUND, 72- *Concurrent Pos:* Rockefeller Found spec fel, Sch Med, Vanderbilt Univ, 42-43; instr, Duke Univ, 43-44; mem food & nutrit bd, Nat Res Coun, 49-71 & steering comt, 55-71; mem sci adv bd, Nat Vitamin Found, 50-54 & tech adv comt, Inst Nutrit Cent Am & Panama, 50-64; mem comt food protection, Interdept Comt Nutrit Nat Develop, 50-71, chmn, 54-71; mem comt consults & dir surv, Philippines, Ethiopia, Ecuador, Lebanon, Jordan & Nigeria, 55-66; mem joint exp comt nutrit, Food & Agr Orgn, WHO, 54, 57, 61 & 66, chmn, 57 & 66, chmn joint comt food additives, 56, mem protein adv group, 56 & 60; mem sci adv comt, Nutrit Found, 58-65, 67-71; mem & chmn adv comt nutrit & metab, Off Surgeon Gen, US Army, 59-60; mem protein adv group, WHO-Food Agr Orgn, UNICEF, 60-62, second citizens' comt, Food & Drug Admin, 61-62 & sci adv comt, United Health Found, 62-70, chmn, 65-70; mem adv comt agr sci, USDA, 63-67 & adv bd, Corn Prod Co, 64-71. *Honors & Awards:* Mead-Johnson Award, Am Inst Nutrit, 47, Osborne-Mendel Award, 62; Order Rodolfo Robles, 59; Star of Jordan, Hashemite Kingdom Jordan, 63; Goldberger Award, AMA, 64; Underwood-Prescott Mem lectr, Mass Inst Technol, 79. *Mem:* Nat Acad Sci; Am Soc Biol Chem; Am Chem Soc; Am Soc Clin Invest; Am Inst Nutrit(pres, 58-59). *Res:* Biochemistry of metabolism and nutrition; clinical nutrition; nutrition surveys and public health nutrition; nutritional anemias; folic acid; zinc metabolism. *Mailing Add:* Dept of Biochem Vanderbilt Univ Sch of Med Nashville TN 37203

DARCEL, COLIN LE Q, b St Helier, Gt Brit; Feb 5, 25; m 48; c 2. VETERINARY VIROLOGY. *Educ:* Royal Vet Col, London, MRCVS, 47, BSc, 48, PhD(vet sci), 52; Cambridge Univ, BA, 49, MA, 54. *Prof Exp:* Pathologist fowl tumors res, Poultry Res Sta, Eng, 49-52 & Imp Cancer Res Fund, 52-55; VIROLOGIST, ANIMAL DIS RES INST, CAN DEPT AGR, 55- *Mem:* Path Soc Gt Brit & Ireland; Brit Soc Immunol; Brit Soc Gen Microbiol; Am Asn Cancer Res; Can Soc Microbiol. *Res:* Immunological and biochemical aspects of pathogenesis of erythroblastosis virus; studies of infectious bovine rhinotracheitis and other cattle viruses. *Mailing Add:* Animal Dis Res Inst PO Box 640 Lethridge Can

DARCEY, TERRANCE MICHAEL, b Oakland, Calif, Nov 12, 50; m 71; c 2. ELECTRICAL ENGINEERING. *Educ:* Univ Calif, Berkeley, BS, 72; Calif Inst Technol, PhD(eng sci), 79. *Prof Exp:* Res asst, Dept Bioinfo Syst, Calif Inst Technol, 72-79; NSF fel, Dept Neurol, Univ Zurich, 79-80 , res biomed engr, Electroencephalogram Inst Zurich, 80-81; RES ASSOC, DEPT NEUROL, SCH MED, YALE UNIV, 81-; BIOMED ENGR, NEUROL SERV, VET ADMIN MED CTR, WEST HAVEN, CONN, 81- *Res:* Application of engineering and mathematical techniques to analysis and modeling of biological systems; application of electric field theory and time-series analysis to localization of electroencephalogram phenomena. *Mailing Add:* 116B1 Vet Admin Med Ctr West Haven CT 06516

D'ARCY, WILLIAM GERALD, b Calgary, Alta, Aug 29, 31; m 81; c 2. BOTANY. *Educ:* Univ Alta, BA, 54; Univ Fla, MS, 68; Wash Univ, PhD(bot), 72. *Prof Exp:* Asst trade comnr Chicago, Govt Can, 55-57; economist mkt anal, Am Can Co, NY, 58-60; proprietor mfg, Tortola Pure Sparkling Water Co, VI, 60-65; herbarium asst bot, Univ Fla, 65-68; RES BOTANIST, MO BOT GARDEN, 69- *Concurrent Pos:* Asst prof, Dept Biol, Univ Mo, 74-; fac assoc biol, Wash Univ, 74-; NSF grants, 71, 77 & 80; ed, Flora Panama Prog, 72- *Mem:* Linnaean Soc London; Am Soc Plant Taxon; Int Asn Plant Taxon. *Res:* Systematics of the Solanaceae; floristics of tropical America, especially Panama. *Mailing Add:* Mo Bot Garden 2345 Tower Grove Ave St Louis MO 63110

DARDEN, COLGATE W, III, b Norfolk, Va, Nov 6, 30; m 52; c 3. NUCLEAR PHYSICS. *Educ:* Univ Va, BEE, 53, MA, 54; Mass Inst Technol, PhD(nuclear physics), 59. *Prof Exp:* Physicist, Savannah River Lab, 58-62; vpres, Columbia Eng, Inc, 62-64; assoc prof physics, 64-77, PROF PHYSICS & ASTRON, UNIV SC, 77- *Mem:* Am Phys Soc. *Res:* Low energy nuclear physics; proton scattering and polarization; astrophysics. *Mailing Add:* Dept of Physics & Astron Univ of SC Columbia SC 29208

DARDEN, EDGAR BASCOMB, JR, b Raleigh, NC, Jan 23, 20; m 69. BIOPHYSICS, HEALTH PHYSICS. *Educ:* Col William & Mary, BS, 41; Univ NC, MS, 50; Univ Tenn, PhD(zool), 57. *Prof Exp:* Instr physics, Col William & Mary, 41-42; from jr biologist to biologist, Oak Ridge Nat Lab, 49-73; mem res staff & radiation safety officer, Univ Tenn-Dept Energy, Comparative Animal Res Lab, 73-81; RADIATION SAFETY OFFICER, OAK RIDGE ASSOC UNIVS, 81- *Mem:* Am Phys Soc; Radiation Res Soc; Health Physics Soc; Sigma Xi; Sci Res Soc. *Res:* Late somatic effects of radiation; metabolism of internally deposited radioisotopes; radiation dosimetry; radiobiology; physiology; radiological physics. *Mailing Add:* Univ Tenn-Dept of Energy 1299 Bethel Valley Rd Oak Ridge TN 37830

DARDEN, GERALDINE C, b Nansemond Co, Va, July 22, 36. ALGEBRA. *Educ:* Hampton Inst, BS, 57; Univ Ill, MS, 60; Syracuse Univ, MS, 65, PhD(math), 67. *Prof Exp:* Teacher, S H Clarke Jr High Sch, Va, 57-59; from instr to assoc prof, 60-71, PROF MATH, HAMPTON INST, 71- *Concurrent Pos:* Lectr, Va Acad Sci, 67- *Mem:* Math Asn Am. *Res:* Abelian group theory. *Mailing Add:* Dept of Math Hampton Inst PO Box 6076 Hampton VA 23668

DARDEN, SPERRY EUGENE, b Chicago, Ill, Aug 16, 28; m 54; c 4. NUCLEAR PHYSICS. *Educ:* Iowa State Col, BS, 50; Univ Wis, MS, 51, PhD(physics), 55. *Prof Exp:* Exchange asst, Univ Basel, 55-56; instr physics, Univ Wis, 56-57; from asst prof to assoc prof, 57-65, PROF PHYSICS, UNIV

NOTRE DAME, 65- *Concurrent Pos:* Sloan fel, 62-64; guest prof, Univ Basel, 65-66 & Mexican Nuclear Ctr, 73. *Mem:* Am Phys Soc. *Res:* Nuclear reactions and scattering processes; polarization effects in nuclear reactions and scattering. *Mailing Add:* Dept Physics Univ Notre Dame Notre Dame IN 46556

DARDEN, WILLIAM H, JR, b Tuscaloosa, Ala, Apr 25, 37; m 59; c 2. ALGOLOGY. *Educ:* Univ Ala, BS, 59, MS, 61; Ind Univ, PhD(bot), 65. *Prof Exp:* From asst prof to assoc prof, 65-73, PROF BIOL, UNIV ALA, 73-, CHMN, 74- *Mem:* Am Soc Cell Biol; Phycol Soc Am. *Res:* Cellular differentiation in algae with emphasis on the chemical control of sexual differentiation. *Mailing Add:* Dept of Biol Box 1927 Univ of Ala University AL 35486

D'ARDENNE, WALTER H, b Jenkintown, Pa, Oct 31, 32; m 57; c 3. NUCLEAR ENGINEERING, MECHANICAL ENGINEERING. *Educ:* Pa State Univ, BS, 59; Mass Inst Technol, PhD(nuclear eng), 64. *Prof Exp:* From asst prof to assoc prof nuclear eng, Pa State Univ, 64-72; MGR BWR PROD STAND, NUCLEAR ENERGY GROUP, GEN ELEC CO, 72- *Concurrent Pos:* Am Soc Eng Educ-Ford Found residency, Atomic Power Equip Dept, Gen Elec Co, 70-71. *Mem:* Am Nuclear Soc. *Res:* Reactor design; nuclear design; thermal-hydraulic design; nuclear safety; system analysis; reactor physics. *Mailing Add:* Nuclear Energy Group Gen Elec Co 175 Curtner Ave San Jose CA 95125

DARDIRI, AHMED HAMED, b Cairo, Egypt, Mar 10, 19; nat US; m 51. VETERINARY VIROLOGY. *Educ:* Cairo Univ, DVM, 40, MVSc, 46; Mich State Univ, MSc, 47, PhD(bact), 50. *Prof Exp:* Dir, Poultry Res Exp Sta, Cairo Univ, 40-46; mem, Egyptian Ed Mission to USA, 46-50; sr lectr, Cairo Univ, 50-55; res assoc animal path, Univ RI, 55-56, from asst prof to assoc prof, 56-61; prin res veterinarian, 61-66, LEADER DIAG INVESTS, PLUM ISLAND ANIMAL DIS LAB, VET RES SCI DIV, AGR RES SERV, USDA, 66- *Concurrent Pos:* Consult, Am Tech Aid to Egypt, Cairo, 51-55; adj prof animal path, Univ RI, 68- *Mem:* Am Vet Med Asn; Am Soc Microbiol; Conf Res Workers Animal Dis; NY Acad Sci; Am Asn Avian Path. *Res:* Microbiology; genetics; veterinary science; poultry pathology and health; foreign diseases of animals. *Mailing Add:* Plum Island Animal Dis Lab PO Box 848 USDA Greenport NY 11944

DARDIS, JOHN G, b Kilkenney, Ireland, May 21, 28; US citizen. ATOMIC PHYSICS, NUCLEAR PHYSICS. *Educ:* Univ Dublin, MA & PhD(physics), 55. *Prof Exp:* Res physicist, Radio Res Sta, Slough, Eng, 55-57; asst prof nuclear physics, Univ Ky, 57-62; res physicist, US Naval Radiol Defense Lab, 62-64, phys sci adminr, Calif, 64-67; physicist, Physics Br, Off Naval Res, 67-76, int rels officer, Off Advan Technol, State Dept, 76-80, PHYSICAL SCI OFFICER, OFF NUCLEAR EXPORT CONTROL, 80- *Mem:* Am Phys Soc; Am Asn Physics Teachers; Brit Inst Physics & Phys Soc; Am Nuclear Soc; Am Geophys Union. *Res:* Radio, cosmic ray, radiation transport, plasma, atomic and molecular physics. *Mailing Add:* 1332 Pinetree Rd McLean VA 22101

DARDOUFAS, KIMON C, b Athens, Greece, Apr 25, 16; US citizen; m 59; c 4. ORGANIC CHEMISTRY, CHEMICAL ENGINEERING. *Educ:* Nat Univ Athens, BA, 35; Darmstadt Tech Univ, BSChE, 37; Dresden Tech Univ, MA, 39. *Prof Exp:* Prod supt, Tannerie-Ganferie Dardoufa SA, 42-47, dir & mem, Bd Dirs, 47-50, proj dir new expansion, 50-54; mgr indust exports, Athens Off, Am Merchandising Corp, 54-56; process engr, Gen Aniline & Film Corp, 56-60, proj leader polymer develop, 60-63; MGR RES PILOT PLANT, TECH CTR, ALLIED FIBERS & PLASTICS CO, 63- *Mem:* Am Inst Chem Eng; Am Chem Soc; fel Am Inst Chemists. *Res:* Process development and economic evaluation in chemical industry; development of synthetic fibers; fiber lubrication; fiber technology. *Mailing Add:* Allied Fibers & Plastics Co Tech Ctr PO Box 31 Petersburg VA 23804

DARE, CHARLES ERNEST, industrial & civil engineering, see previous edition

DARENSBOURG, DONALD JUDE, b Baton Rouge, La, July 5, 41; m 67. INORGANIC CHEMISTRY, ORGANOMETALLIC CHEMISTRY. *Educ:* Calif State Univ, Los Angeles, BS, 64; Univ Ill, PhD(chem), 68. *Prof Exp:* Res chemist, Texaco Res Ctr, Beacon, NY, 68-69; asst prof chem, State Univ NY Buffalo, 69-73; asst prof chem, Tulane Univ, 73-75, assoc prof, 75-78, prof, 78-82; PROF CHEM, TEX A&M UNIV, 82- *Mem:* Am Chem Soc; AAAS. *Res:* Applications of infrared spectroscopy to inorganic and organometallic systems; mechanisms of photochemical and thermal reactions of organometallic compounds, in particular substituted metal carbonyl derivatives. *Mailing Add:* Dept Chem Tex A&M Univ College Station TX 77843

DARENSBOURG, MARCETTA YORK, b Artemus, Ky, May 4, 42; m 67. INORGANIC CHEMISTRY, ORGANOMETALLIC CHEMISTRY. *Educ:* Union Col, Ky, BA, 63; Univ Ill, Urbana, PhD(inorg chem), 67. *Prof Exp:* Asst prof inorg chem, Vassar Col, 67-69; asst prof, State Univ NY Buffalo, 69-71; asst prof, 71-76, assoc prof, 76-79, PROF INORG CHEM, TULANE UNIV LA, 79- *Honors & Awards:* Agnes Faye Morgan Res Award, 81. *Mem:* Am Chem Soc; Sigma Xi. *Res:* Ionpairing effects in transition metal-organic chemistry; metal-bound carbon monoxide reduction. *Mailing Add:* Dept of Chem Tulane Univ New Orleans LA 70118

DAREWYCH, JURIJ WASYL', theoretical physics, atomic physics, see previous edition

DARITY, WILLIAM ALEXANDER, b Flat Rock, NC, Jan 15, 24; m 50; c 2. PUBLIC HEALTH. *Educ:* Shaw Univ, BS, 48; NC Cent Univ, MSPH, 49; Univ NC, PhD(educ & pub health), 64. *Prof Exp:* Community health educator, City Dept Pub Health, Charlotte, NC, 49-50, Dept Pub Health, Danville, Va, 50-52 & AntiTuberculosis League, Norfolk, 52-53; consult, WHO, 53-56, prof health educ, 56-58, regional adv, 58-64; dir prog develop,

NC Fund, 64-65; assoc prof, 65-68, head dept, 69-76, PROF PUB HEALTH, UNIV MASS, AMHERST, 68-, DIR, DIV PUB HEALTH, 76- *Concurrent Pos:* Fac res grant, 66; biomed sci grant, 67; Franklin County biomed sci grant, 69; NIMH grant, 69-70; Nat Inst Child Health & Human Develop grant, 70-72; mem bd dirs, Planned Parenthood Fedn Am, Inc, 67-; mem pub health grant rev comt, NIH, 69-73; mem bd dirs, Drug Abuse Coun, Inc, 72-; assoc, Danforth Found. *Mem:* Am Pub Health Asn; Am Sch Health Asn; Am Nat Coun Health Educ Pub; Int Union Health Educ. *Res:* Barriers to utilization of family planning and other health service. *Mailing Add:* Dept of Pub Health Univ of Mass Amherst MA 01003

DARKAZALLI, GHAZI, b Damascus, Syria, May 20, 45. MECHANICAL ENGINEERING, SOLAR ENERGY. *Educ:* NY Inst Technol, BS, 71; Univ Mass, MS, 72, PhD(mech eng), 77. *Prof Exp:* Mfg engr, Gen Impact Extrusion Mfg, 72-73; res assoc, Energy Alternatives, Univ Mass, 73-76; DIR, SOLAR ENERGY RES FACIL & ASST PROF, DEPT MECH ENG, UNIV TEX, 77- *Concurrent Pos:* Grants, PPG Industs, 76-77 & Lincoln Lab, Mass Inst Technol, 77-; lectr & consult, Energy in Dallas-Ft Worth area, 77- *Mem:* Am Soc Mech Engrs; Int Solar Energy Soc; Am Soc Heating & Air Conditioning Engrs. *Res:* Solar energy related to heating and cooling; wind power for electric generation; thermol properties of materials; energy saving passive solar systems. *Mailing Add:* Dept of Mech Eng Univ of Tex Arlington TX 76019

DARKOW, GRANT LYLE, b Milwaukee, Wis, Jan 7, 28; m 54; c 4. METEOROLOGY. *Educ:* Univ Wis, BSc, 49, MSc, 58, PhD(meteorol), 64. *Prof Exp:* From asst prof to assoc prof, 61-69, PROF ATMOSPHERIC SCI, UNIV MO-COLUMBIA, 69- *Concurrent Pos:* Trustee, Univ Corp Atmospheric Res, 72-74. *Mem:* Am Meteorol Soc; Sigma Xi. *Res:* Dynamics of severe local local storms. *Mailing Add:* Dept of Atmos Sci Univ of Mo Columbia MO 65211

DARLAK, ROBERT, b North Tonawanda, NY, Sept 10, 37; m 66; c 3. ORGANIC CHEMISTRY. *Educ:* Univ Miss, BS, 60; WVa Univ, PhD(phys org chem), 64. *Prof Exp:* Res fel org chem under Dr Mel Newman, Ohio State Univ, 64-66; SR RES CHEMIST, EASTMAN KODAK CO, 66- *Mem:* Am Chem Soc. *Res:* Kinetics and synthesis in heterocyclic chemistry; synthesis in polycyclic aromatic compounds; polymer chemistry. *Mailing Add:* Eastman Kodak Co Res Labs 343 State St Rochester NY 14650

DARLAND, RAYMOND WINSTON, b Codell, Kans, Mar 22, 11; m 33; c 2. ECOLOGY. *Educ:* Ft Hays Kans State Col, BSc, 33, MS, 36; Univ Nebr, PhD(ecol), 47. *Prof Exp:* Instr high sch, Kans, 33-35, prin, 35-41; instr plant ecol, Univ Nebr, 41-44, asst prof biol, 46-48; assoc prof bot, 48-49, prof biol & head dept, 49-52, acad dean, 52-53, provost, 53-76, EMER PROVOST, UNIV MINN, DULUTH, 76- *Concurrent Pos:* VPres & exec dir, Marshall H & Nellie Alworth Mem Fund, 53-; bd dirs, Alice Tweed Tuoky Found, Santa Barbara, 56- & Wilderness Res Found, Chicago, 71-; Paul Harris Fel Rotary Found, 79. *Mem:* Ecol Soc Am. *Res:* Degeneration of grassland; effects of grazing native grasslands; root and soil relationships. *Mailing Add:* 2628 Lindahl Rd Duluth MN 55810

DARLEY, ELLIS FLECK, b Monte Vista, Colo, Nov 2, 15; m 39; c 3. AIR POLLUTION, PLANT PATHOLOGY. *Educ:* Colo State Univ, BS, 38; Univ Minn, PhD(plant path), 45. *Prof Exp:* Asst forestry, Univ Minn, 40-41; instr bot & plant path, Colo State Univ, 41-42; res fel & asst plant path, Univ Minn, 42-45; pathologist, Firestone Plantations Co, Liberia, WAfrica, 45-47; pathologist, Off For Agr Rels, Guatemala, 48-49; from asst plant pathologist to assoc plant pathologist, Citrus Exp Sta, 49-61, lectr plant path, 77-80, PLANT PATHOLOGIST, AIR POLLUTION RES CTR, UNIV CALIF, RIVERSIDE, 61-, EMER LECTR PLANT PATH, 80- *Concurrent Pos:* Guggenheim fel, Germany, 63-64. *Mem:* Air Pollution Control Asn; Am Phytopath Soc. *Res:* Diseases of Hevea rubber; diseases of palms, especially date; air pollution injury to plants; pollution from forest and agricultural burning. *Mailing Add:* Dept of Plant Path Univ of Calif Riverside CA 92502

DARLEY, FREDERIC LOUDON, b Caracas, Venezuela, Nov 25, 18; US citizen; m 45; c 3. SPEECH PATHOLOGY. *Educ:* NMex State Teachers Col, AB, 39; Univ Iowa, MA, 40, PhD(speech path), 50. *Prof Exp:* Instr pub speaking & Eng, Univ Ark, 40-41; instr pub speaking, Univ Calif, Berkeley, 45-47; from instr to assoc prof speech path & audiol, Univ Iowa, 47-61; consult speech path, Mayo Clin, 61-69; PROF SPEECH PATH, MAYO MED SCH, UNIV MINN, 69- *Mem:* Fel Am Speech Lang & Hearing Asn; Acad Aphasia. *Res:* Diagnosis and appraisal of communication disorders; aphasia; motor speech disorders. *Mailing Add:* Mayo Med Sch Univ of Minn Rochester MN 55901

DARLING, BYRON THORWELL, b Napoleon, Ohio, Jan 4, 12; m 46. PHYSICS. *Educ:* Univ Ill, BS, 33, MS, 36; Univ Mich, PhD(physics), 39. *Prof Exp:* Instr math, Mich State Col, 39-41; res physicist, US Rubber Co, Detroit, 41-46; res assoc, Univ Wis & Yale Univ, 46-47; from asst prof to assoc prof physics, Ohio State Univ, 47-53; PROF PHYSICS, LAVAL UNIV, 55- *Mem:* AAAS; Am Asn Physics Teachers; Am Phys Soc; NY Acad Sci; Can Asn Physicists. *Res:* Theory of rubber processing; molecular and nuclear theory; elementary particle theory. *Mailing Add:* Dept of Physics Fac of Sci Laval Univ Quebec Can

DARLING, CHARLES MILTON, b Mineral Wells, Miss, Feb 7, 34; m 54; c 3. PHARMACEUTICAL CHEMISTRY, MEDICINAL CHEMISTRY. *Educ:* Univ Miss, BS, 55, PhD(pharmaceut chem), 66. *Prof Exp:* Mgr, Woods' Pharm, 55-62; sr res chemist, A H Robins Co, 66-69; assoc prof, 69-75, alumni assoc prof pharmaceut chem, 69-79, assoc prof pharm, 78-79, PROF PHARM, AUBURN UNIV, 75-, ASST DEAN, 81- *Mem:* NY Acad Sci; Am Asn Cols Pharm; Am Chem Soc; Am Pharmaceut Asn; Acad Pharmaceut Sci. *Res:* Non-classical histamine antagonists; anticonvulsants. *Mailing Add:* Sch of Pharm Auburn Univ Auburn AL 36830

DARLING, DONALD ALLAN, b Los Angeles, Calif, May 4, 15; m 39; c 1. MATHEMATICAL STATISTICS. *Educ:* Univ Calif, Los Angeles, AB, 40; Calif Inst Technol, PhD(math), 47. *Prof Exp:* Res assoc, Cornell Univ, 47-48; asst prof math, Rutgers Univ, 48-49, Univ Mich, 49-52, Columbia Univ, 52-53 & Univ Mich, 53-55; assoc prof, Univ Chicago, 56-57; from assoc prof to prof, Univ Mich, 57-68; vis prof statist, Univ Calif, Berkeley, 68-69; chmn dept, 73-75, PROF MATH, UNIV CALIF, IRVINE, 69- *Concurrent Pos:* Guggenheim Mem Found fel, 58-59. *Mem:* Am Math Soc; fel Inst Math Statist; Math Asn Am. *Res:* Probability and applications; stochastic processes. *Mailing Add:* Dept of Math Univ of Calif Irvine CA 92717

DARLING, EUGENE MERRILL, JR, b Cambridge, Mass, Jan 13, 25. MATHEMATICS, METEOROLOGY. *Educ:* Harvard Univ, AB, 48; Mass Inst Technol, SM, 53. *Prof Exp:* Meteorologist, Pan Am Grace Airways, Inc, 50-51; lectr meteorol, Univ NMex, 52; atmospheric physicist, Air Force Cambridge Res Ctr, 52-62; aerospace technologist, NIMBUS Proj, Goddard Space Flight Ctr, NASA, 62-63, electronics res task group, NASA Hqs, 64 & Electronics Res Ctr, NASA, 64-70; chief data technol br, Dept Transp, 70-76, chief environ technol br, 77-80; RETIRED. *Res:* Lima, Peru terminal weather prediction research; analysis of meteorological support for United States Air Force aircraft and missiles; operational aspects of NIMBUS satellite cloud pictures; pattern recognition; imagery processing; management of programs in transportation systems modeling, simulation, environmental analysis, traffic safety and data systems. *Mailing Add:* PO Box 199 Lincoln MA 01773

DARLING, GEORGE BAPST, b Boston, Mass, Dec 30, 05; m 31. PUBLIC HEALTH. *Educ:* Mass Inst Technol, BS, 27; Univ Mich, DrPH, 31. *Hon Degrees:* MA, Yale Univ, 47; LLD, Univ Mich, 75. *Prof Exp:* Res assoc, Dept Health, Detroit, 27-32; assoc exec dir, assoc secy & treas, W K Kellogg Found, 32-34, exec dir & mem finance comt, 34-37, mem corp & bd trustees, assoc dir & comptroller, 37, mem admin comt, 38, pres, 40-43; exec secy comts on mil med, Nat Res Coun, 43-44, vchmn div med sci, 44-45; exec secy, Nat Acad Sci & Nat Res Coun, 46; vchmn div med sci, Nat Res Coun, 47-48; dir med affairs, 46-52, prof human ecol, 52-74, EMER PROF HUMAN ECOL, SCH MED, YALE UNIV, 74- *Concurrent Pos:* Trustee, Grace-New Haven Community Hosp, Conn, 46-59; on leave from Yale Univ as dir, Nat Res Coun Atomic Bomb Casualty Comn, Hiroshima, Japan, 57-72; vis prof, Hiroshima Schs Med & Nursing, Japan; resident scholar, NIH Fogarty Int Ctr Advan Studies, 73-74. *Mem:* AAAS; fel Am Pub Health Asn; Int Acad Polit Sci; NY Acad Sci; Radiation Res Soc Japan. *Res:* Public health administration; epidemiology; statistics; medical administration; professional education. *Mailing Add:* 1171 Whitney Ave Hamden CT 06517

DARLING, MARILYN STAGNER, b Boulder, Colo, Apr 20, 35; m 63; c 2. PLANT ECOLOGY. *Educ:* George Washington Univ, BS, 56; Duke Univ, MA, 59, PhD(zool), 66. *Prof Exp:* Instr biol, Hollins Col, Roanoke, 63-64; RES ASSOC PLANT ECOL, DUKE UNIV, 73- *Concurrent Pos:* Instr plant ecol, Duke Univ, 78. *Mem:* Ecol Soc Am; Brit Ecol Soc; Sigma Xi; Bot Soc Am; Am Soc Plant Physiologists. *Mailing Add:* Dept Bot Duke Univ Durham NC 27706

DARLING, SAMUEL MILLS, b Bradenton, Fla, Jan 13, 17; m 40; c 4. CHEMISTRY. *Educ:* Carleton Col, AB, 39; Western Reserve Univ, MS, 43, PhD(chem), 47. *Prof Exp:* Res supvr, 39-67, fuels res supvr, 67-70, supvr lubricant res, 70-75, supvr fuels & lubricant res & develop, 76-77, CORP PROD SAFETY COORDR, STANDARD OIL CO, OHIO, 77- *Mem:* AAAS; Am Soc Lubrication Eng; Am Chem Soc; Soc Automotive Eng; fel Am Inst Chem. *Res:* Halide catalysis; catalytic cracking and reforming; performance of fuels and lubricants; nitrile chemicals and polymers. *Mailing Add:* Standard Oil Co Ohio Midland Bldg Cleveland OH 44115

DARLING, STEPHEN DEZIEL, b Appleton, Wis, May 7, 31; m 60; c 2. ORGANIC CHEMISTRY. *Educ:* Univ Wis, BS, 54; Columbia Univ, MA, 57, PhD(org synthesis), 59. *Prof Exp:* Res fel org chem, Columbia Univ, 59-62; asst prof, Univ Southern Calif, 62-68 & Southern Ill Univ, 68-70; assoc prof, 70-80, PROF ORG CHEM, UNIV AKRON, 80- *Mem:* Am Chem Soc; The Chem Soc. *Res:* New synthetic methods; synthesis of terpenes; stereoselective metal reductions; marine natural products; x-ray crystallographic structure determination. *Mailing Add:* Dept of Chem Univ of Akron Akron OH 44325

DARLINGTON, GRETCHEN ANN JOLLY, b Dayton, Ohio, Jan 24, 42. GENETICS. *Educ:* Univ Colo, BA, 64; Univ Mich, PhD(human genetics), 70. *Prof Exp:* Fel biol, Yale Univ, 70-72, res assoc, 72-74; ASST PROF HUMAN GENETICS, CORNELL UNIV MED COL, 74- *Mem:* Am Soc Human Genetics; AAAS; Tissue Cult Asn; Soc Cell Biol. *Res:* Study of the expression of differentiated functions in somatic cell hybrids between cultured mouse hepatoma and a variety of non-hepatic cells. *Mailing Add:* Cornell Univ Med Col Rm F-209 1300 York Ave New York NY 10021

DARLINGTON, PHILIP JACKSON, JR, b Philadelphia, Pa, Nov 14, 04; m 42; c 1. ENTOMOLOGY. *Educ:* Harvard Univ, AB, 26, MS, 27, PhD(entom), 31. *Prof Exp:* Entomologist, Colombia Div, United Fruit Co, 28-29; asst cur insects, Mus Comp Zool, 32-40, FALI CUR COLEOPTERA, MUS COMP ZOOL, HARVARD UNIV, 40-, ALEXANDER AGASSIZ PROF ZOOL, UNIV, 62- *Concurrent Pos:* Cur insects, Mus Comp Zool, Harvard Univ, 52-64. *Mem:* Nat Acad Sci; assoc Am Ornith Union. *Res:* Taxonomy and distribution of Coleoptera; zoogeography of the world; evolution. *Mailing Add:* Mus of Comp Zool Harvard Univ Cambridge MA 02138

DARLINGTON, SIDNEY, b Pittsburgh, Pa, July 18, 06; m 65; c 2. MATHEMATICS. *Educ:* Harvard Univ, BS, 28; Mass Inst Technol, BS, 29; Columbia Univ, PhD(physics), 40. *Prof Exp:* Mem tech staff, Bell Tel Labs, Inc, 29-71; CONSULT, 71- *Concurrent Pos:* Expert consult off field serv, Off Sci Res & Develop & tech observer, US Army, 44-45; adj prof dept elec eng, Univ NH, 71- *Honors & Awards:* Edison Medal & Medal of Honor, Inst Elec & Electronics Engrs. *Mem:* Nat Acad Sci; Nat Acad Eng; fel Inst Elec &

Electronics Engrs; assoc fel Am Inst Aeronaut & Astronaut. *Res:* Communication network theory; synthesis of networks which produce prescribed characteristics; smoothing and prediction of stochastic processes; guidance and control of missiles and space vehicles. *Mailing Add:* Dept of Elec Eng Univ of NH Durham NH 03824

DARLINGTON, WILLIAM BRUCE, b Wichita, Kans, July 21, 33; m 57; c 4. INORGANIC CHEMISTRY. *Educ:* Baker Univ, AB, 55; Univ Kans, PhD(chem), 61. *Prof Exp:* Chemist, Phillips Petrol Co, 56-57; sr res chemist, Pittsburgh Plate Glass Co, 61-65, res supvr chem div, 65-68, sr supvr, 68-70, HEAD, ELECTROCHEM DEPT, PPG INDUSTS, 70- *Mem:* Am Chem Soc; Electrochem Soc. *Res:* Nonaqueous solution and industrial electrochemistry; fused-salt chemistry; electrometallurgy; alkali metals; halogens. *Mailing Add:* PPG Industs Box 4026 Corpus Christi TX 78408

DARMARA, FALIH NAZMI, b Izmir, Turkey, Feb 4, 11; nat US; m 39, 71; c 3. METALLURGY. *Educ:* Izmir Col, BA, 32; Harvard Univ, MA, 36, PhD(phys chem), 38. *Prof Exp:* Chief metallurgist, Utica Drop Forge & Tool Corp, 41-45; res metallurgist, Nat Adv Comt Aeronaut, 45-47 & Res Lab, US Steel Corp, Del, 47-49; dir res, Utica Drop Forge & Tool Corp, 49-50, asst to pres, 50-52, vpres, 52-58; pres, Metals Div, Kelsey-Hayes Co, 58-61; pres, Spec Metals Corp, 61-76; RETIRED. *Mem:* Fel Am Soc Metals; Metall Soc; Am Inst Mining, Metall & Petrol Engrs. *Res:* Properties of heat resisting alloys; recrystallization behavior of steels; high temperature alloys for gas turbine components and their fabrication; specific heats of gases at low temperatures; vacuum metallurgy. *Mailing Add:* 77 Old Poverty Rd Southbury CT 06488

DARNALL, DENNIS W, b Glenwood Springs, Colo, Dec 14, 41; m 63. BIOCHEMISTRY, BIOINORGANIC CHEMISTRY. *Educ:* NMex Inst Mining & Technol, BS, 63; Tex Tech Col, PhD(chem), 66. *Prof Exp:* NIH fel, Northwestern Univ, 66-68; from asst prof to assoc prof, 68-74, PROF CHEM, N MEX STATE UNIV, 74- *Concurrent Pos:* NIH career develop award, 71-76. *Mem:* AAAS; NY Acad Sci; Am Chem Soc; Am Soc Biol Chemists. *Res:* Physical chemistry and chemical modification of proteins; metalloproteins and enzymes; protein subunit interactions; lanthanide ions as probes of protein structure. *Mailing Add:* Dept Chem NMex State Univ Las Cruces NM 88003

DARNEAL, ROBERT LEE, b Los Gatos, Calif; m. EARTH SCIENCES, CHEMICAL MICROSCOPY. *Educ:* San Jose State Col, AB, 39; Stanford Univ, MS, 55; Calgary Col Technol, PhD(mineral & geochem), 74. *Prof Exp:* Chemist food chem, Calif Prune & Apricot Growers Asn, 39-40; chemist gas anal, Permanente Metals Corp, 41-42; head dept sci & math, Cloverdale Union High Sch, Calif, 42-43; teaching fel mineral, Stanford Univ, 43-44; instr physics & chem, Western Wash Col, 44-46; Royal Victor fel geol, mineral & petrog, Stanford Univ, 46-49; instr chem & earth sci, San Francisco State Col, 49-51; instr geol, Menlo Jr Col, Calif, 52-54; geophysicist, Div Raw Mat, US AEC, 55-57, physicist, Radiol Physics & Instrumentation Br, Div Biol & Med, 57-73; earth scientist environ progs, Div Biomed & Environ Res, US Energy Res & Develop Admin, 73-79; MGR & PROPRIETOR, ANATECH LABS, 79- *Concurrent Pos:* Lectr earth sci, Frederick Community Col, Md, 72- *Mem:* Am Chem Soc; Mineral Soc Am; Meteoritical Soc; Sigma Xi; Geol Soc Am. *Res:* Determinative mineralogy; forensic chemistry and related forensic sciences. *Mailing Add:* Anatech Labs PO Box 444 Mt Airy MD 21771

DARNELL, ALFRED JEROME, b Denton, Tex, Aug 20, 24; m 47; c 1. PHYSICAL INORGANIC CHEMISTRY. *Educ:* San Diego State Col, BA, 50; Univ Calif, Los Angeles, PhD(chem), 64. *Prof Exp:* mem tech staff, 55-57, proj eng, 57-81, PROJ SCIENTIST, ENERGY TECHNOL ENG LAB, ROCKWELL INT, 81- *Concurrent Pos:* Consult physics group, Hughes Res Ctr. *Honors & Awards:* Cattrell res award, 49. *Mem:* AAAS; fel Am Inst Chemists; Am Chem Soc; Am Phys Soc; Int Solar Energy Soc. *Res:* High temperature physical and inorganic chemistry; ultra high pressure physics and chemistry; low temperature physics; super conductivity; solid state physics and chemistry; electrochemistry; metallurgy; air pollution control; biomass conversion; solar conversion; geothermal. *Mailing Add:* Energy Systs Group 8900 Desoto Ave Canoga Park CA 91304

DARNELL, FREDERICK JEROME, b Washington, DC, May 24, 28; m 52; c 3. SOLID STATE PHYSICS. *Educ:* Yale Univ, BS, 50; Carnegie Inst Technol, MS, 51, PhD(physics), 55. *Prof Exp:* Res physicist, 55-62, res supvr, 62-70, assoc dir res, Cent Res & Develop Dept, 70-79, ASSOC DIR ADMIN, E I DU PONT DE NEMOURS & CO, 79- *Concurrent Pos:* Mem comt on educ, Am Phys Soc & corp asn adv comn, Am Inst Physics. *Mem:* Am Phys Soc; Sigma Xi. *Res:* Semiconductors; magnetism. *Mailing Add:* Exp Sta E I du Pont de Nemours & Co Wilmington DE 19898

DARNELL, JAMES EDWIN, JR, b Columbus, Miss, Sept 9, 30. CELL BIOLOGY. *Educ:* Univ Miss, BA, 51; Washington Univ, MD, 55. *Prof Exp:* Sr asst surgeon & virologist, Nat Inst Allergy & Infectious Dis, 56-60; spec fel, Pasteur Inst, Paris, 60-61; from asst prof to assoc prof biol, Mass Inst Technol, 61-64; prof cell biol & biochem, Albert Einstein Col Med, 64-68; prof biol sci, Columbia Univ, 68-74; PROF MOLECULAR CELL BIOL, ROCKEFELLER UNIV, 74- *Mem:* Nat Acad Sci; Am Soc Biol Chem. *Res:* Virology; cellular biology. *Mailing Add:* Rockefeller Univ York Ave & 66th Sts New York NY 10021

DARNELL, REZNEAT MILTON, b Memphis, Tenn, Oct 14, 24; m 51; c 1. ECOLOGY. *Educ:* Southwestern at Memphis, BS, 46; Rice Univ, MA, 48; Univ Minn, PhD(zool), 53. *Prof Exp:* Asst zool, Univ Minn, 48-52; instr, Tulane Univ, 52-55; from asst prof to prof biol, Marquette Univ, 55-69; PROF OCEANOG & BIOL, TEX A&M UNIV, 69- *Concurrent Pos:* Res assoc, Milwaukee Pub Mus, 60-; chmn, Wis State Bd Preserv Sci Areas, 64-68; chmn, Wis Sci Areas Preserv Coun, 68-69; vis prof oceanog, Tex A&M Univ, 68-69. *Mem:* Fel AAAS; Am Soc Ichthyologists & Herpetologists; Am Soc Limnol & Oceanog; Ecol Soc Am; Soc Study Evolution. *Res:* Ecology of streams, estuaries and oceans; subtropical aquatic ecology; community analysis; organic detritus; nitrogen and energy budgets; ecology and systematics of fishes. *Mailing Add:* Dept of Oceanog Tex A&M Univ College Station TX 77843

DARNELL, W(ILLIAM) H(EADEN), b Roanoke, Va, May 14, 25; m 50; c 1. CHEMICAL ENGINEERING. *Educ:* Va Polytech Inst & State Univ, BS, 50; Univ Wis, MS, 51, PhD(chem eng), 53. *Prof Exp:* Asst, Univ Wis, 51-52; res engr process develop, 53-59, tech supt nylon intermediates, 60-63, prod develop mgr, 63-64, prod mgr, 64-69, res mgr, 69-73, lab adminr, 73-76, ENVIRON MGR PROD DIV, CHEM & PIGMENTS DEPT, E I DU PONT DE NEMOURS & CO, 76- *Res:* Atomization; process development; plastics manufacture; safety, health and environmental affairs. *Mailing Add:* 5 Woodchuck Way Kennett Square PA 19348

DARNELL, W(ALTER) THOMAS, b Harrisonburg, Va, Aug 29, 31; m 56; c 3. CHEMICAL ENGINEERING, PHYSICAL CHEMISTRY. *Educ:* Va Polytech Inst, BS, 53; Univ Wis, MS, 54, PhD(chem eng), 57. *Prof Exp:* Engr orlon res, Textile Fibers Dept, Benger Lab, 53, res engr, Polychem Dept, Exp Sta, 57-62, res engr, Plastics Dept, Washington Lab, 62-65, sr res engr, 65-66, res supvr, Com Resins Div, 66-68, asst div supt, 68-69, chief chemist-color, 69, tech div supt, Plastics Dept, Washington Lab, 69-72, chief chemist, 72-75, mfg supt, 75-78, TECH DEPT SUPT, PLASTICS PROD & RESINS DEPT, E I DU PONT DE NEMOURS & CO, INC, 78- *Mem:* Soc Plastics Engrs; Am Inst Chem Engrs. *Res:* Gas flow in spray drying; integrated process development for polymeric materials; drying processes; distillation processes; reactor design; fluid-solid systems; polymer compounding and finishing systems. *Mailing Add:* 18 Ashwood Dr Vienna WV 26105

DAROCA, PHILIP JOSEPH, JR, b New Orleans, La, Nov 14, 42; m 66; c 2. PATHOLOGY. *Educ:* Tulane Univ, BS, 64, MD, 68; Am Bd Path, dipl, 73. *Prof Exp:* Internship, Parkland Mem Hosp, Dallas, Tex, 68-69; residency, Tulane Div, Charity Hosp, 69-73; staff pathologist, Armed Forces Inst Path, 73-75; asst prof, 75-80, ASSOC PROF PATH, TULANE UNIV, 80- *Mem:* Int Acad Pathol. *Mailing Add:* Dept of Path Tulane Med Sch New Orleans LA 70112

DARON, GARMAN HARLOW, b McPherson, Kans, Jan 29, 04; m 29, 43; c 4. ANATOMY. *Educ:* McPherson Col, BS, 24; Univ Chicago, PhD(anat), 32. *Prof Exp:* Instr zool, Univ Wyo, 25-27, 28-29; asst prof, Nebr Wesleyan Univ, 29-30; instr anat, Col Med, NY Univ, 32-38; from asst prof to assoc prof, Sch Med, Georgetown Univ, 38-47; from assoc prof to prof, 47-70, EMER PROF ANAT, SCH MED, UNIV OKLA, 70- *Mem:* Am Asn Anat. *Res:* Vascularity of the uterus; vascular patterns in the brain; cerebellar nuclei. *Mailing Add:* 2741 Plymouth Lane Oklahoma City OK 73120

DARON, HARLOW HOOVER, b Chicago, Ill, Oct 25, 30; m 58; c 4. BIOCHEMISTRY. *Educ:* Univ Okla, BS, 56; Univ Ill, PhD(biochem), 61. *Prof Exp:* NSF res fel biol, Calif Inst Technol, 61-63; asst prof biochem, Tex A&M Univ, 63-67; asst prof, 67-70, ASSOC PROF BIOCHEM, AUBURN UNIV, 70- *Mem:* AAAS; Am Soc Biol Chemists; Am Soc Microbiol. *Res:* Mechanism of enzyme action. *Mailing Add:* Dept of Animal Sci Auburn Univ Auburn AL 36849

DAROSA, EDMUND A, b Viseu, Portugal, Oct 16, 18; nat US; m 40; c 3. AERONAUTICS. *Educ:* Col Sem Sao Jose, Portugal, BA, 36; Aeronaut Univ, BS, 42. *Prof Exp:* Instr, Latin Am Dept, Spartan Sch Aeronaut, 39-40; instr, Lewis Sch Aeronaut, 40-44, dir aviation, Lewis Col, 48-64, assoc prof, 54-64; assoc prof, 64-77, prof aviation technol, 77-80, EMER PROF, AVIATION TECHNOL, SOUTHERN ILL UNIV, 80-, CHMN DEPT, 64- *Concurrent Pos:* Aviation mech examr, Civil Aeronaut Admin, 53, aircraft inspector, 54. *Mem:* Am Inst Aeronaut & Astronaut. *Res:* Transonic aerodynamics and jet powerplant. *Mailing Add:* Dept of Aviation Technol VTI Southern Ill Univ Carbondale IL 62901

DARR, J(ACK) E(DWIN), b Shaffersville, Pa, Jan 23, 21; m 47; c 8. ELECTRICAL ENGINEERING. *Educ:* Pa State Univ, BS, 42, MS, 48. *Prof Exp:* Trainee, Bethlehem Steel Co, 42-43, asst foreman power stas, 43-44; asst, Eng Exp Sta, Pa State Univ, 46-48; asst engr, 48-50, assoc engr, 50-51, eng group leader, 51, sect mgr interceptor armament control systs, Aerospace Div, 51-59, dir eng electronic warfare proj, 59-60, mgr, Astroelectronics Lab, 60-61, mgr airborne weapons control eng, 61-63, proj serv systs opers, 63-65, dep mgr deep submergence systs, 65-67, mgr planning & control, 67-68, mgr opers serv, Underseas Div, 68-71, mem staff ord systs dept, Aerospace & Electronics Systs Div, 71-74, MGR TECH SERVS, OPERS DIV, WESTINGHOUSE ELEC CORP, 74- *Mem:* Inst Elec & Electronics Engrs. *Res:* Project management; military electronic systems. *Mailing Add:* Westinghouse Elec Corp PO Box 1693 MS1690 Baltimore MD 21203

DARRAGH, KIRK VAIL, inorganic chemistry, deceased

DARRAGH, RICHARD T, b Verdun, Que, Apr 30, 31; m 53; c 5. FOOD SCIENCE, PHARMACEUTICAL RESEARCH & DEVELOPMENT. *Educ:* Univ Montreal, BS, 52; Cornell Univ, MFS, 55, PhD(biochem), 57. *Prof Exp:* Asst qual controller, Birds Eye Co, Can, 52; food technologist, Continental Can Co, Can, 53; biochemist, 57-63, sect head food prod develop, 63-68, assoc dir, 68-71, dir indust food prod develop, 71-77, MGR MFG & PROD DEVELOP, SPEC PROD, PROCTER & GAMBLE CO, 77- *Mem:* AAAS; NY Acad Sci. *Res:* Industrial research and development in pharmaceutical and food products; development and management of organizations and programs aimed at new business areas; consumer and market research. *Mailing Add:* 1355 Hollywood Ave Cincinnati OH 45224

DARRAH, WILLIAM CULP, b Reading, Pa, Jan 12, 09; m 34; c 2. PALEOBOTANY. *Educ:* Univ Pittsburgh, BS, 31. *Prof Exp:* Asst paleobot, Univ Pittsburgh, 31-33; asst bot mus, Harvard Univ, 34-35, instr bot, 35-42, tutor & res cur, 36-42; mat engr, Raytheon Mfg Co, Mass, 42-48, admin asst head magnetron res & develop, 48-51; pvt res, writing & lecturing, 51-57; prof, 57-74, EMER PROF BIOL, GETTYSBURG COL, 74- *Concurrent Pos:* Comn Relief Belg Educ Found grant, 35; Univ Lille grant, 35. *Honors & Awards:* LHD, Gettysburg Col, 77. *Res:* Paleobotany of carbonaceous sediments; upper Pennsylvanian stratigraphy; history of science and technology in America; history of nineteenth century photography. *Mailing Add:* RD 1 Spruce Hill Gettysburg PA 17325

DARRELL, JAMES HARRIS, II, b Riverside, NJ, June 27, 42; m 66; c 2. GEOLOGY, PALYNOLOGY. *Educ:* Ohio Wesleyan Univ, BS, 64; Univ Tenn, Knoxville, MS, 66; La State Univ, Baton Rouge, PhD(geol), 73. *Prof Exp:* Res asst, La Water Resources Res Inst, 67-68; ASST PROF GEOL, GA SOUTHERN COL, 70- *Concurrent Pos:* Consult palynology, SC Geol Surv, 74- & Southeastern Environ Consult Group, 75- *Mem:* Geol Soc Am; Soc Econ Paleontologists & Mineralogists; Am Asn Stratig Palynologists; AAAS; Sigma Xi. *Res:* Palynological biostratigraphy and lithostratigraphy of the coastal plain in Georgia and South Carolina; palynomorph distribution in the Mississippi River Delta; quaternary palynology in Georgia; coastal plain riverswamp sedimentation. *Mailing Add:* Dept of Geol Ga Southern Col Statesboro GA 30458

DARROW, FRANK WILLIAM, b Syracuse, NY, Feb 6, 40; m 61; c 2. PHYSICAL CHEMISTRY. *Educ:* Williams Col, BA, 61; Univ Pa, PhD(chem), 65. *Prof Exp:* Vis asst prof chem & Great Lakes Cols Asn teaching intern, Earlham Col, 65-66; asst prof, 66-71, asst to the Provost, 71-72, actg provost, 72-73, provost, 73-76, ASSOC PROF CHEM, ITHACA COL, 71- *Concurrent Pos:* Vis mem fac, Evergreen State Col, Olympia, Wash, 76-77. *Mem:* AAAS; Am Chem Soc; Nat Sci Teachers Asn. *Res:* Properties of electrolyte solutions and fused salt systems. *Mailing Add:* Dept of Chem Ithaca Col Ithaca NY 14850

DARROW, ROBERT A, b Syracuse, NY, July 12, 31; m 62; c 3. ENZYMOLOGY. *Educ:* Amherst Col, AB, 52; Johns Hopkins Univ, PhD(biol), 57. *Prof Exp:* Biochemist, Chem Pharmacol Lab, Nat Cancer Inst, 57-59; Jane Coffin Childs Mem Fund fel, Nat Inst Med Res, London, 59-61; asst biochemist, Mass Gen Hosp, 61-67; assoc biol chem, Harvard Med Sch, 64-67; investr, 67-71, sect head, 71-73, ASST MISSION MGR, CHARLES F KETTERING RES LAB, 73- *Concurrent Pos:* USPHS grant. *Mem:* AAAS; Am Chem Soc; Am Soc Biol Chemists; Am Soc Plant Physiologists. *Res:* Mechanism of enzyme action; control mechanisms and enzyme induction; biological nitrogen metabolism; plant growth regulation. *Mailing Add:* Charles F Kettering Lab Yellow Springs OH 45387

DARROW, THOMAS D, herpetology, see previous edition

D'ARRUDA, JOSE JOAQUIM, b Fall River, Mass, Aug 4, 42; m 65; c 3. THEORETICAL PHYSICS, STATISTICAL MECHANICS. *Educ:* Lowell Technol Inst, BS, 65; Univ Del, MS, 68, PhD(physics), 71. *Prof Exp:* Asst prof physics, Univ Wis Ctr-Richland, 71-74; assoc prof, 74-81, PROF PHYSICS, PEMBROKE STATE UNIV, 81- *Concurrent Pos:* Res assoc, Argonne Nat Lab, 73; vis scientist, Battelle Northwest Lab, 74 & Oak Ridge Nat Lab, 75-81; Energy Workshop Educ leader, US Dept Energy, 76-79; vis assoc prof, Univ Del, 79-80. *Mem:* Am Phys Soc; Am Asn Physics Teachers; Sigma Xi; Arab Phys Soc. *Res:* Quantum statistical mechanics; computer solutions to complex molecular problems. *Mailing Add:* Dept Physics Pembroke State Univ Pembroke NC 28372

DARSOW, WILLIAM FRANK, b Mankato, Minn, May 16, 20; m 62; c 2. MATHEMATICS. *Educ:* Univ Minn, BA, 42; Univ Chicago, PhD, 53. *Prof Exp:* Instr math, Ill Inst Technol, 50-51; from instr to asst prof, De Paul Univ, 52-60; ASSOC PROF MATH, ILL INST TECHNOL, 61- *Mem:* Am Math Soc; Math Asn Am. *Res:* Abstract harmonic analysis; topological algebra. *Mailing Add:* Dept of Math Ill Inst of Technol Chicago IL 60616

DARST, PHILIP HIGH, b Greensboro, NC, June 8, 43; m 68. ECONOMIC ENTOMOLOGY. *Educ:* Wake Forest Univ, BS, 66; Clemson Univ, MS, 68; Purdue Univ, PhD(entom), 71. *Prof Exp:* Asst prof biol, Univ Miss, 71-75; field develop rep, Union Carbide Corp, 75-78; res mgr, Cotton Inc, Raleigh, NC, 78-80; pest control adv, Western Farm Serv, Salinas, Calif, 80-82; VINEYARD CONSULT PEST MGT & PLANT NUTRIT, SALINAS, CALIF, 82- *Mem:* AAAS; Entom Soc Am; Am Inst Biol Sci; Am Reg Prof Entomologists; Sigma Xi. *Res:* Insect behavior. *Mailing Add:* 23085 Guidotti Pl Salinas CA 93908

DARST, RICHARD B, b Chicago, Ill, Oct 5, 34; m 58; c 5. MATHEMATICS. *Educ:* Ill Inst Technol, BS, 57, MS, 58; La State Univ, PhD(math), 60. *Prof Exp:* Instr math, Mass Inst Technol, 60-62; from asst prof to prof, Purdue Univ, 62-73; PROF MATH, COLO STATE UNIV, 71- *Concurrent Pos:* Vis scholar, Stanford Univ, 81-82. *Mem:* Math Asn Am; Am Math Soc. *Res:* Measure and integration; functional analysis; probability and statistics, approximation, real analysis, operations research. *Mailing Add:* Dept Math Colo State Univ Ft Collins CO 80523

DART, JACK CALHOON, b Concord, Mich, Aug 14, 12; m 40; c 4. CHEMICAL ENGINEERING. *Educ:* Albion Col, AB, 34; Univ Mich, BSE, 35, MSE, 37. *Prof Exp:* Res assoc fac res, Univ Mich, 36; chem engr, Universal Oil Prod Co, 36-37 & Pan-Am Refining Corp, Tex, 37-43; instr chem eng exten, Agr & Mech Col, Tex, 41-42; supvr pilot plant develop group, Magnolia Petrol Co, 43-44 & La Div, Esso Labs, Standard Oil Co, NJ, 44-47; dir develop, Houdry Process Corp, 47-52, mgr res & develop div, 52-55; dir, vpres & gen mgr, Chem Div, 55-57, vpres & gen mgr, Sales & Serv Div, 57-62; OWNER, J C DART & ASSOCS, 62- *Concurrent Pos:* Adj prof chem eng, Cath Univ, Am, 69- *Honors & Awards:* Founders Award, Am Inst Chem Engrs, 81. *Mem:* Fel Am Inst Chem; fel Am Inst Chem Engrs; Am Chem Soc. *Res:* Alkylation, isomerization and polymerization of light hydrocarbons; catalytic and thermal cracking of hydrocarbons; hydrocarbon synthesis; azeotropic distillation; hydrogenation; thermal and catalytic reforming; heat transfer, fluid flow, absorption and distillation; ammonia and methanol syntheses; phthalic anhydride. *Mailing Add:* PO Box 34405 Bethesda MD 20034

DART, SIDNEY LEONARD, b Cape Town, SAfrica, Aug 24, 18; m 42; c 4. PHYSICS. *Educ:* Oberlin Col, AB, 40; Univ Notre Dame, MS, 43, PhD(physics), 46. *Prof Exp:* Asst, Univ Notre Dame, 40-43, instr physics, 43-44, res assoc, 44-46; sr physicist, Am Viscose Corp, 46-53; physicist, Dow Chem Co, 53-54; PROF PHYSICS, CLAREMONT MEN'S COL, 54- *Concurrent Pos:* Consult, Dow Chem Co, 56-59; vis prof & head, Postgrad Physics Dept, Am Col Madurai, SIndia, 67-68 & 77-78. *Mem:* AAAS; Am Phys Soc; Soc Rheol; Soc Social Responsibility Sci. *Res:* Fundamental physical properties of high polymers including rubber, cork and textile fiber polymers; biophysics of muscle. *Mailing Add:* Dept of Physics Claremont Men's Col Claremont CA 91711

DARWENT, BASIL DE BASKERVILLE, b Trinidad, BWI, May 20, 13; m 38; c 1. PHYSICAL CHEMISTRY. *Educ:* McGill Univ, BSc, 41, PhD(phys chem), 43. *Prof Exp:* Asst res chemist, Trinidad Leaseholds, Ltd, 36-40; res assoc, McGill Univ, 43-44; res chemist, Nat Res Coun Can, 44-52; mgr dept phys chem, Olin Industs, Inc, 52-55; res prof, 55-57, prof, 57-74, EMER PROF CHEM, CATH UNIV AM, 74- *Mem:* Am Chem Soc; The Chem Soc; Royal Soc Can. *Res:* Kinetics of elementary gas-phase reactions; photochemistry oxidation; reactions of excited species. *Mailing Add:* Lamas Farm Kingston MD 21834

DARWIN, DAVID, b New York, NY, Apr 17, 46; m 68; c 2. STRUCTURAL ENGINEERING, MATERIALS SCIENCE. *Educ:* Cornell Univ, BS, 67, MS, 68; Univ Ill, PhD(civil eng), 74. *Prof Exp:* Officer eng, US Army Corps Engrs, 67-72; asst prof, 74-77, ASSOC PROF CIVIL ENG, UNIV KANS, 77- *Concurrent Pos:* Lectr, George Washington Univ, 71-72; NSF grant, Univ Kans Ctr Res Inc, 76-; mem, Finite Elem Anal & Routing & Clipping & Property of Mats, 78- *Mem:* Am Soc Civil Engrs; Am Concrete Inst; Prestressed Concrete Inst; Post Tensioning Inst; Sigma Xi. *Res:* Structural and materials engineering with emphasis on plain, reinforced and prestressed concrete. *Mailing Add:* Dept of Civil Eng Univ of Kans Lawrence KS 66045

DARWIN, JAMES T, JR, b Decatur, Tex, Apr 13, 33. SIMULATION, HARDWARE-SOFTWARE INTERFACING. *Educ:* Univ Tex, BS, 54, MA, 62, PhD(math), 63. *Prof Exp:* Asst math, Univ Tex, 58-63; asst prof, Auburn Univ, 63-69; assoc prof, Memphis State Univ, 69-75; programmer-analyst, Vitro Labs Div, Automation Industs, Inc, 75-78; PROGRAMMER-ANALYST, MCDONNELL-DOUGLAS TECH SERV CO, 78- *Mem:* Math Asn Am. *Res:* Representation of linear operators on linear spaces; kernels for linear transformations. *Mailing Add:* PO Box 58024 Houston TX 77058

DARWIN, STEVEN PETER, b New Bedford, Mass, Aug 20, 49. BOTANY. *Educ:* Drew Univ, BA, 71; Univ Mass, Amherst, MS, 73, PhD(bot), 76. *Prof Exp:* ASST PROF BIOL, TULANE UNIV, 77- *Concurrent Pos:* Fel, Gray Herbarium, Harvard Univ, 76-77. *Mem:* Int Assoc Plant Taxon. *Res:* Taxonomy of flowering plants, especially systematics of Rubiaceae in the Pacific; biogeography; tropical biology; flora of the southeastern United States. *Mailing Add:* Dept of Biol Tulane Univ New Orleans LA 70118

DARZYNKIEWICZ, ZBIGNIEW DZIERZYKRAJ, b Dzisna, Poland, May 12, 36; m 66; c 2. CELL BIOLOGY, CYTOCHEMISTRY. *Educ:* Med Acad, Warsaw, MD, 60, PhD(cell biol), 65. *Prof Exp:* Physician, Surg Ward, IVth City Hosp, Warsaw, 60-61; res assoc cytochem, Molecular Enzym Unit, State Univ NY, Buffalo, 65-66; sr res asst histol, Med Acad, Warsaw, 66-68; res assoc cytol, Inst Cell Res, Med Nobel Inst, Stockholm, 68-69; staff scientist, Dept Connective Tissue Res, Boston Biomed Res Inst, 69-74; res assoc cytol, Mem Sloan-Kettering Cancer Ctr, 74-76, assoc, 76-78; asst prof, 76-78, ASSOC PROF, GRAD SCH MED SCI, CORNELL UNIV, 78-; ASSOC MEM, MEM SLOAN-KETTERING CANCER CTR, 78- *Concurrent Pos:* Am Cancer Soc grant, 70-72; grants, Nat Cancer Inst & Dept Health & Human Serv, 78-85. *Mem:* AAAS; NY Acad Sci; Soc Anal Cytol. *Res:* Regulation of genome activity in mammalian cells; cell cycle analysis; cell differentiation; flow cytometry. *Mailing Add:* Sloan-Kettering Inst 410 E 68th St New York NY 10021

DAS, BADRI N(ARAYAN), b Calcutta, India, Oct 19, 27; US citizen; m 64; c 2. PHYSICAL METALLURGY. *Educ:* Univ Calcutta, BE, 52; Univ Ill, MS, 58; Ill Inst Technol, PhD(phys metall), 64. *Prof Exp:* Res asst, Univ Ill, 54-60; staff scientist, Tyco Lab, Inc, Mass, 64-67, sr scientist, 67-70; staff metallurgist, Mat Res Ctr, Allied Chem Corp, NJ, 70; METALLURGIST, US NAVAL RES LAB, 70- *Mem:* Am Crystallog Asn; Am Inst Mining, Metall & Petrol Engrs. *Res:* Metal physics; x-ray diffraction; material synthesis and characterization of semiconductor, ferroelectric, dielectric, electro-optic and magnetic compounds and alloys; solidification and crystal growth of metall compounds and alloys; superconductors. *Mailing Add:* Code 6332 US Naval Res Lab Washington DC 20375

DAS, GOPAL DWARKA, b Shikarpur, India, Feb 11, 33; m 61; c 2. NEUROEMBRYOLOGY, NEUROANATOMY. *Educ:* Univ Mysore, BS, 54; Univ Poona, MA, 57; Boston Univ, PhD(exp psychol), 65. *Prof Exp:* Lectr exp psychol, Gujarat Univ, India, 57-61; res asst neuroanat, Mass Inst Technol, 62-63, res assoc, 63-65, lectr, 67-68; res scientist, Max Planck Inst Psychiat, 66-67; asst prof, 68-71, assoc prof, 71-78, PROF NEUROBIOL, PURDUE UNIV, 78- *Mem:* Am Asn Anatomists. *Res:* Neuroembryology in mammals; transplantation of nervous tissue in mammalian brain. *Mailing Add:* Dept of Biol Sci Purdue Univ West Lafayette IN 47906

DAS, KIRON MOY, b Bengal, India, Dec 31, 41; m; c 2. MEDICINE, IMMUNOLOGY. *Educ:* Calcutta Univ, MB, BS, 65, DrMed(internal med), 69; Edinburgh Univ, PhD(internal med), 74; Am Bd Internal Med & Gastroenterol, dipl, 75. *Prof Exp:* Clin instr, Health Sci Ctr, State Univ NY Stony Brook, 73-74; fel gastroenterol, Nassau County Med Ctr, 73-74; attend physician & asst prof, 74-79, ASSOC PROF MED, INTERNAL MED & GASTROENTEROL, ALBERT EINSTEIN COL MED, 79- *Concurrent Pos:* Clin res fel, Western Gen Hosp, Univ Edinburgh, 70-73; consult, Food & Drug Admin, 75 & Am Hosp Formulary Serv, 76; clin investr award, USPHS, 76-79; prin investr, Nat Inst Arthritis, Metab & Diag Dis, 78-81 & Irma T Hirschl career scientist award, 80-85. *Mem:* Royal Col Physicians London; Royal Col Physician Edinburgh; Am Gasteroenterol Asn; Am Fed Clin Res; Am Soc Gastrointestinal Endoscopy. *Res:* Inflammatory bowel diseases; immunological disturbances; etiologic agents; pathogenesis of colonic mucosal injury. *Mailing Add:* Albert Einstein Col of Med 1300 Morris Park Ave Bronx NY 10461

DAS, MIHIR KUMAR, b Purulia, India, Nov 2, 39; m 68; c 1. MACHINE TOOL TECHNOLOGY. *Educ:* Bihar Inst Technol, Ranchi Univ, BS, 61; Birmingham Univ, PhD(mech eng), 65. *Prof Exp:* Gov India res scholar mach tool, Birmingham Univ, 62-66; sr sci officer design & develop, Cent Mech Eng Res Inst, 66-68; chief design engr design & develop, Tech Develop, India, 68-69; Imp Chem Indust res fel mfg, Birmingham Univ, 69-71, sr res fel, 71-81; ASSOC PROF MECH ENG, CALIF STATE UNIV, LONG BEACH, 81- *Concurrent Pos:* Consult, Eng DRD Ltd, 71-81; vis prof, Univ Zulia, Venezuela, 74- & Korea Advan Inst Sci, Seoul, 78- ; exchange vis prof, Warsaw Tech Univ, 80- *Mem:* Am Soc Mech Engrs; Am Soc Eng Educ; Inst Mech Engrs England. *Res:* Dynamic metal cutting; machine tool vibration; bar shearing; metal forming; dynamic impact; high energy rate forming; computer-aided design and manufacture; computer in engineering education. *Mailing Add:* Calif State Univ 1250 Bell Flower Blvd Long Beach CA 90840

DAS, MUKUNDA B, b Khulna, Bangladesh, Sept 1, 31; m 56; c 2. SOLID STATE ELECTRONICS, ELECTRICAL ENGINEERING. *Educ:* Univ Dacca, BSc, 53, MSc, 55; Univ London, PhD(transistor electronics), & Imp Col, dipl, 60. *Prof Exp:* Res asst physics, Univ Dacca, 55-56; lectr elec eng, Imp Col, London, 60-62; sr res officer appl physics, ERegional Lab, Coun Sci & Indust Res, Pakistan, 62-64; from mem sr sci staff to mem prin sci staff semiconductors, Hirst Res Ctr, ASM Ltd, Eng, 64-68; assoc prof, 68-79, PROF ELEC ENG, PA STATE UNIV, 79- *Concurrent Pos:* Specialist lectureship, Chelsea Col Sci & Tech, London, 68; consult, HRB-Singer, Inc, 69 & Device Design, Inst Sci Invest of Venezuela, 76- *Honors & Awards:* Blumlain-Browne-Willan Pemium Award, Inst Elec Engrs, UK, 67. *Mem:* Sr mem Inst Elec & Electronic Engrs; Sigma Xi. *Res:* Design and fabrication of semiconductor devices and integrated circuits; characterization and modeling of metal-oxide-silicon transistors, integrated circuits and GaAs field effect devices; characterization of defects and imperfections in Si and GaAs via electrical measurements on test structures. *Mailing Add:* Dept of Elec Eng Pa State Univ University Park PA 16802

DAS, NABA KISHORE, b Patna, India, Oct 4, 34; m 60; c 1. MICROBIOLOGY, VETERINARY MEDICINE. *Educ:* Bihar Univ, BVS, 59; Univ Mo-Columbia, MS, 63, PhD(microbiol), 67. *Prof Exp:* Vet asst surgeon, Govt Bihar, India, 59-61; asst microbiol, Univ Mo-Columbia, 63-67; sr res microbiologist, Norwich Pharmaceut Co, 67-69; sr res microbiologist, Res Div, W R Grace & Co, 69-79; vet med officer, 79-80, SUPVY RES VET MED OFFICER, DEPT VET MED RES, BUR VET MED, FOOD & DRUG ADMIN, 80- *Mem:* AAAS; NY Acad Sci; Am Soc Microbiol. *Res:* Chemotherapy of bacterial infections in experimental animals for drug evaluation; host-parasite relationship and its pathogenesis in model bacterial infections; anaerobic bacteriology; antibiotic resistance development and transfer by bacteria. *Mailing Add:* 9525 Westwood Dr Ellicott City MD 21043

DAS, NIRMAL KANTI, b Chittagong, EPakistan, Mar 1, 28; US citizen; m 58; c 2. CELL BIOLOGY. *Educ:* Univ Calcutta, BSc, 48, MSc, 50; Univ Wis, PhD(bot), 57. *Prof Exp:* Lectr biol, Midnapore Col, 51-52; res asst cytochem, Carnegie Inst, 52-53; res assoc bot, Univ Wis, 56-58; from asst res zoologist to assoc res zoologist, Univ Calif, Berkeley, 58-73; assoc prof cell biol, Med Col, Univ Ky, 73-78; health scientist adminr, Nat Inst Aging, 78-81, EXEC SECY, ALLERGY, IMMUNOLOGY & TRANSPLANTATION RES COMT, NIH, 81- *Mem:* AAAS; Am Soc Cell Biol. *Res:* Quantitative cytochemistry of nucleic acids and proteins; various aspects of normal and abnormal cell growth, proliferation and development. *Mailing Add:* Nat Inst Allergy & Infectious Dis Rm 706 Westwood Bldg NIH Bethesda MD 20014

DAS, PANKAJ K, b Calcutta, WBengal, India, June 15, 37; US citizen; m 67; c 2. SIGNAL PROCESSING DEVICES, ULTRASOUND. *Educ:* Univ Calcutta, BSc, 57, MSc, 60, PHD(elec eng), 64. *Prof Exp:* Instr, Polytech Inst Brooklyn, 64-65; asst prof, 65-68; assoc prof, Univ Rochester, 68-72; assoc prof, 74-77, PROF, RENSSELAER POLYTECH INST, 77- *Concurrent Pos:* Orgn Am States vis prof, Ctr Invest & Advan Studies, Nat Politech Inst, Mexico City, 72-73; vis prof, Elec Eng Dept, Colo State Univ, 80-81, Dept Appl Physics & Info Sci, Univ Calif, San Diego, 81. *Mem:* Am Phys Soc; Inst Elec & Electronics Engrs; Optical Soc Am; Am Soc Non-destructive Testing; Acoustical Soc Am. *Res:* Electron devices; surface acoustic and charge coupled devices; acousto-optic interaction; hot electron microwave devices; application of ultrasound in bio-engineering and non-destructive testing. *Mailing Add:* Elec Comput & Syst Eng Dept Rensselaer Polytech Inst Troy NY 12181

DAS, PARITOSH KUMAR, b Bangladesh, Dec 10, 42; m 73; c 1. FAST KINETICS, ORGANIC PHOTOCHEMISTRY. *Educ:* Dacca Univ, BSc, 63, MSc, 65; Univ Houston, PhD(chem), 77. *Prof Exp:* Lectr chem, Holy Cross Col, 66-69 & Notre Dame Col, 67-69; prof, Ranaghat Col, 69-73; res fel, Univ Houston, 77-78; res assoc, 78-79, ASST PROF SPECIALIST, UNIV NOTRE DAME, 79- *Mem:* Sigma Xi; Am Chem Soc. *Res:* Molecular spectroscopy, photophysics and photochemistry involving organic systems; mechanistic aspects of electron, proton and hydrogen transfer reactions in condensed systems; laser flash photolysis and pulse radiolysis. *Mailing Add:* Radiation Lab Univ Notre Dame Notre Dame IN 46556

DAS, PHANINDRAMOHAN, b Bholabo, EPakistan, Feb 2, 26; m 55; c 3. ATMOSPHERIC PHYSICS, ATMOSPHERIC DYNAMICS. *Educ:* Univ Dacca, BSc, 47, MSc, 48; Univ Chicago, PhD(meteorol), 63. *Prof Exp:* Res asst physics, Banaras Hindu Univ, 49-51; asst meteorologist, India Meteorol Dept, 51-55; asst prof appl physics, Indian Inst Technol, Kharagpur, 55-59; from asst to res assoc meteorol, Univ Chicago, 59-64; asst prof appl physics, Indian Inst Technol, Kharagpur, 64-67; asst prof meteorol, Tex A&M Univ, 67-68; res physicist, Air Force Cambridge Res Lab, 68-70; assoc prof, 70-81, PROF METEOROL, TEX A&M UNIV, 81- *Concurrent Pos:* Collab res, Univ Hawaii, Hilo, 78, Nat Hurricane Res Lab & Nat Oceanic & Atmospheric Admin, Environ Res Lab, Coral Gables, 80. *Mem:* Am Meteorol Soc; Royal Meteorol Soc. *Res:* Ionospheric physics; radar meteorology; physics and dynamics; mesoscale and tornado dynamics. *Mailing Add:* 1005 Glade St College Station TX 77840

DAS, SALIL KUMAR, b Rangoon, Burma, Dec 21, 40; Indian citizen; m 68; c 1. BIOCHEMISTRY, FOOD SCIENCE. *Educ:* Calcutta Univ, BSc, 58 & 59, MSc, 61, DSc(biochem), 74; Mass Inst Technol, ScD(nutrit biochem), 66. *Prof Exp:* Res asst, Mass Inst Technol, 62-66; res assoc physics, Univ Ariz, 66-67; res assoc chem, Grad Inst Tech, Univ Ark, 67-68 & Duke Univ, 68-69; asst prof, 69-74, assoc prof, 74-81, PROF BIOCHEM, MEHARRY MED COL, 81- *Concurrent Pos:* NIH grant, 72- *Honors & Awards:* Cressy Morrison Award Nat Sci, NY Acad Sci, 67. *Mem:* Fel Am Inst Chemists; Sigma Xi; Am Inst Nutrit; Inst Food Technologists; Int Asn Dent Res. *Res:* Chemistry and metabolism of lipids. *Mailing Add:* Dept of Biochem 1005 18th Ave N Nashville TN 37208

DAS, SUBODH KUMAR, b Bhagalpur, India, June 19, 47; m 70; c 2. METALLURGICAL ENGINEERING. *Educ:* Bihar Inst Technol, India, BSc, 69; Indian Inst Technol, M Tech, 72; Univ Mich, Ann Arbor, PhD(metall eng), 74; Univ Pittsburgh, MBA, 82. *Prof Exp:* Jr res asst metall eng, Indian Inst Technol, Kanpur, 70; res asst, Univ Mich, Ann Arbor, 71-74; engr metall eng, Alcoa Labs, Aluminum Co Am, 74-81; RES CONSULT, ANACONDA ALUMINUM CO, ATLANTIC RICHFIELD CO, 81- *Mem:* Sigma Xi; Am Chem Soc; Metall Soc. *Res:* Extractive metallurgy of metals; process metallurgy of aluminum and aluminum alloys; fused salt electrolysis; coal purification; carbon electrode technology; thermodynamics and structure of ordered and disordered carbons; economic analysis of extractive metallurgical industries technology, forecasting and planning. *Mailing Add:* Anaconda Aluminum Co PO Box 27007 Tuscon AZ 85726

DAS, SURYYA KUMAR, b Calcutta, India; US citizen; m 61; c 2. POLYMER CHEMISTRY, PHYSICAL CHEMISTRY. *Educ:* Calcutta Univ, India, BSc, 48, MSc, 50, PhD(chem), 56. *Prof Exp:* Tech officer chem, Allied Resins & Chem, Calcutta, 60-63; sr res chemist, 63-67, res assoc, 67-73, SR RES ASSOC, PPG INDUSTS, 73- *Concurrent Pos:* Fel, Univ Reading, UK, 56-58 & State Univ NY, Syracuse, 58-60. *Mem:* Am Chem Soc. *Res:* Synthetic polymer chemistry and physical chemistry of polymers. *Mailing Add:* PPG Industs PO Box 9 Allison Park PA 15101

DAS, TARA PRASAD, b India, July 7, 32; US citizen; m 58; c 3. ATOMIC & MOLECULAR PHYSICS. *Educ:* Patna Univ, BS, 49; Univ Calcutta, MS, 51, PhD(physics), 55. *Prof Exp:* Lectr theoret physics, Saha Inst Nuclear Physics, 53-55; res assoc chem, Cornell Univ, 55-56; res assoc physics, Univ Calif, Berkeley, 56-57; reader, Saha Inst Nuclear Physics, 57-58; res asst prof, Univ Ill, 58-59; res assoc chem, Columbia Univ, 59-60; sr res officer, Atomic Energy Estab, Govt India, 60-61; from assoc prof to prof physics, Univ Calif, Riverside, 61-69; prof, Univ Utah, 69-71; PROF PHYSICS, STATE UNIV NY ALBANY, 71- *Concurrent Pos:* NSF grants, 62-; NIH grants, 72- *Mem:* Fel Am Phys Soc; Biophys Soc. *Res:* Electronic structures of atoms, simple molecules, and solid state, including theory of electron-nuclear hyperfine interactions; atomic and molecular scattering theory; electronic structure and properties of biologically important molecules. *Mailing Add:* Dept of Physics State Univ of NY Albany NY 12203

D'ASARO, LUCIAN ARTHUR, physics, see previous edition

DASCH, CLEMENT EUGENE, b Steubenville, Ohio, Nov 28, 25; m 47; c 4. ENTOMOLOGY, TAXONOMY. *Educ:* Cornell Univ, BS, 49, PhD(entom), 53. *Prof Exp:* From asst prof to assoc prof, 53-61, coordr sci div, 66-72 & 76-79, chmn dept, 53-77, PROF BIOL, MUSKINGUM COL, 61- *Concurrent Pos:* NSF res grant, Univ Mich, 63-64; Mack Found & Am Philos Soc res grants, 64, 72, 80 & 81. *Mem:* AAAS; Soc Syst Zool; Am Inst Biol Sci. *Res:* Systematics and ecology of parasitic wasps of the family Ichneumonidae. *Mailing Add:* Dept of Biol Muskingum Col New Concord OH 43762

DASCH, ERNEST JULIUS, b Dallas, Tex, July 9, 32; m 60. GEOCHEMISTRY. *Educ:* Sul Ross State Col, BS, 56; Univ Tex, Austin, MA, 59; Yale Univ, MS, 67, PhD(geochem), 69. *Prof Exp:* Geologist, Magnolia Petrol Co, 56 & W F Guyton & Assoc, Tex, 59-61; res asst geochem, Yale Univ, 63-68; Fulbright vis res fel, Australian Nat Univ, 68-70; asst prof, 70-74, ASSOC PROF GEOL, ORE STATE UNIV, 74- *Mem:* AAAS; Geol Soc Am; Am Geophys Union; Geochem Soc. *Res:* Strontium and lead geochemistry of selected igneous and sedimentary systems; petrology. *Mailing Add:* Dept of Geol Ore State Univ Corvallis OR 97331

DASCH, GREGORY ALAN, b Ithaca, NY, Oct 13, 48; m 76; c 2. RICKETTSIOLOGY, INSECT PHYSIOLOGY. *Educ:* Oberlin Col, AB, 70; Yale Univ, PhD(biol), 75. *Prof Exp:* Res asst insect physiol, Yale Univ, 71-75; microbiologist, Dept Microbiol, 75-77, chemist, 77-79, SUPVR, RICKETTSIAL DIS PROG, NAVAL MED RES INST, 79- *Concurrent Pos:* Nat Res Coun fel, Naval Med Res Inst, 75-76. *Mem:* AAAS; Am Soc Microbiol; NY Acad Sci. *Res:* Intracellular bacteria, particularly rickettsia and the symbiotes of insects: evolution, biochemistry, immunology, and host cell interaction; vaccine development; pathogenic mechanisms. *Mailing Add:* Med Microbiol Br Naval Med Res Inst Bethesda MD 20014

DASCHBACH, JAMES MCCLOSKEY, b Medford, Mass, July 29, 32; m 65; c 8. INDUSTRIAL ENGINEERING. *Educ:* Univ Notre Dame, BS, 54; Southern Methodist Univ, MBA, 61; Okla State Univ, PhD(indust eng), 66. *Prof Exp:* Serv engr, Gen Dynamics, Ft Worth, Tex, 57-60; customer serv engr, Aero Commander Co, 60-64; instr indust eng, Okla State Univ, 64-66; PROF INDUST ENG, COL ENG, NOTRE DAME, 66- *Concurrent Pos:* Vis prof, Nat Defense Univ, Ft McNair, 79-80. *Mem:* Sigma Xi; Am Soc Eng Educ; Am Inst Indust Eng. *Res:* Modelling state court systems; parametric cost estimating models. *Mailing Add:* 53287 N Ironwood Rd South Bend IN 46637

DASCOMB, HARRY EMERSON, b Bath, NY, Aug 12, 16; m 39; c 3. INTERNAL MEDICINE. *Educ:* Colgate Univ, AB, 38; Univ Rochester, MD, 43. *Prof Exp:* Intern med, Univ Rochester, 43; resident physician, Iola Sanatorium, 43-45; intern med, Univ Rochester, 45-46; from instr to assoc prof med & preventive med, Sch Med, La State Univ, New Orleans, 47-59, prof, 59-80, asst dean, 75-78; PROF MED, SCH MED, UNIV NC, CHAPEL HILL, 80- *Concurrent Pos:* Buswell fel, Sch Med & Dent, Univ Rochester, 46-47; dir off hosp infections control, Charity Hosp La, 68-73, med dir, 74-78. *Mem:* AMA; Am Fedn Clin Res; fel Am Col Physicians; Infectious Dis Soc Am. *Res:* Infectious disease. *Mailing Add:* Sch Med Univ NC Chapel Hill NC 27514

DAS GUPTA, AARON, b Nov 20, 43; m 72; c 2. STRUCTURAL MECHANICS, STRESS ANALYSIS. *Educ:* Indian Inst Technol, BTech (Hons), 63; Nova Scotia Tech Col, M Eng, 68; Va Polytech Inst, PhD(mech eng), 75. *Prof Exp:* Asst engr design, Heavy Eng Corp, India, 63-65; electronics engr, electronic prod, Can Marconi, 67-69; prod engr aerospace struct, Whittaker Corp, 69-70; proj engr design develop, Kingsport Press, 73-75; proj engr stress anal, Sundstrand Aviation, 75; SR MECH ENGR BLAST DYNAMICS, BALLISTIC RES LAB, US ARMY, 75- *Concurrent Pos:* Consult, Iron Ore Co, Can, 66; teaching assoc, Va Polytech Inst, 70-74; lectr, NMex State Univ, 71-72; eng consult, Com Fabrication Co, 72; design consult, AAI Corp, 80 & Black & Veatch Corp, 80-81; consult engr, US Army Meradcom, 80- *Mem:* Am Acad Sci; Sigma Xi; NY Acad Sci; Am Soc Mech Engrs. *Res:* Penetration and fracture mechanics; blast dynamics; structural dynamics; finite element and finite difference; analysis containment structures; thermal stress analysis; author and co-author of 50 pubication. *Mailing Add:* 104 John St Perryville Perryville MD 21903

DASGUPTA, ASIM, b Calcutta, India, March 19, 51; m 80. VIROLOGY, MOLECULAR BIOLOGY. *Educ:* Calcutta Univ, India, BS, 70, MS, 72; Univ Nebr-Lincoln, PhD(chem), 78. *Prof Exp:* Grad res asst biochem, Univ Nebr-Lincoln, 74-78; fel assoc virol, Mass Inst Technol, 78-80; ASST PROF MICROBIOL & IMMUNOL, UNIV CALIF, LOS ANGELES, 81- *Concurrent Pos:* Prin investr, NIH grant, 81-84. *Mem:* Am Soc Microbiol; AAAS. *Res:* Mechanism of replication of RNA viruses and the roles of viral and host protein in the process. *Mailing Add:* Dept Microbiol & Immunol Med Sch Univ Calif Los Angeles CA 90024

DASGUPTA, GAUTAM, b Calcutta, WBengal, India, Oct 13, 46; m 70; c 1. COMPUTATIONAL MECHANICS, SINGULAR PHYSICAL PROBLEMS. *Educ:* Bengal Eng Col, India, BEng, 67, MEng, 69; Univ Calif, Berkeley, PhD(civil eng), 74. *Prof Exp:* Teachers trainee appl mech, Bengal Eng Col, India, 67-70; consult math, Berkeley Unified Sch Dist, 71-74; asst res engr civil eng, Univ Calif, Berkeley, 74-77; asst prof, 77-81, ASSOC PROF ENG MECH, COLUMBIA UNIV, 81- *Concurrent Pos:* Lectr appl mech, Govt Polytech, Panaji, Goa, India, 70; consult eng, Bechtel Corp, San Francisco, Calif, 76; prin investr, Grant Columbia Univ, NSF, 77-85. *Mem:* Am Soc Civil Eng; Am Soc Mech Eng; Am Acad Mech. *Res:* Computational mechanics; dynamic analyses of viscoelastic systems; finite element method for unbounded continua; dynamic impacts; kinematics of cranio-facial growth. *Mailing Add:* Dept Civil Eng Columbia Univ 620 SW Mudd New York NY 10027

DAS GUPTA, KAMALAKSHA, b Calcutta, India, Feb 1, 17; m 47; c 1. PHYSICS. *Educ:* Univ Calcutta, MSc, 40; Univ Liverpool, PhD(physics), 52. *Prof Exp:* Lectr physics, Univ Calcutta, 43-47 & 52-56, reader, 59-61; sr res fel physics, Calif Inst Technol, 61-66; consult, Moon Surveyor Proj, Jet Propulsion Lab, 63-80; PROF PHYSICS, TEX TECH UNIV, 66- *Mem:* Am Phys Soc. *Res:* Electro-magnetic interactions in the region of 1 keV to 2 MeV; coherent interaction of electrons and photons in crystals and search for x-ray laser; study of electron states of superconductors, Type II, by the method of soft x-ray emission and absorption spectroscopy; total reflection of x-rays from thin films. *Mailing Add:* Dept of Physics Tex Tech Univ Lubbock TX 79409

DAS GUPTA, SOMESH, b Calcutta, India, Sept 3, 35; m 64; c 1. MATHEMATICAL STATISTICS. *Educ:* Univ Calcutta, BSc, 53, MSc, 56; Univ NC, Chapel Hill, PhD(statist), 62. *Prof Exp:* Res scholar statist, Indian Statist Inst, 57-60; res asst, Univ NC, Chapel Hill, 60-62; from instr to asst prof, Columbia Univ, 62-64; from asst prof to assoc prof, Indian Statist Inst, 64-67; assoc prof, 67-70, chmn statist grad fac, 71-73, PROF STATIST, UNIV MINN, 70- *Concurrent Pos:* Statist consult, Psychomet Unit, Indian Statist Inst, 57-60; dir, Statist Consult Serv, Columbia Univ, 63-64; NSF grant, Univ Minn, 68-70; US Army res grants, 71-73 & 75-79; vis prof, Stanford Univ, 74; vis prof, Indian Statist Inst, 80-81. *Mem:* Fel Inst Math Statist; fel Am Statist Asn; Int Statist Inst. *Res:* Inference in multivariate analysis; classification and discrimination; nonparametric inference; multiple decision theory; probability inequalities; statistical pattern recognition. *Mailing Add:* Theoret Statist Vincent Hall Univ of Minn Minneapolis MN 55455

DASGUPTA, SUNIL PRIYA, b Bangladesh; US citizen. SOLID STATE PHYSICS, CHEMISTRY. *Educ:* Univ Dacca, BSc, 47, MSc, 49; Univ Delhi, PhD(physics), 58. *Prof Exp:* Sr res officer, Nat Phys Lab, New Delhi, India, 56-62; fel solid state physics, Nat Res Coun Can, Ottawa, 62-65; res assoc relaxation mechanism, Princeton Univ, 65-67; res physicist, 67-81, SR RES PHYSICIST, HERCULES INC, 81- *Res:* Dielectric properties; relaxation process and molecular structure; transport properties of semiconducting materials; polymer chemistry and polymer physics; surface chemistry and surface physics. *Mailing Add:* Hercules Res Ctr Hercules Rd Wilmington DE 19899

DASH, HARRIMAN HARVEY, b New York, NY, May 26, 10; m 42; c 1. BIOCHEMISTRY, QUANTUM CHEMISTRY. *Educ:* City Col New York, BS, 33; Univ Chicago, cert, 44; Polytech Inst Brooklyn, MS, 53. *Prof Exp:* Res chemist, Bellevue Hosp, New York, 34-35; proj chemist, Res Labs, Fordham Univ, 35-38; proj chemist, Consumers Labs, 38-42; biochemist med res, Nat Jewish Hosp, Denver, Colo, 46-47; consult chemist high polymers, 47-58; assoc biochemist, Med Lab, North Shore Hosp, Manhasset, NY, 58-62; chief biochemist, Nassau Hosp, Mineola, 62-66 & Variety Children's Hosp, Miami, Fla, 66-68; chief biochemist, Res Div Miami Heart Inst, 68-76. *Concurrent Pos:* Consult, Am Hosp, Miami, 76- *Mem:* AAAS; Am Chem Soc; Am Asn Clin Chemists; Am Inst Physics. *Res:* Clinical biochemistry and application of quantum theory of biochemistry. *Mailing Add:* 5315 SW 111th Ave Miami FL 33165

DASH, JAY GREGORY, b Brooklyn, NY, June 28, 23; m 45; c 3. PHYSICS. *Educ:* City Col New York, BS, 44; Columbia Univ, AM, 49, PhD(physics), 51. *Prof Exp:* Mem staff, Los Alamos Sci Lab, 51-60; actg assoc prof physics, 60-61, assoc prof, 61-63, PROF PHYSICS, UNIV WASH, 63- *Concurrent Pos:* Guggenheim fel, 57-58; consult, Los Alamos Sci Lab, 60- & Boeing Co, 61-64; Louis Susman vis prof, Israel Inst Technol, 74-75; exchange prof, Univ d'Aix-Marseille, 77-78; mem adv comt, Nat Sci Found, 76-80; dir, NATO Advanced Study Inst, 79. *Mem:* Fel Am Phys Soc. *Res:* Low temperature, surface physics; physics of two dimensional matter and the experimental properties of monolayer films adsorbed on solid surfaces; multilayers and the evolution of bulk behavior; applications to sintering and crystal growth. *Mailing Add:* Dept of Physics Univ of Wash Seattle WA 98195

DASH, JOHN, b Hazleton, Pa, June 29, 33; m 68, 79; c 3. PHYSICAL METALLURGY. *Educ:* Pa State Univ, BS, 55, PhD(metall), 66; Northwestern Univ, MS, 60. *Prof Exp:* Res metallurgist, Crucible Steel Co, 55-58; res assoc phase transformations, Res Inst Adv Study, Martin Marietta Corp, Md, 60-63; from asst prof to assoc prof, 66-79, PROF PHYSICS, PORTLAND STATE UNIV, 79- *Mem:* Electron Micros Soc Am; Am Soc Metals; Am Electroplaters Soc. *Res:* Electron microscopy and electron diffraction; electrodeposition of metals. *Mailing Add:* Dept Physics Portland State Univ Box 751 Portland OR 97207

DASHEK, WILLIAM VINCENT, b Milwaukee, Wis, Aug 28, 39; div; c 2. ENVIRONMENTAL HEALTH, GENERAL ENVIRONMENTAL SCIENCES. *Educ:* Marquette Univ, BS, 61, MS, 63, PhD(plant physiol), 66. *Prof Exp:* NIH fel plant physiol & biochem, Mich State Univ, 66-67; asst prof biol, Boston Univ, 67-69; vis asst prof, State Univ NY, Buffalo, 69-70; asst prof, Va Commonwealth Univ, 70-75; vis res biologist, Univ Calif, San Diego, 75-76; sr fel plant biochem, State Univ NY, Syracuse, 76-78; ASST PROF BIOL, DEPT BIOL, WVA UNIV, 78- *Concurrent Pos:* Reviewer, journals & NSF grants, 81- *Mem:* Am Soc Plant Physiol; Soc Plant Physiol Japan; Soc Indust Microbiol; Sigma Xi. *Res:* Cell wall metabolism; pollen physiology and biochemistry; mechanism of action of aflatoxins; quantitation, localization and metabolism of plant hormones; mechanisms of amino acid accumulation in air pollutant-stressed plants. *Mailing Add:* Dept Biol WVa Univ Morgantown WV 26506

DASHEN, ROGER FREDERICK, b Grand Junction, Colo, May 5, 38; m 64; c 2. THEORETICAL PHYSICS. *Educ:* Harvard Univ, AB, 60; Calif Inst Technol, PhD(physics), 64. *Prof Exp:* Res assoc theoret physics, Calif Inst Technol, 64-65; asst prof, 65-66, prof, 66-69; mem staff, 66-69, PROF THEORET PHYSICS, INST ADVAN STUDY, 69- *Concurrent Pos:* Alfred P Sloan Found fel, 66-73; vis prof, Princeton Univ, 66-; mem, Sci Adv Comt, Stanford Linear Accelerator Ctr, 68-72; consult, SRI Int, Jason, 66-, Los Alamos Sci Lab, 74-, Brookhaven Nat Lab, 77-78 & Fermi Nat Accelerator Lab, 72-75. *Res:* Elementary particle theory; quantum field theory; statistical mechanics; waves in random media. *Mailing Add:* Inst for Advan Study Princeton NJ 08540

DASHER, GEORGE FRANKLIN, JR, b Russellville, Ky, Aug 5, 22; m 43; c 4. PHYSICAL CHEMISTRY, SURFACE CHEMISTRY. *Educ:* Kalamazoo Col, BA, 43; Univ Mich, MS, 47, PhD(chem), 49. *Prof Exp:* Chemist, Procter & Gamble Co, 49-61; asst dir res, Clairol Inc, Conn, 61-65, dir prod develop, 65-67, vpres res & develop, 67-73; vpres res & develop, Alberto-Culver Co, 73-77; RETIRED. *Concurrent Pos:* Lectr, Xavier Univ, Ohio, 60-61; trustee, William Rainey Harper Col, 77- *Mem:* AAAS; Am Chem Soc; Rheol Soc. *Res:* Adsorption at phase boundaries; emulsion stability; surface activity in biological systems; mechanical properties of polymers; flow behavior of liquids; viscoelastic behavior of cosmetic materials. *Mailing Add:* 511 Fairway Lane Palatine IL 60067

DASHER, J(OHN) O, b Ky, June 11, 14; m 38; c 3. METALLURGICAL ENGINEERING. *Educ:* Univ Ala, BS, 35. *Prof Exp:* Asst chem engr, Bur Mines, Md & Ala, 37-42; chief res dept, Tin Processing Corp, 42-46; exec officer, Atomic Energy Comn Proj, Mass Inst Technol, 46-51; asst chief metals group, Chem Construct Co, 51-55; res supvr, Crucible Steel Co Am, Pa, 55-63, proj dir procurement, 63-65; PRIN ENGR, BECHTEL GROUP, BECHTEL INVESTMENTS INC, 65- *Concurrent Pos:* Mem adv Bd, Nat Acad Sci, 62. *Mem:* Am Inst Mining, Metall & Petrol Engrs; Asn Iron & Steel Engrs. *Res:* Process metallurgy; mineral dressing; coal; nonmetallics; nonferrous and ferrous metals. *Mailing Add:* Bechtel Investments Inc 50 Beale San Francisco CA 94105

DASHER, PAUL JAMES, b Pleasant Plains, Ill, June 4, 12; m 35; c 2. CHEMISTRY. *Educ:* Univ Ill, BS, 34; Ind Univ, AM, 35, PhD, 37. *Prof Exp:* Res chemist, B F Goodrich Co, 37-39, asst dir rubber res, 39-41, dir develop & eng, Fuel Cell Div, 41-44, tech supt, 44-45, consult, Reclamation Div, 45, dir, New Process Div, 45-46; pres, Merit Chem Co, 46-47 & Summit Indust Prod Co, 46-59; PRES, DASHER RUBBER & CHEM CO, FAIRPORT DEVELOP CO, FAIRPORT TERMINAL CORP, 50-; VPRES, LOWMANS, INC, 50-; CHMN DEPT PHYSICS & PHYS SCI, PALM BEACH JR COL, 69- *Concurrent Pos:* Dir, Lowmans, Inc, 43-50. *Mem:* Am Chem Soc. *Res:* Electrolyte conductance in non-aqueous media; rubber research, emphasizing plant utilization of process; invention of new processes. *Mailing Add:* Dept of Physics & Phys Sci Palm Beach Jr Col Lake Worth FL 33461

DASHMAN, THEODORE, b Brooklyn, NY, Oct 7, 28; m 57; c 3. BIOCHEMISTRY. *Educ:* Brooklyn Col, BS, 50; Fla State Univ, MS, 64; NY Univ, PhD(biol), 77. *Prof Exp:* SR SCIENTIST, HOFFMANN-LA ROCHE INC, 77- *Mem:* AAAS; Am Chem Soc; Am Soc Pharmacol & Exp Therapeut. *Res:* Intermediary metabolism of xenobiotics, inhibition of enzymes by pharmacologically active compounds. *Mailing Add:* Hoffman-La Roche Inc Nutley NJ 07110

DASHNER, PETER ALAN, b Schenectady, NY, April 9, 51. CONSTITUTIVE THEORY, POLYMER RHEOLOGY. *Educ:* Southern Univ NY, Buffalo, BS, 73, MS, 75, PhD(eng sci), 76. *Prof Exp:* Asst prof eng sci & mech, Va Polytech Inst & State Univ, 76-77; asst prof theoret appl mech, Cornell Univ, 88-81; LECTR MECH ENG, CALIF STATE POLYTECH UNIV, 81- *Res:* Theoretical and practical problems relating to the developments of realistic, multiaxial, large deformation constitutive (stress-deformation) models for real materials, both fluid and solid. *Mailing Add:* Dept Mech Eng Calif State Polytech Univ 3801 W Temple Ave Pamona CA 91768

DASKAM, EDWARD, JR, b Detroit, Mich, Mar 1, 20; m 48; c 4. ELECTRICAL ENGINEERING, PHYSICS. *Educ:* Univ Tex, BS, 41; NY Univ, MS, 56. *Prof Exp:* Engr radar, Gen Elec Co, 42-44; engr radio commun, Gen Tel Serv Corp, 46-49, dept head, 49-51; engr, Airborne Instruments Lab, Cutler-Hammer, Inc, 51-52, sect head, 52-58, prog mgr, 58-62, dept head, 68-72, prog mgr, 72-75, dept head, 75-82; CONSULT ENGR, AIL DIV, EATON CORP, DEER PARK, 82- *Mem:* AAAS; sr mem Inst Elec & Electronics Engrs; Am Phys Soc. *Res:* Electronic systems, including antennas, microwaves, solid state circuits and microminiaturization. *Mailing Add:* Eaton Corp Commack Rd/Deer Park Dix Hills NY 11146

DASKIN, W(ALTER), b Passaic, NJ, July 17, 26; m 51; c 2. MECHANICAL ENGINEERING, FLUID MECHANICS. *Educ:* Cooper Union, BME, 45; Univ Mich, MSE, 48. *Prof Exp:* Engr vibration control, Jayburn Eng Co, NY, 46-47; instr mech eng, Johns Hopkins Univ, 49-54; engr fluid mech, Gen Elec Co, Ohio, 54-56, specialist heat transfer, 56; sr scientist reentry physics, Gen Appl Sci Labs, NY, 56-58, proj scientist, 58-60, sci supvr, 60-64, asst dir res, 64-66; consult appl physics, 66-68, mgr, Aeromech & Mat Lab Sect, 68-70, mgr, Technol Eng Sect, Philadelphia, 70-77, mgr cruise missle progs, 78-80, MGR PLANS & ANAL, GEN ELEC CO, LYNN, MASS, 80- *Concurrent Pos:* Res asst, Johns Hopkins Univ, 50-54; consult, Carbide & Carbon Chem Co, Tenn, 52-54 & Gen Elec Co, Ohio, 53-54; adj instr, Polytech Inst Brooklyn, 57. *Mem:* AAAS; Am Soc Mech Engrs; assoc fel Am Inst Aeronaut & Astronaut; Am Phys Soc. *Res:* Heat transfer; fluid mechanics; system optimization techniques; management of research and development. *Mailing Add:* Aircraft Engine Group 1000 Western Ave Lynn MA 01910

DASKIVICH, RICHARD ANTHONY, engineering, see previous edition

DASLER, ADOLPH RICHARD, b Conklin, Mich, Mar 19, 33; m 58; c 3. PHYSIOLOGY. *Educ:* Western Mich Univ, BA & MA, 60; Mich State Univ, PhD(physiol), 66. *Prof Exp:* Instr med technol & physiol, Clin Labs, Hackley Hosp, 55-60; res asst physiol, Mich State Univ, 61; US Navy, 61- res investr, 62-63, proj officer shipboard toxicol opers protectional systs & head thermal stress sect, 63-64, head heat stress facil, 66-73, dep head environ stress div, 70-73, HEAD THERMAL STRESS BR, BUR MED & SURG, NAVAL MED RES UNIT, US NAVY, 63- MIL OFFICER ENVIRON BIOSCI DEPT, 70-, HEAD HEAT STRESS DIV, 73- *Concurrent Pos:* Officer-in-chg shelter habitability, Nat Naval Med Ctr & Bur Med & Surg, 62-64; US Navy rep med adv subcomt thermal factors in environ, Med Sci Div, Nat Acad Sci-Nat Res Coun, 63-65 & med adv comt environ physiol, 66-; consult, Commandant US Marine Corps, 66-, Naval Ships Eng Ctr, 68-, US Navy Environ Health Ctr, 68- & career & prog planning off, Navy Physiologist, 70-; head thermal stress sect, Navy Med Res & Develop Command, 74- *Mem:* AAAS; Am Soc Heat Refrig & Air-Conditioning Eng; NY Acad Sci. *Res:* Environmental physiology; temperature regulation; adaptation and tolerance to heat; etiology, prevention and treatment of heat illnesses. *Mailing Add:* 10005 Wildwood Ct Kensington MD 20795

DASLER, WALDEMAR, b St James, Minn, May 28, 10; m 39; c 3. BIOCHEMISTRY. *Educ:* Univ Wis, BS, 32, MS, 33, PhD(biochem), 38. *Prof Exp:* Chemist, B S Pearsall Co, Ill, 38-41; from res chemist to chief res chemist, Nutrit Res Labs, 41-48; from asst prof to prof, 48-78, EMER PROF, CHICAGO MED SCH, 78-; RETIRED. *Mem:* AAAS; Am Chem Soc; Am Inst Nutrit; Soc Exp Biol & Med. *Res:* Sterols; vitamin D; rickets; osteolathyrism; copper determination; experimental cataract. *Mailing Add:* 4047 N Lawler Ave Chicago IL 60641

DASMANN, RAYMOND FREDRIC, b San Francisco, Calif, May 27, 19; m 44; c 3. ECOLOGY, FISH & WILDLIFE SCIENCES. *Educ:* Univ Calif, AB, 48, MA, 51, PhD(zool), 54. *Prof Exp:* Asst zool, Univ Calif, 48-52; instr biol, Duluth Br, Univ Minn, 53-54; from asst prof to prof & chmn div natural resources, Humboldt State Col, 54-58, prof & chmn div, 62-65; Fulbright scholar, S Rhodesia, 59-60; lectr, Univ Calif, 61-62; dir int progs, Conserv Found, 66-70; sr ecologist, Int Union Conserv Nature, 70-77; PROF ENVIRON STUDIES, UNIV CALIF, SANTA CRUZ, 77- *Concurrent Pos:* Consult, UNESCO, 66-70 & Int Union Conserv Nature, SPac, 79. *Honors & Awards:* Browning Award, 74; Order of Golden Ark, 78; Leopold Award, 79. *Mem:* Wildlife Soc; Ecol Soc Am; Am Soc Mammal; Asn Trop Biol. *Res:* Conservation of natural resources; human and wildlife ecology. *Mailing Add:* Dept of Environ Studies Univ of Calif Santa Cruz CA 95064

DAS SARMA, BASUDEB, b India, Jan 1, 23; m 52; c 2. INORGANIC CHEMISTRY. *Educ:* Univ Calcutta, BS, 44, MS, 46, PhD(chem), 51. *Prof Exp:* Lectr chem, Univ Calcutta, 50-53; res assoc inorg chem, Univ Ill, Urbana, 53-55; lectr chem, Univ Calcutta, 55-57; sr chemist, Geol Surv India, 57-65; assoc prof, 66-69, PROF CHEM, W VA STATE COL, 69- *Concurrent Pos:* Res collabr, Oak Ridge Nat Lab, Tenn, 71-72; exchange prof chem, RI Col, 74. *Honors & Awards:* Outstanding Sci Award, Am Chem Soc, 71. *Mem:* Fel Am Inst Chemists; Am Chem Soc; Fedn Am Scientists; Am Asn Univ Prof. *Res:* Stereo, structural and analytical aspects of coordination chemistry; analytical chemistry and geochemistry of minor and trace metals; solid state reactions in coordination complexes; inorganic pollutants in water; interaction of sulfohydril groups with arsenic compounds; problems and prospects of chemical education in undergraduate colleges; platinum metal complexes with anticancer potential. *Mailing Add:* Dept Chem WVa State Col Institute WV 25112

DASSOW, JOHN ALBERT, b Spokane, Wash, June 30, 17; m 36; c 3. FOOD CHEMISTRY. *Educ:* Univ Wash, BS, 49. *Prof Exp:* Asst fermentation res, Univ Wash, 37-40; asst fish anal, US Fish & Wildlife Serv, 40; fishery technologist, Fisheries Exp Comn, Alaska, 41-45; plant chemist, Dawes Fisheries, 45-46; chemist fish anal & preserv, US Fish & Wildlife Serv, 47-50, chief lab, Alaska, 50-55; supvry chemist fish anal & preserv, US Bur Com Fisheries, 55-70, RES CHEMIST, NAT MARINE FISHERIES SERV, US BUR COM FISHERIES, 70- *Mem:* NY Acad Sci; AAAS; Inst Food Technol. *Res:* Chemical and physical methods of quality measurement; effects of freezing and cold storage on quality; preservation of chilled fish; control of oxidative rancidity; use of fishery resources for protein concentrates and food ingredients. *Mailing Add:* Utilization Res Div 2725 Montlake Blvd E Seattle WA 98112

DATARS, WILLIAM ROSS, b Desboro, Ont, June 14, 32; m 59; c 1. PHYSICS. *Educ:* McMaster Univ, BSc, 55, MSc, 56; Univ Wis, PhD(physics), 59. *Prof Exp:* Sci officer physics, Defence Res Bd Can, 59-62; from asst prof to assoc prof, 62-69, PROF PHYSICS, McMASTER UNIV, 69- *Concurrent Pos:* E W R Steacie res fel, 68-70. *Mem:* Am Phys Soc; Can Asn Physicists; fel Royal Soc Can. *Res:* Electronic properties of solids; properties of semi-metals; far infrared properties of solids. *Mailing Add:* Dept of Physics McMaster Univ Hamilton ON L8S 4L8 Can

DATERMAN, GARY EDWARD, b Freeport, Ill, June 26, 39; m 60; c 3. FOREST ENTOMOLOGY, INSECT ECOLOGY. *Educ:* Univ Calif, Davis, BA, 62; Ore State Univ, MS, 64, PhD(entom), 69. *Prof Exp:* Res scientist entom, 65-74, asst prof entom, Ore State Univ, 71-79, RES ENTOMOLOGIST & PROJ LEADER, PAC NORTHWEST FOREST & RANGE EXP STA, FOREST SCI LAB, US FOREST SERV, 74-, ASSOC PROF ENTOM, ORE STATE UNIV, 79- *Honors & Awards:* Arthur S Fleming Award, 78. *Mem:* Entom Soc Am; Entom Soc Can. *Res:* Forest insect pheromone identifications and applications with major emphasis on development of operational survey and control applications; tussock moths, Orgyia; spruce budworms, Choristoneura; western pine shoot borer, Eucosma sonomana; tip moths, Rhyacionia; insect behavior. *Mailing Add:* Forestry Sci Lab 3200 Jefferson Way Corvallis OR 97331

D'ATRI, DAVID ALBERT, b Amsterdam, NY, Dec 14, 47; m 76. EPIDEMIOLOGY. *Educ:* Boston Col, BS, 69; Yale Univ, MPH, 73, MPhil & PhD(epidemiol), 74. *Prof Exp:* NIH fel, 74-75, asst prof epidemiol, 75-80, SR RES ASSOC & LECTR EPIDEMIOL, SCH MED, YALE UNIV, 80- *Concurrent Pos:* Proj dir, Conn High Blood Pressure Prog, 74-; proj dir health effects of prison environ, Sch Med, Yale Univ, 74-, vis lectr environ design res, Sch Archit, 75-; co-chmn data coord, New Eng Regional Coun on High Blood Pressure, 76- *Mem:* Am Heart Asn; Am Pub Health Asn. *Res:* Role of psychosocial factors in chronic disease with particular emphasis on the effect of the built environment and cardiovascular disease. *Mailing Add:* Dept of Epidemiol & Pub Health Yale Univ Sch of Med New Haven CT 06510

DATSKO, JOSEPH, b Pa, Feb 4, 21; m 46; c 4. MECHANICAL ENGINEERING. *Educ:* Univ Mich, BSME, 43, MSE, 51. *Prof Exp:* Prod engr, Dynamic Tool Co, 43; chief engr & plant mgr, Stevens Mfg Co, 46-49, vpres & plant mgr, 52-53; instr prod eng, 49-52, from asst prof to assoc prof, 53-63, PROF PROD ENG, UNIV MICH, ANN ARBOR, 63- *Concurrent Pos:* Consult, 52- *Mem:* Am Soc Mech Engrs; Am Soc Metals; Am Soc Eng Educ; Am Foundrymens Soc. *Res:* Correlation of microstructures, mechanical properties and fabricability. *Mailing Add:* Dept of Mech Eng Univ of Mich Ann Arbor MI 48104

DATTA, BITHIN, b Kharagpur, India, June 6, 55. ENGINEERING ECONOMICS, OPERATIONS RESEARCH. *Educ:* Indian Inst Technol, India, BTech, Hons, 76, MTech, 78; Purdue Univ, PhD(civil eng), 81. *Prof Exp:* Engr, Irragation & Water Ways Directorate, Govt WBengal, 78; teaching asst, Purdue Univ, 78-79, res asst & David Ross fel, 79-81, grad instr res, 81; RES ASSOC, UNIV WASH, 81- *Mem:* Am Geophys Union; Am Water Resources Asn. *Res:* Scouring around bridge abutments; stochastic optimization models for longterm planning and real time operation of water reservoir systems; rain fall, snowmelt, runoff process modelling; extending optimization models to grain reserve systems. *Mailing Add:* Dept Civil Eng Univ Wash FX-10 Seattle WA 98195

DATTA, DILIP KUMAR, b Jorhat, India, Jan 2, 39; m 68. GEOMETRY. *Educ:* Gauhati Univ, India, BA, 58; Univ Delhi, MA, 60, PhD(math), 63. *Prof Exp:* Lectr math, Assam Eng Col, 63; Brit Govt Commonwealth scholar differential geom, 63-65; asst prof, Univ Calgary, 65-67; from asst prof to assoc prof, 67-80, PROF MATH, UNIV RI, 80- *Mem:* Am Math Soc; Math Soc Can. *Res:* Differential geometry; linear connections; special Riemannian spaces; G-structures. *Mailing Add:* Dept of Math Univ of RI Kingston RI 02881

DATTA, PADMA RAG, b Jorhat, Assam, India, Feb 27, 27; US citizen; m 52; c 2. BIOCHEMISTRY, ECOLOGY. *Educ:* Univ Mass, MS, 50; WVa Univ, PhD(agr biochem), 56. *Prof Exp:* Res assoc biochem, Fels Res Inst, Sch Med, Temple Univ, 56-57; sr res fel anal & phys chem, Am Spice Trade Asn, Eastern Regional Lab, USDA, 57-61; res chemist, Rohm and Haas Co, 61-63; res biochemist, Food & Drug Admin, US Dept Health, Educ & Welfare, 63-70; BIOCHEMIST, OFF PESTICIDES PROGS, ENVIRON PROTECTION AGENCY, 71- *Concurrent Pos:* Res consult biochem, Sch Med, George Washington Univ, 67- *Mem:* AAAS; Am Chem Soc; NY Acad Sci; Int Soc Technol Assessment; World Future Soc. *Res:* Advise on the research, monitoring and regulatory needs for pesticides and other toxic chemicals as they affect environmental ecosystems and human health. *Mailing Add:* 8514 Whittier Blvd Bethesda MD 20034

DATTA, PRASANTA, b Calcutta, India, Oct 10, 29; US citizen; m 57; c 2. BIOCHEMISTRY, MOLECULAR BIOLOGY. *Educ:* Univ Calcutta, BSc, 49, MSc, 51; Univ Wash, PhD(plant biochem), 56. *Prof Exp:* Asst res prof molecular biol, Wash Univ, 61-65; asst prof, 66-68, assoc prof, 68-76, PROF

BIOCHEM, MED SCH, UNIV MICH, ANN ARBOR, 76- *Concurrent Pos:* Playtex Corp fel, Med Sch, Univ Wash, 57-58; Nat Res Coun Can fel, Nat Res Coun Lab, Ottawa, 58-61; NIH spec fel, Salk Inst, Calif, 72-73. *Mem:* AAAS; Am Soc Microbiol; Am Soc Biol Chem; Am Soc Cell Biol. *Res:* Biochemical and genetic studies of enzyme regulation; of eukaryotic membrane. *Mailing Add:* Dept of Biol Chem Univ Mich 4326 Med Sci I Ann Arbor MI 48109

DATTA, RANAJIT K, b Sylhet, Bangladesh, Feb 1, 35. SOLID STATE CHEMISTRY. *Educ:* Univ Calcutta, BSc, 53; Indian Inst Technol, Kharagpur, BS Hons, 56, MTech, 58; Pa State Univ, PhD(geochem), 61. *Prof Exp:* From res asst to res assoc geochem, Pa State Univ, 58-62; res chemist, Large Lamp Eng Sect, 62-64, RES CHEMIST, LAMP DIV, GEN ELEC CO, 64- *Concurrent Pos:* Res liaison, Gen Elec Co, CNRS, Paris, 70-71. *Mem:* Am Ceramic Soc; Sigma Xi. *Res:* Phase equilibria; thermionic emitters; lamp-cathode chemistry; phosphors; alan/ceramic seals. *Mailing Add:* Lamp Bus Group Gen Elec Co Nela Park East Cleveland OH 44112

DATTA, RANAJIT KUMAR, b Munshiganj, Bangladesh, Apr 1, 33; m 64. NEUROCHEMISTRY, NEUROPHARMACOLOGY. *Educ:* Univ Calcutta, BSc, 56, MSc, 58, PhD(biochem), 63, DSc(biochem), 75; Am Bd Clin Chem, dipl. *Prof Exp:* Asst res officer, Inst Postgrad Med Educ & Res, Calcutta, India, 60; lectr chem, Jogamaya Devi Col, 61-6?, asst prof biochem, Bengal Vet Col, 63-64; sr res officer, USDA Proj, Univ Calcutta, 64-65; sr res scientist, NY State Res Inst Neurochem & Drug Addiction, 65-67; res assoc biochem, Col Physicians & Surgeons, Columbia Univ, 67-68; ASSOC BIOPHYSICIST, BETH ISRAEL MED CTR, 68- *Concurrent Pos:* Hon lectr, Dept Agr, Calcutta, 64-65; assoc, Dept Path, Mt Sinai Sch Med, 68-71, asst prof, 71-79; ed, Clinician, 70- *Mem:* Nat Acad Clin Biochem; Am Soc Neurochem; Int Soc Neurochem; Brit Biochem Soc; Indian Soc Biol Chem. *Res:* Metabolism of nucleic acids in brain tissue; biochemical properties of brain ribosomes; drug-induced changes in cerebral macromolecules; protein breakdown processes in the brain; methylation of nucleic acids in cancer; clinical and cancer immunology; immunochemistry. *Mailing Add:* Div of Labs Beth Israel Med Ctr New York NY 10003

DATTA, RATHIN, b Calcutta, India, Nov 11, 48. BIOTECHNOLOGY. *Educ:* Indian Inst Technol, Kanpur, 70; Princeton Univ, MA, 71, PhD(chem eng), 74. *Prof Exp:* Eng assoc, Res & Develop Lab, Merck & Co, 74-78; SR ENGR, EXXON RES & ENG CO, 78- *Mem:* Am Chem Soc; Am Inst Chem Engrs; Soc Indust Microbiol. *Res:* Biotechnology for energy production and conversion; fermentation and separation process development; biomass conversion to fuels and chemicals; economic and energy analysis of renewable resources and energy systems; development of appropriate technology. *Mailing Add:* 629 W 8th St Plainfield NJ 07060

DATTA, SAMIR KUMAR, b Calcutta, India, June 14, 36; m 66; c 1. ELECTRICAL ENGINEERING. *Educ:* Jadavpur Univ, India, BEE, 58; Manchester Univ, MS, 63, PhD(control systs, electronics), 66. *Prof Exp:* Electronic engr, Askania Werke, Ger, 58-60 & Valvo, GmbH, 60-61; sr develop engr, Speed Variator Dept, Gen Elec Co, 67-68; PROF ELEC ENG, CALIF POLYTECH STATE UNIV, SAN LUIS OBISPO, 68- *Mem:* Inst Elec & Electronics Engrs; Sigma Xi. *Res:* Power electronics; solid state energy conversion; electric motor controls; power systems. *Mailing Add:* Dept Electronic & Elec Eng Calif Polytech State Univ San Luis Obispo CA 93407

DATTA, SUBHENDU KUMAR, b Howrah, India, Jan 15, 36; m 66; c 1. ENGINEERING MECHANICS, APPLIED MATHEMATICS. *Educ:* Calcutta Univ, BSc, 54, MSc, 56; Jadavpur Univ, PhD(appl math), 62. *Prof Exp:* Vis asst prof aeronaut, Univ Colo, 64-65; asst prof, Indian Inst Technol, 65-67; asst prof math, Univ Man, 67-68; from asst prof to assoc prof mech, 68-73, PROF MECH, UNIV COLO, 73- *Concurrent Pos:* Prin investr, NSF grant, 70-; prof appl math, Calcutta Univ, 79-80; consult, Nat Bur Standards, 79- *Mem:* Am Acad Mech; Am Soc Mech Engrs; Soc Eng Sci; Soc Indust & Appl Math. *Res:* Wave propagation in elastic and inelastic solids; ultrasonic non-destructive evaluation; earthquake engineering. *Mailing Add:* Dept of Mech Eng Univ of Colo Boulder CO 80309

DATTA, SURINDER P, b Lahore, India, Apr 29, 33; m 63; c 3. GENETICS, IMMUNOLOGY. *Educ:* Panjab Univ, India, BVetSci, 55; Univ Wis-Madison, MS, 59, PhD(genetics, vet sci), 63. *Prof Exp:* Res asst immunogenetics, Indian Vet Res Inst, 55-57 & Univ Wis-Madison, 58-63; res assoc immunol, Albert Einstein Col Med, 63-64; lectr path, Med Col, Monash Univ, Australia, 64-67; assoc scientist, Oak Ridge Assoc Univs, 67-68; asst prof genetics, 68-72, assoc prof life sci, 72-74, PROF LIFE SCI, UNIV WIS-PARKSIDE, 74- *Concurrent Pos:* Res partic, AEC res partic fel, Med Div, Oak Ridge Assoc Univs, 69. *Mem:* Am Inst Biol Sci; Genetics Soc Am. *Res:* Immunogenetic analysis of blood groups in cattle, guinea pigs and marmosets; phytohemagglutinins; kidney transplantation in cattle; development of immune competence. *Mailing Add:* Div of Sci Col of Sci & Soc Univ of Wis-Parkside Kenosha WI 53140

DATTA, TAPAN K, b India, Sept 3, 39; US citizen; m 64; c 2. TRAFFIC OPERATIONS & CONTROL. *Educ:* Bengal Eng Col, India, BEng, 62, dipl town & regional planning, 65; Wayne State Univ, MS, 68; Mich State Univ, PhD(civil eng), 73. *Prof Exp:* Asst engr structural eng, The Kuljian Corp, 62-65, proj engr, 65-67; asst prof, 73-76, assoc prof, 76-78, PROF & CHMN CIVIL ENG, WAYNE STATE UNIV, 79- *Concurrent Pos:* Chief transp engr, Goodell Grivas, Inc, 68-72, vpres eng, 72-79, pres, 79- *Mem:* Am Soc Civil Engrs; Inst Transp Engrs; Am Pub Works Asn; Transp Res Bd. *Res:* Traffic operations and control; traffic and highway safety; training for professionals in traffic and safety. *Mailing Add:* Dept Civil Eng Wayne State Univ 667 Merrick Detroit MI 48202

DATTA, TIMIR, b Sept 14, 47; Indian citizen. CONDENSED MATTER PHYSICS. *Educ:* Calcutta Univ, BS, 67; Boston Col, MS, 74; Tulane Univ, PhD(physics), 79. *Prof Exp:* Vis asst prof, Tulane Univ, 81; ASST PROF, UNIV SC, COLUMBIA, 82- *Concurrent Pos:* Res assoc, Univ NC, Chapel Hill, 79-81. *Res:* Solid state physics experimental and theory; transport and critical properties of low dimensional systems; general relativity; boundary conditions and Mach's principle; plasma physics; non-linear response in dense plasma; amorphous mediums; percolation and transport. *Mailing Add:* Univ SC Columbia SC 29208

D'ATTORRE, LEONARDO, b La Plata, Arg, Feb 2, 20; nat US; m 49. PHYSICS. *Educ:* La Plata Univ, MA, 47, PhD, 52. *Prof Exp:* Instr fluid mech, La Plata Univ, 48-52, assoc prof aerodyn, 52-56; sr res engr, Gen Dynamics/Astroanut, 56-61; prof fluid mech, La Plata Univ, 61-62; staff scientist, Space Sci Lab, Gen Dynamics/Convair, 62-67; STAFF ENGR, TRW SYSTS GROUP, 67- *Concurrent Pos:* Prof, Nat Univ South, Arg, 54-56. *Mem:* Am Math Soc. *Res:* Fluid and classical mechanics; applied mathematics; solution of non-linear systems of partial differential equations, applied to steady and unsteady flows; numerical methods. *Mailing Add:* 230 S Catalina Ave Apt 113 Redondo Beach CA 90277

DATZ, SHELDON, b New York, NY, July 21, 27; m 48; c 2. CHEMICAL PHYSICS, ATOMIC PHYSICS. *Educ:* Columbia Univ, BS, 50, MA, 51; Univ Tenn, PhD(phys chem), 60. *Prof Exp:* Technician, Substitute Alloy Mat Labs, Div War Res, Columbia Univ, 43-44, Dept Physics, 46-50, asst chem, 50-51; chemist, Chem Div, 51-67, leader molecular beam group, 60-67, assoc dir, 67-74, leader atomic & molecular collisions group, 74-81, DISTINGUISHED RES SCIENTIST, OAK RIDGE NAT LAB, 79-, SECT CHIEF ATOMIC PHYSICS, PHYSICS DIV, 81- *Concurrent Pos:* Consult, Gen Atomic Div, Gen Dynamics Corp, 60-62 & Repub Aviation Corp, Long Island, 61-62; guest scientist, Inst Atomic & Molecular Physics, Netherlands, 62-63; guest prof, Inst Physics, Aarhus Univ, Denmark, 70-71; chmn, Gordon Conf Particle Solid Interactions, 70 & Gordon Conf Dynamics Molecular Collisions, 72; guest prof physics dept, Univ Chicago, 72; chmn, V Int Conf Atomic Collisions Solids, 73; guest scientist, Max Planck Inst Plasma Physics, WGer, 74; mem, Nat Res Coun-Nat Acad Sci Comt Atomic & Molecular Physics, 72-75 & 77-; Union Carbide Res fel, 80-; guest distinguished prof, Tex A&M Univ, 81. *Mem:* AAAS; Am Chem Soc; fel Am Phys Soc; Sigma Xi. *Res:* Dynamics of atomic and molecular collisions, chemically reactive collisions; high energy atomic collisions; atomic collisions in solids; particle-surface interactions. *Mailing Add:* Oak Ridge Nat Lab PO Box X Oak Ridge TN 37830

DAU, GARY JOHN, b Lewiston, Idaho, Sept 3, 38; m 61; c 2. NUCLEAR & MECHANICAL ENGINEERING. *Educ:* Univ Idaho, BS, 61; Univ Ariz, PhD(nuclear eng), 65. *Prof Exp:* Sr res scientist, Pac Northwest Labs, Battelle Mem Inst, 64-66, mgr res & develop group, 66-68, mgr nondestructive testing dept, 68-70, mgr appl physics & instrumentation dept, 70-75; prog mgr, 75-80, SR PROG MGR, ELECTRIC POWER RES INST, 81- *Concurrent Pos:* Mem ed adv comt, Nuclear Technol J. *Mem:* Am Nuclear Soc; Nat Soc Prof Engrs. *Res:* Nondestructive testing; applied physics; instrumentation research; electromagnetics; lasers; holography; ultrasonic and thermal testing techniques. *Mailing Add:* Elec Power Res Inst PO Box 10412 Palo Alto CA 94303

DAU, PETER CAINE, b Fresno, Calif, Feb 25, 39; m 65; c 4. IMMUNOLOGY, NEUROLOGY. *Educ:* Stanford Univ, BA, 60, MD, 64. *Prof Exp:* Intern, Los Angeles County Hosp, 64-65; resident neurol, Univ Wis-Madison, 65-66; resident neurol, Univ Chicago, 66-68, fel immunol, 68-69; chief neurol, David Grant US Air Force Hosp, 69-71; sci asst, Ger Cancer Res Ctr, 72-74; assoc neuroimmunologist, Univ Calif, San Francisco, 74-75, instr med, 75-76; res immunologist, Children's Hosp, San Francisco, 75-81; asst clin prof med, Univ Calif, San Francisco, 76-81; HEAD, DIV IMMUNOL, EVANSTON HOSP, ILL, 82-; ASSOC PROF MED & NEUROL, NORTH WESTERN UNIV, 82- *Mem:* AAAS; Am Asn Immunologists. *Res:* Myasthenia gravis; multiple sclerosis; polymyositis; scleroderma; cancer. *Mailing Add:* North Western Univ Evanston IL 60201

DAUB, CLARENCE THEODORE, JR, b Hagerstown, Md, Nov 27, 36; m 63. ASTROPHYSICS. *Educ:* Carleton Col, BA, 58; Univ Wis, PhD(astron), 62. *Prof Exp:* Instr astron, Univ Wis, 62; asst prof physics, Iowa State Univ, 62-67; from asst prof to assoc prof, 67-73, PROF ASTRON, SAN DIEGO STATE UNIV, 73- *Mem:* Am Astron Soc; Sigma Xi; Astron Soc Pac. *Res:* Physical processes in gaseous media. *Mailing Add:* Dept Astron San Diego State Univ San Diego CA 92182

DAUB, EDWARD E, b Milwaukee, Wis, May 17, 24; m 49; c 5. HISTORY OF SCIENCE. *Educ:* Univ Wis, BS, 45, MS, 47, PhD(hist sci), 66; Union Theol Sem, NY, BD, 50, STM, 60. *Prof Exp:* Assoc prof chem eng, Doshisha, Japan, 57-62; from asst prof to assoc prof hist sci, Univ Kans, 65-71; assoc prof, 74, PROF HIST TECHNOL, UNIV WIS-MADISON, 74- *Concurrent Pos:* NSF res grant, 68-70 & 72-74; Danforth Found Underwood fel, 71; Nat Humanities Inst fel, Univ Chicago, 78-79; mem, United Presbyterian Task Force on Sci, Med & Values, 80- & Pub Serv Sci Residency, NSF, 80-81. *Mem:* Soc Hist Technol; Hist Sci Soc; AAAS. *Res:* Relations between science and theology; technology and values; history of chemical engineering; technical Japanese. *Mailing Add:* Col of Eng Univ of Wis Madison WI 53706

DAUB, GUIDO HERMAN, b Milwaukee, Wis, Dec 16, 20; m 48; c 3. ORGANIC CHEMISTRY. *Educ:* Univ Wis, BS, 44, MS, 47, PhD(chem), 49. *Prof Exp:* Chemist, Rohm and Haas Co, 44-45; from asst prof to assoc prof, 49-61, chmn dept, 70-81, PROF CHEM, UNIV NMEX, 61- *Mem:* Fel AAAS; Am Chem Soc. *Res:* Synthesis of polycyclic hydrocarbons and heterocycles; carcinogenic compounds; laser dyes; isotopic labeling with C-13 and N-15. *Mailing Add:* Dept of Chem Univ of NMex Albuquerque NM 87131

DAUBEN, DWIGHT LEWIS, b Ft Smith, Ark, Feb 28, 38; m 63; c 1. PETROLEUM ENGINEERING & TECHNOLOGY. *Educ:* Tex Tech Col, BS, 61; Univ Tulsa, MS, 63; Univ Okla, PhD(eng sci), 66. *Prof Exp:* Petrol engr, Chevron Oil Co, Colo, 62-63; res supvr, Amoco Prod Co, Subsid Stand Oil Ind, 66-81; VPRES, KEPLINGER & ASSOCS, 81- *Mem:* Am Inst Mining, Metall & Petrol Engrs. *Res:* Improved methods of recovering oil, particularly miscible processes and polymer flooding. *Mailing Add:* 8916 S 45th Ave Tulsa OK 74132

DAUBEN, WILLIAM GARFIELD, b Columbus, Ohio; m 47; c 2. PHOTOCHEMISTRY. *Educ:* Ohio State Univ, BA, 41; Harvard Univ, AM, 42, PhD(chem), 44. *Hon Degrees:* Dr, Bordeaux, 80. *Prof Exp:* Fel, Harvard Univ, 44-45; from instr to assoc prof, 45-57, PROF CHEM, UNIV CALIF, BERKELEY, 57- *Concurrent Pos:* Guggenheim Mem Found fels, 51 & 66; NSF fel, 58; mem med chem study sect, NIH, 60-64 & chem panel, NSF, 64-; mem bd dirs, Org Synthesis, 69-; pres, Org Reactions, Inc, 69-; ed in chief, Org Reactions, 69-; mem bd ed, Organometallics in Chem Synthesis, 70-; chmn chem sect, Nat Acad Sci, 77-; mem, Assembly Math & Phys Sci, Nat Res Coun, 77-; Alexander von Humboldt Award, 80. *Honors & Awards:* Award, Am Chem Soc, 59, Guenter Award, 73. *Mem:* Nat Acad Sci; Am Chem Soc; The Chem Soc; Swiss Chem Soc; fel Am Acad Arts & Sci. *Res:* Natural products; organic synthesis; synthetic hormones and drugs; stereochemistry. *Mailing Add:* Dept of Chem Univ of Calif Berkeley CA 94720

DAUBENMIRE, REXFORD, b Coldwater, Ohio, Dec 12, 09; m 38; c 1. PLANT ECOLOGY. *Educ:* Butler Univ, BS, 30; Univ Colo, MS, 32; Univ Minn, PhD(bot), 35. *Prof Exp:* Actg asst prof bot, Univ Tenn, 35-36; from asst prof to prof, 36-75, EMER PROF BOT, WASH STATE UNIV, 75- *Concurrent Pos:* Lectr, Biol Sta, Univ Minn, 37; asst prof, Sci Camp, Univ Wyo, 39; consult, US Forest Serv, Nat Park Serv & Bur Reclamation. *Honors & Awards:* Eminent Ecologist, Ecol Soc Am, 79; Barrington Moore Award, Soc Am Forestry, 80. *Mem:* Ecol Soc Am (pres, 67); Brit Ecol Soc; Soc Trop Ecol. *Res:* Forest classification for Northern Rockies; factors affecting seasonal growth in temperate and tropical trees; causes of forest distribution in Northern Rockies; ecology of grasslands in Columbia drainage; effect of temperature and drought on seedling survival; water requirement of desert plants; productivity of tropical savanna. *Mailing Add:* 636 Interlochen Dr Sorrento FL 32776

DAUBENSPECK, JOHN ANDREW, b Denver, Colo, Nov 3, 42; m 69. BIOMEDICAL ENGINEERING, PHYSIOLOGY. *Educ:* Swarthmore Col, BSME, 66; Dartmouth Col, PhD(eng sci), 72. *Prof Exp:* NIH res fel & res assoc biomed eng, Univ Southern Calif, 72-74; asst prof, 74-80, ASSOC PROF PHYSIOL, DARTMOUTH MED SCH, 80-, ADJ ASST PROF ENG, THAYER SCH ENG, 75- *Concurrent Pos:* Res career develop award, NIH, 76-81. *Mem:* Assoc Sigma Xi; Am Physiol Soc. *Res:* Control of breathing, breathing pattern, respiratory mechanics, application of optimal control principles to biological systems and computer simulations of physiological control processes. *Mailing Add:* Dept of Physiol Dartmouth Med Sch Hanover NH 03755

DAUBENY, HUGH ALEXANDER, b Nanaimo, BC, Dec 6, 31; m 59; c 3. PLANT BREEDING, HORTICULTURE. *Educ:* Univ BC, BSA, 53, MSA, 55; Cornell Univ, PhD(plant breeding), 58. *Prof Exp:* Teaching asst hort, Univ BC, 53-55; res asst plant breeding, Agassiz, BC, 58-73, RES SCIENTIST SMALL FRUIT BREEDING, RES STA, AGR CAN, 73- *Concurrent Pos:* Chmn, Rubus-Riker Working Group, Int Soc Hort Sci. *Mem:* Int Soc Hort Sci; Am Soc Hort Sci; Am Pomol Soc (pres); Agr Inst Can. *Res:* Strawberry and red rasberry breeding with emphasis on disease and insect resistance. *Mailing Add:* Res Sta Agr Can 6660 NW Marine Dr Vancouver BC V6T 1X2 Can

DAUBERT, THOMAS EDWARD, b Pottsville, Pa, Oct 14, 37; m 67; c 2. CHEMICAL ENGINEERING. *Educ:* Pa State Univ, BS, 59, MS, 61, PhD(chem eng), 64. *Prof Exp:* Res asst chem eng, 61, from instr to assoc prof, 61-75, PROF CHEM ENG, PA STATE UNIV, 75- *Concurrent Pos:* Year-in-indust prof, E I du Pont de Nemours & Co, 70-71. *Mem:* Am Chem Soc; Am Inst Chem Engrs; Am Soc Eng Educ. *Res:* prediction and determination of physical, thermodynamic and transport properties of hydrocarbons and organic compounds; characterization and chromatographic separation of petroleum. *Mailing Add:* 165 Fenske Lab Pa State Univ University Park PA 16802

DAUBIN, SCOTT C, b New London, Conn, Sept 20, 22; m 44; c 5. OCEAN ENGINEERING, ACOUSTICS. *Educ:* US Naval Acad, BS, 44; Princeton Univ, MA, 53, PhD(physics), 54. *Prof Exp:* Proj officer, Undersea Warfare Br, Off Naval Res, 54-56; tech aide, 56-57; ship supt, Portsmouth Naval Shipyard, 57-58; asst design supt, 58-61; head marine sci, AC Electronics Defense Res Labs, Gen Motors Corp, 61-67; chmn dept ocean eng, Woods Hole Oceanog Inst, 67-71 & Univ Miami, 71-77; PRES, DAUBIN SYSTS CORP, 77- *Concurrent Pos:* Ed, US Navy J Underwater Acoustics, 54-56; mem deep submergence systs rev group, Adv Comt Secy Navy, 63; adj prof, Univ Miami, 78- *Mem:* Acoustical Soc Am; Am Asn Physics Teachers; Am Soc Mech Engrs; Marine Tech Soc; Soc Naval Architects & Marine Engrs. *Res:* Underwater acoustics; instrumentation systems; signal processing; general underwater technology. *Mailing Add:* Daubin Systs Corp 104 Crandon Blvd Suite 315 Key Biscayne FL 33149

DAUER, DANIEL MARTIN, marine ecology, see previous edition

DAUER, JERALD PAUL, b Toledo, Ohio, Mar 2, 43; m 67; c 3. MATHEMATICS. *Educ:* Bowling Green State Univ, BA, 65; Univ Kans, MA, 67, PhD(math), 70. *Prof Exp:* From asst prof to assoc prof, 70-80, PROF MATH, UNIV NEBR, LINCOLN, 80- *Concurrent Pos:* Vis scholar, Dept Opers Res, Stanford Univ, 75-76. *Mem:* Am Math Soc; Soc Indust & Appl Math; Opers Res Soc Am. *Res:* Optimal control theory; multiobject optimization; operations research; nonlinear optimization. *Mailing Add:* Dept of Math Univ of Nebr Lincoln NE 68588

DAUERMAN, LEONARD, b New York, NY, May 17, 32; m 75; c 4. ENVIRONMENTAL SYSTEMS & TECHNOLOGY. *Educ:* City Col New York, BS, 53; Purdue Univ, MS, 56; Rutgers Univ, PhD(chem), 62, JD, 73. *Prof Exp:* Instr chem, Rutgers Univ, 58-62; res chemist, Dow Chem, 62-63; res assoc chem eng, NY Univ, 63-66; from asst prof to assoc prof, 66-69; ASSOC PROF CHEM & CHEM ENG, NJ INST TECHNOL, 69-, DIR, LAW & TECHNOL CTR, 79- *Mem:* Combustion Inst; Am Chem Soc; Am

Inst Chem Engrs; Am Asn Univ Prof. *Res:* Flue gas desulfurization, magnesia and alkali processes; soot formation in hydrocarbon flames; techniques for detecting low levels of hydrocarbons; development of environmental law. *Mailing Add:* Dept of Chem Eng 323 High St Newark NJ 07102

DAUES, GREGORY W, JR, b St Louis, Mo, Oct 1, 28; m 52; c 4. POLYMER CHEMISTRY, ANALYTICAL CHEMISTRY. *Educ:* Univ St Louis, BS, 50; Univ NMex, MS, 52. *Prof Exp:* Res chemist, 52-59, res group leader, 59-67, mgr res, 67-74, mgr, Polyolefins Res & Mfg, 74-80, GEN SUPT MFG & QUALITY ASSURANCE, MONSANTO CO, 80- *Mem:* Am Chem Soc. *Res:* Plastics applications; spectroscopy. *Mailing Add:* Monsanto Co PO Box 1311 Texas City TX 77590

DAUGHADAY, WILLIAM HAMILTON, b Chicago, Ill, Feb 12, 18; m 45; c 2. MEDICINE. *Educ:* Harvard Univ, AB, 40, MD, 43. *Prof Exp:* Instr med, 50, asst prof med & dir metab div, 51-57, assoc prof, 57-63, PROF MED, SCH MED, WASH UNIV, 63- *Concurrent Pos:* Res fel med, Sch Med, Wash Univ, 47-48, NIH fel biochem, 48-49; consult, Barnes Hosp, 50-; ed, J Lab & Clin Med, 61-66; dir diabetes ctr, Sch Med, Wash Univ, 75; ed, J Clin Endocrin & Metab, 72- *Honors & Awards:* Fred C Koch Medal, Endocrine Soc, 75. *Mem:* Endocrine Soc; Am Soc Clin Invest; Am Fedn Clin Res; Asn Am Physicians; Am Diabetes Asn. *Res:* Pituitary growth hormone somatomcdin; diabetes mellitus. *Mailing Add:* 1414 W Adams Kirkwood MO 63122

DAUGHENBAUGH, RANDALL JAY, b Rapid City, SDak, Feb 10, 48; m 73; c 2. PHYSICAL ORGANIC CHEMISTRY. *Educ:* SDak Sch Mines & Technol, BS, 70; Univ Colo, PhD(chem), 75. *Prof Exp:* res chemist, Air Prod & Chem, Inc, 75-80; MGR PROCESS DEVELOP, CHEM EXCHANGE INDUST, 80- *Mem:* Am Chem Soc. *Res:* Development of new amine products and manufacturing technology; process research and development of petrochemicals and specialty chemicals. *Mailing Add:* 11022 N 66th St Longmont CO 80501

DAUGHERTY, DAVID M, b Warren, Ohio, Mar 29, 28; m 48; c 5. ENTOMOLOGY. *Educ:* Ohio State Univ, BSc, 52, MSc, 53; NC State Univ, PhD(entom), 64. *Prof Exp:* Res fel entom, Ohio State Univ, 52-53; agr specialist, Ohio Dept Agr, 53-56; registr inspector econ poisons, Univ Ky, 56-59; res entomologist, USDA, 61-68, leader oilseed insects invests, 68-71, asst dir, Far East Regional Res Off, New Delhi, India, 71-75; dep dir agr, Bur Int Orgn Affairs, US Dept State, 75-77; USDA liaison officer AID, 77-78, asst chief, Int Progs Staff, Sci & Educ Admin, 78-79, DEP ADMINR INT RES, OFF INT COOP & DEVELOP, USDA, 80- *Concurrent Pos:* Res assoc, Univ Mo-Columbia, 61-64, from asst prof to assoc prof, 64-71; attache, Agr Res, US Embassy, New Delhi, 71- *Mem:* Entom Soc Am. *Res:* Biology, ecology and control of insects affecting cereals and forage crops; parasites, predators and diseases of insects and their utilization in insect control; international research in the agricultural sciences. *Mailing Add:* US Dept Agr Off Int Coop & Develop South Agr Bldg Rm 3047 Washington DC 20250

DAUGHERTY, DON G(ENE), b Mendon, Ill, Nov 14, 35; m 59. ELECTRICAL ENGINEERING. *Educ:* Univ Wis, BS, 57, MS, 58, PhD(elec eng), 64. *Prof Exp:* Instr elec eng, Univ Wis, 59-61; from asst prof to assoc prof, 63-76, PROF ELEC ENG, UNIV KANS, 76- *Mem:* Inst Elec & Electronics Engrs; Am Soc Eng Educ. *Res:* Theory and applications of semiconductor devices; methods of engineering education. *Mailing Add:* 2617 Belle Crest Dr Lawrence KS 66044

DAUGHERTY, FRANKLIN W, b Alpine, Tex, June 20, 27; m 45; c 3. GEOLOGY, HYDROLOGY. *Educ:* Sul Ross State Col, BS, 50; Univ Tex, MA, 59, PhD(geol), 62. *Prof Exp:* Mgr, Big Bend Mineral Explor Co, 54-58; econ geol consult, 62-63; assoc prof geol, WTex State Univ, 63-67, prof geol & coordr earth sci res, 67-77. *Concurrent Pos:* Pres, Pinnacle Resources, Inc, 71; partner, D&F Minerals, Inc, 71-, pres, 80- *Mem:* Am Inst Mining, Metall & Petrol Engrs; Geol Soc Am; Geochem Soc. *Res:* Economic geology; petrography of alkalic igneous rocks; hydrogeology. *Mailing Add:* PO Box 329 Alpine TX 79830

DAUGHERTY, GUY WILSON, b Richmond, Va, Sept 25, 12; m 40; c 4. CLINICAL MEDICINE. *Educ:* Col William & Mary, BS, 37; Med Col Va, MD, 37; Univ Minn, MD, 43. *Prof Exp:* Practicing physician, WVa, 38-41; first asst, 43-44, mem sect med, 47-62, ASSOC CLIN PROF MED, MAYO CLIN, 62-, PROF MED, MAYO MED SCH, 73- *Concurrent Pos:* Fel coun clin cardiol, Am Heart Asn, 70- *Mem:* AMA; fel Am Col Physicians. *Res:* Cardiovascular renal diseases. *Mailing Add:* Mayo Clin 200 First St SW Rochester MN 55901

DAUGHERTY, KENNETH E, b Pittsburgh, Pa, Dec 27, 38; m 61. ANALYTICAL CHEMISTRY. *Educ:* Carnegie Inst Technol, BS, 60; Univ Wash, PhD(anal chem), 64; Claremont Grad Sch, MBE, 71. *Prof Exp:* DIR, TRAC LABS, 81- *Concurrent Pos:* Pres, KEDS Inc & KD Consult, 77-; adj prof chem, NTex State Univ, 77-; adj assoc prof chem, Univ Pittsburgh, 73- *Mem:* Am Chem Soc; Am Inst Chemists; NY Acad Sci; Sigma Xi. *Res:* X-ray fluorescence and diffraction; spectroscopy; cement, forensic and pollution chemistry; instrumental analysis; thermal analysis; materials research; business aspects of research and development; recycling waste materials research. *Mailing Add:* 317 Lakeland Dr Lewisville TX 75067

DAUGHERTY, LEROY ARTHUR, b Scottsbluff, Nebr, Nov 27, 46; m 73; c 1. AGRONOMY, SOIL MORPHOLOGY. *Educ:* Univ Mo-Columbia, BS, 68; Cornell Univ, MS, 72, PhD(soils), 75. *Prof Exp:* Soil scientist, Soil Conserv Serv, USDA, 68-75; ASST PROF SOIL GENESIS, MORPHOL & CLASSIFICATION, NMEX STATE UNIV, 75- *Mem:* Am Soc Agron; Soil Sci Soc Am; Int Soil Sci Soc. *Res:* Study relationships between saturated permeability and soil characteristics; effects of soluble calcium, magnesium and carbonates on organic matter accumulation in soils of New Mexico; relationship of soil moisture to native plant communities for use in soil classification. *Mailing Add:* Dept of Agron Box 3Q NMex State Univ Las Cruces NM 88003

DAUGHERTY, NED ARTHUR, b Ft Wayne, Ind, Sept 27, 34; m 59; c 2. INORGANIC CHEMISTRY. *Educ:* Purdue Univ, BS, 56; Mich State Univ, PhD(chem), 61. *Prof Exp:* Asst prof chem, Purdue Univ, 61-63 & Colo State Univ, 63-64; mem staff, Los Alamos Sci Lab, Univ Calif, 64-66; asst prof, 66-67, ASSOC PROF INORG CHEM, COLO STATE UNIV, 67- *Mem:* Am Chem Soc. *Res:* Kinetics of oxidation-reduction reactions; coordination compounds; vanadium chemistry. *Mailing Add:* Dept of Chem Colo State Univ Ft Collins CO 80523

DAUGHERTY, PATRICIA A, b Mullens, WVa, Oct 24, 22. GENETICS. *Educ:* Seton Hill Col, AB, 44; Columbia Univ, MA, 46; Ohio State Univ, PhD(genetics), 61. *Prof Exp:* Instr biol, Seton Hill Col, 46-48 & WVa Univ, 48-57; ASSOC PROF BIOL, E CAROLINA UNIV, 61- *Mem:* AAAS; Am Genetic Asn; Genetics Soc Am; Am Inst Biol Sci. *Res:* Drosophila. *Mailing Add:* Dept Biol ECarolina Univ Greenville NC 27834

DAUGHERTY, ROBERT M, JR, physiology, internal medicine, see previous edition

DAUGHTERS, GEORGE T, II, b Huntington Park, Calif, July 21, 38; m 60; c 3. BIOMEDICAL ENGINEERING, PHYSIOLOGY. *Educ:* Univ Ill, BS, 61; San Jose State Univ, MS, 67. *Prof Exp:* Res asst solid state physics, Fairchild Semiconductor Corp, 61-66; RES ASSOC BIOENG, PALO ALTO MED RES FOUND, 66- *Concurrent Pos:* Instr bioeng, Univ Santa Clara, 72; instr elec eng, Stanford Univ, 80- *Mem:* Biomed Eng Soc; Cardiovasc Systs Dynamics Soc; Am Heart Asn. *Res:* Cardiovascular dynamics and physiology. *Mailing Add:* Palo Alto Med Res Found 860 Bryant St Palo Alto CA 94301

DAUKSYS, RICHARD JOHN, materials engineering, see previous edition

DAUL, GEORGE CECIL, b Gretna, La, Oct 27, 16; m 40; c 2. ORGANIC CHEMISTRY. *Educ:* Tulane Univ, AB, 37, AM, 40. *Prof Exp:* Teacher high sch, La, 37-41; mem staff, US Weather Bur, 41-42; chief chemist & inspector trinitrotoluene, Longhorn Ord Works, US War Dept, Tex, 42-45; chemist, Chem Properties Sec, Cotton Fiber Res Div, Southern Regional Res Lab, Bur Agr & Indust Chem, USDA, 45-54; chemist, Res Lab, Courtaulds, Inc, 54-62; dir, Eastern Res Div, ITT Rayonier, Inc, 62-81; RETIRED. *Mem:* Am Chem Soc; Am Asn Textile Chemists & Colorists; Fiber Soc. *Res:* Chemical properties and derivatives of cellulose; cross linking of cellulosic fibers and fabrics; rayon spinning technology; cellulosic films; acetate fibers and plastics. *Mailing Add:* 6 Wedgewood Lane Morristown NJ 07960

DAUM, SOL JACOB, b New York, NY, Dec 17, 33; m 54; c 2. ORGANIC CHEMISTRY, MEDICINAL CHEMISTRY. *Educ:* NY Univ, AB, 54; Brooklyn Col, AM, 59; Columbia Univ, AM, 60, PhD(chem), 62. *Prof Exp:* Sr technician, Sloan-Kettering Inst Cancer Res, Mem Hosp, New York, 56-59; asst chem, Columbia Univ, 60; assoc res chemist, 62-67, res chemist, 67-74, SR RES CHEMIST-GROUP LEADER, STERLING WINTHROP RES INST, 74- *Mem:* AAAS; Am Chem Soc. *Res:* Natural products; antibiotics; alkaloids; terpenes. *Mailing Add:* Dept Chem Sterling Winthrop Res Inst Rensselaer NY 12144

DAUNORA, LOUIS GEORGE, b Gary, Ind, Feb 22, 32; m 61; c 4. PHARMACEUTICAL CHEMISTRY, PHARMACY. *Educ:* Purdue Univ, BS, 58. *Prof Exp:* Pharmacist asst mgr, Apollo Drugs, 55-58; pharmacist mgr, Perry Pharm, 59-62; res scientist pharm, Ames Co Div, Miles Labs, 62-81; PHARMACIST, VET ADMIN MED CTR, 81- *Mem:* Am Pharmaceut Asn; Nat Asn Deaf. *Res:* Pharmaceutical solid systems in research and development applications to product development of human diagnostic devices. *Mailing Add:* 13463 W Virginia Dr Lakewood CO 80228

DAUNS, JOHN, algebra, see previous edition

DAUNT, JOHN GILBERT, b Killiney, Ireland, June 30, 13; US citizen. PHYSICS. *Educ:* Oxford Univ, BA, 35, MA & PhD(physics), 37. *Prof Exp:* Demonstr physics, Oxford Univ, 37-39, lectr & demonstr, 40-46, lectr, Exeter Col, 40-46; from asst prof to prof, Ohio State Univ, 46-65; prof physics & elec eng & dir, Cryogenics Ctr, Stevens Inst Technol, 65-78; PROF, QUEEN'S UNIV, ONT, 78- *Concurrent Pos:* Scott scholar, Oxford Univ, 38; vis scientist, Oak Ridge Nat Lab, 49, consult, 50-53; Guggenheim Mem fels, Univ Amsterdam 53 & Harvard Univ, 54 & 58; vis scientist & consult, Los Alamos Sci Lab, Univ Calif, 58-62; mem adv panel physics, Nat Sci Found, 60-63; pres comn low temperatures & mem US nat comn, Int Union Pure & Appl Physics, 60-66; vis prof, Univ Sao Paulo, 61, City Col New York, 64, Columbia Univ, 65, Univ Rio de Janeiro, 74 & Queen's Univ, Ont, 75; adv ed, Physics Condensed Matter & Physics Letters, 62-72; ed & founder, J Low Temperature Physics, 69-; hon fel, Exeter Col, Oxford, 79-; Alexander von Humboldt sr scientist award, 79. *Honors & Awards:* Sr Award, Oxford Univ, 39; Medal, Univ Brussels, 55; Duddell Medal, Brit Inst Physics & Phys Soc, 56. *Mem:* Fel Am Phys Soc; fel Brit Inst Physics & Phys Soc; Int Inst Refrig. *Res:* Low temperature physics; superfluid helium; helium three; superconductivity; production of low tempertures; microwaves and microwave tubes; infrared detectors; noise theory. *Mailing Add:* Physics Dept Queens Univ Kingston ON K7L 3N6

DAUNT, STEPHEN JOSEPH, b Brooklyn, NY, July 3, 47. MOLECULAR SPECTROSCOPY, PLANETARY ATMOSPHERES. *Educ:* Iona Col, NY, BS, 69; Queen's Univ, Ont, PhD(phys chem), 76. *Prof Exp:* Instr math, Dept Math, 75-76, res asst prof, 77-79, ASST PROF ASTRON, DEPT PHYSICS & ASTRON, UNIV TENN, 79-; ASST PROF CHEM, DEPT CHEM, CONCORDIA UNIV, MONTREAL, CAN, 80- *Concurrent Pos:* Res assoc physics, Dept Physics & Astron, Univ Tenn, 75-77; res fel, Dept Chem, Concordia Univ, Montreal, Can, 80-; vis scientist, NASA Goddard Space Flight Ctr, 81- *Mem:* Am Astron Soc; Am Chem Soc; Am Phys Soc; Optical Soc Am; Soc Appl Spectros. *Res:* Molecular spectroscopy; high resolution infrared and Raman spectra of gases; optical instrumentation design and construction; planetary atmospheres; interstellar molecules; air pollution studies; computer simulation of spectra; molecular dynamical calculations; solid state phase transitions. *Mailing Add:* Molecular Spectros Lab Dept Physics & Astron Univ Tenn Knoxville TN 37996

DAUNTON, NANCY GOTTLIEB, b Washington, DC, Sept 9, 42; m 70. NEUROPSYCHOLOGY, NEUROPHYSIOLOGY. *Educ:* George Washington Univ, AB, 64, MA, 66; Stanford Univ, PhD(neuropsychol), 71. *Prof Exp:* Psychologist neurobiol, 67-71, RES SCIENTIST NEUROSCI, AMES RES CTR-NASA, 71- *Concurrent Pos:* Mgr Ames grant prog vestibular & space sickness res, Ames Res Ctr-NASA, 73- & proj scientist vestibular function res proj spacelab, 77- *Mem:* Soc Neurosci. *Res:* Neurophysiological and neurobehavioral studies of vestibular system function; single unit studies of visual- vestibular interactions; etiology of motion sickness and space sickness; efferent control of sensory input. *Mailing Add:* Biomed Res Div N239-7 Ames Res Ctr-NASA Moffett Field CA 94035

DAUPHINAIS, RAYMOND JOSEPH, b Chicago, Ill, May 30, 25. PHARMACY. *Educ:* Univ Ill, BS, 48; Univ Fla, JD, 54; NY Univ, LLM(trade regulation), 56. *Prof Exp:* Lectr pharm law, Univ Fla, 53-54, asst prof, 54-55; lectr pharmaceut econ, Columbia Univ, 55-56; asst prof pharm, Univ Conn, 57-60; dir legal div, Am Pharmaceut Asn, 60-64; asst to dean col pharm, 64-68, PROF PHARM, WAYNE STATE UNIV, 64-, GRAD OFFICER, 81- *Concurrent Pos:* NSF vis scientist, 64-68; Am Asn Cols Pharm vis lectr, 68- *Honors & Awards:* Food Law Inst Award, 55-56. *Mem:* Am Pharmaceut Asn; Nat Health Lawyers Asn; Am Asn Cols Pharm. *Res:* Pharmaceutical economics; trade regulations; food and drug legislation; health-care administration; professional practice law in healing arts; health care law. *Mailing Add:* 635 Health Sci Col Pharm Wayne State Univ Detroit MI 48202

DAUPHINE, T(HONET) C(HARLES), b North Battleford, Sask, Nov 8, 13; US citizen; m 38; c 4. CHEMICAL ENGINEERING. *Educ:* Mass Inst Technol, SB, 35, ScD(chem eng), 39. *Prof Exp:* Instr chem eng, Mass Inst Technol, 36-39; process engr res & develop dept, Standard Oil Co, Calif, 39-43, supv eng, Calif Res Corp, 43-46; eastern mgr prod develop dept, Oronite Chem Co, 46-51; mgr sales develop, Hooker Chem Corp, NY, 51-57, mgr prod develop plastics & polymers, 57-59, sr develop engr, Corp Gen Develop, 59-62; vpres prod & eng, Nease Chem Co, 62-64; consult, 64-65; vpres, Chem Process Corp, Conn, 65-68, process design supvr, Badger Am Inc, 68-76, technol mgr, Badger Energy, Inc, 76-78; PRES & TREAS, DESIGN ENTERPRISES, INC, 78- *Mem:* Am Chem Soc; Am Inst Chem Engrs; Commercial Develop Asn; fel Am Inst Chemists. *Res:* Inventor, insitu retorting process for oil shale using radio frequency energy; process design of synthetic fuel plants for methanol from coal, oil and gas from coal; process design various plants for petroleum and petrochemical products, other chemicals; new product development of synthetic detergents, p, m and o-xylenes, isophthalic acid, chlorendic acid, fire resistant polyesters and rigid urethane foams; process development for various organic chemicals, including aromatic sulfonation and oxidation. *Mailing Add:* 57 Alcott St Acton MA 01720

DAUPHINEE, THOMAS MCCAUL, b Vancouver, BC, July 3, 16; m 40; c 3. PHYSICS. *Educ:* Univ BC, BA, 43, MA, 45, PhD, 50. *Prof Exp:* Instr dept physics, Univ BC, 47-48; res officer physics, 45-67, sr res officer, 67-70, PRIN RES OFFICER PHYSICS, NAT RES COUN CAN, 70- *Concurrent Pos:* Measurement consult, 81; pres, Sea-Met Sci Ltd, 81- *Honors & Awards:* Morris E Leeds Award, Inst Elec & Electronics Engrs, 78. *Mem:* Instrument Soc Am; Can Asn Physicists; Inst Elec & Electronics Engrs; Can Meteorol & Oceanog Soc. *Res:* Thermometry; electrical measurements; instrumentation; thermal and electrical properties of matter; oceanographic measurements. *Mailing Add:* Div of Physics Nat Res Coun of Can Ottawa ON K1A 0R6 Can

DAUPLAISE, DAVID LOUIS, organic chemistry, see previous edition

D'AURIA, JOHN MICHAEL, b New York, NY, Mar 28, 39; m 66; c 2. NUCLEAR CHEMISTRY, TRACE ELEMENT ANALYSIS. *Educ:* Rensselaer Polytech Inst, BS, 61; Yale Univ, MS, 62, PhD(nuclear chem), 66. *Prof Exp:* Res asst chem, Columbia Univ, 66-68; asst prof, 68-72, assoc prof, 72-81, PROF CHEM, SIMON FRASER UNIV, 81- *Concurrent Pos:* Assoc, Cent Europ Orgn Nuclear Res, 75-76. *Mem:* Am Phys Soc; Spectros Soc Can; Can Asn Univ Teachers; Sigma Xi; Chem Inst Can. *Res:* Nuclear spectroscopy; gas jet systems; x-ray fluorescence and trace elements; high energy nuclear reactions. *Mailing Add:* Dept of Chem Simon Fraser Univ Burnaby BC V5A 1S6 Can

DAUTERMAN, WALTER CARL, b Closter, NJ, June 10, 32; m 63; c 2. INSECT TOXICOLOGY, BIOCHEMISTRY. *Educ:* Rutgers Univ, BS, 54, MS, 57; Univ Wis, PhD(entom), 59. *Prof Exp:* Fulbright res fel, Netherlands, 59-60; res assoc, Cornell Univ, 60-62; from asst prof to assoc prof, 62-72, PROF ENTOM, NC STATE UNIV, 72- *Concurrent Pos:* Sabbatical study leave, Ciba-Geigy, Basel, Switz, 72-73. *Mem:* AAAS; Am Chem Soc; Entom Soc Am; Soc Toxicol. *Res:* Mode of action and the selectivity of organophosphorus insecticides. *Mailing Add:* 1519 Gardner Hall NC State Univ Raleigh NC 27650

DAUTLICK, JOSEPH X, b Pittsburgh, Pa, Dec 3, 42; m 66; c 2. CLINICAL BIOCHEMISTRY. *Educ:* Lafayette Col, BS, 64; Bowman Gray Sch Med, MS, 68; Univ Pittsburgh, PhD(biochem), 73. *Prof Exp:* Chief clin chem lab, US Army, Ft Sam Houston, Tex, 68-70; biochemist, 73-75, tech serv supvr, 76-77, tech mgr, Europe, 78-81, WORLDWIDE TECH SERV MGR, AUTOMATIC CLIN ANAL DIV, E I DU PONT DE NEMOURS & CO, INC, 81- *Concurrent Pos:* Mem subcomt assay conditions, Nat Comt Clin Lab Standards, 75-77; corresp ed, J Automated Chem, 80- *Mem:* Am Asn Clin Chem; Am Chem Soc. *Res:* Method development and expanded applications for Du Pont automatic clinical analysis relative to clinical chemistry testing of human body fluids. *Mailing Add:* 35 Decker Dr Newark DE 19711

DAUWALDER, MARIANNE, b Long Beach, Calif, Aug 5, 35; m 62; c 5. CELL BIOLOGY. *Educ:* Occidental Col, BA, 56; Univ Tex, PhD(biol, cytol), 64. *Prof Exp:* Res asst zool, Univ Calif, Los Angeles, 59; RES SCIENTIST ASSOC, CELL RES INST, UNIV TEX, AUSTIN, 63- *Mem:* Am Soc Cell

Biol. *Res:* Cellular differentiation; role of the nucleolus in embryonic development; differential activities of the Golgi apparatus in enzymatic and ultrastructural secretion in developing systems. *Mailing Add:* Dept Bot Univ of Tex Austin TX 78712

DAVANZO, JOHN PAUL, b Seattle, Wash, Jan 14, 27; m 50; c 5. BIOLOGY. *Educ:* Univ Wash, BSc, 49 & 51; Univ NMex, MSc, 55, PhD, 57. *Prof Exp:* Supvr exp surg lab, Sch Med, Univ Wash, 49-51; res assoc & East NJ Heart Asn fel, Princeton Univ, 57-59; mem res div, Upjohn Co, 59-62; head biochem pharmacol, A H Robins Co, 62-68; dir pharmacol, Ortho Res Found, 68-72, exec dir res basic sci, 72-74; vpres res & develop, Purdue Frederick Co, 74-76; PROF PHARMACOL, SCH MED, EAST CAROLINA UNIV, 76- *Concurrent Pos:* Lectr, Med Col, 62-, res assoc, 64-; vis asst prof obstet & gynec, Univ Kans Med Ctr, 74- *Mem:* Am Soc Pharmacol & Exp Therapeut; Am Physiol Soc; Soc Exp Biol & Med; Soc Toxicol; Endocrine Soc. *Res:* Neurochemistry, especially the effects of drugs on the central nervous system. *Mailing Add:* 101 Wesley Dr Greenville NC 27834

DAVAR, K(ERSI) S, b Bombay, India, Oct 3, 23; m 50; c 3. CIVIL ENGINEERING, HYDROLOGY. *Educ:* Univ Poona, India, BE, 46; Colo State Univ, MIE, 57, PhD(civil eng), 61. *Prof Exp:* Asst engr, Damodar Valley Corp, India, 50-55; asst prof hydrol & fluid mech, Univ NB, 61-65; assoc prof, Tex Tech Col, 65-66; assoc prof, 66-68, PROF CIVIL ENG, UNIV NB, 68- *Concurrent Pos:* Mem, Can Nat Comt for Int Hydrol Decade, 66-; mem adv comt, Can Ctr Inland Waters, 69- *Mem:* Int Asn Hydraul Res; Am Soc Civil Engrs; Am Water Resources Asn. *Res:* Hydrology, watershed response, snow hydrology, soil moisture; water resources systems, optimization of multipurpose river systems; hydraulics, dispersive processes in streams and channels, resistance to flow in unsymmetrical channels. *Mailing Add:* Dept of Civil Eng Univ of NB Fredericton NB E3B 5A3 Can

DAVE, BHALCHANDRA A, b Palanpur, India, Dec 10, 31; US citizen; m 65; c 2. MICROBIOLOGY, FOOD SCIENCE. *Educ:* St Xavier's Col, India, BSc, 55, MSc, 58; Univ Calif, Davis, MS, 62, PhD(microbiol), 68. *Prof Exp:* Demonstr, St Xavier's Col, India, 55-58; res asst food sci, Univ Calif, Davis, 59-65, res microbiologist, 66-70; res food scientist, Decco Div, 70-78, SUPVR, RES OPERS, PENNWALT CORP, 78- *Mem:* Inst Food Technologists; Am Soc Microbiol. *Res:* Food microbiology; pectic enzymes; storage of fresh fruits and vegetables; post-harvest pesticide screening, formulation and their Environmental Protection Agency registration; food industry sanitation. *Mailing Add:* Decco Div Pennwalt Corp PO Box 120 1713 S California Ave Monrovia CA 91016

DAVENPORT, ALAN GARNETT, b Madras, India, Sept 19, 32; Can citizen; m 57; c 4. STRUCTURAL ENGINEERING, AERODYNAMICS. *Educ:* Cambridge Univ, BA, 54, MA, 58; Univ Toronto, MASc, 57; Bristol Univ, PhD(eng), 61. *Hon Degrees:* DSc, Univ Lourain. *Prof Exp:* Lectr eng, Univ Toronto, 54-57; asst, Nat Res Coun Can, 57-58; asst, Bristol Univ, 58-61; assoc prof, 61-66, PROF ENG, UNIV WESTERN ONT, 66- *Concurrent Pos:* Consult design, World Trade Ctr, New York, 64-65; mem, Am Soc Civil Eng-Int Asn Bridge & Struct Engrs Joint Comt on Tall Bldgs. *Honors & Awards:* Duggan Prize, Eng Inst Can, 62, Gzowski Medal, 63; Alfred Nobel Prize, Am Soc Civil Engrs, 63. *Mem:* Am Soc Civil Engrs; Eng Inst Can; Royal Meteorol Soc; Int Asn Bridge & Struct Engrs; fel Royal Soc Can. *Res:* Meteorology; wind engineering. *Mailing Add:* Fac of Eng Univ of Western Ont London ON N6A 5B8 Can

DAVENPORT, CALVIN ARMSTRONG, b Gloucester, Va, Jan 15, 28; m 63. BACTERIOLOGY, IMMUNOLOGY. *Educ:* Va State Col, BS, 49; Mich State Univ, MS, 50, PhD(microbiol, pub health), 63. *Prof Exp:* Bacteriologist, Div Labs, State Dept Health, Mich, 52-53, 55-57; assoc prof microbiol, Va State Col, 63-69, head dept, 66-69; assoc prof, 69-72, PROF MICROBIOL, CALIF STATE UNIV, FULLERTON, 72- *Concurrent Pos:* Consult, NIH, Dept Health, Educ & Welfare, 73-; mem bd trustees, Orange County/Long Beach Health Consortium, 72-; mem sr comn, Western Asn Schs & Cols, 76-79 & mem accreditation teams, 72-; mem, Calif State Univ, Fullerton Minority Affairs Coun, 81- & coordr, Med Technol Prog, 69-76; consult, Delst Chem Co, 81- & Anaheim Med Labs, 74-79; mem acad planning comt, Health Manpower Proj, Calif Univs & Cols, 74-76; mem coun, Orange County, Calif, Consort, Nursing Educ, 72-73. *Mem:* Am Soc Microbiol; Am Pub Health Asn; Am Inst Biol Sci; Fedn Am Scientists; AAAS. *Res:* Antibiotic sensitivities of Neisseria gonorrhea; serological and physiological studies of microorganisms. *Mailing Add:* Dept of Biol Sci Calif State Univ Fullerton CA 92634

DAVENPORT, DEREK ALFRED, b Leicester, Eng, Sept 23, 27; m 50. INORGANIC CHEMISTRY, CHEMICAL EDUCATION. *Educ:* Univ London, BSc, 47, PhD, 50. *Prof Exp:* Fel, Ohio State Univ, 51-53; from instr to assoc prof, 53-70, PROF CHEM, PURDUE UNIV, WEST LAFAYETTE, 70- *Concurrent Pos:* Vis prof, Univ Wis-Madison. *Honors & Awards:* Chem Educ Award, Am Chem Soc. *Mem:* Am Chem Soc. *Res:* Borderlands between organic and inorganic chemistry; history of chemistry. *Mailing Add:* Dept of Chem Purdue Univ West Lafayette IN 47907

DAVENPORT, FRED M, b Scranton, Pa, Nov 30, 14; m 41; c 3. INTERNAL MEDICINE, EPIDEMIOLOGY. *Educ:* Columbia Univ, BA, 36, MD, 40, ScMedD, 45. *Prof Exp:* Asst instr path, Col Physicians & Surgeons, Columbia Univ, 46-47; res assoc, Sch Pub Health, 49-51, asst prof epidemiol & internal med, 51-52, from assoc prof to prof, 53-76, chmn dept epidemiol, 69-76, EMER PROF EPIDEMIOL & INTERNAL MED, SCH PUB HEALTH & UNIV HOSP, UNIV MICH, ANN ARBOR, 76- *Concurrent Pos:* Nat Res Coun fel, Rockefeller Inst, 47-49; dir comn influenza, Armed Forces Epidemiol Bd, Off Surgeon Gen, 55-71; mem expert adv panel virus dis, WHO, 58-; chmn US viral dis panel, US-Japan Coop Med Sci Prog, Nat Inst Allergy & Infectious Dis, 69-73; hon mem, Robert Koch Inst, Berlin, Ger. *Honors & Awards:* Mem Medal & Badge of Gamaleya, Inst Epidemiol & Microbiol, Acad Med Sci, USSR. *Mem:* Am Acad Microbiol; Am Asn Immunol; Am Epidemiol Soc (vpres, 71); fel Am Pub Health Asn; Am Soc Clin Invest. *Res:* Virus diseases of the respiratory tract. *Mailing Add:* 1006 Sch Pub Health Univ Mich Ann Arbor MI 48104

DAVENPORT, GUY RODMAN, biochemistry, see previous edition

DAVENPORT, HORACE WILLARD, b Philadelphia, Pa, Oct 20, 12; m 45, 69; c 2. PHYSIOLOGY, GASTROENTEROLOGY. *Educ:* Calif Inst Technol, BS, 35, PhD(biochem), 39; Oxford Univ, BA, 37, BSc, 38, DSc(physiol), 61. *Prof Exp:* Instr physiol, Med Sch, Univ Pa, 41-43; instr, Harvard Med Sch, 43-45; prof physiol & head dept, Col Med, Univ Utah, 45-56; prof, 56-78, WILLIAM BEAUMONT PROF PHYSIOL, MED SCH, UNIV MICH, 78-, CHMN DEPT, 56- *Concurrent Pos:* Lilly fel path, Sch Med, Univ Rochester, 39-40; Sterling fel physiol chem, Yale Univ, 40-41; vis prof physiol, Mayo Clin & Mayo Found, 62-63. *Mem:* Nat Acad Sci; Am Physiol Soc (pres, 61-62). *Res:* Physiology and pathophysiology of the stomach. *Mailing Add:* Dept of Physiol Univ of Mich Ann Arbor MI 48109

DAVENPORT, JAMES WHITMAN, b Indianapolis, Ind, July 8, 45; m 68; c 2. SOLID STATE PHYSICS. *Educ:* Brown Univ, ScB, 67; Princeton Univ, ScM, 68; Univ Pa, PhD(physics), 76. *Prof Exp:* Staff, RCA Labs, 68-71; fel surface physics, Univ Pa, 76-77 & Chalmers Univ Technol, 77-78; asst physicist, 78-80, ASSOC PHYSICIST, BROOKHAVEN NAT LAB, 80- *Mem:* Am Phys Soc. *Res:* Surface physics; chemisoption; photoemission from atoms, molecules and solids; interaction of light and matter. *Mailing Add:* Dept Physics Brookhaven Nat Lab Upton NY 11973

DAVENPORT, JOHN EATON, b Los Vegas, Nev, Aug 26, 44; m 66; c 2. PHYSICAL CHEMISTRY, CHEMICAL PHYSICS. *Educ:* Univ Calif, Santa Barbara, BA, 66, MA, 67; York Univ, PhD(chem), 74. *Prof Exp:* Fel, Molecular Physics Ctr, 73-75, PHYS CHEMIST GAS PHASE KINETICS CHEM LAB, SRI INT, 75- *Mem:* AAAS; Am Chem Soc; Am Phys Soc. *Res:* Gas phase kinetics and dynamics of species and processes important in aeronomy and air-pollution studies. *Mailing Add:* SRI Int (PS 256) 333 Ravenswood Ave Menlo Park CA 94025

DAVENPORT, LEE LOSEE, b Schenectady, NY, Dec 31, 15; m 44; c 2. PHYSICS, TELECOMMUNICATIONS. *Educ:* Union Univ, NY, BS, 37; Univ Pittsburgh, MS, 40, PhD(physics), 46. *Prof Exp:* Res assoc radar, Mass Inst Tech, 41-46; res fel construct cyclotron, Harvard Univ, 46-50; exec vpres, Perkin-Elmer Corp, 50-57; pres, Sylvania Corning Nuclear Corp, 57-60, vpres planning, Sylvania Elec Prod, Inc, 60-62, pres, GTE Labs, Inc, 62-77, V PRES-CHIEF SCIENTIST, GTE CORP, 77- *Concurrent Pos:* Asst dir electronics res lab, Univ Pittsburgh, 46. *Mem:* Nat Acad Eng; fel Am Phys Soc; Sci Res Soc Am; Inst Elec & Electronics Eng; AAAS. *Res:* Research spectroscopy; nuclear physics; microwave radar; particle accelerators; guided missile control system. *Mailing Add:* GTE Corp One Stamford Forum Stamford CT 06904

DAVENPORT, LESLIE BRYAN, JR, b Abingdon, Va, July 10, 28; m 52; c 3. VERTEBRATE ZOOLOGY, ECOLOGY. *Educ:* Col Charleston, BS, 47; Va Polytech Inst, MS, 51; Univ Ga, PhD(zool), 60. *Prof Exp:* Teacher, Porter Mil Acad, SC, 47-49; PROF BIOL & HEAD DEPT, ARMSTRONG STATE COL, 59- *Concurrent Pos:* Wormsloe Found grant ecol res, 64-76. *Mem:* Ecol Soc Am; Am Soc Mammal; Am Ornith Union; Wildlife Soc. *Res:* Dynamics and energy relationships of populations of mammals and birds. *Mailing Add:* Dept Biol Armstrong State Col Savannah GA 31406

DAVENPORT, NANCY JO, cardiovascular physiology, nursing, see previous edition

DAVENPORT, THOMAS LEE, b Bowie, Tex, Oct 16, 47; m 72; c 2. PLANT PHYSIOLOGY, BIOCHEMISTRY. *Educ:* Trinity Univ, BA, 70; Tex A&M Univ, PhD(plant physiol), 75. *Prof Exp:* Fel, 75-77, ASST PROF PLANT PHYSIOL, UNIV FLA, 77- *Honors & Awards:* Wilson Popanoe Award, Am Soc Hort Sci, 79. *Mem:* Am Soc Plant Physiologists; Am Soc Hort Sci; Int Plant Growth Substances Asn; Int Soc Citricult. *Res:* Growth and developmental aspects of flower initiation and young fruit abscission in avocado, Tahiti lime, and other tropical fruit. *Mailing Add:* Agr Res & Educ Ctr 18905 SW 280th St Homestead FL 33031

DAVENPORT, TOM FOREST, JR, b Atlanta, Ga, Apr 25, 30; m 54; c 3. ORGANIC CHEMISTRY, PHARMACEUTICAL CHEMISTRY. *Educ:* Ga Inst Technol, BS, 51; Univ Tex, PhD(chem), 57. *Prof Exp:* Res chemist, Am Oil Co, Tex, 56-60; res chemist, 60-66, prod rep, Com Develop Dept, 66-67, prod mgr, 67-70, mkt develop analyst, Com Develop Dept, 70-74, sr com develop chemist, 74-80, COM DEVELOP ASSOC, ETHYL CORP, 80- *Mem:* Am Chem Soc. *Res:* Organometallics; hydrogenation; nitrogen compounds; synthesis; market research and development on specialty chemical products, including pharmaceutical chemicals. *Mailing Add:* Com Develop Dept Ethyl Corp Baton Rouge LA 70801

DAVENPORT, WILBUR B(AYLEY), JR, b Philadelphia, Pa, July 27, 20; m 45; c 2. COMMUNICATIONS, ELECTRICAL ENGINEERING. *Educ:* Ala Polytech Inst, BEE, 41; Mass Inst Technol, MS, 43, ScD(elec eng), 50. *Prof Exp:* Asst elec eng, Mass Inst Technol, 41-43, instr, Radar Sch, 43, instr, Elec Eng Dept, 46-49, asst prof, 49-53, group leader, Commun Tech Group, Lincoln Lab, 51-55, assoc div head, Commun & Components Div, 55-57, div head, 57-58, head, Info Processing Div, 58-60, prof elec eng, 60-78, asst dir lab, 63-65, assoc head, Dept Elec Eng, 71-72, dir, Ctr Advan Eng Study, 72-74, head, Dept Elec Eng & Comput Sci, 74-78, PROF COMMUN SCI & ENG, MASS INST TECHNOL, 78- *Concurrent Pos:* Vis asst prof, Univ Calif, 50; mem, Carnegie Comn Future of Pub Broadcasting, 77-79. *Honors & Awards:* Pioneer Award, Inst Elec & Electronics Eng, Aerospace & Electronic Systs Soc, 81. *Mem:* Nat Acad Eng; fel AAAS; fel Inst Elec & Electronics Engrs; fel Am Acad Arts & Sci. *Res:* Communications system theory and practice; data networks; satellite communications; communications policy. *Mailing Add:* 325 College Rd Concord MA 01742

DAVENPORT, WILLIAM DANIEL, JR, b Corinth, Miss, Apr 19, 47. ANATOMY. *Educ:* Univ Miss, BS, 69, MS, 71; Registry Med Technologists, cert, 68; Med Col Ga, PhD(anat), 76. *Prof Exp:* Med technologist hematol, Magnolia Hosp, 66-69 & Oxford-Lafayette County Hosp, 69-70; instr zool, Ark State Univ, 71-72; instr, 75-77, ASST PROF ANAT, MED CTR, UNIV

MISS, 77- *Concurrent Pos:* Mem anat sci test construct comt, Coun Nat Bd Exam Am Dent Asn, 78- *Mem:* Am Soc Med Technologists; Int Asn Biol Standardization; Electron Microscopy Soc Am. *Res:* Histology; histochemistry; electron microscopy. *Mailing Add:* Dept of Anat Univ of Miss Med Ctr Jackson MS 39216

DAVERMAN, ROBERT JAY, b Grand Rapids, Mich, Sept 28, 41; m 61; c 2. TOPOLOGY. *Educ:* Calvin Col, AB, 63; Univ Wis-Madison, MA, 65, PhD(math), 67. *Prof Exp:* From asst prof to assoc prof, 67-76, PROF MATH, UNIV TENN, KNOXVILLE, 76- *Concurrent Pos:* Vis assoc prof math, Univ Utah, 73-74; vis prof math, Fla State Univ, 81. *Mem:* Am Math Soc. *Res:* Topology of Euclidean space and of manifolds; flatness and wildness of embeddings; decompositions of manifolds. *Mailing Add:* Dept Math Univ Tenn Knoxville TN 37916

DAVERN, CEDRIC I, b Hobart, Tasmania, Nov 13, 31; m 63; c 3. MOLECULAR GENETICS. *Educ:* Univ Sydney, BSAgr, 53, MSAgr, 56; Calif Inst Technol, PhD(biol), 59. *Prof Exp:* From res officer to sr res offiecer genetics, Commonwealth Sci & Indust Res Orgn, Australia, 54-59; res assoc molecular biol, Lab Quant Biol, Cold Spring Harbor, NY, 64-65, asst dir, 65-67; assoc prof biol, Univ Calif, Santa Cruz, 67-69, exec officer, Div Natural Sci, 74-75, prof biol, 69-76, dean, Col Med, 76-77, PROF GENETICS, UNIV UTAH, 76-, VPRES ACADEMIC AFFAIRS, 77- *Concurrent Pos:* Eccles vis prof microbiol, Sch Med, Univ Utah, 75-76. *Res:* Molecular mechanisms of DNA replication and its regulation. *Mailing Add:* Park Bldg Univ of Utah Salt Lake City UT 84112

DAVES, GLENN DOYLE, JR, b Clayton, NMex, Feb 12, 36; m 59; c 3. ORGANIC CHEMISTRY, BIO-ORGANIC CHEMISTRY. *Educ:* Ariz State Univ, BS, 59; Mass Inst Technol, PhD(org chem), 64. *Prof Exp:* Res chemist org chem, Midwest Res Inst, Mo, 59-61; res assoc bio-org chem, Stanford Res Inst, Calif, 64-67; from asst prof to prof bio-org & org chem, Ore Grad Ctr, 67-81, chmn dept, 72-79; PROF & CHMN, CHEM DEPT, LEHIGH UNIV, 81- *Concurrent Pos:* Affil mem, Dept Biochem, Med Sch, Univ Ore, 72-81. *Mem:* AAAS; Am Chem Soc; Am Soc Mass Spectrometry; Int Soc Heterocyclic Chem. *Res:* Isolation, structure elucidation and synthesis of natural products or other compounds having substantial biological importance; applications of nuclear magnetic resonance and mass spectrometry. *Mailing Add:* Dept of Chem Lehigh Univ Bethlehem PA 18015

DAVES, MARVIN LEWIS, b Lexington, Va, Jan 26, 28; div; c 3. RADIOLOGY. *Educ:* Washington & Lee Univ, BA, 48; Johns Hopkins Univ, MD, 53. *Prof Exp:* Asst radiologist, Clin Ctr, NIH, 57-59; asst prof radiol & actg head dept, Med Ctr, Univ Ark, 59-60; asst prof, 60-62, actg chmn dept, 61-62, chmn dept, 62-77, PROF RADIOL, MED CTR, UNIV COLO, DENVER, 62- *Mem:* Fel Am Col Radiol; Radiol Soc NAm. *Res:* Cardiology; bone dysplasia. *Mailing Add:* Dept of Radiol Univ of Colo Med Ctr Denver CO 80262

DAVEY, CHARLES BINGHAM, b Brooklyn, NY, Apr 7, 28; m 52; c 3. SOIL MICROBIOLOGY. *Educ:* NY State Col Forestry, Syracuse Univ, BS, 50; Univ Wis, MS, 52, PhD(soils), 55. *Prof Exp:* Soil scientist, Agr Res Serv, USDA, 57-62; assoc prof, 62-65, prof soil sci, 65-78, head dept forestry, 70-78, CARL ALWIN SCHENCK PROF FORESTRY, 78- Fel AAAS: fel Am Soc Agron; fel Soil Sci Soc Am (pres, 75-76); Soc Am Foresters; Int Soil Sci Soc. *Res:* Water structure and its relation to biological systems; microbial ecology in soil and rhizosphere; Mycorrhizae; tree nutrition. *Mailing Add:* Dept of Forestry NC State Univ Raleigh NC 27650

DAVEY, FREDERICK K(NOWLES), ceramics, see previous edition

DAVEY, GERALD LELAND, b Salt Lake City, Utah, Apr 9, 30; m 54; c 4. APPLIED MATHEMATICS, SYSTEMS ANALYSIS. *Educ:* Stanford Univ, MS, 54, PhD(math), 59. *Prof Exp:* Employee, Hughes Aircraft Co, Calif, 59-61; consult, Systs Anal Consult, 61; dir bus info systs div, Hughes Dynamics, Inc, 62-65; vpres, Credit Data Corp, Calif & NY, 65-68, pres, NY, 68-70; sr vpres, TRW Info Serv, Inc, 70; pres, Medlab Comput Serv, Inc, 70-73; PRES, DMB FIN SERV, INC & GERALD L DAVEY & ASSOCS, 74-; PRES, SIERRA PROPERTIES CORP, NORTH SAN JUAN, CALIF, 78- *Concurrent Pos:* Instr math, Exten Div, Univ Calif, Los Angeles, 60-65; consult, TRW Info Serv, Inc, 70-72; mem, State Adv Coun Sci & Technol, Utah, 77-80. *Mem:* NY Acad Sci; AAAS; Soc Indust & Appl Math; Math Asn Am; Soc Mining Engrs. *Res:* Systems analysis in placer-mining techniques. *Mailing Add:* 11601 Marjon Dr Nevada City CA 95959

DAVEY, JOHN EDMUND, b Buffalo, NY, July 15, 25; m 50; c 2. PHYSICS. *Educ:* Canisius Col, BS, 49; Univ Notre Dame, MS, 51, PhD(physics), 54. *Prof Exp:* Res physicist, Electron Tubes Br, 54-59, res physicist & sect head, Solid State Electronics Br, 59-69, HEAD SOLID STATE TECHNOL BR, US NAVAL RES LAB, 69- *Mem:* Am Phys Soc; Am Vacuum Soc; sr mem Inst Elec & Electronics Engrs. *Res:* Thermionic, photoelectric and Schottky emission from bulk metals, semiconductors and thin films; structural, electrical and optical properties of thin semiconducting and metal films; x-ray and electron diffration; electron microscopy; high vacuum techniques. *Mailing Add:* Solid State Devices Br Naval Res Lab Washington DC 20390

DAVEY, KENNETH GEORGE, b Chatham, Ont, Apr 20, 32; m 59; c 3. INVERTEBRATE PHYSIOLOGY, PARASITOLOGY. *Educ:* Univ Western Ont, BSc, 54, MS, 55; Cambridge Univ, PhD(zool), 58. *Prof Exp:* Nat Res Coun Can fel, Univ Toronto, 58-59; Drosier fel entom, Gonville & Caius Col, Cambridge Univ, 59-63; assoc prof parasitol, Macdonald Col, McGill Univ, 63-64, dir inst parasitol, 64-67, prof parasitol, 67-74; prof biol & chmn dept, 74-81, DEAN FAC SCI, YORK UNIV, 82- *Concurrent Pos:* Assoc ed, Can J Zool, 70- & Int J Invertebrate Reproduction, 78- *Mem:* Nat Acad Sci (secy, 80-, vpres, 79-81, pres, 81-82); Can Soc Zool; fel Entom Soc Can; Sigma Xi; fel Royal Soc Can. *Res:* Reproduction in arthropods; physiology of insect visceral muscles; neurosecretion in invertebrates; physiology of helminths. *Mailing Add:* Dept of Biol York Univ Downsview ON M3J 1P3 Can

DAVEY, PAUL OLIVER, b West Monroe, La, Apr 5, 31; m 55. PHYSICS. *Educ:* La Polytech Inst, BS, 51; Iowa State Univ, MS, 54; Univ Nebr, PhD(physics), 64. *Prof Exp:* Jr physicist, Ames Lab, AEC, 54-55; asst prof math & physics, Univ Nev, 58-61; assoc prof, 64-74, PROF PHYSICS, STATE UNIV NY COL FREDONIA, 74- *Mem:* Am Phys Soc; Am Inst Physics; Am Asn Physics Teachers. *Res:* Theoretical description of light nuclei; theory of the photodisintegration of light nuclei; theoretical physics. *Mailing Add:* Dept of Physics State Univ of NY Col Fredonia NY 14063

DAVEY, TREVOR B(LAKELY), b Winnipeg, Man, Nov 27, 31; US citizen; m 75; c 4. MECHANICAL & BIOMEDICAL ENGINEERING. *Educ:* Univ Man, BSc, 53; McGill Univ, ME, 57. *Prof Exp:* Engr, Can Gen Elec Co, 53-55; sessional lectr, McGill Univ, 55-57; develop engr, Atomic Energy Can, 57; CHMN DEPT MECH ENG, CALIF STATE UNIV SACRAMENTO, 57-, PROF, 67- *Concurrent Pos:* Consult, Aerojet Gen Corp, 57-64; co-dir, Bioeng Sect, Cardiopulmonary Dept, Sutter Hosps Med Res Found, 63-72, dir, 72-; NSF fac fel, 74-77. *Mem:* Am Soc Mech Engrs; Asn Advan Med Instrumentation. *Res:* Characteristics of fluid flow through prosthetic heart valves; design of heart assists. *Mailing Add:* Dept Mech Eng Calif State Univ 6000 J St Sacramento CA 95819

DAVEY, WILLIAM GEORGE, physics, nuclear physics, see previous edition

DAVEY, WILLIAM ROBERT, b Evanston, Ill, June 8, 43; c 4. ASTROPHYSICS, COMPUTATIONAL PHYSICS. *Educ:* Iowa State Univ, BS, 66; Univ Colo, PhD(astrophys), 70. *Prof Exp:* Fel astrophys, Univ Waterloo, Can, 70-72; sr tutor physics, Univ Queensland, Australia, 72-74; vis asst prof astrophys, Univ NMex, 74-75; MEM TECH STAFF COMPUT PHYSICS, SANDIA LABS, 75- *Concurrent Pos:* Consult astrophys, Los Alamos Sci Lab, 74-75. *Res:* Stability analysis of models for variable stars; nonlinear hydrodynamics of stellar pulsation; periodic solutions of nonlinear partial differential equations; radiation transport; crater formation and ground shock from nuclear explosions. *Mailing Add:* 809 Hermosa Ave Albuquerque NM 87110

DAVEY, WINTHROP NEWBURY, b Jackson, Mich, May 19, 18; m 49; c 3. INTERNAL MEDICINE. *Educ:* Univ Mich, AB, 39, MD, 42. *Prof Exp:* From intern to resident, Hosp, Univ Mich, 44-50, from instr to prof internal med, Sch Med, 44-72, dir med tuberc unit, Hosp, 47-71; assoc dir univ affairs, Training Prog, 71-74, DIR, BUR TRAINING, CTR DIS CONTROL, USPHS, 74- *Concurrent Pos:* Consult tuberc prog, Ctr Dis Control, USPHS, 60-71, mem, Nat Adv Tuberc Control Comt, 61-68, Nat Adv Commun Dis Coun, 68-69 & Nat Adv Heart & Lung Coun, 70-71. *Mem:* Am Col Physicians; Am Pub Health Asn; Asn Am Med Cols; Am Col Chest Physicians; Am Thoracic Soc (pres, 65-66). *Res:* Tuberculosis; pulmonary disease. *Mailing Add:* Bur of Training Ctr for Dis Control Atlanta GA 30333

DAVICH, THEODORE BERT, b McKeenlyville, WVa, Jan 3, 23; m 45; c 2. ECONOMIC ENTOMOLOGY. *Educ:* Ohio State Univ, BSc, 48; Univ Wis, MS, 50, PhD(entom), 53. *Prof Exp:* Asst entom, Univ Wis, 50-53; assoc entomologist, Va Agr Exp Sta, 53-56; entomologist & head lab, Tex Cotton Insects Lab, Agr Res Serv, 56-60, DIR, BOLL WEEVIL RES LAB, SCI & EDUC ADMIN, AGR RES, USDA, 60- *Mem:* Entom Soc Am. *Res:* Insects affecting cotton. *Mailing Add:* Boll Weevil Res Lab Box 5367 Mississippi State MS 39762

DAVID, CARL WOLFGANG, b Hamburg, Ger, June 30, 37; US citizen. PHYSICAL CHEMISTRY. *Educ:* Case Inst Technol, BS, 58; Univ Mich, MS, 60, PhD(chem), 62. *Prof Exp:* Res fel chem, Yale Univ, 62-63; from asst prof to assoc prof chem, 63-74, PROF PHYS CHEM, UNIV CONN, 74- *Mem:* Am Chem Soc. *Res:* Statistical thermodynamics of liquids and liquid mixtures. *Mailing Add:* Dept of Chem Univ of Conn Storrs CT 06268

DAVID, CHELLADURAI S, b Coonoor, India, June 18, 36; US citizen; m 61; c 2. IMMUNOGENETICS. *Educ:* Berea Col, BS, 61; Univ Ky, MS, 62; Iowa State Univ, PhD(immunogenetics), 66. *Prof Exp:* Res assoc immunogenetics, Iowa State Univ, 66-68; res assoc immunogenetics, 68-73, asst res scientist, Med Sch, Univ Mich, Ann Arbor, 73-75; assoc prof genetics, Med Sch, Wash Univ, St Louis, Mo, 75-77; PROF IMMUNOL, MAYO MED SCH, ROCHESTER, 77-; PROF MICROBIOL, MED SCH, UNIV MINN, MINNEAPOLIS, 78- *Mem:* Transplantation Soc; AAAS; Am Asn Immunol; Genetics Soc Am. *Res:* Immunoglobulin allotypes in fowl; mouse immune response genes; mouse histocompatibility system. *Mailing Add:* 311 Guggenheim Bldg Mayo Clin Rochester MN 55901

DAVID, DONALD J, b St Louis, Mo, June 25, 30; m 52; c 1. POLYMERS. *Educ:* St Marys Univ, BS, 52; Univ Dayton, MS, 77, MS, 79, PhD(mat eng), 81. *Prof Exp:* Res group leader & chief chem, Mobay Chem Co, 59-67; mgr res, Tracor, 67-72; sr res group leader & contract mgr, Monsanto Res Corp, Dayton Lab, 72-79, sr res specialist metall, Mound Lab, 77-79, SR RES GROUP LEADER, MONSANTO PLASTICS & RESINS CO, 79- *Concurrent Pos:* Lectr, Thermal Anal Inst, 65-66, Univ Mo, 69. *Mem:* Am Chem Soc; North Am Thermal Anal Soc; Am Soc Metals; AAAS. *Res:* Polymer fundamentals and characterization; analytical characterization techniques; surface chemistry, instrumentation; mathematical modeling and gas chromstography; polymer analytical chemistry and chromatographic instrumentation. *Mailing Add:* Monsanto Plastics & Resins Co 190 Grochmal Indian Orchard MA 01151

DAVID, EDWARD E(MIL), JR, b Wilmington, NC, Jan 25, 25; m 50; c 1. ELECTRICAL ENGINEERING. *Educ:* Ga Inst Technol, BEE, 45; Mass Inst Technol, SM & ScD(elec eng), 50. *Hon Degrees:* DEng, Stevens Inst Technol, 71, Polytech Inst Brooklyn, 71, Univ Mich, 71, Carnegie-Mellon Univ, 72, Lehigh Univ, 73, Univ Ill, Chicago Circle, 73 & Rose-Hulman Inst Technol, 78. *Prof Exp:* Asst, Electronics Res Lab, Mass Inst Technol, 46-50; mem, Hartwell Proj, 50; mem tech staff, Bell Tel Labs, 50-70, exec dir res, 65-70; sci adv to the pres & dir off sci & technol, US Govt, 70-73; exec vpres,

Gould Inc, Ill, 73-77, consult, Ill, 77; PRES, EXXON RES & ENG CO, NJ, 77- *Concurrent Pos:* Chmn bd trustees, Aerospace Corp, Calif, 75-81; mem bd dirs, Mat Res Corp, NY; mem, Exec Comt & Corp & Energy Lab Adv Bd, Mass Inst Technol; mem vis comt, Div Phys Sci, Univ Chicago, mem, Adv Coun Humanities Inst; mem, Marshall Scholarships Adv Coun; mem adv bd, Dept Elec Eng, Univ Calif; mem bd trustees, Carnegie Inst Wash; mem bd, Overseers Fac Arts & Sci, Univ Pa; US rep, Sci Comt, NATO; mem adv resource coun, Princeton Univ. *Honors & Awards:* Anak Award, 58. *Mem:* Nat Acad Sci; Nat Acad Eng; fel AAAS; fel Inst Elec & Electronics Engrs; fel Acoust Soc Am. *Mailing Add:* Exxon Res & Eng Co PO Box 101 Florham Park NJ 07932

DAVID, FLORENCE N, b Hereford, UK, Aug 23, 09. STATISTICS, MATHEMATICS. *Educ:* Univ London, BSc, 31, PhD(statist), 38, DSc(statist), 50. *Prof Exp:* From lectr to prof statist, Univ Col, Univ London, 35-67; prof statist, Univ Calif, Berkeley, 61-62, 64-65; prof statist, Univ Calif, Riverside, 67-75, chmn dept, 68-77; BIOSTATISTICIAN, UNIV CALIF, BERKELEY, 77- *Concurrent Pos:* Sr statistician, Ministry of Home Security, UK, 39-45; consult, US Forest Serv, 63- & Pac State Hosp, Pomona, Calif, 65-; ed, Biometrics, 72-77. *Mem:* Fel Am Statist Soc; fel Inst Math Statist; fel Royal Statist Soc; Int Statist Inst. *Res:* Combinatorial and randomization methods; statistical applications. *Mailing Add:* Dept of Statist Univ of Calif Berkeley CA 94720

DAVID, GARY SAMUEL, b Aurora, Ill, Oct 2, 42; m 69. IMMUNOCHEMISTRY, IMMUNODIAGNOSTICS. *Educ:* Univ Ill, Urbana, BS, 64, PhD(microbiol), 68. *Prof Exp:* US Dept Health, Educ & Welfare fel immunol, City of Hope Med Ctr, 68-70; res assoc, Salk Inst Biol Studies, 70-71; fel, Scripps Clin & Res Found, 71-74, res assoc exp path, 74-77; asst dir, Larson Diagnostics, 78; dir, The Second Antibody, 78-81; sr res scientist, 78-81, PRIN SCIENTIST, HYBRITECH, INC, 81- *Concurrent Pos:* Adv ed, Immunochem, 75-78; adj asst prof, Univ Calif, San Diego, 75-78. *Mem:* Tissue Cult Soc; Clin Ligand Assay Soc; Am Asn Immunologists; Parenteral Drug Asn. *Res:* Immunogenetics; protein chemistry; radioimmunoassay; cellular and developmental immunology; tumor immunology; immunotherapy. *Mailing Add:* Hybritech Inc 11085 Torreyana Rd San Diego CA 92121

DAVID, HERBERT ARON, b Ger, Dec 19, 25; US citizen; m 50; c 1. MATHEMATICAL STATISTICS. *Educ:* Univ Sydney, BSc, 47; Univ London, PhD(statist), 53. *Prof Exp:* Sr lectr statist, Univ Melbourne, 55-57; prof, Va Polytech Inst & State Univ, 57-64; prof, Sch Pub Health, Univ NC, 64-72; DIR & HEAD, STATISTICAL LAB, DEPT STATIST, IOWA STATE UNIV, 72-, DISTINGUISHED PROF, 80- *Concurrent Pos:* Ed, Biometrics, 67-72. *Mem:* Fel Am Statist Asn; fel Inst Math Statist; Int Statist Inst; Biometric Soc (pres, 82-). *Res:* Order statistics; paired comparisons; inference; design of experiments; competing risks. *Mailing Add:* Dept Statist Iowa State Univ Ames IA 50011

DAVID, ISRAEL A, b Philadelphia, Pa, Oct 25, 25; m 51; c 2. ORGANIC POLYMER CHEMISTRY. *Educ:* Univ Pa, BS, 48; Univ Wis, PhD(org chem), 55. *Prof Exp:* From res chemist to sr res chemist, 54-64, res assoc, 65-77, RES CHEMIST, CENT RES & DEVELOP DEPT, E I DU PONT DE NEMOURS & CO, INC, 77- *Mem:* Am Chem Soc. *Res:* Synthesis and modification of polymers. *Mailing Add:* Cent Res & Develop Dept E I du Pont de Nemours & Co Inc Wilmington DE 19898

DAVID, JEAN, b Montreal, Que, Dec 19, 21; m 51; c 3. BIOCHEMISTRY, FOOD TECHNOLOGY. *Educ:* Univ Montreal, LSA, 40; Univ Calif, PhD(biochem), 49. *Prof Exp:* Exten specialist hort, Que Dept Agr, 41-44, food technologist, 49-63; from asst prof to assoc prof, 49-74, registr, 69-79, PROF HORT, MACDONALD COL, MCGILL UNIV, 74-, ASSOC DEAN, FAC AGR, 72- *Res:* Food preservation; cold storage; canning and freezing; physiological and biochemical changes in fruits and vegetables after harvest and during storage. *Mailing Add:* Macdonald Col of McGill Univ Ste Anne de Bellevue Montreal PQ H9X 1C0 Can

DAVID, JOHN R, b Eng, Feb 15, 30; US citizen; m 57; c 2. INTERNAL MEDICINE, IMMUNOLOGY. *Educ:* Univ Chicago, BA, 51, BS & MD, 55. *Prof Exp:* From intern to asst resident, Mass Gen Hosp, 55-57; clin assoc, Nat Inst Arthritis & Metab Dis, 57-59; trainee, Rheumatism Res Unit, Eng, 59-60; resident med, Mass Gen Hosp, 60-61; asst prof med, NY Univ, 64-66; asst prof, 66-69, assoc prof, 69-73, PROF MED, HARVARD MED SCH, 73- *Concurrent Pos:* Univ fel, Sch Med, NY Univ, 61-64. *Mem:* Am Asn Immunol; Am Fedn Clin Res. *Res:* Mechanisms of delayed hypersensitivity and cellular immunity; rheumatology. *Mailing Add:* Robert B Brigham Hosp Harvard Med Sch Boston MA 02115

DAVID, KARL HERBERT, b Salzgitter, Ger, Dec 15, 47; US citizen. ERGODIC THEORY. *Educ:* Univ Richmond, BA, 69; Univ Mass, MA, 74, PhD(math), 78. *Prof Exp:* Asst prof, Union Col, 78-80; ASST PROF MATH, MIDDLEBURY COL, 80- *Mem:* Am Math Soc. *Res:* Full groups and stopping times for measure-preserving transformations. *Mailing Add:* Dept Math Middlebury Col Middlebury VT 05753

DAVID, LARRY GENE, b Searcy, Ark, Apr 11, 38; m 64; c 2. INDUSTRIAL ENGINEERING. *Educ:* Univ Ark, BS, 61, MS, 62; Purdue Univ, PhD(indust eng), 68. *Prof Exp:* Instr, Physics Lab, Univ Ark, 58-60, instr comput prog, 60-61; instr indust eng, Univ Mo-Columbia, 61-64 & Purdue Univ, 67-68; ASSOC PROF INDUST ENG, UNIV MO-COLUMBIA, 68- *Mem:* Am Inst Indust Engrs. *Res:* Manufacturing processes; electric discharge machining; regional blood inventory system; computerized instructional system for classroom supplement. *Mailing Add:* RR 1 Columbia MO 65201

DAVID, PETER P, b Szeged, Hungary, June 9, 32; m 61; c 4. QUATERNARY GEOLOGY. *Educ:* Univ Szeged, dipl, 55; McGill Univ, BSc, 59, MSc, 61, PhD(Pleistocene geol), 65. *Prof Exp:* Lectr, 64, asst prof, 64-69, ASSOC PROF GEOL, UNIV MONTREAL, 69- *Mem:* Can Quaternary Asn; Geol Soc Am; Geol Asn Can; Inst Glaciol Soc; Am Quaternary Asn. *Res:* Quaternary stratigraphy; eolian deposits; development, evolution, morphology, structure and stratigraphy of dunes in Canada; migration rates, absolute chronology and environments; morphology, lithology and stratigraphy of glacial deposits in Gaspe, Quebec; glaciation and deglaciation models. *Mailing Add:* Dept of Geol Univ of Montreal PO Box 6128 Montreal PQ H3C 3J7 Can

DAVIDA, GEORGE I, b Baghdad, Iraq, Aug 2, 44; US citizen. CRYPTOLOGY, DATA SECURITY. *Educ:* Univ Iowa, BS, 67, MS, 69, PhD(elec eng), 70. *Prof Exp:* Asst prof theoret sci, Univ Wis, 70-75, assoc prof, 75-78; prog dir, NSF, 78-79; assoc prof comput sci, Univ Wis, 79-80; prof, Ga Inst Technol, 80-81; PROF ELEC ENG & COMPUT SCI, UNIV WIS-MILWAUKEE, 81- *Concurrent Pos:* Prin investr, NSF grants, 72-; mem, Pub Cryptography Study Group, Am Coun Educ, 79-81. *Mem:* Asn Computing Machinery; sr mem Inst Elec & Electronics Engrs. *Res:* Data security; methods for protecting data in data bases, operating systems and computer networks. *Mailing Add:* Dept Elec Eng & Comput Sci Univ Wis Milwaukee WI 53201

DAVIDIAN, NANCY MCCONNELL, b Philadelphia, Pa, Feb 16, 41. BIOCHEMISTRY, DRUG METABOLISM. *Educ:* Cornell Univ, BA, 62; Univ NC, PhD(biochem), 69. *Prof Exp:* Res asst endocrinol, Sterling-Winthrop Inst, 62-63; NIH fel, 68-69; res assoc biochem, Univ NC, 69-71, instr, 71-74, res assoc pharmacol, 74-77; mem staff, Off Grants Assocs, 77-79, ASST SPEC PROGS OFFICER, OFF EXTRAMURAL RES & TRAINING, NIH, 79- *Mem:* Am Chem Soc; Sigma Xi. *Res:* Effects of drugs and radiation on intracellular pH; effects of drugs and metabolic disturbances on pH of brain; drug metabolizing enzymes of tumor-bearing and normal animals. *Mailing Add:* Off Extramural Res & Training Bldg 31/1B47 NIH Bethesda MD 20205

DAVIDOFF, ROBERT ALAN, b Brooklyn, NY, Oct 5, 34; m 67; c 1. NEUROPHYSIOLOGY, NEUROPHARMACOLOGY. *Educ:* NY Univ, BS, 55, MD, 58. *Prof Exp:* From instr to asst prof psychiat, Sch Med, Ind Univ, 65-69, asst prof neurol, 68-69; from assoc prof to assoc prof pharmacol, 69-76, PROF NEUROL, SCH MED, UNIV MIAMI, 69-, PROF PHARMACOL, 76-, VCHMN NEUROL, 77- *Concurrent Pos:* Res assoc, Vet Admin Hosp, Indianapolis, 65-66, clin investr, 66-69. *Mem:* Am Physiol Soc; Am Soc Neurochem; AAAS; Am Neurol Asn; Soc Neurosci. *Res:* Synaptic transmission; amino acid neurotransmitters. *Mailing Add:* Dept of Neurol Univ of Miami Sch of Med Miami FL 33101

DAVIDON, WILLIAM COOPER, b Fla, Mar 18, 27; m 47, 63; c 3. MATHEMATICAL PHYSICS, NUMERICAL ANALYSIS. *Educ:* Univ Chicago, BS, 47, MS, 50, PhD(physics), 54. *Prof Exp:* Electronics engr, Mines Equip Co, 43-44; dir res, Nuclear Instrument & Chem Corp, 48-54; res assoc, Univ Chicago, 54-56; assoc physicist, Argonne Nat Lab, 56-61; from assoc prof to prof physics, 69-81, PROF MATH, HAVERFORD COL, 81- *Concurrent Pos:* Fulbright-Hays res grant physics, Aarhus Univ, 66-67 & Inst Theoretical Physics, Tromdheim, 76-77. *Mem:* Fedn Am (secy, 60-61); Soc Social Responsibility Sci (pres, 65-67); Am Asn Physics Teachers; Soc Indust & Appl Math. *Res:* Foundations of quantum mechanics and special relativity; numerical optimization. *Mailing Add:* Dept Physics Haverford Col Haverford PA 19041

DAVIDOVITS, PAUL, b Moldava, Czech, Nov 1, 35; Can citizen; m 57; c 2. CHEMICAL PHYSICS. *Educ:* Columbia Univ, BS, 60, MS, 61, PhD(appl physics), 64. *Prof Exp:* Staff engr, Radiation Lab, Columbia Univ, 61-64, res physicist & lectr, 64-65; from asst prof to assoc prof eng & appl sci, Yale Univ, 65-74; PROF CHEM, BOSTON COL, 74- *Mem:* Am Phys Soc. *Res:* Quantum electronics; physics of atomic collisions and recombinations; laser physics; chemical lasers. *Mailing Add:* Dept of Chem Boston Col Chestnut Hill MA 02167

DAVIDOW, BERNARD, b New York, NY, Aug 4, 19; m 42; c 3. TOXICOLOGY, CLINICAL BIOCHEMISTRY. *Educ:* Fordham Univ, BS, 42; Georgetown Univ, MS, 48, PhD, 50. *Prof Exp:* Chief acute toxicity br, Pharmacol Div, Food & Drug Admin, 46-56; dir labs, New Drug Inst, 56-61; chief food & drug lab, 61-71, dep dir, Bur Labs, 71-72, DIR BUR LABS, NEW YORK CITY DEPT HEALTH, 72-, ASST COMNR LAB SERV, 72- *Honors & Awards:* Meritorious Award, FDA, 52; Award Merit, Pub Health Asn New York City, 72. *Mem:* AAAS; Soc Toxicol; Am Soc Pharmacol & Exp Therapeut; Am Pub Health Asn; NY Acad Sci. *Res:* Toxicity and analysis of chemicals used in foods, drugs and cosmetics; detection of drugs subject to abuse in body fluids; detection of toxic metals in body fluids and food; detection drug abuse, trace toxic metals. *Mailing Add:* Bur Labs NY Dept Health 455 First Ave New York NY 10016

DAVIDS, CARY NATHAN, b Edmonton, Alta, Sept 28, 40; m 67; c 2. NUCLEAR PHYSICS, ASTROPHYSICS. *Educ:* Univ Alta, BSc, 61, MSc, 62; Calif Inst Technol, PhD(nuclear physics), 67. *Prof Exp:* Res fel physics, Calif Inst Technol, 67; res assoc, Mich State Univ, 67-69; asst prof, Ctr Nuclear Studies, Univ Tex, Austin, 69-74; MEM STAFF, ARGONNE NAT LAB 74- *Concurrent Pos:* NSF grant, 70-75; Welch grant, 72-74; Alfred P Sloan fel, 72-76; vis scholar, Enrico Fermi Inst, Univ Chicago, 74-75, sr res assoc, 76-79. *Mem:* Am Phys Soc. *Res:* On-line laser spectroscopy of radioactive atoms; isotopes far from line of beta-stability, nuclear masses; nuclear spectroscopy. *Mailing Add:* Argonne Nat Lab 203 9700 S Cass Ave Argonne IL 60439

DAVIDSE, GERRIT, b Grijpskerke, Netherlands, Dec 19, 42; US citizen; m 65; c 3. TAXONOMIC BOTANY. *Educ:* Calvin Col, BS, 65; Utah State Univ, MS, 68; Iowa State Univ, PhD(plant taxon), 72. *Prof Exp:* Asst cur, 72-81, ASSOC CUR, MO BOT GARDEN, 81- *Mem:* Am Soc Plant Taxonomists; Bot Soc Am; Int Soc Plant Taxonomists. *Res:* Taxonomy and biosystematics of the Gramineae. *Mailing Add:* Mo Bot Garden 2345 Tower Grove Ave St Louis MO 63110

DAVIDSEN, ARTHUR FALNES, b Freeport, NY, May 26, 44; m 66; c 2. ASTROPHYSICS, X-RAY ASTRONOMY. *Educ:* Princeton Univ, AB, 66; Univ Calif, Berkeley, MA, 72, PhD(astron), 75. *Prof Exp:* Sci liaison officer x-ray astron, Naval Res Lab, 70-71; from asst prof to assoc prof, 75-80, PROF PHYSICS, JOHNS HOPKINS UNIV, 80- *Concurrent Pos:* Prin investr, Ultraviolet Telescope for Space Shuttle, Johns Hopkins Univ, 79-; dir at large, Asn Univs Res Astron, 79-82; mem, NASA Mgt & Opers Working Group Space Astron, 80-; mem, Advan X-ray Astrophysics Facility Sci Working Group; ed, Astrophys Letters, 76- *Honors & Awards:* Helen B Warner Prize, Am Astron Soc, 79. *Mem:* Am Astron Soc; Int Astron Union; Royal Astron Soc. *Res:* Far-ultraviolet spectroscopy of quasars and galaxies; ultraviolet astronomy; galactic and extragalactic x-ray astronomy; rocket and satellite x-ray observations; ground-based optical observations; clusters of galaxies; the intergalactic medium. *Mailing Add:* Dept of Physics Johns Hopkins Univ Baltimore MD 21218

DAVIDSON, ALEXANDER GRANT, b Moncton, NB, Sept 23, 27; m 53; c 2. FOREST PATHOLOGY. *Educ:* Univ NB, BSc, 48; Univ Toronto, MA, 51, PhD(forest path), 55. *Prof Exp:* Res officer, Forest Biol Lab, Univ NB, 48-58; head forest path invests, Atlantic Prov Res Br, Can Dept Agr, 58-62; assoc coordr, 62-65, asst prog coordr, 65-72, dis specialist, 72-80, SCI ADV, FOREST INSECT & DIS SURV, CAN FORESTRY SERV, 80- *Mem:* Can Inst Forestry. *Mailing Add:* Can Forestry Serv Can Dept of Environ Ottawa ON K1A 1G5 Can

DAVIDSON, ARNOLD B, b Philadelphia, Pa, June 5, 30; m 52; c 2. NEUROPSYCHOPHARMACOLOGY. *Educ:* Brooklyn Col, BA, 51, MA, 53; Temple Univ, EdD(psychol), 64. *Prof Exp:* High sch teacher, New York City Bd Educ, 51-53; sr investr, Smith Kline & French Labs, 55-73; ASST DIR PHARMACOL, HOFFMAN-LA ROCHE INC, 73- *Concurrent Pos:* Instr psychol, Peirce Jr Col, Pa, 66-69. *Mem:* AAAS; fel Am Psychol Asn; Am Soc Pharmacol & Exp Therapeut; Behav Pharmacol Soc. *Res:* Interaction of drugs and behavior; psychophysiology; CNS pharmacology. *Mailing Add:* Hoffmann-La Roche Inc Bldg 76 Nutley NJ 07110

DAVIDSON, ARTHUR CAMPBELL, b Calgary, Alta, July 21, 14; m. APPLIED MECHANICS, STRUCTURAL ENGINEERING. *Educ:* Univ Man, BS, 35, BSc, 36; Univ Toronto, MASc, 49. *Prof Exp:* Field engr, Dom Bridge Co, Ltd, 37-38; demonstr eng drawing, Univ Toronto, 38-40; inspector, Can Inspection & Testing Co, 40-41; lectr civil eng, Univ Toronto, 46-53, asst prof, 53-62, assoc prof, 62-80; RETIRED. *Concurrent Pos:* Subway struct designer, Toronto Transp Comn, 50-51, analyst, 60-62; consult, Defense Construct Ltd, 52-53 & Cent Mortgage & Housing Corp, 54-56; ed booklets, Dept Health, Ont, 63. *Mem:* Fel Eng Inst Can; Can Soc Civil Engrs. *Res:* Concrete technology; nonmetallic mine construction and detection; pressure intensity measuring device for soils; improved truck for railway car; column testing fixtures; stress-strain relations and quantum mechanics; programmed learning for undergraduates. *Mailing Add:* 106 Bideford Ave Downsview ON M3H 1K4 Can

DAVIDSON, BETTY, b Brooklyn, NY, Mar 24, 33; m 60; c 2. BIOCHEMISTRY. *Educ:* Brooklyn Col, BS, 53; Univ Chicago, MS, 61, PhD(biochem), 64. *Prof Exp:* Technician biochem, Mt Sinai Hosp, New York, 54-56, State Univ NY Downstate Med Ctr, 56-58 & Med Sch, Northwestern Univ, 58-59; res assoc, Brandeis Univ, 68-70; RESEARCH ASSOC, HARVARD MED SCH, 70- *Concurrent Pos:* Univ fel biochem, Brandeis Univ, 65-68; res fel, Thyroid Res Unit, Mass Gen Hosp, 70-74; asst med, Thyroid Res Unit, Mass Gen Hosp, 74-78. *Mem:* Am Chem Soc; Biophys Soc; Am Soc Biol Chem. *Res:* Mechanism of enzyme action; protein structure and function. *Mailing Add:* 56 Beals St Brookline MA 02146

DAVIDSON, BRUCE LLOYD, b Sioux City, Iowa, Mar 21, 47; m 71; c 1. PHYTOPATHOLOGY. *Educ:* SDak State Univ, BS, 69, MS, 73. *Prof Exp:* assoc biol, 73-78, proj coordr herbicides, 79-80, PROJ LEADER FUNGICIDE RES, AGR CHEM DIV, FMC CORP, 81- *Mem:* Am Phytopath Soc. *Res:* Fungicide screening and evaluation; herbicide/fungicide/plant regulator field testing; environmental effect of pesticides on soil microorganisms. *Mailing Add:* FMC Corp 100 Niagara St Middleport NY 14105

DAVIDSON, BRUCE M, b Ironwood, Mich, Mar 16, 24; m 49; c 3. TRANSPORTATION ENGINEERING. *Educ:* Univ Mich, BSE, 49; Univ Wis, MS, 51, PhD(eng), 56. *Prof Exp:* Instr civil eng, Univ Wis, 49-51 & 53-55; traffic engr, Wis, 55-56; from asst prof to prof civil eng, Univ Wis, Madison, 56-66, asst dean, 57-62, assoc dean, 62-66; prof & chmn dept, Wash State Univ, 66-71; ACAD DEAN, US NAVAL ACAD, 71- *Concurrent Pos:* Consult, India prog, Agency Int Develop, US Dept State, 69. *Mem:* Am Soc Civil Engrs; Am Soc Eng Educ; Am Rwy Eng Asn. *Res:* Optimization of traffic signal systems; driver response to geometric design of intersections; academic performance of engineering students. *Mailing Add:* US Naval Acad Annapolis MD 21402

DAVIDSON, CHARLES H(ENRY), b Washington, DC, Dec 10, 20; m 52; c 2. COMPUTER SCIENCE, ELECTRICAL ENGINEERING. *Educ:* Am Univ, AB, 41; Univ Wis, PhM, 43, PhD(physics), 52. *Prof Exp:* Instr physics, Mary Washington Col, 46-47; engr, Continental Elec Co, 47-49; proj assoc elec eng, 52-54, asst prof, 54-58, assoc prof, 58-66, PROF ELEC & COMPUT ENG & COMPUT SCI, UNIV WIS, MADISON, 66-, DIR, ENG COMPUT LAB, 61- *Concurrent Pos:* Consult, AC Spark Plug Div, Gen Motors Corp, 59-63; vis prof, Dept Comput Sci, Univ Edinburgh, 68-69. *Mem:* Asn Comput Mach; Am Nat Standards Inst; Inst Elec & Electronics Engrs. *Res:* Computer education; computers and society. *Mailing Add:* Dept of Elec & Comput Eng Univ of Wis Madison WI 53706

DAVIDSON, CHARLES MACKENZIE, b Hamilton, Scotland, June 1, 42; m 65; c 2. FOOD MICROBIOLOGY. *Educ:* Univ Strathclyde, Scotland, BSc, 64; Univ Bath, Eng, PhD(microbiol), 70. *Prof Exp:* Microbiologist qual control, Cerola Fare Ltd, 64-65; microbiologist res & develop, Unilever Res, 65-70; chief microbiologist res & develop, Canada Packers, 70-78; V PRES, SILLIKER LABS CAN, 78- *Mem:* Am Soc Microbiol; Soc Appl Bact. *Res:* Behavior of food borne pathogens in human foods; preservation of food products against microbial spoilage; development of methods for enumeration and identification of bacteria. *Mailing Add:* Silliker Labs of Can 2222 S Sheridan Way Mississauga Can

DAVIDSON, CHARLES NELSON, b Kankakee, Ill, Oct 19, 37; m 59; c 3. NUCLEAR PHYSICS, NUCLEAR WEAPON EFFECTS. *Educ:* The Citadel, BS, 59; Fla State Univ, PhD(nuclear chem), 62. *Prof Exp:* Chem staff officer, Radiol Div, US Army Combat Develop Command, 62-64, physicist, 64-66, physicist, Effects Div, Inst Nuclear Studies, 66-68, sci adv, 68-79, TECH DIR, HQ, US ARMY NUCLEAR & CHEM AGENCY, 79- *Mem:* Am Chem Soc; Am Nuclear Soc. *Res:* Nuclear weapons effects; nuclear defense; radiac instruments; fallout radiation; low energy nuclear physics; nuclear plans and policy. *Mailing Add:* 10838 Greene Dr Lorton VA 22079

DAVIDSON, CHARLES SPRECHER, b Berkeley, Calif, Dec 7, 10. CLINICAL MEDICINE. *Educ:* Univ Calif, AB, 34; McGill Univ, MD & CM, 39. *Hon Degrees:* MA, Harvard Univ, 53. *Prof Exp:* Intern, San Francisco Hosp, 39-40, house officer med, 40-41; asst, 42-45, instr, 45-47, assoc, 47-49, asst prof, 49-51, asst clin prof, 51-52, from assoc prof to prof, 53-73, William B Castle prof med, 73-76, EMER WILLIAM B CASTLE PROF MED, HARVARD MED SCH, 76- *Concurrent Pos:* Res fel, Harvard Med Sch, 41-42; Fogarty scholar, NIH, 72-73; asst, Boston City Hosp, 41-43, from jr vis physician to assoc vis physician, 44-63, vis physician, 64-, from res dir to asst dir 2nd & 4th Med Servs, 43-48, assoc dir, 48-73, from asst resident physician to resident physician, Thorndike Mem Lab, 41-43, from asst physician to assoc physician, 43-63, assoc dir, 63-73; vis prof med & prog dir, Clin Res Ctr, Mass Inst Technol, 74-76, sr lectr, 76-; consult, Cushing Vet Admin Hosp, Framingham, Mass, 50-52, Vet Admin Hosp, Boston, 52-72, Lemuel Shattuck Hosp, 55-, nutrit sect, Off Int Res, NIH, Cambridge City Hosp & Mt Auburn Hosp, Cambridge; trustee, Age Ctr New Eng, 65 & Boylston Med Soc, 61-64. *Mem:* AMA; Am Soc Clin Investr; Am Fedn Clin Res; master Am Col Physicians; Asn Am Physicians. *Res:* Nutrition, metabolism and liver diseases in man. *Mailing Add:* 100 Memorial Dr 5-23-A Cambridge MA 02142

DAVIDSON, CHRISTOPHER, b Boise, Idaho, Feb 10, 44. PLANT ANATOMY, PLANT MORPHOLOGY. *Educ:* Whitman Col, AB, 66; Claremont Grad Sch, MA, 68, PhD(bot), 73. *Prof Exp:* cur, Natural Hist Mus, Los Angeles County, 73-81; DIR, IDAHO BOT GARDEN, 81- *Concurrent Pos:* Ed, Madrono. *Mem:* Int Asn Plant Taxonomists; Int Asn Wood Anatomists; Am Bot Soc; Am Asn Plant Taxonomists; Asn Trop Biol. *Res:* Anatomy and morphology of flowering plants as it relates to problems of phylogeny and biogeography; wood anatomy of tropical forest trees, especially of roots and buttresses. *Mailing Add:* Idaho Bot Garden PO Box 2140 Boise ID 83701

DAVIDSON, CLIFF IAN, b Passaic, NJ, May 9, 50; m 76. ENVIRONMENTAL ENGINEERING, AIR POLLUTION. *Educ:* Carnegie-Mellon Univ, BS, 72; Calif Inst Technol, MS, 73, PhD(environ eng), 77. *Prof Exp:* ASST PROF CIVIL ENG, ENG & PUB POLICY, CARNEGIE-MELLON UNIV, 77- *Concurrent Pos:* Mem comt Lead Human Environ, Environ Studies Bd, Nat Res Coun, 78- *Honors & Awards:* Lincoln T Work Award, Fine Particle Soc, 76. *Res:* Deposition of ambient natural and anthropogenic aerosols onto various surfaces, as functions of particle characteristics, atmospheric state, and surface structure; global atmospheric transport of trace metals; historical trends in air pollutants. *Mailing Add:* Dept of Civil Eng Schenley Park Pittsburgh PA 15213

DAVIDSON, DANIEL LEE, b Columbus, Ohio, Feb 7, 46; m 68, 81; c 2. POLYMER CHEMISTRY. *Educ:* Earlham Col, AB, 68; Univ Akron, PhD(polymer sci), 75. *Prof Exp:* Res chemist, Chem & Plastics Res & Develop, Union Carbide Corp, 74-79; SR RES SCIENTIST, ARCO CHEM CO, 79- *Mem:* Am Chem Soc; Soc Plastics Engrs. *Res:* Chemical and physical modification of polyolefins for specific novel applications; crosslinking chemistry of polyolefins. *Mailing Add:* Arco Chem Co 3801 Westchester Park Newtown Square PA 19073

DAVIDSON, DARWIN ERVIN, b Rockford, Ill, May 5, 43; m 66; c 2. BOTANY, MYCOLOGY. *Educ:* Ore State Univ, BS, 65; Univ Wyo, MS, 67; Duke Univ, PhD(bot), 71. *Prof Exp:* Res assoc mycol, Univ Wyo, 71-74; supvr malting-brewing res, 74-80, MGR BREWING RES, ADOLPH COORS CO, 80- *Mem:* AAAS; Am Soc Brewing Chemists. *Res:* Barley enzyme development during malting and their function during the brewing and fermentation process; product and process improvement; new beverage products. *Mailing Add:* Res & Develop Dept 300 Adolph Coors Co Golden CO 80401

DAVIDSON, DAVID, b Hartford, Conn; m 46; c 1. RADIO SCIENCE, COMMUNICATIONS ENGINEERING. *Educ:* Trinity Col, BS, 39; Univ Mich, MS, 40; Harvard Univ, MA, 49, PhD(appl physics), 55. *Prof Exp:* Staff mem, Radiation Lab Loran Div, Mass Inst Technol, 41-45; res assoc ionospheric physics, Div Appl Sci, Harvard Univ, 46-55; group leader, Hermes Electronics, Cambridge, Mass, 55-62; res mgr, DECO Electronics Inc, Cambridge, Mass, 62-67; mem tech staff, Appl Res Lab, GTE Sylvania Inc, 67-70; MEM TECH STAFF, GTE LABS INC, 70- *Concurrent Pos:* Mem wave propagation comt, Inst Elec & Electronics Engrs, 70- *Mem:* Am Geophys Union; Inst Elec & Electronics Engrs; Sigma Xi; Bioelectromagnetics Soc. *Res:* Radiowave propagation research; transmission research and development; communications satellite systems; electromagnetic bioeffects. *Mailing Add:* GTE Labs Inc 40 Sylvan Rd Waltham MA 02154

DAVIDSON, DAVID EDWARD, JR, b Philadelphia, Pa, Mar 7, 35; m 58; c 2. VETERINARY MEDICINE, RADIOBIOLOGY. *Educ:* Univ Pa, VMD, 59; Univ Rochester, MS, 62; Georgetown Univ, PhD(rad- iation biol), 70. *Prof Exp:* Vet Corps, US Army, 59-, vet lab officer, Dept Radiobiol, US Army Med Res Lab, Ft Knox, 59-61, vet lab officer, Div Med Chem, Walter Reed Army Inst Res, 62-72, chief dept vet med, Seato Med Res Lab, Bangkok, Thailand, 72-75, vet lab officer & chief dept biol, Div Med Chem, 75-78, CHIEF DEPT PARASITOL, DIV EXP THERAPEUT, WALTER REED ARMY INST RES, US ARMY, 78- *Concurrent Pos:* consult sci working group chemother malaria, WHO, 80; US rep Panel VII, NATO, 80-; consult vet pharmacol, Surg Gen Army, 81. *Mem:* Am Vet Med Asn; Sigma Xi. *Res:* Biological testing of pharmaceuticals in laboratory animals; pharmacology and toxicology of antiradiation, antimalarial, antitrypanosomal, antileishmanial and antischistosomal drugs; parasitology. *Mailing Add:* Div Exp Therapeut Walter Reed Army Inst Res Washington DC 20012

DAVIDSON, DAVID FRANCIS, b New York, NY, Aug 9, 23; m 53; c 3. ECONOMIC GEOLOGY. *Educ:* Lehigh Univ, BA, 48. *Prof Exp:* Geologist, US Geol Surv, 48-54; staff geologist, Spencer Chem Co, Mo, 54-56; staff geologist, US Geol Surv, 56-62, chief off exp geol, Br Geochem Census, 62-67, geologist, Br Foreign Geol, 67-68, dep asst chief geologist resources, 68-71, CHIEF BR MID EAST & ASIAN GEOL, US GEOL SURV, 71- *Mem:* Fel Geol Soc Am; Soc Econ Geol. *Res:* Geology and geochemistry of selenium and tellurium; geology of ore deposits of sedimentary origin; automatic data processing of geologic data; geochemistry of phosphate deposits. *Mailing Add:* US Geol Surv Nat Ctr Reston VA 22092

DAVIDSON, DAVID LEE, b Houston, Tex, Apr 22, 35; m 65; c 2. MATERIALS SCIENCE, ELECTRON MICROSCOPY. *Educ:* Rice Univ, BS, 58, MS, 63, PhD(mat sci), 68. *Prof Exp:* Metallurgist, Southwest Res Inst, 63-65, sr metallurgist, 68-70; vis prof mat sci, Univ Fed de Rio de Janeiro, Brazil, 70-71; STAFF SCIENTIST MAT SCI, SOUTHWEST RES INST, 71- *Concurrent Pos:* Instr, Trinity Univ, 69-70, Univ Tex, 72- & Rice Univ, 78; sr vis fel, British Sci Res Coun, 79. *Honors & Awards:* Hetenyi Award, Soc Exp Stress Anal, 81. *Mem:* Am Inst Mining Metall & Petrol Engrs; fel Am Soc Metals; Nat Asn Corrosion Engrs; Microbeam Anal Soc; Electron Micros Soc Am. *Res:* Fatigue; fracture; deformation; dislocations; electron channeling; electron backscattering; surface analysis particulates; stress corrosion. *Mailing Add:* Southwest Res Inst PO Drawer 28510 San Antonio TX 78284

DAVIDSON, DIANE WEST, b New Brighton, Pa, Jan 7, 48. COMMUNITY ECOLOGY, INSECT ECOLOGY. *Educ:* Wilson Col, BA, 69; Univ Denver, MS, 72; Univ Utah, PhD(biol), 76. *Prof Exp:* Inst biol, Dept Zool, Univ Tex, Austin, 76-77; asst prof biol, Dept Biol Sci, Purdue Univ, 77-79; asst prof biol, Dept Biol, 82, ASSOC PROF BIOL, UNIV UTAH, 82- *Concurrent Pos:* NSF grant, 77-79. *Mem:* Ecol Soc Am; Soc Study Evolution; AAAS; Int Union Study Social Insects. *Res:* Evolutionary ecology; geographical ecology, granivory in desert ecosystems; myrmecochory and other ant-plant interactions. *Mailing Add:* Dept Biol Univ Utah Salt Lake City UT 84112

DAVIDSON, DONALD, b Albert Lea, Minn, May 3, 34; m 61; c 5. MECHANICAL ENGINEERING, ELECTRICAL ENGINEERING. *Educ:* Univ Minn, Minneapolis, BS, 57; Washington Univ, St Louis, MSEE, 62, DSc, 77; Univ Mo, Rolla, MS, 70. *Hon Degrees:* Mech Engr, Univ Minn, Minneapolis, 72. *Prof Exp:* Res asst, Heat Transfer Lab, Univ Minn, 56-57; mech engr power plant eng, Iowa Ill Gas & Elec Co, 57; thermodynamics engr design, McDonnell Douglas Corp, 58-74; proj engr design, Pako Corp, 74-78; test engr test mgt, Rosemount Inc, 79-80; DEVELOP ENGR, RES & DEVELOP, GEN MILLS, INC, 80- *Concurrent Pos:* Mgt consult, D Davidson & Assocs, 66- *Mem:* Am Soc Mech Engrs; Inst Elec & Electronics Engrs; Am Soc Heating, Refrigeration & Air Conditioning Engrs; Nat Soc Prof Engrs. *Res:* Electro-mechanics machine design; thermodynamics; heat transfer; research administration and supervision. *Mailing Add:* 3414 M Flag Ave New Hope MN 55427

DAVIDSON, DONALD H(OWARD), b Suffern, NY, Nov 16, 37; m 60; c 1. CHEMICAL ENGINEERING, APPLIED MATHEMATICS. *Educ:* Rensselaer Polytech Inst, BChE, 59; NY Univ, MChE, 62, PhD(chem eng), 67. *Prof Exp:* Chem engr, US Rubber Co, NJ, 60-63, St Regis Paper Co, NY, 63-66 & Petrol & Chem Eng, Shell Develop Co, 67-70; chem engr, Kennecott Copper Corp, 70-78; petrol & chem engr, SAI, 78-79; PETROL & CHEM ENGR, TRW INC, 80- *Mem:* Am Inst Chem Engrs; Am Chem Soc; Soc Petrol Engs. *Res:* Fluid mechanics; heat transfer; applied mechanics; petroleum reservoir engineering. *Mailing Add:* Energy Systs Group TRW Inc 8301 Greensboro Dr McLean VA 22102

DAVIDSON, DONALD MINER, JR, b Minneapolis, Minn, Oct 21, 39; m 66. STRUCTURAL GEOLOGY, TECTONICS. *Educ:* Carleton Col, BA, 61; Columbia Univ, MA, 63, PhD(geol), 65. *Prof Exp:* From asst prof to assoc prof geol, Univ Minn, Duluth, 65-75, prof, 78-81; RES SPECIALIST, EXXON PROD RES, HOUSTON, 81- *Concurrent Pos:* Prof geol & chmn dept, Univ Tex, El Paso. *Mem:* Soc Econ Geol; Geol Soc Am; Am Inst Mining, Metall & Petrol Eng; Sigma Xi; fel Asn Can. *Res:* Landsat imagery analysis (geology, structure, land tectonics); strain analysis. *Mailing Add:* Exxon Prod Res PO Box 2189 Houston TX 77001

DAVIDSON, DONALD WEST, b Moncton, NB, June 25, 25; m 54; c 1. PHYSICAL CHEMISTRY. *Educ:* Univ NB, BSc, 46, MSc, 47; Imp Col, Univ London, dipl, 48; Brown Univ, PhD(phys chem), 51. *Prof Exp:* Fel, 51-53, from asst res officer to assoc res officer, 53-61, sr res officer, 61-73, PRIN RES OFFICER, NAT RES COUN CAN, 73- *Mem:* Am Chem Soc; Am Phys Soc; Chem Inst Can. *Res:* Dielectric and nuclear magnetic resonance studies of solids; clathrates; natural gas hydrates. *Mailing Add:* Div Chem Nat Res Coun Can Ottawa ON K1A 0R6 Can

DAVIDSON, DONALD WILLIAM, b Prairie Grove, Ark, June 8, 36; m 69. ECOLOGY. *Educ:* Univ Minn, BA, 59; Rutgers Univ, PhD(plant ecol), 63. *Prof Exp:* Asst bot, Univ Minn, 56-59 & Rutgers Univ, 59-63; asst prof biol, Univ Ala, 63-65; from asst prof to assoc prof, 65-79, PROF BIOL, UNIV WIS-SUPERIOR, 79- *Mem:* Am Inst Biol Sci; Ecol Soc Am. *Res:* Forest ecology; botany; environment. *Mailing Add:* Dept of Biol Univ of Wis Superior WI 54880

DAVIDSON, DOUGLAS, b North Shields, Eng, Mar 22, 31. CYTOLOGY. *Educ:* Durham Univ, BSc, 53; Oxford Univ, DPhil(cytol), 56. *Prof Exp:* Res fel cytol, Oxford Univ, 56-58; vis biologist, Biol Div, Oak Ridge Nat Lab, 58-61; lectr bot, St Andrew's Univ, 61-64; from asst prof to assoc prof biol, Western Reserve Univ, 64-69; chmn dept, 74-77, PROF BIOL, McMASTER UNIV, 69- *Concurrent Pos:* US AEC grant, 66-68; Nat Res Coun Can grant, 69- *Mem:* Genetics Soc Am; Bot Soc Am; Bot Soc Can; Cell Biol Soc Can. *Res:* Root growth; cell lineage studies in meristems; sensitivity to colchicine and methylxanthines; growth of nuclei; physiology of germination of barley. *Mailing Add:* Dept Biol McMaster Univ Hamilton ON L8S 4K1 Can

DAVIDSON, EDWARD S(TEINBERG), b Boston, Mass, Dec 27, 39; m 64; c 2. ELECTRICAL ENGINEERING, COMPUTER SCIENCE. *Educ:* Harvard Col, BA, 61; Univ Mich, Ann Arbor, MS, 62; Univ Ill, Urbana, PhD(elec eng), 68. *Prof Exp:* Engr, Honeywell, Inc, 62-65; asst prof elec eng, Stanford Univ, 68-73; asst prof, 73-75, ASSOC PROF ELEC ENG, UNIV ILL, 75- *Concurrent Pos:* NSF grant, NAND Network Design, 69-71; NSF grants, prin investr, 69-76; consult, Hewlett Packard, 75-76, Honeywell, 77 & USA-ECOM, Ft Monmouth, 77- *Mem:* AAAS; Asn Comput Mach; Inst Elec & Electronics Engrs; Sigma Xi; Am Fedn Teachers. *Res:* Computer architecture; pipelined and parallel computers; memory organization and management; microprocessors; logic design; automation. *Mailing Add:* Coord Sci Lab Univ of Ill Urbana IL 61801

DAVIDSON, ELIZABETH WEST, b Salem, Ohio, Nov 25, 42; m 68; c 1. INVERTEBRATE PATHOLOGY. *Educ:* Mt Union Col, BSc, 64; Ohio State Univ, MSc, 67, PhD(entom), 71. *Prof Exp:* NIH fel acarology, Ohio State Univ, 71-72; instr biol, Univ Rochester, 73-74; RES ASSOC INSECT PATH, ARIZ STATE UNIV, 74- *Concurrent Pos:* Consult, WHO, 72-; ed, Pathogenesis Microbial Dis, 81. *Mem:* NY Acad Sci; Entom Soc Am; Soc Invert Path; Am Mosquito Control Asn; Int Orgn Biological Control. *Res:* Pathogenesis of bacterial diseases of invertebrates; effect of invertebrate pathogens on non-target organisms; biological control of vector insects. *Mailing Add:* Dept Zool Ariz State Univ Tempe AZ 85287

DAVIDSON, ERIC HARRIS, b New York, NY, Apr 13, 37. MOLECULAR BIOLOGY, DEVELOPMENTAL BIOLOGY. *Educ:* Univ Pa, BA, 58; Rockefeller Inst, PhD(cell biol), 63. *Prof Exp:* Res assoc cell biol, Rockefeller Univ, 63-65, asst prof cell & develop biol, 65-70; assoc prof biol, 71-74, PROF BIOL, CALIF INST TECHNOL, 74- *Res:* Genomic control over cell differentiation; genomic activity underlying early embryological development and oogenesis. *Mailing Add:* Div of Biol Calif Inst of Technol Pasadena CA 91125

DAVIDSON, ERNEST, b Stuttgart, Ger, June 12, 21; US citizen; m 44; c 1. MECHANICAL ENGINEERING. *Prof Exp:* Design engr, Mitchell Camera Corp, 47-51; design engr, Bausch & Lomb, Inc, 51-56, design engr mgr, 56-61, prod mgr, 61-63, eng div mgr, 63, vpres eng, 63-77, vpres & gen mgr, Appl Res Labs, Inc, 73-79, vpres admin, 79-81; MGT CONSULT, 81- *Concurrent Pos:* Lectr, Los Angeles City Col, 59-, mem adv comt, 64- *Mem:* Instrument Soc Am; Optical Soc Am; Am Soc Testing & Mat. *Res:* Instrumentation for spectrochemical analysis. *Mailing Add:* 843 Amherst Dr Burbank CA 91504

DAVIDSON, ERNEST ROY, b West Terre Haute, Ind, Oct 12, 36; m 56; c 4. PHYSICAL CHEMISTRY. *Educ:* Rose Polytech Inst, BS, 58; Ind Univ, PhD(quantum chem), 61. *Prof Exp:* NSF res fel, Theoret Chem Inst, Univ Wis, 61-62; from asst prof to assoc prof, 62-68, PROF CHEM, UNIV WASH, 68- *Concurrent Pos:* Sloan Found fel, 67; Guggenheim Found fel, 73. *Honors & Awards:* Laureate, Int Acad Molecular Quantum Sci, 71. *Mem:* Am Chem Soc; Am Phys Soc. *Res:* Theoretical physical chemistry; quantum mechanics of small molecules. *Mailing Add:* Dept of Chem BG-10 Univ of Wash Seattle WA 98195

DAVIDSON, EUGENE ABRAHAM, b New York, NY, May 27, 30; m 50; c 4. BIOCHEMISTRY. *Educ:* Univ Calif, Los Angeles, BS, 50; Columbia Univ, PhD(biochem), 55. *Prof Exp:* Res assoc, Univ Mich, 55-56, instr biochem, 57-58; from asst prof to prof, Duke Univ, 58-67; PROF BIOL CHEM & CHMN DEPT, MILTON S HERSHEY MED CTR, PA STATE UNIV, 68-, ASSOC DEAN EDUC, 75- *Concurrent Pos:* Consult Nat Cancer Inst, 60-62 & NIH, 63- *Mem:* Am Chem Soc; Am Soc Biol Chem; Am Rheumatism Asn; Brit Biochem Soc. *Res:* Structural chemistry of malignant cells; metabolism of glycoconjugates; hexosamine metabolism and chemistry. *Mailing Add:* Dept of Biol Chem Pa State Univ Milton S Hershey Med Ctr Hershey PA 17033

DAVIDSON, FREDERIC M, b Glens Falls, NY, Feb 11, 41; m 68; c 2. ELECTRICAL ENGINEERING. *Educ:* Cornell Univ, BS, 64; Univ Rochester, PhD(physics), 69. *Prof Exp:* Asst prof elec eng, Univ Houston, 68-70; from asst prof to assoc prof, 70-80, PROF ELEC ENG, JOHNS HOPKINS UNIV, 80- *Concurrent Pos:* Vis assoc prof elec eng, Rice Univ, 78-79. *Mem:* Inst Elec & Electronic Engrs; Optical Soc Am; Am Asn Univ Prof. *Mailing Add:* Dept Elec Eng Johns Hopkins Univ Baltimore MD 21218

DAVIDSON, GILBERT, b Omaha, Nebr, June 10, 34; m 58; c 3. SCIENCE ADMINISTRATION, OPTICS. *Educ:* Mass Inst Technol, SB, 55, PhD(physics), 59. *Prof Exp:* Res assoc physics, Polytech Sch, Paris, 59-60; sr phys scientist, Am Sci & Eng, Inc, 60-64, sr proj dir geophys, 64-67, vpres educ div, 67-69, geophys div, 69-70 & instrument systs div, 70-73; vpres, Infrared Industs, Inc, 73-77; V PRES, PHOTOMETRICS, INC, 77- *Concurrent Pos:* Fulbright scholar, France, 59-60. *Mem:* Am Vacuum Soc;

Am Geophys Union; Instrument Soc Am; Am Phys Soc; Optical Soc Am. *Res:* High-energy physics; atomic physics; geophysics; development of improved opto-electronic devices. *Mailing Add:* Photometrics Inc 4 Arrow Dr Woburn MA 01801

DAVIDSON, GRANT E(DWARD), b Toronto, Ont, Oct 13, 19; m 46; c 3. ELECTRICAL ENGINEERING. *Educ:* Univ Toronto, BASc, 43. *Prof Exp:* Asst testing engr, Illum Lab, Res Div, 46-49, asst res engr, 49-52, res engr, 52-57, illum engr, 57-60, sr illum engr, 60-71, supvry elec inspector & engr, 71-76, CHIEF ELEC INSPECTOR, ONT HYDRO ELEC POWER COMN, 77- *Concurrent Pos:* Spec lectr dept univ exten, Univ Toronto; consult, Ont Dept Transp; mem, Int Illum Comn, 57-78 & Int Electrotech Comn, 59-; mem comt, Can Elec Codes, Part I, Part II and Part III, Can Standards Asn. *Mem:* Fel Am Illum Eng Soc; fel Illum Eng Soc Gt Brit; fel Inst Bldg Serv UK. *Res:* Radiation optics and illumination; electrical safety. *Mailing Add:* Ont Hydro 700 University Ave Toronto ON M5G 1Z5 Can

DAVIDSON, H(AROLD), b Brooklyn, NY, May 2, 21. CHEMICAL ENGINEERING. *Educ:* Columbia Univ, BS, 43, ChE, 48. *Prof Exp:* Chem engr, Kolker Chem Works, 46-47; asst, Columbia Univ, 48-49; chem engr, Metal & Thermit Corp, 49-56; eng statistician, Merck & Co, Inc, 57-60; CONTROL SYSTS REP, IBM CORP, 60- *Mem:* Am Chem Soc; Am Inst Chem Engrs; Am Soc Qual Control; Inst Mgt Sci; Am Statist Asn. *Res:* Chemical engineering and applied mathematics; computer applications and computer control systems. *Mailing Add:* 330 W 28th St Apt 20F New York NY 10001

DAVIDSON, HAROLD, b NJ, July 20, 19; m 50; c 3. LANDSCAPE HORTICULTURE. *Educ:* Univ Calif, BS, 49; Mich State Univ, MS, 53, PhD(hort), 57. *Prof Exp:* Coordr nursery & landscape mgt, 50-57, from asst prof to assoc prof, 57-70, PROF ORNAMENTAL HORT RES, MICH STATE UNIV, 70- *Honors & Awards:* Norman J Coleman Award, Am Asn Nurserymen, 80. *Mem:* Am Soc Hort Sci; Asn Bot Gardens & Arboretums; Am Hort Soc. *Res:* Physiology of woody plants; photo-period; nutrition; propagation; weed control. *Mailing Add:* Dept of Hort Mich State Univ East Lansing MI 48824

DAVIDSON, HAROLD MICHAEL, b Boston, Mass, June 3, 24. BIOCHEMISTRY. *Educ:* Harvard Univ, AB, 44; Univ Ore, MA, 49, PhD(chem), 51. *Prof Exp:* Chemist, Mass Dept Pub Health, 46-47; fel physiol chem, Univ Pa, 50-51; chemist cancer res, Overly Biochem Res Found, 51-52; res assoc, Sch Med, Tufts Univ, 52-59; SCIENTIST-ADMINR RES GRANTS, NIH, 61- *Concurrent Pos:* Am Cancer Soc fel, 53-55; exec secy, Gen Med A Study Sect, Div Res Grants, NIH, 73- *Mem:* AAAS; Am Chem Soc. *Res:* Carbohydrate metabolism; enzymology; cancer; research grants review. *Mailing Add:* 5301 Westbard Circle Bethesda MD 20816

DAVIDSON, IVAN WILLIAM FREDERICK, b Winnipeg, Man, July 31, 26; m 50; c 4. PHYSIOLOGY, PHARMACOLOGY. *Educ:* Univ Man, BSc, 54; Univ Toronto, MA, 56, PhD(physiol), 59. *Prof Exp:* Res assoc, Univ Toronto, 58-59; res assoc, Union Carbide Chem Co, 59-61; asst prof physiol & pharmacol, 61-63, from asst prof to assoc prof pharmacol, 63-70, PROF PHARMACOL, BOWMAN GRAY SCH MED, WAKE FOREST UNIV, 70-, ASSOC PHYSIOL, 63- *Concurrent Pos:* Lederle med fac award, 64-67. *Mem:* AAAS; Am Physiol Soc; Am Pharmacol Soc; NY Acad Sci; Soc Exp Biol & Med. *Res:* Endocrines; diabetes; mechanisms of hormone action, and control metabolism; drug metabolism. *Mailing Add:* Dept of Physiol & Pharmacol B Gray Sch Med Wake Forest Univ Winston-Salem NC 27103

DAVIDSON, J(OHN) P(IRNIE), PHYSICS. *Educ:* Univ Calif, BA, 48; Wash Univ, AM, 51, PhD, 52. *Prof Exp:* Res assoc physics, Columbia Univ, 52-53; asst prof, Brazilian Ctr Phys Res, Rio de Janerio, 53-55; res scientist, Joint Estab Nuclear Energy Res, Norway, 55-57; from asst prof to prof theoret physics, Rensselaer Polytech Inst, 57-66; PROF THEORET PHYSICS, UNIV KANS, 66-, CHMN DEPT, 77- *Concurrent Pos:* Vis scientist-in-residence, Naval Radiol Defense Lab, 64-65; visitor, Los Alamos Sci Lab, 74-75. *Mem:* Am Phys Soc; Am Astro Soc. *Res:* Theoretical physics; astrophysics. *Mailing Add:* Dept Physics & Astron Univ Kans Lawrence KS 66045

DAVIDSON, JACK DOUGAN, b Newark, NJ, Jan 31, 18; m 46; c 4. NUCLEAR MEDICINE. *Educ:* Princeton Univ, AB, 40; Columbia Univ, MD, 43; Am Bd Nuclear Med, cert, 72. *Prof Exp:* Intern med, Bellevue Hosp, 44, resident, 47; instr med, Goldwater Mem Hosp, 50-51; asst prof med, Col Physicians & Surg, Columbia Univ, 53-57; head biochem sect, Lab Chem Pharmacol, Nat Cancer Inst, 57-66; chief dept nuclear med, Clin Ctr, NIH, 66-70; assoc prof, Div Nuclear Med, Med Ctr, Duke Univ, 70-76; SR INVESTR, DEVELOP THERAPEUT PROG, NAT CANCER INST, 77- *Concurrent Pos:* Res fel arteriosclerosis, Goldwater Mem Hosp, 48-50; res fel cancer, Delafield Hosp, 51-57. *Mem:* AAAS; Am Soc Pharmacol; NY Acad Sci; Soc Nuclear Med. *Res:* Nuclear medicine; radioisotopes; anticancer drug research. *Mailing Add:* 5229 Westpath Way Bethesda MD 20816

DAVIDSON, JAMES BLAINE, b Oklahoma City, Okla, Nov 10, 23; m 48; c 3. OCEAN ENGINEERING, ACOUSTICS. *Educ:* US Naval Acad, BS, 46; US Naval Postgrad Sch, BS, 52; Univ Calif, Los Angeles, MS, 53. *Prof Exp:* US Navy, 46-67, anal officer, Key West Testing & Eval Detachment, Oper Testing & Eval Force, 55-57, asst supt, Submarine Construct, Mare Island Naval Shipyard, 57-59, elec officer, Serv Squadron, 7th Fleet, 59-62, proj officer, Off Naval Res, 62-66, dir undersea prog, 66-67; PROF OCEAN ENG, FLA ATLANTIC UNIV, 67- *Concurrent Pos:* Consult, Metallgesellschaft AG, 73-; vis prof, Thorwegian Tech Inst, Norway, 81-82. *Mem:* Am Acoust Soc; Marine Technol Soc; Am Soc Eng Educ. *Res:* Long range, underwater acoustic propagation and submarine detection; submarine target classification; underwater acoustic television; deep ocean mining; manganese nodules. *Mailing Add:* Dept of Ocean Eng Fla Atlantic Univ Boca Raton FL 33431

DAVIDSON, JAMES MELVIN, b The Dalles, Ore, Apr 16, 34; m 57; c 3. SOIL PHYSICS. *Educ:* Ore State Col, BS, 56, MS, 58; Univ Calif, Davis, PhD(soil physics), 65. *Prof Exp:* Res asst soil physics, Ore State Univ, 56-58; lab technician, Univ Calif, Davis, 58-65; from asst prof to prof, Okla State Univ, 65-74; prof soil sci, 74-79, ASST DEAN RES, INST FOOD & AGR SCI, UNIV FLA, 79- *Mem:* Soil Sci Soc Am; fel Am Soc Agron; Am Geophys Union. *Res:* Fluid and solute movement through various porous materials; soil management practices for soil and water conservation and good plant root environment. *Mailing Add:* Dept of Soil Sci 2169 McCarty Univ of Fla Gainesville FL 32611

DAVIDSON, JEFFREY NEAL, b Springfield, Mass, May 7, 50; m 80; c 1. SOMATIC CELL GENETICS. *Educ:* Ind Univ, Bs, 72; Harvard Univ, PhD(biol), 76. *Prof Exp:* Fel sommatic cell genetics, 76-79, INST FEL, ELEANOR ROOSEVELT INST CANCER RES, 79-; ASST PROF MED, HEALTH SCI CTR, UNIV COLO, 80- *Mem:* AAAS; Am Soc Cell Biol; Sigma Xi. *Res:* Biochemical, genetic, and molecular biological techniques are being used to study multifunctional protein which catalyzes the first three steps of pyrimidine biosynthesis in mammalian cells; genes on human chromosome 21. *Mailing Add:* B129 4200 E 9th Ave Denver CO 80262

DAVIDSON, JIMMY LEE, materials science, solid state physics, see previous edition

DAVIDSON, JOHN ANGUS, b Elizabeth, NJ, July 26, 33; m 57; c 2. ENTOMOLOGY. *Educ:* Columbia Union Col, BA, 55; Univ Md, MS, 57, PhD(entom), 60. *Prof Exp:* From instr to assoc prof biol, Columbia Union Col, 60-66; from asst prof to assoc prof, 66-75, PROF ENTOM, UNIV MD, COLLEGE PARK, 75- *Concurrent Pos:* Prof lectr, Am Univ, 63- *Mem:* Entom Soc Am; Soc Syst Zool. *Res:* Biosystematics of scale insects; biology and control of insect pests of ornamental plants; insect taxonomy and morphology. *Mailing Add:* Dept of Entom Univ of Md College Park MD 20742

DAVIDSON, JOHN EDWIN, b Asheville, NC, Oct 27, 37; m 58; c 2. ANALYTICAL CHEMISTRY, INORGANIC CHEMISTRY. *Educ:* Univ Tenn, BSChem, 60, MS, 62, PhD(chem), 65. *Prof Exp:* Asst prof, 65-68, assoc prof, 68-74, PROF CHEM, EASTERN KY UNIV, 74- *Mem:* Am Chem Soc; Sigma Xi. *Res:* Solvent extraction of metal chelates; coordination chemistry; chemical education; experiments in the introductory chemistry laboratory. *Mailing Add:* Dept of Chem Moore 337 Eastern Ky Univ Richmond KY 40475

DAVIDSON, JOHN GERARD NOEL, b Murree, Pakistan, Sept 3, 35; Can citizen; m 74; c 2. PLANT PATHOLOGY. *Educ:* Univ BC, BSF, 57, MSc, 61; Univ Calif, Berkeley, PhD(plant path), 71. *Prof Exp:* RES SCIENTIST PLANT PATH, AGR CAN, 73- *Concurrent Pos:* Fel mycol, Univ Guelph, Ont, 71-72; fel plant path, Univ Toronto, 73. *Mem:* Can Phytopathol Soc; Am Phytopathol Soc. *Res:* Root rots and damping-off of rapeseed and barley; snow molds of grasses, winter cereals and legumes; didymella stem eyespot of fescue; diseases of Saskatoon berries. *Mailing Add:* Agr Can Res Sta Beaverlodge Can

DAVIDSON, JOHN KEAY, III, b Lithonia, Ga, Mar 30, 22; m; c 4. INTERNAL MEDICINE, PHYSIOLOGY. *Educ:* Emory Univ, BS, 43, MD, 45; Univ Toronto, PhD(physiol), 65; Am Bd Internal Med, dipl, 54. *Prof Exp:* Intern surg, Grady Hosp, Atlanta, Ga, 45-46, asst resident internal med, 48-49; chief resident, Emory Univ Hosp, 49-50; resident, New Eng Ctr Hosp, Boston, Mass, 50-51; pvt pract, Columbus, Ga, 51-60; asst prof, Banting & Best Dept Med Res, Univ Toronto, 65-68, res assoc prof physiol, 65-68, res assoc internal med, 65-66, clin teacher, 66-68; PROF MED, SCH MED & DIR DIABETES UNIT, EMORY UNIV, 68- *Concurrent Pos:* Consult, Vet Admin Hosp, Tuskegee, Ala, 51-60; clin asst, Toronto Gen Hosp, 65-68; dir diabetes sect, Grady Mem Hosp, 68- *Honors & Awards:* Starr Medal, Toronto, 63. *Mem:* AMA; Am Diabetes Asn; fel Am Col Physicians; Am Soc Internal Med; Am Physiol Soc. *Res:* Immunologic insulin resistance; insulin immunity in animals and man; pathophysiology and therapy of obesity-induced diabetes mellitus. *Mailing Add:* 1075 Lullwater Rd NE Atlanta GA 30307

DAVIDSON, JOHN MICHAEL, b Covina, Calif, Feb 23, 43; m 70; c 2. NUCLEAR PHYSICS, ASTROPHYSICS. *Educ:* Univ Calif, Berkeley, AB, 67; Univ Md, College Park, MS, 70, PhD(physics), 73. *Prof Exp:* Res assoc physics, Nuclear Res Ctr Univ Alta, 74-76; res fel, 76-78, SR RES FEL PHYSICS, KELLOGG RADIATION LAB, CALIF INST TECHNOL, PASADENA, 78- *Mem:* Am Phys Soc. *Res:* Low energy experimental research in nuclear structure, nuclear astrophysics and weak interactions. *Mailing Add:* Kellogg Radiation Lab 106-38 Calif Inst Technol Pasadena CA 91107

DAVIDSON, JOHN RICHARD, b Derby, Conn, June 17, 29; m 51; c 3. ENGINEERING MECHANICS, APPLIED MECHANICS. *Educ:* Brown Univ, ScB, 51; Va Polytech Inst & State Univ, MS, 59, PhD(eng mech), 68. *Prof Exp:* Design engr, Nat Adv Comt Aeronaut, 51-53, res engr, 53-57, res engr, Nat Aero & Space Admin, 58-65, sect head, 65-70, asst br head, 70-71, BR HEAD, NASA, 71- *Concurrent Pos:* Engr, Vet Admin, 56- *Honors & Awards:* Spec Achievement Award, NASA, 72. *Mem:* Am Soc Mech Engrs; Soc Eng Sci; Am Inst Aeronaut & Astronaut; Sigma Xi. *Res:* Fatigue and fracture of aerospace structural materials; probability theory and its application to structural reliability; heat transfer; dynamics. *Mailing Add:* Mail Stop 188E Langley Res Ctr NASA Hampton VA 23665

DAVIDSON, JOSEPH KILLWORTH, b Columbus, Ohio, Jan 17, 38; m 68. MECHANICAL ENGINEERING. *Educ:* Ohio State Univ, BME & MSc, 60, PhD(mech eng), 65. *Prof Exp:* From instr to asst prof mech eng, Ohio State Univ, 62-73; assoc prof, 73-78, PROF MECH ENG, ARIZ STATE UNIV, 78- *Concurrent Pos:* Vis prof, Monash Univ, Melbourne, Australia, 80. *Mem:* Am Soc Mech Engrs. *Res:* Kinematics and dynamics of machinery; mechanical vibrations; failure prevention; mechanical design. *Mailing Add:* Dept of Mech Eng Ariz State Univ Tempe AZ 85281

DAVIDSON, JULIAN M, b Dublin, Eire, Apr 15, 31; m 60; c 3. NEUROPHYSIOLOGY. *Educ:* Hebrew Univ, Israel, MS, 56; Univ Calif, Berkeley, PhD(physiol), 59. *Prof Exp:* USPHS res fel anat, Sch Med, Univ Calif, Los Angeles, 59-60; res fel neurol, Hadassah Univ Hosp, Israel, 61-62; USPHS res fel psychol, Univ Calif, Berkeley, 62-63; from asst prof to assoc prof, 63-80, PROF PHYSIOL, STANFORD UNIV, 80- *Concurrent Pos:* Co-ed, J Hormones & Behavior, 69-77; mem endocrinol study sect, NIH, 70-74; Guggenheim vis res fel, Dept Human Anat, Oxford Univ, 70-71; vis fel, Battelle Seattle Res Ctr, 74-75. *Mem:* Am Physiol Soc; Endocrine Soc; Int Soc Neuroendocrinol; Int Brain Res Orgn. *Res:* Regulation of gonadotropic hormone secretion; reproductive endocrinology, neural and endocrine determinants of reproductive behavior; psychological correlates of consciousness. *Mailing Add:* Dept of Physiol Stanford Univ Stanford CA 94305

DAVIDSON, KEITH V(ERNON), b Holdrege, Nebr, May 7, 23; m 49; c 2. METALLURGY, MATERIALS SCIENCE. *Educ:* Colo Sch Mines, MetE, 49, MSc, 50. *Prof Exp:* Chemist, Am Smelting & Refining Co, 50-53; staff mem vacuum melting, 5360, staff mem powder metall, 60-70, sect leader, 70-81, ASSOC GROUP LEADER, CHEM & MAT SCI DIV, LOS ALAMOS NAT LAB, 81- *Mem:* Am Soc Metals. *Res:* Preparation of high purity metals, alloys and metal carbides by vacuum melting, arc melting and powder metallurgy; carbide-graphite composite fabrication and physical properties; development and preparation of nuclear fuel materials. *Mailing Add:* 268 Chamisa Los Alamos NM 87544

DAVIDSON, KENNETH LAVERN, b Lake Mills, Iowa, May 13, 40; m 60; c 3. METEOROLOGY. *Educ:* Univ Minn, Minneapolis, BS, 62; Univ Mich, MS, 66, PhD(meteorol), 70. *Prof Exp:* Asst res meteorologist, Great Lakes Res Div, Univ Mich, 65-67 & Dept Meteorol & Oceanog, 67-70; ASSOC PROF METEOROL, NAVAL POSTGRAD SCH, 70- *Mem:* Am Meteorol Soc; Am Geophys Union. *Res:* Properties of turbulent flow in the region adjacent to the earth surface responsible for exchange of heat, moisture and momentum between the atmosphere and boundary (ocean or land). *Mailing Add:* Dept of Meteorol Naval Postgrad Sch Monterey CA 93940

DAVIDSON, KRIS, b Fargo, NDak, Dec 28, 43. ASTROPHYSICS, ASTRONOMY. *Educ:* Calif Inst Technol, BS, 65; Cornell Univ, PhD(astrophys), 70. *Prof Exp:* Fel astron, Princeton Univ, 70-71; asst prof, 71-74; asst prof astrophys, 74-75, ASSOC PROF ASTROPHYS, SCH PHYSICS & ASTRON, UNIV MINN, MINNEAPOLIS, 75- *Concurrent Pos:* Sloan res fel, 75-79. *Mem:* Am Astron Soc; Int Astron Union; Royal Astron Soc; Astron Soc Pac; AAAS. *Res:* quasars; astronomical x-ray sources; crab nebula and other supernova remnants; very massive stars; infrared dwarf stars; extragalactic nebulae; chemical abundances; accretion disks; other astronomical objects. *Mailing Add:* Sch of Physics & Astron 116 Church St SE Minneapolis MN 55455

DAVIDSON, LEON, b New York, NY, Oct 18, 22; m 43; c 3. SOFTWARE SYSTEMS. *Educ:* Columbia Univ, AB, 42, BS, 43, MS, 47, PhD(chem eng), 51. *Prof Exp:* Jr scientist, S A M Labs, Columbia Univ, 43-44; chem engr, Thermal Diffusion Plant, Oak Ridge, 44-45, sr tech engr, Gaseous Diffusion Plant, 45-46; assoc engr, Brookhaven Nat Lab, 47; mem staff, Los Alamos Sci Lab, 49-52; opers analyst, US AEC, 52-53; sr engr, Nuclear Develop Assocs, Inc, 53-58, mgr, Datatron Opers, 58-59; assoc head prog sect, Lab, Gen Precision, Inc, 59-60; sr programmer, Teleregister Corp, 60-61; mgr prog sect, 61-62; mgr adv appl develop, Adv Systs Develop Div, Int Bus Mach Corp, 62-63; adv metroprocessing proj, 63-68, tech dir, Metroprocessing Assoc, 68, PRES, METROPROCESSING CORP AM, 68- *Res:* Alphanumeric computer input via pushbutton telephone dial; formation of bubbles at orifices; isotope separations; nuclear weapons and reactor design; economics of fissionable material productions; digital computer application and programming. *Mailing Add:* Metroprocessing Corp of Am 64 Prospect St White Plains NY 10606

DAVIDSON, LYNN BLAIR, b Grosse Point Farms, Mich, Sept 22, 40; m 65. DECISION ANALYSIS, PETROLEUM ENGINEERING. *Educ:* Stanford Univ, BS, 62, MS, 64, PhD(petrol eng), 66. *Prof Exp:* Sr reservoir engr, Mobil Oil Libya, Ltd, 66; res engr, Chevron Res Co, Standard Oil Calif, 66-70; opers res analyst, Getty Oil Co, 70-79, prof specialist mgt sci, 79-80, prof specialist strategic planning, 80-81. *Mem:* Soc Petrol Engrs. *Res:* Analysis of decision with uncertain consequences; investment analysis; analysis and modelling of large, fuzzy systems; strategic planning. *Mailing Add:* Getty Oil Co 3810 Wilshire Blvd Los Angeles CA 90010

DAVIDSON, MAYER B, b Baltimore, Md, Apr 11, 35; m 61, 80; c 4. ENDOCRINOLOGY, METABOLISM. *Educ:* Swarthmore Col, AB, 57; Harvard Univ, MD, 61. *Prof Exp:* Res internist, US Army Inst Environ Med, 66-69; from asst prof to prof, Sch Med, Univ Calif, Los Angeles, 69-79; DIR DIABETES PROG, CEDARS-LINAI MED CTR, 79- *Concurrent Pos:* Res fel, Dept Endocrinol & Metab, King County Hosp, Univ Wash, 64-65; USPHS fel, Nat Inst Arthritis & Metab Dis, 65-66. *Mem:* Am Diabetes Asn; Endocrine Soc; Am Soc Clin Invest; Sigma Xi; Am Fedn Clin Res. *Res:* Diabetes; insulin antagonism; mechanism of insulin action. *Mailing Add:* Cedars-Linai Med Ctr Bldg 516 8700 Beverly Blvd Los Angeles CA 90048

DAVIDSON, MELVIN G, b Winnipeg, Man, Apr 7, 38; US citizen; m 62; c 2. NUCLEAR PHYSICS. *Educ:* Whitman Col, AB, 60; Rensselaer Polytech Inst, PhD(theoret physics), 64. *Prof Exp:* Res fel theoret physics, Australian Nat Univ, 64-67; from asst prof to assoc prof, 67-74, PROF PHYSICS & DIR, COMPUT CTR, WESTERN WASH UNIV, 74- *Mem:* Am Phys Soc; Am Inst Physics. *Res:* Theoretical nuclear physics; nuclear collective model; elementary particle physics. *Mailing Add:* Dept Systs & Computing Western Wash Univ Bellingham WA 98225

DAVIDSON, NORMAN RALPH, b Chicago, Ill, Apr 5, 16; m 42; c 4. BIOCHEMISTRY. *Educ:* Univ Chicago, BS, 37, PhD(chem), 41; Oxford Univ, BSc, 39. *Prof Exp:* Res assoc, Nat Defense Res Comt proj, Univ Southern Calif, 41, Div War Res, Columbia Univ, 42 & Univ Chicago, 42; instr chem, Ill Inst Technol, 42; re assoc plutonium proj, Univ Chicago, 43-45; res physicist, Radio Corp Am, 45-46; from instr to assoc prof, 46-57, PROF CHEM, CALIF INST TECHNOL, 57- *Concurrent Pos:* Exec off chem, Calif Inst Technol, 67-73. *Honors & Awards:* G N Lewis Award, Am Chem Soc, 54; Peter Debye Award phys chem, Am Chem Soc, 71. *Mem:* Nat Acad Sci; Am Chem Soc; Am Soc Biol Chem. *Res:* Recombinant DNA studies of gene structure and function; electron microscopy of nucleic acids. *Mailing Add:* Dept Chem Calif Inst Technol Pasadena CA 91125

DAVIDSON, PHILIP MICHAEL, b Oakland, Calif, Jan 8, 50. FOOD MICROBIOLOGY. *Educ:* Univ Idaho, BS, 72; Univ Minn, MS, 77; Wash State Univ, PhD(food sci), 79. *Prof Exp:* ASST PROF FOOD MICROBIOL, UNIV TENN, 79- *Mem:* Inst Food Technologists; Am Soc Microbiol; Am Dairy Sci Asn. *Res:* Investigation of the activity and mechanism of action of antimicrobial compounds in foods. *Mailing Add:* Dept Food Technol & Sci PO Box 1071 Univ Tenn Knoxville TN 37901

DAVIDSON, RALPH HOWARD, b Vandalia, Ohio, Jan 19, 08; m 36; c 2. ENTOMOLOGY. *Educ:* Ohio State Univ, BS, 30, MS, 31, PhD(entom), 35. *Prof Exp:* Asst, 30-35, from instr to asst prof, 35-43, res assoc, 43-46, from assoc prof to prof, 58-71, EMER PROF ENTOM, OHIO STATE UNIV, 71- *Concurrent Pos:* Vis prof, Univ Wis & Northern Ariz. *Mem:* Fel AAAS; hon mem Entom Soc Am. *Res:* Leafhopper taxonomy; insect control, morphology, rearing and collecting; economic entomology. *Mailing Add:* 61 Blenheim Rd Columbus OH 43214

DAVIDSON, RICHARD LAURENCE, b Cleveland, Ohio, Feb 22, 41; m 67. GENETICS. *Educ:* Case Western Reserve Univ, BA, 63, PhD, 67. *Prof Exp:* asst prof, Harvard Med Sch, 70-73, assoc prof microbiol & molecular genetics, 73-81, res assoc human genetics, Children's Hosp Med Ctr, Boston,, 70-81; DIR, CTR GENETICS & BENJAMIN GOLDBERG PROF GENETICS, UNIV ILL MED CTR, 81- *Concurrent Pos:* Air Force Off Sci Res-Nat Res Coun fel, 67-68, Ctr Molecular Genetics, Paris, 67-70; ed-in-chief, Somatic Cell Genetics; co-dir, Cell Cult Ctr, Mass Inst Technol, 75-81; mem, Genetics Study Sect, NIH, 75-81. *Mem:* AAAS; Tissue Cult Asn; Cell Biol Asn. *Res:* Control of differentiation and gene expression in mammalian cells. *Mailing Add:* Ctr for Genetics Univ Ill Med Ctr Chicago IL 60612

DAVIDSON, ROBERT A, botany, deceased

DAVIDSON, ROBERT BELLAMY, b New York, NY, Jan 24, 47; c 2. PHYSICAL CHEMISTRY, PHYSICS. *Educ:* City Col New York, BSc, 66; Princeton Univ, MA, 68, PhD(chem), 70. *Prof Exp:* NIH fel chem, Cornell Univ, 69-70; Gibbs instr, Yale Univ, 70-73; asst prof chem, Amherst Col, 73-78; MEM STAFF, R & D ASSOCS, 78- *Mem:* Am Chem Soc; Am Phys Soc; AAAS. *Res:* Modeling, simulation and analysis of physical processes in artificial environments and technological arrtifacts; correlation of molecular electronic structure with chemical and physical properties. *Mailing Add:* R & D Assocs 1401 Wilson Blvd Arlington VA 22209

DAVIDSON, ROBERT W, b Buffalo, NY, Nov 19, 21; m 48; c 1. WOOD SCIENCE, WOOD TECHNOLOGY. *Educ:* Mont State Univ, BS, 48; State Univ NY Col Forestry, Syracuse, MS, 56, PhD(wood physics), 60. *Prof Exp:* Salesman wood prod, Yaw-Kinney Co, Inc, 48-53; res asst, 57-59, from instr to assoc prof, 59-69, asst leader, Org Mat Sci Prog, 69-71, chmn, Dept Wood Prod Eng, 72-79, prog mgr, Trop Timber Info Ctr, 75-79, PROF WOOD PHYSICS, COL ENVIRON SCI & FORESTRY, STATE UNIV NY, 69- *Concurrent Pos:* NSF res grants, 63-64 & 69-71; assoc prof, Col Forestry, Univ Philippines, 64-65; Soc Wood Sci & Technol & NSF vis scientist, 67; NSF & Govt of India exchange scientist, India, 75. *Mem:* Soc Rheol; Forest Prod Res Soc; Soc Wood Sci & Technol. *Res:* Physical properties of wood. *Mailing Add:* Col Environ Sci & Forestry State Univ NY Syracuse NY 13210

DAVIDSON, RONALD CROSBY, b Norwich, Ont, July 3, 41; m 63; c 2. PLASMA PHYSICS. *Educ:* McMaster Univ, BSc, 63; Princeton Univ, PhD(plasma physics), 66. *Prof Exp:* Asst res physicist, Univ Calif, Berkeley, 66-68; from asst prof to assoc prof physics, Univ Md, College Park, 68-73, prof physics & astron, 73-78; ASST DIR APPL PLASMA PHYSICS, OFF FUSION ENERGY, DEPT ENERGY, 78-; PROF PHYSICS & DIR, PLASMA FUSION CTR, MASS INST TECHNOL, CAMBRIDGE, 78- *Concurrent Pos:* Consult, Sci Applications, Inc, 80-; dir, Fusion Power Assocs, 80-; Alfred P Sloan fel, 70-71. *Mem:* Fel Am Phys Soc. *Res:* Plasma turbulence; nonlinear plasma theory; nonneutral plasmas; intense charged particle beams and microwave generation; nonequilibrium statistical mechanics. *Mailing Add:* Plasma Fusion Ctr Mass Inst Technol Cambridge MA 02139

DAVIDSON, RONALD G, b Hamilton, Ont, Oct 24, 33; m 57; c 2. PEDIATRICS, MEDICAL GENETICS. *Educ:* Western Ont Univ, MD, 57. *Prof Exp:* Intern, Vancouver Gen Hosp, BC, 57-58; asst resident pediat, 58-59; asst resident path, Children's Hosp Med Ctr, Boston, 59-60 & pediat, Boston City Hosp, 60-61; asst res prof pediat, State Univ NY Buffalo, 64-67, assoc prof, 67-70, prof pediat & assoc chmn dept, 70-74, dir div human genetics, Children's Hosp, 64-74; PROF PEDIAT, McMASTER UNIV, 75- *Concurrent Pos:* Fel pediat, Johns Hopkins Hosp, 61-63; fel biochem genetics, King's Col, Univ London, 63-64; assoc chief pediat, Roswell Park Mem Inst, 64-67. *Mem:* Am Soc Human Genetics; Soc Pediat Res; Am Pediat Soc; Can Soc Clin Invest. *Res:* Human biochemical genetics; inherited enzyme variants and gene action in the X chromosome. *Mailing Add:* Dept Pediat McMaster Univ Med Ctr Hamilton Can

DAVIDSON, ROSS WALLACE, b Columbus, Kans, Aug 12, 02; m 30; c 1. FOREST PATHOLOGY. *Educ:* Univ Ottawa, BS, 27; Univ Iowa, MS, 28. *Hon Degrees:* DSc, Univ Ottawa, 68. *Prof Exp:* Jr mycologist, USDA, 28-31, from asst mycologist to assoc mycologist, Off Forest Path, 31-44, pathologist, 44-51, forest pathologist, Forest Insect & Dis Lab, Forest Exp Sta, 51-57 & Forest Dis Lab, Plant Indust Sta, 57-61; res pathologist, 61-68, RES SPECIALIST FOREST PATH, COL FORESTRY, COLO STATE UNIV, 68- *Mem:* Bot Soc Am; Am Phytopath Soc. *Res:* Identification of forest fungi from cultural characteristics; fungus damage to wood and wood products. *Mailing Add:* 1205 Lory St Ft Collins CO 80524

DAVIDSON, SAMUEL JAMES, b Chicago, Ill, Mar 9, 37; m 60; c 2. BIOCHEMISTRY, CLINICAL CHEMISTRY. *Educ:* Univ Chicago, AB, 56, BS, 59, PhD(biochem), 64. *Prof Exp:* Res assoc biochem, Univ Chicago, 64; res assoc, Sch Med, Tufts Univ, 67-68, from instr to asst prof physiol, 68-74; res assoc, Bio-Res Inst, 74-76; asst dir, 77-81, ACTG DIR, DEPT CLIN BIOCHEM, BOSTON CITY HOSP, 81- *Concurrent Pos:* NIH fel biochem, Brandeis Univ, 65-67. *Res:* Membranes and dynamics of the vacuolar system; biochemistry of aryl hydrocarbon hydroxylase and chemical carcinogenesis. *Mailing Add:* Dept of Clin Biochem Boston City Hosp 818 Harrison Ave Boston MA 02118

DAVIDSON, STEVE EDWIN, b Dumas, Tex, July 2, 30; m 53; c 3. AGRONOMY. *Educ:* WTex State Col, BS, 51; Iowa State Col, MS, 52; Agr & Mech Col Tex, PhD(agron), 56. *Prof Exp:* Asst, Iowa State Col, 51-52 & Agr & Mech Col Tex, 52-56; soil scientist, Soil Conserv Serv, Plant Indust Sta, USDA, Md, 56-58; asst prof, 58-64, PROF BIOL, EVANGEL COL, 64- *Mem:* Am Soc Agron; Soil Sci Soc Am. *Res:* Soil physics; plant physiology. *Mailing Add:* Dept of Biol Evangel Col Springfield MO 65802

DAVIDSON, THEODORE, b Chicago, Ill, Mar 30, 39; m 62; c 1. MATERIALS SCIENCE, PHYSICAL CHEMISTRY. *Educ:* Cornell Univ, BA, 60; Univ Chicago, MS, 62; Rensselaer Polytech Inst, PhD(phys chem), 68. *Prof Exp:* Asst prof mat sci & chem eng, Northwestern Univ, 67-73; SCIENTIST MAT SCI, XEROX CORP, ROCHESTER, NY, 73- *Concurrent Pos:* Consult scientist, 69-73; exec comt mem, Div Org Coatings & Plastics Chem, Am Chem Soc, 78. *Honors & Awards:* Educ Serv Award, Plastics Inst Am, 75. *Mem:* AAAS; Am Phys Soc; Am Chem Soc; Mats Res Soc. *Res:* Structure of solid polymers in relation to physical properties; physical chemistry of macromolecules; electron and optical microscopy; surface science of polymers; biomaterials; application of physical sciences to archeology. *Mailing Add:* 32 Overbrook Rd Rochester NY 14618

DAVIDSON, THOMAS, JR, soil chemistry, soil fertility, see previous edition

DAVIDSON, THOMAS RALPH, b Alta, Mar 9, 20; m 49; c 2. PLANT PATHOLOGY. *Educ:* Univ Alta, BSc, 43, MSc, 45. *Prof Exp:* Assoc plant pathologist virus diseases, Alta, Can Dept Agr, 44-54, St Catharines, 54-67, res officer, Vineland Sta, Res Sta, 67-80; RETIRED. *Mem:* Agr Inst Can; Can Phytopath Soc. *Res:* Stone and pome fruit diseases. *Mailing Add:* Can Agr Res Sta Vineland-Station ON L0R 2E0 Can

DAVIDSON, WILLIAM JOHN, b Janesville, Minn, May 19, 24; m 46; c 3. PHYSICAL CHEMISTRY. *Educ:* Hamline Univ, BS, 49; Univ Conn, MS, 55. *Prof Exp:* Chemist, Phys Chem Rocket Fuels, US Navy, 51; asst, Univ Conn, 52-54; from chemist to sr res chemist, 54-66, tech serv rep, Spunbonded Prod, Textile Fibers Dept, 66-69, tech serv supvr, 69-72, CARPET TECH SUPVR, CARPET FIBERS & FIBERFILL DIV, TEXTILE FIBERS DEPT, E I DU PONT DE NEMOURS & CO, 72- *Mem:* Am Chem Soc; Am Asn Textile Chemists & Colorists. *Res:* Physical chemistry of high polymers and its application to textile fibers. *Mailing Add:* Textile Fibers Dept Ctr Rd Bldg E I du Pont de Nemours & Co Wilmington DE 19898

DAVIDSON, WILLIAM MARTIN, b Cambridge, Mass, Jan 3, 39; m 64; c 2. ORTHODONTICS. *Educ:* Dartmouth Col, AB, 60; Harvard Univ, DMD, 65; Univ Minn, cert orthod & PhD(anat), 69. *Prof Exp:* Teaching asst anat, Univ Minn, 65-69; asst prof orthod, Univ Conn Health Ctr, Farmington, 69-72, assoc dean dent educ, 72-76, assoc dean grad educ, 73-76; assoc prof orthod & chmn dept, Sch Dent, Univ Miss, 76-78; PROF & CHMN DEPT ORTHOD, UNIV MD, 78- *Concurrent Pos:* Consult, Coun Dent Educ, Am Dent Asn, 74, Am Asn Orthodontists Coun Res. *Mem:* Am Dent Asn; Am Asn Orthod; Int Asn Dent Res. *Res:* Dental education; orthodontics and the future of children's dentistry; bone biology. *Mailing Add:* Dept of Orthod Sch of Dent Univ of Md Baltimore MD 21228

DAVIDSON-ARNOTT, ROBIN, G D, b London, Eng, Mar 2, 47; Can citizen; m 68. GEOMORPHOLOGY, SEDIMENTOLOGY. *Educ:* Univ Toronto, BA Hons, 70, PhD(geog), 75. *Prof Exp:* Asst prof geog, Scarborough Col, Univ Toronto, 75-76; asst prof, 76-80, ASSOC PROF GEOG, UNIV GUELPH, 80- *Mem:* Can Asn Geographers; Soc Econ Paleontologists & Mineralogists; Int Asn Sedimentologists; Geol Asn Can. *Res:* Coastal sedimentology; nearshore processes and sediment transport; sedimentary structures; nearshore sand bars and beach equilibrium-barrier island sedimentation; post-Pleistocene lake and sea level changes. *Mailing Add:* Dept Geog Univ Guelph Guelph ON N1G 2W1 Can

DAVIE, EARL W, b Tacoma, Wash, Oct 25, 27; m 52; c 4. BIOCHEMISTRY. *Educ:* Univ Wash, BS, 50, PhD(biochem), 54. *Prof Exp:* From asst prof to assoc prof biochem, Western Reserve Univ, 56-62; assoc prof, 62-66, PROF BIOCHEM, SCH MED, UNIV WASH, 66-, CHMN DEPT, 77- *Concurrent Pos:* Nat Found Infantile Paralysis fel, Mass Gen Hosp, 54-56; NSF & Commonwealth Fund fel, Inst Molecular Biol, Univ Geneva, 66-67; mem, Nat Bd Med Exam, 71-75; mem res rev comt, Am Nat Red Cross Blood Prog, 73-77; mem, Nat Hemophilia Found Med & Sci Adv Coun, 74-79; mem, Hematology Study Sect, NIH, 75-79. *Mem:* Am Acad Sci; Am Chem Soc; Am Soc Biol Chem (secy, 75-78); Am Soc Hematol; AAAS. *Res:* Protein chemistry and enzymology. *Mailing Add:* Dept Biochem Univ Wash Sch Med Seattle WA 98195

DAVIE, JOSEPH MYRTEN, b LaPorte, Ind, Oct 14, 39; m 60; c 3. IMMUNOLOGY. *Educ:* Ind Univ, AB, 62, MA, 64, PhD(bact), 66; Washington Univ, MD, 68. *Prof Exp:* Fel, Sch Med, Washington Univ, 66-67, intern path, 68-69; staff assoc immunol, Nat Inst Allergy & Infectious Dis, NIH, 69-71, resident path, Nat Cancer Inst, 71-72; assoc prof path & microbiol, 72-75, PROF & HEAD DEPT MICROBIOL & IMMUNOL & PROF PATH, SCH MED, WASHINGTON UNIV, 75- *Concurrent Pos:* Dir grad studies exp path, Sch Med, Washington Univ, 73-75; mem path B study sect, NIH, 74-78; assoc ed, J Immunol, 75- *Mem:* Am Soc Microbiol; Am Asn Immunologists; Am Soc Exp Path; Am Asn Univ Pathologists. *Res:* Cellular basis of immune response and the genetics of immunoglobulin structure. *Mailing Add:* Dept of Microbiol & Immunol Sch of Med Washington Univ St Louis MO 63110

DAVIE, WILLIAM RAYMOND, b Aliquippa, Pa, Mar 16, 24; m 48. ORGANIC CHEMISTRY. *Educ:* Geneva Col, BS, 47; Univ Wis, MS, 49, PhD(org chem), 51. *Prof Exp:* Sampler, J & L Steel Corp, 43-47; asst, Univ Wis, 47-50; asst, 50-51; asst supvr, Agr Res, Pittsburgh Coke & Chem Co, 51-55; supvr, New Prods Res, Chemagro Corp, 55-57; asst supvr, Org Res, Pittsburgh Coke & Chem Co, 57-58, supvr, 59-64; supvr, 64-67, SR RES CHEMIST, APPL RES LAB, GEN ORG RES, CHEM DIV, US STEEL CORP, 67- *Res:* Organic research; agricultural chemical research; resins and protective coatings; phthalocyanine research; dibasic acids and their production; coal carbonization; air and water pollution studies; propagation of trees. *Mailing Add:* 3100 Kane Road Aliquippa PA 15001

DAVIES, CRAIG EDWARD, b Astoria, Ore, Jan 26, 43; m 66; c 3. NUCLEAR ENGINEERING. *Educ:* Ore State Univ, BS, 65; Pa State Univ, MS, 67. *Prof Exp:* Aerodynamics engr, Lockheed Missiles & Space Ctr, 67-69; nuclear plant engr trainee, Westinghouse Elec Corp, Bettis Atomic Power Lab, Naval Reactors Facil, Idaho, 69-70, various mgt position, 70-74, mgr, reactor opers training, 74-75; mgt trainee & student, Westinghouse Elec Corp, Prospective Commanding Officer Sch, Washington, DC, 75; prototype mgr opers & training, 75-78, site mgr overall opers, Naval Reactor Facil, WestinghouseElec Corp, Idaho, 78-81, MGR AVAILABILITY ASSURANCE, WESTINGHOUSE STEAM TURBINE GENERATOR DIV, ORLANDO, FLA, 81- *Concurrent Pos:* Bd dir, Intermountain Sci Exp Ctr, 78- *Mem:* Am Nuclear Soc. *Res:* Testing and performance evaluation of materials and components associated with power generating nuclear reactor plants. *Mailing Add:* Box 95 Rural Route 4 Idaho Falls ID 83401

DAVIES, D K, b Ammanford, Wales, UK, Sept 5, 35; m 62; c 2. PHYSICS. *Educ:* Univ Wales, BSc, 57, PhD(physics), 61. *Prof Exp:* Cent Elec Generating Bd sr res fel physics, Univ Col Swansea, Wales, 60-62; SR PHYSICIST, RES & DEVELOP CTR, WESTINGHOUSE ELEC CORP, 62- *Mem:* Am Phys Soc; fel Brit Inst Physics & Physics Soc. *Res:* Spatial and temporal growth of ionization in gases; atomic collisional processes in gases; vacuum breakdown; analytical spectroscopy; electron transport in gases. *Mailing Add:* Westinghouse Res Labs Beulah Rd Pittsburgh PA 15235

DAVIES, DAVID HUW, b Tredegar, Eng, Oct 29, 42; m 66. PHYSICAL CHEMISTRY. *Educ:* Univ Col, London, BSc, 64, PhD(phys chem), 67; Univ Pittsburgh, MBA, 72. *Prof Exp:* Sr scientist, Westinghouse Elec Corp, 67-72, mgr thin film mat, Res & Develop Ctr, 72-77; mgr eng & dir, Datascreen Corp, Exxon Corp, 77-79, VPRES, KYLEX DIV, EXXON ENTERPRISES, 79- *Mem:* Inst Elec & Electronic Engineers; Electrochem Soc; Optical Soc Am; Soc Info Display. *Res:* Solid state display; thin films; electrical packaging; Optical memory systems; liquid crystals. *Mailing Add:* 328 Gibraltar Dr Sunnyvale CA 94086

DAVIES, DAVID K, b Glamorgan, Wales, Oct 10, 40; m 64; c 2. GEOLOGY. *Educ:* Univ Wales, BSc, 62, PhD(geol), 66; La State Univ, MS, 64. *Prof Exp:* From asst prof to assoc prof geol, Tex A&M Univ, 66-70, asst to dean, 66-70; from assoc prof to prof geol, Univ Mo-Columbia, 70-77; PROF GEOL, CHMN DEPT & DIR RESERVOIR STUDIES INST, TEX TECH UNIV, 77- *Mem:* Am Asn Petrol Geologists; Geol Soc Am; Soc Econ Paleontologists & Mineralogists; fel Brit Geol Soc. *Res:* Reservoir geology; sandstone diagenesis; volcanic sedimentation; paleogeographic reconstruction; quantitative methods. *Mailing Add:* Dept of Geosci Tex Tech Univ Lubbock TX 79409

DAVIES, DAVID R, b Carmarthen, UK, Feb 22, 27; US citizen; m 51; c 2. BIOPHYSICS, CRYSTALLOGRAPHY. *Educ:* Oxford Univ, BA, 49, DPhil(chem crystallog), 52. *Prof Exp:* Noyes fel chem, Calif Inst Technol, 52-54; res scientist, Albright & Wilson, Eng, 54-55; vis scientist molecular biol, NIMH, 55-62, CHIEF SECT MOLECULAR STRUCT, NAT INST ARTHRITIS & METAB DIS, 62- *Mem:* Nat Acad Sci; Am Crystallog Asn; Am Soc Biol Chemists; AAAS; Biophys Soc. *Res:* Application of crystallographic techniques to the determination of structures of biological interest; nucleic acids and proteins; determination of precise crystal structures. *Mailing Add:* NIH Bldg 2 Room 316 Bethesda MD 20205

DAVIES, DONALD HARRY, b Ottawa, Ont, Jan 26, 38; m 78; c 1. PHYSICAL CHEMISTRY. *Educ:* Carleton Univ, BSc, 60; Bristol Univ, PhD(chem), 63. *Prof Exp:* Nat Res Coun Can fel, 63-65; asst prof chem, Dalhousie Univ, 65-69; asst prof, 69-71, chmn dept, 73-78, assoc prof chem, 71-79, PROF CHEM, ST MARY'S UNIV, 79-; PRES, NOVA CHEM, LTD, 78- *Concurrent Pos:* Sessional lectr, Carleton Univ, 65. *Mem:* Chem Inst Can; Royal Soc Chem; Faraday Soc. *Res:* Surface chemistry and thermodynamics; polymer degradation. *Mailing Add:* Dept of Chem St Mary's Univ Halifax NS B3H 3C3 Can

DAVIES, DONALD LESLIE, b Birkenhead, Eng, Jan 26, 24; US citizen; m 47; c 2. FOOD SCIENCE. *Educ:* Roosevelt Col, BS, 50. *Prof Exp:* From res biologist to sect head canned foods grocery div, 50-74, PROJ LEADER NEW PROD, SWIFT & CO, 74- *Mem:* Inst Food Technologists. *Res:* Formulation and development of frozen and canned meat; dehydration of foods; snack food development; sectioned and formed meat items; basic new food product development. *Mailing Add:* Swift & Co Res & Develop Ctr 1919 Swift Dr Oakbrook IL 60521

DAVIES, DOUGLAS MACKENZIE, b Toronto, Ont, May 11, 19; m 48; c 2. ENTOMOLOGY. *Educ:* Univ Toronto, BA, 42, PhD(entom), 49. *Prof Exp:* Res fel parasitol, Ont Res Found, 49-51; sessional lectr, 50-51, from asst prof to assoc prof, 51-63, prof zool, 63-80, PROF BIOL, MCMASTER UNIV, 80- *Mem:* Fel Entom Soc Am; Am Mosquito Control Asn; Entom Soc Can; fel Royal Entom Soc; Can Soc Zool. *Res:* Ecology, behavior physiology and systematics of simuliids, other blood sucking flies and muscids. *Mailing Add:* Dept of Biol McMaster Univ Hamilton ON L8S 4K1 Can

DAVIES, EMLYN B, b Minnedosa, Man, Feb 23, 27; m 62; c 3. PHYSICS. *Educ:* Univ Man, BSc, 48; Pa State Univ, MS, 51, PhD(physics), 53. *Prof Exp:* Sr res geophysicist, 53-70, sect supvr, 70-73, MGR GEOPHYSICS ANAL DEPT, GULF RES & DEVELOP CO, 74- *Mem:* AAAS; Soc Explor Geophys; Acoust Soc Am; Am Phys Soc. *Res:* Elastic wave propagation; information theory. *Mailing Add:* Gulf Res & Develop Co Box 36506 Houston TX 77036

DAVIES, ERIC, b Liverpool, Eng, Aug 24, 39; m 63; c 2. PLANT PHYSIOLOGY. *Educ:* Wye Col, London Univ, BSc, 62; McGill Univ, PhD(bot), 68. *Prof Exp:* Asst prof bot, 68-73, ASSOC PROF LIFE SCI, UNIV NEBR-LINCOLN, 73-, MEM FAC LIFE SCI, 76- *Concurrent Pos:* Res prof, Lab Nuclear Med, Univ Brussels, 75-76. *Mem:* Am Soc Plant Physiologists; Can Soc Plant Physiologists; Scand Soc Plant Physiologists. *Res:* Molecular biology of plant hormones. *Mailing Add:* Sch Life Sci Univ Nebr Lincoln NE 68588

DAVIES, FREDERICK T, JR, b Springfield, Mass, Jan 8, 49. HORTICULTURE, PLANT PHYSIOLOGY. *Educ:* Rutgers Col, BA, 71, MS, 75; Univ Fla, PhD(hort), 78. *Prof Exp:* Grad asst hort, Rutgers Univ, 73-75, Univ Fla, 75-78; ASST PROF HORT, TEX A&M UNIV, 78- *Concurrent Pos:* NJ State fed grant, 74-75. *Mem:* Am Soc Hort Sci; Int Plant Propagators Soc. *Res:* Juvenility-maturity; developmental botany and physiology; plant propagation; plant growth regulators. *Mailing Add:* Dept Hort Sci Tex A&M Univ College Station TX 77843

DAVIES, GEOFFREY, b Stoke-on-Trent, Eng, Feb 6, 42; m 65; c 3. INORGANIC CHEMISTRY, ANALYTICAL CHEMISTRY. *Educ:* Univ Birmingham, BSc, 63, PhD(chem), 66. *Prof Exp:* NIH fel chem, Brandeis Univ, 66-68; res assoc, Brookhaven Nat Lab, 68-69; IMP Chem Industs fel, Univ Kent, 69-71; from asst prof to assoc prof, 71-81, PROF & DIR GRAD AFFAIRS, NORTHEASTERN UNIV, 81- *Concurrent Pos:* Royal Soc traveling fel, 70; fac fel, Inst Chem Anal, Appln & Forensic Sci, Northeastern Univ, 72-; ed consult, John Wiley & Sons, Inc, 73- & Macmillan Co, 74- *Mem:* Am Chem Soc; The Chem Soc; Sigma Xi. *Res:* Kinetics and mechanisms of solution phase reactions; synthesis and characterization of novel inorganic complexes containing oxygen; models for biochemical processes; theoretical studies of electron-transfer; development of new methodology in forensic science. *Mailing Add:* Dept of Chem Northeastern Univ Boston MA 02115

DAVIES, HAROLD WILLIAM, (JR), b Norton, Kans, Aug 2, 30; m 56; c 3. AQUATIC BIOLOGY, PHYCOLOGY. *Educ:* Kans State Teachers Col, BS, 56, MS, 58; Mich State Univ, PhD(bot), 66. *Prof Exp:* Instr biol, Kans State Teachers Col, 57-58; instr & ed consult biol sci, State Dept Sec Educ, New South Wales, 61-63; chmn dept, 64-78, PROF BIOL SCI, PURDUE UNIV, FT WAYNE, 64- *Mem:* Brit Phycol Soc; Phycol Soc Am; Am Micros Soc; Am Inst Biol Sci; Int Phycol Soc. *Res:* Ecology of the phytopsammon; freshwater algae morphology and ecology; limnology. *Mailing Add:* Dept of Biol Sci Purdue Univ Ft Wayne IN 46805

DAVIES, HELEN JEAN CONRAD, b New York, NY, Feb 14, 25; m 61; c 2. BIOCHEMISTRY, MICROBIOLOGY. *Educ:* Brooklyn Col, AB, 44; Univ Rochester, MS, 50; Univ Pa, PhD(biochem), 60. *Prof Exp:* Sci worker biochem, Smith Kline & French Labs, Pa, 53-54; res assoc, Grad Sch Med, 54-56, res assoc microbiol, Sch Med, 62-65, asst prof, 65-71, asst prof community med, 70-71, ASSOC PROF MICROBIOL & PHYS BIOCHEM, UNIV PA, 71- *Concurrent Pos:* Johnson Found res fel, Univ Pa, 60-62; mem bd trustees, Pa State Univ, 73-78. *Mem:* Am Chem Soc; Am Soc Biol Chem; Am Soc Microbiol; Biophys Soc; Asn Women Sci. *Res:* Oxidative enzymes; cytochrome pigments; monoclonal antibodies; respiratory chain systems; enzyme kinetics; steady-state growth of microorganisms; streptococci; recruitment and retention of minority group students and women in biomedical careers. *Mailing Add:* Dept of Microbiol Univ of Pa Philadelphia PA 19104

DAVIES, HUW M, b Newtown, UK, Sept 23, 57; m 80. PLANT BIOCHEMISTRY. *Educ:* Oxford Univ, BA, 74; London Univ, PhD(biochem), 77. *Prof Exp:* Res assoc, Mich State Univ-Dept Energy, Plant Res Lab, 77-80; vis res fel, Plant Growth Lab, Univ Calif, Davis, 80-81; PRIN SCIENTIST, CALGENE, INC, 81- *Mem:* Am Soc Plant Physiologists. *Res:* Plant biochemistry and physiology especially nitrogen and protein metabolism, metabolic regulation and properties of plant cell cultures; enzymology and metabolic pathway dynamics. *Mailing Add:* Calgene Inc 1910 Fifth St Suite F Davis CA 95616

DAVIES, JACK, b Eng, Aug 24, 19; m 46; c 2. ANATOMY, EMBRYOLOGY. *Educ:* Univ Iowa, MD, 43; Cambridge Univ, MA, 46; Univ Leeds, MD, 47. *Prof Exp:* Demonstr anat, Univ Leeds, 43-44; demonstr, Cambridge Univ, 44-49, lectr, 49-51; from asst prof to assoc prof, Univ Iowa, 51-55; from assoc prof to prof, Sch Med, Wash Univ, 55-63; PROF ANAT & CHMN DEPT, SCH MED, VANDERBILT UNIV, 63- *Concurrent Pos:* Fel, Cambridge Univ, 49-51; Markle scholar, 53; consult, USPHS, 58- *Mem:* AAAS; Am Asn Anat; Soc Exp Biol & Med. *Res:* Morphology and physiology of the placenta. *Mailing Add:* Dept of Anat Vanderbilt Univ Med Sch Nashville TN 37240

DAVIES, JACK NEVILLE PHILLIPS, b Devizes, Eng, July 2, 15; m 44, 61; c 3. EPIDEMIOLOGY. *Educ:* Bristol Univ, MB & ChB, 39, MD, 48. *Prof Exp:* Lectr physiol & demonstr pharmacol, Bristol Univ, 41-44; pathologist, Uganda Govt, 45-50; prof path, Med Sch, Makerere Univ Col, Uganda, 50-61; reader morbid anat, Postgrad Med Sch, Univ London, 61-63; PROF PATH, ALBANY MED COL, 63- *Concurrent Pos:* Commonwealth Fund fel, Duke Univ, 49-50; consult pathologist, Uganda Govt, 50-61; mem, EAfrican Med Res Coun, 52-61; mem comt, Int Soc Geog Path, 52-60; mem African cancer comt, Int Union Against Cancer, 55-62; Fox lectr, Bristol Univ, 62; Musser lectr, Tulane Univ, 64. *Mem:* Am Asn Path & Bact; Path Soc Gt Brit & Ireland; Brit Med Asn. *Res:* Morbid anatomy; geographic pathology, especially of cancer and cardiovascular disease. *Mailing Add:* Rowe Road Feura Bush NY 12067

DAVIES, JAMES FREDERICK, b Winnipeg, Man, Dec 5, 24. ECONOMIC GEOLOGY, PETROLOGY. *Educ:* Univ Man, BSc, 46, MSc, 48; Univ Toronto, PhD(geol), 63. *Prof Exp:* Lectr geol, Univ Man, 47; geologist, Man Dept Mines & Natural Resources, 51-57, chief geologist, 57-67; PROF GEOL, LAURENTIAN UNIV, 67- *Concurrent Pos:* Hon lectr, Univ Man, 57-; mem, Nat Adv Comt Res Geol Sci-Can, 58-62. *Honors & Awards:* Barlow Medal, Can Inst Mining & Metall, 65. *Mem:* Fel Geol Asn Can; fel Mineral Asn Can; Soc Econ Geologists; Can Inst Mining & Metall. *Res:* Regional mapping; compilation, analysis and interpretation of regional geology, tectonic features; geochemistry of Pre-Cambrian rocks, mineral deposits and wall-rocks; studies of Pre-Cambrian volcanic rocks; genesis of base metal sulphide deposits; fabrics of sulphides; deformation and remobilization of sulphide deposits. *Mailing Add:* Dept of Geol Laurentian Univ Sudbury ON P3E 2C6 Can

DAVIES, JOHN A, b Milwaukee, Wis, May 4, 31; m 63; c 2. PHYSICS. *Educ:* Univ Md, BS, 53, MS, 54, PhD(physics), 60. *Prof Exp:* Res asst physics, Univ Md, 53-60; vis asst prof, Univ Cincinnati, 63; asst prof, 63-69, ASSOC PROF PHYSICS, CLARK UNIV, 69- *Mem:* Am Phys Soc. *Res:* Mathematical physics; lattice dynamics of ionic crystals. *Mailing Add:* Dept of Physics Clark Univ Worcester MA 01610

DAVIES, JOHN ARTHUR, b Prestatyn, NWales, Mar 28, 27; Can citizen; m 50; c 6. SOLID STATE SCIENCE, ATOMIC PHYSICS. *Educ:* Univ Toronto, BA, 47, MA, 48, PhD(phys chem), 50. *Prof Exp:* Asst res officer phys chem, Chalk River Nuclear Labs, 50-54; Can Ramsey fel polymerization kinetics, Leeds, 54-56; assoc & sr res officer nuclear sci, 56-68, PRIN RES OFFICER, RES CHEM BR, CHALK RIVER NUCLEAR LABS, 68- *Concurrent Pos:* Ammanuensis, Physics Inst, Aarhus Univ, 64-65; guest prof, 69-70; prof physics & eng physics, McMaster Univ, 70- *Honors & Awards:* Noranda Award, Chem Inst Can, 65; T D Callinan Award, 68. *Mem:* Am Vacuum Soc; Royal Danish Acad Sci & Letters; Royal Soc Can; Chem Inst Can. *Res:* Ion transport and diffusion processes in solutions; polymerization kinetics; slowing down behaviour of energetic ions in solids; anodic oxidation of metals; channeling of energetic ion beams in crystals; ion implantation. *Mailing Add:* Chalk River Nuclear Labs Dept of Chem & Mat Div Chalk River Can

DAVIES, JOHN CLIFFORD, b Edmonton, Alta, Sept 30, 32; m 61; c 4. GEOLOGY. *Educ:* Univ Manitoba, BSc, 55, MSc, 56, PhD(petrol & geochem), 66. *Prof Exp:* Geologist, Falconbridge Nickel Mines Ltd, 57 & US Steel Corp, 58-59; res geologist, Ont Dept Mines, 60-68; field geologist, Ont Geol Surv, 68-75; head & asst dir, Econ Geol Div, Geol Surv Botswana, 75-77; SR ECON GEOLOGIST, SASK MINING DEVELOP CORP, 77- *Concurrent Pos:* Field geologist, Ethiopian Ministry Mines, 72-74. *Mem:* Geol Asn Can; Mineral Asn Can; Soc Econ Geologists; Can Inst Mining & Metall. *Res:* Analysis of field data and research programs to identify areas having potential for mineral deposits. *Mailing Add:* 411 Garrison Crescent Saskatoon SK S7H 2Z9 Can

DAVIES, JULIAN ANTHONY, b Middlesex, Eng, Aug 10, 55; m 79. HOMOGENEOUS CATALYSIS, INDUSTRIAL CHEMISTRY. *Educ:* Univ London, Eng, BSc Hons, 76, PhD(chem), 79; Imperial Col Sci & Technol, ARCS, 76. *Prof Exp:* Res fel, Univ Guelph, 79-81; ASST PROF CHEM, UNIV TOLEDO, 81- *Mem:* Royal Soc Chem; Am Chem Soc; AAAS. *Res:* Homogeneous catalytic processes involving transition metal complexes; chemistry of the platinum metals; coordination chemistry; organometallic chemistry; nuclear magnetic resonance spectroscopy. *Mailing Add:* Dept Chem Univ Toledo 2801 W Bancroft St Toledo OH 43606

DAVIES, KENNARD MICHAEL, b Los Angeles, Calif, May 26, 41; m 71. PHYSICS. *Educ:* Loyola Univ Los Angeles, BS, 63; Univ Notre Dame, PhD(physics), 70. *Prof Exp:* ASST PROF PHYSICS, CREIGHTON UNIV, 69- *Mem:* Am Phys Soc; Am Asn Physics Teachers. *Res:* Equilibrium and nonequilibrium statistical physics; phase transitions and interphase surfaces; muscle biophysics. *Mailing Add:* Creighton Univ Omaha NE 68178

DAVIES, KENNETH, b Wales, Jan 28, 28; m 58; c 3. IONOSPHERIC PHYSICS. *Educ:* Univ Wales, BSc, 49, PhD, 53. *Prof Exp:* Team leader, Defence Res Telecommunications Estab, Can, 52-55; asst prof, Brown Univ, 56-58; CHIEF, RES DIV, SPACE ENVIRON LAB, NAT OCEANIC & ATMOSPHERIC ADMIN, 58- *Concurrent Pos:* Adj prof, Univ Colo, 64-; Webster Mem fel, Univ Queensland, 75-76. *Mem:* AAAS; Am Geophys Union; Sigma Xi; Inst Elec & Electronics Engrs; Int Sci Radio Union. *Res:* Upper atmosphere physics; radio propagation; satellite to ground radio propagation; plasmaspheric-ionospheric total electron content. *Mailing Add:* Environ Res Lab Nat Oceanic & Atmospheric Admin Boulder CO 80302

DAVIES, KENNETH THOMAS REED, b Pittsburgh, Pa, Nov 26, 34; m 57; c 3. NUCLEAR PHYSICS, THEORETICAL PHYSICS. *Educ:* Carnegie Inst Technol, BS, 57, MS, 59, PhD(physics), 62. *Prof Exp:* Instr physics, Carnegie Inst Technol, 62; THEORET PHYSICIST, OAK RIDGE NAT LAB, 62- *Mem:* Fel Am Phys Soc; Fedn Am Scientists. *Res:* Fission and heavy-ion reactions; time-dependent Hartree-Fock theory of nuclear collective dynamics. *Mailing Add:* Physics Div Oak Ridge Nat Lab PO Box X Oak Ridge TN 37830

DAVIES, MARCIA A, b Omaha, Nebr, Nov 24, 38; m 71. MOLECULAR SPECTROSCOPY. *Educ:* Duchesne Univ, BA, 61; Univ Notre Dame, PhD(inorg chem), 66. *Prof Exp:* Res assoc, Univ Ariz, 66-67; asst prof, 67-74, ASSOC PROF CHEM, CREIGHTON UNIV, 74- *Mem:* Am Chem Soc; Soc Appl Spectros. *Res:* Metal isotope effects in far infrared spectra of metal complexes; magnetic susceptibilities of metal complexes. *Mailing Add:* Dept of Chem Creighton Univ Omaha NE 68178

DAVIES, MERTON EDWARD, b St Paul, Minn, Sept 13, 17; m 46; c 3. PLANETARY SCIENCES, PHOTOGRAMMETRY. *Educ:* Stanford Univ, AB, 38. *Prof Exp:* Instr math, Univ Nev, 38-39; math group leader, Douglas Aircraft Co, 40-48; MEM SR STAFF, RAND CORP, 48- *Concurrent Pos:* Mem US deleg, Surprise Attack Conf, Geneva, 58; mem, US Observer Team, Antarctic, 67; TV exp teams, Mariner 6 & 7, 69, Mariner 9, 71, Mariner 10, 73, Voyager, 77, Galileo & VOIR. *Honors & Awards:* George W Goddard Award, Soc Photo-Optical Instrument Engineers, 66; Talbert Abrams Award, Am Soc Photogram, 74. *Mem:* AAAS; assoc fel Am Inst Aeronaut & Astronaut; Am Soc Photogram; Am Geophys Union; Am Astron Soc. *Res:* Physics of aerial and space photography; planetary geodesy; inspection for arms control. *Mailing Add:* 1414 San Remo Dr Pacific Palisades CA 90272

DAVIES, MICHAEL SHAPLAND, b Cardiff, Wales, June 6, 39; m 66; c 2. ELECTRICAL ENGINEERING. *Educ:* Cambridge Univ, MA, 61; Univ Ill, MS, 63, PhD(elec eng), 66. *Prof Exp:* Asst prof, 66-74, ASSOC PROF ELEC ENG, UNIV BC, 76- *Mem:* Inst Elec & Electronics Engrs; Can Pulp & Paper. *Res:* Process control systems. *Mailing Add:* Dept Elec Eng Univ BC Vancouver BC V6T 1W5 Can

DAVIES, PETER JOHN, b Sudbury, Eng, Mar 7, 40. PLANT HORMONES, PLANT SENESCIENCE. *Educ:* Univ Reading, BS, 62, PhD(plant physiol), 66; Univ Calif, Davis, MS, 64. *Prof Exp:* Instr biol, Yale Univ, 66-69; asst prof, 69-75, ASSOC PROF PLANT PHYSIOL, CORNELL UNIV, 75- *Mem:* Am Soc Plant Physiol; Int Plant Growth Substance Asn; Scand Soc Plant Physiol; Japanese Soc Plant Physiol. *Res:* Mode of action, biochemistry and transport of plant hormones; physiology of senescence in whole plants; environmental, hormonal and biochemical interrelationships in plant senescence. *Mailing Add:* Div Biol Sci Sect Plant Biol Cornell Univ Ithaca NY 14853

DAVIES, REG, b Nottingham, Eng, May 15, 36; c 2. PARTICLE TECHNOLOGY, CHEMICAL ENGINEERING. *Educ:* Univ London, BS, 59; Loughborough Univ Technol, PhD(particle technol), 77. *Prof Exp:* Scientist coal, Nat Coal Bd, Eng, 53-67; scientist particle res, Ill Inst Technol Res Inst, 67-75; CONSULT PARTICLE PROCESSES, E I DU PONT DE NEMOURS & CO, INC, 75- *Concurrent Pos:* Bd mem, Fine Particle Soc, 73-78; sci bd mem for US, 2nd Europ Conf Particle Technol, 78-79; chmn, Tech Comt, Int Fine Particle Res Inst. *Mem:* Fine Particle Soc (pres, 75-76). *Res:* Powder, slurry, dust and mist technology; particle size analysis; particle characterization, specifically the effect of particle characteristics on chemical processes and products. *Mailing Add:* Eng Serv Div Dupont Co Louviers Bldg Wilmington DE 19898

DAVIES, RICHARD EDGAR, b Schenectady, NY, Jan 5, 15; m 43; c 1. ORGANIC CHEMISTRY, PLASTICS. *Educ:* Union Col, BS, 35; Columbia Univ, PhD(chem), 41. *Prof Exp:* Chemist, Catalin Corp of Am, 42-46, Celanese Corp of Am, 46-57 & Air Reduction Inc, 57-65; chemist, 65-66, asst res mgr, 66-78; assoc dir, Eastern Res Div, ITT Rayonier, Inc, 78-81; RETIRED. *Mem:* Am Chem Soc. *Res:* Organic synthesis; cellulose; hydrogenation; synthetic fibers; high polymers. *Mailing Add:* 46 S Murray Ave Ridgewood NJ 07450

DAVIES, RICHARD GLYN, b Congleton, Eng, Nov 1, 34; m 58; c 3. PHYSICAL METALLURGY. *Educ:* Univ Birmingham, BSc, 56, PhD(phys metall), 59; Univ Mich, MBA, 74. *Prof Exp:* Prof metall, Inst Physics, Nat Univ Cuyo, Bariloche, 59-61; STAFF SCIENTIST, FORD MOTOR CO, 62- *Honors & Awards:* Henry Marion Howe Medal, Am Soc Metals, 72. *Mem:* Am Inst Mining, Metall & Petrol Engrs; Am Soc Metals. *Res:* Relationship of metallurgical structure to deformation behavior in ordered systems; nickel base precipitation hardened alloys and ferrous martensites; martensite morphology; high strength low alloy and dual-phase steels. *Mailing Add:* Metall Dept Sci Res Staff Ford Motor Co PO Box 2053 Dearborn MI 48121

DAVIES, RICHARD O, b Brantford, Ont, July 28, 31; m 54; c 3. MEDICINE, PHARMACOLOGY. *Educ:* Univ Toronto, BSc, 54, MA, 56, PhD(pharmacol), 58, MD, 62. *Prof Exp:* Adj assoc prof med, Thomas Jefferson Univ, Philadelphia, 78- *Concurrent Pos:* Lectr, McGill Univ, 69-76. Concurrent. *Mem:* Can Med Asn; Can Cardiovasc Soc; Am Fedn Clin Res; Am Soc Clin Pharmacol & Therapeut; Am Col Cardiol. *Res:* Clinical pharmacology in cardiovascular areas, especially angina, beta blockade, hypertension, shock, atherosclerosis and lipids; bioavailability and pharmacokinetics; psychopharmacology. *Mailing Add:* Merck Sharp & Dohme Res Labs West Point PA 19486

DAVIES, RICHARD OELBAUM, b New York, NY, Oct 8, 36; m 65. VETERINARY PHYSIOLOGY. *Educ:* Cornell Univ, DVM, 60; Univ Pa, PhD(physiol), 64. *Prof Exp:* Assoc, 64-66, asst prof, 66-69, assoc prof, 69-79, PROF PHYSIOL, SCH VET MED, UNIV PA, 79- *Mem:* AAAS; Am Physiol Soc; Soc Neurosci; Am Soc Vet Physiol & Pharmacol. *Res:* Neurophysiology and respiratory control mechanisms. *Mailing Add:* Dept of Animal Biol Univ of Pa Sch of Vet Med Philadelphia PA 19104

DAVIES, ROBERT DILLWYN, b Bristol, Eng, Mar 22, 39; m 65; c 2. PHYSICS. *Educ:* Univ Wales, BSc, 63, PhD(physics), 66. *Prof Exp:* Asst lectr physics, Univ Wales, 66-67; res physicist, 67-70, sr res physicist, 70-74, RES SUPVR, EXP STA, E I DU PONT DE NEMOURS & CO, INC, 74- *Mem:* Brit Inst Physics & Phys Soc. *Res:* Electrical breakdown in gases and vacuum; x-ray physics; surface physics. *Mailing Add:* 1117 N Dolton Ct Darley Woods Wilmington DE 19810

DAVIES, ROBERT ERNEST, b Lancashire, Eng, Aug 17, 19; m 61. BIOCHEMISTRY, PHYSIOLOGY. *Educ:* Univ Manchester, BS, 41, MS, 42, DS, 52; Univ Sheffield, PhD(biochem), 49; Oxford Univ, MA, 56; Univ Pa, 71. *Prof Exp:* Demonstr chem, Univ Manchester, 41; asst lectr, Univ Sheffield, 42-45, lectr biochem, 48-54; mem sci staff, Med Res Coun, Univ Sheffield & Oxford Univ, 45-56; prof biochem, Med Sch, 56-62 & Sch Vet Med, 62-70, animal biol, Sch Vet Med & grad group molecular biol, 62-73, BENJAMIN FRANKLIN PROF MOLECULAR BIOL & UNIV PROF, SCH VET MED, UNIV PA, 70- *Concurrent Pos:* Guest prof, Univ Heidelberg, 54; mem fac med, Oxford Univ, 56-59. *Mem:* Am Soc Biol Chem; Am Biophys Soc; Am Physiol Soc; fel Royal Soc; Brit Biochem Soc. *Res:* Mechanism of secretion of gastric acid; active transports of ions; energy source for contraction of muscle; origin of life. *Mailing Add:* Labs of Biochem Dept Animal Biol Univ of Pa Sch of Vet Med Philadelphia PA 19104

DAVIES, ROBERT MILTON, b Tulsa, Okla, Aug 11, 44; m 70; c 3. AQUATIC ECOLOGY, WATER CHEMISTRY. *Educ:* Univ Kans, BA, 65; Wichita State Univ, MS, 68; Johns Hopkins Univ, PhD(geog, environ eng), 72. *Prof Exp:* Assoc res scientist geog & environ eng, Johns Hopkins Univ, 72-75; SR BIOLOGIST, HENNINGSON, DURHAM & RICHARDSON, 75-, PROJ MGR, PRIN INVESTR & ACTG DEPT & SECT MGR, NATURAL RESOURCES, 80- *Concurrent Pos:* Consult, Va Gas & Elec Co, 68-71, Pac Gas & Elec Co, 69-70 & Northern States Power Co, 70. *Mem:* Am Nuclear Soc; Am Soc Limnol & Oceanog; Water Pollution Control Fedn; NY Acad Sci; AAAS. *Res:* Marine, estuarine and freshwater ecology of fish, invertebrates and algae with respect to industrial, domestic and agricultural influences on water quality; impacts of recreation, pollution, and groundwater withdrawal upon desert quatic biota; landsat data interpretation. *Mailing Add:* Henningson Durham & Richardson 804 Anacapa St Santa Barbara CA 93101

DAVIES, ROGER, b London, Eng, Aug 29, 48; m 77. ATMOSPHERIC RADIATION, CLIMATE THEORY. *Educ:* Victoria Univ, Wellington, NZ, BSc, 70; Univ Wis, PhD(meteorol), 76. *Prof Exp:* Meteorologist, NZ Meteorol Serv, 71-77; scientist, Meteorol Dept, Univ Wis, 77-79, Space Sci & Eng Ctr, 79-80; ASST PROF ATMOSPHERIC SCI, PURDUE UNIV, 80- *Mem:* Am Meteorol Soc; Am Optical Soc; Am Geophys Union. *Res:* Atmospheric radiation and climate theory, especially the effect of clouds on three dimensional radiative transfer; applications to remote sensing by satellites; developing computer models of climate change. *Mailing Add:* Geosci Dept Purdue Univ West Lafayette IN 47907

DAVIES, RONALD EDGAR, b Victoria, BC, June 23, 32; m 60; c 6. PHOTOBIOLOGY. *Educ:* Univ BC, BSA, 54, MSA, 56; Agr & Mech Col Tex, PhD(biochem, nutrit), 59. *Prof Exp:* Asst prof poultry sci, Agr & Mech Col Tex, 59-62; asst prof, 62-65, res asst prof biochem, 62-75, ASSOC PROF DERMAT, MED SCH, TEMPLE UNIV, 65- *Mem:* Am Soc Photobiol; Biophys Soc; Am Inst Nutrit; Am Inst Biol Sci; NY Acad Sci. *Res:* Cutaneous photobiology and photochemistry; chemical carcinogenesis; photocarcinogenesis; photochemistry of carcinogens. *Mailing Add:* Dept Dermat 3322 N Broad St Philadelphia PA 19140

DAVIES, RONALD WALLACE, b London, Eng, Dec 23, 40; m 63; c 3. ECOLOGY. *Educ:* Univ Col NWales, BSc, 62, Hons, 63, PhD(ecol), 67; Univ Col SWales, dipl ed, 64. *Prof Exp:* Asst lectr zool, Univ Col NWales, 67-68; Can Int Biol Programme fel ecol, Inst Fisheries, Univ BC, 68-69; asst prof, 69-71, assoc prof, 71-80, PROF ZOOL, UNIV CALGARY, 80- *Mem:* Am Soc Limnol & Oceanog; Can Soc Zool; Ecol Soc Am; Brit Ecol Soc. *Res:* Ecology of freshwater ecosystems, with special emphasis on the invertebrate benthic populations. *Mailing Add:* Dept of Biol Univ of Calgary Calgary Can

DAVIES, WALTER GARFIELD, nuclear physics, see previous edition

DAVIES, WARREN LEWIS, b Scranton, Pa, Jan 17, 20; m 46; c 2. MICROBIOLOGY. *Educ:* Pa State Col, BS, 46, MS, 47; Univ Wis, PhD(microbiol), 51. *Prof Exp:* MICROBIOLOGIST, STINE LAB, E I DU PONT DE NEMOURS & CO, 50- *Res:* Viruses and bacteria. *Mailing Add:* 1010 Arc Corner Rd Landenberg PA 19350

DAVIES-JONES, ROBERT PETER, b Leicester, Eng, Feb 15, 43; m 66; c 2. METEOROLOGY. *Educ:* Univ Birmingham, BSc, 64; Univ Colo, PhD(astrogeophys), 69. *Prof Exp:* Fel astrophys, Nat Ctr Atmospheric Res, 69-70; geophysicist, 70-78, METEOROLOGIST, NAT SEVERE STORMS LAB, NAT OCEANIC & ATMOSPHERE ADMIN, 78- *Mem:* Am Meteorol Soc. *Res:* Fluid dynamics of tornadoes and severe thunderstorms. *Mailing Add:* Nat Severe Storms Lab NOAA 1313 Halley Circle Norman OK 73069

DAVIESS, STEVEN NORMAN, b Cedar Rapids, Iowa, Jan 25, 18; m 44; c 2. GEOLOGY. *Educ:* Univ Calif, Los Angeles, BA, 40, MA, 42. *Prof Exp:* From jr geologist to asst geologist, US Geol Surv, 42-46; assoc geologist, Cuban Gulf Oil Co, 46-48, asst geologist, Mozambique Gulf Oil Co, 48-53, staff geologist, Gulf NY Prod Div, 53-56, staff geologist, Gulf Eastern Co, 56-60, area mgr, Spanish Gulf Oil Co, 60-67; geologic adv, Nuclear Fuels Div, Gulf Oil Corp, 67-70; mgr explor, Gulf Energy & Minerals Co, 70-78; CONSULT GEOLOGIST, 78- *Mem:* Fel Geol Soc London; fel Geol Soc Am; Am Asn Petrol Geologists; fel Geol Soc SAfrica. *Res:* Petroleum geology; economic geology. *Mailing Add:* 3961 S Dexter St Englewood CO 80110

DAVIGNON, JEAN, b Montreal, Que, July 29, 35; m 61; c 2. MEDICINE. *Educ:* Univ Paris, BA, 53; Univ Montreal, MD, 58; McGill Univ, MSc, 60; FRCPS(C), 63. *Prof Exp:* Resident, Hotel-Dieu Hosp, 60-61; res asst, Dept Physiol, Mayo Clin & Mayo Found, 62-63; res assoc lipid metab, Rockefeller Univ Hosp, 64-67; SR INVESTR & DIR DEPT LIPID METAB & ATHEROSCLEROSIS RES, CLIN RES INST MONTREAL, 67- *Concurrent Pos:* Nat Res Coun Can med res fel, Dept Clin Res, Hotel-Dieu Hosp, Montreal, 58-60; fel internal med, Mayo Clin & Mayo Found,

Rochester, Minn, 61-62; Que Ministry Educ scholar, 61-65; Markle scholar acad med, 67; assoc physician, Hotel-Dieu Hosp, 67-70, physician, 70-, head sect vascular med, 72-; asst prof, Dept Med, Univ Montreal, 67-71, assoc prof, 71-77, prof, 77-; asst prof & assoc mem, Dept Exp Med, McGill Univ, 70-; fel coun arteriosclerosis, Am Heart Asn, 68. *Mem:* Am Fedn Clin Res; fel Am Col Physicians; fel Am Col Angiol; Am Heart Asn; NY Acad Sci. *Res:* Peripheral vascular diseases; atherosclerosis; lipid and lipoprotein metabolism in hyperlipidemia. *Mailing Add:* Clin Res Inst of Montreal 110 Pine Ave W Montreal PQ H2W 1R7 Can

DAVILA, JULIO C, b Mexico, Dec 1, 21; US citizen; m 48; c 4. CARDIOVASCULAR SURGERY, THORACIC SURGERY. *Educ:* Stanford Univ, BA, 45, MD, 49; Am Bd Surg, dipl, 54; Am Bd Thoracic Surg, dipl, 56. *Prof Exp:* From instr to asst prof surg, Univ Pa, 58-62; clin prof, Sch Med, Temple Univ, 62-65, prof, 65-69; dir cardiopulmonary inst, St Joseph's Hosp, 69-71; chief div thoracic surg, Henry Ford Hosp, 71-76; mem staff, 77-80, CHIEF THORACIC & CARDIOVASC SURGEON, A WARD FORD MEM INST, 80- *Concurrent Pos:* Assoc thoracic surgeon, Presby Hosp, St Christopher's Hosp & Fitzgerald Mercy Hosp, 54-61; dir cardiovasc res, Presby Hosp, 57-61, dir res, 61-62; actg chief thoracic surg, Presby Hosp & St Christopher's Hosp, 61-62; fac assoc & mem sem biomat, Columbia Univ, 66-69; clin prof surg, Sch Med, Univ Mich, 72-; consult, Valley Forge Army Hosp, 62-, Philadelphia Vet Hosp, 64-69 & Letterman Gen Hosp, 69-71. *Mem:* Fel Am Col Surg; fel Am Col Cardiol; fel Am Col Chest Physicians; fel Am Col Angiol; Am Asn Thoracic Surg. *Res:* Cardiac surgery; circulation physiology research; biomaterials; prostheses for circulation especially artificial heart valves. *Mailing Add:* A Ward Ford Mem Inst Cardiovasc Prog 425 Pine Ridge Blvd Suite 203 Wausau WI 54401

DAVINROY, THOMAS BERNARD, b East St Louis, Ill, Nov 16, 32; m 55; c 3. CIVIL & TRANSPORTATION ENGINEERING. *Educ:* Princeton Univ, BSE, 54, MSE, 60; Univ Calif, Berkeley, DEng(transp eng), 66. *Prof Exp:* Instr mech & graphics, Princeton Univ, 59-61; asst prof, 64-69, ASSOC PROF CIVIL ENG, PA STATE UNIV, 69- *Concurrent Pos:* Soils engr, Moran, Proctor Mueser & Rutledge, NY, 58; eng consult, Tanganyika proj, US Peace Corps, 61; transp engr, James C Buckley Inc, NY, 63; consult, Gannett, Fleming, Corddry & Carpenter, Harrisburg, Pa, 68-69 & Bruinette, Gruger, Stoffberg & Hugo, Pretoria, Repub SAfrica, 70-71. *Mem:* Am Soc Civil Engrs. *Res:* Transportation planning; effects of weather and aircraft characteristics on airport design; air transport planning. *Mailing Add:* Dept of Civil Eng 212 Sackett Bldg Pa State Univ University Park PA 16802

DAVIS, A(LVIE) DOUGLAS, b Mo, Apr 29, 45; m, 72; c 1. NUCLEAR PHYSICS. *Educ:* Wichita State Univ, BS, 66; Univ Calif, Los Angeles, MS, 68, PhD(physics), 70. *Prof Exp:* Teaching asst physics, Univ Calif, Los Angeles, 66-70, res asst nuclear physics, 68-70; asst prof, 70-80, ASSOC PROF PHYSICS, EASTERN ILL UNIV, 80- *Concurrent Pos:* Govt bureaucrat US Navy, Div Naval Reactors, US Energy Res & Develop Admin, 71-75; vis assoc prof, Univ Ill, 81-82. *Mem:* Am Asn Physics Teachers. *Res:* Computer assisted instruction in physics; scientific writing; nuclear shell structure; nuclear shape; general relativity. *Mailing Add:* Dept Physics Eastern Ill Univ Charleston IL 61920

DAVIS, ABRAM, b Cleveland, Ohio, Feb 21, 26; m 52; c 4. SPECTROSCOPY, ANALYTICAL CHEMISTRY. *Educ:* Lake Forest Col, AB, 50; Ill Inst Technol, MS, 52. *Prof Exp:* Res chemist, 51-58, group leader instrumental lab, 58-61, supvr, 61-69, supvr anal, Phys & Instrumental Lab, 69-70, asst sect mgr, 70, SR RES ASSOC, CENT RES, HOOKER CHEM CORP, 70- *Mem:* AAAS; Soc Appl Spectros; Am Chem Soc; Coblentz Soc. *Res:* Instrumental analysis of organic compounds; elucidation of structure and development of analytical methods of product control. *Mailing Add:* 1588 Red Jacket Grand Island NY 14072

DAVIS, ALAN, b Chester, Eng, June 18, 32; m 63; c 2. GEOLOGY, PETROLOGY. *Educ:* Univ London, BSc, Imp Col Sci Technol, ARCS, 56; Pa State Univ, MS, 61; Univ Durham, PhD(geol), 65. *Prof Exp:* Geologist mineral explor, John Taylor & Sons, London, 56; prospecting officer coal explor, Opencast Exec, Nat Coal Bd, 57, scientist coal survey, 58, sr res assoc coal res, Dept of Geol, Univ Newcastle, Eng, 61-65; geologist, res & sr geologist, coal petrol, Geol Surv Queensland, 65-73; assoc prof geol, 73-80, PROF GEOL & ASST DIR, COAL RES SECTION, PA STATE UNIV, 80- *Mem:* Int Comt Coal Petrol; Geol Soc Am; Am Soc Testing & Mat; Inst Fuel. *Res:* Coal petrology; coalification processes; coal utilization; coal characterization. *Mailing Add:* 513 Deike Bldg Pa State Univ University Park PA 16802

DAVIS, ALAN, b Gosport, Eng, June 10, 55; m 77. MOLECULAR PHARMACOLOGY. *Educ:* Univ Manchester, Eng, BSc, 76; Southampton Univ, Eng, PhD(neurochem), 79. *Prof Exp:* Res asst pharmacol, Dept Physiol, Southampton Univ, 79; fel, Dept Pharmacol, 80-81, ASST PROF, DEPT PHARMACOL & PSYCHIAT, TORONTO UNIV, 81- *Mem:* Europ Neurosci Asn; Soc Neurosci; Brit Pharmacol Soc. *Res:* Purification, biochemical characterization and antibody generation to dopamine receptors of the central nervous system and antidepressant binding sites of central nervous system and platelets; role of auto-immunity in schizophrenia and endogenous. *Mailing Add:* Dept Psychopharmacol 250 Col St Clarke Inst Psychiat Toronto ON M5T 1R8 Can

DAVIS, ALAN LYNN, b Salt Lake City, Utah, Nov 17, 46; m 73. INTEGRATED CIRCUIT DESIGN. *Educ:* Mass Inst Technol, BS, 69; Univ Utah, PhD(comput sci), 72. *Prof Exp:* Asst prof comput sci, Univ Waterloo, 72-73; consult, Burroughs IRC, 73-77; asst prof, Univ Utah, 77-80; consult, Burroughs Corp, 77-82 & Gen Res Corp, 78-80; ASSOC PROF COMPUT SCI, UNIV UTAH, 80- *Concurrent Pos:* Exchange scholar, Acad Sci, USSR, 76-77; vis prof, Novosibirsk State Univ, USSR, 79; vis scholar, Gesellschaft Math & Datenverarb, 80; vis prof, Tech, Haifa, Israel, 80. *Res:* Data-driven computer system which dynamically exploits concurrency in an extensible multiple resource environment. *Mailing Add:* Comput Sci Dept Univ Utah Salt Lake City UT 84109

DAVIS, ALEXANDER COCHRAN, b Ottawa, Ont, Can, Oct 6, 20; nat US; m 43; c 2. ECONOMIC ENTOMOLOGY. *Educ:* Univ Toronto, BSA, 42; Cornell Univ, PhD(entom), 50. *Prof Exp:* Agr scientist, Div Entom, Can Dept Agr, Ottawa, 46; asst entom, Cornell Univ, 47-50; asst prof, 50-54, assoc prof, 54-76, PROF ENTOM, NY STATE AGR EXP STA, GENEVA, 76-, ASSOC DIR EXP STA & ASST DIR RES, 77- *Mem:* Entom Soc Am. *Res:* Vegetable insect control. *Mailing Add:* 7 Cynthia Dr Geneva NY 14456

DAVIS, ALFRED, JR, b Johnson City, Tex, Feb 10, 19; m 41; c 2. ENGINEERING. *Educ:* Univ Tex, BS, 41. *Prof Exp:* Design engr, Westinghouse Elec Co, Md, 41-45; res engr, Defense Res Lab, 46-62; proj engr, 62-67, SR ENGR, PROD ENG DEPT, TRACOR, INC, 67- *Mem:* Sr mem Inst Elec & Electronics Engrs; Nat Soc Prof Engrs. *Res:* Design of specialized microwave and data recording systems; production engineering of frequency standards and countermeasures systems. *Mailing Add:* 6712 Vine Austin TX 78757

DAVIS, ALVIE LEE, b Richardson, Tex, Jan 22, 31; m 61; c 3. BIOCHEMISTRY. *Educ:* Abilene Christian Col, BS, 55; Univ Tex, PhD(biochem), 60. *Prof Exp:* From asst prof to assoc prof, 59-68, PROF CHEM, ABILENE CHRISTIAN UNIV, 68- *Concurrent Pos:* Robert A Welch Found res grant, 62- *Mem:* Am Chem Soc. *Res:* Metabolic inhibitors; correlation of chemical structure and biological activity; nitrogen heterocycles; cyclic benzohydroxamic acids. *Mailing Add:* Dept of Chem Abilene Christian Col Abilene TX 79601

DAVIS, ALVIN HERBERT, b Buffalo, NY, Jan 26, 29; m 56; c 2. TECHNOLOGY ASSESSMENT, THEORETICAL PHYSICS. *Educ:* Univ Buffalo, BA, 49, MA, 51; Yale Univ, PhD(physics), 55. *Prof Exp:* Physicist, Livermore Radiation Lab, Univ Calif, 55-57, Naval Res Lab, 57-58, Theoret Div, Goddard Space Flight Ctr, Md, 59-66 & Environ Res Corp, Va, 66-69; PHYSICIST, LOS ALAMOS SCI LAB, 69- *Mem:* AAAS; Am Geophys Union; Am Phys Soc; Sigma Xi. *Res:* Technology assessment; geophysics; two-phase flow and fracture in porous media; astrophysics. *Mailing Add:* Los Alamos Nat Lab MS 595 Los Alamos NM 87545

DAVIS, ANDREW MORGAN, b Port Jefferson, NY, May 18, 50; m 81. COSMOCHEMISTRY. *Educ:* Grinnell Col, BA, 71; Yale Univ, MPh, 73, PhD(geochem), 77. *Prof Exp:* Res assoc, Dept Geophys Sci, 76-78, ANALYTICAL CHEMIST, JAMES FRANK INST, UNIV CHICAGO, 78- *Mem:* AAAS; Am Geophys Union; Geochem Soc; Meteoritical Soc. *Res:* Early chemical history of the solar system; trace elements in meteorites. *Mailing Add:* James Frank Inst, Univ Chicago 5640 South Ellis Ave Chicago IL 60637

DAVIS, AUDREY KENNON, physiology, see previous edition

DAVIS, BENJAMIN HAROLD, b Lafayette, Ind, Jan 25, 05; m 33; c 2. PLANT PATHOLOGY. *Educ:* Wabash Col, AB, 28; Cornell Univ, PhD(plant path), 34. *Prof Exp:* Asst plant path, Cornell Univ, 28-29, instr, 29-34; instr sci, Va State Teachers Col, Fredericksburg, 34-35; instr bot, Ohio State Univ, 35-39; from assoc prof to prof, 39-71, chmn dept plant path, 56-63, dept plant biol, 63-71, EMER PROF PLANT PATH, RUTGERS UNIV, 71- *Mem:* Am Phytopath Soc; Mycol Soc Am. *Res:* Diseases of vegetables. *Mailing Add:* 15 MacArthur St High Bridge NJ 08829

DAVIS, BERNARD BOOTH, b Parkersburg, WVa, Sept 12, 32; m 56; c 4. GERIATRICS. *Educ:* Wooster Col, BA, 57; Univ Pittsburgh, MD, 61. *Prof Exp:* Asst prof med, Univ Pittsburgh, 67-70, assoc prof, 70-73, prof, 73-76; PROF MED, ST LOUIS UNIV, 76-; CHIEF MED, VET ADMIN MED CTR, ST LOUIS, 76-, DIR GERIAT, 76- *Concurrent Pos:* Chief of staff, Vet Admin, Pittsburgh, 71-76; dir, Renal Div, St Louis Univ, 76-77. *Mem:* Am Col Physics; AAAS; Am Soc Clin Invest; Am Physiol Soc; Am Soc Nephrol. *Res:* Renal metabolism of hormones, drugs and renobiotics. *Mailing Add:* Vet Admin Med Ctr St Louis MO 63125

DAVIS, BERNARD ERIC, b Milwaukee, Wis, Aug 29, 37; m 64; c 2. METALLURGY, CHEMICAL ENGINEERING. *Educ:* Ore State Univ, BS, 60, MS, 65, PhD(metall eng), 70. *Prof Exp:* Process engr, Org Chem Dept, E I du Pont de Nemours & Co, Inc, 60-61; res metallurgist, Teledyne Wah Chang Albany Corp, Teledyne, Inc, 63-67; tech adv qual control, Naval Nuclear Fuel Div, Babcock & Wilcox Co, 70-80; MEM STAFF, LYNCHBURG RES CTR, 80- *Mem:* Am Inst Mining, Metall & Petrol Engrs; Am Soc Metals; Am Inst Chem Engrs. *Res:* Diffusion in metals; liquid extraction of metals. *Mailing Add:* Lynchburg Res Ctr PO Box 1260 Mt Athos Lynchburg VA 24505

DAVIS, BETTY SCHUCK, zoology, deceased

DAVIS, BILL DAVID, b Junction City, Kans, July 22, 37; m 62; c 2. DEVELOPMENTAL BIOLOGY. *Educ:* Kans State Teachers Col, BS, 59, MS, 61; Purdue Univ, PhD(biol), 65. *Prof Exp:* Teacher, Manhattan Jr High Sch, Kans, 60-62; asst prof, 65-69, ASSOC PROF BIOL SCI, DOUGLASS COL, RUTGERS UNIV, 69- *Mem:* AAAS; Japanese Soc Plant Physiol; Am Soc Plant Physiol; Bot Soc Am; Int Asn Plant Tissue Cult. *Res:* Orientation of the mitotic spindle in fern gametophytes; physiological interactions during seed germinations; plant tissue culture. *Mailing Add:* Dept of Biol Sci Douglass Col Rutgers Univ New Brunswick NJ 08903

DAVIS, BILLY J, b Hobart, Okla, Oct 27, 32; m 53; c 4. ICHTHYOLOGY, WATER POLLUTION. *Educ:* Southwestern State Col, Okla, BS, 54, MS, 57; Okla State Univ, PhD(ichthyol), 66. *Prof Exp:* Pub sch teacher, Okla, 54-63; from asst prof to assoc prof zool, 66-73, PROF ZOOL, LA TECH UNIV, 73- *Mem:* Soc Study Amphibians & Reptiles; Am Soc Ichthyologists & Herpetologists; Herpetologists League; Asn Southwestern Naturalists; Asn Southeastern Biologists. *Res:* Ecological and taxonomic studies of North American freshwater fishes and herptiles, particularly the gross morphology of the cyprinid fish brain in relation to behavior; water pollution biology. *Mailing Add:* Dept of Zool La Tech Univ Ruston LA 71270

DAVIS, BRIAN CLIFTON, b St Louis, Mo, Jan 5, 42; m 66; c 4. PHYSICAL ORGANIC CHEMISTRY. *Educ:* Calif State Univ, Northridge, BS, 67; Univ Wash, PhD(org chem), 72. *Prof Exp:* Res assoc biochem, Chem Dept, Univ Wash, 72-74; res chemist org chem, 74-81, SR RES CHEMIST, SUN OIL CO, 81- *Mem:* Am Chem Soc; Soc Automotive Engrs. *Res:* Synthesis of commercially useful products from raw materials available from petroleum refinery streams; development and evaluation of alternative fuels. *Mailing Add:* Sun Tech Auto Lab PO Box 1135 Marcus Hook PA 19061

DAVIS, BRIAN K, b Sydney, Australia, May 15, 37; US citizen; m 63; c 1. PHYSIOLOGY OF REPRODUCTION. *Educ:* Sch Wool Technol & Pastoral Sci, Univ New SWales, BSc, 58, PhD, 62, DSc, 82. *Prof Exp:* Teaching fel physiol, Sch Wool Technol & Pastoral Sci, Univ New SWales, 58-61; Ford Found fel reproductive physiol, Worcester Found Exp Biol, 62; res fel, Chem Dept, Harvard Univ, 63-65; sci officer, Lab Molecular Biol, Med Res Coun, Cambridge Univ, 65-66; fel chem, McGill Univ, 66-69; staff scientist, Worcester Found Exp Biol, 70-78; res scientist & actg div dir, Long Island Res Inst, 78-80, RES PROF, STATE UNIV NY, STONY BROOK, 80- *Concurrent Pos:* Prin investr grants & contracts, NIH, 73-; contract, Agency Int Develop, State Dept, 74-75; bd dir, Res Found Mental Hygiene, 79. *Mem:* Am Physiol Soc; Biophys Soc; Soc Exp Biol & Med; NY Acad Sci; Am Soc Cell Biol. *Res:* Mammalian fertilization; template-directed polymerization; drug delivery systems; endocrinology; author or coauthor of over 50 publications. *Mailing Add:* Col Arts & Sci State Univ NY Stony Brook NY 11794

DAVIS, BRIAN KENT, b Laramie, Wyo, Dec 2, 39; m 62; c 3. MUTAGENESIS, HUMAN GENETICS. *Educ:* Univ Wis-Madison, BA, 62, MA, 63; Univ Wash, PhD(genetics), 70. *Prof Exp:* Sec sch teacher sci, US Peace Corps, 64-65; res fel genetics, Univ Calif, San Diego, 70-72, asst prof, 72; asst prof genetics, Va Polytech Inst & State Univ, 73-80; asst prof, Col Med, King Faisal Univ, Saudi Arabia, 80-81; RES ASSOC, ALLIED CORP, 81- *Concurrent Pos:* Fel Am Cancer Soc, 70-72. *Mem:* Genetics Soc Am; Am Genetic Asn. *Res:* Drosophila mutagenesis. *Mailing Add:* Allied Corp PO Box 1021R Morristown NJ 07960

DAVIS, BRIANT LEROY, b Brigham City, Utah, Nov 18, 36; m 57; c 4. GEOLOGY, GEOPHYSICS. *Educ:* Brigham Young Univ, BS, 58, MS, 59; Univ Calif, Los Angeles, PhD(geol), 64. *Prof Exp:* Asst res geophysicist, Inst Geophys & Planetary Physics, Univ Calif, Los Angeles, 61-62; from asst prof to assoc prof geol & geol eng, 63-70, asst prof geophys, 70-74, RES PROF GEOPHYS, SDAK SCH MINES & TECHNOL, 75-, RES GEOPHYSICIST, INST ATMOSPHERIC SCI, 66-, SR SCIENTIST & HEAD CLOUD PHYSICS GROUP, INST, 77- *Mem:* AAAS; Am Meteorol Soc; Am Crystallog Soc; Am Geophys Union. *Res:* Petrofabric analysis by means of x-ray techniques; nucleation processes; cloud physics and weather modification; crystallography and x-ray diffraction. *Mailing Add:* Dept of Meteorol SDak Sch of Mines & Technol Rapid City SD 57701

DAVIS, BRUCE ALLAN, b Saskatoon, Sask, Aug 17, 41. ANALYTICAL BIOCHEMISTRY. *Educ:* Univ Sask, BAS, 62; PhD(chem), 66. *Prof Exp:* Res fel org chem, Univ Munich, 66-68; fel mass spectrometry, Univ Cambridge, 68-70; lectr & res fel org chem, Univ Sask, 70-72; LAB SCIENTIST BIOL PSYCHIAT, PSYCHIAT RES DIV, DEPT HEALTH, SASK, 72- *Concurrent Pos:* Mem staff, Dept Org Chem, Univ Sask Hosp. *Mem:* Can Biochem Soc. *Res:* Development and application of analytical methods for trace metals, amines and their acid metabolites in biological materials, particularly in the brain. *Mailing Add:* Dept of Org Chem A508 Univ Hosp Saskatoon SK S7H 0W8 Can

DAVIS, BRUCE W, b Glendale, Calif, July 19, 37; m 64; c 4. PHYSICAL CHEMISTRY. *Educ:* Univ Southern Calif, BS, 60, MS, 62; Univ Calif, Riverside, PhD(phys chem), 64. *Prof Exp:* Teaching asst chem, Univ Southern Calif, 60; Army Res Off Durham assoc critical phenomena, Univ NC, 64-66; asst prof chem, Ga Inst Technol, 66-72; vis asst prof, Cornell Univ, 72-73; sr res chemist, 73-80, SR RES ASSOC, CHEVRON OIL FIELD RES CO, 80- *Concurrent Pos:* Petrol Res Fund grants, 68-71; Army Res Off Durham grants, 68-71. *Mem:* Am Chem Soc; Sigma Xi; Soc Petrol Engrs. *Res:* Statistical mechanics and thermodynamics of the gas, liquid and adsorbed states; interfacial phenomena; properties of fluids in porous media; energy recovery research. *Mailing Add:* Chevron Oil Field Res Co PO Box 446 La Habra CA 90631

DAVIS, BRUCE WILSON, b Owen Co, Ind, Dec 22, 21; m 48; c 3. APPLIED MATHEMATICS. *Educ:* Ind Univ, AB, 48; Purdue Univ, MS, 55. *Prof Exp:* Teacher high sch, Ind, 48-50; mathematician & math consult, Ord Plant, US Navy, 50-55; sr res engr, Allison Div, Gen Motors Corp, Ind, 55-56; asst head math div, Avionics Facil, US Navy, 56-58; engr, head math & comput facil & chief adv studies, Defense Systs & Allison Div, Gen Motors Corp, 58-63; systs anal supvr & proj dir, 63-71, mgr space systs prog off, 72-79, SECT MGR, SPACE SYSTS & APPLN SECT, 79-, DEPT MGR, DEFENSE & SPACE SYSTS DEPT, COLUMBUS LABS, BATTELLE MEM INST, 79- *Mem:* Am Inst Aeronaut & Astronaut; Sigma Xi. *Res:* Control systems; guidance; synthesis of electrical circuitry; operations research; systems analysis; space launch system analyses. *Mailing Add:* Battelle Mem Inst 505 King Ave Columbus OH 43201

DAVIS, BRYAN TERENCE, b Hawkhurst, Eng, Dec 19, 35; m 61; c 3. LUBRICANT & FUEL ADDITIVES. *Educ:* Oxford Univ, BA, 60, BSc, 61, MA, 77. *Prof Exp:* Res chemist, Castrol Ltd, 60-67, sr res chemist, 67-69; sr res chemist, Edwin Cooper Ltd, 69-74, chief chemist res, 74-77; chief chemist res, 75-77, RES SUPVR, PETROLEUM CHEM RES LAB, ETHYL CORP, 77- *Mem:* Am Chem Soc; Soc Automotive Engrs. *Res:* Synthesis evaluation and commercialization of petroleum additives including improved antioxidants; rust inhibitors, antiwear and dispersant additives for lubricants; additives for both lubricants and diesel fuels to prevent malfunction of equipment due to gelation and crystallization at low temperatures. *Mailing Add:* Ethyl Corp 1600 W Right Mile Rd Ferndale MI 48220

DAVIS, BURL EDWARD, b Doniphan, Mo, Aug 30, 35; m 27; c 4. IN-SITU PROCESSES, SYNTHETIC FUEL PROCESS CHEMISTRY. *Educ:* Southern Ill Univ, BA, 64; Univ Wyo, MS, 66. *Prof Exp:* Instr anal chem, Natural Resources Inst, Univ Wyo, 63-66; res chemist, Koppers Co, 66-68; SR PROJ CHEMIST, GULF OIL CO, 68- *Mem:* Am Chem Soc; Sigma Xi. *Res:* Synthetic fuel process chemistry with an emphasis on underground coal gasification; development of the multi-disciplinary technology related to in-situ processes. *Mailing Add:* PO Drawer 2038 Pittsburgh PA 15230

DAVIS, BURNS, b Fulton, Ky, Mar 15, 31; m 54; c 2. POLYMER CHEMISTRY, ORGANIC CHEMISTRY. *Educ:* Murray State Col, BS, 53, MA, 59; Univ Louisville, PhD(polymer chem), 62. *Prof Exp:* Teacher high sch, Ky, 56-58; from res chemist to sr res chemist, 62-71, RES ASSOC, TENN EASTMAN CO, 71- *Mem:* Am Chem Soc. *Res:* Condensation and vinyl polymers. *Mailing Add:* Tenn Eastman Co PO Box 511 Kingsport TN 37662

DAVIS, BURTRON H, b Points, WVa, Dec 21, 34; m 66; c 3. PHYSICAL CHEMISTRY. *Educ:* WVa Univ, BS, 58; St Joseph's Col, Pa, MS, 62; Univ Fla, PhD(chem), 65. *Prof Exp:* Analyst, Atlantic Refining Co, Pa, 59-62; res assoc, Johns Hopkins Univ, 65-66; sr res chemist, Res & Develop Corp, Mobil Oil Corp, NJ, 66-70; assoc prof chem, Potomac State Col, WVa Univ, 70-77; SR CHEMIST, INST MINING & MINERALS RES, UNIV KY, 77-, ADJ PROF, METALL ENG & MAT SCI DEPT, 78- *Mem:* Am Chem Soc; Catalysis Soc. *Res:* Heterogeneous catalysis; coal liquefaction. *Mailing Add:* 102 Lewis Ct Georgetown KY 40324

DAVIS, CARL F, b Milo, Maine, May 12, 19; m 45; c 1. ELECTRICAL ENGINEERING, MATHEMATICS. *Educ:* Univ Maine, BA, 42; US Air Force Inst Technol, BS, 55; Univ Ill, MS, 56, PhD(elec eng), 60. *Prof Exp:* Commun & electronics staff officer, US Air Force, 48-60, assoc prof elec eng, US Air Force Acad, 60-68, chief electronics div, Air Force Weapons Lab, 68-76; SR ASSOC PRIN ENGR, ELEC SYSTS DIV, HARRIS CORP, 76- *Mem:* Inst Elec & Electronics Engrs; NY Acad Sci. *Res:* Nuclear radiation effects on weapon systems; transient radiation effects on electronics; electromagnetic pulse effects on systems; research and exploratory development of arming and fuzing systems for nuclear re-entry vehicles. *Mailing Add:* PO Box 3553 Indialantic FL 32903

DAVIS, CARL LEE, b Dunnville, Ky, Sept 20, 24; m 46; c 5. NUTRITION, BIOCHEMISTRY. *Educ:* Western Ky State Col, BS, 52; Univ Ky, MS, 54; Univ Ill, PhD(dairy sci), 59. *Prof Exp:* Instr dairy sci, Western Ky State Col, 52-53; res assoc, Univ Ky, 53-54; res assoc, 55-59, asst prof, 60-69, PROF NUTRIT, UNIV ILL, URBANA-CHAMPAIGN, 69- *Concurrent Pos:* Am Feed Mfrs Award for Dairy Cattle Res, Am Dairy Sci Asn, 71- *Mem:* Am Dairy Sci Asn; Am Inst Nutrit. *Res:* Nutrition of ruminant animals, especially a as related to milk production. *Mailing Add:* Dept Dairy Sci Univ Ill 1207 W Gregory Urbana IL 61801

DAVIS, CARL O, b Pine Bluff, Ark, June 21, 27; m 51; c 2. DENTISTRY, EDUCATIONAL MEASUREMENT. *Educ:* Univ Ark, BS, 50; Univ Tenn, DDS, 58; Univ Iowa, MS, 70, MA & PhD(educ psychol), 71. *Prof Exp:* Pvt pract, Okla, 58-66; ASSOC PROF EDUC RES & DEVELOP & DIR EVAL, SCH DENT, MED COL GA, 71-, PROF ORAL MED & ASSOC DEAN STUDENTS, 76- *Concurrent Pos:* Partic, USPHS Pilot Prog Model Dent Teacher Training, 68-71. *Mem:* Am Dent Asn; Am Educ Res Asn; Int Asn Dent Res. *Res:* Quality of dentistry and dental education. *Mailing Add:* Sch of Dent Med Col of Ga Augusta GA 30902

DAVIS, CECIL GILBERT, b Los Angeles, Calif, Feb 20, 25; m 57; c 2. THEORETICAL PHYSICS, ASTROPHYSICS. *Educ:* Occidental Col, BA, 50; Univ Calif, Los Angeles, MA, 51, PhD(physics), 57. *Prof Exp:* Staff mem physics, Los Alamos Sci Lab, 57-60, Physics Sect, Convar, 60-61 & Theoret Physics Sect, Gen Atomic, 61-65; STAFF MEM PHYSICS, LOS ALAMOS SCI LAB, 65- *Mem:* Am Astron Soc; Int Astron Union. *Res:* Variable star research; atmospheric sciences. *Mailing Add:* Los Alamos Sci Lab MS420 Los Alamos NM 87544

DAVIS, CHANDLER, b Ithaca, NY, Aug 12, 26; m 48; c 3. MATHEMATICS. *Educ:* Harvard Univ, BS, 45, MA, 47, PhD(math), 50. *Prof Exp:* Teaching fel math, Harvard Univ, 47-48; instr, Univ Mich, 50-54; lectr, Columbia Univ, 55-57; mem, Inst for Advan Study, 57-58; assoc ed, Math Reviews, 58-62; assoc prof, 62-65, PROF MATH, UNIV TORONTO, 65- *Mem:* Soc Indust & Appl Math; Am Math Soc; Can Math Soc; Math Asn Am. *Res:* Linear spaces and operators. *Mailing Add:* 25 Rue des Vinaigriers Paris 75010 France

DAVIS, CHARLES (CARROLL), b Azusa, Calif, Nov 24, 11; m 36; c 2. LIMNOLOGY, INVERTEBRATE ZOOLOGY. *Educ:* Oberlin Col, AB, 33; Univ Wash, MS, 35, PhD(zool), 40. *Prof Exp:* Asst, Scripps Inst, Univ Calif, 38-40; instr sci, Nat Training Sch, Mo, 40-42; biologist, State Dept Res & Educ, Md, 42-43; chemist, US Navy Powder Factory, 43-44; instr biol chem, Jacksonville Jr Col, 44-47; asst prof zool, Univ Miami, 47-48; from asst prof to prof biol, Case Western Reserve Univ, 48-68; prof biol, Mem Univ Nfld, 68-77; RETIRED. *Concurrent Pos:* Instr, San Diego Eve Jr Col, 39; Gjeste prof, Univ Tromso, 75-76. *Mem:* AAAS; Am Soc Limnol & Oceanog; Ecol Soc Am; Int Asn Limnol; Marine Biol Asn UK. *Res:* Crab fishery, marine and fresh-water plankton; pelagic copepoda of the Northeast Pacific Ocean; pollution; Lake Erie ecology; hatching mechanisms; invertebrates; Newfoundland freshwater and marine zooplankton. *Mailing Add:* Dept Biol Mem Univ Nfld St John's NF A1B 3X9 Can

DAVIS, CHARLES A, b Beaumont, Tex, Dec 15, 33; m 56; c 3. WILDLIFE ECOLOGY. *Educ:* Tex A&M Univ, BS, 56, MS, 58; Okla State Univ, PhD(zool), 64. *Prof Exp:* Asst prof biol, Ark State Col, 63-66 & Southwestern State Col, Okla, 66; from asst prof to assoc prof wildlife sci, 67-78, PROF DEPT FISH & WILDLIFE SCI, N MEX STATE UNIV, 78- *Mem:* Wildlife Soc; Cooper Ornith Soc. *Res:* Ecology of birds and mammals. *Mailing Add:* Dept of Fish & Wildlife Sci NMex State Univ Box 4901 Las Cruces NM 88003

DAVIS, CHARLES ALFRED, b Marion, NC, Mar 6, 39; m 62. APPLIED MATHEMATICS. *Educ:* NC State Univ, BS, 61, MApMath, 63, PhD(appl math), 68. *Prof Exp:* Instr math, NC State Univ, 65-67; from asst prof to assoc prof, 67-79, chmn dept, 67-80, PROF MATH, MEREDITH COL, 79-, ASST DEAN & REGISTR, 80- *Res:* Mathematics as applied to heat transfer with particular application of integral transforms. *Mailing Add:* Off Asst Dean & Registr Meredith Col Raleigh NC 27611

DAVIS, CHARLES FREEMAN, JR, b Chicago, Ill, Aug 1, 25; m 56; c 4. PHYSICS. *Educ:* Northwestern Univ, BS, 48, MS, 49; Mass Inst Technol, PhD(physics), 54. *Prof Exp:* Opers analyst, Opers Res Off, Johns Hopkins Univ, 54-56; staff mem res lab electronics, Mass Inst Technol, 56-58; head microwave devices sect, Device Res Dept, Tex Instruments, Inc, 58-60, br mgr microwave & photo sensors, Diode Dept, 60-63; eng mgr microwave diode dept, Sylvania Elec Prod, Inc, Gen Tel & Electronics Corp, Mass, 63-67; prin res scientist, Res Div, Raytheon Corp, 67-69, prin engr, Missile Systs Div, 69-74; mem staff, Physics Dept, Mass Inst Technol, 74-81; SR CONSULT ENGR, AVCO SYSTS DIV, WILMINGTON, MASS, 81- *Mem:* Am Chem Soc; Am Phys Soc; Inst Elec & Electronics Engrs; AAAS; Sigma Xi. *Res:* Nuclear hardening of semiconductors & microwave physics; masers; low temperature techniques; microwave and photosensitive semiconductor devices; lasers. *Mailing Add:* PO Box E Concord MA 01742

DAVIS, CHARLES HOMER, b Glendale, Ariz, Feb 13, 12; m 37; c 2. AGRONOMY. *Educ:* Univ Ariz, BS, 35; Iowa State Col, MS, 36, PhD(plant physiol, crops), 39. *Prof Exp:* Asst agronomist, Exp Sta, Univ Ariz, 37-43; assoc agronomist, Guayule Res Proj, Bur Plant Indust, USDA, 43-45; agronomist, Bur Reclamation, US Dept Interior, 45-52; fieldman, Ariz Fertilizer Inc, 52-62, agronomist, 62-69; chief agronomist, Farm Builders Div, Am Biocult Inc, 69-71; CONSULT AGRONOMIST, 71- *Mem:* Am Soc Agron; Soil Sci Soc Am. *Res:* Water and growth relations of plants; use of water by plants and by irrigation projects in relation to yields; chemical and cultural weed control. *Mailing Add:* 4415 N 31st Dr Phoenix AZ 85017

DAVIS, CHARLES MITCHELL, JR, b Washington, DC, July 2, 25; m; c 4. UNDERWATER ACOUSTICS. *Educ:* Cath Univ Am, BA, 51, MS, 54, PhD, 62. *Prof Exp:* Gen physicist, US Naval Ord Labs, 51-62; from asst prof to prof physics, Am Univ, 62-70; supv res physicist phys acoust, Naval Res Lab, 70-78; CHIEF SCIENTIST, DYNAMIC SYSTS INC, 78- *Concurrent Pos:* Adj prof physics, Am Univ, 71-78. *Mem:* Sigma Xi; Acoust Soc Am; Am Phys Soc; Optical Soc Am. *Res:* Fiber optic sensors; detection of underwater sound by acoustic-optic techniques; radiation and scattering of underwater sound. *Mailing Add:* Dynamic Systs Inc 8200 Greenboro Dr Suite 500 McLean VA 22102

DAVIS, CHARLES PACKARD, b Concord, Mass, May 24, 22; m 46; c 2. MECHANICAL ENGINEERING. *Educ:* Rensselaer Polytech Inst, BSME, 48. *Prof Exp:* Instr, Rensselaer Polytech Inst, 48-53; develop engr, Gen Elec Co, 51-58; prof mech eng, 58-61, head, Aeronaut Eng Dept, 61-74, PROF AERONAUT ENG, CALIF STATE POLYTECH COL, 61-, PROF CIVIL ENG, 76- *Mem:* Am Soc Eng Educ. *Res:* Shock vibration; mechanical design. *Mailing Add:* Dept Aeronaut Eng Calif State Polytech Col San Luis Obispo CA 93407

DAVIS, CHARLES PATRICK, b Dayton, Ohio, Aug 29, 45; m 68; c 1. MICROBIOLOGY. *Educ:* St Edward's Univ, BS, 67; Univ Tex, Austin, MA, 69, PhD(microbiol), 75. *Prof Exp:* Res asst microbiol, US Army Inst Dent Res, 69-71; USPHS fel microbiol, Univ Wis-Madison, 75-76; asst prof, Dept Microbiol, 76-80, ASSOC PROF MICROBIOL, UNIV TEX MED BR GALVESTON, 80- *Mem:* Am Soc Microbiol; Asn Gnotobiotics; Sigma Xi; Am Acad Microbiol. *Res:* Host-parasite relationships in mammalian gastrointestinal tracts; light microscopy, transmission and scanning electron microscopy along with anaerobic culture techniques to discern intimate host-bacterial cell attachments; pathogenic mechanisms of urinary tract pathogens; colostral macrophages. *Mailing Add:* 2521 Holley Ct Galveston TX 77551

DAVIS, CHARLES STEWART, b Akron, Ohio, Apr 22, 35; m 57; c 3. CLINICAL PHARMACOLOGY. *Educ:* WVa Univ, BS, 57; Purdue Univ, MS, 59, PhD(med chem), 61; State Univ NY Upstate Med Ctr, MD, 70. *Prof Exp:* Asst prof med chem, Purdue Univ, 61-63; unit leader, Eaton Labs, Norwich Pharmacal Co, 63-71, asst dir clin pharmacol, 71-73, assoc med dir, 72-75; DIR MED CTR, DRAKES BRANCH, VA, 75- *Concurrent Pos:* Fel, Univ Va, 60-61; NIH res grant, 62. *Mem:* Am Chem Soc. *Res:* Pathophysiology of endocrine diseases and the evaluation of drugs altering these conditions. *Mailing Add:* Med Ctr PO Box 368 Drakes Branch VA 23937

DAVIS, CHESTER L, b Charleston, WVa, July 2, 23; m 51; c 4. COMPUTER SCIENCE, APPLIED MATHEMATICS. *Educ:* Western Mich Univ, AB, 47; Univ Mich, AM, 53; Mich State Univ, PhD, 65. *Prof Exp:* Instr math & eng mech, Gen Motors Inst, 47-55; mathematician, Curtiss-Wright Res Labs, 55-56; sr math programmer, Data Processing Dept, Gen Motors Res Labs, 56-58; prof math & eng mech & chmn dept, Tri-State Col, 58-61; assoc prof mech eng, Univ Toledo, 63-66, dir comput ctr, 64-66; dir, Ogden Col Comput Lab, 70-82, PROF MATH & COMPUT SCI, WESTERN KY UNIV, 67- *Mem:* Am Asn Comput Mach; Comput Soc; Int Elec & Electronics Engrs; AAUP. *Mailing Add:* Dept of Math & Comput Sci Western Ky Univ Bowling Green KY 42101

DAVIS, CLARENCE DANIEL, b Pittsford, NY, Nov 20, 12; m 39; c 3. OBSTETRICS & GYNECOLOGY. *Educ:* Mass Inst Technol, SB, 35; Johns Hopkins Univ, MD, 39; Am Bd Obstet & Gynec, dipl, 49. *Prof Exp:* Rotating intern, Robert Packer Hosp, Pa, 39-40; intern, Genesee Hosp, NY, 40-41; intern obstet & gynec, Univ Minn Hosp, 41-42; asst resident endocrinol, Dept Obstet & Gynec, Duke Univ Hosp, 42, resident, 42-43, instr, 43-46; clin assoc physiol & clin assoc obstet & gynec, Med Sch, Univ Wash & assoc, Div Med Gynec, Mason Clin, 46-50; assoc, Duke Univ Hosp, 50-52, asst prof obstet & gynec, 52-54; prof & chmn dept, Sch Med, Univ Mo, 54-57; from assoc prof to prof, 57-78, EMER PROF OBSTET & GYNEC, SCH MED, YALE UNIV, 78- *Concurrent Pos:* Dir obstet & gynec educ, St Vincent's Hosp, Bridgeport, Conn, 75-77; clin prof obstet & gynec, Univ Calif, San Diego, 78- *Mem:* Fel Am Col Obstet & Gynec; AMA; assoc Med Am Col Legal Med. *Mailing Add:* 17439 Plaza Dolores San Diego CA 92128

DAVIS, CLYDE EDWARD, b Glenns Ferry, Idaho, June 24, 37; m 59; c 2. INORGANIC CHEMISTRY. *Educ:* Col Idaho, BS, 59; Ore State Univ, MS, 62; Colo State Univ, PhD(inorg chem), 68. *Prof Exp:* Teacher chem, Casper Col, 61-64; asst prof, Calif State Polytech Col, 67-68; NIH fel, Res Sch Chem, Australian Nat Univ, 68-69; asst prof, 69-77, ASSOC PROF CHEM, HUMBOLDT STATE COL, 77- *Mem:* Am Chem Soc. *Res:* Kinetics and mechanisms of base hydrolysis of coordination compounds; reactions of coordinated ligands of biological interest; sequential analysis of polypeptides by cobalt complexes. *Mailing Add:* Dept of Chem Humboldt State Univ Arcata CA 95521

DAVIS, CLYDE WILLIAM, JR, b Blairsville, Ga, Mar 24, 40; m 67; c 1. ACTUARIAL SCIENCE. *Educ:* WGa Col, BA, 62; Auburn Univ, MS, 64, PhD(math), 71. *Prof Exp:* Instr math, Auburn Univ, 64-65; from asst prof to prof math, COLUMBUS COL, 65-77; assoc actuary, 77-81, SR VPRES INT OPERS, AM FAMILY ASSURANCE CO, COLUMBUS, 81- *Concurrent Pos:* Adv math progs, Columbus Metro Urban League, 73-; adj prof math, Columbus Col, 77- *Mem:* Soc Indust & Appl Math; Math Asn Am. *Res:* Numerical computation in matrix theory. *Mailing Add:* Am Family Assurance Co PO Box 1459 Columbus GA 31902

DAVIS, COURTLAND HARWELL, JR, b Alexandria, Va, Feb 14, 21; m 42; c 6. NEUROLOGICAL SURGERY. *Educ:* George Washington Univ, BA, 41; Univ Va, MD, 44; Am Bd Neurol Surg, dipl, 54. *Prof Exp:* Rotating intern, US Marine Hosp, New Orleans, La, 44-45; asst resident neurosurg, Univ Va, 45-46; from asst resident to resident neurosurg, Duke Univ, 50-52; from instr to assoc prof, 52-66, PROF SURG, BOWMAN GRAY SCH MED, 66-; MEM STAFF, NC BAPTIST HOSP, 52- *Concurrent Pos:* NIH fel neuropath, Med Ctr, Duke Univ, 48-49 & neurol, 49-50; instr, Duke Hosp, 49-50; co-chmn res comt, Nat Asn Retarded Children, 58; vis prof, Kuala Lumpur, Malaysia & Vellore, Madras, SIndia, 66; vis neurosurg, HOPE, Cartagena, Colombis, SAm, 67 & Jamaica, WI, 71; pres, Bowman Gray Med Found, 62 & Asn Handicapped Children's Ctr, 68; mem bd trustees, Found Int Educ Neurol Surg, Inc, 69-; assoc chief prof serv, NC Baptist Hosps, Inc, 75-; chmn med care eval comt & deleg comt, Piedmont Med Found, 78-; mem bd dirs, Forsyth County Rehab House, Inc & Forsyth County Sheltered Workshop. *Mem:* Fel Am Col Surg; Am Acad Neurol Surg; Asn Res Nervous & Ment Dis; Soc Brit Neurol Surgeons; Soc Neurol Surgeons. *Res:* Applied research in neurology and neurosurgery. *Mailing Add:* Sect of Neurosurg Bowman Gray Sch of Med Winston-Salem NC 27103

DAVIS, CRAIG BRIAN, b Washington, DC, Nov 29, 38; m 70; c 5. ECOLOGY. *Educ:* Colo State Univ, BS, 64, MS, 67; Univ Calif, Davis, PhD(bot), 72. *Prof Exp:* Asst prof biol, Alma Col, 70-73; ASST PROF PLANT ECOL & COORDR ENVIRON STUDIES, IOWA STATE UNIV, 73- *Concurrent Pos:* Consult, ecol, Inst Ecol, 74. *Mem:* Ecol Soc Am; AAAS; Sigma Xi; Int Asn Aquatic Vascular Plant Biologists. *Res:* Vegetative structure and nutrient cycling in aquatic ecosystems; higher vascular plant and substrate components of aquatic ecosystems; environmental impact of pollutants on aquatic ecosystems. *Mailing Add:* Dept of Bot & Plant Path Bessey Hall Iowa State Univ Ames IA 50011

DAVIS, CRAIG H, b Pittsburgh, Pa, Mar 31, 35; m 57; c 2. MOLECULAR BIOLOGY. *Educ:* Ore State Univ, BS, 57; Univ Wash, MS, 62, PhD(biochem), 65. *Prof Exp:* ASST PROF BIOL, SAN DIEGO STATE UNIV, 67- *Mem:* AAAS. *Res:* Episomal nature of Crown-Gall induction. *Mailing Add:* Dept of Biol San Diego State Univ San Diego CA 92182

DAVIS, CRAIG WILSON, b Ypsilanti, Mich, Mar 19, 49; m 73; c 3. MOLECULAR PHARMACOLOGY, NEUROPHARMACOLOGY. *Educ:* Univ Mich, Ann Arbor, BS, 72; Emory Univ, PhD(pharmacol), 77. *Prof Exp:* Staff fel, NIH, 76-79; ASST PROF PHARMACOL, SCH MED, UNIV SC, 80- *Res:* Neurochemical mechanisms involved in the functioning of the nervous system; potential role of cyclic nucleotides. *Mailing Add:* Dept Pharmacol Med Sci Bldg Sch Med Univ SC Columbia SC 29208

DAVIS, CURRY BEACH, b Hornell, NY, Oct 6, 39; m 64; c 4. ORGANIC CHEMISTRY. *Educ:* Alfred Univ, BS, 61; Col Forestry, State Univ NY, PhD(org chem), 69. *Prof Exp:* CHEMIST DEVELOP LAB, ARIZ CHEM CO, 69- *Mem:* Am Chem Soc. *Res:* Tall oil rosin; fatty acids and terpene chemistry. *Mailing Add:* Ariz Chem Co PO Box 2447 Panama City FL 32401

DAVIS, CURTISS OWEN, b Los Angeles, Calif, Jan 1, 45. BIOLOGICAL OCEANOGRAPHY. *Educ:* Univ Calif, Berkeley, BA, 66; Univ Wash, MS, 69, PhD(oceanog), 73. *Prof Exp:* Sr oceanogr, Univ Wash, 73, res assoc oceanog, 73-74; res investr, Great Lakes Res Div, Univ Mich, Ann Arbor, 74-76, asst res oceanographer, 76-79; RES OCEANOGRAPHER & ACTG DIR, TIBURON CTR ENVIRON STUDIES, SAN FRANCISCO STATE UNIV, 80- *Mem:* AAAS; Am Soc Limnol & Oceanog; Estuarine Res Fedn; Phycol Soc Am. *Res:* Phytoplankton nutrient uptake kinetics; continuous culture of phytoplankton; dynamics of coastal marine and estuarine systems. *Mailing Add:* Tiburon Ctr Environ Studies PO Box 855 Tiburon CA 94920

DAVIS, D WAYNE, b Ponce de Leon, Mo, Nov 7, 35; m 65; c 2. ENVIRONMENTAL BIOLOGY. *Educ:* Univ Mo, BS, 61; Univ Sask, MA, 63; Univ Ark, PhD(ecol), 69. *Prof Exp:* From asst prof to assoc prof, 68-74, chmn dept, 78-80, chmn col fac, 80-81, PROF BIOL, SCH OF OZARKS, 74- *Concurrent Pos:* Vis prof, Univ Sask, 78. *Mem:* Nat Audubon Soc; Nature Conservancy. *Res:* Rodent and avian ecology; black walnut and shortleaf pine culture; establishing of native grasses on Ozark glades and prairies; wildlife habitat improvement. *Mailing Add:* Dept of Biol Sch of the Ozarks Point Lookout MO 65726

DAVIS, DANIEL LAYTEN, b Waynesville, NC, Apr 25, 38; m 60; c 3. PLANT PHYSIOLOGY, PLANT GENETICS. *Educ:* Berea Col, BS, 60; Mich State Univ, MS, 62; NC State Univ, PhD(plant physiol), 67. *Prof Exp:* Asst prof physiol, Miss State Univ, 67; from asst prof to assoc prof, 67-77, actg dir, Tobacco & Health Res Inst, 81, PROF AGRON, UNIV KY, 77- *Concurrent Pos:* Univ Ky Res Found tobacco & health res & serv contract, Agr Res Serv, USDA, 68-70. *Mem:* Am Soc Plant Physiol; Am Soc Agron; Crop Sci Soc Am; Phytochem Soc NAm. *Res:* Physiological and biochemical aspects of plant terpenoids, and other natural products as related to tobacco and health research. *Mailing Add:* Dept Agron Univ Ky Lexington KY 40506

DAVIS, DARRELL LAWRENCE, b Corral, Idaho, Feb 17, 27; m 55; c 4. PHYSIOLOGY. *Educ:* Ore State Col, BS, 49, MA, 52; St Louis Univ, PhD(physiol), 56. *Prof Exp:* Asst, Ore State Col, 49-51; asst, St Louis Univ, 51-56; asst res prof, Med Col Ga, 57-60, from asst prof to assoc prof physiol, 60-71; assoc prof, 71-74, PROF PHYSIOL, UNIV S FLA, 74- *Concurrent Pos:* Cardiovasc trainee, Med Col Ga, 56-57. *Mem:* Am Physiol Soc. *Res:* Cardiovascular and temperature regulation. *Mailing Add:* Dept of Physiol Univ of S Fla Tampa FL 33620

DAVIS, DAVID, b Liverpool, Eng. Oct 5, 27; US citizen; m 52; c 3. PSYCHIATRY. *Educ:* Glasgow Univ, MB, ChB, 49, MD, 74; Royal Col Physicians & Surgeons, DPM, 54. *Prof Exp:* House officer, Stobhill Hosp, Glasgow, Scotland, 49-50; registrar psychiat, St Crispin & South Ockendon Hosps, Eng, 52-55; registrar, Bethlem Royal & Maudsley Hosps, London, Eng, 57-59; asst prof, 60-61, assoc prof psychiat & chief sect gen psychiat, 61-68, chmn dept psychiat, 68-69 & 75-76, assoc chmn dept, 71-75, PROF PSYCHIAT, SCH MED, UNIV MO-COLUMBIA, 68-, ASSOC CHMN DEPT, 77-, CHIEF PSYCHIAT, UNIV MED CTR, 77-, DIR PSYCHIAT EDUC, 81- *Concurrent Pos:* Fulbright travel scholar psychiat, Wash Univ, 55-57; Am Fund Psychiat teaching fel, 61-62; Vis fac, Lab Community Psychiat, Harvard Med Sch, 65-67; co-chmn, Inter Forum Educators Community Psychiat, 67-69; Nat Inst Ment Health vis scientist alcohol res, Nat Ctr Prev & Control Alcoholism, 69-70; consult, Vet Admin, Columbia Univ, Mo, 70; vis prof psychiat, Univ Edinburgh, Scotland, 76-77. *Mem:* Fel AAAS; fel Royal Col Psychiat; fel Am Col Psychiat; fel Am Psychiat Asn; fel Royal Soc Health. *Res:* General psychiatry; social and community psychiatry; alcoholism; medical education. *Mailing Add:* Dept of Psychiat Univ of Mo Sch of Med Columbia MO 65201

DAVIS, DAVID, b Poland, Dec 20, 20; nat US; m 46; c 2. PLANT PATHOLOGY. *Educ:* Cornell Univ, BA, 46; Univ Ill, PhD, 50. *Prof Exp:* Plant pathologist, Conn Agr Exp Sta, 50-55; plant pathologist res lab, Merck Sharp & Dohme Div, 55-60; res assoc, NY Bot Garden, 60-70; DIR RES, PHYTA LABS, 70- *Mem:* Am Phytopath Soc; Am Inst Biol Sci. *Res:* Evaluation of pesticides; biological control of plant disease. *Mailing Add:* Phyta Labs Ghent NY 12075

DAVIS, DAVID A, b Springfield, Tenn, Mar 24, 18; m 41; c 2. MEDICINE. *Educ:* Vanderbilt Univ, BA, 38, MD, 41. *Prof Exp:* Instr surg, Tulane Univ, 47-49; assoc prof anesthesiol, Med Col Ga, 49-52; from prof surg in chg anesthesiol to clin prof anesthesiol, Sch Med, Univ NC, Chapel Hill, 52-71; PROF ANESTHESIOL, MED CTR, DUKE UNIV, 71- *Concurrent Pos:* Pres, Monitor Instruments, 69- *Mem:* AMA; Am Soc Anesthesiol; Asn Univ Anesthetists. *Res:* Muscle relaxants; circulatory effects of anesthetic agents; local anesthetic drugs. *Mailing Add:* Dept of Anesthesiol Duke Univ Med Ctr Durham NC 27710

DAVIS, DAVID G, b Dickinson, NDak, July 21, 35; m 72; c 2. PLANT PHYSIOLOGY, TISSUE CULTURE. *Educ:* NDak State Univ, BS, 60, MS, 62; Wash State Univ, PhD(bot), 65. *Prof Exp:* Asst bot, NDak State Univ, 60-62 & Wash State Univ, 62-63 & 63-65; AEC fel, Univ Minn, 65-67; RES PHYSIOLOGIST PLANT PHYSIOL, METAB & RADIATION RES LAB, AGR RES SERV, 67- *Concurrent Pos:* Sabbatical leave, Dept Plant Genetics, Weizmann Inst Sci, Israel, 79-80. *Mem:* Am Asn Plant Physiol; Int Asn Plant Tissue Cult; Weed Sci Soc Am; Scand Soc Plant Physiol; AAAS. *Res:* Metabolism of pesticides; pesticide additives in plant tissue cultures; growth and development of cells, tissues and organs in vitro as affected by pesticides, organic solvents and growth regulators; anatomical and morphological aspects of herbicide application. *Mailing Add:* Metab & Radiation Res Lab Agr Res Serv State Univ Sta Fargo ND 58102

DAVIS, DAVID GALE, b Leicester, NC, July 21, 35; m 57; c 3. GENETICS. *Educ:* Western Carolina Col, BS, 57; Univ NC, MA, 60; Univ Ga, PhD(zool), 63. *Prof Exp:* Asst zool, Univ NC, 57-60 & Univ Ga, 60-61; res assoc, Oak Ridge Nat Lab, 63-64; sr lectr zool, Monash Univ, Australia, 64-67; asst prof, Univ Western Ont, 67-68; NIH spec res fel, Lab Genetics, Univ Wis-Madison, 68-69; ASSOC PROF BIOL, UNIV ALA, TUSCALOOSA, 69- *Mem:* AAAS; Genetics Soc Am; Am Inst Biol Sci; Am Genetic Soc. *Res:* Chromosome mechanics; recombination; developmental genetics. *Mailing Add:* Dept of Biol Univ of Ala PO Box 1927 University AL 35486

DAVIS, DAVID WARREN, b Mankato, Minn, July 6, 30; m 58. PLANT BREEDING, VEGETABLE CROPS. *Educ:* Univ Hawaii, BS, 51; Univ Ill, MS, 56; Ore State Univ, PhD(hort), 63. *Prof Exp:* Res asst genetics, Univ Ill, 55-56; asst-in-training, Exp Sta, Hawaiian Sugar Planter's Asn, 56-57, asst geneticist, 58-61; agriculturist, Lihue Plantation Co, Hawaii, 57-58; res horticulturist, Veg & Ornamental Crops Res Br, Agr Res Serv, USDA, 63-65; assoc prof veg crop breeding, 65-68, PROF HORT, INST AGR, UNIV MINN, ST PAUL, 69- *Mem:* Coun Agr Sci & Technol; Inst Food Technologists; Fel AAAS; Am Soc Hort Sci. *Res:* Genetic improvement of plant populations for adaptability to commercial and consumer needs in vegetable agriculture; pest resistance; raw product quality. *Mailing Add:* Dept Hort Sci Univ Minn St Paul MN 55108

DAVIS, DEAN FREDERICK, b Johnson City, Tenn, May 4, 22; m 47; c 2. ENTOMOLOGY, CHEMISTRY. *Educ:* Univ Tenn, AB, 48, MS, 49. *Prof Exp:* Project leader agr res, USDA, Stored-Prod Insects Lab, 51-58, dir, 58-61, asst br chief, 61-66, asst dir mkt qual res div, 66-70, dir, 70-72, AREA DIR, SCI & EDUC ADMIN-AGR RES, USDA, 72- *Mem:* Entom Soc Am. *Res:* Insect resistant food packaging; pest management. *Mailing Add:* PO Box 14565 Gainesville FL 32604

DAVIS, DENNIS DUVAL, b Cleveland, Ohio, Nov 9, 41; m 63; c 3. ORGANIC CHEMISTRY, ORGANOMETALLIC CHEMISTRY. *Educ:* Case Inst Technol, BS, 63; Univ Calif, Berkeley, PhD(chem), 66. *Prof Exp:* From asst prof to assoc prof, 66-75, PROF CHEM, NMEX STATE UNIV, 76- *Mem:* Am Chem Soc. *Res:* Physical-organic chemistry; electrophilic aliphatic substitution reactions; photochemistry; free radical chemistry; chemistry of organotransition metal compounds. *Mailing Add:* Dept of Chem NMex State Univ Box 3C Las Cruces NM 88001

DAVIS, DENNY CECIL, b Toppenish, Wash, Dec 21, 44; m 72; c 1. AGRICULTURAL ENGINEERING. *Educ:* Wash State Univ, BS, 67; Cornell Univ, MS, 69, PhD(agr eng), 73. *Prof Exp:* Asst prof agr eng, Univ Ga, 73-76; asst prof, 76-80, ASSOC PROF AGR ENG & FOOD SCI & TECHNOL, WASH STATE UNIV, 80- *Concurrent Pos:* Consult, Cornell Univ, 74-75, legal consult, 80-81; res grant, Sci & Educ Admin, USDA, 79-82. *Mem:* Am Soc Agr Engrs; Inst Food Technologists. *Res:* Food processing; energy conservation; solar energy; food texture; storage of agricultural products; dynamics of machinery. *Mailing Add:* Dept Agr Eng Wash State Univ Pullman WA 99164

DAVIS, DICK D, b Hobart, Okla, Aug 7, 33; m 52; c 5. AGRONOMY. *Educ:* Univ Okla, BS, 60; Okla State Univ, MS, 63, PhD(bot), 65. *Prof Exp:* Asst prof, 64-69, assoc prof, 69-77, PROF AGRON, NMEX STATE UNIV, 77- *Mem:* Am Soc Agron; Crop Sci Soc Am. *Res:* Cotton breeding; pest resistant strains and hybrids. *Mailing Add:* Dept of Agron NMex State Univ Las Cruces NM 88001

DAVIS, DONALD ECHARD, b Charleston, Ill, Jan 12, 16; m 40; c 2. PLANT PHYSIOLOGY. *Educ:* Eastern Ill State Col, BEd, 36; Ohio State Univ, MS, 40, PhD(bot), 47. *Hon Degrees:* PedD, Eastern Ill State Col, 56. *Prof Exp:* Inspector, Ravenna Ord Plant, US War Dept, 42-43; instr bot, Ohio State Univ, 46-47; asst prof, Auburn Univ, 48, assoc prof bot, Univ & assoc botanist, Exp Sta, 49-50; AEC agr res fel, Univ Tenn, 51-52; from assoc prof to prof bot, 52-68, assoc botanist, 52-55, ALUMNI PROF BOT & MICROBIOL, AUBURN UNIV, 68-, BOTANIST, EXP STA, 55- *Concurrent Pos:* Vis prof, Univ Ill, 65; mem comt on persistent pesticide residues, Nat Acad Sci-Nat Res Coun, 68-69, mem consult comt to rev the use of 2, 4, 5-T, Nat Acad Sci, 70; mem, Nat Adv Panel Weed Res, 73-; ed, Weed Sci, Weed Sci Soc Am, 73- *Honors & Awards:* Res Award, Weed Sci Soc Am, 74. *Mem:* Fel AAAS; Am Soc Plant Physiol; fel Weed Sci Soc Am; Am Inst Biol Sci. *Res:* Ecological plant physiology; aquatic pollution; physiology of herbicidal action; pesticide problems. *Mailing Add:* Dept Bot Plant Path & Microbiol Auburn Univ Auburn AL 36830

DAVIS, DONALD MILLER, b Ft Knox, Ky, May 7, 45; m 68; c 1. TOPOLOGY. *Educ:* Mass Inst Technol, BS, 67; Stanford Univ, PhD(math), 72. *Prof Exp:* Actg asst prof math, Univ Calif, San Diego, 71-72; asst prof, Northwestern Univ, 72-74; asst prof, 74-78, ASSOC PROF MATH, LEHIGH UNIV, 78- *Concurrent Pos:* NSF res grant, 75-81; vis assoc prof math, Northwestern Univ, 78-79. *Mem:* Am Math Soc. *Res:* Determining for each integer n the smallest Euclidean space in which projective n-space can be immersed, using homotopy theoretic methods. *Mailing Add:* Dept of Math Lehigh Univ Bethlehem PA 18015

DAVIS, DONALD RAY, b Concord, NC, Aug 21, 39; m 63; c 2. PLANETARY SCIENCE, ASTRODYNAMICS. *Educ:* Clemson Univ, BS, 62; Univ Ariz, PhD(physics), 67. *Prof Exp:* Staff scientist & mgr astrodyn, TRW Syst Group, 67-70; res scientist planetary sci, IIT Res Inst, 71-72; SCIENTIST III, PLANETARY SCI INST & SCI APPLN INC, 72- *Concurrent Pos:* NSF fel, 64-65; NASA fel, 65-67; lectr, Dept of Planetary Sci, Univ Ariz, 72-73. *Honors & Awards:* Apollo Achievement Award, NASA, 69; Presidential Medal of Freedom, NASA, 70. *Mem:* Am Astron Soc; Am Inst Aeronaut & Astronaut; Sigma Xi; Am Asn Physics Teachers. *Res:* Origin, evolution and present state of the solar system; dynamical astronomy; hypervelocity impact studies; trajectory analysis; numerical modeling. *Mailing Add:* Planetary Sci Inst 2030 E Speedway Tucson AZ 85719

DAVIS, DONALD RAY, b Oklahoma City, Okla, Mar 28, 34. ENTOMOLOGY. *Educ:* Univ Kans, BA, 56; Cornell Univ, PhD(entom), 62. *Prof Exp:* Assoc cur, 61-64, chmn, Dept Entom, 76-81, CUR LEPIDOPTERA, SMITHSONIAN INST, 64- *Concurrent Pos:* Smithsonian Res Found grant, 66-67 & 73-74. *Honors & Awards:* Smithsonian Res Award, 73, 78, 79, 80 & 81; Jordan Medal Award, Lepidop Soc, 77. *Mem:* Entom Soc Am; Nat Speleol Soc; Soc Syst Zool; Lepidop Soc. *Res:* Systematics, phylogeny and biology of the Microlepidoptera, particularly the superfamily Tineoidea and all members of the Monotrysia; biology of leaf mining Lepidoptera; biology of cave dwelling Lepidoptera. *Mailing Add:* Dept of Entom Smithsonian Inst Washington DC 20560

DAVIS, DONALD ROBERT, b La Jara, Colo, Mar 19, 41; m 80. NUTRITION, BIOCHEMISTRY. *Educ:* Univ Calif, Los Angeles, PhD(chem), 65. *Prof Exp:* NSF fel chem, Calif Inst Technol, 65-67; asst prof, Univ Calif, Irvine, 67-74; RES ASSOC NUTRIT, CLAYTON FOUND BIOCHEM INST, UNIV TEX, AUSTIN, 74- *Concurrent Pos:* Instr part-time, Calif Inst Technol, 65-67. *Mem:* AAAS; Acad Orthomolecular Psychiat; Am Col Nutrit; Soc Nutrit Educ; Int Acad Preventive Med. *Res:* Variability of nutrient requirements; statistics of nutrient allowances; nutritional qualities of foods and diets; unrecognized functions of nutrients. *Mailing Add:* Clayton Found Biochem Inst Univ of Tex Austin TX 78712

DAVIS, DONALD WALTER, b San Francisco, Calif, May 30, 20; m 43; c 6. ENTOMOLOGY. *Educ:* Univ Calif, BS, 41, PhD, 50. *Prof Exp:* Asst entom, Univ Calif, 46-50; res entomologist, Calif Spray-Chem Corp, 50-54; assoc prof entom, Teaching & Exp Sta, 54-67, PROF ENTOM, DEPT BIOL, UTAH STATE UNIV, 67- *Mem:* Entom Soc Am. *Res:* Biology and control of agricultural pests; spider mites of the genus Tetranychus; agricultural entomology. *Mailing Add:* Dept of Biol Utah State Univ Logan UT 84322

DAVIS, DUANE M, b Indianapolis, Ind, July 10, 33; m 57, 75; c 3. AERONAUTICS. *Educ:* Purdue Univ, BS, 55, PhD(aeronaut), 67; Univ Pittsburgh, MS, 57. *Prof Exp:* Engr, Bettis Atomic Power Div, Westinghouse Elec Co, 55-57; from instr to assoc prof aeronaut, US Air Force Acad, 66-73; chief aerospace dynamics br, Air Force Flight Dynamics Lab, 73-75, dep chief structures div, Air Force Flight Dynamics Lab, 75-77, chief eng, Laser Guided Bomb, Systs Proj Off, Air Defense Training Command, 77-78, dir laser guided bombs, 78-79, dep dir precision guided munitions, Systs Proj Off, 79, DIR GUIDED WEAPONS SYSTS PROJ OFF, ARMAMENT DIV, EGLIN AFB, FLA, 79- *Mem:* Am Inst Aeronaut & Astronaut. *Res:* Optimization; weapons system selection and specification; optimal tactics for weapons system employment. *Mailing Add:* Armament Develop Test Ctr/SD4 Eglin AFB FL 32542

DAVIS, E(ARL) JAMES, b St Paul, Minn, July 22, 34; m 78; c 2. CHEMICAL ENGINEERING. *Educ:* Gonzaga Univ, BS, 56; Univ Wash, PhD(chem eng), 60. *Prof Exp:* Design engr, Union Carbide Chem Co, WVa, 56; res engr, Boeing Airplane Co, Wash, 57; from asst prof to assoc prof chem eng, Gonzaga Univ, 60-68; from assoc prof to prof chem eng, Clarkson Col Technol, 68-78, chmn dept, 73-74; prof & chmn, Dept Chem & Nuclear Eng, Univ NMex, 78-80; DIR, ENG DIV & PROF, INST PAPER CHEM, 80- *Concurrent Pos:* Petrol Res Fund grants, 61-65; NSF res grants, 63-64, 66-68 & 69-80, res fel, Imp Col, London, 64-65; Sigma Xi grant, 69; mem, Inst Colloid & Surface Sci, Clarkson Col Technol, assoc dir, 74-78; consult Unilever Res, Port Sunlight, Eng, 74-79, Sandia Nat Lab & Los Alamos Sci Lab, 78-80. *Mem:* Am Chem Soc; Am Inst Chem Engrs; Am Soc Eng Educ; Tech Asn Pulp & Paper Indust. *Res:* Two-phase flow and heat transfer; surface and colloid science; aerosol physics and chemistry; paper making engineering. *Mailing Add:* Inst Paper Chem Appleton WI 54911

DAVIS, EARLE ANDREW, JR, b Aliquippa, Pa, June 1, 19; m 43. NEUROPHYSIOLOGY. *Educ:* Grove City Col, BS, 41; Univ Pittsburgh, MS, 43; Univ Ill, PhD(physiol ecol), 53. *Prof Exp:* Asst prof biol, Elmhurst Col, 46-49; prof, Buena Vista Col, 52-53; prof, West Liberty State Col, 53-55; LECTR ANAT, UNIV CALIF, IRVINE-CALIF COL MED, 55- *Mem:* AAAS; Am Asn Anat; Int Col Surg; Soc Neurosci. *Res:* Human gross and microanatomy; effects of metabolic rate on distribution of animals; sites of action of hallucinogenic drugs in cat brain. *Mailing Add:* Dept of Anat Univ of Calif Col Med Irvine CA 92717

DAVIS, EDWARD ALEX, b Houston, Tex, Jan 2, 31; m 52; c 4. OPERATIONS RESEARCH, ENVIRONMENTAL ASSESSMENT. *Educ:* Rice Univ, BA, 55, MA, 56, PhD(nuclear physics), 61. *Prof Exp:* Proj officer, Nuclear Power Off, US Army Engr Res & Develop Labs, 57-58; res physicist, Texaco, Inc, 61-62; asst prof physics, Okla City Univ, 62-64; mem fac, Eve Sch, 66-71, PRIN STAFF PHYSICIST OPERS RES, JOHNS HOPKINS UNIV, 64- *Mem:* AAAS; Opers Res Soc Am; Am Asn Physics Teachers; Sigma Xi; Inst Mgt Sci. *Res:* cooling towers; nuclear well-logging; tactical military operations analysis; command and control systems; transit systems analysis; applied mathematics; simulation; probabilistic models; air quality; environmental systems; design and analysis of instruction systems; applications of personal computers. *Mailing Add:* Appl Physics Lab Johns Hopkins Univ Laurel MD 20810

DAVIS, EDWARD ALLAN, b San Francisco, Calif, Oct 26, 17; m 56; c 3. MATHEMATICS. *Educ:* Univ Calif, Berkeley, BA, 40, MA, 44, PhD(math), 51. *Prof Exp:* Teaching asst, assoc & jr instr for Army Air Force in math, Univ Calif, Berkeley, 40-47; from instr to asst prof, Univ Nev, 47-55; from asst prof to assoc prof, 55-69, actg dean col sci, 75-76, PROF MATH, UNIV UTAH, 69- *Concurrent Pos:* Fund for Adv Ed res fel, Stanford Univ & Univ Chicago, 53-54; assoc prog dir spec proj in sci educ, NSF, DC, 61-62, consult, 62-67, 71-73, prog dir, Student & Coop Prog, 67-70. *Mem:* Am Math Soc; Math Soc Am; Nat Coun Teachers Math. *Res:* Mathematical economics; teacher training programs in mathematics. *Mailing Add:* Dept of Math Univ of Utah Salt Lake City UT 84112

DAVIS, EDWARD DEWEY, b Philadelphia, Pa, Sept 24, 33. MATHEMATICS. *Educ:* Univ Pa, BA, 55, MA, 57; Univ Chicago, PhD(math), 61. *Prof Exp:* Instr math, Northwestern Univ, 61-62; lectr & res assoc, Yale Univ, 62-64; asst prof, Purdue Univ, 64-67; asst prof, 67-68, assoc prof math, 68-80, PROF MATH, STATE UNIV NY, ALBANY, 80- *Mem:* Am Math Soc. *Res:* Commutative algebra, especially Northerian rings; algebraic geometry. *Mailing Add:* Dept of Math State Univ of NY Albany NY 12222

DAVIS, EDWARD LYON, b Fall River, Mass, July 15, 29. BOTANY. *Educ:* Harvard Univ, BA, 51; Univ Mass, MS, 53; Washington Univ, PhD(bot), 56. *Prof Exp:* Instr bot, Univ Mass, 53; asst, Mo Bot Garden, 54-56; asst prof, 57-61, assoc prof, 61-72, PROF BOT, UNIV MASS, AMHERST, 72-, HEAD DEPT, 75- *Concurrent Pos:* Vis lectr, Smith Col, 58-59. *Mem:* Bot Soc Am. *Res:* Anatomy, systematics and evolution of higher plants; morphogenesis. *Mailing Add:* Dept of Bot Morrill Sci Ctr Univ of Mass Amherst MA 01002

DAVIS, EDWARD MELVIN, b Springfield, Mass, Mar 22, 13; m 40; c 3. ORGANIC CHEMISTRY. *Educ:* Rensselaer Polytech Inst, ChE, 34, MS, 35, PhD(org chem), 38. *Prof Exp:* Res chemist, Joseph E Seagram & Sons, Inc, 39-40; develop chemist, Biofen Labs, 40-41 & Kroger Grocery & Baking Co, Inc, 41-44; vpres mfg, Solo Marx Rubber Co, 44-56; from asst dir to assoc dir chem develop, Hilton-Davis Chem Co Div, Sterling Drug Inc, 56-75, dir chem develop, 75-78; RETIRED. *Concurrent Pos:* Chem processing consult. *Mailing Add:* 2197 Section Rd Cincinnati OH 45237

DAVIS, EDWIN ALDEN, b New Haven, Conn, Dec 28, 23; m 51; c 2. WATERSHED MANAGEMENT. *Educ:* Univ Conn, BS, 45; Yale Univ, PhD(plant physiol), 49. *Prof Exp:* Res fel plant physiol, Carnegie Inst, Dept Plant Biol, Stanford, Calif, 49-52; plant physiologist, Agr Res, Dow Chem Co, 53-57; plant physiologist, Agr Res Serv, 58-63, PRIN PLANT PHYSIOLOGIST, ROCKY MT FOREST & RANGE EXP STA, FOREST SERV, USDA, 63- *Mem:* Bot Soc Am; Am Soc Plant Physiol; Weed Sci Soc; Soil Conserv Soc Am; Agron Soc. *Res:* Water augumentation research to increase stream flow from chaparral watersheds by converting chaparral to plants that use less water; brush control methods and the effects of vegetation conversions on water yield and quality and the environment. *Mailing Add:* Forest Hydrol Lab Ariz State Univ Tempe AZ 85281

DAVIS, EDWIN NATHAN, b Corning, NY, Apr 23, 09; m 36; c 8. MICROBIOLOGY. *Educ:* Cornell Univ, BS, 34. *Prof Exp:* Anal & res chemist, Pleasant Valley Wine Co, NY, 33-36; jr chemist, Bur Agr Chem, USDA, 36-39; asst & instr chem, NY Exp Sta, Geneva, 39-41; prod supt, Mich Wineries, Inc, 41-43; res biochemist, Hiram Walker & Sons, Inc, 43-63; microbiologist, Northern Regional Res Lab, Agr Res Serv, USDA, 63-82. *Mem:* AAAS; Am Soc Microbiol. *Res:* Yeast fermentations, beverage and industrial alcohol; enzymatic starch hydrolysis; biosynthesis; microbial polymers; agripollution control. *Mailing Add:* 710 Bourland Ave Peoria IL 61606

DAVIS, ELDON VERNON, b Burwell, Nebr, Aug 4, 23; m 45; c 1. VIROLOGY. *Educ:* Univ Nebr, BS, 49, MS, 51; Univ Pa, PhD, 57. *Prof Exp:* Jr res scientist, Upjohn Pharmaceut Co, 50-52, scientist & head virus labs, 52-54; asst, Univ Pa, 54-56, res assoc, 56-57, asst prof, 57-58; virologist & head labs, USPHS, 58-63; sr virologist, Midwest Res Inst, 63-64; from virologist to res scientist, 64-69, SR RES SCIENTIST, NORDEN LABS, INC, 69- *Mem:* AAAS; NY Acad Sci; Tissue Cult Asn. *Res:* Cell physiology, tissue culture; growth of mammalian cells in submerged culture; kinetics of viral growth; viral isolation and characterization; vaccines. *Mailing Add:* 7221 South Unit 18 Lincoln NE 68506

DAVIS, ELDRED JACK, b Kelleyville, Okla, Oct 14, 30; m 64; c 5. INTERMEDIARY METABOLISM, BIOENERGETICS. *Educ:* Abilene Christian Col, BSc, 56; Fla State Univ, MSc, 58; McGill Univ, PhD(biochem), 63. *Prof Exp:* Res biochemist, Lederle Labs, Am Cyanamid Co, 58-61; from asst prof to assoc prof, 65-72, PROF BIOCHEM, SCH MED, IND UNIV, INDIANAPOLIS, 72- *Concurrent Pos:* USPHS fel, Lab Biochem, Univ Amsterdam, 63-65; vis asst prof, Univ Amsterdam, 68; vis prof, Univ Oslo, 71-72, Univ Helsinki, 78-79; consult, NIH; sci reviewer, Am Heart Asn, Ind, 73-78; travel fel, NATO, 75-79. *Mem:* AAAS; Am Soc Biol Chemists; Brit Biochem Soc. *Res:* Intermediary metabolism and its regulation: Perfused organs, mitochondria, reconstructed cell-free systems, identification, characterization of new malic enzymes; mitochondria and metabolic control; gluconeogenesis; anaplerotic pathways in mammalian systems. *Mailing Add:* Dept of Biochem Ind Univ Sch of Med Indianapolis IN 46223

DAVIS, ELIZABETH ALLAWAY, b New York, NY, Jan 5, 41; m 68; c 2. DEVELOPMENTAL BIOLOGY, PLANT TISSUE CULTURE. *Educ:* Mt Holyoke Col, BA, 62; Brandeis Univ, PhD(develop biol), 69. *Prof Exp:* Student biol labs, Harvard Univ, 68-69; ASST PROF BIOL, UNIV MASS, BOSTON, 69- *Mem:* AAAS; Am Soc Plant Physiol; Soc Develop Biol. *Res:* Physiology, genetics, multiplication and differentiation of chloroplasts; plant morphogenesis; plant tissue culture. *Mailing Add:* Dept of Biol Harbor Campus Univ of Mass Boston MA 02125

DAVIS, ELIZABETH YOUNG, b Ft Collins, Colo, Apr 23, 20; m 41; c 3. NUTRITION, PHYSIOLOGY. *Educ:* Colo State Univ, BS, 41; Auburn Univ, MS, 57, PhD(nutrit biochem), 64. *Prof Exp:* instr foods & nutrit, Auburn Univ, 57-60; assoc prof nutrit res, Tuskegee Inst, 64-66; prof nutrit, Auburn Univ, 66-73, res coordr home econ, 69-73; group leader human nutrit & social sci, 77-78, ASST DEP ADMINR, HUMAN NUTRIT, FOOD & SOCIAL SCI COOP STATE RES SERV, USDA, 79-, COORDR HOME ECON, COOP RES SCI & EDUC ADMIN, 73- *Mem:* Am Chem Soc; Am Dietetic Asn; Am Inst Nutrit; Inst Food Technol; Am Home Econ Asn. *Res:* Lipid metabolism; biosynthesis of carnitine; incorporation of ethionine ethyl into phospholipids; ethylated ethanolamines in phospholipids; metabolism of N-alkyl amines; cholesterol; diethylstilbestrol; fatty acid relationsips. *Mailing Add:* Coop State Res Serv USDA Washington DC 20250

DAVIS, ELMO WARREN, b Idaho, Sept 9, 20; m 51; c 4. GENETICS, HORTICULTURE. *Educ:* Univ Idaho, BS, 48; Univ Calif, Davis, MS, 49, PhD(genetics), 52. *Prof Exp:* Assoc prof hort & assoc olericulturist, Kans State Univ, 52-53; geneticist, USDA, 53-56, res horticulturist, 57-66; mem jr bd exec, 67-69, dir agr res & develop, Gilroy Foods, Inc, 66-76, mem bd dirs, 70-76; corp agr scientist, 76-80, DIR AGR SCI & TECHNOL, MCCORMICK & CO, 80- *Mem:* Fel Am Soc Hort Sci; Am Genetics Asn; Int Soc Hort Sci. *Res:* Breeding, culture, seed production and dehydration of onions and garlic; horticultural character of allium species; hybrid onions; culinary herbs and spices, sesame, vanilla, onions, garlic, capsicum, basil, etc, in US and foreign. *Mailing Add:* McCormick & Co Inc 11350 McCormick Rd Hunt Valley MD 21031

DAVIS, ELWYN H, b Leon, Iowa, Jan 10, 42; m 63; c 1. COMBINATORICS ALBEBRA. *Educ:* Univ Mo-Columbia, BSE, 64, MA, 66, PhD(math), 69. *Prof Exp:* Assoc prof, 69-77, PROF MATH, PITTSBURG STATE UNIV, 77- *Concurrent Pos:* NSF grant convexity conf, 71; vis instr math, Pa State Univ, 75-76. *Mem:* Am Math Soc; Math Asn Am. *Res:* Projective planes; nearfields and generalizations; construction of finite projective planes via coordinating systems; generalizations of projective planes and the coordinating systems; computer assisted instruction. *Mailing Add:* Dept of Math Pittsburg State Univ Pittsburg KS 66762

DAVIS, ERNST MICHAEL, b Victoria, Tex, Oct 12, 33; div; c 2. AQUATIC BIOLOGY, SANITARY ENGINEERING. *Educ:* NTex State Univ, BA, 56, MA, 62; Univ Okla, PhD(sanit eng), 66. *Prof Exp:* NSF grant, Univ Tex, Austin, 66-67, Fed grant sanit eng, 66-68, Off Water Resources Res grant limnol invests, 67-68, Fed Water Pollution Control Admin grant, 67-69, Tex Water Qual Bd grant, 68, asst prof sanit eng, 69-70; asst prof, 70-73, ASSOC PROF ENVIRON HEALTH, UNIV TEX SCH PUB HEALTH, HOUSTON, 73- *Concurrent Pos:* Tex Water Develop Bd grant, Univ Tex Sch Pub Health, Houston, 70-72, NASA grant, 71-72; consult, Environ Protection Agency, 70-74; res fels, NTex State Univ. *Mem:* Am Acad Environ Engrs; Am Soc Civil Engrs; Water Pollution Control Fedn; Am Water Works Asn; Int Asn Water Pollution Res. *Res:* Water pollution abatement methodology; water resources management. *Mailing Add:* Univ of Tex Sch of Pub Health PO Box 20186 Houston TX 77025

DAVIS, EUGENIA ASIMAKOPOULOS, b Chicago, Ill, Oct 15, 38; m 60; c 2. FOOD SCIENCE, ORGANIC CHEMISTRY. *Educ:* Univ Chicago, BS, 59, MS, 60; Free Univ Brussels, PhD(org chem), 67. *Prof Exp:* Asst scientist chem, Res Inst, Ill Inst Technol, 60-62; res asst, Dept Internal Med, 67-70, res assoc, Dept Foods, 70-72, asst prof, 72-78, ASSOC PROF, DEPT FOOD SCI & NUTRIT, UNIV MINN, 78- *Concurrent Pos:* Agr Exp Sta Proj grant, 75-83; NSF grant, 76-78; co-ed, J Food Microstruct, 81- *Mem:* Am Chem Soc; AAAS; Inst Food Technologists; Am Asn Cereal Chemists; Sigma Xi. *Res:* Heat and mass transfer studies; scanning and transmission; electron microscope ultra structural studies; X-ray microanalysis of foods heated in controlled environment ovens equipped with conventional and microwave heating elements. *Mailing Add:* Dept Food Sci & Nutrit Univ Minn St Paul MN 55108

DAVIS, FLOYD ASHER, b Chester, Pa, June 10, 34; m 62; c 2. NEUROLOGY, NEUROSCIENCES. *Educ:* Franklin & Marshall Col, BS, 56; Univ Pa, MD, 60. *Prof Exp:* Asst prof neurol, Col Med, Univ Ill, 68-71; ASSOC PROF NEUROL & BIOMED ENG, RUSH MED COL, 71- *Concurrent Pos:* From asst attend neurologist to assoc attend neurologist, Presby-St Luke's Hosp, Chicago, 68-74, sr attend neurologist, 74- *Mem:* Am Acad Neurol; Am Neurol Asn; Soc Neurosci; AAAS; NY Acad Sci. *Res:* Pathophysiology of impulse conduction in demyelinated nerve as it relates to multiple sclerosis. *Mailing Add:* Dept of Neurol 1753 W Congress Pkwy Chicago IL 60612

DAVIS, FRANCIS KAYE, JR, b Scranton, Pa, May 4, 18; m 41; c 2. PHYSICAL METEOROLOGY. *Educ:* WChester State Col, BS, 39; Mass Inst Technol, MS, 44; NY Univ, PhD, 57. *Prof Exp:* Asst, Mass Inst Technol, 43-44; PROF PHYSICS, DREXEL UNIV, 46-, DEAN COL SCI, 70- *Concurrent Pos:* Staff meteorologist, WFIL-WFIL-TV, 47-71; meteorol consult, 50-; asst, Johns Hopkins Univ, 54-56; consult, C W Thornthwaite Assocs, 54-, Day & Zimmerman, 55-, City of Philadelphia, 56-, Am Mach & Foundry Co, 57- & Radio Corp Am, 58- *Mem:* Fel Am Meteorol Soc; Am Phys Soc; Am Asn Physics Teachers; Am Geophys Union. *Res:* Storm damage; atmospheric pollution; physics of fog formation; upper atmosphere physics. *Mailing Add:* Col of Sci Drexel Univ Philadelphia PA 19104

DAVIS, FRANK, b New York, NY, Oct 8, 17; m 47; c 3. BIOCHEMISTRY. *Educ:* Brooklyn Col, BA, 40; Va Polytech Inst & State Univ, MS, 41; Univ Md, PhD, 48. *Prof Exp:* Assoc inspector powder & explosives, Radford Ord Works, Va, 41-42; asst poultry nutrit, Exp Sta, Univ Md, 47-48; bacteriologist microbiol, Res Div, Bur Agr & Indust Chem, USDA, 48-50; immunochemist, Nat Naval Med Ctr, Naval Med Res Inst, Md, 50-52; asst chief, Assessment Br, Ralph M Parsons Co, 52-54; asst dir res & develop, Block Drug Co, 54-57; tech dir, Whitehall Labs Div, Am Home Prod, 57-66; vpres & tech dir, J B Williams Co, 67-69; PRES, DAVIS LABS, INC, 69- *Mem:* Am Chem Soc. *Res:* Vitamin deficiencies and respiratory quotient of rat; growth factors of the chick; bacterial nutrition and metabolism; bioorganic studies; enzymes; toxicology; detergents; fungicides; dentifrices; pharmaceuticals; aerosols. *Mailing Add:* Davis Labs Inc 157 N Mansfield Blvd Cherry Hill NJ 08034

DAVIS, FRANK FRENCH, b Pendleton, Ore, July 19, 20; m 48; c 2. BIOCHEMISTRY. *Educ:* Univ Hawaii, BS, 50; Univ Calif, PhD(biochem), 55. *Prof Exp:* Jr res biochemist, Univ Calif, 54-56, asst, 56-57; from asst prof to assoc prof biochem, 57-64, PROF BIOCHEM, RUTGERS UNIV, 64- *Mem:* AAAS; Am Chem Soc; Am Soc Biol Chemists; NY Acad Sci; Sigma Xi. *Res:* Enzyme modification for therapeutic purposes. *Mailing Add:* Dept Biochem Rutgers Univ New Brunswick NJ 08903

DAVIS, FRANKLIN A, b Des Moines, Iowa, Apr 1, 39; m 67. ORGANIC CHEMISTRY. *Educ:* Univ Wis, BS, 62; Syracuse Univ, PhD(org chem), 66. *Prof Exp:* Res asst org chem, Syracuse Univ, 63-66; Welch fel, Univ Tex, 66-68; from asst prof to assoc prof, 68-79, PROF CHEM, DREXEL UNIV, 79- *Mem:* Am Chem Soc. *Res:* Organic sulfur chemistry: synthesis and properties of unusual organic sulfur compounds, sulfenamides, sulfenimines, sulfenic acids; heterocyclic chemistry: oxaziridine; symmetric oxidations. *Mailing Add:* Dept of Chem Drexel Univ Philadelphia PA 19104

DAVIS, FREDERIC WHITLOCK, zoology, wildlife management, see previous edition

DAVIS, GEORGE DIAMENT, b Ithaca, NY, May 7, 26; m 50; c 1. PHYSIOLOGY. *Educ:* Princeton Univ, AB, 46; Yale Univ, PhD(physiol), 51. *Prof Exp:* From instr to assoc prof, 51-63, PROF PHYSIOL, LA STATE UNIV MED CTR, 63- *Concurrent Pos:* Vis prof, La State Univ-Agency Int Develop Contract, Sch Med, Univ Costa Rica, 61-63. *Mem:* AAAS; Am Acad Neurol; Am Physiol Soc; NY Acad Sci. *Res:* Neurophysiology; biophysical instrumentation. *Mailing Add:* La State Univ Med Ctr 1542 Tulane Ave New Orleans LA 70112

DAVIS, GEORGE H, b Detroit, Mich, July 25, 21; m 49, 61; c 1. HYDROLOGY, GEOLOGY APPLIED. *Educ:* Univ Ill, BS, 42. *Prof Exp:* Asst geol, State Geol Surv, Ill, 42-46; geologist, US Geol Surv, 46-68, res hydrologist, 68-79, asst dir, 79-81; CONSULT GEOLOGIST/ HYDROLOGIST, 81- *Concurrent Pos:* First officer, Inst Atomic Energy Agency, Vienna, 66-68; ed, Water Resources Res, 69-76; chmn int hydrol decade work group on ground water, UNESCO, 70-74; vchmn int hydrol decade work group on nuclear techniques in hydrology, Int Atomic Energy Agency, 69-74; chmn work group on water & energy, Int Hydrol Prog, 76-; ed, J Hydrol, 77-; lectr, Univ Md Univ Col, 81. *Honors & Awards:* Meinzer Award, Geol Soc Am, 72. *Mem:* Geol Soc Am; Am Geophys Union; Int Water Resources Asn (treas); Int Asn Hydrogeologists. *Res:* Geologic occurrence of ground water. *Mailing Add:* 10408 Insley St Silver Spring MD 20902

DAVIS, GEORGE HERBERT, b Pittsburgh, Pa, Aug 30, 42; m 65; c 3. STRUCTURAL GEOLOGY. *Educ:* Col Wooster, BA, 64; Univ Tex, Austin, MA, 66; Univ Mich, Ann Arbor, PhD(struct & econ geol), 71. *Prof Exp:* Teaching asst, Univ Tex, Austin, 66; asst prof, 70-75, dir summer field camp, 70-74, ASSOC PROF GEOSCI, UNIV ARIZ, 75- *Mem:* Geol Soc Am. *Res:* Deformational history of strata-bound massive sulfide deposits; monoclines of the Colorado Plateau; gravity gliding; folding and faulting in Southwestern Arizona; structural analysis of metamorphic core complexes. *Mailing Add:* Dept of Geosci Univ of Ariz Tucson AZ 85710

DAVIS, GEORGE KELSO, b Pittsburgh, Pa, July 2, 10; m 36; c 6. ANIMAL NUTRITION. *Educ:* Pa State Univ, BS, 32; Cornell Univ, PhD(nutrit), 37. *Prof Exp:* Asst animal nutrit, Cornell Univ, 34-37; asst chem, Mich State Univ, 37-42; prof nutrit, Inst Food & Agr Sci, 42-79, dir div sponsored res, 70-75, res prof & dir nuclear sci, 60-65, dir biol sci, 65-70, DISTINGUISHED EMER PROF, UNIV FLA, 79- *Concurrent Pos:* Eli Lilly lectr; hon prof, Univ Chile; mem, Frasch Found Awards Comt; mem, Animal Nutrit Comt; mem geochem environ comt, Nat Res Coun; sect convenor, Spec Comt Int Biol Prog; pres, Nat Nutrit Consortium, 77-78; mem, Int Coun Sci Unions. *Honors & Awards:* Borden Award, Am Inst Nutrit, 64; Fla Award, Am Chem Soc; Spencer Award, Am Chem Soc, 80. *Mem:* Nat Acad Sci; Am Chem Soc; Am Inst Nutrit (pres, 75-76); Am Soc Biol Chem; Am Soc Animal Sci; Soc Environ Geochem & Health (pres, 76). *Res:* Relation of nutrition to development of disease, trace substances, vitamins, mineral elements; use of radioactive tracers; metabolism of copper and cardiovascular disorders; trace element metabolism in relation to cardiovascular calcification and urolithiases. *Mailing Add:* 2903 SW Second Ct Gainesville FL 32601

DAVIS, GEORGE MORGAN, b Bridgeport, Conn, May 21, 38; m 61, 75; c 2. MALACOLOGY. *Educ:* Marietta Col, BA, 60; Univ Mich, MS, 62, PhD(zool), 65. *Prof Exp:* Res assoc malacol, Univ Mich, 61-65; chief malacol sect, US Army Med Command, Japan, 65-70; assoc cur malacology, 70-78, CUR MOLLUSCA, ACAD NATURAL SCI PHILADELPHIA, 78-, CHMN DEPT MALACOL, 72- *Concurrent Pos:* Adv, US Educ Comn, Japan, 66-67; consult, Agency Int Develop, Mekong River Proj, 71; partic, US-Japan Coop Med Sci Prog, 71; co-ed-in-chief, Malacologia, Int J Malacol, 72-; exec secy-treas, Int Malacol, 74-; mem steering comt, Am Coun Syst Malacologists, 73-79; adj prof, Univ Pa, 77-; assoc prof, Jefferson Med Univ, 70-81; adj prof, Dept Biol & Pathobiol, Univ Penn; treas, Asn Systs Collections, 77-81, vpres, 81- *Honors & Awards:* US Govt Superior Performance Award, 68, 70. *Mem:* AAAS; Am Inst Biol Sci; Am Soc Zool; Am Malacol Union (pres, 76-77); Japanese Soc Parasitol. *Res:* Systematic studies of freshwater, amphibious, brackish-water snails; medical malacology; morphological, immunochemical and biochemical studies of snails and clams. *Mailing Add:* Dept of Malacol 19th & Pkwy Acad Natural Sci Philadelphia PA 19103

DAVIS, GEORGE THOMAS, b High Point, NC, Sept 30, 32; m 56; c 5. ORGANIC CHEMISTRY. *Educ:* Univ NC, BS, 54; Wash State Univ, MS, 57; Brown Univ, PhD(chem), 60. *Prof Exp:* Res assoc chem, Pa State Univ, 59-60; sr chemist, Melpar, Inc, 60-61 & Food & Drug Admin, 61-62; SR CHEMIST, EDGEWOOD ARSENAL, 62- *Mem:* NY Acad Sci; Am Chem Soc. *Res:* Solution adsorption of pollutants; oxidation and elimination mechanisms; nucleophilic substitution reaction; organophosphorus and fluorine chemistry; chemistry of amines; electrochemistry of nitroaromatics; chemical transformations of pollutants; disposal and detoxification of toxic chemicals including chemical warfare agents. *Mailing Add:* Chem Systs Lab Res Div Edgewood Arsenal Aberdeen Proving Grounds MD 21010

DAVIS, GEORGE THOMAS, b Montour Falls, NY, Oct 20, 33; m 59; c 6. POLYMER CHEMISTRY. *Educ:* Cornell Univ, BChE, 56; Princeton Univ, PhD(chem), 63. *Prof Exp:* Chem engr, Esso Res & Eng Co, 56-60; actg asst prof chem, Univ Va, 63-64; res assoc polymer physics, 64-66, CHEMIST, NAT BUR STAND, 66- *Mem:* Am Chem Soc; Am Phys Soc. *Res:* Secondary oil recovery; diffusion in solids; structure of polymers; polymer crystallization; piezoelectric polymers. *Mailing Add:* 119 Duncannon Rd Bel Air MD 21014

DAVIS, GERALD GORDON, b Owen Sound, Ont, July 7, 37; m 59; c 6. POLYMER CHEMISTRY. *Educ:* Queen's Univ, Ont, BSc, 60, MSc, 61; Oxford Univ, DPhil(chem), 63. *Prof Exp:* Res assoc, Cornell Univ, 63-64; asst prof chem, Queen's Univ, Ont, 64-66; scientist, 66-68, TECH DIR POLYMER CHEM, GLIDDEN CO DIV, SCM(CAN), 70- *Mem:* Am Chem Soc; fel Chem Inst Can. *Res:* Physical chemistry of polymers and coatings. *Mailing Add:* Glidden Co Div SCM(Can) Ltd 351 Wallace Ave Toronto Can

DAVIS, GERALD TITUS, b Kingsport, Tenn, Sept 2, 32; m 52; c 2. PAPER CHEMISTRY. *Educ:* King Col, BA, 54; Univ Tenn, PhD(chem), 58. *Prof Exp:* Res scientist, 58-70, assoc dir res, 70-77, mgr prod develop, 77-80, MGR PROCESS DEVELOP, MEAD CORP, 80- *Res:* Printing and speciality coated papers. *Mailing Add:* 64 N Fork Dr Chillicothe OH 45601

DAVIS, GORDON RICHARD FUERST, zoology, insect physiology, see previous edition

DAVIS, GORDON WAYNE, b Bremerton, Wash, June 7, 45; m 74; c 2. ANIMAL SCIENCE, MEAT SCIENCE. *Educ:* Wash State Univ, BS, 68, 69; Tex A&M Univ, MS, 74, PhD(animal sci), 77. *Prof Exp:* Instr animal sci, Tex A&M Univ, 72-76; asst prof food technol & sci, Univ Tenn, 77-80; ASST PROF ANIMAL SCI, TEX TECH UNIV, 80- *Concurrent Pos:* Res fel, Tex A&M Univ, 76-77. *Mem:* Am Soc Animal Sci; Inst Food Technol; Am Meat Sci Asn; Nat Asn Col Teachers Agr. *Res:* Pork and beef quality; effect of slaughter and processing methods on meat quality; forage finished beef and beef and pork meat blends. *Mailing Add:* Animal Sci Dept Tex Tech Univ Lublock TX 79409

DAVIS, GRAHAM JOHNSON, b Trenton, NC, Oct 5, 25; m 49; c 1. AQUATIC ECOLOGY. *Educ:* ECarolina Col, BS, 49; George Peabody Col, MA, 50; Univ NC, PhD(bot), 56. *Prof Exp:* Asst prof biol, Brenau Col, 50-53 & Univ Tenn, 56-57; plant physiologist, Crops Res Div, USDA, 57-59; from asst prof to assoc prof, 59-63, PROF BIOL, E CAROLINA UNIV, 63- *Mem:* Am Soc Limnol & Oceanog. *Res:* Physiological ecology of aquatic macrophytes; estuarine pollution; upgrading wastewaters with floating vascular plant systems. *Mailing Add:* Dept of Biol ECarolina Univ Greenville NC 27834

DAVIS, GRAYSON STEVEN, Washington, DC, May 29, 47; m 80. MORPHOGENESIS, CELL ADHESION. *Educ:* George Washington Univ, BS, 70; Univ Va, PhD(biol), 81. *Prof Exp:* ASST PROF BIOL, VALPARAISO UNIV, 81- *Res:* Physical analysis of amphibian gastrulation; role of cell-cell adhesion in morphogenesis. *Mailing Add:* Dept Biol Valparaiso Univ Valparaiso IN 46383

DAVIS, GREGORY ARLEN, b Portland, Ore, Jan 29, 35; m 58; c 3. STRUCTURAL GEOLOGY, TECTONICS. *Educ:* Stanford Univ, BS, 56, MS, 57; Univ Calif, Berkeley, PhD(geol), 61. *Prof Exp:* From asst prof to assoc prof, 61-71, PROF GEOL, UNIV SOUTHERN CALIF, 71- *Concurrent Pos:* Vis assoc prof, Univ Wash, 71; consult, Woodward-Clyde Consults, 72-75 & Wash Pub Power Supply Syst, 77-79. *Mem:* Geol Soc Am; Am Geophys Union; Sigma Xi. *Res:* Geotectonics and nature of orogenesis; regional tectonics, North American Cordillera; geology of Klamath Mountains and Mojave Desert, California. *Mailing Add:* Dept of Geol Sci Univ of Southern Calif Los Angeles CA 90007

DAVIS, HALLOWELL, b New York, NY, Aug 31, 96; m 23, 44; c 3. NEUROPHYSIOLOGY, AUDIOLOGY. *Educ:* Harvard Univ, AB & MD, 22. *Hon Degrees:* ScD, Colby Col, 54, Northwestern Univ, 62, Wash Univ, 73, Upstate Med Ctr, Syracuse, 79. *Prof Exp:* From instr to assoc prof physiol, Harvard Med Sch, 23-46, actg head dept, 42-43; res prof otolaryngol, 46-65, EMER PROF PHYSIOL, SCH MED, WASH UNIV, 65-; EMER DIR RES & RES ASSOC, CENT INST FOR DEAF, 65- *Concurrent Pos:* Dir res, Cent Inst for Deaf, 46-65; mem div med sci, Nat Res Coun, 47-53, exec secy comt hearing & bioacoust, Armed Forces, Nat Res Coun, 53-59. *Honors & Awards:* Shambaugh Prize, 53; Beltone Award, 66; Nat Medal Sci, 75. *Mem:* Nat Acad Sci; Am Acad Arts & Sci; Am Physiol Soc (treas, 41-48, pres, 58-59); Acoust Soc Am (pres, 53); Am Electroencephalog Soc (pres, 49). *Res:* Central nervous and auditory physiology; audiology; psychoacoustics; electroencephalography; electric response audiometry. *Mailing Add:* 7526 Cornell Ave University City MO 63130

DAVIS, HAMILTON SEYMOUR, b Pittsburgh, Pa, Oct 28, 20; m 46; c 4. MEDICINE. *Educ:* Colgate Univ, AB, 42; Western Reserve Univ, MD, 45; Am Bd Anesthesiol, dipl, 53. *Prof Exp:* Consult anesthesiologist, Vet Admin Hosp, Grand Junction, 50-52; from asst prof to prof anesthesiol, Sch Med, Western Reserve Univ, 52-66; chmn dept, 65-80, PROF ANESTHESIA, SCH MED, UNIV CALIF, DAVIS, 65-; DIR DEPT ANESTHESIA, SACRAMENTO MED CTR, 66-, CHIEF OF STAFF, 75- *Concurrent Pos:* Temporary chmn dept anesthesia, St Mary's Hosp, Colo, 51-52; attend anesthesiologist, Cleveland City Hosp, Sunny Acres Hosp & Highland View Hosp, 52-66; ed, Anesthesiology, 65- *Honors & Awards:* Maroon Citation, Colgate Univ, 67. *Mem:* AMA; Am Soc Anesthesiol; Am Col Anesthesiol; Asn Univ Anesthetists; fel Int Anesthesia Res Soc. *Res:* Influence of anesthesia on hypovolemic shock; central nervous system effects of anesthetics. *Mailing Add:* Dept of Anesthesia Univ of Calif Sch of Med Davis CA 95616

DAVIS, HARMER E(LMER), b Rochester, NY, July 11, 05; m; c 3. CIVIL & TRANSPORTATION ENGINEERING. *Educ:* Univ Calif, BS, 28, MS, 30. *Prof Exp:* Asst civil eng, 28-30, from instr to assoc prof, 30-48, dir, Inst Transp & Traffic Eng, 48-77, chmn dept, 54-59, prof, 48-73, EMER PROF CIVIL ENG, UNIV CALIF, BERKELEY, 73-, EMER DIR, INST TRANSP & TRAFFIC ENG, 73- *Concurrent Pos:* Res & develop consult, 30-48; vchmn, Hwy Res Bd, Nat Acad Sci-Nat Res Coun, 58, chmn, 59; mem, Div Eng & Indust Res, Nat Res Coun, 60-, mem exec comt, 62-65; consult transp, 73- *Honors & Awards:* Crum Award, Nat Acad Sci-Nat Res Coun, 59 & George S Bartlett Award, 70; James Laurie Prize, Am Soc Civil Engrs, 67; T M Matson Award, Inst Traffic Engrs, 74. *Mem:* Nat Acad Eng; Am Soc Civil Engrs; Am Soc Testing & Mat; Am Concrete Inst. *Res:* Soil mechanics; portland cement concrete; bituminous materials; transportation planning and functioning. *Mailing Add:* Div Transp Eng Univ Calif Berkeley CA 94720

DAVIS, HAROLD, b South Bend, Ind, Mar 13, 24; m 61; c 2. ELECTRICAL ENGINEERING. *Educ:* Univ Calif, Berkeley, BS, 49; Univ Calif, Los Angeles, MS, 50, PhD(eng), 55. *Prof Exp:* Instr eng, Univ Calif, Los Angeles, 54-55, asst prof, 55-61; SR SCIENTIST, HUGHES AIRCRAFT CO, 61- *Concurrent Pos:* Consult, 55- *Mem:* Am Math Soc; Soc Indust & Appl Math; sr mem Inst Elec & Electronics Engrs. *Res:* Noise and random processes in communication and automatic control systems. *Mailing Add:* Hughes Aircraft Co Culver City CA 90230

DAVIS, HAROLD LARUE, b Philadelphia, Pa, Nov 18, 25; m 57. NUCLEAR PHYSICS. *Educ:* Carnegie Inst Technol, BS, 49; Cornell Univ, PhD(physics), 54. *Prof Exp:* Proj engr, Pratt & Whitney Aircraft, 54-57; managing ed, Nucleonics, 57-69; ED PHYSICS TODAY, AM INST PHYSICS, 69- *Concurrent Pos:* Adj asst prof atomic physics, Hartford Grad Ctr, Rensselaer Polytech Inst, 55-57. *Mem:* Am Nuclear Soc; Am Phys Soc. *Res:* Reactor design and development; neutron cross sections; high energy physics and accelerators; particle detectors; scientific data processing. *Mailing Add:* 219 W 22nd St New York NY 10011

DAVIS, HAROLD LLOYD, b Portage, Ohio, Sept 18, 30; m 59; c 2. THEORETICAL SOLID STATE PHYSICS, SURFACE PHYSICS. *Educ:* Bowling Green State Univ, BS, 54; Ohio State Univ, PhD(physics), 59. *Prof Exp:* Mem staff solid state, Sandia Corp, 59-63; mem staff syst anal, Bellcomm Corp, 63-64; SR STAFF MEM & GROUP LEADER THEORY SECT, SOLID STATE DIV, OAK RIDGE NAT LAB, 64- *Concurrent Pos:* Lectr physics, Univ Tenn, 68-72. *Mem:* Fel Am Phys Soc; AAAS. *Res:* Low energy electron diffraction; electronic band structure of metals; magnetism of rare-earth and transition metals; crystal field theory of rare-earth compounds; actinide metals and their compounds. *Mailing Add:* Solid State Div Oak Ridge Nat Lab Oak Ridge TN 37830

DAVIS, HARRY FLOYD, b Colby, Kans, Oct 2, 25; m 61; c 2. MATHEMATICS. *Educ:* Mass Inst Technol, PhD(math), 54. *Prof Exp:* Instr math, Mass Inst Technol, 49-54; asst prof, Miami Univ, 54-55 & Univ BC, 55-58; assoc prof, Royal Mil Col, Can, 58-60; assoc prof, 60-66, PROF MATH, UNIV WATERLOO, 66- *Mem:* Math Asn Am; Soc Indust & Appl Math. *Res:* Applied algebra. *Mailing Add:* Dept Appl Math Univ of Waterloo Waterloo ON N2L 3G1 Can

DAVIS, HARRY GLENWOOD, b Dayton, Wash, June 25, 21; m 48; c 2. ENTOMOLOGY. *Educ:* Eastern Wash State Col, BA, 51; Wash State Univ, PhD(entom), 61. *Prof Exp:* RES ENTOMOLOGIST, SCI & EDUC ADMIN, AGR RES, USDA, 61- *Mem:* Entom Soc Am; Sigma Xi. *Res:* Insect attractants, especially for yellow jackets, sex pheromones of moths and parasites and predators of the alfalfa leaf cutting bees. *Mailing Add:* Yakima Sci & Educ Admin Agr Res USDA 3706 W Nob Hill Blvd Yakima WA 98902

DAVIS, HARRY I, b New York, NY, Dec 2, 09; m 31. ELECTRONIC ENGINEERING. *Educ:* City Col New York, BS, 31, EE, 33; Polytech Inst Brooklyn, MEE, 48. *Hon Degrees:* ScD, Polytech Inst Brooklyn, 73. *Prof Exp:* Proj engr, Daniel Electronic Labs, 33-40; lab chief air navig systs, Watson Lab, US Air Force, 45-50, tech dir, Rome Air Develop Ctr, Air Force Lab, 50-59, spec asst defense dir res & eng, Off Secy Defense, 60-61, dep res, Off Secy Air Force, 61-65, dep asst secy res & develop, 65-69, dep under secy, Air Force Systs Rev, 69-73; PRES, SYSTS REV ASSOCS, INC, 73- *Concurrent Pos:* Consult, Weapons Syst Eval Group, 55-56 & Rand Corp, 55; lectr, Columbia Univ, 56 & Univ Calif, 67-; chmn, Multi-Nat Group Command & Control for NATO, 62; adv, US Air Force Sci Adv Bd, 74- *Honors & Awards:* Harry Diamond Mem Prize, Inst Elec & Electronics Engrs, 68, Man of the Year, 74; George W Goddard Award, Soc Photo-Optical Instrumentations Engrs, 69. *Mem:* Fel Inst Elec & Electronics Engrs; Am Phys Soc; Am Inst Aeronaut & Astronaut; fel Am Optical Soc. *Res:* Radar system design and development; navigation systems; communications; computer applications to command and control; information processing; reconnaissance systems; optical instruments; infrared. *Mailing Add:* 3536 Pinetree Terr Falls Church VA 22041

DAVIS, HARRY JOHN, physics, see previous edition

DAVIS, HARRY L, b Marion, Ill, Mar 8, 21; m 49; c 2. INTERNAL MEDICINE. *Educ:* Southern Ill Univ, BEd, 43, BS, 46; Univ Ill, MD, 50; Univ Minn, Minneapolis, MS, 55; Am Bd Internal Med, dipl & cert pulmonary dis. *Prof Exp:* Pvt pract, Monroe, Wis, 55-57; asst chief pulmonary dis sect, Col Med, Baylor & Jefferson Davis Hosp, Houston, Tex, 57-58; assoc dir cardiopulmonary lab, Baptist Mem Hosp, Memphis, Tenn, 58-64; dir pulmonary labs, 64-68, from asst prof to assoc prof, 61-70, clin assoc prof, 70-71, med dir hosp, 71-80, PROF MED, MED UNITS & CHIEF, PULMONARY DIS DIV, UNIV TENN, MEMPHIS, 71- *Concurrent Pos:* Consult, Baptist Mem Hosp, Memphis, 58- & US Naval Hosp, Millington, 62-69; dir pulmonary lab, St Joseph Hosp, 68- *Mem:* Fel Am Col Chest Physicians; fel Am Col Physicians; Am Thoracic Soc. *Res:* Pulmonary disease and clinical pulmonary physiology; pulmonary stretch receptors; diffuse obstructive pulmonary disease; pulmonary impairment in sickle cell disease. *Mailing Add:* Univ Tenn Col Med 956 Court Ave Rm 3H29 Memphis TN 38163

DAVIS, HARVEY SAMUEL, b Columbus, Ohio, July 6, 36; m 64; c 2. TOPOLOGY. *Educ:* Eastern Ill Univ, BS, 59; Univ Miami, MS, 61; Univ Ill, PhD(math), 65. *Prof Exp:* Asst math, Univ Miami, 59-61; asst, Univ Ill, 61-65; asst prof, 65-69, ASSOC PROF MATH, MICH STATE UNIV, 69- *Mem:* Am Math Soc; Sigma Xi. *Res:* Point set topology; differential manifolds; continuum classification by set functions. *Mailing Add:* Dept of Math Mich State Univ East Lansing MI 48824

DAVIS, HARVEY VIRGIL, b Paces, Va, Dec 19, 32; m 59; c 4. PHARMACOLOGY, OCCUPATIONAL HEALTH. *Educ:* Cent State Col, Wilberforce, Ohio, BS, 55; Wayne State Univ, MS, 66, PhD(pharmacol & physiol), 68. *Prof Exp:* Indust toxicologist, SysteMed Corp, Dayton, Ohio, 68-71; sr toxicologist, Standard Oil Co, Chicago, Ill, 71-76; DIR ENVIRON HEALTH & HYG, VELSICOL CHEM CORP, CHICAGO, 76- *Mem:* Soc Toxicol; NY Acad Sci; AAAS; Am Col Toxicol. *Mailing Add:* 29 West 122 Morris Ct Warrenville IL 60555

DAVIS, HAWTHORNE ANTOINE, b Richmond, Va, Oct 4, 37; m 62; c 1. SOLID STATE PHYSICS. *Educ:* Col William & Mary, BS, 59; Univ Va, MS, 60, PhD(physics), 62. *Prof Exp:* Polymer physicist, 62-69, SR RES PHYSICIST, E I DU PONT DE NEMOURS & CO, INC, 69- *Mem:* Am

Phys Soc. *Res:* Plastic deformation in sodium chloride single crystals; physical properties of crystalline polymers; structure and properties of amorphous and crystalline polymers; mechanical properties of fibers; appearance of fabrics. *Mailing Add:* Rte 1 Box 555 Kinston NC 28501

DAVIS, HENRY MCRAY, b Whitakers, NC, Jan 21, 28; m 49; c 2. ANALYTICAL CHEMISTRY, PHYSICAL CHEMISTRY. *Educ:* NC Col Durham, BS, 52; Howard Univ, MS, 61. *Prof Exp:* Anal chemist, Div Colors & Cosmetics Technol, 60-65, res chemist, Cosmetics Br, 65-68, supvry chemist, Cosmetics Compos Sect, 68-75, chief sect, 70-75, CHIEF PROD COMP BR, DIV COSMETIC TECHNOL, FOOD & DRUG ADMIN, 75- *Mem:* Asn Off Anal Chem; Am Chem Soc; Soc Cosmetic Chem. *Res:* Methodology in cosmetic analysis, adsorption, ion-exchange and partition chromatographic techniques; infrared, ultraviolet and x-ray fluoresence spectorscopy; chrono-potentiometry of the iodide-iodine-triiodide system. *Mailing Add:* Cosmetic Technol Div Food & Drug Admin 5600 Fishers Lane Rockville MD 20852

DAVIS, HENRY MAUZEE, b Sherman, Tex, Oct 25, 02. PHYSICAL CHEMISTRY. *Educ:* Univ Okla, BS, 29, MS, 30; Univ Minn, PhD(phys chem), 34. *Prof Exp:* Asst chem, Univ Okla, 29-30 & Univ Minn, 30-34; in charge dept, Itasca Jr Col, 34-36; asst ceramics, 36-37, res assoc, 37-38, from asst prof to assoc prof, 38-42, from asst prof to prof metall, 42-62, EMER PROF METALL, PA STATE UNIV, 62- *Concurrent Pos:* Dir metall & mat sci div, US Army Res Off, 62-74; adj prof mat eng, NC State Univ, Raleigh, 63- *Mem:* Fel Am Ceramic Soc; Am Chem Soc; fel Am Soc Metals; Am Inst Mining, Metall & Petrol Engrs. *Res:* Phase equilibria in metallic and refractory systems; physical chemistry of metallurgical systems; equilibria and kinetics of gas-metal reactions. *Mailing Add:* New Hope Dr Route 2 Box 350 Chapel Hill NC 27514

DAVIS, HENRY WERNER, b Cambridge, Mass, Aug 31, 36; m 62; c 2. COMPUTER SCIENCE. *Educ:* Rice Univ, BA, 59; Univ Colo, MA, 61, PhD(math), 65. *Prof Exp:* Engr, Martin Co, 62-63; res assoc math, Spec Res Numerical Anal, Duke Univ, 65-67; asst prof, Univ NMex, 67-69; assoc mathematician, Brookhaven Nat Lab, 69-74; asst prof comput sci, Hofstra Univ, NY, 74-75; ASSOC PROF COMPUT SCI, WRIGHT STATE UNIV, DAYTON, OHIO, 75- *Mem:* Asn Comput Mach. *Res:* Data base management systems and artificial intelligence. *Mailing Add:* Dept of Comput Sci Wright State Univ Dayton OH 45431

DAVIS, HERBERT JOHN, b Windsor, Eng, Dec 20, 38; Can citizen; m 60; c 2. PHYSICAL CHEMISTRY, ELECTROCHEMISTRY. *Educ:* London Univ, BSc Hons, 60; ARCS, 60. *Prof Exp:* Sr chemist mat sci, Mullard's Mat Res Labs, 60-62; res scientist fuel cells, Energy Conversion Ltd, 62-63; group leader, Ferranti-Packard Ltd, 63-71; res mgr, Unican Security Systs, Ltd, 71-74; DEPT HEAD PHYS CHEM, NORANDA RES CTR, 74- *Mem:* Electrochem Soc; Chem Inst Can; Inst Elec & Electronic Engrs. *Res:* Dielectrics; electrostatic precipitation; pollution control; batteries; nonaqueous solvents; photovoltaic devices; photoconductive materials; energy transmission and storage; water electrolysis. *Mailing Add:* 414 Halford Rd Beaconsfield PQ H9W 3L4 Can

DAVIS, HERBERT L, JR, b Hendersonville, NC, Aug 18, 35; m 57; c 2. CYTOGENETICS, RADIATION BIOLOGY. *Educ:* Berry Col, BS, 57; Emory Univ, MS, 61. PhD(radiation biol), 65. *Prof Exp:* Instr biol, Western Md Col, 59-61; instr biol & chem, Berry Col, 61-62; from asst prof to assoc prof, 65-80, PROF BIOL, EMORY UNIV, 80-; CHMN DIV NATURAL SCI & MATH, KENNESAW COL, 70- *Concurrent Pos:* McCandless Fund res grant, 66-67. *Mem:* AAAS; Am Soc Biologists. *Res:* Role of metabolic energy compounds on recovery from radiation damage; effects of inhibitors of desoxyribonucleic acid synthesis on recovery from radiation damage. *Mailing Add:* Div of Natural Sci & Math Kennesaw Col Marietta GA 30061

DAVIS, HERBERT THADDEUS, III, b Arcadia, Fla, June 12, 42; m 64. STATISTICS, MATHEMATICS. *Educ:* Univ Fla, BS, 64, MS, 66; Johns Hopkins Univ, PhD(statist), 68. *Prof Exp:* Asst prof, Univ NMex, 69-77, assoc prof math & statist, 77-80; WITH SANDIA NAT LABS, 80- *Mem:* Am Statist Asn; Inst Math Statist; Am Math Soc. *Res:* Time series analysis. *Mailing Add:* Dw 5641 Sandia Nat Labs Albuquerque NM 87185

DAVIS, HORACE RAYMOND, b Clayton, Mo, Oct 8, 22; m 46; c 4. ORGANIC CHEMISTRY. *Educ:* Univ Ill, BA, 43; Univ Minn, PhD(chem), 49. *Prof Exp:* Res chemist, M W Kellogg Co, 49-51, res supvr, 51-57; group supvr, 57-72, MGR CHEM PROCESS DEVELOP, MINN MINING & MFG CO, 72-, GROUP SUPVR, 3-M CTR, 77- *Mem:* AAAS; Am Chem Soc; fel Am Inst Chem; Royal Soc Chem. *Res:* Fluorocarbon chemistry; nucleophilic substitution; chemistry of high polymers; chemical process development. *Mailing Add:* Minn Mining & Mfg Co 3-M Ctr St Paul MN 55101

DAVIS, HOWARD TED, b Hendersonville, NC, Aug 2, 37; m 60. PHYSICAL CHEMISTRY, CHEMICAL PHYSICS. *Educ:* Furman Univ, BS, 59; Univ Chicago, PhD(phys chem), 62. *Prof Exp:* NSF fel, Univ Brussels, 62-63; from asst prof to assoc prof, 63-69, PROF CHEM ENG, MAT SCI & CHEM, UNIV MINN, MINNEAPOLIS, 69-, HEAD CHEM ENG & MAT SCI, 81- *Concurrent Pos:* Sloan Found fel, 67-69, Guggenheim fel, 69-70; consult, Argonne Nat Labs, 70-, Pillsbury Co, 78- & 3M Co, 81- *Mem:* Am Phys Soc; Am Chem Soc; Am Inst Chem Engrs. *Res:* Theoretical and experimental studies of transport processes in low-temperature liquids and fused salts; statistical mechanical studies of fluids, classical and quantum mechanical; electronic structure and radiation chemistry of hydrocarbon liquids and gasses; molecular theoretical studies of low tension interfaces and micellar forms; theoretical and experimental studies of two phase fluid displacement in porous media. *Mailing Add:* Dept of Chem Eng & Chem Univ of Minn Minneapolis MN 55410

DAVIS, HUBERT GREENIDGE, b Brooklyn, NY, July 8, 15; m 45; c 4. PHYSICAL CHEMISTRY, CHEMICAL ENGINEERING. *Educ:* Columbia Univ, BA, 38, PhD(chem), 41. *Prof Exp:* Res chemist, Westvaco Chlorine Prod Co, Calif, 41-42; instr chem, Trinity Col, 42-43; res chemist, Manhattan Dist Proj, SAM Labs, Columbia Univ, 42-45; res chemist, Chem Div, Union Carbide Corp, 45-57, sr res scientist, 58-61, asst dir res & develop, Olefins Div, 62-69, corp sr res fel, 69-80; STAFF SCIENTIST III & PRIN INVESTR, ENERGY & ENVIRON DIV, LAWRENCE BERKELEY LAB, UNIV CALIF, 80- *Concurrent Pos:* Vis lectr, Dept Chem Eng, Univ Calif, 81-; mem bd dirs, Pyrotec, NF, Zoetermeer, Netherlands, 80- *Mem:* Am Chem Soc; Am Inst Chem Eng. *Res:* Pyrolysis, physical properties, chemistry of hydrocarbons; utilization of coal; liquid fuels from biomass and peat. *Mailing Add:* 598 Maureen Lane Pleasant Hill CA 94523

DAVIS, JACK, b New York, NY, May 21, 37; m 59; c 2. PHYSICS. *Educ:* Northeastern Univ, BS, 58, MS, 60; Univ London, DIC & PhD(physics), 67. *Prof Exp:* Res assoc physics, Univ My, 60-61 & Northeastern Univ, 61-63; staff scientist, Avco Corp, 63-67; sr staff scientist, 67-68; sci specialist theoret physics, EG&G, Inc, Mass, 68-70; dept mgr phys sci, 70; SUPVRY RES PHYSICIST & HEAD PLASMA RADIATION THEORY BR, US NAVAL RES LAB, 70- *Concurrent Pos:* Res assoc, Imp Col, Univ London, 65-67, fel, Spectros Lab, 67; adj prof, George Mason Univ, 74-76. *Mem:* AAAS; Am Phys Soc. *Res:* Plasma spectroscopy; atomic collision theory; radiation transport; non-local thermodynamic equilibrium radiation hydrodynamic models applicable to laser and particle beam interactions with matter, exploding wires, tokamaks, and solar and auroral flares; x-ray lasers and atomic processes in ultra-dense plasmas. *Mailing Add:* Code 4707 Plasma Physics Div Naval Res Lab Washington DC 20375

DAVIS, JACK H, b Clinton, SC, Nov 22, 39; m 62; c 2. SOLID STATE PHYSICS. *Educ:* Clemson Univ, BS, 62, PhD(physics), 66. *Prof Exp:* From instr to asst prof, 66-69, ASSOC PROF PHYSICS, UNIV ALA, HUNTSVILLE, 69- *Mem:* Am Phys Soc. *Res:* Metal whiskers growth, strength and electrical properties. *Mailing Add:* Dept of Physics Res Inst Univ of Ala PO Box 1247 Huntsville AL 35899

DAVIS, JAMES ALLEN, b Glasgow, Ky, Oct 17, 40; m 67; c 2. BIOLOGY, ORGANIC CHEMISTRY. *Educ:* W Ky Univ, BS, 62; Univ Akron, MS, 67. *Prof Exp:* Res scientist electrophysiol, Goodyear Aerospace Corp, 64-67; asst res dir, Dept Biochem & Microbiol, Carrtone (Century) Labs, 67-68; group leader microbiol fermentations, Baxter Labs, 68-69; RES SCIENTIST COMPOUNDING & TIRE TECHNOL, FIRESTONE TIRE & RUBBER CO, 69- *Mem:* Am Chem Soc. *Res:* Research programs designed to improve product quality and performance; increased technical knowledge and development of new products and processes. *Mailing Add:* Firestone Cent Res S Main & Wilbeth Rd Akron OH 44317

DAVIS, JAMES ALLEN, b Toledo, Ohio, Jan 18, 30; m 58; c 3. UNDERWATER ACOUSTICS, REACTOR PHYSICS. *Educ:* Univ Toledo, BA, 57; Univ Pittsburgh, PhD(physics), 64. *Prof Exp:* Sr scientist reactor physics, Bettis Atomic Power Lab, 57-67; asst scientist, Woods Hole Oceanog Inst, 67-74; PHYSICIST, US NAVAL OCEANOG OFF, 74- *Res:* Magnetization of thin films; solutions to transport equation in reactor physics; wave propagation using generalized WKB approximation in underwater acoustics problems. *Mailing Add:* Code 6040 US Naval Oceanog Off Washington DC 20373

DAVIS, JAMES AVERY, b New Orleans, La, Aug 13, 39. MATHEMATICAL STATISTICS. *Educ:* Occidental Col, AB, 61; Calif State Col Long Beach, MA, 63; Univ NMex, PhD(math), 67. *Prof Exp:* Res specialist, NAm Aviation, Inc, 62-67; sr assoc probability & statist, Univ Montreal, 67-68; STAFF MEM APPL MATH, SANDIA CORP, 68- *Concurrent Pos:* Fel, Univ Montreal, 67-68. *Mem:* Inst Math Statist; Am Math Soc. *Res:* Probability theory; stochastic processes; convergence rates for sums or random variables; probability; statistics; combinatorial analysis. *Mailing Add:* Appl Math Div 5641 Sandia Labs Albuquerque NM 87115

DAVIS, JAMES HOWELL, b Matoaka, WVa, Aug 17, 24; m 56; c 2. ECONOMIC GEOLOGY, MINING GEOLOGY. *Educ:* Duke Univ, AB, 50; Univ Wis, PhD, 60. *Prof Exp:* Mine geologist, St Joseph Lead Co, 51-56; asst prof geol, Univ Tex, 59-61; mem staff explor, NJ Zinc Co, 61-62; mem staff econ geol, Regional Resource Develop, Tenn Valley Auth, 62-67; CHIEF GEOLOGIST, AMAX LEAD CO OF MO, 67- *Mem:* Geol Soc Am; Soc Econ Geol; Am Inst Mining & Metall Eng. *Res:* Mineral economics; Genesis Mississippi Valley type ore deposits. *Mailing Add:* PO Box 551 Salem MO 65560

DAVIS, JAMES IVEY, QUANTUM OPTICS, LASER APPLICATIONS. *Educ:* Calif Inst Technol, BS, 62; Univ Calif, Los Angeles, MS, 65, PhD(physics), 69. *Prof Exp:* Appl physicist, Hughes Aircraft Co, 62-66; instr advan optics, Univ Ghana, 66-67; grad student physics, Univ Calif, Los Angeles, 67-69, NSF fel, 69-70; dept mgr, Hughes Aircraft Co, 70-74; PROG DIR, LAWRENCE LIVERMORE NAT LAB, 74- *Concurrent Pos:* Master fel, Hughes Aircraft Co, 63-65. *Mem:* Am Phys Soc. *Res:* High technology application; laser isotope separation, fusion, photochemistry and radar; energy laser weapons and low energy laser systems for countermeasures and intelligence gathering; formal scientific training in many-body theory and collective effects; laser-matter interactions and beam propagation; laser physics; quantum electronics; turbulence theory. *Mailing Add:* Lawrence Livermore Nat Lab PO Box 808 L-466 Livermore CA 94550

DAVIS, JAMES NORMAN, b Dallas, Tex, Oct 24, 39; m 65; c 3. NEUROBIOLOGY, CLINICAL NEUROLOGY. *Educ:* Cornell Univ, BA, 61, MD, 65. *Prof Exp:* PROF NEUROL, DUKE UNIV, 72-, ASSOC PROF PHARMACOL, 77-, DIR STROKE CTR, 80-; CHIEF NEUROL, DURHAM VET ADMIN CTR, 74- *Concurrent Pos:* Vis researcher, Univ Goteborg, Sweden, 72; Fulbright fel, 72; consult, NIH, NSF, Can Heart Asn, & Vet Admin, 76- *Mem:* Am Neurol Asn; Soc Neurosci; Am Soc Pharmacol

& Exp Therapeuts; Am Acad Neurol; Am Soc Neurochem. *Res:* Neurobiology of catecholamine neurons and their receptors; neuronal plasticity of noradrenergic neurons in the hippocampus-adrenergic-cholinergic receptor interactions. *Mailing Add:* Med Ctr Duke Univ PO Box 3850 Durham NC 27710

DAVIS, JAMES OTHELLO, b Tahlequah, Okla, July 12, 16; m 41; c 2. PHYSIOLOGY, MEDICINE. *Educ:* Northeastern Okla State Col, BS, 37; Univ Mo, MA, 39, PhD(zool), 42, BS(med), 43; Wash Univ, MD, 45. *Prof Exp:* Asst zool, Univ Mo, 37-42, asst anat, 42-43; intern, Barnes Hosp, St Louis, 45-46; investr, NIH, USPHS & Baltimore City Hosps, 47-49, Lab Kidney & Electrolyte Metab, Nat Heart Inst, 49-57, chief sect exp cardiovasc dis, 57-66; PROF PHYSIOL & CHMN DEPT, SCH MED, UNIV MO-COLUMBIA, 66- *Concurrent Pos:* Fel, Sch Med, Wash Univ, 46; assoc prof, Sch Med, Temple Univ, 55-56; vis assoc prof, Sch Med, Johns Hopkins Univ, 61-64; vis prof, Sch Med, Univ Va, 64; chmn, Nat Coun High Blood Pressure Res, Am Heart Asn, 72-74. *Honors & Awards:* AMA Golden Apple Award, 68; Sigma Xi Res Award, Univ Mo, 71; Modern Med Distinguished Achievement Award, 73; Fac-Alumni Gold Medal Award, Univ Mo, 73; Franz Volhard Award, Int Soc Hypertension, 74; Ciba Award for Hypertension Res, Am Heart Asn, 76; Carl J Wiggers Award, 76. *Mem:* Am Physiol Soc; Am Soc Nephrology; Int Soc Nephrology; Int Soc Hypertension (vpres, 78-, pres, 80-82); Endocrine Soc. *Res:* Cardiovascular, renal and endocrine physiology; physiology of congestive heart failure and hypertension; research administration. *Mailing Add:* Dept Physiol M412 Med Sci Bldg Univ of Mo Sch of Med Columbia MO 65212

DAVIS, JAMES ROBERT, b York, Nebr, Dec 28, 29; m 56; c 3. PLANT PATHOLOGY. *Educ:* Univ Calif, Riverside, AB, 56; Univ Calif, Davis, MS, 61, PhD(plant path), 67. *Prof Exp:* Lab technician I, Univ Calif, Riverside, 56, lab technician II, Univ Calif, Davis, 56-68; from asst prof to assoc prof, 68-77, PROF PLANT PATH, UNIV IDAHO, 77- *Mem:* Am Phytopath Soc. *Res:* Studies in stone fruit pathology relating to canker diseases induced by low temperature, fungi and bacteria; soil-borne diseases of potato. *Mailing Add:* Br Exp Sta Univ Idaho Aberdeen ID 83210

DAVIS, JAMES ROYCE, b Rison, Ark, Apr 6, 38; m 59; c 3. MICROBIAL PHYSIOLOGY, CLINICAL MICROBIOLOGY. *Educ:* Tex Col Arts & Indust, BS, 60; Univ Houston, MS, 62, PhD(microbiol), 65. *Prof Exp:* Lectr microbiol, Univ Houston, 64-65; asst prof, Dent Br, Univ Tex, 65-68; ASST PROF MICROBIOL, BAYLOR COL MED, 68-; DIR MICROBIOL SECT CLIN LAB, METHODIST HOSP, 68-; CHMN COMBINED PROG MED TECHNOL, TEX MED CTR, 70- *Mem:* Am Soc Microbiol. *Res:* Steroid metabolism by microorganisms; streptomycete taxonomy; chemical composition and microbial flora of saliva; rapid and automated techniques for diagnostic microbiology. *Mailing Add:* Dept Path Methodist Hosp 6565 Fannin Houston TX 77030

DAVIS, JAMES WENDELL, b Tulsa, Okla, Aug 22, 27; m 52; c 4. BIOCHEMISTRY, STATISTICS. *Educ:* Univ Tulsa, BS, 49; Ore State Univ, MS, 52, PhD(biochem), 54. *Prof Exp:* Instr chem, Univ Tulsa, 49-50; assoc biochemist, Oak Ridge Nat Lab, 54-57; from sr instr to asst prof, 57-63, ASSOC PROF BIOCHEM, SCH MED, ST LOUIS UNIV, 63-, DIR, CLIN CANCER EDUC PROG, 81- *Mem:* Am Chem Soc; Endocrine Soc; Am Statist Asn; Am Soc Biol Chemists. *Res:* Endocrine control of metabolism; metabolism of bile acids and their possible role in the etiology of colorectal cancer; control of the biosynthesis of catecliolamines in the adrenal medulla. *Mailing Add:* Dept of Biochem St Louis Univ Med Sch St Louis MO 63104

DAVIS, JAY C, b Haskell, Tex, July 12, 42; m 63; c 2. NUCLEAR PHYSICS. *Educ:* Univ Tex, Austin, BA, 63, MA, 64; Univ Wis-Madison, PhD(physics), 69. *Prof Exp:* Teaching asst physics, Univ Tex, Austin, 63-64; teaching asst, Univ Wis-Madison, 64-65, res asst, 65-69, AEC fel nuclear physics, 69-70, res assoc, 70-71; PHYSICIST, LAWRENCE LIVERMORE LAB, 71- *Res:* Fast neutron physics; accelerator technology. *Mailing Add:* L 313 Lawrence Livermore Lab PO Box 808 Livermore CA 94550

DAVIS, JEFFERSON C, b Sulphur Springs, Ark, Dec 8, 32. AEROSPACE MEDICINE. *Educ:* Univ Mo, BS, 55, MD, 57; Univ Calif, MPH, 63. *Prof Exp:* Chief aerospace med, Ellsworth AFB, SDak, 59-61; instr, US Air Force Sch Aerospace Med, Brooks AFB, Tex, 61-62; resident, US Air Force Sch Aerospace Med, Hq Strategic Air Command, Omaha, Nebr & Univ Calif, 62-65; instr altitude & hyperbaric med, US Air Force Sch Aerospace Med, Brooks AFB, Tex, 65-68; comdr, US Air Force Hosp, Phu Cat Air Base, Vietnam, 68-69; dep chief biodynamics & bionics, Aerospace Med Res Lab, Wright-Patterson AFB, Ohio, 69-70; chief aerospace med br, Brooks AFB, Tex, 70-74, chief hyperbaric med br, US Air Force Sch Aerospace Med, 74-77, vcomdr, Aerospace Med Div, 77-79; DIR, HYPERBARIC MED, METHODIST HOSP, SAN ANTONIO, TEX, 79- *Concurrent Pos:* Co-ed, Hyperbaric Oxygen Ther, Undersea Med Soc, Nat Libr Med, 78-; ed, Undersea & Hyperbaric Med, 79-80. *Honors & Awards:* Scientist of the Year, Air Force Asn, 72; Gary Wratten Award, Asn Mil Surgeons, 75. *Mem:* Aerospace Med Asn (pres-elect, 81-82); Undersea Med Soc (vpres, 75-76, pres, 79-80); Soc US Air Force Flight Surgeons (pres, 76-77); Am Col Prevention Med (pres, 81-82). *Res:* Hyperbaric medicine-advanced techniques of treatment of decompression sickness, gas embolism, gas gangrene, carbon monoxide poisoning and wound healing enhancement. *Mailing Add:* 4499 Medical Dr San Antonio TX 78229

DAVIS, JEFFERSON CLARK, JR, b Jacksonville, Fla, Mar 20, 31; m 54; c 3. PHYSICAL CHEMISTRY. *Educ:* Univ Ariz, BS, 53, MS, 54; Univ Calif, PhD(chem), 59. *Prof Exp:* Asst, Lawrence Radiation Lab, Univ Calif, 56-59; from instr to asst prof chem, Univ Tex, 59-65; assoc prof, 65-71, PROF CHEM, UNIV S FLA, 72-, CHMN DEPT, 78- *Concurrent Pos:* Mem adv coun col chem, Int Conf Educ in Chem; ed, Exam Comt, Am Chem Soc, 68-, consult, Multi-Media Proj, 74-; vis prof, Calif Inst Technol, 75. *Mem:* AAAS; Am Chem Soc; Am Inst Chem. *Res:* Application of nuclear magnetic resonance spectroscopy to chemical problems; molecular association in solutions; chemical education. *Mailing Add:* Dept of Chem Univ of SFla Tampa FL 33620

DAVIS, JEFFREY ARTHUR, b Meriden, Conn, July 26, 43; m 76. OPTICS. *Educ:* Rensselaer Polytech Inst, BS, 65; Cornell Univ, PhD(physics), 70. *Prof Exp:* Actg asst prof physics, Univ Calif, Los Angeles, 69-71; asst prof, Ill Inst Technol, 71-77; assoc prof, 77-80, PROF PHYSICS, SAN DIEGO STATE UNIV, 80- *Mem:* Am Phys Soc; Soc Photo-Optical Instrumentation Engrs; Optical Soc Am. *Res:* Optically pumped far infrared lasers; pulsed magnets and experiments studying optical properties of solids in these magnetic fields; development of a highly technical optics education program. *Mailing Add:* Dept Physics San Diego State Univ San Diego CA 92182

DAVIS, JEFFREY ROBERT, b Boise, Idaho, June 22, 35; m 56; c 3. MATHEMATICS. *Educ:* Rensselaer Polytech Inst, BEE, 57, MS, 59; Washington Univ, PhD(math), 63. *Prof Exp:* Instr, Univ Calif, Berkeley, 63-65; asst prof, 65-74, ASSOC PROF MATH, UNIV NMEX, 74- *Mem:* Am Math Soc. *Res:* Toeplitz operators; Wiener-Hopf equations. *Mailing Add:* Dept of Math Univ of NMex Albuquerque NM 87131

DAVIS, JERRY COLLINS, b Richland, Ga, Nov 29, 43; m 66; c 2. ENTOMOLOGY, ZOOLOGY. *Educ:* Mars Hill Col, NC, BS, 65; Univ Tenn, Knoxville, MS, 67; Ohio State Univ, PhD(entomol), 70. *Prof Exp:* Prof biol & vpres develop, Cumberland Col, Ky, 74-77; vpres & prof biol, N Greenville Col, Tigerville, SC, 76-77; PRES, ALICE LLOYD COL, 77- *Concurrent Pos:* Fel, Ohio State Univ, 70; dir, Ky Acad Sci & Appalachian Leadership & Community Outreach, Inc, 77-78. *Mem:* Entomol Soc Am. *Res:* Systematics and biology of a group of tenebrionid beetles. *Mailing Add:* Alice Lloyd Col Pippa Passes KY 41844

DAVIS, JERRY MALLORY, climatology, see previous edition

DAVIS, JIMMY HENRY, b Lexington, Tenn, Mar 22, 48; m 74. ORGANOMETALLIC & PHYSICAL CHEMISTRY. *Educ:* Union Univ, Tenn, BS, 70; Univ Ill, Urbana, PhD(chem), 76. *Prof Exp:* Fel struct chem, Univ Fla, 76-78; ASST PROF PHYS CHEM, UNION UNIV, TENN, 78- *Mem:* Sigma Xi. *Res:* Comparison of the rates and mechanisms of the reactions of hetero-atom pi-bonded organometallic compounds such as pentahapto-(1-methyl pyrrole)chromium tricarbonyl to those of the carbon analog. *Mailing Add:* Dept of Chem & Physics Union Univ Jackson TN 38301

DAVIS, JOE BILL, b Forsyth Co, NC, Dec 2, 33; m 58; c 1. ANALYTICAL CHEMISTRY. *Educ:* Western Carolina Col, BS, 60; Clemson Univ, MS, 63, PhD(anal chem), 65. *Prof Exp:* Lab instr chem, Fla Presby Col, 60-61; asst, Clemson Univ, 62-65; from asst prof to assoc prof, 65-73, PROF CHEM, WINTHROP COL, 73-, CHMN DEPT, 72- *Mem:* Am Chem Soc; fel Am Inst Chem; Am Soc Testing & Mat. *Res:* Analytical instrument design and development; spectroscopy; electro-chemistry; analysis of sulfate and sulfur compounds; analysis via buffer reactions. *Mailing Add:* Dept of Chem Winthrop Col Rock Hill SC 29733

DAVIS, JOHN, b Woodmere, NY, Dec 1, 16; m 47. VERTEBRATE ZOOLOGY. *Educ:* Yale Univ, BA, 37; Univ Calif, PhD(zool), 50. *Prof Exp:* Asst zool, Univ Calif, 47-48, assoc, 49, technician, Mus Vert Zool, 49-50; asst prof biol & cur, Moore Lab Zool, Occidental Col, 50-53; from jr res zoologist to assoc res zoologist, 53-75, RES ZOOLOGIST, HASTINGS NATURAL HIST RESERVATION, 75-, LECTR ZOOL, 62- *Concurrent Pos:* Guggenheim Mem fel, 59. *Mem:* Am Soc Mammal; Am Soc Ichthyologists & Herpetologists; Soc Study Evolution; Cooper Ornith Soc (secy, 53-65); fel Ornith Union. *Res:* Avian systematics; life history studies; gonad cycles; lizard ecology and behavior. *Mailing Add:* Hastings Natural Hist Reserv Star Rte Box 80 Carmel Valley CA 93924

DAVIS, JOHN ALBERT, JR, b Pocatello, Idaho, Apr 22, 36; m 60; c 2. CHEMICAL & PETROLEUM ENGINEERING. *Educ:* Univ Kans, BS, 58, PhD(chem eng), 63; Univ Mich, MSE, 59. *Prof Exp:* Res engr, Marathon Oil Co, Denver, 63-64, adv res engr, 64-70, sr res engr, 70, mgr prod sci dept, 70-72, mgr eng dept, 72-74, res assoc res & chem, 74-77, sr staff engr, Nat Gas Div, 77-79, MGR LIQUEFIED NATURAL GAS, MARATHON OIL CO, 79- *Mem:* Am Inst Chem Engrs; Am Chem Soc; Soc Petrol Engrs. *Res:* Cryogenics; low temperature phase behavior and thermodynamics; secondary oil recovery processes. *Mailing Add:* Marathon Oil Co 539 S Main St Findlay OH 45840

DAVIS, JOHN ARMSTRONG, b Tupelo, Miss, May 4, 50; m 69; c 2. AQUATIC ECOLOGY, WATER CHEMISTRY. *Educ:* Univ Miss, BA, 72, MS, 75; Auburn Univ, PhD(aquatic ecol), 78. *Prof Exp:* Teaching asst zool, Univ Miss, 72-75; res asst water chem, Auburn Univ, 75-77; VPRES & SCI DIR, BREEDLOVE ASSOC, 77- *Mem:* AAAS; Am Fisheries Soc; Am Soc Limnol & Oceanog; Sigma Xi; Am Soc Testing & Mat. *Res:* Effects of pollution on aquatic organisms; indices of water quality. *Mailing Add:* 3444 NW 50th Ave Gainsville FL 32601

DAVIS, JOHN BARNEY, b Dallas, Tex, Dec 13, 17; m 42; c 2. MICROBIOLOGY. *Educ:* NTex State Teachers Col, BS, 38; Univ Tex, Austin, PhD(microbiol), 49. *Concurrent Pos:* City bacteriologist, Dallas, 38-42; instr bact, Univ Tex, 46-48; sr res technologist, 49-57, RES ASSOC, FIELD RES LAB, MOBIL RES & DEVELOP CORP, 57- *Mem:* Am Soc Microbiol; Sigma Xi; Geochem Soc; Am Asn Petrol Geologists. *Res:* Petroleum microbiology; microbial activities related to petroleum geochemistry and geology; microbial oxidation of hydrcarbons; microbial intracellular and extracellular products synthesized from hydrocarbons; Organic geochemistry; pyrolysis-gas chromatography of sedimentary organic matter for oil source rock identification. *Mailing Add:* Mobil Res & Develop Corp Field Res Lab Box 900 Dallas TX 75221

DAVIS, JOHN CHRISTOPHER, b Bristol, Eng, Oct 21, 44; Can citizen; m 67; c 1. ZOOLOGY, WATER POLLUTION. *Educ:* Univ Victoria, BSc, 66; Univ BC, MSc, 68, PhD(zool), 71. *Prof Exp:* Res scientist, Pac Environ Inst, 71-74, head pollutant ecol group, 74-79; actg dir & assoc dir fisheries res, 79-81, DIR, GEN ONT REGION FISHERIES & OCEANS, 81- *Concurrent*

Pos: Res assoc, Univ BC, 73-; adv & review writer, Nat Res Coun Can Assoc Comt Sci Criteria Environ Qual, 74-75; reviewer, Am Pub Health Asn, Am Water Works Asn & Water Pollution Control Fedn, 74-82; mem subcomt water, Nat Res Coun Can, 82- *Mem:* Water Pollution Control Fedn. *Res:* Fish and invertebrate physiology with emphasis on acute and sublethal effects of water pollutants; water quality criteria; testing methodology; field and laboratory investigations. *Mailing Add:* 1940 Four Seasons Dr Burlington ON L7P 2Y1 Can

DAVIS, JOHN CLEMENTS, b Neodesha, Kans, Oct 21, 38; m 78; c 2. GEOLOGY. *Educ:* Univ Kans, BS, 61; Univ Wyo, MS, 63, PhD(geol), 67. *Prof Exp:* Instr stratig, Idaho State Univ, 64-66; res assoc sedimentary petrol, 66-77, SR RES SCIENTIST, KANS GEOL SURV, 77- CHIEF GEOL RES, 70-; PROF CHEM & PETROL ENG, UNIV KANS, 74- *Concurrent Pos:* Vis prof, Wichita State Univ, 69; assoc prof chem & petrol eng, Univ Kans, 70-74, prof, 74-, adj prof geog, 74-; vis sr fel geog, Univ Nottingham, Eng, 72-73; dir, Terradata Inc, 78- *Mem:* Am Asn Petrol Geol; Pattern Recognition Soc; Int Asn Math Geol (treas, 72-); Soc Econ Paleont & Mineral. *Res:* Quantitative analysis of sedimentary rock parameters, especially by statistical means and by optical data processing; probabilistic exploration for petroleum. *Mailing Add:* Kans Geol Surv 1930 Ave A Campus W Lawrence KS 66045

DAVIS, JOHN DUNNING, b Freeport, Maine, June 13, 29; m 55; c 2. ENVIRONMENTAL SCIENCES. *Educ:* Bowdoin Col, AB, 52; Univ Boston, MEd, 54; Univ NH, MS, 61, PhD(zool), 63. *Prof Exp:* Sci teacher high sch, NH, 54-56, 57-60; from instr to asst prof zool, Smith Col, 63-70; VPRES, NORMANDEAU ASSOCS, INC, 70- *Concurrent Pos:* NSF grant, 64. *Mem:* AAAS; Am Soc Zool; Nat Shellfisheries Asn; Ecol Soc Am. *Res:* Systematics and biology of marine Pelecypod mollusks. *Mailing Add:* 25 Old Homestead Rd Westford MA 01886

DAVIS, JOHN EDWARD, JR, b Welch, WVa, Nov 18, 22; m 49; c 1. ZOOLOGY. *Educ:* Univ Va, BA, 48, MA, 50, PhD, 55. *Prof Exp:* Instr biol, Washington & Lee Univ, 49-51; asst, Univ Va, 51-54; instr, Washington & Lee Univ, 54-56; from asst prof to prof, Wake Forest Col, 56-68; prof biol, 68-71, chmn, Dept Biol, 68-71, actg provost, 71-72, dean, Sch Arts & Sci, 72-73, PROF BIOL, JAMES MADISON UNIV, 73-, COORDR PRE-MED STUDIES, 78- *Mem:* AAAS; Sigma Xi; NY Acad Sci. *Res:* Embryology. *Mailing Add:* Dept of Biol James Madison Univ Harrisonburg VA 22807

DAVIS, JOHN GRADY, JR, b Durham, NC, Nov 23, 38; m 60; c 2. ENGINEERING MECHANICS, MECHANICAL ENGINEERING. *Educ:* NC State Univ, BS, 62; Va Polytech Inst & State Univ, MS, 65, PhD(eng), 73. *Prof Exp:* Mat engr thermal protection systs, 62-66, mat engr, 66-81, HEAD, MAT PROCESSING & APPLNS BR, LANGLEY RES CTR, NASA, 76- *Concurrent Pos:* NASA coordr composites prog grant & adj prof, Va Polytech Inst & State Univ, 74-; NASA monitor composites res minority & women, Old Dominion Univ, 75-, mgr casts proj, 76-81. *Mem:* Am Soc Testing & Mat. *Res:* Graphite-polyimide materials; composite structures; materials manufacturing; nondestructive evaluation; stress analysis; environmental effects. *Mailing Add:* Mail Stop 188A Langley Res Ctr NASA Hampton VA 23665

DAVIS, JOHN K, b Webster, Mass, Nov 30, 13; m 40; c 2. OPTICS. *Educ:* Clark Univ, AB, 37; Am Bd Opticianry, Master ophthalmic optics. *Prof Exp:* Mem lens design res dept, Am Optical Co, Southbridge, Mass, 39-49, head optics sect, Appl Res Lab, 49-50, res labs, 50-53, optical comput & serv sect, 53-58, ophthalmic lens sect, New Prod Develop Dept, 59-62, mgr lens technol & design, 62-71, chief ophthalmic sci, Optical Prod Div, 71-75. *Concurrent Pos:* Adj assoc prof physiol optics, Pa Col Optom, 75- *Mem:* AAAS; Am Acad Optom; Optical Soc Am; Nat Acad Opticianry; Asn Res in Vision & Ophthal. *Res:* Geometric optics; ophthalmic lenses; vision; optical instruments; automatic computing; quality control; lens tolerance; standards. *Mailing Add:* Pa Col of Optom 1200 W Godfrey Ave Philadelphia PA 19141

DAVIS, JOHN LITCHFIELD, b Weymouth, Mass, Mar 5, 32; m 61; c 2. SOLID STATE PHYSICS. *Educ:* Bowdoin Col, AB, 53; Univ Md, PhD(physics), 65; George Wash Univ, MEA, 74. *Prof Exp:* Physicist, US Naval Ord Lab, 58-67; physicist, Anal Serv, Inc, 67-81; PHYSICIST, NAVAL SURFACE WEAPONS CTR, 81- *Mem:* AAAS; Am Phys Soc; Oper Res Soc Am; World Future Soc; Soc Advan Med Syst. *Res:* Microwave spectroscopy; physics of solid surfaces; systems analysis; operations research; health systems analysis; infrared detectors; lead salts; epitaxial growth. *Mailing Add:* Naval Surface Weapons Ctr White Oak Lab Silver Spring MD 20910

DAVIS, JOHN M(AXWELL), b Mahomet, Ill, July 18, 19; m 49; c 3. CHEMISTRY, CHEMICAL ENGINEERING. *Educ:* Ill State Norm Univ, 41; Purdue Univ, MS, 45, PhD(org chem, chem eng), 47. *Prof Exp:* Lab asst org chem, Purdue Univ, 41-43; res chemist, Nylon Res Sect, Textile Fibers Dept, 46-55, sr res chemist, 55-64, ENG ASSOC, CHATTANOOGA PLANT TECH SECT, E I DU PONT DE NEMOURS & CO, 64- *Concurrent Pos:* With Off Sci Res & Develop, 44. *Res:* Development of synthetic fibers; production of fluorine compounds; preparation of certain cyclic fluorocarbons and their derivatives. *Mailing Add:* Chattanooga Nylon Plant E I du Pont de Nemours & Co Chattanooga TN 37401

DAVIS, JOHN MARCELL, b Kansas City, Mo, Oct 11, 33; m 60. PSYCHIATRY. *Educ:* Princeton Univ, AB, 56; Yale Univ, MD, 60. *Prof Exp:* Intern, Mass Gen Hosp, 60-61; resident psychiat, Yale Univ, 61-64; clin assoc, NIMH, 64-66; specialist psychopharmacol, 66-69; chief unit clin pharmacol, Lab Clin Sci, NIH, 69-70; assoc prof pharmacol & prof psychiat, Vanderbilt Univ, 70-73; prof psychiat, Sch Med, Univ Chicago, 73-80; GILMAN PROF PSYCHIATRY, SCH MED, UNIV ILL, 80-; DIR RES, ILL STATE PSYCHIAT INST, 73- *Concurrent Pos:* Dir, Clin Div, Tenn Neuropsychiat Inst, Cent State Hosp, 70-73. *Mem:* Am Psychiat Asn; AMA; Am Col Neuropsychopharmacol; Psychiat Res Soc; Am Col Psychiat. *Res:* Biology of depression; psychopharmacology; biochemical factors in mania,

depression and shcizophrenia; catocholamines, scotonin and electrolite in mental disease; lithium treatment of mania sensory deprivation; medical anthropology; computer techniques in psychiatry. *Mailing Add:* 5490 S South Shore Dr Chicago IL 60615

DAVIS, JOHN MILTON, b Red Oak, Iowa, June 2, 18; m 48; c 2. NUCLEAR WASTE MANAGEMENT. *Educ:* Univ Calif, Berkeley, AB, 40. *Prof Exp:* Engr hot lab opers, Atomics Int, 54-63; consult hot lab opers, Kernforschungsanlage, Julich, WGer, 63-66; prin scientist hot lab opers, McDonnell-Douglas Corp, 66-73; sr engr waste mgt, Atlantic Richfield Hanford Co, 73-77; STAFF ENGR WASTE MGT, ROCKWELL HANFORD OPERS, 77- *Mem:* Am Nuclear Soc. *Mailing Add:* Rockwell Hanford Opers PO Box 800 Richland WA 99352

DAVIS, JOHN MOULTON, b Nottingham, UK, Aug 28, 38; US citizen; m 76. SOLAR PHYSICS, X-RAY ASTRONOMY. *Educ:* Univ Leeds, BSc, 60, PhD(physics), 64. *Prof Exp:* Demonstr physics, Univ Leeds, 63-64; res assoc space physics, Lab Nuclear Sci, Mass Inst Technol, 64-67 & Ctr Space Res, 67-70; sr scientist, 70-74, SR STAFF SCIENTIST, AM SCI & ENG, INC, 74- *Mem:* Am Geophys Union; Am Astron Soc. *Res:* Study of the solar corona from observations in the soft x-ray region; solar-terrestrial relations; satellite and rocket instrumentation with emphasis on grazing incidence optics. *Mailing Add:* Am Sci & Eng Inc 955 Massachusetts Ave Cambridge MA 02139

DAVIS, JOHN R(OWLAND), b Minneapolis, Minn, Dec 19, 27; m 47; c 4. AGRICULTURAL ENGINEERING. *Educ:* Univ Minn, BS, 49, MS, 51; Mich State Univ, PhD(agr eng), 59. *Prof Exp:* Hydraul engr, US Geol Surv, 50-51; instr agr eng, Mich State Univ, 51-55; asst prof, Purdue Univ, 55-57; lectr & specialist, Univ Calif, Davis, 57-62; hydraul engr, Stanford Res Inst, 62-64; prof agr eng, Univ Nebr, 64-71, dean, Col Eng & Archit, 65-71; head dept, 71-75, PROF AGR ENG, ORE STATE UNIV, 71-, ASSOC DEAN, SCH AGR & DIR, AGR EXP STA, 75- *Concurrent Pos:* Consult, USDA, 60 & Stanford Res Inst, 64- *Mem:* Am Soc Agr Engrs; Am Soc Civil Engrs; Am Soc Eng Educ. *Res:* Hydrology; hydraulics, irrigation systems; methods of irrigation water application; irrigation feasibility; engineering education; teaching methods. *Mailing Add:* Agr Exp Sta Ore State Univ Corvallis OR 97331

DAVIS, JOHN ROBERT, b Mattoon, Ill, July 10, 29; m 52; c 3. PATHOLOGY. *Educ:* Univ Iowa, BA, 52, MD, 59. *Prof Exp:* Instr path & resident anat path, Col Med, Univ Iowa, 60-63, assoc path, 63-64, asst prof, 64-67; assoc prof, 67-76, PROF PATH, COL MED, UNIV ARIZ, 76- *Concurrent Pos:* Consult pathologist, Vet Admin Hosp, Tucson, 68- *Mem:* AAAS; AMA; Col Am Path; Int Acad Path; Am Soc Cytol; Am Asn Path & Bact. *Res:* Experimental pathology and immunopathology of schistosomiasis, gynecopathology and miscellaneous infectious diseases; surgical pathology; cytopathology computer pattern analysis. *Mailing Add:* Dept of Path Univ of Ariz Col of Med Tucson AZ 85721

DAVIS, JOHN SHELDON, b Fall River, Mass, Aug 24, 46; m 69; c 3. ELECTRICAL ENGINEERING. *Educ:* Southeastern Mass Univ, BS, 68, MS, 75. *Prof Exp:* Staff engr, Naval Underwater Systs Ctr, Middletown, RI, 68-70, proj engr, 70-76, res prog mgr estimation theory, 76-79; SUPVY ENGR, SYSTS ANAL & SYNTHESIS FOR COMBAT CONTROL SYSTS, 79- *Mem:* Inst Elec & Electronics Engrs. *Res:* Application of advanced statistical estimation techniques and modern control theory methods to critical Navy problems; advanced systems synthesis, test and evaluation. *Mailing Add:* 520 Dillon Lane Swansea MA 02777

DAVIS, JOHN STAIGE, IV, b New York, NY, Oct 28, 31; m 56; c 5. INTERNAL MEDICINE. *Educ:* Yale Univ, BA, 53; Univ Pa, MD, 57; Am Bd Internal Med, recert, 78; FACP. *Prof Exp:* From instr to asst prof internal & prev med, 61-67, assoc prof internal med, 67-72, PROF INTERNAL MED, SCH MED, UNIV VA, 72-, HEAD DIV RHEUMATOL, 67- *Concurrent Pos:* Sr investr, Arthritis Found, 64-69; Markle scholar acad med, 64-69; prof invite, Univ Geneva, Switz, 78-79. *Mem:* Am Clin & Climat Asn; Am Rheumatism Asn; Am Fedn Clin Res; AMA; Am Asn Immunol. *Res:* Immune complexes in connective tissue diseases, especially the roles of rheumatoid factors, complement and cryoglobulins. *Mailing Add:* Dept of Internal Med Univ of Va Sch of Med Charlottesville VA 22901

DAVIS, JOHN STEWART, b Fargo, NDak, Nov 11, 52; m 74; c 2. ENDOCRINOLOGY, REPRODUCTION. *Educ:* Minot State Col, BA, 75; Univ NDak, MS, 77, PhD(physiol), 79. *Prof Exp:* Fel reproductive biol & biochem, Endocrine Lab, 79-81, RES ASSOC REPRODUCTIVE ENDOCRINOL, DEPT OBSTET & GYNEC, SCH MED, UNIV MIAMI, 81- *Concurrent Pos:* Chem officer, 227 field artillery brigade, Fla Army Nat Guard, 81- *Mem:* Soc Study Reproduction; Int Soc Neurochem; Sigma Xi. *Res:* Reproductive endocrinology; mechanisms of hormone action; evaluation of local reproductive endocrine regulatory mechanisms and ovarian function; role of membrane phospholipids in ligand-receptor-mediated cell activation. *Mailing Add:* Endocrine Lab D-5 Sch Med Univ Miami PO Box 016960 Miami FL 33101

DAVIS, JOHNNY HENRY, b Crossville, Ala, May 3, 20; m 41; c 2. AGRONOMY. *Educ:* Ala Polytech Inst, BS, 43; Purdue Univ, MS, 52, PhD(plant breeding, genetics), 53. *Prof Exp:* Asst county agent, Ala Agr Exten Serv, 43-50; jr agronomist, Purdue Univ, 50-53; geneticist, Miss Agr Exp Sta, 53-54; agronomist, Tex Res Found, 54-56; assoc head high plains sta, 57-58; asst dir, High Plains Res Found, 59-60; assoc agronomist, 60-68, PROF AGRON, LA STATE UNIV, 68-, SUPT, LA STATE UNIV-IBERIA LIVESTOCK EXP STA, 74- *Concurrent Pos:* Assigned to La State Univ-US AID Mission, Managua, Nicaragua, 71-72. *Mem:* Am Soc Agron; Genetics Soc Am. *Res:* Plant breeding; crop production and management. *Mailing Add:* PO Box 466 Jeanerette LA 70544

DAVIS, JON PRESTON, b Eau Claire, Wis, Nov 26, 45; m 69; c 3. SCATTERING THEORY. *Educ:* Marquette Univ, BS, 68; Columbia Univ, PhD(chem), 75. *Prof Exp:* Fel chem, Univ Alberta, 75-77; lectr, Univ Troms, Norway, 78-79; vis prrof, Univ Mo-Columbia, 79-80; ASST PROF CHEM, PA STATE UNIV, 80- *Mem:* Am Chem Soc. *Res:* Reaction dynamics of small systems forming collision complexes; radiative association of polyatomic molecules. *Mailing Add:* Pa State Univ Ogontz Campus 1600 Woodland Rd Abington PA 19001

DAVIS, JOSEPH HARRISON, b Flushing, NY, Apr 16, 24; m 52; c 7. FORENSIC MEDICINE. *Educ:* Long Island Col Med, MD, 49. *Prof Exp:* Intern surg, Univ Calif Hosp, San Francisco, 49-50, asst resident path, 50-51; asst surgeon, USPHS, 51-52, sr asst surgeon, USPHS Hosp, Seattle, Wash, 52-54, New Orleans, La, 54-55; instr path, Sch Med, La State Univ, 55-56; asst med examr, 56-57, MED EXAMR, MIAMI, 57-; PROF PATH, SCH MED, UNIV MIAMI, 60- *Concurrent Pos:* Consult pathologist, Fed Aviation Agency. 60-80. *Mem:* AMA; Am Acad Forensic Sci; Am Soc Clin Path. *Res:* Accident causation and prevention with emphasis on human factors involved. *Mailing Add:* Dept of Path Med Univ of Miami Sch of Med Miami FL 33136

DAVIS, JOSEPH RICHARD, b Chicago, Ill, May 13, 36; m 58; c 3. TOXICOLOGY, ONCOLOGY. *Educ:* Univ Ill, BS, 56, MD, 58, MS, 59; Baylor Univ, PhD(pharmacol), 61. *Prof Exp:* Instr pharmacol, Col Med, Baylor Univ, 60-61; from asst prof to assoc prof, 61-69, PROF PHARMACOL, STRITCH SCH MED, LOYOLA UNIV CHICAGO, 69- *Concurrent Pos:* Borden Res Award, 58; Am Cancer Soc fel, 58-61; Lederle Med Fac Award, 58; William B Peck Sci Res Award, 70. *Mem:* Am Asn Cancer Res; Am Soc Pharmacol & Exp Therapeut; Am Physiol Soc; Endocrine Soc; Soc Study Reproduction. *Res:* Biochemical approaches to cancer chemotherapy; protein synthesis of the normal and cryptorchid testis; pharmacology of the testicular capsule; urinary delta-aminolevulinic acid in lead poisoning; biology of azopurines; cholesterol and atherosclerosis; pharmacology. *Mailing Add:* Dept Pharmacol Stritch Sch Med Loyola Univ of Chicago Maywood IL 60153

DAVIS, JOYCE S, b Big Spring, Tex, Feb 18, 24; m 46; c 4. MEDICINE, PATHOLOGY. *Educ:* Baylor Univ, BS, 45, MD, 47. *Prof Exp:* Asst path, Col Med, Wash Univ, St Louis, 47-48; res physician, Methodist Hosp, Dallas, Tex, 49; from instr to assoc prof path, Baylor Col Med, 53-75; PROF & HEAD DEPT PATH & LAB MED, TEX A&M COL MED, 75- *Concurrent Pos:* Attend physician, Methodist Hosp, 65-69; Ben Taub Hosp, Houston, 65-75 & Vet Admin Hosp, Houston, 66-75. *Mem:* Am Med Asn; Am Soc Clin Path. *Res:* Diseases of kidney and liver. *Mailing Add:* Dept Path & Lab Med Tex A&M Col Med College Station TX 77843

DAVIS, KAREN PADGETT, b Blackwell, Okla, Nov 14, 42; m 63; c 3. MEDICAL SCIENCE. *Educ:* Rice Univ, BA, 65, PhD(econ), 69. *Prof Exp:* Asst prof econ, Rice Univ, 68-70; econ policy fel social security, Brookings Inst, 70-71, res assoc, 71-74, sr fel, 74-77; asst secy, Dept Planning & Eval Health, HEW, 77-80, adminr, Health Resources Admin, Pub Health Serv, 80-81; PROF, SCH HYG & PUB HEALTH, JOHNS HOPKINS UNIV, 81- *Concurrent Pos:* Mem, Health Tech Study Sect, HEW, 72-76; assoc ed, Milbank Mem Fund Quarterly, 72-77; consult, NSF, 73-74 & Nat Acad Sci, 74-75; vis lectr econ, Harvard Univ, 74-75; mem, Health Adv Panel, US Cong, Off Technol Assessment, 75-77. *Mem:* Nat Inst Med; Am Econ Asn. *Res:* Health economics; health care financing; health care delivery. *Mailing Add:* Sch Hyg & Pub Health Johns Hopkins Univ Baltimore MS 21205

DAVIS, KATHRYN BULLOCK, biostatistics, see previous edition

DAVIS, KENNETH BRUCE, JR, b Texarkana, Ark, Mar 13, 40; m 69. VERTEBRATE PHYSIOLOGY. *Educ:* Univ Ark, BA, 63, MS, 65; La State Univ, PhD(physiol, vert zool), 70. *Prof Exp:* Instr gen zool, La State Univ, 68-69; from asst prof to assoc prof, 69-80, PROF BIOL, MEMPHIS STATE UNIV, 80- *Concurrent Pos:* Res physiologist, Southeastern Fish Cult Lab, US Fish & Wildlife Serv, Marion, Ala, 78-79. *Mem:* AAAS; Am Inst Biol Sci; Am Soc Zool; Am Ornith Union. *Res:* Role of diurnal rhythms of hormones in the regulation of daily and seasonal behavior of sub-mammalian vertebrates, particularly birds; intra-extracellular electrolyte distribution and osmoregulation; stress physiology in fish. *Mailing Add:* Dept of Biol Memphis State Univ Memphis TN 38111

DAVIS, KENNETH JOSEPH, b Spartanburg, SC, Aug 10, 37; m 59; c 4. MATHEMATICS. *Educ:* Wofford Col, BS, 59; Univ Tenn, MA, 62, PhD(math), 63. *Prof Exp:* Res scientist, Marshall Space Flight Ctr, NASA, 63-65; assoc prof math, Old Dom Col, 65-66; assoc prof, 66-77, PROF MATH, E CAROLINA UNIV, 77- *Mem:* Am Math Soc; Math Asn Am. *Res:* Analytic number theory; control theory. *Mailing Add:* Dept of Math E Carolina Univ Greenville NC 27834

DAVIS, KENNETH LEON, b New York, NY, Sept 10, 47; m 72; c 2. PSYCHIATRY. *Educ:* Yale Univ, BA, 69; Mt Sinai Sch Med, MD, 73; Am Bd Psychiat & Neurol, dipl, 80. *Prof Exp:* Res asst, Dept Pharmacol, Mt Sinai Sch Med, 71-73; intern, Stanford Univ, 73-74, fel clin pharmacol, 74-76; clin psychiat consult, Santa Clara Valley Med Ctr, 76-79; ASSOC PROF PSYCHIAT & PHARMACOL, MT SINAI SCH MED, 79-; CHIEF, DEPT PSYCHIAT, VET ADMIN MED CTR, 79- *Concurrent Pos:* Consult, Nassau County Mental Health Bd, 69-73; resident, Sch Med, Stanford Univ, 73-76, life sci res assoc, 75-76; dir & founder, Stanford Comprehensive Care Clin, Stanford Hosp, 74-79; asst dir, Stanford Psychiat Clin Res Ctr, Vet Admin Med Ctr, 75-79, res assoc, 76-79; A E Bennett Clin Sci Res Award, 77; dir, Schizophrenia Biol Res Ctr, Vet Admin Med Ctr, 81- *Mem:* Am Psychiat Asn; Soc Biol Psychiat; Acad Psychosomatic Med; Am Col Neuropsychopharmacol; NY Acad Sci. *Res:* Biological basis of senile dementia of the Alzheimer's type; depression and schizophrenia. *Mailing Add:* Vet Admin Med Ctr 130 W Kingsbridge Rd Bronx NY 10468

DAVIS, KENNETH PICKETT, b Denver, Colo, Sept 2, 06; m 29; c 4. FOREST MANAGEMENT. *Educ:* Univ Mont, BSF, 28; Univ Mich, MF, 32, PhD(forest mgt), 40. *Prof Exp:* Forest ranger, Absaroka Nat Forest, 28-31; jr instr, Univ Mich, 32; silviculturist, Northern Rocky Mountain Forest & Range Exp Sta, US Forest Serv, 33-39, sr silviculturist, Washington, DC, 40-43, chief div forest mgt res, 44-45; dean sch forestry, Univ Mont, 45-49; prof forest mgt, Sch Natural Resources, Univ Mich, 49-67, chmn dept forestry, 50-67, actg dean sch natural resources, 65-66; prof, 67-74, EMER PROF FOREST LAND USE, SCH FORESTRY, YALE UNIV, 74- *Concurrent Pos:* Pres, Mont Conserv Coun, 48-49; chmn wood sect, Mich Natural Resources Coun, 54-61; actg ed, Forest Sci, 57-58; consult ed, McGraw-Hill Encycl Sci & Technol, 61-; mem, Nat Comt Advan Forestry Educ, 62-63, chmn, 64-65; Fulbright lectr, Univ Helsinki, 63. *Honors & Awards:* Univ Helsinki Medal, 63; Sir William Schlich Medal, Soc Am Foresters, 76. *Mem:* Fel Soc Am Foresters (vpres, 68-69, pres, 70-71). *Res:* Silviculture; forest fire control and use; land use. *Mailing Add:* 52 Westerly Dr Mt Carmel CT 06518

DAVIS, L(LOYD) WAYNE, b Medicine Lodge, Kans, July 16, 29; m 63; c 3. CORPORATE MANAGEMENT, PHYSICS. *Educ:* Univ Kans, BS, 52; Univ NMex, MS, 59. *Prof Exp:* Staff mem, Systs Anal Dept, Sandia Corp, 52-56, consult, 56-57; res physicist, Dikewood Corp, 57-60, sr res physicist, 60-64, head, Weapons Effects Div, 64-67, dep tech dir, 67-69, asst vpres, 69-72, vpres, 72-77, secy, 70-80, sr vpres, Dikewood Industs, Inc, 77-80, PRES & CHMN BD, DIKEWOOD CORP, 80- *Mem:* Sr mem Inst Elec & Electronics Engrs; Am Phys Soc; Sigma Xi. *Res:* Nuclear weapons effects and phenomenology effects on personnel and complex military systems. *Mailing Add:* Dikewood Corp 1009 Bradbury Dr SE Albuquerque NM 87106

DAVIS, LANCE A(LAN), b Ridley Park, Pa, Nov 19, 39; m 62; c 3. MATERIALS SCIENCE, PHYSICS. *Educ:* Lafayette Col, BS, 61; Yale Univ, ME, 63, PhD(eng & appl scd), 66. *Prof Exp:* Res staff scientist, Yale Univ, 66-68; res physicist, Mat Res Ctr, 68-74, mgr, Strength Physics Dept, 74-78, mgr, Metglas Develop Sect, Corp Develop Ctr, 78-80, DIR MAT LAB, ALLIED CORP, 81- *Concurrent Pos:* Mem, Comt Technol Potential Amorphous Mat, Nat Mat Adv Bd, 78. *Mem:* Am Phys Soc; Am Soc Metals; Am Inst Mining, Metall & Petrol Engrs; Mat Res Soc. *Res:* Physical properties of materials at high pressure, particularly elastic, anelastic and plastic properties; elasticity, plasticity and fracture of metallic glasses; technology of metallic glasses. *Mailing Add:* Mat Lab Allied Corp PO Box 1021R Morristown NJ 07960

DAVIS, LARRY ALAN, b Delano, Calif, June 1, 40; m 60; c 3. CROP PHYSIOLOGY. *Educ:* La Verne Col, BA, 62; Univ Calif, Davis, MS, 64, PhD(plant physiol), 68. *Prof Exp:* Agronomist & asst mgr, Alina Farms Corp, 64-65; agronomist & mgr, Calcot Pty, Ltd, Australia, 68-70; AGRONOMIST IN CHARGE & PRES, ALINA FARMS CORP, 70- *Concurrent Pos:* Adj lectr biol, Calif State Col, Bakersfield, 72. *Mem:* AAAS; Am Soc Plant Physiol; Am Inst Biol Sci; Am Soc Agron; Crop Sci Soc Am. *Res:* Control of fruit growth and development in the cotton plant by means of plant hormones and the identification and measurement of these hormones by gas-liquid chromatography and other methods. *Mailing Add:* Alina Farms Corp Rte 1 Box 292 McFarland CA 93250

DAVIS, LARRY DEAN, b Marathon, Iowa, June 23, 35; m 58; c 2. HUMAN PHYSIOLOGY. *Educ:* Univ Dubuque, BS, 57; Univ Wis, PhD(physiol), 61. *Prof Exp:* From instr to asst prof, 63-69, assoc prof, 69-75, PROF PHYSIOL, SCH MED, UNIV WIS-MADISON, 75- *Concurrent Pos:* USPHS fel, 61-63. *Mem:* Am Physiol Soc; Soc Exp Biol & Med. *Res:* Cardiac physiology, specifically cellular transmembrane potential changes involved in origin of arrhythmias and antiarrhythmic actions. *Mailing Add:* Dept of Physiol Univ of Wis Sch of Med Madison WI 53706

DAVIS, LARRY E, animal science, animal nutrition, see previous edition

DAVIS, LARRY ERNEST, b New York, NY, Aug 16, 40; m 68; c 2. NEUROLOGY, VIROLOGY. *Educ:* Stanford Univ, BS, 63, MD, 66. *Prof Exp:* Officer virol, Ctr Dis Control, 68-70; instr neurol, Med Sch, Johns Hopkins Univ, 73-75; asst prof, 75-79, ASSOC PROF NEUROL & MICROBIOL, UNIV NMEX, 79- *Honors & Awards:* Moore Award, Am Asn Neuropathologists, 79. *Mem:* Am Neurol Asn; Am Acad Neurol; Am Soc Microbiol; Am Asn Neuropathologists. *Res:* Infections of brain and inner ear; Reye's syndrome. *Mailing Add:* Dept Neurol Univ NMex Albuquerque NM 87131

DAVIS, LARRY WALLACE, mathematics, see previous edition

DAVIS, LAWRENCE CLARK, b London, Eng, Aug 16, 45; US citizen; m 67; c 2. BIOCHEMISTRY, MOLECULAR BIOLOGY. *Educ:* Haverford Col, BS, 66; Yeshiva Col, PhD(molecular biol), 70. *Prof Exp:* Res assoc neurobiol, A Ribicoff Res Ctr, Norwich Hosp, Conn, 71-73; res assoc biochem, Univ Wis-Madison, 73-75; asst prof, 75-80, ASSOC PROF BIOCHEM, KANS STATE UNIV, 80- *Concurrent Pos:* NIH fel, Univ Wis-Madison, 70-71, NSF fel, 75. *Mem:* AAAS; Am Soc Microbiol. *Res:* Gel chromatography of interacting protein systems and natural electron donors; adenosinetriphosphate suppliers for biological nitrogen fixation. *Mailing Add:* Dept Biochem Willard Hall Kans State Univ Manhattan KS 66506

DAVIS, LAWRENCE S, b Missoula, Mont, July 27, 34; m 59; c 3. FOREST ECONOMICS. *Educ:* Univ Mich, BS, 56, MF, 60; Univ Calif, Berkeley, PhD(agr econ), 64. *Prof Exp:* Res forester, US Forest Serv, 56-57; res specialist, Univ Calif, Berkeley, 60-64; from asst prof to assoc prof forest econ, Va Polytech Inst, 64-70; assoc prof forest sci, 70-72, PROF FOREST SCI, UTAH STATE UNIV, 72-, HEAD DEPT FORESTRY & OUTDOOR RECREATION, 70- *Mem:* Soc Am Foresters. *Res:* Resource policy; recreation economics. *Mailing Add:* Dept of Forestry & Outdoor Recreation Utah State Univ Logan UT 84322

DAVIS, LAWRENCE WILLIAM, JR, b Los Angeles, Calif, Oct 21, 30; m 66; c 2. PHYSICS. *Educ:* Pomona Col, BA, 52; Calif Inst Technol, MS, 56; Stanford Univ, PhD(physics), 61. *Prof Exp:* Proj engr, Western Develop Labs, Philco Corp, 60-62, supvr quantum electronics group, 62; sr scientist quantum electronics, Interphase Corp-W, 63-65; res assoc, Stanford Electronics Labs, Stanford Univ, 65-66; lectr elec eng, Univ Calif, Berkeley, 66-68; from asst prof to assoc prof, 68-76, PROF PHYSICS, UNIV IDAHO, 76- *Concurrent Pos:* Vis assoc prof physics, Univ Wash, 74-75 & Quantum Inst, Univ Calif, Santa Barbara, 75; vis fel, Joint Inst Lab Astrophys, Univ Colo, 81-82. *Mem:* Sigma Xi; Am Phys Soc. *Res:* Quantum electronics; laser spectroscopy. *Mailing Add:* Dept of Physics Univ of Idaho Moscow ID 83843

DAVIS, LEODIS, b Stamps, Ark, Sept 25, 33; m 62; c 2. BIOCHEMISTRY. *Educ:* Univ Kansas City, BS, 56; Iowa State Univ, MS, 58, PhD(biochem), 60. *Prof Exp:* Res asst biochem, Iowa State Univ, 60-61; asst prof, Tenn State Univ, 61-63; asst prof, Col Med, Howard Univ, 63-68; vis prof chem, 68-69, assoc prof, 69-76, PROF CHEM, UNIV IOWA, 76-, CHMN CHEM, 79- *Mem:* Am Chem Soc; Am Soc Biol Chem; Sigma Xi. *Res:* Mechanism of pyridoxal phosphate requiring enzymes. *Mailing Add:* Dept of Chem Univ of Iowa Iowa City IA 52240

DAVIS, LEONARD GEORGE, b Chicago, Ill, Nov 23, 46; m 69; c 1. NEUROSCIENCE, NEUROCHEMISTRY. *Educ:* Univ Ill-Urbana, BS, 69; Northwestern Univ, MS, 73; Univ Ill, Chicago, PhD(biochem), 77. *Prof Exp:* Clin res, Beaumont Army Med Ctr, 75-76; res assoc neurochem, Mo Inst Psychiat, Univ Mo-Columbia, 76-80; SCIENTIST, NEUROBIOL GROUP, CENT RES DEPT, E I DU PONT DE NEMOURS CO, 80- *Concurrent Pos:* NIMH traineeship, Northwestern Univ Adminr, 71-73; fel, Ill State Psychiat Inst, 74; USPHS neurosci trainee, Univ Ill Med Ctr Admin, 74-75. *Mem:* Soc Neurosci; Am Soc Neurochem. *Res:* Neuronal membrane structure and function; neuropeptide ligands and membrane interactions; implications of hormones in mental health. *Mailing Add:* E I Du Pont de Nemours Co Inc Cent Res Dept Glenolden Lab 108 Glenolden PA 19036

DAVIS, LEROY THOMAS, b New Castle, Pa, Feb 12, 25; m 48; c 3. FAMILY MEDICINE. *Educ:* Westminster Col, BS, 48; Syracuse Univ, MS, 51, PhD(zool), 54; NY Med Col, MD, 61; Am Bd Family Pract, dipl, 73. *Prof Exp:* Instr physiol, NY Med Col, 54-57; intern, Easton Hosp, Pa, 61-62; pvt pract, Md, 62-72; asst prof med, 71-72, ASSOC PROF FAMILY PRACT, MED SCH, UNIV MD, 72- *Mem:* Fel Am Acad Family Physicians; Soc Teachers Family Pract. *Res:* Classification and computerization of the health problems in family practice. *Mailing Add:* Family Pract Dept Univ of Md Hosp 22 S Greene St Baltimore MD 21201

DAVIS, LEVERETT, JR, b Elgin, Ill, March 3, 14; m 43; c 1. SPACE PHYSICS. *Educ:* Ore State Col, BS, 36; Calif Inst Technol, MS, 38, PhD(physics), 41. *Prof Exp:* Instr & res staff mem, 41-46, from asst prof to assoc prof, 46-56, group supvr, 44-46, prof, 56-81, EMER PROF PHYSICS, CALIF INST TECHNOL, 81- *Concurrent Pos:* NSF sr fel, Max Planck Inst Physics, Univ Gottingen, 57-58; medal exceptional sci achievement, NASA, 70. *Mem:* Am Phys Soc; Am Astron Soc; Am Geophys Union; Int Astron Union. *Res:* Planetary magnetic fields, interplanetary medium; cosmic rays; astrophysics; hydromagnetics; polarization of starlight. *Mailing Add:* Dept Physics 412 Downs Calif Inst Technol Pasadena CA 91125

DAVIS, LLOYD CRAIG, b Council Bluffs, Iowa, May 29, 41; m 63; c 3. PHYSICS. *Educ:* Iowa State Univ, BS, 63, PhD(physics), 66; Calif Inst Technol, MS, 66. *Prof Exp:* Res assoc physics, Iowa State Univ, 66-67; res assoc, Univ Ill, Urbana, 67-69; MEM SCI RES STAFF, PHYSICS DEPT, FORD MOTOR CO, 69- *Concurrent Pos:* NSF fel, Univ Ill, Urbana, 67-68; guest scientist, Deutsches Elektronen-Synchrotron, Hamburg, Ger, 81. *Mem:* Am Phys Soc; Sigma Xi. *Res:* Magnetic levitation of high-speed ground vehicles; electron tunneling in solids; electron energy levels of solids in a magnetic field; sound velocity and lattice vibrations in semiconductors; photoemission, electron energy loss, absorption and Auger spectra of 3d metals. *Mailing Add:* 3212 Katherine Dearborn MI 48124

DAVIS, LLOYD EDWARD, b Akron, Ohio, Aug 23, 29; m 53, 72; c 2. PHARMACOLOGY. *Educ:* Ohio State Univ, DVM, 59; Univ Mo-Columbia, PhD(pharmacol), 63. *Prof Exp:* Instr vet pharmacol, Univ Mo-Columbia, 59-63, assoc prof pharmacol, Sch Med, 63-69; prof, Ohio State Univ, 69-72; vis prof, Univ Nairobi, Kenya, 72-74; prof clin pharmacol, Colo State Univ, 74-78; PROF CLIN PHARAMACOL, UNIV ILL, URBANA, 78- *Concurrent Pos:* Chmn & mem, Adv Panel Vet Med, Gen Rev Comt & Standards Comt, US Pharmacopeia; chmn, Subcomt Vet Pharmacol; ed, Topics Drug Ther, J Am Vet Med Asn. *Mem:* Am Soc Pharmacol & Exp Thrapeut; Soc Exp Biol & Med; Am Col Vet Pharmacol Therapeut (pres, 77-79); Am Asn Vet Clinicians; Am Soc Vet Physiol & Pharmacol. *Res:* Comparative pharmacology; drug metabolism and pharmacokinetics in domestic animals; clinical pharmacology; Species differences in disposition and fate of drugs; influence of disease on drug disposition; evaluation of drug therapy in animal patients; biomedical ethics. *Mailing Add:* Col of Vet Med Univ Ill Urbana IL 61801

DAVIS, LOUIS E(LKIN), b Brooklyn, NY, Sept 10, 18; m 44; c 2. MANAGEMENT, ORGANIZATION. *Educ:* Ga Inst Technol, BSME, 40; Univ Iowa, MS, 42. *Prof Exp:* Asst prof indust eng, Ga Inst Technol, 42-43; supvr, Bell Aircraft Corp, Ga, 43-44; sr indust engr, Western Elec Co, NY, 44-46; asst chief indust eng, Conmar Prods Corp, NJ, 46-47; from asst prof to prof indust eng, Univ Calif, Berkeley, 47-66; prof indust eng, 66-71, chmn, Grad Sch Management, 67-69, 69-71, dir, Ctr Orgn Studies, 71, PROF ORGN SCI, UNIV CALIF, LOS ANGELES, 66- *Concurrent Pos:* Consult, Europ Productivity Agency, France, 57-58, Maritime Transport Res, Nat Acad Sci-Nat Res Coun, 58-62, US Forest Serv, 62-64; adv, Exec Off President, 62-64; Lucas prof, Univ Birmingham, 62-63; comnr, Calif State Comn Manpower, Automation & Technol & Manpower Adv Comn, 63-67; res fel, Tavistock Inst Human Rels, London & Inst Indust Social Res, Norway, 66; res socio-tech scientist, Univ Calif, Los Angeles, 76-; chmn, Ctr Qual Working Life, Inst Indust Rels, 75-82; vis distinguished prof, Univ Queensland, 81. *Honors & Awards:* Hayhow Award, Am Col Hosp Admin. *Mem:* Am Inst Indust Engrs; Human Factors Soc; Brit Ergonomics Res Soc; Brit Inst Indust Psychol; Inst Mgt Sci. *Res:* Human performance skills and measurement; job and organization design; socio-technical systems. *Mailing Add:* Grad Sch of Mgt Univ of Calif Los Angeles CA 90024

DAVIS, LUCKETT VANDERFORD, b Smyrna, Tenn, Oct 16, 32. ENTOMOLOGY, ENVIRONMENTAL BIOLOGY. *Educ:* Mid Tenn State Col, BS, 55; Duke Univ, MA, 58, PhD(zool), 62. *Prof Exp:* Instr biol, Vanderbilt Univ, 60-61; asst prof, Univ Southwestern La, 61-63; asst prof biol sci, Univ of the Pac, 63-64; assoc prof, 64-69, PROF BIOL, WINTHROP COL, 69-, CHMN DEPT, 77- *Mem:* Entom Soc Am; Ecol Soc Am; Am Soc Zool; Am Soc Limnol & Oceanog. *Res:* Ecology of insects of marine-influenced ecosystems. *Mailing Add:* Dept Biol Winthrop Col Rock Hill SC 29733

DAVIS, LUTHER, JR, b Mineola, NY, July 12, 22; m 51; c 3. SOLID STATE ELECTRONICS. *Educ:* Mass Inst Technol, BS, 42, PhD(physics), 49. *Prof Exp:* Mem staff, Radiation Lab, Mass Inst Technol, 42-45, res assoc physics, 45-49; mem staff, 49-64, asst mgr res div, 64-69, GEN MGR RES DIV, RAYTHEON CO, 69- *Mem:* Am Phys Soc; fel Inst Elec & Electronics Engrs. *Res:* Semiconductors; dielectrics; ferromagnetics. *Mailing Add:* Res Div Raytheon Co Waltham MA 02154

DAVIS, MARC, astrophysics, see previous edition

DAVIS, MARGARET BRYAN, b Boston, Mass, Oct 23, 31. PALEOECOLOGY, PALYNOLOGY. *Educ:* Radcliffe Col, AB, 53; Harvard Univ, PhD(biol), 57. *Prof Exp:* Fel, dept biol, Harvard Univ, 57-58, dept geosci, Calif Tech Inst, 59-60; res fel, dept zool, Yale Univ, 60-61; res assoc, dept bot, Univ Mich, 61-64, assoc res biologist, Great Lakes Res Div, 64-70, assoc prof, dept zool, 66-70, res biologist, Great Lakes Res Div & prof zool, 70-73; prof ecol, dept biol, Yale Univ, 73-76; head, dept ecol & behav biol, 76-81, PROF ECOL, UNIV MINN, 76- *Concurrent Pos:* Vis prof, Quaternary Res Ctr, Univ Wash, 73; vis investr, Environ Studies Prog, Univ Calif, Santa Barbara, 81-82. *Mem:* Am Soc Limnologists & Oceanographers; fel Geol Soc Am; fel AAAS; Am Quaternary Asn; Sigma Xi. *Res:* Paleoecology and biogeography of American forest communities, especially Late-Quaternary history as recorded by fossil pollen; watershed-lake interactions and ecosystem development over long time intervals; sedimentary processes in lakes. *Mailing Add:* 108 Zool Bldg Univ Minn 318 Church St Minneapolis MN 55455

DAVIS, MARJORIE, b Elkhart, Kans, Mar 13, 36; m 70; c 1. DEVELOPMENTAL BIOLOGY, INVERTEBRATE ZOOLOGY. *Educ:* Panhandle State Col, BS, 59; Univ Kans, MA, 62; Kans State Univ, PhD(embryol), 70. *Prof Exp:* Instr zool, Mankato State Col, 62-66; asst prof biol, Mo Western Col, 69-71; instr biol, Kans State Univ, 71-75; ASST PROF ANAT, OKLA COL OSTEOPATHIC MED & SURG, 75- *Honors & Awards:* Community Leaders & Noteworthy Americans Award, 78. *Mem:* AAAS; Soc Study Reproduction; Am Asn Anat; NY Acad Sci; Am Soc Zoologists. *Res:* Limnology, especially composition and distribution of zooplankton in various southwest Kansas ponds; differentiation of mammalian limbs; DDT effects in some rodents. *Mailing Add:* 3816 E 105 Tulsa OK 74136

DAVIS, MARSHALL EARL, b Richmond, Calif, Aug 14, 31; m 56; c 2. FUEL TECHNOLOGY. *Educ:* WTex State Col, BS, 57; Purdue Univ, PhD(phys & nuclear chem), 63. *Prof Exp:* Res staff mem, Fission Prod Characterization, Oak Ridge Nat Lab, 62-65; sr chemist, 65-70, SR RES CHEMIST, FUELS RES SECT, TEXACO, INC, 70- *Mem:* Sigma Xi; Am Chem Soc. *Res:* Sorption of high temperature vapors by metal surfaces; fuel and fuel additive development; combustion; air pollution; corrosion. *Mailing Add:* Texaco Inc PO Box 509 Beacon NY 12508

DAVIS, MARTIN (DAVID), b New York, NY, Mar 8, 28; m 51; c 1. MATHEMATICAL LOGIC. *Educ:* City Col New York, BS, 48; Princeton Univ, MA, 49, PhD(math), 50. *Prof Exp:* Res instr math, Univ Ill, 50-51, res assoc control syst lab, 51-52; mem sch math, Inst Advan Study, 52-54; asst prof math, Univ Calif, Davis, 54-55, Ohio State Univ, 55-56 & Rensselaer Polytech Inst, 56-57; assoc prof, Grad Div, Hartford Univ, 57-59; res scientist, Inst Math Sci, NY Univ, 59-60; from assoc prof to prof math, Belfer Grad Sch Sci, Yeshiva Univ, 60-65; PROF MATH, COURANT INST, NY UNIV, 65- *Concurrent Pos:* Vis prof, Belfer Grad Sch Sci, Yeshiva Univ, 70-71, Univ Calif, Berkeley, 76-77 & Univ Calif, Santa Barbara, 78-79. *Honors & Awards:* Chauvenet Prize & Ford Prize, Math Asn Am, 75; Steele Prize, Am Math Soc, 75. *Mem:* Am Math Soc; Asn Symbolic Logic; Asn Comput Mach. *Res:* Recursive functions; Hilbert's tenth problem; theorem proving by computing machine. *Mailing Add:* Courant Inst NY Univ 251 Mercer St New York NY 10012

DAVIS, MARTIN ARNOLD, b Montreal, Que, Apr 24, 30; m 56; c 2. ORGANIC CHEMISTRY, PHARMACEUTICAL RESEARCH. *Educ:* McGill Univ, BSc, 51; Univ London, PhD(org chem), 55. *Prof Exp:* Res chemist, Ayerst Labs, LTD, 55-64, head med chem group, 64-69, dir external projs, 69-75, assoc dir, New Prod Planning & Develop, 75-79, assoc dir res & develop, 79-81; DIR SCI AFFAIRS, PFIZER CAN, INC, 81- *Mem:* Am Chem Soc; fel Chem Inst Can; Royal Soc Chem; Acad Pharmaceut Sci; Israel Chem Soc. *Res:* Medicinal chemistry; drugs affecting the central and autonomic systems; behavioral and spasmolytic agents, anticonvulsants, analgesics; cardiovascular drugs; newer techniques in syntheses; approaches to chemotherapy. *Mailing Add:* 4758 Meridian Ave Montreal PQ H3W 2C1 Can

DAVIS, MARVIN LESTER, b Brockton, Mass, Apr 26, 16; m 62. SYNTHETIC ORGANIC CHEMISTRY. *Educ:* Univ Rochester, BA, 37, MS, 39. *Prof Exp:* Chemist, Eastman Kodak Co, 39-54, supvr synthetic org chem, 54-61, patent liaison synthetic org chem, 62-78; RETIRED. *Mem:* Am Chem Soc. *Res:* Organic synthesis relating to photography. *Mailing Add:* 202 Suburban Ct Rochester NY 14620

DAVIS, MERRITT MCGREGOR, b Ont, Feb 16, 23; m 47; c 2. CIVIL ENGINEERING. *Educ:* Queen's Univ, Ont, BSc, 45; Purdue Univ, MSc, 49. *Prof Exp:* Div maintenance engr, Hwy Dept, Ont, 49-51, res engr, 51-55, design engr, 56; asst prof, 56-61, ASSOC PROF HWY ENG, UNIV TORONTO, 61- *Concurrent Pos:* Assoc mem Hwy Res Bd, Nat Acad Sci-Nat Res Coun. *Mem:* Eng Inst Can; Am Asn Automotive Med. *Res:* Frost action in soils; bituminous pavement mixes; traffic accident causes and crash injury performance. *Mailing Add:* 112 Three Valleys Dr Don Mills Can

DAVIS, MERTON LOUIS, physical chemistry, see previous edition

DAVIS, MICHAEL ALLAN, b Boston, Mass, May 19, 41; m 63; c 2. NUCLEAR MEDICINE, DIAGNOSTIC RADIOLOGY RESEARCH. *Educ:* Worcester Polytech Inst, BS, 62, MS, 64; Harvard Sch Pub Health, SM, 65, ScD(radiobiol), 69; Northeastern Univ, MBA, 79. *Prof Exp:* Res assoc radiol, Harvard Med Sch, 68-70, prin assoc radiol, 70-75, asst prof, 75-78, assoc prof radiol, 78-80; PROF RADIOL & NUCLEAR MED, MED SCH, UNIV MASS, 80- *Concurrent Pos:* Assoc radiol, Peter Bent Brigham Hosp, 68-80; dir radiopharm, Children's Hosp Med Ctr, 71-; clin assoc prof, Col Pharm & Allied Health Professions, Northeastern Univ, 73-77; adj prof radiopharmaceut sci, 77-; consult radiopharm, Brigham & Women's Hosp, 81-; lectr radiol, Harvard Med Sch, 81- *Mem:* Soc Nuclear Med; Am Chem Soc; Radiation Res Soc; Sigma Xi. *Res:* Design, synthesis and biologic evaluation of short-lived radiodiagnostic agents with particular interest in cardiovascular disease; use of radionuclides in all areas of biomedical research; contrast agents for computed tomography and nuclear magnetic resonance. *Mailing Add:* Dept Radiol Mass Med Sch 55 Lake Ave N Worcester MA 01605

DAVIS, MICHAEL E, b Bellefontaine, Ohio, Sept 30, 52; m 81. ANIMAL BREEDING, STATISTICS. *Educ:* Ohio State Univ, BS, 74; Colo State Univ, MS, 77, PhD(animal husbandry), 80. *Prof Exp:* FEL, UNIV WIS, MADISON, 80- *Mem:* Am Soc Animal Sci. *Res:* Beef cattle genetics; estimation of breeding values in beef bulls; examination of selection and inbreeding effects in beef cattle; study of factors affecting lifetime efficiency of beef cows. *Mailing Add:* Dept Meat & Animal Sci Univ Wis 1675 Observ Dr Madison WI 53706

DAVIS, MICHAEL EDWARD, b Jacksonville, Ill, May 17, 22; m 47; c 6. GEOLOGY. *Educ:* Kans State Univ, BS, 50, MS, 51. *Prof Exp:* Instr geol, Kans State Univ, 51-52; asst prof, St Joseph's Col, Ind, 52-54; geologist, Knox-Bergman-Shearer, Colo, 54-57; ASSOC PROF GEOL, ST JOSEPH'S COL, IND, 57-; CHMN DEPT EARTH SCI, 61- *Concurrent Pos:* Glacial geologist, Ind Geol Surv, 62-64. *Mem:* Geol Soc Am; Nat Asn Geol Teachers; Am Asn Petrol Geologists; Asn Prof Geol Scientists. *Res:* Use of photogeologic methods in interpretation of glacial features; photogeologic procedures as applied to geomorphic and structural phenomena; methods of preparation and study of Ostradoda of lower Permian limestones. *Mailing Add:* Dept of Earth Sci St Joseph's Col Rensselaer IN 47978

DAVIS, MICHAEL I, b London, Eng, July 17, 36; m 70; c 1. STRUCTURAL CHEMISTRY. *Educ:* Univ London, BSc, 58, PhD(chem), 62. *Prof Exp:* From instr to asst prof chem, Univ Tex, Austin, 61-68; assoc prof, 68-71, PROF CHEM, UNIV TEX, EL PASO, 71- *Mem:* Am Crystallog Asn; The Chem Soc. *Res:* Molecular structure studies by gas phase lectron diffraction. *Mailing Add:* Dept of Chem Univ of Tex El Paso TX 79999

DAVIS, MICHAEL JAY, b Denver, Colo, Mar 9, 47; m 81. PHYTOBACTERIOLOGY, MYCOPLASMOLOGY. *Educ:* Colo State Univ, BS, 73, MS, 75; Univ Calif, Berkeley, PhD(plant path), 78. *Prof Exp:* Res assoc plant path, Colo State Univ, 73-75; fel, Univ Calif, Berkeley, 78-79; asst prof path, Rutgers Univ, 79-81; ASST PROF PLANT PATH, UNIV FLA, 81- *Mem:* Am Phytopath Soc; Am Soc Microbiol; Sigma Xi. *Res:* Plant pathogenic, fastidious prokaryotes; rickettsia-like bacteria and spiroplasmas; bacterial diseases of plants. *Mailing Add:* Agr Res & Educ Ctr Univ Fla Ft Lauderdale FL 33314

DAVIS, MICHAEL MOORE, b Geneva, NY, Dec 6, 38; m 61; c 4. RADIO ASTRONOMY. *Educ:* Yale Univ, BS, 60; State Univ Leiden, PhD(astron), 67. *Prof Exp:* Asst scientist, Nat Radio Astron Observ, WVa, 67-72; sci coordr, NSF, 72-73; sr res assoc, 74-77, HEAD RADIO ASTRON GROUP, NAT ASTRON & IONOSPHERE CTR, 77- *Concurrent Pos:* mem, NSF Subcomt Radio Astron, Nat Acad Sci Radio Astron Frequency Allocations Subcomt, NASA Sci Working Group on Search for Extraterrestrial Intelligence & Dept Energy/NASA Satellite Power Syst Assessment Subcomt. *Mem:* Int Astron Union; Am Astron Soc. *Res:* Extragalactic radio sources; quasar absorption lines. *Mailing Add:* Arecibo Observ Box 995 Arecibo PR 00612

DAVIS, MICHAEL WALTER, b Norristown, Pa, Apr 26, 49; m 81. TRANSFORMATION GROUPS. *Educ:* Princeton Univ, AB, 71, PhD(math), 75. *Prof Exp:* Moore instr math, Mass Inst Technol, 74-76; mem, Inst Advan Study, 76-77 & 82-83; asst prof math, Columbia Univ, 77-82; ASSOC PROF MATH, OHIO STATE UNIV, 82- *Res:* Transformation groups on homotopy spheres; groups generated by reflections. *Mailing Add:* Math Dept Ohio State Univ Columbus OH 43210

DAVIS, MILFORD HALL, b Chicago, Ill, Aug 20, 25; div; c 2. SPACE PHYSICS. *Educ:* Yale Univ, BS, 49; Calif Inst Technol, MS, 50, PhD(physics), 55. *Prof Exp:* Physicist, Rand Corp, 55-67; physicist, Nat Ctr Atmospheric Res, 67-73; PROG DIR, UNIV SPACE RES ASN, 76- *Mem:* Am Phys Soc. *Res:* Cloud microphysics. *Mailing Add:* PO Box 3006 Boulder CO 80307

DAVIS, MILTON W(ICKERS), JR, b Frederick, Md, Apr 5, 23; m 48; c 2. CHEMICAL ENGINEERING. *Educ:* Johns Hopkins Univ, BE, 43; Univ Calif, Berkeley, MS, 49, PhD(chem eng), 51. *Prof Exp:* Asst radiation lab, Univ Calif, 47-50; res engr atomic energy div, E I du Pont de Nemours & Co,

51-53, res supvr, Savannah River Plant, 54-62; PROF CHEM ENG, UNIV SC, 62-, DIR ENVIRON RES INST, 66- *Mem:* Am Inst Chem Eng; Am Chem Soc. *Res:* Liquid extraction; ion exchange; nuclear chemistry and physics; chemical reaction kinetics; heterogeneous catalysis. *Mailing Add:* PO Box 242 Columbia SC 29202

DAVIS, MONTE V, b Cove, Ore, Apr 29, 23; m 73; c 2. NUCLEAR PHYSICS. *Educ:* Linfield Col, BA, 49; Ore State Univ, MA, 51, PhD(physics), 56. *Prof Exp:* Sr reactor physicist, Gen Elec Co, 51-57; group leader & proj engr, Atomics Int Div, NAm Aviation, Inc, 57-61; prof nuclear eng & dir nuclear reactor lab, Univ Ariz, 61-73; dir, Neely Nuclear Res Ctr, 73-80, PROF NUCLEAR ENG, GA INST TECHNOL, 73- *Concurrent Pos:* Consult, indust & US Govt, 61-; pres, MND Inc, 74- *Mem:* Fel Am Nuclear Soc; Am Phys Soc; Int Solar Energy Soc. *Res:* Direct energy conversion; neutron interactions; nondestructive testing; materials science. *Mailing Add:* 900 Atlantic Dr Atlanta GA 30318

DAVIS, MONTIE GRANT, b Nashville, Tenn, Aug 15, 36; m 62; c 2. PHYSICAL CHEMISTRY, OPTICAL PHYSICS. *Educ:* Vanderbilt Univ, BS, 58; Univ Tenn, MA, 66, PhD(physics), 68. *Prof Exp:* Radiol physicist, Tenn Dept Pub Health, 60-63; res physicist spectroscopy, ARO Inc, 63-69; pvt consult, ARO Inc & US Air Force, 69-71; physics instr, Univ Tenn, 71-75, assoc dean arts & sci, 75-79; prof physics, Utah Space Inst, 79-81; PROF PHYSICS, VOL STATE COMMUNITY COL, 81- *Concurrent Pos:* Consult, ARO Inc & US Air Force, 71-, DuPont, 81- *Mem:* Am Phys Soc; Sigma Xi. *Res:* Spectral characteristics of molecular diatomic spectral, in particular those molecules associated with atmospheric pollution such as nitric oxide. *Mailing Add:* Univ Tenn Tenth & Charlotte Sts Nashville TN 37203

DAVIS, MORRIS SCHUYLER, b Brooklyn, NY, Dec 14, 19; m 45; c 6. ASTRONOMY. *Educ:* Brooklyn Col, BA, 46; Univ Mo, MA, 47; Yale Univ, PhD(astron), 50. *Prof Exp:* Asst instr math, Univ Mo, 46-47; asst astron, Yale Univ, 47-49; from instr to asst prof math & astron, Univ Ky, 50-52, in charge observ, 50-52; from asst prof to assoc prof astron, Univ NC, 52-56; res assoc astron & dir comput ctr, Yale Univ, 56-66; pres & dir, Triangle Univs Comput Ctr, Research Triangle Park, NC, 66-70; MOREHEAD PROF ASTRON, UNIV NC, CHAPEL HILL, 70- *Concurrent Pos:* Tech adv & writer, Morehead Planetarium, 52-56; adj prof, Univ NC, Chapel Hill, NC State Univ & Duke Univ, 66-70; mem bd trustees, Nat Accelerator Lab, 77- *Mem:* AAAS; Am Astron Soc; Int Astron Union. *Res:* Computer science; celestial mechanics; numerical analysis; astrometry. *Mailing Add:* Dept Physics & Astron Univ NC Chapel Hill NC 27514

DAVIS, MORTON DAVID, b Bronx, NY, May 31, 30; m 63; c 2. MATHEMATICS. *Educ:* Univ Colo, AB, 52; Univ Calif, Berkeley, MA, 56, PhD(math), 61. *Prof Exp:* Mathematician, Int Bus Corp, 59-61; asst prof math, Rutgers Univ, 61-65; mem fac, 65-70, assoc prof, 70-78, PROF MATH, CITY COL NEW YORK, 78- *Concurrent Pos:* Res assoc economet, Princeton Univ, 61-63; consult, Mathematica, NJ, 62-65. *Res:* Game theory; infinite games of perfect information; n-person games; game theory models in disarmament. *Mailing Add:* 25 Brinkerhoff Ave Teaneck NJ 07666

DAVIS, MYRTIS, b Bessemer, Ala, Oct 16, 18. MATHEMATICS. *Educ:* Birmingham-Southern Col, AB, 39; La State Univ, MA, 48. *Prof Exp:* Teacher pub schs, Ala, 39-47; asst prof math, Southeastern La Col, 48-49; instr, Miss Southern Col, 49-50; from instr to asst prof, Nicholls State Col, 50-54; assoc prof, Wesleyan Col, Ga, 54-61; assoc prof, 61-63, PROF MATH, GREENSBORO COL, 63-, CHMN DEPT MATH & SCI, 71- *Mem:* Am Math Asn; Nat Coun Teachers Math. *Mailing Add:* Dept of Math & Sci Greensboro Col Greensboro NC 27420

DAVIS, NANCY TAGGART, b Harrisburg, Pa, Mar 30, 44; m 70. PATHOLOGY, ANIMAL BEHAVIOR. *Educ:* Rollins Col, BS, 66; Univ Pa, PhD(path), 73. *Prof Exp:* Res trainee path, Penrose Lab, Philadelphia Zool Garden, 67-73; asst prof, Stockton State Col, 73-78; ADJ RES ASSOC COMP PATH, PENROSE LAB, PHILADELPHIA ZOOL GARDEN, 77-; ASSOC PROF PATH & EPIDEMIOL, STOCKTON STATE COL, 78- *Mem:* Am Heart Asn. *Res:* Comparative pathology; reproductive physiology; relationship between psychosocial stimuli and disease; diet and disease in zoo animals. *Mailing Add:* Dept of Path & Epidemol Stockton State Col Pomona NJ 08240

DAVIS, NEIL CLIFTON, b Duston, Nebr, Apr 5, 18; div; c 1. BIOCHEMISTRY. *Educ:* Nebr Wesleyan Univ, BSc, 39; Univ Nebr, MSc, 41; Iowa State Univ, PhD(chem), 49. *Prof Exp:* Asst res prof biochem, 52-58; assoc prof clin med, Sch Med, Univ Pittsburgh, 58-60; assoc prof res pediat & biochem, 60-71, PROF RES PEDIAT, MED SCH, UNIV CINCINNATI, 71- *Concurrent Pos:* Nat Cancer Inst res fel, Univ Utah, 50-52; fel, Children's Hosp Res Found, 60- *Mem:* Am Asn Immunologists; Am Soc Biol Chemists. *Res:* Purification and study of enzymes; peptides synthesis; fractionation and study of plasma proteins; biochemical approach to teratology. *Mailing Add:* Children's Hosp Res Found Cincinnati OH 45229

DAVIS, NEIL MONAS, b Philadelphia, Pa, Apr 17, 31; m 59; c 2. PHARMACY. *Educ:* Philadelphia Col Pharm, BS, 53, MS, 55, PharmD, 70. *Prof Exp:* Res hosp pharm, Jefferson Med Col Hosp, 53-55, asst dir pharm, 58-61, dir pharm serv, 61-65; instr pharm, Philadelphia Col Pharm & Jefferson Med Col, 61-65; dir pharm serv, Univ Hosp, 65-76, from asst prof to assoc prof, 65-77, PROF PHARM, SCH PHARM, TEMPLE UNIV, 77- *Concurrent Pos:* Ed, Hosp Pharm. *Mem:* Am Pharmaceut Asn; Am Soc Hosp Pharmacist. *Res:* Hospital pharmacy administration and editing; hospital and clinical pharmacy education. *Mailing Add:* 1143 Wright Dr Huntingdon Valley PA 19006

DAVIS, NICHOLAS FALCONER, geochemistry, exploration geology, see previous edition

DAVIS, NORMAN DUANE, b San Diego, Calif, May 7, 28; m 52; c 2. MICROBIOLOGY. *Educ:* Univ Ga, BSc, 53; Ohio State Univ, MSc, 55, PhD, 57. *Prof Exp:* Instr bot, Univ Ga, 57-58; from asst prof to assoc prof, 58-67, PROF BOT & MICROBIOL AUBURN UNIV, 67- *Mem:* AAAS; Am Soc Microbiol; Am Chem Soc. *Res:* Physiology and biochemistry of microbes; industrial and applied microbiology; mycotoxicology. *Mailing Add:* Dept of Bot & Microbiol Auburn Univ Auburn AL 36830

DAVIS, NORMAN RODGER, b Toronto, Ont, June 30, 43. BIOCHEMISTRY. *Educ:* Univ Toronto, BSc, 66, PhD(biochem), 70. *Prof Exp:* Wellcome fel, Meat Res Inst, Langford, Eng, 70-71; asst prof biochem, 71-74, ASSOC PROF DENT, UNIV ALTA, 74- *Res:* Chemistry and structure of collagen crosslinks; mechanism of collagen mineralization; mechanism of desmosine and isodesmosine crosslink formation in elastin. *Mailing Add:* Dept of Oral Biol Fac Dent Univ of Alta Edmonton AB T6G 2E1 Can

DAVIS, NORMAN SEYMOUR, microbiology, biochemistry, see previous edition

DAVIS, NORMAN THOMAS, b DosCabezas, Ariz, Mar 23, 27; m 50; c 4. ENTOMOLOGY. *Educ:* Ariz State Univ, BS, 49; Iowa State Col, MS, 51; Univ Wis, PhD, 54. *Prof Exp:* From instr to assoc prof, 54-68, prof entom, 68-80, PROF BIOL, UNIV CONN, 80- *Mem:* Am Entom Soc. *Res:* Insect morphology; physiology. *Mailing Add:* Biol Sci Group Univ of Conn Storrs CT 06268

DAVIS, OSCAR F, b Oak Park, Ill, June 19, 28; m 51; c 4. PSYCHIATRY, PHARMACOLOGY. *Educ:* Roosevelt Univ, BS, 49; Loyola Univ, Ill, MS, 52, PhD(pharmacol), 54, MD, 58; Am Bd Psychiat, dipl, 66. *Prof Exp:* Assoc pharmacol, Stritch Sch Med, Loyola Univ, Ill, 53-58; intern, Michael Reese Hosp, 58-59; clin instr psychiat, Col Med, Univ Ill, 60-62; clin asst prof, 62-67, CLIN ASSOC PROF PSYCHIAT & PHARMACOL, CHICAGO MED SCH, 67-; DIR CHILD & ADOLESCENT PSYCHIAT, MT SINAI HOSP, 62-; asst prof psychiat, 70-81, ASSOC PROF PSYCHIAT, MED SCH, NORTHWESTERN UNIV, 81- *Concurrent Pos:* Fel, Inst Juvenile Res, Ill, 61-63; resident psychiat, Univ Ill Res & Educ Hosp, 59-62, Passavant Mem Hosp, Children's Mem Hosp & Evanston Hosp; consult pharmacologist, 52-63; sr attend physician, Northwestern Memorial & Evanston Hosps, 76- *Mem:* Am Acad Child Psychiat; fel Am Psychiat Asn; Am Fedn Clin Res; Am Soc Pharmacol & Exp Therapeut. *Res:* Child, adolescent and adult psychiatry; infantile development and psychosomatic diseases in childhood; psychopharmacology; child psychiatry and adolescent. *Mailing Add:* 993 Forest Ave Glencoe IL 60022

DAVIS, P(HILIP) C, b Cornish, Ark, Apr 18, 21; m 44; c 2. CHEMICAL ENGINEERING. *Educ:* Univ Chicago, SB, 43; Univ Kans, BS, 48, MS, 49, PhD(chem eng), 52. *Prof Exp:* Process design engr, 52, engr process develop, 53-55, supvr, 55-59, sr assoc, 59-64, head eng & math sci, 64-67, SR ENG ADV RES & DEVELOP, ETHYL CORP, 74-, ASSOC DIR PROCESS DEVELOP, 81- *Mem:* Am Inst Chem Engrs. *Res:* Vapor-liquid phase equilibria; chemical processes; computer techniques. *Mailing Add:* Ethyl Corp PO Box 341 Baton Rouge LA 70821

DAVIS, PAUL COOPER, b Glenville, WVa, Mar 14, 37; m 60; c 4. ELECTRICAL ENGINEERING. *Educ:* Univ WVa, BSEE, 59; Mass Inst Technol, MS, 61; Lehigh Univ, PhD(elec eng), 68. *Prof Exp:* MEM TECH STAFF, BELL TEL LABS, READING BR, 62- *Mem:* Inst Elec & Electronics Engrs. *Res:* Design of custom linear and digital integrated circuits. *Mailing Add:* 3601 River Rd Reading PA 19605

DAVIS, PAUL JOSEPH, b Chicago, Ill, Oct 28, 37; m 62; c 3. ENDOCRINOLOGY. *Educ:* Westminster Col, Mo, BA, 59; Harvard Univ, MD, 63. *Prof Exp:* Clin assoc endocrinol, Nat Inst Child Health & Human Develop, NIH, 67-69; sr staff assoc, 69-70; head endocrinol div, Baltimore City Hosps, 70-75; HEAD ENDOCRINOL DIV & PROF MED, MED SCH, STATE UNIV NY BUFFALO, 75-; CHIEF MED SERV, VET ADMIN MED CTR, BUFFALO, 80- *Concurrent Pos:* Assoc prof med, Johns Hopkins Univ, 74-75; head, Endocrinol Div, Erie County Med Ctr, 75-; bd sci counr, Nat Inst on Aging, NIH, 77-81. *Mem:* Endocrine Soc; Am Thyroid Asn; Am Diabetes Asn; Am Fedn Clin Res. *Res:* Mechanisms of action of thyroid hormone. *Mailing Add:* Erie County Med Ctr Buffalo NY 14215

DAVIS, PAUL WILLIAM, b Albany, NY, Oct 14, 44; m 66; c 2. APPLIED MATHEMATICS. *Educ:* Rensselaer Polytech Inst, BS, 66, MS, 67, PhD(math), 70. *Prof Exp:* Res mathematician appl math, Tex Instruments Corp, 66; actg chief appl math prog, US Army Res Off, 74-75; from asst prof to assoc prof, 70-80, PROF MATH SCI & HEAD DEPT, WORCESTER POLYTECH INST, 80-, CHMN DEPT, 78- *Concurrent Pos:* Consult, Dept Civil Eng, Worcester Polytech Inst, 71; US Army Res Off, 73 & 74, Dept of Gynec, Mass Gen Hosp, 77; ed, Soc Indust Appl Math News, 75- *Mem:* Soc Indust Appl Math; Am Math Soc; Combustion Inst. *Res:* Analytical techniques for nonlinear diffusion phenomena, especially those arising in combustion theory; measurement system design for electric power systems. *Mailing Add:* Dept of Math Worcester Polytech Inst Worcester MA 01609

DAVIS, PAULS, b Cesis, Latvia, Mar 18, 21; nat US; m 50; c 2. ORGANIC CHEMISTRY. *Educ:* Univ Tübingen, dipl chem, 47, DSc(org chem), 49. *Prof Exp:* Res assoc org chem, Mass Inst Technol, 50-53; res chemist, Burke Res Co, 53-59; from res chemist to sr res chemist, 59-64, res assoc, 64-74, sr res assoc, 74-78, RES FEL, BASF-WYANDOTTE CORP, 78- *Mem:* Am Chem Soc; Sigma Xi; Royal Soc Chem. *Res:* Metalorganic compounds; synthetic fat-soluble vitamines; organic peroxides and ozonides; metalorganic polymerization catalysts; fire retardant polymers; organic halogenous compounds. *Mailing Add:* BASF-Wyandotte Corp Wyandotte MI 48192

DAVIS, PEGGY ANN, see Chun, Peggy Ann Davis

DAVIS, PEYTON NELSON, b Lodi, Calif, Apr 4, 25; m 47; c 2. NUTRITION, BIOCHEMISTRY. *Educ:* Colo State Univ, BSc, 48; Univ Calif, Davis, MSc, 63, PhD(nutrit), 66. *Prof Exp:* Res asst, Exp Sta, Colo State Univ, 48-52; lab technician, Univ Calif, Davis, 52-66; sr scientist, Vivonex Corp, 66-70; sr nutritionist, Dept Food Sci, Stanford Res Inst, 70-74; chief nutritionist, Shaklee Corp, Emeryville, 74-80; MEM STAFF, DEPT NUTRIT, NAT LIVE STOCK & MEAT BOARD, 80- *Mem:* Inst Food Technol; Animal Nutrit Res Coun; Am Inst Nutrit; Soc Nutrit Educ; NY Acad Sci. *Res:* Feeding values of proteins; amino acid requirements; unidentified growth factors; vitamin requirements; pigmentation of shanks; mineral utilization and requirements; effects of chelating agents; chemically defined diets; carbohydrate effect upon atherosclerosis; purine utilization; fabricated foods. *Mailing Add:* Dept Nutrit Nat Live Stock & Meat Bd 444 N Michigan Ave Chicago IL 60611

DAVIS, PHILIP, b Lawrence, Mass, Jan 2, 23; m 44; c 4. MATHEMATICS. *Educ:* Harvard Univ, PhD(math), 50. *Prof Exp:* Mathematician, Nat Bur Standards, 51-58, chief numerical anal, 58-63; PROF APPL MATH, BROWN UNIV, 63- *Concurrent Pos:* Guggenheim fel, 56-57. *Mem:* Am Math Soc. *Res:* Numerical analysis; interpolation and approximation theory. *Mailing Add:* Dept of Appl Math Brown Univ Providence RI 02912

DAVIS, PHILIP K, b Effingham, Ill, Aug 29, 31; m 55; c 2. ENGINEERING MECHANICS. *Educ:* Univ Tex, BS, 58, MS, 59; Univ Mich, MSE & PhD(eng mech), 63. *Prof Exp:* Res engr, Struct Mech Res Lab, Balcones Res Ctr, Univ Tex, 59; stress analyst, Boeing Airplane Co, Kans, 59-60; instr eng mech, Univ Mich, 63-64; asst prof fluid mech, 64-65, prof in chg, 65-67, assoc prof, 67-71, actg dean, Sch Eng & Technol, 78-79, PROF FLUID MECH & CHMN, DEPT ENG MECH & MAT, SOUTHERN ILL UNIV, 71- *Concurrent Pos:* Lectr, Univ Wichita, 59-60; NSF grant, 66-67; NASA grant, 68-70. *Mem:* Am Soc Eng Educ; Am Soc Mech Engrs; Int Asn Hydraul Res; Am Acad Mech; Soc Eng Sci. *Res:* Motion of solid bodies in rotating viscous fluids; viscous and inviscid flows; liquid squeeze film motion; cushioning of large structures against seismic inputs, hydrocyclones and biomechanics. *Mailing Add:* Sch Eng & Technol Dept Eng Mech & Mat Southern Ill Univ Carbondale IL 62901

DAVIS, PHILIP SEALS, b Ft Worth, Tex, Aug 30, 42; m 66; c 2. RESEARCH & DEVELOPMENT MANAGEMENT. *Educ:* Vanderbilt Univ, BA, 64; Rice Univ, PhD(phys chem), 68. *Prof Exp:* Res assoc, Univ Kans, 68-70; res scientist, 70-75, sr res scientist, 75-77, group leader, 77-78, res supvr, 78-80, RES MGR, BETZ LABS, 80- *Mem:* Am Chem Soc; Tech Asn Pulp & Paper Indust. *Res:* Experimental and theoretical determination of the physical and chemical properties of aqueous and gaseous systems, including various ion and particle interactions as well as their associated interfacial phenomena. *Mailing Add:* Betz Labs PO Box 4300 9664 Grogans Mill Rd The Woodlands TX 77380

DAVIS, PHILLIP BURTON, b Owosso, Mich, Oct 11, 51; m 73; c 1. INTEGRATED NATURAL RESOURCE MANAGEMENT. *Educ:* Univ Mich-Flint, BA, 74; Mich State Univ, MS, 75, PhD(resource develop), 79. *Prof Exp:* Teaching asst ecol, Univ Mich-Flint, 71-73; res asst, Wildlife Dept, Mich State Univ, 74-75, res proj coordr, Resource Develop Dept, 76-79, grad teaching asst, Watershed Mgt, 78-79; ASST PROF, NATURAL RESOURCES MGT, DIV RENEWABLE NATURAL RESOURCES, UNIV NEV, RENO, 79- *Concurrent Pos:* Lab asst, Dept Biol, Univ Mich-Flint, 71; mem staff, Inst Sci & Technol, Willow Run Labs, 72; terrestrial ecologist, Mich State Univ, 74. *Mem:* Soc Range Mgt; Wildlife Soc; Soc Am Foresters; Sigma Xi; Nat Wildlife Fedn. *Res:* Coordinated development, use and management of renewable natural resources in accordance with ecological principles for the benefit of man. *Mailing Add:* Renewable Resources Ctr Univ Nev 1000 Valley Rd Reno NV 89512

DAVIS, R(OBERT) E(LLIOT), b Chicago, Ill, Dec 1, 22; m 47; c 4. SOLID STATE PHYSICS, ENGINEERING. *Educ:* Purdue Univ, BSEE, 44, MS, 49. *Prof Exp:* Res physicist, Westinghouse Elec Corp, 49-55, supvr engr solid state device develop & appln, 55, sect mgr, 55-58, dept mgr, 58-60, mgr semiconductor dept, Res Labs, 60-62, mgr adv develop, Semiconductor Div, 62-65; VPRES, ENGR & MEM BD DIRS, PA ELECTRONICS TECHNOL, INC, 65- *Mem:* Inst Elec & Electronics Engrs; Am Physics Soc; Am Ceramic Soc. *Res:* Semiconductor physics; material preparation; electrical and optical measurements on materials and devices; device design and application. *Mailing Add:* Box 13 Murrysville PA 15668

DAVIS, R(ICHARD) S(MITH), b Winnipeg, Man, Mar 1, 26; m 52; c 2. METALLURGY. *Educ:* Univ Toronto, BASc, 51, MASc, 52, PhD(metall), 54. *Prof Exp:* Spec lectr metall, Univ Toronto, 53-54; fel, Div Eng & Appl Physics, Harvard Univ, 54-55, lectr, 55-56, asst prof, 56-59; staff mem, Arthur D Little, Inc, 59-62, vpres, 62-68; prof mat sci & dean, Col Eng & Phys Sci, Univ NH, 68-80; DIR CORP TECHNOL, FMC CORP, 80- *Mem:* Am Inst Mining, Metall & Petrol Engrs; Am Soc Metals; Am Ceramic Soc. *Res:* Mechanical properties of solids; imperfections in solids; oxidation of metals; crystallization of inorganics. *Mailing Add:* FMC Corp 200 E Randolph Chicago IL 60601

DAVIS, RALPH ANDERSON, b Huntington, Ind, Aug 14, 17; m 40; c 2. CHEMISTRY. *Educ:* Huntington Col, AB, 39; Ind Univ, MA, 42. *Prof Exp:* Teacher high sch, Ind, 39-41; asst chem, Ind Univ, 41-42; from res chemist to sr res chemist, 42-74, sr res specialist, 74-80, RES ASSOC, DOW CHEM CO, 80- *Mem:* Am Chem Soc. *Res:* Organic and inorganic fluorides and other halides; catalysis; low temperature distillation; fluorine and high energy oxidizers. *Mailing Add:* 1160 Poseyville Rd RR 7 Midland MI 48640

DAVIS, RALPH LANIER, b Ala, Sept 10, 21; m 43; c 3. GENETICS, PLANT BREEDING. *Educ:* Ala Polytech Inst, BS, 43; Purdue Univ, MS, 48, PhD(genetics, breeding), 50. *Prof Exp:* Asst dean grad sch, 65-71, PROF AGRON, SCH AGR, PURDUE UNIV, 50-, ASSOC DIR DIV SPONSORED PROGS, 66- *Concurrent Pos:* Vis prof, Ore State Univ, 59-60

& NC State Col, 63; ed, Crop Sci, Crop Sci Soc Am, 64-67; patent mgr, Off Patent Mgt, 74-80. *Mem:* Fel AAAS; fel Am Soc Agron; Crop Sci Soc Am (pres-elect & actg pres, 62, pres, 63). *Mailing Add:* Div Sponsored Progs Purdue Res Found Purdue Univ West Lafayette IN 47906

DAVIS, RANDALL T, b Winchester, Va, Jan 9, 36; m 59; c 4. ENGINEERING MECHANICS. *Educ:* Va Polytech Inst, BS, 60; Stanford Univ, MS, 61, PhD(eng mech), 64. *Prof Exp:* From asst prof to prof eng mech, Va Polytech Inst & State Univ, 63-71; PROF AEROSPACE ENG & APPL MECH & HEAD DEPT, UNIV CINCINNATI, 71- *Mem:* Am Soc Mech Engrs; Am Inst Aeronaut & Astronaut. *Res:* Theoretical fluid mechanics, particularly laminar viscous flow; numerical methods applied to viscous flow problems. *Mailing Add:* Dept Aerospace Eng & Appl Mech Univ of Cincinnati Cincinnati OH 45221

DAVIS, RAYMOND, JR, b Washington, DC, Oct 14, 14; m 48; c 5. CHEMISTRY. *Educ:* Univ Md, BS, 37, MS, 40; Yale Univ, PhD(phys chem), 42. *Prof Exp:* Res chemist, Dow Chem Co, Mich, 37-38 & AEC, Ohio, 46-48; SCIENTIST, BROOKHAVEN NAT LAB, 48- Adj prof, Univ Pa, 73- *Honors & Awards:* Boris Prejel Prize, NY Acad Sci, 54; Comstoc Prize, Nat Acad Sci, 78; Award for Nuclear Applns, Am Chem Soc, 79. *Mem:* Fel AAAS; fel Am Phys Soc; Am Geophys Union; Geochem Soc; Meteoritical Soc. *Res:* Nuclear chemistry; meteorites and cosmic rays; neutrino detection; lunar sample studies. *Mailing Add:* 28 Bergen Lane Blue Point NY 11715

DAVIS, RAYMOND E, b Hobbs, NMex, Nov 7, 38; m 60; c 3. PHYSICAL CHEMISTRY. *Educ:* Univ Kans, BS, 60; Yale Univ, PhD(phys chem), 65. *Prof Exp:* Cancer res scientist, Center Crystallog Res, Roswell Park Mem Inst, 64-65, sr cancer res scientist, 65-66; asst prof, 66-70, assoc prof, 70-76, PROF CHEM, UNIV TEX, AUSTIN, 76- *Mem:* Am Crystallog Asn; Am Chem Soc. *Res:* X-ray diffraction; molecular structure studies of organometallic and small ring organic compounds; molecular structure studies of transition metal phosphine complexes and macrocyclic compounds and their complexes. *Mailing Add:* Dept Chem Univ Tex Austin TX 78712

DAVIS, RAYMOND VINCENT, b Chicago, Ill, Feb 3, 27; m 59; c 3. BIOCHEMISTRY, IMMUNOCHEMISTRY. *Educ:* Northwestern Univ, BS, 50; Univ Wis, MS, 57; Univ Mo, PhD(biochem), 65. *Prof Exp:* Res asst, Abbott Labs, 52-55, biochemist, 57-61; res biochemist, Ames Res Labs, Miles Labs, Inc, Ind, 64-70; sr biochemist, 70-80, RES FEL, RES DIV, HOFFMANN-LA ROCHE INC, 80- *Mem:* Am Asn Clin Chem; Am Asn Clin Chemists. *Res:* Immunoadsorbent purification of protein antigens and antibodies; radioimmunoassay research and development; autoimmune diseases; monoclonal antibodies. *Mailing Add:* Res Div Hoffmann-La Roche Inc Nutley NJ 07110

DAVIS, RICHARD, b Gallipolis, Ohio, Oct 17, 32. NEUROBIOLOGY, NEUROPHARMACOLOGY. *Educ:* Kenyon Col, AB, 54; Rice Univ, PhD(biol), 59. *Prof Exp:* Fel cytol, Rockefeller Univ, 59-60; res assoc, 60-70, ASST PROF PHARMACOL, MED SCH UNIV PA, 70- *Mem:* Am Soc Cell Biol; Histochem Soc; Am Inst Biol Sci; Electron Micros Soc Am. *Res:* Cytochemical localization using light microscopic and electron microscopic methods for cholinesterase enzymes in nerve and muscle tissues and the effects of pharmacological agents on their activity. *Mailing Add:* Dept Pharmacol G-3 Med Sch Univ Pa Philadelphia PA 19104

DAVIS, RICHARD A, b Chicago, Ill, June 15, 25; m 60; c 2. NEUROSURGERY, MEDICAL SCIENCES. *Educ:* Princeton Univ, AB, 47; Northwestern Univ, MD, 51, MS, 56. *Prof Exp:* Asst neurol, Nat Hosp, London, 56-57; asst prof, 61-66, ASSOC PROF NEUROSURG, SCH MED, UNIV PA, 66-, RES ASSOC PHYSIOL, 59- *Concurrent Pos:* USPHS res grant, 57-; Am Cancer Soc fel, 62-65; staff surgeon, Hosp Univ Pa, 59- *Mem:* Am Col Surg; Am Asn Neurol Surg. *Res:* Central nervous system control of gastric secretion; clinical research in depth electrode recordings from brain; decerebrate rigidity in animals and man. *Mailing Add:* Dept Neurosurg Univ Pa Univ Hosp Philadelphia PA 19104

DAVIS, RICHARD ALBERT, JR, b Joliet, Ill, Sept 11, 37; m 62; c 2. GEOLOGY. *Educ:* Beloit Col, BS, 59; Univ Tex, MA, 61; Univ Ill, Urbana, PhD(geol), 64. *Prof Exp:* Alumni Res Found fel geol, Univ Wis, 64-65; from asst prof to assoc prof, Western Mich Univ, 65-73; mem fac geol, 73-80, PROF & CHAIRPERSON GEOL, UNIV SFLA, 80- *Concurrent Pos:* Sr Fulbright fel, Univ Melbourne, 76. *Mem:* Soc Econ Paleontologists & Mineralogists; Geol Soc Am; Am Asn Petrol Geologists; Int Asn Great Lakes Res; Int Asn Sedimentologists. *Res:* Physical stratigraphy and sedimentary petrography of Ordovician in Mississippi Valley; nearshore sedimentation and sedimentary structures of United States coasts; beach and nearshore processes. *Mailing Add:* Dept of Geol Univ of SFla Tampa FL 33620

DAVIS, RICHARD ARNOLD, b Cedar Rapids, Iowa, Apr 19, 42; m; c 1. GEOLOGY, PALEONTOLOGY. *Educ:* Cornell Col, BA, 63; Univ Iowa, MS, 65, PhD(geol), 68. *Prof Exp:* NSF fel paleont, Univ Col Swansea, Wales, 68-69; asst prof geol & cur geol, Univ Cincinnati, 69-75; dir sci educ, 75-78, PALEONTOLOGIST, CINCINNATI MUS NATURAL HISTORY, 75-, CUR OF COLLECTIONS, 78- *Mem:* Geol Soc Am; Paleont Soc; Soc Vert Paleont; Paleont Asn; Soc Econ Paleont & Mineral. *Res:* Paleobiology of ammonoid cephalopods; biology and paleobiology of nautiloid cephalopods; problematic fossils. *Mailing Add:* Cincinnati Mus Natural Hist 1720 Gilbert Ave Cincinnati OH 45202

DAVIS, RICHARD B, b Moscow, Idaho, Oct 9, 18; m 40; c 2. VERTEBRATE ECOLOGY, BIOMETRY. *Educ:* Tex Col Arts & Indust, BS(chem) & BS(chem eng), 40; Agr & Mech Col, Tex, MS, 51, PhD(wildlife ecol), 52. *Prof Exp:* Teacher high schs, Tex, 40-41; aircraft engine mech, Army Air Force Tech Training Command, Ill & Miss, 41-43; game & range mgr, Copano Cattle Co & O'Connor Estates, Tex, 52-56; res assoc bat ecol, Johns Hopkins Univ, 56-59; assoc prof wildlife ecol, Tex A&M Univ, 59-64, assoc mem, Statist Inst, 63-64; dir off res, 75-78, res biologist, Entom Res Div, Agr Res Serv, USDA, 64-67; prof & Caesar Kleberg chair wildlife ecol, 67-80, PROF BIOL, TEX A&I UNIV, 80-, DIR RES & DEAN GRAD STUDIES, 78- *Concurrent Pos:* Consult, Tex Game & Fish Comn, 59-64. *Mem:* Ecol Soc Am; Wildlife Soc; NY Acad Sci. *Res:* Ecology of white-tailed deer, bobwhite quail, Mexican free-tailed bats and screwworm flies. *Mailing Add:* Dept of Biol Tex A&I Univ Box 2176 Kingsville TX 78363

DAVIS, RICHARD BRADLEY, b Iowa City, Iowa, Nov 6, 26; m 57; c 3. INTERNAL MEDICINE, HEMATOLOGY. *Educ:* Yale Univ, BS, 49; Univ Iowa, MD, 53; Univ Minn, Minneapolis, PhD(internal med), 64. *Prof Exp:* From instr to asst prof med, Univ Minn, Minneapolis, 59-69; assoc prof, 69-73, actg dir, 73-76, dir, Hemat Div, 76-79, PROF MED, MED SCH, UNIV NEBR, 73-, HEAD HEMAT SECT, DEPT INT MED, 79- *Concurrent Pos:* USPHS res career develop award, 61-69; vis investr, Sir William Dunn Sch Path, Oxford Univ, 64-65. *Mem:* Am Soc Hemat; Am Fedn Clin Res; Endocrine Soc; Soc Exp Biol & Med; Am Soc Exp Path. *Res:* Electron microscopy of blood platelets, platelet aggregating agents, freeze drying of blood platelets. *Mailing Add:* Univ Nebr Hosps Omaha NE 68105

DAVIS, RICHARD FRANCIS, b Keene, NH, Aug 30, 24; m 50; c 2. ANIMAL SCIENCE, DAIRY SCIENCE. *Educ:* Cornell Univ, PhD(animal nutrit), 53. *Prof Exp:* Actg asst prof animal nutrit, Cornell Univ, 53-54; from asst prof to prof dairy husb, 54-74, head dept, 56-74, interim chmn div agr & life sci, 73-74, prof & chmn, Dept Dairy Sci, 74-81, ASSOC PROVOST, DIV AGR & LIFE SCI, UNIV MD, 81- *Concurrent Pos:* Staff scientist, Coop State Res Serv, USDAIO, 74-75. *Mem:* AAAS; Am Soc Animal Sci; Am Dairy Sci Asn; NY Acad Sci; Am Inst Nutrit. *Res:* Rumen physiology; energy evaluation of ruminant feeds; nutritive evaluation of forages. *Mailing Add:* Dept Dairy Sci Univ Md College Park MD 20742

DAVIS, RICHARD HENRY, JR, b Newport News, Va, Nov 18, 43. BIOCHEMISTRY. *Educ:* Temple Univ, BA, 67; Georgetown Univ, MS, 71, PhD(chem), 74. *Prof Exp:* NIH fel, Lab Chem Biol, Nat Inst Arthritis Metab & Digestive Dis, 74-76; RES BIOCHEMIST, CLIN SYSTS DIV, E I DU PONT DE NEMOURS & CO, INC, 76- *Mem:* Sigma Xi. *Res:* Protein chemistry; structure function relationships, enzyme kinetics and immunology; analyses for clinically significant analytes in body fluids. *Mailing Add:* Clin Systs Div Glasgow Site E I du Pont de Nemours & Co Inc Wilmington DE 19898

DAVIS, RICHARD LAVERNE, b Minneapolis, Minn, May 20, 32; m 64; c 3. PATHOLOGY, NEUROPATHOLOGY. *Educ:* Univ Minn, Minneapolis, BA, 53, BS & MD, 56. *Prof Exp:* Intern med, Bellevue Hosp, New York, 56-57; resident path, Univ Minn, Minneapolis, 57-60; Nat Inst Neurol Dis & Blindness training fel neuropath, Armed Forces Inst Path, 60-61; assoc pathologist, Armed Forces Inst Path, 61-65; pathologist, Lab Serv, US Naval Hosp, 65-69; from assoc prof to prof path, Univ Southern Calif, 69-80, chief, Cajal Lab Neuropath, 69-79; PROG PATH, NEUROL SURG & NEUROL, UNIV CALIF, SAN FRANCISCO, 80- *Concurrent Pos:* Nat Cancer Inst training fel, Univ Minn, Minneapolis, 58-60; consult, Washington Hosp Ctr, DC, 61-65, Nat Naval Med Ctr, Md, 62-65, Long Beach Vet Admin Hosp, 70-; clin instr, Sch Med, George Washington Univ, 63-65. *Mem:* Am Asn Neuropath; Am Asn Path; Am Acad Neurol; Soc Exp Biol & Med. *Res:* Histochemistry; Schwartzman phenomenon; experimental tumors; radiation effects on central nervous system; brain tumors. *Mailing Add:* Dept Path HSW 501 Univ Calif San Francisco CA 94143

DAVIS, RICHARD RICHARDSON, b Ala, Dec 7, 23; m 45; c 3. AGRONOMY. *Educ:* Auburn Univ, BS, 47; Purdue Univ, MS, 49, PhD, 50. *Prof Exp:* Res asst, Purdue Univ, 47-50; from asst prof to assoc prof, Ohio Agr Exp Sta, 50-59, prof agron, Ohio Agr Res & Develop Ctr, 59-78, prof, Ohio State Univ, 62-78, assoc chmn, 62-69, asst dir ctr, 69-78; ASST TO V PRES & PROF AGRON, MISS STATE UNIV, 78- *Mem:* AAAS; fel Am Soc Agron; Crop Sci Soc Am (pres, 74); Int Turfgrass Soc (pres, 73). *Res:* Turfgrass management; weed control; pasture management. *Mailing Add:* PO Box 5386 Mississippi State MS 39762

DAVIS, ROBERT, b Delhi, NY, Feb 22, 31; m 56; c 4. INSECT ECOLOGY. *Educ:* Univ Ga, BS, 56, MS, 61, PhD(zool), 63. *Prof Exp:* Entomologist, Ga State Dept Entom, 56; med entomologist, Third US Army Med Lab, 56-59; forest entomologist, Southeastern Forest Exp Sta, USDA, 59-60, res entomologist, Southern Grain Insects Res Lab, 63-65; asst prof entom, Univ Ga, 65-69; DIR STORED-PROD INSECTS RES & DEVELOP LAB, AGR RES SERV, 69- *Mem:* Am Entom Soc. *Res:* Acarology; taxonomy and ecology of eriophyidae; ecology of insects attacking stored products. *Mailing Add:* Stored Prod Insects Res Develop Lab PO Box 22909 Savannah GA 31403

DAVIS, ROBERT A(RTHUR), b Weehawken, NJ, June 15, 26; m 47; c 3; m 62. SPACE SCIENCES, AERODYNAMICS. *Educ:* NY Univ, BAeE, 46, MAeE, 48, DEngSci, 55. *Prof Exp:* Asst aeronaut, Col Eng, NY Univ, 46-47, instr, 47-50; sr engr & group leader aerodyn, Sparrow I Proj, Sperry Gyroscope Co, NY, 50-55; leader satellite opers, Systs Opers Dept, Rand Corp, Calif, 55-62; group dir advan systs, Advan Progs Div, 62-80, PRIN ENGR, ADVAN SYSTS TECH DIV, AEROSPACE CORP, CALIF, 80- *Concurrent Pos:* Consult long range planning & mil space policy to Asst Secy Defense & Defense Sci Bd. *Mem:* AAAS; Am Inst Aeronaut & Astronaut; Am Astronaut Soc. *Res:* Space and missiles research and development; flight test data analysis; operations research; satellite systems analysis; missile systems analysis. *Mailing Add:* Aerospace Corp PO Box 92957 Los Angeles CA 90009

DAVIS, ROBERT BENJAMIN, b Fall River, Mass, June 23, 26; m 58; c 2. MATHEMATICS. *Educ:* Mass Inst Technol, SB, 46, SM, 47, PhD(math), 51. *Prof Exp:* From asst to instr math, Mass Inst Technol, 46-51; asst prof, Univ NH, 51-56; assoc prof math & educ, Syracuse Univ, 56-63, prof & dir math educ, 63-72; DIR CURRIC LAB & ASSOC DIR COMPUT-BASED EDUC RES LAB, UNIV ILL, URBANA, 72-; DIR, MADISON PROJ, 57- *Mem:*

Am Math Soc; Math Asn Am; Am Psychol Asn; AAAS. *Res:* Third order partial differential equations; mathematical physics; mathematics education; computer-assisted instruction. *Mailing Add:* Curric Lab Univ of Ill 1210 W Springfield Ave Urbana IL 61801

DAVIS, ROBERT BERNARD, b Miami, Fla, Dec 4, 35; m 60; c 4. ORGANIC CHEMISTRY, POLYMER CHEMISTRY. *Educ:* Univ Miami, BEd, 57, BS, 59, MS, 61; Mass Inst Technol, PhD(org chem), 65. *Prof Exp:* Res chemist, Textile Fibers Dept, Pioneering Res Div, E I du Pont de Nemours & Co, Del, 65-68; asst prof org chem, Northeastern Univ, 68-72; asst prof, 72-77, assoc dir, FRL, Albany Int Co, 77-80, DIR, ALBANY INT RES CO, 80- *Mem:* Am Chem Soc. *Res:* Materials science; membrane technology; fiber technology; biomaterials; polymer science. *Mailing Add:* Albany Int Res Co Rte 128 Dedham MA 02026

DAVIS, ROBERT CLAY, b Dallas, Tex, June 8, 41; m 67; c 1. PURE MATHEMATICS. *Educ:* Southern Methodist Univ, BA, 63; Tulane Univ, PhD(math), 67. *Prof Exp:* Asst prof, 67-73, ASSOC PROF MATH, SOUTHERN METHODIST UNIV, 73- *Mem:* Math Asn Am. *Res:* Category theory; universal algebra. *Mailing Add:* Dept of Math Southern Methodist Univ Dallas TX 75275

DAVIS, ROBERT DABNEY, b Kershaw, SC, Apr 13, 39. MATHEMATICS. *Educ:* NC State Univ, BS, 61, MS, 63; Fla State Univ, PhD(math), 69. *Prof Exp:* Instr math, Univ Richmond, 63-65; asst prof, 69-74, ASSOC PROF MATH, UNIV NEV RENO, 74- *Mem:* Am Math Soc; Math Asn Am. *Res:* Abstract Algebra; ramification series of ramified v-rings. *Mailing Add:* Dept of Math Univ of Nev Reno NV 89557

DAVIS, ROBERT EDWARD, b Brooklyn, NY, Jan 27, 39; m 62; c 2. PLANT PATHOLOGY, MICROBIOLOGY. *Educ:* Univ RI, BSc, 61; Cornell Univ, PhD(plant path), 67. *Prof Exp:* Lectr plant virol, Univ Minn, 65; resident res assoc, 66-67, RES PLANT PATHOLOGIST, PLANT VIROL LAB, AGR RES SERV, USDA, 67- *Concurrent Pos:* Exchange scientist plant physiol & biochem, Nat Inst Agron Res, Bordeaux, France, 73-74. *Mem:* Am Phytopath Soc; Am Soc Microbiol; AAAS. *Res:* Role of spiroplasmas, mycoplasmas, rickettsium-like organisms, other unusual procaryotes, and viruses in the etiology of plant diseases. *Mailing Add:* 1793 Rochester St Crofton MD 21114

DAVIS, ROBERT ELLIOTT, b Salt Lake City, Utah, Mar 21, 30; m 55; c 3. INORGANIC CHEMISTRY, SYNTHETIC FUELS PROCESS DEVELOPMENT. *Educ:* Univ Utah, AB, 51, PhD(chem), 54. *Prof Exp:* Res anal chemist, M W Kellogg Co, NJ, 54-57; res proj engr, Am Potash & Chem Corp, Calif, 57-60; head new prod sect, 60-63 & process chem sect, Trona Res Lab, 63-67, mgr heavy chem res, 67-69; adminr & res consult, 69-70, mgr chem extraction sect, 70-76; mgr process eng sect, Tech Ctr, 76-79, MGR PROCESS TECHNOL, KERR-MCGEE CORP, 79- *Mem:* Am Chem Soc; Am Inst Mining, Metall & Petrol Engrs; Am Inst Chem Engrs. *Res:* Coordination chemistry; solvent extraction; alkali metals, particularly cesium, rubidium and lithium; chemical process development; synthetic fuel from coal; solution mining; super-critical fluid extraction. *Mailing Add:* Kerr-McGee Corp Tech Ctr PO Box 25861 Oklahoma City OK 73125

DAVIS, ROBERT F(OSTER), b Greensboro, NC, Apr 12, 42; m 69. CERAMIC SCIENCE, CERAMIC ENGINEERING. *Educ:* NC State Univ, BS, 64; Pa State Univ, MS, 66; Univ Calif, Berkeley, PhD(ceramic eng), 70. *Prof Exp:* Res asst mat res, Lawrence Radiation Lab, 67-70; glass scientist, Res Ctr, Corning Glass Works, 70-72; PROF MAT ENG & ENG RES, NC STATE UNIV, 72- *Mem:* Am Ceramic Soc; Sigma Xi; Mat Res Soc. *Res:* Diffusion and high temperature deformation of ceramic materials; crystallization in glasses; growth of high temperature ceramic single crystals. *Mailing Add:* Dept of Mat Eng 109 Page Hall NC State Univ Raleigh NC 27650

DAVIS, ROBERT FOSTER, JR, b Crowell, Tex, Apr 24, 37. PLANT PHYSIOLOGY. *Educ:* North Tex State Univ, BA, 62, MA, 64; Wash State Univ, PhD(bot), 68. *Prof Exp:* Asst bot, zool & physiol, North Tex State Univ, 60-64; asst, Wash State Univ, 64-66; res asst plant physiol, 66-68; NIH trainee, Neurophysiol, Col Physicians & Surgeons, Columbia Univ, 68-69; asst prof, 69-74, ASSOC PROF BOT, RUTGERS UNIV, 74-, CHMN DEPT, 78- *Mem:* AAAS; Am Soc Plant Physiol. *Res:* Ion transport; electrophysiology; water relations; biophysics of flux processes. *Mailing Add:* Dept Bot Rutgers Univ Newark NJ 07102

DAVIS, ROBERT GENE, b Doddsville, Miss, Mar 2, 32; m 54; c 4. PLANT PATHOLOGY. *Educ:* Miss State Univ, BS, 53, MS, 68; La State Univ, Baton Rouge, PhD(plant path), 70. *Prof Exp:* Farm mgr, 57-65; fel plant path, Tex A&M Univ, 70-71; plant pathologist, Miss Agr & Forestry Exp Sta, 71-82; PVT PLANT RES & CONSULT, PLANT SERV, 82- *Mem:* Am Phytopath Soc. *Res:* General plant pathology and plant research; plant growth and protection products. *Mailing Add:* Plant Services PO Box 359 Avon MS 38723

DAVIS, ROBERT HARRY, b Wilkes Barre, Pa, July 16, 27; m 54; c 2. ENDOCRINOLOGY. *Educ:* Kings Col, BS, 50; Rutgers Univ, PhD(endocrinol), 58. *Prof Exp:* Med technician, Wilkes Barre Gen Hosp, 50-51; biologist, Warner-Chilcott Labs, 51-55; asst zool, Rutgers Univ, 55-56; sect head, Wm S Merrell Co, 58-60; sr physiologist, Neuroendocrine Res Unit, Willow Brook State Hosp, Staten Island, NY, 60-63; assoc prof endocrinol, Villanova Univ, 63-66; chief reprod endocrinol, Thomas M Fitzgerald Mercy Hosp, Darby, Pa, 66-69; assoc prof obstet & gynec, physiol & biophys, Hahnemann Med Col, 69-75; PROF PHYSIOL SCI, PA COL PODIATRIC MED, 75- *Concurrent Pos:* Sr reprod teratologist, Merck Inst Therapeut Res, Pa, 66. *Mem:* Am Soc Cytol; Soc Exp Biol & Med; Endocrine Soc; Soc Study Reprod; Am Physiol Soc. *Res:* Nutrition and endocrines; anti-inflammation; physiology of reproduction; endocrinology of mental retardation and pineal gland; peritoneal fluid cytology; teratology. *Mailing Add:* Pa Col Podiatric Med 8th & Race Sts Philadelphia PA 19107

DAVIS, ROBERT HOUSER, b Long Island, NY, Mar 20, 26; m 56. NUCLEAR PHYSICS. *Educ:* Univ Nebr, BS, 49; Univ Wis, MS, 50, PhD(physics), 55. *Prof Exp:* Res assoc nuclear physics, Rice Inst, 55-57; from asst prof to assoc prof physics, 57-64, PROF PHYSICS, FLA STATE UNIV, 64- *Mem:* Am Phys Soc. *Res:* Experimental nuclear physics; high vacuum technology; thin film physics. *Mailing Add:* Dept of Physics Fla State Univ Tallahassee FL 32306

DAVIS, ROBERT IRVING, b Keene, NH, July 1, 22; m 49; c 3. ECONOMIC GEOLOGY, MINING GEOLOGY. *Educ:* Univ NH, BS, 47; Univ Mich, MS, 49, PhD(geol), 54. *Prof Exp:* Geologist, Santa Maria de Oro Mining Co, 49-50 & Penoles Mining Co, 53-58; asst prof geol, St Louis Univ, 59-61; geologist, Am Metal Climax, Inc, 61-68, pres, Amax Explor Inc, 68-73, consult, 73-75; STATE GEOLOGIST, NH, 79- *Concurrent Pos:* Adj prof geol, Univ NH, 75- *Mem:* Geol Soc Am; Soc Econ Geologists; Am Inst Mining, Metall & Petrol Engrs; Mining & Metall Soc Am. *Res:* Geology and economic evaluation of metalliferous mineral deposits. *Mailing Add:* 112 Cutts Rd Durham NH 03824

DAVIS, ROBERT JAMES, b Omaha, Nebr, Oct 26, 29; m 53; c 4. ASTROPHYSICS. *Educ:* Harvard Univ, AB, 51, AM, 56, PhD(astron), 60. *Prof Exp:* ASTROPHYSICIST, SMITHSONIAN ASTROPHYS OBSERV, 56- *Mem:* Am Astron Soc; Int Astron Union. *Res:* Space, television, extragalactic and stellar astronomy; machine-readable astronomical data files. *Mailing Add:* Ctr for Astrophys 60 Garden St Cambridge MA 02138

DAVIS, ROBERT JAQUETTE, JR, soil microbiology, see previous edition

DAVIS, ROBERT LANE, b Henderson, Ky, Oct 23, 36; m 57; c 3. ENGINEERING MECHANICS. *Educ:* Univ Evansville, BS, 58; Univ Md, MS, 62, PhD(mech eng), 65. *Prof Exp:* Staff engr, Naval Ord Lab, 58-62; instr eng, Univ Md, 62-65; PROF ENG MECH, UNIV MO-ROLLA, 65-, ASST DEAN, DEPT ENG, 78- *Concurrent Pos:* Ford Found fel, 63-64; consult, Pressure Sci Inc, 64-66, Nooter Corp, 67-74, D K Eng Assoc, 69-76. *Mem:* Sigma Xi; Am Soc Mech Engrs. *Res:* Materials processing; plasticity; finite element techniques; high pressure mechanics. *Mailing Add:* 101 Eng Res Lab Univ of Mo Rolla MO 65401

DAVIS, ROBERT LLOYD, b New York, NY, May 23, 19; m 49; c 1. MATHEMATICS. *Educ:* Univ Chicago, BS, 49, MS, 51; Univ Mich, PhD(math), 57. *Prof Exp:* Res asst math for social sci, Univ Mich, 51-54, instr math, 54-56; asst prof, Univ Va, 56-59; NSF sci fac fel, Stanford Univ, 59-60; from asst prof to assoc prof, 60-70, PROF MATH, UNIV NC, CHAPEL HILL, 70- *Mem:* Am Math Soc; Math Asn Am. *Res:* Algebra and combinatorial theory; incidence and matrix algebras; theory of relations or graphs; representations. *Mailing Add:* Dept of Math Univ of NC Chapel Hill NC 27514

DAVIS, ROBERT PAUL, b Malden, Mass, July 3, 26; m 53; c 2. BIOCHEMISTRY, MEDICINE. *Educ:* Harvard Univ, AB, 47, MD, 51; Am Bd Internal Med, dipl, 58; Am Bd Internal Med, dipl nephrology, 76. *Hon Degrees:* AM, Brown Univ, 55. *Prof Exp:* Asst protein chem, Univ Lab Phys Chem, Harvard Med Sch, 48-51; med house officer, Peter Bent Brigham Hosp, 51-52, asst med, 52-55, sr asst res physician, 55-56, chief res physician, 56-57; asst prof med, Sch Med, Univ NC, 57-59; from asst prof to assoc prof, Albert Einstein Col Med, 59-67; PROF MED SCI, BROWN UNIV, 67- *Concurrent Pos:* Soc of Fels jr fel phys chem & kinetics, Harvard Univ, 52-55, asst, 55-56, fel med, 56-57; Willard O Thompson Mem traveling scholar, Am Col Physicians, 65; asst vis physician, Bronx Munic Hosp Ctr, 59-65, assoc vis physician, 66-67; career scientist, Health Res Coun City New York, 62-67; physician in chief, Miriam Hosp, 67-74, dir renal & metab dis, 74-78, trustee, Interhosp Organ Bank, 69, treas, 70- *Mem:* Fel AAAS; Am Col Physicians; Am Soc Pediat Nephrology; Am Soc Artificial Internal Organs; Am Soc Nephrology. *Res:* Enzyme kinetics; intermediary metabolism; renal physiology. *Mailing Add:* Div of Biol & Med Sci Brown Univ Providence RI 02906

DAVIS, ROBERT WILSON, b Grinnell, Iowa, Oct 20, 10; m 38; c 4. ANATOMY, PATHOLOGY. *Educ:* Colo State Univ, DVM, 35, MS, 52. *Prof Exp:* Jr vet, US Bur Animal Indust, 35-36; asst to dep state vet, Mont, 35-37; asst prof anat & med, 37-40, assoc prof anat, 41-42, prof, 46-70, head dept, 48-70, CENTENNIAL PROF ANAT, COLO STATE UNIV, 70- *Concurrent Pos:* Prof oral biol, Sch Dent, Univ Colo, 74-75; vis prof anat, Univ Ill, Urbana-Champaign, 75-78; vis prof anat, Purdue Univ, WLafayette, 78; prof anat, Sch Vet Med, Tufts Univ, Boston, 79-81. *Honors & Awards:* Harris T Guard Distinguished Serv Award, 60; Top Prof Award, 62. *Mem:* Am Asn Anatomists; Am Vet Med Asn; Am Asn Vet Anatomists (pres, 54); World Asn Vet Anatomists; Nat Asn Dent Res. *Res:* Anatomy, physiology and pathology dealing with domestic and big game animals; antler and bone growth in deer, emphasis connective and mineralized tissues. *Mailing Add:* Dept of Anat Colo State Univ Ft Collins CO 80521

DAVIS, ROBIN EDEN PIERRE, b Twickenham, Eng, Feb 19, 34; m 61; c 3. HIGH ENERGY PHYSICS. *Educ:* Oxford Univ, BA, 55, MA, 59, DPhil(nuclear physics), 62. *Prof Exp:* Res assoc, Enrico Fermi Inst, Univ Chicago, 62-64; res assoc, Northwestern Univ, 64-66, asst prof, 66-70; assoc prof, 70-76, PROF PHYSICS, UNIV KANS, 76-, PROF ASTRON, 80- *Mem:* Am Phys Soc. *Res:* Experimental high energy physics. *Mailing Add:* Dept of Physics & Astron Univ of Kans Lawrence KS 66044

DAVIS, ROGER (EDWARD), b Milwaukee, Wis, Aug 7, 29; m 58; c 3. BEHAVIORAL BIOLOGY. *Educ:* Univ Mich, BSc & MSc, 54; Univ Wis, PhD(zool), 61. *Prof Exp:* Res assoc, Dept Fisheries, 61-63, from asst res zoologist to assoc res zoologist, 63-69, assoc prof psychol, 69-73, PROF PSYCHOL, UNIV MICH, ANN ARBOR, 74-, RES PSYCHOLOGIST, MENT HEALTH RES INST, 70- *Concurrent Pos:* USPHS training fel, 64-, NIMH res develop award, 68. *Mem:* AAAS; Animal Behav Soc; Am Soc Zoologists. *Res:* Animal behavior; learning, memory physiology; fish brain behavior. *Mailing Add:* Ment Health Res Inst Univ of Mich Ann Arbor MI 48104

DAVIS, RONALD STUART, b Lethbridge, Alta, Aug 3, 41. REACTOR PHYSICS, NUCLEAR PHYSICS. *Educ:* Univ Alta, BS, 63; Univ BC, MS, 65, PhD(physics), 68. *Prof Exp:* Nat Res Coun Can fel theoret physics, Oxford Univ, 68-70; APPL MATHEMATICIAN NUCLEAR REACTORS, CHALK RIVER NUCLEAR LAB, ATOMIC ENERGY CAN LTD, 70- *Res:* Complex energy and angular momenta in nuclear reactions; nuclear three-body problem, especially formalism; applications in particle physics; economics and control of nuclear power reactors; risk of nuclear weapons proliferation. *Mailing Add:* Sta 68 Chalk River Nuclear Labs Chalk River Can

DAVIS, RONALD WAYNE, b Maroa, Ill, July 17, 41; m 69. MOLECULAR GENETICS, ELECTRON MICROSCOPY. *Educ:* Eastern Ill Univ, BS, 64; Calif Inst Technol, PhD(chem), 70. *Prof Exp:* Fel biol, Harvard Univ, 70-72; asst prof, 72-76, ASSOC PROF BIOCHEM, STANFORD UNIV, 76- *Mem:* Am Soc Biol Chemists. *Res:* Higher cell gene isolation and cloning in heterologous cells; transcription and the regulation of gene expression; evolution of DNA sequences; development of electron microscopic and heteroduplex mapping techniques. *Mailing Add:* Dept of Biochem Stanford Univ Sch of Med Stanford CA 94305

DAVIS, ROWLAND HALLOWELL, b Boston, Mass, Dec 8, 33; m. BIOCHEMISTRY, MICROBIOLOGY. *Educ:* Harvard Univ, AB, 54, PhD(biol), 58. *Prof Exp:* Resident tutor, Dunster House, Harvard Univ, 55; NSF res fel biol, Calif Inst Technol, 58-60; from asst prof to prof bot, Univ Mich, Ann Arbor, 60-75; chmn dept, 77-79, PROF MOLECULAR BIOL & BIOCHEM, UNIV CALIF, IRVINE, 75- *Concurrent Pos:* Res grants, 67-75; mem genetic biol panel, NSF, 67-70; assoc ed, Genetics, 71-75, Microbiol Rev, 78- & Molecular Cellular Biol, 81-; mem genetics study sect, NIH, 73-77. *Mem:* Am Soc Biol Chemists; AAAS; Genetics Soc Am; Am Soc Microbiol. *Res:* Biochemical genetics; genetics and compartmentation of metabolic pathways of Neurospora crassa, with emphasis on arginine synthesis; heterokaryosis in Neurospora crassa. *Mailing Add:* Dept of Molecular Biol & Biochem Univ of Calif Irvine CA 92664

DAVIS, RUSS E, b San Francisco, Calif, Mar 8, 41. PHYSICAL OCEANOGRAPHY. *Educ:* Univ Calif, Berkeley, BS, 63; Stanford Univ, PhD(chem eng), 67. *Prof Exp:* Asst res geophysicist, Inst Geophys & Planetary Physics, 67-68, asst prof, 68-74, assoc prof, 74-78, PROF OCEANOG, UNIV CALIF, SAN DIEGO, 78- *Res:* Fluid dynamics, including surface waves; motion in rotating and stratified fluids; statistical analysis of dynamical systems. *Mailing Add:* Scripps Inst Oceanog Univ Calif Box 109 La Jolla CA 92037

DAVIS, RUSSELL PRICE, b Hanford, Calif, Aug 24, 28; m 51; c 2. ZOOLOGY. *Educ:* Univ Redlands, BA, 50; Long Beach State Col, MA, 56; Univ Ariz, PhD(zool), 63. *Prof Exp:* Teacher biol, Santa Ana Col, 56-59; asst prof, Southern Ore Col, 63-64; ASSOC PROF BIOL, UNIV ARIZ, 64- *Mem:* Am Soc Mammal. *Res:* Mammalogy, especially the natural history of bats. *Mailing Add:* Dept of Gen Biol Univ of Ariz Tucson AZ 85721

DAVIS, RUTH MARGARET, b Sharpsville, Pa, Oct 19, 28; m 55. COMPUTER SCIENCES. *Educ:* Am Univ, BA, 50; Univ Md, MA, 52, PhD(math), 55. *Hon Degrees:* DEng, Carnegie-Mellon Univ, 79. *Prof Exp:* Mathematician, US Bur Standards, 50; res assoc inst fluid dynamics & appl math, Univ Md, 52-55; mathematician, David Taylor Model Basin, 55-58, head opers res div, 57-61; staff asst off of spec asst intel & reconnaissance, Off Dir Defense Res & Eng, US Dept Defense, 61-67; assoc dir res & develop, Nat Libr Med, 67-68, dir, Lister Hill Nat Ctr Biomed Commun, 68-70; dir ctr comput sci & technol, Nat Bur Standards, Dept Com, 70-72, dir Inst Comput Sci & Technol, 72-77; dep under secy defense for res & eng, US Dept Defense, 77-79; asst secy of energy, Dept of Energy, 79-81; PRES, PYMATUNING GROUP, 81- *Concurrent Pos:* Lectr, Univ Md, 55-56 & Am Univ, 57-58; consult, Off Naval Res, 57-58; mem, Nat Acad Pub Admin, 74-; mem, Md Govt Sci Adv Comt, 74-77, vchairperson, 75-76; mem nat adv coun, Elec Power Res Inst, 74-78, vchmn, 75-76; adj prof eng, Univ Pittsburg, 81-; mem bd dirs, United Telecommun Inc, Com Credit Corp & Consol Edison, 81-; mem bd overseers, Dartmouth Sch Eng, Harvard Math Dept, Univ Pa Sch Eng & Appl Sci, 81- *Honors & Awards:* Gold Medal for Distinguished Achievement in Fed Serv, Dept Com, 72; Systs Prof of the Year, Asn Systs Mgt, 72; Rockefeller Pub Serv Award for Prof Accomplishment & Leadership, Trustees of Princeton Univ, 73. *Mem:* Nat Acad Eng; AAAS; Coun Libr Resources; Am Math Soc; Math Asn Am. *Res:* Energy development; automation; electronics; computers. *Mailing Add:* Dept of Defense Pentagon Washington DC 20301

DAVIS, SAMUEL HENRY, JR, b Houston, Tex, Dec 19, 30; m 67; c 3. CHEMICAL ENGINEERING, APPLIED MATHEMATICS. *Educ:* Rice Inst, BA, 52, BS, 53; Mass Inst Technol, ScD(chem eng), 57. *Prof Exp:* Engr chem eng, Gen Elec Co, 56-57; PROF CHEM ENG & MATH SCI, RICE UNIV, 57-, CHMN CHEM ENG, 77- *Mem:* Am Inst Chem Engrs. *Res:* Analysis of chemical systems used in atmospheric control in spacecraft. *Mailing Add:* Dept of Chem Eng Rice Univ Houston TX 77001

DAVIS, SARAH FREDERICKA, b Pine Level, Ala, Feb 28, 25; m 56; c 3. PEDIATRICS. *Educ:* Huntingdon Col, AB, 45; Woman's Med Col, Pa, MD, 50; Am Bd Pediat, dipl. *Prof Exp:* Intern, Jefferson-Hillman Hosp, Birmingham, Ala, 50-51, resident pediat, 51-53; from instr to assoc prof, 53-59, PROF PEDIAT, SCH MED, UNIV ALA, BIRMINGHAM, 59- *Mem:* Am Acad Pediat. *Res:* Diseases of the chest and tuberculosis in children. *Mailing Add:* Dept Pediat Sch Med Univ Ala Birmingham AL 35233

DAVIS, SELBY BRINKER, b Washington, DC, Dec 26, 14; m 48; c 3. RESEARCH ADMINISTRATION. *Educ:* George Wash Univ, BS, 37; Harvard Univ, AM, 41, PhD(org chem), 42. *Prof Exp:* Res chemist, Socony-Vacuum Oil Co, 37-39; res fel, Harvard Univ, 42-43; group leader, Chemother Div, Am Cyanamid Co, 43-56, head, Med Chem Dept, Lederle Labs, 56-71, head, Chem Res Dept, Cent Nervous Syst Res Sect, 71-74, dir, Cardiovascular-Renal Res Sect, 74-76, dir Clin Res Info Serv, 76-80; RETIRED. *Mem:* AAAS; Am Chem Soc; NY Acad Sci; Brit Chem Soc. *Res:* Stereochemistry; structure of natural products; chemotherapeutic agents. *Mailing Add:* 56 Birch Lane Greenwich CT 06830

DAVIS, SHERMAN GILBERT, chemistry, food technology, see previous edition

DAVIS, SPENCER HARWOOD, JR, b Philadelphia, Pa, Apr 2, 16; m 45. PLANT PATHOLOGY. *Educ:* Westminster Col, Pa, BS, 37; Univ Pa, PhD(plant path), 44. *Prof Exp:* Asst instr, Univ Pa, 42-43; res assoc, Off Sci Res & Develop, 43-45; asst prof, Univ Del, 46-48; assoc prof, 48-54, extension specialist, 54-80, EMER PROF, RUTGERS UNIV, 80- *Honors & Awards:* Award of Merit, Int Soc Arboriculture, 68. *Mem:* Am Phytopath Soc; Int Soc Arboriculture (vpres, 63, pres, 64); Am Soc Consult Arborists (exec dir, 70-). *Res:* Diseases of ornamentals. *Mailing Add:* Dept of Plant Path Rutgers Univ New Brunswick NJ 08903

DAVIS, STANLEY GANNAWAY, b Hancock Co, Ind, Aug 18, 22. PHYSICAL CHEMISTRY. *Educ:* Purdue Univ, BS, 42; Univ Chicago, PhD(chem), 55. *Prof Exp:* Jr chemist & asst radiation chem, Metall Lab, Univ Chicago, 43-44; jr chemist anal chem, Clinton Eng Works, Tenn Eastman Corp, 45-46; asst res chemist high temperature chem, Inst Eng Res, Univ Calif, 55-57; asst prof chem, 57-63, ASSOC PROF CHEM, RUTGERS UNIV, 63- *Res:* Chemical physics; high-temperature thermodynamics. *Mailing Add:* Dept of Chem Rutgers Univ Camden NJ 08102

DAVIS, STANLEY NELSON, b Rio de Janeiro, Brazil, Aug 6, 24; US citizen; m 49; c 6. HYDROGEOLOGY. *Educ:* Univ Nev, BS, 49; Univ Kans, MS, 51; Yale Univ, PhD(geol), 55. *Prof Exp:* Instr geol, Univ Rochester, 53-54; from asst prof to prof, Stanford Univ, 54-67; prof, Univ Mo-Columbia, 67-73, chmn dept, 70-72; prof, Ind Univ, 73-75; head dept, 75-79, PROF HYDROL & WATER RESOURCES, UNIV ARIZ, 75- *Concurrent Pos:* Vis prof, Univ Chile, 60-61 & Univ Hawaii, 66. *Mem:* AAAS; Geol Soc Am; Am Water Resources Asn; Am Geophys Union; assoc Soc Econ Paleont & Mineral. *Res:* Ground-water geology; isolation of hazardous waste, dating ground water, minor strains induced by ground-water movement and chemistry of ground water. *Mailing Add:* Dept of Hydrol & Water Resources Univ of Ariz Tucson AZ 85721

DAVIS, STARKEY D, b Atlanta, Tex, Jan 29, 31. PEDIATRICS, INFECTIOUS DISEASES. *Educ:* Baylor Univ, BA, 53, MD, 57. *Prof Exp:* Rotating intern, Confederate Mem Med Ctr, Shreveport, La, 57-58; instr prev med, Emory Univ, 58-60; resident pediat, Baylor Univ, 60-62; asst, Sch Med, Univ Wash, 62-64, from instr to prof, 64-75; PROF PEDIAT & MICROBIOL, MED COL WIS, 75-; DIR INFECTIOUS DIS, MILWAUKEE CHILDREN'S HOSP, 75- *Concurrent Pos:* Res fel pediat, Univ Wash, 62-63, spec res fel, 64-65. *Mem:* Am Asn Immunol; Am Soc Microbiol; Infectious Dis Soc Am. *Mailing Add:* Milwaukee Children's Hosp 1700 W Wisconsin PO Box 1997 Milwaukee WI 53201

DAVIS, STEPHEN H(OWARD), b New York, NY, Sept 7, 39; m 66. MATHEMATICS, FLUID DYNAMICS. *Educ:* Rensselaer Polytech Inst, BEE, 60, MS, 62, PhD(math), 64. *Prof Exp:* Teaching asst math, Rensselaer Polytech Inst, 60-61; mathematician, Rand Corp, 64-66; lectr math, Imp Col London, 66-68; from asst prof to prof mech, Johns Hopkins Univ, 68-78; PROF, DEPT ENG SCI & APPL MATH, NORTHWESTERN UNIV, 78- *Concurrent Pos:* Lectr, Univ Calif, Los Angeles, 65 & exten, Univ Southern Calif, 66; asst ed, J Fluid Mech, 69-75, assoc ed, 75-; vis prof, Dept Math, Monash Univ, Melbourne, Australia, 73; vis prof, Dept Chem Eng, Univ Ariz, 77; mem-at-large, US Nat Comt Theoretical & Appl Mech, 78-80. *Mem:* Fel Am Phys Soc; Soc Indust & Appl Mech. *Res:* Theory and applications of hydrodynamic stability, particularly related to unsteady flow; interfacial phenomena, biomechanics. *Mailing Add:* Dept of Eng Sci & Appl Math Northwestern Univ Evanston IL 60201

DAVIS, STEPHEN S(MITH), b Philadelphia, Pa, Oct 24, 10; m 38; c 1. MECHANICAL ENGINEERING. *Educ:* Howard Univ, BSME, 36; Harvard Univ, MSME, 47. *Prof Exp:* Head, Dept Mech Eng, 62-64, dean, Sch Eng & Archit, 64-70, PROF MECH ENG, HOWARD UNIV, 38- *Concurrent Pos:* Asst mech engr, Nat Bur Standards, 43-46; consult engr, Naval Ord Lab, 53-62; vchmn, Bd Dirs, DC Redevelop Land Agency, 68- *Mem:* AAAS; Am Soc Eng Educ; Am Soc Mech Engrs; Nat Soc Prof Engrs. *Res:* Engineering education. *Mailing Add:* 2847 University Terrace NW Washington DC 20016

DAVIS, STEVEN LEWIS, b Pocatello, Idaho, Sept 26, 41; m 63; c 3. ENDOCRINOLOGY. *Educ:* Univ Idaho, BS, 64, MS, 66; Univ Ill, PhD(animal sci), 69. *Prof Exp:* NIH fel, Univ Mich, 69-70; asst prof path, M S Hershey Med Ctr, Pa State Univ, 70-73; ASSOC PROF ANIMAL SCI, UNIV IDAHO, 73- *Concurrent Pos:* NIH res grant, 72-77; consult, Merck, Sharp & Dohme Inst, 75. *Mem:* Am Soc Animal Sci; Endocrine Soc. *Res:* The regulation of prolactin, growth hormone and thyrotropin secretion. *Mailing Add:* Dept of Animal Industs Univ of Idaho Moscow ID 83843

DAVIS, STUART GEORGE, b Lethbridge, Alta, June 15, 17; m 40; c 1. PHYSICAL CHEMISTRY. *Educ:* Univ Alta, BSc, 39, MSc, 40; McGill Univ, PhD(chem), 42. *Prof Exp:* Lectr, 42-43, asst prof, 45-51, ASSOC PROF CHEM, UNIV ALTA, 51- *Honors & Awards:* Prize, Asn Prof Eng, 39; Stiernotte Prize, 39. *Mem:* Am Chem Soc; fel Chem Inst Can. *Res:* Adsorption. *Mailing Add:* Dept of Chem Univ of Alta Edmonton AB T6G 2E8 Can

DAVIS, SUMNER P, b Burbank, Calif. PHYSICS. *Educ:* Univ Calif, Los Angeles, AB, 47; Univ Ill, AM, 48; Univ Calif, Berkeley, PhD(physics), 52. *Prof Exp:* Instr physics, Mass Inst Technol, 52-55, res staff mem, 55-59; lectr, 59-60, from asst prof to assoc prof, 60-67, PROF PHYSICS, UNIV CALIF, BERKELEY, 67- *Concurrent Pos:* NATO sr fel sci, 67-68. *Mem:* Am Phys Soc; Optical Soc Am. *Res:* Optical spectroscopy; molecular spectra; atomic energy level analysis; hyperfine structure in atomic spectra. *Mailing Add:* Dept of Physics Univ of Calif Berkeley CA 94720

DAVIS, TERRY CHAFFIN, b Pearisburg, Va, Apr 12, 32; m 59. FOREST PATHOLOGY. *Educ:* Va Polytech Inst, BS, 59, MS, 61; WVa Univ, PhD(plant path), 65. *Prof Exp:* Asst prof forestry & forest path, 65-70, asst prof bot & plant path, 70-75, ASST PROF BOT & MICROBIOL, AUBURN UNIV, 75- *Mem:* Am Phytopath Soc; Mycol Soc Am. *Res:* Microorganisms which cause tree diseases. *Mailing Add:* Dept Bot & Microbiol Auburn Univ Auburn AL 36830

DAVIS, THOMAS, medicine, physiology, see previous edition

DAVIS, THOMAS ARTHUR, b Columbia, SC, Aug 12, 39; m 62; c 3. CHEMICAL ENGINEERING, BIOMEDICAL ENGINEERING. *Educ:* Univ SC, BS, 61, PhD(eng sci), 67. *Prof Exp:* Jr chem engr, Textile Chem Pilot Plant, Deering Milliken Res Corp, 63-64; asst chem eng, Univ SC, 64-67; res chem engr, Southern Res Inst, 67-68, head, Biomed Eng Sect, 77-78; SR STAFF ENGR, CORP RES LAB, EXXON RES & ENG CO, 78- *Concurrent Pos:* Ann guest lectr, Ctr Prof Advan, 72- *Mem:* Am Inst Chem Engrs; Am Soc Artificial Internal Organs. *Res:* Membrane processes research, particularly electrodialysis for desalination of brackish water, chemical processing and water pollution control; electro-regeneration of ion-exchange resins; development of artificial kidney devices, activated carbon, liquid membrane systems. *Mailing Add:* Exxon Res & Eng Co Corp Res Lab PO Box 45 Linden NJ 07036

DAVIS, THOMAS AUSTIN, b Belgian Congo, May 31, 34; US citizen; m 59; c 2. MATHEMATICS. *Educ:* Denison Univ, AB, 56; Univ Mich, MS, 57; Cambridge Univ, PhD(math), 63. *Prof Exp:* Asst prof math, DePauw Univ, 63-69, assoc prof, asst dean univ & dir grad studies, 69-73; PROF MATH & DEAN UNIV, UNIV PUGET SOUND, 73- *Concurrent Pos:* Am Coun Educ acad admin intern, Princeton Univ, 71-72. *Mem:* Math Asn Am. *Res:* Banach algebras and Fourier analysis. *Mailing Add:* Dept Math Univ Puget Sound Tacoma WA 98416

DAVIS, THOMAS HAYDN, b Philadelphia, Pa, Sept 4, 39; m 71; c 3. PHYSICS. *Educ:* Lehigh Univ, BS, 61; Carnegie-Mellon Univ, MS, 66, PhD(physics), 71. *Prof Exp:* Assoc engr nuclear reactor physics, Westinghouse Bettis Atomic Power Lab, 61-65; PROG MGR ELECTRONICS, MICROWAVES & OPTICS, MAJOR APPLIANCE LAB, GEN ELEC CO, 71-, MGR ENG PHYSICS LAB, 79- *Concurrent Pos:* Adj asst prof, Dept Physics, Univ Louisville, 73-78. *Mem:* Am Phys Soc. *Mailing Add:* Gen Elec Co AP 35-1101 Louisville KY 40225

DAVIS, THOMAS MOONEY, b Claysville, Pa, Mar 12, 34; m 56; c 2. GEOPHYSICS, GEODESY. *Educ:* Pa State Univ, BS, 55, PhD(geophys), 74. *Prof Exp:* Field party chief, Airborne Geomagnetic Surv, 55-66, head, Earth Physics Br, 68-70, HEAD MATH MODELING PROJ, US NAVAL OCEANOG OFF, 70- *Concurrent Pos:* Vis prof, Univ SC, 70. *Honors & Awards:* Meritorious Civilian Serv Award, US Naval Oceanog Off, 74, Navoceano Award, 75; Distinguished Civilian Serv Award, Secy Navy, 76, Secy Defense, 77. *Mem:* Am Geophys Union; Soc Explor Geophysicists. *Res:* Potential fields; mathematical methods of physical geodesy; survey design; Fourier analysis; numerical models of oceanographic data. *Mailing Add:* US Naval Oceanog Off NSTL Sta Bay St Louis MS 39522

DAVIS, THOMAS NEIL, b Greeley, Colo, Feb 1, 32; m 51; c 3. GEOPHYSICS. *Educ:* Univ Alaska, BS, 55, PhD(geophys), 61; Calif Inst Technol, MS, 57. *Prof Exp:* Assoc prof geophys, Geophys Inst, Univ Alaska, 61-64; aerospace technologist, Goddard Space Flight Ctr, NASA, 64-65; asst dir, Geophys Inst, 65-70, actg dir, Geophys Inst & Div Geosci, 76-77, PROF GEOPHYS, GEOPHYS INST, UNIV ALASKA, 65- *Concurrent Pos:* Nat Acad Sci-Nat Res Coun resident res assoc, Goddard Space Flight Ctr, 62-64. *Mem:* AAAS; Int Asn Geomagnetism & Aeronomy; Union. *Res:* Aurora and geomagnetism; low-light-leveling imaging of auroras; rocket and satellite instrumentation; seismology. *Mailing Add:* Geophys Inst Univ of Alaska Fairbanks AK 99701

DAVIS, THOMAS PEARSE, b Kansas City, Mo, May 21, 26; m 74; c 6. RADIATION PHYSICS, OPTICAL PHYSICS. *Educ:* Purdue Univ, BS, 50; Univ Rochester, MS, 55, PhD(biophys), 59. *Prof Exp:* Res asst optics & biophys, Atomic Energy Proj, Univ Rochester, 50-59; from asst prof to assoc prof radiol physics & biophys, Dept Radiation Biol & Biophys, Univ Rochester, 59-67; sr scientist biophys & optics, E H Plesset Assocs, 67-70, sr sci specialist physics & optics, Santa Barbara Div, 70-74, CHIEF SCIENTIST, EG&G, INC, SANTA BARBARA OPERS, 74- *Mem:* Sigma Xi. *Res:* Studies of radiation sensors and data analysis; electro-optics research and laser effects studies. *Mailing Add:* EG&G Inc Santa Barbara Opers PO Box 98 Goleta CA 93116

DAVIS, THOMAS WILDERS, b Nyack, NY, Aug 1, 05; m 42; c 3. PHYSICAL CHEMISTRY. *Educ:* NY Univ, BS, 25, MS, 26, PhD(chem), 28. *Prof Exp:* Res chemist, Combustion Utilities Corp, NJ, 28-29; from instr to prof chem, 29-73, chmn dept, 55-64, EMER PROF CHEM, NY UNIV, 73- *Concurrent Pos:* Instr, Rand Sch Social Sci, 33; res assoc, Metall Lab, Univ Chicago, 42; sr chemist, Clinton Lab, Tenn, 46-47; res chemist, Brookhaven Nat Lab, 48, 50, US Naval Ord Test Sta, 52 & Oak Ridge Nat Lab, 54; res chemist, Argonne Nat Lab, 55, 56, res assoc, 56; vis prof & mem senate, Univ Leeds, 64-65. *Mem:* Am Chem Soc; fel Am Inst Chemists; Radiation Res Soc; Fedn Am Sci. *Res:* Reaction kinetics and mechanisms of reaction; photochemistry and radiation chemistry; thermodynamics; uses of radioactive tracers. *Mailing Add:* Relief Rte 1 Box 190 Green Mountain NC 28740

DAVIS, VERNAM TERRELL, b Long Branch, NJ, July 14, 11; m 36; c 3. PSYCHIATRY. *Educ:* Wash Univ, MD, 36. *Prof Exp:* Asst surgeon drug addiction, USPHS Hosp, Ft Worth, Tex, 39-41, sr asst surgeon clin psychiat, 41-43, exec officer, 43-44; clin dir gen hosp admin, USPHS, Staten Island, NY, 44-45; chief psychiat & neurol, USPHS Hosp, Ellis Island, 45-49; med dir psychiat & Neurol, USPHS, Staten Island, 49-54; clin assoc prof neuropsychiat & asst dir, Psychiat Inst, Univ Wis, 54-56; prof psychiat, Col Med & Dent NJ, Newark, 59-72; DIR PSYCHIAT, WILMINGTON MED CTR, 72- *Concurrent Pos:* Chief med officer, Fed Penitentiary, Lewisburg, Pa, 44; consult, US Immigration Serv, 45-54; dir, Staten Island Ment Health Clin, 53-54; asst dir div ment health, State Dept Pub Welfare, Wis, 54-56; clin dir, Wis Diag Ctr, Madison, 54-56; dir ment health & hosps, NJ, 56-69; WHO fel, 62; clin prof, Med Sch, Rutgers Univ, 68; ment health prog consult, Region II & med dir, NIMH, 69-72; clin prof psychiat & human behav, Jefferson Med Col, 72-76, hon clin prof, 76- *Mem:* Life fel Am Psychiat Asn; Asn Mil Surg US; Am Pub Health Asn; Nat Asn State Ment Health Prog Dirs (pres, 63-65); fel Am Col Psychiat. *Res:* Psychotherapy; psychiatric training; relation of injury to psychiatric illness; relation of psychiatry to employment; psychoanalysis; mental health program administration; forensic psychiatry; psychiatric emergency treatment. *Mailing Add:* Wilmington Med Ctr 501 W 14th Wilmington DE 19801

DAVIS, VIRGINIA EISCHEN, b Okarche, Okla, Nov 9, 25; m 47; c 2. PHARMACOLOGY, BIOCHEMISTRY. *Educ:* Okla State Univ, BS, 47, MS, 49; Rice Univ, PhD(biochem), 60. *Prof Exp:* Biochemist, Res Serv, Vet Admin Hosp, Houston, 49-57; res assoc biochem, Rice Univ, 60-61; res biochemist, Res Serv, 61-63, assoc dir metab res lab, 63-71, DIR NEUROCHEM & ADDICTION RES LAB, VET ADMIN HOSP, 71-; RES ASSOC PROF BIOCHEM & MED, BAYLOR COL MED, 69- *Concurrent Pos:* Res asst prof, Baylor Col Med, 65-69; lectr, Sch Pharm, Univ Houston, 67-69. *Mem:* AAAS; Am Soc Pharmacol & Exp Therapeut; Res Soc Alcoholism; Soc Neurosci; NY Acad Sci. *Res:* Biochemical mechanisms of drug action; neuroamine metabolism; alcoholism. *Mailing Add:* Neurochem & Addiction Res Lab Vet Admin Med Ctr Houston TX 77211

DAVIS, WALLACE, JR, b Pawtucket, RI, Dec 17, 18; m 42; c 3. CHEMISTRY. *Educ:* Brown Univ, ScB, 41; Univ Rochester, PhD(phys chem), 47. *Prof Exp:* Res chemist, Kellex Corp, Tenn, 47; res chemist, Oak Ridge Gaseous Diffusion Plant, 47-58, group leader, 58-72, SR STAFF MEM, OAK RIDGE NAT LAB, UNION CARBIDE CORP, 79- *Concurrent Pos:* Guest scientist, Atomic Energy Res Estab, Harwell, Eng, 65-66. *Mem:* Fel AAAS; fel Am Inst Chem; Am Chem Soc; Am Inst Chem Eng. *Res:* Photochemistry of gases; thermodynamic and phase properties of uranium-fluorine-fluorocarbon systems; isotope separation; gas-solid reaction kinetics; radiation chemistry; radiochemical reprocessing of nuclear fuels; thermodynamics of solvent extraction; foam separation; analysis of environmental impacts of nuclear energy. *Mailing Add:* Union Carbide Corp Oak Ridge Nat Lab Oak Ridge TN 37830

DAVIS, WALTER LEWIS, b Philadelphia, Pa, Sept 30, 42; m 67; c 2. CELL BIOLOGY. *Educ:* Abilene Christian Col, BS, 65; Baylor Univ, MS, 69, PhD(anat, physiol), 71. *Prof Exp:* Instr biol, Eastfield Col, 70-71; fel biochem, Med Sch, Univ Pa, 71-73; ASST PROF HISTOL, BAYLOR COL DENT, 73-, ASST DIR PATH, BAYLOR UNIV MED CTR, 75- *Concurrent Pos:* Consult path, Baylor Univ Med Ctr, 73-; adj prof biol, Southern Methodist Univ, 74- *Mem:* Sigma Xi; AAAS; Am Asn Anatomists; Am Soc Cell Biol; Electron Micros Soc Am. *Res:* The roles of cells and their organelles in the regulation of cellular and extracellular calcium homeostasis; events controlling mineralization phenomena in bones and teeth. *Mailing Add:* Dept of Microscopic Anat Baylor Col of Dent 800 Hall St Dallas TX 75226

DAVIS, WAYNE ALTON, b Ft Macleod, Alta, Nov 16, 31; m 59; c 3. COMPUTER SCIENCE. *Educ:* George Washington Univ, BSE, 60; Univ Ottawa, MSc, 63, PhD(elec eng), 67. *Prof Exp:* Sci officer, Defence Res Bd, Defence Res Telecommun Estab, 60-69; sci officer, Dept Commun, Commun Res Ctr, 69; assoc prof, 69-77, PROF COMPUT SCI, UNIV ALTA, 77- *Concurrent Pos:* Lectr, Univ Ottawa, 65-69; nat leader, Working Panel S-3, Subgroup S, Tech Coop Prog, 66-69; lectr, Carleton Univ, 67; mem reactor safety adv comt, Atomic Energy Control Bd, 67-69; vis scientist, Graphics Sect, Nat Res Coun Can, 75-76. *Mem:* Inst Elec & Electronics Engrs; Asn Comput Mach; Can Info Processing Soc (vpres, 77-78, pres, 78-79). *Res:* Digital image processing; detection of edges; registration; change detection; smoothing of classified images; texture edges; digital pattern recognition in image processing. *Mailing Add:* Dept of Comput Sci Univ of Alta Edmonton AB T6G 2E8 Can

DAVIS, WAYNE HARRY, b Morgantown, WVa, Dec 31, 30; m 58; c 3. MAMMALOGY. *Educ:* WVa Univ, AB, 53; Univ Ill, MS, 55, PhD(zool), 57. *Prof Exp:* Asst zool, Univ Ill, 53-54 & biol, 54-57; res fel, Univ Minn, 57-59; instr biol, Middlebury Col, 59-62; from asst prof to assoc prof, 62-70, prof zool, 70-80, PROF BIOL SCI, UNIV KY, 80- *Mem:* Fel AAAS; Am Soc Mammal. *Res:* Life history of bats; taxonomy of mammals; human ecology. *Mailing Add:* Sch of Biol Sci Univ of Ky Lexington KY 40506

DAVIS, WILBUR MARVIN, b Calumet City, Ill, Apr 13, 31; m 56; c 2. PHARMACOLOGY. *Educ:* Purdue Univ, BS, 52, MS, 53, PhD(pharmacol), 55. *Prof Exp:* From asst prof to prof pharmacol, Sch Pharm, Univ Okla, 55-63; assoc prof, 64-65, PROF PHARMACOL, SCH PHARM, UNIV MISS, 65-, CHMN DEPT, 68- *Honors & Awards:* Lalor Found Award, 58. *Mem:* Soc Toxicol; Am Soc Pharmacol & Exp Therapeut; Acad Pharmaceut Sci; Am Ornith Union; Soc Neurosci. *Res:* Neuropsychopharmacology; behavioral and CNS pharmacology; pharmacology and toxicology of dependence-producing drugs. *Mailing Add:* Dept Pharmacol Sch Pharm Univ Miss University MS 38677

DAVIS, WILFORD LAVERN, b Fairport, Mo, May 6, 30; m 54; c 2. RESEARCH ADMINISTRATION, APPLIED STATISTICS. *Educ:* Univ Mo, BS, 56; NC State Univ, MS, 58. *Prof Exp:* Asst statistician, NC State Col, 56-58; from assoc scientist to scientist, Westinghouse Elec Corp, 58-61; res statistician, Atlantic Richfield, 61-65; chief engr, 65-68, chief comput sci, 68-71, assoc dir systs, 71-73, DIR CORP SYSTS & DATA PROCESSING, OWENS-ILL, INC, 73- *Concurrent Pos:* Lectr, Villanova Univ, 62-65; instr, Univ Toledo, 66-68, adj assoc prof, 71-72. *Mem:* Am Statist Asn; Sigma Xi. *Res:* Mathematical applications; applied and theoretical mathematical statistics; computer application in research and business. *Mailing Add:* Corp Systs & Data Processing Owens-Ill Inc PO Box 1035 Toledo OH 43666

DAVIS, WILLIAM ARTHUR, b East St Louis, Ill, July 29, 47; m 68; c 2. ELECTROMAGNETICS, RADIO ENGINEERING. *Educ:* Univ Ill, BS, 69, MS, 70, PhD(elec eng), 74. *Prof Exp:* Instr electromagnetic radio, Univ Ill, 69-74; asst prof, Air Force Inst Technol, 74-78; ASST PROF ELECTROMAGNETIC RADIO, VA POLYTECH INST & STATE UNIV, 78- *Concurrent Pos:* Engr, Air Force Weapons Lab, 79 & Gen Elec Co, 81; prin investr, Va Polytech Inst & State Univ, 80- *Mem:* Inst Elec & Electronics Engrs. *Res:* Electromagnetic scattering with an emphasis on numerical and transient techniques; radio engineering; nonlinear circuits. *Mailing Add:* 207 Maywood St Blacksburg VA 24060

DAVIS, WILLIAM C, b Red Bluff, Calif, Feb 12, 33; m 56; c 2. MICROBIOLOGY, IMMUNOLOGY. *Educ:* Chico State Col, BA, 55; Stanford Univ, MA, 59, PhD(med microbiol), 67. *Prof Exp:* Fel, Med Ctr, Univ Calif, San Francisco, 66-68; asst prof, 68-73, ASSOC PROF VET MICROBIOL & PATH, COL VET MED, WASH STATE UNIV, 73- *Mem:* AAAS; Transplantation Soc; Am Asn Path & Bact. *Res:* Transplantation immunology; autoimmunity; host defense failure syndromes. *Mailing Add:* Dept of Vet Microbiol & Path Wash State Univ Col Vet Med Pullman WA 99164

DAVIS, WILLIAM CHESTER, b Manchester, NH, Dec 22, 25; div; c 4. PHYSICS, EXPLOSIVES. *Educ:* Tufts Col, BS, 49; Johns Hopkins Univ, PhD(physics), 54. *Prof Exp:* Asst physics, Johns Hopkins Univ, 51-54; MEM STAFF, LOS ALAMOS NAT LAB, 54- *Concurrent Pos:* Vis prof physics, Univ Calif, 57. *Res:* High explosives; shock and detonation waves; ultra-high-speed photography. *Mailing Add:* Los Alamos Nat Lab Los Alamos NM 87545

DAVIS, WILLIAM COURTNEY, b North East, Pa, Feb 8, 20; m 44; c 2. ELECTRICAL ENGINEERING. *Educ:* Ohio State Univ, BEE, 43, MSc, 47. *Prof Exp:* From instr to assoc prof, 46-60, PROF ELEC ENG, OHIO STATE UNIV, 60-, RES ASSOC, RES FOUND, 47- *Concurrent Pos:* Res specialist, NAm Aviation Inc, 61-74. *Mem:* Inst Elec & Electronics Engrs. *Res:* Radar systems; circuit systems. *Mailing Add:* Dept of Elec Eng Ohio State Univ 2015 Neil Ave Columbus OH 43210

DAVIS, WILLIAM DONALD, b Miami, Fla, Aug 6, 21; div; c 5. PHYSICAL CHEMISTRY. *Educ:* Univ Miami, BS, 42; Univ Pittsburgh, PhD(phys chem), 49. *Prof Exp:* Asst phys chem, Off Naval Res Proj, Univ Pittsburgh, 46-48; res assoc phys sect, Knolls Atomic Power Lab, 49-59, PHYSICIST, ELECTRONICS SCI & ENG, RES & DEVELOP CTR, GEN ELEC CO, 59- *Concurrent Pos:* Adj prof, Rensselaer Polytech Inst, 67- *Mem:* AAAS; Am Phys Soc; Am Vacuum Soc; Am Soc Mass Spectrometry. *Res:* Combustion and reaction in solution calorimetry; gas discharges; vacuum and arc physics; diffusion of gases in metals; mass spectroscopy. *Mailing Add:* Res Lab Gen Elec Co Schenectady NY 12301

DAVIS, WILLIAM DUNCAN, JR, b Brookhaven, Miss, Apr 4, 18; m 49; c 3. MEDICINE, GASTROENTEROLOGY. *Educ:* Tulane Univ, BS, 39, MD, 43; Am Bd Internal Med, dipl, 50; Am Bd Gastroent, dipl, 54. *Prof Exp:* Intern, City Hosp, Cleveland, 43; resident, 44-45; instr med, 45-54, from asst prof to assoc prof clin med, 54-65, PROF CLIN MED, TULANE UNIV, 75- *Concurrent Pos:* Mem staff dept internal med, Ochsner Clin & Found Hosp, 45-, head sect gastroenterol, 53-78, head dept internal med, 68-78, trustee, Alton Ochsner Med Found; consult med, Charity Hosp & Vet Admin Hosp, New Orleans & surgeon gen, Army Subcomt Gastroenterol, 63-69. *Mem:* AMA; Fel Am Col Physicians; Am Fedn Clin Res; Am Gastroenterol Asn; Am Asn Study Liver Dis. *Res:* Hemochromatosis; liver disease; gastric secretion. *Mailing Add:* Ochsner Clin 1514 Jefferson Hwy New Orleans LA 70121

DAVIS, WILLIAM EDWIN, JR, b Toledo, Ohio, Nov 17, 36; m 68; c 2. ORNITHOLOGY. *Educ:* Amherst Col, BA, 59; Univ Tex, MA, 62; Boston Univ, PhD(paleont), 66. *Prof Exp:* From instr to asst prof, 65-71, assoc prof sci, 71-80, PROF SCI, BOSTON UNIV, 80- *Mem:* Am Ornithologist Union. *Res:* Research on tropical birds, Belizi, Peru and Trinidad; heron vocalizations; winter bird foraging ecology. *Mailing Add:* 127 East St Foxboro MA 02035

DAVIS, WILLIAM ELLSMORE, JR, b Denver, Colo, June 22, 27; m 54; c 3. CARCINOGENESIS, TOXICOLOGY. *Educ:* Stanford Univ, BS, 51, MS, 53. *Prof Exp:* Biochemist clin res, Vet Admin Hosp, Oakland, Calif, 53-58; radiation biologist, US Naval Radiol Defense Lab, 58-69; res biologist, Vet Admin Hosp, San Francisco, 69-71; cancer biologist, Life Sci Div, 71-80, SR CANCER BIOLOGIST, TOXICOLOGY LAB, SRI INT, 81- *Honors & Awards:* US Naval Radiol Defense Lab Silver Medal Award for Sci Achievement. *Mem:* AAAS; Soc Exp Biol & Med. *Res:* Radiation biology; tissue transplantation; carcinogenesis; toxicology. *Mailing Add:* Life Sci Div SRI Int Menlo Park CA 94025

DAVIS, WILLIAM HATCH, b Holladay, Utah, Mar 9, 25; m 49; c 5. PLANT BREEDING, GENETICS. *Educ:* Utah State Univ, BS, 53, MS, 54; NC State Univ, PhD(plant breeding), 59. *Prof Exp:* Res instr, NC State Univ, 55-59; plant breeder, Great Western Sugar Co, 59-63; dir soybean res & sr res scientist, L Teweles, Seed Co, 63-72; DIR SOYBEAN RES, RING AROUND PRODS, INC, 72- *Mem:* Am Soc Agron. *Res:* Plant breeding, particularly statistical genetics of developing hybrid sugar beets; alfalfa and forage breeding; cytoplasmic male sterility in alfalfa; a source of male sterility in soybeans believed to be a cytoplasmic source. *Mailing Add:* Ring Around Prods Inc PO Box 1629 Plainview TX 79072

DAVIS, WILLIAM HOWARD, b Brockville, Ont, Can, Apr 5, 22; m 48; c 2. PHYSICS. *Educ:* Queen's Univ, Can, BSc, 45, MSc, 46; Brown Univ, PhD(physics), 48. *Prof Exp:* Asst prof physics, Univ Buffalo, 48-54; from asst prof to assoc prof, 54-58, head dept, 58-70, PROF PHYSICS, MARIETTA COL, 58- *Mem:* Am Phys Soc. *Res:* Teaching; theory of atomic spectra. *Mailing Add:* Dept of physics Marietta Col Marietta OH 45750

DAVIS, WILLIAM J, b Portsmouth, Va, Feb 7, 42; m 64; c 4. NEUROSCIENCES. *Educ:* Univ Calif, Berkeley, BA, 64; Univ Ore, PhD(biol), 67. *Prof Exp:* USPHS fel neurobiol, Univ Ore, 67-68; from asst prof to assoc prof biol, 69-79, PROF BIOL & ENVIRON STUDIES, UNIV CALIF, SANTA CRUZ, 79- *Concurrent Pos:* USPHS fel neurobiol, Stanford Univ, 68-70, res grant, 70-81. *Mem:* AAAS; Soc Neurosci; Soc Exp Biol; Am Soc Zool. *Res:* Functional and structural aspects of the neuronal control of behavior; central nervous organization of locomotor systems; developmental neurobiology; neuronal and biochemical substrates of complex behavioral phenomena, including behavioral hierarchies and plasticity; radioactivity in the marine environment. *Mailing Add:* Thimann Labs Univ of Calif Santa Cruz CA 95064

DAVIS, WILLIAM JACKSON, b Warrenton, Va, Sept 29, 30; m 59. AQUATIC BIOLOGY. *Educ:* Va Polytech Inst & State Univ, BS, 53; Univ Kans, PhD(zool), 59. *Prof Exp:* Asst, Kans Biol Surv, 53-57; asst, Univ Kans, 53-59; asst prof biol, St Cloud State Col, 59 & Western Mich Univ, 59-63; assoc marine scientist, VA Inst Marine Sci, 63-68, sr scientist & head dept ichthyol, 68-72, asst dir & head Fisheries & Serv, 72-77; CHIEF SCIENTIST, SOUTH ATLANTIC FISHERY MGT COUN, CHARLESTON, SC, 77- *Mem:* Am Fisheries Soc. *Res:* Fisheries science and management; limnology. *Mailing Add:* PO Box 5202 Hollywood SC 29449

DAVIS, WILLIAM JAMES, b Wilmington, Del, Sept 8, 40; m 63; c 3. PHYSIOLOGY, ENDOCRINOLOGY. *Educ:* Univ Del, AB, 62; Northwestern Univ, MS, 65, PhD(biol), 68. *Prof Exp:* Tech asst rocket propellants, Thiokol Chem Corp, 63; asst biol, Northwestern Univ, 63-67; asst prof zool, Univ Tenn, Knoxville, 68-73; asst prof, 73-76, ASSOC PROF BIOL, LAMBUTH COL, 76- *Concurrent Pos:* Nat Insts Health biomed support grant, 77- *Mem:* Am Soc Zoologists; Am Inst Biol Sci; Sigma Xi. *Res:* General, cellular and comparative physiology; cellular and comparative endocrinology; the biology of pigment cell effectors. *Mailing Add:* Dept of Biol Lambuth Col Jackson TN 38302

DAVIS, WILLIAM POTTER, JR, b Cleveland, Ohio, Aug 27, 24; m 47; c 5. PHYSICS, ACADEMIC ADMINISTRATION. *Educ:* Oberlin Col, AB, 48; Univ Mich, MS, 49, PhD(physics), 54. *Hon Degrees:* MA, Dartmouth Col, 67. *Prof Exp:* From instr to assoc prof, 55-66, assoc provost, 67-70, actg dean, Thayer Sch Eng, 69-70, budget officer, 70-74, PROF PHYSICS, DARTMOUTH COL, 66-, TREAS, 74- *Concurrent Pos:* Assoc prog dir studies & curriculum improv sect, Pre-Col Educ in Sci Div, NSF, 65-66. *Res:* Cosmic rays; gas discharges; plasma physics. *Mailing Add:* 7 Church St Norwich VT 05055

DAVIS, WILLIAM R, b Los Angeles, Calif, Nov 30, 23; m 45; c 6. CONTROL SYSTEMS, ELECTRONICS. *Educ:* Calif Inst Technol, BS, 44, MS, 47; Stanford Univ, PhD(elec eng), 66. *Prof Exp:* Res engr, Hughes Aircraft Co, 47-51 & Santa Barbara Pac Mercury Res Ctr, 51-52; group supvr, Detroit Controls Res Div, 52-56; sr staff scientist, 56-78, prog mgr precision attitude systs, 66-70, mgr spec syst anal, 71-74, proj mgr, Navstar GPS/Satellite Users, 75-79, SYST ENG, REMOTELY PILOTED VEHICLE PROG, LOCKHEED MISSILES & SPACE CO, LOCKHEED AIRCRAFT CORP, 80- *Res:* Development of systems for precise determination and control of space vehicle attitude; optical sensors; gyros; airborne computers, particularly development of space precision attitude reference and pointing system; satellite system synthesis and analysis; satellite guidance and attitude determination. *Mailing Add:* 1359 Belleville Sunnyvale CA 94087

DAVIS, WILLIAM ROBERT, b Oklahoma City, Okla, Aug 22, 29; m 70. PHYSICS. *Educ:* Univ Okla, BS, 53, MS, 54; Hannover Tech Univ, Dr rer nat, 56. *Prof Exp:* Physicist, Trisophia Enterprises, Okla, 56-57; from asst prof to assoc prof, 57-66, PROF PHYSICS, NC STATE UNIV, 66- *Concurrent Pos:* Consult, Trisophia Enterprises, 57-59; Regulus Corp, Okla, 58-59, Lab for Electronics, Inc, Calif, 62-63 & Res Triangle Inst, NC, 64-; Guggenheim fel theoret physics, 70-71. *Mem:* AAAS; fel Am Phys Soc; Am Asn Physics Teachers. *Res:* Theoretical mechanics; electrodynamics; field theory; symmetry properties; the general theory of relativity. *Mailing Add:* Dept of Physics NC State Univ PO Box 5367 State Univ Sta Raleigh NC 27650

DAVIS, WILLIAM S, b Los Angeles, Calif, Sept 16, 30; m 60; c 2. PLANT TAXONOMY, PLANT CYTOGENETICS. *Educ:* Whittier Col, AB, 51, MS, 59; Univ Calif, Los Angeles, PhD(bot), 64. *Prof Exp:* Asst prof, 63-71, PROF BIOL, UNIV LOUISVILLE, 71- *Mem:* AAAS; Am Soc Plant Taxon; Int Asn Plant Taxon; Bot Soc Am. *Res:* Experimental taxonomy and cytotaxonomy of plants. *Mailing Add:* Dept Biol Univ Louisville Louisville KY 40208

DAVIS, WILLIAM SPENCER, b Harrisonburg, Va, Sept 23, 25; m 60; c 2. FISH BIOLOGY, ECOLOGY. *Educ:* Va Polytech Inst, BS, 50, MS, 53. *Prof Exp:* Fishery res biologist, US Bur Commercial Fisheries, NC, 54-59, Wash, 60-67; fishery biologist, Br Resources Mgt, Bur Commercial Fisheries, Dept Interior, 67-70; biol sci administr, 70-76, AQUATIC BIOLOGIST, ENVIRON PROTECTION AGENCY, 76- *Mem:* Am Fisheries Soc; Am Inst Fishery Res Biol; Am Soc Ichthyol & Herpet; Ecol Soc Am; Am Chem Soc. *Res:* Effect of human use of freshwater estuarine, oceanic and great lakes environments on communities of aquatic organisms; develop and evaluate means of abating and preventing pollution there; control of the discharge of dredged or fill material in water. *Mailing Add:* 8523 Durham Court Springfield VA 22151

DAVIS, WILLIAM THOMPSON, b Champaign, Ill, Nov 3, 31; m 52; c 2. VETERINARY MEDICINE. *Educ:* Univ Ill, BS, 56, DVM, 58; Univ Chicago, MBA, 67. *Prof Exp:* Pvt pract, Wyo, 58-62; resident vet, Newhall Land & Farm Co, 62-63 & Abbott Labs, 63-67; asst dir animal health res, Ciba Corp, 67-69; dir animal health clin res, E R Squibb & Sons, Inc, 69-73; DIR LICENSING, AGR, PFIZER INC, 73- *Concurrent Pos:* Mem, Nat Mastitis Coun. *Mem:* Am Vet Med Asn; Indust Vet Asn; NY Acad Sci. *Res:* Animal health research including pharmaceuticals and biologicals, especially final developmental stages, product promotion, liaison with marketing, research organization and management; acquisition of new products, processes and technology from world wide sources for development and marketing. *Mailing Add:* Pfizer Inc 235 E 42nd St New York NY 10017

DAVIS, WILLIAM WIANT, b Parkersburg, WVa, May 26, 46. STATISTICS. *Educ:* Case Western Reserve Univ, BS, 68; Univ Wis-Madison, MS, 71, PhD(statist), 74. *Prof Exp:* ASST PROF STATIST, CARNEGIE-MELLON UNIV, 74- *Mem:* Am Statist Asn; Inst Math Statist. *Res:* Bayesian statistics; linear models; time-series; robustness. *Mailing Add:* Dept of Statist Carnegie-Mellon Univ Pittsburgh PA 15213

DAVISON, ALAN, inorganic chemistry, see previous edition

DAVISON, BEAUMONT, b Atlanta, Ga, May 30, 29; m 52; c 2. ELECTRICAL ENGINEERING. *Educ:* Vanderbilt Univ, BE, 50; Syracuse Univ, MEE, 52, PhD(elec eng), 56. *Prof Exp:* Instr & res assoc, Syracuse Univ, 51-56; asst prof elec eng, Case Inst Technol, 56-59; exec vpres, Indust Electronic Rubber Co, 59-67; chmn dept elec eng, Ohio Univ, 67-69, dean col eng & technol, 69-71, vpres regional higher educ, 71-74; DEAN ENG, CALIF STATE POLYTECH UNIV, POMONA, 74- *Mem:* Am Soc Eng Educ; Inst Elec & Electronics Engrs; Soc Mfg Engrs. *Res:* Microwave devices; electronic circuit component development; rubber technology. *Mailing Add:* Calif State Polytech Univ 3801 W Temple Ave Pomona CA 91768

DAVISON, CLARKE, b Washington, DC, Nov 8, 27; m 53, 64; c 2. FORENSIC CHEMISTRY. *Educ:* George Washington Univ, BSc, 48, MS, 49; Harvard Univ, PhD(biochem), 54. *Prof Exp:* Asst pharmacol, George Washington Univ, 47-49, from asst prof to prof, 53-67; sect head metab chem, Sterling Winthrop Res Inst, 67-76; FORENSIC CHEMIST, LEE COUNTY SHERIFF'S DEPT, FT MYERS, 76- *Mem:* Am Soc Pharmacol & Exp Therapeut. *Mailing Add:* Lee County Sheriff's De Fort Meyers FL 33902

DAVISON, DONALD CRAIG, b Fresno, Calif, Apr 30, 36; m 61; c 3. ACOUSTIC SENSORS, SIGNAL PROCESSING. *Educ:* Stanford Univ, BS, 58; San Diego State Col, MS, 64; Univ Calif, Riverside, PhD(physics), 69. *Prof Exp:* PHYSICIST, US NAVAL OCEAN SYSTS CTR, 64- *Res:* Experimental measurement program to utilize physical oceanography, acoustics, sensors and signal processing to develop the technology base for improved anti-submarine warfare systems. *Mailing Add:* Code 6322 US Naval Ocean Systs Ctr San Diego CA 92152

DAVISON, E(DWARD) J(OSEPH), b Toronto, Ont, Sept 12, 38; m 66; c 4. CONTROL SYSTEM THEORY. *Educ:* Univ Toronto, BASc, 60, MA, 61, PhD(control eng), 64. *Hon Degrees:* ScD, Cambridge Univ, 77. *Prof Exp:* Asst prof elec eng, Univ Toronto, 64-66; asst prof, Univ Calif, Berkeley, 66-68; assoc prof, 68-74, PROF ELEC ENG, UNIV TORONTO, 74- *Concurrent Pos:* E W R Steacie Mem fel, Nat Res Coun Can, 74-77; Killam res fel, 79-80 & 81-82; dir, Elec Eng Consociates Ltd, Toronto, 77- *Mem:* Fel Inst Elec & Electronics Engrs; fel Royal Soc Can. *Res:* Large scale system theory; multivariable systems; computational methods; optimization theory; applications of system theory to biology. *Mailing Add:* Dept Elec Eng Univ Toronto Toronto ON M5S 2R8 Can

DAVISON, FREDERICK CORBET, b Atlanta, Ga, Sept 3, 29; m 52; c 2. VETERINARY PATHOLOGY, PHYSIOLOGY. *Educ:* Univ Ga, DVM, 52; Iowa State Univ, PhD(path, biochem, physiol), 63. *Prof Exp:* Pvt pract vet med, Ga, 52-58; res assoc, Iowa State Univ, 58-59, asst prof physiol, 59-63; asst dir, Dept Sci Activ, Am Vet Med Asn, 63-64; dean, Sch Vet Med, Univ Ga, 64-66; vchancellor, Univ Syst Ga, 66-67; PRES, UNIV GA, 67- *Concurrent Pos:* Assoc, Inst Atomic Res, Iowa State Univ, 58-63; proj leader, US AEC, 59-63; mem prof ed comn, Inst Lab Animal Resources, Nat Acad Sci-Nat Res Coun, 63-; coun biol & therapeut agents, Am Vet Med Asn, 64- *Mem:* Am Soc Vet Physiol & Pharmacol. *Res:* Comparative toxicity of the lanthanide series of rare earths. *Mailing Add:* Univ of Ga Athens GA 30602

DAVISON, J(OSEPH) W(ADE), b Kansas City, Kans, Nov 14, 21; m 51; c 2. CHEMICAL ENGINEERING. *Educ:* Univ Kans, BS, 43. *Prof Exp:* Process design engr, 43-44, process eval mgr, 56-65, dir, Res & Develop Div, 64-71, vchmn & chmn, Operating Comt, 71-75, mgr res & develop, 75-76, vpres res & develop, 76-80, SR VPRES PLANNINNG & DEVELOP, PHILLIPS PETROL CO, 80- *Concurrent Pos:* Mem, US Comt World Petrol Cong, 75-80. *Mem:* Coord Res Coun (pres, 81); Nat Asn Conserv Dist; Indust Res Inst; fel Am Inst Chem Engrs. *Mailing Add:* Phillips Petrol Co Phillips Res Ctr Bartlesville OK 74004

DAVISON, JOHN (AMERPOHL), b Janesville, Wis, June 25, 28; m 50, 65; c 3. PHYSIOLOGY. *Educ:* Univ Wis, BS, 50; Univ Minn, PhD, 55. *Prof Exp:* Instr zool, Wash Univ, 54-57; asst prof, Fla State Univ, 57-60 & La State Univ, 60-64; from asst prof to assoc prof, Rensselaer Polytech Inst, 64-67; ASSOC PROF ZOOL, UNIV VT, 67- *Mem:* Am Soc Zoologists; Soc Gen Physiol. *Res:* Body size and metabolism; cell form; developmental physiology of amphibia and fresh-water invertebrates. *Mailing Add:* Dept of Zool Univ of Vt Burlington VT 05401

DAVISON, JOHN BLAKE, b Waynesboro, Pa, Jan 7, 46; m 74. ORGANOMETALLIC CHEMISTRY, INORGANIC CHEMISTRY. *Educ:* Va Polytech Inst, BS, 67; Univ Md, PhD(inorg chem), 74. *Prof Exp:* Res chemist catalysis, Hooker Chem Corp, 76-78; RES CHEMIST CATALYSIS, OCCIDENTAL RES CORP, 78- *Mem:* Am Chem Soc. *Res:* Organometallic electrocatalysis; homogeneous transition metal catalysts for organic synthesis; synthesis gas chemistry; anchored homogeneous catalysts; organometallic polymers with unusual physical or chemical properties; organometallic chemistry of elemental phosphorus; organosilicon chemistry. *Mailing Add:* 28162 Amable Mission Viejo CA 92692

DAVISON, JOHN PHILIP, b Woodsville, NH, Apr 21, 17; m 46; c 5. BIOCHEMISTRY. *Educ:* Mass Inst Technol, SB, 42; Univ NH, MS, 47; Univ Mich, PhD, 53. *Prof Exp:* Asst chem, Univ NH, 46-47; asst prof biochem, Univ NDak, 51-54; asst prof physiol sci, Dartmouth Med Sch, 54-58; asst prof, 58-61, assoc prof clin path, Med Sch, Univ Va, 61-82; RETIRED. *Mem:* AAAS; Am Chem Soc; NY Acad Sci; Am Asn Clin Chem. *Res:* Clinical biochemistry; methods in clinical chemistry and toxicology; billirubin methodology and metabolism. *Mailing Add:* Box F N Windham ME 04062

DAVISON, KENNETH LEWIS, b Hopkins, Mo, Dec 27, 35; m 57; c 3. NUTRITION, PHYSIOLOGY. *Educ:* Univ Mo, BS, 57; Iowa State Univ, MS, 59, PhD(nutrit), 61. *Prof Exp:* Res assoc nutrit, Cornell Univ, 61-65; RES PHYSIOLOGIST, METAB & RADIATION RES LAB, SCI & EDUC ADMIN, AGR RES, USDA, 65- *Concurrent Pos:* Adj prof, NDak State Univ, 68- *Mem:* Am Soc Animal Sci; Am Dairy Sci Asn; Am Inst Nutrit. *Res:* Accululation of nitrate in plants and toxicity to animals; pesticide metabolism by animals. *Mailing Add:* Metab & Radiation Res Lab USDA Sci & Educ Admin State Univ Sta Fargo ND 58105

DAVISON, LEE WALKER, b Moscow, Idaho, Aug 10, 37. APPLIED MECHANICS. *Educ:* Univ Idaho, BS, 59; NY Univ, MS, 61; Calif Inst Technol, PhD(appl mech), 65. *Prof Exp:* Mem tech staff, Bell Tel Labs, 59-62; res fel, Johns Hopkins Univ, 65-66; staff mem, 66-68, supvr shock wave physics, 68-72, supvr, Explosives Physics Res Div, 72-80, SUPVR, APPL MECHANICS DIV, SANDIA NAT LABS, 80- *Mem:* Am Soc Mech Eng; Am Phys Soc; Soc Eng Sci; Combustion Inst; Am Acad Mech. *Res:* Modern continuum mechanics; propagation of strong shock waves in solids; dynamic fracture; explosives. *Mailing Add:* 7900 Harwood Ave NE Albuquerque NM 87110

DAVISON, PETER FITZGERALD, b London, Eng, Nov 12, 27; m 54; c 2. PHYSICAL CHEMISTRY. *Educ:* Univ London, BSc, 49, PhD(chem), 54. *Prof Exp:* Chemist, Chester Beatty Res Inst, Inst Cancer Res, Eng, 51-56; Indust Cellulose Res Ltd, Can, 56-57 & Dept Biol, Mass Inst Technol, 57-69; DIR DEPT FINE STRUCT RES, BOSTON BIOMED RES INST, 69- *Mem:* Am Chem Soc; Am Soc Biol Chem; AAAS. *Res:* Physical chemistry of nucleoproteins; nucleic acids; proteins and synthetic polymers; collagen organization. *Mailing Add:* Dept of Fine Struct Res Boston Biomed Res Inst Boston MA 02114

DAVISON, RICHARD READ, b Marlin, Tex, Apr 3, 26; m 51; c 3. CHEMICAL ENGINEERING. *Educ:* Tex Tech Col, BS, 49; Tex A&M Univ, MS, 58, PhD(chem eng), 62. *Prof Exp:* Engr gas indust, Lion Oil Co, 49-55; res scientist, 55-61, from instr to assoc prof, 58-68, PROF CHEM ENG, TEX A&M UNIV, 68- *Mem:* Am Chem Soc; Am Inst Chem Engrs; Int Solar Energy Soc. *Res:* Solvent extraction process for conversion of saline water and sewage effluent; aquifer energy storage thermodynamics of solutions and solar energy utilization; methanol as motor fuel. *Mailing Add:* Dept of Chem Eng Tex A&M Univ College Station TX 77843

DAVISON, ROBERT WILDER, b Albany, NY, Dec 30, 20; m 49; c 2. PHYSICAL CHEMISTRY. *Educ:* Union Col, BS, 42; Mass Inst Technol, PhD(phys chem), 50. *Prof Exp:* Res chemist, Res Ctr, Hercules Powder Co, 50-66; from res chemist to sr res chemist, 66-71, RES SCIENTIST, HERCULES RES CTR, HERCULES, INC, 71- *Mem:* Am Chem Soc; Tech Asn Pulp & Paper Indust. *Res:* Surface chemistry; colloidal systems; chemical additives for paper; physical properties of paper. *Mailing Add:* Hercules Res Ctr Hercules Inc Wilmington DE 19899

DAVISON, SOL, b Los Angeles, Calif, Apr 3, 22; m 45; c 2. POLYMER SCIENCE. *Educ:* Pomona Col, BA, 47; Univ Notre Dame, PhD, 51. *Prof Exp:* AEC fel, Univ Notre Dame, 51-52; res assoc radiobiol & phys chem studies on foods, Mass Inst Technol, 52-56; CHEMIST, SHELL DEVELOP CO, 56- *Mem:* Am Chem Soc; Sigma Xi. *Res:* Reaction kinetics and photochemistry; radiation chemistry and radiobiology; testing of polymers; physics and technology of elastomers and reinforced thermoplastics. *Mailing Add:* Shell Develop Co Westhollow Res Ctr Box 1380 Houston TX 77001

DAVISON, SYDNEY GEORGE, b Stockport, Eng, Sept 6, 34; m 59; c 2. SURFACE PHYSICS. *Educ:* Univ Manchester, BSc, 58, MSc, 62, PhD(math), 64. *Prof Exp:* Teacher, Salford Grammer Sch, 58-59; nuclear physicist, Nuclear Power Div, G E C/Simon-Carvers, Eng, 59-60; demonstr math, Univ Manchester, 61-64; fel physics, Univ Waterloo, 64-65; from asst prof to assoc prof, 65-70, dir quantum theory group, 68-70; prof physics, Clarkson Col, 70-72; prof physics, Bartol Res Found, Franklin Inst, 72-74; vis prof, 74-78, PROF APPL MATH, UNIV WATERLOO, 78- *Concurrent Pos:* Ed, Progress Surface Sci, Pergamon, Oxford, 68- *Mem:* Fel Am Phys Soc; fel Brit Inst Physics. *Res:* Quantum theory of crystal surfaces. *Mailing Add:* Dept of Appl Math Univ of Waterloo Waterloo Can

DAVISON, THOMAS MATTHEW KERR, b Scotland, Jan 18, 39; Can citizen; m 64; c 2. MATHEMATICS. *Educ:* Sir George Williams Univ, BSc, 60; Univ Toronto, MA, 62, PhD(math), 65. *Prof Exp:* Asst prof math, Univ Waterloo, 64-66; Nat Res Coun Can res fel, Kings' Col, London, 66-68; from asst prof to assoc prof, 68-81, PROF MATH SCI, MCMASTER UNIV, 81- *Concurrent Pos:* Ed, Ont Math Gazette, 70-73. *Mem:* Am Math Soc; Can Math Cong; Math Asn Am. *Res:* Algebra, number theory, and functional equations. *Mailing Add:* Dept Math McMaster Univ Hamilton ON L8S 4K1 Can

DAVISON, WALTER FRANCIS, b Chicago, Ill, Apr 28, 26; div; c 1. MATHEMATICS. *Educ:* Calif Inst Technol, BS, 51; Univ Va, PhD(math), 56. *Prof Exp:* Instr math, Univ Mich, Ann Arbor, 56-60; sr staff scientist, Collins Radio Co, Tex, 60-61; mem tech staff electronics, Space Gen Corp, Calif, 61-62; branch head electrooptics, Tex Instruments, 62; sr scientist, Int Tel & Tel Fed Labs, Calif, 63-66; ASSOC PROF MATH, CALIF STATE UNIV, NORTHRIDGE, 66- *Concurrent Pos:* Rackham fac fel, Univ Mich, Ann Arbor, 58. *Mem:* Am Math Soc; NY Acad Sci. *Res:* Closure operators; mosaic spaces; frechet equivalence; optical receivers; electrooptical demodulation; noise theory; quasigroups. *Mailing Add:* Dept of Math Calif State Univ Northridge CA 91330

DAVISSON, CHARLOTTE MEAKER, b Phillipston, Mass, Oct 7, 14; m 47; c 1. NUCLEAR SCIENCE. *Educ:* Wellesley Col, BA, 36; Smith Col, MA, 39; Mass Inst Technol, PhD(nuclear physics), 48. *Prof Exp:* Physicist, Eclipse-Pioneer Div, Bendix Aviation Corp, 42-44; res asst, Manhattan Proj, Columbia Univ, 44-46; RES PHYSICIST, RADIATION TECHNOL DIV, US NAVAL RES LAB, DC, 54- *Mem:* Fel AAAS; Am Phys Soc; Am Nuclear Soc; NY Acad Sci. *Res:* Interaction of gamma rays with matter; gamma-ray albedos; computer programming for cyclotron studies, neutron detector efficiency, x-ray analysis and other cyclotron research projects, including ion implantation. *Mailing Add:* 400 Cedar Ridge Dr Oxon Hill MD 20745

DAVISSON, EDWIN ORLANDO, physical chemistry, see previous edition

DAVISSON, LEE DAVID, b Evanston, Ill, June 16, 36; m 57, 75; c 3. ELECTRICAL ENGINEERING. *Educ:* Princeton Univ, BSE, 58; Univ Calif, Los Angeles, MSE, 61, PhD(eng), 64. *Prof Exp:* Res engr, Philco Corp, 60-62; mem tech staff elec eng, Hughes Aircraft Corp, 62-64; from asst prof to assoc prof, Princeton Univ, 64-70; from assoc prof to prof, Univ Southern Calif, 69-76; PROF, UNIV MD, 76-, CHMN DEPT, 80- *Concurrent Pos:* Consult, NASA, 65-70; Bell Tel Labs, 68-69; sr staff engr, Hughes Aircraft Co, 69-74; first vpres, Info Theory Group, 79, pres, 80; co-chmn, Int Info Theory Symp, 79. *Honors & Awards:* Princeton Eng Soc award, 65; outstanding young elec engr award, Eta Kappa Nu, 68; prize paper award, Inst Elec & Electronics Engrs, 76. *Mem:* Fel Inst Elec & Electronics Engrs (2nd vpres, 78). *Res:* Communication theory. *Mailing Add:* Dept Elec Eng Univ Md College Park MD 20742

DAVISSON, M T, b Grafton, WVa, Dec 23, 31; m 55; c 4. CIVIL ENGINEERING. *Educ:* Univ Akron, BCE, 54; Univ Ill, MS, 55, PhD(civil eng), 60. *Prof Exp:* Designer struct eng, Clark, Dietz, Painter & Assocs, 55-56; from instr to assoc prof, 59-71, PROF CIVIL ENG, UNIV ILL, URBANA, 71- *Concurrent Pos:* Indust consult, 60- *Honors & Awards:* Alfred A Raymond Award, 59; Collingwood Prize, Am Soc Civil Engrs, 64. *Mem:* Am Soc Civil Engrs; Am Concrete Inst; Am Rwy Eng Asn; Am Soc Testing & Mat; Nat Soc Prof Engrs. *Res:* Deep foundations; soil dynamics; settlement of structures; waterfront structures; heavy construction. *Mailing Add:* 14 Lake Park Rd Champaign IL 61820

DAVITIAN, HARRY EDWARD, b Flushing, NY, June 19, 45; m 73; c 1. PHYSICS. *Educ:* Mass Inst Technol, BS, 66; Cornell Univ, MS, 69, PhD(appl physics), 73. *Prof Exp:* Res assoc, Cornell Univ, 73; scientist, Inst Energy Anal, Oak Ridge Assoc Univs, 74-75; group leader, Nat Ctr Anal Energy Systs, Brookhaven Nat Lab, NY, 75-80; PRES, ENTEK RES, INC, 80- *Concurrent Pos:* Mem res & develop subgroup, Modeling Resources Group, Comn Nuclear & Alt Energy Resources, Nat Res Coun, 76-77. *Mem:* Int Asn Energy Economists; Int Solar Energy Soc. *Res:* Energy systems analysis. *Mailing Add:* Entek Res Inc 11 Satterly Rd East Setaulut NY 11733

DAVITT, HARRY JAMES, JR, b Philadelphia, Pa, Oct 10, 39; m 64; c 3. CHEMICAL ENGINEERING. *Educ:* Pa State Univ, BS, 61; Purdue Univ, MS, 66, PhD(chem eng), 69. *Prof Exp:* Res engr, Sun Oil Co, 68-73; supt, Oil Sands Technol, Great Can Oil Sands, 73-75; SR PROF ENGR, SUNOCO ENERGY DEVELOP CO, 75- *Res:* Fuel cells; extraction of bitumen from tar sands. *Mailing Add:* Sunoco Energy Develop Co Ste 1500 Box 9 Dallas TX 75251

DAVITT, RICHARD MICHAEL, b Wilmington, Del, Mar 13, 39; m 66; c 2. MATHEMATICS. *Educ:* Niagara Univ, BS, 63; Lehigh Univ, MS, 66, PhD(math), 69. *Prof Exp:* Instr, St Francis de Sales High Sch, Toledo, Ohio, 58-60; asst math, Lehigh Univ, 64-65; from instr to asst prof, Lafayette Col, 67-70; asst prof, 70-74, ASSOC PROF MATH, UNIV LOUISVILLE, 74- *Mem:* Am Math Soc. *Res:* Lattice-ordered groups; finite p-groups. *Mailing Add:* Dept of Math Univ of Louisville Louisville KY 40292

DAW, HAROLD ALBERT, b Granger, Utah, Oct 25, 25; m 53; c 6. PHYSICS. *Educ:* Univ Utah, BS, 48, MA, 52, PhD, 56. *Prof Exp:* Chief lab asst, Elementary Physics Lab, Univ Utah, 47-48, 50-52; res physicist from Utah dept astrophys & phys meteorol, Johns Hopkins Univ, 53-54; from asst prof to assoc prof physics, 54-61, assoc physicist, Phys Sci Lab, 54-61, head dept physics, 61-70, from actg dean to assoc dean arts & sci, 70-74, asst acad vpres, 74-75, PROF PHYSICS, NMEX STATE UNIV, 61-, ASSOC ACAD V PRES, 75- *Mem:* AAAS; Am Phys Soc; Optical Soc Am; Am Asn Physics Teachers; Am Inst Physics. *Res:* Optics; maser optics; physics instructional equipment. *Mailing Add:* Off of Assoc Acad VPres NMex State Univ Las Cruces NM 88003

DAW, JOHN CHARLES, b Tulsa, Okla, July 18, 31; c 7. MEDICAL EDUCATION. *Educ:* Case Western Reserve Univ, BA, 59, PhD(physiol), 66. *Prof Exp:* Res assoc physiol, Univ Va, 66-67; USPHS fel, 67-68; instr, Univ Va, 68; asst prof lab educ, Mt Sinai Sch Med, 68-69, assoc dir lab, 68-71, asst prof med educ & res asst prof physiol, 69-71; ASST PROF PHYSIOL & ASSOC DIR MED SCI TEACHING LABS, SCH MED, UNIV NC, CHAPEL HILL, 71- *Mem:* AAAS; Am Physiol Soc; Asn Multidisicipline Educ in Health Sci. *Res:* Glycogen metabolism; carbohydrate metabolism; cardiac metabolism; experimental shock; experimental burn; surgical research. *Mailing Add:* Med Sci Teaching Labs Univ of NC Med Sch Chapel Hill NC 27514

DAW, NIGEL WARWICK, b London, Eng, Dec 12, 33; US citizen; m 63; c 2. NEUROPHYSIOLOGY, PSYCHOPHYSICS. *Educ:* Cambridge Univ, BA, 56, MA, 61; Johns Hopkins Univ, PhD(biophys), 67. *Prof Exp:* Assoc scientist, Polaroid Corp, 58-63; fel neurobiol, Harvard Med Sch, 67-69, NIH fel, 67-68, spec fel, 68-69; asst prof, 69-72, assoc prof, 72-77, PROF PHYSIOL & OPTHAL, MED SCH, WASHINGTON UNIV, 77- *Concurrent Pos:* Consult visual sci study sect, Div Res Grants, NIH, 70-73; Behav & Neural Sci fel, study sect, 81; ed, J Neurophysiol, 78- *Mem:* AAAS; Am Physiol Soc; Asn Res Vision & Ophthal. *Res:* Effects of synaptic transmitter drugs on the visual system; development of vision; mechanisms of directional sensitivity in the visual system; neurophysiology and psychophysics of color vision. *Mailing Add:* 78 Aberdeen Pl St Louis MO 63105

DAWBER, THOMAS ROYLE, b Duncan, BC, Can, Jan 18, 13; nat US; m 37; c 2. INTERNAL MEDICINE, CARDIOLOGY. *Educ:* Haverford Col, AB, 33; Harvard Univ, MD, 37, MPH, 58. *Prof Exp:* Intern, US Marine Hosps, Va, 37-38, med resident, 38-40, chief med, Mass, 41-42, asst, NY, 42, chief, Mass, 44-49; mem staff diabetes res, Boston City Hosp, 49-50; chief heart dis epidemiol study, US Dept Health, Educ & Welfare, 50-66; prog planning officer, Med Ctr, 66-68, assoc prof, 66-76, PROF MED, SCH MED, BOSTON UNIV, 76- *Mem:* Am Col Chest Physicians; Am Col Physicians; Am Heart Asn. *Res:* Epidemiol of coronary heart disease and hypertension; public health. *Mailing Add:* Dept of Med Boston Univ Med Ctr Boston MA 02118

DAWE, ALBERT ROLKE, b Milwaukee, Wis, June 1, 16; m 42, 73; c 3. COMPARATIVE PHYSIOLOGY. *Educ:* Yale Univ, BA, 38; Harvard Univ, MA, 51; Univ Wis, PhD(zool, physiol), 53. *Prof Exp:* Instr zool, Exten Div, Univ Wis, 46-50, asst prof physiol, Med Sch, 53-56; biologist, Off Naval Res, Chicago, 56-58, chief scientist, 58-67, dep dir & chief scientist, 67-77; RETIRED. *Concurrent Pos:* From adj assoc prof to adj prof physiol, Stritch Sch Med, Loyola Univ, 64-78; chief biol consult, World Book Encycl; mem bd assocs, John Crerar Libr. *Mem:* Am Physiol Soc; Soc Cryobiol; Int Hibernation Soc. *Mailing Add:* 1050 Knollwood Deerfield IL 60015

DAWE, CLYDE JOHNSON, b Easton, Pa, Jan 20, 21; m 47; c 4. PATHOLOGY. *Educ:* Lafayette Col, AB, 42; Johns Hopkins Univ, MD, 45; Univ Minn, PhD, 56; Am Bd Path, dipl, 55. *Prof Exp:* Mem staff surg path, Mayo Clin, 51-54; MED OFFICER, LAB PATH, NAT CANCER INST, 55-, HEAD SECT COMP ONCOL, 69- *Concurrent Pos:* Assoc ed, J Nat Cancer Inst, 57-59; ed, In Vitro, Am Tissue Cult Asn, 65-68; chmn comt comp oncol, Int Union Against Cancer, 70- *Mem:* AAAS; Am Asn Cancer Res; Am Soc Exp Path; Am Asn Path & Bact; Int Acad Path. *Res:* Cancer; experimental carcinogenesis; neoplastic transformation in cell and organ culture; murine leukemias in cell culture; viral carcinogenesis; phylogeny and ontogeny as related to neoplasia. *Mailing Add:* Nat Cancer Inst Bethesda MD 20014

DAWE, HAROLD JOSEPH, b Deckerville, Mich, June 15, 12; m 33; c 4. CHEMISTRY. *Educ:* Cent Mich Col, BS, 32; Univ Mich, MS, 34, PhD(chem), 40. *Prof Exp:* Prod develop engr, Acheson Colloids Co, 40-50, tech dir, 50-56; res dir, Acheson Industs Inc, 56-64, vpres res, 64-76; RETIRED. *Mem:* AAAS; Am Chem Soc; fel Am Inst Chem; Am Soc Lubrication Engrs; fel Chem Inst Can. *Res:* Colloid chemistry of dispersed solids; relation between the stability of suspensions and their interfacial free surface energies. *Mailing Add:* 26 Lake Spur Hendersonville NC 28739

DAWES, CLINTON JOHN, b Minneapolis, Minn, Sept 23, 35; m 62; c 3. PHYCOLOGY, ALGALCYTOLOGY. *Educ:* Univ Minn, Minneapolis, BS, 57; Univ Calif, Los Angeles, MA, 58, PhD(sci), 61. *Prof Exp:* Teaching asst, Bot Labs, Univ Calif, Los Angeles, 57-59; NSF fel, 63-64; asst prof bot, 64-70, assoc prof biol, 70-72, PROF BIOL, UNIV S FLA, 72- *Concurrent Pos:* NSF grants, 65-66, 69-71, 70-72 & 78; Sea grant, 71-73; Fla sea grant, 74, 75 & 76. *Mem:* Bot Soc Am; Phycol Soc Am (pres, 79); Int Phycol Soc; Sigma Xi; Electron Micros Soc Am. *Res:* Algal ultrastructure, especially cell development; cell wall fine structure and cytology of coenocytic algae; physiological studies on economically important algae; floristics of Florida algae. *Mailing Add:* Dept of Biol Univ of S Fla Tampa FL 33620

DAWES, DAVID HADDON, b Cornwall, Ont, Aug 14, 38; m 62; c 5. PHYSICAL CHEMISTRY, POLYMER SCIENCE. *Educ:* McGill Univ, BSc, 59, PhD(phys chem), 62. *Prof Exp:* Nat Res Coun Can fel chem, 62-64; res chemist, E I du Pont de Nemours & Co, 65-67, sr res chemist, 67-74, res mgr, 74-81, MGR, ENVIRON SCI, DU PONT OF CAN, 82- *Mem:* Chem Inst Can. *Res:* Radiolysis of gases; product and process research and development. *Mailing Add:* DuPont Can Inc Front Rd PO Box 5000 Kingston Can

DAWES, JOHN LESLIE, b Olney, Eng, Dec 31, 42; m 69. ORGANOMETALLIC CHEMISTRY, ORGANIC CHEMISTRY. *Educ:* Univ Leicester, BS, 64, PhD(chem), 67. *Prof Exp:* NSF Ctr of Excellence vis asst prof, La State Univ, 67-69; chemist, 69-77, SR RES CHEMIST, TEX EASTMAN CO, 77- *Mem:* Am Chem Soc; Catalysis Soc. *Res:* Inorganic chemistry; homogeneous and heterogeneous catalysis related to the preparation of organic compounds. *Mailing Add:* 115 Fredricks Cts Route 5 Longview TX 75601

DAWES, WILLIAM REDIN, JR, b Charlotte, NC, Oct 10, 40; m 64; c 2. HIGH ENERGY PHYSICS, SOLID STATE PHYSICS. *Educ:* Univ NC, BS, 62; Univ Ariz, MS, 64, PhD(physics), 68. *Prof Exp:* Mem tech staff, Bell Tel Labs, 68-70, supvr, Silicon Device Technol Group, 70-75; SUPVR INTEGRATED CIRCUIT TECHNOL, SANDIA NAT LABS, 75- *Mem:* Sigma Xi. *Res:* Pion-proton elastic scattering at high energy; silicon device technology, especially field effect devices. *Mailing Add:* 7811 Academy Trail NE Albuquerque NM 87109

DAWID, IGOR BERT, b Czernowitz, Romania, Feb 26, 35. BIOCHEMISTRY, DEVELOPMENTAL BIOLOGY. *Educ:* Univ Vienna, PhD(chem), 60. *Prof Exp:* Lab asst chem, Univ Vienna, 59-60; vis lectr biochem, Mass Inst Technol, 60-62; fel, Carnegie Inst, 62-67, mem staff, Dept Embryol, Carnegie Inst Washington, 67-78; HEAD DEVELOP BIOL SECT, LAB BIOCHEM, NAT CANCER INST, 78- *Concurrent Pos:* Vis mem, Max Planck Inst Biol, Univ Tubingen, 65-67; from asst prof to assoc prof biol, Johns Hopkins Univ, 73-; ed-in-chief, Develop Biol, 75-78. *Mem:* Nat Acad Sci; Am Soc Cell Biol; Am Soc Biol Chemists; Int Soc Develop Biologists; AAAS. *Res:* Biochemistry of development; function of nucleic acids in development; gene isolation, ribosomal DNA. *Mailing Add:* Bldg 37 Rm 4D-06 NIH Bethesda MD 20014

DAWKINS, GEORGE S(PANGLER), industrial engineering, operations research, see previous edition

DAWKINS, WILLIAM PAUL, b Houston, Tex, July 25, 34; m 57; c 2. CIVIL ENGINEERING. *Educ:* Rice Univ, BA & BS, 57, MS, 62; Univ Ill, Urbana, PhD(civil eng), 66. *Prof Exp:* Sr engr, Proj Mohole, Brown & Root, Inc, Tex, 62-63; res asst civil eng, Univ Ill, Urbana, 63-65, res assoc, 65-66; asst prof, Univ Tex, 66-69; assoc prof, 69-74, PROF CIVIL ENG, OKLA STATE UNIV, 74- *Mem:* Am Soc Civil Engrs. *Res:* Application of computers to solutions of civil engineering problems, particularly to problems of structural analysis. *Mailing Add:* Sch of Civil Eng Okla State Univ Stillwater OK 74074

DAWSON, ARTHUR DONOVAN, b Wilmington, Del, May 5, 43; m 66. ORGANIC CHEMISTRY. *Educ:* Temple Univ, AB, 67, 68, PhD(org chem), 76. *Prof Exp:* Control analyst, Smith Kline & French Lab, Inc, 68-69; teaching asst, Dept Chem, Temple Univ, 69-72, res fel, 72-76; develop scientist, Household Prod Div, Lever Bros, 75-78; sr prod develop chemist, Johnson & Johnson Personal Prod Co, 78-80; SR RES SCIENTIST, DICKINSON CONSUMER PRODS, 80- *Mem:* Am Chem Soc; Am Oil Chem Soc; Sigma Xi; Royal Soc Chem; Am Diabetes Asn. *Res:* Product development of feminine hygiene products; study of adhesives; non-woven fabrics; surface chemistry; paper & pulp chemistry; product development of otc drugs, devices and diagnostics relating to diabetes and health care. *Mailing Add:* 575 Ridgewood Ave Glen Ridge NJ 07028

DAWSON, CHANDLER R, b Denver, Colo, Aug 24, 30; m 54; c 3. OPHTHALMOLOGY. *Educ:* Princeton Univ, AB, 52; Yale Univ, MD, 56. *Prof Exp:* USPHS epidemiologist, Commun Dis Ctr, 57-60; resident ophthal, 60-63, asst clin prof, 63-66, asst res prof, 66-69, assoc prof in residence, 69-75, PROF OPHTHALMOL, SCH MED, UNIV CALIF, SAN FRANCISCO, 75- *Concurrent Pos:* Fel, Middlesex Hosp Med Sch, London, 63-64; dir, WHO Collab Ctr Prevention Blindness & Trachoma; assoc dir, Francis I Proctor Found, 70- *Honors & Awards:* Knapp Award, AMA, 67 & 69; Medaille Trachome, 78. *Mem:* Am Soc Microbiol; Am Acad Ophthal & Otolaryngol; Asn Res Vision & Ophthalmol. *Res:* Epidemiology of infectious eye diseases and cataracts; prevention of blindness; pathogenesis of virus diseases of the eyes; electron microscropy of eye diseases. *Mailing Add:* Francis I Proctor Found Univ of Calif San Francisco CA 94143

DAWSON, CHARLES ERIC, b Vancouver, BC, Dec 6, 22; nat US; m 45; c 2. ICHTHYOLOGY. *Educ:* Univ Miami, Fla, BSc, 53. *Prof Exp:* Fisheries technician, Univ Miami, Fla, 48-49, oceanog technician, 51; oyster biologist, State of Fla, 49-52, head, Div Oyster Culture, 53-54; res scientist III, Univ Tex, 54-55, res scientist IV, Shrimp Invest, 55, proj dir, 55-56; biologist, Bears Bluff Labs & ichthyologist, Charleston Mus, 57-58; marine biologist & cur, 58-71, SR ICHTHYOLOGIST & CUR, GULF COAST RES LAB MUS, 71-; ASST PROF BIOL, UNIV SOUTHERN MISS, 71- *Concurrent Pos:* Fisheries consult, Arabian Am Oil Co, Saudi Arabia, 57; adj assoc prof, Miss State Univ, 69- *Mem:* Am Fisheries Soc; Am Soc Ichthyologists & Herpetologists; Am Inst Fishery Res Biol; Soc Syst Zool. *Res:* Ichthyology, systematics and distribution of tropical and subtropical shore fishes, especially, syngnathids, gobioids and dactyloscopids. *Mailing Add:* Gulf Coast Res Lab Mus Ocean Springs MS 39564 .

DAWSON, CHARLES H, b Uniontown, Pa, Dec 11, 16; m 38; c 2. ELECTRICAL ENGINEERING, MATHEMATICS. *Educ:* Cornell Univ, EE, 38; Univ Rochester, MS, 41; Iowa State Col, PhD(elec eng), 52. *Prof Exp:* Instr eng, Univ Rochester, 38-42, 45, from asst to assoc prof, 46-58; prof & head dept, Univ RI, 58-59; sr eng specialist, Philco Western Develop Labs, 59-62; sr res engr, Radio Systs Lab, Stanford Res Inst, 62-67; staff scientist, 68-70 & 72-73, STAFF SCIENTIST, RADIO PHYSICS LAB, SRI INT, 74- *Concurrent Pos:* UNESCO assignment, specialist in telecommun, Univ Brasilia, 67-68; prof, Univ PEI, 70-72. *Mem:* Inst Elec & Electronics Engrs; Asn Comput Mach; Am Asn Eng Educ. *Res:* Statistical detection theory; digital computer systems; real time programming; simulation. *Mailing Add:* Radio Physics Lab SRI Int Menlo Park CA 94025

DAWSON, D(ONALD) E(MERSON), b Detroit, Mich, Oct 3, 25; m 52; c 1. ENGINEERING SCIENCE. *Educ:* Wayne State Univ, BS, 48; Pa State Univ, MS, 56, PhD(eng mech), 58. *Prof Exp:* Engr commun, Mich Bell Tel Co, 48-50; physicist aerosol physics, Battelle Mem Inst, 51-52; res assoc, Pa State Univ, 52-53; res engr eng sci, E I du Pont de Nemours & Co, 58-62; res mgr, Armour Res Found, 62-63; assoc prof eng sci, 63-66, PROF MATH & MECH, MICH TECHNOL UNIV, 66- *Mem:* AAAS; Am Phys Soc; Soc Indust & Appl Math. *Res:* Applied and engineering mathematics; dynamics; vibrations. *Mailing Add:* Royalwood Addn US Rte 41 Houghton MI 49931

DAWSON, DANIEL JOSEPH, b Philadelphia, Pa, July 17, 46; m 70. ORGANIC POLYMER CHEMISTRY. *Educ:* Univ NC, Chapel Hill, BS, 67; Calif Inst Technol, PhD(org chem), 71. *Prof Exp:* NIH fel org chem, Harvard Univ, 71-72; sr res chemist & mgr process chem, 72-78, assoc dir process develop, 78-80, DIR CHEM RES & DEVELOP, DYNAPOL, 80- *Mem:* Am Chem Soc. *Res:* Synthesis of high technology functional polymers including polymeric amines, dyes and antioxidants. *Mailing Add:* Dynapol 1454 Page Mill Rd Palo Alto CA 94304

DAWSON, DAVID CHARLES, b Pittsburgh, Pa, Feb 5, 44; m 67; c 2. PHYSIOLOGY. *Educ:* Univ Pittsburgh, BS, 66, PhD(biol), 71. *Prof Exp:* NIH fel membrane physiol & biophys, Sch Med, Yale Univ, 71-73; asst prof physiol & biophys, Sch Med, Univ Iowa, 73-79, assoc prof, 79-80; ASSOC PROF PHYSIOL, SCH MED, UNIV MICH, 81- *Mem:* Am Physiol Soc; Biophys Soc; Am Soc Zoologists; AAAS; Soc Gen Physiologists. *Res:* Ion transport by epithelia and hormonal control; control of amphibian pituitary secretion by light. *Mailing Add:* Med Sci II Univ Mich Med Sch Ann Arbor MI 48109

DAWSON, DAVID FLEMING, b Denton, Tex, Sept 16, 26; m 48; c 6. MATHEMATICAL ANALYSIS. *Educ:* Univ Tex, PhD(math), 57. *Prof Exp:* Asst prof math, Univ Mo, 57-59; from asst prof to assoc prof, 59-64, PROF MATH, N TEX STATE UNIV, 64- *Mem:* Am Math Soc; London Math Soc. *Res:* Analysis; continued fractions; summability theory. *Mailing Add:* 1015 Ector Denton TX 76201

DAWSON, DAVID H, b Brillion, Wis, Sept 21, 19; m 50; c 4. LAND USE PLANNING, SOIL CONSERVATION. *Educ:* Mich State Univ, BS, 48, DF, 57. *Prof Exp:* Plant mat specialist, Agr Res Serv, USDA, US Forest Serv, 57-61, plant geneticist, Rocky Mt Forest & Range Exp Sta, 62-67 & Inst Forest Genetics, 67-70, proj leader, NCent Forest Exp Sta, 70-75, prog mgr, 75-81. *Mem:* Ecol Soc Am; Soc Am Foresters; Int Union Forest Res Orgns. *Res:* Exploring parametecs of maximum yield of woody plants. *Mailing Add:* Forestry Sci Lab Star Rte 2 Rhinelander WI 54501

DAWSON, DAVID LYNN, b Denver, Colo, Sept 16, 42; m 63; c 3. GROSS ANATOMY, PHYSICAL ANTHROPOLOGY. *Educ:* Adams State Col, BA, 64; Southern Ill Univ, MA, 67, PhD(zool), 75. *Prof Exp:* Instr zool, Southern Ill Univ, 71; asst prof & chmn biol, Univ SDak, 71-74; asst prof, 75-80, ASSOC PROF ANAT, SCH MED, MARSHALL UNIV, 80- *Mem:* Am Soc Zoologists; Am Asn Anatomists; Am Asn Phys Anthropologists; Southern Soc Anatomists; Sigma Xi. *Mailing Add:* Dept Anat Sch Med Marshall Univ 1542 Spring Valley Dr Huntington WV 25704

DAWSON, DAVID W(ARFIELD), b Scottdale, Pa, June 20, 28; m 48; c 3. MECHANICAL ENGINEERING. *Educ:* Pa State Univ, BS, 50, MSME, 55. *Prof Exp:* Res mech engr, Cent Res Labs, Borg-Warner Corp, 51-56; sr res engr lab, Gen Motors Corp, 56-69; chief engr develop br, Div Motor Vehicle Res & Develop, Nat Air Pollution Control Admin, HEW, 69-70, chief advan automotive power systs br, 70-71, asst to dir, Div Advan Automotive Power Systs Develop, Off Air Prog, Environ Protection Agency, 71-77; PROJ ENGR, GARRETT INDUST, 77- *Concurrent Pos:* Instr Wayne State Univ, 56-63. *Mem:* Soc Automotive Engrs; Air Pollution Control Asn. *Res:* Automotive emissions research and low emission engine development. *Mailing Add:* 2314 W Sierra St Phoenix AZ 85029

DAWSON, DONALD ANDREW, b Montreal, Que, June 4, 37; m 64. MATHEMATICS, STATISTICS. *Educ:* McGill Univ, BSc, 58, MSc, 59; Mass Inst Technol, PhD(math), 63. *Prof Exp:* Sr engr commun theory, Raytheon Corp, Mass, 62-63; asst prof math, McGill Univ, 63-66; vis asst prof, Univ Ill, 66-67; PROF MATH, CARLETON UNIV, 67- *Concurrent Pos:* Assoc ed, Annals of Probability, 74-79; Vis prof, Univ Wis, 80-81. *Mem:* Am Math Soc; Can Math Soc; Inst Math Statist; Can Statist Soc. *Res:* Probability theory; statistical mechanics; stochastic processes; communications theory; functional analysis; probability theory. *Mailing Add:* Dept of Math Carleton Univ Ottawa ON K1S 5B6 Can

DAWSON, EARL B, b Perry, Fla, Feb 1, 30; m 51; c 4. BIOCHEMISTRY, NUTRITION. *Educ:* Univ Kans, BA, 55; Univ Mo, MA, 60, Tex A&M Univ, PhD(biochem & nutrit), 63. *Prof Exp:* Teacher, Salem Acad, NC, 57-58; technician biochem, R J Reynolds Tobacco Co, 58; lab instr physiol, Univ Mo, 58-60; instr biochem, Tex A&M Univ, 60-63; from instr to asst prof, 63-70, ASSOC PROF BIOCHEM, UNIV TEX MED BR GALVESTON, 70- *Concurrent Pos:* Biochemist consult, Interdept Comt Nutrit Nat Defense, NIH, 65. *Mem:* AAAS; Am Inst Nutrit; Am Soc Clin Nutrit; Am Soc Exp Biol Med; Am Inst Physics. *Res:* Mammalian renal physiology; changes in oxidative enzyme activity associated with cataract formation; placental changes in enzyme activity associated with toxemia of pregnancy; clinical nutrition; trace elements. *Mailing Add:* Dept of Obstet & Gynec Univ of Tex Med Br Galveston TX 77550

DAWSON, FRANK G(ATES), JR, b Alliance, NC, July 6, 25; m 47; c 3. NUCLEAR ENGINEERING. *Educ:* NC State Col, BEE, 50; Univ Wash, PhD(nuclear eng), 73. *Prof Exp:* Test engr, Gen Elec Co, 50-51, sr tech engr, Aircraft Nuclear Propulsion Dept, 51-55, prin engr, 56-60, tech specialist, Hanford Labs, 60, mgr appl physics, 60-63, mgr reactor physics, 63-65; mgr reactor physics, Pac Northwest Labs, 65-68, mgr physics & eng div, 68-71, asst lab dir, 71-73, dir, Battelle Energy Prog, 73-76, DIR, CORP TECH DEVELOP, BATTELLE MEM INST, 76- *Concurrent Pos:* Actg asst prof, Univ Cincinnati, 58-60; mem adv comt reactor physics, Atomic Energy Comn, 64-70; lectr, Univ Calif, Los Angeles, 67-68; mem, Europ-Am Comt Reactor Physics, 70-; US rep, panel on plutonium utilization, Int Atomic Energy Agency, 68, chmn panel on plutonium recycling in thermal power reactors, 71; US deleg, UN Int Conf Peaceful Uses of Atomic Energy, 71. *Res:* Reactor physics and design; energy. *Mailing Add:* Battelle Mem Inst 505 King Ave Columbus OH 43201

DAWSON, GLADYS QUINTY, b Trenton, NJ, Sept 3, 24; m 52. INORGANIC CHEMISTRY. *Educ:* Univ Ill, BS, 46, PhD(chem), 51. *Prof Exp:* Prin chemist chem res, Battelle Mem Inst, 51-52; instr chem, Pa State Univ, 56; patent liaison, E I du Pont de Nemours & Co, 58-63; from teaching assoc to asst prof, 63-71, ASSOC PROF CHEM, MICH TECHNOL UNIV, 71- *Mem:* Am Chem Soc. *Res:* Chemical education. *Mailing Add:* Royalewood Addition Box 39 Houghton MI 49931

DAWSON, GLYN, b New Mills, Eng, Mar 24, 43; m 66; c 2. BIOCHEMISTRY. *Educ:* Univ Bristol, BSc, 64, PhD(biochem), 67. *Prof Exp:* Fel, Univ Pittsburgh, 67-68; res assoc, Mich State Univ, 68-69; from asst prof to assoc prof, 69-75, ASSOC PROF PEDIAT & BIOCHEM, UNIV CHICAGO, 75- *Mem:* AAAS; Am Soc Biol Chem; Soc Complex Carbohydrates; Am Soc Neurochem. *Res:* Regulation of glycosphingolipid glycoprotein and phospholipid metabolism in human cells especially cultured cells-fibroblasts, glial, neuroblastomas by neurotransmitters, hormones etc; inborn errors of metabolism; carbohydrate structure; mass spectrometry. *Mailing Add:* Dept of Pediat & Biochem Box 82 950 E 59th St Chicago IL 60637

DAWSON, HORACE RAY, b Wills Point, Tex, Mar 29, 35; m 56; c 2. PHYSICS. *Educ:* NTex State Univ, BA, 57, MA, 61; Univ Ark, PhD(physics), 68. *Prof Exp:* Instr physics, ETex State Univ, 61-63; assoc prof, 66-76, PROF PHYSICS & HEAD DEPT, ANGELO STATE UNIV, 76- *Mem:* Am Asn Physics Teachers. *Res:* Atomic collisions; radiative lifetimes of atoms; gamma ray spectroscopy. *Mailing Add:* Dept of Physics Angelo State Univ San Angelo TX 76909

DAWSON, J W, b Toronto, Ont, Dec 30, 28; m 52; c 4. INTERNAL MEDICINE, ENDOCRINOLOGY. *Educ:* Univ Toronto, MD, 53; FRCP(C). *Prof Exp:* ASSOC DEAN, UNIV CALGARY, 67-, PROF MED, FAC MED, 68-, DIR DIV CONTINUING MED EDUC, 71- *Concurrent Pos:* Consult internist, Calgary Assoc Clin. *Mem:* Fel Am Col Physicians; Can Soc Clin Invest. *Res:* Pituitary cytology; thyroidology; medical education. *Mailing Add:* Fac of Med Univ of Calgary Calgary AB T2N 1N4 Can

DAWSON, JAMES CLIFFORD, b Toronto, Ont, Apr 19, 41; US citizen; m 71. SEDIMENTOLOGY, COASTAL PROCESSES. *Educ:* Univ Calif, Los Angeles, BS, 65, MS, 67; Univ Wis, Madison, PhD(geol), 70. *Prof Exp:* Asst prof, 70-74, assoc prof geol, 74-80, chmn, Dept Earth Sci, 75-76, PROF ENVIRON SCI, STATE UNIV NY COL, PLATTSBURG, 80-, DIR, INST MAN & ENVIRON, 76- *Concurrent Pos:* Prin investr, State Univ NY Res Found fel & grant-in-aid, 71. *Mem:* AAAS; Nat Asn Environ Educ; Nat Asn Geol Teachers; Sigma Xi; Soc Econ Paleontologists & Mineralogists. *Res:* Carboniferous sedimentology of the Falkland Islands; upper Jurassic and lower Cretaceous sedimentology of the Colorado Plateau; shoreline processes of Lake Champlain; chert petrography; Adrondack wilderness management. *Mailing Add:* Inst for Man & Environ State Univ of NY Col Plattsburgh NY 12901

DAWSON, JAMES THOMAS, b Dover, Ohio, Nov 10, 47; m 76; c 2. PHYCOLOGY. *Educ:* Kent State Univ, BS, 70; Univ Ky, PhD(biol), 77. *Prof Exp:* Technician chem, Dover Chem Corp, 70-71; lab supvr biol, Univ Ky, 77-78; ASST PROF BIOL, PITTSBURGH STATE UNIV, 78- *Mem:* Phycological Soc Am; Sigma Xi; Int Phycol Soc; Brit Phycol Soc. *Res:* Taxonomy and physiology of freshwater algae, particularly the green algae; taxonomy and distribution of higher aquatic plants. *Mailing Add:* Dept of Biol Pittsburg State Univ Pittsburg KS 66762

DAWSON, JEAN HOWARD, b Stacy, Minn, Apr 14, 33; m 54; c 5. WEED SCIENCE. *Educ:* Univ Minn, BS, 55; Univ Calif, MS, 57; Ore State Univ, PhD(weed control), 61. *Prof Exp:* Res asst agron, Univ Calif, 55-57; RES AGRONOMIST & RES LEADER, USDA, 57- *Concurrent Pos:* Consult weed sci, Food & Agr Orgn UN, Alfalfa Improv Proj, Arg, 74-75; coop weed res in Costa Rica & El Salvador, Int Plant Protection Ctr, Ore State Univ, 78; instr & co-dir weed sci course, Food & Agr Orgn, UN, Argentina, 79. *Mem:* Weed Sci Soc Am. *Res:* Principles and practices of weed control in irrigated crops; dodder control in alfalfa; herbicide mode of action and weed biology studies. *Mailing Add:* Irrig Agr Res & Exten Ctr USDA Prosser WA 99350

DAWSON, JEFFREY ROBERT, b Lakewood, Ohio, Oct 5, 41; m 64; c 3. IMMUNOLOGY, BIOCHEMISTRY. *Educ:* Rensselaer Polytech Inst, BS, 64; Case Western Reserve Univ, PhD(biochem), 69. *Prof Exp:* NIH fel biochem, 69-71, instr, 71-72, assoc, 72-74, asst prof, 74-77, ASSOC PROF IMMUNOL, MED CTR, DUKE UNIV, 77- *Mem:* Am Asn Immunol; Sigma Xi; Brit Soc Immunol; Am Asn Cancer Res. *Res:* Human immunity to ovarian cancer. *Mailing Add:* Div Immunol Duke Univ Med Ctr Box 3010 Durham NC 27706

DAWSON, JOHN E, b Hamilton, Ohio, Oct 19, 24; m 69; c 3. REPRODUCTIVE PHYSIOLOGY. *Educ:* Univ Cincinnati, BA, 47, MS, 56, PhD(endocrinol), 62. *Prof Exp:* Teacher high sch, Ky, 47-53 & Ohio, 53-55; asst prof gen zool & sci educ, San Jose State Col, 58-64; asst prof gen biol & physiol, 64-67, prof biol, 64-75, assoc prof physiol, 67-76, prof, 76-82, EMER PROF BIOL, OHIO NORTHERN UNIV, 82- *Concurrent Pos:* Res fel, Univ Wash, 68-69. *Mem:* AAAS; Sigma Xi; Nat Educ Asn; Am Asn Univ Prof. *Res:* Effect of chronic administration of sodium tolbutamide on pregnant albino rats and their offspring; effect of luteinizing hormone on membrane permeability of frog oocytes. *Mailing Add:* 7951 Deer Creek Dr Sacramento CA 95823

DAWSON, JOHN FREDERICK, b Springfield, Ohio, Jan 4, 36; m 58; c 1. PHYSICS. *Educ:* Antioch Col, BS, 58; Stanford Univ, PhD(physics), 63. *Prof Exp:* Res assoc physics, McGill Univ, 62-64; asst prof, Antioch Col, 64-65; vis asst prof, Oberlin Col, 65-66; res assoc, Lowell Technol Inst Res Found, 66-68; from asst prof to assoc prof, 74-80, PROF PHYSICS, UNIV NH, 80- *Mem:* Am Phys Soc. *Res:* Theoretical nuclear physics. *Mailing Add:* Dept of Physics Univ of NH Durham NH 03824

DAWSON, JOHN HAROLD, b Englewood, NJ, Sept 19, 50; m 73. BIO-INORGANIC CHEMISTRY, BIO-ORGANIC CHEMISTRY. *Educ:* Columbia Univ, AB, 72; Stanford Univ, PhD(chem), 76. *Prof Exp:* Res & teaching asst chem, Stanford Univ, 72-76; fel chem, Calif Inst Technol, 76-78; ASST PROF CHEM & BIOCHEM, UNIV SC, 78- *Mem:* Am Chem Soc; Sigma Xi. *Res:* Biochemistry; spectroscopy and mechanism of action of iron and copper oxygen-utilizing metallo-enzymes and model systems; protein electron transfer; membrane bound proteins; magnetic circular dichroism spectroscopy. *Mailing Add:* Dept of Chem Univ SC Columbia SC 29208

DAWSON, JOHN MYRICK, b Champaign, Ill, Sept 30, 30; m 57; c 2. PLASMA PHYSICS. *Educ:* Univ Md, BS, 52, MS, 54, PhD(physics), 56. *Prof Exp:* Res physicist, Proj Matterhorn, Princeton Univ, 56-62, plasma physics lab, 62-64, assoc head theoret group, 64-66, head, 66-73, lectr, 60-73; PROF PHYSICS, UNIV CALIF, LOS ANGELES, 73- *Concurrent Pos:* COnsult, RCA Corp, 62-63 & Boeing Co, 64; Fulbright fel, Inst Plasma Physics, Univ Nagoya, 64-65; sci adv, Dir Naval Res Lab, 69-; chmn plasma physics div, Am Phys Soc, 70-71; consult math sci, Northwestern Univ, 72; consult, TRW, 73- *Honors & Awards:* James Clerk Maxwell Prize in Div Plasma Physics, 77. *Mem:* Nat Acad Sci; Am Phys Soc. *Res:* Plasma, atomic and molecular physics. *Mailing Add:* Dept of Physics 405 Hilgarde Ave Univ Calif Los Angeles CA 90024

DAWSON, JOHN WILLIAM, JR, b Wichita, Kans, Feb 4, 44; m 70. MATHEMATICAL LOGIC. *Educ:* Mass Inst Technol, BS, 66; Univ Mich, PhD(math), 72. *Prof Exp:* Instr math, Pa State Univ, 72-75; asst prof math, 75-81, ASSOC PROF MATH, PA STATE UNIV, YORK CAMPUS, 81- *Mem:* Am Math Soc; Math Asn Am; Asn Symbolic Logic. *Res:* Axiomatic set theory; history of modern logic. *Mailing Add:* 393 Waters Rd York PA 17403

DAWSON, LAWRENCE E, b Mich, July 23, 16; m 45; c 1. FOOD SCIENCE. *Educ:* Mich State Univ, BS, 42, MS, 46; Purdue Univ, PhD(agr mkt), 49. *Prof Exp:* Asst, Purdue Univ, 46-49; PROF FOOD SCI, MICH STATE UNIV, 49-, ACTG CHMN, FOOD & HUMAN NUTRIT DEPT, 79- *Honors & Awards:* Res Achievement Award, Poultry & Egg Nat Bd, 61. *Mem:* Fel Poultry Sci Asn; Inst Food Technol; World Poultry Sci Asn. *Res:* Poultry, egg and fish products technology, flavor, composition and preservation. *Mailing Add:* Dept of Food Sci & Human Nutrit Mich State Univ East Lansing MI 48823

DAWSON, MARCIA ILTON, b Detroit, Mich, May 4, 42; m 70. BIO-ORGANIC CHEMISTRY. *Educ:* Univ Mich, Ann Arbor, BS, 64; Stanford Univ, PhD(org chem), 68. *Prof Exp:* Fel org chem, Calif Inst Technol, 68; NIH fel biochem, Harvard Univ, 69; fel org chem, Calif Inst Technol, 70-71; NIH spec fel, Harvard Univ, 71-72; org chemist, 72-76, sr biochemist, 77-80, PROG DIR, LIFE SCI DIV, SRI INT, 80- *Mem:* Am Chem Soc; Sigma Xi. *Res:* Application of organic synthesis to biochemical problems, particularly in the areas of prostaglandin, retinoid, and biochemistry. *Mailing Add:* SRI Int Life Sci Div Menlo Park CA 94025

DAWSON, MARY (RUTH), b Highland Park, Mich, Feb 27, 31. VERTEBRATE PALEONTOLOGY. *Educ:* Mich State Univ, BS, 52; Univ Kans, PhD(zool), 57. *Prof Exp:* Instr zool, Univ Kans, 56-57; from instr to asst prof, Smith Col, 58-61; asst prog dir, NSF, 61-62; res assoc, 62-63, from asst cur to actg cur, chmn, Earth Sci, 74, 63-71, CUR, CARNEGIE MUS, 71- *Concurrent Pos:* Am Asn Univ Women fel, 57-58. *Honors & Awards:* Arnold Guyot Award, Nat Geog Soc, 81. *Mem:* Paleont Soc; Geol Soc Am; Soc Vert Paleont (pres, 73-74); Paläontologische Ges; Sigma Xi. *Res:* Paleontology of lagomorphs and rodents; early tertiary holarctic faunas; arctic tertiary mammals. *Mailing Add:* Sect of Vert Fossils Carnegie Mus 4400 Forbes Ave Pittsburgh PA 15213

DAWSON, MURRAY DRAYTON, b Christchurch, NZ, Dec 16, 25; US citizen; m 52; c 6. SOILS, PLANT PHYSIOLOGY. *Educ:* Univ NZ, BAgSc, 49, MAgSc, 51; Cornell Univ, MS, 52, PhD(soils), 54. *Prof Exp:* Res scientist field husb, Can Exp Sta, Swift Current, Sask, 50-51; PROF SOILS, ORE STATE UNIV, 54- *Concurrent Pos:* Consult prof, Univ Agr, Bangkok, 59-60; consult, Ford Found, Chiang Mai Univ, 74- *Mem:* Am Soc Agron. *Res:* Legume establishment growth and development on infertile acid soils, with special reference to sulfur nutrition and molybdenum; multiple cropping research. *Mailing Add:* Dept of Soils Ore State Univ Corvallis OR 97331

DAWSON, PETER HENRY, b Derby, Eng, May 28, 37; m 63; c 2. CHEMICAL PHYSICS. *Educ:* Univ London, BSc, 58, PhD(phys chem), 61. *Prof Exp:* Fel, Nat Res Coun Can, 61-63; phys chemist, Res Lab, Gen Elec Co, NY, 63-69; res assoc, Ctr Res Atoms & Molecules, Laval Univ, 69-74; MEM STAFF PHYSICS DIV, NAT RES COUN, CAN, 74- *Mem:* Am Phys Soc; Am Vacuum Soc; Am Soc Mass Spectrometry. *Res:* Mass spectrometry and partial pressure analysis; development of quadrupole field instruments; vacuum techniques; surface physics; secondary ion mass spectrometry of surfaces. *Mailing Add:* 38 Viewmount Dr Neapean K2G 3C5 Can

DAWSON, PETER J, b Wolverhampton, Eng, Feb 17, 28. PATHOLOGY. *Educ:* Cambridge Univ, BA, 49, MB, BCh, 52, MA, 53, MD, 60; Univ London, dipl clin path, 55; Am Bd Path, dipl, 68. *Prof Exp:* House physician, Royal Berkshire Hosp, Reading, Eng, 52-53; house surgeon, Victoria Hosp for Children, London, 53; demonstr path, St George's Hosp Med Sch, London, 53-54, registr morbid anat & asst lectr, Postgrad Med Sch, 58-60; vis asst prof path, Sch Med, Univ Calif, San Francisco, 60-62; lectr, Med Sch, Univ Newcastle, 62-64; from assoc prof to prof path, Med Sch, Univ Ore, 64-76, head div surg path & cytol, 74-76; PROF PATH & DIR LAB SURG PATH, UNIV CHICAGO, 77- *Mem:* Am Asn Cancer Res; Path Soc Gt Brit & Ireland; Royal Col Path; Am Asn Pathologists; Int Acad Path. *Res:* Human and animal malignant lymphomas; virus-induced leukemias. *Mailing Add:* Dept of Path 950 E 59th St Chicago IL 60601

DAWSON, PETER SANFORD, b Philadelphia, Pa, Apr 16, 39; m 59; c 2. POPULATION BIOLOGY, GENETICS. *Educ:* Wash State Univ, BS, 60; Univ Calif, Berkeley, PhD(genetics), 64. *Prof Exp:* Proj asst, Univ Wis, Madison, 65-66; asst prof zool, Univ Ill, Urbana, 66-69; assoc prof, 69-75, PROF ZOOL, ORE STATE UNIV, 75-, CHMN GENETICS PROG, 77- *Mem:* AAAS; Genetics Soc Am; Soc Study Evolution; Am Soc Naturalists. *Res:* Genetic structure of populations; evolution of interspecific competitive ability and cannibalistic behavior in flour beetles; population dynamics and regulation of population size. *Mailing Add:* Dept of Zool Ore State Univ Corvallis OR 97331

DAWSON, PETER STEPHEN SHEVYN, b Birmingham, Eng, Apr 10, 23; m 57; c 2. MICROBIAL BIOCHEMISTRY, PHYSIOLOGY. *Educ:* Birmingham Univ, Eng, BSc, 44 & 47, MSc, 48, Dipl, 49; Univ Sask, PhD(biochem), 64. *Prof Exp:* Res asst chem, Tame & Rae Drainage Bd, Birmingham, Eng, 44-48; sr sci officer microbiol, Chem Res Lab, Dept Sci & Indust Res, Teddington, Eng, 50-57; SR RES OFFICER BIOTECHNOL, PRAIRIE REGIONAL LAB, NAT RES COUN CAN, 57- *Concurrent Pos:* Ed, Microbial Growth, Dowden, Hutchinson & Ross, 74. *Mem:* Assoc Royal Inst Chem; assoc Soc Gen Microbiol. *Res:* Metabolism and physiology of microbes and cells in continuous, asynchronous/synchronous growth; development of rationale, procedures, processes and equipment for fundamental and applied microbiology based upon the cell. *Mailing Add:* Prairie Regional Lab Nat Res Coun Can Saskatoon Can

DAWSON, PETER THOMAS, b Billingham, Eng, May 16, 38; m 65; c 2. SURFACE CHEMISTRY. *Educ:* Univ Birmingham, Eng, BSc, 59; Cambridge Univ, PhD(surface chem), 63. *Prof Exp:* Res assoc chem, Ames Lab, Iowa State Univ, AEC, 63-67; asst prof, 67-73, ASSOC PROF CHEM, McMASTER UNIV, 73- *Concurrent Pos:* Assoc mem, Inst Mat Res & Dept Metall & Mat Sci, McMaster Univ, 67- & Dept Physics, 69- *Mem:* Royal Soc Chem; Am Vacuum Soc. *Res:* Fundamental studies on the interactions between gases and well-characterized surfaces emphasizing systems of catalytic interest; ultra-high vacuum techniques used include field emission, mass spectrometry, low energy electron diffraction and electron spectroscopy. *Mailing Add:* Dept of Chem McMaster Univ Hamilton ON L8S 4L8 Can

DAWSON, ROBERT LOUIS, b Rochester, NY, Oct 18, 36; m 65. POLYMER CHEMISTRY. *Educ:* Univ Rochester, BS, 58; Harvard Univ, PhD(org chem), 62. *Prof Exp:* RES ORG CHEMIST, E I DU PONT DE NEMOURS & CO, INC, 62- *Mem:* Am Chem Soc. *Res:* Preparation of new synthetic elastomers and monomers. *Mailing Add:* 1220 Elderon Dr Wilmington DE 19808

DAWSON, SARA LYNN, b Cleveland, Ohio, Aug 31, 55. ELEMENTARY PARTICLE PHYSICS. *Educ:* Duke Univ, BS, 77; Harvard Univ, AM, 78, PhD(physics), 81. *Prof Exp:* RES ASSOC, FERMI NAT ACCELERATOR LAB, 81- *Res:* Fundamental theories of the strong, weak and electromagnetic interactions and obtaining testable predictions from these theories. *Mailing Add:* Fermi Nat Accelerator Lab PO Box 500 Batavia IL 60510

DAWSON, THOMAS HENRY, mechanics, see previous edition

DAWSON, THOMAS LARRY, b Logan, WVa, Nov 7, 34; m 57; c 2. PHYSICAL CHEMISTRY, POLYMER CHEMISTRY. *Educ:* Berea Col, AB, 56; Univ Ky, MS, 58, PhD(phys chem), 60. *Prof Exp:* Chemist, Am Viscose Corp, 56; chemist, 60-70, res scientist, 70-75, GROUP LEADER & TECHNOL MGR, CHEM & PLASTICS DIVS, UNION CARBIDE CORP, 75- *Mem:* Am Chem Soc. *Res:* Kinetics and mechanisms of reactions in solutions; reactions on polymers; polymer synthesis; kinetics of free radical polymerization. *Mailing Add:* 731 Churchill Dr Charleston WV 25314

DAWSON, WALLACE DOUGLAS, JR, b Louisville, Ky, Mar 15, 31; c 3. GENETICS, EVOLUTION. *Educ:* Western Ky State Col, BS, 54; Univ Ky, MS, 59; Ohio State Univ, PhD(genetics), 62. *Prof Exp:* From asst prof to prof, Univ SC, 62-77, dept head, 74-77, George Bunch chair prof biol, 77-80. *Mem:* AAAS; Am Genetic Asn; Am Soc Mammal; Soc Study Evolution; Genetics Soc Am. *Res:* Developmental genetics and evolution of rodents; speciation and endocrinology of Peromyscus. *Mailing Add:* Dept of Biol Univ of SC Columbia SC 29208

DAWSON, WILFRED KENNETH, b Quebec, Que, Oct 6, 27; m 54; c 2. NUCLEAR PHYSICS. *Educ:* Laval Univ, BScA, 51; Queen's Univ, Can, PhD(physics), 55. *Prof Exp:* Defense serv sci officer nuclear physics, Defense Res Bd, Can, 55-59; from asst prof to assoc prof physics, 59-70, PROF NUCLEAR PHYSICS, UNIV ALTA, 70- *Mem:* Am Phys Soc; Can Asn Physicists. *Res:* Fast neutron time-of-flight spectroscopy; nuclear stripping reactions; photonuclear reactions. *Mailing Add:* Dept of Physics Univ of Alta Edmonton Can

DAWSON, WILLIAM RYAN, b Los Angeles, Calif, Aug 24, 27; m 50; c 3. COMPARATIVE PHYSIOLOGY. *Educ:* Univ Calif, Los Angeles, PhD(zool), 53; Univ Western Australia, DSc(eco-physiol), 71. *Prof Exp:* Asst zool, Univ Calif, Los Angeles, 51-52; USPHS fel, 53; from instr to assoc prof, 53-62, PROF ZOOL, UNIV MICH, ANN ARBOR, 62- *Concurrent Pos:* Guggenheim fel, 62-63; res fel, Australian-Am Educ Found, 69-70. *Mem:* Ecol Soc Am; Am Ornith Union; Cooper Ornith Soc; Am Soc Zool; Am Physiol Soc. *Res:* Temperature regulation and water balance of birds and mammals; reptile physiology; avian paleontology. *Mailing Add:* Div of Biol Sci Univ of Mich Ann Arbor MI 48104

DAWSON, WILLIAM WOODSON, b Nashville, Tenn, May 21, 33; m 55; c 2. PHYSIOLOGY, BIOPHYSICS. *Educ:* Vanderbilt Univ, BA, 55; Fla State Univ, MS, 57, PhD(psychol), 61. *Prof Exp:* Asst res prof psychol, Auburn Univ, 63-64; Joseph P Kennedy prof, George Peabody Col, 64-65; assoc prof ophthal, 65-69, PROF OPHTHAL & PHYSIOL, COL MED, UNIV FLA, 69-, MEM, CTR NEUROBIOL SCI, 66- *Concurrent Pos:* Assoc investr, Nat Inst Neurol Dis & Blindness res grants, 60-61; prin investr, 66-; Army Med Res & Develop Command, 63-64; Consult, Donner Lab Biophys, Univ Calif, Berkeley, 61 & Stanford Res Inst, 62; mem vision comt, Nat Acad Sci-Nat Res Coun, 68-; dir, Ctr Res on Human Prostheses, 71-; mem adv panel, NSF Neurobiol Prog, 72-75. *Mem:* Fel AAAS; Radiation Res Soc; Am Physiol Soc. *Res:* Sense receptor electro-physiology and psychophysics, especially cutaneous quality, vision and receptor biology. *Mailing Add:* Dept of Ophthal Univ of Fla Gainesville FL 32611

DAY, ARDEN DEXTER, b Rutland, Vt, Mar 16, 22; m 45; c 3. PLANT BREEDING. *Educ:* Cornell Univ, BS, 50; Mich State Univ, PhD, 54. *Prof Exp:* Asst prof agron & asst agronomist, 54-56, assoc prof agron & assoc agronomist, 56-59, PROF AGRON & AGRONOMIST, AGR EXP STA, UNIV ARIZ, 59- *Mem:* Fel Am Soc Agron. *Res:* Small grain breeding; environmental pollution control research. *Mailing Add:* Dept of Plant Sci Univ of Ariz Tucson AZ 85721

DAY, BENJAMIN DOWNING, b Nassawadox, Va, July 19, 36; m 58; c 2. THEORETICAL PHYSICS, NUCLEAR PHYSICS. *Educ:* Wesleyan Univ, BA, 58; Cornell Univ, PhD(theoret physics), 64. *Prof Exp:* Res physicist, Univ Calif, Los Angeles, 63-64, asst prof physics, 64-65; resident res assoc, 65-67, asst physicist, 67-69, assoc physicist, 70-79, SR SCIENTIST, ARGONNE NAT LAB, 80- *Concurrent Pos:* Guggenheim fel, 71. *Mem:* Am Phys Soc. *Res:* Theoretical nuclear physics, especially the nuclear many-body problem. *Mailing Add:* Physics Div Bldg 203 Argonne Nat Lab Argonne IL 60439

DAY, BILLY NEIL, b Arthur, WVa, Oct 23, 30; m 53; c 5. ANIMAL SCIENCE. *Educ:* WVa Univ, BS, 52, MS, 54; Iowa State Col, PhD(animal husb), 58. *Prof Exp:* Instr animal husb, Iowa State Col, 57-58; from asst prof to assoc prof, 58-68, PROF ANIMAL SCI, UNIV MO-COLUMBIA, 68- *Mem:* Am Soc Animal Sci; Brit Soc Study Fertil; Endocrine Soc; Soc Study Reproduction. *Res:* Physiology of reproduction in domestic animals. *Mailing Add:* 159 Animal Sci Res Ctr Univ of Mo Columbia MO 65211

DAY, BOYSIE EUGENE, b Haile, La, Sept 9, 17; m 41; c 3. PLANT PHYSIOLOGY. *Educ:* Univ Ariz, BS, 38, MS, 40; Univ Calif, PhD(plant physiol), 50. *Prof Exp:* Prof plant physiol & plant physiologist, Univ Calif, Riverside, 50-70, assoc dir, Agr Exp Sta, Berkeley, 71-72, dir, 72-73, dir citrus res ctr, 68-71, chmn dept hort sci, Riverside, 66-68, PROF PLANT PHYSIOL, UNIV CALIF, BERKELEY, 73- *Concurrent Pos:* Chmn subcomt weeds, Nat Res Coun, 60-70; mem comt on pest control, Nat Acad Sci, 71-75; mem comt pesticide res priorities, NSF, 75- *Mem:* AAAS; Am Soc Plant Physiol; Bot Soc Am; Am Soc Hort Sci; fel Weed Sci Soc Am (pres, 68). *Res:* Chemical weed control; chemistry of herbicidal action. *Mailing Add:* Dept of Plant Path Univ of Calif Berkeley CA 94720

DAY, BRUCE FREDERICK, organic chemistry, see previous edition

DAY, CECIL LEROY, b Dexter, Mo, Oct 4, 22; m 48; c 2. AGRICULTURAL ENGINEERING. *Educ:* Univ Mo, BS, 45, MS, 48; Iowa State Univ, PhD(eng), 57. *Prof Exp:* From instr to assoc prof, 45-62, PROF AGR ENG, UNIV MO-COLUMBIA, 62-, CHMN DEPT, 69- *Mem:* Am Soc Agr Engrs; Nat Soc Prof Engrs. *Mailing Add:* Dept Agr Eng Univ Mo Columbia MO 65211

DAY, D(ELBERT) E(DWIN), b Avon, Ill, Aug 16, 36; m 56; c 2. CERAMICS, MATERIALS SCIENCE. *Educ:* Mo Sch Mines, BS, 58; Pa State Univ, MS, 60, PhD(ceramic tech), 61. *Prof Exp:* Asst prof ceramic eng, Mo Sch Mines, 61-62; from asst prof to assoc prof ceramic eng, 64-67, dir, Indust Res Ctr, 67-72, PROF CERAMIC ENG, UNIV MO-ROLLA, 67-, SR INVESTR, MAT RES CTR, 74- *Honors & Awards:* Prof Achievement Ceramic Eng Award, Nat Inst Ceramic Engrs, 71. *Mem:* Fel Am Ceramic Soc; Am Soc Testing & Mat; Am Soc Eng Educ; Nat Inst Ceramic Engrs; Brit Soc Glass Technol. *Res:* Mass transport, anelasticity, structure and electrical properties of vitreous solids; crystal structure and properties of refractory cements; gaseous corrosion of refractory oxides. *Mailing Add:* Mat Res Ctr Univ Mo Rolla MO 65401

DAY, DAVID ALLEN, b Ann Arbor, Mich, Nov 22, 24; m 45; c 5. ENGINEERING. *Educ:* Cornell Univ, BCE, 45; Univ Ill, MS, 51. *Prof Exp:* Field supt, Raymond Concrete Pile Co, 46-47; tech engr, Gen Paving Co, Ill, 47-48; from instr to assoc prof civil eng & in-charge construct center, Univ Ill, 48-58; prof & chmn dept, Univ Denver, 58-60, dean col eng, 60-68, prof civil eng, 68-74; sr staff civil engr, 74-77, proj civil engr, 77-81, PROJ ENGR, STEARNS-ROGER, INC, 81- *Concurrent Pos:* Consult, State of Ill, 51-58 & Bridge Off, Ill Div Hwys, 52-56; mem proj adv comt, Ill Div Hwys & US Bur Pub Rds, 54-58; assoc, Gen Contractors Am, 59-70; dir, Urban Drainage & Flood Control Dist Bd, 77- *Mem:* Am Soc Civil Engrs; Am Soc Eng Educ; Nat Soc Prof Engrs. *Res:* Construction engineering, structural design problems; economics and planning of construction operations; structural and construction materials. *Mailing Add:* Stearns-Roger Inc PO Box 5888 Denver CO 80217

DAY, DONAL FOREST, b New Brunswick, NJ, Feb 24, 43; m 73; c 2. BIOENGINEERING. *Educ:* Univ NH, BSc, 65; McGill Univ, PhD(microbiol), 73. *Prof Exp:* Fel microbiol, Dept Microbiol & Immunol, McGill Univ, 73-75; asst prof microbiol, Dept Microbiol, Univ Guelph, 75-79; ASST PROF, AUDUBON SUGAR INST, LA STATE UNIV, 79- *Mem:* Am Soc Microbiol; Am Chem Soc; Can Soc Microbiologists; NY Acad Sci; Sigma Xi. *Res:* Ethanol production by immobilized cells, cellulose degradation; use of enzymes in and the development of new industrial processes based on enzymes or microorganisms. *Mailing Add:* Audubon Sugar Inst La State Univ Baton Rouge LA 70803

DAY, DONALD LEE, b Leedey, Okla, Aug 14, 31; m 54; c 3. AGRICULTURAL ENGINEERING. *Educ:* Okla State Univ, BS, 54, PhD(agr eng), 62; Univ Mo, MS, 58. *Prof Exp:* Instr agr eng, Tex Tech Col, 57-58; asst, Univ Mo, 58-59 & Okla State Univ, 59-62; from asst prof to assoc prof, 62-71, PROF AGR ENG, UNIV ILL, URBANA, 71- *Concurrent Pos:* Nat Ctr Urban & Indust Health res grant, 66-69; consult exec, UN WHO, Romania, 73-75. *Honors & Awards:* Cert of Serv, Am Soc Agr Engrs, 75. *Mem:* Am Soc Agr Engrs; Am Soc Eng Educ. *Res:* Livestock housing and environmental factors; livestock waste disposal; recycling agricultural wastes; air pollution in and around livestock buildings. *Mailing Add:* Dept of Agr Eng Univ of Ill Urbana IL 61801

DAY, EDGAR WILLIAM, JR, b New Albany, Ind, Sept 7, 36; m 59; c 4. PESTICIDE RESIDUE, ENVIRONMENTAL CHEMISTRY. *Educ:* Univ Notre Dame, BS, 58; Iowa State Univ, PhD(anal chem), 63. *Prof Exp:* Sr anal chemist, 63-81, RES ASSOC, ELI LILLY & CO, 81- *Mem:* Am Chem Soc; Soc Appl Spectros; Soc Environ Toxicol & Chem. *Res:* gas chromatography; general organic chemical analysis; pesticide formulation and residue analysis; radiochemistry; organic mass spectrometry; high-performance liquid chromatography; environmental fate and risk analysis associated with pesticides. *Mailing Add:* Eli Lilly & Co PO Box 708 Greenfield IN 46140

DAY, ELBERT JACKSON, b Cullman, Ala, Mar 11, 25; m 48; c 3. POULTRY NUTRITION. *Educ:* Ala Polytech Inst, BS, 52, MS, 53, PhD(poultry nutrit), 56. *Prof Exp:* Asst animal nutritionist, Ala Polytech Inst, 55-56; from asst prof to assoc prof poultry sci, 56-59, nutritionist, 56-59, PROF POULTRY SCI, MISS STATE UNIV, 60- *Mem:* Poultry Sci Asn; Am Inst Nutrit. *Res:* Effects of dietary modifications on pigmentation of broilers; proper dietary balance of protein and energy for poultry rations; improvement in performance of poultry rations with feed additives. *Mailing Add:* Dept of Poultry Sci Miss State Univ Box 5188 Mississippi State MS 39762

DAY, EMERSON, b Hanover, NH, May 2, 13; m 37; c 5. INTERNAL MEDICINE. *Educ:* Dartmouth Col, AB, 34; Harvard Univ, MD, 38. *Prof Exp:* Intern, Med Serv, Presby Hosp, New York, 38-40; Libman fel med, Johns Hopkins Hosp, 40-42; asst resident med, NY Hosp, 42; med dir int div, TransWorld Airline, New York, 45-47; from asst prof to assoc prof pub health & prev med, Med Col, Cornell Univ, 47-54, prof prev med & chief div, Sloan-Kettering Div, 54-64, head dept prev med, Mem Ctr, 54-63; dir, Strang Clin, 63-69, pres, Prev Med Inst, 66-69; vpres & med dir, 69-76, SR MED CONSULT, MEDEQUIP INC, 76-; prof med, 76-81, assoc dir, Cancer Ctr, 76-81, EMER PROF MED, MED SCH NORTHWESTERN UNIV, 76- *Concurrent Pos:* Dir, Kips Bay-Yorkville Cancer Detection Ctr, 47-50 & Strang Cancer Prev Clin, 50-63; consult, Off Sci Res & Develop, US Navy, 47-50; attend physician, Mem Hosp, 50-63; assoc, Sloan-Kettering Inst, 52-54, mem, 54-64; mem advan technol comt, Ill Regional Med Prog; mem bd trustees, Prev Med Inst, 66-; dir, Int Health Eval Asn, 73-; attend physician, Northwestern Mem Hosp, 76-81, sr physician, 81-; physician affil staff, Evanston & Glenbrook Hosp, Evanston, Ill, 76-; med dir, Portes Cancer Prev Ctr, 78-79. *Honors & Awards:* Bronze Medal, Am Cancer Soc, 56; Papanicolaou Award, 78. *Mem:* Fel Am Col Physicians; fel Am pub health Systs & Informatics; fel NY Acad Med; fel NY Acad Sci (pres, 65); Am Soc Cytol (pres, 58). *Res:* Preventive medicine; automated multiphase health testing; medical care systems; cancer detection and prevention; cardiology; aviation physiology; neurology; pain mechanisms. *Mailing Add:* 320 Pebblebrook Dr Northbrook IL 60062

DAY, EMMETT E(LBERT), b Paris, Tex, July 21, 15; m 37; c 2. MECHANICAL ENGINEERING. *Educ:* E Tex State Teachers Col, BA, 36; Mass Inst Technol, BS, 45, MS, 47. *Prof Exp:* Instr, Pub Sch, Tex, 36-40; indust specialist, War Prod Bd, 40-42; instrument specialist, San Antonio Arsenal, 42-43; asst instr mech eng, Mass Inst Technol, 44-46, instr, 46-47; from asst prof to assoc prof, 47-54, PROF MECH ENG, UNIV WASH, 54- *Concurrent Pos:* Ed, Mach Design Bull, Am Soc Eng Educ, 54-57. *Mem:* Soc Exp Stress Anal; Am Soc Mech Engrs (vpres, 62-66); Am Soc Eng Educ. *Res:* Experimental stress analysis; materials of engineering. *Mailing Add:* 7520 57th Pl NE Seattle WA 98105

DAY, EUGENE DAVIS, b Cobleskill, NY, June 24, 25; m 46; c 1. IMMUNOLOGY. *Educ:* Union Univ, NY, BS, 49; Univ Del, MS, 50, PhD(biochem), 52. *Prof Exp:* Res assoc, Roscoe B Jackson Mem Lab, Maine, 52-54; sr cancer res biochemist, Roswell Park Mem Inst, 54-58, assoc cancer res biochemist, 58-62, asst res prof chem, Roswell Park Div, Sch Grad Studies, Buffalo, 57-62; assoc prof, 62-65, PROF IMMUNOL, MED CTR, DUKE UNIV, 65-, PROF EXP SURG, 77- *Mem:* Am Soc Neurochem; Am Asn Cancer Res; Am Asn Immunol. *Res:* Cancer immunology; immunochemistry; radio immunoassays; subcellular fractionations; neuroimmunology. *Mailing Add:* Box 3045 Duke Univ Med Ctr Durham NC 27710

DAY, FRANK PATTERSON, JR, b Bristol, Va, July 12, 47; m 69; c 2. ECOLOGY. *Educ:* Univ Tenn, BS, 69; Univ Ga, MS, 71, PhD(ecol), 74. *Prof Exp:* Res asst, Int Biol Prog, Univ Ga, 70-74; asst prof, 74-80, ASSOC PROF BIOL SCI, OLD DOMINION UNIV, 80- *Mem:* Am Inst Biol Sci; Ecol Soc Am; Bot Soc Am; Torrey Bot Club. *Res:* Ecosystem dynamics in Great Dismal Swamp of Virginia; primary productivity and nutrient turnover in the litter layer. *Mailing Add:* Dept Biol Sci Old Dominion Univ Norfolk VA 23508

DAY, GENE F, b Stamford, Tex, June 17, 36; m 59; c 2. MATERIALS SCIENCE. *Educ:* Univ Calif, Berkeley, AB, 58, MS, 60, PhD, 64. *Prof Exp:* Sr engr, Cent Res Lab, 63-69, SR ENGR, ELECTROPHOTOG UNIT, VARIAN ASSOCS, 69- *Mem:* AAAS; Soc Photog Sci & Eng. *Res:* Optical and electronic properties of metals, semiconductors and insulators. *Mailing Add:* 27791 Edgerton Rd Los Alto CA 94002

DAY, HAROLD J, b Milwaukee, Wis, May 22, 29; m 53; c 2. CIVIL ENGINEERING. *Educ:* Univ Wis, BS, 52, MS, 53, PhD(civil eng), 63. *Prof Exp:* Res asst, Hydraul & Sanit Lab, Univ Wis, 52-53, 62-63, instr civil eng, 59-60; proj engr, Scott Paper Co, 53-59; from asst prof to assoc prof civil eng, Carnegie-Mellon Univ, 63-70; chmn dept, 70-76, PROF ENVIRON CONTROL, UNIV WIS-GREEN BAY, 70- *Mem:* Am Geophys Union; Am Soc Civil Engrs. *Res:* Fluid mechanics; hydrology; water resources; hydraulics. *Mailing Add:* Dept of Environ Control Univ of Wis Green Bay WI 54301

DAY, HAROLD R(ANSOM), physics, physical electronics, see previous edition

DAY, HARRY GILBERT, b Monroe Co, Iowa, Oct 8, 06; m 33, 69; c 3. NUTRITIONAL BIOCHEMISTRY. *Educ:* Cornell Col, AB, 30; Johns Hopkins Univ, ScD(biochem), 33. *Hon Degrees:* ScD, Cornell Col, 67. *Prof Exp:* Nat Res fel, Johns Hopkins Univ, 33-34; Gen Educ Bd fel, Yale Univ, 34-36; assoc biochem, Sch Hyg & Pub Health, Johns Hopkins Univ, 36-40; from asst prof to prof, 40-50, chmn dept chem, 52-62, assoc dean res & advan studies, 67-72, prof chem, 50-77, EMER PROF CHEM, IND UNIV, BLOOMINGTON, 76- *Concurrent Pos:* Mem select comt on generally regarded as safe substances, Fedn Am Soc Exp Biol, Bethesda, Md, 73- *Mem:* AAAS; Am Chem Soc; Am Inst Nutrit (pres,71); Am Soc Biol Chem. *Res:* Evaluation of health aspects of food ingredients; history of nutrition. *Mailing Add:* Dept Chem Ind Univ Bloomington IN 47405

DAY, HARVEY JAMES, b Souderton, Pa, Mar 2, 29; m 51; c 3. INTERNAL MEDICINE, HEMATOLOGY. *Educ:* Villanova Univ, BS, 49; Hahnemann Med Col, MD, 53; Am Bd Internal Med, dipl. *Prof Exp:* Intern, Abington Mem Hosp, Pa, 53-54, resident med, 54-56; resident, Ohio State Univ Hosp, 56-57, instr, 57-58; instr hemat, 58-60, assoc med, 61-63, assoc prof, 63-64, PROF MED, SCH MED, TEMPLE UNIV, 66-, DIR HEMAT, 61- *Concurrent Pos:* Consult, Abington Mem Hosp, 59-, chief hemat, 65; res assoc, Inst Thrombosis Res, Riks Hosp, Norway, 66-68; Fulbright res scholar,

Univ Oslo, 66-68. *Mem:* Assoc Am Col Path; fel Am Col Physicians; Am Soc Hemat; Am Fedn Clin Res; Int Soc Hemat. *Res:* Platelets in thrombosis; blood platelets. *Mailing Add:* Dept of Med Temple Univ Sch of Med Philadelphia PA 19140

DAY, HERMAN O'NEAL, JR, b Dallas, Tex, Dec 4, 25; m 52; c 4. PHYSICAL CHEMISTRY. *Educ:* E Tex State Univ, BS, 45; Univ Tex, AM, 48, PhD(phys chem), 51. *Prof Exp:* Asst defense res lab, Univ Tex, 48-50; chemist, Oak Ridge Nat Lab, 51-56; chemist, Plant Tech Sect, Chambers Works, Org Chem Dept, 56-60, Jackson Lab, 60-63, Process Dept, Chambers Works, Org Chem Dept, 63-69, sr process chemist, 69-70, SR CHEMIST, PETROL CHEM DIV TECH SECT, CHAMBERS WORKS, CHEM & PIGMENTS DEPT, E I DU PONT DE NEMOURS & CO, INC, 70- *Mem:* Am Chem Soc. *Res:* The pressure-volume-temperature relationships of gases and liquids; solution chemistry of the heavy elements; radiation corrosion in homogeneous nuclear reactors; manufacture of tetraalkyl lead. *Mailing Add:* Petrol Chem Div Chambers Works E I du Pont de Nemours & Co Inc Deepwater NJ 08023

DAY, IVANA PODVALOVA, b Prague, Czech, Oct 29, 32; m 73. PHARMACOLOGY, BIOLOGY. *Educ:* Charles Univ, Prague, MSc, 64, PhD(pharmacol), 70. *Prof Exp:* Sr pharmacologist, Res Inst Pharm & Biochem, Prague, Czech, 64-70; fel, Inst Mario Negri, Milan, Italy, 71; fel, Univ Minn, 71-73; SR PHARMACOLOGIST, CNS DIS THER SECT, MED RES DIV, AM CYANAMID CO, 73- *Mem:* NY Acad Sci; Am Chem Soc; Am Soc Pharmacol & Exp Therapeut; Collegium Int Neuro-Psychopharmacol. *Res:* Pharmacology of the central nervous system. *Mailing Add:* CNS Dis Ther Sect Med Res Div Am Cyanamid Co Pearl River NY 10965

DAY, JACK CALVIN, b Stamford, Tex, June 17, 36; m 68. ORGANIC CHEMISTRY. *Educ:* Univ Calif, Berkeley, AB, 61; Univ Calif, Los Angeles, PhD(org chem), 67. *Prof Exp:* Res assoc chem, Columbia Univ, 67-68; ASST PROF CHEM, HUNTER COL, 68- *Mem:* Chem Soc London; Am Chem Soc. *Res:* Synthesis and study of new severely hindered organic bases; synthesis of a noncoordinating buffer system; control of orientation in elimination reactions. *Mailing Add:* Dept of Chem Hunter Col 695 Park Ave New York NY 10021

DAY, JAMES HALLIDAY, internal medicine, see previous edition

DAY, JAMES MEIKLE, b Wickham, NB, Oct 20, 24; US citizen; m 51. ENVIRONMENTAL CHEMISTRY. *Educ:* Univ NH, BS, 45; Univ Ill, MS, 52; Univ Ark, PhD(inorg & nuclear chem), 54. *Prof Exp:* Chem engr, E I du Pont de Nemours & Co, NY, 45-46; chemist, Burgess Battery Co, Ill, 46-48; chem engr, Anderson Phys Lab, 48-51; res assoc, Univ Wis, 53-54; radiation chemist, Phillips Petrol Co, Okla, 54-56; nuclear chemist, Idaho, 56-58, reactor core physicist, 58-59; sr res chemist, Indust Reactor Lab, NJ for Am Tobacco Co, Va, 59-62; mgr chem & physics res, Whirlpool Corp, Mich, 62-70, staff chemist, 70-74; SR ENGR, NORTHEAST UTILITIES SERV CO, 75- *Mem:* Am Chem Soc. *Res:* Water chemistry; water treatment, chlorination and other disinfection methods; pollution control. *Mailing Add:* Northeast Utilities Serv Co PO Box 270 Hartford CT 06101

DAY, JANE MAXWELL, b Avon Park, Fla, Mar 12, 37; m 58; c 2. TOPOLOGY. *Educ:* Univ Fla, BA, 58, MS, 61, PhD(math), 64. *Prof Exp:* Asst prof math, Univ Fla, 64-66; Am Asn Univ Women fel, Inst Advan Study, 66-67; from asst prof to assoc prof math, Col Notre Dame, 67-76, chmn dept, 69-71 & 74-75, prof, 76-82; ASSOC PROF MATH, SAN JOSE STATE UNIV, 82- *Concurrent Pos:* Lectr, Women & Math Lectureship Prog; sect officer, Math Asn Am, 75-78. *Mem:* Am Math Soc; Math Asn Am; Asn Comput Mach; Nat Coun Teachers Math; Am Asn Univ Professors. *Res:* Topological algebra, including semigroups and acts with periodic properties, and nonassociative structures. *Mailing Add:* Dept Math San Jose State Univ San Jose CA 95192

DAY, JESSE HAROLD, b Bend, Ore, Oct 27, 16; m 38. PHYSICAL CHEMISTRY. *Educ:* Reed Col, BA, 42; Case Sch Appl Sci, MS, 45, Case Inst Technol, PhD(phys chem), 48. *Prof Exp:* Instr chem, Case Inst Technol, 46-48; from asst prof to assoc prof, 48-58, chmn dept, 58-63, actg dean, 68-69 & 71-72, PROF CHEM, OHIO UNIV, 63-, ASSOC DEAN COL ARTS & SCI, 67-68 & 69- *Concurrent Pos:* Res chemist, Rubber Reserve Bd, 44-45 & Glenn L Martin Co, 46-47; vis prof, Univ Idaho, 64. *Mem:* Fel Am Inst Chem; Am Chem Soc; Soc Plastics Eng (ed, Jour, 45-58); fel NY Acad Sci. *Res:* Thermochromism; vinyl polymerization; chemistry of fulvenes. *Mailing Add:* Col of Arts & Sci Ohio Univ Athens OH 45701

DAY, LAWRENCE EUGENE, b Findlay, Ohio, Feb 12, 33; m 57; c 3. MICROBIOLOGY. *Educ:* Miami Univ, Ohio, AB, 55; Mich State Univ, MS, 60, PhD(microbiol), 63. *Prof Exp:* Res microbiologist, Med Res Lab, Chas Pfizer & Co, Inc, Conn, 63-66; res microbiologist antibiotic develop, 66-70, new fermentation prod team leader, 70-73, MGR ANTIBIOTIC CULT DEVELOP, ELI LILLY & CO, 73- *Concurrent Pos:* Prin investr, Eli Lilly & Co. *Mem:* Am Soc Microbiol. *Res:* Genetics of antibiotic biosynthesis; scale-up and manufacture of human insulin by recombinant DNA technology. *Mailing Add:* Eli Lilly & Co Ky414 Indianapolis IN 46206

DAY, LEROY E(DWARD), b Doswell, Va, Jan 2, 25; m 47; c 3. AERONAUTICAL ENGINEERING. *Educ:* Ga Inst Technol, BAeroEng, 46; Univ Calif, Los Angeles, MS, 55; Mass Inst Technol, MS, 60. *Prof Exp:* Test engr guided missile, US Naval Missile Ctr, 48-51, head controls br develop & testing guid systs, 51-56, head guid div, 56-59, head inertial guid div, develop res testing guid systs missiles, 59-60, dep head, Missile Progs Dept, 60-62; chief, Proj Gemini, NASA, 62-63, dir, Gemini Test Prog, 63-66, dir, Apollo Test, 66-69, mgr space shuttle task group, 69-71, dep dir space shuttle prog, 71-80, DIR SYSTS ENG & INTEGRATION, MANNED SPACE FLIGHT, NASA, 80- *Concurrent Pos:* Lectr, Univ Calif, Los Angeles, 59; consult, 59. *Mem:* Sigma Xi. *Res:* Automatic control and guidance of missiles and space vehicles; manned space flight. *Mailing Add:* 11709 Magruder Lane Rockville MD 20852

DAY, LEWIS RODMAN, b Harrowsmith, Ont, Apr 23, 15; m 43; c 2. FISHERIES MANAGEMENT. *Educ:* Queen's Univ, Ont, BA, 39; Western Ont Univ, MA, 41. *Prof Exp:* Zoologist, Atlantic Herring Invest Comt, 45-48; biologist, Fisheries Res Bd, Can, 48-63, asst dir, 55-63; exec secy, Int Comn Northwest Atlantic Fisheries, 63-79; RETIRED. *Mem:* Fel Maritime Acad. *Res:* Fisheries biology; fisheries management and control; biology of haddock and herring, application of fish dynamics models, selectivity of trawls, bottom fishes, assessment of fish stocks; conservation. *Mailing Add:* 111 Charles St St Andrews NB 30G 2X0 Can

DAY, LOREN A, b Evanston, Ill, Oct 9, 36; m 65; c 2. PHYSICAL CHEMISTRY. *Educ:* Oberlin Col, BA, 58; Yale Univ, PhD(chem), 63. *Prof Exp:* Fel molecular biol div, Max Planck Inst Virus Res, 64-68; assoc, Dept Biochem, 69-75, assoc mem, 76-80, MEM & HEAD DEVELOP & STRUCT BIOL, PUB HEALTH RES INST, NY, 81- *Concurrent Pos:* NIH fel, 64-67; Res Career Develop Award, NIH, 72-77; res assoc prof biochem, Sch Med, NY Univ, 76-; mem, Biophysics & Biophys Chem Study Sect, NIH, 78-82. *Mem:* Biophys Soc; Am Soc Biol Chemists; Am Soc Microbiol; Am Chem Soc. *Res:* Physical chemistry of macromolecules, the structures of viruses and viral nucleic acids, and protein-nucleic acid interactions. *Mailing Add:* Pub Health Res Inst 455 First Ave New York NY 10016

DAY, MAHLON MARSH, b Rockford, Ill, Nov 24, 13; m 39, 52; c 5. MATHEMATICS. *Educ:* Oregon State Col, BS, 35; Brown Univ, ScM, 38, PhD(math), 39. *Prof Exp:* Keene fel, Inst Adv Study, 39-40; from instr to assoc prof math, 40-49, head dept, 58-65, PROF MATH, UNIV ILL, URBANA, 49- *Concurrent Pos:* Res assoc, Brown Univ, 44-46; NSF sr res fel, 56-57. *Mem:* Fel AAAS; Am Math Soc; Math Asn Am. *Res:* Linear spaces; ordered systems; geometry of normed spaces; amenable semigroups. *Mailing Add:* Dept of Math Univ of Ill Urbana IL 61801

DAY, MARION CLYDE, JR, b Malvern, Ark, Aug 7, 27; m 50; c 3. INORGANIC CHEMISTRY, PHYSICAL CHEMISTRY. *Educ:* San Jose State Col, AB, 50; Iowa State Univ, PhD(chem), 55. *Prof Exp:* From asst prof to assoc prof, 55-69, PROF INORG CHEM, LA STATE UNIV, 69- *Mem:* Am Chem Soc. *Res:* Spectroscopic and conductance studies of ion-solvent and ion-ion interactions in solvents of low dielectric constant; alkali metal aluminum alkyls in non-polar and mixed solvent systems. *Mailing Add:* Dept of Inorg Chem La State Univ Baton Rouge LA 70803

DAY, MICHAEL HARDY, b St Louis, Mo, April 4, 50; m 72; c 1. ATOMIC PHYSICS, MOLECULAR PHYSICS. *Educ:* Univ Mo, Columbia, BS, 72; Univ Wis, Madison, PhD(physics), 77. *Prof Exp:* Instr physics, Univ Wis, 77-78; res fel, Univ Sussex, UK Atomic Energy Authority, 78-80; ASST PROF PHYSICS, KANS STATE UNIV, 80- *Mem:* Am Phys Soc. *Res:* Theoretical studies of ionization and charge exchange in ion-atom collisions; interaction of fast ions with solids. *Mailing Add:* Dept Physics Candwell Hall Kans State Univ Manhattan KS 66506

DAY, NOORBIBI KASSAM, US citizen; div; c 2. IMMUNOBIOLOGY. *Educ:* Trinity Col, Dublin, BA, 56; McGill Univ, PhD, 67. *Prof Exp:* Fel pediat, Univ Minn, 67-71, asst prof path, 71-73; assoc prof biol, Cornell Univ, 73-77; lab head, 73-77, ASSOC MEM, MEM SLOAN-KETTERING CANCER CTR, 73- *Concurrent Pos:* NIH spec fel, 70-71; vis scientist molecular path, Scripps Clin, Calif, 71; rheumatoid arthritis fel, 71-73; estab investr, Am Heart Asn, 72-77. *Mem:* Can Soc Immunol; Can Soc Microbiol; Am Soc Microbiol; Am Asn Immunol; Am Soc Exp Path. *Res:* Perturbations of the Complement system in human diseases; isolated deficiencies of the Complement system in man and experimental animals; development of C-phylogenetic and ontogenetic perspectives; effector biology; mouse mammory tumor virus and human breast cancer; feline leukemia and treatment of. *Mailing Add:* Mem Sloan Kettering Cancer Ctr 1275 York Ave New York NY 10021

DAY, PAUL PALMER, b Chicago, Ill, Dec 16, 28; m; c 4. COMPUTER SCIENCES, PHYSICS. *Educ:* Ill Inst Technol, BS, 51, MS, 55. *Prof Exp:* Physicist, Chem Div, 51-68, GROUP LEADER COMPUT SERV, ARGONNE NAT LAB, 68- *Mem:* Asn Comput Mach; Inst Elec & Electronics Engrs. *Res:* irradiation damage in solids; nuclear spectroscopy; nuclear level structure computations; design implementation of on-line multi experiment real time computer facility; design and implement large multicomputer time-sharing network. *Mailing Add:* Chem Div Argonne Nat Lab 9700 S Cass Argonne IL 60439

DAY, PAUL RUSSELL, b Hollister, Calif, Sept 6, 12; m 41; c 3. SOIL PHYSICS. *Educ:* Univ Calif, AB, 35, PhD(soil physics), 41. *Prof Exp:* Assoc soils, Univ Calif, Davis, 41; instr soil physics & jr soil physicist, 41-45, asst prof & asst soil physicist, 45-52, assoc prof & assoc soil physicist, 52-58, chmn dept soils & plant nutrit, 64-70, PROF SOIL SCI & SOIL PHYSICIST, UNIV CALIF, BERKELEY, 58- *Concurrent Pos:* Fulbright sr scholar, Univ Cambridge, 62-63. *Mem:* Fel AAAS; Soil Sci Soc Am; fel Am Soc Agron; Am Geophys Union. *Res:* Thermodynamics of soil-moisture; soil structure; particle size analysis; water movement in soil; soil deformation. *Mailing Add:* Dept of Soil Sci Univ of Calif Berkeley CA 94720

DAY, REUBEN ALEXANDER, JR, b Atlanta, Ga, Feb 3, 15; m 43; c 4. ANALYTICAL CHEMISTRY. *Educ:* Emory Univ, AB, 36, MS, 37; Princeton Univ, PhD(chem), 40. *Prof Exp:* From instr to prof, 40-81, chmn dept, 57-68, EMER PROF CHEM, EMORY UNIV, 81- *Concurrent Pos:* Res assoc, Metall Lab, Univ Chicago, 43; chemist, Clinton Labs, Oak Ridge, Tenn, 43-44; sr chemist, Oak Ridge Nat Lab, Tenn, 48. *Mem:* Am Chem Soc; Electrochem Soc. *Res:* Organic polarography; electrochemistry of organic compounds. *Mailing Add:* Dept of Chem Emory Univ Atlanta GA 30322

DAY, RICHARD ALLEN, b Kellogg, Iowa, Apr 4, 31; m 56; c 2. BIOCHEMISTRY. *Educ:* Iowa State Univ, BS, 53; Mass Inst Technol, PhD(organic chem), 58. *Prof Exp:* Damon Runyon Mem Fund grant biol, Mass Inst Technol, 57-59; from asst prof to assoc prof chem, 59-68, from asst prof to assoc prof biol chem, Col Med, 60-72, PROF CHEM, UNIV CINCINNATI, 68-, PROF BIOL CHEM, COL MED, 72- *Concurrent Pos:* NIH career develop award, 69-74. *Mem:* Am Chem Soc; Am Soc Biol Chem; AAAS. *Res:* Protein structure by gas chromatography and mass spectrometry; affinity labels of active sites; interactions of ionens with DNA and chromatin. *Mailing Add:* Dept of Chem Univ of Cincinnati Cincinnati OH 45221

DAY, ROBERT J(AMES), b Newark, NJ, Feb 2, 10; wid; c 1. PHYSICAL CHEMISTRY, FUEL TECHNOLOGY. *Educ:* Union Univ, NY, BS, 33; Pa State Univ, PhD(fuel tech), 49. *Prof Exp:* Instr petrol prod, Petrol & Nat Gas Eng Dept, Pa State Univ, 38-47; res engr, Consolidation Coal Co, 49-52; res dir chem process & fuel utilization, Philadelphia & Reading Corp, 52-56; chem process develop analyst, Planning Dept, Tex Power & Light Co, 56-58; tech dir water & oil well conditioning, United Chem Corp NMex, 58-59; chief chemist, Chem Eng Co, Inc, Tex, 60; staff engr, Armament Div, Universal Match Corp, 60-61; sr engr-scientist, Missile & Space Systs Div & Aircraft Div, McDonnell Douglas Corp, 61-70; CONSULT, 70- *Concurrent Pos:* Mem res adv comt, Anthracite Inst & Anthracite Res Adv Comt, Pa State Univ, 52-56; mem, Gov Fuel Res Adv Comt, 55. *Mem:* Am Chem Soc; Am Inst Mining, Metall & Petrol Engrs; Am Inst Aeronaut & Astronaut. *Res:* Chemical process development; propellants development; propulsion systems design; reaction kinetics; hydrogenation; gasification; fuels processing and utilization; carbon and graphite properties and production; petroleum production; water conditioning; surfactants; sintering; calcining. *Mailing Add:* Apt 26 3030 Merrill Dr Torrance CA 90503

DAY, ROBERT JAMES, b Los Angeles, Calif, Feb 7, 41. ANALYTICAL CHEMISTRY, ELECTROCHEMISTRY. *Educ:* Univ Of Calif, Riverside, BA, 62; Univ NC, PhD(anal chem), 66. *Prof Exp:* Res chemist, Org Chem Dept, E I du Pont de Nemours & Co, 66-67; mem staff, TRW Systs Group, 67-80, PROJ SCIENTIST, TRW SPACE & TECHNOL GROUP, 80- *Mem:* AAAS; Am Chem Soc. *Res:* Magnetic resonance spectroscopy; electroanalytical chemistry; gas chromatography; electrobiochemistry; exobiology. *Mailing Add:* TRW STG R1 1004 One Space Park Redondo Beach CA 90278

DAY, ROBERT WILLIAM, b Worcester, Mass, Feb 7, 24; m 45; c 2. THERMODYNAMICS. *Educ:* Univ Mass, BS, 48; Rensselaer Polytech Inst, MME, 54. *Prof Exp:* Instr mech eng, Rensselaer Polytech Inst, 48-54; from asst prof to assoc prof, 54-69, prof mech eng, 69-81, PROF & ASSOC DEPT HEAD, MECH ENG, UNIV MASS, AMHERST, 81- *Concurrent Pos:* Engr, Gen Elec Co, NY, 50-52; engr, Boeing Airplane Co, 54; consult, Kollmorgan Optical Co, 57; Western Elec Fund Award, 70. *Mem:* Am Soc Eng Educ; Am Soc Mech Engrs; Sigma Xi; Aerospace Indust Asn Am. *Res:* Application of thermodynamics and heat transfer to aircraft and space vehicles. *Mailing Add:* Dept of Mech Eng Univ of Mass Amherst MA 01002

DAY, ROBERT WINSOR, b Framingham, Mass, Oct 22, 30; c 2. EPIDEMIOLOGY. *Educ:* Univ Chicago, MD, 56; Univ Calif, Berkeley, MPH, 58, PhD(epidemiol), 62. *Prof Exp:* Trainee epidemiol, Univ Calif, Berkeley, 57-60; res specialist ment retardation, Sonoma State Hosp, Calif, 60-62; asst prof prev med, Univ Calif, Los Angeles, 62-64; chief hereditary defects unit, Calif State Dept Pub Health, 64-65, chief bur maternal & child health, 65-66, chief dept dir, 66-67; assoc prof prev med & dir div health serv, 68-70, chmn dept health serv, 70-72, PROF HEALTH SERV, UNIV WASH, 70-, DEAN, SCH PUB HEALTH & COMMUNITY MED, 72-; DIR, FRED HUTCHINSON CANCER RES CTR, SEATTLE, 81- *Concurrent Pos:* Res staff, Pac State Hosp, Pomona, Calif, 62-64; consult, Porterville State Hosp, 62-63 & State Dept Pub Health, Berkeley, 63-64; lectr, Sch Pub Health, Univ Calif, Berkeley, 64-67; assoc clin prof, Univ Calif, San Francisco, 66-67; vis assoc prof, Univ Mich, 68. *Mem:* Am Soc Human Genetics; Am Pub Health Asn; Soc Pediat Res; Am Epidemiol Soc. *Res:* Genetics and epidemiology; population; health services and medical care. *Mailing Add:* Sch Pub Health & Community Med Univ Wash Seattle WA 98195

DAY, STACEY BISWAS, b London, Eng, Dec 31, 27; US citizen; m 52; c 2. MEDICINE, EXPERIMENTAL SURGERY. *Educ:* Royal Col Surgeons, Ireland, MD, 55; McGill Univ, PhD(exp surg), 64; Univ Cincinnati, DSC, 70. *Prof Exp:* Res fel surg & physiol, Univ Minn, 56-60; clin asst med, St George's Hosp, London, Eng, 60-61; demonstr & prosector anat, McGill Univ, 61-62, lectr surg, 64-66; clin investr, Hoechst Pharmaceut, Inc, Ohio, 66-68; regional med dir for New Eng, Hoffmann-La Roche Inc, NJ, 68-69; asst prof res surg, Col Med, Univ Cincinnati, 69-71; assoc prof path & conservator, Bell Mus Path, Univ Minn, Minneapolis, 71-73; prof biol sci, Grad Sch Med Sci, Cornell Univ, 73-80; dir dept biomed commun & med educ, Sloan-Kettering Inst Cancer Res, 73-80; pres, Int Found Biosocial Develop & Human Health, 80; clin prof, Div Behav Med, NY Med Col, 80; RETIRED. *Concurrent Pos:* Asst prof, NJ Col Med, 68-69; assoc dir basic med res, Shriners Hosp, Burns Inst, Cincinnati, 69-71; mem, Inst, Admin Coun & Coun Field Coordr, Sloan-Kettering Inst Cancer Res; mem, World Priorities Pop Comt; consult, Pan-Am Health Orgn; exchange scientist to Soviet Union, US-USSR Agreement for Health, 76; vpres res & sci affairs, Mario Negri Found, NY, 74-80; vpres int health affairs, Am Rural Health Asn, 77-80; ed-in-chief, Biosci Commun & Monograph J Health Commun & Biopsychosocial Health; founding officer & vpres, Am Inst Stress, 79; Consult, dict sci biog, Health Commun, Chile, Inst Creative Health, Lyford Cay. *Honors & Awards:* Moynihan Prize & Medal; Arris & Gale Award, Royal Col Surgeons, 72. *Mem:* Fel Zool Soc London; fel Royal Micros Soc; Asn Surgeons Gt Brit & Ireland; Harvey Soc; Int hon fel Japanese Found Biopsychosocial Health. *Res:* Surgery; physiology; pathobiology; communications and informatics; cultural anthropology. *Mailing Add:* 6 Lomond Ave Spring Valley NY 10977

DAY, STEPHEN MARTIN, b New York, NY, Dec 17, 31; c 6. SOLID STATE PHYSICS. *Educ:* La State Univ, BS, 57; Rice Univ, MA, 59, PhD(physics), 61. *Prof Exp:* From asst prof to assoc prof, 61-71, chmn dept, 69-75, PROF PHYSICS, UNIV ARK, FAYETTEVILLE, 71-, ASSOC DEAN, COL ARTS & SCI, 79- *Mem:* Am Phys Soc; Am Asn Physics Teachers; Sigma Xi. *Res:* Low temperature properties of solids; magnetic resonance phenomena of solids, and superionic properties of solids. *Mailing Add:* Office Dean ARSC VWH-122 Univ Ark Fayetteville AR 72701

DAY, THOMAS BRENNOCK, b New York, NY, Mar 7, 32; m 53; c 9. HIGH ENERGY PHYSICS. *Educ:* Univ Notre Dame, BS, 52; Cornell Univ, PhD(physics), 57. *Prof Exp:* Res assoc, Univ Md, College Park, 57-58, from asst prof to assoc prof, 58-64, prof physics, 64, vchancellor acad planning & policy, 70; PRES, SAN DIEGO STATE UNIV, 78-, PROF PHYSICS, 78- *Concurrent Pos:* Engr, Bendix Aviation Corp, 52-53; consult, US Govt, 58- *Mem:* Am Phys Soc. *Res:* Theoretical investigations in elementary particle physics and quantum mechanics; experimental work in high energy physics. *Mailing Add:* San Diego State Univ San Diego CA 92182

DAY, WALTER R, JR, b Fairfield, Ala, Aug 12, 31; m 58; c 2. ELECTRICAL ENGINEERING. *Educ:* Auburn Univ, BSEE, 53; Ga Inst Technol, MSEE, 57. *Prof Exp:* Sr engr, Sperry Electronic Tube Div, 56-66; mem tech staff, Plasma Physics Lab, Princeton Univ, 66-67; sr scientist, Electron Tube Div, Litton Industs, Inc, 67-78; ENG MGR, SOLID STATE WESTERN DIV, VARIAN ASSOCS, 78- *Mem:* Inst Elec & Electronics Engrs. *Res:* Microwave electron devices including linear beam oscillators and amplifiers; electron beams and focusing systems; solid-state microwave devices and materials. *Mailing Add:* Varian Assocs 611 Hansen Way Palo Alto CA 94303

DAY, WILLIAM H, b Wilmington, Del, Sept 29, 34; m 59; c 1. ECONOMIC ENTOMOLOGY. *Educ:* Univ Del, BS, 55; Cornell Univ, PHD(entom), 65. *Prof Exp:* Res asst entom, Cornell Univ, 55-61; res leader, 71-78, RES ENTOMOLOGIST, PARASITE RES LAB, AGR RES SERV, USDA, 65-71, 78- *Mem:* Entom Soc Am; Am Entom Soc (pres, 71-72). *Res:* Applied biological control of insect pests; population dynamics of insect parasites, predators and pest species; insecticidal control of vegetable insects; plant nutrition vs insect populations; insect sampling and plot design. *Mailing Add:* Parasite Res Lab Agr Res Serv USDA 501 S Chapel Ave Newark DE 19713

DAYAL, RAMESH, b New Delhi, India, July 15, 42; Can citizen; m 72; c 2. NUCLEAR WASTE MANAGEMENT. *Educ:* Univ Stuttgart, Vordiplom, 66, Diplom, 68; Dalhousie Univ, PhD(geochem), 74. *Prof Exp:* Asst prof marine geochem, Marine Sci Res Ctr, State Univ NY Stony Brook, 74-79; GROUP LEADER, LOW LEVEL WASTE RES, DEPT NUCLEAR ENERGY, BROOKHAVEN NAT LAB, 79- *Concurrent Pos:* Adj assoc prof, Marine Sci Res Ctr, State Univ NY Stony Brook, 79-; prin investr, Nuclear Regulatory Comn, 81- *Mem:* AAAS; Int Asn Cosmochem & Geochem; Am Nuclear Soc; Am Chem Soc; AAAS. *Res:* Mineralogy and geochemistry of coastal sediments; sediment pore water studies; silica geochemistry; geochemical aspects of ocean disposal of nuclear wastes and dredge spoil sediments; clay mineralogy. *Mailing Add:* Dept Nulear Energy Brookhaven Nat Lab Upton NY 11973

DAYAN, JASON EDWARD, b Newburgh, NY, Aug 6, 23; m 52; c 3. ORGANIC CHEMISTRY. *Educ:* Yale Univ, BS, 43, PhD(org chem), 49. *Prof Exp:* Lab instr, Yale Univ, 46-47; process develop chemist, Gen Aniline & Film Corp, NY, 48-54, supvr intermediate area, 54-56, azoic area, 56-59, chief chemist, Intermediate Area, NJ, 59-62; asst to plant mgr, Geigy Chem Corp, 62-71, asst to vpres, Prod, Plastics & Additives Div, Ciba-Geigy Corp, 71-74; asst to gen mgr colors & auxiliaries div, 74-77, dir technol colors & intermediates group, 77-78, MFG MGR, COLORS & AUXILIARIES DIV, BASF WYANDOTTE CORP, 78- *Concurrent Pos:* Mem adv comt prof educ, NY State Educ Dept, 58-59. *Mem:* Am Asn Textile Chemists & Colorists; Am Chem Soc. *Res:* Dyes, drugs; drug and dye intermediates; specialty chemicals; textile, leather and paper auxiliaries; ultra violet absorbers; pigments and brightening agents. *Mailing Add:* 41 Fieldston Dr Morristown NJ 07960

DAYANANDA, MYSORE ANANTHAMURTHY, b Mysore City, India, July 1, 34. MATERIALS SCIENCE, METALLURGICAL ENGINEERING. *Educ:* Univ Mysore, BSc hons, 55; Indian Inst Sci, Bangalore, dipl, 57; Purdue Univ, MS, 61, PhD(metall eng), 65. *Prof Exp:* Sr res asst metall, Indian Inst Sci, Bangalore, 57-58; res assoc metall eng, 65-66, from asst prof to assoc prof mat sci & metall eng, 66-75, PROF MAT ENG, PURDUE UNIV, 75- *Concurrent Pos:* Vis prof, Inst Metall, Univ Münster, WGer, 80. *Mem:* Am Inst Mining, Metall & Petrol Engrs; Am Soc Metals; fel Am Inst Chem; Micro-Beam Anal Soc; Am Soc Eng Educ. *Res:* Interactions of diffusing species in multicomponent metallurgical systems; application of electron microprobe and scanning electron microscope in science and engineering. *Mailing Add:* Sch Mat Eng Purdue Univ West Lafayette IN 47907

DAYBELL, MELVIN DREW, b Berkeley, Calif, May 8, 35; m 59; c 2. LOW TEMPERATURE PHYSICS. *Educ:* NMex State Univ, BS, 56; Calif Inst Technol, PhD(physics), 62. *Prof Exp:* Asst prof physics, NMex State Univ, 61-65, assoc prof, 65-68; ASSOC PROF PHYSICS & ENG, UNIV SOUTHERN CALIF, 68- *Concurrent Pos:* Vis staff mem, Los Alamos Sci Lab, 66-68. *Mem:* Am Phys Soc; Inst Elec & Electronics Eng. *Res:* High energy physics; ultra low temperature physics; Kondo effect. *Mailing Add:* Dept of Physics Univ of Southern Calif Los Angeles CA 90007

DAYHOFF, EDWARD SAMUEL, b New York, June 26, 25; m 48; c 2. PHYSICS, MILITARY SYSTEMS. *Educ:* Columbia Univ, AB, 46, MA, 47, PhD(physics), 52. *Prof Exp:* Lab asst, Radiation Lab, Columbia Univ, 48-52; physicist, Bur Standards, 52-55, Naval Ord Lab, 55-66, chief, Div Electronics & Electromagnetics, Naval Surface Weapons Ctr, White Oak, 66-71, res physicist, 71-79; DIR, PRESSURE SCI INC, 80- *Concurrent Pos:* Consult, US Bur Standards, 57-63 & Med Sch, Georgetown Univ, 76-; gen consult, 80- *Mem:* Am Phys Soc; Optical Soc Am. *Res:* Free polarized electrons; spectrum of hydrogen atom; stellar image detection; medical instrumentation; computers; lasers; microwave propagation; magnetic resonances; military surveillance and countermeasures. *Mailing Add:* 1618 Tilton Dr Silver Spring MD 20902

DAYHOFF, MARGARET OAKLEY, b Philadelphia, Pa, Mar 11, 25; m 48; c 2. BIOCHEMISTRY. *Educ:* NY Univ, BA, 45; Columbia Univ, MA, 46, PhD(chem), 48. *Prof Exp:* Asst phys chem, Rockefeller Inst, 48-51; res fel, Univ Md, 57-59; SR RES SCIENTIST, NAT BIOMED RES FOUND, 60-, HEAD DEPT CHEM BIOL, 62-; assoc prof biophysics, 70-78, PROF BIOPHYSICS, SCH MED, GEORGETOWN UNIV, 78- *Concurrent Pos:* Ed, Atlas of Protein Sequence & Struct, 65- *Mem:* Biophys Soc (secy, 71-79, pres, 80-81); Am Soc Biol Chem; Am Chem Soc; Coun Biol Ed; Int Soc Study Origin of Life. *Res:* High-speed computer programs and strategy in protein and nucleic acid sequencing, thermodynamics, protein structure; evolution; genetics; origin of life; protein and nucleic acid sequence data and its organization. *Mailing Add:* 1618 Tilton Dr Silver Spring MD 20902

DAYKIN, PHILIP NORMAN, b Vancouver, BC, Sept 11, 22; m 52; c 2. COMPUTER SCIENCE, MATHEMATICS. *Educ:* Univ BC, BA, 47, MA, 49, PhD(physics), 52. *Prof Exp:* Sr sci officer physics, Res Labs, Gen Elec Co, Eng, 53-57; from asst res physicist to res physicist, BC Res Coun, 57-70; PROF MATH & COMPUT SCI & COORD, UNIV COMPUT CTR, UNIV LETHBRIDGE, 70- *Concurrent Pos:* Nat Res Coun Can overseas fel & Rutherford Mem scholar, 52-53. *Mem:* Asn Comput Mach. *Res:* Theoretical and experimental general physics; physical environment of animals; sensory instrumentation of insects; applied mathematics; applications of computers; computer programming. *Mailing Add:* Dept of Math Sci Univ of Lethbridge Lethbridge AB T1K 3M4 Can

DAYLOR, FRANCIS LAWRENCE, JR, b Fall River, Mass, Dec 17, 32; m 56; c 3. NATURAL PRODUCTS CHEMISTRY, FLAVOR CHEMISTRY. *Educ:* Fordham Univ, BS, 54. *Prof Exp:* Chemist, Beech Nut Life Savers, Inc, 56-59; assoc chemist, 60-63, res chemist, 63-67, sr chemist, 67-69, mgr gen prod, 68-72, MGR FLAVOR DEVELOP, PHILIP MORRIS RES CTR, 72- *Mem:* Inst Food Technologists; Am Soc Heating, Refrig & Air-Conditioning Engrs; Am Chem Soc. *Res:* Flavor research and development; composition of tobacco and smoke to determine flavor; flavor formulation. *Mailing Add:* Philip Morris Inc Res Ctr Po Box 26583 Richmond VA 23261

DAYTON, BRUCE R, b Glen Cove, NY, Oct 11, 37; m 63; c 1. PLANT ECOLOGY. *Educ:* State Univ NY Col Forestry, Syracuse Univ, BSF, 59; Univ NC, Chapel Hill, MA, 65, PhD(bot), 68. *Prof Exp:* Asst prof, 68-70, ASSOC PROF BIOL, STATE UNIV NY COL ONEONTA, 70- *Mem:* Am Museum Natural Hist; Am Inst Biol Sci; Ecol Soc Am. *Res:* Forest ecology; the influence of soils on plant distribution; primary productivity of terrestrial ecosystems; nutrient cycles in terrestrial ecosystems. *Mailing Add:* Dept of Biol State Univ NY Col Oneonta NY 13820

DAYTON, DANIEL FRANCIS, b Hanover, NH, June 26, 19; m 42; c 4. HORTICULTURE. *Educ:* NH Teachers Col, BEd, 42; Univ NH, BS, 49, MS, 50; Univ Ill, PhD(hort), 55. *Prof Exp:* Instr hort, Univ NH, 49-50; instr & first asst plant breeding, 50-55, from asst prof to assoc prof, 55-66, PROF PLANT BREEDING, UNIV ILL, URBANA, 66- *Mem:* Am Soc Hort Sci; Am Pomol Soc. *Res:* Breeding and genetics of deciduous fruit plants. *Mailing Add:* Dept of Hort Univ of Ill Urbana IL 61801

DAYTON, JAMES ANTHONY, JR, b Chicago, Ill, Dec 22, 37; m 65. ELECTRON OPTICS. *Educ:* Ill Inst Technol, BS, 59; Univ Iowa, MS, 60; Univ Ill, PhD(elec eng), 65. *Prof Exp:* Res electronics engr, Aeronaut Lab, Cornell Univ, 65-67; AEROSPACE TECHNOLOGIST, LEWIS RES CTR, NASA, 67- *Concurrent Pos:* Adj prof, Cleveland State Univ, 69- *Mem:* Inst Elec & Electronics Eng. *Res:* Acoustic wave propagation in plasmas; diagnostic techniques in hypersonic flow machines; gas discharge tubes; interaction of nuclear radiation with gases; multi stage depressed collectors; power conditioning; electron beam focusing; microwave tubes. *Mailing Add:* Lewis Res Ctr, NASA 21000 Brookpark Rd MS 54-S Cleveland OH 44135

DAYTON, PETER GUSTAV, b Szigishoava, Rumania, Mar 9, 26; m 53; c 1. PHARMACOLOGY. *Educ:* Mass Inst Technol, BS, 50; Univ Paris, DS, 53. *Prof Exp:* Fel med, Col Med NY Univ, 54-64, res scientist, 65-67; asst prof pharmacol, Emory Univ, 67-71, assoc prof med & chem, 67-72, prof med, 72-78, adj prof chem, 72-78; guest scientist, NY Psychiat Inst, 78-79. *Concurrent Pos:* Chemist, Pharmacol Lab, Nat Heart Inst, Md; vis prof, Dept Psychiat, Univ Pa, 79- *Honors & Awards:* Martini Prize, German Pharmacol Soc, 70. *Mem:* AAAS; Harvey Soc; Am Soc Pharmacol & Therapeut; Am Chem Soc; Soc Exp Biol & Med. *Res:* Chemical pharmacology; carbo-hydrate metabolism; clinical pharmacology; radioimmunoassay. *Mailing Add:* Dept Psychiat Univ Pa Pittsburgh PA 15261

DAYTON, RUSSELL WENDT, b Albany, NY, Sept 16, 10; m 35; c 2. ENGINEERING. *Educ:* Rensselaer Polytech Inst, ChE, 31, MS, 32, PhD(metall), 34. *Prof Exp:* Res engr, Battelle Mem Inst, 34-39, asst supvr, 39-48, supvr, 48-53, asst tech dir, 53-64, asst dir, 64-70, mem corp staff, 71-75; RETIRED. *Mem:* AAAS; Am Nuclear Soc; Am Soc Metals; Am Soc Mech Engrs. *Res:* Physical metallurgy; engineering design and heat transfer; nuclear engineering and metallurgy; bearings; friction and wear; theory and use of metallurgical polarizing microscope. *Mailing Add:* 287 Charleston Ave Columbus OH 43214

DAYTON, SEYMOUR, b New York, NY, Jan 15, 23; m 49; c 2. INTERNAL MEDICINE. *Educ:* Cornell Univ, AB, 42; State Univ NY, MD, 50. *Prof Exp:* Intern med, Maimonides Hosp, 50-51; resident, Goldwater Mem Hosp, 51-52; Life Ins Med Res Fund fel, 52-54; resident med, Vet Admin Ctr, 54-55; resident, Univ Calif, Los Angeles, 55-56, instr, 56-58, asst clin prof, 58-63, assoc prof, 63-68, prof med & vchmn sch med, 68-78; chief med serv, Vet Admin Wadsworth Hosp Ctr, 68-78; PROF MED & ASSOC DEAN SCH MED, UNIV CALIF, SAN DIEGO, 78-; CHIEF OF STAFF, SAN DIEGO VET ADMIN HOSP, 78- *Concurrent Pos:* Jr consult, Student Health Serv, Univ Calif, Los Angeles, 56-58; clin investr, Wadsworth Vet Admin Hosp, 58-59, sect chief, 59-68; mem coun arteriosclerosis & exec bd, Am Heart Asn. *Mem:* Am Fedn Clin Res; Am Soc Clin Invest; Am Inst Nutrit. *Res:* Lipid metabolism and atherosclerosis; coronary heart disease. *Mailing Add:* Chief of Staff San Diego Vet Admin Hosp La Jolla CA 92161

DAYWITT, JAMES EDWARD, b Cedar Rapids, Iowa, Jan 3, 47. COMPUTATIONAL FLUUID DYNAMICS. *Educ:* Iowa State Univ, BS, 70, MS, 74, PhD(aerospace eng), 77. *Prof Exp:* Aerospace engr, McDonnell-Douglas Aircraft Corp, 70-71; res asst, Iowa State Univ, 71-75; res assoc, Ames Res Ctr, NASA, 75-77; vis scientist, Inst Comput Appl Sci & Eng, 77-78; RES ENGR, RE-ENTRY SYSTS DIV, GEN ELEC, CO, 78- *Concurrent Pos:* Adj prof fluid mech, Drexel Univ, 79-80 & numerical methods, Univ Pa, 81- *Mem:* Am Inst Aeronaut & Astronaut. *Res:* Computational techniques with emphasis on finite-difference methods for the analysis of the flow field about supersonic and hypersonic missiles and earth and planetary re-entry vehicles. *Mailing Add:* Gen Elec Re-Entry Systs Div Rm 6098 3198 Chestnut St Philadelphia PA 19101

DAZA, CARLOS HERNAN, b Cali, Colombia, Apr 9, 31; m 60; c 3. NUTRITION, PUBLIC HEALTH. *Educ:* Nat Univ Colombia, MD, 54; Columbia Univ, MS, 62, MPH, 63. *Prof Exp:* Med nutritionist, Nat Inst Nutrit, Colombia, 55; dir, Secy Pub Health, Valle del Cauca, Colombia, 56-57; adv nutrit, Nutrit & Health Educ Prog, Interam Coop Pub Health Serv, Colombia, 58-60; chief med care, Secy Pub Health, Valle del Cauca, Colombia, 63-65; MED OFFICER NUTRIT ADV, PAN-AM HEALTH ORGN-WHO, 66- *Mem:* Am Pub Health Asn; Latin Am Nutrit Soc; Am Inst Nutrit. *Res:* Operational research, development of nutrition manpower and public health nutrition services, formulation and implementation of national food and nutrition policies. *Mailing Add:* 1 Sprinklewood Ct Potomac MD 20854

D'AZZO, JOHN JOACHIM, b New York, NY, Nov 30, 19; m 53; c 1. ELECTRICAL ENGINEERING, CONTROL ENGINEERING. *Educ:* City Col New York, BEE, 41; Ohio State Univ, MS, 50; Univ Salford, PhD(eng), 78. *Prof Exp:* Jr engr qual control, Western Elec Co, NJ, 41-42; proj engr res & develop, Wright Air Develop Ctr, 42-45, PROF ELEC ENG & DEP DEPT HEAD, AIR FORCE INST TECHNOL, WRIGHT-PATTERSON AFB, 47- *Concurrent Pos:* Vis assoc prof, Dayton Campus, Ohio State Univ, 64; vis prof, Univ Salford, 76-79. *Mem:* Am Soc Eng Educ; Inst Elec & Electronics Engrs. *Res:* Feedback control systems; servomechanisms; digital control systems; aircraft flight control systems. *Mailing Add:* AFIT/ENG Dept of Elec Eng Air Force Inst Technol Wright-Patterson AFB OH 45433

DE, NIMAI C, b Vill Sheali, India, July 1, 41; m 71. BIO-ORGANIC CHEMISTRY. *Educ:* Calcutta Univ, MTech, 65; State Univ NY Buffalo, PhD(med chem), 72. *Prof Exp:* Fel kinetics, Univ Southern Calif, Los Angeles, 71-73; res scientist org synthesis, Roswell Park Mem Inst, 73-81; MEM FAC, UNIV UTAH, 81- *Mailing Add:* Dept Med Chem Univ Utah Salt Lake City UT 84112

DEA, PHOEBE KIN-KIN, b Canton, China, June 17, 46; US citizen; m 67; c 2. PHYSICAL CHEMISTRY. *Educ:* Univ Calif, Los Angeles, BS, 67; Calif Inst Technol, PhD(chem), 71. *Prof Exp:* Fel, Nucleic Acid Res Inst, ICN Pharmaceut, Inc, 72-74, head anal & biophys chem, ICN Pharmaceut, Inc, 74-76; asst prof, 76-79, ASSOC PROF CHEM, CALIF STATE UNIV, LOS ANGELES, 79- *Mem:* Sigma Xi; Am Chem Soc. *Res:* Nuclear magnetic resonance spectroscopy; conformational studies on compounds of biological interest; membranes and transport phenomena; applications of analytical instrumentation. *Mailing Add:* Dept Chem Calif State Univ Los Angeles CA 90032

DEACETIS, WILLIAM, b Joliet, Ill, June 1, 28; m 63. ORGANIC CHEMISTRY. *Educ:* Univ Ill, BS, 50; Univ Wis, MS, 52, PhD(chem), 54. *Prof Exp:* Asst alumni res found, Univ Wis, 50-54; fel, Univ Calif, Berkeley, 54-56; res chemist high energy fuels, Olin Mathieson Chem Co, 56-57; res chemist, org chem, Shell Develop Co, Calif, 57-66, prod develop chemist, Shell Chem Co, NY, 66-70; mem staff chem econ handbook, Union Camp Corp, 70-71, mgr surface-active agents sect, 71-73, mkt specialist chem div, 74-80; SR CONSULT, CHEM SYSTS, INC, 80- *Mem:* Am Chem Soc. *Res:* Product and market development; market research; fuel additives; surfactants; resins; commercial development; strategic planning; specialty chemicals. *Mailing Add:* 15 Varian Lane Scarsdale NY 10583

DEACON, JAMES EVERETT, b White SDak, May 18, 34; m 54; c 2. VERTEBRATE ZOOLOGY. *Educ:* Midwestern Univ, BS, 56, PhD(vert zool, bot), 60. *Prof Exp:* Asst, Univ Kans, 56-59, 60; asst prof zool, 60-64, asst res prof, Desert Res Inst, 64-65, assoc prof zool, 65-68, PROF BIOL, UNIV NEV, LAS VEGAS, 68-, CHMN DEPT BIOL SCI, 75- *Concurrent Pos:* NSF res grant, 64-65; US Fish & Wildlife Serv, US Bur Reclamation & Environ Protection Agency res grants, 65- *Honors & Awards:* Jewish War Vet RISSECA Award, 64; Wildlife Conserv Award, Nat Wildlife Fedn, 70. *Mem:* Am Soc Ichthyologists & Herpetologists; Am Fisheries Soc; Desert Fishes Coun. *Res:* Fishes of Nevada; ecology of desert fish; reservoir limnology; use of instream flow methodology and other techniques in the analysis of habitat requirements of fishes and invertebrates; environmental assessments. *Mailing Add:* Dept of Biol Univ of Nev Las Vegas NV 89109

DEADY, MATTHEW WILLIAM, b Chicago, Ill, Oct 22, 53; m 78. ELECTRON SCATTERING, RADIATIVE CORRECTIONS. *Educ:* Univ Ill, BS (math), BS (physics), 75, MS, 77; Mass Inst Technol, PhD(physics), 81. *Prof Exp:* Chief operator, Ill Accelerator Lab, 74-77; res asst, Bates Accelerator Lab, Mass Inst Technol, 77-81; ASST PROF PHYSICS, MOUNT HOLYOKE COL, 81- *Res:* Investigations of electron scattering from nuclei in the region of large energy loss are being done in order to provide insights into the behavior of nucleons in the environment of the nucleus. *Mailing Add:* Dept Physics Mount Holyoke Col South Hadley MA 01075

DEAHL, KENNETH LUVERE, b Pikeville, Ky, Aug 24, 43; c 3. PHYTOPATHOLOGY. *Educ:* Fairmont State Col, BA, 65; WVa Univ, MS, 67, PhD(plant path), 70. *Prof Exp:* RES PLANT PATHOLOGIST, AGR RES SERV, USDA, 71- *Mem:* Am Phytopath Soc; Mycol Soc Am. *Res:* Host-parasite interaction between Phytophthora infestans and Solanum tuberosum; nature of disease resistance; biochemical response to infection; diseases of mushrooms. *Mailing Add:* Agr Res Serv USDA Veg Lab-Beltsville Agr Res Ctr Beltsville MD 20705

DEAL, ALBERT LEONARD, III, b Hickory, NC, Aug 31, 37; m 63. MATHEMATICAL ANALYSIS. *Educ:* Univ NC, BS, 59, MA, 62, PhD(differential equations), 65. *Prof Exp:* From instr to assoc prof, 62-71, PROF MATH, VA MIL INST, 71- *Mem:* AAAS; Soc Indust & Appl Math; Math Asn Am; Am Math Soc. *Res:* Linear differential and difference boundary problems. *Mailing Add:* Dept of Math Va Mil Inst Lexington VA 24450

DEAL, BRUCE ELMER, b Lincoln, Nebr, Sept 20, 27; m 50; c 3. PHYSICAL CHEMISTRY. *Educ:* Nebr Wesleyan Univ, AB, 50; Iowa State Col, MS, 53, PhD(chem), 55. *Prof Exp:* Asst, Ames Lab, AEC, 50-55; res chemist, Kaiser Aluminum & Chem Corp, 55-59; res chemist, Fairchild Semiconductor Corp, Calif, 59-63 & Fairchild Semiconductor, 63-70; DEPT DIR RES & DEVELOP LAB, FAIRCHILD CAMERA & INSTRUMENT CORP, 70- *Concurrent Pos:* Consult prof, Elec Eng Dept, Stanford Univ, 77- *Honors & Awards:* Electronics Div Tech Award, Electrochem Soc, 74; Cert of Merit, Franklin Inst, 75; Dielectrics & Insulation Div Award, Electrochem Soc, 82. *Mem:* AAAS; Int Electrochem Soc; Inst Elec & Electronics Engrs. *Res:* Surface physics and chemistry of solids; electrochemistry; semiconductor materials and processing. *Mailing Add:* Fairchild Camera & Instrument Corp R&D Lab 4001 Miranda Ave Palo Alto CA 94304

DEAL, CARL HOSEA, JR, b Spartanburg, SC, Dec 26, 19; m 44; c 4. PHYSICAL CHEMISTRY. *Educ:* Duke Univ, BS, 41, PhD(chem), 45. *Prof Exp:* Asst chem, Duke Univ, 41-44; chemist, 44-55, SUPVR, SHELL DEVELOP CO, 55-, SR STAFF RES CHEMIST, 72-, RES ASSOC, 80- *Concurrent Pos:* Exchange scientist, Koninklijke Shell Laboratorium, Amsterdam, 62-63; vpres, Tech Fluid Properties Res, Inc, 78-81. *Mem:* Am Chem Soc. *Res:* Physical chemical properties and their relations to separation processes for petrochemical and petroleum; thermodynamic and phase equilibrium properties of imperfect solutions. *Mailing Add:* 5 Lazee Trail Houston TX 77024

DEAL, DON ROBERT, b Dayton, Ohio, Sept 26, 37; m 62; c 2. BOTANY, POMOLOGY. *Educ:* Capital Univ, BA, 60; Miami Univ, MA, 65; Cornell Univ, PhD(plant path). 69. *Prof Exp:* Teacher high schs, Ohio, 60-63; assoc prof, 69-76, PROF BIOL, GLENVILLE STATE COL, 76- *Mem:* Am Inst Biol Sci; Nat Asn Biol Teachers; Sigma Xi. *Res:* New grape, tree-fruit cultivars and rootstocks for productivity, quality and disease resistance in West Virginia test conditions. *Mailing Add:* Dept of Sci Glenville State Col Glenville WV 26351

DEAL, DWIGHT EDWARD, b Staten Island, NY, Apr 18, 38; m 65. ENVIRONMENTAL GEOLOGY. *Educ:* Rensselaer Polytech Inst, BS, 59; Univ Wyo, MS, 63; Univ NDak, PhD(geol), 70. *Prof Exp:* Asst prof geol, Sul Ross State Univ, 67-74; DIR, CHIHUAHUAN DESERT RES INST, 73- *Concurrent Pos:* Chief geologist, Geofactors, Tex, 71-; res scientist assoc, Bur Econ Geol, Univ Tex, Austin, 72-73; asst prof geol, Earlham Col, 81-82. *Mem:* AAAS; Geol Soc Am; Am Asn Petrol Geol; Am Quaternary Asn; Nat Speleol Soc. *Res:* Groundwater, quaternary, environmental and general exploration geology of Mexico and southwestern United States; applied glacial geology in North Dakota; glacial, fluvial and groundwater processes; erosional history of the Rio Conchos-Rio Grande drainages of the Chihuahuan Desert, United State of America and Mexico. *Mailing Add:* PO Box 63 Alpine TX 79830

DEAL, ELWYN ERNEST, b Appling Co, Ga, Oct 10, 36; m 60; c 4. AGRONOMY. *Educ:* Univ Ga, BSA, 58, MS, 60; Rutgers Univ, PhD(turf mgt), 63. *Prof Exp:* Asst turf mgt, Ga Coastal Plain Exp Sta, USDA, 58-60; Rutgers Univ, 60-63 & NC State Univ, 63-64; asst prof, 64-68, ASSOC PROF TURF MGT, UNIV MD, COLLEGE PARK, 68-, ASST DIR PROGS, COOP EXT SERV, 69-, ADMINR EXTEN SERV, COL AGR, 80- *Mem:* Am Soc Agron; Coun Agr Sci & Technol; Sigma Xi. *Res:* Turfgrass management including species selection and adaptation; physiology, ecology, weed control, mowing, fertilization, irrigation and growth control of lawn, golf course and highway roadside turf. *Mailing Add:* Coop Ext Serv Symons Hall Univ of Md College Park MD 20742

DEAL, ERVIN R, US citizen. MATHEMATICS. *Educ:* Nebr Wesleyan Univ, AB, 51; Kans State Univ, MS, 53; Univ Mich, PhD(math), 62. *Prof Exp:* Asst prof, 59-62, ASSOC PROF MATH, COLO STATE UNIV, 62- *Mem:* AAAS; Math Asn Am; Am Math Soc. *Res:* Functional analysis. *Mailing Add:* Dept of Math Colo State Univ Ft Collins CO 80523

DEAL, GLENN W, JR, b Kannapolis, NC, Apr 3, 22; m 41; c 1. CHEMISTRY. *Educ:* Catawba Col, AB, 48; Appalachian State Teachers Col, MS, 56. *Prof Exp:* Student chem analyst, Tidewater Assoc Oil Refinery, 46; chmn dept sci, Ro County High Sch, 46-60; ASSOC PROF CHEM, CATAWBA COL, 60- *Mem:* Am Chem Soc. *Res:* Education; analytical chemistry. *Mailing Add:* Dept of Chem Catawba Col Salisbury NC 28144

DEAL, RALPH MACGILL, b Charlotte, NC, May 29, 31; m 53, 76; c 3. PHYSICAL CHEMISTRY. *Educ:* Oberlin Col, BA, 53; Johns Hopkins Univ, PhD(chem), 58. *Prof Exp:* Res assoc, Monadnock Res Inst, 58-59; Imp Chem Industs Ltd, Univ Keele, 59-61; NIH trainee biophys chem, Univ Ill, 61-62; asst prof, 62-68, assoc prof, 68-79, PROF CHEM, KALAMAZOO COL, 79- *Concurrent Pos:* Consult, Dept Energy, 79- *Mem:* Am Chem Soc; Soc Comput Simulation. *Res:* Modeling thermal energy storage; computer-assisted-learning. *Mailing Add:* Dept of Chem Kalamazoo Col Kalamazoo MI 49001

DEAL, SAMUEL JOSEPH, b Knoxville, Tenn, Mar 9, 25; m 56; c 3. MEDICAL BACTERIOLOGY. *Educ:* Univ Tenn, BS, 49, MS, 50; Univ Minn, PhD(bact), 57. *Prof Exp:* Res bacteriologist, Walter Reed Army Inst Res, 50-52; from instr to asst prof bact, Univ Minn, 57-61; from asst prof to assoc prof, 61-72, PROF BACT, WVA UNIV MED CTR, 72- *Mem:* AAAS; Am Soc Microbiol. *Res:* Bacterial physiology; nutrition and metabolism. *Mailing Add:* Dept of Microbiol WVa Univ Med Ctr Morgantown WV 26506

DEAL, WILLIAM CECIL, JR, b Lake Providence, La, Mar 21, 36; m 57; c 2. PHYSICAL BIOCHEMISTRY. *Educ:* La Col, BS, 58; Univ Ill, Urbana, PhD(phys chem), 62. *Prof Exp:* From asst prof to assoc prof, 62-71, PROF BIOCHEM, MICH STATE UNIV, 71- *Concurrent Pos:* Lectr sch med, Univ Wash, 65; spec res fel, Univ Munich, 69-70. *Mem:* Am Soc Biol Chem; Am Chem Soc. *Res:* Separation and function of human chromosomes and mitotic apparatus; regulation of fatty acid synthetase and phosphofructokinase; computers in biochemistry. *Mailing Add:* Dept Biochem Mich State Univ East Lansing MI 48823

DEAL, WILLIAM E, JR, b Ft Sam Houston, Tex, Sept 24, 25; m 49; c 4. HYDRODYNAMICS, HIGH PRESSURE PHYSICS. *Educ:* Univ Tex, BS, 47, MA, 48, PhD(physics), 51; Univ NMex, MM, 77. *Prof Exp:* Mem staff physics, 50-60, group leader, 60-65, asst div leader, 65-70, alt div leader, 70-72, div leader, 72-79, dep assoc dir, 79-80, CONSULT, LOS ALAMOS NAT LAB, UNIV CALIF, 80- *Mem:* Fel Am Phys Soc. *Res:* Near ultraviolet absorption spectra of polynuclear aromatics; shock hydrodynamics; explosives. *Mailing Add:* Los Alamos Nat Lab Univ Calif PO Box 1663 Los Alamos NM 87544

DE ALBA, ENRIQUE, statistics, mathematics, see previous edition

DE ALBA MARTINEZ, JORGE, b Aguascalientes, Mex, Mar 28, 20; m 43; c 4. REPRODUCTIVE PHYSIOLOGY, ANIMAL HUSBANDRY. *Educ:* Univ Md, BS, 41; Cornell Univ, MS, 42, PhD(animal physiol), 44. *Prof Exp:* Mgr, Hacienda Sierra Hermosa, Mex, 44-49; physiologist, Inter-Am Inst Agr Sci, Costa Rica, 50-51, head dept animal indust, 52-63; dean & founder col agr, Univ Sonora, Mex, 51-52; livestock adv, Bank of Mex, 63-67; Ford Found fel animal sci, Cornell Univ, 67-73; DIR ANIMAL PROD TRAINING CTR, MEX ASN ANIMAL PROD, TAMPICO, 73- *Concurrent Pos:* Guggenheim fel, 56-57; Kellogg authorship grant, 60-61. *Mem:* Mex Asn Animal Prod (first pres, 64-66); Latin Am Asn Animal Prod (first pres, 66-); Am Soc Animal Sci. *Res:* Tropical pasture research for beef and dairy production. *Mailing Add:* Juarez 86 Coyoacan DF 21 Mexico

DE ALVAREZ, RUSSELL RAMON, b New York, NY, June 21, 09; m 43; c 2. OBSTETRICS & GYNECOLOGY. *Educ:* Univ Mich, BS, 31, MD, 35, MS, 40; Am Bd Obstet & Gynec, dipl, 41. *Prof Exp:* Intern, Univ Mich, 35-36, from asst resident to sr resident obstet & gynec, 36-39, instr, Univ Hosp & Med Sch, 38-44; attend gynecologist & asst prof, Univ Hosps, Univ Ore, 46-48; prof obstet & gynec & first chmn, Sch Med, Univ Wash, 48-64; chmn dept, 64-72, PROF OBSTET & GYNEC, MED CTR, TEMPLE UNIV, 64- *Concurrent Pos:* Obstetrician & gynecologist-in-chief, Univ Hosp, Univ Wash & King County Hosp, 48-64 & Temple Univ, 64-; consult, Univ Mich, 41-44, Vet Admin Hosp, Madigan Army Hosp & NIH; consult obstet & gynec, HEW, Rockville, MD & Dept Health, Philadelphia, Pa. *Honors & Awards:* Award, Am Col Obstetricians & Gynecologists, 58. *Mem:* Fel Am Col Obstetritions & Gynecologists; Am Gynec Soc; fel Am Col Surg; Fel Am Gynec & Obstet Soc; AMA. *Res:* Gynecologic cancer; toxemias of pregnancy. *Mailing Add:* 1213 Pine Wood Rd Villanova PA 19085

DEALY, JAMES BOND, JR, b Medford, Mass, Sept 7, 20; wid; c 6. RADIOLOGY. *Educ:* Yale Univ, AB, 42; Columbia Univ, MD, 45; Am Bd Radiol, dipl, 52. *Prof Exp:* Fel med, Harvard Univ, 50-52, fel radiol, 52, asst, 53-54, instr, 55, from asst clin prof to assoc clin prof, 56-66, actg head dept, 56-63, chmn exec comt, 60-63; PROF RADIOL, TUFTS UNIV, 67-; SR RADIOLOGIST, NEW ENG MED CTR HOSP, 75- *Concurrent Pos:* Assoc radiologist, Peter Bent Brigham Hosp, 53-55, actg radiologist in chief, 56, radiologist in chief, 57-66; consult, US Vet Amin, 56-, Brookline Health Dept, 56-66, Mass Ment Health Ctr, 56-66 & Pondville Hosp, 60-; mem comt radiol, Nat Acad Sci-Nat Res Coun, 63-69; chief diag radiol serv, Lemuel Shattuc Hosp, 67-75; mem consult staff, New Eng Med Ctr Hosps, 68-75. *Mem:* Radiol Soc NAm; Asn Univ Radiol; Am Col Radiol; Am Roentgen Ray Soc; Am Radium Soc. *Res:* Diagnostic and therapeutic radiology; biological effects of ionizing irradiation. *Mailing Add:* New Eng Med Ctr Hosp 171 Harrison Ave Boston MA 02111

DEALY, JOHN EDWARD, b Cardiff, Calif, Oct 25, 30; m 55; c 3. WILDLIFE HABITAT ECOLOGY, FOREST ECOLOGY. *Educ:* Ore State Univ, BS, 55, MS, 59, PhD(forestry), 75. *Prof Exp:* Range scientist, 58-63, assoc plant ecologist, 64-72, plant ecologist, 72-79, PRIN PLANT ECOLOGIST, PAC NW FOREST & RANGE EXP STA, FOREST SERV, USDA, 79- *Concurrent Pos:* Assoc prof, Eastern Ore State Col, 69- & Wash State Univ, 75-; referee ed, Wildlife Soc, 77- & Soc Range Mgt, 78- *Mem:* Wildlife Soc; Ecol Soc Am; AAAS. *Res:* Analysis of forest ecosystems; relating wild ungulate behavior to habitat characteristics in order to develop timber harvest options suitable for maintaining optimum ungulate habitat. *Mailing Add:* Rte 2 Box 2321 La Grande OR 97850

DEALY, JOHN MICHAEL, b Waterloo, Iowa, Mar 23, 37; m 64; c 1. RHEOLOGY, POLYMER PHYSICS. *Educ:* Univ Kans, BSChE, 58; Univ Mich, MSE, 59, PhD(chem eng), 63. *Prof Exp:* Fel chem eng, Univ Mich, 64; asst prof, 64-67, assoc prof, 67-73, PROF CHEM ENG, MCGILL UNIV, 73- *Concurrent Pos:* Res vis, Univ Cambridge, 70; vis prof, Univ Del, 78-79. *Mem:* Am Chem Soc; Can Soc Chem Eng; Am Inst Chem Engrs; Soc Rheology; Soc Plastics Engrs. *Res:* Rheological properties of polymer melts and solutions and other fluids; development of new techniques for measuring rheological properties of molten polymers and of relationships between these properties and processing behavior. *Mailing Add:* Chem Eng Dept McGill Univ 3480 Univ St Montreal PQ H3A 2A7 Can

DEAM, JAMES RICHARD, b Springfield, Ohio, Jan 9, 42; m 66; c 1. PROCESS SIMULATION, COMPUTER AIDED ENGINEERING. *Educ:* Univ Cincinnati, BS, 64; Okla State Univ, MS, 66, PhD(chem eng), 69. *Prof Exp:* Coop engr, Int Harvester Co, 60-63; sr res engr, Mgt Info & Systs Dept, Monsanto Co, 68-76; mgr, Mgt Info Systs, Monsanto Can LTD, 76-79; MGR & ENGR, MONSANTO CO, 79- *Mem:* Am Inst Chem Engrs; Am Chem Soc; Sigma Xi; Data Processing Mgt Asn. *Res:* Chemical process simulation; engineering computations; physical property estimation and measurement; process control. *Mailing Add:* Monsanto Co 800 N Lindbergh St Louis MO 63166

DEAMER, DAVID WILSON, JR, b Santa Monica, Calif, Apr 21, 39; m 62; c 3. BIOPHYSICS. *Educ:* Duke Univ, BS, 61; Ohio State Univ, PhD(biochem), 65. *Prof Exp:* Trainee biophys, Univ Calif, Berkeley, 65-66, USPHS fel, 66-67, asst prof zool, 67-70, assoc prof, 70-75, PROF ZOOL, UNIV CALIF, DAVIS, 75- *Res:* Membrane structure; lipid metabolism; cell aging. *Mailing Add:* Dept of Zool Univ of Calif Davis CA 95616

DEAN, ANDREW GRISWOLD, b Rochester, NY, Apr 4, 38; m 63; c 1. EPIDEMIOLOGY. *Educ:* Oberlin Col, AB, 60; Harvard Med Sch, MD, 64; Harvard Sch Pub Health, MPH, 72. *Prof Exp:* Rotating internship, King County Hosp, Seattle, 64-65; Peace Corps physician, USPHS, 65-67; staff mem, Pac Res Sect, Nat Inst Allergy & Infectious Dis, Honolulu, 67-71; epidemiologist, Burkitt's Lymphoma Proj, WHO, Arua, Uganda, 72-73; actg state epidemiologist & actg dir commun dis, Ark Dept Health, 74-76; STATE EPIDEMIOLOGIST & DIR DIS PREV & CONTROL, MINN DEPT HEALTH, 76- *Concurrent Pos:* Epidemic Intel Serv officer, Ctr Dis Control, Atlanta, Ga, 74-76; mem immunol-epidemiol segment, Workin Group Comt, Virus Cancer Prog, Nat Cancer Inst, 75-77; dir, Pac Ctr Geog Dis Res, Honolulu, 76-78. *Mem:* Am Soc Microbiol; Am Soc Trop Med & Hyg. *Res:* A new statewide disease detection system; epidemiology of diseases of public health interest. *Mailing Add:* Minn Dept Health Div Dis Prev & Control 717 SE Delaware St Minneapolis MN 55440

DEAN, ANTHONY MARION, b Savannah, Ga, Aug 26, 44; m 66; c 3. PHYSICAL CHEMISTRY. *Educ:* Spring Hill Col, BS, 66; Harvard Univ, AM, 67, PhD(phys chem), 70. *Prof Exp:* Asst prof phys chem, Univ Mo-Columbia, 70-75, assoc prof, 75-79; SR STAFF CHEMIST, EXXON RES & ENG CO, 79- *Mem:* Am Chem Soc; Combustion Inst; Am Phys Soc. *Res:* Gas phase kinetics; laser diagnostics of flames; kinetics and mechanism of combustion reactions; detailed kinetic modeling of high temperature reactions. *Mailing Add:* Corp Res Lab Exxon Res & Eng Co PO Box 45 Linden NJ 07036

DEAN, BENJAMIN T, b Spickard, Mo, Sept 22, 21; m 48; c 2. ANIMAL SCIENCE. *Educ:* Univ Mo, BS, 47, MS, 59, PhD(animal husb), 61. *Prof Exp:* Swine specialist, Univ Hawaii, 61; livestock adv exten, AID, Santiago, Chile, 62-64; exten prof animal sci, 64-80, EMER PROF, UNIV KY, 80- *Mem:* Am Soc Animal Sci. *Res:* Feeding and management of brood sows during gestation. *Mailing Add:* Box 2280 Bowling Green KY 42101

DEAN, BILL BRYAN, b Omaha, Nebr, Dec 1, 48; m 71; c 3. HORTICULTURE, PLANT PHYSIOLOGY. *Educ:* Wash State Univ, BS, 71, MS, 74, PhD(hort), 76. *Prof Exp:* Asst prof hort, Mich State Univ, 76-78; ASST PROF HORT, WASH STATE UNIV, 78- *Mem:* Am Soc Plant Physiologists; Am Soc Hort Sci. *Res:* Growth regulation of agronomic crop species; biosynthesis of suberin; wound healing in plants. *Mailing Add:* Dept of Hort Wash State Univ Pullman WA 99163

DEAN, BURTON VICTOR, b Chicago, Ill, June 3, 24; m 58; c 3. OPERATIONS RESEARCH. *Educ:* Northwestern Univ, BS, 47; Columbia Univ, MS, 48; Univ Ill, PhD(math), 52. *Prof Exp:* Instr math, Columbia Univ, 47-49 & Hunter Col, 49-50; mathematician, Nat Security Agency, 52-55; res mathematician, Opers Res, Inc, 55-57; assoc prof opers res, 57-65, prof orgn sci, 65-67, chmn opers res group, 65-67, PROF OPERS RES, CASE WESTERN RESERVE UNIV, 67-, CHMN DEPT, 76- *Concurrent Pos:* Indust & govt consult, 57-; vis prof, Dept Indust & Mgt Eng, Israel Inst Technol, 62-63, Inst Mgt, Univ Louvain, Belg & Univ Tel Aviv, Israel, 78-; ed, Mgt Sci, 62-; ed, Studies Mgt, Sci & Systs, North Holland; assoc ed, J Opers Res Soc India, 68-74; assoc, Inst Pub Admin, New York, NY & Washington, DC, 72-; mem coun, Omega Rho; mem bd trustees, Shaker Heights Libr. *Mem:* Fel AAAS (vpres, sect indust sci, 71); Inst Mgt Sci; Opers Res Soc Am; Am Math Soc. *Res:* Applications of operations research to industrial management; zero-base budgeting; research budgeting and corporate growth; production and inventory control; corporate planning; mathematics of management systems; management of research and innovation. *Mailing Add:* 2920 Broxton Rd Shaker Heights OH 44120

DEAN, CHARLES E(ARLE), b Pickens Co, SC, May 23, 98; m 27; c 2. COMMUNICATION ENGINEERING. *Educ:* Harvard Univ, AB, 21; Columbia Univ, AM, 23; Johns Hopkins Univ, PhD(physics), 27. *Prof Exp:* Tech asst, Bell Tel Labs, 21-24; asst physicist, Johns Hopkins Univ, 24-26; tech writer, Am Tel & Tel Co, 27-29; tech writer & ed, Hazeltine Corp, 29-63; ed, Electronics & Commun in Japan, Scripta Publ Corp, Washington, DC, 63-78; RETIRED. *Mem:* Fel Inst Elec & Electronics Eng. *Res:* Electronics engineering. *Mailing Add:* 115 Sherman Ave Takoma Park MD 20912

DEAN, CHARLES EDGAR, b Monticello, Fla, Apr 24, 29; m 57; c 1. PLANT BREEDING, PLANT GENETICS. *Educ:* Univ Fla, BS, 53, MS, 57; NC State Univ, PhD(field crops), 59. *Prof Exp:* From asst agronomist to agronomist, NFla Exp Sta, 59-69, chmn dept, 79, PROF AGRON & AGRONOMIST, UNIV FLA, 70- *Concurrent Pos:* USDA res grant, 64-68. *Mem:* Genetic Asn Am; Am Soc Agron. *Res:* Breeding and genetics of tobacco. *Mailing Add:* Dept of Agron Univ of Fla Gainesville FL 32611

DEAN, CHARLES EDWIN, b Redmesa, Colo, Mar 3, 19; m 43; c 2. MATHEMATICAL STATISTICS, COMPUTER SCIENCE. *Educ:* Brigham Young Univ, BS, 48, MS, 52. *Prof Exp:* Instr, Brigham Young Univ, 49-54; res asst, Surv Res Ctr, Univ Mich, 55-58, head statist serv & data processing sect, Inst Social Res, 58; dir, Comput Res Ctr, Brigham Young Univ, 59-66; acad assoc, Systs Programming Div, Int Bus Mach Corp, Calif, 66-67; assoc prof & chmn dept, 67-77, PROF COMPUT SCI, BRIGHAM YOUNG UNIV, 77- *Concurrent Pos:* Consult sampling techniques, Ford Motor Co, Mich, 58. *Mem:* Am Statist Asn. *Res:* Non-parametric statistical tests; digital computers; programming for computers. *Mailing Add:* Dept of Comput Sci Brigham Young Univ Provo UT 84602

DEAN, CHRISTOPHER, physics, deceased

DEAN, DAVID, b Paterson, NJ, Nov 12, 26; m 49; c 3. BIOLOGICAL OCEANOGRAPHY. *Educ:* Lehigh Univ, AB, 49; Rutgers Univ, PhD(zool), 57. *Prof Exp:* Instr biol, Norwich Univ, 49; from instr to asst prof zool, Univ Conn, 57-66; dir, Darling Ctr, 66-79, prof oceanog, 70-81, PROF ZOOL, UNIV MAINE, 66- *Concurrent Pos:* Co-investr, Maine Yankee Atomic Power Co grants, 69-79; prin investr, Sea Grant Prog, 71- *Mem:* Am Soc Limnol & Oceanog; Marine Biol Asn UK. *Res:* Definition of marine benthic communities and the interrelationships of their components; marine worms; formation and larvae of benthic communities. *Mailing Add:* Ira C Darling Ctr Univ of Maine Walpole ME 04573

DEAN, DAVID CAMPBELL, b Buffalo, NY, Apr 19, 31; m 56; c 3. INTERNAL MEDICINE, CARDIOLOGY. *Educ:* Bowdoin Col, BA, 52; Johns Hopkins Univ, MD, 56; Am Bd Internal Med, dipl, 66; Am Bd Cardiovasc Dis, dipl, 67. *Prof Exp:* Res fel med, Harvard Univ, 59-61; clin instr, 61-65, clin assoc, 65-66, asst prof, 66-72, CLIN ASSOC PROF MED, STATE UNIV NY BUFFALO, 72-; CHIEF CARDIOPULMONARY LAB, VET ADMIN HOSP, 62- *Concurrent Pos:* Res fel cardiol, Mass Gen Hosp, Boston, 60-61; clin asst, Buffalo Gen Hosp, 61-68, clin assoc, 68-74, asst physician, 74-; courtesy staff mem, Deaconess Hosp, 73-75, asst attend, 75-; attend physician, Childrens Hosp, 73-; courtesy staff mem, St Joseph Hosp, 76-78, assoc staff mem, 78-; impartial specialist in cardiol; mem, Workmans Compensation BD, NY. *Mem:* Fel Am Col Physicians; fel Am Col Cardiol; Am Fedn Clin Res; Am Heart Asn; fel Am Col Chest Physicians. *Res:* Electrophysiology of the heart and the electrical control of the heart. *Mailing Add:* 65 Huxley Dr Snyder NY 14226

DEAN, DAVID LEE, b Grand Rapids, Mich, Oct 12, 46. ENVIRONMENTAL SCIENCES, ENVIRONMENTAL HEALTH. *Educ:* Mich State Univ, BS, 67, PhD(chem), 72. *Prof Exp:* Res assoc chem, State Univ NY Buffalo, 72-73; res chemist, E I du Pont de Nemours & Co, Inc, 73-77; asst prof chem, Univ NC, Wilmington, 77-80; ASST PROF CHEM, EASTERN WASHINGTON UNIV, 80- *Mem:* Am Chem Soc. *Res:* Development of instructional laboratory experiments; mechanistic organic chemistry, especially photochemistry, thermolysis, pyrolysis, polymer combustion and diversion of polymer combustion. *Mailing Add:* Dept Chem Eastern Washington Univ Cheney WA 99004

DEAN, DAVID W, mathematics, see previous edition

DEAN, DONALD E, b Flushing, NY, June 3, 27; m 51; c 4. COSMETIC CHEMISTRY, PHARMACEUTICAL CHEMISTRY. *Educ:* Oberlin Col, BA, 50; Stevens Inst Technol, MS, 57. *Prof Exp:* Chemist, Am Cyanamid Co, 50-52, anal method develop, 52-54; mgr, Control & Anal Lab, Shulton, Inc, 54-65; mgr anal & qual control, 65-69 & cosmetic & toiletries res, 69-73, dir prod develop, Leeming /Pacquin Div, 73-75, DIR PROD DEVELOP, CONSUMER PROD OPERS, PFIZER, INC, 75- *Mem:* Am Chem Soc; NY Acad Sci; Soc Cosmetic Chemists. *Res:* Organic analysis; instrumental analysis by infrared and ultra-violet absorption; vapor phase chromatography; development of product forms for use as cosmetics, pharmaceuticals and household products; documentation of product claims through controlled testing. *Mailing Add:* Consumer Prod Opers Pfizer Inc 100 Jefferson Rd Parsippany NJ 07054

DEAN, DONALD HARRY, b San Diego, Calif, Nov 20, 42; m 64; c 1. MOLECULAR GENETICS. *Educ:* Tex Christian Univ, BS, 65, MS, 68; Univ Mich, PhD(cell biol, molecular biol), 72. *Prof Exp:* Fel molecular genetics, Sch Med, Wash Univ, 73 & Rosenstiel Res Ctr, Brandeis Univ, 73-75; asst prof microbiol, 75-79, ASSOC PROF MICROBIOL, OHIO STATE UNIV, 79-, DIR, BACILLUS GENETIC STOCK CTR, 78- *Concurrent Pos:* Ed, Microbial Genetics Bull, 78- *Mem:* Am Soc Microbiol; Soc Insect Path. *Res:* Molecular genetics of Bacillus subtilis and its temperate bacteriophage; restriction enzymes; recombinant molecules; genetic engineering. *Mailing Add:* Dept of Microbiol Ohio State Univ 484 W 12th Ave Columbus OH 43210

DEAN, DONALD L(EE), b Litchfield, Ill, Nov 25, 26; m 49; c 2. ENGINEERING. *Educ:* Univ Mo, BS, 49, MS, 51; Univ Mich, PhD(civil eng), 55. *Prof Exp:* Instr civil eng, Mo Sch Mines, 49-51, admin asst to dean, 52-53, asst prof civil eng, 54-55; assoc prof, Univ Kans, 55-60; prof & chmn civil eng & eng mech, Univ Del, 60-65, . H Fletcher Brown prof civil eng, 62-65; prof & head dept, NC State Univ, 65-78; dean eng, Ill Inst Technol, 78-80. *Concurrent Pos:* Mem, Gov Air Pollution Comn, Del, 61-65. *Honors & Awards:* Walter L Huber Prize, Am Soc Civil Engrs, 67. *Mem:* Fel Am Soc Civil Engrs; Am Soc Eng Educ; Int Asn Shell Struct; Int Asn Bridge & Struct Eng; Sigma Xi. *Res:* Structural design and analysis; latticed and ribbed shells; applied mathematics; mechanics in relation to the behavior of complex structural systems. *Mailing Add:* 1645 Redwood Ave Sarasota FL 33581

DEAN, DONALD STEWART, b Lakewood, Ohio, Nov 21, 16; m 44; c 3. BOTANY. *Educ:* Baldwin-Wallace Col, BS, 38; Univ Mich, MS, 49, PhD(bot), 53. *Prof Exp:* Teacher pub schs, Ohio, 38-42, 45-47; from instr to assoc prof biol, 47-58, PROF BIOL, BALDWIN-WALLACE COL, 58-, CHMN DEPT, 70- *Concurrent Pos:* NSF fac fel, 59-62; staff biologist, Comn Undergrad Educ in Biol Sci, 69-70. *Mem:* AAAS; Nat Asn Biol Teachers; Bot Soc Am; Genetics Asn Am. *Res:* Genetics of grafted plants. *Mailing Add:* Dept of Biol Baldwin-Wallace Col Berea OH 44017

DEAN, DONNA JOYCE, b Danville, Ky, Apr 22, 47. ENDOCRINOLOGY, TOXICOLOGY. *Educ:* Berea Col, BA, 69; Duke Univ, PhD(biochem), 74. *Prof Exp:* Vis res fel biochem, Dept Biol, Princeton Univ, 74-77; res biochemist biochem endocrinol, NIH, 77-79; SCIENTIST/ADMINR, FOOD & DRUG ADMIN, 80- *Concurrent Pos:* Nat Cancer Inst fel, Princeton Univ, 74-77; NIH fel, 77-79; lectr, NIH, 79. *Mem:* AAAS; Grad Women in Sci; Am Chem Soc. *Res:* Glycoprotein biochemistry, endocrinology, cell biology, especially role of glycoproteins and glycolipids in disease processes; toxicology and pharmacology of drugs and food additives. *Mailing Add:* Div Food Animal Additives Bur Foods Food & Drug Admin 200 C St SW Washington DC 20204

DEAN, EUGENE ALAN, b Freeport, Tex, Nov 30, 31; m 56; c 3. PHYSICS. *Educ:* Univ Tex, El Paso, 58; NMex State Univ, MS, 64; Tex A&M Univ, PhD(physics), 69. *Prof Exp:* Physicist, Schellenger Res Lab, 58-61, dir spec proj, 63-65; instr physics, Univ Tex, El Paso, 61-63; asst prof, Tex Southern Univ, 67-69; ASSOC PROF PHYSICS, UNIV TEX, EL PASO, 69- *Concurrent Pos:* Consult, Globe Exploration Co, 65-68; asst prof, Univ Houston, 69. *Mem:* Am Asn Physics Teachers. *Res:* Atmospheric acoustics; plasma physics. *Mailing Add:* Dept of Physics Univ of Tex El Paso TX 79968

DEAN, FREDERICK CHAMBERLAIN, b Boston, Mass, May 22, 27; m 50; c 3. WILDLIFE MANAGEMENT. *Educ:* Univ Maine, BS, 50, MS, 52; State Univ NY, PhD, 57. *Prof Exp:* From asst prof to assoc prof, 54-66, PROF WILDLIFE MGT, UNIV ALASKA, 66-, LEADER, ALASKA COOP PARK STUDIES UNIT, 72- *Concurrent Pos:* Asst leader, Coop Wildlife Res Unit, Univ Alaska, 54-72; head dept wildlife & fisheries, 54-73, ed, Biol Papers, 55-72, assoc dean, Col Biol Sci & Renewable Resources, 72-73; fel systs anal in ecol, Dept Bot, Univ Tenn, 68-69; fel, Oak Ridge Nat Lab, 68-69. *Honors & Awards:* Alaska Sportsmen's Coun Water Conserv Award, Nat Wildlife Fedn, 65; Conserv Educ Award, 71. *Mem:* Ecol Soc Am; Wildlife Soc; Am Soc Mammal; Bear Biol Asn. *Res:* Wildlife management; population ecology; grizzly bears; general ecology; subarctic ecology; wildland park management. *Mailing Add:* 1 1/2 Mile Ballaine Rd SR Box 20971 Fairbanks AK 99701

DEAN, HENRY LEE, b Cumberland, Md, Mar 13, 07. BOTANY. *Educ:* WVa Univ, AB, 29; Univ Iowa, MS, 30, PhD(plant morphol), 36. *Prof Exp:* Asst bot, WVa Univ, 27-29; asst, 30-36, from instr to assoc prof, 37-75, EMER ASSOC PROF BOT, UNIV IOWA, 75- *Mem:* Bot Soc Am; Nat Asn Biol Teachers. *Res:* Host responses and host plants of Cuscuta; biological applications of ultraviolet light; floral variations and anatomy of Lychnis alba; microtechnique and histochemistry; photography. *Mailing Add:* 30 Rocky Shore Dr Iowa City IA 52240

DEAN, HERBERT A, b Damon, Tex, Sept 1, 18; m; c 2. ENTOMOLOGY. *Educ:* Tex A&M Univ, BS, 40, MS, 49. *Prof Exp:* Instr, Tex Agr Exp Sta, Col Sta, Tex A&M Univ, 46-49, from asst entomologist to assoc entomologist, 49-67, assoc prof entom, Agr Res & Ext Ctr, 67-81; RETIRED. *Mem:* Entom Soc Am. *Res:* Citrus mite control with selective miticides; biological control of citrus insects and mites; oil tolerance studies with citrus; citrus pest management through integrated control methods; author of 95 publications. *Mailing Add:* PO Box 942 Weslaco TX 78596

DEAN, JACK HUGH, b Joplin, Mo, Dec 6, 41; m 62; c 3. IMMUNOLOGY, MICROBIOLOGY. *Educ:* Calif State Univ, Long Beach, BS, 65, MS, 68; Univ Ariz, PhD(molecular biol), 72. *Prof Exp:* Microbiologist, Mem Hosp, Long Beach, 65-67; lab supvr, Kaiser Found Hosp, San Diego, 67-68; immunologist, 72-74, assoc dir, 74-76, DIR DEPT IMMUNOL, LITTON BIONETICS, 76- *Concurrent Pos:* Lectr immunol, George Mason Univ, 75-76; mem, NIH Grants Rev Study Sect, 78- *Mem:* Am Soc Microbiol; Am Asn Cancer Res; Am Asn Immunologists; AAAS. *Res:* Tumor immunobiology; study of anti-tumor immunity and general immunocompetence in tumor bearing mice and humans; modulation of immunocompetence by environmental chemicals; regulation and control of cell-mediated immune responses. *Mailing Add:* Litton Dept Immunol 5516 Nicholson Lane Kensington MD 20795

DEAN, JACK LEMUEL, b Keota, Okla, Mar 15, 25; m 49; c 2. PHYTOPATHOLOGY. *Educ:* Okla State Univ, BS, 49, MS, 52; La State Univ, PhD(bot, phytopath), 65. *Prof Exp:* Plant pathologist, Sugar Crops Field Sta, Miss, 51-66, PLANT PATHOLOGIST, SUGARCANE FIELD STA, USDA, CANAL POINT, FLA, 66-; ASSOC PROF PLANT PATH, UNIV FLA, 72- *Mem:* Am Phytopath Soc; Int Soc Sugarcane Technol; Am Inst Biol Sci. *Res:* Pathology of sugarcane and sugar sorghum. *Mailing Add:* US Sugarcane Field Sta Star Route Box 8 Canal Point FL 33438

DEAN, JEFFREY STEWART, b Lewiston, Idaho, Feb 10, 39; m 59; c 2. ARCHAEOLOGY, DENDROCHRONOLOGY. *Educ:* Univ Ariz, BA, 61, PhD(anthrop), 67. *Prof Exp:* Res assoc dendrochronology, 64-66, from instr to asst prof, 66-72, assoc prof, 72-77, PROF DENDROCHRONOLOGY, UNIV ARIZ, 77- *Mem:* AAAS; fel Am Anthrop Asn; Soc Am Archaeol. *Res:* Archaeological theory and method; archaeology of the Southwestern United States; archaeological tree-ring dating; dendroclimatology of the Southwestern United States. *Mailing Add:* Lab of Tree-Ring Res The Univ of Ariz Tucson AZ 85721

DEAN, JOHN AURIE, b Sault Ste Marie, Mich, May 9, 21; m 43; c 5. ANALYTICAL CHEMISTRY. *Educ:* Univ Mich, BS, 42, MS, 44, PhD(chem), 49. *Prof Exp:* Chemist, Chrysler Corp, 44-45; lectr, Univ Mich, 46-48; assoc prof, Univ Ala, 48-50; from asst prof to assoc prof, 50-58, PROF CHEM, UNIV TENN, KNOXVILLE, 58- *Concurrent Pos:* Consult, Nuclear Div, Union Carbide Corp, 53-74 & Stewart Labs, Inc, 68-; mem, Am Schs Orient Res. *Honors & Awards:* Charles H Stone Award, Carolina-Piedmont Sect Am Chem Soc, 74. *Mem:* Am Chem Soc; Soc Appl Spectros; Archaeol Inst Am. *Res:* Flame emission and atomic absorption spectrometry; solvent extraction; instrumental methods of analysis; polarography. *Mailing Add:* 1112 W Nokomis Circle Knoxville TN 37919

DEAN, JOHN GILBERT, b Pawtuxet, RI, Feb 16, 11; m 42; c 3. CHEMISTRY. *Educ:* Brown Univ, PhB, 31, MS, 32; Columbia Univ, PhD(chem), 36. *Prof Exp:* Dir res div, Permutit Co, 36-40; teacher sci, Sarah Lawrence Col, 40-42; Int Nickel Co Sr fel, Mellon Inst, 42-45, in-chg develop & res div, Indust Chem Sect, 46-51; CHEM CONSULT & MGR, DEAN ASSOCS, 52- *Concurrent Pos:* Dir div co-op res, Sch Eng, Columbia Univ, 52-54; dir res & develop div, Nickel Processing Corp Div, Nat Lead Co, 53-60. *Mem:* Am Chem Soc; Am Inst Mining, Metall & Petrol Engrs. *Res:* Management of chemical and metallurgical research; inorganic syntheses; ion exchange; catalysis; air and water pollution control; chemical economics; chemistry and chemical metallurgy of the metals, especially nickel, cobalt, copper, zinc, molybdenum, cadmium, mercury and the precious metals. *Mailing Add:* Elmdale Rd Box 102 Rte 2 North Scituate RI 02857

DEAN, JOHN MARK, b Cedar Rapids, Iowa, Oct 2, 36; m 60; c 2. AQUATIC ECOLOGY. *Educ:* Cornell Col, BA, 58; Purdue Univ, MS, 60, PhD(biol sci), 62. *Prof Exp:* Res assoc, Marine Lab, Duke Univ, 62-63; biol scientist, Hanford Labs, Gen Elec Co, 63-64 & Pac Northwest Labs, Battelle Mem Inst, 65-70; assoc prof marine sci, 73-77, assoc prof biol, 70-77, PROF MARINE SCI & BIOL, BELLE W BARUCH INST MARINE BIOL & COASTAL RES, UNIV SC, 77-, DIR MARINE SCI PROG, 76- *Concurrent Pos:* Mem fac fisheries, Hokkaido Univ, Hakadate, Japan, 77. *Mem:* Fel AAAS; Ecol Soc Am; Am Soc Zoologists; Am Soc Ichthyologists & Herpetologists; Southeastern Estuarine Res Soc; Marine Biol Asn UK. *Res:* Physiological ecology of estuarine fish; age and growth of fish. *Mailing Add:* Belle W Baruch Inst Marine Biol & Coastal Res Univ of SC Columbia SC 29208

DEAN, NATHAN WESLEY, b Johnson City, Tenn, Dec 10, 41; m 63; c 1. SCIENCE AND SOCIETY. *Educ:* Univ NC, BS, 63, Cambridge Univ, PhD(physics), 68. *Prof Exp:* Vis scientist, Europ Orgn Nuclear Res, Geneva, Switz, 67-68; from instr to asst prof physics, Vanderbilt Univ, 68-70; asst prof, Iowa State Univ, 70-74, assoc prof, 74-78, prof physics, 78-80, asst dean sci & humanities & asst dir, Sci & Human Res Inst, 74-80; PROF PHYSICS & ASST VPRES RES, UNIV GA, 80- *Concurrent Pos:* Assoc physicist, Ames Lab, US Dept Energy, 70-74, physicist, 74-78, sr physicist, 78-80; mem admin staff, US Atomic Energy Comn, Germantown, Md, 73. *Mem:* Am Phys Soc. *Res:* Theories of elementary particles and strong interactions; interactions of science with religion and society. *Mailing Add:* Res Dept 608 Grad Studies Univ Ga Athens GA 30602

DEAN, PHILIP ARTHUR WOODWORTH, b Oldham, Lancashire, Eng, June 10, 43; m 65; c 2. INORGANIC CHEMISTRY. *Educ:* Univ London, BSc, 64; Royal Col Sci, London, ARCS, 64; Univ London, PhD(chem), 67; Imperial Col, London, DIC, 67. *Prof Exp:* Asst prof chem, Wash Univ, 70-71; asst prof chem, 71-76, ASSOC PROF CHEM, UNIV WESTERN ONT, 76- *Mem:* Chem Inst Can; Royal Soc Chem; Am Chem Soc. *Res:* Chemistry of metal ions in weakly co-ordinating solvents; inorganic aspects of biological activity of metal ions. *Mailing Add:* Dept Chem Univ Western Ont London Can

DEAN, PHILLIP NOLAN, b Houston, Tex, Aug 28, 34; m 64; c 1. PHYSICS, BIOPHYSICS. *Educ:* Rice Univ, BA, 56, MA, 58. *Prof Exp:* SR STAFF BIOPHYSICIST, LAWRENCE LIVERMORE LAB, 74- *Concurrent Pos:* Chmn intercalibration comt for low-energy photon measurements, Dept of Energy, 70- *Mem:* Cell Kinetics Soc; Soc Anal Cytol. *Res:* Development of instruments for rapid and quantitative analysis of biological cells; applications of computer techniques to biomedical research; health physics research and instrumentation; radiological physics; biological effects of radiation. *Mailing Add:* Lawrence Livermore Lab PO Box 5507 Livermore CA 94550

DEAN, RICHARD A, b Brooklyn, NY, Dec 22, 35; m 57; c 3. MECHANICAL ENGINEERING. *Educ:* Ga Inst Technol, BS, 57; Univ Pittsburgh, MS, 63, PhD, 70. *Prof Exp:* Engr, Westinghouse Nuclear Energy Systs, Pittsburgh, 60-66, mgr thermal-hydraul eng, 66-70; tech dir LWR Fuel Div, Gulf Gen Atomic, 70-71, vpres, 71-74; div dir, 74-76, V PRES, GEN ATOMIC CO, 76- *Mem:* Am Soc Mech Engrs; Am Nuclear Soc. *Res:* Boiling heat transfer and two phase flow; flow instability; nuclear reactor and fuel design and development; nuclear fuel reprocessing; management of uranium litigation; high temperature gas cooled reactor technology. *Mailing Add:* Gen Atomic Co 10955 John Jay Jopkins San Diego CA 92121

DEAN, RICHARD ALBERT, b Columbus, Ohio, Oct 9, 24; m 48, 79; c 1. MATHEMATICS. *Educ:* Calif Inst Technol, BS, 45; Denison Univ, BA, 47; Ohio State Univ, MA, 48, PhD(math), 53. *Hon Degrees:* DSc, Denison Univ, 73. *Prof Exp:* Instr physics, Middlebury Col, 47; Bateman fel math, 54-55, from asst prof to assoc prof, 55-66, PROF MATH, CALIF INST TECHNOL, 66- *Mem:* Am Math Soc; Math Asn Am. *Res:* Abstract algebra; partially ordered sets and lattices; groups; combinatories and finite mathematics. *Mailing Add:* 253-37 Math Dept Calif Inst Technol Pasadena CA 91125

DEAN, RICHARD RAYMOND, b Pittsburgh, Pa, June 23, 40; m 64; c 2. PHARMACOLOGY. *Educ:* Duquesne Univ, BS, 62; Univ Mich, PhD(pharmacol), 66. *Prof Exp:* Res investr, G D Searle & Co, 66-71, sr res investr, 71-72, group leader cardiovasc pharmacol, 72-76, asst dir, Clin Cardiovasc-Renal Sect, 76-78, assoc dir, 78-80; MGR, CARDIOVASC PHARMACOL DEPT, ABBOTT LABS, 80- *Concurrent Pos:* Mem coun basic sci, Am Heart Asn. *Mem:* Am Soc Clin Pharmacol & Therapeut; Am Chem Soc. *Res:* Laboratory and clinical evaluation of drugs on the cardiovascular system. *Mailing Add:* 914 Rosemary Terr Deerfield IL 60015

DEAN, ROBERT BERRIDGE, b San Francisco, Calif, Feb 20, 13; m 39; c 4. COLLOID CHEMISTRY, POLLUTION CONTROL. *Educ:* Univ Calif, AB, 35; Cambridge Univ, PhD(exp zool), 38. *Prof Exp:* Asst colloid sci, Cambridge Univ, 38-39; jr instr, Univ Minn, 40-41; Bristol Meyers fel & res assoc chem, Stanford Univ, 41-44, biol, Off Sci Res & Develop Proj, 42; res assoc synthetic rubber proj, War Prod Bd, 43-44; res assoc oil foam proj, Nat Adv Comt Aeronaut, 44; asst prof chem, Univ Hawaii, 44-47; asst prof, Univ Ore, 47-52; head anal sect, Borden Chem Co, 52-53, mgr develop, 53-63; dir lab res, Advan Waste Treatment, Environ Protection Agency, 64-67, chief ultimate disposal res activities, 67-73, sci adv wastewater res, 73-77; MEM STAFF, LUNDEAN ENVIRONMENTAL CO, 77- *Concurrent Pos:* Vis prof sanitary eng, Denmark Tech Univ, 71. *Mem:* Water Pollution Control Fedn; Int Asn Water Pollution Res. *Res:* Membranes and membrane phenomena, especially accumulation of electrolytes; diffusion; colloids; analytical methods; adhesives; water renovation; treatment and ultimate disposal of sludges and brines; applied statistics of small numbers. *Mailing Add:* 5821 Marlborough Dr Cincinnati OH 45230

DEAN, ROBERT CHARLES, JR, b Atlanta, Ga, Apr 13, 28; m 51; c 5. MECHANICAL ENGINEERING. *Educ:* Mass Inst Technol, SB & SM, 49, ScD(mech eng), 54. *Prof Exp:* Engr, Ultrasonic Corp, Mass, 49-51; asst prof mech eng, Mass Inst Technol, 51-56; head adv eng dept, Ingersoll-Rand Co, NJ, 56-60; consult, Easton, Pa, 60; dir res, Thermal Dynamics Corp, NH, 60-61; founder & pres, Creare Inc, 61-75; founder, chmn & prin engr, Cuave Innovations, 76-79; FOUNDER & PRES, VERAX CORP, 79-; ADJ PROF ENG, THAYER SCH ENG, DARTMOUTH COL, 60- *Concurrent Pos:* Mem turbine & compressor subcomt, Nat Adv Comt Aeronaut, 54-55; venture capital panel, Com Tech Adv Bd, Dept Com. *Honors & Awards:* Prod Eng Master Designer Award, 67; Fluids Eng Dir Award, Am Soc Mech Engrs, 79. *Mem:* Nat Acad Eng; Am Inst Aeronaut & Astronaut; fel Am Soc Mech Engrs; Instrument Soc Am; Soc Automotive Engrs. *Res:* Research and engineering in fluid mechanics and machinery, plasma equipment systems design, alternative fuels, biological production technology, automation and computer control. *Mailing Add:* Verax Corp PO Box B1170 Hanover NH 03755

DEAN, ROBERT G(EORGE), b Laramie, Wyo, Nov 1, 30; m 54; c 2. CIVIL ENGINEERING, OCEANOGRAPHY. *Educ:* Univ Calif, Berkeley, BS, 54; Agr & Mech Col Tex, MS, 56; Mass Inst Technol, DSc(hydrodyn), 59. *Prof Exp:* Asst prof civil eng, Mass Inst Technol, 59-60; res engr coastal res, Calif Res Corp, Standard Oil Co, Calif, 60-63, sr res engr, 63-65; actg assoc prof oceanog, Univ Wash, 65-66; prof coastal & oceanog eng & chmn dept & prof civil eng, Univ Fla, 66-76; PROF DEPT CIVIL ENG, UNIV DEL, 76- *Mem:* Nat Acad Eng; Am Soc Civil Engrs; Am Geophys Union; AAAS. *Res:* Physical oceanography; nonlinear water wave mechanics; interaction of waves with structures; general coastal engineering problems; potential flow applications. *Mailing Add:* Dept of Civil Eng Univ of Del Newark DE 19711

DEAN, ROBERT REED, b Bedford Ind, Apr 18, 14; m 49; c 2. CHEMISTRY. *Educ:* Ind Univ, 34-37; Northwestern Univ, 41. *Prof Exp:* Chemist, Johns-Manville Prod Corp, 38-40 & US Gypsum Res Lab, 40-41; inspector, US Army Ord, 41-42; chemist, Am Cyanamid, 48-49, Diamond Alkali Co, 49-50 & Va Carolina Chem Corp, 50-53; mgr mkt res, Westvaco Chlor-alkali Div, FMC Corp, NY, 53-56, dir mkt res & develop, Res Labs, WVa, 56-58, mgr com develop, 58-59, mgr inorg chem div mkt res develop, 59-71; CONSULT COM DEVELOP & INDUST MKT RES, 71- *Mem:* Am Chem Soc; Am Inst Chem; Am Inst Aeronaut & Astronaut; Chem Mkt Res Asn; Com Chem Develop Asn. *Res:* Introduction and commercial development of new chemicals; application of existing chemicals to new uses; evaluation of markets for all commercial chemicals. *Mailing Add:* 401 Pennsylvania Ave PO Box 426 Avondale PA 19311

DEAN, ROBERT WATERS, b West Chester, Pa, June 6, 29; m 62; c 5. FOOD SCIENCE. *Educ:* Bates Col, BS, 51; Rutgers Univ, MS, 57, PhD(food chem, technol), 59. *Prof Exp:* Chemist gelatin desserts, Standard Brands, Inc, 51-53; technologist, Dessert Prod & Beverages, Gen Foods Corp, 53-55; res chemist, Wilson & Co, 59-61; prod develop chemist, Glidden Co, 61-62; res chemist, Peter Eckrich & Sons, 62-64; asst tech dir, F & F Labs, 64-67; chief chemist, Paradise Fruit Co, 67-70; chemist, Growers Processing Serv, Inc, 71-72; DIR, NUTRIT & TECH SERV STAFF, MIDWEST REGION, FOOD & NUTRIT SERV, USDA, 72- *Mem:* Am Chem Soc; Am Inst Chemists; Inst Food Technologists; AAAS. *Res:* Determination of pigments responsible for color of fresh meat; child nutrition; food stamps; food distribution. *Mailing Add:* Food & Nutrit Div USDA Rm 900 536 S Clark St Chicago IL 60605

DEAN, ROBERT YOST, b Portland, Ore, Jan 13, 21; m 54; c 2. MATHEMATICS. *Educ:* Willamette Col, BA, 42; Calif Inst Technol, MS, 42, PhD(math), 52. *Prof Exp:* Mem staff, Inst Math, Case Inst Technol, 46-48; sr mathematician, Hanford Labs Oper, Gen Elec Co, 52-63, mgr math subsect, 64; math sect, Appl Math Dept, Pac Northwest Labs, Battelle Mem Inst, 64-68; PROF MATH & CHMN DEPT, CENT WASH UNIV, 68- *Concurrent Pos:* Lectr, Ctr Grad Study, Univ Wash, 52- *Mem:* Math Asn Am; Am Math Soc; Soc Indust & Appl Math. *Res:* Applied mathematics. *Mailing Add:* Dept of Math Cent Wash Univ Ellensburg WA 98926

DEAN, SHELDON WILLIAMS, JR, b Flushing, NY, July 3, 35; m 60; c 3. CHEMICAL ENGINEERING, SURFACE CHEMISTRY. *Educ:* Middlebury Col, AB, 58; Mass Inst Technol, SB, 58, ScD(chem eng), 62. *Prof Exp:* Res asst chem eng, Mass Inst Technol, 60-61; mem sr staff res lab, Int Nickel Co, 61-64; eng specialist metal finishing, Metals Res Lab, 64-66, group supvr, metal finishing & bonding, 66-74, group supvr, Corrosion Group, Metals Res Lab, Olin Corp, 74-75; sr corrosion engr, 75-77, MGR MAT ENG, CORPORATE ENG, AIR PROD & CHEM INC, 77- *Honors & Awards:* Sea Horse Inst award, 66; Hamden Jaycee DSA award, 70. *Mem:* Electrochem Soc; Am Inst Chem Eng; Am Chem Soc; Nat Asn Corrosion Eng; Am Soc Testing & Mat. *Res:* Corrosion inhibition. *Mailing Add:* Air Prods & Chem Inc PO Box 538 Allentown PA 18105

DEAN, STEPHEN ODELL, b Niagara Falls, NY, May 12, 36; div; c 3. FUSION ENERGY DEVELOPMENT. *Educ:* Boston Col, BS, 60; Mass Inst Technol, SM, 62; Univ Md, PhD(physics), 71. *Prof Exp:* Physicist, Atomic Energy Comn, 62-68; physicist lasers, Naval Res Lab, 68-72; div dir fusion, Atomic Energy Comn, Energy Res & Develop Admin, Dept Energy, 72-79; PRES, FUSION POWER ASSOCS, 79- *Concurrent Pos:* Dir fusion energy, Sci Appl Inc, 79-; mem exec comt, Fusion Energy Div, Am Nuclear Soc, 81- *Mem:* Am Physical Soc; Am Nuclear Soc. *Res:* Fusion plasmas; laser interactions with plasmas; magnetic fusion programs. *Mailing Add:* Fusion Power Assocs 2 Professional Dr Suite 248 Gaithersburg MD 20879

DEAN, THOMAS SCOTT, b Sherman, Tex, July 6, 24; m 45; c 3. SOLAR TECHNOLOGY, ENGINEERING. *Educ:* N Tex State Univ, BS, 45, MS, 47; Univ Tex, PhD(eng mech), 63. *Prof Exp:* Owner, Thomas Scott Dean, Architect & Engr Dynamics Consult, Tex, 50-60; lectr archit eng, Univ Tex, 60-64; chmn archit sci, Okla State Univ, 64-75, prof archit, 70-75; PROF ARCHIT & ENG, UNIV KANS, 76- *Concurrent Pos:* Lectr, Southern Methodist Univ, 55-59; consult, Tex Indust, Inc, 55-59; fac fel, Latin Am Studies Inst, 63; mem, Hot Weather Res Inst, 63-64; archit eng consult, Brackenridge Field Lab, 63-64; vis prin lectr, NE London Polytech Inst, 73-74; mem prof adv panel, Gen Servs Admin, 77-78; mem, Nat Voluntary Lab Accred Prog Comn, Dept Commerce, 78- *Mem:* Am Inst Archit; Nat Soc Prof Engrs; Am Soc Heat, Refrig & Air-Conditioning Engrs; Am Soc Eng Educ. *Res:* Design criteria for research structures; innovative teaching methods; societal aspects of technology; solar energy systems. *Mailing Add:* Sch Archit & Urban Design Univ Kans Lawrence KS 66045

DEAN, WALTER ALBERT, b Bridgeport, Conn, Feb 5, 05; m 36; c 1. PHYSICAL METALLURGY. *Educ:* Cooper Union, BS, 26; Rensselaer Polytech Inst, MS, 27, PhD(phys metall), 29. *Prof Exp:* Res metallurgist aluminum alloys, Aluminum Co Am, 29-40, asst mgr casting plant, 40-47, works chief metallurgist, 47-57, engr new prod, 57-60, asst dir res, 57-70; RETIRED. *Concurrent Pos:* Chmn, Adv Comt to Metall Div, Nat Bur Standards, 55-58 & Forging & Casting Panel, Mat Adv Bd, 58-61. *Honors & Awards:* Bronze Medal & Citation, Am Ord Asn, 64. *Mem:* Am Inst Mining, Metall & Petrol Engrs; Am Soc Metals. *Res:* High strength aluminum alloys; powder metallurgy; casting techniques; rolling and forging procedures; free machining aluminum alloys. *Mailing Add:* 3623 Muirfield Dr Sarasota FL 33583

DEAN, WALTER E, JR, b Wilkes-Barre, Pa, July 12, 39; m 61; c 2. GEOCHEMISTRY, SEDIMENTOLOGY. *Educ:* Syracuse Univ, AB, 61; Univ NMex, MS, 64, PhD(geol), 67. *Prof Exp:* Res asst geol, Univ NMex, 63-64; res assoc bot, Univ Minn, 67-68; asst prof geol, Syracuse Univ, 68-74, assoc prof, 74-75; GEOLOGIST, US GEOL SURV, COLO, 76- *Mem:* Geol Soc Am; Soc Econ Paleont & Mineral; Am Soc Limnol & Oceanog; Int Asn Sedimentology; AAAS. *Res:* Geochemistry of evaporite and carbonate deposits; geochemistry of lakes and lake sediments; geochemistry of marine sediments. *Mailing Add:* US Geol Surv MS 925 Fed Ctr Br Regional Chem Lakewood CO 80225

DEAN, WALTER KEITH, b Big Timber, Mont, Nov 2, 17; m 41; c 4. INORGANIC CHEMISTRY. *Educ:* Univ Wis, BS, 39; Univ Mo- Rolla, MS, 41. *Prof Exp:* Asst chem, Sch Mines & Metall, Univ Mo-Rolla, 39-41; Chemist, 41-69, res supvr, 69-82, ASSOC SCIENTIST, SCI PROD DIV, MALLINCKRODT CHEM WORKS, 82- *Concurrent Pos:* lectr, Univ Col, Wash Univ, 53-62. *Mem:* Am Chem Soc; Am Soc Testing & Mat. *Res:* Chromatography chemicals; high-purity silicon; rhenium; analytical reagents; ultrapure organic solvents. *Mailing Add:* Sci Prod Div Box 5840 Mallinckrodt Inc St Louis MO 63134

DEAN, WALTER LEE, b Lenoir City, Tenn, Dec 13, 28; m 53; c 3. ORGANIC CHEMISTRY, INORGANIC CHEMISTRY. *Educ:* Maryville Col, BS, 50; Univ Tenn, MS, 53, PhD(org chem), 56. *Prof Exp:* RES CHEMIST, BUCKEYE CELLULOSE CORP, 56- *Mem:* Am Chem Soc; Soc Petrol Engrs. *Res:* Organic chemistry and synthesis; natural products; cellulose derivatives; graft polymer synthesis; nonwoven binders; petroleum recovery; absorbent structures. *Mailing Add:* 5226 Quince Rd Memphis TN 38117

DEAN, WARREN EDGELL, b Richwood, WVa, Aug 1, 32; m 59; c 3. PHYSICAL CHEMISTRY, INORGANIC CHEMISTRY. *Educ:* WVa Inst Technol, BS, 54; WVa Univ, MS, 57, PhD, 59. *Prof Exp:* Instr chem, WVa Univ, 58-59; with Columbia-Southern Chem Corp, 59; supvr process res, 59-74, supt org area, 74-78, tech supt, 79-80, PLANT TECH MGR, CHEM DIV, NATRIUM PLANT, PPG INDUSTS, INC, 80- *Mem:* Am Chem Soc. *Res:* Chelate compounds of alkanol-substituted ethylendiamines; process research; inorganic heavy chemicals. *Mailing Add:* PPG Indust Inc Chem Div New Martinsville WV 26155

DEAN, WILLIAM C(ORNER), b Pittsburgh, Pa, Nov 21, 26; m 50; c 2. ELECTRICAL ENGINEERING. *Educ:* Carnegie Inst Technol, BS, 49, MS, 50, PhD, 52. *Prof Exp:* Res geophysicist, Gulf Res & Develop Co, 52-60; sr eng specialist, United Electrodynamics & Teledyne, Inc, 60-62, proj eng, 62, chief res sect, 62-66, mgr seismic data lab, Teledyne, Inc, 66-70, MGR SEISMIC ARRAY ANAL CTR, TELEDYNE-GEOTECH, 70- *Mem:* Inst Elec & Electronics Engrs; Soc Explor Geophys. *Res:* Circuit theory; information theory; data processing; analog and digital computers; potential fields; wave propagation. *Mailing Add:* Teledyne-Geotech PO Box 334 Alexandria VA 22313

DEANE, DARREL DWIGHT, b Anacortes, Wash, Nov 9, 15; m 43; c 3. DAIRY BACTERIOLOGY. *Educ:* Univ Idaho, BS, 38; Univ Nebr, MSc, 39; Pa State Univ, PhD(bact), 42. *Prof Exp:* Asst prof dairy husb, Univ Nebr, 46-51; asst prof dairy indust, Iowa State Univ, 51-61; from assoc prof to prof, 61-79, EMER PROF DAIRY MFG, UNIV WYO, 79- *Mem:* Am Dairy Sci Asn. *Res:* Production of penicillin from synthetic media; ripening of cheddar cheese; lactic streptococcus bacteriophages; microbial spoilage of cottage cheese; cheese packaging; direct acid manufacture of sour cream and cottage cheese; manufacture of low fat cheese; keeping quality of fluid milk. *Mailing Add:* 3124 Silverwood Dr Fort Collins CO 80525

DEANE, MARGARET, b Calif, Feb 14, 27. BIOSTATISTICS, EPIDEMIOLOGY. *Educ:* Stanford Univ, BA, 49; Univ Calif, Berkeley, MPH, 56. *Prof Exp:* Pub health statistician, 53-68, biostatistician, 68-73, sr res analyst, 73-75, EPIDEMIOLOGIST, CALIF STATE HEALTH DEPT, 76- *Concurrent Pos:* USPHS res fel & vis lectr epidemiol statist, St Thomas' Hosp Med Sch, London, 65-67. *Mem:* Am Pub Health Asn; Soc Epidemiol Res; Int Epidemiol Asn. *Res:* Application of statistical methods and epidemiology to problems of environmental health. *Mailing Add:* 2151 Berkeley Way Berkeley CA 94704

DEANE, NORMAN, b Newark, NJ, Aug 20, 21; m 56; c 2. INTERNAL MEDICINE, PHYSIOLOGY. *Educ:* Temple Univ, BA, 43, MD, 46; Am Bd Internal Med, dipl. *Prof Exp:* Instr physiol, Col Med, NY Univ, 49-51, from instr to asst prof med, Post Grad Med Sch, 53-61, asst prof clin med, 54-56, lectr physiol, Col Med, 55-61, dir clins, Univ Hosp & Med Ctr, 56-60; ASSOC PROF MED & ASSOC ATTEND PHYSICIAN, NEW YORK MED COL, FLOWER & FIFTH AVE HOSPS, 61- *Concurrent Pos:* Vis investr, Med Dept, Brookhaven Nat Lab, 50-51; asst vis physician, Fourth Med Div, NY Univ, 53-61; assoc attend physician, Univ Hosp & Med Ctr, 58-61; Polachek fel med res, 56-61; assoc vis physician, Metrop Hosp, 61-69, vis physician, 70-; attend physician, Lenox Hill Hosp, 67-; mem adv coun, NY State Kidney Dis Inst, 67-70; mem renal dialysis comt, Health & Hosp Planning Coun Southern NY, 67-; mem renal dis subcomt, New York Metrop Regional Med Prog, 68-70; mem hypertension & renal dis comt, NJ Regional Med Prog, 68-74; mem nephrology adv comt, New York Medicaid Prog, 68-; consult physician, Englewood Hosp, 68-78, Hackensack Hosp, 69-76 & St Vincent's Hosp & Med Ctr, 71-; mem med bd, Metrop Hosp, 70-; med dir, Manhattan Kidney Ctr, New York Nephrol Found, 71-; med dir, Nat Nephrology Found, 73- *Mem:* Am Physiol Soc; fel Am Col Physicians; Am Soc Nephrology; Am Soc Artificial Internal Organs; Soc Exp Biol & Med. *Res:* Nephrology; integration of normal cardio-pulmonary, renal and liver function in man and alterations produced by disease; chemical compositon and mechanisms of control of the internal environment of the body. *Mailing Add:* 40 E 30 St New York NY 10016

DEANGELIS, DONALD LEE, b Baltimore, Md, June 7, 44; m 70; c 1. ECOLOGY. *Educ:* Mass Inst Technol, BS, 66; Yale Univ, PhD(plasma physics), 72. *Prof Exp:* Presidential intern ecol, Oak Ridge Nat Lab, Union Carbide, 72-73; res assoc ecol, Inst Soil Sci & Forest Fertil, Goettingen Univ, WGer, 73-74; RES ASSOC ECOL, OAK RIDGE NAT LAB, UNION CARBIDE, 74-, RES STAFF MEM, 76- *Mem:* Ecol Soc Am; AAAS; Am Phys Soc; Sigma Xi. *Res:* Population and ecosystem modeling and the analysis of the mathematical properties of ecological models. *Mailing Add:* Environ Sci Div Oak Ridge Nat Lab PO Box X Oak Ridge TN 37830

DEANHARDT, MARSHALL LYNN, b Anderson, SC, Sept 12, 48; m 70; c 2. ANALYTICAL CHEMISTRY. *Educ:* Clemson Univ, BS, 70; NC State Univ, PhD(anal chem), 75. *Prof Exp:* asst prof, 75-80, ASSOC PROF CHEM, GEORGE MASON UNIV, 80- *Concurrent Pos:* Consult, Naval Res Lab, Washington, DC. *Mem:* Am Chem Soc; Sigma Xi; Electrochem Soc. *Res:* Molten salt and aqueous electrochemistry; chemical instrumentation; computer interfacing of laboratory instrumentation. *Mailing Add:* Dept of Chem George Mason Univ Fairfax VA 22030

DEANIN, RUDOLPH D, b Newark, NJ, June 7, 21; m 46; c 2. POLYMER CHEMISTRY. *Educ:* Cornell Univ, AB, 41; Univ Ill, MS, 42, PhD(org chem), 44. *Prof Exp:* Lab asst org chem, Cornell Univ, 40-41; jr sci aide, Regional Soybean Indust Prod Res Lab, USDA, 41-42; asst chem, Nat Defense Res Comt Proj, Univ Ill, 42, asst instr, 42-43, from res asst to spec res asst, Off Rubber Res, 43-47; res chemist & proj leader, Allied Chem Corp, 47-60; dir chem res & develop, DeBell & Richardson, Inc, Conn, 60-67; PROF PLASTICS, UNIV LOWELL, 67- *Concurrent Pos:* Vis lectr, Univ Mass, 63-64; Brown Univ, 65-66 & Northeastern Univ, 67-68. *Mem:* Am Chem Soc; Soc Plastics Eng. *Res:* Polymerization, compounding, properties, applications and economics of polymers and plastics. *Mailing Add:* Plastics Dept Univ of Lowell Lowell MA 01854

DEANS, HARRY A, b Dallas, Tex, June 17, 32; m 56; c 3. CHEMICAL ENGINEERING. *Educ:* Rice Inst, BA, 53, BS, 54, MS, 56; Princeton Univ, PhD(chem eng), 60. *Prof Exp:* Assoc prof, 59-70, PROF CHEM ENG, RICE UNIV, 70-, ASSOC, BROWN COL, 77- *Concurrent Pos:* Fulbright lectr, Israel, 64; Consult, Esso Prod Res Co. *Mem:* Am Inst Chem Engrs. *Res:* Multiphase, multicomponent fluid flow in porous media; gas-liquid and gas-solid chromatography of chemically reactive systems; chemisorption; bubble-column chromatography; tracer methods in petroleum reservoir evaluation; continuous chromatographic separation technology. *Mailing Add:* Dept of Chem Eng Rice Univ Houston TX 77001

DEANS, ROBERT JACK, b Ft Wayne, Ind, Dec 4, 27; m 50; c 5. ANIMAL HUSBANDRY. *Educ:* Ohio State Univ, BSc, 49; MSc, 50; Mich State Univ, PhD(animal husb), 56. *Prof Exp:* Instr animal husb, Ohio State Univ, 50-52; from instr to assoc prof, 52-74, PROF ANIMAL HUSB, MICH STATE UNIV, 74- *Concurrent Pos:* Adv, Univ Nigeria, 65. *Mem:* Am Soc Animal Sci; Am Meat Sci Asn. *Res:* Effects of endocrine-like substances in meat-animal production; beef and lamb carcass investigations. *Mailing Add:* Dept of Animal Husb Mich State Univ East Lansing MI 48824

DEANS, SIDNEY ALFRED VINDIN, b Montreal, Que, Dec 31, 18; m 59; c 1. ORGANIC CHEMISTRY. *Educ:* McGill Univ, BSc, 39, PhD, 42. *Prof Exp:* Res chemist, Can Industs, Ltd, 42-46; develop chemist, Ayerst, McKenna & Harrison Ltd, 47-56; assoc dir chem develop, Union Carbide Can, Ltd, 56-62; TECH DIR, PFIZER CAN INC, 62- *Mem:* Am Chem Soc; Chem Inst Can. *Res:* Synthesis of ethers; polymerization; penicillin; estrogenic sulfates; tetraethylthiuram disulfide; synthetic organic chemicals; petrochemicals; pharmaceuticals. *Mailing Add:* 361 Lethbridge Ave Montreal PQ H3P 1E6 Can

DEAR, ROBERT E A, b Bristol, UK, June 5, 33; US citizen; m 56; c 3. LUBRICANT ADDITIVES, FLUOROCHEMICAL SPECIALTIES. *Educ:* Univ Western Ont, PhD(org chem), 63. *Prof Exp:* Sr res chemist, Allied Chem Corp, 64-70; group leader, CIBA-GEIGY Corp, 70-79; RES DIR, ELCO CORP, SUBSID OF DETREX CORP, 79- *Mem:* Am Chem Soc; Royal Soc Chem. *Res:* Synthesis and development of lubricant additives in the industrial and automotive fields. *Mailing Add:* PO Box 09168 Cleveland OH 44109

DEARBORN, DELWYN D, b Miller, SDak, Feb 5, 33; m 56; c 3. ANIMAL BREEDING. *Educ:* SDak State Univ, BS, 54, MS, 59; Univ Nebr, PhD(animal sci), 71. *Prof Exp:* Assoc county exten agent, SDak State Univ, 56-59, exten livestock specialist, 59-66; exten livestock specialist, Univ Nebr, 66-70; prof animal sci & head dept, 71-74, DEAN, COL AGR & BIOL SCI, SDAK STATE UNIV, 74- *Mem:* Am Soc Animal Sci; Coun Agr Sci & Technol. *Res:* Beef production. *Mailing Add:* 154 Agr Hall S Dak State Univ Brookings SD 57007

DEARBORN, JOHN HOLMES, b Bangor, Maine, Feb 26, 33; m 60; c 2. MARINE ZOOLOGY, MARINE ECOLOGY. *Educ:* Univ NH, BA, 55; Mich State Univ, MS, 57; Stanford Univ, PhD(biol), 65. *Prof Exp:* Asst, Stanford Univ, 58-64; from asst prof to assoc prof, 66-76, PROF ZOOL, UNIV MAINE, 76- *Concurrent Pos:* NSF fel, 65-66; mem higher inverts adv comt, Smithsonian Oceanog Ctr, 68- *Mem:* AAAS; Am Soc Limnol & Oceanog; Ecol Soc Am; Am Soc Zool; Soc Syst Zool. *Res:* Marine invertebrate zoology and ecology, especially Antarctic benthos; polar and deep sea echinoderms. *Mailing Add:* Dept of Zool Univ of Maine Orono ME 04469

DEARDEN, BOYD L, b Coalville, Utah, Sept 1, 43; m 71; c 1. WILDLIFE ECOLOGY, SYSTEMS ECOLOGY. *Educ:* Univ Utah, BS, 65, MS, 67; Colo State Univ, PhD(syst ecol), 74. *Prof Exp:* Asst prof, 74-78, ASSOC PROF WILDLIFE ECOL, DEPT FORESTRY, WILDLIFE & FISHERIES & GRAD PROG ECOL, UNIV TENN, 78- *Mem:* Wildlife Soc; Am Soc Mammal; Am Inst Biol Sci; Soc for Comput Simulation Ecol. *Res:* Development of systems and analysis and simulation techniques for resource management applications. *Mailing Add:* Dept of Forestry Univ Tenn Knoxville TN 37901

DEARDEN, DOUGLAS MOREY, b Echo, Utah, Aug 25, 23; m 48; c 3. ZOOLOGY, GENETICS. *Educ:* Univ Utah, BA, 47, MA, 49; Univ Calif, Berkeley, 49; Univ Minn, PhD(sci educ, zool), 59. *Prof Exp:* Asst biol & genetics, Univ Utah, 47-49; from instr to assoc prof biol, 51-69, PROF BIOL, UNIV MINN, MINNEAPOLIS, 69- *Mem:* AAAS; Nat Asn Res Sci Teaching. *Res:* Drosophila and human genetics. *Mailing Add:* Dept of Biol Gen Col Univ of Minn Minneapolis MN 55455

DEARDEN, LYLE CONWAY, b Salt Lake City, Utah, Apr 27, 22; m 43; c 3. ANATOMY. *Educ:* Univ Utah, BA, 47, MA, 49, PhD(vert zool), 55. *Prof Exp:* Asst comp anat, Univ Utah, 47-49; asst instr comp anat & embryol, Univ Kans, 49-50; instr zool, Univ Mass, 50-53; instr biol, St Mary of Wasatch Col, 53-54; instr zool, Univ Mass, 54-55; from instr to asst prof anat, Med Sch, Univ Southern Calif, 55-59; assoc prof, Sch Med, George Washington Univ, 59-63; prof, Calif Col Med, 63-66; PROF ANAT, UNIV CALIF, IRVINE-CALIF COL MED, 66-, PROF RADIOL SCI, 77- *Concurrent Pos:* Instr biol, Univ Utah, 53-54; consult, NSF, 59-63, consult, 63-; vis prof, Univ Rome, 73-74. *Mem:* Pan-Am Soc Anat; Am Asn Anat. *Res:* Histology and EM GI system cartilage. *Mailing Add:* Dept of Anat Col Med Univ Calif Irvine CA 92664

DEARLOVE, THOMAS JOHN, b Syracuse, NY, Jan 28, 41; m 64. POLYMER CHEMISTRY. *Educ:* Norwich Univ, BS, 63; Rensselaer Polytechnic Inst, PhD(org chem), 67. *Prof Exp:* Chemist adhesives, Harry Diamond Labs, US Govt, Washington, DC, 67-69; SR STAFF RES SCIENTIST POLYMER COMPOSITES, GEN MOTORS RES LABS, 69- *Mem:* Am Chem Soc; Adhesion Soc; Sigma Xi. *Res:* Fundamental aspects of adhesion; formulation and testing of adhesives; chemistry of silane primers; formulation of polyurethane sealants, the mechanism of tin catalysts in polyurethanes, rapid injection molding of epoxy resins, and the chemistry of chopped fiber composites. *Mailing Add:* Polymers Dept Gen Motors Res Lab Warren MI 48090

DEARMAN, HENRY HURSELL, b Statesville, NC, Aug 28, 34; m 61. PHYSICAL CHEMISTRY. *Educ:* Univ NC, BS, 56; Calif Inst Technol, PhD(chem), 60. *Prof Exp:* Res assoc chem, Enrico Fermi Inst Nuclear Studies, Univ Chicago, 60-61; res chemist, Chemstrand Res Ctr, Inc, Monsanto Co, 61-62; from asst prof to assoc prof chem, 62-74, PROF CHEM, UNIV NC, CHAPEL HILL, 74- *Mem:* Am Chem Soc; Am Phys Soc. *Res:* Paramagnetic resonance spectra; electronic spectra of organic molecules and inorganic transition metal complexes. *Mailing Add:* Dept of Chem Univ of NC Chapel Hill NC 27514

DEARMON, IRA ALEXANDER, JR, b Charlotte, NC, Sept 18, 20; m 50; c 4. STATISTICS. *Educ:* Va Polytech Inst, BS, 43, MS, 48. *Prof Exp:* Sanitarian, State Health Dept, Va, 47-50; statistician, Biomath Div, Ft Detrick, 54-60, res analyst, Chem Corps Opers Res Group, Army Chem Ctr, 60-64, opers res analyst, Opers Res Group, US Army Munitions Command, Edgewood Arsenal, 64-73; opers res analyst, US Army Armament Command, Rock Island, Ill, 73-76; biostatistician, Frederick Cancer Res Ctr, Litton Bionetics, Inc, 76-81; RETIRED. *Concurrent Pos:* Asst prof math, Harford Jr Col, 66-68; exec dir, Pine Bluff Arsenal, Ark, 68-72. *Mem:* Opers Res Soc Am; Biomet Soc; Am Defense Preparedness Asn. *Res:* Planning and coordination of experimental designs for scientific personnel in all areas of cancer research including clinical trials; statistical analyses on data collected in studies to identify candidate carcinogens, on chemotherapy fermentation, on bioassay, on animal health, on animal breeding and in life survival testing. *Mailing Add:* 215 E Second St Frederick MD 21701

DEARMOND, M KEITH, b Ft Wayne, Ind, Dec 10, 35. PHYSICAL CHEMISTRY, INORGANIC CHEMISTRY. *Educ:* DePauw Univ, BA, 58; Univ Ariz, PhD(phys chem), 63. *Prof Exp:* Res assoc magnetic resonance spectros, Univ Ill, 63-64; from asst prof to assoc prof, 64-75, asst head, 75, PROF CHEM, NC STATE UNIV, 75- *Concurrent Pos:* NIH trainee, 63-64; vis prof, Univ Bologna, Italy, 79. *Mem:* Am Chem Soc; Sigma Xi; NAm Photochem Soc. *Res:* Luminescence of transition metal complexes to elucidate nonradiative processes; electrochemical and photoelectrochemical studies of metal complexes; electron spin resonance of transition metal complexes. *Mailing Add:* Dept of Chem NC State Univ Raleigh NC 27607

DEARTH, JAMES DEAN, b Marietta, Ohio, Dec 22, 46. SYNFUELS RESEARCH, COMPUTER MODELING. *Educ:* Univ Calif, Berkeley, BS, 68; Mass Inst Technol, SM, 70, ScD, 79. *Prof Exp:* Sr prin res engr, Atlantic Richfield Co, 74-81; SR STAFF ENGR, EXXON RES & ENG CO, 81- *Mem:* Am Inst Chem Engrs. *Res:* Predevelopment activities on a proprietary process for shale oil generation by thermal pyrolysis of oil shale rock; operations center on a small continuous bench-scale reactor. *Mailing Add:* 2600 Skywalker #2043C Houston TX 77058

DEAS, JANE ELLEN, b New Orleans, La, Mar 9, 33. MEDICAL MICROBIOLOGY, PARASITOLOGY. *Educ:* Loyola Univ, La, BS, 55; La State Univ, MS, 72, PhD(microbiol), 75. *Prof Exp:* Technologist pharmacol, Med Ctr, La State Univ, 55-56; technologist anat, Med Sch, Tulane Univ, 56-59; med res specialist, 59-74, ASST PROF TROP MED, MED SCH, LA STATE UNIV, NEW ORLEANS, 74- *Mem:* Am Soc Trop Med & Hyg; Electron Micros Soc Am; Am Soc Microbiol; Am Soc Parasitologists; Sigma Xi. *Res:* Erythrocyte membrane proteins and their relationships to parasitic mechanisms. *Mailing Add:* Dept of Trop Med & Med Parasitol La State Univ Sch of Med New Orleans LA 70112

DEAS, THOMAS C, b Augusta, Ga, Aug 5, 21; m 43; c 2. ANESTHESIOLOGY. *Educ:* Univ Ga, BS, 42; Ga Sch Med, Md, 45; Am Bd Anesthesiol, dipl, 56. *Prof Exp:* Intern, US Naval Hosp, Parris Island, SC, 45-46, med officer, Post Med Detachment, 46-48; resident anesthesiol, Univ Hosp, Augusta, Ga, 48-49; anesthesiologist, Navy Hosp Ship Consolation, 49-51 & Naval Hosp, Jacksonville, Fla, 51, resident, Philadelphia, 51-52, chief anesthesiol serv, 56-63, anesthesiologist, Bainbridge, Md, 52-55; PROF ANESTHESIOL, TEMPLE UNIV, 63- *Concurrent Pos:* Consult, US Naval Hosp, Philadelphia, 63. *Mem:* Fel Am Col Anesthesiol; Am Soc Anesthesiol; Royal Soc Med; Am Nat Standards Inst; Asn Advan Med Instrumentation. *Mailing Add:* Dept of Anesthesiol Temple Univ Med Ctr Philadelphia PA 19140

DEASON, TEMD R, b York, Ala, Oct 13, 31; m 65; c 2. ALGOLOGY. *Educ:* Univ Ala, BS, 54, MS, 58; Univ Tex, PhD(bot), 60. *Prof Exp:* Asst prof biol sci, Univ Del, 60-61; from asst prof to assoc prof biol, 61-69, PROF BIOL, UNIV ALA, 69- *Honors & Awards:* US Sr Scientist Teaching & Res Award, Alexander von Humboldt Found, W Ger, 74. *Mem:* Am Phycol Soc; Int Phycol Soc. *Res:* Morphology and taxonomy of soil algae; electron microscopy. *Mailing Add:* Dept Biol Univ Ala University AL 35486

DEATH, FRANK STUART, b Winnipeg, Man, Apr 15, 32; m 54; c 5. METALLURGY. *Educ:* Univ BC, BASc, 55, MASc, 56. *Prof Exp:* Engr, Tonawanda Labs, Linde Div, Union Carbide Corp, 56-60, group leader melting & refining process, 60-65, lab div head phys chem steelmaking, Newark Labs, 65-68, asst mgr mkt develop, 68-70, mgr AOD Steelmaking, Tarrytown Labs, 70-73, asst mgr, Gas Prod Div, 73-77, MGR GAS PROD DIV, UNION CARBIDE CORP, 77- *Mem:* Am Inst Mining, Metall & Petrol Engrs. *Res:* Metallurgical science; physical chemistry of steelmaking; thermochemical processes involving new techniques; metal-producing industry. *Mailing Add:* Union Carbide Corp Tarrytown Tech Ctr Tarrytown NY 10591

DEATHERAGE, FRED E, b Waverly, Ill, Dec 30, 13; m 42; c 3. FOOD BIOCHEMISTRY, NUTRITION. *Educ:* Ill Col, AB, 35; Univ Ill, AM, 36; Univ Iowa, PhD(biochem), 38. *Hon Degrees:* DSc, Ill Col, 60. *Prof Exp:* Instr biochem, Univ Iowa, 38-40; Kroger fel agr chem, Ohio State Univ, 40-42; in chg res lab, Food Found, Kroger Co, Cincinnati, 42-46; from asst prof to assoc prof agr biochem, 46-51, prof agr biochem & chmn dept, 51-64, PROF BIOCHEM, OHIO STATE UNIV, 51- *Concurrent Pos:* Prof animal sci, Ohio Agr Res & Develop Ctr, 51-68; mem US Agency Int Develop-Ohio State Univ, Sao Paulo, 64-68; consult, Food Processing Indust; prof food sci, Fac Food Technol, Univ Campinas, Brazil, 74. *Mem:* AAAS; Am Inst Nutrit; Am Chem Soc; Am Soc Animal Sci; Inst Food Technol. *Res:* Processing of meat; fundamental nature of quality in meat; autooxidation of fats; processing of foods; development of army rations; chemistry of coffee; hydrolysis of proteins; use of antibiotics in food preservation; mode of action of antibiotics. *Mailing Add:* Dept of Biochem Ohio State Univ 484 W 12th Ave Columbus OH 43210

DEATLEY, LINDLEY S(HAFER), b Kansas City, Mo, Aug 2, 12; m 37; c 2. CHEMICAL ENGINEERING. *Educ:* Univ Kans, BS, 33. *Prof Exp:* Chemist, Thompson-Hayward Chem Co, 34-36; chem engr, Puritan Compressed Gas Corp, 36-38; chief chemist, Thompson-Hayward Chem Co, 38-42, lab dir, 42-51, dir res & chem eng, 51-53, vpres res & develop, 53-69, sr vpres & dir res & develop, 69-77; RETIRED. *Mem:* AAAS; Am Chem Soc; Am Inst Chem Engrs; Entom Soc Am. *Res:* Synthesis of chlorophenoxyacetic acid herbicides; low volatile esters of 2, 4-D and 2, 4, 5-T; synthesis of non-ionic emulsifiers for pesticides; chlorination of organic compounds; field testing and development of chemicals as pesticides. *Mailing Add:* 8205 Linden Dr Prairie Village KS 66108

DEATLEY, WILLIAM BRANTNER, chemical engineering, metallurgical engineering, see previous edition

DEATON, BOBBY CHARLES, b Pittsburg, Tex, Jan 20, 36; m 60; c 2. SOLID STATE PHYSICS. *Educ:* Baylor Univ, BA, 57, MS, 59; Univ Tex, PhD(physics), 62. *Prof Exp:* Sr res scientist, 61-66, STAFF SCIENTIST, GEN DYNAMICS|FT WORTH, 66- *Concurrent Pos:* Res scientist, Univ Tex, 63-64, adj instr, Univ Tex, Arlington, 64-66; adj assoc prof, Tex Wesleyan Col, 67-, head dept physics, 68-; res grant plate tectonics, Res Corp, 81. *Mem:* Am Phys Soc; Sigma Xi. *Res:* Solid state physics involving Fermi surfaces of metals, superconductivity and study of materials at high pressures and temperatures; plate tectonics of Caribbean Region, especially motion of Polochic Fault. *Mailing Add:* Dept of Physics Tex Wesleyan Col Ft Worth TX 76105

DEATON, EDMUND IKE, b Sulphur Springs, Tex, Aug 18, 30; m 54; c 3. MATHEMATICS. *Educ:* Hardin-Simmons Univ, BA, 50; Univ Tex, MA, 56, PhD(math), 60. *Prof Exp:* Spec instr math, Univ Tex, 56-60; assoc prof, 60-69, PROF MATH, SAN DIEGO STATE UNIV, 69- *Mem:* Am Math Soc; Math Asn Am. *Res:* Partial differential equations. *Mailing Add:* Dept of Math San Diego State Univ San Diego CA 92182

DEATON, JAMES WASHINGTON, b Manning, Ark, June 29, 34; m 56. POULTRY SCIENCE. *Educ:* Univ Ark, BS, 56; Tex A&M Univ, MS, 59, PhD(poultry sci), 64. *Prof Exp:* Poultry serviceman, Paymaster Feed Mills, Tex, 56-58; res asst poultry nutrit, Tex A&M Univ, 58-59, poultry nutrit & genetics, 61-63, res assoc poultry nutrit & statist eval data, 63-64; poultry serviceman, DeKalb Agr Asn, Inc, 59-61; Tex Turkey Fedn grant poultry dis, Tex Agr Exp Sta, 64; res poultry husbandmen, S Cent Res Lab, 64-68, DIR S CENT POULTRY RES LAB, AGR RES SERV, USDA, 68- *Mem:* AAAS; Poultry Sci Asn; Am Genetic Asn; World Poultry Sci Asn; Int Soc Biometeorol. *Res:* Poultry management and environmental research, including poultry nutrition, genetics and disease aspects and physiological relationships. *Mailing Add:* USDA Agr Res Serv PO Box 5367 Mississippi State MS 39762

DEAVEN, DENNIS GEORGE, b Hershey, Pa, Nov 24, 37; m 65; c 2. METEOROLOGY, COMPUTER SCIENCE. *Educ:* Penn State Univ, BS, 68, MS, 70, PhD(meteorol), 74. *Prof Exp:* Res asst meteorol, Penn State Univ, 65-72; scientist, Nat Ctr Atmospheric Res, 72-77; RES METEOROLOGIST, US WEATHER SERV, 77- *Mem:* Am Meteorol Soc; Sigma Xi. *Res:* Numerical weather prediction; dynamic meteorology; atmospheric air quality. *Mailing Add:* World Weather Bldg Develop Div 5200 Auth Rd Camp Springs MD 20233

DEAVEN, LARRY LEE, b Hershey, Pa, Oct 28, 40. CELL BIOLOGY, CYTOGENETICS. *Educ:* Pa State Univ, BS, 62, MS, 64; Univ Tex, PhD(biomed sci), 69. *Prof Exp:* Instr biol, Pa State Univ, 64; fel, M D Anderson Hosp, Univ Tex, 65-69, Nat Cancer Inst fel, 69-71; fel, 71-73, STAFF MEM CELLULAR & MOLECULAR RADIOBIOL, LOS ALAMOS SCI LAB, 73-; GENETICIST, US DEPT ENERGY, 80- *Concurrent Pos:* Assoc ed, Radiation Res, 81- *Mem:* AAAS; Am Chem Soc; Am Soc Cell Biol; Genetics Soc Am; Soc Anal Cytol. *Res:* Chromosome structure and physiology; DNA content and structure in mammalian metaphase chromosomes; automated cytogenetics; chromosome damage by environmental pollutants. *Mailing Add:* Biomed Res Group Los Alamos Nat Lab Los Alamos NM 87545

DEAVER, BASCOM SINE, JR, b Macon, Ga, Aug 16, 30; m 51; c 3. EXPERIMENTAL SOLID STATE PHYSICS. *Educ:* Ga Inst Technol, BS, 52; Wash Univ, MA, 54; Stanford Univ, PhD(physics), 62. *Prof Exp:* Physicist, Air Force Spec Weapons Command, 54-57 & Stanford Res Inst, 57-62; NSF fel, Stanford Univ, 62-63, res assoc low temperature physics, 63-65; assoc prof, 65-73, PROF PHYSICS, UNIV VA, 73- *Concurrent Pos:* Physicist, Stanford Res Inst, 63-65; Alfred P Sloan fel, 66-68. *Mem:* Am Phys Soc. *Res:* Superconductivity; superconducting electronics; low temperature physics. *Mailing Add:* Dept Physics Univ Va McCormick Rd Charlottesville VA 22901

DEAVER, FRANKLIN KENNEDY, b Springdale, Ark, Jan 10, 18; m 45; c 2. MECHANICAL ENGINEERING. *Educ:* Univ Ark, BSChE, 39, MSME, 60; Univ Minn, PhD(mech eng), 69. *Prof Exp:* Asst mgr construct, Pioneer Co, Ark, 39-49, mgr construct, 49-55; from asst prof to assoc prof, 55-69, head dept, 69-80, PROF MECH ENG, UNIV ARK, FAYETTEVILLE, 69- *Mem:* Am Soc Mech Engrs; Am Soc Eng Educ; Nat Soc Prof Engrs. *Res:* Convective heat transfer; solar energy. *Mailing Add:* Rte 9 Box 276 Old Wire Rd N Fayetteville AR 72701

DEAVERS, DANIEL RONALD, b Norman, Ill, Oct 23, 43; m 66. ENVIRONMENTAL PHYSIOLOGY, PHYSIOLOGY. *Educ:* San Diego State Univ, BS, 67, MS, 69; Cornell Univ, PhD(environ physiol), 75. *Prof Exp:* Fel physiol, Dalton Res Ctr, Univ Mo, 75-76; cardiovasc trainee, USPHS, 76-78; instr physiol, Univ Louisville, 78-80; ASST PROF, CELLULAR OSTEOP MED & SURG, DES MOINES, 80- *Mem:* Am Physiol Soc; Am Soc Zool; Am Soc Mammal; Sigma Xi. *Res:* Comparative and regulatory aspects of water and electrolyte metabolism; hormonal control of carbohydrate metabolism and thermogenesis during hypothermia and hibernation. *Mailing Add:* Cellular Osteop Med Surg 3200 Grand Ave Des Moines IA 50312

DEB, ARUN K, b India. ENGINEERING. *Educ:* Univ Calcutta, BS, 57, PhD(civil eng), 68; Univ Wis, MS, 61. *Prof Exp:* USAID fel, Univ Wis, 60-61; asst prof environ eng, Bengal Eng Col, Univ Calcutta, 61-71; sr res fel, Univ Col London, 71-73; vis prof, Univ Notre Dame, 74; MGR ENVIRON SYSTS, WESTON, 77- *Concurrent Pos:* USAID fel, 61; NSF found res grant, 77, 80. *Honors & Awards:* Gold Medal, Inst Engr, Pub Health Engr, 73. *Mem:* Dipl Am Acad Environ Engrs; Am Soc Civil Engrs; Water Pollution Control Fedn; Am Water Works Asn; Inst Engrs India. *Res:* Water and wastewater resources management; mathematical modeling and econometric modeling; systems analysis and optimization of environmental engineering systems; water-distribution systems analysis; water supply, water reuse and wastewater systems planning, evaluation and design. *Mailing Add:* Weston Weston Way West Chester PA 19380

DE BACH, PAUL (HEVENER), b Miles City, Mont, Dec 28, 14; m 40; c 2. ENTOMOLOGY, INSECT ECOLOGY. *Educ:* Univ Calif, BS, 37, PhD(entom), 40. *Prof Exp:* Asst zool, Univ Calif, 37-38, asst entom, Citrus Exp Sta, 38-41, res assoc, 41-42; jr entomologist, USPHS, Calif, 42-43; entomologist, Bur Entom & Plant Quarantine, USDA, Miss, 43-45; from asst entomologist to assoc entomologist, 45-57, ENTOMOLOGIST, UNIV CALIF, RIVERSIDE, 57-, PROF BIOL CONTROL, 61- *Concurrent Pos:* Ed, Sect Biol Control, Biol Abstr, 59; Rockefeller fel & consult, Brazil, 62; Fulbright res fel, Greece, 62-63; mem task force biol control, US Nat Comt

of Int Biol Prog, 67-69; panel mem sect environ biol, NSF, 67-68; int coordr, IBP World Proj Biol Control Scale Insects, 68-; assoc dir, Int Ctr Biol Control, Univ Calif, Berkeley & Riverside, 70-; pres, Int Orgn Biol Control, 71-; fac res lectr, Univ Calif, Riverside, 75- *Mem:* AAAS; Entom Soc Am; Ecol Soc Am; Am Inst Biol Sci; Int Asn Ecol. *Res:* Laboratory and field population studies of insect pests and their natural enemies, biological control; quantitative relations between parasite and host populations; biosystemics of scale insect parasites. *Mailing Add:* Div of Biol Control Univ of Calif Riverside CA 92521

DEBACKER, HILDA SPODHEIM, b Bucharest, Rumania, July 17, 24; US citizen; m 48. NEUROANATOMY, MICROSCOPIC ANATOMY. *Educ:* Cornell Univ, AB, 45; Polytech Inst Brooklyn, MS, 49; Med Col SC, MS, 57, PhD(anat), 67. *Prof Exp:* Res asst chem, Calco Chem Div, Am Cyanamid Co, NJ, 45-46; lab asst polymer chem, Polytech Inst Brooklyn, 48; lit searcher pharmaceut chem, Warner Inst Therapeut Res, NY, 49-50; res librn, Wallace & Tiernan Co, Inc, NJ, 50-52; teaching asst, 53-55, instr, 62-67, assoc, 67-68, asst prof, 68-72, ASSOC PROF ANAT, MED UNIV SC, 72- *Mem:* AAAS; Am Asn Anatomists; Am Chem Soc. *Res:* Microscopic structure and function of living liver; microscopic observations of conjunctival circulation in health and disease in man; conjunctival circulation during cerebral ischemia and during electric shock therapy. *Mailing Add:* Dept of Anat Med Univ of SC Charleston SC 29401

DEBAKEY, LOIS, b Lake Charles, La. INFORMATION SCIENCE, MEDICAL EDUCATION. *Educ:* Tulane Univ, BA, 49, MA, 59, PhD(lit), 63. *Prof Exp:* Instr English, Tulane Univ, 60-63, from asst prof to prof sci commun, Sch Med, 63-68; PROF SCI COMMUN, BAYLOR COL MED, 68- *Concurrent Pos:* Lectr sci commun, Sch Med, Tulane Univ, 68-; dir ann course sci commun, Am Col Surgeons, 69-76; consult, Nat Libr Med, 73-77 & Tex State Tech Inst, 74; mem comt teaching tech & sci writing, Nat Coun Teachers of English; exec coun, Southern Asn Cols & Schs, 75-80; dir, Plain Talk, Inc, 79-; usage panel, The Am Heritage Dict, 80-; nat adv coun, USC Ctr for Continuing Med Educ, 81-; adj prof sci commun, Sch Med, Tulane Univ, 81- *Honors & Awards:* Distinguished Serv Award, Am Med Writers Asn, 70; Bausch & Lomb Sci Award. *Mem:* AAAS; Coun Biol Ed; Soc Tech Commun; Nat Asn Sci Writers; Int Soc Gen Semantics. *Res:* Biomedical communication-writing, editing, publishing, ethics; teaching of scientific communication; linguistics; influence of science on literature and of literature on science. *Mailing Add:* Baylor Col of Med 1200 Moursund Ave Houston TX 77030

DEBAKEY, MICHAEL ELLIS, b Lake Charles, La, Sept 7, 08; m 36, 75; c 5. SURGERY. *Educ:* Tulane Univ, BS, 30, MD, 32, MS, 35. *Hon Degrees:* Numerous from US & foreign univs, 61-76. *Prof Exp:* From instr to assoc prof surg, Tulane Univ, 37-48; vpres med affairs, Univ, 68-69, pres, 69-79, PROF SURG & CHMN DEPT, BAYLOR COL MED, 48-, CHIEF EXEC OFFICER, 68-, CHANCELLOR, 79- *Concurrent Pos:* mem nat adv health coun, NIH, 61-65, mem nat adv gen med sci coun, 65, mem nat adv coun on regional med progs, 65-; mem comt on epidemiol & vet follow-up studies, Nat Res Coun; chmn, President's Comn Heart Dis, Cancer & Stroke, 64; chmn sci adv bd, Delta Regional Primate Res Ctr, Tulane Univ, 65; mem consult staff, Dept Surg, Tex Children's Hosp, Houston, 70-; mem patron's comt, Damon Runyon Mem Fund for Cancer Res, 71; dir, Nat Heart & Blood Vessel Res & Demonstration Ctr, Houston. *Honors & Awards:* Vishnevsky Medal, Inst Surg, Acad Med Sci, USSR, 62; Grand Cros, Order of Leopold, Belg, 62; Lasker Award, 63; Orden Militar del SS, Salvador y Santa Brigida de Suecia Caballero Gran Oficial de Gracia Magistrad, 69; Accademia Internazionale di Pontzen di Lettere Scienze ed Arti Gran Collare Accademico d'Oro, 69; Supreme Red Cross, Hellenic Red Cross, 72. *Mem:* Inst Med-Nat Acad Sci; Am Col Surg; Am Surg Asn; Soc Vascular Surg (pres, 54); Int Cardiovasc Soc (pres, 59). *Res:* Cardiovascular and thoracic surgery; cardiovascular diseases, including aortic diseases; replacement of excised segments of arteries by homografts and plastic prostheses; venous thrombosis; aneurysms and occlusive diseases of arteries; peripheral vascular diseases and development of the artificial heart. *Mailing Add:* Baylor Col of Med Houston TX 77025

DEBAKEY, SELMA, b Lake Charles, La. SCIENTIFIC COMMUNICATIONS. *Educ:* Tulane Univ, BA, 37. *Prof Exp:* Dir dept biomed commun, Alton Ochsner Med Found, 42-68; PROF SCI COMMUN, BAYLOR COL MED, 68- *Concurrent Pos:* Ed, Selected writings from Ochsner Clin, 42-54; ed, Ochsner Clin Reports, 55-58; mem comt judges, Mod Med Monogr Award, 58-60; co-ed, Bull Am Med Writers Asn, 61-64; ed, Cardiovasc Res Ctr Bull, 72- *Mem:* AAAS; Asn Teachers Tech Writing; Soc Tech Commun; Soc Health & Human Values. *Mailing Add:* 1200 Moursund Ave Houston TX 77030

DEBAR, ROGER BRYANT, b Eugene, Ore, Oct 22, 34; m 60. THEORETICAL PHYSICS. *Educ:* Reed Col, BA, 56; Stanford Univ, MS, 57, PhD(physics), 62. *Prof Exp:* PHYSICIST, LAWRENCE LIVERMORE LAB, UNIV CALIF, LIVERMORE, 61- *Mem:* Am Phys Soc. *Res:* Numerical analysis; numerical solution of partial differential equations of physics, especially hydrodynamics; particle physics. *Mailing Add:* Lawrence Livermore Lab Univ of Calif Livermore CA 94550

DEBARDELEBEN, JOHN F, b Houston, Tex, May 19, 37; m 72; c 3. ORGANIC CHEMISTRY, ORGANOPHOSPHORUS COMPOUNDS. *Educ:* Univ Va, BS, 60; Tex A&M, MS, 63; Ga Inst Technol, PhD(chem), 66. *Prof Exp:* Chemist, Monsanto Chem Co, 60-61; instr chem, Ga Inst Technol, 63-65; res scientist, Philip Morris Res Ctr, 66-81; PRES, RICHMOND ORGANICS, INC, 81- *Mem:* Am Chem Soc. *Res:* Organophosphorus chemistry; pyridine chemistry; sesquiterpenes; batch reactions, large scale synthesis; natural products. *Mailing Add:* Richmond Organics Inc 334 S Richardson Rd Ashland VA 23005

DEBAUN, ROBERT MATTHEW, b New York, NY, June 23, 24; m 50; c 4. INFORMATION SCIENCE, STATISTICS. *Educ:* Fordham Univ, BS, 47, MS, 49, PhD(chem), 51. *Prof Exp:* Instr org chem, Col Pharm, St John's Univ, NY, 50-51; assoc scientist, Nat Dairy Res Labs, Inc, 51-54; proj leader, Cent Res Labs, Gen Foods Corp, 54-55; statistician, 55, group leader, Math Anal Group, Stamford Labs, 56-58, ref catalysts group, 58-61, mgr tech comput corp hq, 61-65, adv plan, Corp Data Processing, 65, dir, 65-70, dir opers anal, 70-71, mgr info syst plan, 71-80, DIR INFO SYST, AM/FAR EAST DIV, AM CYANAMID CO, 80- *Mem:* Am Statist Asn; Inst Mgt Sci. *Res:* Applied statistics; management sciences. *Mailing Add:* 15 Lois Ct Wayne NJ 07470

DEBELL, ARTHUR GERALD, b New York, NY, June 10, 12; m 42; c 3. OPTICS. *Educ:* Rensselaer Polytech Inst, ChE, 35. *Prof Exp:* Metall chemist, Adirondack Steel Co, NY, 37-38; instr physics, Siena Col, 38-41; physicist, US Navy Yard, SC, 42-44 & Naval Ord Test Sta, 44-52; physicist, White Develop Corp, 52-55 & Rocketdyne Div, NAm Aviation Inc, 55-67, group scientist, Electrooptical Lab, Autonetics Div, NAm Rockwell Corp, 67-74; RES SPECIALIST, OPTICAL SCI CTR, UNIV ARIZ, 74- *Concurrent Pos:* Consult, Ballistic Missile Radiation Anal Ctr, Univ Mich, 60-64. *Mem:* Optical Soc Am; Soc Photo-Optical Instrumentation Engrs. *Res:* Design of optical, photographic and spectrographic instruments; patents on blackbodies and photographic shutter; infrared and rocket spectroscopy; research and design on solar flux radiometer for pioneer Venus space mission. *Mailing Add:* Optical Sci Ctr Univ Ariz Tucson AZ 85721

DEBELL, DEAN SHAFFER, b Woodbury, NJ, July 6, 42; m 64; c 3. FORESTRY. *Educ:* Juniata Col, BS, 63; Duke Univ, MF, 64, PhD(forest soils, plant physiol), 70. *Prof Exp:* Forester, Gifford Pinchot Nat Forest, US Forest Serv, 64-65, res forester, Southeastern Forest Exp Sta, 65-70; res forester, Cent Res Lab, Crown Zellerbach Corp, 70-75; RES FORESTER & PROJ LEADER SILVICULT, PAC NORTHWEST FOREST & RANGE EXP STA, US FOREST SERV, 75- *Concurrent Pos:* Vis prof forest biol, Belle W Baruch Forest Sci Inst, Clemson Univ, 80-81. *Mem:* Soc Am Foresters; Soil Sci Soc Am; Northwest Sci Asn. *Res:* Silviculture of conifers and hardwoods on the west-side of Cascade Range in Oregon and Washington. *Mailing Add:* Forestry Sci Lab 3625 93rd Ave SW Olympia WA 98502

DEBELL, ROBERT MICHAEL, microbiology, see previous edition

DEBENEDETTI, SERGIO, b Florence, Italy, Aug 17, 12; nat US; m 44; c 3. EXPERIMENTAL PHYSICS. *Educ:* Univ Florence, PhD(physics), 33. *Prof Exp:* Asst prof, Univ Padua, 34-38; fel, Curie Lab, Univ Paris, 38-40; res assoc, Bartol Res Found, 40-43; assoc prof physics, Kenyon Col, 43-44; sr physicist, Monsanto Co, Ohio, 44-45; prin physicist, Clinton Labs, Oak Ridge Nat Lab, 46-48; assoc prof, Wash Univ, 48-49; PROF PHYSICS, CARNEGIE-MELLON UNIV, 49- *Concurrent Pos:* Mem exped cosmic rays, Eritrea, EAfrica, 33; fel, Curie Lab, Univ Paris, 34-35; vis prof, Univ Rio de Janeiro, 52; Fulbright scholar, Univ Turin, 56-57; guest lectr, Brazilian Ctr Phys Sci, 61; lectr, Univ Calif, Berkeley, 63. *Mem:* Fel Am Phys Soc. *Res:* Nuclear and high energy physics; cosmic rays; radioactivity; short-lived isomers; positrons; mesons; Mossbaur spectroscopy; history of science. *Mailing Add:* Dept of Physics Carnegie-Mellon Univ Pittsburgh PA 15213

DEBER, CHARLES MICHAEL, b Brooklyn, NY, Apr 20, 42; m 71. BIOLOGICAL CHEMISTRY. *Educ:* Polytech Inst Brooklyn, BS, 62; Mass Inst Technol, PhD(org chem), 67. *Prof Exp:* NIH res fel, Harvard Med Sch, 67-69, assoc biol chem, 70-74; vis scientist, Inst Enzyme Res, Univ Wis, 75; asst prof, 76-80, ASSOC PROF BIOCHEM DIV, RES INST, HOSP FOR SICK CHILDREN, TORONTO & BIOCHEM DEPT, UNIV TORONTO, 81- *Res:* Conformations of biological macromolecules studied by nuclear magnetic resonance spectroscopy; peptide-cation and peptide-membrane interactions; myelin membrane proteins; cation transport by naturally-occurring and synthetic ionophores. *Mailing Add:* Biochem Dept Res Inst Hosp for Sick Children Toronto ON M5S 2R8 Can

DEBERRY, DAVID WAYNE, b Gonzales, Tex, Feb 5, 46; m 67; c 2. ELECTROCHEMISTRY, CHEMICAL KINETICS. *Educ:* Univ Tex, Austin, BS, 69; Rice Univ, PhD(chem), 74. *Prof Exp:* Res asst, Tracor, Inc, Austin, Tex, 66-69; res scientist, Radian Corp, Austin, Tex, 69-70, sr res scientist, 73-78; PRIN SCIENTIST, SUMX CORP, AUSTIN, TEX, 78- *Mem:* Electrochem Soc; Am Chem Soc; Nat Asn Corrosion Engrs; Sigma Xi. *Res:* Electrochemistry, particularly electrochemical kinetics; photoelectrochemical cell research; corrosion and corrosion inhibition; development of a redox-membrane cell for nox sorbent regeneration. *Mailing Add:* 4001 Knollwood Austin TX 78731

DE BETHUNE, ANDRE JACQUES, b Schaerbeek-Brussels, Belgium, Aug 20, 19; m 49; c 10. CHEMISTRY. *Educ:* St Peter's Col, BS, 39; Columbia Univ, PhD(phys chem), 45. *Prof Exp:* Res chemist, Columbia Univ, 42-45; Nat Res fel, Mass Inst Technol, 45-47; from asst prof to assoc prof, 47-55, chmn, Dept Chem, 65-67 & 74-76, PROF CHEM, BOSTON COL, 55- *Concurrent Pos:* Theoret ed jour, Electrochem Soc, 57-80; Guggenheim fel, Yale Univ, 60-61. *Mem:* Am Chem Soc; Am Phys Soc; Electrochem Soc; Faraday Soc. *Res:* Population kinetics, bioethics of population control; electrochemistry; isotope separation; kinetic theory of gases; statistics of child spacing. *Mailing Add:* Dept of Chem Boston Col Chestnut Hill MA 02167

DEBEVEC, PAUL TIMOTHY, b Cleveland, Ohio, May 30, 46. NUCLEAR PHYSICS. *Educ:* Mass Inst Technol, BS, 68; Princeton Univ, MA, 70, PhD(physics), 72. *Prof Exp:* Res assoc physics, Argonne Nat Lab, 72-74; asst prof, Ind Univ, Bloomington, 74-77; ASSOC PROF PHYSICS, UNIV ILL, URBANA, 77- *Concurrent Pos:* Vis assoc prof, Inst Physics, Louvain-La-Neuve, 79-80; mem subcomt electromagnetic interactions, Nuclear Sci Adv Comt, 81. *Mem:* Am Phys Soc. *Res:* Low and medium energy nuclear reactions and structure. *Mailing Add:* Dept of Physics Univ Ill 1110 W Green St Urbana IL 61801

DEBIAK, TED WALKER, b McKeesport, Pa, Sept 21, 44; m 69; c 1. RADIATION EFFECTS. *Educ:* Pa State Univ, BS, 66; Univ Pittsburgh, PhD(chem), 73. *Prof Exp:* Instr phys chem, 75-76, RES ASSOC NUCLEAR CHEM, STATE UNIV NY STONY BROOK, 74- ; RES SCIENTIST, GRUMMAN AEROSPACE CORP, BETHPAGE, NY, 76- *Mem:* Am Phys Soc; Inst Elec & Electronics Engrs; Am Nuclear Soc. *Res:* Effects of radiation on microwave semiconductor components and modules, infrared detectors and computer control display focal plane arrays, and induced activity due to space radiation in spacecraft. *Mailing Add:* 57 S Windhorst Ave Bethpage NY 11714

DEBIAS, DOMENIC ANTHONY, b Tresckow, Pa, Aug 31, 25; m 51; c 5. PHYSIOLOGY. *Educ:* Temple Univ, AB, 49, AM, 50; Jefferson Med Col, PhD(physiol), 56. *Prof Exp:* Instr & asst biol, Temple Univ, 49-50, instr & asst physiol, Sch Dent, 50-51, res assoc bact, 51; instr physiol, Sch Med, Univ Pa, 55; instr, Sch Dent, Temple Univ, 55; res assoc, Div Endocrine & Cancer Res, Jefferson Med Col, 56-57, from instr to prof physiol, 57-75; PROF PHYSIOL & PHARMACOL & CHMN DEPT, PHILADELPHIA COL OSTEOP MED, 75-, ASST DEAN, 78- *Mem:* Sigma Xi; Am Physiol Soc; Endocrine Soc; Am Heart Asn. *Res:* Physiology of the endocrine glands; endocrine regulation of cardiopulmonary functions; interrelationship of endocrine systems and nervous system; environmental physiology. *Mailing Add:* Dept Physiol & Pharmacol Philadelphia Col Osteop Med Philadelphia PA 19131

DEBITETTO, DOMINICK JOHN, b Barre, Vt, Aug 2, 23; m 51; c 3. EXPERIMENTAL PHYSICS, PHYSICAL OPTICS. *Educ:* Univ Okla, MSME, 46; NY Univ, PhD(physics), 56. *Prof Exp:* Engr power plant anal, Chance Vought Aircraft, United Aircraft Corp, 46-49; lab asst gas discharges, NY Univ, 51-56, instr physics, 53-55; res physicist, Phillips Labs Inc, 56-77; PROF ENG PHYSICS, WESTCHESTER COMMUNITY COL, VALHALLA, NY, 78- *Concurrent Pos:* Mem bd consults, Holographic Industs, Inc, 75- *Mem:* Am Phys Soc; Soc Photo-Optical Instrumentation Engrs; Optical Soc Am. *Res:* Microwave physics; magnetic materials; gas discharges; solid state physics; laser holography; three-dimensional holographic movies. *Mailing Add:* 167 Washburn Rd Briarcliff Manor NY 10510

DE BLAS, ANGEL LUIS, b Madrid, Spain, Jan 31, 50. NEUROBIOLOGY. *Educ:* Univ Madrid, BS & MS, 72; Ind Univ PhD(biochem), 78. *Prof Exp:* Res fel, NIH, 78-81; ASST PROF, STATE UNIV NY STONY BROOK, 81- *Concurrent Pos:* Prin investr, State Univ NY Stony Brook, 81- *Mem:* Soc Neurosci; Am Soc Neurochem; Spanish Biochem Soc. *Res:* Molecular basis of the synaptic functions and synapse formation in the central nervous system of mammals; monoclonal antibodies to synaptic molecules; gaba and benzodiazepine receptors; nerve cells in culture. *Mailing Add:* Dept Neurobiol & Behav State Univ NY Stony Brook NY 11794

DEBLOIS, RALPH WALTER, b Benton Harbor, Mich, Jan 11, 22; m 59; c 3. PHYSICS. *Educ:* Univ Mich, BS, 43, MS, 47; Rensselaer Polytech Inst, PhD(physics), 63. *Prof Exp:* Asst, Manhattan Proj, Columbia Univ, 43-46; fel, Univ Mich, 46-49; instr physics, Am Univ, Beirut, 50-53; PHYSICIST, GEN ELEC RES & DEVELOP CTR, 54- *Honors & Awards:* I-R 100 Award, Indust Res Mag, 70. *Mem:* AAAS; Biophys Soc; Am Phys Soc. *Res:* Ferromagnetic domain structure; submicron particle analysis; molecular-beam epitaxy. *Mailing Add:* 2509 Antonia Dr Schenectady NY 12309

DEBNATH, LOKENATH, b Dacca, India, Sept 30, 35; m 69; c 1. APPLIED MATHEMATICS, PURE MATHEMATICS. *Educ:* Univ Calcutta, BS, 54, MS, 56, PhD(pure math), 64; Imp Col, Univ London, dipl & PhD(appl math), 67. *Prof Exp:* Lectr math, Calcutta & Burdwan Univs, 57-65; res fel appl math, Imp Col, Univ London, 65-67; sr fel, Cambridge Univ, 67-68; assoc prof, 68-69, PROF MATH, E CAROLINA UNIV, 69- *Concurrent Pos:* Ed, Calcutta Math Soc Bulletin, 73-; vis prof, Univ Md, 74; vis prof, Univ Calcutta, 69, 72, 75, 78 & 81, consult, Ctr Advan Study Appl Math, 72-, vis prof Univ Oxford, 80; vis scientist, US-India Exchange of Scientists Prog, NSF, 75; ed, Bulletin of Calcutta Math Soc, 71-; managing ed, J of Math & Math Sci, 77-; reviewer NSF res proposals; 77-; adj prof physics, E Carolina Univ, 77-, res prof, Univ Grants Comn, 78-; sr Fulbright fel oceanic turbulence, 78; dir res conf on spec functions, NSF-Conf Bd of Math Sci, 79; dir grad studies, East Carolina Univ, 79-80. *Mem:* Am Math Soc; Am Phys Soc; Soc Indust & Appl Math; fel British Inst Math. *Res:* Nonlinear waves; dynamics of oceans; complex analysis; generalized functions with applications; fluid dynamics; elasticity-wave motions; vibrations; elements of theory of elliptic and associated functions with applications; elements of general topology; magnetohydrodynamics; rotating and stratified flows; oceanography. *Mailing Add:* Dept of Math E Carolina Univ Greenville NC 27834

DEBNATH, SADHANA, b Jagatpur, India, June 1, 38; m 69; c 1. ANALYTICAL CHEMISTRY, PHYSICAL CHEMISTRY. *Educ:* Gujarat Univ, India, BS, 58, MS, 60; Univ Calcutta, PhD(chem), 64. *Prof Exp:* Fel chem, Univ Minn, 64-67; scientist, Nat Chem Lab, Poona, India, 67-69; res assoc chem, 72-76, INSTR BIOCHEM, SCH MED, E CAROLINA UNIV, 76- *Concurrent Pos:* Fulbright scholar, 64. *Honors & Awards:* Sigma Xi Bislinghoff Res Award, E Carolina State Univ, 74. *Mem:* Indian Asn Cultivation Sci. *Res:* Acid base chemistry; dyes; kinetic study of organic peroxides, and organic synthesis; fatty acids; metabolism; bacterial pigment; pteridine-peptides; polorographic studies in non-acqueous media; acid-base reaction in non-aqueous media; characterization of pigment peptides. *Mailing Add:* 2004 Sherwood Dr Greenville NC 27834

DEBNEY, GEORGE CHARLES, JR, b Beaumont, Tex, Feb 19, 39; m 62, 66; c 3. APPLIED MATHEMATICS, THEORETICAL PHYSICS. *Educ:* Rice Univ, BA, 61; Univ Tex, Austin, PhD(math), 67. *Prof Exp:* Teaching asst math, Univ Tex, Austin, 62-63, res asst relativity theory, Relativity Ctr, 63-64, 65-66; mem tech staff, TRW Systs Group, 66-68; asst prof math, 68-79, ASSOC PROF MATH, VA POLYTECH INST & STATE UNIV, 79- *Concurrent Pos:* Vis prof, Math Inst, Oxford Univ, 76-77. *Mem:* Am Phys Soc; Math Asn Am. *Res:* Differential geometry; exact solutions of the field equations in general relativity theory; mathematical modelling and simulation. *Mailing Add:* Dept of Math Va Polytech Inst & State Univ Blacksburg VA 24061

DEBOER, BENJAMIN, b Grand Rapids, Mich, Sept 13, 11; m 39; c 5. PHARMACOLOGY. *Educ:* Calvin Col, AB, 33; Univ Mo, MA, 39, PhD(physiol), 42. *Prof Exp:* Asst zool, Univ Mo, 34-38, from instr to asst prof pharmacol, 41-46; from asst prof to assoc prof, St Louis Univ, 46-51; prof, 51-76, EMER PROF PHYSIOL & PHARMACOL, SCH MED, UNIV NDAK, 76- *Mem:* Am Physiol Soc; Am Soc Pharmacol; Soc Exp Biol & Med. *Res:* Barbiturate hypnosis; narcotic analgesics; hyperbaric pharmacology. *Mailing Add:* Univ of NDak Sch of Med Grand Forks ND 58202

DEBOER, CHARLES D, photochemistry, see previous edition

DEBOER, FRANK EDWARD, b Grand Rapids, Mich, Feb 15, 27; m 56; c 4. PHYSICAL CHEMISTRY. *Educ:* Calvin Col, AB, 50; Northwestern Univ, PhD(chem), 54. *Prof Exp:* Chemist, Standard Oil Co Ind, 53-56; asst chemist, Argonne Nat Lab, 56-62; sr metallurgist res & develop, Continental Can Co, Inc, 62-66; from asst prof to assoc prof, 66-75, PROF CHEM, N PARK COL, 75- *Mem:* Am Chem Soc. *Res:* Magnetochemistry; catalysis; corrosion. *Mailing Add:* 1104 S Mayfield Ave Chicago IL 60644

DEBOER, GERRIT, b Ureterp, Neth, May 14, 42; Can citizen; m 65; c 3. MEDICAL BIOPHYSICS, BIOSTATISTICS. *Educ:* Univ Western Ont, BSc Hons, 65; Univ Toronto, MSc, 67, PhD(med biophys), 70. *Prof Exp:* Asst physics, Univ Toronto, 65-69; instr phys chem, Johns Hopkins Univ, 70-73; ASST PROF MED BIOPHYS, UNIV TORONTO, 73-; PHYSICIST, ONT CANCER INST, 75-, ACTG HEAD DEPT BIOSTATIST, 75- *Concurrent Pos:* Fel, Med Res Coun Can, 70-73; sr investr demonstration model grant, Ont Ministry Health, 75-78, co-investr, 78- *Mem:* Biophys Soc; Can Asn Advan Comput Health Soc Clin Trails. *Res:* Cancer research; biophysics; ultraviolet photochemistry of nucleic acid derivatives; physical chemistry of nucleic acids; computerized handling of cancer records; computerized medical audits; cancer epidemiology; cost-effectiveness analysis. *Mailing Add:* Dept of Biostatist 500 Sherbourne St Toronto ON M5S 2R8 Can

DEBOER, JELLE, b Zeist, Holland, Aug 23, 34; m 63; c 3. GEOPHYSICS. *Educ:* Univ Utrecht, PhD(geol), 63. *Prof Exp:* Assoc prof geol, 68-74, SENEY PROF GEOL & PROF EARTH & ENVIRON SCI, WESLEYAN UNIV, 74- *Mem:* Geol Soc Am; Am Geophys Union. *Res:* Geotectonics; use of paleomagnetism and rock magnetism for structural analyses. *Mailing Add:* Dept of Geol Wesleyan Univ Middletown CT 06457

DE BOER, JELLE, b Gorredyk, Netherlands, Aug 19, 23; US citizen; m 54. PHYSIOLOGY, RADIOBIOLOGY. *Educ:* Agr & Mech Col, Tex, BS, 54, MS, 55, PhD(physiol), 61. *Prof Exp:* Radiobiologist, Air Force Spec Weapon Ctr, Air Force Weapons Lab, 61-63, mem radiobiol group, Biophys Br, 63-70, sr sci adv & bio-analyst, Bio-Med Group, Anal Div, 70-73, health & syst safety officer, 73-75, environ specialist, 75-81. *Mem:* Sigma Xi; Health Physics Soc. *Res:* Radiation effects of whoe and partial body, proton, neutron, x-ray and gamma irradiation. *Mailing Add:* Air Force Weapons Lab Kirtland AFB NM 87115

DEBOER, KENNETH F, b Verdi, Minn, Nov 6, 38; m 59; c 5. BIOLOGY. *Educ:* Univ Minn, Minneapolis, BA, 61; Mankato State Col, MA, 68; Iowa State Univ, PhD(reproductive physiol), 70. *Prof Exp:* From asst prof to assoc prof biol, Western State Col, Colo, 70-78; PROF ANAT, PALMER COL CHIROPRACTIC, 78- *Concurrent Pos:* Am Philos Soc res grant, 71-73, Found Chiropractic Educ & Res grant, 81-82. *Mem:* Biofeedback Soc Am. *Res:* Clinical efficacy of chiropractic and biofeedback; endocrinology; neurophysiology; biofeedback. *Mailing Add:* Dept of Anat Palmer Col of Chiropractic Davenport IA 52803

DE BOER, P(IETER) C(ORNELIS) TOBIAS, b Leiden, Netherlands, May 21, 30; nat US; m 56; c 3. MECHANICAL & AEROSPACE ENGINEERING. *Educ:* Delft Univ Technol, Ing, 55; Univ Md, PhD(physics), 62. *Prof Exp:* Res asst aerodyn & hydrodyn, Delft Univ Technol, 54-55; res assoc, Inst Fluid Dynamics & Appl Math, Univ Md, 57-62, res asst prof, 62-64; from asst prof to assoc prof, 64-73, grad fac rep, Aerospace Eng & mem fac mech & aerospace eng, 77-80, PROF AEROSPACE ENG, CORNELL UNIV, 73- *Concurrent Pos:* Consult, Conelec, Inc, 65-71 & Allied Chem Automotive Div, 72-; NATO fel, 68; vis prof, von Karman Inst Fluid Dynamics, Belgium, 68 & Cornell Aeronaut Lab, 68-69; engr & consult, Ford Motor Co, 71-72; combustion engr, Gen Elec Co, 78-79. *Mem:* Am Soc Mech Engrs; Int Asn Hydrogen Energy; Am Phys Soc; Am Inst Aeronaut & Astronaut; Netherlands Royal Inst Eng. *Res:* Physics of fluids; ionized gases; relaxation phenomena; pollution by combustion processes. *Mailing Add:* Dept of Eng Cornell Univ Ithaca NY 14853

DE BOER, SOLKE HARMEN, b Haren, Neth, Jan 5, 48; Can citizen; m 78; c 2. PLANT PATHOLOGY, PHYTOBACTERIOLOGY. *Educ:* Univ BC, Bsc, 70, MSc, 72; Univ Wis-Madison, PhD(plant path), 76. *Prof Exp:* Int Agr Ctr fel, Inst Phytopath Res, Neth, 76; Nat Res Coun Can fel, Univ BC, 76-77; RES SCIENTIST PLANT PATH, RES BR AGR CAN, 77- *Mem:* Am Phytopath Soc; Can Phytopathol Soc; Am Soc Microbiol; Potato Asn Am. *Res:* Serology and ecology of plant pathogenic bacteria, especially Erwinia carotovora and Corynebacterium sepedonicum. *Mailing Add:* Agr Can Res Sta 6660 NW Marine Dr Vancouver BC V6T 1X2 Can

DEBOLD, JOSEPH FRANCIS, psychobiology, neuroendocrinology, see previous edition

DEBOLT, HAROLD E(UGENE), electrical engineering, see previous edition

DEBOLT, LAWRENCE CLIFFORD, polymer chemistry, see previous edition

DEBONA, BRUCE TODD, b Medford, Mass, Dec 26, 45; m 73. POLYMER CHEMISTRY, ORGANIC CHEMISTRY. *Educ:* Rensselaer Polytech Inst, BS, 67; Univ Pa, PhD(org chem), 71. *Prof Exp:* Sr res chemist polymer chem, Advan Res Group, Coatings & Resins Div, PPG Industs, 70-74; res chemist, 74-80, RES ASSOC POLYMER CHEM, CORP RES LAB, ALLIED CHEM CORP, 80- *Concurrent Pos:* Res fel, Univ Pa, 67-69. *Mem:* Am Chem Soc; Am Inst Chemists. *Res:* Synthesis of high polymers; structure property relationships; mechanism and stereochemistry of polymer forming reactions; organic synthesis; development of engineering thermoplastics and synthetic fibers. *Mailing Add:* 23 Rose Ave Madison NJ 07940

DEBONO, MANUEL, b Melliha, Malta, Sept 3, 36; US citizen; m 60; c 5. ORGANIC CHEMISTRY. *Educ:* Univ San Francisco, BS, 59; Univ Ore, PhD(chem), 63. *Prof Exp:* RES SCIENTIST, ELI LILLY & CO, 63- *Mem:* Am Chem Soc. *Res:* Natural products; steroids; fertility control agents; photochemical syntheses; structure and modification of antibiotics. *Mailing Add:* Lilly Res Labs Fermentation Prod Div Indianapolis IN 46285

DEBONS, ALBERT FRANK, b Brooklyn, NY, Nov 4, 29; m 55; c 3. PHYSIOLOGY. *Educ:* Syracuse Univ, BS, 53; George Washington Univ, MS, 55, PhD(physiol), 58. *Prof Exp:* Asst med res, George Washington Univ, 53-58; res assoc, Brookhaven Nat Labs, 58-61; prin scientist, Vet Admin Hosp, Birmingham, Ala, 61-64, PRIN SCIENTIST, VET ADMIN HOSP, BROOKLYN, NY, 64- *Mem:* Endocrine Soc; Am Fed Clin Res; Nuclear Med Soc. *Res:* Nuclear medicine; endocrines as related to intermediary metabolism; mechanism of hormone action; obesity studies. *Mailing Add:* Nuclear Med Vet Admin Hosp Brooklyn NY 11209

DEBOO, PHILI B, b Bombay, India, Dec 5, 34; US citizen; m 60; c 1. GEOLOGY, PALEONTOLOGY. *Educ:* Univ Bombay, BSc, 53; La State Univ, MS, 55, PhD(geol), 63. *Prof Exp:* Asst prof geol, Eastern NMex Univ, 63-65; from asst prof to assoc prof, 65-77, PROF GEOL, MEMPHIS STATE UNIV, 77- *Mem:* Geol Soc Am. *Res:* Mid-Tertiary biostratigraphy of the Central Gulf Coastal Plain. *Mailing Add:* Dept of Geol Memphis State Univ Memphis TN 38152

DEBOO, ROBERT FORD, economic entomology, forest entomology, see previous edition

DE BOOR, CARL (WILHELM) REINHOLD, b Stolp, Ger, Dec 3, 37; m 60; c 4. MATHEMATICS. *Educ:* Univ Mich, PhD(numerical anal), 66. *Prof Exp:* Assoc sr res mathematician, Gen Motors Res Labs, 60-64; from asst prof to assoc prof math sci, Purdue Univ, 66-72; PROF MATH & COMPUT SCI, MATH RES CTR, UNIV WIS-MADISON, 72- *Concurrent Pos:* Vis staff mem, Los Alamos Sci Labs, 70- *Mem:* Am Math Soc. *Res:* Numerical analysis; approximation theory; approximation by splines and other piecewise polynomial functions. *Mailing Add:* Math Res Ctr Univ of Wis 610 Walnut St Madison WI 53706

DEBRA, DANIEL BROWN, b New York, NY, June 1, 30; m 54; c 6. ENGINEERING MECHANICS. *Educ:* Yale Univ, BE, 52; Mass Inst Technol, SM, 53, PhD(eng mech), 62. *Prof Exp:* Proj engr boiler auxiliary equip, Thermix Corp, 53-54; supvr dynamics & control anal, Lockheed Missiles & Space Co, 56-64; from res engr to assoc prof guid control, 64-73, DIR GUID & CONTROL LAB, STANFORD UNIV, 64-, PROF AERONAUT & ASTRONAUT, 73- *Concurrent Pos:* Mem comts geod & large space systs technol, Nat Acad Sci; mem US Air Force Sci Adv Bd. *Mem:* Nat Acad Eng; Am Astronaut Soc; Am Astron Soc; Inst Elec & Electronics Engrs; Am Soc Mech Engrs. *Res:* Guidance and attitude control of aerospace vehicles. *Mailing Add:* Dept of Aeronaut & Astronaut Stanford Univ Stanford CA 94305

DE BREMAECKER, JEAN-CLAUDE, b Antwerp, Belg, Sept 2, 23; m 52; c 2. GEOPHYSICS. *Educ:* Univ Louvain, Belg, Mining Engr, 48; La State Univ, MSc, 50; Univ Calif, PhD(geophys), 52. *Prof Exp:* Res scientist geophysics, Inst Sci Res Cent Africa, 52-56, sr scientist, 56-58; from asst prof to assoc prof, 59-65, PROF GEOPHYSICS, RICE UNIV, 65- *Concurrent Pos:* Boese fel, Columbia Univ, 55-56 & Harvard Univ, 58-59; mem Nat Belgium Comt of Geodesy & Geophys, 55-58; vis prof, Univ Petrol & Mining, 80-81. *Mem:* Soc Explor Geophys; Am Geophys Union; Int Asn Seismol & Phys Earth's Interior (secy gen, 71-79). *Res:* Seismology; gravimetry; magnetism; tectonophysics. *Mailing Add:* 2128 Addison Houston TX 77030

DEBREU, GERARD, b Calais, France, July 4, 21; US citizen; m 45; c 2. MATHEMATICAL ECONOMICS. *Educ:* Univ Paris, AGREGATION, 46, DSc, 56. *Hon Degrees:* Dr Rer Pol, Univ Bonn, 77; DSc econ, Univ Lausanne, 80; DSc, Northwestern Univ, 81. *Prof Exp:* Res assoc econ, Ctr Nat Res Sci, Paris, 46-48; res assoc econ, Cowles Comn Res, Univ Chicago, 50-55, Cowles Found, Yale Univ, 55-60; PROF ECON & MATH, UNIV CALIF, BERKELEY, 62- *Concurrent Pos:* Rockefeller fel, US, Swed & Norway, 48-50; fel, Ctr Adv Study Behavioral Sci, Stanford, 60-61; vis prof, Yale Univ, 61, Ctr Oper Res & Economet, Univ Louvain, 68-69, 71-72, Univ Canterbury, Christchurch, New Zealand, 73, Yale Univ, 76; Guggenheim fel, 68-69; Erskine fel, Univ Canterbury, Christchurch, New Zealand, 69; overseas fel, Churchill Col, Cambridge, England, 72; sr US scientist award, Alexander von Humboldt Found, Univ Bonn, 77; res assoc, Cepremap, Paris, 80. *Mem:* Nat Acad Sci; Economet Soc (vpres & pres, 69-71); fel AAAS. *Res:* Theory of general economic equilibrium - preference, utility, and demand theory. *Mailing Add:* Dept Econ Univ Calif Berkeley 94720

DEBRUIN, KENNETH EDWARD, b Oskaloosa, Iowa, May 29, 42; m 69. ORGANIC CHEMISTRY. *Educ:* Iowa State Univ, BS, 64; Univ Calif, Berkeley, PhD(org chem), 67. *Prof Exp:* NIH fel, Princeton Univ, 67-69; asst prof, 69-74, ASSOC PROF CHEM, COLO STATE UNIV, 74- *Mem:* Am Chem Soc; Royal Soc Chem; NY Acad Sci. *Res:* Mechanisms of organic reactions; phosphorus stereochemistry; terpene biosynthesis. *Mailing Add:* Dept of Chem Colo State Univ Ft Collins CO 80521

DEBRUNNER, LOUIS EARL, b Cincinnati, Ohio, Dec 9, 35; m 58; c 2. FOREST ECOLOGY. *Educ:* Univ Cincinnati, BS, 57; Yale Univ, MF, 59; Duke Univ, DFor, 67. *Prof Exp:* ASST PROF FORESTRY, AUBURN UNIV, 61- *Mem:* Soc Am Foresters. *Res:* Regeneration of forest stands; forest recreation. *Mailing Add:* Sch Agr Dept Forestry Auburn Univ Auburn AL 36830

DEBRUNNER, MARJORIE R, b Auburn, Nebr, Feb 21, 27. ORGANIC CHEMISTRY. *Educ:* Nebr State Teachers Col, Kearney, BScEd, 48; Univ Nebr, MS, 51, PhD(chem), 53. *Prof Exp:* Res chemist, 53-72, res div head, 72-76, mgr tech develop, 76-81, TECH MGR, E I DU PONT DE NEMOURS & CO, 81- *Mem:* AAAS; Sigma Xi; Am Chem Soc; The Chem Soc. *Res:* Synthetic hydrocarbon and fluorocarbon elastomers. *Mailing Add:* 11 Binford Lane Wilmington DE 19810

DEBRUNNER, PETER GEORG, b Sitterdorf, Switz, Mar 11, 31; m 55; c 3. PHYSICS. *Educ:* Swiss Fed Inst Technol, PhD(physics), 60. *Prof Exp:* Res assoc, 60-63, res asst prof, 63-68, assoc prof physics, 68-73, PROF PHYSICS UNIV ILL, URBANA, 73- *Mem:* Am Phys Soc; Biophys Soc. *Res:* Angular correlation; Mossbauer and electron paramagnetic resonance spectroscopy; biological physics. *Mailing Add:* Univ Ill Dept of Physics 1110 W Green St Urbana IL 61801

DEBRUNNER, RALPH EDWARD, b Cincinnati, Ohio, Oct 11, 32; m 56; c 2. ORGANIC CHEMISTRY. *Educ:* Univ Cincinnati, BS, 54, PhD(org chem), 60. *Prof Exp:* Res chemist, Chemstrand Corp, Ala, 54-55; res chemist spec proj dept, Monsanto Chem Co, Mass, 60-61, sr res chemist, Dayton Lab, Monsanto Res Corp, Monsanto Co, 61-66, group leader, 66-68, group leader, Chemstrand Res Ctr, NC, 68-72, sr tech serv rep, 72-77, SR GROUP LEADER APPLN RES, NONWOVEN BUS GROUP, MONSANTO TEXTILE CO, 77- *Mem:* Am Chem Soc; Am Soc Testing & Mat; Int Nonwovens Disposables Asn. *Res:* Synthesis of thermally and oxidatively stable polymers, and preparation of high performance composites; applications research for nonwoven fabrics. *Mailing Add:* Monsanto Triangle Pk Develop Ctr PO Box 12274 Research Triangle Park NC 27709

DE BRUYN, PETER PAUL HENRY, b Amsterdam, Holland, July 28, 10; nat US; m 31; c 2. HISTOLOGY. *Educ:* Univ Amsterdam, PhD, 38, MD, 41. *Prof Exp:* Asst, Histol Lab, Univ Amsterdam, 36-39; first asst, Inst Prev Med, Leyden, Holland, 39-40, chief bact dept, 40-41; from instr to assoc prof, 41-52, chmn dept, 46-61, PROF ANAT, UNIV CHICAGO, 52- *Concurrent Pos:* Stokvis-fonds fel, Univ Chicago, 38; mem staff, AEC, 46. *Mem:* AAAS; Am Soc Naturalists; Am Asn Anat; Am Soc Cell Biol; Radiation Res Soc. *Res:* Lipids of leucocytes; locomotion of leucocytes; histopathology of radiation effects; lymphatic tissue; vital staining of nuclei; fine structural studies on transmural migration of blood cells; leukopoietic mechanisms. *Mailing Add:* Dept of Anat Univ Chicago 1025 E 57th St Chicago IL 60637

DE BRUYNE, PIETER, b Middelburg, Netherlands, Mar 7, 28; US citizen; m 60; c 3. ELECTRICAL ENGINEERING. *Educ:* London Univ, BSc, 47; Inst Electronics Technol, London, MIET, 56. *Prof Exp:* Group leader radio lab, Van Der Heem, Holland, 56-58; chief engr nuclear physics, Tracerlab Inc, Europe & US, 58-63; corp app res, Physics Dept, Harvard Univ, 63-68; sr engr, LLTV, RCA Div Burlington, 68-71; mgr prod planning, Philips, Comput Peripherals, Holland, 71-72; RES ASSOC, SWISS FED INST TECHNOL, 72- *Concurrent Pos:* Consult, physics dept, Harvard Univ, 68-71. *Mem:* Sigma Xi; NY Acad Sci. *Res:* High energy physics research with wire spark chambers for inelastic e-P scattering experiments; low light level television target identification and signature analysis; new detection and measurement methods in physics (includ..g space) and in communication; author of over 20 publications. *Mailing Add:* Inst fur Komm Technik ETH-Zentrum-KT Zurich CH 8092 Switzerland

DEBS, ROBERT JOSEPH, b Chicago, Ill, Mar 31, 19; m 46; c 2. MICROWAVE PHYSICS. *Educ:* Mass Inst Technol, PhD(physics), 52. *Prof Exp:* Jr engr, Westinghouse Elec Corp, 42-44; develop engr, Raytheon Mfg Co, 44-46; res assoc electronics & nuclear sci, Mass Inst Technol, 46-52; microwave lab, Stanford Univ, 52-58; res assoc, West Coast Labs, Gen Tel & Electronics Corp, 58-63; RES SCIENTIST, AMES RES CTR, NASA, 63- *Mem:* Inst Elec & Electronics Engrs; Am Phys Soc. *Res:* Low-intensity, low-temperature behavior of solar cells under charged-particle bombardment; superconducting magnetometry; low-level radioactivity counting. *Mailing Add:* 3145 Flowers Lane Palo Alto CA 94306

DE BUHR, LARRY EUGENE, b Rock Rapids, Iowa, Nov 21, 48; m 77; c 1. PLANT SYSTEMATICS, PLANT ANATOMY. *Educ:* Iowa State Univ, BS, 71; Claremont Grad Sch, MA, 73, PhD(bot), 76. *Prof Exp:* Fac mem biol, Cottey Col, 77-80; LEARNING RESOURCES SPECIALIST & ASST PROF BIOL, UNIV MO, KANSAS CITY, 80- *Mem:* Bot Soc Am; Am Soc Plant Taxonomists; Int Asn Plant Taxon; Sigma Xi. *Res:* Plant systematics, anatomy and morphology of Sarraceniaceae, Droseraceae and Crossosomataceae. *Mailing Add:* SASS 212 Univ Mo Kansas City MO 64110

DEBUSK, ARON GIB, b Lubbock, Tex Jan 15, 27; m 47; c 6. GENETICS. *Educ:* Univ Wash, BS, 50; Univ Tex, MA, 52, PhD(genetics), 54. *Prof Exp:* Res scientist, Biochem Inst, Univ Tex, 51-52, Genetics Found, 52-55; instr, Dept Biol Sci, Northwestern Univ, 55-57; from asst prof to assoc prof, 57-69, assoc dir, Inst Molecular Biophys, 62-63, assoc chmn, Dept Biol Sci, 66-67, assoc chmn grad studies, Dept Biol Sci, 72-76, actg chmn dept, 75-76, dir genetics training prog, 62-80, PROF BIOL SCI, FLA STATE UNIV, 69-, CHMN DEPT, 76- *Concurrent Pos:* Vis prof, Southwestern Univ, 54-55; mem staff, Brookhaven Nat Lab, 56; vis fel, Inst Advan Studies, Australian Nat Univ, 68. *Mem:* Am Chem Soc; Biophys Soc; Am Soc Microbiol; Genetics Soc Am; Am Soc Biol Chemists. *Res:* Molecular and biochemical genetics; cellular transport, metabolic chenneling, exoenzymes, mutational phenomena and protein synthesis in Neurospora; biochemical genetics of cystic fibrosis and cellular aging. *Mailing Add:* Genetics Lab Dept of Biol Sci Fla State Univ Tallahassee FL 32306

DEBYE, NORDULF WIKING GERUD, b Czech, Aug 2, 43; US citizen; m 67; c 1. PHYSICAL INORGANIC CHEMISTRY, PHYSICAL CHEMISTRY. *Educ:* Rice Univ, BA, 65; Cornell Univ, PhD(phys chem), 70. *Prof Exp:* Nat Res Coun-Nat Bur Standards res assoc struct inorg chem, Nat Bur Standards, 70-72; asst prof chem, Colo Women's Col, 72-76; ASST PROF CHEM, TOWSON STATE UNIV, 76- *Concurrent Pos:* Vis instr chem, Towson State Col, 75-76. *Mem:* Am Chem Soc; NAm Therm Anal Soc; Am Asn Physics Teachers; Sigma Xi; NY Acad Sci. *Res:* Structural spectrocopy of organometallic compounds, in particular, nuclear quadrupole resonance and Mossbauer spectral techniques applied to solid state samples; scanning calorimetry; thermodynamic properties of organometallics. *Mailing Add:* Dept Chem Towson State Univ Baltimore MD 21204

DEBYLE, NORBERT V, b Green Bay, Wis, May 1, 31; m 54; c 2. FORESTRY, WATERSHED MANAGEMENT. *Educ:* Univ Wis, BS, 53, MS, 57; Univ Mich, PhD(forestry), 62. *Prof Exp:* Conserv aide wildlife mgt, Wis State Dept Conserv, 53-54; res asst forest & wildlife mgt, Univ Wis, 56-57; lectr forestry, Univ Mich, 58-59; res forester, US Forest Serv, Nev, 61-64, RES FORESTER, FORESTRY SCI LAB, INTERMOUNTAIN FOREST & RANGE EXP STA, US FOREST SERV, 64- *Mem:* Fel AAAS; Wildlife Soc; Soil Conserv Soc Am; Ecol Soc Am. *Res:* Water yield and quality improvement from mountain watersheds; aspen autecology; plant nutrient cycling, forest soils; wildlife ecology. *Mailing Add:* Intermountain Forest & Range Exp Sta US Forest Serv 860 N 12th E Logan UT 84321

DE CAMARGO, JOAO LAURO VIANA, b Aracatuba, Brazil, Mar 13, 48; m 70; c 3. ONCOLOGY, NUTRITION. *Educ:* Catholic Univ, Sao Paulo, MD, 71, Univ Sao Paulo, PhD(med), 81. *Prof Exp:* Asst prof path, Sch Med, Univ Sao Paulo, 74-81; VIS SCIENTIST, DEPT NUTRIT FOOD SCI, MASS INST TECHNOL, 81- *Res:* Experimental interactions between cancer and dietary patterns, with emphasis on carcinogenesis; cytological and histological diagnosis of diseases. *Mailing Add:* Mass Inst Technol E18-670B Cambridge MA 02142

DECAMP, MARK RUTLEDGE, b Orange, NJ, Aug 21, 46; m 70; c 2. ORGANIC CHEMISTRY. *Educ:* Williams Col, BA, 68; Princeton Univ, MA, 70, PhD(chem), 72. *Prof Exp:* Fel, Cornell Univ, 72-73; NIH fel, Univ Rochester, 73-75; asst prof, 75-80, ASSOC PROF, DEPT NATURAL SCI, UNIV MICH-DEARBORN, 80- *Mem:* Am Chem Soc. *Res:* Organic synthesis; mechanisms of thermal reactions; reactive intermediates. *Mailing Add:* Dept of Natural Sci Univ of Mich-Dearborn Dearborn MI 48128

DECAMP, PAUL TRUMBULL, b Seoul, Korea, Feb 26, 15; US citizen; m 45; c 6. SURGERY. *Educ:* Wheaton Col, BS, 35; Univ Pa, MD, 41. *Prof Exp:* Asst path, Sch Med, Baylor Univ, 42-44; asst surg, 44-48, from instr to asst prof, 48-59, cancer coordr, 48-50, STAFF SURGEON, OCHSNER CLIN, SCH MED, TULANE UNIV, 50-, ASSOC PROF CLIN SURG, 59- *Mem:* Am Asn Thoracis Surg; Am Col Surg; Soc Vascular Surg; Int Soc Surg; Int Cardiovasc Soc. *Res:* Venous thrombosis and embolism; venous pressure in post-phlebitic and related conditions; cancer of the lung; hypertension due to renal arterial stenosis; cerebrovascular insufficiency. *Mailing Add:* Dept Surg Ochsner Clin 1514 Jefferson Hwy New Orleans LA 70121

DE CAMP, WILSON HAMILTON, b Evanston, Ill, Sept 22, 36; m 77; c 3. PHYSICAL ORGANIC CHEMISTRY. *Educ:* Ind Univ, BS & MS, 60; Univ Md, PhD(chem), 70. *Prof Exp:* Res assoc chem, Clarkson Col, 70; res fel biol, Nat Res Coun Can, 70-72; res assoc chem, Univ Ill, 72-73; res assoc chem, Inst Natural Prod Res, Univ Ga, 73-78; asst prof chem, Cumberland Col, 78-79; CHEMIST, DRUG CHEM DIV, FOOD & DRUG ADMIN, 79- *Mem:* Am Crystallog Asn; Am Chem Soc; AAAS; Sigma Xi. *Res:* Determination of molecular structure by x-ray crystallography; absolute configuration of natural products; molecular mechanisms of drug-receptor interactions; conformational analysis of heterocyclic systems; X-ray powder diffraction. *Mailing Add:* Drug Chem Div 200 C St SW Food & Drug Admin HFO 420 Washington DC 20204

DE CANI, JOHN STAPLEY, b Canton, Ohio, May 8, 24. APPLIED STATISTICS. *Educ:* Univ Wis, BS, 48; Univ Pa, MBA, 51, PhD(statist), 58. *Prof Exp:* Instr statist, Univ Pa, 48-58; from asst prof to assoc prof, 58-72, chmn dept statist & opers res, 71-78, PROF STATIST, UNIV PA, 72- *Concurrent Pos:* Consult, US Naval Air Develop Ctr, 57-; Fulbright grant, Norweg Sch Econ & Bus Admin, 59-60; Consult, McNeil Labs, Inc, 67- & Nat Asn Advan Colored People Legal Defense Fund, Inc, 67-; lectr, Brazilian Inst, 71- *Mem:* Fel Am Statist Asn; Inst Math Statist; Economet Soc; Biomet Soc; Soc Indust & Appl Math. *Res:* Paired comparison experiments; analysis of categorical data; mathematical programming. *Mailing Add:* Dept of Statist Univ of Pa Philadelphia PA 19104

DE CARLO, CHARLES R, b Pittsburgh, Pa, May 7, 21; m 46; c 4. MATHEMATICS, ACADEMIC ADMINISTRATION. *Educ:* Univ Pittsburgh, BE, 43, PhD(math), 51. *Prof Exp:* Lectr math, Univ Pittsburgh, 47-51; from asst dir to dir, Appl Sci Div, Int Bus Mach Corp, 51-57, dir sales serv, 57-58, dir mkt prog, 58, mgr mkt & serv, 58-59, asst gen mgr, Data Systs Div, 59-61, corp dir & ed, 61-63, corp dir & ed, Systs Res & Develop, 63-65, dir automation res, 65-69; PRES, SARAH LAWRENCE COL, 69- *Concurrent Pos:* Fac mem, Am Studies Inst, 68; consult, US Off Educ; mem bd directors, Nat Comn of Resources for Youth, 69- & Inst for Archit & Urban Studies & Comn on Independent Cols & Univs, 74- *Mem:* AAAS; Am Acad Arts & Sci; Soc Indust & Appl Math; Instrument Soc Am; Economet Soc. *Res:* Application of computers and automata to science and business. *Mailing Add:* Off of the Pres Sarah Lawrence Col Bronxville NY 10708

DE CARLO, JOHN, JR, b Philadelphia, Pa, July 9, 18; m 47; c 3. RADIOLOGY. *Educ:* Temple Univ, AB, 40; Jefferson Med Col, MD, 44; Am Bd Radiol, dipl, 50. *Prof Exp:* Dir dept radiol, Baltimore City Hosps, 50-61; DIR RADIOL, ST JOSEPH'S HOSP, 62- *Concurrent Pos:* Asst prof, Univ Md, 50-61; instr, Johns Hopkins Univ, 58-61. *Mem:* AMA; fel Am Col Radiol; Radiol Soc NAm. *Res:* Diagnostic roentgenology. *Mailing Add:* 701 Seabrook Ct Baltimore MD 21204

DECARO, THOMAS F, b Brooklyn, NY, Mar 10, 19; m 50; c 2. CELLULAR & VERTEBRATE PHYSIOLOGY. *Educ:* Rutgers Univ, BS, 48; Univ NH, MS, 50; Univ Pa, PhD, 63. *Prof Exp:* Researcher, Smith, Kline & French Labs, 49-51; instr biol, St Michael's Col, 51-54; asst prof, Villanova Univ, 54-65; assoc prof, Widener Univ, 66-76; ASSOC PROF BIOL, LINCOLN UNIV, 77- *Concurrent Pos:* NIH fel, Sch Med, Univ Pa, 65-66. *Mem:* AAAS; Am Soc Zoologists; Am Soc Cell Biol. *Res:* Muscle physiology. *Mailing Add:* Dept of Biol Lincoln Univ Lincoln University PA 19352

DECASTRO, ARTHUR, b Newark, NJ, July 8, 11; m 51; c 1. ANALYTICAL CHEMISTRY. *Educ:* Newark Col Eng, BS, 31. *Prof Exp:* Chemist, Calco Chem Co, 31-33; control chemist, 33-36, anal res chemist, 36-38, chief chemist, Anal Res Lab, 38-58, LAB DIR ANAL RES & PHYS TESTING LABS, NOPCO CHEM CO, HARRISON, 58- *Concurrent Pos:* Consult, 73- *Mem:* Fel Am Inst Chemists; Am Chem Soc; Am Soc Testing & Mat. *Res:* Surfactants and processed chemicals used in detergent, textile, tanning, paper, paint and metal working. *Mailing Add:* 14 Midvale Dr New Providence NJ 07974

DECELLES, GEORGE ARTHUR, JR, b Derring, NH, Feb 11, 33; m 59; c 3. FOOD SCIENCE. *Educ:* Univ NH, BS, 59; Iowa State Univ, MS, 63, PhD(food technol), 65. *Prof Exp:* Scientist, Refrigerated Foods, Pillsbury Co, 65-67 & Corp Dept, 67-69, sr scientist, 69 & Food Technol Dept, 69-72, sr scientist, Corp Prod Develop, 72-77; mgr, 77-80, DIR TECH DEVELOP, US CONSUMER PROD DIV, INT MULTIFOODS, 80- *Mem:* Inst Food Technologists; Am Asn Cereal Chemists. *Res:* Identify and develop grain, cheese, meat, and potato based consumer products; effects of surfactants on carbohydrate food systems; staling mechanisms; shelf life of consumer products; rehydration technology. *Mailing Add:* Int Multifoods 9449 Sci Ctr Dr New Hope MN 55428

DECELLES, PAUL C, physics, see previous edition

DECESARE, WILLIAM R, b East Orange, NJ, Oct 1, 33; m 71; c 3. RESEARCH ADMINISTRATION. *Educ:* Dartmouth Col, AB, 55; Harvard Med Sch, MD, 58. *Prof Exp:* Intern, Mary Hitchcock Mem Hosp, 58-59; resident internal med, Dartmouth Affiliated Hosp, 59-61, chief resident, 61-62; res fel, Darmouth Med Sch, 62-63; res fel, Med Sch, Georgetown Univ, 63-64, instr, asst dir hemat & asst dir lab diagnosis, 64-66; asst chief & actg chief, GCRC Br, Div Res Facil & Resources, 66-68, CHIEF CLIN RES CTR BR, NIH, 68- *Concurrent Pos:* Mem, Diabetes Coordinating Comt, Clin Trials Comt, NIH, 76-; mem, Diabetes Mellitus Interagency Coordinating Comt, DHHS, 76-; mem, Nutrit Coordinating Comt, NIH, 77-; mem, Cystic Fibrosis Comt, NIH, 78- *Honors & Awards:* Commendation Medal, USPHS, 78. *Mem:* AAAS. *Res:* Neurosciences; diabetes; hypertension; diseases of the newborn. *Mailing Add:* Bldg 31 Rm 5B-51 NIH 9000 Rockville Pike Bethesda MD 20205

DE CHAMPLAIN, JACQUES, b Quebec, Que, Mar 13, 38; m 61; c 2. PHYSIOLOGY, PHARMACOLOGY. *Educ:* Univ Montreal, BA, 57, MD, 62; McGill Univ, PhD(invest med), 65. *Prof Exp:* Vis res assoc, NIMH, 65-67, Med Res Coun Que fel, 67-68; from asst prof to assoc prof, 68-75, EDWARDS FOUND PROF PHYSIOL, UNIV MONTREAL, 75- *Concurrent Pos:* Markle scholar, 68. *Mem:* AAAS; Am Fedn Clin Res; Can Physiol Soc; Int Brain Res Orgn; Int Soc Hypertension. *Res:* Studies on the role of peripheral and central sympathetic nervous system in the regulation of normal blood pressure and in the pathogenesis of hypertensive diseases. *Mailing Add:* Dept of Physiol Univ Montreal Fac Med Montreal Can

DECHARY, JOSEPH MARTIN, b Youngsville, La, Mar 6, 22. ORGANIC CHEMISTRY. *Educ:* Univ La, BS, 43, MS, 47, PhD(chem), 52. *Prof Exp:* CHEMIST, SOUTH REGIONAL RES LAB, USDA, 48-50 & 52- *Concurrent Pos:* Chemist, Sch Med, Tulane Univ, 52-54. *Mem:* Am Chem Soc; Sigma Xi; NY Acad Sci. *Res:* Cottonseed; diazoketones; bromo-2-nitrobenzoic acids; reaction of quinones with ketones; biological antagonists; metabolic pathways in protozoa; spectrophotometry; gossypol chemistry; seed proteins; phytohemagglutinins; seed proteases and protease inhibitors; chemical modification of edestin; optically active gossypol; peanut proteases; peanut proteins determined by gel electrophoresis; blood typing factor from peanuts. *Mailing Add:* 2820 General Pershing St New Orleans LA 70115

DE CHAZAL, L E MARC, b St Denis, Reunion, Nov 23, 21; m 51; c 2. CHEMICAL ENGINEERING, NUCLEAR ENGINEERING. *Educ:* La State Univ, BS, 49, MS, 51, PhD(chem eng), 53. *Prof Exp:* From asst prof to assoc prof, 53-66, PROF CHEM ENG, UNIV MO-COLUMBIA, 66- *Concurrent Pos:* Consult, Mo Farmers Asn, 53-54; prin sci officer, Brit Atomic Res Estab, 59-60; res assoc, Brit AEC, 66-67. *Mem:* AAAS; Am Chem Soc; Am Inst Chem Engrs; Am Soc Testing & Mat. *Res:* Solvent extraction; solids mixing; non-Newtonian fluid mechanics; bubble and drop phenomena. *Mailing Add:* 1506 Wilson Ave Columbia MO 65201

DE CHAZAL, L(OUIS) E(DMOND) MARC, b St Denis, Reunion, Nov 23, 21; m 51; c 2. CHEMICAL ENGINEERING. *Educ:* La State Univ, BS, 49, MS, 51; Okla State Univ, PhD(chem eng), 53. *Prof Exp:* From asst prof to assoc prof chem eng, 53-53, assoc prof chem & nuclear eng, 63-66, PROF CHEM & NUCLEAR ENG, UNIV MO-COLUMBIA, 66- *Concurrent Pos:* Res assoc, Atomic Energy Res Estab, Eng, 59-60 & 66-67; consult, Mo Farmers Asn, Monsanto Co & Esso Standard Oil. *Mem:* AAAS; Am Chem Soc; Am Soc Eng Educ; Am Inst Chem Engrs; Am Soc Testing & Mat. *Res:* Solvent extraction; heat transfer; thermodynamics; applications to nuclear energy; non-Newtonian fluid mechanics. *Mailing Add:* Dept of Chem Eng Univ of Mo Columbia MO 65201

DECHENE, LUCY IRENE, b Petaluma, Calif, Dec 25, 50. COMMUTATIVE RING THEORY. *Educ:* Univ San Francisco, BS, 73; Univ Calif, Riverside, MS, 75, PhD(math), 78. *Prof Exp:* Teaching asst math, Univ Calif, Riverside, 76-77; ASST PROF MATH, FITCHBURG STATE COL, 78- *Mem:* NY Acad Sci; Sigma Xi; Am Math Soc; Math Asn Am; Asm Women Math. *Res:* Adjacent extensions of rings. *Mailing Add:* Fitchburg State Col Box 6167 Fitchburg MA 01420

DECHER, RUDOLF, b Wuerzburg, WGer, Aug 22, 27; US citizen; c 2. SPACE SCIENCE, GRAVITATIONAL PHYSICS. *Educ:* Univ Wuerzburg, WGer, MA, 50, PhD(physics), 54. *Prof Exp:* Res physicist indust res & develop, Dynamit Nobel AG, WGer, 55-60; staff mem syst eng, Astrionic Lab, 60-66, staff of lab dir res & develop planning, 66-69, asst to lab dir space sci, 69-70, CHIEF SPACE PHYSICS DIV, SPACE SCI LAB, NASA-MARSHALL SPACE FLIGHT CTR, 70- *Honors & Awards:* Exceptional Serv Medal, NASA, 77. *Mem:* Am Phys Soc; Am Inst Aeronaut & Astronaut. *Res:* Experimental tests of gravitational theories involving space flight. *Mailing Add:* Marshall Space Flight Ctr ES-61 Huntsville AL 35812

DECICCO, BENEDICT THOMAS, b Rahway, NJ, Feb 7, 38; m 60; c 6. MICROBIAL PHYSIOLOGY. *Educ:* Rutgers Univ, AB, 60, MS, 62, PhD(bact), 64. *Prof Exp:* Asst bact, Rutgers Univ, 60-62; sr lab technician, 62-63, res asst, 63-64; asst prof, 64-68, assoc prof, 69-77, chmn dept, 73-77, PROF BACT, CATH UNIV AM, 78- *Concurrent Pos:* Consult, Richardson-Vick Inc. *Mem:* AAAS; Sigma Xi; Am Soc Microbiol. *Res:* Genetics and metabolism of chemoautotrophs and methylotrophs; limits of bacterial variability; environmental microbiology; single cell protein; antimicrobial agents; microbial resistance. *Mailing Add:* Dept of Biol Cath Univ of Am Washington DC 20064

DECICCO, PETER DONALD, solid state physics, see previous edition

DECIOUS, DANIEL, physical chemistry, see previous edition

DECIUS, JOHN COURTNEY, b San Francisco, Calif, Feb 13, 20; m 48; c 3. PHYSICAL CHEMISTRY. *Educ:* Stanford Univ, AB, 41; Harvard Univ, PhD(chem physics), 47. *Prof Exp:* Res assoc & supvr underwater explosives res lab, Oceanog Inst, Woods Hole, 44-47; res assoc chem, Brown Univ, 47-49; from asst prof to assoc prof, 49-56, PROF CHEM, ORE STATE UNIV, 56- *Concurrent Pos:* Guggenheim fel, Fulbright res scholar, Oxford Univ, 55-56, Sloan Found fel, 56-60; NSF fel, King's Col, London, 63-64. *Mem:* Fel Am Phys Soc; Am Chem Soc. *Res:* Molecular structure; vibrational spectra of solid state; energy transfer in gases. *Mailing Add:* Dept of Chem Ore State Univ Corvallis OR 97331

DECK, CHARLES FRANCIS, b Norfolk, Va, June 5, 30; m 56; c 3. INORGANIC CHEMISTRY, RADIOCHEMISTRY. *Educ:* St Louis Univ, BS, 52; Washington Univ, PhD(chem), 56. *Prof Exp:* Asst, Washington Univ, 52-56; res chemisst, 57-63, sr res chemist, 63-79, RES ASSOC, BASF WYANDOTTE CORP, 79- *Mem:* Am Chem Soc. *Res:* Industrial process study; chemical reaction kinetics. *Mailing Add:* 2805 Trenton Dr Trenton MI 48183

DECK, HOWARD JOSEPH, b Cincinnati, Ohio, Sept 25, 38; m 60; c 2. ELECTRICAL ENGINEERING. *Educ:* Univ Cincinnati, EE, 61, MS, 63; Mich State Univ, PhD(elec eng), 68. *Prof Exp:* Instr elec eng, Mich State Univ, 63-65 & 67-68; asst prof, Ohio Univ, 68-74; ASSOC PROF ELEC ENG, UNIV S ALA, 74- *Mem:* Inst Elec & Electronics Engrs; Am Soc Eng Educ. *Res:* Electromagnetic field theory; antenna and circuit theory; reduction of backscattered energy from receiving antennas; active receiving antennas. *Mailing Add:* Dept of Elec Eng Univ of S Ala Mobile AL 36688

DECK, JAMES DAVID, b Atlanta, Ga, Nov 6, 30; m 55; c 4. HISTOLOGY, EMBRYOLOGY. *Educ:* Davidson Col, BS, 51; Princeton Univ, MA, 53, PhD(biol), 54. *Prof Exp:* From instr to asst prof, 54-62, ASSOC PROF ANAT, SCH MED, UNIV VA, 62- *Concurrent Pos:* USPHS fel anat, Harvard Univ, 65-66. *Mem:* Soc Develop Biol; Am Asn Anat; Am Asn Univ Prof. *Res:* Influence of nerves in amphibian regeneration; experimental production of regenerates in an non-regenerating system by implantations of microinfusions; histamine and antihistamines in regneration; skin structure and response to injury; structure and function of mammalian aortic valves; nerves in mammalian regeneration; scanning and conventional electron microscopy of connective tissues; stress and atherogenesis. *Mailing Add:* Dept of Anat Univ of Va Sch of Med Charlottesville VA 22908

DECK, JOSEPH CHARLES, b Canton, Ohio, July 16, 36; m 61; c 4. PHYSICAL CHEMISTRY. *Educ:* Duquesne Univ, BS, 60; Univ Ill, MS, 64, PhD(phys chem), 66. *Prof Exp:* Chemist, Gulf Res & Develop Co, 60-62; from asst prof to assoc prof chem, 66-70, chmn dept, 75-78, PROF CHEM, UNIV LOUISVILLE, 74- *Concurrent Pos:* Vis prof, Univ Ill, 78-79. *Mem:* Am Chem Soc. *Res:* Magnetic resonance; molecular structure; intermolecular and intramolecular interactions. *Mailing Add:* Dept of Chem Univ of Louisville Louisville KY 40292

DECK, JOSEPH FRANCIS, b St Louis, Mo, Mar 19, 07; m 36; c 3. CHEMISTRY. *Educ:* St Louis Univ, AB, 28, MS, 30; Univ Kans, PhD(chem), 32. *Prof Exp:* Res chemist, Stewart Inso Bd Corp, 32-35; qual supvr, US Gypsum Co, 35; prof chem, 36-77, EMER PROF CHEM, UNIV SANTA CLARA, 77- *Concurrent Pos:* Anal chemist, Richmond-Chase Co, 40- *Mem:* Am Chem Soc. *Res:* Food analyses; synthetic organic chemistry; synthesis of heterocyclic ring compounds; synthesis of stable free radicals. *Mailing Add:* Dept of Chem Univ of Santa Clara Santa Clara CA 95053

DECK, ROBERT THOMAS, b Philadelphia, Pa, Aug 6, 35. QUANTUM OPTICS. *Educ:* La Salle Col, BA, 56; Univ Notre Dame, PhD(physics), 61. *Prof Exp:* Res assoc theoret physics, Bartol Res Found, 61-63; res assoc & instr, Univ Mich, 63-65; from asst prof to assoc prof, 65-74, PROF PHYSICS, UNIV TOLEDO, 74-, PROF ENG PHYSICS, 80- *Mem:* Am Phys Soc; Am Asn Physics Teachers. *Res:* High and low energy theoretical nuclear physics; quantum electrodynamics; elementary particle theory. *Mailing Add:* Dept of Physics Univ of Toledo Toledo OH 43606

DECK, RONALD JOSEPH, b New Orleans, La, May 16, 34. SOLID STATE PHYSICS. *Educ:* Loyola Univ, La, 56; La State Univ, MS, 58, PhD(physics), 61. *Prof Exp:* Asst prof physics, La State Univ, 61-62; assoc physicist, Oak Ridge Nat Lab, 62-63; asst prof, 63-77, ASSOC PROF PHYSICS, TULANE

UNIV LA, 77- *Mem:* Am Inst Physics. *Res:* Galvanomagnetic and thermomagnetic effects in metals at low temperatures; behavior of superconducting alloys. *Mailing Add:* Dept of Physics Tulane Univ of La New Orleans LA 70118

DECKARD, EDWARD LEE, b Cynthiana, Ind, Aug 7, 43; m 67; c 2. CROP PHYSIOLOGY. *Educ:* Purdue Univ, BS, 65; Univ Ill, PhD(agron), 70. *Prof Exp:* Asst prof, 70-77, ASSOC PROF AGRON, N DAK STATE UNIV, 77- *Mem:* Am Soc Agron; Crop Sci Soc Am; Am Soc Plant Physiologists. *Res:* Development of biochemical and physiological selection criteria that could be used by plant breeders in crop improvement; present emphasis on nitrogen metabolism. *Mailing Add:* Dept of Agron NDak State Univ Fargo ND 58102

DECKER, ALVIN MORRIS, JR, b Manocs, Colo, Oct 12, 18; m 43; c 2. AGRONOMY. *Educ:* Colo Agr & Mech Col, BS, 49; Utah State Agr Col, MS, 51; Univ Md, PhD(agron), 53. *Prof Exp:* From instr to assoc prof, 52-67, PROF AGRON, UNIV MD, COLLEGE PARK, 67- *Honors & Awards:* Res Award, Northeast Br, Am Soc Agron, 73; Sigma Xi Res Achievement Award, 77. *Mem:* Fel Am Soc Agron. *Res:* Forage crop management and breeding. *Mailing Add:* Dept of Agron Univ of Md College Park MD 20742

DECKER, ARTHUR JOHN, b Butte, Mont, Oct 16, 41; m 70; c 1. OPTICAL PHYSICS. *Educ:* Univ Wash, BS, 63; Univ Rochester, AM, 66; Case Western Reserve Univ, PhD(elec eng & appl physics), 77. *Prof Exp:* OPTICAL PHYSICIST, NASA LEWIS RES CTR, 66- *Mem:* Optical Soc Am. *Res:* Use of coherent optics for measurements related to aircraft propulsion; holography; speckle interferometry and optical information processing. *Mailing Add:* NASA Lewis Res Ctr 21000 Brookpark Rd Cleveland OH 44135

DECKER, CHARLES DAVID, b Oxnard, Calif, Feb 12, 45; m 68; c 3. LASERS, QUANTUM ELECTRONICS. *Educ:* Wabash Col, AB, 67; Harvard Univ, AM, 69; Rice Univ, PhD(elec eng), 74. *Prof Exp:* Physicist, Arthur D Little, Inc, 68-69; advan res engr, GTE Sylvania Electrooptics Orgn, 73-75, mgr, Res & Develop Dept, 77-79, res mgr, GTE Labs, Inc, 79-82; DIR, RCA ADVAN TECHNOL LABS, 82- *Mem:* Am Phys Soc; Optical Soc Am; Inst Elec & Electronics Engrs; Sigma Xi. *Res:* Dye lasers; nonlinear optics; photochemical interactions; Raman lasers. *Mailing Add:* RCA Advan Technol Labs Front & Cooper Sts Camden NJ 08102

DECKER, CLIFFORD EARL, JR, b Valdese, NC, July 20, 41; m 64; c 2. INDUSTRIAL HYGIENE, ANALYTICAL CHEMISTRY. *Educ:* Univ NC, BS, 63, MSPH, 65. *Prof Exp:* Scientist air pollution, Res Triangle Inst, 65-66; health serv officer, Nat Ctr Air Pollution Control, 66-68; sr scientist, 68-75, DEPT MGR AIR POLLUTION, RES TRIANGLE INST, 75- *Mem:* Air Pollution Control Asn; Am Chem Soc. *Res:* Areas of atmospheric chemistry, air pollution studies in urban and nonurban areas, field measurements, quality assurance, testing and evaluation of instrumentation, and measurement methodology. *Mailing Add:* Res Triangle Inst Box 12194 Research Triangle Park NC 27709

DECKER, DANIEL LORENZO, b Provo, Utah, Sept 22, 29; m 54; c 7. SOLID STATE PHYSICS, HIGH PRESSURE PHYSICS. *Educ:* Brigham Young Univ, BS, 53, MS, 55; Univ Ill, PhD(physics), 58. *Prof Exp:* Asst math, Brigham Young Univ, 52-53, asst physics, 53-55 & asst appl math, 55; asst physics, Univ Ill, 55-56; from asst prof to assoc prof, 58-67, PROF PHYSICS, BRIGHAM YOUNG UNIV, 67- *Concurrent Pos:* Vis staff mem, Los Alamos Sci Lab, 64-70; vis scientist, Argonne Nat Lab, 71-72; res scientist, Centre d'Etudes Nucleaires de Saclay, France, 77-79. *Honors & Awards:* Fel Am Phys Soc, 81. *Mem:* Am Phys Soc; Am Asn Physics Teachers. *Res:* High pressure physics; Mossbauer measurements; diffusion; neutron diffraction; superconductivity. *Mailing Add:* Dept of Physics & Astron Brigham Young Univ Provo UT 84602

DECKER, DAVID GARRISON, b Pittsford, NY, Sept 14, 17; m 41; c 4. OBSTETRICS & GYNECOLOGY. *Educ:* Univ Rochester, AB, 39; Yale Univ, MD, 42; Univ Minn, MS, 51; Am Bd Obstet & Gynec, dipl. *Prof Exp:* Asst biochem & resident obstet, Mary Imogene Bassett Hosp, Cooperstown, NY, 46; fel, Mayo Clin, 47-50; from instr to assoc prof, 53-69, chmn dept, 69-80, PROF OBSTET & GYNEC, MAYO MED SCH, 69-, EMER CHMN DEPT, 80- *Concurrent Pos:* Asst obstet & gynec, Mayo Clin, 49, consult, 50-, head sect obstet & gynec, 69-76. *Mem:* Am Asn Obstet & Gynec; Am Fertil Soc; Am Col Obstet & Gynec; Am Radium Soc; Soc Gynecol Oncologists. *Res:* Infertility and pelvic malignancy. *Mailing Add:* Mayo Clin Rochester MN 55901

DECKER, DAVID RICHARD, solid state devices, see previous edition

DECKER, FRED WILLIAM, b Portland, Ore, July 5, 17; m 42; c 3. PHYSICS. *Educ:* Ore State Col, BS, 40, PhD(physics), 52; NY Univ, MS, 43. *Prof Exp:* Jr meteorologist, US Weather Bur, Calif, 40-41; instr meteorol, NY Univ, 41-44; instr physics, Multnomah Col, 46; from instr to asst prof, Ore State Univ, 46-59, assoc prof physics, 59-81; DEP ASST SECY EDUC, OFF EDUC RES & IMPROVEMENT, WASHINGTON, DC, 81- *Concurrent Pos:* consult to litigants, US Bur Reclamation, 52-, consult, 64-65; consult, Adv Comt Weather Control, 54-57; TV meteorologist, KOIN, Portland, Ore, 68 & KOAC-KOAP, Portland & Corvallis, Ore, 68-70; consult, Fed Water Pollution Control Agency, 68-69 & AEC, 69-70; ed, Universitas, Univ Prof for Acad Order, 75-; atty-gen, Ore, 79-81; prin investr, US Army Res, Nat Sci Found & NASA, 52-81. *Mem:* Fel AAAS; Nat Weather Asn; Univ Prof for Acad Order (pres, 74); Int Asn Statist in Phys Sci; Am Meteorol Soc. *Res:* Atmospheric ozone measurements; meteorological optics; short-period weather forecasting; weather modification evaluation; mesometeorology; weather radar; writer for science museums; meterolog instruction. *Mailing Add:* Off Educ Res & Improvement 400 Maryland Ave SW Washington DC 20202

DECKER, JANE M, b Cleveland, Ohio, June 22, 35; m 59; c 1. PLANT CYTOTAXONOMY. *Educ:* Mt Holyoke Col, AB, 57; Yale Univ, MS, 58, PhD(plant anat), 61. *Prof Exp:* Instr bot, Mass State Col Bridgewater, 60-61; taxonomist, Int Plant Index, 61-62; instr bot, Southern Conn State Col, 62 & Ohio State Univ, 62-64; asst prof, Ohio Wesleyan Univ, 64-66; asst prof bot & plant path, Ohio State Univ, 66-68; vis assoc prof bot, 68-73, asst prof, 73-78, ASSOC PROF BOT, OHIO WESLEYAN UNIV, 78- *Mem:* Bot Soc Am; Am Soc Plant Taxonomists. *Res:* Evolution of ferns; plant tissue culture. *Mailing Add:* Dept of Bot & Bact Ohio Wesleyan Univ Delaware OH 43015

DECKER, JOHN ALVIN, JR, physics, technical management, see previous edition

DECKER, JOHN D, b Middletown, NY, July 10, 22; m 45; c 1. ANATOMY, EMBRYOLOGY. *Educ:* Univ Fla, BS, 50, MS, 52; State Univ NY Upstate Med Ctr, PhD(anat), 65. *Prof Exp:* From instr to assoc prof biol, Hartwick Col, 54-65; res assoc, Washington Univ, 65-67; asst prof, 67-69, ASSOC PROF ANAT, MED CTR, UNIV MO-COLUMBIA, 69- *Res:* Neuroembryology and behavior. *Mailing Add:* Dept of Anat Univ Mo Med Ctr Columbia MO 65201

DECKER, JOHN LAWS, b Brooklyn, NY, June 27, 21; m 54; c 4. RHEUMATOLOGY, INTERNAL MEDICINE. *Educ:* Univ Richmond, BA, 42; Columbia Univ, MD, 51. *Prof Exp:* Instr med, Columbia Univ, 54-55; clin & res fel, Mass Gen Hosp, 55-58; from instr to assoc prof, Univ Wash, 58-65; clin dir, Metab & Digestive Dis, 76-80, CHIEF, ARTHRITIS & RHEUMATISM BR, NAT INST ARTHRITIS, DIABETES, DIGESTIVE & KIDNEY DIS, NIH, 65- *Honors & Awards:* Philip Hench Award, Asn Military Surg US. *Mem:* Am Rheumatism Asn; Am Fedn Clin Res. *Res:* Clinical studies of rheumatoid arthritis and systemic lupus erythematosus. *Mailing Add:* Rm 9N218 Bldg 10 Nat Inst of Health Bethesda MD 20205

DECKER, JOHN P, b Chicago, Ill, Aug 16, 25; m 51; c 2. MOLECULAR PHYSICS, SPECTROSCOPY. *Educ:* Univ Ark, BSEE, 49, MS, 53; Tex A&M Univ, PhD(physics), 64. *Prof Exp:* Engr, Ark Power & Light, 49-51; off engr, F E Woodruff, 52-53; instr physics, Ark Agr & Mech Col, 53-56; from instr to asst prof, Tex A&M Univ, 56-63; from assoc prof to prof, Sam Houston State Col, 63-65; head dept, 65-79, PROF PHYSICS, STEPHEN F AUSTIN STATE UNIV, 65- *Mem:* Am Asn Physics Teachers; Inst Elec & Electronics Engrs. *Res:* Investigations of the ultraviolet absorption spectra of sulfer dioxide with isotopic substitution and of selenium dioxide; development of gas lasers. *Mailing Add:* Dept Physics Stephen F Austin State Univ Nacogdoches TX 75962

DECKER, JOHN PETER, b Ione, Wash, Dec 27, 15; m 40; c 3. APPLIED SYNECOLOGY. *Educ:* Univ Idaho, BS, 38; Duke Univ, AM, 40, PhD(bot), 42; US Air Force Sch Aerospace Med, dipl, 42. *Prof Exp:* Res assoc, Sch Forestry, Duke Univ, 46; asst prof bot, Univ Nebr, 46-47 & NY State Col Forestry, Syracuse, 47-54; chmn audiovisual dept, Brooklyn Bot Garden, 54-55; res physiologist, USDA, 55-63; prof eng, 63-81, EMER PROF ENG, ARIZ STATE UNIV, 81- *Mem:* AAAS; Am Soc Plant Physiol. *Res:* Photosynthesis; transpiration; ergometry; photorespiration; synecology. *Mailing Add:* Col of Eng Sci Ariz State Univ Tempe AZ 85281

DECKER, KENNETH HAROLD, b Kenosha, Wis, Aug 19, 32; m 57; c 3. ANALYTICAL CHEMISTRY. *Educ:* Univ Wis, BS, 54, MS, 59. *Prof Exp:* Instr gen chem, Univ Wis, 56-57; chemist anal res, Morton Chem Co, 59-68, res assoc, 68-70, MGR RES SERV, MORTON-NORWICH PROD, INC, 70- *Res:* Electroanalytical chemistry; polarography. *Mailing Add:* Morton-Norwich Prod Inc 1275 Lake Ave Woodstock IL 60098

DECKER, L(OUIS) H, b Monticello, NY, Nov 23, 13; m 38; c 2. METALLURGY. *Educ:* Rensselaer Polytech Inst, ChE, 35. *Prof Exp:* Mem methods dept, Rome Div, Revere Copper & Brass, Inc, 35-39, metall chemist, Res Dept, 39-43, chief chemist, Refining Div, 43-45, supvr chem & metall sect, Res Dept, 45-64, asst mgr metall dept, Res & Develop Ctr, 64-67, res & develop mgr, New Bedford Div, 67-77, consult, Res & Develop Ctr, 78-80; RETIRED. *Mem:* Am Soc Metals. *Res:* Metallurgy of copper alloys. *Mailing Add:* 6416 Edgewood Dr Rome NY 13440

DECKER, QUINTIN WILLIAM, b Rochester, NY, Aug 22, 30; m 59; c 3. SYNTHETIC ORGANIC CHEMISTRY. *Educ:* Univ Buffalo, BA, 53, MA, 56, PhD(org chem), 58; Univ Charleston, BS, 78. *Prof Exp:* Proj scientist, Eastman Kodak Co, 54-55; proj scientist, Chem & Plastics Div, 57-81, PATENT MGR, UNION CARBIDE CORP, SOUTH CHARLESTON, 81- *Mem:* Am Chem Soc. *Res:* Aliphatic silanes compounds; aliphatic olefin, hydroxyl, carbonyl and amine reactions; hydrogenation reactions and catalysts; dialdehyde tissue fixation; textile chemicals; surfactants. *Mailing Add:* 1006 Sand Hill Dr St Albans WV 25177

DECKER, R(AYMOND) F(RANK), b Afton, NY, July 20, 30; m 51; c 4. METALLURGICAL ENGINEERING. *Educ:* Univ Mich, BS, 52, MS, 55, PhD(metall eng), 58. *Prof Exp:* Asst high temperature metall, Eng Res Inst, Univ Mich, 54-58; res metallurgist, Alloy Studies & Develop, 58-59, sr metallurgist, 59-60, sect head nickel & stainless steels, 60-62, group leader nonferrous metals, 62-67, asst to mgr, Paul D Merica Res Lab, 67-69, asst mgr, 69-76, vpres US res & develop, 76-78, VPRES CORP TECH & DIVERSIFICATION VENTURES, INCO, LTD, 78- *Concurrent Pos:* Adj prof, Polytech Inst Brooklyn, 62-66 & NY Univ, 68; mem res & technol adv panel mat aircraft, NASA, 70-71, NSF, 78-; rep sci bd, Biogen, SAm, 80- *Honors & Awards:* IR-100 Award, 64. *Mem:* Fel Am Soc Metals; Fel Am Inst Chemists; Am Inst Mining, Metall & Petrol Engrs; Sigma Xi; Am Inst Chem Engrs. *Res:* High temperature alloys and transformations; alloy, maraging and stainless steels; cast irons; nickel, copper, aluminum and magnetic alloys; extractive, powder and process metallurgy; welding; electrochemistry, corrosion, ceramics, paints, plastics. *Mailing Add:* INCO Ltd 1 New York Plaza New York NY 10004

DECKER, RICHARD H, b Grand Rapids, Mich, Aug 12, 34; m 60; c 3. BIOCHEMISTRY. *Educ:* Hope Col, AB, 56; Univ Ill, Urbana, MS, 58; Okla State Univ, PhD(biochem), 60. *Prof Exp:* Res assoc & lectr biochem, Mayo Grad Sch Med, Univ Minn, 62-71; head, Sect Infectious Dis, 71-74, RES FEL IMMUNOCHEM, ABBOTT LABS, 74-, HEAD, HEPATITIS RES LABS, 81- *Concurrent Pos:* NIH fel trytophan metab, Sch Med, Univ Wis, 60-62, res career develop award, 66-71. *Mem:* AAAS; Am Chem Soc; Soc Invest Dermat; Am Soc Exp Path; Fedn Am Socs Exp Biol. *Res:* Mechanism of cellular adhesion, acantholysis; phosphoproteins; control of epidermal metabolism; determination of steroids, viral antigens via radioimmunoassay, physical and immunopurification of antibodies, antigens; hepatitis A tissue culture. *Mailing Add:* Abbott Labs North Chicago IL 60064

DECKER, ROBERT DEAN, b Uniondale, Ind, July 7, 33; m 57; c 2. BOTANY, ENVIRONMENTAL BIOLOGY. *Educ:* Purdue Univ, BS, 59, MS, 61; NC State Univ, PhD(bot), 66. *Prof Exp:* Lectr bot, Butler Univ, 61-62; asst prof, 66-69, ASSOC PROF BIOL & BOT, UNIV RICHMOND, 69- *Mem:* Bot Soc Am. *Res:* Plant morphogenesis. *Mailing Add:* Dept of Biol Univ of Richmond Richmond VA 23173

DECKER, ROBERT SCOTT, b Orange, Calif, Oct 9, 42; m 65; c 2. DEVELOPMENTAL BIOLOGY, CELL BIOLOGY. *Educ:* Calif State Col, Long Beach, BA, 65; Univ Iowa, MS, 67, PhD(zool), 70. *Prof Exp:* Vis asst prof biol, Claremont Cols, 70-71; USPHS fel, Univ Calif, San Francisco, 71-73; asst prof cell biol, 73-78, ASSOC PROF CELL BIOL, SOUTHWESTERN MED SCH, UNIV TEX HEALTH SCI CTR DALLAS, 78- *Concurrent Pos:* Mem, Basic Sci Coun, Am Heart Asn; estab investr, Am Heart Asn; spec res fel, Cambridge Univ. *Mem:* AAAS; Am Soc Zool; Soc Develop Biol; Am Soc Cell Biol. *Res:* Role of cell junctions in development; mechanisms of junctional assembly during differentiation; lysosomal alterations during myocardial ischemia. *Mailing Add:* Dept of Cell Biol Med Sch Univ Tex Health Sci Ctr Dallas TX 75235

DECKER, ROBERT WAYNE, b Williamsport, Pa, Mar 11, 27; m 50; c 4. GEOPHYSICS. *Educ:* Mass Inst Technol, BS, 49, MS, 51; Colo Sch Mines, DSc(geol), 53. *Prof Exp:* Asst geologist, Bethlehem Steel Co, 49-50; geologist, New World Explor Co, 52-54; asst prof geol, Univ Ill, 54; from asst prof to assoc prof, Dartmouth Col, 54-67, chmn dept geol, 63-65, prof geophys, 67-79; SCIENTIST-IN-CHG, HAWAIIAN VOLCANO OBSERV, US GEOL SURV, 79- *Concurrent Pos:* Geophysicist, US Geol Surv, 57-, vis scientist, Nat Ctr Earthquake Res, 69-70; assoc prof, Inst Technol Bandung, Indonesia, 59-60; res affil, Hawaii Inst Geophys, Univ Hawaii, 64-; Am Philos Soc-NSF grants, Iceland, 66-77; mem earth sci grants rev panel, NSF, 71-73; pres, Int Asn Volcanology & Chem of the Earth's Interior, 75-79; chmn, Geosci Adv Panel, Los Alamos Nat Lab, 77-79; chmn, Panel Thermal Regimes Continental Sci Drilling Comt, Nat Acad Sci, 80-81; mem bd dir, Hawaii Natural Hist Asn, Hawaii Nat Park, 80-; actg scientist-in-charge, Mount St Helens' Proj, US Geol Surv, 80. *Mem:* AAAS; fel Geol Soc Am; fel Am Geophys Union. *Res:* Physics of volcanoes; structural geology; applied geophysics. *Mailing Add:* Dept of Earth Sci Dartmouth Col Hanover NH 03755

DECKER, ROLAN VAN, b Bartlesville, Okla, Nov 4, 36; m 61; c 3. PHYSICAL BIOCHEMISTRY. *Educ:* Okla State Univ, BS, 58; Purdue Univ, PhD(biochem), 65. *Prof Exp:* From asst prof to assoc prof, 65-74, PROF CHEM, SOUTHWESTERN OKLA STATE UNIV, 74- *Mem:* Am Chem Soc. *Res:* Protein-ion and protein-small molecule interactions and their effects on protein conformation; topology of subcellular particles. *Mailing Add:* RR 1 Box 80 Weatherford OK 73096

DECKER, WALTER JOHNS, b Tannersville, NY, June 13, 33; m 61; c 3. TOXICOLOGY. *Educ:* State Univ NY Albany, BA, 54, MA, 55; George Washington Univ, PhD(biochem), 66. *Prof Exp:* US Army, 55-75, res asst biochem, Walter Reed Army Inst Res, 55-56, res biochemist, 57-60 & 62-65, chief indust hyg sect, 406th Med Gen Lab, Japan, 56-57, chief lab serv, Dept Med Res & Develop, William Beaumont Gen Hosp, 65-71, chief chem, Fifth US Army Area Med Lab, Ft Sam Houston, Tex, 71-75; ASSOC PROF, DEPT PHARMACOL & TOXICOL, UNIV TEX MED BR, 76-, ASSOC PROF, DEPT PEDIAT, 76- *Concurrent Pos:* Consult to surgeon, White Sands Missile Range, 66-71; lectr, Univ Tex, El Paso, 67-71; adj asst prof, Univ Tex Health Sci Ctr, 72-74, adj assoc prof, 74-75. *Mem:* Fel AAAS; Am Chem Soc; sr mem Am Fedn Clin Res; fel Am Inst Chemists; fel Am Acad Clin Toxicol (secy-treas, 78-84). *Res:* Analytical, forensic, and clinical toxicology; industrial hygiene. *Mailing Add:* Dept of Pharmacol & Toxicol Univ of Tex Med Br Galveston TX 78134

DECKER, WAYNE LEROY, b Madison County, Iowa, Jan 24, 22; m 43; c 1. METEOROLOGY. *Educ:* Cent Col, Iowa, BS, 43; Iowa State Univ, MS, 47, PhD(agr climatol), 55. *Prof Exp:* Meteorologist climatol, US Weather Bur, 47-49; agr climatologist, 49-67, PROF ATMOSPHERIC SCI, UNIV MO-COLUMBIA, 67-, CHMN DEPT, 67- *Concurrent Pos:* Adv agr meteorol coop res, Agr Res, Sci & Educ Admin, USDA, 77-79; chmn comt on climate & weather fluctuations & agr product, Nat Acad Sci, 75-76; mem exec comt, Coun Agr Sci & Technol, 80- *Mem:* Am Meteorol Soc; Am Geophys Union; Agron Soc; Int Soc Biomet; AAAS. *Res:* Impact of climate and meteorological variations on agricultural production. *Mailing Add:* Dept of Atmospheric Sci Univ of Mo Columbia MO 65201

DECKER, WINSTON M, b Deckerville, Mich, Jan 10, 23; m 45; c 2. VETERINARY MEDICINE. *Educ:* Mich State Univ, DVM, 46. *Prof Exp:* Pvt pract, 46-47; chief vet, Kalamazoo City County Health Dept, 47-49; pub health vet, Mich Dept Health, 50-55, asst to state health comnr, 55-60; chief spec projs sect, Milk & Food Br, Div Environ Eng & Food Protection, Pub Health Serv, 60-65, prog planning officer, 65-66, asst prog officer, Bur State Serv, 66-67, dir, Off Res & Develop, Bur Dis Prev & Environ Control, 67-69; dir sci activ & asst exec vpres, Am Vet Med Asn, 69-76; WASH REP, AM VET MED ASN & ASN AM VET MED COLS, 77- *Honors & Awards:* Commendation Medal, USPHS, 64. *Mem:* Am Vet Med Asn; Am Pub Health Asn. *Res:* Relationships of environmental factors to cause, control or prevention of chronic and communicable disease and veterinary medicine's capability and productivity in meeting society's requirements upon it. *Mailing Add:* Am Vet Med Asn 1522 K St NW Washington DC 20005

DECKER-JACKSON, JOAN ELISE, protozoology, comparative biochemistry, see previous edition

DECKERS, JACQUES (MARIE), b Antwerp, Belgium, Aug 25, 27; Can citizen; m 58; c 7. PHYSICAL CHEMISTRY. *Educ:* Univ Louvain, Candidat, Sci Chim, 49, Lic Sci Chim, 41, DSc(phys chem), 56. *Prof Exp:* Asst, Univ Louvain, 56-58; res assoc chem eng, Princeton Univ, 58-61; assoc prof, 61-66, PROF CHEM, UNIV TORONTO, 66- *Honors & Awards:* Belgium Govt Travel Award, 57. *Mem:* Am Chem Soc; Am Phys Soc; Chem Inst Can. *Res:* Combustion; ions in in flames; high energy particles in chemical reactions; molecular beams; electric discharges. *Mailing Add:* Dept of Chem Univ of Toronto Toronto Can

DECKERT, CHERYL A, b Philadelphia, Pa, Feb 22, 48. ELECTROCHEMISTRY. *Educ:* Drexel Univ, BS, 69; Univ Ill, MS, 71, PhD(chem), 73. *Prof Exp:* Res assoc molecular biol, Univ Ill, 73-74; staff mem chem, David Sarnoff Res Ctr, RCA Corp, 74-80; MGR PRINTED CIRCUIT RES & DEVELOP, SHIPLEY CO, 80- *Mem:* Am Chem Soc; Sigma Xi; Electrochem Soc; Am Electroplaters Soc. *Res:* Photoresist adhesion to semiconductor devices electroless and electro-plating; chemical etching. *Mailing Add:* Shipley Co Inc 2300 Washington St Newton MA 02162

DECKERT, CURTIS KENNETH, b Whittier, Calif, Jan 3, 39; m 64; c 2. MECHANICAL ENGINEERING, TECHNICAL MANAGEMENT. *Educ:* Univ Ariz, BSME, 60; Univ Southern Calif, MSME, 62, MBA, 68. *Prof Exp:* Assoc engr optical-mech eng, Systs Support Div, Nortronics Co, 60-66; sr engr, Gilfillan Div, Int Tel & Tel Corp, 66 & Calif Comput Prods, 66-70; develop engr, Aeronutronic Div, Ford Motor Co, 72-75; sr mech engr med eng, Diagnostics Div, Abbott Labs, 75-76; PRES, TECH & MGT CONSULT, CURT DECKERT ASSOCS, INC, 76- *Mem:* Soc Photo-optical Instrumentation Engrs; Am Sci Asn; Am Mgt Asn; Asn Mgt Consult; Inst Mgt Consult. *Res:* Market research and management strategy for high technology business; medical systems; optical systems for instrumentation and entertainment; mechanical systems; photographic and other recording systems. *Mailing Add:* 18061 Darmel Pl Santa Ana CA 92705

DECKERT, FRED MANFRED W, b Berlin, Ger, Jan 16, 43; US citizen; m 65; c 2. BIOCHEMICAL TOXICOLOGY, XENOBIOTIC METABOLISM. *Educ:* Gonzaga Univ, BS, 66; Univ Wis-Madison, MS, 68, PhD(biochem), 70. *Prof Exp:* Jr chemist med chem, Cent Res Labs, 3M Co, St Paul, 66; res asst biochem, Univ Wis-Madison, 66-70; res asst biochem pharmacol, Inst Toxicol, Univ Tübingen, Ger, 70-72; res assoc develop pharmacol, Med Ctr, Univ Ill, Chicago, 72-73; group leader biochem pharmacol & drug metab, 73-77, sr group leader biochem toxicol, 77-79, head subchronic, reproductive & biochem toxicol, 79-81, MGR, ANAL & BIOCHEM TOXICOL RES SECT, RES LABS, ROHM & HAAS CO, 81- *Concurrent Pos:* Asst prof pharmacol & toxicol, Dept Pharmacol, Jefferson Med Col, Philadelphia, 77-; lectr, Toxicol Ctr, Rutgers Univ, 81- *Mem:* Soc Toxicol; Int Soc Study Xenobiotic Metab; NY Acad Sci; Int Soc Biochem Pharmacol; Nutrit Today Soc. *Res:* Biochemical-pharmacology and metabolic fate of VACOR; biotransformation and biochemical-toxicology of agricultural and industrial chemicals; biochemistry of 4-hydroxycoumarin anticoagulants; warfarin dicumarol; nutrition and detoxication mechanisms; drug interactions; xenobiotic metabolism; enzyme induction. *Mailing Add:* Toxicol Dept Rohm & Haas Co Res Labs Spring House PA 19477

DECKERT, GORDON HARMON, b Freeman, SDak, May 18, 30; m 51; c 2. PSYCHIATRY, ACADEMIC ADMINISTRATION. *Educ:* Northwestern Univ, BS, 52, MD, 55. *Hon Degrees:* DSc, Albany Med Col, 80. *Prof Exp:* Fel med, Mayo Clin & Found, 56-57; clin investr psychiat, Vet Admin Hosp, Oklahoma City, 63-66; career teacher, NIMH, 66-68; PROF PSYCHIAT & BEHAV SCI & CHMN DEPT, HEALTH SCI CTR, UNIV OKLA, 69- *Concurrent Pos:* Chief of staff, Univ Hosp, Univ Okla, 72-74; chmn psychiat test comt & mem exec comt, Nat Bd Med Examr, 74-78. *Honors & Awards:* Aescalapian Award, 70. *Mem:* Am Psychiat Asn; Asn Am Med Cols; AMA; AAAS; Sigma Xi. *Res:* Psychophysiology of imagery; nonverbal behavior; effectiveness of medical education. *Mailing Add:* Dept of Psychiat & Behav Sci PO Box 26901 Oklahoma City OK 73190

DECKKER, B(ASIL) E(ARDLEY) L(EON), b Ceylon, Sept 25, 18; m 53; c 2. THERMODYNAMICS, FLUID MECHANICS. *Educ:* Birmingham Univ, BSc, 49, PhD(mech eng), 53, DSc, 78. *Prof Exp:* Lectr eng, Univ Glasgow, 53-62; assoc prof, 62-66, PROF ENG, UNIV SASK, 66- *Concurrent Pos:* Mem, Assoc Comn Propulsion, Nat Res Coun, 72; mem, Univ Grants Comt, Nat Res Coun, 72-75, chmn, 74-75; fel, Japan Soc Prom Sci. *Mem:* Fel Brit Inst Mech Engrs. *Res:* Steady and unsteady compressible flows in ducts. *Mailing Add:* Dept Mech Eng Univ Sask Saskatoon SK S7H 0W0 Can

DECLAIRE, GERALD, b Detroit, Mich, Aug 7, 26; m 49; c 4. MECHANICAL ENGINEERING. *Educ:* Wayne State Univ, BSME, 49; Chrysler Inst Eng, MAE, 51. *Prof Exp:* Engr res & develop, Chrysler Corp, 49-56, mgr gas turbine res & develop, 56-62, asst chief engr, 62-67, chief engr power train, 67-70; DIR RES & DEVELOP AUTOMOTIVE, ROCKWELL INT, 70- *Mem:* Soc Automotive Engrs. *Res:* Design and development automotive gas turbine research; automotive production; heavy duty truck drive train. *Mailing Add:* 2361 Eastways Rd Bloomfield Hills MI 48013

DECLARIS, N(ICHOLAS), b Drama, Greece, Jan 1, 31; m 56. ELECTRICAL ENGINEERING, APPLIED MATHEMATICS. *Educ:* Agr & Mech Col, Tex, BS; Mass Inst Technol, ScD. *Prof Exp:* Res engr, Calif Res Corp, 52; asst, Electronic Res Lab, Mass Inst Technol, 52-56; from asst prof to prof elec eng & appl math, Cornell Univ, 56-67; head dept, 67-76, PROF

ELEC ENG & RES PROF, INST FLUID DYNAMICS & APPL MATH, UNIV MD, COLLEGE PARK, 67- *Concurrent Pos:* Consult, Melpar, Inc, 54, Spencer-Kennedy Labs, 55-56, Gen Elec Co, 56-59 & Int Bus Mach Corp, 58-70; assoc ed, Transactions, Inst Elec & Electronics Engrs, 58. *Honors & Awards:* Jones Achievement Award, 52. *Mem:* Am Soc Eng Educ; fel Inst Elec & Electronics Engrs; Sigma Xi; Am Math Soc. *Res:* System theory and engineering; simulation; biomedical engineering. *Mailing Add:* Dept of Elec Eng Col of Eng Univ of Md College Park MD 20740

DECOOK, KENNETH JAMES, b Hebron, Ind, June 7, 25; c 4. GEOLOGY, HYDROLOGY. *Educ:* Univ Ariz, BS, 51, PhD(water resouces admin), 70; Univ Tex, MA, 57. *Prof Exp:* Hydrologic asst, Surface Water Br, US Geol Surv, Ariz Dist, 50-51, geologist, Ground Water Br, Ariz & Tex Dists, 51-58; res assoc, Inst Water Utilization, Univ Ariz, 58-59; consult ground water hydrologist, Water Develop Corp, 58-61; asst dist engr, San Carlos Irrig & Drainage Dist, Ariz, 61-63; geologist & hydrologist, W S Gookin & Assocs, 63-65; res assoc, 65-70, ASSOC HYDROLOGIST, WATER RESOURCES RES CTR, UNIV ARIZ, 70-, ASSOC PROF GEOSCI, 74- *Mem:* Asn Prof Geol Scientists; Am Water Resources Asn; Soc Econ Paleontologists & Mineralogists. *Res:* Arid zone hydrology; cretaceous stratigraphy; ground water geology and hydrology; water resources management; economic water allocation and transfer; legal institutions related to water resources. *Mailing Add:* 5068 E Seneca Tucson AZ 85712

DECORA, ANDREW WAYNE, b Rock Springs, Wyo, July 25, 28; m 53; c 2. PHYSICAL ORGANIC CHEMISTRY, SPECTROSCOPY. *Educ:* Univ Wyo, BS, 50, MS, 57, PhD(kinetics), 62. *Prof Exp:* Chemist, Laramie Petrol Res Ctr, US Bur Mines, 50-51, supvry chemist, 53-59; asst kinetics, Univ Wyo, 59-61; proj leader, 61-74, asst to asst dir explor & extraction, Off Res & Develop, US Dept Interior, Washington, DC, 74; dir, Laramie Energy Technol Ctr, Energy Exec Serv, US Dept Energy, 75-81; PRES, SNOWY RANGE MGT SERV, INC, 81- *Concurrent Pos:* Adj prof chem & chem eng, Univ Wyo, 75-82; consult energy, environ, educ & mgt, 81- *Mem:* AAAS; Am Chem Soc; Soc Appl Spectros; Sigma Xi. *Res:* Gas chromatography; kinetics and mechanisms of organic reactions; thermal and photochemical reactions of sulfur and nitrogen compounds; mass, infrared, nuclear magnetic resonance, spectroscopy; energy development research, particularly in situ processes for oil shale, tar sands, and underground gasification of coal. *Mailing Add:* 1408 Baker St Laramie WY 82070

DECORPO, JAMES JOSEPH, b Lawrence, Mass, Aug 8, 42; m 68; c 1. PHYSICAL CHEMISTRY, ANALYTICAL CHEMISTRY. *Educ:* Northeastern Univ, BS, 64; Pa State Univ, PhD(phys chem), 69. *Prof Exp:* Fel, Rice Univ, 69-70; Nat Acad Sci-Nat Res Coun fel, 70-72; res chemist, 72-75, SUPVRY CHEMIST, NAVAL RES LAB, 75- *Mem:* AAAS; Am Chem Soc; Am Soc Mass Spectrometry. *Res:* Mass spectrometry; development of analytical instrumentation; surface reactions and contaminant characterization; gas phase ion chemistry atmosphere control of enclosed areas and the development of life support system. *Mailing Add:* Naval Res Lab Code 6110 Washington DC 20375

DECOSSE, JEROME J, b Valley City, NDak, Apr 19, 28; m 57; c 5. MEDICINE. *Educ:* Col St Thomas, BS, 48; Univ Minn, MD, 52; State Univ NY Upstate Med Ctr, PhD(anat), 69. *Prof Exp:* Intern surg, Roosevelt Hosp, New York, 52-53, asst resident, 53-55; fel exp med, Sloan-Kettering Inst, 55-56; asst & chief resident, Roosevelt Hosp, 58-60; sr resident Mem Ctr, 60-62; asst, Med Col, Cornell Univ, 62-63; asst prof & cancer coordr, State Univ NY Upstate Med Ctr, 63-66; from assoc prof to prof surg, Sch Med, Case Western Reserve Univ, 66-71; prof surg & chmn dept, Med Col Wis, 71-78; PROF SURG & CHMN DEPT, MEM SLOAN-KETTERING CANCER CTR, 78- *Concurrent Pos:* Markle scholar, 64; consult, NIH, 68- *Honors & Awards:* Borden Award, 52. *Mem:* Am Col Surg; Am Gastroenterol Asn; Am Soc Cell Biol; Soc Surg Alimentary Tract; Soc Head & Neck Surgeons. *Res:* Cancer, cell biology and immunology; gastrointestinal physiology. *Mailing Add:* Mem Sloan-Kettering Cancer Ctr 1275 York Ave New York NY 10022

DECOSTA, EDWIN J, b Chicago, Ill, Mar 25, 06; m 35; c 4. OBSTETRICS & GYNECOLOGY. *Educ:* Univ Chicago, BS, 26, MD, 29; Am Bd Obstet & Gynec, dipl. *Prof Exp:* Mem fac, 46-52, PROF OBSTET & GYNEC, MED SCH, NORTHWESTERN UNIV, CHICAGO, 52- *Concurrent Pos:* Attend obstetrician & gynecologist, Prentice Maternity Hosp, 52-; attend gynecologist, Cook County Hosp, 58. *Mem:* Am Gynec Soc; Am Asn Obstet & Gynec; fel Am Col Surg; fel Am Col Obstet & Gynec. *Res:* Endocrinology. *Mailing Add:* 1540 N Lakeshore Dr Ave Chicago IL 60610

DE COURCY, SAMUEL JOSEPH, JR, b Newport, RI, June 13, 18; m 44; c 1. MEDICAL MICROBIOLOGY. *Educ:* Yale Univ, BMus, 43; Univ RI, BS, 44; Univ Del, MS, 51. *Prof Exp:* Control chemist, US Naval Torpedo Sta, 44-46; fisheries biologist & chief collab, US Fish & Wildlife Serv, 49; microbiologist, Biochem Res Found, Franklin Inst, 51-60; instr, Rutgers Univ, 61-62; staff res microbiologist, Vet Admin Hosp, Philadelphia, 60-72; assoc surg res, Grad Hosp, Univ Pa, 73-74; ASSOC IN BIOSCI, ALBERT EINSTEIN MED CTR, 74- *Concurrent Pos:* Mem staff, Philadelphia Gen Hosp, 64-; dir, Delmont Labs, Inc, 70- *Mem:* Am Soc Microbiol; Am Chem Soc; NY Acad Sci; Reticuloendothelial Soc; Int Soc Quantum Biol. *Res:* Microbial drug resistance; ribosomal vaccines; RES stimulators in immunotherapy of cancer; cell-mediated immunity. *Mailing Add:* 2522 Traynor Ave Northridge Claymont DE 19703

DECOURSEY, DONN G(ENE), b Auburn, Ind, Oct 21, 34; m 57; c 2. HYDROLOGIC MODELING, AGRICULTURAL RESEARCH. *Educ:* Purdue Univ, BS, 57, MS, 58; Ga Inst Technol, PhD(civil eng), 70. *Prof Exp:* Engr, Ind Flood Control & Water Resources Comn, 58-61; res hydraul engr, Southern Plains Watershed Res Ctr, Agr Res Serv, Oxford Miss, 61-71, dir ctr, 71-74, res hydraul engr & dir, Sedimentation Lab, Sci & Educ Admin, 74-81, RES LEADER & NAT TECH ADV, HYDROL RES GROUP, AGR RES SERV, USDA, FT COLLINS, COLO, 81- *Concurrent Pos:* Fel, Colo

State Univ, Ft Collins, 78-79; assoc ed, Am Soc Agr Engrs, Am Soc Civil Engrs & Soil Conserv Soc Am. *Mem:* Am Soc Civil Engrs; Am Soc Agr Engrs; Am Geophys Union; Soil Conserv Soc Am; Sigma Xi. *Res:* Hydrologic, hydraulic, erosion and sedimentation engineering; statistical and process oriented hydrologic model development; agricultural hydrologic systems. *Mailing Add:* 3336 Pineridge Pl Fort Collins CO 80525

DECOURSEY, RUSSELL MYLES, b Indianapolis, Ind, Jan 17, 00; m 30; c 2. ENTOMOLOGY, ZOOLOGY. *Educ:* DePauw Univ, AB, 23; Univ Ill, AM, 25, PhD(entom), 27. *Prof Exp:* Asst prof entom, La Univ, 27-29; from asst prof to prof, 29-70, EMER PROF ENTOM & ZOOL, UNIV CONN, 70- *Mem:* Fel AAAS; Am Soc Zoologists; Entom Soc Am. *Res:* Bionomics of nymphs of Hemiptera; Pentatomidae. *Mailing Add:* 24 Storrs Heights Rd Storrs CT 06268

DECOURSEY, W(ILLIAM) J(AMES), b Rimbey, Alta, Sept 14, 30; m 57; c 4. CHEMICAL ENGINEERING. *Educ:* Univ Alta, BSc, 51; Univ London, DIC & PhD, 55. *Prof Exp:* Process engr, Sherritt Gordon Mines, Ltd, Alta, 55-57, res & develop engr, 57-60; from asst prof to assoc prof, 61-71, PROF CHEM ENG, UNIV SASK, 71- *Mem:* Can Soc Chem Engrs; Am Inst Chem Engrs; Chem Inst Can. *Res:* Mass and heat transfer; fluid mechanics; process development. *Mailing Add:* Dept Chem & Chem Eng Univ Sask Saskatoon SK S7H 0W0 Can

DECRAENE, DENIS FREDRICK, b Geneseo, Ill, Aug 28, 42. ELECTROCHEMISTRY. *Educ:* St Ambrose Col, BS, 64; Univ Ill, PhD(chem), 69. *Prof Exp:* Sr res chemist, Res Dept, Diamond Shamrock, 69-75, asst mgr res & develop, Chemetals Div, 75-78; MGR, RES & DEVELOP, CHEMETALS CORP, 78- *Mem:* Sigma Xi; Am Inst Mining Engrs; Am Soc Metals. *Res:* Electrochemical processes; solid-state inorganic reactions; hydrometallurgy; fused salt electrochemistry; chemistry of manganese; copper and cobalt. *Mailing Add:* Chemetals Corp 711 Pittman Rd Baltimore MD 21226

DECROSTA, EDWARD FRANCIS, b Hudson, NY, Sept 20, 26; m 53; c 2. HEAT TRANSFER, FLUID FLOW. *Educ:* Rensselaer Polytech Inst, BChemEng, 50, MBA, 79; Siena Col, MS, 60. *Prof Exp:* Plant chemist, Universal Watch Corp, 51-64; chemist, Albany Felt Co, 65-69, mgr technol develop, 69-71, dir res & develop, 73-79, dir res & technol develop, Papermaking Prod Group, 80-82, SR SCIENTIST, PAPERMAKING PROD GROUP, ALBANY INT CORP, 82- *Concurrent Pos:* Lectr, Pulp & Paper Asn, 72-81. *Mem:* Am Chem Soc; Can Pulp & Paper Asn; Tech Asn Pulp & Paper Indust. *Res:* Papermachine dryer section ventilation caused by moving fabrics; fluid flow through porous media as related to water removal from paper webs and fabrics on the paper machine; thermally activated electrochemical cells of the concentration type. *Mailing Add:* 28 James St Hudson NY 12534

DEDDENS, J(AMES) C(ARROLL), b Louisville, Ky, Mar 25, 28; m 53; c 4. MECHANICAL & NUCLEAR ENGINEERING. *Educ:* Univ Louisville, BME, 52, MME, 53. *Prof Exp:* Nuclear engr, Atomic Energy Div, Babcock & Wilcox Co, 53-54, nuclear engr & group supvr, 54-58, prof engr, Indian Point Reactor Proj, 58-62, proj mgr, 62-64, asst coordr utility mkt, 64-66, mgr nuclear serv, Nuclear Power Generation Dept, Power Generation Div, 66-74, mgr eng dept, 74-78, mgr proj mgt nuclear power generation div, 78-80, MGR PROJ MGT, MATH BUS INTEGRATION DEPT, BABCOCK & WILCOX CO, 80- *Concurrent Pos:* US observer, Int Conf Peaceful Uses of Atomic Energy, Geneva, Switz, 64. *Mem:* Am Nuclear Soc; Am Soc Mech Engrs. *Res:* Nuclear power plant design and operations; nuclear products marketing. *Mailing Add:* 1523 Club Terrace Lynchburg VA 24503

DEDDENS, JAMES ALBERT, b Cincinnati, Ohio, Sept 7, 43; m 65; c 2. MATHEMATICS, MATHEMATICAL STATISTICS. *Educ:* Univ Cincinnati, BS, 65; Ind Univ, Bloomington, MA, 67, PhD(math), 69. *Prof Exp:* Asst prof math, Univ Mich, Ann Arbor, 69-70; asst prof, 70-75, assoc prof math, Univ Kans, 75-77; assoc prof, 77-78, PROF MATH, UNIV CINCINNATI, 79- *Concurrent Pos:* NSF grants, 69-71 & 72-79; asst prof math, State Univ NY Buffalo, 74-75. *Mem:* Am Math Soc; Am Statist Soc. *Res:* Study of bounded linear operators on Hilbert space; functional analysis. *Mailing Add:* Dept Math Univ Cincinnati Cincinnati OH 45221

DEDECKER, HENDRIK KAMIEL JOHANNES, b Vorst, Belgium, Sept 4, 15; nat US; m 40; c 1. PHYSICAL CHEMISTRY, RESEARCH MANAGEMENT. *Educ:* Univ Amsterdam, BS, 36; Univ Utrecht, PhD(chem), 41. *Prof Exp:* Res chemist, Nat Sci Orgn, Neth, 41-45; head corrosion res, Shell Petrol Co, 45-47, sect head crude distilling, 47-49, dir res, Rubber Stichting, 49-55; mgr polymer res & develop, Tex-US Chem Co, 56-67; planning coordr, Uniroyal Int, 67-71; managing dir, Uniroyal Plastics Europe, 71-74; corp develop mgr, 74-79, CORP STRATEGIC PLANNING MGR, UNIROYAL, INC, 79- *Mem:* Am Chem Soc. *Res:* Polymer research and development; testing of materials; rubber technology; market development. *Mailing Add:* 710A Heritage Village Southbury CT 06488

DEDINAS, JONAS, b Sakiai, Lithuania, Aug 22, 29; US citizen; m 58; c 1. PHYSICAL CHEMISTRY, PHOTOCHEMISTRY. *Educ:* Johns Hopkins Univ, BE, 54; Univ Del, MChE, 58; Carnegie Inst Technol, PhD(chem), 65. *Prof Exp:* Petrol engr, Gulf Res & Develop Co, 56-62; sr res chemist, 65-70, RES ASSOC PHOTOCHEM, EASTMAN KODAK CO, 71- *Honors & Awards:* Frank R Blood Award, Soc Toxicol, 77. *Mem:* Am Chem Soc. *Res:* Petroleum refining and petrochemicals; radiation chemistry of tetramethylsilane; photochemistry of aromatic ketones; mass spectroscopy; reaction mechanisms; plasma chemistry. *Mailing Add:* 174 Golf Ave Pittsford NY 14534

DEDMAN, JOHN RAYMOND, b Washington, DC, Aug 24, 47; m 69; c 3. CELL BIOLOGY, CELL PHYSIOLOGY. *Educ:* Concord Col, BS, 69; NTex State Univ, MS, 72, PhD (zool/biochem), 74. *Prof Exp:* Fel, cell biol, Baylor Col Med, 74-76 & asst prof, 76-80; ASSOC PROF PHYSIOL & CELL BIOL,

MED SCH, UNIV TEX, HOUSTON, 80- *Concurrent Pos:* fel NIH grant, 76; Res Career Develop Award, NIH, 79. *Honors & Awards:* Gail Patrick Verde Award, Am Diabetes Asn, 79. *Mem:* Am Soc Cell Biologists; Am Soc Biol Chemists; Am Chem Soc; NY Acad Sci. *Res:* Understanding the mechanism of action of intracellular calcium, calcium-binding proteins and calcium regulated processes; relating to many diseased states of calcium dysfunction in muscle development and cancer. *Mailing Add:* Dept Physiol & Cell Biol Rm 4100 Med Sch Univ Tex Houston TX 77025

DEDOMINICIS, ALEX JOHN, b New York, NY, May 13, 35; m 70; c 2. POLYMER CHEMISTRY. *Educ:* NY Univ, BS, 56, MS, 61, PhD(org chem), 62. *Prof Exp:* Res chemist, 62-68, res supvr, 68-78, MGR TECHNOL SALES, E I DU PONT DE NEMOURS & CO, INC, 78- *Res:* Thiophene chemistry; fiber forming polymers. *Mailing Add:* 2638 Majestic Dr Brandywood Wilmington DE 19810

DEDRICK, JOHN H, b Milwaukee, Wis, July 10, 13; m 59. METALLURGY. *Educ:* Univ Wis, BS, 35; Mass Inst Technol, DSc(metall), 48. *Prof Exp:* Asst chief metallurgist, Reynolds Metals Co, 41-42; lab mgr, S K Wellman Co, 42-45; asst prof metall, Univ Cincinnati, 47-48; head adv develop sect, Metall Lab, Sylvania Elec Prods, 48-50; lab mgr, Parts Div, Reynolds Metals Co, 50-56, tech asst to vpres, 56-59, staff consult, Metall Div, 59-65, dir basic res, Metall Res Div, 65-71, exec asst to exec vpres res & develop, 71-72, gen dir, Metall Res Div, 72-78; RETIRED. *Mem:* Brit Inst Metals; Sigma Xi; fel Am Inst Chemists; AAAS; Am Inst Mining & Metall Engrs. *Res:* Powder metallurgy; high temperature alloys; aluminum production and fabrication; surface treatments on aluminum and its alloys; aluminum alloys. *Mailing Add:* 7618 Cornwall Rd Richmond VA 23229

DEDRICK, KENT GENTRY, b Watsonville, Calif, Aug 9, 23; m; c 1. THEORETICAL PHYSICS. *Educ:* San Jose State Col, BA, 46; Stanford Univ, MS, 49, PhD(physics), 55. *Prof Exp:* Res asst nuclear reactor technol, Univ Mich, 54-55; res assoc theoret physics, W W Hansen Labs, Stanford Univ, 56-59; staff mem, Stanford Linear Accelerator Ctr, 60-62; math physicist, Stanford Res Inst, 62-75; consult, 75-80; RES SPECIALIST, CALIF STATE LANDS COMN, 80- *Mem:* Am Phys Soc; AAAS. *Res:* Electromagnetic theory; nuclear theory; aerosol scattering; paramagnetic resonance; environmental sciences; high energy physics; applied mathematics; tidal phenomena; estuarine hydraulics. *Mailing Add:* 1559 Ninth Ave Sacramento CA 95818

DEDRICK, ROBERT L(YLE), b Madison, Wis, Jan 12, 33; m 55; c 3. CHEMICAL ENGINEERING. *Educ:* Yale Univ, BE, 56; Univ Mich, MSE, 57; Univ Md, PhD(chem eng), 65. *Prof Exp:* Asst prof mech eng, George Washington Univ, 59-62, asst prof eng & appl sci, 62-63, assoc prof, 65-66; actg chief, 66-67, CHIEF CHEM ENG SECT, BIOMED ENG & INSTRUMENTATION BR, NIH, 67- *Mem:* AAAS; Am Soc Eng Educ; Am Chem Soc; Am Inst Chem Engrs; Am Soc Artificial Internal Organs. *Res:* Pharmacokinetics; cancer chemotherapy; transport, thermodynamics and kinetics in living systems; biomaterials; artificial internal organs; risk estimation. *Mailing Add:* NIH Bethesda MD 90205

DE DUVE, CHRISTIAN RENE, b Thames-Ditton, Eng, Oct 2, 17; Belg citizen; m 43; c 4. BIOCHEMISTRY, CYTOLOGY. *Educ:* Cath Univ Louvain, MD, 41, MSc, 46. *Hon Degrees:* MD, Univ Turin, 69, State Univ Leiden, 70, Univ Sherbrooke, 70, Univ Lille, 73, Cath Univ Chile, 74, Univ Paris V, 74, State Univ Ghent, 75, State Univ Liege, 75, Gustavus Adolphus Col, 75, Univ Rosario, 76, Univ Aix-Marseille II, 79, Univ Keele, 81. *Prof Exp:* Therese & Johan Anderson Stiftelse fel, Stockholm, 46-47; Rockefeller Found fel, Washington Univ, 47-48. *Prof Exp:* Lectr physiol chem, Fac Med, Cath Univ Louvain, 47-51; prof biochem cytol, 62-74, ANDREW W MELLON PROF BIOCHEM CYTOL, ROCKEFELLER UNIV, 74-; PROF PHYSIOL CHEM & HEAD DEPT, FAC MED, CATH UNIV LOUVAIN, 51- *Concurrent Pos:* Vis prof, Albert Einstein Col Med, 61-62, State Univ Ghent, 62-63, Free Univ Brussels, 63-64, Univ Queensland, 72 & State Univ Liege, 72-73; mem adult develop & aging res & training rev comt, Nat Inst Child Health & Human Develop, 70-72; mem adv comt med res, WHO, 74-78; mem sci adv comt, Max Planck Inst Immunobiol, 75-79. *Honors & Awards:* Nobel Prize in Physiol or Med, 74; Prix Pfizer, Royal Acad Med Belg, 57; Prix Francqui, Belg, 60; Spec Award of Merit, Gairdner Found, Can, 67; Prix Quinquennal des Science Medicales, Belg Govt, 67; Dr H P Heineken Prize, Royal Neth Acad Sci, 73. *Mem:* Foreign assoc Nat Acad Sci; Am Acad Arts & Sci; Royal Acad Med Belg; Royal Acad Belg; Leopold Carol Ger Acad Researchers Natural Sci. *Res:* Carbohydrate metabolism; action of insulin and glucagon; tissue fractionation; intracellular distribution of enzymes; lysosomes; peroxisomes. *Mailing Add:* Rockefeller Univ New York NY 10021

DEE, DIANA, b Los Angeles, Calif, Sept 7, 44. PHYSICAL CHEMISTRY. *Educ:* Reed Col, BA, 65; Univ Calif, Los Angeles, PhD(chem), 70. *Prof Exp:* Asst prof chem, Reed Col, 71-72; physicist, R&D Assocs, 72-76; MEM TECH STAFF, TRW SYSTS, 76- *Mem:* Am Phys Soc. *Res:* Effects of high-energy particles on molecules and ions in the upper atmosphere; nuclear weapons effects; high-explosive and incendiary materials; electronic states of diatomic molecules; chemical laser design. *Mailing Add:* TRW Systs One Space Park 01-1070 Redondo Beach CA 90278

DEED, ELEANOR POLK, b Texarkana, Tex, Aug 11, 32; m 56; c 3. MEDICINE, RADIOLOGY. *Educ:* Henderson State Teachers Col, BA, 52; Univ Ark, MD, 56. *Prof Exp:* Intern, 56-57, resident, 57-60, from instr to assoc prof radiol, Med Ctr, Univ Ark, Little Rock, 60-77. *Mem:* Am Col Radiol; Radiol Soc NAm; Am Roentgen Ray Soc; AMA. *Mailing Add:* Tahlequah Radiol Inc 1500 E Downing Tahlequah OK 74464

DEEDS, DONALD G, human physiology, see previous edition

DEEDS, WILLIAM EDWARD, b Lorain, Ohio, Feb 23, 20; wid; c 4. PHYSICS. *Educ:* Denison Univ, AB, 41; Calif Inst Technol, MS, 43; Ohio State Univ, PhD(physics), 51. *Prof Exp:* Asst, Calif Inst Technol, 41-42, jr physicist, 43-46; asst prof physics, Denison Univ, 46-48; asst, Ohio State Univ, 49, Texas Co fels, 51-52; from asst prof to assoc prof physics, 52-59, PROF PHYSICS, UNIV TENN, KNOXVILLE, 59- *Concurrent Pos:* Consult, Redstone Arsenal, 55-56, Chemstrand Corp, 56- & Oak Ridge Nat Lab, 62- *Mem:* Am Phys Soc; Am Asn Physics Teachers. *Res:* Theoretical physics; electromagnetism; molecular spectroscopy; optics; acoustics; DELETE THIS FIELD. *Mailing Add:* Dept of Physics Univ of Tenn Knoxville TN 37916

DEEG, EMIL W(OLFGANG), b Selb, Ger, Sept 20, 26; m 53; c 4. CERAMICS, SOLID STATE PHYSICS. *Educ:* Univ Würzburg, 54, Dr rer nat(phys sci), 56. *Prof Exp:* Res asst glass & ceramics, Max Planck Inst Silicates, 54-59; mem tech staff ceramic eng, Bell Tel Labs, Inc, Pa, 59-60; res assoc glass & ceramics, Jenaer Glaswerk Schott & Gen, Mainz, WGer, 60, dir res, 61-65; assoc prof physics & solid state sci, Am Univ Cairo, 65-67; mgr ceramic res, Am Optical Corp, Southbridge, 67-73, dir mat & process res, 73-77, tech adv glass technol, 77-78; mgr mat res & develop, Anchor Hocking Corp, 78-80; MGR GLASS TECHNOL, BAUSCH & LOMB, 80- *Concurrent Pos:* Mem Ger Standards Comt, 60-65; mem adv comt glass mfg in space, NASA, 70-75. *Mem:* Fel Am Ceramic Soc; Optical Soc Am; Soc Glass Technol; Nat Inst Ceramic Engrs; Soc Advan Mat & Process Eng. *Res:* Theory of ceramic manufacturing processes; physics of highly disordered solids; optical, laser and chalcogenide glasses; mechanical properties of glass and ceramics; diffusion and heat transfer; glass manufacturing in space; strenth of ophthalmic lenses; container and tableware glasses. *Mailing Add:* 5 Stuyvesant Rd Pittsford NY 14534

DEEGAN, MICHAEL J, b Camden, NJ, Sept 23, 42; m; c 2. PATHOLOGY. *Educ:* St Joseph's Col, Pa, BS, 64; Univ Md, MD, 68. *Prof Exp:* Chief clin path serv, Walter Reed Army Med Ctr, Washington, DC, 73-74; asst prof path & dir clin immunol lab, Univ Mich, 74-77, protein chem sect, William Pepper Lab, Univ Hosp, Univ Pa, 77-78; assoc prof path & lab med, Sch Med & dir, Diag Immunol Lab, Univ Hosp, Emory Univ, 78-79; HEAD, IMMUNOPATH DIV, HENRY FORD HOSP, 80- *Concurrent Pos:* Consult path, US Vet Admin Hosp, Ann Arbor, Mich, 74-77; mem inteflex partic fac comt, Med Sch, Univ Mich, 74-77. *Mem:* AAAS; Am Soc Clin Pathologists; Am Fedn Clin Res; Int Acad Path; Am Asn Pathologists. *Res:* Membrane phenotype analysis of malignant lymphomas; cell-mediated immune responses in malignancy; B lymphocyte ontogeny; analysis of autoantibody patterns in disease. *Mailing Add:* Dept Path Henry Ford Hosp 2799 W Grand Blvd Detroit MI 48202

DEEGAN, ROSS ALFRED, b Montreal, Que, Aug 19, 41; m 66; c 1. SOLID STATE PHYSICS. *Educ:* Loyola Col, Montreal, BSc, 61; McGill Univ, BEng, 63; McMaster Univ, PhD(physics), 67; Duquesne Univ, MBA, 74. *Prof Exp:* Nat Res Coun Can overseas fel, Cavendish Lab, Cambridge Univ, 66-68; res asst prof physics, Univ Ill, Urbana, 68-71; res geophysicist, 71-73, dir geophys anal, 73-77, MGR GEOPHYS SCI, GULF RES & DEVELOP CO, 77- *Mem:* Am Phys Soc; Soc Exploration Geophysicists; Can Asn Physicists. *Res:* Solid state theory, especially band theory of transition metals; seismology for petroleum exploration. *Mailing Add:* Gulf Res & Develop Co PO Box 1653 Houston TX 77001

DEEHR, CHARLES STERLING, b Kalamazoo, Mich, Apr 12, 36; m 60; c 4. SPACE PHYSICS. *Educ:* Reed Col, AB, 58; Univ Alaska, MS, 61, PhD(geophys), 68. *Prof Exp:* Asst geophysicist, 64-68, from asst prof to assoc prof, 68-81, PROF GEOPHYSICS, GEOPHYSICS INST, UNIV ALASKA, 81- *Concurrent Pos:* Fel, Royal Norweg Indust & Sci Res Coun, Norweg Inst Cosmic Physics, 69-71 & 79. *Res:* Planetary astrophysics with emphasis on spectrophotometric studies of atmospheric emissions and scattered light. *Mailing Add:* Geophys Inst Univ Alaska Fairbanks AK 99701

DEELY, JOHN JOSEPH, b Cleveland, Ohio, Jan 13, 33; m 55; c 6. MATHEMATICAL STATISTICS. *Educ:* Ga Inst Technol, BEE, 55; Purdue Univ, MS, 58, PhD(math statist), 65. *Prof Exp:* Aeronaut res scientist, Nat Adv Comt Aeronaut, 55-56; asst math, Purdue Univ, 56-58, instr, Ft Wayne exten, 58-60, res asst, 60-61, instr, 61-65; mem tech res staff, Western Elec-Bell Labs, Sandia Corp, 65-68; sr lectr, Dept Math, 68-74, PROF MATH, UNIV CANTERBURY, 74- *Concurrent Pos:* Consult, Naval Avionics Facility, Indianapolis, 63-64. *Mem:* Am Math Soc; Inst Math Statist; Am Statist Asn. *Res:* Applications of statistical decision theory to applied problems, especially multiple decision problems and empirical Bayes procedures; sample surveys. *Mailing Add:* Dept of Math Univ of Canterbury Christchurch New Zealand

DEEM, GARY SPENCER, b Santa Ana, Calif, Apr 4, 39; m 64; c 2. FLUID DYNAMICS, APPLIED MATHEMATICS. *Educ:* Stanford Univ, BS, 61; NY Univ, MS, 64, PhD(math), 69. *Prof Exp:* Mem tech staff atmospheric res, 64-71, MEM TECH STAFF OCEAN ACOUSTICS, BELL LABS, 71- *Mem:* Am Math Soc; Soc Industs & Appl Math; AAAS; NY Acad Sci; Am Phys Soc. *Res:* Turbulence in stratified and non-stratified fluids; wake and shear instabilities; acoustic scattering; numerical simulation of atmosphere; diffusion-reaction kinetics in biological systems. *Mailing Add:* Bell Labs Whippany Rd Whippany NJ 07981

DEEM, MARY LEASE, b Sycamore, Ill, June 10, 37; m 63; c 1. SYNTHETIC CHEMISTRY, PHYSICALORGANIC CHEMISTRY. *Educ:* Univ Mich-Ann Arbor, BA, 58; Univ Wis-Madison, MS, 60, PhD(chem), 64. *Prof Exp:* Mem staff, Union Carbide Corp, 60-61; fel, Univ Wis-Madison, 63-65; instr, Douglass Col, Rutgers Univ, 65-67; mem staff, Air Reduction Co, Inc, 67-68; sr chemist, Union Carbide Corp, 73-78; VIS RES SCIENTIST, LEHIGH UNIV, 79-; VIS FEL, PRINCETON UNIV, 79- *Mem:* Am Chem Soc; Royal Soc Chem; Sigma Xi. *Res:* Chemistry of heterocyles and other nitrogen- and oxygen-containing organic compounds; organometallic chemistry, homogeneous catalysis; synthesis; polymers; chemistry of medium- small- and strained-ring compounds; halohydrocarbon; complexing agents. *Mailing Add:* Sycamore Hill Rd Bernardsville NJ 07924

DEEM, WILLIAM BRADY, b Parkersburg, WVa, Mar 23, 39; m 63. CHEMICAL ENGINEERING. *Educ:* Lehigh Univ, BS, 61; Univ Wis, MS, 62, PhD(chem eng), 65. *Prof Exp:* Res asst chem eng, Univ Wis, 61-65; engr, Esso Res & Eng Co, NJ, 65; chem engr, Feltman Res Labs, Picatinny Arsenal, Dover, 65-66, tech opers officer, Ammunition Eng Directorate, 66-67; eng assoc, 67-81, SECT HEAD, SYSTS ENG DIV, EXXON CORP, 81- *Mem:* Am Inst Chem Engrs; Instrument Soc Am. *Res:* Control of petroleum and petrochemical processes; mathematical modeling; computer control incentives, applications and project implementation. *Mailing Add:* Exxon Res & Engr Co 180 Park Ave Florham Park NJ 07932

DEEMING, TERENCE JAMES, b Birmingham, Eng, Apr 25, 37. PHYSICS. *Educ:* Univ Birmingham, BSc, 58; Cambridge Univ, PhD(astron), 61. *Prof Exp:* Asst observer, Cambridge Univ, 61-62; vis lectr, 62-64, from asst prof to assoc prof astron, Univ Tex, Austin, 67-77; SR SCIENTIST, DIGICON GEOPHYS CORP, HOUSTON, 77- *Mem:* AAAS; Int Asn Univ; Soc Exp Geophysists. *Res:* Geophysics; statistics; data analysis; astrophysics. *Mailing Add:* Digicon Inc 3701 Kirby Dr Houston TX 77098

DEEMS, ROBERT EUGENE, b Zanesville, Ohio, May 23, 27; m 53; c 2. PLANT PATHOLOGY. *Educ:* Marietta Col, AB, 49; Ohio State Univ, MS, 51, PhD(plant path), 56. *Prof Exp:* Plant pathologist, Velsicol Corp, 51-52; PLANT PATHOLOGIST, AM CYANAMID CO, 56- *Mem:* Am Phytopath Soc. *Res:* Plant disease control chemicals; agriculture attendant upon specialty; pesticide development. *Mailing Add:* 13 Lawnside Dr Trenton NJ 08638

DEEN, DENNIS FRANK, b North Platte, Nebr, Apr 22, 44; m 65; c 2. RADIATION BIOLOGY. *Educ:* Chadron State Col, BS, 66; Univ Kans, PhD(radiation biophys), 75. *Prof Exp:* Sci teacher, Syracuse-Dunbar Sch Syst, 66-69 & Wellsville Sch Syst, 69-70; researcher radiation biophysics, 75-77, asst res radiation biophysicist, 77, asst prof, 77-81, ASSOC PROF NEUROL SURG & RADIATION ONCOL, UNIV CALIF, SAN FRANCISCO, 81- *Concurrent Pos:* Vis fel health physics, Brookhaven Nat Lab, Upton, NY, 71; AEC fel radiation sci & protection, 70-73; USPHS trainee, 73-75. *Mem:* AAAS; Radiation Res Soc; Am Asn Cancer Res. *Res:* Radiobiology, particularly drug-radiation interactions in mammalian cell cultures and in animals. *Mailing Add:* Brain Tumor Res Ctr Univ Calif San Francisco CA 94143

DEEN, HAROLD E(UGENE), b Detroit, Mich, Aug 7, 26; m 48; c 4. PETROLEUM CHEMISTRY, CHEMICAL ENGINEERING. *Educ:* Wayne Univ, BS, 48; Purdue Univ, MS, 51. *Prof Exp:* Asst foreman, Rinshed Mason Co, 48-50; engr, Process Res Div, Esso Res & Eng Co, 51-54, engr, Enjay Labs Div, 54-58, group head, 58-61, sr engr, 61-63, sect head, 63-67, mkt coordr, 67-69, sr eng assoc, Esso Res & Eng Co, 69-77, CHIEF SCIENTIST, EXXON CHEM CO, 77- *Mem:* Am Chem Soc; Soc Automotive Engrs. *Res:* Additive research for crank case motor oils; diesel lubricants; automatic transmission fluids. *Mailing Add:* Exxon Chem Co PO Box 536 Linden NJ 07036

DEEN, JAMES ROBERT, b Dallas, Tex, Mar 1, 44; m 71; c 4. REACTOR PHYSICS, THERMAL REACTOR PHYSICS. *Educ:* Univ Tex, Austin, BEngSci, 66, MSME, 70, PhD(nuclear eng), 73. *Prof Exp:* Sr engr boiling water reactor physics, Gen Elec Co, 72-74, sr engr boiling water develop, 74-76; asst nuclear engr reactor physics, 76-80, NUCLEAR ENG, ARGONNE NAT LAB, 80- *Mem:* Am Nuclear Soc; Sigma Xi. *Res:* Reactor physics, especially in research and test reactor reduced enrichment or light-water reactor development. *Mailing Add:* Appl Physics Div 9700 S Cass Ave Argonne IL 60439

DEEN, ROBERT C(URBA), b Henderson, Ky, May 26, 29; m 52; c 2. GEOTECHNICAL ENGINEERING, TRAFFIC ENGINEERING. *Educ:* Univ Ky, BS, 51, MS, 58, JD, 81; Purdue Univ, PhD(civil eng), 64. *Prof Exp:* Res engr, Ky Dept Hwy, 55-58 & Purdue Univ, 58-60; sr res engr, Ky Dept Hwy, 60-63, asst dir res, 63-80; DIR, KY TRANSP RES PROG, UNIV KY, 81- *Concurrent Pos:* Mem, Transp Res Bd, Nat Acad Sci-Nat Res Coun; adj asst prof civil eng, Univ Ky. *Mem:* Nat Soc Prof Engrs; Am Soc Civil Engrs; Am Soc Testing & Mat; Inst Transp Engrs. *Res:* Soils, highway engineering and pavement design and management. *Mailing Add:* 708 Old Dobbin Rd Lexington KY 40502

DEEN, WILLIAM MURRAY, b Seattle, Wash, Jan 30, 47. BIOMEDICAL ENGINEERING, MEMBRANE TRANSPORT. *Educ:* Columbia Univ, BS, 69; Stanford Univ, MS, 71, PhD(chem eng), 73. *Prof Exp:* Nat Kidney Found res fel, Dept Med, Univ Calif & Vet Admin Hosp, 73-75, adj asst prof renal physiol, Depts Physiol & Med, Univ Calif, San Francisco, 75-76; asst prof, 76-80, ASSOC PROF CHEM ENG, MASS INST TECHNOL, 76- *Concurrent Pos:* Western Elec Fund Award, Am Soc Eng Educ, 81-82. *Mem:* Am Physiol Soc; Am Inst Chem Engrs; Am Soc Nephrology. *Res:* Membrane transport processes; renal and microcirculatory physiology; pharmacokinetics and toxicokinetics. *Mailing Add:* Dept of Chem Eng Rm 66-544 Mass Inst of Technol Cambridge MA 94121

DEENEY, ANNE O'CONNELL, b Portland, Ore, Oct 26, 26; m 51. MICROBIOLOGY, BIOCHEMISTRY. *Educ:* Marylhurst Col, BS, 48; Ore State Univ, MS, 59, PhD(microbiol), 63. *Prof Exp:* Technologist, French Hosp, San Francisco, Calif, 49 & Emanuel Hosp, Portland, Ore, 50-53; chief technologist, Good Samaritan Hosp, Corvallis, 54-61; asst prof biochem, 64-74, RES ASSOC AGR CHEM, ORE STATE UNIV, 74- *Mem:* AAAS; Am Chem Soc; Am Soc Microbiol. *Res:* Incidence, nutrition, biochemistry and end-products of Micrococcus radiodurans; ribonucleic acid characterization of avian leukosis virus. *Mailing Add:* Dept of Agr Chem Ore State Univ Corvallis OR 97331

DEEP, IRA WASHINGTON, b Dover, Tenn, July 26, 27; m 52; c 5. PLANT PATHOLOGY. *Educ:* Miami Univ, BA, 50; Univ Tenn, MS, 52; Ore State Univ, PhD(plant path), 56. *Prof Exp:* Instr bot, Ore State Univ, 53-57, from asst prof to assoc prof bot & plant path, 57-68, asst dean grad sch, 65-68; PROF PLANT PATH & CHMN DEPT, OHIO STATE UNIV, 68- *Concurrent Pos:* Staff biologist, Comn Undergrad Educ Biol Sci, Washington, DC, 66-67. *Mem:* AAAS; Am Inst Biol Sci; Am Phytopath Soc. *Res:* Plant diseases caused by bacteria. *Mailing Add:* Ohio State Univ Dept Plant Path 2021 Coffey Rd Columbus OH 43210

DEEPAK, ADARSH, b Sialkot, India, Nov 13, 36. ATMOSPHERIC OPTICS, METEOROLOGY. *Educ:* Delhi Univ, BS, 56, MS, 59; Univ Fla, PhD(aerospace eng), 69. *Prof Exp:* Lectr physics, D B & K M Cols, Delhi Univ, 59-63; instr phys sci, Univ Fla, 65-68, res assoc physics, 70-71; Nat Res Coun fel, Marshall Space Flight Ctr, NASA, 72-74; res assoc prof physics & geophys sci, Old Dominion Univ, 74-77; PRES, INST ATMOSPHERIC OPTICS & REMOTE SENSING, HAMPTON, VA, 77-; PRES, SCI & TECHNOL CORP, HAMPTON, VA, 79- *Concurrent Pos:* Consult eng sci, Wayne State Univ, 70-72; mem panel remote sensing & data acquisition, NASA/OAST Technol Workshop, 75; NSF travel grant to visit Indian insts, 76; adj prof physics, Col William & Mary, 79-80; leader, US Deleg, Int Workshop Appln Remote Sensing Rice Prod, India, 81. *Mem:* Optical Soc Am; Am Meteorol Soc; Air Pollution Control Asn; Am Geophys Union; AAAS. *Res:* Remote sensing of atmospheric particulate and gaseous pollutants and motions, using laser doppler, optical scattering and photographic techniques from space, airborne and ground platforms; theory of radiative transfer in scattering atmospheres, fogs and clouds; inversion methods for remotely sensed data. *Mailing Add:* Inst For Atmospheric Optics PO Box P Hampton VA 23666

DEER, GEORGE WENDELL, b Brookhaven, Miss, Nov 2, 33; m; c 2. MATHEMATICS EDUCATION. *Educ:* Univ Southern Miss, BS, 59, MS, 61; Fla State Univ, EdD(math educ), 69. *Prof Exp:* Asst prof math, William Carey Col, 62-65; assoc prof, 69-80, PROF MATH & HEAD DEPT, MISS COL, 80- *Mem:* Math Asn Am. *Res:* Effects of teaching symbolic logic on students' ability to prove theorems in geometry. *Mailing Add:* Dept of Math Miss Col Clinton MS 39058

DEERE, DON U(EL), b Corning, Iowa, Mar 17, 22; m 44; c 2. ENGINEERING GEOLOGY, CIVIL ENGINEERING. *Educ:* Iowa State Col, BS, 43; Univ Colo, MS, 49; Univ Ill, PhD(civil eng), 55. *Prof Exp:* Jr mine engr, Phelps Dodge Corp, Ariz, 43-44; mine engr explor dept, Potash Co of Am, NMex, 44-47; from asst prof to assoc prof civil eng, Col A&M, Univ PR, 46-50, head dept, 50-51; partner, Found Eng Co, PR, 51-55; from assoc prof to prof civil eng & geol, Univ Ill, Urbana-Champaign, 55-76; PROF CIVIL ENG, UNIV FLA, 76- *Concurrent Pos:* Consult found eng & eng geol, Nat Acad Sci. *Mem:* AAAS; Geol Soc Am; Am Geophys Union; Am Soc Civil Engrs. *Res:* Stability of natural slopes; regional subsidence caused by withdrawal of groundwater, petroleum, or mined products. *Mailing Add:* 6834 SW 35th Way Gainesville FL 32601

DEERING, REGINALD ATWELL, b Brooks, Maine, Sept 21, 32; m 56; c 4. MOLECULAR BIOPHYSICS, DNA ENZYMOLOGY. *Educ:* Univ Maine, BS, 54; Yale Univ, PhD(biophys), 58. *Prof Exp:* Asst prof physics, Southern Ill Univ, 57-58; Fulbright res grant biophys, Univ Oslo, 58-59; res assoc, Yale Univ, 59-61; from asst prof to assoc prof, NMex Highlands Univ, 61-64; assoc prof, 64-69, PhD biophysics, 69-81, PROF MOLECULAR & CELL BIOL, PA STATE UNIV, 81- *Concurrent Pos:* Mem ed bd, Biophys J, 71-74; vis prof, Stanford Univ, 74-75. *Mem:* Biophys Soc; Am Soc Biol Chemists; Am Soc Microbiol; Am Soc Photobiol. *Res:* Genetics, enzymology, and regulation of DNA repair; recombinant DNA; effects of radiation and chemical mutagens on DNA of cells; development of dictyostelium discoideum. *Mailing Add:* Molecular & Cell Biol Pa State Univ 201 Althouse Lab University Park PA 16802

DEERING, WILLIAM DOUGLESS, b Burleson, Tex, Dec 18, 33; m 54; c 3. PHYSICS. *Educ:* Tex Christian Univ, BA, 56; NMex State Univ, MS, 60, PhD(physics), 63. *Prof Exp:* Res assoc atmospheric physics, Grad Res Ctr Southwest, 63-65; asst prof physics, 65-69, ASSOC PROF PHYSICS, NTEX STATE UNIV, 69- *Mem:* Am Phys Soc. *Res:* Statistical mechanics; plasma physics. *Mailing Add:* Dept of Physics NTex State Univ Denton TX 76203

DEES, BOWEN CAUSEY, b Batesville, Miss, July 20, 17; m 37; c 1. PHYSICS, SCIENCE ADMINISTRATION. *Educ:* Miss Col, AB, 37; NY Univ, PhD(physics), 42. *Hon Degrees:* DSc, Miss Col, 63; DL, Lehigh Univ, 76; DL, Philadelphia Col Textiles & Sci, 79; DSc, Temple Univ, 81. *Prof Exp:* Asst, NY Univ, 37-42, instr physics, 42-43; prof, Miss Col, 43-44; staff mem, Radar Sch, Mass Inst Technol, 44-45; asst prof physics, Rensselaer Polytech Inst, 45-47; physicist, Sci & Tech Div, Gen Hqs, Supreme Comdr Allied Powers, Tokyo, 47-50; div chief, NSF, 50-51; prog dir fels, NSF, 51-56, from dep asst dir to asst dir, Sci Personnel & Educ, 56-63, assoc dir, Planning, 63-66; vpres, Univ Ariz, 66-68; provost acad affairs, 68-70; PRES, FRANKLIN INST, 70- *Concurrent Pos:* Mem bd trustees, Sci Serv Inc, Washington, DC, 64-, Argonne Univs Asn, 69-70, Hahnemann Med Col & Hosp, 74-78 & Yarway Corp, 78-; mem sci info coun, NSF, 70-74; mem, Sci Manpower Comn, Washington, DC, 76-74; mem, Coun Foreign Rels, 78- *Mem:* Fel AAAS, fel Royal Soc Arts; Am Phys Soc; Am Asn Physics Teachers. *Res:* Electron scattering; design of special electronic timing equipment; scientific education; science policy studies. *Mailing Add:* Off of the Pres Franklin Inst Philadelphia PA 19103

DEES, SUSAN COONS, b Hancock, Mich, May 26, 09; m 35; c 4. PEDIATRICS. *Educ:* Goucher Col, AB, 30; Johns Hopkins Univ, MD, 34; Univ Minn, MS, 38. *Prof Exp:* House officer med serv, Johns Hopkins Hosp, 34-35, asst dispensary physician, 38-39; asst pediatrician, Duke Hosp, 37-48; asst prof pediat, 48-50, assoc prof pediat & allergy, 50-58, prof, 58-79, EMER PROF PEDIAT & ALLERGY, SCH MED, DUKE UNIV, 79-; CONSULT PEDIAT ALLERGY, 79- *Concurrent Pos:* Asst res, Strong Mem Hosp,

35-36; intern, Baltimore City Hosp, 36-37. *Honors & Awards:* B Ratner Award, Am Acad Pediat. *Mem:* Fel AMA; fel Am Col Allergists; Am Pediat Soc; Am Acad Pediat; Am Acad Allergy. *Res:* Allergy. *Mailing Add:* Dept of Pediat Duke Univ Med Ctr Durham NC 27710

DEESE, DAWSON CHARLES, b Raleigh, NC, Dec 7, 32. BIOCHEMISTRY. *Educ:* Agr & Tech Col NC, BS, 52; Tuskegee Inst, MS, 54; Univ Wis, PhD(chem, biochem), 61. *Prof Exp:* Asst gen chem, Agr & Tech Col NC, 52 & Tuskegee Inst, 53; asst biochem, Univ Wis-Madison, 55-60, res assoc biochem & vet sci, 60-64, instr, 64-68, chmn dept, 69-77, assoc prof nutrit sci, 69-80, ASSOC PROF HUMAN BIOL, UNIV WIS-GREEN BAY, 80- *Mem:* AAAS; Am Chem Soc; Am Inst Biol Sci; NY Acad Sci. *Res:* Digestive enzymes in the ruminant animal and ruminal metabolism of plant macromolecules; pectolytic enzymes in fungal disease and disease resistance of plants; auxin metabolism and plant growth substances; nutritional sciences. *Mailing Add:* Col of Human Biol Univ of Wis Green Bay WI 54302

DEETER, CHARLES RAYMOND, b Norcatur, Kans, Dec 30, 30; m 57; c 2. MATHEMATICAL ANALYSIS. *Educ:* Ft Hays Kans State Col, BS, 52, MS, 56; Univ Kans, PhD(discrete harmonic kernels), 63. *Prof Exp:* From asst prof to assoc prof, 60-70, PROF MATH, TEX CHRISTIAN UNIV, 70- *Mem:* Math Asn Am; Am Math Soc; Soc Indust & Appl Math; Asn Comput Mach. *Res:* Discrete analytic functions; error in energy models. *Mailing Add:* Dept of Math Tex Christian Univ Ft Worth TX 76129

DEETS, GARY LEE, b Sunbury, Pa, Feb 28, 43; m 61; c 3. POLYMER CHEMISTRY. *Educ:* Bloomsburgh State Col, BS, 65; Univ Pittsburgh, PhD(org chem), 69. *Prof Exp:* Sr res chemist, 69-77, RES SPECIALIST, SPRINGFIELD LAB, MONSANTO CO, 77- *Mem:* Am Chem Soc. *Res:* Mechanistic studies in pyridine nitrogen-oxide chemistry; fundamental and exploratory studies of the flame retardancy of styrene based polymeric systems. *Mailing Add:* Springfield Lab 730 Worcester St Indian Orchard MA 01151

DEEVER, DAVID LIVINGSTONE, b Dayton, Ohio, Aug 31, 39; m 61; c 2. PURE MATHEMATICS. *Educ:* Otterbein Col, BA & BS, 61; Ohio State Univ, PhD(math), 66. *Prof Exp:* Asst prof math, Westmar Col, 66-71; ASSOC PROF MATH & CHMN DEPT, OTTERBEIN COL, 71- *Mem:* Math Asn Am; Am Math Soc. *Res:* Set theory and transfinite arithmetic. *Mailing Add:* Dept of Math Otterbein Col Westerville OH 43081

DEEVER, WILLIAM RAY, b Parkersburg, WVa, Sept 30, 33; m 64; c 2. INORGANIC CHEMISTRY, POLLUTION CHEMISTRY. *Educ:* Marietta Col, BS, 61; Univ Wash, PhD(boron chem), 68. *Prof Exp:* Res chemist, Richmond Res Labs, 68-76, RES CHEMIST, PORT ARTHUR RES LABS, TEXACO, INC, 76- *Concurrent Pos:* Lectr, Eve Sch, Va Commonwealth Univ, 68-69. *Res:* Boron hydride compounds; complex compounds as homogenous catalysis; solid waste disposal; physical chemical treatment of wastewater. *Mailing Add:* Texaco Inc Box 1608 Port Arthur TX 77640

DEEVEY, EDWARD SMITH, JR, b Albany, NY, Dec 3, 14; m 38; c 3. BIOLOGY. *Educ:* Yale Univ, BA, 34, PhD(zool), 38. *Prof Exp:* Sterling fel biol, Yale Univ, 38-39; instr, Rice Inst, 39-43; res assoc, Oceanog Inst Woods Hole, 43-46; from asst prof to prof biol, Yale Univ, 46-68, dir geochronomet lab, 51-62; Killam res prof, Dalhousie Univ, 68-71; GRAD RES PROF, FLA STATE MUS, UNIV FLA, 71- *Concurrent Pos:* Ed, J Ecol Soc Am, 50-58; Guggenheim fel, 53-54; Fulbright res award, Denmark, 53-54; ed, Radiocarbon, 58-71; NSF sr fel, Univ NZ, 64-65; prog dir environ biol, NSF, 67-68; mem, Fish Res Bd Can, 69-71; mem, Can Comn Int Biol Prog, 69-71. *Mem:* Nat Acad Sci; Am Soc Limnol & Oceanog (vpres, 50, pres, 74-75); Ecol Soc Am (pres, 69-70); Am Anthrop Asn; fel Geol Soc Am. *Res:* Limnology; ecology; general and Pleistocene ecology; tropical ecology; historical ecology of American tropics; cultural ecology; biogeochemistry. *Mailing Add:* Fla State Mus Univ of Fla Gainesville FL 32611

DEEVEY, GEORGIANA BAXTER, b Pine Orchard, Conn, Feb 24, 14; m 38; c 3. BIOLOGICAL OCEANOGRAPHY. *Educ:* Radcliffe Col, AB, 34; Yale Univ, PhD(zool), 39. *Prof Exp:* Technician, Oceanog Inst, Woods Hole, 45-46; res asst, Bingham Oceanog Lab, Yale Univ, 47-60, res assoc, 60-67; res assoc, Bermuda Biol Sta, 67-71; res assoc, Inst Oceanog, Dalhousie Univ, 68-71; ADJ CUR, FLA STATE MUS, UNIV FLA, 71- *Concurrent Pos:* Mem corp, Bermuda Biol Sta. *Mem:* Marine Biol Asn UK; Crustacean Soc. *Res:* Marine and freshwater zooplankton; invertebrate zoology and ecology; bathypelagic marine copepods and planktonic ostracods. *Mailing Add:* Fla State Mus Univ of Fla Gainesville FL 32611

DEFACIO, W BRIAN, b Palestine, Tex, Dec 14, 36; m 64; c 2. THEORETICAL PHYSICS. *Educ:* Tex A&M Univ, BS, 63, MS, 65, PhD(theoret physics), 67. *Prof Exp:* Asst prof, 67-71, ASSOC PROF PHYSICS, UNIV MO-COLUMBIA, 71- *Concurrent Pos:* Vis assoc prof physics, Iowa State Univ, 74-75; vis assoc prof math & Ames Lab, 79-81; vis scientist, Inst Theoret Physics, Goteborg, Sweden, 81; assoc ed, J Math Physics, 78-81. *Mem:* Sigma Xi; Am Phys Soc; Am Math Soc; Am Asn Univ Profs; Am Asn Physics Teachers. *Res:* mathematical physics. *Mailing Add:* Dept of Physics Univ of Mo Columbia MO 65211

DEFANTI, DAVID R, b Wakefield, RI, Nov 12, 32; m 58; c 2. PHARMACOLOGY. *Educ:* Colgate Univ, AB, 55; Univ RI, MS, 57, PhD(pharmacol), 62. *Prof Exp:* Asst prof, 61-73, PROF PHARMACOL, UNIV RI, 73-, DIR, CRIME LAB, 80- *Concurrent Pos:* Co-prin investr, NIH Grant, 62-64; consult, RI State Labs, Sci Criminal Invest, 63-70, asst dir, 70-73, dir, 73-; prin investr, RI Heart Asn Grant, 64-; prin investr, Law Enforcement Assistance Admin Grant, 70-; dir breath tests alcohol training, State of RI, 70- *Mem:* AAAS; Am Acad Forensic Sci; Int Asn Identification; Int Narcotic Enforcement Officers Asn. *Res:* Cardiovascular pharmacology; medico-legal toxicology. *Mailing Add:* Univ of RI Col of Pharm Kingston RI 02881

DE FAZIO, SALLY RUTH, immunology, see previous edition

DEFELICE, EUGENE ANTHONY, b Beacon, NY, Dec 24, 27; m 57; c 3. INTERNAL MEDICINE. *Educ:* Columbia Univ, BS, 51; Boston Univ, MS, 54, MD, 56. *Prof Exp:* Lectr pharmacol, Sch Med, Boston Univ, 54-57; from assoc prof to prof, New Eng Col Pharm, 56-58; pvt pract internal med, North Miami, Fla, 58-61; asst dir clin res, Warner-Lambert Res Inst, NJ, 61-64; dir clin pharmacol, Bristol Labs, NY, 64-66; dir clin res, Norwich Hosp, Conn, 66-67; dir clin pharmacol, Sandoz Pharmaceut, 67-68, exec dir clin res, 69-70, dir sci affairs & commercial develop, Sandoz-Wander, Inc, 70-73, dir corp-sci affairs, Sandoz Inc, 74, vpres corp-sci develop, 74-77, V PRES INT MED LIAISON, SANDOZ INC, 78-; CLIN ASSOC PROF MED, RUTGERS MED SCH, 77-; CLIN PROF ANESTHESIOL, SCH MED, UNIV CALIF, LOS ANGELES, 78- *Concurrent Pos:* Res assoc anesthesiol, Boston City Hosp, 57; intern, Newton-Wellesley Hosp, 57-58; consult internal med, Morristown, NJ, 61-; consult, Strasenburgh Labs, NY, 66-67; mem bd dirs, Delmark Co, Minneapolis, 73-77 & Vital Assists, Inc, Salt Lake City, 74-77. *Mem:* Am Soc Clin Pharmacol & Therapeut; Asn Advan Med Instrumentation; fel Acad Psychosom Med; fel Am Geriat Soc; fel NY Acad Sci. *Res:* Clinical pharmacology; geriatrics; psychosomatic medicine. *Mailing Add:* 11 Corn Hill Dr Morristown NJ 07960

DE FELICE, LOUIS JOHN, b Morristown, NJ, Aug 17, 40; m 62; c 2. BIOPHYSICS, ELECTROPHYSIOLOGY. *Educ:* Fla State Univ, BS, 62, MS, 64; Univ Calgary, PhD(physics), 67. *Prof Exp:* Med Res Coun Can fels, McGill Univ, 67-69; Med Res Coun Can fel, State Univ Leiden, 69-70, asst prof physiol, 70-71; from asst prof to assoc prof, 71-78, PROF ANAT, EMORY UNIV, 78- *Concurrent Pos:* Asst prof elec eng, Ga Inst Technol, 71-74, assoc prof, 74-; Fulbright-Hayes fel, 78. *Mem:* Biophys Soc; Hist of Sci Soc; Am Physiol Soc. *Res:* Biophysics of biological and synthetic membranes; heart cell membranes and intercellular communication; noise, impendance and single channnel studies in excitable membranes. *Mailing Add:* Dept of Anat Emory Univ Sch of Med Atlanta GA 30322

DEFENBAUGH, RICHARD EUGENE, b Kansas City, Mo, Sept 6, 46; m 78; c 2. MARINE ECOLOGY, INVERTEBRATE ZOOLOGY. *Educ:* Kans State Teachers Col, BA, 67; Tex A&M Univ, MS, 70, PhD(zool), 76. *Prof Exp:* Teaching asst, Tex A&M Univ, 67-74, res asst, 74, lectr biol, 74-75; staff biol oceanogr, 75-81, CHIEF ENVIRON STUDIES, BUR LAND MGT, US DEPT INTERIOR, 81- *Mem:* AAAS. *Res:* General ecology of marine organisms, with emphasis on marine benthic invertebrates; special taxonomic interest in hydroids. *Mailing Add:* Bur Land Mgt 500 Camp St Suite 841 New Orleans LA 70130

DEFENDI, VITTORIO, b Treviglio, Italy, Nov 16, 28; m 55; c 3. PATHOLOGY. *Educ:* Univ Pavia, MD, 51. *Prof Exp:* Instr path dept, Univ Pavia, 51-52; pathologist virus sect, Lederle Labs, NY, 56-58; assoc path, Med Sch, Univ Pa, 58-64, assoc prof, 64-68, Wistar prof, 68-74; PROF PATH & CHMN DEPT, SCH MED, NY UNIV, 74- *Concurrent Pos:* Brit coun scholar, Post-grad Med Sch, Univ London, 52-53; Fulbright fel, Med Sch, Univ Vt, 53-54; res fel, Detroit Inst Cancer Res, 54-56; Leukemia Soc scholar, 62-66; fac res award, Am Cancer Soc, 68-72; assoc mem, Wistar Inst, 58-64, mem staff, 64-74; Am Cancer Soc res prof, 73- *Mem:* Am Soc Cell Biol; Am Soc Exp Path; Histochem Soc; Am Asn Immunol; Am Asn Cancer Res. *Res:* Viral oncology; tumor biology; mechanism of immunological defense. *Mailing Add:* Dept of Path NY Univ Sch of Med New York NY 10016

DEFEO, JOHN JOSEPH, b Southington, Conn, Mar 14, 22; m 55; c 8. PHARMACOLOGY. *Educ:* Univ Conn, BS, 51; Purdue Univ, MS, 53, PhD(pharmacol), 54. *Prof Exp:* From instr to asst prof pharmacol, Univ Pittsburgh, 54-57; assoc prof, 57-64, PROF PHARMACOL, COL PHARM, UNIV RI, 64-, CHMN, DEPT PHARMACOL & TOXICOL, 80- *Mem:* AAAS; Am Soc Pharmacol; Fedn Am Soc Exp Biol; NY Acad Sci. *Res:* Cardio-vascular area. *Mailing Add:* Dept Pharmacol & Toxicol Univ of RI Col of Pharm Kingston RI 02881

DE FEO, VINCENT JOSEPH, b New York, NY, Oct 1, 25; div; c 2. ENDOCRINOLOGY, REPRODUCTIVE BIOLOGY. *Educ:* Juniata Col, BS, 49; Rutgers Univ, MS, 51; Ohio State Univ, PhD(physiol), 54. *Prof Exp:* Asst zool, Rutgers Univ, 50; asst physiol, Ohio State Univ, 50-52, asst prof, 54-55; NIH fel embryol, Carnegie Inst, Washington, DC, 55-57; asst prof anat, Col Med, Univ Ill, 57-63; assoc prof anat & obstet & gynec, Sch Med, Vanderbilt Univ, 63-66; assoc prof, 66-68, chmn dept, 69-73, PROF ANAT & REPRODUCTIVE BIOL, UNIV HAWAII, MANOA, 68- *Mem:* AAAS; Am Asn Anat; Endocrine Soc; Soc Develop Biol; Soc Study Reproduction. *Res:* Anatomy and physiology of reproduction; ovum-uterine relationship; neuroendocrinology; human sexuality. *Mailing Add:* Dept Anat & Reprod Biol Univ of Hawaii Sch of Med Honolulu HI 96822

DEFERRARI, HARRY AUSTIN, b Stoneham, Mass, May 31, 37; m 62; c 3. UNDERWATER ACOUSTICS. *Educ:* Cath Univ Am, BME, 59, PhD(acoust), 66; Mass Inst Technol, MS, 62. *Prof Exp:* Res scientist vibrations anal, David Taylor Model Basin, 61-62; res scientist acoust, Chesapeake Instrument Corp, 65-67; PROF OCEAN ENG, ROSENSTIEL SCH MARINE & ATMOSPHERIC SCI, UNIV MIAMI, 67- *Mem:* Acoust Soc Am. *Res:* Ocean acoustics, the study of acoustical transmission through the ocean; the relationships between acoustic and oceanographic fluctuations. *Mailing Add:* Rosenstiel Sch Marine & Atmos Sci 4600 Rickenbacker Causeway Miami FL 33156

DEFESCHE, CHARLES LEON, b Maastricht, Neth, June 4, 48; m 71; c 2. CLINICAL RESEARCH. *Educ:* Cath Univ Louvain, BS, 69, MD, 73. *Prof Exp:* Private physician, 73-78; med dir, Boots Co, Holland & Belgium, 78-80; DIR MED AFFAIRS, BOOTS PHARMACEUT, 81-; ASST PROF, CLIN PHARMACEUT & THER, LA STATE UNIV MED CTR, 81- *Res:* Clinical research of newly developed pharmaceutical products including clinical pharmacology; anti-inflammatory and analgetic compounds; neuropsychopharmacology; clinical research in cardiovascular medicine. *Mailing Add:* 6540 Line Avenue Shreveport LA 77106

DEFFEYES, KENNETH STOVER, b Oklahoma City, Okla, Dec 26, 31; m 62; c 1. OCEANOGRAPHY. *Educ:* Colo Sch Mines, GeolE, 53; Princeton, MS, 56, PhD(geol), 59. *Prof Exp:* Geologist, Shell Develop Co, Tex, 58-63; asst prof, Univ Minn, 63-64; assoc prof oceanog, Ore State Univ, 65-67; assoc prof geol & geophys sci, 67-74, PROF GEOL & GEOPHYS SCI, PRINCETON UNIV, 74- *Mem:* Mineral Soc Am; Am Asn Petrol Geologists. *Res:* Chemical oceanography; sedimentation. *Mailing Add:* Dept of Geol Princeton Univ Princeton NJ 08544

DE FIEBRE, CONRAD WILLIAM, b Brooklyn, NY, Jan 19, 24; m 46; c 6. MICROBIOLOGY, BIOCHEMISTRY. *Educ:* Rensselaer Polytech Inst, BS, 49; Univ Wis, MS, 50, PhD(bact), 52. *Prof Exp:* Asst bact, Univ Wis, 49-52; res microbiologist, E I du Pont de Nemours & Co, Inc, 52-61; res dir, Wilson Labs Div, Wilson Pharmaceutical & Chem Corp, 61-67, vpres res, 67-69; dir, 69-71, VPRES RES & DEVELOP, ROSS LABS DIV, ABBOTT LABS, 71- *Concurrent Pos:* Chmn bd, Infant Formula Coun, 76-77 & 81- *Mem:* Am Soc Microbiol; Am Chem Soc; fel Am Inst Chemists. *Res:* Bacteriology; fermentation; enzymes; natural products; pharmaceutical development. *Mailing Add:* Res & Develop Ross Labs Div Abbott Labs 625 Cleveland Ave Columbus OH 43216

DEFIGIO, DANIEL A, b Republic, Pa, June 4, 39; m 66; c 2. MYCOLOGY. *Educ:* California State Col, Pa, 61; WVa Univ, MA, 64; Ill State Univ, PhD(mycol), 70. *Prof Exp:* High sch teacher, Pa, 61-64; instr biol, Washington & Jefferson Col, 64-66; teaching asst, Ill State Univ, 66-70; ASSOC PROF BIOL, EDINBORO STATE COL, 70- *Mem:* AAAS; Am Inst Biol Sci; Bot Soc Am. *Res:* Taxonomic analysis of the genus Hymenochaete. *Mailing Add:* Dept of Biol Edinboro State Col Edinboro PA 16444

DE FILIPPI, R(ICHARD) P(AUL), b New York, NY, Mar 26, 36; m 58; c 1. CHEMICAL ENGINEERING. *Educ:* Amherst Col, AB, 57; Mass Inst Technol, SM, 59, ScD(chem eng), 62. *Prof Exp:* Org chemist, Am Cyanamid Co, 56, chem engr, 57-58; chem engr, Arthur D Little Co, Inc, 59; res engr hydrogen processing petrol refining, Calif Res Corp, 62-65; supvr membrane separations sect, Abcor, Inc, 65-66, prog mgr, 66-68, prog dir, 68-70, vpres & gen mgr res & develop div, 70-74; mem spec staff, 74-77, unit mgr, 77-80, PRES, CRITICAL FLUID SYSTS, INC, ARTHUR D LITTLE, 80- *Concurrent Pos:* Mem bd dirs, Abcor, Inc, 72-73; chmn bd dirs, Walden Res Corp, 72-73; vis fel, Imp Col Sci & Technol, London, 73-74; chmn, Cambridge Health Policy Bd, 77-78, mem, 78- *Mem:* AAAS; Am Inst Chem Engrs; Am Soc Artificial Internal Organs; NY Acad Sci; Am Chem Soc. *Res:* Biomedical engineering; membrane technology; mass transfer. *Mailing Add:* Arthur D Little Inc Acorn Park Cambridge MA 02140

DEFILIPPS, ROBERT ANTHONY, b Chicago, Ill, Mar 4, 39. PLANT TAXONOMY. *Educ:* Univ Ill, BS, 60; Southern Ill Univ, MS, 62, PhD(bot), 68. *Prof Exp:* Collabr, Flora Dominica Proj, Smithsonian Inst, 68-69; res assoc, Flora Europaea Proj, Univ Reading, Eng, 69-74; COORDR, ENDANGERED FLORA PROJ, SMITHSONIAN INST, 74- *Mem:* Linnean Soc London; Int Asn Plant Taxon. *Res:* Endangered and threatened plant species of the world. *Mailing Add:* Dept Bot Nat Mus Natural Hist Smithsonian Inst Washington DC 20560

DEFOLIART, GENE RAY, b Stillwater, Okla, June 23, 25; m 50; c 3. ENTOMOLOGY. *Educ:* Okla State Univ, BS, 48; Cornell Univ, PhD(entom), 51. *Prof Exp:* From asst prof to assoc prof entom, Univ Wyo, 51-59; assoc prof, 59-66, chmn dept, 68-76, PROF ENTOM, RUSSELL LABS, UNIV WIS-MADISON, 66- *Mem:* Entom Soc Am; Am Mosquito Control Asn; Am Soc Trop Med & Hyg; AAAS. *Res:* Medical and veterinary entomology. *Mailing Add:* Dept of Entom 545 Russell Labs 1630 Linden Dr Univ of Wis Madison WI 53706

DEFORD, DONALD DALE, b Alton, Kans, Dec 28, 18; m 42; c 2. ANALYTICAL CHEMISTRY. *Educ:* Univ Kans, AB, 40, PhD(chem), 48. *Prof Exp:* From instr to assoc prof chem, 48-60, chmn dept, 62-69, asst to provost, 69-70, assoc dean faculties, 70-71, PROF CHEM, NORTHWESTERN UNIV, 60-, ASST VPRES RES, 71- *Mem:* AAAS; Instrument Soc Am; Am Chem Soc. *Res:* Analytical instrumentation; gas chromatography. *Mailing Add:* Dept of Chem Northwestern Univ Evanston IL 60201

DEFORD, JOHN W, b Lincoln, Nebr, Mar 12, 36; m 58; c 3. SOLID STATE PHYSICS. *Educ:* Carleton Col, BA, 57; Univ Ill, MS, 59, PhD(physics), 62. *Prof Exp:* Asst prof physics, 62-67, ASSOC PROF PHYSICS, UNIV UTAH, 67- *Mem:* Am Phys Soc. *Res:* Radiation damage in metals. *Mailing Add:* Dept of Physics Univ of Utah Salt Lake City UT 84112

DEFOREST, ADAMADIA, b Harrisburg, Pa, July 16, 33; m 57. VIROLOGY. *Educ:* Hood Col, AB, 55; Wash State Univ, MS, 57; Temple Univ, PhD, 68; Am Bd Med Microbiol, dipl. *Prof Exp:* Asst, Wash State Univ, 55-57, sr lab technician, Dept Vet Microbiol, 57-60; res asst & instr, 61-70, ASSOC PROF MICROBIOL, SCH MED, TEMPLE UNIV, 70-; ASSOC PROF PEDIAT IN VIROL, ST CHRISTOPHER'S HOSP FOR CHILDREN, 70- *Concurrent Pos:* Instr pediat virol, St Christopher's Hosp for Children, 67-70. *Mem:* Am Soc Microbiol; Tissue Cult Asn; AAAS; Am Fedn Clin Res; Am Pub Health Asn. *Res:* Protective effects of breast milk against virus infections; bacterial-viral interrelationships in cystic fibrosis; role of cytomegalovirus infections in chronic interstitial pneumonitis of infancy; antibody responses of infants and children to live attenuated virusvaccines; immune status in virus infections. *Mailing Add:* St Christopher's Hosp Children 2600 N Lawrence St Philadelphia PA 19133

DEFOREST, ELBERT M, b Natoma, Kans, July 17, 17; m 42; c 2. PETROLEUM ENGINEERING. *Educ:* Univ Tulsa, BS, 40. *Prof Exp:* Petrol engr, Gulf Oil Corp, 40-41; chemist, E I du Pont de Nemours & Co, 41-42, develop process engr, 42-46; sr process engr, Spencer Chem Co, 46-47, mgr process eng, 47-49; sr proj engr, Pan Am Petrol Corp, Standard Oil Co, Ind, 49-50, supt chem mfg, 50-52; mgr new proj, Frontier Chem Co Div, 52-59,

mgr res & develop, 59-67, V PRES CHEM DIV RES & DEVELOP, VULCAN MAT CO, KANS, 67-, V PRES METALLICS DIV, OHIO, 67- *Mem:* AAAS; Am Inst Chem Engrs; Am Chem Soc; Am Inst Mining, Metall & Petrol Engrs; Electrochem Soc. *Res:* Distillation technology and fluid mechanics; hydrocarbon chlorination technology; chemical plant design. *Mailing Add:* Res & Develop Chems Divs Box 12283 Wichita KS 67277

DEFOREST, PETER RUPERT, b Los Angeles, Calif, Aug 24, 41; m 66; c 2. FORENSIC SCIENCE, CRIMINALISTICS. *Educ:* Univ Calif, Berkeley, BS, 64, DCrim, 69. *Prof Exp:* Asst prof, 69-74, assoc prof criminalistics, 74-80, PROF CRIMINALISTICS, JOHN JAY COL, CITY COL NEW YORK, 80- *Concurrent Pos:* Consult sci interpreter. *Mem:* Am Acad Forensic Sci; Am Chem Soc; NY Acad Sci; AAAS. *Res:* Instrumental methods for the chemical individualization of physical evidence; tagged antibody methods for simultaneous direction of several antigens in dried bloodstains. *Mailing Add:* Dept Sci 445 W 59th St New York NY 10019

DE FOREST, RALPH EDWIN, b Detroit, Mich, Mar 19, 19; m 50; c 3. MEDICINE. *Educ:* Wayne State Univ, BS, 41, MD, 43; Univ Minn, MS, 51. *Prof Exp:* Fel orthop surg, Mayo Found, 44-46, fel phys med & rehab, 48-51; dir dep med physics & rehab, 50-66, dir postgrad progs, 66-70, dir dept med instrumentation, 70-72, asst dir dept grad med educ, 72-77, DIR DEPT CONTINUING MED EVAL, AMA, 77- *Concurrent Pos:* Chmn, President's Task Force on Physically Handicapped, 69-70; secy, Liaison Comt Continuing Med Educ, 77- *Mem:* Am Acad Phys Med & Rehab; Sigma Xi; Am Cong Rehab Med. *Res:* Internal derangements of the knee; effects of physical agents on lymph flow; effects of ultrasound on bone. *Mailing Add:* 535 N Dearborn Chicago IL 60610

DEFOTIS, GARY CONSTANTINE, b Chicago, Ill, June 30, 47. PHYSICAL CHEMISTRY. *Educ:* Univ Ill, BSc, 68; Univ Chicago, PhD(phys chem), 77. *Prof Exp:* Res asst chem, Argonne Nat Lab, 68 & Univ Chicago, 69-76; res assoc, Univ Ill, 77-78; asst prof chem, Mich State Univ, 78-80; ASST PROF CHEM, COL WILLIAM & MARY, 80- *Mem:* Am Chem Soc; Am Phys Soc. *Res:* Solid state chemistry; paramagnetism, ferromagnetism and antiferromagnetism; crystallographic phase transformations; thermodynamic properties at low temperatures. *Mailing Add:* Dept of Chem Col William & Mary Williamsburg VA 23185

DEFOUW, DAVID O, b Grand Rapids, Mich, June 3, 45; m 67; c 1. ANATOMY, PHYSIOLOGY. *Educ:* Hope Col, BA, 67; Mich State Univ, MS, 70, PhD(anat), 72. *Prof Exp:* From instr to asst prof, 72-78, ASSOC PROF ANAT, NJ MED SCH, NEWARK, 78- *Mem:* Microcirc Soc; Am Asn Anatomists. *Res:* Pulmonary ultrastructure and function; neurogenic control of the microcirculation, especially the pulmonary circulation. *Mailing Add:* Dept of Anat NJ Med Sch Newark NJ 07103

DEFRANCE, JON FREDRIC, b Battle Creek, Mich, Mar 17, 43; m 73; c 2. NEUROPHYSIOLOGY, NEUROPHARMACOLOGY. *Educ:* Mich State Univ, BS, 67; Wayne State Univ, PhD(neurophysiol), 73. *Prof Exp:* From instr to asst prof anat, Wayne State Univ, 73-76; ASSOC PROF NEUROBIOL, MED SCH, UNIV TEX, 76-, ASSOC PROF ANAT, 80- *Mem:* Soc Neurosci. *Res:* Electrophysiology of limbic system. *Mailing Add:* Univ of Tex Health Sci Ctr 6400 W Cullen Houston TX 77030

DE FRANCE, JOSEPH J, b New York, NY, Aug 22, 09; m 35; c 2. AUDIO COMMUNICATIONS. *Educ:* City Col New York, BS, 30, EE, 31. *Prof Exp:* Lab engr, City Col New York, 31-39; instr high sch, NY, 39-43; prof radio, electronics, Signal Corps Training Sch, 42-43; chief engr, Int Div, Trans World Airline, 46-47; dept head electronic technol, 47-64, prof electronics, 64-74, EMER PROF ELECTRONICS, NEW YORK CITY COMMUNITY COL, 74- *Concurrent Pos:* Consult, Cleveland Inst Electronics, Ohio, 62-; mem adv bd, NY Inst Technol, 64- *Mem:* Am Soc Eng Educ; Am Tech Educ Asn; Inst Elec & Electronics Engrs. *Res:* Electronics communications; technical textbooks and pamphlets. *Mailing Add:* 143 Jackson St Garden City NY 11530

DE FRANCESCO, LAURA, b Arlington, Mass, Sept 22, 48. CYTOPLASMIC INHERITANCE, CELLULAR BIODYNAMICS. *Educ:* Tufts Univ, BS, 70; Univ Calif, San Diego, PhD(biol), 75. *Prof Exp:* NIH fel, Calif Inst Technol, 76-77, Am Cancer Soc fel, 77-79; ASST RES SCIENTIST, BIOL DIV, CITY HOPE RES INST, 80- *Mem:* Am Soc Cell Biol. *Res:* Mechanisms governing the expression and inheritance of the mitochondrial genome of animal cells, with particular emphasis on recombination, and the role it may play in maintaining homogeny of this highly repeated genome. *Mailing Add:* City Hope Res Inst 1450 E Duarte Rd Duarte CA 91001

DEFRANCO, RONALD JAMES, b Baltimore, Md, Feb 18, 43; m 74. APPLIED MATHEMATICS. *Educ:* Univ Dubuque, BS, 65; Univ Ariz, MS, 68, PhD(math), 73. *Prof Exp:* Instr math, Univ Ariz, 73-76; asst prof math, Univ Portland, 76-78; programmer & analyst, 78-80, TECH SPECIALIST, CUBIC CORP, 80- *Mem:* Am Math Soc; Math Asn Am. *Res:* Numerical solutions for multiple Volterra integral equations. *Mailing Add:* 8024 Linda Vista Rd Apt 2D San Diego CA 92111

DE FREITAS, ANTHONY S, biochemistry, physiology, see previous edition

DE FREMERY, DONALD, biochemistry, see previous edition

DEFRIES, JOHN CLARENCE, b Delrey, Ill, Nov 26, 34; m 56; c 2. BEHAVIORAL GENETICS. *Educ:* Univ Ill, BS, 56, MS, 58, PhD(genetics), 61. *Prof Exp:* Asst prof genetics in dairy sci, Univ Ill, 61-63; USPHS res fel genetics, Univ Calif, Berkeley, 63-64; from asst prof to assoc prof genetics in dairy sci, Univ Ill, Urbana, 64-67; assoc prof, 67-70, PROF BEHAV GENETICS, UNIV COLO, BOULDER, 70-, PROF PSYCHOL, 76-, DIR, INST BEHAV GENETICS, 80- *Concurrent Pos:* Co-founder & ed, Behavior Genetics, 70-78; affil grad fac mem, Dept Genetics, Univ Hawaii, 74- *Mem:*

AAAS; Soc Study Social Biol; Am Soc Naturalists; Behav Genetics Asn (secy, 74-77, pres-elect, 81-82). *Res:* Genetics of specific cognitive abilities and reading disability. *Mailing Add:* Inst Behav Genetics Univ Colo Boulder CO 80309

DEGANI, MEIR HERSHTENKORN, b Warsaw, Poland, Jan 4, 09; nat 44; m 48; c 2. METEOROLOGY, PHYSICS. *Educ:* Mass Inst Technol, BS, 32, MS, 41, ScD(phys meteorol), 42. *Prof Exp:* Asst meteorol, Mass Inst Technol, 41; from instr to asst prof geophys, Pa State Col, 42-43; chief instr meteorol, Am Export Airlines, Inc, 43-44; asst prof physics, 46-47, chmn sci dept, 47-73, PROF PHYSICS, STATE UNIV NY MARITIME COL, 73- *Mem:* AAAS; Am Phys Soc; Am Meteorol Soc; Am Geophys Union; Am Asn Physics Teachers. *Res:* Long wave radiation emitted by atmosphere; atmospheric heat balance. *Mailing Add:* Dept of Sci State Univ NY Maritime Col New York NY 10465

DEGASPARIS, AURELIO ALFONSO A, geophysics, meteoritics, see previous edition

DEGEETER, MELVIN JOSEPH, b Bancroft, Iowa, Feb 11, 40; m 64; c 3. ANIMAL NUTRITION. *Educ:* Iowa State Univ, BS, 66, MS, 68; Univ Ky, PhD(animal sci), 70. *Prof Exp:* staff scientist nutrit & health, Upjohn Co, 70-81; SR RES GROUP LEADER, MONSANTO CO, 81- *Mem:* Am Soc Animal Sci; Am Poultry Sci Asn; AAAS; Am Dairy Sci Asn. *Res:* Disease control in animals; disease and nutrition interrelationship; increased weight gain or improved feed utilization in animals as a result of improved health or administration of exogenous materials. *Mailing Add:* Monsanto Co 800 N Lindbergh Blvd St Louis MO 63166

DEGEISO, RICHARD CHARLES, analytical chemistry, see previous edition

DEGEN, VLADIMIR, b Prague, Czech, Apr 24, 31; Can citizen; m 61; c 4. AERONOMY, ASTROPHYSICS. *Educ:* Univ Toronto, BA, 58, MA, 60; Univ Western Ont, PhD(physics), 66. *Prof Exp:* NASA fel, Lab Atmospheric & Space Physics, Univ Colo, Boulder, 67-70; asst prof, 70-74, ASSOC PROF PHYSICS, UNIV ALASKA, FAIRBANKS, 74- *Mem:* Am Geophys Union. *Res:* Spectroscopy of earth's auroral and airglow emissions. *Mailing Add:* Geophys Inst Univ of Alaska Fairbanks AK 99701

DEGENFORD, JAMES EDWARD, b Bloomington, Ill, June 11, 38; m 59; c 6. ELECTRICAL ENGINEERING. *Educ:* Univ Ill, BS, 60, MS, 61, PhD(elec eng), 64. *Prof Exp:* Res asst elec eng, Univ Ill, Urbana-Champaign, 60-64, res assoc, 64-65; sr engr, appl physics sect, 65-69, fel engr, microwave physics group, 69-78, ADV ENGR, WESTINGHOUSE ELEC CORP, 78- *Mem:* Inst Elec & Electronics Engrs; Microwave Theory & Techniques Soc (secy-treas, 75). *Res:* Investigation of transmission systems and detection techniques suitable for use at submillimeter wavelengths; microwave integrated circuits and monolithic microwave circuits. *Mailing Add:* Westinghouse Elec Corp PO Box 1521 MS 3717 Baltimore MD 21203

DEGENHARDT, KEITH JACOB, b Goodsoil, Sask, Jan 18, 50; m 73; c 1. PLANT PATHOLOGY. *Educ:* Univ Alta, BS, 71, MS 73; Univ Sask, PhD(plant path), 78. *Prof Exp:* Lectr biol sci, Kelsey Inst Appl Arts & Sci, 77-78; RES SCIENTIST CEREAL PATH, RES BR, AGR CAN, 78- *Mem:* Can Phytopath Soc; Am Phytopath Soc. *Res:* The biology, epidemiology, and control of the Tilletia species (bunt) and Urocystis species (stem smut) on wheat and rye; biology and control of other cereal and oil seed deseases. *Mailing Add:* Res Sta Agr Can Lethbridge Can

DEGENHARDT, WILLIAM GEORGE, b Queens Co, NY, Apr 16, 26; m 58. VERTEBRATE ZOOLOGY. *Educ:* Syracuse Univ, AB, 50; Northeastern Univ, MS, 53; Tex A&M Univ, PhD(zool), 60. *Prof Exp:* Teaching fel, Northeastern Univ, 51-53; grad asst, Tex A&M Univ, 53-54, instr, 55-60; from asst prof to assoc prof, 60-75, PROF BIOL, UNIV NMEX, 75- CUR REPTILES & AMPHIBIANS, MUS SOUTHWESTERN BIOL, 61- *Concurrent Pos:* Collabr, Nat Park Serv, 55-59, 64-, ranger-naturalist, 60. *Mem:* Am Soc Naturalists; Am Soc Ichthyologists & Herpetologists; Ecol Soc Am. *Res:* Herpetology; vertebrate ecology. *Mailing Add:* Dept Biol Univ NMex Albuquerque NM 87131

DEGENKOLB, HENRY JOHN, b Peoria, Ill, July 13, 13; m 39; c 5. STRUCTURAL ENGINEERING. *Educ:* Univ Calif, Berkeley, BSCE, 36. *Prof Exp:* With var eng firms, 36-46; chief engr & partner, John J Gould & H J Degenkolb, Engrs, San Francisco, 46-61, CHMN BD, H J DEGENKOLB & ASSOCS ENGRS, 61- *Concurrent Pos:* Lectr, Univ Calif Exten, 47-58; mem, Presidential Task Force Earthquake Hazard Reduction, 70-71, Calif Bldg Standards Comn, 71- & Calif Seismic Safety Comn, 75-77; mem eng criteria rev bd, Bay Conserv & Develop Comn, 70-76. *Honors & Awards:* Moiseiff Award, Am Soc Civil Engrs, 53, Ernest E Howard Award, 67. *Mem:* Nat Acad Eng; hon mem Am Soc Civil Engrs; Earthquake Eng Res Inst (pres, 74-78); Am Concrete Inst; Am Consult Engrs Coun. *Mailing Add:* H J Degenkolb & Assocs Engrs 350 Sansome St Rm 500 San Francisco CA 94104

DE GENNARO, LOUIS D, b New York, June 1, 24; m 49; c 5. ZOOLOGY. *Educ:* Fordham Univ, BS, 48; Boston Col, MS, 50; Syracuse Univ, PhD, 59. *Prof Exp:* Asst, Boston Col, 48-49; from instr to assoc prof zool, 49-62, PROF ZOOL, LE MOYNE COL, 62- *Concurrent Pos:* Adj res prof, State Univ NY Upstate Med Ctr, 74-, adj prof, Col Forestry, 80- *Mem:* Aerospace Med Asn; Soc Develop Biol. *Res:* Experimental embryology; tissue and organ culture; electron microscopy. *Mailing Add:* Dept of Biol Le Moyne Col Syracuse NY 13214

DEGGINGER, EDWARD R, b Chicago, Ill, Oct 12, 26; m 49; c 2. ORGANIC CHEMISTRY. *Educ:* Univ Ill, BS, 49; Univ Wis, MS, 51, PhD(chem), 52. *Prof Exp:* Res supvr, Solvay Process Div, 52-67, tech assoc, Corp, 67-72, RES GROUP LEADER, ALLIED CHEM CORP, 72- *Mem:* Am Chem Soc. *Res:* Urethanes, pesticides and flame retardants; nylon composites. *Mailing Add:* PO Box 186 Convent Station NJ 07961

DEGHETT, VICTOR JOHN, b New York, NY, May 26, 42. ETHOLOGY. *Educ:* Univ Dayton, BA, 64; Bowling Green State Univ, PhD(animal behav), 72. *Prof Exp:* Instr psychol, Univ Dayton, 66-67; from instr to asst prof, 71-77, ASSOC PROF PSYCHOL, STATE UNIV NY POTSDAM, 77- *Mem:* Animal Behav Soc; Am Soc Naturalists; Am Soc Mammal; Sigma Xi. *Res:* Vertebrate behavioral and morphological development; quantitative methods in ethology; rodent ultrasound production; evolution of behavior. *Mailing Add:* Dept of Psychol State Univ of NY Potsdam NY 13676

DEGIOVANNI-DONNELLY, ROSALIE F, b Brooklyn, NY, Nov 22, 26; m 61; c 2. MICROBIAL GENETICS, BIOCHEMISTRY. *Educ:* Brooklyn Col, BA, 47, MA, 53; Columbia Univ, PhD(zool), 61. *Prof Exp:* Mem staff, Allergy Lab, Univ Hosp, Bellevue Med Ctr, New York, 47-51; technician, Sch Pub Health, Columbia Univ, 52-54, asst microbial genetics & biochem of nucleic acids, Col Physicians & Surgeons, 54-62; sr scientist, Bionetics Res Labs, Inc, Va, 62-67; asst prof lectr, 68-71, asst res prof, 71-77, ASSOC PROF LECTR MICROBIOL, MED CTR, GEORGE WASHINGTON UNIV, 77-; RES BIOLOGIST, GENETIC TOXICITY BR, BUR SCI, FOOD & DRUG ADMIN, 68- *Honors & Awards:* Food & Drug Admin Award of Merit. *Mem:* AAAS; Am Soc Microbiol; NY Acad Sci; Environ Mutagen Soc; Sigma Xi. *Res:* Genotypic and phenotypic effects of specific chemicals on microbes; mutation mechanisms. *Mailing Add:* Food & Drug Admin 5600 Fishers Lane Rockville MD 20852

DE GIUSTI, DOMINIC LAWRENCE, b Treviso, Italy, March 31, 11; nat US; m 38, 74; c 3. PARASITOLOGY. *Educ:* St Thomas Col, Minn, BS, 36; Univ Mich, MS, 38; Univ Wis, PhD(zool), 42. *Prof Exp:* Instr biol, Col St Thomas, 36-38; teaching asst, Biol Sta, Univ Mich, 40-41; asst prof biol, Col St Thomas, 42-43; asst prof prev med, Col Med, NY Univ, 43-45; asst prof biol, Col St Thomas, 46-47; res assoc pharmacol, Univ Minn, 47; asst prof biol, Catholic Univ, 47-49; assoc prof, 49-58, chmn dept biol, 67-72, chmn dept comp med, Sch Med, 78-79, prof parasitol, Lib Arts Col & prof parasitol & microbiol, 59-79, prof comp med, Sch Med, 74-79, prof immunol-micorbiol, 79-81, EMER PROF, WAYNE STATE UNIV, 81- *Concurrent Pos:* Markle Found fel, Cent Am; lectr, Med Sch, Georgetown Univ, 47-48; consult, USPHS, 48, Off Surgeon-Gen, 48-49, Off Sci Res & Develop & Vet Admin Hosp, 73-; Fulbright fel, Zool Sta, Univ Naples, 52-53; univ assoc, Dept Path, Detroit Gen Hosp & Dept Med & Path, Hutzel Hosp & Vet Admin Hosp, 72- *Mem:* Am Soc Parasitologists; Am Zool Soc; Am Soc Trop Med & Hyg; fel NY Acad Sci; fel AAAS. *Res:* Life cycles of acanthocephala; histology and cytology of trematodes; blood protozoa of cold blooded vertebrates; life cycles of gregarines. *Mailing Add:* Dept Immunol-Microbiol Sch of Med Wayne State Univ Detroit MI 48201

DEGNAN, JOHN JAMES, III, b Philadelphia, Pa, Dec 10, 45; m 69; c 2. PHYSICS. *Educ:* Drexel Inst Technol, BS, 68; Univ Md, MS, 70, PhD(physics), 79. *Prof Exp:* Physicist CO_2 laser commun, 68-72, sr physicist, 72-75, sr physicist laser ranging & lidar, 75-79, HEAD, ADVAN ELECTRO-OPTICAL INSTRUMENT SECT, NASA-GODDARD SPACE FLIGHT CTR, 79- *Honors & Awards:* Spec Achievement Award, NASA-Goddard Space Flight Ctr, 76. *Mem:* Optical Soc Am; Am Inst Physics. *Res:* Lasers, optics, lidar, spectroscopy, CO_2 laser communications; short pulse laser ranging. *Mailing Add:* Code 723 Instrument Electro-Optics Br NASA Goddard Space Flight Ctr Greenbelt MD 20771

DE GOES, LOUIS, b Maui, Hawaii, June 23, 14; m 44; c 3. ENGINEERING GEOLOGY. *Educ:* Colo Sch Mines, GeolE, 41; Stanford Univ, MS, 50. *Prof Exp:* Master navigator, USAF, 41-44, chief navigator, Pac Div Mil Air Transp Serv, 45-48, assoc prof, USAF Inst Technol, 50-53 & Res Studies Inst, Air Univ, 54-56, dir terrestrial sci lab, Air Force Cambridge Res Labs, 57-61, dep technol & subsysts, Foreign Technol Div, Air Force Systs Command, 62-66; exec secy, Polar Res Bd, Nat Acad Sci, 67-81; CONSULT, 81- *Concurrent Pos:* Mem, Southeast Asia Geog Exped, 55-56; panels earth physics, oceanog & polar res, US Dept Defense, 57-61, arctic adv comt, 70; proj scientist, Fletcher's Ice Island Res Prog, Int Geophys Yr, 57-58. *Honors & Awards:* Antarctic Serv Medal, 70. *Mem:* Fel Geol Soc Am; fel Arctic Inst NAm; Int Glaciol Soc; AAAS; Am Geophys Union. *Res:* Site selection and construction in permafrost; polar geomorphology; applied glaciology; polar logistics; technical writing; climate dynamics; polar mineral and living resource development. *Mailing Add:* 4727 38th St N Arlington VA 22207

DEGOWIN, RICHARD LOUIS, b Iowa City, Iowa, May 14, 34; m 57; c 2. INTERNAL MEDICINE. *Educ:* Univ Chicago, MD, 59. *Prof Exp:* Nat Heart Inst fel, 62-63; from res asst to res assoc internal med, Univ Chicago, 63-65, asst prof med, 65-68; assoc prof med & radiation res, 68-73, PROF MED & RADIOL, UNIV IOWA HOSP, 73-, PROF RADIOBIOL, RADIATION RES LAB, COL MED, 68-, DIR, CANCER CTR, 78- *Concurrent Pos:* Proj supvr hemat, Argonne Cancer Res Hosp, 65-68; USPHS career develop, 68-69; consult physician, Vet Admin Hosp, 69- *Mem:* Am Soc Clin Invest; fel Am Col Physicians; Am Soc Hemat; Radiation Res Soc; Int Soc Exp Hemat. *Res:* Hematology and radiobiology; hemopoietic stem cell kinetics; erythropoietin and erythropoiesis; postirradiation recovery of hemopoiesis; bone marrow stromal cells; drug-induced hemolysis; malaria. *Mailing Add:* Dept of Med Univ of Iowa Hosp Iowa City IA 52242

DE GRAAF, ADRIAAN M, b Naaldwijk, Neth, Aug 4, 35; m 64; c 2. SOLID STATE PHYSICS. *Educ:* Swiss Fed Inst Technol, PhD(physics), 62. *Prof Exp:* Vis prof, Univ Sao Paulo, 62-64; vis prof, Centro Brasileiro de Pesquisas Fisicas, Rio de Janeiro, 64-65; sr res scientist, Sci Lab, Ford Motor Co, 65-68; assoc prof, 68-74, PROF PHYSICS, WAYNE STATE UNIV, 74-, PROF ASTRON, 80-, MEM RES INST ENG SCI, 80- *Concurrent Pos:* Ford Found grant, 64-65; NSF grant, 72- *Mem:* Fel Am Phys Soc. *Res:* Theoretical solid state physics; properties of noncrystalline materials. *Mailing Add:* Dept of Physics Wayne State Univ Detroit MI 48202

DEGRAAF, DONALD EARL, b Grand Rapids, Mich, June 17, 26; m 48; c 3. PHYSICS, PHYSICS EDUCATION. *Educ:* Univ Mich, PhD(physics), 57. *Prof Exp:* From instr to assoc prof, 56-67, PROF PHYSICS, UNIV MICH, FLINT, 67- *Concurrent Pos:* Pres, Crystal Press. *Mem:* AAAS; Am Sci Affiliation; Am Asn Physics Teachers. *Res:* Physics education and curriculum design; helical physics. *Mailing Add:* 1909 Proctor St Flint MI 48504

DEGRAFF, ARTHUR CHRISTIAN, b Paterson, NJ, Dec 3, 99; m 26; c 3. MEDICINE. *Educ:* NY Univ, BS, 20, MD, 21. *Prof Exp:* Instr med, Col Med, NY Univ, 23-24; lectr physiol, Western Reserve Univ, 24-25; instr physiol, 25-27 & med, 27-30, asst prof therapeut, 30-32, SAMUEL A BROWN PROF THERAPEUT, SCH MED, NY UNIV, 32- *Concurrent Pos:* Crile fel, Western Reserve Univ, 24-25; from intern to res physician, Bellevue Hosp, 21-24, adj asst vis physician, 27-30, from asst vis physician to assoc vis physician, 30-36, vis physician, 36-, chmn comt drugs & formulary, 36-; res, Univ Col, Univ London, 32; mem rev comt, US Pharmacopoeia, 40-, pres, US Pharmacopoeial Conv, Inc, 65-70, chmn scope comt, 65-70; sr Serv, Univ Hosp, NY Univ Med Ctr. *Mem:* AMA; Soc Exp Biol & Med; fel Am Col Physicians; Am Soc Clin Pharmacol (pres, 48); Am Soc Pharmacol & Exp Therapeut. *Res:* Therapeutics; physiology of the heart and circulation; diseases of the heart. *Mailing Add:* Dept of Therapeut 550 First Ave New York NY 10016

DEGRAFF, BENJAMIN ANTHONY, b Columbus, Ohio, Dec 23, 38; m 60; c 2. CHEMICAL KINETICS. *Educ:* Ohio Wesleyan Univ, BA, 60; Ohio State Univ, MS, 63, PhD(phys chem), 65. *Prof Exp:* Fel, Harvard Univ, 65-67; asst prof phys chem, Univ Va, 67-72; assoc prof, 72-76, head dept, 76-80, PROF CHEM, JAMES MADISON UNIV, 76- *Mem:* Am Chem Soc; Am Phys Soc. *Res:* Kinetics of fast reactions; energy transfer processes; photochemistry. *Mailing Add:* Dept of Chem James Madison Univ Harrisonburg VA 22807

DEGRANDE, GARY GASTON, b Moline, Ill, July 22, 47; m 69; c 3. ORGANIC CHEMISTRY, PROCESS DEVELOPMENT. *Educ:* Univ Ill, BS, 70; Univ Minn, PhD(org chem), 74. *Prof Exp:* Med chemist, Pfizer Cent Res, 74; sr med chemist, 74-76, prod develop chemist, BS&CP, 76-78, process develop chemist/supvr, 78-81, MGR, CHEMICAL DEVELOP, RIKER LABS, 3M CO, 81- *Res:* Medicinal organic chemistry; process development chemistry and technical management. *Mailing Add:* Riker Labs 3M Ctr Bldg 218-1 St Paul MN 55101

DE GRANDPRE, JEAN LOUIS, b Montreal, Que, May 25, 29; c 3. SYSTEMS ANALYSIS. *Educ:* Univ Montreal, BA, 48, BSc, 52, MSc, 54. *Prof Exp:* Engr, Spec Weapons Dept, Canadair Ltd, 54-55, coordr systs, 55-57, engr, Sparrow II 6-D Digital Simulation, 57-59, engr, Flight Simulation, 59-60; systs coordr & chief programmer, Sperry Gyroscope Can Ltd, 60-61; comp coordr, Adv Prog Develop, Reentry Syst Anal, Missiles & Space Systs Div, Douglas Aircraft, 61-65, sect chief, 63-64, br mgr methodology, 64-65; MEM TECH STAFF, GEN RES CORP, 65- *Mem:* Inst Elec & Electronics Engrs; Am Inst Aeronaut & Astronaut; Asn Comput Mach; Can Asn Physicists; assoc mem Opers Res Soc Am. *Res:* US and Soviet defense systems evaluation; radars and interceptor evaluations; tracking and filtering; theoretical discrimination; counter-insurgency analysis; simulation of radars, interceptors, tank breakup, defense systems, maneuvering reentry vehicles; non-nuclear kill defense systems; tactical simulation design and implementation. *Mailing Add:* Gen Res Corp 307 Wynn Dr Huntsville AL 35805

DEGRASSE, ROBERT W(OODMAN), b Yakima, Wash, July 4, 29; m 52; c 4. ELECTRONICS, DATA PROCESSING. *Educ:* Calif Inst Technol, BS, 51; Stanford Univ, MS, 54, PhD(elec eng), 58. *Prof Exp:* Res engr guided missile develop, Jet Propulsion Lab, Calif Inst Technol, 51-53; asst electronics res lab, Stanford Univ, 53-55, res assoc microwave tube res, 55-57; mem tech staff, Bell Tel Labs, 57-60; dir res & develop, Microwave Electronics Corp, 60-64; vpres, Quantum Sci Corp, 64-69; vpres & tech dir, Quantor Corp, 69-78; DIR RES & DEVELOP, NCR MICROGRAPHICS DIV, 78- *Mem:* Inst Elec & Electronics Engrs. *Res:* Microfilm and electronic data processing information systems; input-output theory data base for technology forecasting; satellite communications microwave masers, memories, solid state devices and tubes. *Mailing Add:* NCR Micrographics Div 520 Logue Ave Mountain View CA 94043

DEGRAW, JOSEPH IRVING, JR, b Washington, DC, May 26, 33; m 57; c 2. MEDICINAL CHEMISTRY. *Educ:* Univ Calif, Berkeley, BS, 56; Stanford Univ, PhD(org chem), 61. *Prof Exp:* Org chemist, Merck & Co, 56-57; org chemist, Cancer Chemother & Med Chem, 57-74, PROG MGR, MED CHEM, STANFORD RES INST, 74- *Mem:* Am Chem Soc; NY Acad Sci; Int Soc Heterocyclic Chem. *Res:* Folic acid antagonists; components of white snakeroot, indole alkylating agents; indole compounds; tryptamines, pyrimidines, pteridines, analgesics, histamine releasers and piperidines; synthesis of alkaloids; antileprotic drugs. *Mailing Add:* 880 Hanover Ave Sunnyvale CA 94087

DEGRAW, WILLIAM ALLEN, b Washington, DC, Apr 26, 39; m 61; c 3. ZOOPHYSIOLOGY, ENDOCRINOLOGY. *Educ:* Allegheny Col, BS, 61; Colo State Univ, MS, 65; Wash State Univ, PhD(zoophysiol), 72. *Prof Exp:* Jr biologist pharmacol, Wallace & Tiernan, Inc, 61-62; from asst prof to assoc prof, 69-80, PROF BIOL, UNIV NEBR, OMAHA, 80- *Mem:* Am Ornithologist's Union; Cooper Ornith Soc; Inland Bird Banders Asn. *Res:* Avian physiology and endocrinology: seasonal adaptations in lipid metabolism, plasma volume changes during molting, seasonal fluctuations in responsiveness to glucagon. *Mailing Add:* Dept of Biol Univ of Nebr Omaha NE 68182

DE GRAY, RONALD WILLOUGHBY, b Hartford, Conn, Feb 10, 38. MATHEMATICS. *Educ:* Univ Conn, BA, 60, MA, 62; Syracuse Univ, PhD(math), 69. *Prof Exp:* Asst prof math, Utica Col, 69-75; ASST PROF MATH, DENISON UNIV, 75- *Concurrent Pos:* Vis asst prof math, Saint Joseph Col, 81. *Mem:* AAAS; Am Math Soc; Math Asn Am; Sigma Xi. *Res:* Probability. *Mailing Add:* Dept of Math Denison Univ Granville OH 43023

DEGROAT, WILLIAM CHESNEY, JR, b Trenton, NJ, May 18, 38; m 59; c 3. PHARMACOLOGY. *Educ:* Philadelphia Col Pharm, BSc, 60, MSc, 62; Univ Pa, PhD(pharmacol), 65. *Prof Exp:* Lab instr, Philadelphia Col Pharm, 60-62; USPHS fel pharmacol, Sch Med, Univ Pa, 65-66; hon fel physiol, John Curtin Sch Med Res, Australian Nat Univ, 66-68; from asst prof to assoc prof, 68-77, actg chmn dept, 78-80, PROF PHARMACOL, SCH MED, UNIV PITTSBURGH, 77- *Concurrent Pos:* Chemist, Vet Admin Hosp, Philadelphia, 61-62; NSF fel, 66; Riker Int fel pharmacol, 66-67; pharmacol test comt, Nat Bd Med Examrs. *Mem:* AAAS; Am Soc Pharmacol & Exp Therapeut; NY Acad Sci; Soc Neurosci; Urodynamics Soc. *Res:* Central autonomic mechanisms; nervous control of the urinary bladder and pharmacology of transmission in peripheral autonomic ganglia. *Mailing Add:* Dept Pharmacol Sch Med Univ Pittsburgh Pittsburgh PA 15213

DE GROOT, JACK, b Bandoeng, Java, Apr 24, 21; nat US; m 49; c 3. ANATOMY, ENDOCRINOLOGY. *Educ:* Univ Amsterdam, BM, 47, Drs, 48, PhD(neuroanat), 52. *Prof Exp:* Instr histol, Univ Leiden, 49-51; res assoc, Brain Res Inst, Holland, 51-53; res assoc anat, Univ Calif, Los Angeles, 55-56; asst prof gross anat & neuroanat, Univ Utrecht, 56-57; asst prof physiol, Col Med, Baylor Univ, 57-59; from asst prof to assoc prof, 59-69, PROF ANAT, UNIV CALIF, SAN FRANCISCO, 69- *Concurrent Pos:* USPHS sr res fel, 59-64, career develop award, 64. *Mem:* AAAS; Endocrine Soc; Am Asn Anat; Am Physiol Soc; Soc Exp Biol & Med. *Res:* Anatomical and functional interrelationships between endocrine system, hypothalamus and rhinencephalon. *Mailing Add:* Dept of Anat Univ of Calif Med Ctr San Francisco CA 94143

DEGROOT, LESLIE JACOB, b Ft Edward, NY, Sept 20, 28; m; c 5. ENDOCRINOLOGY. *Educ:* Union Col, NY, BS, 48; Columbia Univ, MD, 52. *Prof Exp:* Intern & asst res med, Presby Hosp, New York, 52-54; pub health physician, US Oper Mission, Afghanistan, Nat Cancer Inst, 55-56; resident, Mass Gen Hosp, 57-58; asst, Harvard Med Sch, 58-59, instr, 59-62, assoc, 62-66; assoc prof exp med, Mass Inst Technol & assoc dir dept nutrit & food sci, Clin Res Ctr, 66-68; PROF ENDOCRINOL & CHIEF SECT, THYROID STUDY UNIT, PRITZKER SCH MED, UNIV CHICAGO, 68- *Concurrent Pos:* Clin fel, Nat Cancer Inst, 54-55; clin & res fel med, Mass Gen Hosp, 56 & 58-60, asst, 60-64, asst physician, 64-66. *Mem:* Asn Am Physicians; Am Thyroid Asn; Endocrine Soc; Am Soc Clin Invest; Am Fedn Clin Res. *Mailing Add:* Thyroid Study Unit Univ of Chicago Chicago IL 60637

DEGROOT, MORRIS H, b Scranton, Pa, June 8, 31; m 79; c 2. STATISTICS. *Educ:* Roosevelt Univ, BS, 52; Univ Chicago, MS, 54, PhD(statist), 58. *Prof Exp:* Asst prof math, 57-63, assoc prof math & indust admin, 63-66; head dept statist, 66-72, PROF STATIST, CARNEGIE-MELLON UNIV, 66- *Concurrent Pos:* Prof, Inst Advan Studies in Mgt, Belg, 71; assoc ed, J Am Statist Asn, 70-74, book rev ed, 71-75, theory & methods ed, 76-78, assoc ed, Ann Statist, 74-75; mem assembly behav & soc sci, Nat Res Coun, 73-78 & 80-, mem comt nat statist, 75-79, assoc chmn, 78-79, mem comt environ monitoring, 75; mem coun, Inst Math Statist, 75-78 & 81- *Mem:* Fel Am Inst Math Statist; fel AAAS; Int Statist Inst; fel Am Statist Asn; fel Royal Statist Soc. *Res:* Statistics and probability. *Mailing Add:* Dept of Statist Carnegie-Mellon Univ Pittsburgh PA 15213

DEGROOT, RODNEY CHARLES, b Racine, Wis, Dec 24, 34; m 54; c 3. PLANT PATHOLOGY, MYCOLOGY. *Educ:* Univ Wis, BS, 58, MS, 60; State Univ NY Col Forestry, PhD(forest path), 63. *Prof Exp:* Instr bot, Syracuse, 62-63; sr scientist bot, NY State Mus & Sci Serv, 63-68; prin pathologist, Forest & Wood Prod Dis Lab, 68-77, plant pathologist, Prod Lab, 77-78, PROJ LEADER WOOD PROTECTION RES, US FOREST SERV, 79- *Mem:* Mycol Soc Am; Forest Prod Res Soc; Am Phytopath Soc. *Res:* Forest pathology; wood decay. *Mailing Add:* US Forest Serv PO Box 5130 Madison WI 53704

DE GROOT, SYBIL GRAMLICH, b Evanston, Ill, Feb 28, 28; div; c 3. HUMAN FACTORS ENGINEERING, INDUSTRIAL ENGINEERING. *Educ:* Ohio State Univ, BA, 47, MA, 49, PhD(eng psychol), 68. *Prof Exp:* Res asst human performance, Inst Coop Res, Johns Hopkins Univ, 50-51; psychophysicist of vision submariners' vision, US Naval Med Res Lab, New London, Conn, 51-52; staff psychologist exp psychol & syst design, Dunlap & Assocs, Inc, Darien, Conn, 58-62; res assoc children's vision, Bur Educ Res & Serv, Ohio State Univ, 62-66; res assoc human performance, Div Info & Comput Sci, Ohio State Univ, 67-68; asst prof human factors psychol, Mont State Univ, 68-72; assoc prof psychol, 72-74, ASSOC PROF INDUST SYSTS, DIV INDUST ENG TECHNOL, FLA INT UNIV, 74- *Concurrent Pos:* Proj dir, HEW grant, 64-66; NSF grant, 67-68; consult, Mont State Off Water Resources, 71-72; res dir, Univ grant to Sch Hotel, SFla Hotel Owner's Asn, 73-74; prin investr, Air Force Off Sci Res grant, 77-78; consult, Pratt & Whitney, GPD Div, West Palm Beach, Fla, 78- *Mem:* Human Factors Soc; Int Ergonomics Asn; Am Soc Eng Educr; Am Psychol Asn; Soc Women Engrs. *Res:* Human performance; training and system design; professional and managerial women in industry; human perception; sensor displays and controls; human factors engineering; industrial safety and health. *Mailing Add:* Dept of Indust Systs Fla Int Univ Miami FL 33199

DE HAAN, FRANK P, b Paterson, NJ, Nov 1, 34; m 58; c 4. PHYSICAL CHEMISTRY, INORGANIC CHEMISTRY. *Educ:* Calvin Col, AB, 57; Purdue Univ, PhD(chem), 61. *Prof Exp:* From asst prof to assoc prof, 61-74, chmn dept, 70-74, PROF CHEM, OCCIDENTAL COL, 74- *Concurrent Pos:* NSF sci fac fel, 68-69. *Mem:* Am Chem Soc; AAAS; Sigma Xi. *Res:* Mechanisms of Friedel-Crafts and related reactions. *Mailing Add:* Dept of Chem Occidental Col Los Angeles CA 90041

DEHAAN, ROBERT LAWRENCE, b Chicago, Ill, Nov 18, 30; m 57; c 2. BIOLOGY, EMBRYOLOGY. *Educ:* Univ Calif, Los Angeles, BA, 52, MA, 54, PhD(zool), 56. *Prof Exp:* Jr res physiologist, Univ Calif, Los Angeles, 54-56; res embryologist, Carnegie Inst Wash, 56-73; prof anat & physiol, 73-76, WILLIAM P TIMMIE PROF EMBRYOL, DEPT ANAT, EMORY UNIV, 76- *Concurrent Pos:* Instr, Woods Hole Marine Biol Lab, 62-64 & 65; from assoc prof to prof biol, Johns Hopkins Univ, 64-73; mem biol study sect, NIH, 70-74; extramural res assoc, Carnegie Inst Wash, 73-; southern regional res rev & adv subcomt, Am Heart Asn, 75-79; foreign investr, Deleg Gen Res

Sci & Tech, Univ Paris-Sud, Orsay, France, 80-81; consult, US Senate Comt Human Resources, 79; fac scholar, Josiah Macy Found, 80-81. *Mem:* Am Soc Cell Biol; Biophys Soc; Soc Develop Biol; Tissue Cult Asn; Int Soc Develop Biol (int secy, 72-81). *Res:* Embryonic development of the heart; cell migration and morphogenetic movements; biophysics of excitable cells; differentiation and physiology of cardiac pacemakers; heart cell culture. *Mailing Add:* Dept of Anat Emory Univ Atlanta GA 30322

DE HAAS, HERMAN, b Northbridge, Mass, Jan 6, 24; m 51; c 4. BIOLOGICAL CHEMISTRY. *Educ:* Westminster Col, Pa, BS, 47; Univ Mich, MS, 50, PhD(biol chem), 55. *Prof Exp:* Asst, Univ Mich, 47-52, res assoc biochem, 54-55; from asst prof to assoc prof chem, Westminster Col, 55-59; from asst prof to assoc prof, 59-71, PROF BIOCHEM, UNIV MAINE, 71- *Mem:* Am Chem Soc; Am Sci Affiliation. *Res:* Protein nutrition; amino acids of marine gastropods. *Mailing Add:* Dept of Biochem 202 Hitchner Hall Univ of Maine Orono ME 04469

DEHART, ARNOLD O('DELL), b Davy, WVa, May 8, 26; m 51; c 3. BEARING TECHNOLOGY, TRIBOLOGY. *Educ:* Univ WVa, BSME, 50. *Prof Exp:* Sr res engr, 51-64, supvry res engr, 64-76, sr engr, 76-77, RES ENGR, DEPT MECH DEVELOP, RES LABS, GEN MOTORS CORP, 77- *Mem:* Soc Automotive Engrs; Am Soc Lubrication Engrs. *Res:* General bearing, fluid film and rolling contact hydrodynamics; hydrostatics; tribology; system kinematics; mechanisms; sliding surface bearings; lubrication. *Mailing Add:* Mech Develop Dept Res Labs GM Tech Ctr Warren MI 48090

DEHART, ROBERT C(HARLES), b Laramie, Wyo, Aug 16, 17; m 41, 70; c 2. STRUCTURAL ENGINEERING. *Educ:* Univ Wyo, BS, 38; Ill Inst Technol, MS, 40, PhD(civil eng), 55. *Prof Exp:* Design engr, Standard Oil Co, Ind, 40-46; assoc prof civil eng, Mont State Univ, 46-53; struct analyst, Armed Forces Spec Weapons Proj, 53-58; mgr, struct mech, 58-59, dir struct res dept, 59-70, VPRES, SOUTHWEST RES INST, 70- *Concurrent Pos:* Lectr, George Washington Univ, 55-58. *Mem:* NY Acad Sci; Am Soc Mech Engrs; Am Soc Civil Engrs; Sigma Xi. *Res:* Structural dynamics; theoretical and applied mechanics; air, underwater and underground shock; underwater vehicles. *Mailing Add:* Southwest Res Inst 8500 Culebra Rd San Antonio TX 78206

DE HARVEN, ETIENNE, b Brussels, Belg, Mar 5, 28; m 53; c 3. CYTOLOGY, BIOLOGICAL STRUCTURE. *Educ:* Univ Brussels, MD, 53. *Prof Exp:* Asst, Free Univ Brussels, 55-62 & in chg cytol, Electron Micros Lab, Anat Inst, 58-62; asst prof cytol, 62-69, PROF BIOL, SLOAN-KETTERING DIV, CORNELL UNIV, 69-; MEM DIV CYTOL, SLOAN-KETTERING INST CANCER RES, 68- *Concurrent Pos:* Fel, Inst Cancer, France, 55-56; Belg Am Educ Found & Damon Runyon res fels, 56-57; vis res fel, Sloan-Kettering Inst Cancer Res, 56-57, vis assoc, 59 & 61, assoc, 62-64, assoc mem, 64-68; assoc, Nat Fund Sci Res, Belg, 59-61; guest investr, Rockefeller Inst, 62. *Mem:* Electron Micros Soc Am; NY Acad Sci; Int Soc Cell Biol. *Res:* Virology; electron microscope cytology; viruses associated with murine cancers. *Mailing Add:* Dept Path Univ Toronto Banting Inst Toronto ON M5G 1L5

DE HASETH, PIETER LOURENS, biophysical chemistry, see previous edition

DEHAVEN, DIANE LOUISE, b East Stroudsburg, Pa, Aug 3, 54. NEUROCHHEMISTRY, NEUROTOXICOLOGY. *Educ:* Millersville State Col, BA, 76; Syracuse Univ, PhD(biophyschol), 81. *Prof Exp:* FEL, BIOL SCI RES CTR, UNIV NC, 81- *Mem:* Soc Neurosci. *Res:* Effects of environmental toxicants on central nervous system chemistry and function; neurochemical and behavioral sequelae of toxicant exposure. *Mailing Add:* Biol Sci Res Ctr 220H Univ NC Sch Med Chapel Hill NC 27514

DE HEER, JOSEPH, b Eindhoven, Neth, Jan 24, 22; nat US. PHYSICAL CHEMISTRY. *Educ:* Delft Inst Technol, Chem Eng, 47; Univ Amsterdam, PhD(physics, math), 50. *Prof Exp:* Res assoc physics & astron, Ohio State Univ, 50-52; from asst prof to assoc prof, 52-63, PROF CHEM, UNIV COLO, BOULDER, 63- *Concurrent Pos:* Guggenheim fel, Quantum Chem Group, Univ Uppsala, 59-60; Fulbright res scholar, Univ Copenhagen, 63-64. *Mem:* Fel Am Phys Soc. *Res:* Quantum mechanics of molecules; valence theory; thermodynamics. *Mailing Add:* Dept of Chem Univ of Colo Boulder CO 80309

DE HERTOGH, AUGUST ALBERT, b Chicago, Ill, Aug 24, 35; m 57; c 3. PLANT PHYSIOLOGY, HORTICULTURE. *Educ:* NC State Col, BS, 57, MS, 61; Ore State Univ, PhD(plant physiol), 64. *Prof Exp:* Asst plant physiologist, Boyce Thompson Inst, 64-65; from asst prof to prof hort, Mich State Univ, 65-78; PROF & HEAD DEPT HORT SCI, NC STATE UNIV, 78- *Mem:* Int Soc Hort Sci; fel Am Soc Hort Sci; Sigma Xi. *Res:* Influence of environmental and growth regulator factors on growth and development of bulbous plants. *Mailing Add:* Dept Hort Sci NC State Univ Sch Agr Raleigh NC 27650

DEHL, RONALD, physical chemistry, see previous edition

DEHLINGER, PETER, b Berlin, Ger, Oct 3, 17; nat US; m 41; c 2. GEOPHYSICS, OCEANOGRAPHY. *Educ:* Univ Mich, BS, 40; Calif Inst Technol, MS, 43, PhD(geophysics), 50. *Prof Exp:* Seismologist, Shell Oil Co, Inc, 43-48; geophysicist, Battelle Mem Inst, 50-53; from assoc prof to prof geophys, Tex A&M Univ, 54-62; prof geophys oceanog, Ore State Univ, 62-68; dir marine sci inst, 68-75, PROF GEOPHYS, UNIV CONN, 68-, MEM MARINE SCI INST, 76- *Concurrent Pos:* Indust consult, 57-; with US Geol Surv, 57-68; head geophys prog, Ocean Sci & Technol Div, Off Naval Res, Washington, DC, 66-68; adj prof, Am Univ, 66-67. *Mem:* AAAS; fel Geol Soc Am; Am Geophys Union; Seismol Soc Am; Soc Explor Geophys. *Res:* Gravity and seismic measurement at sea; tectonics of oceanic crustal and mantle structures. *Mailing Add:* Dept of Geol & Geophys Univ of Conn Storrs CT 06268

DEHM, DAVID CO, organic chemistry, polymer chemistry, see previous edition

DEHM, HENRY CHRISTOPHER, b Newark, NJ, Apr 1, 21; m 48, 67; c 2. ORGANIC CHEMISTRY. *Educ:* Univ Denver, BS, 48, MS, 49; Univ Wis, PhD(chem), 54. *Prof Exp:* Asst chem, Univ Denver, 48-49; asst chem, Univ Wis, 49-52; res chemist, Res Ctr, Hercules Powder Co, 54-61, tech specialist, 61-66, SR TECH SPECIALIST, CHEM PROPULSION DIV, HERCULES INC, 66- *Concurrent Pos:* Lectr, Brigham Young Univ, 63-; adj prof chem eng, Univ Utah, 67- *Mem:* Am Chem Soc; Sigma Xi. *Res:* Synthesis and stereochemistry of steroids; organic synthesis; halogenation; catalysis; metal complexes; polymers; ultrahigh energy compounds; fundamental chemistry of solid propellants; surface chemistry as it affects propellant mechanical and ballistic properties; alternate energy systems. *Mailing Add:* Hercules Inc Magna UT 84044

DEHM, RICHARD LAVERN, b Pontiac, Ill, Sept 11, 27; m 52; c 3. ELECTROPHOTOGRAPHY. *Educ:* Ill Wesleyan Univ, BS, 50; Univ Ill, MS, 52, PhD(chem), 54; Univ Rochester, MBA, 69. *Prof Exp:* Asst, Univ Ill, 51-54; anal chemist, 54-60, tech assoc, 60-65, asst dir indust lab, 65-70, asst supt photochem div, 70-72, DIR PROJ DEVELOP DIV, EASTMAN KODAK CO, 72- *Mem:* Am Chem Soc; Soc Appl Spectros. *Res:* Emission, x-ray and absorption spectroscopy; x-ray diffraction; concentration techniques; trace element analysis; microprobe; spark source mass spectroscopy. *Mailing Add:* 6 Bittersweet Rd Fairport NY 14450

DEHMELT, HANS GEORG, b Goerlitz, Ger, Sept 9, 22. EXPERIMENTAL PHYSICS. *Educ:* DrRerNat, Gottingen, 50. *Prof Exp:* Res assoc, Duke Univ, 52-55; vis asst prof physics, 55-56, from asst prof to assoc prof, 56-61, PROF PHYSICS, UNIV WASH, 61- *Concurrent Pos:* Res fel, Univ Goettingen, 50-52; consult, Varian Assocs, 56-80. *Honors & Awards:* Davisson-Gerner Prize, Am Phys Soc, 70; Humboldt Prize, Alexander von Humboldt Stiftung, 74. *Mem:* Nat Acad Sci; Am Acad Arts & Sci; AAAS; Am Phys Soc. *Res:* Nuclear quadrupole resonance; nuclear and electron paramagnetic resonance; optical detection of free atom orientation; spin exchange resonance; spectroscopy of stored ions; free electron/positron magnetic moment from geonium spectroscopy. *Mailing Add:* Dept of Physics Univ of Wash Seattle WA 98105

DEHMER, JOSEPH LEONARD, b St Charles, Mo, Jan 21, 45; m 70. CHEMICAL PHYSICS, ATOMIC PHYSICS. *Educ:* Wash Univ, BS, 67; Univ Chicago, PhD(chem physics), 71. *Prof Exp:* Res assoc, 71-80, from asst physicist to physicist, 73-80, SR PHYSICIST, ARGONNE NAT LAB, 80- *Concurrent Pos:* Consult, Nat Bur of Standards, 80- *Mem:* fel Am Phys Soc; Am Chem Soc; Radiation Res Soc. *Res:* Theory of photoionization of atoms and molecules; measurement of photoionization branching ratios and photoelectron angular distributions; multiphoton processes in atoms and molecules; effects of radiation interactions with matter; systematics of atomic properties. *Mailing Add:* Bldg 203 Argonne Nat Lab Argonne IL 60439

DEHMER, PATRICIA MOORE, b Chicago, Ill, Sept 18, 45; m 70. CHEMICAL PHYSICS, MOLECULAR PHYSICS. *Educ:* Univ Ill, BS, 67; Univ Chicago, PhD(chem physics), 72. *Prof Exp:* Res assoc, 72-75, asst chemist, 75-78, CHEMIST, ARGONNE NAT LAB, 78- *Mem:* Am Chem Soc; Am Phys Soc. *Res:* Experimental atomic and molecular photoionizaton; vacuum ultraviolet spectroscopy and the analysis of molecular spectra; molecular beam scattering and determination of intermolecular potentials; chemical reactions and kinetics; ion-molecule reactions. *Mailing Add:* Argonne Nat Lab Bldg 203 Argonne IL 60439

DEHN, JAMES THEODORE, b New York, NY, Oct 24, 30; m 68; c 3. CHEMICAL PHYSICS, PHYSICAL MATHEMATICS. *Educ:* Fordham Univ, AB, 55; Georgetown Univ, MS, 59, PhD(physics), 61. *Prof Exp:* NASA physics grant, 62-64; instr physics, St Peter's Col, 65-66; res assoc, Pa State Univ, 66-68; PHYSICIST, BALLISTICS RES LAB, 68- *Mem:* Am Phys Soc; Sigma Xi; Combustion Inst. *Res:* Mathematical and chemical physics involved in terminal ballistics; vulnerability and survivability. *Mailing Add:* Dept of Physics Ballistics Res Lab Aberdeen Proving Ground MD 21005

DEHN, JOSEPH WILLIAM, JR, b Brooklyn, NY, Feb 18, 28; m 53; c 2. ORGANIC CHEMISTRY. *Educ:* Columbia Col, BA, 49; Stevens Inst Technol, MS, 53; Polytech Inst Brooklyn, PhD(org chem), 64. *Prof Exp:* Sr org chemist, Cent Res Labs, Interchem Corp, 49-64; group leader org chem, Wallace & Tiernan, Inc, 65-67; sr scientist, Cent Res Labs, Shulton Inc, 68-70; SR ORG CHEMIST, NOPCO DIV, DIAMOND-SHAMROCK CHEM CO, MORRISTOWN, NJ, 71- *Mem:* AAAS; Am Chem Soc; Am Inst Chemists; NY Acad Sci. *Res:* Synthesis of dyes, pigments, organic intermediates and heterocyclic and organometallic compounds; polymers; surfactants; leather tanning compounds; textile chemicals. *Mailing Add:* 52 Berkshire Rd Great Neck NY 11023

DEHN, RUDOLPH A(LBERT), b East Rutherford, NJ, Aug 12, 19; m 45; c 3. ELECTRICAL ENGINEERING. *Educ:* Newark Col Eng, BSEE, 41. *Prof Exp:* Develop engr, 41-45, res assoc, 45-60, consult engr, 60-66, mgr tube res, microwave tube bus sect, 66-72, MEM ENG STAFF, RES & DEVELOP, GEN ELEC CORP, 72- *Mem:* Inst Elec & Electronics Engrs. *Res:* New methods of generating microwaves; design of attendant transmission networks; application of microwave energy for materials processing. *Mailing Add:* Gen Elec Co PO Box 8 Schenectady NY 12301

DEHNE, EDWARD JAMES, b Ft Clark, NDak, June 28, 11; m 32; c 3. OCCUPATIONAL MEDICINE, PUBLIC HEALTH. *Educ:* Univ NDak, BS, 35; Univ Ore, MD, 37; Johns Hopkins Univ, MPH, 41, DPH, 55; Am Bd Prev Med, dipl & cert pub health, 49, cert occup med, 55; Am Bd Indust Hyg, cert, 62. *Prof Exp:* Indust med pract, Idaho, 38-39; dir, Coos County Health Dept, Ore, 39-41; asst post surgeon, US Army, Ft McDowell, Calif, 41-43, health officer, Mil Govt Pub Health, Eng, 43-44 & Civil Affairs Ctr, Europ Civil Affairs Div, Eng, 44, chief prev med, Europ Theater Opers, 44, chief surg, Forward Echelon, France, 44, exec officer, Western Europe, 44-45, chief prev med, Off Mil Govt, Ger, 45-47, dir off occup health, Edgewood Arsenal, Md, 48-50, dir off occup health, Hq, Third US Army, Ga, 50-51, dir off occup health, Caribbean, CZ, 51-55, comdr, US Army Environ Hyg Agency, 55-59, chief prev med, Second US Army, 59-60 & Brooke Army Med Ctr, 60-63, dir health & welfare, US Civil Admin, Ryukyu Islands, 63-65, dir health, Fifth US Army, 65-66; health officer, State of Nev, 66-68; med dir WVa regional med prog, Med Ctr, Univ WVa, 68-69; dir NJ tuberc serv, State of NJ Dept Health, 69-71; CHIEF MED CONSULT OFFICER, STATE OF NEV, 71- Concurrent Pos: Consult, Off Surgeon Gen, 57; mem fac Vietnam surv, Sch Pub Health, Univ Calif, Los Angeles, 68-69. Honors & Awards: Mem, Order of Leopold, Belg; mem, Order of Pub Health, France; Pro Mundi Beneficio, Brazil. Mem: Fel Am Col Physicians; fel Am Col Prev Med; fel Am Pub Health Asn; fel Am Occup Med Asn; Int Health Soc. Res: Identifying, evaluating and minimizing environmental health hazards; industrial hygiene; rehabilitation; effects of environmental temperature upon susceptibility to toxic agents; international health and behavioral sciences. Mailing Add: 250 Tahoe Dr Carson City NV 89701

DEHNE, GEORGE CLARK, b Pittsburgh, Pa, Oct 2, 37; m 58; c 2. ANALYTICAL CHEMISTRY, INORGANIC CHEMISTRY. Educ: Allegheny Col, BS, 59; Purdue Univ, MS, 61, PhD(anal chem), 63. Prof Exp: From asst prof to assoc prof, 63-74, chmn dept, 69-74, PROF CHEM, CAPITAL UNIV, 74-, DIR DATA PROCESSING, 80- Concurrent Pos: Vis res assoc, Col Pharm, Ohio State Univ, 72-77. Mem: AAAS; Am Chem Soc; Am Soc Testing & Mat. Res: Absorption spectroscopy; analytical instrumentation and spectrophotometry; heteropoly chemistry; computer applications in chemistry. Mailing Add: Dept of Chem Capital Univ Columbus OH 43209

DEHNEL, PAUL AUGUSTUS, b Pomona, Calif, Dec 31, 22; m 43, 71; c 2. COMPARATIVE PHYSIOLOGY, INVERTEBRATE ZOOLOGY. Educ: San Diego State Col, BA, 43; Univ Calif, Berkeley, MA, 48; Univ Calif, Los Angeles, PhD, 54. Prof Exp: Instr zool, San Diego State Col, 48-50; assoc, Univ Calif, Los Angeles, 53-55; from asst prof to assoc prof, 55-65, PROF MARINE INVERT, UNIV BC, 65- Res: Electrolyte balance; water regulation; respiration marine invertebrates. Mailing Add: 830 Burley Dr West Vancouver BC V7T 1Z6 Can

DEHNER, EUGENE WILLIAM, b Burlington, Iowa, May 26, 14. ZOOLOGY. Educ: St Benedict's Col, BSc, 37; Cornell Univ, MSc, 43, PhD(zool), 46. Prof Exp: From instr to prof biol, St Benedict's Col, 46-71, chmn dept, 53-71, PROF BIOL & CHMN DEPT, BENEDICTINE COL, 71- Concurrent Pos: Res assoc, Clayton Found Biochem Inst, Univ Tex, 66-67. Mem: AAAS; Wilson Ornith Soc; Am Soc Zoologists; Sigma Xi. Res: Functional anatomy of birds, especially the adaptation of bodily dimensions to the habits of these animals; wing dimensions of two doves of different flight habits; respiratory volume and specific gravity of diving and surface feeding ducks. Mailing Add: Dept of Biol Benedictine Col N Campus Atchison KS 66002

DEHNHARD, DIETRICH, b Rengshausen, Ger, Apr 29, 34; m 58; c 3. NUCLEAR PHYSICS. Educ: Univ Marburg, dipl, 61, DrPhil(nuclear physics), 64. Prof Exp: Resident res assoc nuclear res, Argonne Nat Lab, 64-66; from asst prof to assoc prof, 66-77, PROF, SCH PHYSICS & ASTRON, UNIV MINN, MINNEAPOLIS, 77- Concurrent Pos: Visitor, Max Planck Inst Nuclear Physics, Heidelberg, Ger, 71-72 & Suisse Inst Nuclear Res, Villigen, Switz, 81. Mem: Am Phys Soc. Res: Nuclear structure studies by use of intermediate energy pions and protons and low energy light and heavy ions. Mailing Add: Sch of Physics & Astron Univ of Minn Minneapolis MN 55455

DE HOFF, GEORGE R(OLAND), b Baltimore, Md, Oct 16, 23; m 48; c 3. CHEMICAL & PLASTICS ENGINEERING. Educ: Johns Hopkins Univ, BE, 48, MS, 50. Prof Exp: Chem engr, Nat Plastics Prod Co, 50-53; res engr plastics dept, 53-62, tech rep, 62-67, consult, 67-72, sr engr, 72-79, STAFF ENGR, PLASTIC PRODS & RESINS DEPT, MFG DIV, WASHINGTON WORKS, E I DU PONT DE NEMOURS & CO, INC, 79- Mem: Soc Plastics Engrs. Res: Behavior of various thermoplastics in processing equipment, including relating the rheological properties of a resin to its processing characteristics; thermoplastic polymer processing. Mailing Add: Plastic Prod & Resins Dept E I du Pont de Nemours & Co Inc Parkersburg WV 26101

DEHOFF, PAUL HENRY, JR, b York Twp, Pa, Mar 12, 34; m 56; c 1. SOLID MECHANICS. Educ: Pa State Univ, BS, 56, MS, 58; Purdue Univ, PhD(solid mech), 65. Prof Exp: Mech engr, York Div, Bendix Corp, 58-61; instr aeronaut & astronaut eng sci, Purdue Univ, 61-65; res engr, exp sta, E I du Pont de Nemours & Co, Del, 65-66; asst prof mech eng, Bucknell Univ, 66-71, assoc prof & coordr grad studies, 71-78; PROF & CHAIR, ENG SCI, MECH & MAT, UNIV NC, CHARLOTTE, 78- Concurrent Pos: Consult, Scott Paper Co, Philadelphia, 73-78 & Med Col Ga, 77- Mem: Soc Rheol; Am Soc Mech Engrs; Am Soc Eng Educ; Sigma Xi; Am Acad Mech. Res: Solid deformations of polymeric material; creep and relaxation behavior under large strains; anisotropic behavior of polymers; biomechanical response of soft biological tissues; stress analysis of dental devices. Mailing Add: Dept Eng Sci Mech & Mat Univ of NC Charlotte NC 28223

DEHOFF, ROBERT THOMAS, b Sharon, Pa, Jan 15, 34; m 57; c 2. METALLURGY. Educ: Youngstown State Univ, BE, 55; Carnegie-Mellon Univ, MS, 58, PhD(metall eng), 59. Prof Exp: From asst prof to assoc prof, 59-70, PROF METALL ENG, UNIV FLA, 70- Concurrent Pos: Consult, Hanford Labs, Gen Elec Co, Wash, 63-64 & Bausch & Lomb, 76-78; ed, Bull Int Soc Stereology, 64-67. Honors & Awards: Sigma Xi fac res award, 64. Mem: Am Inst Mining, Metall & Petrol Engrs; Int Soc Stereol (vpres, 75-); Am Soc Metals; Int Metallog Soc; Sigma Xi. Res: Quantitative microscopy, sintering, multicomponent diffusion; thermodynamics; microstructural processes. Mailing Add: Dept of Mat Sci & Eng Univ of Fla Gainesville FL 32611

DE HOFFMANN, FREDERIC, b Vienna, Austria, July 8, 24; nat US; m 53. PHYSICS. Educ: Harvard Univ, BS, 45, MA, 47, PhD(physics), 48. Prof Exp: Staff mem, Los Alamos Sci Lab, 44-46; consult, AEC, 47-48; staff mem, Los Alamos Sci Lab, 48-55; vpres, Gen Dynamics Corp, Calif, 55-67, gen mgr, Gen Atomic Div, 55-59, pres, 59-67; vpres, Gulf Oil Corp, 67-69, pres, Gulf Gen Atomic, 67-69; chancellor, 70-71, PRES & CHIEF EXEC SALK INST BIOL STUDIES, 72-, CHMN & CHIEF EXEC, INDUST ASSOCS, 81- Concurrent Pos: Alt asst dir, Los Alamos Sci Lab, 50-51; hon prof theoretical physics, Univ Vienna, 68-; mem governing bd, Courant Inst Math, NY Univ, 68-; pres, Conf Future Sci & Technol, Austria, 72; mem adv comt mgt & technol, Int Inst Appl Systs Anal, Nat Acad Sci, 76-; mem bd dirs, Am Seminar, Salzburg, Austria, 78-81; mem, Sci & Technol Publ Adv Bd, Singapore Govt, 80- Honors & Awards: Great Golden Decoration of Merit, Repub Austria, 78; Great Commander Cross Medal & Cross for Sci & Arts, Repub Austria. Mem: Fel Am Phys Soc; fel Am Nuclear Soc. Res: Fission process; theory of chain reactions, neutron diffusion; magnetohydrodynamic shocks; meson theory. Mailing Add: 9736 La Jolla Farms Rd La Jolla CA 92037

DEHOLLANDER, WILLIAM ROGER, b Grand Rapids, Mich, Nov 15, 18; m 47; c 5. PHYSICAL CHEMISTRY. Educ: Univ Wash, PhD(phys chem), 51. Prof Exp: Sr scientist, Hanford Atomic Prods Oper, 51-59, specialist, Atomic Prod Equip Dept, 59-67, mgr process develop, Nuclear Fuels Dept, 67-75, consult engr, Boiling Water Reactor Systs Dept, 75-77, mgr chem eng, 77-81, CONSULT ENGR, GEN ELEC CO, 81- Mem: Am Chem Soc. Res: Gas chromatography; pyrophoricity; gas-solid reactions; kinetics; thermodynamics; reactor fuels and materials computer process control; hydraulics; radiation buildup and control. Mailing Add: Nuclear Fuels Dept Gen Elec Co 175 Curtner San Jose CA 95125

DEHORITY, BURK ALLYN, b Peoria, Ill, Sept 3, 30; m 53; c 4. RUMINANT NUTRITION, MICROBIOLOGY. Educ: Blackburn Col, BA, 52; Univ Maine, MS, 54; Ohio State Univ, PhD(biochem), 57. Prof Exp: Asst prof animal nutrit, Univ Conn, 57-58; from asst prof to assoc prof, 59-70, PROF ANIMAL SCI, OHIO AGR RES & DEVELOP CTR, 70-, ASSOC CHMN, 81- Mem: Am Soc Microbiol; Am Soc Animal Sci; Am Dairy Sci Asn. Res: Rumen microbiology. Mailing Add: Dept of Animal Sci Ohio Agr Res & Develop Ctr Wooster OH 44691

DEIBEL, ROBERT HOWARD, b Chicago, Ill, Dec 20, 24; m 49; c 4. BACTERIOLOGY. Educ: Univ Chicago, MS, 52, PhD, 62. Prof Exp: Bacteriologist, Am Meat Inst Found, 52-64; assoc prof bact, Cornell Univ, 64-66; assoc prof, 66-69, PROF BACT, UNIV WIS-MADISON, 69- Mem: Am Soc Microbiol; Can Soc Microbiol; Brit Soc Gen Microbiol. Res: Bacterial metabolism and taxonomy; food microbiology. Mailing Add: Dept of Bact Univ of Wis Madison WI 53706

DEIBEL, RUDOLF, b Berlin, Ger, Apr 27, 24; US citizen; m 57; c 3. PEDIATRICS, VIROLOGY. Educ: Univ Berlin, Cand Med, 50; Univ Freiburg, Dr Med, 53. Prof Exp: Intern med, Wenckebach Hosp, Berlin, 53-55; asst path, Inst Path, Univ Freiburg, 55-56, res asst pediat & virol, Children's Hosp, 56-58; vis scientist virol, NY State Dept Health, 58-59; res asst pediat & virol, Children's Hosp, 59-61; assoc med virologist, 62-67, DIR VIRUS LABS, NY STATE DEPT HEALTH, 67- Concurrent Pos: Asst prof pediat & microbiol, Albany Med Col, 65-69, assoc prof, 69-78, prof, 78- Mem: Am Asn Immunol; Am Pub Health Asn; Am Soc Microbiol; Am Soc Trop Med & Hyg; NY Acad Sci. Res: Pathogenesis, immunology and epidemiology of virus infections in man. children. Mailing Add: Div of Labs & Res NY State Dept of Health Albany NY 12201

DEIBERT, MAX CURTIS, b Lansing, Mich, May 19, 37; m 61; c 2. CHEMICAL ENGINEERING, ENVIRONMENTAL ENGINEERING. Educ: Cornell Univ, BChE, 60; Mass Inst Technol, ScD(chem eng), 64. Prof Exp: Asst prof chem eng, Mass Inst Technol, 64-70; tech dir, Anacon, Inc, 70-71; chief scientist, Environ Res & Technol Inc, 71-76, mgr, Billings Mont Off, 76-81; DIR QUAL ASSURANCE, NORTHERN TIER PIPELINE CO, 81- Concurrent Pos: Ford fel, 64-66; sr res chem engr, Monsanto Res Corp, Mass, 64-69; res group leader, Ionics, Inc, Mass, 69-70. Mem: Am Chem Soc; Am Inst Chem Engrs; Electrochem Soc; Am Pollution Control Asn. Res: Process instrumentation; electrochemistry; surface chemistry; process control; materials properties; infrared technology; instrumentation science and technology; pollution control systems development; drilling fluids development; energy development consulting. Mailing Add: 1009 Princeton Ave Billings MT 59102

DEIFT, PERCY ALEC, b Durban, SAfrica, Sept 10, 45. MATHEMATICAL PHYSICS. Educ: Univ Natal, MSc, 71; Princeton Univ, PhD(math physics), 76. Prof Exp: instr, 76-78, asst prof, 78-81, ASSOC PROF MATH, COURANT INST MATH SCI, NY UNIV, 81- Mem: Am Math Soc. Res: Application of the methods of functional analysis to spectral theoretic problems in mathematical physics; inverse spectral problems. Mailing Add: NY Univ 251 Mercer St New York NY 10012

DEILY, FREDRIC H(ARRY), b Evanston, Ill, June 9, 26; m 47; c 2. MECHANICAL ENGINEERING. Educ: Northwestern Univ, BS, 47, PhD(mech eng), 51. Prof Exp: Asst, Nat Defense Res Coun-Off Sci Res & Develop Proj, Northwestern Univ, 46-47, dept mech eng, 47-51; res engr, Carter Oil Co, Standard Oil Co, NJ, 51-58, group head, Jersey Prod Res Co, 58-59, res assoc, 60-63; eng adv, Imp Oil Ltd Can, 59-60, drilling adv, Int Petrol Co, Peru, 63-64, RES ASSOC, EXXON PROD RES CO, TEX, 64- Concurrent Pos: Mem, Drilling Domain Adv Comt, Am Petrol Inst, 60-63; Soc Petrol Engrs. Res: Oil well drilling research and engineering; rock behavior and failure; underground stress distribution; drilling fluid rheology and mechanics; drilling optimization. Mailing Add: Exxon Prod Res Co PO Box 2189 Houston TX 77001

DEINES, PETER, b Münden, Ger, Apr 2, 36. GEOCHEMISTRY. *Educ:* Pa State Univ, MSc, 64, PhD(geochem), 67. *Prof Exp:* Res asst geochem, 66-67, from asst prof to assoc prof geochem, 67-80, PROF GEOCHEM & MINERALOGY, PA STATE UNIV, UNIVERSITY PARK, 80- *Res:* Isotope geochemistry; variations in stable isotopes of carbon, oxygen, and hydrogen. *Mailing Add:* Dept Geosci 207 Deike Bldg Pa State Univ University Park PA 16802

DEINET, ADOLPH JOSEPH, b Elberfeld, Ger, Oct 29, 20; nat US; m 42; c 2. ORGANIC CHEMISTRY. *Educ:* Univ Va, BS, 43, PhD(chem), 46. *Prof Exp:* Res chemist antimalarials, Off Sci Res Develop, 44-46; res chemist, 46-70, supvr synthetic org res & develop, Heyden Div, 70-75, group leader, 75-78, LAB MGR, PROCESS DEVELOP LAB, ORG & POLYMERS DIV, TENNECO CHEM, INC, 78- *Mem:* Am Chem Soc. *Res:* General synthetic organic research and development. *Mailing Add:* 52 Valley Forge Dr East Brunswick NJ 08816

DEININGER, ROBERT WADE, b Monroe, Wis, Aug 15, 27; m 60; c 2. GEOLOGY, PETROLOGY. *Educ:* Univ Wis, BS, 50, MS, 57; Rice Univ, PhD(geol), 64. *Prof Exp:* Geologist, US Army Engrs, 51-53, engr, 53-54; geologist, Tidewater Oil Co, 57-58; instr geol, Univ Conn, 60-62; from instr to asst prof, Univ Ala, 62-66; from asst prof to assoc prof, 66-75, PROF GEOL, MEMPHIS STATE UNIV, 75- *Mem:* Geol Soc Am; Geochem Soc; Int Asn Geochem & Cosmochem. *Res:* Relationships among tectonics, metamorphism and igneous activity. *Mailing Add:* Dept of Geol Memphis State Univ Memphis TN 38152

DEININGER, ROLF A, b Ulm, Ger, Feb 13, 34; nat US; m 61; c 2. CIVIL ENGINEERING, ENVIRONMENTAL HEALTH. *Educ:* Stuttgart Tech Univ, Dipl Ing, 58; Northwestern Univ, MS, 61, PhD(civil eng), 65. *Prof Exp:* From asst prof to assoc prof, 63-72, PROF ENVIRON HEALTH, SCH PUB HEALTH, UNIV MICH, ANN ARBOR, 73- *Concurrent Pos:* Consult, UN, WHO, UNESCO, Environ Protection Agency, Pan Am Health Orgn. *Mem:* Am Soc Civil Eng; Am Water Works Asn; Opers Res Soc Am; Asn Comput Mach; Water Pollution Control Fedn. *Res:* Computer aided design of waste water collection and treatment systems; design of water distribution systems; optimal lake level control. *Mailing Add:* Dept Environ Health Univ of Mich Ann Arbor MI 48109

DEINKEN, HERMAN PORTER, physics, see previous edition

DEINZER, MAX LUDWIG, b Weehauken, NJ, June 19, 37; m 68; c 2. ORGANIC CHEMISTRY. *Educ:* Rutgers Univ, BS, 60; Univ Ariz, MS, 63; Univ Ore, PhD(org chem), 69. *Prof Exp:* Res chemist, E I du Pont de Nemours & Co, 69-71 & Environ Protection Agency, 71-73; ASSOC PROF AGR CHEM, ORE STATE UNIV, 73- *Mem:* Am Chem Soc; AAAS; Am Soc Mass Spectrometry. *Res:* Environmental and agricultural chemistry. *Mailing Add:* Dept of Agr Chem Ore State Univ Corvallis OR 97331

DEIRMENDJIAN, DIRAN, b Adapazari, Turkey, Nov 13, 17; nat US. ATMOSPHERIC PHYSICS. *Educ:* Univ Calif, Los Angeles, BA, 50, MA, 52, PhD(meteorol), 56. *Prof Exp:* Asst meteorol, Univ Calif, Los Angeles, 51, jr res meteorologist, 51-56, lectr, 56-57; PHYS SCIENTIST, SR STAFF, RAND CORP, 56- *Mem:* Am Astron Soc; Am Geophys Union; Optical Soc Am. *Res:* Radiation; em scattering of visible through mm wave radiation by atmospheric particles; cloud microphysics; radiative transfer in planetary atmospheres. *Mailing Add:* Rand Corp 1700 Main St Santa Monica CA 90406

DEIS, DANIEL WAYNE, b Martinez, Calif, May 9, 43. SOLID STATE PHYSICS. *Educ:* Stanford Univ, BS, 64; Duke Univ, PhD(physics), 68. *Prof Exp:* Instr physics, Duke Univ, 67-68; sr engr cyrogenics, Westinghouse Res & Develop Ctr, 68-73, fel eng cryogenics, 73-75; mech engr, Lawrence Livermore Lab, 75-79, fel eng electrotechnol, 79-81, MGR, HIGH CURRENT SYSTS, WESTINGHOUSE RES & DEVELOP CTR, 81- *Res:* Cryogenics; superconductivity; fusion magnets; machine design. *Mailing Add:* Westinghouse Res & Develop Ctr Beulah Rd Pittsburgh PA 15235

DEISCHER, CLAUDE KNAUSS, b Emmaus, Pa, Oct 14, 03; m 29; c 1. CHEMISTRY. *Educ:* Muhlenberg Col, BS, 25; Univ Pa, MS, 28, PhD(chem), 33. *Prof Exp:* Teacher pub schs, 21-24 & 25-27; from instr to assoc prof, 28-71, asst chmn dept, 52-65, EMER PROF CHEM, UNIV PA, 71- *Concurrent Pos:* Actg cur, E F Smith Mem Libr, 55-71. *Mem:* Am Inst Chemists; Am Chem Soc; Hist Sci Soc. *Res:* Quantitative inorganic analysis; history and literature of chemistry; chemistry of rare elements. *Mailing Add:* 158 Idris Rd Merion Station PA 19066

DEISHER, ROBERT WILLIAM, b Bradford, Ill, Aug 20, 20; m 48; c 3. MEDICINE, PEDIATRICS. *Educ:* Knox Col, AB, 41; Univ Wash, MD, 44. *Prof Exp:* From instr to assoc prof, 49-62, PROF PEDIAT, SCH MED, UNIV WASH, 62- *Mem:* Soc Pediat Res; Am Acad Pediat. *Res:* Child growth and development; adolescence; school problems; delinquency; mental retardation. *Mailing Add:* Dept of Pediat Univ of Wash Seattle WA 98195

DEISS, WILLIAM PAUL, JR, b Shelbyville, Ky, Feb 1, 23; m 48; c 3. INTERNAL MEDICINE. *Educ:* Univ Notre Dame, BS, 42; Univ Ill, MD, 45. *Prof Exp:* Intern, Univ Wis, 45-46, resident internal med, 48-51; Arthritis & Rheumatism Found res fel, 51-54; from asst prof to assoc prof med & biochem, Duke Univ, 54-58; from assoc prof to prof, Ind Univ, Indianapolis, 56-68; PROF MED & CHMN DEPT, UNIV TEX MED BR GALVESTON, 68- *Concurrent Pos:* In chg med serv, Durham Vet Admin Hosp, 56-58; consult, NIH, 60-64 & 68-72. *Mem:* Fel Am Col Physicians; Am Soc Clin Invest; Am Fedn Clin Res; Asn Am Physicians; Endocrine Soc. *Res:* Endocrinology and metabolism; bone and thyroid chemistry and physiology. *Mailing Add:* Dept of Med Univ of Tex Med Br Galveston TX 77550

DEISSLER, ROBERT G(EORGE), b Greenville, Pa, Aug 1, 21; m 50; c 4. FLUID DYNAMICS, HEAT TRANSFER. *Educ:* Carnegie Inst Technol, BS, 43; Case Inst Technol, MS, 48. *Prof Exp:* Engr mat develop, Goodyear Aircraft Corp, Ohio, 43-44; aerospace res spec fluid dynamics & chief fundamental heat transfer br, 47-72, STAFF SCIENTIST & SCI CONSULT FLUID PHYSICS, LEWIS RES CTR, NASA, 72- *Honors & Awards:* Max Jacob Award, Am Soc Mech Engrs & Am Inst Chem Engrs, 75. *Mem:* AAAS; Am Phys Soc; Am Inst Aeronaut & Astronaut; Am Soc Mech Engrs; Soc Natural Philos. *Res:* Fluid turbulence; turbulent heat transfer; thermal radiation; vortex flows; heat transfer in powders; meteorological and astrophysical flows. *Mailing Add:* NASA Lewis Res Ctr 21000 Brookpark Rd Cleveland OH 44135

DEIST, ROBERT PAUL, b Reading, Pa, Nov 28, 28; m 55; c 3. PHARMACEUTICAL CHEMISTRY. *Educ:* Albright Col, BS, 50. *Prof Exp:* Chemist, Allied Chem Co, 50-51; CHEMIST & SR RES SCIENTIST, WYETH LABS INC, AM HOME PROD CORP, 53- *Mem:* Am Chem Soc. *Mailing Add:* PO Box 565 West Chester PA 19380

DEITCH, ARLINE D, b New York, NY, Mar 12, 22; m 42. CELL BIOLOGY, CYTOPATHOLOGY. *Educ:* Brooklyn Col, BA, 44; Columbia Univ, MA, 46, PhD, 54. *Prof Exp:* Asst zool, 44-48, lectr, 49-50, asst surg, 53-55, vis fel, 55-56, from res assoc surg to res aasoc microbiol, 58-62, from asst prof microbiol to asst prof path, 62-73, ASSOC PROF PATH, COLUMBIA UNIV, 73- *Concurrent Pos:* USPHS fel, Nat Inst Neurol Dis & Blindness, 55-56. *Mem:* Am Soc Cell Biol; Histochem Soc; Tissue Cult Asn; Sigma Xi. *Res:* Flow cytometry, cytochemistry and cytopathology of cultured human and animal cells exposed to viruses and toxic chemical agents; tumor cell chemotherapy. *Mailing Add:* Dept of Path Columbia Univ New York NY 10032

DEITERMAN, LOUIS HENRY, JR, b Temple, Tex, Dec 14, 32; m 56; c 2. PHYSICS. *Educ:* Univ Tex, Austin, BS, 54, MA, 57, PhD(physics), 65. *Prof Exp:* Nuclear engr, Gen Dynamics Corp, 55-58; systs engr, Bendix Systs Div, 58-59; res physicist, Tex Instruments, Inc, 60-62; res scientist, Defense Res Labs, Univ Tex, Austin, 62-63; proj nuclear physicist, Gen Dynamics Corp, 65; STAFF PHYSICIST, SCOTT & WHITE MEM HOSP, 65- *Concurrent Pos:* Consult, Vet Admin Hosp, Temple, Tex, 68- *Mem:* Am Asn Physicists in Med; Sigma Xi. *Res:* Dosimetry of intense pulsed radiation fields; electroencephalograph effects due to auditory stimuli. *Mailing Add:* Dept of Res Scott & White Clin 2901 S 31st St Temple TX 76501

DEITERS, JOAN A, b Cincinnati, Ohio, Apr 28, 34. INORGANIC CHEMISTRY. *Educ:* Col Mt St Joseph, BA, 63; Univ Cincinnati, PhD(chem), 67. *Prof Exp:* Fel chem, Univ Mass, Amherst, 67-68; from instr to asst prof, Col Mt St Joseph, 68-73, assoc prof, 73-77, prof chem, 77-80; ASSOC PROF, VASSAR COL, 80- *Concurrent Pos:* Petrol Res Found-Am Chem Soc res grant, 69-71; vis lectr, Vassar Col, 78-80. *Mem:* Am Chem Soc; Sigma Xi. *Res:* Ion-molecule hydrogen bonds; spectroscopy and structure of pentacoordinated compounds; interaction of halide ions with carbon tetrahalides; computer simulation of structures of phosphorus compounds. *Mailing Add:* Dept Chem Vassar Col Poughkeepsie NY 12601

DEITRICH, L(AWRENCE) WALTER, b Pittsburgh, Pa, Oct 17, 38; m 64; c 1. MECHANICAL & NUCLEAR ENGINEERING. *Educ:* Cornell Univ, BME, 61; Rensselaer Polytech Inst, MS, 63; Stanford Univ, PhD(mech eng), 69. *Prof Exp:* Engr, Knolls Atomic Power Lab, Gen Elec Co, 61-64; asst mech engr, 69-72, mech engr, reactor anal & safety div, 72-79, mgr, fuel behav sect, 74-79, sect asst off dir, 79-80, ASSOC DIR, REACTOR ANAL & SAFETY DIV, ARGONNE NAT LAB, 80- *Honors & Awards:* Mat Sci & Technol Award of Recognition, Am Nuclear Soc, 78. *Mem:* Am Nuclear Soc; Am Soc Mech Engrs. *Res:* Nuclear reactor safety and design; heat transfer; fluid mechanics; engineering mechanics; modeling and analysis of reactor fuel elements; analysis of hypothetical reactor accidents. *Mailing Add:* Reactor Anal & Safety Div 9700 S Cass Ave Argonne IL 60439

DEITRICH, RICHARD ADAM, b Monte Vista, Colo, Apr 22, 31; m 54; c 3. PHARMACOLOGY, BIOCHEMISTRY. *Educ:* Univ Colo, BS, 53, MS, 54, PhD(pharmacol), 59. *Prof Exp:* Nat Heart Inst fel physiol chem, Sch Med, Johns Hopkins Univ, 59-61, instr, 61-63; asst prof, 63-69, assoc prof, 69-76, PROF PHARMACOL, UNIV COLO MED CTR, DENVER, 76- *Concurrent Pos:* Lederle fac award med, 63-65; Nat Inst Neurol Dis & Blindness res grant, 63-66; Nat Inst Gen Med Sci res career develop award, 65-75; Nat Inst Alcohol Abuse & Alcoholism res grants, 66-78; Nat Coun Alcoholism res grant, 73-74; vis prof, Inst Med Chem, Univ Berne, 73-74; dir, Univ Colo Alcohol Res Ctr, 77- *Mem:* Am Chem Soc; Res Soc Alcoholism (pres, 81-83); Am Soc Pharmacol & Exp Therapeut; Am Soc Biol Chem; Am Soc Neurochem. *Res:* Mechanism of enzyme action; biochemical basis of drug action; metabolic pathways for aldehydes; mechanism of sedative addiction; behavioral pharmacogenetics. *Mailing Add:* Dept of Pharmacol Univ of Colo Sch of Med Denver CO 80262

DEITZ, LEWIS LEVERING, b Harford Co, Md, June 22, 44. SYSTEMATICS, HOMOPTERA. *Educ:* Univ Md, BS, 67, MS, 68; NC State Univ, Raleigh, PhD(entom), 73. *Prof Exp:* Res asst entom, NC State Univ, 71-73, res assoc, 73-75; hemipterist, Dept Sci & Indust Res, Auckland, New Zealand, 75-79; res assoc, 79-80, ASST PROF, ENTOM DEPT & CUR INSECT COLLECTION, NC STATE UNIV, 80- *Mem:* Entom Soc Am; Entom Soc NZ; Sigma Xi; Systs Asn NZ. *Res:* Systematic research on homopterous insects, treehoppers, scale insects, and New Zealand planthoppers; identification and biology of soybean arthropods, classification of New World treehoppers and W M Maskells Homoptera. *Mailing Add:* Dept Entom Box 5215 NC State Univ Raleigh NC 27650

DEITZ, PAUL HAMILTON, b Philadelphia, Pa, Dec 29, 42; m 70; c 2. OPTICS. *Educ:* Gettysburg Col, BA, 64; Univ Wash, MS, 71, PhD(elec eng), 73. *Prof Exp:* Res physicist atmospheric optics, 64-76, res physicist weapons eng, 76-79, res physicist, Interactive Comput Graphics, 79-81, SUP

PHYSICIST, BR CHIEF VULNERABILITY METHODOLOGY, VULNERABILITY/LETHALITY DIV, US ARMY BALLISTIC RES LABS, 81-,. *Mem:* Inst Elec & Electronics Engrs; Optical Soc Am; Sigma Xi. *Res:* Weapons systems engineering for performance estimates and optimization of a new class of anti-tank devices which utilize both passive and active self-targeting schemes; interactive computer graphics for generation, display and modification of three dimensional target descriptions. *Mailing Add:* Ballistic Res Labs DRDAR-BLB Aberdeen Proving Ground MD 21005

DEITZ, VICTOR REUEL, b Downingtown, Pa, Apr 13, 09; m 40; c 4. SURFACE CHEMISTRY. *Educ:* Johns Hopkins Univ, PhD(chem), 32. *Prof Exp:* Asst, Johns Hopkins Univ, 32-33; Nat Res Coun fel, Univ Ill, 33-35, spec res assoc, 36-37; with res lab, Gen Elec Co, 37-38; res assoc, US Bur Stand, US Cane Sugar Res Proj, 39-46, chemist, 46-63; chemist, 63-73, RES CONSULT, US NAVAL RES LAB, 73- *Concurrent Pos:* Guggenheim fel, Imp Col, Univ London, 57-58. *Mem:* Am Chem Soc; Sugar Indust Technologists. *Res:* Adsorption and adsorbents; carbon fibers; sugar refining with bone char; carbon filters and charcoal adsorbents. *Mailing Add:* 3310 Winnett Rd Chevy Chase MD 20015

DEITZ, WILLIAM HARRIS, b Amsterdam, NY, June 14, 25; m 46; c 2. MICROBIOLOGY, BACTERIOLOGY. *Educ:* Hartwick Col, BS, 49; Univ Mass, MS, 51. *Prof Exp:* Res asst bact, Sterling Winthrop Res Inst, 52-62, res assoc, 62-68, res biologist, 68-70; DIR ALUMNI RELS, HARTWICK COL, 70- *Mem:* Am Soc Microbiol; assoc mem Sigma Xi. *Res:* Antibacterial agents; methods of bioassay; antibiotics; mode of action of nalidixic acid. *Mailing Add:* Hartwick Col Oneonta NY 13820

DEITZER, GERALD FRANCIS, b Buffalo, NY, June 5, 42; m 66; c 1. PHOTOBIOLOGY, CHRONOBIOLOGY. *Educ:* State Univ NY, Buffalo, BA, 66; Univ Ga, PhD(bot), 71. *Prof Exp:* Teaching asst plant anat, State Univ NY, Buffalo, 66-67; teaching asst biol, Univ Ga, 67-70; res asst photobiol, Univ Freiburg, WGer, 71-75; PLANT PHYSIOLOGIST PHOTOBIOL, SMITHSONIAN-RADIATION BIOL LAB, 75- *Mem:* Am Soc Plant Physiologist; Am Soc Photobiol. *Res:* Molecular mechanisms regulating the control of plant reproduction by light; interaction of light with the biological clock that determines photoperiodic sensitivity. *Mailing Add:* 12441 Parklawn Dr Rockville MD 20852

DEJAIFFE, ERNEST, b Fernwood, Pa, Mar 28, 12; m 35; c 1. CIVIL ENGINEERING. *Educ:* Pa State Univ, BS, 33, MS, 47. *Prof Exp:* Teacher, Altoona Sch Dist, Pa, 35-46 & 47-52; from instr to prof eng, Pa State Univ, 46-76; RETIRED. *Concurrent Pos:* Design engr, Gwin Engrs, 64. *Honors & Awards:* English Speaking Union Award, 61. *Mem:* Am Soc Eng Educ. *Res:* Engineering education and technical institutes. *Mailing Add:* 214 21st Ave Altoona PA 16601

DEJARNETTE, FRED ROARK, b Rustburg, Va, Oct 21, 33; m 51; c 2. AEROSPACE ENGINEERING. *Educ:* Ga Inst Technol, BS, 57, MS, 58; Va Polytech Inst, PhD(aerospace eng), 65. *Prof Exp:* Aerodyn engr, Douglas Aircraft Co, Inc, 58-61; asst prof aerospace eng, Va Polytech Inst, 61-63; aerospace engr, Langley Res Ctr, NASA, 63-65; assoc prof aerospace eng, Va Polytech Inst, 65-70; assoc prof mech & aerospace eng, 70-71, PROF MECH & AEROSPACE ENG, NC STATE UNIV, 71-, GRAD ADMINR, 73-, ASSOC HEAD MECH & AEROSPACE ENG, 80- *Concurrent Pos:* Consult, Langley Res Ctr, 66- & McDonnell Douglas Corp, 77- *Mem:* Am Inst Aeronaut & Astronaut. *Res:* Aerodynamics and high temperature gas dynamics. *Mailing Add:* Dept of Mech & Aerospace Eng NC State Univ Raleigh NC 27650

DEJMAL, ROGER KENT, b Hubbell, Nebr, Dec 26, 40; m 70; c 2. PHYSIOLOGY. *Educ:* Westmont Col, BA, 63; Ore State Univ, MS, 67, PhD(insect physiol), 69. *Prof Exp:* Asst prof physiol, Sioux Falls Col, 69-70; vol food biochemist, Inst Fisheries Develop, Peace Corps, Santiago, Chile, 70-72; MEM FAC CHEM & LIFE SCI FOR NURSING STUDENTS, UMPQUA COMMUNITY COL, 72- *Mem:* Am Sci Affil. *Res:* Protein synthesis and deposition during egg formation in insects; protein-lipid interaction in fish meat. *Mailing Add:* Dept of Chem & Life Sci Umpqua Community Col Box 967 Roseburg OR 97470

DEJONG, DIEDERIK CORNELIS DIGNUS, b Haarlem, Netherlands, Apr 23, 31; Am citizen; m 66. PLANT TAXONOMY. *Educ:* Univ Guelph, BSA, 58, MSA, 60; Mich State Univ, PhD(bot), 64. *Prof Exp:* From instr to asst prof bot, Miami Univ, 63-66; asst prof, McMicken Col Arts & Sci, 66-71, asst prof biol & bot, Raymond Walters Gen & Tech Col, 71-74, ASSOC PROF BIOL & BOT, RAYMOND WALTERS GEN & TECH COL, UNIV CINCINNATI, 74- *Res:* Taxonomic studies in the Angiosperms of Iceland. *Mailing Add:* Dept of Biol Raymond Walters Gen & Tech Col Cincinnati OH 45221

DEJONG, DONALD WARREN, b Doon, Iowa, Oct 14, 30; m 52; c 5. PLANT CYTOCHEMISTRY, AGRICULTURAL BIOTECHNOLOGY. *Educ:* Calvin Col, AB, 51; Univ Ga, PhD(bot), 65. *Prof Exp:* Jr high sch teacher, 51-54, sr high sch teacher, Mich, 54-55; high sch teacher, Guam, 55-57; instr biol, Pac Island Cent, Truk, 57-59; high sch instr, Mont, 59-61; instr, NSF Inst Sci Teachers, 61-62; res asst histochem, Univ Ga, 63-64; res biologist, Plant Enzyme Pioneering Res Lab, Agr Res Serv, USDA, 65-68, res chemist, Mid-Atlantic Area, Southern Region, 68-79; assoc prof bot, NC State Univ, 68-79; ASSOC STAFF SCIENTIST PLANT BIOCHEM, INT HARVESTER CO, CHICAGO, 79- *Concurrent Pos:* Nat Acad Sci-Nat Res Coun resident associateship, 65-67; Phi Sigma Soc grad res award, 65. *Mem:* Am Sci Affiliation; Am Inst Biol Sci; Am Soc Plant Physiol; Phytochem Soc NAm; Am Chem Soc. *Res:* Enzyme levels and isoenzyme patterns associated with physiological stages of growth in plants; biochemical properties of subcellular organelles during senescence of leaves; leaf protein fractionation and utilization. *Mailing Add:* USDA Mid-Atlantic Area Southern Region Agr Res Serv Oxford NC 27565

DE JONG, GARY JOEL, b Bellingham, Wash, June 21, 47; m 67; c 2. ANALYTICAL CHEMISTRY. *Educ:* Univ Calif, Riverside, BS, 69; Ore State Univ, PhD(anal chem), 73. *Prof Exp:* SCIENTIST CHEM, BRISTOL RES LABS, ROHM AND HAAS CO, 73- *Mem:* Am Chem Soc. *Res:* chromatographic methods for particle size analysis; instrumentation automation; instrumental-computer interfaces; thermal analysis of polymers; polymer analysis by spectroscopic and chromatographic methods; gel permeation chromatography; evaluation of hazardous materials by thermal methods. *Mailing Add:* Rohm and Haas Co Bristol Res Labs PO Box 219 Bristol PA 19007

DE JONG, MARVIN LEE, radio astronomy, see previous edition

DE JONG, PETER J, b Zeeland, Mich, July 22, 37; m 59; c 2. MICROBIOLOGY. *Educ:* Hope Col, BA, 59; Univ Wis, PhD(bacteriol), 64. *Prof Exp:* Res microbiologist, Procter & Gamble Co, 64-68; prof biol, Saginaw Valley State Col, 68-76; PROF BIOL, COE COL, 76- *Mem:* Am Soc Microbiol; Am Inst Biol Sci; AAAS. *Res:* Physiology of the streptomycetes, more specifically sporulation and germination of the spores of the streptomycetes. *Mailing Add:* Dept of Biol Coe Col Cedar Rapids IA 52402

DE JONG, RUDOLPH H, b Amsterdam, Netherlands, Aug 10, 28; US citizen; m 56, 76. MEDICINE, ANESTHESIOLOGY. *Educ:* Stanford Univ, BS, 51, MD, 54; Am Bd Anesthesiol, dipl, 61. *Prof Exp:* Asst prof anesthesia, Med Ctr, Univ Calif, San Francisco, 61-65; assoc prof anesthesiol & pharmacol, Sch Med, Univ Wash, 65-70, prof, 70-76; sr ed, JAMA, 76-78; Richard Saltonstall prof res anesthesiol, Sch Med, Tufts Univ, 78-82; PROF ANESTHESIOL & PHARMACOL, SCH MED, UNIV CINCINNATI, 82- *Concurrent Pos:* Consult, Med Serv, Vet Admin & US Navy, 61-76; res career develop award, Univ Wash, 66-76. *Mem:* AAAS; AMA; Am Soc Anesthesiol. *Res:* Physiology and pharmacology of central and peripheral nervous system, especially problems related to pain. *Mailing Add:* Dept Anesthesiol Univ Cincinnati Med Ctr Cincinnati OH 45267

DEJONG, RUSSELL NELSON, b Orange City, Iowa, Mar 12, 07; m 38; c 3. NEUROLOGY. *Educ:* Univ Mich, AB, 29, MD, 32, MS, 36. *Prof Exp:* From instr to prof, 35-76, chmn dept, 50-76, EMER PROF NEUROL, UNIV MICH, ANN ARBOR, 76- *Concurrent Pos:* Consult & adv, Selective Serv Syst, Mich, 40-45; consult, Vet Admin Hosp, Ft Custer, 46- & Ann Arbor, 53-; surgeon gen, Far East Command, US Dept Army, 51 & Ypsilanti State Hosp, 51-; ed in chief, Neurology, 51-76. Fulbright fel, Nat Hosp, London, 54-55; pres, Am Bd Psychiat & Neurol, 58. *Mem:* Am Neurol Asn (pres, 64-65); Asn Res Nerv & Ment Dis; Am Acad Neurol; Am Epilepsy Soc (pres, 54); Am Psychiat Asn. *Res:* Clinical neurology and neurologic complications of systemic disease. *Mailing Add:* Dept of Neurol Univ Hosp Ann Arbor MI 48104

DE JONG, SYBREN HENDRIK, b East Kildonan, Man, Oct 20, 08; m 38; c 4. GEODESY. *Educ:* Univ Man, BSc, 31, MSc, 40; Ohio State Univ, PhD, 68. *Prof Exp:* Eng clerk, Topog Surv Can, 36-38, chief surv party, 39-40; instr civil eng, Univ Toronto, 40-44, lectr surv, 44-45; from assoc prof to prof civil eng, 45-75, EMER PROF CIVIL ENG, UNIV BC, 75- *Mem:* Eng Inst Can; hon mem Can Inst Surv (pres, 69); Asn Prof Engrs BC. *Res:* Electronic surveying measurements; crustal deformations of the earth. *Mailing Add:* 5649 Ash St Vancouver Can

DEJONGH, DON C, b Burnips, Mich, May 10, 37; m 60; c 3. ORGANIC CHEMISTRY. *Educ:* Hope Col, BA, 59; Univ Mich, MS, 61, PhD, 63. *Prof Exp:* Res assoc, Mass Inst Technol, 62-63; from asst prof to prof chem, Wayne State Univ, 63-72; vis prof, 71, prof chem, Univ Montreal, 72-78; PRES, FINNIGAN INST, 78- *Mem:* Am Chem Soc; Am Soc Mass Spectrometry; AAAS; Can Inst Chem. *Res:* Application of mass spectrometry to structure problems in chemistry, biological sciences, and environmental sciences. *Mailing Add:* Finnigan Inst 11 Triangle Park Dr Cincinnati OH 45246

DEJU, RAUL A, b Havana, Cuba, Mar 14, 46; US citizen; m 68, 79; c 1. NUCLEAR MANAGEMENT, HYDROLOGY. *Educ:* NMex Inst Mining & Technol, BS, 66, PhD(geosci), 69. *Prof Exp:* Res asst metall, State Bur Mines & Mineral Resources, NMex Inst Mining & Technol, 62-65; res asst comput sci, NMex Inst Mining & Technol, 66-69; vis assoc prof hydraul, Grad Sch Eng & Chmn Dept Geohydraul & Geochem, Inst Geophys, Univ Mex, 69-70; res geochemist, Gulf Res & Develop Co, 70-73; prof hydrol, Wright State Univ, 73-75; res assoc, Atlantic Richfield Hanford Co, 75, mgr ground water hydrol, 75-77, DIR WASTE ISOLATION, ROCKWELL HANFORD, 77- *Concurrent Pos:* Lectr, Univ Pittsburgh, 70-; consult, 73-75. *Mem:* Am Inst Mining, Metall & Petrol Eng; Am Asn Petrol Geologists; Am Geophys Union; Assoc Prof Geol Scientists. *Res:* Groundwater hydrology; petroleum engineering; geology; pollution problems; water management; flow through porous media; environmental control and management techniques. *Mailing Add:* PO Box 800 Rockwell Hanford Richland WA 99352

DEKAZOS, ELIAS DEMETRIOS, b Merkovouni, Greece, Sept 14, 20; US citizen; m 55; c 3. PLANT PHYSIOLOGY, FOOD SCIENCE. *Educ:* Univ Thessaloniki, dipl, 44; Univ Calif, MS, 53, PhD(plant physiol), 57. *Prof Exp:* Prof agr, Pedagogical Acad Tripolis, Greece, 49-51; tech adv, Agr Bank, Greece, 45-54; res assoc & instr bot, Univ Chicago, 58-60; lectr biochem, Loyola Univ, Ill, 61-62; plant physiologist, Mkt Qual Res Div, USDA, Beltsville, 63-67, plant physiologist, Human Nutrit Res Div, Agr Res Ctr, 67-70, PLANT PHYSIOLOGIST, RUSSELL AGR RES CTR, USDA, 70- *Mem:* Am Soc Hort Sci; Am Soc Plant Physiol; Inst Food Technologists; NY Acad Sci; Sigma Xi. *Res:* Fruit production and postharvest horticulture; control of flowering; anthocyanins; objective methods of quality evaluation; color and texture; quality sorting; growth regulators in fruit production; fruit maturity; storage; postharvest ripening of immature fruit; dehydration-explosion puffing. *Mailing Add:* Russell Agr Res Ctr USDA Agr Res Serv PO Box 5677 Athens GA 30604

DE KIMPE, CHRISTIAN ROBERT, b Brussels, Belgium, Aug 1, 37; Can citizen; m 64; c 3. PHYSICAL CHEMISTRY, MINERALOGY. *Educ:* Univ Louvain, Ing Chim & Ind Agr, 59, Dr Sc Agr(phys chem & clay mineral), 61. *Prof Exp:* Res assoc clay mineral, Fonds Nat De Recherche Sci, 63-65; res asst clay genesis, Ministere Educ Nat, 65-67; RES SCIENTIST SOIL GENESIS, AGR CAN, 67- *Concurrent Pos:* Ed, Can J Soil Sci, 80-82; lectr, McGill Univ, 80-82. *Mem:* Can Soc Soil Sci: Clay Minerals Soc; Int Soc Soil Sci; Soil Sci Soc Am; Int Asn Study of Clays. *Res:* Soil genesis, clay formations; relations between soil; physical condition, water movement and natural fertility; effect of amorphous substances and organic matter on soil aggregation. *Mailing Add:* Agr Can Res Sta 2560 Blvd Hochelaga Ste-Foy PQ G1V 2J3 Can

DEKIRMENJIAN, HAROUTUNE, biochemistry, see previous edition

DEKKER, CHARLES ABRAM, b Chicago, Ill, Apr 9, 20; m 47; c 5. BIOCHEMISTRY. *Educ:* Calvin Col, AB, 41; Univ Ill, PhD(biochem), 47. *Prof Exp:* Asst biochem, Univ Ill, 41-43, teaching asst chem, 43-44, biochem, 46-47; res asst, Yale Univ, 47-49; fel Am Cancer Soc, Cambridge Univ, 49-51; from asst prof to assoc prof & from lab asst to assoc res biochemist, 51-62, PROF BIOCHEM & RES BIOCHEMIST, VIRUS LAB, UNIV CALIF, BERKELEY, 62-, MAJOR ADV, DEPT BIOCHEM, 80- *Mem:* Am Chem Soc; Am Soc Biol Chem. *Res:* Chemistry and enzymology of nucleic acids and their derivatives. *Mailing Add:* Dept of Biochem Univ of Calif Berkeley CA 94720

DEKKER, DAVID BLISS, b Evanston, Ill, May 28, 19; m 42; c 2. MATHEMATICS. *Educ:* Univ Calif, AB, 41, PhD(math), 48; Ill Inst Technol, MS, 43. *Prof Exp:* Asst math, Ill Inst Technol, 41-43; mathematician, Lockheed Aircraft Corp, Calif, 43-44; asst math, Univ Calif, 46-48; instr, 48-51, asst prof, 51-59, ASSOC PROF MATH & COMPUT SCI, UNIV WASH, 59- *Concurrent Pos:* Dir, Comput Ctr, Univ Wash, 56-66. *Mem:* Am Math Soc. *Res:* Foundations of geometry; metric differential geometry; hypergeodesic curvature and torsion; generalizations of hypergeodesics; numerical analysis. *Mailing Add:* Dept of Math Univ of Wash Seattle WA 98195

DEKKER, EUGENE EARL, b Highland, Ind, July 23, 27; m 58; c 3. BIOCHEMISTRY. *Educ:* Calvin Col, AB, 49; Univ Ill, MS, 51, PhD(biochem), 54. *Prof Exp:* Res assoc biochem, Univ Ill, 54; instr, Sch Med, Univ Louisville, 54-56; from instr to assoc prof, 56-70, PROF BIOCHEM, SCH MED, UNIV MICH, ANN ARBOR, 70-, ASST CHMN DEPT, 75- *Concurrent Pos:* Life inst med res fel, Med Sch, Univ Mich, Ann Arbor, 56-58; Lederle med fac award, 58-61; NIH res fel, Univ Calif, Berkeley, 65-66; NIH res fel, Scripps Clin & Res Found, La Jolla, Calif, 73-74. *Mem:* Am Chem Soc; Am Soc Biol Chem; Am Soc Plant Physiol. *Res:* Mechanism of action and comparative biochemistry of enzymes, especially aldolases; metabolism of nitrogen compounds in animals, plants and bacteria; enzyme structure-function relationships. *Mailing Add:* Dept of Biochem Univ of Mich Med Sch Ann Arbor MI 48109

DEKKER, JACOB CHRISTOPH EDMOND, b Hilversum, Neth, Sept 6, 21; nat US; m 50. MATHEMATICS. *Educ:* Syracuse Univ, PhD(math), 50. *Prof Exp:* Instr math, Univ Chicago, 51-52; from instr to asst prof, Northwestern Univ, 52-55; vis asst prof, Univ Chicago, 55-56; mem, Inst Advan Study, 56-58; assoc prof, Univ Kans, 58-59; from asst prof to assoc prof, 59-61, PROF MATH, RUTGERS UNIV, 61- *Concurrent Pos:* Lectr, Nat Univ Mex, 61; consult, Int Bus Mach Corp, 58 & 60; mem, Inst Advan Study, 67-68. *Mem:* Math Asn Am; Am Math Soc; Asn Symbolic Logic. *Res:* Recursive functions; combinatorial theory. *Mailing Add:* Dept of Math Rutgers Univ New Brunswick NJ 08903

DEKLOET, SIWO R, b Maarssen, Neth, Feb 22, 33; m 64; c 2. BIOCHEMISTRY, MOLECULAR GENETICS. *Educ:* Univ Utrecht, BS, 53, MS, 56, PhD(biophys, chem), 61. *Prof Exp:* Res assoc cell biol, Rockefeller Univ, 61-62; res scientist, Philips Res Labs, Eindhoven, Neth, 63-67; assoc prof, 67-80, PROF BIOL SCI, INST MOLECULAR BIOPHYS, FLA STATE UNIV, 80- *Res:* Metabolism and properties of nucleic acids; genetics of fungi; metabolism of nucleotide analogues; mechanism of action of antibiotics. *Mailing Add:* Dept of Biol Sci Fla State Univ Tallahassee FL 32306

DE KOCK, CARROLL WAYNE, b Oskaloosa, Iowa, Apr 14, 38; m 59; c 2. INORGANIC CHEMISTRY. *Educ:* Calvin Col, BS, 60; Iowa State Univ, PhD(chem), 65. *Prof Exp:* Fel chem, Argonne Nat Lab, 65-67; assoc prof, 67-80, PROF CHEM, ORE STATE UNIV, 80- *Mailing Add:* Dept of Chem Ore State Univ Corvallis OR 97331

DEKOCK, ROGER LEE, b Oskaloosa, Iowa, Oct 4, 43; m 65; c 2. STRUCTURE & BONDING. *Educ:* Calvin Col, BA, 65; Univ Wis-Madison, PhD(inorg chem), 70. *Prof Exp:* Res assoc, Univ Fla, 69-70, Univ Birmingham, Eng, 70-72; asst prof inorg chem, Am Univ, Beirut, 72-76; assoc prof, 76-80, PROF CHEM, CALVIN COL, 80- *Concurrent Pos:* Vis prof, Univ Notre Dame. *Mem:* Am Chem Soc. *Res:* Proton affinity studies of cluster molecules using semiempirical molecular orbital methods; electronic structure and bonding of hydrocarbon fragments in organometallic cluster molecules; theoretical studies of cluster-surface analogy. *Mailing Add:* Dept Chem Calvin Col Grand Rapids MI 49506

DEKORNFELD, THOMAS JOHN, b Iregszemcse, Hungary, June 19, 24; US citizen; m 52; c 4. ANESTHESIOLOGY. *Educ:* George Washington Univ, BS, 48, MS, 49; Harvard Med Sch, MD, 53. *Prof Exp:* Instr anesthesiol, Sch Med, Univ Wis, 56-57; from asst chief to chief, Baltimore City Hosp, Md, 57-63; dir clin therapeut, Parke, Davis & Co, Mich, 63-64; assoc prof anesthesiol, 64-68, PROF ANESTHESIOL, MED SCH, UNIV MICH, ANN ARBOR, 68- *Mem:* AMA; Am Soc Anesthesiol; Am Soc Pharmacol. *Res:* Clinical pharmacology; clinical and laboratory investigation of new narcotic and non-narcotic analgesics. *Mailing Add:* Dept of Anesthesiol Univ of Mich Med Ctr Ann Arbor MI 48104

DE KORTE, AART, b Rotterdam, Neth, Sept 4, 34; US citizen. PHYSICAL CHEMISTRY. *Educ:* NY Univ, BA, 58; Yale Univ, MS, 60, PhD(chem), 65. *Prof Exp:* Instr chem, Queens Col, NY, 64-66; asst prof, 66-71, assoc prof, 71-77, chmn dept, 78-81, PROF CHEM, FAIRLEIGH DICKINSON UNIV, 77- *Mem:* Am Chem Soc; NY Acad Sci. *Res:* Fluorescence. *Mailing Add:* Dept of Chem Fairleigh Dickinson Univ Rutherford NJ 07070

DEKORTE, JOHN MARTIN, b Grand Rapids, Mich, Sept 20, 40; m 63; c 2. INORGANIC CHEMISTRY. *Educ:* Hope Col, BA, 62; Purdue Univ, PhD(inorg chem), 69. *Prof Exp:* From asst prof to assoc prof, 66-79, PROF CHEM, NORTHERN ARIZ UNIV, 80- *Concurrent Pos:* Res grant, Petrol Res Fund-Am Chem Soc, 68; res grant, Res Corp, 70. *Mem:* Am Chem Soc; Sigma Xi. *Res:* Kinetics and mechanisms of inorganic oxidation-reduction reactions. *Mailing Add:* Dept of Chem Box 5698 Northern Ariz Univ Flagstaff AZ 86001

DE KORVIN, ANDRE, b Berlin, Ger, Dec 13, 35; US citizen; m 67. MATHEMATICS. *Educ:* Univ Calif, Los Angeles, BA, 62, MA, 63, PhD(math), 67. *Prof Exp:* Mathematician, IBM Corp, San Jose, Calif, 63-64, res mathematician, Sci Ctr, Los Angeles, 64-67; asst prof math, Carnegie-Mellon Univ, 67-69; vis asst prof, 68-69, from asst prof to assoc prof, 69-75, PROF MATH & COMPUT SCI, IND STATE UNIV, TERRE HAUTE, 75- *Concurrent Pos:* Vis prof, Ind Univ-Purdue Univ, 80-81. *Mem:* AAAS; Am Math Soc; Math Asn Am; NY Acad Sci. *Res:* Functional analysis; algebra of operators; vector measures; information sciences; computer sciences; probability theory. *Mailing Add:* 1474 Spruce Dr Carmel IN 46032

DE KRASINSKI, JOSEPH S, b Mszana, Poland, June 15, 14; m 47; c 4. FLUID MECHANICS. *Educ:* Univ London, BSc, 44, PhD(aeronaut), 64. *Prof Exp:* Res scientist, Royal Aircraft Estab, Farnborough, Eng, 44-46; head aerodyn res, Argentine Aeronaut Res Inst, 47-67; assoc prof, 66-76, PROF FLUID MECH, UNIV CALGARY, 76- *Concurrent Pos:* Prof, Univ Cordoba, 55-67. *Mem:* Am Inst Aeronaut & Astronaut. *Res:* Aerodynamics; gas dynamics; boundary layer theory; separated flows; atmospheric aerodynamics; compressible boundary layers; wind tunnelling; experimental techniques in wind tunnels; wind tunnel design. *Mailing Add:* Eng Dept Univ Calgary Calgary AB T2N 1N4 Can

DELABARRE, EVERETT MERRILL, JR, b Boston, Mass, Mar 3, 18; m 53; c 4. MEDICINE. *Educ:* Columbia Univ, BA, 40, MD, 43. *Prof Exp:* Asst path, Columbia Univ, 44; clin instr med, Yale Univ, 54-57; assoc chief med, Mem Med Ctr, Williamson, WVa, 57-64; asst chief, Vet Admin Hosp, 64-65; asst prof, 65-70, ASSOC PROF PHYS MED & REHAB, TUFTS UNIV, 70- *Mem:* Am Thoracic Soc; Asn Mil Surg US; Am Col Physiol. *Res:* Chest disease rehabilitation. *Mailing Add:* Vet Admin Med Ctr 150 S Huntington Ave Boston MA 02130

DE LA BURDE, ROGER Z, b Katowice, Poland, Sept 22, 31; US citizen; m 58; c 2. RESEARCH ADMINISTRATION. *Educ:* Jagiellonian Univ, MS, 52, PhD(org chem), 59; Aachen Tech Univ, PhD(chem eng), 61; Cracow Tech Univ, MChE, 56. *Prof Exp:* Mgr int tech dept, Cracow Mfg Co, 52-56; chemist, Roswell Park Mem Inst, 56-59; proj leader, Armour & Co, 59-61; MGR PROJ & SR RES SCIENTIST, PHILIP MORRIS USA RES CTR, INC, 61- *Concurrent Pos:* Dir, Fed Inst Indust Res, Ministry of Industs, Nigeria, 68-69; adv, UN Indust Develop Orgn. *Honors & Awards:* Polish Nat Award, 55; US Nat Hide Asn Award, 61; Philip Morris Patent Medals, 67, 70 & 75; Indust Award, Nigeria, 69. *Mem:* AAAS; Am Chem Soc; Sigma Xi. *Res:* Development of chemical industries, business planning and international marketing; management of research and development; new product development in tobacco, foodstuffs, natural products; research on proteins and drugs. *Mailing Add:* Philip Morris USA Res Ctr PO Box 26583 Richmond VA 23261

DELACERDA, FRED G, b Natchitoches, La, Sept 19, 37; m 72. HUMAN FACTORS, BIOMECHANICS. *Educ:* La Tech Univ, BS, 60; La State Univ, MS, 69, PhD(exercise physiol), 71; Univ Tenn, BS, 73; Okla State Univ, BS, 79. *Prof Exp:* Syst analyst indust, Tex Eastern Gas Transmission, Inc, 61-62; instr math & physics, Sabine Parish Sch Syst, 64-67; asst prof health, Tenn Technol Univ, 71-72 & Univ Southwestern La, 73-75; asst prof, 75-80, ASSOC PROF HEALTH, OKLA STATE UNIV, 80- *Concurrent Pos:* Gooch Allied Health Scholarship, Med Ctr, Univ Tenn, 72-73; consult physiotherapy, Teachers' Conf Phys Disabled Children, La State Univ, Eunice, 74-75, Wagoner Community Hosp, 76-77, Logan County Mem Hosp, 76-77, Williams Clin, Pawnee Manor Nursing Home, 77-, Hominy City Hosp, 76- & Okla Dept Corrections. *Mem:* Am Soc Biomech; Am Soc Mech Engrs; Human Factor Soc; Am Inst Aeronaut & Astronaut. *Res:* Biomechanics and human factor engineering. *Mailing Add:* Colvin Ctr Rm 124-E Okla State Univ Stillwater OK 74074

DE LA CHAPELLE, CLARENCE EWALD, b New York, NY, Dec 6, 97; m 25; c 2. MEDICINE. *Educ:* NY Univ, BS, 21, MD, 22. *Prof Exp:* Intern & house physician, Bellevue Hosp, 22-24; instr path, Col Med, 24-26, instr med, 26-32, asst prof, 32-38, actg chmn dept, 37-38, prof clin med, 34-48, asst dean, 42-45, assoc dean, 45-63, dir postgrad div, 45-48, dean, Postgrad Med Sch, 48-64, PROF MED, NY UNIV, 45- *Concurrent Pos:* Physician, Sch Nursing, Bellevue Hosp, 25-45, asst physician, Outpatient Dept & from adj asst vis physician to vis physician, Hosp, 25-; actg dir, 3rd Med Div, 37-38; chief cardiac clin, Lenox Hill Hosp, 33-48, assoc vis physician, 33-45, attend cardiologist, 45-48, dir med, 48-60, consult med, 60-; consult physician, St Lukes Hosp, Newburgh, NY, 33-48; consult & adv prof educ, US War Dept, 42-44; consult cardiologist, Community Hosp, Glen Cove, 45-49, 58- & New Rochelle Hosp, 47-; consult, Flushing Hosp, Long Island, 46-48, Fitkin Mem Hosp, NJ, 46-53 & Vassar Bros Hosp, 47-55; dir regional hosp div, NY Univ-Bellevue Med Ctr, 47-63, consult, 63-; nat consult, Surgeon Gen, US Air Force, 58-64; mem med adv panel, Fed Aviation Agency, 65-68; consult cardiovasc dis. *Honors & Awards:* Pres Citation, NY Univ, 63. *Mem:* Fel Am Col Physicians; fel Am Heart Asn; Am Asn Path & Bact; fel NY Acad Med; Int Acad Path. *Res:* Cardiovascular pathology; correlation of clinical and pathological data in cardiovascular diseases; post-graduate and graduate medical education. *Mailing Add:* Dept of Med NY Univ Med Ctr New York NY 10016

DE LA FUENTE, ROLLO K, b Mt Province, Philippines, Oct 6, 33; m 61; c 2. PLANT PHYSIOLOGY. *Educ:* Univ Philippines, BS, 55; Univ Hawaii, MS, 59, PhD(bot) 64. *Prof Exp:* From asst instr to instr bot, Univ Philippines, 55-61; res asst, Univ Hawaii, 63-64; res fel plant physiol, Purdue Univ, 64-69; asst prof, 69-74, ASSOC PROF PLANT PHYSIOL, KENT STATE UNIV, 74- *Concurrent Pos:* Mem adv panel, Physiol Cell Metab Biol Sect, NSF, 81-84. *Mem:* Sigma Xi; Am Soc Plant Physiologists; AAAS. *Res:* Mechanism and significance of the plant hormone indoleacetic acid; the possible role that calcium plays in regulating this pheonomenon. *Mailing Add:* Dept of Biol Sci Kent State Univ Kent OH 44242

DELAGI, EDWARD F, b New York, NY, Nov 4, 11; m 41; c 2. MEDICINE. *Educ:* Fordham Univ, BS, 34; Hahnemann Med Col, MD, 38. *Prof Exp:* Asst chief paraplegic sect, Vet Admin Hosp, Bronx, 51-53, chief ward sect phys med & rehab, 51-56; adj, Jewish Hosp Chronic Dis, Brooklyn, 56-58; assoc prof, 59-64, PROF REHAB MED, ALBERT EINSTEIN COL MED, 64- *Concurrent Pos:* Attend physician, Vet Admin Hosp, Bronx, 56-; dir, Frances Schervier Hosp & Home, Riverdale, 56-; vis physician, Bronx Munic Hosp Ctr, 56-; chief, St Josph's Hosp, Yonkers, 57- & Misericordia Hosp, Bronx, 58- *Mem:* AAAS; fel AMA; fel Am Acad Phys Med & Rehab; fel Am Cong Rehab Med; fel Am Col Physicians. *Res:* Physical medicine and rehabilitation; kinesiology; electromyography; electrodiagnostic methods. *Mailing Add:* Dept of Rehab Med Albert Einstein Col of Med New York NY 10461

DE LA HABA, GABRIEL LUIS, b PR, June 29, 26; m 61. BIOLOGICAL CHEMISTRY. *Educ:* Johns Hopkins Univ, AB, 46, PhD(biol), 50. *Prof Exp:* USPHS fel, NY Univ, 51-52; USPHS fel, Yale Univ, 52-53; instr biochem, 53-54, asst prof, 54-55; sr asst scientist, USPHS, 55-58; res assoc, Johns Hopkins Univ, 58-59; res assoc anat, Univ, 59-68, ASSOC PROF ANAT, SCH MED, UNIV PA, 68- *Mem:* Am Soc Biol Chemists. *Res:* Biochemistry of development. *Mailing Add:* Dept of Anat Univ of Pa Sch of Med Philadelphia PA 19174

DELAHAY, PAUL, b Sas Van Gent, Neth, Apr 6, 21; nat US; m 62. CHEMICAL PHYSICS. *Educ:* Univ Brussels, BS, 41, MS, 45, Liege, 44; Univ Ore, PhD(chem), 48. *Prof Exp:* Instr chem, Univ Brussels, 45-46; res assoc, Univ Ore, 48-49; from asst prof to Boyd prof, La State Univ, 49-65; PROF CHEM, NY UNIV, 65-, FRANK G GOULD PROF SCI, 74- *Concurrent Pos:* Guggenheim fels, Cambridge Univ, 55 & NY Univ, 71-72; Fulbright prof, Univ Paris, 62-63. *Honors & Awards:* Heyrovsky Medal, Czech Acad Sci; Turner Prize, Electrochem Soc, 51, Palladium Medal Award, 67; Award in Pure Chem, Am Chem Soc, 55, Southwest Award, 59. *Mem:* AAAS; Am Chem Soc; Am Phys Soc. *Res:* Photoelectron emission spectroscopy of solutions; electron scattering in gases; solvated electron. *Mailing Add:* Dept Chem NY Univ 4 Washington Pl Rm 514 New York NY 10003

DELAHAYES, JEAN, b Rouen, France, June 9, 36; m 57; c 1. PHYSIOLOGY. *Educ:* Univ Paris, Lic es Sci, 64, Dipl, 66, Dr es Sci(physiol), 68. *Prof Exp:* Teaching asst physiol, Univ Paris, 65-68; from instr to asst prof, Ohio State Univ, 69-74; ASSOC PROF PHYSIOL, MED COL GA, 74- *Concurrent Pos:* Head pharmacol, Clin-Midy Res Ctr, Montpellier, France, 75-78. *Res:* Movements of ions across the cell membrane in heart during activity; problems of excitation cantiaction coupling; movements of Ca-45 associated with heart activity. *Mailing Add:* Dept of Physiol Med Col Ga Augusta GA 30912

DELAHUNTA, ALEXANDER, b Concord, NH, Dec 3, 32; m 55; c 4. VETERINARY ANATOMY, NEUROLOGY. *Educ:* State Univ NY Vet Col, DVM, 58; Cornell Univ, PhD(vet anat), 64; Am Col Vet Internal Med, dipl neurol. *Prof Exp:* Vet practr, Cilley's Animal Hosp, NH, 58-60; from instr to assoc prof, 60-73, PROF VET ANAT, STATE UNIV NY VET COL, CORNELL UNIV, 73-, CHMN DEPT CLIN SCI, 77- *Mem:* Am Vet Med Asn; Am Asn Vet Anatomists; Am Asn Anatomists; Am Asn Vet Neurologists. *Res:* Clinical neurology; neuropathology; neuroanatomy. *Mailing Add:* State Univ of NY Vet Col Cornell Univ Ithaca NY 14850

DELAHUNTY, GEORGE, b Upper Darby, Penn, May 5, 52; m 78. ICHTHYOLOGY. *Educ:* Duquesne Univ, BS, 74; Marquette Univ, PhD(biol), 79. *Mem:* Am Soc Zoologists; AAAS; Am Soc Icthyologists & Herpetologists. *Res:* Environmental control of metabolism and reproduction in teleosts; role of the pineal organ as possible tranducer of photo period information; the role of the pineal in the circadian organization of the animal. *Mailing Add:* Dept Biol Goucher Col Towson MD 21204

DE LA IGLESIA, FELIX ALBERTO, b Cordoba, Arg, Nov 27, 39; m 64; c 3. EXPERIMENTAL PATHOLOGY, TOXICOLOGY. *Educ:* Nat Univ Cordoba, BSc, 56, MD, 63. *Prof Exp:* Instr path, Nat Univ Cordoba, 59-62, res asst electron micros, 63-64; res fel, Hosp Sick Children, Toronto, 64-66; scientist, 66-68, dir toxicol, 68-72, dir, Warner Lambert Res Inst Can, 72-76; dir, Dept Toxicol, 77-81, DIR, DEPT PATH & EXP TOXICOL, PHARMACEUT RES DIV, PARKE DAVIS & CO, WARNER-LAMBERT CO, 81- *Concurrent Pos:* Mem, Int Study Group Res in Cardiac Metab; Med Res Coun Can res fel; adj prof path, Univ Toronto Fac Med, 81-; ed, Current Topics Toxicol, Drug Metab Rev, 81- *Honors & Awards:* J Carveth Wells Award. *Mem:* Int Acad Path; Am Col Toxicol; Soc Toxicol Pathologists; Am Asn Pathologists; Soc Toxicol. *Res:* Liver diseases; nutrition and pathology; adverse hepatic effects of therapeutic agents; chemical carcinogenesis; drug safety evaluation; subcellular pathology and toxicology. *Mailing Add:* Pharmaceut Res Div Parke Davis & Co Warner-Lambert Co 2800 Plymouth Rd Ann Arbor MI 48105

DELAITSCH, DALE M, b Colfax, Wis, Dec 18, 22; m 45; c 2. ORGANIC CHEMISTRY. *Educ:* Univ Chicago, BS, 44; St Olaf Col, AB, 46; Univ Minn, PhD(chem), 50. *Prof Exp:* From asst prof to assoc prof, 50-63, PROF CHEM, UNIV SOUTHWESTERN LA, 63- *Mem:* Am Chem Soc. *Res:* Protection of hydroxyl and sulfhydryl groups. *Mailing Add:* Dept of Chem Univ of Southwestern La Lafayette LA 70501

DE LA MARE, HAROLD ELISON, b Burley, Idaho, Aug 5, 22; m 52; c 6. ORGANIC CHEMISTRY, POLYMER CHEMISTRY. *Educ:* Utah State Univ, BS, 44; Purdue Univ, PhD(org chem), 51. *Prof Exp:* Chemist, Eastman Kodak Co, NY, 44-46; asst org chem, Purdue Univ, 46-48 & 49-50, instr chem, 50-51; res chemist, 51-72, sr staff res chemist, 72-80, RES ASSOC, SHELL DEVELOP CO, 80- *Mem:* Am Chem Soc; NY Acad Sci. *Res:* Organic peroxide chemistry and oxidation reactions; free radical-metal ion interactions; coordination complex catalysis in elastomer synthesis; anionic polymerization; epoxy and photocure resins, epoxy reaction injection molding, thermostat composites. *Mailing Add:* Shell Develop Co PO Box 1380 Houston TX 77001

DELAMATER, EDWARD DOANE, b Plainfield, NJ, Jan 24, 12; m 43; c 5. MICROBIOLOGY, ELECTRON MICROSCOPY. *Educ:* Johns Hopkins Univ, MA, 37; Columbia Univ, PhD(bact, dermat), 41, MD, 42. *Prof Exp:* Asst bot, Johns Hopkins Univ, 33-36; asst dermat, Columbia Univ, 36-42, mycologist, Vanderbilt Clin, Med Ctr, 36-42; fel dermat, Mayo Found, Univ Minn, 46-47, asst prof bact & mycol, 47-48; mycologist, Mayo Clin, 46-48; assoc res prof dermat, Sch Med, Univ Pa, 48-51, from assoc res prof to res prof microbiol, 50-63, res prof dermat, 51-63, dir sect cytol & cytochem, 53-63, consult, Pepper Lab Hosp, 48-63; prof & chmn dept microbiol, New York Med Col, 63-66; hosp epidemiologist, New York City Dept Health, 65-66; prof microbiol & dean col sci, Fla Atlantic Univ, 66-68, distinguished prof sci, 68-78. *Concurrent Pos:* Consult, Smith, Kline & French Lab, 48-51, Off Surgeon Gen, 48-63, Children's Hosp, Philadelphia, 49-63 & Skin & Cancer Hosp, 58-63; Guggenheim fel, 53; mem med staff, Eastern Shore Hosp Ctr, Cambridge, 77- *Mem:* Mycol Soc Am; Am Col Physicians; Bot Soc Am; Genetics Soc Am; Am Soc Trop Med & Hyg. *Res:* Cytology and cytochemistry of micro-organisms; medical mycology; life cycles of spirochetes; structure and ultrastructure of fish scales. *Mailing Add:* Rte 1 Box 97 Oxford MD 21654

DELAMATER, GEORGE (BEARSE), b Oneonta, NY, Mar 12, 22; m 48; c 2. INDUSTRIAL CHEMISTRY. *Educ:* Cornell Univ, BChE, 44; Harvard Univ, PhD(phys org chem), 48. *Prof Exp:* Res chemist, Nat Defense Res Comt, Cornell Univ, 43-45; res engr, Explosives Res Lab, Pa, 45; from res chemist to dir res, Mallinckrodt Chem Works, 48-66; dir res & mgr spec projs, 66-79, MGR INVENTION LIAISON, AIR PROD & CHEM INC, 79- *Mem:* Am Chem Soc; Fel AAAS. *Res:* Process development; general industrial chemistry; chemical engineering; research administration. *Mailing Add:* Air Prod & Chem Inc Box 538 Allentown PA 18105

DE LAMIRANDE, GASTON, b Montreal, Que, Dec 22, 23; m 50; c 3. BIOLOGICAL CHEMISTRY. *Educ:* Univ Montreal, BA, 43, BSc, 46, MSc, 47, PhD(chem), 49. *Prof Exp:* Lectr org chem, Univ Montreal, 46-49; res assoc biochem, Montreal Cancer Inst, Nat Cancer Inst Can, Notre Dame Hosp, 49-60; res assoc prof biol chem, 60-67, RES PROF BIOL CHEM, FAC MED, UNIV MONTREAL, 67-, VDEAN, FAC MED, 75- *Concurrent Pos:* Damon Runyon Found Cancer Res fel, 52-55; res scientist, Montreal Cancer Inst, Nat Cancer Inst Can, Notre Dame Hosp, 60-67, assoc dir, 67-75. *Mem:* AAAS; Am Asn Cancer Res; NY Acad Sci; Can Physiol Soc; Can Biochem Soc. *Res:* Chemistry and metabolism of nucleic acids and proteins; enzymology; cancer. *Mailing Add:* Univ of Montreal PO Box 6207 Montreal Can

DE LA MONEDA, FRANCISCO HOMERO, b Dec 20, 39. SOLID STATE DEVICE MODELING. *Educ:* Rensselaer Polytech Inst, BS, 61, Syracuse Univ, MS, 65; Univ Fla, PhD(elec eng), 70. *Prof Exp:* Staff engr, Syst Commun Div, 70-74, adv engr, Data Syst Div, 74-78, Gen Technol Div, 78-81, ADV ENGR, GEN PROD DIV, IBM, 81- *Mem:* Inst Elec & Electronics Engrs. *Res:* Analytical and numerical models for bipolar and metal-oxide-semiconductor transitors and development of measurement techniques for constants and parameter of such models. *Mailing Add:* 3660 N San Sebastian Dr Tucson AZ 85715

DE LANCEY, GEORGE BYERS, b Cresson, Pa, Oct 19, 40; m 63; c 2. CHEMICAL ENGINEERING. *Educ:* Univ Pittsburgh, BS, 62, MS, 65, PhD(chem eng), 67. *Prof Exp:* Res engr, Jones & Laughlin Steel Corp, 63-65, consult, 65-66; res assoc math, Nat Bur Stand, 67-68; asst prof, 68-77, PROF CHEM ENG, STEVENS INST TECHNOL, 77- *Mem:* Am Inst Chem Engrs. *Res:* Interfacial mass transfer and heterogeneous catalysis. *Mailing Add:* Dept of Chem & Chem Eng Castle Point Sta Hoboken NJ 07030

DELAND, ANDRE N, b St Johns, Que, Feb 6, 26; m 56; c 1. GEOLOGY. *Educ:* Univ Montreal, BA, 51; McGill Univ, MSc, 52; Yale Univ, PhD(geol), 55. *Prof Exp:* Field geologist, Que Dept Mines, 55-65; ASST PROF GEOL, CONCORDIA UNIV, 65- *Concurrent Pos:* Assoc prof geol, Concordia Univ, 65- *Mem:* Geol Soc Can; Can Inst Mining & Metall. *Res:* Petrology; industrial minerals; field geology. *Mailing Add:* Dept of Geol Concordia Univ Montreal Can

DELAND, EDWARD CHARLES, b Lusk, Wyo, May 16, 22; m 52. MATHEMATICS. *Educ:* SDak Sch Mines & Technol, BS, 43; Univ Calif, Los Angeles, PhD(math), 56. *Prof Exp:* Engr, Corning Glass Works, 43-46; asst prof physics, San Diego State Col, 46-48; sr scientist, Rand Corp, 56-72; ADJ PROF THORACIC SURG, ANESTHESIOL & BIOMATH, UNIV CALIF, LOS ANGELES, 72- *Concurrent Pos:* Dir analog comput facil, Univ Calif, Los Angeles, 53-56, instr eng, 56-62; res colloid sci, Univ Cambridge, 65; NIH spec res resources bd fel, 67-68; consult, Nat Ctr Health Serv Res & Develop, 68-70, Nat Lab Med, Nat Bur Standards & NASA. *Mem:* Math Asn Am; Asn Comput Mach; Int Asn Analog Comput; Soc Advan Med Systs; Bioeng Soc. *Res:* Computer design and applications; applied mathematics; pedagogy; physiology; computer systems; mathematical models; biochemistry of heart cells; hemoglobin. *Mailing Add:* Div of Thoracic Surg Univ of Calif Ctr for Health Sci Los Angeles CA 90024

DELAND, FRANK H, b Jackson, Mich, July 2, 21; m 49; c 4. NUCLEAR MEDICINE. *Educ:* Univ Mich, Ann Arbor, BS, 47; Univ Louisville, MD, 52; Univ Minn, St Paul, MS, 56. *Prof Exp:* Fel path, Mayo Found, 53-56; dir lab med, Lakeland, Fla, 57-67; assoc prof nuclear med, Johns Hopkins Univ, 67-70; prof, Univ Fla, 70-74; PROF RADIATION MED, MED CTR, UNIV KY, 74- *Concurrent Pos:* Instr path, Ohio State Univ, 65-67; NIH fel, Johns Hopkins Univ, 66-67; res grants, US Dept Health, Educ & Welfare, 67-71 & Vet Admin, 71-; ed, J Nuclear Med, 75- *Mem:* Am Soc Clin Path; Col Am Path; Int Acad Path; Soc Nuclear Med. *Res:* Application of radionuclides for in-vivo study and diagnosis of neoplastic, inflammatory and congenital disease; automation of microbiology by means of in-vitro radionuclide methodology. *Mailing Add:* Dept of Radiation Med Univ of Ky Med Ctr Lexington KY 40506

DELANEY, CHARLES MACGREGOR, b Ottawa, Can, July 16, 22; nat US; m. PHYSICAL CHEMISTRY. *Educ:* Univ Detroit, AB, 43; Syracuse Univ, MSc, 47, PhD(phys chem), 52. *Prof Exp:* Plastics engr, Eng Div, Chrysler Corp, 44-45; asst & asst instr chem, Syracuse Univ, 45-52; res chemist, Houston Res Lab, Shell Oil Co, 52-54; Gulf Found fel, Mellon Inst, 54-56; lectr, Univ Pittsburgh, 55, asst prof, 56-58; assoc prof, 58-63, PROF CHEM, WELLS COL, 64- *Concurrent Pos:* Fulbright lectr, Vidyodaya Univ Ceylon, 64-65. *Mem:* Am Chem Soc. *Res:* Vapor pressure of solutions by differential manometry; thermal cracking; catalysis; olefin polymerization; thermodynamics. *Mailing Add:* Dept Chem Wells Col Aurora NY 13026

DELANEY, EDWARD JOSEPH, b Evergreen Park, Ill, Apr 28, 53; m 77. CHEMISTRY. *Educ:* Loyola Univ, Bs, 74, Univ Ill Med Ctr, PhD(med chem), 80. *Prof Exp:* Teaching asst gen chem, Univ Ill Med Ctr, 74-80; FEL, NORTHWESTERN UNIV, 80- *Mem:* Am Chem Soc; Sigma Xi. *Mailing Add:* 1724 W Greenleaf Chicago IL 60626

DELANEY, JOHN P, b St Paul, Minn, Oct 1, 30; m 60; c 2. SURGERY, PHYSIOLOGY. *Educ:* Univ Minn, BS, 53, MD, 55, PhD(physiol), 63. *Prof Exp:* Univ fel, 59-67, from asst prof to assoc prof, 67-80, PROF SURG, UNIV MINN, MINNEAPOLIS, 80- *Concurrent Pos:* USPHS fel, 63- *Res:* Splanchnic blood flow; cause of peptic ulcer. *Mailing Add:* Dept Surg Univ Minn Minneapolis MN 55455

DELANEY, PATRICK FRANCIS, JR, b Fall River, Mass, Mar 11, 33; m 54; c 4. METABOLISM, ACADEMIC ADMINISTRATION. *Educ:* Providence Col, AB, 54; Brown Univ, AMT, 61, PhD(biol), 64. *Prof Exp:* Teacher, Mass High Schs, 55-59, chmn dept math, 60-61; asst biol, Brown Univ, 61-63; asst prof biochem & physiol, Col Holy Cross, 64-67, assoc prof biol, 67-69; prof biol & chmn dept, Lindenwood Cols, 69-71, dean, Lindenwood Col For Men, 71-79; VPRES ACAD AFFAIRS, FITCHBURG STATE COL, 79- *Concurrent Pos:* Nat Inst Arthritis & Metab Dis res grant, 64-70; consult, Dept Internal Med, Med Sch, St Louis Univ, 70-71. *Mem:* AAAS; NY Acad Sci; Am Asn Higher Educ; Sigma Xi. *Res:* Renal metabolism; mitochondrial protein synthesis; hormonal control of metabolism; effect of acidosis on kidney metabolism. *Mailing Add:* Fitchburg State Col Fitchburg MA 01420

DELANEY, ROBERT, b Pittsfield, Mass, May 20, 28; m 53; c 8. BIOCHEMISTRY. *Educ:* Boston Col, BS, 52; Albany Med Col, PhD(biochem), 63. *Prof Exp:* Res scientist, Div Labs & Res, NY State Dept Health, 60-63; Nat Inst Arthritis & Metab Dis fel, Med Ctr, Duke Univ, 63-66, res assoc biochem, 65-66; from asst prof to assoc prof, 66-74, PROF BIOCHEM, SCH MED, UNIV OKLA, 74- *Mem:* Am Soc Immunol; Am Soc Biol Chem. *Res:* Protein structure of acid proteases carboxylated proteins and bacterial toxins. *Mailing Add:* Dept Biochem & Molecular Biol Univ of Okla Health Sci Ctr Oklahoma City OK 73190

DELANEY, ROBERT MICHAEL, b Wood River, Ill, Nov 13, 31. THEORETICAL PHYSICS. *Educ:* St Louis Univ, BS, 53, PhD(physics), 58. *Prof Exp:* From asst prof to assoc prof, 56-68, PROF PHYSICS, ST LOUIS UNIV, 68- *Mem:* Am Phys Soc; Sigma Xi. *Res:* Thermal neutron scattering; relativistic wave equations; high energy physics; scattering of polarized particles; resonant states in quantum mechanics. *Mailing Add:* Dept of Physics St Louis Univ St Louis MO 63103

DELANGE, ROBERT J, b Richfield, Utah, Mar 30, 37; m 60; c 6. BIOCHEMISTRY, PROTEIN CHEMISTRY. *Educ:* Brigham Young Univ, BS, 61; Univ Wash, PhD(biochem), 65. *Prof Exp:* Fel, 65-67, asst prof, 67-71, assoc prof, 71-77, PROF BIOL CHEM, SCH MED, UNIV CALIF, LOS ANGELES, 77- *Concurrent Pos:* Guggenheim fel, 73-74. *Mem:* Am Soc Biol Chem; AAAS. *Res:* Structure-function relationships of chromosomal and other proteins; amino acid sequences; role of naturally occurring derivatives of amino acids. *Mailing Add:* Dept of Biol Chem Univ of Calif Sch of Med Los Angeles CA 90024

DELANGLADE, RONALD ALLAN, b Indianapolis, Ind, May 20, 36; m 62; c 1. PLANT MORPHOLOGY. *Educ:* Wabash Col, BA, 58; Purdue Univ, MS, 61, PhD(morphol), 64. *Prof Exp:* Instr biol, Wabash Col, 61-64; from asst prof to assoc prof, Eastern Ky Univ, 64-67; asst prof, 67-70, chmn dept, 74-76, assoc prof, 70-77, PROF BIOL, WITTENBERG UNIV, 77- *Mem:* AAAS; Bot Soc Am. *Res:* Plant succession in old-fields; leaf morphogenesis. *Mailing Add:* Dept of Biol Wittenberg Univ Springfield OH 45501

DELANNEY, LOUIS EDGERTON, b Omaha, Nebr, Feb 2, 12; wid; c 1. ZOOLOGY, BIOLOGY. *Educ:* Univ Calif, Los Angeles, BA, 35, MA, 36; Stanford Univ, PhD(embryol), 40. *Prof Exp:* Asst, Univ Calif, Los Angeles, 35-36; from asst to instr biol, Stanford Univ, 36-41; from instr to asst prof physiol, San Jose State Col, 41-46; asst prof biol, Notre Dame Univ, 46-49; from assoc prof to prof zool, Wabash Col, 49-66; prof biol, Ithaca Col, 66-77, chmn dept, 66-73; affil investr, Pac Northwest Res Found, 77-78; res assoc, The Jackson Lab, 78-81; SCIENTIST, INST MED RES, 81- *Concurrent Pos:* Ford Found fac fel, 55-56; fel, Carnegie Inst, 57. *Mem:* AAAS; Am Soc Naturalists; Am Soc Zoologists; Soc Develop Biol; Tissue Cult Asn. *Res:* Neoplasia in urodeles; ontogeny of immune response; amphibian embryology; role of ectoderm in determination of pigmentation; embryology of the spleen and thymus; biological specificity and development. *Mailing Add:* Inst Med Res 751 S Bascom Ave San Jose CA 95128

DELANO, ERWIN, b New York, NY, June 27, 26; m 55. OPTICS. *Educ:* Yale Univ, BS, 50; Univ Rochester, MS, 56, PhD(optics), 66. *Prof Exp:* Engr, Bausch & Lomb Optical Co, 51-53, sect head optical design, 53-58, dept head optical design & comput, Bausch & Lomb Inc, 58-63; from asst prof to assoc prof, 63-69, chmn dept, 66-72 & 74-81, PROF PHYSICS, ST JOHN FISHER COL, 69- *Mem:* Fel Optical Soc Am. *Res:* Geometrical optics, theory and practice of lens design; methods of synthesis for dielectric multilayer interference filters; primary aberrations of fresnel lenses. *Mailing Add:* Dept of Physics St John Fisher Col 3690 East Ave Rochester NY 14618

DELANO, RALPH B(ENJAMIN), JR, b Nov 18, 19; m 46; c 2. ELECTRICAL ENGINEERING, MANAGEMENT SCIENCE. *Educ:* Mass Inst Technol, BS, 41. *Prof Exp:* Elec & ultrasonic develop, Sperry Prods, Inc, 41-48; sr engr, Res Ctr, Int Bus Mach Corp, 49-61, mgr patent eng, Components Div, 61-69; fel, Ctr Advan Eng, Mass Inst Technol, 69-70; SR ENGR, GEN TECHNOL DIV, IBM CORP, HOPEWELL JUNCTION, 70- *Honors & Awards:* IBM Invention Award, 61, 71 & 79. *Res:* Cryogenic technology; digital computers; components; operations research; decision theory; information systems; patents; computer aided design. *Mailing Add:* Lane Gate Rd Cold Spring NY 10516

DE LA NOUE, JOEL JEAN-LOUIS, b Ferryville, Tunisia, Mar 18, 38; m 59, 80; c 3. CELL PHYSIOLOGY, NUTRITION. *Prof Exp:* Asst prof biol, Laval Univ, 64-68; fel cell physiol, Univ Sheffield, 68-69; res assoc zool, Univ Wash, 69-70; adj prof biol, 70-72, assoc prof, 72-80, PROF BIOL, LAVAL UNIV, 80-, DIR NUTRIT, CTR RES NUTRIT, 78- *Concurrent Pos:* NATO fel, 68-70. *Mem:* Can Soc Zoologists; AAAS; French Can Asn Advan Sci; Nutrit To-Day Soc. *Res:* Wastewater treatment through selective biological utilization of nutrients; invertebrate and fish nutrition. *Mailing Add:* Dept Biol Laval Univ Ste Foy Quebec PQ C1K 7P4 Can

DELANSKY, JAMES F, b Philipsburg, Pa, July 27, 34; m 59. ELECTRICAL ENGINEERING. *Educ:* Pa State Univ, BS, 62; Cornell Univ, MS, 64, PhD(elec eng, math), 68. *Prof Exp:* Technician, Electronic Tube Div, Westinghouse Elec Corp, 57 & Remington Rand Corp, 58; asst prof elec eng, 68-74, ASSOC PROF ELEC ENG, PA STATE UNIV, 74- *Mem:* Inst Elec & Electronics Engrs. *Res:* Circuit theory; synthesis of passive and active networks, including networks of several variables. *Mailing Add:* Dept of Elec Eng Pa State Univ University Park PA 16802

DELANY, ANTHONY CHARLES, atmospheric chemistry, cosmochemistry, see previous edition

DE LA PAZ, ARMANDO, chemical engineering, see previous edition

DE LA PENA, ARMANDO, b San Antonio, Tex, Apr 2, 31; m 59; c 1. CLINICAL CHEMISTRY, CHEMISTRY. *Educ:* Trinity Univ, BS, 53; St Mary's Univ, Tex, MS, 65. *Prof Exp:* ASSOC FOUND SCIENTIST CLIN CHEM, SOUTHWEST FOUND RES & EDUC, 63- *Concurrent Pos:* Consult, Bioregional Ref Lab, San Antonio, 73-76. *Mem:* Am Chem Soc; Am Asn Clin Chemists; Clin Radioassay Soc. *Res:* Radioimmunoassay of oral contraceptive drugs such as ethynyl estradiol, mestranol and norethinedrone; radioimmunoassays of steroids and gonadotropins in plasma. *Mailing Add:* Southwest Found for Res & Educ PO Box 28147 San Antonio TX 78284

DE LA PENA, RAMON SERRANO, b San Jacinto, Pangasinan, Philippines, Oct 2, 36; US citizen; m 63; c 4. AGRONOMY, PLANT PHYSIOLOGY. *Educ:* Univ Philippines, BSc, 58; Univ Hawaii, MSc, 64, PhD(agron), 67. *Prof Exp:* Asst agronomist, 67-76, ASSOC AGRONIMIST, UNIV HAWAII, 76- *Concurrent Pos:* Rice Training Off, Rice Training Ctr, Univ Hawaii, 68-72; dir econ develop, County of Kauai, 73-74; vis sci, Philippine Root Crop Res Ctr, 76; prin investr, Coop State Res Serv USDA, 76-79; consult, AID, Thailand, 74, World Bank, Thailand, 78, Universe Tankships, 80 & Nat Acad Sci, Indonesia, 81. *Mem:* Am Soc Agron; Soil Sci Soc Am; Weed Sci Soc Am; Int Soil Sci Soc; Int Soc Trop Root Crops. *Res:* Management, production and physiology of tropical root and tuber crops, legumes and cereals; weed control in tropical root crops with emphasis on taro, Colocasia esculenta. *Mailing Add:* Kauai Br Sta Univ of Hawaii Rte 1 Box 278-A Kapaa HI 96746

DELAPPE, IRVING PIERCE, b Boston, Mass, Oct 28, 15; m 42; c 3. SCIENCE ADMINISTRATION. *Educ:* Harvard Univ, BS, 42, AM, 46, PhD, 53. *Prof Exp:* Asst epidemiol, Sch Pub Health, 48; asst prof bact & pub health, Mich State Univ, 48-54; adminstr, Am Cyanamid Co, 54-60; exec secy microbiol panel, 60-62, asst chief fel & career awards, 62-65, chief biochem & physiol br, 65-76, chief parasitol & med entomol, 74-76, CHIEF MOLECULAR MICROBIOL & PARASITOL, PHYSIOL BR, NAT INST ALLERGY & INFECTIOUS DIS, NAT INSTS HEALTH, 77- *Res:* Physiology of Histomonas meleagridis, Trichomonas gallinarum, Entamoeba histolytica studies. *Mailing Add:* 8907 Ridge Pl Bethesda MD 20817

DE LA SIERRA, ANGELL O, b Santurce, PR; US citizen; m 60; c 5. CELL BIOPHYSICS, CHEMISTRY. *Educ:* Univ PR, Rio Piedras, BS, 54; City Univ New York, MS, 58; St John's Univ, NY, PhD(cell biophys), 63. *Prof Exp:* Res analyst biophys, Smithsonian Inst, 63-64; res chemist, Armed Forces Radiobiol Res Inst, Dept Defense, 64-65; NIH fel biophys, Col Med, Georgetown Univ, 65-67; vis prof, Col Med, Univ PR, San Juan, 67, mem fac, 67-68; DIR FAC NATURAL SCI, UNIV PR, CAYEY, 68- *Mem:* Biophys Soc; Am Chem Soc; Radiation Res Soc; NY Acad Sci. *Res:* Learning and affect computer charracterization of putative synaptic transmitters; neuropharmacology of behavior. *Mailing Add:* Fac of Natural Sci Univ of PR Cayey PR 00633

DELATE, EDWARD JOSEPH, applied statistics, deceased

DE LA TORRE, JACK CARLOS, b Paris, France, Dec 2, 37; US citizen; m 62. NEUROPHARMACOLOGY, NEUROSURGERY. *Educ:* Am Univ, BS, 61; Univ Madrid, SM, 63; Univ Geneva, PhD(neuroanat), 68; Univ Juarez, MD, 79. *Prof Exp:* Res asst opthal, Int Eye Bank, Washington, DC, 59-61; head microbiol, Armour & Co, Cent Res Lab, Ill, 64-65; clin bacteriologist, Chicago Bd Health, Ill, 65-66; instr neurol surg, Pritzker Sch Med, Univ Chicago, 69, asst prof, 69-75, assoc prof, 75-78; assoc prof, Univ Miami Sch Med, 79-82; ASSOC PROF NEUROL SURG, MED SCH, NORTHWESTERN UNIV, 82- *Concurrent Pos:* NIH res grant, 70- *Mem:* AAAS; Asn Res Nerv & Ment Dis; Soc Neurosci; Am Acad Neurol; Int Brain Res Orgn. *Res:* Experimental head, spinal cord injury; basal ganglia disorders; cerebral stroke, CNS lesions, cerebral blood flow mechanisms, brain death; central nervous system regeneration. *Mailing Add:* Northwestern Univ Med Sch 303 E Chicago Ave Chicago IL 60611

DE LATOUR, CHRISTOPHER, b Nov 24, 47; US citizen; m 70. ENVIRONMENTAL PHYSICS. *Educ:* Georgetown Univ, BS, 69; Mass Inst Technol, SM, 71, PhD(physics), 74. *Prof Exp:* Staff res scientist environ physics, Francis Bitter Nat Magnet Lab, Mass Inst Technol, 75-77; LECTR, PHYSICS DEPT, CALIF POLYTECH STATE UNIV, 77- *Mem:* Am Phys Soc; Sigma Xi. *Res:* Improvement and maintenance of environmental quality; development of advanced methods of water purification. *Mailing Add:* Dept of Physics Calif Polytech State Univ San Luis Obispo CA 93407

DE LAUBENFELS, DAVID JOHN, b Pasadena, Calif, Dec 5, 25; m 54; c 4. GEOGRAPHY, BOTANY. *Educ:* Colgate Univ, AB, 49; Univ Ill, AM, 50, PhD(geog), 53. *Prof Exp:* From asst prof to assoc prof geog & geol, Univ Ga, 53-59; assoc prof, 59-71, PROF GEOG, SYRACUSE UNIV, 71- *Concurrent Pos:* Bowman fel, Johns Hopkins Univ, 55-56. *Mem:* Asn Am Geogrs; Am Geog Soc; Bot Soc Am; Ecol Soc Am; Int Soc Plant Morphologists. *Res:* Vegetation geography; morphology and taxonomy of conifers; climatology. *Mailing Add:* Dept of Geog Syracuse Univ Syracuse NY 13210

DELAUER, R(ICHARD) D(ANIEL), b Oakland, Calif, Sept 23, 18; m 40; c 1. AERONAUTICS. *Educ:* Stanford Univ, AB, 40; US Naval Post-Grad Sch, BS, 49; Calif Inst Technol, PhD(aeronaut), 53. *Prof Exp:* Exp eng officer, Naval Aeronaut Sch, NJ, 50-51; missile aerodyn sect head, Bur Aeronaut, US Navy, 53-54; mem, mil staff, Los Alamos Sci Lab, Calif, 54-57; warhead res officer, Naval Air Spec Weapon Facility, 57-58; dir, Vehicle Develop Lab, TRW Inc, 58-60, dir, Titan Weapon Syst, 60-63, vpres & dir, Systs Eng & Integration, 63-68, vpres & gen mgr, exec vpres, 70-81; UNDER SECY DEFENSE, RES & ENG, DEPT DEFENSE, 81- *Concurrent Pos:* Instr, Univ NMex, 55 & Univ Calif, 59; consult, Los Alamos Sci Lab, Calif, 57- *Mem:* Nat Acad Engrs; AAAS; Am Inst Aeronaut & Astronaut. *Res:* Hypersonic aerodynamics; nuclear propulsion; space vehicle development. *Mailing Add:* 1101 S Arlington Ridge Rd 402 Arlington VA 22202

DELAVAULT, ROBERT EDMUND, b Edmonton, Alta, Dec 3, 07; m; c 2. GEOCHEMISTRY, METALLURGY. *Educ:* Univ Paris, Lic es Sci, 28, DSc(phys sci), 36. *Prof Exp:* Mem res staff, Mineral Lab, Mus Natural Hist, Paris, 41-43, lectr geochem, 43-46; res assoc geol, Univ BC, 47-64, assoc prof, 64-74; VIS PROF GEOSCI, UNIV BRAZILIA, 76- *Mem:* Geol Soc Am; Geochem Soc; Asn Explor Geochemists. *Res:* Chemistry of magnesium metallurgy; etch figures of crystals; trace metal analysis; biogeochemistry; geochemistry of ore deposits; applications of geochemistry to prospecting. *Mailing Add:* Dept of Geosci Univ of Brazilia Brasilia Brazil

DELAWARE, DANA LEWIS, b Gardiner, Maine, Mar 16, 51; m 79; c 1. CARBOHYDRATE CHEMISTRY, ANTIBIOTICS. *Educ:* Marist Col, BA, 73; Purdue Univ, PhD(med chem & pharmacog), 78. *Prof Exp:* Teaching asst chem, Purdue Univ, 73-75, res asst, 76; res asst, Univ Ariz, 76-78; res asst, Univ Ill, 78-80, vis asst prof, 78-79; ASST PROF ORG CHEM, NORTHEAST MO STATE UNIV, 80- *Mem:* Am Chem Soc; AAAS; Sigma Xi. *Res:* Investigation of structural activity-relationships of carbohydrate derived antibiotics and synthesis of inhibitors of Aldolase enzymes. *Mailing Add:* 1404 S Riggen Kirksville MO 63501

DE LAY, ROGER LEE, b Waukee, Iowa, Aug 3, 45; m 67; c 2. RUMINANT NUTRITION. *Educ:* Iowa State Univ, BS, 67; Colo State Univ, MS, 69, PhD(ruminant nutrit), 72. *Prof Exp:* Res nutritionist, 72-76, develop mgr ruminant prods, 76-80, DEVELOP MGR ANIMAL PRODS, INT, AM CYANAMID CO, 80- *Mem:* Am Soc Animal Sci. *Res:* Growth promotion and feed utilization in beef cattle and sheep; animal feed and health products that will result in improved meat production. *Mailing Add:* Am Cyanamid Co PO Box 400 Princeton NJ 08540

DELAYEN, JEAN ROGER, b Auchel, France, Apr 27, 47; m 73; c 2. CRYOGENICS, PARTICLE ACCELERATORS. *Educ:* ENS Arts & Metiers, France, Ingenieur, 70; Calif Inst Technol, MS, 71, PhD(appl sci), 78. *Prof Exp:* Scientist, 77-80, sr scientist, 80, MEM PROF STAFF, CALIF INST TECHNOL, 81- *Res:* Applications of RF superconductivity; design development of superconducting particle accelerators. *Mailing Add:* Sloan 63-37 Calif Inst Technol Pasadena CA 91125

DELBECQ, CHARLES JARCHOW, b Toledo, Ohio, Aug 19, 21; m 47; c 3. SOLID STATE CHEMISTRY. *Educ:* Univ Toledo, BS, 43; Univ Ill, PhD(chem), 49. *Prof Exp:* Assoc chemist, 49-62, SR CHEMIST, ARGONNE NAT LAB, 62- *Mem:* Am Phys Soc; Sigma Xi. *Res:* Study of imperfections and impurities, and the trapping of electrons and holes in solids, especially the alkali halides. *Mailing Add:* SSS-223 Argonne Nat Lab Argonne IL 60439

DEL BEL, ELSIO, b Worthington, Ont, Can, Jan 28, 20; US citizen. ORGANIC CHEMISTRY. *Educ:* Clarkson Tech Col, BS, 41; Columbia Univ, MA, 48; Pa State Univ, PhD(fuel technol), 51. *Prof Exp:* Metallurgist, Rochester Ord Dist, War Dept, 41-42; chemist pharmaceut prod, Ayerst Labs, 45-47; res org chemist, Res Div, Consol Coal Co, 51-71; supvry chem engr, Pittsburgh Energy Res Ctr, BOM, 72-74, SUPVRY CHEM ENGR, PITTSBURGH ENERGY RES CTR, ENERGY RES & DEVELOP ADMIN, 74- *Res:* Chemistry of phenolic compound, aryl mercaptans and coal chemicals; conversion of coal and organic waste to liquid fuels. *Mailing Add:* 5697 Library Rd Bethel Park PA 15102

DEL BENE, JANET ELAINE, b Girard, Ohio, June 3, 39. THEORETICAL CHEMISTRY. *Educ:* Youngstown State Univ, BS, 63, BA, 65; Univ Cincinnati, PhD(chem), 68. *Prof Exp:* Fel chem, Theoret Chem Inst, Univ Wis, 68-69 & Mellon Inst, 69-70; asst prof, 70-73, assoc prof, 73-76, PROF CHEM, YOUNGSTOWN STATE UNIV, 76- *Concurrent Pos:* Grants, Am Chem Soc, 72, Nat Inst Gen Med Sci, 74, Camille & Henry Dreyfus Found, 74 & Nat Inst Gen Med Sci, 80; consult basic med sci, Col Med, Northeastern Ohio Univ, 76, res prof molecular path & biol, 77-; mem grad fac, Molecular Path & Biol Area Comt, Kent State Univ, 78- *Honors & Awards:* Agnes Fay Morgan Award, Iota Sigma Pi, 72. *Mem:* AAAS; Am Chem Soc; AAAS; NY Acad Sci; Sigma Xi. *Res:* Molecular orbital theory of chemical bonding, structure, and spectroscopy; computers in chemistry; molecular orbital theory of hydrogen bonding and ion-molecule interactions. *Mailing Add:* Dept of Chem Youngstown State Univ Youngstown OH 44555

DEL BIANCO, WALTER, b Firenze, Italy, Feb 28, 33; m 67. NUCLEAR PHYSICS. *Educ:* Univ Rome, Dr, 58; Univ Pa, PhD, 61. *Prof Exp:* Res assoc, Univ Pa, 61-62; res physicist, Nuclear Physics Div, Max Planck Inst Chem, 62-65; from asst prof to assoc prof, 65-77, PROF PHYSICS, UNIV MONTREAL, 77- *Mem:* Am Phys Soc; Can Asn Physicists. *Res:* Photonuclear reactions. *Mailing Add:* Dept of Physics Univ of Montreal Montreal PQ H3C 3J7 Can

DELBRUCK, MAX, biology, deceased

DELCAMP, ROBERT MITCHELL, b Lexington, Ky, Apr 18, 19; m 40; c 3. ORGANIC CHEMISTRY. *Educ:* Transylvania Col, AB, 39; Univ Cincinnati, MA, 41, PhD(chem), 54. *Prof Exp:* Shift supvr, E I du Pont de Nemours & Co, 41-44; shift supvr, Tenn Eastman Corp, 44-45; instr, 45-48, from asst prof to prof, 48-58, asst dean, 62-67, assoc dean, 67-78, actg dean, 76-78, prof org chem, 58-65, PROF CHEM ENG, UNIV CINCINNATI, 65- *Concurrent Pos:* Consult, Darling & Co, 47-48, Charles Straus & Assocs, 49-51 & Tanner's Coun Res Lab, Cincinnati, 54-68. *Mem:* Am Chem Soc; Am Soc Eng Educ; Am Inst Chem Engrs. *Res:* Base-catalyzed condensation of aromatic aldehydes with compounds containing active hydrogen; enzymatic assay using epidermis as substrate; microbiological conversion of raw materials into useful organic chemicals; resin modification of leather; fermentation processes. *Mailing Add:* Col Eng Univ of Cincinnati Cincinnati OH 45221

DEL CASTILLO, JOSE, b Salamanca, Spain, Dec 25, 20; US citizen; m 55; c 2. NEUROPHYSIOLOGY. *Educ:* Lit Univ Salamanca, MB, 45; Univ Madrid, MD, 47. *Prof Exp:* Asst prof physiol, Fac Med, Lit Univ Salamanca, 45-46; Sandoz res fel, Physiol Inst, Bern, 48-50; asst lectr, Univ Col, Univ London, 50-52, lectr biophys, 52-53, lectr, 53-56; vis prof physiol, State Univ NY Downstate Med Ctr, 56-57; chief sect clin neurophysiol, Nat Inst Neurol Dis & Blindness, Md, 57-59; assoc prof pharmacol, 59-60, PROF PHARMACOL & HEAD DEPT, SCH MED, UNIV PR, 60-, DIR LAB NEUROBIOL, 67- *Concurrent Pos:* Nat Inst Neurol Dis & Blindness career res prof grant, 62. *Mem:* Am Physiol Soc; Int Brain Res Orgn; Brit Physiol Soc. *Res:* Synaptic physiology and pharmacology; comparative neurophysiology. *Mailing Add:* Univ PR Sch Med Lab Neurobiol PO Box 5067 Old San Juan PR 00936

DEL CERRO, MANUEL (PEREZ), b Buenos Aires, Arg, Aug 20, 31; m 57; c 2. NEUROSCIENCES, DEVELOPMENTAL BIOLOGY. *Educ:* Univ Buenos Aires, MD, 58. *Prof Exp:* Sr instr histol, Sch Med, Univ Buenos Aires, 58-61, assoc prof, 61-64; res assoc neuroanat, 65-69, sr res assoc, 69-71, assoc prof, 71-80, PROF NEUROL, CTR BRAIN RES & CTR VISUAL SCI, STRONG MEM HOSP, UNIV ROCHESTER, 80-, ASSOC PROF ANAT & OPHTHALMOL, 80- *Concurrent Pos:* Lectr, Nat Res Coun, Arg, 62 & 63. *Mem:* AAAS; Am Asn Anat; Am Asn Neuropath; Am Soc Cell Biol; Int Brain Res Asn. *Res:* Brain research; microscopical, ultrastructural and biochemical study of neurogenesis; growth and regeneration of central nervous system; action of drugs, hormones and viruses on neural development; transplantation of nervous tissue and immune response to it. *Mailing Add:* Sch Med & Dent Med Ctr Univ Rochester Rochester NY 14642

DELCO, EXALTON ALFONSO, JR, b Houston, Tex, Sept 4, 29; m 52; c 4. VERTEBRATE ECOLOGY. *Educ:* Fisk Univ, AB, 49; Univ Mich, MS, 50; Univ Tex, PhD(zool), 62. *Prof Exp:* From instr to assoc instr biol, Tex Southern Univ, 50-57; res asst zool, Univ Tex, 58-60; from asst prof to assoc prof, 59-63, PROF BIOL, HUSTON-TILLOTSON COL, 63-, DEAN, 67- *Concurrent Pos:* Co-investr, NSF Grant, 58-62. *Honors & Awards:* Stoye Prize, Am Soc Ichthyologists & Herpetologists, 60. *Mem:* Fel AAAS; Am Fisheries Soc; Am Soc Ichthyologists & Herpetologists; Ecol Soc Am. *Res:* Vertebrate speciation and ethology, especially isolating mechanisms in the vertebrate group. *Mailing Add:* Dept of Biol Huston-Tillotson Col Austin TX 78702

DELCOMYN, FRED, b Copenhagen, Denmark, June 4, 39; US citizen; m 69; c 3. NEUROSCIENCE. *Educ:* Wayne State Univ, BS, 62; Northwestern Univ, MS, 64; Univ Ore, PhD(physiol), 69. *Prof Exp:* Res assoc zool, Univ Glasgow, 69-71; lectr physiol, Inst Physiol, Univ Glasgow, 71-72; asst prof entom, 72-77, ASSOC PROF ENTOM, UNIV ILL, 77- *Concurrent Pos:* Assoc prof, Dept Physiol, Univ Ill, 77- *Mem:* Soc Exp Biol; AAAS; Am Soc Zoologists; Soc Neurosci. *Res:* Physiological basis of behavior in invertebrates; neural basis of coordination; locomotion. *Mailing Add:* Univ Ill Dept Entom 505 S Goodwin Urbana IL 61801

DELCOURT, HAZEL ROACH, quaternary paleoecology, palynology, see previous edition

DELCOURT, PAUL ALLEN, b Clifford, Mich, Feb 10, 49; m 71. QUATERNARY PALEOECOLOGY, GEOLOGY. *Educ:* Albion Col, BA, 71, La State Univ, MS, 74; Univ Minn, PhD(geol), 78. *Prof Exp:* ASST PROF QUATERNARY PALEOECOLOGY, DEPT GEOL SCI & GRAD PROG ECOL, UNIV TENN, KNOXVILLE, 78- *Honors & Awards:* Res Award, Asn Southeastern Biologists, 74; Murray Buell Award, Ecol Soc Am, 78. *Mem:* Int Comn Palynology; Am Asn Stratig Palynologists; Ecol Soc Am; Am Quaternary Asn. *Res:* Quantitative landscape development; Quaternary paleovegetation, geomorphology and paleoclimatology; modern vegetation-pollen calibrations; pollen and plant-macrofossil identification. *Mailing Add:* Ctr for Quaternary Studies of Dept of Geol Sci Univ of Tenn Knoxville TN 37916

DEL DUCA, BETTY SPAHR, b Warren, Ohio, Nov 12, 30; div; c 2. PHYSICAL CHEMISTRY. *Educ:* Case Western Reserve Univ, AB, 52, MS, 54, PhD(chem), 57, MSM, 73. *Prof Exp:* Aerospace scientist chem kinetics, Lewis Res Ctr, NASA, Cleveland, 57-62, aerospace scientist energy conversion & electrochem, 62-73; sr analyst, 73-75, staff asst to vpres supply & distrib, 75-77, MGR INT CRUDE OIL OPERS, STANDARD OIL CO OF OHIO, 77- *Res:* Trace element concentrations in biological material; heat transfer; chemistry of comets and upper atmosphere; electrochemistry-kinetics of electrode processes. *Mailing Add:* 1052 Guildhall Bldg Cleveland OH 44115

DELEANU, ARISTIDE ALEXANDRU-ION, b Pitesti, Romania, Apr 12, 32; US citizen; m 56. ALGEBRAIC TOPOLOGY, CATEGORY THEORY. *Educ:* Bucarest Univ, MS, 55, PhD(math), 61; Inst Civil Eng, MS, 55. *Prof Exp:* Asst prof math, Univ Bucarest, 55-58; res fel, Inst Math, Romanian Acad, 60-66, Div head, 66-68; vis assoc prof, 68-71, PROF MATH, SYRACUSE UNIV, 71- *Concurrent Pos:* NSF res grant, 73-75. *Honors & Awards:* Simion Stoilow Prize, Romanian Acad Sci, 66. *Mem:* Am Math Soc. *Res:* Generalized completions in the sense of J Frank Adams with applications to localizations and completions in homotopy theory; categorical aspects of the theory of shape in the sense of Karol Borsuk. *Mailing Add:* Dept of Math Syracuse Univ 200 Carnegie Hall Syracuse NY 13210

DELEEUW, J H, b Amsterdam, Netherlands, Jan 4, 29; Can citizen; m 59; c 3. AEROSPACE ENGINEERING. *Educ:* Delft Univ Technol, Dipl eng, 53; Ga Inst Technol, MS, 52; Univ Toronto, PhD(aerophys), 58. *Prof Exp:* Res engr aerodyn, Nat Aeronaut Res Inst, Netherlands, 52-53; from asst prof to prof aerospace eng, 58-76, asst dir res, 70-76, PROF & DIR INST AEROSPACE STUDIES, UNIV TORONTO, 76- *Mem:* Am Inst Aeronaut & Astronaut; Can Aeronaut & Space Inst. *Res:* Rarefied plasma and gasdynamics; rocket sounding of upper atmosphere. *Mailing Add:* Inst for Aerospace Studies Univ of Toronto Toronto ON M5S 1A1 Can

DELEEUW, SAMUEL LEONARD, b Grand Rapids, Mich, Aug 2, 34; m 56; c 3. ENGINEERING MECHANICS, CIVIL ENGINEERING. *Educ:* Mich State Univ, BS, 56, MS, 58, PhD(appl mech), 61. *Prof Exp:* Asst prof civil eng, Yale Univ, 60-65; PROF CIVIL ENG & CHMN DEPT, UNIV MISS, 65- *Concurrent Pos:* Int Bus Mach Corp res assoc, Mass Inst Technol, 62-63. *Mem:* Am Soc Civil Engrs; Am Soc Eng Educ; Am Soc Mech Engrs; Nat Soc Prof Engrs. *Res:* Bending and buckling of viscoelastic columns and plates with large deflections; transportation; water resources. *Mailing Add:* Dept Civil Eng Univ Miss University MS 38677

DE LEMOS, CARMEN LORETTA, b Santo Domingo, Dominican Repub, May 6, 37. CELL BIOLOGY. *Educ:* Hunter Col, BA, 60; NY Univ, MS, 66, PhD(biol, basic med sci), 72. *Prof Exp:* Asst res scientist, 60-72, instr cell biol, 72-77, RES ASST PROF, NY UNIV, 77- *Mem:* Am Soc Cell Biol; Am Asn Anat; Am Soc Zool; Soc Develop Biol. *Res:* Development of human gastric mucosa; topography of membrane glyco proteins of subcellular organelles by fractionation, electrophoresis, enzymatic analysis and electron microscopic lectin binding techniques. *Mailing Add:* Dept of Cell Biol NY Univ 550 First Ave New York NY 10016

DELEON, MORRIS JACK, b Seattle, Wash, June 21, 41; div; c 2. NUMBER THEORY. *Educ:* Univ Calif, Los Angeles, BA, 63; Univ Ill, MS, 64; Pa State Univ, PhD(math), 68. *Prof Exp:* ASSOC PROF MATH, FLA ATLANTIC UNIV, 68- *Mem:* Am Math Soc; Math Asn Am. *Mailing Add:* Dept of Math Fla Atlantic Univ Boca Raton FL 33431

DE LEONIBUS, PASQUALE S, b Chester, Pa, Jan 13, 26; m 63; c 1. OCEANOGRAPHY, METEOROLOGY. *Educ:* NY Univ, BS, 52, MS, 55. *Prof Exp:* Chief scientist, US Naval Oceanog Off, 54-75; oceanogr, Nat Oceanic & Atmospheric Admin, 75-78; OCEANOGR SEASAT PROJ, NAT ENVIRON SATELLITE SERV, WORLD WEATHER BLDG, WASHINGTON, DC, 78- *Concurrent Pos:* Expert adv, Comn Maritime Meteorol, 70-; US mem, Int Ships Struct Cong, 81- *Honors & Awards:* Henry S Kaminski Mem Award, Res Soc Am, 72. *Mem:* Am Geophys Union; Am Meteorol Soc. *Res:* Air-sea interactions; ocean wave research; development of air-sea boundary layer model from the point of view of ocean wave generation and wave forecasting. *Mailing Add:* S3X1 World Weather Bldg 5200 Auth Rd Washington DC 20233

DELERAY, ARTHUR LOYD, b Sonora, Calif, June 27, 36; m 61; c 2. CHEMICAL & NUCLEAR ENGINEERING. *Educ:* Univ Calif, Berkeley, BSE, 59; Princeton Univ, MSE & MA, 62, PhD(chem eng), 66. *Prof Exp:* Staff chem engr, MB Assocs, 64-70; PROF, CHABOT COL, VALLEY CAMPUS, 70- *Concurrent Pos:* Consult solar energy. *Res:* Fast neutron moderation; pyrotechnics; unique radar reflectors; miniature rocketry; solar heating applications. *Mailing Add:* 5171 Oakview Ct Pls Pleasanton CA 94566

DELEVIE, ROBERT, b Amsterdam, Holland, July 21, 33; m 60; c 2. ELECTROCHEMISTRY, BIOPHYSICS. *Educ:* Univ Amsterdam, Drs 60, PhD, 63. *Prof Exp:* Vis asst prof, La State Univ, 63-65; from asst prof to assoc prof, 65-73, PROF CHEM, GEORGETOWN UNIV, 73- *Concurrent Pos:* US ed, J Electroanal Chem, 70-80. *Mem:* Am Chem Soc; Biophys Soc; Electrochem Soc; Royal Neth Chem Soc; Royal Dutch Acad Sci. *Res:* Mechanisms of electrode kinetics; phenomena of nucleation and growth; double layer effects; ion transport through membranes; electrochemical and biophysical instrumentation. *Mailing Add:* Dept of Chem Georgetown Univ Washington DC 20057

DELEVORYAS, THEODORE, b Chicopee Falls, Mass, July 22, 29; m 81; c 5. PALEOBOTANY. *Educ:* Univ Mass, BS, 50; Univ Ill, MS, 51, PhD, 54. *Prof Exp:* Rockefeller fel, Nat Res Coun, Univ Mich, 54-55; asst prof bot, Mich State Univ, 55-56; from instr to asst prof, Yale Univ, 56-60; assoc prof, Univ Ill, 60-62; from assoc prof to prof biol, Yale Univ & from assoc cur to cur paleobot, Peabody Mus Natural Hist, 62-72; chmn dept, 74-80, PROF BOT, UNIV TEX, AUSTIN, 72- *Concurrent Pos:* Pres, Int Orgn Palaeobotany, 78-81. *Mem:* AAAS; Int Soc Plant Morphologists; Paleont Soc; Brit Palaeont Asn; Bot Soc Am (treas, 67-72, vpres, 73, pres, 74). *Res:* Morphology and evolution of fossil and living vascular plants. *Mailing Add:* Dept of Bot Univ of Tex Austin TX 78712

DELFIN, ELISEO DAIS, b San Andreas, Manila, Phillipines, Sept 28, 25; m 64. BIOLOGY, ENTOMOLOGY. *Educ:* Cent Philippines Univ, BS, 49, BSE, 51; Univ Colo, Boulder, MA, 54; Ohio State Univ, PhD(entom), 60. *Prof Exp:* Instr biol, Cent Philippines Univ, 49-52, asst prof, 60-64, chmn dept life sci, 62-64; fel acarology, Univ Calif, Berkeley, 64-65; asst prof zool, San Jose State Col, 65-67; assoc prof, 67-71, chmn dept, 69-77, prof biol, Ind Cent Col, 71-80, PROF BIOL, IND CENT UNIV, 80- *Concurrent Pos:* Consult, Philippines Bur Plant Indust, Iloilo City Br, 60-64. *Mem:* AAAS; Am Inst Biol Sci. *Res:* Biology of mites and ticks and of central Indiana; leafhoppers, especially Cicadellidae. *Mailing Add:* Dept of Biol Ind Cent Univ Indianapolis IN 46227

DELFLACHE, ANDRE P, b Brussels, Belg, 1923; nat US; m 50; c 4. CIVIL ENGINEERING, GEOPHYSICS. *Educ:* Univ Brussels, CEngMines, 47, ScD(soil mech), 64. *Prof Exp:* Asst prof eng geol, Univ Brussels, 47-48; vis prof geol, La State Univ, 48-49; engr, Explor Div, Petrofina, Brussels, 49-54; seismologist, United Geophys Co, Calif, 54; Europ mgr subsurface explor in Europe & NAfrica, Independent Explor Co, Tex, 54-58; PROF CIVIL ENG, LAMAR UNIV, 58- *Concurrent Pos:* Consult soils eng & found, 58; NSF res grant, 73-78. *Mem:* Am Soc Civil Engrs. *Res:* Geotechnique; marine geophysics; determination of geotechnical properties of soils and sediments by seismic methods; land subsidence in the Houston-Galveston region of Texas. *Mailing Add:* Dept of Civil Eng Lamar Univ Beaumont TX 77710

DEL FOSSE, ERNEST SHERIDAN, entomology, aquatic ecology, see previous edition

DELGADO, JAIME NABOR, b El Paso, Tex, July 28, 32; m 54; c 1. PHARMACEUTICAL CHEMISTRY, MEDICINAL CHEMISTRY. *Educ:* Univ Tex, BS, 54, MS, 55; Univ Minn, PhD(pharmaceut chem), 60. *Prof Exp:* Asst pharmaceut chem, Univ Minn, 55-57; from asst prof to assoc prof, 59-72, PROF PHARMACEUT CHEM, COL PHARM, UNIV TEX, AUSTIN, 72- *Concurrent Pos:* Mem res rev comt, Nat Inst Drug Abuse, HEW, 77- *Mem:* AAAS; Am Pharmaceut Asn; Am Chem Soc; Acad Pharmaceut Sci; Sigma Xi. *Res:* Synthesis of organic medicinals and structure-activity studies; natural products; mechanisms of drug-receptor interactions; anticholinergics. *Mailing Add:* Dept of Pharmaceut Chem Univ of Tex Austin TX 78712

DELGASS, W NICHOLAS, b Jackson Heights, NY, Oct 14, 42; m 67; c 2. CATALYSIS, KINETICS. *Educ:* Univ Mich, BS, 64; Stanford Univ, MS, 66, PhD(chem eng), 69. *Prof Exp:* Asst prof eng & appl sci, Yale Univ, 69-74; assoc prof, 74-78, PROF CHEM ENG, PURDUE UNIV, 78- *Concurrent Pos:* Consult, Am Cyanamid Co, 70-76 & Amoco Oil, Inc, 77- *Mem:* Am Inst Chem Engrs; Am Chem Soc. *Res:* Heterogeneous catalysis, especially application of Mossbauer and photoelectron spectroscopy, secondary ion mass spectrometry and transient kineteics to the study of catalysts and interactions of gases with catalytically active surfaces. *Mailing Add:* Sch Chem Eng Purdue Univ West Lafayette IN 47907

DEL GRECO, FRANCESCO, b Italy, Aug 23, 23; nat US; m 56; c 1. MEDICINE. *Educ:* Univ Rome, Italy, MD, 46. *Prof Exp:* Res fel exp med, Cleveland Clin, 51-52, res assoc, 52-54, asst staff, 55-57; from intern to chief med resident, Passavant Mem Hosp, Chicago, 58-60, dir metab unit, 58-61; dir, Clin Res Ctr, 61-81, PROF MED, MED SCH, NORTHWESTERN UNIV, 67-, DIR, DIALYSIS CTR, 64-, ATTEND PHYSICIAN, 64-, CHIEF, SECT NEPHROLOGY-HYPERTENSION, 73- *Concurrent Pos:* Danish govt scholar, 51; Nat Heart Inst fel, NIH, 52-53; vol asst, Postgrad Med Sch, London, 55; hon res fel, St Thomas' Hosp, 55; vis attend physician, Vet Admin Lakeside Med Ctr, Chicago, 60-; asst to assoc prof, Northwestern Univ, 60-67; chmn med adv bd, Kidney Found Ill, 75-79; mem cardiovasc & renal study sect, Nat Heart & Lung Inst, 75-79; mem coun circulation, coun arteriosclerosis, coun kidney in cardiovasc dis & coun high blood pressure res, Am Heart Asn. *Mem:* Am Physiol Soc; Soc Exp Biol & Med; Am Soc Nephrology; Am Col Physicians; Int Soc Hypertension. *Res:* Renal and cardiovascular physiology; hypertension. *Mailing Add:* Wesley Pavilion Northwestern Mem Hosp 250 E Chicago Ave Chicago IL 60611

DEL GROSSO, VINCENT ALFRED, b Newark, NJ, Aug 9, 25; m 51; c 5. PHYSICAL OCEANOGRAPHY. *Educ:* Northeastern Univ, BS, 47; Cath Univ Am, PhD, 68. *Prof Exp:* Phys chemist, 48-52, physicist & head ultrasonics sect, 52-72, physicist & head, Ocean Instrumentation Sect, 72-74, CONSULT, OCEAN TECHNOL DIV, NAVAL RES LAB, 74- *Concurrent Pos:* Res assoc, Univ Calif, Los Angeles, 70-71. *Mem:* Inst Elec & Electronics Engrs; sr mem Am Chem Soc; fel Acoust Soc Am; Soc Photo-Optical Instrumentation Engrs. *Res:* Ultrasonics; underwater sound; physical chemistry; underwater optics and imaging. *Mailing Add:* PO Box 226 Rt 1 Edelen Dr Bryantown MD 20617

DEL GUERCIO, LOUIS RICHARD M, b New York, NY, Jan 15, 29; m 57; c 8. SURGERY, PHYSIOLOGY. *Educ:* Fordham Univ, BS, 49; Yale Univ, MD, 53. *Prof Exp:* From instr to prof surg, Albert Einstein Col Med, 60-71, assoc dir clin res ctr, 63-67, dir, 67-71; prof surg, Col Med & Dent NJ & dir surg, St Barnabas Med Ctr, 71-76; PROF & CHMN DEPT SURG, NY MED COL, 76- *Concurrent Pos:* Am Thoracic Soc teaching & res fel, 59-60; Health Res Coun NY res grants, 64-66 & career scientist award, 66; res grants, Am Heart Asn, 65-68 & NIH, 65-70; from assoc attend to attend, Bronx Munic Hosp Ctr, 60-65, pres med bd, 69; mem tech rev comt artificial heart test & eval facil, NIH, 68, mem surg study sect, Div Res Grants, 70; mem comt on shock, Nat Acad Sci-Nat Res Coun, 69-; mem merit rev bd surg, US Vet Admin, 72-; consult surg devices, Food & Drug Admin, 74- & health care technol study sect, Nat Ctr Health Serv Res, Dept Health & Human Serv, 80- *Mem:* AAAS; Am Surg Asn; Am Thoracic Soc; AMA; fel Am Col Surgeons; Soc Univ Surgeons. *Res:* Cardiorespiratory physiology in clinical practice; thoracic surgery; surgery of biliary pancreatic system. *Mailing Add:* Dept of Surg NY Med Col Munger Pavilion Valhalla NY 10595

D'ELIA, CHRISTOPHER FRANCIS, b Bridgeport, Conn, Aug 7, 46; m 73. MARINE ECOLOGY, BIOLOGY. *Educ:* Middlebury Col, AB, 68; Univ Ga, PhD(zool), 74. *Prof Exp:* Scholar biol, Univ Calif, Los Angeles, 73-75; vis asst prof, Univ Southern Calif, 75; fel biol, Woods Hole Oceanog Inst, 75-77; ASST PROF BIOL, CHESAPEAKE BIOL LAB, UNIV MD, 77- *Mem:* AAAS; Am Soc Limnol & Oceanog; Estuarine Res Fedn. *Res:* Marine and estuarine nutrient dynamics; coral reef ecology; algal endosymbiosis; aquaculture. *Mailing Add:* Chesapeake Biol Lab Univ Md Solomons MD 20688

DELIA, THOMAS J, b Brooklyn, NY, Nov 19, 35; m 64; c 4. ORGANIC CHEMISTRY, MEDICINAL CHEMISTRY. *Educ:* Col Holy Cross, BS, 57; Va Polytech Inst, MS, 59, PhD(org chem), 62. *Prof Exp:* Res assoc bio-org chem, Sloan-Kettering Inst Cancer Res, 62-66; from asst prof to assoc prof, 66-70, PROF CHEM, CENT MICH UNIV, 70- *Concurrent Pos:* Nat Acad Sci fel, Czech, 71-72. *Mem:* NY Acad Sci; Am Chem Soc; Int Soc Heterocyclic Chem. *Res:* Synthesis of heterocyclic compounds as antitumor, antiviral and antimalarial agents. *Mailing Add:* Dept of Chem Cent Mich Univ Mt Pleasant MI 48859

DELIHAS, NICHOLAS, b New York, NY, Sept 22, 32; m 61; c 3. MOLECULAR BIOLOGY. *Educ:* Queens Col, NY, BS, 54; Yale Univ, PhD(biophys), 61. *Prof Exp:* Jr tech specialist, Biol Dept, Brookhaven Nat Lab, 54-57; res asst biophys, Yale Univ, 57-58; res assoc, Sloan-Kettering Inst Cancer Res, 60-62; from assoc scientist to scientist, Med Dept, Brookhaven Nat Lab, 62-71; asst prof, 71-74, assoc prof & dir multidisciplinary labs, Sch Basic Health Sci, 74-80, ASSOC DEAN & ASSOC PROF, SCH MED, STATE UNIV NY STONY BROOK, 81- *Concurrent Pos:* Res assoc, Sloan-Kettering Div, Cornell Univ, 61-62; NIH spec fel, Ciba Res Labs, Basel, Switz, 64-65; adj prof biol, Southampton Col, 70-; univ grant-in-aid, State Univ NY, 73; Nat Inst Gen Med Sci res grant, 73- *Mem:* Am Soc Biol Chemists; Am Soc Microbiol; Biophys Soc; Am Soc Cell Biol; AAAS. *Res:* RNA and ribosome structure and function. *Mailing Add:* Sch of Basic Health Sci State Univ of NY Stony Brook NY 11794

DE LILLO, NICHOLAS JOSEPH, b New York, NY, July 14, 39; m 66; c 4. MATHEMATICAL LOGIC, COMPUTER SCIENCE. *Educ:* Manhattan Col, BS, 60; Fordham Univ, MA, 62; NY Univ, PhD(math), 71. *Prof Exp:* From instr to asst prof, 63-73, ASSOC PROF MATH, MANHATTAN COL, 73- *Concurrent Pos:* Adj asst prof math, Lehman Col, 72-73; adj assoc prof, 73- *Mem:* Math Asn Am; Am Math Soc; Asn Symbolic Logic; Asn Comput Mach; Sigma Xi. *Res:* Model theory; theory of abstract computability. *Mailing Add:* Dept Math & Comput Sci Manhattan Col New York NY 10471

DELINGER, WILLIAM GALEN, b Hyannis, Nebr, Apr 29, 39. SOLID STATE PHYSICS. *Educ:* Chadron State Col, BS, 61; SDak Sch Mines & Technol, MS, 65; Univ Iowa, PhD(physics), 72. *Prof Exp:* Teacher physics, Western Ill Univ, 63-66; NASA trainee physics, Univ Iowa, 68-72; asst prof, 72-80, ASSOC PROF PHYSICS, NORTHERN ARIZ UNIV, 80- *Mem:* Am Asn Physics Teachers; Int Solar Energy Soc; Asn Comput Mach; Am Inst Aeronaut & Astronaut. *Res:* Solar energy; mathematical modeling to describe the performance of solar collectors and storage systems as well as solar instrumentation. *Mailing Add:* Dept of Physics Northern Ariz Univ Box 6010 Flagstaff AZ 86011

D'ELISCU, PETER NEAL, b Riverside, Calif, July 27, 46; m 67; c 1. MARINE ECOLOGY, PARASITOLOGY. *Educ:* Univ Calif, Irvine, BS, 68; San Jose State Univ, MS, 70; Univ Ariz, PhD(biol), 74. *Prof Exp:* Lectr biol, San Jose State Univ, 70-71 & Univ Ariz, 73; biochemist & supvr biol, NASA, Moffett Field Naval Air Sta, 74; ASST PROF BIOL, UNIV SANTA CLARA, 74- *Mem:* AAAS; Am Soc Zoologists; Sigma Xi. *Res:* Estuarine ecosystem balances, including phyto and zooplankton productivity; invertebrate symbiosis, including physiological-behavioral parasitism; human and other vertebrate parasite interactions; vector control; invertebrate zoology; effects of pollutants in aquatic habitats. *Mailing Add:* Dept of Biol Univ of Santa Clara Santa Clara CA 95053

DE LISI, CHARLES, b New York, NY, Dec 9, 41; m 68; c 2. BIOPHYSICS. *Educ:* City Col New York, BA, 63; NY Univ, PhD(physics), 69. *Prof Exp:* Engr, Sperry Rand Corp, 64-65; fel biophysics, Yale Univ, 69-72, sr lectr eng & appl sci, 71-72; staff scientist biophys, Los Alamos Sci Lab, Univ Calif, 72-77; vis scientist, 75-77, spec asst off dir, NIH, 79-80, SR INVESTR BIOPHYSICS, NAT CANCER INST, NIH, 77-, CHIEF, SECT THEORET IMMUNOL, 81- *Honors & Awards:* Gordon Res Conf Award, Soc Math Biol. *Res:* Theoretical immunology; physical chemical properties of biopolymers. *Mailing Add:* Lab Theoret Biol Nat Cancer Inst NIH Bethesda MD 20014

DELISI, DONALD PAUL, b Pittsburgh, Pa, Nov 15, 44; m 71; c 1. OCEANIC INTERNAL WAVES, OCEANIC TURBULENCE. *Educ:* Princeton Univ, BS, 66; Univ Calif, Berkeley, MS, 67, PhD(mech eng & fluid mech), 72. *Prof Exp:* Nat res coun resident res assoc, Geophys Fluid Dynamics Lab, Nat Oceanic & Atmospheric Admin, 72-74; res scientist, Flow Res Co, 74-77; STAFF SCIENTIST, PHYS DYNAMICS, INC, 77- *Mem:* Am Geophys Union; Am Meteorol Soc; Am Phys Soc. *Res:* Physical oceanography of the upper ocean (from the surface to approximately 300 meters depth) including the study of internal waves, shear, turbulence and fine and micro-structure. *Mailing Add:* PO Box 3027 Bellevue WA 98009

DELISLE, CLAUDE, b Quebec, Que, Nov 15, 29; m 58; c 5. OPTICS. *Educ:* Univ Montreal, BA, 51; Laval Univ, BScA, 58, PhD(optics), 63. *Prof Exp:* Lectr physics, Laval Univ, 62-63; res assoc optics, Inst Optics, NY, 63-65; from asst prof to assoc prof, 65-73, PROF PHYSICS, LAVAL UNIV, 73- *Concurrent Pos:* Nat Res Coun Can grants, 66-; consult, Ctr Psychol Res Inc, Montreal, 69-71; prof consult, Ministry of Educ, Que, 73-74. *Mem:* Fel Optical Soc Am; Can Asn Physicists; Fr-Can Asn Advan Sci. *Res:* Coherence, interferometry, photocounting; hybrid bistability with piezo electric Fabry-Perot and acousto-optic modulator in multimode laser light; computer modeling of carbon dioxide laser; metrology. *Mailing Add:* LROL Physics Dept Laval Univ Quebec PQ G1K 7P4 Can

DELIYANNIS, PLATON CONSTANTINE, b Athens, Greece, Aug 21, 31. MATHEMATICS. *Educ:* Nat Tech Univ Athens, dipl eng, 54; Univ Chicago, MS, 55, PhD(math), 63. *Prof Exp:* Res asst, Univ Chicago, 55-56; from instr to asst prof math, Ill Inst Technol, 61-65; dir, Ctr Advan Studies, Greek Atomic Energy Comn, 66-69; asst prof, 69-74, chmn dept, 75-80, ASSOC PROF MATH, ILL INST TECHNOL, 74- *Mem:* Am Math Soc; Math Asn Am; NY Acad Sci; Soc Indust & Appl Math. *Res:* Functional analysis and operator algebras; topological groups and representations; abstract quantum theory. *Mailing Add:* Dept of Math Ill Inst of Technol 3300 S Federal St Chicago IL 60616

DELKER, GERALD LEE, b Portland, Ore, Dec 9, 47; m 72; c 3. INORGANIC CHEMISTRY. *Educ:* Univ Calif, Riverside, BS, 70, Univ Ill, Champaign-Urbana, PhD(inorganic chem), 76. *Prof Exp:* Fel, Univ Calif, Davis, 76-77; Occidental Col, Los Angeles, 77-79; SR CHEMIST & LAB SUPVR, ANAL RES LABS, INC, 79- *Mem:* Am Chem Soc. *Res:* Methods development for the analysis of various substances or environments; general chemical analyses. *Mailing Add:* 3046 Treefern Dr Duarte CA 91010

DELL, CURTIS G(EORGE), b Buffalo, NY, Mar 18, 24; m 49; c 4. ELECTRICAL ENGINEERING. *Educ:* Rutgers Univ, BS, 48; Cornell Univ, MEE, 51. *Prof Exp:* Engr, 48-51, instrument engr, eng dept, design div, 51-53, res engr, eng res lab, appl physics sect, 53-58, res proj engr, 58-59, res proj supvr, 59-61, sr res engr, 61-64, sr appln engr, develop dept, 64-67, eng supvr, 67-69, res supvr, photo prod dept, 69-77, develop assoc, 77-80, SR DEVELOP ASSOC, PHOTO PROD DEPT, E I DU PONT DE NEMOURS & CO, 80- *Concurrent Pos:* Lectr, Univ Del, 52-54. *Mem:* Sigma Xi; Instrument Soc Am; Inst Elec & Electronics Engrs. *Res:* Industrial research, development and marketing of laboratory and process analytical instruments. *Mailing Add:* Photo Prods Dept E I du Pont de Nemours & Co Wilmington DE 19898

DELL, GEORGE F, JR, b Columbus, Ohio, Dec 28, 31; m 65; c 2. HIGH ENERGY PHYSICS, SOLID STATE PHYSICS. *Educ:* Ohio State Univ, BSc, 53, MSc, 55, PhD(physics), 62. *Prof Exp:* Res assoc nuclear physics, Purdue Univ, 63-65; res fel high energy physics, Harvard Univ, 65-70; asst physicist, 70-73, assoc physicist, 73-77, physicist, 77-78, physics assoc solid state physics, 78-80, PHYSICS ASSOC, ACCELERATOR DEPT, BROOKHAVEN NAT LAB, 80- *Mem:* Am Phys Soc. *Res:* Neutron induced damage in insulators; high energy interactions; detector development for high energy physics. *Mailing Add:* Accelerator Dept Bldg 902 Upton NY 11973

DELL, M(ANUEL) BENJAMIN, b Chelsea, Mass, Apr 12, 19. CARBON ELECTRODES, ALUMINUM SMELTING. *Educ:* Tufts Col, BS, 40; Pa State Col, MS, 50, PhD(fuel technol), 51. *Prof Exp:* Res chemist bituminous prod, Barrett Div, Allied Chem & Dye Corp, 47-48; res investr emulsions, Flintkote Co, 51-53; res chemist, 53-60, sci assoc, 60-81, TECH CONSULT, METAL DIVISION LABS, ALUMINUM CO AM, 81- *Mem:* AAAS; Am Inst Mining, Metall & Petrol Engrs; Am Chem Soc. *Res:* Fuels; chemistry of coal tar, asphalt, coal; carbon electrodes; aluminum smelting; clay-stabilized emulsions. *Mailing Add:* 144 Woodshire Dr Pittsburgh PA 15215

DELL, ROGER MARCUS, b Los Angeles, Calif, Oct 20, 36; m 62; c 3. MATHEMATICAL ANALYSIS. *Educ:* Calif State Univ Long Beach, BS, 59, MA, 62; Univ Calif, Los Angeles, PhD(math), 71. *Prof Exp:* Engr, Douglas Aircraft Co, 56-58; comput scientist, Hughes Aircraft Co, 59-60; instr math & physics, Calif State Univ, Long Beach, 60-62; comput scientist, Gen Elec Co, 62-63; instr math & physics, Deep Springs Col, 63-66; teaching asst math, Univ Calif, Los Angeles, 67-69; instr math & physics, Deep Springs Col, 70-74; ASSOC PROF MATH, LINFIELD COL, 74- *Mem:* Math Asn Am. *Mailing Add:* Dept of Math Linfield Col McMinnville OR 97128

DELL, TOMMY RAY, b New Orleans, La, May 21, 37; m 57; c 2. FOREST BIOMETRY. *Educ:* La State Univ, BS, 59; Univ Ga, MS, 64, PhD, 69. *Prof Exp:* Res forester, Southlands Exp Forest, Int Paper Co, Ga, 60-61; chief biomet br, 63-77, PROJ LEADER, SOUTHERN FOREST EXP STA, US FOREST SERV, NEW ORLEANS, 77- *Concurrent Pos:* Mem adv bd, Forest Sci, 73-77. *Mem:* Soc Am Foresters; Biomet Soc; Am Statist Asn. *Res:* Design and analysis of studies on biological topics, particularly forest resources; research on biometrical procedures, timber growth and yield forecasting. *Mailing Add:* Rm T-10210 Southern Forest Exp Sta 701 Loyola Ave New Orleans LA 70113

DELLA-FERA, MARY ANNE, b Wilmington, Del, Mar 29, 54. NEUROPHYSIOLOGY. *Educ:* Univ Del, BA, 75; Univ Pa, VMD, 79, PhD(physiol), 80. *Prof Exp:* Fel neurosci, NIH, 80-81; res assoc, 81, RES ASST PROF, UNIV PA, 82- *Concurrent Pos:* Alfred P Sloan Found Fel, 81. *Honors & Awards:* Donald Lindsley Prize, Soc Neurosci, 81. *Mem:* AAAS; Am Vet Med Asn; Soc Neurosci; Am Physiol Soc. *Res:* Role of the central nervous system in the control of food intake and regulation of energy balance; importance of particular brain peptides in feeding behavior; central nervous system control of gastrointestinal function. *Mailing Add:* Sch Vet Med Univ Pa New Bolton Ctr 382 W Street Rd Kennett Square PA 19348

DELLA TORRE, EDWARD, b Milan, Italy, Mar 31, 34; US citizen; m 56; c 3. ELECTRICAL ENGINEERING, PHYSICS. *Educ:* Polytech Inst Brooklyn, BEE, 54; Princeton Univ, MA, 56; Rutgers Univ, MS, 61; Columbia Univ, DEngSc(elec eng), 64. *Prof Exp:* Assoc prof elec eng, Rutgers Univ, 56-67; mem staff, Bell Tel Labs, 67-68; assoc prof, McMaster Univ, 68-70, assoc chmn dept, 70-72, chmn dept, 72-78, prof elec eng, 70-79; prof & chmn, Elec & Comput Eng, Wayne State Univ, 79-82; PROF ELEC ENG & COMPUT SCI, GEORGE WASHINGTON UNIV, 82- *Mem:* Inst Elec & Electronics Engrs; Sigma Xi; Am Physics Soc; fel Inst Elec & Electronics Engrs. *Res:* Theoretical and experimental study of magnetic materials; electromagnetic theory; application of information and computer sciences; numerical solutions of partial differential equations. *Mailing Add:* Wayne State Univ Dept Elec & Comp Engr Detroit MI 48202 Can

DELLENBACK, ROBERT JOSEPH, b Los Angeles, Calif, June 3, 28; m 58; c 4. MEDICAL PHYSIOLOGY, ACADEMIC ADMINISTRATION. *Educ:* Univ Calif, Los Angeles, BA, 50, MA, 53, PhD(zool, physiol), 55. *Prof Exp:* Asst zool & physiol, Univ Calif, Los Angeles, 50-55; from instr to asst prof physiol, Col Physicians & Surgeons, Columbia Univ, 56-71; assoc prof biochem, Dent Sch, Fairleigh Dickinson Univ, 72-74; admin cordr, Elizabeth Morrow Sch, 74-78; PRES INVESTMENTS, R G DELL CORP, 78- *Concurrent Pos:* Eli Lilly fel & Nat Res Coun fel, Zool Inst, Univ Würzburg, 55-56. *Mem:* Am Physiol Soc; Soc Exp Biol & Med; Harvey Soc; Am Soc Zoologists; Undersea Med Soc. *Res:* Hemorrhage; cardiac output; blood volume. *Mailing Add:* Montgomery St R G Dell Corp PO Box 1748 Lakeville CT 06039

DELLER, JOHN JOSEPH, JR, b Pittsburgh, Pa, Nov 3, 31; m 53; c 3. INTERNAL MEDICINE, ENDOCRINOLOGY. *Educ:* Univ Pittsburgh, BSc, 53, MD, 57; Am Bd Internal Med, dipl, 67. *Prof Exp:* US Army, 56-76, resident internal med, Walter Reed Gen Hosp, DC, 58-61; chief gen med serv, Letterman Gen Hosp, 64-68, asst chief dept med, 68-70, chief dept med, Letterman Army Med Ctr, 70-76; dir primary care internal med res prog, Univ Calif, San Francisco, 76-77; dir educ & res, 78-81; PRACTR INTERNAL MED & ENDOCRINOL, EISENHOWER MED CTR, RANCHO MIRAGE, CALIF, 81- *Concurrent Pos:* Fel endocrinol & metab, Univ Calif, San Francisco, 63-64; asst clin prof, 67-72, assoc clin prof, 72-77. *Mem:* Fel Am Col Physicians; Endocrine Soc; Am Geriat Soc. *Mailing Add:* 34 Sierra Madre Way Rancho Mirage CA 92270

DELLEUR, JACQUES W(ILLIAM), b Paris, France, Dec 30, 24; nat US; m 57; c 2. HYDRAULIC ENGINEERING, HYDROLOGY. *Educ:* Nat Univ Colombia, SAm, CE & MinE, 49; Rensselaer Polytech Inst, MSCe, 50; Columbia Univ, DEngSc, 55. *Prof Exp:* Engr, R J Tipton & Assocs Inc, 50-51; asst civil eng & eng mech dept, Columbia Univ, 52-53, instr civil eng, 53-55; from asst prof to assoc prof hydraul eng, 55-63, head hydromech & water resources area, 65-76, PROF HYDRAUL ENG, SCH CIVIL ENG, PURDUE UNIV, 63-, ASSOC DIR, WATER RESOURCES RES CTR, 71-, HEAD HYDROL & SYSTS ENG AREA, 81- *Concurrent Pos:* Consult, Res Staff, Gen Motors Corp, 57-62; deleg, Univs Coun Water Resources, 64-; researcher, French Nat Hydraulics Lab, France, 68-69, 76-77; tech adv, Nationwide Urban Runoff Prog, Environ Protection Agency/US Geol Survey, 79- *Mem:* Am Soc Civil Engrs; AAAS; Int Asn Sci Hydrol; Am Geophys Union; Int Asn Hydraul Res. *Res:* Hydrology of water resources, stochastic and urban hydrology, hydraulic engineering; turbulence; open channel hydraulics. *Mailing Add:* Sch of Civil Eng Purdue Univ Lafayette IN 47907

DELLICOLLI, HUMBERT THOMAS, b Utica, NY, July 8, 44; m 67; c 1. PHYSICAL CHEMISTRY, AGRICULTURAL CHEMISTRY. *Educ:* Clarkson Col Technol, BS, 66, PhD(chem), 71. *Prof Exp:* Res chemist phys chem, Edgewood Arsenal, US Army, 71-73; res chemist lignin chem, Charleston Res Ctr, 73-75, PROD DEVELOP MGR AGR CHEM, POLYCHEM DEPT, WESTVACO CORP, 75- *Concurrent Pos:* Consult, US Army Chem Systs Lab, 71- *Mem:* Am Chem Soc; AAAS. *Res:* Colloid and surface science; macromolecular chemistry; biocolloids; pesticide formulation chemistry; controlled release of bioactive materials; agricultural chemistry. *Mailing Add:* 7 Campanella Ct Hanahan SC 29410

DELLINGER, THOMAS BAYNES, b Crawfordsville, Ind, Jan 31, 26; m 52; c 4. PETROLEUM ENGINEERING. *Educ:* Purdue Univ, BS, 48; Univ Tulsa, MS, 62, PhD(petrol eng), 70. *Prof Exp:* Engr, Creole Petrol Corp, 48-59; res engr, Jersey Prod Res Co, 60-62; engr, Fenix & Scisson, Inc, 63-67; RES ENGR, MOBIL RES & DEVELOP CORP, 70- *Mem:* Soc Petrol Engrs. *Mailing Add:* 1010 Springwood Ln PO Box 163 Duncanville TX 75116

DELLMANN, HORST-DIETER, b Berlin, Ger, June 6, 31; m 55; c 2. HISTOLOGY, NEUROENDOCRINOLOGY. *Educ:* Nat Vet Sch, Alfort, France, DVM, 54, MS, 55; Univ Munich, PhD(anat, histol & embryol), 61. *Prof Exp:* Mem staff vet med, Chemie Gruenenthal, Stolberg, Ger, 55-57; res asst anat, histol & embryol vet fac, Univ Munich, 57-61; pvt docent, 62-63; univ docent, 64; vis prof & actg chmn dept fac vet med, Cairo Univ, 63-64; from assoc prof to prof anat, histol & embryol, Sch Vet Med, Univ Mo-Columbia, 64-75; PROF VET ANAT, PHARMACOL & PHYSIOL, COL VET MED, IOWA STATE UNIV, 75- *Concurrent Pos:* Mem, Int Comn Vet Anat Nomenclature, 59-; Fulbright travel grant, 64-65; assoc prof, Louis Pasteur Univ, Strasbourg, France, 70-71 & Univ Marseille, France, 81-82.

Mem: Am Asn Anatomists; World Asn Vet Anat; Europ Asn Vet Anat; Ger Anat Soc; Europ Soc Comp Endocrinol. *Res:* Hypothalamus; neurosecretion; hypothalamo-hypophyseal systems; pars tuberalis; circumventricular organs; secretory activity of nerve cells in extrahypothalamic areas. *Mailing Add:* Dept Vet Anat Iowa State Univ Col of Vet Med Ames IA 50011

DELL'ORCO, ROBERT T, b St Louis, Mo, Jan 12, 42; m 67; c 3. CELL BIOLOGY. *Educ:* Rockhurst Col, BA, 63; Univ Kans, PhD(microbiol), 69. *Prof Exp:* Nat Cancer Inst Can fel, 69-70; res biologist, 70-73, asst scientist, 73-77, assoc scientist, 77-81, SCIENTIST, SAMUEL ROBERTS NOBLE FOUND, INC, 81-, HEAD, CELL BIOL SECT, 73- *Mem:* Soc Exp Biol & Med; Tissue Cult Asn; Am Soc Cell Biol; Genontological Soc Am. *Res:* Metabolism and physiology of human diploid cells maintained in culture as applicable to their use as a model system for the study of senescence on a cellular level. *Mailing Add:* Samuel Roberts Noble Found Inc Rte 1 Ardmore OK 73401

DELLUVA, ADELAIDE MARIE, b Bethlehem, Pa, Sept 2, 20. BIOCHEMISTRY. *Educ:* Bucknell Univ, BS, 39, MS, 40; Univ Pa, PhD(physiol chem), 46. *Prof Exp:* Asst instr physiol chem, 43-46, instr, Sch Med, 46-54, asst prof biochem, 54-69, from asst prof to assoc prof, Sch Vet Med, 69-78, assoc chmn, Dept Animal Biol, 71-73, actg chmn, 73-75, PROF BIOCHEM, SCH VET MED, UNIV PA, 78- *Mem:* Am Soc Biol Chemists; AAAS. *Res:* Organic synthesis of compounds with C-13 and C-14 for use in researches in physiological chemistry; various phases of metabolism using isotopes; carbon dioxide assimilation; adrenaline biosynthesis; lactate metabolism; energy source for contraction of muscle; alanine metabolism; gastric urease; anion transport in mitochondria. *Mailing Add:* Dept of Animal Biol Univ of Pa Sch of Vet Med Philadelphia PA 19104

DELLWIG, LOUIS FIELD, b Washington, DC, Feb 13, 22; m 48; c 3. REGIONAL GEOLOGY, REMOTE SENSING. *Educ:* Lehigh Univ, BA, 43, MS, 48; Univ Mich, PhD(geol), 54. *Prof Exp:* Instr, Univ Mich, 51-53; from asst prof to assoc prof, 53-63, dir, Remote Sensing Lab, 75-76, PROF GEOL, UNIV KANS, 63- *Concurrent Pos:* Fulbright grant, Univ Heidelberg, 71. *Mem:* Am Asn Petrol Geol; Soc Econ Paleont & Mineral; Am Soc Photogram. *Res:* Evaporites; use of radar in geologic mapping. *Mailing Add:* Dept of Geol Univ of Kans Lawrence KS 66044

DELMASTRO, ANN MARY, b Brooklyn, NY, Nov 29, 45; m 75; c 1. ANALYTICAL CHEMISTRY. *Educ:* Fordham Univ, BS, 67; Cornell Univ, MS, 69, PhD(anal chem), 71. *Prof Exp:* SR CHEMIST ANAL CHEM, ALLIED CHEM CORP, 72- *Mem:* Am Chem Soc; Soc Appl Spectros; Am Soc Mass Spectrometry; Sigma Xi. *Res:* Development of analytical methods in x-ray spectrometry, emission spectrometry, and mass spectrometry for the analysis of samples related to the chemical reprocessing of nuclear fuels. *Mailing Add:* 1849 Grandview Dr Idaho Falls ID 83402

DELMASTRO, JOSEPH RAYMOND, b Joliet, Ill, Sept 10, 40; m 75; c 1. ANALYTICAL CHEMISTRY. *Educ:* Northern Ill Univ, BS, 62; Northwestern Univ, PhD(anal chem), 67. *Prof Exp:* Res chemist electrochem, Idaho Nuclear Corp, 67-71; sr chemist, Allied Chem Corp, 71-73, assoc scientist, 73-76, group leader, 76-79; GROUP LEADER, EXXON NUCLEAR IDAHO CO, 79- *Res:* Theory of electroanalytical techniques; coulometry; electroanalysis; general analytical chemistry methods development; thermal analysis; chromatography. *Mailing Add:* Exxon Nuclear Idaho Co PO Box 2800 Idaho Falls ID 83401

DELMER, DEBORAH P, b Indianapolis, Ind, Dec 7, 41; m 65. PLANT PHYSIOLOGY, BIOCHEMISTRY. *Educ:* Ind Univ, AB, 63; Univ Calif, San Diego, PhD(biol), 68. *Prof Exp:* NIH fel chem, Univ Colo, 68-69; NIH fel biol, Univ Calif, San Diego, 69-70, asst res biologist, 70-73; from asst prof to assoc prof biochem, 74-80, PROF, DEPT BIOCHEM, MICH STATE UNIV, 80- *Mem:* Am Soc Microbiol; Am Soc Plant Physiol. *Res:* Biochemistry of sucrose synthesis and metabolism in higher plants; circadian rhythms in fungi; biosynthesis of cellulose and other plant polysaccharides; glycoprotein synthesis in higher plants. *Mailing Add:* MSU/DOE Plant Res Lab Mich State Univ East Lansing MI 48824

DELMONTE, DAVID WILLIAM, b Auburn, NY, May 29, 30; m 58; c 6. ORGANIC CHEMISTRY, POLYMER CHEMISTRY. *Educ:* Villanova Univ, BS, 52; Univ Notre Dame, PhD(org chem), 57. *Prof Exp:* Chemist, Pioneering Res Lab, Textile Fibers Dept, E I du Pont de Nemours & Co, Inc, 52-53; asst, Univ Notre Dame, 53-54; res chemist, 56-69, mkt develop rep, 69-73, mkt develop supvr, 73-75, develop mgr, 75-81, MGR, FIBERS TECH CTR, HERCULES INC, 81- *Mem:* Am Chem Soc. *Res:* Condensation polymerization of esters and phosphorus compounds; isocyanate chemistry; polyurethane foam preparation and characterization; adhesives; polymer syntheses; terpenes and rosin acids chemistry; printing inks; polyolefin fibers. *Mailing Add:* Hercules Inc PO Box 8 Oxford GA 30267

DELMONTE, LILIAN, b Hamburg, Ger, Mar 19, 28; US citizen. HEMATOLOGY. *Educ:* Mt Holyoke Col, AB, 50; NY Univ, MSc, 52; Sorbonne Univ, Dr es Sci(hemat), 57. *Prof Exp:* Hemat lab supvr, Dept Pharmacol, Hoffmann-La Roche, 58-59; med writer, Cyanamid Int, Am Cyanamid Co, 59-62; from instr to asst prof anat, Baylor Col Med, 64-74; vis investr, 74-78, RES ASSOC, SLOAN-KETTERING INST, 78- *Concurrent Pos:* USPHS spec fel anat, Baylor Col Med, 62-64; Int Cancer Soc-Eleanor Roosevelt-Am Cancer Soc fel; Nat Cancer Inst spec fel, 72-73; sr vis scientist, Cancer Res Inst, Walter & Eliza Hall Inst Med Res, Melbourne, Australia, 71-73. *Mem:* Am Med Writers Asn; Am Soc Hemat; Int Soc Exp Hemat; Sigma Xi. *Res:* Hemopoietic self-regulatory mechanisms; leukemic cell regulation; transplantation immunology. *Mailing Add:* 440 E 62nd New York NY 10021

DEL MORAL, ROGER, b Detroit, Mich, Sept 13, 43; m 80; c 2. ECOLOGY. *Educ:* Univ Calif, Santa Barbara, BA, 65, MA, 66, PhD(biol), 68. *Prof Exp:* From asst prof to assoc prof, 68-82, PROF BOT, UNIV WASH, 82- *Concurrent Pos:* Del, Int Bot Cong, 69 & 75; NSF grants, 70-72, 79-81 & 81-84; consult, King County Design Comn, 71-73, AEC, 72-75, Seattle Parks Dept, 73-75 & 79-80, US Forest Serv, 75, Northern Tier Pipeline Co, 78, Nat Park Serv, 78 & 80 & King County Parks Dept, 79-80; sr res fel, CSIRO & Univ Melbourne, 76-77. *Mem:* Brit Ecol Soc; Bot Soc Am; Ecol Soc Am. *Res:* Allelopathy and competition; statistical ecology; phytosociology; vegetation structure; vegetation control. *Mailing Add:* Dept Bot AJ-10 Univ of Wash Seattle WA 98195

DELNORE, VICTOR ELI, b Yuba City, Calif, July 20, 43; m 70; c 2. REMOTE SENSING. *Educ:* Rensselaer Polytech Inst, BEE, 65; Univ Miami, MS, 67; Old Dominion Univ, PhD(phys oceanog), 76. *Prof Exp:* Res oceanographer, Nat Oceanic & Atmospheric Admin, 70-74; asst prof phys oceanog, Rutgers Univ, 76-79; SR CONSULT ENGR ENVIRON ENG, KENTRON INT, 79- *Concurrent Pos:* NSF fel, Univ Miami, 66-67; prin investr, Storms Response Exp, Univ Wash, NASA & Nat Oceanic & Atmospheric Admin, 80- *Mem:* Am Geophys Union. *Res:* Microwave remote sensing of the earths oceans and atmosphere. *Mailing Add:* Kentron Int Inc 3221 N Armistead Ave Hampton VA 23666

DELOACH, BERNARD COLLINS, JR, b Birmingham, Ala, Feb 19, 30; m 51; c 2. PHYSICS. *Educ:* Ala Polytech Inst, BS, 51, MS, 52; Ohio State Univ, PhD(physics), 56. *Prof Exp:* Mem tech staff, 56-63, head, Gallium Arsenide Laser Dept, 63-80, HEAD, SOLID STATE MAT & DEVICES DEPT, BELL LABS, 80- *Honors & Awards:* David Sarnoff Award, Inst Elec & Electronics Engrs, 75; Stuart Ballantine Award, Franklin Inst, 75. *Mem:* Inst Elec & Electronics Engrs. *Res:* Solid state millimeter wave sources; semiconductor junction electroluminescence; solid state physics; microwave applications; gallium arsenide solid state lasers. *Mailing Add:* Bell Labs Murray Hill NJ 07974

DELOACH, CULVER JACKSON, JR, b Greensboro, NC, July 25, 32; m 57; c 3. ENTOMOLOGY. *Educ:* Auburn Univ, BS, 54, MS, 60; NC State Univ, PhD(entom), 64. *Prof Exp:* Asst prof entom, Univ Hawaii in Japan, 64-65; res entomologist, Biol Control Insects Lab, Mo, 65-71 & Biol Control Aquatic Weeds Lab, Hurlingham, Arg, 71-74, RES ENTOMOLOGIST, GRASSLAND SOIL & WATER RES LAB, AGR RES SERV, USDA, 74- *Mem:* Entom Soc Am; Weed Sci Soc Am; Int Orgn Biol Control; Hyacinth Control Soc. *Res:* Biological control of weeds and brush in rangelands utilizing insects and pathogens. *Mailing Add:* Grassland-Forage Res Ctr USDA PO Box 748 Temple TX 76501

DELOACH, JOHN ROOKER, Humboldt, Tenn, July 5, 46; m 68; c 1. DRUG CARRIERS. *Educ:* Union Univ, BS, 68; Memphis State Univ, PhD(biochem), 75. *Prof Exp:* Res assoc med biochem, Sch Med, Univ Pittsburgh, 75-77; vis asst prof, Tex A&M Col Med, 77-78; RES CHEMIST, VET TOXICOL ENTOM RES LAB, USDA, 78- *Concurrent Pos:* Consult, Int Atomic Energy Agency, 80-81. *Mem:* AAAS; NY Acad Sci; Entom Soc Am; Sigma Xi. *Res:* Drug, pesticide, enzyme encapsulation in erythrocytes; lysosome involvement in insect metamorphosis; physiology of blood digestion by arthropods. *Mailing Add:* USDA Vet Toxicol Entom Res Lab PO Drawer GE College Station TX 77841

DELOATCH, EUGENE M, b Piermont, NY, Feb 3, 36; m 67; c 1. CONTROLS. *Educ:* Tougaloo Col, BS, 59; Lafayette Col, BS, 59; Polytech Inst Brooklyn, MS, 67, PhD(bio eng), 71. *Prof Exp:* Systs Eng, NY State Elec & Gas Co, 59-60; fac, 60, Assoc Prof, CHMN, ELEC & BIO ENGR, HOWARD UNIV, 75- *Concurrent Pos:* Chmn math, Urban Ctr Manhattan, Staten Univ NY, 68-69; consult, City Univ NY, 70; sci rev bd, Lister Hill-Ctr Biomed Comn, NIH, 80-83; mem acad adv bd, Indust Res Inst, 81-84; mem tech adv bd, Whirlpool Corp, 82-83. *Mem:* AAAS; Am Soc Eng Educ; Sigma Xi. *Res:* Engineering applications in the areas of biology and medicine. *Mailing Add:* Sch Eng Howard Univ Washington DC 20059

DE LONG, CHESTER WALLACE, b Seattle, Wash, Feb 27, 25; m 56; c 3. BIOCHEMISTRY, PHYSIOLOGY. *Educ:* Univ Washington, BS, 48; State Col Washington, PhD(chem), 56. *Prof Exp:* Biochemist isotope metab, Hanford Atomic Power Labs, Gen Elec Co, 48-52; asst chem, State Col Washington, 54-55; biochemist, US Govt, 56-68; chief training grants & career develop prog, Educ Serv, 68-71, chief prog & career develop rev div, Med Res Serv, 71-74, chief, Rev Div, Manpower Grants Serv, 74-79, COORDR, REV & LIAISON, OFF ACAD AFFAIRS, DEPT MED SURG, US VET ADMIN, 79- *Concurrent Pos:* Vis res assoc, Phys Biol Lab, Nat Inst Arthritis & Metab Dis, 62-63; ex officio Vet Admin rep, Nat Adv Res Resources Coun, 73-80. *Mem:* Sigma Xi; Asn Mil Surgeons of US; fel AAAS; Am Chem Soc. *Res:* Intermediary metabolism; radioisotope toxicology and metabolism; chemistry of penicillin formation; electron paramagnetic resonance of biological materials; biochemistry of amino acids; research training; health manpower education; program management. *Mailing Add:* Off Acad Affairs 14D 810 Vermont Ave NW Washington DC 20420

DELONG, KARL THOMAS, b Philadelphia, Pa, July 18, 38; m 63; c 3. ECOLOGY. *Educ:* Oberlin Col, AB, 60; Univ Calif, Berkeley, PhD(ecol), 65. *Prof Exp:* Asst prof biol, Ripon Col, 65-66; from asst prof to assoc prof, 66-70, PROF BIOL, GRINNELL COL, 70- *Mem:* Ecol Soc Am; Am Soc Mammalogy. *Res:* Population ecology of small mammals. *Mailing Add:* Dept of Biol Grinnell Col Grinnell IA 50112

DELONG, ROBERT FRANCIS, b Seattle, Wash, June 17, 16; m 41; c 3. BACTERIOLOGY. *Educ:* Lawrence Col, BA, 38; Univ Wis, MS, 40. *Prof Exp:* Lab asst bact, Inst Paper Chem, 40-41; microbiologist, Nat Aluminate Corp, 41-45; group leader microbiol packaging, Paper Prod Res, Am Can Co, 45-66, supvr packaging sect, Paper Prod Res & Develop, 66-70, supvr prod eval, Lab Serv, Packaging Tech Serv, 70-75, sr res assoc, Packaging Res & Develop, 75-77; RETIRED. *Concurrent Pos:* Mem food irradiation, Mil Personnel Supplies, Nat Res Coun, 73- *Mem:* Am Soc Microbiol; Tech Asn Pulp & Paper Indust. *Res:* Control growth of microorganisms in pulp and paper systems; retard spoiling of packaged foods; food packaging materials. *Mailing Add:* PO Box 683 Neenah WI 54956

DELONG, STEPHEN EDWIN, b Evansville, Ind, Sept 22, 43; m 65; c 3. PETROLOGY. *Educ:* Oberlin Col, AB, 65; Univ Tex, Austin, MA, 69, PhD(geol), 71. *Prof Exp:* Res fel geochem, Calif Inst Technol, 71-72; asst prof geol, 73-79, assoc vpres acad affairs, 79-81, actg vpres acad affairs, 81-82, ASSOC PROF GEOL, STATE UNIV NY ALBANY, 79- *Mem:* Am Geophys Union. *Res:* Petrology, geochemistry and tectonics of oceanic crust and subduction zones. *Mailing Add:* Dept Geol Sci State Univ NY Albany NY 12222

DE LORENZO, EUGENE JOSEPH, b Niagara Falls, NY, Aug 25, 30; m 62. PHYSICAL CHEMISTRY. *Educ:* Niagara Univ, BS, 52; NY Univ, PhD(phys chem), 64. *Prof Exp:* Res chemist, Olin Mathieson Chem Corp, 52-56; group leader borane chem, 56-59; assoc res scientist, Eng Res Div, Grad Sch, NY Univ, 59-61, res asst quantum chem, 61-64, asst res scientist, 64-65; sr chemist, Itek Corp, 65-71, mem sci staff, 71-74, plant mgr, Lithographic Systs, 74-75, SR MEM SCI STAFF, CENT RES LABS, ITEK CORP, 74-, GROUP MGR, 75- *Concurrent Pos:* Prog consult cosmic ray proj, NY Univ, 64-66. *Mem:* Am Chem Soc; Soc Photog Sci & Eng. *Res:* Spectral sensitization of photoresponse; development of lithographic and photographic systems; characterization of thick film inks; abrasion-resistant coatings for plastics. *Mailing Add:* Cent Res Labs 10 Maguire Rd Lexington MA 02173

DELORENZO, ROBERT JOHN, b Clifton, NJ, June 26, 47; c 3. NEUROSCIENCE, NEUROLOGY. *Educ:* Yale Univ, BS, 69, PhD(neuropharmacol), 73, MD, 74, MPH, 74. *Prof Exp:* Resident, Neurol Dept, Yale Univ, 74-76, chief resident, 76-77, asst prof, 77-80, ASSOC PROF NEUROL, MED SCH, YALE UNIV, 80- *Concurrent Pos:* mem staff res career develop grant, NIH, 76-81; mem, Epilepsy Res Found, 77; Consult, West Haven Veterans Hosp, 77-, Conn Mental Health Ctr, 79- & Parent Educ Res; prin investr, NIH res grant, 77-; attend physician, Yale New Haven Hosp, 77-; vis prof, Sch Med, Wash Univ, 81. *Honors & Awards:* Fisk Award. *Mem:* Am Soc Neurochem; Soc Neurosci; Int Soc Neurochem; Am Acad Neurol; NY Acad Sci. *Res:* Mechanisms involved in mediating the effects of calcium on synaptic function; antivulsant and neuroleptic drugs; role of calmodulin in synaptic function. *Mailing Add:* Dept Neurol Yale Med Sch 333 Cedar St New Haven CT 06510

DELORENZO, RONALD ANTHONY, b Schenectady, NY, Sept 28, 41; m 67; c 2. PHYSICAL INORGANIC CHEMISTRY. *Educ:* St John's Univ, BS, 63; Lowell Technol Inst, PhD(chem), 70. *Prof Exp:* Asst prof, 70-77, ASSOC PROF CHEM, MID GA COL, 77-, COMPUT COORDR, 73- *Concurrent Pos:* Feature ed, J Chem Educ. *Mem:* Am Chem Soc; AAAS; Am Asn Univ Prof. *Res:* Thermodynamic studies of coordination compounds in mixed solvents; electron paramagnetic resonance studies of photochemically generated radicals; random number generation; chemical education. *Mailing Add:* Dept of Chem Mid Ga Col Cochran GA 31014

DELORENZO, WILLIAM F, b Newark, NJ, Dec 22, 19. BACTERIOLOGY, CHEMOTHERAPY. *Educ:* Univ Ill, BS, 43, MS, 47, PhD(bact), 51. *Prof Exp:* Asst bact, Univ Ill, 46-50, fel, 50-52; med bacteriologist, Chem Corps, Camp Detrick, Md, 53-54; SR BACTERIOLOGIST, HOFFMANN-LA ROCHE, INC, 54- *Mem:* Am Soc Microbiol; Sigma Xi; NY Acad Sci. *Mailing Add:* Hoffmann-La Roche Roche Park Nutley NJ 07110

DELORIT, RICHARD JOHN, b Door Co, Wis, May 22, 21; m 42; c 2. WEED SCIENCE. *Educ:* Univ Wis-River Falls, BS, 42; Univ Wis-Madison, MS, 48, PhD(agron), 59. *Prof Exp:* Teacher, Wis High Schs, 42-53; critic teacher voc agr, Univ Wis-River Falls & River Falls High Sch, 53-55; asst prof agron, 56-57, dean col agr, 57-64, VCHANCELLOR, UNIV WIS-RIVER FALLS, 64- *Concurrent Pos:* Mem, Coun Agr Sci & Technol. *Mem:* Weed Soc Am; Am Soc Agron. *Res:* Weed science; botany; ecology. *Mailing Add:* Dept of Plant & Earth Sci Univ of Wis River Falls WI 54022

DELOS, JOHN BERNARD, b Ann Arbor, Mich, Mar 24, 44; m 65; c 3. MOLECULAR PHYSICS, THEORETICAL CHEMISTRY. *Educ:* Univ Mich, BSChem, 65; Mass Inst Technol, PhD(chem), 70. *Prof Exp:* Fel chem, Univ Alta, 70 & Univ BC, 70-71; asst prof physics, 71-77, ASSOC PROF PHYSICS, COL WILLIAM & MARY, 77- *Res:* Atomic and molecular collision theory; structure and properties of small molecules. *Mailing Add:* Dept of Physics Col of William & Mary Williamsburg VA 23185

DE LOS REYES, B WILLIAM, space physics, see previous edition

DELOUCHE, JAMES CURTIS, b La, Oct 30, 30; m 54; c 3. BOTANY. *Educ:* Southwestern La Inst, BS, 51; Iowa State Univ, MS, 52, PhD(econ bot), 55. *Prof Exp:* From asst agronomist to assoc agronomist, 57-65, agronomist seed technol, 65-77, PROF AGRON, MISS STATE UNIV, 65- *Concurrent Pos:* State seed analyst, Miss Dept Agr, 58-77. *Mem:* Am Soc Agron; Asn Off Seed Anal. *Res:* Economic botany; quality evaluation of seed; seed physiology; dissemination and germination of weed seeds. *Mailing Add:* Dept of Agron Miss State Univ Mississippi State MS 39762

DELP, CHARLES JOSEPH, b St Louis, Mo, May 9, 27; m 49; c 4. PLANT PATHOLOGY, FUNGICIDE DEVELOPMENT MANAGEMENT. *Educ:* Colo State Univ, BS, 50; Univ Calif, PhD(plant path), 53. *Prof Exp:* Res asst, Univ Calif, Davis, 50-53; sr res investr plant path, 53-68, res supvr, 68-79, MGR FUNGICIDE DEVELOPMENT, E I DU PONT DE NEMOURS & CO, INC, 80- *Concurrent Pos:* Consult fungicide resistance problems. *Mem:* Am Phytopath Soc; Am Inst Biol Sci. *Res:* Environmental influence on grape powdery mildew; discovery and development of chemicals to control plant diseases. *Mailing Add:* Biochem Dept E I du Pont de Nemours & Co Inc Wilmington DE 19898

DELPHIA, JOHN MAURICE, b Kans, Mar 29, 25; m 49; c 5. VERTEBRATE MORPHOLOGY. *Educ:* St Benedicts Col, BS, 49; Kans State Col, MS, 50; Univ Nebr, PhD(zool, anat), 59. *Prof Exp:* Instr zool, NDak Agr Col, 50-51, comp anat, embryol & histol, 52-54, asst prof, 55; asst prof, 64-70, ASSOC PROF ANAT, COL MED, OHIO STATE UNIV, 70-*Concurrent Pos:* NIH grants, 57, 58 & 59. *Mem:* Am Asn Anatomists. *Res:* Developmental and gross anatomy of avian lungs and airsacs; abnormalities in bovine endocrine glands. *Mailing Add:* Dept of Anat Ohio State Univ Col of Med Columbus OH 43210

DEL PICO, JOSEPH, chemical engineering, see previous edition

DEL REGATO, JUAN A, b Camaguey, Cuba, Mar 1, 09; US citizen; m 39; c 3. RADIOLOGY. *Educ:* Univ Paris, MD, 37. *Hon Degrees:* DSc, Colo Col, 67. *Prof Exp:* Asst roentgentherapist, Radium Inst Paris, 36-37; asst radiotherapist, Chicago Tumor Inst, 37-38; radiotherapist, Warwick Cancer Clin, Washington, DC, 39-40, Nat Cancer Inst, Baltimore, Md, 41-42 & Ellis Fischel Cancer Hosp, 43-49; prof clin radiol, Univ Colo, Colorado Springs, 49-74; PROF RADIOL, COL MED, UNIV SOUTH FLA, 74- *Concurrent Pos:* Dir, Penrose Cancer Hosp, 49-74; distinguished physician, Vet Admin; mem adv comt, PR Nuclear Ctr & Nat Adv Cancer Coun; mem nat adv cancer coun & lung cancer task force, SFla Cancer Found, 67-; mem adv comt, Milheim Found Cancer Res; trustee, Am Bd Radiol, 74- *Honors & Awards:* Laureat, French Acad Med, 48 & 79; Order of Carlos Finlay, 55; Gold Medals, Inter-Am Col Radiol, Am Col Radiol, Radiol Soc NAm & Am Soc Therapeutic Radiologists; Prix Bruninghaus, French Acad Med, 79; Beclere Medal, Ctr Antoine Beclere, Paris, 80. *Mem:* Inter-Am Col Radiol (pres, 67-71); fel Am Col Radiol; Am Roentgen Ray Soc; Radiol Soc NAm (vpres, 59-60); Am Radium Soc (vpres, 63-64, treas, 65, pres, 68-69). *Res:* Therapeutic radiology; radiotherapy of cancer of the maxillary sinuses; transvaginal roentgentherapy for cancer of the cervix; total body irradiation for chronic leukemia; pathways of spread of malignant tumors; radiotherapy of soft tissue sarcomas; radiotherapy of inoperable cancer of the prostate; treatment of cancer of the breast. *Mailing Add:* Dept Radiol Univ Southern Fla Col Med Tampa FL 33612

DELSANTO, PIER PAOLO, b Torino, Italy, Mar 14, 41; m 70; c 2. NUCLEAR & THEORETICAL PHYSICS. *Educ:* Univ Torino, Italy, Dr(physics), 63, specialization nuclear physics, 65. *Prof Exp:* Fel physics & instr math, Univ Torino, Italy, 64-66, Alexander von Humboldt Stiftung fel physics, Univ Frankfurt, 66-68, res assoc, 69; from asst prof to assoc prof, 69-77, PROF PHYSICS, UNIV PR, MAYAGUEZ, 77- *Concurrent Pos:* Scientist I, PR Nuclear Ctr, 70-75; vis prof, Univ Melbourne, 73 & Univ Cagliari, Sardinia, 75-76. *Honors & Awards:* Libera Docenza, Italian Govt, Rome, 71. *Mem:* Am Phys Soc; Europ Phys Soc. *Res:* Nuclear reaction theory; intermediate energy nuclear physics; calculations of photonuclear reaction cross sections. *Mailing Add:* Dept of Physics Univ of PR Mayaguez PR 00708

DELSEMME, ARMAND HUBERT, b Verviers, Belg, Feb 1, 18; m; c 3. ASTROPHYSICS. *Educ:* Univ Liege, BA, 38, MA & MEd, 40, PhD(physics), 51. *Prof Exp:* Res worker, Res Labs, Belge de l' Azote Corp, Belg, 46-51, head phys res lab, 51-53, mgr & head res, 53-56; dir, Belgian Congo Astron Observ & sci adv, Belgian Inst Sci Res Cent Africa, 56-61; head basic studies div, Directorate Sci Affairs, Orgn Econ Coop & Develop, France, 61-66; PROF ASTROPHYS, UNIV TOLEDO, 66- *Concurrent Pos:* Corresp mem, Belg Nat Comt Astron, 58-64, assoc mem, 64-68; prof, Belg State Univ, Elizabethville, Congo, 60; guest investr, CRB adv fel, Mt Wilson & Palomar Observ, 60-61; chmn int govt comn, Int Ctr Geothermal Res, 64-66; vpres comn 15 for phys study of comets, Int Astron Union, 70-73, pres comn 15 for phys study of comets, minor planets and meteorites, 73-76, chmn comt world inventory cometary archives, 75-79; consult, Var NASA & Nat Acad Sci Panels. *Mem:* Am Astron Soc; Int Astron Union; Astron Soc France; Belg Phys Soc; Royal Belg Acad Overseas Sci. *Res:* Molecular spectroscopy; thermodynamics; geophysics; volcanology; stellar astrophysics; cometary phenomena; air glow. *Mailing Add:* Dept of Physics & Astron Univ of Toledo Toledo OH 43606

DELSON, ERIC, b New York, NY, Jan 18, 45; m 67; c 1. PHYSICAL ANTHROPOLOGY, PRIMATOLOGY. *Educ:* Harvard Univ, AB, 66; Columbia Univ, PhD(geol), 73. *Prof Exp:* Asst prof anthrop, Univ Pittsburgh, 72-73; asst prof, 73-75, assoc prof, 76-79, PROF ANTHROP, LEHMAN COL, 80- *Concurrent Pos:* Res grants, Wenner-Gren Found Anthrop Res, 71, 78 & 80, Nat Geog Soc, 71, NSF, 74 & 79-82, City Univ New York Res Award Prog, 75-82, L S B Leakey Found, 78 & 80 & Found Res Origin Man, 80; asst prof, assoc prof & prof anthrop, City Univ New York Grad Ctr, 74-; res assoc, Dept Vertebrate Paleont, Am Mus Natural Hist, 75-; paleoanthrop deleg to People's Repub China, Nat Acad Sci, 75; vis prof, Yale Univ, 80; mem, Anthrop Adv Panel, NSF, 80-82; J S Guggenheim Mem fel, 81-82; consult, AMS Press, 80- & Stonehenge Press, 81; assoc ed, Contributions to Primatology, 80- *Mem:* Am Quaternary Asn; Am Asn Phys Anthropologists; Int & Am Primatol Soc; Soc Study Evolution. *Res:* Primate paleontology and primatology, especially Cercopithecidae; biological and cultural evolution of humans; later Tertiary stratigraphy; evolutionary biology and systematic methodology; primate classification and systematics; vertebrate paleontology. *Mailing Add:* Dept of Anthrop Lehman Col Bronx NY 10468

DELTON, MARY HELEN, b Troy, NY, Mar 6, 46. ORGANIC CHEMISTRY. *Educ:* Ariz State Univ, BS, 67; Univ Calif, Los Angeles, MS & PhD(org chem), 70. *Prof Exp:* NSF fel, Northwestern Univ, 70-71; asst prof chem, Mt Holyoke Col, 71-76; adj asst prof, Wayne State Univ, 76-78; ASST PROF CHEM, OAKLAND UNIV, 78- *Mem:* Am Chem Soc. *Res:* Organic photochemistry, both mechanistic and synthetic applications; new synthetic methods. *Mailing Add:* Dept of Chem Oakland Univ Rochester MI 48063

DEL TORO, VINCENT, b New York, NY, Sept 17, 23; m 65. ELECTRICAL ENGINEERING, CONTROL SYSTEMS. *Educ:* City Col New York, BEE, 46; Polytech Inst Brooklyn, MEE, 50. *Prof Exp:* Tutor, 46-50, from instr to assoc prof, 50-62, asst dean, 62-65, PROF ELEC ENG, CITY COL NEW YORK, 63-, ASSOC DEAN SCH ENG, 65- *Concurrent Pos:* Consult control systs, Gen Dynamics/Convair, 57-59; consult, Bendix Corp, 77-78. *Mem:* Sr mem Inst Elec & Electronics Engrs; Am Soc Eng Educ. *Res:* Self-adaptive control systems; feedback and nonlinear control systems; synchronous induction motors; analog computers. *Mailing Add:* Dept of Elec Eng City Col of New York New York NY 10031

DE LUCA, CHESTER, b Bristol, Pa, Sept 7, 27; m 54; c 5. BIOCHEMISTRY, CELL BIOLOGY. *Educ:* Georgetown Univ, BS, 52; Johns Hopkins Univ, PhD(biochem), 56. *Prof Exp:* Jr instr biol, Johns Hopkins Univ, 52-54, Nat Cancer Inst fel, 54-56; Am Cancer Soc fel, Rockefeller Inst, 56-59; instr pediat, Johns Hopkins Univ, 59-62; sr cancer res scientist, Roswell Park Mem Inst, 62-65; asst prof, 65-71, ASSOC PROF ORAL BIOL, SCH DENT, STATE UNIV NY BUFFALO, 71- *Concurrent Pos:* Res assoc pediat, Sinai Hosp, Baltimore, Md, 59-62. *Mem:* AAAS; Am Chem Soc; Am Soc Cell Biol; Nutrit Today Soc; Tissue Cult Asn. *Res:* Biochemical parameters of neutrophil function; biochemical and genetic control mechanisms; nutrition. *Mailing Add:* Dept of Oral Biol State Univ NY 4510 Main St Buffalo NY 14226

DE LUCA, DONALD CARL, b Amsterdam, NY, May 24, 36; m 66; c 2. ORGANIC CHEMISTRY, BIOCHEMISTRY. *Educ:* Rensselaer Polytech Inst, BS, 57; Univ Minn, PhD(org chem), 63. *Prof Exp:* Res fel biochem, Sch Med, Johns Hopkins Univ, 64-66; asst prof biochem, Sch Med, 66-75, ASSOC PROF BIOCHEM, COL MED, UNIV ARK MED SCI, LITTLE ROCK, 75- *Mem:* AAAS; Am Chem Soc; Royal Soc Chem. *Res:* Photochemical oxidations; chemical and biological oxidative processes of nitrogen containing compounds; biochemistry of behavior. *Mailing Add:* Dept of Biochem Univ of Ark for Med Sci Little Rock AR 72201

DELUCA, HECTOR FLOYD, b Pueblo, Colo, Apr 5, 30; m 54; c 4. BIOCHEMISTRY. *Educ:* Univ Colo, BA, 51; Univ Wis, MS, 53, PhD, 55. *Hon Degrees:* DSc, Univ Colo, Boulder, 74; DSc, Med Col Wis, 80. *Prof Exp:* Res asst biochem, 51-55, proj assoc, 55, fel, 56-57, from instr to assoc prof, 57-65, PROF BIOCHEM & HARRY STEENBOCK RES PROF, 65-, CHMN DEPT, 70- *Concurrent Pos:* Vis scientist, Strangeways Res Labs, Eng, 60; lectr, Royal Col Physicians & Surgeons Can, 77; Lenore Richards vis prof, Northwestern Hosp, Minneapolis, Minn, 77; distinguished lectr med sci, Mayo Clin, Rochester, 78. *Honors & Awards:* Andre Lichtwitz Prize, 68; Mead Johnson Award, 68; Nicolas Andry Award, 71; Osborne & Mendel Award, Am Inst Nutrit, 73; Roussel Prize of France, 74; Gairdner Found Award from Can, 74; Dixon Medal, Irish Med Coun, 75; Distinguished lectr Med Sci, Mayo Clin, 78; Plenary lectr, 5th Int Cong Hormonal Steroids, New Delhi, 78; Atwater Award, 79; William Rose lectr, 80; Harvey lectr, 80. *Mem:* Am Chem Soc; Am Soc Biol Chemists; Am Inst Nutrit; Endocrine Soc; Am Acad Arts & Sci. *Res:* Mechanism of action and metabolism of vitamins and hormones, especially vitamin D. *Mailing Add:* Dept Biochem Univ Wis Madison WI 53706

DELUCA, JOHN ANTHONY, solid state chemistry, see previous edition

DE LUCA, LUIGI M, b Maglie, Italy, Feb 25, 41; m 65; c 2. BIOCHEMISTRY. *Educ:* Univ Pavia, PhD(org chem), 64. *Prof Exp:* Res assoc, Maggiore Hosp, Milan, 64-65; from res assoc to instr nutrit & food sci, Mass Inst Technol, 65-71, vis lectr, 71-75; sr staff scientist, 71-73, head differentiation control lung cancer, 73-75, head differentiation control exp path, 75-81, HEAD, DIFFERENTIATION CONTROL SECT, LAB CELLULAR CARCINOGENESIS & TUMOR PROM, NAT CANCER INST, NIH, 81- *Concurrent Pos:* Japan Soc Promotion Sci vis prof, Univ Tokyo, 76. *Honors & Awards:* Mead-Johnson Award, Am Inst Nutrit, 78. *Mem:* Soc Complex Carbohydrates; Am Inst Nutrit; Am Soc Biol Chemists; Am Chem Soc; Fedn Am Scientists. *Res:* Molecular involvement of vitamin A in biological processes involved in structure and function of epithelial tissues and investigation of biochemical targets of chemical carcinogens. *Mailing Add:* Nat Cancer Inst NIH 9000 Rockville Pike Bethesda MD 20205

DELUCA, MARLENE, b La Crosse, Wis, Nov 10, 36; m 59, 67; c 1. BIOCHEMISTRY. *Educ:* Hamline Univ, BS, 58; Univ Minn, PhD(biochem), 63. *Prof Exp:* Fel biol, McCollum-Pratt Inst, 62-65, asst prof, Johns Hopkins Univ, 65-70; asst prof biochem, Schs Med & Dent, Georgetown Univ, 70-72; assoc prof, 72-78, PROF CHEM, UNIV CALIF, SAN DIEGO, 78- *Mem:* Am Soc Biol Chem; Sigma Xi; Am Chem Soc. *Res:* Firefly luciferase, oxidative phosphorylation, enzyme mechanisms and energy transductions. *Mailing Add:* Dept of Chem Univ of Calif San Diego La Jolla CA 92037

DELUCA, PATRICK JOHN, b Springfield, Mass, July 27, 44; m 66; c 2. MICROBIOLOGY, CYTOLOGY. *Educ:* St Michael's Col, Vt, BA, 66; Fordham Univ, MS, 68, PhD(biol), 75. *Prof Exp:* Lab asst biol, Fordham Univ, 66-69, teaching fel, 69-70; asst prof, 70-77, assoc prof biol, 77-80, PROF BIOL, MT ST MARY COL, NY, 80-, PRE-MED ADV, 77- *Concurrent Pos:* Instr, Dutchess Community Col, 75. *Mem:* Am Inst Biol Sci; Sigma Xi; Torrey Bot Club. *Res:* Ultrastructural characteristics of certain green soil algae and how these characteristics might be used for taxonomic purposes. *Mailing Add:* Dept of Biol Mt St Mary Col Newburgh NY 12550

DELUCA, PATRICK PHILLIP, b Scranton, Pa, Sept 7, 35; m 56; c 6. PHARMACEUTICS. *Educ:* Temple Univ, BS, 57, MS, 60, PhD(pharm), 63. *Prof Exp:* Jr anal chemist, Smith Kline & French Labs, 57-59; sr res pharmacist, Ciba Pharmaceut Co, 63-66, plant mgr, Somerville Opers, 66-69, plant mgr, Cormedics Corp, 69-70, dir develop & control, 70; assoc prof, 70-75, PROF PHARM, UNIV KY, 75-, ASST DEAN COL PHARM, 71- *Concurrent Pos:* Mem, US Pharm-FDA Nat Coord Comt on Large Vol Parenterals. *Honors & Awards:* Lunsford-Richardson Pharm Award, 60 & 62. *Mem:* Am Pharmaceut Asn; fel Acad Pharmaceut Sci; NY Acad Sci. *Res:* Pharmaceutical technology; kinetics and stabilization; lyophilization; sterile products; intravenous administration. *Mailing Add:* Univ of Ky Col of Pharm Lexington KY 40506

DELUCA, PAUL MICHAEL, JR, b Albany, NY, Apr 22, 44; m 66; c 2. MEDICAL PHYSICS, NUCLEAR PHYSICS. *Educ:* LeMoyne Col, BS, 66; Univ Notre Dame, PhD(physics), 71. *Prof Exp:* Fel radiol, 71-73, adj asst prof, 73-75, asst prof radiol, 75-81, ASSOC PROF MED PHYSICS, UNIV WIS-MADISON, 81- *Mem:* Am Inst Physics; Health Physics Soc; Am Asn Physicists Med. *Res:* Fast neutron physics; high linear energy transfer therapy beams; dosimetry and charged particle spectroscopy. *Mailing Add:* Univ Wis Dept Med Physics 1300 University Ave Madison WI 53706

DELUCA, ROBERT D(AVID), b Passaic, NJ, Jan 11, 41; m 63; c 4. METALLURGY, SOLID STATE PHYSICS. *Educ:* Stevens Inst Technol, BE, 62, MS, 64, PhD(metall), 66. *Prof Exp:* Sr metallurgist, Corning Glass Works, 66-76; SR RES SCIENTIST, JOHNSON & JOHNSON DENTAL PRODS CO, 76- *Mem:* Am Phys Soc; Electrochem Soc; Am Inst Mining, Metall & Petrol Engrs. *Res:* Strengthening mechanisms in metals; physical metallurgy; dental materials; amalgam alloys; metal-ceramic systems; manufacturing processes for high strength, lowloss, optical waveguide fibers; electronic materials; semiconducting glass-ceramics; metal-glass systems. *Mailing Add:* Johnson & Johnson Dent Prod Co 20 Lake Dr East Windsor NJ 08520

DE LUCCIA, JOHN JERRY, b Philadelphia, Pa, Mar 15, 35; m 57; c 3. MATERIALS SCIENCE, CORROSION. *Educ:* Drexel Univ, BSc, 61; Univ Pa, MSc, 67, PhD(metall & mat sci), 76. *Prof Exp:* Instr metall eng, Drexel Univ, 61-63; metallurgist, 63-72, SUPVRY MAT ENGR, AERO MAT LAB, NAVAL AIR DEVELOP CTR, 72- *Concurrent Pos:* Adj prof mat & metall eng, Evening Col, Drexel Univ, 66-; N Am Coordr Corrosion Fatigue Coop Study, Adv Group for Aerospace Res & Develop, NATO, 77-; vis prof mat eng, Drexel Univ, 78-79. *Honors & Awards:* Templin Award, Am Soc Testing & Mat, 70; Sci Achievement Award, Naval Air Develop Ctr, 78. *Mem:* Fel Am Soc Metals; Nat Asn Corrosion Engrs; Naval Civilian Adminr Asn. *Res:* Corrosion and degradation of aerospace materials; stress corrosion cracking and hydrogen embrittlement of high strength alloys. *Mailing Add:* Drexel Univ Mat & Metall Eng Dept 32 & Chestnut St Philadelphia PA 19104

DE LUCIA, FRANK CHARLES, b St Paul, Minn, June 21, 43; m 65. MOLECULAR PHYSICS, QUANTUM ELECTRONICS. *Educ:* Iowa Wesleyan Col, BS, 64; Duke Univ, PhD(physics), 69. *Prof Exp:* From instr & res assoc to asst prof, 69-76, ASSOC PROF PHYSICS, DUKE UNIV, 76- *Mem:* AAAS; Am Phys Soc. *Res:* Microwave spectroscopy; millimeter and submillimeter waves. *Mailing Add:* Dept of Physics Duke Univ Durham NC 27706

DELURY, DANIEL BERTRAND, b Walker, Minn, Sept 19, 07; Can citizen; m 41; c 2. MATHEMATICS, STATISTICS. *Educ:* Univ Toronto, BA, 29, MA, 30, PhD(math), 36. *Prof Exp:* Instr math, Univ Sask, 31-34; lectr, Univ Toronto, 36-43, asst prof, 43-45; from assoc prof to prof statist, Va Polytech Inst, 45-47, dir dept math statist, Ont Res Found, 47-58; prof math, 58-77, EMER PROF MATH, UNIV TORONTO, 77- *Concurrent Pos:* Chmn dept math, Univ Toronto, 58-68. *Mem:* Can Statist Soc; fel Am Statist Asn; Am Math Soc; Inst Math Statist; Biomet Soc. *Res:* Population dynamics; estimation of biological populations. *Mailing Add:* 35 Owen Blvd Willowdale ON M2P 1G2 Can

DELUSTRO, FRANK ANTHONY, b Brooklyn, NY, May 8, 48; m 74. CELLULAR IMMUNOLOGY. *Educ:* Fordham Univ, BS, 70; State Univ NY, PhD(immunol), 76. *Prof Exp:* Res assoc immunol, Dept Basic & Clin Immunol & Microbiol, 76-78, instr immunol, Div Rheumatol & Immunol, 78-80, ASST PROF, MED DIV, MED UNIV SC, 80- *Concurrent Pos:* Am Cancer Soc fel, 76-78. *Mem:* Sigma Xi; Am Asn Immunol; Reticuloendothelial Soc; Soc Exp Biol Med. *Res:* Elucidation of immune responses in rheumatic disease, especially as cell-mediated immunity and monocyte function relate to autoimmunity and fibrosis. *Mailing Add:* Div Rheumatol & Immunol Dept of Med Med Univ SC Charleston SC 29425

DELVAILLE, JOHN PAUL, b Riverside, Calif, Oct 5, 31; div; c 1. PHYSICS. *Educ:* Univ Calif, Berkeley, BA, 54; Cornell Univ, PhD(exp physics), 62. *Prof Exp:* Instr & res assoc physics, Cornell Univ, 62-63, actg asst prof, 63-64, asst prof, 64-70; res mem, Ctr Space Res, Mass Inst Technol, 70-74, res affil, 74-80; PHYSICIST, CTR ASTROPHYS, SMITHSONIAN ASTROPHYS OBSERV, 74- *Mem:* AAAS; Am Asn Physics Teachers; Am Phys Soc. *Res:* Cosmic rays; extensive air showers; gamma-ray and x-ray astronomy; atomic collisions. *Mailing Add:* Smithsonian Ctr for Astrophys 60 Garden St Cambridge MA 02138

DEL VECCHIO, ANTHONY JOSEPH, b Philadelphia, Pa, Dec 9, 40; m 64; c 1. FOOD CHEMISTRY, LIPID CHEMISTRY. *Educ:* Drexel Univ, BS, 63, MS, 65. *Prof Exp:* Res chemist colloid chem, Atlas Chem Indust Inc, 65-68, develop scientist foods, 68-70; sect head food technol, C J Patterson Co, 71-73, mgr prod develop foods, 73-75, tech dir food & cosmetics, 75-76; mgr fats, oils & emulsifier develop, 76-80, DIR, TECHNOL LICENSING, PILLSBURY CO, 80- *Mem:* Am Asn Cereal Chemists; Inst Food Technologists; Am Oil Chemists Soc; Licensing Exec Soc. *Res:* Fats and oils; surface-active agents in foods; food science; colloid chemistry. *Mailing Add:* 311 Second St SE Minneapolis MN 55414

DEL VECCHIO, VITO GERARD, b Dunmore, Pa, May 13, 39. BIOCHEMICAL GENETICS. *Educ:* Univ Scranton, BS, 61; St John's Univ, NY, MS, 63; Hahnemann Med Col, PhD(biochem genetics), 67. *Prof Exp:* USPHS res fel microbiol, Univ Geneva, 66-68; assoc prof biol, Stonehill Col, 68-69; from asst prof to assoc prof, 73-77, PROF BIOL, UNIV SCRANTON, 77- *Mem:* AAAS; Genetics Soc Am; Am Soc Microbiol. *Res:* Tyrosinase genetics; biochemistry and immunochemistry of Neurospora crassa morphogenesis; biochemical control of morphogenesis of Neurospora isozymes of Neurospora crassa. *Mailing Add:* Dept of Biol Univ of Scranton Scranton PA 18510

DELVIGS, PETER, b Riga, Latvia, June 28, 33; US citizen; m 65. ORGANIC POLYMER CHEMISTRY. *Educ:* Western Reserve Univ, BA, 59; Univ Minn, Minneapolis, PhD(org chem), 63. *Prof Exp:* Res assoc biochem, Cleveland Clin Found, 63-67; AEROSPACE CHEMIST, NASA LEWIS RES CTR, CLEVELAND, 67- *Mem:* AAAS; Am Chem Soc; NY Acad Sci. *Res:* Synthesis, characterization and properties of new thermally stable polymers; development of fiber-reinforced resin composites. *Mailing Add:* 21290 Parkwood Ave Fairview Park OH 44126

DEL VILLANO, BERT CHARLES, b Yeadon, Pa, Apr 9, 43; m 63; c 1. IMMUNOLOGY, CANCER. *Educ:* Lehigh Univ, BA, 65; Univ Pa, PhD(microbiol), 71. *Prof Exp:* Fel immunol, Scripps Clin Res Found, 71-73, asst, 73-75; mem staff immunol, Cleveland Clin, 75-80; DIR, CANCER DIV, CEMTOCOR, 81- *Honors & Awards:* Basil O'Connor grant, March of Dimes Nat Found, 74. *Mem:* Am Soc Microbiol; Int Asn Comp Res Leukemia & Related Dis; Am Asn Immunologists. *Res:* Expression of viral proteins in normal and malignant tissues and the immune response against these viral proteins; tumor markers. *Mailing Add:* Cancer Div Cemtocor 244 Great Valley Pkwy Malverm PA 19355

DELWICHE, CONSTANT COLLIN, b Wis, Nov 26, 17; m 43; c 4. COMPARATIVE BIOCHEMISTRY. *Educ:* Univ Wis, BS, 40; Univ Calif, PhD, 49. *Prof Exp:* Chmn dept soils & plant nutrit, 65-72, PROF GEOBIOL, DEPT LAND, AIR & WATER RESOURCES, UNIV CALIF, DAVIS, 60- *Mem:* AAAS; Am Soc Plant Physiologists; Am Soc Microbiologists. *Res:* Inorganic nitrogen transformation; nitrogen fixation; inorganic energy metabolism; isotope distribution; mass spectrometry. *Mailing Add:* Dept of Land Air & Water Resources Univ of Calif Davis CA 95616

DELWICHE, EUGENE ALBERT, b Green Bay, Wis, Nov 26, 17; m 49; c 4. BACTERIOLOGY. *Educ:* Univ Wis, BS, 41; Cornell Univ, PhD, 48. *Prof Exp:* From asst prof to assoc prof, 48-55, PROF BACT, CORNELL UNIV, 55- *Concurrent Pos:* Consult, Oak Ridge Nat Labs, 51-59; Guggenheim fel, Karolinska Inst, Sweden, 64. *Mem:* Am Soc Biol Chemists; Am Acad Microbiol; Am Soc Microbiol; Can Soc Microbiol. *Res:* Physiology, biochemistry, nutrition and intermediary metabolism of bacteria and other microorganisms. *Mailing Add:* Stocking Hall Cornell Univ Ithaca NY 14850

DEMAGGIO, AUGUSTUS EDWARD, b Malden, Mass, Apr 22, 32; m 54; c 3. BOTANY, PHYSIOLOGY. *Educ:* Mass Col Pharm, BS, 54, MS, 56; Harvard Univ, AM, 58, PhD, 60. *Hon Degrees:* AM, Dartmouth Col, 70. *Prof Exp:* From asst prof to assoc prof pharmacog, Col Pharm, Rutgers Univ, 59-64; from asst prof to assoc prof 64-66, PROF BIOL, DARTMOUTH COL, 66- *Concurrent Pos:* Waksman Found fel, France; univ fac fel, Rutgers Univ & mem staff, Nat Ctr Agr Res, France, 62-63; res fel, Harvard Univ, 69-70; vis prof, Yale Univ, 73-74. *Mem:* Fel AAAS; Bot Soc Am; Am Soc Plant Physiol; Torrey Bot Club; Am Soc Pharmacog. *Res:* Experimental botany; morphogenesis; chloroplast biochemistry; plant chemistry. *Mailing Add:* Dept of Biol Sci Dartmouth Col Hanover NH 03755

DEMAIN, ARNOLD LESTER, b Brooklyn, NY, Apr 26, 27; m 52; c 2. INDUSTRIAL MICROBIOLOGY. *Educ:* Mich State Univ, BS, 49; MS, 50; Univ Calif, PhD(microbiol), 54. *Prof Exp:* Asst yeast physiol, Univ Calif, 52-54; res microbiologist, Merck, Sharp & Dohme Res Labs, 54-64, head fermentation res, 64-69; PROF INDUST MICROBIOL, MASS INST TECHNOL, 69- *Concurrent Pos:* Labatt lectr, Univ Western Ont, 77. *Honors & Awards:* Waksman Award, Am Soc Microbiol, 75; Charles Thom Award, Soc Indust Microbiol, 78; Hotpack Award, Can Soc Microbiol, 78. *Mem:* Soc Indust Microbiol; Am Soc Microbiol. *Res:* Microbial nutrition; penicillin and cephalosporin biosynthesis; pectic enzymes; protein synthesis; nucleotide biosynthesis; regulation of fermentation processes. *Mailing Add:* Dept of Nutrit & Food Sci Mass Inst of Technol Rm 56-123 Cambridge MA 02139

DE MAINE, PAUL ALEXANDER DESMOND, b Koster, SAfrica, Oct 11, 24; US citizen; m 55. COMPUTER SCIENCE. *Educ:* Univ Witwatersrand, BA, 48; Univ BC, PhD(chem), 56. *Prof Exp:* Res spectros, Univ Chicago, 54-55; res math & chem, Univ Cambridge, 55-56; res spectros, King's Col, London, 56; res electrochem, Univ Ottawa, Ont, 57; from assoc prof to prof chem, State Univ Col Educ, Albany, 57-60; prof, Univ Miss, 60-63; vis scientist, Univ Ill, 63-64; assoc specialist, Univ Calif, Santa Barbara, 64-65; assoc specialist, Ctr Comput Sci & Technol, Nat Bur Standards, 65-67; assoc prof comput sci, Pa State Univ, University Park, 68-70, prof, 70-81; PROF COMPUT SCI, UNIV ALA, HUNTSVILLE, 81- *Concurrent Pos:* A von Humboldt Found sr US scientist award, 74-75 & 76-77. *Mem:* Am Chem Soc; Asn Comput Mach; Inst Elec & Electronics Engrs. *Res:* Computerized information storage and retrieval; data processing; transportable software; deductive systems for chemistry. *Mailing Add:* Comput Sci Dept Univ Ala Huntsville AL 35899

DEMAN, JOHN MARIA, b Rotterdam, Neth, Apr 13, 25; Can citizen; m 54; c 3. FOOD CHEMISTRY. *Educ:* Univ Neth, Chem Eng, 51; Univ Alta, PhD(dairy chem), 59. *Prof Exp:* Res chemist, Unilever Res Labs, Holland, 49-54; res asst, Univ Alta, 54-59, asst prof, 59-64, assoc prof dairy & food chem, 64-69; chmn dept, 69-80, PROF FOOD SCI, UNIV GUELPH, 69- *Honors & Awards:* Dairy Res Inc Award, Am Dairy Sci Asn, 74; W J Eva Award, Can Inst Food Sci & Technol, 75. *Mem:* Can Inst Food Technol (past pres); Inst Food Technologists; Am Oil Chemists' Soc; Am Dairy Sci Asn; Brit Soc Rheol. *Res:* Food texture and rheology; instrumentation for food texture measurement; fat crystallization and polymorphism; triglyceride composition and structure; food contaminants; cereal and oilseed technology. *Mailing Add:* Dept of Food Sci Univ of Guelph Guelph ON N1G 2W1 Can

DEMANCHE, EDNA LOUISE, b Marionville, Mo, Aug 1, 15. SCIENCE EDUCATION, PLANT PHYSIOLOGY. *Educ:* Col Mt St Vincent, BS, 40; Univ Notre Dame, MS, 64, PhD(plant physiol), 69. *Prof Exp:* Parochial sch teacher, Hawaii, 40-59; sci consult, 59-67; admin tech & prof asst educ res & develop, Foundational Approaches in Sci Prog, Univ Hawaii, 67-73, dir, Hawaii Nature Study Proj, 73-80; RETIRED. *Concurrent Pos:* Consult sci fair projs, pub & pvt schs, Hawaii, 59-68; traveling team lectr, Hawaii, 65-66; planning facilitator, Hawaii State Dept Educ, 75. *Honors & Awards:* Nat Asn Soil Conserv Dists Cert Merit, 74. *Mem:* AAAS; Sigma Xi; Nat Asn Biol Teachers; Nat Sci Teachers Asn. *Res:* Factors associated with changes in phyllotaxy; development of new laboratory-oriented procedures in ecology centered on local environmental phenomena and accompanying procedures for classroom implementation. *Mailing Add:* 3351 Kalihi St Honolulu HI 96819

DEMAR, ROBERT E, b Keene, NH, Nov 7, 31; m 59. VERTEBRATE PALEONTOLOGY. *Educ:* Harvard Univ, AB, 53; Univ Chicago, MS, 60, PhD(vert paleont), 61. *Prof Exp:* Geologist, US Geol Surv, 53-54; asst, 56-58, from instr to assoc prof, 58-74, PROF GEOL, UNIV ILL, CHICAGO CIRCLE, 74-, ACTG HEAD DEPT, 79- *Concurrent Pos:* Assoc ed, Paleobiol, 75-80. *Mem:* AAAS; Soc Study Evolution; Geol Soc Am; Soc Vert Paleont; Paleont Soc. *Res:* Late Paleozoic vertebrates; jaw mechanics of synapsid reptiles; functional and evolutionary models in paleobiology; jaw mechanics and the organization of dentitions. *Mailing Add:* Dept of Geol Sci PO Box 4348 Chicago IL 60680

DE MARCO, F(RANK) A(NTHONY), b Italy, Feb 14, 21; nat US; m 48; c 11. CHEMICAL ENGINEERING. *Educ:* Univ Toronto, BASc, 43, MASc, 43, PhD(chem eng), 51. *Prof Exp:* Instr, Univ Toronto, 43-46; from asst prof to prof chem & head dept, Assumption Univ, 46-57, actg head eng dept, 57-59, assoc dean arts & sci, 58; dean fac appl sci, 59-64, vpres univ, 63-76, PROF CHEM & CHEM ENG, UNIV WINDSOR, 70-, SR V PRES UNIV, 76- *Concurrent Pos:* Chmn staff comt, Essex Col, Assumption, 56-59, prin, 59-63; chmn bd gov, St Clair Col Appl Arts & Technol. *Mem:* Am Soc Eng Educ; fel Chem Inst Can; Eng Inst Can. *Res:* Coordination compounds; electrorefining of copper; glueline studies; cyanine dye synthesis; solubilization of hydrocarbons. *Mailing Add:* Dept of Chem Univ of Windsor Windsor Can

DEMARCO, JOHN GREGORY, b New York, NY, May 13, 39; m 62; c 6. ORGANIC CHEMISTRY. *Educ:* Iona Col, BS, 62; Fordham Univ, PhD(org chem), 67. *Prof Exp:* Res chemist textile, Bound Brook, NJ, 66-71; develop chemist, Charlotte, NC, 71-73, sales rep intermediate chem, 73-77, CHIEF CHEMIST SPECIALITY CHEM, AM CYANAMID, 77- *Res:* Reaction mechanism and kinetics of reductive triazolation. *Mailing Add:* Am Cyanamid Co Willow Island WV 26190

DEMARCO, RALPH RICHARD, b Brooklyn, NY, Oct 18, 48; m 78. PHYSICS, MATHEMATICAL STATISTICS. *Educ:* Polytech Inst Brooklyn, BSc, 70; Univ Va, PhD(physics), 76. *Prof Exp:* Team leader data anal, Comput Sci Corp, 76-77; SR STAFF PHYSICIST SUBMARINE DATA ANAL, APPL PHYSICS LAB, JOHNS HOPKINS UNIV, 77- *Mem:* Am Phys Soc. *Mailing Add:* Appl Physics Lab Johns Hopkins Rd Laurel MD 20810

DE MARCO, RONALD ANTHONY, b Newark, NJ, Apr 10, 44; m 68; c 2. FLUORINE CHEMISTRY. *Educ:* Montclair State Col, BA, 66; Univ Idaho, MS, 69, PhD(chem), 72. *Prof Exp:* RES CHEMIST FLUORINE CHEM, NAVAL RES LAB, 72-, HEAD, ADVAN INORG MAT, 76- *Mem:* Am Chem Soc; Sigma Xi. *Res:* Synthesis, characterization and chemistry of fluorine-containing compounds of non-metallic elements; synthesis and characterization of conducting polymers, chemistry of non-implantation into covalent materials. *Mailing Add:* Code 6130 Naval Res Lab 4555 Overlook Ave Washington DC 20375

DE MARCO, THOMAS JOSEPH, b Farmingdale, NY, Feb 12, 42; m 66; c 3. PHARMACOLOGY, PERIODONTOLOGY. *Educ:* Univ Pittsburgh, BS, 62, DDM, 65; Boston Univ, cert periodont & PhD(pharmacol), 68. *Prof Exp:* Nat Inst Dent Res fel, Boston Univ, 63-68; from asst prof to assoc prof pharmacol & periodont, Sch Dent, 68-73, asst prof pharmacol, Sch Nursing, 71-72, assoc dean sch dent, 72-75, PROF PHARMACOL & PERIODONT, SCH DENT, CASE WESTERN RESERVE UNIV, 73-, DEAN, SCH DENT, 76-, ASST PROF PHARMACOL, SCH MED, 69- *Mem:* Am Chem Soc; Am Acad Periodont; Am Dent Asn; Am Col Dentists. *Res:* Lymphatic drug absorption from the gastrointestinal tract and the sublingual area of the mouth. *Mailing Add:* Sch of Dent Case Western Reserve Univ Cleveland OH 44106

DEMARCUS, WENDELL CARDEN, b Anderson Co, Tenn, May 9, 24; m 54; c 2. PHYSICS. *Educ:* Univ Ky, BS, 47; Yale Univ, MS, 50, PhD(physics), 51. *Prof Exp:* Physicist, Carbide & Carbon Chem Co, 51-52, sr physicist, 52-56, prin physicist, 56-57; assoc prof, 57-58, PROF PHYSICS, UNIV KY, 58- *Concurrent Pos:* Consult, Union Carbide Nuclear Co, 57- *Mem:* Am Phys Soc; Am Astron Soc; Int Astron Union; fel Royal Astron Spc. *Res:* Astrophysics; solid state physics. *Mailing Add:* Dept of Physics Univ of Ky Lexington KY 40506

DEMAREE, GALE E, pharmacology, see previous edition

DEMAREE, RICHARD SPOTTSWOOD, JR, b Akron, Ohio, July 1, 42; m 65. CYTOLOGY, PARASITOLOGY. *Educ:* Purdue Univ, BS, 64; Ind State Univ, MA, 66; Colo State Univ, PhD(zool), 69. *Prof Exp:* Head, Electron Micros Br, Path Div, US Army Med Res & Nutrit Lab, Fitzsimons Gen Hosp, Denver, Colo, 69-72; from asst prof to assoc prof biol sci, 72-80, PROF BIOL SCI, CALIF STATE UNIV, 80- *Mem:* NY Acad Sci; Electron Micros Soc Am; Am Soc Parasitol; Soc Protozool. *Res:* Parasite ultrastructure and morphogenesis; ultrastructural cytology and pathology; high altitude research. *Mailing Add:* Dept of Biol Sci Calif State Univ First & Normal St Chico CA 95926

DEMAREST, HAROLD HUNT, JR, b New York, NY, Dec 20, 46; m 68; c 1. ROCK PHYSICS, EQUATIONS OF STATE. *Educ:* Reed Col, BA, 69; Columbia Univ, MA, 71; Univ Calif, Los Angeles, PhD(planetary physics), 74. *Prof Exp:* Scholar geophys, Univ Calif, Los Angeles, 74-75; res assoc

geophys, Univ Chicago, 75-79; ASST PROF GEOL, ORE STATE UNIV, 79- *Concurrent Pos:* Vis staff mem, Los Alamos Sci Lab, 72-75. *Mem:* AAAS; Am Geophys Union. *Res:* Physical properties of rocks and minerals; geophysics; application of statistics to geological and geophysical problems; elasticity; equations of state. *Mailing Add:* Dept Geol Ore State Univ Corvallis OR 97331

DE MARGERIE, JEAN-MARIE, b Prud'homme, Sask, Dec 11, 27; m 55; c 5. OPHTHALMOLOGY. *Educ:* Univ Ottawa, BA, 47; Laval Univ, BEd, 49, MD, 52; Oxford Univ, DPhil(ophthal), 59; FRCPS(C), 61. *Prof Exp:* Asst prof, Queen's Univ, 60-66; head dept ophthal, 66-77, vdean res fac med, 73-80, PROF OPHTHAL, UNIV SHERBROOKE, 66- *Concurrent Pos:* Consult, Ont Hosp, 60-66 & Armed Forces Hosp, Can, 64-66; head dept ophthal, Hotel-Dieu Hosp, Kingston, Ont, 64-66; mem exec med res coun Can & health res coun Que, 74- *Mem:* Can Med Asn; Can Ophthal Soc; fel Am Col Surgeons; fel Acad Ophthal & Otolaryngol; Asn Res Vision & Ophthal. *Res:* Anatomy and pathology of ocular fundus; arterial hypertension; toxic retinopathies; ocular photography; fluorescein photography of the eye; diabetic retinopathies. *Mailing Add:* Dept of Ophthal Univ of Sherbrooke Sherbrooke Can

DEMARIA, ANTHONY JOHN, b Italy, Oct 30, 31; US citizen; m 53; c 1. APPLIED & LASER PHYSICS. *Educ:* Univ Conn, BSEE, PhD, 65; Rensselaer Polytech Inst, MS, 60. *Prof Exp:* Res acoustic engr, Anderson Labs, Conn, 56-57; staff physicist phys electronics, Hamilton Standard Div, 57-58, prin scientist & group leader, res labs, 58-70, chief scientist, Electromagnetics Labs, 70-73, mgr electromagnetic & physics labs, 73-81, ASST DIR RES ELECTRONICS & ELECTRO-OPTICS TECHNOLS, UNITED TECHNOLS RES CTR, 81- *Concurrent Pos:* Adj prof, Rensselaer Polytech Inst, 68-77; mem bd dirs, Laser Indust Asn; consult lasers, Nat Acad Sci; consult, Nat Bur Standards, 76-79; ed, J Quantum Electronics, 77-; chmn bd adv group electronic devices, Dept Defense, 79- *Honors & Awards:* RPI Davies Medal & Award, 80; Lieberman Award, Inst Elec & Electronic Engrs, 79. *Mem:* Nat Acad Eng; Am Phys Soc; fel Optical Soc Am (pres, 79-82); fel Inst Elec & Electronics Engrs. *Res:* Utilization of laser devices; interaction of elastic waves with coherent light radiation; generation, measurement and application of picosecond light pulses; gas laser research and applications; acoustic-optics; laser physics and devices; optics. *Mailing Add:* United Technol Res Ctr East Hartford CT 06108

DE MARIA, F JOHN, b Sliema, Malta, Apr 30, 28; Can citizen; m 58; c 4. OBSTETRICS & GYNECOLOGY. *Educ:* Royal Univ Malta, MD, 52; FRCS(C), 63. *Prof Exp:* House officer obstet & gynec, Postgrad Med Sch, Univ London, 54-56; registr, Durham & Newcastle, 57-59; Ramsay res fel physiol, Univ St Andrew's, 59-61; asst prof obstet & gynec, Univ BC, 61-66; ASSOC PROF OBSTET & GYNEC, MED SCH, UNIV WIS, 66- *Concurrent Pos:* Los Angeles County res fel, 60-61; obstetrician & gynecologist, Vancouver Gen Hosp, 61-66. *Mem:* Fel Am Col Obstet & Gynec; Royal Col Obstet & Gynec. *Res:* Neuroendocrinology; placental enzymes and pre-eclampsia; temporal correlation between the hypothalamus and uterus; surgery of infertility. *Mailing Add:* 9155 SW Barnes Rd Suite 201 Portland OR 97225

DEMARINIS, ROBERT MICHAEL, organic chemistry, see previous edition

DEMARQUE, PIERRE, b Fez, Morocco, July 18, 32; Can citizen; m 58; c 2. ASTROPHYSICS. *Educ:* McGill Univ, BSc, 55; Univ Toronto, MA, 57, PhD(astron), 60. *Hon Degrees:* MA, Yale Univ, 68. *Prof Exp:* Mem staff appl math, Canadair Ltd, Mont, 55-56; asst prof astron, La State Univ, 59-60 & Univ Ill, 60-62; from asst prof to assoc prof, Univ Toronto, 62-66; from assoc prof to prof, Univ Chicago, 66-68; chmn dept astron, 68-74, PROF ASTROPHYS, YALE UNIV, 68- *Honors & Awards:* Warner Prize, Am Astron Soc, 67. *Mem:* Am Astron Soc; Royal Astron Soc; Int Astron Union. *Res:* Stellar structure and evolution; stellar atmospheres; star clusters and galaxies; cosmology. *Mailing Add:* Yale Univ Observ Box 2023 Yale Sta New Haven CT 06520

DEMARR, RALPH ELGIN, b Detroit, Mich, Jan 17, 30. MATHEMATICS. *Educ:* Univ Idaho, BS, 52; Wash State Univ, MA, 54; Univ Ill, PhD(math), 61. *Prof Exp:* Mem tech staff math, Bell Tel Labs, Inc, 54-56; Ford Found study grant, Moscow State Univ, 61-62; asst prof, Univ Wash, 62-68; assoc prof, 68-73, PROF MATH, UNIV NMEX, ALBUQUERQUE, 73- *Concurrent Pos:* Vis lectr, Leningrad State Univ, 69 & Tashkent State Univ, 70. *Mem:* Am Math Soc. *Res:* Functional analysis; probability; statistics. *Mailing Add:* Dept of Math Univ of NMex Albuquerque NM 87131

DE MARS, CLARENCE JOHN, JR, forest entomology, insect ecology, see previous edition

DEMARS, ROBERT IVAN, b New York, NY, Apr 10, 28. MICROBIOLOGY. *Educ:* City Col New York, BS, 49; Univ Ill, PhD(bact), 53. *Prof Exp:* Res fel biol, Calif Inst Technol, 53-54; instr microbiol, Med Sch, Washington Univ, 54-56; microbiologist, NIH, 56-59; from asst prof to assoc prof, 59-69, PROF MED GENETICS, UNIV WIS-MADISON, 69- *Res:* Intermediate stages in the multiplication of bacterial viruses; genetics of cultivated animal cells; differentiation in early embryos. *Mailing Add:* Dept of Med Genetics Univ of Wis-Madison Madison WI 53706

DEMARTINI, EDWARD EMILE, b San Francisco, Calif, Aug 12, 46; m 73. BEHAVIORAL ECOLOGY, ICHTHYOLOGY. *Educ:* Univ San Francisco, BSc, 68, MSc, 70; Univ Wash, Seattle, PhD(zool), 76. *Prof Exp:* Sr scientist & prin investr marine biol, Lockheed Marine Biol Lab, 76-77; independent consult marine biol, Army Corp Engrs, 77-78; asst res biologist, 78-81, ASSOC RES BIOLOGIST, MARINE SCI INST, UNIV CALIF, SANTA BARBARA, 81- *Concurrent Pos:* NSF fel, 70-73. *Mem:* Am Soc Naturalists; Ecol Soc Am; Soc Study Evolution. *Res:* Behavioral ecology and evolution of the lower vertebrates, especially studies of the spacing patterns, mating systems and interspecific associations among marine reef fishes. *Mailing Add:* Univ Calif Santa Barbara 533 Stevens Ave Solana Beach CA 92075

DEMARTINI, JOHN, b San Francisco, Calif, Oct 11, 33; m 55; c 7. INVERTEBRATE ZOOLOGY. *Educ:* Humboldt State Col, BA, 55, MA, 60; Ore State Univ, PhD(zool), 64. *Prof Exp:* Instr high sch, Calif, 56-59; instr zool, bot & plant taxon, Humboldt State Col, 59-61, from asst prof to assoc prof zool, 63-72, PROF BIOL, HUMBOLDT STATE UNIV, 72- *Concurrent Pos:* Mem adv bd underwater parks & reserves, Calif Dept Parks & Recreation, 68-, chmn, 72-73, spec consult, 75; mem ad hoc comt abalone res, Calif Dept Fish & Game, 71-73, mem sea otter sci adv comt, 78- *Mem:* Nat Shellfisheries Asn; Marine Biol Asn UK; Wildlife Dis Asn; Am Soc Parasitologists. *Res:* Comparative and functional invertebrate morphology; marine ecology and invertebrate reproductive cycles; parasitology. *Mailing Add:* Fred Telonicher Marine Lab Humboldt State Univ Box A-E Trinidad CA 95570

DEMARTINIS, FREDERICK DANIEL, b Philadelphia, Pa, Dec 10, 24; m 66; c 3. PHYSIOLOGY. *Educ:* Temple Univ, BA, 48, MA, 50; Jefferson Med Col, PhD(physiol), 59. *Prof Exp:* Asst biol, Temple Univ, 48-50, instr physiol, Sch Dent, 50-54; asst, Jefferson Med Col, 57-58; instr, 58-61, assoc, 61-62, from asst prof to assoc prof, 62-77, PROF PHYSIOL, MED COL PA, 77- *Honors & Awards:* Lindbach Found Award Distinguished Teaching, 65. *Mem:* AAAS; Am Physiol Soc; NY Acad Sci. *Res:* Control of adipose tissue development; regulation of adipocyte growth in tissue culture; regulation of thyroid gland function. *Mailing Add:* Dept of Physiol Med Col of Pa Philadelphia PA 19129

DEMARTINO, RONALD NICHOLAS, b Bayonne, NJ, Jan 14, 43; m 68; c 2. CHEMISTRY. *Educ:* Fairleigh Dickinson Univ, BS, 64; Fordham Univ, PhD(org chem), 69. *Prof Exp:* Res chemist, Nat Starch & Chem Corp, 68-73; SR RES CHEMIST, CELANESE CORP, 73- *Concurrent Pos:* Mem chem technol adv, Comt Union County Tech Inst, 75- *Mem:* Am Chem Soc; Nat Geog Soc. *Res:* Synthesis of modified polysaccharides and wholly aromatic liquid crystalline polymers; surface modification of polyethylene terephthalate to improve comfort and stain release properties. *Mailing Add:* 7 Crest Ct Wayne NJ 07470

DEMAS, JAMES NICHOLAS, b Washington, DC, Dec 28, 42; m 65; c 2. PHOTOCHEMISTRY. *Educ:* Univ NMex, BS, 64, PhD(chem), 70. *Prof Exp:* Res assoc chem, Univ Southern Calif, 70-71; ASSOC PROF CHEM, UNIV VA, 71- *Concurrent Pos:* NSF fel, 70. *Mem:* Am Chem Soc; Sigma Xi; Comn Int de l'Eclairage. *Res:* Photochemistry and luminescence of transition metal complexes and organic dyes; chemical, instrumental and mathematical methods for measuring or evaluating photochemical and optical properties of materials; microcomputers. *Mailing Add:* Dept of Chem Univ of Va Charlottesville VA 22901

DEMASON, DARLEEN AUDREY, b Battle Creek, Mich, June 4, 51. PLANT MORPHOLOGY, PLANT ANATOMY. *Educ:* Univ Mich, BS, 73; Univ Calif, Berkeley, MS, 76, PhD(bot), 78. *Prof Exp:* ASST PROF BOT, UNIV CALIF, RIVERSIDE, 78- *Mem:* Bot Soc Am; Am Mus Natural Hist; Sigma Xi. *Res:* Development and control of development in plant systems with special emphasis on unique structural features of monocotyledons. *Mailing Add:* Dept Plant Sci Univ Calif Riverside CA 92521

DEMASSA, THOMAS A, b Detroit, Mich, Nov 6, 37; m 59; c 3. ELECTRICAL ENGINEERING, SOLID STATE ELECTRONICS. *Educ:* Univ Mich, BS, 60, MS, 61 & 63, PhD(elec eng), 66. *Prof Exp:* Res assoc, Univ Mich, 64-66; from asst prof to assoc prof solid state electronics, 66-73, PROF SOLID STATE ELECTRONICS, ARIZ STATE UNIV, 73- *Concurrent Pos:* Consult, Udylite Corp, Mich; lectr, Dickson Electronics & Honeywell & AiResearch. *Mem:* Am Soc Eng Educ; Inst Elec & Electronics Engrs. *Res:* Solid state devices. *Mailing Add:* Dept of Eng Sci Ariz State Univ Tempe AZ 85281

DEMASTER, DOUGLAS PAUL, b Sheboygan, Wis, Mar 27, 51; m 75. POPULATION DYNAMICS, MARINE MAMMALOGY. *Educ:* Univ Wis-Madison, BA, 73; Univ Minn, Minneapolis, 78. *Prof Exp:* Res asst, Antarctic Seal Prog, Univ Minn, 73-79; res biologist, US Fish & Wildlife Serv, 79-80; RES BIOLOGIST, NAT MARINE FISHERIES SERV, 80- *Concurrent Pos:* US Rep, Antarctic Seal Conf, 77, prin investr, Off Polar Prog, NSF, 78-81. *Mem:* Wildlife Soc; Am Soc Mammologists. *Res:* Population dynamics of marine mammals that occur off the coast of California; population assessment of California sea lions, harbor seal, and pilot whales. *Mailing Add:* Southwest Fisheries Ctr PO Box 271 La Jolla CA 92038

DE MASTER, EUGENE GLENN, b Sheboygan, Wis, Oct 20, 43; m 68; c 2. BIOCHEMISTRY. *Educ:* Dordt Col, Iowa, BA, 65; Wayne State Univ, PhD(biochem), 72. *Prof Exp:* CHEMIST ALCOHOLISM, MINNEAPOLIS VET MED CTR, 73- *Mem:* Am Chem Soc; Res Soc Alcoholism. *Res:* Alterations in biochemical processes induced by chronic alcohol consumption; role of vanadium oxyanions and tungstic acids in biological systems; drug alcohol interactions. *Mailing Add:* Vet Admin Hosp Minneapolis MN 55417

DEMASTUS, HOWARD LESLIE, b St Joseph, Mo, June 5, 29. SOLAR ASTROPHYSICS. *Prof Exp:* Astrophysicist, Harvard Col Observ, 54-67, ASTROPHYSICIST, AIR FORCE GEOPHYS LAB, SACRAMENTO PEAK OBSERV, 67- *Mem:* Am Astron Soc; AAAS; Am Meteorol Soc. *Res:* Solar atmospheres; solar surface phenomena; spectroscopy; solar terrestrial relationships. *Mailing Add:* Air Force Geophys Lab Sacramento Peak Observ Sunspot NM 88349

DE MATTE, MICHAEL L, b Bridgeport, Ohio, Nov 3, 37; m 62; c 1. ORGANIC CHEMISTRY. *Educ:* Wheeling Col, BS, 59; WVa Univ, MS, 61, PhD(org chem), 66. *Prof Exp:* Res chemist, 66-73, SR RES CHEMIST, WESTVACO, INC, 73- *Mem:* Am Chem Soc. *Res:* Polyaromatic synthesis; reaction mechanisms in heterocyclic N-oxides; chemistry of paper coatings. *Mailing Add:* Laurel Res Ctr Johns Hopkins Rd Laurel MD 20810

DE MAURIAC, RICHARD ARTHUR, organic chemistry, see previous edition

DE MAYO, BENJAMIN, b Atlanta, Ga, Aug 4, 40; m 71. EXPERIMENTAL SOLID STATE PHYSICS. *Educ:* Emory Univ, BS, 62; Yale Univ, MS, 64; Ga Inst Technol, PhD(physics), 69. *Prof Exp:* Res assoc metal physics, Univ Ill, Urbana-Champaign, 69-71; asst prof physics, 71-75, assoc prof, 75-81, PROF PHYSICS, WEST GA COL, 81- *Concurrent Pos:* vis prof, Ga Tech, 81-82. *Mem:* AAAS; Am Phys Soc; Am Soc Metals. *Res:* Metals and alloys; magnetism; low temperature physics; Mossbauer spectroscopy; hydrogen in metals. *Mailing Add:* Dept of Physics West Ga Col Carrollton GA 30118

DE MAYO, PAUL, b London, Eng, Aug 8, 24; m 49; c 2. ORGANIC CHEMISTRY, PHOTOCHEMISTRY. *Educ:* Univ London, BSc, 44, MSc, 52, PhD(chem), 54; Univ Paris, Dr es Sci, 70. *Prof Exp:* Res fel chem, Univ Col Hosp, London, Eng, 50-52, Birkbeck Col, London, 52-53, asst lectr, 54-55; lectr, Glasgow Univ, 55-57 & Imp Col, Univ London, 57-59; dir photochem unit, 69-73, PROF CHEM, UNIV WESTERN ONT, 59- *Honors & Awards:* Lect Award, Merck, Sharp & Dohme, 66. *Mem:* Am Chem Soc; Chem Inst Can; fel Royal Soc Can; fel Royal Soc; Royal Soc Chem. *Mailing Add:* Dept of Chem Univ of Western Ont London Can

DEMBER, ALEXIS BERTHOLD, b Dresden, Ger, May 30, 12; nat US; m 43; c 2. PHYSICS. *Educ:* German Univ, Prague, PhD(physics), 35. *Prof Exp:* Instr & asst physics, Istanbul Univ, 35-36; res fel, Calif Inst Technol, 37-44; chief res sect, Friez Instrument Div, Bendix Aviation Corp, Md, 44-47; chief radiation br, Eng Res & Develop Labs, Va, 47-48; head photog develop br, US Naval Ord Test Sta, 48-49, head instrument develop div, 49-56, asst head test dept, 56-59; tech consult to dir test & eval, US Naval Missile Ctr, Pac Missile Range, 59, dep head, Astronaut Dept, 59-60, head, 60-69, head, Electro-Optics Div, Lab Dept, 69-76; RETIRED. *Concurrent Pos:* Mem working group optical instrumentation, Panel Test Range Instrumentation, Res & Develop Bd, 48-51, chmn, 51-52; mem inter-range instrument group, 56-58, vchmn, 58-59; consult, Spec Comt Adequacy Range Facil, Dept Defense, 57-58; mem starlight study group naval appln space technol, 62; sea bed study group adv, Sea-based Deterrent Systs, 64. *Mem:* Am Phys Soc; Optical Soc Am; Inst Elec & Electronics Engrs; Sigma Xi. *Res:* Visible and infrared optics; ballistic and meteorological instrumentation; low temperature crystal physics; semiconductors; military space systems. *Mailing Add:* 4275 Varsity St Ventura CA 93003

DEMBICKI, HARRY, JR, b Poughkeepsie, NY, Oct 18, 51; m 70. ORGANIC GEOCHEMISTRY. *Educ:* State Univ NY Col, New Paltz, BS, 73; Ind Univ, PhD(org geochem), 77. *Prof Exp:* Res asst geochem, Ind Univ, 73-74; assoc instr, 74-76; geochem consult, Ind Geol Surv, 76-77; RES SCIENTIST ORG GEOCHEM, EXPLOR RES DIV, CONTINENTAL OIL CO, 77- *Mem:* Geochem Soc. *Res:* Application of biological marker hydrocarbons to petroleum exploration; thermodynamics and kinetics of the pyrolysis of kerogen; computer systems for data management; design of specialized analytical systems. *Mailing Add:* Explor Res Div PO Box 1267 Ponca City OK 74601

DEMBITZER, HERBERT, b New York, NY, June 18, 34; m 61; c 3. CELL BIOLOGY, EXPERIMENTAL PATHOLOGY. *Educ:* NY Univ, AB, 55, MS, 58, PhD(biol), 67. *Prof Exp:* Res asst biol, NY Univ, 58-62, asst res scientist, 62-63; electron microscopist, 63-67, RES ASSOC, MONTEFIORE HOSP, 67-, ASST PROF PATH, ALBERT EINSTEIN COL MED, 73- *Mem:* Am Soc Cell Biol; Electron Miscros Soc Am. *Res:* Fine structure and histochemistry of cellular development; structure and development of cell junctions. *Mailing Add:* Montefiore Hosp Dept of Path 111 E 210th St Bronx NY 10467

DEMBURE, PHILIP PITO, b Chilimanzi, Rhodesia, Dec 15, 41; US citizen; m 70; c 1. BIOCHEMISTRY. *Educ:* Xavier Univ, La, BS, 68; State Univ NY, Buffalo, MA, 74, PhD(biochem), 78. *Prof Exp:* Res asst biochem genetics, State Univ NY, Buffalo, 70-78; instr pediat, 78-80, ASST PROF, SCH MED, EMORY UNIV, 81- *Mem:* AAAS; Sigma Xi. *Res:* Regulation of hemoglobin synthesis; biochemical basis of disease. *Mailing Add:* Div of Med Genetics Box 23344 Atlanta GA 30322

DEMEDICIS, E M J A, b Etterbeek, Belg, Dec 17, 37; m 62; c 3. BIOCHEMISTRY, ORGANIC CHEMISTRY. *Educ:* Univ Louvain, Lic in Sci, 59. PhD(org chem), 62. *Prof Exp:* Asst org chem, Lab Gen & Org Chem, Univ Louvain, 63-67; asst lectr, Dept Chem, Fac Sci, 67-69, PROF BIOCHEM, FAC MED, UNIV SHERBROOKE, 71- *Concurrent Pos:* Fel biochem, Fac Med, Univ Sherbrooke, 69-71. *Mem:* Chem Soc Belgium; Can Biochem Soc; Chem Inst Can. *Res:* Structure and function of proteases; halophilic enzymes. *Mailing Add:* Univ Hosp Ctr Univ of Sherbrooke Sherbrooke Can

DEMEIO, JOSEPH LOUIS, b Hurley, Wis, Sept 9, 17; m 41; c 1. MEDICAL MICROBIOLOGY. *Educ:* Marquette Univ, BS, 50, MS, 53; Univ Wis, PhD(med microbiol), 58. *Prof Exp:* Virologist, Naval Med Res Unit 4, 51-54, immunologist, 57-58; asst, Univ Wis, 54-57; asst chief diag reagents, Commun Dis Ctr, USPHS, 58-59; res assoc, Merrell-Nat Labs, 59-77; MEM STAFF, SALK INST, 78- *Concurrent Pos:* Assoc, Moravian Col, 73-75. *Mem:* AAAS; NY Acad Sci; Am Pub Health Asn; Soc Exp Biol & Med; Am Asn Immunol. *Res:* Antigenic relationships among arboviruses. *Mailing Add:* Govt Serv Div Salk Inst Swiftwater PA 18370

DE MELLO, W CARLOS, b Florianopolis, Brazil, Sept 11, 31; m 56; c 4. PHYSIOLOGY. *Educ:* Univ Rio de Janeiro, MD, 55. *Prof Exp:* Asst prof physiol, Sch Med, Univ Rio de Janeiro, 57-58, assoc researcher physiol & biophys, 58-66; vis assoc prof, 63-64, assoc prof, 66-70, PROF PHARMACOL, SCH MED, UNIV PR, 70-, CHMN DEPT, 72- *Concurrent Pos:* Guest fel physiol, State Univ NY, 58-59; Rockefeller Found fel physiol, Nat Inst Med Res, Eng, 65-66; Nat Heart Inst res grants, 65-76. *Mem:* Am Physiol Soc; NY Acad Sci. *Res:* Electrophysiology of the heart; ionic mechanisms of cardiac electrogenesis; excitatory and inhibitory processes in Ascaris; membrane biophysics and physiology. *Mailing Add:* Univ of PR Sch of Med PO Box 4509 San Juan PR 00905

DE MEMBER, JOHN RAYMOND, b Elmira, NY, Oct 30, 42; m 64; c 4. ORGANIC CHEMISTRY. *Educ:* Niagara Univ, BS, 64; George Washington Univ, PhD(chem), 68. *Prof Exp:* Instr, Mt Vernon Col, 64-68; instr, Case Western Reserve Univ, 68-69; fel, 68-70; scientist chem, 70-76, SR SCIENTIST CHEM, POLAROID CORP, 76- *Mem:* Sigma Xi; Am Chem Soc. *Res:* Electronic energy transfer; carbonium ions; Raman and nuclear magnetic resonance spectroscopy; chemistry of photographic systems. *Mailing Add:* 750M-3 Res Labs Polaroid Corp Cambridge MA 02139

DEMENT, WILLIAM CHARLES, b Wenatchee, Wash, July 29, 28; m 56; c 3. NEUROPHYSIOLOGY. *Educ:* Univ Wash, BS, 51; Univ Chicago, MD, 55, PhD(physiol), 57. *Prof Exp:* Intern, Mt Sinai Hosp, 57-58; assoc prof, 63-67, PROF PSYCHIAT, SCH MED, STANFORD UNIV, 67-, DIR SLEEP RES LABS, DEPT PSYCHIAT, 63-, DIR SLEEP DISORDERS CLIN & LAB, 70- *Concurrent Pos:* Res fel psychiat, Mt Sinai Hosp, 58-63; chief ed & founder, Sleep Rev Proj, Brain Info Serv. *Honors & Awards:* Hofheimer Prize, Am Psychiat Asn, 64; Thomas W Salmon Medal, NY Acad Med, 69; Intra-Sci Res Found Medalist, 81. *Mem:* Am Psychiat Asn; Asn Sleep Disorders Ctr (first pres, 76-); Asn Psychophysiol Study Sleep; Psychiat Res Soc; Am Col Neuropsychopharmacol. *Res:* Physiology of dreaming and sleep; electroencephalography. *Mailing Add:* Dept Psychiat Stanford Univ Sch Med Stanford CA 94305

DEMENTI, BRIAN ARMSTEAD, b Richmond, Va, Mar 3, 38; c 2. BIOCHEMISTRY, TOXICOLOGY. *Educ:* Hampden-Sydney Col, BS, 61; Univ Richmond, MS, 64; Med Col Va, PhD(biochem), 77. *Prof Exp:* Teacher sci, Henrico County Pub Sch Syst, Va, 67-68; res polymer chemist, Fibers Div, Allied Chem Corp, 68-73; TOXICOLOGIST, STATE VA HEALTH DEPT, 77- *Mem:* Am Chem Soc; Soc Occup & Environ Health. *Res:* Enzyme regulation; regulation of key hepatic glycolytic and gluconeogenic enzymes; synthesis of novel pyri- midines as potential antiviral and antileukemic agents; polyester polymer chemistry. *Mailing Add:* 7519 Oakmont Dr Richmond VA 23228

DE MEO, EDGAR ANTHONY, b Yonkers, NY, Jan 14, 42; m 68; c 2. ELECTRICAL ENGINEERING, SOLID STATE PHYSICS. *Educ:* Rensselaer Polytech Inst, BEE, 63; Brown Univ, ScM, 65, PhD(elec eng), 68. *Prof Exp:* Mem tech staff, Bell Tel Labs, 63; res asst elec eng, Brown Univ, 64-66; instr, US Naval Acad, 67-69; asst prof, Brown Univ, 69-75, assoc prof, 75-76; proj mgr, Solar Energy Prog, 76-79, MGR, SOLAR POWER SYSTS PROG, ELEC POWER RES INST, 80- *Mem:* Inst Elec & Electronics Engrs; AAAS. *Res:* Millimeter wave devices; anisotropic magnetic materials; magnetic resonance investigations; far infrared spectroscopy; photovoltaic devices. *Mailing Add:* Elec Power Res Inst 3412 Hillview Ave Palo Alto CA 94304

DEMERJIAN, KENNETH LEO, b Cambridge, Mass, Sept 10, 45; m 68; c 2. PHYSICAL CHEMISTRY, ATMOSPHERIC SCIENCE. *Educ:* Northeastern Univ, BS, 68; Ohio State Univ, MS, 70, PhD(phys chem), 73. *Prof Exp:* Teaching asst phys chem, Ohio State Univ, 68-72; res assoc, Calspan Corp, 73-74; br chief physchem & atmospheric sci, 74-81, DIR, METEOROL LAB, NAT OCEANIC & ATMOSPHERIC ADMIN, US ENVIRON PROTECTION AGENCY, 81- *Concurrent Pos:* Mem working group, Alternative Methods Assessing Oxidant Control Strategies, 76-77, President's Interagency Task Force Environ Data & Monitoring, Air Pollution Data & Monitoring, 77-79, Oxidant Criteria Doc, 76-78; adv comt, Elec Power Res Inst, 76- *Mem:* AAAS; Am Chem Soc; Am Meteorol Soc. *Res:* Chemistry and mechanistic processes of clean and polluted tropospheres; rates and decomposition pathways of photolytic species in sunlight irradiation; computer models for simulating air quality over a variety of space and time scales. *Mailing Add:* 1005 Bayfield Dr Raleigh NC 27606

DEMERS, JEAN-MARIE, animal physiology, animal nutrition, see previous edition

DEMERS, LAURENCE MAURICE, b Lawrence, Mass, May 9, 38; m 62; c 4. CLINICAL PATHOLOGY, ENDOCRINOLOGY. *Educ:* Merrimack Col, AB, 60; State Univ NY Upstate Med Ctr, PhD(biochem), 70. *Prof Exp:* Lalor Found fel, Lab Human Reprod & Reprod Biol, Harvard Med Sch, 70-73; ASSOC PROF PATH, ASSOC DIR DIV CLIN PATH & DIR CLIN CHEM, HERSHEY MED CTR, PA STATE UNIV, 74- *Mem:* AAAS; Am Soc Clin Pathologists; NY Acad Sci; Am Asn Clin Chem; Endocrine Soc. *Res:* Biochemical endocrinology with particular emphasis on hormonal regulation of carbohydrate metabolism in reproductive tissue; mechanism of action of the prostaglandins. *Mailing Add:* Dept of Path M S Hershey Med Ctr Hershey PA 17033

DEMERS, PIERRE (A E), b Deal, Eng, Nov 8, 14. PHOTOGRAPHY, COLOR SCIENCE. *Educ:* Univ Montreal, BA, 33, LSc, 35, MSc & LSc, 36; Univ Paris, DSc, 50. *Prof Exp:* Physicist, CIL Res & Develop Lab, 40-43 & Nat Res Coun Can, 43-47; assoc prof, 47-50, PROF NUCLEAR PHYSICS, FAC SCI, UNIV MONTREAL, 50- *Concurrent Pos:* Mem, Coun Arts Que; guest prof, Univ Frankfurt, 70-71; pres, Quebec Mus Color, 75. *Mem:* Am Phys Soc; Can Asn Physicists (treas, 50); fel Royal Soc Can; Ger Soc Photog; Color Soc Can. *Res:* Scientific photography and ionography; theory of knowledge, noise and environment; color; relativity; physiology vision and audiology. *Mailing Add:* Fac of Sci Univ of Montreal Montreal PQ H3C 3J7 Can

DEMERS, PIERRE-PAUL, b Quebec, Que, Sept 14, 28; m 63; c 2. PEDIATRICS, CARDIOLOGY. *Educ:* Laval Univ, BA, 48, MD, 53; FRCP(C), 58. *Prof Exp:* Assoc prof, 69-71, prof pediat & head dept, 71-77, DIR OF PROF, DEPT PEDIATRICS, UNIV SHERBROOKE, 77- *Mailing Add:* Dept of Pediat Univ of Sherbrooke Fac of Med Sherbrooke Can

DEMERSON, CHRISTOPHER, b St John, NB, May 16, 42; m 72; c 3. MEDICINAL CHEMISTRY. *Educ:* Univ NB, BSc, 64, PhD(chem), 68. *Prof Exp:* Fel, Univ NB, 68-69; res chemist, 69-72, res assoc, 72-80, SECT HEAD, AYERST LABS, 80- *Concurrent Pos:* Mem adv bd chem technol, Dawson Col, 75- *Mem:* Am Chem Soc; Chem Inst Can. *Res:* Synthesis of the alkaloid delphinine; development of synthetic methods; medicinal chemistry and the structure-activity relationship of drugs. *Mailing Add:* Ayerst Labs PO Box 6115 Montreal Can

DEMET, EDWARD MICHAEL, b Elmhurst, Ill, July 27, 49. BIOCHEMISTRY, PSYCHOPHARMACOLOGY. *Educ:* Univ Ill, BS, 71; Ill Inst Technol, PhD(biochem), 76. *Prof Exp:* Res technician pharmacol, Univ Chicago, 72-73; res technician toxicol, 73-75; sr res technician, 75-76, res assoc, 76-77, instr, 77-78, res asst prof psychiat, 78-80; res chemist, VA Med Ctr, Brentwood, 80-; ASST PROF, NEUROPSYCHIATRIC INST, UNIV CALIF, LOS ANGELES, 80- *Concurrent Pos:* USPHS fel, Univ Chicago, 76-77, 78-79; NSF-KKI sci exchange fel, Budapest, Hungary, 77. *Mem:* Int Soc Supramolec Biol; Am Soc Microbiol; Am Chem Soc; Fedn Am Scientists; Soc Neurosci. *Res:* Neurochemistry of psychiatric disorders and subcellular biochemistry. *Mailing Add:* 6425 Reseda #226 950 E 59th St Chicago IL 60637

DEMETRESCU, M, b Bucharest, Romania, May 23, 29; m 69; c 1. NEUROPHYSIOLOGY, BIOMEDICAL ENGINEERING. *Educ:* Bucharest Polytech Inst, MEE, 54; Romanian Acad Sci, PhD(electrophysiol), 57. *Prof Exp:* Prin investr neurophysiol & EEG, Inst Endocrinol, Romanian Acad Sci, 58-66; fel neurophysiol, Brain Res Inst, Univ Calif, Los Angeles, 66-67; asst res physiologist, 67-71, assoc res physiologist, 78-79, ASST PROF PHYSIOL, MED SCH, UNIV CALIF-IRVINE, 72-, ASSOC CLIN PROF, 79- *Honors & Awards:* Victor Babes Prize, Romanian Acad Sci, 62. *Mem:* AAAS; sr mem Inst Elec & Electronic Engrs; Am Physiol Soc; Soc Neurosci. *Res:* Neurophysiology of active inhibition at thalamo-cortical level; control of cortical excitability by diffuse subcortical mechanisms; clinical electroencephalography; electrophysiology of bladder stimulation in paraplegics; new electronic-electrophysiologic research methods. *Mailing Add:* Dept of Physiol Univ of Calif Med Sch Irvine CA 92715

DEMETRIADES, STERGE THEODORE, b Athens, Greece, June 30, 28; US citizen; m 56; c 3. SCIENCE ADMINISTRATION, PLASMA PHYSICS. *Educ:* Bowdoin Col, AB, 50; Mass Inst Technol, MS, 51; Calif Inst Technol, ME, 58. *Prof Exp:* Res engr, Mass Inst Technol, 51-53; ord engr, Ballistic Res Labs, US Army Ord Corps, 53-54; res engr, Lear, Inc, 54-55; res engr, Astronaut Dept, Aerojet-Gen Corp, 58-59; res engr, Northrop Corp, 59-60, head space propulsion & power lab, 60-62, head plasma labs, 62-63; chief scientist, Res Labs, Rocket Power Inc, 63-64; PRES & DIR, STD RES CORP, 64-, PRES STD INT RES & DEVELOP CORP, 69- *Concurrent Pos:* Consult, Aerojet-Gen Corp, 55-62, Air Logistics Corp, 58-59, Hughes Tool Co, 59-60, Marquardt Corp, 60, McGraw-Hill, Inc, 61-, Jet Propulsion Lab, Calif Inst Technol, 62-63 & Space Sci Lab, Litton Industs, Inc, 63-64. *Mem:* Assoc fel Am Inst Aeronaut & Astronaut. *Res:* Electrostreaming birefringence; powered space flight; plasma accelerators and propulsive fluid accumulator engines; experimental magnetogasdynamics; measurement of plasma properties and energy conversion; magnetohydrodynamic power generation; scientific technology development; research and development program assessment and national science and technology planning. *Mailing Add:* STD Res Corp 150 E Foothill Blvd Arcadia CA 91006

DEMETRIOU, JAMES A, b Santa Ana, Calif, Dec 26, 23; m 53; c 4. CLINICAL CHEMISTRY, BIOCHEMISTRY. *Educ:* Univ Southern Calif, BA, 48, PhD(biochem), 56. *Prof Exp:* Fel endocrinol, Col Med, Univ Utah, 57-58; asst prof biochem, Sch Med, Univ Southern Calif, 58-63; mem sr res bioastronaut, Northrop Corp Labs, 63-67; sr res scientist, 67-70, asst dir res dept, 70-74, DIR ENDOCRINOL DEPT, BIO-SCI LABS, 74- *Mem:* AAAS; Am Asn Clin Chem; Am Chem Soc. *Res:* Development of analytical methods for measurement of products in body fluids, application of these methods for detection of disease states, pathological processes or abnormal physiological states; analytical methodologies, technical literature, quality control and operational aspects of a service department dealing with hormone assays. *Mailing Add:* Bio-Sci Labs 7600 Tyrone Ave Van Nuys CA 91405

DEMETS, DAVID L, biostatistics, mathematics, see previous edition

DEMEYER, FRANK R, b San Francisco, Calif, Nov 7, 39; m 67. MATHEMATICS. *Educ:* Univ Seattle, BS, 61; Univ Ore, MA, 63, PhD(math), 65. *Prof Exp:* Asst prof math, Purdue Univ, 65-68; from asst prof to assoc prof, 68-75, PROF MATH, COLO STATE UNIV, 75- *Mem:* Math Asn Am. *Res:* Mathematical economics; abstract algebra; decision problems in welfare economics. *Mailing Add:* Dept of Math Colo State Univ Ft Collins CO 80523

DEMILLO, RICHARD A, b Hibbing, Mich, Jan 26, 47; m 69; c 3. MATHEMATICS, COMPUTER SCIENCE. *Educ:* Col St Thomas, BA, 69; Ga Inst Technol, PhD(comput sci), 72. *Prof Exp:* Res asst comput sci, Los Alamos Sci Lab, Univ Calif, 69-70; res assoc, Ga Inst Technol, 69-72; asst prof, Univ Wis-Milwaukee, 72-76; assoc prof, 76-80, PROF COMPUT SCI, GA INST TECHNOL, 80- *Concurrent Pos:* Consult, US Army Electronics Command, Commun/ADP Lab, 74-, US Army Comput Systs Command, Army Instr Res Mgt, Info & Comput Sci, Mgt Sci Am, Math Res Ctr, Univ Wis & UNESCO, Off Naval Res. *Mem:* Am Math Soc; Math Asn Am; Soc Indust & Appl Math; AAAS; Asn Symbolic Logic. *Res:* Theoretical computer science; software engineering; privacy, security, and cryptography. *Mailing Add:* Sch of Info & Comput Sci Ga Inst of Technol Atlanta GA 30332

DEMING, JOHN MILEY, b Prescott, Ariz, May 28, 25; m 51; c 5. PROCESS DEVELOPMENT, FORMULATION OF PESTICIDES. *Educ:* Univ Ariz, BS, 48, MS, 49; Purdue Univ, PhD(agron, soil physics & chem), 51. *Prof Exp:* Agronomist, 51-58, group leader, 53-58, biophys group leader, 58-65, sr res group leader, 76-79, RES FEL FORMULATION, SOILS & FIELD RES, MONSANTO CO, 79- *Res:* Biophysical investigation and formulation of commercial pesticides; controlled release; micro encapsulation; process development. *Mailing Add:* 1295 Woodcrest Dr St Louis MO 63042

DEMING, QUENTIN BURRITT, b New York, NY, July 24, 19; m 49; c 2. MEDICINE. *Educ:* Dartmouth Col, AB, 41; Columbia Univ, MD, 43. *Prof Exp:* From intern to asst resident med, Presby Hosp, 44-48, from instr to asst prof, Stanford Univ, 50-53; from asst prof to assoc prof, Columbia Univ, 53-59; assoc prof, 59-64, PROF MED, ALBERT EINSTEIN COL MED, 64- *Concurrent Pos:* Res fel, Sch Med, Stanford Univ, 48-50; Markle Found scholar, 50-55; asst vis physician, Goldwater Mem Hosp, Columbia, 53-; vis physician, Bronx Munic Hosp Ctr, 59- *Mem:* Am Soc Clin Invest; Harvey Soc; Am Fedn Clin Res; Am Heart Asn. *Res:* Hormonal aspects of edema formation; hypertension; atherosclerosis. *Mailing Add:* Dept of Med Albert Einstein Col of Med New York NY 10461

DEMING, ROBERT W, b Wabasha, Minn, Apr 5, 28; m 60; c 2. MATHEMATICS. *Educ:* Univ Minn, BS, 52, MA, 60; NMex State Univ, PhD(math), 65. *Prof Exp:* Instr math, Univ Minn, Duluth, 57-62; asst prof, Idaho State Univ, 65-67; assoc prof math, 67-77, PROF MATH & COORDR APPL MATH ECON, STATE UNIV NY COL OSWEGO, 77- *Mem:* Math Asn Am; Am Math Soc. *Res:* Applications of algebraic topology to the theory of uniform and uniform-like spaces. *Mailing Add:* Dept of Math State Univ of NY Col Oswego NY 13126

DEMING, STANLEY NORRIS, b Corpus Christi, Tex, May 7, 44; m 67; c 2. ANALYTICAL CHEMISTRY. *Educ:* Carleton Col, BA, 66; Purdue Univ, MS, 70, PhD(chem), 71. *Prof Exp:* Asst prof chem, Emory Univ, 70-74; asst prof, 74-76, ASSOC PROF CHEM, UNIV HOUSTON, 76- *Mem:* AAAS; Am Chem Soc. *Res:* Automated development of analytical chemical methods; optimization in chemistry; process optimization; laboratory scale continuous flow processes; high performance liquid chromatography. *Mailing Add:* Dept Chem Univ Houston Cent Campus 4800 Calhoun Houston TX 77004

DEMING, WILLIAM EDWARDS, b Sioux City, Iowa, Oct 14, 00; m 32; c 3. MATHEMATICAL STATISTICS. *Educ:* Univ Wyo, BS, 21; Univ Colo, MS, 24; Yale Univ, PhD(physics), 28. *Hon Degrees:* LLD, Univ Wyo, 58. *Prof Exp:* Instr elec eng, Univ Wyo, 21-22; from instr to asst prof physics, Colo Sch Mines, 22-24; asst prof, Univ Colo, 24-25; instr, Yale Univ, 25-27; from asst physicist to physicist, Bur Chem & Soils, USDA, 27-39; head mathematician & math adv, US Bur Census, 39-46; prof statist, 46-76, EMER PROF STATIST, NY UNIV, 76- STATIST CONSULT, 48- *Concurrent Pos:* Spec lectr, Bur Standards, 30-41; head dept math & statist, USDA Grad Sch, 33-53; adv sampling, US Bur Budget, 45-53; consult to various countries, 40-; lectr, Univ Kiel, Inst Social Res, Frankfurt, Tech Acad, Wuppertal-Elberfeld, Nürnberg Tech Univ & Australian Inst Econ Res, Vienna, 53. *Honors & Awards:* Shewhart Medal, Am Soc Qual Control, 56; Second Order of the Sacred Treasure, Emperor Japan, 60. *Mem:* AAAS; Math Asn Am; fel Am Statist Asn (vpres, 41); fel Inst Math Statist (pres, 45); Opers Res Soc Am. *Res:* Fundamentals of statistical inference; statistical logic in administration; applications in demography, sociology, medicine and industry; statistical theory of failure; application to depreciation; application to complex apparatus; schizophrenia. *Mailing Add:* 4924 Butterworth Pl Washington DC 20016

DE MIRANDA, PAULO, b Goa, India; m 66; c 4. PHARMACOLOGY, BIOCHEMISTRY. *Educ:* Univ Oporto, Lic, 60; Univ Wis, MS, 63; Marquette Univ, PhD(pharmacol), 65. *Prof Exp:* Instr pharmacol, Sch Med, Marquette Univ, 66; asst prof, Fac Med, Univ Valle, Colombia, 66-69; sr res biochemist, Wellcome Res Labs, 69-78, GROUP LEADER, BURROUGHS WELLCOME CO, 79- *Mem:* AAAS; Am Soc Pharmacol & Exp Therapeut; Am Chem Soc. *Res:* Biochemistry of nucleic acid antagonists; drug disposition; pharmacokinetics; antiviral chemotherapy. *Mailing Add:* Wellcome Res Labs Research Triangle Park NC 27709

DEMIREL, T(URGUT), b Bursa, Turkey, Mar 2, 24; m 50; c 2. GEOTECHNICAL ENGINEERING, MATERIAL SCIENCE. *Educ:* Univ Ankara, ChemEng, 49; Iowa State Univ, MSc, 59, PhD(soil eng), 62. *Prof Exp:* Hwy mat engr, Gen Directorate Turkish Hwys, 49-51; sr res engr, 51-56; asst soil eng, 57-58; res assoc, 58-63; from asst prof to assoc prof, 63-70, PROF SOIL ENG, IOWA STATE UNIV, 70- *Concurrent Pos:* Assoc mem, Hwy Res Bd, Nat Acad Sci-Nat Res Coun, 51; vis prof, Mid East Tech Univ, Ankara, 72-73; consult, UN, UNESCO, 77-78. *Mem:* d; Am Soc Civil Engrs. *Res:* Load bearing capacity and physiocochemical properties of soils; effects of chemical treatments on load bearing capacity of soils; soil-water interaction. *Mailing Add:* Dept of Civil Eng Iowa State Univ Ames IA 50011

DEMIS, DERMOT JOSEPH, b New York, NY, Apr 19, 29. DERMATOLOGY, PHARMACOLOGY. *Educ:* Union Univ, NY, BS, 50; Univ Rochester, PhD(pharmacol), 53; Yale Univ, MD, 57. *Prof Exp:* Chief dept dermat, Walter Reed Army Inst Res, Washington, DC, 60-64; assoc prof med & dir div dermat, Sch Med, Wash Univ, 64-67; PROF DERMAT, ALBANY MED COL, 67- *Concurrent Pos:* Mem pharmacol & exp therapeut study sect, NIH, 60-68, mem med study sect, 68-72; mem subcomt dermat, US Army Surgeon Gen Adv Comt Med, 63-64; consult, Barnes & Jewish Hosps, St Louis, Mo & Scott Air Force Base, Ill, 64-67; Albany Med Ctr Hosp, 67-, Albany Mem Hosp, 67- & Child Hosp, 67-; USPHS res career develop award, 65. *Mem:* Am Soc Clin Invest; Am Dermat Asn; NY Acad Sci; Am Soc Pharmacol & Exp Therapeut; Am Col Physicians. *Res:* Investigative dermatology; role of vasoactive amines in pathophysiologic processes; physiologic control and pathologic alterations of microcirculation; mucopolysaccharide metabolism. *Mailing Add:* 105 S Lake Ave Albany NY 12208

DEMITRAS, GREGORY CLAUDE, b Pittsburgh, Pa, Dec 21, 29. INORGANIC CHEMISTRY. *Educ:* La Salle Col, AB, 52, MA, 53; Univ Pa, MS, 58, PhD(chem), 65. *Prof Exp:* Teacher, La Salle Col High Sch, 53-60; teacher & prefect discipline, Trinity High Sch, Pa, 64-65; from asst prof to assoc prof chem, 65-75, PROF CHEM, LA SALLE COL, 75- *Mem:* Am Chem Soc. *Res:* Synthesis of inorganic fluorides. *Mailing Add:* Dept of Chem La Salle Col Philadelphia PA 19144

DEMKOVICH, PAUL ANDREW, b Zborova, Czech, Nov 19, 22; nat US; m 47; c 5. PETROLEUM CHEMISTRY, ANALYTICAL CHEMISTRY. *Educ:* Univ Chicago, BS, 47, MS, 48. *Prof Exp:* Group leader, Res & Develop Dept, 47-65, supvr anal lab, 65-74, supt lab inspection, 74-81, MGR, LAB SERV DIV, AMOCO OIL CO, STANDARD OIL CO IND, 81- *Mem:* Am Chem Soc. *Mailing Add:* 7520 Magoun Ave Hammond IN 46324

DEMMERLE, ALAN MICHAEL, b Port Jefferson, NY, Nov 4, 33; m 61; c 2. ELECTRONIC ENGINEERING. *Educ:* Carnegie Inst Technol, BS, 55; Columbia Univ, MS, 58. *Prof Exp:* Engr circuit design, Westinghouse Elec, 55-56; engr, US Naval Res Lab, 57-60; engr telemetry processing, Goddard Space Flight Ctr, NASA, 60-66; CHIEF COMPUT SYSTS LAB, NIH, 66- *Concurrent Pos:* Dir, Aspin Res Inst, 81- *Res:* New applications of the computer technology to facilitate laboratory & clinical biomedical research; on-line laboratory automation and real time clinical evaluation and care. *Mailing Add:* Rm 2035 Bldg 12A Nat Inst Health Bethesda MD 20205

DEMOISE, CHARLES FRANCIS, cancer, see previous edition

DE MONASTERIO, FRANCISCO M, b Buenos Aires, Arg, Jan 26, 44; US citizen; m 75. NEUROPHYSIOLOGY, NEUROANATOMY. *Educ:* Fed Univ Rio de Janeiro, Brazil, MD, 69, DSc, 72. *Prof Exp:* Vis scientist, 73-80, MED OFFICER & CHIEF, SECT VISUAL PROCESSING, NAT EYE INST, NIH, 81- *Concurrent Pos:* Pres, assembly scientist, Nat Eye Inst, NIH, 77-78; ad hoc mem, Visual Disorders Study Sect, NIH, 79-80. *Mem:* Brazilian Soc Physiol; Asn Res in Vision & Ophthalmol; AAAS; Found Advan Educ Sci. *Res:* Anatomical and physiological properties of neurons of the visual system of primates and other mammals; clinical electrophysiology and psychophysics of the visual system. *Mailing Add:* Bldg 9 Rm 1E108 Sect Visual Processing Clin Br Nat Eye Inst NIH Bethesda MD 20205

DEMOND, JOAN, b Los Angeles, Calif. MARINE BIOLOGY, INVERTEBRATE ECOLOGY. *Educ:* Univ Calif, Los Angeles, BA; Mills Col, MA. *Prof Exp:* Fishery aide, Nat Oceanic & Atmospheric Admin, Nat Fisheries Serv, Honolulu; sci asst, Inter-Am Trop Tuna Comn; res biologist, Scripps Inst Oceanog, Univ Calif; marine zoologist, Div Mollusks, US Nat Mus; res assoc, Univ Calif, Los angeles, mus scientist, Dept Earth & Space Sci & instr phys sci; marine biologist ecol. *Concurrent Pos:* NSF grant; consult marine zool, Univ Hawaii & Pac Sci Bd Projs. *Mem:* AAAS; Underwater Photog Soc; Western Soc Naturalists; Western Soc Malacologists; Am Malacol Union. *Res:* Ecology, systematics of Indo-Pacific reef-dwelling mollusks; zoogeographical distribution; phylogenetic and areal abundance of zooplankton of central Pacific; ecology & taxonomy of mollusks of Gulf of Mexico, west coast of North America and Hawaii; ocean ecology and environmental impacts upon marine ecosystems; ecology, systematics and zoogeography of the South Pacific. *Mailing Add:* 202 Bicknell Ave No 8 Santa Monica CA 90405

DEMONEY, FRED WILLIAM, b Oak Park, Ill, Nov 25, 19; m 44; c 5. PHYSICAL METALLURGY, CRYOGENICS. *Educ:* Ill Inst Technol, BS, 41; Univ Minn, MS, 51, PhD(phys metall), 54. *Prof Exp:* Design engr, Kimberly-Clark Corp, 41-44; asst, Ill Inst Technol, 44-45; engr, Parten Mach Co, 45-47; prod eng supt, Maico Co, Inc, 47; instr phys metall, Univ Minn, 47-51, res assoc mech & metals, 51-54; res metallurgist, Magnesium Dept, Dow Chem Co, 54-55; res engr, DMR, Kaiser Aluminum & Chem Corp, 55-57, br head mech metall & tech supvr mech metall, Fabrication & Appln Res Dept, 66-69, tech supvr, 69-71, prog mgr, 71-72; PRES, MONT COL MINERAL SCI & TECHNOL, 72- *Concurrent Pos:* Consult, Twin City Testing & Eng Lab, 51-54; vchmn, Cryogenic Eng Conf, 66-69; pres & chmn bd, Mont Energy & MHD Res & Develop Inst, 77-78. *Honors & Awards:* Award of Merit, Am Soc Mech Engrs, 69. *Mem:* Am Soc Metals; Am Inst Mining, Metall & Petrol Engrs; Am Soc Mech Engrs; Sigma Xi; NY Acad Sci. *Res:* Engineering properties of aluminum for cryogenic service; pressure vessel materials and applications; rolling and extrusion technology; formability; terminal ballistics; aluminum armor; dynamic response of materials; properties of materials at cryogenic temperature; effect of microstructure on properties of metals; MHD. *Mailing Add:* Mont Col Mineral Sci & Technol Butte MT 59701

DEMONSABERT, WINSTON RUSSEL, b New Orleans, La, June 12, 15; m 55; c 1. CHEMISTRY, RESEARCH ADMINISTRATION. *Educ:* Loyola Univ, BS, 37; Tulane Univ, AM, 45, PhD(chem), 52. *Prof Exp:* Prof, Warren Easton High Sch, 40-44 & Behrman High Sch, 44-48; from assoc prof to prof chem, Loyola Univ, La, 48-66; phys scientist adminr, Proj Off & chief chemist, Community Studies Div, Pesticides Prog, Nat Commun Dis Ctr, Ga, 66-69, health scientist adminr & dir contract liaison br, Nat Ctr Health Serv Res & Develp, 69-73, head extramural prog, bur drugs, 73-79, SCI COORD INTERAGENCY AFFAIRS, OFF COMNR, FOOD & DRUG ADMIN, DEPT HEALTH & HUMAN SERV, 79- *Concurrent Pos:* Assoc prof, Tulane Univ, 57-58; prof lectr anal chem, Cath Univ Am, 75-76. *Mem:* Fel AAAS; fel Am Inst Chemists; Soc Res Adminr; Am Chem Soc; Sigma Xi. *Res:* Health services research; chemical instrumentation, gas chromatography, spectrophotometry, and polarography; zirconium chemistry; complex-ion formation; chemical toxicology; drug research. *Mailing Add:* 604 Cobblestone Ct Silver Spring MD 20904

DEMOOY, CORNELIS JACOBUS, b Rotterdam, Netherlands, July 1, 26; m 53; c 2. SOIL FERTILITY, PLANT NUTRITION. *Educ:* Univ Wageningen, BS, 51, MS, 53; Iowa State Univ, PhD(soil fertil), 65. *Prof Exp:* Assoc soil surv classification & genetis, Univ Wageningen, 52-53; res scientist, Commonwealth Sci & Indust Res Orgn, 53-60; res assoc soil fertil, Iowa State Univ, 60-65; asst prof soil sci, Univ Utrecht, 65-67; from asst prof to assoc prof soil fertil, Iowa State Univ, 67-72, PROF AGRON, COLO STATE UNIV, 72- *Concurrent Pos:* Consult, Sir Alexander Gibb & Partners, Cent Africa, 66; agr res adv, US AID Mission to Pakistan, 72-76; consult, Castlewood Corp, Littleton, Colo, 79; Mich State Univ, WAfrica, 79, Colo State Univ, Indonesia, 80, Mich State Univ, Senegal, 80 & Nigeria, Botswania, 81; interdisciplinary environ res award, Colo State Univ, 78. *Mem:* Am Soc

Agron; Netherlands Royal Soc Agr Sci; Int Soil Sci Soc; Sigma Xi. *Res:* Soil-plant-water relationships; nutritional requirements of crops; optimum fertilization; soil classification and genesis; quantitative evaluation of soil properties and soil fertility factors in terms of land use potentialities. *Mailing Add:* Dept of Agron Colo State Univ Ft Collins CO 80523

DEMOPOULOS, HARRY BYRON, b New York, NY, Feb 14, 32; m 55; c 4. EXPERIMENTAL PATHOLOGY. *Educ:* State Univ NY, MD, 56. *Prof Exp:* Intern, Kings County Hosp, Brooklyn, NY, 56-57; resident path, Bellevue Hosp, New York, 57-60, asst pathologist, 60-61; from asst prof to assoc prof path, Univ Southern Calif, 63-67; dir cancer ctr planning, 73-76, ASSOC PROF PATH, SCH MED, NY UNIV, 67- *Concurrent Pos:* NIH res training grant, Sch Med, NY Univ, 57-61; Nat Cancer Inst res career develop award, Sch Med, Univ Southern Calif, 63-66. *Mem:* Am Chem Soc; Am Soc Exp Path. *Res:* Melanoma metabolism; molecular pathology of membranes; role of free radical reactions in altering lipids, proteins and associated nucleic acids; free radical pathology in aging, central nervous system disorders, cancer and arteriosclerosis. *Mailing Add:* Dept Path NY Univ Sch Med New York NY 10016

DEMOPOULOS, JAMES THOMAS, b New York, NY, Dec 26, 28; m 69; c 3. PHYSICAL MEDICINE & REHABILITATION. *Educ:* NY Univ, BS, 50; State Univ NY, MD, 56. *Prof Exp:* From intern to resident, Kings County Hosp, Brooklyn, NY, 56-58; resident rehab med, Inst Rehab Med, NY Univ Med Ctr, 59-61, assoc dir outpatient serv, 61-65; assoc dir, Dept Rehab Med, City Hosp, Elmhurst, 65-67; DIR DEPT REHAB MED, HOSP JOINT DIS & MED CTR, 67-; PROF REHAB MED, MT SINAI SCH MED, 72-; DIR DEPT REHAB MED, BETH ISRAEL MED CTR, 76- *Concurrent Pos:* Fel stroke coun, Am Heart Asn, 69-; chmn adv comt amputee, orthotic, neuromuscular & pediat-orthop progs, New York Dept Health, 70-; consult, New York Bur Handicapped Children, 70-; fel, Arthritis Found, 72- *Mem:* Fel Am Acad Phys Med & Rehab; fel Am Cong Rehab Med; fel Am Rheumatism Asn. *Res:* Prosthetic and orthotic devices; development of predictors of outcome in rehabilitation as guides to management. *Mailing Add:* 1919 Madison Ave New York NY 10035

DEMORT, CAROLE LYLE, b Independence, Mo, Apr 1, 42. PHYCOLOGY, ECOLOGY. *Educ:* Park Col, BA, 64; Univ Mo-Kansas City, MS, 66; Ore State Univ, PhD(bot), 69. *Prof Exp:* Asst prof biol, St Mary's Col, Ind, 69-74; ASSOC PROF NAT SCI, UNIV N FLA, 74- *Mem:* Am Inst Biol Sci; Phycol Soc Am; Int Phycol Soc; Bot Soc Am; Am Soc Limnol & Oceanog. *Res:* Relative nutritional value of phytoplankton species as food for shellfish and shrimp larvae; developmental morphology and biochemical analysis of estuarine phytoplankton species; toxic effects of heavy metals on marine phytoplankton species. *Mailing Add:* Dept of Natural Sci Univ of NFla Jacksonville FL 32216

DEMOS, CHRISTOPHER HARRY, b Chatham, NY, Apr 23, 25; m 49; c 2. MEDICINE. *Educ:* Albany Med Col, MD, 47. *Prof Exp:* Intern, Fordham Hosp, NY, 47-48, resident med, 51-52; from intern to asst resident, Univ Hosp, 48-50; pvt pract med, 52-53; assoc dir dept clin pharmacol & assoc dir prof serv, Lederle Labs, Am Cyanamid Co, 53-60; dir clin res, Syntex Labs, 60-61; med dir, Squibb Inst Med Res, 61-68, clin res dir, NJ, 62-68; med dir, Beecham, Inc, 68-72; ASSOC DIR MED RES, HOFFMANN-LA ROCHE, 72- *Concurrent Pos:* Fel allergy, Univ Hosp, New York, 50-51; assoc prof med, NJ Col Med & Dent, 72- *Mem:* AMA; Am Rheumatism Asn; Am Acad Allergy; NY Acad Sci; Am Col Allergists. *Res:* Clinical evaluation of new drugs in the fields of endocrinology, anti inflammatory agents and antiinfective agents. *Mailing Add:* Hoffmann-La Roche Med Res Dept 340 Kingsland St Nutley NJ 07110

DEMOS, PETER THEODORE, b Toronto, Ont, Can; m 41; c 3. PHYSICS. *Educ:* Queen's Univ, Ont, BSc, 41; Mass Inst Technol, PhD(physics), 51. *Hon Degrees:* LLD, Trent Univ, Ont, 81. *Prof Exp:* Instr math & physics, Queen's Univ, Ont, 41-42; mem, Ballistics Res Staff, Nat Res Lab, Ont, 42-44; mem staff, Can Army Res Estab, Que, 44-46; asst physics, 46-51, mem staff, Lab Nuclear Sci, 51-52, lectr & assoc dir lab, 52-61, dir, 61-75, PROF PHYSICS, MASS INST TECHNOL, 61-, DIR, BATES LINEAR ACCELERATOR, 75- *Mem:* AAAS; Am Phys Soc; Am Acad Arts & Sci. *Res:* Linear accelerator development; electro and photonuclear studies. *Mailing Add:* Dept Physics Mass Inst Technol Cambridge MA 02139

DEMOSS, RALPH DEAN, b Danville, Ill, Dec 29, 22; m 46, 75; c 4. MICROBIOLOGY. *Educ:* Ind Univ, AB, 48, PhD(bact), 51. *Prof Exp:* AEC fel, Brookhaven Nat Labs, 51-52; asst prof biol, Johns Hopkins Univ, 52-56; assoc prof bact, 56-59, PROF MICROBIOL, UNIV ILL, URBANA, 59-, HEAD DEPT, 71- *Concurrent Pos:* NSF sr fel, Lab Genetic Physiol, Nat Ctr Sci Res, France, 62-63; ed, J Bact, 65-70; chmn microbiol training comt, Nat Inst Gen Med Sci, 69-71. *Mem:* Am Soc Microbiol; Am Soc Biol Chem; Brit Soc Gen Microbiol. *Res:* Structure and function of tryptophanase; tryptophanase in gnotobiotic animals; intestinal microbiology of mosquitoes. *Mailing Add:* Dept of Microbiol Univ of Ill Urbana IL 61801

DEMOTT, BOBBY JOE, b Kans, Nov 6, 24; m 47; c 5. DAIRY CHEMISTRY. *Educ:* Kans State Univ, BS, 49; Univ Idaho, MS, 51; Mich State Univ, PhD(dairy), 54. *Prof Exp:* Instr, Milk Factory Tests, Univ Idaho, 49-51; asst market milk, buttermaking & cheese, Mich State Univ, 51-54; asst prof dairy indust, Colo State Univ, 54-57; ASSOC PROF DAIRY INDUST, UNIV TENN, KNOXVILLE, 57- *Mem:* Nutrit Today Soc; Am Dairy Sci Asn; Packaging Inst; Inst Food Technologists; Int Asn Milk Food & Environ Sanitarians. *Res:* Homogenized milk; adding iron to milk; Xanthine oxidase in milk; whey utilization. *Mailing Add:* PO Box 1071 Knoxville TN 37901

DEMOTT, HOWARD EPHRAIM, b Bloomsburg, Pa, Oct 24, 13; m 40; c 1. BOTANY. *Educ:* Bloomsburg State Col, BS, 35; Bucknell Univ, MS, 40; Univ Va, PhD, 65. *Prof Exp:* Teacher high schs, NY, 35-48; From instr to prof, 48-80, EMER PROF BIOL, SUSQUEHANNA UNIV, 81- *Mem:* Bot Soc Am. *Res:* Plant morphology and morphogenesis. *Mailing Add:* Dept of Biol Susquehanna Univ Selinsgrove PA 17870

DEMOTT, LAWRENCE LYNCH, b Arlington, NJ, Jan 16, 22; m 49; c 1. GEOLOGY, PALEONTOLOGY. *Educ:* Oberlin Col, BA, 43; Univ Chicago, MA, 47; Harvard Univ, MA, 53, PhD(geol), 64. *Prof Exp:* Instr eng, State Col Wash, 47-51; instr geol, Oberlin Col, 54-62; from instr to assoc prof, 62-74, PROF GEOL, KNOX COL, ILL, 74- *Mem:* AAAS; Geol Soc Am; Paleont Soc; Am Asn Geol Teachers. *Res:* Middle Ordovician trilobite faunas of North America. *Mailing Add:* Dept of Geol Knox Col Galesburg IL 61401

DEMPESY, COLBY WILSON, b Chicago, Ill, Mar 12, 31; m 52; c 5. PHYSICS, NEUROBIOLOGY. *Educ:* Oberlin Col, BA, 52; Rice Inst, MA, 55, PhD(physics), 57. *Hon Degrees:* MA, Amherst Col, 67. *Prof Exp:* From instr to assoc prof, 57-67, chmn dept, 72-74, PROF PHYSICS, AMHERST COL, 67-, MEM FAC, NEUROSCI PROG, 74- *Concurrent Pos:* Fulbright res fel to Japan, 65-66; vis prof, Tulane Univ, 74-; res scientist, Charity Hosp, New Orleans, 74. *Mem:* Am Phys Soc; Am Asn Physics Teachers; AAAS. *Res:* Low temperature physics; neurophysiology. *Mailing Add:* Dept Physics Amherst Col Amherst MA 01002

DEMPSEY, ALVIN HUGH, b Jackson, Ga, Feb 17, 20; m 48; c 2. HORTICULTURE. *Educ:* Univ Ga, BSA, 42, MSA, 47; Ohio State Univ, PhD(hort), 53. *Prof Exp:* From asst horticulturist to assoc horticulturist, 48-56, HORTICULTURIST, GA EXP STA, 56- *Mem:* Am Soc Hort Sci. *Res:* Genetics; cytogenetics; breeding of vegetables. *Mailing Add:* Ga Exp Sta Univ of Ga Experiment GA 30212

DEMPSEY, BARRY J, b Galesburg, Ill, Mar 17, 38; m 63; c 2. CIVIL ENGINEERING. *Educ:* Univ Ill, Urbana, BS, 60, MS, 66, PhD(civil eng), 69. *Prof Exp:* Asst resident engr hwy construct, State Ill Hwy Dept, 60 & 63-64; res asst, 64-69, asst prof, 69-74, assoc prof civil eng, 74-79, PROF CIVIL ENG, UNIV ILL, URBANA, 79- *Concurrent Pos:* Prin investr, Ill Div Hwy, 68-; consult, NY State Dept Transp, 70-71; mem, Transp Res Bd, Nat Res Coun-Nat Acad Sci, 70-; US Army Corps Engrs, Monsanto, 73- & Fed Hwy Admin, 76- *Honors & Awards:* A W Johnson Mem Award, 70; K B Woods Award, 78. *Mem:* Am Soc Civil Engrs; Soc Am Mil Engrs; Soil Sci Soc Am. *Res:* Transportation materials with major emphasis on the investigation of the influence climatic factors have on construction, design, behavior and performance of pavement systems. *Mailing Add:* 111 Talbot Lab Dept Civil Eng Univ of Ill Urbana IL 61801

DEMPSEY, DANIEL FRANCIS, b Buffalo, NY, July 23, 29; m 60; c 3. PHYSICS. *Educ:* Canisius Col, BS, 51; Univ Notre Dame, PhD(physics), 57. *Prof Exp:* From asst prof to assoc prof physics, 56-77, PROF PHYSICS, CANISIUS COL, 77- *Mem:* Am Phys Soc. *Res:* Focusing trajectories for charged and neutral particles; general nuclear physics and particle accelerators. *Mailing Add:* 6641 Powers Rd Orchard Park NY 14127

DEMPSEY, JOHN NICHOLAS, b St Paul, Minn, June 16, 23; m 48; c 3. PHYSICAL CHEMISTRY. *Educ:* Col St Thomas, BS, 48; Univ Iowa, PhD(phys chem), 51. *Prof Exp:* Asst, Univ Iowa, 48-50; res chemist, Ethyl Corp, 51-52; res physicist, Minneapolis Honeywell Regulator Co, 52-56, res sect head, 56-60, from asst dir res to dir res, Honeywell Inc, 60-65, vpres, Corp Res Ctr, 65-67, vpres sci & eng, 67-72; vpres tech serv, 72-75, VPRES SCI & TECHNOL, BEMIS CO, INC, 75- *Concurrent Pos:* Mem Patent & Trademark Adv Comt, US Dept Com, 76. *Mem:* Am Inst Chemists; Am Chem Soc; Indust Res Inst. *Res:* X-ray crystal structures of coordination; complex compounds; intermetallic compounds and bond orders. *Mailing Add:* Bemis Co Inc 800 Northstar Ctr Minneapolis MN 55402

DEMPSEY, MARTIN E(WALD), b Chicago, Ill, Mar 28, 21; m 45; c 3. SURFACE ACOUSTIC WAVE TECHNOLOGY, ULTRASONICS. *Educ:* Purdue Univ, BS, 48, MS, 49, PhD(elec eng), 55. *Prof Exp:* Engr voice commun lab, Purdue Univ, 48-49, chief engr, 50-55; mem tech staff, Bell Tel Labs, 49-50; dir aid to hearing res, Zenith Radio Corp, 55-59; dir psychoacoust res, Beltone Res Labs, 59-61; mgr advan phys develop, GTE Automatic Elec Labs, 61-71; mgr, 71-78, PRIN INVESTR, GTE LABS, WALTHAM RES CTR, 78- *Concurrent Pos:* Consult dept commun disorders, Northwestern Univ, 58-62. *Mem:* Acoust Soc Am; Am Vacuum Soc; Electrochem Soc; NY Acad Sci; Optical Soc Am. *Res:* Communication engineering; psychoacoustics; materials science. *Mailing Add:* GTE Labs 40 Sylvan Rd Waltham MA 02154

DEMPSEY, MARY ELIZABETH, b St Paul, Minn, Sept 23, 28. BIOCHEMISTRY. *Educ:* St Catherine Col, BS, 50; Wayne State Univ, MS, 52; Univ Minn, PhD(enzym), 61. *Prof Exp:* Res biochemist, Minneapolis Vet Admin Hosp, 52-56; instr clin biochem, 56-58, from instr to assoc prof biochem, 61-75, PROF BIOCHEM, MED COL, UNIV MINN, MINNEAPOLIS, 75- *Concurrent Pos:* Am Heart Asn res fel, 61-63; res grants, Minn Heart Asn, 61-64 & 77-78, Nat Heart Inst, 64-80, Muscular Dystrophy Asn Am, Inc, 65-70, NSF, 70-74 & Am Heart Asn, 71-74. *Mem:* Am Chem Soc; Am Soc Biol Chem; Soc Exp Biol & Med. *Res:* Enzymology; steroid and sterol; arteriosclerosis; bioenergetics muscle contraction; oxygen-18 methodology; cholesterol biosynthesis; regulation of lipid biosynthesis. *Mailing Add:* Box 68 Mayo Bldg Univ of Minn Minneapolis MN 55455

DEMPSEY, WALTER B, b San Francisco, Calif, Nov 21, 34; m 57; c 4. BIOCHEMISTRY. *Educ:* Univ San Francisco, BS, 56; Univ Mich, MS, 58, PhD(biol chem), 60. *Prof Exp:* NSF fel, 60-62; USPHS res grants, 63-68 & 69-; fel, Univ Edinburgh, 73-74. *Concurrent Pos:* Res chemist, Vet Admin Hosp, Dallas, 67-75. Concurrent. *Mem:* AAAS; Fedn Am Socs Exp Biol; Am Soc Microbiol; Am Chem Soc; Am Soc Biol Chemists. *Res:* Mechanisms for and control of transfer of R factors and other bacterial plasmids; bacterial genetics; microbiology of pyridoxine. *Mailing Add:* Dept of Biochem Univ Tex Health Sci Ctr Dallas TX 75235

DEMPSEY, WESLEY HUGH, b Waltham, Mass, Dec 2, 26; m 51; c 4. GENETICS, PLANT BREEDING. *Educ:* Cornell Univ, BS, 49; Univ Calif, MS, 50, PhD(genetics), 54. *Prof Exp:* Res asst genetics & plant breeding, Univ Calif, 51-54; PROF BIOL, CALIF STATE UNIV, CHICO, 54- *Concurrent*

Pos: NSF sci fac fel, Univ Wis, 63-64; adj prof plant breeding, Pa State Univ, 70-71; vis prof bot, Bot Dept, Univ Canterbury, Christchurch, NZ, 80-81. *Mem:* Am Soc Hort Sci; Bot Soc Am; AAAS; Am Inst Biol Sci. *Res:* Tomato genetics, inheritance on consistency; red cotyledon in lettuce; pectic substances in tomatoes; electron microscopy of tomato mutants; population cytogenetics of Trimerotropis. *Mailing Add:* Dept of Biol Calif State Univ Chico CA 95926

DEMPSKI, ROBERT E, b Centermoreland, Pa, July 3, 34; m 66; c 3. PHARMACEUTICS. *Educ:* Philadelphia Col Pharm, BS, 56; Univ Wis, PhD(pharm), 60. *Prof Exp:* Instr pharm, Univ Wis, 56-58; res assoc pharm res, Merck & Co, Inc, 60-66, unit head, West Point, 66-72, SR RES FEL PHARM RES, MERCK SHARP & DOHME, WEST POINT, 72- *Mem:* Am Pharmaceut Asn; Acad Pharmaceut Sci. *Res:* Design of new dosage forms for medicinals; study of new methods of dermatologic therapy; solid dosage form research and development. *Mailing Add:* 1629 Arran Way Dresher PA 19025

DEMPSTER, ARTHUR PENTLAND, b Toronto, Ont, Oct 8, 29; m 57; c 3. STATISTICS. *Educ:* Univ Toronto, BA, 52, MA, 53; Princeton Univ, PhD(math statist), 56. *Hon Degrees:* Harvard Univ, AM, 61. *Prof Exp:* Lectr math, Univ Toronto, 56-57; mem tech staff, Bell Tel Labs, 57-58; from asst prof to assoc prof statist, 58-64, chmn dept, 69-75 & 77-80, PROF THEORET STATIST, HARVARD UNIV, 64- *Mem:* Am Statist Asn; Inst Math Statist; Biomet Soc. *Res:* Theoretical statistics. *Mailing Add:* Harvard Univ Dept of Statist 1 Oxford St Cambridge MA 02138

DEMPSTER, GEORGE, b Edinburgh, Scotland, June 28, 17; m 42; c 2. MEDICAL MICROBIOLOGY. *Educ:* Univ Edinburgh, MB, ChB, 40, BSc, 41, MD, 52. *Prof Exp:* Intern, Peel Hosp, Scotland, 40; asst, Pub Health Lab, Edinburgh, 41-42, lectr bact, 42-46 & 48-50; res assoc, Connaught Med Res Lab, Toronto, 50-55; head dept, 56-72, prof virol, 55-77, PROF MICROBIOL, UNIV SASK, 77- *Concurrent Pos:* Dir bact, Univ Hosp, Saskatoon, 55-72, virologist, 55- *Mem:* Can Soc Microbiol; Can Med Asn; Can Pub Health Asn. *Res:* Virology; epidemic respiratory disease; influenza; atypical pneumonia and adenoviruses; neuro-tropic viruses, particularly Coxsackie viruses. *Mailing Add:* Dept of Microbiol Univ of Sask Med Col Saskatoon SK S7H 0W0 Can

DEMPSTER, LAURAMAY TINSLEY, b El Paso, Tex, May 11, 05; m 27; c 2. TAXONOMIC BOTANY. *Educ:* Univ Calif, MA, 27. *Prof Exp:* Asst bot, 33-35, herbarium botanist, 51-61, res geneticist bot, NSF grants, 59-69, RES ASSOC, DEPT BOT, UNIV CALIF, BERKELEY, 69- *Mem:* Am Soc Plant Taxon; Soc Bot Mex. *Res:* Taxonomy of flowering plants; currently the genus Galium in western North America, Mexico and South America. *Mailing Add:* Jepson Herbarium Univ of Calif Dept of Bot Berkeley CA 94720

DEMSKEY, SIDNEY, b Brooklyn, NY, Oct 4, 24; m 49; c 3. STATISTICAL ANALYSIS. *Educ:* Brooklyn Col, BA, 48; City Col New York, MBA, 53. *Prof Exp:* Statistician, Dept Health, NY, 48-50; sales analyst, Nestle-LeMur Co, 50-51; statistician & admin asst, Schenley Industs, 51-59; statistician, Aerojet Gen Corp, 59-60; SUPVRY STATISTICIAN, REENTRY SYSTS DEPT, GEN ELEC CO, 60- *Concurrent Pos:* Lectr eve sch, City Col New York, Drexel Inst Technol & Villanova Univ, 68-70. *Mem:* Am Statist Asn; fel Am Soc Qual Control. *Res:* Business and industrial statistics; mathematics; estimation and/or demonstration method for reliability or deterministic system/models; statistical system for shelf life estimation. *Mailing Add:* 3198 Chestnut St Philadelphia PA 19104

DEMSKI, JAMES WILLARD, plant pathology, see previous edition

DEMSKI, LEO STANLEY, b Pittsburgh, Pa, Mar 29, 43; m 65. NEUROANATOMY, ANIMAL BEHAVIOR. *Educ:* Miami Univ, AB, 65; Univ Rochester, PhD(anat, neurobiol), 69. *Prof Exp:* Asst prof anat, Sch Med, Univ NMex, 71-74; assoc prof, Sch Med, La State Univ, 74-77; ASSOC PROF, DEPT BIOL SCI, UNIV KY, 77- *Concurrent Pos:* NIMH fel, Am Mus Natural Hist, NY, 69-71. *Mem:* Animal Behav Soc; Am Soc Ichthyologists & Herpetologists; Am Asn Anatomists; Am Soc Zool; Am Inst Biol Sci. *Res:* Identification of neural systems controlling sound production and sexual, feeding and aggressive behavior in fishes. *Mailing Add:* Dept of Biol Sci 101 T H Morgan Bldg Lexington KY 40506

DEMUTH, GEORGE RICHARD, b Sherwood, Ohio, Nov 16, 25; m 51; c 4. PEDIATRICS. *Educ:* Univ Cincinnati, MD, 50. *Prof Exp:* From instr to assoc prof, 56-65, assoc dean, 68-81, dir integrated premed prog, 73-75, PROF PEDIAT, UNIV MICH, ANN ARBOR, 65-, MED SCIENTIST TRAINING PROG, 79- *Mem:* AAAS; Soc Pediat Res; Asn Am Med Cols. *Mailing Add:* Univ of Mich Med Sch Ann Arbor MI 48109

DEMUTH, HOWARD B, b Junction City, Kans, June 22, 28; m 51; c 4. ELECTRICAL ENGINEERING, COMPUTER SCIENCE. *Educ:* Univ Colo, BS, 49; Stanford Univ, MS, 54, PhD(elec eng), 57. *Prof Exp:* Staff mem electronic comput, Los Alamos Sci Lab, 49-53; res asst network synthesis, Stanford Univ, 53-54; res engr, Stanford Res Inst, 54-56; proj engr, Int Bus Mach Res Lab, 56-58; staff mem digital comput & control systs, Los Alamos Nat Lab, 58-80; PROF ELEC ENG, UNIV TULSA, 80- *Concurrent Pos:* Prof, Univ NMex, 58-; vis lectr, Univ Colo, 62-63; vis prof, Univ Hawaii, 68-69. *Mem:* Inst Elec & Electronics Engrs. *Res:* Digital data communication; digital control systems; information and communication theory. *Mailing Add:* Dept Elec Eng Univ Tulsa 600 S College Ave Tulsa OK 74104

DEMUTH, JOHN ROBERT, b St Louis, Mo, Nov 15, 24. ORGANIC CHEMISTRY. *Educ:* Washington Univ, BA, 49; Univ Ill, MS, 52, PhD(chem), 55. *Prof Exp:* Asst, Washington Univ, 49-50; asst, Univ Ill, 50-55; assoc prof, 55-72, chief adv dept chem, 75-80, PROF CHEM, UNIV NEBR, LINCOLN, 72- *Mem:* Am Chem Soc. *Mailing Add:* 731 Hamilton Hall Univ of Nebr Lincoln NE 68588

DEMYER, MARIAN KENDALL, b Greensburg, Ind; m; c 3. CHILD PSYCHIATRY, PSYCHIATRY. *Educ:* Ind Univ, BS, 49, MD, 52; Am Bd Psychiat & Neurol, cert psychiat, 59, cert child psychiat, 60. *Prof Exp:* Intern med & surg, Detroit Receiving Hosp, Mich, 52-53; resident psychiat, Univ Med Ctr, 53-56, from instr to assoc prof psychiat, 57-69, dir clin res ctr early childhood schizophrenia, 61-74, actg coordr child psychiat, 74, chief clin res sect, 74-80, PROF PSYCHIAT, INST PSYCHIAT RES, IND UNIV-PURDUE UNIV, INDIANAPOLIS, 69-, PRIN INVESTR, 80- *Concurrent Pos:* Fel child psychiat, Eastern Pa Psychiat Inst, 56-57; NIMH fel, Ind Univ, 61-74; Ind Dept Ment Health fel, Ind Univ-Purdue Univ, Indianapolis, 74-77; dir children's serv, Carter Hosp, Indianapolis, 57-61; mem ed bd, Schizophrenia, 70-; assoc ed, J Child Schizophrenia & Autism, 71-76. *Mem:* Am Psychiat Asn. *Res:* Neurological correlates mental illness; neurochemical correlates of mental illness. *Mailing Add:* Inst for Psychiat Res Ind Univ-Purdue Univ Indianapolis IN 46202

DE MYER, WILLIAM ERL, b South Charleston, WVa, Aug 7, 24; m 52; c 2. NEUROLOGY. *Educ:* Ind Univ, BS, 49, MD, 52; Am Bd Psychiat & Neurol, dipl, 56, cert child neurol, 68. *Prof Exp:* Intern, Univ Mich Hosp, 52-53; resident neurol, Med Ctr, 53-56; from instr to assoc prof, 54-68, PROF NEUROL, SCH MED & DIR NEUROANAT LAB, IND UNIV, 68- *Concurrent Pos:* NIH spec fel, 62; mem med fac training prog, Univ Pa, 56-57; consult, LaRue Carter Hosp, Wishard Mem Hosp & Vet Admin Hosp, Indianapolis, 65- *Mem:* AAAS; Int Soc Cranio-Facial Biol; Am Asn Neuropath; World Fedn Neurol; fel Am Acad Neurol; Child Neurol Soc. *Res:* Quantitative neuroanatomy; relation of congenital malformations of face and brain; developmental neuroanatomy and teratology. *Mailing Add:* Dept Neurol Ind Univ Sch Med Indianapolis IN 46223

DENARIEZ-ROBERGE, MARGUERITE MARIE, lasers, see previous edition

DE NAULT, KENNETH J, b Los Angeles, Calif, Apr 3, 43; m 68; c 2. GEOLOGY, MINERALOGY. *Educ:* Stanford Univ, BS, 65, PhD(geol), 74; Univ Wyo, MS, 67. *Prof Exp:* Geologist uranium explor, Getty Oil Co, 68-69 & Union Oil Co, 70; asst prof, 73-79, ASSOC PROF GEOL, UNIV NORTHERN IOWA, 80- *Concurrent Pos:* US Inst Airways res fel, 81. *Mem:* Am Asn Petrol Geologists; Geol Soc Am; Sigma Xi; Mineral Soc Am; Am Fern Soc. *Res:* Mineralogy, petrology, and crystallography; investigating the mineralogy and petrology of the Rattlesnake Hills eruptive center, Wyoming. *Mailing Add:* Dept Earth Sci Univ Northern Iowa Cedar Falls IA 50613

DENAVARRE, MAISON GABRIEL, b Poland, Mar 27, 09; nat US; m 38; c 2. COSMETIC CHEMISTRY. *Educ:* Wayne Univ, PhC, 29, BS, 30, MSc, 57. *Prof Exp:* Apprentice pharmacist, C G Meyer, Mich, 27-29, regist pharmacist, 29-30; regist pharmacist, Willis Pharmacy, 30-34; consult chemist, 30-47; vpres charge mfg & res, Cosmetic Labs, Inc, div Beauty Counselors, Inc, 47-55, dir, 55-68, pres, 56-58; pres res & develop, Vanda Beauty Counr, Dart Industs Inc, 68-78; VPRES, TERRY CORP, 78- *Concurrent Pos:* Spec instr, Wayne Univ; vpres & dir, Helfrich Labs, Can, Ltd, 55, Beauty Counselors Can, Ltd, Beauty Counselors London, Ltd, 61 & Beauty Counr Int, 63; tech ed & ed dir, Am Perfumer; hon mem, Ital Comt Esthetics & Cosmetics. *Honors & Awards:* Medal, Soc Cosmetic Chemists, 51. *Mem:* Am Chem Soc; Am Pharmaceut Asn; fel Soc Cosmetic Chemists (pres, 45, ed jour, 46-61); fel Am Inst Chemists; fel NY Acad Sci. *Res:* Cosmetic emulsions; ultraviolet absorption; chemical anticorrosive agents; chemical heating mixture; production, control and analysis of cosmetics; cosmetic microbiology; preservatives. *Mailing Add:* 7130 S Orange Blossom Trail Orlando FL 32809

DENAVIT, JACQUES, b Paris, France, Oct 1, 30; US citizen; m 54; c 3. ENGINEERING. *Educ:* Univ Paris, Baccalaureat, 49, cert, 51; Northwestern Univ, MS, 53, PhD, 56. *Prof Exp:* Instr, Dept Mech Eng, 58-60, assoc prof mech eng & astronaut sci, 60-65, PROF MECH ENG & ASTRONAUT SCI, NORTHWESTERN UNIV, 65- *Mem:* Am Soc Mech Engrs; fel Am Phys Soc. *Res:* Plasma physics and kinetic theory. *Mailing Add:* 623 Milburn Evanston IL 60201

DENBER, HERMAN C B, b New York, NY, Oct 9, 17; m 44; c 1. PSYCHIATRY, BIOCHEMICAL PHARMACOLOGY. *Educ:* NY Univ, BA, 38, MS, 63, PhD(biol), 67; Univ Geneva, BMS, 41, MD, 43; Am Bd Psychiat & Neurol, dipl, 55. *Prof Exp:* Assoc res scientist, Manhattan State Hosp, 54-55, dir psychiat res, 55-72, prof psychiat & pharmacol, Col Med, Univ Fla, 72-74; PROF PSYCHIAT, SCH MED, UNIV LOUISVILLE, 74- *Concurrent Pos:* Instr psychiat, Col Physicians & Surgeons, Columbia Univ, 56-60; assoc clin prof, New York Med Col, 60-66, prof, 66-72. *Honors & Awards:* Chevalier de l'Ordre de la Sante, France, 60. *Mem:* Am Col Psychiatrists; fel AAAS; NY Acad Sci; Sigma Xi; hon mem Royal Belg Soc Ment Med. *Res:* Psychopharmacology; clinical psychiatry; molecular biology; psychoanalysis; social psychiatry; electroencephalography; neuropathology. *Mailing Add:* Dept of Psychiat Sch of Med Univ of Louisville PO Box 1055 Louisville KY 40201

DEN BESTEN, IVAN EUGENE, b Corsica, SDak, Jan 11, 33; m 60; c 2. PHYSICAL CHEMISTRY. *Educ:* Calvin Col, AB, 57; Northwestern Univ, PhD(chem), 61. *Prof Exp:* Instr chem, 61-62, from asst prof to assoc prof, 62-70, PROF CHEM, BOWLING GREEN STATE UNIV, 70- *Mem:* AAAS; Am Chem Soc; NY Acad Sci. *Res:* Catalysis by metals and metal oxides; photocatalysis and photochemistry; reactions in discharges; surface reactions. *Mailing Add:* Dept of Chem Bowling Green State Univ Bowling Green OH 43402

DENBO, JOHN RUSSELL, b Evansville, Ind, June 12, 47; m 71. PHYSIOLOGY, NEUROANATOMY. *Educ:* Eastern Ill Univ, BS, 69; Southern Ill Univ, MA, 72, PhD(physiol), 74. *Prof Exp:* asst prof, 74-80, ASSOC PROF PHYSIOL, DEPT BIOL, GRINNELL COL, 80- *Mem:* Sigma Xi; AAAS. *Res:* Elucidation of the controlling mechanisms of movement in the acellular slime mold Physarum polycephalum. *Mailing Add:* Dept of Biol Grinnell Col Grinnell IA 50112

DENBOW, CARL (HERBERT), b Zanesville, Ohio, Dec 13, ll; m 39; c 3. MATHEMATICS. *Educ:* Univ Chicago, BS, 32, MS, 34, PhD(math), 37. *Prof Exp:* From instr to assoc prof math, Ohio Univ, 36-46; assoc prof math & mech, US Naval Postgrad Sch, 46-50; chmn math dept, 54-55 & 66-67, PROF MATH, OHIO UNIV, 50- *Concurrent Pos:* Ford fac fel, Harvard Univ, 55-56; coordr, Int Teacher Training Prog, 61, 62; chmn AID surv team, Cambodia, 62; dir training prog, Peace Corps, Cameroon, 63, 64. *Mem:* Am Math Soc; Math Asn Am. *Res:* Applied mathematics; foundations of mathematics; philosophy of science and mathematics. *Mailing Add:* Dept of Math Ohio Univ Athens OH 45701

DENBURG, JEFFREY LEWIS, b Brooklyn, NY, Oct 5, 44; div; c 3. NEUROBIOLOGY, BIOCHEMISTRY. *Educ:* Amherst Col, BA, 65; Johns Hopkins Univ, PhD(biol), 70. *Prof Exp:* Fel neurobiol, Cornell Univ, 70-72; res fel, Australian Nat Univ, 72-77; ASST PROF ZOOL, UNIV IOWA, 77- *Concurrent Pos:* NIH res develop award, 79- *Mem:* AAAS; Soc Neurosci. *Res:* Identification of the genetic mechanisms responsible for the formation of neuronal connections and the isolation of macromolecules mediating these mechanisms. *Mailing Add:* Dept Zool Univ Iowa Iowa City IA 52240

DENBY, LYALL GORDON, b Regina, Sask, Oct 4, 23. POMOLOGY. *Educ:* Univ BC, BSA, 45, MSA, 50. *Prof Exp:* Nursery sales & mgt, Hyland Barnes Nursery, 47-50; head veg crops, 50-59, head veg & ornamentals, 59-70, RES SCIENTIST POMOL & GRAPES, SUMMERLAND RES STA, CAN DEPT AGR, 70- *Honors & Awards:* Sadler Mem Gold Medal, 45; Can Hort Coun Award Merit, 72. *Mem:* Am Soc Hort Sci; Am Pomol Soc. *Res:* Tree fruit varieties; rootstocks and tree training; grape culture and breeding. *Mailing Add:* Agr Can Res Sta Summerland BC V0H L2O Can

DENCE, MICHAEL ROBERT, b Sydney, Australia, June 17, 31; m 67; c 2. GEOLOGY, METEORITICS. *Educ:* Univ Sydney, BSc, 53. *Prof Exp:* Geologist, Falconbridge Nickel Mines, Ltd, 53-54; res asst tectonics, Geophys Lab, Univ Toronto, 56-58; tech officer, Dept Mines & Tech Surv, 59-61, res scientist, Dom Observ, 62-70, res scientist, 70-81, RES MGR, DEPT ENERGY, MINES & RESOURCES, GOVT CAN, 81- *Mem:* Am Geophys Union; fel Meteoritical Soc; fel Geol Asn Can; fel Royal Soc Can; AAAS. *Res:* Meteor crater studies; meteoritics; rock deformation; metamorphism; rock physics; tectonophysics; planetary sciences; lunar sample studies; nuclear waste disposal. *Mailing Add:* Gravity Div Earth Phys Br Dept Energy Mines & Resources Ottawa ON K1A 0Y3 Can

DENDINGER, JAMES ELMER, b Long Beach, Calif, Nov 13, 43. INVERTEBRATE PHYSIOLOGY. *Educ:* Calif State Univ, Long Beach, BA, 69, MS, 71; Univ Mass, PhD(zool), 75. *Prof Exp:* Mem res & develop staff biol, Hyland Labs, Costa Mesa, Calif, 68-69; biomed res technician, Vet Admin Hosp, Long Beach, 69-70; asst physiol, Dept Biol, Calif State Univ, Long Beach, 70-71; res asst parasitol, Dept Zool, Univ Mass, 71-75; asst prof, 75-81, PROF BIOL, JAMES MADISON UNIV, 81- *Concurrent Pos:* Technician immunohemat, Walter Reed Army Med Ctr, Washington, DC, 65-67 & Georgetown Univ Med Ctr, 66-67. *Mem:* Am Soc Zoologists; AAAS; Sigma Xi. *Res:* Regulation of intermediary metabolism in invertebrate animals; crustacean physiology. *Mailing Add:* Dept of Biol James Madison Univ Harrisonburg VA 22807

DENDINGER, RICHARD DONALD, b Minot, NDak, Feb 21, 36; m 57; c 3. INORGANIC CHEMISTRY, NUCLEAR CHEMISTRY. *Educ:* Minot State Col, BS, 58; NDak State Univ, MS, 66; SDak State Univ, PhD(inorg chem & nuclear chem), 74. *Prof Exp:* Chem, physics, math & biol teacher, Bottineau Spec Sch Dist, NDak, 58-62; assoc prof inorg, nuclear & gen chem, 65-80, PROF CHEM, ST CLOUD STATE UNIV, 80- *Concurrent Pos:* Chem traineeship, NSF, 62. *Mem:* Am Chem Soc. *Res:* Photochemical effects on polar solutions of tungsten, vanadium and molybdenum polydentate chelate compounds, a method of preparation of lower oxidation state compounds by photoredox. *Mailing Add:* Dept of Chem St Cloud State Univ St Cloud MN 56301

DENDY, JOEL EUGENE, JR, b Anderson, SC, Mar 24, 45; m 67; c 1. NUMERICAL ANALYSIS. *Educ:* Rice Univ, BA, 67, PhD(math), 71. *Prof Exp:* Asst prof math, Univ Denver, 71-73; STAFF MEM MATH, LOS ALAMOS NAT LAB, 73- *Mem:* Soc Indust & Appl Math. *Res:* Finite difference and finite element methods for the numerical solution of partial differential equations. *Mailing Add:* 2877 Woodland Rd Los Alamos NM 87544

DENEAU, GERALD ANTOINE, b Oxford, Mich, May 9, 28; m 52; c 3. PHARMACOLOGY. *Educ:* Univ Western Ontario, BA, 50, MS, 52; Univ Mich, PhD(pharmacol), 57. *Prof Exp:* Instr pharmacol, Med Ctr, Univ Mich, 57-65; sr pharmacologist, Southern Res Inst, 65-72; assoc prof pharmacol, Sch Med, Univ Calif, Davis, 72-75; RES SCIENTIST, NY STATE ASST SECY ARMY, BROOKLYN, 76- *Mem:* Am Soc Pharmacol. *Res:* Physical dependence and tolerance development to addicting drugs; general pharmacology of all centrally-acting drugs. *Mailing Add:* NY State Asst Secy Army 80 Hanson Pl Brooklyn NY 11217

DENEKAS, MILTON OLIVER, b Dempster, SDak, Apr 20, 18; m 49; c 3. CHEMISTRY. *Educ:* Hope Col, BA, 40; Univ Mich, PhD(chem), 47. *Prof Exp:* Jr res chemist, Upjohn Co, Mich, 45-47; from instr to asst prof chem, Univ Tulsa, 47-57; res chemist, Esso Prod Res Co, 57-74, sr res chemist, 74-79, RES SPECIALIST, EXXON PROD RES CO, 79- *Mem:* Soc Petrol Engrs; Am Inst Mech Engrs; Am Chem Soc. *Res:* Isoaromatization studies; drugs for amebiasis; amino acids and protein hydrolysates; synthesis of omega-omega diaminoalkanes; petroleum reservoir wettability studies; geochemistry; tertiary petroleum recovery; secondary petroleum recovery; oil well drilling. *Mailing Add:* Exxon Prod Res Co PO Box 2189 Houston TX 77001

DENELL, ROBIN ERNEST, b Peoria, Ill, Aug 6, 42; m 66; c 2. GENETICS. *Educ:* Univ Calif, Riverside, BA, 65; Univ Tex, Austin, MA, 68, PhD(genetics), 69. *Prof Exp:* NIH trainee, Univ Tex, Austin, 69-70; NIH fel genetics, Univ Calif, San Diego, 70-72; Ford Found fel genetics, Univ Edinburgh, 72-73; asst prof biol, 73-76, ASSOC PROF BIOL, KANS STATE UNIV, 77- *Mem:* AAAS; Soc Develop Biol; Am Soc Naturalists; Genetics Soc Am. *Res:* Cytogenetics and developmental genetics of Drosophila. *Mailing Add:* Div of Biol Kans State Univ Manhattan KS 66506

DENENBERG, VICTOR HUGO, b Apr 3, 25; m 50, 75; c 4. NEUROSCIENCES. *Educ:* Bucknell Univ, BA, 49; Purdue Univ, MS, 51, PhD(psychol), 53. *Prof Exp:* Res assoc human res off, George Washington Univ, 52-54; from asst prof to prof psychol, Purdue Univ, 54-69; PROF PYSCHOBIOL, UNIV CONN, 69- *Concurrent Pos:* Carnegie fel, Roscoe B Jackson Mem Lab, 55, vis investr, 56-; NIH spec fel, Cambridge Univ, 63-64. *Mem:* AAAS; Am Psychol Asn; Int Soc Develop Psychobiol (pres, 70). *Res:* Experimental developmental psychology; ontogeny of behavior; animal behavior and early experience. *Mailing Add:* Dept of Biobehav Sci U-154 Univ of Conn Storrs CT 06268

DENES, PETER B, b Budapest, Hungary, Nov 9, 20. COMMUNICATION SCIENCES, ELECTRICAL ENGINEERING. *Educ:* Manchester Univ, England, BSc, 41, MSc, 43; Univ London, PhD(eng), 60. *Prof Exp:* Demonstr elec eng, Manchester Col, 41-44; res engr, Welwyn Elec Labs, 44-46; lectr phonetics, Univ Col, Univ London, 46-61; mem tech staff, 61-67, head Speech & Commun Res Dept, 67-81, HEAD, COMPUT ENHANCED COMMUN RES DEPT, BELL LABS, 81- *Concurrent Pos:* Mem, med & sci comt, Nat Inst for Deaf, London, 47-61; mem subcomt hearing aids & audiometers, Brit Standards Inst, 52-61; physicist, audiol unit, Royal Nat Throat, Nose & Ear Hosp, London, Eng, 52-61; vis fel, Columbia Univ, 53; assoc ed, Acoust Soc Am J, 69-75. *Mem:* Fel Acoustical Soc Am. *Res:* Speech communication; automatic speech recognition; speech synthesis; hearing and deafness; graphics; digital type settings; man-machine interface. *Mailing Add:* Bell Labs Inc Murray Hill NJ 07974

DE NEVERS, NOEL HOWARD, b San Francisco, Calif, May 21, 32; m 55; c 3. CHEMICAL ENGINEERING. *Educ:* Stanford Univ, BS, 54; Univ Mich, MS, 56, PhD(chem eng), 59. *Prof Exp:* Res engr, Calif Res Corp, Standard Oil Co Calif, 58-63; PROF CHEM ENG, UNIV UTAH, 63- *Concurrent Pos:* Officer air progs, Environ Protection Agency, 71-72. *Mem:* Am Inst Chem Engrs; Air Pollution Control Asn. *Res:* General and multifluid flow; thermodynamics and thermodynamic properties; interaction of technology and society; teaching of technology to nontechnologists; air pollution control technology. *Mailing Add:* Dept of Chem Eng Univ of Utah Salt Lake City UT 84112

DENFORD, KEITH EUGENE, b London, Eng, Feb 10, 46; Can citizen; m 68; c 2. PHYTOCHEMISTRY. *Educ:* Univ London, BSc, 67, PhD(chemosystematics), 70. *Prof Exp:* Fel phytochem, 70-71, asst prof, 71-76, ASSOC PROF PHYTOCHEM, UNIV ALTA, 76- *Concurrent Pos:* Forensic consult, Royal Can Mounted Police, 71- *Mem:* Can Bot Soc; Phytochem Soc; Linnean Soc London. *Res:* Phytochemical studies of vascular plant populations with respect to their evolutionary relationships with special reference to glaciation and glacial refugia in western North America. *Mailing Add:* Dept of Bot Univ of Alta Edmonton Can

DENGO, GABRIEL, b Heredia, Costa Rica, Mar 9, 22; m 50; c 3. PETROLOGY, STRUCTURAL GEOLOGY. *Educ:* Univ Costa Rica, BS, 44; Univ Wyo, BA, 45, MA, 46; Princeton Univ, MA, 48, PhD(geol), 49. *Prof Exp:* Res instr, Princeton Univ, 50; geologist, Direccion de Geol, Ministerio de Minas e Hidrocarburos, Venezuela, 50-52 & Union Oil Co Calif, 53-62; consult, Orgn Am States, 62-64; dep secy gen, Permanent Secretariat Cent Am Econ Integration Treaty, 64; mem res staff, 65-70, assoc dir, 70-75, DIR, CENT AM RES INST INDUST TECHNOL, 75- *Mem:* Geol Soc Am; Mineral Soc Am; Asn Petrol Geologists; Ger Geol Asn; Soc Econ Geologists. *Res:* Economic geology; regional geology of Central America and Northern South America; tectonics. *Mailing Add:* Apartado 468 Guatemala City Guatemala

DENHAM, JOSEPH MILTON, b Port Jervis, NY, Jan 21, 30; m 51; c 2. ORGANIC CHEMISTRY. *Educ:* Pa State Univ, BS, 51; Ohio Univ, MS, 56, PhD(chem), 59. *Prof Exp:* Instr math & chem, Orange County Community Col, 51-52, 54; from asst prof to assoc prof chem, 58-69, PROF CHEM, HIRAM COL, 69- *Concurrent Pos:* Vis asst prof, Ohio Univ, 60; NSF res partic, Univ Fla, 63, vis asst prof, 64; res fel, Col Pharm, Ohio State Univ, 71-72; vis prof chem, Case Western Reserve Univ, 78-81. *Mem:* Am Chem Soc; AAAS; Smithsonian Assocs; Sigma Xi. *Res:* Synthesis, organophosphorus compounds; heterocyclic; small ring compounds. *Mailing Add:* Dept of Chem Hiram Col Hiram OH 44234

DENHARD, E(LBERT) E(DWIN), JR, b Baltimore, Md, June 4, 20; m 44; c 3. MECHANICAL & METALLURGICAL ENGINEERING. *Educ:* Purdue Univ, BS, 41; Johns Hopkins Univ, MS, 57. *Prof Exp:* Inspector stainless steels, 41-43, jr combustion engr, 43-48, res engr, 48-57, SR RES ENGR STAINLESS STEELS, ARMCO STEEL CORP, 57- *Mem:* Am Soc Testing & Mat; Nat Asn Corrosion Engrs; Electrochem Soc; Am Soc Metals. *Res:* Corrosion research in stainless steels; alloy development; specifications, mechanical properties, patents and commercial development of stainless steels. *Mailing Add:* 703 Stone Barn Rd Baltimore MD 21204

DENHARDT, DAVID TILTON, b Sacramento, Calif, Feb 25, 39; m 61; c 3. MOLECULAR BIOLOGY. *Educ:* Swarthmore Col, BA, 60; Calif Inst Technol, PhD(biophys, physics), 65. *Prof Exp:* From instr to asst prof biol, Harvard Univ, 64-70; assoc prof, 70-77, PROF BIOCHEM, McGILL UNIV, 77- *Mem:* Am Microbiol Soc; Am Soc Biol Chem; Can Biochem Soc. *Res:* Mechanism of replication of bacteriophage OX174; biochemistry of the replication, repair and synthesis of deoxyribonucleic acid; structure and evolution of the cell; control of eucaryote DNA replication. *Mailing Add:* Dept of Biochem McGill Univ McIntyre Med Bldg Montreal PQ H3A 2T5 Can

DEN HARTOG, J(ACOB) P(IETER), b Ambarawa, Java, July 1901; nat US; m 26; c 2. ENGINEERING MECHANICS. *Educ:* Delft Univ Technol, EE, 24; Univ Pittsburgh, PhD(math), 29. *Hon Degrees:* DrEng, Carnegie Tech, 62; DrApplSc, Univ Ghent, 65; DrTechSc, Univ Delft, 66; ScD, Univ Salford, Eng, 70 & Univ Newcastle, Tyne, 75. *Prof Exp:* Res labs, Westinghouse Elec & Mfg Co, East Pittsburgh, 24-30 & 31-32; from asst prof to assoc prof appl mech, Harvard Univ, 32-41; prof mech eng, Mass Inst Technol, 45-69, head dept, 54-58, emer prof & sr lectr, 69-75; CONSULT ENGR, 75- *Concurrent Pos:* Lectr, Univ Pittsburgh, 28 & Harvard Univ, 31-32. *Mem:* Nat Acad Sci; hon mem Am Soc Mech Engrs; fel Am Inst Aeronaut & Astronaut; fel Brit Inst Mech Engrs; hon mem Japan Soc Mech Engrs. *Res:* Dynamics and mechanical vibration; elasticity. *Mailing Add:* 150 Barnes Hill Rd Concord MA 01742

DENHOFF, ERIC, b Brooklyn, NY, June 5, 13; m 45; c 3. MEDICINE. *Educ:* Univ Vt, BS, 34, MD, 38; Am Bd Pediat, dipl, 46. *Hon Degrees:* DSc, Brown Univ, 80. *Prof Exp:* Dir clin lab, 47-56, DIR PHYSIOL & BIOL RES, EMMA P BRADLEY HOME, 56-; MEM INST RES HEALTH & SCI, BROWN UNIV, 58- *Concurrent Pos:* Consult, Roger Williams Gen, Providence Lying-In & Bradley Hosps & Crippled Children & Adults of RI, 47; med dir, Meeting State Sch Children's Rehab, 47; lectr, Univ RI, 50-51, Col Physicians & Surgeons, Columbia Univ, 52-58, Med Sch, Syracuse Univ, 52-57, Postgrad Sem, Univ Conn, 52-53 & 58, Ohio State Univ, 55-56 & United Cerebral Palsy Sem, 56; chief pediat & exec comt staff, Miriam Hosp, 54; physician, RI Hosp, 56; clin prof pediat, Brown Univ; adj prof spec educ, RI Col. *Mem:* Fel Am Acad Cerebral Palsy (pres, 63-64); fel AMA; fel Am Acad Pediat; assoc Am Acad Neurol; assoc mem Am Psychiat Asn. *Res:* Abnormal and normal child growth and development, particularly cerebral dysfunction. *Mailing Add:* Gov Med Ctr 293 Governor St Providence RI 02912

DENHOLM, ALEC STUART, b Glasgow, Scotland, Aug 24, 29; US citizen; m; c 1. ELECTRICAL ENGINEERING. *Educ:* Univ Glasgow, BSc, 50, PhD(elec eng), 56. *Prof Exp:* Assoc res officer elec eng, Nat Res Coun Can, 54-59; sr engr, Ion Physics Corp, 59-63, dir eng & develop, 63-68, vpres, 68-69; V PRES, ENERGY SCI INC, 70-, CHIEF RES EXEC, 76- *Mem:* Am Inst Aeronaut & Astronaut; Inst Elec & Electronics Engrs; Brit Inst Elec Engrs. *Res:* Electrical discharges in vacuum and gases; development of high voltage equipment. *Mailing Add:* Energy Sci Inc 213 Burlington Rd Bedford MA 01730

DENINE, ELLIOT PAUL, b Marlboro, Mass, Sept 9, 35; m 65; c 3. TOXICOLOGY, PHARMACOLOGY. *Educ:* Memphis State Univ, BS, 59; Boston Univ, PhD(path), 71. *Prof Exp:* Lab technician toxicol, Worcester Found Exp Biol, 61-62; assoc pathologist, Worcester Mem Hosp Res Lab, 62-65; mem staff toxicol lab, Arthur D Little, Inc, 65-71; chief pathologist, Foster D Snell, Inc, 71-73; sr pharmacologist toxicol, Southern Res Inst, 73-81; CHIEF PATH-TOXICOL SECT, NORWICH-EATON PHARMACEUTS, 81- *Mem:* Soc Toxicol; Soc Pharmacol & Environ Pathologists; Am Asn Cancer Res. *Res:* Toxicological-pathological action of chemotherapeutics, industrial chemicals, nutrients and prostheses, especially potential hazard of interactions resulting from combined exposure. *Mailing Add:* RD 2 Box 48 Brookview Dr Hamilton NY 13346

DENIS, GUSTAVE, nephrology, metabolism, see previous edition

DE NISCO, STANLEY GABRIEL, b New York, NY, Sept 24, 18; m 41; c 4. NUTRITION. *Educ:* Fordham Univ, BA, 40; NY Univ, MA, 46, PhD, 61. *Prof Exp:* Chemist charge qual control, Sheffield Farms, Inc, 40-42; chemist res veg oils, Best Foods, Inc, 42-44; asst dir appl res, Stand Brands, Inc, 44-51; admin asst tech serv, Chas Pfizer & Co, Inc, 51-53; VPRES & DIR SCI DEPT, TED BATES & CO, INC, 53- *Mem:* AAAS; Am Chem Soc; Inst Food Technol; NY Acad Sci; NY Acad Med. *Res:* Biochemistry; food chemistry; food technology. *Mailing Add:* 643 Pelham Rd New Rochelle NY 10803

DENISEN, ERVIN LOREN, b Austin, Minn, Nov 10, 19; m 43; c 3. HORTICULTURE. *Educ:* Univ Minn, BS, 41; Iowa State Univ, MS, 47, PhD(hort, plant physiol), 49. *Prof Exp:* Voc agr instr high sch, Minn, 41-42; from instr to assoc prof hort, 46-65, chmn dept, 67-73, PROF HORT, IOWA STATE UNIV, 65- *Concurrent Pos:* Consult, US AID, Uruguay, 63 & Proj Unicorn, Inc; chmn small fruits sect, Nat Clonal Repository, USDA, 75-77. *Honors & Awards:* Medal of Appreciation, Univ Bologna, 74. *Mem:* Fel AAAS; Am Pomol Soc; fel Am Soc Hort Sci; Am Soc Plant Physiol; Int Soc Hort Sci. *Res:* Small fruits breeding; physiology of horticulture crops; chemical weed control; air pollution; mechanical harvesting of strawberries. *Mailing Add:* 2137 Friley Rd Ames IA 50010

DENISON, ARTHUR B, b Oakland, Calif, June 17, 36; m 60; c 3. EXPERIMENTAL PHYSICS, MOLECULAR PHYSICS. *Educ:* Univ Calif, Berkeley, AB, 59; Univ Colo, PhD(physics), 63. *Prof Exp:* From asst prof to assoc prof physics, 63-73, PROF PHYSICS, UNIV WYO, 73- *Concurrent Pos:* Vis prof, Max Planck Inst Med Res, 67, 68, & 69. *Mem:* Am Inst Physics. *Res:* Nuclear magnetic resonance, electron paramagnetic resonance and ultrasonic nuclear magnetic resonance in solids; nuclear magnetic resonance of paraffin hydrocarbons in liquid and solid state; excited state molecular physics optically modified mass spectra; muon physics. *Mailing Add:* Dept of Physics & Astron Univ of Wyo Laramie WY 82071

DENISON, FRANK WILLIS, JR, b Temple, Tex, Jan 5, 21; m 48; c 4. MICROBIOLOGY. *Educ:* Univ Tex, PhD(bact), 52. *Prof Exp:* Sr res microbiologist, Abbott Labs, 52-55, group leader microbiol, 55-63, asst mgr microbiol physiol, 63-64, mgr microbial chem, 64-74, mgr admin & sci servs, 75-76, assoc dir licensing, 76-79, dir licensing, 79; TECHNOL DEVELOP LIAISON MGR, UPJOHN CO, 80- *Concurrent Pos:* Lectr, Lake Forest Col, 58-61. *Mem:* Am Chem Soc. *Res:* Antibiotics and submerged fermentations with special reference to pilot plant equipment; chemistry of microbial products and intermediary metabolism. *Mailing Add:* 9809-88-55 Upjohn Co 7000 Portage Rd Kalamazoo MI 49001

DENISON, JACK THOMAS, b Gainesville, Fla, Mar 8, 26; m 78; c 1. PHYSICAL CHEMISTRY. *Educ:* Univ Calif, Los Angeles, BS, 48, PhD(chem), 51. *Prof Exp:* Res chemist, 51-57, from res supvr to sr res supvr, 57-70, RES ASSOC, PLASTICS DEPT, E I DU PONT DE NEMOURS & CO, INC, 70- *Mem:* Am Chem Soc; Sigma Xi; Soc Plastics Engrs. *Res:* Thermodynamics of electrolytes in nonaqueous media; high polymers; high temperature chemistry; digital computation; process research in low and high pressure polyethylene synthesis. *Mailing Add:* 2300 Sunset Orange TX 77630

DENISON, JOHN SCOTT, b Waco, Tex, June 18, 18; m 41; c 2. ELECTRICAL ENGINEERING. *Educ:* NMex State Univ, BSEE, 48; Agr & Mech Col, Tex, MSEE, 49. *Prof Exp:* From instr to assoc prof 49-67, acting head dept elec eng, 66-67, dir elec power inst, 67-76, PROF ELEC ENG, TEX A&M UNIV, 67- *Concurrent Pos:* Consult, 51- *Mem:* Inst Elec & Electronics Engrs. *Res:* Electrical transmission and distribution. *Mailing Add:* Dept of Elec Eng Tex A&M Univ College Station TX 77843

DENISON, ROBERT HOWLAND, b Somerville, Mass, Nov 9, 11; m 40, 65; c 3. VERTEBRATE PALEONTOLOGY. *Educ:* Harvard Univ, AB, 33; Columbia Univ, AM, 34, PhD(vert paleont), 38. *Prof Exp:* Asst cur mus, Dartmouth Col, 37-47, instr zool, 38-43, asst prof, 43-47; paleontologist, Univ Calif African Exped, 47-48; cur fossil fishes, Field Mus Natural Hist, 48-70, res assoc, 71-; ASSOC, MUS COMP ZOOL, HARVARD UNIV, 73- *Concurrent Pos:* Guggenheim fel, Europe, 53-54; lectr, Univ Chicago, 65- *Honors & Awards:* Morrison Prize, 37. *Mem:* AAAS; Soc Vert Paleont (secy-treas, 59-60, pres, 62-63); Paleont Soc. *Res:* Fossil fishes; early fossil vertebrates. *Mailing Add:* Todd Pond Rd Lincoln MA 01773

DENISON, RODGER ESPY, b Ft Worth, Tex, Nov 11, 32; m 57; c 2. GEOLOGY. *Educ:* Univ Okla, BS, 54, MS, 58; Univ Tex, PhD, 66. *Prof Exp:* Geologist, Okla Geol Surv, 58-61 & Crustal Studies Lab, Tex, 62-64; geologist, Mobil Oil Corp, 64-68, sr res geologist, Mobil Res & Develop Corp, Field Res Lab, 68-74; CONSULT GEOLOGIST, 74- *Mem:* Am Asn Petrol Geologists; Geol Soc Am. *Res:* Petrology and geochronology of basement rocks in southern midcontinent and their influence on later geologic history. *Mailing Add:* One Energy Sq Dallas TX 75206

DENISON, WILLIAM CLARK, b Rochester, NY, June 1, 28; m 48; c 4. BOTANY. *Educ:* Oberlin Col, AB, 50, AM, 52; Cornell Univ, PhD(mycol), 56. *Prof Exp:* Asst prof bot, Swarthmore Col, 55-58; vis asst prof, Univ NC, 58-59; asst prof biol, Swarthmore Col, 59-66; ASSOC PROF BOT & CUR MYCOL HERBARIUM, ORE STATE UNIV, 66- *Mem:* Mycol Soc Am; Int Lichenological Asn. *Res:* Mycology, especially Pezizales, lichens; forest ecology. *Mailing Add:* Dept of Bot Ore State Univ Corvallis OR 97331

DENK, RONALD H, b Buffalo, NY, Sept 17, 37. ORGANIC CHEMISTRY, LASERS. *Educ:* Canisius Col, BS, 59; Villanova Univ, MS, 61; Va Polytech Inst, PhD(chem), 67. *Prof Exp:* Chemist, Texaco, Inc, 66-67, sr chemist, 67-70; asst prof chem, Genesee Community Col, 70-79; chem safety officer, Roswell Park Mem Inst, 79-81; RES MGR, NUCLEAR SCI & TECHNOL FACIL, STATE UNIV NY BUFFALO, 82- *Concurrent Pos:* Coordr lasers & holographics, Buffalo Mus Natural Sci, 75-; founder & current pres, Western NY Holographers Asn. *Mem:* Am Chem Soc; Sigma Xi; Am Inst Chemists. *Res:* Synthesis of potential anticarcinogenic agents; mechanism of the thermal decomposition of 1-bromo-2-(1-naphthyl) naphthyl carbinol and related diarylcarbinols; Ziegler-Natta copolymerization of alpha-olefins. *Mailing Add:* 100 Colden Ct Cheektowaga NY 14225

DENKER, MARTIN WILLIAM, b Paterson, NJ, June 20, 43; m 69; c 2. PSYCHIATRY. *Educ:* Johns Hopkins Univ, BA, 65, MD, 68. *Prof Exp:* Asst prof psychiat, 72-75, actg chmn, 73-75, ASSOC PROF PSYCHIAT, COL MED, UNIV S FLA, 75- *Concurrent Pos:* Dir, Lab for Appl Math in Behav Systs, 75- & prog dir, Evaluation of Mental Health Care Delivery Systs Proj, Col Med, Univ S Fla, 76- *Mem:* AAAS; Soc Gen Systs Res; Nat Coun Family Rels. *Res:* Family sociology research-mathematical models and computer simulation; clinical family therapy; mental health services delivery research. *Mailing Add:* Dept of Psychiat Col of Med 12901 N 30th St Tampa FL 33612

DENKO, CHARLES W, b Cleveland, Ohio, Aug 12, 16; m 50; c 3. BIOCHEMISTRY. *Educ:* Geneva Col, BS, 38; Pa State Col, MS, 39, PhD(physiol chem), 43; Johns Hopkins Univ, MD, 51; Am Bd Nutrit, dipl, 52. *Prof Exp:* Asst physiol chem, Pa State Univ, 40-43; instr biochem, Sch Med, Univ WVa, 43; res chemist, Res Lab, SMA Corp, Ohio, 44-45; prof chem, Geneva Col, 48; intern, Univ Ill, 51-52; resident, Dept Med, Univ Chicago, 52-53, res assoc, 55-56; from instr to asst prof internal med, Med Sch, Univ Mich, 56-59; asst prof med, Ohio State Univ, 59-66, with div rheumatic dis, Univ Hosp, 59-66, res assoc, Res Ctr, 66-68; DIR RES, FAIRVIEW GEN HOSP, 68-; asst prof, 70-77, ASSOC PROF CLIN MED, SCH MED, CASE WESTERN RESERVE UNIV, 77- *Concurrent Pos:* Fel, Univ Chicago, 53-55; sr investr, Arthritis & Rheumatism Found; vis res fel, Australian Nat Univ, 74-75. *Honors & Awards:* Distinguished Serv Award, Geneva Col, 69. *Mem:* AAAS; Am Chem Soc; Am Rheumatism Asn; Am Soc Clin Pharmacol & Therapeut; NY Acad Sci. *Res:* Synthesis and biochemical effects of organic gold compounds; nutritional biochemistry; metabolism of connective tissue; clinical rheumatology; experimental arthritis pharmacology; clinical pharmacology; prostaglandin pharmacology; endorphine physiology. *Mailing Add:* Scott Res Lab Fairview Gen Hosp Cleveland OH 44111

DENKO, JOHN V, b Ellwood City, Pa, July 22, 23; m 47; c 3. PATHOLOGY. *Educ:* Univ Chicago, BS, 46, MD, 47; Am Bd Path, dipl, 52. *Prof Exp:* From intern to resident path, St Luke's Hosp, Chicago, 47-49; instr, Col Med, Univ Ill, 50-52; clin instr path, Univ Wash, 52-54; PATHOLOGIST & DIR LABS, NORTH WEST TEX HOSP, 54-; ASSOC PROF PATH, SCH MED, TEX TECH UNIV, 73-, ASSOC CLIN PROF, 74- *Concurrent Pos:* Dep chief path, USPHS Hosp, Seattle, 52-54; consult, Vet Admin Hosp, Amarillo, 54-; ed med bull, Panhandle Dist Med Soc, 58-; pres, Amarillo Found Health & Sci Educ, Inc, 67-; counr, Tex Med Asn, 72-; mem bd dirs, Health Systems Agency, Tex Dist One, 76- *Mem:* Fel Am Soc Clin Path; fel Col Am Path; AMA; Soc Nuclear Med. *Res:* Clinical pathology and surgical diagnostic pathology. *Mailing Add:* 2507 Harmony Amarillo TX 79106

DENLINGER, DAVID LANDIS, b Lancaster, Pa, Nov 20, 45; m 67; c 2. INSECT PHYSIOLOGY. *Educ:* Pa State Univ, BS, 67; Univ Ill, PhD(entom), 71. *Prof Exp:* Netherlands Ministry Agr & Fisheries res fel entom, Agr Univ, Wageningen, 71-72; NIH res scientist entom, Int Centre Insect Physiol & Ecol, Nairobi, Kenya, 72-74; res fel biol, Harvard Univ, 74-76; ASST PROF ENTOM, OHIO STATE UNIV, 76- *Mem:* Entom Soc Am. *Res:* Environmental and physiological mechanisms regulating insect dormancy and reproduction; tropical biology. *Mailing Add:* Dept of Entom Harvard Univ 16 Divinity Ave Columbus OH 02138

DENMAN, EUGENE D(ALE), b Farmington, Mo, Mar 15, 28; m 52; c 2. ELECTRICAL ENGINEERING, SYSTEMS ENGINEERING. *Educ:* Washington Univ, St Louis, BS, 51; Vanderbilt Univ, MS, 55; Univ Va, DSc, 63. *Prof Exp:* Engr electronic equip, Magnavox Co, 51-52; engr, Sperry Gyroscope Co, 54-56; sr engr, Midwest Res Inst, 56-60; sr physicist, res labs eng sci, Univ Va, 60-63; asst prof elec eng, Vanderbilt Univ, 63-69; PROF ELEC & SYSTS ENG, UNIV HOUSTON, 69- *Concurrent Pos:* Consult, Lockheed Electronics Co, 74-78. *Mem:* Inst Elec & Electronics Engrs. *Res:* Electromagnetic propagation, microwave tubes; radiological systems; system engineering; numerical methods in engineering; mathematical modeling. *Mailing Add:* Cullen Col of Eng Univ of Houston Houston TX 77004

DENMAN, HARRY HARROUN, b Riverside, NJ, Jan 7, 25; m 50; c 4. THEORETICAL MECHANICS, MATHEMATICAL PHYSICS. *Educ:* Drexel Inst Technol, BSEE, 48; Univ Cincinnati, MS, 50, PhD(theoret physics), 52. *Prof Exp:* Mem res staff, Digital Comput Lab, Mass Inst Technol, 52-54; from asst prof to assoc prof physics, 54-70, PROF PHYSICS, WAYNE STATE UNIV, 71- *Concurrent Pos:* Consult, Avco Corp, 56, Gen Elec Co, 59 & Ford Motor Co, 66-; ed, J Indust Math Soc, 66-69. *Mem:* Am Phys Soc; Sigma Xi. *Res:* Applied mathematics; group theory; nonlinear problems. *Mailing Add:* Dept of Physics Wayne State Univ Detroit MI 48202

DENMARK, HAROLD ANDERSON, b Lamont, Fla, July 3, 21; m 47; c 2. ACAROLOGY. *Educ:* Univ Fla, BSA, 52, MS, 53. *Prof Exp:* Interim instr, Univ Fla, 53; entomologist, 54-55, actg chief entomologist, 56-58, CHIEF ENTOM, FLA DEPT AGR & CONSUMER SERV, 58- *Mem:* Entom Soc Am. *Res:* Phytoseiidae; monographs and description of new species of phytoseiid mites in relation to ecological and biological control projects. *Mailing Add:* 10930 NW 12th Pl Gainesville FL 32601

DENN, MORTON M(ACE), b Passaic, NJ, July 7, 39; m 62; c 3. CHEMICAL ENGINEERING. *Educ:* Princeton Univ, BSE, 61; Univ Minn, PhD(chem eng), 64. *Prof Exp:* Fel chem eng, Univ Del, 64-65, asst prof chem eng & comput sci, 65-68, from assoc prof to prof chem eng, 68-77, Allan P Colburn prof chem, 77-81; PROF CHEM ENG, UNIV CALIF, BERKELEY, 81- *Concurrent Pos:* Guggenheim fel, 71-72; Fulbright lectr & Harry Pierce prof technol, Israel, 79-80; vis Chevron energy prof, Calif Inst Technol, 80; vis lectr chem eng, Mass Inst Technol, 78-; adj prof chem eng, Univ Del, 81- *Honors & Awards:* Prof Progress Award in Chem Eng, Am Inst Chem Engrs, 77; William H Lacey lectr, Calif Inst Technol, 79; P C Reilly lectr, Univ Notre Dame, 80. *Mem:* Soc Rheol; Am Inst Chem Engrs; Am Chem Soc; Brit Soc Rheol. *Res:* Polymer processing; rheology; non-Newtonian fluid mechanics; process simulation; stability and control; coal gasification. *Mailing Add:* Dept Chem Eng Univ Calif Berkeley CA 94720

DENNEAU, MONTY MONTAGUE, b Newark, NJ, Dec 24, 48; m 70. COMPUTERS. *Educ:* Mass Inst Technol, BS, 70; Boston Univ, MA, 72; Univ Ill, Urbana-Champaign, MS & PhD(math), 78. *Prof Exp:* MEM RES STAFF COMPUTER SCI, IBM WATSON RES CTR, 78- *Res:* High performance computer architecture and design. *Mailing Add:* Thomas J Watson Res Ctr IBM Box 218 Yorktown NY 10598

DENNEN, DAVID W, b Clarks Summit, Pa, Mar 20, 32; m 54; c 3. BIOCHEMISTRY, MICROBIOLOGY. *Educ:* Mass Inst Technol, BS, 54; Ind Univ, MS, 64, PhD(microbiol), 66. *Prof Exp:* Assoc phys chemist, Res Labs, Eli Lilly & Co, 54-56, phys chemist, 59-64, sr microbiologist, Analyt Develop, Greenfield Labs, 66-67 & Antibiotic Develop Div, 67-69, mgr, 69-71, dir 71-73; mgr dir, Lilly Pharmachemie GmbH, 73-75; dir, Antibiotic Tech Serv, Antibiotic Mfg & Develop Div, 75-79, MANAGING DIR, LILLY RES CTR, ELI LILLY & CO, ENGLAND, 80- *Mem:* Am Chem Soc; Am Soc Microbiol. *Res:* Reaction kinetics; control mechanisms in cellular systems; enzyme regulation during morphogenesis; biosynthesis of antibiotics. *Mailing Add:* Eli Lilly & Co PO Box 618 Indianapolis IN 46206

DENNEN, WILLIAM HENRY, b Gloucester, Mass, Apr 8, 20; m 44; c 3. GEOLOGY, GEOCHEMISTRY. *Educ:* Mass Inst Technol, SB, 42, PhD(geol), 49. *Prof Exp:* From instr to assoc prof geol, Mass Inst Technol, 49-67; chmn dept, 67-74, actg dean, Grad Sch & coordr res, 70-72, chmn dept, 67-74 & 77-81, PROF GEOL, UNIV KY, 67- *Mem:* Geol Soc Am; Geochem Soc. *Res:* Applications of spectrography to petrological problems; mineral exploration; engineering geology. *Mailing Add:* Dept of Geol Univ of Ky Lexington KY 40506

DENNERT, GUNTHER, b Hettstedt, Ger, Oct 7, 39; m 68; c 2. IMMUNOLOGY, MOLECULAR BIOLOGY. *Educ:* Univ Koln, Ger, PhD(genetics, biochem & physiol), 67. *Prof Exp:* Asst genetics, Max Planck Inst Biol, Tubingen, Ger, 66-68; fel biochem, Univ Uppsala, Sweden, 68-69; fel immunol, Univ Koln, Ger, 69-70; res assoc immunol, 70-73, ASSOC RES PROF IMMUNOL, SALK INST, 78- *Concurrent Pos:* Fel, Deutsche Forschungsgemeinschaft, 68-69; Jane Coffins Child Mem Fund, 70-72 & Edna McConnel Clark Found, 72-73; Nat Cancer Inst grant, 73- *Mem:* Am Asn Immunologists; Ger Asn Biochemists. *Res:* Cellular immunology; tumor immunology; lymphocytes: functional heterogeneity, interactions, specificity, antigen receptors; immunostimulatory drugs. *Mailing Add:* Salk Inst 10010 N Torrey Pines Rd La Jolla CA 92037

DENNETT, ROBERT KINGSLEY, b Honolulu, Hawaii, Oct 18, 21; m 47; c 6. GENETICS. *Educ:* Cornell Univ, BS, 48; Univ Hawaii, MS, 50; Pa State Univ, PhD(genetics), 52. *Prof Exp:* Asst olericulturist, Univ Hawaii, 48-50; asst, Pa State Univ, 50-52; hybridizer, Bodger Seeds Ltd, 53-59; mgr, Alpha Seeds, 59-62; agronomist, Hunt Foods & Indust, Inc, 62-68; plant breeder, Peto Seed Co, Inc, 68-72; PLANT BREEDER, GOLDSMITH SEEDS INC, 72- *Mem:* Am Soc Hort Sci; Am Genetic Asn; Am Soc Agron; Soil Sci Soc Am. *Res:* Genetics and breeding in tomato, zinnia and petunia plants. *Mailing Add:* Rte 1 Box 2145 Davis CA 95616

DENNEY, DONALD BEREND, b Seattle, Wash, Apr 3, 27; m 56. ORGANIC CHEMISTRY. *Educ:* Univ Wash, BS, 49; Univ Calif, PhD(chem), 52. *Prof Exp:* Asst, Univ Calif, 49-51; res chemist, E I du Pont de Nemours & Co, 52-53; fel Hickrill Chem Res Found, 53-54; instr chem, Yale Univ, 54-55; from asst prof to assoc prof, 55-62, PROF CHEM, RUTGERS UNIV, 62- *Concurrent Pos:* Fel, A P Sloan Found, 55-59; mem NIH med panel B, 65-67, 75. *Mem:* Am Chem Soc. *Res:* Organic reaction mechanisms; organo phosphorus compounds; hypervalent molecules; polymeric adsorbents. *Mailing Add:* Sch of Chem Rutgers Univ New Brunswick NJ 08903

DENNEY, DONALD DUANE, b Boone, Iowa, Nov 30, 30; m; c 3. PSYCHIATRY. *Educ:* Willamette Univ, BA, 53; Univ Ore, MS & MD, 57. *Prof Exp:* Resident psychiat, 59-62, from instr to assoc prof, 63-74, resident internal med, 68-70, PROF PSYCHIAT, SCH MED, UNIV ORE, 74- *Prof Exp:* USPHS career teachers' award, 62-64, career develop award, 64-68. *Mem:* Am Psychiat Asn. *Res:* Neurophysiology; psychiatric consultation in internal medicine. *Mailing Add:* Dept of Psychiat Univ of Ore Med Sch Portland OR 97201

DENNEY, DONALD JOHN, b Philadelphia, Pa, Dec 7, 20; m 56; c 3. PHYSICAL CHEMISTRY. *Educ:* Univ Pa, BS, 50; Brown Univ, PhD(chem), 54. *Prof Exp:* Res chemist, E I du Pont de Nemours & Co, 54-55; res assoc, Brown Univ, 55-57; from asst prof to assoc prof chem, 57-68, PROF CHEM, HAMILTON COL, 68- *Mem:* Am Chem Soc; Am Phys Soc. *Res:* Dielectric and flow properties of liquids. *Mailing Add:* Dept of Chem Hamilton Col Clinton NY 13323

DENNEY, JOSEPH M(YERS), b Auburn, Wash, May 25, 27; m 50; c 3. PHYSICS, METALLURGY. *Educ:* Calif Inst Technol, BS, 51, MS, 52, PhD(metall, physics), 54. *Prof Exp:* Res engr solid state physics, Atomics Int, 52-54; res assoc phys metall, Gen Elec Res Lab, 55-57; res fel, Calif Inst Technol, 57-59; dir solid state physics lab, TRW Space Technol Labs, 59-69; PRES, DIGITAL DEVELOP CORP, SAN DIEGO, 69- *Concurrent Pos:* Head radiation effects, Hughes Res Labs, 58-59; consult, Nat Acad Sci, Washington, DC, 70. *Mem:* Assoc fel Am Inst Aeronaut & Astronaut; sr mem Inst Elec & Electronics Engrs; Sigma Xi. *Res:* Radiation effects in solids; alloy theory; physics of semiconductors; space environment; satellite and spacecraft design and development; electronics. *Mailing Add:* 408 Via Almar Palos Verdes Estates CA 90274

DENNEY, RICHARD MAX, b Portland, Ore, Jan 28, 46; c 2. HUMAN GENETICS, IMMUNOCHEMISTRY. *Educ:* Reed Col, Ore, BA, 68; Stanford Univ, Calif, PhD, 73. *Prof Exp:* Fel, Oxford Univ, Eng, 73-75; fel, Yale Univ, 75-77; ASST PROF HUMAN GENETICS, DEPT HUMAN BIOL CHEM & GENETICS, UNIV TEX MED BR, GALVESTON, 77- *Mem:* AAAS; Am Soc Cell Biol. *Res:* Immunochemistry of human monoamine oxidase and of the human secretory component of secretory immunoglobulin A. *Mailing Add:* Dept Human Biol Chem & Genetics Univ Tex 408 Gail Borden Galveston TX 77550

DENNING, DOROTHY ELIZABETH ROBLING, b Grant Rapids, Mich, Aug 12, 45; m 74. CRYPTOGRAPHY, DATA SECURITY. *Educ:* Univ Mich, AB, 67, AM, 69; Purdue Univ, PhD(comput sci), 75. *Prof Exp:* asst prof, 75-80, ASSOC PROF COMPUT SCI, PURDUE UNIV, WEST LAFAYETTE, 80- *Mem:* Asn Comput Mach; Inst Elec & Electronics Engrs; Sigma Xi. *Res:* Cryptography and related protection mechanisms that control access to and the dissemination of information in computer systems. *Mailing Add:* Dept of Comput Sci Purdue Univ West Lafayette IN 47907

DENNING, GEORGE SMITH, JR, b Chicago, Ill, Dec 4, 31; m 55; c 5. BIO-ORGANIC CHEMISTRY. *Educ:* Washington & Lee Univ, BS, 54; Cornell Univ, PhD(org chem), 60. *Prof Exp:* From res assoc to instr biochem, Med Col, Cornell Univ, 60-62; res assoc peptide chem, 62-71, chief, Amino Acid Chem Sect, 71-80, CHIEF, ORG CHEM SECT, NORWICH-EATON PHARMACEUT, 80- *Concurrent Pos:* Scholar, Dept Biol Chem, Sch Med, Univ Calif, Los Angeles, 69-70. *Mem:* AAAS; Am Chem Soc; The Chem Soc. *Res:* Chemistry of amino acids and peptides; organic synthesis; method development for drug analysis. *Mailing Add:* 158 N Broad St Norwich NY 13815

DENNING, JACK, biology, zoology, see previous edition

DENNING, PETER JAMES, b New York, NY, Jan 6, 42; m 64; c 2. ELECTRICAL ENGINEERING, COMPUTER SCIENCE. *Educ:* Manhattan Col, BEE, 64; Mass Inst Technol, MS, 65, PhD(elec eng), 68. *Prof Exp:* Asst prof elec eng, Princeton Univ, 68-72; assoc prof comput sci, 72-75, PROF COMPUT SCI, PURDUE UNIV, 75-, DEPT HEAD, 79- *Concurrent Pos:* Ed, Elsevier Ser on Operating & Prog Systs, 73-; assoc ed, ACTA Informatica, 73-; lectr, Technol Transfer, Inc, 76-; ed-in-chief, Comput Survs, J Asn Comput Mach, 77-79. *Honors & Awards:* Best paper award, Asn Comput Mach, 70 & Am Fedn Info Processing Socs, 72. *Mem:* NY Acad Sci; sr mem Inst Elec & Electronics Engrs; Asn Comput Mach (vpres, 78-80). *Res:* Computer system organization; analysis of queueing phenomena; parrallel computation; data security and reliabltiy. *Mailing Add:* Dept of Comput Sci Purdue Univ West Lafayette IN 47907

DENNING, RICHARD SMITH, b Plainfield, NJ, Apr 20, 40; m 63; c 2. NUCLEAR ENGINEERING. *Educ:* Cornell Univ, BS, 63; Univ Fla, MSE, 65, PhD(nuclear eng), 67. *Prof Exp:* Researcher nuclear eng, 67-75, assoc sect mgr, 75-77, res leader, 77-81, SR RES LEADER, NUCLEAR ENG, COLUMBUS LABS, BATTELLE MEM INST, 81- *Mem:* AAAS; Am Nuclear Soc. *Res:* Reactor safety and risk research including core meltdown behavior, reactor kinetics, transient thermal-hydraulics; criticality and shielding analysis. *Mailing Add:* Columbus Labs Battelle Mem Inst 505 King Ave Columbus OH 43201

DENNIS, CLARENCE, b St Paul, Minn, June 16, 09; m 39, 77; c 4. SURGERY, PHYSIOLOGY. *Educ:* Harvard Univ, BS, 31; Johns Hopkins Univ, MD, 35; Univ Minn, MS, 38, PhD(surg, physiol), 40. *Prof Exp:* Instr physiol, Univ Minn, 38-39, from instr to prof surg, 40-47; prof surg, State Univ NY Downstate Med Ctr, 51-72, chmn dept, 52-72; spec asst technol, Off Dir, Nat Heart & Lung Inst, 72-74; PROF SURG, STATE UNIV NY STONY BROOK, 74- *Concurrent Pos:* Dir surg, Univ Div, Kings County Hosp, 51-59, surgeon-in-chief, 59-72, Univ Hosp, 67-72; mem, Surg Study Sect, NIH, 62-66; mem bd dirs, Nat Soc Med Res, 67-, pres, 77-; pres US chap, Int Soc Surg, 74-77; clin prof surg, Georgetown Univ Sch Med, 72-75, prof lectr, 75-; assoc chief staff res & develop, Vet Hosp, Northport, NY, 75- *Mem:* Soc Univ Surgeons (secy, 50-52); Am Surg Asn (vpres, 71-72); Soc Clin Surg; Soc Vascular Surg (pres, 65-66); Am Soc Artificial Internal Organs (past pres). *Res:* Mechanical support in acute heart failure; artificial heart; gastrointestinal physiology. *Mailing Add:* Dept of Surg State Univ NY Stony Brook NY 11794

DENNIS, CLIFFORD JOHN, entomology, see previous edition

DENNIS, DAVID THOMAS, b Preston, Eng, Nov 2, 36; m 60; c 2. PLANT BIOCHEMISTRY, PLANT PHYSIOLOGY. *Educ:* Univ Leeds, BSc, 59, PhD(biophys), 62. *Prof Exp:* Fel, Biosci Div, Nat Res Coun Can, 62-63; fel chem, Univ Calif, Los Angeles, 63-65; scientist, Unilever Res Inst, Colworth House, Eng, 65-68; assoc prof, 68-76, PROF PLANT PHYSIOL, QUEEN'S UNIV, ONT, 76- *Mem:* Am Chem Soc; Can Biochem Soc; Can Soc Plant Physiol; Am Soc Plant Physiologists; Am Soc Biol Chemists. *Res:* Regulation of metabolism in plants; extraction, purification and kinetics of plant enzymes; isoenzymes and cell compartments in plants. *Mailing Add:* Dept of Biol Queen's Univ Kingston ON K7L 3N6 Can

DENNIS, DON, b Baltimore, Md, Feb 22, 30; m 49; c 4. BIOCHEMISTRY. *Educ:* Univ Md, BS, 52; Brandeis Univ, PhD(biochem), 59. *Prof Exp:* Biologist pharmacol, Nat Cancer Inst, 52-55; NIH fel & biochemist org chem, Harvard Univ, 59-61; asst prof, 61-70, ASSOC PROF CHEM, UNIV DEL, 70- *Mem:* Fedn Am Socs Exp Biol. *Res:* Enzymology; mechanism of action of enzymes. *Mailing Add:* Dept of Chem Univ of Del Newark DE 19711

DENNIS, EDWARD A, b Chicago, Ill, Aug 10, 41; m 69; c 3. BIOCHEMISTRY, PHYSICAL ORGANIC CHEMISTRY. *Educ:* Yale Univ, BA, 63; Harvard Univ, MA, 65, PhD(chem), 68. *Prof Exp:* NIH res fel, Harvard Med Sch, 67-69; asst prof chem, 70-75, assoc prof, 75-81, PROF CHEM, UNIV CALIF, SAN DIEGO, 81- *Mem:* Am Soc Biol Chemists; Biophys Soc; NY Acad Sci; Am Chem Soc; Sigma Xi. *Res:* Detailed mechanism of enzyme catalysis; nuclear magnetic resonance studies of phospholipids and membrane structure; enzymes of phospholipid biosynthesis; phospholipid biosynthesis; mechanism of organo-phosphorus reactions and phosphate ester hydrolysis, pseudo-rotation. *Mailing Add:* Dept of Chem Univ of Calif at San Diego La Jolla CA 92093

DENNIS, EMERY WESTERVELT, b Oklahoma City, Okla, Dec 19, 05; m 31; c 2. BACTERIOLOGY, PARASITOLOGY. *Educ:* Oklahoma City Univ, AB, 27; Univ Calif, AM, 29, PhD(protozool, bact), 31. *Prof Exp:* Assoc, Univ Calif, Los Angeles, 30-31; adj prof bact, Sch Med, Am Univ Beirut, 31-35, from assoc prof to prof, 35-45, chmn depts bact & parasitol, 31-46; assoc dir biol res, 46-50, dir biol div, 50-71, CONSULT, STERLING-WINTHROP RES INST, 71- *Concurrent Pos:* Rockefeller Found fel, Harvard Med Sch, 34-35. *Honors & Awards:* Medaille d'Honneur Merite Libanaise, 43. *Mem:* Soc Exp Biol & Med; Am Soc Trop Med & Hyg; Am Soc Microbiol; Am Asn Immunol; Fedn Am Socs Exp Biol. *Res:* Piroplasmosis; life cycle of Babesia; bacterial toxins in blood dyscrasias; immunization against echinococcus; mechanism of invasion of streptococci; typhoid toxin and leukocidin; rickettsioses; malaria; tuberculosis; amebiasis; schistosomiasis. *Mailing Add:* Sterling-Winthrop Inst Rensselaer NY 12144

DENNIS, EMMET ADOLPHUS, b Bassa, Liberia, June 3, 39; m 63; c 2. PARASITOLOGY. *Educ:* Cuttington Col, Liberia, BS, 61; Ind Univ, Bloomington, MA, 65; Univ Conn, PhD(parasitol), 67. *Prof Exp:* Chmn div sci & math, Cuttington Col, Liberia, 67-69; asst prof, 69-74, ASSOC PROF ZOOL, RUTGERS UNIV, NEW BRUNSWICK, 74- *Concurrent Pos:* Assoc investr, NIH Training Grant, 70-74; dir, Liberian Inst Biomed Res, Liberia, 75- *Mem:* Am Soc Parasitologists; Sigma Xi. *Res:* Pathogenesis in host-trematode interactions with particular reference to nutritional balance or imbalance and cellular resistance. *Mailing Add:* Dept of Zool Rutgers Univ New Brunswick NJ 08903

DENNIS, FRANK GEORGE, JR, b Lyons, NY, Apr 12, 32; m 54. POMOLOGY, PLANT PHYSIOLOGY. *Educ:* Cornell Univ, BS, 55, PhD(pomol), 61. *Prof Exp:* NSF fel, 61-62; from asst prof to assoc prof pomol, NY State Agr Exp Sta, Cornell Univ, 62-68; assoc prof, Dept Hort, 68-72, PROF, DEPT HORT, MICH STATE UNIV, 72- *Concurrent Pos:* Vis prof, Univ Bristol, 74-75. *Mem:* Fel Am Soc Hort Sci; Sigma Xi; Am Soc Hort Sci; Am Soc Plant Physiol. *Res:* Fruit set and development; dormancy; flowering; plant growth substances; cold hardiness. *Mailing Add:* Dept of Hort Mich State Univ East Lansing MI 48824

DENNIS, JACK BONNELL, b Elizabeth, NJ, Oct 13, 31; m 56; c 1. COMPUTER SCIENCE. *Educ:* Mass Inst Technol, SB & SM, 54, ScD(elec eng), 58. *Prof Exp:* Asst, 54-58, from instr to assoc prof, 58-69, PROF ELEC ENG, MASS INST TECHNOL, 69- *Mem:* Inst Elec & Electronics Engrs; Asn Comput Mach. *Res:* Design and programming problems in general purpose multiprogrammed computation systems. *Mailing Add:* Dept of Elec Eng Mass Inst of Technol Cambridge MA 02139

DENNIS, JOE, b Sherman, Tex, Dec 5, ll; m 35; c 3. BIOCHEMISTRY. *Educ:* Austin Col, AB, 33; Univ Tex, AM, 37, PhD(biol chem), 42. *Hon Degrees:* DSc, Austin Col, 65. *Prof Exp:* Tutor biol chem, Sch Med, Univ Tex, 34-36, instr, 36-38; from instr to assoc prof chem, 38-47, head dept, 50-69, prof, 47-76, EMER PROF CHEM, TEX TECH UNIV, 76- *Mem:* AAAS; Am Chem Soc; Am Inst Chemists. *Res:* Protein denaturation; blood potassium and calcium. *Mailing Add:* Dept of Chem Tex Tech Univ Lubbock TX 79409

DENNIS, JOHN EMORY, JR, b Coral Gables, Fla, Sept 24, 39; m 60; c 1. MATHEMATICS. *Educ:* Univ Miami, BS, 62, MS, 64; Univ Utah, PhD(math), 66. *Prof Exp:* Asst prof math, Univ Utah, 66-68; from asst prof to prof comput sci, Col Eng, Cornell Univ, 68-79; PROF MATH SCI, RICE UNIV, 79- *Mem:* Am Math Soc; Soc Indust & Appl Math; Asn Comput Mach; Math Prog Soc. *Res:* Numerical analysis. *Mailing Add:* Dept Math/Sci Rice Univ Houston TX 77001

DENNIS, JOHN GORDON, b Berlin, Ger, June 28, 20; m 66; c 2. STRUCTURAL GEOLOGY, TECTONICS. *Educ:* Univ London, BSc, 48; Columbia Univ, AM, 56, PhD(geol), 57. *Prof Exp:* Geologist, Mines Develop Syndicate, Nigeria, 48-49; mining geologist, SW Africa Co, 50-52; consult, 52-53; asst geol, Columbia Univ, 53-56; asst prof, Tex Tech, 56-62; from asst prof to assoc prof, 62-71, PROF GEOL, CALIF STATE UNIV, LONG BEACH, 71- *Concurrent Pos:* Geologist, Vt Geol Surv, 54-59; NSF grant, 62-65; ed, NAm Neues Jahrbuch Geol & Paleont. *Mem:* Geol Soc Am; Am Geophys Union; Am Asn Petrol Geologists; Geol Soc London. *Res:* Structural control of ore deposits; evolution of orogenic belts; rock cleavage. *Mailing Add:* Dept of Geol Sci Calif State Univ Long Beach CA 90840

DENNIS, KENT SEDDENS, b New Eagle, Pa, June 25, 28. PHYSICAL CHEMISTRY. *Educ:* Grove City Col, BS, 50; Western Reserve Univ, MS, 53, PhD(phys chem), 54. *Prof Exp:* Res assoc, Western Reserve Univ, 51-54; phys chemist, 54-62, proj leader, 62-65, sr res chemist, 65-73, res specialist, 73, sr res specialist, 73-81, RES ASSOC, DOW CHEM CO, 81- *Mem:* Am Chem Soc; Sigma Xi; fel Am Inst Chemists; NY Acad Sci. *Res:* Polymer chemistry; anionic polymerization; polymer characterization; new polymer development; polymer flammability; block ploymers. *Mailing Add:* 5800 Highland Dr Midland MI 48640

DENNIS, MARTHA GREENBERG, b New Haven, Conn, Dec 17, 42; m 69; c 1. COMPUTER SCIENCE. *Educ:* Smith Col, BA, 64; Harvard Univ, MS, 68, PhD(appl math), 71. *Prof Exp:* Sr mem tech staff, Comput Sci Corp, San Diego, Calif, 70-72; sr systs analyst, Systs, Sci & Software, La Jolla, 72-74; sr systs analyst, Computervision Corp, San Diego, 74-76; SR SCIENTIST, LINKABIT CORP, SAN DIEGO, 76- *Mem:* Sigma Xi; Asn Comput Mach; Inst Elec & Electronics Engrs. *Res:* Multi-task minicomputer systems; computer indexing methods for chemical and biochemical literature. *Mailing Add:* 2731 Glenwick Pl La Jolla CA 92037

DENNIS, MARY, b Toledo, Ohio, June 11, 26. INORGANIC CHEMISTRY. *Educ:* Madonna Col, BA, 55; Creighton Univ, MS, 59; Univ Notre Dame, PhD(chem), 62. *Prof Exp:* From instr to assoc prof, 62-76, PROF CHEM, MADONNA COL, 76- *Mem:* Am Chem Soc. *Res:* Coordination compounds. *Mailing Add:* Dept of Chem Madonna Col Livonia MI 48150

DENNIS, MICHAEL JOSEPH, neurobiology, see previous edition

DENNIS, PATRICK P, b Minneapolis, Minn, Nov 19, 42; m 69; c 2. MOLECULAR BIOLOGY, BIOCHEMISTRY. *Educ:* Univ Wis-Eau Claire, BSc, 65; Univ Minn, PhD(genetics), 69. *Prof Exp:* Res assoc, Roswell Park Mem Inst, Buffalo, NY, 70-71; Univ Tex, Dallas, 71-73 & Enzyme Inst, Univ Wis-Madison, 73-75; asst prof microbiol, 75-77, ASST PROF BIOCHEM, UNIV BC, 77- *Concurrent Pos:* Vis prof, Microbiol Inst, Univ Copenhagen, 76 & 78. *Res:* Regulation of ribosome synthesis in Escherichia Coli; ribosome genetics; molecular mechanisms of antibiotic action. *Mailing Add:* Dept of Biochem Univ of BC Vancouver BC V6T 1W5 Can

DENNIS, ROBERT E, b Adrian, Mich, Oct 15, 20; m 48; c 3. AGRONOMY. *Educ:* Mich State Univ, BS, 42, MS, 53, PhD(plant sci), 58. *Prof Exp:* Teacher pub schs, Mich, 46-51; instr agron, Mich State Univ, 51-59; PROF AGRON & EXTEN AGRONOMIST, UNIV ARIZ, 59- *Concurrent Pos:* Consult, Mex, Pakistan, Saudi Arabia, Sudan & Niger. *Mem:* Am Soc Agron; Am Soc Sugar Beet Technol. *Res:* Production of agronomic plants in an irrigated desert environment. *Mailing Add:* Dept of Plant Sci Univ of Ariz Tucson AZ 85721

DENNIS, TOM ROSS, b Macon, Ga, Jan 17, 42; m 69. ASTRONOMY. *Educ:* Univ Mich, BA, 63; Princeton Univ, PhD(astrophys), 70. *Prof Exp:* Asst prof, 70-78, ASSOC PROF ASTRON, MT HOLYOKE COL, 78- *Mem:* Am Astron Soc; AAAS. *Res:* Observational optical astronomy; photometry of galaxy clusters. *Mailing Add:* Williston Observatory Mt Holyoke Col South Hadley MA 01075

DENNIS, WARREN HOWARD, b Louisville, Ky, Aug 15, 25; m 51; c 5. PHYSIOLOGY, BIOPHYSICS. *Educ:* Univ Louisville, BChE, 47, MS, 53, PhD(phys chem, biophys), 59. *Prof Exp:* Lectr med math, Univ Louisville, 53-59, instr community health, 59-61, from asst prof to assoc prof physiol, 61-64; from assoc prof to prof physiol, 64-77, ASSOC PROF PHYSIOL & PREVENTIVE MED, UNIV WIS-MADISON, 77- *Concurrent Pos:* Estab investr, Am Heart Asn, 61-66. *Mem:* AAAS; Am Physiol Soc; Biophys Soc; Biomet Soc. *Res:* Electro-physiology of ion transporting systems with emphasis on gastric secretion; chemical biomedical engineering applications to mass transfer systems. *Mailing Add:* Dept of Physiol Serv Mem Inst Univ of Wis-Madison Madison WI 53706

DENNIS, WILLIAM ERIC, metallurgy, physical chemistry, see previous edition

DENNISON, BRIAN KENNETH, b Louisville, Ky, Aug 14, 49. RADIO ASTRONOMY. *Educ:* Univ Louisville, BS, 70; Cornell Univ, MS, 74, PhD(astron), 76. *Prof Exp:* Res asst, Nat Astron & Ionosphere Ctr, 71-74, Cornell Univ, 74-76; res assoc, 76-77, asst prof, 77-82, ASSOC PROF PHYSICS, VA POLYTECH INST, 82- *Concurrent Pos:* Comt mem, User's Comt, Nat Radio Astron Observ, 81-83. *Mem:* Am Astron Soc; Int Astron Union. *Res:* Observational study of low-frequency variability in extragalactic radio sources; theoretical and observational studies of the intracluster medium of clusters of galaxies. *Mailing Add:* Physics Dept Va Polytech Inst & State Univ Blacksburg VA 24061

DENNISON, BYRON LEE, b Clarksburg, WVa, Dec 8, 30; m 54; c 2. ELECTRICAL ENGINEERING. *Educ:* Univ WVa, BSEE, 53; Va Polytech Inst, MSEE, 62; Worcester Polytech Inst, PhD(elec eng), 67. *Prof Exp:* Sr elec engr, Govt & Indust Div, Philco Corp, 53-58; assoc prof elec eng, Va Polytech Inst, 58-66; prof elec eng, Lowell Technol Inst, 66-74, actg head dept, 67-68, head dept, 68-72; vis prof, Va Polytech Inst & State Univ, 77-79, Southeastern Mass Univ, 79-81, ADJ PROF, UNIV LOWELL, 81- *Concurrent Pos:* Consult, Polysci Corp, 62-63; mem, Simulation Coun, Inc, 64-; vis prof, Va Polytech Inst & State Univ, 77-79 & Southeastern Mass Univ, 79-81; adj prof, Univ Lowell, 81- *Mem:* Inst Elec & Electronics Engrs; Am Soc Eng Educ; Soc Comput Simulation. *Res:* Application of control system theory and simulation techniques to the study of biological systems, particularly to the study of the pupillary control system. *Mailing Add:* 70 Patten Rd Rte 4 Lowell Technol Inst Lowell MA 01854

DENNISON, CLIFFORD C, b Riffle, WVa, Mar 26, 22; m 42; c 5. ZOOLOGY. *Educ:* Marshall Col, BA, 52; Marshall Univ, MA, 61; Univ Fla, EdD(biol curriculum & develop), 69. *Prof Exp:* Teacher biol, Lee Col, Tenn, 55-61; assoc prof life & phys sci, Monroe Community Col, 64-65; ASSOC PROF LIFE & PHYS SCI, LEE COL, TENN, 65- *Concurrent Pos:* Head res & develop, Clean Water Soc, Ltd, 74-75; pres, Dennison Technol, Inc. *Mem:* AAAS; Am Inst Biol Sci. *Res:* Comparative evaluation of two approaches to teaching physical science materials to junior high school students; water purification equipment and processes. *Mailing Add:* Lee Col Cleveland TN 37311

DENNISON, DAVID KEE, b Monett, Mo, July 15, 52; m 74. HUMAN ANATOMY. *Educ:* William Jewell Col, BA, 74; Univ Kans, PhD(anat), 78. *Prof Exp:* assoc investr immunol, Howard Hughes Med Inst, 78-80; DIR, FLOW CYTOMETRY LAB CELL BIOL, COL MED, BAYLOR UNIV, 80- *Mem:* Am Asn Immunologists. *Res:* Regulation of cell mediated immune responses; flow cytometry. *Mailing Add:* Dept Cell Biol Col Med Baylor Univ Houston TX 77030

DENNISON, DAVID SEVERIN, b Ann Arbor, Mich, Mar 19, 32; m 54; c 2. BIOPHYSICS. *Educ:* Swarthmore Col, BA, 54; Calif Inst Technol, PhD(biophys), 58. *Prof Exp:* Asst, Calif Inst Technol, 54-58; from instr to assoc prof biol, 58-70, PROF BIOL, DARTMOUTH COL, 70- *Concurrent Pos:* NSF sci fac fel, 64; NIH spec res fel, 69. *Mem:* Biophys Soc; Am Soc Photobiology; AAAS. *Res:* Sensory physiology; stimulus-response relationships in phycomyces sporangiophores. *Mailing Add:* 19 Dresden Rd Hanover NH 03755

DENNISON, JOHN MANLEY, b Keyser, WVa, Apr 13, 34; m 57, 81; c 1. GEOLOGY. *Educ:* WVa Univ, BS, 54, MS, 55; Univ Wis, PhD(geol), 60. *Prof Exp:* From asst prof to assoc prof geol, Univ Ill, 60-65; assoc prof, Univ Tenn, 65-67; chmn dept, 69-74, PROF GEOL, UNIV NC, CHAPEL HILL, 67- *Concurrent Pos:* Coop geologist, WVa Geol Surv, 60- *Mem:* Geol Soc Am; Am Asn Petrol Geologists; Paleont Soc. *Res:* Appalachian structural geology and stratigraphy; palinspastic maps; energy resources. *Mailing Add:* Dept Geol Univ NC Chapel Hill NC 27514

DENNISON, RAYMOND ALEXANDER, b Sedalia, Ind, July 12, 14; m 42; c 3. FOOD SCIENCE. *Educ:* Miami Univ, AB, 36; Univ Iowa, MS, 40, PhD(plant physiol), 42. *Prof Exp:* Assoc horticulturist, Inst Food & Agr Sci, Univ Fla, 46-53, horticulturist, 53-56, head food technol & nutrit dept, 56-66, chmn food sci dept, 66-78. *Mem:* AAAS; Inst Food Technol; Am Soc Plant Physiol; Am Soc Hort Sci; Am Chem Soc. *Res:* Food chemistry; processing fruits and vegetables; food composition. *Mailing Add:* Inst of Food & Agr Sci Univ of Fla Gainesville FL 32611

DENNISTON, JOSEPH CHARLES, b Mineola, NY, June 3, 40; m 63; c 1. MEDICAL PHYSIOLOGY. *Educ:* Univ Pa, VMD, 67; Baylor Col Med, PhD(cardiovasc physiol), 74. *Prof Exp:* Asst chief lab animal med, Pine Bluff Arsenal, US Army, 67-68, adv large animal dis, AID, South Vietnam, 68-69, res microbiologist infectious dis, Med Res Inst Infectious Dis, 69-71, res physiologist high altitude res, Res Inst Environ Med, 74-76, res physiologist, Aviation Med, US Army Aeromed Ctr, 72nd Med Detachment, 76-78 & Med Res & Develop Command, 78-81, CHEM DEFENSE STAFF OFFICER, US ARMY, 81- *Concurrent Pos:* Vis assoc prof physiol, Baylor Col Med, 75-; consult to Surgeon Gen, Dept of Army, 75- *Mem:* Am Vet Med Asn; AAAS; Am Asn Vet Anesthesiol; Sigma Xi. *Res:* Incidence and eyidence of ischemic heart disease in the military; effects of high altitude on cardiac mechanics and performance; pathophysiology of high altitude pulmonary edema; interaction of carbon monoxide and altitude in aviator performance; medical aspects of chemical defense. *Mailing Add:* 204 Wyngate Dr Frederick MD 21701

DENNISTON, ROLLIN H, II, b Chicago, Ill, Dec 16, 14; m 41; c 3. ANIMAL BEHAVIOR. *Educ:* Univ Wis, BA, 36, MA, 37; Univ Chicago, PhD(zoophysiol), 41. *Prof Exp:* Instr zool & physiol, Univ Ariz, 41-43; from instr zool, physiol & physics to asst prof zoophysiol, Univ Wyo, 43-48, from assoc prof to prof physiol, 48-70, dir res & develop, 65-70, chief of party, AID-Univ Wyo, Kabul, Afghanistan, 70-73, PROF ZOOL & PHYSIOL, UNIV WYO, 73- *Concurrent Pos:* New York Zool Soc grants, 47-52; Ford Found grant & fel psychol, Yale Univ, 52-53; NIMH grant, 53-60, sr res fel neurophysiol, 60-61; NSF-Nat Res Coun conf grant, 60-61; dir dept, NDEA, 60-; res consult, Jackson Lab, 63. *Honors & Awards:* High Medal for Educ, Govt Afghanistan, 73. *Mem:* Am Psychol Asn; Am Soc Zoologists; Am Physiol Soc; Animal Behav Soc; Psychonomic Soc. *Res:* Endocrinology; behavior; reproduction neurophysiology; vertebrate ecological ethology. *Mailing Add:* Dept of Zool & Physiol Univ of Wyo Laramie WY 82071

DENNO, KAHLIL I, b Baghdad, Iraq, July 1, 33; US citizen; m 61; c 3. ALTERNATIVE ENERGY SOURCES. *Educ:* Univ Baghdad, BSc, 55; Rensselaer Polytech Inst, MEE, 59; Iowa State Univ, PhD(elec eng), 67. *Prof Exp:* Fac mem elec eng, Univ Baghdad, 59-64; asst prof, Univ La, 67-68; assoc prof, 69-74, PROF ELEC ENG, NJ INST TECHNOL, 74- *Concurrent Pos:* Researcher, Found NJ Inst Technol, 69- *Mem:* Fel Inst Elec Engrs; sr mem Inst Elec & Electronics Engrs; Am Soc Eng Educ; Sigma Xi; Plasma & Nuclear Sci Soc. *Res:* Modes of advanced alternative energy sorces including: magnetohydrodynamics using exhaust plasma of fusion reactors and characterization of ferromagnetic fluids for redox batteries as insulation barriers. *Mailing Add:* 68 Ridgeway Ave West Orange NJ 07052

DENNY, CHARLES STORROW, b Brookline, Mass, Sept 17, 11; m; c 3. GEOLOGY. *Educ:* Harvard Univ, AB, 34, PhD(geol), 38. *Prof Exp:* Instr geol, Dartmouth Col, 38-42; asst prof, Wesleyan Univ, 42-44; assoc geologist, US Geol Surv, 44-47, geologist, 47-81. *Mem:* Fel Geol Soc Am. *Res:* Glacial geology; geomorphology. *Mailing Add:* 7906 Cypress Place Chevy Chase MD 20815

DENNY, CLEVE B, b Dallas, Tex, Oct 12, 25; m 51; c 2. FOOD MICROBIOLOGY. *Educ:* Univ Tex, BA, 49. *Prof Exp:* From jr bacteriologist to asst chief bacteriologist, 49-65, head bact sect, 65-73, asst to dir res serv, 73-75, mgr res servs, 75-78, DIR RES SERVS, WASH LAB, NAT FOOD PROCESSORS ASN, 78- *Concurrent Pos:* Assoc referee for bact testing of canned foods, Asn Off Anal Chemists, 68-, for microbiol methods sugar & sugar prod, 74-; mem, Am Pub Health Asn Intersoc/Agency Comt Microbiol Exam Foods, 72-76; delete this line; chmn, Food Processors Inst Curric Comt, 78- & Comt Microbiol Food, Nat Res Coun Adv Bd, Mil Personnel Supplies, 82-84. *Mem:* Am Soc Microbiol; AAAS; Inst Food Technologists; Am Pub Health Asn; Am Soc Mech Eng. *Res:* Antibiotic preservation of food; radiation sterilization of food; food poisoning; canned food spoilage organisms; heat inactivation of bacterial toxins; hydrogen peroxide sterilization of food containers. *Mailing Add:* Nat Food Processors Asn 1133 20th St NW Washington DC 20036

DENNY, FLOYD WOLFE, JR, b Hartsville, SC, Oct 22, 23; m 46; c 3. PEDIATRICS. *Educ:* Wofford Col, BS, 44; Vanderbilt Univ, MD, 46; Am Bd Pediat, dipl. *Prof Exp:* Asst prof pediat, Univ Minn, 52-53; asst prof, Sch Med, Vanderbilt Univ, 53-55; from asst prof to assoc prof prev med & pediat, Western Reserve Univ, 55-60; prof pediat & chmn dept, 60-73, ALUMNI DISTINGUISHED PROF PEDIAT & CHMN DEPT, SCH MED, UNIV NC, CHAPEL HILL, 73- *Concurrent Pos:* Asst to pres, Armed Forces Epidemiol Bd, 55-57, mem comn streptococcal dis, 54-70; dep dir, 59-63; mem comn acute respiratory dis, 60-73, dep dir, 63-67, dir, 67-73. *Mem:* Am Pediat Soc; Am Soc Clin Invest; Am Soc Microbiol; Infect Dis Soc Am; Soc Pediat Res (pres, 68-69). *Res:* Streptococcal infections; rheumatic fever; viral infections; mycoplasma infections. *Mailing Add:* Dept of Pediat Univ of NC Sch of Med Chapel Hill NC 27514

DENNY, GEORGE HUTCHESON, b Westfield, NJ, May 30, 28; m 67; c 2. ORGANIC CHEMISTRY. *Educ:* Washington & Lee Univ, BS, 50; Johns Hopkins Univ, MA, 51, PhD(chem), 54. *Prof Exp:* Jr instr chem, Johns Hopkins Univ, 51-53; res chemist, Nylon Res Div, E I du Pont de Nemours & Co, 56-58; USPHS fel chem, Wayne State Univ, 58-59; asst prof, Arlington State Col, 59-60; asst prof, Va Polytech Inst & State Univ, 60-63; assoc prof, Peabody Col, 63-64; res assoc, 64-65, sr chemist, 65-70, RES FEL, MERCK SHARP & DOHME RES LABS, 70- *Mem:* AAAS; Am Chem Soc. *Res:* Medicinal chemistry. *Mailing Add:* 125 Rosewood Dr Lansdale PA 19446

DENNY, J(OHN) P(ALMER), b Pittsburgh, Pa, Mar 7, 21; m 45; c 3. METALLURGY. *Educ:* Colo Sch Mines, EMet, 42; Univ Utah, MS, 48, PhD, 50. *Prof Exp:* Res engr, Battelle Mem Inst, 45-47; phys metallurgist, Gen Elec Co, NY, 50-59; sect chief, Beryllium Corp, 59-69; mgr beryilium develop, Berylco Div, Kawecki Berylco Industs, Inc, 69-80, MGR PROD DEVELOP, CABOT CORP, 80- *Mem:* Am Soc Metals; Am Inst Mining, Metall & Petrol Engrs. *Res:* Physical metallurgy; alloy development; precipitation hardening; low melting alloys; high temperature materials. *Mailing Add:* Cabot Corp Berylco Div PO Box 1462 Reading PA 19607

DENNY, JOHN LEIGHTON, b Birmingham, Ala, Oct 11, 31; m 56. PROBABILITY. *Educ:* Stanford Univ, BA, 53, Univ Calif, Berkeley, PhD(statist), 62. *Prof Exp:* Asst prof, Ind Univ, 62-64; asst prof, Univ Calif, Riverside, 65-66; assoc prof, 67-69, PROF MATH, UNIV ARIZ, 70- *Concurrent Pos:* Actg head statists, Univ Ariz, 82; invited lectr, Inst Math Statist, 79-82. *Mem:* Am Math Soc; Inst Math Statist; Int Statist Inst; Am Statist Asn. *Res:* Extreme points of convex sets of measures; stochastic differential equations; mathematical economics. *Mailing Add:* Dept Math Univ Ariz Tucson AZ 85721

DENNY, WAYNE BELDING, b Oberlin, Ohio, Feb 4, 14; m 39; c 2. PHYSICS. *Educ:* Oberlin Col, AB, 35; Yale Univ, PhD(ed), 41. *Prof Exp:* Instr high sch, NY, 35-38; ed, Univ Conn, 40-41; instr physics, Emory Univ, 41-43; vis lectr, Oberlin Col, 43-46, asst prof, 46-48; assoc prof physics, Grinnell Col, 48-55, prof, 55-79; RETIRED. *Concurrent Pos:* Fulbright prof, Robert Col, Istanbul, 58-59; Ahmednagar Col, India, 65-66; vis prof physics, Silliman Univ, Philippines, 71-72. *Mem:* Audio Eng Soc. *Res:* Electronics; acoustics. *Mailing Add:* Dept of Physics Grinnell Col Grinnell IA 50112

DENNY, WILLIAM F, b Tryon, Okla, Aug 15, 27; m 49; c 2. HEMATOLOGY, INTERNAL MEDICINE. *Educ:* Cent State Col, Okla, BS, 49; Univ Okla, MD, 53. *Prof Exp:* Intern, George Washington Univ Hosp, 53-54; resident med, Sch Med, Univ Okla, 54-56, instr, 56, chief resident, 56-57; asst prof, Sch Med, Univ Ark, 61-67; assoc prof med, 67-80, PROF INTERNAL MED, COL MED, UNIV ARIZ, 80-; CHIEF MED SERVS, VET ADMIN HOSP, 67- *Concurrent Pos:* Clin res investr, Consol Vet Admin Hosp, Ark, 61-64, chief hemat sect, Med Serv, 64-67. *Mem:* AAAS; AMA; Am Fedn Clin Res. *Res:* Erythropoietin measurements in anemic and non-anemic individuals; non-immune hemolytic mechanisms. *Mailing Add:* Dept of Internal Med Univ of Ariz Tucson AZ 85724

DENNY-BROWN, DEREK ERNEST, medicine, deceased

DENO, NORMAN C, b Chicago, Ill, Feb 15, 21; m 44; c 3. PHYSICAL ORGANIC CHEMISTRY. *Educ:* Univ Ill, BS, 42; Univ Mich, MS, 46, PhD(chem), 48. *Prof Exp:* Asst chem, Univ Mich, 42-45; res assoc, Ohio State Univ, 48-50; prof chem, 50-81, EMER PROF, PA STATE UNIV, 81- *Res:* Reaction mechanisms. *Mailing Add:* Dept of Chem Pa State Univ University Park PA 16802

DENONCOURT, ROBERT FRANCIS, b Manchester, NH, Sept 13, 32; m 55; c 6. AQUATIC ECOLOGY, ICHTHYOLOGY. *Educ:* Springfield Col, BS, 55, MEd, 57; Union Col, NY, MS, 61; Cornell Univ, PhD(vert zool, ichthyol), 69. *Prof Exp:* Teacher sci, Gilboa-Conesville Cent Sch, NY, 57-59; asst prof zool, Ithaca Col, 59-65; teaching & res asst ichthyol, Cornell Univ, 66-68; res ichthyologist aquatic ecol, Ichthyol Assocs, 68-69; PROF BIOL & ZOOL, YORK COL PA, 69- *Concurrent Pos:* Biol consult fishes, Pa Power & Light Co, 71-82; biol consult aquatic fauna, P H Glatfelter Co, 75-82 & USDA, Environ Impact Studies, Soil Conserv Serv, US Corps Engrs, Dept Interior, 74-80. *Mem:* Am Fisheries Soc; Am Soc Ichthyol & Herpetol; Ecol Soc Am; Am Inst Biol Sci; Nat Geog Soc. *Res:* Taxonomy, distribution and life history of freshwater fishes, particularly West Virginia and Pennsylvania; studies of fishes and macroinvertebrates as affected by natural and man-caused disturbances, flood, warm water, toxic chemicals and sewage; environmental impact studies. *Mailing Add:* York Col of Pa Country Club Rd York PA 17405

DENOON, CLARENCE ENGLAND, JR, b Richmond, Va, Feb 25, 15; m 42; c 2. ORGANIC CHEMISTRY. *Educ:* Univ Richmond, BS, 34, MS, 35; Univ Ill, PhD(org chem), 38. *Prof Exp:* Asst, Univ Ill, 35-37; res chemist, Exp Sta, E I du Pont de Nemours & Co, 38-42; res dir, Landers Corp, 42-45; mgr spec prod dept, Rohm & Haas Co, 45-58, asst mgr chem & plastics div, 58-62, mgr indust chem div, 62-65, mkt mgr chem div, 65-66, vpres, 66-76, dir, 72-76; DIR, SARTOMER INDUST, 76-; VPRES, TRI-EX CORP, 78- *Res:* High polymers; corporate management. *Mailing Add:* Wycombe PA 18980

DE NOTO, THOMAS GERALD, b Rochester, NY, Apr 2, 43. CHEMICAL ENGINEERING. *Educ:* Univ Rochester, BS, 64, MS, 67, PhD(chem eng), 72. *Prof Exp:* Engr, Res Div, 71-72, chem engr, Res Div, 72-74, sr engr, 74-80, PRIN ENGR, FILMS DIV, POLAROID CORP, 80- *Concurrent Pos:* Vis scholar, Univ Calif, Berkeley, 68-70 & Argonne Nat Lab, 70; NATO fel, 73 & 76; reviewer, Am Inst Chemists Jour, 78- *Mem:* Am Inst Chem Engrs. *Res:* Filtration of polymeric fluids, agitation of fluids and scale-up criteria. *Mailing Add:* Polaroid Corp 1265 Main St W-8 Waltham MA 02154

DENOYER, JOHN M, b Kalaw, Burma, May 19, 26; US citizen; m 51; c 4. GEOPHYSICS. *Educ:* Chico State Col, AB, 53; Univ Calif, MA, 55, PhD(geophys), 58. *Prof Exp:* Asst seismol, Univ Calif, 54-57; from instr to assoc prof geol, Univ Mich, 57-65, actg head acoust & seismics lab, 63-65; dep dir nuclear test detection off, Advan Res Projs Agency, Dept Defense, Washington, DC, 65-67; asst dir res, US Geol Surv, Dept Interior, 67-69; dir earth observations prog, NASA, 69-72; dir earth observations syst prog, 72-79, RES GEOPHYSICIST, US GEOL SURV, DEPT INTERIOR, 79- *Concurrent Pos:* Mem staff, Inst Defense Anal, Washington, DC, 62-63. *Honors & Awards:* Henry Russel Award, 64; Except Serv Medal, NASA, 72; Meritorious Serv Award, US Dept Interior, 77; William T Pecora Award, NASA & US Dept Interior, 79. *Mem:* AAAS; Geol Soc Am; Acoust Soc Am; Seismol Soc Am; Am Geophys Union. *Res:* Wave propagation; signal processing; energy in seismic waves; strain energy in crustal deformation; crustal structure; remote sensing; gravity and magnetic fields. *Mailing Add:* 4835 Drummond Ave Chevy Chase MD 20815

DENOYER, LINDA KAY, b Hollywood, Calif. ASTROPHYSICS. *Educ:* Univ Wis, BA; Cornell Univ, PhD(astrophys), 72. *Prof Exp:* Instr astron, Univ Toronto, 69-71 & Cornell Univ, 71-72; res assoc, Univ Ill, 72-75; asst prof physics, Colgate Univ, 75-76; Am Asn Univ Women fel, Cavendish Lab, Cambridge, 76-77; lectr & res assoc, 77-80, SR RES ASSOC & FEL, CORNELL UNIV, 80- *Mem:* Am Astron Soc. *Res:* Molecular abundances and excitation conditions in shocked clouds. *Mailing Add:* CRSR Space Sci Bldg Cornell Univ Ithaca NY 14853

DENSEN, PAUL M, b New York, NY, Aug 1, 13; m 39; c 2. BIOSTATISTICS. *Educ:* Brooklyn Col, BA, 34; Johns Hopkins Univ, DSc(hyg), 39. *Prof Exp:* Instr in charge biostatist, Dept Prev Med & Pub Health, Sch Med, Vanderbilt Univ, 39-41, from asst prof to assoc prof, 41-46; chief med res statist div, US Vet Admin, 47-49; assoc prof biostatist, Grad Sch Pub Health, Univ Pittsburgh, 49-52, prof biomet, 52-54; dir res & statist, Health Ins Plan Greater New York, 54-59; dep comnr health, New York City Health Dept, 59-66, dep health serv adminr, 66-68; DIR CTR COMMUNITY HEALTH & MED CARE, HARVARD MED SCHOOL, 68- *Honors & Awards:* Lowell J Reed Award, Am Public Health Asn, 79. *Mem:* Inst of Med of Nat Acad Sci; fel Am Statist Asn; fel Am Pub Health Asn; Am Epidemiol Soc. *Res:* MeMedical, hospital, public health statistics; health services. *Mailing Add:* Ctr Community Health & Med Care 643 Huntington Ave Boston MA 02115

DENSHAW, JOSEPH MOREAU, b Trenton, NJ, Jan 26, 29; m 53; c 6. ELECTRICAL ENGINEERING. *Educ:* Univ Pa, BS, 52, MS, 63. *Prof Exp:* Engr, Minneapolis Honeywell Regular Co, 52-56; engr, Missile & Space Div, Gen Elec Co, 56-62, mgr, 62-64, develop engr, 64-65, mgr electro-optics, 65-70, prod develop engr, Reentry & Environ Systs Div, 70-74; instrument engr, United Engrs & Constructors Inc, 74-76; prof engr, 76-80, MGR PROD ASSURANCE, HONEYWELL, INC, 80- *Mem:* Inst Elec & Electronics Engrs (secy, 62-63, treas, 63-64, vchmn, 64-65); Optical Soc Am; Am Inst Physics; Instrument Soc Am. *Res:* Synthesize and analyze information systems, particularly development of new techniques in signal processing and control theory applications; instrumentation engineering; development of microprocessor based control systems for radiation monitoring; coal gasification; methane reforming; naphtha hydrotreating. *Mailing Add:* 907 Jode Rd Audubon PA 19403

DENSLOW, JOHN STEDMAN, b Hartford, Conn, Dec 19, 06; m 34; c 3. OSTEOPATHY. *Educ:* Kirksville Col, DO, 29. *Hon Degrees:* DSc, Chicago Col Osteop, 41. *Prof Exp:* Asst dir clin, Chicago Col Osteop, 30-32, dir, 32-38; prof & chmn dept osteop technol, 38-65, dir res affairs, 45-65, VPRES, KIRKSVILLE COL OSTEOP MED, 65- 65-, CONSULT TO PRES, 77- *Concurrent Pos:* Pvt pract, Ill, 33-38; mem, Mo State Bd Health, 68-, chmn, 71; mem proj rev comt, Mo Regional Med Prog, 68-; mem, Mo Gov Adv Coun Comprehensive Health Planning, 71-76; mem gov body, Area II Health Systs Agency of Mo, Inc, 76- *Mem:* AAAS; Am Osteop Asn; Am Asn Cols Osteop Med (pres, 73-74); Am Physiol Soc; NY Acad Sci. *Res:* Reflex activity of the spinal cord; neuromuscular physiology; reflex and postural muscle contraction. *Mailing Add:* Kirksville Col of Osteop Med Kirksville MO 63501

DENSON, COSTEL D, chemical engineering, see previous edition

DENSON, DONALD D, b Beverly, Mass, July 11, 45. PHARMACOLOGY, BIOCHEMISTRY. *Educ:* Univ Ga, BS, 67, PhD(org chem), 70. *Prof Exp:* Res chemist, Air Force Rocket Propulsion Lab, 70-71 & Air Force Mat Lab, 71-72; res chemist, Stanford Res Inst, 72-78; ASST PROF ANESTHESIA & DIR ANESTHESIA RES, UNIV CINCINNATI MED SCH, 78- *Concurrent Pos:* Consult, Div Res Pediat & Neurophysiol, Univ Cincinnati Med Sch, 71- *Mem:* Am Soc Anesthesiologists; Am Heart Asn; NY Acad Sci; Am Soc Regional Anesthesia. *Res:* Chemistry of anesthetic drugs; anesthetic metabolism; pharmacokinetics of local anesthetics; drug interactions. *Mailing Add:* Dept Anesthesia MSB 3562 231 Bethesda Ave Cincinnati OH 45267

DENT, BRIAN EDWARD, b Binghamton, NY, June 29, 43; m 69. GEOPHYSICS. *Educ:* Rensselaer Polytech Inst, BS, 65; Calif State Univ, Northridge, MS, 67; Stanford Univ, PhD(geophys), 74. *Prof Exp:* Instr physics, State Tech Univ, Chile, 67-69; res geophysicist seismol, Newmont Mining Ltd, 74-75; RES GEOPHYSICIST SEISMOL, CITIES SERV CO, 75- *Mem:* Soc Explor Geophysicists; Europ Asn Explor Geophysicists; Am Geophys Union. *Res:* Seismology applied to petroleum exploration, especially statics and migration; borehole seismology; gravity modeling; tectonophysics, especially impact cratering. *Mailing Add:* Cities Serv Co Box 3908 Tulsa OK 74102

DENT, JAMES (NORMAN), b Martin, Tenn, May 10, 16; div; c 2. ZOOLOGY. *Educ:* Univ Tenn, AB, 38; Johns Hopkins Univ, PhD(zool), 41. *Prof Exp:* Asst anat, Johns Hopkins Univ, 38-41, res assoc, 41-42; asst prof biol, Marquette Univ, 45-46 & Univ Pittsburgh, 46-49; assoc prof zool, 49-58, PROF ZOOL, UNIV VA, 58- *Concurrent Pos:* Mem Johns Hopkins Univ exped, Jamaica, BWI, 41; consult, Biol Div, Oak Ridge Nat Lab, 55-70; Guggenheim fel, Univ St Andrews, 59-60; US AID, Philippines, 63; USPHS spec res fel, Harvard Univ, 69-70; Fulbright lectr, Banaras Hindu Univ, 76 & Univ Calcutta, 76; vis fel, Univ Calif, Berkeley, 77. *Mem:* AAAS; Am Soc Zoologists; Am Asn Anatomists. *Res:* Developmental physiology; comparative endocrinology. *Mailing Add:* Dept of Biol Gilmer Hall Univ of Va Charlottesville VA 22901

DENT, PETER BORIS, b Prague, Czech, May 16, 36; Can citizen; m 62; c 3. IMMUNOLOGY, PEDIATRICS. *Educ:* Univ Toronto, MD, 60; FRCP(C), 65. *Prof Exp:* From instr to asst prof pediat, Univ Minn, 64-68; from asst prof to assoc prof, 68-76, PROF PEDIAT, McMASTER UNIV, 76- *Concurrent Pos:* Consult, Ont Cancer Treat & Res Round, 75- *Mem:* Can Soc Immunol; Am Asn Immunol; Am Asn Cancer Res; Can Soc Clin Oncol; Am Soc Clin Oncol. *Res:* Nature of tumor antigens and the host response to such antigens with particular emphasis on clinical implications of tumor immunology. *Mailing Add:* 4H17 McMaster Univ Med Ctr Hamilton ON L8S 4L8 Can

DENT, SARA JAMISON, b Lockhart, SC, Feb 5, 22. ANESTHESIOLOGY. *Educ:* Univ SC, MD, 45. *Prof Exp:* From asst prof to assoc prof, 55-65, PROF ANESTHESIOL, DUKE UNIV, 65-, STAFF ANESTHESIOLOGIST, UNIV HOSP, 55- *Concurrent Pos:* Attend, Vet Admin Hosp, 55- *Mem:* Am Soc Anesthesiol; AMA. *Res:* General anesthesiology. *Mailing Add:* Dept of Anesthesiol Duke Univ Box 3094 Durham NC 27710

DENT, THOMAS CURTIS, b Canton, Ohio, June 6, 28; m 48; c 2. BOTANY, PLANT TAXONOMY. *Educ:* Univ Akron, BAEd, 62; Univ Okla, MNS, 64, PhD(plant taxon), 69. *Prof Exp:* Teacher, Hoover High Sch, Ohio, 61-68; instr biol, Kent State Univ, 68-69; PROF BIOL, GORDON COL, 69-, CHMN DEPT, 72- *Mem:* Am Inst Biol Sci; Am Soc Plant Taxon; Nat Asn Biol Teachers; Am Forestry Asn. *Res:* Relationships of two isolated groups of sugar maple in central Oklahoma to eastern and western species. *Mailing Add:* Dept of Biol Gordon Col Wenham MA 01984

DENT, WARREN THOMAS, statistics, economics, see previous edition

DENT, WILLIAM HUNTER, JR, b Philadelphia, Pa, Sept 30, 36; m 59; c 3. MATHEMATICS. *Educ:* Maryville Col, BA, 57; Univ Ky, MS, 62; Univ Tenn, PhD(math), 72. *Prof Exp:* Instr math, Univ Ky, 60-64; from instr to asst prof, 64-72, ASSOC PROF MATH, MARYVILLE COL, 72-, CHMN DEPT MATH & PHYSICS, 77- *Mem:* Math Asn Am; Nat Coun Teachers Math. *Res:* Topology. *Mailing Add:* 107 Hummingbird Dr Maryville TN 37801

DENTON, ARNOLD EUGENE, b Remington, Ind, Mar 18, 25; m 50; c 3. BIOCHEMISTRY. *Educ:* Purdue Univ, BS, 49; Univ Wis, MS, 50, PhD, 53. *Prof Exp:* Head pet food res div, Res Lab, Swift & Co, 53-55, head biochem res div, 55-58; dir basic res, 58-66, vpres basic res, 66-70, vpres, Tech Admin, 70-78, VPRES RES & TECHNOL, CAMPBELL SOUP CO, 70-, PRES, CAMPBELL INST RES & TECHNOL, 78- *Mem:* Am Chem Soc; Inst Food Technol; Am Inst Nutrit; NY Acad Sci. *Res:* Amino acid and vitamin assays; vitamin stability in foods and feeds; protein digestibility; by-product utilization; commercial applications of enzymes; meat tenderness; chemistry of flavors; nutritional value of foods. *Mailing Add:* Campbell Soup Co Campbell Pl Camden NJ 08101

DENTON, JOHN JOSEPH, b Newkirk, Okla, Nov 24, 15; m 49; c 3. MEDICINAL CHEMISTRY. *Educ:* Okla Agr & Mech Col, BS, 37; Univ Ill, PhD(org chem), 41. *Prof Exp:* Asst chem, Univ Ill, 37-40, spec asst, Off Sci Res & Develop, 40-41; res chemist, Calco Chem Div, Am Cyanamid Co, 41-45, group leader pharmaceut res, 45-50, sect dir, 50-52, dir, Bound Brook, 52-54, tech dir fine chem div, NY, 54-56, dir org chem res, Lederle Labs, 56-71, dir cardiovasc-renal res, 71-73, dir new prod acquisitions, 73-81; RETIRED. *Mem:* Am Chem Soc; NY Acad Sci; Royal Soc Chem. *Res:* Medicinal chemistry. *Mailing Add:* 565 Upper Blvd Ridgewood NJ 07450

DENTON, MELINDA FAY, b Horton, Kans, Mar 27, 44. PLANT SYSTEMATICS. *Educ:* Kans State Teachers Col, BS, 65; Univ Mich, AM, 67, PhD(bot), 71. *Prof Exp:* Vis asst prof & actg cur bot, Mich State Univ, 71-72; asst prof, 72-78, ASSOC PROF BOT, UNIV WASH, 78-, CUR, 72-, ASSOC CHMN, 79- *Concurrent Pos:* Assoc ed, Am Midland Naturalist, 78-81. *Honors & Awards:* George R Cooley Award, Am Soc Plant Taxonomists, 78. *Mem:* Am Soc Plant Taxonomists (secy, 76-79); Int Asn Plant Taxon; Bot Soc Am; Soc Study Evolution; Asn Trop Biol. *Res:* Systematic studies of vascular plants; phytogeography; evolutionary biology; floristics of the Pacific Northwest. *Mailing Add:* Dept of Bot Univ of Wash Seattle WA 98195

DENTON, RICHARD T, b York, Pa, July 13, 32; m 53; c 11. ELECTRICAL ENGINEERING, SOLID STATE PHYSICS. *Educ:* Pa State Univ, BS, 53, MS, 54; Univ Mich, PhD(elec eng), 60. *Prof Exp:* Res asst comput circuits, Pa State Univ, 53-54; mem tech staff, Bell Tel Labs, Inc, 54-56; res assoc solid state physics res inst, Univ Mich, 56-59; mem tech staff, 59-68, head, Shore Technol Dept, 68-76, HEAD, UNDERSEA TECHNOL DESIGN DEPT, BELL TEL LABS, 76- *Mem:* Am Phys Soc; fel Inst Elec & Electronics Engrs. *Res:* Digital signal processing; microwave properties of magnetic materials; microwave ultrasonic devices and study of ultrasonic properties of solids; optical processing; undersea cable transmission system. *Mailing Add:* Bell Labs Whippany NJ 07981

DENTON, TOM EUGENE, b Montgomery, Ala, May 29, 37; m 59; c 2. GENETICS. *Educ:* Huntington Col, BA, 59; Univ Ala, MS, 63, PhD(biol), 66. *Prof Exp:* From asst prof to assoc prof, 65-74, PROF BIOL, SAMFORD UNIV, 74- *Mem:* Sigma Xi; AAAS. *Res:* Human genetics and cytogenetics. *Mailing Add:* Dept of Biol Samford Univ Birmingham AL 35209

DENTON, WILLIAM IRWIN, b Paterson, NJ, July 5, 17; m 41; c 5. CHEMICAL ENGINEERING. *Educ:* Case Western Reserve Univ, BS, 38, MS, 39. *Prof Exp:* Res engr, Am Gas Asn, 39-40; sr chemist, Socony-Mobil Oil Co, 40-53; sect chief org chem res dept, 53-59, dir process develop, 59-70, dir process technol, 71-75, SAFETY & HAZARD MGR, OLIN CORP, 76- *Concurrent Pos:* Vpres, Sprayed Reinforced Plastics Co, 59-60. *Mem:* Am Chem Soc; Am Inst Chem Engrs; Soc Plastics Engrs; Instrument Soc Am. *Res:* New chemical processes; catalytic processes; petrochemicals; urethanes; alkoxylations; isocyanates; hazard identification. *Mailing Add:* Oil Corp 275 Winchester Ave New Haven CT 06504

DE NUCCIO, DAVID JOSEPH, b Lawrence, Mass, May 29, 35; m 60; c 2. MEDICAL PHYSIOLOGY. *Educ:* Merrimack Col, BA, 59; Boston Col, MS, 61; Univ Tenn, Memphis, PhD(med sci), 69. *Prof Exp:* From instr to assoc asst prof human anat & physiol, 64-77, PROF HUMAN ANAT & PHYSIOL, CENT CONN STATE COL, 77-, CHIEF HEALTH PROFESSIONS ADV & COORDR, MED TECHNOL PROG, 75- *Concurrent Pos:* Consult health educ. *Mem:* AAAS; Am Soc Zoologists; Asn Adv Health Professions; Sigma Xi. *Res:* Neuroendocrine regulation of mammary gland function with emphasis on the measurement and biophysics of milk ejection; mammary compliance; nervous regulation of duct tone and gland capacity. *Mailing Add:* 25 Sequin St Newington CT 06111

DENYES, HELEN ARLISS, b Kingston, Ont, Sept 17, 22. ENVIRONMENTAL BIOLOGY & EVOLUTION. *Educ:* Queen's Univ, Ont, BA, 45; Univ Mich, MS, 46, PhD(ecol), 51. *Prof Exp:* From instr to asst prof physiol, Fla State Univ, 49-56; from asst prof to assoc prof biol, Queen's Univ, Ont, 56-64; assoc prof, Mankato State Col, 66-67; assoc prof, 67-77, chairperson dept, 74-80, PROF BIOL, SACRED HEART UNIV, 77- . *Concurrent Pos:* Ecol adv, Conserv Adv Comn, City of Bridgeport, Conn, 70- *Mem:* AAAS; Am Inst Biol Sci; Am Soc Zoologists; Ecol Soc Am. *Res:* Physiological-ecological adaptations in fish and mammals; lipid metabolism in cold exposed and hibernating mammals. *Mailing Add:* Dept of Biol Sacred Heart Univ Bridgeport CT 06604

DENZEL, GEORGE EUGENE, b Seattle, Wash, Nov 1, 39; m 58; c 3. MATHEMATICS. *Educ:* Univ Wash, BS, 60, MS, 63, PhD(math), 65. *Prof Exp:* Res instr math, Dartmouth Col, 65-67; asst prof statist, Univ Mo-Columbia, 67-70; ASSOC PROF MATH, YORK UNIV, 70- *Mem:* Am Math Soc; Inst Math Statist. *Res:* Markov processes and potential theory; Martingale theory. *Mailing Add:* York Univ Dept of Math 4700 Keele St Downsview ON M3J 1P3 Can

DEODHAR, SHARAD DINKAR, b Poona, India, Nov 17, 29; US citizen; m 55; c 3. PATHOLOGY, BIOCHEMISTRY. *Educ:* Pa State Univ, MS, 52; Western Reserve Univ, PhD, 56, MD, 60. *Prof Exp:* Res biochemist, Mt Sinai Hosp, Cleveland, Ohio, 56-60; pathologist, 64-69, DIR IMMUNOL, CLEVELAND CLIN FOUND, 69- *Concurrent Pos:* Res fel path, Univ Hosps Cleveland, 60-64; Am Col Cardiol young investr award, 63- *Res:* Immunopathology; experimental hypertension. *Mailing Add:* Cleveland Clin Found 2020 E 93rd St Cleveland OH 44106

DEONIER, D L, b La Russell, Mo, June 27, 36; m 65; c 2. ENTOMOLOGY, ECOLOGY. *Educ:* Kans State Col Pittsburg, BS, 59; Iowa State Univ, MS, 61, PhD(entom), 66. *Prof Exp:* Med entomologist, US Army, SEATO Med Res Lab, Thailand, 65-66, instr med entom, Brooke Army Med Ctr, Ft Sam Houston, Tex, 66; asst prof zool, 66-71, ASSOC PROF ZOOL, MIAMI UNIV, 71- *Mem:* Entom Soc Am; Soc Syst Zool; Royal Entom Soc London; NAm Benthological Soc (treas, 75-80, pres-elect, 81). *Res:* Systematics of Diptera; taxonomy and ecology of Ephydridae; insect ecology. *Mailing Add:* Dept Zool Miami Univ Oxford OH 45056

DEONIER, RICHARD CHARLES, b Lakeport, Calif, Apr 9, 42; m 74. MOLECULAR GENETICS, PLASMID MOLECULAR BIOLOGY. *Educ:* Okla State Univ, BS, 64; Univ Wis, PhD(chem), 70. *Prof Exp:* Fel, Calif Inst Technol, 71-73; asst prof chem, 73-77, asst prof molecular biol, 77-79, ASSOC PROF MOLECULAR BIOL, UNIV SOUTHERN CALIF, 79- *Mem:* Am Chem Soc; AAAS; Am Soc Microbiol. *Res:* Molecular genetics of movable elements in prokaryotes; the organization of genes in bacterial systems, with emphasis on sequence relationships among plasmids and episomes; specialized recombination. *Mailing Add:* Molecular Biol Dept Biol Sci Univ of Southern Calif Los Angeles CA 90007

DE PACE, DENNIS MICHAEL, b Monticello, NY, Jan 19, 47. ANATOMY. *Educ:* State Univ NY Buffalo, BA, 68, PhD(anat), 74. *Prof Exp:* ASST PROF ANAT, HAHNEMANN MED COL & HOSP PHILADELPHIA, 74- *Res:* Autonomic nervous system including morphology, histochemistry and electron microscopy of autonomic neurons; autonomic innervation of the bone marrow. *Mailing Add:* Dept of Anat Hahnemann Med Col & Hosp of Philadelphia 230 N Broad Philadelphia PA 19102

DE PAGTER, JAMES KEITH, physics, see previous edition

DE PAIVA, HENRY ALBERT RAWDON, b Edmonton, Alta, Feb 29, 32; m 64; c 3. CIVIL ENGINEERING. *Educ:* Univ Alta, BS, 55; Univ Ill, MSc, 60, PhD(civil eng), 61. *Prof Exp:* Res bridge engr, Bridge Dept, Dept Hwys, Alta, 55-57; from asst prof to assoc prof, 61-68, asst dean, 65-67, actg dean, 67-68, head dept, 69-72, actg vpres capital resources, 71-72, PROF CIVIL ENG, UNIV CALGARY, 68-, V PRES SERV, 72- *Concurrent Pos:* Nat Res Coun sr res fel, 68-69. *Honors & Awards:* Gznoski Medal, Eng Inst Can, 71; State of Art of Civil Eng Award, Am Soc Civil Engrs, 74. *Mem:* Am Concrete Inst; Am Soc Civil Engrs; Eng Inst Can; Can Soc Civil Engrs. *Res:* Reinforced and prestressed concrete structures. *Mailing Add:* V Pres Serv Univ of Calgary Calgary AB T2N 1N4 Can

DEPALMA, JAMES JOHN, b Rochester, NY, Oct 30, 27; m 52; c 4. OPTICS, MATHEMATICS. *Educ:* Univ Rochester, BS, 55, MS, 57. *Prof Exp:* Sr res physicist, 52-66, lab head, 66-77, SR LAB HEAD, PHYSICS DIV, RES LABS, EASTMAN KODAK CO, 77-, MEM SR STAFF, 67- *Concurrent Pos:* Instr, Rochester Inst Technol, 57-67. *Honors & Awards:* Jour Award, Soc Motion Picture Picture & TV Engrs, 68; Optical Soc Am Award, 62. *Mem:* Optical Soc Am; Soc Photog Sci & Eng. *Res:* Optical and photographic physics, image science, and photometry; psychophysics; optical filters; emulsion optics. *Mailing Add:* Rochester NY 14650

DEPALMA, PHILIP ANTHONY, b Boston, Mass, Mar 2, 30; m 63; c 1. MEDICAL MICROBIOLOGY. *Educ:* Boston Univ, AB, 60, AM, 62, PhD(microbiol), 66. *Prof Exp:* From instr to asst prof biol, Boston Univ, 65-75; asst prof, 75-78, ASSOC PROF BIOL, SALEM STATE COL, 78- *Mem:* AAAS; Am Soc Microbiol. *Res:* Biochemistry of morphogenesis in fungi; biochemistry and electron microscopy of the cell wall of Candida albicans; relationship between virulence and morphology in the fungal pathogen, Candida albicans. *Mailing Add:* Dept Biol Salem State Col Salem MA 01970

DEPALMA, RALPH G, b New York, NY, Oct 29, 31; m 55; c 4. SURGERY. *Educ:* Columbia Univ, AB, 53; NY Univ, MD, 56. *Prof Exp:* Intern, Columbia-Presby Hosp, New York, 56-57; asst resident, St Lukes Hosp, 57-58 & 61-62; resident, Univ Hosps Cleveland, 62-64; from instr to assoc prof, 64-71, PROF SURG, CASE WESTERN RESERVE UNIV, 71-; ASSOC SURGEON, UNIV HOSPS CLEVELAND, 70- *Concurrent Pos:* Fel Coun Atherosclerosis, Am Heart Asn, 70- *Mem:* Am Col Surg; Soc Univ Surg; Am Heart Asn; Europ Soc Exp Surg. *Res:* Vascular surgery, atherogenesis; lipid metabolism; cellular and subcellular changes in shock; electron microscopy. *Mailing Add:* Univ Hosps of Cleveland 2065 Adelbert Rd Cleveland OH 44106

DEPAMPHILIS, MELVIN LOUIS, b Pittsburgh, Pa, Apr 15, 43. MOLECULAR BIOLOGY. *Educ:* Univ Pittsburgh, BS, 64; Univ Wis, PhD(biochem), 70. *Prof Exp:* Fel biochem, Univ Wis, 70-71 & Stanford Univ Med, 71-73; asst prof, 73-78, ASSOC PROF BIOL CHEM, HARVARD MED SCH, 78- *Concurrent Pos:* Established investr, Am Heart Asn, 74-79. *Mem:* Am Soc Biol Chemists; Am Soc Virol; Sigma Xi. *Res:* To understand at the molecular level how mammalian cells replicate their chromosomes and how chromosome replication is related to the control of cell proliferation. *Mailing Add:* Dept Biol Chem Harvard Med Sch Boston MA 02115

DE PANGHER, JOHN, b Oakland, Calif, Apr 6, 18; m 45; c 3. PHYSICS. *Educ:* Univ Calif, Berkeley, AB, 41, PhD(physics), 53. *Prof Exp:* Physicist, Radiation Lab, Univ Calif, Berkeley, 42-45; physicist, Naval Ord Test Sta, China Lake, Calif, 45-46; physicist, Radiation Lab, Univ Calif, Berkeley, 50-53; sr physicist, Gen Elec Co, 53-62; staff scientist, Lockheed Missiles & Space Co, 62-70; SR HEALTH PHYSICIST, STANFORD UNIV, 70- *Mem:* Am Phys Soc; Health Physics Soc; Am Nuclear Soc. *Res:* Neutron dosimetry; radiological and radiation damage physics. *Mailing Add:* 809 Newell Rd Palo Alto CA 94303

DEPAOLA, DOMINICK PHILIP, b Brooklyn, NY, Dec 29, 42; m 69. DENTAL RESEARCH, NUTRITION. *Educ:* St Francis Col, NY, BS, 64; NY Univ, DDS, 69; Mass Inst Technol, PhD(nutrit biochem), 74. *Prof Exp:* Fel, Mass Inst Technol, 70-74; clin instr oral diag, Sch Dent Med, Tufts Univ, 73-74; assoc prof nutrit & prev dent, Sch Dent, Med Col Va, Va Commonwealth Univ, 74-78; prof pharmacol & oral biol, Sch Dent, Fairleigh Dickinson Univ, 78-81, dir, Div Oral Biol, dir res & grants admin & dir nutrit, Oral Health Res Ctr, 78-81; PROF, DEPT COMMUNITY DENT & ASST DEAN POSTGRAD AFFAIRS & RES, HEALTH SCI CTR, UNIV TEX, 81- *Concurrent Pos:* Chmn, Comt Nutrit Dent & Med Educ, Va Coun Health & Med Care, 75-; Dept Health & Human Serv res grants, Nat Inst Dent Res, 75- & 78- *Mem:* AAAS; Int Asn Dent Res; Teratolog Soc; Nutrit Today Soc; Am Dent Asn. *Res:* Biochemical development of the cranio-facial complex; the effects of nutrition on development; the effects of nutrition on the etiology, progression and therapy of oral disease. *Mailing Add:* Dept Community Dent Univ Tex Health Sci Ctr San Antonio TX 78284

DEPAOLI, ALEXANDER, b Italy, Mar 20, 36; US citizen; m 61; c 2. VETERINARY PATHOLOGY. *Educ:* Mich State Univ, BS, 59, DVM, 61; Univ Calif, MS, 67; George Washington Univ, PhD(comp path), 74. *Prof Exp:* Resident vet path, US Army Med Unit, 63-65; staff pathologist, Div Vet Path, Armed Forces Inst Path, 67-69; asst chief exp path, Dept Path, SEATO Med Lab, 70-72; asst chief vet path, Armed Forces Inst Path, 72-74, chief, Div Vet Path, 74-76; CHIEF, PATH DIV, US ARMY INST INFECTIOUS DIS, 76- *Concurrent Pos:* Consult comp path, WHO, 75. *Mem:* Am Vet Med Asn; Am Asn Pathologists; Am Col Vet Pathologists; Int Acad Path; Soc Toxicol Pathologists. *Res:* Pathogenesis of bacterial and viral diseases. *Mailing Add:* Path Div Ft Detrick Frederick MD 21701

DE PASQUALI, GIOVANNI, b Theresienstadt, Czech, Jan 20, 17; US citizen; m 46. INORGANIC CHEMISTRY, RADIOCHEMISTRY. *Educ:* Univ Vienna, Bachelor Law, 38; Vienna Tech Univ, MS, 43, dipl eng, 47. *Prof Exp:* Asst prof mineral, Tech Inst Appl Mineral & Petrog, Austria, 49-50; res asst, 53-57, res asst prof, 61-73, RES ASSOC PROF PHYSICS, UNIV ILL, URBANA, 73- *Res:* Mossbauer spectroscopy; biomolecules; preparation of inorganic and organic compounds for Mossbauer spectroscopy and biochemistry; one and two dimensional conductors. *Mailing Add:* Dept of Physics Univ of Ill 110 W Green Urbana IL 61801

DEPASS, LINVAL R, b Kingston, Jamaica, Jan 14, 48; US citizen. TOXICOLOGY, CARCINOGENESIS. *Educ:* Georgetown Univ, BS, 68; Univ Miami, MS, 73; Univ Ark, PhD(toxicol), 78. *Prof Exp:* Toxicologist, Carnegie-Mellon Univ, 78-79; MGR, BUSHY RUN RES CTR, UNION CARBIDE CORP, 79- *Concurrent Pos:* Adj asst prof, Univ Pittsburgh. *Mem:* Sigma Xi; AAAS; NY Acad Sci. *Res:* Oral and dermal toxicology; acute, subchronic and chronic toxicity tests, reproduction studies and carcinogenesis bioassays. *Mailing Add:* Bushy Run Res Ctr Union Carbide Corp RD 4 Mellon Rd Export PA 15632

DEPATIE, DAVID A, b St Albans, Vt, Mar 24, 34; m 58; c 2. LASER PHYSICS, NONLINEAR OPTICS. *Educ:* Univ Vt, BA, 56, MS, 58; Yale Univ, PhD(physics), 64. *Prof Exp:* Instr physics, Univ Vt, 57-58; res asst, Yale Univ, 62-64; asst prof, Amherst Col, 64-66; vis staff mem, Los Alamos Sci Lab, 66-67; asst prof physics, Univ Vt, 67-72; RES PHYSICIST, US AIR FORCE WEAPONS LAB, 73- *Mem:* Am Phys Soc. *Res:* Experimental studies of nonlinear opitcal properties of matter and applications to phase conjugation; laser spectroscopy; atmospheric propagation; opto-acoustic spectroscopy. *Mailing Add:* Air Force Weapons Lab/ARAA KAFB Albuquerque NM 87117

DE PENA, JOAN FINKLE, b Lincoln, Nebr, Dec 3, 23; div; c 2. BIOLOGICAL ANTHROPOLOGY, PHYSICAL ANTHROPOLOGY. *Educ:* Univ Nebr, BA, 45; Ind Univ, PhD(anthrop), 58. *Prof Exp:* From instr to asst prof anthrop, St Louis Univ, 58-63, asst prof anat & orthod, Med & Dent Schs, 63-66; ASSOC PROF ANTHROP, UNIV MAN, 66-, HEAD DEPT ANTHROP, 81- *Concurrent Pos:* Consult & lectr health orgn res prog, St Louis Univ, 58-66 & Peace Corps training progs Latin Am, 60-63; consult, Nat Asn Home Builders, St Louis, Mo & Washington, DC, 63-64; Can Comn Int Biol Prog grant human adaptability, Igloolik Proj, Univ Man, 68-75, coordr comt human develop, 72- *Mem:* AAAS; fel Am Anthrop Asn; NY Acad Sci; Am Asn Phys Anthropologists; fel Royal Anthrop Inst Gt Brit & Ireland. *Res:* Physical growth and skeletal maturation; human adaptability; human evolution. *Mailing Add:* Dept of Anthrop Univ of Man Winnipeg MB R3B 2E9 Can

DE PENA, ROSA G, b Bairamcea, Rumania, Sept 1, 21; Arg citizen; m 46; c 2. ATMOSPHERIC CHEMISTRY, CLOUD PHYSICS. *Educ:* Univ Buenos Aires, PhD(chem), 50. *Prof Exp:* Instr phys chem, Univ Buenos Aires, 55-60, from instr to assoc prof meteorol, 60-67; res assoc, 69-73, assoc prof, 73-78, PROF METEOROL, PA STATE UNIV, UNIVERSITY PARK, 78- *Concurrent Pos:* Sci investr, Arg Coun Sci & Technol Res, 61-67; Arg Nat Coun Sci & Technol Res fel, Univ Clermont-Ferrand, 63-64; sabbatical leave, Univ Frankfurt, 78-79. *Mem:* Am Geophys Union; Sigma Xi; Advan Meteorol Soc. *Res:* Nucleation and growth of particles from gas phase reactions; scavenging of gases and particles by clouds and raindrops; chemistry of precipitation. *Mailing Add:* Dept of Meteorol Pa State Univ University Park PA 16802

DE PERCIN, FERNAND, b New Brunswick, NJ, June 8, 21; m 45; c 4. PHYSICAL GEOGRAPHY, METEOROLOGY. *Educ:* Rutgers Univ, BSc, 43; Calif Inst Technol, MSc, 47; Harvard Univ, PhD(climat, geog), 58. *Prof Exp:* Instr meteorol, Pa State Col, 47-48; chief, Qm Res & Develop Field Off, Dept of Army, 48-53, chief, Polar & Mountain Sect, Environ Protection Div, Qm Res & Develop Command, 53-60, chief, Polar Br, Army Res Off, Off Chief Res & Develop, Hq, 60-61; assoc prog dir, Phys Sci Facil, NSF, 61-63; chief, Spec Proj Br, Environ Sci Div, HQ, Dept of Army, 63-70, chief, Atmospheric Sci Br, 70-74, staff asst to cheif, Res & Develop Off, DAEN-RDM, 74-80; RETIRED. *Mem:* Am Meteorol Soc; Am Polar Soc; Sigma Xi; Asn Am Geogrs; Arctic Inst NAm. *Res:* Climatology; field investigations; physical environment of the arctic, subarctic and polar regions; climatology and microclimatology. *Mailing Add:* 5328 Wapakoneta Rd Bethesda MD 20016

DEPEW, CREIGHTON A, b Minneapolis, Minn, Mar 30, 31; m 52; c 5. MECHANICAL ENGINEERING. *Educ:* Univ Calif, Berkeley, BS, MS, 57, PhD(mech eng), 60. *Prof Exp:* From asst prof to assoc prof, 60-72, PROF MECH ENG, UNIV WASH, 72- *Res:* Heat transfer and fluid mechanics. *Mailing Add:* Dept of Mech Eng Univ of Wash Seattle WA 98195

DEPEYSTER, FREDERIC A, b Chicago, Ill, Nov 8, 14; m 48; c 2. MEDICINE. *Educ:* Williams Col, BA, 36; Univ Chicago, MD, 40. *Prof Exp:* From asst instr to prof, Col Med, Univ Ill, 46-71; PROF SURG, RUSH MED COL, 71- *Concurrent Pos:* Asst attend surgeon, Presby Hosp, 48-58, assoc attend surgeon, Presby-St Luke's Hosp, 58-62, attend surgeon, 62-; from assoc attend surgeon to attend surgeon, Cook County Hosp, 48-, clin prof, Cook County Grad Sch Med, 59- *Mem:* AMA; Am Col Surgeons; Am Asn Cancer Res; Int Soc Surg. *Res:* Surgery of the gastrointestinal tract; cancer of colon and rectum; behavior of experimental cancer in animals. *Mailing Add:* Dept of Surg Rush Med Col Chicago IL 60612

DEPHILLIPS, HENRY ALFRED, JR, b New York, NY, Apr 16, 37; m 59; c 3. PHYSICAL CHEMISTRY. *Educ:* Fordham Univ, BS, 59; Northwestern Univ, PhD(chem), 65. *Prof Exp:* From asst prof to assoc prof chem, 63-73, chmn dept, 71-76, PROF CHEM, TRINITY COL, CONN, 73- *Concurrent Pos:* Mem corp, Marine Biol Lab, Woods Hole. *Mem:* AAAS; Am Chem Soc; Soc Appl Spectros. *Res:* Physical biochemistry; spectrophotometric study of liquid water and effect of electrolytes on structure of aqueous solutions; structure-function relationships in respiratory proteins. *Mailing Add:* Dept of Chem Trinity Col Hartford CT 06106

DE PILLIS, JOHN, b New York, NY, Dec 21, 36; m 60; c 3. MATHEMATICS. *Educ:* Stevens Inst Technol, ME, 58; Univ Calif, Berkeley, MA, 62, PhD(math), 65. *Prof Exp:* Asst prof math, San Francisco State Col, 62-65; from asst prof to assoc prof, 65-73, chmn dept, 70-76, PROF MATH, UNIV CALIF, RIVERSIDE, 73- *Concurrent Pos:* Vis assoc mathematician, Brookhaven Nat Lab, 68-69; vis res fel, Math Inst, Florence, Italy, 72-73. *Mem:* Am Math Soc; Soc Indust & Appl Math; Math Asn Am. *Res:* Functional analysis; operator algebras; convexity; iterative analysis; complexity of computation; acceleration of convergence schemes; multilinear algebra; computer science. *Mailing Add:* Dept of Math Univ of Calif Riverside CA 92521

DEPINTO, JOHN A, b Youngstown, Ohio, Jan 4, 37; m 62; c 3. MICROBIOLOGY, BIOCHEMISTRY. *Educ:* Youngstown Univ, BA, 58; Univ Ill, PhD(microbiol), 65. *Prof Exp:* Nat Acad Sci-Agr Res Serv fel microbiol chem, Northern Regional Res Lab, USDA, Ill, 65-66; from asst prof to assoc prof, 66-75, PROF BIOL, BRADLEY UNIV, 75-, ASSOC DEAN, LIB ARTS & SCI, 78- *Mem:* Am Soc Microbiol. *Res:* Mechanism of action of microbial amylases. *Mailing Add:* Dept of Biol Bradley Univ Peoria IL 61606

DE PLANQUE, GAIL, b Orange, NJ, Jan 15, 45. RADIATION PHYSICS. *Educ:* Immaculata Col, AB, 67; Newark Col Eng, MS, 73. *Prof Exp:* PHYSICIST, ENVIRON MEASUREMENTS LAB, US DEPT ENERGY, 67- *Concurrent Pos:* Chmn health physics soc stand working group, Am Nat Stand Inst, 73-75 & 80-, co-chmn, Comt for Int Intercomparison of Environ Dosimeters, 74-, US expert deleg, Int Orgn Stand Comt for Develop of an Int Stand on Thermoluminescence Dosimetry. *Mem:* Am Phys Soc; Asn Women Sci; Am Nuclear Soc; Health Physics Soc. *Res:* Physics of radiation, radiation shielding and transport, radiation protection solid state dosimetry, reactor and personnel monitoring; design and testing of radiation instrumentation and calibration facilities. *Mailing Add:* Environ Measurements Lab 376 Hudson St New York NY 10014

DEPOCAS, FLORENT, b Montreal, Que, Jan 1, 23; m 52; c 2. PHYSIOLOGY. *Educ:* Univ Montreal, BSc, 46, PhD(biochem), 51. *Prof Exp:* Biochemist, Sacred Heart Hosp, Montreal, 51-52; asst res officer, Div Biosci, 52-58, assoc res officer, 58-61, sr res officer, 61-69, asst dir, Div Biol Sci, 69-79, ASSOC DIR, DIV BIOL SCI, NAT RES COUN CAN, 79- *Mem:* Am Physiol Soc; Can Physiol Soc; Can Biochem Soc. *Res:* Biochemistry and physiology of acclimation to cold in small mammals; noradrenaline-induced calorigenesis. *Mailing Add:* Nat Res Coun Div of Biol Sci Montreal Rd Ottawa ON K1A 0R6 Can

DEPOE, CHARLES EDWARD, b Southampton, NY, Sept 18, 27; m 52. BOTANY, FRESH WATER ECOLOGY. *Educ:* NC State Col, BS(ornamental hort) & BS(zool), 56, MS, 58, PhD(bot), 61. *Prof Exp:* Tech asst, Long Island Agr & Tech Inst, 53-54; asst prof biol, 61-66, ASSOC PROF BIOL, NORTHEAST LA UNIV, 66- *Concurrent Pos:* Chmn, La Jr Acad Sci, 66- *Honors & Awards:* Asn Acads Sci Distinguished Serv Award, 74. *Mem:* Fel AAAS; Bot Soc Am; Soc Study Evolution; Ecol Soc Am; Am Soc Plant Taxonomists. *Res:* Distribution, ecology and productivity of aquatic macrophytes. *Mailing Add:* Dept of Biol Northeast La Univ Monroe LA 71209

DEPOMMIER, PIERRE HENRI MAURICE, b Montcy-St-Pierre, France, Dec 15, 25; m 56; c 3. NUCLEAR PHYSICS. *Educ:* Univ Lille, Lic es Sci, 46; Univ Paris, Lic es Sci, 48; Univ Grenoble, PhD(physics), 61. *Prof Exp:* Lectr, Fac Sci, Univ Grenoble, 61-65, prof, 65-69; PROF, FAC SCI, UNIV MONTREAL, 69-, DIR LAB NUCLEAR PHYSICS, 69- *Mem:* Am Phys Soc; Brit Inst Physics & Phys Soc; Fr Phys Soc. *Res:* Weak interactions at low and intermediate energies. *Mailing Add:* Lab of Nuclear Physics Univ of Montreal Montreal Can

DEPP, JOSEPH GEORGE, b Pittsburgh, Pa, Dec 13, 43; m 68; c 2. RESEARCH & DEVELOPMENT MANAGEMENT. *Educ:* Carnegie Inst Technol, BS, 65, MS, 66; Carnegie-Mellon Univ, PhD(nuclear theory), 70. *Prof Exp:* Physicist radio physics, 71-76, mgr electro optics prog, 76-79, DIR, SPEC SYSTS OFF, SRI INT, 79- *Mem:* Am Phys Soc. *Res:* Apply state-of-the-art technology across the electromagnetic spectrum to the design and development of sensor systems. *Mailing Add:* 4815 Blue Ridge Dr San Jose CA 95129

DEPREE, DAVID OTTE, b Amoy, China, Sept 17, 18; m 42; c 2. ORGANIC CHEMISTRY. *Educ:* Hope Col, AB, 40; Univ Mass, MS, 42. *Prof Exp:* Res chemist dielectrics, Gen Elec Co, 42-44; res chemist fuel additives, Ethyl Corp, 46-61; sr chemist, Aerojet Gen Corp, 61-67, scientist, 67-71, SCIENTIST, AEROJET SOLID PROPULSION CO, 71- *Mem:* Am Chem Soc; Sigma Xi. *Res:* Development of solid propellants for rocket motors; fundamental research on alkali metal organic compounds; development of new antioxidants for hydrocarbon fuels; development of new water demineralization process. *Mailing Add:* Aerojet Solid Propulsion Co Dept 5440 Bldg 0525 PO Box 13400 Sacramento CA 95813

DEPREE, JOHN DERYCK, b Zeeland, Mich, Dec 5, 33; m 54; c 3. MATHEMATICS. *Educ:* Hope Col, BA, 55; Univ Colo, MS, 58, PhD(math), 62. *Prof Exp:* Inst appl math, Univ Colo, 57-62; asst prof math, Ore State Univ, 62-65; assoc prof, Va Polytech Inst & State Univ, 65-68; PROF MATH, N MEX STATE UNIV, 68-, HEAD DEPT, 75- *Mem:* Am Math Soc; Math Asn Am. *Res:* Theory of analytic functions; entire functions; integral equations. *Mailing Add:* Dept of Math NMex State Univ Las Cruces NM 88001

DEPRIESTER, CORAL LEE, b Jackson, Mich, Apr 24, 22; m 46; c 2. CHEMICAL ENGINEERING, PETROLEUM ENGINEERING. *Educ:* Univ Mich, BS, 47, MS, 48. *Prof Exp:* Res engr, Calif Res Corp, 48-58; chief engr, Richmond Explor Co, Venezuela, 58-62; sr eng assoc, Chevron Res Co, 62-68, sr staff engr, 68-79, licensing exec, 79-82; CONSULT, 82- *Mem:* AAAS; Am Inst Chem Engrs; Soc Petrol Engrs. *Res:* Light hydrocarbon vapor-liquid equilibrium; applied chemistry and physics for improving oil and gas well performance; analysis of oil, formation water and sedimentary rock to develop advanced practical technology. *Mailing Add:* 142 Selborne Way Moraga CA 94556

DEPRIMA, CHARLES RAYMOND, b Paterson, NJ, July 10, 18; m 43, 51. APPLIED MATHEMATICS. *Educ:* NY Univ, AB, 40, PhD(math), 43. *Prof Exp:* Instr math, Washington Sq Col, NY Univ, 41-43; lectr, Grad Sch, 43-46, res scientist, Appl Math Panel, 42-46; from asst prof to prof appl mech, 46-64, PROF MATH, CALIF INST TECHNOL, 64- *Concurrent Pos:* Vis prof, Univ Calif, Los Angeles, 48-; vis math br, Off Naval Res, 51-52; vis prof, NY Univ, 63-64; ed, Pac J Math, 73- *Mem:* Am Math Soc; Soc Indust & Appl Math; Math Asn Am. *Res:* Partial differential equations; mathematical theory of compressible gases and supersonic nozzle flows; water waves; functional analysis. *Mailing Add:* Dept of Math Calif Inst of Technol Pasadena CA 91125

DEPRISTO, ANDREW ELLIOTT, b Newburgh, NY, Nov 3, 51; m 73; c 2. SURFACE CHEMISTRY, CHARGE TRANSFER PROCESSES. *Educ:* State Univ NY, Oneonta, BA, 72; Univ Pittsburgh, MS, 73; Univ Md, PhD(chem physics), 76. *Prof Exp:* Teaching asst physics, Dept Physics, Univ Pittsburgh, 72-73; teaching & res asst physics & chem, Dept Physics & Chem, Univ Md, 73-76; NSF fel chem, Dept Chem, Princeton Univ, 76-77, res assoc, 77-79; ASST PROF CHEM, UNIV NC, 79- *Mem:* Am Phys Soc; Am Chem Soc. *Res:* Quantum number scaling properties in dynamics; charge transfer in gas and liquid phase reactions; gas-solid surface energy transfer and reaction dynamics. *Mailing Add:* Dept Chem Univ NC Chapel Hill NC 27514

DEPRIT, ANDRE A(LBERT) M(AURICE), b St Servais, Belg, Apr 10, 26; m 59; c 1. ASTRONOMY. *Educ:* Univ Louvain, MA, 48, MSc, 53, PhD(math), 57. *Prof Exp:* Lectr celestial mech, Lovanium Univ, Congo, 57-58; lectr, Univ Louvain, 58-62, prof, 62-64; mem staff, Boeing Sci Res Labs, 64-71; prof astron, Univ South Fla, 71-72; prof math sci, Univ Cincinnati, 78-79; MATHEMATICIAN, NAT BUR STANDARDS, 79- *Concurrent Pos:* NATO advan res fel, 63; vis lectr, Univ Wash, 65-67; vis prof, Univ Liege, 70; Nat Acad Sci sr res fel, 71; C P Taft prof, Univ Cincinnati, 79; vis prof, Univ Namur, 81. *Honors & Awards:* Agathon De Potter Prize, Royal Acad Sci, Belg, 57; Adolphe Wattrems Prize, 71; James Craig Watson Golden Medal, Nat Acad Sci. *Mem:* AAAS; fel Am Inst Aeronaut & Astronaut; Royal Astron Soc; Am Astron Soc; Int Astron Union. *Res:* Celestial and analytical mechanics; periodic orbits in the three body problem; axiomatic foundations of Hamiltonian formalisms; computer science. *Mailing Add:* Dept of Math Univ of Cincinnati Cincinnati OH 45221

DEPROSPO, NICHOLAS DOMINICK, b New York, NY, July 16, 23; m 60; c 1. ANATOMY, ACADEMIC ADMINISTRATION. *Educ:* NY Univ, BA, 46, MA, 47, PhD(biol ed), 57. *Prof Exp:* From instr to assoc prof biol, 47-57, actg dean, Col Arts & Sci, 71-74, actg asst vpres acad affairs, 72-73, dean, Col Arts & Sci, 74-79, PROF BIOL, SETON HALL UNIV, 74-79, VPRES PLANNING, 79- *Concurrent Pos:* Mem, Health Professions Educ Adv Coun NJ, 71-; mem, State Panel of Sci Adv, NJ, 81. *Mem:* Am Soc Zoologists; Am Inst Biol Sci. *Res:* Interrelationships between the pineal gland and other endocrine glands; comparative vertebrate anatomy; mammalian endocrinology. *Mailing Add:* Off of the Dean Seton Hall Univ Col of Arts & Sci South Orange NJ 07079

DEPUE, ROBERT HEMPHILL, b Pittsburgh, Pa, Aug 15, 31; m 56; c 2. CANCER. *Educ:* Carnegie Inst Technol, BS, 53; Hahnemann Med Col, PhD(microbiol), 63. *Prof Exp:* Res asst biochem, Univ Ill, 53-54; fel biophysics, Mellon Inst, 62-65; USPHS OFFICER, NAT CANCER INST, 65- *Concurrent Pos:* Vis assoc prof epidemiol, Univ Southern Calif, 58-80. *Mem:* Soc Epidemiol Res. *Res:* Enzymology; molecular biology; biophysics of muscle proteins; electron microscopy; viral oncology; research administration; cancer epidemiology. *Mailing Add:* Nat Cancer Inst Rm 11A04 Bldg 31 Bethesda MD 20014

DEPUIT, EDWARD J, DISTURBED LAND REHABILITATION, RANGE PLANT ECOLOGY. *Educ:* Mich Technol Univ, BS, 70; Utah State Univ, MS, 73, PhD(range sci), 74. *Prof Exp:* Res assoc reclamation, Mont State Univ, 74-80; ASST PROF RANGE MGT, UNIV WYO, 80- *Concurrent Pos:* Comt mem, Steering Comt Soil & Water Resources, Res Priorities for the Nation, 81- *Mem:* Soc Range Mgt; Soil Conserv Soc Am; Can Land Reclamation Asn. *Res:* Rehabilitation of drastically disturbed lands, with emphasis on western mined land reclamation; range plant ecology, ecophysiology and improvements. *Mailing Add:* Range Mgt Div Univ Wyo PO Box 3354 Laramie WY 82071

DE PUY, CHARLES HERBERT, b Detroit, Mich, Sept 10, 27; m 49; c 4. ORGANIC CHEMISTRY. *Educ:* Univ Calif, Berkeley, BS, 48; Columbia Univ, AM, 52; Yale Univ, PhD(chem), 53. *Prof Exp:* Res fel, Univ Calif, Los Angeles, 53-54; from asst prof to prof chem, Iowa State Univ, 54-64; chmn dept, 66-68, PROF CHEM, UNIV COLO, BOULDER, 64- *Concurrent Pos:* NIH fel, Univ Basel, 69-70; vis prof, Univ Ill, 54 & Univ Calif, Berkeley, Guggenheim fel, 77-78; 60; consult, Marathon Oil Co. *Mem:* Am Chem Soc; The Chem Soc. *Res:* Organic reaction mechanisms and stereochemistry; organic gas-phase ion molecule chemistry. *Mailing Add:* Dept of Chem Univ of Colo Boulder CO 80302

DERANLEAU, DAVID A, b Seattle, Wash, Apr 9, 34. BIOPHYSICS. *Educ:* San Francisco State Col, BA, 56; Stanford Univ, MS, 58; Univ Wash, PhD(biochem), 63. *Prof Exp:* NIH fel biochem, Univ Wash, 63-65; NIH fel, Swiss Fed Inst Technol, 65-67, Ciba res fel, 67-68; asst prof biochem, Univ Wash, 69-75; dir res, Hayes Prod, 76; asst prof biochem, 77-80, RES ASSOC, UNIV BERNE, 80- *Mem:* Am Chem Soc; Am Soc Biol Chemists. *Res:* Multiple equilibria; radiationless energy transfer in biological systems; optically detected magnetic resonance; biophysics of blood platelet activation. *Mailing Add:* Theodor Kocher Inst Univ Berne CH3000 Berne 9 Switzerland

DERBY, ALBERT, b Antwerp, Belg, Nov 12, 39; US citizen; m 62; c 3. DEVELOPMENTAL BIOLOGY, ENDOCRINOLOGY. *Educ:* City Col New York, BS, 61; NY Univ, MS, 64; City Univ New York, PhD(biol), 69. *Prof Exp:* Teacher gen sci, New York Bd Educ, 62-64; NIH training grant develop biol, Yale Univ, 68-70; ASSOC PROF BIOL, UNIV MO-ST LOUIS, 70- *Mem:* AAAS; Am Soc Zool; Soc Develop Biol. *Res:* Developmental study, both in vivo and in vitro of the biochemistry and endocrinology of amphibian metamorphosis; wound healing. *Mailing Add:* Dept Biol Univ Mo 8001 Natural Bridge Rd St Louis MO 63121

DERBY, BENNETT MARSH, b Brooklyn, NY, May 5, 29; div. NEUROPATHOLOGY, NEUROLOGY. *Educ:* Hamilton Col, AB, 52; Univ Va, MD, 56. *Prof Exp:* From intern to asst resident, Univ Va Hosp, 56-58; asst resident, NY Hosp, 58-59; res infectious dis, Vanderbilt Univ Hosp, 59-60, resident neurol, 60-61; vis fel, Neurol Inst NY, 61-63; res & clin fel neuropath, Mass Gen Hosp, 63-65; resident path & neuropath, Bellevue Med Ctr, 68-69; PROF CLIN NEUROL, SCH MED, NY UNIV, 71- *Concurrent Pos:* Dir neurol, Vet Admin Hosp, NY, 65- & neuropathologist, 66-; attend neurologist, Univ Hosp, 65-; vis neurologist, Bellevue Hosp, 65- *Mem:* Asn Res Nervous & Ment Dis; AAAS. *Res:* Long-term delineation of inter-relation of systemic and neurological disease, using sophisticated techniques of internal medicine and clinical-pathological correlation with adjunct electron microscopy. *Mailing Add:* Dept of Neurol Vet Admin Hosp New York NY 10016

DERBY, JAMES VICTOR, b Keene, NH, Sept 11, 44. PROJECT MANAGEMENT, ANALYTICAL CHEMISTRY. *Educ:* Oberlin Col, BA, 66; Univ Hawaii, PhD(anal chem), 70. *Prof Exp:* Anal develop chemist, 70-74, chief anal develop chemist, 74-77, supt metall control, Smelting Div, St Joe Zinc Co, 77-79, MGR RES, ST JOE MINERALS CORP, 79- *Mem:* Am Chem Soc; Am Soc Testing & Mat; Am Inst Mining Engrs. *Res:* Project management of new non-ferrous processes plus management of professional services including analytical labs, engineering, and library; specific experience in analytical chemistry, wet and instrumental, quality assurance, and project trouble-shooting. *Mailing Add:* Smelting Div St Joe Zinc Co Monaca PA 15061

DERBY, PALMER, b Washington, DC, May 23, 20; m 41; c 2. ELECTRICAL ENGINEERING. *Prof Exp:* Proj engr magnetron develop lab, 42-52, head develop eng sect, 52-54, mgr, Microwave Power Tube Div, 54-59, asst mgr, Spencer Lab, 59-60, mkt mgr, 61-62, asst gen mgr, 62-76, VPRES, MICROWAVE & POWER TUBE DIV, RAYTHEON CO, 67-, DIR, NEW BUS ANAL, 76- *Res:* Microwave electron tubes; microwaves. *Mailing Add:* Exec Offs Raytheon Co 141 Spring St Lexington MA 02173

DERBY, STANLEY KINGDON, b Bangor, Mich, Sept 12, 20; m 43; c 3. ATOMIC SPECTROSCOPY. *Educ:* Univ Chicago, BS, 44; Univ Mich, MS, 48, PhD, 57. *Prof Exp:* From asst to prof, 55-64, PROF PHYSICS, WESTERN MICH UNIV, 64- *Mem:* Am Asn Physics Teachers. *Res:* Faraday effects; analysis of biological material by ultraviolet emission spectroscopy; holography. *Mailing Add:* Dept of Physics Western Mich Univ Kalamazoo MI 49001

DERBYSHIRE, JOHN BRIAN, b Manchester, Eng, Apr 15, 33; m 55; c 2. VETERINARY VIROLOGY. *Educ:* Univ London, BSc, 55, PhD(microbiol), 60; Royal Col Vet Surgeons, MRCVS, 55. *Prof Exp:* Asst lectr vet path, Univ London, 55-56; sci officer path, Agr Res Coun, Inst Res Animal Dis, 56-64; assoc prof vet sci, Univ Wis, 64-65; prin sci officer microbiol, Agr Res Coun, 65-71; PROF VIROL, UNIV GUELPH, 71- *Concurrent Pos:* Bd mem, WHO/Food & Agr Orgn Prog Comp Virol, 75-79. *Mem:* Soc Gen Microbiol; Can Soc Microbiologists; Path Soc Gt Brit; Can Vet Med Asn; Conf Res Workers Animal Dis (pres, 80). *Res:* Immunological responses of swine to enteric viruses; immune response to rabies virus; immunological studies with bovine respiratory viruses. *Mailing Add:* Dept of Vet Microbiol & Immunol Univ of Guelph Guelph ON N1G 2W1 Can

DERBYSHIRE, WILLIAM DAVIS, b Paterson, NJ, June 26, 24; m 47; c 2. PHYSICS. *Educ:* Stevens Inst Technol, ME, 45; Purdue Univ, MS, 51, PhD(physics), 58. *Prof Exp:* Engr, Gen Elec Co, 45-47; instr physics, Stevens Inst Technol, 47-48; asst, Purdue Univ, 48-56; asst prof, 56-61, ASSOC PROF PHYSICS, COLO STATE UNIV, 61- *Mem:* Am Phys Soc. *Res:* Ferromagnetism; statistical physics. *Mailing Add:* Dept of Physics Colo State Univ Ft Collins CO 80521

DERDERIAN, EDMOND JOSEPH, b Sofia, Bulgaria, June 23, 42; m 73; c 2. PHYSICAL CHEMISTRY, SURFACE SCIENCE. *Educ:* Colby Col, AB, 66; Pa State Univ, PhD(chem), 74. *Prof Exp:* PROJ SCIENTIST, UNION CARBIDE CORP, 76- *Concurrent Pos:* Assoc, ERDA, Ames Labs, Iowa State Univ, 74-76. *Mem:* Am Chem Soc. *Res:* Microemulsions, surface and colloid science; heterogeneous catalysis; solution properties of polymers. *Mailing Add:* Res & Develop Dept Union Carbide Corp South Charleston WV 25303

DEREMER, RUSSELL JAY, b Bell, Calif, May 2, 40; div; c 2. PHYSICS. *Educ:* Occidental Col, AB, 61; Ind Univ, MS, 63, PhD(high energy physics), 66. *Prof Exp:* From asst prof to assoc prof physics, Calif State Col, San Bernardino, 66-78, assoc dean activ & housing, 68-78; ASSOC PROF PHYSICS & DEAN OF STUDENTS, WHITMAN COL, 78- *Mem:* Am Phys Soc; Am Asn Physics Teachers. *Res:* High energy physics. *Mailing Add:* Phys Dept Whitman Col Walla Walla WA 99362

DERENIAK, EUSTACE LEONARD, b Standish, Mich, Dec 29, 41; m 68; c 2. INFRARED ASTRONOMY, OPTICAL DESIGN. *Educ:* Mich Technol Univ, BS, 63; Univ Mich, MS, 65; Univ Ariz, PhD(optics), 76. *Prof Exp:* Engr, Rockwell Int, 65-72, Ball Brother Res, 72-73; tech asst fourier optics, Univ Ariz, 73-76; res assoc radiol imaging, Ariz Health Ctr, 76-78; PROF CORONA CURRENT DETECTORS, UNIV ARIZ, 78- *Concurrent Pos:* Vis prof, Hanscom Air Force Base, Lexington, Mass, 81. *Mem:* Optical Soc; Soc Photo-Optical Instrumentation Engrs; Radiol Soc; Optical Soc Am. *Res:* Infrared detectors with emphasis on understanding physics; schottky barrier diodes; charge transfer devices, used in the infrared spectrum. *Mailing Add:* 528 N Martin Tucson AZ 85719

DE RENZO, EDWARD CLARENCE, b Passaic, NJ, Sept 29, 25; m 50; c 4. BIOCHEMISTRY. *Educ:* Fordham Univ, BS, 45, MS, 47, PhD(biochem), 50. *Prof Exp:* Instr chem, Fordham Univ, 45-50; res chemist, 51-54, group leader & sr res biochemist, 54-68, head metab chemother dept, 68-71, dir metab ther res, 71-77, DIR ADMIN SERV LEDERLE LABS DIV, AM CYANAMID CO, 77- *Mem:* Am Soc Biol Chem. *Res:* Activation of plasminogen; streptokinase; fibrinolysis; metabolism. *Mailing Add:* Admin Serv Lederle Labs Am Cyanamid Co Pearl River NY 10965

DERENZO, STEPHEN EDWARD, b Chicago, Ill, Dec 31, 41; m 66; c 2. NUCLEAR MEDICINE. *Educ:* Univ Chicago, BS, 63, MS, 65, PhD(physics), 69. *Prof Exp:* Res asst, Enrico Fermi Inst, 64-68; PHYSICIST, LAWRENCE BERKELEY LAB, UNIV CALIF, 68- *Concurrent Pos:* Lectr, Univ Calif, Berkeley, 69-70 & 79- *Mem:* Am Phys Soc; Soc Nuclear Med. *Res:* Muon decay; strong interaction resonances; instrumentation for particle detection and radionuclide computed tomography. *Mailing Add:* Donner Lab Univ Calif Berkeley CA 94720

DE REPENTIGNY, JACQUES, b Montreal, Que, May 15, 20; m 46; c 1. BACTERIOLOGY, IMMUNOLOGY. *Educ:* Univ Montreal, BSc, 44, MSc, 45, PhD(org chem), 48. *Prof Exp:* From res asst to res assoc microbiol, Inst Microbiol & Hyg, 47-64, assoc prof bact & immunol, Fac Med, 64-66, PROF MICROBIOL & IMMUNOL, FAC MED, UNIV MONTREAL, 66-, ASST DIR DEPT, 77-, CONSULT, INST MICROBIOL & HYG, 64- *Concurrent Pos:* Univ Montreal fel biochem, Univ Paris, 52-53 & immunol, Nat Inst Med Res, London, Eng, 53-54. *Honors & Awards:* Can Soc Microbiol Award, 69. *Mem:* Am Soc Microbiol; Chem Inst Can; Can Biochem Soc; Can Pub Health Asn; Can Soc Microbiol (pres, 71). *Res:* Purification of antigens and antibodies; antigenic structure of microorganisms; immunofluorescence and fluorescence microscopy; nucleic acids and virulence in bacteria; metabolism and pathogenicity in pyogenic bacteria. *Mailing Add:* Univ of Montreal Fac of Med PO Box 6128 Montreal PQ H3C 3J7 Can

DERESIEWICZ, HERBERT, b Czechoslovakia, Nov 5, 25; nat US; m 55; c 3. THEORETICAL MECHANICS, APPLIED MECHANICS. *Educ:* City Col New York, BME, 46; Columbia Univ, MS, 48, PhD(mech), 52. *Prof Exp:* Res engr, Sr Staff, Appl Physics Lab, Johns Hopkins Univ, 50-51; res assoc civil eng, 51-53, asst prof, 53-55, from asst prof to assoc prof mech eng, 55-62, PROF MECH ENG, COLUMBIA UNIV, 62-, CHMN DEPT, 81- *Concurrent Pos:* Fulbright sr res scholar, Italy, 60-61; Fulbright lectr, Israel, 66-67, vis prof, 73-74. *Mem:* AAAS; Am Soc Mech Eng; Seismol Soc Am; NY Acad Sci. *Res:* Theory of elasticity; vibrations of crystals; thermoelasticity; elastic contact theory; mechanics of granular media; wave propagation in porous media; soil consolidation. *Mailing Add:* Dept Mech Eng Columbia Univ New York NY 10027

DERFER, JOHN MENTZER, b Navarre, Ohio, Aug 9, 20; m 44. INDUSTRIAL ORGANIC CHEMISTRY. *Educ:* Col Wooster, AB, 42; Ohio State Univ, PhD(org chem), 46. *Prof Exp:* Asst, Ohio State Univ, 42-45, res assoc & ed res proj, Am Petrol Inst, 45 & Air Res & Develop Command Proj 572, 45-47; res assoc, Univ Res Found, 47-55, assoc dir petrol inst res proj, 55-59; mgr res labs, Glidden Co, 59-61, dir res, Org Chem Div, 61-66, mgr explor res, Org Chem Group, Glidden-Durkee Div, 66-71, asst tech dir org chem group, 71-75, ASST DIR RES & DEVELOP, ORG CHEM DIV, SCM CORP, 75- *Honors & Awards:* Dwight P Joyce Award, SCM Corp, 67. *Mem:* Am Chem Soc; Tech Asn Pulp & Paper Indust; Am Oil Chemists Soc; NY Acad Sci. *Res:* Synthesis of low molecular weight hydrocarbons; synthesis and infrared spectra of cyclic hydrocarbons; knocking characteristics of hydrocarbons; pre-flame reactions of fuels; terpene chemistry; rosin; fatty acids; naval stores; essential oils; flavor and perfume chemicals. *Mailing Add:* 9136 August Rd Star Rte Box 107 Jacksonville FL 32226

DERGARABEDIAN, PAUL, b Racine, Wis, Jan 19, 22; m 47; c 4. MECHANICAL ENGINEERING, PHYSICS. *Educ:* Univ Wis, BS, 48, MS, 49; Calif Inst Technol, PhD(mech eng, physics), 52. *Prof Exp:* Actg head hydrodyn br, US Naval Ord Test Sta, 52-55; mgr syst design and anal dept, 55-65, STAFF MGR, TRW SYSTS, REDONDO BEACH, 65- *Concurrent Pos:* Vis prof, Calif Inst Technol, 71-72. *Mem:* Am Astron Soc (pres, 69-71). *Res:* Mechanism of cavitation; water-entry impact; rotational non-viscous flow; missile systems design and analysis; powered-flight mechanics; space technology; meteorology and theoretical analysis of tornadoes and hurricanes. *Mailing Add:* 18 Poppy Trails Rolling Hills CA 90274

DERGE, G(ERHARD) (JULIUS), b Lincoln, Nebr, Feb 11, 09; m 37; c 2. EXTRACTIVE METALLURGY. *Educ:* Amherst Col, AB, 30; Princeton Univ, PhD(phys chem), 34. *Prof Exp:* Metallurgist, metals res lab, 34-39, from asst prof to assoc prof metall, 39-49, prof, 49-51, Jones & Laughlin prof, 51-64, prof, 64-77, EMER PROF METALL, CARNEGIE-MELLON UNIV, 77- *Concurrent Pos:* Ed, Metall Trans, 58- *Mem:* Am Chem Soc; Am Inst Mining, Metall & Petrol Engrs; fel Am Soc Metals; fel Metall Soc; Am Ceramic Soc. *Res:* Kinetics and mechanisms of slag-metal reactions, especially ferrous systems, constitution and properties of non-aqueous melts, including slag, matte, fused salts and related high temperature systems; especially by electrochemical measurements, diffusion in such melts. *Mailing Add:* Carnegie-Mellon Univ Schenley Park Pittsburgh PA 15213

DERICKSON, WILLIAM KENNETH, b Jacksonville, Fla, Nov 9, 42. INTERNATIONAL TRAINING, ENVIRONMENTAL ASSESSMENTS. *Educ:* Univ Del, BA, 68, MS, 70; Kans State Univ, PhD(biol), 74. *Prof Exp:* asst ecologist, 74-79, proj leader, 78-80, terrestrial biol group leader & ecologist, 79-80, EDUC COORD & PROG MGR, NON-NUCLEAR INT PROGS, ARGONNE NAT LAB, 81- *Concurrent Pos:* Vis scholar, Univ Chicago, 77-78; consult, Asian Develop Bank, 80-; training specialist, Korea Inst Energy & Resources, 80-; consult, Gov Turkey, 81- *Mem:* AAAS; Am Mus Natural Hist; NY Acad Sci; Sigma Xi. *Res:* Environmental assessment of non-nuclear and nuclear energy technologies; international training programs in non-nuclear and nuclear energy technologies; computer modelling; physiological ecology; population ecology. *Mailing Add:* Argonne Nat Lab Div Educ Progs 9700 S Cass Ave Argonne IL 60439

DERIEG, MICHAEL E, b Jan 24, 35; US citizen; m 62; c 3. ORGANIC CHEMISTRY. *Educ:* Univ Nebr, BS, 56, MS, 58, PhD(org chem), 60. *Prof Exp:* Asst org chem, Univ Nebr, 55-59; res chemist, Celanese Corp, 60-61; appointee, Mass Inst Technol, 61-62; sr chemist, 62-71, tech coordr, Div Animal Health, 71-73, asst dir animal health res, 73-75, ASST DIR CHEM RES, HOFFMANN-LA ROCHE INC, 75- *Mem:* Am Chem Soc; The Chem Soc; fel Am Inst Chemists; NY Acad Sci. *Res:* Naphthenic acids; exocyclic olefins; macrocyclic and pyrimidine nucleoside antibiotics; reaction mechanisms; heterocyclic chemistry, especially benzodiazepines, benzodiazocines, quinazolines; polyether antibiotics, anthelmintics and coccidiostats. *Mailing Add:* Hoffmann-La Roche Inc Nutley NJ 07110

DE RIJK, WALDEMAR G, b Venlo, Neth, Mar 5, 45; US citizen; m 74; c 2. DENTISTRY, ATOMIC PHYSICS. *Educ:* Univ Amsterdam, BA, 68; Univ Nebr, PhD(physics), 74, DDS, 77. *Prof Exp:* Res asst, Lab Atomic Physics, Found Fundamental Res on Matter, Amsterdam, 62-68; res asst atomic physics, Univ Nebr, 68-74; ASST PROF DENT, CREIGHTON UNIV, 77- *Concurrent Pos:* Staff dentist, Plaza Dent Group, Lincoln, 77- *Honors & Awards:* E Hatton Award, Int Asn Dent Res, 76. *Mem:* AAAS; Int Asn Dent Res; Am Phys Soc. *Res:* Restorative dentistry; diagnostic procedures and dental materials, particularly myography of masticatory muscles and adaptation of dental direct restorative materials. *Mailing Add:* Creighton Univ Sch of Dent 2500 California St Omaha NE 68178

DERINGER, MARGARET K, b Spangler, Pa, Aug 16, 15; m 49, 77; c 4. CANCER, BIOLOGY. *Educ:* Hood Col, AB, 36; Johns Hopkins Univ, MA, 38, PhD(biol), 42. *Hon Degrees:* DSc, Hood Col, 76. *Prof Exp:* Res asst tissue cult, Dept Embryol, Carnegie Inst, Washington, DC, 38-40; res asst anat, John Hopkins Med Sch, 41-42; res fel biol, genetics, 42-66, biologist, 46-61, res biologist, 61-65, biologist, 71-80, GUEST WORKER, REGISTRY OF EXP CANCERS, NAT CANCER INST, 71- *Concurrent Pos:* Panel mem, Bd US Civil Serv Examiners, 50-55; mem spec fel bd, Nat Cancer Inst, 57-63. *Mem:* Am Asn Cancer Res; Am Genetic Asn. *Res:* Storage and retrieval of pathologic material and data on cancers and lesions of laboratory animals; use of information for research and educational purposes. *Mailing Add:* Nat Cancer Inst Landow Bldg Rm 1D16 Bethesda MD 20205

DERISI, MARY CHRISTINE, b Schenectady, NY, Sept 14, 05; m 38. DENTISTRY. *Educ:* Univ Pa, DDS, 27. *Prof Exp:* From instr to assoc prof prosthetic dent, 28-66, PROF PROSTHODONT, SCH DENT, GEORGETOWN UNIV, 66- *Mem:* Fel Am Col Dent; Am Dent Asn; Asn Am Women Dentists (secy-treas, 54, pres, 56). *Res:* Prosthetic dentistry. *Mailing Add:* 2849 29th Pl NW Washington DC 20008

DERKITS, GUSTAV, b Philadelphia, Pa, Apr 19, 50; m 75; c 1. SEMICONDUCTOR PHYSICS, SEMICONDUCTOR DEVICE PHYSICS. *Educ:* St Joseph's Col, Philadelphia, BS, 72; Univ Pittsburgh, MS, 76, PhD(physics), 80. *Prof Exp:* Res assoc, Dept Physics, Univ Pittsburgh, 80-82; MEM TECH STAFF, BELL LABS, MURRAY HILL, 82- *Mem:* Am Phys Soc; Inst Elec & Electronics Engrs; Sigma Xi. *Res:* Semiconductor physics, especially low temperature uses of tunnelling to examine impurity states; device-related physics. *Mailing Add:* 1707 Wallace St Philadelphia PA 19130

DERMAN, CYRUS, b Philadelphia, Pa, July 16, 25; m 61; c 2. MATHEMATICAL STATISTICS, OPERATIONS RESEARCH. *Educ:* Univ Pa, AB, 48, AM, 49; Columbia Univ, PhD(math statist), 54. *Prof Exp:* Instr math, Syracuse Univ, 54; prof indust eng, 55-68, PROF OPERS RES, COLUMBIA UNIV, 68- *Concurrent Pos:* Vis prof, Israel Inst Technol, 61-62, Stanford Univ, 65-66, Univ Calif, Davis, 75-76 & Univ Calif, Berkeley, 79. *Mem:* Fel Inst Math Statist; fel Am Statist Asn. *Res:* Applied probability theory. *Mailing Add:* 302A SW Mudd Bldg Columbia Univ New York NY 10027

DER MATEOSIAN, EDWARD, b New York, NY, Aug 6, 14; m 47; c 2. NUCLEAR PHYSICS. *Educ:* Columbia Univ, BA, 35, MA, 41. *Prof Exp:* Res chemist, Barrett Co, 38-41; asst physics, Ind Univ, 41-42; physicist, US Naval Res Lab, 42-46 & Argonne Nat Lab, 47-49; PHYSICIST, BROOKHAVEN NAT LAB, 49- *Mem:* Fel Am Phys Soc. *Res:* Radioactive decay; nuclear energy levels; high spin states and deexcitation of compound nucleus following heavy ion reactions. *Mailing Add:* Brookhaven Nat Lab Upton NY 11973

DERMER, OTIS CLIFFORD, b Hoytville, Ohio, Nov 11, 09; m 35; c 3. INDUSTRIAL ORGANIC CHEMISTRY. *Educ:* Bowling Green State Univ, BS, 30; Ohio State Univ, PhD(chm), 34. *Hon Degrees:* DSc, Bowling Green State Univ, 60. *Prof Exp:* From instr to prof, 34-72, head dept, 49-71, Regents Serv prof, 72-75, EMER PROF CHEM, OKLA STATE UNIV, 75- *Mem:* Am Chem Soc; AAAS; Royal Soc Chem. *Res:* Chemicals from petroleum and natural gas; organic nomenclature; chemical literature. *Mailing Add:* Dept of Chem Okla State Univ Stillwater OK 74078

DERMIT, GEORGE, b Istanbul, Turkey, Feb 9, 25; US citizen; m 50; c 2. SOLID STATE PHYSICS, ELECTRONICS. *Educ:* Robert Col, Istanbul, BS, 47; Cornell Univ, MS, 49; Polytech Inst Brooklyn, PhD(physics), 61. *Prof Exp:* Engr, Sylvania Elec Prod, Inc, 52-54; sr engr, Link Aviation, Inc, 54-56; chief scientist, Gen Transistor Corp, 56-59; sect head, Gen Tel & Electronics Lab, Inc, 59-63; OWNER, G DERMIT ELECTRONICS, 63- *Mem:* Inst Elec & Electronics Engrs. *Res:* Semiconductor devices; metals and alloys. *Mailing Add:* G Dermit Electronics 198-31 27th Ave Flushing NY 11358

DERMODY, WILLIAM CHRISTIAN, b Lompoc, Calif, Sept 22, 41; m 64; c 1. ONCOLOGY, ENDOCRINOLOGY. *Educ:* Calif State Polytech Univ, BS, 64; Utah State Univ, MS, 68, PhD(animal physiol), 69. *Prof Exp:* NIH fel reproductive physiol, Cornell Univ, 69-70; res physiologist, Endocrinol Dept, Parke, Davis & Co, 70-73; sr res physiologist, 73-76; head, Hormone Markers Sect, Biol Markers Lab, Frederick Cancer Res Ctr, 76-81; HEAD, ONCOLOGY RES & DEVELOP, AM DADE, MIAMI, FLA, 81- *Concurrent Pos:* Consult, Dept Anat, Med Sch & Dept Pediat & Commun Dis, Univ Med Ctr, Univ Mich, 71-76. *Mem:* NY Acad Sci. *Res:* Molecular endocrinology; oncology. *Mailing Add:* Am Dade 1851 Delaware Pkwy Miami FL 33125

DERMOTT, STANLEY FREDERICK, b Ormskirk, Eng, Aug 14, 42; m 65; c 2. PLANETARY SCIENCE, ASTRONOMY. *Educ:* Univ Col London, BSc, 64; Univ London, PhD(physics), 75. *Prof Exp:* Demonstr physics, Royal Mil Col Sci, 67-71; sr demonstr, Univ Newcastle upon Tyne, 72-74; sr res assoc, 75-76; res assoc & lectr, 77-80, SR RES ASSOC, CTR RADIOPHYSICS & SPACE RES, CORNELL UNIV, 80- *Mem:* Fel Royal Astron Soc. *Res:* Dynamical evolution of the solar system; dynamics of planetary rings; tidal and resonant interactions between planets and satellites; structure of the asteroid belt. *Mailing Add:* Ctr for Radiophysics & Space Res Cornell Univ Space Sci Bldg Ithaca NY 14853

DE ROCCO, ANDREW GABRIEL, b Westerly, RI, July 31, 29; m; c 1. CHEMICAL PHYSICS, BIOPHYSICS. *Educ:* Purdue Univ, BS, 51; Univ Mich, MS, 53, PhD(chem physics), 56. *Prof Exp:* Instr chem, Univ Mich, 54-56, Nat Acad Sci fel physics, 56-57, instr chem, 57-60, asst prof, 60-62; from asst prof to prof, Inst Molecualr Physics, Univ Md, College Park, 63-76, prof chem, Inst Phys Sci & Technol, 76-79; PROF NATURAL SCI & DEAN FAC, TRINITY COL, 79- *Concurrent Pos:* Vis prof, Univ Colo, 62-63 & Tufts Univ, 68-69; distinguished vis prof, US Air Force Acad, 75-76, mem, Defense Educ Study Group, 76-77; mem staff, phys sci lab, Div Comput Res & Technol, NIH, 69-79. *Mem:* fel AAAS; Sigma Xi; Biophys Soc; Am Phys Soc. *Res:* Statistical mechanics, especially liquid crystals; membrane phase transitions; circadian clocks; mathematical biology. *Mailing Add:* Dept Nat Sci Trinity Col Hartford CT 06106

DEROME, JACQUES FLORIAN, b Montreal, Que, Apr 20, 41; m 67. DYNAMIC METEOROLOGY. *Educ:* McGill Univ, BS, 63, MS, 64; Univ Mich, PhD(meteorol), 68. *Prof Exp:* Res fel meteorol, Mass Inst Technol, 68-69; res scientist, Dynamic Prediction Res Unit, Can Atmospheric Environ Serv, 69-72; ASSOC PROF METEOROL, McGILL UNIV, 72- *Mem:* Can Meteorol Soc; prof mem Am Meteorol Soc. *Res:* Numerical weather predictions; effects of energy sources and sinks in numerical models of the atmosphere; structure and stability of large-scale waves in the atmosphere. *Mailing Add:* Dept of Meteorol 805 Sherbrooke W Montreal PQ H3A 2K6 Can

DEROOS, FRED LYNN, b Minneapolis, Minn, Oct 23, 47; m 76. ANALYTICAL CHEMISTRY, MASS SPECTROMETRY. *Educ:* Univ SDak, Vermillion, BA, 69; Univ Nebr-Lincoln, PhD(anal chem), 76. *Prof Exp:* Asst prof & dir mass spectrometry, Univ Pa, 76-77; RES CHEMIST ANAL MASS SPECTROMETRY, BATTELLE MEM INST, 77- *Mem:* Am Chem Soc; Am Soc Mass Spectrometry. *Res:* Analytical mass spectrometry; chemical instrumentation design and modification; kinetic energy release accompanying metastable transitions in the mass spectrometer; chemical ionization mass spectrometry. *Mailing Add:* Battelle Mem Inst 505 King Ave Columbus OH 43201

DEROOS, ROGER MCLEAN, b Fresno, Calif, Aug 11, 30; m 55; c 3. ZOOLOGY. *Educ:* Univ Calif, Berkeley, BA, 55, PhD(zool), 61; Utah State Univ, MS, 58. *Prof Exp:* From asst prof to assoc prof zool, 61-70, PROF BIOL SCI, UNIV MO-COLUMBIA, 70- *Concurrent Pos:* Assoc dir, Div Biol Sci, Univ Mo, 71. *Mem:* AAAS; Soc Exp Biol & Med. *Res:* Comparative endocrinology; adrenal cortex functions and control; reproductive physiology. *Mailing Add:* 14 Eubank Ct Columbia MO 65201

DEROSE, ANTHONY FRANCIS, b Chicago, Ill, June 7, 20; m 52; c 6. MEDICINAL CHEMISTRY, PHARMACEUTICAL CHEMISTRY. *Educ:* Univ Ill, BS, 41, MS, 43. *Prof Exp:* Asst pharmacog & pharmacol, Col Pharm, Univ Ill, 41-43; res biochemist, Res Div, 46-60, supvr res serv, 60-64, mgr dept sci bldg serv, Sci Div, 64-66, res pharmaceut chemist, New Prod Div, 66-70, chief pharmacist & mgr res & develop pilot plant opers, 70-80, SR RES PHARMACIST, HOSP PROD DIV, ABBOTT LABS, 80- *Mem:* AAAS; Am Chem Soc. *Res:* Chemical consitution; pharmacognosy and pharmacology of medical plants; isolation and chemistry of substances of biochemical origin; antibiotic and vitamin research; pharmaceuticals. *Mailing Add:* Res & Develop Hosp Prod Div Abbott Labs AP4 North Chicago IL 60064

DEROSIER, DAVID J, b Milwaukee, Wis, Feb 22, 39; m 62; c 2. BIOPHYSICS, MOLECULAR BIOLOGY. *Educ:* Univ Chicago, BS, 61, PhD(biophys), 65. *Prof Exp:* Visitor, Lab Molecular Biol, Cambridge Univ, 65-69; from asst prof to assoc prof, Univ Tex, Austin, 69-73; assoc prof, 73-78, prof physics, 78-79, PROF BIOL, ROSENSTIEL BASIC MED SCI RES CTR, BRANDEIS UNIV, 79- *Concurrent Pos:* Air Force Off Sci Res fel, 65-66; Am Cancer Soc fel, 66-67; NSF fel, 67-68. *Res:* Determination and interpretation of the three-dimensional structure of complexes of biological macromolecules, in particular multi-enzyme complexes and actin containing structures. *Mailing Add:* Rosenstiel Basic Med Sci Res Ctr Brandeis Univ Waltham MA 02254

DEROSSET, ARMAND JOHN, b New York, NY, Jan 10, 15; m 39; c 5. CHEMISTRY. *Educ:* Lafayette Col, BS, 36; Univ Wis, PhD(chem), 39. *Prof Exp:* Jr chemist, State Hwy Comn Wis, 36-39; res chemist, Universal Oil Prod Co, 36-64, asst dir res, 64-74, assoc dir res, 74-76, dir separation res, Corp Res Ctr, 76-80; CONSULT, 80- *Mem:* Am Chem Soc; Newcomen Soc. *Res:* Process and catalyst research in the petroleum refining and petrochemical field of hydrotreating and separation via adsorbents; sulfur removal from stack gases; coal liquefaction. *Mailing Add:* 3223 Village Green Dr Sarasota FL 33579

DE ROSSET, WILLIAM STEINLE, b Chicago, Ill, Apr 1, 42; m 71; c 3. PHYSICS, BALLISTICS. *Educ:* Johns Hopkins Univ, BA, 64; Univ Ill, MS, 66, PhD(physics), 70. *Prof Exp:* RES PHYSICIST BALLISTICS, BALLISTICS RES LAB, ARMY ARMAMENT MAT READINESS COMMAND, 71- *Honors & Awards:* Res & Develop Award, US Army, 77. *Mem:* Am Phys Soc. *Res:* Penetration mechanics; shock physics; material properties at high strain rates; modeling of dynamic material failure mechanisms; ballistic testing. *Mailing Add:* Ballistics Res Lab Attn: DRDAR-BLT Aberdeen Proving Ground MD 21005

DEROTH, GERARDUS CABBLE, zoology, see previous edition

DEROTH, LASZLO, b Budapest, Hungary, Oct 26, 41; m 70; c 3. PHYSIOLOGY, CARDIOLOGY. *Educ:* Univ Montreal, DVM, 72; Univ Guelph, MSc, 75, PhD(biomed), 77. *Prof Exp:* Lectr physiol, 72-75, asst prof biomed, 75-80, chmn, Dept Med, 81-82, ASSOC PROF BIOMED, FAC VET MED, UNIV MONTREAL, 80-, ASSOC DEAN RES, 81- *Honors & Awards:* Scherring Award, 72. *Mem:* Am Asn Vet Physiologists, Pharmacologists & Biochemists; Am Physiol Soc; Int Bee Res Asn; World Asn Vet Physiologists, Pharmacologists & Biochemists. *Res:* Veterinary clinical physiology; veterinary cardiology; fetal and neonatal physiology; autonomic pharmacology. *Mailing Add:* Fac of Vet Med Univ of Montreal St-Hyacinthe PQ H3C 3J7 Can

DEROUSSEAU, C(AROL) JEAN, b Rice Lake, Wis, Aug 29, 47. OSTEOLOGY. *Educ:* Univ Chicago, BA, 70; Northwestern Univ, MA, 74, PhD(anthrop), 78. *Prof Exp:* Instr anthrop, Northwestern Univ, 74-78; staff assoc ophthal, Columbia Univ, 78-80; adj asst prof anthrop, Hunter Col, City Univ New York, 80; ASST PROF ANTHROP, NEW YORK UNIV, 80- *Concurrent Pos:* Co-prin investr NIH grant. *Mem:* Am Asn Phys Anthropologists; Human Biol Coun; Paleopath Asn; NY Acad Sci. *Res:* Documentation of age-changes in the adult rhesus monkey including joint degeneration, loss of bone, presbyopia and other age-related disorders; rates of aging are species-specific. *Mailing Add:* Dept Anthrop NY Univ 25 Waverly Pl New York NY 10003

DEROW, MATTHEW ARNOLD, b New York, NY, Apr 29, 09; m 41; c 2. MICROBIOLOGY. *Educ:* City Col New York, BS, 29; Columbia Univ, AM, 30; Boston Univ, MD, 34, PhD(med sci, biochem), 41; Army Med Sch, dipl, 43. *Prof Exp:* Teaching fel biochem, 35-37, instr bact & immunol, 36-56, from asst prof to assoc prof, 57-75, PROF MICROBIOL, SCH MED, BOSTON UNIV, 75- *Concurrent Pos:* Chemist & bacteriologist, Natick, Mass, 35-53; vis physician, Allergy Clin, Mass Mem Hosp, 36-43; path consult, Norfolk County Hosp, 42-; China Med Bd fel trop med, 56. *Mem:* NY Acad Sci. *Res:* Vitamin assays; blood groups; immunochemistry; allergy; chemotherapeutic agents and antibiotics; bacterial toxins and enzymes; medical parasitology. *Mailing Add:* Dept of Microbiol Sch Med Boston Univ 80 E Concord St Boston MA 02118

DERR, JOHN SEBRING, b Boston, Mass, Nov 12, 41; c 3. GEOPHYSICS. *Educ:* Amherst Col, BA, 63; Univ Calif, Berkeley, MA, 65, PhD(geophys), 68. *Prof Exp:* Field asst geol mapping, US Geol Surv, 62-63; geophysicist, Pan Am Petrol Corp, 64; res assoc lunar seismol, Mass Inst Technol, 68-70; res scientist geophys, Martin Marietta Aerospace, 70-74; chief opers seismol, 74-79, CHIEF TECH REPORTS UNIT, NAT EARTHQUAKE INFO SERV, US GEOL SURV, 80- *Concurrent Pos:* Co-investr seismol, Pioneer Venus '78, Comp Atmospheric Struct Exp, 66- *Mem:* Sigma Xi; Am Geophys Union; Seismol Soc Am; Royal Astron Soc. *Res:* Seismology, free oscillations; seismicity; earthquake prediction; planetary seismology. *Mailing Add:* US Geol Surv MS 51 345 Middlefield Rd Menlo Park CA 94025

DERR, ROBERT FREDERICK, b Philadelphia, Pa, Feb 15, 34; m 68; c 3. BIOCHEMISTRY. *Educ:* Pa State Univ, BS, 55; Univ Minn, MS, 58, PhD(biochem), 61. *Prof Exp:* Fel, Univ Minn, 61-62; biochemist, Northern Grain Insects Res Lab, 62-64 & Minneapolis Vet Hosp, 64-69; Nat Inst Gen Med Sci spec fel, 69-71; RES BIOCHEMIST, MINNEAPOLIS VET HOSP, 71- *Mem:* Am Soc Biol Chemists; Am Inst Nutrit. *Res:* Total intravenous nutrition; etiology of alcoholism. *Mailing Add:* Rte 3 Kenyon MN 55946

DERR, RONALD LOUIS, b Chicago, Ill, July 13, 38; m 76; c 3. COMBUSTION ENGINEERING. *Educ:* Purdue Univ, BS, 60, MS, 62, PhD(mech eng), 67. *Prof Exp:* Res asst, Purdue Univ, 61-62; develop engr solid propellant combustion res, Aerojet Corp, 62-63; res asst, Purdue Univ, 63-67; tech specialist, Lockheed Aircraft Corp, 67-72, chief combustion sect, 72-73; assoc head aerothermochem div, 73-75, HEAD AEROTHERMOCHEM DIV, NAVAL WEAPONS CTR, 75- *Concurrent Pos:* Mem steering comt, Joint Army-Navy-NASA-Air Force Combustion Working Group, 74-, chmn steering comt, 75-77, chmn, Propulsion Syst Hazards Subcomt, 79- *Mem:* Assoc fel Am Inst Aeronaut & Astronaut. *Res:* Basic and applied research in the area of solid propellant combustion including ignition, steady state combustion, combustion instability, and deflagration to detonation phenomena. *Mailing Add:* Aerothermochem Div Naval Weapons Ctr Code 388 China Lake CA 93555

DERR, VERNON ELLSWORTH, b Baltimore, Md, Nov 22, 21; m 43; c 4. ATMOSPHERIC PHYSICS. *Educ:* St Johns Col, AB, 48; Johns Hopkins Univ, PhD, 59. *Prof Exp:* Asst appl physics lab, Johns Hopkins Univ, 50, res assoc, Radiation Lab, 51-59; prin res scientist, Martin Co, 59-67; res scientist, 67-77, chief atmospheric spectro, Wave Propagation Lab, 67-81, DEP DIR, ENVIRON RES LABS, NAT OCEANIC & ATMOSPHERIC ADMIN, 81- *Concurrent Pos:* Adj prof, Rollins Col, 59-67 & Univ Colo, 71- *Mem:* Inst Elec & Electronics Engrs; Am Geophys Union; Optical Soc Am; Am Meteorol Soc. *Res:* Microwave, infrared and optical spectroscopy; atmospheric radiation and climate; atmospheric optics; cloud physics; statistical decision theory; statistical mechanics; lidar development. *Mailing Add:* R453 Wave Propagation Lab Nat Oceanic & Atmospheric Admin Boulder CO 80302

DERR, WILLIAM FREDERICK, b Reading, Pa, June 27, 39; m 61; c 2. PLANT ANATOMY. *Educ:* Lebanon Valley Col, BS, 60; Univ Wis, MS, 62, PhD(bot), 64. *Prof Exp:* Asst bot, Univ Wis, 60-64; from asst prof to assoc prof, 64-72, PROF BIOL, CALIF STATE UNIV, CHICO, 72- *Concurrent Pos:* NSF res grant, 65-67. *Mem:* AAAS; Bot Soc Am. *Res:* Seasonal development of cambium, ontogeny, and structure of phloem; histochemical studies of differentiating cells. *Mailing Add:* Dept of Biol Calif State Univ Chico CA 95929

DERRICK, FINNIS RAY, b Ballentine, SC, May 1, 11; m 37; c 2. ZOOLOGY. *Educ:* Univ SC, BS, 34, MS, 37, PhD(zool), 55. *Prof Exp:* Teacher pub sch, SC, 38-41; instr biol, Augusta Jr Col, 41-46; head dept, 46-73, PROF BIOL, APPALACHIAN STATE UNIV, 46- *Res:* Aquatic biology; conservation. *Mailing Add:* Kellwood 4 Boone NC 28607

DERRICK, JOHN RAFTER, b Clayton, Ga, Jan 17, 22; m 51; c 6. SURGERY. *Educ:* Clemson Col, BS, 43; Tulane Univ, MD, 46. *Prof Exp:* Instr chest & cardiovasc surg, Sch Med, Emory Univ, 56-57; assoc prof thoracic surg & actg chief div thoracic & cardiovasc surg, 57-67, PROF THORACIC SURG & CHIEF DIV THORACIC & CARDIOVASC SURG, UNIV TEX MED BR, GALVESTON, 67- *Mem:* Am Asn Thoracic Surg; Am Col Angiol; Am Col Cardiol; Am Col Surgeons; Am Fedn Clin Res. *Res:* Cardiovascular and thoracic surgery. *Mailing Add:* Div of Thoracic & Cardiovasc Surg Univ of Tex Med Br Galveston TX 77550

DERRICK, M ELIZABETH, b Augusta, Ga, Oct 11, 41. PHYSICAL CHEMISTRY. *Educ:* ECarolina Univ, AB, 63; Emory Univ, MS, 65, PhD(chem), 70. *Prof Exp:* Instr gen & phys chem, Salem Col, NC, 65-67; teacher gen & org chem & chmn sci dept, Davidson County Community Col, 70-76; assoc prof, 76-78, PROF CHEM, VALDOSTA STATE COL, 78- *Concurrent Pos:* teaching fel, Univ Ga, 79 & 80; vis lectr, Univ Ga, 80. *Mem:* Am Chem Soc; Sigma Xi; Am Asn Univ Prof. *Res:* Thermodynamics of solutions, including measurement of excess free energies of mixing using light-scattering techniques; physical properties of micromuscions. *Mailing Add:* Dept of Chem Valdosta State Col Valdosta GA 31698

DERRICK, MALCOLM, b Hull, Eng, Feb 15, 33; m 57, 65; c 1. EXPERIMENTAL HIGH ENERGY PHYSICS. *Educ:* Univ Birmingham, BSc, 54, PhD(physics), 59; Oxford Univ, MA, 61. *Prof Exp:* Instr physics, Carnegie Inst Technol, 57-60; sr res officer nuclear physics, Oxford Univ, 60-63; from asst physicist to sr physicist, Argonne Nat Lab, 63-74, dir, High Energy Physics Div, 74-81. *Mem:* Fel Am Phys Soc. *Res:* Elementary particle interactions and decays; neutrino physics; construction and development of techniques for colliding electron-positron beam experiments. *Mailing Add:* Argonne Nat Lab 9700 S Cass Ave Argonne IL 60439

DERRICK, WILLIAM RICHARD, b Oklahoma City, Okla, May 18, 38; m 60; c 3. MATHEMATICS. *Educ:* Okla State Univ, BS, 58, MS, 60; Ind Univ, PhD(math), 66. *Prof Exp:* Programmer, Int Bus Mach Corp, 60-61; asst prof math, Univ Utah, 66-71; vis assoc prof, Ariz State Univ, 71-72; assoc prof, 72-

75, PROF MATH, UNIV MONT, 75- *Concurrent Pos:* Fulbright fel, 75. *Mem:* Am Math Soc. *Res:* Complex analysis, particularly quasiconformal mappings in space and differential equations. *Mailing Add:* Dept of Math Univ of Mont Missoula MT 59812

DERRICK, WILLIAM SHELDON, b Millville, Pa, Mar 5, 16; m 42; c 2. ANESTHESIOLOGY. *Educ:* George Washington Univ, BA, 40, MD, 42. *Prof Exp:* Head anesthesiol sect, Peter Bent Brigham Hosp, 48-54; prof anesthesiol & head dept, Univ Tex M D Anderson Hosp & Tumor Inst Houston, 54-77; EMER PROF, UNIV TEX, HOUSTON, 77- HEAD DEPT, UNIV TEX M D ANDERSON HOSP & TUMOR INST HOUSTON, 54- *Concurrent Pos:* Assoc anesthesia, Harvard Med Sch, 48-54; sr consult, Vet Admin Hosps, Rutland Heights, Mass, 50-54 & West Roxbury, 53-54; consult, Murphy Army Hosp, 50-54, Cancer Yearbk, 54-77, St Joseph's Hosp, 55- & St Luke's Episcopal Hosp, 56-59. *Mem:* Am Soc Anesthesiol; Am Heart Asn; AMA; NY Acad Sci; Int Anesthesia Res Soc. *Res:* Respiratory physiology. *Mailing Add:* 2808 University Blvd Houston TX 77005

DERRICKSON, CHARLES M, b Simpson, Ky, Apr 26, 27; m 49; c 3. ANIMAL SCIENCE. *Educ:* Univ Ky, BS, 51, MS, 56; Mich State Univ, PhD(animal sci), 65. *Prof Exp:* Asst county agent exten, Univ Ky, 52-57, supt, Robinson Agr Exp Substa, 57-65; assoc prof, 65-70, PROF ANIMAL SCI & DEAN, SCH APPL SCI & TECHNOL, MOREHEAD STATE UNIV, 75-, HEAD DEPT AGR, 68- *Concurrent Pos:* Mem, Ky State Bd Agr, 70- *Mem:* Am Soc Animal Sci. *Res:* Basic and applied research in the field of animal nutrition. *Mailing Add:* 405 Edgewood Dr Morehead KY 40351

DERRINGER, CAROL VENTRESCA, b Columbus, Ohio; m 81; c 5. CHEMICAL WARFARE DEFENSE. *Educ:* Ohio State Univ, BS, 78, MS, 81. *Prof Exp:* Tech staff, Metrek Div, Mitre Corp, 78; RES SCIENTIST, BATTELLE MEM INST, 79- *Mem:* Opers Res Soc Am; Mil Opers Res Soc. *Res:* Chemical warfare defense and chemical threat analysis, including the behavior of chemical agents after their deployment; analysis of the use of screening smokes against enemy detection by both visual and electrooptical means. *Mailing Add:* Defense Syst Anal Sect Battelle Mem Inst 505 King Ave Columbus OH 43201

DERRY, DUNCAN RAMSAY, b Eng, June 27, 06; Can citizen; m 35; c 2. GEOLOGY. *Educ:* Cambridge Univ, BA, 27; Univ Toronto, MA, 28, PhD(geol), 31. *Prof Exp:* Lectr geol, Univ Toronto, 31-35; geologist, Ventures, Ltd & assoc co, 35-47, chief geologist, 47-54; vpres explor, Rio Tinto Mining Co Can, 54-60; consult geologist & pres, Duncan R Derry, Ltd, 60-69; PARTNER, DERRY, MICHENER & BOOTH, 69- *Honors & Awards:* Gold Medal, Brit Inst Mining & Metall; Logan Medal, Geolog Asn Can; Blaylock Medal, Can Inst Mining & Metall. *Mem:* Fel Geol Soc Am; Am Soc Econ Geol; fel Geol Asn Can; Can Inst Mining & Metall; fel Brit Geol Soc. *Res:* Mining geology; pegmatites; ore deposits. *Mailing Add:* 401 Bay St Suite 2302 Toronto ON M5H 2Y4 Can

DERRYBERRY, OSCAR MERTON, b Columbia, Tenn, June 12, 10; m 35; c 3. OCCUPATIONAL MEDICINE, PUBLIC HEALTH. *Educ:* Univ Tenn, AB & MD, 34; Johns Hopkins Univ, MPH, 40; Am Bd Prev Med, dipl, 50; Am Bd Occup Med, dipl, 56. *Prof Exp:* Rotating intern, John Gaston Hosp, Tenn, 35-36; field med staff, 36-48, asst dir health, 48-51, dir health, 51-69, mgr health & environ sci, 69-72, CONSULT OCCUP & ENVIRON HEALTH, TENN VALLEY AUTHORITY, 73-, LECTR PREVENTIVE MED, 80- *Concurrent Pos:* Consult prev & indust med, Baroness Erlanger Hosp & Mem Hosp, 52-; lectr prev med, Univ Tenn, 54-69; temporary consult, WHO, 60, 65 & 67. *Mem:* Fel AMA; fel Am Col Prev Med; fel Am Acad Occup Med; fel Am Pub Health Asn. *Res:* Industrialization and medicine; employee health and safety; environemntal hygiene; mass screening techniques; malaria control; fluorides and worker health. *Mailing Add:* 621 Miss Ave Signal Mountain TN 37377

DERSHEM, HERBERT L, b Troy, Ohio, Mar 26, 43; m 68; c 3. COMPUTER SCIENCE. *Educ:* Univ Dayton, BS, 65; Purdue Univ, MS, 67, PhD(comput sci), 69. *Prof Exp:* From asst prof to assoc prof, 69-81, PROF MATH & COMPUT SCI, HOPE COL, 81-, CHMN, DEPT COMPUT SCI, 77- *Concurrent Pos:* Res Corp res grant, 70. *Mem:* Asn Comput Mach; Math Asn Am; Inst Elec & Electronic Engrs. *Res:* Computer science education; programming languages; programming techniques; mathematical software. *Mailing Add:* Dept of Comput Sci Hope Col Holland MI 49423

DERUDDER, RONALD DEAN, geology, see previous edition

DERUSSO, PAUL M(ADDEN), b Albany, NY, Sept 9, 31; m 53; c 3. ELECTRICAL & SYSTEMS ENGINEERING. *Educ:* Rensselaer Polytech Inst, BEE, 53, MEE, 55; Mass Inst Technol, EE, 58, ScD(elec eng), 59. *Prof Exp:* From asst prof to assoc prof, 59-64, chmn syst eng div, 67-74, PROF ELEC ENG, RENSSELAER POLYTECH INST, 64-, ASSOC DEAN ENG, 74- *Concurrent Pos:* Consult, Gen Elec Co, 60-; Du Pont Year-In-Indust prof, 66-67; field reader, off educ, US Dept HEW, 70-; ad hoc vis, Eng Coun Prof Develop, 77- *Mem:* Inst Elec & Electronics Engrs. *Res:* Systems engineering, especially automatic control systems. *Mailing Add:* Jonsson Eng Ctr Rensselaer Polytech Inst Troy NY 12181

DERVAN, PETER BRENDAN, b Boston, Mass, June 28, 45; m 75. ORGANIC CHEMISTRY. *Educ:* Boston Col, BS, 67; Yale Univ, PhD(chem), 72. *Prof Exp:* NIH fel chem, Stanford Univ, 72-73; asst prof, 73-79, ASSOC PROF CHEM, CALIF INST TECHNOL, 79- *Concurrent Pos:* Alfred P Sloan fel, Alfred P Sloan Found, 77; Camille & Henry Dreyfus teacher scholar, Camille & Henry Dreyfus Found, 78. *Honors & Awards:* Wolfgang Prize, Yale Univ, 72. *Mem:* Sigma Xi. *Res:* Physical organic, especially reaction mechanisms, diradicals and I, I-Diazenes; biophysical organic, especially DNA polyintercalators, nucleic acid and crosslinking reagents. *Mailing Add:* Dept of Chem Calif Inst of Technol Pasadena CA 91125

DERZKO, NICHOLAS ANTHONY, b Kapuskasing, Ont, Jan 19, 40; m 66. APPLIED MATHEMATICS. *Educ:* Univ Toronto, BS, 62; Calif Inst Technol, PhD(math, physics), 65. *Prof Exp:* Asst prof, 65-70, ASSOC PROF MATH, UNIV TORONTO, 70- *Mem:* Soc Indust & Appl Math; Am Math Soc; Can Math Cong. *Res:* Matrix theory; mathematical scattering theory; Monte Carlo methods; mathematical economics. *Mailing Add:* Dept of Math Univ of Toronto Toronto ON Can

DE SA, RICHARD JOHN, b New York, NY, Aug 4, 38; m 59; c 3. ENZYMOLOGY. *Educ:* St Bonaventure Univ, BS, 59; Univ Ill, PhD(biochem), 64. *Prof Exp:* Trainee biochem, Johnson Res Found, Univ Pa, 64-65 & Cornell Univ, 65-68; from asst prof to assoc prof biochem, Univ Ga, 68-74; PRES, ON-LINE INSTRUMENT SYSTS, 80- *Mem:* Am Soc Biol Chemists. *Res:* Bioluminescence of marine organisms; enzyme kinetics, particularly flavin enzymes; instrumental design and construction. *Mailing Add:* Rte 2 Box 239A Jefferson GA 30549

DESAI, BIPIN C, b Rangoon, Burma, Oct 28, 59; Can citizen; m 74; c 3. DATABASE SYSTEMS. *Educ:* Jodhpur Univ, BEE, 62; Purdue Univ, MSEE, 65; McGill Univ, PhD(elec eng), 77. *Prof Exp:* Program engr, Gen Electric, 63-64; systs engr, Xerox Corp, 65-66 & CAE Electronics Ltd, 66-70; ASST PROF COMPUT SCI, CONCORDIA UNIV, 70- *Concurrent Pos:* Sessional lectr, Loyola Col, 67-70. *Mem:* Inst Elec & Electronics Engrs; Asn Comput Mach; Brit Comput Soc. *Res:* Architecturial improvement for database operating system and office automation applications. *Mailing Add:* Concordia Univ 7141 Sherbrooke St W Montreal PQ H3G 1M8 Can

DESAI, BIPIN RATILAL, b Hansot, India, Oct 5, 35; m 61. HIGH ENERGY PHYSICS. *Educ:* Univ Bombay, BSc, 54; Univ Ill, MS, 57; Univ Calif, Berkeley, PhD(physics), 61. *Prof Exp:* Physicist, Lawrence Radiation Lab, Univ Calif, Berkeley, 61; res assoc physics, Ind Univ, 61-63 & Univ Wis, 63-64; asst res physicist, Univ Calif, Los Angeles, 64-65; from asst prof to assoc prof, 65-71, PROF PHYSICS, UNIV CALIF, RIVERSIDE, 71- *Concurrent Pos:* Prin investr, Dept Energy contract. *Mem:* fel Am Phys Soc. *Res:* Regge poles; Dispersion relations; s-matrix theory; quark confinement; quantum chromo dynamics. *Mailing Add:* Dept Physics Univ Calif Riverside CA 92502

DESAI, INDRAJIT DAYALJI, b Nairobi, Kenya, Jan 7, 32; Can citizen. NUTRITION, BIOCHEMISTRY. *Educ:* Nat Dairy Res Inst, India, IDD, 50; Gujarat Univ, India, BSc, 54, MSc, 58; Univ Calif, Davis, PhD(nutrit), 63. *Prof Exp:* Instr dairy sci, Gujarat Univ, India, 54-55; res assoc nutrit, Cornell Univ, 63-64; res assoc biochem, 65-67, asst prof human nutrit, 67-70, assoc prof nutrit, 70-74, chmn div human nutrit, 71-72, DIR CONTINUING EDUC NUTRIT & DIETETICS, HEALTH SCI CTR, UNIV BC, 71-, PROF NUTRIT, UNIV, 74- *Concurrent Pos:* Vis prof, Med Sch, Univ Sao Paulo, Ribeirao Preto, Brazil, 77- *Honors & Awards:* Gilmore Award, Univ Calif, Davis, 63. *Mem:* Am Inst Nutrit; Nutrit Today Soc; Can Soc Nutrit Sci; Indian Dairy Sci Asn; Sigma Xi. *Res:* Dietary aspects of vitamins; nutritional role of vitamin E; lipid peroxidation; ceroids and biology of aging; food habits and assessment of nutritional status; biochemical and nutritional studies of vitamin E, selenium and antioxidants; international studies on malnutrition in developing countries. *Mailing Add:* Div of Human Nutrit Univ of BC Vancouver BC V6T 1W5 Can

DESAI, KANTILAL PANACHAND, b Mota-Samadhiala, India, Feb 7, 29; m 60; c 3. EXPLORATION GEOPHYSICS. *Educ:* Univ Bombay, BS, 52; Colo Sch Mines, GpE, 56, MS, 57; Univ Tulsa, PhD(petrol eng), 68. *Prof Exp:* Trainee well logging, Seismog Serv Corp, 58, log analyst, Birdwell Div, 58-61, area engr, 61-62; from geophysicist to sr res geophysicist, Res Ctr, Sinclair Oil Co, 62-69, sr res engr, Atlantic Richfield Co, 69; SR RES ENGR, FIELD RES LAB, MOBIL OIL CORP, 69- *Mem:* Soc Prof Well Log Analysts (pres, 74-75). *Res:* Design and development of laboratory measuring systems which precisely and sequentially measure both the longitudinal and shear velocities of a rock sample under triaxial pressure. *Mailing Add:* 6006 Hunters View Dallas TX 75232

DESAI, NITIN, b Bangalore, India, June 19, 48. EMULSION SCIENCE, TECHNOLOGY. *Educ:* Bangalore Univ, India, BSc, 68; Mysore Univ, India, MSc, 71; Ohio State Univ, MS, 76, PhD(food sci), 79. *Prof Exp:* Scientist, 79-80, SR SCIENTIST, PILLSBURY CO, 80- *Mem:* Am Chem Soc; AAAS. *Res:* Food stabilizers; protein-carbohydrate interactions; separation of polymers. *Mailing Add:* Res & Develop Pillsbury Co 311 2nd St SE Minneapolis MN 55414

DESAI, PRAMOD D, b Sangamner, India, Sept 11, 39; US citizen; m 67; c 3. THERMOPHYSICS. *Educ:* Tex A&M Univ, PhD(chem), 68. *Prof Exp:* Res assoc thermodynamics, Univ Calif, Berkeley, 68-72; ASSOC SR RES THERMOPHYSICS, PURDUE UNIV, 73- *Mem:* Am Chem Soc; Sigma Xi. *Res:* Collection, correlation analysis and synthesis of thermodynamic and thermophysical properties of metals, alloys, steels, polymers, minerals, rocks and other technologically important materials; generation of reference data values. *Mailing Add:* 1011 Devon St West Lafayette IN 47906

DESAI, PRATEEN V, b Baroda, India, Aug 14, 36. MECHANICAL ENGINEERING. *Educ:* Univ Baroda, BEng, 59; Va Polytech Inst, MS, 63; Tulane Univ, PhD(mech eng), 67. *Prof Exp:* Asst engr, Nat Mach Mfrs, India, 59-61; asst prof, 66-71, ASSOC PROF MECH ENG, GA INST TECHNOL, 71- *Concurrent Pos:* Consult, Lockheed-Ga Co, 68- *Mem:* Am Soc Eng Educ. *Res:* Thermal sciences; turbulent boundary layers; fluid vibrations; fluidics; biomechanics; whiplash studies. *Mailing Add:* Sch of Mech Eng Ga Inst of Technol Atlanta GA 30332

DESAI, RAJENDRA G, b Junagadh, India, Nov 7, 23; US citizen; m 55; c 4. HEMATOLOGY. *Educ:* Univ Bombay, MB, BS, 49; Boston Univ, PhD(physiol), 55. *Prof Exp:* Indian Coun Med Res fel hemat, 49-52; res fel, New Eng Ctr Hosp, Boston, 52-55; Fulbright scholar, 52-55; Damon Runyon fel, 53-55; hematologist, Nat Med Col, India, 56-57; res assoc hemat, Sch Med, Stanford Univ, 57-62; asst prof med, Sch Med, Boston Univ & Univ Hosp, 62-65; chief hemat, Orange County Gen Hosp, 65-69; DIR ONCOL, MERCY GEN HOSP, 78-; ASST CLIN PROF, SCH MED, UNIV CALIF, IRVINE, 69- *Concurrent Pos:* Anna Fuller Fund travel award, Far East, 60. *Mem:* Am Fedn Clin Res; fel Am Col Angiol; Microcirculatory Soc; fel Int Soc Hemat. *Res:* Microcirculation; transplantation immunity; kinetics of cell transfer across placenta; clinical and therapeutic aspects of various blood disorders. *Mailing Add:* 11100 Warner Ave Suite 150 Fountain Valley CA 92708

DESAI, RASHMI C, b Amod, India, Nov 21, 38; m 63; c 2. STATISTICAL MECHANICS, CHEMICAL PHYSICS. *Educ:* Univ Bombay, BSc, 57; Cornell Univ, PhD(appl physics), 66. *Prof Exp:* Trainee physics, Atomic Energy Estab Trombay, Bombay, India, 57-58, sci officer theoret physics, 58-62; res assoc statist physics, Mass Inst Technol, 66-68; from asst prof to assoc prof, 68-78, PROF PHYSICS, UNIV TORONTO, 78- *Concurrent Pos:* Vis assoc, Calif Inst Technol, 75; vis scientist, IBM Res Lab, San Jose, Calif, 81-82. *Mem:* Am Phys Soc; Am Asn Physics Teachers; Can Asn Physicists; NY Acad Sci. *Res:* Nonequilibrium and equilibrium statistical mechanics; molecular transport phenomena in liquids and gases; surface physics; dynamics of phase transitions; inelastic neutron and light scattering; kinetic theory of molecular fluids. *Mailing Add:* Dept of Physics Univ of Toronto Toronto ON M5S 2R8 Can

DESAI, VINODRAI RANCHHODJI, b Bulsar, India, Oct 14, 39; m 63; c 2. ORGANIC POLYMER CHEMISTRY. *Educ:* Gujarat Univ, India, MSc, 62; Univ St Andrews, PhD(chem), 68. *Prof Exp:* Sr chemist, Atlil Prod, Bulsar, India, 63-65; fel chem, George Washington Univ, 68-70; sr res assoc polymer chem, NC State Univ, 70-73; group leader, North Chem Co, Marietta, Ga, 73-75; res & develop group leader, Polymer Industs Inc, 75-77; MEM STAFF, INTEX PROD, INC, 77- *Mem:* Am Chem Soc; Am Asn Textile Chemists & Colorists. *Res:* Solution and emulsion polymerization of acrylic vinyl acetate/crotonic VAc/IBMA co-polymers; radiation induced polymerization of vinyl ethers. *Mailing Add:* Intex Prod Inc PO Box 6648 Greenville SC 29606

DE SALVA, SALVATORE JOSEPH, b New York, NY, Jan 14, 24; m 48; c 8. NEUROLOGY, PHARMACOLOGY. *Educ:* Marquette Univ, BS, 47, MS, 49; Loyola Univ, PhD, 57. *Prof Exp:* Asst anat, Marquette Univ, 47-49; asst neuroanat, Sch Med, Univ Ill, 50-51, instr, 51-52; asst prof anat & physiol, Chicago Col Optom, 51-53; pharmacologist, Armour Lab, 53-59; head pharmacol sect, Biol Res Lab, 59-66, sr res assoc, 66-72, mgr pharmacol & toxicol, 72-76, ASSOC DIR RES, COLGATE-PALMOLIVE CO, 76- *Concurrent Pos:* Biochemist, Milwaukee County Gen Hosp, 50-51; lectr pharmacol, Stritch Sch Med, Loyola Univ, 57- *Mem:* AAAS; Soc Exp Biol & Med; NY Acad Sci; Soc Pharmacol & Exp Therapeut; Inst Elec & Electronics Engrs. *Res:* Forebrain of primate; cytoarchitectonic of cerebral cortex in man, primate and squirrel; anti-convulsion and brain excitability; brain excitability and endocrine; interdependencies; pulmonary pharmacology; analgesimetry; dental pharmacology; experimental toxicology of surfactants; experimental dermatology. *Mailing Add:* Res & Develop Dept Colgate-Palmolive Co Piscataway NJ 08854

DE SANDO, RICHARD JOHN, b Haverhill, Mass, Apr 18, 32; m 65. PHYSICAL CHEMISTRY, X-RAY CRYSTALLOGRAPHY. *Educ:* Univ Mass, BS, 54; Purdue Univ, MS, 57; Univ Cincinnati, PhD(phys & inorg chem), 61. *Prof Exp:* Sr res chemist, 61-65, res specialist, 65-69, group leader, 69-73, advan develop mgr, 73-76, MAT DEVELOP MGR, MONSANTO RES CORP, 76- *Mem:* Am Chem Soc; Am Crystallog Asn. *Res:* X-ray diffraction studies of liquids and solutions, and metals and alloys. *Mailing Add:* Monsanto Res Corp Mound Ave Miamisburg OH 45342

DESANTIS, MARK EDWARD, b Vineland, NJ, May 9, 42; m 69; c 1. MORPHOLOGY, NEUROBIOLOGY. *Educ:* Villanova Univ, BS, 63; Creighton Univ, MS, 66; Univ Calif, Los Angeles, PhD(anat), 70. *Prof Exp:* Res assoc neurophysiol, Naval Aerospace Med Res Inst, 70-71; from instr to assoc prof anat, Georgetown Univ, 71-78; ASSOC PROF BIOL SCI, WASH, ALASKA, MONT & IDAHO MED EDUC PROG UNIV IDAHO, 78- *Concurrent Pos:* Res assoc, Nat Res Coun, 70-71; mem, Biological & Neurosci Subcomt, Nat Inst Mental Health, 80. *Mem:* AAAS; Soc Neurosci; Am Assoc Anatomists; Sigma Xi. *Res:* Degeneration and regeneration of nervous tissue; structure and function of muscle receptors and their central nervous system projections. *Mailing Add:* Dept Biol Sci & WAMI Med Prog Univ of Idaho Moscow ID 83843

DESANTO, DANIEL FRANK, b New Rochelle, NY, June, 21, 30; m 65. FLUID-STRUCTURE INTERACTION, SCALING LAWS. *Educ:* NY Univ, BAeroE, 52, MAeroE, 53, DEngSc, 61. *Prof Exp:* Res asst, Col Eng, NY Univ, 52-56, assoc res scientist, 59-63; flight test res engr, Grumman Aircraft Eng Corp, 56-59; prin aerodynamicist, Cornell Aeronaut Lab, Inc, 63-70; SR ENGR, WESTINGHOUSE RES & DEVELOP CTR, 70- *Concurrent Pos:* Instr, Manhattan Col, 56; adj asst prof, Col Eng, NY Univ, 62-63. *Mem:* Am Soc Mech Engrs; Am Inst Aeronaut & Astronaut. *Res:* Experimental and theoretical studies of flow-induced vibrations and dynamic response of structures to unsteady forcing functions including fluid coupling. *Mailing Add:* 15 Morris St Export PA 15632

DESANTO, JOHN ANTHONY, b Wilkes-Barre, Pa, May 25, 41; m 64; c 3. THEORETICAL PHYSICS, ACOUSTICS. *Educ:* Villanova Univ, BS & MA, 62; Univ Mich, MS, 63, PhD(physics), 67. *Prof Exp:* Res physicist, Acoust Div, Naval Res Lab, 67-78, res physicist, Ocean Sci Div, 78-81; SR SCIENTIST & PROG MGR THEORET PHYSICS, ELECTRO MAGNETIC APPLICATIONS, INC, 81- *Concurrent Pos:* Exchange scientist, Admiralty Res Lab, Teddington, UK, 74-75. *Mem:* Fel Acoust Soc Am; Am Phys Soc; Soc Indust & Appl Math; Sigma Xi; Inst Elec & Electronics Engrs. *Res:* Sound scattering from periodic surfaces and from random rough surfaces; propagation of sound in both deterministic and stochastic waveguides; theoretical foundations of acoustics and oceanography; electromagnetic scattering and propagation and theory. *Mailing Add:* Electro Magnetic Applications Inc 1978 S Garrison St Denver CO 80226

DESANTO, ROBERT SPILKA, b New Rochelle, NY, Sept 21, 40; m 64; c 2. ENVIRONMENTAL MANAGEMENT, ECOLOGY. *Educ:* Tufts Univ, BS, 62; Columbia Univ, PhD, 67. *Prof Exp:* Lectr zool, Columbia Univ, 62-64; asst prof, Conn Col, 68-72, dir summer marine sci prog, 69-72; chief ecol scientist, C E Maguire, Inc, 72-74; staff assoc, 74; co-founding dir & chief ecol scientist, Environ Serv, Comsis Corp, 74-77; CHIEF ECOLOGIST, DeLEUW, CATHER CO, 77- *Concurrent Pos:* Pres, Thomas Sci Ctr, 72-73; ed-in-chief, Environ Mgt, 74-, ed, 79- *Mem:* Ecol Soc Am; AAAS; Am Soc Zool; Soc Scholarly Publ. *Res:* Environmental monitoring, analysis, and management relative to environmental impacts and applied ecology. *Mailing Add:* 8 Sylvan Glen East Lyme CT 06333

DE SAPIO, RODOLFO VITTORIO, b New York, NY, Aug 16, 36. MATHEMATICS. *Educ:* Univ Chicago, MS, 61, PhD(math), 64. *Prof Exp:* Instr math, Stanford Univ, 64-66; asst prof, Univ Calif, Los Angeles, 66-69; assoc prof, Belfer Grad Sch Sci, Yeshiva Univ, 69-71; ASSOC PROF MATH, UNIV CALIF, LOS ANGELES, 71- *Concurrent Pos:* Mem, Inst Advan Study, 68-69; NSF grants. *Mem:* Am Math Soc; Math Asn Am; NY Acad Sci. *Res:* Topology and geometry of manifolds; algebraic topology, including homotopy theory and homology theory as applied to classification questions in differential topology. *Mailing Add:* Dept of Math Univ of Calif Los Angeles CA 90024

DE SAUSSURE, GERARD, b Geneva, Switz, Nov 22, 24; US citizen; m 55; c 2. NUCLEAR PHYSICS. *Educ:* Swiss Fed Inst Technol, dipl, 49; Mass Inst Technol, PhD(physics), 54. *Prof Exp:* Res asst physics, Mass Inst Technol, 52-54; PHYSICIST, NEUTRON PHYSICS DIV, OAK RIDGE NAT LAB, 55- *Mem:* Am Phys Soc; Am Nuclear Soc; Ital Phys Soc. *Res:* Measurement of neutron transport parameters by the pulsed neutron source technique; measurement of neutron cross sections, especially of fissionable isotopes, by the time of flight technique. *Mailing Add:* 100 Windham Rd Oak Ridge TN 37830

DESAUSSURE, RICHARD LAURENS, JR, b Macon, Ga, Dec 29, 17; m 48; c 3. NEUROSURGERY. *Educ:* Univ Va, AB, 39, MD, 42; Am Bd Neurol Surg, dipl, 51. *Prof Exp:* Intern, Univ Va Hosp, 42-43, resident neurol surg, 46-49; resident neuropath & neurophysiol, Cincinnati Gen Hosp, 47-48; asst chief neurosurg, Kennedy Vet Admin Hosp, 49-50, chief, 50; asst prof, 50-65, clin assoc prof, 65-70, PROF NEUROSURG, MED SCH, UNIV TENN, MEMPHIS, 70- *Concurrent Pos:* Pvt pract, 50-; mem exec comt, Baptist Mem Hosp, 62 & 65-67; mem, Am Bd Neurol Surg, 66-72, secy, 70-73. *Mem:* AMA; Cong Neurol Surg (pres, 61-62); Am Col Surgeons; Am Acad Neurol Surg; Am Asn Neurol Surg (pres-elect). *Res:* Concussion experiments. *Mailing Add:* Semmes-Murphey Clin 920 Madison Ave Suite 201N Memphis TN 38103

DESAUTELS, EDOUARD JOSEPH, b Winnipeg, Man, Jan 18, 38; m 61; c 3. COMPUTER SCIENCES. *Educ:* Univ Man, BSc, 60; Univ Ottawa, MSc, 64; Purdue Univ, PhD(comput sci), 69. *Prof Exp:* Sci programmer comput sci, IBM Sci Ctr, Ottawa, 60-62; systs programmer comput sci, Coop Comput Lab, Mass Inst Technol, 70; fel comput sci, IBM Systs Res Inst, New York, 63-64; instr comput sci, Purdue Univ, 66-69; asst prof, 69-74, ASSOC PROF COMPUT SCI, UNIV WIS-MADISON, 74- *Concurrent Pos:* Consult, Bur Purchases & Serv, Printing Bur, State of Wis, 75. *Mem:* Asn Comput Mach; Inst Elec & Electronics Engrs; Can Info Processing Soc. *Res:* Programming systems; minicomputer and microcomputer systems; computer networks; intelligent terminals; personal computers; managing computing. *Mailing Add:* Comput Sci Dept Univ Wis Madison WI 53706

DESBOROUGH, GEORGE A, b Panama, Ill, Jan 15, 37; m 66. GEOLOGY, MINERALOGY. *Educ:* Southern Ill Univ, BA, 59, MA, 60; Univ Wis, PhD(geol), 66. *Prof Exp:* Res assoc geol, Univ Wis, Madison, 64-66, fel, 66; geologist, Br Astrogeol, 66-67, GEOLOGIST, BR CENT MINERAL RESOURCES, US GEOL SURV, 67- *Concurrent Pos:* Consult, Ray-O-Vac Res & Develop, 62 & US Forest Serv Regional Off, 64; assoc prof, Dept Geol, Colo State Univ, 70; Mineral Soc Am rep, Int Comn Ore Micros, 71-73, secy, Comn, 74-78, chmn, Comn, 78-82; assoc ed, Am Mineral, 79-80. *Mem:* Fel Mineral Soc Am; fel Geol Soc Am; Mining Soc Gt Brit; Soc Econ Geologists; Am Inst Mining, Metall & Petrol Eng. *Res:* Mineralogy and origin of ore deposits. *Mailing Add:* Br of Cent Mineral Resources Bldg 25 Fed Ctr Denver CO 80225

DESBOROUGH, SHARON LEE, b Carbondale, Ill, Dec 22, 35. PLANT GENETICS. *Educ:* Southern Ill Univ, BA, 58, MA, 59; Univ Wis, PhD(genetics), 67. *Prof Exp:* Res assoc genetics, Univ Wis, 60-62, fel hort, 68-69; res fel, 69-72, asst prof, 72-76, ASSOC PROF HORT, UNIV MINN, 76- *Mem:* Am Genetics Asn; Genetics Soc Am; Am Potato Asn; Europ Potato Asn. *Res:* Potato-biochemical genetics, improvement of potato protein, isoenzymes and proteins from tubers; evolutionary species relationships. *Mailing Add:* Hort Sci & Landscape Archit Univ Minn St Paul MN 55108

DESCARRIES, LAURENT, b Montreal, Que, Jan 27, 39; m 62; c 3. NEUROBIOLOGY, NEUROANATOMY. *Educ:* Univ Paris, BA, 56; Univ Montreal, MD, 61; FRCP(C), 66. *Prof Exp:* Intern med, Maisonneuve Hosp, Montreal, 60-61; resident, Notre Dame Hosp, 61-62 & Maisonneuve Hosp, 62-63; from asst prof to assoc prof, 69-77, PROF PHYSIOL, FAC MED, UNIV MONTREAL, 77-, MEM CTR RES SCI NEUROL, 70- *Concurrent Pos:* Fel neurol & neuropath, Mass Gen Hosp, Boston, 63-67; clin & res fel neurol, Harvard Med Sch, 63-64, res fel neuropath, 64-65 & exp neuropath, 65-67; Med Res Coun Can fel, 63-67, centennial fel, 67-69, scholar, 69-74; fel neurobiol, Commissariat Atomic Energy, Ctr Nuclear Studies, France, 67-69. *Mem:* Can Neurol Soc; French Soc Electron Micros; Can Asn Anat; Am Asn Anat; Soc Neurosci. *Res:* Neurocytology; transmitters and modulators; monoaminergic systems; neuronal metabolism. *Mailing Add:* Ctr for Res in Neurol Sci Univ of Montreal Montreal PQ H3C 3J7 Can

DESCH, MICHAEL DANIEL, b East Orange, NJ, May 28, 47; m 81. RADIO ASTRONOMY, PLANETARY MAGNETOSPHERES. *Educ:* Providence Col, BS, 69; Univ Fla, PhD(astron), 76. *Prof Exp:* Fel, Nat Res Coun, 78-80 & Univ Md, 80-81; RADIO ASTRONR, GODDARD SPACE FLIGHT CTR, NASA, 81- *Res:* analysis and interpretation of data from spaceborne radio astronomy experiments, especially related to the planets Earth, Jupiter and Saturn. *Mailing Add:* Code 695 Goddard Space Flight Ctr Greenbelt MD 20771

DESCHAMPS, GEORGES ARMAND, b Vendome, France, Oct 18, 11; US citizen; m 43; c 3. ELECTRICAL ENGINEERING, APPLIED MATHEMATICS. *Educ:* Univ Paris, Licence, 33, Agrege(math), 34. *Prof Exp:* Sr scientist fed telecom lab, ITT Corp, 58; PROF ELEC ENG & DIR ELECTROMAGNETICS LAB, UNIV ILL, 58- *Concurrent Pos:* Chmn US comn B fields & waves, Int Union Radio Sci, 79- *Mem:* Nat Acad Eng; Am Phys Soc; fel Inst Elec & Electronics Engrs. *Res:* Physics; electromagnetics. *Mailing Add:* Dept of Eng Univ of Ill Urbana IL 61801

DESCHENES, JEAN MARC, b Quebec, Que, Aug 9, 41; m 64; c 2. ECOLOGY, AGRONOMY. *Educ:* Laval Univ, BS, 63; Rutgers Univ, MS, 65, PhD(ecol), 68. *Prof Exp:* RES SCIENTIST, RES BR, AGR CAN, 67- *Mem:* Ecol Soc Am; Weed Sci Soc Am; Sigma Xi. *Res:* Weed surveys and crop losses due to weeds; reproductive and growth strategies of weeds; population dynamics of weeds versus agricultural practices. *Mailing Add:* Res Sta Agr Can 2560 Boul Hoche Laga Ste-Foy Quebec PQ G1R 4X6 Can

DESCHERE, ALLEN R(ICHARD), b New York, NY, Sept 1, 17; m 45; c 4. MECHANICAL ENGINEERING. *Educ:* Worcester Polytech Inst, BSME, 38; Lehigh Univ, MSIE, 40. *Prof Exp:* Instr, Lehigh Univ, 38-40; indust engr & supvr, E I du Pont de Nemours & Co, Inc, 40-43; from asst prof to assoc prof mech eng, Univ Colo, 46-51; head rocket develop sect, Rohm and Haas Co, 51-54, dir res, Redstone Div, 54-56, gen mgr, 56-63, asst dir res, Res Div, Springhouse, 63-70, dir info serv, 70-76; AUTOMATED SYSTS COORDR, NAT LIBR SERV FOR BLIND & PHYS HANDICAPPED, US LIBR CONG, 76- *Concurrent Pos:* Consult, Gates Rubber Co, 51. *Mem:* Am Soc Mech Engrs; Sigma Xi. *Res:* Administration; library and office automation. *Mailing Add:* 4609 Bel Pre Rd Rockville MD 20853

DE SCHMERTZING, HANNIBAL, b Budapest, Hungary, Aug 21, 16; US citizen; m 59; c 1. ANALYTICAL CHEMISTRY. *Educ:* Pazamany Univ, Budapest, MS, 38, PhD(anal chem), 43. *Prof Exp:* Asst anal chem, Eotvos Lorand Univ, Budapest, 40-43; chief chemist, Testing Lab, Mid Slovakian Ironworks, 47-48; interpreter transl, Counter Intel Corps, 48-49; res chemist, Austrian Nitrogen Work, 49-50; bookkeeping, construct, Cie Africaine Emballage et Conditionement, 50-51; chief chem sect, Porter Urquhardt Skidmore Owings & Merrill Assocs, 51-53; head cent lab, Mediter Div, US Army Corps Engrs, Morocco, 53-56; res chemist, Allied Chem Co, 56-59; sr scientist, Melpar Inc, 60-68; SR SCIENTIST, GODDARD SPACE FLIGHT CTR, NASA, 68- *Mem:* Am Chem Soc; Am Soc Testing & Mat; Am Inst Aeronaut & Astronaut. *Res:* Titrimetry; gravimetry; colorimetry; qualitative and quantitative micro analysis; thin layer chromatography; x-ray diffraction and fluorescence analysis; gas chromatography and mass spectroscopy. *Mailing Add:* 1025 Towlston Rd McLean VA 22101

DESCHNER, ELEANOR ELIZABETH, b Jersey City, NJ, Oct 18, 28; m 75; c 2. CELL KINETICS, CARCINOGENESIS. *Educ:* Notre Dame Col, Staten Island, BA, 49; Fordham Univ, MS, 51, PhD(biol), 54. *Prof Exp:* Asst, Fordham Univ, 51-52; jr tech specialist, Brookhaven Nat Lab, 52, res collabr, 54; USPHS fel, Nat Cancer Inst & Brit Empire Cancer Campaign, Res Unit Radiobiol, Mt Vernon Hosp, Eng, 54-57; res assoc, Columbia Univ, 58-59; res assoc, 60-63, asst prof radiol, 63-76, ASSOC PROF RADIOBIOL IN MED, CORNELL UNIV, 76-; ASSOC MEM, SLOAN-KETTERING INST CANCER RES, 75- *Concurrent Pos:* AEC fel, 52-54; assoc, Sloan-Kettering Inst Cancer Res, 71-75, assoc mem & head, Lab Digestive Tract Carcinogenesis, 75-; asst radiobiologist, Mem Hosp Cancer & Allied Dis, 72-78, assoc radiobiologist, 78-; mem path subcomt, Nat Large Bowel Cancer Proj; sci comt cancer res unit, Clin St Michel, Brussels, Belg, 77-80; mem, Int Study Group Gastric Cancer, 78- *Honors & Awards:* Auxiliary Lectr, Am Col Gastroenterol, 81. *Mem:* AAAS; Radiation Res Soc; Sigma Xi; Am Asn Cancer Res; Am Gastroenterol Asn. *Res:* Carcinogenesis; autoradiographic methods for early detection of colon cancer; cell kinetic studies of the gastrointestinal tract during carcinogenesis; nutritional modification of cell proliferation and tumor igenesis. *Mailing Add:* Mem Sloan-Kettering Cancer Ctr 1275 York Ave New York NY 07306

DESELM, HENRY RAWIE, b Columbus, Ohio, Nov 1, 24; m 48; c 2. PLANT ECOLOGY. *Educ:* Ohio State Univ, PhD(bot), 53. *Prof Exp:* Asst bot, Ohio State Univ, 50-53, asst instr, 54; instr biol, Mid Tenn State Col, 54-56; instr & res asst bot, 56-60, from asst prof to assoc prof, 60-73, PROF BOT, UNIV TENN, KNOXVILLE, 73- *Mem:* Fel AAAS; Ecol Soc Am; Bot Soc Am. *Res:* Natural vegetation distribution and control; primary production; mineral and fission product cycling; calciphiles; ecological races; remote sensing of environment. *Mailing Add:* Dept of Bot & Grad Prog Ecol Univ of Tenn Knoxville TN 37916

DE SELMS, ROY CHARLES, b San Pedro, Calif, Dec 17, 32; m 59; c 2. ORGANIC CHEMISTRY. *Educ:* Univ Wash, BS, 54; Stanford Univ, PhD(chem), 59. *Prof Exp:* Res chemist, Res Labs, Eastman Kodak Co, NY, 59-62; fel alkaloid biosynthesis, Univ Calif, Berkeley, 62-63; res chemist, Ortho Div, Chevron Chem Co, 63-66; sr res chemist, 66-70, RES ASSOC, EASTMAN KODAK CO, 70- *Concurrent Pos:* Instr, Univ Calif, Berkeley, 64-76; assoc instr, Eve Exten, Univ Rochester, 67- *Mem:* Am Chem Soc. *Res:* Organic chemistry of heterocyclics, carbenes, alicyclics, pesticides and photoreproduction. *Mailing Add:* Eastman Kodak Res Labs B82 Kodak Park Rochester NY 14650

DESER, STANLEY, b Poland, Mar 19, 31; nat US. THEORETICAL PHYSICS. *Educ:* Brooklyn Col, BS, 49; Harvard Univ, MA, 50, PhD(physics), 53. *Hon Degrees:* DPhil, Stockholm Univ, 78. *Prof Exp:* Mem & Jewett fel, Inst Advan Study, Princeton, 53-55; NSF fel, Inst Theoret Physics, Denmark, 55-57; lectr physics, Harvard Univ, 57-58; from assoc prof to prof, 58-80, ANCELL PROF PHYSICS, BRANDEIS UNIV, 80- *Concurrent Pos:* Res assoc, Radiation Lab, Univ Calif, 54; Fulbright & Guggenheim fels, 66-67; vis prof, Univ Sorbonne, 66-67, 71-72; Fulbright prof, Univ of Repub, Uruguay, 70; Loeb lectr, Harvard Univ, 75-76; NATO sr res fel, 76; vis sr scientist, Europ Orgn Nuclear Res, Geneva, 76 & 80-81; vis prof, Col France, 76. *Mem:* Fel Am Phys Soc; fel Am Acad Arts & Sci. *Res:* Elementary particle physics; field theory; relativity. *Mailing Add:* Dept of Physics Brandeis Univ Waltham MA 02254

DE SERRES, FREDERICK JOSEPH, b Dobbs Ferry, NY, Sept 24, 29; m 54; c 6. ENVIRONMENTAL HEALTH, MICROBIAL GENETICS. *Educ:* Tufts Univ, BS, 51; Yale Univ, MS, 53, PhD(bot), 55. *Prof Exp:* Res assoc, Biol Div, Oak Ridge Nat Lab, 55-57, sr staff biologist, 57-72, coordr environ mutagenesis prog, 69-72, lectr, Univ Tenn-Oak Ridge Grad Sch Biomed Sci, 71-72; chief environ mutagenesis br, 72-76, ASSOC DIR GENETICS, NAT INST ENVIRON HEALTH SCI, 76- *Concurrent Pos:* mem comt for RBE of neutrons, Int Comn Radiol Protection Task Group, 69-72; adv comt, Environ Mutagen Info Ctr, 69-72; comt assessment nitrate accumulation in environ, Agr Bd, Div Biol & Agr, Nat Res Coun, 70-72, Genetics Soc Am rep, 70-73, mem comt radiation preserv of food, Nat Acad Sci-Nat Res Coun, 72-75; mem, Mammalian Genetics Panel, Sci Adv Bd, NCTR, 72-74; chmn panel mutagenesis & carcinogenesis, US-Japan Coop Med Sci Prog, 72-; US coordr biol & genetic consequences proj, US-USSR Environ Protection Agreement, 72-; chmn subcomt environ mutagenesis, Dept Health, Educ & Welfare Comt to Coord Toxicol & Related Progs, 72-; assoc ed, Mutation Res, 73-; adj prof path, Univ NC, Chapel Hill, 73-; mem ad hoc adv group on pre-mkt predictive testing, Off Technol Assessment, 74; consult, Genetics Study Sect, Div Res Grants, NIH, 67, NASA Biosci Exp Surv, 68, Joint Food & Agr Orgn-Int Atomic Energy Agency-WHO Expert Comt Irradiated Food, 69, DDT Adv Comt, Environ Protection Agency, 71 & Panel Vapor Phase Org Air Pollutants, Nat Acad Sci-Nat Res Coun, 71-75; chmn, Coord Comt, Int Prog Evaluation Short-Term Tests Carcinogenicity, 78-; mem, Steering Comt & Assessment Panel, Gene-Tox Prog, Off Toxic Substances, Environ Protection Agency, 79- *Mem:* AAAS; Radiation Res Soc; Environ Mutagen Soc (vpres, 72-73, pres, 73-76); Genetics Soc Am; Am Asn Cancer Res. *Res:* Environmental mutagenesis; mutagenicity of carcinogens, radiation and chemical mutagenesis; space biology; author or co-author of 215 publications. *Mailing Add:* Nat Inst Environ Health Sci PO Box 12233 Research Triangle Park NC 27709

DE SESA, MICHAEL ANTHONY, b Boston, Mass, Feb 21, 27; m 53; c 2. RESEARCH ADMINISTRATION. *Educ:* Boston Col, BS, 49; Mass Inst Technol, PhD(anal chem), 53. *Prof Exp:* Res chemist, Raw Mat Develop Lab, AEC, 53-54, anal group leader, 54-58, chem group leader, 58-59, dept head inorg process develop, Feed Mat Prod Ctr, 59-62, asst tech dir uranium chem & metall, 62-63, assoc tech dir, 64; asst sect chief mech, chem & thermal properties, Res & Adv Develop Div, Avco Corp, 64-67; head anal & phys res dept, 67-73, dir cent res lab, 70-75, DIR RES & DEVELOP, INDUST CHEM DIV, NL INDUSTS, INC, 76- *Mem:* Am Chem Soc; Soc Appl Spectros; Asn Res Dirs; alt mem Indust Res Inst. *Res:* Instrumental methods of analysis; uranium hydrometallurgy; uranium compounds and metal; ablative plastics; development of chemical products; process development. *Mailing Add:* 33 Haddon Park Fair Haven NJ 07701

DESESSO, JOHN MICHAEL, b Phillipsburg, NJ, Mar 8, 47; m 73; c 4. TERATOLOGY, TOXICOLOGY. *Educ:* Hamilton Col, AB, 68; Va Commonwealth Univ, PhD(anat), 75. *Prof Exp:* asst prof anat, Sch Med, Univ Cincinnati, 75-81; SYSTS SCIENTIST, THE MITRE CORP, 81- *Concurrent Pos:* Adj asst prof anat, Sch Med, Univ Cincinnati, 81-; ad hoc mem, Study Sect, Nat Inst Occup Safety & Health, 81- *Mem:* Am Asn Anatomists; Am Soc Cellular Biol; Teratology Soc; Soc Toxicol; Soc Study Reproduction. *Res:* Experimental and human teratology, especially mechanisms of drug teratogenicity; embryology and experimental production of malformations; regulatory mechanisms in development; toxicological mechanisms; risk assessment. *Mailing Add:* The MITRE Corp 1820 Dolly Madison Blvd McLean VA 22102

DESFORGES, JANE FAY, b Melrose, Mass, Dec 18, 21; m 48; c 2. MEDICINE. *Educ:* Wellesley Col, BA, 42; Tufts Univ, MD, 45. *Prof Exp:* Intern path, Mt Auburn Hosp, 45-46; from intern to resident med, Boston City Hosp, 46-50, res fel hematol, 50-52; from asst prof to assoc prof, 52-70, PROF MED, SCH MED, TUFTS UNIV, 70-; SR PHYSICIAN & HEMATOLOGIST, NEW ENG MED CTR HOSP, 72- *Concurrent Pos:* NIH res fel hemat, Salt Lake City Hosp, 47-48; physician in-chg immunohemat lab, Hosp, Tufts Univ, 52-68, asst dir I & III Med Serv, 52-68, assoc dir, 68-72, actg dir clin labs, 67-69; assoc dir, Tufts Univ Hemat Labs, Boston City Hosp, 56-72; assoc ed, New Eng J Med, 60-; mem adv comt, Oak Ridge Assoc Univs, 72-; mem drug experience comt, Food & Drug Admin, Bur Drugs, 72-; mem automation med lab sci rev comt, Nat Inst Gen Med Sci, 71-, chmn, 74; comt on hemat, Am Bd Internal Med, 76-; mem, NIH, NIHLB, Blood Dis & Resources Adv Comt, 77-, chmn, 78- *Mem:* Am Fedn Clin Res; Am Soc Hemat; Int Soc Hemat; Am Soc Exp Path; Asn Am Physicians. *Res:* Hematology. *Mailing Add:* New Eng Med Ctr Hosp 171 Harrison Ave Boston MA 02111

DESHA, CAROLYN MCFALL, b Ft Worth, Tex, Oct 4, 41; c 2. INDUSTRIAL MICROBIOLOGY, RADIATION BIOLOGY. *Educ:* Tex Woman's Univ, BA, 62, MS, 64, PhD(radiation biol), 71. *Prof Exp:* Asst prof biol, Savannah State Col, 71-73; asst prof radiation biol & microbiol, Skidmore Col, 73-77; RES ASSOC INDUST MICROBIOL, UNION CARBIDE, OAK RIDGE NAT LAB, 77- *Concurrent Pos:* Fac res fels, Energy Res & Develop Admin, Oak Ridge Nat Lab, 76 & Dept Energy, 77. *Mem:* Soc Indust Microbiol; Sigma Xi. *Res:* Biological treatment of industrial waste water; identification of microbial contamination in aquatic environments; effects of toxic chemicals and radiation on biological systems. *Mailing Add:* Bldg 1505 Oak Ridge Nat Lab Oak Ridge TN 37830

DESHAW, JAMES RICHARD, b Monticello, Iowa, June 19, 42; m 65; c 1. BIOLOGY, ENVIRONMENTAL BIOLOGY. *Educ:* Loras Col, BS, 65; Tex A&M Univ, MS, 67, PhD(biol), 70. *Prof Exp:* Asst prof, 70-73, ASSOC PROF BIOL, SAM HOUSTON STATE UNIV, 73-, DIR FAC RES & GRANTS, 81- *Mem:* AAAS; Am Soc Indust Microbiol; Am Soc Microbiol; Sigma Xi. *Res:* Primary productivity, physical-chemical and biological aspects of streams and reservoirs. *Mailing Add:* Dept of Life Sci Sam Houston State Univ Huntsville TX 77341

DE SHAZER, LARRY GRANT, b Washington, DC, Nov 3, 34; m 60, 73; c 5. PHYSICS. *Educ:* Univ Md, BS, 56; Johns Hopkins Univ, PhD(physics), 63. *Prof Exp:* Physicist, Aerospace Group, Hughes Aircraft Co, 63-66; from asst prof to assoc prof physics, elec eng & mat sci, Univ Southern Calif, 66-78; sr staff physicist, 78-80, HEAD LASER OPTICAL MATERIALS, HUGHES RES LABS, 80- *Mem:* Royal Inst Gt Brit; Am Phys Soc; Soc Photo-Optical Instrumentation Engrs; Sigma Xi; fel Optical Soc Am. *Res:* Solid state lasers; spectroscopy of rare-earth ions and organic dyes; nonlinear absorption spectroscopy; propagation of high-power optical beams; physics of dielectric thin films; fiber optics. *Mailing Add:* Hughes Res Labs 3011 Malibu Canyon Rd Malibu CA 90265

DESHAZO, MARY LYNN DAVISON, b Carthage, Tex, Aug 14, 29; m 64. BIOCHEMISTRY. *Educ:* ETex Baptist Col, BS, 49; Univ Houston, MEd, 57; Tex A&M Univ, PhD(biochem), 68. *Prof Exp:* Teacher pub schs, Tex, 51-57; asst prof, 57-67, assoc prof, 68-72, PROF CHEM, SAM HOUSTON STATE UNIV, 72- *Mem:* Am Chem Soc; Sigma Xi. *Res:* Proteolytic enzymes of Aeromonas proteolytica. *Mailing Add:* Dept of Chem Sam Houston State Univ Huntsville TX 77341

DESHMUKH, DIWAKAR SHANKAR, b Nagpur, India, Aug 16, 36; m 67; c 2. BIOCHEMISTRY. *Educ:* Univ Nagpur, BSc, 59, MSc, 61; Indian Inst Sci, Bangalore, PhD(biochem), 68. *Prof Exp:* Sr res fel biochem, Indian Inst Sci, Bangalore, 66-68; fel nutrit, Nat Res Coun Can, 68-69; fel biochem, Med Sch, Temple Univ, 69-73, instr, 73-74; SR RES SCIENTIST NEUROCHEM, NY STATE BASIC RES INST MENT RETARDATION, 74- *Mem:* AAAS; NY Acad Sci; Sigma Xi; Am Soc Neurochem; Int Soc Neurochem. *Res:* Biogenesis of myelin membrane of central nervous system under normal and diseased conditions by studying metabolism of the myelin-specific compounds during different stages of myelin development. *Mailing Add:* Dept of Neurochem State Basic Res Inst Ment Retard Staten Island NY 10314

DESHOTELS, WARREN JULIUS, b New Orleans, La, Jan 3, 26; m 51; c 11. PHYSICS, SOLAR ENERGY. *Educ:* Tulane Univ, BS, 45, MS, 47; St Louis Univ, PhD(physics), 53. *Prof Exp:* Dir physics, Xavier Univ, La, 48-53; chief instrumentation engr, Jackson & Church Co, Mich, 53-55; sr physicist, Clevite Res Ctr, Ohio, 55-64; chmn dept, 65-77, ASSOC PROF PHYSICS, MARQUETTE UNIV, 64- *Mem:* AAAS; Am Phys Soc; Am Asn Physics Teachers. *Res:* Solid state and electron physics. *Mailing Add:* Dept of Physics Marquette Univ Milwaukee WI 53233

DESHPANDE, ACHYUT BHALCHANDRA, Indian citizen; m 68; c 3. POLYMER CHEMISTRY, POLYMER TECHNOLOGY. *Educ:* Univ Poona, BS, 55, BS Hons, 56, MS, 57, PhD(polymer chem), 64. *Prof Exp:* Sr sci asst polymer, Nat Chem Lab, India, 62-68, scientist A, 68-73; SR RES CHEMIST POLYMER, GAYLORD RES INST, WHIPPANY, 73- *Concurrent Pos:* Jr res fel, Coun Sci & Indust Res, New Delhi, 59-62; trainee Colombo plan, Overseas Tech Coop Agency, Japan, 66-68; res assoc, Polytech Inst New York, 74-75. *Mem:* Am Chem Soc. *Res:* Linear and stereo regular polymerization with Ziegler-Natta polymerization catalysts and charge transfer complex catalysts and other initiating systems; synthesis of flame resistant fiber polymers, coating composition, contact lens composition, emulsion polymerization and telomerization. *Mailing Add:* 70 S Munn Ave Apt 1012B East Orange NJ 07018

DESHPANDE, KRISHNANATH BHASKAR, b India, Nov 1, 21; m 50; c 2. PHYSICAL CHEMISTRY, INORGANIC CHEMISTRY. *Educ:* Bombay Univ, BS, 43, MS, 46, PhD(phys chem), 51. *Prof Exp:* Instr chem, Bombay Univ, 43-46, lectr inorg & phys chem, 47-57; curators grant, Univ Mo, 57, Am Petrol Inst fel, 57-60; res assoc phys chem, Univ NC, 60-65; dir NSF acad year inst, 69-71, PROF CHEM, FISK UNIV, 61-, COORDR ADVAN INSTNL DEVELOP PROG, 74- *Concurrent Pos:* Chadraseniya Kayastha Prabhu scholar, 57-60; Fulbright travel grant, US Dept State, 57-60; Am Petrol Inst fel, Oak Ridge Inst Nuclear Studies, 60; res chemist, US AEC, 60-65; dir US Off Educ-Inst Advan Studies in Phys Sci, 70-72; consult, Univ Tenn-AEC Agr Res Lab, Tenn. *Mem:* Am Chem Soc; Clay Minerals Soc. *Res:* Colloid chemistry of systems containing soaps and organic solvents; electrochemistry of clay-electrolyte systems; surface chemistry; ion exchange in inorganic exchangers using radioisotopes; ion exchange thermodynamics. *Mailing Add:* Dept Chem Fisk Univ Nashville TN 37203

DESHPANDE, MOHAN DHONDORAO, b Shirhatti, India, Apr 30, 45. FLUID MECHANICS, BIOMECHANICS. *Educ:* Ga Inst Technol, PhD(aerospace eng), 77. *Prof Exp:* Res asst aerospace eng, Ga Inst Technol, 70-77; res assoc biomech, 77-78, ASST PROF MECH ENG, CATH UNIV AM, 77- *Mem:* Sigma Xi; Eng Sci Soc; Am Soc Mech Engrs. *Res:* Laminar and turbulent flow computations; turbulent flow modelling; flow measurements; thermal sciences. *Mailing Add:* Dept of Mech Eng Cath Univ of Am Washington DC 20064

DESHPANDE, NARAYAN V(AMAN), b Bhadwan, India, May 4, 38; m 66; c 3. MECHANICAL ENGINEERING, APPLIED MECHANICS. *Educ:* Univ Poona, BEng, 61; Univ Rochester, MS, 64, PhD(fluid mech), 66. *Prof Exp:* Eng asst, Tata Thermal Power Co, India, 61-62; res assoc fluid instabilities, Culham Lab, UK Atomic Energy Authority, 66-67; asst prof mech & aerospace sci, Univ Rochester, 67-73; scientist, 73-75, SR SCIENTIST, XEROX CORP, ROCHESTER, 75- *Concurrent Pos:* Ctr Naval Anal res grant, 68-70; consult, Xerox Corp, 72-73. *Mem:* Am Soc

Mech Engrs; Am Acad Mech; Sigma Xi. *Res:* Fluid mechanics and magnetohydrodynamics; the stability of magnetohydrodynamic boundary layer type flows and the two-stream instability; study of a boundary layer over a moving surface; air bearings; heat transfer; contact problems in elasticity; magnetic recording technology. *Mailing Add:* Xerox Corp Xerox Sq W114 Rochester NY 14644

DESHPANDE, NILENDRA GANESH, b Karachi, Pakistan, Apr 18, 38; m 60; c 2. ELEMENTARY PARTICLE PHYSICS. *Educ:* Madras Univ, BSc, 59, MA, 60, MSc, 61; Univ Pa, PhD(physics), 65. *Prof Exp:* Res fel theoret physics, Imp Col, Univ London, 65-66; mem, Inst Math Sci, Madras, India, 66; res assoc physics, Northwestern Univ, Evanston, 66-67, asst prof, 67-73; assoc prof, Univ Tex, Austin, 73-75; ASSOC PROF PHYSICS, UNIV ORE, 75- *Concurrent Pos:* Vis prof, Univ Warsaw, Poland, 74-75 & Chalmers Inst, Gothenburg, Sweden, 75. *Mem:* Am Phys Soc. *Res:* Spontaneous breakdown of symmetry; chiral symmetry breaking and sum rules; current algebra; weak interactions and gauge theories; grand unified theories. *Mailing Add:* Dept of Physics Univ of Ore Eugene OR 97403

DESIDERATO, ROBERT, JR, b New York, NY, Aug 21, 39; m 68; c 2. PHYSICAL CHEMISTRY. *Educ:* Columbia Univ, AB, 61; Rice Univ, PhD(chem), 66. *Prof Exp:* Res assoc crystallog, Univ Pittsburgh, 65-66; asst prof, 66-74, ASSOC PROF CHEM, N TEX STATE UNIV, 75- *Mem:* Am Chem Soc; Am Crystallog Asn. *Res:* X-ray structure and analysis of biologically important compounds and transition metal complexes; computer programming. *Mailing Add:* Dept of Chem NTex State Univ Denton TX 76203

DESIDERIO, ANTHONY MICHAEL, b Philadelphia, Pa, Sept 26, 43; m 66; c 2. SYSTEMS ANALYSIS, APPLIED RESEARCH. *Educ:* La Salle Col, BA, 65; Univ Notre Dame, MA, 67, PhD(physics), 70. *Prof Exp:* Mem prof staff, Ctr Naval Anal, 71-78; MEM RES STAFF, SYST PLANNING CORP, 78- *Mem:* Am Phys Soc; Sigma Xi; Opers Res Soc Am. *Res:* Analysis of real world problems related to optimization of systems; analysis of factors and cost-benefit analysis. *Mailing Add:* 1817 Opalocka Dr McLean VA 22101

DESIDERIO, DOMINIC MORSE, (JR), b McKees Rocks, Pa, Jan 11, 41; m 65; c 2. BIOCHEMISTRY, MASS SPECTROMETRY. *Educ:* Univ Pittsburgh, BA, 61; Mass Inst Technol, SM, 64, PhD(anal chem), 65. *Prof Exp:* Organic control chemist, Pittsburgh Coke & Chem Co, 58-60; res chemist, Univ Pittsburgh, 60-61; teaching asst, Mass Inst Technol, 61-62, res asst, 62-65; res chemist, Am Cyanamid Co, 66-67; from asst prof to assoc prof chem, Inst Lipid Res & Dept Biochem, Baylor Col Med, 67-78; PROF NEUROL & DIR STOUT NEUROSCI MASS SPECTROMETRY, DEPT NEUROL, UNIV TENN CTR HEALTH SCI, 78- *Concurrent Pos:* Intra-Sci Res Found fel, 71-75. *Mem:* Am Chem Soc; Am Soc Mass Spectrometry; AAAS; Am Soc Biol Chemists. *Res:* Structural elucidation of molecules of biological origin including peptides, prostaglandins, macrolides by means of mass spectrometry. *Mailing Add:* Univ Tenn Ctr Health Sci 800 Madison Ave Memphis TN 38163

DESIENO, ROBERT P, b Scranton, Pa, Sept 1, 33; m 62; c 2. PHYSICAL CHEMISTRY. *Educ:* Union Col, NY, BS, 55, MS, 62; Univ Calif, Davis, PhD(chem), 66. *Prof Exp:* Chemist, Gen Elec Co, 57-62; res asst, Univ Calif, 62-65; sr chemist, Rohm and Haas Corp Res Labs, 65-68; asst prof, 68-72, assoc prof chem, Westminster Col, Pa, 72-80; PROF CHEM & DIR, COMPUT CTR, DAVIDSON COL, NC, 80- *Mem:* AAAS; Am Chem Soc. *Res:* Science and literature; spectroscopic properties of electrically exploded wires; computers in science education; history of science. *Mailing Add:* Dept of Chem Westminster Col New Wilmington PA 16142

DE SIERVO, AUGUST JOSEPH, b Passaic, NJ, Feb 4, 40; m 73; c 3. MICROBIOLOGY. *Educ:* Rutgers Univ, BA, 63, MS, 66, PhD(microbiol), 68. *Prof Exp:* Asst scientist microbiol, Warner Lambert Res Inst, 63-64; instr, Med Sch, NY Univ, 68-69; asst prof, 70-76, ASSOC PROF MICROBIOL, UNIV MAINE, ORONO, 76- *Mem:* Am Soc Microbiol; Sigma Xi; AAAS. *Res:* Membrane biosynthesis and function; role of phospholipids and phospholipid-associated enzymes in membrane structure and function. *Mailing Add:* Dept of Microbiol Univ of Maine Orono ME 04469

DESILETS, BRIAN H, b Leominster, Mass, Oct 7, 27; m 70; c 1. PHYSICS. *Educ:* Marist Col, BA, 50; St John's Univ, NY, MS, 54; NY Univ, MS, 58; Cath Univ Am, PhD(physics), 64. *Prof Exp:* Teacher, Bishop Dubois High Sch, 50-54; instr math & physics, Marist Col, 54-56, asst prof physics, 56-60; lectr elec eng, Cath Univ Am, 63-64; from asst prof to prof physics, Marist Col, 65-74; ADV ENGR, IBM CORP, 74- *Concurrent Pos:* Res assoc, Cath Univ Am, 62-64; consult, X-Ray Labs, IBM Corp, NY, 57-60. *Mem:* Am Asn Physics Teachers. *Res:* Solid state physics; x-ray studies; microwave attenuation; photoconductivity. *Mailing Add:* 6 Lake Oniad Dr Wappingers Falls NY 12590

DESILVA, ALAN W, b Los Angeles, Calif, Feb 8, 32; m 59; c 3. PLASMA PHYSICS. *Educ:* Univ Calif, Los Angeles, BS, 54; Univ Calif, Berkeley, PhD(physics), 61. *Prof Exp:* Res physicist, Lawrence Radiation Lab, Univ Calif, Berkeley, 61-62; Nat Sci fel plasma spectros, Culham Lab, UK Atomic Energy Authority, 62-63, res assoc, 63-64; from asst prof to assoc prof, 64-74, PROF PHYSICS, UNIV MD, COLLEGE PARK, 74- *Mem:* Am Phys Soc; Inst Elec & Electronics Engrs. *Res:* Plasma physics, including hydromagnetic wave phenomena and radiations from plasmas; interactions of electromagnetic radiation with plasmas; collision free shockwaves and turbulence in plasmas; diagnostics. *Mailing Add:* Dept Physics & Astron Univ Md College Park MD 20742

DESILVA, CARL NEVIN, b British Guiana, Aug 6, 23; US citizen; m 54; c 6. ENGINEERING MECHANICS. *Educ:* Columbia Univ, BS, 49, MS, 50; Univ Mich, PhD(mech), 55. *Prof Exp:* Res asst, Univ Mich, 52-55, res assoc, 55-57; unit chief mech res, Boeing Airplane Co, 57-60; from assoc prof to prof aeronaut & eng mech, Univ Minn, 60-66; chmn dept mech eng sci, 66-76, PROF MECH ENG, WAYNE STATE UNIV, 66- *Concurrent Pos:* Consult, Boeing Airplane Co, 60-62, Honeywell Corp, 62-63, Gen Mills, Inc, 63-64 & Geophysics Corp Am, 65-66. *Mem:* Am Math Soc; Am Soc Mech Engrs; Soc Natural Philos. *Res:* Solutions of problems in the classical theory of elastic shells; development of nonlinear theories of elastic shells and of non-Newtonian fluids; constitutive equations of viscoelastic materials with memory; analysis of fluid suspensions as applied to blood flow. *Mailing Add:* Dept of Mech Eng Sci Wayne State Univ Detroit MI 48202

DE SILVA, JOHN ARTHUR F, b Colombo, Ceylon, Sept 23, 33; US citizen; m 59; c 1. ANALYTICAL CHEMISTRY, PHARMACEUTICAL CHEMISTRY. *Educ:* Univ Ceylon, BSc, 56; Rutgers Univ, MS, 58, PhD(soil chem), 61. *Prof Exp:* Res chemist, Agr Div, Am Cyanamid Co, NJ, 61-63; sr res chemist, Dept Clin Pharmacol, 63-70, res group chief, Bioanal Method Develop, 70-74, res sect head bioanal methods develop, 74-78, asst dir, Dept Biochem & Drub Metab, 78-79, ASST DIR DEPT PHARMACOUINETICS & BIOPHARMACEUTICS, HOFFMANN-LA ROCHE INC, 79- *Mem:* Am Chem Soc; fel Am Inst Chem; Sigma Xi; Am Pharmaceut Asn. *Res:* Drug analysis in biological fluids; biopharmaceutics; pharmacokinetics. *Mailing Add:* Dept Pharmacouinetics Hoffmann-La Roche Inc Bldg 86/802C Nutley NJ 07110

DE SIMONE, DANIEL V, b Chicago, Ill, May 4, 30; m 55; c 3. SCIENCE POLICY. *Educ:* Univ Ill, BS, 56; NY Univ, JD, 60. *Prof Exp:* Staff mem commun technol, Bell Tel Labs, 56-62; consult technol innovation, Asst Secy Sci & Technol, US Dept Com, 62-64; dir, Off Invention & Innovation, Nat Bur Standards, 64-69; dir technol assessment, US Metric Study for Cong, 69-71; sci policy asst, Off Sci & Technol, Exec Off of the President, 71-73, exec secy, Fed Coun Sci & Technol, 72-73; DEP DIR, CONG OFF TECHNOL ASSESSMENT, 73- *Concurrent Pos:* Mem & rapporteur, Interagency Comt East-West Trade, 63; exec dir, Nat Inventors Coun, 63-69; exec secy, Panel on Invention & Innovation, US Dept Com, 65-67; consult, Nat Comn Technol, Automation & Econ Progress, 66 & Arms Control & Disarmament Agency, 66-69; mem, Panel on Venture Capital, US Dept Com, 68-70; adv, Dept Sci Affairs, Orgn Am State, 68-70. *Honors & Awards:* Gold Medal Distinguished Achievement Fed Serv, US Dept Com, 69; Career Serv Award, Nat Civil Serv League, 72. *Mem:* Inst Elec & Electronics Engrs; Am Soc Eng Educ. *Res:* Technology assessments concerning energy, natural resources, health care, transportation, food, agriculture, nutrition, telecommunications, electronic funds transfer, international trade and development, national security, and federal research and development programs and priorities. *Mailing Add:* Off of Technol Assessment Cong of the US Washington DC 20510

DESIO, PETER JOHN, b Boston, Mass, June 29, 38. ORGANOMETALLIC CHEMISTRY. *Educ:* Boston Col, BS, 60; Univ NH, PhD(org chem), 64. *Prof Exp:* Asst gen & org chem, Univ NH, 60-63; res assoc, Mat Div, Mass Inst Technol, 64-66; assoc prof org chem, 66-80, chmn, Chem Dept, 76-80, actg dir fire sci, 77-78, PROF ORG CHEM, UNIV NEW HAVEN, 80- *Mem:* Am Chem Soc; Am Inst Chem; NY Acad Sci; Royal Soc Chem; Sigma Xi. *Res:* Structure, particularly ring-chain tautomerism in acids and alcohols; organo-cadmium reactions as well as other organometallics. *Mailing Add:* Dept of Chem Univ of New Haven West Haven CT 06516

DESJARDINS, CLAUDE, b Fall River, Mass, June 13, 38; m 62; c 3. PHYSIOLOGY. *Educ:* Univ RI, BS, 60; Mich State Univ, MS, 64, PhD(animal physiol), 67. *Prof Exp:* Instr reproductive physiol, Mich State Univ, 60-67; assoc staff scientist, Jackson Lab, Maine, 67-68; asst prof physiol, Okla State Univ, 68-70, assoc prof, 70-71; assoc prof, 71-75, PROF PHYSIOL, UNIV TEX, AUSTIN, 75- *Concurrent Pos:* Consult reproductive endocrinol, NIH, NASA, Nat Sci Found. *Mem:* Soc Exp Biol & Med; Soc Study Reproduction (secy, 77-80, pres, 81-82); Brit Soc Study Fertil; Am Physiol Soc; Endocrine Soc. *Res:* Endocrinology; control systems affecting the secretion of reproductive hormones; hypothalamo-hypophyseal-gonadal interrelationships; testicular function and physiology of the male reproductive system. *Mailing Add:* Dept Zool Inst Reproductive Biol Univ of Tex Patterson Labs Austin TX 78712

DESJARDINS, PAUL ROY, b Cheyenne, Wyo, Aug 7, 19; m 47; c 3. PLANT PATHOLOGY. *Educ:* Colo State Univ, BS, 42; Univ Calif, Berkeley, PhD(plant path), 52. *Prof Exp:* Res asst, Univ Calif, Berkeley, 47-50, jr plant pathologist, Univ Calif, Riverside, 52-53, asst plant pathologist, 53-59, assoc prof, 61-70, PROF PLANT PATH, UNIV CALIF, RIVERSIDE, 70- *Concurrent Pos:* Res assoc, Nat Acad Sci-Nat Res Coun, 64-65. *Mem:* AAAS; Am Phys Soc; Electron Micros Soc Am; Torrey Bot Club. *Res:* Seed transmission; electron microscopy, purification and serological studies of plant viruses; cytological studies of virus infected tissues; virus structure and morphology; virus nucleic acid and disease of citrus, avocado and other plants. *Mailing Add:* 4168 Quail Rd Riverside CA 92507

DESKIN, WILLIAM ARNA, b Mo, Aug 16, 24; m 49; c 3. INORGANIC CHEMISTRY. *Educ:* Northeast Mo State Teacher Col, BS & AB, 48; Univ Mo, MA, 50; Univ Iowa, PhD(chem), 57. *Prof Exp:* Phys chemist, Chem Labs, US Army Chem Ctr, Md, 50-51; prof chem & physics, Upper Iowa Univ, 52-54; from asst prof to assoc prof, 56-63, chmn dept, 61-70, PROF CHEM, CORNELL COL, 63- *Concurrent Pos:* Resident res assoc, Argonne Nat Lab, 63-64. *Mem:* Am Chem Soc; AAAS. *Res:* Coordination compounds of transition metals with sulfur containing ligands. *Mailing Add:* Dept of Chem Cornell Col Mt Vernon IA 52314

DESKINS, WILBUR EUGENE, b Morgantown, WVa, Feb 20, 27; m 53; c 2. MATHEMATICS. *Educ:* Univ Ky, BS, 49; Univ Wis, MS, 50, PhD(math), 53. *Prof Exp:* Instr math, Univ Wis, 53; from instr to asst prof, Ohio State Univ, 53-56; from asst prof to prof, Mich State Univ, 56-71; PROF MATH & CHMN DEPT, UNIV PITTSBURGH, 71- *Concurrent Pos:* Staff assoc, Comprehensive Sci Math Prog, Cent Midwestern Regional Educ Lab, 69-80. *Mem:* Am Math Soc; Math Asn Am; AAAS. *Res:* Algebra; group theory. *Mailing Add:* Dept of Math Univ of Pittsburgh Pittsburgh PA 15261

DESLATTES, RICHARD D, JR, b New Orleans, La, Sept 21, 31; m 56; c 5. RADIOLOGY, PHYSICS. *Educ:* Loyola Univ, La, BS, 52; Johns Hopkins Univ, PhD(physics), 59. *Prof Exp:* Instr, Loyola Univ, La, 54-55; res assoc physics, Fla State Univ, 56-58 & Cornell Univ, 58-62; physicist, 62-68, CHIEF QUANTUM METROL GROUP & SR RES FEL, CTR ABSOLUTE PHYS QUANTITIES, NAT BUR STAND, 68- *Concurrent Pos:* Consult, Air Force Cambridge Res Ctr, 60-62. *Mem:* AAAS; Am Phys Soc. *Res:* X-ray spectroscopy of solids; atomic spectroscopy of high excited systems; x-ray diffraction microscopy. *Mailing Add:* Ctr Absolute Phys Quantities Nat Bur of Stand Washington DC 20234

DESLAURIERS, ROXANNE MARIE LORRAINE, b Montreal, Que, Oct 2, 47; m 70; c 2. PHYSICAL BIOCHEMISTRY. *Educ:* Univ Laval, BSc, 68; Univ Ottawa, PhD(biochem), 72. *Prof Exp:* asst res officer, 72-80, ASSOC RES OFFICER BIOCHEM, NAT RES COUN CAN, 80- *Concurrent Pos:* Asst prof, Dept Physiol & Biophys, Univ Ill Med Ctr, 75- *Mem:* Biophys Soc. *Res:* Structural and metabolic studies on live organisms using nuclear magnetic resonance spectroscopy. *Mailing Add:* Div of Biol Sci Rm 2095 100 Sussex Dr Nat Res Coun Can Ottawa ON K1A 0R6 Can

DESLOGE, EDWARD AUGUSTINE, b St Louis, Mo, Aug 31, 26; m 58. PHYSICS. *Educ:* Univ Notre Dame, BS, 47; St Louis Univ, MS, 55, PhD(physics), 57. *Prof Exp:* Instr physics, Yale Univ, 58-59; from asst prof to assoc prof, 59-69, PROF PHYSICS, FLA STATE UNIV, 69- *Mem:* Am Phys Soc. *Res:* Mechanics; thermal and statistical physics. *Mailing Add:* Dept of Physics Fla State Univ Tallahassee FL 32306

DESLONGCHAMPS, PIERRE, b St Lin, Que, May 8, 38; m 60; c 2. ORGANIC CHEMISTRY. *Educ:* Univ Montreal, BSc, 59; Univ NB, PhD(org chem), 64. *Prof Exp:* Res fel chem, Harvard Univ, 64-65; asst prof, Univ Montreal, 66-67; adj prof, 67, assoc prof, 68-72, PROF CHEM, UNIV SHERBROOKE, 72- *Concurrent Pos:* A P Sloan fel, 70-72; Sci Prize of Que, 71-72; E W R Steacie fel, 71-74; Guggenheim Found fel, 79- *Honors & Awards:* Medaille Pariseau, Fr-Can Asn Advan Sci, 79. *Mem:* Am Chem Soc; Royal Soc Can; fel Chem Inst Can; AAAS; Fr-Can Asn Advan Sci. *Res:* Synthesis in organic chemistry and studies on the mechanism of hydrolysis reactions. *Mailing Add:* Dept of Chem Univ of Sherbrooke Sherbrooke PQ J1K 2R1 Can

DES MARAIS, DAVID JOHN, b Richmond, Va, Jan 12, 48; m 70; c 2. GEOCHEMISTRY, BIOCHEMISTRY. *Educ:* Purdue Univ, BS, 69; Ind Univ, Bloomington, MS, 72, PhD(geochem), 74. *Prof Exp:* Assoc geochem, Ind Univ, 74-75; res fel, Inst Geophys & Planetary Physics, Univ Calif, Los Angeles, 75-76; RES CHEMIST GEOCHEM, NASA-AMES RES CTR, 76- *Concurrent Pos:* Mem bd dirs, Cave Res Found, Yellow Springs, Ohio, 73-75 & 78-81; lunar sample prin investr, NASA, 77-79. *Mem:* Geochem Soc. *Res:* Geochemistry of carbon, nitrogen and hydrogen in lunar materials; light isotope analytical chemistry; light isotope organic geochemistry; biochemical fractionation of light isotopes; geochemical cycle of carbon. *Mailing Add:* NASA-Ames Res Ctr Mail Stop 239-12 Moffett Field CA 94035

DESMARTEAU, DARRYL D, b Garden City, Kans, May 25, 40; m 62; c 3. INORGANIC CHEMISTRY, FLUORINE CHEMISTRY. *Educ:* Wash State Univ, BS, 63; Univ Wash, PhD(chem), 66. *Prof Exp:* Asst prof chem, Univ Wash, 66-67 & Northeastern Univ, 67-71; from asst prof to assoc prof, 71-77, PROF CHEM, KANS STATE UNIV, 77- *Concurrent Pos:* Alexander von Humboldt res fel, 79-80. *Mem:* Am Chem Soc; Sigma Xi. *Res:* Synthesis and properties of nonmetal fluorine compounds, fluorocarbon derivatives of non-metals, and compounds of phosphorus, sulfur and strong oxidizers such as peroxides, fluoroxides, hypohalites, and xenon compounds. *Mailing Add:* Dept Chem Kans State Univ Manhattan KS 66506

DESMOND, MARY ELIZABETH, b La Junta, Colo, May 29, 40. DEVELOPMENTAL BIOLOGY, NEUROBIOLOGY. *Educ:* Marquette Univ, BA, 63; Univ Colo, Boulder, MA, 71, PhD(biol), 73. *Prof Exp:* Res technician clin med, Med Sch, Univ Colo, 64-68, res technician cell biol, Dept Anat, 68-69, teaching asst biol dept, 68-72, instr biol & continuing educ, 72-73; chmn dept sci, St Scholastica Acad, 73-75; fel develop biol, Dept Zool, Austin Tex, 75-77; asst prof embryol & anat, 77-80, ASST PROF COMPARATIVE VERTEBRATE ANATOMY & DEVELOP BIOL, VILLANOVA UNIV, 80- *Concurrent Pos:* Co-investr grant, Carnegie Embryol Lab, Davis, Calif, 77. *Mem:* Sco Develop Biologists; Int Soc Develop Biologists; AAAS. *Res:* Mechanisms involved in the morphogenesis of the vertebrate brain; growth parameters of the human brain during embryogenesis. *Mailing Add:* Dept of Biol Villanova Univ Villanova PA 19085

DESMOND, MURDINA MACFARQUHAR, b Isle of Lewis, Scotland, Nov 14, 16; nat US; m 48; c 2. PEDIATRICS. *Educ:* Smith Col, BA, 38; Temple Univ, MD, 42. *Prof Exp:* From instr to assoc prof, 48-64, PROF PEDIAT, BAYLOR COL MED, 64- *Concurrent Pos:* Fel pediat, Sch Med, George Washington Univ, 47-58. *Mem:* Soc Pediat Res; Am Pediat Soc; Am Acad Ment Deficiency. *Res:* Neonatology; transition of infant from intrauterine to extrauterine life; relation newborn area to later development. *Mailing Add:* Dept of Pediat Baylor Col of Med Houston TX 77025

DESNOYERS, JACQUES EDOUARD, b Ottawa, Ont, Jan 28, 35; m 64; c 3. PHYSICAL CHEMISTRY. *Educ:* Univ Ottawa, Can, BSc, 58, PhD(phys chem), 61. *Prof Exp:* NATO & Ramsay fels, Battersea Col Tech & Manchester Univ, Eng, 61-62; lectr, 62-63, from asst prof to assoc prof, 63-71, PROF PHYS CHEM, UNIV SHERBROOKE, 71- *Honors & Awards:* Lash Miller Award, Electrochem Soc, 70; Huffman Mem Award, Calorimetry Conf, 78; Brit Petrol Prize, 80. *Mem:* Am Chem Soc; Electrochem Soc; Chem Inst Can. *Res:* Theoretical and experimental studies of thermodynamic properties of aqueous solutions and colloidal solutions and in particular surfactants and microemulsions; extractions of bitumen from oil sands. *Mailing Add:* Dept of Chem Univ de Sherbrooke Sherbrooke PQ J1K 2R1 Can

DE SOBRINO, R(ICARDO), b Cadiz, Spain, Mar 22, 21; US citizen; c 3. SYSTEMS ENGINEERING, COMMUNICATIONS. *Educ:* Span Navy Postgrad Sch, EE, 47; Polytech Inst Brooklyn, MEE, 51; Columbia Univ, DEngSci(info theory), 53. *Prof Exp:* Res engr, Naval Bur, Madrid, 53-57; engr, Nat Inst Indust, 57-59; mem staff commun acoust, RCA Labs, NJ, 59-62; staff scientist eng systs, SRI Int, 62-77; SR STAFF ENGR, ADVAN PROGS, LOCKHEED MISSILES & SPACE, SUNNYVALE, 77- *Concurrent Pos:* Prof, Span Navy Postgrad Schs, 53-58. *Mem:* Sr mem Inst Elec & Electronics Engrs. *Res:* Engineering systems; nuclear power; speech recognition; communication acoustics; operations research; oceanography; underwater acoustics. *Mailing Add:* Lockheed Missiles & Space PO Box 504 Sunnyvale CA 94088

DESOER, CHARLES A(UGUSTE), b Brussels, Belg, Jan 11, 26; nat US; m 51; c 3. ENGINEERING, SYSTEMS THEORY. *Educ:* Univ Liege, Belg, Dipl, 49; Mass Inst Technol, ScD, 53. *Hon Degrees:* DSc, Univ Liege, 77. *Prof Exp:* Mem tech staff, Bell Tel Labs, Inc, 53-58; assoc prof elec eng, 58-62, PROF ELEC ENG, UNIV CALIF, BERKELEY, 62- *Concurrent Pos:* Guggenheim fel, 70-71. *Mem:* Nat Acad Eng; fel AAAS; Am Math Soc; Soc Indust & Appl Math; fel Inst Elec & Electronics Engrs. *Res:* System theory; control and circuits. *Mailing Add:* Dept Elec Eng & Comput Sci Univ Calif Berkeley CA 94720

DESOMBRE, EUGENE ROBERT, b Sheboygan, Wis, May 6, 38; m 60; c 2. BIOCHEMISTRY, ENDOCRINOLOGY. *Educ:* Univ Chicago, BS, 60, MS, 61, PhD(org chem), 63. *Prof Exp:* Res assoc, 63-65, from instr to asst prof, 66-73, assoc prof, PROF, BEN MAY LAB CANCER RES & DIR, BIOMED COMPUT FACIL, UNIV CHICAGO, 80- *Mem:* AAAS; Endocrine Soc; Am Asn Cancer Res; Am Chem Soc. *Res:* Organophosphorous chemistry; steroid mechanism of action; estrogen endocrinology; hormone dependent cancer. *Mailing Add:* Ben May Lab for Cancer Res Univ of Chicago Chicago IL 60637

DESOR, JEANNETTE ANN, b Baltimore, Md, July 11, 42. PSYCHOPHYSICS. *Educ:* Cornell Univ, AB, 64; PhD(exp psychol), 69. *Prof Exp:* Res asst psychol, Dept Psychol, Yale Univ, 65; teaching asst psychol, Cornell Univ, 65-69; staff scientist exp psychol, Monell Chem Senses Ctr, Univ Pa, 70-75; mgr sensory eval, res & develop, Warner-Lambert Co, 75-78; MGR BEHAV SCI, RES & DEVELOP, GEN FOODS CORP, 78- *Concurrent Pos:* Fel chemoreception, Univ Pa, 70-72; NIH fel, 71 & 72 & consult, Oral & Pharyngeal Develop Sect, 73; res investr, Vet Admin Hosp, Philadelphia, 73-75; consult, Dept Oral Med, Sch Dent, Univ Pa, 73-75, asst prof, Dept Otorhinol & Human Commun, Sch Med, 73-, staff therapist, Behav Weight Control Prog, Dept Psychiat, Hosp Univ Pa, 74-75. *Mem:* Am Psychol Asn; AAAS; Asn Chemoreception Sci; Eastern Psychol Asn. *Res:* Human sensory systems; development of human taste preferences; clinical assessment of taste; functions of taste and olfaction in nutrition; measurement techniques for sensory evaluation; crowding; product development. *Mailing Add:* Tech Ctr Gen Foods Corp White Plains NY 10625

DESOWITZ, ROBERT, b New York, NY, Jan 2, 26; m 54; c 2. PARASITOLOGY, IMMUNOLOGY. *Educ:* Univ Buffalo, BA, 48; Univ London, PhD(parasitol), 51, DSc(parasitol), 60. *Prof Exp:* Prin sci officer, Colonial Med Res Serv, WAfrican Inst Trypanosomiasis Res, 51-60; prof parasitol & head dept, Univ Singapore, 60-65; chief dept parasitol, SEATO Med Res Lab, Bangkok, Thailand, 65-68; PROF TROP MED & PUB HEALTH, LEAHI HOSP, SCH MED, UNIV HAWAII, MANOA, 68- *Concurrent Pos:* Mem expert comt parasitic dis, WHO, 64- *Mem:* Am Soc Parasitol; fel Royal Soc Trop Med & Hyg; hon fel Malaysian Soc Trop Med. *Res:* Host-parasite relationships, especially malaria; immunologic response to malaria, trypanosomiasis and filariasis. *Mailing Add:* Leahi Hosp Univ of Hawaii Sch of Med Honolulu HI 96816

DESPAIN, ALVIN M(ARDEN), b Salt Lake City, Utah, July 2, 38; m 57; c 2. COMPUTER SCIENCE, ELECTRICAL ENGINEERING. *Educ:* Univ Utah, BS, 60, MS, 64, PhD(elec eng), 66. *Prof Exp:* Engr trainee elec eng, Southern Calif, Edison Co, 57; res asst elec eng & physics, Univ Utah, 57-60, res engr, 60-66, asst res prof elec eng, 66-67; asst prof, Utah State Univ, 66-69, asst dir electrodyn labs, 67-73, assoc prof elec eng, 69-76; assoc prof, 76-80, PROF COMPUT SCI, DIV ELEC ENG & COMPUT SCI, UNIV CALIF, BERKELEY, 80- *Concurrent Pos:* Vis assoc prof, Stanford Univ, 72-73. *Mem:* Inst Elec & Electronics Engrs; Am Soc Eng Educ; Asn Comput Mach; AAAS; Sigma Xi. *Res:* Communication-information theory; data communications, computer design, computer architecture, microprocessors and computer hardware. *Mailing Add:* Dept of Comput Sci Univ of Calif Berkeley CA 94720

DESPAIN, LEWIS GAIL, b Salt Lake City, Utah, Feb 7, 28; m 56; c 4. SPACE PHYSICS. *Educ:* Univ Utah, BS, 55, MS, 57, PhD(physics), 62. *Prof Exp:* Sr scientist, Space Sci Div, Jet Propulsion Lab, Calif Inst Technol, 61-64, group supvr, 64-66, assoc proj scientist, 66-67; supvr, Space Physics Group, Boeing Co, Seattle, 67-73, dir, Radiation Effects Lab, 73-76, staff scientist, Inertial Upper Stage Syst Integration, 76-78 & Solar Elec Power Syst, 79, adv, Defense Missile Early Warning Syst, 80, STAFF SCIENTIST SHORT RANGE ATTACK MISSILE ADVAN CONCEPTS, BOEING AEROSPACE CO, 81- *Mem:* Am Asn Physics Teachers. *Res:* Direction of specialized group which conducts theoretical and experimental research in space physics. *Mailing Add:* Boeing Aerospace Co 20403 68th St Kent WA 98031

DESPER, CLYDE RICHARD, b Greenwood, Ark, Dec 14, 37. POLYMER SCIENCE. *Educ:* Mass Inst Technol, BS, 59, MS, 60; Univ Mass, Amherst, PhD(chem), 67. *Prof Exp:* Res assoc, Fabric Res Labs, Inc, Mass, 60-62; res chemist, US Army Natick Labs, Mass, 66-68; RES CHEMIST POLYMERS, US ARMY MAT & MECH RES CTR, 68- *Mem:* Am Phys Soc; Am Chem Soc; Am Crystallog Asn; Sigma Xi. *Res:* Investigation of solid state morphology and properties in polymers, primarily by x-ray diffraction; crystallography; preferred orientation effects; microphase segregation. *Mailing Add:* Army Mat & Mech Res Ctr Watertown MA 02172

DESPOMMIER, DICKSON, b New Orleans, La, June 5, 40; m 63; c 1. PARASITOLOGY, IMMUNOLOGY. *Educ:* Fairleigh Dickinson, BS, 62; Columbia Univ, MS, 64; Univ Notre Dame, PhD(microbiol), 67. *Prof Exp:* Asst parasitol, Sch Pub Health & Admin Med, Columbia Univ, 62-63; asst biol, Univ Notre Dame, 64-65; USPHS guest investr parasitol, Rockefeller Univ, 67-70; asst prof parasitol, Sch Pub Health, 70-75, ASSOC PROF PARASITOL, SCH PUB HEALTH, COLUMBIA UNIV, 75- *Concurrent Pos:* NIH career develop award, 71-76. *Mem:* AAAS; Am Soc Parasitol; Am Soc Cell Biol; Am Soc Trop Med & Hyg. *Res:* Effects of the immune state in the biology of nematode parasites in mammalian hosts; molting and morphogenesis of nematodes in culture; pathology and molecular biology of the muscle phase of trichinosis; mechanisms of host immunity to trichinosis. *Mailing Add:* Dept of Trop Med Columbia Univ Sch of Pub Health New York NY 10032

DESPRES, THOMAS A, b Grand Rapids, Mich, Nov 13, 32; m 59; c 2. MECHANICAL & METALLURGICAL ENGINEERING. *Educ:* Univ Mich, BSIE, 56, MSME, 59, PhD(mech eng), 64. *Prof Exp:* Test & eval missile components, Redstone Arsenal, 57-58; teaching fel mech & metall eng, 58-63, from asst prof to assoc prof, 63-76, PROF MECH ENG, UNIV MICH, DEARBORN, 76- *Res:* Metallurgical and solid state research in fatigue of metals; mechanical properties of metals and application of electron microscopy to metallurgical and mechanical properties study. *Mailing Add:* Sch of Eng Univ of Mich Dearborn MI 48128

DES PREZ, ROGER MOISTER, b Chicago, Ill, Mar 14, 27; m 65; c 7. INTERNAL MEDICINE, PULMONARY DISEASES. *Educ:* Dartmouth Col, AB, 51; Columbia Univ, MD, 54; Am Bd Internal Med, dipl, 62. *Prof Exp:* Intern, asst med resident & chest med resident, NY Hosp, 54-57; physician, Ft Defiance Tuberc Sanatorium, 57-59; from instr to asst prof med, Med Col, Cornell Univ, 57-63; assoc prof, 63-68, PROF MED, SCH MED, VANDERBILT UNIV, 68- *Concurrent Pos:* Teaching fel, Am Trudeau Soc, 56-57; Edward L Trudeau fel, 59-63; physician outpatients, NY Hosp, 59-63; chief med serv, Vet Admin Hosp, Nashville, Tenn, 63-; ed chest sect, Yearbk Med, Asn Am Physicians. *Mem:* Asn Vet Admin Chiefs Med; Am Soc Clin Invest; Am Orthop Asn; Asn Am Physicians. *Res:* Patterns if tissue injury; immunologic injury to rabbit platelets. *Mailing Add:* Dept of Med Vanderbilt Univ Sch of Med Nashville TN 37240

DESROCHERS, ALAN ALFRED, b Northampton, Mass, June 1, 50. CONTROL SYSTEMS ENGINEERING. *Educ:* Univ Lowell, BSEE, 72; Purdue Univ, MSEE, 73, PhD(elec eng), 77. *Prof Exp:* Assoc engr, Lockheed Missiles & Space Co, 73-75; asst prof comput & syst eng, Boston Univ, 77-80; ASST PROF COMPUT & SYST ENG, RENSSELAER POLYTECH INST, 80- *Concurrent Pos:* Fac res assoc, Auburn Univ, 78. *Mem:* Inst Elec & Electronics Engrs; Am Soc Eng Educ. *Res:* Simplification and design of nonlinear control systems with application to manufacturing, automation and flight control systems. *Mailing Add:* Elec Comput & Syst Eng Dept Rensselaer Polytech Inst Troy NY 12181

DESROSIERS, JOSEPH A JACQUES, b Matane, Que, Jan 30, 31; m 56; c 2. OBSTETRICS & GYNECOLOGY, PHYSIOLOGY. *Educ:* Laval Univ, BA, 53, MD, 58; Med Col Can, med lic, 58; FRCPS(C), 63. *Prof Exp:* Asst prof, 64-70, AGGREGATE PROF OBSTET & GYNEC, UNIV MONTREAL, 70- *Concurrent Pos:* Pvt pract, Maissonneuve Hosp, Montreal, 64-; lectr, Nurses Sch; sr consult, Inst Cardiol, Montreal, 65-; lectr, Inst Marguerite Youville, Montreal. *Mem:* Sr mem Am Fertil Soc; Can Med Asn; Can Soc Fr Speaking Obstet & Gynec; Fedn Socs Fr Speaking Gynec & Obstet; Can Fertil Soc. *Res:* Family planning; effective therapy, physiopathology, anatomy and histology of the underdeveloped uterus in young women. *Mailing Add:* Dept of Obstet & Gynec Univ of Montreal Montreal PQ H3C 3J7 Can

DESS, HOWARD MELVIN, b Chicago, Ill, Dec 23, 29; m 51; c 3. INORGANIC CHEMISTRY. *Educ:* Ind Univ, BS, 51; Univ Mich, MS, 53, PhD(chem), 55. *Prof Exp:* Res chemist, Electrometall Co, 55-56 & Pennsalt Chem Corp, 56-58; res chemist, Union Carbide Corp, 58-63, group leader crystal prod res, Speedway Lab, Linde Div, 63, res & develop supvr, Crystal Prod Dept, Electronics Div, 63-68, group mgr, 68; asst tech dir, Nat Lead Co, 68, dir res, Hightstown Cent Res Lab, 68-70, MGR COM CRYSTALS DEPT, TITANIUM PIGMENT DIV, NL INDUSTS, INC, 70- *Mem:* Am Chem Soc; Am Asn Crystal Growers; Am Ceramic Soc; Electrochem Soc. *Res:* Crystal growth. *Mailing Add:* 316 Goldfinch Dr Bridgewater NJ 08807

DESSAUER, HERBERT CLAY, b New Orleans, La, Dec 30, 21; m 50; c 3. BIOCHEMISTRY. *Educ:* La State Univ, PhD(biochem), 52. *Prof Exp:* Teaching fel biochem, Sch Med, 49-50, asst, 50-51, from instr to assoc prof, 51-63, actg head dept, 77-78, PROF BIOCHEM, SCH MED, LA STATE UNIV MED CTR, NEW ORLEANS, 63- *Concurrent Pos:* Consult, Vet Admin Hosp, New Orleans, La, 62-; mem panel for advan sci educ, NSF, 65-67, mem panel for systematics, 72-; mem alpha helix exped to New Guinea, 69; mem task force fluoridation, New Orleans Health Planning Coun, 71-72; mem nat comt resources herpet, 73-75; res assoc, Dept Herpet, Am Mus Nat Hist. *Mem:* AAAS; Am Physiol Soc; Am Soc Ichthyologists & Herpetologists; Sigma Xi; Herpetologists League. *Res:* Biochemistry of the lizard Anolis carolinensis; comparative biochemistry; blood proteins; protein taxonomy. *Mailing Add:* 7100 Dorian St New Orleans LA 70126

DESSAUER, JOHN HANS, b Aschaffenburg, Ger, May 13, 05; nat US; m 36; c 3. CHEMISTRY, CHEMICAL ENGINEERING. *Educ:* Munich Tech Inst, BS, 26; Aachen Tech Inst, Master, 27; DIngSc, 29. *Hon Degrees:* LHD, Le Moyne Col, 63; DSc, Clarkson Col, 75. *Prof Exp:* Res chemist, Ansco, NY, 29-35; res chemist & dir, Haloid Co, 35-51, vpres in chg res & prod develop & dir, 46-58, exec vpres res & eng, Xerox Corp, 59-66, vchmn bd & exec vpres res & advan eng, 66-70, dir, 59-73, dir, Rank Xerox Ltd, 59-70; TRUSTEE, NY STATE SCI & TECHNOL FOUND, 72- *Concurrent Pos:* Emer trustee, Fordham Univ. *Honors & Awards:* Phillipp Medal, Inst Elec & Electronic Engrs, 74; Indust Res Inst Medal, 68. *Mem:* Nat Acad Eng; fel NY Acad Sci; fel Am Inst Chemists; Am Chem Soc; Am Phys Soc. *Res:* Photo research; organic chemistry; xerography. *Mailing Add:* 37 Parker Dr Pittsford NY 14534

DESSAUER, ROLF, b Nurnberg, Ger, Nov 3, 26; nat US; m 68; c 2. ORGANIC CHEMISTRY. *Educ:* Univ Chicago, BS, 48, MS, 49; Univ Wis, PhD(chem), 52. *Prof Exp:* From res chemist to sr res chemist, Org Chem Dept, 52-68, res assoc, 69-78, RES ASSOC, CHEM, DYES & PIGMENTS DEPT, PHOTO PROD DEPT, E I DU PONT DE NEMOURS & CO, INC, 78- *Mem:* Am Chem Soc; Soc Photog Sci & Eng. *Res:* Steroids; dyes; photochemistry; photochromism; imaging systems; liquid crystals; chemical marketing. *Mailing Add:* Box 3796 Greenville DE 19807

DESSEL, NORMAN F, b Ida Grove, Iowa, July 9, 32; m 55; c 3. PHYSICS. *Educ:* Univ Iowa, BA, 57, MA, 58, PhD(physics, sci educ). 61. *Prof Exp:* From asst prof to assoc prof physics, 61-68, chmn dept phys sci, 69-73, prof physics & phys sci, 68-76, PROF NATURAL SCI, SAN DIEGO STATE UNIV, 76- *Concurrent Pos:* Consult, US Naval Electronics Lab, 62-69; mgr grad traineeships & fels, NSF, 76-77. *Mem:* AAAS; Optical Soc Am; Am Asn Physics Teachers. *Res:* Coherent optical information processing and holography, laser communications, physics education and energy research and development. *Mailing Add:* Dept of Natural Sci San Diego State Univ San Diego CA 92182

DESSER, SHERWIN S, b Winnipeg, Man, Sept 2, 37; m 63; c 3. ZOOLOGY, PARASITOLOGY. *Educ:* Univ Man, BSc, 59, MSc, 63; Univ Toronto, PhD(protozool), 67. *Prof Exp:* Res fel parasitol, Univ Toronto, 67 & Hebrew Univ, Israel, 67-68; from asst prof to assoc prof, 68-81, PROF PARASITOL, UNIV TORONTO, 81- *Mem:* Am Soc Parasitol; Soc Protozool; Royal Soc Trop Med & Hyg. *Res:* Protozoology; Haemosporidia. *Mailing Add:* Dept Zool Univ of Toronto Fac of Med Toronto ON M5S 2R8 Can

DESSLER, ALEXANDER JACK, b San Francisco, Calif, Oct 21, 28; m 52; c 4. SPACE PHYSICS. *Educ:* Calif Inst Technol, BS, 52; Duke Univ, PhD(physics), 56. *Prof Exp:* Res assoc, Duke Univ, 55-56; mem staff, Lockheed Missile & Space Co, 56-62; prof, Southwest Ctr Advan Studies, 62-63; chmn dept space sci, 63-69, mgr campus business affairs, 74-76, PROF SPACE PHYSICS & ASTRON, RICE UNIV, 63-, CHMN DEPT, 78- *Concurrent Pos:* Mem, US Nat Comt, Int Sci Radio Union, 60-63 & 67-70; co-ed, J Geophys Res, 65-69; sci adv, Nat Aeronaut & Space Coun, 69-70; co-ed, Rev Geophys & Space Physics, 69-74; consult, NSF, 76. *Honors & Awards:* James B Macelwane Award, Am Geophys Union, 63. *Mem:* Fel AAAS; fel Am Geophys Union; Int Sci Radio Union; Univs Space Res Asn (pres, 75-81); Int Asn Geomagnetism & Aeronomy (vpres, 79-). *Res:* Geomagnetism; theory of planetary magnetospheres; plasma physics; hydromagnetism; interplanetary physics; low temperature physics. *Mailing Add:* Dept of Space Physics & Astron Rice Univ Houston TX 77001

DESSOUKY, DESSOUKY AHMAD, b Mitgamr, UAR, Jan 18, 32; m 69; c 1. ANATOMY, ELECTRON MICROSCOPY. *Educ:* Ain Shams Univ, Cairo, MD, 56, MS, 60; Tulane Univ, PhD(anat), 64. *Prof Exp:* Instr anat, Sch Med, Ain Shams Univ, 57-61; from instr to asst prof, 64-67, resident obstet & gynec, 67-70, asst prof, 70-74, ASSOC PROF OBSTET & GYNEC, GEORGETOWN UNIV, 74- *Mem:* AAAS; Am Asn Anat; Am Col Obstet & Gynec; Am Fertil Soc. *Res:* Fine structure of corpus luteum, uterine wall and uterine blood vessels in normal and abnormal pregnancy; electron microscopy of female reproductive system. *Mailing Add:* Dept of Obstet & Gynec Georgetown Univ Hosp Washington DC 20007

DESSOUKY, MOHAMED IBRAHIM, b Cairo, Egypt, Dec 20, 26; US citizen; m 58; c 4. INDUSTRIAL ENGINEERING. *Educ:* Cairo Univ, BSc, 48; Purdue Univ, MS, 54; Ohio State Univ, PhD(indust eng), 56. *Prof Exp:* Res fel, oper res, Case Inst Technol, 56-57; asst prof indust eng, Cairo Univ, 57-63; assoc prof oper res, Thayer Sch Eng, Dartmouth Col, 64-65; prof mgt sci, Nat Inst Mgt Develop, 65-68; ASSOC PROF INDUST ENG, UNIV ILL, URBANA, 68- *Concurrent Pos:* Consult, UN Indust Develop Orgn, 65- & Construction Eng Res Lab, 71-78; vis prof, Univ Khartoum, 67-68; sr scientist, Kuwait Inst Sci Res, 78- *Mem:* Sr mem, Am Inst Indust Eng; Oper Res Soc Am; Inst Mgt Sci; Proj Mgt Inst; Egyptian Engrs Soc. *Res:* Project network analysis, scheduling, simulation, multiple criteria decision making, failure diagnosis, and applications of operations research in developing countries, especially in national planning. *Mailing Add:* 1106 Mitchem Dr Urbana IL 61801

DESSUREAUX, LIONEL, b Ste-Genevieve de Batiscan, Que, June 28, 17; m 44; c 5. AGRONOMY, GENETICS. *Educ:* St Joseph Col, BA, 40; Laval Univ, BScA, 44; Univ Wis, MS, 45, PhD(agron, genetics), 47. *Prof Exp:* Asst agron, Univ Wis, 44-47; plant breeder, Dom Exp Farm, Que, 47-65; plant breeder, Ottawa Res Sta, Cent Exp Farm, Can Dept Agr, 65-66; geneticist, 66-79; SPEC ADV, RES BR, AGR CAN, 79- *Mem:* Agr Inst Can; Can Soc Agron; Genetics Soc Can. *Res:* Breeding methods in legumes; combining ability in legumes; biometrical genetics of tetraploids; breeding methods. *Mailing Add:* Ottawa Res Sta Cent Exp Farm Ottawa Can

DESSY, RAYMOND EDWIN, b Reynoldsville, Pa, Sept 3, 31. CHEMICAL INSTRUMENTATION. *Educ:* Univ Pittsburgh, BS, 53, PhD, 56. *Prof Exp:* Fel & instr, Ohio State Univ, 56-57; from asst prof to assoc prof chem, Univ Cincinnati, 57-66; PROF CHEM, VA POLYTECH INST & STATE UNIV, 66- *Concurrent Pos:* Sloan fel, 62-64; NSF sr fel, 63-64. *Mem:* Am Chem Soc. *Res:* Design and automation of new chemical instruments for spectroscopy and chromotography; solid state detector development; development of courses to teach small computer automation to chemists. *Mailing Add:* Dept of Chem Va Polytech Inst & State Univ Blacksburg VA 24061

DESTEFANO, ANTHONY JOSEPH, b Middletown, Conn, June 6, 49. PHYSICAL CHEMISTRY. *Educ:* Villanova Univ, BS, 71; Cornell Univ, MS, 73, PhD(chem), 76. *Prof Exp:* STAFF CHEMIST MASS SPECTROMETRY, MIAMI VALLEY LABS, PROCTER & GAMBLE CO, 76- *Mem:* AAAS; Am Chem Soc; Am Soc Mass Spectrometry. *Res:* Organic mass spectrometry including GC/MS, field desorption, field ionization and chemical ionization. *Mailing Add:* Miami Valley Labs PO Box 39175 Cincinnati OH 45247

DESTEVENS, GEORGE, b Tarrytown, NY, Aug 21, 24; m 50. ORGANIC CHEMISTRY. *Educ:* Fordham Univ, BS, 49, MS, 50, PhD, 53. *Prof Exp:* Instr chem, Fordham Univ, 52-53; lectr org chem, Marymount Col, NY, 52; res chemist, Remington Rand Corp, 53-55; sr res scientist, CIBA Pharmaceut Co, Ciba-Geigy Pharmaceut Res Labs, 55-61, dir med chem res, 62-66, dir chem res, Chem Res Dept, CIBA Pharmaceut Prod Inc, 66-67, vpres res, CIBA Pharmaceut Co, 67-70, exec vpres & dir res, 70-79; RES PROF CHEM, DREW UNIV, 79-E. *Honors & Awards:* Walter J Hartung Memorial Award Oustanding Contrib Med Res, 79. *Mem:* Am Chem Soc; fel NY Acad Sci. *Res:* Cyanine dyes as therapeutics; diuretics; analgesics; tranquilizers; chemistry of heterocyclics; spectral properties or organic compounds. *Mailing Add:* 2 Warwick Rd Summit NJ 07901

DESU, MANAVALA MAHAMUNULU, b Ongole, India, Nov 12, 31; m 58; c 2. STATISTICS. *Educ:* Andhra Univ, India, BA, 50; Madras Univ, MA, 53; Univ Minn, PhD(statist), 66. *Prof Exp:* Lectr math, SSN Col, Narasaraopet, India, 53-55, math & statist, SV Univ Tirupati, India, 59-62; lectr, 65-66, asst prof, 66-69, ASSOC PROF STATIST, STATE UNIV NY BUFFALO, 69- *Mem:* Inst Math Statist; Am Statist Asn; Royal Statist Soc; Biomet Soc. *Res:* Nonparametric methods; survival data analysis; biostatistics; ranking and selection procedures. *Mailing Add:* Dept of Statist State Univ NY Ridge Lea Campus Amherst NY 14226

DESUA, FRANK CRISPIN, b Monessen, Pa, Oct 26, 21; m 45; c 1. MATHEMATICS. *Educ:* Univ Pittsburgh, BS, 44, PhD(math), 56. *Prof Exp:* Instr math, Univ Pittsburgh, 44-54; asst prof, Ohio Univ, 54-56 & Univ Pittsburgh, 56-57; mem tech staff, Bell Tel Labs, 57-58; assoc prof math, Col William & Mary, 58-60; prof & chmn dept, Simmons Col, 60-70 & Sweet Briar Col, 70-75; PROF MATH, FLA INST TECHNOL, 75- *Mem:* Am Math Soc; Math Asn Am. *Res:* Foundations of mathematics; symbolic logic; meta-mathematics; point-set topology. *Mailing Add:* Dept of Math Fla Inst of Technol Melbourne FL 32901

DE SYLVA, DONALD PERRIN, b Rochester, NY, July 20, 28; m 50; c 2. BIOLOGICAL OCEANOGRAPHY, ICHTHYOLOGY. *Educ:* Cornell Univ, BS, 52, PhD(vert zool), 58; Univ Miami, MS, 53. *Prof Exp:* Asst fish collection, Cornell Univ, 51-52, asst oceanog, 52; asst zool, Univ Miami, 52-53; asst biomet & statist, Univ Calif, 53-54; res instr oceanog, Univ Miami, 54, res instr fisheries, 54-56; asst vert zool, Cornell Univ, 56-57; asst prof biol sci, Univ Del, 58-61; from asst prof to assoc prof marine sci, 61-75, PROF MARINE SCI, UNIV MIAMI, 75- *Concurrent Pos:* Res aide, Univ Miami, 53; scientist chg, Pac Billfish Exped, Lou Marron & Univ Miami, Chile, 56; consult, Dr Edward C Raney, Cornell Univ, 57 & Comt on the Effects of Herbicides in Vietnam, Nat Acad Sci, 71-73; mem atomic safety & licensing bd, USAEC/US Nuclear Regulatory Comn, 71- *Mem:* AAAS; Am Fisheries Soc; Coun Biol Educ; Am Soc Ichthyol & Herpet; Am Inst Fisheries Res Biol. *Res:* Life history, systematics and ecology of marine and estuarine fishes; fisheries and estuarine ecology; ecology of mangrove fishes; early life history of fishes; ecology of poisonous fishes and pelagic fishes. *Mailing Add:* Sch Marine & Atmospheric Sci Univ Miami Miami FL 33149

DE TAKACSY, NICHOLAS BENEDICT, b Budapest, Hungary, Feb 24, 39; Can citizen; m 62; c 3. NUCLEAR PHYSICS. *Educ:* Loyola Col, Can, BSc, 59; Univ Montreal, MSc, 63; McGill Univ, PhD(nuclear theory), 66. *Prof Exp:* Lectr physics, Loyola Col, Can, 61-63; res fel nuclear theory, Calif Inst Technol, 66-67; asst prof, Loyola Col, Que, 67-68; from asst prof to assoc prof nuclear theory, 68-77, PROF NUCLEAR THEORY, McGILL UNIV, 77-, CHMN DEPT PHYSICS, 79- *Concurrent Pos:* Res fel, McGill Univ, 67-68. *Mem:* Am Phys Soc; Can Asn Physicists. *Res:* Nuclear structure of transitional nuclei; low energy pion-nucleon interaction; quark model. *Mailing Add:* Dept of Physics 3600 University St Montreal PQ H3A 2T8 Can

DETAR, DELOS FLETCHER, b Kansas City, Mo, Jan 18, 20; m 43; c 4. ORGANIC CHEMISTRY. *Educ:* Univ Ill, BS, 41; Univ Pa, MS, 43, PhD(org chem), 44. *Prof Exp:* Res chemist, Pioneering Res Sect, Rayon Dept, Tech Div, E I du Pont de Nemours & Co, 44-46; fel, Univ Ill, 46; from instr to asst prof chem, Cornell Univ, 46-53; from assoc prof to prof, Univ SC, 53-60; PROF CHEM, FLA STATE UNIV, 60- *Concurrent Pos:* NSF sr fel, Harvard Univ, 56-57; vis prof, Univ Calif, Berkeley, 60. *Mem:* Am Chem Soc; fel The Chem Soc. *Res:* Mechanisms of organic reactions; peptides and enzyme models; computer techniques; molecular mechanics. *Mailing Add:* Dept of Chem Fla State Univ Tallahassee FL 32306

DETAR, REED L, b Oil City, Pa, May 14, 32; m 59; c 4. PHYSIOLOGY. *Educ:* Susquehanna Univ, AB, 54; Hahnemann Med Col, MS, 59; Univ Mich, PhD(physiol), 68. *Prof Exp:* Assoc scientist, Warner-Lambert Res Inst, 59-63; asst prof physiol, 69-75, assoc prof physiol, 75-80, RES ASSOC PROF PHARMACOLOGY, 80- *Mem:* Assoc mem Am Physiol Soc. *Res:* Local control of vascular smooth muscle. *Mailing Add:* Dept of Physiol Dartmouth Med Sch Hanover NH 03755

DETELS, ROGER, b Brooklyn, NY, Oct 14, 36; m 63; c 2. EPIDEMIOLOGY. *Educ:* Harvard Univ, BA, 58; New York Univ, MD, 62; Univ Wash, MS, 66. *Prof Exp:* Med officer, US Naval Med Res, Taiwan, 66-69, Epidemiol Br, Nat Inst Neurolog Dis & Stroke, NIH, 69-71; assoc prof epidemiol, 71-73, actg head, Div Epidemiol, 71-72, div head, 72-80, PROF EPIDEMIOL, SCH PUB HEALTH, UNIV CALIF, LOS ANGELES, 73-, DEAN, 80- *Concurrent Pos:* Prin investr, Epidemiol Study Chronic Obstructive Respiratory Dis, Nat Inst Pub Health Serv, Calif, 72-, Studies Immune Factors in Multisclerosis, 75-; prog dir, Cancer Epidemiol Training Prog, Nat Cancer Inst, 75-, Nat Inst Environ Health Sci, 78-; co-prin investr, Health Status Am Men, Nat Inst Child Health & Human Develop, 79-, Epidemiol Study Phenoxy Herbicide incl Agent Orange, 81-; mem, Adv Panel Clin Sci, Nat Res Coun, 81-, Sci Rev Panel Health Res Environ Protection Agency, 80- *Mem:* Am Public Health Asn; Soc Epidemiol Res (pres, 77-78); Am Epidemiol Soc; Int Epidemiol Soc; Am Thoraic Soc. *Res:* Epidemiologic research into factors causing and which determining the clinical course of multiplesclerosis; relationship between chronic exposure to air pollution and lung function; health outcomes of vasectomy; control of hypertension. *Mailing Add:* Sch Pub Health Univ Calif Los Angeles CA 90024

DETEMPLE, THOMAS ALBERT, b New York, NY, Sept 2, 41; m 66; c 2. ELECTRICAL ENGINEERING, QUANTUM ELECTRONICS. *Educ:* San Diego State Univ, BS, 65, MS, 69; Univ Calif, Berkeley, PhD(elec eng), 71. *Prof Exp:* Res physicist, Navy Electronics Lab Ctr, San Diego, 66-69; res asst elec eng, Univ Calif, Berkeley, 69-71; asst prof optical sci, Optical Sci Ctr, Univ Ariz, 71-72; asst prof, 72-74, assoc prof, 74-79, PROF ELEC ENG, UNIV ILL, 79- *Mem:* Inst Elec & Electronics Engrs; Am Inst Physics. *Res:* Quantum optics; gaseous electronics; superradiance, far infrared sources and techniques; gas lasers. *Mailing Add:* Dept Elec Eng Univ Ill 200 Eerl Urbana IL 61801

DETENBECK, ROBERT WARREN, b Buffalo, NY, Feb 11, 33; m 54; c 2. PHYSICS, OPTICS. *Educ:* Univ Rochester, BS, 54; Princeton Univ, PhD(nuclear physics), 62. *Prof Exp:* Instr physics, Princeton Univ, 58-59; asst prof, Univ Md, 59-67; assoc prof, 67-70, PROF PHYSICS, UNIV VT, 70- *Mem:* AAAS; Am Phys Soc; Am Asn Physics Teachers; Optical Soc Am; Inst Elec & Electronics Engrs. *Res:* Quantum optics; instrumentation; light scattering from aerosols. *Mailing Add:* Dept of Physics Univ of Vt Burlington VT 05401

DETERLING, RALPH ALDEN, JR, b Williamsport, Pa, Apr 29, 17; m 47; c 4. SURGERY. *Educ:* Stanford Univ, BA, 38, MD, 42; Univ Minn, MS, 46, PhD(surg), 47. *Prof Exp:* From asst prof to assoc prof surg, Col Physicians & Surgeons, Columbia Univ, 48-53, assoc prof clin surg & dir surg res labs, 53-59; chmn dept surg, 59-75, PROF SURG, SCH MED, TUFTS UNIV, 59- *Concurrent Pos:* From asst attend surgeon to assoc attend surgeon, Presby Hosp, 48-59; consult surg, Manhattan Vet Admin Hosp & Paterson Gen Hosp, US Naval Hosp, 52-59, Boston Vet Admin Hosp, 60-, St Elizabeth's Hosp, Brighton, 61-, Mt Auburn Hosp, Cambridge, 62-, Nashoba Community Hosp, Ayer, 75-, Framingham Union Hosp & Emerson Hosp, Concord, 76-; vis surgeon, Francis Delafield Hosp, 53-59; dir first surg serv, Boston City Hosp, 59-70; surgeon-in-chief, Tufts-New Eng Med Ctr Hosps, 59-75; surg consult, Lemuel Shattuck Hosp, Boston, 59- & Choate Hosp & Waltham Hosp, 78. *Honors & Awards:* Malmo Surg Found Award, 63; Outstanding Achievement Award, Univ Minn, 64. *Mem:* Am Surg Soc; Int Cardiovasc Soc (secy-gen, 63, pres, 71); Int Soc Surg; AMA; Am Acad Arts & Sci. *Res:* Blood vessel replacement; cardiovascular surgical technics; application of hypothermia to cardiac surgery; extracorporeal circulation for cardiac surgery; surgical applications of laser; organ homotransplantation. *Mailing Add:* 171 Harrison Ave Boston MA 02111

DE TERRA, NOEL, b New York, NY, Dec 31, 33; m 62. CELL BIOLOGY. *Educ:* Barnard Col, Columbia Univ, BA, 55; Univ Calif, Berkeley, PhD(zool), 59. *Prof Exp:* Fel, Rockefeller Inst, 59-61, res assoc biochem genetics, 61-62; asst res zoologist, Univ Calif, Los Angeles, 62-63, asst res biophysicist, Lab Nuclear Med & Radiation Biol, Sch Med, 63-67; asst mem, Inst Cancer Res, 67-75; res assoc prof anat, Hahnemann Med Col, 75-81; INDEPENDENT INVESTR, MARINE BIOL LAB, 81- *Mem:* Am Soc Cell Biol; Soc Protozool. *Res:* The role of the cell surface in control of cell division and morphogenesis in the eiliate Stentor; the role of the cell surface in determining the position of the macronucleus in Stentor. *Mailing Add:* Marine Biol Lab Woods Hole PA 02543

DETERS, DONALD W, b Quincy, Ill, Dec 20, 44. BIOENERGETICS, MITOCHONDRIAL BIOGENESIS. *Educ:* St Louis Univ, BS, 66; Univ Calif, Irvine PhD(chem), 72. *Prof Exp:* Fel biochem, Cornell Univ, 72-74; asst scientist biochem, Bioctr, Univ Basel, Switz, 74-78; ASST PROF MICROBIOL, UNIV TEX, AUSTIN, 79- *Mem:* Am Soc Microbiol; AAAS. *Res:* Enzymes, particularly those in mitochrondria that participate in oxidation of nutrients and adenosine triphosphate synthesis. *Mailing Add:* Dept Microbiol Univ Tex Austin TX 78712

DETERT, FRANCIS LAWRENCE, b San Diego, Calif, Apr 13, 23. ORGANIC CHEMISTRY. *Educ:* Univ Santa Clara, BS, 44; Stanford Univ, MS, 48, PhD(org chem), 50. *Prof Exp:* Researcher, Hickrill Chem Res Found, 50-52; res chemist, Calif Res Corp, 52-62; mem staff petrochem prod develop, Calif Chem Co, 62-65; petrochem prod tech specialist, Chevron Chem Co, 65-71, chem mkt res, 71-80; RETIRED. *Mem:* Am Chem Soc. *Res:* Diazonium coupling of furans; chemistry of cycloheptatrienone; synthetic detergents; chemical process development; gas odorants, xylenes and polybutenes; chemical market research and economics. *Mailing Add:* 6127 Outlook Ave Oakland CA 94605

DETHIER, BERNARD EMILE, b Boston, Mass, June 5, 26; m 52; c 6. METEOROLOGY. *Educ:* Calif Inst Tech, BS, 46, MS, 47; Johns Hopkins Univ, PhD(geog), 58. *Prof Exp:* Dir Climat Div, Patterson Weather Serv, 47-48; from asst prof to assoc prof math, Nazareth Col, 48-52; from asst prof to assoc prof agr climatol, 58-69, PROF METEOROL, CORNELL UNIV, 69- *Concurrent Pos:* Climatologist & dir, NY Climate Prog, 82-; dir, Northeast Regional Climate Prog, 81- *Mem:* Am Meteorol Soc; Sigma Xi. *Res:* Impact of climate variability on agriculture and climatology of the Northeast. *Mailing Add:* Div of Atmospheric Sci Cornell Univ Ithaca NY 14850

DETHIER, VINCENT GASTON, b Boston, Mass, Feb 20, 15; m 60; c 2. INSECT PHYSIOLOGY. *Educ:* Harvard Univ, AB, 36, AM, 37, PhD(biol), 39. *Hon Degrees:* ScD, Providence Col, 64, Ohio State Univ, 70. *Prof Exp:* Entomolgist, G W Pierce Lab, NH, 37-38; asst, Cruft Physics Lab, Harvard Univ, 39; from instr to asst prof biol, John Carroll Univ, 39-41; res physiologist, Army Chem Corps, 46; prof zool & entom, Ohio State Univ, 47; from assoc prof to prof biol, Johns Hopkins Univ, 48-58; prof zool & psychol, Univ Pa, 58-67, assoc, Inst Neurol Sci, Sch Med, 58-67; Class 1877 prof biol, Princeton Univ, 67-75; GILBERT WOODSIDE PROF ZOOL, UNIV MASS, AMHERST, 75- *Concurrent Pos:* Res fel, Atkins Inst, Cuba, 39-40; Belg-Am Educ Found fel, Belgian Congo, 52; Fulbright sr scholar, London Sch Hyg & Trop Med, 54-55; Guggenheim fels, State Agr Univ, Wageningen, 64-65 & Univ Sussex, Eng, 72-73. *Mem:* Nat Acad Sci; Am Philos Soc; Royal Entom Soc London; Am Soc Zool; Am Acad Arts & Sci. *Res:* Chemoreception in insects; chemistry of food plant choice by larvae; life histories of Lepidoptera. *Mailing Add:* Dept of Zool Univ of Mass Amherst MA 01003

DETHLEFSEN, LYLE A, b Oakes, NDak, Feb 27, 34; m 57; c 2. RADIOBIOLOGY, ONCOLOGY. *Educ:* Colo State Univ, BS, 60, DVM, 62; Univ Pa, PhD(molecular biol), 66. *Prof Exp:* Lectr radiation biol, St Joseph's Col (Pa), 65; asst prof radiology, Sch Vet Med, Univ Pa, 66-72, asst prof radiological sci, Sch Med, 68-72; assoc prof, 72-76, PROF RADIOL, COL MED, UNIV UTAH, 76- *Concurrent Pos:* USPHS res career develop award, 69-; consult, Breast Cancer Task Force, Nat Cancer Inst, NIH, 74-77 & Exp Therapeut Study Sect, NIH, 77-81; res prof anat, Univ Utah, 79; assoc ed, Radiation Res J, 77-80 & Cancer Res, 81-84. *Mem:* AAAS; Radiation Res Soc; Am Soc Cell Biol; Am Asn Cancer Res. *Res:* Cell biology; tumor growth; tumor cell kinetics. *Mailing Add:* Dept of Radiol Univ of Utah Med Ctr Salt Lake City UT 84132

DETHLEFSEN, ROLF, b Niebuell, Ger, Aug 30, 34; US citizen; m; c 4. PLASMA PHYSICS, ELECTRICAL POWER ENGINEERING. *Educ:* Braunschweig Tech Univ, Dipl Ing, 61; Mass Inst Technol, MS, 62, ScD(physics of fluids), 65. *Prof Exp:* Staff scientist space sci lab, Convair Div, Gen Dynamics Corp, Calif, 65-68; assoc dir, Advan Tech Ctr, Allis Chalmers Mfg Co, 68-72; consult engr, Res & Develop, Gould Brown Boveri, 72-79, SR PROJ MGR, BROWN BOVERI ELEC CORP, 79- *Concurrent Pos:* NATO fel, N Atlantic Treaty Orgn, 61-62. *Mem:* Am Vac Soc; Inst Elec & Electronics Engrs; Asn Ger Engrs. *Res:* Electric arcs; circuit breakers; electrical power equipment. *Mailing Add:* Brown Boveri Elec Corp 100 County Line Rd Colmar PA 18915

DETIG, ROBERT HENRY, b Pittsburgh, Pa, Oct 6, 35. ELECTRONICS, ELECTRICAL ENGINEERING. *Educ:* Carnegie Inst Technol, BS, 57, MS, 58, PhD(elec eng), 62. *Prof Exp:* Staff engr, satellite commun agency, US Army, 62-63; asst prof elec eng, Carnegie Inst Technol, 63-65; scientist, res div, Xerox Corp, 65-68; mgr electronics res br, Olivetti Corp Am, 68-72; treas, Med Graph Inc, 72-73; self employed, 74-76; PROJ ENGR, ELECTRONICS FOR MED, 76- *Mem:* Inst Elec & Electronics Engrs. *Res:* Reprographics; non-impact printing; information display; chemical and surface physics; medical electronics; electrostatics. *Mailing Add:* Honeywell Elec Med 1 Campus dr Pleasantville NY 10570

DETITTA, GEORGE THOMAS, b Jersey City, NJ, Nov 29, 47; m 69. CRYSTALLOGRAPHY, BIOPHYSICS. *Educ:* Villanova Univ, BS, 69; Univ Pittsburgh, PhD(crystallog, biochem), 73. *Prof Exp:* RES SCIENTIST MOLECULAR BIOPHYS, MED FOUND BUFFALO RES LABS INC, 73- *Concurrent Pos:* Prin investr, NIH grants, 77- *Honors & Awards:* Sidhu Award, Pittsburgh Diffraction Conf, 78. *Mem:* AAAS; Am Chem Soc; Am Crystallog Asn. *Res:* Elucidation of the relationships between molecular structure and molecular function in the biological milieu. *Mailing Add:* Med Found of Buffalo 73 High St Buffalo NY 14203

DETMERS, PATRICIA ANNE, b Riverside, Calif, Nov 13, 53; m 81. CELL BIOLOGY, CELL MOTILITY. *Educ:* Pomona Col, BA, 74; Univ Pa, PhD(biol), 79. *Prof Exp:* Fel, biol dept, Washington Univ, 79-81; FEL, ANAT DEPT, ALBERT EINSTEIN COL MED, 81- *Concurrent Pos:* Lectr, Univ Pa Col Gen Studies, 79, Albert Einstein Col Med, 82. *Mem:* Am Soc Cell Biol. *Res:* Actin polymerization in cell motility; factors that regulate actin polymerization during mating of Chlamydomonas reinhardi gametes. *Mailing Add:* Albert Einstein Col Med 1300 Morris Park Ave Bronx NY 10461

DETOMA, ROBERT PAUL, b Milton, Mass, Sept 5, 44; m 73. PHYSICAL CHEMISTRY, MOLECULAR SPECTROSCOPY. *Educ:* St Anselm's Col, BA, 66; Johns Hopkins Univ, PhD(chem), 73. *Prof Exp:* Assoc res scientist, Dept Biol, Johns Hopkins Univ, 73-77; asst prof chem, Univ Richmond, 77-78; ASST PROF CHEM, LOYOLA COL, 78- *Concurrent Pos:* NIH fel, 75-77. *Mem:* Sigma Xi; Am Chem Soc; Am Phys Soc; Am Soc Photobiol. *Res:* Time-dependent spectroscopy, excited state solvation, radiationless transitions, adiabatic photophysical reactions, biological application of fluorescence, photophysics, diffusion limited processes, chemometrics. *Mailing Add:* Dept Chem Loyola Col Baltimore MD 21210

DE TOMMASO, GABRIEL LOUIS, b Providence, RI, Aug 19, 34; m 56; c 4. ORGANIC CHEMISTRY, POLYMER CHEMISTRY. *Educ:* Univ RI, BS, 56; Univ Ill, PhD(org chem), 60. *Prof Exp:* Org polymer chemist, Air Reduction Co, Inc. 59-62; sr chemist, 62-76, proj leader, 76-80, SECT MGR, ROHM AND HAAS CO, INC, SPRING HOUSE, 80- *Res:* Organic synthesis; solution, suspension and emulsion polymerization of vinyl monomers; films; plastics; polymer structure; application of aqueous coatings for coil, metal decorating, general product finishing and building products. *Mailing Add:* 249 Laurel Lane Lansdale PA 19446

DE TOROK, DENES GABOR, b Sopron, Hungary, May 27, 31; US citizen; m 59; c 3. BIOLOGY. *Educ:* Eotvos Lorand Univ, Budapest, 53, MSc, 54, PhD(biol), 56. *Prof Exp:* Head cytol lab, Plant Breeding Inst, Hungarian Nat Acad Sci, 55-56; asst prof plant biochem, Budapest Tech Univ, 56-57; res asst, Mich State Univ, 57-58; res assoc, Roscoe B Jackson Mem Lab Biomed Res, Univ Maine, 58-59; officer instr & res fel, Harvard Univ, 59-62; asst prof bot, Pa State Univ, 62-68, prof biol sci, 68-74; DIR, MED RES, MAYVIEW STATE HOSP, BRIDGEWATER, PA, 74- *Concurrent Pos:* Consult, Am Polymer & Chem Co, 62; prin investr, Sigma Xi res grants, 63-64; dir res proj, NSF Instnl Grant, 63-64; prin investr, Am Cancer Soc grant, 63-65; chmn, Photosynthesis Study Group & consult, Comn Undergrad Educ Biol Sci, NSF, 65-; vis prof, Carnegie-Mellon Univ, 68-; Commonwealth Pa med res scientist, Mayview State Hosp, 68-74; prin investr, Scaife Found res grants, 69-71; res dir biochem & genetics studies alcoholism, M Hamilton & C Hagan Found grants, 69-71. *Mem:* AAAS; Int Asn Plant Tissue Cult; Scand Soc Plant Physiol. *Res:* Etiology of plant tumors; using cell and tissue cultures for the study of differences between normal and tumor chromosome numbers; nutritional requirements and base ratios; biochemistry and genetics of alcoholism; chromosomal and enzymatic studies on alcoholics. *Mailing Add:* Med Res Dept Mayview State Hosp Bridgewater PA 15017

DETRA, RALPH W(ILLIAM), b Thompsontown, Pa, Mar 23, 25; m 47; c 2. AERONAUTICAL ENGINEERING. *Educ:* Cornell Univ, BS, 46, MAeroE, 51; Swiss Fed Inst Technol, DrScTech, 53. *Prof Exp:* Flight test proj engr, US Naval Air Test Ctr, Md, 46-49; instr mech eng, Cornell Univ, 53-55; prin res scientist, Avco-Everett Res Lab, 55-59, vpres missile prog, Avco Res & Adv Develop Div, 59-65, vpres & asst gen mgr missile systs, 65-66, vpres & gen mgr, Avco Systs Div, 66-71, pres, Tyco Labs, Inc, 71-72, vpres energy technol, Avco-Everett Res Lab, Inc, 72-81, EXEC VPRES, AVCO-EVERETT RES LAB, INC, AVCO CORP, 81- *Mem:* Am Inst Aeronaut & Astronaut. *Res:* Hypervelocity flight; high temperature gasdynamics. *Mailing Add:* AERL Inc Avco Corp 2385 Revere Beach Pkwy Everett MA 02149

DETRAY, DONALD ERVIN, b Napoleon, Ohio, Nov 9, 17; m 40; c 2. VETERINARY MEDICINE. *Educ:* Ohio State Univ, DVM, 40. *Prof Exp:* Pvt pract, 40-47; vet, Mex-US Comn Eradication Foot & Mouth Dis, 47-48; res vet, USDA, 49-51, E Africa, 51-61, asst to dir, Animal Dis & Parasite Res Div, Agr Res Serv, Md, 61-63, from asst dir to assoc dir, 63-66; regional livestock adv, USAID, Lagos, Nigeria, 66-68, Nairobi, Kenya, 68-70, Ethiopia, 70-73; CONSULT, USDA, 73-; CONSULT, USAID, 73- *Mem:* Am Vet Med Asn; US Animal Health Asn; Conf Res Workers Animal Dis; Asn Advan Agr Sci Africa. *Res:* Bovine and porcine brucellosis; rinderpest of cattle and African swine fever; research administration in animal diseases and parasites. *Mailing Add:* PO Box 3404 Central Point OR 97502

DETRE, THOMAS PAUL, b Budapest, Hungary, May 17, 24; m 56; c 2. PSYCHIATRY. *Educ:* Gym Piarist Fathers, BA, 42; Univ Rome, MD, 52; Am Bd Psychiat & Neurol, dipl, 59. *Prof Exp:* Consult psychologist, Salvator Mundi Int Hosp, Rome, Italy, 51-53; chief resident psychiat, 57-58, from instr to prof, Sch Med, Yale Univ, 57-72, dir psychiat inpatient serv, Yale-New Haven Hosp, 60-68, psychiatrist-in-chief, 68-72; PROF PSYCHIAT & CHMN DEPT, UNIV PITTSBURGH, 72- *Concurrent Pos:* Consult, Fairfield Hosp, Newton, Conn, 58-61, Vet Admin Hosp, West Haven, 61-72 & Norwich Hosp, 62-72; dir, Western Psychiat Inst & Clin, 72-; assoc examr, Am Bd Psychiat & Neurol; chmn res scientist develop review comt, NIMH, 81- *Mem:* AAAS; fel Am Psychiat Asn; fel Am Col Psychiatrists; Am Col Neuropsychopharmacol; Pan-Am Med Asn. *Res:* Clinical research in psychopharmacology; hospital psychiatry. *Mailing Add:* Dept Psychiat 3811 O'Hara St Pittsburgh PA 15261

DETRICK, JOHN K(ENT), b Denver, Colo, Mar 10, 20; m 47; c 1. CHEMICAL ENGINEERING. *Educ:* Univ Denver, BS, 41; Univ Cincinnati, MS, 43. *Prof Exp:* Res engr, East Lab, Res & Develop Div, Explosives Dept, E I Du Pont De Nemours & Co, Inc, 42-47 & Burnside Lab, 47-49, supvr, East Lab, 49-53, tech asst res & develop staff, Del, 53-57, supt, Repauno Develop Lab, 57-67 & East Lab Lab, 67-68, spec asst dept eng sect, 68-70, res assoc, Exp Sta, Petrochem Dept, 70-78, sr financial analyst, 78-79; FINANCIAL CONSULT, 79- *Mem:* Am Chem Soc. *Res:* Process development in polymer intermediates. *Mailing Add:* 731 Park Ave Woodbury Heights NJ 08097

DETRICK, ROBERT SHERMAN, b Denver, Colo, Feb 3, 18; m 41, 74; c 4. CHEMISTRY. *Educ:* Univ Denver, BS, 39; Rensselaer Polytech Inst, MChE, 40. *Prof Exp:* From jr fel to sr fel, Mellon Inst, 40-51; mgr tar prod res, 51-54, from asst mgr to mgr lab res, 54-57, asst mgr tech planning, 57-58, mgr applns eval res, 58-66, mgr develop, Assoc Opers, 66-67, mgr systs develop, 67-71, mgr environ health & safety, 71-79, MGR EXTERNAL RES, RES DEPT, KOPPERS CO, INC, 79- *Mem:* Am Chem Soc; Soc Plastics Eng. *Res:* Reinforced plastics and environmental control. *Mailing Add:* Koppers Co Inc Res Dept 440 College Park Dr Monroeville PA 15146

DETRIO, JOHN A, b Miami, Fla, June 13, 37; m 63; c 3. SOLID STATE PHYSICS. *Educ:* Spring Hill Col, BS, 59; Univ Ala, MS, 61. *Prof Exp:* Res asst, Univ Ala, 59-61; physicist, Army Rocket & Guided Missile Agency, Ala, 61; physicist, Army Munition Command, Picatinny Arsenal, 61-66; res physicist, Univ Dayton, 66-75, RES GROUP LEADER OPTICAL MAT, RES INST, UNIV DAYTON, 75- *Mem:* Optical Soc Am; Sigma Xi; Am Phys Soc; Am Soc Testing & Mat. *Res:* Electroluminescence; solid state lasers; optical properties of solids; photoconductivity; atomic spectra; electrical properties of solids; infrared, ultra violet and visible spectroscopy and photometry. *Mailing Add:* Res Inst Univ of Dayton Dayton OH 45409

DETROY, ROBERT WILLIAM, b Jasper, Ind, Aug 20, 41; m 64; c 2. BIOCHEMISTRY, MICROBIOLOGY. *Educ:* Ind State Univ, BS, 62; Univ Wis, MS, 65, PhD(bact biochem), 67. *Prof Exp:* Res chemist, 67-76, RES LEADER, AGR MICROBIOL RES GROUP, NORTHERN REGIONAL RES LAB, USDA, 76- *Concurrent Pos:* Fel chem, Univ Manchester, Eng, 70-71; res assoc, Sch Med, Univ Ill; external staff appointment, Peoria Sch Med, 74- *Mem:* Am Soc Microbiol; Sigma Xi. *Res:* Fungal metabolism and synthesis of secondary metabolites; biological insecticides; fungal virology; bioconversion of animal waste and lignocellulosic residues; alternative energy resources from agriculture. *Mailing Add:* Northern Regional Res Lab USDA 1815 N University St Peoria IL 61604

DETTBARN, WOLF DIETRICH, b Berlin, Ger, Jan 30, 28; US citizen; m 60; c 2. NEUROCHEMISTRY, NEUROPHARMACOLOGY. *Educ:* Univ Gottingen, Dr med, 53. *Prof Exp:* Intern, Med Sch, Univ Gottingen, 54; res assoc, Ciba, Switz, 54-55; res assoc, Physiol Inst Med Sch, Univ Saarland, 55-58; res assoc neurol, Col Physicians & Surgeons, Columbia Univ, 58-61, from asst prof to assoc prof, 61-68; PROF PHARMACOL, SCH MED, VANDERBILT UNIV, 68- *Concurrent Pos:* Mem Marine Biol Lab Corp, Woods Hole, 63. *Mem:* Am Soc Pharmacol & Exp Therapeutics; Am Physiol Soc; Soc Gen Physiol; Am Soc Neurochem; Soc Neurosci. *Res:* Neurophysiology; trophic function of the neuron; peripheral nerve; ion flux; membrane permeability. *Mailing Add:* Dept of Pharmacol Vanderbilt Univ Sch of Med Nashville TN 37203

DETTINGER, DAVID, b Little Falls, NY, June 1, 19; m 52; c 2. RADIO ENGINEERING. *Educ:* St Lawrence Univ, BS, 41. *Prof Exp:* Engr, Hazeltine Electronics Corp, 42-45 & Teleregister Corp, 45-47; vpres & chief engr, Wheeler Labs, 47-61; head, commun dept, 61-75, FAC MEM, MITRE INST, MITRE CORP, 75- *Mem:* Sr mem Inst Elec & Electronics Engrs. *Res:* Communications engineering; microwaves; antennas; communication systems. *Mailing Add:* Three Penn Rd Winchester MA 01890

DETTMAN, JOHN WARREN, b Oswego, NY, July 14, 26; m 50; c 3. MATHEMATICAL ANALYSIS. *Educ:* Oberlin Col, AB, 50; Carnegie Inst Technol, MS, 52, PhD(math), 54. *Prof Exp:* Instr math, Carnegie Inst Technol, 53-54; mem tech staff, Bell Tel Labs, 54-56; from asst prof to assoc prof math, Case Inst Technol, 56-64; PROF MATH, OAKLAND UNIV, 64- *Concurrent Pos:* NSF fac fel, 62-63; sr res fel, Univ Glasgow, 70-71; NSF grants, 68, 70, 72, 74 & 77. *Mem:* Soc Indust & Appl Math; Am Math Soc; Math Asn Am; Sigma Xi. *Res:* Differential equations; functional analysis. *Mailing Add:* Dept of Math Oakland Univ Rochester MI 48063

DETTRE, ROBERT HAROLD, b Philadelphia, Pa, Aug 20, 28; m 57; c 2. PHYSICAL CHEMISTRY. *Educ:* Lafayette Col, BS, 52; Johns Hopkins Univ, MA, 54, PhD(phys chem), 57. *Prof Exp:* From res chemist to sr res chemist, 57-70, RES ASSOC, E I DU PONT DE NEMOURS & CO, INC, 70- *Mem:* AAAS; Am Chem Soc. *Res:* Thermodynamics of solutions; calorimetry; surface chemistry. *Mailing Add:* 509 Brentwood Dr Wilmington DE 19803

DETTWILER, HERMAN ANDREW, b Monroe, Wis, Mar 1, 10; m 40; c 5. BACTERIOLOGY. *Educ:* Univ Wis, BS, 35; Ohio State Univ, MS, 37, PhD(bact), 39. *Prof Exp:* Asst, Christ Hosp Inst Med Res, Cincinnati, 39-40; bacteriologist, Eli Lilly & Co, 40-46, from asst dir to dir biol prod div, 46-64, dir biol prod develop & control div, 64-69, res adv, Greenfield Labs, 69-72; RETIRED. *Mem:* AAAS; Am Soc Microbiol; Am Soc Trop Med & Hyg; Am Asn Immunol. *Res:* Chemotherapy of the pneumococcus; viruses and rickettsiae; development and production of typhus, poliomyelitis and influenza vaccines and biological products. *Mailing Add:* 304 Hawthorn Lane Greenfield IN 46140

DETTY, WENDELL EUGENE, b Bemidji, Minn, June 30, 22; m 45; c 4. ORGANIC CHEMISTRY. *Educ:* Am Univ, BA, 44; Georgetown Univ, MS, 49; Univ Okla, PhD(chem), 53. *Prof Exp:* Lab asst, Nat Bur Stand & Am Petrol Inst, Washington, DC, 42-44; biochemist, Nat Cancer Inst, USPHS, 47-50; res chemist, Southern Dyestuff Corp, 53-59; prof chem, Belmont Abbey Col, 54-59; PROF CHEM & CHMN DEPT, CATAWBA COL, 59- *Mem:* Am Chem Soc. *Res:* Chromatographic analysis of podophyllin; preparattion of new compounds for use in chemotherapy of cancer; amperometric titrations of flavonoid pigments with metal salts; infrared spectra of flavonoids, derivatives and their metal complexes. *Mailing Add:* Dept of Chem Catawba Col Salisbury NC 28144

DETWEILER, DAVID KENNETH, b Philadelphia, Pa, Oct 23, 19; m; c 6. PHYSIOLOGY, PHARMACOLOGY. *Educ:* Univ Pa, VMD, 42, MS, 49. *Hon Degrees:* DSc, Ohio State Univ, 66; DVM, Univ Vienna, 68 & Univ Torino, 69. *Prof Exp:* Asst instr physiol & pharmacol, 42, instr, 43-45, assoc, 45-47, asst prof, 47-51, assoc prof physiol, 51-62, prof physiol & pharmacol & head lab, 62-68, chmn dept vet med sci, Grad Sch Med, 56-70, assoc prof, Grad Sch Arts & Sci & Grad Sch Med, 56-62, PROF PHYSIOL & HEAD LAB, SCH VET MED, UNIV PA, 68-, CHMN, GRAD GROUP COMP MED SCI, 71-, DIR COMP CARDIOVASC STUDIES UNIT, 60- *Concurrent Pos:* Guggenheim fel, Univ Zurich, 55-56; consult, WHO, 58, Food & Drug Admin, 70-; guest prof, Univ Munich, 63, Univ Berlin, 68, Agr Orgn, 63- & Hannover Vet Sch, Ger, 73; mem, Expert Panel Vet Educ, Food & Agr Orgn, 63-; mem, Physiol Training Grant Comt, Nat Inst Gen Med Sci, 67-70; mem, Coun Basic Sci, Am Heart Asn. *Honors & Awards:* Gaines award & medal, Am Vet Med Asn. *Mem:* Nat Inst Med; fel AAAS; Am Physiol Soc; Am Vet Med Asn. *Res:* Comparative cardiology; electrocardiography; cardiovascular physiology; cardiovascular toxicology. *Mailing Add:* Sch of Vet Med Univ of Pa 3800 Spruce St Philadelphia PA 19104

DETWEILER, W KENNETH, b Quakertown, Pa, Jan 27, 23; m 44; c 2. ORGANIC CHEMISTRY. *Educ:* Ursinus Col, BS, 47; Lehigh Univ, MS, 49, PhD(chem), 51. *Prof Exp:* Group leader org chem res, Union Carbide & Carbon Chem Corp, 51-55; sect head new uses & new areas res, 55-66, asst dir lubricants & petrol specialties, 66-67, coordr hq mkt, 67-68, COORDR PROD RES, EXXON RES & ENG CO, EXXON CORP, 68- *Mem:* Am Chem Soc; Soc Automotive Eng; Am Inst Chem Eng. *Res:* Synthesis and characterization of heterocyclic nitrogen derivatives, acyl aldehydes, polyglycol ethers, alcohols and phosphate esters; study of the effect of structure upon plasticizing action; synthetic lubricants; diesel fuels and diesel lubricants; recruiting; industrial lubricants and greases; new uses and new areas research; worldwide petroleum research management. *Mailing Add:* 205 Sylvania Pl Westfield NJ 07090

DETWILER, DANIEL PAUL, b Woodbury, Pa, Feb 16, 27; m 49; c 3. SOLID STATE PHYSICS. *Educ:* Swarthmore Col, AB, 49; Yale Univ, MS, 50, PhD(physics), 52. *Prof Exp:* Res physicist, Lab, Franklin Inst, 52-54; from asst prof to assoc prof physics, State Univ NY Col Ceramics, Alfred, 54-60, chmn dept, 59-60; prof, Wilkes Col, 60-66, chmn dept, 61-66, chmn div natural sci & math & dir res & grad ctr, 63-66; physics specialist, NSF-India Liaison Off, New Delhi, 66-69; staff physicist, Comn Col Physics, 69-70; chmn, Dept Physics, 70-79, PROF PHYSICS, CALIF STATE COL, BAKERSFIELD, 79- *Mem:* AAAS; Am Asn Physics Teachers; Am Phys Soc; Sigma Xi. *Res:* Low temperature physics; semiconductivity; dielectrics; internal friction. *Mailing Add:* Dept of Physics Calif State Col Bakersfield CA 93309

DETWILER, JOHN STEPHEN, b Pittsburgh, Pa, Sept 23, 46; m 67; c 2. BIOMEDICAL ENGINEERING. *Educ:* Carnegie Inst Technol, BSEE, 67; Carnegie-Mellon Univ, MS, 68, PhD(elec eng), 71. *Prof Exp:* Biomed engr, Vet Admin Hosp, Pittsburgh, 71-76; asst prof eng med, Carnegie-Mellon Univ, 71-79; res asst prof obstet, Res Instr Med, Univ Pittsburgh, 76-79; MGR SYST ENG, BROWN BOVERI CONTROL SYSTS, 80- *Mem:* Inst Elec & Electronics Engrs. *Res:* Neural control of fetal heart rate and information extraction from clinical measurement of heart rate variability. *Mailing Add:* Brown Boveri Control Systs 564 Alpha Dr Pittsburgh PA 15238

DETWILER, PETER BENTON, b Stamford, Conn, Apr 17, 44; div; c 1. PHYSIOLOGY, BIOPHYSICS. *Educ:* St Lawrence Univ, BS, 66; Georgetown Univ, PhD(pharmacol), 70. *Prof Exp:* Staff fel physiol, NIH, 71-75; res fel biophys, Univ Cambridge, Eng, 76-78; asst prof, 78-81, ASSOC PROF PHYSIOL & BIOPHYS, UNIV WASH, 81- *Res:* Sensory physiology. *Mailing Add:* Dept of Physiol & Biophys Univ of Wash Seattle WA 98195

DETWILER, THOMAS C, b Hannibal, Mo, Dec 28, 33; m 62; c 2. BIOCHEMISTRY. *Educ:* Univ Ill, BS, 57, PhD(nutrit), 60. *Prof Exp:* Res assoc, Oak Ridge Nat Lab, 60-61; res assoc, Philadelphia Gen Hosp, Pa, 61-63; res assoc, McCollum-Pratt Inst, Johns Hopkins Univ, 63-65; from instr to assoc prof, 65-75, PROF BIOCHEM, STATE UNIV NY DOWNSTATE MED CTR, 75- *Concurrent Pos:* Vis assoc prof biochem, Univ Wash, 72-73. *Mem:* Am Soc Biol Chem; Am Asn Univ Prof; AAAS; NY Acad Sci; Sigma Xi. *Res:* Cellular regulatory mechanisms; biochemistry of platelets. *Mailing Add:* Dept Biochem SUNY Downstate Med Ctr 450 Clarkson Ave Brooklyn NY 11203

DETWYLER, ROBERT, b Middletown, NY, Apr 16, 29; m 51; c 2. ZOOLOGY. *Educ:* State Univ NY Col New Paltz, BS, 54; Univ NH, MS, 59, PhD(zool), 63. *Prof Exp:* Instr campus elem sch, NY State Teachers Col, New Paltz, 54-55; teacher pub sch, 55-57; instr, Univ NH, 62-63; asst prof biol, Nasson Col, 63-65; from asst prof to prof, 65-75, chmn dept, 68-78, CHARLES A DANA PROF BIOL, NORWICH UNIV, 75- *Mem:* Am Inst Biol Sci; AAAS; Am Fisheries Soc; Oceanic Soc; Sigma Xi. *Res:* Intertidal ecology; fish embryology; biology of the sea snail, Liparis atlanticus. *Mailing Add:* Dept of Biol Norwich Univ Northfield VT 05663

DETZ, CLIFFORD M, b New York, NY, Dec 16, 42; m 66; c 2. RESEARCH MANAGEMENT, HYDROMETALLURGY. *Educ:* Brown Univ, AB, 64; Univ Chicago, MS, 66, PhD(chem physics), 70. *Prof Exp:* Sr res scientist, Res Dept, Linde Div, Union Carbide Corp, 70-75, group leader, 75-78; GROUP LEADER, CHEVRON RES CO, STANDARD OIL OF CALIF, 78- *Mem:* Am Chem Soc; Am Inst Chem Engrs; Soc Mining Engrs. *Res:* Mineral processing and extractive metallurgy; separations and purification processes; petroleum processing. *Mailing Add:* Chevron Res Co 576 Standard Ave Richmond CA 94802

DEUBEN, ROGER R, b Detroit, Mich, Sept 9, 38; m 66; c 3. PHARMACOLOGY, PHYSIOLOGY. *Educ:* Mich State Univ, BS, 60, MS, 64; Univ Pittsburgh, PhD(pharmacol), 69. *Prof Exp:* Physiologist, Mich State Univ, 61-63; instr physiol, Sch Dent Med, Univ Pittsburgh, 65-66, from asst prof to assoc prof pharmacol, 69-77; ASSOC PROF PHYSIOL & PHARMACOL & CHMN DEPT, SCH DENT, UNIV DETROIT, 77- *Mem:* AAAS; Int Asn Dent Res; Soc Exp Biol & Med; Am Asn Dent Schs. *Res:* Studies on the central effects of angiotensin II and its possible role in the etiology of hypertension; regulation of anterior pituitary hormone secretion; role of prostaglandins in the above fields. *Mailing Add:* Dept Physiol & Pharmacol 2985 E Jefferson Ave Detroit MI 48207

DEUBERT, KARL HEINZ, b Weissensee, Ger, Feb 1, 29; nat US; m 50. ENVIRONMENTAL CHEMISTRY. *Educ:* Univ Halle, MS, 53, PhD(agr zool), 55. *Prof Exp:* Asst agr zool, Univ Halle, 53-60; sr asst phytopath, Cent Biol Inst, Berlin, Ger, 61-65; prof biol, Nat Univ Honduras, 65-67; res assoc phytopath, 67-74, asst prof residue anal, 74-81, assoc prof residue anal, 72-81, PROF RESIDUE ANAL, CRANBERRY EXP STA, UNIV MASS, 81- *Mem:* Am Inst Biol Sci; Soc Europ Nematol. *Res:* Pesticide residues in soil, water and tissues; compounds interfering with identification of pollutants. *Mailing Add:* Cranberry Exp Sta PO Box 569 Univ of Mass East Wareham MA 02538

DEUBLER, EARL EDWARD, JR, b Sayre, Pa, May 19, 27; m 51; c 4. ICHTHYOLOGY. *Educ:* Moravian Col, BS, 50; Cornell Univ, PhD(vert zool), 55. *Prof Exp:* Asst, Cornell Univ, 50-55; asst fisheries res biol, US Fish & Wildlife Serv, 55-56; from asst prof to assoc prof zool, Inst Fisheries Res, Univ NC, 56-61; assoc prof biol, Hartwick Col, 61-62, fisheries biol, Univ Mass, 62-63 & zool, Inst Fisheries Res, Univ NC, 63-67; assoc prof biol, 67-69, from actg chmn dept to chmn dept, 70-75, chmn fac, 75-76, actg pres, 76-77, PROF BIOL, HARTWICK COL, 69-, DEAN FAC, 80- *Mem:* NY Acad Sci; Am Inst Fishery Res Biologists; Sigma Xi. *Res:* Systematic ichthyology; ecology; life histories of marine and brackish water fishes. *Mailing Add:* Dept Biol Hartwick Col Oneonta NY 13820

DEUBLER, MARY JOSEPHINE, b Philadelphia, Pa, May 4, 17. VETERINARY MEDICINE. *Educ:* Univ Pa, VMD, 38, MS, 41, PhD(path), 44. *Prof Exp:* Asst instr vet path, Sch Vet Med, Univ Pa, 40-44; res assoc parasitol, Jefferson Med Col, 44-46; instr bact, 46-51, ASST PROF MED PATH, SCH VET MED, UNIV PA, 51- *Mem:* Am Vet Med Asn; Sigma Xi. *Res:* Virus, feline enteritis; anatomy and histology of the horse's eye; veterinary clinical bacteriology and mycology. *Mailing Add:* 2811 Hopkinson House Washington Square S Philadelphia PA 19106

DEUBNER, RUSSELL L(EIGH), b Jamestown, Ohio, Aug 10, 19; m 44; c 2. ELECTRONICS ENGINEERING. *Educ:* Ohio State Univ, BMetE, 42. *Prof Exp:* Asst metall, Ohio State Univ, 40-42; res engr & asst to supvr Res Div, graphic arts, Battelle Mem Inst, 45-50, mgr, Battelle Develop Corp, 50-58, admin dept econ, Battelle Mem Inst, 57-58; gen mgr, Chrome Plating Div, Gen Develop Corp, 58-61 & Ohio Semiconductors, Inc, 61-62; chmn & treas,

Sci Columbus Inc, Div Esterline Corp, 62-69, pres, 69-81; RETIRED. *Mem:* Am Soc Metals. *Res:* Metallurgy of case hardening chromium alloys; improvements in photo-engraving processes; development of xerography; printing; electroplating; patent and invention management; diversification studies and new product development; semiconductor product sales and production; Hall effect and thermoelectric devices and systems; corporate financing; electric power measurement (transducers and meters). *Mailing Add:* 2420 Donna Dr Columbus OH 43220

DEUPREE, JEAN DURLEY, b Washington, DC, Nov 9, 42. PHARMACOLOGY. *Educ:* Ferris State Col, BS, 65; Mich State Univ, PhD(biochem), 70. *Prof Exp:* Res fel pharmacol, Med Ctr, Univ Wis, 70-72; asst prof, 72-79, ASSOC PROF PHARMACOL, UNIV NEBR MED CTR, 79- *Mem:* AAAS; Am Soc Pharmacol & Exp Therapeut; Am Soc Neurochem; Sigma Xi; Soc Neurosci. *Res:* Epilepsy; mechanism of action of anticonvulsant drugs; neurotransmitter receptors; uptake, storage and release of neurotransmitters from storage granules. *Mailing Add:* Dept Pharmacol 42nd & Dewey Omaha NE 68105

DEUPREE, ROBERT G, b Washington, DC, Aug 5, 46; m 68; c 2. COMPUTER HYDRODYNAMICAL MODELLING. *Educ:* Univ Wis, BA, 68; Univ Colo, MS, 70; Univ Toronto, PhD(astron), 74. *Prof Exp:* Fel astron res, Dept Astrophys Sci, Princeton Univ, 74-75; staff mem, Los Alamos Sci Lab, 75-78; asst prof astron, Boston Univ, 78-80; STAFF MEM RES, LOS ALAMOS NAT LAB, 80- *Concurrent Pos:* Consult, Los Alamos Nat Lab, 78-80. *Mem:* Am Astron Soc; Int Astron Union. *Res:* Numerical fluid dynamic modelling of geophysical and astrophysical hydrodynamic events. *Mailing Add:* ESS-5 MS-665 Los Alamos Nat Lab PO Box 1663 Los Alamos NM 87545

DEUPREE, ROBERT GASTON, b Washington, DC, Aug 5, 46; m 68; c 1. ASTROPHYSICS, PHYSICS. *Educ:* Univ Wis, BA, 68; Univ Colo, MS, 70; Univ Toronto, PhD(astron), 74. *Prof Exp:* Fel astron, Princeton Univ, 74-75 & Los Alamos Sci Lab, 75-77; staff mem weapons physics, Los Alamos Sci Lab, 77-78; fac mem astron, Boston Univ, 78-80; STAFF MEM, LOS ALAMOS NAT LAB, 80- *Concurrent Pos:* Consult, Los Alamos Sci Lab, 78-; NSF grant, 78-79. *Mem:* Am Astron Soc; Int Astron Union. *Res:* Stellar interiors; stellar pulsation; stellar convection; high enthalpy flow; geophysical modelling. *Mailing Add:* ESS-5 MS-665 Los Alamos Nat Lab PO Box 841 Los Alamos NM 87545

DEURBROUCK, ALBERT WILLIAM, b Kansas City, Mo, Jan 2, 32; m 61; c 2. MINING ENGINEERING, MINERAL DRESSING. *Educ:* Univ Idaho, BS, 57. *Prof Exp:* Mining engr, US Bur Mines, 57-61, supvry mining methods res engr, 61-64, supvry mining engr, 64-77; CHIEF COAL PREP RES GROUP, DEPT ENERGY, 77- *Concurrent Pos:* US del, Int Coal Prep Cong, 77- *Mem:* Soc Mining Engrs; Am Mining Cong. *Res:* Research on flotation characteristics of American coals; pyritic sulfur reduction potential of conventional and non-conventional coal washing devices; liquid-solid separation; mineral benefication. *Mailing Add:* Dept of Energy 4800 Forbes Ave Pittsburgh PA 15213

DEUSCHLE, KURT W, b Kongen, Ger, Mar 14, 23; nat US; m 75; c 3. MEDICINE. *Educ:* Kent State Univ, BS, 44; Univ Mich, MD, 48; Am Bd Internal Med, dipl. *Prof Exp:* Intern med, Colo Med Ctr, 48-49; asst resident internal med, Syracuse Med Ctr, 49-50; resident, Col Med, State Univ NY Upstate Med Ctr, 50-52, instr, 51-52 & 54-55, dir tumor clin & cancer coordr, 54-55; chief tuberc, Ft Defiance Indian Hosp, USPHS, 52-54; asst prof pub health & prev med & dir, Navajo-Cornell Field Health Proj, Med Col, Cornell Univ, 55-60; prof community med & chmn dept, Med Col, Univ Ky, 60-68; prof, 68-69, ETHEL H WISE PROF COMMUNITY MED, MT SINAI SCH MED, 69-, CHMN DEPT, 68- *Concurrent Pos:* Consult, Off Technol Assessment, Cong US, 79- *Mem:* Am Col Prev Med; Am Pub Health Asn; Inst Med; Asn Teachers Prev Med; Int Epidemiol Asn. *Res:* Clinical investigations of antituberculous chemotherapeutic agents; cross-cultural medical research in areas of low economic development. *Mailing Add:* Dept of Community Med Mt Sinai Sch of Med New York NY 10029

DEUSER, WERNER GEORG, b Duesseldorf, Ger, Oct 31, 35; m 59; c 2. MARINE GEOCHEMISTRY. *Educ:* Univ Bonn, Vordiplom, 57; Pa State Univ, MS, 61, PhD(geochem), 63. *Prof Exp:* Consult geochemist, Nuclide Corp, 61-63; res scientist, Geol Surv WGer, 63-64; res geochemist, Nuclide Corp, 64-66; res assoc, 66-67, ASSOC SCIENTIST GEOCHEM, WOODS HOLE OCEANOG INST, 67- *Mem:* AAAS; Geochem Soc. *Res:* Mass spectrometry applied to geological problems; isotope geology; radioactive age determinations; stable isotope geochemistry, chemical and geological oceanography. *Mailing Add:* Dept of Chem Woods Hole Oceanog Inst Woods Hole MA 02543

D'EUSTACHIO, DOMINIC, b Pittsburgh, Pa, Feb 19, 04; m 45; c 2. PHYSICS. *Educ:* Columbia Univ, BS, 26; NY Univ, PhD(physics), 36. *Prof Exp:* Res assoc, Columbia Univ, 27-28; asst & instr physics, NY Univ, 29-35; instr, Polytech Inst Brooklyn, 36-42; chief crystal res sect, Ft Monmouth, NJ, 42-44; res dir, Bliley Mfg Co, 44-47; head physics res, Pittsburgh-Corning Corp, 47-60, res dir res & eng ctr, 60-65, vpres res, 65-69; prof mat sci, Univ PR, Mayaguez, 69-75; CONSULT, 75- *Mem:* AAAS; Acoust Soc Am; Am Phys Soc. *Res:* Hyperfine structure; surface properties of crystalline solids; high vacuum techniques; physical properties of glass; thermal conductivity at low temperatures; acoustics; portland cement and related materials; energy conservation, particularly as it applies to housing; use of solar energy. *Mailing Add:* 1431 Arboretum Dr Chapel Hill NC 27514

DEUSTER, RALPH W(ILLIAM), b Paterson, NJ, June 28, 20; m 46; c 3. MECHANICAL ENGINEERING, NUCLEAR PHYSICS. *Educ:* Purdue Univ, BSME, 42; Princeton Univ, MS, 50; Univ Pittsburgh, Cert Bus Mgt, 67. *Prof Exp:* Proj mgr, Armour Res Found, Ill, 54-55; with Babcock & Wilcox Co, 55-70; vpres & gen mgr, Reactor Fuels Div, 70-73, PRES, NUCLEAR FUEL SERV, INC, 73- *Mem:* Am Nuclear Soc; Am Soc Mech Engrs. *Res:* Economics of nuclear reactor fuels; beta spectroscopy. *Mailing Add:* Nuclear Fuel Serv Inc 6000 Executive Blvd Rockville MD 20852

DEUTCH, BERNHARD IRWIN, b New York, NY, Sept 29, 29; m 63; c 2. PHYSICS. *Educ:* Cornell Univ, BA, 51, MS, 53; Univ Pa, PhD(physics), 59. *Prof Exp:* Asst biophys, Cornell Univ, 51-53; asst nuclear physics, Univ Pa, 54-58; physicist, Bartol Res Found, 58-62; amanuensis physics, Univ Aarhus, 62-64; physicist, Nobel Inst Physics, 64-65; lectr, 65-70, DEPT LEADER PHYSICS, UNIV AARHUS, 70- *Concurrent Pos:* Vis, Orsay, Brookhaven Nat Lab, 67, Niels Bohr Inst, 69, Shanghai Met Inst, 74, Yale Univ, 76 & Fu Tan Univ, Shanghai, 78. chmn, Int Hyperfine Conf, Aarhus, 71; assoc ed, J Nuclear Physics, 73-; ed, J Hyperfine interactions, 74- *Mem:* AAAS; Am Phys Soc. *Res:* Atomic and nuclear polarization; nuclear structure; hyperfine interactions; biophysics. *Mailing Add:* Inst of Physics Univ of Aarhus DK-8000 Aarhus C Denmark

DEUTCH, JOHN MARK, b Brussels, Belg, July 27, 38; US citizen; m 63; c 3. PHYSICAL CHEMISTRY, STATISTICAL MECHANICS. *Educ:* Amherst Col, BA, 61; Mass Inst Technol, BEng, 61, PhD(phys chem), 66. *Hon Degrees:* DSc, Amherst Col, 78. *Prof Exp:* Systs analyst, Off Secy Defense, 61-65; Nat Acad Sci-Nat Res Coun fel, Nat Bur Stand, 65-66; asst prof chem, Princeton Univ, 66-70; assoc prof, 70-72, chmn dept, 77-78, dir energy res, 78-79, PROF CHEM, MASS INST TECHNOL, 72-,. *Concurrent Pos:* Consult, Bur Budget, Exec Off President, 66-68; mem, Defense Sci Bd, 75- & Army Sci Adv Panel, 76-78; Undersecy Energy, 79-80; mem, Urban Inst, Univ Res Assocs & President's Nuclear Safety Oversight Comt, 80-81. *Mem:* Am Phys Soc; Am Chem Soc. *Res:* Liquids; transport processes; light scattering; polymer theory. *Mailing Add:* Dept Chem Room 6-123 Mass Inst Technol Cambridge MA 02139

DEUTSCH, DANIEL HAROLD, b New York, NY, Aug 29, 22; m 46; c 2. ORGANIC CHEMISTRY, NUCLEAR CHEMISTRY. *Educ:* Calif Inst Technol, BS, 48, PhD(chem, math), 51. *Prof Exp:* Fel cyclobutane chem, Calif Inst Technol, 51; pres & dir, Calif Found Biochem Res, 51-73; CONSULT, CALBIOCHEM, 70-; PRES & DIR, DANIEL H DEUTSCH LABS, INC, 77- *Concurrent Pos:* Vpres, Calbiochem, 58-70, dir, 58-72. *Mem:* Am Chem Soc; NY Acad Sci; AAAS; Am Nuclear Soc. *Res:* Commercial production of research biochemicals; medicinal chemistry; physical chemistry; ion-exchange resin kinetics; limitations on the second law of thermodynamics; isotope separation methodology; variant model for the stellar red shift; the liquid state; turbulence in liquids. *Mailing Add:* Daniel H Deutsch Labs Inc 141 Kenworthy Dr Pasadena CA 91105

DEUTSCH, EDWARD ALLEN, b New York, NY, July 13, 42; m 63; c 2. INORGANIC CHEMISTRY. *Educ:* Univ Rochester, BS, 63; Stanford Univ, PhD(inorg chem), 67. *Prof Exp:* USPHS fel, Univ Calif, San Diego, 67-68; asst prof inorg chem, Univ Chicago, 68-73; assoc prof, 73-78, PROF INORGANIC CHEM, UNIV CINCINNATI, 78- *Concurrent Pos:* Vis scientist, Argonne Nat Lab, 69- & Brookhaven Nat Lab, 80- *Mem:* NY Acad Sci; Am Chem Soc; Soc Nuclear Med. *Res:* Kinetics and mechanisms of homogeneous reactions; catalytic processes; electron transfer reactions; chemistry of transuranium elements; chemistry of vitamin B12; inorganic models for biochemical systems; chemistry of technetium as applied to nuclear medicine. *Mailing Add:* Dept of Chem Univ of Cincinnati Cincinnati OH 45221

DEUTSCH, ERNST ROBERT, b Frankfurt, Ger, May 13, 24; Can citizen; m 49; c 3. GEOPHYSICS. *Educ:* Univ Toronto, BA, 46, MA, 49; Univ London, PhD(geophys) & DIC, 54. *Prof Exp:* Seismic explor, Texaco Explor Co, Alta, 49-51; res asst physics, Imp Col, Univ London, 54-57; res engr, Imp Oil Ltd, Alta, 57-63; assoc prof, 63-68, PROF GEOPHYS, MEM UNIV NEWF, 68- *Concurrent Pos:* Vis lectr, Univ Western Ont, 57; mem assoc comt geod & geophys, Nat Res Coun Can, 64-70; assoc ed, J Can Soc Exp Geophys, 78- *Mem:* Soc Explor Geophys; Can Asn Physicists; Can Geophys Union; Am Geophys Union; Soc Geomagnetism & Geoelec Japan. *Res:* Magnetic properties and domain structure of rocks; palaeomagnetism and application to hypotheses of polar wandering and plate tectonics ; paleogeography of the North Atlantic; gravity studies and crustal structure. *Mailing Add:* Dept of Physics Mem Univ of Newf St John's NF A1B 3X7 Can

DEUTSCH, GEORGE C, b Budapest, Hungary, Apr 19, 20; US citizen; m 42; c 3. MATERIALS SCIENCE, METALLURGY. *Educ:* Case Western Reserve Univ, BS, 42. *Prof Exp:* Metallurgist, Copperweld Steel Co, 42-44; res metallurgist, Lewis Res Ctr, NASA, 46-60, asst dir res mat sci & eng, 60-70, dir, Mat & Struct Div, Off Advan Res & Technol, 70-81, dir res & technol, 73-81; CONSULT ENGR, 81- *Concurrent Pos:* Mem, Nat Mat Adv Bd, 62-65; coordr comt mat res & technol, Fed Coun Sci & Technol, 63-69; chmn interagency comt mat, Nat Acad Sci, 70-71. *Honors & Awards:* NASA exceptional serv medal, 67. *Mem:* Fel Am Soc Metals; Am Inst Mining, Metall & Petrol Engrs. *Res:* High temperature nickel and cobalt base alloys; powder metallurgy; refractory metals; cermets. *Mailing Add:* 8303 Whitman Dr Bethesda MD 20817

DEUTSCH, HAROLD FRANCIS, b Sturgeon Bay, Wis, Sept 2, 18; m 42; c 2. CHEMISTRY. *Educ:* Univ Wis, PhB, 40, PhD(physiol chem), 44. *Prof Exp:* Asst cancer res, McArdle Lab, 40-41, teaching asst physiol chem, 42-44, res assoc, Sch Med, 44-45, asst prof, 45-46, assoc prof, 47-56, PROF PHYSIOL CHEM, SCH MED, UNIV WIS-MADISON, 56- *Concurrent Pos:* Rockefeller Found fel natural sci, Univ Stockholm, 50-51; vis prof, Univ Brazil, 50, Univ Sao Paulo, 54, Univ Hokkaido, 71 & Tech Univ Munich, 74-75; vis scientist, Rockefeller Found, 60, Max-Planck Inst Biochem, Munich, 60 & 64 & Univ Hokkaido, 81. *Mem:* Am Chem Soc; Am Soc Biol Chem. *Res:* Separation and characterization of plasma, erythrocyte and tissue protein; immunochemistry. *Mailing Add:* Dept Physiol Chem Sch Med Univ Wis Madison WI 53706

DEUTSCH, JAMES WILLIAM, biochemistry, neurobiology, see previous edition

DEUTSCH, JOHN LUDWIG, b New York, NY, May 5, 38; m 61. PHYSICAL CHEMISTRY, SPECTROSCOPY. *Educ:* Tulane Univ, BS, 59; Oxford Univ, DPhil(ultraviolet spectros), 63. *Prof Exp:* NSF fel & tutor chem, Oxford Univ, 63-64; vis asst prof, Pomona Col, 64-66; actg chmn dept, 74-75, assoc prof, 66-77, PROF CHEM, STATE UNIV NY COL GENESEO, 77- *Concurrent Pos:* Vis researcher, Phys Chem Lab, Oxford Univ, 80 & 81. *Mem:* AAAS; Am Chem Soc; Royal Soc Chem; Sigma Xi; NY Acad Sci. *Res:* Electronic spectra of simple molecules and nuclear magnetic resonance spectroscopy. *Mailing Add:* Dept Chem State Univ NY Col Geneseo NY 14454

DEUTSCH, LAURENCE PETER, b Boston, Mass, Aug 7, 46. INFORMATION SCIENCE. *Educ:* Univ Calif, Berkeley, BA, 69, PhD(comput sci), 73. *Prof Exp:* Programmer comput sci, Univ Calif, Berkeley, 65-68; syst architect, Berkeley Comput Corp, 68-71; mem res staff, Comput Sci, 71-79, PRIN SCIENTIST, XEROX PALO ALTO RES CTR, 79- *Res:* Programming languages and environments; filing systems; automatic programming; user interfaces. *Mailing Add:* Xerox Palo Alto Res Ctr 3333 Coyote Hill Rd Palo Alto CA 94304

DEUTSCH, MARSHALL EMANUEL, b New York, NY, Aug 17, 21; m 47; c 3. CLINICAL CHEMISTRY, NUTRITION. *Educ:* City Col New York, BS, 41; NY Univ, PhD(physiol sci), 51. *Prof Exp:* Asst & assoc biochem, NY Univ-Bellevue Med Ctr, 47-51; jr assoc, Henry Ford Hosp, 51-53; head chem microbiol, Warner-Chilcott Res Labs, 53-55, sr scientist biochem, 55-58; dir prod develop, G W Carnrick Co, 58-59, dir res & develop, 59-60; dir life sci res, Becton, Dickinson & Co, 60-66; tech dir, NEN-Picker Radiopharmaceut, 66-68; consult, Farbwerke Hoechst AG, 68, tech dir, Picker-Hoechst, Inc, 69-70; vpres & tech dir, Mead Diag, Inc, 70-72; VPRES & TECH DIR, THYROID DIAG, 72- *Concurrent Pos:* Vpres & tech dir, CIS Radiopharmaceut, 72-75; consult, United Nations Capital Develop Fund, 77. *Mem:* Soc Environ Geochem & Health; fel AAAS; Soc Nuclear Med; Am Asn Clin Chem; Sigma Xi. *Res:* Thyroid and anti-thyroid drugs; effects of viricides; chemical kinetics; diagnostic reagents; pharmaceutical products; nutrition. *Mailing Add:* 41 Concord Rd Sudbury MA 01776

DEUTSCH, MARTIN, b Vienna, Austria, Jan 29, 17; nat US; m 39; c 2. PHYSICS. *Educ:* Mass Inst Technol, BS, 37, PhD(physics), 41. *Prof Exp:* Instr physics, Mass Inst Technol, 41-45; scientist, Los Alamos Sci Lab, Univ Calif, 44-46; from asst prof to assoc prof, 45-53, dir lab nuclear sci, 75-80, PROF PHYSICS, MASS INST TECHNOL, 53- *Mem:* Nat Acad Sci; AAAS; fel Am Phys Soc. *Res:* Study of radioactive radiations; study of the fission process; nuclear spectroscopy; elementary particle physics. *Mailing Add:* Dept of Physics Mass Inst of Technol Cambridge MA 02138

DEUTSCH, MIKE JOHN, b Denver, Colo, Apr 4, 20; m 42; c 5. BIOCHEMISTRY. *Educ:* Univ Denver, BS, 42. *Prof Exp:* Biochemist, 57-61, SUPVRY BIOCHEMIST, FOOD & DRUG ADMIN, 61- *Mem:* Asn Off Agr Chemists. *Res:* Vitamin methodology. *Mailing Add:* Food & Drug Admin Div of Nutrit 200 C St SW Washington DC 20204

DEUTSCH, ROBERT W(ILLIAM), b Far Rockaway, NY, Mar 21, 24; m 49; c 2. NUCLEAR ENGINEERING. *Educ:* Mass Inst Technol, BS, 48; Univ Calif, PhD(physics), 53. *Prof Exp:* Physicist high energy nuclear physics, Radiation Lab, Univ Calif, 50-53; res assoc theoret nuclear physics, Knolls Atomic Power Lab, 53-57; chief physicist, Gen Nuclear Eng Corp, 57-61; consult physics, Martin Co, 61-63; prof & chmn dept nuclear sci & eng, Cath Univ, 63-71; PRES, GEN PHYSICS CORP, 66- *Mem:* AAAS; fel Am Nuclear Soc; Am Soc Eng Educ; Sigma Xi. *Mailing Add:* Gen Physics Corp 1000 Century Plaza Columbia MD 21044

DEUTSCH, S(ID), b New York, NY, Sept 19, 18; m 41; c 3. BIOENGINEERING, ELECTRICAL ENGINEERING. *Educ:* Cooper Union, BEE, 41; Polytech Inst Brooklyn, MEE, 47, DEE, 55. *Prof Exp:* Technician elec motor, Rite-Way Fur Machine Co, 35-40; designer electro-mech equip, Otis Elevator Co, 40-41 & Allied Process Engrs, 41-43; instr physics, Hunter Col, 43-44; instr TV, Madison Inst Technol, 46-50; engr electronics, Polytech Res & Develop Co, 50-54; instr commun, Polytech Inst Brooklyn, 51-56, proj engr electronics, Microwave Res Inst, 54-60, prof elec eng, 56-72; prof, Rutgers Med Sch, 72-79; adj prof, Rutgers Univ, 72-79; PROF BIOMED ENG, TEL AVIV UNIV, 79- *Concurrent Pos:* Designer, Fairchild Camera & Instrument Co, 43-44; instr, City Col New York, 55-57; consult, Polytech Res & Develop Co, 57, Budd Electronics Co, 58-60 & Rockefeller Inst, 61-64. *Mem:* Fel Inst Elec & Electronics Engrs; fel Soc Info Display. *Res:* Communications and electronics; information and network theory; biomedical electronics. *Mailing Add:* Tel Aviv Univ Sch Eng Ramat Aviv Israel

DEUTSCH, STANLEY, b Brooklyn, NY, Apr 4, 30; m 54; c 2. ANESTHESIOLOGY, PHARMACOLOGY. *Educ:* NY Univ, BA, 50; Boston Univ, MA, 51, PhD(physiol), 55, MD, 57; Am Bd Anesthesiol, dipl. *Prof Exp:* Rotating intern, Grad Hosp, Univ Pa, 57-58; resident anesthesiol, Hosp Univ Pa, 58-61, assoc, 63-64, asst prof, Univ Pa, 63-65; assoc in anesthesia, Harvard Med Sch, 65-68, asst prof, 68-69; assoc surg, Peter Bent Brigham Hosp, 68-69; prof anesthesiol, Univ Chicago & chmn dept, Michael Reese Hosp, 69-71; PROF ANESTHESIOL & CHMN DEPT, SCH MED, UNIV OKLA HEALTH SCI CTR, 71- *Concurrent Pos:* Consult, Vet Admin Hosp, Philadelphia, Pa, 60-61 & 63-; mem sect anesthesia, Nat Acad Sci-Nat Res Coun, 70-72. *Mem:* AAAS; NY Acad Sci; Am Soc Anesthesiol; Asn Univ Anesthetists. *Res:* Cardiovascular and renal effects of anesthesia and surgery; pharmacology of anesthetics and drugs used in association with anesthesia; cardiovascular and renal physiology. *Mailing Add:* 800 NE 13th St Oklahoma City OK 73190

DEUTSCH, THOMAS, b Vienna, Austria, Apr 24, 32; nat US. LASERS. *Educ:* Cornell Univ, BEngPhys, 55; Harvard Univ, AM, 56, PhD(appl physics), 61. *Prof Exp:* From sr res scientist to prin res scientist, Res Div, Raytheon Co, Mass, 60-74; STAFF MEM, LINCOLN LAB, MASS INST

TECHNOL, 74- *Mem:* Fel Am Phys Soc; Inst Elec & Electronics Engrs. *Res:* Laser processing of materials; laser induced photochemistry; gas and chemical lasers. *Mailing Add:* Rm C-128 Lincoln Lab Mass Inst Technol Lincoln Lab Lexington MA 02173

DEUTSCHER, MURRAY PAUL, b New York, NY, Sept 1, 41; m 66; c 2. BIOCHEMISTRY, MOLECULAR BIOLOGY. *Educ:* City Col New York, BS, 62; Albert Einstein Col Med, PhD(biochem), 66. *Prof Exp:* Am Cancer Soc fel, Stanford Univ, 66-68; from asst prof to assoc prof biochem, 68-75, PROF BIOCHEM, UNIV CONN HEALTH CTR, 75- *Concurrent Pos:* Vis scientist, Weizmann Inst Sci, 69 & Nat Inst Med Res, London, 75; mem ed, Nucleic Acids Res, 79- *Mem:* AAAS; Am Soc Biol Chemists; Am Chem Soc. *Res:* Protein biosynthesis; enzymology of nucleic acid metabolism. *Mailing Add:* Dept of Biochem Univ of Conn Health Ctr Farmington CT 06032

DEUTSCHMAN, ARCHIE JOHN, JR, b Chicago, Ill, Nov 21, 17; m 46; c 5. ORGANIC CHEMISTRY. *Educ:* Univ Ill, BS, 39; Lawrence Col, MS, 41, PhD(chem), 43. *Prof Exp:* Spec asst, Univ Ill, 44-45; chief chemist, Graham, Crawley & Assocs, Chicago, 45-46; sr res chemist, Phillips Petrol Co, Okla, 46-47; dir chem res, Spencer Chem Co, 47-57; prof agr biochem, 57-75, PROF NUTRIT & FOOD, UNIV ARIZ, 75- *Mem:* Am Chem Soc; Sigma Xi. *Res:* High pressure reactions; vapor phase and solution; furfural polymer control; butadiene chemistry; polymerizations; electrical conductivity of paper; hydrothermal crystal growth; copper recovery. *Mailing Add:* Dept of Nutrit & Food Univ of Ariz Tucson AZ 85721

DEV, PARVATI, b New Delhi, India, Dec 6, 46; m 75; c 1. BIOMECHANICS, COMPUTER SIMULATION. *Educ:* Indian Inst Technol, Kharagpur, BTech, 68; Stanford Univ, MS, 69, PhD(elec eng), 75. *Prof Exp:* Staff scientist, Neurosci Res Prog, Mass Inst Technol, 72-76; asst prof biomed eng, Col Eng, Boston Univ, 76-78; RES SCIENTIST, DEVELOP CTR, VET ADMIN MED CTR, PALO ALTO, CALIF, 79- *Concurrent Pos:* Res assoc, Dept Psychol, Mass Inst Technol, 73-76; assoc ed, Transactions Biomed Eng, Inst Elec & Electronic Engrs, 80- *Mem:* Inst Elec & Electronic Engrs; Soc Neurosci; Biomed Eng Soc; Am Asn Artificial Intel. *Res:* Mathematical analysis and quantitative modelling of neuromuscular systems; biomechanics of the hand. *Mailing Add:* 3340 Ross Rd Palo Alto CA 94303

DEV, VAITHILINGAM GANGATHARA, b Kalayarkurichi, India, Mar 8, 37; m 66; c 2. GENETICS, CYTOGENETICS. *Educ:* Univ Madras, BVSc, 59; Univ Mo, MS, 61, PhD(animal husbandry), 65. *Prof Exp:* Mem scientists pool, Coun Sci & Indust Res, India, 66-69; res assoc, Columbia Univ, 72-73, asst prof human genetics & develop, 74-77; asst prof path, Univ Tex Health Sci Ctr, Dallas, 78-81; ASSOC PROF MED GENETICS, UNIV SALA, MOBILE, 81- *Concurrent Pos:* Trainee, Columbia Univ, 70-72. *Res:* Chromosome structure; polymorphisms; linkage. *Mailing Add:* Dept Med Genetics Univ SAla Mobile AL 36617

DEV, VASU, b Lahore, Punjab, Mar 18, 33; m 63; c 2. ORGANIC CHEMISTRY, MEDICINAL CHEMISTRY. *Educ:* Punjab Univ, BSc, 51, Hons, 53, MSc, 54; Univ Calif, Davis, PhD(chem), 62. *Prof Exp:* Chemist, Drug Res Lab, India, 55-56 & Govt Med Col, India, 56-59; res assoc org chem, Univ Chicago, 63-64; asst prof med chem, Univ Tenn, 64-65; from asst prof to assoc prof chem, 65-72, chmn dept, 70-78, PROF CHEM, CALIF STATE POLYTECH UNIV, POMONA, 73- *Mem:* Am Chem Soc; Royal Soc Chem. *Res:* Reaction mechanisms, natural products and organic synthesis; synthesis and study of products possessed with pharmacodynamic properties. *Mailing Add:* Dept of Chem Calif State Polytech Univ Pomona CA 91768

DEVALL, WILBUR BOSTWICK, b Phelps, NY, Mar 17, 15; m 38; c 1. FORESTRY. *Educ:* Syracuse Univ, BS, 37; Univ Fla, MS, 41. *Prof Exp:* Field asst, Northeastern Forest Exp Sta, Cooperstown, NY, 37; from instr to asst prof, Univ Fla, 41-43; assoc forester, US Forest Serv, Fla, 43-45 & Southern Forest Exp Sta, 45-46; assoc prof, 46-78, head dept, 71-78, EMER PROF FORESTRY, AUBURN UNIV, 78- *Concurrent Pos:* Pres, Proxy Serv Ltd, 78-; vchmn, Ala Surface Mining Reclamation Comn, 81- *Mem:* Soc Am Foresters; Forest Farmers Asn (pres, 74-75). *Res:* Forest ecology of Florida and Alabama; taxonomy of Pinus caribaea in Florida; visual aids for teaching dendrology. *Mailing Add:* 757 Cary Dr Auburn AL 36830

DEVANEY, JOSEPH JAMES, b Boston, Mass, Apr 29, 24; m 54; c 1. LASERS, MATHEMATICAL PHYSICS. *Educ:* Mass Inst Technol, SB, 47, PhD(theoret physics), 50. *Prof Exp:* Mem staff, Theoret Div, 50-72, mem staff, Laser Div, 72-80, MEM STAFF, MONTE CARLO GROUP, LOS ALAMOS NAT LAB, 80- *Concurrent Pos:* Adj prof math, Univ NMex, 56-59, adj prof physics, 59-; mem, Gov Policy Bd Air & Water Pollution, 70. *Mem:* Am Phys Soc; Am Nuclear Soc. *Res:* Theoretical nuclear physics; laser systems analysis; Monte Carlo particle transport. *Mailing Add:* X6 MS 226 Los Alamos Nat Lab Los Alamos NM 87545

DEVANEY, RICHARD G(EORGE), b Sharpsburg, Pa, May 21, 23; m 46; c 2. ELECTRICAL ENGINEERING, ELECTRONIC PHYSICS. *Educ:* Pa State Univ, BSEE, 43. *Prof Exp:* Tech supvr magnetic separation, Manhattan Proj, Clinton Eng Works, Tenn, 43-45; proj engr elec, 45-46, res engr electronics & physics, 46-56, sr res engr dielectrics, 56-66, sr res engr & lab supvr, 66-68 & 70-72, new prods analyst, 68-70 & 73-75, SR RES ENGR, TENN EASTMAN CO, 75- *Concurrent Pos:* Mem, conf elec insulation, Nat Res Coun-Nat Acad Sci; exec comt, Int Wire & Cable Symp. *Mem:* Nat Soc Prof Engrs; Inst Elec & Electronics Engrs; Am Chem Soc. *Res:* Dielectric properties of new insulating materials; design and development of new scientific instruments; solid state infrared detectors; semi-permeable membranes. *Mailing Add:* Res Labs B-150B Tenn Eastman Co PO Box 511 Kingsport TN 37662

DEVARTANIAN, DANIEL VARTAN, b Boston, Mass, July 16, 33; m 64; c 2. BIOCHEMISTRY. *Educ:* Boston Univ, AB, 56; Northeastern Univ, MSc, 59; Univ Amsterdam, 65. *Prof Exp:* Res fel biochem, Univ Amsterdam, 61-65; res assoc, Univ Wis-Madison, 65-68; asst prof, 68-73, assoc prof, 73-78, PROF BIOCHEM, UNIV GA, 78- *Concurrent Pos:* Res career develop award, Nat Inst Gen Med Sci, 71-76; mem, Int Union Pure & Appl Chem & Int Union Biochem subcomt Cytochrome Nomenclature, 73- *Mem:* Am Soc Microbiol; Am Soc Biol Chem; Brit Biochem Soc. *Res:* Role of respiratory chain in energy conservation; function and structure of iron containing proteins by electron spin resonance spectroscopy; study of bacterial mutants in energy coupling. *Mailing Add:* Dept of Biochem Boyd Grad Studies Res Univ of Ga Athens GA 30602

DE VAUCOULEURS, GERARD HENRI, b Paris, France, Apr 25, 18; m. ASTRONOMY. *Educ:* Univ Paris, BSc, 36, Lic es sci, 39, D Univ, 49; Australian Nat Univ, DSc, 57. *Prof Exp:* Res fel, Inst Astrophys, Nat Ctr Sci Res, France, 45-50 & Australian Nat Univ, 51-54; observer, Yale-Columbia Southern Sta, Australia, 54-57; astronr, Lowell Observ, Ariz, 57-58; res assoc, Harvard Col Observ, 58-60; assoc prof, 60-65, prof, 65-81, ASHBEL SMITH PROF ASTRON, UNIV TEX, AUSTIN, 81- *Honors & Awards:* Herschel Medal, Royal Astron Soc, 80. *Mem:* Am Astron Soc; Royal Astron Soc; Soc Astron France; French Phys Soc; Int Astron Union. *Res:* Extragalactic research. *Mailing Add:* Dept of Astron RLM Hall 16-316 Univ of Tex Austin TX 78712

DEVAULT, DON CHARLES, b Battle Creek, Mich, Dec 10, 15; m 48; c 2. BIOPHYSICS, PHYSICAL CHEMISTRY. *Educ:* Calif Inst Technol, BS, 37; Univ Calif, Berkeley, PhD(chem), 40. *Prof Exp:* Jr res assoc chem, Stanford Univ, 40-42, assoc investr, Off Sci Res & Develop Cyclotron Proj, Dept Physics, 42; instr chem, Inst Nuclear Studies, Univ Chicago, 46-48; assoc prof chem & physics, Col of the Pac, 49-58; consult, Biophys Electronics, Inc & Bionic Instruments, Inc, 59-63; fel biophys, Johnson Res Found, Med Sch, Univ Pa, 63-64, assoc, 64-67, asst prof, 67-77; VIS ASSOC PROF BIOPHYS, UNIV ILL, URBANA-CHAMPAIGN, 77- *Concurrent Pos:* NSF grants, 67-69 & 71-83. *Mem:* Biophys Soc; Am Soc Biol Chemists; Am Soc Photobiol. *Res:* Electron transport phenomena in biology; energy transduction from electron transport as in respiration and photosynthesis. *Mailing Add:* Dept Physiol & Biophys Univ Ill 524 Burrill Hall 407 S Goodwin Ave Urbana IL 61801

DEVAULT, GUILLAUME PIERRE, physics, see previous edition

DEVAY, JAMES EDSON, b Minneapolis, Minn, Nov 23, 21; m 47; c 6. PLANT PATHOLOGY. *Educ:* Univ Minn, BS, 49, PhD(plant path), 53. *Prof Exp:* Asst plant path, Univ Minn, 49-52, from instr to assoc prof, 53-57; from asst prof to assoc dean, Div Biol Sci, 76-79, PROF PLANT PATH, UNIV CALIF, DAVIS, 65-, CHMN DEPT, 80- *Mem:* Fel AAAS; fel Am Phytopath Soc; Mycol Soc; Scand Soc Plant Physiol. *Res:* Physiology and biochemistry of host-parasite relationships; diseases of cotton. *Mailing Add:* Dept of Plant Path Univ of Calif Davis CA 95616

DE VEBER, LEVERETT L, b Toronto, Ont, Jan 27, 29; m 54; c 6. HEMATOLOGY, IMMUNOLOGY. *Educ:* Univ Toronto, MD, 53; FRCP(C), 61. *Prof Exp:* Jr intern, St Michael's Hosp, Toronto, 53-54; sr intern med, Shaughnessey Hosp, Univ BC, 54-55; sr house officer pediat, Univ Manchester, 57-58; registr, Univ Liverpool, 58; jr asst resident, NY Univ, 59-60; asst resident pediat & path, Univ Toronto, 60-61; lectr, 62-65, from asst prof to assoc prof pediat & path chem, 65-74, PROF PEDIAT, UNIV WESTERN ONT, 74-, DIR Rh RES LAB, 64- *Concurrent Pos:* Mead-Johnson fel immunohemat, Univ Man, 61-62; Can Life Ins Co fel, 62-64; dir immunohemat div, Rh Serv & Blood Bank, Victoria Hosp, London, 62-74; Western Can Rh Prev Prog investr, 64-; Nat Health & Welfare res investr, 64-68, chief investr, 68- *Mem:* Can Soc Immunol (treas, 68-); Can Fedn Biol Sci. *Res:* Prevention of Rh sensitization with Rh immune globulin; detection of early Rh sensitization with serological and lymphocyte culture techniques; detection of Rh antigen on amniotic cells with fluorescent antibody technique; cellular immunity in children with acute lymphoblastic leukemia; families of children with cancer, specifically death in children. *Mailing Add:* Dept of Pediat Univ of Western Ont London ON N6A 3K7 Can

DEVENEY, JAMES KEVIN, b Boston, Mass, Feb 28, 45; m 70. PURE MATHEMATICS. *Educ:* Boston Col, BS, 70; Fla State Univ, PhD(math), 74. *Prof Exp:* Vis prof math, Kans State Univ, 74; asst prof, 74-80, ASSOC PROF MATH, VA COMMONWEALTH UNIV, 81- *Concurrent Pos:* Vis prof math, La State Univ, 80. *Mem:* Am Math Soc; Math Asn Am. *Res:* Structure of field extensions and related p-adic fields, with an emphasis on Galois theory. *Mailing Add:* Dept of Math Va Commonwealth Univ Richmond VA 23284

DEVENS, W(ILLIAM) GEORGE, b Ft Eustis, Va, Mar 2, 26; m 48; c 8. ENGINEERING & EDUCATION. *Educ:* US Mil Acad, BS, 46; Univ Ill, Urbana-Champaign, MS, 53. *Prof Exp:* Dep commandant cadets, Norwich Univ, 66-67; asst prof eng & assoc dir, 67-69, PROF ENG & DIR DIV ENG FUNDAMENTALS, VA POLYTECH INST & STATE UNIV, 69- *Mem:* Soc Am Mil Engrs; Am soc Eng Educ; Nat Soc Prof Engrs. *Res:* Educational technology. *Mailing Add:* Div of Eng Fundamentals Va Polytech Inst & State Univ Blacksburg VA 24061

DEVENUTO, FRANK, b Giovinazzo, Italy, July 28, 28; nat US; m 57; c 4. ORGANIC CHEMISTRY, BIOLOGICAL CHEMISTRY. *Educ:* Univ Rome, PhD(org chem, biol chem), 51. *Prof Exp:* Asst org res, Univ Rome, 48-51; sr chemist antibiotic res, Leo-Penicillin Co, 51-52; consult, chemist abrasive res, Ace Abrasive Labs, NY, 52-53; chief sect, Steroid Hormones Res, US Army Med Res Lab, 53-74; SUPV RES CHEMIST, LETTERMAN ARMY INST RES, 74- *Mem:* AAAS; Soc Exp Biol & Med; NY Acad Sci; Am Soc Biol Chemists. *Res:* Metabolism and mechanism of action of steroid hormones; carbohydrate metabolism; blood research; hemoglobin and blood substitutes. *Mailing Add:* Blood Res Div Letterman Army Inst of Res San Francisco CA 94129

DEVENY, C(HARLES) A(LBERT), JR, b Corsicana, Tex, Mar 2, 24; m 64; c 1. MECHANICAL ENGINEERING. *Educ:* Univ Tex, BS, 48. *Prof Exp:* Sr staff engr, 48-65, operating supvr, 65-70, mech supvr, Maintenance & Construct Div, 70-73, PROJ ENGR, EXXON CO, USA, 73- *Mem:* Am Soc Mech Engrs. *Res:* Engineering and design of oil refinery equipment and processes. *Mailing Add:* 2108 N Fisher Courts Pasadena TX 77502

DEVER, DAVID FRANCIS, b Quebec, Que, Oct 9, 31; m 57; c 4. PHYSICAL CHEMISTRY. *Educ:* Spring Hill Col, BS, 53; Fla State Univ, MS, 55; Ohio State Univ, PhD(phys chem), 59. *Prof Exp:* Off Naval Res fel thermodyn, Ohio State Univ, 60-61; univ fel molecular spectros, 62-63; asst prof chem, Univ Miami, 61-62; res photochemist, US Bur Mines, 63-64; proj leader air pollution res, 64-66; chmn dept chem, Col Petrol & Minerals, Dharhan, Saudi Arabia, 66-69; chmn div natural sci & math, 69-72, PROF CHEM, MACON JR COL, 72- *Honors & Awards:* M D Marshall Award, 53; Nat Award, Mfg Chemists Asn, 79. *Mem:* AAAS; Am Chem Soc. *Res:* Thermodynamics; photochemistry; kinetics; IR laser chemistry. *Mailing Add:* Dept Chem Macon Jr Col Macon GA 31206

DEVER, DONALD ANDREW, b Sudbury, Ont, Sept 18, 26; m 47; c 2. PLANT SCIENCE. *Educ:* Ont Agr Col, BSA, 49; Univ Wis, MSc, 50, PhD(entom plant path), 53. *Prof Exp:* Tech asst, Dom Parasite Lab, Can Sci Serv, Ont, 45-48, proj leader, 49; asst, Univ Wis, 49-53, asst prof, 53-56; dist res entomologist, Res & Develop, Calif Spray-Chem Corp, 56-62; tech dir, Niagara Brand Chem Div, FMC Mach & Chem Ltd, 62-68, mgr int develop, Niagara Chem Div, FMC Corp, NY, 68-69; SECY-GEN, CAN GRAINS COUN, 69- *Concurrent Pos:* Dir, Man Res Coun; Western Transportation Adv Coun, Vancouver; Dir, Biomass Energy Inst, Winnipeg. *Mem:* Entom Soc Am; Can Entom Soc; Can Agr Chem Asn (pres, 67-68). *Res:* Administration; maximize export and domestic sales of Canadian grain through market analysis and development. *Mailing Add:* Can Grains Coun 360-760 Main St Winnipeg Can

DEVER, G E ALAN, b Kingston, Ont, June 9, 41; m 63; c 2. PUBLIC HEALTH ADMINISTRATION. *Educ:* State Univ NY Buffalo, BA, 67, MA, 68; Univ Mich, PhD(geog), 70. *Prof Exp:* Asst prof, Univ Md, Baltimore, 70-71; asst prof, Ga State Univ, 71-74, res grants, 72-77; chief epidemiologist & dir, Health Serv Res & Statist Sect, 72-77, dir, Health Serv Anal, Div Phys Health, Ga Dept Human Resources, 77-81; ASSOC PROF EPIDEMIOL, MED SCH, MERCER UNIV, 81- *Concurrent Pos:* Consult, Appl Statist Training Inst, Nat Ctr Health Statist, US Dept Health, Educ & Welfare, 74-; pres & dir, Health Serv Anal, Inc, 81- *Mem:* Am Pub Health Asn; Can Pub Health Asn; Pop Ref Bur. *Res:* Health program planning and evaluation; epidemiology; nutrition. *Mailing Add:* 1623 Hidden Hills Pkwy Stone Mountain GA 30088

DEVER, JOHN E, JR, b Camden, NJ, Sept 24, 32; m 52; c 2. PLANT PHYSIOLOGY, BIOCHEMISTRY. *Educ:* Rutgers Univ, BA, 60; Ore State Univ, MS, 62; Mich State Univ, PhD(plant physiol, biochem), 67. *Prof Exp:* Lectr biol, Flint Col, Mich, 67; asst prof bot, 67-74, ASSOC PROF BIOL, FT LEWIS COL, 74- *Mem:* Am Soc Plant Physiol; Am Inst Biol Sci; Scand Soc Plant Physiol. *Res:* Cell wall structure and metabolism; exocellular enzymes in root cell walls. *Mailing Add:* Dept of Biol Ft Lewis Col Durango CO 81301

DEVERALL, LAMAR IVAN, b Taylorsville, Utah, Nov 9, 24; m 63. APPLIED MATHEMATICS, APPLIED MECHANICS. *Educ:* Univ Utah, BS, 46, MS, 48, PhD(math), 54. *Prof Exp:* Instr math, Univ Utah, 48-53; mathematician, Dugway Proving Ground, 53-56, Phillips Petrol Co, 56-57 & Radiation Lab, Univ Calif, 57-62; MATHEMATICIAN, UNITED TECHNOL CTR, UNITED AIRCRAFT CORP, 62- *Res:* Theory of elasticity; finite element analysis methods; numerical methods for engineering analysis; random vibration analysis. *Mailing Add:* United Technol Ctr United Aircraft Corp PO Box 358 Sunnyvale CA 94086

DEVEREUX, OWEN FRANCIS, b Lexington, Mass, Aug 23, 37; m 57, 69. CORROSION, METALLURGY. *Educ:* Mass Inst Technol, SB, 59, SM, 60, PhD(metall), 62. *Prof Exp:* Res chemist, Chevron Res Corp, 62-64, Corning Glass Works, 64-66 & Chevron Res Corp 66-68; assoc prof metall, 68-76, PROF METALL, INST MAT SCI, UNIV CONN, 68- *Mem:* Metall Soc; Electrochem Soc; Corrosion Soc. *Res:* Thermodynamics; transport phenomena; oxidation corrosion. *Mailing Add:* Dept of Metall Univ of Conn Storrs CT 06268

DEVILLEZ, EDWARD JOSEPH, b Covington, Ky, Apr 12, 39; m 59; c 4. COMPARATIVE PHYSIOLOGY, COMPARATIVE BIOCHEMISTRY. *Educ:* Xavier Univ, Ohio, BS, 59; Univ Miami, MS, 61; Univ Ill, Urbana, PhD(physiol), 64. *Prof Exp:* Res assoc comp digestive enzym & NSF fel, Friday Harbor Labs, Univ Wash, 64-65; from asst prof to assoc prof, 65-72, PROF ZOOL, MIAMI UNIV, 72- *Mem:* Am Soc Zoologists; Am Physiol Soc. *Res:* histochemical localization of digestive enzymes in annelids, arthropods and fish. *Mailing Add:* Dept of Zool Miami Univ Oxford OH 45056

DEVIN, CHARLES, JR, b New York, NY, Mar 29, 24. ACOUSTICS, HYDRODYNAMICS. *Educ:* George Washington Univ, BS, 53, MS, 57; Cath Univ Am, PhD(appl physics), 70. *Prof Exp:* Meteorol aide, US Weather Bur, 46-47; weather observr, 47-52; jr physicist, Phys Res Div, 52-54; asst proj mgr, Ship Acoustics Dept, Naval Ship Res & Develop Ctr, 54-57, proj mgr, 57-60, sr proj mgr, 60-61, supvry physicist, Hydrodynamic Noise Sect, 61-72, mem staff, Ship Acoust Dept, 72-80; WITH HYDROTONICS INC, 80- *Concurrent Pos:* Lectr eve session, George Washington Univ, 63-64. *Honors & Awards:* Superior Accomplishment Award, US Navy, 64 & 65. *Mem:* AAAS; Acoust Soc Am; Am Asn Physics Teachers; Am Meteorol Soc. *Res:* Sonar, signal processing, sound propagation, bubble noise, turbulent boundary layer noise, noise radiated by marine propellers. *Mailing Add:* Hydrotonics Inc 7929 Jones Br Rd Ste 500 McLean VA 22102

DEVINATZ, ALLEN, b Chicago, Ill, July 22, 22; m 52, 56; c 2. MATHEMATICS. *Educ:* Ill Inst Technol, BS, 44; Harvard Univ, AM, 47, PhD(math), 50. *Prof Exp:* Instr math, Ill Inst Technol, 50-52; NSF fel, Inst Advan Study, 52-53, mem, 53-54; asst prof math, Univ Conn, 54-55; from asst prof to assoc prof, Wash Univ, 55-60; NSF sr fel, 60-61; prof, Wash, Univ, 61-67; PROF MATH, NORTHWESTERN UNIV, EVANSTON, 67- *Concurrent Pos:* Vis mem, Weizmann Inst, 80. *Mem:* Am Math Soc. *Res:* Analysis. *Mailing Add:* Dept of Math Northwestern Univ Evanston IL 60201

DEVINCENZI, DONALD LOUIS, exobiology, biochemistry, see previous edition

DEVINE, CHARLES JOSEPH, JR, b Norfolk, Va, Feb 23, 23; c 5. SURGERY. *Educ:* Washington & Lee Univ, BA, 43; George Washington Univ Sch Med, MD, 47. *Prof Exp:* Intern, Brady Inst, Johns Hopkins Hosp, 47-48; urol fel, Cleveland Clinic, 48-50; urol residency, US Navy Hosp, Pa, 51-52; chmn dept surg, DePaul Hosp, 65-66; pres med staff, Med Ctr Hosp, Inc, 69-70; PROF & CHMN UROL, EASTERN VA MED SCH, 70-; CHIEF UROL, CHILDREN'S HOSP OF THE KING'S DAUGHTERS, 77- *Concurrent Pos:* Chief urol, Med Ctr Hosp, Inc, 79-80; lectr urol, Navy Med Ctr, 70-, Aukland, Wellington, New Zealand; Melborne & Adelaide, Australia, 82; asst ed, J Urol, 78-; found lectr & sect guest, Royal Australasian Col Surgeons, 82; consult, Proj Hope, Univ Alexandria, Egypt, 77. *Mem:* AAAS; AMA; Am Urol Asn; Am Asn Genitourinary Surgeons; Soc Int D'Urologie. *Res:* Reconstructive surgery of the genitourinary tract. *Mailing Add:* 100 Hague Med Ctr 400 W Brambleton Ave Norfolk VA 23510

DEVINE, JOHN EDWARD, b Du Bois, Pa, Feb 14, 23; m 53; c 5. MECHANICAL ENGINEERING. *Educ:* Carnegie Inst Technol, BS, 48. *Prof Exp:* Res engr, Alcoa Labs, 48-60, construct proj engr, Alcoa Bldg, 60-65, head bldg serv dept, Alcoa Tech Ctr, 65-67, eng adv, 67-69, MGR FACIL ENG DEPT, ALCOA LABS, ALUMINUM CO AM, 70- *Mem:* Am Soc Mech Engrs; Sigma Xi; Am Soc Heating Refrig & Air Conditioning Engrs. *Res:* Quenching of metals; design of laboratory buildings, systems and equipment. *Mailing Add:* Alcoa Tech Ctr Aluminum Co of Am Alcoa Center PA 15069

DEVINE, MARJORIE M, b East Machias, Maine, May 19, 34. NUTRITION. *Educ:* Univ Maine, BS, 56, MS, 62; Cornell Univ, PhD(nutrit), 67. *Prof Exp:* Teacher high sch, Conn, 56-58 & high sch, Maine, 58-62; instr food sci, Univ Maine, 62-64; asst prof, 67-73, assoc prof human nutrit & food, 73-78, PROF NUTRIT SCI, CORNELL UNIV, 78-, COORDR UNDERGRAD PROG, 74-, ASSOC DIR ACAD AFFAIRS, DIV NUTRIT SCI, 76- *Res:* Ascorbic acid metabolism; nutrition education. *Mailing Add:* Div of Nutrit Sci Cornell Univ Ithaca NY 14853

DEVINE, ROBERT T, electrodynamics, see previous edition

DEVINE, THOMAS EDWARD, b NY. PLANT GENETICS, PLANT BREEDING. *Educ:* Fordham Univ, BS; Pa State Univ, MS; Iowa State Univ, PhD(plant breeding), 67. *Prof Exp:* Asst prof plant breeding, Cornell Univ, 67-69; RES GENETICIST, SCI & EDUC ADMIN-AGR RES, USDA, 69- *Honors & Awards:* Award, Am Soc Agron, 81. *Mem:* Coun Am Genetics Asn; Crop Sci Soc Am; Am Soc Agron; Am Genetic Asn. *Res:* Development of air pollution resistant plant population and anthracnose resistant alfalfa; genetics and breeding of nitrogen fixation by soybeans; interaction of soybean cultivars with nitrogen fixing Rhizobium; extension of the range of adaptation of soybeans to marginal edaphic environments; evolution and symbiosis. *Mailing Add:* Cell Cult & Nitrogen Fixation Lab Agr Res Ctr-West US Dept of Agr Beltsville MD 20705

DEVINE, THOMAS MAURICE, JR, b Boston, Mass, Aug 4, 48; m 70; c 2. METALLURGY, CORROSION. *Educ:* Mass Inst Technol, BS, 71, MS, 71, PhD(metall), 74. *Prof Exp:* METALLURGIST, CORP RES & DEVELOP CTR, GEN ELEC CO, 74- *Honors & Awards:* Joseph Vilella Award, Am Soc Testing & Mat, 79; Marcus Grossman Award, Am Soc Metals, 81. *Mem:* Nat Asn Corrosion Engrs; Electrochem Soc Am; Am Soc Metals; Am Inst Mining, Metall & Petrol Engrs. *Res:* Stress corrosion cracking; phase transformations; fracture; influence of metallurgical microstructure on the corrosion and stress corrosion cracking behavior of metallic alloys; structure of metal-electrolyte interface. *Mailing Add:* Corp Res & Develop Ctr Gen Elec Co PO Box 8 Schenectady NY 12301

DEVINEY, MARVIN LEE, JR, b Kingsville, Tex, Dec 5, 29; m 58, 75; c 3. SURFACE CHEMISTRY, PHYSICAL CHEMISTRY. *Educ:* Southwest Tex State Col, BS, 49; Univ Tex, MA, 52, PhD(phys chem), 56. *Prof Exp:* Develop chemist, Plant Lab, Celanese Corp Am, Tex, 56-58; res chemist, Indust Chem Res Lab, Shell Chem Co, 58-66; sr scientist, United Carbon Co Div, 66-68, mgr phys & anal res, Ashland Chem Co Div, 68-70, mgr phys chem res sect, 70-78, RES ASSOC & SUPVR APPL SURFACE CHEM, RES & DEVELOP DIV, ASHLAND CHEM CO DIV, ASHLAND OIL, INC, 78- *Concurrent Pos:* Mem sci adv comt, Am Petrol Inst Res Proj, 60; mem chem educ adv comts, Columbus Tech Inst, Ohio, 74- & Cent Ohio Tech Col, 75- *Honors & Awards:* Best Paper Awards, Rubber Div, Am Chem Soc, 67 & 70. *Mem:* Am Chem Soc; fel Am Inst Chem; Sigma Xi; NAm Catalysis Soc. *Res:* Surface chemistry; heterogeneous catalysis; electron spectroscopy for chemical analysis; composite interfacial research; rubber and carbon technology; industrial petrochemicals; physical separation methods; homogeneous catalysis; electrochemistry; chromatography; physico-chemical measurements; radiochemical methods; quality improvement; vapor liquid equilibria; electron microscopy; textile chemicals; pressure-volume-temperature relations. *Mailing Add:* R & D Div Ashland Chem Co Div Ashland Oil Inc PO Box 2219 Columbus OH 43216

DEVINS, DELBERT WAYNE, b Warwick, Okla, Sept 6, 34; m 66. NUCLEAR PHYSICS. *Educ:* Fresno State Col, BS, 58; Univ Southern Calif, MS, 62, PhD(physics), 64. *Prof Exp:* Vis asst prof physics, Univ Southern Calif, 64-65; from asst prof to assoc prof, 65-76, PROF PHYSICS, IND UNIV, BLOOMINGTON, 76- *Concurrent Pos:* Sr sci officer, Rutherford High Energy Lab, Eng, 65-66; vis prof physics, Macquarie Univ, Australia, 78- *Mem:* AAAS; Am Phys Soc; Am Asn Physics Teachers. *Res:* Intermediate energy reactions; knock-out, transfer reactions; neutron polarization; sequential decay; reaction mechanisms. *Mailing Add:* Dept of Physics Ind Univ Bloomington IN 47401

DEVINY, EDWARD JOHN, b Owatonna, Minn, July 14, 39; m 61; c 3. INDUSTRIAL ORGANIC CHEMISTRY, RADIATION CHEMISTRY. *Educ:* Hamline Univ, BS, 61; Univ Calif, Berkeley, PhD(org chem), 65. *Prof Exp:* Res specialist, 65-73, PROD DEVELOP MGR, MINN MINING & MFG CO, 73- *Mem:* Am Chem Soc. *Res:* Synthetic and mechanistic organic chemistry; organic photochemistry; non-conventional imaging processes; radiation curing; development and application of new organic polymers. *Mailing Add:* 2814 Merrill St St Paul MN 55113

DE VITA, JOSEPH MICHAEL, ecology, see previous edition

DEVITA, VINCENT T, JR, b Bronx, NY, Mar 7, 35; m 57; c 1. INTERNAL MEDICINE, PHARMACOLOGY. *Educ:* Col William & Mary, BS, 57; George Washington Univ, MD, 61; Am Bd Internal Med, dipl, 68 & 74, cert hemat, 72, cert oncol, 73 & 74. *Prof Exp:* Intern med, Med Ctr, Univ Mich, 61-62; resident, Gen Hosp, Med Serv, George Washington Univ, 62-63; clin assoc, Lab Chem Pharmacol, Nat Cancer Inst, 63-65; resident med, Yale New Haven Med Ctr, 65-66; sr investr, Med Br, 66-68, chief solid tumor serv, 68-71, chief med br, 71-74, dir, Div Cancer Treatment, 74-80, CLIN DIR, NAT CANCER INST, 75-, DIR, NAT CANCER PROG, 80- *Concurrent Pos:* Prof, Sch Med, George Washington Univ, 75-; assoc ed, Jour Nat Cancer Inst, 68-74; sci ed, Cancer Chemother Reports, 70-74; adv ed, J Radiation Oncol, Biol & Physics, 75-; assoc ed, Cancer Clin Trials, 77-; mem bd med/sci consult, Cancer Nursing, 77-; mem bd sci coun, Cancer Chemother & Pharmacol, 77-; assoc ed, Am J Med, 78-81; adv panel mem, WHO, 76-; mem panel consults clin oncol, Int Union Against Cancer, 79-82; mem, Awards Assembly, Gen Motors Cancer Res Found, 81- *Honors & Awards:* Albert & Mary Lasker Med Res Award, 72; Esther Langer Award, 76; Jeffrey Gottlieb Award, 76; Karnofsky Prize, 79; Griffuel Prize, Asn Develop Res Cancer, Paris, 80. *Mem:* Am Asn Cancer Res; fel Am Col Physicians; Am Soc Clin Invest; Soc Surg Oncol. *Res:* Pharmacology of anti tumor agents in relation to tumor cell kinetics; chemotherapy of the lymphomas. *Mailing Add:* Div Cancer Treat Bldg 31 Nat Cancer Inst Bethesda MD 20205

DEVITO, CARL LOUIS, b New York, NY, Oct 21, 37; m 65; c 1. MATHEMATICAL ANALYSIS. *Educ:* City Col New York, BS, 59; Northwestern Univ, PhD(math), 67. *Prof Exp:* Instr math, DePaul Univ, 65-67; asst prof, 67-71, ASSOC PROF MATH, UNIV ARIZ, 71- *Concurrent Pos:* Invited speaker, Liege Colloquium, Belg, 70. *Mem:* Am Math Soc. *Res:* Theory of locally convex, topological vector spaces, particularly the completions of these spaces for various topologies and the relations among these completions, and study of the weakly compact subsets of these spaces; applications of mathematics to certain aspects of space science. *Mailing Add:* Dept of Math Univ of Ariz Tucson AZ 85721

DEVITO, JUNE LOGAN, b Alta, Jan 12, 28; m 53; c 4. NEUROANATOMY, NEUROPHYSIOLOGY. *Educ:* Univ BC, BA, 47, MA, 49; Univ Wash, PhD(physiol), 54. *Prof Exp:* Asst embryol & physiol, Univ BC, 47-49; res assoc physiol & biophys, 54-55, actg instr, 55-58, res instr, 58-60, instr, 60-63, res instr neurosurg, 63-65, res staff mem, Regional Primate Res Ctr, 71-78, res asst prof, 65-78, RES ASSOC PROF NEUROL SURG, SCH MED, UNIV WASH, 78- *Concurrent Pos:* USPHS fel, 61-62. *Mem:* AAAS; Am Asn Anat; Soc Neurosci. *Res:* Central pathways subserving weight discrimination; effects of sensory stimulation on activity; supplementary motor area projections; corticothalamic connections of sensory cortices; septo-hippocampal pathways; autonomic nervous system; basal ganglia connections. *Mailing Add:* Regional Primate Res Ctr SJ 50 Univ of Wash Seattle WA 98105

DE VLAMING, VICTOR LYNN, comparative endocrinology, see previous edition

DEVLETIAN, JACK H, b Boston, Mass, May 23, 41; m 69; c 3. WELDING RESEARCH. *Educ:* Univ Mass, BS, 63; Univ Wis, MS, 66, PhD(metall eng), 72. *Prof Exp:* Equip develop engr, Union Carbide Corp, Linde Div, 63-64; mat & standards engr, Raytheon Missile Systems Div, 66-67; welding engr, Rocketdyne Div Rockwell Int, 67-68; assoc prof mat sci, Youngstown State Univ, 72-79; ASSOC PROF MAT SCI, ORE GRAD CTR, 79- *Honors & Awards:* Charles H Jennings Mem Award, Am Welding Soc, 76. *Mem:* Am Welding Soc; Am Foundrymen's Soc. *Res:* Physical metallurgy of weldments and solidification mechanics. *Mailing Add:* Ore Grad Ctr 19600 NW Walker Rd Beaverton OR 97006

DEVLIN, JOHN F, b Rockville Centre, NY, Nov 24, 44. METAL PHYSICS. *Educ:* Harpur Col, State Univ NY, Binghamton, BA, 66; Mich State Univ, MS, 68, PhD(physics), 70. *Prof Exp:* Res assoc, Univ Groningen, Netherlands, 70-72; staff physicist, Battelle Mem Inst, 72-76; asst prof, 76-82, ASSOC PROF PHYSICS, UNIV MICH, DEARBORN, 82- *Mem:* Am Phys Soc; Am Asn Physics Teachers; AAAS; Sigma Xi. *Res:* Theoretical solid state physics; structural properties of metals and alloys. *Mailing Add:* Dept Natural Sci Univ Mich 4901 Evergreen Rd Dearborn MI 48128

DEVLIN, JOSEPH PAUL, b Hale, Colo, Jan 11, 35; m 57; c 3. PHYSICAL CHEMISTRY. *Educ:* Regis Col, Colo, BS, 56; Kans State Univ, PhD(phys chem), 60. *Prof Exp:* Res assoc spectros, Univ Minn, 60-61; from asst prof to assoc prof, 61-70, chmn dept, 76-81, PROF PHYS CHEM, OKLA STATE UNIV, 70- *Concurrent Pos:* AEC grant, 66-71; NSF grant, 62-82. *Mem:* Am Chem Soc. *Res:* Vibrational spectra and structures of disordered solids; matrix idolated high temperature species, solid state charge transfer complexes and proton transfer in protic solids. *Mailing Add:* Dept of Chem Okla State Univ Stillwater OK 74074

DEVLIN, RICHARD GERALD, JR, b Philadelphia, Pa, Aug 4, 42; m 65; c 2. IMMUNOLOGY, CLINICAL PHARMACOLOGY. *Educ:* LaSalle Col, BA, 64; Villanova Univ, MS, 66; Univ Md, PhD(immunol), 69. *Prof Exp:* Asst biol, Villanova Univ, 64-66; asst zool, Univ Md, 66-69; NIH fel biol, Univ Pa, 69-71; sr scientist, 71-74, sr investr biochem, Mead Johnson & Co, 74-75; mem staff, Merck Inst Therapeut Res, 75-78; asst dir clin pharmacol, 78-80, ASSOC DIR CLIN PHARMACOL, SQUIBB INST MED RES, 81-. *Concurrent Pos:* Vis asst prof, Dept Pharmacol, Rutgers Col Pharm, 80-81. *Mem:* Am Soc Immunologists; AAAS; Can Soc Immunol; Am Col Clin Pharm; Am Asn Clin Pharm & Ther. *Res:* Developmental, transplantation and radiation biology; cell physiology; tumor immunology; immunopharmacology; cellular immunology. *Mailing Add:* D2217 Squibb Inst Princeton NJ 08540

DEVLIN, ROBERT B, b Denver, Colo, Mar 31, 47; m 75; c 1. BIOLOGY, GENETICS. *Educ:* Univ Tex, El Paso, BS, 69; Univ Va, PhD(biol), 76. *Prof Exp:* ASST PROF BIOL, EMORY UNIV, 79- *Mem:* Soc Develop Biol; Am Soc Cell Biologists; AAAS. *Res:* Factors responsible for control of gene expression during development and differentiation; muscle differentiation and drosophila development as model systems. *Mailing Add:* Dept Biol Emory Univ Atlanta GA 30322

DEVLIN, ROBERT MARTIN, b US citizen; Oct 13, 31; m; c 3. PLANT PHYSIOLOGY. *Educ:* State Univ NY Albany, BS, 59; Dartmouth Col, MA, 61; Univ Md, PhD(biol), 63. *Prof Exp:* Asst prof plant physiol, NDak State Univ, 63-65; assoc prof, 65-74, PROF PLANT PHYSIOL, AGR EXP STA, LAB EXP BIOL, UNIV MASS, 74- *Mem:* Am Soc Plant Physiologists; Am Soc Hort Sci; Int Platform Asn; Plant Growth Regulator Working Group (pres, 74-75); Weed Sci Soc Am. *Res:* Plant hormone effects, herbicide metabolism and nature of seed dormancy. *Mailing Add:* Dept Plant Physiol Lab Exp Biol Univ of Mass Agr Exp Sta East Wareham MA 02538

DEVLIN, THOMAS MCKEOWN, b Philadelphia, Pa, June 29, 29; m 53; c 2. BIOCHEMISTRY. *Educ:* Univ Pa, BA, 53; Johns Hopkins Univ, PhD(physiol chem), 57. *Prof Exp:* Asst org chem, Sharples Corp, Pa, 47-49; asst biophys, Johnson Found, Univ Pa, 49-53; res assoc enzyme chem, Merck Inst, 57-61, sect head, Biol Cancer Res, 61-66, dir enzymol, 66-67; PROF & CHMN DEPT BIOL CHEM, HAHNEMANN MED COL & HOSP, 67- *Concurrent Pos:* Vis res scientist, Brussels, 64-65; actg dean, Col Allied Health Prof, Hahnemann Med Col & Hosp, 72-74 & 80-81. *Mem:* Soc Exp Biol & Med; Am Soc Biol Chemists; Am Asn Cancer Res; Biochem Soc; Am Soc Cell Biol. *Res:* Oxidative phosphorylation and electron transport; mitochondrial physiology and biogenesis, ion transport mechanisms; biochemistry of membranes; biochemical control mechanisms; intermediary metabolism of malignant tissues. *Mailing Add:* Dept of Biol Chem Hahnemann Med Col Philadelphia PA 19102

DEVOE, ARTHUR GERARD, b Seattle, Wash, Mar 24, 09; m 39; c 3. OPHTHALMOLOGY. *Educ:* Yale Univ, AB, 31; Cornell Univ, MD, 35; Columbia Univ, DMSc, 40. *Prof Exp:* Assoc ophthal, Col Physicians & Surgeons, Columbia Univ, 40-50; prof, Post-Grad Med Sch, NY Univ-Bellevue Med Ctr & dir eye serv, Bellevue & Univ Hosps, 50-59; prof opthal, 59-70, chmn dept, 59-74; Edward S Harkness prof, 70-74; EMER PROF, COL PHYSICIANS & SURGEONS, COLUMBIA UNIV, 74- *Concurrent Pos:* Consult, Presby Hosp, 74- *Mem:* AMA; Am Ophthal Soc; Am Acad Ophthal & Otolaryngol; Am Col Surgeons; Asn Res Vision & Ophthal. *Res:* Diseases of the eye. *Mailing Add:* Dept of Ophthal Columbia Univ New York NY 10032

DEVOE, HOWARD JOSSELYN, b White Plains, NY, Dec 10, 32; div; c 3. PHYSICAL CHEMISTRY. *Educ:* Oberlin Col, AB, 55; Harvard Univ, PhD(chem), 60. *Prof Exp:* Univ fel, Univ Calif, Berkeley, 60-61; res chemist, Phys Chem Sect, NIMH, 61-68; ASSOC PROF CHEM, UNIV MD, COLLEGE PARK, 68- *Mem:* AAAS; Am Chem Soc. *Res:* Molecular interactions in nucleic acids; dye aggregation; hydrophobic interactions; theory of optical properties of molecular aggregates and biopolymers; solubility and partitioning of nonpolar solutes. *Mailing Add:* Dept of Chem Univ of Md College Park MD 20742

DEVOE, IRVING WOODROW, b Brewer, Maine, Oct 4, 36; m 60; c 4. MEDICAL MICROBIOLOGY, ELECTRON MICROSCOPY. *Educ:* Aurora Col, BS, 64; Univ Ore, PhD(microbiol), 68. *Prof Exp:* Fel, Macdonald Col, McGill Univ, 68-69; asst prof microbiol, Aurora Col, 69-70; from asst prof to assoc prof microbiol, MacDonald Col, McGill Univ, 70-78; ASSOC PROF & CHMN DEPT MICROBIOL & IMMUNOL, FAC MED, McGILL UNIV, 78- *Concurrent Pos:* Res assoc, Argonne Nat Lab, 69-70; consult shoreline surv, Fisheries Res Bd Can, 71; med scientist, Dept Med & Microbiol, Royal Victoria Hosp, Montreal. *Mem:* AAAS; Am Soc Microbiol; Can Soc Microbiol. *Res:* Bacterial physiology; role of inorganic ions in gram-negative bacterial cell walls; carrier mediated transport; phagocytosis of bacterial pathogens; pathogenesis of meningococcus; role of iron in microbiol injections. *Mailing Add:* Dept of Microbiol & Immunol Fac of Med McGill Univ 3775 University St Montreal Can

DEVOE, JAMES ROLLO, b Sterling, Ill, Sept 27, 28; m 56; c 3. RADIOCHEMISTRY. *Educ:* Univ Ill, BS, 50; Univ Minn, MS, 52; Univ Mich, PhD(chem), 59. *Prof Exp:* Consult, Subcomt Radiochem, Nat Acad Sci-Nat Res Coun, 60-61; phys chemist, Anal & Inorg Chem Div, 61-63, chief radiochem sect, Anal Chem Div, 63-66, chief activation anal sect & radiochem anal sect, 66-69, chief tech support group & radiochem anal sect, 69-73, CHIEF SPEC ANAL INSTRUMENTATION SECT, NAT BUR STANDARDS, 73-, LEADER, INSTRUMENT DEVELOP GROUP, CTR ANAL CHEM, 80- *Concurrent Pos:* Mem subcomt low background counting, Nat Acad Sci-Nat Res Coun, 63-69; working comt lunar probe, NASA, 64-65. *Honors & Awards:* Distinguished Serv Award, Nat Bur Standards, 64. *Mem:* Am Chem Soc. *Res:* Radioisotope techniques in analysis; Mossbauer effect; activation analysis; low level radiation detection; analytical radiochemistry; laboratory automation with digital computers; spectroscopic techniques; laser spectroscopy. *Mailing Add:* 17708 Parkridge Dr Gaithersburg MD 20760

DEVOE, RALPH GODWIN, physics, see previous edition

DEVOE, ROBERT, b White Plains, NY, Oct 7, 34; m 60; c 2. PHYSIOLOGY, BIOPHYSICS. *Educ:* Oberlin Col, AB, 56; Rockefeller Inst, PhD(biophys), 61. *Prof Exp:* From instr to asst prof, 61-69, dir year I prog, 70-73 & 75-76, ASSOC PROF PHYSIOL, SCH MED, JOHNS HOPKINS UNIV, 69-, ASSOC PROF NEUROSCI, 80- *Concurrent Pos:* Alexander von Humboldt Found sr US scientist award, 73-74; guest prof, Inst Zool, Technische Hochschule, Darmstadt, 77 & 80. *Mem:* AAAS; Soc Neurosci; Asn Res Vision & Ophthal; Biophys Soc. *Res:* Electrophysiology of vision; arthropod color vision; motion detection. *Mailing Add:* Sch of Med Johns Hopkins Univ Baltimore MD 21205

DEVOL, ALLAN HOUSTON, biological oceanography, chemical oceanography, see previous edition

DE VOLPI, ALEXANDER, b New York, NY, Feb 28, 31; m 55, 78; c 4. REACTOR PHYSICS. *Educ:* Washington & Lee Univ, BA, 53; Va Polytech Inst, MS, 58, PhD(physics), 67. *Prof Exp:* PHYSICIST, ARGONNE NAT LAB, 60- *Mem:* AAAS; Am Phys Soc; Am Nuclear Soc. *Res:* Nuclear parameters of use in nuclear reactor physics design, especially fission parameters; development of a fast neutron hodoscope used in nuclear reactor safety research; environmental aspects of nuclear power; relationships between science and society. *Mailing Add:* Reactor Anal & Safety Div Argonne Nat Lab D208 Argonne IL 60439

DEVONS, SAMUEL, b Bangor, NWales, UK, Sept 30, 14; m 38; c 4. HISTORY OF PHYSICS. *Educ:* Cambridge Univ, BA, 35, MA, 39, PhD(physics), 39. *Hon Degrees:* MSc, Univ Manchester, 59. *Prof Exp:* Sci officer, Air Ministry, Ministry Supply, 39-45; fel & dir studies, Trinity Col, Cambridge, 46-49; prof physics, Imp Col, Univ London, 50-55; Langworthy prof & dir phys labs, Univ Manchester, 55-60; chmn dept, 63-67, PROF PHYSICS, COLUMBIA UNIV, 60- *Concurrent Pos:* Lectr, Cambridge Univ, 46-49; UNESCO tech aide, Mission to Arg, 57; vis prof, Columbia Univ, 59-60; Royal Soc vis prof, Andhra Univ, India, 67-68; dir, Barnard Col-Columbia Univ Hist Physics Lab, vis prof, Barnard Col, 69-; Racah vis prof, Hebrew Univ, Jerusalem, 73-74. *Honors & Awards:* Rutherford Medal & Prize, Brit Inst Physics & Phys Soc, 70. *Mem:* Fel Am Phys Soc; fel Royal Soc; Brit Inst Physics & Phys Soc (vpres, 53-55). *Res:* Radar; nuclear and elementary particle physics; history of physics. *Mailing Add:* Dept Physics Columbia Univ New York NY 10027

DEVONSHIRE, LEONARD NORTON, inorganic chemistry, analytical chemistry, see previous edition

DEVOR, ARTHUR WILLIAM, b El Paso Co, Colo, Apr 13, 11; m 38; c 2. BIOCHEMISTRY. *Educ:* McPherson Col, BS, 35; Kans State Col, MS, 37; Univ Southern Calif, PhD(biochem), 47. *Prof Exp:* Asst, Kans State Col, 36-41; instr chem, Erie Ctr, Univ Pittsburgh, 41-43; instr, Adelphi Col, 43-45; asst biochem, Univ Southern Calif, 45-46; assoc, Univ SDak, 47; prof chem & head dept, NDak State Teachers Col, Minot, 47-48; from asst prof to assoc prof biochem, SDak State Col, 48-51; from asst prof to prof physiol chem, Col Med, Ohio State Univ, 52-75, emer prof physiol chem, 75-79; prof chem, SDak State Univ, 80-81, dir, Water Resource Lab, 81. *Mem:* AAAS; Am Chem Soc. *Res:* Oxidation of monosaccharides; dehydration of bile acids; blood proteins; chemical education; sulfonated alpha-naphthol as carbohydrate test; dialysis; lyophilization; cerebrosides; sulfonated resorcinol as carbohydrate test; studies on nondialyzable materials in human urine. *Mailing Add:* PO Box 264 Brookings SD 57006

DEVOR, KENNETH ARTHUR, b Erie, Pa, Feb 15, 43. BIOCHEMISTRY. *Educ:* Ohio State Univ, BS, 65; Univ Calif, Riverside, MS, 67, PhD(biochem), 70. *Prof Exp:* Fel biochem, Johns Hopkins Univ, 70-72; Inst Genetics, Cologne, WGer, 72-73 & Max Planck Inst Biol, 73-74; ASST PROF BIOCHEM, CALIF STATE UNIV, LOS ANGELES, 74- *Mem:* Am Chem Soc; AAAS. *Res:* Structure, synthesis and metabolism of biological membranes; phospholipid metabolism. *Mailing Add:* Dept of Chem Calif State Univ 5151 State University Dr Los Angeles CA 90032

DEVORE, GEORGE WARREN, b Laramie, Wyo, Apr 29, 24; m 52; c 2. GEOLOGY. *Educ:* Univ Wyo, BA, 46; Univ Chicago, PhD(geol), 52. *Prof Exp:* From instr to asst prof geol, Univ Chicago, 50-60; assoc prof, 60-64, PROF GEOL & CHMN DEPT, FLA STATE UNIV, 64- *Concurrent Pos:* Geologist, US Geol Surv, 48-60. *Mem:* Mineral Soc Am; Am Clay Minerals Soc. *Res:* Geochemistry and petrology; the distribution of elements in minerals and materials in rocks. *Mailing Add:* Dept of Geol Fla State Univ Tallahassee FL 32306

DEVORE, THOMAS CARROLL, b Muscatine, Iowa, Mar 25, 47; m 69; c 2. HIGH TEMPERATURE CHEMISTRY, PHYSICAL CHEMISTRY. *Educ:* Univ Iowa, BS, 69; Iowa State Univ, PhD(phys chem), 75. *Prof Exp:* Asst prof chem, Univ Iowa, 75-76; res chem, Univ Fla, 76-77; ASST PROF CHEM, JAMES MADISON UNIV, 77- *Mem:* AAAS; Am Chem Soc. *Res:* Vibrational infrared and electronic spectrum of high temperature molecules (molecule stable at high temperatures); structure and bonding of high temperature molecules. *Mailing Add:* Dept of Chem James Madison Univ Harrisonburg VA 22807

DEVOTO, RALPH STEPHEN, b San Francisco, Calif, Oct 23, 34; m 59; c 3. PLASMA PHYSICS. *Educ:* Mass Inst Technol, SB, 58, SM, 60; Stanford Univ, PhD(aeronaut eng), 65. *Prof Exp:* Asst prof aeronaut eng, Stanford Univ, 66-67 & 69-72; assoc prof mech eng, Ga Inst Technol, 72-74; PHYSICIST, LAWRENCE LIVERMORE NAT LAB, 74- *Concurrent Pos:* NSF fel, Institut fur Plasmaphysik, Munich, 67-69. *Mem:* Am Physical Soc; Am Nuclear Soc. *Res:* Confinement and production of plasmas for production power by nuclear fusion. *Mailing Add:* 1338 Lexington Way Livermore CA 94550

DEVREOTES, PETER NICHOLAS, b Long Branch, NJ, April 22, 48; m 80. CELL-CELL INTERACTIONS, CHEMOTAXIS. *Educ:* Univ Wis, BS, 71; Johns Hopkins Univ, PhD(biophysics), 77. *Prof Exp:* Res fel, Univ Chicago, 77-79; ASST PROF BIOCHEM, DEPT PHYSIOL CHEM, JOHNS HOPKINS UNIV, 79- *Mem:* Sigma Xi. *Res:* Dictyostelium; discoideum as a model system for investigation of chemotaxis, cell-cell interactions and transmembranesignal transduction. *Mailing Add:* Dept Physiol Chem Johns Hopkins Univ 725 N Wolfe St Baltimore MD 21205

DE VRIES, ADRIAAN, b Harderwijk, Neth, June 21, 31; m 57; c 3. X-RAY CRYSTALLOGRAPHY, PHYSICAL CHEMISTRY. *Educ:* State Univ Utrecht, BS, 52, Drs(chem), 57, PhD(chem), 63. *Prof Exp:* Asst phys chem, State Univ Utrecht, 54-58, scientist x-ray crystallog, 58-59; res assoc, Roswell Park Mem Inst, 59-61; scientist x-ray crystallog & phys chem, State Univ Utrecht, 61-62, scientist first class, 62-65; res assoc, 65-71, SR RES FEL X-RAY STUDIES LIQUID CRYSTALS, LIQUIDS & CRYSTALS, LIQUID CRYSTAL INST, KENT STATE UNIV, 71- *Concurrent Pos:* Mem ed adv bd, Advances in Liquid Crystals, Acad Press, 71-; adj assoc prof physics dept, Kent State Univ, 75-; chmn, 6th Int Liquid Crystal Conf, 76; mem planning & steering comt, Int Liquid Crystal Conf, 76- *Mem:* Am Crystallog Asn; Sigma Xi; Am Chem Soc. *Res:* Study of the structure of liquid crystals, liquids and crystals, mainly through x-ray diffraction techniques; classification of liquid crystals on the basis of structure; phase transition phenomena. *Mailing Add:* Liquid Crystal Inst Kent State Univ Kent OH 44242

DEVRIES, ARTHUR LELAND, b Conrad, Mont, Dec 12, 38; m 68; c 1. COMPARATIVE PHYSIOLOGY, BIOCHEMISTRY. *Educ:* Univ Mont, BA, 60; Stanford Univ, PhD(biol), 68. *Prof Exp:* Assoc res physiologist, Scripps Inst Oceanog, 70-76; asst prof, 76-80, ASSOC PROF PHYSIOL & BIOPHYS, UNIV ILL, URBANA, 80- *Mem:* AAAS; Soc Cryobiol; Am Soc Zoologists. *Res:* Cryobiology, especially the role of peptide and glycopeptide antifreezes in the survival of polar fishes; cold adaptation in the lower vertebrates; research known for the discovery of the glycopeptide and peptide antifreeze in cold-water fishes. *Mailing Add:* Dept of Physiol Univ of Ill 524 Burrill Hall Urbana IL 61801

DEVRIES, DAVID J, b Grand Rapids, Mich, Sept 22, 42; m 65. MATHEMATICS. *Educ:* Calvin Col, AB, 65; Pa State Univ, MA, 66, PhD(math), 69. *Prof Exp:* Asst prof math, Hobart & William Smith Cols, 69-71; asst prof, 71-74, chmn dept math & physics, 71-76, ASSOC PROF MATH, MARS HILL COL, 74-, COORDR INFO SYSTS, 76- *Mem:* Am Math Soc; Math Asn Am. *Res:* General prime number theory; algebraic number theory. *Mailing Add:* Dept of Math Mars Hill Col Mars Hill NC 28754

DEVRIES, FREDERICK WILLIAM, b New York, NY, Feb 5, 30; m 59; c 3. CHEMICAL ENGINEERING. *Educ:* Columbia Univ, AB, 49, BS, 50, MS, 51. *Prof Exp:* From jr engr to prod asst, 51-53, process supvr, 53-55, sr supvr & engr, 56-61, supvr, 61-64, semiworks supvr, 64-66, eng supvr, 66-71, tech rep, 71-78, TECH SERV CONSULT, E I DU PONT DE NEMOURS & CO, INC, 78- *Mem:* Am Chem Soc; Am Inst Chem Engrs; Soc Mining Engrs; Sigma Xi; Geothermal Resources Coun. *Res:* Hydrogen peroxide in mineral processing; recovery of uranium mineral leaching processes; sodium cyanide in mineral processing; process design and economic evaluation; applications research. *Mailing Add:* Chem & Pigments Dept E I du Pont de Nemours & Co Inc Wilmington DE 19898

DE VRIES, GEORGE HENRY, biochemistry, neurochemistry, see previous edition

DE VRIES, JOHN EDWARD, b Fenton, Ill, Oct 4, 19; m 46; c 2. CHEMISTRY. *Educ:* Hope Col, AB, 41; Univ Ill, PhD(chem), 44. *Prof Exp:* Asst chem, Univ Ill, 41-44; res chemist, Manhattan Proj, Stand Oil Co, Ind, 44-46; from asst prof to assoc prof chem, Kans State Univ, 46-51, head gen anal res sect, Naval Ord Test Sta, 51-55; sr chemist & mgr anal serv, Stanford Res Inst, 55-64; PROF CHEM, CALIF STATE UNIV, HAYWARD, 64- *Mem:* AAAS; Am Chem Soc. *Res:* Organic analytical reagents; spectroscopy in chemical analysis; spectrophotometry; analytical applications of phenanthrolinium and related compounds; analysis of rocket propellants; nitrogen compounds; polarography; environmental analysis; pesticide residue analysis; gas chromatography. *Mailing Add:* 886 Garland Dr Palo Alto CA 94303

DEVRIES, K LAWRENCE, b Ogden, Utah, Oct 27, 33; m 58; c 2. MECHANICAL ENGINEERING, MATERIALS SCIENCE. *Educ:* Univ Utah, BS, 59, PhD(physics), 62. *Prof Exp:* Design engr hydraulics, Convair Aircraft, Tex, 57; from asst prof to assoc prof, 60-68, chmn dept, 70-81, PROF MECH ENG, UNIV UTAH, 68- *Concurrent Pos:* Consult, 60-; dir polymer prog, NSF, 75-76. *Mem:* AAAS; Am Soc Mech Engrs; Am Phys Soc; Soc Exp Stress Anal; Am Chem Soc. *Res:* Mechanical behavior of materials; molecular phenomena associated with deformation and failure; biomedical and dental materials. *Mailing Add:* MEB 3008 Univ Utah Salt Lake City UT 84112

DEVRIES, MARVIN FRANK, b Grand Rapids, Mich, Oct 31, 37; m 59; c 3. COMPUTER AIDED MANUFACTURING. *Educ:* Calvin Col, Mich, BS, 60; Univ Mich, BSME, 60, MSME, 61; Univ Wis, Madison, PhD(mech eng), 66. *Prof Exp:* Instr, 62-66, asst prof, 66-70, assoc prof, 70-77, PROF MECH ENG, UNIV WIS, MADISON, 77- *Concurrent Pos:* Assoc dir, Indust Res Prog, Univ Wis, 75-77; vis prof, Cranfield Inst Technol, Eng, 79-80. *Mem:* Soc Mfg Engrs (secy-treas, 81-82); Am Soc Mech Engrs; Int Inst Prod Res; Numerical Control Soc. *Res:* Manufacturing processes; material removal processes and computer-aided manufacturing; microscopic aspects of manufacturing; macroscopic approach to manufacturing systems. *Mailing Add:* Dept Mech Eng Univ Wis 1513 Univ Ave Madison WI 53706

DEVRIES, RALPH MILTON, b Los Angeles, Calif, Apr 16, 44. NUCLEAR PHYSICS. *Educ:* Univ Calif, Los Angeles, BS, 65, PhD(physics), 71. *Prof Exp:* Fel nuclear physics, Ctr Nuclear Studies, Saclay, France, 71-72 & Univ Wash, 73; asst prof nuclear physics, Univ Rochester, 74-76, assoc prof, 76-78; MEM STAFF, LOS ALAMOS NAT LAB, 78- *Mem:* Am Phys Soc. *Res:* Heavy-ion interactions; instrument development; complex computer calculations of theoretical reaction models; antiproton-nucleus interactions. *Mailing Add:* Los Alamos Nat Lab MS 456 Los Alamos NM 87545

DE VRIES, RICHARD N, b Cortland, Nebr, May 24, 32; m 58; c 2. ENVIRONMENTAL ENGINEERING, WATER RESOURCES. *Educ:* Univ Nebr, BS, 58, MS, 63; Utah State Univ, PhD(water resources eng), 69. *Prof Exp:* Draftsman, Lincoln Tel & Tel Co, 54; storage engr, Northern Natural Gas Co, Nebr, 58-60; dist engr & mgr, Sanit Dist 1, Lancaster County, 60-62; asst prof civil eng, Univ Nebr, Lincoln, 63-66, 68-69; assoc prof, 69-77, PROF CIVIL ENG, OKLA STATE UNIV, 77- *Concurrent Pos:* Co-investr, Res Grants, 64-66; prin investr res grants, Univ Nebr, 68-69, Okla State Univ, 69-70 & Okla Water Resources Res Inst, 70-71. *Mem:* Am Soc Civil Engrs; Nat Soc Prof Engrs; Am Geophys Union; Am Water Resources Asn; Am Soc Eng Educ. *Res:* Bioenvironmental and water resources engineering; hydrology; hydraulics; urban planning. *Mailing Add:* Sch of Civil Eng Okla State Univ Stillwater OK 74074

DEVRIES, ROBERT CHARLES, b Evansport, Ohio, Oct 10, 22; m 43; c 5. MINERALOGY. *Educ:* ePauw Univ, BA, 48; Pa State Univ, PhD(mineral), 53. *Prof Exp:* From asst to res assoc mineral, Pa State Univ, 50-54; mem tech staff, Metall & Ceramic Div, Res Lab, Gen Elec Co, 54-61; assoc prof ceramics, Rensselaer Polytech Inst, 61-65; MEM TECH STAFF, PHYS CHEM LAB, RES & DEVELOP CTR, GEN ELEC CO, 65- *Concurrent Pos:* Coolidge fel, Res & Develop Ctr, Gen Elec Co, 81. *Mem:* Fel Am Ceramic Soc; Am Mineral Soc; Am Chem Soc; AAAS; Am Asn Crystal Growth. *Res:* Phase equilibria studies at high temperature and pressures and crystal-chemical relationships in silicate, titanate and fluoride systems of geologic and ceramic interest; crystal growth; microstructure; property relationships in ceramics; diamond synthesis. *Mailing Add:* Gen Elec Res & Develop Ctr The Knolls Schenectady NY 12301

DEVRIES, RONALD CLIFFORD, b Chicago, Ill, Dec 4, 36; m 63; c 3. ELECTRICAL ENGINEERING, COMPUTER SCIENCE. *Educ:* Northwestern Univ, BS, 59; Univ Ariz, MS, 62, PhD(elec eng), 68. *Prof Exp:* Coop student, Wells-Gardner & Co, 56-58; jr engr, Data-Stor Div, Cook Elec Co, 59-60; asst prof elec eng, San Diego State Col, 64-66; asst prof, 67-72, assoc prof elec eng, 72-80, PROF ELEC & COMPUT ENGR, UNIV NMEX, 80- *Concurrent Pos:* Consult, Sandia Nat Lab, 77- *Mem:* Inst Elec & Electronic Engrs, Computer Soc; Sigma Xi. *Res:* Logic design; minimization, computer organization and arithmetic; iterative circuits and cellular arrays; decomposition; fault detection and tolerance; nuclear safety and security; writing, debugging and documenting of computer programs. *Mailing Add:* Dept Elec Eng & Comput Sci Univ NMex Albuquerque NM 87131

DEW, JESS (EDWARD), b Okemah, Okla, July 18, 20; m 44; c 3. CHEMICAL ENGINEERING. *Educ:* Univ Okla, BS, 43; Mass Inst Technol, SM, 48. *Prof Exp:* Asst chem engr, Humble Oil & Ref Co, 43-47; chem engr, Stanolind Oil & Gas Co, 48-52; sr engr, Chem Co Div, Deere & Co, 52-53, asst chief engr, 53-56, chief engr, 56-61, vpres, 61-63, prod supt, Planter Works Div, 63-64, gen supt, 64-65; Helena Plant mgr, Ark-La Gas Co, 65-67; vpres fertilizer opers, Ark-La Chem Corp, 67-69; proj mgr chem, Construct Corp, 69-74; consult engr, 74-78; CONSTRUCT MGR, W R HOLWAY & ASSOCS, 78- *Mem:* Am Inst Chem Engrs; Am Soc Mech Engrs. *Res:* Process and general engineering; petrochemicals; ammonia; urea; phosphatic fertilizers. *Mailing Add:* 120 South Prairie Okmulgee OK 74447

DEW, JOHN N(ORMAN), b Okemah, Okla, Feb 27, 22; m 53; c 5. CHEMICAL ENGINEERING. *Educ:* Univ Okla, BS, 43; Univ Mich, MSE, 49, PhD(chem eng), 53. *Prof Exp:* Res engr, Res & Develop Div, NMex Sch Mines, 43-47; prod res, 53-54, sr res engr, 54-55, res group leader, 55-57, supvr res engr, 57-61, supv res scientist, 61-66, asst dir prod res div, 66-67, asst mgr prod res div, 67-68, mgr proj develop, 68-74, dir fuels technol, 74-78, DIR SPEC PROJ, RES & DEVELOP DEPT, CONOCO INC, 78- *Concurrent Pos:* Asst, Univ Okla, 47-48. *Mem:* Am Soc Petrol Engrs; Am Inst Chem Engrs. *Res:* Reaction kinetics; technological forecasting research planning and coordination project evaluationa; oil shale technology and economics. *Mailing Add:* 800 Dalewood Ave Ponca City OK 74601

DEW, WILLIAM CALLAND, b Belle Valley, Ohio, Dec 30, 16; m 42; c 2. DENTISTRY. *Educ:* Ohio State Univ, DDS, 41. *Prof Exp:* Intern prosthodontics, 41-42, from instr to assoc prof, 42-60, asst dean, Col Dent, 64-70, assoc dean, 70-76, PROF DENT, COL DENT, OHIO STATE UNIV, 60-, SECY, 59- *Concurrent Pos:* Mem, Dent Alumni Asn Quart, 77-; chmn, Callahan Mem Comn; mem, Boucher Prosthodontic Conf. *Mem:* Pierre Fauchard Acad; Am Dent Asn; Am Col Dent. *Res:* Fixed and removable prosthodontics; operative dentistry; dental materials. *Mailing Add:* Col of Dent Ohio State Univ Columbus OH 43210

DE WALD, CHARLES G(RIFFITH), operations research, applied mathematics, see previous edition

DEWALD, GORDON WAYNE, b Jamestown, NDak, July 22, 43; m 65; c 3. CYTOGENETICS. *Educ:* Jamestown Col, BS, 65; Univ NDak, MS, 68, PhD(cytogenetics), 72. *Prof Exp:* From res asst to res assoc, 72-77, assoc consult, 77-78, CONSULT, MAYO CLIN, 79-, ASSOC PROF, MAYO MED SCH, 80- *Concurrent Pos:* Nat Defense fel, 68-71; March of Dimes, Basil O'Connor Starter Res Grant, 74-77; NIH, Res Career Develop Grant. *Mem:* Sigma Xi; Am Soc Human Genetics. *Res:* Chromosomes in malignant pleural effusions and in hematologic disorders: leukemics and lymphomas; development of improved methods in laboratory cytogenetics. *Mailing Add:* Cytogenetics Lab Mayo Clin Rochester MN 55905

DEWALD, HORACE ALBERT, b Emlenton, Pa, Oct 25, 22; m 55; c 6. ORGANIC CHEMISTRY. *Educ:* Allegheny Col, BS, 44; Univ Ill, PhD(chem), 50. *Prof Exp:* Chemist, Eastman Kodak Co, 44-46; res chemist, Gen Aniline & Film Corp, 50-52; Parke Davis & Co fel med chem, Mellon Inst, 52-57; from res chemist to sr res chemist, 57-72, SR RES ASSOC WARNER-LAMBERT/PARKE-DAVIS, 72- *Mem:* Am Chem Soc. *Res:* Addition of Grignard reagents to olefinic hydrocarbons; synthesis of new detergents; preparation of potential chemotherapeutic agents. *Mailing Add:* Warner-Lambert/Parke-Davis 2800 Plymouth Rd Ann Arbor MI 48103

DEWALD, ROBERT REINHOLD, b Twining, Mich, Aug 31, 35; m 63; c 1. PHYSICAL CHEMISTRY. *Educ:* Cent Mich Univ, BS, 58; Mich State Univ, PhD(chem), 63. *Prof Exp:* From asst prof to assoc prof, 65-77, PROF CHEM, TUFTS UNIV, 77- *Mem:* Am Chem Soc. *Res:* Kinetics of fast reactions in solution; properties of metal nonaqueous solutions. *Mailing Add:* Dept of Chem Tufts Univ Medford MA 02155

DE WALL, GORDON, b Muskegon, Mich, Feb 6, 41; m 63; c 3. ORGANIC CHEMISTRY. *Educ:* Calvin Col, BS, 62; Univ Mich, MS, 64, PhD(chem), 67. *Prof Exp:* Res chemist, 67-70, res mgr, 70-72, dir prod, 72-77, V PRES PROD, BURDICK & JACKSON LABS, INC, 77- *Concurrent Pos:* Mem res & develop exec comt, Nat Safety Coun, 73- *Mem:* Am Chem Soc. *Res:* Synthesis of organic compounds; small chemical plant operations. *Mailing Add:* 1752 Kregel Ave Muskegon MI 49442

DEWALL, RICHARD A, b Appleton, Minn, Dec 16, 26; c 3. THORACIC SURGERY, CARDIOVASCULAR SURGERY. *Educ:* Univ Minn, BA, 49, BS, 50, MB, 52, MD, 53, MS, 61. *Prof Exp:* From instr to asst prof surg, Univ Minn, 59-62; prof & chmn dept, Chicago Med Sch & Mt Sinai Hosp, 62-66; chief surg, Cox Heart Inst, 66-75; coordr surg residency, Kettering Hosp, 66-75; CLIN PROF SURG, WRIGHT STATE UNIV, 75- *Concurrent Pos:* Estab investr, Am Heart Asn, 60-65. *Mem:* AMA; Am Col Surgeons; Soc Univ Surg; Am Asn Thoracic Surgeons. *Res:* Open heart surgery. *Mailing Add:* 421 Thornhill Rd Dayton OH 45419

DEWALLE, DAVID RUSSELL, b St Louis, Mo, June 18, 42; m 65; c 3. FOREST MICROCLIMATOLOGY, WATERSHED MANAGEMENT. *Educ:* Univ Mo-Columbia, BS, 64, MS, 66; Colo State Univ, PhD(watershed mgt), 69. *Prof Exp:* assoc prof, 69-80, PROF FOREST HYDROL, PA STATE UNIV, 80-, CHMN, FOREST SCI PROG, SCH FOREST RESOURCES, 80- *Concurrent Pos:* Vis fel, Sch Forestry, Univ Canterbury, NZ, 79. *Mem:* Am Geophys Union; Soc Am Foresters; Am Meteorol Soc; Am Water Resources Asn. *Res:* Windbreaks and shade trees in home energy conservation; effects of clear cutting on water quality and quantity; characteristics of acid snowpacks and effects of acid snowmelt on stream quality; water quality in urban areas; tree growth in artificially heated soil; snow hydrology. *Mailing Add:* 106 Land & Water Res Bldg Pa State Univ University Park PA 16802

DEWAMES, ROGER, b Menin, Belg, Dec 9, 31; US citizen; m 56; c 6. SOLID STATE PHYSICS. *Educ:* St Mary's Univ, Tex, BS & BA, 56; Tex Christian Univ, MA, 58; Tex A&M Univ, PhD(physics), 61; Pepperdine Univ, MBA, 81. *Prof Exp:* Mem tech staff theoret physics, Sci Ctr, NAm Aviation, Inc, 61-74, prog develop mgr, Sci Ctr, 74-75, DIR PHYSICS & CHEM, ROCKWELL INT CORP, 75-, DIR RES & TECHNOL, 81- *Mem:* Fel Am Phys Soc; Sigma Xi. *Res:* Particle scattering; lattice dynamics; magnetism; molecular spectroscopy; collective excitation in solids; signal processing. *Mailing Add:* Rockwell Int ESG 8900 DeSoto Ave Canoga Park CA 91304

DEWAN, EDMOND M, b Forest Hills, NY, Feb 17, 31; m 59; c 2. THEORETICAL PHYSICS, APPLIED MATHEMATICS. *Educ:* Duke Univ, BS, 53; Yale Univ, PhD(theoret physics), 57. *Prof Exp:* Physicist, Microwave Physics Lab, Air Force Cambridge Res Labs, 59-63; adj asst prof biol, Brandeis Univ, 63; theoret physicist, Data Sci Lab, US Air Force Cambridge Res Labs, 64-72, THEORET PHYSICIST, AERONOMY DIV, AIR FORCE GEOPHYSICS LAB, HANSCOM AFB, 72- *Concurrent Pos:* Res asst, Yale Univ, 53-57; res assoc, Brandeis Univ, 61-63; consult psychiat res, Mass Gen Hosp, Boston, 63-64, res assoc, 64; res assoc, Harvard Med Sch, 64. *Honors & Awards:* Aerospace Educ Found 1st Prize, Nat Air Force Symp Sci, 63. *Mem:* AAAS; Inst Elec & Electronics Engrs; Am Geophys Union; Am Soc Cybernet (vpres, 68-); Sigma Xi. *Res:* Plasma physics; special relativity; mathematics of nonlinear oscillations and applications to physical and biological oscillations; theory of sleep and rapid eye movement state; electroencephalographic analysis; control of human ovulation cycles by photic stimulation; atmospheric physics; vertical transport in the stratosphere; turbulence and waves in stratified media. *Mailing Add:* Aeronomy Div Hanscom AFB Bedford MA 01731

DEWAR, MICHAEL JAMES STEUART, b Ahmednagar, India, 18; Brit & US citizen; m 44; c 2. CHEMISTRY. *Educ:* Oxford Univ, BA, 40, PhD(chem), 42, MA, 43. *Prof Exp:* Imp Chem Industs res grant, Oxford Univ, 42-45 & fel, 45; phys chemist, Courtaulds Ltd, 45-51; prof chem & head dept, Queen Mary Col, London, 51-59; prof, Univ Chicago, 59-63; ROBERT A WELCH PROF CHEM, UNIV TEX, AUSTIN, 63- *Concurrent Pos:* Reilly lectr, Univ Notre Dame, 51; Tilden lectr, Brit Chem Soc, 54; vis prof, Yale Univ, 57; Falk Plaut lectr, Columbia & Daines Mem lectr, Univ Kans, 63; Glidden Co lectr, Western Reserve Univ & William Pyle Philips vis, Haverford Univ, 64; Arthur D Little vis prof, Mass Inst Technol & Marrhan vis lectr, Newcastle-upon-Tyne, Eng, 66; Glidden Co lectr, Kent State Univ, 67; Grehm lectr, Eidg Technische Hochschule, Zurich, 68; Barton lectr, Univ Okla, 69; Kahlbaum lectr, Univ Basel & Benjamin Rush lectr, Univ Pa, 71; Kharasch vis prof, Univ Chicago, 71; Venable lectr, Univ NC, Chapel Hill, 71; Firth vis prof, Univ Sheffield, Eng, 72; Foster lectr, State Univ NY Buffalo, 73; Five-Col lectr, Mass, 73; spec lectr, Univ London, 74; Sprague lectr, Univ Wis, 74; consult, Monsanto Chem Ltd, Eng, 54-59 & Monsanto Co, US, 59-; Distinguished Bicentennial prof, Univ Utah, 76; Bircher lectr, Vanderbilt Univ, 76; Pahlavi lectr, Iran, 77; Michael Faraday lectr, Northern Ill Univ, 77. *Honors & Awards:* Howe Award, Am Chem Soc, 62; Robert Robinson Medal & lectr, The Chem Soc, 74; Priestly lectr, Pa State Univ, 80. *Mem:* Am Chem Soc; fel Am Acad Arts & Sci; Brit Chem Soc (hon secy, 57-59); fel Royal Soc. *Res:* Interpretation of structure and chemical reactivity in terms of fundamental physical theory; organic, inorganic, physical and theoretical chemistry. *Mailing Add:* Dept of Chem Univ of Tex Austin TX 78712

DEWAR, NORMAN ELLISON, b Rochester, NY, Nov 14, 30; m 55; c 3. MICROBIOLOGY, BIOCHEMISTRY. *Educ:* Syracuse Univ, BS, 52; Purdue Univ, MS, 55, PhD(microbiol, biochem), 59. *Prof Exp:* Head div microbiol, Vestal Labs, Inc, 59-62, dir res, Vestal Div, 62-69, vpres res, Vestal Div, 69-76, VPRES & TECH DIR, VESTAL DIV, CHEMED CORP, 76- *Concurrent Pos:* Chmn disinfectant & sanitizers div, Chem Specialties Mfrs Asn, 71-72; mem antimicrobial prog adv comt, Environ Protection Agency, 73-74. *Mem:* Fel Royal Soc Health; Am Soc Testing & Mat; Am Soc Microbiol; Soc Indust Microbiol; Am Chem Soc. *Res:* Physiology and biochemistry of microorganisms; chemoautotrophic carbon dioxide assimilation; development of environmental biocidal agents; environmental microbiology. *Mailing Add:* 7145 Westmoreland Dr St Louis MO 63130

DEWAR, ROBERT LEITH, b Melbourne, Australia, Mar 1, 44; m 69; c 1. PLASMA PHYSICS. *Educ:* Univ Melbourne, BSc, 65, MSc, 67, PhD(astrophys sci, plasma physics), 70. *Prof Exp:* Fel, Ctr Theoret Physics, Dept Physics & Astron, Univ Md, 70-71; res assoc, Plasma Physics Lab, Princeton Univ, 71-73; res fel, Dept Theoret Physics, Res Sch Phys Sci, Australian Nat Univ, 74-76, sr res fel, 76-77; mem prof res staff, 77-79, res physicist, 79-81, PRIN RES PHYSICIST, PLASMA PHYSICS LAB, PRINCETON UNIV, 81- *Mem:* Fel Am Phys Soc; Australian Inst Physics. *Res:* Theoretical plasma physics; hydromagnetic stability; canonical transformations; turbulence. *Mailing Add:* Plasma Physics Lab Princeton Univ PO Box 451 Princeton NJ 08540

DEWART, GILBERT, b New York, NY, Jan 14, 32. GEOPHYSICS. *Educ:* Mass Inst Technol, BS, 53, MS, 54; Ohio State Univ, PhD(geol), 68. *Prof Exp:* Seismologist, US-Int Geophys Yr Antarctic Exped, Arctic Inst NAm, Calif Inst Technol, 56-58, res engr, Seismol Lab, 58-59, exchange scientist with Soviet Antarctic Exped, 59-61, res engr, Seismol Lab, 61-63; prin investr seismol gravimetry, Inst Polar Studies, Ohio State Univ, 64-70, res assoc, 68-71, adj asst prof geol, 69-71; GEOPHYS CONSULT, 72- *Honors & Awards:* Antarctic Serv Cert, US Nat Comt, Int Geophys Yr, 56-58. *Mem:* AAAS; Soc Explor Geophys; Seismol Soc Am; Am Geophys Union; Am Inst Prof Geologists. *Res:* Seismic study of earth's crust; seismic effects of underground nuclear explosions; seismic properties of glacier ice; gravity and magnetic surveys in polar regions; geotechnical applications of acoustic emission. *Mailing Add:* PO Box 331 Pasadena CA 91102

DE WEER, PAUL JOSEPH, b Avelgem, Belg, July 15, 38; m 65; c 3. BIOPHYSICS, PHYSIOLOGY. *Educ:* Cath Univ Louvain, BS, 59, MD, 63, MS, 64; Univ Md, Baltimore, PhD(biophys), 69. *Prof Exp:* Res assoc endocrinol, Med Sch, Cath Univ Louvain, 63-65; from instr to asst prof biophys, Sch Med, Univ Md, Baltimore, 70-73; assoc prof, 73-78, PROF PHYSIOL & BIOPHYS, SCH MED, WASHINGTON UNIV, 78- *Concurrent Pos:* NIH res career develop award, 70-73. *Mem:* Biophys Soc; Am Physiol Soc. *Res:* Active transport of ions through cell membranes. *Mailing Add:* Dept of Physiol & Biophys Washington Univ Sch Med St Louis MO 63110

DEWEES, ANDRE AARON, b Herrin, Ill, Feb 17, 39; m 63; c 3. POPULATION GENETICS. *Educ:* Southern Ill Univ, BA, 61, MA, 63; Purdue Univ, PhD(genetics), 68. *Prof Exp:* From asst prof to assoc prof, 61-75, PROF BIOL, SAM HOUSTON STATE UNIV, 75- *Mem:* AAAS; Genetics Soc Am; Biomet Soc. *Res:* Insect population genetics; role of crossing over between linked genes in evolution. *Mailing Add:* Dept of Biol Sam Houston State Univ Huntsville TX 77340

DEWEESE, DAVID D, b Columbus, Ohio, Mar 16, 13; m 38, 75; c 2. OTOLARYNGOLOGY, SURGERY. *Educ:* Univ Mich, AB, 34, MD, 38; Am Bd Otolaryngol, dipl, 43. *Prof Exp:* Resident & instr otolaryngol, Med Sch, Univ Mich, 42-44; chmn dept, Portland Clin, 44-62; prof & chmn dept, 62-79, EMER PROF OTOLARYNGOL, MED SCH, UNIV ORE, 79- *Concurrent Pos:* Asst examr, Am Bd Otolaryngol, 57-59, mem bd dirs, 60-79, pres, 72-76; mem res training comt communicative dis, NIH, 63-67; mem adv coun, Nat Inst Neurol Dis & Stroke, 68-69; mem bd regents, Maryhurst Col. *Honors & Awards:* Am Acad Ophthal & Otolaryngol Award, 59. *Mem:* Am Acad Ophthal & Otolaryngol; Am Otol Soc; Am Laryngol, Rhinol & Otol Soc (pres, 74-75); Am Laryngol Asn; Am Broncho-Esophagol Asn. *Res:* Deafness and hearing loss; vertigo and dizziness; diseases of ear, throat and nose. *Mailing Add:* Dept of Otolaryngol Univ of Ore Med Sch Portland OR 97201

DEWEESE, JAMES A, b Kent, Ohio, Apr 5, 25; m 50, 62; c 6. SURGERY. *Educ:* Univ Rochester, MD, 49. *Prof Exp:* From instr to assoc prof surg, 55-69, dir surg res, 58-62, PROF SURG, MED CTR, UNIV ROCHESTER, 69-, SURGEON, 68-, CHMN DIV CARDIOTHORACIC SURG, 75- *Concurrent Pos:* Asst surgeon, Strong Mem Hosp, 56-58, assoc surgeon, 58-75, surgeon, 75-; consult, Rochester Gen Hosp, 59- & Batavia & Bath Vet Hosps, 63- *Mem:* fel Am Col Surgeons; Soc Vascular Surg (pres, 77-78); Int Cardiovasc Soc. *Res:* Cardiovascular diseases; hypothermia in cardiac surgery; venous thrombosis, phlebography, arterial reconstructions and venous reconstructions. *Mailing Add:* Dept Surg Univ Rochester Med Ctr Rochester NY 14620

DEWEESE, MARION SPENCER, b Corydon, Ind, Aug 17, 15; m 41; c 3. SURGERY. *Educ:* Kent State Univ, AB, 35; Univ Mich, MD, 39, MS, 48. *Prof Exp:* From instr to asst prof surg, Univ Mich, 48-51; pvt pract, Calif, 51-53; assoc prof surg, Univ Mich, 53-64; prof surg & chmn dept, Sch Med, Univ Mo-Columbia, 64-74; CLIN PROF SURG, UNIV MICH, ANN ARBOR, 74- *Concurrent Pos:* Chief surg serv, Ann Arbor Vet Admin Hosp, 53-56; consult, 56-64; mem, Am Bd Surg; pvt pract surg, Ann Arbor, 74-; chief staff, St Joseph Mercy Hosp, Ann Arbor, 79-81. *Mem:* AMA; Am Surg Asn; fel Am Col Surgeons. *Res:* Vascular disease; diseases of aorta and peripheral arteries; thromboembolism; thermal injury and wound healing. *Mailing Add:* 2229 Glendaloch Ann Arbor MI 48104

DEWEIN, LOUIS F, physiology, see previous edition

DEWERD, LARRY ALBERT, b Milwaukee, Wis, July 18, 41; m 63; c 3. MEDICAL PHYSICS, SOLID STATE PHYSICS. *Educ:* Univ Wis-Milwaukee, BS, 63; Univ Wis-Madison, MS, 65, PhD(physics, radiol), 70. *Prof Exp:* Res assoc mat sci, Univ Wash, 70-72, res asst prof dosimetry, 72-75; vis asst prof, Ctr Radiol Physics, 75-76, clin asst prof med physics, 76-79, CLIN ASSOC PROF MED PHYSICS & DIR, MIDWEST CTR RADIOL PHYSICS, UNIV WIS-MADISON, 79- *Concurrent Pos:* Mem screening & diag, Wis Coun Cancer Control, 77-; mem, Radiotherapy, Mammography, Chamber Calibration Tech Group, 78- *Mem:* Am Asn Physicists Med; Health Physics Soc; Am Phys Soc; Soc Photo-Optical Instrumentation Engrs; Am Asn Physics Teachers. *Res:* Radiological systems in diagnostic radiology-medical physics; electrophotographic imaging; mammography; solid state dosimetry; luminescence and physics of the solid state. *Mailing Add:* Med Physics 1530 MSC Univ Wis 1300 University Ave Madison WI 53706

DEWET, JAN M J, b Vredefort, SAfrica, July 4, 27; m 50; c 2. GENETICS. *Educ:* Univ Pretoria, BSc, 49; Univ Calif, Berkeley, PhD(genetics), 52. *Prof Exp:* Prof officer, Div Hort, Dept Agr, SAfrica, 52-54, sr prof officer, Div Bot, 54-59; Nat Res Coun Can fel, 59-60; from asst prof to assoc prof exp taxon, Okla State Univ, 60-67; PROF CYTOGENETICS, UNIV ILL, URBANA, 67- *Concurrent Pos:* NSF res grants, 60-; Guggenheim fel, 69-70. *Mem:* Bot Soc Am; Am Soc Plant Taxon; Int Asn Plant Taxon; Asn Taxon Study Trop African Flora. *Res:* Experimental taxonomy of the Gramineae; experimental control of reproduction; genetics of apomixis; chromosome pairing; ethnobotany; origin and evolution of cultivated plants. *Mailing Add:* Dept of Agron Univ of Ill Urbana IL 61801

DEWET, PIETER D, b Caledon, SAfrica, Nov 3, 27; m 53; c 3. NEUROSCIENCE. *Educ:* Agr Col Grootfontein, SAfrica, dipl agr, 49; Univ Pretoria, DVM, 53; Univ Minn, PhD(neuroanat), 66. *Prof Exp:* State vet, Div Vet Serv, Dept Agr SAfrica, 54-55; vet pvt pract, 55-61; asst prof vet histol & vet anat, Col Vet Med, Univ Pretoria, 62-63; res asst neuroanat, Col Vet Med, Univ Minn, 63-66; assoc prof vet histol & anat, Univ Pretoria, 67-69; assoc prof, 69-74, PROF NEUROL SCI, COL VET MED, OHIO STATE UNIV, 74- *Concurrent Pos:* NIH grant, 69-70; Ohio State Univ Col Vet Med rep, Multimedia Prog Tech Conf, Purdue Univ. *Mem:* World Asn Anat; Med & Vet Asn Anat SAfrica; SAfrica Vet Med Asn; Neurol Soc SAfrica. *Res:* Comparative basic neurology. *Mailing Add:* Dept of Vet Anat Ohio State Univ Columbus OH 43210

DE WETTE, FREDERIK WILLEM, b Bussum, Neth, June 29, 24; m 52; c 3. SOLID STATE PHYSICS. *Educ:* State Univ Utrecht, Drs, 50, Dr(theoret physcis), 59. *Prof Exp:* Res assoc, State Univ Utrecht, 50-52; vis lectr physics, Brown Univ, 52-53; res assoc chem, Univ Md, 53-55; asst prof, State Univ Utrecht, 55-60; res asst prof physics, Univ Ill, 60-62; res physicist, Neth Reactor Ctr, 62-63; resident res assoc, Solid State Sci Div, Argonne Nat Lab, 63-65; chmn, Dept Physics, 69-74, assoc dean, Col Nat Sci, 76-80, PROF PHYSICS, UNIV TEX, AUSTIN, 65-, . *Concurrent Pos:* Consult, Argonne Nat Lab, 65-72; trustee, Argonne Univs Asn, 72-74; vis prof, State Univ Utrecht, 74-75. *Mem:* Fel Am Phys Soc. *Res:* Surface physics, dynamical, thermodynamical and scattering properties of crystals and crystal surfaces. *Mailing Add:* Dept Physics Univ Tex Austin TX 78712

DEWEY, BRADLEY, JR, b Pittsburgh, Pa, Apr 10, 16; m 40; c 5. CHEMICAL ENGINEERING. *Educ:* Harvard Univ, BS, 37; Mass Inst Technol, ScD(chem eng), 41. *Prof Exp:* Indust res, Dewey & Almy Chem Co, 40-43, dir develop dept, 45-50, vpres, 50-56; pres, Cryovac Div, W R Grace & Co, 56-64, sr vpres chem group, 64-70; pres & treas, Thermal Dynamics Co, 70-80; RETIRED. *Mem:* Am Chem Soc; Am Inst Chem Engrs. *Res:* Creaming of latex; colloid chemistry. *Mailing Add:* 43 Ocean Ridge Hanover NH 03755

DEWEY, C(LARENCE) FORBES, JR, b Pueblo, Colo, Mar 27, 35; m 63. FLUID MECHANICS, LASER PHYSICS. *Educ:* Yale Univ, BE, 56; Stanford Univ, MS, 57; Calif Inst Technol, PhD(aeronaut), 63. *Prof Exp:* Mem tech staff aerodyn, Aeronutronic Div, Philco Corp, 57-59; NSF fel aeronaut, Calif Inst Technol, 59-63; asst prof aerospace sci, Univ Colo, 63-68; assoc prof mech eng, 68-76, PROF MECH ENG, MASS INST TECHNOL, 76- *Concurrent Pos:* Consult, Rand Corp, 60-76, Swissident, Inc, 64-65, adv group aerospace res & develop, NATO, 66-67, Eng & Develop Co Colo, 66-68, Xenon Corp, 69-, Sausum Clin, 70 & others; lectr, Univ Calif, Los Angeles, 64; vis scientist, Inst Plasmaphysik, Ger, 66-67; chmn bd, Sensoresearch Corp, 72-79; trustee, Cardiovasc Trust of Boston, 74-80; consult med, Mass Gen Hosp, 76-80; vis prof path, Harvard Med Sch, 78-79; chmn bd, Mass Comput Corp, 81- *Mem:* Am Phys Soc; Am Inst Aeronaut & Astronaut. *Res:* Gas physics; ionization and collision phenomena; applied laser technology using wavelength-tunable lasers; fluid mechanics in biomedical engineering, including noninvasive diagnostic techniques; intelligent systems. *Mailing Add:* Dept of Mech Eng Rm 3-250 Mass Inst of Technol Cambridge MA 02139

DEWEY, DONALD HENRY, b Geneva, NY, Apr 25, 18; m 47; c 2. HORTICULTURE, POMOLOGY. *Educ:* Cornell Univ, BS, 39, PhD(veg crops), 50. *Prof Exp:* Jr olericulturist, Cheyenne Hort Field Sta, USDA, 39-45, horticulturist, Fresno Lab, 45-51; actg chmn dept, 77-78, PROF HORT, MICH STATE UNIV, 51- *Concurrent Pos:* Orgn Europ Econ Coop sr vis fel, Ditton Lab, Eng, 60; vis prof, Technion Univ, Israel, 80. *Mem:* Fel Am Soc Hort Sci; Int Soc Hort Sci. *Res:* Harvesting; handling and storage of fruits and vegetables; controlled atmosphere storage of fruit; physiology of maturation, ripening and senescence. *Mailing Add:* Dept Hort Mich State Univ East Lansing MI 48824

DEWEY, DOUGLAS R, b Brigham City, Utah, Oct 23, 29; m 49; c 3. CYTOGENETICS, PLANT BREEDING. *Educ:* Utah State Univ, BS, 51, MS, 54; Univ Minn, PhD(plant genetics), 56. *Prof Exp:* Res agronomist, 56-62, RES GENETICIST, US DEPT AGR, 62- *Mem:* Am Soc Agron; Bot Soc Am; Crop Sci Soc Am. *Res:* Genetics, cytology, interspecific and intergeneric hybridization of species of the Triticeae tribe of grasses. *Mailing Add:* Crops Res Lab Utah State Univ Logan UT 84322

DEWEY, FRED MCALPIN, b Akron, Ohio, Sept 9, 39; m 59; c 7. ORGANIC CHEMISTRY. *Educ:* Colo State Univ, BS, 61; Univ Colo, PhD(chem), 65. *Prof Exp:* Res chemist, Harry Diamond Labs, DC, 65-67 & Air Force Rocket Propulsion Lab, Calif, 67-68; asst prof, 68-74, assoc prof, 74-78, PROF CHEM, METROPOLITAN STATE COL, 78- *Mem:* Am Indust Hyg Asn. *Res:* Synthesis; stereochemistry. *Mailing Add:* Metropolitan State Col Dept Chem 1006 11th St Denver CO 80204

DEWEY, J(OHN) L(YONS), b Savannah, Ga, Sept 24, 19; m 46; c 1. CHEMICAL ENGINEERING. *Educ:* Ga Inst Technol, BS, 42. *Prof Exp:* Chem engr res dept, Tenn Copper Co, 42-46; Tex Gulf Sulfur asst, Univ Ill, 47-48; asst prof chem eng, Univ Cincinnati, 48-49; sr chem engr, Battelle Mem Inst, 50-53; sect head res dept, Maxwell House Coffee Div, Gen Foods Co, 53-54; sect head reduction res lab, 54-68, eng dir, Alumina Res Div, 68-76, RES ASSOC, ALUMINA RES DIV, REYNOLDS METALS CO, 76- *Honors & Awards:* Best Contribution 1965-66, Extractive Metall Div, Am Inst Mining, Metall & Petrol Engrs, 67. *Mem:* Am Inst Chem Engrs; Am Chem Soc. *Res:* Application of chemical engineering to extractive metallurgy; iodide titanium; thermal and electrolytic aluminum; alumina from clay, other native ores; mass transfer at high temperatures and reduced pressures; digital control systems. *Mailing Add:* Reynolds Metals Co Alumina Res Div PO Box 97 Bauxite AR 72011

DEWEY, JAMES EDWIN, b Geneva, NY, Jan 15, 17; m 43; c 1. ENTOMOLOGY. *Educ:* Cornell Univ, BS, 40, PhD(entom), 44; Univ Tenn, MS, 41. *Prof Exp:* Instr exten entom, 44-45, from asst prof to assoc prof, 45-54, PROF INSECT TOXICOL, NY STATE COL AGR & LIFE SCI, CORNELL UNIV, 54-, LEADER CHEM-PESTICIDES PROG, 64- *Mem:* Entom Soc Am; Am Chem Soc. *Res:* Insect toxicology; insect resistance to insecticides; synergism; bioassay; insecticide formulation; fruit insect control. *Mailing Add:* Dept of Entom NY State Col of Agr & Life Sci Ithaca NY 14853

DEWEY, JOHN FREDERICK, b London, Eng, May 22, 37; m 61; c 2. STRUCTURAL GEOLOGY. *Educ:* Univ London, BSc, 58, DIC & PhD(struct geol), 60; Cambridge Univ, MA, 64. *Prof Exp:* From asst lectr to lectr geol, Univ Manchester, 60-64; lectr, Cambridge Univ, 64-70; PROF GEOL, STATE UNIV NY ALBANY, 70- *Concurrent Pos:* Sr res assoc, Lamont-Doherty Geol Observ, 67-; commonwealth fel, Mem Univ, 70; comt mem, Int Geodynamics Proj, 71-; assoc ed bull, Geol Soc Am. *Honors & Awards:* Daniel Pidgeon Fund Award, Geol Soc London, 64 & Murchison Fund Award, 71. *Mem:* Fel Geol Soc London; fel Geol Asn Can; Am Geophys Union. *Res:* Stratigraphic-structural evolution of the Appalachian-Caledonian orogen and the Alpine orogen of Europe; significance of plate tectonics for the evolution of continental margins and orogenic belts. *Mailing Add:* Dept of Geol Sci State Univ of NY Albany NY 12222

DEWEY, JOHN MARKS, b Portsmouth, Eng, Mar 23; 30; m 51; c 2. PHYSICS, FLUID DYNAMICS. *Educ:* Univ London, BSc, 50, PhD(physics), 64. *Prof Exp:* Sci master physics, De La Salle Col, Channel Islands, 50-53, head sci dept, 53-56; scientist, Planning & Reporting Sect, Suffield Exp Sta, Can, 56-58, scientist, Physics Sect, 58-63, leader aerophys group, 63-64, head aerophys & shock tube sect, 64-65; from asst prof to assoc prof, 65-72, dean acad affairs, 73-77, PROF PHYSICS, UNIV VICTORIA BC, 72-, DEAN GRAD STUDIES & RES, 77- *Mem:* Am Phys Soc; fel Inst Physics; Can Asn Physicists. *Res:* Physics of blast waves; effect of blast waves; shock tube flows; measurement techniques in high speed fluid flows; high speed photography. *Mailing Add:* Dept of Physics Univ of Victoria Victoria BC V8W 2Y2 Can

DEWEY, KENNETH FREDERIC, meteorology, see previous edition

DEWEY, MAYNARD MERLE, b Hickory Corners, Mich, June 26, 32; m 55; c 2. ANATOMY. *Educ:* Kalamazoo Col, AB, 54; Univ Mich, MS, 56, PhD, 58. *Prof Exp:* Asst, A M Todd Co, Mich, 51-54; instr anat, Univ Mich, 58-60, from asst prof to assoc prof, 60-66; prof & chmn dept, Med Col Pa, 66-71; dean pro tem, Sch Basic Health Sci, 78-80, PROF ANAT & CHMN DEPT, HEALTH SCI CTR, UNIV NY, STONY BROOK, 71- *Mem:* AAAS; Histochem Soc; Soc Gen Physiol; Am Physiol Soc; Biophys Soc; Am Asn Anatomists. *Res:* Electron microscopy; cytochemistry; membrane structure; intracellular communication; muscle. *Mailing Add:* Dept of Anat Sci Health Sci Ctr State Univ of NY Stony Brook NY 11790

DEWEY, THOMAS GREGORY, b Pittsburgh, Pa, June 2, 52. BIOCHEMISTRY. *Educ:* Carnegie-Mellon Univ, BSc, 74; Univ Rochester, MS, 77, PhD(chem), 79. *Prof Exp:* NIH fel, Cornell Univ, 79-81; ASST PROF, UNIV DENVER, 81- *Mem:* Am Chem Soc. *Res:* Thermodynamic and kinetic investigations are being pursued on membrane bound enzymes that catalyze the coupling of chemiosmotic gradients to chemical synthesis. *Mailing Add:* Dept Chem Univ Denver Denver CO 80208

DEWEY, WADE G, b Los Angeles, Calif, Aug 10, 27; m 51; c 4. PLANT BREEDING, GENETICS. *Educ:* Utah State Univ, BS, 53; Cornell Univ, PhD(plant breeding), 56. *Prof Exp:* Asst prof agron, Utah State Univ, 56-58; geneticist, USDA, 58-59; from asst prof to assoc prof, 59-66, PROF AGRON, UTAH STATE UNIV, 66- *Mem:* Am Soc Agron. *Res:* Plant breeding and genetics of the cereal crops, particularly winter wheat. *Mailing Add:* Dept of Plant Sci Utah State Univ Logan UT 84321

DEWEY, WILLIAM CORNET, radiobiology, see previous edition

DEWEY, WILLIAM LEO, b Albany, NY, Oct 21, 34; m 60; c 6. PHARMACOLOGY, BIOCHEMISTRY. *Educ:* St Bernardine of Siena Col, BS, 57; Col St Rose, MS, 64; Univ Conn, PhD(pharmacol), 66. *Prof Exp:* Asst res biologist, Sterling-Winthrop Res Inst, 59-64; asst pharmacol, Sch Pharm, Univ Conn, 64-66; from instr to asst prof, Schs Med & Pharm, Univ NC, Chapel Hill, 68-72; assoc prof, 72-76, PROF PHARMACOL, MED COL VA, VA COMMONWEALTH UNIV, 76-, HEAD CNS DIV, 78-

Concurrent Pos: Fel pharmacol, Sch Med & Pharm, Univ NC, Chapel Hill, 66-68. *Mem:* AAAS; Am Soc Pharmacol & Exp Therapeut; Am Pharmaceut Asn; Am Chem Soc. *Res:* Agents that affect the central nervous system, especially hallucinogens, analgesics, stimulants and tranquilizers. *Mailing Add:* 1715 Chadwick Dr Richmond VA 23229

DEWHIRST, LEONARD WESLEY, b Marquette, Kans, Sept 28, 24; m 46; c 3. VETERINARY PARASITOLOGY. *Educ:* Kans State Col, BS, 49, MS, 50, PhD(parasitol), 57. *Prof Exp:* Res asst parasitol, Kans State Col, 49-52, instr zool, 52-57; asst prof & asst animal pathologist, Univ Ariz, 57-60, assoc prof, 60-63, prof vet sci & animal pathologist, Agr Exp Sta, 63-74; prof vet microbiol & asst dean students, Col Vet Med, Univ Mo-Columbia, 74-76; PROF VET SCI, ASSOC DEAN, COL AGR & DIR AGR EXP STA, UNIV ARIZ, 76- *Mem:* AAAS; Am Soc Parasitol; Am Micros Soc; Am Soc Trop Med & Hyg. *Res:* Agricultural parasitology; biology, treatment and control of parasites of domestic animals. *Mailing Add:* Col of Agr Univ of Ariz Tucson AZ 85721

DEWHURST, HAROLD AINSLIE, b Ottawa, Ont, June 18, 24; m 48; c 4. PHYSICAL CHEMISTRY. *Educ:* McGill Univ, BS, 46, PhD(phys chem), 50. *Prof Exp:* Res chemist, Can Atomic Energy Proj, 47-50; res fel, Univ Edinburgh, 50-52; res assoc phys chem, Univ Notre Dame, 52-54; res lab, Gen Elec Co, 54-60, liaison scientist chem, 60-61, personnel & admin, metall & ceramics res, 62-64, mgr struct & reactions studies, 64-65, mgr gen chem lab, Res & Develop Ctr, 65-68, mgr mat sci & eng, 68; mgr res group, 68-72, dir corp res & develop, 72-75, dir res & develop explor res, 75-78, dir strategic tech planning, 78-80, DIR SCIENTIFIC AFFAIRS, OWENS-CORNING FIBERGLAS CORP, 80- *Mem:* Am Chem Soc; Faraday Soc. *Res:* Kinetics of reactions; photochemistry of aqueous solutions; electric discharge chemistry; physical radiation chemistry; polymers; metallurgy; inorganic metals; glass fibers; textiles. *Mailing Add:* Tech Ctr Owens-Corning Fiberglas Corp Granville OH 43023

DEWING, STEPHEN BRONSON, b Princeton, NJ, Dec 18, 20; m 43; c 1. RADIOLOGY. *Educ:* Princeton Univ, AB, 42; Columbia Univ, MD, 45; Am Bd Radiol, dipl, 53. *Prof Exp:* Dir radiol, Hunterdon Med Ctr, Flemington, NJ, 53-65; assoc prof radiol, WVa Univ, 65-69; ASSOC RADIOL, STEPHENS MEM HOSP, NORWAY, MAINE, 69- *Concurrent Pos:* Assoc clin prof, NY Univ, 53-65; dir radiol, North Cumberland Mem Hosp, Bridgton, 69-74. *Mem:* AMA; Radiol Soc NAm. *Res:* Clinical radiology. *Mailing Add:* RFD 2 Harrison ME 04040

DEWIRE, JOHN WILLIAM, b Milton, Pa, June 12, 16; m 43; c 2. NUCLEAR PHYSICS. *Educ:* Ursinus Col, BS, 38; Ohio State Univ, PhD(physics), 42. *Hon Degrees:* DSc, Ursinus Col, 79. *Prof Exp:* Assoc scientist, Nat Defense Res Comt, Princeton, 42-43 & Los Alamos Sci Lab, NMex, 43-46; res assoc, 46-47, from asst prof to assoc prof, 47-58, PROF PHYSICS, CORNELL UNIV, 58-, ASSOC DIR LAB NUCLEAR STUDIES, 68- *Concurrent Pos:* NSF sr fel, Frascati, Italy, 60-61; Fulbright scholar & vis prof, Univ Bonn, 68; US sr scientist award, Ger Fed Repub, 74-75; trustee, Assoc Univs, Inc, 75- *Mem:* AAAS; Am Phys Soc. *Res:* High energy electron and meson physics; accelerators. *Mailing Add:* Lab of Nuclear Studies Cornell Univ Ithaca NY 14853

DE WIT, MICHIEL, b Amsterdam, Netherlands, June 6, 33; US citizen; m 57; c 5. LASERS. *Educ:* Ohio Univ, BS, 54; Yale Univ, PhD(physics), 60. *Prof Exp:* MEM TECH STAFF, TEX INSTRUMENTS, INC, 59- *Concurrent Pos:* Mem res associateships eval panel, Nat Res Coun, 74 & 76. *Mem:* Am Phys Soc; Optical Soc Am; Inst Elec & Electronic Engrs. *Res:* Studies of defects in solids via electron paramagnetic resonance, luminescence, Zeeman and Raman spectroscopy; laser and nonlinear optical device development; design and development of transversal filters with charge coupled devices. *Mailing Add:* Cent Res Lab MS 134 Tex Instruments Inc PO Box 5936 Dallas TX 75222

DEWIT, ROLAND, b Amsterdam, Netherlands, Feb 28, 30; US citizen; m 54; c 2. DISLOCATION THEORY, FRACTURE MECHANICS. *Educ:* Ohio Univ, BS, 53; Univ Ill, MS, 55, PhD(physics), 59. *Prof Exp:* Asst, Univ Ill, 53-59, res assoc, 59; asst res physicist, Univ Calif, Berkeley, 59-60; PHYSICIST, NAT BUR STANDARDS, 60- *Mem:* Am Phys Soc; Metall Soc; Am Soc Metals; Am Soc Mech Engr; Am Soc Testing & Mat. *Res:* Theory of dislocations and fracture mechanics. *Mailing Add:* Fracture & Deformation Div Nat Bur Standards Washington DC 20234

DEWITT, BERNARD JAMES, b Oak Harbor, Wash, Jan 29, 17; m 42; c 2. CHEMISTRY. *Educ:* Hope Col, AB, 37; Carnegie Inst Technol, DSc(phys chem), 41. *Concurrent Pos:* Res chemist, Pittsburgh Plate Glass Co, 40-51; sr supvr anal & phys chem, Columbia-South Chem Corp, 51-59, mgr, 59-64; asst dir res, 64-78, DIR ANALYTICAL & ELECTROCHEM RES, PPG INDUST, 78- *Mem:* Am Chem Soc; Am Indust Hyg Asn; Am Soc Testing & Mat. *Res:* Chlorination aliphatic organics; silica pigments; physical testing of rubber products; analysis of chlorinated hydrocarbons and particle size analysis; environmental chemistry. *Mailing Add:* PPG Indust Barberton OH 44203

DEWITT, BRYCE SELIGMAN, b Dinuba, Calif, Jan 8, 23; m 51; c 4. THEORETICAL PHYSICS. *Educ:* Harvard Univ, BS, 43, MA, 47, PhD(physics), 50. *Prof Exp:* Mem, Inst Advan Study, NJ, 49-50; Fulbright fel, Tata Inst Fundamental Res, India, 51-52; sr physicist, Radiation Lab, Univ Calif, 52-55; res prof physics, Univ NC, Chapel Hill, 56-59, prof, 60-64, Agnew Hunter Bahnson, Jr prof, 64-72, dir res, Inst Field Physics, 56-72; PROF PHYSICS, UNIV TEX, AUSTIN & DIR CTR RELATIVITY, 73- *Concurrent Pos:* Mem, Inst Advan Study, 54, 64; Fulbright lectr, France, 56; consult, Gen Atomic Div, Gen Dynamics Corp, 59; mem, Int Comt Relativity & Gravitation, 59-72; NSF sr fel, 64; Fulbright lectr, Japan, 64-65; leader, Tex-Mauritanian Eclipse Exped, 73; mem fels panel, Nat Res Coun, 74-; Guggenheim vis res fel, All Souls Col, Oxford, 75-76; group leader, Inst Theoret Physics, Univ Calif, Santa Barbara, 80-81. *Mem:* Fel Am Phys Soc; Explorers Club. *Res:* Non-Abelian gauge field theory; quantum theory of gravity; astrophysics. *Mailing Add:* Dept of Physics Univ of Tex Austin TX 78712

DEWITT, CALVIN BOYD, physiological ecology, see previous edition

DEWITT, CHARLES WAYNE, JR, b Akron, Ohio, Oct 16, 21; m 46; c 3. IMMUNOLOGY. *Educ:* Morris Harvey Col, BS, 49; Ohio State Univ, MS, 51, PhD(bact), 52. *Prof Exp:* Res scientist bact, Upjohn Co, 52-55, res assoc infect dis, 55-61; asst prof, Depts Microbiol & Surg, Sch Med, Tulane Univ, 61-62, from assoc prof to prof surg, 62-68; PROF PATH & SURG, MED CTR, UNIV UTAH, 68- *Concurrent Pos:* Mem ed bd, Transplantation. *Mem:* AAAS; Am Soc Microbiol; fel Am Acad Microbiol; Am Asn Immunol; Transplantation Soc. *Mailing Add:* Dept of Path Univ of Utah Med Ctr Salt Lake City UT 84132

DEWITT, DAVID P, b Bethlehem, Pa, Mar 2, 34; m 57; c 3. HEAT TRANSFER. *Educ:* Duke Univ, BS, 55; Mass Inst Technol, SM, 57; Purdue Univ, PhD(mech eng), 63. *Prof Exp:* Instr thermodyn, Col Eng, Duke Univ, 57-59; physicist, Nat Bur Standards, 63-64; dep dir, Thermophys Properties Res Ctr, 65-72, assoc prof, 72-78, PROF MECH ENG, PRUDUE UNIV, 78- *Concurrent Pos:* Guest worker, Nat Phys-Technol Inst, Bur Standards, Brunswick, Ger, 70-71. *Mem:* Am Soc Mech Eng; Am Inst Aeronaut & Astronaut; Sigma Xi. *Res:* Thermophysical properties of matter, especially thermal radiation properties of materials, experimental procedures and techniques. *Mailing Add:* Sch of Mech Eng Purdue Univ West Lafayette IN 47907

DEWITT, ELMER JOHN, b Grand Junction, Mich, Aug 6, 24; m 50; c 4. ORGANIC POLYMER CHEMISTRY. *Educ:* Univ Maine, BS, 50; Univ NH, MS, 53; Emory Univ, PhD(org chem), 55. *Prof Exp:* Technologist, 55-57, jr technologist, 57-58, sr technologist, 58-64, sr res chemist, 64-80, RES ASSOC, B F GOODRICH CO, 80- *Mem:* Am Chem Soc. *Res:* Polymer derivatives; organic oxidations; organic boron chemistry; emulsion polymerizations and plastics; polymer toughening and polymer properties; reaction injection molding; polymer chlorinations. *Mailing Add:* Res Ctr B F Goodrich Co 9921 Brecksville Rd Brecksville OH 44141

DE WITT, HOBSON DEWEY, b New Bern, NC, July 12, 23; m 48; c 3. ORGANIC CHEMISTRY. *Educ:* Erskine Col, BA, 44; Vanderbilt Univ, PhD(chem), 51. *Prof Exp:* Chemist, E I du Pont de Nemours & Co, 44; res chemist, Southland Paper Mills, 50-52; res chemist, The Chemstrand Corp, 52-56; PROF CHEM & CHMN DEPT, WESTMINSTER COL, 56- *Mem:* Am Chem Soc; Sigma Xi; fel Am Inst Chem. *Res:* Synthesis of amino acid derivatives; monomers; polymers of textile interest; resolution of optically active compounds. *Mailing Add:* Dept of Chem Westminster Col New Wilmington PA 16142

DE WITT, HUGH EDGAR, theoretical physics, see previous edition

DE WITT, HUGH HAMILTON, b San Jose, Calif, Dec 28, 33; m 56, 81; c 3. ICHTHYOLOGY, MARINE BIOLOGY. *Educ:* Stanford Univ, BA, 55, MA, 60, PhD(biol), 66. *Prof Exp:* Res assoc biol sci, Hancock Found, Univ Southern Calif, 62-67; asst prof marine biol, Univ SFla, 67-69; asst prof zool, 69-70, from asst prof oceanog to prof oceanog, 70-81, chmn, Dept Oceanog, 76-79, PROF ZOOL, UNIV MAINE, ORONO, 81- *Concurrent Pos:* mem biomass working party of fish biol, Spec Comt Atlantic Res & Sci Comt Oceanic Res. *Mem:* Am Soc Ichthyologists & Herpetologists (secy, 74-79); Sigma Xi; Ichthyol Soc Japan; Soc Systematic Zool; Soc Francaise Ichtyologie. *Res:* Freshwater fishes of southeastern Asia; polar marine fishes; taxonomy, biology and zoogeography of Antarctic fishes and of deep-water fishes of western north Atlantic. *Mailing Add:* Dept Zool Univ of Maine Orono ME 04469

DE WITT, JOHN WILLIAM, JR, b Pawhuska, Okla, Dec 16, 22; m 47; c 1. FISHERIES, LIMNOLOGY. *Educ:* Ore State Univ, PhD, 63. *Prof Exp:* Fishery biologist, US Fish & Wildlife Serv, 48-49; chmn dept, 75-78, PROF FISHERIES, HUMBOLDT STATE UNIV, 49- *Concurrent Pos:* Dir fisheries training & overseas support progs, Peace Corps, Chile, 66-69; fishery biologist, Lake Nasser Develop Ctr, Food & Agr Orgn UN, UAR, 69-71; mem, Calif State Regional Water Qual Control Bd, 73- *Mem:* Am Fisheries Soc; Water Pollution Control Fedn; Am Soc Ichthyol & Herpet; Am Soc Limnol & Oceanog; Sigma Xi. *Mailing Add:* Dept of Fisheries Humboldt State Univ Arcata CA 95521

DE WITT, ROBERT MERKLE, b Wolcott, NY, May 31, 15. ZOOLOGY. *Educ:* Univ Mich, BS, 40, MS, 41, PhD, 53. *Prof Exp:* Teacher high schs, NY, 41-46; asst prof biol, Sampson Col, 46-49; teaching asst, Univ Mich, 49-50, teaching fel, 50-52, instr, 52-54, Lloyd fel, 53-54; asst prof, 54-59, actg chem dept, 69-71, assoc prof biol, 59-80, EMER ASSOC PROF ZOOL, UNIV FLA, 80-, VCHMN DEPT, 80- *Mem:* AAAS; Am Malacol Union; Am Micros Soc; Ecol Soc Am; Am Soc Zool. *Res:* Morphological and physiological factors of adaptation in amphibious snails; reproduction, ecology, population biology and systematics of fresh-water mollusks. *Mailing Add:* Dept of Zool Univ of Fla Gainesville FL 32601

DEWITT, WILLIAM, b Washington, DC, Nov 28, 39. MICROBIOLOGY, BIOCHEMISTRY. *Educ:* Williams Col, BA, 61; Princeton Univ, MA, 63, PhD(biol), 66. *Prof Exp:* Res assoc biochem, Mass Inst Technol, 66-67; asst prof biol, 67-74, assoc prof, 74-77, PROF BIOL & CHMN DEPT, WILLIAMS COL, 77- *Res:* Genetic control of colicin synthesis in enteric bacteria; synthesis of hemoglobin and other specific proteins during amphibian development. *Mailing Add:* Dept of Biol Williams Col Williamstown MA 01267

DEWITT-MORETTE, CECILE, b Paris, France, Dec 21, 22; m 51; c 4. THEORETICAL PHYSICS. *Educ:* Univ Caen, Lic es sci, 43; Univ Paris, dipl, 44, PhD(theoret physics), 47. *Prof Exp:* Mem, Inst Advan Studies, Ireland, 46-47, Univ Inst Theoret Physics, Denmark, 47-48 & Inst Advan Study, Princeton, 48-50; teacher res, Inst Henri Poincare, France, 50-51; res assoc & lectr, Univ Calif, 52-55; vis res prof, Univ NC, Chapel Hill, 56-67, dir inst field physics, 58-66, lectr physics, 67-71; PROF ASTRON, UNIV TEX,

AUSTIN, 72- *Concurrent Pos:* Dir & founder, Summer Sch Theoret Physics, Les Houches, France, 51-72. *Honors & Awards:* Chevalier Ordre National Du Merite, France, 81. *Res:* Theory of field; elementary particles; mathematical physics; gravitation. *Mailing Add:* Dept of Astron Univ of Tex Austin TX 78712

DE WOLF, DAVID ALTER, b Dordrecht, Neth, July 23, 34. THEORETICAL PHYSICS, ELECTRICAL ENGINEERING. *Educ:* Univ Amsterdam, BSc, 55, MSc, 59; Univ Eindhoven, Dr Tech, 68. *Prof Exp:* Res physicist, Nuclear Defense Lab, Edgewood Arsenal, Md, 62; MEM TECH STAFF, DAVID SARNOFF RES CTR, RCA CORP, 62- *Concurrent Pos:* ed, J Optical Soc Am, 69- *Mem:* AAAS; Inst Elec & Electronics Engrs; Optical Soc Am; Neth Phys Soc. *Res:* Wave propagation and multiple scattering (in random media). *Mailing Add:* David Sarnoff Res Ctr RCA Corp Princeton NJ 08540

DEWOLF, GORDON PARKER, JR, b Lowell, Mass, Aug 17, 27; m 55. TAXONOMIC BOTANY. *Educ:* Univ Mass, BSc, 50; Tulane Univ, MSc, 52; Univ Malaya, MSc, 54; Cambridge Univ, PhD, 59. *Prof Exp:* Asst bot, Tulane Univ, 50-52; asst, Bailey Hortorium, Cornell Univ, 53-54, res assoc, 54-56; sr sci officer, Royal Bot Gardens, Eng, 59-61; assoc prof bot, Ga Southern Col, 61-64, prof, 64-67, actg head dept biol, 66-67; hort taxonomist, Arnold Arboretum, Harvard Univ, 67-70, horticulturist, 70-75; COORDR, HORT PROG, MASS BAY COMMUNITY COL, 76- *Concurrent Pos:* Hort consult, Horticulture Magazine. *Mem:* Int Asn Plant Taxonomists. *Res:* Ficus of Africa and America; taxonomy of cultivated plants. *Mailing Add:* Arnold Arboretum Arborway Jamica Plain MA 02021

DEWOLF, JOHN T, b Oakland, Calif, Jan 12, 43; m 68; c 2. STRUCTURAL ANALYSIS, STRUCTURAL DESIGN. *Educ:* Univ Hawaii, BSCE, 66; Cornell Univ, ME, 67, PhD(struct eng), 73. *Prof Exp:* Struct engr, Albert Kahn Assoc, Detroit, 67-69; ASSOC PROF CIVIL ENG, UNIV CONN, 73- *Concurrent Pos:* Acad vis, Imp Col, London, 79. *Mem:* Am Soc Civil Engrs; Am Concrete Inst. *Res:* Structural engineering and applied mechanics, with major emphasis on application to structural design. *Mailing Add:* Dept Civil Eng Univ Conn Box U-37 Storrs CT 06268

DEWOLFE, BARBARA BLANCHARD OAKESON, b San Francisco, Calif, May 14, 12; m 50, 60. VERTEBRATE ZOOLOGY. *Educ:* Univ Calif, AB, 33, PhD(zool), 38. *Prof Exp:* Asst zool, Univ Calif, 33-35, 36-37; Palmer fel, Wellesley Col, 38-39; instr, Placer Jr Col, 39-42; instr zool, Col Agr & jr zoologist, Exp Sta, Univ Calif, 42-43; instr zool, Smith Col, 43-45; lectr, 46, from asst prof to prof, 46-77, EMER PROF ZOOL, UNIV CALIF, SANTA BARBARA, 77- *Mem:* Cooper Ornith Soc; fel Am Ornith Union. *Res:* Environment, annual cycle and migration in white-crowned sparrows; vertebrate cycles and microclimates; song dialects. *Mailing Add:* Dept of Biol Sci Univ of Calif Santa Barbara CA 93106

DEWS, EDMUND, b Medford, Ore, Oct 1, 21; m 53, 59; c 4. ATMOSPHERIC CHEMISTRY, ATMOSPHERIC PHYSICS. *Educ:* Stanford Univ, BA, 43; Univ Wash, dipl, 44; Univ Calif, Los Angeles, MA, 47; Oxford Univ, BA, 51, MA, 54; Air War Col, dipl, 70. *Prof Exp:* Chief air weather serv upper air forecast sect, Oper Crossroads, Kwajalein-Bikini, 46; instr math & physics, Southern Ore State Col, 46; res meteorologist, Air Force Cambridge Res Ctr, 55-56, br chief & aeronaut res adminstr geophys, 57-58; vpres & managing ed, Pergamon Press, Inc, 59-60; asst head, 64-66, MEM ECON DEPT, RAND CORP, 60- *Concurrent Pos:* Mem, Secy of Air Force's Spec Study Group on Air Power in Southeast Asia, 67-68. *Res:* Hurricane meteorology, dynamics of vertical motions, political economy of research and development; research and development organization and decision making; history of science; information storage and retrieval; military systems analysis; tactical air warfare. *Mailing Add:* Rand Corp 1700 Main St Santa Monica CA 90406

DEWS, PETER BOOTH, b Ossett, Eng, Sept 11, 22; nat US; m 49; c 4. PSYCHOBIOLOGY. *Educ:* Univ Leeds, MB, ChB, 44; Univ Minn, PhD(physiol), 52. *Hon Degrees:* MA, Harvard Univ, 59. *Prof Exp:* Lectr pharmacol, Univ Leeds, 46-47; Wellcome res fel, Wellcome Res Lab, 48-49; Mayo Found fel, Univ Minn, 50-51, res assoc biomet, Mayo Found, 52; from instr to assoc prof pharmacol, 53-62, STANLEY COBB PROF PSYCHIAT & PSYCHOBIOL, HARVARD MED SCH, 62- *Mem:* Am Soc Pharmacol; Am Physiol Soc; Brit Pharmacol Soc; Physiol Soc Gt Brit; AAAS. *Res:* Pharmacology of the central nervous system; psychobiology. *Mailing Add:* 25 Shattuck St Boston MA 02115

DEWSBURY, DONALD ALLEN, b Brooklyn, NY, Aug 11, 39; m 63; c 2. ANIMAL BEHAVIOR. *Educ:* Bucknell Univ, AB, 61; Univ Mich, PhD(psychol) 65. *Prof Exp:* Fel psychol, Univ Calif, Berkeley, 65-66; from asst prof to assoc prof, 66-73, PROF PSYCHOL, CTR NEUROBIOL SCI, UNIV FLA, 73- *Mem:* Animal Behav Soc (treas, 73-78, pres, 76-80); fel Am Psychol Asn; Am Soc Zoologists; Psychonomic Soc; Sigma Xi. *Res:* Evolution and adaptive significance of animal behavior; evolution of reproduction behavior in muroid rodents and the role of behavior in reproductive success. *Mailing Add:* Dept Psychol Univ Fla Gainesville FL 32611

DEWYS, WILLIAM DALE, b Zeeland, Mich, Sept 14, 39; m 61; c 3. ONCOLOGY, INTERNAL MEDICINE. *Educ:* Calvin Col, BS, 60; Univ Mich, MD, 64. *Prof Exp:* Res assoc, Nat Cancer Inst, 66-68; resident & fel, Univ Rochester, 68-71, asst prof, 71-73; assoc prof, Sch Med, Northwestern Univ, 73-78, prof med, 78-79, chief, Med Oncol Sect, 73-79; HEAD, NUTRIT SECT & CHIEF CLIN INVEST BR, NAT CANCER INST, 80- *Concurrent Pos:* Am Cancer Soc clin fel, 70-71 & jr fac clin fel, 71-73; assoc physician, Strong Mem Hosp, 71-73; asst attend physician, Rochester Gen Hosp, 71-73; attend staff physician, Northwestern Mem Hosp, 73-79 & Vet Admin Res Hosp, 73-79; affil staff physician, Evanston Hosp, 73-79; chmn clin task force progs, Ill Cancer Coun, 75-79; mem cancer clin invest rev comt, Nat Cancer Inst, 76-80. *Mem:* Am Asn Cancer Res; Am Fedn Clin Res; Am Soc Clin Oncol. *Res:* Adverse systemic effects of cancer; experimental chemotherapy of cancer. *Mailing Add:* Clin Invest Br Landow Bldg Rm 4A04 Nat Cancer Inst Bethesda MD 20850

DEXTER, DAVID LAWRENCE, theoretical solid state physics, deceased

DEXTER, DEBORAH MARY, b Oakland, Calif, Sept 28, 38. MARINE ZOOLOGY, ECOLOGY. *Educ:* Stanford Univ, BA, 60, MA, 62; Univ NC, Chapel Hill, PhD(zool), 67. *Prof Exp:* From asst prof to assoc prof, 67-73, PROF ZOOL, SAN DIEGO STATE UNIV, 73- *Mem:* Am Soc Limnol & Oceanog; Ecol Soc Am. *Res:* Marine invertebrate zoology and ecology; population ecology of benthic invertebrates; sandy beach ecology. *Mailing Add:* Dept of Zool San Diego State Univ San Diego CA 92182

DEXTER, MORRIS W, medicine, see previous edition

DEXTER, RALPH WARREN, b Gloucester, Mass, Apr 7, 12; m 38; c 2. ECOLOGY, HISTORY OF BIOLOGY. *Educ:* Mass State Col, BS, 34; Univ Ill, PhD(ecol), 38. *Prof Exp:* Asst zool, Univ Ill, 34-37; from instr to assoc prof, 37-48, PROF BIOL, KENT STATE UNIV, 48- *Concurrent Pos:* Res contract, US AEC, 56-62; vis prof, Stone Lab, Ohio State Univ, 53-55, 67-69 & 71. *Mem:* Life mem Marine Biol Asn India; Life mem Ecol Soc Am; Am Malacol Union (vpres, 64-65 & pres, 65-66); Am Ornith Union; Wilson Ornith Soc. *Res:* Ecology of marine communities, mollusca and crustacea (anostracan phyllopods) ; life history of chimney swift; history of nineteenth century American naturalists; studies of bird-banding; history of biology. *Mailing Add:* 1228 Fairview Dr Kent OH 44240

DEXTER, RICHARD JOHN, physics, see previous edition

DEXTER, RICHARD NEWMAN, b Port Huron, Mich, Sept 2, 33; m 61; c 2. INTERNAL MEDICINE. *Educ:* Harvard Univ, AB, 55; MD, Cornell Univ, 59; Am Bd Internal Med, dipl, 67, 74 & 80, cert endocrinol & metab, 73. *Prof Exp:* From intern to resident internal med, Univ Minn Hosps, 59-62; res assoc, NIH, Bethesda, 62-64; resident, Peter Bent Brigham Hosp, Boston, 64-65; fel endocrinol & instr med, Sch Med, Vanderbilt Univ, 65-67; from asst prof to assoc prof, 67-73, PROF MED, SCH MED, IND UNIV, INDIANAPOLIS, 73-, ASST DEAN & DIR, DIV CONTINUING MED EDUC, 81- *Mem:* Endocrine Soc; fel Am Col Physicians; Am Fedn Clin Res. *Res:* Endocrinology; metabolism. *Mailing Add:* Dept of Med Ind Univ Med Ctr Indianapolis IN 46202

DEXTER, RICHARD NORMAN, b Ashland, Wis, Nov 22, 27; m 58; c 4. SOLID STATE PHYSICS. *Educ:* Mich State Univ, BS, 49; Univ Wis, MS, 51, PhD(physics), 55. *Prof Exp:* Staff microwave res, Lincoln Lab, Mass Inst Technol, 52-55, solid state physics, 53-55; asst from asst prof to assoc prof, 55-61, PROF PHYSICS, UNIV WIS-MADISON, 61- *Concurrent Pos:* Alfred P Sloan Found fel, 55-59. *Mem:* AAAS; fel Am Phys Soc. *Res:* Experimental solid state physics; energy band structure determinations; optical properties in vacuum ultraviolet. *Mailing Add:* Dept of Physics Sterling Hall Univ of Wis Madison WI 53706

DEXTER, STEPHEN C, b East Orange, NJ, Sept 18, 42; m 71; c 2. MATERIALS SCIENCE, CORROSION. *Educ:* Univ Del, BS, 65, MAS, 68, PhD(metall), 71. *Prof Exp:* Investr, Woods Hole Oceanog Inst, 71-72, asst scientist corrosion & fouling, 72-75; asst prof, 76-80, ASSOC PROF OCEANOG ENG, UNIV DEL, 81- *Concurrent Pos:* Res grants, Off Sea Grant, Nat Oceanic Atmospheric Admin, 71-76, 80-, Nat Data Buoy Off, 72-74, Alcoa Found, 73-74, Dept Energy, 76-78 & Off Naval Res, 77- *Mem:* Am Soc Metals; Nat Asn Corrosion Engrs. *Res:* Interactions of structural materials with seawater; electrochemical corrosion; surface chemistry of microbiological fouling; fouling. *Mailing Add:* Col Marine Studies Univ Del LeWes DE 19958

DEXTER, THEODORE HENRY, b Preston, Cuba, June 1, 23; US citizen; m 52; c 3. INDUSTRIAL INORGANIC CHEMICALS, ELECTROCHEMICALS. *Educ:* Tulane Univ, BS, 44, MS, 47; Univ Ill, PhD(chem), 50. *Prof Exp:* Asst chem, Tulane Univ, 43-44; chemist, E I du Pont de Nemours & Co, 44-45; asst chem, Tulane Univ, 46-47; Gen Aniline asst, Illinois, 47-49; chief inorg res sect, Chem Div, Olin Mathieson prog leader res & develop mineral prods, 75-76, SR RES CHEMIST, RES & DEVELOP ELECTROCHEM, HOOKER CHEM & PLASTICS CORP, 76- *Mem:* Am Chem Soc; Electrochem Soc; Sigma Xi. *Res:* Inorganic specialty and heavy chemicals; applications to detergents, pulp, paper textiles, leather; fused salts; coordination compounds; chemistry of non-metallic elements, especially nitrogen, phosphorus, oxygen, sulfur, fluorine and chlorine. *Mailing Add:* 850 Hillside Dr Lewiston NY 14092

DEY, ABHIJIT, b Patna, India, Oct 2, 45. GEOPHYSICS. *Educ:* Indian Inst Technol, Kharagpur, BSc Hons, 65, MSc, 67; Univ Calif, Berkeley, PhD(eng geosci), 72. *Prof Exp:* Assoc res geophysicist, Univ Calif, Berkeley, 72-77; SR GEOPHYSICIST GEOTHERMAL DIV, CHEVRON RESOURCES CO, 77- *Concurrent Pos:* Consult var mining co & geotech eng co, 72-77. *Mem:* Soc Explor Geophysicists; Europ Asn Explor Geophysicists; AAAS; Australian Soc Explor Geophysicists. *Res:* Interpretation of electrical, electromagnetic, seismic and pot field data; mineral and geothermal exploration; quantitative numerical modelling of two and three-dimensional geological structures. *Mailing Add:* Chevron Resources Co PO Box 3722 San Francisco CA 94111

DEY, SUDHANSU KUMAR, b Calcutta, India, Nov 8, 44; m 70; c 1. REPRODUCTIVE BIOLOGY, ENDOCRINOLOGY. *Educ:* Univ Calcutta, BSc, 65, MSc, 67, PhD(physiol), 72. *Prof Exp:* Lectr physiol, City Col Calcutta, 70-72; Ford Found fel reproductive biol, 73-75, res assoc, 75-77, asst prof gynec & obstet, 77-81, ASST PROF PHYSIOL, KANS UNIV MED CTR, 79-, ASSOC PROF GYNEC & OBSTET, 81- *Concurrent Pos:* Sr res fel reproductive biol, Dept Physiol, Univ Calcutta, 72. *Mem:* Brit Soc Study Fertil; Soc Study Reproduction; Am Physiol Soc. *Res:* Physiology and metabolism of preimplantation and early postimplantation mammalian embryos; physiology and mechanism of ovum implantation. *Mailing Add:* Dept Gynec & Obstet Univ Kans Med Ctr Kansas City KS 66103

DEYOE, CHARLES W, b Two Buttes, Colo, Mar 12, 33; m 56; c 5. BIOCHEMISTRY, NUTRITION. *Educ:* Kans State Univ, BS, 55; Tex A&M Univ, MS, 57, PhD(biochem), 59. *Prof Exp:* Asst prof biochem & poultry nutrit, Tex A&M Univ, 60-62; from asst prof to prof feed technol, 62-68, PROF GRAIN SCI, KANS STATE UNIV, 68-, HEAD DEPT GRAIN SCI & INDUST & DIR, FOOD & FEED GRAIN INST, 77- *Concurrent Pos:* Feed technol res scientist, Agr Exp Sta, Kans State Univ, 75-; dir, Int Grain Prog, 80. *Mem:* Am Chem Soc; Am Soc Animal Sci; Poultry Sci Asn; Am Asn Cereal Chemists; Inst Food Technologists. *Res:* Nutrition of farm animals and biochemistry related to animal processes; feed technology and chemical relationships between foodstuffs and nutritive values. *Mailing Add:* Dept of Grain Sci & Indust Kans State Univ Manhattan KS 66506

DE YOUNG, DAVID SPENCER, b Colorado Springs, Colo, Nov 29, 40. THEORETICAL ASTROPHYSICS. *Educ:* Univ Colo, BA, 62; Cornell Univ, PhD(physics). 67. *Prof Exp:* Res scientist, Los Alamos Sci Lab, 67-69; scientist, Nat Radio Astron Observ, 69-80; ASTRONOMER, KITT PEAK NAT OBSERV, 80- *Concurrent Pos:* Consult, Los Alamos Sci Lab, 70-74; mem exec comt, Bd Trustees, Aspen Ctr Physics, 74-80, mem adv bd, 80-; chmn, Radio Astron Exp Selection Panel, 79- *Mem:* Int Astron Union; Am Astron Soc; Am Phys Soc; Int Union Radio Sci. *Res:* Origin and evolution of extended extragalactic radio sources; physics of galactic nuclei and quasi-stellar objects; evolution of galaxies and galaxy clusters; solar flares and interplanetary disturbances. *Mailing Add:* Kitt Peak Nat Observ 950 N Cherry Ave Tucson AZ 85726

DE YOUNG, DONALD BOUWMAN, b Grand Rapids, Mich, July 29, 44; m 66; c 3. SOLID STATE SCIENCE. *Educ:* Mich Technol Univ, BS, 66, MS, 68; Iowa State Univ, PhD(physics), 72. *Prof Exp:* Teaching asst physics, Mich Technol Univ, Houghton, 66-68; res worker, Inst Atomic Res, AEC, Ames, Iowa, 68-72; ASSOC PROF PHYSICS, GRACE COL, WINONA LAKE, IND, 72- *Mem:* Sigma Xi; Am Asn Physics Teachers; Am Phys Soc. *Res:* Mossbauer effect studies of transition metal borides. *Mailing Add:* Physics Dept Grace Col Winona Lake IN 46590

DEYOUNG, EDWIN LAWSON, b Milwaukee, Wis, Jan 14, 29; m 56. ORGANOMETALLIC CHEMISTRY. *Educ:* Univ Louisville, BS, 52, MS, 53; Univ Ill, PhD(org chem), 56. *Prof Exp:* Res chemist, Reynolds Metals Co, Ky, 52-53, Minn Mining & Mfg Co, 54, Shell Develop Co, Colo, 55, Whiting Res Labs, Standard Oil Co Ind, 56-60, R B & P Chem Co, Wis, 60-62 & Universal Oil Prod Co, Des Plaines, 62-68; chmn, Dept Phys Sci, 68-80, PROF CHEM, CHICAGO CITY COL, LOOP BR, 68- *Mem:* Am Inst Chem; Sigma Xi. *Res:* Metal organic compounds; synthesis and reactions; pi-complexes and metal aromatic compounds. *Mailing Add:* Dept of Phys Sci Chicago City Col Loop Br Chicago IL 60601

DEYOUNG, JACOB J, b Grand Rapids, Mich, May 14, 26; m 57; c 4. ORGANIC CHEMISTRY. *Educ:* Hope Col, AB, 50; Wayne State Univ, MS, 52, PhD, 58. *Prof Exp:* Chemist, Merck Chem Co, 52-53; from asst prof to assoc prof, 57-77, PROF CHEM, ALMA COL, 77- *Mem:* Am Chem Soc. *Res:* Organic synthesis; isolation and synthesis of natural products from plants. *Mailing Add:* Dept of Chem Alma Col Alma MI 48801

DEYOUNG, JOYCE LEWIS, pharmaceutics, see previous edition

DE YOUNG, LAWRENCE MARK, skin biology, cancer, see previous edition

DE YOUNG, MARVIN, b Grand Rapids, Mich, Nov 23, 26; m 48; c 7. PHYSICS. *Educ:* Calvin Col, AB, 48; Univ SDak, MA, 61; Univ of Pac, PhD(chem), 65. *Prof Exp:* Teacher high sch, 48-58; instr chem, 58-61, from asst prof to assoc prof chem & physics, 61-70, PROF PHYSICS, DORDT COL, 70-, DIR AUXILIARY SERV, 77- *Mem:* Nat Sci Teachers Asn. *Mailing Add:* Dept of Physics Dordt Col Sioux Center IA 51250

DEYRUP, JAMES ALDEN, b Englewood, NJ, Oct 13, 36; m 61; c 1. ORGANIC CHEMISTRY. *Educ:* Swarthmore Col, BA, 57; Univ Ill, PhD(org chem), 61. *Prof Exp:* NSF fel, Univ Zurich, 61-62; instr chem, Harvard Univ, 62-65; from asst prof to assoc prof chem, 65-74, asst dean preprof educ, 71-74, asst dean, Cols Med & Dent, 74-80, PROF CHEM, UNIV FLA, 74- *Res:* Chemistry of heterocyclic compounds including macromolecular heterocyclic catalysis. *Mailing Add:* Dept of Chem Univ of Fla Gainesville FL 32611

DEYRUP, MARK AMIDON, b New York, NY, Apr 12, 47; m 73; c 3. ENTOMOLOGY. *Educ:* Cornell Univ, BS, 68; Univ Wash, MS, 73, PhD(entom), 76. *Prof Exp:* Volunteer agr develop, US Peace Corps, 68-70; grad asst, Tundra Biome, Univ Alaska, 71; res asst, Coniferous Biome, Univ Wash, 72-76, actg asst prof, 76-77; ASST PROF ENTOM, PURDUE UNIV, 77- *Mem:* Am Entom Soc; Entom Soc Am; Coleopterists Soc. *Res:* Taxonomy and ecology of insects, with special reference to insects inhabiting dead trees. *Mailing Add:* Dept of Entom Purdue Univ West Lafayette IN 47907

DEYRUP-OLSEN, INGRITH JOHNSON, b Nyack, NY, Dec 22, 19; m 62. ZOOLOGY. *Educ:* Columbia Univ, AB, 40, PhD(physiol), 44. *Prof Exp:* Instr physiol, Col Physicians & Surgeons, Columbia Univ, 42-47, lectr zool, Barnard Col, 47, from asst prof to prof, 47-64; res prof, 64-69, PROF ZOOL, UNIV WASH, 69- *Concurrent Pos:* Guggenheim fel, 53-54; Fulbright fel Denmark, 53-54. *Mem:* AAAS; Soc Gen Physiol; Am Soc Zool; Am Physiol Soc; NY Acad Sci. *Res:* Physiology; circulation; kidney; circulatory changes following subcutaneous injection of histamine in dogs; water and electrolyte exchange of tissue slices; fluid exchange in molluscs. *Mailing Add:* Dept of Zool Univ of Wash Seattle WA 98195

DEYSACH, LAWRENCE GEORGE, b Milwaukee, Wis, July 9, 36; m 66. MATHEMATICAL BIOLOGY. *Educ:* Marquette Univ, BS, 57; Harvard Univ, AM, 63. *Prof Exp:* Lectr math biol, Univ Chicago, 67-69; med statistician, 69-80, SR BIOSTATISTICIAN, G D SEARLE & CO, SKOKIE, 80- *Mem:* Am Statist Asn; Biomet Soc; Sigma Xi. *Res:* Topological dynamics; mathematical ecology and biophysics; experimental design of clinical trials; pharmacokinetics; stochastic processes. *Mailing Add:* 944 Wesley Evanston IL 60202

DE ZAFRA, ROBERT LEE, b White Plains, NY, Feb 15, 32; m. EXPERIMENTAL ATOMIC PHYSICS, ATOMOSPHERIC CHEMISTRY. *Educ:* Princeton Univ, AB, 54; Univ Md, PhD(physics), 58. *Prof Exp:* Res asst physics, Princeton Univ, 55; res asst, Univ Md, 57-58; instr, Univ Pa, 58-61; asst prof, 61-64, ASSOC PROF PHYSICS, STATE UNIV NY STONY BROOK, 64- *Concurrent Pos:* Nat Res Coun sr fel, NASA, 70-71. *Mem:* Am Phys Soc; AAAS. *Res:* Atomic and molecular physics; upper atmospheric research; radio astronomy. *Mailing Add:* Dept of Physics State Univ of NY Stony Brook NY 11790

DE ZEEUW, CARL HENRI, b East Lansing, Mich, Dec 6, 12; m 39; c 5. WOOD TECHNOLOGY, MECHANICS. *Educ:* Mich State Col, BA, 34, BS, 37; State Univ NY Col Forestry, Syracuse Univ, MS, 39, PhD(wood anat), 49. *Prof Exp:* From instr to assoc prof wood technol, 47-61, PROF WOOD PROD ENG, STATE UNIV NY COL ENVIRON SCI & FORESTRY, 61- *Concurrent Pos:* Consult, Col Forestry, Univ Philippines, State Univ NY & US Int Coop Admin, 59-61, Food , Agr Orgn, Philippines, 66, Venezuela, 68, Arg, 71, Brazil, 77 & Burma, 80. *Mem:* Forest Prod Res Soc; Am Soc Testing & Mat; Int Asn Wood Anat; Soc Wood Sci & Technol; fel Int Acad Wood Sci. *Res:* Interrelationship of gross wood anatomy, ultra structure and composition of the woody cell wall and the physical properties of wood; descriptive anatomy of tropical woods. *Mailing Add:* 319 E Genesee Fayetteville NY 13066

DE ZEEUW, JOHN ROBERT, b Brooklyn, NY, Apr 6, 28; m 50; c 2. BIOCHEMISTRY. *Educ:* Cornell Univ, BS, 49, PhD(biochem), 54. *Prof Exp:* Chemist, Chas Pfizer & Co, Inc, 49-50; asst, Cornell Univ, 50-53; biochemist, 54-64, mgr microbiol res, 64-67, asst dir microbiol res, 67-72, RES ADV, PFIZER, INC, 72- *Mem:* Genetics Soc Am; Am Soc Microbiol. *Res:* Microbial genetics. *Mailing Add:* Montauk Ave Stonington CT 06378

DEZELSKY, THOMAS LEROY, b Saginaw, Mich, Mar 3, 34; m 71; c 2. HEALTH SCIENCE. *Educ:* Cent Mich Univ, BS, 56; Univ Mich, MA, 59; Ind Univ, HSD, 66. *Prof Exp:* Teacher, Copemish High Sch, Mich, 56-57 & Mt Pleasant Jr High, Mich, 57-61; asst prof health & phys educ, Wis State Univ-Oshkosh, 61-66; assoc prof, Brigham Young Univ, 66-68; ASSOC PROF HEALTH SCI, ARIZ STATE UNIV, TEMPE, 68- *Mem:* Am Sch Health Asn; Am Pub Health Asn. *Res:* Suicide behavior; drug and substance abuse; mental health problems of aged populations. *Mailing Add:* 1778 W Mesquite St Chandler AZ 85224

DEZENBERG, GEORGE JOHN, b Tientsin, China, Jan 12, 35; US citizen; m 60; c 4. ELECTRICAL ENGINEERING. *Educ:* Auburn Univ, BEE, 60; Univ Ark, MS, 62; Ga Inst Technol, PhD(elec eng), 66. *Prof Exp:* RES ELECTRONIC ENGR, PHYS SCI LAB, US ARMY MISSILE COMMAND, 65- *Mem:* Inst Elec & Electronic Engrs; Optical Soc Am. *Res:* Carbon dioxide laser research, including Q-switching, mode locking, multipath, and mode control techniques. *Mailing Add:* 910 San Ramon Ave Huntsville AL 35802

DE ZOETEN, GUSTAAF A, b Tjepoe, Indonesia, July 5, 34; m 61; c 3. PLANT PATHOLOGY, PLANT VIROLOGY. *Educ:* Univ Wageningen, MSc, 60; Univ Calif, Davis, PhD(plant path), 65. *Prof Exp:* Tech asst plant physiol, Western Prov Res Sta, SAfrica, 57-58; lab technician plant path, Univ Calif, Davis, 62 & 64-65, asst res plant pathologist, Univ Calif, Berkeley, 65-67; asst prof, 67-70, assoc prof, 70-74, PROF PLANT PATH, UNIV WIS-MADISON, 74- *Concurrent Pos:* Vis prof, Dept Plant Pathol, Univ Calif, Davis, 78-79. *Mem:* Am Phytopath Soc; Royal Soc Agr Sci Neth. *Res:* Physiology and cytology of virus host relationships; electron microscopy; plant virus replication. *Mailing Add:* 3570 Talley Ho Lane Madison WI 53705

DHALIWAL, AMRIK S, b Punjab, India, Nov 17, 34; m 62; c 2. HORTICULTURE, VIROLOGY. *Educ:* Punjab Univ, India, BSc, 55; Utah State Univ, MSc, 59, PhD(biol), 62. *Prof Exp:* Res assoc plant virol, Utah State Univ, 62-65, asst prof bot, 65-66; asst prof, 66-72, assoc prof, 72-75, PROF BIOL, LOYOLA UNIV CHICAGO, 75- *Mem:* AAAS; Am Inst Biol Sci; Am Physiol Soc. *Res:* Cytogenetics and plant breeding of field and horticultural crops; post harvest physiology, pathology and biochemistry and in vitro synthesis of plant viruses. *Mailing Add:* Dept of Biol Loyola Univ 6525 N Sheridan Rd Chicago IL 60626

DHALIWAL, RANJIT S, b Bilaspur, India, June 21, 30; m 58; c 1. APPLIED MATHEMATICS. *Educ:* Punjab Univ, India, BA, 51; Indian Inst Technol, Kharagpur, PhD(appl math), 60. *Prof Exp:* Lectr math, Guru Nanak Col Dabwali, Punjab, India, 55-56, lectr math, Guru Nanak Eng Col, Ludhiana, 56-61; lectr math, Indian Inst Technol, New Delhi, 61-63, asst prof, 63-66; assoc prof, 66-71, PROF MATH, UNIV CALGARY, 71- *Concurrent Pos:* Visitor, Imp Col, Univ London, 64-65; vis prof, City Univ London & sr res assoc, Glasgow Univ, 71-72. *Mem:* Am Acad Mech; Am Math Soc; Soc Indust & Appl Math; Can Math Cong; Indian Math Soc. *Res:* Theory of plates; elastodynamics; viscoelasticity; thermoelasticity. *Mailing Add:* Dept of Math Univ of Calgary Calgary Can

DHALLA, NARANJAN SINGH, b Punjab, India, Oct 10, 36. PHYSIOLOGY, PHARMACOLOGY. *Educ:* Univ Pa, MS, 63; Univ Pittsburgh, PhD(pharmacol), 65; Inst Chem, India, FIC. *Prof Exp:* Res assoc biochem, Sch Med, St Louis Univ, 66, asst prof pharmacol, 66-68; from asst prof to assoc prof, 68-74, PROF PHYSIOL, FAC MED, UNIV MAN, 74- *Concurrent Pos:* Secy gen, Int Soc Heart Res. *Mem:* Am Soc Pharmacol & Exp Therapeut; Am Physiol Soc; Can Physiol Soc; Pharmacol Soc Can; fel Inst Chem India. *Res:* Pathophysiology of heart, muscle contraction, membrane transport and autonomic nervous system. *Mailing Add:* Dept of Physiol Univ of Man Fac of Med Winnipeg Can

DHAMI, KEWAL SINGH, b Punjab, India, Jan 10, 33; US citizen; m 59; c 1. ORGANIC CHEMISTRY, POLYMER CHEMISTRY. *Educ:* Panjab Univ, India, BSc, 54, MSc, 55; Univ Western Ont, PhD(org chem), 64. *Prof Exp:* US Air Force assoc chem, Ohio State Univ, 64-65; sr res chemist, Res & Develop Div, Polymer Corp Ltd, Ont, 65-69; SR RES CHEMIST, ITT WIRE & CABLE DIV, INT TEL & TEL CORP, 69- *Mem:* Am Chem Soc; fel The Chem Soc; Soc Plastic Engrs. *Res:* C13 nuclear magnetic resonance studies of organic compounds; preparation and properties of new polymers; mechanical and physical properties of polymers; degradation of polymeric compounds; synthesis of new sulfur compounds; irradiation crosslinking of polymers; preparation of new high temperature radiation sensitive crosslinking agents. *Mailing Add:* Res & Develop Div ITT Surprenant Int Tel & Tel Corp Clinton MA 01510

DHANAK, AMRITLAL M(AGANLAL), b Bhavnagar, India, July 13, 25; nat US; m 54; c 3. MECHANICAL ENGINEERING, SOLAR ENERGY. *Educ:* Univ Calif, MS, 51, PhD(mech eng), 56. *Prof Exp:* Res engr, Univ Calif, 52-56; proj engr, Gen Elec Co, 56-58; assoc prof, Rensselaer Polytech Inst, 58-61; PROF MECH ENG, MICH STATE UNIV, 61- *Concurrent Pos:* Sr staff scientist & consult, Avco Mfg Corp, 59-62. *Mem:* Sigma Xi; Am Soc Mech Engrs (chmn, Technol & Soc Div, 78-79); Int Solar Energy Soc. *Res:* Heat transfer; thermodynamics and fluid dynamics with specializations in solar energy. *Mailing Add:* Dept of Mech Eng Mich State Univ East Lansing MI 48823

DHAR, SACHIDULAL, b Muktagachha, Bangladesh, July 16, 43. HIGH ENERGY PHYSICS, SOFTWARE SYSTEMS DESIGN. *Educ:* Univ Dacca, BSc, 64, MSc, 65; Duke Univ, PhD(physics), 74. *Prof Exp:* Sci officer physics, Pakistan Atomic Energy Comn, 65-67; lectr & res assoc, State Univ NY. Albany, 74-75; res assoc physics, Univ Mass, Amherst, 75-79; software engr, Raytheon Co, Wayland, 80-81; MEM TECH STAFF, MITRE CORP, BEDFORD, 81- *Res:* Experimental and phenomenological study of elementary particle interactions at high energies. *Mailing Add:* Mitre Corp Mail Stop E200 PO Box 208 Bedford MA 01730

DHESI, NAZAR SINGH, b Dhesian Kahna, India, Sept 2, 23; Can citizen; m 55; c 2. SEED TESTING. *Educ:* Punjab Univ-Lahore, BSc, 45; Utah State Univ, MS, 50; Kans State Univ, PhD(agron), 52. *Prof Exp:* Asst veg botanist plant breeding, Punjab Agr Dept, 55-58, seed testing officer, 58-60, veg botanist plant breeding, 60-64, dep dir agr, exten, 64-65; biologist seed testing, Agr Can, 65-71, BIOLOGIST METHOD DEVELOP SEED TESTING, AGR CAN, 72- *Concurrent Pos:* Vis fel, Ohio State Univ, 59; assoc grad fac dept crop sci, Guelph Univ, Ont, 78-79. *Mem:* Am Soc Agron; Can Seed Grower's Asn. *Res:* Development of laboratory test methods for the identification of crop cultivars required for monitoring the genetic purity of seed lots offered for sale in Canada or produced for export. *Mailing Add:* Lab Serv Div Carling Ave Ottawa Can

DHILLON, BALBIR SINGH, b Jhaj, India, Aug 5, 47; m 79. RELIABILITY ENGINEERING, INDUSTRIAL ENGINEERING. *Educ:* Univ Wales, BSc, 72, MSc, 73; Univ Windsor, PhD(indust eng), 75. *Prof Exp:* Fel reliability eng, Univ Windsor, 75-76; reliability engr, C A E Electronics Ltd, 76-77; tech supvr reliability eng, Ont Hydro, 77-79; ASST PROF, UNIV OTTAWA, 80- *Concurrent Pos:* Adv ed, Microelectronic & Reliability, 77-; referee, Inst Elec & Electronics Engrs on Reliability, 76- & Can Univs res grants comt, Nat Res Coun Can, 78-; organizer, Ann Modeling & Simulation Conf, Univ Pittsburgh, 78- *Res:* Reliability, especially common cause failures; reliability of multi state devices and reliability modeling. *Mailing Add:* Dept Mech Eng Univ Ottawa Ottawa ON K1N 6N5 Can

DHINDSA, DHARAM SINGH, b Nov 25, 34; m 61; c 3. REPRODUCTIVE ENDOCRINOLOGY, CARDIOLOGY. *Educ:* Punjab Univ, DVM, 56; Mont State Univ, MS, 63; Univ Ill, Urbana, PhD(physiol), 67. *Prof Exp:* Vet asst surgeon, Punjab State Govt, India, 56-57; lectr physiol, Punjab Vet Col, 57-58, in-chg rabies vaccine prep, 58-59, lectr parasitol, 59-61; res asst animal sci, Mont State Univ, 61-63; res asst, Univ Ill, 63-66, res assoc, Col Vet Med, 67; res fel, Heart Res Lab, Sch Med, Univ Ore, 67-72, res assoc, Dept Med, 71-74, instr, Health Sci Ctr, 74-75; EXEC SECY, REPRODUCTIVE BIOL, NIH, 75- *Concurrent Pos:* Chmn, Dept Animal Sci, Ore Zool Res Ctr, 71-75. *Mem:* AAAS; Soc Study Reproduction; Am Physiol Soc; Int Primatological Soc; Am Soc Animal Sci. *Res:* Physiology, especially reproductive endocrinology, cardiovascular pre- and postnatal; reproductive biology. *Mailing Add:* Div of Res Grant NIH Westwood Bldg Bethesda MD 20014

DHINDSA, K S, b India, Jan 24, 32; Can citizen; m 60. CELL BIOLOGY. *Educ:* Panjab Univ, India, BSc, 51, Hons, 53, MSc, 54. Univ Helsinki, PhD(zool), 70. *Prof Exp:* Demonstr zool, Panjab Univ, 53-56, lectr, Col Faridkot, 55-61, sr lectr biol, Dairy Sci Col, 61-62; asst zool, Univ Calif, Los Angeles, 62-63; asst biol, Inst Biol Res, Culver City, Calif, 63-65; asst prof zool, Panjab Agr Univ India, 65-66; asst prof, 67-74, ASSOC PROF BIOL, LOYOLA CAMPUS, CONCORDIA UNIV, 73- *Concurrent Pos:* Res grant, Loyola Col Montreal, 69; Nat Res Coun Can res grants, 69 & 71-72. *Mem:* AAAS; fel Royal Micros Soc; Am Soc Zoologists; Can Soc Cell Biol. *Res:* Effect of psychotherapeutic drugs and food additives on brain and endocrine metabolism; RNA synthesis in brain and other tissues in mammals using histochemical and radiographic methods. *Mailing Add:* Dept Biol Loyola Campus Concordia Univ 7141 Sherbrooke St W Montreal PQ H4B 1R6 Can

DHIR, SURENDRA KUMAR, b Sonekatch, India, Aug 9, 37; m 65; c 2. ENGINEERING MECHANICS, PHYSICS. *Educ:* Birla Inst Technol & Sci, Ranchi, India, BS, 60; Munich Tech Univ, Dr Ing, 64. *Prof Exp:* Design engr, Allgemeine Elektricitätsgesellschaft, Frankfurt, 64-65; sr proj engr struct dept, 65-71, HEAD NUMERICAL STRUCT MECH BR, DAVID TAYLOR NAVAL SHIP RES & DEVELOP CTR, 71- *Mem:* Sigma Xi. *Res:* Theoretical and experimental mechanics; coherent optics; computer application in numerical mechanics. *Mailing Add:* David Taylor Naval Ship Res & Develop Ctr Bethesda MD 20084

DHIR, VIJAY KUMAR, b Giddarbaha, India, Apr 4, 43; m 73; c 2. ENGINEERING. *Educ:* Punjab Eng Col, BSc, 65; Indian Inst Technol, Kanpur, MTech, 68; Univ Ky, PhD(mech engr), 72. *Prof Exp:* Asst develop engr pump design, Jyoti Pumps, Ltd, 68-69; engr auto part design, TATA Eng & Locomotive Co, 69; res assoc & lectr, Univ Ky, 72-74; asst prof, 74-78, ASSOC PROF ENG, UNIV CALIF, LOS ANGELES, 78- *Concurrent Pos:* Res grants, US Nuclear Regulatory Comn, 76- & Elec Power Res Inst, 78- *Mem:* Am Soc Mech Engrs; Am Nuclear Soc; Am Inst Astronaut & Aeronaut; Sigma Xi. *Res:* Nuclear engineering; thermal and hydraulics of nuclear reactors and reactor safety; heat transfer during phase change; boiling and condensation, thermal and hydrodynamic instability. *Mailing Add:* 2445 22nd St Santa Monica CA 90405

DHOPESHWARKAR, GOVIND ATMARAM, b Dharwar, India, Dec 13, 24; nat US; m 52; c 2. NEUROCHEMISTRY. *Educ:* Univ Bombay, India, PhD(biochem), 54. *Prof Exp:* Res assoc chem, Columbia Univ, 57-59; res assoc biol chem, Univ Calif, Los Angeles, 59-62; sr sci officer, Radiation Med Ctr, Atomic Energy Estab Govt, India, Trombay, Bombay, 63-66; asst res biochemist, Lab Nuclear Med & Radiation Biol, 66-70, assoc res biochemist, 70-76, lectr nutrit, Dept Environ & Nutrit Sci, Sch Pub Health, 71-74, assoc prof, 74-76, RES BIOCHEMIST, LAB NUCLEAR MED & RADIATION BIOL, UNIV CALIF, LOS ANGELES, 76-, ADJ PROF NUTRIT, DEPT ENVIRON & NUTRIT SCI, SCH PUB HEALTH, 76- *Mem:* AAAS; Am Oil Chemists' Soc; Am Soc Biol Chemists; Am Soc Neurochem. *Res:* Metabolism of brain lipids; uptake of fatty acids and other lipids by the brain with reference to blood-brain-barrier; biosynthetic pathways of essential fatty acids in the brain. *Mailing Add:* Lab Nuclear Med & Radiation Biol Univ of Calif 900 Veteran Ave Los Angeles CA 90024

DHOPLE, ARVIND MADHAV, clinical biochemistry, microbial physiology, see previous edition

DHRUV, ROHINI ARVIND, b Bombay, Maharashtra, Mar 26, 50; m 74; c 1. BIOANALYTICAL RESEARCH. *Educ:* St Xavier's Col, Univ Bombay, BSc, 71; EStroudsburg State Col, Pa, Med, 73; Rutgers Univ, PhD(microbiol), 80. *Prof Exp:* Asst chem, E Stroudsburg State Col, 71-72; res intern immunol, Rutgers Univ, 72-73, teaching asst biol, 73-77; instr biol, Montclair State Col, 78; RES INVESTR BIOANALYTICAL RES & DEVELOP, E R SQUIBB & SONS, 78- *Mem:* Am Soc Microbiol. *Res:* Chemical and/or microbiological assays for the detection of different antibiotics in tissues, biological fluids, pharmaceutical formulations, water and feeds using a wide variety of techniques. *Mailing Add:* 25 Dutch Rd East Brunswick NJ 08816

DHUDSHIA, VALLABH H, b Shahpur, India, July 1, 39; US citizen; m 65; c 2. RELIABILITY, MAINTAINABILITY. *Educ:* Gujarat Univ, BS, 63; Ill Inst Technol, MS, 65; New York Univ, PhD(indust eng & opers res), 73. *Prof Exp:* Res engr solid mech, Foster Wheeler Corp, 65-72; eng specialist reliability, 72-79, MEM RES STAFF, XEROX CORP, 79- *Mem:* Am Soc Mech Engrs; Am Soc Qual Control. *Res:* Reliability of advanced marking technology; reliability and maintainability assurance, management, assessment, and evaluation. *Mailing Add:* 2605 Graphic Pl Plano TX 75075

DHURANDHAR, HAMIDA NINA, b Bombay, India, Jan 6, 37; m 63; c 2. PATHOLOGY, CYTOLOGY. *Educ:* G S Med Col, Bombay, MB, 62; Univ London, DCP, 65; Am Bd Path, dipl anat path, 73. *Prof Exp:* Instr, 66-68, asst prof, 73-79, ASSOC PROF PATH, SCH MED, TULANE UNIV, 79- *Concurrent Pos:* Vis pathologist, Charity Hosp of New Orleans, 73-, dir autopsy path, 75-78; staff pathologist, Tulane Med Ctr Hosp, 76- *Mem:* Int Acad Path; Am Soc Cytol. *Res:* Role of platelet micro-aggregates in stored blood in the production of pulmonary insufficiency; study of the pathophysiology of human corpus luteum and its relationships to various ovarian and extra-ovarian hormones; warty dyskeratosis of cervix; etiology and natural history; touch imprint cytology as an aid to frozen section diagnosis. *Mailing Add:* Dept of Path Tulane Univ Sch of Med New Orleans LA 70112

DHYSE, FREDERICK GEORGE, b Hinkley, Utah, June 23, 18; m 50; c 2. BIOCHEMISTRY, INFORMATION SCIENCE. *Educ:* Univ Calif, BA, 41. *Prof Exp:* Chemist control & prod res, Cutter Labs, Calif, 41-46; chemist vitamins in canned foods, Gerber Prods Co, 46-47; biochemist endocrinol sect, Nat Cancer Inst, 48-50, res analyst document sect, 50-63, biochemist cancer studies, 53-66, SCI INFO OFFICER, NAT INST CHILD HEALTH & DEVELOP, NIH, 66- *Mem:* AAAS; Am Chem Soc. *Res:* Vitamin function; biotin; hormonal activity; antivitamins, antimetabolites in cancer; machine and punch-card applications to problems of scientific literature. *Mailing Add:* 8603 Bunnell Dr Rockville MD 20854

DIAB, IHSAN M, b Jaffa, Palestine, Aug 26, 33; US citizen; m 61; c 2. PHARMACOLOGY, BIOCHEMISTRY. *Educ:* Roosevelt Univ, BS, 60; Univ Ill, Chicago, PhD(pharmacol), 68. *Prof Exp:* Instr med technol, Chicago Sch Med Technicians, 55-60; asst instr biochem, Med Sch, Cairo Univ, 60-63; asst instr pharmacol, Univ Ill Med Sch, 63-67; asst prof psychiat & pharmacol & res assoc, Univ Chicago Med Sch, 68-74, assoc prof pharmacol, physiol sci & psychiat, 74-78; assoc prof, 78-80, PROF PHYSIOL & PHARMACOL, COL OSTEOP MED & SURG, DES MOINES, 80- *Concurrent Pos:* Fel USPHS; mem, Nat Res Coun, Nat Acad Sci, 82. *Mem:* AAAS; Am Soc Pharmacol & Exp Therapeut; Sigma Xi; Soc Neurosci; Am Col Clin Pharmacologists. *Res:* Neuropharmacology; cytopharmacology; biochemical pharmacology; drug abuse; histochemistry; autoradiography; drug localizations; morphine agonists and antagonists; opiate receptors; endorphins and enkephalins. *Mailing Add:* Col Osteop Med & Surg 3200 Grand Ave Des Moines IA 50312

DIACHUN, STEPHEN, b Phenix, RI, Aug 20, 12; m 38; c 2. PLANT PATHOLOGY. *Educ:* RI State Col, BS, 34; Univ Ill, MS, 35, PhD(plant path), 38. *Prof Exp:* Asst bot, Univ Ill, 34-37; asst plant path, 37-46, from asst prof to assoc prof, 47-53, PROF PLANT PATH, EXP STA, UNIV KY, 53- *Concurrent Pos:* Assoc plant pathologist, Exp Sta, Univ Ky, 46-50. *Mem:*

AAAS; Am Phytopath Soc; Bot Soc Am. *Res:* Relation of environment to bacterial and fungus leaf spots of tobacco; growth of bacteria on roots; distribution of tobacco mosaic virus in plants; inoculation methods with streak virus of tobacco; virus diseases of forage legumes. *Mailing Add:* Dept of Plant Path Univ of Ky Lexington KY 40506

DIACONIS, PERSI, b New York, NY, Jan 31, 45. MATHEMATICAL STATISTICS. *Educ:* City Col New York, BS, 71; Harvard Univ, MA, 73, PhD(statist), 74. *Prof Exp:* Asst prof, 74-80, ASSOC PROF STATIST, STANFORD UNIV, 80- *Res:* Probabilistic number theory; data analysis; foundations of inference. *Mailing Add:* Dept of Statist Stanford Univ Stanford CA 94305

DIACUMAKOS, ELAINE G, b Chester, Pa, Aug 11, 30; m 58. CELL BIOLOGY. *Educ:* Univ Md, BS, 51; NY Univ, MS, 55, PhD(biol), 58. *Prof Exp:* Lab instr microsurg, NY Univ, 56-58, res assoc, 58-66; from res assoc to assoc, Sloan-Kettering Inst Cancer Res, 58-71; res assoc, Sloan-Kettering Div, Grad Sch Med Sci, Cornell Univ, 59-63, instr, 63-71; SR RES ASSOC, ROCKEFELLER UNIV, 71-, HEAD LAB, 76- *Concurrent Pos:* Guest investr, Rockefeller Inst, & USPHS spec fel, 62-64; consult molecular hematol br, Nat Heart, Lung, Blood Inst, 77-; consult cell biol, Nat Cancer Inst, 78- *Mem:* AAAS; Am Soc Cell Biol; Genetics Soc Am; NY Acad Sci; Harvey Soc. *Res:* Cancerigenesis; somatic cell and biochemical genetics; congenital malformations; microsurgery and microinjection; automation. *Mailing Add:* Lab of Cytobiol Rockefeller Univ New York NY 10021

DIAKOW, CAROL, b New York, NY. ANIMAL BEHAVIOR. *Educ:* City Col New York, BS, 63; NY Univ, MS, 67, PhD(biopsychol), 69. *Prof Exp:* Lectr biol, City Col New York, 63; fel biopsychol, Dept Animal Behav, Am Mus Natural Hist, 63-69; fel neurophysiol & neuroendocrinol, Inst Animal Behav, Rutgers Univ, 69-71; fel neurophysiol & behav, Rockefeller Univ, 71, res assoc neuroanat & behav, 71-73; asst prof, 73-77, ASSOC PROF BIOL, ADELPHI UNIV, 77- *Concurrent Pos:* Staff assoc, Psychobiol Prog, Nat Sci Found, 81-82. *Honors & Awards:* Sergei Zlinkoff Award Med Res. *Mem:* Animal Behav Soc; NY Acad Sci; Int Soc Psychoneuroendocrinol; Soc Neurosci; AAAS. *Res:* Neuroendocrine bases of mating behavior in female vertebrates. *Mailing Add:* Dept of Biol Adelphi Univ Garden City NY 11530

DIAL, NORMAN ARNOLD, b Kell, Ill, June 17, 26; m 58; c 4. ZOOLOGY. *Educ:* Ill Col, AB, 49; Univ Ill, MS, 52, PhD(zool), 60. *Prof Exp:* PROF, LIFE SCI DEPT, IND STATE UNIV & ADJ PROF ANAT, SCH MED, TERRE HAUTE CTR MED EDUC, 60- *Res:* Effects of heavy metals and toxic chemicals on embryonic development. *Mailing Add:* Dept of Life Sci Ind State Univ Terre Haute IN 47802

DIAL, WILLIAM RICHARD, b Washington Court House, Ohio, Aug 30, 14; m 36; c 1. ORGANIC CHEMISTRY. *Educ:* Ohio Wesleyan Univ, AB, 36; Univ Ill, PhD(org chem), 39. *Prof Exp:* Org chemist, Columbia Chem Div, Pittsburgh Plate Glass Co, 39-52; org chemist, Columbia-Southern Chem Corp, 52-59, mgr appl org res, Chem Div, Pittsburgh Plate Glass Co, 59-64, asst dir res, 64-69, asst dir res, Chem Div, PPG Industs, Inc, 69-77; RETIRED. *Mem:* Am Chem Soc; Soc Plastic Engrs; Soc Plastic Indust. *Res:* Synthetic resins and plastics; plasticizers; casting synthetic resins; structure of gossypol; chlorinated hydrocarbons; polymerization catalysts; reinforcing rubber and paper fillers; phosgene derivatives. *Mailing Add:* 438 Roslyn Ave Akron OH 44320

DIAMANTE, JOHN MATTHEW, b New York, NY, Jan 14, 40; m 81. SATELLITE REMOTE SENSING, TIDAL DYNAMICS. *Educ:* New York Univ, BA, 61, MS, 63, PhD(aeronaut & astronaut), 69. *Prof Exp:* Asst res scientist, Dept Meteorol, NY Univ, 67-69; head, Anal Sect Command Control & Commun Dept, Systs Group TRW Inc, 69-71; sr scientist, Wolf Res & Develop Group, Wash Anal Sci Ctr, EG&G, Inc, 71-74; sr staff scientist, Bus & Technol Systs Inc, 74-77; TECH ADVR, TIDES & WATER LEVELS DIV, NAT OCEAN SURV, NAT OCEANIC & ATMOSPHERIC ADMIN, 77- *Mem:* Am Geophys Union; Am Meterol Soc; AAAS; Sigma Xi. *Res:* Measurement and modeling of ocean tides using satellite radar altimeter data; application of satellite radar altimeter data to determination of ocean geoid and mean sea surface. *Mailing Add:* 1614 Sherwood Rd Silver Spring MD 20902

DIAMANTIS, WILLIAM, b New York, NY, May 27, 23; m 50; c 2. PHARMACOLOGY. *Educ:* Fordham Univ, BS, 44, MS, 55, PhD(biol), 59. *Prof Exp:* Asst instr physiol & pharmacol, Col Pharm, Fordham Univ, 44-45, instr pharmacog, 45-58, asst prof pharmacog, microbiol & physiol, 58-60; srogist, 60-78, sect leader pharmacol, 78-80, DIR PHARMACOL, WALLACE LABS DIV, CARTER-WALLACE, INC, 80- *Mem:* AAAS; NY Acad Sci; Am Soc Pharmacol & Exp Therapeut; Am Pharm Asn. *Res:* Autonomic pharmacology; gastrointestinal pharmacology; inflammation; antipyresis; chemical mediators in anaphylaxis; pulmonary pharmacology; pharmacology of platelet function. *Mailing Add:* Wallace Labs Div Carter-Wallace Inc Cranbury NJ 08512

DIAMENT, PAUL, b Paris, France, Nov 14, 38; US citizen; m 63; c 3. ELECTRICAL ENGINEERING, PHYSICS. *Educ:* Columbia Univ, BS, 60, MS, 61, PhD(elec eng), 63. *Prof Exp:* PROF ELEC ENG, COLUMBIA UNIV, 63- *Concurrent Pos:* Res assoc, Stanford Univ, 66-67; vis assoc prof, Tel Aviv Univ, 70-71; consult, Appl Sci Labs, 70-71; Air Force Cambridge Res Labs, 73-74, State Univ NY Downstate Med Ctr, 74-75 & Riverside Res Inst, 77-78. *Mem:* Am Phys Soc; Inst Elec & Electronics Engrs; Optical Soc Am. *Res:* Relativistic electron beams; optics; laser radiation statistics; nonlinear wave interactions; microwaves; antennas; signal processing; electromagnetic theory; plasma physics. *Mailing Add:* Dept of Elec Eng Columbia Univ New York NY 10027

DIAMOND, BRUCE I, b Far Rockaway, NY, June 7, 45; m 76; c 1. PHARMACOLOGY. *Educ:* Bradley Univ, BA, 67; Long Island Univ, MS, 69; Chicago Med Sch, PhD(pharmacol), 75. *Prof Exp:* Res asst psychopharmacol, Cent Islip State Hosp, 67-70; res scientist, Neuropsychiatric Hosp, Borda, Arg, 70-71; res assoc anesthesia, Mt Sinai Hosp, Chicago, 72-81; asst prof pharmacol, Rush-St Lukes-Presby Med Ctr, 78-81; ASSOC PROF PSYCHIAT, MED COL GEORGIA, 81- *Concurrent Pos:* Asst prof, Chicago Med Sch, 77-81; res pharmacol, Augusta, Va, 81-; Ill Dept Mental Health grants, 78-81. *Mem:* Soc Neurosci; Am Soc Anesthesiologists; Sigma Xi. *Res:* Neuropharmacology and mechanisms of action of central nervous system agents and putative neurotransmitters; animal models of neuropsychiatric diseases. *Mailing Add:* Dept Psychiat Med Col Georgia Augusta GA 30912

DIAMOND, DAVID J(OSEPH), b New York, NY, Dec 31, 40; m 62; c 3. REACTOR SAFETY, REACTOR PHYSICS. *Educ:* Cornell Univ, BEP, 62; Univ Ariz, MS, 64; Mass Inst Technol, PhD(nuclear eng), 68. *Prof Exp:* Nuclear engr, Westinghouse Astronuclear Lab, 63-64; res asst reactor physics, 65, NUCLEAR ENGR, BROOKHAVEN NAT LAB, 68- *Concurrent Pos:* Adj prof, Polytech Inst New York, 77-78. *Mem:* Am Nuclear Soc. *Res:* Reactor safety; responsible for modification, evaluation and application of computer codes for tha analysis of light water reactor transients. *Mailing Add:* Brookhaven Nat Lab Upton NY 11973

DIAMOND, EARL LOUIS, b Tiffin, Ohio, Nov 8, 28; m 60; c 1. BIOSTATISTICS EPIDEMIOLOGY. *Educ:* Univ Miami, AB, 50; Univ NC, MA, 52, PhD(statist), 58. *Prof Exp:* Asst math statist, Univ NC, 52-54, biostatist, 56-57, asst prof, 57-59; sr asst sanitarian, Commun Dis Ctr, USPHS, 54-56; asst prof, 59-64, assoc prof, 64-69, PROF EPIDEMIOL & BIOSTATIST, SCH HYG & PUB HEALTH, JOHNS HOPKINS UNIV, 69- *Mem:* AAAS; Am Statist Asn; Biomet Soc; Inst Math Statist; Soc Epidemiol Res. *Res:* Biostatistics; epidemiology. *Mailing Add:* Sch Hyg & Pub Health Johns Hopkins Univ Baltimore MD 21205

DIAMOND, HAROLD GEORGE, b Wurtsboro, NY, Feb 15, 40; m 63; c 2. MATHEMATICS. *Educ:* Cornell Univ, AB, 61; Stanford Univ, PhD(math), 65. *Prof Exp:* NSF fel, Swiss Fed Inst Technol, 65-66 & Inst Adv Study, 66-67; from asst prof to assoc prof, 67-71, PROF MATH, UNIV ILL, URBANA, 71- *Concurrent Pos:* Sabbatical vistor, Univ Nottingham, 73-74 & Univ Texas, 81-82. *Mem:* Am Math Soc. *Res:* Analytic number theory; mathematical analysis; asymptotic distribution of multiplicative arithmetical functions; application of Banach algebras and harmonic analysis in number theory. *Mailing Add:* Dept of Math 374 Altgeld Hall Univ of Ill Urbana IL 61801

DIAMOND, HERBERT, b Chicago, Ill, July 28, 25; m 48; c 1. NUCLEAR CHEMISTRY. *Educ:* Univ Chicago, PhB, 47, BS, 48. *Prof Exp:* From asst chemist to assoc chemist, 49-72, CHEMIST NUCLEAR CHEM, ARGONNE NAT LAB, 72- *Mem:* Am Chem Soc; Am Phys Soc. *Res:* Production and characterization of new nuclides; nuclear half-lives; cross sections; decay schemes; nuclear aspects of cosmic and geochemical problems; separations chemistry; nuclear waste management. *Mailing Add:* Argonne Nat Lab Bldg 200 M119 Argonne IL 60439

DIAMOND, HOWARD, b Detroit, Mich, Aug 11, 28; m 51; c 4. ELECTROCHEMISTRY, PHYSICAL CHEMISTRY. *Educ:* Univ Mich, BS, 52, MS, 54, PhD(physics & elec eng), 60. *Prof Exp:* Res assoc, Eng Res Inst, Univ Mich, 57-59, from instr to assoc prof, 58-70; PRES, TRANSIDYNE-GEN CORP, 67-, CHMN, 80- *Concurrent Pos:* NSF grant, 62-63; consult, Lear Siegler Inc, Mich, 60-62 & Electrovoice Corp, 63- *Mem:* Nat Acad Sci; AAAS; Am Phys Soc. *Res:* Semiconductor and dielectric theory; theory of ferroelectricity and piezoelectricity. *Mailing Add:* Transidyne Gen Corp 903 Airport Dr Ann Arbor MI 48106

DIAMOND, ISRAEL, b Flint, Mich, Aug 1, 14; c 1. PATHOLOGY. *Educ:* City Col New York, BSc, 34. *Prof Exp:* Instr path, Harvard Univ, 48-52; assoc prof, Sch Med, Univ Louisville, 52-60; dir labs, Lutheran Med Ctr, 60-68; clin assoc prof path, NY Med Col, 64-68; PROF PATH, BROWN UNIV, 68-; DIR LABS, ROGER WILLIAMS GEN HOSP, 68- *Concurrent Pos:* Fel embryol, Boston Univ, 46-48; assoc pathologist, Children's Med Ctr, Mass, 48-52; dir labs, Children's Hosp, Ky, 52-60; dir tumor clin, 55-60; consult, Muscatatuck Children's Inst, 54-55; Kosair Crippled Children's Hosp, 53-60, Vet Admin Hosp, Ky, 54-60, Ireland Army Hosp, 55-60 & Nat Inst Neurol Dis & Blindness, 63, 64; clin assoc prof, State Univ NY Downstate Med Ctr, 60-64. *Mem:* Fel Am Soc Clin Path; fel Col Am Path. *Res:* Pediatric pathology; morphology of malnutrition; toxicology. *Mailing Add:* Roger Williams Gen Hosp 825 Chalkstone Ave Providence RI 02908

DIAMOND, IVAN, b Brooklyn, NY, May 7, 35; m 62; c 2. NEUROANATOMY. *Educ:* Univ Chicago, AB, 56, BS, 57, MD, 61, PhD(neuroanat), 67. *Prof Exp:* Intern med, New Eng Ctr Hosp, Boston, Mass, 61-62; resident neurol, Univ Chicago, 62-65, instr, Sch Med, 65-67; asst, Beth Israel Hosp, Boston, 67-69; from asst prof to assoc prof, 68-80, PROF NEUROL & PEDIAT, MED CTR, UNIV CALIF, SAN FRANCISCO, 80- *Concurrent Pos:* USPHS res fel neurol, Univ Chicago, 64-65, spec res fel biol chem, Harvard Med Sch, 67-69 & career development award, 69. *Honors & Awards:* Joseph A Capps Prize, Inst Med Chicago, 66. *Mem:* AAAS; Am Acad Neurol; Am Fedn Clin Res. *Res:* Bilirubin metabolism and neurotoxicity; biochemistry of synaptic function; regulation of receptor function. *Mailing Add:* Dept of Neurol & Pediat Univ of Calif Med Ctr San Francisco CA 94133

DIAMOND, JACK, pharmacology, see previous edition

DIAMOND, JACOB JOSEPH, b New York, NY, July 25, 17; m 44; c 2. PHYSICAL CHEMISTRY, SCIENCE ADMINISTRATION. *Educ:* Brooklyn Col, BA, 37. *Prof Exp:* Chemist, Nat Bur Standards, 40-70, mgr protective equip prog, Law Enforcement Standards Lab, 70-72, chief, Law

Enforcement Standards Lab, 72-79; RETIRED. *Concurrent Pos:* Assoc, George Washington Univ, 47-48; ed, Bibliog High Temperature Chem & Physics of Mat in Condensed State, 57-70; assoc mem, Comn High Temperatures & Refractories, Int Union Pure & Appl Chem, 59-67; mem, Nat Adv Comt Law Enforcement Equip & Technol, 76-79. *Honors & Awards:* Student Medal, Am Inst Chem, 37; Silver Medal, Dept of Com, 76. *Mem:* Fel AAAS; Am Chem Soc; Am Ceramic Soc; Int Asn Chiefs of Police. *Res:* Performance standards and guidelines for law enforcement equipment; protective, communications, security and investigative equipment; instrumental methods of chemical analysis; analysis of silicates; optical glass; flame photometry; image-furnace research; vaporization of refractory materials; high temperature chemistry. *Mailing Add:* 109 Ridgewood Dr Longwood FL 32750

DIAMOND, JARED MASON, b Sept 10, 37. PHYSIOLOGY, ECOLOGY. *Educ:* Harvard Col, BA, 58; Cambridge Univ, Eng, PhD(physiol), 61. *Prof Exp:* Fel, Trinity Col, Cambridge Univ, Eng, 61-62; jr fel, Harvard Univ, 62-65; assoc, Harvard Med Sch, 65-66; assoc prof, 66-68, PROF PHYSIOL, MED CTR, UNIV CALIF, LOS ANGELES, 68- *Mem:* Nat Acad Sci; fel Am Acad Arts & Sci. *Res:* Membrane biophysics and physiology; ecology and evolution of species communities. *Mailing Add:* Sch of Med Dept of Physiol Univ of Calif Med Ctr Los Angeles CA 90024

DIAMOND, JULIUS, b Philadelphia, Pa, Apr 12, 25; m 53; c 3. MEDICINAL CHEMISTRY. *Educ:* Univ Pa, BS, 45; Temple Univ, MA, 53, PhD(chem), 55. *Prof Exp:* Org res chemist, Wyeth Labs, 50-56; dir labs, G F Harvey Co, NY, 56-57; proj leader, Wallace Labs, NJ, 57-59; tech dir, Lincoln Labs, Ill, 59-62; group leader, William H Rorer Inc, 62-67, mgr org chem dept, 67-69, asst dir res, 69-73; DIR BASIC RES, COOPER LABS, INC, NJ, 73- *Concurrent Pos:* Lectr, Pa State Univ, 64-65. *Mem:* Am Chem Soc; fel Am Inst Chemists; Acad Pharmaceut Sci; Sigma Xi. *Res:* Pharmaceuticals; medicinal chemistry; drug metabolism; gastrointestinal drugs; antiinflammatory drugs; cardiovascular drugs; synthetic analgesics; bronchopulmonary drugs; dental antiplaque agents. *Mailing Add:* Box 246 Morris Plains NJ 07950

DIAMOND, LEILA, b Newark, NJ, July 19, 25. CHEMICAL CARCINOGENESIS, CELL BIOLOGY. *Educ:* Univ Wis-Madison, BA, 45; Cornell Univ, PhD(biol), 61. *Prof Exp:* From asst prof to assoc prof, 64-77, PROF, WISTAR INST, 78- *Concurrent Pos:* USPHS fel, Inst Virol, Univ Glasgow, 61-63; assoc prof path, Sch Med, Univ Pa, 73-; mem, Exp Therapeut Study Sect, NIH, 74-78; assoc ed, Cancer Res, 77-; mem adv comt, Biochem & Chem Carcinogens, Am Cancer Soc, 80-83. *Mem:* Am Asn Cancer Res; Am Soc Cell Biol; Environ Mutagen Soc. *Res:* Tissue culture; cell transformation; mutagenesis; tumor virology. *Mailing Add:* Wistar Inst 36th St & Spruce Philadelphia PA 19104

DIAMOND, LOUIS, b Baltimore, Md, July 13, 40; m 67; c 2. PHARMACOLOGY. *Educ:* Univ Md, BSc, 61, MSc, 64, PhD(pharmacol), 67. *Prof Exp:* From asst prof to assoc prof, 67-80, PROF PHARMACOL, UNIV KY, 80- *Concurrent Pos:* Nat Heart Inst fel, 68; NSF grant, 68-70. *Mem:* AAAS; Am Soc Pharmacol & Exp Therapeut; NY Acad Sci. *Res:* Pulmonary pharmacology. *Mailing Add:* Dept of Pharmacol Univ of Ky Lexington KY 40506

DIAMOND, LOUIS KLEIN, b New York, NY, May 11, 02; m 29; c 2. MEDICINE, PEDIATRICS. *Educ:* Harvard Univ, AB, 23, MD, 27. *Prof Exp:* Asst pediat & path, Harvard Med Sch, 30-32, asst pediat, 32-33, instr, 33-35, assoc, 35-41, from asst prof to prof, 41-68; assoc prof, 68-70, resident prof, 70-76, ADJ PROF PEDIAT, MED SCH, SAN FRANCISCO MED CTR, UNIV CALIF, 76- *Concurrent Pos:* Res fel pediat, Harvard Med Sch, 27-28; mem res staff, Children's Hosp, 28-30, asst physician, 31, assoc physician, 32-33, assoc vis physician, 34-38, sr physician, 38-45, assoc physician-in-chief, 46-; med dir, Nat Blood Prog, Am Nat Red Cross, 48-50; mem hemat study sect, NIH, 49-53 & human embryo & develop study sect, 54-59, 64-68; mem subcomt blood & related problems, Nat Res Coun. *Honors & Awards:* Mead-Johnson Award, Am Acad Pediat, 46; Carlos J Findlay Gold Medal, Cuba, 51; Merit AWard, Netherlands Red Cross, 59; Karl Landsteiner Award, 62; Theodore Roosevelt Award, 64; George R Minot Award, 65. *Mem:* Am Acad Pediat; Soc Pediat Res; Am Pediat Soc; Am Soc Clin Invest; AMA. *Res:* Children's diseases, especially diseases of the blood. *Mailing Add:* Dept of Pediat Univ of Calif Med Sch San Francisco CA 94143

DIAMOND, LOUIS STANLEY, b Philadelphia, Pa, Feb 6, 20; m 39; c 3. ZOOLOGY, ENTOMOLOGY. *Educ:* Univ Pa, AB, 40; Univ Mich, MS, 41; Univ Minn, PhD, 58. *Prof Exp:* Wildlife res biologist, Patuxent Res Refuge, US Fish & Wildlife Serv, 51-53; vet parasitologist, Animal Dis & Parasite Res Br, Agr Res Serv, USDA, 53-58; MED PARASITOLOGIST SEC CHIEF, LAB PARASITIC DIS, NAT INST ALLERGY & INFECTIOUS DIS, NIH, US DEPT HEALTH & HUMAN SERV, 59- *Concurrent Pos:* Guest scientist & founding mem, Centro de Estudios sobre Amibiasis, Mex City, 77; sr vis scientist & consult, Sch Med, Keio Univ, Tokyo, 78; consult, expert adv panel parasitic dis, WHO, 68- *Mem:* Am Soc Parasitol; Am Micros Soc; Am Soc Trop Med & Hyg; Soc Protozoologists. *Res:* Axenic cultivation of entamoeba and trichomonads of human and veterinary importance; pathobiology of human pathogen entamoeba histolytica; host parasite relationships of indigenous viruses of E histolytica; cryobiology. *Mailing Add:* Rm 225 Bldg 5 Lab Parasitic Dis Nat Inst Allergy & Infect Dis NIH Bethesda MD 20014

DIAMOND, MARIAN C, b Glendale, Calif, Nov 11, 26; m 50; c 4. NEUROBIOLOGY. *Educ:* Univ Calif, Berkeley, AB, 48, MA, 49, PhD(anat), 53. *Prof Exp:* Res asst neurobiol, Harvard Col, 52-53; res asst & instr, Cornell Univ, 54-58; lectr anat, Sch Med, San Francisco, 59-61, res assoc psychol, Berkeley, 61-65, from asst prof to assoc prof anat, 65-74, from asst dean to assoc dean, Col Letters & Sci, 68-72, PROF ANAT, UNIV CALIF, BERKELEY, 74- *Concurrent Pos:* Res grants, NSF, 61-62, 66-71 & 71-74, NIH, 66-69, WHO, 78 & biomed, Univ Calif, Berkeley, 78-80. *Mem:* Fel AAAS; Soc Neurosci; Int Soc Psychoneuroendocrinol; Am Asn Anat; Int Soc Develop Neurosci. *Res:* Environmentally induced anatomical and chemical brain changes; pituitary hormones and brain development. *Mailing Add:* Dept of Anat Univ of Calif Berkeley CA 94704

DIAMOND, MARTIN J, b New York, NY, June 10, 20; m 64; c 1. ORGANIC CHEMISTRY. *Educ:* Univ Wis, BA, 41; Stanford Univ, PhD(org chem), 53. *Prof Exp:* Res chemist, Chem Process Co, 51-52; sr res chemist, Calif Spray Chem Co, 53-58; RES CHEMIST, WESTERN REGIONAL RES CTR, AGR RES SERV, USDA, 59- *Mem:* Am Chem Soc; Royal Soc Chem. *Res:* Synthetic organic chemistry; stereochemistry; pesticides; fatty acids; graft polymers; textile finishes; flame retardants. *Mailing Add:* Western Regional Res Ctr USDA 800 Buchanan St Berkeley CA 94710

DIAMOND, MILTON, b New York, NY, Mar 6, 34; m 55; c 4. SEXOLOGY, REPRODUCTIVE BIOLOGY. *Educ:* City Col New York, BS, 55; Univ Kans, PhD(anat & psychol), 62. *Prof Exp:* From instr to asst prof anat, Sch Med, Univ Louisville, 62-67; assoc prof anat, 67-71, PROF ANAT & REPROD BIOL, SCH MED, UNIV HAWAII, 71- *Concurrent Pos:* NIH grant, Univ Louisville & Univ Hawaii, 62-; Lederle med fac award, 68-71; Pop Coun grant, Univ Hawaii, 72-73; consult, State of Hawaii Dept Educ, 71-; res prof psychiat & behav sci, State Univ NY Stony Brook, 75-78. *Mem:* Soc Study Reprod; fel Soc Sci Study Sex; fel Int Acad Sex Res; Am Asn Sex Educ, Counr & Therapists; Brit Soc Study Fertil. *Res:* Sexology; reproduction; contraception and abortion; sex education. *Mailing Add:* Dept Anat & Reprod Biol Univ Hawaii Sch Med Honolulu HI 96822

DIAMOND, RAY BYFORD, b Louisa, Ky, Jan 10, 33; m 57; c 3. SOIL FERTILITY. *Educ:* Ohio State Univ, BS, 54; Univ Fla, MSA, 61, PhD(soils), 63. *Prof Exp:* Agriculturist, Tenn Valley Authority, 63-64, agronomist fertilizer usage, 64-76, fertilizer use specialist, USAID contract, 74-76; regional coordr, Africa, 76-79, CHIEF COORDR MKT DEVELOP & FERTILIZER EVALUATIONS, INT FERTILIZER DEVELOP CTR, 79- *Mem:* Am Soc Agron; Soil Sci Soc Am; Int Soil Sci Cong. *Res:* Evaluation of agronomic properties of new fertilizer products under a variety of soil, climatic and cropping conditions; data collection and analysis and technical assistance on fertilizer marketing; distribution and usage relevant to developing countries. *Mailing Add:* Rt 8 Box 107 Florence AL 35630

DIAMOND, RICHARD MARTIN, b Los Angeles, Calif, Jan 7, 24; m 50; c 4. NUCLEAR SPECTROSCOPY. *Educ:* Univ Calif, Los Angeles, BS, 47; Univ Calif, PhD(nuclear chem), 51. *Prof Exp:* Instr chem, Harvard Univ, 51-54; asst prof, Cornell Univ, 54-58; MEM STAFF, LAWRENCE BERKELEY LAB, UNIV CALIF, 58- *Concurrent Pos:* Guggenheim fel, Denmark, 66-67; fel Japan Soc Promotion Sci, 81. *Honors & Awards:* Tom W Bonner Award, Am Physical Soc, 80. *Mem:* Am Chem Soc; Am Phys Soc. *Res:* Nuclear spectroscopy; coulomb excitation; ion exchange resin and solvent extraction mechanisms; solution chemistry. *Mailing Add:* Lawrence Berkeley Lab Univ of Calif Berkeley CA 94720

DIAMOND, SEYMOUR, b Chicago, Ill, Apr 15, 25; m 48; c 3. NEUROLOGY, CLINICAL PHARMACOLOGY. *Educ:* Chicago Med Sch, BM, 48, MD, 49. *Prof Exp:* DIR NEUROL, DIAMOND HEADACHE CLIN, LTD, 73- *Concurrent Pos:* Adj clin assoc neurol, Chicago Med Sch, 70-; exec dir, Nat Migraine Found, Am Asn Study of Headache, 80,; exec officer res group on headache & head pain, World Fedn Neurol, 80-; pres, Interstate Postgrad Med Asn, 81. *Honors & Awards:* Physicians Recognition Award, AMA, 70-73 & 74-77; Outstanding Serv Award, Am Asn Study Headache, 70. *Mem:* AMA; Am Soc Clin Pharmacol & Therapeut; Int Asn Study Pain; World Fedn Neurol; Am Asn Study Headache (past pres). *Res:* Research using pharmaceutical preparations for the prophylactic and abortive treatment of headache; behavioral modification and pain. *Mailing Add:* 5252 N Western Ave Chicago IL 60625

DIAMOND, SIDNEY, b New York, NY, Nov 10, 29; m 53; c 2. ENGINEERING MATERIALS, CHEMISTRY. *Educ:* Syracuse Univ, BS, 50; Duke Univ, MF, 51; Purdue Univ, PhD(soil chem), 63. *Prof Exp:* Hwy res engr, US Bur Pub Roads, 53-62; asst, Purdue Univ, 62-63; res chemist, US Bur Pub Roads, 64-65; assoc prof, 65-70, PROF ENG MAT, PURDUE UNIV, 70- *Concurrent Pos:* Ed, Cement & Concrete Res, 76-; pres, Sidney Diamond & Assocs, Inc, 77-; mem, Panel on Status of Res & Devel US Cement & Concrete Industs, Nat Mat Adv Bd, 77-80; chmn, Fourth Int Conf Effect Alkalies, 78, Seventh Int Cong Chem of Cement, Paris, 80 & Symp Effects Flyash in Cement & Concrete, Boston, 81. *Mem:* Fel Am Ceramic Soc (trustee, 78-81); Am Concrete Inst; Clay Minerals Soc; Am Soc Testing & Mat; Mat Res Soc. *Res:* Physics and chemistry of cement and concrete; microstructural characterization of inorganic systems by scanning electron microscopy; cement hydration; concrete durability; clay mineralogy; soil stabilization. *Mailing Add:* Sch of Civil Eng Purdue Univ West Lafayette IN 47907

DIAMOND, STEVEN ELLIOT, b Brooklyn, NY, Sept 15, 49; m 79. INORGANIC CHEMISTRY, CATALYSIS. *Educ:* Rensselaer Polytech Inst, BS, 71; Stanford Univ, PhD(chem), 75. *Prof Exp:* RES ASSOC, CORP RES LAB, ALLIED CORP, 75- *Mem:* Am Chem Soc; NY Acad Sci. *Res:* Inorganic chemistry and organometallic chemistry as applied to catalysis; coordination chemistry; homogeneous and heterogeneous catalysis. *Mailing Add:* Allied Corp PO Box 1021R Morristown NJ 07960

DIANA, JOHN N, b Lake Placid, NY, Dec 19, 30; m 54, 66; c 3. PHYSIOLOGY. *Educ:* Norwich Univ, BA, 52; Univ Louisville, PhD(physiol), 65. *Prof Exp:* Biochemist, Inst Med Res, Louisville, Ky, 54-56; physiologist, US Army Med Res Lab, Ft Knox, Ky, 56-58; from res asst to res assoc cardiovasc physiol, Sch Med, Univ Louisville, 58-65; asst prof, Col Human Med, Mich State Univ, 66-68; assoc prof physiol & biophys, Col Med, Univ Iowa, 68-74, prof, 74-78; PROF & CHMN PHYSIOL & BIOPHYS, SCH MED, LA STATE UNIV, 78- *Concurrent Pos:* Fel, Sch Med, Univ Okla, 65-66; Am Heart Inst fel, 65-67; fel coun circulation, Am Heart Asn, 71- *Mem:* AAAS; Am Fedn Clin Res; Am Physiol Soc; Microcirc Soc. *Res:* Cardiovascular research, especially venomotor activity, transcapillary fluid movement and capillary permeability in skeletal muscle, intestine and myocardium during infusion of vasoactive agents; effects of hypertension, hypotension, shock and heart failure on capillary permeability. *Mailing Add:* Dept Physiol & Biophys La State Univ Sch Med Shreveport LA 71130

DIANA, LEONARD M, b Columbia, Pa, Jan 26, 23; m 50, 80; c 3. PHYSICS. *Educ:* Ga Inst Technol, BS, 48; Univ Pittsburgh, PhD(physics), 53. *Prof Exp:* Asst, Univ Pittsburgh, 48-50, instr, 49-52, res assoc, 51-53; proj physicist res & develop, Standard Oil Co, 53-59; physicist, Am Tobacco Co, 59-62; assoc prof physics, Univ Richmond, 62-65; assoc prof, 65-71, assoc dean, Col Sci, 75-81, PROF PHYSICS, UNIV TEX, ARLINGTON, 71- *Concurrent Pos:* Va state chmn, Vis Scientists Prog Physics, High Schs, 63-65; specialist, US Agency Int Develop, India, 66. *Mem:* Fel AAAS; Am Phys Soc; Am Asn Physics Teachers. *Res:* Experimental nuclear physics; theoretical physics; computing; instrumentation; positron annihilation; defects in metals; liquid structure. *Mailing Add:* Dept Physics Univ of Tex Arlington TX 76019

D'IANNI, JAMES DONATO, b Akron, Ohio, Mar 11, 14; m 40; c 1. POLYMER CHEMISTRY. *Educ:* Univ Akron, BS, 34; Univ Wis, PhD(org chem), 38. *Prof Exp:* Asst chem, Univ Wis, 34-37; res chemist, Goodyear Tire & Rubber Co, 38-51, asst to vpres res & develop, 52-61, chem prod liaison, 61-63, assoc dir res, 63-65, asst dir, 65-68, dir res, 65-77, asst to vpres res, 78; CONSULT, 78- *Concurrent Pos:* Instr, Univ Akron, 41-46; chief polymer res br, Off Rubber Reserve, Reconstruct Finance Corp, 46-47; chmn, Gordon Res Conf Elastomers, 52. *Mem:* Am Chem Soc; Am Inst Chem; Am Inst Chem Eng. *Res:* Catalytic hydrogenation of hydroxyamides and lignin; synthesis of polymerizable monomers; synthetic rubber; vinyl resin; chemical derivatives of rubbers. *Mailing Add:* 860 Sovereign Rd Akron OH 44303

DIAS, JERRY RAY, b Oakland, Calif, Oct 26, 40; m 58; c 3. PHYSICAL ORGANIC CHEMISTRY, CHEMICAL ENGINEERING. *Educ:* San Jose State Univ, BS, 65; Ariz State Univ, PhD(phys & org chem), 70. *Prof Exp:* Test technician, Fuel Filtration Filters, Inc, 59-61; engr asst semiconductors, Amelco, Inc, 61-62; supvr electroplating, Huggins Microwave Labs, 62-64; res asst chem, San Jose State Univ, 64-66; engr electrochem, Fairchild Corp, Mountain View, 66-67; NIH fel chem, Ariz State Univ, 68-70; fel, Stanford Univ, 70-72; asst prof, 72-78, ASSOC PROF CHEM, UNIV MO-KANSAS CITY, 78- *Concurrent Pos:* Consult, Mobay Chem Corp, 78 & Region VII, Environ Protection Agency, 79 & 80; Fulbright-Hays sr scholar, Yugoslavia, 81. *Mem:* Am Chem Soc; Am Electroplaters Soc; Am Soc Testing & Mat; Electrochem Soc; Nat Soc Prof Engrs. *Res:* Organic chemical mechanisms and synthesis; material science; electrochemical methods of organic synthesis; electrode mechanisms, mass spectrometry, structural elucidation, natural products and chemical graph theory. *Mailing Add:* Dept Chem Univ Mo Kansas City MO 64110

DIASIO, ROBERT BART, b New York, NY, Jan 20, 46; m 70; c 3. ONCOLOGY, PHARMACOLOGY. *Educ:* Univ Rochester, BA, 67; Yale Univ, MD, 71. *Prof Exp:* Intern internal med, Strong Mem Hosp, Univ Rochester, 71-72, resident, 72-73; clin assoc med oncol, Nat Cancer Inst, 73-75, res assoc cancer pharmacol, 75-76; ASST PROF MED & PHARMACOL, MED COL VA, 76- *Mem:* Am Fedn Clin Res; Am Soc Clin Oncol; Am Asn Cancer Res; Am Chem Soc. *Res:* Biochemical and clinical pharmacology of antineoplastic drugs. *Mailing Add:* Dept of Med & Pharmacol Med Col of Va Box 540 Richmond VA 23298

DIASSI, PATRICK ANDREW, b Morristown, NJ, July 1, 26; m 52. ORGANIC CHEMISTRY. *Educ:* St Peter's Col (NJ), BSc, 46; Rutgers Univ, MSc, 50, PhD(chem), 51. *Prof Exp:* Asst, Rutgers Univ, 47-50; res assoc, 51-63, res supvr, 63-66, sr res assoc, 66-68, asst dir dept org chem, 68-71, dir dept chem process develop, 71-72, dir chem & microbiol, 72-77, ASSOC DIR SQUIBB INST MED RES, 72-, V PRES CHEM, RES & DEVELOP, 77- *Mem:* AAAS; Am Chem Soc; The Chem Soc. *Res:* Chemistry of natural products. *Mailing Add:* 744 Norgate Westfield NJ 07090

DIAUGUSTINE, RICHARD PATRICK, b Hackensack, NJ, Jan 15, 42; m 65; c 2. ONCOLOGY, MOLECULAR PHARMACOLOGY. *Educ:* Northeastern Univ, BS, 64; Tulane Univ, PhD(pharmacol & biochem), 68. *Prof Exp:* NIH fel pharmacol, Sch Med, Univ Iowa, 68-70; staff fel biochem, 70-74, res chemist molecular pharmacol & biochem, 74-77, HEAD ENDOCRINOL GROUP LAB PULMONARY FUNCTION & TOXICOL, NAT INST ENVIRON HEALTH SCI, NIH, 77- *Concurrent Pos:* Adj asst prof med, Med Ctr, Duke Univ, 75- *Mem:* Am Soc Pharmacol & Exp Therapeut. *Res:* Formation and secretion of polypeptide hormones by chemically-induced lung carcinomas; early modulation of gene expression in chemical oncogenesis; secretions and secretory cells of the terminal airways of the lung. *Mailing Add:* Nat Inst of Environ Health Sci PO Box 12233 Research Triangle Park NC 27709

DIAZ, ARTHUR FRED, b Calexico, Calif, Dec 25, 38; m 62; c 4. ORGANIC CHEMISTRY. *Educ:* San Diego State Univ, BS, 60; Univ Calif, Los Angeles, PhD(chem), 65. *Prof Exp:* Res assoc, Univ Calif, Los Angeles, 65-69; mem prof res staff, TRW Inc, 69-70; asst prof, Univ Calif, San Diego. 70-74; prog mgr, NSF, 74-75; MEM RES STAFF, IBM CORP, 75- *Res:* Thin polymer films on electrode surfaces. *Mailing Add:* 3864 Wellington Sq San Jose CA 95136

DIAZ, CARLOS MANUEL, b Chile, Apr 16, 32; m 56; c 5. EXTRACTIVE METALLURGY, PYROMETALLURGY. *Educ:* Columbia Univ, MSc, 58; Univ London, PhD(extractive metall), 66. *Prof Exp:* Asst prof extractive metall, Univ Chile, 54-58, assoc prof, 58-66, prof, 67-75, head, Dept Mines, 67-73, dir, Sch Eng, 69-75; process engineer 75-78, SECT HEAD PYROMETAL, J ROY GORDON RES LAB, INCO METALS CO, 78- *Concurrent Pos:* Dir mining & extractive metall, Latin Am Prog Adv Sci & Technol, 70-72; vis prof, Nat Univ Eng, Peru, 70, Nat Univ, Columbia, 70-78 & Univ San Luis Potosi, Mex, 78; consult, UNESCO, 79. *Honors & Awards:* Ismael Valdes Prize, Chilean Inst Engrs, 57. *Mem:* Chilean Inst Mining Engrs; Can Inst Mining. *Res:* Pyrometallurgical operations for treating sulfide and oxide nickel and copper ores with the objective of improving existing processes of developing new processes. *Mailing Add:* J R Gordon Res Lab INCO Metals Co Sheridan Park Mississauga ON L5K 1Z9 Can

DIAZ, LUIS FLORENTINO, b Lima, Peru, Apr 20, 46; US citizen; m 68; c 1. ENVIRONMENTAL ENGINEERING, HEAT TRANSFER. *Educ:* San Jose State Univ, BS, 72; Univ Calif, Berkeley, MS, 73, PhD(environ eng), 76. *Prof Exp:* Engr, Pac Gas & Elec Co, 68-72; res asst, Univ Calif, Berkeley, 72-75; PRES, CAL RECOVERY SYSTS INC, 75- *Concurrent Pos:* Consult, WHO, 78, Calif Solid Waste Mgt Bd, 76, City of Berkeley, 75, World Bank, Asian Develop Bank, US Aid & UN Indust Develop Orgn. *Mem:* Am Soc Mech Engrs; Sigma Xi. *Res:* Material and energy recovery from wastes; composting; biogasification and waste heat utilization. *Mailing Add:* Cal Recovery Systs Inc 160 Broadway Richmond CA 94804

DIAZ, PEDRO MIGUEL, b Mayaguez, PR, May 12, 36; c 2. ANESTHESIOLOGY. *Educ:* Univ PR, BS, 57, MD, 60. *Prof Exp:* Asst prof anesthesiol, Sch Med, Univ PR, 67-71; asst prof, 71-75, ASSOC CLIN PROF ANESTHESIOL, SCH MED, UNIV MIAMI, 75- *Concurrent Pos:* Res fel, Col Physicians & Surgeons, Columbia Univ, 65-67; co-dir dept anesthesia, PR Med Ctr, 67-71; NIH res award, 68; consult, Vet Admin Hosp, San Juan, PR, 69-71 & Vet Admin Hosp, Miami, Fla, 72-; attend anesthesiologist, Jackson Mem Hosp, Miami, 71-; NSF res award, 74. Am Soc Anesthesiologists; Am Fedn Clin Res; Am Thoracic Soc; Int Anesthesia Res Soc. *Res:* Brain biogenic amines; convulsants; anticonvulsants; cardiovascular physiology; anesthesia equipment; thermography. *Mailing Add:* PO Box 2544 Boca Raton FL 33432

DIAZ, ROBERT JAMES, b Chester, Pa, Oct 16, 46; m 71; c 2. MARINE ECOLOGY. *Educ:* La Salle Col, BA, 68; Univ Va, MS, 71, PhD(marine biol), 76. *Prof Exp:* Res asst ecol & pollution, 71-74, asst marine sci, 74-76, res marine biol, Corps Engrs, Waterways Exp Sta, 77-78, ASSOC MARINE SCI, VA INST MARINE SCI, 78-; ASST PROF, COL WILLIAM & MARY, 78- *Res:* Tidal freshwater and estuarine ecology; application of multivariate methods in ecology; taxonomy of oligochaetes; habitat evaluation; secondary productivity. *Mailing Add:* Va Inst of Marine Sci Gloucester Point VA 23062

DI BARTOLO, BALDASSARE, b Trapani, Italy, Jan 5, 26; m 68; c 2. SOLID STATE PHYSICS. *Educ:* Univ Palermo, DSc(indust eng), 50; Inst Telecommun, Rome, dipl, 51; Mass Inst Technol, PhD(physics), 64. *Prof Exp:* Design engr, Microlambda, Italy, 53-56; microwave engr, Studio Tecnico di Consulenza Elettronica, 56-57; vis fel physics, Mass Inst Technol, 57-58, res staff mem, Lab Insulation Res, 58-63; sr scientist & dir Spectros Lab, Mithras Div, Sanders Assocs, Inc, 64-68; assoc prof, 68-75, PROF PHYSICS, BOSTON COL, 75- *Concurrent Pos:* Lectr, Cybernetics Study Ctr, Naval Inst, Naples, 54-56; dir, Int Sch Atomic & Molecular Spectros, 73- *Mem:* AAAS; Am Phys Soc; Ital Phys Soc; Int Photochem Soc; Am Chem Soc. *Res:* Solid state and molecular spectroscopy; maser and laser theory; theory of atomic and crystal spectra; information theory; microwave technique; flash photolysis; photoacoustic spectroscopy. *Mailing Add:* Dept of Physics Boston Col Chestnut Hill CA 02167

DIBB, DAVID WALTER, b Draper, Utah, July 4, 43; m 66; c 4. SOIL FERTILITY. *Educ:* Brigham Young Univ, BS, 70; Univ Ill, PhD(soil fertil & plant nutrit), 74. *Prof Exp:* Res assoc soils, NC State Univ, 74-75; southern midwest dir mkt develop & res, Potash Inst, 75-77, SOUTHCENTRAL DIR, RES, EDUC & MKT DEVELOP, POTASH & PHOSPHATE INST, 77- *Mem:* Am Soc Agron; Soil Sci Soc Am. *Res:* Corn growth as affected by form of nitrogen; subsoil management and its effect on soybean growth; crop management for maximum economic yields. *Mailing Add:* Rte 10 Box 448 Columbia MO 65202

DIBBEN, MARTYN JAMES, b Gosport, Eng, Jan 26, 43; m 68; c 2. SYSTEMATIC BOTANY, LICHENOLOGY. *Educ:* Univ London, BSc, 65, MA, 66; Duke Univ, PhD(bot), 74. *Prof Exp:* Instr bot, Duke Univ, 72-74; res fel lichenology, Harvard Univ, 74-75; CHMN, DEPT BOT, MILWAUKEE PUB MUS, 75- *Concurrent Pos:* Mem, Int Standing Comt Mycological Nomenclature, 75-78 & Wis State Sci Areas Preserv Coun, 75-; adj prof, Univ Wis-Milwaukee; dep dir, Org Flora Neotropica, UNESCO Comn, 80-; ed newsletter, Int Asn Lichenol, 81- *Mem:* Am Bryological & Lichenological Soc; Am Inst Biol Sci; Int Asn Plant Taxon; Mycol Soc Am; Sigma Xi. *Res:* Taxonomy of bryophytes, fleshy fungi and lichens; biochemical systematics of lichens; edible and poisonous mushrooms; lichen flora of the neotropics; world distribution and systematics of pertinence. *Mailing Add:* Head-Bot Div Milwaukee Pub Mus 800 W Wells St Milwaukee WI 53233

DIBBLE, JOHN THOMAS, b Kenosha, Wis, Apr 28, 50. POLLUTANTS, RESOURCE RECOVERY. *Educ:* Univ Wis, Stevens Pt, BS, 72; Western Ky Univ, MS, 74; Rutgers Univ, PhD(microbiol), 78. *Prof Exp:* Lab tech, Western Ky Univ, 74; res intern appl environ microbiol, Cook Col, Rutgers Univ, 74-78; PROJ MICROBIOLOGIST, TEXACO RES, 78- *Concurrent Pos:* Consult, 77-78. *Mem:* Am Soc Microbiol; Soc Indust Microbiol. *Res:* Treatment and disposal of waste water and solid waste; permit negotiations, public comment and proposed legislation; environmental assessment, oil spill response and the restoration of perturbed ecosystems. *Mailing Add:* Texaco Res PO Box 1608 Port Arthur TX 77627

DIBBLE, MARJORIE VEIT, b Brooklyn, NY, Jan 11, 28; m 54; c 2. NUTRITION, FOOD SCIENCE. *Educ:* Hunter Col, BS, 49; Univ Tenn, Knoxville, MS, 50. *Prof Exp:* Instr foods & nutrit, Syracuse Univ, 51-57; instr foods, Teachers Col, Columbia Univ, 57-58; from asst prof foods & nutrit to assoc prof nutrit & food sci, 58-73, dean, Col Human Deveop, 73-74, PROF NUTRIT & FOOD SCI, SYRACUSE UNIV, 73-, CHMN DEPT, 63- *Mem:* Am Dietetic Asn; fel Am Pub Health Asn; Inst Food Technologists. *Res:* Nutritional status surveys of adolescent and older age adults; relationship of nutrition to growth and development. *Mailing Add:* Dept of Nutrit & Food Sci 200 Slocum Hall Syracuse Univ Syracuse NY 13210

DIBBLE, WILLIAM E, b Schenectady, NY, Dec 25, 30. PHYSICS. *Educ:* Calif Inst Technol, BS, 54, PhD(physics), 60. *Prof Exp:* From asst prof to assoc prof, 61-71, PROF PHYSICS, BRIGHAM YOUNG UNIV, 71- *Mem:* AAAS; Am Phys Soc. *Res:* Small-angle x-ray scattering. *Mailing Add:* Dept of Physics Brigham Young Univ Provo UT 84601

DIBELER, VERNON HAMILTON, b Elizabeth, NJ, July 20, 18; m 43; c 3. CHEMICAL PHYSICS. *Educ:* Duke Univ, BS, 39, MA, 40; Columbia Univ, PhD(chem), 50. *Prof Exp:* Asst chemist, Duke Univ, 39-41; asst phys chemist, Nat Bur Stand, 42-45, phys chemist, 45-75; RETIRED. *Honors & Awards:* Meritorious Serv Award, 52; Gold Medal Award, Dept Com, 69. *Mem:* AAAS; Am Chem Soc; Am Phys Soc; Am Inst Chemists. *Res:* Separation and use of isotopes in chemical research; mass spectrometry, theory and analytical application; bond dissociation energies and dissociation of isotopically-substituted molecules by electron and photon impact. *Mailing Add:* PO Box 151 Bethany Beach DE 19930

DIBELIUS, NORMAN RICHARD, b Richmond Hill, NY, Dec 24, 22; m 46; c 2. MECHANICAL ENGINEERING. *Educ:* Polytech Inst Brooklyn, BME, 53; Rensselaer Polytech Inst, MSME, 60. *Prof Exp:* Engr, Gas Turbine Dept, 53-55 & Gen Eng Lab, 55-59, proj engr, Advan Tech Labs, 59-65, proj engr, Res & Develop Ctr, 65-69, mgr combustion & control develop, Gas Turbine Develop Eng, 69-72, MGR ENVIRON EFFECTS & SPEC PROJ, GAS TURBINE DEVELOP ENG, GEN ELEC CO, 73- *Mem:* Am Soc Mech Engrs. *Res:* Development of combustion systems for gas turbines to burn various fuels with minimum atmospheric pollution; assess environmental effect of gas turbines e on ambient air quality. *Mailing Add:* Gas Turbine Opers Bldg 53-322 One River Rd Schenectady NY 12345

DIBELLA, EUGENE PETER, b New York, NY, June 19, 28; m 50; c 4. ORGANIC CHEMISTRY. *Educ:* Fordham Univ, BS, 48, MS, 50, PhD(chem), 53. *Prof Exp:* Asst chem, Fordham Univ, 49-53; res chemist, Heyden Chem Corp, 53-66, supvr, Heyden Chem Div, 66-70, group leader org synthesis, Intermediates Div, 70-75, supvr specialty chem, 75-77, LAB MGR ORG SYNTHESIS, RES & DEVELOP, TENNECO CHEM INC, 77- *Concurrent Pos:* Instr, Fairleigh Dickinson Univ, 53- *Mem:* Am Chem Soc; AAAS. *Res:* Synthetic organic chemistry; flame retardants; chlorination technology; organophosphates. *Mailing Add:* 19 Ralston Ave Piscataway NJ 08854

DIBENEDETTO, ANTHONY T, b New York, NY, Oct 27, 33; m 55; c 5. CHEMICAL ENGINEERING, MATERIALS SCIENCE. *Educ:* City Col New York, BChE, 55; Univ Wis, MS, 56, PhD(chem eng), 60. *Prof Exp:* Chem engr, Bakelite Co, Union Carbide Corp, 54-55; from instr to assoc prof chem eng, Univ Wis, 56-66; from assoc prof to prof, Wash Univ, 66-71, dir, Mat Res Lab, 68-71; prof & head chem eng, 71-76, vpres grad educ & res, 79-81, VPRES ACAD AFFAIRS, UNIV CONN, 81- *Mem:* Soc Plastics Engrs; Am Inst Chem Engrs. *Res:* Physical properties of organic high polymers; polymer composite materials. *Mailing Add:* Dept of Chem Eng Univ of Conn Storrs CT 06268

DIBENNARDO, ROBERT, b New York, NY, Oct 19, 41; m 69; c 1. MORPHOMETRICS, FORENSIC ANTHROPOLOGY. *Educ:* Hunter Col, BA, 63, MA, 66; City Univ New York, PhD(anthrop), 73. *Prof Exp:* Lectr, Hunter Col, 65-68; lectr, 68-73, asst prof, 73-81, ASSOC PROF ANTHROP, LEHMAN COL, CITY UNIV NEW YORK, 81- *Concurrent Pos:* Vis Scientist, Am Mus Natural Hist, 77-; coordr, Anthrop-Biol Prog, Lehman Col, 75-; asst dir, Metro Forensic Anthrop Team, 80- *Mem:* Am Asn Phys Anthropologists. *Res:* Multivariate morphometrics; forensic anthropology; human genetics; dental anthropology; quantitative methods. *Mailing Add:* Dept of Anthrop Lehman Col Bedford Park Blvd W Bronx NY 10468

DIBERARDINO, MARIE A, b Philadelphia, Pa, May 2, 26. DEVELOPMENTAL BIOLOGY, DEVELOPMENTAL GENETICS. *Educ:* Chestnut Hill Col, BS, 48; Univ Pa, PhD(zool), 62. *Prof Exp:* Res assoc embryol, Inst Cancer Res, 60-64, asst mem, 64-67; assoc prof, 67-71, PROF ANAT, MED COL PA, 71-, PROF PHYSIOL, 81- *Concurrent Pos:* Prin investr, Nat Sci Found, 68-77 & NIH, 78-84. *Honors & Awards:* Linnback Award, Med Col Pa, 78. *Mem:* Am Soc Zoologists; Soc Develop Biol (treas, 75-78); fel AAAS; Am Soc Cell Biol; Int Soc Develop Biologists. *Res:* Genetic potential of nuclei during normal differentiation and cancer being studied by means of nuclear transplantation into eggs and oocytes. *Mailing Add:* Dept Physiol & Biochem Med Col of Pa Philadelphia PA 19129

DIBIANCA, FRANK ANTHONY, experimental high energy physics, see previous edition

DI BIASE, STEPHEN AUGUSTINE, b Rochester, NY, Apr 6, 52; m 75; c 1. ORGANIC CHEMISTRY. *Educ:* St John Fisher Col, BS, 74; Pa State Univ, PhD(org chem), 78. *Prof Exp:* Anal technician photographic chem, Eastman Kodak Co, 72-74; res chemist, 78-81, RES SUPVR LUBRICANT ADDITIVES, LUBRIZOL CORP, 81- *Mem:* Am Chem Soc. *Res:* Development of new synthetic methods with subsequent application to the preparation of lubricant additives and other synthetic intermediates. *Mailing Add:* Lubrizol Corp 29400 Lakeland Blvd Wickliffe OH 44092

DIBLE, WILLIAM TROTTER, JR, b Oakmont, Pa, Sept 7, 25; m 48; c 4. CHEMISTRY. *Educ:* Pa State Col, BS, 49; Univ Wis, PhD, 52. *Prof Exp:* Asst, Univ Wis, 49-52; prod planning mgr, Int Minerals & Chem Corp, 52-64, dir mkt, 64; PRES, TERRA CHEMS, INTL, 64- *Res:* Boron determination in plants and soils; response of alfalfa to and its distribution in the plant. *Mailing Add:* Terra Chems Intl PO Box 1828 Sioux City IA 51102

DIBNER, MARK DOUGLAS, b New York, NY, Nov 7, 51. NEUROBIOLOGY, NEUROPHARMACOLOGY. *Educ:* Univ Pa, BA, 73; Cornell Univ, PhD(neurobiol), 77. *Prof Exp:* Fel pharmacol, Med Sch Univ Colo, 77-79, res fel & lectr, Univ Calif, San Diego, 79-80; PRIN SCIENTIST NEUROBIOL, E I DU PONT DE NEMOURS & CO, 80- *Concurrent Pos:* Instr Phychol, Metrop State Col, Denver, 79 & Nat Univ, San Diego, 80; vis lectr, Univ Del, 81- *Mem:* Soc Neurosci; AAAS; Sigma Xi; Am Soc Pharmacol & Exp Therapeut. *Res:* Receptors for neurotransmitters in brain and on cultured cells and ways drugs and other factors regulate these receptors. *Mailing Add:* Cent Res Dept Rm 107 Du Pont Glenolden Labs Glenolden PA 19036

DIBOLL, ALFRED, b San Diego, Calif, Aug 30, 30; m 67; c 3. DEVELOPMENTAL ANATOMY, PLANT ANATOMY. *Educ:* San Diego State Col, BS, 56; Claremont Grad Sch, MA, 59; Univ Tex, PhD(bot), 64. *Prof Exp:* Sr lab technician, Univ Calif, Riverside, 51-53, asst prof bot, Univ Calif, Los Angeles, 63-68; head fac biol, 68-72, CHMN DIV NATURAL SCI & MATH, MACON JR COL, 72- *Mailing Add:* Div of Natural Sci & Math Macon Jr Col Macon GA 31297

DIBONA, PETER JAMES, b Philadelphia, Pa, Dec 31, 41; m 71; c 4. SOLID STATE PHYSICS, SURFACE PHYSICS. *Educ:* Villanova Univ, BS, 64; Univ Del, MS, 67, PhD(physics), 74. *Prof Exp:* physicist explosives, Naval Surface Weapons Ctr, 76-80; PRIN DEVELOP ENGR, HONEYWELL, INC, 80- *Concurrent Pos:* Resident res assoc, Nat Res Coun, Picatinny Arsenal, 73-75. *Honors & Awards:* Civilian Commendation, Picatinny Arsenal, 74. *Mem:* Am Phys Soc. *Res:* X-ray photoelectron spectroscopy; detonation physics; radiation damage; explosives applications; flash radiography; weapons design; weapons development. *Mailing Add:* Honeywell Inc 5901 S County Rd 18 Edina MN 55436

DICARLO, ERNEST NICHOLAS, b Philadelphia, Pa, Jan 27, 36; m 75; c 4. CHEMICAL PHYSICS. *Educ:* St Joseph's Univ, Pa, BS, 58; Princeton Univ, PhD(chem), 62. *Prof Exp:* Asst chem, Princeton Univ, 58-59, res asst, 60-62; res chemist, Gulf Res & Develop Co, 62-63; from asst prof to assoc prof, 63-69, PROF CHEM, ST JOSEPH'S COL, PA, 69. *Mem:* Am Chem Soc. *Res:* Dipole moments; microwave absorption of liquids; nuclear magnetic resonance; electron spin resonance. *Mailing Add:* Dept Chem St Joseph's Univ 54th & City Line Ave Philadelphia PA 19131

DI CARLO, FREDERICK JOSEPH, b New York, NY, Nov 24, 18; m 43; c 3. CHEMISTRY, PHARMACOLOGY. *Educ:* Fordham Univ, BS, 39, MS, 41; NY Univ, PhD(org chem), 45. *Prof Exp:* Asst chem, NY Univ, 41-44; res assoc, Squibb Inst Med Res, 44-45; res chemist, Fleischmann Labs, Standard Brands, Inc, 45-46, dept head, 47-53, head biochem div, 53-60; sr res assoc, Warner-Lambert Res Inst, 60-70, dir, Dept Drug Metab, 70-77; CONSULT, OFF TOXIC SUBSTANCES, US ENVIRON PROTECTION AGENCY, 77- *Concurrent Pos:* Adj prof, Col St Elizabeth, 68-77; ed-in-chief, Drug Metab Rev. *Mem:* Am Soc Biol Chem; Am Soc Pharmacol & Exp Therapeut; Reticuloendothelial Soc (secy-treas, 65-67 & pres, 69); Am Chem Soc; Int Soc Biochem Pharmacol. *Res:* Drug metabolism; mechanisms of toxicity; penicillin; nucleic acids; amylases; fermentation; yeast derivatives; natural products; host defense mechanisms. *Mailing Add:* Xenobiotics Inc PO Box 361 Denville NJ 07834

DICARLO, JAMES ANTHONY, b Buffalo, NY, Jan 15, 38; m 66; c 5. SOLID STATE PHYSICS, MATERIALS SCIENCE. *Educ:* Canisius Col, BS, 59; Univ Pittsburgh, PhD(physics), 65. *Prof Exp:* Res assoc solid state physics, Brookhaven Nat Lab, 65-67; PHYSICIST, LEWIS RES CTR, NASA, 67- *Mem:* Metall Soc; AAAS; Am Phys Soc. *Res:* Crystal imperfections and their interactions in metals; radiation effects in solids; deformation and fracture of fiber-reinforced metal matrix composites. *Mailing Add:* Lewis Res Ctr MS106-1 Nat Aeronaut & Space Admin Cleveland OH 44135

DICE, J FRED, b Fowler, Calif, Aug 16, 47. CELL BIOLOGY, BIOCHEMISTRY. *Educ:* Univ Calif, Santa Cruz, BA, 69; Stanford Univ, PhD(biol), 73. *Prof Exp:* Res assoc physiol, Med Sch, Harvard Univ, 73-75; asst prof biol, Univ Calif, Santa Cruz, 74-78; ASST PROF PHYSIOL & BIOPHYS, MED SCH, HARVARD UNIV, 78- *Mem:* NY Acad Sci; AAAS; Am Soc Cell Biol. *Res:* Intracellular protein degradation; regulation by hormones, mechanisms of breakdown, influence of protein conformation on degradative rates. *Mailing Add:* Dept of Physiol 25 Shattuck St Boston MA 02115

DICE, JOHN RAYMOND, b Ann Arbor, Mich, Jan 11, 21; m 44; c 4. MEDICINAL CHEMISTRY. *Educ:* Univ Mich, BS, 41, MS, 42, PhD(chem), 46. *Prof Exp:* Shift foreman, Manhattan Proj, Tenn Eastman Co, 44-45; asst prof chem, Univ Tex, 46-51; from res chemist to sr res chemist, 51-61, lab dir, 61-62, group dir, 63-69, asst dir chem res, 70-76, DIR CHEM DEPT, WARNER-LAMBERT/PARKE-DAVIS PHARMACEUT RES DIV, ANN ARBOR, 76- *Mem:* Am Chem Soc; NY Acad Sci. *Res:* Chemistry of phenanthrenes; chemotherapy of virus diseases and cancer; chemistry of peptides and protein; drugs affecting the central nervous system. *Mailing Add:* Warner-Lambert/Parke-Davis Chem Dept 2800 Plymouth Rd Ann Arbor MI 48105

DICE, STANLEY FROST, b Pittsburgh, Pa, July 26, 21. MATHEMATICS. *Educ:* Oberlin Col, AB, 42; Univ Pittsburgh, MLitt, 51, PhD(math), 58. *Prof Exp:* Instr math & physics, WLiberty State Col, 51-52; instr math, Univ Detroit, 52-55; from instr to asst prof, Bucknell Univ, 55-62; asst prof, Carleton Col, 62-66; ASSOC PROF MATH, WITTENBERG UNIV, 66- *Mem:* Am Math Soc; Math Asn Am. *Res:* Summability of divergent series. *Mailing Add:* Dept of Math Wittenberg Univ Springfield OH 45501

DICELLO, JOHN FRANCIS, JR, b Bradford, Pa, Dec 18, 38; m 62; c 2. MEDICAL BIOPHYSICS, NUCLEAR PHYSICS. *Educ:* St Bonaventure Univ, BS, 60; Univ Pittsburgh, MS, 62; Tex A&M Univ, PhD(physics), 68. *Prof Exp:* Instr physics, St Bonaventure Univ, 62-63; res scientist, 67-69, res assoc radiol physics, Columbia Univ, 69-73; MEM STAFF, LOS ALAMOS NAT LAB, 73-; INSTR, UNIV NMEX, LOS ALAMOS, 81- *Mem:* Am Asn Physicists Med; Radiation Res Soc; Am Phys Soc; Am Cancer Soc. *Res:* Medical physics; microdosimetry; nuclear structure; biophysics. *Mailing Add:* MP-3 Los Alamos Nat Lab Los Alamos NM 87545

DICENZO, COLIN D, b Hamilton, Ont, July 26, 23; m 50; c 6. ELECTRICAL ENGINEERING. *Educ:* Univ NB, BSc, 52, MSc, 57; Imp Col, London, dipl elec eng, 53. *Prof Exp:* Lectr elec eng, Royal Mil Col, Ont, 54-57; dep head, Sonar Group, Royal Can Naval Hq, Ottawa, 57-60, head, Underwater Fire Control, 60-62, proj engr, Hydrofoil Ship HMCS Bras d'Or,

64-65; assoc prof elec eng, McMaster Univ, 65-72, dir undergrad stud, Fac Eng, 68-75, prof elec eng, 72-79, prof elec & comput eng, 79-80; PROF & DEAN ENG & APPL SCI, MEM UNIV NFLD, 80- *Concurrent Pos:* Nat Res Coun res grants, 66-70; assoc ed, Inst Elec & Electronics Engrs trans IECI, 75-78. *Honors & Awards:* Julian C Smith Medal, Eng Inst Can. *Mem:* sr mem & fel, Inst Elec & Electronics Engrs; fel Eng Inst Can (sr vpres, 78, pres, 79); Can Soc Elec Eng (pres, 76-78). *Res:* Underwater acoustic systems; fire-control systems; application and design of permanent magnet devices; engineering and management systems. *Mailing Add:* Mem Univ Nfld St Johns ON L9A 2T4 Can

DICHTER, MICHAEL, b Jan 15, 12; US citizen; m 39; c 1. PETROLEUM CHEMISTRY, POLYMER CHEMISTRY. *Educ:* Polish Acad Sci, PhD, 33; Lvov Polytech Inst, MSc, 36. *Prof Exp:* Sr engr, Petrol Refineries, Poland, 36-41 & USSR, 41-44; dir petrochem prod, Trzebinia, Poland, 45-48; dir planning, Ministry For Trade, Warsaw, 48-55, dep for trade secy, 55-56; dir res, Cent Lab, Petrol Prod, 57-62; mem staff, Inst Petrol Technol, Cracow-Warsaw, 63-69; dir res, 69-75, V PRES RES & RECRUITING CONTACT, POLYMER RES CORP, 75-, CHIEF RES EXEC, COAL & BATTERY DIV, 77- *Honors & Awards:* Golden Award Merit, Polish Govt, 47; Order Polonia Restituta 2nd Class, 54, 1st class, 64. *Res:* New high quality lubricants and fuels for modern engines and machines; corrosion and water pollution prevention in petroleum refineries; Groft polymerization; polymer modification of solving problems, specifically surface modification, adhesion, nonflammable textiles and improving additives for petroleum products. *Mailing Add:* Polymer Res Corp 2186 Mill Ave Brooklyn NY 11234

DICIANNI, NICHOLAS M, b Fall River, Mass, Feb 22, 39; m 63. COMPUTER SCIENCE, SYSTEMS PROGRAMMING. *Educ:* Providence Col, BS, 60; Notre Dame Univ, PhD(chem), 65. *Prof Exp:* Asst prof comput sci, Notre Dame Univ, 65-68; staff consult to vpres systs programming, Univac Div, Sperry Rand Corp, 68-70, dir applns software, 70-76, DIR STRATEGIC PLANNING, SPERRY UNIVAC, 76- *Mem:* Asn Comput Mach; Sigma Xi. *Res:* Design of computer operating systems; programming language processors; industry oriented computer applications; computeer and business statistics. *Mailing Add:* Sperry Univac PO Box 500 Blue Bell PA 19424

DICK, BERTRAM GALE, b Portland, Ore, June 12, 26; m 56; c 3. PHYSICS. *Educ:* Reed Col, BA, 50; Oxford Univ, MA, 57; Cornell Univ, PhD(physics), 58. *Prof Exp:* Res assoc physics, Univ Ill, 57-59; from asst prof to assoc prof, 59-65, from actg chmn dept to chmn, 64-67, PROF PHYSICS, UNIV UTAH, 65- *Concurrent Pos:* Consult, Minn Mining & Mfg Co, 60-67; vis prof, Munich Tech Univ, 67-68; vis scientist, Max-Planck-Inst Solid State Res, Stuttgart, 76-77. *Mem:* Fel Am Phys Soc; AAAS; Fedn Am Scientists. *Res:* Solid state physics; ionic crystals; phonons and phonon-defect interactions; paraelectric defects; color centers. *Mailing Add:* Dept of Physics Univ of Utah Salt Lake City UT 84112

DICK, CHARLES EDWARD, b Fort Wayne, Ind, Apr 24, 37; m 58; c 2. ATOMIC AND MOLECULAR PHYSICS. *Educ:* Ill Benedictine Col, BS, 58; Univ Notre Dame, PhD(physics), 63. *Prof Exp:* PHYSICIST, NAT BUR STAND, 62- *Mem:* AAAS; Sigma Xi; Am Phys Soc; Soc Photo-Optical Instrumentation Engrs. *Res:* Low energy electron scattering; bremstrahlung production; low energy electromagnetic interactions; x-ray analysis; applications of x-rays; medical and industrial radiographic systems. *Mailing Add:* Ctr for Radiation Res Nat Bur of Stand Washington DC 20234

DICK, DONALD EDWARD, b Little Rock, Ark, Apr 23, 42; m 63. BIOMEDICAL ENGINEERING, ELECTRICAL ENGINEERING. *Educ:* Calif Inst Technol, BS, 64; Univ Wis-Madison, MS, 65, PhD(elec eng), 68. *Prof Exp:* Res asst elec eng, Univ Wis-Madison, 64-66; asst prof elec eng, Univ Colo, Boulder, 68-73; asst prof phys med & rehab, Med Ctr, Univ Colo, Denver, 68-73; sect head res & develop, Unirad Corp, 73-75; res assoc anat, Bioeng Sect, Med Ctr, Univ Colo, Denver, 76-78; sr engr, Life Instruments Corp, 78-; MGR ENG, ARMCO AUTOMETRICS, 80- *Concurrent Pos:* NIH grant biomed sci, 69-70. *Mem:* Inst Elec & Electronics Engrs. *Res:* Advanced ultrasonic instrumentation for medical diagnostic use; high resolution image storage and retrieval systems; biomedical simulation and computer-aided patient monitoring in cardiovascular intensive care units; microprocessors and minicomputers and process control. *Mailing Add:* Life Instruments Corp 2300 Central Ave Boulder CO 80302

DICK, ELLIOT C, b Miami, Fla, June 30, 26; m 50, 67; c 4. MICROBIOLOGY, EPIDEMIOLOGY. *Educ:* Univ Minn, BA, 50, MS, 53, PhD(bact), 55; Univ Wis, cert epidemiol, 65; Am Bd Med Microbiol, dipl, 68. *Prof Exp:* Asst prof bact, Univ Kans, 55-59; asst prof med, Sch Med, Tulane Univ, 59-61; from asst prof to assoc prof, 61-72, PROF PREV MED, UNIV WIS-MADISON, 72- *Concurrent Pos:* Grant, Univ Kans, 56-59, Kans State Bd Health grant, 57-58; USPHS grants, Univ Wis, 61-70 & 71-, S C Johnson, Inc grants, 66-67 & 70-, Smith Kline & French grants, 66-71 & 74, NASA grants, 67- & NSF grants, 76-; USPHS career develop award, 64-68; vis scientist, Delta Regional Primate Ctr, Tulane Univ, 67; mem, WHO Collab Comts Rhinoviruses; consult, S C Johnson & Son, Inc, 62-, Smith Kline & French Labs, 65-, NIH, 65-, NASA, 65-, Abbott Labs, 65-, Sterling Drug Co, Albany, NY, 73-, NSF, 80- & Kimberly-Clark Corp, 81- *Honors & Awards:* Elizabeth M Watkins Res Award, Univ Kans, 58. *Mem:* Soc Exp Biol & Med; fel Infectious Dis Soc Am; NY Acad Sci; Am Soc Microbiol; fel Explorers Club. *Res:* Etiology, pathogenesis and epidemiology of respiratory infections; role of viruses in asthma; transmission of respiratory viruses in isolated Antarctic populations; virology. *Mailing Add:* Dept of Prev Med Univ of Wis-Madison Madison WI 53706

DICK, GEORGE W, b Toronto, Ont, June 12, 31; m 53; c 3. ELECTRONICS ENGINEERING. *Educ:* Univ Toronto, BASc, 53, MASc, 57, PhD(eng), 60. *Prof Exp:* Mem staff elec res & develop, Apparatus Engr Lab, Can Gen Elec Co, 53-55; mem staff commun res, 59-65, MEM TECH STAFF, BELL TEL LABS, 68- *Concurrent Pos:* Assoc prof elec eng, Univ Toronto, 65-68. *Mem:* Assoc Inst Elec & Electronics Engrs. *Res:* Communication principles; display communications techniques including gas plasma display panels, light emitting diodes and associated data transmission electronics. *Mailing Add:* Supvr Bell Tel Lab Roberts Rd Holmdel NJ 07733

DICK, HENRY JONATHAN BIDDLE, petrology, see previous edition

DICK, HENRY MARVIN, b Duchess, Alta, June 1, 31; m 57; c 3. ORAL PATHOLOGY. *Educ:* Univ Alta, DDS, 57; Univ Man, MSc, 68. *Prof Exp:* Gen pract dent, 57-66; assoc prof, 68-77, PROF ORAL PATH & ACTG CHMN DEPT, UNIV ALTA, 77- *Res:* Immunopathology of periodontal disease. *Mailing Add:* 3632 118 St Edmonton Can

DICK, JAMES GARDINER, b Perth, Scotland, Oct 22, 20; Can citizen; m 56; c 2. ANALYTICAL CHEMISTRY, ELECTROCHEMISTRY. *Prof Exp:* Chief chemist & metallurgist, Can Bronze Co, Ltd, 47-54, dist mgr prod, res & sales, Montreal Bronze, Ltd, 54-58, mgr mfg prod, control & res, Can Bronze Co, Ltd, 58-63; from asst prof to assoc prof chem & mat sci, 63-71, vchmn dept, 71-74, chmn dept, 74-76, PROF CHEM, CONCORDIA UNIV, 71-, DIR SCI INDUST RES, 75- *Concurrent Pos:* Mgr, Roast Labs Registered, 41-47; lectr, Sir George Williams Univ, 47-63; pres, Technitrol Ltd, 63-68, consult, 68-; consult, Can Metal Co Ltd, Metals & Alloys Cp Ltd & Ingot Medal Co Ltd, 68-; pres, Methodologies Consult Ltd, 81- *Mem:* Am Foundryman's Soc; Am Soc Testing & Mat; Chem Inst Can; Spectros Soc; Am Chem Soc. *Res:* X-ray spectrochemical analysis; environmental chemistry; electrochemical kinetics; polarography. *Mailing Add:* Dept of Chem Concordia Univ Montreal PQ H3G 1M8 Can

DICK, JERRY JOEL, b Langdon, NDak, May 12, 42; m 65; c 5. PHYSICS, MATERIAL SCIENCE. *Educ:* Ore State Univ, BA, 63; Southern Ore Col, MA, 70; Wash State Univ, PhD(physics), 74. *Prof Exp:* Exp physicist shockwaves in solids, Stanford Res Inst, 66-69 & Physics Int Co, 69; asst physicist, Wash State Univ, 74-77; STAFF MEM DETONATION PHYSICS, LOS ALAMOS SCI LAB, 77- *Res:* Shock initiation of detonation in reactive solids; dynamic failure and elastic-plastic wave propagation in solids; phase transition and transport phenomena under dynamic high pressure. *Mailing Add:* Los Alamos Sci Lab PO Box 1663 M-3 MS-960 Los Alamos NM 87545

DICK, JOHN WALTER, avian pathology, see previous edition

DICK, KENNETH ANDERSON, b Vancouver, BC, July 30, 37; m 59; c 2. PHYSICS. *Educ:* Univ BC, BSc, 60, MSc, 63, PhD(physics), 66. *Prof Exp:* Res assoc physics, Johns Hopkins Univ, 66-69, asst physicist, Kitt Peak Nat Observ, 69-74; vis res scientist, Johns Hopkins Univ, 74-75; vis assoc prof, Inst Phys Sci & Technol, Univ Md, 74-78; STAFF SCIENTIST, BENDIX CORP, 78- *Mem:* Optical Soc Am. *Res:* Atomic and molecular spectroscopy; terrestrial aeronomy and planetary astronomy; atmospheric optics. *Mailing Add:* Environ & Process Instruments Div 1400 Taylor Ave Baltimore MD 21204

DICK, RICHARD DEAN, b Angola, Ind, Sept 27, 30; m 56; c 3. SHOCK WAVE PHYSICS, EQUATION OF STATE. *Educ:* Ariz State Univ, BS, 57, MS, 60, PhD(physics), 68. *Prof Exp:* Staff mem condensed matter physics, Los Alamos Sci Lab, 59-75, dep group leader shock & weapon physics, 75-81, STAFF MEM ROCK FRAGMENTATION, LOS ALAMOS NAT LAB, 81- *Mem:* Am Phys Soc; Am Geophys Union. *Res:* Dynamic high pressure equation of state properties of solids and liquids; radiography of high speed events using a 30 mega electron volts flash x-ray machine; fragmentation of oil shale using explosives. *Mailing Add:* Los Alamos Nat Lab Box 1663 MS 335 Los Alamos NM 87545

DICK, RICHARD IRWIN, b Sanborn, Iowa, July 18, 35; m 58; c 4. ENVIRONMENTAL ENGINEERING, CIVIL ENGINEERING. *Educ:* Iowa State Univ, BS, 57; Univ Iowa, MS, 58; Univ Ill, Urbana, PhD(sanit eng), 65. *Prof Exp:* Sanit engr, Clark, Daily, Dietz & Assocs, Consult Engrs, 60-62; from instr to prof sanit eng, Univ Ill, Urbana-Champaign, 62-70; vis engr, Water Pollution Res Lab, Eng, 70-71; prof civil eng, Univ Del, 72-77; JOSEPH P RIPLEY PROF ENG, CORNELL UNIV, 77- *Honors & Awards:* Harrison Prescott Eddy Medal, Water Pollution Control Fedn, 68. *Mem:* Asn Environ Eng Prof (pres, 73); Int Asn Water Pollution Res. *Res:* Unit operations and processes used in water and waste water treatment; treatment and disposal of wastewater sludges. *Mailing Add:* Dept of Environ Eng Cornell Univ Ithaca NY 14853

DICK, RONALD STEWART, b Queens, NY, Jan 14, 34; m 58; c 2. MATHEMATICAL STATISTICS. *Educ:* Queens Col, BS, 55; Columbia Univ, MA, 57, PhD(math statist), 68. *Prof Exp:* Math statistician, US Census Bur, Washington, DC, 56-57; lectr math, Queens Col, NY, 57-62; sr mem tech staff, ITT Defense Commun, NJ, 60-68; asst prof math, C W Post Col, Long Island Univ, 63-68; assoc prof mgt, George Washington Univ, 68-75; supvr opers anal, Social Security Admin, 75-80; STATISTICIAN, CHI ASSOC, 80- *Concurrent Pos:* Asst, Columbia Univ, 56-57; engr, Sperry Gyroscope Co, NY, 57-59; reliability engr, Am Bosch Arma, 59-60; vis lectr, Stevens Inst Technol, 63. *Mem:* Opers Res Soc Am; Inst Math Statist; Am Statist Asn. *Res:* Queueing theory with balking; reliability of repairable complex systems. *Mailing Add:* 956 W Monroe Arlington MD 20904

DICK, STANLEY, b Brooklyn, NY, Aug 13, 36. FUNGAL GENETICS & MORPHOGENESIS. *Educ:* Brooklyn Col, AB, 56; Harvard Univ, MA & PhD(biol), 60. *Prof Exp:* Northern Atlantic Treaty Orgn fel, Dept Bot, Univ Col, Univ London, 60-61; USPHS fel, Bot Inst, Univ Cologne, 61-62; res assoc biol, Harvard Univ, 62-64; asst prof bot, Ind Univ, Bloomington, 64-71; from asst prof to assoc prof, 71-78, PROF BIOL, FITCHBURG STATE COL, 78-, CHMN DEPT, 73- *Concurrent Pos:* NSF res fel, Orgn Trop Studies, San Jose, Costa Rica, 70; vis prof biol, Harvard Univ, 72, 73 & 74; vis res assoc bot, Univ Wis-Madison, 76 & 77, vis prof & NSF fel, 78. *Mem:* AAAS; Genetics Soc Am; Mycol Soc Am; Am Soc Microbiol. *Res:* Genetics, physiology and morphogenesis in higher basidiomycetes; hormonal, chemical and mechanical induction of fruiting bodies and tumors; fungal phenoloxidases; mutation expression and somatic recombination in heterokaryons; biochemical genetics of incompatibility. *Mailing Add:* Dept of Biol Fitchburg State Col Fitchburg MA 01420

DICK, T(HOMAS) M(ILNE), b New Stevenston, Scotland, Dec 11, 31; Can citizen; m 56; c 4. HYDRAULICS. *Educ:* Glasgow Univ, BSc, 53; Univ Strathclyde, ARTC, 54; Queen's Univ, Ont, MSc, 60, PhD(hydraul), 69. *Prof Exp:* Engr, City Port Arthur, Ont, 53-55; design engr, C D Howe Co Ltd, 55-58; res asst hydraul, Queen's Univ, Ont, 58-60; engr, Dept Pub Works, 60-61 & Dept Transport, 61-64; res officer, Nat Res Coun Can, 64-69; head hydraul, Dept Energy, Mines & Resources, 69-70; CHIEF HYDRAUL, DEPT ENVIRON, 70- *Concurrent Pos:* Lectr, Queen's Univ, Ont, 66-67. *Mem:* Am Geophys Union; Int Asn Hydraul Res; Int Asn Great Lakes Res. *Res:* Coastal engineering; transportation; river hydraulics; ice in rivers; sediment transport. *Mailing Add:* Can Ctr Inland Waters 867 Lakeshore Rd Box 5050 Burlington ON L7R 4A6 Can

DICK, WILLIAM EDWIN, JR, b Waynesboro, Va, Oct 31, 36; m 58; c 3. CHEMISTRY. *Educ:* NC State Univ, BS, 58; Purdue Univ, MS, 62, PhD, 66. *Prof Exp:* CHEMIST, NORTHERN UTILIZATION RES LAB, USDA, 65- *Mem:* Am Chem Soc; Sigma Xi. *Res:* Characterization of microbiol polysaccharides, and development of analytical methodology. *Mailing Add:* Northern Utilization Res Lab 1815 N University Ave Peoria IL 61604

DICKAS, ALBERT BINKLEY, b Sidney, Ohio, Sept 4, 33; m 62; c 4. RESEARCH ADMINISTRATION, GEOLOGY. *Educ:* Miami Univ, BA, 55, MS, 56; Mich State Univ, PhD(geol), 62. *Prof Exp:* Develop geologist, Magnolia Petrol Co, 56-59; instr geol, Mich State Univ, 59-62; explor geologist, Standard Oil Co Calif, 63-66; from asst prof to assoc prof, 66-76, PROF GEOL, UNIV WIS-SUPERIOR, 76- DIR, OFF EXTRAMURAL PLANNING, 69- *Mem:* Am Asn Petrol Geologists; Soc Econ Paleontologists & Mineralogists; Int Asn Great Lakes Res. *Res:* Social, economic, physical and biological aspects of present and future development of the Lake Superior Basin. *Mailing Add:* Off Extramural Planning Univ Wis Superior WI 54880

DICKASON, ALAN FREDERICK, organic chemistry, see previous edition

DICKASON, ELVIS ARNIE, b Ore, Oct 9, 19; m 46; c 2. ENTOMOLOGY. *Educ:* Ore State Univ, BS, 47, MS, 49; Mich State Univ, PhD(entom), 59. *Prof Exp:* From instr to assoc prof entom, Ore State Univ, 49-70; interim dir, Int Progs, 73-75, PROF ENTOM & HEAD DEPT, UNIV NEBR, LINCOLN, 70- *Concurrent Pos:* Grant-in-aid entom, IRI Res Inst, Salvador, Brazil, 66-67. *Mem:* Entom Soc Am. *Res:* Applied entomology; insect ecology. *Mailing Add:* Dept of Entom Univ of Nebr Lincoln NE 68583

DICKASON, WILLIAM CHARLES, organic chemistry, see previous edition

DICKE, FERDINAND FREDERICK, b New Bremen, Ohio, Aug 25, 99; m 29; c 3. ENTOMOLOGY. *Educ:* Ohio State Univ, BS, 27. *Prof Exp:* Field asst, Bur Entom & Plant Quarantine, USDA, Mich, 27-28; jr entomologist, 28-29, asst entomologist, Va, 29-33, Arlington Farm, 33-42 & Beltsville Res Ctr, 42, assoc entomologist, Ohio, 42-50, entomologist, Entom Res Div, Agr Res Serv, 50-63; assoc prof entom, 57-61, PROF ENTOM, IOWA STATE UNIV, 61-; ENTOMOLOGIST, PIONEER HI-BRED INT INC, 63- *Mem:* AAAS; Entom Soc Am; Sigma Xi. *Res:* Development of crop varieties resistant to insects; corn insect vectors of diseases. *Mailing Add:* 1430 Harding Ave Ames IA 50010

DICKE, ROBERT HENRY, b St Louis, Mo, May 6, 16; m 42; c 3. ASTROPHYSICS. *Educ:* Princeton Univ, AB, 39; Univ Rochester, PhD(physics), 41. *Hon Degrees:* DSc, Univ Edinburgh, Scotland, 72, Univ Rochester & Ohio Northern Univ, 81. *Prof Exp:* Staff mem radiation lab, Mass Inst Technol, 41-46; from asst prof to prof physics, 46-57, Cyrus Fogg Brackett prof, 57-75, chmn dept physics, 68-70, ALBERT EINSTEIN UNIV PROF SCI, PRINCETON UNIV, 75- *Concurrent Pos:* Vis prof, Harvard Univ, 54-55; mem adv panel physics, NSF, 59-61, chmn adv comt radio astron, 67-69; chmn adv comt atomic physics, Nat Bur Standards, 61-63; mem comt physics, NASA, 63-70, chmn, 63-66, mem lunar ranging exp team, 66-; chmn physics panel, Adv to Comt Int Exchange of Persons, Fulbright Fels, 64-66; mem, Nat Sci Bd, 70-76; mem vis comt, Nat Bur Stand, 75-, chmn, 78. *Honors & Awards:* Rumford Premium Award, Am Acad Arts & Sci, 67; Nat Medal Sci, 71; Comstock Prize, Nat Acad Sci & Medal Exceptional Sci Achievement, NASA, 73; Cresson Medal, Franklin Inst, 74. *Mem:* Nat Acad Sci; fel Am Acad Arts & Sci; fel Am Phys Soc; fel Am Geophys Union; Royal Astron Soc. *Res:* Gravitation; relativity; astrophysics; solar physics; cosmology. *Mailing Add:* Joseph Henry Labs Dept Physics Jadwin Hall Princeton Univ Princeton NJ 08544

DICKEL, HELENE RAMSEYER, b Cambridge, Mass, Mar 19, 38; m 61; c 2. ASTRONOMY. *Educ:* Mt Holyoke Col, BA, 59; Univ Mich, MA, 61, PhD(astron), 64. *Prof Exp:* Res assoc astron, Univ Ill Observ, Urbana, 65-70; vis scientist astron, Div Radio Physics, Commonwealth Sci & Indust Res Orgn, Australia, 70-71; res assoc astron, 71-77, RES ASSOC PROF ASTRON, UNIV ILL OBSERV, URBANA, 77- *Concurrent Pos:* Vis astronomer, Huygens Lab, Leiden, Neth, 77-78, Harlow Shapley vis lectr, 81-82. *Mem:* Int Astron Union; Int Sci Radio Union; Am Astron Soc; Astron Soc Pac. *Res:* Optical and radio studies of physical conditions in interstellar gas clouds which are composed of ionized hydrogen and/or dust and molecules. *Mailing Add:* 341 UI Astron Bldg 1011 W Springfield Urbana IL 61801

DICKENS, BRIAN, b Manchester, Eng, Mar 15, 37; US citizen; m 62; c 2. PHYSICAL CHEMISTRY. *Educ:* ARIC, London, 58; Univ Minn, MS, 60, PhD(phys chem), 62. *Prof Exp:* Res assoc chem, Harvard Univ, 60-62; chemist, Chloride Tech Serv, Manchester, Eng, 62-64; phys chemist, Naval Propellant Plant, Md, 64-66; PHYS CHEMIST, NAT BUR STANDARDS, 66- *Concurrent Pos:* Res chemist, Am Dent Asn, 73-74. *Mem:* Am Chem Soc; Royal Soc Chem. *Res:* Polymer degradation; polymer oxidation; thermogravimetry; chemiluminescence; computer automation and optimization of experiments; computer prediction of epitaxy and twinning; crystal structures of calcium phosphates by x-ray and neutron diffraction; hydrates and hydrogen bonding. *Mailing Add:* Nat Bur of Standards Washington DC 20234

DICKENS, CHARLES HENDERSON, b Thomasville, NC, Nov 22, 34; m 65; c 2. SCIENCE POLICY, SCIENCE EDUCATION. *Educ:* Duke Univ, BS, 57, MEd, 64, DEduc(math educ), 66. *Prof Exp:* Res technician, Nat Security Agency, 57-58 & 60-62; teacher high sch, NC, 62-63; instr educ, Wake Forest Col, 65-66, asst prof math & educ, 66-67; planning specialist, Planning & Eval Unit Off Assoc Dir Educ, 67-69, assoc prog dir, Stud-Originated Studies Prog, Div Undergrad Educ Sci, 69-73, prog mgr, Exp Projs & Prob Assessment Group, Off Exp Projs & Progs, 73, study dir, 73-80, SR STUDY DIR, SUPPLY & EDUC ANAL GROUP, DIV SCI RESOURCES STUDIES, NSF, 80- *Concurrent Pos:* Consult, Am Political Sci Asn & US Civil Serv Comn Cong fel, 71-72; NSF rep, Higher Educ Adv Panel, Nat Ctr Educ Statist, 81- *Mem:* AAAS; Am Educ Res Asn. *Res:* Statistics of higher education; research activity of science and engineering faculty; supply of scientists and engineers. *Mailing Add:* Supply & Educ Anal Group Nat Sci Found Washington DC 20550

DICKENS, ELMER DOUGLAS, JR, b Charleston, WVa, Dec 26, 42; c 2. POLYMER SCIENCE. *Educ:* Morris Harvey Col, BS, 65; WVa Univ, MS, 67, PhD(physics), 70. *Prof Exp:* From res physicist to sr res physicist, 70-74, group leader new prod, 74-76, sect leader new ventures, 76-78, sect mgr, 78-81, MGR CORP RES, B F GOODRICH RES CTR, 81- *Mem:* Combustion Inst; Am Inst Physics. *Res:* Mathematical models of physical systems; polymer combustion; smoke generation from polymers; modeling of fires; flammability testing; polymer physics; group theory; theoretical physics. *Mailing Add:* BF Goodrich R & D Ctr 9921 Breeksville Rd Breeksville OH 44141

DICKENS, JUSTIN KIRK, b Syracuse, NY, Nov 2, 31; m 57; c 4. NUCLEAR PHYSICS. *Educ:* Univ Southern Calif, AB, 55, PhD(physics), 62; Univ Chicago, MS, 56. *Prof Exp:* PHYSICIST, LOW ENERGY NUCLEAR PHYSICS, OAK RIDGE NAT LAB, 62- *Mem:* AAAS; Am Phys Soc; Am Nuclear Soc; Sigma Xi. *Res:* Nuclear reaction mechanisms, experimental and theoretical; experimental reactor safety research; adminstration of scientific programs. *Mailing Add:* Oak Ridge Nat Lab Oak Ridge TN 37830

DICKENS, LAWRENCE EDWARD, b North Kingstown, RI, Dec 8, 32; m 52; c 7. ELECTRICAL & ELECTRONIC ENGINEERING. *Educ:* Johns Hopkins Univ, BSEE, 60, MSEE, 62, DEng, 64. *Prof Exp:* Field Engr Radio Div, Bendix Corp, 53-56, asst proj engr, 56-58, proj engr, 58-60; res staff asst electronic design, Radiation Lab, Johns Hopkins Univ, 60-62 res assoc microwave semiconductors, 62-64, res scientist, 64-65; res scientist, Advan Technol Corp, 65-69; ADV ENGR, WESTINGHOUSE ELEC CORP, 69- *Concurrent Pos:* Consult, Radio Div, Bendix Corp, 60-63, Appl Microwave Elec Corp, 61, Am Electronics Labs, Inc, 63, Res Div, Electronic Commun, Inc, 63-64 & Pinkerton Electro-Security Co, 65-66. *Mem:* Inst Elec & Electronics Engrs. *Res:* Development of low noise communications systems and components; microwave and millimeter wave semiconductor components and their applications. *Mailing Add:* Advan Technol Labs Box 1521 MS-3717 Baltimore MD 21203

DICKENS, LESTER EMERT, b Palisade, Colo, Nov 18, 19; m 45. PLANT PATHOLOGY. *Educ:* Colo State Univ, BS, 50, MS, 53; Cornell Univ, PhD, 57. *Prof Exp:* Asst prof bot & plant path & asst plant pathologist, 57-63, exten plant pathologist, 63-70, exten prof plant path, 70-77, PROF BOT & PLANT PATH, COLO STATE UNIV, 77- *Concurrent Pos:* Partic, workshop plant path, Tech Task Force Comt, Great Plains Agr Coun, 69- *Mem:* AAAS; Am Phytopath Soc; Sigma Xi. *Res:* Extension plant pathology. *Mailing Add:* Dept of Plant Path Colo State Univ Ft Collins CO 80521

DICKENS, MICHAEL STEPHEN, biochemistry, carcinogenesis, see previous edition

DICKENSON, DONALD DWIGHT, b Paris, Ill, Jan 15, 25; m 46; c 4. CROP BREEDING, AGRONOMY. *Educ:* Univ Ill, BS, 49, MS, 50; Univ Minn, PhD(grass breeding), 57. *Prof Exp:* Plant breeder, 53-62, asst dir agr res, 62-66, dir agr res, 66-81, AGR RES COORDR, HOLLY SUGAR CORP, 81- *Mem:* Am Soc Agron; Am Soc Sugar Beet Technol; Am Phytopath Soc; Am Genetics Asn; Crop Sci Soc Am. *Res:* Assessment of agronomic problems with appropriate action-all areas; coordinate state & federal research for agronomic problems. *Mailing Add:* 4515 Ridgeglen Rd Colorado Springs CO 80907

DICKER, DANIEL, b Brooklyn, NY, Dec 30, 29; m 51; c 2. AEROELASTICITY, PARTIAL DIFFERENTIAL EQUATIONS. *Educ:* City Col New York, BCE, 51; NY Univ, MCE, 55; Columbia Univ, EngScD(appl mech), 61. *Prof Exp:* Engr, Bogert-Childs, 51-52 & 54-55; proj engr, Praeger-Kavanagh, 55-58; res asst eng, Columbia Univ, 59-60, from instr to asst prof, 60-62; from asst prof to assoc prof, 62-68, asst dean, Grad Sch, 65-69, exec officer, Col Eng, 70-71, dir postgrad exten prog, Col Eng, 74-78, PROF APPL MATH, STATE UNIV NY STONY BROOK, 68- *Concurrent Pos:* NSF grant, 63-70; NATO fel, Imp Col, Univ London, 69-70; hon res fel, Harvard Univ, 78-79. *Honors & Awards:* Norman Medal, Am Soc Civil Engrs, 67, Arthur M Wellington Prize, 72. *Mem:* fel Am Soc Civil Engrs; Soc Indust & Appl Math; fel NY Acad Sci. *Res:* Hydrodynamics; approximate solutions of boundary value problems; heat conduction; structural dynamics; transient flow in porous media. *Mailing Add:* Dept Appl Math & Statistics State Univ of NY Stony Brook NY 11790

DICKER, PAUL EDWARD, b Philadelphia, Pa, June 17, 25; m 53; c 4. ELECTRICAL ENGINEERING. *Educ:* Swarthmore Col, BSc, 45; Ohio State Univ, MSc, 48. *Prof Exp:* Asst math, Ohio State Univ, 46-47; instr elec eng, 47-48; instr, Princeton Univ, 48-51; res assoc, Eng Res Inst, Univ Mich, 51-54; from asst prof to assoc prof elec eng, Vanderbilt Univ, 54-59; instr elec eng, Tenn State Univ, 59-64; chief engr, Aladdin Electronics, 59-65, asst gen mgr, 65-67, mgr opers & dir prod develop, 67-70, vpres, Telecommun Prod, 70-79, VPRES MKT & PROD DEVELOP, AIE, DIV VERNITRON, 79-; PRES, QUAL ASSURANCE DATA ELECTRONICS, INC, 69- *Concurrent Pos:* plant engr, Kaiser-Frazer Corp, 52-; consult, Avco Mfg Co, Miniature Electronic Components & Essex Electronics. *Mem:* Sr mem Inst Elec & Electronics Engrs. *Res:* Electronics; magnetic components. *Mailing Add:* 6110 Elizabethan Dr Nashville TN 37205

DICKERHOOF, DEAN W, b Akron, Ohio, Nov 9, 35; m 58; c 2. INORGANIC CHEMISTRY. *Educ:* Univ Akron, BS, 57; Univ Ill, MS & PhD(inorg chem), 61. *Prof Exp:* From asst prof to assoc prof, 61-73, PROF CHEM, COLO SCH MINES, 74- *Mem:* Am Chem Soc; The Chem Soc. *Res:* Synthesis and characterization of inorganic and organometallic compounds. Analysis of coal and coal-derived liquids. *Mailing Add:* Dept of Chem Colo Sch of Mines Golden CO 80401

DICKERMAN, CHARLES EDWARD, b Carbondale, Ill, Mar 9, 32; m 54; c 4. NUCLEAR SCIENCE. *Educ:* Southern Ill Univ, BA, 51, MA, 52, Univ London, DIC, 53; Univ Iowa, PhD(physics), 57. *Prof Exp:* PHYSICIST, ARGONNE NAT LAB, 57- *Mem:* Am Phys Soc; Am Nuclear Soc. *Res:* Nuclear safety of fast reactors. *Mailing Add:* React Anal Safe Div Argonne Nat Lab 9700 S Cass Ave Argonne IL 60439

DICKERMAN, HERBERT W, b New York, NY, Aug 3, 28; m 63; c 3. BIOCHEMISTRY, INTERNAL MEDICINE. *Educ:* State Univ NY, MD, 52; Johns Hopkins Univ, PhD(biol), 60. *Prof Exp:* Instr med, Sch Med, Johns Hopkins Univ, 60-63; investr clin biochem, Nat Heart Inst, 63-66; assoc prof med, Sch Med, Johns Hopkins Univ, 66-75; MEM STAFF, DIV LAB & RES, NY STATE DEPT HEALTH, 75-; PROF BIOCHEM, ALBANY MED COL, 77- *Concurrent Pos:* Estab investr, Am Heart Asn, 60-66; NIH res career develop award, 66- *Mem:* Am Soc Biol Chemists; Endocrine Soc. *Res:* Folate and vitamin B-12 metabolism; biochemical control mechanisms; ribonucleic acid metabolism; steroid hormone mechanism of action; hematopoesis. *Mailing Add:* Div Lab & Res NY State Dept Health Albany NY 12201

DICKERMAN, RICHARD CURTIS, b Chicago, Ill, Jan 31, 34; m 60; c 2. GENETICS, ZOOLOGY. *Educ:* Col Wooster, BA, 56; Univ Tex, PhD(genetics), 62. *Prof Exp:* Asst, Genetics Found, Univ Tex, 60-62; asst prof biol, Kans State Teachers Col, 62-65; resident res assoc, Div Biol & Med Res, Argonne Nat Lab, 65-67; asst prof, 67-69, ASSOC PROF BIOL, CLEVELAND STATE UNIV, 69-, DIR ADMIS & REC, 79- *Mem:* AAAS; Genetics Soc Am. *Res:* Genetic studies of x-irradiated Drosophilia oocytes; genetic studies of irradiated Drosophilia populations; radiation and chemical induced mutations in Drosophilia. *Mailing Add:* Dept Biol Cleveland State Univ Cleveland OH 44115

DICKERSON, CHARLESWORTH LEE, b Fredericksburg, Va, Dec 14, 27; m 59; c 2. ORGANIC CHEMISTRY. *Educ:* Col William & Mary, BS, 49; Univ Va, MS, 51, PhD(org chem), 54. *Prof Exp:* Res chemist, Am Enka Corp, 54-55; sr chemist appl res, 57-65, prod res, 65-67, tech librn-info specialist, 67, sr res chemist & info specialist, 67-74, toxicol coordr, 74-78, SR PROD SAFETY COORDR, S C JOHNSON & SON, INC, 78- *Mem:* AAAS; Am Chem Soc; Spec Libr Asn (treas, 68-73, vpres, 73-74 & pres, 74-75); Nat Microfilm Asn. *Res:* Action of Grignard reagents on 2, 3-unsaturated-1, 4-diketones and related furans; high polymer compositions and properties; synthesis of insecticides. *Mailing Add:* 1525 Howe St Racine WI 53403

DICKERSON, CHESTER T, JR, b Lewes, Del, Apr 26, 39; m 60; c 2. WEED SCIENCE, OLERICULTURE. *Educ:* Univ Del, BS, 62, MS, 64; Cornell Univ, PhD(weed sci), 68. *Prof Exp:* Supvr weed sci, Monsanto Co, 68-71, tech mgr, 71-73, reg mgr prod develop, 73-75, res mgr, Monsanto Japan Ltd, 75-81, DIR AGR AFFAIRS, MONSANTO CO, POTOMAC, MD, 81- *Mem:* Weed Sci Soc Am. *Res:* Herbicide research and development. *Mailing Add:* 11313 Willowbrook Dr Oldfield Potomac MD 20851

DICKERSON, DONALD ROBERT, b Champaign, Ill, Jan 21, 25; m 51; c 2. ORGANIC GEOCHEMISTRY. *Educ:* Univ Ill, BS, 50, MS, 59, PhD(food sci), 62. *Prof Exp:* Chemist, Clark Microanal Lab, Urbana, Ill, 50-52, chief chemist, 52-53; asst chemist, 53-62, assoc chemist, 62-69, chemist, 69-70, ORGANIC CHEMIST, ILL STATE GEOL SURV, URBANA, 70- *Mem:* Am Chem Soc. *Res:* Organic geochemistry of coal and black shale; organic matter as environmental pollutants. *Mailing Add:* Ill State Geol Surv 615 E Peabody Champaign IL 61820

DICKERSON, DORSEY GLENN, b Indianapolis, Ind, Mar 1, 41; m 61; c 3. PHOTOGRAPHIC CHEMISTRY. *Educ:* Purdue Univ, BS, 63; Univ Wash, PhD(chem), 67. *Prof Exp:* Sr res chemist, 67-73, lab head, Photog Res Div, 73-79, RES ASSOC, EMULSION RES DIV, EASTMAN KODAK CO, 79- *Mem:* Am Chem Soc. *Res:* Design, fabrication and evaluation of novel photographic materials and processes. *Mailing Add:* Res Labs Eastman Kodak Co Kodak Park Rochester NY 14650

DICKERSON, GEORGE FIELDEN, applied physics, see previous edition

DICKERSON, GORDON EDWIN, b La Grande, Ore, Jan 30, 12; m 33; c 4. ANIMAL BREEDING. *Educ:* Mich State Univ, BS, 33; Univ Wis, MS, 34, PhD(animal genetics), 37. *Prof Exp:* Asst genetics, Univ Wis, 34-35, instr genetics & dairy records, 35-39, instr genetics & dairy husb, 39-41; geneticist, Regional Swine Breeding Lab, USDA, 41-47; prof animal husb, Univ Mo, 47-52; geneticist, Kimber Farms, 52-65; geneticist, Res Br, Can Dept Agr, 65-67; PROF ANIMAL SCI, UNIV NEBR, LINCOLN & GENETICIST,

US MEAT ANIMAL RES CTR, AGR RES SEA, USDA, 67- *Honors & Awards:* Breeding-Genetics Award, Am Soc Animal Sci, 70, Morrison Award, 78. *Mem:* Fel AAAS; fel Am Soc Animal Sci; Genetics Soc Am; Am Genetic Asn; Biomet Soc. *Res:* Animal genetics; experimental design; effectiveness of selection and breeding systems in swine, dairy and beef cattle, poultry, mice. *Mailing Add:* 225 Baker Hall Univ of Nebr Lincoln NE 68583

DICKERSON, JAMES PERRY, b Bunn, NC, May 8, 39; m 70. ORGANIC CHEMISTRY. *Educ:* Univ NC, Chapel Hill, BS, 62; Wayne State Univ, PhD(org chem), 66. *Prof Exp:* Sr res chemist, Ash Stevens Inc, 66-68; sr res chemist, 68-78, group leader, R J Reynolds Industs, Inc, 78-80, MGR RES & DEVELOP, R J REYNOLDS TOBACCO CO, 80- *Mem:* Am Chem Soc; Sigma Xi. *Res:* Carbohydrates; organic synthesis; natural products; amino sugars; tobacco science. *Mailing Add:* Res & Develop R J Reynolds Tobacco Co Winston-Salem NC 27102

DICKERSON, L(OREN) L(ESTER), JR, b Fitzgerald, Ga, May 11, 18; m 53; c 3. ELECTRONIC ENGINEERING, PHYSICS. *Educ:* Emory Univ, BS, 39; Mass Inst Technol, ScD(chem eng), 42. *Prof Exp:* Res chem engr, Arthur D Little, Inc, 42-44; res assoc metall, Mass Inst Technol, 44-45; res supvr process metall, Reynolds Metals Co, 45-46, proj engr process develop, 46-48; pvt consult & mfg printing & embroidering methods, 48-53; dir reduction res, Reynolds Metals Co, 53-57, assoc dir & leader fundamental res dept, 57-60; consult & prin sci investr, Army Missile Command, 60-70; aerospace engr & coordr nuclear effects studies, Safeguard Syst Command, 70-76, physicist, Army Metrol & Calibration Ctr, 76-77 & Army Standards Lab, 77-78, ELECTRONICS ENGR, DEVELOP EVAL & COORDR, LONG-RANGE RES & DEVELOP PLAN, ARMY ARMAMENTS RES & DEVELOP COMMAND, DEPT DEFENSE, DOVER, 78- *Mem:* Fel AAAS; Am Inst Mining, Metall & Petrol Engrs; Am Chem Soc; Electrochem Soc; Int Soc Gen Semantics. *Res:* Electrical and control engineering; electronics; automation by computers; instrumentation; chemical, metallurgical and nuclear engineering. *Mailing Add:* 167 Diamond Spring Rd Denville NJ 07834

DICKERSON, MARVIN HUBERT, meteorology, see previous edition

DICKERSON, OTTIE J, b Mulberry, Ark, Sept 4, 33; m 55; c 2. ADMINISTRATION, PLANT PATHOLOGY. *Educ:* Univ Ark, BS, 55, MS, 56; Univ Wis, PhD(plant path), 61. *Prof Exp:* From asst prof to prof nematol, Kans State Univ, 61-78, chmn crop protection curric comt, 72-78; HEAD DEPT PLANT PATH & PHYSIOL, CLEMSON UNIV, 78- *Mem:* Am Phytopath Soc; Soc Nematol. *Res:* Biology and control of plant parasitic nematodes. *Mailing Add:* Dept Plant Path & Physiol Clemson Univ Clemson SC 29631

DICKERSON, R(ONALD) F(RANK), b Middletown, NY, Jan 27, 22; m 44; c 2. METALLURGICAL ENGINEERING. *Educ:* Va Polytech Inst, BS, 47, MS, 49. *Prof Exp:* Prin metallurgist reactor mat, Battelle Mem Inst, 48-53, asst div chief, 53-56, div chief, 56-62, asst mgr metall & physics dept, 62-64, staff mgr, Pac Northwest Lab, 64-68, asst dir BMI Int, 68-70, mgr spec projs, 70-72, VPRES & GEN MGR, BATTELLE DEVELOP CORP, 72- *Mem:* Am Soc Metals. *Res:* Fuel alloy development for reactor cores, melting and casting or uranium, zirconium, thorium, niobium, molybdenum and other rare metals; metallography of these materials and irradiation damage. *Mailing Add:* Battelle Develop Corp 505 King Ave Columbus OH 43201

DICKERSON, RICHARD EARL, b Casey, Ill, Oct 8, 31; m 56; c 5. BIOCHEMISTRY, MOLECULAR EVOLUTION. *Educ:* Carnegie Inst Technol, BS, 53; Univ Minn, PhD(phys chem), 57. *Prof Exp:* NSF fel, Univ Leeds, 57-58 & Cavendish Lab, Cambridge Univ, 58-59; asst prof phys chem, Univ Ill, 59-63; from assoc prof to prof chem, Calif Inst Technol, 63-81; PROF CHEM & GEOPHYSICS, UNIV CALIF, LOS ANGELES, 81- *Mem:* AAAS; Am Inst Physics; Am Soc Biol Chem; Am Crystallog Asn. *Res:* X-ray crystallography and molecular structure of DNA and complexes with drugs and proteins; evolution at the molecular level; molecular biology. *Mailing Add:* Div Chem & Chem Eng Calif Inst of Technol Pasadena CA 91125

DICKERSON, ROGER WILLIAM, JR, b Louisville, Ky, Dec 8, 31; m 56; c 3. FOOD ENGINEERING & TECHNOLOGY, HEAT TRANSFER. *Educ:* Univ Ky, BS, 57, MS, 58. *Prof Exp:* Instr, Univ Ky, 57-58; assoc engr missile guidance, Sperry Rand Corp, 58-59; tech engr theoret heat transfer, Gen Elec Co, 59-61; chief, Food Process Eval Br Milk Pasteurization, USPHS, 61-69; CHIEF, FOOD ENG BR, US FOOD & DRUG ADMIN, 69- *Concurrent Pos:* Vchmn, Comt Thermal Properties Foods, Am Soc Heating, Refrig & Air Conditioning Engrs, 70-; mem, Comt Environ Heat Transfer, Am Soc Mech Engrs, 72-76. *Mem:* Int Asn Milk, Food & Environ Sanitarians; Am Soc Mech Engrs; Am Soc Heating, Refrig & Air Conditioning Engrs. *Res:* Heat transfer and thermal properties related to processes for pasteurization and/or sterilization of foods. *Mailing Add:* 1090 Tusculum Ave Cincinnati OH 45226

DICKERSON, STEPHEN L(ANG), b Rockford, Ill, Jan 6, 40; m 62; c 2. MECHANICAL ENGINEERING. *Educ:* Ill Inst Technol, BS, 62; Univ Calif, Berkeley, MS, 63; Mass Inst Technol, ScD(eng), 65. *Prof Exp:* From asst prof to assoc prof, 65-73, PROF MECH ENG, GA INST TECHNOL, 74- *Concurrent Pos:* Pres, Urban Transp Co, 75- *Mem:* Am Soc Mech Engrs; Soc Automotive Engrs. *Res:* Automatic control; system design; transportation systems; robotics. *Mailing Add:* Sch of Mech Eng Ga Inst of Technol Atlanta GA 30332

DICKERT, HERMAN A(LONZO), b Newberry, SC, Jan 16, 03; m 27; c 2. ENGINEERING, MATERIALS SCIENCE. *Educ:* Newberry Col, AB, 23, ScD, 55; Univ NC, MA, 25. *Prof Exp:* Res chemist, Food & Nutrit Lab, State Dept Agr, NC, 24-25; res chemist, Cellulose & Rayon, E I du Pont de Nemours & Co, 25-31; supvry work, Rayon Div, 34-45; dir, A French Textile Sch, 45-58, prof textile eng, 58-70, EMER PROF TEXTILE ENG, GA INST TECHNOL, 70- *Concurrent Pos:* Pres, Nat Coun Textile Sch Deans, 52;

Fulbright lectr, Tech Sch Indust Eng, Barcelona, 63-64; consult & lectr, Israel Inst Technol, 64; consult, Int Exec Serv Corp, Fortaleza, Brazil, 73. *Res:* Food and nutrition studies; motion picture film base; synthetic and natural fibers including manufacturing processes for synthetics, fabricating, dyeing, finishing and application to plastic laminates; industrial chemistry. *Mailing Add:* 374 E Paces Ferry Rd NE Atlanta GA 30305

DICKES, ROBERT, b New York, NY, Apr 15, 12; m 38; c 2. PSYCHIATRY. *Educ:* City Col NY, BS, 33; Emory Univ, MS, 34, MD, 38. *Prof Exp:* From asst prof to assoc prof, 49-63, actg chmn dept, 66-67 & 71-72, PROF PSYCHIAT, STATE UNIV NY DOWNSTATE MED CTR, 63-, TRAINING & SUPV ANALYST, PSYCHOANAL INST, 65-, DIR, CTR SEXUAL DYSFUNCTION, 74-, PSYCHIATRIST-IN-CHIEF, UNIV HOSP, 70- *Concurrent Pos:* Commonwealth fel med, 41-42; consult, Vet Admin, 46-51 & Bur Hearings & Appeals, Dept Health, Educ & Welfare, 64-67; dir & psychiatrist-in-chief, Kings County Psychiat Hosp, 66-71, chmn, Dept Psychiat, 75-78. *Mem:* Fel Am Col Physicians; fel Am Psychiat Asn; Am Psychoanal Asn; fel Am Col Psychiatrists. *Res:* Psychoanalysis; human depth psychology; problems of human sexuality. *Mailing Add:* State Univ NY Downstate Med Ctr Box 1203 450 Clarkson Ave Brooklyn NY 11203

DICKEY, D(AVID) F(ARIS), metallurgy, deceased

DICKEY, DANA H, b Easton, Maine, May 16, 30; m 58; c 3. SOLID STATE PHYSICS. *Educ:* Univ Maine, BS, 52; Mass Inst Technol, PhD(physics), 57. *Prof Exp:* MEM STAFF, LINCOLN LAB, MASS INST TECHNOL, 57- *Mem:* Am Phys Soc. *Res:* Development of far infrared techniques and infrared sensor systems. *Mailing Add:* Tower Rd Lincoln MA 01773

DICKEY, DAYTON DELBERT, b Des Moines, Iowa, June 1, 27; m 54; c 3. GEOLOGY. *Educ:* Iowa State Univ, BS, 50. *Prof Exp:* Geologist, Fed Power Comn, 50; geologist, Mineral Deposits & Eng Br, 52-61, geologist spec proj br, 61-75, GEOLOGIST, ENG BR, US GEOL SURV, 75- *Concurrent Pos:* Engr, Res & Develop Lab, US Army, 50-52. *Mem:* AAAS; Geol Soc Am; Asn Eng Geol; Am Geophys Union; Seismol Soc Am. *Res:* Stress and strain of earth associated with faulting and underground nuclear explosions; general engineering geology. *Mailing Add:* 1680 S Iris Way Denver CO 80226

DICKEY, E(DWARD) T(HOMPSON), b Oxford, Pa, Nov 16, 96; m 44; c 2. ELECTRONICS. *Educ:* City Col New York, BS, 18. *Prof Exp:* Engr, Radio Res, Radio Corp Am, 18-24, sample testing & equip develop, T & T Dept, 24-29, field res radio competitive anal, 29-40, admin asst radio ed work on res projs, 41-61; pub acquisition, Libr, Plasma Physics Lab, 62-66, film scanner, Jadwin Hall, Princeton Univ, 68-72. *Mem:* Sr mem, Inst Elec & Electronics Engrs; fel Radio Club Am. *Res:* Development of radio test equipment; hi-speed transoceanic reception equipment; radio receiver circuit development; Poulsen arc research. *Mailing Add:* 104 Jefferson Rd Princeton NJ 08540

DICKEY, FRANK R(AMSEY), JR, b San Antonio, Tex, Apr 10, 18; m 44; c 3. ELECTRICAL ENGINEERING. *Educ:* Univ Tex, BS, 39; Harvard Univ, MS, 46, PhD(appl physics), 51. *Prof Exp:* Engr, Gen Elec Co, 50-53; mem res staff, Melpar, Inc, 53-54; consult engr, 54-76, SR CONSULT ENGR, HEAVY MIL ELECTRONICS DEPT, GEN ELEC CO, 76- *Mem:* Fel Inst Elec & Electronics Engrs. *Res:* Radar and communication systems. *Mailing Add:* 112 Cornwall Dr Dewitt NY 13214

DICKEY, FREDERICK PIUS, b Zanesville, Ohio, Sept 1, 16; m 42; c 3. PHYSICS. *Educ:* Muskingum Col, BS, 38; Ohio State Univ, MS, 39, PhD(physics), 46. *Prof Exp:* From instr to assoc prof, 46-60, PROF PHYSICS, OHIO STATE UNIV, 60- *Mem:* Am Phys Soc. *Res:* Infrared; microwaves; lasers. *Mailing Add:* Dept of Physics Ohio State Univ Columbus OH 43210

DICKEY, HOWARD CHESTER, b Durand, Mich, June 26, 13; m 39; c 4. DAIRY HUSBANDRY. *Educ:* Mich State Univ, BS, 34; WVa Univ, MS, 36; Univ Iowa, PhD(dairy husb), 39. *Prof Exp:* Asst dairy husb, WVa Univ, 34-36; asst, Iowa State Univ, 36-39; from asst prof to assoc prof animal husb, Colo State Univ, 39-45; assoc prof dairy husb, Univ Vt, 45-47; prof & head dept animal indust, 47-57, prof & head dept, 57-77, EMER PROF ANIMAL SCI, UNIV MAINE, 77- *Concurrent Pos:* Animal nutrit consult, Jackson Lab. *Mem:* Am Dairy Sci Asn; Am Genetic Soc; Am Soc Animal Sci. *Res:* Dairy cattle nutrition and inheritance; animal nutrition; relationship between the curd tension in milk and its rate and percentage of digestibility. *Mailing Add:* Dept of Animal & Vet Sci Univ of Maine Rogers Hall Orono ME 04473

DICKEY, JAMES MILLS, statistics, see previous edition

DICKEY, JOAN MARION, physics, nuclear engineering, see previous edition

DICKEY, JOHN SLOAN, JR, b Washington, DC, Jan 24, 41; m 63; c 1. PETROLOGY. *Educ:* Dartmouth Col, AB, 63; Univ Otago, NZ, MSc, 66; Princeton Univ, PhD(geol), 69. *Prof Exp:* Field geologist, Brit Newf Explor Co Ltd, 63-64; res assoc lunar geol, Smithsonian Astrophys Observ, 69-70; res fel petrol, Geophys Lab, Carnegie Inst Wash, 70-72; asst prof geol, Mass Inst Technol, 72-76, assoc prof, 76-79; prog dir, NSF, 79-81; CHMN DEPT & JESSIE PAGE HEROY PROF GEOL, SYRACUSE UNIV, 81- *Concurrent Pos:* NSF res grant, 71-76. *Mem:* Geochem Soc; Mineral Soc Am; Am Geophys Union; AAAS. *Res:* Petrology of mafic and ultramafic igneous rocks; economic petrology; experimental petrology. of. *Mailing Add:* 204 Heroy Geol Lab Syracuse Univ Syracuse NY 13210

DICKEY, JOSEPH FREEDMAN, b Orange County, NC, Apr 1, 34; m 59; c 2. REPRODUCTIVE PHYSIOLOGY, ELECTRON MICROSCOPY. *Educ:* NC State Col, BS, 56, MS, 62; Pa State Univ, PhD(dairy sci), 65. *Prof Exp:* From asst prof to assoc prof, 69-75, PROF DAIRY SCI, CLEMSON UNIV, 75- *Mem:* Am Dairy Sci Asn; Am Soc Animal Sci; Soc Study Reproduction; Am Asn Univ Professors; Sigma Xi. *Res:* Physiology and endocrinology of reproduction in mammals; histochemistry and electron microscopy of reproductive tissues; causes of embryonic mortality. *Mailing Add:* Dept of Dairy Sci Clemson Univ Clemson SC 29631

DICKEY, LELAND CLAUDE, b Kansas City, Mo, June 18, 42. CHEMICAL ENGINEERING. *Educ:* Univ Cincinnati, BS, 65; Ohio State Univ, MS, 68; NC State Univ, PhD(chem eng), 74. *Prof Exp:* Sr res engr, Northern Nat Gas Co, 76-80, PRIN RES ENGR PROCESS DEVELOP, INTERNORTH, 80- *Mem:* Am Inst Chem Engrs. *Res:* Chemical reaction engineering. *Mailing Add:* Internorth 4840 F St Omaha ON 68117 N1G 2W1

DICKEY, PARKE ATHERTON, b Chicago, Ill, Mar 3, 09; m 35; c 4. PETROLEUM GEOLOGY. *Educ:* Johns Hopkins Univ, PhD(geol), 32. *Prof Exp:* Petrographer, Lago Petrol Corp, Venezuela, 30-31; geologist, Trop Oil Co, Colombia, 32-38; geologist chg oil & gas, Pa State Geol Surv, 38-42; geologist, Forest Oil Corp, 42-44; prod engr, Quaker State Oil Ref Co, 44-46; head geol res, Carter Oil Co, 46-56, asst chief res, 56-58; geologist, Creole Petrol Corp, Venezuela, 58-60; mgr geol div, Jersey Prod Res Co, 60-61; prof geol & head geol earth sci, 61-72, EMER PROF GEOL, UNIV TULSA, 74- *Mem:* Am Inst Mining, Metall & Petrol Engrs; Am Asn Petrol Geol; fel Geol Soc Am; Am Geophys Union. *Res:* Petroleum geology including exploration, production and research. *Mailing Add:* Rte 1 Box 1193 Owasso OK 74055

DICKEY, RICHARD PALMER, b Napoleon, Ohio, Feb 10, 35; m 57; c 4. OBSTETRICS & GYNECOLOGY. *Educ:* Ohio State Univ, BA, 56, MMSc, 65, PhD, 70; Western Reserve Univ, MD, 60; Am Bd Obstet & Gynec, dipl, 67; Am Bd Reproductive Med, Cert, 76. *Prof Exp:* Res assoc obstet & gynec, Ohio State Univ, 65-70, asst prof, 70-72, instr pharmacol, dir div reprod endocrinol & dir family planning, 71-72; assoc prof obstet & gynec & chief sect reprod endocrinol, La State Univ Med Ctr, New Orleans, 72-76. *Concurrent Pos:* NIH trainee gynec endocrinol, 63-66; mem adv comt obstet & gynec devices, Food & Drug Admin; chmn subcomt conception control devices, 74-77. *Mem:* AAAS; AMA; Am Col Obstet & Gynec. *Res:* Reproductive endocrinology; infertility; population control and family planning; mechanisms of actions of steroids in contraception; neuropharmacology of gonadotropic secretion. *Mailing Add:* 5640 Read Rd New Orleans LA 70127

DICKEY, ROBERT SHAFT, b Riverside, Calif, Jan 18, 21; m 46; c 3. PLANT PATHOLOGY. *Educ:* Univ Calif, BS, 48, PhD(plant path), 54. *Prof Exp:* Asst plant path, Univ Calif, 48-51; from asst prof to assoc prof, 52-69, PROF PLANT PATH, CORNELL UNIV, 69- *Concurrent Pos:* Adj prof plant path, Pa State Univ, 74- *Mem:* Am Inst Biol Sci; Am Soc Microbiol; Am Phytopath Soc. *Res:* Bacterial diseases of plants; phytopathogenic bacteria. *Mailing Add:* Dept of Plant Path Cornell Univ Ithaca NY 14853

DICKEY, RONALD WAYNE, b Compton, Calif, Mar 12, 38; m 65. APPLIED MATHEMATICS. *Educ:* Univ Calif, Los Angeles, AB, 59; NY Univ, MS, 62, PhD(math), 65. *Prof Exp:* Vis mem math, Courant Inst, NY Univ, 65-67; from asst prof to assoc prof, 67-74, PROF MATH, UNIV WIS-MADISON, 74- *Concurrent Pos:* Sci Res Coun sr vis fel, Univ Newcastle, 71-72. *Mem:* Am Math Soc; Soc Indust & Appl Math. *Res:* Nonlinear differential and integral equations and their relations to problems in elasticity. *Mailing Add:* Dept of Math Univ of Wis Madison WI 53706

DICKEY, WILLIAM DARYL, b Vernon, Tex, Sept 16, 50. CELLULAR IMMUNOLOGY, CONNECTIVE TISSUE BIOLOGY. *Educ:* West Tex State Univ, BS, 74; Univ Tex Med Br Galveston, PhD(genetics), 79. *Prof Exp:* MCLAUGHLIN FEL, IMMUNOLOGY, UNIV TEX MED BR GALVESTON, 79- *Mem:* Sigma Xi; NY Acad Sci; AAAS. *Res:* Factors which control the adherence, deformability and movement of eucaryotic cells with particular emphasis on lymphocytes and epthelial cells. *Mailing Add:* Univ Tex Med Br PO Box 203 Galveston TX 77550

DICKHAUS, DONALD WILLIAM, b St Louis, Mo, Apr 9, 25; m 60; c 2. INTERNAL MEDICINE, CARDIOLOGY. *Educ:* Univ Mo, AB, 50, BS, 54; Tulane Univ, MD, 56. *Prof Exp:* From intern to asst resident med, St Louis City Hosp, Mo, 56-59; chief cardiol, Denver Vet Admin Hosp, 61-66; assoc prof, 66-77, PROF MED, UNIV MO-COLUMBIA, 77- *Concurrent Pos:* Twenty-Thirty Int fel cardiol, Univ Calif, San Francisco, 59-61. *Res:* Arteriosclerotic heart disease. *Mailing Add:* 401 Keene St Columbia MO 65201

DICKHOFF, WALTON WILLIAM, b Watertown, Wis, Apr 8, 47; c 3. ENDOCRINOLOGY, PHYSIOLOGY. *Educ:* Univ Calif, Berkeley, AB, 70, PhD(physiol), 76. *Prof Exp:* Actg asst prof, 77-78, 80 & 81, RES ASSOC ZOOL, UNIV WASH, 75- *Concurrent Pos:* NIH fel, Univ Wash, 76-77. *Mem:* Am Soc Zoologists; AAAS; Endocrine Soc. *Res:* Evolution of endocrine and neuroendocrine control systems; hormonal control of development in lower vertebrates; comparative physiology; finfish aquaculture. *Mailing Add:* Dept of Zool NJ-15 Univ of Wash Seattle WA 98195

DICKIE, HELEN AIRD, b North Freedom, Wis, Feb 19, 13. MEDICINE. *Educ:* Univ Wis, BA, 35, MD, 37. *Prof Exp:* From instr to assoc prof, 42-54, PROF MED, SCH MED, UNIV WIS-MADISON, 54- *Mem:* AMA; master Am Col Physicians; Am Thoracic Soc; Am Fedn Clin Res. *Res:* Bacillus Calmette-Guerin vaccination for prevention of tuberculosis; pulmonary resection in tuberculosis; sarcoidosis and diffuse interstitial disease. *Mailing Add:* Dept of Med Univ of Wis Sch of Med Madison WI 53711

DICKIE, JOHN PETER, b Waseca, Minn, Apr 4, 34; div; c 4. BIOCHEMISTRY, ORGANIC CHEMISTRY. *Educ:* Univ Minn, BA, 56; Univ Wis, MS, 58, PhD(biochem), 60. *Prof Exp:* Wis Alumni Res Found fel chem, Univ Wis, 60-61; res fel, Mellon Inst, 61-68; group mgr, Res Dept, Koppers Co, Inc, 68-74; dir basic res, Carnation Co, 75-78; PRES, JOHN P DICKIE ASSOCS, 81- *Mem:* Am Chem Soc. *Res:* Antimycins; chemistry and origin of natural bitumens; antibiotic structure; mechanism of antibiotic action. *Mailing Add:* 533 Mears Pk Pl 410 Sibley St St Paul MN 55101

DICKIE, LLOYD MERLIN, b Canning, NS, Mar 6, 26; m 52; c 3. MARINE BIOLOGY. *Educ:* Acadia Univ, BSc, 46; Yale Univ, MSc, 48; Univ Toronto, PhD(zool), 53. *Prof Exp:* Asst biol, Acadia Univ, 43-46; asst, Yale Univ, 46-48; demonstr, Univ Toronto, 48-51; asst scientist biol, Biol Sta, St Andrews Univ, 51-53, in chg clam & scallop invest, 53-57, assoc scientist in chg population dynamics studies, Groundfish Invest, 57-65, dir, Marine Ecol Lab, Fisheries Res Bd Can, 65-74, RES SCIENTIST MARINE ECOL LAB, BEDFORD INST OCEANOG, 74- *Concurrent Pos:* Assoc prof biol, Dalhousie Univ, 65-74, prof oceanog & chmn dept, 74-77, adj prof, 78- *Mem:* Ecol Soc Am; Brit Ecol Soc. *Res:* Marine ecology; population dynamics of molluscan shellfish and marine demersal species; fisheries biology. *Mailing Add:* Marine Ecol Lab Bedford Inst of Oceanog Dartmouth NS B2Y 3Y1 Can

DICKIE, RAY ALEXANDER, b Minot, NDak, Jan 19, 40; m 65; c 2. POLYMER CHEMISTRY, ORGANIC COATINGS. *Educ:* Univ NDak, BS, 61; Univ Wis-Madison, PhD(phys chem), 65. *Prof Exp:* Res fel, Glasgow Univ, 66; chemist, Stanford Res Inst, 67-68; STAFF SCIENTIST, ENG & RES STAFF, FORD MOTOR CO, 68- *Mem:* Am Chem Soc; Soc Rheol. *Res:* Structure and mechanical properties of polymer blends and elastomers; chemistry and physics of organic coatings and corrosion protection; polymer and surface characterization. *Mailing Add:* Eng & Res Staff Ford Motor Co Box 2053 Dearborn MI 48121

DICKINSON, ALAN CHARLES, b New Britain, Conn, Jan 10, 40; m 63; c 3. PHYSICAL CHEMISTRY. *Educ:* Tufts Univ, BS, 61; Ind Univ, PhD(phys chem), 65. *Prof Exp:* Teacher chem pub schs, Springfield, Mass, 65-68; asst prof, 68-74, ASSOC PROF CHEM, AM INT COL, 75- *Concurrent Pos:* Fel, Univ Ala, 78-79. *Mem:* Am Chem Soc. *Res:* Photochemistry and electron spin resonance spectroscopy. *Mailing Add:* Dept of Chem Am Int Col Springfield MA 01109

DICKINSON, ALICE B, b New York, NY, Apr 11, 21; m 44; c 2. MATHEMATICS. *Educ:* Univ Mich, AB, 41, PhD(math), 52; Columbia Univ, MA, 47. *Prof Exp:* Asst proj engr, Sperry Gyroscope Co, 42-44; mem staff, Radiation Lab, Mass Inst Technol, 44-45; instr, Pa State Univ, 50-56; assoc prof, 59-70, prof, 70-81, dean col, 75-78, EMER PROF MATH, SMITH COL, 81- *Concurrent Pos:* Lectr, Univ Baroda, 68. *Honors & Awards:* Founder's Award, Hampshire Col, 70. *Mem:* Math Asn Am. *Res:* Topology. *Mailing Add:* PO Box 235 Ashfield MA 01330

DICKINSON, BRADLEY WILLIAM, b St Mary's, Pa, Apr 28, 48. SIGNAL PROCESSING, SYSTEM THEORY. *Educ:* Case Western Reserve Univ, BS, 70; Stanford Univ, MSEE, 71, PhD(elec eng), 74. *Prof Exp:* Asst prof, 74-80, ASSOC PROF ELEC ENG, DEPT ELEC ENG & COMPUT SCI, PRINCETON UNIV, 80- *Concurrent Pos:* Assoc ed, Transaction on Automatic Control, Inst Elec & Electronics Engrs, 80-81. *Mem:* Inst Elec & Electronic Engrs; Sigma Xi. *Res:* Applicatons of system theory and statistical analysis to signal processing; system identification, signal analysis and applied linear algebra. *Mailing Add:* Dept Elec Eng & Comput Sci Princeton Univ Princeton NJ 08544

DICKINSON, CLIFFORD LEE, JR, b Freeport, Ill, Nov 11, 30; m 52; c 3. ORGANIC CHEMISTRY. *Educ:* Univ Ill, BS, 52; Univ Rochester, PhD(chem), 56. *Prof Exp:* Lab instr org chem, Univ Rochester, 52-54; res chemist, 56-70, res supvr, 70-74, res mgr, 74-77, PLANNING CONSULT, CENT RES & DEVELOP DEPT, E I DU PONT DE NEMOURS & CO, INC, 77- *Mem:* Am Chem Soc. *Res:* Cyanocarbon chemistry; heterocyclic compounds; medicinal and agricultural chemistry; toxicology; industrial hygiene. *Mailing Add:* CR&D DuPont Exp Sta Wilmington DE 19898

DICKINSON, DALE FLINT, b Galveston, Tex, Oct 11, 33; m 63; c 2. PHYSICS. *Educ:* Univ Tex, BS, 55; Univ Calif, PhD(physics), 65. *Prof Exp:* Res assoc radio astron lab, Univ Calif, 66-67; res assoc, Smithsonian-Harvard Ctr Astrophysics, 67-78, lectr astron, Harvard Univ, 75-78; vis assoc prof physics, Williams Col, 78-80; WITH JET PROPULSION LAB, 80- *Mem:* Am Astron Soc. *Res:* Spectral line radio astronomy; interstellar molecules, maser emission in long-period variable stars; galactic structure studies. *Mailing Add:* Jet Propulsion Lab TR 1166 4800 Oak Grove Dr Pasadena CA 91109

DICKINSON, DAVID (JAMES), b Denver, Colo, Sept 16, 20; m 44; c 2. MATHEMATICS. *Educ:* Univ Denver, BA, 42; Columbia Univ, AM, 47; Univ Mich, PhD(math), 54. *Prof Exp:* Mem staff radiation lab, Mass Inst Technol, 42-45; lectr, Columbia Univ, 45-46; instr math, Pa State Univ, 50-58; prof, 58-81, EMER PROF MATH, UNIV MASS, AMHERST, 81- *Mem:* Am Math Soc. *Res:* Classical analysis; special functions; orthogonal polynomials; theoretical linguistics. *Mailing Add:* PO Box 235 Ashfield MA 01330

DICKINSON, DAVID BUDD, b New York, NY, Jan 10, 36; m 61. PLANT PHYSIOLOGY. *Educ:* Univ NH, BS, 57; Univ Ill, PhD(hort), 62. *Prof Exp:* From instr to assoc prof, 61-74, PROF PLANT PHYSIOL, UNIV ILL, URBANA, 74- *Mem:* AAAS; Am Chem Soc; Am Soc Plant Physiol; Am Soc Hort Sci. *Res:* Plant carbohydrate metabolism; plant cell wall biogenesis; metabolic transformations in germinating pollen and mechanisms regulating germination. *Mailing Add:* Dept of Hort Univ of Ill Urbana IL 61801

DICKINSON, DAVID F(RANKLIN), b Coffeyville, Kans, Jan 28, 14; m 50; c 1. CHEMICAL ENGINEERING. *Educ:* Kans State Teachers Col, AB, 34, MS, 36; Iowa State Col, PhD(chem eng), 41. *Prof Exp:* Res chemist, Maytag Co, 41-43 & Benson Process Eng Co, NY, 43; jr chem engr, Mathieson Alkali Works, NY, 43-46; chem engr, Armour Res Found, Ill, 46-47; asst prof chem eng, Mich State Col, 47-50; chmn dept chem eng, Ind Technol Col, 50-54; mem staff, Chem Eng Dept, Univ Tulsa, 54-56; prof, Univ NMex, 56-57; resident res assoc, Argonne Nat Lab, 57-58; prof nuclear eng & chmn dept, 58-77, EMER PROF NUCLEAR ENG, UNIV NEV, RENO, 77- *Mem:* Am Chem Soc; Am Soc Metals; Am Inst Chem Engrs; Am Nuclear Soc. *Res:* Drying; coal tar; mechanism of drying of ideal porous materials. *Mailing Add:* Dept of Nuclear Eng Univ of Nev Reno NV 89507

DICKINSON, DEAN RICHARD, b Highland Park, Ill, May 21, 28. CHEMICAL ENGINEERING. *Educ:* Cornell Univ, BChE, 51; Univ Wis, MS, 54, PhD(chem eng), 58. *Prof Exp:* Sr chem engr, Hanford Labs, Gen Elec Co, 58-64 & Pac Northwest Lab, Battelle Mem Inst, 65-71; PRIN ENGR, WESTINGHOUSE HANFORD CO, 71- *Mem:* Am Inst Chem Engrs; Am Nuclear Soc. *Res:* Coolant systems of nuclear reactors; corrosion, fluid flow and heat transfer; gas entrainment, liquid mixing and thermal striping in nuclear reactors. *Mailing Add:* Westinghouse Hanford Co Box 1970 Richland WA 99352

DICKINSON, DEANNE, applied mathematics, see previous edition

DICKINSON, EDWIN JOHN, b Carlisle, Eng, Oct 15, 33; m 59; c 5. FLUID MECHANICS. *Educ:* Cambridge Univ, BA, 55, MA, 58; Laval Univ, PhD(fluid mech), 65. *Prof Exp:* Engr servomechanisms, A V Roe, Manchester, 56-58; res asst aeronaut, Laval Univ, 59-61, teaching asst fluid mech, 61-63; res asst boundary layers, Univ Poitiers, 63-64; asst prof appl math, 64-67, ASSOC PROF APPL MATH, LAVAL UNIV, 67- *Concurrent Pos:* Defense Res Bd Can res grant, 65. *Mem:* Assoc fel Royal Aeronaut Soc; Can Aeronaut & Space Inst. *Res:* Experimental determination of turbulent skin friction, particularly the development of floating element skin friction balances for this purpose. *Mailing Add:* Dept of Mech Eng Fac of Sci Laval Univ Quebec Can

DICKINSON, ERNEST MILTON, b Boston, Ohio, May 12, 05; m 27; c 2. VETERINARY MEDICINE. *Educ:* Ohio State Univ, DVM, 27; Ore State Univ, MS, 35. *Prof Exp:* Asst poultry pathologist & asst prof vet med, Ore State Univ, 27-36; jr veterinarian, Univ Calif, 36-38; assoc prof vet med & assoc veterinarian, 38-41, prof vet med & veterinarian, 41-73, head dept, 55-73, EMER PROF VET MED, ORE STATE UNIV, 73- *Mem:* Fel AAAS; Am Vet Med Asn; Am Asn Avian Path. *Res:* Poultry diseases; coccidiosis; erysipelas infection in turkeys; salmonellosis in chickens and turkeys; ornithosis. *Mailing Add:* 231 N W 30th St Corvallis OR 97330

DICKINSON, FRANK N, b Boston, Mass, July 25, 30; m 57; c 3. GENETICS, STATISTICS. *Educ:* Univ Mass, BS, 53; Univ Ill, MS, 58, PhD(dairy sci), 61. *Prof Exp:* Dairy husbandman, Agr Res Serv, USDA, Univ Ill, 57-61; anal statistician, Biomet Serv, Md, 61-65; asst prof animal sci, Univ Mass, 65-68; invest leader, Dairy Herd Improv Invests, 67-72, CHIEF, ANIMAL IMPROV PROGS, AGR RES CTR, 72- *Mem:* Am Soc Animal Sci; Am Dairy Sci Asn. *Res:* Biological statistics; improvement of production in dairy cattle. *Mailing Add:* Animal Imp Progs Lab Bldg 263 Agr Res Ctr East Beltsville MD 20705

DICKINSON, FRED EUGENE, b Beltrami Co, Minn, Dec 29, 12; m 38; c 3. FOREST PRODUCTS. *Educ:* Univ Minn, BS, 38; Mich State Univ, MS, 41; Yale Univ, PhD(forest prods econ), 51. *Prof Exp:* Forestry foreman & dir civilian conserv corps enrollees, US Forest Serv, 38-39; asst wood utilization lab, Mich State Univ, 39-41; dir dept forestry, Lassen Jr Col, Calif, 41-42; technologist, Forest Prods Lab, US Forest Serv, 42-45, packaging technician, US War Dept, France, 45; from asst prof to assoc prof lumbering, Yale Univ, 45-52; prof wood utilization & chmn dept wood tech, Univ Mich, 52-55; prof & dir, 55-80, EMER PROF, FOREST PROD LAB, UNIV CALIF, BERKELEY, 80- *Concurrent Pos:* Mem adv comt prevention deterioration, Nat Res Coun, 54-57; US del, Food & Agr Orgn, Conf Wood Technol, 63; comt forestry res, Agr Bd, Nat Res Coun-Nat Acad Sci, 64-66; chmn proj group terminology, Div 5, Int Union Forest Res Orgns, 66-73, chmn, S6.03. 04, Info Retrieval for Forest Prods, 74-76. *Honors & Awards:* Heinrich Christian Burckhardt Medal, Univ Gottingen, 70. *Mem:* AAAS; fel Soc Am Foresters; Forest Prod Res Soc (pres, 63-64); fel Int Acad Wood Sci (pres, 69-75); Soc Wood Sci & Technol. *Res:* Physical processing of wood. *Mailing Add:* Forest Prod Lab Univ of Calif Berkeley CA 94804

DICKINSON, HELEN ROSE, b Skowhegan, Maine, Feb 6, 45. BIOPHYSICS, PHYSICAL CHEMISTRY. *Educ:* Univ Maine, BS, 67; Ore State Univ, PhD(biophys), 72. *Prof Exp:* Res assoc chem, Ill Inst Technol, 73-77; res assoc biophys, Case Western Reserve Univ, 77-81; SR CHEMIST, MARINE COLLOIDS DIV, FMC CORP, 81- *Concurrent Pos:* Nat Inst Gen Med Sci, NIH fel, 75-77. *Mem:* Am Chem Soc; Biophys Soc; Soc Complex Carbohydrates. *Res:* Conformations of polysaccharides and proteins; interactions of biological molecules; physical chemistry. *Mailing Add:* Marine Colloids Div FMC Corp Box 308 Rockland ME 09841

DICKINSON, JAMES M(ILLARD), b Waterloo, Iowa, July 31, 23; m 47; c 3. PHYSICAL METALLURGY. *Educ:* Iowa State Univ, BS, 49, PhD(phys chem & metall), 53. *Prof Exp:* Jr chemist, Phys Metall Res, Atomic Energy Comn, Ames Lab, Iowa State Col, 46-53; metallurgist & mem staff, 53-74, asst group leader, 74-81, GROUP LEADER MAT TECHNOL, LOS ALAMOS NAT LAB, UNIV CALIF, 81- *Mem:* Am Soc Metals; Am Inst Mining & Metall Engrs. *Res:* General physical metallurgy of the less common metals; very high temperature metallurgy; phase diagrams, metal reduction, casting and fabrication; graphite fabrication, properties and structure; powder metallurgy; ceramics. *Mailing Add:* 354 El Viento Los Alamos NM 87544

DICKINSON, JOHN G, inorganic chemistry, see previous edition

DICKINSON, JOHN OTIS, b Champaign, Ill, Aug 29, 24; m 47; c 3. VETERINARY PHARMACOLOGY. *Educ:* Univ Ill, BS, 48 & 61, DVM, 63, MS, 65, PhD(vet med sci), 68. *Prof Exp:* Instr vet physiol & pharmacol, Univ Ill, 63-64; Nat Inst Arthritis & Metab Dis fel, 64-66; from asst prof to assoc prof, 66-77, PROF VET PHYSIOL & PHARMACOL, WASH STATE UNIV, 77- *Mem:* Am Soc Vet Physiol & Pharmacol; Soc Study Reproduction; Am Col Vet Toxicologists; Am Vet Med Asn. *Res:* Oral histamine metabolism in ruminants; effect of chlorinated hydrocarbon pretreatment on toxicity of carbamate insecticides; mechanism of allium poisoning; cacodylic acid and monososium acid methane arsonate toxicity in cattle; pyrrolizidine alkaloids and milk transfer. *Mailing Add:* Col of Vet Med Wash State Univ Pullman WA 99163

DICKINSON, JOSHUA CLIFTON, JR, b Tampa, Fla, Apr 28, 16; m 36; c 3. ORNITHOLOGY. *Educ:* Univ Fla, BS, 40, MS, 46, PhD, 50. *Prof Exp:* Asst biol, Univ Fla, 40-42, instr biol & geol, 46-50, from asst prof to assoc prof zool, 50-79, cur biol sci, Fla State Mus, 53-59, actg dir, 59-61, dir & cur ornith, Fla State Mus, 61-79, PROF ZOOL, UNIV FLA, 73-, EMER DIR, FLA STATE MUS, 79- *Concurrent Pos:* Mem, Univ Fla Exped, Honduras, 46; Mus comp zool res fel & Gen Ed Bd fel, Harvard Univ, 51-52; vis investr, Woods Hole Oceanog Inst, 52; mem, Fla State Mus Exped, Baffin Island, 55, Bahamas Islands, 58, 59, 60, 61, 66, & 67, Sombrero Island, 64 & Navassa Island, 67; mem mus adv panel, Nat Endowment Arts, 70-72, co-chmn, 72-74; mem, Nat Coun Arts, 76-82. *Mem:* Fel AAAS; Am Soc Zoologists; Am Ornithologists Union; Am Asn Mus (secy, 70-73); Asn Systs Collections, Inc (pres, 72-75). *Res:* Taxonomy and zoogeography; general ecology. *Mailing Add:* Fla State Mus Dickinson Hall Univ Fla Gainesville FL 32611

DICKINSON, KENDELL A, sedimentary petrology, see previous edition

DICKINSON, LEONARD CHARLES, b Glasgow, Ky, Dec 12, 41; m 66; c 2. PHYSICAL CHEMISTRY, BIOPHYSICAL CHEMISTRY. *Educ:* Bellarmine Col, Ky, AB, 63; Univ Wis-Madison, PhD(phys chem), 69. *Prof Exp:* Sci res fel, Univ Leicester, 69-70; asst prof chem, 70-73, sr res fel, 73-75, PROJ DIR, UNIV MASS, AMHERST, 75-, ASST PROF CHEM, 76- *Mem:* Sigma Xi; Am Chem Soc; AAAS. *Res:* Magnetic resonance line shapes; active site structures of hematin enzymes; metal replacement in hematin enzymes; artificial polymeric enzymes; photosynthetic reaction center tetrapyrrole function; single crystal water soluble polymers; electron paramagnetic resonance of metalloenzymes. *Mailing Add:* Dept of Chem Univ of Mass Amherst MA 01002

DICKINSON, PETER CHARLES, b London, Eng, Sept 30, 39; m 65; c 1. STATISTICS. *Educ:* Univ London, BS, 65; Rutgers Univ, MS, 67, PhD(statist), 69. *Prof Exp:* Engr, Res & Develop Labs, E M I Ltd, Eng, 58-64; teaching asst statist, Rutgers Univ, 65-69; asst prof, 69-76, ASSOC PROF STATIST, UNIV SOUTHWESTERN LA, 76- *Mem:* Biomet Soc; Inst Math Statist; Am Statist Asn; Am Soc Qual Control. *Res:* Non-parametric statistics; experimental design; order statistics. *Mailing Add:* Dept of Statist Univ of Southwestern La Lafayette LA 70504

DICKINSON, ROBERT GERALD, geology, see previous edition

DICKINSON, STANLEY KEY, JR, b Clarksburg, WVa, Feb 16, 31; c 1. GEOCHEMISTRY, SOLID STATE SCIENCE. *Educ:* WVa Univ, BS, 53, MS, 55; Harvard Univ, PhD(geol), 68. *Prof Exp:* Res develop officer, Magnetics Sect, Solid State Sci Lab, Air Force Cambridge Res Ctr, 54-56, phys scientist, 62-77, PHYS SCI ADMINR, DIRECTORATE SCI, DIR LABS, HQ AIR FORCE SYSTS COMMAND, 77- *Concurrent Pos:* Vis scientist, Diamond Res Lab, Johannesburg, 72. *Mem:* Sigma Xi. *Res:* Inorganic equilibria and phase relationships; solid state science; thermodynamics; physical inorganic chemistry; mineral synthesis and stability relations; general inorganic geochemistry; crystallography; x-ray diffraction analysis; stratigraphy; paleontology. *Mailing Add:* Solid State Sci Lab Hanscom AFB Bedford MA 01731

DICKINSON, WADE, b Hickory Twp, Pa, Oct 29, 26; m 52; c 3. BIOPHYSICS, NUCLEAR PHYSICS. *Educ:* US Mil Acad, BS, 49. *Prof Exp:* Proj officer aircraft nuclear propulsion, Wright Air Develop Ctr, 51-53; nuclear physicist, Rand Corp, 53-54; PRIN ENGR & CONSULT, BECHTEL CORP, 54-; pres & chief exec, W W Dickinson Corp, 62-71; PRES & CHIEF EXEC, AGROPHYSICS, INC, 68-, PETROLPHYSICS, LTD, 76- & BIOPHYSICS, LTD, 80- *Concurrent Pos:* Consult, Rand Corp, 54-56; tech consult, 85th Cong Joint Comt Atomic Energy, 57-58. *Mem:* Am Phys Soc; Soc Petrol Engrs; Am Soc Mech Engrs. *Res:* Weight gain stimulation and behavior control in meat animals by internal devices; human contaceptive devices; ultrasonic measurement of heart performance; high speed, precision seed planters; nondestructive tests of seed vigor and genotype; nuclear engineering and physics; petroleum drilling technology. *Mailing Add:* 187 Steuart St San Francisco CA 94105

DICKINSON, WILLIAM BORDEN, b Norfolk, Va, Jan 20, 26. MEDICINAL CHEMISTRY. *Educ:* Emory Univ, AB, 46, MS, 47; Univ Wis, PhD, 50. *Prof Exp:* Res assoc, 50-57, assoc mem-res chemist, 57-65, group leader, 58, SR RES CHEMIST, STERLING-WINTHROP RES INST, 65- *Mem:* Am Chem Soc. *Res:* Ester condensations; hindered ketones; steroids; heterocyclic compounds; synthetic therapeutic agents; organic nomenclature. *Mailing Add:* Sterling-Winthrop Res Inst Rensselaer NY 12144

DICKINSON, WILLIAM CLARENCE, b St Joseph, Mo, Mar 15, 22; m 47; c 2. ENERGY CONVERSION. *Educ:* Univ Calif, AB, 45; Mass Inst Technol, PhD(physics), 50. *Prof Exp:* Asst physics, Mass Inst Technol, 48-50; mem staff, Physics Div, Los Alamos Sci Lab, 50-54; prof physics & head dept, Univ Indonesia, 54-57; mem staff, Neutronics Div, Lawrence Radiation Lab, 57-61, mem staff, Test Div, Lawrence Radiation Lab, 61-73, SOLAR PROJS LEADER, LAWRENCE LIVERMORE LAB, UNIV CALIF, LIVERMORE, 73- *Concurrent Pos:* Lectr, Univ NMex, 53-54. *Mem:* Am Phys Soc; Am Asn Physics Teachers; Int Solar Energy Soc. *Res:* Nuclear magnetic resonance; nuclear reactions; neutron physics; nuclear radiation detectors; solar thermal collectors; solar thermal conversion. *Mailing Add:* 54 Panoramic Way Berkeley CA 94704

DICKINSON, WILLIAM JOSEPH, b Pasadena, Calif, June 17, 40; m 63; c 2. DEVELOPMENTAL GENETICS. *Educ:* Univ Calif, Berkeley, BA, 63; Johns Hopkins Univ, PhD(biol), 69. *Prof Exp:* Sci investr, Cellular Radiobiol Br, US Navy Radiol Defense Lab, Calif, 63-65; asst prof biol, Reed Col, 69-72; from asst prof to assoc prof, 72-81, PROF BIOL, UNIV UTAH, 81- *Concurrent Pos:* Vis scientist, Dept Zool, Univ BC, 71 & Dept Genetics, Univ Hawaii, 78-79. *Mem:* AAAS; Genetics Soc Am; Soc Develop Biol; Am Soc Naturalists; Am Soc Zoologists. *Res:* Genetics of aldehyde oxidase and related enzymes in Drosophila; genetic regulation of differential enzyme synthesis; evolution of patterns of gene regulation. *Mailing Add:* Dept Biol Univ Utah Salt Lake City UT 84112

DICKINSON, WILLIAM RICHARD, b Tenn, Oct 26, 31; m 53, 70; c 4. GEOLOGY. *Educ:* Stanford Univ, BS, 52, MS, 56, PhD(geol), 58. *Prof Exp:* From asst prof to prof geol, Stanford Univ, 58-79; PROF GEOSCI, UNIV ARIZ, 79- *Concurrent Pos:* Guggenheim fel, 65. *Mem:* AAAS; Geol Soc Am; Soc Econ Paleontologists & Mineralogists; Am Geophys Union; Am Asn Petroleum Geologists. *Res:* Petrology; structural geology; sedimentology; plate tectonics. *Mailing Add:* Dept Geol Univ Ariz Tucson AZ 85721

DICKINSON, WILLIAM TREVOR, b Toronto, Ont, Aug 30, 39; m 63; c 2. AGRICULTURAL ENGINEERING, SOIL SCIENCE. *Educ:* Univ Toronto, BSA, 61, BASc, 62, MSA, 64; Colo State Univ, PhD(hydroll hydraul), 67. *Prof Exp:* Lectr eng, 63-64, from asst prof to assoc prof hydrol, 67-78, PROF HYDROL, UNIV GUELPH, 78- *Concurrent Pos:* Comt mem & newsletter ed, Assoc Comt Hydrol, Nat Res Coun, 75-78. *Res:* Characterization of hydrological variables; development of watershed response modes; soil erosion and fluvial sedimentation models. *Mailing Add:* Sch of Eng Univ Guelph Guelph ON N1G 2W1 Can

DICKISON, HARRY LEO, b Ashland, Ky, Sept 3, 12; m 35; c 2. PHARMACOLOGY. *Educ:* Vanderbilt Univ, AB, 35, MS, 36, PhD(org chem), 39. *Prof Exp:* Asst pharmacol, Med Sch, Vanderbilt Univ, 39-41, res assoc, 41-45, asst prof, 45-47; dir pharmacol res, Bristol Labs, 47-58, asst dir res, 51-58, dir labs, 58-66, dir res US, 66-68, gen mgr vet prod, 68-76; RETIRED. *Concurrent Pos:* Lectr, State Univ NY Syracuse, 49-76. *Mem:* Am Soc Pharmacol & Exp Therapeut; Am Fedn Clin Res; Am Chem Soc; Soc Toxicol. *Res:* Hypnotics; anesthetics; analgetics; metabolic fate of drugs; antibiotics; antihistaminics; terpenoid amines; isomeric thujyl amines. *Mailing Add:* 4639 Prince Edward Rd Jacksonville FL 32210

DICKISON, WILLIAM CAMPBELL, b Jamaica, NY, Mar 12, 41; m 63; c 1. PLANT MORPHOLOGY, PLANT ANATOMY. *Educ:* Western Ill Univ, BSEd, 62; Ind Univ, AM, 64, PhD(bot), 66. *Prof Exp:* Asst prof, Va Polytech Inst & State Univ, 66-69; asst prof, 69-74, ASSOC PROF BOT, UNIV NC, CHAPEL HILL, 74- *Mem:* Bot Soc Am; Int Soc Plant Morphol; Int Soc Plant Taxon. *Res:* Morphology and phylogeny of vascular plants; comparative morphology and relationships of the Dilleniaceae and allies. *Mailing Add:* Dept of Bot Univ of NC Chapel Hill NC 27514

DICKMAN, ALBERT, b Lake Placid, NY, Nov 3, 03; m 28; c 1. LABORATORY MEDICINE. *Educ:* Johns Hopkins Univ, AB, 24; Univ Pa, MS, 31, PhD(bact), 33; Am Bd Microbiol, dipl. *Prof Exp:* Teacher pub schs, Md, 24-25; asst to cur, Com Mus, Pa, 25-26; teacher biol, Pub Schs, 28-41; DIR, DICKMAN LABS, 33- *Concurrent Pos:* Mem ad comt lab procedures, Pa Dept Health & nat adv serol coun, USPHS; mem, Conf State & Prov Pub Health Dirs. *Mem:* Fel Am Pub Health Asn; Am Asn Clin Chem; Am Chem Soc; Am Soc Microbiol. *Res:* Medical laboratory science; serology; general clinical laboratory field. *Mailing Add:* Foxcroft Square Apt Jenkintown PA 19046

DICKMAN, JOHN THEODORE, b Hamilton, Ohio, Oct 27, 27; m 56; c 2. BIOCHEMISTRY. *Educ:* Ohio State Univ, BS, 50, MS, 57, PhD(physiol chem), 60. *Prof Exp:* Instr high sch, Ohio, 50-53; asst ed, Biochem Sect, 60-63, asst dept head, Biochem Edit Dept, 63-64, dept head, 64-65, asst managing ed, Abstract Issues, 65-69, mgr ed, 69-71, asst managing ed publ, 71-79, SR ASST ED OPERS, CHEM ABSTRACTS SERV, 79- *Concurrent Pos:* Teaching assoc, Ohio State Univ, 65-71. *Mem:* Am Chem Soc; Coun Biol Ed; Asn Earth Sci Ed. *Res:* Science education; toxicology; lipid chemistry; chemical documentation. *Mailing Add:* Chem Abstracts Serv PO Box 3012 Columbus OH 43210

DICKMAN, MICHAEL DAVID, b Pittsburgh, Pa, June 30, 40; m 62; c 2. LIMNOLOGY, AQUATIC BIOLOGY. *Educ:* Univ Calif, Santa Barbara, BA, 62; Univ Ore, MSc, 65; Univ BC, PhD(limnology), 68. *Prof Exp:* Asst prof, Univ Ottawa, 69-74; ASSOC PROF BIOL, BROCK UNIV, 74- *Concurrent Pos:* Thord Gray fel, Univ Uppsala, 69; dir, Lower Rideau River Pollution Abatement Prog, Ottawa-Carleton Regional Munic, 73-75; chmn, Pollution Abatement Standing Comt, Welland Canals Preserv Asn, 78-; exec mem, Welland River Conserv Proj, Niagara Regional Conserv Authority, 78-; Nat Sci & Eng Res Coun Can travel award, Univ Istanbul, 78. *Mem:* Am Soc Limnology & Oceanog; Int Soc Theoret & Appl Limnology; Soc Canadian Limnologists (vpres, 81). *Res:* Paleolimnology of Canadian shield lakes and the Black Sea; acid rain and Lake Meromixis. *Mailing Add:* Dept of Biol Brock Univ St Catharines ON L2S 3A1 Can

DICKMAN, RAYMOND F, JR, b Cincinnati, Ohio, July 8, 37; m 63. TOPOLOGY. *Educ:* Univ Miami, BS, 61, MS, 63; Univ Va, PhD(math), 66. *Prof Exp:* From asst prof to assoc prof math, Univ Miami, 66-71; assoc prof, 71-74, asst vpres acad affairs, 74-75, PROF MATH, VA POLYTECH INST & STATE UNIV, 74- *Mem:* Am Math Soc; Math Asn Am. *Res:* Mappings; extensions of spaces and mappings; compactifications; unicoherence. *Mailing Add:* Dept of Math Va Polytech Inst & State Univ Blacksburg VA 24061

DICKMAN, ROBERT LAURENCE, b New York, NY, May 16, 47; m 75; c 2. ASTROPHYSICS, MICROWAVE ENGINEERING. *Educ:* Columbia Col, AB, 69; Columbia Univ, MA, 72, PhD(physics), 76. *Prof Exp:* Res assoc physics, Rensselaer Polytech Inst, 75-78; mem tech staff physics, Aerospace corp, Los Angeles, 78-80; FAC RES ASSOC RADIO ASTRON, UNIV MASS, AMHERST, 80- *Mem:* Am Phys Soc; Am Astron Soc. *Res:* Molecular radio astronomy; star formation; interstellar cloud dynamics; millimeter-wave receiver design and engineering. *Mailing Add:* Five Col Radio Observ Grad Res Ctr Univ MA Amherst MA 01003

DICKMAN, SHERMAN RUSSELL, b Buffalo, NY, Jan 15, 15; m 41; c 3. BIOCHEMISTRY. *Educ:* Pa State Col, BS, 36; Univ Ill, MS, 37, PhD(soil chem), 40. *Prof Exp:* First asst soil serv anal, Univ Ill, 40-41, spec asst chem, 41-45; asst chem, Argonne Nat Lab, Chicago, 45-46; res assoc med biochem, Col Physicians & Surgeons, Columbia Univ, 46-47; from asst prof to assoc prof, 47-67, PROF BIOCHEM, SCH MED, UNIV UTAH, 67- *Mem:* AAAS; Am Chem Soc; Am Soc Biol Chemists; Sigma Xi. *Res:* Nutrition wellness. *Mailing Add:* Col Med Univ Utah 410 Chipeta Way Salt Lake City UT 84108

DICKS, JOHN BARBER, JR, b Natchez, Miss, Mar 10, 26; m 50; c 6. PHYSICS. *Educ:* Univ of the South, BS, 48; Vanderbilt Univ, PhD(physics), 55. *Prof Exp:* Assoc prof physics, Tenn Polytech Inst, 53; from asst prof to assoc prof, Univ of the South, 54-63; PROF PHYSICS, UNIV TENN SPACE INST, 63-. DIR ENERGY CONVERSION, 72- *Concurrent Pos:* Pres, J B Dicks & Assocs, 67-; assoc ed, J Am Inst Aeronaut & Astronaut, 74-75. *Mem:* Am Phys Soc; assoc fel Am Inst Aeronaut & Astronaut; Am Soc Mech Engrs. *Res:* Magnetohydrodynamics; open-cycle magnetohydrodynamic power generation; fossil fuels. *Mailing Add:* 114 Noblitt Ct Tullahoma TN 37388

DICKSON, ARTHUR DAVID, b Londonderry, Northern Ireland, Mar 2, 25; m 52; c 2. REPRODUCTIVE BIOLOGY, MEDICAL EDUCATION. *Educ:* Queen's Univ Belfast, MB, BCh, BAO, 49, MD, 54. *Prof Exp:* Demonstr anat, Queen's Univ Belfast, 50-51, asst lectr, 51-54; univ demonstr, Cambridge Univ, 54-56; lectr, Aberdeen Univ, 56-63; assoc prof, Dalhousie Univ, 63-66; from assoc prof to prof, Univ Western Ont, 66-68; mem, Med Res Coun, 68-71, from asst dean to assoc dean med educ, 70-75, prof anat, 68-80, PROF DIV MORPHOL SCI, UNIV CALGARY, 80- *Concurrent Pos:* Res grants, Dept Sci & Indust Res, UK, 59-60, Pop Coun, 63-68 & Can Med Res Coun, 65- *Mem:* Am Asn Anat; Can Asn Anat (vpres, 69-71, pres, 71-73); Soc Study Reproduction; Anat Soc Gt Brit & Ireland; Brit Soc Endocrinol. *Res:* Ovo-implantation and placentation. *Mailing Add:* Div of Morphol Sci Univ of Calgary Calgary Can

DICKSON, ARTHUR DONALD, b Lowellville, Ohio, Apr 26, 27; m 52; c 7. PHYSICAL CHEMISTRY, PHYSICS. *Educ:* Carnegie Inst Technol, BSc, 50; Univ Minn, PhD(phys chem), 55. *Prof Exp:* Naval Ord res fel, Univ Minn, 54-55; res chemist, Electrochem Dept, E I du Pont de Nemours & Co, Inc, 55-57; RES CHEMIST, MINN MINING & MFG CO, 57- *Concurrent Pos:* Dir, Aquamotion, Inc, Minneapolis. *Mem:* Am Vacuum Soc. *Res:* Infrared spectroscopy; high pressure gas absorption spectra; colorimetry of fluorescent pigments; thermographic reaction kinetics; vacuum deposition of dielectric films; durable pavement markings. *Mailing Add:* 2593 Western Ave St Paul MN 55113

DICKSON, CHARLES RAY, b Henefer, Utah, Aug 20, 29; m 52; c 2. METEOROLOGY. *Educ:* Univ Utah, BS, 51, MS, 57. *Prof Exp:* Meteorologist, US Marine Corps, 52-54; res asst, Univ Utah, 54-57; meteorologist, Trans World Airlines, 57-58; RES METEOROLOGIST, AIR RESOURCES LABS, NAT OCEANIC & ATMOSPHERIC ADMIN, 58- *Concurrent Pos:* Consult, Dept Energy, 65-, Environ Protection Agency, 70-, NASA, 70, Nuclear Regulatory Comn, 75- & Atomic Indust Forum, 74-; mem, Coord Res Coun, 70- *Mem:* Am Meteorol Soc; AAAS. *Res:* Organizes research to describe and predict, quantitatively, concentrations of atmospheric pollutants as a function of horizontal and vertical distance; theoretical development and modification of dispersion formulae and new and unique mathematical formulae. *Mailing Add:* Air Resources Labs 550 Second St Idaho Falls ID 83401

DICKSON, DAVID ROSS, b Chicago, Ill, Oct 22, 31; m 71; c 4. SPEECH PATHOLOGY. *Educ:* Grinnell Col, BA, 53; Northwestern Univ, MA, 54, PhD(speech path), 61. *Prof Exp:* Assoc prof speech path, Sch Speech, Northwestern Univ, 58-68; lectr cleft palate, Dent Sch, 65-68; prof speech & anat, Univ Pittsburgh, 68-75; PROF PEDIAT, UNIV OF MIAMI & DIR DIV SPEECH & HEARING, MAILMAN CTR FOR CHILD DEVELOPMENT, 75- *Mem:* Am Speech & Hearing Asn; Am Cleft Palate Asn; Sigma Xi. *Res:* Speech science; cleft palate; anatomy and physiology; computed tomography. *Mailing Add:* Box 016820 Miami FL 33101

DICKSON, DON ROBERT, b Devil's Slide, Utah, May 19, 25; m 53; c 7. METEOROLOGY. *Educ:* Univ Utah, BS, 50, MS, 53. *Prof Exp:* Lectr meteorol, Univ NMex, 51-52; physicist, US Geol Surv, 53-55; asst prof meteorol, Okla State Univ, 55-57; asst prof, 57-65, actg head dept, 63-67, chmn dept, 67-72, ASSOC PROF METEOROL, UNIV UTAH, 65- *Concurrent Pos:* Consult, Kennecott Copper Corp, 67-73 & Hales & Co, 71- *Mem:* Am Meteorol Soc; Am Geophys Union; Int Soc Biometeorol; Royal Meteorol Soc; Sigma Xi. *Res:* Physical meteorology; neurometeorology studies; microclimatology; meteorological instruments; atmospheric pollution; severe storm damage. *Mailing Add:* Dept of Meteorol Univ of Utah Salt Lake City UT 84112

DICKSON, DONALD WARD, b Dickson, Tenn, Dec 9, 38; m 62; c 2. NEMATOLOGY, PLANT PATHOLOGY. *Educ:* Austin Peay State Univ, BS, 63; Okla State Univ, MS, 63; NC State Univ, PhD(plant path), 68. *Prof Exp:* Plant pathologist, 68-70, NEMATOLOGIST, UNIV FLA, 70- *Mem:* Soc Nematol (secy, 77-80, vpres, 80-81, pres, 81-82); Am Phytopath Soc. *Res:* Nematode control; biology of root-knot nematodes and comparative biochemistry of nematodes. *Mailing Add:* Dept Entom & Nematol Bldg 78 Univ of Fla Gainesville FL 32611

DICKSON, DOUGLAS GRASSEL, b Montclair, NJ, Nov 11, 24; m 52; c 2. MATHEMATICAL ANALYSIS. *Educ:* Wesleyan Univ, BA, 47; Harvard Univ, AM, 49; Columbia Univ, PhD(math), 58. *Prof Exp:* Instr math, Dartmouth Col, 48-49; lectr, Hunter Col, 49-51; lectr, Columbia Univ, 51-52, instr, 52-57; from asst prof to assoc prof, 58-74, PROF MATH, UNIV MICH, 74- *Mem:* Am Math Soc. *Res:* Complex analysis. *Mailing Add:* Dept of Math Univ of Mich Ann Arbor MI 48109

DICKSON, DOUGLAS HOWARD, b St Thomas, Ont, Feb 16, 42; m 69; c 2. MICROSCOPIC ANATOMY. *Educ:* Univ Western Ont, BA, 65, MSc, 68, PhD(anat), 71. *Prof Exp:* Med Res Coun Can fel, Dept Ophthal, Univ Melbourne, 71-72; assoc prof, 72-81, PROF ANAT, DALHOUSIE UNIV, 81- *Mem:* Can Fedn Biol Soc; Can Asn Anat; Am Asn Anat; Micros Soc Can; Asn Res Vision & Ophthal. *Res:* Fine structural, by transmission and scanning electron microscopy, studies of normal and pathological ocular tissues. *Mailing Add:* Dept of Anat Dalhousie Univ Halifax NS B3H 3J5 Can

DICKSON, FRANK WILSON, b Oplin, Tex, Nov 29, 22; m 45; c 4. GEOLOGY. *Educ:* Univ Calif, Los Angeles, BA, 50, BS, 53. *Prof Exp:* Res geologist, Univ Calif, Los Angeles, 52-55 & Shell Develop Co, Tex, 55-56; from asst prof to assoc prof geol, Univ Calif, Riverside, 56-69; prof geochem, Stanford Univ, 69-79, chmn dept, 76-79; STAFF SCIENTIST, OAK RIDGE NAT LAB, 79- *Concurrent Pos:* Shell Oil fel, 53-54; Fulbright res scholar, 62-63; Guggenheim fel, 62-63. *Mem:* Geol Soc Am; Geochem Soc; Nat Asn Geol Teachers; Soc Econ Geol. *Res:* Field and laboratory genesis of ore deposits; equilibria in systems of metal sulfides and water, as functions of temperature and pressure; rock-aqueous solution reactions and geochemical applications. *Mailing Add:* Oak Ridge Nat Lab Oak Ridge TN 37830

DICKSON, GEORGE, b Henryville, Ind, Mar 11, 16; m 42; c 3. DENTAL MATERIALS. *Educ:* DePauw Univ, AB, 38; Ind Univ, MA, 40. *Prof Exp:* PHYSICIST DENT MAT, NAT BUR STANDARDS, 40- *Mem:* Am Phys Soc; AAAS; Int Asn Dent Res. *Res:* Physical properties of dental and medical materials. *Mailing Add:* Dent & Med Mat Sect Nat Bur of Standards Washington DC 20234

DICKSON, HOWARD WESLEY, b Grove City, Pa, June 5, 42; m 61; c 4. HEALTH PHYSICS, RADIATION BIOLOGY. *Educ:* Slippery Rock State Col, BS, 64; Univ Tenn, Knoxville, MS, 67; Am Bd Health Physics, cert, 72. *Prof Exp:* Res assoc, Oak Ridge Assoc Univs, 67-72, res assoc radiation res, Health Physics Div, 72-76, actg sect chief assessment & technol, 76-77, group leader dosimetry, Health & Safety Res Div, 77-80, HEAD, HEALTH PHYSICS DEPT, OAK RIDGE NAT LAB, 80- *Honors & Awards:* Elda E Anderson Award, Health Physics Soc, 81. *Mem:* Health Physics Soc (treas, 81-83); Int Radiation Protection Asn; Radiation Res Soc. *Res:* Radiation dosimetry; research reactor operation; technology assessments; decontamination and decommissioning of nuclear facilities. *Mailing Add:* Oak Ridge Nat Lab PO Box X Oak Ridge TN 37830

DICKSON, JAMES FRANCIS, III, b Boston, Mass, May 4, 24. MEDICINE, ELECTRICAL ENGINEERING. *Educ:* Dartmouth Col, AB, 44; Harvard Med Sch, MD, 47; Am Bd Surg, dipl, 56. *Prof Exp:* Res assoc, Mass Inst Technol, 61-65; dir eng in biol & med, NIH, 65-70, dep asst secy health, Dept Health, Educ & Welfare, 75-77, actg asst secy health, 77, asst surg gen, 78-81. *Concurrent Pos:* NIH spec fel eng, Mass Inst Technol, 61-65; mem, President's Comn Technol, Automation & Econ Progress, 65; mem, President's Adv Coun Mgt Improv, 71. *Mem:* Inst Med-Nad Acad Sci; Am Col Surg. *Res:* Surgery; control systems engineering; science and technology policy. *Mailing Add:* Off of Asst Secy for Health Dept of Health, Educ & Welfare Washington DC 20201

DICKSON, JAMES GARY, b Chattanooga, Tenn, Apr 26, 43; m 71; c 1. WILDLIFE MANAGEMENT, FORESTRY. *Educ:* Univ of the South, BS, 65; Univ GA, MS, 67; La State Univ, PhD(forestry), 74. *Prof Exp:* Res asst, La State Univ, 72-74; asst prof, La Tech Univ, 74-76; RES WILDLIFE BIOLOGIST, SOUTHERN FOREST EXP STA, USDA FOREST SERV, 76- *Concurrent Pos:* Mem, Nongame Subcomt Southeast Sect Wildlife Soc, 76-; grad fac, Stephen F Austin State Univ, 77- *Mem:* Wildlife Soc; Am Ornithologists Union; Sigma Xi; Am Soc Mammalogists. *Res:* Seasonal populations and vertical distribution of bird communities; bird-habitat relationships, specifically effects of snags, edge, herbicides, etc on bird habitat and populations. *Mailing Add:* USDA Forest Serv PO Box 7600 SFA Nacogdoches TX 75962

DICKSON, KENNETH LYNN, b Jacksboro, Tex, Nov 20, 43; m 66; c 2. AQUATIC BIOLOGY, ENVIRONMENTAL SCIENCES. *Educ:* NTex State Univ, BS, 66, MS, 68; Va Polytech Inst & State Univ, 71. *Prof Exp:* From asst prof to assoc prof zool, Va Polytech Inst & State Univ, 70-78, asst dir, Ctr Environ Studies, 70-78; res scientist, 78-79, PROF, DEPT BIOL SCI, NTEX STATE UNIV, 81-, DIR, INST APPL SCI, 79- *Concurrent Pos:* Consult, Nat Acad Sci, 71- *Mem:* Am Fisheries Soc; Soc Environ Toxicol & Chem. *Res:* Limnology of reservoirs and rivers; microbiotic cycles in reservoirs; development of biological pollution monitoring systems; effects of pollution on aquatic organisms; biological diversity indices of community structure; effects of carbon, nitrogen and phosphorus on aquatic communities; fate and effects of chemicals in aquatic life. *Mailing Add:* Inst of Appl Sci Box 13078 NTex State Univ Denton TX 76203

DICKSON, LAWRENCE JOHN, b Seattle, Wash, Oct 25, 47. MATHEMATICAL ANALYSIS, APPLIED MATHEMATICS. *Educ:* Seattle Univ, BS, 68; Princeton Univ, PhD(math), 71. *Prof Exp:* Mathematician, Naval Torpedo Sta, Keyport, Wash, 68; instr math, Purdue Univ, West Lafayette, 71; teaching fel, Univ New South Wales, 73-74; sr engr, Boeing Com Airplane Co, Subsid Boeing Co, 75-78; consult, 78-81; PROGRAMMER, SUPERSET, INC, 81- *Concurrent Pos:* NSF fel, 68. *Mem:* Am Math Soc; Math Asn Am. *Res:* Aerodynamic flow analysis; curve and surface fitting; generalized Poisson kernel on unbounded domains in complex vector spaces; convex set theory; hyperbolic geometry models. *Mailing Add:* 3522 Burke Ave N Seattle WA 98103

DICKSON, LAWRENCE WILLIAM, b Saskatoon, Sask, Dec 1, 56. CHEMICAL KINETICS, PLASMA CHEMISTRY. *Educ:* Univ Sask, BSc, 77; Univ Toronto, PhD(phys chem), 82. *Prof Exp:* ASST RES OFFICER, RES CO, ATOMIC ENERGY CAN, LTD, 81- *Mem:* Am Phys Soc; Chem Inst Can. *Res:* Fundamental chemistry relating to the removal of gas phase radionuclides using the corona discharge scrubbes. *Mailing Add:* Atomic Energy Can Ltd Pinawa MB R0E 1L0 Can

DICKSON, LEROY DAVID, b New Brighton, Pa, June 26, 34; m 54; c 4. ELECTRICAL ENGINEERING. *Educ:* Johns Hopkins Univ, BES, 60, MSE, 62, PhD(elec eng), 68. *Prof Exp:* Res assoc optical data processing, Barton Lab, Johns Hopkins Univ, 61-68; mem tech staff laser atmospheric transmission, Bell Tel Labs, NJ, 68; staff engr, 68-74, adv engr, 74-81, SR ENGR, COMPUT APPLN LASER TECHNOL, IBM CORP, 81- *Mem:*

Optical Soc Am; Soc Photo-Optical Instrumentation Engrs; Laser Inst Am. *Res:* Optical data processing; holography; laser technology; applications of laser and laser systems to information processing. *Mailing Add:* 4805 Connell Dr Raleigh NC 27612

DICKSON, MICHAEL HUGH, b Eng, Apr 2, 32; nat US; m 58; c 3. PLANT BREEDING. *Educ:* McGill Univ, BS, 55; Mich State Univ, MS, 56, PhD(veg breeding), 58. *Prof Exp:* Asst prof hort, Univ Guelph, 58-64; from asst prof to assoc prof, 64-76, PROF HORT, NY STATE AGR EXP STA, GENEVA-CORNELL, 76- *Mem:* Am Soc Hort Sci; Am Soc Agron. *Res:* Breeding and genetics of snap beans, with special emphasis on disease resistance and plant efficiency; breeding cabbage, especially high dry matter, insect resistance and male sterility. *Mailing Add:* Dept of Veg Crops NY State Exp Sta Geneva NY 14456

DICKSON, PAUL WESLEY, JR, physics, see previous edition

DICKSON, PHILIP F, b Huron, SDak, Aug 5, 36; m 56; c 3. CHEMICAL ENGINEERING. *Educ:* SDak Sch Mines & Technol, BS, 58; Univ Minn, PhD(chem eng), 62. *Prof Exp:* Res engr, Esso Res & Eng Co, 58-59 & Humble Prod Res Div, Humble Oil & Ref Co, 62-63; assoc prof chem eng, 63-70, prof, 70-72, HEAD CHEM & PETROL REFINING ENG, COLO SCH MINES, 72- *Mem:* Am Inst Chem Engrs; Am Soc Eng Educ; Asn Asphalt Paving Technol. *Res:* Mass and heat transfer; chemical reactor analysis; heat transferred during asphalt paving operations; oil shale and shale oil. *Mailing Add:* Dept of Chem & Petrol Refining Colo Sch of Mines Golden CO 80401

DICKSON, RICHARD EUGENE, b Carbondale, Ill, Sept 13, 32; m 56; c 3. TREE PHYSIOLOGY. *Educ:* Southern Ill Univ, BS, 60, MS, 62; Univ Calif, Berkeley, PhD(plant physiol), 68. *Prof Exp:* Res asst, Univ Calif, Berkeley, 62-68; res plant physiologist, NCent Forest Exp Sta, 68-70, RES PLANT PHYSIOLOGIST, FORESTRY SCI LAB, US FOREST SERV, 70- *Mem:* AAAS; Am Soc Agron; Ecol Soc Am; Crop Sci Soc Am; Am Soc Plant Physiol. *Res:* Water relations studies on ecology of bottomland hardwoods; water and oxygen relationships of swamp trees and herbaceous plants; water relations studies on walnut; translocation of organic compounds; physiology of wood formation. *Mailing Add:* Forestry Sci Lab PO Box 898 Rhinelander WI 54501

DICKSON, ROBERT CARL, b Coevr d'Alene, Idaho, Apr 22, 43. MOLECULAR BIOLOGY. *Educ:* Univ Redlands, BS, 65; Univ Calif, Los Angeles, PhD(molecular biol), 70. *Prof Exp:* Fel phage assembly, Calif Inst Technol, 70-72, med microbiol, Univ Calif, Los Angeles, 72-73 & genetic regulation, Univ Calif, San Diego, 73-75; asst prof, 75-79, ASSOC PROF BIOCHEM, COL MED, UNIV KY, 79- *Mem:* Sigma Xi; Am Soc Microbiol; AAAS; Am Soc Biol Chemists. *Res:* Eucaryatic gene regulation. *Mailing Add:* Dept Biochem Col Med Univ KY Lexington KY 40536

DICKSON, ROBERT CLARK, b St Marys, Ont, Sept 24, 08; m 39; c 3. INTERNAL MEDICINE. *Educ:* Univ Toronto, MD, 34; FACP, 49, FRCP(C); FRCP, 72, MACP, 74. *Prof Exp:* From jr demonstr to sr demonstr med, Univ Toronto, 45-48, assoc, 48-50, from asst prof to assoc prof, 50-55; prof med & head dept, 56-74, EMER PROF MED, DALHOUSIE UNIV, 74- *Concurrent Pos:* Consult physician, Sunnybrook Hosp, Dept Vet Affairs, 46, Camp Hill Hosp, 56, Royal Can Navy, 56 & Halifax Childrens Hosp, 56; head dept med, Victoria Gen Hosp, 56-69, sr consult physician, 69-; pres, Royal Col Physicians & Surgeons Can, 70-72. *Honors & Awards:* Off Order Brit Empire, 45; App Queens Hon Physician, 71, reapp, 74; Officer, Order of Can, 78. *Mem:* Am Gastroenterol Asn; master Am Col Physicians; Can Med Asn; Can Cardiovasc Soc; Can Asn Gastroenterol (pres, 63). *Res:* Medicine; gastroenterology; infection; metabolism. *Mailing Add:* Dept of Med Dalhousie Univ Halifax Can

DICKSON, SPENCER E, b Topeka, Kans, Dec 17, 38; div; c 3. MATHEMATICS. *Educ:* Univ Kans, BA, 60; NMex State Univ, MS, 61, PhD(math), 63. *Prof Exp:* From asst prof to assoc prof math, Univ Nebr, 63-67; on leave from Univ Nebr, Off Naval Res res assoc, Univ Ore, 66-67; assoc prof, Univ Southern Calif, 67-68; assoc prof, 68-71, PROF MATH, IOWA STATE UNIV, 71- *Mem:* Am Math Soc; Math Asn Am. *Res:* Homological algebra with applications to ring theory and theory of modules. *Mailing Add:* Dept of Math Iowa State Univ Ames IA 50011

DICKSON, STANLEY, b New York, NY, Sept 3, 27; m 50; c 3. SPEECH PATHOLOGY, AUDIOLOGY. *Educ:* Brooklyn Col, BA, 50, MA, 54; Univ Buffalo, EdD, 61. *Prof Exp:* Speech clinician, New York City Bd Educ, 50-51; speech clinician, Rochester Bd Educ, 51-52; exec dir, Rochester Hearing & Speech Ctr, 52-56; assoc prof, 56-60, PROF SPEECH PATH & AUDIOL, STATE UNIV NY COL BUFFALO, 60- *Concurrent Pos:* Speech clinician, Cerebral Palsey Ctr Rochester, 51-52; coordr workshop audiol, State Univ NY Col Geneseo, 54; lectr, Univ Rochester & Nazareth Col, 54-56; consult, Edith Hartwell Clin, LeRoy, NY, 54-56; consult, Children's Rehab Ctr, Buffalo, NY, 63-64, audiol consult, 68-81. *Mem:* Am Speech & Hearing Asn; fel Am Speech-Lang-Hearing Asn; NY Acad Sci; Am Acad Sci. *Res:* Developmental speech and hearing disorders and factors related to its inception and remediation. *Mailing Add:* 34 Park Lane Ct Williamsville NY 14221

DICKSON, WILLIAM MORRIS, b Denver, Colo, Oct 22, 24; m 46, 79; c 2. VETERINARY PHYSIOLOGY. *Educ:* Colo Agr & Mech Col, DVM, 49; State Col Wash, MS, 53; Univ Minn, PhD, 61. *Prof Exp:* Instr vet physiol & pharmacol, State Col Wash, 49-53, asst prof, 53-55; instr, Univ Minn, 55-57; from asst prof to assoc prof, 57-66, chmn dept, 72-76, PROF VET PHYSIOL & PHARMACOL, WASH STATE UNIV, 66- *Concurrent Pos:* Endocrinol consult, Hanford Biol Lab, 62-63. *Mem:* Am Physiol Soc; Soc Study Reproduction. *Res:* Veterinary endocrinology; reproductive physiology. *Mailing Add:* Dept Vet Physiol Wash State Univ Pullman WA 99163

DICKSTEIN, JACK, b Philadelphia, Pa, Dec 14, 25; m 50; c 3. ORGANIC CHEMISTRY, POLYMER CHEMISTRY. *Educ:* Pa State Univ, BS, 46; Temple Univ, MA, 51; Rutgers Univ, PhD(polymer chem), 58. *Prof Exp:* Res chemist, Lederle Labs, Am Cyanamid Co, 46-48; asst, Temple Univ, 49-51; chemist, Parenteral Formulations, E R Squibb & Sons Div, Olin Mathieson Chem Corp, 51-56; prof org chem, Alma White Col, 57-58; group leader adhesives, Borden Chem Co, 58-60, develop mgr, Monomer Polymer Labs, 60-61, develop mgr, Thermoplastics Div, 61-67, dir res, 67-74; group mgr & dir res & develop, Haven Chem Co, 74-77; vpres & dir res & develop, Seal Inc, 77-79; PRES, DEPT MONOMER-POLYMER, DAJAC LABS, 79- *Concurrent Pos:* Mem, Smithsonian Inst. *Mem:* AAAS; Am Chem Soc; Franklin Inst; Am Inst Chem; NY Acad Sci. *Res:* High polymers; emulsions; medicinals; adhesives; physical chemistry; research and development in specialty monomers and polymers and medicinal and diagnostic agents. *Mailing Add:* 318 Keats Rd Huntingdon Valley PA 19006

DICORLETO, PAUL EUGENE, b Hartford, Conn, May 19, 51; m 75; c 1. VASCULAR CELL BIOLOGY, MEMBRANE BIOCHEMISTRY. *Educ:* Rensselaer Polytech Inst, BS, 73; Cornell Univ, PhD(biochem), 78. *Prof Exp:* Res fel, Dept Path, Sch Med, Univ Wash, 78-81; PROJ SCIENTIST, DEPT CARDIOVASC RES, CLEVELAND CLIN FOUND, 81- *Mem:* Am Soc Cell Biologists; NY Acad Sci. *Res:* Interaction of growth factors with the cells of the artery wall and the degree to which cell-cell interactions play a role in the development of the atherosclerotic plaque. *Mailing Add:* Res Div Cleveland Clin Found 9500 Euclid Cleveland OH 44106

DI CUOLLO, C JOHN, b Scotch Plains, NJ, Jan 1, 35. BIOCHEMISTRY, MICROBIOLOGY. *Educ:* Va Polytech Inst, BS, 56; Rutgers Univ, PhD(biochem), 60. *Prof Exp:* Sr res biochemist, Colgate Palmolive Co, 60-63; sr res biologist, 63-67, asst dir microbiol, 67-71, mgr bioanal sect, 71-73, MGR DEVELOP OPER, ANIMAL HEALTH PRODS, SMITH-KLINE CORP, 73- *Mem:* AAAS; Am Soc Microbiol; Am Chem Soc; Am Inst Chemists; assoc Am Col Vet Toxicologists. *Res:* Applications of radioisotopes to biological problems; metabolic fate of drugs; development of automation in the field of microbiology; development of tissue residue methods; perform safety studies on potential animal health products. *Mailing Add:* 353 Colonial Ave Collegeville PA 19426

DICUS, DUANE A, b Okanogan, Wash, Nov 23, 38; m 57; c 3. ELEMENTARY PARTICLE PHYSICS. *Educ:* Univ Wash, BS, 61, MS, 63, Univ Calif, Los Angeles, PhD(physics), 68. *Prof Exp:* Res scientist, Boeing Co, 63-64; asst prof, Univ Calif, Los Angeles, 68-69; res assoc, Mass Inst Technol, 69-71, Univ Rochester, 71-73; asst prof, 73-78, ASSOC PROF PHYSICS, UNIV TEX, AUSTIN, 78- *Mem:* Am Phys Soc. *Res:* Fundamental and phenomenological studies of the field theories of strong, electromagnetic, and weak interactions and the application of particle physics to astrophysics and cosmology. *Mailing Add:* Physics Dept Univ Tex Austin TX 78712

DIDDLE, ALBERT W, b Hamilton, Mo, July 1, 09; m 42; c 2. OBSTETRICS & GYNECOLOGY. *Educ:* Univ Mo, AB, 30, MA, 33; Yale Univ, MD, 36. *Prof Exp:* Asst anat, Univ Mo, 31-33; asst, Yale Univ, 33-36; instr obstet & gynec, Univ Iowa, 39-40, assoc, 40-42; assoc prof, Southwestern Med Sch, Univ Tex, 45-48; regional consult, Vet Admin, Ga, 48-55; clin prof, 56-68, chmn dept, 56-72, prof obstet & gynec, 68-72, EMER CLIN PROF OBSTET & GYNEC, UNIV TENN, KNOXVILLE, 72- *Concurrent Pos:* Consult, Vet Admin, Tex, 46-48 & Oak Ridge Hosp, 49- *Honors & Awards:* Humanitarian Award, Res Gynec & Obstet, Univ Tenn, 81. *Mem:* Am Asn Obstet & Gynec; fel Am Col Obstet & Gynec; Continental Gynec Soc. *Res:* Anatomy; endocrinology; oncology. *Mailing Add:* 7209 Sheffield Dr Knoxville TX 37919

DIDIO, LIBERATO JOHN ALPHONSE, b Sao Paulo, Brazil, May 7, 20; m 60; c 4. ANATOMY. *Educ:* Univ Sao Paulo, BS, 39, MD, 45, DSc(anat), 49, PhD(anat), 52. *Prof Exp:* Instr physiol, Fac Med, Univ Sao Paulo, 42-43, from instr to assoc prof anat, 43-53; prof topog anat & head dept, Cath Univ Minas Gerais, 53-54, prof anat & chmn dept, Med Sch, Fed Univ Minas Gerais, 54-63; prof, Med, Dent & Grad Sch, Northwestern Univ, Chicago, 63-67; PROF ANAT & CHMN DEPT, MED COL OHIO, 67-, DEAN GRAD SCH, 72- *Concurrent Pos:* Rockefeller Found fel, Sch Med, Univ Wash; intern, Hosp Med Sch, Univ Sao Paulo, 44-45; vis prof, Univ Messina, 55, Sch Med, Univ Brazil, 57 & Univ Parma, 58; mem Nat Coun Sci Res, Brazil, 56-60; guest investr, Rockefeller Inst Med Res, NY & Harvard Med Sch, 60-61; Brazilian del, Int Cong Electron Micros, Philadelphia, 62; treas, Brazilian Asn Schs Med, 62-64, secy, 64-66; mem, Order Med Merit Presidency Brazilian Repub, Int Anat Nomenclature Comt. *Honors & Awards:* Medal Sci Merit, Govt State Minas Gerais; Star Solidarity Italy & Medal Cult Merit, 62, Presidency Repub Italy; William H Rorer Award, 70; Ipiranga Medal, Govt State, Sao Paulo, Brazil, 79. *Mem:* Am Asn Anat; Electron Micros Soc; NY Acad Sci; Pan Am Asn Anat (pres, 69-72, hon pres, 72-). *Res:* Gross anatomy; surgical anatomy; coronary circulation; electron microscopy of the prostate; pineal body and heart musculature. *Mailing Add:* Dept of Anat Med Col of Ohio CS10008 Toledo OH 43699

DIDISHEIM, PAUL, b Paris, France, June 3, 27; US citizen; m 52; c 3. HEMATOLOGY, CARDIOVASCULAR DISEASES. *Educ:* Princeton Univ, BA, 50; Johns Hopkins Univ, MD, 54. *Prof Exp:* Life Ins Med Res Fund fel, Sch Med, Univ Pittsburgh, 55-57; Nat Heart Inst spec res fel, Nat Blood Transfusion Ctr, Paris, France, 57-58; from instr to asst prof med, Col Med, Univ Utah, 58-65; mem staff, Sect Clin Path, Thrombosis Res Lab, 65-70, asst prof exp path, 66-70, assoc prof clin path, Mayo Grad Sch Med, 70-73, assoc prof lab med, 73-75, PROF LAB MED, MAYO MED SCH, 75-, MEM STAFF, DEPT LAB MED, MAYO CLIN, 71-, DIR, THROMBOSIS RES LAB, 65- *Concurrent Pos:* Chief coagulation lab & assoc physician, Salt Lake County Gen Hosp, 58-65; chief coagulation subdiv, Div Hemat, Dept Med, Col Med, Univ Utah, 58-65; attend, Salt Lake City Vet Admin Hosp, Utah, 59-65; mem med adv coun, Nat Hemophilia Found, 65-77, mem res rev panel, 70-74; mem ad hoc comt standardization human antihemophilic factor assay,

Nat Acad Sci-Nat Res Coun, 63; mem comp plasma fractionation & coagulation res, Am Nat Red Cross, 67-72; mem adv bd, Coun on Circulation, Am Heart Asn, 68-, mem orgn comt coun thrombosis, 70-71, mem exec comt, 71-, mem path res study comt, 73-76; mem contract rev panels, Nat Heart & Lung Inst, 74-; mem ed bd, Artery, 74- & Platelets, 74-; mem NIH site visit teams, Prog Proj & Clin Res Ctrs, 75- *Honors & Awards:* Borden Award, Johns Hopkins Univ, 54. *Mem:* Am Fedn Clin Res; Am Asn Pathologists; Am Soc Hemat; Int Soc Hemat; Soc Exp Biol & Med. *Res:* Blood coagulation; hemostasis; thrombosis; hemorrhagic diseases. *Mailing Add:* Dept of Lab Med Mayo Clin Rochester MN 55901

DIDOMENICO, MAURO, JR, b New York, NY, Jan 12, 37; m 64; c 2. SOLID STATE PHYSICS. *Educ:* Stanford Univ, BS, 58, MS, 59, PhD(elec eng), 63. *Prof Exp:* Supvr, 66, dept head, 70, MEM TECH STAFF, BELL LABS, 62- *Mem:* fel Am Phys Soc; fel Inst Elec & Electronics Engrs. *Res:* Quantum electronics; lasers; nonlinear optical phenomena; ferroelectricity; luminescence in semiconductors; optical communications. *Mailing Add:* Bell Labs 600 Mountain Ave Murray Hill NJ 07974

DIDONATO, ARMIDO RICHARD, b Pittsburgh, Pa, June 8, 22; m 71; c 4. MATHEMATICS, PHYSICS. *Educ:* Duquesne Univ, BS, 50; Mass Inst Technol, SM, 51; Carnegie-Mellon Univ, PhD(math), 72. *Prof Exp:* Mathematician, E I du Pont de Nemours & Co, Inc, 51-53 & Melpar Inc, 53-54; MATHEMATICIAN, NAVAL SURFACE WEAPONS LAB, 54- *Concurrent Pos:* Adj prof, Va Polytech Inst, 72- *Mem:* Math Asn Am; Soc Indust & Appl Math. *Res:* Numerical analysis with applications to computers from the fields of math and physics. *Mailing Add:* Box 405 Dahlgren VA 22448

DIDWANIA, HANUMAN PRASAD, b Bhagalpur, India, Mar 13, 35; US citizen; m 69; c 2. PHYSICAL CHEMISTRY, POLYMER CHEMISTRY. *Educ:* Univ Bihar, Bsc, Hons, 55; Inst Paper Chem, MS, 65, PhD(chem), 68; Rider Col, MBA, 71. *Prof Exp:* Shift-in-charge pulp & paper mfg, Orient Paper Mills Ltd, India, 55-61; tech supt, Sirpur Paper Mills Ltd, 61-63; Inst Int Educ develop fel, 65-66; res scientist, Union Camp Corp, 68-73; res assoc, 73-77, MGR NEW PROD DEVELOP, AM CAN CO, 77- *Concurrent Pos:* consult, UN Tokten Proj, 81. *Mem:* AAAS; Am Chem Soc; Tech Asn Pulp & Paper Indust; assoc Am Inst Chem Engrs; Indian Inst Eng. *Res:* Pulping, bleaching, soda recovery; physics and chemistry of papermaking; chemical modification of cellulose; effect of hydroxyethylation of fibers on strength properties of paper; paper product development; tissue and towel manufacturing; fiber technology systems; paperboard manufacturing. *Mailing Add:* Am Can Co 1915 Marathon Ave Neenah WI 54956

DIEBEL, ROBERT NORMAN, b Chico, Calif, May 15, 27; m 51; c 3. ANALYTICAL CHEMISTRY, RADIOCHEMISTRY. *Educ:* Univ Ore, BS, 50, MS, 54. *Prof Exp:* Chemist, Hanford Labs, Gen Elec Co, 60-65; sr scientist, Pac Northwest Labs, Battelle Mem Inst, 65-71; lead chemist, Atlantic Richfield Hanford Co, 71-77, SR CHEMIST, HANFORD OPERS, ROCKWELL INT, 77- *Mem:* AAAS; Am Chem Soc; Sigma Xi. *Res:* Electron magnetic resonance studies of free radicals produced by irradiation of water solutions; nuclear chemical analytical techniques; quality assurance and chemical standards; chemical assay and impurity analysis on plutonium and uranium; thermal ionization isotope ratio mass spectrometry. *Mailing Add:* 1925 Everest Richland WA 99352

DIEBOLD, GERALD JOSEPH, b Louisville, Ky, May 20, 43; m 77. PHYSICAL & ANALYTICAL CHEMISTRY. *Educ:* Univ Notre Dame, BS, 65; Boston Col, PhD(physics), 74. *Prof Exp:* Fels, Boston Col, 74-75, Columbia Univ, 76-77 & Stanford Univ, 77-78; ASST PROF PHYS CHEM, BROWN UNIV, 78- *Mem:* Am Chem Soc; Am Phys Soc. *Res:* Chemical reaction dynamics, especially the use of lasers in determining state-to-state reaction rates; optoacoustics effect; trace detection techniques. *Mailing Add:* Dept of Chem Brown Univ Providence RI 02912

DIEBOLD, ROBERT ERNEST, b Rhinelander, Wis, Aug 31, 37; m 57; c 4. HIGH ENERGY PHYSICS. *Educ:* Univ NMex, BS, 58; Calif Inst Technol, MS, 60, PhD(physics), 63. *Prof Exp:* NSF fel, Europ Orgn Nuclear Res, Geneva, Switz, 62-64; res assoc, Stanford Linear Accelerator Ctr, 64-69; physicist, 69-75, assoc dir, high energy physics div, 77-79, assoc lab dir high energy physics, 79-80, SR PHYSICIST, ARGONNE NAT LAB, 75-, DIR, HIGH ENERGY PHYSICS DIV, 81- *Concurrent Pos:* Mem, High Energy Adv Comt, Brookhaven Nat Lab, 72-74, Prog Adv Comt, Fermi Nat Accelerator Lab, 73-76 & Stanford Linear Accelerator Ctr, 74-76; high energy physics rev comt, Lawrence Berkeley Lab, 74-78 & High Energy Physics Adv Panel, Energy Res & Develop Admin, 75-78, subpanel on Accelerator Res & Develop & Review & Planning for US High Energy Physics Prog, 80. *Mem:* Am Phys Soc; AAAS. *Res:* Experimental high energy physics using spectrometer systems to study hadronic interactions; design of proton storage rings. *Mailing Add:* Argonne Nat Lab Argonne IL 60439

DIECK, RONALD LEE, US citizen. INORGANIC CHEMISTRY, POLYMER CHEMISTRY. *Educ:* Ripon Col, AB, 68; Ariz State Univ, PhD(chem), 72. *Prof Exp:* Res chemist, Res & Develop Ctr, Armstrong Cork Co, 73-77; specialist prod develop, Valox Bus Sect, Gen Elec Co, 77-79, mgr qual control & anal, 79-80; tech dir, Thermofit Bus Sect, 80-81, BUS DEVELOP MGR, MED PROD GROUP, RAYCHEM CORP, 81- *Mem:* AAAS; Soc Plastics Engrs; Am Chem Soc; Sigma Xi. *Res:* Synthesis and characterization of compounds of the lanthanides and of inorganic polymers and oligomers; processing and physical properties of engineering thermoplastics; radiation cured polymer systems; polymer formulation; medical devices. *Mailing Add:* Raychem Corp 300 Constitution Dr Menlo Park CA 94025

DIECKE, FRIEDRICH PAUL JULIUS, b June 27, 27; m 55; c 2. PHYSIOLOGY. *Educ:* Univ Würzburg, Dr rer nat, 53. *Prof Exp:* Jr res zoologist, Univ Calif, Los Angeles, 53-55; asst comp physiol, Univ Würzburg, 55-56; from instr to asst prof, Col Med, Univ Tenn, Memphis, 56-59; guest investr, Rockefeller Inst, 59; assoc prof physiol, Sch Med, George Washington Univ, 59-63; prof physiol & biophys, Col Med, Univ Iowa, 63-75; PROF PHYSIOL & CHMN DEPT, COL MED & DENT NJ-NJ MED SCH, 75- *Concurrent Pos:* Actg head, Col Med, Univ Iowa, 73. *Mem:* AAAS; Biophys Soc; Fedn Am Socs Exp Biol; Soc Neurosci; Am Physiol Soc. *Res:* Ion transport in nerve and smooth muscle; excitation-contraction coupling and muscle. *Mailing Add:* Dept Physiol Col Med & Dent NJ-NJ Med Sch Newark NJ 07103

DIECKERT, JULIUS WALTER, b Houston, Tex, June 15, 25; m 50; c 4. BIOCHEMISTRY. *Educ:* Agr & Mech Col, Tex, BS, 49, MS, 51, PhD(biochem), 55. *Prof Exp:* Biochemist, Res Found, Agr & Mech Col, Tex, 53-55; res chemist, Southern Utilization Res Br, USDA, 55-60; assoc prof, 60-70, PROF BIOCHEM & NUTRIT, TEX A&M UNIV, 70- *Concurrent Pos:* Asst prof, Med Sch, Tulane Univ, 59. *Honors & Awards:* USDA Award, 58. *Mem:* Am Chem Soc; Sigma Xi; Am Soc Plant Physiol. *Res:* Chemistry of natural products, isolation and identification of lipides, saponins and proteins; glass paper chromatography, theory and application of natural products; plant cytochemistry, histochemical and cytochemical organization of seeds. *Mailing Add:* Dept of Biochem & Biophysics Tex A&M Univ College Station TX 77848

DIEDRICH, DONALD FRANK, b Passaic, NJ, May 17, 32; m 58; c 1. BIOCHEMICAL PHARMACOLOGY. *Educ:* Univ Ill, BS, 54; Univ Wis, MS, 56, PhD(biochem), 59. *Prof Exp:* Res fel physiol, Col Med, Univ Cincinnati, 59; res instr, Col Med & Dent, Univ Rochester, 59-63; from asst prof to assoc prof pharmacol, 63-74, acad ombudsman, 73-74, PROF PHARMACOL, COL MED & DENT, UNIV KY, 74- *Concurrent Pos:* Vis scientist, Max Planck Inst Biophys, 71; Fulbright award, 71; vis prof, Eidgenossische Technische Hochschule, Zurich, 78-79. *Mem:* AAAS; Am Chem Soc; Am Soc Pharmacol & Exp Therapeut; NY Acad Sci; Am Asn Univ Professors. *Res:* General cellular biology; transport of metabolites across cell membranes; carbohydrate chemistry; drug-receptor interrelationships. *Mailing Add:* Dept Pharmacol Univ Ky Col Med Lexington KY 40506

DIEDRICH, JAMES LOREN, b St Paul, Minn, Jan 13, 25; m 50; c 6. POLYMER CHEMISTRY. *Educ:* Univ Minn, BChem, 45; Ind Univ, AM, 47, PhD(chem), 49. *Prof Exp:* Res assoc, Northwestern Univ, 49-50; instr chem, Loyola Univ, Ill, 50-51; res chemist, A B Dick Co, 51-52 & Minn Mining & Mfg Co, 52-58; serv engr, Northwest Orient Airlines, Inc, 58-60; proj leader, Borden, Inc, Mass, 60-67; SR RES ASSOC POLYMERS, H B FULLER CO, 67- *Mem:* Am Chem Soc. *Res:* Emulsion polymerization. *Mailing Add:* H B Fuller Co 2267 Como Ave St Paul MN 55108

DIEFENDORF, RUSSELL JUDD, b Mount Vernon, NY, Aug 28, 31; m 52; c 4. PHYSICAL CHEMISTRY, MATERIALS SCIENCE. *Educ:* Univ Rochester, BS, 53; Univ Toronto, PhD(phys chem), 58. *Prof Exp:* Scientist graphite, missile & ord dept, Gen Elec Co, 58-59, scientist vapor deposition, Res Lab, 60-65; assoc prof, 65-71, PROF MAT SCI, RENSSELAER POLYTECH INST, 71- *Honors & Awards:* Humboldt-Preis, Alexander von Humboldt-Stiftung, 74. *Mem:* Am Chem Soc; Am Ceramic Soc; Am Soc Metals. *Res:* Mechanical properties; structure to properties; graphite; pyrolytic materials; boron and carbon fibers; composites; high temperature materials; electrochemical power sources; gas phase kinetics. *Mailing Add:* Dept of Mat Eng Rensselaer Polytech Inst Troy NY 12181

DIEGLE, RONALD BRUCE, b Marion, Ohio, Jan 17, 47; m 69; c 2. CORROSION SCIENCE, INORGANIC ELECTROCHEMISTRY. *Educ:* Case Inst Technol, BS, 69; Rensselaer Polytech Inst, MS, 72, PhD(mat eng), 74. *Prof Exp:* Assoc staff, Gen Elec Corp, Res & Develop Ctr, 69-74; sr res metallurgist, Battelle Mem Inst, 74-81; DIV SUPVR, SANDIA NAT LAB, 81- *Honors & Awards:* A B Campbell Award, Nat Asn Corrosion Engrs, 76. *Mem:* Electrochem Soc; Nat Asn Corrosion Engrs. *Res:* Application of corrosion science and electrochemical techniques to the study of localized and general corrosion of alloys used in energy and weapons systems; corrosion of amorphous alloys. *Mailing Add:* Orgn 5841 Sandia Nat Lab Albuquerque NM 87185

DIEGNAN, GLENN ALAN, b Paterson, NJ, Aug 12, 47. PHYSICAL ORGANIC CHEMISTRY, ANALYTICAL CHEMISTRY. *Educ:* Bucknell Univ, BS, 69; Duke Univ, PhD(phys org chem), 73. *Prof Exp:* Mgr anal chem, Biometric Testing Inc, 74-75; sr anal chemist pharmaceut anal, Hoechst-Roussel Pharmaceut Inc, 75-76; sr scientist pharmaceut anal, Hoffmann-La Roche Inc, 76-79; SR SCIENTIST II, BIOPHARMACEUTICS, CIBA-GEIGY CORP, 79- *Mem:* Am Chem Soc; AAAS; Sigma Xi. *Res:* Biopharmaceutics; organic structure determination by spectroscopic methods; development of chromatographic methods for identification and quantification of drugs; metabolism; automated analysis. *Mailing Add:* 42 Pine St Morristown NJ 07960

DIEHL, ANTONI MILLS, b Minneapolis, Minn, Nov 5, 24; m 48; c 4. PEDIATRICS, CARDIOLOGY. *Educ:* Univ Minn, BS, 46, MB, 47; MD, 48; Am Bd Pediat, dipl & cert cardiol, 53. *Prof Exp:* Intern, Univ Mich, 47-48; resident pediat, Univ Minn Hosp, 48-50, fel pediat cardiol, 50-51; instr pediat cardiol, 53-55, from asst prof to prof pediat, 55-78, CLIN PROF PEDIAT, MED SCH, UNIV MO-KANSAS CITY, 78- *Concurrent Pos:* Med Dir, Children's Cardiac Ctr, 53-64; pvt pract cardiol, 78-; teacher, Children's Mercy Hosp, Kansas City, Mo, 79- *Mem:* Am Heart Asn; fel Am Acad Pediat; fel Am Col Cardiol; fel Am Col Chest Physicians; AMA. *Res:* Pediatric cardiology; rheumatic fever. *Mailing Add:* 618 Med Plaza 4320 Wornall Rd Kansas City MO 64111

DIEHL, FRED A, b Staunton, Va, Aug 15, 36; m 58; c 4. DEVELOPMENTAL BIOLOGY. *Educ:* Bridgewater Col, BA, 60; Western Reserve Univ, PhD(biol), 65. *Prof Exp:* NIH fel biol, Univ Brussels, 64-65; res fel, Univ Va, 65-66; instr, Western Reserve Univ, 66-67; asst prof, 69-73, ASSOC PROF BIOL, UNIV VA, 73- *Mem:* Am Soc Zoologists; Soc Develop Biol. *Res:* Studies of form genesis and regulation in cnidaria; specific pathways of cellular differentiation, cellular migration and controlling mechanisms of morphogenesis examined in Hydra, Cordylophora and various other hydroids. *Mailing Add:* Dept Biol Univ Va Charlottesville VA 22903

DIEHL, HARVEY, b Detroit, Mich, Nov 2, 10; m 36; c 6. ANALYTICAL CHEMISTRY. *Educ:* Univ Mich, BS, 32, PhD(chem), 36. *Prof Exp:* Instr anal chem, Cornell Univ, 36-37; instr, Purdue Univ, 37-39; from asst prof to assoc prof anal chem, 39-47, distinguished prof sci & humanities, 65-81, PROF ANAL CHEM, IOWA STATE UNIV, 47-, EMER PROF SCI & HUMANITIES, 81- *Honors & Awards:* Anachem Award, Asn Anal Chemists, Detroit, Mich, 66; Fisher Award, Am Chem Soc, 56, Gold Medal, 61. *Mem:* AAAS; Am Chem Soc. *Res:* Coordination and chelate ring compounds; electro analysis; tridentate compounds of cobalt; chemical structure of vitamin B12; organic reagents for iron, copper, calcium, magnesium, cobalt and beryllium; perchlorate chemistry; high-precision coulometric titrations; the value of the Faraday. *Mailing Add:* Dept Chem Iowa State Univ Ames IA 50011

DIEHL, JOHN EDWIN, b Sunbury, Pa, Feb 7, 29; m 53; c 4. BIOCHEMISTRY. *Educ:* Susquehanna Univ, AB, 52; Pa State Univ, MS, 54, PhD(biochem), 60. *Prof Exp:* Sr res biochem, Va Inst Sci Res, 59-64; asst prof chem, Dickinson Col, 64-65; from asst prof to assoc prof, 65-73, PROF CHEM & HEAD DEPT, SHEPHERD COL, 73- *Concurrent Pos:* Gen chmn, Tobacco Chemists' Res Conf, Va, 62. *Mem:* AAAS; Am Chem Soc; NY Acad Sci. *Res:* Enzymes; sheep erythrocyte sphingolipides and tobacco leaf proteins; histone chemistry and neurochemistry. *Mailing Add:* Dept of Chem Shepherd Col Shepardstown WV 25443

DIEHL, JOHN RICHARD, reproductive physiology, animal production, see previous edition

DIEHL, WILLIAM PAUL, b Reading, Pa, Mar 3, 33; m 55; c 3. MICROBIAL GENETICS. *Educ:* Univ Ariz, BS, 55; Univ Calif, Los Angeles, PhD(genetics of phage lambda), 68. *Prof Exp:* ASSOC PROF BIOL, SAN DIEGO STATE UNIV, 68- *Mem:* Genetics Soc Am. *Res:* Control mechanisms and functions in bacteriophage lambda. *Mailing Add:* Dept of Biol San Diego State Univ San Diego CA 92182

DIEHN, BODO, b Hamburg, Ger, June 22, 34. BIOPHYSICAL CHEMISTRY, RADIOCHEMISTRY. *Educ:* Univ Hamburg, BS, 60; Univ Kans, PhD(phys chem), 64. *Prof Exp:* Res assoc biochem, Univ Ariz, 64-66; from asst prof to prof chem, Univ Toledo, 66-79; PROF ZOOL, MICH STATE UNIV, 80-; DIR, LEGIS SCI OFF, STATE OF MICH, 79- *Concurrent Pos:* Adj assoc prof biochem, Med Col Ohio Toledo, 70-75; adj prof, 75-79. *Honors & Awards:* Outstanding Res Award, Sigma Xi, 78. *Mem:* Am Chem Soc; Biophys Soc; Am Soc Photobiol; Fedn Am Scientists. *Res:* Radio and hot-atom chemistry; photosynthesis and phototaxis; origin of life; membrane phenomena. *Mailing Add:* Legis Sci Off State Mich PO Box 30036 Lansing MI 48909

DIEHR, PAULA K, b Philadelphia, Pa, Sept 26, 41. BIOSTATISTICS. *Educ:* Harvey Mudd Col, BS, 63; Univ Calif, Los Angeles, MS, 67, PhD(biostatist), 70. *Prof Exp:* Sci programmer, ITT Fed Labs, 63-66; instr, 70-72, asst prof, 72-79, ASSOC PROF BIOSTATIST, UNIV WASH, 79- *Concurrent Pos:* Researcher health serv qual res, Nat Ctr Health Serv Res, HEW, 75-76. *Mem:* Am Statist Asn; Biomet Soc; Am Pub Health Asn. *Res:* Statistical methods in health services research; evaluation of health care technology; utilization of health and mental health services; statistical re-evaluation of common health problems. *Mailing Add:* SC-32 Dept Biostatist Univ of Wash Seattle WA 98195

DIEKE, SALLY HARRISON, b Belvoir, Va, Feb 7, 13; m 38. ASTRONOMY. *Educ:* Johns Hopkins Univ, PhD(chem), 38. *Prof Exp:* Asst chem, Johns Hopkins Univ, 42-43, instr psychobiol, 43-47, instr, 47-53; vis lectr astron, Goucher Col, 50-59, adj prof, 59-69; RES FEL ASTRON, JOHNS HOPKINS UNIV, 66- *Mem:* Hist Sci Soc; Am Astron Soc. *Res:* General astronomy; variable stars; biological effects of thiourea derivatives; hair growth and color in rats; history of astronomy, especially 19th century and early 20th century astronomers. *Mailing Add:* Hist of Sci Dept Johns Hopkins Univ Baltimore MD 21218

DIEKHANS, HERBERT HENRY, b West Palm Beach, Fla, Mar 4, 25; m 55; c 2. MATHEMATICS. *Educ:* Univ Ala, BS, 50, MA, 51; Univ Ill, Urbana, PhD(math), 64. *Prof Exp:* Instr math, Ohio Univ, 55-60; instr, Univ Ill, Urbana, 64; assoc prof, 64-70, PROF MATH, IND STATE UNIV, TERRE HAUTE, 70- *Mem:* Am Math Soc; Math Asn Am. *Res:* Mathematical analysis. *Mailing Add:* Dept of Math Ind State Univ Terre Haute IN 47803

DIEKMAN, JOHN DAVID, b Bridgeport, Conn, Jan 1, 43; m 68. ORGANIC CHEMISTRY. *Educ:* Princeton Univ, AB, 65; Stanford Univ, PhD(chem), 69. *Prof Exp:* Res fel, Australia Nat Univ, 69-70; sr chemist, 70-71, proj mgr prod develop, 71-72, mgr toxical & regist, 72-73, dir prod develop, 73-75, VPRES RES & DEVELOP, ZOECON CORP, 75-, VPRES & GEN MGR, INT DIV, 81- *Mem:* Am Chem Soc; Entom Soc; AAAS. *Res:* Innovative approaches to pest control. *Mailing Add:* Zoecon Corp 975 Calif Ave Palo Alto CA 94304

DIEKMAN, ROBERT, b Elgin, Ill, Apr 29, 22; m 47; c 2. CHEMICAL ENGINEERING. *Educ:* Northwestern Univ, BS, 44, MS, 48. *Prof Exp:* Chem engr process div, Res Dept, Standard Oil Co, Ind, 47-51, group leader, 51-61, head engr process eng div, Eng Dept, Am Oil Co, 61-66, supvr long-range planning, Mfg Dept, 66-68, supt tech serv, Whiting Refinergy, 68-72, coordr mgt develop, 73-75; mgr prod design, 75-77, mgr opers, Whiting Refinery, 77-78, MGR ENG, TECH DIV, AMOCO OIL CO, 78- *Mem:* Am Inst Chem Engrs; Am Chem Soc. *Mailing Add:* Nat Inst Environ Health Sci Whiting TN 46394

DIEL, JOSEPH HENRY, b Tulsa, Okla, Aug 3, 37; m 68; c 2. BIOMEDICAL RESEARCH, COMPUTER PROGRAMMING. *Educ:* Univ Tulsa, BS, 59, MS, 60; NMex State Univ, PhD(math), 74. *Prof Exp:* Physicist, Phys Sci Lab, NMex State Univ, 60-65; PHYSICIST, LOVELACE BIOMED & ENVIRON RES INST, INC, 75- *Concurrent Pos:* Adj prof,

Univ NMex, 80-81. *Mem:* Am Math Soc; Soc Indust & Appl Math; AAAS; Radiation Res Soc. *Res:* Metabolism, dosimetry and toxicity of internally deposited radioactive materials; use of computerized data collection and analysis; computer simulation of biological systems. *Mailing Add:* 337 Rhode Island Northeast Albuquerque NM 87108

DIEM, HUGH EGBERT, b Arendtsville, Pa, Mar 31, 22; m 48; c 2. SPECTROSCOPY. *Educ:* Ohio Wesleyan Univ, AB, 47; Ohio State Univ, MA, 49. *Prof Exp:* Asst chem, Ohio State Univ, 47-49; res chemist, Colgate-Palmolive-Peet Co, 50-51; develop engr, B F Goodrich Chem Co, 51-54, res chemist, 57-58, proj leader, 59-61, sect leader olefin rubbers, 61, RES ASSOC, B F GOODRICH CO, 63- *Mem:* AAAS; Am Chem Soc; Coblentz Soc. *Res:* Polymer chemistry; polymerization mechanisms; relation of polymer properties to physical structure; polymer reactions; infrared spectroscopy. *Mailing Add:* Res Ctr B F Goodrich Co Brecksville OH 44141

DIEM, JOHN EDWIN, b Bridgeport, Conn, Dec 7, 37; m 63; c 2. STATISTICS. *Educ:* Pa State Univ, BA, 61, MA, 62; Purdue Univ, PhD(math), 65. *Prof Exp:* Asst prof math, 66-72, assoc prof biostat, 73-80, PROF STATIST, TULANE UNIV, 81- *Mem:* Am Statis Asn; Biometric Soc; Am Thoracic Soc; Soc Epidemol Res; AAAS. *Res:* Biostatistics; pulmonary disease; epidemiology. *Mailing Add:* Dept of Math Tulane Univ New Orleans LA 70118

DIEM, KENNETH LEE, b Milwaukee, Wis, Apr 17, 24; m 50; c 2. ZOOLOGY. *Educ:* Lawrence Col, BS, 48; Utah State Univ, MS, 52, PhD(wildlife mgt), 58. *Prof Exp:* Game technician, N Kaibab Deer Herd, Ariz Game & Fish Comn, 51-54; from asst prof to assoc prof, 57-65, PROF ZOOL & GAME MGT, UNIV WYO, 65- *Concurrent Pos:* Nat Res Coun grant, Univ Wyo, 58; NY Zool Soc grant, 61-63; US Nat Park Serv grant, 63; consult environ impact assessment, Thorne Ecol Inst, 70-; vchmn conserv & land use study comn, Wyo, 73-75. *Mem:* Fel AAAS; Am Ornith Union; Wildlife Soc; Am Soc Mammal; Ecol Soc Am. *Res:* Animal ecology; dynamics of wildlife populations; big game and avian populations. *Mailing Add:* 22 Corthell Rd Laramie WY 82070

DIEM, MAX, b Karlsruhe, WGer, Nov 6, 47; m 74; c 2. CHEMICAL INSTRUMENTATION, COMPUTER INTERFACING. *Educ:* Univ Karlsruhe, BS, 70; Univ Toledo, MS, 75, PhD(chem), 76. *Prof Exp:* Res assoc & fel phys chem, Syracuse Univ, 76-78; asst prof chem, Southeast Mass Univ, 78-79; ASST PROF PHYS CHEM & BIOPHYS CHEM, CITY UNIV NEW YORK, HUNTER COL, 79- *Concurrent Pos:* Consult, SAM Instruments, 81- *Mem:* Sigma Xi; Am Chem Soc. *Res:* Elucidation of solution structures of biogically interesting molecules in newly developed spechoscopic techniques. *Mailing Add:* Dept Chem Hunter Col NY City Univ New York Box 315 695 Park Ave New York NY 10021

DIEMER, EDWARD DEVLIN, b Pittsburgh, Pa, Nov 4, 33; m 56; c 6. METEOROLOGY. *Educ:* St Louis Univ, BS, 55, M Pr Gph, 60, PhD(meteorol, math), 65. *Prof Exp:* Forecaster, US Weather Bur, Mo, 59-64, asst regional meteorologist, Utah, 65-66, chief sci serv div, 66-71, METEOROLOGIST-IN-CHARGE, WEATHER SERV FORECAST OFF, ALASKAN REGION, NAT WEATHER SERV, NAT OCEANIC & ATMOSPHERIC ADMIN, 71- *Concurrent Pos:* Lectr math, Univ Alaska, 66- *Mem:* Nat Weather Asn. *Res:* Weather forecasting; synoptic meteorology. *Mailing Add:* 5326 Wandering Dr Anchorage AK 99502

DIEMER, F(ERDINAND) P(ETER), b New York, NY, Oct 16, 20; m 52; c 9. ELECTRICAL ENGINEERING, SYSTEMS DESIGN & SCIENCE. *Educ:* Cooper Union, BSEE, 48; NY Univ, MSEE, 50, PhD(studies). *Prof Exp:* Commun engr, Telephonics Corp, 41-44; group leader instruments & electronics, Celanese Corp, NJ, 46-49; asst mgr res lab & staff adv to vpres, Fleischman Labs, Standard Brands, Inc, 49-51; sr develop engr control inst div, Burroughs Corp, 51-52; proj coordr & sr res engr, Am Bosch Arma Corp, 52-54; mgr appl physics, G M Giannini & Co, Inc, 54-57, tech dir, Giannini Res Lab, Calif, 56-57; dir eng & tech consult, Cal-Tronics Corp, 57-58; proj mgr & sr staff engr, Hughes Aircraft Co, 58-60; vpres & dir eng, Daystrom, Inc, 60-61; asst dir advan prog & dir eng, Martin-Marietta Corp, 61-66; exec engr, TRW Systs, Inc, Washington, DC, 66-67, mgr command & control, 67-71; phys sci adminr ocean sci, Off Naval Res, Arlington, Va, 71-80; DIR PLANS & DEVELOP, ENERGY INFO ADMIN, US DEPT ENERGY, 80- *Concurrent Pos:* Consult, Indust Eng Dept, Columbia Univ, 50-61, Electrodata Div, Burroughs Corp, 57 & Macro Econ Anal; lectr, Univ Southern Calif, 56-, Univ Calif, Los Angeles, 57- & Am Univ. *Mem:* Inst Elec & Electronics Engrs; Am Inst Aeronaut & Astronaut; Asn Comput Mach; Indust Math Soc; Soc Indust & Appl Math. *Res:* Information and control systems; data processing computer technology; program management; technical consultation; military weapons systems; ocean science. *Mailing Add:* 5307 Springlake Way Baltimore MD 21212

DIEN, CHI-KANG, b China, Sept 18, 24; nat US; m 52; c 3. ORGANIC CHEMISTRY. *Educ:* Nat Fuh Tan Univ, BS, 47; Univ Tex, PhD(chem), 53. *Prof Exp:* Res chemist, China Textile Industs Inc, 47-49; fel, Univ Va, 53-56; res chemist, Nat Aniline Div, Allied Chem Corp, 56-68; sr scientist, Specialty Chem Div, 68-76; SR SCIENTIST, SUN CHEM CORP, 76- *Mem:* Am Chem Soc. *Res:* Conjugated systems; furan derivatives; heterocyclic compounds; anthraquinone and azo dyestuffs; organic pigment and intermediates. *Mailing Add:* 41 Cornell Dr Livingston NJ 07039

DIENA, BENITO B, bacteriology, veterinary medicine, see previous edition

DIENEL, GERALD ARTHUR, b Boston, Mass, Sept 19, 45. NEUROCHEMISTRY. *Educ:* Pa State Univ, Bs, 67; Harvard Univ, MA, 69, PhD(biochem), 78. *Prof Exp:* fel, 78-81, INSTR BIOCHEM, DEPT NEUROL, CORNELL UNIV MED COL, 81- *Mem:* Soc Neurosci; Am Soc Neurochem. *Res:* Brain development and metabolism in disease states; effects of brain injury or disease of protein synthesis and degradation. *Mailing Add:* Cornell Univ Med Col 1300 York Ave New York NY 10021

DIENER, ROBERT G, b Brookville, Pa, Apr 12, 38; m 61. AGRICULTURAL ENGINEERING. *Educ:* Pa State Univ, BS, 60, MS, 63; Mich State Univ, PhD(agr eng), 66. *Prof Exp:* Technol & develop engr, Int Harvester Co, Ill, 60-61; asst, Pa State Univ, 61-62 & Mich State Univ, 63-65; asst prof agr eng, Mich State Univ, 65-68; from asst prof to assoc prof, 68-77, PROF AGR ENG, W VA UNIV, 77- *Concurrent Pos:* Agr engr, USDA, 65-68. *Mem:* Am Soc Agr Engrs; Soc Rheol. *Res:* Mechanical viscoelastic behavior of engineering; agricultural materials; mechanization of harvest of fruits and vegetables. *Mailing Add:* Dept of Agr Eng WVa Univ Morgantown WV 26506

DIENER, ROBERT MAX, b Zurich, Switz, Jan 15, 31; US citizen; m 54; c 4. TOXICOLOGY, PATHOLOGY. *Educ:* Cornell Univ, BS, 53; Mich State Univ, DVM, 60, MS, 61; Am Col Vet Path, dipl. *Prof Exp:* Instr clin vet med, Mich State Univ, 60-61; sr vet, 61-62, asst dir toxicol, 63-69, dir, 69-77, EXEC DIR TOXICOL & PATH, CIBA PHARMACEUT CO, 77- *Mem:* Am Vet Med Asn; Am Asn Lab Animal Sci; fel Am Col Vet Toxicol; Soc Toxicol; Int Acad Path. *Res:* Animal toxicology, pathology and teratology. *Mailing Add:* CIBA Pharmaceut Co 556 Morris Ave Summit NJ 07901

DIENER, THEODOR OTTO, b Zurich, Switz, Feb 28, 21; nat US; m 50, 68; c 3. VIROLOGY. *Educ:* Swiss Fed Inst Technol, Dr sc nat(plant path), 48. *Prof Exp:* Asst, Swiss Fed Inst Technol, 46-48; plant pathologist, Swiss Fed Exp Sta, Wine, Fruit & Hort, Waedenswil, 49; asst plant pathologist, RI State Col, 50; from asst plant pathologist to assoc plant pathologist, Wash State Univ, 50-59; RES PLANT PATHOLOGIST, PLANT VIROL LAB, USDA, 59- *Concurrent Pos:* Assoc ed, Virology, 64-67 & 74-76, ed, 68-71; regents' lectr, Univ Calif, 70; mem ed comt, Annual Rev Phytopath, 70-74; Andrew D White prof-at-large, Cornell Univ, 79-; mem, Leopoldina, Ger Acad Nat Scientists, 80. *Honors & Awards:* Campbell Award, Am Inst Biol Sci, 68; Super Serv Award, USDA, 69; Alexander Von Humbolt Award, Alexander Von Humboldt Found, 75; Ruth Allen Award, Am Phytopath Soc, 76; Distinguished Serv Award, USDA, 77. *Mem:* Nat Acad Sci; Am Acad Arts & Sci; AAAS; fel Am Phytopath Soc; fel NY Acad Sci. *Res:* Plant viruses and virus diseases; physiology of virus diseases; nature and properties of viroids, a novel class of pathogens. *Mailing Add:* Plant Virol Lab Agr Res Ctr US Dept Agr Beltsville MD 20705

DIENER, URBAN LOWELL, b Lima, Ohio, May 26, 21; m 56. PHYTOPATHOLOGY. *Educ:* Miami Univ, AB, 43; Harvard Univ, AM, 45; NC State Univ, PhD(plant path), 53. *Prof Exp:* Indust mycologist, Sindar Corp, 45-47; asst plant pathologist, SC Agr Exp Sta, 47-48; asst plant pathologist, 52-57, assoc prof, 57-63, PROF PLANT PATH, AUBURN UNIV, 63- *Concurrent Pos:* Chmn, Task Force on mycotoxins, Coun Agr Sci & Technol, 79. *Mem:* Fel AAAS; Phytopath Soc; Am Soc Microbiol; Int Soc Plant Path. *Res:* Mycotoxicology; fungus ecology; aflatoxin in peanuts and corn and other mycotoxins of food crops; author or co author of 50 publications. *Mailing Add:* Dept of Bot & Microbiol Auburn Univ Auburn AL 36830

DIENES, GEORGE JULIAN, b Budapest, Hungary, Apr 28, 18; nat US; m 40; c 1. SOLID STATE PHYSICS. *Educ:* Carnegie Inst Technol, BS, 40, MS, 42, DSc(phys chem), 47; Columbia Univ, MA, 46. *Prof Exp:* Instr chem, Wash & Jefferson Col, 40-41; asst, Carnegie Inst Technol, 41-43; res chemist, Ridbo Labs, NJ, 43-44; group leader, Physics Div, Bakelite Corp, 44-49; res specialist, NAm Aviation, 49-51; SR PHYSICIST, BROOKHAVEN NAT LAB, UPTON, 51- *Concurrent Pos:* Mem solid state sci panel, Nat Acad Sci-Nat Res Coun, 53-; assoc ed, J Phys Chem Solids, 74- *Mem:* AAAS; Soc Rheol (secy-treas, 49-53); fel Am Phys Soc; Radiation Res Soc. *Res:* Theory of diffusion in crystals; flow and mechanical properties of high polymers; molecular weight distributions; solid state physics; imperfections in crystals; radiation effects in solids; phase transitions; shock waves; equation of state. *Mailing Add:* PO Box 435 Stony Brook NY 11790

DIENHART, CHARLOTTE MARIE, b Sioux Falls, SDak, Aug 14, 23. ANATOMY. *Educ:* Col St Catherine, BS, 45; State Univ Iowa, MS, 47; Mich State Univ, PhD(anat), 60. *Prof Exp:* Res asst nutrit, Univ Minn, 47-48; instr anat, physiol & nutrit, Col St Catherine, 48-57; teaching asst physiol, Univ Minn, 57-58; teaching asst anat, Mich State Univ, 58-60; ASST PROF ANAT & ASSOC PROF ALLIED HEALTH, EMORY UNIV, 60- *Mem:* AAAS; NY Acad Sci. *Res:* Gross anatomy. *Mailing Add:* Dept of Anat Emory Univ Atlanta GA 30322

DIERCKS, FREDERICK O(TTO), b Rainy River, Ont, Sept 8, 12; US citizen; m 37; c 2. PHOTOGRAMMETRY, CARTOGRAPHY. *Educ:* US Mil Acad, BS, 37; Mass Inst Technol, MS, 39; Syracuse Univ, MS, 50. *Prof Exp:* Corps Engrs, US Army, 37-67, engr photogram res, Wright Field, Ohio, 37-38, co comdr photomapping, Ft Belvoir, Va, 39-41, topog engr, Ft Jackson, SC, 41-42, officer-in-chg hydrographic surv, Nicaragua Canal Surv, 42, batallion comdr, Eng Aviation Batallion, Geiger Field, Wash, 42-44, topog engr batallion, France & Ger, 44-45, officer-in-chg topog eng res, Ft Knox, Ky, 45-47, batallion comdr geod surv, Philippines, 47-48, officer-in-chg eng intel & mapping, Gen Hq, Far East Command, Tokyo, 48-49, topog engr ed, Ft Belvoir, 50-52, engr intel mapping, Hq, US Army Europe, Heidelberg, 53-56, commanding officer, Map Serv, DC, 57-61, asst dir mapping, charting & geod, Defense Intel Agency, 61-63, dep engr, Eng Sect, Korea, 63-64, dir, Coastal Eng Res Ctr, 64-67; assoc dir aeronaut charting & cartog, 67-74, CONSULT, NAT OCEAN SURVEY, NAT OCEANIC & ATMOSPHERIC ADMIN, 75- *Concurrent Pos:* Lectr, Catholic Univ, 50-51; mem nat atlas comt & adv comt on cartog, Nat Acad Sci, 57-61; US mem comt cartog, Pan-Am Inst Geog & Hist, Orgn Am States, 61-67, alt US mem, dir coun & vchmn, US Nat Sect, 70-74, exec secy, 75- *Honors & Awards:* Grand Cross, Order of King George II, Greece, 59; Comdr, Most Exalted Order of White Elephant, Thailand, 68; Luis Struck Award, Am Soc Photogram, 69; Colbert Medal, Soc Am Mil Engrs, 72. *Mem:* Am Soc Civil Engrs; Soc Am Mil Engrs; Am Soc Photogram (pres, 70-71); Am Cong Surv & Mapping. *Res:* Geodetic and topographic surveying and mapping instruments and methods; photogrammetric plotting equipment and techniques; wave theory, shore processes, tides, inlet and estuary dynamics; coastal works design and construction techniques. *Mailing Add:* 9313 Christopher St Fairfax VA 22031

DIERENFELDT, KARL EMIL, b Eureka, SDak, Mar 17, 40. PHYSICAL CHEMISTRY, NUCLEAR CHEMISTRY. *Educ:* SDak State Univ, BS, 62; Univ Calif, Davis, PhD(phys chem), 66. *Prof Exp:* Asst prof, 66-73, ASSOC PROF CHEM, CONCORDIA COL, MOORHEAD, MINN, 73- *Mem:* Am Chem Soc. *Res:* Production of light fragments in high energy nuclear reactions; free radicals in solid organic glasses. *Mailing Add:* Dept of Chem Concordia Col Moorhead MN 56560

DIERKS, RICHARD ERNEST, b Flandreau, SDak, Mar 11, 34; m 56; c 3. VIROLOGY, VETERINARY MICROBIOLOGY. *Educ:* Univ Minn, BS, 57, DVM, 59, MPH & PhD(microbiol), 64; Am Col Vet Prev Med, dipl; Am Col Vet Microbiol, dipl. *Prof Exp:* Field vet, Minn State Livestock Sanit Bd, 59; NIH fel, Univ Minn, 59-64; vet officer in chg rickettsial dis lab, Spec Projs Unit, Lab Br Commun Dis Ctr, USPHS, Ga, 64-66, chief rabies invests lab, Vet Pub Health Sect, Epidemiol Br, 66-68; from assoc prof to prof vet med, Vet Med Res Inst, Col Vet Med, Iowa State Univ, 68-74; prof vet med & head vet res lab, Col Agr, Mont State Univ, 74-76; DEAN COL VET MED, UNIV ILL, URBANA, 76- *Concurrent Pos:* Nat Inst Allergy & Infectious Dis grants, 68-71 & 73-75; Air Force Off Sci res grant, 69-71; NIH res career develop award, 69-74; Agr Res Serv, USDA grant, 70-72; vis prof, Fed Res Inst Animal Virus Dis, Tübingen, WGer, 71-72; Jensen Salbery grant, 73-75. *Mem:* Am Vet Med Asn; Am Asn Avian Path; Am Soc Microbiol; Soc Exp Biol & Med; Am Asn Immunol. *Res:* Rabies; Rhabdoviruses; bovine respiratory viruses; rickettsial diseases; viral immunology; equine viruses; purification and concentration of viruses and subviral proteins. *Mailing Add:* Col of Vet Med Univ of Ill Urbana IL 61801

DIERKS-VENTLING, CHRISTA, b Switz, July 28, 30; US citizen; m 59; c 2. CELL BIOLOGY. *Educ:* Univ Lausanne, dipl chem, 54; Oxford Univ, DPhil(biochem), 57. *Prof Exp:* Res asst biochem, Oxford Univ, 57; res asst, Univ Iowa, 57-58, res assoc surg, Col Med, 58-60; chief chemist, Iowa Lutheran Hosp, Des Moines, 60-61, res assoc internal med, Hopkins Hosp, Baltimore, Md, 63-65; lab scientist, Rosewood State Hosp, 65-71; RES SCIENTIST, FRIEDRICH MIESCHER-INST, SWITZ, 71- *Concurrent Pos:* Instr sch med, Univ Md, 65-67, asst prof, 67-71. *Mem:* Am Soc Cell Biol. *Res:* Regulation of transcription in eukaryotes; regulation of storage proteins in cereals. *Mailing Add:* Friedrich Miescher-Inst PO Box 273 Basel Switzerland

DIERMANN, JOACHIM, b Leipzig, Ger, Apr 7, 32; US citizen. ELECTRONIC ENGINEERING. *Educ:* Aachen Tech Univ, Dipl Ing, 56. *Prof Exp:* Design engr, Atlas Werke AG, Ger, 56-60; design engr, Raytheon Co, Mass, 60-61, sect head marine radar, Calif, 61-64; sr engr, RS Electronics Corp, Calif, 64-66; mem res staff, 66-69, mgr electron beam recording sect, 69-76, CHIEF ENGR, AUDIO VIDEO SYSTS DIV, AMPEX CORP, 76- *Mem:* Soc Motion Picture & TV Engrs. *Res:* Electron and laser beam technology; recording technology. *Mailing Add:* 738 Torreya Ct Palo Alto CA 94303

DIERMEIER, HAROLD FREDERICK, physiology, deceased

DIEROLF, JACK, b Rock Island, Ill, Sept 14, 25; m 46; c 2. PHYSICAL CHEMISTRY. *Educ:* Augustana Col (Ill), BA, 53. *Prof Exp:* Res chemist, Rock Island Arsenal, Ord Dept, US Army, 52-56; res chemist, US Naval Ord Test Sta, Naval Weapons Ctr, 56-59, gen engr, 59-63, res chemist, 63-70, comput programmer, 70-82, comput systs analyst, 73-82. *Res:* Packaging materials; rocket propulsion; solid, liquid and hybrid rocket propellants; explosives. *Mailing Add:* Mgt Data Processing Code 0840 Naval Weapons Ctr China Lake CA 93555

DIERSCHKE, DONALD JOE, b Rowena, Tex, Nov 30, 34; m 56; c 2. REPRODUCTIVE BIOLOGY. *Educ:* Tex A&M Univ, BS, 56; Mont State Univ, MS, 57; Univ Calif, Davis, PhD(reprod endocrinol), 65. *Prof Exp:* Assoc prof biol, Oklahoma City Univ, 65-69; USPHS spec res fel physiol, Sch Med, Univ Pittsburgh, 69-71, res asst prof, 71-73; PROF, WIS REGIONAL PRIMATE RES CTR & PROF MEAT & ANIMAL SCI, UNIV WIS, 73- *Concurrent Pos:* NIH res grants, 67-69, 75-78, 77-; Eli Lilly res grant, 68-69. *Mem:* Am Soc Animal Sci; Soc Study Reproduction; Am Physiol Soc; Endocrine Soc; Int Soc Neuroendocrinol. *Res:* Endocrine mechanisms regulating ovarian function; neuroendocrine regulation of gonadotropin secretion; the involvement of hemodynamic mechanisms in the control of reproductive function; hormonal/neural control of puberty. *Mailing Add:* Wis Regional Primate Res Ctr 1223 Capitol Ct Madison WI 53706

DIERSSEN, GUNTHER HANS, b Hamburg, Ger, Jan 10, 26; US citizen; m 59; c 4. CRYSTAL CHEMISTRY, PHYSICS. *Educ:* Tech Univ Denmark, MS, 54. *Prof Exp:* Develop engr biochem, Danish Fermentation Indust, Ltd, 54-58; advan prod engr, Gen Elec Co, 56-60 & Harshaw Chem Co, 60-63; sr res physicist, 63-68, res specialist, 68-74, sr res specialist mat sci, 74-81, STAFF SCIENTIST, CENT RES LAB, 3M CO, 81- *Mem:* Am Asn Crystal Growth; Am Inst Chem Engrs. *Res:* Materials science and processing. *Mailing Add:* Process Technol Labs 3M Ctr 208-1 St Paul MN 55144

DIESCH, STANLEY L, b Blooming Prairie, Minn, May 16, 25; m 56; c 2. VETERINARY PUBLIC HEALTH, VETERINARY MICROBIOLOGY. *Educ:* Univ Minn, St Paul, BS, 51, DVM, 56; Univ Minn, Minneapolis, MPH, 63. *Prof Exp:* Teacher veterans agr training, Belle Plaine Schs, Minn, 51-52; pvt pract, 57-62; USPHS traineeship, 62-63; asst prof prev med & environ health, Col Med, Univ Iowa, 63-66; asst prof vet microbiol & pub health, Col Vet Med, 66-70, assoc prof vet microbiol & pub health, Col Vet Med & epidemiol, Sch Pub Health, 70-73, PROF VET MICROBIOL & PUB HEALTH, COL VET MED, UNIV MINN, 73-, PROF EPIDEMIOL, SCH PUB HEALTH, 73- *Concurrent Pos:* Chmn epidemiol sect, Leptospirosis Res Conf, 66-67; consult, Meat Hyg Training Ctr, Chicago, 67-68; adv vet pub health to Venezuela, Pan-Am Health Orgn, 68; USPHS res grant, 68-76; mem, Coun Pub Health & Regulatory Vet Med, Am Vet Med Asn, 77-78, chmn, 77. *Mem:* Am Vet Med Asn; Am Col Vet Prev Med; Am Pub Health Asn; Conf Pub Health Vets; Asn Teachers Vet Pub Health & Prev Med. *Res:* Epidemiology of leptospirosis in animals and man; zoonotic diseases. *Mailing Add:* Dept of Vet Clin Sci Univ of Minn Col Vet Med St Paul MN 55108

DIESEM, CHARLES D, b Galion, Ohio, July 5, 21; m 45; c 3. VETERINARY ANATOMY. *Educ:* Ohio State Univ, DVM, 43, MSc, 49, PhD(anat), 56. *Prof Exp:* From instr to assoc prof, 47-61, PROF VET ANAT, OHIO STATE UNIV, 61- *Concurrent Pos:* Health comnr, Ohio, 54-76. *Mem:* Am Asn Anat; Am Vet Med Asn; Conf Res Workers Animal Dis; Sigma Xi. *Res:* Gross anatomy and histology; ophthalmology and hematology. *Mailing Add:* 1872 Berkshire Rd Columbus OH 43221

DIESEN, CARL EDWIN, b Cloquet, Minn, Aug 21, 21; m 49; c 2. NUMERICAL ANALYSIS. *Educ:* Univ Minn, Minneapolis, BA, 42, MA, 49. *Prof Exp:* Mgr electronic data processing, Bell Aircraft Corp, 51-60, eng systs, Hughes Aircraft Co, 60-61, electronic data processing, Gen Dynamics\Astronaut, 61-64, digital comput, Telecomput Serv, Inc, 64-66 & data processing & comput, Ling-Temco-Vought, Inc, 66-67; CHIEF COMPUT CTR DIV, US GEOL SURV, 67- *Mem:* Asn Comput Mach; Math Asn Am; Data Processing Mgt Asn. *Res:* Numerical analysis for digital computation and for business information systems design and data processing. *Mailing Add:* 8617 Red Coat Lane Rockville MD 20854

DIESEN, RONALD W, b Highland, Ill, Oct 16, 31; m 51; c 2. PHYSICAL CHEMISTRY. *Educ:* Southern Ill Univ, BA, 53; Univ Wash, PhD(phys chem), 58. *Prof Exp:* From res chemist to sr res chemist, 58-72, SR RES SPECIALIST, DOW CHEM CO, 72- *Mem:* Am Chem Soc; Sigma Xi. *Res:* High temperature kinetics; shock tube applications; free radical and combustion reactions; mass spectrometry; laser photochemistry; photochemical recoil spectroscopy; atmospheric chemistry; oxidative catalysis. *Mailing Add:* 1776 Bldg Dow Chem Co Midland MI 48640

DIESENDRUCK, LEO, b Budweis, Czech, July 1, 20; nat US; m 42; c 4. PHYSICS. *Educ:* Univ Cincinnati, BA, 41; Johns Hopkins Univ, PhD(physics), 50. *Prof Exp:* Jr instr physics, Johns Hopkins Univ, 41-43; physicist theoret aerodyn, Nat Adv Comt Aeronaut, 44-46; from assoc prof to prof physics, Univ RI, 49-60; prin scientist, Gen Dynamics Electronics, 59-63; PROF PHYSICS, QUEENS COL, NY, 63- *Mem:* Am Phys Soc. *Res:* Aerodynamics of perfect fluids; theory of nuclear reactions; upper air measurements of solar radiation; normal mode theory of sound transmission; relativistic electrodynamics and Cherenkov effect. *Mailing Add:* Dept Physics Queens Col Flushing NY 11367

DIESTEL, JOSEPH, b Westbury, NY, Jan 27, 43; m 64; c 2. MATHEMATICS. *Educ:* Univ Dayton, BS, 64; Cath Univ Am, PhD(math), 68. *Prof Exp:* Res scientist, Tech Opers Res, Inc, Washington, DC, 67-68; sr scientist, Consultec, Inc, 68; asst prof math WGa Col, 68-70; fel, Univ Fla, 70-71; assoc prof, 71-75, PROF MATH, KENT STATE UNIV, 75- *Concurrent Pos:* Eng consult, Southwire Int, Inc, Ga, 69-70; Fulbright fel, Univ Col, Dublin, 77-78. *Mem:* Am Math Soc; Irish Math Soc. *Res:* Functional analysis; measure and integration. *Mailing Add:* Dept of Math Kent State Univ Kent OH 44242

DIESTLER, DENNIS JON, b Ames, Iowa, Oct 23, 41. THEORETICAL CHEMISTRY. *Educ:* Harvey Mudd Col, BS, 64; Calif Inst Technol, PhD(chem), 68. *Prof Exp:* Asst prof chem, Univ Mo, St Louis, 67-69; asst prof, 69-72, assoc prof, 72-79, PROF CHEM, PURDUE UNIV, 79- *Honors & Awards:* Sr US Scientist Award, Alexander Von Humboldt Found, 75. *Mem:* Am Chem Soc; Am Phys Soc. *Res:* Theoretical studies in molecular relaxation. *Mailing Add:* Dept of Chem Purdue Univ Lafayette IN 47907

DIETER, GEORGE E(LLWOOD), JR, b Philadelphia, Pa, Dec 5, 28; m 52; c 2. ENGINEERING METALLURGY. *Educ:* Drexel Inst Technol, BS, 50; Carnegie Inst Technol, DSc(metall), 53. *Prof Exp:* Res coordr, Ballistics Res Lab, Aberdeen Proving Ground, 53-55; res engr, Eng Res Lab, E I du Pont de Nemours & Co, 55-58, res supvr, 58-62; prof metall eng & head dept, Drexel Univ, 62-69, dean col eng, 69-73; prof eng, Carnegie-Mellon Univ, 73-77; DEAN COL ENG, UNIV MD, 77- *Concurrent Pos:* Mem Mat Adv Bd, Metalworking Processes & Equip Comt. *Mem:* Am Soc Metals; Am Inst Mining, Metall & Petrol Engrs; Am Soc Eng Educ; Nat Soc Prof Engrs. *Res:* Mechanical metallurgy; fracture; materials processing; engineering design. *Mailing Add:* Col of Eng Univ of Md College Park MD 20742

DIETER, MICHAEL PHILLIP, b Joplin, Mo, Jan 1, 38; m 62; c 3. ENVIRONMENTAL PHYSIOLOGY, TOXICOLOGY. *Educ:* Notre Dame Univ, BS, 60; Univ Mo, MA, 65, PhD(zool), 68. *Prof Exp:* Asst zool, Univ Mo, 62-67; staff fel physiol, NIH, 67-69, sr staff fel, 69-71; physiologist, US Dept Interior, 71-77; health scientist adminr, Nat Inst Aging, 78-79, Nat Cancer Inst, 79-80, HEALTH SCIENTIST ADMINR, NAT INST ENVIRON HEALTH SCI, NIH, 80- *Mem:* AAAS; Am Physiol Soc; Am Soc Exp Biol & Med. *Res:* Effects of industrial, pharmaceutical and environmental chemicals on mammalian physiology; petroleum hydrocarbons; heavy metals; industrial pollutants; comparative toxicology; immunotoxicology; blood and tissue enzymes; adrenal and gonadal steroid hormones; carcinogenesis. *Mailing Add:* Nat Inst Environ Health Sci Box 12233 Research Triangle Park NC 27514

DIETER, RICHARD KARL, b Philadelphia, Pa, Apr 21, 51; m 79. PHOTOCHEMISTRY. *Educ:* Lehigh Univ, BA, 73; Univ Pa, PhD(chem), 78. *Prof Exp:* Fel chem, Cornell Univ, 78-79; ASST PROF CHEM, BOSTON UNIV, 79- *Mem:* Am Chem Soc. *Res:* Organic synthesis; new synthetic methodology; organic photochemistry; isolation and structure elucidation of biologically active compounds. *Mailing Add:* Dept Chem Boston Univ 685 Commonwealth Ave Boston MA 02215

DIETER-CONKLIN, NANNIELOU, radio astronomy, see previous edition

DIETERICH, DAVID ALLAN, b Cleveland, Ohio, Sept 9, 46; m 68; c 2. PHOTOGRAPHIC SCIENCE. *Educ:* Col Wooster, BA, 68; Univ Ill, PhD(org & phys chem), 73. *Prof Exp:* Sr res chemist, 73-80, RES LAB HEAD, RES LABS, EASTMAN KODAK CO, 80- *Mem:* Am Chem Soc; Royal Soc Chem; Am Crystallog Asn; AAAS. *Mailing Add:* 228 Overbrook Rd Rochester NY 14618

DIETERICH, ROBERT ARTHUR, b Salinas, Calif, Mar 22, 39; m 67; c 2. WILDLIFE DISEASES. *Educ:* Univ Calif, Davis, BS, 61, DVM, 63. *Prof Exp:* Private practice, Calif, 63-67; vet & zoophysiologist, 67-76, PROF VET SCI, INST ARCTIC BIOL, UNIV ALASKA, 77- *Concurrent Pos:* Proj mgr, Wildlife Dis Proj, United Nations, Kabete, Kenya, 74-75. *Mem:* Am Vet Med Asn; Wildlife Dis Asn; Am Asn Lab Animal Sci; Am Soc Lab Animal Practitioners. *Res:* Wild animal diseases; control of brucellosis in Alaskan reindeer; various pathological lesions found in arctic mammals; animal facility management. *Mailing Add:* Inst of Arctic Biol Univ of Alaska Fairbanks AK 99701

DIETERT, MARGARET FLOWERS, b Pittsfield, Mass, July 16, 51; m 75. PLANT TISSUE CULTURE, BRYOLOGY. *Educ:* Mt Holyoke Col, AB, 73; Univ Tex, PhD(bot), 77. *Prof Exp:* assoc fel plant path, 77-80, RES ASSOC PLANT PATH, CORNELL UNIV, 80- *Concurrent Pos:* Consult, Corning Glass, 80-81. *Mem:* Bot Soc Am; Int Asn Plant Tissue Culture; Sigma Xi. *Res:* Bryophyte ecology; plant-parasite interactions; plant tissue culture. *Mailing Add:* Dept of Plant Pathol Cornell Univ Ithaca NY 14853

DIETERT, RODNEY REYNOLDS, b Ft Lee, Va, Dec 6, 51; m 75. IMMUNOGENETICS, IMMUNOTOXICOLOGY. *Educ:* Duke Univ, BS, 74; Univ Tex, PhD(zool), 77. *Prof Exp:* ASST PROF IMMUNOGENETICS, CORNELL UNIV, 77- *Mem:* Genetics Soc Am; Poultry Asn Am; Soc Exp Biol & Med; Am Asn Immunologists; Am Genetics Asn. *Res:* Avian immunogenetics; cell surface antigens; genetic regulation of chicken fetal antigen expression; chicken onco-developmental antigen system; avian immunotoxicology. *Mailing Add:* Dept of Poultry Sci Cornell Univ Ithaca NY 14853

DIETERT, SCOTT EDWARD, anatomy, pathology, see previous edition

DIETHORN, WARD SAMUEL, b Waukegan, Ill, Sept 8, 27; m 53; c 2. NUCLEAR ENGINEERING, CHEMISTRY. *Educ:* Lake Forest Col, BS, 50; Carnegie Inst Technol, MS, 53, PhD(chem), 56. *Prof Exp:* Asst div chief, Radio-isotope & Radiation Div, Battelle Mem Inst, 56-60; from asst prof to assoc prof, 60-64, PROF NUCLEAR ENG, PA STATE UNIV, 64- *Mem:* AAAS; Am Chem Soc; Am Nuclear Soc. *Res:* Radiation damage; nuclear reactor materials; radioisotope technology. *Mailing Add:* Dept of Nuclear Eng Pa State Univ University Park PA 16802

DIETLEIN, LAWRENCE FREDERICK, b New Iberia, La, Feb 9, 28; m 58; c 3. MICROSCOPIC ANATOMY, INTERNAL MEDICINE. *Educ:* La State Univ, BS, 48; Harvard Univ, MA, 49, MD, 55. *Prof Exp:* From intern to asst resident, Harvard Med Serv, Boston City Hosp, 55-57; instr med, Sch Med, Tulane Univ, 57-59; from resident to chief med res, USPHS Hosp, New York, 59-61, chief outpatient serv, New Orleans, La, 61-62; chief space med br, 62-65, asst div chief, Crew Systs Div, 65-66, chief, Biomed Res Off, 66-68, asst dir res, med res & opers directorate, Manned Space Craft Ctr, 68-72, DEP DIR LIFE SCI, JOHNSON SPACE CTR, NASA, 72- *Concurrent Pos:* Res fel, Sch Med, Tulane Univ, 57-59; mem comt hearing & bioacoust, Nat Res Coun, 62- *Honors & Awards:* Commendation Award, NASA, 71, Except Serv Medal, 74; Hubertus Strughold Award, Aerospace Med Asn, 75; Melbourne W Boynton Award, Am Astronaut Soc, 75; John Jeffries Award, Am Inst Aeronaut & Astronaut, 75. *Mem:* AMA; NY Acad Sci; Aerospace Med Asn; corresp mem Int Acad Astronaut. *Res:* Human physiology, particularly cardiovascular, as affected by the space environment; histology and histochemistry of endocrines and their target organs. *Mailing Add:* 7702 Glenheath Houston TX 77061

DIETMEYER, DONALD L, b Wausau, Wis, Nov 20, 32; m 57; c 4. COMPUTER ENGINEERING. *Educ:* Univ Wis, BS, 54, MS, 55, PhD(elec eng), 59. *Prof Exp:* From asst prof to assoc prof, 58-67, PROF ELEC ENG, UNIV WIS-MADISON, 67- *Concurrent Pos:* Sr assoc engr, Int Bus Mach Corp, 63-64, consult, 64- *Honors & Awards:* Am Soc Elec Eng Western Elec Fund Award, 72. *Mem:* Inst Elec & Electronics Engrs; Asn Comput Mach. *Res:* Digital computer use and design; design automation computer hardware description languages. *Mailing Add:* Dept of Elec & Comput Eng Univ of Wis Madison WI 53706

DIETRICH, DANIEL DAVID, atomic physics, see previous edition

DIETRICH, DAVID EDWARD, b New York, NY, Jan 16, 43. COMPUTATIONAL FLUID DYNAMICS, METEOROLOGY. *Educ:* NCent Col, BS, 65; Fla State Univ, MS, 67, PhD(geophys fluid dynamics), 72. *Prof Exp:* Asst prof meteor, McGill Univ, 72-74; staff scientist comput fluid dynamics, Sci Applns, Inc, 74-75; staff scientist comput fluid dynamics, Jaycor, 75-80; sr scientist, 80-82. *Mem:* Can Meteorol Soc; Am Meteorol Soc; Japanese Meteorol Soc. *Res:* Dynamic meteorology. *Mailing Add:* 8450 Via Sonoma La Jolla CA 92037

DIETRICH, FRANK S, nuclear physics, see previous edition

DIETRICH, J(OSEPH) R(OBERT), b Miles City, Mont, Aug 25, 14; m 43; c 3. PHYSICS. *Educ:* Col William & Mary, BS, 35; Univ Va, MS, 37, PhD(physics), 39. *Prof Exp:* Head ignition res sect, Lewis Lab, Nat Adv Comt Aeronaut, 43-45, rockets sect, 45-46; engr anal power pile div, Oak Ridge Nat Lab, 47-48; engr naval reactor physics sect, Argonne Nat Lab, 49-53, assoc dir reactor eng div, 54-56; vpres & dir physics dept, Gen Nuclear Eng Corp, 56-64; chief scientist nuclear power, Combustion Eng, Inc, 64-80. *Concurrent Pos:* Ed, Power Reactor Tech, 57-64. *Mem:* Fel Am Nuclear Soc; Nat Acad Eng. *Res:* Design and development of nuclear reactors; reactor physics. *Mailing Add:* 19 Diggis Dr Newport News VA 23602

DIETRICH, JOHN WILLIAM, b Syracuse, NY, June 28, 46; m 69; c 2. PHARMACOLOGY, ENDOCRINOLOGY. *Educ:* LeMoyne Col, BS, 68; Univ Dayton, MS, 70; Univ NC, Chapel Hill, PhD(pharmacol), 74. *Prof Exp:* Fel, Univ Rochester, 74 & Health Ctr, Univ Conn, 74-76; ASST PROF PHARMACOL, PEORIA SCH MED, UNIV ILL, 76- *Concurrent Pos:* Nat

Inst Dent Res fel, 74-76; reviewer, Ill Heart Asn, 77-; grants, Pharmaceut Mfg Asn Found, 77- & NIH, 78-81. *Mem:* AAAS; Sigma Xi; Am Soc Bone & Mineral Res. *Res:* Effects of hormones and drugs on calcium and bone metabolism, including skeletal demineralization and collagen synthesis. *Mailing Add:* Peoria Sch of Med 123 SW Glendale Ave Peoria IL 61605

DIETRICH, JOSEPH JACOB, b Bismarck, NDak, Oct 31, 32; m 59. ORGANIC CHEMISTRY. *Educ:* Iowa State Univ, PhD, 57. *Prof Exp:* Sr res chemist, Columbia-South Corp, 57-59; res chemist, Spencer Chem Co, 60, sr staff mem, 61-63; sr res engr, Diamond Alkali Co, 64-66, group leader, T R Evans Res Ctr, 66-69, mgr org prod & processes, 69-71, assoc dir org polymers, 71-73, dir res, 73-77, DIR TECH DEV, ELECTROLYTIC SYSTS DIV, DIAMOND SHAMROCK CORP, 77- *Mem:* Am Chem Soc; Soc Plastics Engrs; Electrochem Soc. *Res:* Heterocyclic compounds; organometallic compounds; condensation polymers; high pressure polymerization; polymer development. *Mailing Add:* T R Evans Res Ctr Diamond Shamrock Corp PO Box 348 Painesville OH 44077

DIETRICH, MARTIN WALTER, b Chicago, Ill, Feb 2, 35; m 60; c 3. ENVIRONMENTAL CHEMISTRY, ANALYTICAL CHEMISTRY. *Educ:* Northwestern Univ, BA, 57; Washington Univ, St Louis, PhD(chem), 62. *Prof Exp:* Res chemist, 61-67, GROUP LEADER, MONSANTO CO, 67- *Mem:* Am Chem Soc; Sci Res Soc Am. *Res:* Toxicology; mass spectrometry; environmental science; radiochemistry. *Mailing Add:* Monsanto Co 800 N Lindbergh St Louis MO 63166

DIETRICH, RICHARD VINCENT, b La Fargeville, NY, Feb 7, 24; m 46; c 3. PETROLOGY. *Educ:* Colgate Univ, AB, 47; Yale Univ, MS, 50, PhD(geol), 51. *Prof Exp:* Geologist, State Geol Surv, Iowa, 47; from asst prof to prof geol, Va Polytech Inst, 51-69, assoc mineral technologist, 52-56, assoc dean col arts & sci, 66-69; dean arts & sci, 69-75, PROF GEOL, CENT MICH UNIV, 69- *Concurrent Pos:* Fulbright vis scholar, Mineral-Geol Mus, Univ Oslo, Norway, 58-59. *Mem:* Fel Geol Soc Am; Soc Econ Geol; fel Mineral Soc Am; Geol Soc Finland; Norweg Geol Soc. *Res:* Petrology of northwestern Adirondacks; geology of Blue Ridge; petrology of Migmatites and banded gneisses; dolomite-chert petrogenesis; feldspar geothermometry; Zr under high T-P conditions. *Mailing Add:* Brooks Hall Cent Mich Univ Mt Pleasant MI 48858

DIETRICH, SHELBY LEE, b Lexington, Ky, Apr 27, 24; m 51; c 3. PEDIATRICS. *Educ:* Univ Mich, BA, 45; Univ Mich, MD, 49. *Prof Exp:* Dir pediat, Calif Pediat Ctr, 57-60; dir, Hemophilia Projs, 64-68, asst med dir pediat, 70-75, dir dept res & spec prog, 70-78, actg asst med dir, 74-75, ASST MED DIR OUTPATIENT SERV, ORTHOP HOSP, 78- *Concurrent Pos:* Consult pediatrician & sch physician, Pasadena Unified Sch Dist, 51-70; mem adv comt, Genetically Handicapped Persons Prog, Calif, 75-; assoc clin prof pediat, Univ Southern Calif, 76-; consult ed, Phys Ther, Am Phys Ther Asn, 76- *Honors & Awards:* Physicians Recognition Award, AMA, 74. *Mem:* Fel Am Acad Pediat; fel Am Acad Cerebral Palsy; Ambulatory Pediat Soc; Orthop Res Soc. *Res:* Effectiveness of various treatment methods in hemophilia; multidisciplinary treatment of spina bifida; bone architecture and biosynthesis of collagen in osteogenesis imperfecta. *Mailing Add:* Orthop Hosp PO Box 60132 Terminal Annex Los Angeles CA 90060

DIETRICH, WILLIAM EDWARD, b Easton, Pa, Nov 20, 42; m 66; c 3. PLANT PHYSIOLOGY. *Educ:* LaSalle Col, BA, 64; Univ Pa, PhD(biol), 70. *Prof Exp:* Res assoc photosynthesis, Brookhaven Nat Lab, 69-71; asst prof, 71-75, ASSOC PROF BIOL, INDIANA UNIV PA, 75- *Mem:* Am Soc Plant Physiologists; Sigma Xi; AAAS. *Res:* Tree photosynthesis and adaptations of the leaf to light; photosynthetic endosymbiosis. *Mailing Add:* Dept of Biol Indiana Univ of Pa Indiana PA 15701

DIETRICK, HARRY JOSEPH, b Cleveland, Ohio, Aug 15, 22; m 43; c 2. PHYSICAL CHEMISTRY. *Educ:* Western Reserve Univ, BS, 48, MS, 50, PhD(chem), 51. *Prof Exp:* Anal chemist, Cosma Labs Co, 40-43 & 46-49; asst phys chem, Western Reserve Univ, 49-51, res assoc, 51-53; tech mgr, 53-55, sr tech mgr, 55-59, sect leader, 59-63, mgr aerospace & indust prod res, 63-64, mgr tire res, 65-74, dir tech admin & spec asst to vpres technol, 74-80, DIR, TIRE RES & DEVELOP ADMIN, B F GOODRICH TIRE CO, 80- *Mem:* Fel AAAS; Am Chem Soc; Acoust Soc Am; fel Am Inst Chem. *Res:* Electrode potentials; primary batteries; ultrasonics; physical chemistry of high polymers; space materials; tires. *Mailing Add:* 7354 Brookside Pkwy Cleveland OH 44130

DIETSCHY, JOHN MAURICE, b Alton, Ill, Sept 23, 32; m 59; c 4. INTERNAL MEDICINE, GASTROENTEROLOGY. *Educ:* Wash Univ, AB, 54, MD, 58. *Prof Exp:* Asst med, Sch Med, Boston Univ, 62-63; fel metab, 63-65, from asst prof to assoc prof internal med, 65-69, PROF MED, UNIV TEX HEALTH SCI CTR DALLAS, 71- *Concurrent Pos:* USPHS trainee gastroenterol, Sch Med, Boston Univ, 61-63; Markle scholar acad med, 66-71; consult metab study sect, NIH, 71, 74-78; consult, Monsanto Co, 75-; mem NIH task force eval, Nat Inst Arthritis, Metab, Diabetes & Digestive Dis, 78-79; ed, Clin Gastroenterol Monograph Series, ed-in-chief, Sci & Pract Clin Med. *Mem:* AAAS; Am Fedn Clin Res; Am Gastroenterol Asn; Am Soc Clin Invest; Gastroenterol Res Group. *Res:* Mechanisms of control of cholesterol synthesis in liver and other tissues mechanisms of lipoprotein transport; mechanisms of intestinal absorption of bile acids; intestinal transport of sugars. *Mailing Add:* 5411 Stonegate Dallas TX 75209

DIETZ, ALBERT (GEORGE HENRY), b Lorain, Ohio, Mar 7, 08; m 36; c 2. STRUCTURAL ENGINEERING, MATERIALS SCIENCE. *Educ:* Miami Univ, AB, 30; Mass Inst Technol, SB, 32, ScD(mat), 41. *Prof Exp:* Designer & job foreman, Peter Dietz, Lorain, Ohio, 32-33; mill foreman, Nat Tube Co, 33-34; asst, 34-36, instr, 36-41, asst prof struct eng, Dept Bldg Eng & Construct, 41-45, assoc prof struct design, 45-51, prof struct eng, 51-53, prof bldg eng & construct, Dept Civil Eng & Dept Archit, 53-73, EMER PROF BLDG ENG & CONSTRUCT & SR LECTR, DEPT ARCHIT, MASS INST TECHNOL, 73- *Concurrent Pos:* Sr consult engr, Forest Prod Lab, USDA, 42; mem, Eng Ed Mission, Japan, 51; bldg res adv bd, Nat Acad Sci-Nat Res Coun; sr res fel, East-West Ctr, Honolulu, Hawaii, 73-75; vis prof, Univ Hawaii, Honolulu, 74-75 & Univ Mich, Ann Arbor, 76. *Honors & Awards:* Templin Award, Am Soc Testing & Mat, Award of Merit, 57, Voss Award, 74; Derham Int Award, Plastics Inst Australia, 62; New Eng Award, Eng Socs New Eng, 69; Int Award Plastics Sci & Eng, Soc Plastics Engrs, 71; Construct Man of the Quarter Century, Bldg Res Adv Bd, Nat Acad Sci-Nat Acad Eng, 77. *Mem:* Fel AAAS; fel & hon mem Am Soc Civil Engrs; fel & hon mem Am Soc Testing & Mat; Soc Plastics Engrs; fel Am Acad Arts & Sci. *Res:* Construction materials, especially wood, plastics, and composites; materials for developing countries; industrialized buildings; solar energy for buildings. *Mailing Add:* 19 Cambridge St Winchester MA 01890

DIETZ, ALBERT ARNOLD CLARENCE, b Port Huron, Mich, Aug 15, 10; m 37; c 2. BIOCHEMISTRY. *Educ:* Univ Toledo, BS, 32, MS, 33; Purdue Univ, PhD(org chem), 41. *Prof Exp:* Asst, Dept Chem, Univ Toledo, 30-33; biochemist, Enza-Vita Labs, Ohio, 33-39; mem staff, US Rubber Co, 42-43; biochemist, Inst Med Res, Toledo Hosp, Ohio, 43-59; biochemist, Armour & Co, 59-60; supvry biochemist, 60-64; assoc prof biochem & biophysics, Stritch Sch Med, Loyola Univ Chicago, 69-74; PRIN SCIENTIST, VET ADMIN HOSP, 74-; PROF BIOCHEM & BIOPHYS, STRITCH SCH MED, LOYOLA UNIV CHICAGO, 74- *Concurrent Pos:* Off Sci Res & Develop-Nat Defense Res Comt fel, Purdue Univ, 41-42; asst prof, Chicago Med Sch, 62-69; co-ed, Chicago Clin Chemist, 68-77; consult lab eval, Dept Pub Health, Ill, 68- *Honors & Awards:* Natelson Award, Am Asn Clin Chem, 77. *Mem:* Fel AAAS; Am Chem Soc; fel Am Inst Chemists; Am Asn Clin Chemists (pres-elect, 78, pres, 79); NY Acad Sci. *Res:* Electrophoresis; enzymology; proteins. *Mailing Add:* Res Serv Vet Admin Hosp Hines IL 60141

DIETZ, ALBERT J, JR, clinical pharmacology, biochemistry, see previous edition

DIETZ, ALFRED, entomology, apiculture, see previous edition

DIETZ, CONRAD P, b Beach, NDak, May 30, 36; m 56; c 7. COMPUTER SCIENCE, MATHEMATICS. *Educ:* Dickinson State Col, BS, 59; Univ NDak, MS, 61; cert, Inst Cert Comput Prof, 71. *Prof Exp:* Instr math, Univ NDak, 60-61; numerical analyst, NAm Aviation, Rocketdyne, 61-63; supvr, Aerospace Corp, 63-67; ASSOC PROF & DIR, COMPUT CTR, UNIV NDAK, 67- *Concurrent Pos:* Instr, Univ Calif, Riverside, 66; consult, Reiss Davis Child Health, 65-66, San Bernardino County, 67 & NDak Regional Med Prog, 63-74. *Mem:* Asn Comput Mach. *Mailing Add:* Comput Ctr Univ NDak Grand Forks ND 58202

DIETZ, DAVID (HENRY), b Cleveland, Ohio, Oct 6, 97; m 18; c 3. SCIENCE WRITING. *Educ:* Western Reserve Univ, AB, 19. *Hon Degrees:* LittD, Western Reserve Univ, 48; LLD, Bowling Green State Univ, 54. *Prof Exp:* Mem ed staff, Cleveland Press, 15-77. *Concurrent Pos:* Sci ed, Scripps-Howard Newpapers, 21-77; lectr, Western Reserve Univ, 27-50; mem comt publicity, Div Med Sci, Nat Res Coun, 39-46; consult, Surgeon Gen, US Army, 44-47; sci commentator, Nat Broadcasting Co, 45-50. *Honors & Awards:* Pulitzer Prize in Journalism, 37; Goodrich Award, 40; Westinghouse Distinguished Sci Writers Award, 46; Lasker Award, Am Pub Health Asn, 54; Grady Award, Am Chem Soc, 61. *Mem:* AAAS; Nat Asn Sci Writers (pres); Am Astron Soc; fel Am Geog Soc; fel Royal Astron Soc. *Res:* Scientific journalism; history of science; popularization of sciences and medicine; history of atomic energy. *Mailing Add:* 2891 Winthrop Rd Shaker Heights OH 44120

DIETZ, DENNIS DONNELLY, toxicology, pharmacology, see previous edition

DIETZ, EARL D, ceramics, mineralogy, see previous edition

DIETZ, EDWARD ALBERT, JR, b Pa, Oct 2, 45; m 67; c 2. ANALYTICAL CHEMISTRY. *Educ:* Geneva Col, Pa, BS, 67; Univ Mich, Ann Arbor, PhD(chem), 70. *Prof Exp:* Res chemist stable isotope geochem, Gulf Oil Corp, 70-71; Welch fel, Univ Tex, Arlington, 71-72; sr anal chemist, Ansul Co, 72-76; res chemist, 76-80, SR RES CHEMIST, HOOKER CHEM CORP, 80- *Mem:* Am Chem Soc. *Res:* Separation science, environmental analyses and development of analytical techniques for use in corporate research and development effort; trace analyses for organic materials in air, water, and soil. *Mailing Add:* 3325 Baseline Rd Grand Island NY 14072

DIETZ, ELEANOR JACQUELIN, b Philadelphia, Pa, Oct 5, 51; m 79. MATHEMATICAL STATISTICS. *Educ:* Oberlin Col, AB, 73; Univ Conn, MS, 75, PhD(statist), 78. *Prof Exp:* ASST PROF STATIST, NC STATE UNIV, 78- *Mem:* Am Statist Asn; Biomet Soc; Asn Women Math. *Res:* Nonparametric statistical methods in multivariate analysis especially with application to problems in biology. *Mailing Add:* Dept Statist Box 5457 NC State Univ Raleigh NC 27650

DIETZ, FRANK TOBIAS, b Bridgeport, Conn, Aug 13, 20; m 45; c 2. ACOUSTICS, ACADEMIC ADMINISTRATION. *Educ:* Bates Col, BS, 42; Wesleyan Univ, MA, 46; Pa State Univ, PhD(physics), 51. *Prof Exp:* Asst physics, Wesleyan Univ, 42-44; mem staff, Radiation Lab, Mass Inst Technol, 45; asst, Wesleyan Univ, 45-47; instr physics, Pa State Univ, 47-49, asst, 49-51; res assoc, Woods Hole Oceanog Inst, 51-54; asst prof marine physics & res assoc phys oceanog, Narragansett Marine Lab, 54-56, from asst prof to assoc prof physics, 56-64, assoc dean, Col Arts & Sci, 74-76, prof oceanography, 68-76, PROF PHYSICS, UNIV RI, 64- *Concurrent Pos:* Vis assoc prof, Inst Marine Sci, Univ Miami, Fla, 63-64. *Mem:* Am Asn Physics Teachers; fel Acoust Soc Am; Am Geophys Union. *Res:* Underwater acoustics. *Mailing Add:* Dept of Physics Univ RI Kingston RI 02881

DIETZ, GEORGE ROBERT, b Schofield Barracks, Hawaii, Jan 15, 31; m 52; c 4. NUCLEAR SCIENCE. *Educ:* US Mil Acad, BS, 52; Ga Inst Technol, MSNS, 62. *Prof Exp:* Proj officer, AEC food irradiation prog, US Army Radiation Lab, Mass, 60-64; chief facilities eng sect, Div Isotopes Develop, AEC, 64-69; asst vpres opers, Radiation Mach Corp, 69-70, mgr radiation serv, Nuclear Div, Radiation Int, Inc, 70-73; PRES, ISOMEDIX, INC, 73- *Mem:* Am Nuclear Soc. *Res:* Preservation of foods by ionizing energy and related processing facilities; all aspects of radioisotope applications to commercial radiation facilities and processing. *Mailing Add:* Isomedix Inc 80 S Jefferson Rd Whippany NJ 07981

DIETZ, GEORGE WILLIAM, JR, b New York, NY, Apr 14, 38. BIOCHEMISTRY, MOLECULAR BIOLOGY. *Educ:* Williams Col, BA, 59; Yale Univ, PhD(biochem), 65. *Prof Exp:* NSF fel, Inst Biophys & Biochem, Paris, 65-67; mem staff res, Dept Biochem & Molecular Biol, Med Col, Cornell Univ, 67-69, asst prof biochem, 69-77; ASST RES SCIENTIST, DIV NEUROSCI, CITY OF HOPE RES INST, 78- *Mem:* AAAS; Am Chem Soc; Am Soc Microbiol; Harvey Soc; Am Soc Biol Chemists. *Res:* Neurochemistry, metabolism of neurotransmitters; control mechanisms in the expression of transport processes; biochemistry of transport in microorganisms. *Mailing Add:* City of Hope Med Ctr Duarte CA 91010

DIETZ, JOHN W, b Rainelle, WVa, Dec 17, 34; m 62; c 3. CHEMICAL ENGINEERING, METALLURGICAL ENGINEERING. *Educ:* WVa Univ, BS, 56; Cornell Univ, PhD(chem eng), 60. *Prof Exp:* Res chem engr, Exp Sta, 60-68, res supvr, 68-73, tech supt, 73-78, PLANNING ASSOC, E I DU PONT DE NEMOURS & CO, INC, 78- *Mem:* Am Inst Chem Engrs. *Res:* High temperature inorganic chemistry; process development. *Mailing Add:* Chem & Pigments Dept E I du Pont de Nemours & Co Inc Wilmington DE 19898

DIETZ, LEONARD ALLAN, b Manistee, Mich, Nov 18, 22; m 50; c 3. PHYSICS. *Educ:* Univ Mich, BS, 49, MS, 50. *Prof Exp:* Develop engr mass spectrometry, Gen Eng Lab, 50-55, physicist, Knolls Atomic Power Lab, 55-66, mgr mass spectrometer res & develop, 66-74, mgr mass spectrometry, 74-79, MGR, ADVAN CHEM SUPPORT & MICROCHEMICAL CHARACTERIZATION, KNOLLS ATOMIC POWER LAB, GEN ELEC CO, 79- *Mem:* Am Phys Soc; Am Soc Mass Spectros; AAAS. *Res:* Mass spectrometry of solids; electron multipliers and pulse counting; secondary electron emission; ion microprobe. *Mailing Add:* Knolls Atomic Power Lab River Rd Niskayuna NY 12309

DIETZ, PAUL LUTHER, JR, b Pittsburgh, Pa, Mar 31, 30. PHYSICAL CHEMISTRY, ELECTROCHEMISTRY. *Educ:* Univ Pittsburgh, BS, 51, PhD(phys chem), 55. *Prof Exp:* Sr res chemist, Pittsburgh Plate Glass Co, 55-60, res assoc, 60-62, supvr phys chem res, 62-68, sr supvr, 68-69, SR RES ASSOC, PPG INDUSTS, INC, 69- *Mem:* Am Chem Soc. *Res:* Kinetics of nucleation and crystal growth; linear crystallization velocities of sodium acetate in supersaturated solutions. *Mailing Add:* Res Lab PPG Industs Inc PO Box 31 Barberton OH 44203

DIETZ, RICHARD DARBY, b Rahway, NJ, Sept 28, 37. ASTRONOMY. *Educ:* Calif Inst Technol, BS, 59; Univ Colo, PhD(astrogeophys), 65. *Prof Exp:* Asst astronomer, Univ Hawaii, 65-69; asst prof astron, 69-73, assoc prof earth sci, 73-77, PROF ASTRON, UNIV NORTHERN COLO, 77- *Mem:* AAAS; Astron Soc Pac; Am Astron Soc; Am Asn Physics Teachers. *Res:* Theoretical studies in radiative transfer and atomic physics and their application to problems of stellar atmospheres. *Mailing Add:* Dept of Earth Sci Univ of Northern Colo Greeley CO 80639

DIETZ, ROBERT AUSTIN, b New York, NY, Feb 14, 22; m 60; c 4. CYTOTAXONOMY, ECOLOGY. *Educ:* Washington Univ, PhD(bot, zool), 52. *Prof Exp:* Instr bot, Univ Tenn, 52-54; assoc prof biol, 54-70, PROF BOT, TROY STATE UNIV, 70- *Concurrent Pos:* Bache fel, Nat Acad Sci, 57. *Mem:* AAAS; NY Acad Sci. *Res:* Variation in southeastern liliaceous genera; orchid genetics; historical ecology; coastal plain historical ecology; Central American orchid speciation. *Mailing Add:* Dept of Biol Troy State Univ Troy AL 36081

DIETZ, ROBERT E, b Joplin, Mo, May 8, 31; m 56; c 2. SOLID STATE PHYSICS. *Educ:* Tex Tech Col, BS, 56; Northwestern Univ, PhD(phys chem), 60. *Prof Exp:* MEM TECH STAFF, CRYSTAL PHYSICS DEPT, BELL LABS, 59- *Mem:* Am Phys Soc. *Res:* Effect of chemisorbed gases on the magnetic properties of small ferromagnetic particles; optical spectroscopy of crystals, including semiconductors and insulators; magneto-optic effects; solid state lasers; spectroscopic studies of magnetically ordered crystals; electron energy loss spectroscopy of solids; high-resolution, low-energy electron reflection spectroscopy from solid surfaces. *Mailing Add:* Crystal Physics Dept Bell Labs Murray Hill NJ 07974

DIETZ, ROBERT SINCLAIR, b Westfield, NJ, Sept 14, 14; m 55; c 2. GEOLOGY, OCEANOGRAPHY. *Educ:* Univ Ill, BS, 37, MS, 39, PhD(geol), 41. *Prof Exp:* Asst, Ill State Geol Surv, 35-37 & Scripps Inst Oceanog, Univ Calif, San Diego, 37-39; oceanogr, Navy Electronics Lab, 46-52, 54-58; oceanogr, US Coast & Geod Surv, 58-65; oceanogr, Inst Oceanog, Environ Sci Serv Admin, Nat Oceanic & Atmospheric Admin, Md, 65-67, Fla, 67-70, oceanogr, Atlantic Oceanog & Meteorol Labs, 70-77; PROF GEOL, ARIZ STATE UNIV, 77- *Concurrent Pos:* Fulbright scholar, Univ Tokyo, 52-53; Alexander von Humboldt scholar, WGer, 78; mem, London Br, Off Naval Res, 54-58; lectr, Scripps Inst Oceanog, Univ Calif, San Diego. *Honors & Awards:* Bucher Medal, Am Geophys Union, 72; Gold Medal, US Dept Com, 72; Shepard Medal for Marine Geol, 79. *Mem:* Geol Soc Am; Am Geophys Union; Meteoritical Soc; hon mem Geol Soc London; Mineral Soc Am. *Res:* Marine geology plate tectonics, metrorities and oceanography; underwater sound; sediments and structure of sea floor; submarine processes; nature of continental shelves and slopes; bathyscaph and deep submersibles; selenography and meteoritics; astroblemes; plate tectonics; sea floor spreading; continental drift. *Mailing Add:* Dept of Geol Ariz State Univ Tempe AZ 85281

DIETZ, RUDOLPH JOHN, inorganic & nuclear chemistry, see previous edition

DIETZ, SHERL M, b Ames, Iowa, Nov 29, 27; m 51; c 2. PLANT PATHOLOGY. *Educ:* Ore State Univ, BS, 50; Wash State Univ, PhD(plant path), 63. *Prof Exp:* Agr res aide plant path, USDA, 54-57, res plant pathologist, 57-66, regional coordr plant introd, 66-74, RES LEADER & TECH ADV PLANT GERMPLASM, AGR RES SERV, USDA, 74- *Concurrent Pos:* Consult, US Agency Int Develop Germplasm, Pakistan, 81; mem, Plant Explor Comt, US Drug Admin. *Mem:* Am Phytopath Soc; Soc Econ Bot. *Res:* Stem smut of grasses; screening plants for disease resistance; plant germ plasm. *Mailing Add:* Regional Plant Introd Sta Rm 59 Johnson Hall Wash State Univ Rm 59 Pullman WA 99164

DIETZ, THOMAS HOWARD, b Tacoma, Wash, Jan 22, 40; m 62; c 2. ANIMAL PHYSIOLOGY. *Educ:* Wash State Univ, BS, 63, MS, 65; Ore State Univ, PhD(physiol), 69. *Prof Exp:* Instr zool, Ore State Univ, 68-69; NIH fel biophys, Cardiovascular Res Inst, Univ Calif, San Francisco, 69-71; asst prof, 71-75, ASSOC PROF ZOOL & PHYSIOL, LA STATE UNIV, BATON ROUGE, 75- *Mem:* Am Physiol Soc; Sigma Xi; AAAS; Am Soc Zool; Soc Study Amphibians & Reptiles. *Res:* Osmotic and ionic regulation in animals; mechanism of ion transport; control of ion and water balance. *Mailing Add:* Dept of Zool & Physiol La State Univ Baton Rouge LA 70803

DIETZ, WILLIAM H, b Philadelphia, Pa, Oct 6, 44; m 66; c 2. PEDIATRICS. *Educ:* Wesleyan Univ, BA, 66; Univ Pa, MD, 70; Mass Inst Technol, PhD(nutrit), 81. *Prof Exp:* ASST DIR, CLIN RES CTR, MASS INST TECHNOL, 78- *Concurrent Pos:* Asst med, Boston Children's Hosp, 79- *Mem:* Am Acad Pediat; Am Soc Trop Med Hyg. *Res:* Childhood obesity, identification, morbidity, therapy; body composition, protein and glucose metabolism among obese adolescents; assessment of nutritional status. *Mailing Add:* Mass Inst Technol Clin Res Ctr E18 473 50 Ames St Cambridge MA 02142

DIFATE, VICTOR GEORGE, b Mt Vernon, NY, Aug 5, 43; m 66. ORGANIC CHEMISTRY, ANTIMICROBIOL CHEMISTRY. *Educ:* Iona Col, BS, 65; NY Univ, MS, 67, PhD(chem), 71. *Prof Exp:* Instr chem, Grad Sch Arts & Sci, NY Univ, 71-74; sr res chemist, 74-79, proj leader, 79, COMMERCIAL DEVELOP MGR, MONSANTO CO, 79- *Concurrent Pos:* Assoc res scientist, NY Univ, 71-74. *Mem:* Am Chem Soc. *Res:* Development of new applications for sorbates; widely used food and feed preservatives; food microbiology; development of environmentally acceptable antimicrobial compounds that are biodegradable and of lower toxicity to higher organisms; organic reaction mechanisms; organic synthesis; animal nutrition; food and feed preservatives. *Mailing Add:* Monsanto Co 800 N Lindbergh Blvd St Louis MO 63166

DIFAZIO, LOUIS T, b Brooklyn, NY, Jan 22, 38; m 61; c 2. DRUG METABOLISM, PHARMACEUTICAL CHEMISTRY. *Educ:* Rutgers Univ, BS, 59; Univ RI, PhD(pharmaceut chem), 64. *Prof Exp:* Res scientist, Colgate-Palmolive Co, 64-65; res scientist, E R Squibb & Sons, Inc, 66-67, sect head gen pharm, 67-71 & preformulation studies, 71-73, asst dir clin pharmacol, Squibb Inst Med Res, 73-75, dir drug metab, 75-77, DIR QUAL CONTROL, SQUIBB INST MED RES, E R SQUIBB & SONS, 77- *Mem:* Am Chem Soc; Am Pharmaceut Asn; Am Col Clin Pharmacol. *Res:* Synthesis of potential psychotherapeutic agents; factors effecting bioavailability of drugs; physical-chemical studies of pharmaceutical agents and products; factors effecting absorption, blood levels and distribution of drugs; product quality control. *Mailing Add:* E R Squibb & Sons Inc 5 Georges Rd New Brunswick NJ 08903

DIFEO, DANIEL RICHARD, JR, b Baltimore Md, July 10, 48; m 78; c 3. ANALYTICAL CHEMISTRY, PLANT CHEMISTRY. *Educ:* Bloomsburg State Col, BA, 70; Univ Tex, Austin, PhD(bot), 77. *Prof Exp:* Fel phytochem, La State Univ, 77; res assoc biomolecular anal, Univ Tex Med Sch, 77-80; mkt engr, Finnigan Mat Corp, 80-82; MASS SPECTRONOMY MGR, SOUTHERN PETROL LABS, 82- *Mem:* Am Soc Mass Spectrometry; Phytochem Soc NAm; Am Soc Pharmacog; Water & Waste Water Anal Asn. *Res:* Analysis of biomolecules and drugs by means of gas chromatography/mass spectronometry; structural elucidation of plant natural products and their pharmacology; analysis of environmental and petroleum samples by gas chromatography and mass spectronomy. *Mailing Add:* 7502 Carew Houston TX 77074

DI FERRANTE, DANIELA TAVELLA, b Rome, Italy, Feb 2, 49; m 76. BIOLOGY, BIOCHEMISTRY. *Educ:* Univ Rome, PhD(biol sci), 71. *Prof Exp:* Fel, Dept Pediat, Univ Rome, 71-72, asst prof, 72-76; res assoc genetic dis metab, 76-80, INSTR, DEPT BIOCHEM, BAYLOR COL MED, 80- *Concurrent Pos:* Fel, Dept Biochem, Baylor Col Med, 73-75. *Mem:* Soc Complex Carbohydrates. *Res:* Inherited diseases affecting connective tissue; biochemistry of glycosaminoglycans; role of glycosaminoglycans in the etiopathogenesis of atherosclerosis. *Mailing Add:* Dept Biochem Baylor Col Med 1200 Moursund Ave Houston TX 77030

DI FERRANTE, NICOLA MARIO, b Fontana Liri, Italy, Jan 26, 25; US citizen; m 76; c 4. MEDICINE, BIOCHEMISTRY. *Educ:* Univ Rome, MD, 48; Univ Rochester, PhD(biochem), 61. *Prof Exp:* Asst med, Inst Med Path, Rome, 50-52; asst biochem, Rockefeller Inst & Hosp, 53-56; assoc scientist, Brookhaven Nat Lab, 56-57; from asst prof to assoc prof physiol, Univ Cincinnati, 61-64; assoc biochem, Retina Found, 64-65; PROF BIOCHEM, DEPTS BIOCHEM & MED & DIV ORTHOP SURG, TEX MED CTR, BAYLOR COL MED, 65- *Concurrent Pos:* Asst, United Hosps, Rome, Italy, 50-51; res assoc, 1st Superior Sanita, Italy, 51-52; Helen Hay Whitney Found res fel, 60-63; sci collabr, Brookhaven Nat Lab, NY, 63-; estab investr, Am Heart Asn, 63-68; consult, Vet Admin Hosp, Houston, Tex, 71- *Mem:* AAAS; Am Soc Biol Chemists; Am Soc Human Genetics; Biochem Soc. *Res:* Connective tissue, glycoproteins and glycosaminoglycans; metabolism, immunochemistry of components of ground substance; labeling of glycosaminoglycans with isotopes. *Mailing Add:* Dept of Biochem Baylor Col of Med Houston TX 77030

DIFFENDAL, ROBERT FRANCIS, JR, b Hagerstown, Md, June 20, 40; m 67. INVERTEBRATE PALEONTOLOGY, GEOLOGY. *Educ:* Franklin & Marshall Col, Pa, AB, 62; Univ Nebr, MS, 64, PhD(geol), 71. *Prof Exp:* From instr to asst prof geol, St Dominic Col, 66-70; asst prof, 70-75, ASSOC PROF GEOL, DOANE COL, NEBR, 75-, CHMN SCI DIV, 78- *Concurrent Pos:* Res geologist, Nebr Geol Surv, Univ Nebr, 75- *Mem:* Geol Soc Am; Nat Asn Geol Teachers; Paleont Soc; AAAS; Sigma Xi. *Res:* Classification of Middle Devonian Brachiopods from Ontario; classification and stratigraphic distribution of microfossils from Pennsylvanian rocks in Nebraska; geologic mapping of Pliocene outcrops in Western Nebraska. *Mailing Add:* Dept of Geol Doane Col Crete NE 68333

DIFFLEY, PETER, b St Paul, Minn, Mar 15, 46; m 74; c 1. IMMUNOPARASITOLOGY. *Educ:* Tulane Univ, BS, 68; Univ Mont, MA, 74; Univ Mass, Amherst, PhD(zool), 78. *Prof Exp:* Fel, Yale Sch Med, 78-81; ASST PROF, TEX TECH UNIV, 81- *Mem:* Am Soc Parasitologists; Am Soc Microbiol; AAAS; Sigma Xi. *Res:* Effector immune responses to infectious disease agents and tumor and parasite/tumor evasion strategies, specifically, the models being used to study these relationships include rodent responses to African trypanosomissis, leishmaniasis and murine melanoma. *Mailing Add:* Dept Biol Sci Tex Tech Univ Lubbock TX 79409

DIFFORD, WINTHROP CECIL, b East Liverpool, Ohio, Nov 12, 21; m 44; c 3. GEOLOGICAL OCEANOGRAPHY. *Educ:* Mt Union Col, BS, 43; WVa Univ, MS, 47; Syracuse Univ, PhD(geol), 54. *Prof Exp:* Asst geol, Ohio State Univ, 42-43; instr, WVa Univ, 47-48; asst area geologist, US Bur Reclamation, Nebr, 48-49, area geologist, Colo, 50-51; from asst prof to prof geol, Dickinson Col, 54-66; assoc prof geol, asst dean & dir grad studies, Col Arts & Sci, Univ Bridgeport, 66-68; dean grad col & dir summer session, 68-78, PROF GEOL, UNIV WIS-STEVENS POINT, 68- *Concurrent Pos:* Am Geol Inst vis scientist, 63-65; intern acad admin, Ellis L Phillips Found, 65-66. *Mem:* Fel Geol Soc Am; Marine Tech Soc; fel Royal Soc Arts; fel Explorers Club. *Res:* Oceanography; engineering geology. *Mailing Add:* Dept Geog Geol Univ of Wis Stevens Point WI 54481

DI FRANCO, ROLAND B, b New York, NY, July 26, 36; m 65; c 2. DIFFERENTIAL EQUATIONS. *Educ:* Fordham Univ, BS, 58; Rutgers Univ, MS, 60; Ind Univ, PhD(math), 65. *Prof Exp:* Asst prof math, Fordham Univ, 65-66 & Swarthmore Col, 66-72; assoc prof, 72-78, chairperson dept, 75-78, PROF MATH, UNIV OF THE PAC, 78- *Concurrent Pos:* NSF sci fac fel, Univ Calif, Berkeley, 69-70; Danforth assoc, 70-; vis scholar, Univ Calif, Berkeley, 77. *Mem:* Am Math Soc; Math Asn Am. *Res:* Extending a norm residue symbol to inseparable extensions. *Mailing Add:* Dept of Math Univ of the Pac Stockton CA 95211

DI GANGI, FRANK EDWARD, b West Rutland, Vt, Sept 29, 17; m 46; c 2. CHEMISTRY. *Educ:* Rutgers Univ, BSc, 40; Western Reserve Univ, MSc, 42; Univ Minn, PhD(pharmaceut chem), 48. *Prof Exp:* From asst prof to assoc prof, 48-57, asst dean student affairs, 69-77, PROF MED CHEM, COL PHARM, UNIV MINN, MINNEAPOLIS, 57-, ASSOC DEAN ADMIN AFFAIRS, 78- *Mem:* Fel Am Pharmaceut Asn; Am Asn Univ Prof; fel Am Chem Soc; Am Asn Cols Pharm; Sigma Xi. *Res:* Synthesis of organic medicinals and phytochemistry. *Mailing Add:* Col Pharm Univ Minn Minneapolis MN 55455

DIGAUDIO, MARY ROSE, b Brooklyn, New York. PROTOZOOLOGY, ALGOLOGY. *Educ:* St John's Univ, BS, 61; Fordham Univ, MS, 63; NY Univ, PhD(biol), 75. *Prof Exp:* ASST PROF, ST FRANCIS COL, NY, 77- *Mem:* Sigma Xi; Am Soc Cell Biol; NY Acad Sci; AAAS; Soc Protozoologists. *Res:* Pollutants and their effect on aquatic biota. *Mailing Add:* 1038 85th St Brooklyn NY 11228

DIGBY, JAMES F(OSTER), b Aug 11, 21. SYSTEMS ANALYSIS, INTERNATIONAL AFFAIRS. *Educ:* La Polytech Inst, BS, 41; Stanford Univ, MA, 42. *Prof Exp:* Res engr, Watson Labs, US Air Force, 45-49; res engr, Rand Corp, 49, head opers dept, 55-59, spec asst to head eng div, 59-60, assoc mem res coun, 61-62, prog mgr, Int Security Affairs, 63-65; asst to pres, NATO Force Planning, 65-66, PROG MGR & PROJ LEADER, NATO, 66- *Concurrent Pos:* Consult & comt mem, President's Sci Adv Comt, Fed Aviation Agency & Dept Defense; mem President's task force on air traffic control, 61; exec dir, Calif Sem on Int Security & Foreign Policy, 76-; dir, European-Am Inst for Security Res, 75- *Res:* Evaluation of defense weapon systems; military strategy. *Mailing Add:* 20773 Big Rock Dr Malibu CA 90265

DIGBY, PETER SAKI BASSETT, b London, Eng, Jan 15, 21; m 47; c 4. MARINE BIOLOGY, PHYSIOLOGY. *Educ:* Cambridge Univ, BA, 43, MA, 47; Univ London, DSc, 67. *Prof Exp:* Res asst agr entom, Agr Adv Serv, Cambridge Univ, 42-46; res marine biol, Marine Lab, Plymouth & Exped to Spitsbergen, 46-48; entom, Oxford Univ, 48-50; in field res grant, Marine Plankton Exped to Greenland, 50-51; entom, Oxford Univ, 51-52; from lectr to sr lectr biol, St Thomas's Hosp, Med Sch, 52-67; PROF ZOOL, McGILL UNIV, 67- *Concurrent Pos:* Res grants, Develop Comn, 46-48, Agr Res Coun, 48-50, Browne Fund, 50-51 & Percy Sladen Mem Fund, 56. *Mem:* AAAS; Marine Biol Asn UK; Soc Exp Biol & Med; Am Physiol Soc; Biophys Soc. *Res:* Marine biology, ecology and physiology; plankton; geographical aspects of biology, especially in arctic; physiological mechanisms, especially pressure sensitivity; physiology of calcification in marine plants and animals and in bone and teeth and its apparent electrochemical basis; organic semiconductors; general physiology and ecology of insects and marine organisms. *Mailing Add:* Dept of Biol McGill Univ Montreal Can

DIGENIS, GEORGE A, b Athens, Greece, Sept 28, 35; US citizen; m 61; c 3. MEDICINAL CHEMISTRY, NUCLEAR MEDICINE. *Educ:* Am Univ Beirut, BSc, 59; Univ Wis-Madison, MSc, 62, PhD(med chem), 64. *Prof Exp:* Asst prof pharmaceut chem, Am Univ Beirut, 64-67; from asst prof to assoc prof, 67-74, PROF PHARMACEUT CHEM, COL PHARM & ASSOC PROF NUCLEAR MED, COL MED, UNIV KY, 74- *Mem:* Am Pharmaceut Asn. *Res:* Natural products chemistry; organic and medicinal chemistry; biochemistry; bio-organic chemistry; radiopharmaceuticals. *Mailing Add:* Col of Pharm Univ of Ky Lexington KY 40506

DI GEORGE, ANGELO MARIO, b Philadelphia, Pa, Apr 15, 21; m 51; c 3. ENDOCRINOLOGY, PEDIATRICS. *Educ:* Temple Univ, AB, MD, 46, MS, 52. *Prof Exp:* Intern, Temple Univ Hosp, 47; pediat resident, Temple Univ Hosp & St Christopher's Hosp for Children, 49-52; instr pediat, Sch Med, Temple Univ, 52-57, assoc, 57-58, from asst prof to assoc prof, 58-67; from asst attend pediatrician & endocrinologist to assoc attend pediatrician & endocrinologist, 52-61, CHIEF ENDOCRINE & METAB SERV, ST CHRISTOPHER'S HOSP FOR CHILDREN, 61-, DIR CLIN RES CTR, 63-; PROF PEDIAT, SCH MED, TEMPLE UNIV, 67- *Concurrent Pos:* Nat Inst Arthritis & Metab Dis fel, Jefferson Med Col, 52-54; asst chief pediat, Philadelphia Gen Hosp, 56-66; consult & lectr, US Naval Hosp, Philadelphia, 67- *Mem:* Am Pediat Soc; Am Soc Human Genetics; Am Acad Pediat; Endocrine Soc; Am Diabetes Asn. *Res:* Endocrinologic, metabolic and genetic disorders of growth and development. *Mailing Add:* St Christopher's Hosp for Children 2600 N Lawrence St Philadelphia PA 19133

DIGGINS, MAUREEN RITA, b Omaha, Nebr, July 17, 42. FRESH WATER ECOLOGY, COMPARATIVE PHYSIOLOGY. *Educ:* Mt Marty Col, BA, 66; Northwestern Univ, MS, 68, PhD(biol sci), 71. *Prof Exp:* Instr, St Agnes Sch, 62-65; from instr to asst prof, 67-74, ASSOC PROF BIOL, MT MARTY COL, 74-, CHAIRPERSON, DIV NATURAL SCI, 78- *Mem:* AAAS; Ecol Soc Am; NAm Benthological Soc; Sigma Xi. *Res:* Eutrophication of prairie lakes; benthic life of South Dakota rivers; species diversity of benthos; quality of rural drinking water in South Dakota. *Mailing Add:* Dept of Biol Mt Marty Col Yankton SD 57078

DIGGS, CARTER LEE, b Deltaville, Va, Dec 31, 34; m 56; c 3. IMMUNOLOGY. *Educ:* Randolph Macon Col, BS, 56; Med Col Va, MD, 60; Johns Hopkins Univ, PhD(immunol), 68. *Prof Exp:* Intern & resident path, Med Col Va, 60-62; researcher parasitic dis, Dept Med Zool, Walter Reed Army Inst Res, 62-64; fel microbiol, Johns Hopkins Univ, 64-68; chief, Dept Parasitic Dis, SEATO Med Res Lab, Bangkok, 68-70; dep dir, Div Commun Dis & Immunol, 70-73, CHIEF IMMUNOL, WALTER REED ARMY INST RES, 73- *Concurrent Pos:* Lectr, Johns Hopkins Univ, 73-78; mem study group trop med & parasitol, NIH, 78-80. *Mem:* Am Asn Immunologists; Am Soc Trop Med & Hyg; Soc Exp Biol & Med; AAAS; Am Soc Microbiol. *Res:* Effector mechanisms of immunity against Malaria and trypanosomiasis, especially the role oc complement; experimental immunization. *Mailing Add:* Walter Reed Army Inst of Res Washington DC 20012

DIGGS, DONALD R(OGER), b Richmond, Va, June 28, 24; m 47; c 4. MECHANICAL ENGINEERING. *Educ:* Northwestern Univ, BS, 44, MS, 47, PhD(mech eng), 53. *Prof Exp:* Res engr, Nat Adv Comt Aeronaut, 44-46; instr mech eng, Northwestern Univ, 47-50; mech engr, Combustion Res Group, Petrol Lab, 50-53, supvr engine test group, 53-56, tech asst, 56-58, supvr combustion res group, 58-59, head combustion div, 59-61, tech asst, Petrol Chem Div, 61-64, asst tech mgr, 64-70, TECH DIR, PETROL CHEM DIV, E I DU PONT DE NEMOURS & CO, INC, 70- *Mem:* Soc Automotive Engrs. *Res:* Internal combustion engines; combustion; fuel and lubricant additives. *Mailing Add:* Petrol Chem Div E I du Pont de Nemours & Co Inc Wilmington DE 19898

DIGHE, SHRIKANT VISHWANATH, b Murud, India, Nov 29, 33; m 64; c 2. ORGANIC CHEMISTRY, BIOPHARMACEUTICS. *Educ:* Univ Bombay, BSc, 55, MSc, 57; Univ Cincinnati, PhD(org chem), 65. *Prof Exp:* Res asst med drugs, Haffkine Inst, India, 57-58; res chemist, W R Grace & Co, 65-71; res assoc, Sch Med, Johns Hopkins Univ, 71-73; chemist, 73-79, CHIEF BIOPHARMACEUT REV BR, DIV BIOPHARMACEUT, FOOD & DRUG ADMIN, 80- *Mem:* Am Chem Soc; NY Acad Sci; fel Am Inst Chem. *Res:* Organometallic chemistry; chemistry of metal carbonyls, sulfur compounds and polymer synthesis; coordination chemistry; organic and organometallic synthesis; biopharmaceutics; pharmacokinetics. *Mailing Add:* 9811 Wildwood Rd Bethesda MD 20814

DI GIACOMO, ARMAND, b NY, Jan 26, 29; m 54; c 4. POLYMER CHEMISTRY. *Educ:* Long Island Univ, BS, 50; Princeton Univ, MA, 52, PhD(chem), 53. *Prof Exp:* SR RES CHEMIST, E I DU PONT DE NEMOURS & CO INC, 53- *Res:* Polymer physical chemistry; polymerization theories, mechanisms and kinetics; glass and crystallization transitions; solution properties; structure-property relations; kinetics over solid catalysts. *Mailing Add:* 1140 Webster Dr Wilmington DE 19803

DIGIORGIO, JOSEPH BRUN, b San Francisco, Calif, Aug 4, 32; m 57; c 6. PHYSICAL ORGANIC CHEMISTRY. *Educ:* Johns Hopkins Univ, BE, 54, MA, 57, PhD, 60. *Prof Exp:* Res assoc org chem, Johns Hopkins Univ, 59, NIH fel, 60-61; NIH fel, vis scientist & Nat Res Coun Can fel, Nat Res Coun Can, Ottawa, 61-63; res assoc, Johns Hopkins Univ, 63-64; from asst prof to assoc prof, 64-70, PROF CHEM, CALIF STATE UNIV, SACRAMENTO, 70- *Mem:* AAAS; Am Chem Soc; The Chem Soc; Sigma Xi. *Res:* Steroids and natural products; relationship between reactivity and geometry; conformational analysis; infrared and Raman spectroscopy of complex organic compounds. *Mailing Add:* Dept of Chem Calif State Univ 6000 J St Sacramento CA 95819

DIGIOVANNA, CHARLES V, organic chemistry, see previous edition

DI GIROLAMO, RUDOLPH GERARD, b Brooklyn, NY, Jan 26, 34; m 64, 78; c 1. MARINE BIOLOGY, MICROBIOLOGY. *Educ:* Mt St Mary's Col, Md, BS, 55; Univ Wash, PhD(marine biol, microbiol), 69. *Prof Exp:* Res assoc microbiol, St John's Univ, NY, 55-56; res assoc microbiol & virol, Univ Wash, 64-69, res assoc prof sanit eng, 69; from asst prof to prof biol & environ sci, Col Notre Dame, Calif, 70-80, chmn dept, 73-80; INSTR BIOL SCI, SACRAMENTO CITY COL, 80-; CONSULT MARINE RESOURCES, 80- *Concurrent Pos:* Chmn comt environ sci, Col Notre Dame, Calif, 70-80, dir marine resources ctr, 73-80; consult fish dis remedies, Halox-Am Corp, 73-; mem task force shellfish in San Francisco Bay, Asn Bay Area Govts, 77; mem comn mussel quarantine in San Francisco Bay, Calif Dept Pub Health, 77.

Mem: Am Soc Malacologists; Am Soc Microbiol; Am Fisheries Soc; NY Acad Sci; Int Oceanog Found. *Res:* Uptake and survival of enteroviruses and bacteria in shell fish and other marine food products; diseases of marine tropical fish; aquatic microbial pollution. *Mailing Add:* 343 Zephyr Ranch Dr Sacramento CA 95831

DIGIUSEPPE, MICHAEL ANTHONY, inorganic chemistry, see previous edition

DIGMAN, ROBERT V, b Wendel, WVa, Jan 9, 30; m 53; c 4. ORGANIC CHEMISTRY. *Educ:* Alderson-Broaddus Col, BS, 51; Univ Maine, MS, 53; Pa State Univ, PhD(chem), 63. *Prof Exp:* Instr chem, Alderson-Broaddus Col, 54-56; res asst petrol chem, Pa State Univ, 56-59; from asst prof to assoc prof chem, Marshall Univ, 59-65; chmn, Dept Natural & Appl Sci, 65-78, PROF CHARLES MCCLUNG SWITZER CHAIR CHEM, ALDERSON-BROADDUS COL, 65-, DEAN INSTR, 75- *Mem:* Am Chem Soc; AAAS; fel Am Inst Chemists. *Res:* Vapor-phase oxidation of hydrocarbons; reactions of epoxides. *Mailing Add:* Div of Natural Sci Alderson-Broaddus Col Philippi WV 26417

DIGNAM, MICHAEL JOHN, b Toronto, Ont, May 25, 31; m 53; c 5. SURFACE CHEMISTRY, ELECTROCHEMISTRY. *Educ:* Univ Toronto, BA, 53, PhD(phys chem), 56. *Prof Exp:* Demonstr chem, Univ Toronto, 53-54; res chemist, Aluminum Labs, Ltd, 56-58; lectr chem, Univ, 58-59, from asst prof to assoc prof, 59-66, PROF CHEM, UNIV TORONTO, 66- *Concurrent Pos:* Assoc ed, J Electrochem Soc, 76-81. *Mem:* Electrochem Soc; Am Chem Soc; Royal Soc Chem; Chem Inst Can; Can Asn Physicists. *Res:* Surface science and catalysis; ellipsometric and conventional spectroscopy of adsorbed species; solar energy conversion. *Mailing Add:* Dept Chem Univ Toronto Toronto ON M5S 2R8 Can

DIGNAM, WILLIAM JOSEPH, b Manchester, NH, Aug 11, 20; m 47; c 4. OBSTETRICS & GYNECOLOGY. *Educ:* Dartmouth Col, AB, 41; Harvard Univ, MD, 43. *Prof Exp:* Intern, Boston City Hosp, 44; resident obstet & gynec, Univ Kans, 47-50; resident endocrinol, Duke Univ, 48; instr obstet & gynec, Univ Calif, San Francisco, 51-53; from asst prof to assoc prof, 53-66, PROF OBSTET & GYNEC, CTR HEALTH SCI, SCH MED, UNIV CALIF, LOS ANGELES, 66- *Mem:* AMA; Am Fedn Clin Res; Endocrine Soc; Am Gynec Soc; Soc Gynec Invest. *Res:* Gynecologic endocrinology. *Mailing Add:* Sch of Med Univ Calif Ctr for Health Sci Los Angeles CA 90024

DI GREGORIO, GUERINO JOHN, b Philadelphia, Pa, May 11, 40; m 63. PHARMACOLOGY. *Educ:* Pa State Univ, BS, 62; Hahnemann Med Col, PhD(pharmacol), 66, MD, 78. *Prof Exp:* From instr to assoc prof, 66-80, PROF PHARMACOL, HAHNEMANN MED COL, 80- *Mem:* Am Soc Exp Path; Am Soc Clin Toxicol; Am Chem Soc. *Res:* Isolation of biologically active compounds from plants; structure activity relationships of autonomic nervous system; synthesis of quinoline compounds; pharmacokinetics of drugs of abuse; salivary secretion of drugs; drug analysis and toxicology. *Mailing Add:* Dept of Pharmacol Hahnemann Med Col Philadelphia PA 19102

DIILIO, CHARLES CARMEN, b Philadelphia, Pa, May 10, 12; m 37; c 3. MECHANICAL ENGINEERING. *Educ:* Pa State Univ, BS, 34, MS, 35. *Prof Exp:* Machine designer, Yale & Towne Mfg Co, 35-37; instr mech eng, Rensselaer Polytech, 37-41; from asst prof to prof, 41-46, mem grad sch faculty, 49-76, EMER PROF MECH ENG, PA STATE UNIV, 76- *Concurrent Pos:* Examr mech eng, Pa State Registr Bd Prof Engrs, 58-62; consult, Consumers Res Inc, 50-56, Curtis Wright Corp & Fairchild Stratos Corp. *Mem:* Am Soc Mech Engrs. *Res:* Heat power; thermodynamics; refrigeration; air conditioning; internal combustion engines; rocket motors; fluid mechanics; heat transfer. *Mailing Add:* 430 Philmont Dr Lancaster PA 17601

DIKE, PAUL ALEXANDER, b Mt Vernon, Iowa, Nov 26, 12; m 45; c 3. GEOLOGY. *Educ:* Johns Hopkins Univ, BA, 37, Bryn Mawr Col, MA, 50. *Prof Exp:* Instr geol, Univ Pa, 46-53; master parochial sch, Pa, 53-54; foreman phys testing lab, E L Conwell & Co, Pa, 54-55; asst prof geol & dir dept, Temple Univ, 55-62; asst prof sci, 62-70, chmn dept phys sci, 71-77, ASSOC PROF GEOL, GLASSBORO STATE COL, 70- *Concurrent Pos:* Lectr, Drexel Inst Technol, 48-62; tutor, Bryn Mawr Col, 50-55; consult, E L Conwell & Co, 55-, Ambric Testing & Eng Assocs, Inc, 56-, Rowle & Henderson, 57- & Asphalt Technol, 62-; lectr, Gloucester County Col, 68-70. *Res:* Field studies with magnetometer, earth resistivity and seismology locating mineral deposits; geology of Central Delaware County, Pennsylvania; Coastal Plains materials. *Mailing Add:* Dept of Phys Sci Glassboro State Col Glassboro NJ 08028

DI LAVORE, PHILIP, III, b Lawrence, Mass, Apr 24, 31; m 53; c 4. PHYSICS. *Educ:* Dakota Wesleyan Univ, AB, 54; Univ Mich, MS, 61, PhD(physics), 67. *Prof Exp:* Teacher high schs, SDak, 53-54 & Mich, 56-58; lectr physics, Univ Mich, 62 & 64; asst prof, Univ Md, 65-71, assoc chmn dept physics & astron, 69-71; assoc prof, 71-75, assoc dean, Sch Grad Studies, 76-77, PROF PHYSICS, IND STATE UNIV, 75-, ASST VPRES ACAD AFFAIRS, 77- *Concurrent Pos:* Staff physicist, Comn Col Physics, 67-69; coordr, Nat Tech Physics Proj, 72-76; ed, Physics of Technol Modules, 74-75. *Mem:* Am Asn Physics Teachers; Am Phys Soc. *Res:* Level-crossing spectroscopy; optical pumping; quantum electronics; nuclear physics; lasers, optics, musical acoustics. *Mailing Add:* Dept Physics Ind State Univ Terre Haute IN 47809

DILCHER, DAVID L, b Cedar Falls, Iowa, July 10, 36; m 61. PALEOBOTANY. *Educ:* Univ Minn, BS, 58, MS, 60; Yale Univ, PhD(biol), 64. *Prof Exp:* Instr biol, Yale Univ, 65-67; from asst prof to assoc prof bot, 67-77, PROF PALEOBOT, IND UNIV, BLOOMINGTON, 77- *Concurrent Pos:* Sigma Xi grants-in-aid, 61, 62 & 66; NSF fel, 64-65, res grants, 66-; Guggenheim fel, 72-73; distinguished vis res scholar, Adelaide Univ, 80.

Mem: Int Asn Paleobot; Int Union Biol Sci; AAAS; Bot Soc Am; Am Inst Biol Sci. *Res:* Cretaceous and Tertiary plant fossils of North America; Angiosperm evolution with particular reference to foliar and reproductive anatomy and morphology of fossil and modern plants. *Mailing Add:* Dept of Biol Ind Univ Bloomington IN 47401

DILENGE, DOMENICO, b Grassano, Italy, June 11, 25; m 69. RADIOLOGY. *Educ:* Univ Bari, BA, 43; Univ Naples, MD, 49, Med Specialist, 53; Univ Pisa, Docente, 64; Univ Paris, MMSc, 64; FRCP(C), 74. *Prof Exp:* Asst neuroradiol, St Anne Hosp, Paris, 53-60; asst neuroradiol, Pitie Hosp, 60-66; assoc prof angioneuroradiol, Univ Nantes, 66-68; res assoc prof radiol, Wash Univ, 68; chmn dept, 68-77, PROF RADIOL, UNIV SHERBROOKE, 68- *Concurrent Pos:* Int Brain Res Orgn Coordr, Int Round Table Cerebral Circulation, Paris, 67. *Mem:* Laureat French Acad Med; sr mem Am Soc Neuroradiol; Am Col Radiol; Can Asn Radiol; hon mem French Neurol Soc & Soc Neurol & Electroencephalog, Luxembourg. *Res:* Cerebral circulation; angiography of cerebral and spinal circulation; clinical neuroradiology; ophthalmic angiography; gas myelography. *Mailing Add:* Dept of Radiol Univ of Sherbrooke Sherbrooke Can

DILEONE, GILBERT ROBERT, b Providence, RI, Oct 30, 35; m 65; c 2. IMMUNOLOGY. *Educ:* Boston Univ, AB, 58; Univ RI, MS, 60, PhD(biol sci), 64. *Prof Exp:* Res assoc immunol, Brown Univ, 64-66; ASSOC BIOL, DEPT CANCER RES, RI HOSP, PROVIDENCE, 66- *Mem:* AAAS; Am Soc Microbiol; Tissue Cult Asn; Reticuloendothelial Soc. *Res:* Nature of recognition of antigens and synthesis of antibodies; cellular immunology; nature of antigen sensitive memory cells; tumor immunology. *Mailing Add:* 24 Old Lyme Dr Warwick RI 02886

DILGEN, ST FRANCIS, b Brooklyn, NY, Feb 27, 24. ORGANIC CHEMISTRY. *Educ:* St John's Univ, NY, BS, 53; Fordham Univ, MS, 55, PhD(chem), 59. *Prof Exp:* Asst, Fordham Univ, 53-57; instr chem, 57-58, from instr to assoc prof, 58-70, PROF CHEM & CHMN DEPT, ST JOSEPH'S COL, NY, 70- *Mem:* Am Chem Soc; NY Acad Sci. *Res:* Reactions of B-epoxy ketones and related compounds with organometallic compounds and ring opening reagents. *Mailing Add:* Dept of Chem St Joseph's Col Brooklyn NY 11205

DILGER, WILLIAM C, vertebrate zoology, see previous edition

DILIDDO, BART A(NTHONY), b Cleveland, Ohio, Mar 5, 31; m 55. CHEMICAL ENGINEERING. *Educ:* Fenn Col, BS, 54, Ill Inst Technol, MS, 56, Case Inst Technol, PhD(chem eng), 60. *Prof Exp:* Mem tech staff, Independence Tech Ctr, BF Goodrich Co, 56-58, res engr, 60-62, sr res engr, Avon Lake Tech Ctr, 62-64, res sect leader, 64-67, proj mgr, 67-70, process mgr, Orange Plant, 70-72; dir, Latex & Specialty Chemicals, Cleveland, BF Goodrich Co, 72-73, res & develop, 73-75, div vpres, Akron Corp, 75-78, Special Projs, Cleveland, 78, Plastics, 78-79, sr vpres & gen mgr, Plastics, 79-80; PRES CHEM GROUP & EXEC VPRES, BF GOODRICH CO, 80- *Mem:* Am Inst Chem Engrs. *Res:* New chemical processes. *Mailing Add:* BF Goodrich Chem Group 6100 Oak Tree Blvd Cleveland OH 44131

DILIDDO, REBECCA MCBRIDE, b Canton, Ohio, June 25, 51; m 78. ROOT PHYSIOLOGY, CELL MOTILITY. *Educ:* Milligan Col, BS, 77; Ohio State Univ, PhD(bot), 77. *Prof Exp:* Asst prof bot & cell biol, Eastern Ore State Col, 78-79; ASST PROF BOT & CELL BIOL, SUFFOLK UNIV, 81- *Concurrent Pos:* Asst prof, Hiran Col, 78-80; assoc, Mass Inst Technol, 80-81. *Mem:* Am Soc Plant Physiologists. *Res:* Hormonal, environmental, physiological plantgrowth; root growth and the roles of auxin and hydrogen plus ions in the control of elongation and geotropism. *Mailing Add:* Suffolk Univ Beacon Hill Boston MA 02108

DILIELLO, LEO RALPH, b Baltimore, Md, Jan 17, 32; m 54; c 3. MICROBIOLOGY. *Educ:* Univ Md, BS, 54, MS, 56, PhD, 58. *Prof Exp:* Res asst, Univ Md, 54-58; assoc prof, 58-68, PROF MICROBIOL, STATE UNIV NY AGR & TECH COL FARMINGDALE, 68- *Mem:* Am Soc Microbiol; Sigma Xi; Am Inst Food Technol. *Res:* Veterinary medicine; oral bacteria; dairy and food microbiology; medical microbiology; medical-veterinary aspects; human-animal diseases involving Vibrios; synergistic etiologies of human disease. *Mailing Add:* Dept of Biol Sci State Univ of Ny Agr & Tech Col Farmingdale NY 11735

DILKS, ELEANOR, b Richmond, Ind, Jan 29, 21. ZOOLOGY. *Educ:* Earlham Col, AB, 42; Univ Wis, MS, 44, PhD(zool), 48. *Prof Exp:* Instr biol, Earlham Col, 42-43; asst zool, Univ Wis, 43-45; instr, Drury Col, 45-47; from instr to asst prof, Univ Buffalo, 47-52; assoc prof biol, 52-61, PROF ZOOL, ILL STATE UNIV, 61- *Concurrent Pos:* NSF fac fel, 57-58, particip, Conf Marine Biol & Trop Ecol, PR, 64. *Mem:* Am Soc Zool; AAAS; Marine Biol Asn UK; Am Micros Soc; Soc Develop Biol. *Res:* Serology; precipitin formation; embryology; endocrinology; invertebrate zoology. *Mailing Add:* Dept of Biol Sci Ill State Univ Normal IL 61761

DILL, ALOYS JOHN, b Jersey City, NJ, Jan 8, 40; m 62; c 2. ELECTROCHEMISTRY. *Educ:* Hunter Col, AB, 62; City Col New York, MA, 64; City Univ New York, PhD(chem), 68. *Prof Exp:* res chemist, Paul D Merica Res Lab, 67-80, SR SCIENTIST, INCO RES & DEVELOP CTR, INT NICKEL CO, INC, 80- *Mem:* Am Chem Soc; Electrochem Soc; Am Electroplaters Soc. *Res:* Electrodeposition of metals. *Mailing Add:* Inco Res & Develop Ctr Sterling Forest Suffern NY 10901

DILL, CHARLES WILLIAM, b Greenville, SC, June 1, 32; m 54; c 3. FOOD SCIENCE, ORGANIC CHEMISTRY. *Educ:* Berea Col, BS, 54; NC State Col, MS, 57, PhD(food sci), 62. *Prof Exp:* Instr food chem, NC State Col, 59-62; asst prof dairy sci, Univ Nebr, 62-66; assoc prof, 66-75, PROF ANIMAL SCI, TEX A&M UNIV, 75- *Mem:* AAAS; Inst Food Technol; Am Dairy Sci Asn; Sigma Xi. *Res:* Thermal denaturation and degradation of proteins; instrumentation and control in systems for heating fluid products; flavor stability of fats and oils. *Mailing Add:* Dept of Animal Sci Tex A&M Univ College Station TX 77843

DILL, DALE ROBERT, b Towanda, Kans, Jan 10, 34; m 55; c 3. ORGANIC CHEMISTRY, PHARMACEUTICAL CHEMISTRY. *Educ:* Univ Kans, BS, 55, PhD(pharmaceut chem), 58. *Prof Exp:* Res assoc pharmaceut chem, Univ Kans, 58-59; sr res chemist, 59-63, res specialist, 63-67, group leader, 67-74, SR GROUP LEADER, MONSANTO CO, 74- *Concurrent Pos:* NIH grant, 58-59. *Mem:* Am Chem Soc; NY Acad Sci; Tech Asn Pulp & Paper Indust. *Res:* Anti-hypertensive drugs; plasticizers; paper chemicals; cancer drugs. *Mailing Add:* Monsanto Co 800 N Lindbergh Blvd St Louis MO 63166

DILL, DAVID BRUCE, b Eskridge, Kans, Apr 22, 91; m 45; c 2. PHYSIOLOGY. *Educ:* Occidental Col, BS, 13; Stanford Univ, MA, 14, PhD(biochem), 25. *Hon Degrees:* DSc, Occidental Col, 59; LHD, Univ Nev, Las Vegas, 72. *Prof Exp:* High sch teacher, 14-18; asst chemist, Bur Chem, USDA, 18-22, assoc chemist, 22-25; Nat Res Coun fel chem, Harvard Univ, 25-27, asst prof biochem, 27-36, assoc prof indust physiol, 36-38, prof, 38-47, dir res, Fatigue Lab, 27-47; sci dir, Chem Corps, Med Labs, Army Chem Ctr, Md, 47-61; res scholar, Ind Univ, 61-66; res prof, Lab Environ Pathophysiol, Desert Res Inst, 66-77, RES PROF PHYSIOL, UNIV NEV, LAS VEGAS, 77- *Concurrent Pos:* Vis lectr, Harvard Univ, 50-61; leader physiol explor expeds, Andes, CZ & Colo Desert. *Honors & Awards:* Legion of Merit. *Mem:* Am Chem Soc; Am Soc Biol Chemists; Am Physiol Soc (treas, 46-50, pres, 50); hon fel Am Col Cardiol; Am Col Sports Med (pres, 60-61). *Res:* Physico-chemical properties of blood; physiology of exercise; environmental physiology; physiology of aging. *Mailing Add:* Desert Biol Res Ctr Univ of Nev Las Vegas Boulder City NV 89005

DILL, EDWARD D, b Salt Lake City, Utah, July 6, 41; m 63; c 4. INORGANIC CHEMISTRY, PHYSICAL CHEMISTRY. *Educ:* Southwestern State Col, BS, 63; Univ Ark, PhD(chem), 69. *Prof Exp:* ASSOC PROF CHEM, SOUTHWESTERN OKLA STATE UNIV, 68-, CHMN, DEPT CHEM, 79- *Mem:* Am Chem Soc. *Res:* Inorganic synthesis; x-ray structure analysis. *Mailing Add:* Dept of Chem Southwestern Okla State Univ Weatherford OK 73096

DILL, ELLIS HAROLD, b Pittsburgh Co, Okla, Dec 31, 32; m 53; c 2. CIVIL ENGINEERING. *Educ:* Univ Calif, PhD(civil eng), 57. *Prof Exp:* Prof aeronaut & astronaut, Univ Wash, 56-77; DEAN ENG, RUTGERS UNIV, 77- *Mem:* Soc Natural Philos. *Res:* Applied mechanics. *Mailing Add:* Rutgers Univ PO Box 909 Piscataway NJ 08854

DILL, FREDERICK H(AYES), JR, b Sewickley, Pa, Mar 1, 32. ELECTRICAL ENGINEERING, PHYSICS. *Educ:* Carnegie Inst Technol, BS, 54, MS, 56, PhD(elec eng), 58. *Prof Exp:* MEM RES STAFF, THOMAS J WATSON RES CTR, IBM CORP, 58- *Concurrent Pos:* Mackay vis lectr, Univ Calif, Berkeley, 68-69. *Res:* Semiconductor junction phenomena and devices. *Mailing Add:* Old Town Rd Carmel NY 10512

DILL, JAMES DAVID, b Okla City, Okla, Feb 24, 49; m 71, 81. THEORETICAL CHEMISTRY. *Educ:* Harvard Univ, BA, 71; Princeton Univ, MA, 73, PhD(chem), 76. *Prof Exp:* Fel, Univ Basel, 76-77; fel anal chem, Cornell Univ, 77-78; DIR QUANTUM CHEM, MOLECULAR DESIGN LTD, 78- *Mem:* Am Chem Soc; Am Soc Mass Spectrometrists. *Res:* Computational modelling and designing of organic compounds; development of chemical information technology and software. *Mailing Add:* Molecular Design Ltd 1122 B St Hayward CA 94541

DILL, JAMES F, b Cleveland, Ohio, Jan 4, 45. CHEMICAL PHYSICS, MATERIALS SCIENCE. *Educ:* John Carroll Univ, Bs, 67, MS, 69; Cath Univ Am, PhD(physics), 73. *Prof Exp:* Fel, Dept Physics, Cath Univ Am, 73-75; RES PHYSICIST, AIR FORCE AERO PROPULSION LAB, 75- *Res:* Tribiology; lubricant dynamics in elastohydrodynamic contacts; high pressure properties of lubricants; high speed rolling element bearing performance and rotodynamics of rotating systems. *Mailing Add:* Air Force Aero Propulsion Lab Wright-Patterson AFB OH 45433

DILL, JOHN C, b Vancouver, BC, Nov 20, 39; m 62; c 3. COMPUTER SCIENCE, COMPUTER GRAPHICS. *Educ:* Univ BC, BASc, 62; NC State Univ, MS, 64; Calif Inst Technol, PhD(info sci), 70. *Prof Exp:* Comput scientist, Res Labs, Gen Motors Tech Ctr, 70-80; SR RES ASSOC, COL ENG, CORNELL UNIV, 80- *Mem:* Asn Comput Mach; Inst Elec & Electronics Engrs. *Res:* Computer graphics; computer-aided design. *Mailing Add:* Col Eng Cornell Univ Ithaca NY 14853

DILL, KENNETH AUSTIN, b Oklahoma City, Okla, Dec 11, 47. POLYMER CHEMISTRY. *Educ:* Mass Inst Technol, SB & SM, 71; Univ Calif, San Diego, PhD(biol), 78. *Prof Exp:* Res asst biomed eng, Mass Inst Technol, 70-71; res asst biol, Univ Calif, San Diego, 71-78; Damon Runyon-Walter Winchell fel, 79-81, FEL CHEM, STANFORD UNIV, 78-; ASST PROF CHEM, UNIV FLA, 81- *Mem:* Am Chem Soc; Am Phys Soc; Biophys Soc. *Res:* Physical properties of membranes, micelles, macromolecules. *Mailing Add:* Dept Chem Univ Fla Gainesville FL 32611

DILL, LAWRENCE MICHAEL, b Vancouver, BC, Apr 4, 45; m 67; c 2. BEHAVIORAL ECOLOGY. *Educ:* Univ BC, BSc, 66, MSc, 68, PhD(ecol), 72. *Prof Exp:* Biologist, Dept Fisheries, Can, 67-69; asst prof ecol, York Univ, Toronto, 72-74; ASSOC PROF ECOL & ETHOLOGY, SIMON FRASER UNIV, BURNABY, 74- *Concurrent Pos:* Hon assoc prof animal resource ecol, Univ BC, 80-; mem, Pop Biol Grant Selection Comt, Natural Sci & Eng Res Coun, Can, 81-83; chmn, Can Comt Int Ethological Congress, 81-83. *Mem:* Can Soc Biologists; Asn Study Animal Behav; Ecol Soc Am. *Res:* Behavioral tactics used by animals, particulary in predator-prey interactions and intraspecific competition (utilizing) fish as experimental subjects. *Mailing Add:* Dept Biol Sci Simon Fraser Univ Burnaby BC V5A 1S6 Can

DILL, NORMAN HUDSON, b Wilmington, Del, Apr 6, 38. BOTANY, PLANT ECOLOGY. *Educ:* Univ Del, BA, 60; Rutgers Univ, MS, 62, PhD(plant ecol), 64. *Prof Exp:* Prof biol, 64-66, PROF BIOL & NATURAL RESOURCES, DEL STATE COL, 66- *Concurrent Pos:* Consult, USAID-NSF Sci Educ Improv Prog for India, 68 & 69; mem bd experts, Rachel Carson Trust for Living Environ. *Mem:* AAAS; Ecol Soc Am; Am Inst Biol Sci; Am Nature Study Soc; Nat Asn Biol Teachers. *Res:* Forest productivity; vegetation management; plant geography; use of wild shrubs in songbird management; effects of periodic cicada on forest ecosystems; plants for noise and air pollution abatement; agricultural drainage effects. *Mailing Add:* Dept of Biol & Natural Resources Del State Col Dover DE 19901

DILL, ROBERT FLOYD, b Denver, Colo, May 25, 27; m 45; c 4. MARINE GEOLOGY. *Educ:* Univ Southern Calif, BS, 50, MS, 52; Univ Calif, San Diego, PhD, 64. *Prof Exp:* Oceanogr, US Navy Electronics Lab, 51-68, marine geologist, Naval Undersea Res & Develop Ctr, 68-71; marine geologist, Nat Oceanic & Atmospheric Admin, 71-74 & Dept Interior, US Geol Surv, 74-75; dir, West Indies Lab, Fairleigh Dickenson Univ, 75-81; MEM STAFF, NAT OCEANIC & ATMOSPHERIC ADMIN, 81- *Concurrent Pos:* Consult & owner, Gen Oceanog Inc, 53-71; mem fac, San Diego State Col, 68-71; investr, Inst Oceanog Res, Univ Baja Calif; dipl, Mex Comt Eng for Ocean Resources, 70; adj prof, George Washington Univ, 71-74; mem, Gov Comn Water Resources Virgin Islands. *Honors & Awards:* Leverson Award, Am Asn Petrol Geologists, 69. *Mem:* Fel Geol Soc Am; Marine Technol Soc; Am Asn Petrol Geologists; Soc Econ Paleontologists & Mineralogists. *Res:* Marine sedimentation, erosion, and sediment distribution patterns in present and ancient seas; mass physical properties of sediments, Pleistocene sea level fluctuations, comparative studies of ancient and recent carbonate reefs; submarine canyons; scientific application of scuba and submersibles; deep sea mineral development. *Mailing Add:* Off Ocean Minerals & Energy Nat Oceanic & Atmospheric Admin Rockville MD 20852

DILL, RUSSELL EUGENE, b Rising Star, Tex, July 27, 32; m 54; c 3. PHYSIOLOGY, NEUROANATOMY. *Educ:* NTex State Col, BA, 53, MS, 57; Univ Ill, PhD(physiol), 60. *Prof Exp:* Instr anat, Univ Tex Med Br Galveston, 61-65; from asst prof to assoc prof, 65-74, PROF ANAT, COL DENT, BAYLOR UNIV, 74-, CHMN DEPT MICROS ANAT, 74- *Concurrent Pos:* Fel anat, Univ Tex Med Br Galveston, 60-61. *Mem:* AAAS; Am Asn Anat; Soc Neurosci. *Res:* Experimental neurology; extrapyramidal motor systems; central nervous system pharmacology. *Mailing Add:* Dept Micros Anat Baylor Univ Col Dent Dallas TX 75246

DILLARD, BEVERLY MINCEY, see Mincey, Beverly Jean

DILLARD, CLYDE RUFFIN, b Norfolk, Va, Apr 17, 20. INORGANIC CHEMISTRY. *Educ:* Va Union Univ, BS, 40; Univ Chicago, MS, 48, PhD, 49. *Prof Exp:* Res chemist, Manhattan Proj, Chicago, 43-45, asst chem, 45-48; prof, Tenn Agr & Indust State Univ, 48-53 & Morgan State Col, 53-59; assoc prof, 59-69, PROF CHEM, BROOKLYN COL, 69-, ASSOC DEAN FACULTIES, 70- *Concurrent Pos:* Asst ed, Appl Spectros, Soc Appl Spectros, 63-; Fulbright res scholar, Osaka Univ, 65-66. *Mem:* AAAS; Am Chem Soc; NY Acad Sci; Soc Appl Spectros. *Res:* Chemistry of volatile hydrides; organotin compounds; infrared spectroscopy; radiochemistry and isotopic tracer techniques. *Mailing Add:* Dept of Chem Brooklyn Col Brooklyn NY 11210

DILLARD, DAVID HUGH, b Spokane, Wash, May 14, 23; m 48; c 7. SURGERY. *Educ:* Whitman Col, AB, 46; Johns Hopkins Univ, MD, 50; Am Bd Surg, dipl, 59; Bd Thoracic Surg, dipl, 61. *Hon Degrees:* Dr Sci, Witman Col, 79. *Prof Exp:* Intern, Johns Hopkins Hosp, 51; instr, 54-57, resident, 58, instr, 58, assoc prof, 57-69, chief, Div Cardiothoracic Surg, 72-78, PROF SURG, SCH MED, UNIV WASH, 69- *Res:* Esophageal and cardiovascular research; thoracic surgery. *Mailing Add:* Dept of Surg Univ of Wash Sch of Med Seattle WA 98195

DILLARD, EMMETT URCEY, b Sylva, NC, Aug 12, 17; m 40; c 4. ANIMAL GENETICS. *Educ:* Berea Col, BSA, 40; NC State Col, MS, 48; Univ Mo, PhD(animal husb), 53. *Prof Exp:* From asst county supvr to county supvr, Farm Security Admin, USDA, 40-44; instr animal husb, Bur Animal Indust, 47-49, asst prof, 49-60, assoc prof, 60-69, EMER ASSOC PROF ANIMAL HUSB, NC STATE UNIV, 79- *Concurrent Pos:* Livestock res adv, NC Agr Res Mission to Peru, 58-60 & 67-68. *Mem:* Am Soc Animal Sci; Sigma Xi. *Res:* Livestock, improvement through breeding and management; selection and crossbreeding in beef cattle improvement. *Mailing Add:* 1110 Dogwood Lane NC State Univ Raleigh NC 27607

DILLARD, GARY EUGENE, b Ridgway, Ill, Apr 26, 38; m 59; c 2. PHYCOLOGY, AQUATIC ECOLOGY. *Educ:* Southern Ill Univ, BA, 60, MS, 62; NC State Univ, PhD(bot), 66. *Prof Exp:* Asst taxon, Southern Ill Univ, 59-60, bot, 60-62; asst phycol, NC State Univ, 62-65; asst prof bot, Clemson Univ, 65-68; assoc prof biol, 68-74, PROF BIOL, WESTERN KY UNIV, 74- *Mem:* Phycol Soc Am; Am Micros Soc; Int Phycol Soc. *Res:* Taxonomy and ecology of freshwater algae, especially Chlorophyceae of Southeastern United States. *Mailing Add:* Dept of Biol Western Ky Univ Bowling Green KY 42102

DILLARD, JAMES WILLIAM, b Pueblo, Colo, Feb 26, 48; m 75. ANALYTICAL CHEMISTRY, ELECTROCHEMISTRY. *Educ:* Univ Ariz, BS, 70; NC State Univ, PhD(anal chem), 76. *Prof Exp:* Fel, Colo State Univ, 75-77; ANAL CHEMIST RADIOCHEM, TENN VALLEY AUTHORITY, 77- *Mem:* Am Chem Soc; Sigma Xi. *Res:* Finite difference simulation of electron transfer reactions; application of electrochemical techniques to environmental radiochemistry; implementation of computer-based acquisition and data handling systems for analytical laboratories. *Mailing Add:* Tenn Valley Authority PO Box 99 Vonore TN 37885

DILLARD, JOHN GAMMONS, b Kermit, Tex, Nov 1, 38; m 63; c 2. INORGANIC CHEMISTRY, PHYSICAL CHEMISTRY. *Educ:* Austin Col, BA, 61; Kans State Univ, PhD(chem), 66. *Prof Exp:* Asst chem, Okla State Univ, 61-63 & Kans State Univ, 63-66; fel Rice Univ, 66-67; from asst prof to assoc prof, 67-78, PROF CHEM, VA POLYTECH INST & STATE UNIV, 78- *Mem:* Am Chem Soc; Am Soc Mass Spectrometry. *Res:* Mass spectrometry, corrosion, surface chemistry oceanography. *Mailing Add:* 201 Craig Dr Blacksburg VA 24060

DILLARD, JOSEPH KING, b Westminster, SC, May 10, 17; m 39; c 2. ELECTRICAL ENGINEERING. *Educ:* Ga Inst Technol, BSEE, 47; Mass Inst Technol, MSEE, 50. *Prof Exp:* Instr elec eng, Mass Inst Technol, 47-50; elec utility eng mgr, 50-56, mgr elec utility eng, 56-69, GEN MGR ADVAN SYSTS TECHNOL, WESTINGHOUSE ELEC CORP, 69- *Concurrent Pos:* Chmn nat adv bd, Ga Tech Univ. *Mem:* Nat Acad Eng; fel Inst Elec & Electronics Engrs (pres, 76); Nat Soc Prof Engrs. *Mailing Add:* Westinghouse Elec Corp Advan Systs Technol 777 Penn Ctr Blvd Pittsburgh PA 15235

DILLARD, MARGARET BLEICK, b Newark, NJ; m 68; c 1. RADIOLOGICAL PHYSICS, MATHEMATICAL PHYSICS. *Educ:* Mt Holyoke Col, AB, 61; Univ NC, Chapel Hill, PhD(physics), 67. *Prof Exp:* Res assoc physics, Duke Univ, 67-68; instr & res assoc, Univ NC, Chapel Hill, 68-69; assoc prof physics & math, St Augustine's Col, NC, 69-71; comput programmer, NC Mem Hosp, Chapel Hill, 73-75; ASST PROF RADIOL, SCH MED, UNIV NC, CHAPEL HILL, 75- *Mem:* Am Phys Soc; Am Asn Physics Teachers. *Res:* Changes in radiation dose due to blocking of high energy x-ray beams used in radiation therapy. *Mailing Add:* 3106 Buckingham Rd Durham NC 27707

DILLARD, MARTIN GREGORY, b Chicago, Ill, July 7, 35; m 58; c 3. NEPHROLOGY. *Educ:* Univ Chicago, BA, 56, BS, 57; Howard Univ, MD, 65. *Prof Exp:* Asst prof med, 70-76, chief hemodialysis unit nephrol, Freedmen's Hosp, 70-73, asst chmn postgrad educ, 73-76, ASSOC PROF, 74- & ASSOC DEAN CLIN AFFAIRS, COL MED, HOWARD UNIV, 76- *Concurrent Pos:* Mem, Nat Adv Coun, Regional Med Prog, 76-78. *Mem:* Am Soc Nephrol; Am Fedn Clin Res; Int Soc Nephrol; Am Col Physicians. *Res:* Clinical-pathological correlations in renal disease; protein handling by the intact and damaged nephron; insulin binding in renal disease. *Mailing Add:* Renal Div Howard Univ Hosp 2041 Georgia Ave Washington DC 20059

DILLARD, MORRIS, JR, b York, Ala, Apr 27, 27. METABOLISM, INTERNAL MEDICINE. *Educ:* Birmingham-Southern Col, AB, 49; Emory Univ, PhD(anat), 54, MD, 59. *Prof Exp:* From instr to asst prof med, 63-69, ASSOC PROF CLIN MED, SCH MED, YALE UNIV, 69- *Concurrent Pos:* Fels, Yale Univ, 61-62 & 63-64. *Mailing Add:* Dept of Clin Med Yale Univ Sch of Med New Haven CT 06520

DILLAWAY, ROBERT BEACHAM, b Washington, DC, Nov 10, 24; m 47, 71; c 6. PHYSICS, MECHANICAL ENGINEERING. *Educ:* Univ Mich, BS(math) & BS(mech eng), 45; Univ Ill, MS, 51, PhD(mech), 53. *Prof Exp:* Develop engr, Carrier Corp, 45-46 & Eng Res Assocs, Inc, 47-48; instr mech eng, Univ Ill, 48-53; sr res engr, Rocketdyne Div, NAm Aviation, Inc, 53-54, res specialist, 54-56, supvr basic studies, 56-57, group leader basic studies & nuclear propulsion, 57-58, mgr nucleonics subdiv, Space Power Res & Develop, 58-64, corp dir res & tech mkt planning, 64-68; dep dir & dep for systs anal, Off Prog Appraisal Secy Navy Staff, 68-69; dep foreign labs, Lab & Res Mgt, US Army Mat Command, 69-75; sr vpres, Consol Diesel Elec Corp, 75-76; staff dir, Spec Invest, US House of Rep Sci & Technol Comn, 76-77; CONSULT & PRES, GLOBAL DEFENSE & COMMUN CORP, 77- *Concurrent Pos:* Exten lectr, Univ Calif, 53-; indust consult, Proj Rover, Los Alamos Sci Lab, 54-55; astronaut comn del, Int Aeronaut Fedn, 60-64; chmn, Intersoc Comt on Transp, 71-73. *Mem:* Am Soc Mech Engrs; Am Inst Aeronaut & Astronaut; Soc Exp Stress Anal; Brit Interplanetary Soc. *Res:* Fluid mechanics; heat transfer and thermodynamics; nuclear reactors for propulsion; transient fluid flow and boundary layer behavior; high speed temperature measurement. *Mailing Add:* 1306 Ballantrae Ct McLean VA 22101

DILLE, JOHN ROBERT, b Waynesburg, Pa, Sept 2, 31; m 55; c 2. AEROSPACE MEDICINE. *Educ:* Waynesburg Col, BS, 52; Univ Pittsburgh, MD, 56; Harvard Univ, MIH, 60; Am Bd Prev Med, dipl & cert aerospace med, 64. *Prof Exp:* Resident aerospace med, US Air Force Sch Aviation Med, Harvard Univ, 59-62, prog adv officer, Civil Aeromed Res Inst, 63-65, regional flight surgeon, Western Region, Los Angeles, 65, CHIEF CIVIL AEROMED INST, FED AVIATION ADMIN, 65- *Concurrent Pos:* Assoc prof, Sch Med, Univ Okla, 62- *Honors & Awards:* Theodore C Lyster Award, Aerospace Med Asn, 78. *Mem:* Fel Aerospace Med Asn; Civil Aviation Med Asn; fel Am Col Prev Med; Sigma Xi; Flying Physicians Asn. *Res:* Aircraft accident investigation; pulmonary physiology; toxicity of drugs and pesticides; penetrating eye injuries. *Mailing Add:* Civil Aeromed Inst Fed Aviation Admin Box 25082 Oklahoma City OK 73125

DILLE, KENNETH LEROY, b Caldwell, Idaho, May 9, 25; m 52; c 4. ORGANIC CHEMISTRY, PETROLEUM CHEMISTRY. *Educ:* Col Idaho, BA, 50; Ore State Col, MA, 52, PhD(org phys chem), 54. *Prof Exp:* Asst org chem, Ore State Col, 50-52; res chemist, 54-62, group leader chem res, 62-64, group leader fuels res, 64-68, asst supvr, 68-73, supvr, Fuels Res Sect, 73-80, coordr, Environ Affairs, 80-81, COORDR, INDUST HYGIENE & TOXICOL, TEXACO, INC, BEACON, 81- *Concurrent Pos:* Texaco proj leader with US Govt, 60-62. *Mem:* Am Chem Soc; Sigma Xi. *Res:* Synthesis and development of additives for improving motor and aviation gasolines, diesel and jet fuels and antifreezes; product development of petrochemicals. *Mailing Add:* 9 Sherrywood Rd Wappingers Falls NY 12590

DILLE, ROGER MCCORMICK, b Caldwell, Idaho, Apr 19, 23; m 55; c 1. CHEMISTRY. *Educ:* Col Idaho, BS, 44. *Prof Exp:* Chemist, Texaco Refinery, 44-51 & Montebello Res Lab, Texaco, Inc, 51-58, from res chemist to sr res chemist, 58-70, supvr anal & testing, Richmond Res Lab, Va, 70-76, SUPVR CUSTOMER SERVS SECT, PORT ARTHUR RES LABS, TEXACO, INC, 76- *Mem:* Am Chem Soc; Am Petrol Inst; Am Soc Testing Mat. *Res:* Petrochemicals; synthetic fuels; partial oxidation; environmental problems; coal gasification. *Mailing Add:* 4449 Lakeshore Port Arthur TX 77640

DILLEMUTH, FREDERICK JOSEPH, physical chemistry, see previous edition

DILLENIUS, MARNIX FRITZ EUGEN, b Bandung, Java, Nov 6, 38; US citizen. AERONAUTICAL ENGINEERING. *Educ:* Univ Calif, Berkeley, BS, 62, MS, 64, PhD(mech eng), 68. *Prof Exp:* Res asst heat transfer, Dept Mech Eng, Univ Calif, Berkeley, 63-68; res engr aerodyn & heat transfer, 69-80, SCIENTIST, NIELSEN ENG & RES, 80- *Mem:* Am Inst Aeronaut & Astronaut; assoc mem Sigma Xi. *Res:* Low and high speed flow aerodynamics of aircraft and missiles; radiation heat transfer. *Mailing Add:* Nielsen Eng & Res Inc 510 Clyde Ave Mountain View CA 94043

DILLER, EROLD RAY, b New Stark, Ohio, May 4, 22; m 52; c 2. BIOCHEMISTRY, PHARMACOLOGY. *Educ:* Bowling Green State Univ, BA, 49; Ind Univ, MS, 51. *Prof Exp:* Res assoc biochem, Ind Univ, 49-51; sr scientist, 51-66, res scientist, 66-71, RES ASSOC, LILLY RES LABS, 71- *Mem:* NY Acad Sci; Sigma Xi; Soc Exp Biol & Med. *Res:* Intermediary metabolism and metabolic control mechanisms; lipid and sterol metabolism and metabolic control mechanisms; lipid and sterol metabolism; biochemical pharmacology; absorption. *Mailing Add:* Lilly Res Labs 307 E McCarty St Indianapolis IN 46285

DILLER, KENNETH RAY, b Wooster, Ohio, Nov 20, 42; m 67; c 3. THERMODYNAMICS, HEAT TRANSFER. *Educ:* Ohio State Univ, BME, 66, MSc, 67; Mass Inst Technol, ScD, 72. *Prof Exp:* Res assoc biomed eng, Mass Inst Technol, 72-73; asst prof, 73-79, ASSOC PROF MECH ENG, UNIV TEX, AUSTIN, 79- *Mem:* AAAS; Am Soc Mech Eng; Soc Cryobiol (treas, 74-75); Microcirculation Soc; Am Ceramic Soc. *Res:* Study of energy processes in living systems involving transport of heat and mass; applications include microscopic evaluation of burn injury process and frozen preservation of living tissues and organs; computer modelling and computerized analysis of biomedical images. *Mailing Add:* Biomed Eng Ctr ENS 612 Univ Tex Austin TX 78712

DILLER, THOMAS EUGENE, b Orrville, Ohio, Sept 10, 50; m 77; c 1. HEAT & MASS TRANSFER, FLUID MECHANICS. *Educ:* Carnegie-Mellon Univ, BS, 72; Mass Inst Technol, SM, 74, ScD, 77. *Prof Exp:* Sr engr, Res & Develop, Polaroid Corp, 76-79; ASST PROF MECH ENG, VA POLYTECH INST & STATE UNIV, 79- *Concurrent Pos:* Prin investr res grants, Whitaker Found, 81-, US Dept Energy , 82- *Mem:* Am Soc Mech Engrs; Am Inst Chem Engrs; AAAS; Sigma Xi. *Res:* Fundamental analysis and experimentation jet impingement heat transfer, heat transfer in unsteady and separated flows, and mass transfer in flowing blood; application of result in areas such as drying, heat exchanger design, and atherosclerosis. *Mailing Add:* Dept Mech Eng Va Polytech Inst & State Univ Blacksburg VA 24061

DILLER, VIOLET MARION, b Cincinnati, Ohio, Feb 7, 14. BIOPHYSICS. *Educ:* Univ Cincinnati, BA, 34, BE, 35, MS, 45, PhD(physics), 47. *Prof Exp:* Instr physics, Univ Cincinnati, 43-44, from asst prof to assoc prof biophys, 47-76, PROF BIOPHYS, GRAD SCH, UNIV CINCINNATI, 76- *Mem:* Fel AAAS; Int Phycol Soc; Am Asn Physics Teachers; Phycol Soc Am; Biophys Soc. *Res:* Production of mutants in microorganisms by physical methods; metabolism of nonfilamentous algae; metabolism of liverworts. *Mailing Add:* Dept of Physics Univ of Cincinnati Cincinnati OH 45221

DILLER, WILLIAM FREY, JR, b Lancaster, Pa, July 26, 02; m 38. PROTOZOOLOGY. *Educ:* Franklin & Marshall Col, AB, 23; Univ Pa, PhD, 28. *Prof Exp:* Instr zool, Univ Pa, 23-25, Franklin & Marshall Col, 25-27 & Univ Pa, 27-30; Sterling fel, Yale Univ, 30-31; from instr to asst prof zool, Dartmouth Col, 31-39; from instr to prof, 39-72, EMER PROF ZOOL, UNIV PA, 72- *Mem:* AAAS; Am Soc Zool; Soc Protozool; Am Soc Parasitol; Micros Soc Am. *Res:* Nuclear behavior and life history of ciliated Protozoa. *Mailing Add:* Dept of Biol Univ of Pa Philadelphia PA 19104

DILLERY, DEAN GEORGE, b Fremont, Ohio, Nov 18, 28; m 51; c 4. ZOOLOGY. *Educ:* Ohio State Univ, BS, 52, MS, 55, PhD(ornith), 61. *Prof Exp:* Instr zool, Ohio Wesleyan Univ, 59-60; assoc prof, 60-73, chmn dept, 76-82, PROF BIOL, ALBION COL, 73- *Res:* Biology and behavior of arthropods; population biology and behavior of amphipods. *Mailing Add:* Dept Biol Albion Col Albion MI 49224

DILLEY, DAVID ROSS, b South Haven, Mich, Mar 10, 34; m 56; c 3. PLANT PHYSIOLOGY. *Educ:* Mich State Col, BS, 55; Mich State Univ, MS, 57; NC State Col, PhD(bot), 60. *Prof Exp:* Technician, 56-57, from asst prof to assoc prof, 60-67, PROF HORT, MICH STATE UNIV, 67- *Concurrent Pos:* Chmn Gordon Res conf Post Harvest Physiol, 72; consult, United Fruit Co & Cent Am Res Inst Indust; consult, Gen Foods Corp, 74, Grumman Allied Industs, Inc, 75- & Union Carbide Corp, 75-; lectr, Nato Adv Studies Inst, Greece, 81. *Honors & Awards:* Dow Chem Award, Am Soc Hort Sci. *Mem:* Am Soc Plant Physiol; fel Am Soc Hort Sci. *Res:* Physiology and biochemistry of fruits during growth, maturation and senescence; handling, transportation and storage of perishable commodities; design and manufacturing gas analysis and gas atmosphere control systems. *Mailing Add:* Dept of Hort Mich State Univ East Lansing MI 48823

DILLEY, JAMES PAUL, b Athens, Ohio, Feb 19, 34. THEORETICAL PHYSICS. *Educ:* Ohio Univ, AB, 55, MS, 56; Syracuse Univ, PhD(physics), 64. *Prof Exp:* From asst prof to assoc prof, 63-76, PROF PHYSICS, OHIO UNIV, 76- *Concurrent Pos:* Res fel, Theoret Physics Inst, Univ Alta, 68-69; vis assoc prof, Univ Colo, 71-72; vis prof, Univ Ariz, 79-80. *Mem:* Am Phys Soc; Am Asn Physics Teachers; Am Geophys Union; Am Astron Soc; AAAS. *Res:* Planets. *Mailing Add:* Dept of Physics Ohio Univ Athens OH 45701

DILLEY, JAMES V, toxicology, inhalation toxicology, deceased

DILLEY, RICHARD ALAN, b South Haven, Mich, Jan 12, 36; m 60; c 4. BIOCHEMISTRY, PLANT PHYSIOLOGY. *Educ:* Mich State Univ, BS, 58, MS, 59; Purdue Univ, PhD(biochem, plant physiol), 63. *Prof Exp:* NIH, C F Kettering Res Lab, 63-64; vis asst prof biophys, Univ Rochester, 65; staff scientist, C F Kettering Res Lab, 66-68, investr, 69-71; assoc prof, 71-75, PROF BIOL SCI, PURDUE UNIV, 75- *Mem:* AAAS; Am Soc Plant Physiol;

Am Inst Biol Sci; Am Soc Biol Chemists. *Res:* Membrane biochemistry in energy transducing systems; ion and electron transport; photophosphorylation and membrane structure in the photosynthetic apparatus; quinones of plants. *Mailing Add:* Dept Biol Sci Purdue Univ West Lafayette IN 47906

DILLEY, WILLIAM G, b Van Nuys, Calif, Sept 21, 42; m 65; c 2. CELL BIOLOGY, ONCOLOGY. *Educ:* Univ Calif, Berkeley, AB, 65, MA, 67, PhD(endocrinol), 70. *Prof Exp:* Asst prof anat, Col Physicians & Surgeons, Columbia Univ, 70-76; ASST PROF EXP SURG, DUKE UNIV MED CTR, 76-, DIR CLIN RES, UNIT LAB, 78- *Mem:* AAAS. *Res:* Breast cancer; thyroid-parathyroid endocrinology. *Mailing Add:* Duke Univ Med Ctr Box 3966 Durham NC 27710

DILLING, WENDELL LEE, b Bluffton, Ind, June 16, 36; m 58; c 1. ORGANIC CHEMISTRY. *Educ:* Manchester Col, BA, 58; Purdue Univ, PhD(org chem), 62. *Prof Exp:* Org res chemist, 62-68, SR RES CHEMIST, DOW CHEM CO, 68- *Mem:* Am Chem Soc; AAAS; Inter-Am Photochem Soc; Am Soc Photobiol; The Chem Soc. *Res:* Carbonium ion and pentacyclodecane chemistry; reaction mechanisms; spectroscopy; organic and atmospheric photochemistry; environmental chemistry. *Mailing Add:* 1810 Norwood Dr Midland MI 48640

DILLINGHAM, ELWOOD OLIVER, toxicology, see previous edition

DILLMAN, LOWELL THOMAS, b Huntington, Ind, Aug 31, 31; m 54; c 4. NUCLEAR PHYSICS. *Educ:* Manchester Col, BA, 53; Univ Ill, MS, 55, PhD(physics), 58. *Prof Exp:* Asst, Univ Ill, 53-57; from asst prof to assoc prof physics, 58-68, PROF PHYSICS, OHIO WESLEYAN UNIV, 68- *Concurrent Pos:* Consult, Health and Safety Res Div, Oak Ridge Nat Lab, 67- *Mem:* Am Phys Soc; Am Asn Physics Teachers; Health Physics Soc. *Res:* Health physics internal dosimetry. *Mailing Add:* Dept of Physics Ohio Wesleyan Univ Delaware OH 43015

DILLMAN, RICHARD CARL, b Ft Dodge, Iowa, Sept 4, 31; m 64; c 2. VETERINARY PATHOLOGY. *Educ:* Iowa State Univ, BS, 59, DVM, 61; Kans State Univ, MS, 64, PhD(path), 68. *Prof Exp:* Instr vet path, Kans State Univ, 64-68; from asst prof to assoc prof, Iowa State Univ, 68-75; PROF VET PATH, NC STATE UNIV, 75- *Mem:* Sigma Xi. *Res:* Clinical pathology; serum proteins; bovine respiratory diseases; reproductive disorders of domestic livestock; avian respiratory diseases. *Mailing Add:* Sch Vet Med NC State Univ Raleigh NC 27650

DILLON, HENRY KENNETH, analytical chemistry, physical chemistry, see previous edition

DILLON, HUGH C, JR, b Auburn, Ala, July 4, 30. MEDICINE. *Educ:* Ala Polytech Inst, BS, 51; Med Col Ala, MD, 55. *Prof Exp:* From intern to resident pediat, Univ Hosp, Birmingham, 55-57; pvt pract, Ala, 60-61; from asst prof to assoc prof pediat, 63-69, asst prof pub health & epidemiol, 66-70, assoc prof microbiol, 70-77, PROF PEDIAT, SCH MED, UNIV ALA, BIRMINGHAM, 69-, ASSOC PROF PUB HEALTH & EPIDEMIOL, 70-, PROF MICROBIOL, 77-, DIR DIV INFECTIOUS DISEASES, UNIV HOSP & CHILDRENS'S HOSP, 66- *Concurrent Pos:* Fel, Univ Hosp, Univ Minn, 57-58, Nat Found fel, Dept Pediat, 61-63; co-chmn comt infections, Univ Hosp, Univ Ala, 63-68, chmn, 68-69, mem, 69-, dir pediat out-patient clin, Children's Hosp, 64-65, dir sr teaching prog, Sch Med, 64-67, dir pediat postgrad prog, 64-67, consult clin microbiol sect, 66-, mem comt admissions, 69-, consult dent caries study, Sch Dent, 67-, coursemaster, Integrative Concepts Sect, Basic Med Sci Curriculum, Schs Med & Dent, 70-; mem comt prophylaxis streptococcal infections, Armed Forces Epidemiol Bd, 66-, assoc mem comt streptococcal & staphylococcal dis, 68-69, full mem, 69-; mem comt rheumatic fever, Am Heart Asn, 69- *Mem:* Am Acad Pediat; Am Fedn Clin Res; Soc Pediat Res; Am Soc Microbiol; Infectious Dis Soc Am. *Mailing Add:* Dept of Pediat Univ of Ala Sch of Med Birmingham AL 35294

DILLON, JOHN HENRY, b Ripon, Wis, July 10, 05; m 35, 63; c 2. POLYMER PHYSICS. *Educ:* Ripon Col, AB, 27; Univ Wis, PhD(physics), 31. *Hon Degrees:* ScD, Ripon Col, 50; MSc, Lowell Textile Inst, 51; DSc, Southeastern Mass Univ, 71. *Prof Exp:* Asst physics, Univ Wis, 27-31; physicist, Firestone Tire & Rubber Co, 31-37, head physics res div, 37-44, asst dir res, 44-46; dir res, Textile Found & Textile Res Inst, 46-51, dir, Textile Res Inst, 51-59, pres, 59-70, EMER PRES, TEXTILE RES INST, 70-, CONSULT PHYSICIST & LECTR, 70- *Concurrent Pos:* Vis lectr, Princeton Univ, 46-71; chmn, Gordon Res Conf Textiles, 59; vpres, Nat Coun Textile Educ, 57-58, pres, 58-59; Edward R Schwartz mem lectr, Am Soc Mech Eng, 69; hon fel Textile Res Inst, 71; trustee, Philadelphia Col Textiles & Sci & Ripon Col; mem panel carpet & rug indust consumer action, 73-75; Gossett Mem lectr, Sch Textiles, NC State Univ, 72. *Honors & Awards:* Harold DeWitt Smith Medal, Am Soc Testing & Mat, 55. *Mem:* Am Chem Soc; fel Am Phys Soc; Soc Rheology, (vpres, 39-41, 53-57, pres, 57-59); hon mem Fiber Soc (vpres, 60-61, pres, 61-62); hon mem & fel Textile Inst Eng. *Res:* Chemistry and physics of high polymers, rubbers and fibers; rubber and textile products; applied radioactivity; spark breakdown; photoelectric properties of zinc single crystals. *Mailing Add:* 121 Houston St PO Box 1661 Clemson SC 29631

DILLON, JOHN JOSEPH, III, b Emmitsburg, Md, Jan 15, 47; m 72; c 1. BIOCHEMISTRY. *Educ:* Mt St Mary Col, BS, 68; Univ Pittsburgh, MS, 70; Univ Del, PhD(chem), 78. *Prof Exp:* Instr chem, Va Mil Inst, 70-73; vis prof chem, Buknell Univ, 78-79; ASST PROF CHEM, SAINT MARY'S COL, 79- *Mem:* Am Chem Soc; AAAS. *Res:* Enzymology; mechanism of RNA polymerase; gene regulation; molecular biology. *Mailing Add:* Chem Dept St Marys Col Notre Dame IN 46556

DILLON, JOHN THOMAS, b Ft Worth, Tex, Dec 17, 47. STRUCTURAL GEOLOGY. *Educ:* Calif State Univ, Los Angeles, BS, 70; Univ Calif, Santa Barbara, PhD(geol), 76. *Prof Exp:* Geologist, Dept Interior, US Geol Surv, 72-74; marine geologist, Dept of Interior, Bur Land Mgt, 76-77; MINING GEOLOGIST, ALASKA DIV GEOL & GEOPHYS SURV, 77- *Concurrent Pos:* Adj assoc prof geol, Univ Alaska, 78- *Mem:* Geol Soc Am; Am Geophys Union; Sigma Xi; Am Asn Petrol Geologists; AAAS. *Res:* The San Andreas fault in southeasternmost California; how to identify and avoid geologic hazards to petroleum development of the Outer Continental Shelf; stratigraphy in Franciscan rocks; geologic history of the Brooks Range; seismicity in Alaska; solar energy in Alaska. *Mailing Add:* PO Box 80007 College AK 99708

DILLON, JOSEPH FRANCIS, JR, b Flushing, NY, May 25, 24; m 46; c 2. MAGNETISM, MAGNETO-OPTICS. *Educ:* Univ Va, AB, 44, AM, 48, PhD(physics), 49. *Prof Exp:* Physicist, Naval Ord Lab, 48 & Brit Agr Res Coun Lab, USDA, 49-52; MEM TECH STAFF, BELL TEL LABS, 52- *Concurrent Pos:* Vis scientist, Inst Solid State Physics, Univ Tokyo, 66-67, vis prof, 78; Guggenheim fel, 66-67. *Honors & Awards:* Distinguished lectr, Magnetic Soc, 81. *Mem:* Am Phys Soc; Magnetic Soc; Conf Magnetism & Magnetic Mat. *Res:* Ferromagnetism; ferrites; crystal growth; ferrimagnetic resonance; ferrimagnetic garnets; optical properties of solids; magnetic domains; optical study of metamagnetic transitions; critical phenomena. *Mailing Add:* Bell Labs Rm 1 D-328 Murray Hill NJ 07974

DILLON, LAWRENCE SAMUEL, b Reading, Pa, Apr 6, 10; m 32; c 1. EVOLUTION. *Educ:* Univ Pittsburgh, BS, 33; Agr & Mech Col Tex, MS, 50, PhD(entomol), 54. *Prof Exp:* Chemist, Glidden Co, 34-37; cur entomol, Reading Pub Mus, 37-48; from instr to prof, 48-75, EMER PROF BIOL, TEX A&M UNIV, 75- *Concurrent Pos:* NSF sci fac fel, Queensland, Australia, 59-60. *Mem:* Fel AAAS; NY Acad Sci; Am Soc Zoologists; Soc Study Evolution; Acad Zool. *Res:* Evolution and phylogeny of living things; pleistocene paleoecology and bioclimatology; systematic zoology; speciation; evolution of mammalian brain; neuroanatomy. *Mailing Add:* Rockwood Park Estates 1904 Cedarwood Dr Bryan TX 77801

DILLON, MARCUS LUNSFORD, JR, b Charleston, WVa, Feb 7, 24; m 47; c 8. SURGERY. *Educ:* Duke Univ, BS & MD, 48. *Prof Exp:* Intern surg, Duke Univ Hosp, 47-49, from jr asst res to sr asst res, 49-55, resident surg, 55-56, from instr to assoc prof, 53-71; PROF SURG, UNIV KY, 71- *Concurrent Pos:* Asst chief surg serv, Vet Admin Hosp, Durham, 56-71; chief thoracic surg, 64-71; asst chief surg serv & chief thoracic & cardiovasc surg, Vet Admin Hosp, Lexington, 71- *Mem:* Am Col Surg; Am Asn Thoracic Surg; Soc Thoracic Surg; AMA. *Res:* Hypothermia; extracorporeal circulation and coagulation; cardiovascular disease and hypothermia; infections; cancer. *Mailing Add:* Vet Admin Hosp Lexington KY 40511

DILLON, OSCAR WENDELL, JR, b Franklin, Pa, May 27, 28; m 60; c 4. ENGINEERING MECHANICS. *Educ:* Univ Cincinnati, AeroEng, 51; Columbia Univ, MS, 55, DrEngSc, 59. *Prof Exp:* Aeronaut engr, Cornell Aeronaut Lab, 53-54; asst prof mech, Johns Hopkins Univ, 58-63; lectr aerospace eng, Princeton Univ, 63-65; assoc prof, 65-67, chmn dept, 67-72, PROF ENG MECH, UNIV KY, 67- *Honors & Awards:* Res Award, Am Soc Eng Educ, 67 & Univ Ky, 68. *Mem:* Soc Natural Philos; Am Soc Mech Engrs. *Res:* Theoretical and experimental mechanics of solids, especially in the inelastic range. *Mailing Add:* Dept of Eng Mech Univ of Ky Lexington KY 40506

DILLON, RAYMOND DONALD, b Superior, Wis, Apr 19, 25; m 50; c 3. ZOOLOGY. *Educ:* Wis State Univ, Superior, BS, 49; Syracuse Univ, MS, 51; Univ Wis, PhD(zool), 55. *Prof Exp:* Asst prof biol, Nebr State Teachers Col, 54-60; asst prof, Ball State Teachers Col, 60-62; asst prof zool & Physiol, Univ Nebr, 62-65; prof zool & chmn dept, 65-69, PROF BIOL, UNIV SDAK, 69- *Concurrent Pos:* Partic, NSF US Antarctic Res Prog, 67-69, Arctic Biome Prog, Naval Arctic Res Lab, Alaska, 71-72; vis res scholar, Ind Univ, 80-81. *Mem:* AAAS; Soc Protozool; Nat Asn Biol Teachers; Am Inst Biol Sci; Am Micros Soc. *Res:* Protozoology; research in free-living and parasitic protozoa. *Mailing Add:* Dept Biol Univ SDak Vermillion SD 57069

DILLON, RICHARD THOMAS, b Pocatello, Idaho, May 2, 28; m 51; c 4. RADIATION GENETICS, SYSTEMS ANALYSIS. *Educ:* Idaho State Col, BS, 52; Univ Ore, MS, 54, PhD(abstr harmonic anal), 58. *Prof Exp:* Staff mem systs anal, 58-61; staff mem of dir advan systs study, 61-69 & planetary quarantine, 69-72, STAFF MEM BIOSYSTS STUDIES, SANDIA LABS, 72- *Mem:* Am Microbiol Soc; Am Inst Biol Sci; AAAS; NY Acad Sci; Sigma Xi. *Res:* Experimentally determining the inactivating and mutagenic effects of heat and ionizing radiation separately and in combination on various cellular systems, recently with dry spores including the effect of relative humidity. *Mailing Add:* 5808 Pojoaque Rd NE Albuquerque NM 87110

DILLON, ROBERT MORTON, b Seattle, Wash, Oct 27, 23; m 43; c 3. BUILDING RESEARCH. *Educ:* Univ Wash, BArch, 49; Univ Fla, MAArch, 54. *Prof Exp:* Asst prof archit, Clemson Col, 49-50; instr, Univ Fla, 50-52, asst prof, 52-55; staff architect, Bldg Res Adv Bd, Nat Res Coun-Nat Acad Sci, 55-57, proj dir, 57-58, exec dir, 58-77; EXEC ASST TO PRESIDENT, NAT INST BLDG SCI, 78- *Concurrent Pos:* Designer-draftsman, SC, 49-50; architect, Fla, 52-55; lectr, Cath Univ Am, 57-63; consult, Educ Facilities Labs, Inc, NY, 58-71; ed reports & publ, Bldg Res Adv Bd, 58-77; adv bd dirs, Washington Ctr Metrop Studies, 58-60; mem sub-panel housing, White House Panel Civilian Technol, 61-62; exec secy, US Nat Comt for Int Coun Bldg Res, Studies & Documentation, Nat Res Coun, Nat Acad Sci-Nat Acad Eng, 62-74; mem adv comt low income housing demonstration prog, HUD, 64-66; mem, Am Inst Archit adv comt, Voc Rehab Admin, HEW, 67-68; mem, ERIC-CEF Adv Coun, Univ Wis, 67-69; mem, Nat Adv Coun Res in Energy Conserv, 75-78. *Mem:* Corp mem Am Inst Archit; Am Soc Civil Engrs; Am Inst Steel Construct; Am Real Estate & Urban Econ Asn; Nat Acad Code Admin. *Res:* Housing, building and city planning. *Mailing Add:* Nat Inst Bldg Sci 1015 15th St NW Washington DC 20005

DILLON, ROY DEAN, b Peoria, Ill, Dec 10, 29; m 53; c 3. AGRICULTURE. *Educ:* Univ Ill, BS, 52, EdM, 58, EdD, 65. *Prof Exp:* Teacher high schs, Ill, 52-53 & 54-61; asst dir safety, Ill Agr Asn, 61-62; assoc prof agr, Morehead State Univ, 64-67; assoc prof, 67-70, prof sec educ, 70-80, PROF AGR, UNIV NEBR, LINCOLN, 70- *Res:* Knowledges and abilities required in agriculture by workers in off-farm agricultural occupations. *Mailing Add:* 302 Agr Hall Univ of Nebr Lincoln NE 68506

DILLON, THOMAS ANDREW, b White Plains, NY, June 30, 44; m 68; c 2. PHYSICS, CHEMISTRY. *Educ:* Harvard Univ, AB, 66; Univ Colo, PhD, 69. *Prof Exp:* Res physicist, Off Telecommun, Boulder, Colo, 67-69; physicist, Nat Bur Standards, Dept Com, 69-71, sect chief, 71-73, prog analyst, 74, sr prog analyst, 75-76; dep div dir, Nuclear Res & Appln Div, Dept Energy, 76-77, actg dir, Advan Systs & Mat Prod Div, 77-78; dep dir, Nat Bur Standards, Dept Com, 78-80, dep asst secy, Nuclear Reactor Progs, Dept Energy, 80-81, PRIN DEP ASST SECY, NUCLEAR ENERGY, NAT BUR STANDARDS, 81- *Honors & Awards:* Super Performance Award, Nat Bur Standards, Dept Com, 72 & Outstanding Achievement Award, 74; Meritorious Serv Award, Dept Energy, 77. *Mem:* Am Phys Soc; AAAS. *Res:* Theoretical calculations of molecular collision processes, particularly line broadening and volocity-volume energy transfer rates. *Mailing Add:* Nat Bur Standards Washington DC 20234

DILLON, WILLIAM PATRICK, b Fall River, Mass, Dec 13, 36; m 61; c 3. GEOLOGICAL OCEANOGRAPHY. *Educ:* Bates Col, BS, 58; Rensselaer Polytech Inst, MS, 61; Univ RI, PhD(geol oceanog), 69. *Prof Exp:* Res assoc marine geol, Narragansett Marine Lab, Univ RI, 61-64, instr oceanog, Sch Oceanog, 68-69; asst prof geol, San Jose State Col, 69-71; MARINE GEOLOGIST, US GEOL SURV, 71- *Concurrent Pos:* Consult, Mystic Oceanog Co, Conn, 68-69. *Mem:* Geol Soc Am; Sigma Xi; Am Geophys Union. *Res:* Structure and development of continental margins; US eastern margin south of Cape Hatteras; coastal evolution. *Mailing Add:* Off of Marine Geol US Geol Surv Woods Hole MA 02543

DILLS, CHARLES E, b La Moure, NDak, Apr 20, 22; m 61; c 1. PHYSICAL CHEMISTRY, ORGANIC CHEMISTRY. *Educ:* NDak State Univ, BS, 49; George Washington Univ, MS, 51; Harvard Univ, PhD(chem), 56. *Prof Exp:* Res assoc org chem, Columbia Univ, 54-56; res chemist, Nat Res Corp, Mass, 56-58; instr chem, Northwest Mo State Col, 58-59, asst prof, 59-60; asst ed res, Chem & Eng News, 60-61; prof sci, Deep Springs Col, 61-63; asst prof chem, 63-67, assoc prof, 67-80, PROF CHEM, CALIF POLYTECH STATE UNIV, SAN LUIS OBISPO, 80- *Res:* Mechanisms of organic reactions. *Mailing Add:* Dept of Chem Calif Polytech State Univ San Luis Obispo CA 93407

DILORENZO, JAMES V, b New York, NY, Feb 27, 41; m 63; c 2. PHYSICAL CHEMISTRY, INORGANIC CHEMISTRY. *Educ:* Hofstra Univ, BS, 62; State Univ NY Stony Brook, MS, 62, PhD(chem), 67. *Prof Exp:* Fel chem, Yale Univ, 67-68; mem tech staff, 68-73, supvr microwave mat & processes group, 73-80, HEAD, SPEC MAT & DEVICES DEPT, BELL LABS, 80- *Mem:* Electrochem Soc. *Res:* Epitaxial growth of compound semiconductors; growth of gallium arsenide as epitaxial structures for microwave device applications; semiconductor device physics and fabrication with particular attention to microwave field effect transitors and high speed III-V devices. *Mailing Add:* Bell Labs Murray Hill NJ 07971

DIL PARE, ARMAND LEON, b New York, NY, Aug 12, 32; m 52; c 1. MACHINE DESIGN, AUTOMATIC CONTROL SYSTEMS. *Educ:* City Col New York, BME, 53; Columbia Univ, MSME, 57, PhD(kinematics mechanisms), 65. *Prof Exp:* Instr mech eng, City Col New York, 53; struct engr, Repub Aviation Corp, 53-56; mem tech staff, Bell Tel Labs, NY, 56-62; div engr, Lundy Electronics & Systs Inc, 62-65; asst prof mech eng, Columbia Univ, 65-70; assoc dir res & develop, Defense Systs Div, Lundy Electronics & Systs, Inc, 70-75; DIR COOP ENGR SCI PROGS, JACKSONVILLE UNIV, 78- *Concurrent Pos:* Consult, Lundy Electronics & Systs, Inc, 65-70; assoc prof mech eng, Fla Inst Technol, 75-78, prof, 78- *Mem:* Am Soc Mech Engrs; Am Soc Eng Educ. *Res:* Kinematic analysis and synthesis of mechanisms; dynamics of machinery; computer-aided-design. *Mailing Add:* Jacksonville Univ Jacksonville FL 32211

DILS, ROBERT EARL, b Ohio, July 6, 19; m 42; c 3. ACADEMIC ADMINISTRATION, RESOURCE MANAGEMENT. *Educ:* Colo Agr & Mech Col, BSF, 46, MF, 47; Mich State Col, 52. *Prof Exp:* Res asst forestry, Colo Agr Exp Sta, 46-47; timber mgt asst, Helena Nat Forest, Mont, 47; from instr to assoc prof forestry, Mich State Col, 47-55; assoc prof forestry, Univ Mich, 55-58; assoc dean col forestry & natural resources, 65-69, prof watershed mgt, 58-80, EMER PROF EARTH RESOURCES, COLO STATE UNIV, 80-, DEAN COL FORESTRY & NATURAL RESOURCES, 69- *Concurrent Pos:* Cooperator, Coweeta Hydrol Lab, Ga, 52-56; collabr, Mich Hydrol Res Proj, 53-55, Lake States Forest Exp Sta, US Forest Serv, 53-58 & Rocky Mt Forest & Range Exp Sta, 59-; leader watershed mgt unit, 58-65, Col Forestry & Natural Resources, Colo; Fulbright res scholar, NZ, 64-65; consult, Food & Agr Orgn, UN, Arg; assoc ed, J Forestry, Soc Am Foresters; dir forest environ res, USDA Forest Serv, Washington, DC, 77- *Mem:* Fel Soc Am Foresters; Am Geophys Union; fel Soil Conserv Soc Am; Am Soc Agron; Soil Sci Soc Am. *Mailing Add:* Col Forestry & Nat Resources Colo State Univ Ft Collins CO 80521

DILS, ROBERT JAMES, b Dayton, Ohio, Oct 2, 19; m 47; c 4. SCIENCE EDUCATION. *Educ:* Eastern Ky Univ, BS; Marshall Univ, MA, 60. *Prof Exp:* Teacher high sch, Ky, 48-51; instr chem, Ashland Jr Col, 51-57; chmn dept sci, Paul G Blazer High Sch, 57-62; coord sci, Sec Sch, Ashland, Ky, 62-63; asst prof, 64-67, ASSOC PROF PHYS SCI, MARSHALL UNIV, 67- *Mem:* AAAS; Am Asn Higher Educ. *Res:* Science education and curriculum development in college and secondary schools. *Mailing Add:* Dept of Phys Sci Marshall Univ Huntington WV 25701

DILTS, JOSEPH ALSTYNE, b Sommerville, NJ, Sept 12, 42. INORGANIC CHEMISTRY. *Educ:* Ohio Wesleyan Univ, BA, 64; Northwestern Univ, PhD(chem), 69. *Prof Exp:* Fel Ga Inst Technol, 68-70; asst prof, 70-78, ASSOC PROF CHEM, UNIV NC, GREENSBORO, 78- *Concurrent Pos:* Vis prof chem, Col William & Mary, 76-77. *Mem:* Am Chem Soc; The Chem Soc; NAm Thermal Anal Soc. *Res:* Organometallic and hydride chemistry of the main group elements; application of thermal analysis techniques to organometallic chemistry. *Mailing Add:* Dept of Chem Univ of NC Greensboro NC 27412

DILTS, PRESTON VINE, JR, b Louisiana, Mo, Jan 16, 34; m 57; c 3. OBSTETRICS & GYNECOLOGY. *Educ:* Wash Univ, BA, 55; Northwestern Univ, MD, 59, MS, 61; Am Bd Obstet & Gynec, dipl, 69, cert fetal & maternal med, 75. *Prof Exp:* From asst prof to assoc prof obstet & gynec, Sch Med, Univ Ky, 68-72; prof & chmn dept, Sch Med, Univ NDak, 73-75; PROF OBSTET & GYNEC & CHMN DEPT, SCH MED, UNIV TENN, 75- *Concurrent Pos:* Examr, Am Bd Obstet & Gynec; USPHS fel reprod physiol, Sch Med, Univ Calif, Los Angeles, 67. *Mem:* Am Col Obstet & Gynec; Am Col Surg; Soc Gynec Invest; Soc Obstet Anesthesia & Perinatology. *Res:* Reproductive physiology, specifically the placental transfer of drugs and trace metals. *Mailing Add:* Dept of Obstet & Gynec Univ Tenn Sch Med Memphis TN 38163

DILTS, ROBERT VOORHEES, b Plainfield, NJ, June 18, 29. ANALYTICAL CHEMISTRY. *Educ:* Wesleyan Univ, AB, 51; Princeton Univ, MA, 53, PhD(chem), 54. *Prof Exp:* From instr to asst prof chem, Williams Col, 54-60; asst prof, 60-68, ASSOC PROF CHEM, VANDERBILT UNIV, 68- *Concurrent Pos:* Dir undergrad prog chem, Vanderbilt Univ, 67-69; vis assoc prof, Univ Kans, 69-70; dir undergrad prog chem, Vanderbilt Univ, 74- *Mem:* Am Chem Soc; Sigma Xi. *Res:* Coulometric titrations; atomic absorption spectroscopy; complexometric titrations. *Mailing Add:* Dept of Chem Vanderbilt Univ Nashville TN 37235

DI LUZIO, NICHOLAS ROBERT, b Hazleton, Pa, May 4, 26; m 48; c 3. PHYSIOLOGY. *Educ:* Univ Scranton, BS, 50; Univ Tenn, PhD(physiol), 54. *Prof Exp:* From instr to prof physiol & biophys, Med Units, Univ Tenn, 55-68, chmn dept, 64-68; PROF PHYSIOL & CHMN DEPT, SCH MED, TULANE UNIV, 68- *Concurrent Pos:* Lederle med fac award, 58-61; mem Tenn adv comt atomic energy, 58-68; consult, Riker Lab, 61-70; mem sci adv comt, Nat Coun Alcoholism, 63-68; consult, Uniroyal, 68-70 & NIH, 70-75; ed, Advan Exp Med & Biol, Jour. *Honors & Awards:* Res Award, Reticuloendothelial Soc, 64. *Mem:* Am Physiol Soc; Soc Exp Biol & Med; Am Asn Study Liver Dis; Reticuloendothelial Soc; Am Heart Asn. *Res:* Metabolism of lipids and radioactive colloids; host defense mechanisms and neoplasia; hepatic cell function, liver injury; physio-pathology of reticuloendothelial system. *Mailing Add:* Dept of Physiol Tulane Univ Sch of Med New Orleans LA 70112

DILWORTH, BENJAMIN CONROY, b Monroe, La, Sept 29, 31; m 55; c 3. POULTRY NUTRITION, BIOCHEMISTRY. *Educ:* Miss State Univ, BS, 59, MS, 62, PhD(poultry nutrit), 66. *Prof Exp:* Res asst poultry nutrit, 59-66, asst prof poultry sci, 66-73, assoc prof poultry nutrit & poultry sci, 73-78, prof poultry nutrit, 78-80, PROF POULTRY SCI, MISS STATE UNIV, 78- *Mem:* Poultry Sci Asn; Sigma Xi; World Poultry Sci Asn. *Res:* Calcium, phosphorus and vitamin D3 interrelationships and requirements of poultry; protein quality of feedstuffs; sodium requirement of poultry. *Mailing Add:* Dept of Poultry Sci Miss State Univ PO Box 5188 Mississippi State MS 39762

DILWORTH, ROBERT HAMILTON, III, b Bryson City, NC, Aug 6, 30; m 53; c 4. TECHNICAL VENTURE MANAGEMENT. *Educ:* Univ Tenn, BS, 52. *Prof Exp:* Chief engr, Spec Instruments Lab, Inc, Tenn, 54-55; instrument engr, Oak Ridge Inst Nuclear Studies, 55-56, develop engr, Oak Ridge Nat Lab, 56-62, chief electronics engr, Ortec, Inc, 62-66, prod mgr electronics, 66-68, mgr life sci prod, 68-76; head mgt sect, Fusion Energy Div, 76-81, TECH ASST, CENT MGT OFF, OAK RIDGE NAT LAB, 81. *Mem:* Inst Elec & Electronics Engrs. *Res:* Analysis and management of new technological ventures; modular nuclear instrumentation for physics research; engineering and product line management; research management. *Mailing Add:* I200 4500N Oak Ridge Nat Lab PO Box X Oak Ridge TN 37830

DILWORTH, ROBERT PALMER, b Hemet, Calif, Dec 2, 14; m 40; c 2. MATHEMATICS. *Educ:* Calif Inst Technol, BS, 36, PhD(math), 39. *Prof Exp:* Sterling res fel, Yale Univ, 39-40, instr math, 40-43; from asst prof to assoc prof, 43-51, PROF MATH, CALIF INST TECHNOL, 51- *Mem:* Am Math Soc; Math Asn Am. *Res:* Lattice theory; mathematical statistics; structure and arithmetical theory of noncommutative residuated lattices. *Mailing Add:* Dept of Math Calif Inst Technol Pasadena CA 91125

DIMAGGIO, ANTHONY, III, b New Orleans, La, Aug 17, 35; m 60; c 2. BIOCHEMISTRY. *Educ:* Loyola Univ, La, BS, 56; La State Univ, PhD(biochem), 61. *Prof Exp:* Asst prof chem, 61-64, ASSOC PROF CHEM, LOYOLA UNIV, LA, 64-, CHMN DEPT, 67- *Concurrent Pos:* Consult, Photo-Dek, Inc, 64-66; dir res strontium fallout in tooth study, 64-66, co-prin investr, 66-68; chmn grad coun, Loyola Univ, 68-70; consult legal, 77- *Mem:* AAAS; Am Chem Soc; Am Soc Ichthyologists & Herpetologists. *Res:* Comparative biochemistry of reptiles, especially the lizard, Anolis carolinensis, particularly its endocrinology and metabolism; nutrition and social issues. *Mailing Add:* Dept of Chem Loyola Univ New Orleans LA 70118

DI MAGGIO, FRANK LOUIS, b New York, NY, Sept 2, 29; m 63; c 2. STRUCTURAL MECHANICS. *Educ:* Columbia Univ, BS, 50, MS, 51, PhD(civil eng), 54. *Prof Exp:* PROF CIVIL ENG, COLUMBIA UNIV, 56- *Concurrent Pos:* Consult, Weidlinger Assocs, 56-; tech consult, Implements & Bal Comn, US Golf Asn, 58-66; NSF sr fel, Turin Polytech Inst, Italy, 62-63. *Mem:* Fel Am Soc Civil Engrs; Sigma Xi. *Res:* Structural dynamics; fluid-structure interaction; constitutive equations for geological materials. *Mailing Add:* Dept of Civil Eng Columbia Univ New York NY 10027

DI MAIO, VINCENT J M, b Brooklyn, NY, Mar 22, 41; c 2. FORENSIC MEDICINE. *Educ:* State Univ NY Downstate Med Ctr, MD, 65; Am Bd Path, cert anat & clin path, 70 & cert forensic path, 71. *Prof Exp:* Chief, Legal Med Sect, Armed Forces Inst Path, 70-71 & Wound Ballistics Sect, 71-72; med examr, Dallas County, 72-81; assoc prof path, Med Sch Univ Tex, Dallas, 75-81; PROF PATH, UNIV TEX, SAN ANTONIO, 81- *Concurrent Pos:* Chief med examr, Bexar County, 81- *Mem:* Am Acad Forensic Sci; Am Soc Clin Pathologists; Col Am Pathologists. *Res:* Gunshot wounds; wound ballistics. *Mailing Add:* Univ Tex San Antonio TX 78228

DIMARCO, G ROBERT, b Camden, NJ, July 31, 27; m 49; c 5. FOOD SCIENCE & TECHNOLOGY. *Educ:* Rutgers Univ, BS, 54, PhD(plant pathol), 59. *Prof Exp:* From asst prof to prof food sci, Ruters Univ, 59-74; dir, Basic & Health Sci, 75-77, DIR, CENT RES, GEN FOODS CORP, 77- *Concurrent Pos:* Hon prof food sci, Cook Col, Ruters Univ, 75-; Comt mem, Adv Bd Mil Personnel Supplies, Nat Res Coun, 78-81 & Food Indust Liaison Adv Panel, AMA, 78- *Mem:* Fel Inst Food Technologists. *Res:* Res administration in nutrition; physiology; biochemistry; physical chemistry; engineering; research from very basic to totally applied. *Mailing Add:* Gen Foods Tech Ctr 250 North St White Plains NY 10625

DI MARIA, DONELLI JOSEPH, b Waterbury, Conn, Mar 18, 46. SOLID STATE PHYSICS. *Educ:* Lehigh Univ, BS, 68, MS, 70, PhD(physics), 73. *Prof Exp:* Fel, 73-74, RES STAFF MEM INSULATOR PHYSICS, THOMAS J WATSON RES CTR, IBM CORP, 73- *Res:* Optical and electrical properties of insulators and their interfaces with other materials. *Mailing Add:* Thomas J Watson Res Ctr IBM Corp PO Box 218 Yorktown NY 10598

DIMARTINI, RAYMOND, b Jersey City, NJ. ELECTROOPTICAL MATERIALS. *Educ:* St Peters Col, BS, MS, 61; Stevens Inst Technol, PhD(chem), 64. *Prof Exp:* DIR, RES DYNAMICS, INC, 74-; PROF CHEM, LONG ISLAND UNIV, 75-; PROF CHEM, MANHATTAN COL, 81- *Concurrent Pos:* Mem staff, Bell Labs, 72-74; fel res scientist, Port Authority NY & NJ, 64-72; consult, Res Dynamics, Inc, 74- *Mem:* Am Chem Soc; Am Physiol Soc; NY Acad Sci; Sigma Xi; Soc Photo-Optical Instrumentation Engrs. *Res:* Chemical instrumentation, data processing and collection; electronic materials, electronic instrumentation and photonics; computer software and hardware. *Mailing Add:* Res Dynamics Inc Village Sta PO Box 65 New York NY 10014

DIMARZIO, EDMUND ARMAND, b Philadelphia, Pa, Mar 23, 32; m 56; c 3. PHYSICS. *Educ:* St Joseph's Col, Pa, BS, 55; Univ Pa, MS, 60; Cath Univ Am, PhD, 67. *Prof Exp:* Physicist, Am Viscose Co, 56-62; mem tech staff theoret chem, Bell Tel Labs, 62-63; PHYSICIST, NAT BUR STAND, 63- *Honors & Awards:* High Polymer Physics Prize, 67; Stratton Award, 71. *Mem:* Fel Am Phys Soc. *Res:* Helixcoil transition in biological macromolecules; glass transition in polymers; liquid crystal phase transitions; surface polymers; kinetics of crystallization. *Mailing Add:* Polymer Physics Sect Nat Bur of Stand Washington DC 20034

DIMASI, GABRIEL JOSEPH, b Harrison, NJ, July 11, 36; m 62; c 5. ELECTROCHEMISTRY, CHEMICAL ENGINEERING. *Educ:* Newark Col Eng, BSChE, 58, MS, 63. *Prof Exp:* Chem engr primary batteries, US Army Electronics Command Labs, 58-60, engr fuel cells, 60-63, engr magnesium batteries, 63-65, res engr, 66-67, group leader electrode kinetics, 67-72, chmn dept chem, educ & training, 66-72, GROUP LEADER ELECTRONICS TECHNOL & DEVICES LAB, US ARMY ELECTRONICS COMMAND, 72-, CHMN DEPT MAT SCI & ENG, 72- *Concurrent Pos:* Lectr, Rensselaer Polytech Inst, 71. *Honors & Awards:* Spec Awards, US Army Electronics Command, 68, 69 & 70. *Mem:* Electrochem Soc; Am Inst Chem Eng; Am Inst Chem; Int Soc Electrochem. *Res:* Optimum design for lithium-sulfurdioxide cells; determination of the iron-moisture cycle in lithium-sulfurdioxide cells; analytical methods for determining the water content carbon cathode porosity and electrical capacity in lithium-sulfurdioxide cells; techniques for fabricating and analyzing high rate cathodes for non-agueous systems. *Mailing Add:* 24 Pal Dr Wayside Ocean NJ 07712

DIMAURO, SALVATORE, b Verona, Italy, Nov 14, 39; m 68; c 2. NEUROLOGY. *Educ:* Univ Padova, Italy, MD, 63, Specilization neurol, 67. *Prof Exp:* Inst gen path, Univ Padova, Italy, 64-68; fel neurol, Univ Pa, 68-69, instr & asst prof, 72-74; assoc prof, 74-78, PROF NEUROL, COLUMBIA UNIV, 78- *Mem:* Am Neurol Asn; Am Acad Neurol; Soc Neurosci; AAAS. *Res:* Biochemical research in neuromuscular diseases, with particular emphasis on hereditary disorders of muscle metabolism; metabolic mypathies; mitochondrial mypathies. *Mailing Add:* 4-420 Col Physicians & Surgeons Columbia Univ 630 W 168th St New York NY 10032

DIMEFF, JOHN, b Detroit, Mich, July 2, 21; m 44; c 2. PHYSICS. *Educ:* Harvard Univ, BS, 42. *Prof Exp:* Radio engr, Naval Res Lab, 43-44 & 45-46; physicist, Ames Res Ctr, NASA, 46, aeronaut res scientist, 46-53, chief wind tunnel instrument br, 56-59, asst chief, Instrumentation Div, 59-67, chief, 67-71, asst dir instrumentation res, 71-75; PRES, DIMEFF ASSOCS, 75-; PRES, SIGNATHICS, 77- *Concurrent Pos:* Adj prof dent, Univ Calif, San Francisco, 75- *Res:* Sensors; instrumentation; electronics; data processing. *Mailing Add:* Dimeff Assocs 5346 Greenside Dr San Jose CA 95127

DIMENT, WILLIAM HORACE, b Oswego, NY, Oct 15, 27; m 58; c 3. GEOPHYSICS. *Educ:* Williams Col, AB, 49; Harvard Univ, AM, 51, PhD(geophys), 54. *Prof Exp:* Explor geophysicist, Calif Co, 53-56; geophysicist, US Geol Surv, 56-60, chief, Br Theoret Goephys, 60-62, res geophysicist, 62-65; prof geol, Univ Rochester, 65-73; RES GEOPHYSICIST, US GEOL SURV, 73- *Concurrent Pos:* NSF sr fel, Yale Univ, 64-65. *Mem:* AAAS; Geol Soc Am; Seismol Soc Am; Am Geophys Union; Soc Explor Geophysicists. *Res:* Terrestrial heat flow; seismology; gravity; limnology. *Mailing Add:* US Geol Surv Box 25046 MS 966 Denver Fed Ctr Denver CO 80225

DIMICCO, JOSEPH ANTHONY, b New Haven, Conn, June 13, 47. PHARMACOLOGY, NEUROBIOLOGY. *Educ:* Tufts Univ, BS, 69; Georgetown Univ, PhD(pharmacol), 78. *Prof Exp:* Staff fel, Lab Clin Sci, NIMH, 78-80; ASST PROF PHARMACOL, SCH MED, IND UNIV, 80- *Mem:* AAAS; Soc Neurosci. *Res:* CNS control of cardiovascular function; neuropharmacology of central and peripheral cardiovascular control mechanisms. *Mailing Add:* Dept Pharmacol Ind Univ Sch Med 1100 W Michigan St Indianapolis IN 46223

DIMICHELE, LEONARD VINCENT, b Williamsport, Pa, Sept 12, 52; m 79. ICHTHEOLOGY. *Educ:* Villanova Univ, BA, 74; Univ Del, MS, 77, PhD(physiol), 80. *Prof Exp:* NIH FEL ANIMAL PHYSIOL, JOHNS HOPKINS UNIV, 80- *Mem:* AAAS; Am Soc Zoologists; Am Soc Icthyologists & Herpetologists. *Res:* Ways Teleosts adapt to their environment; mechanism of hatching in Teleosts and the relationship between polymorphic genes and the development, growth and physiological performance of Fundulus heteroclitus. *Mailing Add:* Biol Dept Johns Hopkins Univ Baltimore MD 21218

DIMICHELE, WILLIAM ANTHONY, b Wilmington, Del, May 13, 51; m 72; c 1. PALEOBOTANY, PLANT PALEOECOLOGY. *Educ:* Drexel Univ, BS, 74; Univ Ill, Urbana, MS, 76, PhD(bot), 79. *Prof Exp:* ASST PROF BOT, UNIV WASH, 79- *Concurrent Pos:* Vis lectr bot, Univ Ill, Urbana, 78; res assoc, Coal Sect, Ill State Geol Surv, 79; vis res scholar, Ind Univ, 80. *Honors & Awards:* Isbella C Cookson Award, Bot Soc Am, 79. *Mem:* Sigma Xi; Bot Soc Am; Soc Study Evolution; Geol Soc Am; Soc Econ Palcontoogists & Mineralogists. *Res:* Terrestrial paleoecology, particularly investigation of Carboniferous plant communities and patterns of change in vegetation through time; relationships among community paleoecological parameters, species-level variability and evolutionary patterns. *Mailing Add:* Dept Bot AJ-10 Univ Wash Seattle WA 98195

DIMICK, PAUL SLAYTON, b Burlington, Vt, Sept 15, 35; m 58; c 3. FOOD SCIENCE. *Educ:* Univ Vt, BS, 58, MS, 60; Pa State Univ, PhD(dairy sci), 64. *Prof Exp:* Asst dairy sci, Univ Vt, 58-60; asst dairy sci, 61-63, res asst, 63-64, res assoc, 64-66, from asst prof to assoc prof food sci, 66-75, PROF FOOD SCI, PA STATE UNIV, 75- *Mem:* Am Dairy Sci Asn; Inst Food Technol. *Res:* Ruminant lipid metabolism, especially milk fat synthesis; flavor research, especially lipid precursors. *Mailing Add:* 116 Borland Lab Pa State Univ University Park PA 16802

DI MILO, ANTHONY J, b Philadelphia, Pa, May 6, 24; m 48, 70; c 3. POLYMER CHEMISTRY. *Educ:* Temple Univ, AB, 48; Mass Inst Technol, PhD(org chem), 53. *Prof Exp:* Res chemist, Atlantic Ref Co, 53-58; from chemist to sr chemist, Aerojet Solid Propulsion Co, 58-66, chem supvr, 66-78; MX proj engr, 78-82, STAFF SCIENTIST, TRW SYSTS, 82- *Concurrent Pos:* Adj prof Drexel Inst, 55-58. *Mem:* Am Chem Soc; Sci Res Soc Am. *Res:* Reaction kinetics; petrochemicals; chemistry of solids rocket propellants; chemistry of isocyanates, epoxides and aziridines. *Mailing Add:* Space Syst Div TRW Inc One Space Park Redondo Beach CA 90278

DIMITMAN, JEROME EUGENE, b New York, NY, Sept 24, 20; m 44; c 3. PLANT PATHOLOGY. *Educ:* Univ Calif, BS, 43, MS, 49, PhD, 58. *Prof Exp:* Assoc plant pathologist, State Dept Agr, Calif, 47-49; chmn dept biol sci, 49-73, PROF BIOL, CALIF STATE POLYTECH UNIV, POMONA, 49- *Mem:* Am Phytopath Soc; Bot Soc Am; Asn Trop Biol. *Res:* Citrus diseases, viruses; Phytophthora physiology; subtropical plants; crop diseases; Phytophthora citrophthora host range studies; citrus virus studies; Exocortis virus effect on callus formation. *Mailing Add:* Dept Biol Sci Calif State Polytech Univ Pomona CA 91768

DIMITRIJEVICH, SLOBODAN DAN, b Novi Vrbas, Yugoslavia, Aug 13, 40; Brit citizen; m 68; c 1. ANTIVIRAL CHEMOTHERAPY. *Educ:* Nat Coun Technol Awards, Eng, dipl, 64; Bath Univ, Eng, BSc, 66, PRD(carbohydrates), 69. *Prof Exp:* Asst exp officer, bio-org chem, Sch Biol Sci, Bath Univ, Eng, 67-69; fel, dept chem, Univ Alta, 69-71; syntex fel, Inst Molecular Biol Syntex Res, Calif, 71-73; res fel, Glycoprotein Res Unit, dept bot, Univ Durham, 73-74; sr res officer, org chem, dept chem, Birkbeck Col, Univ London, 74-76; sr res chemist & head anal dept, Nucleic Acid Res Inst ICN Pharmaceut, Inc, 76, tech dir, Chem & Radiosotopes Div, 76-79; RES ASST PROF, BIOL APPLICATIONS ISTOPIC LABELING, DEPT BIOPHYS SCI FAC HEALTH SCI, STATE UNIV NY, BUFFALO, 79- *Concurrent Pos:* Chem res consult, Corp Drug Develop & Regulatory, Affairs Dept, ICN Pharmaceut, Inc, 78-79. *Mem:* Am Chem Soc; Royal Soc Chem. *Res:* Synthesis, structure and activity of novel nucleosides and carbohydrates exhibiting antivirel activity; carbohydrate components of glycoproteins involved in virus-host cell interaction; stable istopes in biochemical studies. *Mailing Add:* Dept Biophys Sci Fac Health Sci 118 Cary Hall State Univ NY Buffalo NY 14214

DIMITROFF, EDWARD, b Nancy, France, Feb 27, 27; US citizen; m 51; c 2. ORGANIC CHEMISTRY, PHYSICAL CHEMISTRY. *Educ:* Univ Denver, BS, 56; St Mary's Univ, Tex, MS, 65. *Prof Exp:* Res chemist, US Naval Ord Test Sta, 56-59; from assoc res chemist to sr res chemist, 59-66, staff scientist, 66-69, mgr petrol technol, 70-78, asst dir energy technol, 78-80, DIR PETROL RES, SOUTHWEST RES INST, 80- *Mem:* Am Chem Soc; fel Am Inst Chemists; Soc Automotive Eng; Am Soc Testing & Mats. *Res:* Mechanisms of dispersancy in oil media; engine sludge, varnish, rust formation; liquid fuels crystallization; development of synthetic fuels, lubricants and novel energy systems; technical management. *Mailing Add:* 8530 Pendragon San Antonio TX 78250

DIMITROFF, GEORGE ERNEST, b New York, NY, July 22, 38; m 61; c 3. ALGEBRA. *Educ:* Reed Col, BA, 60; Univ Ore, MA, 62, PhD(math), 64. *Prof Exp:* Asst prof math, Knox Col, Ill, 64-73; MEM FAC, EVERGREEN STATE COL, 73- *Mem:* Am Math Soc; Math Asn Am. *Res:* Partially ordered topological spaces. *Mailing Add:* Evergreen State Col Olympia WA 98505

DIMMEL, DONALD R, b Waseca Co, Minn, May 26, 40; m 60; c 3. ORGANIC CHEMISTRY. *Educ:* Univ Minn, Minneapolis, BS, 62; Purdue Univ, PhD(org chem), 66. *Prof Exp:* NIH fel photochem, Cornell Univ, 66-67; asst prof org chem, Marquette Univ, 67-74; from res chemist to sr res chemist, Hercules, Inc, 74-78; RES ASSOC & ASSOC PROF CHEM, INST PAPER CHEM, 78- *Mem:* Am Chem Soc. *Res:* Mechanisms for the delignification of wood; terpene chemistry; wood extractives. *Mailing Add:* Inst of Paper Chem PO Box 1039 Appleton WI 54912

DIMMICK, HENRY M, b Canton, Ohio, Sept 27, 22; m 58; c 2. ELECTRONICS. *Educ:* Pa State Univ, BS, 48. *Prof Exp:* Res physicist, Preston Labs, Pa, 48-51, chief engr instrument develop, 51-52; prod engr, Brockway Glass Co, 52-53; owner, Dimmick Assocs, Pa, 53-61; vpres eng & develop instrument design, 61-76, PRES, AM GLASS RES, INC, 76- *Mem:* Soc Motion Picture & TV Engrs; Audio Eng Soc. *Res:* Fracture of brittle materials; electronic, mechanical and optical instrument systems for research or industrial process control. *Mailing Add:* Am Glass Res Inc PO Box 149 Butler PA 16001

DIMMICK, JOHN FREDERICK, b Thomson, Ill, Aug 7, 21; m 46; c 2. ANIMAL PHYSIOLOGY. *Educ:* Western Ill Univ, BS, 48, MS, 49; Univ Ill, PhD(mammalian physiol), 60. *Prof Exp:* Teaching asst biol, Western Ill Univ, 48-49; teacher high schs, Ill, 49-59; res asst physiol, Univ Ill, 59-60 , USDA fel, 60-61; TEACHER & RES ANIMAL PHYSIOL & GEN BIOL, WAKE FOREST UNIV, 61- *Concurrent Pos:* Vis lectr, NC Acad Sci, 63-; dir training ctr high sch teacher's inserv training proj, NSF-NC Acad Sci, 64-68. *Mem:* Assoc mem Am Physiol Soc; Nat Sci Teachers Asn; Nat Asn Biol Teachers. *Mailing Add:* Dept Biol Wake Forest Univ PO Box 7325 Winston-Salem NC 27109

DIMMICK, RALPH W, b Chicago, Ill, Nov 18, 34; m 54; c 2. ANIMAL ECOLOGY, WILDLIFE MANAGEMENT. *Educ:* Southern Ill Univ, BA, 57, MA, 61; Univ Wyo, PhD(zool), 64. *Prof Exp:* Asst prof animal ecol, Tenn Tech Univ, 64-66; asst prof, 66-71, assoc prof forestry, 71-78, PROF WILDLIFE FISHERIES SCI, UNIV TENN, KNOXVILLE, 79- *Mem:* Wildlife Soc. *Res:* Ecology and management of wildlife resources. *Mailing Add:* Dept Forestry Wildlife & Fisheries Univ Tenn Knoxville TN 37916

DIMMICK, ROBERT LEWELLYN, b Parkersburg, WVa, Jan 4, 20; m 42; c 1. MICROBIAL PHYSIOLOGY. *Educ:* Marietta Col, AB, 47; Purdue Univ, MS, 49, PhD, 53. *Prof Exp:* Asst, Purdue Univ, 47-52; from asst res bacteriologist to res bacteriologist, Naval Biol Labs, Univ Calif, Berkeley, 53-68; prof biol & dir, Ctr Advan Med Technol, San Francisco State Col, 68-71; res bacteriologist, Naval Biomed Res Labs, 71-75, chmn, Dept Aerosol Sci, Naval Biosci Lab, 75-81; RETIRED. *Mem:* AAAS; Am Chem Soc; Am Soc Microbiol; fel Am Acad Microbiol; Int Soc Study Origins of Life. *Res:* Survival of bacteria in air; aerosols; airborne microbes; respiratory deposition. *Mailing Add:* 765 Colusa Ave El Cerrito CA 94530

DIMMIG, DANIEL ASHTON, b Lansdale, Pa, Mar 5, 24; m 54; c 2. ORGANIC POLYMER CHEMISTRY, INDUSTRIAL ORGANIC CHEMISTRY. *Educ:* Muhlenberg Col, BS, 45; Univ Pa, MS, 48; Univ Pittsburgh, PhD(org chem), 63. *Prof Exp:* Res chemist, Nitrogen Div, Allied Chem Corp, 48-55; US Steel jr fel utilization of coal tar chem, Mellon Inst, 55-63; sr res chemist, Pennsalt Chem Corp, 63-67, PROJ LEADER, PENNWALT CORP, 67- *Mem:* Am Chem Soc. *Res:* Synthesis of new organic addition and condensation polymers; photochemistry of sulfur compounds; heterogeneous catalytic synthesis of sulfur compounds. *Mailing Add:* Res & Develop Dept Pennwalt Corp 900 First Ave King of Prussia PA 19406

DIMMLER, D(IETRICH) GERD, b Karlsruhe, Ger, Nov 14, 33; m 57; c 2. SYSTEM ARCHITECTURE, SYSTEM DEVELOPMENT. *Educ:* Karlsruhe Tech Univ, Elec Eng, 62. *Prof Exp:* Electronics engr logic design, Karlsruhe Nuclear Res Ctr, 62-66; assoc elec engr systs develop, Brookhaven Nat Lab, 66-69; prin mem tech staff systs planning, Xerox Corp, El Segundo, Calif, 70-71; mgr software develop, Process Control Systs Develop, Rank Xerox Corp, Munchen, Ger, 71-72; SR SCIENTIST, BROOKHAVEN NAT LAB, 72-, ASSOC DIV HEAD, 80- *Mem:* Inst Elec & Electronics Engrs; AAAS. *Res:* Architectures, hardware and software of real-time systems and computer networks in data acquisition, experiment control and process control-specific interest; distributed function computer networks; architectures of intelligent systems. *Mailing Add:* Brookhaven Nat Lab Upton NY 11973

DIMMOCK, JOHN O, b Garden City, NY, Nov 24, 36; m 58, 74; c 4. PHYSICS. *Educ:* Yale Univ, BS, 58, PhD(physics), 62. *Prof Exp:* Res scientist solid state physics, Raytheon Co, 62-63; mem staff, Lincoln Lab, Mass Inst Technol, 63-66, leader appl physics group, 66-71, leader appl optics group, 71-74; dir electronic & solid state sci prog, 74-81, DEP DIR TECHNOL PROGS, OFF NAVAL RES, 81- *Mem:* fel Am Phys Soc; Inst Elec & Electronics Engrs. *Res:* Theoretical and experimental solid state physics; magnetism and semiconductors. *Mailing Add:* Off Naval Res 800 N Quincy St Arlington VA 22217

DIMMOCK, JONATHAN RICHARD, b Southampton, Eng, July 6, 37; m 68. MEDICINAL CHEMISTRY. *Educ:* Univ London, BPharm, 59, PhD(pharmaceut chem), 63. *Prof Exp:* Org res chemist, Chesterford Park Res Sta, Saffron Waldon, Eng, 63-67; from asst prof to assoc prof, 67-76, PROF PHARMACEUT CHEM, UNIV SASK, 76- *Concurrent Pos:* Res grants, Can Found for Advan Pharm, 68, Nat Res Coun Fund, 68-70 & Smith Kline & French Labs, Pa, 71; Med Res Coun grant, 72- *Mem:* Pharmaceut Soc Gt Brit. *Res:* Design, synthesis and evaluation of novel compounds screened against cancers and respiration in mebochondria; antiparasitic agents; anti-epileptic compounds. *Mailing Add:* Dept Med Chem Col Pharm Univ Sask Saskatoon SK S7N 0W0 Can

DIMOCK, DIRCK L, b Braintree, Mass, June 23, 30; m 52; c 3. PHYSICS. *Educ:* Antioch Col, BS, 52; Johns Hopkins Univ, PhD(physics), 57. *Prof Exp:* Mem res staff, Plasma Physics Lab, Princeton Univ, 57-62; vis scientist, Max Planck Inst Physics & Astrophys, 62-63; assoc head, Exp Div, 63-77, PRIN RES PHYSICIST, PLASMA PHYSICS LAB, PRINCETON UNIV, 76- *Concurrent Pos:* Lectr astrophys sci, 63-66; consult, Princeton Appl Res Corp, 64-65 & EMR Corp, 80. *Mem:* AAAS; Am Phys Soc. *Res:* Plasma physics; spectroscopic and optical plasma diagnostics, and atomic structure. *Mailing Add:* Plasma Physics Lab Princeton Univ PO Box 451 Princeton NJ 08540

DIMOCK, RONALD VILROY, JR, b Melrose, Mass, Apr 11, 43; m 66; c 2. INVERTEBRATE ZOOLOGY, PHYSIOLOGICAL ECOLOGY. *Educ:* Univ NH, BA, 65; Fla State Univ, MS, 67; Univ Calif, Santa Barbara, PhD(invert zool), 70. *Prof Exp:* Asst prof, 70-76, ASSOC PROF BIOL, WAKE FOREST UNIV, 76- DIR, BELEWS LAKE BIOL STA, 75- *Mem:* Am Soc Zool; Am Micros Soc; Ecol Soc Am. *Res:* Invertebrate chemical communication; physiological ecology of marine invertebrates; dynamics of host-symbiont interactions. *Mailing Add:* Dept of Biol Wake Forest Univ Winston-Salem NC 27109

DIMOND, EDMUNDS GREY, b St Louis, Mo, Dec 8, 18; m 44; c 3. CARDIOLOGY. *Educ:* Ind Univ, BS, 42, MD, 44. *Hon Degrees:* DSc, Hahnemann Grad Sch & Med Col. *Prof Exp:* Lectr, Sch Aviation Med, Randolph Field, 49; dir cardiovasc lab, Med Ctr, Univ Kans, 50-60, prof med & chmn dept, Sch Med, 53-60; dir Inst Cardiopulmonary Dis, Scripps Clin & Res Found, 60-68; DISTINGUISHED PROF MED, UNIV MO-KANSAS CITY, 68-, PROVOST HEALTH SCI, 70- *Concurrent Pos:* Med consult, US Bur Labor, 55-60; Fulbright prof, Neth, 56; vis prof, Nat Heart Inst, London, 59; State Dept Am Specialists Abroad Prog, Philippines & Taiwan, 61; Columbia & Chile, 63 & Czech, Ceylon, Indonesia & Vietnam, 64; res assoc, Univ Calif, San Diego, 64-67, prof med-in-residence, 67-68; spec consult med educ to Under Secy Health, Dept Health, Educ & Welfare, 68-69; ed-in-chief, ACCEL, J in Cardiol, Am Col Cardiol, 69-77; Am specialist cardiol, People's Repub China, 71-72 & 74-78; scholar-in-residence, Rockefeller Found Ctr, Bellagio, Italy, 78. *Mem:* Am Col Physicians; corresponding mem Brit Cardiac Soc; Am Col Cardiol (pres, 61). *Res:* Cardiovascular physiology. *Mailing Add:* 2220 Holmes St Kansas City MO 64108

DIMOND, HAROLD LLOYD, b Paterson, NJ, May 1, 22; m 49; c 2. ORGANIC CHEMISTRY. *Educ:* NY Univ, AB, 48; Carnegie Inst Technol, MS, 52, PhD(chem), 53. *Prof Exp:* Asst chem, Carnegie Inst Technol, 48-50; res chemist, Pittsburgh Coke & Chem Co, 53-56 & Gulf Res & Develop Co, 56-66; from res chemist to sr res chemist, Hilton-Davis Chem Co, Sterling Drug, Inc, 66-69; sr res chemist, 69-77, SR SCIENTIST, DRACKETT CO, BRISTOL-MYERS CO, 77- *Mem:* Am Chem Soc; AAAS; Am Inst Chem; Sigma Xi. *Res:* Preparation of 3-pyrrolidones; industrial work on preparation of derivatives of coal tar chemicals; alkylation; petrochemicals; detergents; oxidation; general synthetic work; process development; product evaluation; new product and process development of household products. *Mailing Add:* Drackett Co, Bristol-Myer Co R&D Dept 5020 Spring Grove Ave Cincinnati OH 45232

DIMOND, JOHN BARNET, b Providence, RI, July 20, 29; m 55; c 2. ENTOMOLOGY, ECOLOGY. *Educ:* Univ RI, BS, 51, MS, 53; Ohio State Univ, PhD(entom), 57. *Prof Exp:* Sr entomologist, Maine State Forest Serv, 56-59; from asst prof to assoc prof entom, 59-66, PROF ENTOM, UNIV MAINE, 66-, CHMN DEPT, 74-, COOP PROF FOREST RES, 77- *Mem:* AAAS; Entom Soc Am; Entom Soc Can. *Res:* Medical insects; insect nutrition; forest insects; insect ecology; populations. *Mailing Add:* 313 Derring Hall Univ of Maine Orono ME 04473

DIMOND, MARIE THERESE, b Valdez, Alaska, Nov 13, 16. ZOOLOGY. *Educ:* Trinity Col, DC, AB, 38; Cath Univ, MS, 52, PhD(biol), 54. *Prof Exp:* Instr Ger, Trinity Col, DC, 38-39; teacher high schs, Md & Pa, 39-48; from instr to assoc prof, 48-70, PROF BIOL, TRINITY COL, DC, 60- *Concurrent Pos:* NSF sci fac fel marine biol, Marine Lab, Duke Univ, 59, Plymouth Lab, 60 & Hopkins Marine Sta, Stanford Univ; 61; res assoc, Univ BC, 70; vis prof, Bhopal Univ, India, 79. *Mem:* AAAS; assoc Am Physiol Soc; Am Soc Zoologists; World Pop Soc; Sigma Xi. *Res:* Thyroid, pituitary, parathyroids, ultimobranchial, gonads and gonoducts; turtles: embryological development, histology, incubation and hatching of eggs, juvenile growth as related to diet, drugs and temperature. *Mailing Add:* Dept of Biol Trinity Col Washington DC 20017

DIMOPOULLOS, GEORGE TAKIS, b Flushing, NY, Nov 24, 23; m 45; c 1. MICROBIOLOGY. *Educ:* Pa State Univ, BS, 49, MS, 50; Mich State Univ, PhD(bact), 52; Am Bd Med Microbiol, dipl. *Prof Exp:* Lab asst bact, Pa State Univ, 47-48, asst, 49; asst virol, Mich State Univ, 50-52; res assoc, Univ Wis, 52-53; virologist animal dis & parasite res div, Agr Res Serv, USDA, 53-57; prof vet sci, La State Univ, 57-75; PROF BIOL SCI & CHMN DEPT, WRIGHT STATE UNIV, 75- *Concurrent Pos:* Spec fel, NIH, 64-65. *Mem:* Fel AAAS; Am Acad Microbiol; Am Soc Med Technol; Am Soc Microbiol; Soc Exp Biol & Med. *Res:* Finite purification of vacines; immunochemistry; autoimmunity. *Mailing Add:* Dept of Biol Sci Wright State Univ Dayton OH 45435

DIMROTH, ERICH, b Wurzburg, Ger, Apr 14, 34. GEOLOGY. *Educ:* Univ Munich, dipl geol, 58, Dr rer nat(geol), 61. *Prof Exp:* Res assoc geol, McGill Univ, 61-63; geologist, Prov Que Dept Natural Resources, 63-74; guest prof, 75-79, PROF, UNIV QUE, CHICOUTIMI, 80- *Concurrent Pos:* Pres, Int Geol Correlation Prog Proj 160 (Precambrian exogenic processes), 79-81. *Mem:* Ger Geol Asn; Geol Asn Can; Geol Soc Am; Am Geophys Union. *Res:* Tectonic and Paleotectonic evolution of Precambrian geosynclines in Quebec; sedimentology of Precambrian cherty iron formation; evolution of Precambrian atmosphere; volcanology and sedimentology of subaqueous volcanic rocks; tectonic evolution of high-grade gueiss terrain in Grenville province. *Mailing Add:* Dept of Earth Sci Univ of Que Chicoutimi PQ G7H 2B1 Can

DIMSDALE, BERNARD, b Sioux City, Iowa, Aug 3, 12; m; c 2. MATHEMATICS. *Educ:* Univ Minn, BCh, 33, AM, 35, PhD(math), 40. *Prof Exp:* Instr, Univ Idaho, 38-42; assoc instr, US War Dept, 42-43; instr math, Purdue Univ, 46; mathematician, Ballistic Res Lab, Aberdeen Proving Ground, 47-51 & Raytheon Mfg Co, Waltham, Mass, 51-56; sr mathematician, IBM Corp, 56-61, mgr, 61-69, indust consult, 69-77; CONSULT APPL MATH & DATA PROCESSING, 77- *Concurrent Pos:* Indust fel, IBM Corp, 74. *Mem:* Am Math Soc; Asn Comput Mach; Soc Indust & Appl Math. *Res:* Approximation theory; numerical analysis; optimization techniques; numerical geometry. *Mailing Add:* 319 9th St Santa Monica CA 90402

DINA, STEPHEN JAMES, b Bronx, NY, May 2, 43; m 65; c 3. PLANT ECOLOGY. *Educ:* Mt Union Col, BS, 65; Ohio State Univ, MS, 67; Univ Utah, PhD(biol), 70. *Prof Exp:* Asst prof, 70-75, ASSOC PROF BIOL, ST LOUIS UNIV, 75- *Concurrent Pos:* Environ Protection Agency grant, 73; Nat Endowment for the Humanities curric develop grant, 75-80. *Mem:* AAAS; Ecol Soc Am; Brit Ecol Soc; Am Inst Biol Sci; Am Soc Plant Physiol. *Res:* Implications of vascular plant distribution patterns expressed through understanding of the differential effects of the environment on plant physiology; water relations; organic energy balance; environmental stress conditions. *Mailing Add:* Dept Biol St Louis Univ 3507 Laclede Ave St Louis MO 63103

DINAN, FRANK J, b Buffalo, NY, Dec 3, 33; m 54; c 2. ORGANIC CHEMISTRY, ANALYTICAL CHEMISTRY. *Educ:* State Univ NY Buffalo, BA, 59, PhD(chem), 64. *Prof Exp:* Jr chemist anal chem, Carborundum Metals Co, 53-59; chemist, Hooker Chem Corp, 59-61; res chemist org chem, E I du Pont de Nemours & Co, 63-64; res assoc anal chem, Cornell Univ, 64-66; from asst prof to assoc prof chem, 66-74, chmn dept, 70-74, PROF CHEM, CANISIUS COL, 74- *Mem:* Am Chem Soc. *Res:* Heterocyclic chemistry and instrumental methods of analysis and structure determination. *Mailing Add:* Dept of Chem Canisius Col Buffalo NY 14208

DINAPOLI, FREDERICK RICHARD, b Providence, RI, Nov 19, 40; m 61; c 3. ACOUSTICS. *Educ:* Univ RI, BS, 62, MS, 65, PhD(elec eng), 69. *Prof Exp:* Scientist comput, Pratt & Whitney Aircraft, 62-63; res scientist acoust, Raytheon Marine Res Lab, 67-68; RES SCIENTIST ACOUST, NAVAL UNDERWATER SYSTS CTR, 70- *Concurrent Pos:* Adj prof acoust, Univ RI, 71- *Mem:* Assoc Acoust Soc Am. *Res:* All aspects of the study and prediction of the transmission of underwater acoustic energy. *Mailing Add:* Environ Model & Acoust Prediction Code TA113 Naval Underwater Systs New London CT 06320

DINARDI, SALVATORE ROBERT, b New York City, NY, July 3, 43; m 79; c 2. INDOOR AIR POLLUTION, INDUSTRIAL HYGIENE. *Educ:* Hofstra Univ, BA, 65; Univ Mass, PhD(phys chem), 71. *Prof Exp:* Instr environ health, 70-71, asst prof, 71-75, ASSOC PROF ENVIRON HEALTH & INDUST HYGIENE, UNIV MASS, 75- *Concurrent Pos:* Vis prof, Univ NC, 79-80; indust hygiene consult, Several Nat Corp, 79-; indust ventilation design continuing educ, Ten Major Univ eastern US, 79-; fel, Univ NC, 79-80. *Mem:* Nat Environ Health Asn; Am Indust Hygiene Asn; Am Public Health Asn; Soc Occupational Environ Health; Am Chem Soc. *Res:* Characterizing the quality of indoor air and controlling indoor air pollution in private residences; impact of passive solar design on air quality; industrial hygiene. *Mailing Add:* Div Public Health Univ Mass Amherst MA 01003

DINBERGS, KORNELIUS, b Riga, Latvia, June 5, 25; nat; m 58. ORGANIC POLYMER CHEMISTRY. *Educ:* Ukrainian Tech Inst, Ger, MagPharm, 49; Baylor Univ, MA, 51; Purdue Univ, PhD(org chem), 56. *Prof Exp:* From tech man to sr tech man, 56-61; SR RES CHEMIST, B F GOODRICH CO, 61- *Mem:* Am Chem Soc. *Res:* Polyurethanes, polymerization, structure-property relationships; diisocyanate and polyester preparation and stability; peroxide cures; vinyl chloride polymerization. *Mailing Add:* Res & Develop Ctr B F Goodrich Co Brecksville OH 44141

DINDAL, DANIEL LEE, b Findlay, Ohio, Sept 17, 36; m 58; c 3. ECOLOGY. *Educ:* Ohio State Univ, BS(wildlife mgt) & BS(sci educ), 58, MA, 61, PhD(ecol), 67. *Prof Exp:* Teacher high sch, Ohio, 58-63; teaching asst zool & ecol, Ohio State Univ, 63-64; US Fish & Wildlife Serv res assoc, 64-66; asst prof terrestrial invertebrate ecol, 67-71, assoc prof, 71-77, prof terrestrial invertebrate ecol, 77-80, PROF, DEPT ENVIRON & FOREST BIOL, COL ENVIRON SCI & FORESTRY, STATE UNIV NY, 80- *Concurrent Pos:* Acarology Inst traineeship adv acarine taxon, Ohio State Univ, 68 & 70; AEC res grant, 68-73; New Eng Interstate Water Pollution Control Comn res grant, 72-73; US Forest Serv res grant, 72-74. *Mem:* Ecol Soc Am; Soil Sci Soc Am; Am Soc Zoologists; Entom Soc Am; Acarological Soc Am. *Res:* Ecology of soil invertebrates in natural and manipulated terrestrial microcommunities; effects of dichloro-diphenyl-trichloroethane on invertebrate microcommunities and species diversity; effects of municipal wastewater disposal and urban street salting on soil invertebrates; succession and interspecific relationships of invertebrates in bird nests, carrion and soil litter. *Mailing Add:* State Univ of NY Col of Environ Sci & Forestry Syracuse NY 13210

DINEEN, CLARENCE FRANCIS, b DeGraff, Minn, Apr 1, 16; m 43; c 4. ZOOLOGY, ECOLOGY. *Educ:* Minn State Teachers Col, BE, 39; Univ Minn, MS, 48, PhD, 50. *Prof Exp:* Asst prof biol, Univ Notre Dame, 50-56; chmn dept biol, 56-77, PROF BIOL, ST MARY'S COL, IND, 74- *Mem:* AAAS; Ecol Soc Am; Am Soc Zoologists. *Res:* Osteology of fishes; aquatic ecology. *Mailing Add:* Dept of Biol St Mary's Col Notre Dame IN 46556

DINEEN, EUGENE JOSEPH, organic chemistry, analytical chemistry, see previous edition

DINEGAR, ROBERT HUDSON, b New York, NY, Dec 18, 21; wid; c 3. PHYSICAL CHEMISTRY. *Educ:* Cornell Univ, AB, 42; Columbia Univ, AM, 48, PhD(phys chem), 51, Col Santa Fe, AB, 76. *Prof Exp:* Asst chem, Columbia Univ, 46-50; RES PHYS CHEMIST, LOS ALAMOS NAT LAB, UNIV CALIF, 50- *Concurrent Pos:* Adj prof chem, Univ NMex, Northern Br Col, 70-77; staff mem, Northern NMex Community Col, 77-78; mem, Shroud Turin Res Proj. *Mem:* Am Chem Soc; fel Am Inst Chem; prof mem Am Meteorol Soc; Sigma Xi. *Res:* Kinetics of phase changes and explosions; physics and chemistry of explosives; properties and reactivity of small particles. *Mailing Add:* 2317 46th St Los Alamos NM 87544

DINER, BRUCE AARON, b New York, NY, Nov 7, 45; m 68. BIOPHYSICS, BIOCHEMISTRY. *Educ:* City Col New York, BS, 66; Rockefeller Univ, PhD, 72. *Prof Exp:* Helen Hay Whitney res fel photosynthesis, 72-75, Joliot-Curie fel photosynthesis, Comn Atomic Energy, 75-76, CHARGE DE RECHERCHE, NAT CTR SCI RES, INST BIOL PHYS CHEM, PARIS, 76- *Honors & Awards:* Prix Fanny Evaden, Academie de Sci, Paris, 80. *Res:* Identification of electron transport components in photosystem II of photosynthesis using detergent-solubilized photoactive particles; study of mechanism of electron transport and oxygen production in this photosystem. *Mailing Add:* Inst Biol Phys Chem 13 rue Pierre et Marie Curie Paris France

DINER, WILMA CANADA, b Monaville, WVa, Jan 21, 26; m 55; c 3. RADIOLOGY. *Educ:* Univ Ky, BS, 46; Duke Univ, MD, 50. *Prof Exp:* Intern med, Duke Hosp, 50; asst resident path, Mass Gen Hosp, Boston, 51; asst res resident radiol, 52-54; assoc radiologist, St Luke's Hosp, New Bedford, 55-56; from asst prof to assoc prof, 56-70, PROF RADIOL, MED CTR, UNIV ARK, LITTLE ROCK, 70-, DIR DIAG SECT, DEPT RADIOL & DIR DIAG RADIOL RESIDENCY PROG, 74- *Concurrent Pos:* Consult, Ark Children's Hosp, Little Rock, 62-65 & Little Rock AFB Hosp, 62-65. *Mem:* Fel Am Col Radiol; Asn Univ Radiol; Am Roentgen Ray Soc; Radiol Soc NAm; Soc Gastrointestinal Radiologists. *Res:* Diagnostic radiology, especially gastrointestinal and mammography; Cronkhite-Canada syndrome. *Mailing Add:* Dept of Radiol Univ Ark Med Sci Little Rock AR 72205

DINERSTEIN, ROBERT ALVIN, b New York, NY, Jan 4, 19; m 41; c 3. CHEMISTRY. *Educ:* City Col New York, BS, 39; Pa State Univ, MS, 40. *Prof Exp:* Chemist, Am Oil Co, 46-52, from group leader to sect leader, 52-62, mgr info & commun, 62-68, dir anal res, 68-70, mgr compensation & orgn, Am Oil Co, 70-73; dir orgn planning, 73-76, DIR ORGN & DOMESTIC COMPENSATION, STANDARD OIL CO, IND, 76- *Concurrent Pos:* Harvey Washington Wiley lectr, Purdue Univ, 57. *Mem:* AAAS; Am Chem Soc. *Res:* Hydrocarbon reactions, properties, separation and analysis; distillation; chromatography; information science; documentation. *Mailing Add:* Standard Oil Co Box 5910 A Chicago IL 60680

DINERSTEIN, ROBERT JOSEPH, b Little Rock, Ark, Mar 5, 44; m 76. PHARMACOLOGY, HISTOCHEMISTRY. *Educ:* Harvard Univ, BA, 66; Univ Ore, PhD(org chem), 71; Univ Chicago, MD, 76. *Prof Exp:* Res assoc, 76-78, ASST PROF PHARMACOL, DEPT PHARMACOL & PHYSIOL SCI, UNIV CHICAGO, 78- *Mem:* Am Chem Soc; Soc Neurosci. *Res:* Cytopharmacology; cellular identification of neurosecretory substances; autoradiography of pharmacological agents; microspectrofluorometry. *Mailing Add:* Dept of Pharmacol & Physiol Sci Univ of Chicago Chicago IL 60637

DINES, ALLEN I, b Pittsburgh, Pa, Dec 16, 29; m 53; c 2. PHARMACEUTICAL CHEMISTRY, MEDICINAL CHEMISTRY. *Educ:* Univ Pittsburgh, BS, 51; Ohio State Univ, MS, 53, PhD(pharmaceut chem), 58. *Prof Exp:* Assoc dir prod develop, Flint Labs, Baxter Labs, Inc, Ill, 58-60; group leader pharmaceut res & develop, Miles Prod Div, Miles Labs, Inc, Ind, 60-64; lab dir, Warren-Teed Pharmaceut Inc, Rohm and Haas Co, 64-69; dir res, Strong Cobb Arner, Inc, 69-70; dir res & develop, Mylan Pharmaceut, Inc, 71-76; TECH MGR DEVELOP PROD, VICK INT, WESTPORT, CONN, 76- *Mem:* Am Chem Soc; Am Pharmaceut Asn; Acad Pharmaceut Sci. *Res:* Pharmaceutical research and development; pharmaceutics. *Mailing Add:* 27 Ironwood Dr Danbury CT 06810

DINES, MARTIN BENJAMIN, b Pittsburgh, Pa, May 9, 43; m 64; c 1. ORGANOMETALLIC CHEMISTRY, INORGANIC CHEMISTRY. *Educ:* Carnegie-Mellon Univ, BS, 64; Univ Ill, PhD(chem), 68. *Prof Exp:* Researcher chem, Exxon Res & Eng Co, Linden, NJ, 68-77; GROUP LEADER, OCCIDENTAL RES CORP, 77- *Mem:* Am Chem Soc. *Res:* New materials, especially solid-state, having application in areas of catalysis and energy storage; layered compounds, and separations. *Mailing Add:* Occidental Res Corp PO Box 19601 Irvine CA 92713

DINESS, ARTHUR M(ICHAEL), b New York, NY, Apr 21, 38; m 63; c 2. ENGINEERING SCIENCE, TECHNICAL MANAGEMENT. *Educ:* NY Univ, BA, 58; Pa State Univ, MS, 60, PhD(solid state sci), 66. *Prof Exp:* Asst chem, Pa State Univ, 58-60, mat res lab, 60-64; res specialist mat res, Appl Res Lab, Philco Corp, 64-65; supvr, Solid State Mat Sect, 65-66; chemist, Metall Prog, 66-77, dir, Metall & Ceramics Prog, 78-80, dir, Mat Sci Div, 80, ASSOC DIR RES ENG SCI, OFF NAVAL RES, 81- *Concurrent Pos:* Res scientist, Ford Sci Lab, Pa, 66; guest scientist, Nat Bur Stand, 72-; liaison scientist, Off Naval Res, Tokyo, 78. *Mem:* Fel Am Ceramic Soc; Am Chem Soc; AAAS. *Res:* Materials research and engineering; ceramics and glasses. *Mailing Add:* Metall & Ceramics Prog Off Naval Res Arlington VA 22217

DINGA, GUSTAV PAUL, b Haugen, Wis, Oct 6, 22; m 48; c 4. INORGANIC CHEMISTRY. *Educ:* St Olaf Col, BA, 47; Univ Louisville, MS, 49; Univ Wyo, PhD(inorg chem), 62. *Prof Exp:* Asst, Univ Ky, 49-50; instr chem, Ill Wesleyan Univ, 50-51 & St Cloud Teachers Col, 51-53; from asst prof to assoc prof, 53-64, chmn dept, 69-72, PROF CHEM, CONCORDIA COL, MOORHEAD, MINN, 64-, CHMN DEPT, 81- *Concurrent Pos:* Researcher, Univ Utah, 60 & Nuclear Sci Inst, Wash State Univ, 62; resident res assoc, Argonne Nat Lab, 63; vis prof, Augustana Col, SDak, 64, 65 & 66; fac res appointee, Pac Northwest Labs, Battelle Mem Inst, 68-69; mem grad fac,

NDak State Univ, 71; Ames lab res, Iowa State Univ, 77. *Mem:* Am Chem Soc; fel Am Inst Chem; Sigma Xi. *Res:* Inorganic and organic chemistry; synthesis and identification of organic foam inhibiting compounds and p-tolylmethyl ether; determination of physical constants for non-aqueous solvents at very low temperature; zirconium compounds and complexes. *Mailing Add:* Dept Chem Concordia Col Moorhead MN 56560

DINGEE, DAVID AARON, plasma physics, reactor physics, see previous edition

DINGELL, JAMES V, b Detroit, Mich, Oct 10, 31; m 80; c 2. PHARMACOLOGY, CHEMISTRY. *Educ:* Georgetown Univ, BS, 54, MS, 57, PhD(chem), 62. *Prof Exp:* Chemist, Lab Chem Pharmacol, Nat Heart Inst, 55-62; from instr to assoc prof pharmacol, Sch Med, Vanderbilt Univ 62-79; mem staff, Lab Chem Pharmacol, Nat Cancer Inst, 76-79; SCIENTIST ADMINR, NAT HEART, LUNG & BLOOD INST, 79- *Mem:* Am Soc Pharmacol & Exp Therapeut; Am Col Neuropsychopharmacol. *Res:* Drug metabolism, distribution in tissues, assay and mechanism of action, especially in area of psychotherapeutic agents. *Mailing Add:* Rm 304 Cardiac Functions Br Fed Bldg NHLBI Bethesda MD 20205

DINGER, ANN ST CLAIR, b Eau Claire, Wis, Oct 16, 45. ASTROPHYSICS. *Educ:* Vassar Col, AB, 67; Northwestern Univ, MS, 68, PhD(astron), 71. *Prof Exp:* Asst prof physics, Univ Wis-Eau Claire, 71-74; asst prof astron, Wellesley Col, 74-78; vis lect astron, Williams Col, 78-79; RES AFFIL, JET PROPULSION LAB, 79- *Mem:* Am Astron Soc; Royal Astron Soc; Sigma Xi. *Res:* Computer models of the interior structure and evolution of helium stars, matching the models to the observed stars; radio molecular line observations of cool stars and interstellar gas clouds. *Mailing Add:* Jet Propulsion Lab T1166 4800 Oak Grove Dr Pasadena CA 91109

DINGES, DAVID FRANCIS, b Hays, Kans, May 30, 49; m 71; c 1. PSYCHOPHYSIOLOGY, BIOLOGICAL RHYTHMS. *Educ:* St Benedicts Col, AB, 71; St Louis Univ, MS, 74, PhD(psychol), 76. *Prof Exp:* Instr psychol, Florrisant Valley Community Col, 74-75; res psychol, Nat Med Ctr, Childrens Hosp, 75-79; RES PSYCHOL, INST PA HOSP, 79-; CLIN ASST PROF PSYCHOL, UNIV PA, 81- *Concurrent Pos:* Asst prof & lectr, George Wash Univ, 76-79; prin investr, Off Naval Res, 80-; co-dir, Unit Exp Psychiat, Pa Hosp, 82- *Mem:* AAAS; Am Psychol Asn; Asn Psychophysiol Study Sleep; Soc Psychophysiol Res. *Res:* Human (infant and adult) psychophysiology, primarily in the study of sensory systems and sleep, wake cycles; sleep deprivation, napping, and studies of hypnosis. *Mailing Add:* Unit Exp Psychiat Inst Pa Hosp 111 N 48th St Philadelphia PA 19139

DINGLE, ALBERT NELSON, b Bismarck, NDak, May 22, 16; m 41; c 2. METEOROLOGY, CLOUD PHYSICS. *Educ:* Univ Minn, BS, 39; Iowa State Col, MS, 40; Mass Inst Technol, ScD, 47. *Prof Exp:* Asst prof physics, Hampton Inst, 41-42; res assoc meteorol, Mass Inst Technol, 43-47; asst prof physics & meteorol, Ohio State Univ, 47-54; assoc res meteorologist, Eng Res Inst, 54-56, assoc prof, 56-63, PROF METEOROL, UNIV MICH, 63- *Concurrent Pos:* Res assoc, Mapping & Charting Res Lab, Ohio State Univ Res Found, 50-54; consult & expert witness, NASA, 74-81. *Mem:* fel AAAS; Am Meteorol Soc; Am Geophys Union. *Res:* Rain cleansing of the atmosphere; drop-size distributions in rain; study of convective storms by use of tracer indium; air and precipitation chemistry; waste disposal capacity of the atmosphere; cloud microphysics and modeling of convective rain-generating systems. *Mailing Add:* Dept Atmospheric & Oceanic Sci Univ Mich 200 Res Activ Bldg Ann Arbor MI 48109

DINGLE, ALLAN DOUGLAS, b Hamilton, Ont, May 3, 36; m 62. DEVELOPMENTAL BIOLOGY. *Educ:* McMaster Univ, BSc, 58; Univ Ill, MSc, 60; Brandeis Univ, PhD(biol), 64. *Prof Exp:* NIH trainee develop biol, 64-65; asst prof, 65-75, ASSOC PROF BIOL, MCMASTER UNIV, 75- *Mem:* AAAS; Am Soc Cell Biol; Soc Develop Biol; Can Soc Cell Biol. *Res:* Development of flagella and their basal bodies during cell differentiation; pigment cell differentiation and development of pigment patterns in fish. *Mailing Add:* Dept of Biol McMaster Univ Hamilton Can

DINGLE, RAYMOND, b Perth, Australia, Sept 5, 35; m 58; c 3. DEVICE PHYSICS. *Educ:* Univ Western Australia, BSc, 55, Hons, 57, PhD(chem), 65. *Prof Exp:* Sr demonstr phys chem, Univ Western Australia, 59-62; fel chem, Univ Col, London, 62-63; amanuensis phys chem, Copenhagen Univ, 63-66 & lektor solid state chem, 64-66; mem tech staff solid state physics, 66-79, SUPVR, EXPLOR HIGH SPEED III-V DEVICE GROUP, BELL LABS, 79- *Concurrent Pos:* Sr fel, Dept Solid State Physics, Res Sch Phys Sci, The Australian Nat Univ, 72-73. *Mem:* AAAS; Am Phys Soc. *Res:* Electronic properties of solids; III-V semiconductor device studies; III-V integrated circuit technology; quantum effects in ultra thin semiconductor hetero-structures. *Mailing Add:* Bell Labs Murray Hill NJ 07974

DINGLE, RICHARD DOUGLAS HUGH, b Penang, Malaya, Nov 4, 36; US citizen; m 59; c 3. ANIMAL BEHAVIOR, ECOLOGY. *Educ:* Cornell Univ, BA, 58; Univ Mich, MSc, 59, PhD(zool), 62. *Prof Exp:* Instr zool, Univ Mich, 61-62; NSF fel, Cambridge Univ, 62-63; NIMH training fel, Univ Mich, 63-64; from asst prof to assoc prof, 64-72, PROF ZOOL, UNIV IOWA, 72- *Concurrent Pos:* NIH fel, Univ Nairobi, 69-70. *Mem:* AAAS; Am Soc Zool; Am Soc Naturalists; Animal Behav Soc; Ecol Soc Am. *Res:* Insect and crustacean behavior and populations; insect migration. *Mailing Add:* Dept of Zool Univ of Iowa Iowa City IA 52242

DINGLE, RICHARD WILLIAM, b Bismarck, NDak, Jan 5, 18; m 47; c 2. SILVICULTURE. *Educ:* Univ Minn, BS, 41; Yale Univ, MF, 47, PhD(forestry), 53. *Prof Exp:* Instr forestry, Univ Mo, 48-53; from asst prof to assoc prof, 53-69, PROF FORESTRY, WASH STATE UNIV, 69- *Mem:* AAAS; Am Forestry Asn; Soc Am Foresters. *Res:* Artificial regeneration and grafting of ponderosa pine in eastern Washington; vegetative regeneration of conifers; windbreak establishment and culture in Columbia Basin and Eastern Washington drylands; Christmas tree production and culture; forest ecology; forest tree physiology; forest genetics; silviculture. *Mailing Add:* Dept of Forestry & Range Mgt Wash State Univ Pullman WA 99164

DINGLE, THOMAS WALTER, b Burnaby, BC, Aug 6, 36; m 63. THEORETICAL CHEMISTRY. *Educ:* Univ Alta, BSc, 58, PhD(phys chem), 65. *Prof Exp:* Ramsay Mem fel chem, Math Inst, Oxford Univ, 64-66; fel, Univ Ottawa, 66-67; ASST PROF CHEM, UNIV VICTORIA, 67- *Res:* Molecular orbital calculations. *Mailing Add:* 8893 Marshall Victoria BC V8W 2Y2 Can

DINGLEDINE, RAYMOND J, b Celina, Ohio, Dec 17, 48; m 71; c 2. NEUROPHYSIOLOGY, NEUROPHARMACOLOGY. *Educ:* Mich State Univ, BS, 71; Stanford Univ, PhD(pharmacol), 75. *Prof Exp:* Fel neuropharmacol, Med Res Coun Neurochem, Pharmacol Unit, Univ Cambridge, Eng, 75-77; fel neurophysiol, Neurophysiol Inst, Univ Oslo, Norway, 77-78; res assoc neurophysiol, Dept Physiol, Duke Univ, 78; ASST PROF NEUROPHARMACOL, UNIV NC, CHAPEL HILL, 78- *Mem:* Soc Neurosci; Am Soc Pharmacol & Exp Therapeut. *Res:* Cellular mechanisms (electrophysiology) of opioid actions; synaptic pathology in experimental models of epilepsy. *Mailing Add:* Dept Phamacol Univ NC Bldg 231 H Chapel Hill NC 27514

DINGLEDY, DAVID PETER, b Youngstown, Ohio, Mar 11, 19; m 44; c 8. PHYSICAL CHEMISTRY, PHOTOCHEMISTRY. *Educ:* John Carroll Univ, BS, 40; Marquette Univ, MS, 42; Ohio State Univ, PhD(phys chem), 62. *Prof Exp:* Res chemist, Owens-Corning Fiberglas, 43-53; res assoc cryog, Res Found, Ohio State Univ, 53-55; teacher high schs, Ohio, 55-57; instr chem, Ohio Wesleyan Univ, 57-59; ASSOC PROF CHEM, STATE UNIV NY COL FREDONIA, 62- *Mem:* Am Chem Soc; Sigma Xi. *Res:* Physical chemistry of glass; structure of inorganic glasses. *Mailing Add:* Dept of Chem State Univ of NY Col Fredonia NY 14063

DINGMAN, CHARLES WESLEY, II, b Springfield, Mass, June 2, 32; m 54; c 3. CELL BIOLOGY, PSYCHIATRY. *Educ:* Dartmouth Col, AB, 54; Univ Rochester, MD, 59. *Prof Exp:* Res assoc neurochem, Dept Psychiat, Sch Med & Dent, Univ Rochester, 57-58; res assoc biochem, Nat Inst Neurol Dis & Blindness, 60-64; res med officer, Nat Cancer Inst, 64-75; resident in psychiat, Northern Va Ment Health Inst, 75-77; STAFF PSYCHIATRIST, CHESTNUT LODGE, INC, 77- *Mem:* AAAS; Am Soc Biol Chem; Am Psychiat Asn. *Res:* Biochemical studies of nucleic acid synthesis and metabolism; effect of carcinogens on nucleic acid structure and metabolism; DNA repair mechanisms. *Mailing Add:* 10113 Bevern Lane Potomac MD 20854

DINGMAN, JANE VAN ZANDT, b Summit, NJ, Jan 5, 31; m 53, 74; c 2. EVOLUTIONARY BIOLOGY, PSYCHOBIOLOGY. *Educ:* Wellesley Col, BA, 53; Yale Univ, PhD(zool), 57. *Prof Exp:* NSF fel, Oxford Univ, 57-58; instr zool, Mt Holyoke Col, 58-59; res assoc biol, Amherst Col, 59-71; res dir, Mass Pub Interest Res Group, 72-73, environ res consult, 73-75; lectr biol, Univ NH, 76-78, res assoc, Family Res Lab, 79-80; RES CONSULT, 81- *Concurrent Pos:* NIH spec fel, Oxford Univ, 63-64; mem bd dirs, Conn River Ecol Action Corp; chmn, Conn River Task Force; mem sci adv group, Conn River Basin Prog-New Eng River Basins Comn; sci adv, New Eng Coal-Coalition Nuclear Pollution & For Land's Sake; spec adv, Restoration of Atlantic Salmon in Am, 70-74 & Strafford County Task Force on Family Violence, 78-79. *Mem:* Am Soc Naturalists; Lepidopterists Soc; Sigma Xi. *Res:* Origin and maintenance of mimicry in butterflies; ecological genetics of natural populations; interaction of social and biological aspects of human menstrual cycle. *Mailing Add:* RFD Canney Rd Durham NH 03824

DINGMAN, REED (OTHELBERT), b Rockwood, Mich, Nov 4, 06; m 32; c 3. PLASTIC SURGERY. *Educ:* Univ Mich, BA, 28, DDS, 31, MS, 32, MD, 36. *Prof Exp:* Maxillofacial & plastic surgeon, Geisinger Mem Hosp, 37-39; from asst prof to assoc prof oral surg, 40-66, from asst prof to assoc prof surg, 53-66, prof surg & head sect plastic surg, 66-77, EMER PROF SURG, DEPT SURG, MED SCH, UNIV MICH, ANN ARBOR, 77- *Concurrent Pos:* Staff surg plastic surg, St Joseph Mercy Hosp, Ann Arbor. *Mem:* Am Col Surg; Am Asn Plastic Surg; Am Soc Plastic & Reconstruct Surg (past pres); Am Soc Maxillofacial Surg (past pres). *Res:* Plastic surgery; facial trauma and reconstruction; cleft palate and facial deformities. *Mailing Add:* 221 N Ingalls St Ann Arbor MI 48104

DINGMAN, STANLEY LAWRENCE, b Jersey City, NJ, Jan 31, 39; m 73; c 2. HYDROLOGY, RESOURCE MANAGEMENT. *Educ:* Dartmouth Col, AB, 60; Harvard Univ, AM, 61, PhD(geol), 70. *Prof Exp:* Res hydrologist, US Army Cold Regions Res & Eng Lab, 63-69; vis asst prof environ studies & earth sci, Dartmouth Col, 69-72; dir res water resources, Dubois & King, Inc Environ Engrs, 72-73; sr resource planner, Conn River Basin Prog, New Eng River Basins Comn, 73-75; ASSOC PROF WATER RESOURCES, INST NATURAL & ENVIRON RESOURCES, UNIV NH, 75-; VPRES, HYDROSCI ASSOCS, INC, 80- *Mem:* Am Geophys Union; AAAS; Am Water Resources Asn; Sigma Xi. *Res:* Hydrology of New England; water quantity/quality management; hydrology of arctic and subarctic regions. *Mailing Add:* RFD Canney Rd Durham NH 03824

DINGUS, RONALD SHANE, b Appleton City, Mo, Sept 17, 38; m 58; c 2. HIGH TEMPERATURE PHYSICS & CHEMISTRY. *Educ:* Univ Mo, BS, 60; Iowa State Univ, PhD(nuclear physics), 65. *Prof Exp:* Res asst, Ames Lab, Iowa State Univ, 60-65, res assoc, 65; res assoc, Physics Inst, Aarhus Univ, 65-66 & Nuclear Physics Lab, Univ Colo, Boulder, 66-68; MEM STAFF, LOS ALAMOS NAT LAB, 68- *Concurrent Pos:* Fulbright travel grant, Physics Inst, Aarhus Univ. *Mem:* Am Phys Soc; Sigma Xi; AAAS. *Res:* X-ray and gamma-ray spectroscopy; x-ray vulnerability of strategic reentry vehicle systems; dynamic response of materials to pulsed heating. *Mailing Add:* MS 948 Los Alamos Nat Lab Los Alamos NM 87545

DINKINS, REED LEON, b Whitehall, Ark, June 10, 38; m 60; c 1. ENTOMOLOGY. *Educ:* Ark Polytech Col, BS, 62; Univ Ark, MS, 66; Miss State Univ, PhD(entom), 69. *Prof Exp:* Surv entomologist, Miss State Univ, 66-69; assoc prof, 69-80, PROF ZOOL & ENTOM, PITTSBURG STATE UNIV, 80- *Mem:* Entom Soc Am; Cent States Entom Soc. *Res:* Insect pests of the Pecan. *Mailing Add:* Dept Biol Pittsburg State Univ Pittsburg KS 66762

DINMAN, BERTRAM DAVID, b Philadelphia, Pa, Aug 9, 25; m 50; c 4. OCCUPATIONAL MEDICINE, ENVIRONMENTAL MEDICINE. *Educ:* Temple Univ, MD, 51; Univ Cincinnati, ScD(occup med), 57; Am Bd Prev Med, dipl, 60. *Prof Exp:* From asst prof to prof prev med, Col Med, Ohio State Univ, 57-65; prof environ & indust health, Univ Mich, Ann Arbor, 65-73; med dir, 73-78, VPRES HEALTH & SAFETY, ALUMINUM CO AM, 78- *Concurrent Pos:* Mem comn environ hyg, Armed Forces Epidemiol Bd, 65-73; mem comt toxicol, Nat Res Coun, 65-70, chmn, 72-77, mem comt biol effects of atmospheric pollutants, 69-71; dir, Inst Environ & Indust Health, Univ Mich, Ann Arbor, 70-73; expert advisor, WHO, 71- *Mem:* Fel Am Acad Occup Med (pres, 73-75); fel Am Col Prev Med; Soc Toxicol. *Res:* Cellular toxicology; enzymatic response to chemical injury; environmental toxicology. *Mailing Add:* VPres Health & Safety Aluminum Co of Am Pittsburgh PA 15219

DINNEEN, GERALD PAUL, b Elmhurst, NY, Oct 23, 24; m 47; c 3. MATHEMATICS. *Educ:* Queens Col, BS, 47; Univ Wis, MS, 48, PhD(math), 52. *Prof Exp:* Teaching asst math, Univ Wis, 47-51; sr develop engr, Goodyear Aircraft Corp, Ohio, 51-53; staff mem, Lincoln Lab, Mass Inst Technol, 53-58, sect leader data processing group, 58, from asst leader to leader, 58-60, assoc head info processing div, 60-63 & commun div, 63-64, head, 64-66, from asst dir to assoc dir, 66-70, dir, 70-77, prof elec eng, Mass Inst Technol, 71-77; asst secy defense for commun, command, control & intelligence, Dept Defense, 77-81; CORP VPRES SCI & TECHNOL, HONEYWELL, INC, 81- *Concurrent Pos:* Consult, Air Force Sci Adv Bd, 59-60, mem electronics panel, 60-65 & chmn info processing panel, 63-65; mem, Defense Intel Agency Sci Adv Comt, 65-66, vchmn, 66-73; mem, Defense Sci Bd Panels, 66-67; chmn, US Air Force Sci Adv Bd, 75-77. *Honors & Awards:* Decoration Exceptional Civilian Serv, US Air Force, 66 & 77. *Mem:* Nat Acad Eng; Am Math Soc. *Res:* Matrix algebra; probability theory; logical design of digital computers; military systems design; satellite communications. *Mailing Add:* 7611 Gleason Rd Edina MN 55435

DINNEEN, GERALD UEL, b Denver, Colo, May 6, 13; m 38; c 2. CHEMISTRY. *Educ:* Univ Denver, BS, 34. *Prof Exp:* Chemist, Richards Labs, Colo, 34-38; soil conserv serv, USDA, NMex, 38-42 & US Customs Serv, Calif, 42-44; chemist in charge lab invests, US Maritime Comn, 44-45; res chemist & supvr, Laramie Energy Res Ctr, US Bur Mines, 45-64, res dir, 64-75; CONSULT ENGR FOSSIL FUELS, 75- *Mem:* AAAS; Am Inst Chem Eng; Am Chem Soc; Geochem Soc. *Res:* Composition and reactions of shale oil and petroleum; chemistry of hydrocarbons and organic nitrogen, sulfur and oxygen compounds; origin of petroleum and oil shale; recovery and processing of shale oil. *Mailing Add:* 2993 S Columbine St Denver CO 80210

DINNER, ALAN, b Newton, Mass, Sept 30, 44; m 81. ORGANIC CHEMISTRY, ANALYTICAL CHEMISTRY. *Educ:* Mass Inst Technol, BS, 66; Ind Univ, Bloomington, PhD(org chem), 70. *Prof Exp:* Teaching asst org chem, Ind Univ, Bloomington, 66-67, res asst med chem, 67-69, fel dept chem, 70-71; fel sch pharm, Univ Calif, San Francisco, 71-73; sr anal chemist org & anal chem, 74-78, res scientist, 78-79, MGR DRY PROD DEVELOP, ELI LILLY & CO, 79- *Concurrent Pos:* Lectr chem, Butler Univ, 75- *Mem:* Am Chem Soc; AAAS. *Res:* The study of drug stability and the isolation and identification of trace contaminants in new drugs; development of new drug dosage forms. *Mailing Add:* Eli Lilly & Co IC740 Indianapolis IN 46285

DINNING, JAMES SMITH, b Franklin, Ky, Sept 28, 22; m 44; c 4. NUTRITION. *Educ:* Univ Ky, BS, 46; Okla State Univ, MS, 47, PhD(biochem), 48. *Hon Degrees:* DSc, Mahidol Univ, Thailand, 74. *Prof Exp:* Asst prof, Med Sch, Univ Ark, 48-52, assoc prof biochem, 53-58, prof & head dept, 59-63; mem staff, Rockefeller Found, 63-75, assoc dir, 75-78; RES SCIENTIST, DEPT FOOD SCI & HUMAN NUTRIT, UNIV FLA, 78- *Concurrent Pos:* Asst prof, Univ Pittsburgh, 52-53; spec consult, USPHS; assoc ed, Nutrit Rev, ed, J Nutrit. *Honors & Awards:* Lederle Med Fac Award, 55; Mead-Johnson Award, Am Inst Nutrit, 64. *Mem:* Soc Exp Biol & Med; Am Soc Biol Chemists; Am Inst Nutrit. *Res:* Metabolic effects of vitamin deficiencies; blood cell formation. *Mailing Add:* Dept Food Sci & Human Nutrit Univ of Fla Gainesville FL 32611

DINOS, NICHOLAS, b Tamaqua, Pa, Jan 15, 34; m 55; c 3. CHEMICAL ENGINEERING. *Educ:* Pa State Univ, BS, 55; Lehigh Univ, MS, 66, PhD(chem eng), 67. *Prof Exp:* Chem engr, E I du Pont de Nemours & Co, Inc, 55-57, res engr nuclear eng, Savannah River Lab, SC, 57-62, reactor engr nuclear safety, 62-64; teaching asst chem eng, Lehigh Univ, 64-65; ceramics engr, Bethlehem Steel Corp, Pa, 65; assoc prof, 66-72, PROF CHEM ENG, OHIO UNIV, 72-, CHMN DEPT, 77- *Mem:* AAAS; Am Chem Soc; Am Inst Chem Engrs. *Res:* Applications of chemical engineering to biology and vice versa; transport phenomena, mathematics. *Mailing Add:* Dept of Chem Eng Ohio Univ Athens OH 45701

DINOWITZ, MARSHALL, microbiology, see previous edition

DINSE, GREGG ERNEST, b Rochester, NY, Nov 9, 54; m 81. SURVIVAL ANALYSIS, NONPARAMETRIC STATISTICS. *Educ:* Bucknell Univ, BS, 76; State Univ NY, Buffalo, MS, 78; Harvard Univ, ScD, 81. *Prof Exp:* Res fel biostatist, Sch Pub Health, Harvard Univ, 81-82; STAFF FEL BIOMET, NAT INST ENVIRON HEALTH SCI, 82- *Mem:* Am Statist Asn; Biomet Soc; Royal Statist Soc. *Res:* Statistical analysis of incomplete observations, such as censored survival data and tumor prevalence and onset data, applied in various clinical, epidemiological and laboratory investigations. *Mailing Add:* 888-A Cedar Fork Trail Chapel Hill NC 27514

DINSMORE, BRUCE HEASLEY, b Indiana, Pa, Sept 18, 15; m 39; c 3. ECOLOGY, AQUATIC BIOLOGY. *Educ:* Ind Univ Pa, BS, 37; Columbia Univ, MA, 41; Univ Pittsburgh, MS, 54, PhD(ecol), 58. *Prof Exp:* Teacher pub schs, Pa & NY, 37-47; from asst prof to assoc prof, 47-71, prof biol & chmn dept biol sci, 71-78, EMER PROF BIOL, CLARION STATE COL, 78- *Mem:* Ecol Soc Am; Am Inst Biol Sci. *Res:* Ecological studies of plant and animal communities of strip mine ponds in Pennsylvania; ecology of streams receiving acid mine drainage. *Mailing Add:* 203 South St Clarion PA 16214

DINSMORE, CHARLES EARLE, b Lisbon Falls, Maine, Oct 10, 47; m 72; c 2. DEVELOPMENTAL BIOLOGY, EXPERIMENTAL MORPHOGENESIS. *Educ:* Bowdoin Col, BA, 70; Brown Univ, PhD(biol), 74. *Prof Exp:* Asst prof biol, Emmanuel Col, 74-76; ASST PROF ANAT, COL MED, RUSH UNIV, 76- *Mem:* AAAS; Am Asn Anatomists; Sigma Xi; Am Soc Zoologists; Fedn Am Scientists. *Res:* Urodele limb and tail regeneration; ultrastructure of the urodelespinal cord; pattern regulation in regenerating systems. *Mailing Add:* Dept Anat Col Med 600 S Paulina Chicago IL 60612

DINSMORE, HOWARD LIVINGSTONE, b Patton, Pa, May 27, 21; m 42; c 7. ANALYTICAL CHEMISTRY. *Educ:* Johns Hopkins Univ, AB, 42; Univ Minn, PhD(phys chem), 49. *Prof Exp:* Chemist, US Naval Res Lab, 42-46; res assoc phys chem, Brown Univ, 49-50; chemist, Smith Kline & French Labs, 50-51, Com Solvents Corp, 51-54 & M W Kellogg Co, 54-56; prof chem, Bethel Col, 56-66; PROF CHEM, FLA SOUTHERN COL, 66- *Concurrent Pos:* Chemist, Agr Res Corp, Lakeland, Fla, 74- *Mem:* Am Chem Soc. *Res:* Infrared and mass spectroscopy applied to chemical analysis; pesticide trace analysis by gas chromatography. *Mailing Add:* 730 S Mississippi Ave Lakeland FL 33801

DINSMORE, JAMES JAY, b Owatonna, Minn, Feb 25, 42; m 64; c 4. ORNITHOLOGY. *Educ:* Iowa State Univ, BS, 64; Univ Wis, MS, 67; Univ Fla, PhD(zool), 70. *Prof Exp:* Asst prof zool, Univ Fla, 70-71; asst prof biology, Univ Tampa, 71-75; assoc prof, 75-81, PROF ANIMAL ECOL, IOWA STATE UNIV, 81- *Mem:* Am Ornith Union; Cooper Ornith Soc; Wilson Ornith Soc. *Res:* Ethology of colonial seabirds; foraging behavior of birds; biology of marsh birds. *Mailing Add:* Dept of Animal Ecol Iowa State Univ Ames IA 50011

DINSMORE, R(AY) P(UTNAM), chemical engineering, deceased

DINTZIS, HOWARD MARVIN, b Chicago, Ill, May 28, 27; m 51; c 3. BIOPHYSICS. *Educ:* Univ Calif, Los Angeles, BS, 48; Harvard Univ, PhD(med sci), 53; Lawrence Univ, DSc, 64. *Prof Exp:* Lilly res fel, Harvard Univ, 52-53; NSF fel, Yale Univ, 53-54; fel, Univ Cambridge, 54-56; asst prof chem, Calif Inst Technol, 56-58; sr res assoc biol, Mass Inst Technol, 58-61; PROF BIOPHYS & DIR DEPT, SCH MED, JOHNS HOPKINS UNIV, 61- *Mem:* Am Chem Soc. *Res:* Structure and biosynthesis of proteins and nucleic acids. *Mailing Add:* Dept of Biophys Sch of Med Johns Hopkins Univ Baltimore MD 21218

DINTZIS, RENEE ZLOCHOVER, b New York, NY; m 51; c 3. CELL BIOLOGY, HISTOLOGY. *Educ:* Hunter Col, BA, 48; Harvard Univ, PhD(biochem), 53. *Prof Exp:* Fel physiol, Yale Med Sch, 53-54, biochem, Cambridge Univ, 54-56; instr, 71-73, ASST PROF CELL BIOL, ANAT & BIOPHYSICS, MED SCH, JOHNS HOPKINS UNIV, 74- *Res:* Mechanism of stimulation of the immunoresponsive cell. *Mailing Add:* Dept Cell Biol & Anat Med Sch Johns Hopkins Univ 725 N Wolfe St Baltimore MD 21205

DINUNNO, CECIL MALMBERG, b Washington, DC, Aug 2, 49; m 76. ORGANIC CHEMISTRY. *Educ:* Gettysburg Col, BA, 71; Univ NH, MS, 74. *Prof Exp:* Res chemist, SISA Inc, 74-76; asst res scientist, 76-78, RES SCIENTIST CHEM, SOUTHWEST FOUND RES & EDUC, 78- *Mem:* Am Chem Soc; Sigma Xi; AAAS. *Res:* Organic synthesis of biologically significant compounds; steroids, analgesics and narcotic antagonists and polyfunctional macrocycles. *Mailing Add:* Southwest Found Res & Educ W Loop 410 & Military Dr San Antonio TX 78284

DINUNZIO, JAMES E, b Buffalo, NY, Sept 26, 50; m 75. ANALYTICAL CHEMISTRY. *Educ:* Utica Col, BS, 72; Southern Ill Univ, PhD(anal chem), 77. *Prof Exp:* Res assoc chem, Univ Ariz, 77-78; ASST PROF CHEM, WRIGHT STATE UNIV, 78- *Mem:* Am Chem Soc. *Res:* Separations, environmental trace analysis. *Mailing Add:* Dept of Chem Wright State Univ Dayton OH 45435

DINUS, RONALD JOHN, b Ford City, Pa, Feb 19, 40; m 64. FOREST GENETICS, DISEASE RESISTANCE. *Educ:* Pa State Univ, BS, 61; Univ Wash, MS, 63; Ore State Univ, PhD(forest genetics), 67. *Prof Exp:* Res plant geneticist, Inst Forest Genetics, Southern Forest Exp Sta, Forest Serv, USDA, 68-72, res leader, 72-77; MGR, WESTERN FOREST RES CTR, INT PAPER CO, 77- *Concurrent Pos:* Mem task force basic res needs in forestry, USDA, 79. *Mem:* Am Inst Biol Sci; Soc Am Foresters; Sigma Xi; Am Phytopath Soc. *Res:* Characterization of intraspecific variation in photoperiodic responses of Douglas-fir populations from several geographic areas; selection, progenytesting and breeding of slash and loblolly pines resistant to fusiform rust; Douglas-fir genetics, regeneration and silviculture. *Mailing Add:* Int Paper Co 34937 Tennessee Rd Lebanon OR 97355

DINUSSON, WILLIAM ERLING, b Svold, NDak, Apr 28, 20; m 44; c 2. ANIMAL NUTRITION, ANIMAL HUSBANDRY. *Educ:* Okla Agr & Mech Col, BS, 41; Purdue Univ, PhD(animal nutrit), 49;Am Soc Animal Sci, cert animal nutritionist, 75. *Prof Exp:* Asst, Tex A&M Univ, 41-42; asst, Purdue Univ, 46-48; asst prof animal husb, Exp Sta, SDak State Col, 48-49; assoc prof, 49-56, PROF ANIMAL HUSB, EXP STA, NDAK STATE UNIV, 56- *Concurrent Pos:* Fulbright res scholar, Iceland, 60-61; mem subcomt sheep, Nat Res Coun, 55-75. *Honors & Awards:* Fac Lectr Award, 66. *Mem:* Fel AAAS; Am Soc Animal Sci; animal nutrition; ruminant nutrition. *Res:* Sunflower seed oil meal for livestock; protein and energy sources for beef cattle and swine; use of adjuvants in beef cattle. *Mailing Add:* Dept Animal Sci NDak State Univ Fargo ND 58105

DINWIDDIE, JOSEPH GRAY, JR, b Penns Grove, NJ, Oct 7, 22; m 45; c 4. ORGANIC CHEMISTRY. *Educ:* Randolph-Macon Col, BS, 42; Univ Va, PhD(chem), 49. *Prof Exp:* From asst prof to prof chem, Clemson Univ, 48-68; DEAN, AUGUSTA COL, 68- *Mem:* Fel AAAS; Am Chem Soc. *Res:* Synthetic medicinals; stereochemistry; molecular rearrangements. *Mailing Add:* 3606 St Croix Ct Augusta GA 30909

DIOKNO, ANANIAS CORNEJO, b San Luis, Batangas, Philippines, Aug 13, 42; m 67; c 4. UROLOGY. *Educ:* Univ Santo Tomas, Manila, MD, 65. *Prof Exp:* Fel, 70-71, from instr to asst prof, 71-76, ASSOC PROF UROL, UNIV MICH, 76- *Concurrent Pos:* Consult urol, Wayne Co Gen Hosp & Vet Admin Hosp, Ann Arbor, 70-; consult, drugs for bladder dysfunction, AMA, 78, urol res Marion Labs, 72- & Eli Lilly Co, 78-; med adv, Mideast Region Int Asn Entro-stomach ther, 77-, Hydrodyn Comt, Urodyn Soc, 78-; contribr continuing med educ prog, Am Urol Asn, 77-78. *Honors & Awards:* Sci Exhib Award, Am Urol Asn, 75; Clin Res Award, 75; Silver Medal Award, Sci Exhib Cong Phys Med & Rehab, 75. *Mem:* Urodyn Soc; AMA; Am Col Surgeons; Philippine-Am Urol Soc (pres, 77-78); Am Cong Rehab. *Res:* Lower urinary tract dysfunctions (urodynamics) and sexual dysfunctions. *Mailing Add:* C5117 Outpatient Bldg Univ Hosp Ann Arbor MI 48105

DION, ANDRE R, b Quebec, Que, May 3, 26; m 59; c 3. PHYSICS. *Educ:* Laval Univ, BScA, 49, MSc, 50, DSc(physics), 53. *Prof Exp:* Defense res sci officer, Defense Res Bd, Can, 53-60; MEM STAFF, LINCOLN LAB, MASS INST TECHNOL, 60- *Mem:* Inst Elec & Electronics Eng. *Res:* Electromagnetic waves; microwaves; antennas; propagation. *Mailing Add:* 600 Hayward Mill Rd Concord MA 01742

DION, ARNOLD SILVA, b Laconia, NH, June 26, 39; m 61; c 4. BIOCHEMISTRY. *Educ:* Univ NH, BS, 64, MS, 66, PhD(biochem), 69. *Prof Exp:* NIH fel, Univ Pa, 68-70, res assoc biochem, 70-71; asst biochemist, 71-72, ASSOC BIOCHEMIST & HEAD, MOLECULAR BIOL DEPT, INST MED RES, NJ, 72- *Concurrent Pos:* Adj assoc prof path, NY Med Col, 81- *Mem:* AAAS; Am Soc Microbiol; Sigma Xi; NY Acad Sci. *Res:* Correlations between polyamine and nucleic acid synthesis during development in Drosophila melanogaster and in bacteriophage infected cells; biochemical characterization of oncornaviruses, including RNA-dependent DNA polymerase; SV40 integration sites. *Mailing Add:* Inst for Med Res Copewood St Camden NJ 08103

DIONNE, GERALD FRANCIS, b Montreal, Que, Feb 5, 35; m 63; c 1. MAGNETISM, NEAR-MILLIMETER WAVES. *Educ:* Concordia Univ, BSc, 56; McGill Univ, BEng, 58, PhD(physics), 64; Carnegie-Mellon Univ, MS, 59. *Prof Exp:* Engr I, Bell Tel Co Can, 58-59; jr engr, Int Bus Mach Corp, NY, 59-60; sr engr, Gen Tel & Electronics Semiconductor Div, Sylvania Elec Prod, Inc, Mass, 60-61; res asst physics, Eaton Electronics Res Lab, McGill Univ, 63-64; res assoc, Advan Mat Res & Develop Lab, Pratt & Whitney Aircraft Div, United Aircraft Corp, 64-66; sr res assoc, 66; STAFF MEM, LINCOLN LAB, MASS INST TECHNOL, 66- *Concurrent Pos:* Asst, Carnegie-Mellon Univ, 58-59. *Mem:* Am Phys Soc; sr mem Inst Elec & Electronics Eng. *Res:* Magnetism and ferrimagnetic materials; magneto-elastic phenomena; electron and ion emission; electron spin resonance and relaxation; far infrared spectroscopy and laser optics; millimeter-wave radiometry; thermionic energy conversion; semiconductor devices. *Mailing Add:* 182 High St Winchester MA 01890

DIONNE, JEAN-CLAUDE, b Luceville, Que, Jan 3, 35; m 66; c 3. GEOLOGY, GEOGRAPHY. *Educ:* Univ Moncton, BA, 57; Univ Montreal, MA, 61; Univ Paris, PhD(geog), 70. *Prof Exp:* Res officer geomorphol, Bur Amenagement l'Est Que, Mont-Joli, 64-66; ares officer geomorphol, Dept Forestry & Rural Develop, Can, 66-70; res scientist, Land Div, Environ Can, Que, 70-80; PROF, DEPT GEOG, UNIV LAVAL, QUE, 80- *Concurrent Pos:* Prof coastal morphol & photo-interpretation, Laval Univ, 66-67; consult, Urban Planning Off Que, 66-68. *Mem:* Geol Asn Can; Soc Econ Paleont & Mineral. *Res:* Geomorphology; physical geography; quaternary geology; sedimentology; coastal and marine geology; oceanography; photo-interpretation. *Mailing Add:* 2761 Valcourt Quebec PQ G1W 1V9 Can

DIONNE, RAYMOND A, b Providence, RI, Dec 25, 46; m 71. CLINICAL PHARMACOLOGY, PAIN. *Educ:* Univ Conn, BA, 68; Georgetown Univ, DDS, 72; Med Col Va, PhD(pharmacol), 80. *Prof Exp:* Fel, 75-78, ASST CLIN PROF ORAL SURG, MED COL VA, VA COMMONWEALTH UNIV, 78-; STAFF FEL, NAT INST DENT RES, NIH, 78- *Mem:* Int Asn Study of Pain; Int Asn Dent Res; Soc Neurosci; Am Pain Soc. *Res:* Assessment of relationship between clinical efficacy and toxicity of drugs used to control pain and apprehension in outpatients. *Mailing Add:* Bldg 10 Rm 2B-05 Nat Inst Dent Res 9000 Rockville Pike Bethesda MD 20205

D'IORIO, ANTOINE, b Montreal, Que, Apr 22, 25; m 50; c 7. BIOCHEMISTRY. *Educ:* Univ Montreal, BSc, 46, PhD(biochem), 49. *Prof Exp:* Lectr physiol, Univ Montreal, 49-51, asst prof, 52-56; fel enzymol, Univ Wis, 51-52; fel pharmacol, Oxford Univ, 56-57; assoc prof physiol, Univ Montreal, 57-61; head dept biochem, 61-69, dean sci, 69-76, PROF BIOCHEM, UNIV OTTAWA, 61-, VICE-RECTOR ACAD, 76- *Mem:* Am Chem Soc; Am Asn Biol Chemists; Soc Exp Biol & Med; Can Physiol Soc (treas, 58-61); Can Fedn Biol Soc (hon treas, 62-66). *Res:* Physiology and biochemistry of catecholamines. *Mailing Add:* Off of the Vice-Rector Univ of Ottawa Ottawa Can

DIOSY, ANDREW, b Szarvas, Hungary, Mar 27, 24; Can citizen; m 55; c 2. INTERNAL MEDICINE. *Educ:* Univ Szeged, MD, 50; Univ Man, MSc, 59; FRCP(C). *Prof Exp:* Asst prof physiol, Univ Szeged, 50-52; res fel, Aviation Hosp, Budapest, Hungary, 52-56; res asst, Univ Man, 57-59; jr intern med, Winnipeg Gen Hosp, Man, 59-60; sr intern, Deer Lodge Hosp, 60-61; resident med, St Michael's Hosp, Toronto, Ont, 62-63; res assoc pharmacol, Univ Toronto, 63-65; dir clin res, 65-70, MED DIR, WARNER-LAMBERT CAN LTD, 70- *Concurrent Pos:* Res fel endocrinol, St Michael's Hosp, Toronto, Ont, 61-62. *Honors & Awards:* E L Drewry Mem Award, 59. *Mem:* Am Col Physicians; Can Med Asn; NY Acad Sci; Royal Soc Med. *Res:* Clinical pharmacology; new drug research. *Mailing Add:* Warner-Lambert Can Ltd 2200 Eglinton Ave E Scarborough Can

DIPALMA, JOSEPH RUPERT, b New York, NY, Mar 21, 16; m 48; c 5. PHARMACOLOGY. *Educ:* Columbia Univ, BS, 36; Long Island Col Med, MD, 41. *Prof Exp:* Instr physiol & pharmacol, Long Island Col Med, 41-42, asst med, 44-48; assoc physiol & pharmacol, 46-48, asst prof med, 48-50; head dept, 50-67, PROF PHARMACOL, HAHNEMANN MED COL, 50-, SR VPRES ACAD AFFAIRS & DEAN MED COL, 67- *Concurrent Pos:* Fel, Harvard Med Sch, 46; consult malaria, Surgeon Gen, 67-69. *Mem:* Am Physiol Soc; Am Soc Clin Invest; Harvey Soc; AMA; Am Soc Pharmacol & Exp Therapeut. *Res:* Heart muscle; antifibrillatory drugs; chemical welfare agents; anthocyanins. *Mailing Add:* 230 N Broad St Philadelphia PA 19102

DI PAOLA, JANE WALSH, b Brooklyn, NY, Sept 17, 17; m 42; c 3. COMBINATORICS, GEOMETRY. *Educ:* St Joseph's Col, NY, BA, 39; Brooklyn Col, MA, 62; City Univ New York, PhD(math), 67. *Prof Exp:* Struct engr appl math, Cornell Aeronaut Lab, Buffalo, NY, 42-45; instr math, New York City Community Col, 64-65; asst prof, NY Univ, 67-71; ADJ PROF MATH, FLA ATLANTIC UNIV, 71- *Concurrent Pos:* Assoc ed, Am Math Monthly, Math Asn Am, 71-76. *Mem:* Sigma Xi; Math Asn Am; Can Soc Hist & Philos of Math. *Res:* Combinatorial mathematics with particular attention to graph theory, block designs, Steiner triple systems, algebraic structures from combinatorial designs, finite geometries. *Mailing Add:* Dept of Math Fla Atlantic Univ Boca Raton FL 33432

DIPAOLO, JOSEPH AMADEO, b Bridgeport, Conn, June 13, 24; m 52; c 2. GENETICS. *Educ:* Wesleyan Univ, AB, 48; Western Reserve Univ, MS, 49; Northwestern Univ, PhD(genetics), 51. *Prof Exp:* Asst instr genetics & biol, Northwestern Univ, 49-51; asst instr, Dept Biol, Loyola Univ, 51-53; asst instr clin & exp path, Med Sch, Northwestern Univ, 53-55; sr cancer res scientist, Roswell Park Mem Inst, NY, 55-63; asst res prof biol, Grad Sch, State Univ NY Buffalo, 55-63; head cytogenetics & cytol sect, 63-77, CHIEF LAB BIOL, BIOL BR, NAT CANCER INST, 77- ASSOC PROFESSIONAL LECTR ANAT, GEORGE WASHINGTON UNIV, 65- *Concurrent Pos:* Co-chmn US-USSR joint working group mammalian somatic cell genetics related to Neoplasia; consult, US-Poland Cancer Prog. *Mem:* Fel AAAS; Am Asn Cancer Res; Am Soc Human Genetics; Genetics Soc Am; fel NY Acad Sci. *Res:* Experimental cancer research; cell biology. *Mailing Add:* 6605 Melody Lane Bethesda MD 20034

DI PAOLO, ROCCO JOHN, b Brooklyn, NY. ORTHODONTICS. *Educ:* Long Island Univ, BS, 44; Univ Mo, DDS, 49; Am Bd Orthodont, dipl, 68; Univ Mo, cert pedodont. *Prof Exp:* Asst prof, 65-72, PROF ORTHODONT, CHMN DEPT & DIR, PROF & DIR ORAL REHAB CTR, SCH DENT, FAIRLEIGH DICKINSON UNIV, 72- *Concurrent Pos:* Consult, Bard-Parker Div Becton Dickinson Corp, 72-; univ grant, Sch Dent, Fairleigh Dickinson Univ, 73-74; consult & lectr, Oral Facial Rehab Ctr, St Barnabas Hosp, 74-; lectr, Sch Dent, Columbia Univ, 74-; dir, Int Dento-Facial Asn Abnormalities; consult, St Joseph Hosp, Paterson, NJ. *Mem:* Am Asn Orthodont; Am Cleft Palate Asn; Sigma Xi; fel Am Col Dent; fel Int Col Dent. *Res:* Cephalometric analysis; biomechanics; orthodontic development; cleft palate; oral facial rehabilitation; surgical orthodontics; birth defects; orthodontic diagnosis. *Mailing Add:* Fairleigh Dickson Univ Rutherford NJ 07070

DI PASQUALE, ALBERT MARTIN, cell biology, see previous edition

DIPASQUALE, GENE, b New York, NY, July 17, 32; m 62; c 2. BIOLOGY, PHYSIOLOGY. *Educ:* Iona Col, BS, 54; Long Island Univ, MS, 60; NY Univ, PhD, 70. *Prof Exp:* from asst scientist to sr res assoc, Dept Pharmacodynamics, Warner-Lambert Res Inst, 57-75, assoc dir, 71-77; SECT MGR IMMUNSPHARMACOL, STUART PHARMACEUT, 77- *Mem:* Endocrine Soc; NY Acad Sci; Am Soc Pharmacol & Exp Therapeut; Soc Exp Biol & Med. *Res:* Connective tissue metabolism in relation to inflammation, wound healing and atherosclerosis, especially effects of drugs in these areas; drugs and their relation to pregnancy and general endocrine interrelations; search for compounds which possess anti-fertility and anti-inflammatory properties; dermatopharmacology; pharmacology, especially as related to osteoarthritis and rheumatoid arthritis. *Mailing Add:* Pharmacol Dept ICI Am Wilmington DE 19803

DIPERT, ARNOLD WILLIAM, electrical engineering, see previous edition

DI PIETRO, DAVID LOUIS, b Philadelphia, Pa, Jan 16, 32; m 61; c 3. BIOCHEMISTRY. *Educ:* Temple Univ, BA, 55, MA, 57, PhD(biochem), 61. *Prof Exp:* Res fel med, Harvard Med Sch, 61-62; res assoc biochem, Div Res, Lankenau Hosp, Philadelphia, 62-63; res instr, Sch Med & res investr, Fels Res Inst, Temple Univ, 63-66, res asst prof, 66-68; ASST PROF OBSTET & GYNEC, SCH MED, VANDERBILT UNIV, 68- *Mem:* Am Chem Soc; Am Soc Biol Chemists; Brit Biochem Soc. *Res:* Enzymes of carbohydrate metabolism in liver and placenta; metabolism of estrogens in pregnancy. *Mailing Add:* Dept Obstet & Gynec Sch Med Vanderbilt Univ Nashville TN 37232

DI PIPPO, ASCANIO G, b Providence, RI, Jan 21, 32; m 61; c 4. ORGANIC CHEMISTRY, CLINICAL CHEMISTRY. *Educ:* Univ RI, BS, 54, MS, 58, PhD(chem), 61. *Prof Exp:* Sr res chemist, Labs, Olin Mathieson Chem Corp, 61 & Nat Labs Res & Testing, 61-62; from asst prof to assoc prof, 62-69, PROF ORG CHEM, SALVE REGINA COL, 69- *Concurrent Pos:* Consult, Newport Hosp, RI, 64- & Johns Hopkins Med Lab, 66-; chem eng, Raytheon, Submarine Signal Div, 68- *Mem:* Am Chem Soc. *Res:* Organic mechanisms; organoboron compounds; effects of radiation on organic compounds. *Mailing Add:* Dept of Chem Salve Regina Col Newport RI 02840

DIPIPPO, RONALD, b Providence, RI, June 2, 40; m 62, 80; c 3. MECHANICAL ENGINEERING, THERMODYNAMICS. *Educ:* Brown Univ, ScB, 62, ScM, 64, PhD(eng), 66. *Prof Exp:* Mech engr res dept, US Naval Underwater Systs Ctr, 66-67; assoc prof, 67-74, PROF MECH ENG & CHMN DEPT, SOUTHEASTERN MASS UNIV, 74- *Concurrent Pos:* Mem adv comt, Mass Bd Higher Educ, 70-71; adj prof eng res, Brown Univ;

consult, Stone & Webster Eng Corp; mem, Geotherm Resources Coun. *Mem:* Am Soc Eng Educ; Am Soc Mech Engrs. *Res:* Measurement and correlation of transport properties of gases; propulsion systems; geothermal energy conversion systems. *Mailing Add:* Dept of Mech Eng Southeastern Mass Univ North Dartmouth MA 02747

DIPIRRO, MICHAEL JAMES, b Haverhill, Mass, July 26, 51; m 79. LOW TEMPERATURE PHYSICS. *Educ:* Clarkson Col Technol, NY, BS, 73; State Univ NY, Buffalo, PhD(physics), 79. *Prof Exp:* Res assoc, Nat Bur Standards, 79-80; PHYSICIST, GODDARD SPACE FLIGHT CTR, NASA, 80- *Mem:* Am Phys Soc. *Res:* Physics of liquid helium including properties of 3Helium on the surface of 4Helium; properties of 4Helium near the lambda point; porous plug containment of 4Helium in space. *Mailing Add:* Code 713 NASA Goddard Space Flight Ctr Greenbelt MD 20771

DIPPEL, WILLIAM ALAN, b Jersey City, NJ, June 12, 26; m 52; c 5. ANALYTICAL CHEMISTRY. *Educ:* Princeton Univ, AB, 50, PhD(chem), 54. *Prof Exp:* Res chemist, Res Div, Explosives Dept, 54-59, anal supvr, 59-62, anal supt, 62-72, res supvr res & develop, Polymer Intermediates Dept, 72-78, res supvr, 78-79, RES MGR, RES & DEVELOP DIV, PETROCHEM DEPT, E I DUPONT DE NEMOURS & CO, 79- *Mem:* Am Chem Soc; Am Inst Chem. *Res:* Analytical research and development; analytical methods in process development and environmental quality gas and liquid chromatography; wet chemistry. *Mailing Add:* 203 Alapocas Dr Alapocas Wilmington DE 19803

DIPPELL, RUTH VIRGINIA, b Huntington, Ind, June 25, 20. CELL BIOLOGY, GENETICS. *Educ:* Ind Univ, Bloomington, PhD(zool), 49. *Prof Exp:* Asst zool, 42-45, res assoc, 45-67, ASSOC PROF ZOOL, IND UNIV, BLOOMINGTON, 67- *Concurrent Pos:* Adj prof, Ind State Univ, 66-67. *Honors & Awards:* Newcomb Prize, AAAS, 46. *Mem:* Fel AAAS; fel Am Asn Univ Women; Soc Protozool (vpres, 65-66); Am Soc Cell Biol; Int Soc Cell Biol. *Res:* Inheritance and morphogenesis of cell organelles, chromosomal organization and behavior in ciliate Protozoa. *Mailing Add:* Dept of Biol Ind Univ Jordan Hall 220 Bloomington IN 47405

DIPPLE, ANTHONY, b Eng, Feb 9, 40. CANCER. *Educ:* Univ Birmingham, BSc, 61, PhD(chem), 64. *Prof Exp:* Fel oncol, McArdle Lab, Univ Wis-Madison, 64-66; lectr, Chester Beatty Res Inst, Inst Cancer Res, London, 66-75; sect head molecular aspects carcinogenesis, 75-81, ASSOC DIR CHEM CARCINOGENESIS PROG, 81- *Mem:* The Chem Soc; Brit Asn Cancer Res; Am Asn Cancer Res. *Res:* Studies of the mechanism of action of chemical carcinogens. *Mailing Add:* 713 Midway Dr Frederick MD 21701

DIPPREY, DUANE F(LOYD), b Minneapolis, Minn, Dec 22, 29; m 52; c 2. MECHANICAL ENGINEERING. *Educ:* Univ Minn, BS, 51, MSME, 53; Calif Inst Technol, PhD(mech eng, physics), 61. *Prof Exp:* Develop engr, 53-56, sr develop engr, 56-60, eng group supvr, 60-62, asst sect mgr liquid rockets, 62-64, sect mgr liquid propulsion, 64-72, sect mgr advan concepts, 72-74, dep div mgr propulsion, 74-76, dep div mgr control & energy conversion, 76-78, DIV MGR APPLIED MECH, JET PROPULSION LAB, CALIF INST TECHNOL, 78- *Concurrent Pos:* Lectr, Univ Southern Calif, 63-65. *Mem:* Assoc fel Am Inst Aeronaut & Astronaut. *Res:* Heat transfer from roughened surfaces to flowing fluids; propulsion systems analysis. *Mailing Add:* Appl Mech Div 4800 Oak Grove Dr Pasadena CA 91103

DI PRIMA, RICHARD CLYDE, b Terre Haute, Ind, Aug 9, 27; m 54; c 2. APPLIED MATHEMATICS. *Educ:* Carnegie Inst Technol, BS, 50, MS, 51, PhD(math), 53. *Prof Exp:* Res assoc, Mass Inst Technol, 53-54; res fel, Harvard Univ, 54-56; physicist, Hughes Aircraft Co, Calif, 56-57; from asst prof to assoc prof, 57-62, assoc dean grad sch, 68-72, chmn fac coun, 69-70, chmn, Dept Math Sci, 72-81, prof math, 62-79, ELIZA RICKETTS FOUND PROF, RENSSELAER POLYTECH INST, 79- *Concurrent Pos:* Fulbright lectr, Weizmann Inst, Israel; mem coun, Conf Bd Math Sci, 75-78; bd trustees, Soc Indust & Appl Math, 77-; mem sci coun, Inst Comput Appln Sci & Eng, Langley Res Ctr, NASA, 77-, chmn, 81-; mem, Comt Recommendations, US Army Basic Sci Res, Nat Acad Sci-Nat Res Coun, 76-, chmn, 81- *Mem:* Am Math Soc; Math Asn Am; Soc Indust & Appl Math (pres, 79-81); fel Am Acad Mech (pres, 76-77); fel Am Soc Mech Engrs. *Res:* Hydrodynamics stability; fluid mechanics; singular perturbation theory; lubrication. *Mailing Add:* Dept Math Sci Rensselaer Polytech Inst Troy NY 12181

DIRECTOR, STEPHEN WILLIAM, b Brooklyn, NY, June 28, 43; m 65; c 4. ELECTRICAL ENGINEERING. *Educ:* State Univ NY Stony Brook, BS, 65; Univ Calif, Berkeley, MS, 67, PhD(elec eng), 68. *Prof Exp:* From asst prof to prof, Univ Fla, 68-77; PROF ELEC ENG, CARNEGIE-MELLON UNIV, 77-, U A & HELEN WITAKER PROF, ELEC & ELECTRONICS ENGR, 80-, PROF COMPUT SCI, 81- *Concurrent Pos:* Consult, IBM Corp, Intel Corp, Tex Instruments, Inc & Harris Corp; consult ed, McGraw Hill Book Co, 76- *Honors & Awards:* F E Terman Award, Am Soc Eng Educ, 76. *Mem:* Fel Inst Elec & Electronics Engrs; Inst Elec & Electronics Circuits & Systs Soc (pres, 80). *Res:* Computer aided design; network theory. *Mailing Add:* Dept of Elec Eng Carnegie-Mellon Univ Pittsburgh PA 15213

DIRENDE, JOSEPH S(ICILIANO), engineering, see previous edition

DI RIENZI, JOSEPH, b Brooklyn, NY, Aug 12, 47; m 76; c 1. RADIATION PHYSICS, NUCLEAR ENERGY. *Educ:* Polytech Inst NY, BS, 68, MS, 72, PhD(physics), 75. *Prof Exp:* Adj instr physics, Polytech Inst NY, 72-76, NY Inst Technol, 74-76; ASSOC PROF & CHMN PHYSICS & MATH, COL NOTRE DAME, 76- *Concurrent Pos:* Adj fac & mem adv comt, Sch Nuclear Med Technol, St Joseph Hosp, 81- *Mem:* Am Asn Physics Teachers; Sigma Xi. *Res:* Studies in the theory of nuclear structure; application of the intermediate coupling theory in the unified nuclear model on certain odd-mass nuclei. *Mailing Add:* Col Notre Dame 4701 N Charles St Baltimore MD 21210

DIRIGE, OFELIA VILLA, b Manila, Philippines, July 14, 40. NUTRITION. *Educ:* Univ Philippines, BSHE, 59; Univ Hawaii, MS, 68; Univ Calif, Los Angeles, DrPH(nutrit), 72. *Prof Exp:* Res asst nutrit, Sch Pub Health, Univ Calif, Los Angeles, 68-69, teaching asst, 69-71, res asst, 71-72, res assoc, 72-74; NUTRITIONIST, LOS ANGELES COUNTY COMMUNITY HEALTH SERV, 74- *Concurrent Pos:* Instr, Pepperdine Univ, 75- *Mem:* Am Dietetic Asn; Am Pub Health Asn; Am Home Econ Asn. *Res:* Biochemical assessment of nutritional status in pregnant women and malnourished children; transketolase activity in chronic uremia and in experimental uremia of rats; dietary assessment of nutritional status of pregnant women. *Mailing Add:* Hubert H Humphrey Health Ctr 5850 S Main Los Angeles CA 90003

DIRKS, BRINTON MARLO, b Newton Kans, July 20, 20; m 44; c 2. AGRICULTURAL BIOCHEMISTRY. *Educ:* Kans State Col, BS & MS, 48; Univ Minn, PhD(agr biochem), 53. *Prof Exp:* Chemist, Moundridge Milling Co, 38-40; chief operator, Tenn Eastman Corp, 45-46; head biochem res sect Pillsbury Mills, Inc, 52-56; group leader food prod develop, 56-60, head flavor develop sect, 60-68, head flour technol sect, 68-74, HEAD REGULATORY RELAT SECT, PROCTER & GAMBLE CO, 74- *Mem:* Am Chem Soc; Am Asn Cereal Chem; Inst Food Technol. *Res:* Enzymes of cereal grains, fungi and related materials; bio-chemistry of prepared baking mixes and other food products; flavor chemistry and application. *Mailing Add:* 8862 Woodview Dr Cincinnati OH 45231

DIRKS, JOHN HERBERT, b Winnipeg, Man, Aug 20, 33; m 61; c 4. MEDICINE, NEPHROLOGY. *Educ:* Univ Man, BSc & MD, 57; FRCPS(C), 63; FACP, 75. *Prof Exp:* Vis scientist, NIH, 64-65; asst prof med, Royal Victoria Hosp, 65-68, assoc physician, 68-71; asst prof, 68-69, ASSOC PROF PHYSIOL, McGILL UNIV, 70-, PROF MED, 73-, ASSOC PROF MED, ROYAL VICTORIA HOSP, 68-, SR PHYSICIAN, 71-, DIR RENAL & ELECTROLYTE DIV, UNIV CLIN, 65-; ERIC W HAMBER PROF MED & HEAD DEPT MED, UNIV BC, 76- *Concurrent Pos:* Med Res Coun fels, McGill Univ, 60-61, NIH fel, 62-64; grants, Med Res Coun, 65-, NIH, 66-68, Life Ins Med Res Fund, 67-, Banting Res Found & Can Cystic Fibrosis Found, 70-71, Can Arthritis & Rheumatism Soc & Hoechst Pharmaceut Co, 70- & Que Med Res Coun, 71-; ed renal & electrolyte sect, Am J Physiol, 73- *Mem:* Am Heart Asn; Am Fedn Clin Res; Am Physiol Soc; Am Soc Clin Invest; Can Soc Clin Invest (secy-treas, 72-75, pres & past pres, 75-78). *Res:* Renal physiology, primarily using micropuncture research; sodium, calcium and magnesium reabsorption by proximal and distal tubules in different physiological conditions; effects of diuretics on Na and K transport; clearance and micropuncture studies of magnesium transport in the renal tubule; micropuncture studies in Ca and P transport. *Mailing Add:* Dept Med Univ of BC 700 W 10th Ave Vancouver Can

DIRKS, LESLIE C, b New Ulm, Minn, Mar 7, 36; m 59; c 3. ENGINEERING. *Educ:* Mass Inst Technol, BS, 58; Oxford, BS, 60. *Prof Exp:* Instr physics, Phillips Acad, Mass, 60-61; tech staff, 61-76, DEP DIR SCI & TECHNOL, CENT INTELLIGENCE AGENCY, 76- *Honors & Awards:* Annual Award, Inst Elec & Electronics Engrs, 80. *Mem:* Nat Acad Eng. *Mailing Add:* 4451 Greenwich Parkway NW Washington DC 20007

DIRKS, RICHARD ALLEN, b Belmond, Iowa, Nov 11, 37; m 65; c 2. DYNAMIC METEOROLOGY. *Educ:* Wheaton Col, Ill, BS, 59; Drake Univ, MA, 62; Cornell Univ, MST, 65; Colo State Univ, PhD(atmospheric sci), 70. *Prof Exp:* Instr physics, Southeast Mo State Col, 62-64; jr meteorologist, Colo State Univ, 68-69; from asst prof to assoc prof atmospheric resources, Univ Wyo, 69-75; prog mgr environ res & technol, 75-77, PROG DIR ATMOSPHERIC SCI, NSF, 77- UNIV WYO, 69-, RES METEOROLOGIST, 70- *Mem:* AAAS; Am Meteorol Soc; Sigma Xi. *Res:* Observation and modeling of small scale airflow including such areas as convective circulations, thunderstorms, mountain airflow, urban circulations and boundary layer flow; airflow studies employing meteorological satellites. *Mailing Add:* Dept Atmospheric Sci NSF Washington DC 20550

DIRKS, VICTOR ALEXANDER, b Aug 11, 21; Can citizen. PLANT PROTECTION, CROP ROTATION ANALYSIS. *Educ:* Univ Man, BSA, 43, MSc, 45, PhD(genetics), 71. *Prof Exp:* From asst to assoc agronomist, South Dakota State Univ, 47-61; res asst, Univ Minn, 61-66, res assoc, 67-70; RES SCIENTIST, HARROW RES STA, AGR CAN, 73- *Mem:* Agr Inst Can; Am Soc Agron; Biomet Soc; Can Phytopath Soc; Genetics Soc Am. *Res:* Design, analysis and evaluation of agricultural experiments in SW Ontario region; crop management on clay soils; tobacco quality and inheritance; greenhouse tomato wilt; plant parasitic nematodes; tree fruit disease problems. *Mailing Add:* Agr Can Res Sta Harrow ON N0R 1G0 Can

DIRKSE, THEDFORD PRESTON, b Holland, Mich, Jan 5, 15; m 42; c 4. CHEMISTRY, ELECTROCHEMISTRY. *Educ:* Calvin Col, AB, 36; Ind Univ, AM, 37, PhD(gen & phys chem), 39. *Prof Exp:* Instr chem, Iowa State Col, 39-41; asst prof, Hamline Univ, 41-42; chemist, US Naval Res Lab, Wash, 42-46; asst prof, Hamline Univ, 46-47; assoc prof, 47-51, prof, 51-80, EMER PROF CHEM, CALVIN COL, 80- *Mem:* Am Chem Soc; Electrochem Soc; Int Soc Electrochem. *Res:* Electroplating from nonaqueous media; electrical conductance of solutions; alkaline batteries; conductance of salts in monoethanolamine; electrode kinetics. *Mailing Add:* Dept of Chem Calvin Col Grand Rapids MI 49506

DIRKSEN, CHRISTIAAN, b Leeuwarden, Neth, July 18, 36; US citizen; m 59; c 4. SOIL PHYSICS. *Educ:* State Agr Univ Wageningen, BS, 57, Agr Eng, 59; Cornell Univ, PhD(soil physics), 64. *Prof Exp:* Res engr hydrol, State Agr Univ Wageningen, 59; res assoc agron, Cornell Univ, 59-60; res physicist reservoir mech, Gulf Res & Develop Co, Pa, 63-68; soil scientist, Agr Res Serv, USDA, Madison, Wis, 68-73, soil scientist physics, Riverside, Calif, 73-78; ASSOC PROF SOIL PHYSICS, AGR UNIV WAGENINGEN, THE NETHERLANDS, 78- *Mem:* Am Soc Agron; Soil Sci Soc Am; Int Soc Soil Sci; European Geophys Soc; Nederl Bodemk Ver. *Res:* Interactions of water, salts and other environmental factors with growth of crops of irrigation agriculture under arid and semi-arid conditions; physics of subsurface watershed hydrology. *Mailing Add:* Salverdaplein 10 PB 9101 6700 HB Wageningen Netherlands

DIRKSEN, ELLEN ROTER, b Lagow, Poland, May 10, 29; US citizen; m 56; c 1. CELL BIOLOGY, DEVELOPMENTAL BIOLOGY. *Educ:* Univ Ariz, BS, 49; Univ Ill, MS, 53; Univ Calif, Berkeley, PhD(zool), 61. *Prof Exp:* Res asst, Rheumatic Fever Res Inst, Sch Med, Northwestern Univ, Chicago, 49-51; assoc res physiologist, Cancer Res Inst, Univ Calif, San Francisco, 61-75, assoc prof anat, 74-75; ASSOC PROF ANAT, UNIV CALIF, LOS ANGELES, 75- *Mem:* AAAS; Am Soc Cell Biol; Soc Develop Biol; Soc Study Reproduction; Am Inst Biol Sci. *Res:* Origin, composition and formation of centrioles, basal bodies and cilia; ciliary activity in metazoan epithelia; structure of oncogenic viruses and function as they relate to human cancers. *Mailing Add:* Dept of Anat Univ Calif Sch of Med Los Angeles CA 90024

DIRKSEN, THOMAS REED, b Pekin, Ill, Nov 5, 31; m 55; c 6. DENTISTRY, BIOCHEMISTRY. *Educ:* Bradley Univ, BS, 53; Univ Ill, DDS, 57; Eastman Dent Ctr, cert pedodontics, 60; Univ Rochester, MS, 61, PhD(biochem), 68. *Prof Exp:* Assoc prof oral biol, Sch Dent & assoc prof biochem, Sch Med, coordr biochem dent, 67-78, 67-71, assoc prof cell & molecular biol, Sch Med, 71-73, PROF CELL & MOLECULAR BIOL, SCH MED, 73-, ASSOC DEAN BIOL SCI, 78- *Concurrent Pos:* Nat Inst Arthritis & Metab Dis study grant, 68-74; Nat Inst Dent Res Caries Study, 75-78; Juvenile Diabetes res grant, 76-78. *Mem:* Am Asn Dent Schs; Am Dent Asn; Int Asn Dent Res; Am Inst Nutrit; Am Asn Dent Res. *Res:* Lipid synthesis by bone and bone cell cultures; lipid constituents of calcified structure; pH of carious cavities. *Mailing Add:* Dept of Oral Biol Med Col of Ga Sch of Dent Augusta GA 30902

DIRLAM, JOHN PHILIP, b Eugene, Ore, Oct 3, 43; m 65; c 2. ORGANIC CHEMISTRY, MEDICINAL CHEMISTRY. *Educ:* Pac Lutheran Univ, BS, 65; Univ Calif, Los Angeles, PhD(org chem), 69. *Prof Exp:* Fel, Univ Lund, 70-71; NSF fel, Yale Univ, 71-72; res chemist, 72-76, sr res scientist med chem, 76-81, INVESTR ORG CHEM, PFIZER INC, 81- *Mem:* Am Chem Soc. *Res:* Synthesis of natural products; antibiotic research; heterocyclic chemistry. *Mailing Add:* Pfizer Cent Res Eastern Point Rd Groton CT 06340

DIRR, MICHAEL ALBERT, ornamental horticulture, see previous edition

D'ISA, FRANK ANGELO, b Youngstown, Ohio, Mar 30, 21; m 50; c 1. MECHANICAL ENGINEERING. *Educ:* Youngstown Univ, BS, 43; Carnegie Inst Technol, MS, 47; Univ Pittsburgh, PhD(mech eng), 60. *Prof Exp:* From asst prof to assoc prof, 47-60, PROF MECH ENG, YOUNGSTOWN STATE UNIV, 60-, CHMN DEPT, 56- *Mem:* Am Soc Mech Engrs; Nat Soc Prof Engrs; Am Soc Eng Educ; Sigma Xi. *Res:* Strength of materials, elasticity, plasticity, creep, impact, fatigue; engineering mechanics, dynamics of machinery, vibrations. *Mailing Add:* Dept of Mech Eng Youngstown State Univ 410 Wick Ave Youngstown OH 44555

DI SABATO, GIOVANNI, b Venice Italy, Mar 2, 29; m 63. IMMUNOLOGY. *Educ:* Univ Padua, MD, 54. *Prof Exp:* Res fel biochem, Univ Milan, 54-58 & Brandeis Univ, 59-61, sr res assoc, 61-63; Am Cancer Soc scholar, Carlsberg Lab, Copenhagen Denmark, 63-65; res asst prof, Brandeis Univ, 65-66; asst prof, 66-68, ASSOC PROF BIOCHEM, VANDERBILT UNIV, 68- *Concurrent Pos:* Vis prof, Dept Path, Univ of Minn, 72-73. *Mem:* AAAS; Am Soc Biol Chem. *Res:* Control of the immunologic response; biochemical aspects of cellular immunology. *Mailing Add:* Dept Molecular Biol Vanderbilt Univ Nashville TN 37203

DISALVO, ARTHUR F, b New York, NY, May 16, 32; m 58; c 1. MICROBIOLOGY. *Educ:* Univ Ariz, BS, 54, MS, 58; Med Col Ga, MD, 65; Am Bd Microbiol, dipl & cert med mycol, 71. *Prof Exp:* Jr bacteriologist, Ariz State Lab, 56-58; lab dir & bacteriologist, Milledgeville State Hosp, 58-59; res asst, Med Col Ga, 59-63; fel med microbiol, Nat Commun Dis Ctr, 66-68; CHIEF, BUR LABS, SC DEPT HEALTH & ENVIRON CONTROL, 68-; CLIN ASSOC PROF LAB MED, MED UNIV SC, 78-; clin assoc prof, Sch Med, Univ SC, 76-80. *Concurrent Pos:* Asst clin prof microbiol, Sch Med, Univ SC, 71-78; consult microbiol subcomt, Food & Drug Admin, 75-81; adj prof med microbiol, Sch Med, Univ SC, 80- *Mem:* AMA; Am Soc Microbiol; AAAS; Int Soc Human & Animal Mycol; Med Mycol Soc Americas (secytreas, 79-). *Res:* Medical mycology. *Mailing Add:* SC Dept Health & Environ Control Bur Labs 2600 Bull St Columbia SC 29201

DI SALVO, FRANCIS JOSEPH, b Montreal, Can, July 20, 44; US citizen; m 66; c 2. SOLID STATE PHYSICS, CHEMISTRY. *Educ:* Mass Inst Technol, BS, 66; Stanford Univ, PhD(appl physics), 71. *Prof Exp:* MEM TECH STAFF RES, BELL LABS, 71- *Mem:* Am Phys Soc; Am Chem Soc. *Res:* Preparation and properties, mainly electrical and magnetic, of new materials. *Mailing Add:* Bell Labs Rm 10-257 Murray Hill NJ 07974

DI SALVO, JOSEPH, b Brooklyn, NY, July 1, 35; m 70; c 3. CARDIOVASCULAR PHYSIOLOGY. *Educ:* NY Univ, BA, 66; Cornell Univ, PhD(physiol), 69. *Prof Exp:* NIH fel, Mich State Univ, 69-70; res assoc pharmacol, Squibb Inst Med, Res, 70-71; asst prof physiol, Ball State Univ, 71-72; asst prof physiol & internal med, 72, assoc prof physiol, 73-78, PROF PHYSIOL, SCH MED, UNIV CINCINNATI, 78- *Mem:* Soc Exp Biol & Med; Am Physiol Soc. *Res:* Neurohumoral regulation of peripheral blood flow; vosoactive peptides; vascular smooth muscle; agonist-receptor interactions in vascular smooth muscle. *Mailing Add:* Dept of Physiol Univ Cincinnati Sch of Med Cincinnati OH 45267

DI SALVO, NICHOLAS ARMAND, b New York, NY, Nov 2, 20; m 45; c 2. ORTHODONTICS, PHYSIOLOGY. *Educ:* City Col New York, BS, 42; Columbia Univ, DDS, 45, PhD(physiol), 52; Am Bd Orthodont, dipl, 66. *Prof Exp:* Dent intern, Mem Hosp, 45; asst prof physiol, Col Physicians & Surgeons, 52-57, assoc prof & dir div orthod, 57-58, PROF ORTHOD & DIR DIV, SCH DENT & ORAL SURG, COLUMBIA UNIV, 58- *Concurrent Pos:* Attend dent surgeon, Presby Hosp, New York, 72-; consult orthod, New York City & NY State Dept Health; consult dent educ, Proj Hope, Egypt & Vet Admin Hosp, Kingsbrook, Bronx, NY. *Mem:* Fel NY Acad Sci; Am Asn Orthod; NE Soc Orthod (pres); Angle Soc Orthod (pres); Int Soc Cranio-Facial Biol (pres). *Res:* Posture and movement of jaws; growth and development of jaws and teeth. *Mailing Add:* Sch of Dent & Oral Surg Columbia Univ New York NY 10032

DISALVO, WALTER A, b Harrison, NJ, Dec 23, 20; m; c 2. CHEMICAL ENGINEERING. *Educ:* Newark Col Eng, BS, 47, MS, 51. *Prof Exp:* Technician, Nopco Chem Co, 39-47, head pilot lab, 47-53; sr res engr, Colgate-Palmolive Co, 53-64, sect head, 64-66, res coordr, 66-70, sr res assoc, 70-73; DIR RES & DEVELOP, INT PLAYTEX INC, 74- *Mem:* Am Chem Soc. *Res:* Process development of pharmaceuticals such as vitamins and hormones; product and process development of detergents, paper and plastics; development of personal care products. *Mailing Add:* 237 Prospect Ave North Arlington NJ 07032

DI SANT'AGNESE, PAUL EMILIO ARTOM, b Rome, Italy, Apr 23, 14; nat US; m 43; c 2. PEDIATRICS. *Educ:* Univ Rome, MD, 38; Columbia Univ, ScD(med), 48; Am Bd Pediat, dipl. *Hon Degrees:* DrMed, Univ Giessen, 62. *Prof Exp:* Intern, NY Post-Grad Hosp, 40-41; from asst resident to chief resident, 42-44; intern, Willard-Parker Hosp, 41-42; instr pediat, Col Physicians & Surgeons, Columbia Univ, 44-46, assoc, 46-51, asst prof & head, Cystic Fibrosis & Celiac Prog, 51-59; CLIN PROF PEDIAT, MED SCH, GEORGETOWN UNIV, 60-; CHIEF, PEDIAT METAB BR, NIH, 60- *Concurrent Pos:* Asst pediat, Presby Hosp, New York, 44-46, asst attend pediatrician, 48-59; chief, Pediat Div, Vanderbilt Clin, 44-53; instr pediat, Johns Hopkins Univ, 60-63; dir cystic fibrosis care res & teaching ctr, Children's Hosp, DC, 60-67, mem acad staff & consult, 60-; from vchmn to chmn & trustee, Gen Med & Sci Adv Coun, Nat Cystic Fibrosis Res Found, 62-67, mem exec comt & chmn res comt, 67-; founder trustee & mem exec comt, Int Cystic Fibrosis Asn, 65-, chmn sci med adv coun, 65-69; consult, Cystic Fibrosis Subcomt, Nat Acad Sci, 72-76; mem, Sr Exec Serv US, 79- *Mem:* Am Pediat Soc; Soc Pediat Res; Am Acad Pediat; AMA; Am Inst Nutrit. *Res:* Cystic fibrosis; pediatric gastroenterology; glycogen storage disease; immunology in children. *Mailing Add:* 4928 Sentinel Dr 406 Bethesda MD 20816

DI SANZO, CARMINE PASQUALINO, b Saracena, Italy, Apr 16, 33; US citizen; m 69; c 2. NEMATOLOGY. *Educ:* Univ Bari, Italy, Doctorate, 61; Univ Mass, PhD(plant path), 67. *Prof Exp:* Sr res biologist, 67-80, SR RES ASSOC, AGR CHEM DIV, FMC CORP, 80- *Concurrent Pos:* Leader task force develop stands for screening nematicides, Am Soc Testing & Mat, 72. *Mem:* Am Phytopath Soc; Soc Nematologists; Orgn Trop Am Nematologists; Europ Soc Nematologists. *Res:* Field of nematicides to discover new nematode control agents. *Mailing Add:* FMC Corp 100 Niagara St Middleport NY 14105

DISCH, RAYMOND L, b Lynbrook, NY, June 10, 32. PHYSICAL CHEMISTRY. *Educ:* Colgate Univ, AB, 54; Harvard Univ, AM, 56, PhD(phys chem), 59. *Prof Exp:* NIH fel phys chem, Oxford Univ & Nat Phys Lab, Eng, 59-63; asst prof chem, Columbia Univ, 63-68; ASSOC PROF CHEM, QUEENS COL, NY, 68- *Mem:* Optical Soc Am. *Res:* Experimental physical chemistry; electric, magnetic and optical properties of fluids; molecular physics. *Mailing Add:* Dept of Chem Queens Col Flushing NY 11367

DISCHE, ZACHARIAS, b Sambor, Russia, Feb 18, 95; nat US; div; c 2. BIOCHEMISTRY. *Educ:* Univ Vienna, MD, 21. *Prof Exp:* Res asst, Inst Physiol, Univ Vienna, 23-30, res assoc & head biochem lab, 31-38; res assoc, 43-48, mem fac, 48-59, prof, 59-63, EMER PROF BIOCHEM, COL PHYSICIANS & SURGEONS, COLUMBIA UNIV, 63- *Honors & Awards:* Proctor Medal, Am Asn Res Ophthal, 65. *Mem:* Nat Acad Sci; Am Soc Biol Chemists; Am Soc Develop Biol; Harvey Soc. *Mailing Add:* Dept of Ophthal Columbia Univ 630 W 168th St New York NY 10032

DISCHER, CLARENCE AUGUST, b Oshkosh, Wis, July 22, 12; m 41. PHYSICAL CHEMISTRY, INORGANIC CHEMISTRY. *Educ:* Oshkosh Teachers Col, EdB, 35; Ind Univ, MA, 45, PhD(chem), 47. *Prof Exp:* Teacher sch, Wis, 36-37; lab asst chem, Oshkosh Teachers Col, 38-39; powder inspector, Kankakee Ord Works, US War Dept, 42; chemist, Interlake Pulp & Paper Wis, 42-43; instr chem, Oshkosh Teachers Col, 43; instr, Preflight Sch, US Air Force, 43-44; asst chem, Ind Univ, 44-47; from asst prof to prof, 47-73, EMER PROF CHEM, COL PHARM, RUTGERS UNIV, 73- *Mem:* Am Chem Soc. *Res:* Theoretical electrochemistry; instrumental methods of analysis; inorganic pharmaceutical chemistry. *Mailing Add:* Rte 1 Box 176 Birnamwood WI 54414

DISHART, KENNETH THOMAS, b Pittsburgh, Pa, July 31, 31. ORGANIC CHEMISTRY. *Educ:* Univ Pittsburgh, BSc, 53, PhD(chem), 58. *Prof Exp:* Res chemist, 58-68, supvr fuels performance group, 68-70, head chem div, Del, 70-74, TECH MGR, PETROL CHEM DIV, E I DU PONT DE NEMOURS & CO, INC, 74- *Mem:* Am Chem Soc; Am Soc Testing & Mat. *Res:* Organic synthesis; fluorine chemistry; petroleum chemicals; automotive emissions. *Mailing Add:* 140 Exp Sta Bldg 336 E I DuPont De Nemours & CO Wilmington DE 19898

DISINGER, JOHN FRANKLIN, b Lockport, NY, July 7, 30; m 60; c 2. CONSERVATION. *Educ:* State Univ NY Teachers Col Brockport, 52; Univ Rochester, EdM, 60; Ohio State Univ, PhD(educ), 71. *Prof Exp:* Teacher pub schs, Rochester, NY, 56-70; from asst prof to assoc prof, 71-80, PROF NATURAL RESOURCES, OHIO STATE UNIV, 80- *Concurrent Pos:* Res assoc, Info Anal Ctr Sci, Math & Environ Educ, Educ Resource Info Ctr, 71-74, assoc dir, 74- *Mem:* AAAS; Conserv Educ Asn; Nat Asn Environ Educ; Nat Sci Teachers Asn. *Res:* Simulation as an instructional technique for natural resources management; objectives and methodology relative to environmental management education. *Mailing Add:* Sch Natural Resources Ohio State Univ Columbus OH 43210

DISKO, MILDRED ANNE, b Athens, Ala, Mar 24, 27; m 47; c 1. MATHEMATICS, STATISTICS. *Educ:* Univ Ala, BS, 48; Ohio Univ, MS, 69, PhD(educ res math), 73. *Prof Exp:* High sch teacher sci & math, Jackson Co, Ohio, 48-49 & Athens Co, Ohio, 62-65; instr, Ohio Univ, 65-72; asst prof, Morris Harvey Col, 73-74; ASST PROF MATH, GLENVILLE STATE COL, 74- *Mem:* Math Asn Am; Asn Women Math. *Res:* Measurement of mathematics processing skills. *Mailing Add:* Dept of Math PO Box 128 Glenville WV 26351

DISMUKES, EDWARD BROCK, b Georgiana, Ala, Oct 9, 27; m 54; c 2. PHYSICAL CHEMISTRY. *Educ:* Birmingham-Southern Col, BS, 49; Univ Wis, MS, 51, PhD(chem), 53. *Prof Exp:* Asst phys chem, Univ Wis, 49-52; chemist, Phys Div, 53-58, sr chemist, 58-59, head phys chem sect, 59-66, head chem defense sect, 66-71, head phys chem sect, 71-78, SR RES ADV, SOUTHERN RES INST, 78- *Concurrent Pos:* Lectr, Birmingham-Southern Col, 55-60. *Mem:* Am Chem Soc; Sigma Xi. *Res:* Analysis of pollutants in air and water; properties of molten silicates; properties of aqueous complex ion systems; electrochemistry; colloid chemistry; infrared spectrophotometry; kinetics of chemical reactions; electrostatic precipitation of fly ash. *Mailing Add:* 2321 Lane Circle Birmingham AL 36203

DISMUKES, GERARD CHARLES, b Boston, Mass, July 30, 49. PHYSICAL CHEMISTRY. *Educ:* Lowell Technol Inst, BSc, 71; Univ Wis-Madison, PhD(phys chem), 75. *Prof Exp:* Fel Biophys, Univ Calif Lab Chem Biodynamics, Lawrence Berkeley Lab, 75-77; ASST PROF CHEM, PRINCETON UNIV, 77- *Mem:* Sigma Xi; Am Chem Soc. *Res:* Elucidation of the primary photophysical and photochemical processes involved in photosynthesis; effect of ionizing radiation on organic solids. *Mailing Add:* Dept of Chem Princeton Univ Princeton NJ 08541

DISMUKES, ROBERT KEY, b Dahlonega, Ga, June 21, 43. NEUROSCIENCE. *Educ:* NGa Col, BS, 64; Vanderbilt Univ, MA, 66; Pa State Univ, PhD(biophysics), 71. *Prof Exp:* Fel, Johns Hopkins Univ Sch Med, 72-73; staff fel, NIH, 73-75; vis scientist, Free Univ, Netherlands, 75-76; staff scientist, Neurosci Res Prog, Mass Inst Technol, 77-79; STUDY DIR, COMT VISION, NAT ACAD SCI, 79- *Concurrent Pos:* Fel, Inst Soc, Ethics & Life Sci, 76-77. *Mem:* Soc Neurosci; Int Brain Res Orgn; AAAS. *Res:* Neurochemistry and psychopharmacology; conceptual research on brain function and behavior. *Mailing Add:* Nat Acad Sci 2101 Constitution Ave NW Washington DC 20418

DISNEY, RALPH L(YNDE), b Baltimore, Md, Feb 27, 28; m 55; c 3. PROBABILITY. *Educ:* Johns Hopkins Univ, BE, 52, MSE, 55, DEng(indust eng), 64. *Prof Exp:* Engr, Indust Diecraft, Inc, 53-55; res analyst, Opers Res Off, 55-56; asst prof eng, Lamar State Col Technol, 56-59; assoc prof, Univ Buffalo, 59-63; vis assoc prof, Univ Mich, 63-64, assoc prof, 64-68, prof indust eng, 68-77; CHARLES O GORDON PROF ENG, VA POLYTECH INST & STATE UNIV, 77- *Concurrent Pos:* Vis lectr, Univ Mich, 62-63; Orgn Am States vis prof, Inst Aeronaut Technol, Brazil, 70-71; sr ed, Am Inst Indust Engrs, 72-; distinguished vis prof, Grad Sch, Ohio State Univ, 74-75. *Honors & Awards:* David F Baker Distinguished Res Award, Am Inst Indust Engrs, 72. *Mem:* fel Am Inst Indust Engrs; Soc Indust & Appl Math; Am Math Asn; Inst Math Statist; Opers Res Soc Am. *Res:* Stochastic networks and processes; operations research. *Mailing Add:* Dept of Indust Eng & Opers Res Va Polytech Inst & State Univ Blacksburg VA 24061

DISNEY, RALPH WILLARD, b Kansas City, Mo, Mar 13, 23; m 44; c 4. GEOLOGY. *Educ:* Univ Okla, BS, 48, MS, 50, PhD(geol), 60. *Prof Exp:* From instr to asst prof geol, Univ Okla, 49-55; staff geologist, Sinclair Oil & Gas Co, 60-65; res assoc, 65-67; independent consult geologist, 67-69; vpres & mgr explor, Western Diversified Industs, Ind, 69-74; div geologist, 74-80, CHIEF GEOLOGIST, SOUTHPORT EXPLOR, INC, 80- *Mem:* Am Asn Petrol Geologists. *Res:* Petroleum exploration. *Mailing Add:* Southport Explor Inc 320 S Boston The Mezzanine Tulsa OK 74103

DI STEFANO, HENRY SAVERIO, b Palermo, Italy, Jan 1, 20; US citizen; m 51; c 2. ANATOMY. *Educ:* Brooklyn Col, BA, 41; Columbia Univ, MA, 46, PhD(zool), 48. *Prof Exp:* Instr anat, Col Med, Syracuse Univ, 48-51; from instr to prof, 51-76, MEM ANAT FAC, STATE UNIV NY UPSTATE MED CTR, 76- *Mem:* Histochem Soc; Am Asn Anat; Am Soc Cell Biol; Electron Micros Soc Am. *Res:* Cytochemistry and electron microscopy; viral induced avian and murine leukemias. *Mailing Add:* Dept of Anat State Univ of NY Upstate Med Ctr Syracuse NY 13210

DISTEFANO, JOSEPH JOHN, III, b Brooklyn, NY, Apr 30, 38. BIOCYBERNETICS, CONTROL SYSTEMS. *Educ:* City Col New York, BEE, 61; Univ Calif, Los Angeles, MS, 64, PhD(control systs, biocybernet), 66. *Prof Exp:* PROF ENG, COMPUT SCI & MED, UNIV CALIF, LOS ANGELES, 66- *Concurrent Pos:* NATO fel clin med, Radiol Lab, Univ Rome, 67-68; Fulbright scholar, 80. *Mem:* Inst Elec & Electronics Engrs; Endocrine Soc; Am Thyroid Asn; Am Soc Clin Res. *Res:* Control system theory and applications; computer applications and simulation; bioengineering systems; modeling of biological regulatory systems and biochemical phenomena. *Mailing Add:* BH 4731 Univ of Calif Los Angeles CA 90024

DISTEFANO, THOMAS HERMAN, b Philadelphia, Pa, Dec 21, 42; m 75; c 2. SOLID STATE PHYSICS. *Educ:* Lehigh Univ, BS, 64; Stanford Univ, MS, 65, PhD(appl physics), 70. *Prof Exp:* Staff mem, Stanford Linear Accelerator Ctr, Stanford Univ, 69-70; staff mem, T J Watson Res Ctr, 70-74, mgr interface physics, 74-77, tech planning staff res, 77-78, MGR OPTICAL STORAGE, IBM RES, IBM CORP, 78- *Concurrent Pos:* Consult, Synvar Assocs, 69-70. *Mem:* Inst Elec & Electronics Engrs; AAAS; Am Phys Soc. *Res:* Optical storage technology and materials; photoemission spectroscopy; non-destructive testing including acoustic microscopy and photovoltaic imaging; internal photoemission and interfaces. *Mailing Add:* T J Watson Res Ctr IBM Corp PO Box 218 Yorktown Heights NY 10598

DISTEFANO, VICTOR, b Rochester, NY, Mar 17, 24; m 47; c 5. PHARMACOLOGY. *Educ:* Univ Rochester, AB, 49, PhD(pharmacol), 53. *Prof Exp:* Instr pharmacol, Sch Med, Marquette Univ, 53-54; from instr to assoc prof pharmacol, 54-72, assoc prof toxicol & radiation biol, 70-72, PROF PHARMACOL & TOXICOL, SCH MED, UNIV ROCHESTER, 72-, PROF RADIATION BIOL & BIOPHYS, 76- *Mem:* Am Soc Pharmacol. *Res:* Autonomics; antiradiation; central nervous system. *Mailing Add:* Dept of Pharmacol & Toxicol Univ of Rochester Sch of Med Rochester NY 14642

DISTERHOFT, JOHN FRANCIS, b Marengo, Iowa, June 9, 44. NEUROBIOLOGY. *Educ:* Loras Col, BA, 66; Fordham Univ, MA, 68, PhD(psychol), 71. *Prof Exp:* USPHS training grant, Calif Inst Technol, 70-73; asst prof anat, 73-78, ASSOC PROF ANAT, MED SCH, NORTHWESTERN UNIV, CHICAGO, 78- *Mem:* AAAS; Am Asn Anat; Soc Neurosci. *Res:* Neurophysiological and neuroanatomical foundations of plasticity in mammalian central nervous system. *Mailing Add:* Dept of Anat Med Sch Northwestern Univ Chicago IL 60611

DISTLER, RAYMOND JEWEL, b Paducah, Ky, July 3, 30; m 51; c 4. ELECTRICAL ENGINEERING. *Educ:* Univ Ky, BSEE, 51, MSEE, 60, PhD(math, elec eng), 64. *Prof Exp:* Mem tech staff, Bell Tel Labs, NJ, 51-58; from instr to asst prof, 58-66, ASSOC PROF ELEC ENG, UNIV KY, 66- *Mem:* Inst Elec & Electronics Engrs. *Res:* Circuit analysis and design; logical design; microprocessors. *Mailing Add:* Dept of Elec Eng Univ of Ky Lexington KY 40506

DITARANTO, ROCCO A, b Philadelphia, Pa, Aug 12, 26; m 56; c 4. ENGINEERING MECHANICS, MECHANICAL ENGINEERING. *Educ:* Drexel Inst Tech, BS, 47; Univ Pa, MS, 50, PhD(eng mech), 61. *Prof Exp:* Jr engr, Philco Corp, 48-50; sr engr, Vertol Helicopter Co, 50-53; anal engr, Aviation Gas Turbine Div, Westinghouse Elec Co, 53-55, shock & vibration consult, RCA Defense Electronics Prod, 55-59; assoc prof mech eng, Drexel Inst Technol, 59-62; PROF ENG, WIDENER COL, 62- *Concurrent Pos:* Eng consult, US Navy Marine Eng Lab, 61-; vis prof, Inst Sound & Vibration, Univ Southampton, 69-70; acoustical specialist, Environ Protection Agency, 73; mech consult, Scott Paper Co, 75- *Mem:* Am Soc Mech Engrs; Am Soc Eng Educ; Am Inst Aeronaut & Astronaut; Acoust Soc Am; Sigma Xi. *Res:* Shock and vibrations; vibration damping; dynamics of structures and shells; mechanics of laminated structures; acoustic noise survey and design abatement. *Mailing Add:* Dept of Eng Widener Col Chester PA 19013

DITCHEK, BRIAN MICHAEL, b New York, NY, Jan 31, 51; m 75. MATERIALS SCIENCE, PHYSICAL METALLURGY. *Educ:* State Univ NY, Stony Brook, BE, 73; Northwestern Univ, PhD(mat sci), 77. *Prof Exp:* Res asst spinodol decomposition, Northwestern Univ, 73-77; fel, Nat Bur Standards, 77-78; res scientist ceramics, Martin Marietta Labs, 78-81; MEM TECH STAFF, GEN TEL & ELECTRONICS CORP LABS, 81- *Concurrent Pos:* Vchmn comt fatigue res, Am Soc Testing & Mat, 78-; assoc Nat Res Coun, Nat Bur Standards, 77-78. *Mem:* Am Soc Metals; Am Soc Testing & Mat; Am Inst Mining, Metall & Petrol Engrs; Sigma Xi; AAAS. *Res:* Role of phase transformations in improving material properties; modulated structures; fatigue processes in metals; sintering and strengthening behavior of high temperature ceramics; directional solidification. *Mailing Add:* 24 Hancock St Milford MA 01757

DITMAN, JOHN GORDON, b Kenton, Ohio, Jan 20, 09; wid; c 1. PHYSICAL CHEMISTRY. *Educ:* Wooster Col, AB, 31; NY Univ, PhD(phys chem), 35. *Prof Exp:* Asst, NY Univ, 31-35; asst chemist, Standard Oil Develop Co, 35-37; head lubricating oil group, Petrol Tech Serv Lab, Esso Standard Oil Co, 37-48; lab & pilot plant coordr, 48-76, consult, Process Plants Div, Wheeler Corp, 76-80, CONSULT, FOSTER WHEELER DEVELOP CO, 80- *Concurrent Pos:* Instr, Polytech Inst, Brooklyn, 53-54. *Res:* Rates of thermal decomposition; refining of heavy petroleum oils. *Mailing Add:* Apt 9-D 35 Manor Dr Newark NJ 07106

DITMARS, JOHN DAVID, b Trenton, NJ, Oct 16, 43; m 66; c 4. CIVIL ENGINEERING, ENVIRONMENTAL SCIENCES. *Educ:* Princeton Univ, BSE, 65; Calif Inst Technol, MS, 66, PhD(civil eng), 71. *Prof Exp:* Vis asst prof civil eng, Mass Inst Technol, 70-72; asst prof civil eng & marine studies, Univ Del, 72-77; ENGR & MGR, WATER RESOURCES SECT, ENERGY & ENVIRON SYSTS DIV, ARGONNE NAT LAB, 77- *Concurrent Pos:* Consult var eng & indust firms, 70-; res assoc, Energy & Environ Systs Div, Argonne Nat Lab, 76-77. *Mem:* Am Soc Civil Engrs. *Res:* Mixing and transport processes in hydrologic environments; wastewater jets and air-bubble plumes; model verification with prototype data; environmental impacts of advanced ocean energy systems. *Mailing Add:* Energy & Environ Systs Div Argonne Nat Lab Argonne IL 60439

DI TORO, MICHAEL JOHN, electrical engineering, acoustics, deceased

D'ITRI, FRANK M, b Flint, Mich, Apr 25, 33; m 55; c 4. ANALYTICAL CHEMISTRY, WATER CHEMISTRY. *Educ:* Mich State Univ, BS, 55, MS & PhD(anal chem), 68. *Prof Exp:* Technologist, Dow Chem Co, 60-62; asst anal chem, 62-68, from asst prof to assoc prof water chem, 68-77, PROF WATER CHEM, INST WATER RES, MICH STATE UNIV, 77- *Concurrent Pos:* NIH fel, 67-68; prin investr, Off Water Resources Res, US Dept Interior, 69-; adv environ mercury pollution, Mich House Rep, 70-; mem critical pollution mat comt, Mich Water Resources Comn, 71-; adv, Revision Water Qual Criteria Publ, Nat Acad Sci, 71-; Rockefeller scholar, 72 & 75; Japan Soc for Promotion of Sci fel, 80. *Mem:* Am Chem Soc. *Res:* Analytical aspects of water and sediment chemistry with special interest on the transformation and translocation of mercury; phosphorus, nitrogen, heavy metals, and hazardous organic chemicals in the environment. *Mailing Add:* Rm 334 Natural Resources Bldg Mich State Univ East Lansing MI 48824

DITTBERNER, PHILLIP LYNN, b Riverside, Calif, Feb 27, 44; m 66; c 3. RANGE ECOLOGY, WILDLIFE ECOLOGY. *Educ:* WTex State Univ, BS, 67; NMex State Univ, MS, 71; Colo State Univ, PhD(range ecol), 73. *Prof Exp:* Ecologist, Nat Park Serv, 72-75; PLANT ECOLOGIST, US FISH & WILDLIFE SERV, 75- *Concurrent Pos:* Mem, Publ Comt, Soc Range Mgt, 74-76 & Colo Sect Rangeland Ref Comt, 75-76. *Mem:* Soc Range Mgt; Ecol Soc Am; Am Soc Agron; Soil Sci Soc Am; Sigma Xi. *Res:* Wildlife habitat reclamation; resource management systems; soil-plant-animal relationships; reclamation of surface disturbed areas; plant and animal species adaptation to site conditions on reclaimed mine and other disturbed lands; designing reclamation plans for specific post mining land uses. *Mailing Add:* US Fish & Wildlife Serv 2625 Redwing Rd Ft Collins CO 80521

DITTERLINE, RAYMOND LEE, b Mesquite, NMex, July 29, 41; m 63; c 3. PLANT BREEDING, AGRONOMY. *Educ:* NMex State Univ, BS, 63, MS, 70; Mont State Univ, PhD(agron), 73. *Prof Exp:* From instr to asst prof, 73-77, ASSOC PROF AGRON, MONT STATE UNIV, 77- *Mem:* Am Soc Agron; Crop Sci Soc Am; Nat Alfalfa Improv Conf. *Res:* Breeding forage legumes, including alfalfa, sainfoin and birdsfoot trefoil; nodulation of legumes; disease and insect resistance; seedling vigor; fertility; forage nutritive value. *Mailing Add:* Dept Plant & Soil Sci Mont State Univ Bozeman MT 59715

DITTERT, LEWIS WILLIAM, b Philadelphia, Pa, Jan 22, 34; m 57; c 2. PHARMACY. *Educ:* Temple Univ, BS, 56; Univ Wis, MS, 60, PhD(pharm), 61. *Prof Exp:* Sr res pharmacist, Smith Kline & French Labs, 61-67; from asst prof to prof pharm, Col Pharm, Univ Ky, 67-78; DEAN, SCH PHARM, UNIV PITTSBURGH, 78- *Mem:* Am Pharmaceut Asn; fel Acad Pharmaceut Sci; Am Asn Col Pharm. *Res:* Physical pharmacy; biopharmaceutics; performance of pharmaceutical products in humans, absorption of drugs from gastrointestinal tract; drug metabolism; clinical pharmacokinetics. *Mailing Add:* Sch Pharm Univ Pittsburgh 501 Terr St Pittsburgh PA 15261

DITTFACH, JOHN HARLAND, b St Paul, Minn, Apr 17, 18; m 44; c 5. MECHANICAL ENGINEERING. *Educ:* Univ Minn, BSME, 47, MSME, 48. *Prof Exp:* Instr mech eng, Univ Minn, 47-48; from asst prof to assoc prof, 48-70, PROF MECH ENG, UNIV MASS, AMHERST, 70- *Res:* Experimental testing techniques; energy conversion. *Mailing Add:* Dept of Mech Eng Univ of Mass Amherst MA 01003

DITTMAN, FRANK W(ILLARD), b Pittsburgh, Pa, July 22, 18; m 46; c 4. CHEMICAL ENGINEERING. *Educ:* Univ Pittsburgh, BS, 40; Cornell Univ, MChE, 43, PhD(chem eng), 44. *Prof Exp:* Asst chem eng, Cornell Univ, 40-44, instr math, 43-44; process engr, Koppers Co, Inc, 46-52; process engr, Rust Process Design Co, 52-55, chief chem process consult, 55-58; res technologist, Appl Res Lab, US Steel Corp, Pa, 58-62; PROF CHEM ENG, RUTGERS UNIV, 62- *Concurrent Pos:* Res engr, Rubber Reserve Co, 43-44; instr, Carnegie Inst Technol, 47-50; coun mem & former mayor, Bridgewater, NJ; chmn, Energy Mgt Coun, Somerset Co, NJ. *Honors & Awards:* Serv to Soc Award, Am Inst Chem Eng, 77. *Mem:* Am Inst Chem Engrs; Filtration Soc. *Res:* Mass, heat and momentum transfer, including distillation, extraction, drying, reverse osmosis, and filtration; design, construction and economics of chemical plants; distillation, extraction, drying, filtration, decomposition of residual organics in wastewater. *Mailing Add:* Col Eng Busch Campus PO Box 909 Piscataway NJ 08854

DITTMAN, RICHARD HENRY, b Sacramento, Calif, July 5, 37; m 62; c 2. SURFACE PHYSICS. *Educ:* Univ Santa Clara, BS, 59; Univ Notre Dame, PhD, 65. *Prof Exp:* Guest scientist, Fritz-Haber-Inst, W Berlin, 65-66; asst prof, 66-71, chmn dept physics, 72-75, assoc dean col letters & sci, 75-77, ASSOC PROF PHYSICS, UNIV WIS-MILWAUKEE, 71- *Mem:* Am Asn Physics Teachers. *Res:* Field electron emission microscopy; flash filament spectrometry; classical gravitation experiments. *Mailing Add:* Dept Physics Univ Wis Milwaukee WI 53201

DITTMANN, JOHN PAUL, b Winfield, Kans, Nov 28, 48; m 69; c 3. OPERATIONS RESEARCH, INDUSTRIAL ENGINEERING. *Educ:* Univ Mo-Columbia, BS, 70, MS, 71, PhD(indust eng), 73. *Prof Exp:* Opers res analyst, 73-75, mgr mkt res, 75-76, MGR DISTRIB OPERS MGT SCI, WHIRLPOOL CORP, 76- *Mem:* Am Inst Indust Engrs; Nat Coun Phys Distrib Mgt. *Res:* Management science. *Mailing Add:* Whirlpool Admin Ctr US 33 N Benton Harbor MI 49022

DITTMER, DONALD CHARLES, b Quincy, Ill, Oct 17, 27. ORGANIC CHEMISTRY. *Educ:* Univ Ill, BS, 50; Mass Inst Technol, PhD(org chem), 53. *Prof Exp:* Fel chem, Harvard Univ, 53-54; from instr to asst prof, Univ Pa, 54-61; E I du Pont de Nemours & Co fel, 61-62; assoc prof, 62-66, PROF CHEM, SYRACUSE UNIV, 66- *Mem:* Am Chem Soc; Royal Soc Chem; AAAS; Sigma Xi. *Res:* Model enzyme systems; small-ring heterocyclic chemistry; organic reaction mechanisms; organometallic chemistry. *Mailing Add:* Dept Chem Syracuse Univ Syracuse NY 13210

DITTMER, HOWARD JAMES, b Pekin, Ill, Jan 29, 10; m 41; c 1. BOTANY, MORPHOLOGY. *Educ:* Univ NMex, AB, 33, AM, 34; Univ Iowa, PhD(plant morphol), 38. *Prof Exp:* Prof sci, Chicago Teachers Col, 38-43; from assoc prof to prof, 43-75, asst dean, 56-70, assoc dean, Col Arts & Sci, 70-75, EMER PROF BIOL, UNIV NMEX, 75- *Concurrent Pos:* Environ consult, Kennecott Copper Co, 70-75. *Mem:* AAAS (past pres, Southwestern & Rocky Mt Div); Bot Soc Am; Ecol Soc Am. *Res:* Investigation of subterranean plant parts; quantitative study of roots and root hairs and their relation to physics of soil; flora of New Mexico; lawn problems of the southwest; phylogeny and form in the plant kingdom; root biomass; biomass of desert plants; root systems. *Mailing Add:* Biol Dept Univ NMex Albuquerque NM 87131

DITTMER, JOHN EDWARD, b Colesburg, Iowa, May 10, 39; m 62; c 2. DEVELOPMENTAL BIOLOGY. *Educ:* Ariz State Univ, BS, 62; Brown Univ, MAT, 66, PhD(develop biol), 70. *Prof Exp:* Instr high sch, Kans, 62-65; asst prof anat, 69-77, ASSOC PROF ANAT, SCH MED, BOSTON UNIV, 77- *Mem:* AAAS; Am Soc Zoologists. *Res:* Transplantation immunology. *Mailing Add:* Dept of Anat Sch Med Boston Univ Boston MA 02118

DITTMER, KARL, b Hebron, NDak, Jan 18, 14; m 49; c 3. CHEMISTRY. *Educ:* Jamestown Col, BA, 37; Univ Colo, MA, 39; Cornell Univ, PhD(biochem), 44. *Prof Exp:* Fel antibiotins & penicillin assay methods, Biochem Dept, Med Col, Cornell Univ, 44-45; from asst prof to assoc prof chem, Univ Colo, 45-49; prof & head dept, Fla State Univ, 49-58; head div grants & fels prog adminr petrol res fund, Am Chem Soc, 58-64; vpres acad affairs, Fla State Univ, 64-66; dean, Col Sci, 66-79, prof chem & coordr environ sci, 74-79, EMER DEAN & PROF CHEM, PORTLAND STATE UNIV, 79- *Mem:* AAAS; Am Chem Soc; Am Soc Biol Chemists. *Res:* Structural basis for antimetabolites; antivitamins; antibiotins; antiamino acids synthesis and properties; amino acid metabolism of rats and bacteria; biosynthesis of vitamins and amino acids; synthesis of nucleosides and derivatives; microbiological study of structural specificity of biotin. *Mailing Add:* Col of Sci Portland State Univ Portland OR 97207

DITTNER, PETER FRED, b Vienna, Austria, Mar 24, 37; US citizen; m 80; c 2. ATOMIC PHYSICS. *Educ:* NY Univ, BS, 58, PhD(physics), 65. *Prof Exp:* Res assoc chem, 65-76, RES STAFF MEM II, OAK RIDGE NAT LAB, 76- *Concurrent Pos:* Humboldt sr sci fel, 72-73. *Mem:* Am Phys Soc. *Res:* Atomic beams; atom-surface interactions; channeling; transuranium elements. *Mailing Add:* Chem Div Oak Ridge Nat Lab PO Box X Oak Ridge TN 37830

DIUGUID, LINCOLN ISAIAH, b Lynchburg, Va, Feb 6, 17; m 52; c 4. ORGANIC CHEMISTRY. *Educ:* WVa State Col, BS, 38; Cornell Univ, MS, 39, PhD(org chem), 45. *Prof Exp:* Head chem dept, Ark State Col, 39-43; anal chemist, Pine Bluff Arsenal, Chem Warfare Serv, US Army, 42-43; Merrill res fel, Cornell Univ, 43-45, Off Sci Res & Develop res fel, 45-46, res assoc, 46-47, B F Goodrich Rubber res fel, 47; prof chem, 54-74, chmn dept phys sci, 70-74, PROF PHYS SCI, HARRIS-STOWE COL, 74-, CHMN DEPT, 77-; RES DIR, DU-GOOD CHEM LAB, 47- *Concurrent Pos:* Cancer res, Jewish Hosp, St Louis, 59-; mem, Leukemia Res Proj, 61-63; vpres, Leukemia Guild, Mo & Ill, 64- *Mem:* Am Chem Soc; fel Am Inst Chemists; Asn Consult Chemists & Chem Eng. *Res:* New method synthesis of primary aliphatic alcohols, large carbon ring compounds and benzothiazole derivatives; new micromethods for organic quantitative analyses; industrial development. *Mailing Add:* Dept of Phys Sci 3026 Laclede Ave St Louis MO 63103

DIVADEENAM, MUNDRATHI, b Pulukurthy, India, June 21, 35; US citizen; m 64; c 2. NUCLEAR PHYSICS. *Educ:* Osmania Univ, India, BSc, 54, MSc, 56; Duke Univ, PhD(nuclear physics), 67. *Prof Exp:* Lectr physics, Osmania Med Col, India, 56-57; jr sci asst physics, Int Geophys Year Sponsored, 57-58; from res asst to res assoc nuclear physics, 60-69; asst prof physics, Prairie View Agr & Mech Col, 69-70; asst prof physics, NC Cent Univ & Duke Univ, 70-74; PHYSICIST, NAT NUCLEAR DATA CTR, BROOKHAVEN NAT LAB, 74- *Mem:* Am Phys Soc. *Res:* Average and high resolution neutron total cross sections; strength functions; optical model; doorway states; intermediate structure; analog states; nuclear structure; neutron resonance parameters; thermal cross sections; neutron induced reactions. *Mailing Add:* Nat Nuclear Data Ctr Brookhaven Nat Lab B 197D Upton NY 11973

DIVELBISS, JAMES EDWARD, b Pueblo, Colo, Oct 12, 33; m 54; c 4. ZOOLOGY. *Educ:* Westmar Col, BA, 55; Univ Iowa, MS, 59, PhD(zool, genetics), 61. *Prof Exp:* From asst prof to assoc prof, 61-71, PROF BIOL, WESTMAR COL, 71- *Concurrent Pos:* NSF sr fac fel, 71-72. *Mem:* AAAS; Am Inst Biol Sci; Genetics Soc Am; Am Genetic Asn; Nat Asn Biol Teachers. *Res:* Fine structure of gene in Drosophila; pteridine of Drosophila. *Mailing Add:* Dept of Biol Westmar Col Le Mars IA 51031

DIVELEY, WILLIAM RUSSELL, b Royal Center, Ind, June 13, 21; m 49; c 1. ORGANIC CHEMISTRY. *Educ:* Manchester Col, BS, 43; Purdue Univ, MS, 50, PhD(chem), 52. *Prof Exp:* Res chemist, 52-63, sr res chemist, 63-71, RES SCIENTIST, HERCULES, INC, 71- *Mem:* Am Chem Soc. *Res:* Synthetic organic chemistry; agricultural chemicals and pesticides; Organophosphorous chemistry. *Mailing Add:* 3713 Valleybrook Rd Oakwood Hills Wilmington DE 19808

DIVEN, BENJAMIN CLINTON, b Chico, Calif, Jan 5, 19; m 51; c 3. NUCLEAR PHYSICS. *Educ:* Univ Calif, AB, 41; Univ Ill, MS, 48, PhD(physics), 50. *Prof Exp:* MEM STAFF LOS ALAMOS SCI LAB, UNIV CALIF, 43-45, 50- *Mem:* Fel Am Phys Soc. *Res:* Experimental nuclear physics. *Mailing Add:* 4730 Sandia Dr Los Alamos NM 87544

DIVEN, WARREN FIELD, b St Louis, Mo, Oct 10, 31; m 54; c 3. BIOCHEMISTRY. *Educ:* Hastings Col, BA, 52; Univ Nebr, MS, 60, PhD(chem), 62. *Prof Exp:* NIH fel, Univ Wis, 62-64; asst prof biochem, 64-71, ASSOC PROF PATH & BIOCHEM, SCH MED, UNIV PITTSBURGH, 71- *Mem:* Am Chem Soc; Am Asn Biol Chemists; Am Asn Clin Chem; NY Acad Sci. *Res:* Clinical biochemistry; enzyme defects in inborn errors of metabolism; enzymology; molecular mechanisms of metabolic control. *Mailing Add:* Dept of Biochem Univ Pittsburgh Sch of Med Pittsburgh PA 15261

DIVETT, ROBERT THOMAS, b Salt Lake City, Utah, Nov 4, 25; m 53; c 6. INFORMATION SCIENCE, HISTORY OF MEDICINE. *Educ:* Brigham Young Univ, BS, 53; George Peabody Col, MA, 55; Univ Utah, EdD(educ admin & media), 68. *Prof Exp:* Teacher-librn, Idaho Jr High Sch, 53-54; first asst, Med Libr, Vanderbilt Univ, 54-56; asst prof libr sci & med librn, Univ Utah, 56-62; med sci librn, 63-77, ASSOC PROF MED BIBLIOG, UNIV NMEX, 63- *Concurrent Pos:* Consult, Okla Med Ctr, 66 & Mayo Clin, 68; dir, Health Sci Info & Commun Ctr, 68-71; vis assoc prof, Univ Wash, 69; contribr, Third Int Cong Med Librarianship, Amsterdam, 69. *Honors & Awards:* Murray Gottlieb Prize, Med Libr Asn, 59 & 62. *Mem:* Med Libr Asn; Spec Libr Asn; Am Soc Info Sci. *Res:* Computer file structures for on-line storage and retrieval of literature citations and other biomedical data and information; history of medicine on the American frontier, particularly in the mountain West; patterns of acquisition and use of biomedical information by medical practitioners in small New Mexico communities. *Mailing Add:* Med Ctr Libr Univ of NMex Albuquerque NM 87131

DIVILBISS, JAMES LEROY, b Parsons, Kans, Jan 17, 30. INFORMATION SCIENCE. *Educ:* Kans State Univ, BS, 52; Univ Ill, MS, 55, PhD(elec eng), 62. *Prof Exp:* Res assoc elec eng, Coord Sci Lab, Univ Ill, 55-63; mem tech staff elec eng, Bell Tel Labs, Inc, 63-65; sr res engr, Dept Comput Sci, 65-70, ASSOC PROF, GRAD SCH LIBR SCI & SR RES ENGR, COORD SCI LAB, UNIV ILL, URBANA-CHAMPAIGN, 70- *Mem:* Inst Elec & Electronics Engrs; Am Soc Info Sci. *Res:* Logical design of computers; computer music; information retrieval; library automation; systems analysis. *Mailing Add:* 1912 Robert Dr Champaign IL 61820

DIVINCENZO, GEORGE D, b Rochester, NY, Sept 18, 41; m 62; c 2. BIOCHEMISTRY. *Educ:* St John Fisher Col, BS, 63; State Univ NY Buffalo, PhD(biochem), 69. *Prof Exp:* BIOCHEM TOXICOLOGIST, HEALTH, SAFETY & HUMAN FACTORS LAB, EASTMAN KODAK CO, 68- *Mem:* AAAS; Am Chem Soc; Am Indust Hyg Asn; Soc Toxicol. *Res:* Metabolic fate of foreign compounds; biologic monitoring of industrial chemicals; mechanisms of toxicity. *Mailing Add:* Health, Safety & Human Factors Lab Bldg 320 Eastman Kodak Co Kodak Park Rochester NY 14650

DIVINE, JAMES R(OBERT), b Stockton, Calif, Mar 11, 39. CHEMICAL ENGINEERING. *Educ:* Univ Calif, Berkeley, BS, 61; Ore State Univ, PhD(chem eng), 65. *Prof Exp:* Chem engr food processing, Western Regional Res Labs, USDA, 61; sr res engr Corrosion, 65-74, JOINT CTR GRAD STUDIES, PAC NORTHWEST LABS, 65-, SR RES ENGR CORROSION, 78- *Concurrent Pos:* Mem staff, Westinghouse-Hanford, 74-78. *Mem:* Nat Asn Corrosion Engrs; Am Inst Chem Engrs; Sigma Xi; Nat Asn Prof Engrs. *Res:* Corrosion transport of corrosion products through coolant systems; decontamination. *Mailing Add:* Pac NW Lab Box 999 Richland WA 99352

DIVINSKY, NATHAN JOSEPH, b Winnipeg, Man, Oct 29, 25; m 47; c 3. MATHEMATICS. *Educ:* Univ Man, BSc, 46; Univ Chicago, MSc, 47, PhD(math), 50. *Prof Exp:* Res assoc math, Cowles Comn, Chicago, 49-50; asst prof, Ripon Col, 50-51; from asst prof to assoc prof, Univ Man, 51-59; assoc prof, 59-64, asst dean sci, 69-79, PROF MATH, UNIV BC, 64- *Concurrent Pos:* Royal Soc Can scholar, 57-58; Can Coun fel vis prof, Queen Mary Col, Univ London, 65-66 & 72-73. *Mem:* Am Math Soc; London Math Soc. *Res:* Power-associative algebras; theory of rings; radicals. *Mailing Add:* Dept Math Univ BC Vancouver BC V6T 1W5 Can

DIVIS, ALLAN FRANCIS, b Chicago, Ill, Mar 23, 46; m 67; c 3. GEOLOGY, CHEMISTRY. *Educ:* Univ Calif, BS, 68; Scripps Inst Oceanog, PhD(earth sci), 75. *Prof Exp:* Lab asst chem, Scripps Inst Oceanog, 64-68; comn officer eng, Nat Oceanic & Atmospheric Admin, 68-71; res asst geol, Scripps Inst Oceanog, 71-74; lectr, Univ Calif, Riverside, 74-75; asst prof, Colo Sch Mines, 75-77; consult geol, Resource Serv Int, Inc, 77-78; CONSULT GEOL, 78- *Concurrent Pos:* Penrose grant, Geol Soc Am, 72-73; consult, Lawrence Livermore Lab, 74-75; NSF grant, 75-77. *Mem:* Geol Soc Am; Am Geophys Union; Soc Mining Engrs. *Res:* Physical and chemical evolution of magma systems and its relationship to the formation of ore deposits; geophysical and geochemical exploration; reclamation of mine sites. *Mailing Add:* 12001 W 32nd Dr Wheat Ridge CO 80033

DIVIS, ROY RICHARD, b Berwyn, Ill, July 23, 28; m 51; c 4. FOAM EXTRUSION. *Educ:* Morton Jr Col, BGEd, 48; St Mary's Col, Minn, BS, 50; Univ Detroit, MS, 53. *Prof Exp:* Chemist L R Kerns Co, 52-53 & Amphenol-Borg Electronics, 53-55; chief chemist, Alkalon Corp, 55-59, head plastics & elastomers res, 59-60; mgr res, Plastic Container Div, Continental Can Co, 60-66; dir appln develop, Foster Grant Co, 66-79; VPRES TECHNOL, U C INDUSTS, 79- *Mem:* Am Chem Soc; Soc Plastics Eng. *Res:* Polymer properties and resins fabrication technology. *Mailing Add:* U C Industs Box 37 Tallmadge OH 44278

DIWAN, BHALCHANDRA APPARAO, b Sangli, India, Apr 28, 37; m 66; c 2. BIOLOGY, MEDICAL RESEARCH. *Educ:* Univ Poona, BSc, 59, MSc, 61, PhD(zool), 64. *Prof Exp:* Asst prof biol, Vivekanand Col, 66-67; sci officer, Cancer Res Inst, 67-71; res assoc, Jackson Lab, 73-74; PRIN SCIENTIST LIFE SCI, MELOY LABS, 76- *Concurrent Pos:* Fel, Indian Coun Med Res, 64-66; fel trainee, Jackson Lab, 71-73; spec fel, Leukemia Soc Am, 74-76. *Mem:* Am Asn Cancer Res; AAAS. *Res:* Chemical carcinogenesis; viral and chemical cocarcinogenesis; embryology; teratology; genetics. *Mailing Add:* Meloy Labs 6715 Electronic Dr Springfield VA 22151

DIWAN, JOYCE JOHNSON, b Brooklyn, NY, Dec 25, 40; m 70. CELL BIOLOGY. *Educ:* Mt Holyoke Col, AB, 62; Univ Ill, Chicago, PhD(physiol), 67. *Prof Exp:* USPHS fel, Johnson Res Found, Univ Pa, 66-69; asst prof, 69-75, ASSOC PROF BIOL, RENSSELAER POLYTECH INST, 75- *Concurrent Pos:* Mem exec comt, US Bioenergetics Group, 80-83. *Mem:* AAAS; Am Soc Cell Biol; Biophys Soc; Am Soc Biol Chemists. *Res:* Physiology of intra-cellular membranes, particularly mechanisms of solute transport and related metabolic processes in isolated mitochondria. *Mailing Add:* Dept of Biol Rensselaer Polytech Inst Troy NY 12181

DIX, CHARLES HEWITT, b Los Angeles, Calif, Mar 27, 05; m 70. GEOPHYSICS. *Educ:* Calif Inst Technol, BS, 27; Rice Inst, AM, 28, PhD(math), 31. *Prof Exp:* Instr math, Rice Inst, 29-34; res geophysicist, Humble Oil & Refinery Co, 34-37; geophysicist, Socony-Vacuum Oil Co, 39-41; chief seismologist & vpres, United Geophys Co, 41-47; from assoc prof to prof, 48-73, EMER PROF GEOPHYS, CALIF INST TECHNOL, 73- *Concurrent Pos:* Civilian consult, US Navy, 44; consult, 48-; French Inst Petrol, Univ Paris, 52; Fulbright fel, Univ Tokyo, 63-64. *Honors & Awards:* Ewing Medal, Soc Explor Geophys, 74. *Mem:* AAAS; Am Phys Soc; hon mem Seismol Soc Am; hon life mem Soc Explor Geophys; Am Geophys Union. *Res:* Potential theory; theory of elastic wave propagation. *Mailing Add:* Geol & Planetary Sci Div Calif Inst of Technol Pasadena CA 91125

DIX, JAMES SEWARD, b Colton, Calif, Jan 6, 32; m 79; c 2. ORGANIC CHEMISTRY. *Educ:* Univ Iowa, BS, 54; Univ Ill, PhD(org chem), 57. *Prof Exp:* Res chemist, Phillips Petrol Co, 57-66, mgr fiber additives sect, Res & Develop Dept, 66-70, proj mgr, Phillips Fibers Corp, 70-77, res chemist, Phillips Petrol Co, 77-78, develop engr, 78-80, SECT SUPVR, PHILLIPS CHEM CO, 80- *Mem:* AAAS; Am Chem Soc; Soc Plastics Engrs. *Res:* Polymer stabilization; fiber modifications; fiber finishes; plastics compounding. *Mailing Add:* Phillips Petrol Co Res Ctr Bartlesville OK 74004

DIX, MARY ELLEN, forest entomology, biology, see previous edition

DIX, ROLLIN CUMMING, b New York, NY, Feb 8, 36; m 60. MECHANICAL ENGINEERING. *Educ:* Purdue Univ, BS, 57, MS, 58, PhD(mech eng), 63. *Prof Exp:* Sr engr, Bendix Mishawaka Div, 62-64; asst prof, 64-68, assoc prof, 64-80, PROF MECH ENG, ILL INST TECHNOL, 80-, ASSOC DEAN COMPUT, 81- *Mem:* Am Soc Eng Educ; Am Soc Mech Engrs. *Res:* Heat transfer, mechanical and biomedical design; numerical computation and design optimization. *Mailing Add:* MMAE Dept Ill Inst of Technol Chicago IL 60616

DIXIT, AJIT SURESH, b Nadiad, India, Sept 30, 50; m 81. CHROMATOGRAPHY, PAPER TECHNOLOGY. *Educ:* Univ Bombay, BS, 70; Indian Inst Technol, MSc, 72; Univ Maine, Orono, MS, 75; Univ Miss, PhD(chem), 80. *Prof Exp:* Res assoc pharmaceut chem, Univ Kans, 80-81; SR RES CHEMIST, ORGANIC CHEM, ECUSTA PAPER & FILM GROUP, OLIN CORP, 81- *Mem:* Am Chem Soc; Sigma Xi; Royal Chem Soc. *Res:* Synthetic organic chemistry; amino acids and peptides; paper and tobacco industrial research; analytical chemistry; chromatography; cellulose chemistry. *Mailing Add:* PO Box 991 Brevard NC 28712

DIXIT, BALWANT N, b Kerawade, India, Jan 7, 33; m 69; c 2. PHARMACOLOGY. *Educ:* Univ Poona, BS, 54, Hons, 55, MS, 56; Univ Baroda, MS, 62; Univ Pittsburgh, PhD(pharmacol), 65. *Prof Exp:* Res asst pharmacol, Indian Coun Med Res, Med Col, Univ Baroda, 56-59, res asst, 63-65, asst prof, 65-68, asst chmn dept, 68-73, assoc prof, 68-75, atg dean, 76-78, PROF PHARMACOL, SCH PHARM, UNIV PITTSBURGH, 75-, CHMN DEPT & ASSOC DEAN, 74- *Concurrent Pos:* Sr res fel, Coun Sci & Indust Res, Univ Baroda, 60-62. *Mem:* AAAS; Am Soc Pharmacol & Exp Therapeut; NY Acad Sci; Soc Neurosci. *Res:* Autonomic and biochemical pharmacology; neuroendocrinology; drug interactions; analytical biochemistry. *Mailing Add:* Dept Pharmacol 1100 Salk Hall Univ Pittsburgh Sch of Pharm Pittsburgh PA 15261

DIXIT, MADHU SUDAN, b Nagpur, India, July 10, 42; Can citizen; m 71; c 2. WEAK INTERACTIONS, INTERMEDIATE ENERGY PHYSICS. *Educ:* Vikram Univ, India, BSc, 61; Univ Delhi, MSc, 63; Univ Chicago, PhD(physics), 71. *Prof Exp:* Asst res physicist, Univ Calif, Los Angeles, 71-73; res assoc, Carleton Univ, Ottawa, 73-75; sr res fel, Univ Victoria, Vancouver, 76-79; ASSOC RES OFFICER, NAT RES COUN, OTTAWA, 79- *Concurrent Pos:* Vis staff mem, Los Alamos Meson Physics Facil, Univ Calif, Los Angeles, 71-73. *Mem:* Am Phys Soc. *Res:* Pionic and muonic x-ray; elementary particle physics, weak interactions; rare and ultra-rare decays of pion and muon. *Mailing Add:* High Energy Physics Nat Res Coun Ottawa ON K1A 0R6

DIXIT, PADMAKAR KASHINATH, b Calcutta, India, Aug 7, 21; m 48; c 3. ANATOMY, NUTRITIONAL BIOCHEMISTRY. *Educ:* Univ Bombay, BSc, 42, MSc, 46, PhD(nutrit biochem), 48. *Prof Exp:* Asst res officer, Nutrit Res Lab, Coonoor, India, 49-59; from res assoc to assoc prof anat, 61-70, PROF ANAT, SCH MED, UNIV MINN, MINNEAPOLIS, 70- *Concurrent Pos:* Raptakos-Brett res fel, Nutrit Res Lab, Coonoor, India, 48-49; Tech Coop Mission fel, Western Reserve Univ, 52-54; res fel, Dept Anat, Sch Med, Univ Minn, Minneapolis, 59-61. *Mem:* Am Asn Anat; Soc Biol & Exp Med. *Res:* Diabetes, especially quantitative histochemistry as applied in pancreatic islets; studies on pancreatic islet adenoma; studies in experimental rickets; studies on nutritional deficiencies; microtechnics. *Mailing Add:* Dept Anat Med Sch 4-143 Jackson Hall 321 Church St SE Minneapolis MN 55455

DIXIT, SARYU N, b Sehud, India, Aug 8, 37; US citizen; m 56; c 2. BIOCHEMISTRY, ORGANIC CHEMISTRY. *Educ:* Agra Univ, BS, 56, MS, 58; Banaras Hindu Univ, PhD(org chem), 62. *Prof Exp:* Res assoc org chem, Univ Ill & Univ Chicago, 63-67; asst prof med chem, Banaras Hindu Univ, 67-70; res assoc biochem, Case Western Reserve Univ, 70-72; asst prof, 72-78, ASSOC PROF, VET ADMIN HOSP & UNIV TENN, 78-, RES CHEMIST, 72- *Mem:* Am Chem Soc; Sigma Xi; Am Soc Biol Chemists. *Res:* Biochemistry of interstitial and basement membrane collagens. *Mailing Add:* Vet Admin Hosp 1030 Jefferson Memphis TN 38104

DIXON, ANDREW DERART, b Belfast, Northern Ireland, Oct 27, 25; m 48; c 3. ANATOMY, DENTISTRY. *Educ:* Queen's Univ, Belfast, BDS, 49, MDS, 53, BSc, 54, DSc, 65; Univ Manchester, PhD(anat), 58. *Prof Exp:* Demonstr dent prosthetics, Queen's Univ, Belfast, 48-49; lectr anat, Univ Manchester, 54-62, sr lectr, 62-63; vis assoc prof, Univ Iowa, 59-61; prof oral biol & anat, Sch Med, Univ NC, Chapel Hill, 63-73, asst dean & coordr dent res, 66-73, dir dent res ctr, 67-73, assoc dean res, Sch Dent, 69-73; dean, Sch Dent, 73-80, PROF ORTHOD, UNIV CALIF, LOS ANGELES, 80- *Concurrent Pos:* Fulbright travel award, 59-61; Commonwealth Fund traveling fel, 61. *Mem:* Nat Inst Med-Nat Acad Sci; Am Soc Cell Biol; Am Asn Anat; Am Dent Asn; fel AAAS. *Res:* Development and growth of the jaws; innervation of oral tissues; electron microscopy of nerve tissue. *Mailing Add:* Sch of Dent Univ of Calif Los Angeles CA 90024

DIXON, ARTHUR EDWARD, b Woodstock, NB, Nov 16, 38; m 63; c 3. PHYSICS. *Educ:* Mt Allison Univ, BSc, 60; Dalhousie Univ, MSc, 62; McMaster Univ, PhD(solid state physics), 66. *Prof Exp:* Asst prof, 66-72, ASSOC PROF PHYSICS, UNIV WATERLOO, 72-, ASSOC DIR CORRESP PROG, 76- *Mem:* Am Phys Soc. *Res:* Electronic properties of solids; solar energy. *Mailing Add:* Dept of Physics Univ of Waterloo Waterloo ON N2L 3G1 Can

DIXON, CARL EUGENE, solid state physics, see previous edition

DIXON, CARL FRANKLIN, b La Junta, Colo, Sept 14, 26; m 60; c 3. PARASITOLOGY, ZOOLOGY. *Educ:* Univ Colo, BA, 50; Kans State Univ, PhD(parasitol), 60. *Prof Exp:* Vet parasitologist, USDA, 60-64; asst prof parasitol, 64-70, ASSOC PROF PARASITOL, AUBURN UNIV, 70- *Mem:* Am Soc Parasitol. *Res:* Interrelationship of helminth parasites and nutrition as a cause of disease in domestic animals. *Mailing Add:* Dept of Zool-Entom Auburn Univ Auburn AL 36849

DIXON, DALE DAVID, organic chemistry, polymer chemistry, see previous edition

DIXON, DAVID ALLEN, b Waukegan, Ill, Sept 19, 40; m 64; c 2. OCEAN ENGINEERING, PETROLEUM ENGINEERING. *Educ:* Northwestern Univ, BS, 63, MS, 64, PhD(struct mech), 66. *Prof Exp:* Res engr, Amoco Prod Co, 66-76, eng group supvr, Res Ctr, Amoco Int Oil Co, 76-78, CHIEF ENGR, AMOCO NORWAY OIL CO, 79- *Mem:* Am Soc Civil Engrs; Soc Petrol Engrs. *Res:* Offshore petroleum production. *Mailing Add:* Amoco Norway Oil Co Box 388 4001 Stavanger Norway

DIXON, DENNIS MICHAEL, b Richmond, Va, Sept 4, 51. BIOLOGY, MEDICAL MYCOLOGY. *Educ:* Univ Richmond, BS, 73; Va Commonwealth Univ, PhD(microbiol), 78. *Prof Exp:* A D Williams fel microbiol, Va Commonwealth Univ, 74-75, teaching asst, 75-77, res asst, 77-78; ASST PROF BIOL, LOYOLA COL, 78- *Mem:* Am Soc Microbiol; Mycol Soc Am; Med Mycol Soc Am; Int Soc Human & Animal Mycol; Med Mycol Soc NY. *Res:* Distribution of zoopathogenic fungi in nature and ultrastructural studies of conidial ontogeny for use in taxonomy. *Mailing Add:* Dept of Biol 4501 N Charles St Baltimore MD 21210

DIXON, DWIGHT R, b Fairfield, Idaho, June 16, 19; m 49; c 6. NUCLEAR PHYSICS. *Educ:* Utah State Univ, BSc, 42; Univ Calif, Berkeley, PhD(nuclear physics), 55. *Prof Exp:* Mem staff electronics, Radiation Lab, Mass Inst Technol, 42; proj engr, Sperry Co, NY, 42-46; physicist, Radiation Lab, Univ Calif, Berkeley, 48-55; sr engr missile eng, Utah Eng Lab, Sperry Gyroscope Co, 57-58, eng sect head, 58-59; from asst prof to assoc prof, 59-66, PROF PHYSICS, BRIGHAM YOUNG UNIV, 66- *Mem:* Sigma Xi; Am Asn Physics Teachers; Am Phys Soc. *Res:* Study of nuclear structure physics by means of radiative proton capture and inelastic neutron scattering reactions; study of energy loss and multiple scattering of charged particles in matter. *Mailing Add:* Dept Physics & Astron Brigham Young Univ Provo UT 84602

DIXON, FRANK JAMES, b St Paul, Minn, Mar 9, 20; m 46; c 3. IMMUNOLOGY. *Educ:* Univ Minn, BS, 41, MB, 43, MD, 44. *Prof Exp:* Intern, US Naval Hosp, Ill, 43-44; res fel path, Harvard Univ, 46-48; from instr to asst prof, Wash Univ, 48-51; prof & chmn dept, Med Sch, Univ Pittsburgh, 51-60; chmn dept exp path, 61-74, chmn dept biomed res, 70-74, DIR, SCRIPPS CLIN & RES FOUND, 74- *Concurrent Pos:* Adj prof, Univ Calif, San Diego, 61-; mem expert adv panel immunol, WHO, Sci Adv Comt, Helen Hay Whitney Found, Am Cancer Soc & Comt Res Nat Found, sci adv bd, Nat Kidney Found, Nat Cancer Adv Bd & Sci Adv Bd, St Jude Children's Res Hosp, vis comt biol div, Calif Inst Technol & Nat Arthritis Comn; Pahlavi lectr, Iran. *Honors & Awards:* Theobald Smith Award, 52; Parke-Davis Award, 57; Award Distinguished Achievement, Mod Med, 61; Martin E Rehfuss Award, 66; Von Pirquet Medal, Annual Forum Allergy, 67; Bunim Gold Medal, Am Rheumatism Asn, 68; Mayo Soley Award, West Soc Clin Res, 69; Gairdner Found Int Award, 69; Albert Lasker Basic Med Res Award; Dickson Prize in Med, Univ Pittsburgh. *Mem:* Nat Acad Sci; NY Acad Sci; Am Soc Exp Path (pres, 66); Am Asn Immunol (pres, 71); Am Asn Cancer Res. *Res:* Immunopathology. *Mailing Add:* Dept of Immunopath Scripps Clin & Res Found La Jolla CA 92037

DIXON, GARY EDWARD, b Delta, Colo, Aug 26, 51; m 75; c 2. FOREST BIOMETRY, STATISTICS. *Educ:* Colo State Univ, BS, 73, MS, 74, PhD(forest biomet), 77. *Prof Exp:* RES FORESTER & BIOMETRICIAN SAMPLE DESIGN, ROCKY MOUNTAIN FOREST & RANGE EXP STA, FOREST SERV, USDA, 76- *Res:* Renewable resource inventory techniques; statistical estimation; sample design; plot design; forest growth modelling; disease spread modelling; resource interaction modelling. *Mailing Add:* 240 W Prospect Ft Collins CO 80526

DIXON, GEORGE DOUGLASS, polymer chemistry, see previous edition

DIXON, GEORGE SUMTER, JR, b Asheville, NC, Mar 28, 38; m 66; c 1. SOLID STATE PHYSICS, MAGNETISM. *Educ:* Univ Ga, BS, 60, MS, 63, PhD(physics), 67. *Prof Exp:* Asst prof physics, Tenn Technol Univ, 67-68; AEC fel, Solid State Div, Oak Ridge Nat Lab, 68-70; asst prof, 70-75, ASSOC PROF PHYSICS, OKLA STATE UNIV, 75- *Mem:* Am Phys Soc. *Res:* Phase transitions; biophysics; spin-phonon interactions. *Mailing Add:* Dept of Physics Okla State Univ Stillwater OK 74078

DIXON, GORDON H, b Durban, SAfrica, Mar 25, 30; Can citizen; m 54; c 4. MOLECULAR BIOLOGY, DEVELOPMENTAL BIOLOGY. *Educ:* Cambridge Univ, BA, 51; Univ Toronto, PhD(biochem), 56. *Prof Exp:* Assoc biochem, Univ Wash, 55-56, asst prof, 56-58; Med Res Coun mem, Oxford Univ, 58-59; res assoc, Univ Toronto, 59-60, from asst prof to assoc prof, 60-63; from assoc prof to prof biochem, Univ BC, 63-72; prof & head biochem group, Univ Sussex, 72-74; PROF, DIV MED BIOCHEM, FAC MED, UNIV CALGARY, 74- *Concurrent Pos:* Vis scientist, Med Res Coun Lab Molecular Biol, Cambridge Univ, 70-71. *Honors & Awards:* Steacie Prize, 66; Ayerst Award, Can Biochem Soc, 66. *Mem:* Am Soc Biol Chemists; fel Royal Soc; Can Biochem Soc; Royal Soc Can. *Res:* Biochemistry of differentiation; structure and function of chromosomal proteins; protamines and histones; biochemistry of spermatogenesis; sequence analysis of messenger RNA; protein evolution. *Mailing Add:* Div of Med Biochem Fac of Med Health Sci Ctr Univ of Calgary Calgary AB T2N 1N4 Can

DIXON, HARRY S(TERLING), b Woodland, Calif, Nov 30, 10; m 37; c 4. ELECTRICAL ENGINEERING. *Educ:* Stanford Univ, BA, 31, EE, 36; Purdue Univ, PhD, 52. *Prof Exp:* Asst engr, Reclamation Dist No 108, Calif, 34-37; instr elec eng, Purdue Univ, 37-42; elec test engr, Douglas Aircraft, Calif, 42-44; elec design engr, NAm Aviation, Inc, 44-45; prof elec eng & chmn dept, NDak Agr Col, 45-51; lectr, Univ Calif, Berkeley, 51-52; prof & chmn dept, Newark Col Eng, 52-56; lectr, Univ Calif, Berkeley, 56-57; CONSULT ENGR, 57- *Concurrent Pos:* UNESCO int expert, Lagos, Nigeria, 64-65. *Mem:* AAAS; Inst Elec & Electronics Engrs; Nat Soc Prof Engrs; Am Soc Eng Educ; Illum Eng Soc. *Res:* Engineering education; aircraft electrical design; illumination design; electrical power transmission; electrical control; gaseous electrical phenomena; safety; fires and explosions, causes. *Mailing Add:* Harry S Dixon PhD Engrs 130 Jessie St San Francisco CA 94105

DIXON, HELEN ROBERTA, b Belvidere, Ill, Aug 13, 27. GEOLOGY. *Educ:* Carleton Col, BA, 49; Univ Calif, MA, 56; Harvard Univ, PhD(geol), 69. *Prof Exp:* GEOLOGIST, US GEOL SURV, 55- *Mem:* AAAS; Geol Soc Am; Mineral Soc Am; Am Geophys Union. *Res:* Igneous and metamorphic petrology; Precambrian of central Wyoming; metamorphics of eastern Connecticut. *Mailing Add:* US Geol Surv Denver Fed Ctr Bldg 25 Denver CO 80225

DIXON, HENRY MARSHALL, III, b New York, NY, June 4, 29. PHYSICS. *Educ:* Univ Va, BA, 50, MS, 52, PhD(physics), 54. *Prof Exp:* Asst prof physics, Tulane Univ, 54-55; physicist, White Sands Signal Agency, 55-57; asst prof physics, NMex State Col, 56-57; from asst prof to assoc prof, 57-65, PROF PHYSICS, BUTLER UNIV, 65- *Mem:* AAAS; Am Phys Soc; Sigma Xi; Inst Elec & Electronics Engrs. *Res:* Electronics and chemical physics. *Mailing Add:* Dept of Physics Butler Univ Indianapolis IN 46208

DIXON, JACK EDWARD, b Nashville, Tenn, June 16, 43. BIOCHEMISTRY. *Educ:* Univ Calif, Los Angeles, BA, 66, Santa Barbara, PhD(chem), 71. *Prof Exp:* Res asst chem, Univ Calif, Santa Barbara, 68-71, NSF fel biochem, San Diego, 71-73; asst prof, 73-78, ASSOC PROF BIOCHEM, PURDUE UNIV, WEST LAFAYETTE, 78- *Mem:* Am Chem Soc; AAAS; Am Soc Biol Chemist. *Res:* Mechanisms of biosynthesis and degradation of peptide hormones and releasing factors; molecular biology of peptide hormones. *Mailing Add:* Dept of Biochem Purdue Univ West Lafayette IN 47906

DIXON, JACK RICHARD, b Mich, Oct 29, 25; m 50; c 3. PHYSICS. *Educ:* Western Reserve Univ, BS, 48, MS, 50; Univ Md, PhD, 56. *Prof Exp:* Asst physics, Western Reserve Univ, 48-50; physicist chem & radiation lab, US Army Chem Corps, 50-52; res asst physics, Univ Md, 52-55; res physicist, US Naval Ord Lab, 55-75, HEAD MAT DIV, NAVAL SURFACE WEAPONS CTR, 75- *Concurrent Pos:* Assoc prof, Univ Md, 63- *Mem:* Am Phys Soc. *Res:* Theoretical weapons analysis; study of decay rates of metastable noble atoms; experimental solid state physics. *Mailing Add:* 422 Hillsboro Dr Silver Spring MD 20902

DIXON, JAMES EDWARD, b Schenectady, NY, Sept 9, 41; m 63; c 2. ORGANIC CHEMISTRY. *Educ:* St Bonaventure Univ, BS, 63, MS, 65; State Univ NY Albany, PhD(chem), 74. *Prof Exp:* RES CHEMIST ELECTROPHOTOG, EASTMAN KODAK RES LABS, 74- *Mem:* Am Chem Soc. *Res:* Investigation of xerographic behavior of sensitized polymeric systems. *Mailing Add:* 29 Everwild Lane Rochester NY 14616

DIXON, JAMES FRANCIS PETER, b Eng; US citizen; m 68; c 1. EXPERIMENTAL PATHOLOGY. *Educ:* Calif State Univ, Los Angeles, BS, 69; Univ Southern Calif, PhD(exp path), 75. *Prof Exp:* Res assoc, Children's Hosp, Los Angeles, 64-68; fel cancer res, Los Angeles County-Univ Southern Calif Cancer Ctr, 75-77, ASST PROF PATH, SCH MED, UNIV SOUTHERN CALIF, 77- *Concurrent Pos:* Consult & lectr histochem, City of Hope Med Ctr, Duarte, Calif, 69-72. *Mem:* AAAS; Brit Inst Med Lab Sci; Royal Micros Soc; Am Asn Pathologists; NY Acad Sci. *Res:* Control of cell proliferation; mechanisms of lymphocyte transformation; histochemistry of metabolic diseases. *Mailing Add:* Dept of Path Sch Med Univ Southern Calif Los Angeles CA 90033

DIXON, JAMES RAY, b Houston, Tex, Aug 1, 28; m 53; c 5. HERPETOLOGY. *Educ:* Howard Payne Col, BS, 50; Tex A&M Univ, MS, 57, PhD(zool), 61. *Prof Exp:* Cur reptiles, Ross Allen Reptile Inst, 54-55; asst prof vet med, Tex A&M Univ, 56-61; asst prof wildlife mgt, NMex State Univ, 61-65; cur herpet, Life Sci Div, Los Angeles County Mus, 65-67; assoc prof wildlife sci, 67-71, PROF WILDLIFE & FISHERIES SCI, TEX A&M UNIV, 71- *Concurrent Pos:* Sigma Xi res grants, 60 & 73; consult, NMex State Dept Game & Fish, 64-65; NSF grants, 64-66, 78-79 & 80; chmn bd scientists, Chihuahuan Desert Res Inst, 81- *Mem:* Am Soc Ichthyologists & Herpetologists; Zool Soc London; Soc Study Amphibians & Reptiles; Herpetologists League. *Res:* Zoogeography, systematics and ecology of lizards of the family Gekkonidae; systematics of reptiles and amphibians of southwestern United States, Mexico and South America, especially Peru; ecology of fish in impounded waters; general natural history of vertebrates. *Mailing Add:* Dept of Wildlife Sci Tex A&M Univ College Station TX 77843

DIXON, JOE BORIS, b Clinton, Ky, Nov 15, 30; m 52; c 2. SOIL SCIENCE. *Educ:* Univ Ky, BS, 52, MS, 56; Univ Wis, PhD(soil sci), 58. *Prof Exp:* NSF fel soil sci, 58-59; assoc prof, Auburn Univ, 59-68; PROF SOIL MINERAL, TEX A&M UNIV, 68- *Mem:* fel AAAS; fel Am Soc Agron; fel Soil Sci Soc Am; Mineral Soc Am; Int Soil Sci Soc. *Res:* Clay mineralogy of soils; soil genesis and classification; weathering of minerals in soils and rocks; surface properties of clays; mine spoil reclamation. *Mailing Add:* Dept Soil & Crop Sci Tex A&M Univ College Station TX 77843

DIXON, JOHN ALDOUS, b Provo, Utah, July 16, 23; m 44; c 3. SURGERY, PHYSIOLOGY. *Educ:* Univ Utah, BS, 44, MD, 47; Am Bd Surg, dipl, 54. *Prof Exp:* Exec vpres & prof surg, Col Med, 70-77, dean, 72-77, VPRES HEALTH SCI, UNIV UTAH, 73- *Concurrent Pos:* Chief surg, Johnson Air Force Hosp, Honshu, Japan & surg consult, Far East Air Force, 52-53. *Mem:* Fel Am Col Surg; Am Gastroenterol Asn; Soc Surg Alimentary Tract; Am Soc Gastrointestinal Endoscopy; Soc Am Gastrointestinal Endoscopic Surg. *Res:* Gastrointestinal surgery and diseases; motility of intestine; absorption and secretion; laser surgery and research. *Mailing Add:* Univ of Utah Col of Med Salt Lake City UT 84112

DIXON, JOHN CHARLES, b Chicago, Ill, July 21, 31; m 63; c 2. ENTOMOLOGY. *Educ:* Beloit Col, BS, 53; Univ Wis, MS, 55, PhD(entom, zool), 61. *Prof Exp:* Entomologist, Southeast Forest Exp Sta, Forest Serv, USDA, 59-64; asst prof biol, Chicago State Col, 64-68; asst prof, 68-70, ASSOC PROF BIOL, UNIV WIS-EAU CLAIRE, 70- *Mem:* AAAS; Entom Soc Am. *Res:* Ecological studies of defoliating insects; population studies and ecology of pine bark beetles. *Mailing Add:* Dept of Biol Univ of Wis Eau Claire WI 54701

DIXON, JOHN D(OUGLAS), b Buffalo, Minn, July 29, 24; m 49; c 4. ELECTRICAL ENGINEERING. *Educ:* Univ Minn, BEE, 49; Univ Mo, MS, 52. *Prof Exp:* From instr to asst prof elec eng, Univ Mo, 49-53; from asst prof to assoc prof, 53-63, PROF ELEC ENG, UNIV NDAK, 63-, CHMN DEPT, 79- *Mem:* Am Soc Eng Educ; Inst Elec & Electronics Engrs. *Res:* Control systems; computers. *Mailing Add:* Dept Elec Eng Univ NDak Grand Forks ND 58202

DIXON, JOHN DOUGLAS, b Ewell, Eng, Jan 18, 37; m 61; c 3. GROUP THEORY, ANALYSIS OF ALGORITHMS. *Educ:* Univ Melbourne, BS, 57, MA, 59; McGill Univ, PhD(math), 61. *Prof Exp:* Instr math, Calif Inst Technol, 61-64; sr lectr, Univ New South Wales, 64-67, assoc prof, 68; assoc prof, 68-71, PROF MATH, CARLETON UNIV, ONT, 71- *Mem:* London Math Soc; Am Math Soc; Math Asn Am; Math Can; Australian Math Soc. *Res:* Algebra and number theory; theory of linear groups and representation theory; design and analysis of algorithms in algebra and combinatorics. *Mailing Add:* Dept of Math Carleton Univ Ottawa ON K1S 5B6 Can

DIXON, JOHN E(LVIN), b Roseburg, Ore, Mar 23, 27; m 48; c 2. AGRICULTURAL ENGINEERING. *Educ:* Ore State Univ, BS(agr eng) & BS(agr), 51; Univ Idaho, MS, 57; Mich State Univ, PhD(agr eng), 79. *Prof Exp:* Instr agr eng, Colo State Univ, 51-54; from instr to assoc prof, Univ Idaho, 54-67; agr eng adv, Kans State Univ at Hyderabad, India, 67-69; dir prof adv serv ctr, 69-71, assoc prof, 69-79, PROF AGR ENG, UNIV IDAHO, 69- *Concurrent Pos:* Fallout shelter analyst instr, Defense Civil Protection Agency, 70-; res asst, Mich State Univ, 72-74. *Mem:* Am Soc Agr Engrs; Am Soc Eng Educ; Nat Soc Prof Engrs; Prof Soc Nuclear Defense. *Res:* Farm structures with emphasis on environmental control; poultry housing; crop storage; water quality; farmstead energy use and storage. *Mailing Add:* Dept of Agr Eng Univ of Idaho Moscow ID 83843

DIXON, JOHN FRANCIS CLEMOW, b Ottawa, Ont, Mar 1, 19; m 46; c 4. INDUSTRIAL CHEMISTRY. *Educ:* McGill Univ, BSc, 42, PhD(chem), 47. *Prof Exp:* Res chemist high polymers, Ont Res Found, 42-44; res chemist high polymers & explosives, Cent Res Lab, 47-53; group leader explosives, 53-56, asst, Explosives Div, 56-58, res mgr, 58-60, tech mgr, Chem Div, 61-65, gen sales mgr, Can Industs Ltd, 65-69, EDUC RELS MGR, CIL INC, 69- *Concurrent Pos:* Lectr, Sir George Williams Col, 46 & Concordia Univ, 74-79. *Mem:* Chem Inst Can. *Res:* Cellulose chemistry; protective coatings; chemistry of chlorine and derivatives; manufacture of heavy chemicals. *Mailing Add:* CIL Inc PO Box 200 Sta A Willowdale ON M2N 6H2 Can

DIXON, JOHN MICHAEL SIDDONS, b Derby, Eng, Aug 22, 28; m 52; c 2. MEDICAL MICROBIOLOGY. *Educ:* Univ Wales, MB, BCh, 50, MD, 60; Univ London, dipl bact, 57; FRCPS(C), 69; FRCPath, 71. *Prof Exp:* Dir, Pub Health Lab, Ipswich, Eng, 59-66; chief bact, Wellesley Hosp, Toronto, Ont, 66-67; PROF BACT, UNIV ALTA, 67- *Concurrent Pos:* Prov bacteriologist, Alta, 67-; dir, Prov Lab Pub Health, Edmonton & Calgary, 67-; consult bacteriologist, Univ Alta Hosp, Edmonton, 67-; chmn, Can Nat Adv Comt Immunization, 72-; chmn, Grants Comt Microbiol & Infectious Dis, Med Res Coun Can, 73-76. *Mem:* Can Asn Med Microbiol (pres, 70-72); Am Soc Microbiol; Am Pub Health Asn; Can Microbiol; Infectious Dis Soc Am. *Res:* Bacteria of the intestine; antibiotic resistance of streptococci and pneumococci. *Mailing Add:* Prov Lab Pub Health Univ of Alta Edmonton AB T6G 2E8 Can

DIXON, JOHN R, b Akron, Ohio, Oct 19, 30; m 51; c 1. MECHANICAL ENGINEERING. *Educ:* Mass Inst Technol, BS, 52, MS, 53; Carnegie Inst Technol, PhD(mech eng), 60. *Prof Exp:* Engr, Jarl Extrusions, Inc, NY, 55-57; proj engr, Joseph Kaye & Co, Mass, 57-58; asst prof mech eng, Carnegie Inst Technol, 60-61; assoc prof, Purdue Univ, 61-65 & Swarthmore Col, 65-66; head dept, 66-71, PROF MECH ENG, UNIV MASS, AMHERST, 66-, HEAD DEPT, 81- *Concurrent Pos:* Pres, Dixon Energy Systs, Inc. *Mem:* AAAS; fel Am Soc Mech Engrs; Am Soc Heating, Refrig & Airconditioning Engrs. *Mailing Add:* Dept of Mech & Aerospace Eng Univ of Mass Amherst MA 01002

DIXON, JOSEPH ARDIFF, b Philadelphia, Pa, Nov 4, 19; m 42; c 2. ORGANIC CHEMISTRY. *Educ:* Pa State Univ, BS, 42, MS, 45, PhD(org chem), 47. *Prof Exp:* Chemist, USDA, 42-44; instr chem, Pa State Univ, 47-51; chemist, Calif Res Corp, 51-52; assoc prof chem, Lafayette Col, 52-55; assoc prof, 55-60, PROF CHEM, PA STATE UNIV, UNIVERSITY PARK, 60-, HEAD DEPT, 71- *Mem:* AAAS; Am Chem Soc. *Res:* Correlation of properties with molecular structures; synthesis and properties of hydrocarbons; organo-lithium chemistry. *Mailing Add:* Dept of Chem Pa State Univ University Park PA 16802

DIXON, JULIAN THOMAS, b Birmingham, Ala, Nov 3, 13. ELECTRONICS ENGINEERING, COMMUNICATIONS ENGINEERING. *Educ:* Ga Inst Technol, BSEE, 35. *Prof Exp:* Electronics engr radio monitoring, Fed Commun Comn, 40-44; electronics officer radar design, US Naval Res Lab, -46; chief, FM Broadcasting Br, Fed Commun Comn, 46-50, TV Broadcasting Br, 50-54, Tech Standards Br, 54-60, Tech Res Div, 60-74, chief, Res Standards Div, 74-80, dep chief scientist, 80-81; CONSULT COMMUN, 81- *Concurrent Pos:* Tech adv, Int Electrotech Comn, 65-; mem, Elec & Electronics Standards Mgt Bd, Am Nat Standards Inst, 68-; Int Chmn, Study Group 1, Int Radio Consult Comt, 74- *Res:* All kinds of radio electronic systems, especially improvement of system performance by application of advanced technology, improved radio frequency spectrum utilization, new systems, and related matters. *Mailing Add:* 300 S 81st St Birmingham AL 35206

DIXON, KEITH LEE, b El Centro, Calif, Jan 20, 21; m 49; c 1. VERTEBRATE ZOOLOGY. *Educ:* San Diego State Col, AB, 43; Univ Calif, MA, 48, PhD(zool), 53. *Prof Exp:* Mus technician, Mus Vert Zool, Univ Calif, 47-52, asst zool, 47-49; from asst prof to assoc prof wildlife mgt, Agr & Mech Col Tex, 52-58; asst res zoologist, Hastings Natural Hist Reservation, 58-59; from asst prof to assoc prof, 59-67, PROF ZOOL, UTAH STATE UNIV, 67- *Concurrent Pos:* Asst ed, Cooper Ornith Soc, 49-52; leader Mex expeds, Agr & Mech Col Tex, 53-54; ed bull, Wilson Ornith Soc, 55-58; mem field expeds, Calif, Mont, Ariz & Tex. *Mem:* Am Soc Mammal; fel Am Ornith Union; Cooper Ornith Soc; Wilson Ornith Soc; Ecol Soc Am. *Res:* Ecology, social behavior and distribution of birds and mammals. *Mailing Add:* Dept of Biol Utah State Univ Logan UT 84322

DIXON, KEITH R, b Portsmouth, Eng, Dec 4, 40; m 66. INORGANIC CHEMISTRY. *Educ:* Cambridge Univ, BA, 63; Univ Strathclyde, PhD(fluorine chem), 66. *Prof Exp:* Fel inorg chem, Univ Western Ont, 66-68; asst prof inorg chem, 68-74, ASSOC PROF CHEM, UNIV VICTORIA, 74- *Mem:* Chem Inst Can; The Chem Soc. *Res:* Chemistry of complex fluorides; organometallic chemistry of the precious metals. *Mailing Add:* Dept of Chem Univ of Victoria Victoria BC V8W 2Y2 Can

DIXON, KENNETH RANDALL, b Madison, Wis, Aug 2, 42; m 65. SYSTEMS ECOLOGY, WILDLIFE MANAGEMENT. *Educ:* Univ Fla, BSF, 64, MSF, 68; Univ Mich, PhD(wildlife mgt), 74. *Prof Exp:* Res ecologist ecosyst anal, Oak Ridge Nat Lab, 73-76; ASST PROF WILDLIFE ECOL, APPALACHIAN ENVIRON LAB, UNIV MD, 76- *Concurrent Pos:* Consult, Md Dept Natural Resources, 76- & Fed Energy Regulatory Comn, 78- *Mem:* AAAS; Am Inst Biol Sci; Ecol Soc Am; Wildlife Soc. *Res:* Effects of pollutants on environment; wildlife as monitors; wildlife population dynamics. *Mailing Add:* Appalachian Environ Lab Frostburg State Col Campus Frostburg MD 21532

DIXON, LINDA KAY, b Brownsville, Pa, Aug 20, 40. BEHAVIORAL GENETICS. *Educ:* California State Col, Pa, BS, 62; Univ Calif, Berkeley, MS, 64; Univ Ill, Urbana, 67. *Prof Exp:* Res assoc, Inst Behav Genetics, Univ Colo, Boulder, 68; assoc prof genetics, 69-76, assoc prof biol, 76-80, PROF BIOL, UNIV COLO, DENVER, 80- *Concurrent Pos:* Behav genetics training grant, Inst Behav Genetics, Colo, 68-69. *Mem:* AAAS; Genetics Soc Am; Am Inst Biol Sci; Behav Genetics Asn. *Res:* Developmental genetics of mouse behavior; relationships between chromosomal aberrations and behavioral differences. *Mailing Add:* Div of Natural & Phys Sci Biol Univ of Colo 1100 14th St Denver CO 80202

DIXON, LYLE JUNIOR, b Osborne, Kans, Feb 28, 24; m 42; c 3. MATHEMATICS. *Educ:* Okla State Univ, BS, 48, MS, 50; Univ Kans, PhD, 63. *Prof Exp:* Instr math, Okla State Univ, 47-48 & Southwestern State Col, 49-50; asst instr, Univ Kans, 50-51; asst prof, Ark State Col, 51-53, supvr sci & math areas, Gen Educ, 53-57, registr, 57-58, dir res, 58-59, assoc prof math, 59-63; assoc prof, 63-67, PROF MATH, KANS STATE UNIV, 67- *Mem:* Math Asn Am. *Res:* Algebra; matrix theory; mathematics education. *Mailing Add:* Dept of Math Kans State Univ Manhattan KS 66502

DIXON, MARK ADRIAN, geology, ichthyology, see previous edition

DIXON, MARVIN PORTER, b Kansas City, Mo, Nov 10, 38; m 61; c 3. ORGANIC CHEMISTRY, PHYSICAL ORGANIC CHEMISTRY. *Educ:* William Jewell Col, BA, 60; Univ Ill, Urbana, MS, 63, PhD, 65. *Prof Exp:* From asst prof to assoc prof, 65-75, PROF CHEM, WILLIAM JEWELL COL, 75-, CHMN DEPT, 74- *Concurrent Pos:* Kans City Regional Coun Higher Educ Fac develop grant. *Mem:* Midwest Asn Chem; Teachers Lib Arts Cols; Am Chem Soc. *Res:* Ambident ion chemistry; kinetics; reaction mechanisms; organometallic chemistry. *Mailing Add:* Dept of Chem William Jewell Col Liberty MO 64068

DIXON, MICHAEL JOHN, b Chicago, Ill, July 1, 41. COMPLEX ANALYSIS, APPROXIMATION THEORY. *Educ:* Col St Thomas, BA, 63; Purdue Univ, MS, 65; Univ Calif, San Diego, PhD(math), 76. *Prof Exp:* Asst prof, 67-72, assoc prof, 75-80, PROF MATH & CHMN DEPT, CALIF STATE UNIV, CHICO, 80- *Concurrent Pos:* NASA trainee, Purdue Univ, 63-66; vis res scientist, Univ Amsterdam, 77. *Mem:* Math Asn Am. *Res:* Complex approximation theory. *Mailing Add:* Dept of Math Calif State Univ Chico CA 95929

DIXON, PEGGY A, b Cleveland, Ohio, June 9, 28; m 50; c 3. PHYSICS. *Educ:* Western Reserve Univ, AB, 50; Univ Md, MS, 54, PhD(physics), 59. *Prof Exp:* Physicist munitions res, Chem Corps, US Army, 50-52; asst physics, Univ Md, 52-58, res assoc, 58-61; from asst prof to assoc prof, 59-70, PROF PHYSICS & ENG, MONTGOMERY COL, 70- *Concurrent Pos:* NSF res fel, 62; chmn panel on physics in two-year col, Comn Col Physics, 68-69; vis prof, Univ Md, 70-71. *Mem:* AAAS; Am Asn Physics Teachers. *Res:* Solid state theory; ferromagnetism; lattice vibration theory. *Mailing Add:* Dept of Physics Montgomery Col Takoma Park MD 20012

DIXON, PETER STANLEY, b Redcar, Eng, Nov 29, 28; m 55; c 3. PHYCOLOGY. *Educ:* Univ Manchester, BSc, 49, MSc, 50, PhD(bot), 52, DSc(bot), 78. *Prof Exp:* Asst lectr bot, Univ Liverpool, 54-56, lectr, 56-64, sr lectr, 64-65; assoc prof, Univ Wash, 65-67; chmn dept pop & environ biol, 69-72, 75-76, PROF BIOL SCI, UNIV CALIF, IRVINE, 67- *Res:* Developmental morphology, ecology and taxonomy of algae, particularly Rhodophyta. *Mailing Add:* Dept of Pop & Environ Biol Univ of Calif Irvine CA 92664

DIXON, RICHARD WAYNE, b Hubbard, Ore, Sept 25, 36; m 70. SOLID STATE PHYSICS. *Educ:* Harvard Univ, AB, 58, MA, 60, PhD(appl physics), 64. *Prof Exp:* Res fel appl physics, Univ Harvard, 64-65; staff mem, 65-68, supvr, 68-79, DEPT HEAD, APPL PHYSICS, BELL TEL LABS, INC, 79- *Mem:* AAAS; Am Phys Soc; fel Inst Elec & Electronics Eng. *Res:* Research and development of acoustooptic, electroluminescent, and injection laser materials and devices. *Mailing Add:* Bell Tel Labs Inc Murray Hill NJ 07974

DIXON, ROBERT JEROME, JR, b Seattle, Wash, Apr 26, 31; m 52; c 2. AERODYNAMICS, HYDRODYNAMICS. *Educ:* Univ Wash, BS, 58, MS, 60. *Prof Exp:* PRIN ENGR HYDRODYN & PROPULSION, BOEING CO, 59- *Mem:* Sigma Xi. *Res:* Viscous flows; separated flows; test simulation. *Mailing Add:* Boeing Marine Systs PO Box 3707 Seattle WA 98124

DIXON, ROBERT LELAND, b Sumter, SC, July 2, 40. RADIOLOGICAL PHYSICS. *Educ:* Univ SC, BS, 63, PhD(physics), 70. *Prof Exp:* Instr reactor physics, US Naval Nuclear Power Sch, 64-68; assoc prof, 70-80, PROF RADIOL PHYSICS, BOWMAN GRAY SCH MED, WAKE FOREST UNIV, 80- *Mem:* Am Asn Physicists Med; Am Col Radiol. *Res:* Nuclear magnetic resonance applications in biophysics; thermoluminescence phosphor research in dosimetry; computer applications in medicine. *Mailing Add:* Dept Radiol Bowman Gray Sch Med Wake Forest Univ Winston-Salem NC 27103

DIXON, ROBERT LOUIS, b Sacramento, Calif, Feb 9, 36; m 58; c 3. PHARMACOLOGY, BIOCHEMISTRY. *Educ:* Idaho State Univ, BS, 58; Univ Iowa, MS, 61, PhD(pharmacol), 63. *Prof Exp:* Sr investr, Nat Cancer Inst, 63-65; from asst prof to assoc prof pharmacol, Sch Med, Univ Wash, 65-69; chief lab toxicol-chemother, Nat Cancer Inst, 69-72, chief, Environ Toxicol Lab, 72-80, CHIEF, REPROD & DEVLOP TOXICOL LAB, NAT INST ENVIRON HEALTH SCI, 80- *Concurrent Pos:* Sci policy analyst, Off Sci & Technol Policy, Exec Off of the President, 77-78. *Mem:* AAAS; Am Asn Cancer Res; Soc Exp Biol & Med; Am Soc Pharmacol & Exp Therapeut; Soc Toxicol. *Res:* Environmental toxicology; biochemical pharmacology; developmental and reproductive pharmacology. *Mailing Add:* Nat Inst of Environ Health Sci PO Box 12233 Research Triangle Park NC 27709

DIXON, ROGER L, b Pecos, NMex, Aug 14, 47; m 68; c 1. PHYSICS. *Educ:* NMex Highlands Univ, BS, 70; Purdue Univ, MS, 72, PhD(physics), 75. *Prof Exp:* Res assoc physics, Cornell Univ, 75-77; PHYSICIST PHYSICS, FERMILAB, 77- *Mem:* Am Phys Soc; Sigma Xi. *Res:* High energy particle accelerators, particularly extraction, beam lines and superconducting applications; high energy physics. *Mailing Add:* Fermilab PO Box 500 Batavia IL 60510

DIXON, SAMUEL, JR, b Six, WVa, Oct 16, 27; m 59; c 2. ELECTRONIC ENGINEERING, PHYSICS. *Educ:* WVa State Col, BS, 49; Monmouth Col, MS, 72. *Prof Exp:* Physicist components, Electron Rest Develop Command, 58-80, SR ELECTRONICS ENGR, ELECTRON TECHNOL & DEVICES LAB, US ARMY ELECTRONICS COMMAND, FT MONMOUTH, 80- *Mem:* Inst Elec & Electronics Engrs. *Res:* Investigation and design of milllimeter-wave components in high resistivity, high permittivity dielectrics used as waveguides; evaluate new technologies related to millimeter-wave integrated circuits. *Mailing Add:* Electron Technol & Devices Lab US Army Electronics Command Ft Monmouth NJ 07703

DIXON, STUART EDWARD, b Minto, NB, Oct 11, 22; nat; m 55; c 3. ENTOMOLOGY. *Educ:* McMaster Univ, BA, 47; Univ Toronto, MSA, 51; Cornell Univ, PhD(entom), 55. *Prof Exp:* Lectr entom, 47-55, from asst prof to assoc prof zool, 55-77, PROF BIOL UNIV GUELPH, 77- *Mem:* Can Soc Zool. *Res:* Growth, development and physiology of insects; insect morphology. *Mailing Add:* Dept Environ Biol Univ of Guelph Guelph ON N1G 2W1 Can

DIXON, THOMAS F(RANCIS), b Nashville, Tenn, Mar 15, 16; m 43; c 4. AERONAUTICAL ENGINEERING. *Educ:* Vanderbilt Univ, BS, 38; Univ Mich, BS, 39, MS, 40; Calif Inst Technol, MS, 45. *Prof Exp:* Develop engr, Am Maize Prods Co, Ind, 40-41 & Westinghouse Elec Co, Pa, 41-42; extrusion officer, Naval Powder Factory, US Navy, Md, 42-43, div head solid propellant rocket res & develop dept, Bur Ord, Washington, DC, 43-44, liaison officer, Calif Tech Liaison, 44-45, div head propellant rocket progress, Bur Ord, 45; group leader propulsion & dir, Eng Propulsion Ctr, 46-55, chief engr, Rocketdyne Div, 55-59, dir eng, 59-60, vpres res & eng, 60; dep assoc adminstr, NASA, 61-63; vpres mkt planning, N Am Aviation, Inc, 63-67; chmn bd, Airtronics, Inc, 67-69, pres, 69-75; PRES, TELEDYNE MCCORMICK SELPH, 76- *Honors & Awards:* Goddard Mem Award, 57; Lewis W Hill Space Transp Award, 60. *Mem:* Fel Am Inst Aeronaut & Astronaut; Soc Automotive Engrs; Aerospace Indust Asn Am. *Res:* Liquid and solid propellant rocket engines. *Mailing Add:* 7 Via Las Encinas Carmel Valley CA 93924

DIXON, THOMAS PATRICK, b San Antonio, Tex, Feb 21, 22; m 44; c 3. ELECTRONIC ENGINEERING, OPTICAL PHYSICS. *Educ:* Univ Southern Calif, BSEE, 50. *Prof Exp:* Supvr elec res & develop labs, Technicolor Motion Picture Corp, 50-57; group supvr, electronic systs, Radioplane Co, 57-59; sr mem tech staff, ITT Aerospace, 59-63, exec engr, 63-66, dept dir electrooptical systs, 66-67, DIR ELECTROOPTICAL SYSTS, ITT AEROSPACE/OPTICAL DIV, INT TEL & TEL CORP, 67- *Mem:* Inst Elec & Electronics Engrs; Soc Photo-Optical Instrument Engrs. *Res:* Electro-optical systems for guidance and navigation of space vehicles; laser communication, ranging and tracking, color picture analysis and synthesis; optical surveillance and low-light-level imaging systems. *Mailing Add:* 7821 Orion Ave Van Nuys CA 91409

DIXON, WALLACE CLARK, JR, b Winston-Salem, NC, Dec 18, 22; m 46; c 2. PHYSIOLOGY. *Educ:* Eastern Nazarene Col, AB, 46; Boston Univ, AM, 47, PhD(biol), 56. *Prof Exp:* From instr to asst prof biol, Eastern Nazarene Col, 48-54; from asst prof to prof basic studies & grad sch, Boston Univ, 56-68; prof biol & chmn, Natural Sci Dept, Cent Univ Col, 68-79, ASSOC DEAN, COL NATURAL & MATH SCI, EASTERN KY, 79- *Mem:* Asn Gen & Lib Studies. *Res:* Cellular physiology; endocrinology; science in general education. *Mailing Add:* Col Natural & Math Sci Eastern Ky Univ Richmond KY 40475

DIXON, WILFRID JOSEPH, b Portland, Ore, Dec 13, 15; div; c 2. BIOMATHEMATICS. *Educ:* Ore State Col, BA, 38; Univ Wis, MA, 39; Princeton Univ, PhD(math statist), 44. *Prof Exp:* Asst, Princeton Univ, 39-41 & Nat Defense Res Comt Proj, 41-42; from instr to asst prof math, Univ Okla, 42-44; res assoc & consult, Joint Target Group, Air Corps & Air Serv, Intel & Opers Analyst, 20th Air Force, 44-45; assoc prof math, Univ Okla, 45-46; assoc prof, Univ Ore, 46-52, prof, 52-55; PROF BIOSTATIST, UNIV CALIF, LOS ANGELES, 55-, PROF BIOMATH, 67- *Concurrent Pos:* Assoc ed, Biomet, 52-66 & Annals Math Statist, 55-58; consult, Off Naval Res, Rand Corp, Vet Admin, State Dept Ment Hyg, Calif & NIH; chief statist res, Brentwood Vet Admin Hosp, 72- *Mem:* Fel Royal Statist Soc; fel Am Statist Asn; fel Inst Math Statist; Biomet Soc. *Res:* Mathematical theory of serial correlation; sensitivity experiments; inefficient statistics; computers in medical research. *Mailing Add:* Dept of Biomath Sch of Med Univ of Calif Ctr for Health Sci Los Angeles CA 90024

DIXON, WILLIAM BRIGHTMAN, b Fall River, Mass, Dec 18, 35; m 57; c 2. PHYSICAL CHEMISTRY, LABORATORY COMPUTER INTERFACING. *Educ:* Wheaton Col (Ill), BS, 57; Harvard Univ, AM, 59, PhD(phys chem), 61. *Prof Exp:* NSF fel, Nat Res Coun, Ottawa, 61-62, Nat Res Coun Can fel, 62-63; from asst prof to assoc prof chem, Wheaton Col (Ill), 63-68; assoc prof, 68-69, PROF CHEM, STATE UNIV NY COL ONEONTA, 69- *Concurrent Pos:* Fulbright student, Copenhagen, 60-61; vis prof, Dartmouth Col, 77-78. *Mem:* AAAS; Am Chem Soc. *Res:* Molecular spectroscopy. *Mailing Add:* Dept Chem State Univ of NY Col Oneonta NY 13820

DIXON, WILLIAM GORDON, JR, b Sedalia, Mo, Nov 28, 31; m 54; c 5. GEOLOGY. *Educ:* Ind Univ, BS, 58, AM, 66. *Prof Exp:* Geologist found explor, Soil Testing Serv, Inc, 58-59, dam found studies, Harza Eng Co, 61-63, Layne-Western Co, 63-64; eng geologist, Testing Serv Corp, 64-74; field engr earthwork control, Dames & Moore, 74-75; ASSOC GEOLOGIST, HYDROGEOL & GEOPHYS SECT, ILL STATE GEOL SURV, 75- *Mem:* Asn Eng Geologists; Am Inst Prof Geologists. *Res:* Engineering geology; hydrogeology. *Mailing Add:* Ill State Geol Surv PO Box I Warrenville IL 60555

DIXON, WILLIAM ROSSANDER, b Sask, July 3, 25; m 73. NUCLEAR PHYSICS. *Educ:* Univ Sask, BA, 45, MA, 47; Queen's Univ, PhD(physics), 55. *Prof Exp:* RES OFFICER X-RAYS & NUCLEAR RADIATIONS, NAT RES COUN CAN, 50- *Mem:* Can Asn Physicists; Am Phys Soc. *Res:* Gamma rays produced in charged-particle nuclear reactions to elucidate nuclear structure; radioactivity; radiation dosimetry. *Mailing Add:* X-ray & Nuclear Radiations Nat Res Coun Ottawa ON K1A 0R6 Can

DIZENHUZ, ISRAEL MICHAEL, b Toronto, Ont, May 20, 31. PSYCHIATRY. *Educ:* Univ Toronto, MD, 55; Am Asn Psychiat Clin Children, cert career child psychiat, 60; Am Bd Psychiat & Neurol, dipl & cert psychiat, 62, cert child psychiat, 65. *Prof Exp:* Rotating gen intern, E J Meyer Mem Hosp, Buffalo, NY, 55-56; resident psychiat, Ont Hosp, Hamilton, 56-57; resident, Col Med, Univ Cincinnati, 57-58, fel, 59-60, from instr to asst prof child psychiat, Col Med, 61-69, from asst dir to assoc dir child psychiat, Cent Psychiat Clin, 63-70, assoc prof child psychiat, 69-78; DIR PSYCHIAT, THE JEWISH HOSP, CINCINNATI, 78- *Concurrent Pos:* Staff child psychiatrist, Child Guid Home, Cincinnati, 61; consult, Family Serv Cincinnati, 63-67 & Jewish Family Serv, 63-68; lectr, Vol Training for Community Ment Health Serv, Cincinnati, 63-68; attend child psychiatrist & clinician child psychiat, Cincinnati Gen Hosp; mem bd trustees, Hamilton Co Diagnostic Ctr Ment Retarded, 63-; psychiatrist, Consult Staff, Children's Hosp, Cincinnati, 66; chmn MidE reg comt on pub educ, Am Asn Psychiat Clin for Children, 66, mem nat comt on pub educ, 66-; lectr, Univ Cincinnati, 67; asst examiner, Child Psychiat Exam, Am Bd Psychiat & Neurol, 67-69; mem prof adv comt, United Serv for Handicapped of Cincinnati; mem, Citizen's Comt, Area Task Force on Ment Retardation; mem res team, Family Serv of Cincinnati, 75- *Mem:* Fel Am Psychiat Asn; Am Orthopsychiat Asn; fel Am Acad Child Psychiat. *Res:* Community psychiatry. *Mailing Add:* The Jewish Hosp Cincinnati OH 45229

DI ZIO, STEVEN F(RANK), b Newark, NJ, Dec 15, 38; m 58; c 1. CHEMICAL ENGINEERING. *Educ:* Oregon State Univ, BS, 61; Rensselaer Polytech, PhD(chem eng), 64. *Prof Exp:* Texaco fel, Rensselaer Polytech, 61-62, Procter & Gamble fel, 62-63, Lummus Co fel, 63-64; asst prof chem eng, Rensselaer Polytech Inst, 64-68, assoc prof, 68-69, chmn dept biomed eng, 67-69; vpres, 69-72, pres & dir, Aero Vac Corp, 72-74; PRES, CHIEF EXEC OFFICER & DIR, SES INC, 74- *Concurrent Pos:* Adj assoc prof, Rensselaer Polytech Inst, 69- *Mem:* AAAS; Am Inst Chem Engrs; Am Chem Soc; Am Soc Eng Educ; Soc Cryobiol. *Res:* Application of engineering principles to medicine; development of a coherent academic program to train bioengineers. *Mailing Add:* SES Inc Tralee Ind Park Newark DE 19711

DIZON, ANDREW EDWARD, b Minneapolis, Minn, Sept 12, 42; m 64; c 1. FISH BIOLOGY. *Educ:* Univ Wis, BS, 64, MS, 67, PhD(zool), 71. *Prof Exp:* FISHERY BIOLOGIST, NAT MARINE FISHERIES SERV, 71- *Concurrent Pos:* Affil prof, Univ Hawaii, 72- *Mem:* Am Fisheries Soc. *Res:* Studies of the behavioral and physiological responses of tunas to environmental factors to develop predictive models of distribution, abundance and availability to the fishery. *Mailing Add:* Nat Marine Fisheries Serv Honolulu Lab PO Box 3830 Honolulu HI 96812

DJANG, ARTHUR H K, b Lio-Yuan, China, Feb 12, 25; US citizen; m 58; c 4. PATHOLOGY, NUCLEAR MEDICINE. *Educ:* Harbin Med Univ, China, MD, 44; Univ Minn, Minneapolis, MPH, 51; Univ Calif, Los Angeles, PhD(infectious dis), 55; Am Bd Path, dipl, 62; Am Bd Nuclear Med, dipl, 74. *Prof Exp:* Clin instr infectious dis, Sch Med, Univ Calif, Los Angeles, 50-55; asst prof microbiol, Sch Med & Sch Trop Med, Univ PR, San Juan, 56; dir div chronic dis & actg dir div communicable dis control, NMex State Dept Pub Health, 57-58; dir microbiol & virus lab, St Francis Hosp, Wichita, Kans, 58-61; chief pathologist & dir labs, Mem Gen Hosp, Las Cruces, NMex, 62-71; pres & dir, Bio-Med Sci Labs, Las Cruces & Albuquerque, NMex, 63-75; CHMN DEPT PATH & NUCLEAR MED, JAMESTOWN GEN HOSP, 75- *Concurrent Pos:* Consult prof path, NMex State Univ, University Park, 63-71; consult, Holloman AFB Hosp, NMex, 63-73; med exam-coroner, Dona Ana County, NMex, 67-70; prof biol sci, Western NMex Univ, 67-75; clin prof, Univ Fredomia, 77-; vpres & dir res, Am Heart Asn, 79- *Mem:* Col Am Pathologists; Am Soc Clin Pathologists; Soc Nuclear Med; Am Soc Cytol; Am Soc Microbiol. *Res:* Immunotherapy and chemotherapy of cancers; radioimmunoassay of hormones, isoenzymes and epidemiology of cardiovascular diseases and tumors. *Mailing Add:* 51 Glasgow Ave Jamestown NY 14701

DJERASSI, CARL, b Vienna, Austria, Oct 29, 23; nat US; div; c 2. ORGANIC CHEMISTRY. *Educ:* Kenyon Col, AB, 42; Univ Wis, PhD(org chem), 45. *Hon Degrees:* DSc, Nat Univ Mex, 53, Kenyon Col, 58, Fed Univ Rio de Janeiro, 69, Worcester Polytech Inst, 72, Wayne State Univ, 74 & Columbia Univ, 75, Uppsala Univ, 77, Coe Col & Univ Geneva, 78. *Prof Exp:* Res chemist, Ciba Pharmaceut Prod, Inc, 42-43, 45-49; assoc dir chem res, Syntex, SA, Mex, 49-52; from assoc prof to prof, Wayne State Univ, 52-59; PROF CHEM, STANFORD UNIV, 59- *Concurrent Pos:* Vpres, Syntex, SA, 57-60, pres, Syntex Res Div, 68-72; pres, Zoecon Corp, 69-; chmn bd sci & int technol develop, Nat Acad Sci, 68-75. *Honors & Awards:* Pure Chem Award, Am Chem Soc, 58, Baekeland Medal, 59, Fritzsche Medal, 60 & Chem Invention Award, 73; Intrasci Res Found Award, 70; Freedman Patent Award, Am Inst Chemists, 71 & Chem Pioneer Award, 73; Nat Medal of Sci, 73; Perkin Medal, Soc Chem Indust, 75; Nat Inventors Hall of Fame & Wolf Prize in Chem, 78. *Mem:* Nat Acad Sci; Inst of Med of Nat Acad Sci; fel Am Acad Arts & Sci; Am Chem Soc; hon fel The Chem Soc. *Res:* Chemistry of steroids; structure of alkaloids; antibiotics and terpenoids; synthesis of drugs, particularly antihistamines, oral contraceptives, antiinflammatory agents; optical rotatory dispersion and circular dichroism studies, organic mass spectrometry; magnetic circular dichroism of organic compounds; applications of computer artificial intelligence techniques to chemical structure elucidation. *Mailing Add:* Dept of Chem Stanford Univ Stanford CA 94305

DJERASSI, ISAAC, b Bulgaria, July 27, 21; nat US; m 54; c 2. HEMATOLOGY. *Educ:* Hebrew Med Sch, Israel, MD, 51. *Hon Degrees:* DH, Villanova Univ, 77. *Prof Exp:* Resident pediat, Hadassah Hosp, Israel, 53-54; assoc path, Children's Med Ctr, Children's Cancer Res Found, 55-60; assoc dir clin labs & dir blood bank & donor ctr, Children's Hosp Philadelphia, 60-69; DIR DONOR CTR & RES HEMAT, MERCY CATH MED CTR, 69- *Concurrent Pos:* Res assoc, Harvard Med Sch, 57-60; asst prof pediat, Sch Med, Univ Pa, 60-69; consult, Children's Cancer Res Found, Boston, Mass, 61-77; mem, Acute Leukemia Task Force, Nat Cancer Inst. *Honors & Awards:* Prize, Cong Hemat, 56; Lasker Award, 72; Golden Plate Award, 77. *Mem:* Soc Pediat Res; Am Asn Cancer Res; Am Soc Exp Path. *Res:* Pediatric hematology and hemostasis. *Mailing Add:* Fitzgerald Mercy Div Lansdowne Ave & Bailey Rd Darby PA 19023

DJORDJEVIC, MILAN S, b Belgrade, Yugoslavia, Aug 22, 13; m 38. MECHANICAL ENGINEERING. *Educ:* Univ Belgrade, BS, 36; Univ Munich, PhD(mech eng), 39. *Prof Exp:* From asst prof to prof mech eng, Univ Belgrade, 46-64; prof, Duke Univ, 64-66; PROF MECH ENG, UNIV ALA, TUSCALOOSA, 66- *Concurrent Pos:* Chmn motor inst, Serbian Acad Sci, 48-58; consult, State of Ala Bd Planning & Indust Develop, 68. *Mem:* Am Soc Mech Engrs. *Res:* Internal combustion engines; thermodynamics and heat transfer. *Mailing Add:* Dept of Mech Eng PO Box 6307 University AL 35486

DJURIC, DUSAN, b Novi Sad, Yugoslavia, Jan 17, 30; m 55; c 2. METEOROLOGY. *Educ:* Univ Belgrade, Dipl, 53, DrSc(meteorol), 60. *Prof Exp:* Asst meteorol, Col Sci, Univ Belgrade, 54-60, docent, 60-65; vis scientist, Nat Ctr Atmospheric Res, Colo, 65-66; asst prof meteorol, 66-68, ASSOC PROF METEOROL, TEX A&M UNIV, 68- *Concurrent Pos:* Docent, Dept Meteorol, Darmstadt Tech, 62-63; prof, Free Univ Berlin, 74-75. *Mem:* Am Meteorol Soc; Meteorol Soc Serbia; Meterol Soc Ger; Royal Meteorol Soc. *Res:* Numerical weather forecasting. *Mailing Add:* Dept Meteorol Tex A&M Univ College Station TX 77843

DJURIC, STEVAN WAKEFIELD, b Leicester, Eng, Jan 5, 54; m 78. MEDICINAL CHEMISTRY. *Educ:* Univ Leeds, BSc, 76, PhD(org chem), 79. *Prof Exp:* Res fel org chem, Ohio State Univ, 80-81; RES INVESTR MED CHEM, G D SEARLE & CO, 81- *Mem:* Am Chem Soc. *Res:* New drugs to interact with the cardiovascular system, especially in the area of platelet dysfunction; chemistry and biology of prostanoids; new organic synthetic methodology. *Mailing Add:* 535 Michigan Ave Evanston IL 60202

DJURICKOVIC, DRAGINJA BRANKO, b Belgarde, Serbia, Yugoslavia, Jan 1, 40; US citizen; m 63; c 2. IMMUNOLOGY, PARASITOLOGY. *Educ:* Univ Belgrade, DVM, 63, MSc, 67. *Prof Exp:* Vet milk hyg, Vet Inst Serbia, Yugoslavia, 63-65; lectr res & develop irradiated vaccines, Inst for Appln Nuclear Energy in Agr Vet Sci & Forestry, Yugoslavia, 65-57; res asst immunol studies E Coli, Dept Immunol, Ont Vet Col, Can, 67-70, immune response gnotobiotic animals, Dept Biomed Studies, 70-71; vet clinician small animal pract, Leawood Animal Hosp, Kansas City, Mo, 72-75; SCIENTIST, IMMUNOL CANCER RES, NAT CANCER INST, FREDERICK CANCER RES FACIL, FREDERICK, MD, 76- *Concurrent Pos:* Dep State Vet, Mo. *Mem:* Am Vet Med Asn; Tissue Cult Asn. *Res:* Immunological studies on prevention of spontaneous and chemically induced cancer; development of potential vaccines; experimental surgeries; pathology; radiobiology. *Mailing Add:* Frederick Cancer Res Facil Nat Cancer Inst PO Box B Frederick MD 21701

DLAB, VLASTIMIL, b Bzi, Czech, Aug 5, 32; m 59; c 2. PURE MATHEMATICS. *Educ:* Charles Univ, Prague, RNDr, 56, CSc, 59, DSc, 66; Univ Khartoum, PhD(algebra), 62. *Prof Exp:* Sr lectr math, Charles Univ, Prague, 57-59, reader, 64-65; sr lectr, Univ Khartoum, 59-64; sr res fel, Inst Adv Studies, Australian Nat Univ, 65-68. chmn dept, 71-74, PROF MATH, CARLETON UNIV, 68- *Concurrent Pos:* Nat Res Coun Can grants, 69-; Can Coun fel, 74; vis prof, Univ Paris, Brandeis Univ & Univ Bonn, 74-75, Univ Tsukuba & Univ Sao Paulo, 76, Univ Stuttgart, 77 & Univ Portiers, 78. *Honors & Awards:* Dipl of Honours, Czech Math Union, 62. *Mem:* Am Math Soc; Math Asn Am; fel Royal Soc Can; Can Math Cong; London Math Soc. *Res:* Theory of groups; theory of rings and modules; general algebra; representation theory. *Mailing Add:* Dept Math Carleton Univ Ottawa Can

DLOTT, DANA D, b Los Angeles, Calif, Sept 11, 52. PICOSECOND LASERS. *Educ:* Columbia Univ, BA, 74; Stanford Univ, PhD(chem), 79. *Prof Exp:* ASST PROF CHEM, UNIV ILL, URBANA-CHAMPAIGN, 79- *Res:* Excited state dynamics of molecular crystals, particularly vibrational relaxation; photochemistry and energy transport, using picosecond lasers. *Mailing Add:* 505 S Mathews Ave Noyes Lab Box 37 Urbana IL 61820

DMOWSKI, W PAUL, b Lodz, Poland, May 17, 37; m 67; c 1. OBSTETRICS & GYNECOLOGY, REPRODUCTIVE ENDOCRINOLOGY. *Educ:* Warsaw Acad Med, Poland, MD, 62; Med Col Ga, PhD(endocrinol), 71. *Prof Exp:* Res fel endocrinol, Med Col Ga, 67-71; asst prof obstet/gynec, Univ Chicago, 71-74, assoc prof, 74-79; prof obstet/gynec, Univ Ark, 79-81; PROF OBSTET & GYNEC, DIR REPROD ENDOCRINOL & INFERTILITY & SR ATTEND, RUSH PRESBY ST LUKE'S MED CTR, 81- *Concurrent Pos:* Attend physician obstet/gynec, Michael Reese Hosp & Med Ctr, Chicago, 71-79, dir fertil unit reproductive endocrinol & infertil, 73-79. *Honors & Awards:* Prize Award, Am Col Obstet & Gynec, 75. *Mem:* Am Fertil Soc; Endocrine Soc; Soc Study Reproduction; Am Col Obstet & Gynec; Soc Gynec Invest. *Res:* Clinical research in the area of reproductive endocrinology and infertility; animal studies on implantation and implantation control; clinical and experimental research on the effect of synthetic steroids on reproductive process; studies on immunologic aspects of endometriosis. *Mailing Add:* Rush Presby St Luke's Med Ctr 600 S Paulina St Chicago IL 60612

DMYTRYSZYN, MYRON, b St Louis, Mo, Dec 26, 24; m 47; c 2. CHEMICAL ENGINEERING. *Educ:* Washington Univ, BS, 47, MS, 49, DSc, 57. *Prof Exp:* Res chem engr, Monsanto Co, 47-57, proj leader, Econ & Eng Eval Group, 57-58, group leader, 58-60, eng specialist, 60-64, proj mgr eng develop, 64-65, eng mgr, Cost & Eval Eng, Cent Eng Dept, 65-68, mgr eng, 68-69, dir eng sci, 69-70, dir design & construct, Corp Eng Dept, 70-75, proj dir, Major Joint Venture, 76-77, GEN MGR, TECHNOL DIV, MONSANTO CHEM INTERMEDIATES CO, 77- *Mem:* Fel Am Inst Chem Engrs; Am Chem Soc; Nat Soc Prof Engrs. *Res:* Process development. *Mailing Add:* Monsanto Chem Intermediates Co 800 N Lindbergh Blvd St Louis MO 63166

DOAK, GEORGE OSMORE, b Prince Albert, Sask, Dec 25, 07; nat US; m 33; c 2. PHARMACEUTICAL CHEMISTRY. *Educ:* Univ Sask, BA(chem), 29, BA(pharm), 30; Univ Wis, AM, 32, PhD(chem), 34. *Prof Exp:* Asst, Univ Wis, 32-33; asst chemist, NDak Regulatory Dept, Bismarck, 34-36; res chemist, George A Breon Co, 36-38; chemist, USPHS, 38-51, from asst dir to assoc dir VD exp lab, 51-61; prof chem, 61-73, EMER PROF CHEM, NC STATE UNIV, 73- *Concurrent Pos:* Instr med, Johns Hopkins Hosp, 38-46; res assoc, Johns Hopkins Univ, 46-48; assoc prof, Sch Pub Health, Univ NC, 48-61. *Mem:* Am Chem Soc. *Res:* Synthesis of organometallic compounds, particularly those of arsenic, antimony and bismuth; preparation of organophosphorus compounds; biochemistry of treponemata; stereochemistry of trigonal bipyramids. *Mailing Add:* Dept of Chem NC State Univ Raleigh NC 27607

DOAK, KENNETH WORLEY, b Gallatin, Mo, Jan 27, 16; m 45; c 3. POLYMER CHEMISTRY. *Educ:* Cent Col, Mo, AB, 38; Johns Hopkins Univ, PhD(phys org chem), 42. *Prof Exp:* Res chemist, US Rubber Co, 42-55; res assoc, Res Ctr, Koppers Co Inc, 55-57, mgr plastics res, 58-60; asst dir polymer res, Rexall Chem Co, NJ, 60-65, dir cent res, 65-70; mgr plastics res, Res Ctr, Koppers Co, Inc, Arco Polymers, Inc, mgr polymer res, 74-76, tech adv, 77-80; CONSULT POLYMERS, 81- *Mem:* Am Chem Soc; Acad Appl Sci; fel Am Inst Chemists. *Res:* Theory of polymerization; ionic and free-radical processes; polymer structure and properties; polyethylene; polypropylene; polystyrene; foam; block and graft copolymers. *Mailing Add:* 3469 Burnett Dr Murrysville PA 15668

DOAN, ARTHUR SUMNER, JR, b Ft Wayne, Ind, July 29, 33; m 60; c 3. PHYSICAL CHEMISTRY & METALLURGY. *Educ:* Wabash Col, AB, 55; Iowa State Univ, MS, 58; Colo Sch Mines, DSc, 63. *Prof Exp:* Chemist, Ames Lab, Atomic Energy Comn, 55-59; physicist, US Army Biol Res Lab, Md, 59-61; physicist refractory mat, Lewis Res Ctr, 62-68, PHYS CHEMIST, GODDARD SPACE FLIGHT CTR, NASA, 68- *Mem:* AAAS; Am Chem

Soc; Meteoritical Soc; Am Soc Mass Spectrometry. *Res:* Lunar and meteorite mineral and metals analysis; electron microprobe and computerized data reduction; planetary atmospheric analysis; mass spectrometry, gas chromatography, trace component enrichment. *Mailing Add:* Goddard Space Flight Ctr NASA Code 962 Greenbelt Rd Greenbelt MD 20771

DOAN, DAVID BENTLEY, b State College, Pa, Jan 9, 26; m 54; c 4. EARTH SCIENCE. *Educ:* Pa State Univ, BS, 48, MS, 49. *Prof Exp:* Asst mineral, Pa State Univ, 48-49, instr geol, 49; geologist, US Geol Surv, 49-62; opers analyst, Res Anal Corp, 62-68; treas, Earth Sci Group, Inc, Washington, DC, 68-73; DIR, BOBCAT PROPERTIES, INC, 73- *Concurrent Pos:* Consult geologist, 62-; consult to many US & foreign indust & govt orgn & var pvt explor progs; vis prof geol, Univ Md, College Park, 76- *Mem:* AAAS; Geol Soc Am; Am Inst Prof Geologists; Am Asn Petrol Geologists; Sigma Xi. *Res:* Physical geology; petroleum; terrain analysis; engineering geology; mineral exploration; geology of Pacific Basin and Southeast Asia; equilibria in fluvial processes; hydraulic fracturing of rock. *Mailing Add:* 5635 Bent Branch Rd Bethesda MD 20016

DOANE, BENJAMIN KNOWLES, b Philadelphia, Pa, May 9, 28; Can citizen; m 61; c 2. PSYCHIATRY. *Educ:* Princeton Univ, AB, 50; Dalhousie Univ, MA, 52, MD, 62; McGill Univ, PhD(psychol), 55; FRCP(C), 67; FACP, 76. *Prof Exp:* Res officer psychol, Defense Res Bd Can, 51-53; res assoc, Montreal Neurol Inst, McGill Univ, 55-57; McLaughlin fel, Maudsley Hosp, London, Eng, 64-65; Med Res Coun fel, Univ Montreal, 65-66; lectr physiol, 66-75, asst dean med, 73-75, from asst prof to assoc prof, 66-75, head dept, 75-81, PROF PSYCHIAT, DALHOUSIE UNIV, 75- *Mem:* Can Psychiat Asn; Can Med Asn; fel Am Col Psychiatrists. *Res:* Neurosciences. *Mailing Add:* Dept of Psychiat Dalhousie Univ Fac of Med Halifax Can

DOANE, CHARLES CHESLEY, b Bradford, Ont, July 19, 25; US citizen; m 53. ENTOMOLOGY. *Educ:* Ont Agr Col, BS, 49; Univ Wis, MS, 51, PhD, 53. *Prof Exp:* Mem staff prod develop dept, Shell Chem Corp, 53-56; asst entomologist, Conn Agr Exp Sta, 56-60, assoc entomologist, 60-70, entomologist, 70-77; RETIRED. *Concurrent Pos:* Mem, Int Orgn Biol Control Noxious Animals & Plants; agr consult & field res mgr, Controlled Release Div, Albany Int Co. *Mem:* Soc Invert Path; Entom Soc Am; Entom Soc Can. *Res:* Sex pheromones of insects for their control; insect behavior; biological control and insect pathology. *Mailing Add:* 5934 E Calle Del Sud Phoenix AZ 85018

DOANE, ELLIOTT P, b Ill, July 11, 29; m; c 4. CHEMICAL ENGINEERING. *Educ:* Harvard Univ, AB, 51; Univ Ill, MS, 53, PhD(chem eng), 55. *Prof Exp:* Chem engr, Hooker Chem Co, NY, 54-57, supvr pilot plant, 57-60; res engr, Tex Butadiene & Chem Co, 61, dir res lab, 62; res engr, Phillips Petrol Co, 63-66, mgr hydrocarbon processes br, 66-69; mgr process develop dept, Western Res Ctr, 69-76, DIR TECHNOL PLANNING DEPT, STAUFFER CHEM CO, 77- *Mem:* Am Chem Soc; Am Inst Chem Engrs; Sigma Xi. *Res:* High pressure studies; kinetics; absorption; catalysis. *Mailing Add:* Stauffer Chem Co Westport CT 06880

DOANE, FRANCES WHITMAN, b Halifax, NS, Aug 30, 28. VIROLOGY, ELECTRON MICROSCOPY. *Educ:* Dalhousie Univ, BSc, 50; Univ Toronto, MA, 62. *Prof Exp:* Res asst ophthal, Univ & Hosp for Sick Children, 53-57, res asst virol, Univ, 57-62, lectr & asst prof, 62-69, head unit, 62-80, ASSOC PROF VIROL, DEPT MICROBIOL & PARASITOL, UNIV TORONTO, 69- *Concurrent Pos:* Consult electron micros, Hosp for Sick Children, 71- *Mem:* Micros Soc Can; Can Soc Microbiol; Am Soc Microbiol; Electron Micros Soc Am; NY Acad Sci. *Res:* Electron microscopy applied to diagnostic virology; immunoelectron microscopy; ultrastructural aspects of viral-induced cytopathology and transformation. *Mailing Add:* Dept of Microbiol & Parasitol Fac of Med Univ of Toronto Toronto ON M5S 1A1 Can

DOANE, JOHN FREDERICK, b Newmarket, Ont, Apr 14, 30; m 63; c 2. ENTOMOLOGY, ANIMAL BEHAVIOR. *Educ:* Ont Agr Col, BSA, 54; Univ Wis, MS, 56, PhD(entom), 58. *Prof Exp:* Res officer entom, 58-65, RES SCIENTIST ENTOM, RES BR, AGR CAN, 65- *Mem:* Entom Soc Can; Entom Soc Am. *Res:* Investigation of the biology, ecology, population dynamics and the orientation and feeding behavior of wireworms pests of grain crops in the Prairie Provinces of Canada. *Mailing Add:* Res Sta 107 Science Cres Saskatoon Can

DOANE, MARSHALL GORDON, b Syracuse, NY, June 11, 37. BIOPHYSICS, BIOMEDICAL ENGINEERING. *Educ:* Univ Rochester, BS, 59, MS, 61; Univ Md, PhD(biophys), 67. *Prof Exp:* Res asst phys optics, Univ Rochester, 59-61; optical physicist, Aerojet-Gen Corp, 61; physicist, Bausch & Lomb, Inc, 61-62; res fel corneal res, 67-69, res assoc, 69-71, ASSOC STAFF SCIENTIST, EYE RES INST, RETINA FOUND, 71- *Concurrent Pos:* Instr, Dept Ophthal, 75-79, ASSOC PROF OPHTHAL, HARVARD MED SCH, 79- *Mem:* Asn Res Vision & Ophthal. *Res:* Pyridine nucleotide fluorescence in nerve cells; corneal physiology and metabolism; active transport and dehydration mechanisms in the cornea; corneal prostheses; bioinstrumentation; optics; corneal wetting and lid/tear-film interactions; lid dynamics during blinking. *Mailing Add:* Eye Res Inst 20 Staniford St Boston MA 02114

DOANE, TED H, b Fairview, Okla, May 12, 30; m 54; c 1. ANIMAL BREEDING. *Educ:* Okla State Univ, BS, 52; Kans State Univ, MS, 53, PhD(animal breeding), 60. *Prof Exp:* Exten county agt, 55-56, exten livestock specialist, 56-58 & 60-64, assoc prof animal sci, Agr Exten, 62-74, assoc prof, 75-78, PROF ANIMAL SCI, UNIV NEBR-LINCOLN, 78- *Concurrent Pos:* Prof agr, Exten Admin, Univ Nebr-Ataturk Univ Contract, Turkey, 64-66; prof animal sci & adv, Kabul Univ-Univ Nebr Contract, 75-77. *Mem:* Am Soc Animal Sci. *Res:* Animal production and management; sheep breeding. *Mailing Add:* Dept of Animal Sci Univ of Nebr Lincoln NE 68588

DOANE, WILLIAM, b Bayard, Nebr, Apr 26, 35; m 58; c 2. LIQUID CRYSTALS, NUCLEAR MAGNETIC RESONANCE. *Educ:* Univ Mo, BS, 58, MS, 62, PhD(physics), 65. *Prof Exp:* From asst prof to assoc prof, 65-74, PROF PHYSICS, KENT STATE UNIV, 74-, ASSOC DIR, LIQUID CRYSTAL INST, 79- *Concurrent Pos:* Res prof, Molecular Path & Biol, Col Med, Northeastern Ohio Univ; assoc mem, Stefan Inst, Ljubljana, Yugoslavia, 74- *Mem:* Am Phys Soc; Am Asn Physics Teachers; Biophys Soc; Sigma Xi. *Res:* Nuclear magnetic resonance studies in liquid crystals and biological membranes. *Mailing Add:* Dept of Physics Kent State Univ Kent OH 44242

DOANE, WILLIAM M, b Covington, Ind, Sept 26, 30; m 52; c 4. ORGANIC CHEMISTRY. *Educ:* Purdue Univ, BS, 52, MS, 60, PhD(biochem), 62. *Prof Exp:* Teacher, Sec Sch, Ind, 54-55; res chemist, Northern Mkt & Nutrit Res Lab, 62-70, leader nonstarch prod invests, 70-75, res leader derivatives & polymer exploration, 75-79, LAB CHIEF, BIOMAT CONVERSION, NORTHERN REGIONAL RES LAB, USDA, 80- *Concurrent Pos:* Instr chem, Bradley Univ, 64- *Honors & Awards:* IR-100 Award, 78. *Mem:* Am Chem Soc; AAAS; Weed Sci Soc; Controlled Release Biologically Active Chemists. *Res:* Reaction mechanisms in carbohydrate chemistry; sulfur derivatives of carbohydrates; synthesis and characterization of starch derivatives; starch graft copolymers; encapsulation of biologically active chemicals. *Mailing Add:* USDA Northern Regional Res Lab 1815 N University Peoria IL 61604

DOANE, WINIFRED WALSH, b New York, NY, Jan 7, 29; m 53; c 1. DEVELOPMENTAL GENETICS. *Educ:* Hunter Col, BA, 50; Univ Wis, MS, 52; Yale Univ, PhD(zool), 60. *Prof Exp:* Asst zool, Univ Wis, 50-51; asst prof biol, Millsaps Col, 54-55; lab asst genetics, Yale Univ, 56-58, NIH res trainee, 60-62, res assoc develop genetics, 62-75, lectr, 65-75, assoc prof biol, 75-77; PROF ZOOL, ARIZ STATE UNIV, 77- *Concurrent Pos:* Mem genetics study sect, NIH, 74-77; assoc ed, Develop Genetics, 79-; mem, Genetic Basis Dis Rev Comt, Nat Inst Gen Med Sci, NIH, 80- *Mem:* Am Soc Cell Biol; Am Soc Naturalists; Genetics Soc Am; Am Soc Zoologists; Int Soc Develop Biologists. *Res:* Developmental, physiological and biochemical genetics of eukaryotes, especially Drosophila and other insects; regulatory mechanisms in cellular differentiation and development with emphasis on genetic and endocrine controls; amylases in Drosophila. *Mailing Add:* Dept of Zool Ariz State Univ Tempe AZ 85281

DOBAY, DONALD GENE, b Cleveland, Ohio, Sept 12, 24; m 45, 66; c 5. POLYMER CHEMISTRY, CHEMICAL ENGINEERING. *Educ:* Oberlin Col, AB, 44; Univ Mich, MS, 45, PhD(colloid chem), 48. *Prof Exp:* Res chemist, Union Carbide Corp, 48-51; sr res chemist, B F Goodrich Res Ctr, Ohio, 51-60, tech coordr, B F Goodrich Sponge Prod, Conn, 60-62, mgr polymer develop, 62-74; tech mgr & res dir, Grand Sheet Metal Sponge Rubber Prod, 74-75; consult, 75-78, PROCESS MGR & DIR LAB, CRAWFORD & RUSSELL, INC, STAMFORD, 78- *Mem:* Am Chem Soc; NY Acad Sci; Am Inst Chemists; Soc Plastics Engrs. *Res:* Environmental engineering; polymerization; process engineering; chemical processing; rubber and plastics production; polymer characterization; latex properties and processing; flammability; analytical test methods; pollution control; thermal and acoustic insulation; cellular properties. *Mailing Add:* Crawford & Russell Inc 17 Amelia Pl Stamford CT 06904

DOBBELSTEIN, THOMAS NORMAN, b Wyandotte, Mich, Oct 14, 40; m 60; c 3. ANALYTICAL CHEMISTRY. *Educ:* Eastern Michigan, BS, 64; Iowa State Univ, MS, 66, PhD(anal chem), 67. *Prof Exp:* Asst prof, 67-72, assoc prof, 72-81, PROF CHEM, YOUNGSTOWN STATE UNIV, 81-, CHMN DEPT, 74- *Mem:* Am Chem Soc; Sigma Xi. *Res:* Ion-responsive membranes. *Mailing Add:* Dept of Chem Youngstown State Univ Youngstown OH 44555

DOBBEN, GLEN D, b Fremont, Mich, Sept 25, 28; m 54; c 5. RADIOLOGY. *Educ:* Calvin Col, BS, 50; Marquette Univ, MD, 53. *Prof Exp:* Intern med, Blodgett Mem Hosp, Grand Rapids, Mich, 53-54; res radiol, Henry Ford Hosp, Detroit, Mich, 54-55, 57-59; instr, Univ Chicago, 59-61; res fel neuroradiol, Univ Lund, 61-62; from asst prof to assoc prof radiol, Univ Chicago, 62-72; PROF NEURORADIOL, COL MED, UNIV ILL, CHICAGO, 73-, PROF NEUROSURG, 76- *Concurrent Pos:* Dir, Div Radiol, Cook County Hosp, 69-72. *Mem:* Asn Univ Radiologists. *Res:* Diagnostic radiological sciences as applied to neuroradiology. *Mailing Add:* PO Box Two South Holland IL 60473

DOBBINS, B(ILLY) D(OUGLAS), b Lufkin, Tex, Mar 5, 22; m 43. SYSTEMS ENGINEERING. *Educ:* John Tarleton Agr Col, AS, 41; Southern Methodist Univ, BS, 48. *Prof Exp:* Prin prof staff & group supvr guid syst develop, 48-66, asst supvr, Missile Systs Div, 66-73, ASST SUPVR TECH COORD, FLEET SYSTS DEPT, APPL PHYSICS LAB, JOHNS HOPKINS UNIV, 73- *Concurrent Pos:* Chmn advan tech objectives working group fleet defense, Dir Navy Labs; chmn, Navy Net Tech Assessment Ocean Surveillance, Dept Navy, 74-75. *Res:* Electronic systems; guidance and control of missiles; weapon system countermeasures. *Mailing Add:* Johns Hopkins Univ Appl Physics Lab Johns Hopkins Rd Laurel MD 20810

DOBBINS, CHARLES NELSON, JR, b Yadkinville, NC, Jan 23, 29; m 51; c 2. VETERINARY MEDICINE. *Educ:* NC State Col, BS, 51; Univ Ga, DVM, 58. *Prof Exp:* Vet, J D Jewell, Inc, 58-60; HEAD EXTEN VET DEPT, COOP EXTEN SERV, UNIV GA, 60- *Concurrent Pos:* Assoc dean serv, Col Vet Med, Univ Ga, 75- *Honors & Awards:* Exten Vet of Yr. Am Asn Exten Vets, 73. *Mem:* Am Vet Med Asn; Am Asn Exten Vets (pres, 67). *Res:* Co-developed a process to convert food waste into a safe, nutritious, palatable animal feed ingredient. *Mailing Add:* 320 Pinewood Circle Athens GA 30606

DOBBINS, DAVID ROSS, b Indianapolis, Ind, Aug 9, 41; m 64; c 1. BOTANY. *Educ:* Franklin Col Ind, BA, 63; Univ Mass, MA, 67, PhD(bot), 71. *Prof Exp:* Nat Res Coun Can fel, Univ Lethbridge, 70-72; asst prof bot, Dept Biol Sci, Wellesley Col, 72-77; asst prof, 77-80, ASSOC PROF BOT, DEPT BIOL, MILLERSVILLE STATE COL, 80- *Mem:* Bot Soc Am; Am

Soc Plant Physiologists; Int Soc Plant Morphologists; Soc Develop Biol; Am Hort Soc. *Res:* Developmental anatomy and morphogenesis; investigations on regulation of vascular cambium, factors affecting the plane of cell division and the structural mode of parasitism in flowering plant parasites. *Mailing Add:* Dept of Biol Millersville State Col Millersville PA 17551

DOBBINS, JAMES TALMAGE, JR, b Chapel Hill, NC, June 13, 26; m 51; c 2. ANALYTICAL CHEMISTRY. *Educ:* Univ NC, BS, 47, PhD(anal chem), 58. *Prof Exp:* Chief indust hyg sect, Dept Chem, 406th Med Gen Lab, US Army, 54-56, head dept chem, 56; res chemist, R J Reynolds Industs, 58-66, head anal instrumentation sect, 67-72, mgr anal div, 72-75, MASTER SCIENTIST, APPL RES & DEVELOP DEPT, R J REYNOLDS TOBACCO CO, 75- *Mem:* AAAS; Soc Appl Spectroscopy; NY Acad Sci; Am Chem Soc. *Res:* Atomic absorption and emission spectroscopy by inductively coupled argon plasma (ICP); analytical chemistry of tobacco and tobacco products. *Mailing Add:* Appl Res & Develop Dept R J Reynolds Tobacco Co Winston-Salem NC 27102

DOBBINS, RICHARD ANDREW, b Burlington, Mass, July 15, 25; m 53; c 2. FLUID DYNAMICS, AEROSOL SCIENCE. *Educ:* Harvard Univ, SB, 48; Northeastern Univ, MS, 58; Princeton Univ, PhD, 61. *Prof Exp:* Res engr, Arthur D Little, Inc, 50-53; sr engr, Sylvania Elec Prod Inc, 53-57; from asst prof to assoc prof eng, 60-68, PROF ENG, BROWN UNIV, 68- *Concurrent Pos:* Vis res assoc, Calif Inst Technol, 67-68 & Univ Essex, Eng, 71; assoc ed, Combustion Sci & Technol, 69-73; vis prof, Abadan Inst Technol, Iran, 75; consult, various govt & indust orgns; sr scientist, Nat Bur Standards, 81-82. *Mem:* AAAS; Am Soc Mech Engrs; Combustion Inst; Am Phys Soc; Am Meteorol Soc. *Res:* Nucleation and condensation dynamics; aerosol science and technology; high temperature effects in fluid dynamics; heat transfer; atmospheric fluid mechanics; air pollution. *Mailing Add:* 11 President Ave Providence RI 02906

DOBBINS, ROBERT JOSEPH, b Buffalo, NY, Aug 16, 40; m 64; c 4. CELLULOSE CHEMISTRY. *Educ:* Fordham Univ, BS, 62; State Univ NY Buffalo, PhD(phys chem), 66. *Prof Exp:* Res chemist, Indust Chem Div, Am Cyanamid Co, 66-72; SR RES CHEMIST & GROUP LEADER PAPERMAKING DEVELOP, ST REGIS PAPER CO, 72- *Mem:* Am Chem Soc; Tech Asn Pulp & Paper Indust. *Res:* Cellulose-water-electrolyte interactions; adsorption from aqueous solutions; chemistry of pulping and bleaching processes; mechanisms of inorganic reactions; coordination chemistry. *Mailing Add:* St Regis Tech Ctr West Nyack NY 10994

DOBBINS, THOMAS EDWARD, b Frankfort, NY, Oct 10, 13; m 45; c 3. FOREST PRODUCTS. *Educ:* Syracuse Univ, BS, 39. *Prof Exp:* Chemist paper mfg, Hamersley Mfg Co, 39-41; chemist, Container Tech Serv Dept, Am Can Co, 41-50, supvr, Tech Serv Dept, 50-64, sr res assoc paper prod res, 64-79; CONSULT. *Mem:* Am Chem Soc; Tech Asn Pulp & Paper Indust. *Res:* Technology of pulp and paper, plastics, adhesives, and petroleum waxes; packaging engineering; materials testing, specifications, and quality control; new products development. *Mailing Add:* 310 Cresent Dr Neenah WI 54956

DOBBS, CARROLL R, b Mt Pleasant, Ark, Jan 31, 39. ANALYTICAL CHEMISTRY, RADIATION CHEMISTRY. *Educ:* Ark Polytech Col, BS, 60; Ohio State Univ, MS, 67; Va Polytech Inst, PhD(chem), 73. *Prof Exp:* Chemist, US Food & Drug Admin, New Orleans, La, 60-62; med lab officer path, US Air Force Med Ctr, Lackland AFB, Tex, 62-65; Air Force Inst Technol fel, Ohio State Univ, 65-67; sr biomed scientist US space prog, Brooks Aerospace Med Div, San Antonio, Tex, 67-74; chief clin chem, US Air Force Hosp, Wiesbaden, Ger, 74-78; RES CHEMIST RADIATION CHEM, ARMED FORCES RADIOBIOL RES INST, 78- *Concurrent Pos:* Instr chromatography, Fisk Inst, 72. *Mem:* Brit Biochem Soc; Am Chem Soc; fel Am Inst Chemists; Sigma Xi; Am Soc Med Technol. *Res:* Effects of ionizing radiation on biological systems; analysis of trace level biometabolites by chromatographic and mass spectrometric systems; radiation chemistry and product analysis. *Mailing Add:* Defense Nuclear Agency AFRRI Nat Naval Med Ctr Bethesda MD 20014

DOBBS, DAVID EARL, b Winnipeg, Man, Feb 4, 45; m 65; c 2. ALGEBRA. *Educ:* Univ Man, BA, 64, MA, 65; Cornell Univ, PhD(math), 69. *Prof Exp:* Vis prof math, Univ Calif, Los Angeles, 69-70; asst prof, Rutgers Univ, 70-75; assoc prof, 75-80, PROF MATH, UNIV TENN, 80- *Concurrent Pos:* Res assoc, Off Naval Res, Univ Calif, Los Angeles, 69-70. *Mem:* Am Math Soc; Math Asn Am. *Res:* Commutative algebra; homological algebra. *Mailing Add:* Dept Math Univ Tenn Knoxville TN 37916

DOBBS, FRANK W, b Chicago, Ill, Sept 8, 32; m 58; c 3. PHYSICAL CHEMISTRY. *Educ:* Univ Chicago, BA, 53, MS, 55; Mass Inst Technol, PhD(phys chem), 61. *Prof Exp:* From asst prof to assoc prof, 59-67, chmn dept, 71-77, PROF CHEM, NORTHEASTERN ILL UNIV, 67-, DEAN COL ARTS & SCI, 78- *Mem:* AAAS; Am Chem Soc. *Res:* Molecular orbitals. *Mailing Add:* 2728 Noyes Evanston IL 60201

DOBBS, GARY HOBSON, III, b Birmingham, Ala, Mar 25, 48. HISTOLOGY, PHYSIOLOGY. *Educ:* Washington & Lee Univ, BS, 70; Univ Calif, San Diego, PhD(marine biol), 74. *Prof Exp:* asst prof, 75-80, ASSOC PROF BIOL, WASHINGTON & LEE UNIV, 80- *Concurrent Pos:* Res assoc, Med Sch, Duke Univ, 75 & Med Sch, Univ Chicago, 76. *Mem:* Fisheries Soc Brit Isles. *Res:* Energy dispersive x-ray analysis of ion transport in biological systems; renal function in marine vertebrates; the kidneys' role in freezing resistance in Antarctic bony fishes; scanning electron microscopy of fish tissues. *Mailing Add:* Dept of Biol Washington & Lee Univ Lexington VA 24450

DOBBS, GREGORY MELVILLE, b Teaneck, NJ, Aug 19, 47; m 76; c 2. PHYSICAL CHEMISTRY, COMPUTER SCIENCE. *Educ:* Dartmouth Col, AB, 69; Princeton Univ, MA, 71, PhD(chem), 75. *Prof Exp:* Systs programmer, Kiewit Computation Ctr, Hanover, NH, 66-69; resident res fel physics, Cent Res Dept, E I du Pont de Nemours & Co, Inc, 69; asst in instr chem, Princeton Univ, 70-73; res assoc chem, Mass Inst Technol, 74-76; RES SCIENTIST, UNITED TECHNOLOGIES RES CTR, 76- *Concurrent Pos:* Adj instr comput sci, Hartford Grad Ctr, 79- *Mem:* Am Chem Soc; Am Phys Soc. *Res:* Chemical physics; molecular spectroscopy and energy transfer; application of lasers to chemistry and combustion science. *Mailing Add:* United Technologies Res Ctr Silver Lane East Hartford CT 06108

DOBBS, HARRY DONALD, b Atlanta, Ga, Nov 23, 32; m 53; c 3. BIOLOGY. *Educ:* Emory Univ, AB, 53, MS, 54, PhD(biol), 67. *Prof Exp:* Res asst parasitol, Emory Univ, 54-55; from asst prof to assoc prof biol, 55-70, PROF BIOL, WOFFORD COL, 70- *Mem:* Am Soc Zoologists; Am Inst Biol Sci. *Res:* Parasitology, especially trichiniasis in mice; anatomical and physiological adaptations of invertebrates. *Mailing Add:* Dept of Biol Wofford Col N Church St Spartanburg SC 29301

DOBBS, ROBERT CURRY, b Seattle, Wash, Nov 9, 35; Can citizen; m 55, 75; c 4. SILVICULTURE. *Educ:* Univ Wash, BSc, 59, PhD(tree biol), 66; Yale Univ, MFor, 60. *Prof Exp:* Forester, US Forest Serv, Seattle, 59, res forester, Klamath, Calif, 60-61; res scientist silvicult, Can Forestry Serv, Winnipeg, 66-70, Victoria, 70-77, RES MGR SILVICULT, CAN FORESTRY SERV, OTTAWA, 77- *Concurrent Pos:* Weyerhaeuser fel Univ Wash, 61-62. *Mem:* Can Inst Forestry; Sigma Xi. *Res:* Silviculture, particularly reforestation problems; research and development relating to production of forest biomass for conversion to energy. *Mailing Add:* 23 - 3205 Uplands Dr Ottawa ON Can

DOBBS, THOMAS LAWRENCE, b Los Angeles, Calif, Apr 9, 43; m 64; c 3. AGRICULTURAL ECONOMICS. *Educ:* SDak State Univ, BS, 65; Univ Md, PhD(agr econ), 69. *Prof Exp:* Asst prof agr econ, Univ Wyo, 69-74; agr economics, US AID, 74-78; ASSOC PROF AGR ECON, SDAK STATE UNIV, 78- *Mem:* Am Agr Econ Asn. *Res:* Community and rural development; natural resource economics. *Mailing Add:* Dept of Econ SDak State Univ Brookings SD 57007

DOBELBOWER, RALPH RIDDALL, JR, b Bellefonte, Pa, Mar 23, 40; m 63; c 3. RADIATION THERAPY. *Educ:* Pa State Univ, BS, 62, AB, 63; Jefferson Med Col, MD, 67, PhD(radiation biol), 75; Am Bd Radiol, dipl, 75. *Prof Exp:* Instr radiation ther & nuclear med, Thomas Jefferson Univ Hosp, 74-75, asst prof & coordr, Outreach Prog Radiation Ther, 75-79, assoc prof, 79-80, dir, Gastrointestinal Radiother Serv, 75-80; ASSOC PROF RADIOL & DIR RADIATION ONCOL, MED COL OHIO, TOLEDO, 80-; PROG ADV RADIATION THER TECHNOL, MICHAEL J OWENS TECH COL, 80- *Concurrent Pos:* Jr fac clin fel, Am Cancer Soc, 74-77; asst dir, Am Col Radiol, 74-79; asst attend physician, Radiation Ther, Bryn Mawr Hosp, 75-79; mem adv bd, Sch Radiation Ther Technol, Gwynedd-Mercy Col, 77-79. *Mem:* Am Soc Therapeut Radiologists; Am Radium Soc; Radiol Soc NAm; Sigma Xi; Am Asn Physicists Med. *Res:* Radiation treatment of gastronintestinal malignancies; cancer of the pancreas; intraoperative radiation treatment. *Mailing Add:* Div Radiation Oncol Med Col Ohio Toledo OH 43699

DOBELLE, WILLIAM HARVEY, b Pittsfield, Mass, Oct 24, 41; m 72. BIOMEDICAL ENGINEERING. *Educ:* Johns Hopkins Univ, BA, 64, MA, 67; Univ Utah, PhD(physiol), 74. *Prof Exp:* Res assoc, Dept Biophys, Johns Hopkins Univ, 61-68; dir, Neuroprostheses Prog, Inst Biomed Eng, Univ Utah, 69-76, assoc dir, 73-76; dir, Div Artificial Organs, Dept Surg, Col Physicians & Surgeons, Columbia Univ, 76-81; CHMN, INST FOR ARTIFICIAL ORGANS, NEW YORK CITY, 82- *Concurrent Pos:* Exec dir, Med Eye Bank, Md, 64-67 & Intermountain Organ Bank, Salt Lake City, 69-70; mem bd dirs, NY Regional Transplant Prog, Inc, 78-80. *Honors & Awards:* Kusserow Award, Am Soc Artificial Internal Organs, 76 & 78. *Mem:* Int Soc Artificial Organs; Am Soc Artificial Internal Organs. *Res:* Sensory prostheses for the blind and deaf; 'hybrid' and mechanical artificial pancreas; cardiac assist devices and artificial heart; organ banking and transplantation. *Mailing Add:* One Lincoln Plaza #37R New York NY 10023

DOBERENZ, ALEXANDER R, b Newark, NJ, Aug 17, 36; m 58; c 2. NUTRITION. *Educ:* Tusculum Col, BS, 58; Univ Ariz, MS, 60, PhD(biochem), 63. *Prof Exp:* Res assoc biophys, Univ Ariz, 63-69; vis assoc prof nutrit, Univ Hawaii, 69; assoc prof nutrit, Univ Wis-Green Bay, 69-71, asst dean col human biol, 69-71, assoc dean cols, 71-74, prof nutrit sci, 71-76, prof growth & develop, 75-76; PROF FOOD SCI & HUMAN NUTRIT & DEAN COL HUMAN RESOURCES, UNIV DEL, 76-, COORDR HOME ECON RES, DEL EXP STA, COL AGR SCI, 78- *Concurrent Pos:* Nat Inst Dent Res fel, 63-66, res career develop award, 66-69; consult, Northeastern Wis Health Planning Coun, 74-, Bellin Hosp Obesity Clin, 75- & Gen Foods Corp, 78-; mem home econ res subcomt, Exp Sta Comt on Orgn & Policy, 78-; mem, Nat Coun Adminrs Home Econ. *Mem:* Soc Exp Biol Med; Am Home Econ Asn; Am Chem Soc; Sigma Xi; Am Inst Nutrit. *Res:* Calcified tissue; mineral metabolism. *Mailing Add:* Col Human Resources Univ Del Newark DE 19711

DOBERNECK, RAYMOND C, b Milwaukee, Wis, June 17, 32; m 57; c 6. SURGERY. *Educ:* Marquette Univ, BS, 53, MD, 56; Univ Minn, Minneapolis, PhD(surg), 65. *Prof Exp:* From asst prof to assoc prof surg, Sch Med, Creighton Univ, 65-70, PROF SURG & VCHMN DEPT, SCH MED, UNIV NMEX, 70- *Concurrent Pos:* John & Mary R Markle Found scholar acad med, 66. *Mem:* Am Col Surg; Soc Univ Surg; Asn Acad Surg; Am Gastroenterol Asn; Soc Head & Neck Surg. *Res:* Head and neck tumors; hepatic hemosiderosis in surgical states; deglutition after oral and pharyngeal resection for cancer. *Mailing Add:* Dept of Surg Univ of NMex Sch of Med Albuquerque NM 87106

DOBERSEN, MICHAEL J, b Bay Village, Ohio, May 13, 49. IMMUNOPATHOLOGY, AUTOIMMUNITY. *Educ:* Kent State Univ, BS, 71; Univ Miami, PhD(microbiol), 76. *Prof Exp:* Intern, St Thomas Hosp, 70-71; teaching asst biol, Dept Biol, Kent State Univ, 71-72; grad student & res asst microbiol, Dept Microbiol, Sch Med, Univ Miami, 72-76, investr, 76-

77, staff fel, 77-81; SR STAFF FEL & ASSOC INVESTR, LAB ORAL MED, NAT INST DENT RES, NIH, 81- *Mem:* AAAS; Am Soc Microbiol. *Res:* Role of autoantibodies in the pathogenesis of insulin; dependent diabetes mellitus including the isolation and biochemical characterization of the corresponnding pancreatic antigens. *Mailing Add:* Lab Oral Med Nat Inst Dent Res NIH Bldg 30 Rm 227 Bethesda MD 20205

DOBIE, JAMES, forest economics, forest products, see previous edition

DOBINSON, FRANK, b Bolton, Eng, Oct 4, 31; nat US; m 77; c 3. ORGANIC CHEMISTRY, POLYMER CHEMISTRY. *Educ:* Univ Birmingham, BS, 53, PhD(chem), 56. *Prof Exp:* Res fel ozone org chem, Dept Mining, Univ Birmingham, 56-59; fel chem, Univ Tex, 59-61; res chemist, 61-69, group leader, Monsanto Textiles Co, 69-76, SUPVR, MONSANTO CHEM INTERMEDIATES CO, 76- *Res:* Reactions of ozone with organic compounds; new organic polymers with special properties. *Mailing Add:* 201 Shoreline Dr Gulf Breeze FL 32561

DOBKIN, ALLEN BENJAMIN, anesthesiology, see previous edition

DOBKIN, DAVID PAUL, b Pittsburgh, Pa, Feb 29, 48. ALGORITHMS ANALYSIS, COMPUTER GRAPHICS. *Educ:* Mass Inst Technol, BS, 70; Harvard, MS, 71, PhD(appl math), 73. *Prof Exp:* Asst prof comput sci, Yale Univ, 73-78; assoc prof, Univ Ariz, 78-81; PROF ELEC ENG & COMPUT SCI, PRINCETON UNIV, 81- *Concurrent Pos:* Consult, Bell Lab, 78; vis scientist, Xerox, Palo Alto Res Ctr, 81. *Mem:* Soc Indust & Appl Math; Asn Comput Mach. *Res:* Application of techniques from the analysis of algorithms area to problems of practical importance; computer geometry and graphics; distributed computing and computer security. *Mailing Add:* Elec Eng & Comput Sci Dept Eng Quadrangle Princeton Univ Princeton NJ 08544

DOBKIN, SHELDON, b New York, NY, Nov 12, 33; m 59; c 3. BIOLOGICAL OCEANOGRAPHY, INVERTEBRATE ZOOLOGY. *Educ:* City Col New York, BS, 57; Univ Miami, MS, 60, PhD(marine biol), 65. *Prof Exp:* Res aide, Rosenstiel Sch Marine & Atmospheric Scis, Univ Miami, 58-61, res instr, 61-63, instr marine biol, 63-64; from asst prof to assoc prof, 64-74, PROF ZOOL, FLA ATLANTIC UNIV, 74- *Mem:* Am Soc Zoologists; World Maricult Soc; AAAS. *Res:* Larval development of decapod crustaceans, particularly the caridean and penaeidean shrimps; taxonomy of caridean shrimps; larval development of marine invertebrates; shrimp and prawn culture. *Mailing Add:* Dept of Biol Sci Fla Atlantic Univ Boca Raton FL 33432

DOBO, EMMERICK JOSEPH, b Szeged, Hungary, Oct 23, 19; US citizen; m 50; c 3. CHEMICAL ENGINEERING. *Educ:* Univ Mich, BS, 42; Univ Wash, MS, 48; Univ Tex, PhD(chem eng), 54. *Prof Exp:* Develop chem engr, Crown Zellerbach Corp, Wash, 48-51; sr develop chem engr, Chemstrand Corp, Ala, 54-57, group leader chem eng, 57-62; group leader explor eng, 62-70, eng fel, 70-76, SR FEL, MONSANTO CO, 76- *Mem:* Am Inst Chem Engrs; Am Chem Soc. *Res:* Engineering and chemistry related to high polymers and fibers, to nonwovens, and to gas separations. *Mailing Add:* Monsanto Develop Ctr Inc Triangle Park NC 27709

DOBRATZ, CARROLL J, b Park Rapids, Minn, Oct 13, 15; m 42; c 4. CHEMICAL ENGINEERING. *Educ:* Univ Minn, BChE, 38; Univ Cincinnati, PhD(chem eng), 43. *Prof Exp:* Instr chem eng, Univ Cincinnati, 41-43; sr res chemist, Shell Oil Co, Tex, 43-46; res & develop engr, Dow Chem Co, 46-74; PROCESS ENG SPECIALIST, KALAMA CHEM INC, 74- *Mem:* Am Chem Soc; Am Inst Chem Eng. *Res:* Heat and mass transfer; applied kinetics; thermodynamics. *Mailing Add:* Kalama Chem Inc PO Box 113 Kalama WA 98625

DOBRIN, MILTON BURNETT, b Vancouver, BC, Apr 7, 15; m 44, 48; c 5. GEOPHYSICS. *Educ:* Mass Inst Technol, BS, 36; Columbia Univ Pittsburgh, MS, 41; Columbia Univ, PhD(geophys), 50. *Prof Exp:* Asst physics, Univ Columbia, 37; asst geophysicist, Gulf Res & Develop Co, 37-40, geophysicist, 40-42; physicist, Naval Ord Lab, 42-49; sr res technologist, Field Res Labs, Magnolia Petrol Co, 49-55; sr interpretation geophysicist, Triad Oil Co, Can, 56-61; chief geophysicist, United Geophys Corp, 61-69, vpres, 67-69; W S Farish vis prof geophys, Univ Tex, Austin, 69; PROF GEOL, UNIV HOUSTON, 69- *Concurrent Pos:* Britton scholar, Univ Columbia, 47-48, lectr, 48-49; mem atomic bomb test, Bikini, 46 & Arctic Res Lab, 48; mem, US Nat Comt Geol, 70-74, chmn, 73-74; Esso vis lectr, Australia, 78. *Mem:* AAAS; Soc Explor Geophys (vpres, 61-62, pres, 69-70); Geol Soc Am (chmn, Geophysics Div, 77-78); Am Asn Petrol Geologists; Am Geophys Union; European Asn Explor Geophys. *Res:* Seismic prospecting; experimental geology; underwater acoustics; seismic exploration of atolls; seismic surface waves; seismic data processing; use of laser light for optical filtering of geophysical data; seismic studies of stratigraphy. *Mailing Add:* Geol Dept Univ of Houston Houston TX 77004

DOBRIN, PHILIP BOONE, b Passaic, NJ, Dec 21, 34; m 61; c 3. MEDICAL PHYSIOLOGY, CARDIOVASCULAR PHYSIOLOGY. *Educ:* NY Univ, BA, 58; Conn Col, MA, 62; Loyola Univ Chicago, PhD(physiol), 68, MD, 74. *Prof Exp:* Res asst psychopharmacol, Chas Pfizer Res Labs, 59-63; asst prof med physiol, 68-74, adj asst prof med physiol & surg resident, 74-80, ASST PROF SURG, STRITCH SCH MED, LOYOLA UNIV, CHICAGO, 80- *Concurrent Pos:* Consult, NIH, 68-; adj assoc prof physiol, Stritch Sch Med, Loyola Univ, Chicago, 80- *Mem:* Am Physiol Soc; Asn Acad Surg. *Res:* Biomechanics of the arterial wall; physiology of vascular smooth muscle; physiology of the circulation; balloon embolectomy catheters; endotracheal tubes. *Mailing Add:* Dept of Physiol Loyola Univ Stritch Sch of Med Maywood IL 60153

DOBRINSKA, MICHAEL R, b Shawano, Wis, Apr 16, 49; m 71; c 2. PHARMACOKINETICS, BIOPHARMACEUTICS. *Educ:* Univ Wis, BS, 72, MS, 75, PhD(pharmaceut), 77. *Prof Exp:* RES FEL, MERCK, SHARP & DOHME RES LAB, MERCK & CO, INC, 77- *Mem:* Am Pharmaceut Asn; Acad Pharmaceut Sci; Int Soc Study Xenobiotics. *Res:* Study of the pharmacokinetics and biopharmaceutics of drugs in laboratory animals and in man. *Mailing Add:* Merck Sharp & Dohme Res Labs West Point PA 19486

DOBROGOSZ, WALTER JEROME, b Erie, Pa, Sept 3, 33; m 53; c 4. MICROBIOLOGY, BIOCHEMISTRY. *Educ:* Pa State Univ, BS, 55, MS, 57, PhD(bact biochem), 60. *Prof Exp:* NIH fel microbiol, Univ Ill, 60-62; from asst prof to assoc prof, 62-71, PROF MICROBIOL, NC STATE UNIV, 71- *Concurrent Pos:* NIH career develop award, 63-, res grant, 64-; NSF res grant, 64-; AEC res grant, 68-; mem ed bd, J Bacteriol, 71-76. *Mem:* Am Soc Microbiol. *Res:* Metabolic regulatory mechanisms in bacteria and higher organisms including studies on regulation of carbohydrate metabolism and nucleic acid and enzyme synthesis formation and the role of cyclic AMP in these processes. *Mailing Add:* Dept of Microbiol NC State Univ Raleigh NC 27607

DOBROTT, ROBERT D, b Guymon, Okla, Sept 28, 32; m 62; c 3. CRYSTALLOGRAPHY, PHYSICAL CHEMISTRY. *Educ:* Univ Wichita, BS & MS, 59; Harvard Univ, PhD(phys chem), 64. *Prof Exp:* Anal chemist, Cessna Aircraft, Kans, 54-59; mem tech staff, Tex Instruments Inc, 64-68, mgr characterization serv, 68-72, mem tech staff, 73-80; SR RES SCIENTIST, PACKAGE MAT RES, MOSTER INC, 80- *Mem:* Am Chem Soc; Am Crystallog Asn. *Res:* X-ray and electron diffraction; x-ray fluorescence; SEM, TEM and optical microscopy; auger and ion scattering spectroscopy; ion probe and electron probe microanalysis; microanalysis standards fabrication; environment testing; failure analysis. *Mailing Add:* 1429 Lamp Post Lane Richardson TX 75222

DOBROV, WADIM (IVAN), b Masur, Russia, July 14, 26; nat US; m 56; c 4. SOLID STATE PHYSICS. *Educ:* Univ Calif, PhD(physics), 56. *Prof Exp:* Res asst, Univ Calif, 54-56; res scientist, 56-65, staff scientist, 65-66, SR STAFF SCIENTIST SOLID STATE PHYSICS, LOCKHEED RES LAB, 66- *Mem:* Am Phys Soc; Inst Elec & Electronics Engrs. *Res:* Nuclear moments; paramagnetic resonance; ferroelectricity; microwave ultrasonics; lasers and infrared technology. *Mailing Add:* Lockheed Res Labs 3251 Hanover St Palo Alto CA 94304

DOBROVOLNY, CHARLES GEORGE, b Budapest, Hungary, July 19, 02; nat US; m 32; c 1. VIROLOGY, PUBLIC HEALTH. *Educ:* Univ Mont, AB, 28; Kans State Univ, MS, 33; Univ Mich, PhD(parasitol, zool), 38. *Prof Exp:* High sch teacher, Idaho, 28-29; instr zool, Kans State Univ, 29-35; instr, Univ Mich, 35-40; asst prof, Univ NH, 40-45, assoc prof, 45-48, chmn div biol sci, 47-48; parasitologist, Div Trop Dis, NIH, 48-51, consult schistosomiasis control, WHO, Brazil, 51-57, consult yellow fever & trop virus invest, Guatemala, 57-59, trop virus studies, Panama, 59-60, malaria studies, Malaya & Atlanta, Ga, 61-64, consult int demonstration proj for commun dis control, Tex, 65-66, pesticide studies, 66-67, proj officer pesticides prog, 67-68, proj officer, Food & Drug Admin, 68-70, proj officer, Environ Protection Agency, 70-75; RETIRED. *Mem:* AAAS; Am Soc Parasitol; Am Micros Soc; Am Soc Trop Med & Hyg; Am Pub Health Asn. *Res:* General and experimental parasitology; malarian chemotherapy; schistosomiasis; tropical virology; pesticides; virology; parasitology. *Mailing Add:* 1366 Vistaleaf Dr Decatur GA 30033

DOBROVOLNY, ERNEST, b Delmont, SDak, Aug 27, 12; m 40; c 4. GEOLOGY. *Educ:* Kans State Col, BS, 35; Univ Mich, MS, 40. *Prof Exp:* Chem analyst, E I du Pont de Nemours & Co, 35-37; asst geol, Univ Mich, 38-40; asst geologist, State Hwy Comn Kans, 40-42; regional geologist, 43-44; asst hwy engr, Pub Rds Admin, Alaska, 42-43; geologist, US Geol Surv, Ariz, 44, NMex, 45-46, Mont, 46-48, Colo, 48-54, asst chief eng geol br, 49-54, geologist-in-chg munic geol & eng, La Paz, Bolivia, 54-55, res geologist, Nev Test Site, 56-59, consult eng geol earthquake studies, Chilean Geol Surv, 60, geologist mapping proj, Ky, 60-61, res geologist, Sci & Eng Task Force, Fed Reconstruct & Develop Planning Comn, US Geol Surv, Alaska, 64-76; CONSULT GEOLOGIST, 76- *Concurrent Pos:* Mem comt Alaska Earthquake, Nat Acad Sci, chmn comt eng geol, Hwy Res Bd, 63- *Mem:* Geol Soc Am; Asn Eng Geol. *Res:* Stratigraphy; military geology; civil engineering; mapping geology. *Mailing Add:* 2210 S Corona Denver CO 80210

DOBROVOLNY, JERRY S(TANLEY), b Chicago, Ill, Nov 2, 22; m 47; c 2. CIVIL ENGINEERING. *Educ:* Univ Ill, BS, 43, MS, 47. *Prof Exp:* From instr to assoc prof, 45-59, PROF GEN ENG & HEAD DEPT, UNIV ILL, URBANA, 59- *Concurrent Pos:* Civil Engr, Ill State Hwy Dept, 48-54; consult, 55-59; mem, State of Ill Adv Coun Voc Educ, 69-72 & Nat Adv Coun Voc Educ, 70-72; examr, Comn Insts Higher Educ, NCent Asn Cols & Sec Schs. *Honors & Awards:* Arthur L Williston Award, Am Soc Eng Educ. *Mem:* Fel AAAS; Am Soc Civil Engrs; Am Soc Eng Educ; Hist Sci Soc; Nat Soc Prof Engrs (nat dir, 74-82). *Res:* Engineering geology and technology; soil mechanics. *Mailing Add:* Col of Eng Univ of Ill Urbana IL 61801

DOBROVOLSKIS, ANTHONY R, planetary science, celestial mechanics, see previous edition

DOBROWOLSKI, JERZY ADAM, b Katowice, Poland, May 9, 31; Can citizen; m 59; c 3. PHYSICAL OPTICS. *Educ:* Univ London, BSc, 53, MSc & dipl, Imp Col, 54, PhD, 55. *Prof Exp:* Nat Res Coun Can fel, 55-56; from asst res officer to assoc res officer, 56-71, SR RES OFFICER, DIV PHYSICS, NAT RES COUN CAN, 71- *Mem:* Optical Soc Am; Am Vacuum Soc. *Res:* Design and fabrication of optical thin film systems; optical filters. *Mailing Add:* Div Physics Nat Res Coun Ottawa ON K1A 0R6 Can

DOBRY, ALAN (MORA), b Chicago, Ill, Mar 19, 27; m 50; c 2. PHYSICAL CHEMISTRY. *Educ:* Univ Chicago, PhB & SB, 45, SM, 48, PhD(chem), 50; Univ Pittsburgh, MLitt, 56. *Prof Exp:* Fel calorimetry peptide reactions, Yale Univ, 51; res engr phys chem lubrication, Westinghouse Elec Co, 52-56; RES CHEMIST, AMOCO OIL CO, 56- *Mem:* Am Chem Soc; The Chem Soc. *Res:* Emulsions; particle size distributions; adsorption from solutions; physical chemistry of lubrication; high pressure chemistry; radiochemistry; fertilizers. *Mailing Add:* Res & Develop Dept Amoco Oil Co PO Box 400 Naperville IL 60566

DOBRY, REUVEN, b Bialistock, Poland, Apr 13, 30; nat US; m 60; c 2. CHEMICAL ENGINEERING. *Educ:* Syracuse Univ, BChE, 54; Univ Ill, PhD(chem MS, 55; Cornell Univ, PhD(chem eng), 58. *Prof Exp:* Res chem engr, Bioferm Corp, 58-63; sr chem engr, Battelle Mem Inst, 63-67; sr proj leader, Standard Brands Inc, 67-69; eng res group leader, 69-73, MGR RES & DEVELOP, QUALITY ASSURANCE, BEECHNUT INC, 73- *Mem:* Am Chem Soc; Am Inst Chem Engrs; Inst Food Technologists. *Res:* Special techniques for isolation and purification of biochemicals; engineering research and process/product development, related to foods and beverages; quality control; quality assurance. *Mailing Add:* Tetley Inc 100 Commerce Dr Shelton CT 06484

DOBSON, ALAN, b London, Eng, Dec 20, 28; m 54; c 4. VETERINARY PHYSIOLOGY, GASTROENTEROLOGY. *Educ:* Cambridge Univ, BA, 52, MA, 70; Aberdeen Univ, PhD(physiol), 56. *Prof Exp:* From sci officer to prin sci officer, Dept Physiol, Rowett Res Inst, Scotland, 52-64; assoc prof physiol, 64-70, PROF VET PHYSIOL, NY STATE COL VET MED, CORNELL UNIV, 70- *Concurrent Pos:* Vis prof, NY State Col Vet Med, Cornell Univ, 61-62; Wellcome fel, Vet Sch, Cambridge Univ, 70-71, vis worker Physiol Lab, 77-78, 79, 80. *Mem:* Am Physiol Soc; Brit Physiol Soc; Brit Biochem Soc. *Res:* Physiology of the ruminant digestive tract; homeostasis in the ruminant; control of absorption; peripheral blood flow; perfusion and ventilation in the horse. *Mailing Add:* Dept Physiol NY State Col Vet Med Cornell Univ Ithaca NY 14853

DOBSON, DAVID A, b Oakland, Calif, Mar 28, 37; m 57. NUCLEAR PHYSICS, ATOMIC PHYSICS. *Educ:* Univ Calif, Berkeley, BS, 59, PhD(physics), 64. *Prof Exp:* Physicist, Lawrence Radiation Lab, Livermore, 64-69; asst prof, 69-72, assoc prof, 72-78, PROF PHYSICS, BELOIT COL, 80- *Mem:* AAAS; Am Phys Soc. *Res:* Investigation of weak interactions by a study of asymmetries and angular correlations in beta decay of polarized nuclei. *Mailing Add:* 1211 Bushnell Beloit WI 53511

DOBSON, DONALD C, b Central, Idaho, Sept 18, 26; m 49; c 9. POULTRY SCIENCE. *Educ:* Utah State Univ, BS, 54; Cornell Univ, MS, 55; Utah State Univ, PhD(nutrit, biochem), 61. *Prof Exp:* Res asst biochem, Univ Utah, 55-57; res asst nutrit biochem, 57-60, asst prof turkey res, 60-70, assoc prof animal sci, 70-80, ASSOC PROF ANIMAL SCI & VET, UTAH STATE UNIV, 80- *Mem:* Poultry Sci Asn. *Res:* Poultry nutrition and management, especially turkeys. *Mailing Add:* Dept of Animal Sci Utah State Univ Logan UT 84322

DOBSON, ERNEST L, physiology, biophysics, deceased

DOBSON, GERARD RAMSDEN, b Lynbrook, NY, May 4, 33; m 62; c 3. ORGANOMETALLIC CHEMISTRY, CHEMICAL KINETICS. *Educ:* Fla Southern Col, BS, 55; Temple Univ, MEd, 58; Fla State Univ, PhD(chem), 64. *Prof Exp:* High sch teacher, Pa, 55-58; asst prof inorg chem, Univ Ga, 63-67; assoc prof chem, Univ SDak, 67-69; assoc prof, 69-72, PROF PHYS CHEM, NORTH TEX STATE UNIV, 72- *Mem:* Am Chem Soc; Royal Soc Chem; Sigma Xi; Am Inst Chemists. *Res:* Organotransition metal chemistry; kinetics and mechanism of reactions of metal carbonyls and derivatives; physical methods of molecular structure determination. *Mailing Add:* Dept of Chem N Tex State Univ Denton TX 76203

DOBSON, HAROLD LAWRENCE, b Liberty Co, Tex, May 10, 21; m 45; c 4. BIOCHEMISTRY, INTERNAL MEDICINE. *Educ:* Baylor Univ, BS, 43, MD, 46, MS, 56. *Prof Exp:* Intern, Salt Lake County Hosp, Utah, 46-47; instr biochem, 47-48, from instr to assoc prof internal med, 53-70, CLIN ASSOC PROF, BAYLOR COL MED, 71-; CLIN PROF MED & INTERNAL MED, UNIV TEX MED SCH HOUSTON, 73- *Concurrent Pos:* USPHS fel biochem & internal med, Col Med, Baylor Univ, 48-50; resident, Vet Admin Hosp, Houston, 50-51; fel coun on atherosclerosis, Am Heart Asn; head, Diabetic Clin, Hermann Hosp, Univ Tex Med Sch Houston, 73-80. *Mem:* AAAS; AMA; Am Col Cardiol; Am Soc Pharmacol & Exp Therapeut; Am Soc Nephrol. *Res:* Metabolic disease; diabetes; computer use for clinical records. *Mailing Add:* 2210 Maroncal Suite 304 Houston TX 77030

DOBSON, JAMES GORDON, JR, b Waterbury, Conn, Jan 23, 42; m 71; c 1. PHYSIOLOGY, BIOCHEMISTRY. *Educ:* Cent Conn State Col, BS, 65; Wesleyan Univ, MA, 67; Univ Va, PhD(physiol), 71. *Prof Exp:* Res pharmacologist, Univ Calif, San Diego, 71-73; asst prof, 73-77, ASSOC PROF PHYSIOL, MED SCH, UNIV MASS, 77- *Concurrent Pos:* Fel, Univ Calif, San Diego, 71-72, Giannini Found fel, 72-73. *Mem:* Am Heart Asn; Am Physiol Soc; Biophys Soc; Int Soc Heart Res; AAAS. *Res:* Cardiovascular physiology; particularly the mechanisms involved in the regulation of contractile and metabolic function in the myocardium of the normal, ischemic and hypoxic heart. *Mailing Add:* Dept of Physiol Med Sch 55 Lake Ave N Worcester MA 01605

DOBSON, MARGARET VELMA, b Burbank, Calif, June 8, 48; m 75; c 2. VISUAL SCIENCES, CHILD DEVELOPMENT. *Educ:* Fla State Univ, BA, 70; Brown Univ, ScM, 73, PhD(psychol), 75. *Prof Exp:* Res scientist ophthal, Tufts-New Eng Med Ctr, 74-75; NIH fel, 75-78, res assoc, 77-78, res asst prof, 78-82, RES ASSOC PROF PSYCHOL, UNIV WASH, 82- *Concurrent Pos:* Prin investr, NIH res grant, 78- & Children's Eye Care Found grant, 80-; affiliate, Child Develop & Mental Retardation Ctr, Univ Wash, 81- *Mem:* Am Res Vision & Ophthal; Soc Res Child Develop; AAAS. *Res:* Development and use of behavioral methods for the assessment of visual acuity in infants and young children in laboratory and clinical settings. *Mailing Add:* Dept Psychol Univ Wash Seattle WA 98195

DOBSON, PETER N, JR, b Baltimore, Md, Sept 15, 36; m 57; c 3. THEORETICAL HIGH ENERGY PHYSICS. *Educ:* Mass Inst Technol, BS, 58; Univ Md, 60-64, PhD(physics), 65. *Prof Exp:* Physicist, Raytheon Corp, 58-59; physicist, Westinghouse Elec Corp, 59-60; from asst prof to assoc prof physics, 65-74, actg chmn dept, 75-76, PROF PHYSICS & ASTRON, UNIV HAWAII, 74- *Mem:* Am Phys Soc. *Res:* Theory of elementary particles and their interactions at high energy. *Mailing Add:* Dept of Physics & Astron Univ of Hawaii Honolulu HI 96822

DOBSON, R LOWRY, b Beijing, China, Nov 2, 19; US citizen; m 43; c 5. MEDICAL RESEARCH, RADIOBIOLOGY. *Educ:* Univ Calif, Berkeley, AB, 41, PhD(biophys), 50; Univ Calif, San Francisco, MD, 44. *Prof Exp:* Teaching asst, Univ Calif, Berkeley, 41-42; intern, Univ Calif Hosp, San Francisco, 44-45; resident physician, Permanente Found Hosp, 45-46; physician & res fel, Donner Lab, Univ Calif, 46-47, dir med servs, Lawrence Radiation Lab, 47-58; chief med officer, radiation & isotopes, WHO, Geneva, Switzerland, 58-67; SR SCIENTIST, BIOMED SCI DIV, LAWRENCE LIVERMORE NAT LAB, UNIV CALIF, LIVERMORE, 67-, LEADER REPRODUCTIVE BIOL SECT, 80- *Concurrent Pos:* Med physics physician to Univ & lectr & assoc res med physicist, Univ of Calif, 48-58, instr & res assoc med physics, Donner Lab, 47-48; consult, Int Comn Radiol Protection & Int Comn Radiol Units & Meas, 59-60, US Dept Com, 71-72 & WHO, 78; adj prof radiol, Sch Med Univ Calif, Davis, 77- *Mem:* Radiation Res Soc; Environ Mutagen Soc; AAAS; Sci Res Soc N Am. *Res:* Biological and health effects of exposure to environmental agents, radiation, radionuclides and chemicals, especially on certain mammalian cell populations during development; radiobiology; toxicology; teratology; cell biology; reproductive and developmental biology. *Mailing Add:* Lawrence Livermore Nat Lab PO Box 5507 Univ Calif Livermore CA 94550

DOBSON, RICHARD CECIL, b Florence, Mont, Dec 29, 19; m 45; c 3. VETERINARY ENTOMOLOGY, ECONOMIC ENTOMOLOGY. *Educ:* Univ Wis, BS, 46, MS, 47; Ore State Col, PhD, 53. *Prof Exp:* Res asst entom, Univ Wis, 45-47; instr biol, NMex State Univ, 48-50, entomologist, Fruit Insects Div, USDA, 50-51; asst entom, Ore State Col, 51-53; asst, Exten Serv, NMex State Univ, 53-54; state entomologist, Plant Quarantine Serv, 54-55, res entomologist, Dept Bot & Entom, 55-58; prof entom, Purdue Univ, West Lafayette, 58-76; ASSOC DEAN & DIR RESIDENT INSTR, COL AGR, UNIV IDAHO, 76- *Concurrent Pos:* Mem forest pest action comt, Ariz & NMex, 53-58. *Mem:* AAAS; Entom Soc Am; Sigma Xi. *Res:* Livestock insect research. *Mailing Add:* Col of Agr Univ of Idaho Moscow ID 83843

DOBSON, RICHARD LAWRENCE, b Boston, Mass, Apr 12, 28; m 50; c 3. DERMATOLOGY. *Educ:* Univ Chicago, MD, 53; Am Bd Dermat, dipl, 59. *Prof Exp:* From instr to asst prof dermat, Univ NC, 57-61; from assoc prof to prof, Med Sch, Univ Ore, 61-72; prof derm & chmn dept, Sch Med, State Univ NY, Buffalo, 72-79; PROF DERMAT, MED UNIV SC, 80- *Concurrent Pos:* NIH res fel, 56-57; attend physician, Univ Sch, Ore Hosps, 61-72; consult, Vet Admin Hosp, Portland, 61-72; scientist, Ore Regional Primate Ctr, 63-68; asst chief ed, Arch Dermat, 64-69; mem gen med study sect, NIH, 65-69, chmn, 70-72; vis prof, Univ Nijmegen, Netherlands, 69-70; head dept dermat, Buffalo Gen Hosp, E J Meyer Hosp, Buffalo. *Mem:* Am Asn Cancer Res; Am Acad Dermat; Soc Invest Dermat (pres, 76); Am Col Physicians; Am Dermat Asn. *Res:* Cutaneous carcinogenesis; physiology of eccrine sweat gland. *Mailing Add:* Dept of Dermatol State Univ NY Sch Med Buffalo NY 14202

DOBY, RAYMOND, b New York, NY, Oct 9, 23; m 49; c 2. CONTINUUM & FLUID MECHANICS. *Educ:* NY Univ, BME, 47, MS, 51; Univ Pa, PhD(eng mech), 62. *Prof Exp:* Sr engr steam div, Westinghouse Elec Corp, 53-62; sr staff scientist, Avco Corp, 62-63; adv engr astronuclear labs, Westinghouse Elec Corp, 63-66; assoc prof eng, Swarthmore Col, 66-71; PRES & CONSULT, RADO ASSOCS, 72- *Concurrent Pos:* Adj asst prof, Evening Col, Drexel Inst, 56-62. *Mem:* AAAS; Am Soc Mech Engrs; Soc Indust & Appl Math; Sigma Xi. *Res:* Gas dynamics; boundary layer analysis; heat and mass transfer; biomechanics; interaction of science and society; elastic waves in bounded media; seismic structural analysis. *Mailing Add:* Rado Assocs Box 2708 Cherry Hill NJ 08034

DOBY, TIBOR, b Budapest, Hungary, Aug 23, 14; US citizen; m 48. RADIOLOGY, NUCLEAR MEDICINE. *Educ:* Univ Budapest, MD, 38; Am Bd Radiol, dipl, 62. *Prof Exp:* Resident internal med, Med Sch Hosp, Univ Budapest, 38-44, asst prof, 44-48, asst prof radiol, 48-50; assoc radiologist, Trade Union & Rwy Employees Hosp, Budapest, 50-56; resident, St Raphael's Hosp, New Haven, Conn, 57-59; instr, Med Sch, Yale Univ, 59-60; assoc radiologist, 60-65, dir radiol dept, 65-80, CHIEF RADIOL & ISOTOPE SCANNING & EMER CHIEF DIAG RADIOL, MERCY HOSP, PORTLAND, MAINE, 80- *Mem:* Fel Am Col Radiol; NY Acad Sci; Radiol Soc NAm; Soc Nuclear Med. *Res:* Circulatory shock; hemodynamics; history of medicine. *Mailing Add:* Dept of Radiol Mercy Hosp 144 State St Portland ME 04101

DOBYNS, BROWN M, b Jacksonville, Ill, May 14, 13; m 40; c 3. SURGERY. *Educ:* Ill Col, BA, 35; Johns Hopkins Univ, MD, 39; Univ Minn, MS, 44, PhD, 46; Am Bd Surg, dipl. *Prof Exp:* Intern surg, Johns Hopkins Hosp, 39-40; resident, Kahler Hosp, Mayo Clin, 43-45, resident, Mayo Clin, 45-46, asst to surg staff, 46; asst prof surg, Med Sch, Harvard Univ, 48-51; assoc prof, 51-58, PROF SURG, SCH MED, CASE WESTERN RESERVE UNIV, 58-; ASSOC CHIEF SURG SERV, CLEVELAND METROP GEN HOSP, 67- *Concurrent Pos:* Res fel surg, Med Sch, Harvard Univ, 46-48; asst, Mass Gen Hosp, 46-51; asst chief surg serv, Cleveland Metrop Gen Hosp, 51-66; asst surgeon, Univ Hosps, Cleveland, 51-; mem courtesy staff, St Luke's Hosp, Cleveland, 51-; mem staff, Lutheran Hosp, 75- *Honors & Awards:* Van Meter Prize, Am Thyroid Asn, 46, Merit Award, 54. *Mem:* Am Surg Asn; Soc Univ Surg; Am Col Surg; Am Soc Clin Invest; Am Thyroid Asn (pres, 56-57). *Res:* Thyroid physiology. *Mailing Add:* Cleveland Metrop Gen Hosp 3395 Scranton Rd Cleveland OH 44109

DOBYNS, LEONA DANETTE, b Shelby, Mont, Jan 28, 30. PHYSICAL CHEMISTRY. *Educ:* Col Great Falls, BS, 58; Univ Notre Dame, PhD(phys chem), 64. *Prof Exp:* From asst prof to assoc prof chem, Seattle Univ, 64-72; assoc prof, 72-78, PROF CHEM, CALIF STATE UNIV, DOMINGUEZ HILLS, 78- *Concurrent Pos:* Res grant, Univ Notre Dame, 68. *Mem:* Am Chem Soc; Am Phys Soc. *Res:* Microwave spectroscopy and molecular structure. *Mailing Add:* Dept of Chem Calif State Univ Dominguez Hills CA 90747

DOBYNS, ROY A, b Bristol, Va, Jan 31, 31; m 55; c 2. MATHEMATICS. *Educ:* Carson-Newman Col, BA, 53; Vanderbilt Univ, MA, 54; George Peabody Col, PhD(math), 63. *Prof Exp:* Asst prof math, La Col, 56-58; from asst prof to prof, McNeese State Col, 58-68; prof & chmn dept, Georgetown Col, 68-73; chmn div natural sci & math, Clayton Jr Col, 73-75; ACAD DEAN, CARSON-NEWMAN COL, 75- *Mem:* Math Asn Am. *Mailing Add:* Carson-Newman Col Jefferson City TN 37760

DOBYNS, SAMUEL WITTEN, b Norton, Va, Mar 7, 20; m 45; c 3. CONSTRUCTION MANAGEMENT, STRUCTURAL ENGINEERING. *Educ:* Va Mil Inst, BS, 41; Lehigh Univ, MS, 49. *Prof Exp:* Sr instrumentman, E I du Pont de Nemours & Co, 46; from instr to assoc prof civil eng, 46-60, dir eve col, 67-74, PROF CIVIL ENG, VA MIL INST, 60- *Concurrent Pos:* Dir, Robert A Marr Sch Surv & Comput Clin, 50-72; partner, Dobyns & Morgan Consult Engrs, 52-64; NASA fac fel, Manned Spacecraft Ctr, Univ Houston, Tex A&M Univ, 67; Off Civil Defense fel, WVa Univ, 69; consult, Thompson & Litton, 70-75; consult engr & land survr, 75- *Mem:* Am Soc Civil Engrs; Am Soc Photogram; Am Cong Surv & Mapping; Am Soc Eng Educ. *Res:* Bridge design; structural analysis; construction management computer programming and applications; project management; photogrammetry; solid waste; surveying; nuclear defense. *Mailing Add:* Dept of Civil Eng Va Mil Inst Lexington VA 24450

DOCHERTY, JOHN JOSEPH, b Youngstown, Ohio, Dec 5, 41; m 65; c 2. VIROLOGY, MICROBIOLOGY. *Educ:* Youngstown Univ, BA, 64; Miami Univ, Ohio, MS, 66; Univ Ariz, PhD(microbiol), 70. *Prof Exp:* Fel virol, Dept Microbiol, Sch Med, 70-72, asst prof microbiol, 72-76, ASSOC PROF MICROBIOL, DEPT MICROBIOL, COL SCI, PA STATE UNIV, 76- *Concurrent Pos:* Consult, Hercules Chem Co, Wilmington, Del, 73 & Frederick Cancer Res Ctr, Frederick, Md, 75; res fel virology, Univ Glasgow, Scotland, 80. *Mem:* Am Soc Microbiol; Sigma Xi; AAAS. *Res:* Cancer virology and immunology; mechanism of cell transformation by herpes simplex viruses; herpes simplex virus latency; detection of herpes viruses markers by immunological methods. *Mailing Add:* Dept of Microbiol 101 S Frear Bldg Pa State Univ University Park PA 16802

DOCHINGER, LEON S, b Woodbridge, NJ, Aug 30, 24; m 53; c 2. PLANT PATHOLOGY. *Educ:* Rutgers Univ, BS, 50, PhD(plant path), 56; Cornell Univ, MS, 52. *Prof Exp:* Asst, Cornell Univ, 50-52; plant pathologist, 56-70, proj leader, 70-77, PRIN PLANT PATHOLOGIST, US FOREST SERV, 77- *Mem:* Soc Am Foresters; Am Phytopath Soc. *Res:* Relationship of air pollution to forests in the eastern United States. *Mailing Add:* US Forest Serv US Dept Agr Delaware OH 43015

DOCKEN, ADRIAN (MERWIN), b Holt, Minn, Nov 17, 13; m 41; c 4. SYNTHETIC ORGANIC CHEMISTRY. *Educ:* Luther Col, BA, 37; Univ Wis, PhD(org chem), 41. *Prof Exp:* Asst, Univ Wis, 37-41; res assoc, Northwestern Univ, 41-42; head dept chem, 42-70 & 77-78, PROF CHEM, LUTHER COL, 42- *Concurrent Pos:* Fac fel, Ford Found, Yale Univ, 54-55; fac fel, Imp Col, Univ London, 61-62; Am Chem Soc Petrol Fund fac award, Stanford Univ, 67-68; vis scholar, Univ Calif, Los Angeles, 74-75. *Mem:* AAAS; Am Chem Soc; The Chem Soc. *Res:* Organic synthesis; philosophy and history of science. *Mailing Add:* Dept of Chem Luther Col Decorah IA 52101

DOCKERY, JOHN T, b Cleveland, Ohio, May 2, 36; m 61; c 3. PHYSICS, OPERATIONS RESEARCH. *Educ:* John Carroll Univ, BS, 58; Fla State Univ, MS, 62, PhD(physics), 65. *Prof Exp:* Physicist, US Naval Weapons Lab, Va, 60-61; engr, Boeing Aerospace, Wash, 63-64; res physicist, Bendix Aerospace Systs, Mich, 65-66; sr scientist, Res Inst, Ill Inst Technol, 66-68; opers res analyst, Weapons-Systs Anal, Off Chief of Staff, US Army, 68-73; opers res analyst, Md, 73-80, OPERS RES BR CHIEF, SHAPE TECH CTR, US ARMY CONCEPTS ANAL AGENCY, HOLLAND, 80- *Concurrent Pos:* Mem, Army Math Steering Comt, 68-73; mem, Europ Working Group Multi-Criteria Decision Theory, 75-78. *Mem:* Am Phys Soc; Am Geophys Union; Am Inst Aeronaut & Astronaut; Asn Comput Mach; Opers Res Soc Am. *Res:* Large-scale simulation; Fuzzy Set theory; multi-criteria decision theory; weapon systems analysis; computational physics. *Mailing Add:* US Radco Stc Hague Netherlands APO New York NY 09159

DOCKS, EDWARD LEON, b Detroit, Mich, Jan 14, 45; m 69; c 2. NONMETALLIC MATERIAL EVALUATION. *Educ:* Wayne State Univ, BS, 67; Univ Calif, Los Angeles, PhD(chem), 72. *Prof Exp:* NIH res fel, 72-74; res chemist, 74-79, SR RES CHEMIST, US BORAX RES CORP, 79- *Mem:* Am Chem Soc; Nat Asn Corrosion Engrs. *Res:* Test, evaluate, and specify nonmetallic materials such as, fiberglass reinforced plastic, lined pipe, rubber and brick; research and development changes. *Mailing Add:* US Borax Res Corp 412 Crescent Way Anaheim CA 92801

DOCKTER, MICHAEL EDWARD, b Carmel, Calif, July 29, 49; m 69; c 2. BIOCHEMISTRY, BIOPHYSICS. *Educ:* Calif State Col, Sonoma, BS, 71; Wash State Univ, PhD(biochem), 75. *Prof Exp:* Res asst, Univ Basel, 75-77; ASST MEM BIOCHEM, ST JUDE CHILDREN'S RES HOSP, 77-; ASST PROF, UNIV TENN MED UNITS, 78- *Concurrent Pos:* Fel, Europ Molecular Biol Orgn, 75-76. *Mem:* AAAS; Am Chem Soc; NY Acad Sci; Am Soc Biol Chemists. *Res:* Studies of membrane structure and function using biochemical and biophysical approaches; the protein complexes of oxidative phosphorylation. *Mailing Add:* St Jude Children's Res Hosp PO Box 318 Memphis TN 38101

DOCTOR, NORMAN J(OSEPH), b Brooklyn, NY, Oct 5, 29; m 56; c 3. ORDNANCE ENGINEERING. *Educ:* Purdue Univ, BS, 51. *Prof Exp:* Physicist, Nat Bur Standards, 51-53; physicist, Diamond Ord Fuze Labs, 53-56, res & develop supvr, 56-63, res & develop supvr, Harry Diamond Labs, 63-69, chief electron devices br, 69-70, chief electron timing br, Army Materiel Command 70-81, CHIEF POWER SUPPLY & MAT BR, US ARMY ELECTRONICS RES & DEVELOP COMMAND,, HARRY DIAMOND LABS, 81- *Honors & Awards:* Arthur S Flemming Award, 62. *Mem:* Inst Elec & Electronics Engrs. *Res:* Dielectric and magnetic measurements; printed circuit technology; microelectronics; thin films; ammunition electronics; electronic timing; ordnance electrochemical and electromechanical power supplies. *Mailing Add:* Power Supply & Mat Br 2800 Powder Mill Rd Adelphi MD 20783

DOCTOR, VASANT MANILAL, b Surat, India, Mar 19, 26; m 53; c 3. BIOCHEMISTRY. *Educ:* Royal Inst Sci, India, 46 & 48; Univ Wis, MS, 51; Tex Agr & Mech Col, PhD, 53. *Prof Exp:* Fel biochem, Tex Agr Exp Sta, 53-54; Hite fel exp med, M D Anderson Hosp & Tumor Inst, Univ Tex, 54-55, from asst biochemist to assoc biochemist, 55-62, USPHS res career develop award, Dent Br, 59-62; chief biochemist, Hindustan Antibiotics, Ltd, 62-65; assoc prof chem, Univ Houston, 65-68; PROF CHEM, PRAIRIE VIEW AGR & MECH UNIV, 68- *Mem:* AAAS; Am Soc Biol Chemists; Soc Exp Biol & Med. *Res:* Model enzyme systems; active site of nucleases; blood clotting mechanisms; cancer chemotherapy. *Mailing Add:* Dept of Chem Prairie View Agr & Mech Univ Prairie View TX 77445

DODD, CHARLES GARDNER, b St Louis, Mo, Jan 26, 15; m 43; c 4. PHYSICAL CHEMISTRY, MATERIALS SCIENCE. *Educ:* Rice Inst, BS, 40; Univ Mich, MS, 45, PhD(phys chem), 48. *Prof Exp:* Halliburton prof petrol eng, Univ Okla, 56-62; chief advan mat res, Owens-Ill, Inc, 62-68; assoc prin scientist, Philip Morris, Inc, 68-74; sr res assoc, Warner-Lambert Co, Milford, 74-80; PRES, CONN TECHNOL CONSULTS, INC, 80- *Mem:* Fel AAAS; fel Am Inst Chemists; Am Mineral Soc; Am Soc Metals; Microbeam Anal Soc. *Res:* Ion implantation for the surface modification of materials; surface physics and chemistry; scanning electron microscopy; soft x-ray spectroscopy and chemical bonding; thin films. *Mailing Add:* Conn Technol Consults Inc PO Box 524 Stratford CT 06497

DODD, CURTIS WILSON, b Fulton, Mo, Nov 4, 39; m 63; c 1. ELECTRICAL ENGINEERING. *Educ:* Univ Mo-Rolla, BS, 63, MS, 64; Ariz State Univ, PhD(control theory), 68. *Prof Exp:* Fac assoc elec eng, Ariz State Univ, 64-66; asst prof elec sci, 67-77, ASSOC PROF ELEC SCI, SOUTHERN ILL UNIV, CARBONDALE, 77- *Res:* Optimal control of distributed parameter systems. *Mailing Add:* Sch of Technol Southern Ill Univ Carbondale IL 62901

DODD, DAVID CEDRIC, b Sydney, Australia, Mar 18, 22; m 47. VETERINARY PATHOLOGY. *Educ:* Univ Sydney, BVSc, 46. *Hon Degrees:* MA, Univ Pa, 71. *Prof Exp:* Med registr vet med, Univ Sydney, 46-47; pvt pract, 48-51; vet res off, Dept Agr, NZ, 51-63; pathologist vet path, Pitman-Moore Div, Dow Chem Co, 64-65; from asst prof to assoc prof, Univ Pa, 65-70, prof path, 70-75; prof vet path & head, Okla State Univ, 75-79; DIR PATH, G D SEARLE & CO, 79- *Concurrent Pos:* Ed, Vet Path, Am Col Vet Pathologists, 70-79. *Mem:* Am Col Vet Pathologists; Int Acad Path; Am Soc Exp Path; NY Acad Sci; AAAS. *Res:* Toxicologic pathology-pharmaceutical compounds as potential compounds. *Mailing Add:* G D Searle & Co Box 5110 Chicago IL 60680

DODD, EDWARD ELLIOTT, b Rochester, NY, June 27, 22; m 64; c 2. SPACE TELECOMMUNICATIONS SYSTEMS. *Educ:* Univ Rochester, BS, 43; Univ Calif, PhD(physics), 52. *Prof Exp:* Physicist, Nat Bur Stand, 52-53; physicist, Naval Ord Lab, 53-54; physicist, Motorola Inc, 54-63; res specialist, Lockheed Missiles & Space Co, 63-66, ADVAN SYSTS ENGR, LOCKHEED ENG & MGT SERV CO, 66- *Mem:* Am Phys Soc; Audio Eng Soc. *Res:* Missile guidance systems; ranging and inertial sensors; computer information systems; space telecommunications systems design. *Mailing Add:* PO Box 57622 Webster TX 77598

DODD, EVERETT E, protozoology, cytology, see previous edition

DODD, GERALD DEWEY, JR, b Oaklyn, NJ, Nov 18, 22; m 46; c 7. RADIOLOGY. *Educ:* Lafayette Col, Pa, BA, 45; Jefferson Med Col, MD, 47. *Prof Exp:* Intern, Fitzgerald Mercy Hosp, 47-48; resident radiol, Jefferson Med Col Hosp, 48-50, asst radiologist, 52-55; assoc prof radiol, Univ Tex Postgrad Sch Med & assoc radiologist & head sect diag radiol, M D Anderson Hosp & Tumor Inst, 55-61; clin prof radiol & asst radiologist, Jefferson Med Col, 61-66; prof diag radiol & dir prog, Univ Tex Med Sch, Houston, 71-74, PROF DIAG RADIOL & HEAD DEPT, UNIV TEX SYST CANCER CTR, M D ANDERSON HOSP & TUMOR INST HOUSTON, 66- *Concurrent Pos:* Mem comt atlas tumor radiol, Am Col Radiol, 66-, chmn div postgrad educ, 76-, mem bd chancellors, 77-, vchmn comn diag radiol, 77-; mem adv comt cancer, Am Col Surgeons, 73-; deleg-at-large, Am Cancer Soc, 77. *Honors & Awards:* Silver Medal, Am Roentgen Ray Soc, 56. *Mem:* Fel Am Col Radiol; Am Roentgen Ray Soc; Radiol Soc NAm; Int Soc Lymphology. *Mailing Add:* Dept of Radiol M D Anderson Hosp & Tumor Inst Houston TX 77030

DODD, JACK GORDON, (JR), b Spokane, Wash, June 19, 26; m 51; c 2. ATOMIC PHYSICS. *Educ:* Ill Inst Technol, BS, 51; Univ Ark, MS, 57, PhD, 65. *Prof Exp:* Res technician physics, Argonne Nat Lab, 51-53; pub sch teacher, 53-55, prin, 56-57; asst physics, Univ Ark, 55-56; asst prof, Drury Col, 57-60; assoc prof & chmn dept, Ark Polytech Col, 62-67; assoc prof, Univ Tenn, Knoxville, 67-71; CHARLES A DANA PROF PHYSICS, COLGATE UNIV, 71- *Concurrent Pos:* Consult, McCrone Assocs, 61- & Honeywell, Inc, 64- *Mem:* Am Phys Soc; Am Asn Physics Teachers; Am Astron Soc. *Res:* Optical instrumentation and physical optics; atomic beams, shocks and detonations. *Mailing Add:* Dept of Physics Colgate Univ Hamilton NY 13346

DODD, JAMES ROBERT, b Bloomington, Ind, Mar 11, 34; m 56; c 2. PALEOECOLOGY. *Educ:* Ind Univ, AB, 56, AM, 57; Calif Inst Technol, PhD(geobiol), 61. *Prof Exp:* Ford Found fel oceanog, Calif Inst Technol, 61; geologist res labs, Texaco Inc, Tex, 61-63; asst prof geol, Case Western Reserve Univ, 63-66; assoc prof, 66-73, PROF GEOL, IND UNIV, BLOOMINGTON, 73- *Mem:* AAAS; Geol Soc Am; Soc Econ Paleontologists & Mineralogists; Paleontologic Soc; Sigma Xi. *Res:* Quantitative paleoecology and biogeochemistry; carbonate petrology; paleoecology and biogeochemistry. *Mailing Add:* Dept of Geol Ind Univ Bloomington IN 47401

DODD, JERROLD LOWELL, range ecology, see previous edition

DODD, JIMMIE DALE, b Esbon, Kans, Aug 6, 31; m 54; c 4. PLANT ECOLOGY, SOILS. *Educ:* Ft Hays Kans State Col, AB, 56, MS, 57; Univ Sask, PhD(plant ecol, soils), 60. *Prof Exp:* Asst prof forestry, Ariz State Col, 60-61; asst bot, NDak State Univ, 61-63; from asst prof to assoc prof range & forestry, 63-70, prof, 70-80, PROF RANGE SCI, TEX A&M UNIV, 80- *Concurrent Pos:* Secy range sci educ coun, Southwestern Naturalist. *Mem:* Ecol Soc Am; Bot Soc Am; Am Soc Range Mgt. *Res:* Soil-plant relationships in native vegetation; effects of prescribed fire on native vegetation; use of radionuclides in the study of ecological systems; native vegetation manipulation to increase production. *Mailing Add:* Dept of Range Sci Tex A&M Univ College Station TX 77843

DODD, JOHN DURRANCE, b Tarrytown, NY, Mar 15, 17; m 40; c 3. BOTANY. *Educ:* Syracuse Univ, BS, 38; Univ Vt, MS, 40; Columbia Univ, PhD(bot), 47. *Prof Exp:* Teaching asst & asst bot, Univ Vt, 38-41; asst morphol lab, Columbia Univ, 41-43 & 46-47; instr bot, Univ Wis, 47-49; from asst prof to assoc prof dept bot & plant path, 49-60, PROF BOT, DEPT BOT & PLANT PATH, IOWA STATE UNIV, 60- *Mem:* Bot Soc Am. *Res:* Interspecific grafts in Viola; cell shape; plant morphology; freshwater algae; diatoms; aquatic plant biology. *Mailing Add:* Dept of Bot & Plant Path Iowa State Univ Ames IA 50011

DODD, MATTHEW CHARLES, b Circleville, Ohio, Mar 24, 10; m 33; c 3. BACTERIOLOGY. *Educ:* Ohio State Univ, AB, 33; Univ Mich, PhD(bact), 41. *Prof Exp:* Asst pharmacologist, Parke, Davis & Co, Mich, 33-37; asst instr bact, Med Sch, Univ Mich, 37-41; chief dept bact & pharmacol, Eaton Labs, NY, 41-46; from asst prof to assoc prof bact, 46-54, prof, 54-80, chmn dept microbiol, 67-70, PROF MICROBIOL, OHIO STATE UNIV, 80- *Mem:* Am Soc Microbiol; Am Asn Immunol; Soc Exp Biol & Med; Am Fedn Clin Res; Tissue Cult Asn. *Res:* Nitrofuran chemotherapy; immunology of hemolytic anemia; autoimmunity; antibodies to nucleic acids; inhibitors of Rh antibody; immunology of cancer. *Mailing Add:* Dept Microbiol Ohio State Univ 484 W 12th Ave Columbus OH 43210

DODD, RICHARD ARTHUR, b Eng, Feb 11, 22; m 47; c 3. METALLURGY. *Educ:* Univ London, BS, 44, MS, 47, DSc(metall), 74; Univ Birmingham, PhD(metall), 50. *Prof Exp:* Res metallurgist, Rolls Royce Ltd, Eng, 44-47; sr lectr, Univ Witwatersrand, SAfrica, 50-54; res metallurgist, Dept Mines, Ottawa, 54-56; asst prof metall eng, Univ Pa, 56; chmn dept, 74-80, PROF METALL ENG, UNIV WIS-MADISON, 56- *Mem:* Am Inst Mining, Metall & Petrol Engrs; Am Soc Metals; Brit Iron & Steel Inst; Brit Inst Metals; fel Royal Inst Chemists. *Res:* General physical metallurgy. *Mailing Add:* Dept of Mining & Metals Univ of Wis Col of Eng Madison WI 53706

DODD, ROBERT TAYLOR, b Bronx, NY, July 11, 36; m 58; c 3. MINERALOGY, PETROLOGY. *Educ:* Cornell Univ, AB, 58; Princeton Univ, MA, 60, PhD(geol), 62. *Prof Exp:* Spec scientist, Air Force Cambridge Res Labs, 62-65, gen phys scientist, 65; from asst prof to prof mineral, 73-77, PROF EARTH SCI, STATE UNIV NY STONY BROOK, 77- *Mem:* AAAS; Geol Soc Am; Mineral Soc Am; Am Geochem Soc; Meteoritical Soc. *Res:* Igneous and metamorphic petrology; petrology and mineralogy of meteorites. *Mailing Add:* Dept of Earth & Space Sci State Univ of NY Stony Brook NY 11794

DODDS, ALVIN FRANKLIN, b Starkville, Miss, Jan 20, 19; m 43; c 3. BIOCHEMISTRY, PHARMACEUTICAL CHEMISTRY. *Educ:* Miss State Univ, BS, 40; Northwestern Univ, MS, 42, PhD(biochem), 43; Med Col SC, BS, 49. *Prof Exp:* Asst biochem, Dent Sch, Northwestern Univ, 40-43; res chemist, Pan Am Refinery Corp, Tex, 43-45; asst prof pharmaceut chem, Loyola Univ (La), 45-47; assoc prof, 47-52, prof, 52-81, EMER PROF PHARMACEUT CHEM, MED UNIV SC, 81- *Mem:* Am Chem Soc; Am Pharmaceut Asn. *Res:* Synthesis of local anesthetics; toxicity of synthetic vitamin K; metabolism of mouth bacteria; medicinal chemistry. *Mailing Add:* 425 Geddes Ave Charleston SC 29407

DODDS, DONALD GILBERT, b North Rose, NY, Oct 4, 25; m 45; c 2. WILDLIFE BIOLOGY, ECOLOGY. *Educ:* Cornell Univ, BSc, 53, MSc, 55, PhD(wildlife mgt), 60. *Prof Exp:* Asst, Cornell Univ, 53-55 & 58-60; wildlife biologist, Dept Mines & Resources, Nfld, 55-58; big game biologist, Dept Lands & Forests, NS, 60-63, asst dir wildlife conserv, 63-64, actg dir, 64-65; vis prof, 61-64, assoc prof wildlife biol, 64-70, assoc prof biol, 70-75, dean sci, 75-79, PROF WILDLIFE BIOL, ACADIA UNIV, 70- *Concurrent Pos:* Food & Agr Orgn ecologist, Zambia, 66-67, 72, 74 & 81; resource consult, Eastern Can, 67-; pres, Eastern Ecol Res Ltd, 73-80. *Mem:* Wildlife Soc; Can Soc Wildlife & Fishery Biol; Can Soc Zool. *Res:* Population ecology study of snowshoe hare; general ecological and management studies of white-tailed deer, moose, weasel, fox, Hungarian partridge, beaver and lynx; forest-wildlife interrelationships and population ecology; resource and environmental planning studies. *Mailing Add:* Dept of Biol Acadia Univ Wolfville Can

DODDS, DONALD JAMES, b Everett, Wash, Jan 20, 34; c 6. GEOTECHNICAL ENGINEERING, CIVIL ENGINEERING. *Educ:* Ore State Univ, BS, 60, MS, 70. *Prof Exp:* Engr, Bechtel Corp, 60-63; field engr construct, Paul Hardeman Co, 63-65; sr engr, Leeds Hill & Jewitt Co, 65-66; res engr, Lockheed Construct Co, 66-67; VPRES, FOUND SCI, INC, 67- *Mem:* Am Soc Civil Engrs; Am Soc Testing Mat; Consult Engr Coun; Int Soc Rock Mech. *Res:* In situ testing of rock and soil; support of underground caverns. *Mailing Add:* Found Sci Inc 1630 SW Morrison Portland OR 97205

DODDS, JAMES ALLAN, b Sunderland, UK, June 29, 47. PLANT VIROLOGY. *Educ:* Leeds Univ, BSc, 69; McGill Univ, MSc, 72, PhD(plant path), 74. *Prof Exp:* Nat Res Coun Can fel, Agr Can Res Sta, Vancouver, 74-76; asst plant pathologist virol, Conn Agr Exp Sta, 76-80; ASST PROF, UNIV CALIF, RIVERSIDE, 80- *Mem:* Am Phytopathological Soc; Can Phytopathological Soc. *Res:* Viruses of algae and fungi and their use in biological control; consequences of mixed virus infections on viruses and plants; cross protection, induced resistance, vegetable and citrus viruses. *Mailing Add:* Dept Plant Path Univ Calif Riverside CA 92521

DODDS, STANLEY A, b Toledo, Ore, Jan 26, 47. SOLID STATE PHYSICS. *Educ:* Harvey Mudd Col, BS, 68; Cornell Univ, PhD(physics), 75. *Prof Exp:* Asst res physicist, Univ Calif, Los Angeles, 74-77; asst prof, 77-82, ASSOC PROF PHYSICS, RICE UNIV, 82- *Mem:* Am Phys Soc. *Res:* Muon spin rotation in metallic systems. *Mailing Add:* Physics Dept Rice Univ Houston TX 77251

DODDS, WELLESLEY JAMISON, b Faulkton, SDak, Oct 18, 15; m 37; c 4. ELECTRICAL ENGINEERING. *Educ:* SDak State Col, BS, 38; Univ Kans, MS, 41. *Prof Exp:* Asst physics, SDak State Col, 38-39, Univ Kans, 39-40 & Univ Ill, 41-42; power tube design engr, Victor Div, Radio Corp Am, Pa, 42-44, res engr, Labs Div, NJ, 45-54, mgr microwave solid state eng, 63-66, mem staff electronic components & devices, 66-70, mem tech planning staff, Picture Tube Div, 70-76, dir, prod quality, safety & reliability assurance & dir, prod qual, oper & analysis, 76-81; CONSULT QUAL ASSURANCE & RELIABILITY, 81- *Concurrent Pos:* Consult, US Dept Defense, 55- & Nat Acad Sci, 63. *Mem:* AAAS; Inst Elec & Electronics Engrs. *Res:* Invention and research in microwave radio; electrets; biophysics of nerve. *Mailing Add:* RCA Corp Picture Tube Div New Holland Pike Lancaster PA 17604

DODERER, GEORGE CHARLES, b Monticello, NY, Aug 3, 28; m 58; c 4. CHEMISTRY. *Educ:* Union Univ (NY), BS, 50; Univ Louisville, MS, 73. *Prof Exp:* Asst physics prog, Gen Elec Co, NY, 50-51, spectroscopist metals, Mass, 51-52, researcher vacuum insulation, Pa, 52-54, instrumental analyst, Ky, 54-55; guest worker polymers, Nat Bur Stand, 56-57; instrumental chem analyst, 58-68, mgr anal chem, 68-71, mgr chem develop, 71-77, mgr chem res & develop, 77-79, MGR ENG CHEM, GEN ELEC CO, 80- *Mem:* Soc Appl Spectros; Am Chem Soc; Sigma Xi. *Res:* Instrumental chemical analysis; chemistry of hermetic refrigerating systems; flat panel vacuum thermal insulation; vacuum technology; chemistry of laundering and dishwashing. *Mailing Add:* Gen Elec Co Appliance Park 35-1101 Louisville KY 40225

DODGE, ALICE HRIBAL, b Fullerton, Calif; c 2. ANATOMY, CELL BIOLOGY. *Educ:* Univ Calif, Berkeley, AB, 48, MA, 51; Stanford Univ, PhD(anat), 69. *Prof Exp:* Res asst, 60-68, RES ASSOC ANAT, SCH MED, STANFORD UNIV, 70- *Concurrent Pos:* Nat Cancer Inst grant, 71-76; from instr to assoc prof, Calif Col Podiat Med, 69-78, prof, 78- *Mem:* AAAS; NY Acad Sci; Am Soc Cell Biol; Histochem Soc; Am Asn Cancer Res. *Res:* Subcellular localization of enzymes; light and electron microscopic, electrophoretic, cytogenetic and immunohistolcyto chemical study of androgen/estrogen and estrogen induced hamster tumors and hamster fetal tissues. *Mailing Add:* 2038 Maryland St Redwood City CA 94061

DODGE, AUSTIN ANDERSON, b Waukesha Co, Wis, Aug 27, 06; m 38. PHARMACY. *Educ:* Valparaiso Univ, PhC, 28; Univ Wis, BS, 38, PhD(pharmaceut chem), 41. *Prof Exp:* From instr to assoc prof pharm, Philadelphia Col Pharm, 41-48; prof pharmaceut chem, Sch Pharm, 48-60, prof pharmacog, 60-72, assoc dean, 63-72, EMER ASSOC DEAN PHARM, UNIV MISS, 72- *Mem:* Am Inst Hist Pharm; Am Pharmaceut Asn; AAAS. *Res:* Plant chemistry; volatile oils; derivatives of isophorone; applications of the aerosol wetting agents in pharmaceutical formulations for creams and lotions. *Mailing Add:* 808 S 11th St Oxford MS 38655

DODGE, CARROLL WILLIAM, b Danby, Vt, Jan 20, 95; m 25; c 2. BOTANY. *Educ:* Middlebury Col, AB, 15, AM, 16; Washington Univ, PhD(bot), 18. *Hon Degrees:* Hon Dr, Univ Guatemala, 42 & Univ Chile, 50. *Prof Exp:* From instr to asst prof bot, Brown Univ, 19-21; instr, Harvard Univ, 21-24, asst prof & cur Farlow Libr & Herbarium, 24-31; prof, 31-63, EMER PROF BOT, SHAW SCH BOT, WASHINGTON UNIV, 63-; PROF BOT, UNIV VT, 63- *Concurrent Pos:* Asst prof, Univ Calif, 21; mem Harvard bot exped, Gaspe Peninsula, 23; fel, Inst Res Trop Am, 25; Guggenheim fel, Costa Rica, 29-30, Europe, 30-31; mycologist, Mo Bot Garden, 31-63; mem Washington Univ bot exped, Panama, 34-35 & Costa Rica, 36; US exchange prof, Univ Guatemala, 40-42, La State Univ, 49, Univ Chile, 50 & Univ Brazil, 59-60; vpres sect mycol, Int Cong Microbiol, 50. *Mem:* AAAS; Bot Soc Am; Am Micros Soc (pres, 38); Am Phytopath Soc; Mycol Soc Am. *Res:* Mycology; Hymenogastraceae; Plectascales; fungi pathogenic to man; systematic lichenology; flora of tropical America, Africa and Antarctica. *Mailing Add:* Dept of Botany Univ of Vt Burlington VT 05401

DODGE, CHARLES FREMONT, b Dallas, Tex, May 28, 24; m 50; c 2. GEOLOGY. *Educ:* Southern Methodist Univ, BS, 49, MS, 52; Univ NMex, PhD, 67. *Prof Exp:* Valuation engr, T Y Pickette, 47-48; instr geol, Arlington Col, 48-50; geologist, Concho Petrol Co, 50-52 & Intex Oil Co, 52-53; district geologist, Am Trading & Prod Corp, 53-57; from assoc prof to prof geol, Univ Tex, Arlington, 57-77, chmn dept, 74-76; SR SCIENTIST, ISEM-SMU, 77- *Concurrent Pos:* Consult, Core Labs, 58, McCord & Assocs & Lewis Eng, 59, Atlantic Refining Co, 59-61, Sun Oil Co, 66-67, Coastal Plains Oil, 68, Tex Steel, 69 & Sonatrach (Algeria), 69-70; NSF sci fac fel, 65-66; res proj 91A, Am Petrol Inst, 66-70; vpres explor, Arkomagas Co, 77- *Mem:* Am Asn Petrol Geol; Soc Econ Paleontologists & Mineralogists; Am Inst Prof Geol; Soc Explor Geophys; Soc Independent Prof Earth Sci. *Res:* Reservoir geology; clastic sedimentology. *Mailing Add:* 1301 Briarwood Arlington TX 76013

DODGE, DONALD W(ILLIAM), b Worcester, Mass, Aug 29, 28; m 50; c 2. CHEMICAL ENGINEERING. *Educ:* Worcester Polytech Inst, BS, 50, MS, 52; Univ Del, PhD(chem eng), 58. *Prof Exp:* Chem engr, Arthur D Little, Inc, 52-53; res engr, 57-60, staff engr, 60-62, supvr res, 62-63, mgr, 63-66, tech supt, 66-67, mfg supt, 67-68, prod mgr film dept, 68-71, tech mgr, 71-75, BUS MGR, POLYMER PROD DEPT, E I DU PONT DE NEMOURS & CO, 75- *Mem:* Am Inst Chem Engrs; NY Acad Sci. *Res:* Plastics processing and technology; fluid mechanics; rheology. *Mailing Add:* Polymer Prod Dept E I du Pont de Nemours & Co Wilmington DE 19898

DODGE, E(LDON) R(AYMOND), b Eland, Wis, June 17, 10; m 39; c 3. CIVIL ENGINEERING. *Educ:* Univ Wis, BS, 32, MS, 35, PhD(civil eng), 42. *Prof Exp:* Engr, Wis Hwy Comn, 32-33; asst, Univ Wis, 33-35; instr civil eng, Case Inst Technol, 35-37 & Univ Wis, 37-43; div engr, Fairbanks, Morse

& Co, 43-46; prof civil eng & eng mech, 46-76, EMER PROF CIVIL ENG & ENG MECH, MONT STATE UNIV, 76- *Mem:* Fel Am Soc Civil Engrs; Am Soc Eng Educ. *Res:* Hydraulics; hydrology. *Mailing Add:* 3755-3 Vista Campana N Oceanside CA 92056

DODGE, FRANKLIN C W, b Oakland, Calif, Sept 18, 34; m 53; c 5. GEOLOGY. *Educ:* Univ Calif, Berkeley, BA, 59; Stanford Univ, MS, 60, PhD(geol), 63. *Prof Exp:* GEOLOGIST, US GEOL SURV, 63- *Mem:* Geol Soc Am; Mineral Soc Am; Mineral Asn Can; Norweg Geol Soc. *Res:* Geochemical and mineralogical study of the Sierra Nevada batholith, California. *Mailing Add:* US Geol Surv 345 Middlefield Rd Menlo Park CA 94025

DODGE, FRANKLIN TIFFANY, b Uniontown, Pa, Nov 11, 36; m 68; c 2. MECHANICAL ENGINEERING, FLUID MECHANICS. *Educ:* Univ Tenn, BS, 60; Carnegie Inst Tech, MS, 61, PhD(mech eng), 63. *Prof Exp:* Coop engr, Pittsburgh DesMoines Steel Co, 56-59; res asst fluid mech, Carnegie Inst Tech, 60-61; sr res engr dept mech sci, Southwest Res Inst, 63-70, group leader fluid mech & eng anal, 70-71; asst prof mech & aerospace eng, Univ Tenn, Knoxville, 71-73; STAFF ENGR, SOUTHWEST RES INST, 73- *Mem:* Assoc fel Am Inst Aeronaut & Astronaut; fel Am Soc Mech Engrs. *Res:* Hydrodynamics; nuclear reactor safety; lubrication; tanker ship safety; fluid dynamics of pollution; spacecraft propellant management. *Mailing Add:* Div of Eng Sci 6220 Culebra Rd San Antonio TX 78284

DODGE, HAROLD T, b Seattle, Wash, May 20, 24; m 51; c 2. INTERNAL MEDICINE, CARDIOLOGY. *Educ:* Harvard Univ, MD, 48. *Prof Exp:* Intern med, Peter Bent Brigham Hosp, Mass, 48-49; resident, King County Hosp, Wash, 49-50; asst, Sch Med, Univ Wash, 50-51; clin investr, Nat Heart Inst, Md, 51-56; asst prof, Sch Med, Duke Univ, 56-57; from asst prof to prof, Sch Med, Univ Wash, 57-66; prof & dir cardiovasc div, Med Ctr, Univ Ala, 66-69; PROF MED & DIR CARDIOVASC RES & TRAINING CTR, SCH MED, UNIV WASH, 69-, CO-DIR DIV CARDIOL, 71- *Concurrent Pos:* Res fel med, Sch Med, Univ Wash, 50-51; fel cardiol, Emory Univ, 52-53; instr, Sch Med, Georgetown Univ, 53-56; chief cardiol, Durham Vet Admin Hosp, 56-57 & Seattle Vet Admin Hosp, 57-66. *Mem:* Am Fedn Clin Res; Am Soc Clin Invest; Asn Univ Cardiol; Asn Am Physicians. *Res:* Cardiovascular research; physiological aspects of heart disease; epidemiology of cardiovascular disease; drug research. *Mailing Add:* Dept of Med Univ of Wash Sch of Med RG-20 Seattle WA 98195

DODGE, JAMES STANLEY, b Washington, DC, June 22, 39; m 61; c 2. COLLOID CHEMISTRY, RHEOLOGY. *Educ:* Case Inst Technol, BS, 61, MS, 66; Case Western Reserve Univ, PhD(macromolecular sci), 69. *Prof Exp:* Res engr, TRW, Inc, 61-63; sr res chemist, Sherwin-Williams Co, 69-74, staff scientist, 74-76; res assoc, 76-80, SR RES & DEVELOP ASSOC, B F GOODRICH CHEM CO, 80- *Mem:* Am Chem Soc; Soc Rheol. *Res:* Colloidal properties of polymer latexes; rheology of polymers and colloids. *Mailing Add:* B F Goodrich Chem Co Tech Ctr PO Box 122 Avon Lake OH 44012

DODGE, PATRICK WILLIAM, b Sleepy Eye, Minn. June 2, 36; m 62; c 3. PHARMACOLOGY. *Educ:* Univ Minn, BS, 59, PhD(pharmacol), 67. *Prof Exp:* Scientist drug metab, 67-69; from group leader to head anti-inflammatory analgesic sect, 69-73, dept mgr pharmacodynamics, 73-74, dept mgr pharmacol, 74-75; dept mgr pharmacol & med chem, 75-77, DEPT MGR PHARMACOL ABBOTT LABS, 77- Planning and administration of research associated with discovery of medicinal agents for therapeutic use in cardiovascular diseases, inflammation, and diseases of the central nervous system. *Mem:* Am Soc Pharmacol & Exp Therapeut; Sigma Xi. *Mailing Add:* D-464 AP-9 Abbott Labs 1400 Sheridan Rd North Chicago IL 60064

DODGE, PHILIP ROGERS, b Beverly, Mass, Mar 16, 23; m 47; c 3. PEDIATRICS. *Educ:* Univ Rochester, MD, 48. *Prof Exp:* From instr to asst prof neurol, Harvard Med Sch, 57-67; PROF PEDIAT & NEUROL & HEAD EDWARD MALLINCKRODT DEPT PEDIAT, SCH MED, WASH UNIV, 67- *Concurrent Pos:* Pediat neurologist, Boston Lying-In Hosp, 61-67; investr, J P Kennedy, Jr Lab Study Ment Retardation, 63-67; consult, Fernald State Sch Retarded Children, 63-67; mem, Surgeon Gen Comt Epilepsy, USPHS, 66-70, mem child develop & ment retardation rev comt, 66-70, mem gen clin res ctrs comt, 71-74; med dir, St Louis Children's Hosp, 67-; assoc neurologist, Barnes & Allied Hosps, 67-; mem, Ment Health Comn, State of Mo, 74-78 & Nat Adv Child Health & Human Develop Coun, NIH, 74-77. *Honors & Awards:* Hower Award, Child Neurol Soc, 78. *Mem:* Am Acad Neurol; Am Neurol Asn; Soc Pediat Res; Am Pediat Soc. *Res:* Pediatric neurology; clinical and laboratory investigations of neurologic disorders of childhood, especially infectious, nutritional and metabolic diseases. *Mailing Add:* Dept of Pediat PO Box 14871 St Louis MO 63178

DODGE, RICHARD E, b Machias, Maine, Mar 4, 47; m 73; c 2. CORAL REEF ASSESSMENT. *Educ:* Univ Maine, BA, 69; Yale Univ, MPhil, 73, PhD(geol & geophys), 78. *Prof Exp:* Cur paleontol, Peabody Mus Natural Hist, Yale Univ, 78; asst prof, 78-81, ASSOC PROF OCEAN SCI, NOVA UNIV OCEAN SCI CTR, 81- *Concurrent Pos:* Geol Soc Am grant, 74-75; NSF grants, 75-77 & 79-81, Environ Protection Agency grant, 80-82, Nat Oceanic Atmospheric Admin grant, 80-82 & Exxon, Bermuda Biol Sta grant, 81-82; subcontract, Dept Energy-Ocean Thermal Energy Conversion, Univ Miami, 80-81; field work, Red Sea-Saudia Arabia, Vicques, Puerto Rico, St Croix & US Virgin Islands. *Res:* Ecology, paleoecology, paleoclimatology, and paleobiology of corals and coral reefs; relation of coral growth rate to the environment for recent and fossil ecology studies; geology of coral reefs to include structure, zonation, morphology, dating, sea level changes. *Mailing Add:* Nova Univ Ocean Sci Ctr 8000 N Ocean Dr Dania FL 33004

DODGE, RICHARD PATRICK, b Wichita, Kans, Mar 17, 32. PHYSICAL CHEMISTRY. *Educ:* Univ Wichita, BS, 54; Univ Calif, PhD, 58. *Prof Exp:* Asst chem, Univ Calif, 54-55, assoc, 55-56, asst, Lawrence Radiation Lab, 56-58; res chemist, Union Carbide Res Inst, 58-64; asst prof chem, 64-69,

assoc prof, 69-78, PROF CHEM, UNIV OF THE PAC, 78- *Mem:* AAAS; Am Crystallog Soc. *Res:* X-ray diffraction; molecular structure; quantum chemistry; computer calculations. *Mailing Add:* Dept of Chem Univ of the Pac Stockton CA 95211

DODGE, WARREN FRANCIS, b Scottsdale, Pa, May 5, 28; m 49; c 2. PEDIATRICS, PREVENTIVE MEDICINE. *Educ:* Univ Tenn, BS, 53, MD, 55. *Prof Exp:* Intern, Jefferson Davis Hosp, 55-56; resident pediat, Baylor Col Med, 56-58; from asst prof to assoc prof, 60-72, PROF PEDIAT, UNIV TEX MED BR GALVESTON, 72- *Concurrent Pos:* Jessie Jones fel, 58; fel renal dis of childhood, Baylor Col Med, 58-60. *Mem:* Soc Pediat Res; Am Soc Pediat. *Res:* Clinical pharmacology; epidemiology of renal disease and hypertension; delivery of health care. *Mailing Add:* Dept of Pediat Univ of Tex Med Br Galveston TX 77550

DODGE, WILLIAM HOWARD, b Moss Point, Miss, Feb 20, 43; div; c 1. ONCOLOGY. *Educ:* Millsaps Col, BS, 65; Univ Miss, MS, 67, PhD(microbiol), 70. *Prof Exp:* Asst prof microbiol, Winston-Salem State Univ, 73-75; res asst prof med, 75-81, ASSOC PROF EXP MED, BOWMAN GRAY SCH MED, WAKE FOREST UNIV, 81- *Concurrent Pos:* Fel, Vet Admin Hosp & Sch Med, Univ Fla, 70-73; vis scientist, Tumor Biol Lab, Nat Cancer Inst, 76. *Mem:* Int Asn Comparative Res Leukemia; Int Soc Exp Hematol; Am Asn Cancer Res; Sigma Xi. *Res:* Factors which regulate the growth and differentiation of hematopoietic cells; how alterations in the levels of various factors contribute to leukemia progression; leukemogenic oncornaviruses. *Mailing Add:* Hemat/Oncol Sect Dept of Med Bowman Gray Sch of Med Winston-Salem NC 27103

DODGE, WILLIAM R, b Oregon City, Ore, Mar 21, 29; m 55. PHYSICS. *Educ:* Stanford Univ, BS, 56, PhD(physics), 62. *Prof Exp:* PHOTONUCLEAR PHYSICIST, NAT BUR STAND, 61- *Mem:* Am Phys Soc. *Res:* Electron and photon induced nuclear disintegration reactions; semiconductor radiation detectors; linear accelerator physics. *Mailing Add:* 8200 Raymond Lane Potomac MD 20854

DODGEN, CHARLES LEE, biochemistry, deceased

DODGEN, DURWARD F, b Winnsboro, Tex, Apr 10, 31; m 54; c 2. CHEMISTRY. *Educ:* N Tex State Univ, BS, 52; Univ Miss, MS, 57. *Prof Exp:* Res chemist, Phillips Petrol Co, 52-55; anal chemist, Am Pharmaceut Asn Lab, 57-59; med serv rep, Chas Pfizer & Co, Inc, 59-60; pub coordr, Warren-Teed Pharmaceut Div, Rohm and Haas Co, 60-61; asst dir, Food Chem Codex, Nat Acad Sci-Nat Res Coun, 61-65, assoc dir, 65-66; asst dir nat formulary & asst dir sci div, Am Pharmaceut Asn, 66-69, assoc ed, J Pharmaceut Sci, 67-69; dir, Food Chem Codex, Dir GRAS & Food Additives Surv & Staff Officer, Food & Nutrit Bd, Div Biol Sci, Nat Acad Sci-Nat Res Coun, 69-81; STAFF SCIENTIST, KELLER & HECKMAN LAW OFFICES, 81- *Concurrent Pos:* Observer, Joint Expert Comt Food Additives, Food & Agr Orgn, WHO, 64, 65, 67 & 69-72, mem, 73-; mem, Nat Formulary Bd, 66-75; mem, US Adopted Names Coun, 67-69 & 74-77; mem adv panel pharmaceut ingredients, US Pharmacopoeia, 70-75; assoc mem food additives comt, Int Union Pure & Appl Chem, 71-75, titular mem, 75-80; mem-at-large, US Pharmacopeial Conv, 80-; mem fac, Toxicol Forum, 81; mem adv comt, Int Prog Chem Safety, Food & Drug Admin, 81. *Mem:* Am Chem Soc; Inst Food Technologists. *Res:* Food additive specifications and patterns of use; pharmaceutical analysis; standards for food additives and drugs. *Mailing Add:* Keller & Heckman Law Offices 1150 17th St NW Washington DC 20036

DODGEN, HAROLD WARREN, b Blue Eye, Mo, Aug 31, 21; m 45; c 3. CHEMICAL PHYSICS. *Educ:* Univ Calif, BS, 43, PhD(phys chem), 46. *Prof Exp:* Asst, Manhattan Dist Proj, Univ Calif, 43-46; Inst Nuclear Studies fel, Univ Chicago, 46-48; from asst prof to assoc prof, 48-59, dir nuclear reactor proj, 55-68, chmn chem physics prog, 68-77, PROF CHEM, WASH STATE UNIV, 59- *Mem:* Am Chem Soc; Am Phys Soc; AAAS; Sigma Xi. *Res:* Theory of ammonium chloride phase transition; complex ions of iron and thorium with fluoride; neutron scattering; radioactive exchange; quenching of fluorescence; application of radioisotopes in physical chemistry; spectrochemical analysis; nuclear magnetic and quadrupole resonance. *Mailing Add:* Dept Chem Wash State Univ Pullman WA 99164

DODINGTON, SVEN HENRY MARRIOTT, b Vancouver, BC, May 22, 12; nat US; m 40; c 3. NAVIGATION, ELECTRONICS. *Educ:* Stanford Univ, AB, 34. *Prof Exp:* From jr engr to head elec dept, Scophony Ltd, London, 35-41; dept head, Int Tel & Tel Fed Labs, 41-50, div head, 51-54, lab dir, 54-58, vpres, 58-69, asst tech dir, 69-75, AVIONICS CONSULT, INT TEL & TEL CORP, 75- *Honors & Awards:* Pioneer Award, Inst Elec & Electronics Engrs, 80. *Mem:* Assoc fel Am Inst Aeronaut & Astronaut; fel Inst Elec & Electronics Engrs; Am Inst Navig. *Res:* Navigation; countermeasures; television; microelectronics. *Mailing Add:* Int Tel & Tel Corp 320 Park Ave New York NY 10022

DODSON, B C, b Magnolia, Ark, Dec 6, 24; m 46; c 3. INORGANIC CHEMISTRY, SCIENCE EDUCATION. *Educ:* Ark State Teachers Col, BSE, 48; Univ Ark, MS, 58; Kans State Teachers Col, EdS, 61; Univ Okla, EdD, 69. *Prof Exp:* High sch teacher, Ark, 48-54 & Tex, 54-55; teacher, Ark, 55-60, sci coordr, 56-60; asst prof chem, 60-70, actg head dept chem, 66-69, chmn div sci & math, 70-73, PROF CHEM & SCI EDUC, SOUTHERN ARK UNIV, 70-, DEAN, SCH SCI & TECHNOL, 77- *Concurrent Pos:* NSF sci fac fel, 65-66. *Mem:* Am Chem Soc; Nat Sci Teachers Asn; Nat Educ Asn; Asn Educ Teachers Sci (treas, 70-71). *Res:* Analysis of the objectives, materials and methods used in the introductory college chemistry course in selected colleges and universities; evaluation of individualized science modules. *Mailing Add:* Southern Ark Univ PO Box 1397 Magnolia AR 71753

DODSON, CHARLES LEON, JR, b Knoxville, Tenn, Mar 15, 35; m 58; c 1. PHYSICAL CHEMISTRY. *Educ:* Emory & Henry Col, BS, 57; Univ Tenn, MS, 62, PhD(chem), 63. *Prof Exp:* Asst prof chem, Univ Ala, Huntsville, 66-67, head dept, 68-70, assoc prof, 67-81; TECH SUPPORT SPECIALIST, BECKMAN INSTRUMENTS, INC, 81- *Concurrent Pos:* European Off, US Off Aerospace Agency grant, Univ Birmingham, 63-64; Nat Res Coun fel, Can, 64-66; vis, Dept Theoret Chem, Univ Oxford, 72-73. *Mem:* AAAS; Am Chem Soc; Am Phys Soc. *Res:* Infrared, microwave and electron spin resonance spectroscopy; liquid scintillation. *Mailing Add:* Dept of Chem Univ of Ala Huntsville AL 35807

DODSON, CHESTER LEE, b Eastland, Tenn, Dec 18, 21; m 47; c 2. GEOLOGY, HYDROLOGY. *Educ:* WVa Univ, BS, 50, MS, 53. *Prof Exp:* Geologist, US Geol Surv, 52-63; ASST PROF HYDROL & DIR WATER RES INST, WVA UNIV, 63- *Mem:* AAAS; Geol Soc Am; Am Geophys Union; Nat Water Well Asn; Am Water Resources Asn. *Res:* Groundwater geology; geology of mineral deposits; water resources. *Mailing Add:* Water Res Inst WVa Univ Morgantown WV 26506

DODSON, EDWARD O, b Fargo, NDak, Apr 26, 16; m 40; c 6. EVOLUTIONARY BIOLOGY, GENETICS. *Educ:* Carleton Col, BA, 39; Univ Calif, PhD(zool), 47. *Prof Exp:* Asst zool, Univ Calif, 39-46; instr, Dominican Col, 46-47; from instr to assoc prof, Univ Notre Dame, 47-57; assoc prof, 57-59, PROF BIOL, UNIV OTTAWA, 59- *Concurrent Pos:* Lectr, Univ Calif, Los Angeles, 45; vis prof, Univ Montreal, 62, Fondation Teilhard de Chardin, Paris, 71-72, Sta Zool, Italy, 79, Lab Arago, France, 79, Sta biol d'Arcachon, France, 79 & Sta biol de Roscoff, France, 79; vis res prof, Roswell Park Mem Inst, 64-65. *Mem:* AAAS; Genetics Soc Am; Soc Study Evolution; Genetics Soc Can. *Res:* Chromosomes of vertebrates; evolution; mutation; tissue culture. *Mailing Add:* Dept of Biol Univ of Ottawa Ottawa Can

DODSON, NORMAN ELMER, b Gregory, Ky, Oct 18, 09; m 36; c 1. MATHEMATICS. *Educ:* Berea Col, AB, 33; Univ Ala, AM, 47. *Prof Exp:* High sch teacher, Ky, 33-34 & 35-37; headmaster & teacher math, Jefferson Mil Col, 38-42; assoc prof, Newberry Col, 42-45; asst, Univ Ala, 45-46, asst prof statist, 46-47; assoc prof math, Lenoir-Rhyne Col, 47-57; from asst prof to assoc prof, Wittenberg Univ, 57-75; adj prof math, 75-77, INSTR MATH, LANDER COL, 79-; RETIRED. *Concurrent Pos:* High sch teacher, Fla, 37-39. *Mem:* Math Asn Am. *Res:* Algebra and new trends in mathematical education. *Mailing Add:* 139 Ridgewood Circle Greenwood SC 29646

DODSON, PETER, b Ross, Calif, Aug 20, 46; m 68; c 2. PALEOBIOLOGY, VERTEBRATE ANATOMY. *Educ:* Univ Ottawa, BSc, 68; Univ Alta, MSc, 70; Yale Univ, PhD(geol), 74. *Prof Exp:* Curatorial assoc vert paleont, Peabody Mus Nat Hist, Yale Univ, 73-74; assoc anat, 74-75, ASST PROF VET ANAT, SCH VET MED, UNIV PA, 75- *Mem:* Soc Vert Paleont; Paleont Soc; Am Soc Ichthyol & Herpet; Soc Study Evolution; Soc Syst Zool. *Res:* Relationships of morphometric anatomy to function, behavior and ecology of living and extinct vertebrates; taphonomic biases in the fossil record; dinosaurs. *Mailing Add:* Lab Anat Dept Animal Biol Sch of Vet Med Univ of Pa Philadelphia PA 19104

DODSON, RAYMOND MONROE, b West Hazleton, Pa, July 8, 20; m 43; c 4. ORGANIC CHEMISTRY. *Educ:* Franklin & Marshall Col, BS, 42; Northwestern Univ, PhD(org chem), 47. *Prof Exp:* Asst prof org chem, Univ Minn, 47-51; chemist, G D Searle & Co, 51-55, asst to dir chem res, 55-60; PROF CHEM, UNIV MINN, MINNEAPOLIS, 60- *Concurrent Pos:* Mem endocrinol study sect, NIH, 62-66. *Mem:* AAAS; fel Am Chem Soc; NY Acad Sci; The Chem Soc. *Res:* Heterocyclic compounds; organic sulfur-containing compounds; steroids; stereochemistry of cholesterol and its derivatives; fermentation of steroids; reactions of sulfur monoxide and disulfur monoxide. *Mailing Add:* Dept of Chem Univ of Minn Minneapolis MN 55455

DODSON, RICHARD WOLFORD, b Kirksville, Mo, Jan 15, 15; m 37; c 2. PHYSICAL CHEMISTRY. *Educ:* Calif Inst Technol, BS, 36; Johns Hopkins Univ, PhD(chem), 39. *Prof Exp:* Am Can Co fel, Johns Hopkins Univ, 36-40; Nat Res fel, Calif Inst Technol, 40, mem staff, Nat Defense Res Comt Proj, Calif Inst Technol & Northwestern Univ, 40-43; group leader & later asst div leader, Los Alamos Lab, NMex, 43-45; asst prof chem, Calif Inst Technol, 46-47; chmn dept chem, 47-68, SR CHEMIST, BROOKHAVEN NAT LAB, 48-, PROF CHEM, COLUMBIA UNIV, 53- *Concurrent Pos:* Assoc prof chem, Columbia Univ, 47-53; secy, Gen Adv Comt, AEC, 51-56. *Mem:* AAAS; Am Phys Soc; Am Chem Soc. *Res:* Reaction kinetics; radiochemistry. *Mailing Add:* Dept of Chem Brookhaven Nat Lab Upton NY 11973

DODSON, ROBIN ALBERT, b Palmer, Alaska, Dec 15, 40; m 60; c 5. PHARMACOLOGY. *Educ:* Eastern Wash Univ, BS, 70; Wash State Univ, PhD(pharmacol sci), 78; Idaho State Univ, BS, 81. *Prof Exp:* Ward supvr, Eastern State Hosp, 65-71; bio-lab coordr, Eastern Wash Univ, 70-71; teaching asst pharmacol, Wash State Univ, 72-75; asst prof, 75-80, ASSOC PROF PHARMACOL, COL PHARM, IDAHO STATE UNIV, 80- *Concurrent Pos:* Consult, State Idaho, Dept Health & Welfare, Substance Abuse & Drug Abuse Prev, 76-; consult, Alcohol Rehab, Ctr I, 76- *Mem:* AAAS; Am Asn Col Pharm; Sigma Xi. *Res:* Pharmacology of commonly used chemicals on various aspects of the central nervous system; how ethanol and barbiturates effect the biochemistry of the brain. *Mailing Add:* Col of Pharm Idaho State Univ Pocatello ID 83209

DODSON, RONALD FRANKLIN, b Paris, Tex, Feb 14, 42; m 65. ELECTRON MICROSCOPY, CYTOLOGY. *Educ:* ETex State Univ, BA, 64, MA, 65; Tex A&M Univ, PhD(biol electron micros), 69. *Prof Exp:* Asst instr biol, ETex State Univ, 64-65; instr, Electron Micros Ctr, Tex A&M Univ, 65-69; res assoc anat, Med Sch, Univ Tex, San Antonio, 69-70; asst prof neurol, Baylor Col Med, 70-77; CHIEF, DEPTS CELL BIOL & ENVIRON SCI, UNIV TEX HEALTH CTR, 77- *Concurrent Pos:* Res fel, Electron Micros Ctr, Tex A&M Univ, 65-69; fel stroke coun, Am Heart Asn. *Mem:* AAAS; Am Chem Soc; Am Thoracic Soc; Int Acad Path; NY Acad Sci. *Res:* Ultrastructural studies of experimental pathology in respiratory diseases and environmental sciences and cerebrovascular diseases. *Mailing Add:* Depts of Cell Biol & Environ Sci PO Box 2003 Tyler TX 75710

DODSON, VANCE HAYDEN, JR, b Oklahoma City, Okla, June 12, 22; m 53. INORGANIC CHEMISTRY. *Educ:* Univ Toledo, BChE, 44, MS, 47; Purdue Univ, PhD(chem), 52. *Prof Exp:* Mat engr, Curtiss-Wright Corp, 44-45; from instr to assoc prof chem, Univ Toledo, 45-57; asst instr, Purdue Univ, 48-50; res chemist, Elec Autolite Co, Ohio, 57-58, res mgr, Battery Div, 58-61; res mgr construct specialties, 61-63, dir res, Construct Mat Div, 63-70, TECH SERV DIR, DEWEY & ALMY CHEM CO, CAMBRIDGE, 70- *Mem:* Am Chem Soc; Am Ceramic Soc; Am Concrete Inst; Am Soc Testing & Mat. *Res:* Silicates; elastomers; organic coatings; lead alloys; electrochemical sources of energy; portland cement; concrete. *Mailing Add:* W R Grace & Co 62 Whittemore Ave Cambridge MA 02140

DODSON, VERNON N, b Benton Harbor, Mich, Feb 19, 23; m 55; c 5. TOXICOLOGY, BIOCHEMISTRY. *Educ:* Marquette Univ, MD, 51; Univ Mich, BS, 52; Am Bd Prev Med, cert occup med, 69. *Prof Exp:* Asst pathologist, Sch Med, Johns Hopkins Univ, 53-54; asst resident internal med, Univ Hosp, Univ Mich, Ann Arbor, 54-55, resident, 55-56, jr clin instr, 56-57; instr internal med, Univ Mich, 57-61, asst prof internal & indust med & toxicol, 61-64, assoc prof, 65-71; prof med & environ med, Med Col Wis, 71-72; vis prof prev med, Med Sch, Univ Wis, 73-74; prof prev med, Grad Sch, Univ Minn, Rochester-Minneapolis, 74-77; PROF PREV MED, MED SCH, UNIV WIS-MADISON, 77-, DIR UNIV HOSP EMPLOYEE HEALTH SERV, 77-, ACTG DIR CTR ENVIRON TOXICOL, HEALTH SCI DIV, 78- *Concurrent Pos:* Lectr, Inst Social Work, Univ Mich, 57-58, Sch Dent, 57-58, Sch Nursing, 58-60 & Dept Postgrad Med, 59, res assoc, Clin Radioisotope Unit, Med Sch, 50-60, res assoc, Inst Indust Health, 60-71; attend physician internal med, US Vet Admin Hosp, Ann Arbor, 63-71; consult, Gen Motors Corp Tech Ctr, Warren, Mich, 63-65 & 72-; mem numerous comts, Univ Mich Med Ctr, 63-71; med dir, Delco Electronics Div, Gen Motors Corp, Wis, 71-72; assoc physician, Trinity Mem Hosp, Cudahy, Wis, 71-73; mem comt toxicity determinants & lists, Bur Occup Safety & Health, USPHS, HEW, 71-72; consult, Atty Gen, Dept Natural Resources & Dept Health & Social Servs, State of Wis, 73-74, Oscar Mayer Co, Madison, 73-74, Forest Prod Div, Forest Serv, USDA, 73- & Nat Inst Occup Safety & Health, Bethesda, Md, 74-; consult plant physician, IBM Co, Rochester, Minn, 76-77; consult occup & environ health, Dept Health & Social Servs, State of Wis, 77-, mem gov's task force occup health & safety, 78-; consult prev med & internal med, Mayo Clin, 74-77, mem res comt, Div Prev Med, Dept Med, 74-77, mem educ comt, 74-77, chmn, 74-75, chmn ad hoc toxicol comt, 74-77, mem comt occup safety & health, 76-77; mem educ comt, Ctr Environ Toxicol, Health Sci Div, Univ Wis, 78-, mem infectious dis control comt, Univ Hosp, 78- *Mem:* AMA; Am Fedn Clin Res; Brit Biochem Soc; fel Am Col Physicians; fel Am Col Prev Med. *Res:* Auto-immunity; immunotoxicology; clinical medicine; thyroid metabolism and diseases; electrophoresis; rheumatology. *Mailing Add:* Dept of Prev Med Univ Wis Med Ctr Madison WI 53706

DOE, BRUCE, b St Paul, Minn, Apr 24, 31; m 58. GEOLOGY. *Educ:* Univ Minn, BS & BGeol E, 54; Mo Sch Mines, MS, 56; Calif Inst Technol, PhD(geol), 60. *Prof Exp:* Fel isotope chem, Geophys Lab, Carnegie Inst, 60-61; geologist, Washington, DC, 61-63, Colo, 63-68, Switz, 68-69, Washington, DC, 69-71, Colo, 71-81, chief, Br Isotope Geol, Colo, 76-81, CHIEF, BR ISOTOPE GEOL, US GEOL SURV, VA, 81- *Concurrent Pos:* Vis investr, Geophys Lab, Carnegie Inst, 61-62 & Japan-US Sci Coop Prog, 65; acad guest, Swiss Fed Inst Technol, Zurich, 68-69; staff scientist, Lunar Sample Prog, NASA, 69-71, mem lunar sample anal planning team, Houston, 70-71, vchmn, 72-73; mem, Comet & Asteroid Missions Adv Panel, 71-72; mem, Comet & Asteroid SciWorking Group, 72-73; coordr earth sci exhibs trailer, US Geol Surv, 72-73, Vernadsky Mem Lectr, Moscow-Leningrad, 76; reporter isotopes, US Geodynamics Comt, Nat Acad Sci, 77-81. *Mem:* AAAS; fel Geol Soc Am; Geochem Soc; Soc Econ Geologists. *Res:* Trace element and isotope geochemistry; radiogenic tracer analysis; volcanology; ore genesis. *Mailing Add:* MS 981 US Geol Surv Reston VA 22092

DOE, FRANK JOSEPH, b Dover, NH, July 14, 37; m 73; c 2. GENETICS. *Educ:* Spring Hill Col, BS, 62; Brandeis Univ, PhD(biol), 68. *Prof Exp:* ASSOC PROF BIOL, UNIV DALLAS, 69- *Mem:* Genetics Soc Am. *Res:* Genetics of the mating-type loci in the yeast, Schizosaccharomyces pombe; general genetics of neurospora. *Mailing Add:* Dept Biol Univ Dallas Irving TX 75061

DOE, RICHARD P, b Minneapolis, Minn, July 21, 26; m 50; c 2. ENDOCRINOLOGY, INTERNAL MEDICINE. *Educ:* Univ Minn, BS, 49, MB, 51, MD, 52, PhD, 66. *Prof Exp:* Instr med, 52-66, assoc prof, 66-69, head endocrine sect, 69-76, PROF MED, MED SCH, UNIV MINN, MINNEAPOLIS, 69- *Concurrent Pos:* Chief chem sect, Minneapolis Vet Admin Hosp, 55-60, chief metab & endocrine sect, 60-69, mem endocrine sect, 76- *Mem:* Endocrine Soc; Am Fedn Clin Res; Am Soc Clin Invest; Cent Soc Clin Res. *Res:* Role of glucocorticoid receptors in modulation of the human immune system; isolation; characterization and measurement of transcortin thyroxine-binding globulin and thyroxine-binding protein; cell mediated immunity in diabetes mellitus. *Mailing Add:* Endocrine Sect Med Ctr Minneapolis Vet Admin Hosp Minneapolis MN 55417

DOEBBLER, GERALD FRANCIS, b San Antonio, Tex, June 27, 32; m 57; c 7. BIOCHEMISTRY. *Educ:* Univ Tex, BS, 53, MA, 54, PhD(chem), 57. *Prof Exp:* Scientist, Biochem Inst Tex, 53-55; res chemist, Linde Co Div, 57-60, sr res chemist, 60-68, sr res chemist, Ocean Systs, Inc, 68-69, res assoc, 69-71, sr res scientist, Corp Res Dept, 71-76, SR RES SCIENTIST, CENT SCI LAB, UNION CARBIDE CORP, 76- *Mem:* Am Chem Soc; Am Soc Microbiol. *Res:* Biophysics, physiology of inert gases and decompression sickness; cryobiology; blood and cell preservation; analytical biochemistry; enzymology; low temperature spectroscopy; sulfur metabolism; biochemical individuality; analytical chemistry. *Mailing Add:* Cent Sci Lab Tech Ctr Union Carbide Corp Saw Mill River Rd Tarrytown NY 10591

DOEDE, JOHN HENRY, b Chicago, Ill, Sept 29, 37; div; c 3. RESOURCE MANAGEMENT. *Educ:* Harvard Univ, AB, 59; Univ Chicago, MS, 62, PhD(chem), 63. *Prof Exp:* Res assoc high energy physics, Argonne Nat Lab, 63-64, asst physicist, 64-66; mgr prog, EMR Comput Div, Electro-Mech Res, Inc, 66-67; pres, Data Int Inc, Minn, 67-70; vpres, Heizer Corp, 70-72; VPRES, FIRST CAPITAL CORP, FIRST CHICAGO INVESTMENT CORP, 72-, DIR, 75- *Mem:* Am Phys Soc; Sigma Xi. *Res:* Weak interaction particle physics; laser development and applications; computer applications and data reduction; monetary investment to support economically viable and applicable research. *Mailing Add:* First Capital Corp Suite 2628 One First Nat Plaza Chicago IL 60670

DOEDEN, GERALD ENNEN, b Onarga, Ill, Oct 16, 18; m 42; c 1. ANALYTICAL CHEMISTRY. *Educ:* Cent Normal Col (Ind), BS, 40; Ind Univ, MA, 50, PhD(anal chem), 65. *Prof Exp:* High sch teacher, Ind, 40-41; analyst, E I du Pont de Nemours & Co, Inc, 41-43; high sch teacher, Ariz, 45-46 & Ind, 46-56; from asst prof to assoc prof chem, 56-70; prof, 70-81, EMER PROF CHEM, BALL STATE UNIV, 81- *Mem:* Fel Am Inst Chem; Am Chem Soc; Soc Appl Spectros. *Res:* Coulometric analysis; gas chromatography; spectrophotometry. *Mailing Add:* Dept of Chem Ball State Univ Muncie IN 47306

DOEDENS, DAVID JAMES, b Milwaukee, Wis, July 2, 42; m 66; c 3. TOXICOLOGY. *Educ:* Univ Wis, BS, 65; Univ Ill, PhD(pharmacol), 71; Am Bd Forensic Toxicol, dipl. *Prof Exp:* Res assoc pharmacol, Sch Med, Ind Univ, Indianapolis, 70-71; res assoc toxicol, 71-72, lectr, 72-74, instr, 74-76, ASST PROF TOXICOL, IND STATE DEPT TOXICOL & TOXICOL DIV, DEPT PHARMACOL, SCH MED, IND UNIV, INDIANAPOLIS, 76-, ASST DIR, IND STATE DEPT TOXICOL, 75- *Mem:* Am Acad Forensic Sci; Sigma Xi. *Res:* Development of analytical methods for drugs; mechanisms of drug toxicity; drug stability in biological media. *Mailing Add:* Dept of Pharmacol Sch of Med Ind Univ 1100 W Michigan St Indianapolis IN 46223

DOEDENS, ROBERT JOHN, b Milwaukee, Wis, Dec 15, 37; m 61; c 2. PHYSICAL CHEMISTRY, INORGANIC CHEMISTRY. *Educ:* Univ Wis-Milwaukee, BS, 61; Univ Wis-Madison, PhD(chem), 65. *Prof Exp:* Res asst & instr chem, Northwestern Univ, 65-66; asst prof, 66-72, assoc prof, 72-78, PROF CHEM, UNIV CALIF, IRVINE, 78- *Mem:* Am Chem Soc; Am Crystallog Asn; The Chem Soc. *Res:* Structural inorganic chemistry; x-ray crystallography; crystal and molecular structures of coordination and organometallic compounds of the transition elements; structure and magnetism in magnetically condensed systems. *Mailing Add:* Dept of Chem Univ of Calif Irvine CA 92664

DOEG, KENNETH ALBERT, b Weehawken, NJ, Aug 5, 31; m 57; c 2. BIOCHEMISTRY. *Educ:* NJ State Teachers Col, AB, 52; Rutgers Univ, PhD(zool), 57. *Prof Exp:* Smith, Kline & French fel, Rutgers Univ, 57-58; fel enzyme inst, Univ Wis, 58-61; asst prof clin sci, Sch Med, Univ Pittsburgh, 61-64; asst prof zool, 64-69, assoc prof, 69-77, PROF BIOL, UNIV CONN, 77- *Mem:* AAAS; Am Chem Soc; Soc Study Reproduction; Endocrine Soc; Am Soc Biol Chem. *Res:* Mechanisms of hormone action; mitochondrial enzymology. *Mailing Add:* Sect of Biochem & Biophys Box U-125 Univ of Conn Storrs CT 06268

DOEGE, THEODORE CHARLES, b Lincoln, Nebr, Dec 11, 28; m 57; c 2. EPIDEMIOLOGY, PUBLIC HEALTH. *Educ:* Oberlin Col, AB, 50; Univ Rochester, MD, 58; Univ Wash, MS, 65; Am Bd Prev Med, dipl. *Prof Exp:* Intern med, Salt Lake County Gen Hosp, Utah, 58-59; asst resident pediat, Univ Hosps, Seattle, 61-63; chief resident, King County Hosp, 63; instr prev med, Sch Med, Univ Wash, 63-65, asst prof, 65-67; assoc prof prev med, Univ Ill Col Med, 67-77, ASSOC PROF EPIDEMIOL, SCH PUB HEALTH, UNIV ILL, 72-; DIR, DEPT ENVIRON, PUB & OCCUP HEALTH, AMA, CHICAGO, 77- *Concurrent Pos:* Fel prev med, Sch Med, Univ Wash, 63-65; fel trop med, La State Univ, 66; vis assoc prof, Chiengmai Univ, Thailand, 67-70. *Mem:* Fel Am Pub Health Asn; Am Col Prev Med; Am Col Epidemiol. *Res:* Injuries; epidemiology of community health problems. *Mailing Add:* 535 N Dearborn St Chicago IL 60610

DOEHLER, ROBERT WILLIAM, b Mt Olive, Ill, Aug 7, 29; m 54; c 2. MINERALOGY. *Educ:* Univ Ill, BS, 51, MS, 53, PhD(geol), 57. *Prof Exp:* Res geologist, Jersey Prod Res Co, 57-60; dir chem res, Am Colloid Co, 60-69; assoc prof, 69-80, PROF GEOL, NORTHEASTERN ILL UNIV, 80- *Concurrent Pos:* Vis prof, Notre Dame, 73; res assoc, Argonne Nat Lab, 77 & 78. *Mem:* Mineral Soc Am; AAAS; Sigma Xi. *Res:* Production and industrial applications of non-metallic minerals; mineralogy and geochemistry of sediments; geology and geochemistry of coal. *Mailing Add:* Dept of Geol Northeastern Ill Univ Chicago IL 60625

DOEHRING, DONALD O, b Milwaukee, Wis, Sept 8, 35; m 58; c 2. GEOMORPHOLOGY, GEOENVIRONMENTAL SCIENCE. *Educ:* Univ Calif, Berkeley, AB, 62; Claremont Grad Sch & Univ Ctr, MA, 65; Univ Wyo, PhD(geol), 68. *Prof Exp:* Instr geol, Univ Wyo, 67-68; vis asst prof, Pomona Col, 68-69 & Washington & Lee Univ, 69-70; fel, State Univ NY Binghamton, 70-71; asst prof, Univ Mass, Amherst, 71-75; ASSOC PROF EARTH RESOURCES, COLO STATE UNIV, 75- *Mem:* AAAS; Geol Soc Am; Nat Asn Geol Teachers; Am Inst Prof Geologists; Am Geophys Union. *Res:* Arid region geomorphology; quantitative modeling and analysis of landforms; slope process studies; environmental geomorphology; environmental geology, particularly the application of geology to land use planning. *Mailing Add:* Dept of Earth Resources Colo State Univ Ft Collins CO 80523

DOELL, RICHARD RAYMAN, b Oakland, Calif, June 28, 23; m 50; c 2. GEOPHYSICS. *Educ:* Univ Calif, AB, 52, PhD(geophysics), 55. *Prof Exp:* Lectr geophysics, Univ Toronto, 55-56; asst prof, Mass Inst Technol, 56-59; GEOPHYSICIST, US GEOL SURV, 59- *Concurrent Pos:* Co-chmn comt mineral resources & environ, mem panel environ aspects of submarine mining & appraisal of mineral resource base, mem nat mat adv bd, Nat Acad Sci.

Honors & Awards: Vetlesen Prize, 71. *Mem:* Nat Acad Sci; Geol Soc Am; fel Royal Astron Soc. *Res:* General geophysics, especially the earth's magnetic field; remnant magnetism in rocks. *Mailing Add:* US Geol Surv 345 Middlefield Rd Menlo Park CA 94025

DOELL, RUTH GERTRUDE, b Vancouver, BC, Mar 24, 26; nat US; m 50; c 2. BIOLOGY. *Educ:* Univ Calif, AB, 52, PhD(comp biochem), 56. *Prof Exp:* Instr physiol, Med Sch, Tufts Univ, 56-59; res assoc biochem, Sch Med, Stanford Univ, 59-60; res assoc pediat, 60-65, res assoc med microbiol, 65-67; lectr, 67-69, assoc prof, 69-74, PROF BIOL, SAN FRANCISCO STATE UNIV, 74- *Res:* Viral and chemical carcinogenesis; immunology. *Mailing Add:* Dept Biol 1600 Holloway San Francisco CA 94132

DOELLGAST, GEORGE JOHN, biochemistry, see previous edition

DOELLING, HELLMUT HANS, b New York, NY, July 25, 30; m 60; c 7. ECONOMIC GEOLOGY. *Educ:* Univ Utah, BS, 56, PhD(geol), 64. *Prof Exp:* Geologist, Utah Geol & Mining Surv, 64; asst prof geol, Midwestern Univ, 64-66; ECON GEOLOGIST, UTAH GEOL & MINERAL SURV, 66- *Mem:* AAAS; Soc Econ Geologists. *Res:* Coal, uranium, clay deposits, copper, mercury and bituminous sands. *Mailing Add:* 606 Blackhawk Way Research Park Salt Lake City UT 84114

DOELP, LOUIS C(ONRAD), JR, b Philadelphia, Pa, Jan 8, 28; m 50; c 2. CHEMICAL ENGINEERING. *Educ:* Univ Pa, BS, 50; Villanova, MS, 72. *Prof Exp:* Plant engr, Am Foam Rubber Corp, 50-51; chem engr develop, 51-55, proj dir process develop, 55-61, sect head, 61-69, DIR RES & DEVELOP, CATALYSTS & PROCESSES, HOUDRY PROCESS & CHEM CORP DIV, AIR PROD & CHEM, INC, 69- *Mem:* Am Chem Soc. *Res:* Hazard and risk analysis. *Mailing Add:* Air Prod & Chem Inc PO Box 538 Allentown PA 18105

DOEMEL, WILLIAM NAYLOR, b Pittsburgh, Pa. MICROBIAL ECOLOGY, SAINCE POLICY. *Educ:* Heidelberg Col, BS, 66; Ind Univ, PhD(microbiol), 70. *Prof Exp:* Asst prof, 70-78, ASSOC PROF BIOL, WABASH COL, 78- *Concurrent Pos:* Lilly fac fel, 77-78. *Mem:* AAAS; Am Soc Microbiol; Nat Asn Biol Teachers; Am Soc Limnol & Oceanog. *Res:* Physiological ecology of micro-organisms existing in extreme environments including thermal effluents, acid effluents and polluted streams; scientists and the public. *Mailing Add:* Dept of Biol Wabash Col Crawfordsville IN 47933

DOEMLING, DONALD BERNARD, b Chicago, Ill, Nov 20, 30; m 59; c 2. PHYSIOLOGY. *Educ:* St Benedict's Col, BS, 52; Univ Ill, MS, 54, PhD(physiol), 58. *Prof Exp:* Asst physiol, Univ Ill, 52-57; instr physiol & pharmacol, Dent Sch, Northwestern Univ, Chicago, 57-59, asst prof, 59-60; from instr to assoc prof, Jefferson Med Col, 61-68; PROF PHYSIOL & PHARMACOL & CHMN DEPT, SCH DENT, LOYOLA UNIV CHICAGO, 68- *Mem:* AAAS; Am Physiol Soc; Am Asn Dent Schs. *Res:* Lymph flow and composition; intestinal absorption, secretion and motility. *Mailing Add:* Dept Physiol & Pharmacol Loyola Univ Sch Dent Maywood IL 60153

DOEPKER, RICHARD DUMONT, b Findlay, Ohio, Jan 22, 33; m 59, 76; c 4. PHYSICAL CHEMISTRY. *Educ:* Xavier Univ, Ohio, BS, 55, MS, 57; Carnegie Inst Technol, MS, 60, PhD(chem), 61. *Prof Exp:* Nat Acad Sci-Nat Res Coun res assoc photoradiation chem, Nat Bur Stand, 63-65; from asst prof to assoc prof, 65-80, PROF CHEM, UNIV MIAMI, 80- *Mem:* AAAS; Am Soc Photobiol; Am Chem Soc. *Res:* Photoradiation chemistry; reaction of hot radicals; modes of decomposition of highly excited molecules produced through vacuum ultraviolet photolysis and electron impact; photo-ionization; H-atom reactions; Lyman absorption technique; environmental chemical analysis and exhaust emission methodology. *Mailing Add:* Dept Chem Univ Miami Coral Gables FL 33124

DOERDER, F PAUL, b Boone, Iowa, June 4, 45. GENETICS. *Educ:* Dana Col, BS, 67; Univ Ill, PhD(cell biol), 72. *Prof Exp:* Fel genetics, Univ Iowa, 72-73; asst prof biol, Univ Pittsburgh, 73-79; vis res scientist, Univ Ill, 79-81; ASSOC PROF BIOL, CLEVELAND STATE UNIV, 81- *Mem:* Genetics Soc Am; Soc Protozoologists; Am Genetic Asn; AAAS; Am Soc Zoologists. *Res:* Immunogenetics of surface antigens in Tetrahymena; cytogenetics; aging; population genetics of ciliates; developmental genetics of cell cycle. *Mailing Add:* Dept Biol Cleveland State Univ 1983 E 24 St Pittsburgh PA 15260

DOERFLER, THOMAS EUGENE, b Dayton, Ohio, Feb 16, 37; m 68; c 2. STATISTICS. *Educ:* Univ Dayton, BS, 59; Iowa State Univ, MS, 62, PhD(stat), 65. *Prof Exp:* Analyst-programmer statist, Res Inst, Univ Dayton, 55-59; res asst, Statist Lab, Iowa State Univ, 59-65; consult, Booz-Allen Appl Res Inc, 65-70; dir mgt sci, Columbia House Div, Columbia Broadcasting Systs, 70-73; MGR STATIST SECT, ARTHUR D LITTLE INC, 73- *Mem:* Am Stat Asn. *Res:* Statistical methods and applications; design and analysis of experiments; optimization techniques. *Mailing Add:* Arthur D Little Inc Acorn Park 20-329 Cambridge MA 02140

DOERFLER, WALTER HANS, b Weissenburg, WGer, Aug 11, 33; m 60; c 1. VIROLOGY, MOLECULAR BIOLOGY. *Educ:* Univ Munich, MD, 59. *Prof Exp:* Res fel, Max Planck Inst Biochem, 61-63 & Dept Biochem, Sch Med, Stanford Univ, 63-66; asst prof virol, Rockefeller Univ, 66-69, assoc prof, 69-71, adj prof virol, 71-78; PROF GENETICS, UNIV COLOGNE, 72- *Concurrent Pos:* City of New York Health Res Coun career scientist, 69-71; guest prof, Univ Uppsala, 71-72 & Stanford Univ, 78; ed, J Gen Virol, 77- *Mem:* Am Soc Biol Chemists; Am Soc Microbiol; AAAS. *Res:* Structure and function of nucleic acids; molecular biology of virus infected cells; interaction between viral and host genomes; DNA medley-lation; regulation of expression of integrated viral genes in transformed cells; molecular biology of baculoviruses; linguistics and genetic code. *Mailing Add:* Inst Genetics Univ of Cologne 121 Weyertal 5 Koln Germany

DOERING, CHARLES HENRY, b Munich, WGer, Jan 7, 35; US citizen; m 61; c 4. BIOCHEMISTRY, PSYCHOENDOCRINOLOGY. *Educ:* Univ San Francisco, BSc, 56; Univ Munich, MSc, 59; Univ Calif, San Francisco, PhD(biochem), 64. *Prof Exp:* Asst biochem, Univ Calif, San Francisco, 59-63; res fel, Harvard Med Sch, 63-67; res assoc psychiat, Stanford Univ Sch Med, 67-71, sr res scientist, 71-76; chief, Chem Labs, 76-80, SR RES SCIENTIST PSYCHOENDOCRINOL GROUP, LONG ISLAND RES INST, 76- *Concurrent Pos:* Assoc res prof psychiat, State Univ NY Sch Med, Stony Brook, 77- *Mem:* AAAS; Endocrine Soc; Am Psychosom Soc; Am Chem Soc. *Res:* Biosynthesis of steroid hormones and its genetic control; influence of steroid hormones on behavior; correlation between androgens and aggressiveness; developmental psychoendocrinology. *Mailing Add:* Health Sci Ctr Dept Psychiat Long Island Res Inst Stony Brook NY 11794

DOERING, EUGENE J(OHNSON), b Plankinton, SDak, Aug 28, 28; m 54; c 2. AGRICULTURAL ENGINEERING. *Educ:* SDak State Univ, BS, 52, MS, 58. *Prof Exp:* Engr, Boeing Airplane Co, Kans, 52; agr engr, Soil Conserv Serv, 54-56, agr engr, Sci & Educ Admin-Agr Res, Calif, 58-65, AGR ENGR, NORTHERN GREAT PLAINS RES CTR, AGR RES SERV, USDA, NDAK, 65- *Mem:* Am Soc Agr Engrs; Am Soc Agron; Nat Soc Prof Engrs. *Res:* Salinity in agriculture; reclamation; irrigation; drainage; flow of water in saturated and unsaturated soil. *Mailing Add:* Northern Great Plains Res Ctr USDA PO Box 459 Mandan ND 58554

DOERING, JEFFREY LOUIS, b Chicago, Ill, May 26, 49; m 74; c 2. GENE CLONING, CHROMATIN STRUCTURE. *Educ:* Univ Chicago, BA, 71, PhD(develop biol), 75. *Prof Exp:* Res asst, Univ Chicago, 71-75; fel embryol, Carnegie Inst, 75-77; ASST PROF BIOL SCI, NORTHWESTERN UNIV, 78- *Concurrent Pos:* Res fel, NIH, 75-77. *Mem:* Am Soc Cell Biol. *Res:* Molecular genetics of human collagen disorders; chromatin structure and control of gene expression; characterization of human complex repetitive DNAs. *Mailing Add:* Dept Biochem, Molecular & Cell Biol Northwestern Univ Evanston IL 60201

DOERING, JOHN P, chemical physics, see previous edition

DOERING, ROBERT DISTLER, b Peoria, Ill, Feb 23, 25; m 52; c 3. INDUSTRIAL ENGINEERING, MECHANICAL ENGINEERING. *Educ:* Univ Southern Calif, BE, 50, MS, 59 & 65, PhD(eng), 68. *Prof Exp:* Sales eng mfg, Allis Chalmers Mfg Co, 50-51; plant eng process res div, Union Oil Co, 51-60, supvr opers engr, Distrib Dept, 60-61; chief engr space simulation, Honeywell, Inc, 61-64; sr proj engr cryogenics, res & develop div, 64-67, sr staff head systs, Hughes Aircraft, 67-69; assoc prof bus & econ, Calif State Univ, Fullerton, 69; PROF ENG, UNIV CENT FLA, 69- *Concurrent Pos:* Ford Found fel, 66-68; consult, Hughes Aircraft Ground Systs Group, 69-70, Walt Disney World, 70-, Red Lobster Inns Am, 74-78, Dawkins & Assoc, 71-, Cent Fla Eng Serv, 71-; pres, Omega Systs Group, 71-; dir, Crime Watch Cent Fla, Inc, 71- *Mem:* Am Inst Indust Engrs; Nat Soc Prof Engrs; Am Mgt Asn; Am Soc Mech Engrs. *Res:* Command and control public safety operations analysis, police and fire; energy conservation and management systems; cogeneration plant operations optimization; engineering management; project administration and economic evaluation; safety hazard analysis; accident investigation. *Mailing Add:* Col of Eng PO Box 25000 Orlando FL 32816

DOERING, WILLIAM VON EGGERS, b Ft Worth, Tex, June 22, 17; div; c 3. PHYSICAL ORGANIC CHEMISTRY. *Educ:* Harvard Univ, BS, 38, PhD(org chem), 43. *Hon Degrees:* DSc, Tex Christian Univ, 74. *Prof Exp:* Res chemist Nat Defense Res Comt proj, Harvard Univ, 41-42; res chemist, Polaroid Corp, Mass, 43; from instr to assoc prof org chem, Columbia Univ, 43-52; prof, Yale Univ, 52-67, dir div sci, 62-65; prof org chem, 67, MALLINCKRODT PROF ORG CHEM, HARVARD UNIV, 68- *Concurrent Pos:* Dir res, Hickrill Chem Res Found, NY, 47-59; consult, Upjohn Co, 56-; co-chmn, Coun Livable World, 62-78; hon prof, Fudan Univ, 80. *Honors & Awards:* Scott Award, 45; Pure Chem Award, Am Chem Soc, 53, Synthetic Chem Award, 63; Hoffman Medal, Ger Chem Soc, 62. *Mem:* Nat Acad Sci; Am Acad Arts & Sci; Am Chem Soc. *Res:* Mechanism of thermal rearrangements, Cope, Diels-Alder; vinylcyclobutane; vinylcyclopropane; methylenecyclopropane; energy flow in chemically activated molecules; conjugative interaction. *Mailing Add:* Dept of Chem Harvard Univ Cambridge MA 02138

DOERMANN, AUGUST HENRY, b Blue Island, Ill, Dec 7, 18; m 47; c 2. BIOLOGY, BACTERIAL VIRUS GENETICS. *Educ:* Wabash Col, AB, 40; Univ Ill, MA, 41; Stanford Univ, PhD(biol), 46. *Hon Degrees:* DSc, Wabash Col, 75. *Prof Exp:* Fel bacteriophage res, Vanderbilt Univ, 45-47, vis instr biol, 46; fel, Carnegie Inst Genetics Res Unit, 47-49; biologist, Oak Ridge Nat Lab, 49-53; from assoc prof to prof biol, Univ Rochester, 53-58; prof, Vanderbilt Univ, 58-64; PROF GENETICS, UNIV WASH, 64- *Concurrent Pos:* Vis res fel, Calif Inst Technol, 49; vis prof, Univ Cologne, 57-58; sci assoc, Basel Inst Immunol, 70-71. *Mem:* Nat Acad Sci; AAAS; Nat Acad Sci; Am Acad Arts & Sci. *Res:* Microbiological and biochemical genetics; viral morphogenesis; radiation genetics of bacteriophage. *Mailing Add:* Dept of Genetics Univ of Wash Seattle WA 98195

DOERNER, WILLIAM A(LLEN), b Pullman, Wash, Feb 24, 20; m 50; c 4. CHEMICAL ENGINEERING, MATHEMATICS. *Educ:* Ore State Col, BS, 42; Univ Mich, MSE, 47, MS, 49, ScD(chem eng), 52. *Prof Exp:* Res engr cent res dept, 51-66, develop supvr photo prod dept, 66-69, GROUP LEADER, CENT RES DEPT, EXP STA, E I DU PONT DE NEMOURS & CO, 69- *Mem:* AAAS; Am Chem Soc; Am Inst Chem Engrs. *Res:* Thermodynamics of power fluids; process chemistry engineering research. *Mailing Add:* 19 Baynard Blvd Wilmington DE 19803

DOERR, MARVIN LEROY, organic chemistry, see previous edition

DOERR, PHILLIP DAVID, b Ft Gordon, Ga, Oct 29, 42; m 65; c 2. WILDLIFE ECOLOGY. *Educ:* Colo Col, BA, 64; Colo State Univ, MS, 68; Univ Wis, Madison, PhD(wildlife ecol), 73. *Prof Exp:* Res asst wildlife ecol, Univ Wis, 68-73; asst prof, 73-78, ASSOC PROF ZOOL, NC STATE UNIV, 78- *Mem:* Am Ornithologists Union; Cooper Ornith Soc; Wilson Ornith Soc; Wildlife Soc. *Res:* Population studies of American woodcock in North Carolina; population studies of redcockaded woodpecker and American alligator in North Carolina; relationships of avian predator and prey populations. *Mailing Add:* Dept of Zool Box 5577 NC State Univ Raleigh NC 27607

DOERR, ROBERT GEORGE, b Winona, Minn, Jan 26, 41; m 70. ORGANIC CHEMISTRY, ANALYTICAL CHEMISTRY. *Educ:* St Mary's Col (Minn), BA, 63; Pa State Univ, PhD(chem), 67. *Prof Exp:* Fel, Pa State Univ, 67; prof chem, Luther Col (Iowa), 67-68; CHEMIST, WATKINS PROD INC, 68- *Mem:* Am Chem Soc. *Mailing Add:* Watkins Prod Inc Winona MN 55987

DOERSCH, RONALD ERNEST, b Cleveland, Wis, Sept 13, 35; m 57; c 4. WEED SCIENCE. *Educ:* Univ Wis, BS, 58, MS, 61, PhD(soils), 63. *Prof Exp:* From asst prof to assoc prof, 62-71, PROF WEED CONTROL, UNIV WIS-MADISON, 71-; EXTEN SPECIALIST, USDA, 62-, PEST MGT EDUC COORDR, 78- *Mem:* Weed Sci Soc Am; Am Soc Agron. *Res:* Weed control in field crops; the influence of soil properties upon soil-applied herbicides and their responses in terms of total crop management. *Mailing Add:* Dept of Agron Univ of Wis Madison WI 53706

DOERSCHUK, ALBERT PETER, b Kansas City, Mo, Dec 13, 23; m 49; c 4. ORGANIC CHEMISTRY, ECONOMICS. *Educ:* Univ Pittsburgh, BS, 43, PhD(chem), 49; NY Univ, MBA, 59. *Prof Exp:* Instr chem, Columbia Univ, 48-51; group leader biochem, Chem Process Improv Dept, Lederle Labs, Am Cyanamid Co, 51-54, head, 54-57, asst to plant mgr, 57, asst to dir res, 57-58, mgr pharmaceut prod develop sect, 58-60, tech dir fine chem dept, 60-64, sr mgt analyst, Commercial Develop Div, 64-66; asst to dir planning, Lederle Labs Div, 66-69; asst dir, G D Searle & Co, 69-71, assoc dir diversification, 71-75; vpres & gen mgr, Nichols Inst Diag, San Pedro, Calif, 75-76; mgr new prod develop, Hyland Div, Costa Mesa, Calif, 77, PROD MGR, CLIN ASSAYS DIV, BAXTER TRAVENOL, 78- *Mem:* AAAS; Am Chem Soc; Am Pharmaceut Asn; NY Acad Sci. *Res:* Chemistry, radiochemistry, chemical physics; drugs; natural products; instrumentation; economics; acquisitions; management. *Mailing Add:* Clin Assays 600 Memorial Dr Cambridge MA 02139

DOETSCH, GERNOT SIEGMAR, b Berlin, Ger, May 25, 40; US citizen; m 66; c 2. NEUROSCIENCE. *Educ:* DePauw Univ, BA, 62; Duke Univ, PhD(psychol), 67. *Prof Exp:* Res psychol, 6571st Aeromed Res Lab, Holloman AFB, 67-70; fel neurophysiol, Dept Physiol & Biophys, Univ Wash, 70-72; asstprof, 72-77, assoc prof surg & asst prof physiol, 77-81, ASSOC PROF SURG & PHYSIOL, MED COL GA, 81- *Mem:* Sigma Xi; Soc Neurosci; Soc Exp Biol & Med; AAAS; Asn Am Volunteer Physicians. *Res:* Physiology of sensory systems; sensory and motor functions of cerebral cortex; information processing in neuronal populations; neural plasticity. *Mailing Add:* Dept Physiol Med Col of Ga Augusta GA 30912

DOETSCH, RAYMOND NICHOLAS, b Chicago, Ill, Dec 5, 20; m 48; c 3. BACTERIOLOGY. *Educ:* Univ Ill, BS, 42; Ind Univ, AM, 43; Univ Md, PhD(bact), 48. *Prof Exp:* Asst bacteriologist, Ind Univ, 42-43; bacteriologist, Nat Dairy Res Lab, Baltimore, 43-45; asst bact, 45-46, from instr to assoc prof, 46-60, PROF BACT, UNIV MD, COLLEGE PARK, 60- *Concurrent Pos:* Guggenheim fel, Rowett Inst, Aberdeen, 56; vis lectr, Inst Hist Med, Johns Hopkins Univ, 63. *Mem:* AAAS; Am Soc Microbiol; NY Acad Sci; Am Acad Microbiol; Am Asn Hist Med. *Res:* Bacterial cytology; general microbiology; history of science and microbiology; bacterial motility systems. *Mailing Add:* Dept Microbiol Univ Md College Park MD 20742

DOETSCHMAN, DAVID CHARLES, b Aurora, Ill, Nov 24, 42; m; c 2. CHEMICAL PHYSICS. *Educ:* Northern Ill Univ, BS, 63; Univ Chicago, PhD(chem), 69. *Prof Exp:* Res fel chem, Australian Nat Univ, 69-74; res fel, Univ Leiden, 74-75; asst prof, 75-82, ASSOC PROF CHEM, STATE UNIV NY BINGHAMTON, 82- *Mem:* Sigma Xi; Am Phys Soc; Am Chem Soc. *Res:* Applications of time-resolved electron paramagnetic resonance and optical-magnetic double resonance techniques to the study of chemical reaction mechanisms in solids at low temperatures. *Mailing Add:* Dept of Chem State Univ NY Binghamton NY 13901

DOFF, SIMON DAVID, b Russia, Oct 12, 11; nat US; m 43; c 3. MEDICINE, PUBLIC HEALTH. *Educ:* Univ Pittsburgh, BS, 32; Long Island Col Med, MD, 39; Columbia Univ, MPH, 51; Am Bd Prev Med, dipl. *Prof Exp:* Clin instr med, Sch Med, Yale Univ, 43-48; asst dir bur tuberc control, Fla State Bd Health, 49-51, dir div heart dis control, 51-58, dir bur maternal & child health, 58-60, dir bur spec health serv, 60-65; chmn dept community med & outpatient serv, Univ Hosp, Jacksonville, 65-77; clin assoc prof med, Col Med, 74-77, DIR DEPT COMMUNITY MED & OUTPATIENT SERV & SR ATTEND PHYSICIAN, UNIV FLA, 77- *Concurrent Pos:* Fel, WHO, 63; epidemiologist, New Haven Health Dept, 43-48; consult, Heart Dis Control Prog, USPHS, 56-59; sr attend physician, Univ Hosp, Jacksonville. *Mem:* Am Thoracic Soc; fel Am Col Cardiol; fel Am Col Chest Physicians; Am Soc Internal Med. *Res:* Epidemiology chronic disease; preventive medicine. *Mailing Add:* Dept of Clin Med Univ of Fla Gainesville FL 32601

DOGGER, JAMES RUSSELL, b Milwaukee, Wis, July 31, 23; m 46; c 3. ENTOMOLOGY. *Educ:* Univ Wis, BS, 47, MS, 48, PhD(entom), 50. *Prof Exp:* Instr econ entom, Univ Wis, 48-49; asst prof entom, Okla Agr & Mech Col, 50-52; from asst prof to assoc prof, NC State Col, 52-58; prof entom & chmn dept, NDak State Univ, 58-69; asst chief stored prod, Mkt Qual Res Div, 69-72, asst area dir, GA-SC area, Agr Res Serv, 72-75, area dir, Ches-Pot area, Sci & Educ Admin, 76-78, ASST TO REGIONAL ADMIN, NORTH EAST REGION, AGR RES SERV, USDA, 79- *Concurrent Pos:* State entomologist, NDak, 58-69; Fulbright prof, Univ Nat Trujillo, Peru, 67-68.

Mem: Entom Soc Am; Sigma Xi. Res: Insects affecting stored products, forage and related crops; immature insects; taxonomic, Coleoptera, Elateridae, Carabidae. Mailing Add: Northeast Region Agr Res Serv USDA Rom 325 Bldg 003 Barc-W Beltsville MD 20705

DOGGETT, LEROY ELSWORTH, b Waterloo, Iowa, Oct 22, 41; m 65. DYNAMICAL ASTRONOMY, NAVIGATION. Educ: Univ Mich, BS, 64; Georgetown Univ, MA, 70; NC State Univ, PhD, 81. Prof Exp: ASTRONR, NAUTICAL ALMANAC OFF, US NAVAL OBSERV, 65- Concurrent Pos: Consult ed, Archaeoastron, 81. Mem: Am Astron Soc; Inst Navig. Res: Planetary theory; archaeoastronomy. Mailing Add: US Naval Observ Washington DC 20390

DOGGETT, WESLEY OSBORNE, b Brown Summit, NC, Jan 24, 31; m 53; c 8. PLASMA PHYSICS. Educ: NC State Col, BS, 52, BS, 53; Univ Calif, Berkeley, MA, 54, PhD(physics). 56. Prof Exp: Res assoc physics, Radiation Lab, Univ Calif, 54-56; tech proj coordr, Air Force Nuclear Eng Test Reactor, Wright Air Develop Ctr, 56-58; from asst prof to assoc prof physics, 58-62, asst dean sch phys sci & appl math, 64-68, PROF PHYSICS, NC STATE UNIV, 62- Concurrent Pos: Consult, Repub Aviation Corp, 56-59, Res Triangle Inst, 62-, NASA, Langley Field, 63, Off Civil Defense, 63-65 & Becton, Dickinson & Co, 76-; dir, Troxler Electronics, Inc, 62-76. Mem: AAAS; Am Phys Soc; Am Soc Eng Educ; Am Inst Physics; Am Nuclear Soc. Res: Nuclear reactor physics; development and analysis of statistical methods for investigating half-lives; theoretical analysis of gammaray penetration in matter; relativistic electron beam studies. Mailing Add: NC State Univ Dept of Physics PO Box 5342 Raleigh NC 27650

DOHANY, JULIUS EUGENE, b Banatski Karlovac, Yugoslavia, May 28, 26; nat US; m 51; c 2. POLYMER CHEMISTRY. Educ: Budapest Tech, MChE, 50; Swiss Fed Inst Technol, ScD, 63. Prof Exp: Supvr plant, Coal Chem Co, Hungary, 51-53, mgr, 53-56; supvr pilot plant, Viscose Co, Switz, 56-58, res lab, 58-59; res chemist, Cryovac Div, W R Grace & Co, 63-64; sr res chemist, 64-66, proj leader, 66-67, group leader, 67-81, DIR RES & DEVELOP, PENNWALT CORP, 81- Mem: Am Chem Soc; Soc Plastics Eng. Res: Synthesis and characterization of polymers; fluorine containing polymers, coatings, film, polymer rheology; vicose fiber process; synthetic fibers; textile chemistry; tar distillation; coal carbonization; gas desulfurization. Mailing Add: 480 Howellville Rd Berwyn PA 19312

DOHERTY, JAMES EDWARD, III, b Newport, Ark, Nov 22, 23; div; c 2. INTERNAL MEDICINE, CARDIOLOGY. Educ: Univ Ark, BS, 44, MD, 46; Am Bd Internal Med, dipl, 55; Am Bd Cardiovasc Dis, dipl, 59. Prof Exp: Intern, Columbus City Hosp, Ga, 46-47; resident med, 49-52, from instr to assoc prof, 52-68, PROF MED, SCH MED, UNIV ARK, LITTLE ROCK, 68-, PROF PHARM, 69-; DIR CONTINUING MED EDUC & DIR CARDIOVASC RES, CARDIOL, UNIV ARK MED CTR-VET ADMIN HOSPS, 77- Concurrent Pos: Chief cardiol, Little Rock Vet Admin Hosp, 57-69; dir div cardiol, Univ Ark Med Ctr-Vet Admin Hosps, 69-77. Honors & Awards: Wellcome lectr, 81. Mem: Am Fedn Clin Res; Soc Nuclear Med; Am Col Physicians; Am Col Cardiol; fel Am Heart Asn. Res: Cardiovascular disease, primarily the metabolism of radioactive digoxin and cholesterol. Mailing Add: 48 Wingate Dr Little Rock AR 72205

DOHERTY, LOWELL RALPH, b San Diego, Calif, Mar 12, 30. ASTROPHYSICS. Educ: Univ Calif, Los Angeles, BA, 52; Univ Mich, MS, 54, PhD(astron), 62. Prof Exp: Lectr astron & res fel, Harvard Univ, 57-63; from asst prof to assoc prof, 63-76, PROF ASTRON, UNIV WIS-MADISON, 76- Mem: Am Astron Soc; Sigma Xi; Int Astron Union; AAAS. Res: Stellar photometry and spectroscopy; theory of stellar atmospheres. Mailing Add: 3202 Knollwood Way Madison WI 53713

DOHERTY, PAUL MICHAEL, b Boston, Mass, July 7, 48. SOLID STATE PHYSICS. Educ: Mass Inst Technol, BS, 70, PhD(physics), 74. Prof Exp: ASST PROF PHYSICS, OAKLAND UNIV, 74- Mem: Am Asn Physics Teachers; Sigma Xi. Res: Laser intensity fluctuation spectroscopy of biological macromolecules and turbulent flow. Mailing Add: Dept of Physics Oakland Univ Rochester MI 48065

DOHLMAN, CLAES HENRIK, b Uppsala, Sweden, Sept 11, 22; m 48; c 6. OPHTHALMOLOGY. Educ: Univ Lund, Lic Med, 50, Med Dr & docent, 57. Prof Exp: Resident ophthalmol, 50-52, asst surgeon, Univ Eye Clin, Univ Lund, 55-57; dir cornea serv, 64-75; CHIEF EYE SERV, MASS EYE & EAR INFIRMARY, 74-; PROF OPHTHAL, CHMN DEPT & DIR HOWE LAB OPHTHAL, HARVARD MED SCH, 74- Concurrent Pos: Res fel ophthal, Johns Hopkins Hosp, 52-53; res fel, Retina Found, 53-54; fel, Mass Eye & Ear Infirmary, 58-63. Res: Diseases of the cornea of the eye. Mailing Add: Mass Eye & Ear Infirmary 243 Charles St Boston MA 02114

DOHM, GERALD LYNIS, b Colby, Kans, Mar 1, 42; m 63; c 2. BIOCHEMISTRY, PHYSIOLOGY. Educ: Kans State Univ, BS, 65, MS, 66, PhD(biochem), 69. Prof Exp: Captain biochem, US Army Med Res & Nutrit Lab Fitzsimons Gen Hosp, Denver, 69-72; ASSOC PROF BIOCHEM, SCH MED, E CAROLINA UNIV, GREENVILLE, NC, 72- Mem: Am Physiol Soc; Soc Exp Biol Med; Sigma Xi. Res: Primary research involves biochemical adaptation to exercise; also control of muscle protein turnover. Mailing Add: Dept of Biochem E Carolina Univ Greenville NC 27834

DOHMS, JOHN EDWARD, b New York, NY, Apr 5, 48. AVIAN MEDICINE, AVIAN IMMUNOLOGY. Educ: Bowling Green State Univ, BS, 70, MS, 72; Ohio State Univ, PhD(poultry sci), 77. Prof Exp: Tech res assoc, Ohio Agr Res & Develop Ctr, Ohio State Univ, 72-74; res asst, Grad Sch, 74-77; ASST PROF AVIAN IMMUNOL, DEPT ANIMAL SCI & AGR BIOCHEM, UNIV DEL, 77- Mem: Am Soc Microbiologists; Poultry Sci Asn. Res: Host parasite relationships of domestic poultry and economically important avian pathogens; immunology of the upper respiratory tract of domestic birds. Mailing Add: Dept Animal Sci & Agr Biochem Univ Del Newark DE 19711

DOHNANYI, JULIUS S, b Budapest, Hungary, Aug 29, 31; US citizen; m 60; c 1. THEORETICAL PHYSICS. Educ: Fla State Univ, MS, 55; Ohio State Univ, PhD(physics), 60. Prof Exp: Mem staff, Sandia Corp, 60-63; mem tech staff, Bell Comm, Inc, 63-72, MEM STAFF, BELL TEL LABS, INC, 72- Mem: Am Phys Soc; Am Geophys Union. Res: Physics of interplanetary debris; nuclear magnetic resonance; superconductivity; statistical models of the nucleus. Mailing Add: Bell Tel Labs Inc Holmdel NJ 07733

DOHOO, ROY MCGREGOR, b Essex, Eng, Sept 3, 19; Can citizen; m 49; c 2. ELECTRICAL ENGINEERING, SATELLITE COMMUNICATIONS. Educ: Cambridge Univ, BA, 41, MA, 44. Prof Exp: Exp officer radar, Air Ministry, UK, 47-48; sci officer electronic fuzing, Armament Design Estab, 48-52; sci officer, Defence Res Telecommun Estab, Defence Res Bd Can, 52-55, sect leader radar systs, 55-57; res engr, Rand Corp, Calif, 57-59; sci officer, Defence Res Bd Can, 59-62, sect leader microwave propagation, Commun Res Ctr, 62-67, supt, Commun Lab, 67-69; dir, Nat Commun Lab, Commun Res Ctr, Dept Commun, 69-74, dir, Gen Space Prog, 74-77; PRES, ROY M DOHOO LTD, 77- Mem: Sr mem Inst Elec & Electronics Engrs; fel Brit Inst Elec Engrs; assoc fel Aeronaut & Space Inst. Res: Telecommunications; radar systems; electronic fuzing; microwave propagation; satellite communications. Mailing Add: 2092 Woodcrest Rd Ottawa ON K1H 6H8 Can

DOI, KUNIO, b Tokyo, Japan, Sept 28, 39; m 62; c 2. MEDICAL PHYSICS, OPTICS. Educ: Waseda Univ, Japan, BSc, 62, PhD, 69. Prof Exp: Chief radiography res, Kyokko Res Labs, Dai Nippon Toryo Co, Ltd, Japan, 62-69; asst prof, 69-72, assoc prof, 72-77, PROF RADIOL, UNIV CHICAGO, 77-; DIR KURT ROSSMANN LAB RADIOL IMAGE RES, 77- Concurrent Pos: Instr, Fac Med, Tohoku Univ, Japan, 66-69. Honors & Awards: Award, Japanese Appl Physics Soc, 68; Award, Japanese Soc Instrument & Control Engrs, 72. Mem: Am Asn Physicists in Med; Optical Soc Am; Soc Nondestructive Testing; Japanese Appl Physics Soc; Phys Soc Japan. Res: Image quality of radiologic imaging systems; solid state inorganic luminescent materials. Mailing Add: Dept of Radiol Univ of Chicago Chicago IL 60637

DOI, ROY HIROSHI, b Sacramento, Calif, Mar 26, 33; m 58; c 2. MICROBIOLOGY. Educ: Univ Calif, Berkeley, AB, 53 & 57; Univ Wis, MS, 58, PhD(bact), 60. Prof Exp: USPHS fel, 60-63; asst prof bact & bot, Syracuse Univ, 63-65; from asst prof to assoc prof, 65-69, chmn dept biochem & biophys, 74-77, PROF BIOCHEM, UNIV CALIF, DAVIS, 69- Concurrent Pos: NSF sr fel, 71-72; mem microbiol training comt, Nat Inst Gen Med Sci, 68-71; mem microbial chem study sect, NIH, 75-79; vis prof, Max Planck Inst Biochem, Munich, 78-79; sr US scientist award, Alexander von Humboldt Found, 78-79. Mem: Am Soc Microbiol; Am Soc Biol Chemists. Res: Isolaation, cloning, and charaterization of bacillus subtilis genes; structure and function of RNA polymerase of sporulating bacteria. Mailing Add: Dept of Biochem & Biophys Univ of Calif Davis CA 95616

DOIG, MARION TILTON, III, b Charleston, SC, Sept 29, 43; m 66; c 2. BIOCHEMISTRY, ENVIRONMENTAL CHEMISTRY. Educ: Col Charleston, BS, 66; Univ SFla, MS, 71, PhD(chem), 73. Prof Exp: Anal chemist environ chem, Environ Protection Agency, 65-69; vis asst prof clin chem, Univ SFla, 73-74; asst prof, 74-79, ASSOC PROF CHEM, COL CHARLESTON, 80- Mem: Am Chem Soc. Res: Marine toxicology; folate metabolism; cancer chemotherapy; applications of flow microcalorimetry to biochemical problems. Mailing Add: Dept of Chem Col Charleston Charleston SC 29401

DOIG, RONALD, b Montreal, Que, Feb 14, 39. GEOLOGY, GEOPHYSICS. Educ: McGill Univ, BSc, 60, MSc, 61, PhD(geol). 64. Prof Exp: Mem staff gamma-ray spectrometry, Geophys Div, Geol Surv Can, 62-64; lectr isotope geol & geophys, 64-66, asst prof geol sci, 66-70, assoc prof, 70-78, chmn dept, 75-80, PROF GEOL SCI, MCGILL UNIV, 78- Mem: Geol Soc Am; Geol Asn Can. Res: Isotope geology; geochronology; gamma-ray spectrometry. Mailing Add: Dept of Geol Sci McGill Univ Montreal PQ H3A 2T5 Can

DOIGAN, PAUL, b Greenfield, Mass, June 8, 19; m 53; c 3. PHYSICAL CHEMISTRY. Educ: Univ Conn, BS, 41; NY Univ, BS, 43, PhD(chem), 50; Univ Mass, MS, 46. Prof Exp: Res assoc chem, Atomic Res Inst, Iowa State Col, 46; instr chem, Univ Mass, 46-47; instr chem, Univ Conn, 50-51; res chemist, 51-55, prof personnel, 55-58, consult engr & mgr personnel placement & facility planning, 59-60, mgr eng admin, missile & space vehicle dept, 60-62 & spacecraft dept, 62-64, consult specialist, 66-66, proj mgr col placement coun, 66-67, mgr doctoral & int recruiting, 67-79, mgr entry level recruiting, 75-79, MGR TECH RECRUITING, GEN ELEC CO, 79- Concurrent Pos: Mem conf elec insulation, Nat Res Coun. Mem: AAAS; Am Chem Soc; Inst Elec & Electronics Engineers; fel Am Inst Chemists; Am Soc Eng Educ. Res: Engineering administration; space vehicles; manned space laboratory. Mailing Add: 2242 Pine Ridge Rd Schenectady NY 12309

DOIRON, THEODORE DANOS, b New Orleans, La, Aug 14, 48; m 71; c 1. PHYSICS. Educ: Univ New Orleans, BS, 70, MS, 72; Duke Univ, PhD(physics), 77. Prof Exp: Fel physics, Duke Univ, 77-78; Nat Res Coun fel, Nat Bur Standards, 78-80; ASST PROF PHYSICS, VA COMMONWEALTH UNIV, 80- Mem: Am Phys Soc; Am Asn Physics Teachers; Sigma Xi. Res: Properties of matter near phase transitions; including static and dynamic properties of fluids, fluid mixtures and currently metals near the superconducting transition. Mailing Add: Physics Dept Va Commonwealth Univ Richmond VA 23284

DOISY, EDWARD ADELBERT, b Hume, Ill, Nov 13, 93; m 18, 65; c 4. PHYSIOLOGY, BIOCHEMISTRY. Educ: Univ Ill, AB, 14, MS, 16; Harvard Univ, PhD(biochem), 20. Hon Degrees: ScD, Wash Univ, 40, Yale Univ, 40, Univ Chicago, 41, Cent Col, 42, Univ Ill, 60, Gustavus Adolphus Col, 63; Dr, Univ Paris, 45; LLD, St Louis Univ, 55. Prof Exp: Asst biochem, Harvard Med Sch, 15-17; instr, Sch Med, Wash Univ, 19-20, assoc, 20-22, assoc prof, 22-23; prof & dir dept, 23-65, prof, 51, distinguished serv prof, 51-65, EMER PROF BIOCHEM & EMER DIR EDWARD A DOISY DEPT BIOCHEM, SCH MED, ST LOUIS UNIV, 65- Concurrent Pos: Numerous hon lectr,

31-46; mem comt standardization sex hormones, League of Nations, 32-35; mem comt biol & med, AEC; with Nat Adv Cancer Coun, 41-43 & 48-51. *Honors & Awards:* Co-winner Nobel Prize, 43; Gold Medal, St Louis Med Soc, 35; Conne Medal, 35; Gibbs Medal, 41; Award, Am Pharmaceut Mfg Asn, 42; Squibb Award, 44; Fleur de Lis, St Louis Univ, 51; Com Solvents Award, 52; Illini Achievement Award, Univ Ill, 58; Barren Found Medal, 72. *Mem:* Nat Acad Sci; AAAS; Am Soc Biol Chemists (vpres, 41, pres, 43-45); Endocrine Soc (pres, 49); Soc Exp Biol & Med (vpres, 47-49, pres, 49-51). *Res:* Metabolism; insulin; blood buffers; isolation and chemical characterization of theelin, theelol and dihydro-theelin; ovarian hormones and estrogenic substances; gonadotropic and thyrotropic principles; vitamin K; antibiotics; bile acids; metabolism of steroids. *Mailing Add:* Dept of Biochem St Louis Univ Sch of Med St Louis MO 63104

DOISY, RICHARD JOSEPH, b St Louis, Mo, Jan 30, 26; m 50; c 2. BIOCHEMISTRY. *Educ:* Univ Mo, BS, 46; Univ Nebr, MS, 51; Syracuse Univ, PhD(biochem), 54. *Prof Exp:* Asst chem, Univ Nebr, 48-51; from instr to assoc prof, 56-73, PROF BIOCHEM, STATE UNIV NY UPSTATE MED CTR, 73- *Concurrent Pos:* Res fel biochem, State Univ NY, 51-54; Am Cancer Soc fel, Enzyme Inst, Univ Wis, 54-56. *Mem:* Am Diabetes Asn; Soc Environ Geochem & Health. *Res:* Insulin assay; adipose tissue metabolism; glucose tolerance; chromium; diabetes; nutrition. *Mailing Add:* 601 Waldorf Pkwy Syracuse NY 13224

DOKU, HRISTO CHRIS, b Istanbul, Turkey, Apr 17, 28; US citizen; m 58; c 1. ORAL SURGERY. *Educ:* Univ Istanbul, DDS, 51; Tufts Univ, DMD, 58, MDS, 60. *Prof Exp:* From instr to assoc prof, 58-67, PROF ORAL SURG, SCH DENT MED, TUFTS UNIV, 67-, CHMN DEPT, 65-, ASSOC DEAN, 67- *Concurrent Pos:* USPHS trainee, 58-60; prin investr, USPHS. *Honors & Awards:* Hatton Award, Chicago, 60. *Mem:* Am Dent Asn; Am Soc Oral Surg; Int Asn Dent Res. *Res:* Blood clotting factors; thromboplastic activity and its relation to saliva; wound healing; age and dentition. *Mailing Add:* Dept of Oral Surg Tufts Univ Sch of Dent Med Boston MA 02111

DOLAN, DESMOND DANIEL, b Nelson-Miramichi, NB, Nov 19, 16; nat US; m 49; c 4. PLANT PATHOLOGY. *Educ:* McGill Univ, BSc, 37, MSc, 39; Cornell Univ, PhD(plant breeding), 46. *Prof Exp:* Veg pathologist, Dom Path Lab, 38-41; asst, Cath Univ Am, 41-42; asst plant breeding & veg crops, Cornell Univ, 42-46; assoc res prof hort, Univ RI, 46-53; COORDR & HORTICULTURIST-IN-CHG PLANT INTROD, NY STATE AGR EXP STA, PLANT SCI RES DIV, USDA, 53- *Concurrent Pos:* Assoc prof, Cornell Univ, 55- *Mem:* Am Soc Hort Sci; Am Phytopath Soc; Am Soc Agron; Am Chem Soc; Bot Soc Am. *Res:* Fungus causing stem-streak on melons; breeding Iroquois muskmelon, Rhode Island Red watermelon and Rhode Island Early and Summer Sunrise tomatoes; plant germ plasm for the Northeast; discovery of first all female gynoecious cucumber. *Mailing Add:* Plant Introd Sturtevant Hall NY State Agr Exp Sta Rm 201 Geneva NY 14456

DOLAN, JAMES MICHAEL, zoology, see previous edition

DOLAN, JOSEPH EDWARD, b Sterling, Colo, May 21, 45; m 67; c 2. ARTHROPOD ZOOLOGY, AQUATIC BIOLOGY. *Educ:* Colo State Univ, BS, 67, MS, 69; Univ Northern Colo, DA(biol sci), 78. *Prof Exp:* Instr zool, 69-75, DIV CHMN LIFE & PHYS SCI & INSTR ZOOL, CENT WYO COL, 76- *Mem:* Assoc mem Sigma Xi; Nat Asn Biol Teachers; Am Mus Natural Hist. *Res:* Aquatic insects of running water. *Mailing Add:* Div of Life & Phys Sci Cent Wyo Col Riverton WY 82501

DOLAN, JOSEPH FRANCIS, b Rochester, NY, Sept 17, 39; m 71; c 2. ASTRONOMY, ASTROPHYSICS. *Educ:* St Bonaventure Univ, BS, 61; Harvard Univ, AM, 63, PhD(astrophys), 66. *Prof Exp:* Physicist, Smithsonian Astrophys Observ, 65-66; sr scientist, Jet Propulsion Lab, Calif Inst Technol, 66-68; asst prof astron, Case Western Reserve Univ, 68-75; Nat Res Coun sr res assoc, 75-77, ASTROPHYSICIST, LAB ASTRON & SOLAR PHYSICS, NASA GODDARD SPACE FLIGHT CTR, 77- *Mem:* Am Astron Soc; Int Astron Union. *Res:* X-ray and gamma ray astronomy; astronomical polarization. *Mailing Add:* Code 681 Goddard Space Flight Ctr Greenbelt MD 20771

DOLAN, KENNETH WILLIAM, b Yakima, Wash, July 23, 40; m 63; c 3. NUCLEAR PHYSICS. *Educ:* Univ Wash, BS, 62; Univ Ore, MS, 64, PhD(nuclear physics), 68. *Prof Exp:* Res asst, Univ Ore, 66-68; tech staff mem physics, 68-77, MEM SCI STAFF, SANDIA LABS, 77- *Mem:* Am Phys Soc. *Res:* Experimental low energy nuclear physics. *Mailing Add:* Sandia Labs PO Box 969 Livermore CA 94550

DOLAN, LOUISE ANN, b Wilmington, Del, Apr 5, 50. THEORETICAL HIGH ENERGY PHYSICS. *Educ:* Wellesley Col, BA, 71; Mass Inst Technol, PhD(physics), 76. *Prof Exp:* Asst physics, Mass Inst Technol, 72-76; jr fel physics, Soc Fels, Harvard Univ, 76-79; ASST PROF, ROCKEFELLER UNIV, 79- *Concurrent Pos:* Vis scientist, Ecole Normale, Paris, 77; vis fel, Princeton Univ, 78. *Mem:* Am Phys Soc; Sigma Xi. *Res:* Coherent phenomena in quantum field theory including phase transitions, critical phenomena ; spontaneous symmetry breakdown and nonabelian gauge theories; loop space; hidden symmetry; exactly integrable systems; spin systems; Kramers Wannier duality; transfer matrix; non-perturbative analysis. *Mailing Add:* 1230 York Ave Physics Dept Rockefeller Univ New York NY 10021

DOLAN, THOMAS J(AMES), b Chicago, Ill, Dec 29, 06; m 29; c 2. MECHANICAL ENGINEERING. *Educ:* Univ Ill, BS, 29, MS, 32. *Prof Exp:* Asst & instr theoret & appl mech, Univ Ill, Urbana-Champaign, 29-37, from asst prof to assoc prof, 37-42, res prof, 45-52, head dept eng mech, 52-70; CONSULT ENGR, 73- *Concurrent Pos:* Mem, Nat Res Develop Bd, 48; eng adv bd mem, NSF, 52-57; mem, Nat Res Coun, 55-; eng consult & mem bd dirs, Packer Eng; Am ed, Appl Mat Res, 62-73. *Honors & Awards:* Dudley Medal, Am Soc Testing & Mat, 52, Templin Award, 54; Distinguished Serv

Eng, Univ Ill, 74. *Mem:* Fel Am Soc Mech Engrs (vpres, 58-60); fel Am Soc Testing & Mat; hon mem Soc Exp Stress Anal (pres, 51); Am Soc Eng Educ. *Res:* Fatigue of metals; photoelastic stress analysis; properties of metals; mechanical vibrations; metallurgy; failure analysis; product liability. *Mailing Add:* 510 S Highland Ave Champaign IL 61820

DOLBEAR, GEOFFREY EMERSON, b Richmond, Calif, June 1, 41; m 61; c 2. FUEL SCIENCE. *Educ:* Univ Calif, Berkeley, BS, 62; Stanford Univ, PhD(inorg chem), 66. *Prof Exp:* Res chemist, Film Res Lab, E I du Pont de Nemours & Co, Inc, Del, 65-68, Cracking Catalyst Res Dept, 68-70, Automotive Exhaust Res Dept, 70-73 & Res Div, W R Grace & Co, 73-75; sr res chemist, 75-76, group leader, 76-79, MGR, OCCIDENTAL RES CORP, 79- *Mem:* AAAS; Am Chem Soc; Catalysis Soc. *Res:* Chemistry of processes for manufacture of chemicals and fuels from coal; characterization of coal and coal derived liquids and solids. *Mailing Add:* PO Box 19601 Irvine CA 92713

DOLBIER, WILLIAM READ, JR, b Elizabeth, NJ, Aug 17, 39; m 61; c 3. ORGANIC CHEMISTRY. *Educ:* Stetson Univ, BS, 61; Cornell Univ, PhD(org chem), 65. *Prof Exp:* Fel org chem, Yale Univ, 65-66; assoc prof chem, 66-77, PROF CHEM, UNIV FLA, 77- *Concurrent Pos:* A P Sloan fel, 70-72. *Mem:* Am Chem Soc. *Res:* Thermal rearrangement of small ring hydrocarbons; kinetic and deuterium isotope effect studies of nomechanism reactions; carbene chemistry; reactive organometallic intermediates. *Mailing Add:* Dept of Chem Univ of Fla Gainesville FL 32601

DOLBY, JAMES LOUIS, b Philadelphia, Pa, Apr 29, 26; m 50; c 5. APPLIED STATISTICS. *Educ:* Dartmouth Col, AB, 46; Wesleyan Univ, MA, 49; Stanford Univ, PhD(statist), 66. *Prof Exp:* Mgr math, Eng Lab, Gen Elec Co, 51-60; consult engr, Lockheed Missile & Space Co, 60-64; consult, Corp Econ & Indust Res, 64-65; partner, R&D Consults Co, 65-77; assoc prof math, 66-77, PROF MATH, SAN JOSE STATE UNIV, 77- *Concurrent Pos:* Vis statistician, Univ Newcastle, Eng, 65-66 & Princeton Univ, 66-67. *Mem:* Bernoulli Soc Math Statist & Probability; Am Statist Asn; Am Libr Asn; Math Asn Am; Am Soc Info Sci. *Res:* Data analysis; pattern recognition; linguistic computation. *Mailing Add:* Dept of Math 125 S Seventh St San Jose CA 95192

DOLBY, LLOYD JAY, b Elgin, Ill, Oct 5, 35; m 56; c 3. ORGANIC CHEMISTRY, NATURAL PRODUCTS CHEMISTRY. *Educ:* Univ Ill, BS, 56; Univ Calif, Berkeley, PhD(chem), 59. *Prof Exp:* NSF fel chem, Univ Wis, 59-60; from asst prof to assoc prof, 60-69, PROF CHEM, UNIV ORE, 69- *Concurrent Pos:* Sloan Found res fel, 65-67. *Mem:* Am Chem Soc. *Res:* Synthesis of natural products; reaction mechanisms. *Mailing Add:* Dept of Chem Univ of Ore Eugene OR 97403

DOLCH, WILLIAM LEE, b Kansas City, Mo, July 11, 25; m 48; c 2. PHYSICAL CHEMISTRY. *Educ:* Purdue Univ, BSChE, 47, MS, 49, PhD(chem), 56. *Prof Exp:* Asst hwy engr, 47-56, res assoc & asst prof, 56-60, assoc prof, 60-65, PROF ENG MAT, SCH CIVIL ENG, PURDUE UNIV, WEST LAFAYETTE, 65- *Concurrent Pos:* Mem, Transp Res Bd, Nat Acad Sci-Nat Res Coun. *Honors & Awards:* Dudley Medal, Am Soc Testing & Mat, 66; Wason Medal, Am Concrete Inst, 68. *Mem:* Fel Am Soc Testing & Mat; Am Concrete Inst. *Res:* Physico-chemical properties of engineering materials; concrete and concrete aggregates; problems of concrete. *Mailing Add:* Sch of Civil Eng Purdue Univ West Lafayette IN 47907

DOLE, HOLLIS MATHEWS, b Paonia, Colo, Sept 4, 14; m 43; c 2. ECONOMIC GEOLOGY. *Educ:* Ore State Col, BS, 40, MS, 42; Univ Utah, PhD(geol), 54. *Hon Degrees:* DrEng, Mont Tech Col Mineral Sci & Technol, 71. *Prof Exp:* Mining engr, US Bur Mines, 42-43; geologist, US Geol Surv, 46; state geologist & dir state dept geol & mineral indust, Ore, 46-69; asst secy mineral resources, US Dept Interior, 69-73; gen mgr colony develop oper, Atlantic Richfield Co, 73-76; mgr, Washington Off, 76-79; CONSULT ENERGY & MINERALS, 79- *Honors & Awards:* Gold Medal Honor, US Dept Interior, 72. *Mem:* Am Asn Petrol Geologists; Am Inst Mining, Metall & Petrol Eng; Geol Soc Am; Soc Econ Geol. *Res:* Ultrabasics; oil shale development. *Mailing Add:* 75 Condolea Way Lake Oswego OR 97034

DOLE, JIM, b Phoenix, Ariz, May 28, 35; m 57; c 3. VERTEBRATE ECOLOGY. *Educ:* Ariz State Univ, BA, 57; Univ Mich, MS, 59, PhD(zool), 63. *Prof Exp:* Instr zool, Univ Mich, 62-63; from asst prof to assoc prof biol, 63-70, PROF BIOL, CALIF STATE UNIV, NORTHRIDGE, 70- *Mem:* AAAS; Ecol Soc Am; Am Soc Ichthyologists & Herpetologists. *Res:* Vertebrate ecology and behavior; population ecology. *Mailing Add:* Dept of Biol Calif State Univ Northridge CA 91330

DOLE, MALCOLM, b Melrose, Mass, Mar 4, 03; m 28; c 2. PHYSICAL CHEMISTRY. *Educ:* Harvard Univ, AB, 24, AM, 26, PhD(chem), 28. *Prof Exp:* Asst Rockefeller Inst, 28-30; from instr to assoc prof phys chem, 30-45, prof chem, 45-69, prof mat sci, 64-69, chmn mat res ctr, 64-68, EMER PROF CHEM & MAT SCI, NORTHWESTERN UNIV, 69-; ROBERT A WELCH PROF CHEM, BAYLOR UNIV, 69- *Concurrent Pos:* Hon fac mem, Univ Chile, 51 & Univ San Marcos, Peru, 55; mem bd trustees, Gordon Res Conf, 58-61; chmn chem rev comt, Argonne Nat Lab, 57-63; mem adv panel, Off Inst Prog, NSF, 62-65. *Honors & Awards:* Army-Navy Cert Appreciation, 47; Southwest Regional Award, Am Chem Soc, 79. *Mem:* AAAS; Am Chem Soc; Am Phys Soc; cor mem Peruvian Chem Soc; cor mem Nat Acad Exact, Phys & Natural Sci Argentina. *Res:* Physical and radiation chemistry of high polymers. *Mailing Add:* Dept Chem Baylor Univ Waco TX 76798

DOLE, VINCENT PAUL, b Chicago, Ill, May 8, 13; m 42; c 3. MEDICINE. *Educ:* Stanford Univ, AB, 34; Harvard Univ, MD, 39. *Prof Exp:* Intern, Mass Gen Hosp, Boston, 40-41; from asst resident to resident, 41-46, assoc mem & assoc physician, 47-51, MEM & PHYSICIAN, ROCKEFELLER INST & HOSP, 51-, PROF MED, ROCKEFELLER UNIV, 59- *Concurrent Pos:* Co-ed, J Exp Med, 56-65. *Mem:* Nat Acad Sci; AAAS; Am Soc Clin Invest; Soc Exp Biol & Med; Asn Am Physicians. *Res:* Cardiovascular and metabolic research. *Mailing Add:* Dept of Med Rockefeller Univ New York NY 10021

DOLECEK, ELWYN HAYDN, b Lubbock, Tex, Mar 1, 46; m 70. RADIOLOGICAL PHYSICS. *Educ:* Valparaiso Univ, BS, 68; Rutgers Univ, MS, 71, PhD(radiol physics), 75. *Prof Exp:* Oceanogr, Naval Oceanog Off, 67-69; radiol physicist health physics, Rutgers Univ, 71-77; HEALTH PHYSICIST, ARGONNE NAT LAB, 77- *Mem:* Nat Health Physics Soc. *Res:* Thermoluminescent dosimetry with emphasis on lithium fluoride dosimeters as well as the development of DNA as a practical thermoluminescent dosimeter for measuring human exposure to ionizing radiation. *Mailing Add:* OHS/HP Argonne Nat Lab 9700 Cass Ave Argonne IL 60439

DOLEN, RICHARD, theoretical physics, elementary particle physics, see previous edition

DOLENKO, ALLAN JOHN, b Winnipeg, Man, June 24, 42; m 65; c 2. ORGANIC POLYMER CHEMISTRY. *Educ:* Univ Man, BSc, 64, MSc, 65; Queen's Univ, PhD(chem), 70. *Prof Exp:* Sr chemist, Chemco Ltd, 70 & Actol Chem Ltd, 71; RES SCIENTIST, EASTERN FOREST PROD LAB, ENVIRON CAN, 71- *Mem:* Forest Prod Res Soc. *Mailing Add:* 2043 Kingsgrove Cresent Gloucester Can

DOLES, JOHN HENRY, III, b Youngstown, Ohio, Nov 20, 43. OCEAN ACOUSTICS, SYSTEMS ENGINEERING. *Educ:* Case Inst Technol, BS, 65; Mass Inst Technol, PhD(math), 69. *Prof Exp:* mem tech staff geophys, Bell Tel Labs, 69-81, SYSTS ENGR, BELL LABS, 81- *Mem:* Soc Indust & Appl Math; Am Geophys Union. *Res:* Computational physics; ionospheric physics; ocean acoustics. *Mailing Add:* Bell Labs Whippany NJ 07981

DOLEZAL, VACLAV J, b Ceska Trebova, Czech, May 21, 27; m 63; c 3. APPLIED MATHEMATICS. *Educ:* Tech Univ Prague, Ing, 49; Czech Acad Sci, CSc(appl math), 56, DrSc(appl math), 66. *Prof Exp:* Res assoc math, Math Inst, Czech Acad Sci, 51-56, mathematician, 56-65; vis prof appl math, Eng Col, State Univ NY Stony Brook, 65-66; mathematician, Math Inst, Czech Acad Sci, 66-68; PROF APPL MATH, STATE UNIV NY STONY BROOK, 68- *Concurrent Pos:* Vis prof, Univ Linz, Austria, 74-75. *Res:* Operator-theoretic analysis of nonlinear systems; optimal digital filters. *Mailing Add:* Dept Appl Math & Statist State Univ NY Stony Brook NY 11794

DOLEZALEK, HANS, b Berlin, Ger, May 14, 12; US citizen; m 51; c 3. MARITIME REMOTE SENSING, COASTAL GEOGRAPHY. *Educ:* Aachen Tech Univ, Diplom, 56. *Prof Exp:* Chief int rels, Dept Foreign Acad, Charlottenburg, Ger, 32-41; physicist, Aeronaut Commun Res Inst, Oberpfaffenhofen, 44-45; scientist with Dr H Israel, Aachen, 50-57; asst head, Meteorol Observ, 57-61; group leader atmospheric physics, Space Systs Div, Avco Corp, 61-66; consult, Boston Col, 66-67; PHYSICIST, OFF NAVAL RES, 67- *Concurrent Pos:* Chmn subcomt I, Int Comn Atmospheric Elec, 63-75, secy, 64-75, chmn subcomt VII, 75-; chmn comt atmospheric & space elec, Am Geophys Union, 69-74, mem, 74-; mem working group atmospheric elec, Comn Atmospheric Sci, World Meteorol Orgn, 68-78, US deleg session V, 70, rapporteur atmospheric elec, 74-78, US deleg session Caracas, 75; hon mem, Int Comn Atmospheric Elec, chmn subcomt VII, 76-, chmn res study group maritime remote sensing NATO/ORG/III, 78-80, US delegate, 80- *Mem:* AAAS; Am Meteorol Soc; Am Geophys Union; NY Acad Sci. *Res:* Theoretical and experimental research on basic problems of atmospheric electricity; consulting and guidance for research projects and initiation of coordinated efforts in atmospheric electricity and in coastal geography and in maritime remote sensing on national and international scale. *Mailing Add:* 1812 Drury Lane Alexandria VA 22307

DOLFINI, JOSEPH E, b Middletown, NY, July 11, 36; m 62. ORGANIC CHEMISTRY, MEDICINAL CHEMISTRY. *Educ:* Univ Mich, BS, 57, MS, 61, PhD(chem), 62. *Prof Exp:* NIH fel org chem, Columbia Univ, 61-63; asst prof chem, Purdue Univ, West Lafayette, 63-65; res supvr, Squibb Inst, 65-73; head dept org chem, Merrell-Nat Labs, 73-78, assoc dir drug develop, 78-81; PRES & SCI CONSULT, NOBILENT INC, CINCINNATI, 81- *Mem:* Am Chem Soc; Royal Soc Chem; NY Acad Sci. *Res:* Synthetic organic chemistry; heterocyclic and carbocyclic synthesis; new reaction mechanisms; natural products synthesis. *Mailing Add:* Suite 133 Nobilent Inc 10999 Reed Hartman Hwy Cincinnati OH 45242

DOLGIN, MARTIN, b New York, NY, Apr 12, 19; m 50; c 3. CARDIOLOGY, INTERNAL MEDICINE. *Educ:* NY Univ, AB, 40, MD, 43; Am Bd Internal Med, dipl, 51 & 74; Am Bd Cardiovasc Dis, dipl, 56. *Prof Exp:* Intern & asst resident med, Lincoln Hosp, New York, 43-45; from instr to assoc prof, 48-73, PROF CLIN MED, SCH MED, NY UNIV, 73-; CHIEF CARDIOL SECT, NEW YORK VET ADMIN HOSP, 54- *Concurrent Pos:* Fel internal med, Lahey Clin, Boston, 45-47; fel cardiovasc dis res, Michael Reese Hosp, Chicago, 47-48; lectr med, Columbia Univ, 48-68; consult cardiol, Will Rogers Hosp, Saranac, NY, 61-71 & Columbus Hosp, New York, 68-72; attend physician, Bellevue Hosp & Univ Hosp, New York, 73- *Mem:* Am Heart Asn; fel Am Col Physicians; fel Am Col Cardiol; Am Fedn Clin Res. *Res:* Clinical electrocardiography. *Mailing Add:* New York Vet Admin Hosp 24th St & First Ave New York NY 10010

DOLGOFF, ABRAHAM, b New Brunswick, NJ, Aug 10, 33; m 56. ENGINEERING GEOLOGY, PETROLEUM GEOLOGY. *Educ:* City Col New York, BS, 53; NY Univ, MS, 58; Rice Univ, PhD(geol), 60. *Prof Exp:* Jr civil engr, Bd Water Supply, City New York, 53-55, asst civil engr, Dept Pub Works, 55-58; res geologist, Rice Univ, 60-61 & Bellaire Labs, Texaco, Inc, 61-66; specialist eng geol of dams, Gerard Eng Inc, 66-71 & eng geol of dams & tunnels, Harza Eng Co, 71-74; sr geologist, 72-77, SR SPECIALIST GEOL, SARGENT & LUNDY, ENGRS, 77- *Concurrent Pos:* Lectr, Hunter Col, 70; gen chmn, Annual Meeting, Asn Eng Geologists, 76-79; qual assurance expert, Sargent & Lundy, 81- *Honors & Awards:* Cert of Appreciation, Asn Eng Geologists, 76. *Mem:* Geol Soc Am; Am Asn Petrol Geol; Asn Eng Geol. *Res:* Applied geology-geologic, environmental, seismic aspects, siting and construction engineering works (nuclear power plants, waste disposal facilities); regional factors, petroleum accumulation; quality assurance and administration. *Mailing Add:* Sargent & Lundy Engrs 55 E Monroe St Chicago IL 60603

DOLHINOW, PHYLLIS CAROL, b Elgin, Ill, Nov 6, 33; m 68; c 1. PHYSICAL ANTHROPOLOGY. *Educ:* Beloit Col, AB, 55; Univ Chicago, AM, 60, PhD(anthrop), 63. *Prof Exp:* Lectr anthrop, Univ Calif, Berkeley, 61-62; asst prof, Columbia Univ, 63-64; asst prof, Univ Calif, Davis, 64-66; from asst prof to assoc prof, 66-71, PROF ANTHROP, UNIV CALIF, BERKELEY, 71- *Concurrent Pos:* Fel, Ctr Advan Study Behav Sci, 62-63; asst res anthropologist, Nat Ctr Primate Biol, 64-66; Wenner-Gren Found anthrop res grant primatology in Africa, 66; NSF grant, Primate Behav Unit, Univ Calif, Berkeley, 67-71, NIMH grant, 73-77, Miller prof, 75-76. *Mem:* Fel AAAS; Sigma Xi; fel Am Anthrop Asn; Ecol Soc Am; Animal Behav Soc. *Res:* Primate social behavior and ecology in Asia and Africa; human evolution and behavior; attachment and social bonds. *Mailing Add:* Dept Anthrop Univ Calif Berkeley CA 94720

DOLIN, MORTON IRWIN, b Brooklyn, NY, Dec 24, 20. BIOCHEMISTRY. *Educ:* City Col New York, BS, 42; Univ Ky, MS, 44; Ind Univ, PhD(bact), 50. *Prof Exp:* Res fel, Univ Ill, 50-52; biochemist, Oak Ridge Nat Lab, 52-69; vis investr, Agr Univ, Wageningen, 70-71; NIH spec fel, Dept Biochem, 71-73, RES ASSOC MICROBIOL, UNIV MICH, ANN ARBOR, 73- *Concurrent Pos:* Guggenheim fel, 59-60. *Mem:* Am Soc Microbiol; Am Soc Biol Chemists. *Res:* Electron transport reactions; pyridine nucleotides. *Mailing Add:* Dept of Microbiol Univ of Mich Ann Arbor MI 48105

DOLIN, RICHARD, b Brooklyn, NY, May 16, 21; m 45; c 3. ELECTRICAL ENGINEERING. *Educ:* NY Univ, BS, 47, MS, 50. *Prof Exp:* Instr elec eng, NY Univ, 47-51; engr-in-charge commun & control systs, Res Labs, Sylvania Elec Prod, NY, 51-56; prin engr reconnaissance & electronic systs, Bulova Res & Develop Labs, 56-58; sr res engr, Fairchild Camera & Instrument Co, 58-59; consult, Airborne Instruments Lab Div, Cutler-Hammer Inc, 59-61; assoc prof eng sci, 61-70, chmn dept, 68-70 & 77-80, PROF ENG SCI, HOFSTRA UNIV, 70-, DIR TECHNOL & PUB POLICY, 79- *Mem:* Sr mem Inst Elec & Electronics Engrs; Am Soc Eng Educ. *Res:* Analysis and design of communications and reconnaissance systems. *Mailing Add:* 941 Alice Ct North Bellmore NY 11710

DOLL, EUGENE CARTER, b Ft Benton, Mont, Feb 15, 21; m 47; c 3. SOIL FERTILITY. *Educ:* Mont State Col, BS, 49, MS, 51; Univ Wis, PhD(soils), 53. *Prof Exp:* Asst, Mont State Col, 50-51; from asst agronomist to assoc agronomist soil fertil, Univ Ky, 53-60, assoc prof soils, 58-60; from assoc prof soils to prof soil sci, Mich State Univ, 60-74; agronomist, Int Staff, Tenn Valley Authority, 74-75; soil scientist, Int Fertilizer Develop Ctr, 75-76; int training, USDA, 78-80; SUPT, LAND RECLAMATION RES CTR, NDAK STATE UNION RECLAMATION, 81- *Concurrent Pos:* Regional maize adv, Int Atomic Energy Agency, 66; regional dir, NC State Univ Proj for AID, Ecuador & Panama, 70-71. *Mem:* Fel Am Soc Agron; fel Soil Sci Soc Am. *Res:* Nitrogen, phosphorus and potash requirements of general farm crops; phosphorus availability in tropical and subtropical soils and the evaluation of various sources of phosphate fertilizers, including phosphate rock; reclamation techniques for returning stripmined lands to full agricultural productivity. *Mailing Add:* NDak State Union Reclamation PO Box 459 Mandan ND 58554

DOLL, JERRY DENNIS, b Pocahontas, Ill, Oct 26, 43; m 73; c 3. PLANT SCIENCE, WEED SCIENCE. *Educ:* Univ Ill, BS, 65; Mich State Univ, MS, 66, PhD(crop sci), 69. *Prof Exp:* Vol, Peace Corps, 69-71; weed scientist, Int Ctr Trop Agr, 71-76; WEED SCIENTIST, UNIV WIS, MADISON, 77- *Mem:* Weed Sci Soc Am; Am Soc Agron; hon mem Colombian Weed Sci Soc (vpres, 74, pres, 75); Int Weed Sci Soc; Latin Am Weed Sci Soc. *Res:* Perennial weed research, including allelopathy studies. *Mailing Add:* Dept of Agron Univ of Wis Madison WI 53706

DOLL, JIMMIE DAVE, b San Diego, Calif, Oct 19, 45; m 66; c 1. PHYSICAL CHEMISTRY. *Educ:* Univ Kans, BS, 67; Harvard Univ, PhD(phys chem), 71. *Prof Exp:* From asst prof to assoc prof chem, State Univ NY, Stony Brook, 75-80; staff mem, 79-81, FEL, LOS ALAMOS NAT LAB, 81- *Concurrent Pos:* NSF fel, 71-72; Sloan Found fel, 76-78; vis staff mem, Los Alamos Sci Lab, 77- *Mem:* Am Phys Soc. *Res:* Theoretical chemistry; surface chemistry. *Mailing Add:* Los Alamos Nat Lab CNC 2/MS 738 Los Alamos NM 87545

DOLLAHITE, JAMES WALTON, b Center Point, Tex, May 1, 11; m 34; c 2. VETERINARY TOXICOLOGY. *Educ:* Agr & Mech Col Tex, DVM, 33, MS, 61; Am Bd Vet Toxicol, dipl. *Prof Exp:* Pvt pract, 33-34; jr vet dis control, Bur Animal Indust, USDA, 34-36 & Path Div, 36-39; pvt pract, 39-42 & 46-52; supt animal dis invest lab, Tex Agr Exp Sta, 52-61; mem res staff, Col Vet Med, Tex A&M Univ, 61-64, from assoc prof to prof vet path, 64-67, prof physiol & pharmacol, 67-68, prof toxicol, 68-75; vet med officer, vet toxicol & entom res lab, Agr Res Serv, USDA, 75-77; RETIRED. *Mem:* Fel AAAS; Am Col Vet Toxicologists (pres, 69-71); NY Acad Sci; Am Vet Med Asn; Soc Toxicol. *Res:* Toxic plants. *Mailing Add:* 4200 Milam St Bryan TX 77801

DOLLAHON, JAMES CLIFFORD, b Roswell, NMex, Sept 27, 30; m 54. ANIMAL BREEDING. *Educ:* NMex State Univ, BS, 52; Univ Fla, MS, 56, PhD(animal husb), 58. *Prof Exp:* Asst, Univ Fla, 55-58; asst prof animal husb, Miss State Univ, 58-60; PROF ANIMAL SCI, UNIV WIS-RIVER FALLS, 60-, DEAN COL AGR, 64- *Mem:* Am Soc Animal Sci; Am Asn Univ Agr Adminrs (pres, 75-77); Am Genetic Asn. *Res:* Population; physiological and statistical genetics; differential and integral calculus. *Mailing Add:* Off of Dean Col of Agr Univ of Wis River Falls WI 54022

DOLLAHON, NORMAN RICHARD, b Gallup, NMex, Apr 22, 44; m 66; c 1. PROTOZOOLOGY, PARASITOLOGY. *Educ:* Univ NMex, BS, 66, MS, 68; Univ Nebr-Lincoln, PhD(zool), 71. *Prof Exp:* USPHS trainee parasitol, Rutgers Univ, 72-73; ASST PROF BIOL, VILLANOVA UNIV, 73- *Mem:* Am Soc Parasitologists; Soc Protozoologists. *Res:* Study of infections of insects, reptiles and mammals with trypanosomatid flagellates. *Mailing Add:* Dept of Biol Villanova Univ Villanova PA 19085

DOLLAR, ALEXANDER M, b Vancouver, BC, Apr 7, 21; US citizen; m 44; c 1. ANIMAL NUTRITION, FOOD BIOCHEMISTRY. *Educ:* Univ Calif, Berkeley, BS, 48, MS, 49; Reading Univ, PhD(nutrit & biochem), 58. *Prof Exp:* From asst prof to assoc prof food sci, Col Fisheries, Univ Wash, 59-67; supvr, Hawaii Develop Irradiator, Hawaii Dept Agr, 67-76; PROF ENVIRON HEALTH SCI, UNIV HAWAII, 76- *Mem:* AAAS; Am Chem Soc; Inst Food Technologists; Brit Biochem Soc; Am Indust Hyg Asn. *Mailing Add:* 700 Richards St Apt 1504 Honolulu HI 96813

DOLLARD, JOHN D, b New Haven, Conn, Jan 19, 37. PHYSICS, MATHEMATICS. *Educ:* Yale Univ, BA, 58; Princeton Univ, MA, 60, PhD(physics), 63. *Prof Exp:* Res assoc physics, Princeton Univ, 63-65; asst prof math, Univ Rochester, 65-68; vis asst prof math & physics, Yale Univ, 68-69; assoc prof, 69-79, PROF MATH, UNIV TEX, AUSTIN, 79- *Mem:* Am Phys Soc; Am Math Soc; Math Asn Am. *Res:* Quantum mechanical scattering theory. *Mailing Add:* Dept of Math Univ of Tex Austin TX 78712

DOLLHOPF, WILLIAM EDWARD, b Pittsburgh, Pa, June 13, 42; m 64; c 2. NUCLEAR PHYSICS. *Educ:* Thiel Col, AB, 64; Western Reserve Univ, MS, 67; Col William & Mary, PhD(physics), 75. *Prof Exp:* Instr physics, Alliance Col, 66-69; accelerator scientist, Space Radiation Effects Lab, Newport News, 74-75; asst prof physics, Wabash Col, 75-80; ASST PROF PHYS, WITTENBERG UNIV, 80- *Concurrent Pos:* Beam transp consult, Space Radiation Effects Lab, Newport News, 74-75. *Mem:* Am Asn Physics Teachers; Am Phys Soc. *Res:* Quasi-elastic nuclear reactions at intermediate energies to determine the structure of clusters within nuclei; charged particle beam transport systems. *Mailing Add:* Dept Physics Wittenberg Univ Springfield OH 45501

DOLLING, DAVID STANLEY, b Bournemouth, UK, Mar 21, 50. HIGH SPEED EXTERNAL AERODYNAMICS. *Educ:* London Univ, BSc, 71, PhD(aerospace sci), 77; von Karman Inst, Belg, dipl, 74. *Prof Exp:* Aerodynamicist, Hawker Siddeley Dynamics, UK, 71-73; MEM RES STAFF & LECTR VISCOUS FLOWS, MECH & AEROSPACE ENG DEPT, PRINCETON UNIV, 76- *Mem:* Am Inst Aeronaut; Royal Aeronaut Soc. *Res:* Supersonic fluid dynamics; interactions of shock waves with turbulent boundary layers. *Mailing Add:* Gas Dynamics Lab Forrestal Campus Princeton Univ Princeton NJ 08544

DOLLING, GERALD, b Dunstable, Eng, Nov 21, 35; m 59; c 3. SOLID STATE PHYSICS. *Educ:* Cambridge Univ, BA, 57, PhD(physics), 61. *Prof Exp:* RES OFFICER PHYSICS, ATOMIC ENERGY CAN LTD, 61-, HEAD, NEUTRON & SOLID STATE PHYSICS BR, 79- *Mem:* Fel Am Phys Soc; Can Asn Physicists. *Res:* Lattice and magnetic dynamics; neutron scattering from condensed systems; ferroelectricity. *Mailing Add:* 17 Cabot Pl Chalk River Nuclear Labs Deep River ON K0J 1P0 Can

DOLLINGER, ELWOOD JOHNSON, b Lynchburg, Ohio, Apr 20, 20; m 55; c 2. CYTOGENETICS, PLANT BREEDING. *Educ:* Ohio State Univ, BSc, 44; Pa State Univ, MSc, 47; Columbia Univ, PhD(cytogenetics, bot), 53. *Prof Exp:* Agt, US Regional Pasture Res Lab, 44-47; asst, Columbia Univ, 47-48 & Univ Ill, 49-50; res assoc, Carnegie Inst, 50-51 & Brookhaven Nat Lab, 51-53; USPHS fel, Nat Cancer Inst, 53-55; PROF CYTOGENETICS, OHIO AGR RES & DEVELOP CTR, 55- *Mem:* Genetics Soc Am; Am Genetic Asn; Am Soc Agron. *Res:* Cytogenetics of maize; radiation induced mutation of maize; corn breeding. *Mailing Add:* Dept Agron Ohio Agr Res & Develop Ctr Wooster OH 44691

DOLLWET, HELMAR HERMANN ADOLF, b Merzig, Ger, Jan 20, 29; US citizen; div; c 4. PLANT PHYSIOLOGY, PLANT BIOCHEMISTRY. *Educ:* Univ Mich, BS, 58; Univ Calif, Riverside, MS, 67, PhD(plant sci & physiol), 69. *Prof Exp:* Asst prof, 70-80, ASSOC PROF BIOL, UNIV AKRON, 80- *Res:* Antiinflamatory properties of copper in rheumatoid diseases. *Mailing Add:* Dept Biol Univ Akron Akron OH 44304

DOLLY, EDWARD DAWSON, b Davenport, Iowa, July 29, 40; m 60; c 2. GEOLOGY. *Educ:* Univ Ill, BS, 63; Univ Okla, MS, 65, PhD(geol), 69. *Prof Exp:* Explor geologist, Shell Oil Co, 69-73; explor geologist oil & gas, Filon Explor Corp, 73-78; INDEPENDENT GEOLOGIST, 78- *Honors & Awards:* Leverson Award, Am Asn Petrol Geologists, 80. *Mem:* Am Asn Petrol Geologists; Sigma Xi. *Res:* Oil, gas and mineral exploration worldwide. *Mailing Add:* Rte 7 Box 340B Evergreen CO 80439

DOLMAGE, VICTOR, geology, deceased

DOLMAN, CLAUDE ERNEST, b Portleven, Eng, May 23, 06; m 31, 55; c 6. MEDICAL MICROBIOLOGY. *Educ:* Univ London, MB, BS, 30, DPH, 31, PhD(bact), 35; FRCP; FRCP(C). *Prof Exp:* House surgeon, St Mary's Hosp, 29; clin asst, Royal Chest Hosp & Hosp Sick Children, London, 30; res scholar, St Mary's Hosp Inst Path & Res, 31; clin assoc & res asst, Connaught Labs, Toronto, 31-33, res & clin assoc, 33-35, demonstr hyg & prev med, 33-35, res mem, 35-73; EMER PROF MICROBIOL, UNIV BC, 71- *Concurrent Pos:* Assoc prof bact & prev med & actg head dept, Univ BC, 35-36, prof & head dept, 36-51, prof bact & immunol & head dept, 51-65, res prof microbiol, 65-71; actg head dept nursing & health, 35-43, prof & head dept, 43-51; dir div labs, Dept Health, BC, 35-56; hon consult bacteriologist, Vancouver Gen Hosp, 36- *Honors & Awards:* Coronation Medal, 53; Jubilee Medal, 78. *Mem:* Fel Am Pub Health Asn; hon life mem Can Pub Health Asn; fel Royal Soc Can (pres, 69-70); hon life mem Can Asn Med Microbiologists (pres, 64-66); hon mem, Am Soc Microbiologists. *Res:* Staphylococcus toxins; botulinum toxins; brucellosis; cholera; salmonellosis; bacterial food poisoning; history of bacteriology and microbiology. *Mailing Add:* 1611 Cedar Crescent Vancouver BC V6J 2P8 Can

DOLOVICH, JERRY, b Winnipeg, Ont, Can, Apr 2, 36; m 63; c 3. ALLERGY. *Educ:* Univ Man, MD, 59. *Prof Exp:* PROF, DEPT PEDIAT, FAC HEALTH SCI, MCMASTER UNIV, 78- *Mailing Add:* Health Sci Ctr Rm 3V41 McMaster Univ Hamilton ON L8S 4J9 Can

DOLPH, CHARLES LAURIE, b Ann Arbor, Mich, Aug 27, 18; m 44; c 2. APPLIED MATHEMATICS. *Educ:* Univ Mich, BA, 39; Princeton Univ, MA, 41, PhD(math), 44. *Prof Exp:* Asst, Nat Defense Res Comt, Princeton Univ, 41-42, instr math, 42; theoret physicist, Naval Res Lab, Washington, DC, 43-45; mem tech staff, Math Group, Bell Tel Labs, 45-46; from asst prof to assoc prof math, 46-59, math res, Eng Res Inst, 46-64, head theoret & comput div, Willow Run Res Ctr, 52-64, PROF MATH, UNIV MICH, ANN ARBOR, 59- *Concurrent Pos:* Consult, Ramo-Wooldridge, 54-57 & Bendix Aviation Corp, 59-; Guggenheim fel, 57; mem Nat Acad Sci-Nat Res Coun adv comt math, Off Naval Res, 64-66; vis res prof, Army Math Res Ctr, Wis, 65; vis prof, Univ Stuttgart, 72. *Honors & Awards:* Thompson Prize, Inst Elec & Electronics Engineers. *Mem:* AAAS; Am Math Soc. *Res:* Nonlinear integral equations; antenna theory; theory of compressible flow; stochastic processes; vibration theory; anomalous propagation theory; transform theory. *Mailing Add:* Dept of Math Univ of Mich Ann Arbor MI 48109

DOLPH, GARY EDWARD, b Binghamton, NY, Oct 17, 46; m 70, 82; c 2. PALEOBOTANY. *Educ:* State Univ NY Binghamton, BA, 68; Ind Univ, MA, 73, PhD(bot), 74. *Prof Exp:* Asst prof, 74-78, ASSOC PROF PLANT SCI, IND UNIV, 78- *Concurrent Pos:* Ed, Int Asn Angiosperm Paleobotanists; grants, Exxon Educ Found & NSF Comprehensive Asst Undergrad Sci Educ. *Mem:* Paleont Soc; Bot Soc Am; Sigma Xi; Biomet Soc; Int Asn Angio Paleobotany. *Res:* Multivariate statistics in analyzing the gross morphology and cuticular structure of modern and fossil leaves; contruction of a data bank containing information on modern and fossil leaves. *Mailing Add:* Ind Univ 2300 S Washington St Kokomo IN 46901

DOLPHIN, DAVID HENRY, b London, Eng, Jan 15, 40; m 63; c 3. BIO-ORGANIC CHEMISTRY, BIOINORGANIC CHEMISTRY. *Educ:* Nottingham Univ, BSc, 62, PhD(chem), 65. *Prof Exp:* Res fel chem, Harvard Univ, 65-66, from instr to assoc prof, 66-74; assoc prof, 74-79, PROF CHEM, UNIV BC, 79- *Concurrent Pos:* Guggenheim fel, 80; vis prof, Harvard Univ, 80. *Mem:* Am Chem Soc; The Chem Soc; Royal Inst Chem; Chem Inst Can. *Res:* Structure, synthesis, chemistry and biochemistry of porphyrins, vitamin B12, and related macrocycles. *Mailing Add:* Dept of Chem Univ of BC 2075 Wesbrook Pl Vancouver Can

DOLPHIN, JOHN MICHAEL, b Mahanoy City, Pa, Nov 21, 23; m 50; c 3. PATHOLOGY. *Educ:* Hahnemann Med Col, MD, 47. *Prof Exp:* Resident path, Hahnemann Med & Hosp, 49-50, 52-54; resident path, Pa Hosp, 54-55; from asst prof to assoc prof path, Hahnemann Med Col, 63-74; LAB DIR LAB PROCEDURES, UPJOHN CO, 74- *Mem:* AMA; Col Am Path. *Res:* Pathology of tumors; hypertensive vascular lesions. *Mailing Add:* Lab Procedures Upjohn Co 1075 First Ave King of Prussia PA 19406

DOLPHIN, LAMBERT TYLER, JR, b Shoshone, Idaho, May 24, 32. PHYSICS. *Educ:* San Diego State Col, AB, 54. *Prof Exp:* Asst mgr, Radio Physics Lab, Stanford Res Inst, 56-68; consult & lectr, 68-72; SR PHYSICIST, RADIO PHYSICS LAB, SRI INT, 72- *Mem:* AAAS; Am Geophys Union; Acoust Soc Am; Am Sci Affil; Soc Explor Geophysicists. *Res:* Radio communication and propagation; geophysics; archaeology; remote sensing. *Mailing Add:* 21111 Grenola Dr Cupertino CA 95014

DOLPHIN, PETER JAMES, b Derby, Eng, Mar 5, 47; Can citizen. BIOCHEMISTRY. *Educ:* Southampton Univ, UK, BSc hons, 68, PhD(biochem endocrinol), 71. *Prof Exp:* Res scientist, Nat Inst Med Res, London, UK, 71-72; Can Heart Found fel biochem, McGill Univ, 72-75, res assoc, 75-76, res scholar & asst prof biochem, 76-78; asst prof, 78-82, ASSOC PROF BIOCHEM, DALHOUSIE UNIV, 82- *Concurrent Pos:* Mem, Grant Rev Comt, Can Heart Found, 80- *Mem:* Fel Am Heart Asn; Can Soc Clin Invest; Can Biochem Soc; Electromoresis Soc. *Res:* The influence of dietary and hormonal factors on the sub-cellular assembly secretion and metabolism of plasma lipoproteins in animal models of atherosclerosis; human disorders of lipoprotein metabolism. *Mailing Add:* Dept Biochem Dalhousie Univ Halifax NS B3H 4H7 Can

DOLPHIN, ROBERT EARL, b Worcester, Mass, Oct 4, 29; m 49; c 2. ENTOMOLOGY. *Educ:* San Jose State Col, BA, 58; Purdue Univ, West Lafayette, PhD(entom), 66. *Prof Exp:* Mgr entom, Mosquito Abatement Dist, Calif, 58-61; instr agr entom, Agr Exp Sta, Purdue Univ, West Lafayette, 61-65; res entomologist, Entom Res Div, 65-68, supvr res entomologist & res leader, 68-75, ASSOC AREA DIR, MID-GREAT PLAINS AREA, NCENT REGION, AGR RES SERV, USDA, 75- *Mem:* AAAS; Sigma Xi; Entom Soc Am. *Res:* Biological control and ecology of deciduous fruit insects. *Mailing Add:* 1107 Ridge Rd Columbia MO 65201

DOLPHIN, WARREN DEAN, b Philadelphia, Pa, Feb 17, 40; m 63; c 2. CELL PHYSIOLOGY, SCIENCE EDUCATION. *Educ:* W Chester State Col, BS, 62; Ohio State Univ, PhD(cell biol), 68. *Prof Exp:* Res fel zool, Univ Maine, 68-69; asst prof, 69-70; asst prof, 70-75, assoc prof, 75-79, PROF ZOOL, IOWA STATE UNIV, 79-, EXEC OFFICER BIOL, 77- *Concurrent Pos:* NIH grant, 68-70; NSF grants, 76-79 & 81-83; consult, Am Col Testing Prog, 78. *Mem:* AAAS; Soc of Protozool; Sigma Xi; Int Cong Individualized Instr (pres). *Res:* Nitrogen metabolism in Acanthamoeba; multivariate analysis of student achievement in self-paced instructional systems. *Mailing Add:* Dept of Zool Iowa State Univ Ames IA 50011

DOLUISIO, JAMES THOMAS, b Bethlehem, Pa, Sept 28, 35; m 69; c 3. PHARMACEUTICS. *Educ:* Temple Univ, BS, 57, MS, 59; Purdue Univ, PhD(phys pharm), 62. *Prof Exp:* From asst to assoc prof pharm, Philadelphia Col Pharm & Sci, 61-67; prof & asst dean, Col Pharm, Univ Ky, 67-73; PROF PHARM & DEAN COL PHARM, UNIV TEX, 73- *Concurrent Pos:* NSF fel, Am Found Pharmaceut Educ; consult, Hoechst-Roussel Pharmaceut, Inc & Nat Inst Drug Abuse, 73- *Mem:* Sigma Xi; Am Found Pharmaceut Educ; Am Asn Col Pharm; AAAS; Acad Pharmaceut Sci (vpres elect, 75). *Res:* Bioequivalence as a measure of therapeutic equivalence; factors affecting drug absorption; pharmacokinetic studies in animals and in man. *Mailing Add:* Col of Pharm Univ of Tex Austin TX 78712

DOLYAK, FRANK, b Statford, Conn, Nov 13, 27; m 51; c 3. PHYSIOLOGY. *Educ:* Univ Conn, BA, 50; Univ Kans, PhD(zool), 55. *Prof Exp:* Asst instr zool, Univ Kans, 51-54; from instr to assoc prof physiol, Univ Conn, 54-65; assoc prof biol & chmn dept, Augusta Col, 65-66; chmn dept, 67-73 & 79-81, PROF BIOL, RI COL, 66- *Mem:* AAAS; NY Acad Sci. *Res:* Serology; radiation biology; immunogenetics. *Mailing Add:* Dept of Biol RI Col Providence RI 02908

DOMAGALA, JOHN MICHAEL, b Detroit, Mich, Feb 26, 51; m 72; c 1. ANTI-INFECTIVES. *Educ:* Univ Detroit, BS, 73; Wayne State Univ, PhD(org chem), 77. *Prof Exp:* Res chemist catalysts, Chrysler Corp, 72-73; RES CHEMIST ANTI-INFECTIVES, PARKE DAVIS CO, WARNER-LAMBERT, 79- *Concurrent Pos:* Consult, BASF Wayandotte Corp, 76-77. *Mem:* Am Chem Soc. *Res:* Organic mechanism; rearrangements of epoxides; carbonyl compounds and carbonyl ions; theoretical chemistry; molecular orbital calculations; mechanism of action of anti-infectives; quinoline anti-infectives; totally synthetic anti-infectives. *Mailing Add:* Parker Davis & Co Warner-Lambert Co 2800 Plymouth Rd PO Box 1047 Ann Arbor MI 48106

DOMAGALA, ROBERT F, b Chicago, Ill, Jan 23, 29; m 51; c 3. PHYSICAL METALLURGY. *Educ:* Ill Inst Technol, BS, 50, MS, 54. *Prof Exp:* Mgr metall serv, IIT Res Inst, 50-66; assoc prof metall, 66-72, PROF METALL, UNIV ILL, CHICAGO CIRCLE, 72- *Mem:* Am Soc Metals. *Res:* Determination of binary and more complex phase diagrams; high temperature properties of metals. *Mailing Add:* Dept of Mat Eng Univ of Ill at Chicago Circle Chicago IL 60680

DOMAILLE, PETER JOHN, b Swan Hill, Australia, Aug 10, 48. MOLECULAR SPECTROSCOPY. *Educ:* Monash Univ, Australia, BSc, 69, PhD(chem), 73. *Prof Exp:* Fel chem, Univ Canterbury, 73-75; fel chem, Univ Calif, Santa Barbara, 75-78; MEM STAFF, CENT RES & DEVELOP DEPT, E I DU PONT DE NEMOURS & CO, INC, 78- *Res:* Laser spectroscopy of small molecules and molecular structure determination; nuclear magnetic resonance of organometallics and paramagnetic complexes. *Mailing Add:* Cent Res & Develop Dept E356-B33 E I du Pont de Nemours & Co Inc Wilmington DE 19898

DOMAN, ELVIRA, b New York, NY. BIOCHEMISTRY, ENZYMOLOGY. *Educ:* Hunter Col, BA, 55; NY Univ, MS, 59; Columbia Univ, MA, 60; Rutgers Univ, PhD(physiol, biochem), 65. *Prof Exp:* Jr technician, NY Univ Hosp, 55-56; sr technician cancer chemother, Sloan Kettering Inst Cancer Res, 56-57; sr technician endocrinol, Col Physicians & Surgeons, Columbia Univ, 57, res asst, 58; res asst phys chem, Sloan Kettering Inst Cancer Res, 60-61; Pop Coun fel endocrinol, Rockefeller Univ, 65-66, res assoc, 66-68; lectr, Dept Biol Sci, Douglass Col, Rutgers Univ, 70-73; asst prof biol, Seton Hall Univ, 73-77; asst prog dir, 78-81, PROG DIR REGULATORY BIOL, NSF, 81- *Mem:* AAAS; Am Chem Soc; NY Acad Sci. *Res:* Isolation and characterization of enzymes in respiratory chain of beef heart, of enzymes in rat liver related to endocrinology, and of enzymes involved in the growth of yeast cells and callus tissue. *Mailing Add:* Nat Sci Found 1800 G St NW Washington DC 20550

DOMANIK, RICHARD ANTHONY, b Racine, Wis, Oct 13, 46; m 72; c 2. BIOCHEMISTRY, INSTRUMENTATION. *Educ:* Ripon Col, Wis, BA, 68; Northwestern Univ, Evanston, PhD(chem), 74. *Prof Exp:* Res assoc biophys, Univ Conn, 72-75; asst prof chem, Cent Mich Univ, 75-79; INSTRUMENTATION SCIENTIST, ABBOTT LABS, 79- *Mem:* Am Chem Soc; Biophys Soc; Sigma Xi; Soc Photo-Optical Instrumentation Engrs. *Res:* Development of instrument based systems for clinical diagnostics. *Mailing Add:* Dept 93F Bldg AP9 Abbott Labs North Chicago IL 60064

DOMANSKI, JOHN JOSEPH, JR, b Philadelphia, Pa, Feb 21, 43. TOXICOLOGY, PESTICIDE TOXICOLOGY. *Educ:* Philadelphia Col Textiles & Sci, BS, 66; NC A&T State Univ, MS, 74; NC State Univ, PhD, 75. *Prof Exp:* Res asst entom, 70-75; res plant physiologist, 75-76, TOXICOLOGIST, HERCULES INC, 76- *Mem:* Am Chem Soc; AAAS; Soc Toxicol; Am Col Toxicol; Am Acad Clin Toxicol. *Res:* Physiological mode of action and toxicology of insecticides, herbicides and plant growth regulators. *Mailing Add:* Med Dept Hercules Inc Wilmington DE 19899

DOMANSKI, THADDEUS JOHN, b Jersey City, NJ, June 14, 11; m 34; c 1. CHEMICAL & PHYSICAL CARCINOGENESIS. *Educ:* NY Univ, BS, 32, MS, 36, PhD(col sci teaching), 49. *Prof Exp:* Chemist, Path Dept, Med Ctr, Jersey City, NJ, 35-43; biochemist, Lab Serv, 8th Gen Hosp, US Air Force, 44-45, chief, Bur Labs, Dept Pub Health & Welfare, Hqs, Korea, 46-47, biochemist, Sch Aviation Med, 50, chief lab, 50-54, chief lab serv & actg chief dept path, 54-57, rep, Off Air Force Surgeon Gen, US Army Biol Labs, Ft Detrick, Md, 57-58, chief epidemiol lab, Aerospace Med Ctr, Tex, 58-61, chief toxicol br, Armed Forces Inst Path, 61-66, assoc chief clin biores lab sci, Biomed Sci Corps, 65-66; scientist adminr pharmacol & toxicol, Res Grants Br, Nat Inst Gen Med Sci, 66-67; chief cause & prevention br & prog dir carcinogenesis, 67-78, CHIEF CHEM & PHYS CARCINOGENESIS BR & PROG DIR SPEC PROJS, DIV CANCER CAUSE & PREV, NAT CANCER INST, 78- *Mem:* Aerospace Med Asn; assoc Soc Clin Path; Sigma Xi. *Res:* Extramural, research grants program development in chemical carcinogenesis. *Mailing Add:* 5924 Rudyard Dr Bethesda MD 20814

DOMANY, EYTAN, physics, see previous edition

DOMASK, W(ILLIAM) G(ERHARD), b Port Arthur, Tex, Mar 11, 20; m 48; c 6. CHEMICAL ENGINEERING. *Educ:* Tex A&M Univ, BS, 42, MS, 48; Univ Tex, PhD(chem eng), 53. *Prof Exp:* Res chemist, Jefferson Chem Co, 45-46; sr chem engr, Humble Oil & Refining Co, 52-60, mgr southwest region sales eng, 60-65, tech adv, Hq Mkt, 66-77; GOVT REGULATIONS ADV, MKT DEPT, EXXON CO, USA, 77- *Mem:* AAAS; Soc Automotive Engrs; Am Chem Soc; Sigma Xi; Am Inst Chem Engrs. *Res:* Synthesis of chlorinated hydrocarbons; process engineering research; chemicals, plastics and petroleum products development; products research coordination, and toxicologicol aspects of products. *Mailing Add:* Mkt Dept PO Box 2180 Houston TX 77001

DOMB, ELLEN RUTH (COLMER), b Morristown, NJ, Aug 18, 46; m 68. EXPERIMENTAL SOLID STATE PHYSICS. *Educ:* Mass Inst Technol, BS, 68; Univ Pa, MA, 69; Temple Univ, PhD(physics), 74. *Prof Exp:* Res assoc physics, Univ Nebr-Lincoln, 74-76; asst prof physics, Harvey Mudd Col, 76-79; sr physicist, Pomona Div, Gen Dynamics, 79-81; TECH STAFF SPECIALIST, AEROJET ELECTRO SYSTEMS CORP, 81- *Concurrent Pos:* Vis assoc, Calif Inst Technol, 77- *Mem:* Am Phys Soc. *Res:* Electrical and magnetic properties of limited dimensionality materials, including spin-glass alloys and layered compounds; properties of amorphous ferromagnetic and superconducting materials; fiber optics. *Mailing Add:* 2443 Oceanview Dr Upland CA 91786

DOMBRO, ROY S, b Brooklyn, NY, Oct 21, 33; m 67; c 2. BIOCHEMISTRY. *Educ:* Brooklyn Col, BS, 54; Univ Wis, MS, 56, PhD(biochem), 58. *Prof Exp:* Res assoc biochem, Rockefeller Inst, 58-64; mem staff, Inst Muscle Dis, 64-65; assoc, Dept Surg, Albert Einstein Col Med, 65-67; asst prof biochem, 67-70; res scientist surg, Med Sch, 70-75, RES ASST PROF SURG, SCH MED, UNIV MIAMI, 75- *Concurrent Pos:* Res chemist, Vet Admin Hosp, Miami. *Mem:* AAAS; Am Chem Soc. *Res:* Design and synthesis of antimetabolites neurochemistry; amino acid metabolism; vasoactive amines and peptides. *Mailing Add:* Dept of Surg Sch of Med Univ of Miami Miami FL 33125

DOMBROWSKI, GEORGE E(DWARD), b Bayonne, NJ, Feb 22, 27; m 54; c 5. ELECTRONICS. *Educ:* Cooper Union, BEE, 49; Univ Mich, MSE, 50, PhD(elec eng), 57. *Prof Exp:* Jr engr, Raytheon Mfg Co, 50-51; proj engr, Sperry Gyroscope Co, 51-52; res assoc, Univ Mich, 52-57; sr engr, Raytheon Co, 57-61; assoc prof elec eng, Univ Conn, 61-71, prof eng, 71-79; CONSULT, 79- *Res:* Microwave electronics; microwave electron tubes, high power levels with crossed electric and magnetic fields; magnetrons and amplitrons; plasma electronics; computer simulation. *Mailing Add:* 69 Birchwood Height Rd Storrs CT 06268

DOMBROWSKI, HENRY S(TEPHEN), b Bayonne, NJ, Sept 27, 25; m 51; c 3. CHEMICAL ENGINEERING. *Educ:* Cooper Union, BChE, 47; Univ Mich, MSChE, 48, PhD(chem eng), 52. *Prof Exp:* Res engr, 52-59, RES SUPVR, E I DU PONT DE NEMOURS & CO, 59- *Res:* Fluid flow through porous media; process development; reactive metals; silicon; oxides for magnetic tape. *Mailing Add:* Photo Prod Dept E I du Pont de Nemours & Co Newport DE 19804

DOMBROWSKI, JOANNE MARIE, b Detroit, Mich, Aug 14, 46. MATHEMATICAL ANALYSIS. *Educ:* Marygrove Col, BS, 68; Purdue Univ, MS, 70, PhD(math), 73. *Prof Exp:* Asst prof, 73-78, ASSOC PROF MATH, WRIGHT STATE UNIV, 78- *Mem:* Am Math Soc; Math Asn Am. *Res:* Bounded linear operators defined on Hilbert spaces. *Mailing Add:* Dept Math Wright State Univ Dayton OH 45435

DOMENICALI, CHARLES ANGELO, b Albuquerque, NMex, Dec 27, 17; m 44; c 3. SOLID STATE PHYSICS. *Educ:* Univ NMex, BS, 39; Mass Inst Technol, PhD(physics), 49. *Prof Exp:* Physicist ballistics, Univ NMex, 42; physicist radar, US Naval Res Lab, 42-45; physicist electronic rocket sights, Calif Inst Technol, 45; res assoc physicist magnetism, Mass Inst Technol, 47-49; assoc prof physics & chmn dept, Alfred, 49-52; res physicist solid state physics, Franklin Inst, 52-55; res physicist & head solid state physics sect, Honeywell Res Ctr, 55-57, sr staff physicist, 57-61; prof physics, Ariz State Univ, 61-63; res physicist, Union Carbide Res Inst, NY, 63-64; chmn dept physics, 65-68, PROF PHYSICS, TEMPLE UNIV, 65- *Concurrent Pos:* Vis lectr elec eng, Univ Minn, 59- *Mem:* Am Asn Physics Teachers; NY Acad Sci; Am Phys Soc. *Res:* Irreversible thermodynamics; magnetism; thermoelectricity: Mossbauer effect. *Mailing Add:* Dept of Physics Temple Univ Philadelphia PA 19122

DOMENICONI, MICHAEL JOHN, b San Francisco, Calif, Sept 22, 46; m 74; c 2. PHYSICAL CHEMISTRY, ELECTROCHEMISTRY. *Educ:* Univ San Francisco, BS, 68; Univ Calif, Berkeley, PhD(chem), 75. *Prof Exp:* Sr chemist, Electrochimica Corp, Mt View, Calif, 75-76; mem tech staff electrochem, GTE Labs, Inc, 76-79; TECH DIR SPEC PROJS, ALTUS CORP, SAN JOSE, 79- *Mem:* Am Chem Soc; Electrochem Soc; AAAS; Sigma Xi; Int Soc Electrochem. *Res:* Exploratory physical-chemical and electrochemical investigations in non-aqueous solvents; applied research and development of advanced battery systems. *Mailing Add:* 1610 Crane Ct San Jose CA 95112

DOMER, FLOYD RAY, b Cedar Rapids, Iowa, July 12, 31; m 65. PHARMACOLOGY. *Educ:* Univ Iowa, BS, 54, MS, 56; Tulane Univ, PhD(pharmacol), 59. *Prof Exp:* Asst pharm, Univ Iowa, 54-55, asst pharmacol, 55-56; asst, Tulane Univ, 56-59; US Air Force res contract, Istituto Superiore Sanita, Italy, 60-61; asst prof pharmacol, Col Med, Cincinnati, 61-62; from asst prof to assoc prof, 63-74, PROF PHARMACOL, TULANE UNIV, 74- *Concurrent Pos:* Life Ins Med Res Fund fel, Nat Inst Med Res, Eng, 59-60; hon res fel, Univ Col, Univ London, 71-72; consult, Pan-Am Sanit Bur Regional Off, Arg, WHO, 71. *Mem:* AAAS; Soc Exp Biol & Med; Am Soc Pharmacol & Exp Therapeut; Soc Neurosci. *Res:* Transport systems, ways of affecting them, particularly the blood-brain barrier; pharmacology of hemicholiniums. *Mailing Add:* Dept of Pharmacol Tulane Univ New Orleans LA 70112

DOMER, JUDITH E, b Millersville, Pa, Apr 9, 39; m 65. MEDICAL MICROBIOLOGY, MYCOLOGY. *Educ:* Tusculum Col, BA, 61; Tulane Univ, PhD(microbiol), 66; Am Bd Med Microbiol, dipl, 81. *Prof Exp:* Asst prof biol, St Mary's Dominican Col, 67-68; res assoc microbiol, 68-71, asst prof, 72-77, ASSOC, PROF MICROBIOL, SCH MED, TULANE UNIV,

77- *Concurrent Pos:* NIH fel, Tulane Univ, 66-67; Wellcome Trust fel immunol, Kennedy Inst Rheumatology, London, Eng, 71-72; mem bact & mycol study sect, NIH, 75-79; assoc ed, Exp Mycol J, 78-80. *Mem:* Am Soc Microbiol; Med Mycol Soc of the Americas; Int Soc Human & Animal Mycol; Am Asn Immunol; Infectious Dis Soc Am. *Res:* Biochemistry of fungal cell walls; immunology of the systemic mycoses; host-parasite interactions in experimental marine candidiasis and cryptococcosis, with emphasis on cellular immune mechanisms; biochemistry of fungal cell walls, especially those of dimorphic organisms. *Mailing Add:* Dept of Microbiol Tulane Univ Sch of Med New Orleans LA 70112

DOMERMUTH, CHARLES HENRY, JR, b St Louis, Mo, Nov 16, 28; m 52; c 3. VETERINARY MICROBIOLOGY. *Educ:* Elmhurst Col, BS, 51; Univ Ky, MS, 55; Va Polytech Inst, PhD(microbiol), 62. *Prof Exp:* Asst prof, 54-70, PROF VET SCI, VA POLYTECH INST & STATE UNIV, 70- CHMN, DIV AGR & URBAN PRACT, 80- *Concurrent Pos:* Res microbiologist, Statens Serum Inst, Denmark, 62-63, EAfrican Vet Res Orgn, Kenya, 64-66 & USDA, 64- *Mem:* Am Soc Microbiol; Am Asn Avian Pathologists; Asn Am Vet Med Cols; Res Workers Animal Dis; Int Orgn Mycoplasmology. *Res:* Electron microscopy of infected tissue; studies of Mycoplasmataceae and viruses and diseases caused by them. *Mailing Add:* Col Vet Med Va Polytech Inst & State Univ Blacksburg VA 24061

DOMESHEK, S(OL), b New York, NY, Dec 6, 20; m 42; c 2. DISPLAY SYSTEMS, NAVIGATION. *Educ:* City Col New York, BS, 41; NY Univ, BME, 56. *Prof Exp:* Jr engr, US Geol Surv, 42-44; proj engr, US Naval Training Device Ctr, 46-51, sr engr, 51-57, head visual systs br, 57-61, staff eng consult, 61-64, head phys sci lab, 64-66; dir instrumentation, Avionics Lab, US Army Electronics Command, 66-72, chief, Navig Div, 73-81, CHIEF SYSTS MGT OFF, US AVIONICS RES & DEVELOP ACTIV, FT MONMOUTH, 81- *Mem:* Nat Soc Prof Engrs; Optic Soc Am; Am Soc Photogram; Inst Navig. *Res:* Patents in photogrammetry; display technology; positioning and navigation; radar mapping; cockpit instrumentation; geographic orientation. *Mailing Add:* 2320 Edgewood Terrace Scotch Plains NJ 07076

DOMHOLDT, LOWELL CURTIS, b Tyler, Minn, Mar 17, 34; m 55; c 4. MECHANICAL ENGINEERING. *Educ:* Univ Minn, BS, 55, MS, 57; Case Inst Technol, PhD(fluid mech), 63. *Prof Exp:* Instr mech eng, Ohio State Univ, 58; from instr to assoc prof, Case Inst Technol, 60-67; assoc prof, 67-73, PROF MECH ENG, CLEVELAND STATE UNIV, 73- *Honors & Awards:* Ralph R Teetor Award, Soc Automotive Engrs, 67. *Mem:* Soc Automotive Engrs; Am Soc Mech Engrs; Am Soc Eng Educ; Nat Soc Prof Engrs; AAUP. *Mailing Add:* Dept of Mech Eng Cleveland State Univ Cleveland OH 44115

DOMIER, KENNETH WALTER, b Norquay, Sask, Aug 30, 33; m 56; c 2. AGRICULTURAL ENGINEERING. *Educ:* Univ Sask, BE, 55, MSc, 57; Mich State Univ, PhD(agr eng), 67. *Prof Exp:* Fuels & lubricants engr, Federated Cooperatives Ltd, 55-58; asst prof agr eng, Univ Man, 58-69; chmn dept, 69-74, PROF AGR ENG, UNIV ALTA, 69- *Concurrent Pos:* Vis prof, Swed Inst Agr Eng, 74-75. *Mem:* Am Soc Agr Engrs; Can Soc Agr Engrs; Agr Inst Can. *Res:* Fuels; lubricants; tractors; machinery. *Mailing Add:* Dept of Agr Eng Univ of Alta Edmonton AB T6G 2E8 Can

DOMINGO, WAYNE ELWIN, b Weeping Water, Nebr, June 30, 16; m 37; c 4. CROP BREEDING. *Educ:* Univ Nebr, BS, 38; Utah State Col, MS, 40; Univ Ill, PhD(plant breeding), 42. *Prof Exp:* Assoc, Univ Ill, 42-43; assoc plant breeder, Bur Plant Indust, Soils & Agr Eng, USDA, 43-45, agronomist, 45-46; dir oilseeds prod div, Baker Castor Oil Co, 46-74; consult agronomist, NL Industs, 75-81; RETIRED. *Mem:* Am Soc Agron; Soc Econ Bot. *Res:* Hybridization of forage grasses; genetics of soybean; breeding condiment, insecticide and drying oil plants; domestic and foreign production of oilseeds. *Mailing Add:* 10002 County View Rd La Mesa CA 92041

DOMINGOS, HENRY, b Massena, NY, Sept 17, 34; m 58; c 2. SOLID STATE ELECTRONICS. *Educ:* Clarkson Technol Univ, BEE, 56; Univ Southern Calif, MSEE, 58; Univ Wash, Seattle, PhD(elec eng), 63. *Prof Exp:* Mem tech staff electronics, Hughes Aircraft Co, 56-58; asst prof elec eng, Univ Nev, 58-60; actg instr, Univ Wash, Seattle, 60-63; ASSOC PROF ELEC & COMPUT ENG, CLARKSON COL TECHNOL, 63- *Mem:* Am Phys Soc; Inst Elec & Electronics Engrs; Am Soc Eng Educ. *Res:* Semiconductor devices and integrated circuits. *Mailing Add:* Dept of Eng Clarkson Col of Technol Potsdam NY 13676

DOMINGUE, GERALD JAMES, b Lafayette, La, Mar 2, 37; m 58, 81; c 5. BACTERIOLOGY, IMMUNOLOGY. *Educ:* Univ Southwestern La, BS, 59; Tulane Univ, PhD(med microbiol, immunol), 64. *Prof Exp:* Teaching asst bact, Univ Southwestern La, 58-59; asst res instr pediat, Sch Med, State Univ NY Buffalo, 64-66; instr microbiol, Sch Med, St Louis Univ, 66-67; from asst prof to assoc prof surg, microbiol & immunol, 67-74, PROF, UROL, MICROBIOL & IMMUNOL, SCH MED, TULANE UNIV, 74- *Concurrent Pos:* USPHS fel, Children's Hosp, Buffalo, NY, 64-66; dir microbiol, Snodgras Lab Path & Bact, St Louis City Hosp, 66-67; lectr, Sch Dent, Wash Univ, 66-67; consult bacteriologist, Southern Baptist Hosp, New Orleans, 68-; consult res scientist, Vet Admin Hosp, New Orleans, 69-72; consult & mem tech adv bd, Analytab Prod Inc, New York, 72-78; consult, Armour Pharmaceut, 75-77; consult bacteriologist, Tulane Med Ctr Hosp, 78; div lectr microbiol, Am Soc Microbiol Found. *Mem:* Fel Am Acad Microbiol; NY Acad Sci; Soc Exp Biol & Med; Am Soc Microbiol; fel Infectious Dis Soc Am. *Res:* Significance of cell wall deficient microorganisms in renal and other chronic infections; biological studies on common enterobacterial antigens; immune response in urinary tract infections; chorionic gonadotropin producing bacteria and malignancies. *Mailing Add:* Dept of Urol 1430 Tulane Ave New Orleans LA 70112

DOMINGUEZ, CESAREO AUGUSTO, b Buenos Aires, Argentina, Oct 1, 42; m 68; c 2. HADRONIC SYMMETRIES, WEAK INTERACTIONS. *Educ:* Univ Buenos Aires, MS, 68, PhD(physics), 71. *Prof Exp:* Instr physics, Univ Buenos Aires, 68-71; res assoc, Stanford Linear Accelerator Ctr, 71-72; prof physics, Centro de Investigacion Del I P N, 72-78; ASSOC PROF PHYSICS, TEX A&M UNIV, 78- *Concurrent Pos:* NSF exchange, Rockefeller Univ, 74-80; vis mem staff, Los Alamos Sci Lab, 79-; co-prin investr, US Dept Energy grant, 79- *Mem:* Mex Acad Sci. *Res:* Calculation of chiral-symmetry breaking in elementary particle and nuclear physics; chirality in quantum chromodynamics. *Mailing Add:* Dept Physics Tex A&M Univ College Station TX 77843

DOMINH, THAP, b Hanoi, NVietnam, Dec 25, 38; US citizen; m 64; c 2. PHOTOCHEMISTRY, PHOTOGRAPHIC CHEMISTRY. *Educ:* Univ Chicago, MS, 62, PhD(photochem), 66. *Prof Exp:* G Swift fel photochem, Univ Chicago, 64-65; Nat Res Coun fel, Univ Alta, 66-68, res assoc, 68-69; mem tech staff chem res, Bell Labs, 69-71; RES ASSOC, KODAK RES LABS, 71- *Mem:* Am Chem Soc; AAAS; Soc Photog Scientists & Engrs. *Res:* Reactive intermediates; carbenes, carbynes, free radicals, carbonyl and azomethine ylides; dynamic nuclear polarization; catalysis involving transition metal complexes; organic and organometallic photochemistry, photochromism, photopolymerization, photocatalysis, unconventional imaging systems. *Mailing Add:* Kodak Res Labs Eastman Kodak Co 1669 Lake Ave Rochester NY 14650

DOMINIANNI, SAMUEL JAMES, b New York, NY, Sept 21, 37; m 68. ORGANIC CHEMISTRY. *Educ:* Queens Col, NY, BS, 58; Univ Mass, MS, 60; Univ NC, PhD(org chem), 64. *Prof Exp:* Res assoc fel chem, Iowa State Univ, 64-66; SR ORG CHEMIST, ELI LILLY & CO, 66- *Mem:* AAAS; Am Chem Soc; Royal Soc Chem. *Res:* Heterocyclic synthesis; organic photochemistry. *Mailing Add:* Eli Lilly & Co Res Labs 307 East McCarty St Indianapolis IN 46285

DOMINICK, WAYNE DENNIS, b Chicago, Ill, Oct 19, 46; m 71; c 2. COMPUTER SCIENCE. *Educ:* Ill Inst Technol, BS, 68; Northwestern Univ, MS, 74, PhD(comput sci), 75. *Prof Exp:* Systs analyst comput sci, US Army Data Support Command, 69-70; systs programmer, Vogelback Comput Ctr, Northwestern Univ, 71-74, res asst, Dept Comput Sci, 74-75; asst prof, 75-77, assoc prof comput sci, Univ Southwestern La, 77-81; PRES, EXEC SYST INC, 81- *Concurrent Pos:* Grants, US Army Corps Engrs, 74-77; consult, US Army Corps Engrs, 75-77, La State Natural Resources & Energy Div, 75-77, Battelle Columbus Labs, 76-, OCLC, Inc, 77- & La State Dept Educ, 77-; NSF grants, 76-; vpres, Info Mgt Inc, 78- *Honors & Awards:* Royal E Cabell Sci Award, Northwestern Univ, 74. *Mem:* Am Soc Info Sci; Asn Comput Mach. *Res:* Data base management system design; information storage and retrieval system design; software monitoring; system performance measurement and evaluation; user-system interfacing; interactive graphics; computer systems analysis. *Mailing Add:* Exec Syst, Inc PO Box 51637 OCS Lafayette LA 70505

DOMINO, EDWARD FELIX, b Chicago, Ill, Nov 20, 24; m 48; c 5. PHARMACOLOGY. *Educ:* Univ Ill, BS, 48, MD & MS, 51. *Prof Exp:* Rotating intern, Presby Hosp, Chicago, 51-52; instr pharmacol, Univ Ill, 52-53; from instr to assoc prof, 53-62, PROF PHARMACOL, UNIV MICH, ANN ARBOR, 62-, DIR, NEURO-PSYCHOPHARMACOL RES LAB, 66- *Concurrent Pos:* Vis prof psychiat, Wayne State Univ, 65-; mem neuropharmacol sect, Int Brain Res Orgn; rep, US Pharmacopeia, 76- *Honors & Awards:* Sigma Xi Prize, 51; Award, Mich Soc Neurol & Psychiat, 55; First Prize, Am Soc Anesthesiol, 63; Nikolai Pavlovich Kravkov Mem Medal, Acad Bd Inst Pharmacol & Chemother, Acad Med Sci, USSR, 68. *Mem:* Am Soc Pharmacol; NY Acad Sci; Soc Psychophysiol Res; fel Am Col Neuropsychopharmacol (vpres, 76); AMA. *Res:* Experimental and clinical neuropharmacology and psychopharmacology as a means of understanding brain function; central neural transmitters, especially cholingeric substances and interaction of various psychoactive drugs with neural transmitters; biology of mental disease, particularly schizophrenia. *Mailing Add:* Dept of Pharmacol Univ of Mich Ann Arbor MI 48109

DOMINY, BERYL W, b Davison, Mich, Apr 2, 41. ORGANIC CHEMISTRY, INFORMATION SCIENCE. *Educ:* Mich State Univ, BS, 63; Univ Mich, PhD(chem), 67. *Prof Exp:* Org chemist, 67-73, INFO SCIENTIST, PFIZER INC, 73- *Mem:* Am Chem Soc. *Res:* Heterocyclic chemistry; computer utilization in pharmaceutical research and development. *Mailing Add:* Pfizer Inc Groton CT 06340

DOMKE, CHARLES J, b Chicago, Ill, Nov 4, 14; m 45; c 1. AIR POLLUTION. *Educ:* Loyola Univ, Ill, BS, 41. *Prof Exp:* Res chemist, Burgess Battery Co, 41; from asst chemist to chemist, Standard Oil Co (Ind), 41-48, from asst proj automotive engr to proj automotive engr, 49-65; sr proj automotive engr, Am Oil Co, 66-67; procedures & standards coordr, Environ Protection Agency, 67-69, chief, Surveillance Br, 67-76, proj mgr, Characterization & Appl Br, 76-79, proj mgr inspection & maintenance staff, 79-80; RETIRED. *Concurrent Pos:* Leader vapor lock prog, Coord Res Coun, 64-65 & expression for fuel volatility panel, 64- *Mem:* Soc Automotive Eng. *Res:* Design and use of motor fuels under extreme environmental conditions, and/or in high compression engines; development of engine to run without crankcase lubrication; use of ammonia and hydrazine as fuels for spark ignition and compression ignition engines; automation and automatic data logging. *Mailing Add:* 41181 Crestwood Dr Plymouth MI 48170

DOMKE, HERBERT REUBEN, b Hillsboro, Kans, Apr 6, 19; m 46; c 4. PUBLIC HEALTH. *Educ:* Univ Chicago, SB, 39, MD, 42; Harvard Univ, MPH, 48, DrPH, 59. *Hon Degrees:* DSc Cent Methodist Col, Fayette, Mo, 75. *Prof Exp:* Chief med officer, Chicago Health Dept, 44-47; health comnr, St Louis County Health Dept, Mo, 49-58; dir, Pittsburgh-Allegheny County Health Dept, Pa, 59-66; hosp comnr & dir health & hosps, City of St Louis, Mo, 66-71; dir, 71-79, DIR, SECT MED CARE, MO DIV HEALTH, 79-; PROF COMMUNITY HEALTH & MED PRACT, UNIV MO-

COLUMBIA, 71- *Concurrent Pos:* Asst anat, Univ Chicago, 44-46; asst prof prev med & pub health, Wash Univ, 49-58, prof pub health in prev med & prof med, 66; clin prof prev med in internal med, St Louis Univ, 66. *Honors & Awards:* Presidential Award, Nat Med Asn, 67; St Louis City Mayors Civic Award, 70; Mo Nursing Home Asn Award, 71. *Mem:* AAAS; Asn State & Territorial Health Officers; Conf State & Prov Health Authorities NAm. *Res:* Epidemiology and public health administration. *Mailing Add:* Mo Div of Health 221 W High St Jefferson City MO 65101

DOMMERT, ARTHUR ROLAND, b Crowley, La, Apr 3, 37; m 63; c 4. VETERINARY MICROBIOLOGY. *Educ:* Tex A&M Univ, BS, 60, DVM, 61; La State Univ, MS, 63, PhD(microbiol, biochem), 66; Am Col Vet Microbiol, dipl, 69. *Prof Exp:* NIH fel microbiol & biochem, La State Univ, 61-66; assoc prof vet microbiol, Univ Mo-Columbia, 66-71; prof vet microbiol & parasitol & head dept, 71-81, PROF VET MICROBIOL & PARASITOL & ASSOC VICE CHANCELLOR, ACAD AFFAIRS, LA STATE UNIV, BATON ROUGE, 81- *Concurrent Pos:* Mem, Exec Coun Conf Res Workers in Animal Dis, 80- *Mem:* Am Vet Med Asn; Am Soc Microbiol; Conf Res Workers Animal Dis; Asn Am Vet Med Cols. *Res:* Changes in animal tissues due to obligate anaerobic bacteria; isolation and identification of obligate anaerobic bacteria; curriculum development in veterinary medicine; academic administration. *Mailing Add:* Dept Vet Microbiol & Parasitol Sch of Vet Med La State Univ Baton Rouge LA 70803

DOMNING, DARYL PAUL, b Biloxi, Miss, Mar 14, 47. EVOLUTIONARY BIOLOGY, PALEOECOLOGY. *Educ:* Tulane Univ, BS, 68; Univ Calif, Berkeley, MA, 70, PhD(paleont), 75. *Prof Exp:* Res biologist, Inst Nat Pesquisas da Amazonia, Manaus, Brazil, 76-78; ASST PROF ANAT, HOWARD UNIV, WASHINGTON, DC, 78- *Concurrent Pos:* Res assoc, Univ Calif Mus Paleont, 76-78 & Smithsonian Inst, 79-; marine mammal specialist, Int Union Conserv Nature & Natural Resources, 79-; mem manatee tech adv coun, Dept Natural Resources, Fla, 81-; sci adv, US Marine Mammal Comn, 82-85. *Mem:* Soc Vert Paleont; Soc Study Evolution; Am Soc Mammalogists; Soc Syst Zool. *Res:* Morphology, systematics, functional anatomy, ecology, paleoecology, fossil and recent distribution, evolution, conservation, and bibliography of the Sirenia and Desmostylia; herbivorous marine mammals. *Mailing Add:* Dept Anat Howard Univ Washington DC 20059

DOMOKOS, GABOR, b Budapest, Hungary, Mar 5, 33; US citizen; m 67. ELEMENTARY PARTICLE PHYSICS. *Educ:* Eotvos Lorand Univ, Budapest, dipl physics, 56; Joint Inst Nuclear Res, USSR, Dr(math sci, physics), 63. *Prof Exp:* Res assoc cosmic rays, Cent Res Inst Physics, Budapest, 56-60; mem res staff elementary particle physics, Joint Inst Nuclear Res, USSR, 61-63; vis scientist, Europ Orgn Nuclear Res, Switz, 63-64; sr res staff mem, Cent Res Inst Physics, Budapest, 64-65; lectr, Johns Hopkins Univ, 65-66; res scientist, Univ Calif, Berkeley, 66-67; sr res scientist, Cent Res Inst Physics, Budapest, 67-68; PROF PHYSICS, JOHNS HOPKINS UNIV, 68- *Concurrent Pos:* Consult, Rutherford Lab, Chilton, Eng, 73; vis sci staff mem, Europ Orgn Nuclear Res, Switz, 75-76; Alexander von Humboldt sr vis scientist award, Deutsches Electronen-Synchrotron, Hamburg, Ger, 76; vis prof, Univ Florence, Italy, 78. *Mem:* Am Math Soc; fel Am Phys Soc; Ital Phys Soc; Europ Phys Soc. *Res:* Interactions of elementary particles at high energies; quantum gravity; cosmology. *Mailing Add:* Dept of Physics Johns Hopkins Univ Baltimore MD 21218

DOMROESE, KENNETH ARTHUR, b Vincennes, Ind, May 23, 33; m 57; c 3. PHYSIOLOGY. *Educ:* Concordia Teachers Col, Ill, BS, 55; DePaul Univ, MS, 62; Northwestern Univ, PhD(biol sci), 63. *Prof Exp:* Asst prof, 61-64, assoc prof biol sci, 64-77, PROF, CONCORDIA COL, 77- *Concurrent Pos:* Res fel, Med Sch, Loyola Univ, 72-73. *Mem:* AAAS; Am Soc Zool; Sigma Xi. *Res:* Lipid metabolism in insect flight muscle; invertebrate endocrinology; cardiovascular physiology. *Mailing Add:* Dept of Biol Concordia Teachers Col River Forest IL 60305

DOMSKY, IRVING ISAAC, b Racine, Wis, Feb 3, 30; m 64; c 4. ANALYTICAL CHEMISTRY. *Educ:* Univ Wis, BS, 51, PhD(anal org chem), 59. *Prof Exp:* Anal chemist, Qm Food & Container Inst, Ill, 54; res asst chem, Yale Univ, 58-60; res assoc, Div Oncol, Chicago Med Sch, 60-64; anal chemist, Abbott Labs, 64-67; sr anal chemist, Armour Dial, Inc, 67-73; sr anal group leader, Quaker Oats Co, 73-74; sr anal res chemist, Chem Prod Div, Chemetron Corp, 75-77; PRES & LAB DIR, ALLIED LABS, LTD, 77- *Mem:* Am Water Works Asn; Mem: AAAS; Am Chem Soc; Am Oil Chemists Soc. *Res:* Gas chromatography; new analytical methods. *Mailing Add:* 7404 N Talman Ave Chicago IL 60645

DON, CONWAY J, b Newcastle, UK, Dec 1, 22; m 49; c 5. RADIOLOGY. *Educ:* Univ London, MB, BS, 46; Royal Col Physicians, dipl med radiodiag, 49; FRCR, 53; FRCP(C), 70; FRCP, 71. *Prof Exp:* House physician, Univ Col, London, 46; house physician & house surgeon, Addenbrooke's Hosp, Cambridge, Eng, 47; resident med officer, Univ Col, London, 48-49, med registr, 50-51, registr x-ray dept, 51-54, sr registr, 55-56; DIR X-RAY DEPT, OTTAWA GEN HOSP, 57-; PROF & HEAD DEPT RADIOL, UNIV OTTAWA, 57- *Concurrent Pos:* Teaching fel, Harvard Col, 56-57; clin fel, Mass Gen Hosp, Boston, 56-57; vis fel, 69; Ont Heart Found grants, 61-63; consulting radiologist, St Vincent's Hosp, Ottawa, Ottawa Civic Hosp, Ottawa Clinic, Ont Cancer Found; vis prof radiol, Vanderbilt Univ, 77 & King Abdul Aziz Univ, Jeddah, Saudi Arabia, 80. *Mem:* Can Asn Radiologists; Can Med Asn; Asn Univ Radiologists; Radiol Soc NAm; Can Prof Radiol. *Res:* renal arterial disease in hypertension; radiological changes in pulmonary edema. *Mailing Add:* 20 Rideau Terr Ottawa ON K1M 1Z9 Can

DONABEDIAN, AVEDIS, b Beirut, Lebanon, Jan 7, 19; nat US; m 45; c 3. PUBLIC HEALTH. *Educ:* Am Univ, Beirut, BA, 40, MD, 44; Harvard Univ, MPH, 55. *Prof Exp:* Physician & actg supt, Eng Mission Hosp, Jerusalem, 45-47; asst dermat & venerology, Am Univ, Beirut, 48-54, instr physiol, 48-50, univ physician, 49-51, dir univ health serv, 51-54; res assoc med care, Sch Pub Health, Harvard Univ, 55-57; from asst prof to assoc prof prev med, New York Med Col, 57-61; from assoc prof to prof pub health econ, 61-66, prof, Med Care Orgn, 66-78, NATHAN SINAI DISTINGUISHED PROF PUB HEALTH, SCH PUB HEALTH, UNIV MICH, ANN ARBOR, 79- *Concurrent Pos:* Med assoc, Med Care Eval Studies, United Community Serv, Boston, 55-57; vis lectr, Sch Pub Health, Harvard Univ, 57-58. *Honors & Awards:* Elizur Wright Award, Am Risk & Ins Asn, 78. *Mem:* Nat Inst Med; fel Am Pub Health Asn; Asn Teachers Prev Med. *Res:* Medical care organization. *Mailing Add:* Sch of Pub Health Univ of Mich Ann Arbor MI 48109

DONACHIE, MATTHEW J(OHN), JR, b Orange, NJ, Oct 23, 32; m 55; c 4. PHYSICAL METALLURGY. *Educ:* Rensselaer Polytech Inst, BMetE, 54; Mass Inst Technol, SM, 55, MetE, 57, ScD(x-ray & lattice strains), 58. *Prof Exp:* Metallurgist, Adv Metals Res Corp, 58; res scientist, Res Labs, United Aircraft Corp, 58-59; group leader high temperature metall, Gen Dynamics/Elec Boat, 59-61; supvr phys metall, Chase Brass & Copper Co, 61-63; gen supvr metall eng, 63-67, develop metallurgist, 67-69, PROJ MAT ENGR, PRATT & WHITNEY AIRCRAFT GROUP, UNITED TECHNOLOGIES CORP, 69- *Concurrent Pos:* From adj asst prof to adj assoc prof, Hartford Grad Ctr, 58-68, adj prof, 68- *Mem:* Am Soc Metals; Am Soc Testing & Mat. *Res:* Metallurgy of high temperature alloys; x-ray metallurgy; mechanical behavior of metals; environmental effects in metals; electron microscopy and metallography; creep and fatigue. *Mailing Add:* Pratt & Whitney Aircraft Mail Stop EB3B Main St East Hartford CT 06108

DONADY, JOHN JAMES, b Hempstead, NY, June 21, 38; m 62; c 1. DEVELOPMENTAL GENETICS. *Educ:* State Univ NY Stony Brook, BS, 62; Univ Iowa, PhD(zool), 69. *Prof Exp:* NIH fel genetics, City of Hope Med Ctr, 69-70, jr res scientist develop genetics, 71-72; asst prof genetics, 73-79, asst prof biol, 77-80, ASSOC PROF BIOL, WESLEYAN UNIV, 80- *Concurrent Pos:* Res grant, NIH Child Health & Human Develop & Sci Found, 74, 78 & 79. *Mem:* Genetics Soc; AAAS; Tissue Cult Asn; Am Inst Bsol Sci; Sigma Xi. *Res:* Genetic approach to problems of cell differentiation, embryonic development and maternal information in development; combines Drosophila genetics, mutants and in vitro culturing of embryonic cells; emphasis on muscle protein genes, their organization and regulation. *Mailing Add:* Dept of Biol Wesleyan Univ Middletown CT 06457

DONAGHY, JAMES JOSEPH, b Cumberland, Ky, Mar 13, 35; m 60. PHYSICS. *Educ:* Univ Fla, BS, 59; Univ NC, PhD(physics), 65. *Prof Exp:* Opers analyst, Univ NC, 64-65; asst prof physics, Va Mil Inst, 65-66; opers analyst, US Govt, 66-67; asst prof, 67-72, assoc prof, 72-79, PROF PHYSICS, WASHINGTON & LEE UNIV, 79- *Concurrent Pos:* Vis prof, 66. *Mem:* Am Phys Soc; Am Asn Physics Teachers. *Res:* Positron annihilation in solids; Fermi surface in metals. *Mailing Add:* Dept Physics Washington & Lee Univ Lexington VA 24450

DONAGHY, RAYMOND MADIFORD PEARDON, b Eastman, PQ, Aug 18, 10; nat US; m 41; c 4. NEUROSURGERY. *Educ:* Univ Vt, BS, 33, MD, 36. *Prof Exp:* Intern neurol, Montreal Gen Hosp, Can, 36-37, asst resident internal med, 37-38; resident gen surg, Children's Mem Hosp, 38-39; asst resident neurosurg, Mass Gen Hosp, 39-40; resident psychiat, McLean Hosp, 40-41; resident, Mass Gen Hosp, 42-43; assoc prof, 46-52, PROF NEUROSURG, COL MED, UNIV VT, 52- *Concurrent Pos:* Fel neurosurg, Lahey Clin, 41-42; Dalton scholar, Mass Gen Hosp, 42. *Mem:* Fel Am Col Surgeons; Soc Neurol Surgeons; Am Asn Neurol Surgeons; Acad Neurol Surgeons; Can Neurol Soc. *Res:* Brain abscess; spastic element in cerebral thrombosis; neurovascular surgery; microsurgery; spinal cord and brain trauma. *Mailing Add:* Med Ctr Hosp Univ of Vt Burlington VT 05401

DONAHOE, FRANK J, b Ashland, Pa, Mar 12, 22; m 43; c 2. SOLID STATE PHYSICS. *Educ:* La Salle Col, BA, 43; Univ Pa, PhD(physics), 54. *Prof Exp:* Instr math & phys chem, La Salle Col, 48-49; asst, Univ Pa, 49-51; res physicist, Franklin Inst, 51-64; assoc prof physics, 64-68, PROF PHYSICS, WILKES COL, 68- *Mem:* AAAS; Inst Elec & Electronics Engineers; Am Phys Soc; Am Asn Physics Teachers. *Res:* Low temperature physics of metals; order-disorder in ferromagnetic alloys; thermoelectricity; cosmogony. *Mailing Add:* Dept of Physics Wilkes Col Wilkes Barre PA 18703

DONAHOE, JOHN PHILIP, b Hagerstown, Md, Dec 1, 44; m 70; c 2. VETERINARY MEDICINE. *Educ:* Univ Ga, BS, 67, DVM, 70, PhD(microbiol), 77. *Prof Exp:* ASST PROF VET MED, OHIO STATE UNIV, 76- *Mem:* Am Vet Med Asn; AAAS; Am Asn Avian Pathologists; Asn Vet Med Col; World Vet Poultry Asn. *Res:* Mechanisms of viral immune suppression as well as molecular basis of animal oncogenic herpesviral cellular transformation. *Mailing Add:* 1900 Coffey Rd Columbus OH 43210

DONAHOO, PAT, b Van Buren, Ark, July 22, 28; m 65; c 2. ANALYTICAL CHEMISTRY, FOOD SCIENCE. *Educ:* Hendrix Col, BS, 50; Okla State Univ, MS, 52, PhD(chem), 55. *Prof Exp:* Chemist, Tex Co, 52-53; res chemist, Lion Oil Co Div, Monsanto Co, 55-56 & Inorg Chem Div, 56-60; res chemist, Griffiths Labs, Inc, 60-62; chief chemist, 62-66; tech mkt mgr, 66-71; dir grocery prod develop, Anderson Clayton Foods, 71-77; V PRES RES & QUAL CONTROL, RICH-SEAPAK CORP, 77- *Mem:* Am Chem Soc; Inst Food Tech; Soc Adv Food Serv Res. *Res:* Seasonings for food products; soy proteins; hydrolyzed plant proteins; oil based grocery products; spices; frozen seafood products. *Mailing Add:* Rich-SeaPak Corp PO Box 667 St Simons Island GA 31522

DONAHUE, DOUGLAS JAMES, b Wichita, Kans, Oct 26, 24; m 48; c 5. NUCLEAR PHYSICS. *Educ:* Univ Ore, BS, 47, MS, 48; Univ Wis, PhD, 52. *Prof Exp:* Physicist, Hanford Labs, Gen Elec Co, 52-57; from asst prof to assoc prof physics, Pa State Univ, 57-63; assoc prof, 63-64, PROF PHYSICS, UNIV ARIZ, 64- *Mem:* Fel Am Phys Soc. *Res:* Low energy nuclear physics; reactor physics; atomic physics; medical physics. *Mailing Add:* Dept of Physics Univ of Ariz Tucson AZ 85721

DONAHUE, FRANCIS M(ARTIN), b Philadelphia, Pa, May 8, 34; m 60; c 5. ELECTROCHEMICAL ENGINEERING. *Educ:* La Salle Col, BA, 56; Univ Calif, Los Angeles, PhD(eng), 65. *Prof Exp:* Res chemist, Tasty Baking Co, 56-59; group leader corrosion res, Betz Labs, Inc, 59-61; electrochemist, Stanford Res Inst, 61-63; res engr, Univ Calif, Los Angeles, 63-65; asst prof chem eng, 65-69, assoc prof chem eng, 69-79, PROF CHEM ENG, UNIV MICH, 79- *Concurrent Pos:* Vis prof, Swiss Fed Inst Technol, Zurich, 72-73. *Mem:* Electrochem Soc; Nat Asn Corrosion Engrs; Int Soc Electrochem. *Res:* Corrosion and corrosion inhibition; electrochemical energy conversion; electrocatalysis; electrosynthesis; electrodeposition; electroless plating. *Mailing Add:* Col of Eng Univ of Mich Ann Arbor MI 48109

DONAHUE, HAYDEN HACKNEY, b El Reno, Okla, Dec 4, 12; m 47; c 3. PSYCHIATRY, GENERAL ENGINEERING. *Educ:* Univ Kans, BS, 39, MD, 41. *Prof Exp:* Intern, Univ Hosps, Univ Ga, 41-42, instr med & psychiat, Sch Med, 42; lectr hosp admin & psychiat, Residency Prog & asst mgr, Vet Admin Hosp, North Little Rock, Ark, 46-49; dir educ & res, Ark State Hosp, 49-51; asst med dir, Tex State Bd Hosps & Spec Schs, 51-53; dir ment health, State of Okla, 53-59; asst supt, Ark State Hosp, 59-61; dir dept ment health, State of Okla, 70-78; supt, Cent State Griffen Mem Hosp, 61-79; DIR, OKLA INST MENT HEALTH EDUC & TRAINING, 79- *Concurrent Pos:* Assoc prof psychiat, Sch Med, Univ Ark, 49-51 & 60-61; consult, Ark State Dept Health, 49-51; lectr legal med, Sch Law, Univ Tex, 52; lectr, Homicide Inst, Univs Okla & Tex, 53-; consult asst prof neurol & psychiat, Univ Okla, 54-58, assoc prof psychiat, 58-67, clin prof, 67-; adv, Okla Comt, President's Comt Employ Handicapped, 57-59 & 61-71, vchmn, Okla Comt, White House Conf Children & Youth, 59; instr, Okla State Univ, 58-59; mem, Okla Gov Comn, White House Conf Aging, 59-60, Ark Gov Comn, 60-61 & nat adv comt, 59-61, chmn sect ment health & aging, 60-61; mem bd dirs, Pan Am Training Exchange Prog Psychiat, 61-63, treas, 63; mem, Am Psychiat Asn-Pan Am Exchange rep, Latin Am Sem Ment Health, WHO, Buenos Aires, 63; secy sect psychopharmacol, Am Mex Joint Ment Health Conf, Mexico City, 64; co-chmn sect pvt & pub ment hosps; Nat Conf Ment Illness & Health, Chicago, 64; chief consult, Okla State Penitentiary, 63-; consult, Okla State Crime Bur, 63-; consult, Base Hosp, Tinker Field, 64-; lectr, Univ Okla, 64-70; mem state, county & local adv comts & coun ment health. *Honors & Awards:* Bowis Award, Am Col Psychiat. *Mem:* Fel Am Psychiat Asn (treas, 68-72); fel Am Geriat Soc; fel Am Col Psychiat (regent, 65, treas, 66-71); Am Col Psychiat (pres, 75); Am Asn Med Supt Ment Hosps (pres, 74-75). *Res:* War neurosis; tuberculosis; narcosynthesis; problems of the aged; psychological selection and training of professional, technical and ancillary hospital personnel; hospital operations and management problems; use of special drugs in treatment of mental patients and rehabilitative therapies in care and treatment of institutionalized patients. *Mailing Add:* 107 State Dr Norman OK 73071

DONAHUE, JACK DAVID, b Chicago, Ill, Nov 21, 38; m 65; c 2. STRATIGRAPHY. *Educ:* Univ Ill, Urbana, BA, 60; Columbia Univ, PhD(geol), 67. *Prof Exp:* Lectr geol, Queens Col, NY, 64-67, asst prof, 67-70; asst prof, 70-74, ASSOC PROF GEOL, UNIV PITTSBURGH, 74-, ASSOC PROF ANTHROPOL, 78- *Mem:* AAAS; Geol Soc Am; Soc Econ Paleontologists & Mineralogists; Paleont Soc; Int Asn Sedimentology. *Res:* Paleozoic sedimentary depositional environments; evolution and environments of Paleozoic marine benthic communities; geology of archeological sites. *Mailing Add:* Dept Geol & Planetary Sci Univ of Pittsburgh Pittsburgh PA 15260

DONAHUE, JAMES EDWARD, b Trenton, Mich, Sept 9, 47; m 69. COMPUTER SCIENCE. *Educ:* Univ Mich, BA, 69; Rutgers Univ, MS, 71; Univ Toronto, PhD(comput sci), 75. *Prof Exp:* Mem tech staff, Bell Tel Labs, 69-71; comput scientist, Combustion Eng, Inc, 71-72; ASST PROF COMPUT SCI, CORNELL UNIV, 75- *Mem:* Asn Comput Mach. *Res:* Programming language design and definition. *Mailing Add:* Dept of Comput Sci Cornell Univ Ithaca NY 14853

DONAHUE, JOSEPH E, b Milwaukee, Wis, Oct 2, 23; m 61; c 2. CHEMISTRY, TEXTILE CHEMISTRY. *Educ:* Agr & Mech Col Tex, BS, 48. *Prof Exp:* Chemist, Tenn, 48-51, chemist anal chem, Ga, 51-53, area supvr radiation chem, 53-56, process supvr, NY, 56-61, res chemist textile fibers, Va, 61-62, res chemist, 62-80, SR RES CHEMIST TEXTILE FIBERS, TEXTILE RES LAB, E I DU PONT DE NEMOURS & CO, INC, 80- *Res:* Analytical chemistry. *Mailing Add:* Chestnut Run Textile Res Lab E I du Pont de Nemours & Co Inc Wilmington DE 19898

DONAHUE, ROGER PURTEE, medical genetics, see previous edition

DONAHUE, SHEILA, b Northolt, Eng, Nov 1, 16; US citizen. PATHOLOGY, NEUROPATHOLOGY. *Educ:* MRCS & LRCP, 43; FRCPath, 63; Am Bd Path, dipl, 57. *Prof Exp:* House physician, Elizabeth Garret Anderson Hosp, Eng, 43; house surgeon, Royal Surrey County Hosp, 44; asst, NY Univ, 48-51, instr, 53-55; spec trainee, Sect Neurocytol, Nat Inst Neurol Dis & Stroke, 58; assoc neuropath, Col Physicians & Surgeons, Columbia Univ, 58-60, asst prof, 60-63; from asst prof to assoc prof path, Sch Med, Ind Univ, 63-70; assoc res scientist, NY State Inst Basic Res Ment Retardation, 70-76; RETIRED. *Concurrent Pos:* Fel path, Col Med, NY Univ, 47-48; fel neuropath, Bellevue Hosp, 55-56 & Col Physicians & Surgeons, Columbia Univ, 56-58; resident, Bellevue Hosp, NY, 48-50, asst pathologist, 50-51 & 53-55. *Mem:* Fel Col Am Path; assoc Am Acad Neurol; Electron Micros Soc Am; Am Asn Path & Bact; Am Asn Neuropath. *Res:* Structure and function of the nervous system in the normal and diseased states including the morphology as it appears in the electron microscope. *Mailing Add:* 458 S Wood Dr Marietta GA 30060

DONAHUE, THOMAS MICHAEL, b Healdton, Okla, May 23, 21. PHYSICS. *Educ:* Rockhurst Col, AB, 42; Johns Hopkins Univ, PhD(physics), 48. *Hon Degrees:* DSc, Rockhurst Col, 81. *Prof Exp:* Asst Prof physics, Johns Hopkins Univ, 49-50; from assoc prof to prof, Univ Pittsburgh, 50-74; CHMN DEPT ATMOSPHERIC & OCEANIC SCI, UNIV MICH, 77- *Concurrent*

Pos: Vis prof, Univ Paris, 60, 80 & 81 & Harvard Univ, 71-72. *Honors & Awards:* Henry K Arctowski Medal, Nat Acad Sci, 81; John Adam Fleming Medal, Am Geophys Union, 81. *Mem:* Fel Am Geophys Union; fel AAAS; fel Am Phys Soc. *Res:* Atmospheric chemistry and physics; atomic and molecular physics. *Mailing Add:* Dept Atmospheric & Oceanic Sci Univ Mich Ann Arbor MI 48109

DONALD, ELIZABETH ANN, b Edmonton, Alta, Feb 14, 26. NUTRITION. *Educ:* Univ Alta, BSc, 49; Wash State Univ, MS, 55; Cornell Univ, PhD(nutrit), 62. *Prof Exp:* Dietitian, Univ Alta, 50-51; actg jr home economist, Wash State Univ, 55-59; from asst prof to assoc prof foods & nutrit, Cornell Univ, 62-69; assoc prof, 69-74, PROF FOODS & NUTRIT, UNIV ALTA, 74- *Mem:* AAAS; NY Acad Sci; Am Inst Nutrit; Can Nutrit Soc; Am Dietetic Asn. *Res:* Foods; nutritional status; vitamin B-6; vitamin B-6 requirement of young women using anovulatory steroids; energy balance in the elderly female; nutritional status of elderly. *Mailing Add:* Fac of Home Econ Univ of Alta Edmonton AB T6G 2M8 Can

DONALD, MERLIN WILFRED, b Montreal, PQ; c 2. NEUROPSYCHOLOGY. *Educ:* McGill Univ, PhD(psychol), 68. *Prof Exp:* Asst prof psychol, Dept Neurol, Yale Univ Sch Med, 70-72; neuropsychologist, Vet Admin Hosp, West Haven, Conn, 70-72; ASSOC PROF PSYCHOL, DEPT PSYCHOL, QUEEN'S UNIV, ONT, 73- *Concurrent Pos:* Nat Res Coun fel, Neuropsychol Lab, Vet Admin Hosp, West Haven & res assoc, Dept Psychiat, Yale Univ Sch Med, 68-70. *Mem:* Can Psychol Asn; Am Psychol Asn; Soc Neurosci; Int Neuropsychol Soc. *Res:* Neural models of selective attention; medical applications of human psychobiology; neurolinguistics. *Mailing Add:* Dept of Psychol Queen's Univ Kingston ON K7L 3N6 Can

DONALD, WILLIAM DAVID, b Donalds, SC, Apr 27, 24; m 48; c 4. MEDICINE. *Educ:* Erskine Col, AB, 45; Vanderbilt Univ, MD, 47. *Prof Exp:* Instr pediat, Sch Med, Vanderbilt Univ, 50-51; from asst prof to assoc prof, Sch Med, Univ Ala, 53-59; assoc prof, Med Col Ga, 59-60; ASSOC PROF PEDIAT, SCH MED, VANDERBILT UNIV, 60- *Mem:* AAAS; Am Acad Pediat; Am Fedn Clin Res. *Res:* Infectious diseases in children. *Mailing Add:* Dept of Pediat Vanderbilt Univ Nashville TN 37203

DONALD, WILLIAM WALDIE, b Freeport, NY, Feb 16, 50; m 74; c 1. WEED SCIENCE, PLANT PHYSIOLOGY. *Educ:* State Univ NY, Stony Brook, BS, 72; Univ Minn, St Paul, MS, 74; Univ Wis, Madison, PhD(agron), 77. *Prof Exp:* Fel weed sci, USDA Metab & Radiation Lab, 77-78; asst prof weed sci, Colo State Univ, Ft Collins, 78-80; RES AGRONOMIST, METAL & RADIATION LAB, USDA, 80- *Mem:* Weed Sci Soc Am; Am Soc Agron; Crop Sci Soc Am; Am Soc Plant Physiologists; Sigma Xi. *Res:* Mode of action of herbicides; applied weed control of foxtails and Canada thistle in wheat; chemical fallow. *Mailing Add:* Metab & Radiation Lab USDA Fargo ND 58105

DONALDSON, ALAN C, b Northampton, Mass, Oct 23, 29; m 57; c 4. GEOLOGY. *Educ:* Amherst Col, BA, 51; Univ Mass, MS, 53; Pa State Univ, PhD(geol), 59. *Prof Exp:* From asst prof to assoc prof, 57-69, PROF GEOL, WVA UNIV, 69-, CHMN DEPT, 71- *Mem:* Soc Econ Paleontologists & Mineralogists; Am Asn Petrol Geologists; fel Geol Soc Am. *Res:* Modern sediments and their depositional environments, sedimentary rocks, stratigraphy and sedimentation. *Mailing Add:* Dept of Geol WVa Univ Morgantown WV 26506

DONALDSON, COLEMAN DUPONT, b Philadelphia, Pa, Sept 22, 22; m 45; c 5. AERONAUTICAL ENGINEERING. *Educ:* Rensselaer Polytech Inst, BAeroE, 43; Princeton Univ, MA, 54, PhD(aeronaut eng), 57. *Prof Exp:* Mem staff, Nat Adv Comt Aeronaut, 43-44, head aerophys sect, 46-52; aeronaut engr, Bell Aircraft Corp, 46; PRES & SR CONSULT, AERONAUT RES ASSOCS OF PRINCETON, INC, 54- *Concurrent Pos:* Consult, Martin-Marietta Corp, 55-72, Gen Elec Co, 56-72, Gen Precision Equip Corp, 57-67, Thompson Ramo Wooldridge Inc, 58-61 & Grumman Aerospace Corp, 64-72; mem, Res & Adv Subcomt Fluid Mech, NASA & Vehicle Response Group, Defense Atomic Support Agency; Robert H Goddard vis lectr, Princeton Univ, 70-71, mem adv coun; indust prof adv comt, Pa State Univ, 70-77; chmn, Naval Res Adv Comn, Air Warfare Bd, 72-77. *Mem:* Am Phys Soc; assoc fel Am Inst Aeronaut & Astronaut. *Res:* Fluid and gas dynamics; viscous and other transport phenomena; turbulence and turbulent transport phenomena; chemical aspects of high temperature gas flows. *Mailing Add:* Aeronaut Res Assocs of Princeton Inc 50 Washington Rd PO Box 2229 Princeton NJ 08540

DONALDSON, DAVID MILLER, b Ogden, Utah, Oct 2, 24; m 47; c 4. BACTERIOLOGY, IMMUNOLOGY. *Educ:* Univ Utah, BS, 50, MS, 52, PhD(bact), 54. *Prof Exp:* Lab fel, Univ Utah, 50-52, asst, 52-54, res instr, 54-55; prof bact, 55-68, PROF MICROBIOL, BRIGHAM YOUNG UNIV, 68- *Mailing Add:* Dept of Microbiol Brigham Young Univ Provo UT 84602

DONALDSON, DONALD JAY, b Toledo, Ohio, Feb 15, 40; m 60. HUMAN ANATOMY, DEVELOPMENTAL BIOLOGY. *Educ:* Univ Toledo, BEd, 62; Tulane Univ, PhD(anat), 68. *Prof Exp:* Instr histol & embryol, 68-70, asst prof anat, 70-75, ASSOC PROF ANAT, CTR HEALTH SCI, UNIV TENN, MEMPHIS, 75- *Mem:* Am Asn Anatomists. *Res:* Control of growth and differentiation-regeneration of appendages in Amphibia; epidermal cell migration. *Mailing Add:* Dept of Anat Univ Tenn Ctr for Health Sci Memphis TN 38163

DONALDSON, EDWARD ENSLOW, b Wenatchee, Wash, Mar 7, 23; m 46; c 1. ATOMIC PHYSICS, MOLECULAR PHYSICS. *Educ:* Wash State Univ, BS, 48, PhD, 53. *Prof Exp:* Physicist radiol physics, Hanford Labs, Gen Elec Co, 53-57; from asst prof to assoc prof physics, 57-67, actg chmn dept, 64-67, chmn dept, 67-74 & 80-82, PROF PHYSICS, WASH STATE UNIV, 67- *Concurrent Pos:* Vis prof, Univ Liverpool, 68. *Mem:* AAAS; Am Asn Physics Teachers; sr mem Am Vacuum Soc; Am Phys Soc. *Res:* Physics and chemistry of surfaces. *Mailing Add:* Dept Physics Wash State Univ Pullman WA 99164

DONALDSON, EDWARD MOSSOP, b Whitehaven, Eng, June 25, 39; Can citizen; m 64. COMPARATIVE ENDOCRINOLOGY, FISHERIES. *Educ:* Sheffield Univ, BSc, 61, DSc(zool), 75; Univ BC, PhD(zool), 64. *Prof Exp:* USPHS fel steroid biochem, Univ Minn, Minneapolis, 64-65; scientist, West Vancouver Lab, Fisheries Res Bd Can, 65-75; prog head nutrit & endocrinol, 75-81, SECT HEAD, FISH CULT RES, RESOURCE SERV BR, DEPT FISHERIES & OCEANS, FISHERIES & MARINE SERVICE, 81- *Concurrent Pos:* Consult zool, Univ Calif, Berkeley, 68; mem orgn comt, Int Symp Comp Endocrinol, 69-; vis res scientist, Oceanic Inst, Hawaii, 69; res assoc, Univ BC, 69-; consult, Int Develop Res Ctr, 73- & Can Exec Serv Overseas, 80. *Mem:* Can Soc Zool; Am Soc Zool; Am Fisheries Soc. *Res:* Purification of gonadotropin; endocrinology and hormonal control of sex differentiation, ovulation and growth in fish; stress in salmonids; diet development and testing in salmon; resource enhancement and aquaculture of Pacific salmon; effects of wastes pollutants on reproduction and corticosteroidogenesis. *Mailing Add:* Resource Serv Br 4160 Marine Dr West Vancouver BC V7V 1N6 Can

DONALDSON, ERLE C, b Tela, Honduras, Dec 30, 26; m 54; c 5. CHEMICAL ENGINEERING, PETROLEUM ENGINEERING. *Educ:* The Citadel, BS, 53; Univ SC, MS, 55; Univ Houston, BS, 61; Univ Tulsa, PhD(chem eng), 75. *Prof Exp:* Anal chemist, Signal Oil & Gas Co, 55-59, chem engr, 59-61; proj leader, US Bur Mines, 61-73; proj mgr environ aspects oil recovery, 73-80, CHIEF, RESERVOIR EVALUATION SECT, US DEPT ENERGY, 80- *Mem:* Am Inst Chem Engrs; Soc Petrol Engrs. *Res:* In situ determination of oil saturation, reservoir porosity, permeability and lithology; determine the surface chemical and physical reactions of oil-water-rock systems; production of petroleum using chemical compounds to enchance recovery. *Mailing Add:* Res Ctr US Dept Energy PO Box 1398 Bartlesville OK 74003

DONALDSON, JAMES A, b Madison, Fla, Apr 17, 41. MATHEMATICS. *Educ:* Lincoln Univ, Pa, AB, 61; Univ Ill, MS, 63, PhD(math), 65. *Prof Exp:* Asst prof math, Howard Univ, 65-66; Univ Ill, Chicago Circle, 66-70; assoc prof, Univ NMex, 70-71, PROF MATH, HOWARD UNIV, 71-, CHMN DEPT, 72- *Concurrent Pos:* Vis mem, Courant Inst Math Sci, NY Univ, 76-77. *Mem:* Math Asn Am; Am Math Soc; Nat Asn Mathematicians; Soc Indust & Appl Mathematicians. *Res:* Differential equations; scattering theory; perturbation theory. *Mailing Add:* Dept of Math Howard Univ Washington DC 20059

DONALDSON, JAMES ADRIAN, b St Cloud, Minn, Jan 22, 30; m 50; c 5. OTOLOGY. *Educ:* Univ Minn, BA, 50, BS, 52, MD, 54, MS, 61. *Prof Exp:* Clin instr otolaryngol, Univ Southern Calif, 60-61; from asst prof to assoc prof otolaryngol & maxillofacial surg, Col Med, Univ Iowa, 61-65; head dept, 65-75, PROF OTOLARYNGOL, SCH MED, UNIV WASH, 65- *Mem:* Am Acad Ophthal & Otolaryngol; fel Am Otol Soc; fel Am Laryngol, Rhinol & Otol Soc; fel Am Col Surg; AMA. *Res:* Surgical anatomy of the temporal bone. *Mailing Add:* Univ Hosp Univ of Wash Seattle WA 98195

DONALDSON, JOHN ALLAN, b Chatham, Ont, Oct 15, 33; m 57; c 2. GEOLOGY. *Educ:* Queen's Univ, Ont, BSc, 56; Johns Hopkins Univ, PhD(geol), 60. *Prof Exp:* Geologist, Geol Surv Can, 59-65, res scientist, 65-68; assoc prof, 68-74, PROF GEOL, CARLETON UNIV, ONT, 74-, CHMN DEPT, 80- *Mem:* Soc Econ Paleontologists & Mineralogists; Geol Asn Can; Int Asn Sedimentol. *Res:* Dispersal patterns in sedimentary rocks; Precambrian sedimentation; primitive life. *Mailing Add:* Dept Geol Carleton Univ Rideau River Campus Ottawa ON K1S 5B6 Can

DONALDSON, JOHN RILEY, b Dallas, Tex, Nov 24, 25; m 51; c 4. NUCLEAR PHYSICS. *Educ:* Rice Inst, BS, 45, MA, 47; Yale Univ, MS, PhD(physics), 51. *Prof Exp:* Nuclear physicist, Calif Res & Develop Co, 50-53; assoc prof physics, Univ Ariz, 53-54; assoc prof, Fresno State Col, 56-67, PROF PHYSICS, CALIF STATE UNIV, FRESNO, 67- *Concurrent Pos:* Mem, Fresno County Bd Supvrs, 73-80, chmn, 77-78. *Mem:* Sigma Xi; AAAS; Am Asn Physics Teachers; Am Phys Soc. *Res:* General and nuclear physics. *Mailing Add:* Dept of Physics Calif State Univ Fresno CA 93740

DONALDSON, LAUREN RUSSELL, b Tracy, Minn, May 13, 03; m 27; c 2. BIOLOGY. *Educ:* Intermountain Union Col, AB, 26; Univ Wash, MS, 31, PhD(fisheries), 39. *Hon Degrees:* DSc, Rocky Mountain Col, 58 & Hamline Univ, 65. *Prof Exp:* Prin & teacher high sch, Mont, 26-30; from asst to prof fisheries, 32-73, dir lab radiation biol, 58-66, dir appl fisheries lab, 43-57, EMER PROF FISHERIES, COL FISHERIES, UNIV WASH, 73- *Concurrent Pos:* Consult fish & wildlife serv, US Dept Interior, 35-40, Gen Elec Co, 47- & Gen Mills Inc; biologist, State Dept Fisheries, Wash, 42-43; chief div radiobiol, Radiol Safety Sect, Oper Crossroads, Bikini, 46, chief div radiobiol, Bikini Sci Resurv, 47-48 & Bikini-Eniwetok Resurv, 49; biologist, Oper Ivy, 52; lectr, Univ Oslo, 52, Univ Helsinki, 59 & Tokyo Fish Univ, 73; rep, AEC, Japan, 54; dir radiobiol studies, Pac Weapons Testing Prog, 54- *Mem:* Am Fisheries Soc (vpres, 39); Radiation Res Soc. *Res:* Fisheries management; fresh water biology; radiobiology; genetics of salmonoid fishes; nutrition of the chinook salmon, particularly histological changes. *Mailing Add:* Col of Fisheries Univ of Wash Seattle WA 98195

DONALDSON, MERLE RICHARD, b Silverdale, Kans, Apr 7, 20; m 43; c 2. ELECTRICAL ENGINEERING. *Educ:* Ga Inst Technol, BEE, 46, MS, 47, PhD(elec eng), 59. *Prof Exp:* Instr elec eng, Ga Inst Technol, 46-50, asst prof, 50-51; engr, Oak Ridge Nat Lab, 51-55, sr engr in chg res & develop cyclotrons, 55-57; proj engr, Basic Study Projs, Norden-Ketay Corp, 57; res engr, Electronic Commun, Inc, 57-58, sr staff engr, Advan Technol Group, 58-60, prin eng scientist, 60, mgr, Advan Develop Sect, 60-61, dir, Advan Develop Lab, 61-63; acad supvr, Off-Campus Grad Ctr & assoc prof elec eng, Univ Fla, 62-64; PROF ELEC ENG & CHMN DEPT, UNIV S FLA, 64- *Concurrent Pos:* Consult, Univ Colo, 57, Am Lava Corp, 59, Capital Radio Eng Inst, 60- & Sperry Microwave Electronics Co, 63-70; newsletter ed, Inst Elec & Electronics Engrs, 58-59, ed, Transactions, 59-60. *Mem:* AAAS; fel Inst Elec & Electronics Engrs. *Res:* Microwave theory and techniques. *Mailing Add:* Dept of Elec Eng Univ of SFla Col of Eng Tampa FL 33620

DONALDSON, PATRICIA LYNN, b Wichita, Kans, Jan 12, 51. BRAIN & BEHAVIOR. *Educ:* Duke Univ, BS, 73; Univ Calif, Irvine, PhD(biol sci), 77. *Prof Exp:* Res assoc biol, Dept Develop & Cell Biol, Univ Calif, Irvine, 77-78; res fel zool, Dept Zool, Univ Nottingham, Eng, 78-80; ASSOC PHYSIOL, DEPT PHYSIOL & BIOPHYS, UNIV IOWA, 81- *Mem:* Soc Neurosci; Am Soc Zoologists; Soc Exp Biologists. *Res:* Neurophysiology, including peripheral nerve connections to muscle, development of neuronal innervation, and the excitability of muscle cells. *Mailing Add:* Dept Physiol & Biophys Univ Iowa Iowa City IA 52242

DONALDSON, PAUL, b Ephrata, Wash, July 4, 16; m 40; c 2. MICROBIOLOGY, IMMUNOLOGY. *Educ:* Univ Wash, BS, 39; Univ Wis, MS, 45, PhD(med microbiol), 47. *Prof Exp:* Asst prof microbiol, Tulane Med Sch, 47-51; asst prof, Univ Tex Southwestern Med Sch, 51-67; assoc prof & head dept, Northwestern La State Univ, 67-73; ASSOC PROF MICROBIOL & IMMUNOL, SCH MED, LA STATE UNIV, SHREVEPORT, 73- *Mem:* Am Soc Microbiol; Reticuloendothelial Soc. *Res:* Immune and nonimmune phagocytosis; nonprofessional phagocytes; immediate hypersensitivities in mice. *Mailing Add:* Dept of Microbiol & Immunol La State Univ Sch of Med Shreveport LA 71130

DONALDSON, RAYMOND EDWIN, chemistry, see previous edition

DONALDSON, ROBERT E(DWARD), b Indianapolis, Ind, Sept 2, 22; m 44; c 3. CHEMICAL ENGINEERING. *Educ:* Purdue Univ, BS, 43. *Prof Exp:* Pilotplant operator, Process Develop Sect, Gulf Res & Develop Co, 43-44, supvr pilot plant opers, 44-47, proj leader, 47-53, group leader, 53-57, asst sect head, 57-61, sect head, 61-65, staff engr, Pa, 65-68, supv engr process, Pac Gulf Oil, Ltd, Japan, 68-70; process design engr, Korea Lubricants Co, Ltd, 70-77; process engr, 77-80, PROCESS MGR, GULF SCI & TECHNOL CO, 80- *Mem:* Am Chem Soc; Am Inst Chem Engrs. *Res:* Petroleum refining; process development work; catalytic cracking; hydrogenation; lubricating oil processing; catalyst development and evaluation; process design of petroleum refining, and lube oil blending plants. *Mailing Add:* Gulf Sci & Technol Co 6003 Green Terrace Lane Houston TX 77088

DONALDSON, ROBERT M, JR, b Hubbardston, Mass, Aug 1, 27; m 50; c 2. INTERNAL MEDICINE, GASTROENTEROLOGY. *Educ:* Yale Univ, BS, 49; Boston Univ, MD, 52. *Prof Exp:* Asst prof med, Sch Med, Boston Univ, 59-64; assoc prof, Univ Wis, 64-67; from assoc prof to prof med, Sch Med, Boston Univ, 67-73; PROF MED & VCHMN DEPT INTERNAL MED, SCH MED, YALE UNIV, 73-; CHIEF MED SERV, VET ADMIN HOSP, 73- *Concurrent Pos:* USPHS fel, Harvard Med Sch, 57-59; chmn gastroenterol res eval comt, Vet Admin, 68-71; chmn gastroenterol & nutrit training comt, NIH, 69-73; ed J, Am Gastroenterol Asn, 70- *Mem:* Am Gastroenterol Asn (pres, 79); Asn Am Physicians; Am Soc Clin Invest. *Res:* Gastric; secretion; intestinal absorption; gastrointestinal bacteriology. *Mailing Add:* Vet Admin Hosp W Spring St West Haven CT 06516

DONALDSON, ROBERT PAUL, b Berkeley, Calif, Oct 15, 41; m 64, 78; c 2. PLANT BIOCHEMISTRY. *Educ:* Univ Tex, Austin, BA, 64; Miami Univ, Ohio, MS, 66; Mich State Univ, PhD(biochem), 71. *Prof Exp:* Res assoc, lysosome res, Rockefeller Univ, NY City, 71-73; res assoc, glyxysomal membrane res, Univ Calif, Santa Cruz, 73-76; ASST PROF PLANT CELL BIOL TEACHING & RES, GEORGE WASHINGTON UNIV, 77- *Mem:* Am Soc Plant Physiologists; AAAS. *Res:* Flavoproteins and cytochromes in the membranes of organelles such as glyoxysomes and peroxisomes; anaerobic metabolism in germinating seeds. *Mailing Add:* Dept Biol Sci George Washington Univ Washington DC 20052

DONALDSON, ROBERT RYMAL, b Hornell, NY, Feb 27, 17; m 42; c 3. SCIENCE EDUCATION, PHYSICS. *Educ:* Syracuse Univ, BA, 40, MA, 43; Cornell Univ, PhD(sci educ), 55. *Prof Exp:* Teacher pub sch, 40-43, 46-51 & 54-55; PROF PHYSICS, COL ARTS & SCI, STATE UNIV NY COL PLATTSBURGH, 55- *Concurrent Pos:* Ed consult spec proj, Ford Found, Ankara, Turkey, 64-65. *Mem:* AAAS; Am Asn Physics Teachers; Nat Sci Teachers Asn. *Res:* Introductory courses in physics and physical science; meteorology; astronomy; science education. *Mailing Add:* Dept of Physics Col Arts & Sci State Univ of NY Col Plattsburgh NY 12901

DONALDSON, SUE KAREN, b Detroit, Mich, Sept 16, 43; c 1. MUSCLE PHYSIOLOGY. *Educ:* Wayne State Univ, BSN, 65, MSN, 66; Univ Wash, PhD(physiol & biophysics), 73. *Prof Exp:* Asst assoc prof physiol & nursing, Univ Wash, 73-78; ASSOC PROF PHYSIOL & NURSING, RUSH UNIV, ILL, 78-, DIR CLIN NURSING RES PROG, 80- *Concurrent Pos:* Prin investr, Wash State Heart Asn grant, 73-74, NIH grants, 73-, USPHS Div Nursing grant, 80- & Muscular Dystrophy Asn grant, 81- *Mem:* Am Nurses Asn; Biophys Soc; Am Heart Asn; Coun Nurse Researchers. *Res:* Animal studies of excitation-contraction-coupling mechanisms in mammalian ventricular and skeletal muscle fibers, including alterations in muscle properties associated with ontogenetic differentiation and disease. *Mailing Add:* Dept Physiol Rush Univ Med Ctr 1753 W Harrison Chicago IL 60612

DONALDSON, TERRENCE LEE, b Franklin, Pa, Apr 20, 46. CHEMICAL ENGINEERING, BIOENGINEERING. *Educ:* Pa State Univ, BS, 68; Univ Pa, PhD(chem eng), 74. *Prof Exp:* Asst prof chem eng, Univ Rochester, 74-80, assoc prof, 80; GROUP LEADER, BIOPROCESS RES & DEVELOP, OAK RIDGE NAT LAB, 81- *Concurrent Pos:* Lectr chem eng, Univ Tenn, 81. *Mem:* Am Inst Chem Engrs; Am Chem Soc; Sigma Xi. *Res:* Mass transfer; carrier transport in synthetic membranes; enzyme catalysis; separations and kinetics; biochemical engineering. *Mailing Add:* Oak Ridge Nat Lab Box X Oak Ridge TN 37830

DONALDSON, VIRGINIA HENRIETTA, b Glen Cove, NY, Oct 3, 24. MEDICINE. *Educ:* Univ Vt, AB, 47, MD, 51. *Prof Exp:* Intern, Strong Mem Hosp, Rochester, NY, 51-53, asst res pediat, Strong Mem & Genessee Hosps, 53-54; asst res pediat, Buffalo Children's Hosp, 54-55; from instr to sr instr med, Western Reserve Univ, 62-67; assoc prof med, 67-71, PROF PEDIAT

& MED, COL MED, UNIV CINCINNATI, 71- Concurrent Pos: Res fel pediat, Sch Med, Western Reserve Univ, 55-57, res fel med, 57-62; asst attend pediat & asst dir, Outpatient Dept, Babies' & Children's Hosp, Cleveland, Ohio, 56-57; assoc, Res Div, Cleveland Clin, 57-62, asst mem staff, 62-63; mem res staff, St Vincent Charity Hosp, 63-67, estab investr, Am Heart Asn, 64-69; dir hemat, Cincinnati Shrine Burn Inst, 67-70. Mem: AAAS; Am Fedn Clin Res; Am Soc Hemat; Am Soc Clin Invest; Asn Am Physicians. Res: Studies of hydrolytic enzymes of human blood as related to blood coagulation; fibrinolysis; action of first component of complement and relation of fibrinolytic mechanisms to complement action. Mailing Add: Children's Hosp Res Found Univ of Cincinnati Col of Med Cincinnati OH 45229

DONALDSON, W(ILLIS) LYLE, b Cleburne, Tex, May 1, 15; m 38; c 4. ELECTRICAL ENGINEERING. Educ: Tex Tech Univ, BS, 38. Prof Exp: Distribution engr, Tex Elec Serv Co, 38-42, distribution supvr, 45-46; from asst prof to assoc prof elec eng, Lehigh Univ, 46-54; sr res engr, 54-55, mgr commun res, 55-59, dir elec & electronics dept, 59-63, vpres, 64-72, vpres planning & prog develop, 72-74, SR V PRES PLANNING & PROG DEVELOP, SOUTHWEST RES INST, 74- Mem: Sigma Xi; fel Am Soc Nondestructive Testing; fel Inst Elec & Electronics Engrs; Nat Soc Prof Engrs; Am Optical Soc. Res: Radio direction finding; communications; system engineering; electronic instrumentation and control; sonics; military physics; bioengineering; nondestructive testing of materials; new techniques for testing ferrous metals; design work on receivers, transmitters and industrial electronic devices. Mailing Add: Southwest Res Inst PO Drawer 28510 San Antonio TX 78284

DONALDSON, WILLIAM EMMERT, b Baltimore, Md, Dec 19, 31; m 55; c 6. POULTRY NUTRITION. Educ: Univ Md, BS, 53, MS, 55, PhD(poultry nutrit), 57. Prof Exp: Asst poultry nutrit, Univ Md, 53-57; asst prof, Univ RI, 57-62; from asst prof to assoc prof, 62-68, prof poultry nutrit, 68-80, PROF POULTRY SCI, NC STATE UNIV, 80- Honors & Awards: Am Feed Mfg Nutrit Res Award, 76. Mem: AAAS; Am Inst Nutrit; Poultry Sci Asn. Res: Fat metabolism, especially fatty acid biosynthesis and interconversion. Mailing Add: Dept of Poultry Sci NC State Univ Raleigh NC 27650

DONALDSON, WILLIAM TWITTY, b Statesboro, Ga, June 26, 27; m 48; c 2. ANALYTICAL CHEMISTRY. Educ: Univ Ga, BS, 48. Prof Exp: Develop chemist, Ethyl Corp Develop Lab, 48-51; res supvr, Savannah River Lab, E I duPont Co, 51-63, lab supvr, Martinsville Nylon Plant, 63-66; chief chem serv, US Federal Water Pollution Control Admin Southeast Water Lab, 66-69; chief anal chem, 69-78, DEP DIR, US ENVIRON PROTECTION AGENCY ENVIRON RES LAB, 78- Mem: Am Chem Soc; Am Soc Testing Mat; Asn Official Anal Chemists; Sigma Xi. Res: Applied analytical chemistry. Mailing Add: US Environ Protection Agency College Station Rd Athens GA 30605

DONART, GARY B, b Howard, Kans, Sept 6, 40; m 61; c 3. RANGE SCIENCE. Educ: Ft Hays Kans State Col, BS, 62, MS, 63; Utah State Univ, PhD(range sci), 68. Prof Exp: Asst prof range mgt, Humboldt State Col, 65-68; asst prof range sci, Tex A&M Univ, 68-72; assoc prof, 72-79, PROF RANGE SCI, NMex State Univ, 79- Concurrent Pos: Consult, Nat Parks, 65-66. Mem: Am Soc Range Mgt; Am Soc Agron; Crop Sci Soc Am; Am Inst Biol Sci. Res: Ecology and management of range lands; poison plant problems; livestock management; forage plant physiology; soil-plant relations. Mailing Add: Dept Range Sci NMex State Univ Las Cruces NM 88003

DONARUMA, L GUY, b Utica, NY, Sept 6, 28; m 50; c 3. ORGANIC CHEMISTRY. Educ: St Lawrence Univ, BS, 49; Carnegie Inst Technol, PhD(org chem), 53. Prof Exp: Sr chemist explosives dept, Eastern Lab, E I du Pont de Nemours & Co, Inc, 53-55, res chemist, 55-57, sr res chemist, 57-60, res assoc & supvr, 60-62; asst prof chem, 62-64, assoc prof & exec off dept, 65-67, prof, 67-73, assoc dean grad sch, 68-73, dean grad sch & dir res, Clarkson Col Technol, 73-75; prof chem & dean math, sci & eng, Calif State Univ, Fullerton, 75-77; vpres acad affairs, NMex Inst Mining & Technol, 77-81, prof chem, 77-81; PROVOST, POLYTECH INST NY, 81- Mem: Am Chem Soc; NY Acad Sci; The Chem Soc. Res: Synthetic polymer chemistry, medicinal and polymer chemistry; polymer drugs, novel polymer systems, polymers for enhanced oil recovery. Mailing Add: 28 Eldorado Blvd Plainview NY 11803

DONATH, ERNEST E, b Sternberg, Austria-Hungary, Nov 4, 02; nat US; m 27; c 2. PHYSICAL CHEMISTRY. Educ: Tech Univ Breslau, Dipl Ing, 24, Dr Ing, 26. Prof Exp: Chemist, group leader & chief chemist for res, High Pressure Dept, Badische Anilin & Soda-Fabrik Plant, I G Farbenindustrie, Ludwigshafen, 26-46; sci adv, Synthetic Liquid Fuels Sta, Bur Mines, Mo, 47-49; mgr fuels res, Tech Planning & Contract Res Sect, Koppers Co, Inc, 49-64; RES CONSULT, 64- Mem: Am Inst Chem Engrs; Am Chem Soc. Res: Synthetic liquid fuels; high pressure reactions; coal carbonization and gasification; hydrocarbon conversion. Mailing Add: PO Box 1068 Christiansted VI 00820

DONATH, FRED ARTHUR, b St Cloud, Minn, July 11, 31; m 52; c 2. APPLIED GEOLOGY, GEOLOGIC DEFORMATION. Educ: Univ Minn, BA, 54; Stanford Univ, MS, 56, PhD(geol), 58. Prof Exp: Asst prof geol, San Jose State Col, 57-58; from asst prof geol to prof, Columbia Univ, 58-67; head dept, Univ Ill, Urbana-Champaign, 67-77, prof geol, 67-80; PRES, CGS INC, 80- Concurrent Pos: Vis lectr, Am Geol Inst, 66-70; lectr, continuing educ prog, Am Asn Petrol Geol, 65-78; ed, Annual Rev Earth & Planetary Sci, 70-80. Honors & Awards: Semicentennial Medallion, Rice Univ, 62. Mem: Fel AAAS; fel Geol Soc Am; Am Geophys Union; Am Asn Petrol Geol; fel Geol Soc London. Res: Structural geology; experimental rock deformation; mechanics of earth deformation. Mailing Add: CGS Inc 104 W University Urbana IL 61801

DONATI, EDWARD JOSEPH, b Wilkes-Barre, Pa, Sept 9, 24; m 48. ANATOMY. Educ: King's Col, Pa, BA, 51; Univ Md, PhD(anat), 64. Prof Exp: Technician, Med Labs, US Army Chem Ctr, 52-56, biologist-histologist, 56-60; sect chief microanat-cytol, Directorate Med Res, Edgewood Arsenal, 60-67, actg chief path br, Med Res Labs, 67-68; asst prof, 68-71, ASSOC PROF ANAT, SCH MED, UNIV MD, BALTIMORE', 71- Mem: Electron Micros Soc Am; Am Asn Anat. Res: Electron microscopy of renal lymphatics and murine tumors. Mailing Add: Sch of Med Univ of Md Baltimore MD 21201

DONATI, ROBERT M, b Richmond Heights, Mo, Feb 28, 34. NUCLEAR MEDICINE. Educ: St Louis Univ, BS, 55, MD, 59. Prof Exp: Intern, St Louis City Hosp, 59-60; asst resident, John Cochran Hosp, St Louis, 60-62; from instr to assoc prof, 63-74, PROF MED, MED SCH, ST LOUIS UNIV, 74-, DIR DIV NUCLEAR MED, 68- Concurrent Pos: Fel nuclear med, Med Sch, St Louis Univ, 62-63; staff physician, St Louis Univ & John Cochran Hosp, 63-; chief nuclear med serv, St Louis Vet Admin Hosp, 68-79; consult, Walter Reed Army Inst Res, 68-75; nuclear med res prog specialist, Reg Res Adv Group, 73-74, Res Adv Comt, 73-76, Vet Admin Cent Off, Washington, DC; mem, Presidents Adv Comn Vet Admin, 72, Radiation Task Force, HEW, 78-79; actg chief staff, St Louis Vet Admin Hosp, 76-77. Mem: Am Physiol Soc; Soc Nuclear Med; NY Acad Sci; Cent Soc Clin Res; fel Int Soc Hemat. Res: Control of cellular proliferation in a variety of systems; clinical investigation in nuclear medicine. Mailing Add: Vet Admin Med Ctr 11JC St Louis MO 63125

DONAWICK, WILLIAM JOSEPH, b Troy, NY, Aug 18, 40; m 61; c 2. TRANSPLANTATION BIOLOGY, VETERINARY SURGERY. Educ: Cornell Univ, DVM, 63; Am Col Vet Surg, dipl, 72; Univ Pa, MS, 73. Prof Exp: Vet intern clin med & surg, 64-66, USPHS res fel transplantation biol, 66-69, asst prof surg, 69-72, assoc prof, 72-78, PROF SURG, UNIV PA, 78- Concurrent Pos: NIH career develop award, 73-77. Mem: Am Col Vet Surgeons (pres, 82-83). Res: Veterinary clinical surgical investigation. Mailing Add: Univ of Pa New Bolton Ctr Kennett Square PA 19348

DONCHIN, EMANUEL, b Tel Aviv, Israel, Apr 3, 35; m 55; c 3. PHYSIOLOGICAL PSYCHOLOGY. Educ: Hebrew Univ, Israel, BA, 61; Univ Calif, Los Angeles, MA, 63, PhD(psychol), 64. Prof Exp: Res asst psychol, Univ Calif, Los Angeles, 61-64, res assoc, 64-65; res assoc neurol, Sch Med, Stanford Univ, 65-67; res assoc neurobiol, Ames Res Ctr, NASA, 66-69; assoc prof psychol, 69-73, PROF PSYCHOL, UNIV ILL, URBANA-CHAMPAIGN, 73-, HEAD, DEPT PHYSIOL, 80- Mem: Am Electroencephalog Soc; Psychonomic Soc; Soc Psychophysiol Res (pres, 79-80); fel Am Pschol Asn; fel AAAS. Res: Physiological mechanisms of attention and perception; computer analysis of brain waves. Mailing Add: Dept Psychol Univ Ill Champaign IL 61820

DONDERO, NORMAN CARL, b Somerville, Mass, May 22, 18; m 52; c 1. MICROBIOLOGY, WATER POLLUTION. Educ: Univ Mass, BS, 41; Univ Conn, MS, 43; Cornell Univ, PhD(bact), 52. Prof Exp: Instr animal dis, Univ Conn, 46-48; res assoc bact, Cornell Univ, 51-53, asst prof, 53-54; assoc, Inst Microbiol, Rutgers Univ, 54-56, asst prof sanit, 56-59, assoc prof, 59-63, prof environ sci, 63-66, chmn microbiol sect, 63-65; PROF APPL MICROBIOL, CORNELL UNIV, 66- Mem: Am Soc Microbiol; Soc Appl Bact; Soc Gen Microbiol; Am Soc Limnol & Oceanog; Am Acad Microbiol. Res: Aquatic microbiology; water pollution. Mailing Add: Dept of Microbiol Cornell Univ Ithaca NY 14853

DONDERSHINE, FRANK HASKIN, b Newark, NJ, Dec 29, 31; m 58. MICROBIOLOGY. Educ: Seton Hall Univ, AB, 55. Prof Exp: Asst hematologist, Martland Med Ctr, NJ, 51-54; microbiologist, Warner-Lambert Res Inst, 57-62; microbiologist, Ethicon, Inc, 62-70; sr microbiologist, Cosan Chem Corp, 70-71; MGR, MICROBIOL DEPT, CARTER-WALLACE, INC, 71- Concurrent Pos: Lectr, Ctr Prof Advan. Mem: AAAS; Am Soc Microbiol; Soc Indust Microbiol. Res: Antimicrobial product evaluations; general antimetabolite and clinical evaluations; antiseptics, disinfectants and sterilizers development; ultrasonics; aerosols; antibiotics; dental research; quality control. Mailing Add: Wallace Labs Div Carter-Wallace Inc Half Acre Rd Cranbury NJ 08512

DONDES, SEYMOUR, b New York, NY, Apr 3, 18; m 45; c 3. PHYSICAL CHEMISTRY. Educ: Brooklyn Col, BA, 39; Rensselaer Polytech Inst, MS, 50, PhD(chem), 54. Prof Exp: Res scientist radiation chem, 52-70, assoc prof, 70-73, PROF CHEM, RENSSELAER POLYTECH INST, 73- Mem: AAAS; Am Chem Soc. Res: Radiation chemistry; photochemistry; kinetics of gas reactions; nuclear reactor technology. Mailing Add: Dept of Chem Rensselaer Polytech Inst Troy NY 12181

DONE, ALAN KIMBALL, b Salt Lake City, Utah, Sept 23, 26; m 47; c 10. PEDIATRICS, CLINICAL PHARMACOLOGY. Educ: Univ Utah, BA, 49, MD, 52. Prof Exp: From intern to assoc pediatrician, Salt Lake County Gen Hosp, 53-58; from res instr to res asst prof pediat, Col Med, Univ Utah, 56-58; asst prof, Stanford Univ, 58-60; from assoc res prof to prof pediat, Col Med, Univ Utah, 60-71; spec asst to dir, Bur Drugs, Food & Drug Admin, 71-74; PROF PEDIAT & PHARMACOL, COL MED, WAYNE STATE UNIV, 75-, ADJ PROF CLIN PHARM, 80- Concurrent Pos: Am Heart Asn fel, 54-57; adj prof pharmacol, Col Med, Univ Utah, 69-71, prof clin pharmacol, Col Pharm, 70-71. Mem: Am Pediat Soc; Soc Pediat Res; fel Am Acad Pediat; Soc Exp Biol & Med. Res: Developmental pharmacology. Mailing Add: Dept of Pediat Wayne State Univ Detroit MI 48202

DONEFER, EUGENE, b Brooklyn, NY, Jan 2, 33; m 53; c 3. ANIMAL NUTRITION. Educ: Cornell Univ, BS, 55, MS, 57; McGill Univ, PhD(nutrit), 61. Prof Exp: From asst prof to assoc prof, 61-74, PROF ANIMAL SCI, McGILL UNIV, MACDONALD CAMPUS, 75- Concurrent Pos: Consult, Beef Prod Proj Caribbean, Barbados; res assoc, Int Develop Res Centre, Ottawa, 72-73; proj dir, Sugarcane Feeds Ctr, Trinidad, 76-81. Mem: Am Soc Animal Sci; Am Inst Nutrit; Nutrit Soc Can. Res: Ruminant nutrition; nutritive evaluation of forages; improving low-quality forages; utilization of sugar cane feeds. Mailing Add: Dept of Animal Sci McGill Univ Macdonald Campus Ste Anne de Bellevue PQ H9X 1C0 Can

DONELAN, MARK ANTHONY, b Grenada, West Indies, Mar 27, 42; m 67; c 3. PHYSICAL OCEANOGRAPHY, METEOROLOGY. *Educ:* McGill Univ, BEng, 64; Univ BC, PhD(oceanog), 70. *Prof Exp:* Proj engr, Procter & Gamble Can, 64-66; fel, Dept Appl Math & Theoret Physics, Cambridge Univ, 70-71; RES SCIENTIST, ENVIRON CAN, FED GOVT CAN, 71- *Concurrent Pos:* Adj prof, Dept Appl Math, Univ Waterloo, 79-; assoc ed, Atmosphere-Ocean, 78- *Mem:* Can Meteorol & Oceanog Soc; Am Meteorol Soc. *Res:* Air-water interaction, surface gravity waves, turbulence. *Mailing Add:* Can Ctr Inland Waters PO Box 5050 Burlington ON L7R 4A6 Can

DONELSON, JOHN EVERETT, b Ogden, Iowa, May 23, 43; m 66; c 2. BIOCHEMISTRY. *Educ:* Iowa State Univ, BSc, 65; Cornell Univ, PhD(biochem), 71. *Prof Exp:* Teacher math & chem, sec sch, Am Peace Corps, Ghana, WAfrica, 65-67; fel molecular biol, Med Res Ctr, Lab Molecular Biol, Cambridge, Eng, 71-73; fel biochem, Med Ctr, Stanford Univ, 73-74; from asst prof to assoc prof, 74-80, PROF BIOCHEM, UNIV IOWA, 80- *Res:* Sequence and function of intercistronic regions of eukaryotic DNA molecules; biochemical mechanisms of antigenic variation in tryparosomes. *Mailing Add:* Dept Biochem Sch Med Univ Iowa Iowa City IA 52242

DONER, LANDIS WILLARD, b Winona, Minn, Aug 31, 41; m 72. CARBOHYDRATE CHEMISTRY. *Educ:* Winona State Univ, BA, 64; NDak State Univ, MS, 66; Purdue Univ, PhD(biochem), 71. *Prof Exp:* Fel biochem, Purdue Univ, 71; fel chem, Dundee Univ, Scotland, 71-73; fel biochem, Purdue Univ, 73-74; RES CHEMIST BIO-ORG CHEM, EASTERN REGIONAL RES CTR, USDA, 74- *Mem:* Am Chem Soc; AAAS. *Res:* Organic and biochemistry of sugars and polysaccharides; instrumental methods of sugar analysis; honey; applications of stable isotope ratio analysis in food science. *Mailing Add:* USDA Eastern Regional Res Ctr 600 E Mermaid Lane Philadelphia PA 19118

DONEY, DEVON LYLE, b Franklin, Idaho, Mar 31, 34; m 58; c 5. PLANT GENETICS. *Educ:* Utah State Univ, BS, 60, MS, 61; Cornell Univ, PhD(plant breeding, genetics), 65. *Prof Exp:* Tomato breeder, Libby, McNeil & Libby, 64-65; RES GENETICIST, AGR RES SERV, USDA, 65- *Mem:* Crop Sci Soc Am; Am Soc Sugarbeet Technologists. *Res:* Physiological genetics of sugarbeet; selection methods; alcohol fuel from beets. *Mailing Add:* Crops Res Lab Utah State Univ Logan UT 84321

DONG, RICHARD GENE, b Sacramento, Calif, Mar 16, 35. STRUCTURAL MECHANICS, SEISMIC ENGINEERING. *Educ:* Univ Calif, Berkeley, BS, 57, MS, 59, PhD(civil eng), 64. *Prof Exp:* Develop engr, Aerojet-Gen Corp, Calif, 59-61; ENGR, LAWRENCE LIVERMORE NAT LAB, UNIV CALIF, 63- *Res:* Equipment qualification for nuclear power plants; fragilities of equipment and structures; material behavior and properties; technical bases for nuclear power plant licensing; seismic design methodology; fluid structure interaction. *Mailing Add:* 38 Hornet Ct Danville CA 94526

DONG, STANLEY B, b Canton, China, Apr 2, 36; US citizen; m 64; c 3. STRUCTURAL MECHANICS, STRUCTURAL DYNAMICS. *Educ:* Univ Calif, Berkeley, BS, 57, MS, 58, PhD(struct mech), 62. *Prof Exp:* Sr res engr, Aerojet-Gen Corp, 62-65; from asst prof to assoc prof eng, 65-73, PROF ENG, UNIV CALIF, LOS ANGELES, 73- *Concurrent Pos:* Off Naval Res-Am Inst Aeronaut & Astronaut res scholar struct mech, 70. *Mem:* Am Soc Civil Engrs; Am Soc Mech Engrs; AAAS. *Res:* Analysis of structural composites, structural dynamics of plates and shells. *Mailing Add:* 6731 Boelter Hall Eng & Appl Sci Univ of Calif Los Angeles CA 90024

DONGIER, MAURICE HENRI, b Sorgues, France, Nov 27, 25; Can citizen; m 52; c 4. PSYCHIATRY, PSYCHOANALYSIS. *Educ:* Univ Aix-Marseille, MD, 51; McGill Univ, dipl psychiat, 53. *Prof Exp:* Res asst psychiat, McGill Univ, 51-52; chef de clin adj neuro psychiat, Univ Aix-Marseille, 54-57, chef de clin tit psychiat, 57-60; res psychiatrist neurophysiol, Hosp Timone, Marseille, 60-63; prof psychiat & chmn dept, Univ Liege, 63-71; PROF PSYCHIAT, McGILL UNIV, 71-, CHMN DEPT, 74-; DIR, ALLAN MEM INST, 71- *Concurrent Pos:* Res award, Med Res Sci Found, Belg, 65-70; res award, Med Res Coun Can, 73-75, mem behav sci grant comt, 76- *Mem:* Can Psychiat Asn; Am Psychiat Asn; Am Psychopath Asn; Am Psychosomatic Soc. *Res:* Psychosomatics, especially coronary heart disease; brief dynamic psychotherapy; electroencehalography in psychiatry. *Mailing Add:* Allan Mem Inst 1025 Pine Ave W Montreal Can

DONIACH, SEBASTIAN, b Paris, France, Jan 25, 34; m 55; c 4. THEORETICAL PHYSICS. *Educ:* Cambridge Univ, BA, 54; Univ Liverpool, PhD(theoret physics), 58. *Prof Exp:* Imp Chem Industs fel theoret physics, Univ Liverpool, 58-60; lectr physics, Queen Mary Col, Univ London, 60-64 & Imp Col, 64-66, reader, 67-69; PROF APPL PHYSICS, STANFORD UNIV, 69- *Concurrent Pos:* Vis scientist, Europ Orgn Nuclear Res, Geneva, 63; consult, Atomic Energy Res Estab, Harwell, Eng, 66-69, Bell Tel Res Labs, 67, 70 & 71, Dept Physics, Univ Calif, San Diego, 68 & Argonne Nat Lab, AEC, 70-; res assoc, Dept Physics, Harvard Univ, 67-68; dir, Stanford Synchrotron Radiation Proj, 73-78; prof assoc, Univ Paris, 75-76. *Mem:* Brit Inst Physics & Phys Soc; Am Phys Soc. *Res:* Cooperative phenomena in condensed matter physics; biophysics; x-ray spectroscopy. *Mailing Add:* Dept Appl Physics Stanford Univ Stanford CA 94305

DONIGER, JAY, b Brooklyn, NY, Mar 22, 44; m 67; c 2. MOLECULAR BIOLOGY. *Educ:* Brooklyn Col, BS, 65; Purdue Univ, PhD(biol), 72. *Prof Exp:* Res assoc biochem, Brandeis Univ, 72-75; asst biologist, Brookhaven Nat Lab, 75-77; EXPERT SCIENTIST, NAT CANCER INST, 77- *Res:* DNA repair mechanisms in Mammalian cells. *Mailing Add:* Bldg 37 Rm 2A19 Nat Cancer Inst 9000 Rockville Pike Bethesda MD 20205

DONIKIAN, MARC ROUPEN, b Harar, Ethiopia, July 2, 14; US citizen; m 39; c 2. PHARMACEUTICAL CHEMISTRY, CLINICAL PATHOLOGY. *Educ:* Am Univ, Beirut, PhG, 37, PhC, 38, cert pub anal, 43, MD, 52. *Prof Exp:* Instr pharmaceut chem, Sch Pharm, Am Univ, Beirut, 38-43, instr chem & asst prof bot, Sch Arts & Sci, 42-43; owner & dir, Clin Lab & Mfg Pharm, 44-59; res biologist, 59-68, sr res biologist & dir, Clin Path Labs, 68-79, SECT HEAD CLIN CHEM & HEMATOL, DEPT TOXICOL, STERLING-WINTHROP RES INST, RENSSELAER, 79- *Concurrent Pos:* Consult forensic med, Lebanese Govt, 56-57. *Mem:* AAAS; NY Acad Sci; assoc mem Am Soc Clin Path. *Res:* Clinical pathological study of new drugs. *Mailing Add:* A 023388 Sterling-Winthrop Res Inst Rensselaer NY 12144

DONINGER, JOSEPH EUGENE, b Chicago, Ill, Aut 18, 39; m 61; c 3. CHEMICAL ENGINEERING, INORGANIC CHEMISTRY. *Educ:* Univ Ill, BS, 61; Northwestern Univ, MS, 62, PhD, 65. *Prof Exp:* Res engr, 64-69, chem eng specialist, 69-72, tech mgr, 72-74, dir develop, 74-76, gen mgr resins, 76-78, gen mgr, Olivine, 78-80, GEN MGR MINERALS, INT MINERALS & CHEM CORP, 80- *Mem:* Am Inst Chem Engrs; Nat Paint & Coatings Soc; Am Foundry Soc. *Res:* Process control and optimization; cryogenics; pollution control; refractories; carbon products; ferroalloys and metals; foundry resins and mineral binders; paint and coatings resins; olivine sand and fluxes; oil well drilling minerals. *Mailing Add:* IMC Indust Group 666 Garland Pl Des Plaines IL 60016

DONISCH, VALENTINE, b Novocherkassk, Russia, Nov 29, 19; Can citizen; m 45. BIOCHEMISTRY. *Educ:* Univ Bonn, MD, 47; Univ Western Ont, PhD(biochem), 65; FRCP(C), 77. *Prof Exp:* Physician, Extrapulmonal Tuberc Sanitorium, 47-52; physician, Lutheran Mission Hosp, Eket, Nigeria, 52-54; physician govt hosps, Accra & Kumasi, Ghana, 55-59; physician, Victoria Hosp, London, Ont, 59-61; from instr to asst prof, 66-73, ASSOC PROF BIOCHEM, MED SCH, UNIV WESTERN ONT, 73- *Concurrent Pos:* Fel, Victoria Hosp, London, Ont, 65-66. *Res:* Extrapulmonal tuberculosis; phospholipids and cancer. *Mailing Add:* Dept of Biochem Univ of Western Ont Med Sch London ON N6A 5B8 Can

DONIVAN, FRANK FORBES, JR, b Inglewood, Calif, Oct 19, 43; m 66; c 2. RADIO ASTRONOMY, SPACECRAFT NAVIGATION. *Educ:* Univ Calif, Los Angeles, BA, 66; Univ Fla, PhD(astron), 70. *Prof Exp:* Asst dean, Grad Sch, Univ Fla, 71-73, asst prof, 70-76, assoc prof phys sci & astron, 77-79; MEM TECH STAFF, JET PROPULSION LAB, CALIF INST TECHNOL, PASADENA, 79- *Mem:* Am Astron Soc; Sigma Xi. *Res:* Radio investigation of clusters of galaxies; quasars and solar energy; developing technique for using very long baseline interferometry; navigation of interplanetary (deep space) probes. *Mailing Add:* Jet Propulsion Lab 4800 Oak Grove Dr Pasadena CA 91103

DONKER, JOHN D, b New Brunswick, NJ, Mar 2, 20; m 48; c 1. ANIMAL SCIENCE. *Educ:* Univ Calif, BS, 48; Univ Minn, PhD(reproductive physiol), 52. *Prof Exp:* Dir dairy cattle nutrit lab, Univ Ga, 54-56; assoc prof dairy husb, 56-65, PROF DAIRY HUSB, UNIV MINN, MINNEAPOLIS, 65- *Concurrent Pos:* Fel, Am Inst Indian Studies, 64. *Mem:* Am Dairy Sci Asn; Am Soc Animal Sci. *Res:* Nutrition of dairy cows; evaluation of energy contents of forages and/or rations; lactational physiology. *Mailing Add:* Col Agr Univ Minn Minneapolis MN 55455

DONLEY, DAVID EDWARD, b Morgantown, WVa, Nov 7, 28; m 52; c 3. ENTOMOLOGY, ZOOLOGY. *Educ:* Waynesburg Col, BS, 50; WVa Univ, MS, 51; Ohio State Univ, PhD(entom), 59. *Prof Exp:* Prev med specialist, US Air Force, 52-55; RES ENTOMOLOGIST, US FOREST SERV, 56-, RES PROJ LEADER FOREST INSECT ECOL, 62- *Mem:* Entom Soc Am; Ecol Soc Am. *Res:* Ecology of forest and forest plantation insects. *Mailing Add:* 287 W Heffner St Delaware OH 43015

DONN, BERTRAM (DAVID), b Brooklyn, NY, May 25, 19. ASTRONOMY. *Educ:* Brooklyn Col, AB, 40; Harvard Univ, PhD(astron), 53. *Prof Exp:* Physicist, Elec Testing Labs, 40-41; asst physicist, Signal Corps Labs, 41-43; res assoc radiation lab, Columbia Univ, 43-46; from instr to assoc prof physics & astron, Wayne State Univ, 50-59; head, Astrochem Br, 59-75, SR SCIENTIST, GODDARD SPACE FLIGHT CTR, NASA, 75- *Concurrent Pos:* Res assoc, Inst Nuclear Studies, Chicago, 54-56; vis prof astron, Cornell Univ, 74-75. *Mem:* AAAS; Am Phys Soc; Am Astron Soc; Am Geophys Union; Int Astron Union. *Res:* Interstellar matter; comets; cosmic chemistry. *Mailing Add:* NASA Goddard Space Ctr Code 691 Greenbelt MD 20771

DONN, CHENG, b Chungking, China, Nov 24, 38; US citizen; m 64; c 1. ELECTRICAL ENGINEERING, ELECTROMAGNETISM. *Educ:* Chengkung Univ, BS, 60; Wichita State Univ, MS, 68; Univ Kans, PhD(elec eng), 73. *Prof Exp:* Res assoc antennas, Electrosci Lab, Ohio State Univ, 69-73; electromagnetic pulse analyst, Intelcom Rad Tech, 73-74; mem tech staff, TRW Defense & Space Systs Group, 74-77; sr staff engr antennas, Martin Marietta Aerospace, Denver Div, 77-80; ADV SYSTS PROG ENGR, GEN DYNAMICS, 80- *Mem:* Inst Elec & Electronics Engrs; Sigma Xi. *Res:* Electromagnetic theory and antenna systems. *Mailing Add:* Gen Dynamics PO Box 80847 San Diego CA 92138

DONN, WILLIAM L, b Brooklyn, NY, Mar 2, 18; m 60; c 2. CLIMATOLOGY, AERONOMY. *Educ:* Brooklyn Col, BA, 39; Columbia Univ, MA, 46, PhD(geol, geophys), 51. *Prof Exp:* Geologist, Del Aqueduct Proj, 41 & US Engrs, 42; from instr to prof geol, Brooklyn Col, 46-63; prof geol, City Col New York, 63-77; SR RES SCIENTIST, LAMONT-DOHERTY GEOL OBSERV, COLUMBIA UNIV, 51- *Concurrent Pos:* Res consult, Oceanog Inst, Woods Hole, 46-47; chief scientist, Microseismol Eval Study, Off Naval Res, 49-52; dir tornado warning proj, Res Corp, 55-56; dir storm surge proj, Eng Found, 55-57; dir & chief scientist, US Atlantic Island Observs Prog, Int Geophys Year, 58-59 & Int Geophys Coop, 59-60; NSF sr fel, 59-60; dir atmospheric acoustic & gravity wave proj, NSF, 59-79; dir climate change proj, US Steel Found, 59-79; distinguished nat lectr, Am Asn Petrol Geologists & Soc Explor Geophysicists, 60; prin investr, Atmospheric Infra-sound proj, Army Res Off, 68-79; prin investr, Arctic Climate Change Proj, NSF, 69; prin investr wave propagation neutral atmosphere & ionosphere, US Army Electronics Command, 69-76; prin investr, Sonic Boom Proj, Fed Aviation Admin, 77-79; prin investr, Thermodyn Climate

Forecasting Proj, Nat Oceanic & Atmospheric Admin, 79-; mem, White House Panel, Evaluation of Possible Nuclear Test in Southern Hemisphere, 79. *Mem:* Fel AAAS; Am Meteorol Soc; fel Geol Soc Am; Seismol Soc Am; Am Geophys Union. *Res:* Geological and geophysical education; physical oceanography; microseisms; ocean waves and wave forecasting; sea level change; climate change and Ice ages; gravity and acoustic wave propagation in the atmosphere; pregeologic earth history; infrasound used to probe the atmosphere; climate forecasting. *Mailing Add:* Lamont-Doherty Geol Observ Palisades NY 10964

DONNALLEY, JAMES R, JR, b Camden, NJ, June 6, 18; m 46; c 3. CHEMICAL ENGINEERING. *Educ:* Pa State Univ, BS, 39; Cornell Univ, PhD(chem eng), 44. *Prof Exp:* Res assoc silicones, Res Lab, 43-46, group leader silicone process develop, Chem Div, 46-48, mgr, Waterford Plant, 48-52 & Mfg Silicone Prod Dept, 52-60, gen mgr, Insulating Mat Dept, 60-66 & Semiconductor Prod Dept, 66-74, mgr lighting res & tech serv oper, Lamp Bus Div, 74-80, VPRES ENVIRON ISSUES, GEN ELEC CO, FAIRFIELD, 80- *Mem:* Am Chem Soc; Am Inst Chem Engrs. *Res:* Silicates for adsorption and catalyses; process research on freeze-preservation of food; chemical process research on chlorosilanes and silicones; chemical research high temperature polymers. *Mailing Add:* 2730 Burr St Fairfield CT 06431

DONNALLY, BAILEY LEWIS, b Deatsville, Ala, June 22, 30; m 55; c 3. ATOMIC PHYSICS. *Educ:* Auburn Univ, BS, 51, MS, 52; Univ Minn, PhD(physics), 61. *Prof Exp:* Instr physics, Col St Thomas, 56-61; from asst prof to assoc prof, 61-66, chmn dept, 71-80, PROF PHYSICS, LAKE FOREST COL, 66- *Concurrent Pos:* Vis fel, Yale Univ, 66-67. *Mem:* AAAS; fel Am Phys Soc; Am Asn Physics Teachers (pres). *Res:* Mass spectrometry; polarized proton sources; nuclear scattering with polarized protons; atomic collision processes; development of experiments for advanced undergraduate laboratories. *Mailing Add:* Dept of Physics Lake Forest Col Lake Forest IL 60045

DONNAN, WILLIAM W, b Keystone, Iowa, June 15, 11; m 35; c 3. ENGINEERING, AGRICULTURE. *Educ:* Iowa State Univ, BS, 34, CE, 46. *Prof Exp:* Jr engr soil conserv serv, USDA, 34-39, assoc engr, Calif, 39-41, res engr, 41-53, sr res engr agr res serv, 53-57, res invest leader, 57-61, br chief SW br soil & water conserv res, 61-71; CONSULT ENGR, 71- *Concurrent Pos:* Grant, Western Europe, 58; mem, Soil & Water Conserv Cultural Exchange Group, USSR, 58 & Tech Activ Comt, Int Comn Irrig & Drainage, 60-65; consult, Indus Basin, WPakistan, 60, Khusistan Basin, Iran, 66, Upper Ferat Basin, Turkey, 69 & Tisza River Basin, Hungary, 71; team leader consult group, FAD Tech Assistance to Egypt on Nile Delta Drainage Probs, 75-76. *Honors & Awards:* Hancock Drainage Eng Award, Am Soc Agr Engrs, 66; R J Tipton Medal, Am Soc Civil Engrs, 71. *Mem:* Fel Am Soc Civil Engrs; Am Soc Agr Engrs. *Res:* Drainage of irrigated land including the spacing and depth of drains and criteria for the design of drainage systems. *Mailing Add:* 3521 Yorkshire Rd Pasadena CA 91107

DONNAY, GABRIELLE (HAMBURGER), b Landeshut, Ger, Mar 21, 20; nat US; m 49; c 2. CRYSTALLOGRAPHY. *Educ:* Univ Calif, Los Angeles, BA, 41; Mass Inst Technol, PhD(crystallog), 48. *Prof Exp:* Res chemist, Mass Gen Hosp, 44-45; div indust coop staff mem, Mass Inst Technol, 45-46, Arthur D Little fel, 48-49; fel, Johns Hopkins Univ, 49-50; fel, Geophys Lab, Carnegie Inst, 50-52; physicist, US Geol Surv, 52-54; crystallogr, Geophys Lab, Carnegie Inst, 55-70; PROF CRYSTALLOG, MCGILL UNIV, 70-, ASSOC CHEMIST, 72- *Concurrent Pos:* Guest scientist, Sorbonne, 58-59; scholar, Johns Hopkins Univ, 70; assoc ed, Can Mineralogist, 76-79. *Mem:* Am Crystallog Asn; Mineral Soc Am; Fr Soc Mineral & Crystallog; Mineral Asn Can; Brit Mineral Soc. *Res:* Structural interpretation of solid solutions; crystal structure and chemistry. *Mailing Add:* Dept of Geol Sci McGill Univ Montreal PQ H3A 2A7 Can

DONNAY, JOSEPH DESIRE HUBERT, b Grandville, Belg, June 6, 02; nat 39; m 31, 49; c 4. CRYSTALLOGRAPHY, MINERALOGY. *Educ:* Univ Liege, EM, 25; Stanford Univ, PhD(geol), 29. *Prof Exp:* Engr & geologist, Syndicat des Petroles au Maroc, French Morocco, 29-30; teaching fel mineral & res assoc geol, Stanford Univ, 30-31; assoc mineral, Johns Hopkins Univ, 31-39; prof crystallog & mineral, Laval Univ, 39-45; prof crystallog & mineral, 45-71, EMER PROF CRYSTALLOG & MINERAL, JOHNS HOPKINS UNIV, 71- *Concurrent Pos:* Res chemist, Hercules Powder Co, 42-45; prof, Univ Liege, 46-47; Fulbright lectr, Sorbonne, Paris, 58-59; guest prof, Univ Marburg, 66; lectr, Univ Montreal, 70-72, guest prof, 72-76; US deleg, Int Union Crystallog Cong, USA, 48, Sweden, 51, France, 54, Can, 57 & USSR, 66; res assoc, McGill Univ, 75- *Honors & Awards:* Roebling Medal, Mineral Soc Am, 71; Trasenster Medal, Asn Ing Univ Liege, 77; Can Silver Jubilee Medal, 77. *Mem:* Fel Geol Soc Am (vpres, 54); fel Mineral Soc Am (vpres, 49, 52, pres, 53); Am Crystallog Asn (secy-treas, Crystallog Soc Am, 44, secy, 45-46, vpres, 46, 48, 55, pres, 49, 56); fel Mineral Soc Gt Brit & Ireland; hon mem Soc Fr Mineral (vpres, 49). *Res:* Crystallography, especially crystal optics and relationships between crystal morphology and structure. *Mailing Add:* 320 Cote Saint-Antoine Montreal PQ H3Y 2J4 Can

DONNELL, GEORGE NINO, b Shanghai, China, Feb 21, 19; US citizen; m 42; c 3. PEDIATRICS. *Educ:* Pomona Col, BA, 40; Wash Univ, MD, 44; Am Bd Pediat, dipl, 50. *Prof Exp:* Asst pediat, Sch Med, Wash Univ, 45-46; from instr to assoc prof, 45-61, PROF PEDIAT, UNIV SOUTHERN CALIF, 61-, CO-CHMN, DEPT PEDIAT, 80- *Concurrent Pos:* Mem & consult, Nat Kidney Dis Found, chmn sci adv coun, Southern Calif Chap, 58-59. *Mem:* AAAS; Am Acad Pediat; Soc Pediat Res; Am Pediat Soc; fel Royal Soc Med. *Res:* Biochemical genetics; galactose metabolism; disorders of organic acid metabolism; disorders of amino acid metabolism. *Mailing Add:* Children's Hosp of Los Angeles 4650 Sunset Blvd Los Angeles CA 90054

DONNELL, HENRY DENNY, JR, b Vandalia, Ill, June 21, 35; m 58; c 3. EPIDEMIOLOGY. *Educ:* Greenville Col, AB, 57; Wash Univ, MD, 60; Univ Calif, Berkeley, MPH, 65; Am Bd Prev Med, dipl, 70. *Prof Exp:* Intern, Butterworth Hosp, Grand Rapids, Mich, 60-61, asst resident surg, 61-62; asst chief prev med, Ft Leonard Wood, Mo, 62-63, chief, 63-64; resident epidemiol, Calif State Dept Health, Berkeley, 65-66; asst prof, Sch Med, Univ Mo-Columbia, 66-71, clin asst prof, Dept Commun Health & Med Pract, 66-71; dir, Bur Commun Dis Control, 71-73, DIR SECT EPIDEMIOL & DIS SURVEILLANCE, DIV OF HEALTH OF MO, 73- *Concurrent Pos:* Chief prog methodology unit, Mo Regional Med Prog, 69-71, consult, 71-; dir grad study community health, Univ MoColumbia. 69-70. *Mem:* AAAS; Am Pub Health Asn; Asn Teachers Prev Med; Royal Soc Health. *Res:* Studies of distribution of disease, especially heart, cancer, stroke and infectious diseases; distribution of health manpower in relationship to distribution of population and various influencing variables. *Mailing Add:* Div of Health of Mo PO Box 570 Jefferson City MO 65101

DONNELLAN, J(AMES) EDWARD, JR, molecular biophysics, see previous edition

DONNELLY, A(ARON) V(AN), b Bonaparte, Iowa, June 2, 16. ELECTRICAL ENGINEERING. *Educ:* Univ Iowa, BS, 39, MS, 40, PhD(elec eng), 47; Columbia Univ, MA, 41. *Prof Exp:* Asst, Univ Iowa, 39-40; inspection engr, Day & Zimmermann, 41-42; instr eng sci & mgt war training, Univ Iowa, 42-43, instr elec eng, 43-44; res engr, Stromberg-Carlson Co, NY, 44-45 & Collins Radio Co, Iowa, 45-47; asst prof elec eng, Univ Iowa, 47-55; tech consult, Pac Missile Range, 55-62; assoc prof elec eng, 62-67, prof eng, 67-79, EMER PROF ENG, ARIZ STATE UNIV, 79- *Mem:* Inst Elec & Electronics Engrs; Sigma Xi. *Res:* Microwave and electronic systems; electrical networks. *Mailing Add:* Col of Eng Sci Ariz State Univ Tempe AZ 85281

DONNELLY, BRENDAN JAMES, b Dublin, Ireland, July 6, 37; US citizen; m 66. FOOD CHEMISTRY. *Educ:* Nat Univ Ireland, BSc, 60, PhD(chem), 65; Trinity Col, Dublin, MSc, 62; St Louis Univ, MBA, 75. *Prof Exp:* USDA fel chem, Exp Sta, Colo State Univ, 65-68; sr res chemist, Corn Prod Div, Anheuser-Busch Inc, 68-75; assoc prof cereal chem, Cereal Chem & Tech Dept, NDak State Univ, 75-79; Cereal Qual Lab mgr, North Am Plant Breeders, Colo, 79-82; DIR, NORTHERN CROPS INST, NORTH DAK STATE UNIV, 82- *Concurrent Pos:* Consult, US Wheat Assocs, Washington, DC, 77-; mem, Nat Wheat Improv Comt, 80-; assoc ed, Cereal Chem, Am Asn Cereal Chemists, 80-; affil prof, Dept Food Sci & Nutrit, Colo State Univ, 81- *Mem:* Inst Food Technologists; Am Asn Cereal Chemists; Am Chem Soc; Phytochem Soc NAm; AAAS. *Res:* Isolation and identification of naturally occurring polyphenols (flavonoid family); precursors of haze and sediment formation in fruit juice; chemical components of cereal grain (wheat and barley) quality; high fructose syrup prroduction from corn starch. *Mailing Add:* Northern Crops Inst North Dak State Univ Fargo ND 58105

DONNELLY, EDWARD DANIEL, b Birmingham, Ala, Dec 5, 19; m 47; c 3. PLANT BREEDING. *Educ:* Auburn Univ, BS, 46, MS, 48; Cornell Univ, PhD(plant breeding), 51. *Prof Exp:* Res asst & instr forage crops, 47-48, assoc plant breeder, 51-58, PROF AGRON & SOILS, AUBURN UNIV, 58- *Concurrent Pos:* Res asst, Cornell Univ, 48-51. *Mem:* Fel Am Soc Agron. *Res:* Forage crops breeding; improving for disease and root-knot nematode; increased palatability and nutritive value; earlier development and larger seeded; reseeding winter annual legumes. *Mailing Add:* Dept of Agron & Soils Auburn Univ Auburn AL 36849

DONNELLY, GRACE MARIE, b Providence, RI, Apr 5, 29. CELL BIOLOGY. *Educ:* Univ RI, BS, 52; Brown Univ, MS, 56; Univ Conn, PhD(cytol), 62. *Prof Exp:* Res librarian, Citrus Exp Sta, Univ Fla, 52-54; biol fel, Brookhaven Nat Lab, 62-64; res assoc biol, City of Hope Med Ctr, 64-67; from instr to asst prof cell biol, Univ Ky, 67-72, bioassay proj leader, 72-75, SR RES BIOLOGIST, TOBACCO & HEALTH RES INST, UNIV KY, 75- *Mem:* AAAS; Genetics Soc Am; Am Soc Cell Biol; Am Genetic Asn; Radiation Res Soc. *Res:* Cytology of the domestic fowl; radiosensitivity of amphibians; chromosome cytology; cellular requirements for ribonucleic acid synthesis; effect of environmental agents on cells. *Mailing Add:* Tobacco & Health Res Inst Univ of Ky Lexington KY 40506

DONNELLY, JOHN, b Liverpool, Eng, June 9, 14; nat US; m 49; c 2. PSYCHIATRY. *Educ:* Univ Liverpool, MB, ChB, 38; Royal Col Physicians & Surgeons, DPM, 48; Am Bd Psychiat & Neurol, dipl, 52. *Hon Degrees:* ScD, Trinity Col, Conn, 79. *Prof Exp:* Sr registr, Cane Hill Hosp, Eng, 48-49; chief serv psychiat, 49-52, clin dir, 52-56, med dir, 56-65, psychiatrist-in-chief, 65-79, SR CONSULT, INST LIVING, 79- *Concurrent Pos:* Asst clin prof psychiat, Med Sch, Yale Univ, 52-64, assoc clin prof, 64-68, lectr, 58-80; ed, Digest of Neurol & Psychiat, Inst Living, 63-79; prof psychiat, Sch Med, Univ Conn, 77- *Mem:* Life Fel Am Psychiat Asn; fel Am Col Physicians; fel Royal Soc Med; fel Royal Col Psychiat. *Res:* Psychodynamic and biophysical correlates; forensic aspects of psychiatry. *Mailing Add:* Inst of Living 200 Retreat Ave Hartford CT 06106

DONNELLY, JOHN KINDELAN, b Terre Haute, Ind, July 16, 43; m 65. CHEMICAL ENGINEERING. *Educ:* Univ Alta, BSc, 65, PhD(chem eng), 68. *Prof Exp:* Asst prof, 68-70, ASSOC PROF CHEM ENG, UNIV CALGARY, 70- *Mem:* Am Inst Chem Engrs; Can Soc Chem Engrs. *Res:* Applied mathematics; chemical reactor engineering; oil sands technology; in situ combustion. *Mailing Add:* Dept of Chem Eng Univ of Calgary Calgary AB T2N 1N4 Can

DONNELLY, JOSEPH P(ETER), b Brooklyn, NY, May 10, 39; m 68; c 5. ELECTRICAL ENGINEERING, SEMICONDUCTOR PHYSICS. *Educ:* Manhattan Col, BEE, 61; Carnegie Inst Tech, MS, 62, PhD(elec eng), 66. *Prof Exp:* NATO fel, Imp Col, London, 65-66; STAFF MEM APPL PHYSICS, LINCOLN LAB, MASS INST TECHNOL, 67- *Concurrent Pos:* Nat lectr, Inst Elec & Electronics Engrs, Electron Device Soc, 79. *Mem:* Inst Elec & Electronics Engrs; Bohmische Physical Soc. *Res:* Ion implantation in compound semiconductors; photodiodes; lasers and LED's; integrated optics; infrared detectors; microwave devices; semiconductor heterojunctions. *Mailing Add:* Lincoln Lab Mass Inst of Technol PO Box 73 Lexington MA 02173

DONNELLY, KENNETH GERALD, b Brooklyn, NY, Jan 17, 37; m 62; c 4. AUDIOLOGY, SPEECH PATHOLOGY. *Educ:* Cath Univ Am, BA, 60, MA, 61; Univ Pittsburgh, PhD(audiol), 64. *Prof Exp:* Instr speech path, Gallaudet Col, 61-62, from asst prof to assoc prof audiol, 64-66; dir speech & hearing clin, St Charles Hosp, Port Jefferson, NY, 66-67; assoc prof audiol & speech path, 67-69, prof, 69-70, HEAD DEPT SPEECH, UNIV CINCINNATI, 70- *Concurrent Pos:* Study, Off Voc Rehab, 68-69; proj dir, US Off Educ, HEW, 68-72; training grant, Vet Admin, 69-73; develop grant, Merrill Trust Fund, 69-70; fel, Am Speech & Hearing Asn, 69. *Mem:* Acad Rehab Audiol; Am Speech & Hearing Asn; Soc Int D'Audiologie. *Res:* Hearing disorders in children; methods of determining best fit for hearing aids; academic placement techniques for deaf children. *Mailing Add:* Dept of Commun Speech & Theatre Mail Location 379 Cincinnati OH 45221

DONNELLY, PATRICIA VRYLING, b Memphis, Tenn, July 23, 33. MICROBIOLOGY. *Educ:* Tex Woman's Univ, BA, 55; Univ Mo, MS, 63. *Prof Exp:* Bacteriologist, Dallas Pub Health Lab, 55-57; lab dir, La Rabida Hosp, 57-58; microbiologist, Water Reed Army Hosp, 58-59 & US Air Force Aerospace Med Ctr, 59-62; biologist, Marine Lab, Fla Bd Conserv, 63-67; SR RES ASST DEPT BIOCHEM, BAYLOR COL MED, 67- *Mem:* Am Soc Microbiol; AAAS. *Res:* Biochemical genetics; tissue culture. *Mailing Add:* Dept of Biochem Baylor Col of Med Houston TX 77030

DONNELLY, RUSSELL JAMES, b Hamilton, Ont, Apr 16, 30; m 56; c 1. PHYSICS. *Educ:* McMaster Univ, BSc, 51, MSc, 52; Yale Univ, MS, 53, PhD(physics), 56. *Prof Exp:* Instr, dept physics & James Franck Inst, Univ Chicago, 56-57, from asst prof to prof, 57-66; chmn dept, 66-72, PROF PHYSICS, UNIV ORE, 66- *Concurrent Pos:* Alfred P Sloan res fel, 59-63; consult, Gen Motors Res Labs, 58-68 & NSF, 68-73; mem adv panel physics, NSF, 70-73 & 79-, chmn, 71-72; vis prof, Niels Bohr Inst, Copenhagen, Denmark, 72, Univ Birmingham, Eng, 80 & Univ Calif, Santa Barbara, 81; sr vis fel, Sci Res Coun, Eng, 78. *Honors & Awards:* Gov Northwest Sci Award, Ore Mus Sci & Indust; Otto LaPorte Mem Lectr, Am Phys Soc, 74. *Mem:* AAAS; fel Am Phys Soc; Am Asn Physics Teachers. *Res:* Experimental and theoretical low temperature physics, especially superfluidity; fluid dynamics; hydrodynamic stability; turbulence. *Mailing Add:* Dept of Physics Univ of Ore Eugene OR 97403

DONNELLY, THOMAS EDWARD, JR, b Chelsea, Mass, Sept 16, 43; m 75; c 2. PHARMACOLOGY, BIOCHEMISTRY. *Educ:* Mass Col Pharm, BS, 66; Harvard Univ, MA, 68; Yale Univ, PhD(pharmacol), 72. *Prof Exp:* Pharmacologist, Leo Pharmaceut Prod, 73-74; ASSOC PROF PHARMACOL, UNIV NEBR MED CTR, 74- *Mem:* Am Soc Pharmacol & Exp Therapeut. *Res:* Regulation of cyclic nucleotide metabolism; regulation of nuclear function; drug-induced cardiac supersensitivity. *Mailing Add:* Dept Pharmacol Univ Nebr Med Ctr Omaha NE 68105

DONNELLY, THOMAS HENRY, b Endicott, NY, Apr 20, 28; m 55; c 4. BIOPHYSICAL CHEMISTRY. *Educ:* Rensselaer Polytech Inst, BS, 50; Cornell Univ, PhD, 55. *Prof Exp:* Phys chemist, Swift & Co, Oak Brook, 55-67, mgr gelatin & stabilizers res, 67-71, gen mgr sci & serv, 72-77, res mgr appl chem, res & develop ctr, 77-79; vis prof chem, 79-81, ASST CHMN, DEPT CHEM, UNIV CHICAGO, LOYOLA, 81- *Concurrent Pos:* Fac fel, Ill Benedictine Col, 70-; mem educ comt, Nat Confectioners Asn, 73-75; instr, Mundelein Col, 79- *Mem:* AAAS; Am Chem Soc; Inst Food Technologists. *Res:* Physical chemistry of proteins and polymers; ultracentrifugation, gelatin; food chemistry. *Mailing Add:* 4633 Grand Ave Western Springs IL 60558

DONNELLY, THOMAS WALLACE, b Detroit, Mich, Dec 23, 32; m 56; c 3. GEOLOGY. *Educ:* Cornell Univ, BA, 54; Calif Inst Technol, MS, 56; Princeton Univ, PhD(geol), 59. *Prof Exp:* From asst prof geol to assoc prof, Rice Univ, 59-66; assoc prof, 66-69, PROF GEOL, STATE UNIV NY BINGHAMTON, 69- *Concurrent Pos:* Res assoc, Fla State Collection Arthropods, 66- *Mem:* Geol Soc Am. *Res:* Geology of island arcs; geochemistry of volcanic rocks; geology of Caribbean area and Guatemala; deep-sea sediment chemistry; aquatic entomology. *Mailing Add:* Dept of Geol State Univ of NY Binghamton NY 13901

DONNELLY, THOMAS WILLIAM, theoretical nuclear physics, see previous edition

DONNER, DAVID BRUCE, b New York, NY, Oct 17, 45. ENDOCRINOLOGY. *Educ:* Queens Col, BA, 66; Rensselaer Polytech Inst, PhD(chem), 72. *Prof Exp:* Fel biochem, Cornell Univ, 72-73; res assoc, Sloan-Kettering Inst, 73-78; instr, 73-78, ASST PROF BIOCHEM, GRAD SCH MED SCI, CORNELL UNIV, 78- *Concurrent Pos:* Assoc biochem, Sloan-Kettering Inst, 78- *Mem:* Am Chem Soc. *Res:* Peptide hormone regulation of cell growth and differentiation; signal transmission in biological membranes; insulin and growth, hormone action in cells; peptide hormone-receptor binding. *Mailing Add:* Sloan-Kettering Inst 1275 York Ave New York NY 10021

DONNER, MARTIN W, b Leipzig, Ger, Sept 5, 20; US citizen; m 51; c 3. MEDICINE, RADIOLOGY. *Educ:* Univ Leipzig, MD, 45. *Prof Exp:* Intern, Leipzig Hosp, 45-46, resident med, 46-50; resident radiol, Radiol Ctr, Cologne, Ger, 50-54; resident, Mt Park Hosp, St Petersburg, Fla, 54-57; fel, Johns Hopkins Univ Hosp, 57-58, from instr to assoc prof, 58-66, prof radiol & radiologic sci & chief, Div Diag Roentgenol, 66-72, CHMN DEPT RADIOL & RADIOL SCI & RADIOLOGIST-IN-CHIEF, SCH MED & HOSP, JOHNS HOPKINS UNIV, 72-, DIR, JOHNS HOPKINS SWALLOWING CTR, 81- *Concurrent Pos:* Vis investr, Carnegie Inst, 62-72; consult, Good Samaritan Hosp, Rosewood State Hosp, Baltimore City Hosps & Vet Admin Hosp, Baltimore. *Mem:* AAAS; AMA; fel Am Col Radiol; Asn Univ Radiol; corresp mem Ger Radiol Soc. *Res:* Hematology; metabolitic joint diseases; radiotherapy and blood coagulation; cineradiography of intestinal motility; roentgen diagnosis of gastrointestinal diseases and abdominal calcifications; radioangiography of placental circulation; radiography of diabetic complications and diseases involving the hands; Roentgen tomography. *Mailing Add:* Dept of Radiol Johns Hopkins Univ Sch Med Baltimore MD 21205

DONNER, W(ALTER), b Pasadena, Calif, May 10, 25; m 43; c 2. PHYSICS, ELECTRONICS. *Educ:* Pasadena City Col; Univ Calif, Los Angeles. *Prof Exp:* Res technician, electronic engr & proj engr, 46-53, chief engr mass spectrom res, 53-59, proj mgr, 59-62, mgr space eng dept, 62-65, tech mgr, 65-71, opers mgr advan technol opers, 71-80, mgr electrochem, 80-81, MGR, MICROCIRCUIT PROD, BECKMAN INSTRUMENTS, INC, 81- *Mem:* Inst Elec & Electronics Engrs; Instrument Soc Am; Soc Appl Spectros; Am Inst Aeronaut & Astronaut. *Res:* Mass spectrometry; infrared spectrophotometry; electronic research. *Mailing Add:* Microcircuit Prod 2500 Harbor Blvd Fullerton CA 92634

DONOGHUE, JOHN FRANCIS, b Roslyn, NY, Nov 30, 50; m 73; c 1. PHYSICS. *Educ:* Univ Notre Dame, BS, 72; Univ Mass, Amherst, PhD(physics), 76. *Prof Exp:* Res assoc physics, Carnegie-Mellon Univ, 76-78; RES ASSOC PHYSICS, CTR THEORET PHYSICS, MASS INST TECHNOL, 78- *Mem:* Am Phys Soc. *Res:* Weak interactions, quarks. *Mailing Add:* Ctr for Theoret Physics Mass Inst of Technol Cambridge MA 02139

DONOGHUE, JOSEPH F, b Philadelphia, Pa, Mar 23, 47. SEDIMENTOLOGY. *Educ:* Princeton Univ, BSc, 69; Univ Southern Calif, PhD(geol), 81. *Prof Exp:* Oakley fel, Dept Geol Sci, Univ Southern Calif, 76-79; Smithsonian fel & res assoc, Nat Mus Natural Hist, Washington, DC, 79-80; GEOLOGIST, ADV COMT REACTOR SAFEGUARDS, WASHINGTON, DC, 81- *Concurrent Pos:* Collabr, Sedimentology Lab, Smithsonian Inst, Washington, DC, 81- *Mem:* Geol Soc Am; Soc Econ Paleontologists & Mineralogists; Am Geophys Union; Estuarine Res Soc; AAAS. *Res:* Sediment dynamics; sediment-water interactions; environmental geochemistry; radiosotopic tracers; estuarine and coastal marine geology; nuclear waste disposal. *Mailing Add:* EG-2 Nat Mus Natural Hist Smithsonian Inst Washington DC 20560

DONOGHUE, TIMOTHY R, b Milton, Mass, May 3, 36; m 64; c 2. NUCLEAR PHYSICS. *Educ:* Boston Col, BS, 57; Univ Notre Dame, PhD(physics), 63. *Prof Exp:* Instr physics, Univ Notre Dame, 62-63; fel, 63-64, from asst prof to assoc prof, 64-75, PROF PHYSICS, OHIO STATE UNIV, 75-, ASSOC DEAN RES, GRAD SCH, 79- *Concurrent Pos:* Vis staff scientist, Los Alamos Sci Labs, 71-74; mem, Ind Univ Cyclotron User's Comt, 79-81; mem int prog adv comt, 5th Int Symp in Polarization Phenomena, 79-80. *Honors & Awards:* Fritz Thyssen Stiftung, 81. *Mem:* Am Phys Soc; AAAS. *Res:* Investigation of fundamental symmetries in physics including time reversal invariance, parity non-conservation and search for neutral weak currents; nuclear astrophysics including nuclear aspects of solar neutrino problem; polarized beam investigations of nuclear reaction mechanisms and nuclear level structure. *Mailing Add:* Dept of Physics Ohio State Univ Columbus OH 43210

DONOGHUE, WILLIAM F, JR, b Rochester, NY, Sept 7, 21; m 74. MATHEMATICS. *Educ:* Univ Rochester, AB, 47, MSc, 48; Univ Wis, PhD(math), 51. *Prof Exp:* Assoc mathematician, appl physics lab, Johns Hopkins Univ, 51-52; from asst prof to assoc prof math, Univ Kans, 52-62; temp mem, Courant Inst Math Sci, NY Univ, 63-64; vis prof math, Mich State Univ, 64-66; PROF MATH, UNIV CALIF, IRVINE, 66- *Concurrent Pos:* Guggenheim fel, 58-59. *Res:* Linear topological spaces; Eigenvalue problems. *Mailing Add:* Dept of Math Univ of Calif Irvine CA 92717

DONOHO, ALVIN LEROY, b Humphreys, Mo, Nov 20, 36; m 64; c 3. BIOCHEMISTRY. *Educ:* Univ Mo, BS, 58, MS, 60, PhD(biochem), 65. *Prof Exp:* Res scientist, 64-80, RES ADV BIOCHEM, ELI LILLY & CO, 80- *Mem:* Am Chem Soc; AAAS. *Res:* Metabolism, degradation, and assay of drugs and agrichemicals. *Mailing Add:* 9281 Sacramento Dr Greenfield IN 46140

DONOHO, CLIVE WELLINGTON, JR, b Nashville, Tenn, Jan 16, 30; m 55; c 4. HORTICULTURE, PLANT PHYSIOLOGY. *Educ:* Univ Ky, BS, 52; NC State Univ, MS, 58; Mich State Univ, PhD(hort), 60. *Prof Exp:* From asst prof to prof res hort, Ohio Agr Res & Develop Ctr & Ohio State Univ, 60-67; prof hort sci & head dept, NC State Univ, 67-73; ASSOC DIR, OHIO RES & DEVELOP CTR, 73-, PROF HORT, OHIO STATE UNIV, 80- *Mem:* Fel Am Soc Hort Sci; Int Soc Hort Sci; Sigma Xi. *Res:* Fruit physiology; natural auxins; absorption, translocation and metabolism of synthetic growth regulators; influence of pesticide chemicals on fruit physiology; water relations in fruit crops. *Mailing Add:* Ohio Agr Res & Develop Ctr Wooster OH 44691

DONOHO, PAUL LEIGHTON, physics, see previous edition

DONOHOO, HORRIE VAN WALDO, b Tucumcari, NMex, June 7, 14; m 33; c 2. GEOPHYSICS. *Prof Exp:* Computer, Stanolind Oil & Gas Co, Okla, 39-40 & Phillips Petrol Co, 40-41; instr mech, Cornell Univ, 41-43; instr geophys, Colo Sch Mines, 46-47; asst prof, Univ Utah, 47-51; geophys engr, Columbia-Geneva Div, US Steel Corp, 53-57; mgr mining explor & chief geophysicist, Tex Gulf Sulfur Co, 57-66, gen mgr, Potash Div, Texasgulf Inc, 66, vpres, Agr Div, 67-73, exec vpres, 73-79; RETIRED. *Concurrent Pos:* Res engr, Columbia Univ, 47; consult, New Park Mining Co, Utah, 48. *Honors & Awards:* Distinguished Achievement Medal, Colo Sch Mines. *Mem:* Am Inst Mining, Metall & Petrol Engrs; Soc Explor Geophysicists; Am Soc Econ Geologists; Europ Asn Explor Geophysicists; Mining & Metall Soc Am. *Res:* Raw materials exploration, development and production management. *Mailing Add:* 22 Wardwell Dr New Canaan CT 06840

DONOHOO, JOHN T, b St Louis, Mo, Feb 26, 19. ZOOLOGY, CELL PHYSIOLOGY. *Educ:* Marquette Univ, MS, 52; Univ Notre Dame, PhD(biol), 56. *Prof Exp:* Instr chem, physics & aeronaut, Chaminade Col, Mo, 40-44; instr sci & athletic dir, Don Bosco High Sch, Wis, 44-50; instr chem, 50-52, chmn dept, 56-77, PROF BIOL, ST MARY'S UNIV, SAN ANTONIO, 56- *Mem:* AAAS; Nat Asn Biol Teachers; Am Soc Microbiol. *Res:* Radiation effects on bacterial viruses and inorganic chemical protectors. *Mailing Add:* Dept of Biol St Mary's Univ One Camino Santa Maria San Antonio TX 78284

DONOHUE, DAVID ARTHUR TIMOTHY, b Montreal, Que, Apr 11, 37; US citizen; m 61; c 1. PETROLEUM. *Educ:* Univ Okla, BS, 59; Pa State Univ, PhD(petrol eng), 63; Boston Col, JD, 71. *Prof Exp:* Prod engr, Imp Oil Ltd, Can, 58, res engr, 63-64; from asst prof to assoc prof petrol & natural gas eng, Pa State Univ, 64-69; PRES, INT HUMAN RESOURCES DEVELOP CORP, 69-; PRES, HONEOYE STORAGE CORP, 73- *Concurrent Pos:* Chmn, Pa-NY Chap, Petrol Inst, 67-68; partner, Donohue Anstem & Morrill, 76-; pres, Arlington Explor Co, 78- *Honors & Awards:* Cedric K Ferguson Medal, Soc Petrol Engrs, 68. *Mem:* Am Inst Mining, Metall & Petrol Engrs; Soc Petrol Engrs; Am Inst Chem Engrs; Am Soc Eng Educ; Am Asn Petrol Geologists. *Res:* Experimental and theoretical research dealing with developing new methods and improving old methods of producing crude oil from underground formations; analysis and development of underground gas storage reservoirs; training of international petroleum industry personnel; oil and gas exploration and development. *Mailing Add:* 17 Allen Rd Wellesley MA 02181

DONOHUE, JERRY, b Sheboygan, Wis, June 12, 20; m 45; c 2. CRYSTALLOGRAPHY. *Educ:* Dartmouth Col, AB, 41, MA, 43; Calif Inst Technol, PhD(chem), 47. *Prof Exp:* Instr chem, Dartmouth Col, 41-43, Nat Res Coun fel, 46-47, asst, 43-47, res fel, 47-52, Guggenheim fel, 52-53; from asst prof to prof chem, Univ Southern Calif, 53-66; PROF CHEM, UNIV PA, 66- *Concurrent Pos:* NSF fel, 59-60. *Mem:* Am Crystallog Asn. *Res:* X-ray crystal structures; structures of compounds of biological interest; hydrogen bonds; structures of the elements. *Mailing Add:* Dept of Chem Univ of Pa Philadelphia PA 19104

DONOHUE, JOHN J, b Totowa, NJ, Feb 17, 19; m 45; c 3. MARINE GEOLOGY, GEOENVIRONMENTAL SCIENCE. *Educ:* Univ Maine, BA, 44, MSc, 49; Rutgers Univ, PhD(geol sci), 51. *Prof Exp:* Field geologist, State Geol Surv Maine, 47-49; proj dir & consult, Off Naval Res, 51-54; sr res & explor geologist, Arabian Am Oil Co, 54-61; dir & consult, Geo-Tek Assocs, 61-64; prof phys sci, Bennett Col, NY, 64-77, chmn sci-math dept, 67-77, dir, Kettering Sci Ctr, 70-77; sr mgr environ assessments, Camp Dresser & McKee, Inc, Environ Engrs, Boston, 77-79; MINERAL RESOURCES CONSULT & PRES, GEO-TEK ASSOCS, LTD, 79- *Concurrent Pos:* Asst, Univ Maine, 48-49; sr res marine geologist, head sect & assoc prof, marine lab, Univ RI, 51-54; res consult, Davison Chem Div, W R Grace Co, 61-73 & Valumet Corp, 75-; sr staff consult, United Aircraft Res Labs, 67-71. *Mem:* Geol Soc Am; Am Asn Petrol Geol; Am Geophys Union. *Res:* Geoenvironmental research, geotechnical and ocean engineering; environmental systems and technology; mineralogy; mining and petroleum geology; strategic mineral resources exploration and evaluation. *Mailing Add:* 45 Locust St Danvers MA 01923

DONOHUE, JOYCE MORISSEY, b Holyoke, Mass, Jan 27, 40; m 73; c 4. BIOCHEMISTRY, NUTRITION. *Educ:* Framingham State Col, BSEd, 61; Univ Mass, MS, 64; Univ NH, PhD(biochem), 72. *Prof Exp:* Teacher chem & biol, W Springfield High Sch, 62-66; instr chem & nutrit, Framingham State Col, 66-68, assoc prof biochem, 71-73; ASSOC PROF & LECTR NUTRIT, FOOD SCI & CHEM, NORTHERN VA COMMUNITY COL, 74- *Concurrent Pos:* Hood fel, Univ Mass, 61-62; NSF fel, Yale Univ, 65-66; Nat Defense Educ Act fel, Univ NH, 68-71. *Mem:* AAAS. *Res:* Protein structure. *Mailing Add:* Northern Va Community Col 8333 Little River Turnpike Annandale VA 22003

DONOHUE, MARC DAVID, b Watertown, NY, Sept 10, 51; m 74. CHEMICAL ENGINEERING. *Educ:* Clarkson Col Technol, BS, 73; Univ Calif, Berkeley, PhD(chem eng), 77. *Prof Exp:* asst prof chem eng, Clarkson Col Technol, 77-79; ASST PROF CHEM ENG, JOHNS HOPKINS UNIV, 79- *Mem:* Am Inst Chem Engrs. *Res:* Thermodynamics and phase transitions. *Mailing Add:* Dept Chem Eng Johns Hopkins Univ Baltimore MD 21218

DONOHUE, PAUL CHRISTOPHER, b Brooklyn, NY, June 28, 38; m 66; c 2. SOLID STATE CHEMISTRY, INORGANIC CHEMISTRY. *Educ:* St John's Univ, NY, BS, 60; Univ Conn, MS, 63, PhD(inorg chem), 65. *Prof Exp:* RES CHEMIST, PHOTO PROD DEPT, E I DU PONT DE NEMOURS & CO, INC, 65- *Mem:* AAAS. *Res:* Synthesis of new solid state oxides sulfides and phosphides and structural studies by x-ray crystallography; synthesis and evaluation of heterogeneous catalysts; preparation and characterization of thick film materials for hybrid microcircuit electronics. *Mailing Add:* Photo Prod Dept E I du Pont de Nemours & Co Inc Wilmington DE 19898

DONOHUE, ROBERT J, b Chicago, Ill, Jan 31, 34; m 57; c 4. SPECTROSCOPY, PHYSICAL OPTICS. *Educ:* DePaul Univ, BS, 55, MS, 57. *Prof Exp:* Res asst physics, DePaul Univ, 54-56; res physicist, Gen Motors Res Labs, 56-61, sr res physicist, 61-74, MEM ENVIRON ACTIVITIES STAFF, AUTOMOTIVE SAFETY ENG, GEN MOTORS TECH CTR, 74- *Mem:* Optical Soc Am. *Res:* Plasma spectroscopy; nuclear physics; geometrical and physical optics; illumination and lighting systems. *Mailing Add:* Automotive Safety Eng Gen Motors Tech Ctr Warren MI 48090

DONOHUE, WILLIAM LESLIE, b Niagara Falls, Ont, Aug 8, 06; m 40; c 3. PATHOLOGY. *Educ:* Univ Toronto, BA, 29, MD, 32, MA, 36; FRCPSC, 62. *Prof Exp:* Intern, Hamilton Gen Hosp, Ont, 32-33; resident path, Hosp Sick Children, 33-34; mem staff, Nat Hosp Nerv Dis, London, Eng, 37-38; asst pathologist, 38-47; prof path, 65-77, EMER PROF PATH, UNIV TORONTO, 77-; CHIEF PATH, HOSP SICK CHILDREN, 47- *Concurrent Pos:* Fel path, Univ Toronto, 34-36 & Col Physicians & Surgeons, Columbia Univ, 36-37. *Mem:* Am Asn Path & Bact; Am Soc Pediat. *Res:* Pediatric pathology. *Mailing Add:* Dept of Path Univ of Toronto Toronto Can

DONOIAN, HAIG CADMUS, b Ramallah, Palestine, Apr 8, 30; US citizen; m 57; c 2. PHYSICAL CHEMISTRY, COLLOID CHEMISTRY. *Educ:* Lowell Technol Inst, BS, 52; Clark Univ, MA, 54, PhD(chem), 58. *Prof Exp:* Res chemist, Am Cyanamid Co, 57-63, Cabot Corp, Mass, 63-67 & Org Chem Div, Am Cyanamid Co, 67-72; SCIENTIST, XEROX CORP, 72- *Honors & Awards:* Roon Award, Fedn Socs Paint Technol, 67. *Mem:* Am Chem Soc. *Res:* Diffusion of substances in solution; colloidal chemistry and optical properties of carbon black. *Mailing Add:* 1195 Severn Rd Webster NY 14580

DONOVAN, ALLEN F(RANCIS), b Onondaga, NY, Apr 22, 14; m 40, 53; c 3. AERONAUTICAL ENGINEERING. *Educ:* Univ Mich, BSE & MS, 36. *Hon Degrees:* DEng, Univ Mich, 64. *Prof Exp:* Stress analyst, Curtiss Aeroplane & Motor Co, NY, 36-38; sr stress analyst, Glenn L Martin Co, Md, 38-39; asst chief struct, Stinson Aircraft Div, Aviation Mfg Corp, Mich, 39-40; chief struct, Nashville Div, Vultee Aircraft Corp, 40-41; asst chief exp design engr, Airplane Div, Curtiss Wright Corp, NY, 41-42, asst head struct dept, Res Lab, 42-44, head, 44-46; head aero mech dept, Cornell Aero Lab, Cornell Univ, 46-55; dir aero res & develop staff, Space Tech Labs, Inc, 55-58, vpres, 58-60; sr vpres tech, Aerospace Corp, 60-78; RETIRED. *Concurrent Pos:* Mem, US Air Force Sci Adv Bd, 48-57 & 59-68, chmn propulsion panel, 59-60 & 63-68; US deleg, Geneva Conf Suspension of Nuclear Test, consult, President's Sci Adv Comt, 59; & Sci & Technol Off, NSF, 73-76. 57-72. *Honors & Awards:* US Air Force Assoc Sci Award, 61, Medal for Exceptional Civilian Serv, 68. *Mem:* Nat Acad Eng; fel Am Inst Aeronaut & Astronaut. *Res:* Space and ballistic missile system design and development. *Mailing Add:* 4030 Aladdin Dr Huntington Beach CA 92649

DONOVAN, EDWARD FRANCIS, b Columbus, Ohio, Nov 20, 18; m 43; c 5. VETERINARY MEDICINE. *Educ:* Ohio State Univ, DVM, 49. *Prof Exp:* Pvt pract, Ohio, 49-52; assoc dir clin res, Am Cyanamid Co, 52-56; from asst prof to assoc prof vet med, 56-62, PROF VET CLIN SCI, COL VET MED & GRAD SCH, OHIO STATE UNIV, 62-, LECTR OPHTHAL, COL MED, 65- *Concurrent Pos:* Morris Animal Found res dir, 62-; mem comt prof educ, Inst Lab Animal Resources, Nat Acad Sci, 66- *Mem:* Am Vet Med Asn. *Res:* Veterinary ophthalmology; retinal diseases; animal endocrinology. *Mailing Add:* Dept of Vet Med Ohio State Univ Columbus OH 43210

DONOVAN, GERALD ALTON, b Hartford, Conn, Feb 10, 25; m 48; c 3. POULTRY NUTRITION, BIOCHEMISTRY. *Educ:* Univ Conn, BS, 50, MS, 52; Iowa State Univ, PhD(poultry nutrit, biochem), 55. *Prof Exp:* Asst poultry res, Univ Conn, 51-52; res assoc, Iowa State Univ, 52-55; in-chg poultry nutrit res, Agr Res Dept, Charles Pfizer & Co, Inc, 55-60; assoc prof poultry sci, Univ Vt, 60-66, prof animal sci, 66-73, assoc dir agr exp sta, 66-67, assoc dir col agr & home econ, 67-73, actg dean, Col Agr & Home Econ, 70-73; PROF ANIMAL SCI, DEAN COL RESOURCE DEVELOP, DIR AGR EXP STA & DIR COOP EXTEN SERV, UNIV RI, 73-, DIR, INT CTR MARINE RESOURCE DEVELOP, 75- *Mem:* Sigma Xi; Asn Univ Dirs Int Agr Progs; Am Inst Nutrit. *Res:* Vitamins, particularly vitamin A; antibiotics; hormones; chemotherapeutic agents. *Mailing Add:* Col of Resource Develop Univ of RI Kingston RI 02881

DONOVAN, GERARD ANTHONY, b Cork, Ireland, Nov 28, 37. MICROBIOLOGY, BIOCHEMISTRY. *Educ:* Nat Univ, Ireland, BS, 60, MS, 61; Univ Calif, Davis, Phd(microbiol), 65. *Prof Exp:* Res demonstr microbiol, Univ Col, Cork, 60-61; asst, Univ Calif, Davis, 62-65; lectr bact, Univ Calif, Berkeley, 65-66, Am Cancer Soc fel molecular biol, 66-68; asst prof, 68-71, ASSOC PROF BIOCHEM, BIOPHYS & GENETICS, TEX A&M UNIV, 72- *Concurrent Pos:* Founder & chmn, Gulf Coast Molecular Biol Conf, 69-; prin investr, Int Collab NATO Res Grant Basic Sci, 70-75; Robert A Welch chem res grant, Tex A&M Univ, 70-78. *Mem:* AAAS; Am Soc Microbiol; Brit Biochem Soc; Genetics Soc Am. *Mailing Add:* Dept Biochem & Biophys Tex A&M Univ College Station TX 77843

DONOVAN, JAMES, b Vancouver, Wash, Oct 26, 06; m 31; c 2. CHEMICAL ENGINEERING. *Educ:* Mass Inst Technol, BS, 28. *Prof Exp:* Instr chem eng, Mass Inst Technol, 28-29; chem engr, Hird & Connor, Inc, 29-32 & Acme Indust Equip Co, 32-34; chief engr & exec, Artisan Metal Prods, Inc, 34-61, chief engr & exec, Artisan Indust Inc, 61-76, PRES & TREAS, ARTISAN INDUST INC, 76- *Concurrent Pos:* Exec, Jet-Vac Corp, Kontro Co, Inc & Anyl-Ray Corp. *Mem:* Am Inst Chem Engrs; Am Chem Soc; Am Welding Soc; Inst Food Technol. *Res:* Chemical engineering process; evaporation, distillation and reaction costs. *Mailing Add:* Artisan Industs Inc 73 Pond St Waltham MA 02154

DONOVAN, JOHN FRANCIS, b St John, NB, Nov 11, 35; m 63; c 2. ECONOMIC GEOLOGY, EARTH SCIENCES. *Educ:* St Francis Xavier Univ, BSc, 57; Univ Iowa, MS, 59; Cornell Univ, PhD(geol), 63. *Prof Exp:* Resident geologist, Ont Dept Mines, 63-68; assoc prof geol & earth sci, Winona State Col, 68-80, PROF GEOL & EARTH SCI, WINONA STATE UNIV, 80- *Mem:* Geol Soc Am; Soc Econ Geol. *Res:* Study of iron formations-sedimentary deposits of Archean age, Precambrian areas of Canadian Shield. *Mailing Add:* 1515 W Fifth St Apt 308 Winona MN 55987

DONOVAN, JOHN JOSEPH, b Lynn, Mass; c 5. MANAGEMENT INFORMATION SYSTEMS, COMPUTER SCIENCE. *Educ:* Tufts Univ, BS, 63; Mass Inst Technol, BS, 63; Yale Univ, MEng, 64, MS, 65, MPh & PhD(comput), 66. *Prof Exp:* Assoc prof elec eng, 66-73, PROF MGT SCI, SLOAN SCH MGT, MASS INST TECHNOL, 73- *Concurrent Pos:* Ford fel, Mass Inst Technol, 66; pres, Int Comput Inc, 67-69; chmn bd, Mitrol, 70-71; clin prof pediat, Med Sch, Tufts Univ, 74-, dir financial publ, 75, dir, Ctr Birth Defects Info Systs, 77- *Res:* Computer based information systems. *Mailing Add:* Sloan Sch of Mgt Mass Inst Technol Cambridge MA 02139

DONOVAN, JOHN LEO, b Rochester, NY, Apr 1, 29; m 53; c 4. NUCLEAR PHYSICS. *Educ:* Univ Rochester, BS, 51; Univ Pittsburgh, MS, 53; Univ Mich, PhD(nuclear sci), 64. *Prof Exp:* Instr, NY Univ, 53-56; sr res physicist, Curtiss-Wright Corp, 56-59; SR RES PHYSICIST, EASTMAN KODAK CO, 64- *Concurrent Pos:* Assoc lectr, Univ Rochester, 66- *Mem:* AAAS; Am Nuclear Soc; Soc Photog Sci & Eng; Sigma Xi; Am Phys Soc. *Res:* Nonsilver image forming systems and their application to radiography, including measurement of intrinsic efficiency of phosphors irradiated with x-rays. *Mailing Add:* Eastman Kodak Co Physics Res Lab Kodak Park Rochester NY 14650

DONOVAN, JOHN RICHARD, b St Louis, Mo, Aug 7, 17; m 40; c 3. CATALYSIS, INORGANIC CHEMISTRY. *Educ:* Wash Univ, BS, 39, MS, 53. *Prof Exp:* Jr engr reinforced plastics, Burkhart Mfg Co, 39-40; control chemist, asst mfg supvr, eng, inorganics & organic intermediates, Monsanto Co, W G Krummrich Plant, Sauget, Ill, 40-45; sr engr nuclear reactors, Clinton Nat Lab, Oak Ridge, Tenn, 45-47; group leader inorganics, Monsanto-Krummrich Plant, 47-56, group leader catalyst & inorganic res, Monsanto Co, St Louis, 57-63, asst plant mgr & qual control mgr, copper powder, Kans City Plant, 63-64, sr eng specialist sulfuric acid & catalyst, St Louis Off, 64-70, mgr process design, 70-73, MGR TECHNOL SULFURIC ACID & CATALYST, MONSANTO ENVIRO-CHEM SYSTS, INC, 73- *Concurrent Pos:* Mem nat comn Am Soc Testing & Mat, 60-63, Nat Mat Adv Bd, 77-78; consult Bunker Hill Co & Kennecott Copper Co, 74-75. *Mem:* Am Inst Chem Engrs; Am Chem Soc; Air Pollution Control Asn; fel Am Inst Chem Engrs. *Res:* Sulfuric acid, all phases, major emphasis on process and engineering aspects; sulfur and inorganic sulfur compounds; air pollution control oxidation catalysts, major emphasis on vanadium. *Mailing Add:* Monsanto Enviro-Chem Syst Inc PO Box 14547 St Louis MO 63178

DONOVAN, JOHN W, b Boston, Mass, June 7, 29; m 61; c 4. PHYSICAL CHEMISTRY. *Educ:* Boston Col, BS, 50; Col Holy Cross, MS, 53; Cornell Univ, PhD(chem), 59. *Prof Exp:* Fel chem, Univ Rochester, 59-61; trainee molecular biol, virus lab, Univ Calif, Berkeley, 61-63; res assoc chem, Univ Ore, 63-65; MEM STAFF, WESTERN REGIONAL RES LAB, USDA, 65- *Mem:* Am Chem Soc; Am Soc Biol Chemists. *Res:* Physical chemistry of proteins and starch; absorption spectrophotometry; scanning calorimetry. *Mailing Add:* Western Regional Res Lab USDA Berkeley CA 94710

DONOVAN, LEO F(RANCIS), b East Orange, NJ, Apr 12, 32; m 60; c 2. AERONAUTICAL ENGINEERING, CHEMICAL ENGINEERING. *Educ:* Lehigh Univ, BS, 54; Rensselaer Polytech Inst, MChE, 57, PhD(chem eng), 65. *Prof Exp:* Chem engr, Res Lab, Mobil Oil Co, 57-59; nuclear chem engr, Nuclear Power Eng Dept, Alco Prod Inc, 59-62; AEROSPACE ENGR, LEWIS RES CTR, NASA, 65- *Mem:* Am Inst Chem Engrs. *Res:* Fluid mechanics; numerical analysis; numerical flow visualization; computer time sharing. *Mailing Add:* NASA Lewis Res Ctr 21000 Brook Park Cleveland OH 44135

DONOVAN, RICHARD C, b McKees Rocks, Pa, May 15, 41; m 64; c 2. MANUFACTURING TECHNOLOGY. *Educ:* Univ Pittsburgh, BS, 62, MS, 64, PhD(mech eng), 67. *Prof Exp:* Asst prof mech eng, Univ Pittsburgh, 67-68; mem res staff, 68-71, res leader, 71-78, supvr technol planning, 78-80, ASST DIR INTERCONNECTION & SEMICONDUCTOR PROCESS TECHNOL, ENG RES CTR, WESTERN ELEC CO, 80- *Mem:* Am Soc Mech Engrs; Inst Elec & Electronics Engrs; Soc Plastics Engrs. *Res:* Semiconductor processing; plasma processes for silicon, crystal and epitaxial growth of III-V compounds; interconnection assembly technology; soldering materials and processes; automated assembly; polymer processes and materials recylcing processes; research and technical management. *Mailing Add:* Western Elec Co Eng Res Ctr PO Box 900 Princeton NJ 08540

DONOVAN, ROSS GRANT, b Niagara Falls, Ont, Sept 20, 30; m 52; c 2. BIOCHEMISTRY. *Educ:* Univ Toronto, BA, 52, MA, 54, PhD(biochem), 65. *Prof Exp:* Chief chemist, Collis Leather Co, Ltd, Ont, 53-60; group leader, Res Ctr, 63-80, RES MGR, CAN PACKERS, INC, 80- *Mem:* Am Sci Affil; Am Leather Chemists Asn; fel Chem Inst Can; Can Biochem Soc; Brit Soc Leather Trades Chem. *Mailing Add:* 17 Markland Dr Etobicoke ON M9C 1M8 Can

DONOVAN, SANDRA STERANKA, b Cleveland, Ohio, Sept 20, 42; m 66; c 1. PHYSICAL CHEMISTRY, ELECTROCHEMISTRY. *Educ:* Western Reserve Univ, BA, 64, MS, 66, Case Western Reserve Univ, PhD(electrochem), 69. *Prof Exp:* Res chemist mat, Hercules Inc, 69-70; sr res assoc, Horizons Res Inc, 71-73, group leader mat, 73-76, mgr mat sci & contract res & develop, 76-78; prog mgr bus develop, 78-80, MGR PROG, VISTRON CORP, STANDARD OIL OHIO, 81- *Concurrent Pos:* mem bd overseers, Case Western Reserve, 72-78; dir, Mather Col Alumnae Asn, 73-79. *Mem:* Electrochem Soc; Sigma Xi. *Res:* Electrochemically fabricated oxides and protective coatings; electrochemical kinetics, materials, petrochemicals and derivatives; commercial development of petrochemicals. *Mailing Add:* 246 Hawthorne Dr Chagrin Falls OH 44022

DONOVAN, TERENCE M, b Chicago, Ill, Dec 7, 31; m 55; c 3. PHYSICS. *Educ:* San Jose State Col, BS, 56; Stanford Univ, MS, 61, PhD, 70. *Prof Exp:* Physical chemist, Chem Div, US Naval Ord Test Sta, 56-60, chem physicist, 61-65, RES PHYSICIST, PHYSICS DIV, MICHELSON LAB, NAVAL WEAPONS CTR, 70- *Concurrent Pos:* Assoc chemist, Shockley Transistor Corp, 60-61. *Mem:* Am Phys Soc. *Res:* Optical properties of solids; optical properties and photoemission; electronic structure of amorphous and crystalline solids; optical coatings for high energy lasers. *Mailing Add:* Code 6018 Naval Weapons Ctr China Lake CA 93555

DONOVAN, TERRENCE JOHN, b Waterbury, Conn, July 27, 36; m 56; c 3. GEOLOGY. *Educ:* Midwestern Univ, BS, 61; Univ Calif, Riverside, MA, 63; Univ Calif, Los Angeles, PhD(geol), 72. *Prof Exp:* Geologist petrol explor, Mobil Oil Corp, 63-68; asst prof geol, Midwestern Univ, 68-72; GEOLOGIST & PROG CHIEF RES, US GEOL SURV, 72- *Honors & Awards:* A I Levorsen Award, Am Asn Petrol Geologists, 71. *Mem:* Fel Geol Soc Am; Am Asn Petrol Geologists; AAAS. *Res:* Petroleum geology and geochemistry; research into the geochemical basis for remote sensing exploration for energy resources, especially petroleum and natural gas. *Mailing Add:* US Geol Surv 2255 Gemini Dr Flagstaff AZ 86001

DONOVAN, THOMAS ARNOLD, b Galesburg, Ill, July 11, 37; m 60; c 3. INORGANIC CHEMISTRY. *Educ:* Knox Col (Ill), BA, 59; Univ Ill, PhD(inorg chem), 62. *Prof Exp:* Asst prof chem, Ind State Col, 62-64; asst prof chem, Knox Col (Ill), 64-68; from asst prof to assoc prof, 68-81, PROF CHEM, STATE UNIV NY COL BUFFALO, 81- *Mem:* Am Chem Soc. *Res:* Preparation, characterization and properties of new coordination compounds; biological applications of coordination chemistry. *Mailing Add:* Dept of Chem State Univ NY Col 1300 Elmwood Ave Buffalo NY 14222

DONOVICK, PETER JOSEPH, b Champaign, Ill, Jan 14, 38; m 62, 81; c 2. BIOPSYCHOLOGY. *Educ:* Lafayette Col, BA, 61; Univ Wis, MS, 63, PhD(psychol), 67. *Prof Exp:* Asst prof psychol, Harpur Col, 66-71, assoc prof, 71-76, PROF PSYCHOL, STATE UNIV NY BINGHAMTON, 76-, CHMN DEPT, 78- *Concurrent Pos:* Spec res fel anat & vis asst prof, Hershey Med Ctr, Pa State Univ, 70-71. *Mem:* Am Psychol Asn; NY Acad Sci; Soc Neurosci; Behavior Genetics Asn. *Res:* Genetic and environmental influences of the response to lesions of the limbic system of the brain; impact of environmental toxims, parasites and nutrition on behavior; lifespan developmental psychobiology and behavior genetics. *Mailing Add:* Dept of Psychol State Univ of NY Binghamton NY 13901

DONOVICK, RICHARD, b Minneapolis, Minn, July 8, 11; m; c 4. BACTERIOLOGY. *Educ:* Univ Calif, Los Angeles, BA, 34, MA, 36; Univ Ill, PhD(bact), 40; Am Bd Microbiol, dipl. *Prof Exp:* Asst bact, Univ Calif, Los Angeles, 34-36 & Univ Ill, 36-40; res fel, col physicians & surgeons, Columbia Univ, 40-41; pathologist, virus div, Lederle Labs, NY, 41-42; sr bacteriologist & head typhus dept, Reichel Labs, Pa, 42-44; res assoc div microbiol, Squibb Inst Med Res, 44-46, assoc mem, 46-49, head dept microbiol res & develop, 49-50, dir div, 50-69; res proj dir & mem exec comt, Life Sci, Inc, 69-73; dir, Am Type Cult Collection, 73-80; RETIRED. *Concurrent Pos:* Mem Sci Adv Bd, US Air Force; consult, Life Sci, Inc, 73- *Mem:* Fel AAAS; Am Soc Microbiol (treas, 62-64); Soc Exp Biol & Med; Am Chem Soc; fel Am Acad Microbiol. *Res:* Experimental infections of virus and rickettsial diseases; several aspects for antibiotics; fermentation; chemotherapy of number of experimental bacteriological infections; various biosynthesis including biosynthesis of steroids. *Mailing Add:* 11135 Carla Dr Largo FL 33540

DONSKER, MONROE DAVID, b Burlington, Iowa, Oct 17, 24; m 46. MATHEMATICS. *Educ:* Univ Minn, BA, 44, MA, 46, PhD(math), 49. *Prof Exp:* Asst math, Univ Minn, 44-46, instr, 46-48; instr, Cornell Univ, 48-50; from asst prof to prof, Univ Minn, 50-59; Fulbright sr res scholar, Denmark, 59-61; prof, Courant Inst Math Sci, 62-77, PROF MATH, NY UNIV, 77- *Concurrent Pos:* Mem, Comt Int Exchange of Persons; chmn postdoctoral comt, Off Naval Res; chmn, Fulbright Screening Panel in Math. *Mem:* Am Math Soc; Math Asn Am. *Res:* Stochastic processes; analysis. *Mailing Add:* Dept of Math NY Univ Washington Sq New York NY 10003

DONTA, SAM THEODORE, b Aliquippa, Pa, Aug 9, 38; m 59; c 4. INFECTIOUS DISEASES. *Educ:* Allegheny Col, BS, 59; Albert Einstein Col Med, MD, 63. *Prof Exp:* Intern & resident, Univ Pittsburgh Hosps, 64-65; fel biochem, Brandeis Univ, 67-70; res assoc infectious dis, Univ Hosp, Boston, 70-71; asst prof, 71-74, assoc prof, 74-77, PROF MED, UNIV IOWA, 78- *Concurrent Pos:* Clin investr, Vet Admin Hosp, 75-78; mem, Bact & Mycol Study Sect, NIH, 76-80. *Mem:* Infectious Dis Soc Am; Am Fedn Clin Res; AAAS; Am Soc Microbiologists. *Res:* Mechanisms of action of cholera and Escherichia coli enterotoxins on cultured adrenal cells; toxin-membrane interactions; tissue culture models of infectious disease; bacterial adherence. *Mailing Add:* Dept of Internal Med Univ of Iowa Iowa City IA 52242

DOOB, JOSEPH LEO, b Cincinnati, Ohio, Feb 27, 10; m 31; c 3. MATHEMATICS. *Educ:* Harvard Univ, AB, 30, AM, 31, PhD(math), 32. *Prof Exp:* Nat Res fel math, Columbia Univ, 32-34, assoc theoret statist & Carnegie Corp fel, 34-35; from assoc math to assoc prof, 35-45, PROF MATH, UNIV ILL, URBANA-CHAMPAIGN, 45- *Honors & Awards:* Foreign assoc, Acad Sci, Paris, 75. *Mem:* Nat Acad Sci; Am Acad Arts & Sci; Am Math Soc (pres, 63-64); fel Inst Math Statist (vpres, 45, pres, 50). *Res:* Probability and potential theory. *Mailing Add:* Dept of Math Univ of Ill Urbana IL 61801

DOODY, JOHN EDWARD, b Chicago, Ill, Mar 30, 25. PHYSICAL CHEMISTRY. *Educ:* St Mary's Col, BS, 46; St Louis Univ, MS, 50, PhD(phys chem), 53. *Prof Exp:* Mil high sch teacher, Mo, 46-53; instr, 53-54, PROF CHEM, CHRISTIAN BROS COL, 54-, DIR GRANTS, 80- *Concurrent Pos:* Cottrell res grant, 54; NSF grant, 54, res grant, 62; AEC res grant, 55-66; Tenn heart res grant, 62 & 63; Am Chem Soc petrol res grant, 63; dir, NSF Insts Sci Teachers, 67-75; dir, Dept Health, Educ & Welfare Inst Minority Cult, 69 & 71. *Mem:* Am Chem Soc; Am Inst Chemists; AAAS. *Res:* Heavy metal ions; transport across membranes and reactions with nucleic acids and derivatives; electrochemistry. *Mailing Add:* Dept of Chem Christian Bros Col 650 E Pkwy Memphis TN 38104

DOOLEN, GARY DEAN, b Billings, Mont, June 7, 39; m 62; c 2. NUCLEAR FUSION, PLASMA MODELLING. *Educ:* Purdue Univ, BS, 61, MS, PhD(physics), 67. *Prof Exp:* Res assoc atomic physics, Goddard Space Flight Ctr, NASA, 67-69; asst prof physics, Tex A&M Univ, 69-75; STAFF MEM PHYSICS, LOS ALAMOS NAT LAB, 75- *Mem:* Am Phys Soc. *Res:* Nuclear fusion with special interest in pure fusion; energy transport; atomic and nuclear excited states; nuclear properties; computer modelling of plasmas; plasma radiation interactions. *Mailing Add:* MS 420 Los Alamos Nat Lab Los Alamos NM 87545

DOOLEY, DAVID MARLIN, b Tulare, Calif, May 13, 52; m 78. INORGANIC CHEMISTRY. *Educ:* Univ Calif, San Diego, BA, 74; Calif Inst Technol, PhD(chem), 79. *Prof Exp:* Res asst, Calif Inst Technol, 74-78; ASST PROF CHEM, AMHERST COL, 78- *Concurrent Pos:* NIH fel, 74-78; vis scientist, Mass Inst Technol, 81; vis scholar, Stanford Univ, 82. *Mem:* Am Chem Soc. *Res:* Spectroscopic studies of the electronic structure and bonding in transition metal complexes; ligand field theory; applications to bioinorganic chemistry; copper proteins; inorganic photochemistry. *Mailing Add:* Dept of Chem Amherst Col Amherst MA 01002

DOOLEY, DOUGLAS CHARLES, b Chicago, Ill, Mar 5, 46. BONE MARROW CULTURE, CELL PHYSIOLOGY. *Educ:* Univ Calif, Berkeley, BA, 67; Univ Wash, PhD(microbiol), 72. *Prof Exp:* Fel cell physiol, Worcester Found Exp Biol, 72-76; res assoc cell physiol, 76-77, HEAD, TISSUE CULT LAB, RED CROSS BLOOD RES LAB, 77- *Mem:* Int Soc Exp Hematol; AAAS; Soc Cryobiol. *Res:* Long term culture of bone marrow and regulation of hematopoiesis. *Mailing Add:* Am Nat Red Cross 9312 Old Georgetown Rd Bethesda MD 20014

DOOLEY, ELMO S, b Davidson, Tenn, Feb 23, 24; m 45; c 3. PHYSIOLOGY. *Educ:* Tenn Polytech Inst, BS, 52; Univ Tenn, MS, 55, PhD, 57. *Prof Exp:* Consult microbiol, Cumberland Med Ctr, 57-58; chief microbiol br, US Army Med Res Lab, 58-61; sr scientist, US Aerospace Med Res Lab, 61-63; chmn dept biol, 64-66, PROF BIOL, TENN TECHNOL UNIV, 64- *Mem:* Aerospace Med Asn; Am Soc Microbiol; Am Fedn Clin Res; fel Royal Soc Health. *Res:* Aerospace and cardiovascular physiology. *Mailing Add:* Dept of Biol Tenn Technol Univ Cookeville TN 38501

DOOLEY, GEORGE JOSEPH, III, b Greenwich, Conn, Aug 8, 41; m 63; c 3. MATERIALS SCIENCE. *Educ:* Univ Notre Dame, BS, 63; Iowa State Univ, MS, 66; Ore State Univ, PhD(mat sci), 69. *Prof Exp:* Res metallurgist, Albany Metall, Res Ctr, Bur Mines, 66-68; res scientist, Aerospace Res Labs, US Air Force Systs Command, 68-73; DIR METALL & PROCESS RES & DEVELOP, OREGON METALL CORP, 74- *Mem:* Am Soc Metals; Am Inst Mining, Metall & Petrol Eng; Am Vacuum Soc; Am Phys Soc. *Res:* Process and production metallurgy, ingot manufacture and mill products aspects of titanium metal production; surface chemistry and surface physics of both single crystal and polycrystalline materials using the techniques of low energy electron diffraction and auger electron spectroscopy. *Mailing Add:* Ore Metall Corp PO Box 580 Albany OR 97321

DOOLEY, JAMES KEITH, b Steubenville, Ohio, Aug 8, 41; m 64; c 2. SYSTEMATIC ICHTHYOLOGY, AQUATIC ECOLOGY. *Educ:* Univ Miami, BS, 64; Univ S Fla, MA, 70; Univ NC, Chapel Hill, PhD(zool), 74. *Prof Exp:* Res asst ichthyol, Inst Marine Sci, Univ Miami, 64-67; asst prof, 73-80, ASSOC PROF BIOL, ADELPHI UNIV, 80- *Concurrent Pos:* Res fisheries consult, Biol Consult, Inc, 73-75; adj assoc prof ichthyol, Dowling Col, 74; consult, NY State Dept Environ Conserv, 75. *Mem:* Am Soc Ichthyologists & Herpetologists; Ecol Soc Am; Fisheries Soc Brit Isles; Soc Syst Zoologists; Sigma Xi. *Res:* Systematics and biology of the tilefishes, Branchiostegidae and Malacanthidae; ecology of littoral fishes; heavy metals in fishes; ecological aspects of New York Fishes. *Mailing Add:* Dept Biol Adelphi Univ Garden City NY 11530

DOOLEY, JOHN RAYMOND, JR, b Denver, Colo, Dec 12, 25; m 52; c 5. NUCLEAR PHYSICS. *Educ:* Regis Col (Colo), BS, 49; Univ Denver, MS, 51. *Prof Exp:* Engr, Colo State Hwy Dept, 49-51; instr physics, guided missile training, Lowry AFB, Colo, 51-52; staff mem nuclear physics, Sandia Corp, 52-53; PHYSICIST, ISOTOPE GEOL BR, US GEOL SURV, 53- *Res:* Natural radioactivity and uranium geochemistry; uranium and thorium disequilibrium; health physics; uranium-234 fractionation; fission tracks; uranium-lead dating of uranium deposits, developing the radioluxograph for autoradiography of uranium and induced-particle autoradiography of lithium. *Mailing Add:* Isotope Geol Br US Geol Survey Denver Fed Ctr Denver CO 80225

DOOLEY, JOSEPH FRANCIS, b New York, NY, Oct 3, 41; m 63; c 2. CLINICAL CHEMISTRY, TOXICOLOGY. *Educ:* Fordham Univ, BS, 63; Univ Minn, Minneapolis, PhD(org chem), 67. *Prof Exp:* Res chemist, E I du Pont de Nemours & Co, Inc, 67-70; staff scientist, Med Res Labs, 70-74, sr res scientist, 74-77, SR RES INVESTR, PFIZER CENT RES, PFIZER INC, 77-; ASSOC PROF TOXICOL & MED LAB SCI, QUINNIPIAC COL, HAMDEN, CONN, 77- *Concurrent Pos:* Clin assoc prof, Dept Lab Med, Sch Med, Univ Conn, 76-; sr partner, Med Lab & Consult, Biomed Assoc, 80-; nat comt chmn, Clin Lab Testing in Chem & Drug Safety Eval, Am Asn Clin Chemistry, 76-; mem comt, Effects of Drugs in Clin Lab Tests, Int Fed Clin Chemistry. *Mem:* AAAS; Am Chem Soc; Am Asn Clin Chemistry; Soc Toxicol. *Res:* Hematology; enzymology; effects of drugs on kidney function and liver metabolism; radioimmunoassay; toxicology; laboratory instrumentation. *Mailing Add:* Pfizer Cent Res Pfizer Inc Groton CT 06340

DOOLEY, THOMAS JOSEPH, organic chemistry, see previous edition

DOOLEY, WALLACE T, b Conway, Ark, June 15, 17; m 39; c 4. ORTHOPEDIC SURGERY. *Educ:* Univ Kans, AB, 39, MA, 41; Meharry Med Col, MD, 47. *Prof Exp:* Rockefeller Found fel, 51-52; Nat Polio Found fel, 51-55; DIR PHYS MED, GEORGE W HUBBARD HOSP, 55-, PROF ORTHOP SURG, MEHARRY MED COL, 67-, HEAD DIV, 60- *Concurrent Pos:* Chief orthop surg, Riverside Sanitarium & Hosp, 55-; assoc prof, Meharry Med Col, 60-67; prog dir rehab med, 63-67. *Mem:* Am Cong Rehab Med. *Mailing Add:* Dept of Surg Meharry Med Col Nashville TN 37208

DOOLEY, WILLIAM PAUL, b Richmond, Va, Aug 2, 15; m 41; c 2. CHEMISTRY, CHEMICAL ENGINEERING. *Educ:* Univ Richmond, BS, 38; Mass Inst Technol, SM, 40. *Prof Exp:* Tech & admin asst to gen mgr, Am Viscose Corp, 40-45, asst supt, Staple Develop Plant, 45-46, supt, 46-50, head, Develop Serv Dept, 50-55, corp prod tech supt, 55-60; mkt specialist, Sun Oil Co, 60-67, asst to dir, Com Develop, 67-70, proj mgr, 70-78; TECH & VENTURE CONSULT, 78- *Mem:* Am Chem Soc; Am Inst Chem Engrs; Chem Mkt Res Asn. *Res:* Manufacture of viscose and viscose rayon products; technical support of sales programs; petrochemicals market research and development; research, development and new venture development. *Mailing Add:* 2 Salette Lane The Landings Skidaway Island Savannah GA 31411

DOOLIN, PAUL F, b Jacksonville, Ill, May 17, 26. NEUROBIOLOGY. *Educ:* Ill Col, AB, 50; Univ Ill, MS, 53; Western Reserve Univ, PhD(chem cytol), 58; Loyola Univ Chicago, MD, 78. *Prof Exp:* Res asst cytol & histol, Univ Ill, 50-53; res assoc cytochem, Inst Path, Western Reserve Univ, 53-58; asst prof, Washington & Jefferson Col, 59-60; assoc prof zool, Ill State Univ, 60-64; assoc prof anat & path, Stritch Sch Med, Loyola Univ Chicago, 64-76; RESIDENT DIAG RADIOL, UNIV ILL HOSPS, 78- *Concurrent Pos:* Res biologist & chief electron micros lab, Neuropath Res Sta, Vet Admin Hosp, Hines, Ill, 64-67, res chemist, 67-74. *Res:* Cellular and developmental biology; neurological ultrastructure; blood brain barrier and cerebrospinal fluid barrier systems. *Mailing Add:* 3001 Thatcher Ave River Grove IL 60171

DOOLITTLE, CHARLES HERBERT, III, b Holyoke, Mass, July 18, 39; m 61; 71; c 2. CLINICAL PHARMACOLOGY. *Educ:* Univ Mass, Amherst, BS, 62, MA, 65; George Washington Univ, PhD(pharmacol), 70; Brown Univ, MD, 75. *Prof Exp:* Res asst clin pharmacol, Sch Med, Yale Univ, 64-66; USPHS res fel biochem pharmacol, Brown Univ & Roger Williams Gen Hosp, 69-75, intern, Roger Williams Gen Hosp, 75-76; resident, Roger Williams Gen Hosp, 76-77; chief oncology sect, 77-80, PRIN INVESTR, DEPT MED & SURG, VET ADMIN, PROVIDENCE, 80- *Mem:* AAAS. *Res:* Anti-neoplastic agents. *Mailing Add:* 32 Brookwood Rd Attleboro MA 02703

DOOLITTLE, DONALD PRESTON, b Torrington, Conn, May 14, 33; m 57; c 2. GENETICS. *Educ:* Univ Conn, BS, 54; Cornell Univ, MS, 56, PhD(animal genetics), 59. *Prof Exp:* Asst, Cornell Univ, 54-58; fel, Roscoe B Jackson Mem Lab, 58-60; asst res prof biomet, Grad Sch Pub Health, Univ Pittsburgh, 60-65; asst prof genetics & asst geneticist, WVa Univ, 65-67, ASSOC PROF ANIMAL SCI, PURDUE UNIV, 67- *Mem:* Am Genetics Asn; Genetics Soc Am. *Res:* Quantitative genetics; mammalian genetics; biometry. *Mailing Add:* Dept of Animal Sci Purdue Univ West Lafayette IN 47907

DOOLITTLE, J(ESSE) S(EYMOUR), b Bethany, Conn, Sept 20, 03; m 27. MECHANICAL ENGINEERING. *Educ:* Tufts Univ, BS, 25; Pa State Univ, MS, 37. *Prof Exp:* Student engr, Gen Elec Co, Mass, 25-27; instr mech eng, Case Inst Technol, 27-31; from instr to assoc prof, Pa State Univ, 31-47; prof & dept grad adminr, 47-73, EMER PROF MECH ENG, NC STATE UNIV, 73- *Concurrent Pos:* Extensive consulting. *Honors & Awards:* G Edwin Burks Award, 70. *Mem:* AAAS; fel Am Soc Mech Engrs; Am Soc Eng Educ; Sigma Xi. *Res:* Thermodynamics; heat transfer; power; author of 4 textbooks. *Mailing Add:* Dept of Mech Eng NC State Univ Raleigh NC 27650

DOOLITTLE, JOHN H(ENRY), b Foster, Mo, Feb 8, 20; m 41; c 4. ELECTRONICS. *Educ:* Univ Kans, BS, 42. *Prof Exp:* From jr electronics engr to head phys systs sect, Cornell Aeronaut Lab, NY, 46-57; from dept head to dir res div, Radiation, Inc, Fla, 57-61; from asst dept head to assoc dir, Electronics Div, Cornell Aeronaut Lab, Inc, 61-73; VPRES, ELECTROSCI FOR MED INC, 73- *Mem:* Sr mem Inst Elec & Electronics Engrs. *Res:* Radar; electron circuits; remote control systems for aircraft and guided missiles; navigation; data links; space navigation and control man-machine interface; application of electronics to medical problems. *Mailing Add:* ElectroSci for Med Inc 4100 Barton Rd Clarence NY 14031

DOOLITTLE, ROBERT FREDERICK, II, b Chicago, Ill, Dec 21, 25; m 55; c 2. PHYSICS. *Educ:* Oberlin Col, AB, 48; Univ Mich, MS, 50, PhD(physics), 58. *Prof Exp:* Asst, Univ Mich, 50-58; asst prof physics, San Diego State Col, 58-60; mem tech staff, Space Physics Dept, TRW Space Tech Labs, 60-66, mem tech staff, Space Sci Lab, TRW Systs, 66-70, staff scientist, Instrument Systs Lab, 70-78, proj scientist, High Energy Astron Observ, 78-81, PROJ SCIENTIST, GAMMA RAY OBSERV, SR STAFF SCIENTIST, SOFTWARE & INFO SYSTS DIV, TRW DEFENSE & SPACE SYSTS GROUP, REDONDO BEACH, 82- *Mem:* AAAS; Am Phys Soc; Am Astron Soc; Res & Engr Soc Am. *Res:* High energy astronomy and cosmic ray physics. *Mailing Add:* TRW Defense & Space Systs Group One Space Park Redondo Beach CA 90278

DOOLITTLE, RUSSELL F, b New Haven, Conn, Jan 10, 31; m 55; c 2. BIOCHEMISTRY. *Educ:* Wesleyan Univ, BA, 52; Trinity Col (Conn), MA, 57; Harvard Univ, PhD(biochem), 62. *Prof Exp:* Instr biol, Amherst Col, 61-62; Nat Heart Inst fel, 62-64; asst res biologist, 64-65, from asst prof to assoc prof chem, 67-72, PROF BIOCHEM, UNIV CALIF, SAN DIEGO, 72- *Concurrent Pos:* Mem corp, Marine Biol Lab, 62-69; career develop award, USPHS, 69-74; mem, NIH Blood Adv Comt, 74-78; mem coun thrombosis, Am Heart Asn. *Mem:* Am Soc Biol Chemists. *Res:* Protein chemistry and molecular evolution; structure of fibrinogen. *Mailing Add:* Dept of Chem Univ of Calif San Diego La Jolla CA 92093

DOOLITTLE, WARREN FORD, III, b Urbana, Ill, Feb 21, 42; m 67; c 1. MOLECULAR BIOLOGY. *Educ:* Harvard Col, BA, 63; Stanford Univ, PhD(biol sci), 69. *Prof Exp:* NIH fel, Nat Jewish Hosp, Denver, Colo, 69-70, res assoc molecular biol, 70-71; asst prof biochem, 71-76, ASSOC PROF BIOCHEM, DALHOUSIE UNIV, 76-, MED RES COUN CAN SCHOLAR, 71- *Mem:* Am Soc Microbiol. *Res:* Molecular biology and genetics of blue-green algae; ribosome maturation; control of gene expression. *Mailing Add:* 47 Albion Rd Halifax B3P 1P8 Can

DOOLITTLE, WARREN TRUMAN, b Webster City, Iowa, July 24, 21; m 42; c 3. SILVICULTURE, FOREST SOILS. *Educ:* Iowa State Univ, BS, 46; Duke Univ, MF, 50; Yale Univ, PhD, 55. *Prof Exp:* Res forester, Southeastern Forest & Range Exp Sta, US Forest Serv, USDA, 46-57, Washington, DC, 57-59, asst dir, Northeastern Forest Exp Sta, 59-70, dir, 70-74, dir, Timber Mgt Res, 74-75, assoc dep chief, 75-80; CONSULT, INT SOC TROP FORESTERS, 80- *Concurrent Pos:* Mem, Nat Comt, UNESCO & Biosphere Prog, 76- *Honors & Awards:* Outstanding serv to forestry, Soc of Am Forestry, 75. *Mem:* AAAS; Soc Am Foresters; Soil Conserv Soc Am; Am Forestry Asn. *Res:* Forest management and soils. *Mailing Add:* 9004 Nomini Lane Alexandria VA 22309

DOOMES, EARL, b Washington, La, Feb 8, 43; m 65; c 3. ORGANIC CHEMISTRY. *Educ:* Univ Nebr, PhD(chem), 69. *Prof Exp:* Res assoc chem, Northwestern Univ, Evanston, 68-69; asst prof, 69-74, assoc prof chem, Macalester Col, 74-77; ASSOC PROF CHEM, SOUTHERN UNIV, 77- *Concurrent Pos:* NSF sci fac fel, Fla State Univ, 75-76. *Mem:* Am Chem Soc. *Res:* Interaction of small organic molecules with nucleic acids; synthetic approaches to cyclophanes and related conjugated polyenes, nonbenzenoid and unusual bridged aromatics, and nucleophilic substitution reactions of allyl systems. *Mailing Add:* Dept of Chem Southern Univ Baton Rouge LA 70813

DOORENBOS, HAROLD E, b Morrison, Ill, Oct 4, 25; m 49; c 2. ORGANIC CHEMISTRY. *Educ:* Cent Col (Iowa), BS, 49; Univ Ark, MS, 56; Univ Del, PhD(chem), 62. *Prof Exp:* Instr chem, Pa State Univ, 55-56; chemist, USDA, Md, 58 & E I du Pont de Nemours & Co, 61-62; CHEMIST, DOW CHEM CO, 62- *Mem:* AAAS; Am Chem Soc; Sigma Xi. *Res:* Organic synthesis; pharmaceutical, polymer, chlorine and fluorine chemistry. *Mailing Add:* 2102 Sylvan Lane Midland MI 48640

DOORENBOS, NORMAN JOHN, b Flint, Mich, May 13, 28; m 51, 79; c 7. CHEMISTRY PHARMACOGNOSY, MEDICINAL CHEMISTRY. *Educ:* Univ Mich, BS, 50, MS, 51, PhD(chem), 53. *Prof Exp:* Sr res chemist sensitizing dyes, Ansco, 53-56; from asst prof to prof pharmaceut chem, Univ Md, 56-65; prof med chem, Univ Miss, 65-77, prof pharmacog & chmn dept, 67-77; PROF PHYSIOL & DEAN COL SCI, SOUTHERN ILL UNIV, CARBONDALE, 77- *Concurrent Pos:* Vis scientist, Am Asn Cols Pharm, 63-73; consult, Malinckrodt Chem Works, 63-71; Merck Sharp & Dohme lectr, WVa Univ, 64; NSF Sci Curric Proj, Univ Ill, 64-65. *Mem:* AAAS; Am Chem Soc (treas, 49, chmn, 50); Soc Econ Bot (pres, 77-78); Acad Pharmaceut Sci; Am Soc Pharmacog. *Res:* Medical chemistry; steroids; heterocyclic steroids; alkaloids; natural products; biopharmaceutics; pharmacology; drug abuse; marijuana and phytochemistry; food toxins and bioactive marine substances. *Mailing Add:* Col of Sci Southern Ill Univ Carbondale IL 62901

DOORNENBAL, HUBERT, b Utrecht, Neth, Apr 19, 27; Can citizen; m 56; c 3. PHYSIOLOGY, MEAT SCIENCE. *Educ:* Univ BC, BSA, 52, MSA, 56; Cornell Univ, PhD(physiol, meats), 61. *Prof Exp:* Res asst beef cattle, 54-56, res officer beef cattle & swine nutrit, 56-59, RES SCIENTIST PHYSIOL & MEATS, RES STA, CAN DEPT AGR, 61- *Mem:* Am Soc Animal Sci; Can Soc Animal Sci; Agr Inst Can. *Res:* Physiology; endocrinology; nutrition; radiation biology; meat science. *Mailing Add:* Agr Can Res Sta Lacombe AB T0C 1S0 Can

DOR, LEONARD ELIEZER, b Magnitogorsk, USSR, Oct 16, 42; Israel citizen; m 71; c 1. MATHEMATICS. *Educ:* Tel Aviv Univ, BSc, 64, MSc, 69; Ohio State Univ, PhD(math), 75. *Prof Exp:* Vis lectr math, Univ Ill, Urbana, 75-78; ASST PROF MATH, WAYNE STATE UNIV, 78- *Mem:* Am Math Soc. *Res:* Geometry of Banach spaces; classical Banach spaces; projections; bases. *Mailing Add:* Dept of Math Wayne State Univ Detroit MI 48202

DORAIN, PAUL BRENDEL, b New Haven, Conn, Aug 30, 26; m 50; c 2. PHYSICAL CHEMISTRY. *Educ:* Yale Univ, BS, 50; Ind Univ, PhD, 54. *Prof Exp:* Mem, Enrico Fermi Inst Nuclear Studies, Univ Chicago, 54-56; mem, Aeronaut Res Lab, Ohio, 56-58; from asst prof to prof chem, Brandeis Univ, 58-81, from co-chmn to chmn dept, 71-74; DEAN FAC & VPRES ACAD AFFAIRS, COLBY COL, 81- *Concurrent Pos:* Trustee, Lowell Technol Inst, Mass, 72-74; Tallman vis prof chem & physics, Bowdoin Col, 74-75; vis fel, Yale Univ, 79-80. *Mem:* Am Phys Soc; Sigma Xi; AAAS. *Res:* Paramagnetic resonance; optical spectra of 4d and 5d transition metal ions; solid state; surface enhanced Raman scattering. *Mailing Add:* Colby Col Waterville ME 04901

DORAI-RAJ, DIANA GLOVER, b Rochester, NY, Sept 24, 38; c 4. CHEMISTRY. *Educ:* Univ Rochester, BS, 60; Univ Ore, PhD(chem), 67. *Prof Exp:* Lectr chem, Univ Waterloo, 66-67; instr, Seneca Col Arts & Technol, 68-69; ASSOC PROF CHEM, STILLMAN COL, 80- *Mailing Add:* 932 35th Ave Tuscaloosa AL 35401

DORAN, DAVID JAMES, parasitology, see previous edition

DORAN, DONALD GEORGE, b Los Angeles, Calif, Oct 2, 29; m 50; c 4. SOLID STATE PHYSICS, METAL PHYSICS. *Educ:* Wash State Univ, BS, 51, MS, 55, PhD(physics), 60. *Prof Exp:* Eng asst, Hanford Works Div, Gen Elec Co, 51-53; aeronaut res scientist, Ames Aeronaut Lab, Nat Adv Comt Aeronaut, 55; physicist, Poulter Res Labs, Stanford Res Inst, 55-58 & 60-62, sr physicist, 62-64, head solid state group, 64-65, dir shock wave physics div, 65-67; res assoc mat res sect, Pac Northwest Lab, Battelle Mem Inst, 67-70; res assoc, Mat Technol Dept, Wadco Corp, 70-72; fel scientist, 72-77, mgr irradiation effects, 77-79, MGR IRRADIATION TECHNOL, WESTINGHOUSE-HANFORD CO, 79- *Concurrent Pos:* Fel scientist, Westinghouse-Hanford Co, 72- *Mem:* Am Phys Soc; Am Nuclear Soc; Am Soc Testing & Mat. *Res:* Analysis of damage in metals irradiated with fission and fusion neutrons, ions and electrons; analytical and computer modeling of damage mechanisms. *Mailing Add:* 1853 Mahan Ct Richland WA 99352

DORAN, J CHRISTOPHER, b Dayton, Ohio, May 26, 45; m 70; c 1. ATMOSPHERIC PHYSICS. *Educ:* Fordham Univ, BS, 66; Yale Univ, PhD(physics), 71; Univ Utah, MS, 76. *Prof Exp:* Res assoc & assoc instr physics, Univ Utah, 71-73, asst res prof, 73-74; res scientist atmospheric sci, 76-78, SR RES SCIENTIST ATMOSPHERIC SCI, BATTELLE NORTHWEST, 78- *Mem:* Am Meteorol Soc. *Res:* Boundary layer meteorology; micrometeorology; diffusion studies; deposition studies; turbulence; wind energy. *Mailing Add:* 1516 Johnston Ave Richland WA 99352

DORAN, PETER COBB, b Bronxville, NY, Nov 23, 36; m 64; c 3. HEALTH SCIENCES. *Educ:* Colby Col, AB, 58; Southern Ill Univ, MA, 60, PhD(health, psychol), 66. *Prof Exp:* Instr health educ, Southern Ill Univ, 61-66, supvr student teachers, Dept Health Educ, 63-66; consult psychologist & dir ment health educ, Maine Bur Ment Health, 66-67; exec dir, Maine Comn Rehab Needs, 67-70 & Maine Health Coun, 70-72; prof spec educ, 71-73, dir health educ ctr, 72-73, chmn dept, 73-80, PROF HEALTH SCI, UNIV MAINE, FARMINGTON, 73- *Concurrent Pos:* Coordr health training, Peace Corps Projs, Southern Ill Univ, 64; chmn, Nat Comt Ment Health Educ, 67, historian, 67-; res consult, Maine's Regional Med Prog, 70-71; secy, Maine's Health Educ Consortium, 73-76; consult, Nat Instrnl TV, 74-76; trustee, Maine's Health Syst Agency, 75-76. *Mem:* Am Pub Health Asn; Am Psychol Asn; Nat Rehab Asn. *Res:* Attitudinal effects of rural preceptorships on medical and dental students in a health maintenance organization; dynamics of activating patients toward preventive health practices; mental health education. *Mailing Add:* Dept of Health Sci Univ of Maine Farmington ME 04938

DORAN, THOMAS J, JR, b Brooklyn, NY, Dec 31, 42; m 64; c 4. ORGANIC CHEMISTRY. *Educ:* Case Inst Technol, BS, 62; Western Reserve Univ, PhD(chem), 67. *Prof Exp:* Sr res chemist, 66-77, RES SUPVR BIOCHEM, CHEM DIV, PPG INDUSTS, INC, 77- *Mem:* Am Chem Soc. *Res:* Organic synthesis; nuclear magnetic resonance spectroscopy; environmental chemistry; metabolism; agricultural chemicals. *Mailing Add:* 496 Parkway Blvd Norton OH 44203

DORAN, WILLIAM THOMAS, b New York, NY, July 31, 10; m 32, 50; c 4. OCCUPATIONAL MEDICINE, PUBLIC HEALTH. *Educ:* Dartmouth Col, AB, 30; Cornell Univ, MD, 34; Johns Hopkins Univ, DPH, 51; Am Bd Prev Med, dipl, 59. *Prof Exp:* Intern med & surg, Bellevue Hosp, New York, 34-36; resident surg, Lawrence Hosp, Bronxville, 36-37; practicing surgeon, 37-42; chief ed, Dept Med & Surg, Vet Admin, 46-50; med dir occup health, Social Security Admin, Bur Old Age & Survivors Ins, 51-56; med dir, US Army Engr Ctr & Develop Labs, 56-62; chief physician oper health & safety, AEC, 62-66, chief occup med staff, Div Oper Health & Safety, 66-71; CHIEF OCCUP HEALTH & EMPLOYEE HEALTH, ST ELIZABETH'S HOSP, NIMH, 71- *Concurrent Pos:* Mem, President's Comt Med Rec, Bur Budget, 47-50; consult, Div Prev Med, Army Surgeon Gen Off, 50-51; lectr, Sch Hyg & Pub Health, Johns Hopkins Univ, 52-54; chmn arrangements, Am Indust Health Conf, 64, chmn prog, 65, mem long range prog planning comt, 64-66; mem bd dirs, Va State Ment Health Asn, 76, Northern Va Ment Health Asn, Mt Vernon Community Ment Health Ctr & Am Cancer Soc, DC, 75. *Mem:* Fel Am Col Prev Med; fel Am Occup Med Asn; fel Am Pub Health Asn. *Res:* National medical program planning in fields of medical administration, public health, occupational health, nuclear medicine, medical education and medical care. *Mailing Add:* St Elizabeth's Hosp 2700 Martin Luther King Ave SE Washington DC 20032

DORATO, PETER, b New York, NY, Dec 17, 32; m 56; c 4. ELECTRICAL ENGINEERING. *Educ:* City Col New York, BEE, 55; Columbia Univ, MSEE, 56; Polytech Inst Brooklyn, DEE, 61. *Prof Exp:* Instr elec eng, City Col New York, 56-57; assoc prof, Polytech Inst Brooklyn, 57-72; prof, Univ Colo, Colorado Springs, 72-76; PROF ELEC & COMPUT ENG & CHMN DEPT, UNIV NMEX, 76- *Concurrent Pos:* Vis prof, Univ Colo, Boulder, 69-70. *Mem:* Fel Inst Elec & Electronics Engrs. *Res:* Control theory; stability; systems analysis; solar energy systems. *Mailing Add:* Dept of Elec Eng & Comput Sci Univ of NMex Albuquerque NM 87131

D'ORAZIO, VINCENT T, b Joliet, Ill, Dec 28, 29; m 54; c 2. ORGANIC CHEMISTRY. *Educ:* Univ Ill, BS, 52; Mich State Univ, PhD(org chem), 63. *Prof Exp:* Supv chemist, US Rubber Co, 52-54; SR RES CHEMIST, S C JOHNSON & SON, INC, 63- *Mem:* AAAS; fel Am Inst Chem; Am Chem Soc; Royal Soc Chem. *Res:* Synthesis of heterocyclic organic compounds; synthesis of insecticides related to pyrethrins, pyrethrum cultivation extraction and technology; development of insecticidal products and insect repellents. *Mailing Add:* S C Johnson & Son Inc 1525 Howe St Racine WI 53406

DORCHESTER, JOHN EDMUND CARLETON, b Vancouver, BC, Aug 18, 17; nat US; m 44; c 3. PHYSIOLOGY, BIOCHEMISTRY. *Educ:* Univ BC, BA, 47, MA, 48; Univ Toronto, PhD(physiol, biochem), 52. *Prof Exp:* Asst, Univ Toronto, 49-52; from instr to asst prof physiol, Jefferson Med Col, 53-60; vchmn dept, 65-67, prof sci, 60-80, PROF BIOL, WEST CHESTER STATE COL, 80- *Mem:* Am Physiol Soc. *Res:* Thermal tolerance in fish; gastrointestinal hormones; hormonal assay methods; gastrointestinal innervation and relation to structure and hormones; effects of tranquilizers on gastrointestinal motility. *Mailing Add:* Box 195 Pine Creek Rd Chester Springs PA 19425

DORDICK, HERBERT S(HALOM), b Philadelphia, Pa, Oct 20, 25; m 48; c 2. ELECTRICAL ENGINEERING, SYSTEMS ANALYSIS. *Educ:* Swarthmore Col, BSEE, 49; Univ Pa, MSEE, 57. *Prof Exp:* Res & develop engr, Leeds & Northrup Co, Pa, 49-54; systs engr & mgr advan proj, Radio Corp Am, 54-62; dir eng, Electronic Instruments Div, Burroughs Corp, 62-64; group leader & sr mem res staff, Rand Corp, 64-68; dep dir res & spec projs, Syst Develop Corp, 68-69; pres, Info Transfer Corp, 69-71; dir, Off Telecommun, City New York, 71-73; ASSOC PROF COMMUN SCI & ASSOC DIR CTR COMMUN POLICY RES, ANNENBERG SCH COMMUN, UNIV SOUTHERN CALIF, 73- *Concurrent Pos:* Contrib researcher, President's Task Force Telecommun Policy, 44-46; vis scholar, Ctr Int Studies, Mass Inst Technol, 78-79; consult to indust, govt, educ insts, and nat and int foundations, 61- *Mem:* AAAS; Inst Elec & Electronics Engrs; Am Inst Aeronaut & Astronaut; Opers Res Soc Am. *Res:* Communications policy and planning; cable television; broadcast and common carrier policy; computer networks; information systems and services; communications engineering; public television; educational television; diffusion of innovation. *Mailing Add:* Annenberg Sch of Commun Univ of Southern Calif Los Angeles CA 90007

DORDICK, ISADORE, b Riga, Latvia, June 14, 11; US citizen; m 54. MEDICAL GEOGRAPHY. *Educ:* Univ Pa, BA, 33, MA, 37; Johns Hopkins Univ, PhD(geog), 52. *Prof Exp:* Res assoc physiol, Mt Sinai Hosp, 38-39, res ed, 40-42; librn, Libr Cong, 42-44; biologist, Off Quarter Master Gen War Dept, 44-45; res analyst, Dept State, 45-47; climatologist, Am Meteorol Soc, 52-58; consult bioclimat, Sales Productivity Serv, 58-62; CLIMATOLOGIST, AM METEOROL SOC, 62- *Concurrent Pos:* Consult climat, 62- *Mem:* Am Meteorol Soc; Asn Am Geog. *Res:* Bioclimatolog with pecticular regard to the effect of climate on human work; medical climatology; applied climatology in business and engineering. *Mailing Add:* Apt 1804 900 N Lake Shore Dr Chicago IL 60611

DOREMUS, ROBERT HEWARD, b Denver, Colo, Sept 16, 28; m 56; c 4. GLASS SCIENCE, FRACTURE. *Educ:* Univ Colo, BS, 50; Univ Ill, MS, 51, PhD(phys chem), 53; Cambridge Univ, PhD(phys chem), 56. *Prof Exp:* Phys chemist, res lab, Gen Elec Co, 55-71; NEW YORK STATE PROF GLASS & CERAMICS, RENSSELAER POLYTECH INST, 71- *Honors & Awards:* Purdy Award, Am Ceramic Soc. *Mem:* AAAS; fel Am Ceramic Soc. *Res:* Glass science; crystallization from solution; optical properties of metals; diffusion; precipitation in metals; ionic binding to polyelectrolytes; biomaterials. *Mailing Add:* Materials Sci Dept Rensselaer Polytech Inst Troy NY 12181

DORENBUSCH, WILLIAM EDWIN, b Hamilton, Ohio, Mar 14, 36; m 64. NUCLEAR PHYSICS. *Educ:* Univ Notre Dame, BS, 58, PhD(nuclear physics), 62. *Prof Exp:* Instr physics, Univ Notre Dame, 62-63; instr, Mass Inst Technol, 63-65, asst prof, 65-69; ASSOC PROF PHYSICS, WAYNE STATE UNIV, 69- *Mem:* Am Phys Soc. *Res:* Ion-solid interactions; charged particle spectroscopy with nuclear reactions. *Mailing Add:* Dept of Physics Wayne State Univ Detroit MI 48202

DORENFELD, ADRIAN C, b Brooklyn, NY, Dec 16, 19; m 42; c 3. METALLURGICAL & MINING ENGINEERING. *Educ:* Columbia Univ, BS, 40, EM, 41. *Prof Exp:* Operator, Utah Copper Co, 41; metallurgist, US Vanadium Co, 41-42; mill supt, Callahan Zinc-Lead Co, 42; chief metallurgist, Mammoth-St Anthony Co, 42-43; metallurgist, Combined Metals Co, 43-45; foreman, Phelps Dodge Corp, 45-50; from asst prof to assoc prof mineral eng, Univ Ala, 51-54; sr mineral engr, C F Braun & Co, 54-56; gen mgr mines, Roberts & Assocs, 56-60; ASSOC PROF MINERAL ENG, UNIV MINN, MINNEAPOLIS, 60- *Concurrent Pos:* Consult, Pac Uranium Inc, 55-60; Israel Mining Industs, 56-62,Tec Trans Int Ltd, 75- & Harbridge House Inc, 77-; Consult to various companies. *Mem:* Am Inst Mining, Metall & Petrol Engrs; Can Inst Mining & Metall. *Res:* Examination, management and design of mineral projects; application of statistics to mineral processing; mineral economics and feasibility studies. *Mailing Add:* 5337 Sailor Lane Minneapolis MN 55429

DORER, CASPER JOHN, b Cleveland, Ohio, Sept 25, 22; m 46; c 2. FUEL SCIENCE & TECHNOLOGY. *Educ:* Case Western Reserve Univ, BS, 43. *Prof Exp:* Res assoc res & develop chem, Case Western Reserve Univ, 44-48 & Carl F Prutton & Assocs, 48-50; vpres, Cleveland Indust Res, 50-72; prof mgr fuel additives, 72-77, proj mgr & admin asst res & develop, 77-81, MGR RES FUEL ADDITIVES, LUBRIZOL CORP, 81- *Mem:* Am Chem Soc. *Res:* Additives for fuels and lubricants. *Mailing Add:* 4852 Fairlawn Rd Lyndhurst OH 44124

DORER, FREDERIC EDMUND, b Cleveland, Ohio, Aug 24, 33; m 61; c 3. BIOCHEMISTRY. *Educ:* Case Western Reserve Univ, AB, 55, MS, 56; State Univ NY, PhD(biochem), 61. *Prof Exp:* Fel biochem, Sch Med, Univ Wis, 61-63; chemist, radioisotope serv, Vet Admin Hosp, 63-68; sr instr biochem, 69-73, ASST PROF BIOCHEM, CASE WESTERN RESERVE UNIV, 73-; RES CHEMIST, VET ADMIN HOSP, 68- *Mem:* Am Soc Biol Chemists; AAAS; Am Chem Soc; NY Acad Sci; Am Soc Pharmacol & Exp Ther. *Res:* Experimental renal hypertension; occurrence and metabolism of biologically active peptides. *Mailing Add:* Vet Admin Hosp 10701 East Blvd Cleveland OH 44106

DOREY, CHERYL KATHLEEN, b Wellsville, NY, Sept 7, 44; m 67. CELL BIOLOGY, HISTOCHEMISTRY. *Educ:* State Univ NY Buffalo, BA, 66; Univ Mass, MA, 68; Georgetown Univ, PhD(cell biol & histochem), 75. *Prof Exp:* Res asst electron microscopy, Litton Bionetics, Inc, 69-72, scientist histochem, 72-75; fel biochem & develop biol, Univ Southern Calif, 75-78; ASST PROF RES OPTHAL, SCH DENT MED, SOUTHERN ILL UNIV, 78- *Mem:* Am Soc Cell Biol; Tissue Cult Asn; Am Histochem Soc; Int Asn Dent Res. *Res:* Control of the endothelial cell cycle by a cartilage factor; diabetic microangiopathy; osteogenesis. *Mailing Add:* Dept of Biomed Sci Southern Ill Univ Edwardsville IL 62026

DORF, MARTIN EDWARD, b Bound Brook, NJ, May 16, 44; m 76; c 1. IMMUNOGENETICS. *Educ:* Rutgers Univ, BA, 66; Duke Univ, MA & PhD(immunogenetics), 72. *Prof Exp:* Exchange fel immunogenetics, Hosp St Louis, Paris, 71-72; res fel, 72-73; instr, 74-75, asst prof path, 75-77, ASSOC PROF PATH, HARVARD MED SCH, 77- *Mem:* Am Asn Immunologists; Am Asn Pathologists; Transplantation Soc; AAAS. *Res:* Analysis of the mechanisms and genetic control of immune responses and immunoregulation with emphasis on the roles of the major histocompatibility and immunoglobulin gene complexes. *Mailing Add:* Dept Path Harvard Med Sch 25 Shattuck St Boston MA 02115

DORF, RICHARD C, b New York, NY, Dec 27, 33; m 56; c 2. ELECTRICAL ENGINEERING. *Educ:* Clarkson Tech Univ, BSEE, 55; Univ Colo, MSEE, 57; US Naval Postgrad Sch, PhD(elec eng), 61. *Prof Exp:* Instr elec eng, Clarkson Tech Univ, 56-58; res assoc, Univ NMex, 58-59; instr, US Naval Postgrad Sch, 59-61; lectr, Univ Edinburgh, 61-62; assoc prof, US Naval Postgrad Sch, 62-63; from assoc prof to prof, Univ Santa Clara, 63-69, chmn dept, 63-69; dean col eng & & vpres educ serv, 69-72; dean extended learning, 72-81, PROF ELEC ENG, UNIV CALIF, DAVIS, 72-, PROF, GRAD SCH ADMIN, 81- *Mem:* Fel Inst Elec & Electronics Engrs; Am Soc Eng Educ. *Res:* Analysis and design of automatic control systems; design of digital control systems; engineering management. *Mailing Add:* Dept Extended Learning Univ Calif Davis CA 95616

DORFMAN, ALBERT, b Chicago, Ill, July 6, 16; m 40; c 2. BIOCHEMISTRY, PEDIATRICS. *Educ:* Univ Chicago, BS, 36, PhD(biochem), 39, MD, 44. *Prof Exp:* Asst biochem, 37-40, res assoc, 40-43, from instr to prof pediat, 48-64, prof pediat & biochem, 64-65, chmn dept, 62-72, RICHARD T CRANE DISTINGUISHED SERV PROF PEDIAT & BIOCHEM, SCH MED, UNIV CHICAGO, 65-; DIR JOSEPH P KENNEDY, JR MENT RETARDATION RES CTR, 65- *Concurrent Pos:* With Off Sci Res & Develop, 44; chief biochem, US Army Med Dept Res & Grad Sch, 46-48; dir res, La Rabida Jackson Park Sanitarium, 50-; dir, La Rabida-Univ Chicago Inst, 57-69; mem coun rheumatic fever, Am Heart Asn; mem comt genetics. *Honors & Awards:* Mead Johnson Award, 57; Borden Award, 70. *Mem:* Nat Inst Med; Am Chem Soc; Am Soc Biol Chem; Am Pediat Soc; Am Acad Arts & Sci. *Res:* Bacterial nutrition and metabolism; mechanism of drug action; chemistry of connective tissue; developmental biology; human genetics; rheumatic fever. *Mailing Add:* Dept of Pediat Univ of Chicago Sch of Med Chicago IL 60637

DORFMAN, DONALD, b Bronx, NY, Mar 5, 34; m 54; c 4. FRESH WATER & MARINE BIOLOGY. *Educ:* Monmouth Col (NJ), BS, 66; Univ Conn, MS, 68; Rutgers Univ, PhD(environ sci), 70. *Prof Exp:* Res asst fisheries, Univ Conn, 66-68; res asst environ sci, Rutgers Univ, 68-70; ASSOC PROF BIOL, MONMOUTH COL, NJ, 70- *Concurrent Pos:* Chmn, Environ Assessment Coun, 73-; adj prof, Rutgers Univ, 74- *Mem:* Am Fisheries Soc. *Res:* Effect of lead on growth of brook trout; responses of anadromous fishes to increased temperature and decreased oxygen concentration; fish scrum proteins. *Mailing Add:* Dept of Biol Monmouth Col West Long Branch NJ 07764

DORFMAN, EDWIN, organic chemistry, polymer chemistry, deceased

DORFMAN, HOWARD DAVID, b New York, NY, July 20, 28; m 52; c 3. PATHOLOGY. *Educ:* NY Univ, BA, 47; State Univ NY, MD, 51. *Prof Exp:* Intern, Maimonides Hosp Brooklyn, 51-52; resident path & microbiol, Mt Sinai Hosp, New York, 52-54; resident surg path, Columbia Presby Med Ctr, 54-58; pathologist & dir labs, Sharon & New Milford Hosps, Conn, 58-59; asst pathologist, Sinai Hosp Baltimore, 59-61, assoc pathologist, 62-64; dir labs & pathologist, Hosp Joint Dis & Med Ctr, 64-77; ASSOC PROF PATH & ORTHOP SURG, SCH MED, JOHNS HOPKINS UNIV, 77- *Concurrent Pos:* Asst surgery, Col Physicians & Surgeons, Columbia Univ, 57-58, asst prof, 65-67; asst prof, Med Sch, Johns Hopkins Univ, 63-64; staff pathologist, Johns Hopkins Hosp, 63-64; from assoc prof to prof clin path, Mt Sinai Sch Med, 67-74; mem staff, Sinai Hosp Baltimore, 74-; consult, Nat Cancer Inst. *Mem:* Orthop Res Inst; fel NY Acad Med; Int Acad Path; fel Am Soc Clin Path; Int Skeletal Soc. *Res:* Pathology of bone tumors and joint diseases with particular reference to rheumatoid athritis, neoplasms, secondary to pre-existing bone disease, osteoblastic tumors and vascular tumors of the bone. *Mailing Add:* Sinai Hosp Baltimore Belvedere Ave at Greenspring Baltimore MD 21215

DORFMAN, JAY ROBERT, b Pittsburgh, Pa, May 20, 37; m 60; c 3. THEORETICAL PHYSICS, STATISTICAL MECHANICS. *Educ:* Johns Hopkins Univ, BA, 57, PhD(physics), 61. *Prof Exp:* Res assoc physics, Rockefeller Inst, 61-64; from asst prof to assoc prof, dept physics & astron & Inst Fluid Dynamics & Applied Math, 64-72, PROF DEPT PHYSICS & ASTRON & INST FLUID DYNAMICS & APPLIED MATH, UNIV MD, COLLEGE PARK, 72- *Concurrent Pos:* Vis assoc prof, Rockefeller Univ, 69-70. *Mem:* Am Phys Soc. *Res:* Kinetic theory; theory of transport processes. *Mailing Add:* Dept of Physics & Astron Univ of Md College Park MD 20742

DORFMAN, LEON MONTE, b Winnipeg, Man, June 9, 22; nat US; m 48; c 3. CHEMICAL KINETICS, RADIATION CHEMISTRY. *Educ:* Univ Man, BSc, 44; Univ Toronto, MA, 45, PhD(chem), 47. *Prof Exp:* Fel, Univ Rochester, 47-48; instr chem, 48-50; res assoc, Knolls Atomic Power Lab, Gen Elec Co, 50-57; sr chemist, Argonne Nat Lab, 57-64; chmn dept, 68-77, PROF CHEM, OHIO STATE UNIV, 64- *Concurrent Pos:* Consult, Argonne Nat Lab, 64-65 & Gen Dynamics Corp, 64-67; prof, Univ Toronto, 67; vis res scientist, Hebrew Univ, Jerusalem, 69; Guggenheim fel, 71-72; consult, Westinghouse Res Ctr, 74-76. *Honors & Awards:* Spinks lectr, Univ Sask, 81. *Mem:* Am Chem Soc; Am Phys Soc; Radiation Res Soc; Am Asn Univ Professors. *Res:* Chemical kinetics; fast reactions; radiation chemistry; spectroscopy of reactive transients. *Mailing Add:* Dept of Chem Ohio State Univ 140 W 18th Ave Columbus OH 43210

DORFMAN, LESLIE JOSEPH, b Montreal Que, Can, Sept 11, 43. NEUROLOGY, CLINICAL NEUROPHYSIOLOGY. *Educ:* McGill Univ, BSc, 64; Albert Einstein Col Med, MD, 68. *Prof Exp:* Fel electromyography, Nat Hosp, Queen Square, London, 74; instr neurol, 73-74, asst prof, 74-80, ASSOC PROF NEUROL, STANFORD UNIV MED CTR, 80- *Concurrent Pos:* Stanford dir, Lab Electromyography, Evoked Potential Lab, Multiple Sclerosis Clinic, Adult Neuromuscular Disorders Clinic, 74-; attend physician, Standford Univ Hosp, 74-; consult neurol, Palo Alto Vet Admin Med Ctr, 74-; consult neurol, Rehab Eng Res & Develop Ctr, Palo Alto, 79- *Mem:* AAAS; Am Acad Neurol; Can Neurol Soc; Am Asn Electromyography & Electrodiagnosis; Am EEG Soc. *Res:* Application of signal processing techniques to clinical electrophysiology for diagnosis of neurological disorders. *Mailing Add:* Dept Neurol Rm C338 Stanford Univ Med Ctr Stanford CA 94305

DORFMAN, MYRON HERBERT, b Shreveport, La, July 3, 27; c 2. GEOTHERMAL ENGINEERING, PETROLEUM GEOLOGY. *Educ:* Univ Tex, Austin, BS, 50, MS, 74, PhD(petrol eng), 75. *Prof Exp:* Engr & geologist, Sklar Oil Co, 50-56, mgr prod exp, 56-57, vpres, 57-59; owner, Dorfman Oil Properties, 59-71; from asst prof to prof petrol eng, 74-80, H B Harkins prof, 80, DIR GEOTHERMAL STUDIES, CTR ENERGY STUDIES, UNIV TEX, AUSTIN, 74-, CHMN, DEPT PETROL ENG, 78- *Concurrent Pos:* Prin investr, Geopressured Geothermal Energy Prog, Dept Energy, 74-81; mem steering comt, Geothermal Adv Comt, Dept Energy, 75-, Geothermal Reservoir Mgt Prog, 76- & Geothermal Well Logging Prog, Sandia Nat Lab, 77- *Mem:* Nat Acad Sci; AAAS; Am Asn Petrol Geologists; fel Geol Soc Am; Soc Petrol Engrs. *Res:* Geopressured geothermal energy; well-logging in hostile environments underground. *Mailing Add:* PEB 211 Univ Tex Austin TX 78712

DORFMAN, RALPH ISADORE, b Chicago, Ill, June 30, 11; m 33; c 2. BIOCHEMISTRY. *Educ:* Univ Ill, BS, 32; Univ Chicago, PhD(physiol chem, pharmacol), 34. *Prof Exp:* Asst physiol chem, Univ Chicago, 33-35; instr pharmacol, Sch Med, La State Univ, 35-36; from instr to asst prof physiol chem, Yale Univ, 36-41; asst prof biochem, Western Reserve Univ & chemist, Brush Found, 41-49, assoc prof, 49-51; from assoc dir to dir labs, Worcester Found Exp Biol, 51-64; dir, Inst Hormone Biol, Syntex Res Div, Syntex Corp, 64-69, from sr vpres to exec vpres, 64-73, pres, 73-76; CONSULT PROF, SCH MED, STANFORD UNIV, 73- *Concurrent Pos:* Res prof, Boston Univ, 51-67; affil prof, Clark Univ, 56-64; vis prof, Sch Med, Stanford Univ, 67-73; consult, Adv Panel Metab Biol, Div Biol & Med Sci, NSF & sub-chmn comt standardization of androgens, US Pharmacopoeia; mem endocrinol panel, Cancer Chemother Nat Serv Ctr, USPHS chmn subcomt biol activ, Endocrinol Panel; mem sci adv comt, Nat Better Bus Bur, Inc, exec & prog comts, 2nd Int Cong Endocrinol & Int Comt Steroid Hormones. *Mem:* Nat Acad Sci; fel AAAS; fel Am Acad Arts & Sci; Am Chem Soc; fel NY Acad Sci. *Res:* Steroid biochemistry; bioassay; endocrinology; reproductive physiology. *Mailing Add:* 1046 S Berkshire Dr Los Altos Hills CA 94022

DORFMAN, S(TEVEN) D(AVID), b Brooklyn, NY, Sept 26, 35; m; c 1. ELECTRICAL ENGINEERING. *Educ:* Univ Fla, BSEE, 57; Univ Southern Calif, MSEE, 59. *Prof Exp:* Mem tech staff, 57-61, staff engr, 62, sect head, 62-64, proj mgr, 65-67, mgr earth observation systs, Advan Proj Labs, Space Systs Div, 67-69, mgr advan prog, Space & Commun Group, NASA Prog Div, 69-74, mgr, Pioneer Venus Prog, 74-78, asst mgr, 78-81, ASSOC MGR, NASA SYSTS DIV, SPACE & COMMUN GROUP, HUGHES AIRCRAFT CO, 81- *Res:* Management of technical projects; systems design analysis and engineering; infrared sensing systems. *Mailing Add:* NASA Systs Div S41-B355 PO Box 92919 El Segundo CA 90245

DORGAN, WILLIAM JOSEPH, b Davenport, Iowa, Dec 27, 38; m 65; c 2. DEVELOPMENTAL BIOLOGY, CELL BIOLOGY. *Educ:* St Ambrose Col, BA, 61; Creighton Univ, MS, 63; Univ Colo, PhD(anat), 68. *Prof Exp:* From asst prof to assoc prof zool, 68-80, ASSOC PROF ANAT, MONT STATE UNIV, 80- *Mem:* AAAS; Soc Develop Biol; Am Asn Univ Prof. *Res:* Programmed death in embryonic development and abnormal development; programmed death in rat placental giant cells in vitro; studies on the photodynamic action of vital dyes in embryonic systems. *Mailing Add:* Dept of Biol Mont State Univ Bozeman MT 59715

DORHEIM, FREDRICK HOUGE, b Bedger, Iowa, Nov 12, 12; m 39; c 1. ECONOMIC GEOLOGY. *Educ:* Iowa State Col, BS, 38, MS, 50. *Prof Exp:* Chief geologist, Iowa State Hwy Comn, 46-50 & B L Anderson, Inc, 50-56; geologist, 56-69, chief econ geol, 56-75, CHIEF GEOLOGIST, IOWA GEOL SURV, 75-; consult, Indust Minerals & Sanit Landfills, 57-78; RETIRED. *Concurrent Pos:* Chmn, Forum Geol Indust Minerals, 72. *Mem:* Am Inst Prof Geol Sci; Am Asn Petrol Geologists. *Res:* Geophysical study of sand and gravel resources in northwest Iowa; geophysical study of area of gypsum occurrence in the Fort Dodge area; geology of Floyd County, Iowa. *Mailing Add:* 3322 Hanover Ct Iowa City IA 52240

DORIAN, WILLIAM D, b Timisoara, Romania, Mar 4, 21; Can citizen; m 44; c 2. INTERNAL MEDICINE. *Educ:* Univ Cluj, Romania, MD, 48; FRCPC(c), 70. *Prof Exp:* EXEC DIR MED RES, MERCK FROSST LABS, 73- *Concurrent Pos:* Staff physician, St Mary's Hosp, Montreal, 66-; affil, Montreal Gen Hosp, 67-; lectr, Dept Med, McGill Univ, 70- *Mem:* NY Acad Sci; Am Acad Allery. *Res:* Clinical pharmacology; cardiovascular, antiinflammatory, antibiotic agents. *Mailing Add:* Merck Frosst Labs PO Box 1005 Pointe Claire-Dorval PQ H9R 4P8 Can

DORITY, GUY HIRAM, b Canandaigua, NY, Jan 2, 33. ORGANIC CHEMISTRY. *Educ:* Oglethorpe Univ, BS, 54; Univ NC, MA, 59; Univ Hawaii, PhD(chem), 65. *Prof Exp:* From instr to asst prof chem, 63-71, ASSOC PROF CHEM, UNIV HAWAII, HILO, 71- *Concurrent Pos:* Vis scientist, Nat Biol Inst, Indonesia, 70-71; leader, training course natural prod chem, SE Asian Ministries of Educ Orgn. *Mem:* Am Chem Soc; Sigma Xi. *Res:* Aromatic and heterocyclic fluorine compounds; natural products from Polynesian and Southeast Asian medicinal plants. *Mailing Add:* Dept of Chem Univ of Hawaii Hilo HI 96720

DORKO, ERNEST A, b Detroit, Mich, Sept 16, 36. ORGANIC CHEMISTRY, PHYSICAL CHEMISTRY. *Educ:* Univ Detroit, BChE, 59; Univ Chicago, MS, 61, PhD(org chem), 64. *Prof Exp:* Res chemist, Phys Sci Lab, US Army Missile Command, Redstone Arsenal, Ala, 64-67; from asst prof to assoc prof, 67-77, PROF CHEM, AIR FORCE INST TECHNOL, 77- *Concurrent Pos:* Consult, Wright-Patterson AFB, 68- & Wright Aeronaut Labs, 75- *Mem:* AAAS; Am Chem Soc. *Res:* Synthesis of small ring organic compounds; infrared and normal coordinate analysis; shock-tube kinetics of pollution reactions; chemiluminescence reactions in flow tubes; laser dyes. *Mailing Add:* AFIT/ENP Air Force Inst Technol Wright-Patterson AFB OH 45433

DORMAAR, JOHAN FREDERIK, b Djakarta, Indonesia, Feb 16, 30; Can citizen; m 55; c 3. SOIL CHEMISTRY. *Educ:* Univ Toronto, BSA, 57, MSA, 58; Univ Alta, PhD(soil chem), 61. *Prof Exp:* Asst soil chem, Univ Alta, 58-61, lectr, 61-62; res scientist, Agr Res Sta, Can Dept Agr, 62-75, SR RES SCIENTIST, RES STA, AGR CAN, 75- *Mem:* Soil Sci Soc Am; Can Soc Soil Sci; Int Asn Quaternary Res; Am Quaternary Asn; Soc Archaeol Sci. *Res:* Organic matter of chernozemic soils, formation and present properties as influenced by parent material, various grass species and man-induced pressures; lignin chemistry as related to soil organic matter; effect of pseudo-gley on soil organic matter; palaeosols. *Mailing Add:* Soil Sci Sect Res Sta Agr Can Lethbridge Can

DORMAN, CLIVE EDGAR, b Granite City, Ill, Nov 30, 42; m 67; c 1. PHYSICAL OCEANOGRAPHY, METEOROLOGY. *Educ:* Univ Calif, Riverside, BA, 65; Ore State Univ, MS, 72, PhD(phys oceanog), 74. *Prof Exp:* Assoc prof oceanog, 74-80, ASSOC PROF GEOL, SAN DIEGO STATE UNIV, 80- *Mem:* Am Meteorol Soc; Am Geophys Union. *Res:* Air-sea interaction; climatology; coastal oceanography. *Mailing Add:* Dept of Geol Sci San Diego State Univ San Diego CA 92182

DORMAN, DOUGLAS EARL, b Burbank, Calif, Mar 9, 40; m 68; c 2. SPECTROCHEMISTRY. *Educ:* Univ Calif, Los Angeles, BS, 63; Brandeis Univ, MA, 65, PhD(org chem), 67. *Prof Exp:* NIH fel biogenesis, Univ Sussex, 67-68; NIH fel nuclear magnetic resonance, Calif Inst Technol, 68-71; mem tech staff, Bell Labs, 71-73; sr phys chemist nuclear magnetic resonance, 73-75, RES SCIENTIST, MOLECULAR STRUCT, LILLY RES LABS, 75- *Mem:* Am Chem Soc; The Chem Soc. *Res:* Determination of molecular structure by physical and chemical methods. *Mailing Add:* MCM 525 Lilly Res Lab Indianapolis IN 46206

DORMAN, HENRY JAMES, b Chicago, Ill, Mar 21, 28; m 57; c 2. GEOPHYSICS. *Educ:* Carleton Col, BA, 49; Northwestern Univ, MS, 51; Columbia Univ, PhD(geophys), 61. *Prof Exp:* Res scientist, Lamont-Doherty Geol Observ, Columbia Univ, 60-63, sr res assoc, 63-72, asst dir, 65-72, lectr geol, Univ, 66-72; prof geophys, Univ Tex Med Br, 72-74; RES SCIENTIST, MARINE SCI INST, UNIV TEX, GALVESTON, 74-, PROF GEOL SCI, 75-, PROF MARINE SCI, 76- *Concurrent Pos:* Mem, Panel Solid Earth Probs, Geophys Res Bd, Nat Acad Sci, 62-63; lectr geol, Univ Wis, 63; mem, Village Planning Bd, Pomona, NY, 67-72; consult, Consol Edison Co, New York, 68-; mem, Mayor Lindsay's Oceanog Adv Comt, 69-73; adj prof geol, Rice Univ, 74-78. *Mem:* Soc Explor Geophysicists; AAAS; Seismol Soc Am; Am Geophys Union; fel Geol Soc Am. *Res:* Structural geology; exploration seismology; long-period surface waves and free oscillations; model seismology; seismic inverse problem; crust and mantle structure; microearthquake studies; seismicity; lunar seismology; numerical analysis and computer applications. *Mailing Add:* Univ of Tex Marine Sci Inst Geophys Lab 700 The Strand Galveston TX 77550

DORMAN, HOMER LEE, b Denton, Tex, Sept 23, 30; m 52; c 4. PHYSIOLOGY, BIOCHEMISTRY. *Educ:* NTex State Univ, BA, 50, MA, 51; Univ Ill, PhD(physiol), 57. *Prof Exp:* From asst prof to assoc prof, 57-62, PROF PHYSIOL, BAYLOR COL DENT, 62-, CHMN DEPT, 69- *Concurrent Pos:* Consult, Baylor Univ Med Ctr, 60-63, artificial heart-lung operator, 60-63; consult, Sammons Res Inst, 63-71; abstractor, Am Dent Asn, 65. *Mem:* AAAS; Am Physiol Soc; Int Asn Dent Res. *Res:* Cardiovascular and metabolic factors involving the oral cavity; pain; remodeling of bone by pressures. *Mailing Add:* Dept Physiol Baylor Col Dent 3302 Gaston Ave Dallas TX 75246

DORMAN, LEROY MYRON, b Virginia, Minn, Oct 15, 38; m 59; c 3. GEOPHYSICS. *Educ:* Ga Inst Technol, BS, 60; Univ Wis, MS, 69, PhD(geophys), 70. *Prof Exp:* Asst res physicist, Ga Inst Technol, 63-66; res asst geophys, Univ Wis, 66-69; Carnegie fel, Carnegie Inst, 69-71; res geophysicist, Atlantic Oceanog & Meteorol Lab, Nat Oceanic & Atmospheric Admin, 71-73; asst res geophysicist & lectr, 73-75, assoc res geophysicist & lectr, 75-77, ASSOC PROF GEOPHYS, SCRIPPS INST OCEANOG, UNIV CALIF, SAN DIEGO, 78- *Mem:* Am Geophys Union; Seismol Soc Am; Soc Explor Geophysicists. *Res:* Theoretical and experimental seismology; isostasy; marine geophysics. *Mailing Add:* Scripps Inst of Oceanog A-015 Univ of Calif at San Diego La Jolla CA 92093

DORMAN, LINNEAUS CUTHBERT, b Orangeburg, SC, June 28, 35; m 58; c 2. MEDICINAL CHEMISTRY. *Educ:* Bradley Univ, BS, 56; Ind Univ, PhD(org chem), 61. *Prof Exp:* Res chemist, 60-68, sr res chemist, 68-72, res specialist, 72-76, sr res specialist, Cent Res-Plastics Lab, 76-79, RES ASSOC, POLYMER RES LAB, DOW CHEM CO, 79- *Mem:* AAAS; Am Chem Soc; Sigma Xi. *Res:* Organic synthesis; pharmaceutical chemistry; synthesis of heterocyclic compounds; diagnostic reagents; peptide synthesis; materials science. *Mailing Add:* Cent Res-Polymer Labs 1712 Bldg Dow Chem Co Midland MI 48640

DORMAN, ROBERT VINCENT, b Niles, Mich, July 2, 49; m 76; c 2. BIOCHEMISTRY. *Educ:* Villanova Univ, BS, 71; Ohio State Univ, PhD(physiol chem), 76. *Prof Exp:* Res chemist neurobiol, Vet Admin, 76-78; res assoc neurochem, Ohio State Univ, 78-81; ASST PROF, DREXEL UNIV, 81- *Concurrent Pos:* NIH fel, 77-78. *Mem:* Am Soc Neurochem. *Res:* Phospholipid metabolism in nerve and muscle tissue, especially to phospholipases during development and pathoological conditions. *Mailing Add:* Dept Biol Sci Drexel Univ Philadelphia PA 19104

DORMANT, LEON M, b Paris, France, Oct 1, 40; US citizen. ENHANCED OIL RECOVERY. *Educ:* Drexel Inst, BS, 64; Univ Southern Calif, PhD(phys chem), 69, MS, 81. *Prof Exp:* Sr scientist, chem div, 3M Co, 68-70; sr scientist, Aerospace Corp, 71-75; sr scientist, Occidental Res Corp, 76-81; SR ENGR, HUSKY OIL LTD, 81- *Concurrent Pos:* Unilever fel, Bristol Univ, 70-71. *Mem:* AAAS; Am Chem Soc; Soc Petrol Engrs. *Res:* Surface and colloid chemistry; lubrication; enhanced oil recovery; physical adsorption. *Mailing Add:* Husky Oil LTD PO Box 1869 Santa Maria CA 93456

DORMER, KENNETH JOHN, b Ashland, Pa, Mar 10, 44; m 66; c 3. CARDIOVASCULAR PHYSIOLOGY, NEUROPHYSIOLOGY. *Educ:* Cornell Univ, BS, 66; Univ Calif, Los Angeles, MS, 69, PhD(biol), 74. *Prof Exp:* Fel cardiovasc control, Marine Biomed Inst, Univ Tex Med Br, 74-77; ASST PROF PHYSIOL, UNIV OKLA HEALTH SCI CTR, 77-, CLIN NEUROPHYSIOLOGIST, COCHLEAR IMPLANT CLINIC, CENT EAR RES INST, 79- *Concurrent Pos:* Nat Heart, Lung & Blood Inst fel, Univ Tex Med Br, 74-77; NIH grants, 78-81 & 81-84. *Mem:* Am Physiol Soc; Soc Exp Biol & Med; Am Sci Affil; Soc Neurosci; Von Bekesy Soc. *Res:* Neural control of the cardiovascular system; mechanisms of hypertension; auditory neuroprostheses (cochlear implant). *Mailing Add:* Dept Physiol & Biophysics PO Box 26901 Oklahoma City OK 73190

DORN, CHARLES RICHARD, b London, Ohio, June 12, 33; m 64; c 3. VETERINARY PREVENTIVE MEDICINE. *Educ:* Ohio State Univ, DVM, 57; Harvard Univ, MPH, 62; Am Bd Vet Pub Health, dipl. *Prof Exp:* Staff vet, Stark Animal Hosp, Canton, Ohio, 57-58; vet inspector, Cincinnati Health Dept, 60-61; USPHS trainee, 61-62; res specialist cancer, Calif State Dept Pub Health, 62-68; prof vet microbiol & community health & med pract, Univ Mo-

Columbia, 68-75; PROF VET PREV MED & CHMN DEPT, OHIO STATE UNIV, 75- *Concurrent Pos:* Lectr vet med, Univ Calif, Davis, 67-68; consult, Calif State Dept Pub Health, 68-70; vis scientist epidemiol, Nat Cancer Inst, 75-76. *Mem:* Am Vet Med Asn; fel Am Pub Health Asn; Conf Pub Health Vet; Asn Teachers Prev Med; Int Asn Comp Res Leukemia & Related Dis. *Res:* Cancer morbidity in dogs, cats and man; temporal and spatial distribution of leukemia and other malignancies; heavy metal contamination of foods; epidemiology of salmonellosis and other zoonoses. *Mailing Add:* Dept of Vet Prev Med Ohio State Univ Col of Vet Med Columbus OH 43210

DORN, CONRAD PETER, JR, b Baltimore, Md, Jan 15, 37; m 60; c 3. PHARMACEUTICAL CHEMISTRY. *Educ:* Univ Md, BS, 58, MS, 61, PhD(pharmaceut chem), 63. *Prof Exp:* Res fel, 62-80, SR RES FEL, MERCK SHARP & DOHME RES LABS, MERCK & CO, 80- *Res:* Steroid and heterocyclic steroid chemistry; synthesis of non-steroidal anti-inflammatory agents, non narcotics analgesics, vaccine adjuvants, pro-drugs, immunoregulants and protease inhibitors. *Mailing Add:* Merck Sharp & Dohme Res Labs 126 Lincoln Ave Rahway NJ 07065

DORN, DAVID W, b Detroit, Mich, June 25, 30; m 54; c 4. THEORETICAL NUCLEAR PHYSICS, RESEARCH ADMINISTRATION. *Educ:* Purdue Univ, BS, 52, PhD(physics), 59. *Prof Exp:* From res physicist to group leader physicist, 59-69, staff asst to assoc dir nuclear design, 69-72, prog mgr, Environ Studies Group, 72-75, prog mgr, Technol Appln Group, 75-78, PROG MGR ENERGY & RESOURCES PLANNING GROUP, LAWRENCE LIVERMORE NAT LAB, 78- *Concurrent Pos:* Mem tech subcomt, explosives tagging, alcohol, tobacco & firearms, US Dept Treas, 73-75; mem solar technician training prog adv comt, Univ Calif, 78- *Mem:* Am Phys Soc. *Res:* Utilization of results from scientific and engineering research; assessment of possible outcomes of adoption of technology; national and regional energy and resource problems; long range stategic planning. *Mailing Add:* Lawrence Livermore Nat Lab Univ Calif Livermore CA 94550

DORN, GORDON LEE, b Chicago, Ill, June 8, 37; m 59; c 1. MICROBIOLOGY. *Educ:* Purdue Univ, BS, 58, MS, 60, PhD(genetics), 61. *Prof Exp:* NSF fel, 61-63; univ res fel genetics, Albert Einstein Col Med, 63, asst prof, 64-68; chmn dept microbiol, Baylor Univ, 68-69; CHMN DEPT MICROBIOL & DIR CLIN MICROBIOL LABS, WADLEY INST MOLECULAR MED, 69- *Concurrent Pos:* Adj prof, NTex State Univ, 75-; pres, Dorn Microbiol Assocs Dallas, 78- *Mem:* AAAS; Am Genetic Asn; Genetics Soc Am; Am Soc Microbiol. *Res:* Phosphatases-esterases; gene enzymes; clinical microbiology diagnostics; interferon production from human leucocytes; fine genetic analysis; fermentation and antibiotics; microbiology; inventor of new blood culture device, Dupont isolator. *Mailing Add:* Wadley Inst of Molecular Med 9000 Harry Hines Blvd Dallas TX 75235

DORN, WILLIAM S, b Pittsburgh, Pa, July 12, 28; m 52; c 3. COMPUTER EDUCATION, NUMERICAL METHODS. *Educ:* Carnegie Inst Technol, BS, 51, PhD(math), 55. *Prof Exp:* Mgr mech & eng syst comput, Gen Elec Co, 55-57; res scientist, NY Univ, 57-59; mathematician, IBM Corp, 59-65, mgr comput ctr, 65-67, asst dir math sci, 67-68; chmn dept, 74-79, PROF MATH, UNIV DENVER, 68- *Concurrent Pos:* Fulbright scholar, Comn on Int Exchange of Persons, 72-73; vis prof comput scici, Open Univ, Eng, 79- *Mem:* Fel AAAS; Asn Comput Mach (ed-in-chief, Comput Surveys, 68-72); Soc Indust & Appl Math (secy, 64); Math Asn Am. *Res:* Educational technology; digital computers and their application; numerical analysis; computer-assisted instruction. *Mailing Add:* Dept of Math Univ of Denver Denver CO 80208

DORNBUSH, RHEA L, b New York, NY. HEALTH SCIENCES. *Educ:* Queen's Col, BA, 62, MA, 63; City Univ New York, PhD(exp psychol), 67; Columbia Univ, Sch Pub Health, MPH, 81. *Prof Exp:* Lectr, teaching fel & res assoc psychol, Queen's Col, City Univ New York, 63-65; asst prof psychol, Rutgers Univ, 65-68; from asst prof to assoc prof biol psychiat, New York Med Col, 68-76; sr res scientist, Reproductive Biol Res Found, 76-78; assoc prof psychiat, 78-80, assoc dir, Div Biol Psychiat, 78-80, PROF PSYCHIAT & DIR GRAD PROG MED PSYCHOL, NEW YORK MED COL, 80- *Concurrent Pos:* Clin lectr med psychol, Dept Psychiat, Washington Univ, 76-78. *Mem:* AAAS; Soc Biol Psychiat; Am Psychol Asn; Int Neuropsychol Soc; Geront Soc. *Res:* Psychophysiological and behavioral correlates of psychoactive substances; research design, methodology and statistical analysis in medical research. *Mailing Add:* NY Med Col Dept of Psychiat Munger Pavilion Valhalla NY 10595

DORNE, ARTHUR, b Philadelphia, Pa, Apr 6, 17; m 39; c 1. ENGINEERING. *Educ:* Univ Pa, BA, 38, BS, 39. *Prof Exp:* Radio engr, Glenn D Gillett, consult radio engr, Washington, DC, 40-42; engr, Fed Tel & Tel, NJ, 42-43; antenna group leader & res assoc, Radio Res Lab, Harvard Univ, 43-45; supvr engr antenna group, Airborne Inst Lab, NY, 45-47; pres, Dorne & Margolin, Inc, 47-69 & Granger Asn, 69-70; PRES, DORNE CONSULT, 71- *Mem:* AAAS; fel Inst Elec & Electronics Engrs; Mineral Soc Am. *Res:* Telecommunications; radio navigation; antennas. *Mailing Add:* 1668 S Forge Mountain Dr Valley Forge PA 19481

DORNER, ROBERT WILHELM, b Bern, Switz, Oct 22, 24; nat US; div; c 2. BIOCHEMISTRY, IMMUNOLOGY. *Educ:* Univ Lausanne, dipl, 48; Univ Calif, PhD(biochem), 53. *Prof Exp:* Asst biochem, Univ Calif, 49-51, asst virus lab, 51-53; res assoc zool, Univ Southern Calif, 53-54; jr res botanist, Univ Calif, Los Angeles, 55-56, asst res botanist, 56-57; asst insect toxicol entom, Citrus Exp Sta, Univ Calif, Riverside, 57-62; asst prof biochem, 62-77, ASSOC PROF BIOCHEM & INTERNAL MED, ST LOUIS UNIV, 77- *Concurrent Pos:* Spec investr, Arthritis Found, 64-67. *Mem:* AAAS; Am Asn Clin Chem; Am Chem Soc; Am Rheumatism Asn; fel Nat Acad Clin Biochem. *Res:* Biochemistry of connective tissues; immunology of rheumatoid arthritis. *Mailing Add:* Sect Arthritis Sch Med St Louis Univ St Louis MO 63104

DORNETTE, WILLIAM HENRY LUEDERS, b Cincinnati, Ohio, June 22, 22; m 45; c 2. ANESTHESIOLOGY. *Educ:* Univ Cincinnati, BS, 44, MD, 46, JD, 69. *Prof Exp:* Fel anesthesiol, Med Ctr, Georgetown Univ, 49-51; from instr to asst prof anesthesiol, Univ Wis, 52-55; asst prof, Univ Calif, Los Angeles, 55-57; prof & chmn dept, Col Med, Univ Tenn, Memphis, 58-65; chief anesthesiol, Vet Admin Hosp, Cincinnati, Ohio, 66-71; dir educ, Div Anesthesiol, Cleveland Clin, 72-76; consult anesthesia & hosp safety, 76-81; DIR RISK MGT, ARMED FORCES HOSP, 82- *Concurrent Pos:* Anesthesiologist-in-chief, John Gaston Hosp; asst clin prof, Col Med, Univ Cincinnati, 65-71, assoc clin prof med jurisprudence, 73-80; ed, J Legal Med, 72-76. *Mem:* Am Soc Anesthesiol; fel Am Col Legal Med; Nat Fire Protection Asn; Int Anesthesia Res Soc. *Res:* Instrumentation in anesthesiology; pathology of anesthetic complications; fire and electrical safety in hospitals; legal problems related to medicine; hospital and medical risk management. *Mailing Add:* Armed Forces Inst Path Washington DC 20306

DORNEY, ROBERT STARBIRD, b Milwaukee, Wis, Apr 1, 28; m 50; c 5. ENVIRONMENTAL SCIENCES. *Educ:* Univ Wis, BS, 49, MS, 52, PhD, 59. *Prof Exp:* Conserv biologist, Wis Conserv Dept, 49-57; asst dept vet sci, 57-58, instr parasitol, 58-59, asst prof biol, biol exten, 59-62, assoc prof, Univ Wis, 63-64; sci adv, Pan Am Union, 64-67; assoc prof biol, 67-69, PROF, SCH URBAN & REGIONAL PLANNING & DEPT BIOL, UNIV WATERLOO, 69- *Concurrent Pos:* Chmn bd, Ecoplans Ltd; pres, Natural Woodland Nursery Ltd. *Mem:* Wildlife Soc; Ecol Soc Am; Can Inst Planning; Wildlife Dis Asn. *Res:* Epizootiology of protozoan and helminth diseases; ecology of game birds and mammals; ecology of human settlements and impact of development activities on temperate ecosystems. *Mailing Add:* Sch of Urban & Regional Planning Univ of Waterloo Waterloo ON N2L 3G1 Can

DORNFELD, ERNST JOHN, b Milwaukee, Wis, Apr 6, 11; m 45; c 5. CELL BIOLOGY. *Educ:* Marquette Univ, BS, 33; Univ Wis, AM, 35, PhD(zool), 37. *Prof Exp:* Asst zool, Univ Wis, 35-37; instr histol & embryol, sch med, Univ Okla, 37-38; from instr to prof zool, 38-76, chmn dept, 52-76, EMER PROF ZOOL, ORE STATE UNIV, 76- *Mem:* AAAS; Am Soc Zool; Am Soc Cell Biol; Am Soc Gen Physiol; Lepidopterists' Soc. *Res:* Experimental cytology of the adrenal gland; cytology and embryology of the ovary; role of nucleic acids in cell growth and differentiation; cytochemistry; physiology of mitosis; comparative vertebrate histology; Lepidoptera of Pacific Northwest. *Mailing Add:* Dept Zool Ore State Univ Corvallis OR 97331

DORNFEST, BURTON S, b New York, NY, Oct 31, 30; m 54; c 2. HEMATOLOGY, ANATOMY. *Educ:* NY Univ, BA, 52, MS, 54, PhD(physiol), 60. *Prof Exp:* Mem staff biostatist, Mem Hosp Cancer & Allied Dis, New York, 52-53; asst biol, NY Univ, 53-54, 56-58, instr gen sci, 58-63; instr anat, NY Med Col, 63-64; from instr to asst prof, 64-73, ASSOC PROF ANAT, STATE UNIV NY DOWNSTATE MED CTR, 73- *Concurrent Pos:* Vis assoc prof anat, City Univ New York, 74-78; adj assoc prof hemat, Sch Health Sci, Hunter Col, 78-79. *Mem:* AAAS; NY Acad Sci; Am Soc Hemat; Am Asn Anat. *Res:* Problems relating to reticuloendothelial system function and hemopoiesis; reticuloendothelial system function in the leukemic rat and blood cell production, release and destruction in the rat. *Mailing Add:* Dept of Anat & Cell Biol State Univ NY Downstate Med Ctr Brooklyn NY 11203

DORNHOFF, LARRY LEE, b Minden, Nebr, Apr 13, 42; m 68; c 1. MATHEMATICS. *Educ:* Univ Nebr, Lincoln, BS, 62; Univ Chicago, MS, 63, PhD(math), 66. *Prof Exp:* Instr math, Yale Univ, 66-68; asst prof, 68-74, ASSOC PROF MATH, UNIV ILL, URBANA, 74- *Mem:* Math Asn Am; Am Math Soc. *Res:* Finite group theory; group representations; representations of finite groups, especially solvable groups; solvable permutation groups. *Mailing Add:* Dept of Math Univ of Ill Urbana IL 61801

DORNING, JOHN JOSEPH, b Bronx, NY, Apr 17, 38; m 63; c 3. MATHEMATICAL PHYSICS, NUCLEAR ENGINEERING. *Educ:* US Merchant Marine Acad, BS, 59; Columbia Univ, MS, 63, PhD(nuclear sci & eng), 67. *Prof Exp:* Ensign marine engr, US Navy, 59-60, marine engr, Merchant Marine, 60-62; fel nuclear sci & eng, AEC, 63-66; asst physicist reactor theory, Brookhaven Nat Lab, 67-69, assoc physicist & group leader, 69-70; assoc prof, 70-75, PROF NUCLEAR ENG, UNIV ILL, URBANA, 75- *Concurrent Pos:* Consult, Brookhaven Nat Lab, Argonne Nat Lab, Los Alamos Nat Lab & Sci Appln, Inc, 74-; Nat Res Coun vis prof math physics, Ital Nat Res Coun, 75-76; physicist plasma physics, Lawrence Livermore Lab, 77-78. *Honors & Awards:* Mark Mills Award, Am Nuclear Soc, 67. *Mem:* Fel Am Nuclear Soc; Am Phys Soc; Soc Indust & Appl Math. *Res:* Fission reactor theory, neutron transport theory, fission reactor kinetics, kinetic theory of gases, plasma physics, computational and numerical methods for fluid flow and particle transport. *Mailing Add:* Nuclear Eng Lab Univ of Ill Urbana IL 61801

DORNY, CARL NELSON, b Washington, DC, Jan 20, 37; m 60; c 5. ELECTRICAL & SYSTEMS ENGINEERING. *Educ:* Brigham Young Univ, BES, 61; Stanford Univ, MSEE, 62, PhD(elec eng), 65. *Prof Exp:* Engr, Westinghouse Res Labs, 63-64; asst prof 65-69, assoc prof elec eng, 70-79, assoc dean, 79-80, PROF SYSTS ENG, UNIV PA, 79-, CHMN SYSTS ENG, 80- *Concurrent Pos:* White House fel, spec asst to Secy, USDA, 69-70; NSF res initiation grant, 67-69; consult, Westinghouse Res Labs, Pa, 66-, Hewlett-Packard, 75-76, BDS Technol, 78-79, & Interspec, Inc, 78-; assoc dir, Valley Forge Res Ctr, Univ Pa, 75-80. *Mem:* Sigma Xi; Systems, Man and Cybernetics Soc (vpres, 74-76); Inst Elec & Electronics Engrs; Am Soc Eng Educ. *Res:* High resolution imaging with microwaves and acoustic waves; radar; large adaptive arrays; computer optimization; applied mathematics; mathematical programming; numerical analysis; control theory; system engineering; operations research; optimization of distributed systems. *Mailing Add:* 369 Moore Sch Univ of Pa Philadelphia PA 19104

DOROTHY, ROBERT GLENN, chemical physics, see previous edition

DOROUGH, GUS DOWNS, JR, b Los Angeles, Calif, Mar 5, 22; m 70; c 3. PHYSICAL CHEMISTRY. *Educ:* Univ Calif, BS, 43, PhD(chem), 47. *Prof Exp:* Asst chem, Univ Calif, 43-44; res chemist, Manhattan Atomic Bomb Proj, 44-46; Nat Res fel, Washington, DC, 46-47; from instr to asst prof chem, Washington Univ, 47-54; chemist & div leader, Lawrence Radiation Lab, Univ Calif, 54-67; head dept chem, 67-71; dep dir res & advan technol, US Dept Defense, Washington, DC, 71-73; ASSOC DIR, LAWRENCE LIVERMORE NAT LAB, 73- *Honors & Awards:* Civilian Meritorious Serv Award, US Dept of Defense, 73. *Mem:* Am Chem Soc. *Res:* Chemical explosives; material research and development. *Mailing Add:* Lawrence Livermore Nat Lab PO Box 808 Livermore CA 94550

DOROUGH, H WYMAN, b Notasulga, Ala, Dec 23, 36; m 57; c 5. TOXICOLOGY, PESTICIDE CHEMISTRY. *Educ:* Auburn Univ, BS, 59, MS, 60; Univ Wis, PhD(toxicol), 63. *Prof Exp:* Lab asst entom, Auburn Univ, 56-59, res asst, 59-61; res asst, Univ Wis, 61-63; from asst prof to assoc prof entom, Tex A&M Univ, 63-69; assoc prof, 69-70, PROF TOXICOL & ENTOM, UNIV KY, 70-, DIR, GRAD CTR TOXICOL, 77- *Concurrent Pos:* USPHS & Environ Protection Agency res grant, 65-81; consult, Nat Ctr Toxicol Res, 80-81. *Mem:* Soc Toxicol; Soc Environ Toxicol & Chemistry; Entom Soc Am; Am Chem Soc. *Res:* Chemistry and toxicology of pesticides. *Mailing Add:* Grad Ctr for Toxicol (00916) Univ of Ky Lexington KY 40306

DORR, JOHN ADAM, JR, b Grosse Pointe Park, Mich, Oct 25, 22; m 43; c 3. VERTEBRATE PALEONTOLOGY. *Educ:* Univ Mich, BS, 47, MS, 49, PhD(vert paleont), 51. *Prof Exp:* Asst vert paleont, Univ Mich, 48-51; asst cur, Carnegie Mus, Pittsburgh, 51-52; from instr to assoc prof, 52-64, chmn dept, 66-71, dir, Rocky Mountain Field Sta, 65-78, PROF HIST GEOL, UNIV MICH, ANN ARBOR, 64- *Concurrent Pos:* Res assoc, Mus Paleont, Univ Mich. *Mem:* Soc Vert Paleont (past pres); Soc Study Evolution; Paleont Soc; Geol Soc Am. *Res:* Mammalian vertebrate paleontology; Cenozoic stratigraphy; Tectonic history of the Middle Rockies. *Mailing Add:* Dept of Geol & Mineral Univ of Mich Ann Arbor MI 48109

DORR, JOHN VAN NOSTRAND, II, b New York, NY, May 16, 10; m 46; c 3. GEOLOGY. *Educ:* Harvard Univ, BS, 32; Colo Sch Mines, GeolE, 37. *Hon Degrees:* DSc, Univ Minas Gerais, 66. *Prof Exp:* Geologist, Superior Oil Co, Calif, 37-38; from jr geologist to staff geologist, 38-71, actg chief, Br Latin Am & African Geol, Off Int Geol, US Geol Surv, 71-72; CONSULT GEOLOGIST, 74- *Concurrent Pos:* Vpres working group & comn on manganese, Int Asn Genesis Ore Deposits, 70-75. *Honors & Awards:* Medal, State of Minas Gerais, Brazil, 62; Bonifacio Medal, Brazilian Geol Soc, 64. *Mem:* Fel AAAS; fel Geol Soc Am; Soc Econ Geol; fel Brazilian Geol Soc (vpres, 56); Geol Mining & Metall Soc India. *Res:* Economic geology; ore deposits; tungsten; nickel; manganese; iron. *Mailing Add:* Apt 304 4982 Sentinel Dr Bethesda MD 20816

DORRANCE, WILLIAM HENRY, b Highland Park, Mich, Dec 3, 21; m 46; c 4. PHYSICAL CHEMISTRY, GAS DYNAMICS. *Educ:* Univ Mich, BS, 47, MS, 48; Occidental Univ St Louis, ScD(physics), 78. *Prof Exp:* Res engr, Aeronaut Res Ctr, Univ Mich, 47-49, aerodyn group leader, 49-51; sr aerodyn engr, Convair Div, Gen Dynamics Corp, 51-53, aerodyn group supvr astronaut div, 53-55, asst to dir sci res, Gen Off, 55-58, sr staff scientist, 58-61; head gas dynamics dept, Aerospace Corp, 61-62, group dir adv planning div, 62-64; vpres, Conductron Corp, 64-69, group exec, 64-67, mem bd dirs, 65-67, 68-69; chmn bd dirs, Interface Systs Corp, 67-69, chmn & chief exec, 69-70; PRES, ENG & CONSULT CO, 70-; PRES & MEM BD DIRS, ORGN CONTROL SERV, INC, 71- *Mem:* Am Inst Aeronaut & Astronaut; AAAS; Fedn Am Scientists. *Res:* Systems and operations analysis; high speed aerodynamics; compressible gas dynamics; hypersonic flow; nonsteady flow phenomena; thermal protection systems; high performance missile design; thermochemical cycles for producing fuels. *Mailing Add:* Orgn Control Serv Inc 1925 Pauline Plaza Ann Arbor MI 48103

DORRELL, DOUGLAS GORDON, b Clinton, BC, Oct 14, 40; m 63; c 2. PLANT CHEMISTRY. *Educ:* Univ BC, BSA, 62; Univ Sask, MSc, 63; Mich State Univ, PhD(crop sci), 68. *Prof Exp:* Res officer plant breeding, 63-65; res asst crop sci, Mich State Univ, 66-68; res scientist lipid chem, 68-78, adv planning & evaluation directorate, 78-79, DIR, WINNIPEG RES STA, RES BR, CAN DEPT AGR, 80- *Concurrent Pos:* Mem, Can Comt Grain Qual, 74-76; adv, Nat Defence Col, 79-80. *Mem:* Am Soc Agron; Crop Sci Soc Am; Agr Inst Can; Can Soc Agron. *Res:* Identification and modification of the concentration of chemical components in flax and sunflower seeds to improve quality; identification of specific components in new crop plants that have commercial value. *Mailing Add:* 100 Cornell Dr Winnipeg Can

DORRENCE, SAMUEL MICHAEL, b Rock Springs, Wyo, May 21, 39; m 60; c 3. FOSSIL FUEL CHEMISTRY, ORGANIC CHEMISTRY. *Educ:* Univ Utah, BA, 61, PhD(org chem), 64. *Prof Exp:* Res chemist, Celanese Chem Co, 64-67, group leader, 67; res chemist, Laramie Petrol Res Ctr, US Bur Mines, 67-70, res chemist, 70-73, proj leader, 73-77, chem res assoc, 77-80, MGR PHYSICAL SCI DIV, LARAMIE ENERGY TECHNOL CTR, US DEPT ENERGY, 80- *Concurrent Pos:* Adj prof fuels eng, Univ Utah, 75- *Mem:* Am Chem Soc; Sigma Xi. *Res:* Chemical structrure and physical property determinations of tar sands bitumens, shale oils and materials derived from fossil fuel raw materials during recovery experiments; analyses of nitrogen, sulfer, and metals in crudes and syncrudes; in situ recovery experiments in tar sands; hydrocarbon oxidation; syncrude upgrading. *Mailing Add:* 1410 La Prele Laramie WY 82070

DORRINGTON, KEITH JOHN, b London, Eng, Oct 26, 39; m 60; c 3. BIOCHEMISTRY, IMMUNOLOGY. *Educ:* Univ Sheffield, BSc, 61, PhD(biochem), 64. *Prof Exp:* Res biochem, Univ Sheffield, 61-64, fel, 64-66; vis fel, Duke Univ Med Ctr, 66-67; sr scientist molecular pharmacol, Univ Cambridge, Eng, 67-70; assoc prof, 70-75, PROF BIOCHEM, UNIV TORONTO, 75-, CHMN DEPT, 77-, ASSOC DEAN RES, FAC MED, 81- *Concurrent Pos:* Mem, Immunol & Transplantation Comt, Med Res Coun Can, 75-79; sect ed, J Immunol, Am Asn Immunologists, 75-81. *Mem:* Am Asn Immunologists; Am Soc Biol Chemists; Brit Biochem Soc; Can Biochem Soc; Can Soc Immunol. *Res:* Chemical, physical and biological properties of proteins with special reference to the immunoglobulins. *Mailing Add:* Dept of Biochem Univ of Toronto Toronto ON M5S 2R8 Can

DORRIS, GILLES MARCEL, b Varennes, Que, May 23, 52; m 77; c 1. SURFACE & COLLOID CHEMISTRY. *Educ:* Univ Que, BSc, 75; McGill Univ, PhD(chem), 79. *Prof Exp:* Fel, 79-81, ASST SCIENTIST, PULP & PAPER INST CAN, 81- *Mem:* Chem Inst Can; Can Pulp & Paper Asn. *Res:* Surface chemistry of polymers; physical measurements by inverse gas chromatography; flocculation and sedimentation studies on colloidal suspensions. *Mailing Add:* Paprican 570 St Johns Blvd Pointe Claire PQ H9R 3J9 Can

DORRIS, KENNETH LEE, b Baytown, Tex, Sept 26, 35; m 57; c 1. PHYSICAL CHEMISTRY. *Educ:* Univ Tex, BS, 61, PhD(microwave spectros), 66. *Prof Exp:* Asst prof chem, 65-69, ASSOC PROF CHEM, LAMAR UNIV, 69- *Concurrent Pos:* Robert A Welch res grant, 67-70. *Mem:* Am Chem Soc. *Res:* Spectroscopic studies of heterocyclic and N-acyl compounds, especially structure, symmetry and forces in the molecule. *Mailing Add:* Dept of Chem Lamar Univ Beaumont TX 77710

DORRIS, PEGGY RAE, b Holly Bluff, Miss, Feb 27, 33. ZOOLOGY. *Educ:* Miss Col, BS, 56; Univ Miss, MS, 63, PhD(zool), 67. *Prof Exp:* Asst biol, Univ Miss, 63-66; from asst prof to assoc prof, 66-74, PROF BIOL, HENDERSON STATE UNIV, 74-, CHMN DEPT, 72- *Res:* Spiders of Mississippi and Arkansas. *Mailing Add:* 125 Evonshire Dr Arkadelphia AR 71923

DORRIS, ROY LEE, b Choctaw, Okla, Oct 2, 32; m 56; c 3. PHARMACOLOGY. *Educ:* Bethany Nazarene Col, BS, 59; Peabody Teachers Col, MA, 60; Vanderbilt Univ, PhD(pharmacol), 69. *Prof Exp:* Asst prof pharmacol, Univ Tex Southwestern Med Sch Dallas, 69-74; asst prof, 74-76, ASSOC PROF PHARMACOL, BAYLOR COL DENT, DALLAS, 76- *Mem:* AAAS; Am Soc Exp Pharmacol & Therapeut; Sigma Xi. *Res:* Effects of drugs on uptake, storage and release of catecholamines, with particular emphasis on dopamine-containing centers in the brain. *Mailing Add:* Dept of Pharmacol Baylor Col Dent Dallas TX 75246

DORRIS, TROY CLYDE, b West Frankfort, Ill, Apr 6, 18; m 43; c 2. LIMNOLOGY, WATER POLLUTION. *Educ:* Univ Ill, PhD(zool, limnol), 53. *Prof Exp:* Assoc prof biol sci, Quincy Col, 47-56; assoc prof zool, 56-61, PROF ZOOL, OKLA STATE UNIV, 61-, DIR RESERVOIR RES CTR, RES FOUND, 67- *Res:* Biological effects of oil refinery effluents; biological parameters for water quality criteria; primary productivity of tropical waters. *Mailing Add:* Dept of Zool Okla State Univ Stillwater OK 74078

DORROH, JAMES ROBERT, b Marion, Ala, Apr 20, 37; m 59; c 1. MATHEMATICS. *Educ:* Univ Tex, BA, 58, MA, 60, PhD(math), 62. *Prof Exp:* From asst prof to assoc prof math, 67-71, PROF MATH, LA STATE UNIV, BATON ROUGE, 71-, VCHMN ADMIN, DEPT MATH, 80- *Mem:* Am Math Soc; Math Asn Am. *Res:* Functional analysis; semigroups of linear and nonlinear transformations. *Mailing Add:* Dept of Math La State Univ Baton Rouge LA 70803

DORSCHNER, KENNETH PETER, b Appleton, Wis, Sept 7, 21; m 51; c 2. AGRONOMY. *Educ:* Univ Wis, BS, 49, MS, 51, PhD, 54. *Prof Exp:* Res asst, Univ Wis, 49-51 & 52-54; asst plant physiologist, Miss State Col, 51-52; biologist, Niagara Chem Div, FMC Corp, 54-59, supvr biol labs, 59-62, prod mgr herbicides, 62-67; res supvr pesticides, W R Grace & Co, Md, 67-69; mgr agr chem res, Glidden-Durkee Div, SCM Corp, 69-72; CHIEF PLANT STUDIES BR, CRITERIA & EVAL DIV, ENVIRON PROTECTION AGENCY, 72- *Mem:* Weed Sci Soc Am. *Res:* Synthetic plant hormones as herbicidal compounds. *Mailing Add:* 14th St & Independence SW Washington DC 20250

DORSCHNER, TERRY ANTHONY, b Moultrie, Ga, June 29, 43; m 65; c 2. LASER GYROSCOPES, MAGNETO-OPTICS. *Educ:* Mass Inst Technol, BS, 65; Univ Wis, MS, 67, PhD(elec & electronics), 71. *Prof Exp:* Teaching asst elec & electronics, Univ Wis, 68-69, res asst, 65-71, lectr, 74; res assoc, Institut fur Hochfrequenztechnik, Tech Univ, Braunschweig, 71-73; SR RES SCIENTIST, RAYTHEON RES DIV, 74- *Mem:* Inst Elec & Electronic Engrs; Optical Soc Am. *Res:* Development of lasers for inertial measurement applications, particularly ring laser gyroscopes; optics; magneto-optics; quantum electronics; electromagnetic field theory; thin film devices; applications of hyperbolic geometry. *Mailing Add:* Res Div Raytheon Co 131 Spring St Lexington MA 02273

DORSET, DOUGLAS LEWIS, b York, Pa, Aug 29, 42; m 67; c 1. CRYSTALLOGRAPHY, BIOLOGICAL STRUCTURE. *Educ:* Juniata Col, BS, 64; Sch Med, Univ Md, Baltimore City, PhD(biophysics), 71. *Prof Exp:* Res assoc membrane biophysics, Dept Biol Sci, State Univ NY Albany, 70-72; NIH fel electron diffraction, Roswell Park Mem Inst, 72-73; ASSOC RES SCIENTIST ELECTRON DIFFRACTION, MOLECULAR BIOPHYSICS DEPT, MED FOUND BUFFALO, 73- *Concurrent Pos:* Adj prof chem eng, State Univ NY Buffalo, 78-80; guest prof, Microbiol Dept, Biozentrum der Universitat Basel, Switz, 80-81. *Mem:* NY Acad Sci; Am Crystallog Asn; Biophys Soc; Electron Micros Soc Am; Sigma Xi. *Res:* Solid state packing of biomembrane components and linear polymers determined from electron diffraction and electron microscopy data. *Mailing Add:* Dept of Molecular Biophysics Med Found of Buffalo 73 High St Buffalo NY 14203

DORSEY, CLARK L(AWLER), JR, b Lakota, Va, Apr 22, 23; m 45; c 4. CHEMICAL ENGINEERING. *Educ:* Va Polytech Inst, BS, 45, MS, 46; Purdue Univ, PhD(chem eng), 49. *Prof Exp:* Mem staff, Textile Fibers Dept, Acetate & Orlon Div, EI Du Pont De Nemours & Co, Inc, 49-56, Nylon Div, 57-60, New Prod Div, 61-64 & Develop Dept, 65-67, planning mgr, Org Chem Dept, 68-74, prin consult, 75-81; PRIVATE CONSULT, STRATEGIC PLANNING, 81- *Res:* Venture analysis and development; corporate planning; management sciences. *Mailing Add:* Rte 1 Box 121 Lancaster VA 22503

DORSEY, GEORGE FRANCIS, b Chattanooga, Tenn, Dec 15, 42; m 66; c 3. POLYMER CHEMISTRY. *Educ:* Univ Chattanooga, AB, 64; Univ Tenn, PhD(chem), 69. *Prof Exp:* DEVELOP CHEMIST, NUCLEAR DIV, UNION CARBIDE CORP, 69- *Mem:* Am Chem Soc. *Res:* Polymers; adhesives; foamed epoxy resins; polyurethanes; protective coatings. *Mailing Add:* Union Carbide Corp Nuclear Div PO Box Y Bldg 9202 Oak Ridge TN 37830

DORSEY, ROBERT T, b Cleveland, Ohio, Feb 28, 18; m 45; c 1. ELECTRICAL ENGINEERING. *Educ:* Mass Inst Technol, SB, 40. *Prof Exp:* Supvr ord, Naval Ord Lab, 40-43 & Mine Test Sta, 43-45; supvr lighting appln, 48-66, MGR LIGHTING DEVELOP, GEN ELEC CO, 66- *Concurrent Pos:* Mem, Int Comn Illum, 57-, vpres, 67; chmn, US Comt Appln, 64- *Mem:* Fel AAAS; fel Illum Eng Soc (pres-elect, 71). *Res:* Illuminating engineering; new lighting techniques; design and application of new lamps; development on vision and visual performance. *Mailing Add:* Lamp Dept Gen Elec Co Nela Park Cleveland OH 44112

DORSEY, THOMAS EDWARD, b New York, NY, June 6, 40. BIOCHEMISTRY. *Educ:* Queens Col, BA, 63, MA, 65; City Univ New York, PhD(biochem), 75. *Prof Exp:* Mem fac, Univ Inst Oceanog, City Col New York, 74-77; SR BIOCHEMIST, USV PHARMACEUT CORP REVLON INC, 77- *Concurrent Pos:* Res scientist, Lamont-Doherty Geol Observ, Columbia Univ, 75-76. *Mem:* Am Chem Soc; NY Acad Sci; Sigma Xi. *Res:* Pharmacokinetics and biopharmaceutics of drugs including enzyme kinetic studies and metabolic studies. *Mailing Add:* USV Pharmaceut Corp 1 Scarsdale Rd Tuckahoe NY 10707

DORSEY, W(ILLIAM) SMITH, b Revelstoke, BC, Dec 28, 19. COMPUTER & INFORMATION SCIENCE. *Educ:* Iowa State Univ, BS, 40; Calif Inst Technol, PhD(org chem), 50. *Prof Exp:* MEM TECH STAFF, ELECTRONICS GROUP, AUTONETICS DIV, ROCKWELL INT, 68- *Mem:* Asn Comput Mach; Am Chem Soc; Am Inst Chem Engrs; Am Soc Info Sci. *Res:* Applications of computer processing and information science to literature problems of research and engineering. *Mailing Add:* 1018 North Glenhaven Ave Fullerton CA 92635

DORSEY, WILLIAM RAOUL, b St Louis, Mo, Oct 4, 18; m 44; c 2. CHEMICAL lk ENGINEERING. *Educ:* Univ Calif, BS, 40. *Prof Exp:* Chem engr, Basic Veg Prod, Inc, 49; chief chemist, Vacu- Dry Co, 49-53, dir res, 53-59, vpres ress & develop div, 59-65; pres, Chelan Packing Co, 65-71; PRES, COLUMBIA PROD INC, 71- *Mem:* Assoc Am Chem Soc; assoc Inst Food Technologists. *Res:* Food process engineering. *Mailing Add:* Columbia Prod Inc PO Box 1807 Wenatchee WA 98801

DORSKY, JULIAN, b New York, NY, May 11, 16; m 40; c 3. CHEMISTRY. *Educ:* Brooklyn Col, AB, 36; Pa State Univ, MS, 37; Purdue Univ, PhD(org chem), 39. *Prof Exp:* Group leader, develop sect, Ethyl Corp La, 39-47; sr fel, Mellon Inst, 47-51; chemist, 51-59, res assoc, 59-64, res adminr, 64-66, from asst res dir to dir res, 66-71, vpres res, 71-77, VPRES RES & DEVELOP, GIVAUDAN CORP, 77- *Mem:* AAAS; Am Chem Soc; Soc Cosmetic Chemists; NY Acad Sci. *Res:* Organic chemistry. *Mailing Add:* 125 Delawanna Ave Clifton NJ 07014

DORSON, WILLIAM JOHN, JR, b Nashua, NH, May 9, 36; m 58; c 2. CHEMICAL & BIOMEDICAL ENGINEERING. *Educ:* Rensselaer Polytech Inst, BChE, 58, MChE, 60; Univ Cincinnati, PhD(chem eng, biomed), 67. *Prof Exp:* Coop engr, Gen Elec Co, 56-58, develop engr, Knolls Atomic Power Lab, 58-64, res & develop engr, Space Power & Propulsion Dept, 64-65; instr chem eng, Univ Cincinnati, 65-66; assoc prof biomed eng, 66-71, PROF BIOMED ENG, ARIZ STATE UNIV, 71-, PROF CHEM ENG, 80- *Concurrent Pos:* Consult, Gen Elec Co, Randam Electronics, Inc & Hunkar Instrument Develop Labs, Inc; mem, Int Conf Med & Biol Eng, 67. *Mem:* Am Chem Soc; Am Soc Mech Engrs; Am Inst Chem Engrs; Asn Advan Med Instrumentation. *Res:* Development of medical diagnostic and prosthetic methods; body fluid rheology; transport phenomena; radioactive tracer techniques; two-phase flow and heat transfer; nucleonics. *Mailing Add:* Dept of Chem Eng Ariz State Univ Tempe AZ 85287

DORST, JOHN PHILLIPS, b Cincinnati, Ohio, July 8, 26; m 50; c 4. MEDICINE, RADIOLOGY. *Educ:* Cornell Univ, MD, 53. *Prof Exp:* Intern, Univ Iowa Hosps, 53-54, resident radiol, 55-58; fel pediat radiol, Childrens Hosp, Univ Cincinnati, 58-59, from asst prof to assoc prof radiol, 59-66, asst prof pediat, 65-66; assoc prof radiol, 66-69, assoc prof pediat, 67-78, PROF PEDIAT, JOHNS HOPKINS UNIV, 78-, PROF RADIOL, 70- *Mem:* Soc Pediat Radiol; fel Am Col Radiol; Radiol Soc NAm; Am Roentgen Ray Soc. *Res:* Pediatric radiology; functional craniology; chondrodysplasias. *Mailing Add:* Dept of Radiol Johns Hopkins Hosp Baltimore MD 21205

DORT, WAKEFIELD, JR, b Keene, NH, July 16, 23; m 54, 67; c 1. QUATERNARY GEOLOGY, GEOMORPHOLOGY. *Educ:* Harvard Univ, BSc, 44; Calif Inst Technol, MSc, 48; Stanford Univ, PhD(geol), 55. *Prof Exp:* Field geologist, Bunker Hill & Sullivan, Idaho, 47 & 49; field geologist, US Geol Surv, 48; instr geomorphol & econ geol, Duke Univ, 48-50; asst prof, Pa State Univ, 52-57; assoc prof, 57-70, PROF GEOL, UNIV KANS, 70- *Concurrent Pos:* Consult engr geol, 50-52 & ground water & petrol geol, 52-57; geol ed, Petrol & Natural Gas Digest, 53-56; mem visual educ comt, Am Geol Inst, 55-63 & earth sci curric proj, 63-64; assoc ed, Monitor, 56-59, Oil & Gas Abstr, 59-61 & Mining Abstr, 59-61; mem Antarctic expeds, US, 65, 66 & 69, Japan, 67. *Mem:* AAAS; Geol Soc Am; Am Geog Soc; Asn Am Geog; Soc Am Archaeol. *Res:* Geomorphology; glacial and Pleistocene geology; late Cenozoic paleoclimatology; geology of Idaho; geology of archaeological sites; geomorphology of Antarctica; quaternary history of central Great Plains. *Mailing Add:* Dept of Geol Univ of Kans Lawrence KS 66044

DORUS, ELIZABETH, b Parsons, Kans, Dec 6, 40; m 68; c 1. BEHAVIORAL GENETICS. *Educ:* Valparaiso Univ, BA, 62; Univ Chicago, PhD(personality & psychopath), 71; Univ Pa, MA, 75. *Prof Exp:* Intern clin psychol, Duke Univ Med Ctr, 64-65; trainee, Westside Vet Admin Ment Hyg Clin, 65-67; consult psychologist, Ment Health Div, Chicago Bd of Health, 67-71; instr psychol, Univ Pa, 72-73; res fel, Ill State Psychiat Inst, 74-75; RES ASSOC & ASST PROF PSYCHIAT, UNIV CHICAGO, 77- *Concurrent Pos:* Fel Found Fund Res Psychiat, 72-73; NIH fel, 75-76; NIMH fel, 77-81. *Mem:* Am Psychol Asn; Am Soc Human Genetics; AAAS; Behavior Genetics Asn; Social Biol Asn. *Res:* Genetics of psychiatric disorders; studies of lithium; human genetics. *Mailing Add:* Dept of Psychiat Univ of Chicago Chicago IL 60637

DORWARD, RALPH C(LARENCE), b Viking, Alta, July 31, 41; m 64; c 2. METALLURGY, MATERIALS SCIENCE. *Educ:* Univ Alta, BSc, 62, MSc, 64; McMaster Univ, PhD(metall), 67. *Prof Exp:* Res assoc metall, Univ Alta, 64; sr res metallurgist, 67-69, staff res metallurgist, 69-77, SR STAFF METALLURGIST, KAISER ALUMINUM & CHEM CORP, 77- *Mem:* Am Soc Metals; Am Soc Testing & Mat. *Res:* Physical metallurgy of aluminum alloys; thermodynamics of solutions, phase transformations and phase equilibria; electrochemistry of corrosion and aluminum extraction; alloy development; stress corrosion; properties of ceramics. *Mailing Add:* Metals Res Div Kaiser Ctr for Technol Pleasanton CA 94566

DORWART, BONNIE BRICE, b Petersburg, Va, Jan 27, 42; m 63; c 2. RHEUMATOLOGY. *Educ:* Bryn Mawr Col, AB, 64; Sch Med, Temple Univ, MD, 68. *Prof Exp:* From intern to resident, Lankenau Hosp, Philadelphia, 68-72; fel rheumatology, Sch Med, Univ Pa, 72-74; instr med, 74-76, ASST PROF MED, JEFFERSON MED COL, PHILADELPHIA, 76-; ASST PHYSICIAN CONNECTIVE TISSUE DIS, LANKENAU HOSP, 74- *Mem:* Rheumatism Asn; Am Col Physicians. *Res:* Clinical correlates of cervical spondylosis; pathogenesis of edema in rheumatoid arthritis; hypothyroid arthropathy. *Mailing Add:* Lankenau Med Bldg Suite 41 Philadelphia PA 19151

DORY, ROBERT ALLAN, b St Paul, Minn, June 7, 36; m 67; c 3. MATHEMATICAL PHYSICS. *Educ:* Univ NDak, BS, 58; Univ Wis, MS, 60, PhD(physics), 62. *Prof Exp:* Res asst physics, Midwestern Univ Res Asn, 60-62; instr, Univ Wis, 62-64; physicist, 64-73, group leader, 73-75, asst sect leader, 75-79, SECT LEADER, OAK RIDGE NAT LAB, 79- *Mem:* Fel Am Phys Soc. *Res:* Thermonuclear research; plasma theory. *Mailing Add:* Oak Ridge Nat Lab PO Box Y Oak Ridge TN 37830

DOSANJH, DARSHAN S(INGH), b Sultanwind, India, Feb 21, 21; m 57; c 2. AERONAUTICAL ENGINEERING. *Educ:* Punjab Univ, BSc, 44, MSc, 45; Univ Mich, MSE, 48; Johns Hopkins Univ, PhD(aeronaut), 53. *Prof Exp:* Jr instr mech eng, Johns Hopkins Univ, 49-50, asst, Aeronaut Dept, 50-54; res assoc, Inst Fluid Dynamics & Appl Math, Univ Md, 55-56; assoc prof mech eng, 56-62, PROF MECH & AEROSPACE ENG, SYRACUSE UNIV, 62- *Concurrent Pos:* Vis prof, Col Aeronaut Eng, 61-62; NATO sr fel, 67; Fulbright-Hays sr fac res fel & vis prof, Southampton Univ, 71-72. *Mem:* Acoust Soc Am; assoc fel Am Inst Aeronaut & Astronaut; Am Phys Soc; Am Soc Mech Engrs; Am Soc Eng Educ. *Res:* High speed gas dynamics; aerodynamics; aerodynamic noise; bioacoustics. *Mailing Add:* Dept of Mech & Aerospace Eng Syracuse Univ Syracuse NY 13214

DOSCHEK, GEORGE A, b Pittsburgh, Pa, Sept 3, 42; m 68. SOLAR PHYSICS, ATOMIC SPECTROSCOPY. *Educ:* Univ Pittsburgh, BS, 63, PhD(physics), 68. *Prof Exp:* Teaching asst physics, Univ Pittsburgh, 63-64, res assoc astrophys, Univ Pittsburgh at E O Hulburt Ctr Space Res, 68-70, astrophysicist, 70-79, HEAD, SOLAR TERRESTRIAL RELATIONSHIPS BR, E O HULBURT CTR SPACE RES, US NAVAL RES LAB, 79- *Mem:* Am Astron Soc; Int Astron Union; fel Optical Soc Am. *Res:* Astrophysics; ultraviolet and x-ray spectroscopy of high temperature astrophysical and laboratory plasmas. *Mailing Add:* 4170 E O Hulburt Ctr Space Res US Naval Res Lab Washington DC 20375

DOSCHEK, WARDELLA WOLFORD, b Sewickley, Pa, May 18, 44; m 68. RESEARCH ADMINISTRATION. *Educ:* Univ Pittsburgh, BS, 63, PhD(phys chem), 68. *Prof Exp:* Res scientist photosynthesis, Res Inst Advan Studies, 68-70; asst prog dir regulatory biol prog, NSF, 70-78. *Mem:* Sigma Xi. *Res:* Photosynthesis. *Mailing Add:* 8221 Coach St Potomac MD 20854

DOSCHER, MARILYN SCOTT, b New York, NY, July 1, 31. BIOCHEMISTRY. *Educ:* Cornell Univ, BA, 53; Univ Wash, PhD(biochem), 59. *Prof Exp:* Chemist, Schering Corp, NJ, 53-55; asst prof, 67-72, ASSOC PROF BIOCHEM, SCH MED, WAYNE STATE UNIV, 73- *Concurrent Pos:* NIH fel, Yale Univ, 60-62; univ fel, 62-64; Am Cancer Soc res assoc grant, Brookhaven Nat Lab, 64-67. *Mem:* Am Chem Soc. *Res:* Protein structure. *Mailing Add:* Dept of Biochem Wayne State Univ Sch of Med Detroit MI 48202

DOSHAN, HAROLD DAVID, b New York, NY, Oct 30, 41; m; c 2. CLINICAL PHARMACOLOGY, DRUG METABOLISM. *Educ:* Cornell Univ, BA, 62; Stanford Univ, PhD(org chem), 67. *Prof Exp:* Res assoc org chem, Johns Hopkins Univ, 67-68, NIH fel pharmacol, Sch Med, 68-70; sr res scientist, Cent Res Labs, Pfizer, Inc, 70-80; ASST DIR, CLIN PHARMACOL, REVLON HEALTH CARE GROUP, 80- *Mem:* Am Chem Soc; Tissue Culture Asn. *Res:* Clinical research; clinical pharmacology and drug disposition; pharmacokinetics; natural products; biosynthetic pathways; strained ring systems and their reaction. *Mailing Add:* Revlon Health Care Group Tuckahoe NY 10707

DOSHI, MAHENDRA R, b India, May 6, 41; US citizen; m 71; c 2. PULP AND PAPER, MEMBRANE PROCESSES. *Educ:* Bombay Univ, BS, 65; Clarkson Col, MS, 68, PhD(chem eng), 70. *Prof Exp:* Res assoc chem eng, Clarkson Col Technol, 70-71; vis asst prof, State Univ NY, Buffalo, 71-77; ASSOC PROF ENG, INST PAPER CHEM, 77- *Mem:* Am Inst Chem

Engrs; Sigma Xi; Tech Asn Pulp & Paper Indust. *Res:* Recycled paper processing; screening; hydrocyclones; deinking; separation processes; solid-liquid separation; membrane processes; reverse osmosis; ultrafiltration; filtration; flotation; sedimentation; fluid mechanics; heat and mass transfer. *Mailing Add:* Inst Paper Chem Box 1039 Appleton WI 54912

DOSIER, LARRY WADDELL, b Waynesboro, Va, Mar 26, 44. PLANT MORPHOGENETICS, CROP BREEDING. *Educ:* Col William & Mary, BS, 66; Univ Va, MA, 71, PhD(biol), 74. *Prof Exp:* Asst plant variety examr, 75-76, PLANT VARIETY EXAMR, PLANT VARIETY PROTECTION OFF, LMGS DIV, AGR MKT SERV, USDA, 76- *Concurrent Pos:* Mem rev bd, Nat Grass Variety, 77-79, 79-81; mem rev bd, Nat Clover Variety, 78-79, inaugural mem, 79-81 & 81-83. *Mem:* Bot Soc Am. *Res:* Developmental phenomena of Elodea trichoblasts as they relate to plant cell differentiation. *Mailing Add:* Plant Variety Protection Off Rm 500 Nat Agr Libr Beltsville MD 20705

DOSKOTCH, RAYMOND WALTER, b Husiatyn, Western Ukraine, May 23, 32; Can citizen; m 55; c 2. PHARMACOGNOSY, BIOCHEMISTRY. *Educ:* McMaster Univ, BSc, 55; Univ Wis, MS, 57, PhD(biochem), 59. *Prof Exp:* Res assoc, Enzyme Inst, Univ Wis, 59-60; unit head, Mich Dept Health Labs, 60-61; asst prof res, Sch Pharm, Univ Wis, 61-63; from asst prof to assoc prof pharmacog, Col Pharm, 63-70, PROF BIOCHEM, COL BIOL SCI & PROF NATURAL PROD CHEM & PHARMACOG, COL PHARM, OHIO STATE UNIV, 70- *Mem:* Am Soc Pharmacog; Am Chem Soc; The Chem Soc. *Res:* Isolation of biologically active natural products and structure determination biosynthesis of natural products. *Mailing Add:* Med Chem & Pharmacog Col Pharm Ohio State Univ Columbus OH 43210

DOSS, JAMES DANIEL, b Reading, Pa, Mar 9, 39; m 58; c 2. ELECTRICAL ENGINEERING, BIOMEDICAL ENGINEERING. *Educ:* Ky Wesleyan Col, BS, 64; Univ NMex, MSEE, 69. *Prof Exp:* MEM STAFF BIOMED ENG, LOS ALAMOS SCI LAB, 64-; MEM SCI STAFF BERNALILLO COUNTY MED CTR, 75- *Concurrent Pos:* Assoc prof elec eng, Univ NMex, 69-71, instr radio, Sch Med, 75-76. *Honors & Awards:* IR-100 Award, Indust Res Develop Mag, 78. *Mem:* Asn Advan Med Instrumentation. *Res:* Tissue hyperthermia; electrosurgery; ophthalmology; oncology, especially veterinary and human clinical applications. *Mailing Add:* Group MP-3 MS-844 Los Alamos Sci Lab Los Alamos NM 87545

DOSS, NAGIB A, organic chemistry, see previous edition

DOSS, RAOUF, b Cairo, Egypt, Sept 9, 15; m 52; c 3. MATHEMATICS. *Educ:* Univ Paris, Lic es sc, 38; Cairo Univ, PhD(math), 44. *Prof Exp:* Lectr math, Univ Alexandria, 43-50, assoc prof, 50-54; prof, Cairo Univ, 54-65; vis prof, Univ Ill, Urbana, 65-66; PROF MATH, STATE UNIV NY STONY BROOK, 66- *Concurrent Pos:* Mem, Inst Advan Study, 49-50. *Honors & Awards:* State Prize Sci, Egypt, 51 & 64; Prix France-Egypte, 52. *Res:* Abstract harmonic analysis. *Mailing Add:* Dept of Math State Univ of NY Stony Brook NY 11790

DOSS, RICHARD COURTLAND, b Omaha, Nebr, Nov 14, 26; c 4. APPLIED CHEMISTRY. *Educ:* Creighton Univ, BSChem, 50, MS, 52. *Prof Exp:* Sr res chemist, 52-77, SR PATENT DEVELOP CHEMIST, CHEM APPLN, PHILLIPS PETROL CO, 77- *Mem:* Am Chem Soc. *Res:* Petrochemicals-aimed towards organic adhesives, coatings and sealants. *Mailing Add:* Phillips Petrol Co Bartlesville OK 74004

DOSSEL, WILLIAM EDWARD, b St Louis, Mo, Apr 16, 20; m 55; c 2. HISTOLOGY, EMBRYOLOGY. *Educ:* Ill Col, BA, 48; Marquette Univ, MS, 50; Johns Hopkins Univ, PhD(zool), 54. *Prof Exp:* Asst zool, Marquette Univ, 48-50; fr instr, Johns Hopkins Univ, 40-53; from instr to asst prof anat, Sch Med, Univ NC, 54-60; assoc prof, 60-69, actg chmn dept, 69-70, PROF ANAT, SCH MED, CREIGHTON UNIV, 69-, CHMN DEPT, 70- *Concurrent Pos:* Asst, Marine Biol Lab, Woods Hole, Mass, 52-54. *Mem:* Am Asn Anat; Electron Micros Soc Am. *Res:* Functional and morphological development of chick endocrine organs; fine structure chick embryonic organs. *Mailing Add:* Dept of Anat Creighton Univ Sch of Med Omaha NE 68178

DOSSETOR, JOHN BEAMISH, b Bangalore, India, July 19, 25; Can citizen; m 57; c 4. TRANSPLANTATION IMMUNOLOGY, NEPHROLOGY. *Educ:* Oxford Univ, BA, 46, MA & BM, BCh, 50; McGill Univ, PhD, 61; FRCP(C), 57. *Prof Exp:* Asst prof med & exp surg, McGill Univ, 61-69; PROF MED, HEAD DIV NEPHROLOGY & DIR CLIN & TRANSPLANTATION IMMUNOL GROUP, UNIV ALTA, 69- *Mem:* Fel Am Col Physicians; Can Soc Clin Invest; Am Soc Nephrology; Can Soc Immunol; Transplantation Soc. *Mailing Add:* Clin Sci Bldg Univ of Alta Edmonton AB T6G 2E1 Can

DOSSO, HARRY WILLIAM, b Gull Lake, Sask, Jan 9, 32; m 56; c 4. GEOPHYSICS. *Educ:* Univ BC, BA, 55, MSc, 57, PhD, 67. *Prof Exp:* From instr to assoc prof physics, 57-69, head dept, 69-75, PROF PHYSICS, UNIV VICTORIA (BC), 69- *Concurrent Pos:* Res tech officer, Pac Naval Lab, Defence Res Bd Can, 58-63; Nat Res Coun & Defence Res Bd Can grants, 65- *Mem:* Can Asn Physicists; Am Geophys Union; Can Geophys Union. *Res:* Electromagnetic fields; geomagnetic micropulsations and magnetotelluric modelling; analytical and analogue methods of studying electromagnetic variations at the earth's surface. *Mailing Add:* Dept of Physics Univ of Victoria Victoria BC V8W 2Y2 Can

DOST, FRANK NORMAN, b Seattle, Wash, Mar 24, 26; m 50; c 2. PHYSIOLOGY, TOXICOLOGY. *Educ:* Wash State Univ, BS & DVM, 51; Kans State Univ, MS, 59. *Prof Exp:* Pvt pract, 51-56; instr physiol & pharmacol, Kans State Univ, 56-59; Mark L Morris Found fel & jr vet, Dept Vet Physiol & Pharmacol, Wash State Univ, 59-62; asst prof chem, pharmacol & vet med, 62-67, assoc prof vet med, Environ Health Serv Ctr, 67-75, prof agr chem, Vet Med, Environ Health Sci Ctr, 75-80, PROF AGR CHEM &

EXTENSION TOXICOLOGIST, ORE STATE UNIV, 80- *Concurrent Pos:* Consult, Adv Comt, Environ Protection Agency, 70- & US Forest Serv, 76-; mem ad hoc panel toxicol hydrazines, Nat Acad Sci-Nat Res Coun, 71-; mem, Ore State Bd Educ, 77- *Mem:* Soc Toxicol; Am Soc Pharmacol & Exp Therapeut. *Res:* Effects of intoxicants on biochemical and physiological mechanisms and metabolic fate of intoxicants; methods of hazard assessment. *Mailing Add:* Dept Agr Chem Ore State Univ Corvallis OR 97331

DOSTAL, HERBERT C, b Ludington, Mich, Oct 9, 30; m 51; c 6. PLANT PHYSIOLOGY, HORTICULTURE. *Educ:* Mich State Univ, BS, 60, MS, 62, PhD(hort), 63. *Prof Exp:* Asst prof, Univ Idaho, 63-64; asst prof, 64-70, ASSOC PROF HORT, PURDUE UNIV, 70- *Mem:* Am Soc Hort Sci. *Res:* Biochemistry and physiology of ripening and senescence of fruit tissues. *Mailing Add:* Dept of Hort Purdue Univ West Lafayette IN 47907

DOSWELL, CHARLES ARTHUR, III, b Elmhurst, Ill, Nov 5, 45; m 75; c 2. METEOROLOGY. *Educ:* Univ Wis, BSc, 67; Univ Okla, MSc, 69, PhD(meteorol), 76. *Prof Exp:* Res meteorologist, Nat Severe Storms Lab, 74-76; RES METEOROLOGIST, TECHNIQUES DEVELOP UNIT, NAT SEVERE STORMS FORECAST CTR, 76- *Mem:* Am Meteorol Soc. *Res:* Severe thunderstorm forecasting; severe thunderstorm dynamics; objective analysis. *Mailing Add:* Techniques Develop Unit Rm 1728 Fed Bldg 601 E 12th St Kansas City MO 64106

DOTT, ROBERT HENRY, b Sioux City, Iowa, Jan 8, 96; m 22; c 2. GEOLOGY. *Educ:* Univ Mich, BSF, 17, AM, 20. *Prof Exp:* Asst mineral, Univ Mich, 16-17, asst geol, 19-20; geologist, Empire Gas & Fuel Co, 17-19; geologist, foreign prod dept, Standard Oil Co NJ, 20-22, Carter Oil Co, 22-26 & Mid-Continent Petrol Corp, 26-29; chief geologist, Sunray Oil Co, 29-31; consult geologist, 31-35; dir, Okla Geol Surv, 35-52; distinguished lectr, 51 & 57; exec dir, 52-63, ED CONSULT, AM ASN PETROL GEOLOGISTS, 63- *Concurrent Pos:* Mem, Int Geol Cong, 33, 56 & 60. *Mem:* Hon mem Am Asn Petrol Geologists (assoc ed, 31-51, secy-treas, 51); fel Geol Soc Am; hon mem Asn Am State Geologists. *Res:* Economic geology of petroleum and industrial minerals; stratigraphy, especially of mid-continent region. *Mailing Add:* 2550 E 24th St Tulsa OK 74114

DOTT, ROBERT HENRY, JR, b Tulsa, Okla, June 2, 29; m 51. SEDIMENTOLOGY, TECTONICS. *Educ:* Univ Mich, BS, 50, MS, 51; Columbia Univ, PhD, 55. *Prof Exp:* Field asst, US Geol Surv, 47-48; asst struct geol, Univ Mich, 50-51; geologist, Humble Oil & Refining Co, 54-58; assoc prof geol, 58-66, chmn dept geol & geophys, 74-77, PROF GEOL, UNIV WIS-MADISON, 66- *Concurrent Pos:* With Cambridge Res Ctr, US Air Force, 56-57; mem, Comn on Educ in Geol Sci, 67-69; consult, Roan Selection Trust, Zambia, 67; vis prof, Univ Calif, Berkeley, 69; lectr, Tulsa Univ, 69; NSF sci fac fel, Stanford Univ & US Geol Surv, Calif, 78 & Univ Colo, 79. *Honors & Awards:* Pres Award, Am Asn Petrol Geologists, 56. *Mem:* Geol Soc Am; Am Asn Petrol Geologists; Soc Econ Paleontologists & Mineralogists (secy-treas, 70-72, vpres, 72-73, pres, 81-82); Int Asn Sedimentol. *Res:* Sedimentology and tectonics of mobile belts, particularly Pacific Northwest, Southern Chile, Antarctic Peninsula and Lake Superior-Precambrian; sedimentology Great Lakes region; Pennsylvanian age rocks of Nevada; submarine sliding; clastic intrusions; shallow marine and eolian deposits in western United States; history of geology. *Mailing Add:* Dept of Geol & Geophys Univ of Wis Madison WI 53706

DOTTERWEICH, FRANK H(ENRY), b Baltimore, Md, Dec 11, 05; m 46. CHEMICAL ENGINEERING. *Educ:* Johns Hopkins Univ, BE, 28, PhD(chem eng), 37. *Prof Exp:* From cadet engr to asst gen supt gas opers, Consol Gas, Elec Light & Power Co, 28-34; instr & coach, Johns Hopkins Univ, 34-37; assoc prof eng, 37-41, dir div, 46-64, dean eng, 64-71, PROF ENG, TEX A&I UNIV, 41- *Concurrent Pos:* Tech consult, Petrol Admin War, 42-45 & Nat Gas & Gasoline. *Mem:* Am Chem Soc; Am Inst Mining, Metall & Petrol Engrs; Am Inst Chem Engrs; Am Gas Asn. *Res:* Processing of gas-condensate reservoirs; chemicals from gas. *Mailing Add:* Sch of Eng Tex A&I Univ Kingsville TX 78363

DOTY, COY WILLIAM, b Cleveland, Ala, Sept 18, 31; m 51; c 4. AGRICULTURAL ENGINEERING, SOIL CONSERVATION. *Educ:* Auburn Univ, BSAE, 58; SDak State Univ, MSAE, 68. *Prof Exp:* Res agr engr, Sedimentation Lab, Soil & Water Conserv Res Div, Agr Res Serv, Miss, 58-64 & SDak, 64-68, AGR ENGR, COASTAL PLAINS SOIL & WATER CONSERV RES CTR, USDA, 68- *Concurrent Pos:* Mem, US Comt Irrig, Drainage & Flood Control. *Mem:* Am Soc Agr Engrs; Soil Conserv Soc Am. *Res:* Investigations on sediment yield and delivery, soil erosion, runoff, moisture conservation, tillage, irrigation and drainage on agricultural lands; water conservation and underground storage for surface and subsurface irrigation. *Mailing Add:* Coastal Plains Soil & Water Conserv Res Ctr PO Box 3039 Florence SC 29502

DOTY, MAXWELL STANFORD, b Portland, Ore, Aug 11, 16; m 40; c 3. PHYCOLOGY. *Educ:* Ore State Col, BS, 40, MS, 42; Stanford Univ, PhD(biol), 45. *Prof Exp:* Asst bot, Ore State Col, 39-41; asst bot, Stanford Univ, 41-45; instr bot, Northwestern Univ, 45-46, asst prof, 46-50; assoc prof, 50-54, chmn dept, 54-80, PROF BOT, UNIV HAWAII, 54- *Concurrent Pos:* Head dept bot, marine biol lab, Woods Hole Oceanog Inst, 46-51; chmn, Pac Sci Assoc, Sci Comn on Pac botany; chmn, Int Adv Comn for Int Seaweed Symposia. *Mem:* AAAS; Int Phys Soc; Brit Phys Soc; Phys Soc France; Philippine Phys Soc. *Res:* Marine algae; marine algal production ecology and marine agronomy. *Mailing Add:* Dept of Bot Univ of Hawaii Honolulu HI 96822

DOTY, PAUL MEAD, b Charleston, WVa, June 1, 20; m 42, 54; c 4. BIOCHEMISTRY. *Educ:* Pa State Univ, BS, 41; Columbia Univ, MA, 43, PhD(chem), 44. *Prof Exp:* Instr chem, Polytech Inst Brooklyn, 43-45, asst prof, 45-46; asst prof, Notre Dame Univ, 46-48; from asst prof phys chem to assoc prof chem, 48-56, prof chem, 56-68, chmn dept, 67-70, prof biochem & molecular biol, 68-80, MALLINCKRODT PROF BIOCHEM,

HARVARD UNIV, 80- *Concurrent Pos:* Ed, J Polymer Sci, 45-61; Rockefeller fel, Cambridge Univ, 46-47; Harvey Lectr, 59-60; ed, J Molecular Biol, 59-63; chmn sci adv comt, Soviet-Am exchanges, Nat Acad Sci, 61-63; mem, President's Sci Adv Comt, 61-65; consult, US Arms Control & Disarmament Agency, 61-; chmn comt rev gen ed, Harvard Univ, 62-64; mem, Coun Foreign Relations, 62- *Honors & Awards:* Pure Chem Award, Am Chem Soc, 56. *Mem:* Fel Nat Acad Sci; Am Chem Soc; Fedn Am Sci; Am Soc Biol Chem; fel Am Acad Arts & Sci. *Res:* Molecular biology; structure, properties and function of nucleic acids and proteins. *Mailing Add:* Dept of Biochem & Molecular Biol Harvard Univ Cambridge MA 02138

DOTY, RICHARD LEROY, b Boulder, Colo, Oct 14, 44. BEHAVIORAL BIOLOGY, PSYCHOPHYSICS. *Educ:* Colo State Univ, BS, 66; Calif State Univ, San Jose, MA, 68; Mich State Univ, PhD(psychol), 71. *Prof Exp:* Res asst psychophys, Ames Res Ctr, NASA, 67-68; fel, Univ Calif, Berkeley, 72-73; head, Human Olfaction Sect & assoc mem, Monell Chem Senses Ctr, 73-78, ASST PROF, DEPT OTORHINOLARYNGOL & HUMAN COMMUN, MED SCH, UNIV PA, 73-, RES ASSOC DEPT PHYSIOL, 78-; RES SCIENTIST, VET ADMIN HOSP, PHILADELPHIA, 78-; DIR, SMELL & TASTE CLINIC, UNIV PA HOSP & SCI DIR, SMELL & TASTE RES CTR, UNIV PA, 80- *Concurrent Pos:* Res assoc, Dept Oral Med, Philadelphia Gen Hosp, 73-78. *Mem:* AAAS; Am Soc Zoologists; Am Soc Mammalogists; Animal Behav Soc; Europ Chemoreception Res Orgn. *Res:* Endocrine-sensory physiology interactions; biological rhythms; chemoreception; evolutionary processes; animal behavior; trigeminal detection of chemical vapors. *Mailing Add:* 408 S 47th St Philadelphia PA 19143

DOTY, ROBERT BRUCE, b Ironton, Ohio, Apr 16, 28; m 58; c 3. BACTERIOLOGY. *Educ:* Univ Md, BS, 50; Univ Fla, MS, 56; Pa State Univ, PhD(bact), 62. *Prof Exp:* Lab technician, USPHS, 50-51; asst bact, Univ Fla, 56-57; from instr to asst prof microbiol, Pa State Univ, 62-74; ASST PROF BIOL, WILKES COL, 75- *Mem:* AAAS; Am Soc Microbiol; Sigma Xi. *Res:* Early laboratory diagnosis of caseous lymphadenitis in sheep and goats; history of microbiology. *Mailing Add:* Dept of Biol Wilkes Col Wilkes-Barre PA 18703

DOTY, ROBERT L, b Missouri Valley, Iowa, Aug 2, 18. ELECTRICAL ENGINEERING. *Educ:* Univ Iowa, BS, 48; Iowa State Univ, PhD, 55. *Prof Exp:* From instr to asst prof elec eng, Iowa State Univ, 53-59; sect chief preliminary eng, Data Systs Div, Autonetics Div, N Am Aviation, Inc, 59-62, chief engr, 62-65, DIR ADVAN ANAL, AUTONETICS DIV, ROCKWELL INT, 65- *Res:* Control theory; inertial navigation; digital computers. *Mailing Add:* 1506 W Flippen Ct Anaheim CA 92802

DOTY, ROBERT WILLIAM, b New Rochelle, NY, Jan 10, 20; m 41; c 4. NEUROPHYSIOLOGY, NEUROPSYCHOLOGY. *Educ:* Univ Chicago, BS, 48, MS, 49, PhD(physiol), 50. *Prof Exp:* USPHS fel neurophysiol, Neuropsychiat Inst, Univ Ill, 50-51; asst prof physiol, Col Med, Univ Utah, 51-56; from asst prof to assoc prof, Med Sch, Univ Mich, 56-61; PROF PHYSIOL & PSYCHOL, CTR BRAIN RES, SCH MED, UNIV ROCHESTER, 61- *Concurrent Pos:* Mem, Nat Eye Inst Visual Sci Study Sect, 68-72, Int Brain Res Orgn, bd sci counselors, NIMH & bd sci advisors, Yerkes Primate Ctr; ed, Neurosci Transl, 63-70, Exp Neurol, 65-75, Acta Neurobiologiae Experimentalis, J Physiol (Paris) & Pavlovian J Biol Sci. *Mem:* Fel AAAS; Am Physiol Soc; Soc Neurosci (pres, 76); fel Am Psychol Asn; Int Primatological Soc. *Res:* Visual cortex; reflex deglutition; conditioned reflexes. *Mailing Add:* Ctr for Brain Res Univ Rochester Sch of Med Rochester NY 14642

DOTY, STEPHEN BRUCE, b Dekalb, Ill, Nov 20, 38; m. ANATOMY. *Educ:* Rice Univ, BA, 61, MA, 63, PhD(biol), 65. *Prof Exp:* Assoc prof orthop surg res, Sch Med, Johns Hopkins Univ, 65-75; res biologist, NIH, 75-78; ASSOC PROF ANAT, COL PHYSICIANS & SURGEONS, COLUMBIA UNIV, 78- *Concurrent Pos:* Fel, Dept Path, Nat Cancer Inst, NIH, 72-73. *Mem:* NY Acad Sci; Microbeam Anal Soc. *Res:* Tissue culture, electron microscopy and cell physiology studies of mineralizing tissues; hormonal and bio-electrical controls governing bone formation; role of phagocytic processes. *Mailing Add:* BB 1401 Columbia Univ 630 W 168th St New York NY 10032

DOTY, W(ILLIAM) D'ORVILLE, b Rochester, NY, Mar 11, 20; m 45; c 2. METALLURGY, MATERIALS ENGINEERING. *Educ:* Rensselaer Polytech Inst, BMetE, 42, MMetE, 44, PhD(metall), 46. *Prof Exp:* Welding res fel & asst, Rensselaer Polytech Inst, 42-46, supvr, 46-47; welding metallurgist, Carnegie-Ill Steel Corp, 47-52; welding metallurgist, 52-57, div chief bar, plate & forged prod, 58-66, res consult steel prod develop, Appl Res Lab, 66-73, chief staff engr, 73-75, chief res engr, 75-77, SR RES CONSULT, US STEEL CORP, 77- *Concurrent Pos:* With Off Sci Res & Develop, 44; chmn pressure vessel res comt, Welding Res Coun; mem heavy sect steel technol comt, Atomic Energy Comn-Oak Ridge Nat Lab; mem adv comt, Ship Hull Res Comt, Nat Res Coun. *Mem:* Am Inst Mining, Metall & Petrol Engrs; fel Am Soc Metals; hon mem Am Welding Soc; Am Soc Mech Engrs; Brit Inst Welding. *Res:* Development and application of new and improved carbon, high-strength low-alloy and high-yield-strength alloy steels; weldability of steels, especially quenched and tempered carbon and alloy steels; design, material selection and fabrication of pressure vessels and structures. *Mailing Add:* Res Lab US Steel Corp Monroeville PA 15146

DOTZENKO, ALEXANDER DANIEL, b Sandpoint, Idaho, Feb 8, 20; m 41; c 4. AGRONOMY. *Educ:* Univ Idaho, BSc, 41; Rutgers Univ, PhD(crops), 50. *Prof Exp:* Asst, Rutgers Univ, 49-50; asst prof & asst agronomist, NMex State Univ, 50-52; assoc prof agron & assoc agronomist, 52-67, PROF AGRON & AGRONOMIST, COLO STATE UNIV, 67-, MEM EGYPTIAN WATER USE & MGT PROJ, BULAK, CAIRO, ARAB REPUB EGYPT, 77- *Concurrent Pos:* Vis lectr, Lincoln Col, Canterbury, NZ, 67; res assoc, Queen's Univ Belfast, 70; mem design team, EAfrica, 80-; mem, Int Ex Serv Corps, Brazil, 80. *Mem:* Am Soc Agron; Soil Conserv Soc Am. *Res:* Forage crops; production, genetics and physiological factors related to forage grasses and legumes; sugarbeet production systems; environmental studies on heavily used recreational areas. *Mailing Add:* Dept of Agron Colo State Univ Ft Collins CO 80521

DOUB, WILLIAM BLAKE, b Rocky Mt, NC, Dec 10, 24; m 64. NUCLEAR PHYSICS. *Educ:* Univ Calif, Los Angeles, PhD(nuclear physics), 56. *Prof Exp:* SR SCIENTIST, BETTIS ATOMIC POWER LAB, WESTINGHOUSE ELEC CORP, WEST MIFFLIN, 57- *Mem:* Am Phys Soc; Am Nuclear Soc. *Res:* Nucleon-nucleon low energy scattering; reactor physics. *Mailing Add:* 628 Rolling Green Dr Bethel Park PA 15102

DOUBEK, DENNIS LEE, b Chicago, Ill, June 15, 44. BIOCHEMISTRY, ORGANIC CHEMISTRY. *Educ:* Univ Ill, PhD(biochem), 77. *Prof Exp:* Fac res assoc, 76-78, SR RES CHEMIST NATURAL PROD CHEM, CANCER RES INST, ARIZ STATE UNIV, 78- *Mem:* AAAS. Mem: AAAS. *Res:* Isolation and characterization of antineoplastic agents from marine organisms. *Mailing Add:* Cancer Res Inst Ariz State Univ Tempe AZ 85281

DOUBLEDAY, CHARLES E, JR, b Corpus Christi, Tex, July 29, 44. PHYSICAL ORGANIC CHEMISTRY. *Educ:* Univ Kans, AB, 66; Univ Chicago, PhD(chem), 73. *Prof Exp:* Res chem, Univ Tex, Austin, 73-75; ASST PROF CHEM, STATE UNIV NY BUFFALO, 75- *Mem:* Am Chem Soc. *Res:* Chemically induced dynamic nuclear polarizations; potential surfaces of excited states of organic molecules. *Mailing Add:* Dept of Chem State Univ NY 112 Acheson Hall Buffalo NY 14214

DOUDNEY, CHARLES OWEN, b Dallas, Tex, Nov 5, 25; m; c 1. BIOCHEMISTRY, GENETICS. *Educ:* Univ Tex, PhD(genetics), 53. *Prof Exp:* Res biologist, Univ Tex, 51-53; assoc biologist, Oak Ridge Nat Lab, 53-55; res assoc, Univ Pa, 55-56; from assoc biologist to biologist, Univ Tex M D Anderson Hosp & Tumor Inst, 56-67, chief, Sect Genetics, 56-67, assoc prof biol, Post-grad Sch Med, 57-67, assoc, Grad Sch Biomed Sci, 63-67; head, Dept Genetics, Albert Einstein Med Ctr, 67-74; RES SCIENTIST, NY STATE DEPT HEALTH, 74- *Mem:* Genetics Soc Am; Am Soc Microbiol. *Res:* Biochemistry and genetics of neurospora; radiation protection and recovery of microorganisms; mutation; macromolecular synthesis; ultraviolet effects on microorganisms; human genetics; medical genetics; mutation in mammalian cell lines and carcinogenesis; mutation induction in microorganisms. *Mailing Add:* NY State Dept of Health Albany NY 12201

DOUDOROFF, PETER, b Libau, Russia, June 22, 13; nat US; m 38, 48, 68; c 1. ZOOLOGY. *Educ:* Stanford Univ, AB, 35; Univ Calif, PhD(zool), 41. *Prof Exp:* Asst biologist, US Bur Fisheries, 34; asst biol, Stanford Univ, 34-35; asst oceanog, Scripps Inst, Univ Calif, 35-41; biologist, La State Dept Conserv, 41-45; aquatic biologist, US Fish & Wildlife Serv, Wash & Ore, 46-47; biologist, USPHS, Ohio, 47-53, supvry fishery res biologist, Ore, 53-65; prof fisheries, 54-76, EMER PROF FISHERIES, ORE STATE UNIV, 77- *Concurrent Pos:* Consult biologist, 69- *Mem:* AAAS; Am Fisheries Soc; Water Pollution Control Fedn. *Res:* Ecology, physiology and toxicology of fresh-water and marine fishes; inland fisheries biology; water pollution. *Mailing Add:* Dept of Fisheries & Wildlife Ore State Univ Corvallis OR 97331

DOUEK, MAURICE, b Cairo, Egypt, Nov 2, 48; Can citizen; m 75; c 2. PHYSICAL CHEMISTRY. *Educ:* McGill Univ, BSc, 70, PhD(chem), 75. *Prof Exp:* Fel chem, 75-77, ASSOC SCIENTIST CHEM, PULP & PAPER RES INST CAN, 77- *Mem:* Can Pulp & Paper Tech Asn Pulp & Paper Indust. *Res:* Wood resin problems in the pulp and paper industry; control of deposit formation in mills. *Mailing Add:* 570 St John's Blvd Pointe Claire PQ H9R 3J9 Can

DOUGAL, ARWIN A(DELBERT), b Dunlap, Iowa, Nov 22, 26; m 51; c 4. ELECTRICAL ENGINEERING, PHYSICAL ELECTRONICS. *Educ:* Iowa State Col, BS, 52; Univ Ill, MS, 55, PhD(elec eng), 57. *Prof Exp:* Engr, Collins Radio Co, 52; asst elec eng, Univ Ill, 52-56, res assoc, 56-57, from asst prof to assoc prof, 57-61; dir labs, Electronics & Rel Sci Res, 64-67, dir electronics res ctr, 71-77, PROF ELEC ENG, UNIV TEX, AUSTIN, 61- *Concurrent Pos:* Asst dir defense res & eng for res, Dept of Defense, DC, 67-69. *Mem:* Fel Am Phys Soc; fel Inst Elec & Electronics Engrs; Soc Eng Sci; Am Soc Eng Educ; Optical Soc Am. *Res:* Electrical gaseous discharge and plasma physics; magnetohydrodynamics; controlled thermonuclear fusion; electron physics of the gaseous state; ionization phenomena and physics of the earth-earth's upper atmosphere; science and technology of lasers and coherent electro-optics; holography; scientific research administration. *Mailing Add:* Dept of Elec Eng Univ of Tex Austin TX 78712

DOUGALIS, VASSILIOS, b Athens, Greece, Mar 19, 49; m 76. NUMERICAL ANALYSIS, PARTIAL DIFFERENTIATION EQUATIONS. *Educ:* Princeton Univ, BSE, 71; Harvard Univ, SM, 73, PhD(appl math), 76. *Prof Exp:* ASST PROF, DEPT MATH, UNIV TENN, 76- *Concurrent Pos:* Vis prof, Dept Math, Univ Crete, Greece, 80. *Mem:* Soc Indust & Appl Math; Am Math Soc. *Res:* Numerical methods for nonlinear partial differential equations of hyperbolic and parabolic type occuring mainly in fluid mechanics. *Mailing Add:* Dept Math Univ Tenn Knoxville TN 37916

DOUGALL, DONALD K, b Perth, Western Australia, Dec 3, 30; m 56, 69. BIOCHEMISTRY, EXPERIMENTAL MORPHOLOGY. *Educ:* Univ Western Australia, MSc, 54; Oxford Univ, DPhil, 56. *Prof Exp:* Nat Res Coun Can fel, 56-57; proj assoc biochem, Univ Wis, 56-59; lectr, Univ Sydney, 59-63; asst prof, Ohio State Univ & Agr Exp Sta, 63-67, assoc prof bot & biochem, univ, 67-71; SR SCIENTIST, W ALTON JONES CELL SCI CTR, 71- *Mem:* Am Soc Plant Physiol; Int Asn Plant Tissue Cult (secy, 70-74); NY Acad Sci. *Res:* Biosynthesis of amino acids; control of metabolism in plants; growth and morphogenesis in plant cell cultures; cryogenic storage of plant cells. *Mailing Add:* W Alton Jones Cell Sci Ctr Old Barn Rd Lake Placid NY 12946

DOUGALL, RICHARD S(TEPHEN), b Schenectady, NY, Apr 22, 37; m 67; c 3. HEAT TRANSFER, FLUID MECHANICS. *Educ:* Union Col, NY, BSME, 59; Mass Inst Technol, SM, 60, ME & ScD, 63. *Prof Exp:* Res asst, Heat Transfer Lab, Mass Inst Technol, 60-63; asst prof mech eng, 63-68, ASSOC PROF MECH ENG, UNIV PITTSBURGH, 68- *Concurrent Pos:*

Consult, adv bd on hardened elec power systs, Nat Acad Sci, 64-66 & Westinghouse Nuclear Energy Systs, 67- *Mem:* Am Soc Mech Engrs; Am Soc Eng Educ; Am Nuclear Soc; Soc Natural Philos. *Res:* Boiling heat transfer and two-phase flow in engineering systems; convection and radiation heat transfer. *Mailing Add:* Dept of Mech Eng 4200 Fifth Ave Pittsburgh PA 15261

DOUGH, ROBERT LYLE, SR, b Ft Lauderdale, Fla, Aug 5, 31; m 53; c 5. SCIENCE EDUCATION. *Educ:* Guilford Col, BS, 53; NC State Univ, MS, 56, PhD(appl physics), 62. *Prof Exp:* Instr physics, NC State Col, 56-60; assoc nuclear engr, Astra, Inc, 60-61; asst prof physics, NC State Univ, 62-67; assoc prof sci educ, 68-77, PROF SCI EDUC, E CAROLINA UNIV, 77- *Concurrent Pos:* Vis asst prof, Ctr Res in Col Instr Sci & Math, Fla State Univ, 67-68. *Mem:* Nat Sci Teachers Asn; Am Asn Physics Teachers. *Res:* Introductory physics education; science and society; history of physics. *Mailing Add:* Dept of Sci Educ E Carolina Univ Greenville NC 27834

DOUGHERTY, CHARLES MICHAEL, b Sept 16, 44; US citizen. ORGANIC CHEMISTRY. *Educ:* Williams Col, AB, 66; Pa State Univ, PhD(chem), 72. *Prof Exp:* Asst prof, 73-78, ASSOC PROF, DEPT CHEM, LEHMAN COL, 78- *Concurrent Pos:* NSF vis fac fel, Columbia Univ, 80-81. *Mem:* NY Acad Sci; Sci Res Soc NAm; Am Chem Soc; The Chem Soc. *Res:* Development of new synthetic methods especially as applied to systems of potential biological and/or pharmaceutical activity. *Mailing Add:* Dept Chem Lehman Col Bronx NY 10468

DOUGHERTY, DENNIS A, b Harrisburg, Pa, Dec 4, 52; m 73; c 1. ORGANIC CHEMISTRY. *Educ:* Bucknell Univ, BS, 74, MS, 74; Princeton Univ, PhD(chem), 78. *Prof Exp:* Fel chem, Yale Univ, 78-79; ASST PROF CHEM, CALIF INST TECHNOL, 79- *Mem:* Am Chem Soc. *Res:* Physical organic chemistry; strained hydrocarbons and related structures; biradicals; photochemistry; sterochemistry and conformational analysis; theoretical and computational organic chemistry. *Mailing Add:* Dept Chem 164-30 Calif Inst Technol Pasadena CA 91125

DOUGHERTY, HARRY L, b San Jose, Costa Rica, Sept 22, 26; US citizen; m 52; c 4. ANATOMY, ORTHODONTICS. *Educ:* Univ Calif, Berkeley, AB, 51, MA, 53; Univ Calif, San Francisco, DDS, 57. *Prof Exp:* Assoc clinician, Children's Hosp, Los Angeles, 58-60; chief sci, Orthop Hosp, 60-64; ASSOC PROF ORTHOD & CHMN DEPT, SCH DENT, UNIV SOUTHERN CALIF, 60- *Mem:* AAAS; Am Asn Orthod. *Res:* Cleft palate research. *Mailing Add:* Dept of Orthod Univ Southern Calif Sch of Dent Los Angeles CA 90007

DOUGHERTY, JAMES G(REGG), JR, b New York, NY, Jan 13, 26; m 49; c 2. ELECTRICAL ENGINEERING. *Educ:* Princeton Univ, BSEE, 48, MSEE, 49. *Prof Exp:* Engr & sect leader, Vitro Labs, 48-55, group leader systs eval, 55-57 & acoust res group, 57-59, head, Dept Res & Studies, 59-67 & Develop Eng Dept, 67-69, asst head res dept, 69-71, SR STAFF ENGR, RES & DEVELOP BR, VITRO LABS, 71- *Mem:* Inst Elec & Electronics Engrs. *Res:* Electronics; acoustics; operations research; data processing. *Mailing Add:* 7016 Beechwood Dr Chevy Chase MD 20015

DOUGHERTY, JOHN A, b Shreveport, La, Jan 5, 43. BEHAVIORAL PHARMACOLOGY, BEHAVIORAL TOXICOLOGY. *Educ:* Univ Minn, BA, 69, PhD(psychol & pharmacol), 73. *Prof Exp:* ASSOC PROF, DEPT PSYCHIAT, COL MED, UNIV KY, 73-, ASST PROF, DEPT PHARMACOL, 75-, ASST PROF GRAD CTR TOXICOL, 82- *Concurrent Pos:* Staff psychologist, Vet Admin Ctr, Lexington, Ky, 73- *Mem:* Soc Neurosci; Behav Pharmacol Soc; Am Psychol Asn. *Res:* Behavioral effects of opioids, stimulants, nicotine and herbicides. *Mailing Add:* Dept Psychiat MN 368 Univ Ky Med Ctr Lexington KY 40536

DOUGHERTY, JOHN E, b Lindsay, La, Feb 2, 22; m 44; c 4. PHYSICS. *Educ:* La State Univ, BS, 42; Univ Mich, PhD(physics), 50. *Prof Exp:* Radio physicist, US Naval Res Lab, 42-43; instr physics, La State Univ, 43-44; mem staff electronics, Univ Calif, 44-45; mem staff, Physics Lab, Johns Hopkins Univ, 45-46; asst, Univ Mich, 46-50; MEM STAFF PHYSICS, LOS ALAMOS SCI LAB, UNIV CALIF, 50- *Mem:* Am Phys Soc. *Res:* Nuclear and neutron physics; ferroelectrics; mechanics. *Mailing Add:* 3548 Arizona Ave Los Alamos NM 87544

DOUGHERTY, JOHN JAMES, b Philadelphia, Pa, Aug 15, 24; m 47; c 7. DC TRANSMISSION, POWER CABLE ENGINEERING. *Educ:* Villanova Univ, BSEE, 50. *Prof Exp:* Proj mgr, Oper Res Proj, 63-69; engr in chg energy distrib res, Philadelphia Elec Co, 72-75; DIR, ELEC SYST DIV, ELEC POWER RES INST, 75- *Concurrent Pos:* Mem, Comt Solar Power Satellites, Nat Acad Eng, 79-81. *Mem:* Fel Inst Elec & Electronics Engrs; Am Nat Standards Inst. *Res:* Direct current transmission and its integration into large alternating current power networks; cable engineering; synthetic polymers. *Mailing Add:* 4766 Calle de Lucia San Jose CA 95124

DOUGHERTY, JOHN WILLIAM, b Jerome, Ariz, Oct 13, 25; m 47; c 4. GENERATOR DESIGN. *Educ:* Univ Calif, Berkeley, BS, 47; Polytech Inst Brooklyn, PhD(syst sci), 69. *Prof Exp:* Test engr, 47-48, design engr medium steam turbine, Generator & Gear Dept, 48-55, design anal engr, 55-58, design methods engr, 58-60, consult eng ed, Corp Eng, 60-71, sr engr test facil, Turbine Div Facil Planning, 71-72, tech leader test integration, 72-76, TECH LEADER ELECTROMAGNETICS & DESIGN, LARGE STEAM TURBINE-GENERATOR DEPT, GEN ELEC CO, 77- *Mem:* Inst Elec & Electronics Engrs. *Res:* Synchronous generator design; computerized design; Chebyshev approximation theory; finite element analysis. *Mailing Add:* 62 Fredericks Rd Scotia NY 12302

DOUGHERTY, JOSEPH PATRICK, electrooptics, see previous edition

DOUGHERTY, RALPH C, b Dillon, Mont, Jan 31, 40; m 60; c 3. PHYSICAL ORGANIC CHEMISTRY, BIOCHEMISTRY. *Educ:* Mont State Col, BS, 60; Univ Chicago, PhD(phys org chem), 63. *Prof Exp:* Resident res assoc, Argonne Nat Lab, 63-65; asst prof chem, Ohio State Univ, 65-69; assoc prof, 69-77, PROF CHEM, FLA STATE UNIV, 77- *Concurrent Pos:* Mem, Nat Res Coun Comt on Anal Chem, 75-78. *Mem:* Am Soc Andrology; Am Chem Soc; The Chem Soc; Am Phys Soc; Am Soc Mass Spectrometry. *Res:* Organic mass spectrometry; pollution chemistry; ion-molecule reactions; biochemical epidemiology; molecular orbital theory; analytical toxicology. *Mailing Add:* Dept Chem Fla State Univ Tallahassee FL 32306

DOUGHERTY, ROBERT MALVIN, b Long Branch, NJ, May 25, 29; m 50; c 2. MICROBIOLOGY, VIROLOGY. *Educ:* Rutgers Univ, BS, 52, MS, 54, PhD(microbiol), 57. *Prof Exp:* Instr microbiol, Sch Med & Dent, Univ Rochester, 57-60; Nat Cancer Inst spec res fel virol, Imp Cancer Res Fund, London, Eng, 60-62; assoc prof, 62-69, PROF MICROBIOL, STATE UNIV NY UPSTATE MED CTR, 69- *Mem:* AAAS; Am Soc Microbiol; Soc Exp Biol & Med; Am Asn Immunol; Brit Soc Gen Microbiol. *Res:* Virology; virus immunology; viral oncology. *Mailing Add:* Dept Microbiol State Univ NY Upstate Med Ctr Syracuse NY 13210

DOUGHERTY, ROBERT WATSON, b Newcomerstown, Ohio, Feb 5, 04; m 48; c 2. VETERINARY MEDICINE. *Educ:* Iowa State Univ, BS, 27; Ohio State Univ, DVM, 36; Ore State Univ, MS, 42. *Prof Exp:* Instr vet med, Ore State Univ, 37-39, from asst prof to assoc prof, State Col Wash, 46-48; prof, State Univ NY Vet Col, Cornell Univ, 48-61; actg head dept vet physiol, 53-54; leader physiopath invests, Nat Animal Disease Lab, 61-74. *Concurrent Pos:* Fulbright scholar, NZ, 56-57; prof, Iowa State Univ, 62-; chmn orgn & ed comt, Int Symposium Physiol Digestion in Ruminant, 64; vis prof, Univ Wis-Madison. *Honors & Awards:* Distinguished Alumnus award, Ohio State Univ, 65; Borden Award, Am Vet Med Asn, 63. *Mem:* AAAS; NY Acad Sci; Conf Res Workers Animal Dis (pres, 71); distinguished fel Am Col Vet Pharmacol & Therapeut; Am Soc Vet Physiologists & Pharmacologists. *Res:* Reproductive physiology in ruminants; bovine spermatozoa and the vaginal pH of the female; formation and absorption of toxins from the bovine rumen; hematological changes in certain pathological conditions in ruminants; physiological studies of acute tympanites in ruminants. *Mailing Add:* Rte 2 Ames IA 50010

DOUGHERTY, THOMAS JOHN, b Buffalo, NY, Aug 2, 33. RADIOBIOLOGY. *Educ:* Canisius Col, BS, 55; Ohio State Univ, PhD(org chem), 59. *Prof Exp:* Res chemist, film dept, Yerkes Res & Develop Lab, E I du Pont de Nemours & Co, Inc, 59-67, staff scientist, 67-70; from cancer res scientist to assoc cancer res scientist, 70-75, PRIN CANCER RES SCIENTIST, ROSWELL PARK MEM INST, 75-, HEAD, DIV RADIOBIOL, DEPT RADIOL, 76- *Concurrent Pos:* Assoc prof, State Univ NY Buffalo, 75- *Honors & Awards:* Benjamin Franklin Award, 81. *Mem:* AAAS; Am Chem Soc; Am Asn Cancer Res; Sigma Xi; Am Soc Photobiol. *Res:* Radiobiology, especially photochemically induced in vivo reactions; photoradiation therapy for cancer treatment. *Mailing Add:* 2306 W Oakfield Rd Grand Island NY 14072

DOUGHERTY, WILLIAM J, b Brooklyn, NY, June 3, 34; m 58; c 2. CELL BIOLOGY, HISTOLOGY. *Educ:* St Joseph's Col, Pa, BS, 56; Princeton Univ, MA, 61, PhD(biol), 63. *Prof Exp:* Biochemist, State Univ NY Downstate Med Ctr, 56-59; USPHS fel, Harvard Univ, 63-64; from asst prof to assoc prof, 64-77, PROF ANAT, MED UNIV SC, 77- *Concurrent Pos:* Vis prof anat, McGill Univ, 74-75. *Mem:* Am Soc Cell Biol; Am Soc Zoologists; Electron Micros Soc Am; Am Asn Anat; Histochem Soc. *Res:* Cytochemical and electron microscope study of cells and tissues, especially mechanisms of mitosis and cytokinetics and effects of heavy metals and other poisons on mitochondrial structure and function; muscle ultrastructure and cytochemistry; tooth mineralization. *Mailing Add:* Dept of Anat Med Univ of SC Charleston SC 29403

DOUGHMAN, DONALD JAMES, b Des Moines, Iowa, Sept 26, 33; m 71; c 4. OPHTHALMOLOGICAL SURGERY. *Educ:* Drake Univ, BME, 55; State Univ Iowa, MD, 61. *Prof Exp:* Instr ophthal, State Univ Iowa Hosps, 68; fel corneal dis, Mass Eye & Ear Infirmary, Boston, 68-72 & Retina Found, Boston, 70-72; asst prof, 72-75, assoc prof, 75-80, PROF & HEAD, DEPT OPTHALMOL, UNIV MINN, 80- *Concurrent Pos:* Chief ophthal, USPHS Hosp, Boston, 68-70. *Mem:* Asn Res Vision & Ophthal; Am Acad Ophthal Otolaryngol; fel Am Col Surgeons. *Res:* Corneal transplantation; methods of corneal preservation utilizing organ culture incubation as a method of long term storage. *Mailing Add:* Dept of Ophthal Univ Minn Box 493 Mayo Mem Bldg Minneapolis MN 55455

DOUGHTY, CHARLES CARTER, b Alamosa, Colo, Dec 12, 15; m 44; c 2. HORTICULTURE. *Educ:* Kans State Univ, BS, 52; Wash State Univ, PhD(hort), 59. *Prof Exp:* Supt & asst hort, Coastal Wash Res & Exten Unit, 54-65, assoc horticulturist, Western Wash Res & Exten Ctr, 67-75, HORTICULTURIST, WESTERN WASH RES & EXTEN CTR, WASH STATE UNIV, 75- *Honors & Awards:* Dow Chem Co Award, 68. *Mem:* AAAS; Am Soc Hort Sci. *Res:* Effects of growth regulators on hardiness and freeze injury in small fruits; herbicide activity and nutrition of horticultural crops. *Mailing Add:* Western Wash Res & Exten Ctr Puyallup WA 98371

DOUGHTY, CLYDE CARL, b Hutchinson, Kans, July 21, 24; m 51; c 4. BIOCHEMISTRY. *Educ:* Univ Kans, BA, 48, MA, 50; Ill Inst Technol, PhD(microbiol biochem), 56. *Prof Exp:* Asst, Rheumatic Fever Inst, Northwestern Univ, 51-53; asst, Ill Inst Technol, 53-56; res biochemist, Charles F Kettering Found, 56-59; res assoc biol chem, 59-62, asst prof, 62-66, assoc prof biol chem & prev med, 66-76, PROF BIOL CHEM & PREV MED, UNIV ILL COL MED, 76- *Mem:* AAAS; Am Soc Microbiol; Am Soc Biol Chem. *Res:* Enzymology; microbial cell wall; microbial metabolism; immunochemistry. *Mailing Add:* Dept of Biol Chem Univ of Ill at the Med Ctr Chicago IL 60612

DOUGHTY, JULIAN O, b Tuscaloosa, Ala, June 11, 33; m 56; c 2. FLUID MECHANICS, RHEOLOGY. *Educ:* Miss State Univ, BS, 56, MS, 60; Univ Tenn, PhD(eng sci), 66. *Prof Exp:* Design engr, McDonnell Aircraft Co, 56-57; instr eng graphics, Miss State Univ, 57-60; instr & res asst basic eng & eng mech, Univ Tenn, 60-66; asst prof aerospace eng, 66-70, ASSOC PROF AEROSPACE ENG, UNIV ALA, TUSCALOOSA, 70- *Concurrent Pos:* NASA res grant, 71. *Mem:* Am Inst Aeronaut & Astronaut; Am Soc Mech Engr; Am Soc Eng Educ. *Res:* Aerodynamics; viscoelastic fluids. *Mailing Add:* Dept Mech Eng Univ of Ala University AL 35486

DOUGHTY, MARK, b Hull, Eng, Dec 20, 21; m 49; c 7. ORGANIC CHEMISTRY. *Educ:* Univ London, BSc, 49, PhD(org chem), 51. *Prof Exp:* Res dir org chem lab, Fothergill & Harvey, Eng, 51-54; lectr chem, Mt St Mary's Col, Eng, 54-61; lectr chem & physics, Staffordshire Col Technol, Eng, 62-63; asst prof, 63-65, ASSOC PROF CHEM & CHMN DEPT, CONCORDIA UNIV, CAN, 65- *Res:* Stereochemistry; cellulose derivatives; mechanism of organic reactions; philosophy of science. *Mailing Add:* Concordia Univ 7141 Sherbrooke St West Montreal PQ H4B 1R6 Can

DOUGHTY, SAMUEL PRESTON, JR, b Corpus Christi, Tex, May 31, 40; m 62; c 1. MECHANICS, APPLIED MATHEMATICS. *Educ:* Univ Tex, Austin, BES, 63, MS, 65, PhD(mech eng), 68. *Prof Exp:* Instr math & physics, Southwestern Univ, Tex, 64-65; res engr, Tracor, Inc, 65-66; asst prof mech eng, Univ Tex, Austin, 68-69 & NC State Univ, 69-70; sr staff physicist, Hamilton Watch Co, 70-71; asst prof physics, Tex Lutheran Col, 71-77; mem staff, Radian Corp, 77-79; MEM STAFF, DEPT MECH ENG, TEX A&M UNIV, 79- *Mem:* Am Soc Mech Engrs. *Res:* Classical mechanics; engineering applications of elasticity, vibration theory, rigid body dynamics; dynamics of mechanisms, torsional vibrations of machinery trains. *Mailing Add:* 5802 Marilyn Dr Austin TX 78731

DOUGLAS, ALEXANDER EDGAR, molecular spectroscopy, deceased

DOUGLAS, ALLAN STANLEY, b Boston, Mass, Dec 27, 39; m 62; c 5. CHEMICAL ENGINEERING, POLYMER CHEMISTRY. *Educ:* Mass Inst Technol, SB, 61, SM, 63, ScD(chem eng), 66. *Prof Exp:* Proj engr, Dynatech Corp, Mass, 62-65; fel eng & asst prof chem eng, Mass Inst Technol, 66-68; staff assoc, Gulf Gen Atomic Inc, Calif, 68-70; dir membrane develop, Millipore Corp, 70-73; sr res engr, Stauffer Chem Co, 73-74; sr re engr, Pall Corp, 74-77, sr staff scientist, 77-79; consult, 79-82; PROF CHEM ENG, MANHATTEN COL, 82- *Concurrent Pos:* Lectr, San Diego State Col, 68-69. *Mem:* Am Inst Chem Engrs; Inst Environ Sci. *Res:* Structure-property relations of polymers; controlled porosity polymer membranes; reverse osmosis; air pollution control; filtration; process design. *Mailing Add:* 85 8th Ave Sea Cliff NY 11579

DOUGLAS, ALVIN GENE, agronomy, plant breeding, see previous edition

DOUGLAS, BEN HAROLD, b Wesson, Miss, Feb 20, 35; m 53; c 2. PHYSIOLOGY. *Educ:* Miss Col, BS, 56; Univ Miss, PhD(physiol), 64. *Prof Exp:* Instr basic electronics, Keesler AFB, Miss, 56-57; teacher physics, Copiah-Lincoln Jr Col, 57-60; chief instr, Sch Nursing, St Dominics Hosp, Miss, 62-63; from inst to asst prof, 64-68, ASSOC PROF PHYSIOL & BIOPHYSICS, UNIV MISS, 68-, PROF ANAT, 77-, ASST VCHANCELLOR, 81- *Concurrent Pos:* Estab investr, Am Heart Asn, 72-; vis investr, Blood Pressure Unit, Western Infirmary, Glasgow, Scotland, 73-74. *Mem:* AAAS; Am Heart Asn; Am Physiol Soc; Am Fedn Clin Res; Am Soc Study Reproduction. *Res:* Hypertension and hypertension effects on pregnancy. *Mailing Add:* Dept of Anat Univ of Miss Med Ctr Jackson MS 39216

DOUGLAS, BODIE EUGENE, b New Orleans, La, Dec 31, 24; m 45; c 4. INORGANIC CHEMISTRY. *Educ:* Tulane Univ, BS, 44, MS, 47; Univ Ill, PhD(chem), 49. *Prof Exp:* Asst, Tulane Univ, 46-47; res assoc chem, Pa State Univ, 49-50, asst prof, 50-52; from asst prof to assoc prof, 52-63, PROF CHEM, UNIV PITTSBURGH, 63- *Concurrent Pos:* Fulbright lectr, Univ Leeds, 54-55; vis prof, Osaka Univ, 70. *Mem:* fel AAAS; Am Chem Soc. *Res:* Coordination compounds; spectroscopy. *Mailing Add:* Dept of Chem Univ of Pittsburgh Pittsburgh PA 15260

DOUGLAS, BRUCE L, b New York, NY, July 14, 25; m 74; c 4. DENTISTRY, ORAL SURGERY. *Educ:* Princeton Univ, AB, 47; NY Univ, DDS, 48; Columbia Univ, dipl oral surg, 51, MA, 55, dipl higher educ, 57; Univ Calif, MPH, 62; Am Bd Oral & Maxillofacial Surg, dipl, 57. *Prof Exp:* Intern dent, Queens Gen Hosp, Jamaica, NY, 48-49; dent officer, US Navy, 51-53; resident oral surg, Queens Hosp Ctr, 53-54; pvt pract, 54-59; Fulbright prof oral surg, Col Dent, Okayama Univ, Japan, 59-61; assoc prof oral med & coordr social aspects dent, Col Dent & assoc prof prev med, Col Med, Univ Ill Med Ctr, 63-67, prof prev med, Col Med & prof community dent, Col Dent, 67-72, prof health admin, Sch Pub Health, 71-79; CHIEF, DENT DEPT, GRANT HOSP, CHICAGO, 81- *Concurrent Pos:* Assoc attend oral surgeon & dir oral surg training prog, New York City Hosp, Elmhurst, 56-59; attend oral surgeon, Chigaco Cent Hosp, 64-, chief, Dept Dent, 66-70, chmn, 78-80; dir dent dept, Mile Sq Health Ctr, Presby-St Luke's Hosp, 67-68; attend oral surgeon, Rush-Presby-St Luke's Med Ctr, Chicago, 67-77, dir, Dept Dent & Oral Surg, 68-75; mem, Ill House Rep, 71-74; prof dent & oral surg, Rush Med Col, 71-77; planning consult, Ill State Comprehensive Health Planning Agency, 75; dir, Off Dent Manpower Distrib, Ill Dept Pub Health, 75-76, chief, Div Dent Health, 76-77 & Health Manpower Develop, 77-78; Am Dent Asn; Sigma Xi; fel Am Pub Health Asn; fel Am Dent Soc Anesthesiol (pres); Am Asn Hosp Dentists (pres); prof surg, Chicago Med Sch, 79- *Res:* New methods of providing dental care to the chronically ill and aged; impact of water fluoridation on dental practice. *Mailing Add:* 1608 N Wells Chicago IL 60614

DOUGLAS, BRYCE, b Glasgow, Scotland, Jan 6, 24; m 55; c 3. MEDICINAL CHEMISTRY. *Educ:* Glasgow Univ, BS, 44; Univ Edinburgh, PhD(chem), 48. *Prof Exp:* Res chemist, J F MacFarlan & Co, Scotland, 44-46; asst, Royal Col Physicians Lab, 47-49; dept biol chem, Aberdeen Univ, 49; Nat Res Coun Can fel, 49-51; fel, Harvard Med Sch, 52-53; res assoc natural prod, Ind Univ, 53-56, vis res assoc, Univ Malaya, 56-58; group leader to sect head, 58-67, dir res macrobiol, 67-71, vpres, 71-80, pres, 80-81, res & develop, Pharmaceut Prod, VPRES, SCI & TECHNOL, SMITH KLINE & FRENCH LABS, 81- *Concurrent Pos:* Mem, Study Comn on Pharm, 73-75. *Mem:* AAAS; Am Chem Soc; Soc Chem Indust; fel Royal Inst Chem; The Chem Soc. *Res:* Alkaloids; chemotherapy; heterocyclic compounds; management science. *Mailing Add:* Smith Kline & French Labs 1500 Spring Garden St Philadelphia PA 19101

DOUGLAS, CARROLL REECE, b Knoxville, Tenn, Sept 3, 32; m 51; c 1. POULTRY NUTRITION. *Educ:* Univ Tenn, BS, 55, PhD(animal nutrit), 66; Univ Fla, MSA, 59. *Prof Exp:* Asst poultry nutrit, Univ Tenn, 56-57; interim asst, Univ Fla, 57-59; farm mgr, Am Develop Corp, Fla, 60; asst mgr & mgr chick hatchery, Fla State Hatcheries, 60-62; nutritionist & supvr, Loret Mills, Tenn, 62; asst poultry nutrit, Univ Tenn, 62-66, poultryman & leader exten poultry, Agr Exten Serv, 66-69; asst prof poultry mgt & asst scientist, 69-73, assoc prof, 73-79, PROF POULTRY MGT & EXTEN POULTRYMAN, UNIV FLA, 79- *Mem:* AAAS; Poultry Sci Asn; World Poultry Sci Asn. *Res:* Protein, amino acid, energy and mineral requirements of broilers and laying hens; xanthophyll utilization by the chicken; management systems for growing chickens; nutrition of growing pullet. *Mailing Add:* Dept of Poultry Sci Univ of Fla Gainesville FL 32601

DOUGLAS, CHARLES FRANCIS, b Tucson, Ariz, July 16, 30; m 52; c 2. AGRONOMY. *Educ:* Univ Ill, BS, 56, MS, 57; Purdue Univ, PhD(agron), 61. *Prof Exp:* Agr consult, Tenn Valley Authority, 61-65, supvr agr & indust educ progs on fertilizer mfr & use, Midwestern & New Eng States, 65-69; HEAD DEPT AGRON, COASTAL PLAIN EXP STA, UNIV GA, 69- *Mem:* Am Soc Agron. *Res:* Crop physiology and ecology; fertilizer education; experimental fertilizer use. *Mailing Add:* Dept Agron Coastal Plain Exp Sta Univ Ga PO Box 748 Tifton GA 31793

DOUGLAS, CHARLES HERBERT, b Loughman, Fla, Dec 2, 26; m 49; c 2. RESEARCH ADMINISTRATION. *Educ:* Converse Col, BM, 49, MM, 58; Fla State Univ, PhD(music), 65. *Prof Exp:* Teacher pub schs, SC, 49-50; instr, US Vet Rehab Sch, La, 50-51; teacher parochial & pvt schs, La, 53-57; asst prof music, Converse Col, 57-61; from asst prof to assoc prof music, 61-67, asst dean arts & sci, 67-68, asst vpres all areas, 68-71, ASST VPRES RES & DIR GEN RES, UNIV GA, 71- *Concurrent Pos:* Mem, Nat Coun Univ Res Adminr & Nat Conf Admin Res, 68- *Mem:* Am Soc Cybernet; Am Soc Info Sci; Nat Oceanog Asn. *Res:* Developing research programs in natural and social sciences, humanities and fine arts. *Mailing Add:* Off of VPres for Res Univ of Ga Athens GA 30602

DOUGLAS, CHARLES LEIGH, b Danville, Ill, Aug 2, 30; m 77; c 2. MAMMALIAN ECOLOGY. *Educ:* Antioch Col, AB, 59; Dartmouth Col, MS, 61; Univ Kans, PhD(zool), 67. *Prof Exp:* Biologist, Wetherill Mesa Archeol Proj, Mesa Verde Nat Park, 61-64; res scientist biol, Tex Mem Mus, Univ Tex, Austin, 66-69; assoc prof, Prescott Col, 69-73; assoc prof, 73-78, PROF, DEPT BIOL SCI, UNIV NEV, LAS VEGAS, 79-, RES SCIENTIST & UNIT LEADER, NAT PARK SERV COOP RESOURCES STUDIES UNIT, 73- *Concurrent Pos:* Collabr, Mesa Verde Nat Park, 65-70; chmn fac, Prescott Col, 70-71, chmn, Ctr Man & Environ, 71-73; partner, Southwestern Environ Consult, 72-74. *Mem:* Am Soc Mammalogists; Ecol Soc Am; Wildlife Soc. *Res:* Ecology of desert bighorn sheep and feral burros; analysis and interpretation of faunal remains from archeological sites; microanatomy of hair; aging parameters in southwestern mammals. *Mailing Add:* Dept of Biol Sci Univ of Nev Las Vegas NV 89154

DOUGLAS, DAVID LEWIS, b Seattle, Wash, Jan 22, 20; m 48; c 2. PHYSICAL CHEMISTRY. *Educ:* Calif Inst Technol, BS, 47, PhD(phys chem), 51. *Prof Exp:* Res assoc, Knolls Atomic Power Lab, Gen Elec Co, 51-55, phys chemist, Res Lab, 55-60, mgr fuel cell eng, Aircraft Accessory Turbine Dept, 60-62, tech planning, Direct Energy Conversion Oper, 62-64; dir res & develop, Gould-Nat Batteries, Inc, Gould Inc, 64-66, vpres res, 66-70, vpres & dir energy tech lab, 70-74, vpres contract res, 74-79; TECH MGR, ELEC POWER RES INST, 79- *Mem:* Fel AAAS; fel Am Inst Chem; Am Phys Soc; Am Chem Soc; Electrochem Soc. *Res:* Electrochemistry; fuel cells; batteries. *Mailing Add:* 4237 Ponce Dr Palo Alto CA 94306

DOUGLAS, DEXTER RICHARD, b Benton, Ohio, Nov 14, 37; m 62; c 2. PLANT PATHOLOGY, BOTANY. *Educ:* Kent State Univ, BS, 62; Univ Wyo, MS, 65; Univ Minn, PhD(plant path), 68. *Prof Exp:* Res pathologist, USDA, Res & Exten Ctr, Univ Idaho, 68-75; dir res, Chem Supply Co Inc, Twin Falls, Idaho, 76-78; pres, Hi-Alta, Inc, 78-80; AREA MGR, IDAHO CROP IMPROVEMENT ASN INC, 80- *Concurrent Pos:* Agr consult, 76-78. *Mem:* Am Potato Asn; Am Phytopath Soc. *Res:* Control of potato resistance and control of post-harvest pathogens. *Mailing Add:* Box 188 Idaho Crop Improvement Asn Inc Idaho Falls ID 83401

DOUGLAS, DONALD WILLS, JR, b Washington, DC, July 3, 17; m 39, 50; c 2. AEROSPACE ENGINEERING. *Prof Exp:* Engr, Douglas Aircraft Co, Inc, Calif, 39-43, chief flight test group in chg testing models, 43-51, dir contract admin, 48, in chg res labs, Santa Monica Div, 49, vpres mil sales, 51-57, pres, 57-67, pres, Douglas Aircraft Co Div, McDonnell Co, 67-68, vpres admin, McDonnell Douglas Corp, 68-73, sr corp vpres, 71-73, pres, Douglas Aircraft Co Can, Ltd, 68-71, DIR, MCDONNELL DOUGLAS CORP, 67-, CHMN, DOUGLAS AIRCRAFT CO CAN, LTD, 71- *Concurrent Pos:* Pres, Douglas Develop Co, Calif, 72-74; chmn & chief exec officer, La Fleur Cryogenics Co, Calif, 74-; sr consult mkt develop, Biphase Energy Systs. *Honors & Awards:* Chevalier, Legion of Honor, France; Officiale, Order of Merit, Repub of Italy. *Mem:* Nat Acad Eng; Aerospace Industs Asn; Nat Defense Transp Asn; Am Ord Asn; Newcomen Soc. *Mailing Add:* 707 Brooktree Rd Pacific Palisades CA 90272

DOUGLAS, DOROTHY ANN, b Bennington, Vt, May 13, 51. ECOLOGY, BOTANY. *Educ:* Oberlin Col, BA, 72; Univ Calif, Berkeley, PhD(bot), 77. *Prof Exp:* ASST PROF BIOL, EARLHAM COL, 77- *Concurrent Pos:* NSF fel, 72-75; Sigma Xi grants, 75 & 76; Prof Develop Fund grant, Earlham Col, 78- *Mem:* Ecol Soc Am; Bot Soc Am; Brit Ecol Soc. *Res:* Plant ecology; reproductive ecology and demography; arctic and alpine ecology. *Mailing Add:* Dept of Biol Earlham Col Box 57 Richmond IN 47374

DOUGLAS, EDWARD CURTIS, b Greensburg, Pa, July 27, 40; m 73; c 2. ELECTRICAL ENGINEERING. *Educ:* Col Wooster, BA, 62; NY Univ, MEE, 64, PhD(elec eng), 69. *Prof Exp:* Mem tech staff elec eng, David Sarnoff Res Lab, 69-79, MGR, ADVAN PROCESS TECHNOL DEVELOP, SOLID STATE TECHNOL CTR, RCA CORP, 79- *Mem:* Inst Elec & Electronics Engrs; Electrochem Soc. *Res:* Technology development for very-large-scale integration in areas of ion implantation, plasma etching, direct step on vafe, photolithography, low pressure chemical vapor deposition, direct digital controlled furnaces, and advanced iox photo masks. *Mailing Add:* RCA Solid State Technol Ctr Rte 202 MS 111 Somervville NJ 08876

DOUGLAS, GORDON WATKINS, b Midlothian, Va, June 2, 21; m 54; c 4. OBSTETRICS & GYNECOLOGY. *Educ:* Princeton Univ, AB, 42; Johns Hopkins Univ, MD, 45. *Prof Exp:* Asst, 49-52, asst prof, 53-56, PROF OBSTET & GYNEC & CHMN DEPT, SCH MED, NY UNIV, 56- *Concurrent Pos:* Markle scholar, 52; dir, Am Bd Obstet & Gynec, 64- *Mem:* Am Col Obstet & Gynec; Am Col Surg; Asn Profs Gynec & Obstet; Harvey Soc; Am Gynec Soc. *Res:* Immunology. *Mailing Add:* Dept of Obstet & Gynec NY Univ Sch of Med New York NY 10016

DOUGLAS, HOWARD CLARK, b Los Angeles, Calif, July 4, 10; m 36; c 3. MICROBIOLOGY. *Educ:* Univ Calif, AB, 36, PhD(microbiol), 49. *Prof Exp:* From instr to assoc prof, 41-58, PROF MICROBIOL, UNIV WASH, 58-, PROF IMMUNOL & GENETICS, 77- *Mem:* Am Soc Microbiol; Brit Soc Gen Microbiol. *Res:* Bacterial taxonomy and biochemistry; physiology genetics of yeast. *Mailing Add:* Dept of Genetics Univ of Wash Seattle WA 98195

DOUGLAS, HUGH, b Salisbury, SRhodesia, Oct 28, 27; m 53; c 4. NATURAL RESOURCES ECONOMICS. *Educ:* Amherst Col, AB, 49; Columbia Univ, MA, 51. *Prof Exp:* Geologist, AEC, 51 & Tex Gulf Sulphur Co, 51-55; sr geologist & asst to mgr, Am Overseas Petrol Ltd, Turkey, 55-59 & Libya, 59-62; consult, Oil Shale Corp & Swan Petrol Ltd, 62-63; secy treas, Thermonetics, Inc, 63-65; indust economist energy & natural resources & mgr mining & mineral econ, Stanford Res Inst, 65-71; mgr mineral planning, Utah Int Inc, 71-76; PRES, HUGH DOUGLAS & CO, RESOURCES ECON CONSULTS, 76- *Concurrent Pos:* Consult prof mineral econ, Stanford Univ. *Mem:* Mining & Metall Soc Am; Corp Planners Asn; Am Inst Mining, Metall & Petrol Engrs; Am Asn Petrol Geologists; Soc Econ Geologists. *Res:* Metals and minerals substitutes; economic analysis of world metals and minerals industries. *Mailing Add:* 2108 Baker San Francisco CA 94115

DOUGLAS, J(AMES) M(ERRILL), b Aurora, Ill, July 27, 33; m; c 2. CHEMICAL ENGINEERING. *Educ:* Johns Hopkins Univ, BE, 54; Univ Del, PhD(chem eng), 60. *Prof Exp:* Res chem engr, Atlantic Refining Co, Pa, 60-62, res assoc, 62-65; asst prof chem eng, Univ Del, 65; assoc prof, Univ Rochester, 65-68; PROF CHEM ENG, UNIV MASS, AMHERST, 68- *Concurrent Pos:* Atlantic Refining Co res grant, Imp Col, Univ London, 64. *Mem:* Am Inst Chem Engrs. *Res:* Process dynamics and control; optimization theory; reaction kinetics; reactor design. *Mailing Add:* Dept of Chem Eng Univ of Mass Amherst MA 01003

DOUGLAS, JAMES, b Uvalde, Tex, Oct 1, 14; m 41; c 4. CIVIL ENGINEERING. *Educ:* US Naval Acad, BS, 38; Rensselaer Polytech Inst, BCE & MCE, 43; Stanford Univ, PhD(civil eng), 63. *Prof Exp:* Instr construct, 61-63, assoc prof, 63-75, PROF CIVIL ENG, STANFORD UNIV, 75- *Concurrent Pos:* Chmn comt construct mgt, Hwy Res Bd, 70. *Honors & Awards:* Thomas Fitch Rowland Prize, 69 & Construct Mgt Award, 75, Am Soc Civil Engrs. *Mem:* Fel Am Soc Civil Engrs; Am Soc Eng Educ. *Res:* Economics of construction equipment ownership, obsolescence, depreciation, standardization; simulation of construction equipment operations using statistical-computer solution. *Mailing Add:* Dept of Civil Eng Sch of Eng Stanford Univ Stanford CA 94305

DOUGLAS, JAMES NATHANIEL, b Dallas, Tex, Aug 14, 35; div; c 3. RADIO ASTRONOMY. *Educ:* Yale Univ, BS, 56, MS, 58, PhD(astron), 61. *Prof Exp:* Instr astron, Yale Univ, 60-61, from asst prof to assoc prof, 61-71, PROF ASTRON, UNIV TEX, AUSTIN, 71- *Concurrent Pos:* Mem Comn 5, Int Sci Radio Union, 63-; mem, Int Astron Union, 64-; mem, Adv Panel for Astron, NSF, 71-74. *Mem:* Fel AAAS; Am Astron Soc; Am Geophys Union. *Res:* Studies of decametric radiation from Jupiter and from discrete radio sources. *Mailing Add:* Dept of Astron Univ of Tex Austin TX 78712

DOUGLAS, JOCELYN FIELDING, b Delta, Utah, Jan 25, 27; m 51; c 3. BIOCHEMISTRY. *Educ:* Univ Ill, BS, 48; Columbia Univ, MA, 50, PhD(chem), 53. *Prof Exp:* Asst chem, Columbia Univ, 48-52; res chemist, Johnson & Johnson, 52-54, proj leader, 54-58; dir biochem, Wallace Labs, 58-74; SCI CONSULT, 74- *Concurrent Pos:* Expert, Nat Cancer Inst, 76-80 & dep dir, Carcinogenesis Testing Prog, 79- *Mem:* AAAS; Am Soc Pharmacol & Exp Therapeut; Am Chem Soc; Int Soc Biochem Pharmacol; NY Acad Sci. *Res:* Metabolism; hypocholestermic agents; chemical carcinogenesis toxicology; drug analysis; scientific consulting; biopharmaceutics; scientific management. *Mailing Add:* Hermitage Farm PO Box 533 Front Royal VA 22630

DOUGLAS, JOHN EDWARD, b Normal, Ill, June 29, 26; m 51; c 3. PHYSICAL CHEMISTRY. *Educ:* Univ Chicago, BS, 47, MS, 48; Univ Wash, PhD(chem), 52. *Prof Exp:* Instr chem, Univ Wyo, 52-56; phys chemist, Stanford Res Inst, 56-60; assoc prof, 60-66, chmn dept, 73-76, PROF CHEM, EASTERN WASH UNIV, 66-, ACTG VPROVOST ACAD AFFAIRS, 80- *Mem:* Am Chem Soc. *Res:* Gas phase kinetics; energetics of complex formation; application of molecular orbital methods to molecular interactions. *Mailing Add:* Acad Affairs Off Eastern Wash Univ Cheney WA 99004

DOUGLAS, JOSEPH FRANCIS, b Indianapolis, Ind, Oct 31, 26; m 50; c 4. ELECTRICAL ENGINEERING. *Educ:* Purdue Univ, BSEE, 48; Univ Mo, MSEE, 62. *Prof Exp:* Proj engr elec eng, USDA, 48-56; asst prof, Southern Univ, 56-62, assoc prof & head dept, 62-64; training coordr, Atomics Div, Am Mach & Foundry Co, 64-66; group leader elec technol & eng, 66-74, app assoc dean acad instr, 74-77, asst prof eng, 66-70, ASSOC PROF ENG, PA STATE UNIV, YORK, 70-, ASSOC PROF ELEC TECHNOL, BACHELOR TECHNOL PROG, 77- *Mem:* Sr mem Inst Elec & Electronics Engrs. *Res:* Low speed with reasonable torque output from electrical induction motors of the wound rotor class. *Mailing Add:* Pa State Univ Off W-252 Capitol Campus Rte 20 Middletown PA 17057

DOUGLAS, KENNETH THOMAS, bio-organic chemistry, see previous edition

DOUGLAS, LARRY JOE, b Oklahoma City, Okla, Mar 3, 37; m 69; c 5. PHYSICAL CHEMISTRY, ELECTROCHEMISTRY. *Educ:* Univ Denver, BS, 58, PhD(phys chem), 70. *Prof Exp:* Assoc res engr, Nat Cash Register Co, Calif, 58-61, res engr, 62-64; res scientist, Denver Res Ctr, Marathon Oil Co, 70-76; SR PROG MGR ALCOHOL FUELS, SOLAR ENERGY RES INST, 78- *Mem:* AAAS; Sigma Xi; Electrochem Soc; Soc Petrol Engrs. *Res:* Mass transport mechanisms in oxide crystals; electrochemistry of alloy deposition; liquid/liquid and liquid/solid interfacial properties; adsorption into and from micellar solutions; electrokinetic behavior of non-electrolytic fluids. *Mailing Add:* 1747 S Field Ct Denver CO 80226

DOUGLAS, LOWELL ARTHUR, b Durango, Colo, June 17, 26; m 53; c 2. CLAY MINERALOGY, SOIL GENESIS. *Educ:* Utah State Univ, BS, 52, MS, 59; Rutgers Univ, PhD(soils), 61. *Prof Exp:* Soil chemist, US Salinity Lab, 54-56; from instr to assoc prof, 59-69, PROF SOILS, RUTGERS UNIV, 69-, DIR GRAD PROG IN SOILS & CROPS, 76- *Concurrent Pos:* Ed, Soil Sci, 79- *Mem:* Soil Sci Soc Am; Clay Minerals Soc; Mineral Soc Am; Int Soc Soil Sci. *Res:* Clay mineralogy, soil micromorphology; soil chemistry; soils and faulting; clay mineral genesis and alteration. *Mailing Add:* Dept of Soils & Crops Rutgers The State Univ New Brunswick NJ 08903

DOUGLAS, MATTHEW M, b East Grand Rapids, Mich, Apr 3, 49; m 73; c 2. THERMOREGULATORY ECOLOGY. *Educ:* Univ Mich, Ann Arbor, BA, 72; Eastern Mich Univ, MS, 74; Univ Kans, PhD(entomol), 78. *Prof Exp:* Asst prof entom, Calif State Univ, Fresno, 77-78; asst prof, Boston Univ, 78-80; WRITER & RESEARCHER, 81- *Concurrent Pos:* Lectr, Marine Prog, Boston Univ, 79; Consult, Arthur D Little, Inc, 79, Boston Mus Sci, 80; asst prof zool, Harvard Univ, 79; adj asst prof entom & biophys ecol, Boston Univ, 81-82; adj sr res scientist, Univ Kans, 82- *Mem:* AAAS; Soc Study Evolution; Lepidopterists Soc; Entom Soc Am. *Res:* Behavioral and physiological thermoregulatory strategies of insects, especially the Lepidoptera; fern defenses, chemical and other, against insect attack. *Mailing Add:* 1503 Woodland St Jenison MI 49428

DOUGLAS, MICHAEL GILBERT, b Perth, Western Australia, June 9, 45; US citizen; m 73; c 2. BIOCHEMISTRY, MOLECULAR BIOLOGY. *Educ:* Southwestern Univ, BS, 67; St Louis Univ, PhD(biochem), 74. *Prof Exp:* Res assoc, Dept Biochem, Health Sci Ctr, Univ Tex, Dallas, 73-75; Swiss State fel, Biozentrum, Dept Biochem, Univ Basel, 75-77; ASST PROF BIOCHEM, HEALTH SCI CTR, UNIV TEX, 77- *Concurrent Pos:* NIH fel, Univ Tex, Dallas, 74-75; NIH grant, 78-81. *Mem:* Am Soc Cell Biol; Am Soc Chem; AAAS; NY Acad Sci. *Res:* Biochemical genetics and assembly of intracellular organelle membranes. *Mailing Add:* Dept Biochem Univ Tex Health Sci Ctr San Antonio TX 78284

DOUGLAS, NEIL HARRISON, b Moorefield, WVa, Feb 17, 32; m 58; c 2. SYSTEMATIC ICHTHYOLOGY. *Educ:* Okla State Univ, BS, 55, MS, 59, PhD(zool), 62. *Prof Exp:* Asst zool, Okla State Univ, 57-59, asst water pollution, 59-62; from asst prof to assoc prof, 62-72, prof zool, 72-80, PROF BIOL, NORTHEAST LA UNIV, 80- *Mem:* Am Fisheries Soc; Am Soc Icthyologists & Herpetologists. *Res:* Taxonomy of freshwater fishes; herpetology; fresh water fishes of Louisiana. *Mailing Add:* Dept of Biol Northeast La Univ Monroe LA 71209

DOUGLAS, RICHARD HERBERT, b Edmonton, Alta, Sept 20, 19; m 44; c 2. ATMOSPHERIC PHYSICS, AGRICULTURAL METEOROLOGY. *Educ:* Univ Alta, BSc, 41; Univ Toronto, MA, 45, PhD(meteorol), 57. *Prof Exp:* Meteorologist, Meteorol Serv Can, 41-51, res meteorologist, 51-60; res assoc meteorol, McGill Univ, 57-60, assoc prof, 60-65; chmn dept, 65-76, PROF AGR PHYSICS, MACDONALD COL, MCGILL UNIV, 65- *Concurrent Pos:* Field dir, Alta Hail Studies, 56-65, sci dir, 65-69. *Mem:* Can Meteorol & Oceanog Soc; Sigma Xi. *Res:* Cloud and precipitation physics; severe storms, particularly hail; agrometeorology; in-crop climate; crop-atmosphere interaction. *Mailing Add:* Dept Agr Chem & Physics Macdonald Campus McGill Univ Ste Anne de Bellevue Quebec PQ H9X 1C0 Can

DOUGLAS, ROBERT ALDEN, b High Point, NC, Dec 4, 25; m; c 3. MECHANICS, MATERIALS SCIENCE. *Educ:* Purdue Univ, BS, 51, MS, 52, PhD(mech), 56. *Prof Exp:* Mgr res & develop, Danly Mach Specialties, 56-58; from assoc prof to prof mech, 58-74, assoc head dept eng mech & mgr themis res prog, 67-74, PROF CIVIL ENG, NC STATE UNIV, 76- *Concurrent Pos:* Dep dir, US Eng Team, Afghanistan, 64-66. *Mem:* Soc Exp Stress Anal; Am Soc Eng Educ; Am Soc Civil Engrs; Soc Eng Sci. *Res:* Wave propagation; the behavior of solids during impact; biomechanics; wave velocities in human tissue. *Mailing Add:* Dept of Civil Eng 208 Mann Hall NC State Univ Raleigh NC 27650

DOUGLAS, ROBERT GORDON, JR, b New York, NY, Apr 17, 34; m 56; c 3. INTERNAL MEDICINE, INFECTIOUS DISEASES. *Educ:* Princeton Univ, AB, 55; Cornell Univ, MD, 59. *Prof Exp:* Intern med, NY Hosp, 59-60, asst resident, 60-61; asst resident, Johns Hopkins Hosp, 61-62; chief resident, NY Hosp, 62-63; clin assoc & clin investr, Lab Clin Invest, Nat Inst Allergy & Infectious Dis, 63-66; from instr to assoc prof microbiol & med, Bayler Col

Med, 66-70; assoc prof med & microbiol, Univ Rochester, 70-74, prof, 74-82, head, Infectious Dis Unit, Sch Med & Dent, 70-82, sr assoc dean educ, 79-82; PROF MED & CHMN DEPT, MED COL, CORNELL UNIV, 82-; PHYSICIAN IN CHIEF, NEW YORK HOSP, 82- *Mem:* Am Soc Clin Invest; Am Soc Microbiol; Am Asn Immunol; Am Fedn Clin Res; fel Am Col Physicians. *Res:* Pathogenesis of respiratory viral infections; influenza; vaccines; antiviral chemotherapy; secretory antibody; clinical virology. *Mailing Add:* Cornell Med Ctr New York Hosp 525 E 68th St New York NY 10021

DOUGLAS, ROBERT HAZARD, b Miami, Fla, Feb 23, 47. REPRODUCTIVE PHYSIOLOGY. *Educ:* WVa Univ, BS, 69, MS, 72; Univ Wis, PhD(endocrinol, reproductive physiol), 75. *Prof Exp:* Asst prof reproductive physiol, Mich State Univ, 75-78; mem staff, 78-80, ASST PROF VET SCI, UNIV KY, 80- *Mem:* Am Asn Animal Sci. *Res:* Control of luteolysis and induction of ovulation in large domestic farm species. *Mailing Add:* Dept of Vet Sci Univ of Ky Lexington KY 40506

DOUGLAS, ROBERT JAMES, b Seattle, Wash, Dec 4, 37. MATHEMATICS. *Educ:* Univ Wash, BS, 61, MS, 66, PhD(math), 68. *Prof Exp:* Res assoc, Univ NC, Chapel Hill, 68-69; asst prof, 69-74, assoc prof, 74-77, PROF MATH, SAN FRANCISCO STATE UNIV, 77- *Mem:* Am Math Soc; Math Asn Am. *Res:* Combinatorial analysis; graph theory. *Mailing Add:* Dept Math Sch Natural Sci San Francisco State Univ San Francisco CA 94132

DOUGLAS, ROBERT JOHN, b Toronto, Ont, May 3, 25; m 47; c 3. MICROBIOLOGY. *Educ:* Univ Toronto, BSA, 49, MSA, 50; Mich State Univ, PhD, 55. *Prof Exp:* Lectr bact, 50-56, from asst prof to assoc prof, 56-70, PROF RES, DEPT MICROBIOL, ONT AGR COL, UNIV GUELPH, 70- *Mem:* Am Soc Microbiol; Can Soc Microbiol; Can Fedn Biol Sci. *Res:* Physiology and serology of streptomyces; immunology. *Mailing Add:* Dept of Microbiol Ont Agr Col Univ of Guelph Guelph ON N1G 2W1 Can

DOUGLAS, ROBERT JOHN WILSON, geology, deceased

DOUGLAS, RONALD GEORGE, b Osgood, Ind, Dec 10, 38; c 3. MATHEMATICS. *Educ:* Ill Inst Technol, BS, 60; La State Univ, PhD(math), 62. *Prof Exp:* From res instr to assoc prof math, Univ Mich, 62-69; chmn dept, 71-73, PROF MATH, STATE UNIV NY STONY BROOK, 69-, CHMN DEPT, 81- *Concurrent Pos:* Mem, Inst Advan Study, 65-66; Sloan fel, 68-74; sr res fel, Newcastle Univ, Eng, 74. *Mem:* Am Math Soc; Math Asn Am. *Res:* Operator theory; functional analysis; measure theory; abstract harmonic analysis. *Mailing Add:* Dept of Math State Univ of NY Stony Brook NY 11794

DOUGLAS, ROY RENE, b Chicago, Ill, Oct 8, 38; m 66; c 2. TOPOLOGY. *Educ:* Northwestern Univ, BA, 60; Univ Calif, Berkeley, MA, 63, PhD(math), 65. *Prof Exp:* Res asst, Univ Calif, Berkeley, 63-65; asst prof, 65-69, ASSOC PROF MATH, UNIV BC, 69- *Concurrent Pos:* Nat Res Coun Can grant, 67- *Mem:* Am Math Soc; Can Math Cong. *Res:* Algebraic topology; H-spaces and rational homotopy theory. *Mailing Add:* Dept of Math Univ of BC Vancouver Can

DOUGLAS, STEVEN DANIEL, b Jamaica, NY, Feb 28, 39. MEDICINE, IMMUNOLOGY. *Educ:* Cornell Univ, AB, 59, MD, 63. *Prof Exp:* Intern med, Mt Sinai Hosp, NY, 63-64, asst resident, 66-67; staff assoc surgeon, Lab Exp Path, Nat Inst Arthritis, Metab & Digestive Dis, 64-66; NIH fel immunol & hemat, Dept Med, Univ Calif, San Francisco, 67-69; from asst prof to assoc prof med, Mt Sinai Sch Med, 69-74; assoc prof, 74-76, prof med & microbiol, Sch Med, Univ Minn, 76-80; DIR, DIV ALLERGY-IMMUNOL, CHILDREN'S HOSP PHILADELPHIA, 80-; PROF PEDIAT & MICROBIOL, SCH MED, UNIV PA, 80- *Concurrent Pos:* Asst attend physician, Mt Sinai Med Sch, 69-73; Nat Heart & Lung Inst grant, 69-74; Nat Inst Allergy & Infectious Dis grant, 74-; rep, Am Bd Med Lab Immunol, 74- *Honors & Awards:* Redway Award, Med Soc State NY, 77; Emil Conason Mem Award, Mt Sinai Sch Med, 70; William Hammond Award, NY State J Med, 80. *Mem:* Am Soc Clin Invest; Am Acad Microbiol; Am Asn Immunologists; Soc Exp Biol & Med; Soc Cell Biol. *Res:* Cellular immunology, cell biology and genetics, arthritis; differentiation of mononuclear phagocytes; author of over 50 scientific publications. *Mailing Add:* Children's Hosp Philadelphia 34th & Civic Ctr Blvd Philadelphia PA 19104

DOUGLAS, TOMMY CHARLES, b Durant, Okla, Sept 29, 46. GENETICS, IMMUNOLOGY. *Educ:* Princeton Univ, AB, 69; Calif Inst Technol, MS, 70, PhD(immunol), 74. *Prof Exp:* Fel immunogenetics, Calif Inst Technol, 74; mem staff, Basel Inst Technol, 74-76; ASST PROF MED GENETICS, UNIV TEX HEALTH SCI CTR, 76- *Mem:* Sigma Xi; Am Asn Immunologists. *Res:* Genetically determined variation in mammals, particularly with respect to cell surface antigens, immune responsiveness, immunoglobulins, and the major histocompatability complex. *Mailing Add:* Med Genetics Ctr UTGSBS PO Box 20334 Astrodome Sta Houston TX 77025

DOUGLAS, W J MURRAY, b Briercrest, Sask, Feb 15, 27; c 1. CHEMICAL ENGINEERING. *Educ:* Queen's Univ, Ont, BSc, 48; Univ Mich, MSE, 52, PhD(chem eng), 58. *Prof Exp:* Develop engr, Polymer Corp, Ont, 48-51; from asst prof to assoc prof, 58-69, PROF CHEM ENG, MCGILL UNIV, 69-, CHMN DEPT, 77- *Concurrent Pos:* Consult, Pulp & Paper Res Inst Can, 62- *Mem:* AAAS; Am Inst Chem Engrs; Chem Inst Can. *Res:* Transport processes, including transport of heat, mass and momentum; chemical reaction and diffusion; mixing. *Mailing Add:* Dept of Chem Eng McGill Univ Montreal PQ H3A 2T6 Can

DOUGLAS, WALTER S, b Cranford, NJ, Jan 22, 12; m 38; c 3. CIVIL & TRANSPORTATION ENGINEERING. *Educ:* Dartmouth Col, BA, 33; Harvard Univ, MS, 35. *Prof Exp:* Partner, 52-56, pres, 59-66, chmn, 66-77, SR PARTNER, PARSONS BRINCKERHOFF QUADE & DOUGLAS,

INC, 66-, ASSOC CONSULT, 77- *Honors & Awards:* Moles Award, Am Soc Civil Engrs, James Laurie Prize; Hon Award, Newcomen Soc N Am. *Mem:* Nat Acad Eng; Am Inst Consult Eng; Soc Am Mil Engrs; fel Am Soc Civil Engrs. *Mailing Add:* Parsons Brinckerhoff 1 Penn Plaza New York NY 10001

DOUGLAS, WILLIAM H, b Saranac Lake, NY, Nov 1, 41; m 63; c 3. ANATOMY. *Educ:* State Univ NY, Plattsburgh, BS, 63; Brown Univ, MAT, 67, PhD(biomed sci), 70. *Prof Exp:* Assoc prof biol, Edinboro Col, 70-71; assoc dir & sr scientist cell culture, W Alton Jones Cell Sci Ctr, 71-78; ASSOC PROF ANAT, SCH MED, TUFTS UNIV, 78- *Concurrent Pos:* Fel, Div Biol & Med Sci, Brown Univ, 70; consult, Dept Med, Mem Hosp, Pawtucket, RI, 73-78; grants, Am Lung Asn, 73-75, NIH, 74-78 & United Cerebral Palsy Res & Educ Found, 75-78. *Mem:* Am Asn Anatomists; Histochem Soc; Am Thoracic Soc; Am Soc Cell Biol; Tissue Cult Asn. *Res:* Isolation and culture of diploid epithelial cells from lung, liver and prostate; ultrastructural and biochemical characterization of these cultures. *Mailing Add:* Dept of Anat Sch of Med Tufts Univ Boston MA 02111

DOUGLAS, WILLIAM KENNEDY, b Estancia, NMex, Sept 5, 22; m 46; c 1. MEDICINE, AEROSPACE MEDICINE. *Educ:* Col Mines & Metal, Tex, BS, 46; Univ Tex, MD, 48; Johns Hopkins Univ, MPH, 54; Am Bd Prev Med, dipl & cert aviation med, 56. *Prof Exp:* Command flight surgeon, Hq, Northeast Air Command, US Air Force, 50-52, base surgeon, Harmon AFB, Nfld, 52-53, res aviation med, Johns Hopkins Univ & Langley AFB, 53-55, chief prof serv, Hq, Mil Air Transport Serv, 55-57, chief aircrew effectiveness br, Off Surgeon Gen, 57-59, flight surgeon, Proj Mercury Astronauts, NASA, 59-62, from asst dep bioastronaut hq, Air Force Missile Test Ctr to dir bioastronaut, Hq, Air Force Eastern Test Range, Patrick AFB, Fla, 62-66, asst dep chief staff bioastronaut & med, Hq, Systs Command, 66-68, chief cent aeromed serv, Hq, Europe, 68-71, vcomdr aerospace med div, Systs Command, US Air Force, 71-77; DIR PROG ENG-LIFE SCI, McDONNELL DOUGLAS ASTRONAUT CO, 77- *Concurrent Pos:* Mem, US Air Force Sci Adv Bd, 79- *Honors & Awards:* Louis H Bauer Found Award, Aerospace Med Asn, 64; John Jefferies Award, Am Inst Aeronaut & Astronaut, 65. *Mem:* fel Am Col Physicians; AMA; fel Aerospace Med Asn; Am Inst Aeronaut & Astronaut; Int Acad Astronaut. *Mailing Add:* McDonnell Douglas Astronaut Co 5301 Bolsa Ave Huntington Beach CA 90740

DOUGLAS, WILLIAM WILTON, b Glasgow, Scotland, Aug 15, 22; m 54; c 2. NEUROPHARMACOLOGY, NEUROENDOCRINOLOGY. *Educ:* Univ Glasgow, MB, ChB, 46, MD, 49. *Prof Exp:* Houseman, Glasgow West Infirmary, 46; houseman, Law Hosp, Carluke, 47; lectr physiol, Aberdeen Univ, 47-48; staff mem med res coun, Physiol & Pharmacol Div, Nat Inst Med Res, Eng, 50-56; vis assoc pharmacol, Col Physicians & Surg, Columbia Univ, 52-53; assoc prof, Albert Einstein Col Med, 56-58, prof, 58-68; PROF PHARMACOL, SCH MED, YALE UNIV, 68- *Mem:* Am Physiol Soc; Soc Pharmacol & Exp Therapeut; Pharmacol Soc Can; Brit Pharmacol Soc; Brit Physiol Soc. *Res:* Pharmacology and physiology of the neurohumoral transmission; cellular mechanisms of release of nervous and neuroendocrine secretions. *Mailing Add:* Dept of Pharmacol Yale Univ Sch of Med New Haven CT 06520

DOUGLASS, CARL DEAN, b Little Rock, Ark, Apr 27, 25; m 46; c 2. BIOCHEMISTRY. *Educ:* Hendrix Col, BS, 45; Univ Okla, MS, 49, PhD(chem), 52. *Prof Exp:* Asst, Univ Okla, 47; from instr to assoc prof biochem, Sch Med, Univ Ark, 52-59; chief nutrit res br, US Food & Drug Admin, 59-61; nutrit prog officer, Nat Inst Arthritis & Metab Dis, 61-64; chief res & training div, Nat Libr Med, 64-66, chief facil & resources div, 66-67; assoc dir prog develop, Div Res Facil & Resources, 67-69; assoc dir, Div Res Resources, 69-70, assoc dir, Statist, Anal & Res Eval, 70-71, dep dir, Div Res Grants, 71-77, DIR, DIV RES GRANTS, NIH, 77- *Mem:* Fel AAAS; Am Chem Soc; Soc Exp Biol & Med; Am Inst Nutrit; Am Inst Biol Sci. *Res:* Intermediary metabolism of drugs; metabolism of plant pigments. *Mailing Add:* Div of Res Grants NIH Bethesda MD 20014

DOUGLASS, CLAUDIA BETH, b Detroit, Mich, Oct 29, 50; m 78. BIOLOGY EDUCATION. *Educ:* Ind Univ, Bloomington, BS, 72, MAT, 74; Purdue Univ, W Lafayette, PhD(biol educ), 76. *Prof Exp:* Res asst biol educ, Purdue Univ, 74-75, instr physiol, 75-76, vis instr inst design, 76; asst prof biol, 76-79, ASSOC PROF BIOL, CENTRAL MICH UNIV, 80- *Concurrent Pos:* Consult mat develop, Univ Elem Sch, Bloomington, 73-74, Indianapolis Sickle Cell Found, 75-76; NSF grant, 77-79, book reviewer, Sci & Children, Am Biol Teacher, 73-; statist consult, Nat Inst Educ grant, 79; sci educ consult, Bilalian Child Develop Ctr, 80. *Mem:* Nat Asn Res Sci Teaching; Nat Asn Biol Teachers; Nat Sci Teachers Asn; Sch Sci & Math Asn. *Res:* Cognitive style, learning theory and motivation related to the development of instructional materials; individualized instruction including audio-tutorial, inquiry based and mastery learning techniques for high school, especially urban disadvantaged students. *Mailing Add:* Dept of Biol Cent Mich Univ Mt Pleasant MI 48859

DOUGLASS, DAVID HOLMES, b Bangor, Maine, Feb 12, 32; m 53; c 3. PHYSICS, ASTROPHYSICS. *Educ:* Univ Maine, BS, 55; Mass Inst Technol, PhD(physics), 59. *Prof Exp:* Res scientist physics, Lincoln Lab, Mass Inst Technol, 59-61, instr, 61-62; from asst prof to prof, Univ Chicago, 62-68; PROF PHYSICS, UNIV ROCHESTER, 68- *Concurrent Pos:* Alfred P Sloan res fel, 64-68. *Mem:* AAAS; Am Phys Soc; Int Soc Gen Relativity & Gravitation; Am Asn Physics Teachers; Am Astron Soc. *Res:* Liquid helium; superconductivity; low temperature, solid state, condensed matter and gravitation physics; gravitation waves; elementary particles; quarks. *Mailing Add:* Dept of Physics Univ of Rochester Rochester NY 14627

DOUGLASS, IRWIN BRUCE, b Des Moines, Iowa, Sept 2, 04; m 31; c 2. ENVIRONMENTAL CHEMISTRY. *Educ:* Monmouth Col, BS, 26, DSc, 58; Univ Kans, PhD(org chem), 32. *Prof Exp:* Teacher, Ill High Sch, 26-28; teacher, Kans City Jr Col, 30-31; asst chem, Univ Kans, 29-32; asst prof, NDak Agr Col, 32-33; asst prof, Northern Mont Col, 33-37; res asst, Yale

Univ, 37-38; prof, Northern Mont Col, 38-40; from asst prof to prof, 40-70, actg head dept, 41-46, head dept, 46-52, head planning off, 69-72, res prof, 72-74, EMER PROF CHEM, UNIV MAINE, 70- *Concurrent Pos:* Mem, Maine Bd Environ Protection, 74-77. *Mem:* AAAS; Am Chem Soc. *Res:* Kraft pulping odor control; organic sulfur compounds. *Mailing Add:* 904 Rt 2A Williston VT 05495

DOUGLASS, JAMES EDWARD, b Bessemer, Ala, Nov 3, 28; m 53; c 2. FORESTRY. *Educ:* Auburn Univ, BS, 51; Mich State Univ, MS, 55. *Prof Exp:* Conserv forester, Int Paper Co, 53-54; RES FORESTER, SOUTHEASTERN FOREST EXP STA, US FOREST SERV, ASHVILLE, 56-; MEM STAFF, COWEETA HYDROLOGIC LAB, 71- *Mem:* Soc Am Foresters; Soil Sci Soc Am. *Res:* Soil moisture-vegetative relations; forest hydrology using control and treatment experimental watershed approach. *Mailing Add:* Coweeta Hydrologic Lab Rte 1 Box 216 Otto NC 28763

DOUGLASS, JAMES EDWARD, b Corpus Christi, Tex, May 18, 30; m 55; c 2. ORGANIC CHEMISTRY. *Educ:* Rice Univ, BA, 52; Univ Tex, PhD(chem), 59. *Prof Exp:* Hickrill Chem Res Found res fel, 58-59; asst prof, Univ Ky, 60-65; assoc prof, 65-68, PROF CHEM, MARSHALL UNIV, 68- *Mem:* AAAS; Am Chem Soc. *Res:* Pyrimidinium ylide chemistry; heterocyclic synthesis. *Mailing Add:* Dept of Chem Marshall Univ Huntington WV 25701

DOUGLASS, KENNETH HARMON, b Rochester, NY. MEDICAL PHYSICS, NUCLEAR MEDICINE. *Educ:* Univ Rochester, BS, 64; Carnegie-Mellon Univ, MS, 66, PhD(physics), 69. *Prof Exp:* Asst prof physics, Pa State Univ, Schuylkill Campus, 69-71; res assoc biophysics, Johns Hopkins Univ, 71-74; instr, 74-80, ASST PROF NUCLEAR MED, JOHNS HOPKINS MED INST, 80- *Res:* Non-invasive studies of cardiac function; computerized image-processing. *Mailing Add:* Div Nuclear Med Johns Hopkins Med Inst Baltimore MD 21205

DOUGLASS, MATTHEW MCCARTNEY, b Port of Spain, Trinidad, Sept 21, 26; US citizen; m 54; c 5. CIVIL ENGINEERING, ENGINEERING EDUCATION. *Educ:* McGill Univ, BEng, 52; George Washington Univ, MSE, 62; Okla State Univ, PhD(civil eng), 66. *Prof Exp:* Jr engr, Kilborn Eng Co, Ont, 52; asst engr, Dept Works & Hydraul, Trinidad, 53-55; exec engr, 55-57; asst designer, E Lionel Pavlo, Consult Engrs, 57; from instr to asst prof civil eng, Howard Univ, 57-66; ASSOC PROF CIVIL ENG, CONCORDIA UNIV, 66- *Concurrent Pos:* Examr, Order Engrs of Quebec, 77- *Honors & Awards:* Western Elec Fund Award, Am Soc Eng Educ, 78-79. *Mem:* Am Soc Civil Engrs; Am Soc Eng Educ; Can Soc Civil Engrs. *Res:* Elastic-plastic buckling of columns; application of complementary potential energy to the analysis of space frameworks; curved-girder orthotropic bridges. *Mailing Add:* 91 Rockwyn Ave Pointe Claire Can

DOUGLASS, PRITCHARD CALKINS, b Jamestown, NY, Mar 22, 13; m 38; c 3. ANALYTICAL CHEMISTRY. *Educ:* Houghton Col, BS, 35. *Prof Exp:* Chemist, G C Murphy Co, 37-42; chemist, Bausch & Lomb Optical Co, 42-48; fel, Mellon Inst Indust Res, 48-51; microscopist cotton properties, Coats & Clark Res Labs, 51-53; chemist & head anal chem & controls, 53-63, chemist specialist, 63-78, CONSULT, BAUSCH & LOMB, INC, 78- *Mem:* Am Chem Soc; Electrochem Soc; Am Inst Chemists; Am Soc Testing & Mat. *Res:* Application of analytical and electrochemistry to chemical processes and materials; microscopy; environmental chemistry; instrumentation applied to metal finishing, glass, lubrication and polycrystalline materials. *Mailing Add:* 31 Pickford Dr Rochester NY 14618

DOUGLASS, RAYMOND CHARLES, b San Francisco, Calif, Mar 30, 23; m 48; c 2. INVERTEBRATE PALEONTOLOGY. *Educ:* Stanford Univ, BS, 50, PhD, 57; Univ Nebr, MS, 52. *Prof Exp:* Field asst, 47-48, GEOLOGIST, US GEOL SURV, 52- *Concurrent Pos:* Asst, Univ Nebr, 50-51; mem fac, USDA Grad Sch, 57-; from instr to assoc prof math, NY Univ, 50-56; assoc res prof, 56-58, PROF MATH, UNIV MD, COLLEGE PARK, 58- *Mem:* Am Math Soc; Math Asn Am. *Res:* Partial differential equations. *Mailing Add:* Dept of Math Univ of Md College Park MD 20742

DOUGLASS, ROBERT L, b Weiser, Idaho, July 25, 21; m 45; c 2. SPEECH PATHOLOGY. *Educ:* Univ Redlands, AB, 46, MA, 48; Univ Southern Calif, PhD, 51. *Prof Exp:* Speech therapist, Children's Hosp, Los Angeles, 50-51; from asst prof to assoc prof, 51-60, chmn dept speech & drama, 66-69, PROF SPEECH, CALIF STATE UNIV, LOS ANGELES, 60- *Concurrent Pos:* Res consult, Children's Speech & Hearing Ctr, 60-; speech consult, Lawrence Sch Except Children, 62- *Mem:* Am Psychol Asn; Am Speech & Hearing Asn. *Res:* Audiology; clinical psychology. *Mailing Add:* Dept of Speech & Drama Calif State Univ Los Angeles CA 90032

DOUGLASS, ROGER THACKREY, mathematics, see previous edition

DOUGLASS, TERRY DEAN, b Jackson, Tenn, Oct 26, 42; m 64; c 3. ELECTRONIC ENGINEERING, PHYSICS. *Educ:* Univ Tenn, BS, 65, MS, 66, PhD, 68. *Prof Exp:* Sr scientist, Life Sci Dept, 68-76, div mgr & vpres, 76-80, PRES, EG&G, ORTEC, INC, 80- *Mem:* Inst Elec & Electronics Engrs. *Res:* Optimization of time measurement in nuclear instrumentation; emission computed tomography; nuclear medicine. *Mailing Add:* Ortec Inc 100 Midland Rd Oak Ridge TN 37830

DOUGLIS, AVRON, b Tulsa, Okla, Mar 14, 18; m 41; c 2. MATHEMATICS. *Educ:* Univ Chicago, AB, 38; NY Univ, MS, 48, PhD(math), 49. *Prof Exp:* Res fel, Calif Inst Technol, 49-50; from instr to assoc prof math, NY Univ, 50-56; assoc res prof, 56-58, PROF MATH, UNIV MD, COLLEGE PARK, 58- *Mem:* Am Math Soc; Math Asn Am. *Res:* Partial differential equations. *Mailing Add:* Dept of Math Univ of Md College Park MD 20742

DOUKAS, HARRY MICHAEL, b Washington, DC, July 30, 19; m 47; c 4. ORGANIC CHEMISTRY, BIOCHEMISTRY. *Educ:* Univ Md, BS, 42; Georgetown Univ, MS, 52, PhD(chem), 53. *Prof Exp:* Asst, Univ Md, 46-48; chemist, Bur Agr & Indust Chem, Biol Active Compounds Div, USDA, 48-52, res chemist, Eastern Utilization Res Br, 53-55; sr investr, Georgetown Univ, 52-53; head org sect, Chem Corps Biol Lab, US Army, 55-58; prog dir fels, NSF, 58-65; asst chief fels, Career Develop Rev Br, Div Res Grants, NIH, 65-72, chief, 72-73, chief, Off Res Manpower, 73-75; ASST DEAN SPONSORED RES, MED CTR, GEORGETOWN UNIV, 75- *Mem:* Am Chem Soc; Sigma Xi; Nat Coun Univ Res Adminr; Soc Res Adminr; Asn Am Med Col. *Res:* Natural and synthetic plant growth hormones; unsaturated naphthylenic acids; isolation and characterization of plant alkaloids; substituted pyridine compounds; health science administration. *Mailing Add:* 9920 Brixton Lane Bethesda MD 20817

DOULL, JOHN, b Baker, Mont, Sept 13, 22; m 58. PHARMACOLOGY. *Educ:* Mont State Col, BS, 44; Univ Chicago, PhD(pharmacol), 50, MD, 53. *Prof Exp:* Asst, Toxicity Lab, Univ Chicago, 46-51, res assoc, 51-53, from asst prof to assoc prof pharmacol, Univ, 53-57; res assoc, US Air Force Radiation Lab, 53-54, asst dir, 54-67; PROF PHARMACOL & TOXICOL, MED CTR, UNIV KANS, 67- *Mem:* Soc Exp Biol & Med; Am Soc Pharmacol & Exp Therapeut; Am Chem Soc; Soc Toxicol; Am Indust Hyg Asn. *Res:* Pesticides; biological aspects of ionizing radiation; toxicology. *Mailing Add:* Dept of Pharmacol Univ of Kans Med Ctr Kansas City KS 66103

DOUMA, JACOB H, b Hanford, Calif, May 30, 12. CIVIL ENGINEERING. *Educ:* Univ Calif, BS, 35. *Prof Exp:* With US Army Corps Engrs, 35-36 & US Bur Reclamation, 36-39; mem staff, 39-55, CHIEF HYDRAUL ENGR, US ARMY CORPS ENGRS, 55- *Concurrent Pos:* Hydraul consult pvt eng firms & foreign govts. *Mem:* Nat Acad Eng; fel Am Soc Civil Eng. *Res:* Irrigation, drainage and flood control. *Mailing Add:* 1001 Manning St Great Falls VA 22066

DOUMANI, GEORGE ALEXANDER, b Acre, Palestine, Apr 16, 29; US citizen; m 57; c 3. PETROLEUM GEOLOGY, STRATIGRAPHY. *Educ:* Univ Calif, Berkeley, BA, 56, MA, 57. *Prof Exp:* Petrol inspector, Arabian Am Oil Co, Saudi Arabia, 50-52; geologist, Hersey Inspection Bur, 57-58; geologist & glaciologist, Nat Acad Sci & NSF, Antarctic, 58-60; res assoc geol, Inst Polar Studies, Ohio State Univ, 60-63; sect head arctic & antarctic bibliog, Cold Regions Sect, Sci & Technol Div, Libr of Cong, Washington, DC, 63-66; specialist earth sci & oceanog, Sci Policy Res Div, Cong Res Serv, 66-75; pres, ADAR Corp, 75-77; pres, Tech Transfer Int Corp, 77-79; VPRES, TECH TRANSFER, HRM INC, 79- *Honors & Awards:* Doumani Peak & Mount Doumani in Antarctica named by Nat Bd Geog Names; Antarctic Serv Medal, US Dept Defense; Knight, Nat Order of Cedars, Lebanon Repub. *Mem:* Am Asn Petrol Geologists; fel Geol Soc Am; Am Polar Soc; Sigma Xi; Antartican Soc. *Res:* Stratigraphic paleontology; earth sciences and oceanography; national science policy issues; antarctic geology; technology transfer; technology assessment; energy policy. *Mailing Add:* 9702 Culver St Kensington MD 20895

DOUMAS, A(RTHUR) C(ONSTANTINOS), b Fredericksburg, Va, Jan 31, 32; div; c 5. CHEMICAL ENGINEERING. *Educ:* Va Polytech Inst, PhD(chem eng), 55. *Prof Exp:* Proj leader, 55-70, mgr, 70-77, SR PROCESS SPECIALIST, DOW CHEM CO, FREEPORT, 77- *Mem:* Am Chem Soc; Am Soc Metals; Am Soc Qual Control; Am Inst Chem Eng. *Res:* Chemical process; applications; electrochemistry; heat transmission; engineering statistics; unit operations. *Mailing Add:* 217 Narcissus Lake Jackson TX 77566

DOUMAS, BASIL T, b Argos Orestikon, Greece, July 16, 30; US citizen; m 57; c 3. CLINICAL CHEMISTRY. *Educ:* Univ Thessaloniki, BS, 52; Univ Tenn, MS, 60, PhD(biochem), 62. *Prof Exp:* Consult path, Baptist Mem Hosp, Memphis, 60-62; head dept clin chem, 62-64; asst prof path, Med Col & asst dir clin chem, Univ Hosp, Univ Ala, 64-65; assoc dir clin chem, Univ Hosp, 65-70, assoc prof path, Med Col, 68-70; assoc prof, 70-75, PROF PATH, MED COL WIS, 75- *Concurrent Pos:* Instr, Univ Tenn, 63-64; chmn subcomt human albumin, Nat Comt Clin Lab Standards, 75- *Mem:* AAAS; Am Asn Clin Chemists; Am Chem Soc; NY Acad Sci; Acad Clin Lab Physicians & Scientists. *Res:* Electrophoresis of serum proteins and dye binding; bacterial metabolism pyrimidines; clinical chemistry methodology, standards, instrumentation and quality control. *Mailing Add:* Dept of Path Med Col of Wis Milwaukee WI 53226

DOUMAS, MENELAOS, b Greece, Jan 26, 23; US nat; m 51; c 2. MECHANICAL ENGINEERING. *Educ:* City Col New York, BSME, 47; Columbia Univ, MSME, 49. *Prof Exp:* Sect head, Cent Res Labs, Gen Foods Corp, 47-55, fel engr, 55-58, supvr thermal hydraulic & mech design nuclear reactors, 58-78; MGR IRRADIATIONS, BETTIS ATOMIC POWER LAB, WESTINGHOUSE ELEC CORP, 55- *Mem:* Am Soc Mech Engrs; Am Nuclear Soc; Am Inst Chem Engrs. *Res:* Development work on food processing and equipment; spray drying; atomization of liquids; thermal, hydraulic and mechanical design of nuclear reactors; design of high pressure and temperature irradiation facilities; remote handling and examination equipment. *Mailing Add:* 760 Pinetree Rd Pittsburgh PA 15243

DOUMAUX, ARTHUR ROY, JR, b Little Neck, NY, Mar 15, 38; m 62; c 2. ORGANIC CHEMISTRY. *Educ:* Lehigh Univ, BS, 61; Yale Univ, PhD(org chem), 66. *Prof Exp:* Res & develop chemist, 66-73, proj scientist, 73-76, RES SCIENTIST, UNION CARBIDE CORP, 76- *Mem:* Am Chem Soc. *Res:* Photosensitized autooxidation of heterocyclic dienes, especially those relating to naturally found substances; metal-ion catalyzed oxidations with peroxidic materials; chemistry of ethylene oxide adducts; systhesis gas chemistry. *Mailing Add:* 1401 Wilkie Dr Charleston WV 25314

DOUMIT, CARL JAMES, b New Iberia, La, Jan 11, 45; m 69; c 1. INORGANIC CHEMISTRY, ANALYTICAL CHEMISTRY. *Educ:* Univ Southwestern La, BS, 67; Tulane Univ, MS, 70, MAT, 71, PhD(inorg chem), 73. *Prof Exp:* Instr chem, Tulane Univ, 68-70; assoc prof phys sci, 73-80, PROF CHEM, MISS UNIV WOMEN, 80- *Mem:* Am Chem Soc; Sigma Xi. *Res:* Coordination chemistry; bioinorganic chemistry; analytical chemistry. *Mailing Add:* Dept of Phys Sci PO Box W-40 Miss Univ for Women Columbus MS 39701

DOUPLE, EVAN BARR, b Hershey, Pa, Sept 16, 43; m 66; c 2. RADIOBIOLOGY, ONCOLOGY. *Educ:* Millersville State Col, BS, 64; Kans Univ, PhD(radiation biophysics), 72. *Prof Exp:* Sci teacher biol & chem, Lebanon Sr High Sch, 64-67; lectr radiation biophysics, Kans Univ, 70-72; instr radiobiol, 73-74, asst prof, 74-80, ASSOC PROF RADIOBIOL, DARTMOUTH MED SCH, 80- *Concurrent Pos:* Adj asst prof, Thayer Sch Eng, Dartmouth Col, 76-80, adj assoc prof, 80- *Mem:* Sigma Xi; Radiation Res Soc; Am Soc Therapeutic Radiologists; Am Asn Physicists Med; AAAS. *Res:* Radiobiology of in vitro and animal tumor models; hyperthermia and radiation; radiation-platinum coordination complex interactions in vitro and in transplantable animal tumors. *Mailing Add:* Radiobiology Lab Dartmouth-Hitchcock Med Ctr Hanover NH 03755

DOUPNIK, BEN LEE, JR, b Agenda, Kans, Aug 13, 39; m 61; c 3. FIELD CROPS, MYCOTOXINS. *Educ:* Kans Wesleyan Univ, AB, 62; Univ Nebr, MS, 64; La State Univ, PhD(plant path), 67. *Prof Exp:* Asst prof plant path, Coastal Plain Exp Sta, Univ Ga, 67-72; ASSOC PROF, S CENT STA, UNIV NEBR, 72- *Mem:* Am Phytopath Soc; Am Soc Microbiol; Sigma Xi. *Res:* Control of field crop diseases, grain deterioration and mycotoxin studies, and general extension plant pathology. *Mailing Add:* Univ of Nebr S Cent Sta Box 66 Clay Center NE 68033

DOUROS, JOHN DRENKLE, b Reading, Pa, Dec 26, 30; m 54; c 2. MICROBIOLOGY. *Educ:* Duke Univ, BA, 52; Rutgers Univ, MS, 55; Pa State Univ, PhD(bact), 58. *Prof Exp:* Assoc microbiologist, Parke, Davis & Co, 57-60 & Sun Oil Co, 60-63; sr chemist & microbiologist, Esso Res & Eng Co, 63-68; mgr microbiol res & develop, Gates Rubber Co, 68-72; chief natural prod br, Nat Cancer Inst, 72-81; ASST DIR RES, BRISTOL LABS, 80- *Mem:* Am Soc Microbiol; Am Chem Soc; Soc Indust Microbiol; NY Acad Sci; Am Cancer Soc. *Res:* Mechanism of action of antibiotics; degradation of organic compounds by microorganisms; fermentation and natural products research. *Mailing Add:* Nat Cancer Inst NIH Bethesda MD 20205

DOUSA, THOMAS PATRICK, b Prague, Czech, Dec 13, 37; m 66; c 3. INTERNAL MEDICINE, PHYSIOLOGY. *Educ:* Charles Univ, Prague, MD, 62; Czech Acad Sci, PhD(biochem), 68. *Prof Exp:* From intern to resident & res assoc, Inst Cardiovasc Dis, Prague Tech Univ, 62-65; attend physician, Community Med Ctr, 65-68; clin investr & attend physician, Dept Med I, Charles Univ, 68-69; AMA fel molecular endocrinol, Inst Biomed Res, Univ Chicago, 69-70; asst prof physiol, Med Sch, Northwestern Univ, 70-72; asst prof, 72-74, assoc prof, 74-77, PROF MED & PHYSIOL, UNIV MINN & MAYO CLIN FOUND, 77- *Concurrent Pos:* Estab investr, Am Heart Asn, 74-79, fel high blood pressure coun. *Honors & Awards:* Czech Acad Sci Prize, 69. *Mem:* Am Fedn Clin Res; Am Soc Clin Invest; Am Physiol Soc; Endocrine Soc. *Res:* Cellular action of vasopressin and other hormones in the kidney; hormonal regulation of water and phosphate excretion. *Mailing Add:* Dept Med Div Nephrol Mayo Clin Mayo Med Sch Rochester MN 55901

DOUTHART, RICHARD JAMES, b Chicago, Ill, June 11, 35; m 59; c 2. MOLECULAR BIOLOGY. *Educ:* Little Rock Univ, BS, 61; Univ Ill, Urbana, PhD(phys chem), 68. *Prof Exp:* Chemist, IIT Res Inst, 62-64; RES SCIENTIST, LILLY RES LABS, 68- *Mem:* AAAS; Am Chem Soc. *Res:* Physical chemistry of nucleic acids and virus; interferon induction; DNA replication, interaction of nucleic acids with small molecules; DNA sequencing; computer gene analysis; molecular biology, recombinant DNA. *Mailing Add:* Lilly Res Labs 307 E McCarty St Indianapolis IN 46206

DOUTHAT, DARYL ALLEN, b Nescopeck, Pa, Nov 3, 42; m 67. PHYSICAL CHEMISTRY, CHEMICAL PHYSICS. *Educ:* Pa State Univ, BS, 65; Univ Chicago, MS, 72, PhD(chem), 74. *Prof Exp:* Instr, Kennedy-King Col, 72-76, asst prof chem, 77-80; ASST PROF, DEPT PHYSICS & CHEM, UNIV ALASKA, 81- *Concurrent Pos:* Consult, Radiol & Environ Res Div, Argonne Nat Lab, 74-; vis fel, Centre Interdisciplinary Studies in Chem Physics, Univ Western Ont, 76-77, mem int adv panel, 78- *Mem:* Am Chem Soc; Radiation Res Soc. *Res:* Theory of electron transport; electron energy degradation in matter; calculation of the initial yields of ions and exited states produced in matter exposed to penetrating charged particles of photons. *Mailing Add:* Dept Physics & Chem Univ Alaska 3221 Providence Dr Anchorage AK 99504

DOUTHETT, ELWOOD MOSER, b Pottstown, Pa, Oct 4, 15; m 49, 77; c 5. NUCLEAR CHEMISTRY. *Educ:* Pa State Col, BS, 36; Ohio State Univ, MS, 47; Univ Calif, PhD(nuclear chem), 51. *Prof Exp:* Engr, Gen Elec Co, 36-39 & Gen Steel Castings Co, 39-41; air tech liaison officer, US Air Force, Am Embassy, The Hague, 47-48 & Mem Tech Appln Ctr, US Air Force, Washington, DC, 51-54, dir, McClellan Cent Lab, 54-58, chief weapons develop br, Hq, 59-60, chief res div, 60-61, dir geophys res directorate, Cambridge Res Labs, 61-62, mgr, SNAP-50 nuclear auxiliary space power prog, AEC, 62-65, comdr, Air Force Rocket Propulsion Lab, Edwards AFB, Calif, 65-69; dir effects eval div, US Energy Res & Develop Admin, 69-77; dir, Phys & Life Sci Div, US Dept Energy, 78-79, dir, Environ Sci Div, 79-80; RETIRED. *Res:* Ranges of fission products; radiochemistry of fission products. *Mailing Add:* 3165 S Batavia Las Vegas NV 89102

DOUTHIT, HARRY ANDERSON, JR, b Raymondville, Tex, June 18, 35; m 59; c 1. MOLECULAR BIOLOGY. *Educ:* Univ Tex, BA, 61, PhD(bot), 65. *Prof Exp:* Fel molecular biol, Univ Wis, 64-67; asst prof, 67-73, assoc prof cell & molecular biol, 73-80, ASSOC PROF BIOL SCI, UNIV MICH, 80- *Mem:* AAAS; Am Soc Microbiol. *Res:* Enzymology, including the nature and relevance of thiaminase I; differentiation including the contributions and interactions of nucleic acids in bacterial differentiation. *Mailing Add:* Dept of Cell & Molecular Biol Univ of Mich Ann Arbor MI 48109

DOUTHIT, THOMAS D NATHAN, b Lubbock, Tex, July 9, 18; m 48; c 2. GEOPHYSICS, ENGINEERING MANAGEMENT. *Educ:* Tex Tech Col, BS, 51; St Louis Univ, MS, 59; Univ Chicago, MBA, 62. *Prof Exp:* Geophysicist, Air Force Cambridge Res Labs, US Air Force, 56-61, prog coordr, 62-64, dir, Space Physics Lab, 64-68, dir, Ionospheric Physics Lab, 68-69; geophysicist, Weston Observ, 69-70; prog coordr, Air Force Cambridge Res Labs, 70-72; chief res & develop plans, 72-77, chief scientist biotechnol, 77-80, BIOTECHNOL RES & DEVELOP PLANS OFFICER, AEROSPACE MED DIV, BROOKS AFB, 80- *Concurrent Pos:* Chmn working group, Int Years Quiet Sun, 63-66, deleg, Madrid, Spain, 65 & London, Eng, 67; mem, Comt Solar-Terrestrial Res, Nat Acad Sci, 64-69; deleg, Int Years Active Sun, London, Eng, 69. *Mem:* Soc Explor Geophysicists; Am Geophys Union; Am Geol Inst; Seismol Soc Am; NY Acad Sci. *Res:* Engineering management; seismology; space physics; ionospheric physics; arctic terrain research. *Mailing Add:* Aerospace Med Div Brooks AFB TX 78235

DOUTT, RICHARD LEROY, b La Verne, Calif, Dec 6, 16; m 42, 79; c 2. ENTOMOLOGY, ENVIRONMENTAL SCIENCES. *Educ:* Univ Calif, BS, 39, MS, 40, PhD(entom), 46, LLB, 59, JD, 68. *Prof Exp:* Jr entomologist, 46-48, from asst prof to prof, 48-75, chmn dept, 64-69, actg dean col agr sci & actg assoc dir agr exp sta, 69-70, EMER PROF BIOL CONTROL & ENTOM, DIV BIOL CONTROL LABS AT ALBANY, UNIV CALIF, BERKELEY, 75- *Concurrent Pos:* Prin scientist, Ecosci Div Henningson, Durham & Richardson, Inc, 75-; entomologist, Santa Barbara County, 81- *Mem:* Am Entom Soc; Ecol Soc Am. *Res:* Taxonomy of Chalcidoidea; biology of entomophagous insects. *Mailing Add:* 1781 Glen Oaks Dr Santa Barbara CA 93108

DOUTY, RICHARD T, b Williamsport, Pa, June 12, 30; m 59; c 4. STRUCTURAL ENGINEERING. *Educ:* Lehigh Univ, BS, 56; Ga Inst Technol, MS, 57; Cornell Univ, PhD(struct eng), 64. *Prof Exp:* Engr trainee, Bethlehem Steel Co, 57-58; res assoc, Cornell Univ, 61-62; from asst prof to assoc prof civil eng, 62-68, PROF CIVIL ENG, UNIV MO-COLUMBIA, 68- *Concurrent Pos:* Partic, NSF Proj Use of Comput & Math Optimization Tech in Eng Design, 65; sr fel, Univ Pa, 69-70; mem eval panel, Associateship Prog, Nat Res Coun, 71. *Mem:* Am Soc Civil Engrs; Int Asn Bridge & Struct Engrs. *Res:* Computer techniques in engineering design. *Mailing Add:* Col of Eng Univ of Mo Columbia MO 65201

DOUVILLE, PHILLIP RAOUL, b Hartford, Conn, June 24, 36; m 59; c 3. PHYSICAL CHEMISTRY. *Educ:* Univ Conn, BA, 59, PhD(phys chem), 69. *Prof Exp:* Asst instr chem, Univ Conn, 63-65; asst prof, 65-70, ASSOC PROF CHEM, CENT CONN STATE COL, 70- *Mem:* AAAS; Am Chem Soc. *Res:* Chemical information; computer based information systems. *Mailing Add:* Dept of Chem Cent Conn State Col New Britain CT 06050

DOUVRES, FRANK WILLIAM, animal science, see previous edition

DO-VAN-QUY, DOMINIC, b Nam-Dinh, NVietnam, Jan 19, 27. CANCER, MOSQUITO GENETICS. *Educ:* St Joseph Sem & Col, NY, BA, 51; Fordham Univ, MS, 57, PhD(biol), 60. *Prof Exp:* Chief entom sect, Admin Gen Malaria Eradication, Ministry Health, Saigon, 60-63; chief entom-parasitol & plague labs, Pasteur Inst Vietnam, 63-68; asst prof genetics & cell physiol, Fairleigh Dickinson Univ, 69-70; res adminr, 70-72, RES ADMINR, ANAL & PROJ PROG, AM CANCER SOC, INC, 72- *Concurrent Pos:* Prof zool, Univ Hue, 62-68; prof parasitol, Univ Saigon & prof entom, Sch Agr, 66-68; prof zool, Univ Can-tho, 67-68; adv ed, Ca-A Cancer J for Clinicians, 75- *Res:* Mosquito taxonomy of Vietnam, particularly mosquito genetics, ecology and control; insecticide resistance studies of mosquitoes and fleas; plague and infectious diseases in Vietnam; research on cancer: data bank, data processing and information retrieval of all aspects of cancer, analysis and projection. *Mailing Add:* Am Cancer Soc 777 Third Ave New York NY 10017

DOVE, A(LLAN) B(URGESS), b Ayr, Scotland, Apr 9, 09; m 34, 63; c 3. CHEMICAL ENGINEERING, METALLURGICAL ENGINEERING. *Educ:* Queen's Univ, Ont, BSc, 32. *Prof Exp:* Chem engr, Steel Co Can Ltd, 32-38, engr, Montreal Plants, 38-40, supt, Lachine Plant, 46-53, supt develop & res, 53-67, sr develop metallurgist, Wire & Fastener Div, 67-74; CONSULT ENG, 74- *Honors & Awards:* Awards, Am Iron & Steel Inst, 60, Wire Asn, 37, 49, 55, 64, 69, 70 & 72; Eng Medal, Asn Prof Engrs, 79. *Mem:* Fel Am Soc Metals; fel Chem Inst Can; fel Eng Inst Can; NY Acad Sci; Wire Asn Int (pres, 58-60). *Res:* Wood fastenings; corrosion of metals; scale formation and removal; protective coatings; concrete reinforcing; cold working of metals; operational research; heat treatment and cold working of steel; Stelmor process; continuous electroplating; special fasteners and nails; prestressed concrete tendons, specs, manufacture and use. *Mailing Add:* 933 Glenwood Ave Burlington ON L7T 2K1 Can

DOVE, DEREK BRIAN, b Middlesex, Eng, Jan 12, 32; m 54; c 2. PHYSICS. *Educ:* Imp Col, Univ London, BSc, 53, PhD(crystallog), 56. *Prof Exp:* Sci officer, Atomic Energy Res Estab, Eng, 55-59, sr sci officer, 59; Nat Res Coun Can fel, 59-61; mem tech staff, Bell Tel Labs, Inc, 61-67; assoc prof, Univ Fla, Gainesville, 67-71, prof mat sci eng & elec eng, 71-77; MGR, IBM WATSON RES CTR, YORKTOWN HEIGHTS, NY, 77- *Mem:* Am Vacuum Soc. *Res:* Magnetic films; structure of amorphous film using electron diffraction; surface analysis; luminescent materials. *Mailing Add:* IBM Watson Res Ctr Yorktown Heights NY 10598

DOVE, JOHN EDWARD, b Minneapolis, Minn, Aug 11, 30; m 62; c 3. CHEMICAL KINETICS. *Educ:* Oxford Univ, BA, 52, BSc, 54, MA & DPhil(chem), 59. *Prof Exp:* Sr sci officer, Div Chem Eng, Atomic Energy Res Estab, UK Atomic Energy Auth, 58-60; asst prof, 62-66, assoc prof, 66-75, PROF CHEM, UNIV TORONTO, 75-, CHMN, PHYS SCI DIV, 77- *Concurrent Pos:* Commonwealth Fund Harkness fel, Harvard Univ, 60-62; vis scientist, Univ Gottingen, 69-70 & 76-77. *Mem:* Am Phys Soc; Combustion Inst; Chem Inst Can; Royal Soc Chem. *Res:* High temperature reaction kinetics and molecular energy transfer processes in gases; ionization in gases; combustion chemistry; chemistry and physics of shock waves and detonations. *Mailing Add:* Dept of Chem Univ of Toronto Toronto ON M5S 1A1 Can

DOVE, LEWIS DUNBAR, b Savannah, Ga, Oct 8, 34; m 58; c 1. PLANT PHYSIOLOGY. *Educ:* Univ Md, BS, 57, MS, 59; Duke Univ, PhD(bot), 64. *Prof Exp:* Phys sci aid, Plant Indust Sta, USDA, Md, 57; instr bot, Newcomb Col, Tulane Univ, 61-65, asst prof biol, 65-69; assoc prof, 69-74, PROF BIOL, WESTERN ILL UNIV, 74-, FAC DEVELOP ASSOC, 80- *Concurrent Pos:* Soc Sigma Xi res grant in aid, 65-66; res grants, NSF, 67-69 & 81- & Ill State Acad Sci, 71-72. *Mem:* Am Soc Plant Physiol; Sigma Xi; Asn Develop Computer-Based Instrnl Syst. *Res:* Effects of environmental stress on metabolism in plants; plant proteins; computer-assisted instruction; faculty development. *Mailing Add:* Dept of Biol Sci Western Ill Univ Macomb IL 61455

DOVE, MICHAEL ROGER, Hartford, Conn, Dec 26, 49. HUMAN ECOLOGY, RURAL DEVELOPMENT. *Educ:* Northwestern Univ, BA, 71; Stanford Univ, MA, 72, PhD(anthrop), 81. *Prof Exp:* Instr anthrop, Stanford Univ, 78; fel, 79-81, RES FEL RURAL DEVELOP, ROCKEFELLER FOUND, 81- *Concurrent Pos:* Investr res grant, NSF, 74-76; consult, Pop Studies Ctr, Gadjah Mada Univ, 79-81, Environ Studies Ctr, 81-, vis prof, Fac Arts & Forestry, 79- *Mem:* Royal Anthrop Inst; AAAS; Am Anthrop Asn; Am Ethiol Asn. *Res:* Economy and ecology of swidden agricultural system in West Kalimantan; agricultural intensification and forest grassland succession in South Kalimantan; perception and exploitation of natural resources, especially forests and grasslands, throughout Indonesia. *Mailing Add:* Rockefeller Found PO Box 63 Yogyakarta DIY Indonesia

DOVE, RAY ALLEN, b Rockmart, Ga, Aug 17, 21; m 47; c 4. CHEMISTRY. *Educ:* Univ Akron, BS, 47, MS, 53. *Prof Exp:* Chemist, 53-58, from jr res chemist to sr res chemist, 58-75, SECT HEAD, GOODYEAR TIRE & RUBBER CO, 75- *Mem:* Am Chem Soc. *Res:* Polarography; ultraviolet spectrophotometry; nonaqueous titrimetry; solid-liquid gas and ion-exchange chromatography; flame photometry; atomic absorption spectroscopy. *Mailing Add:* Dept 455B Res Bldg Goodyear Tire & Rubber Co Akron OH 44316

DOVE, WILLIAM FRANCIS, b Washington, DC, July 30, 33; m 61; c 2. PLASMA PHYSICS. *Educ:* Pa State Univ, BS, 56; Univ Calif, Berkeley, PhD(physics), 68. *Prof Exp:* Res assoc physics & astron, Univ Md, 68-74; MEM STAFF, DIV CONTROLLED THERMONUCLEAR RES, US DEPT OF ENERGY, 74- *Mem:* Am Phys Soc. *Res:* High Mach number plasma flow, magnetic diffusion, shock wave propagation and turbulent ion heating; non-equilibrium plasma transport properties and measurement of thermoelectric coefficient. *Mailing Add:* Div Control Thermonuclear Res US Dept of Energy Washington DC 20545

DOVE, WILLIAM FRANKLIN, b Bangor, Maine, June 20, 36; m 64; c 3. GENETICS, CELL BIOLOGY. *Educ:* Amherst Col, AB, 58; Calif Inst Technol, PhD(chem), 61. *Prof Exp:* From asst prof to assoc prof, 64-73, prof oncol, 73-77, PROF ONCOL & GENETICS, MCARDLE LAB, UNIV WISMADISON, 77- *Concurrent Pos:* A A Noyes fel, Calif Inst Technol, 61-62; NSF fel, Cambridge Univ, 62-63; NIH fel, Stanford Univ, 64; Guggenheim fel, Pasteur Inst, 75-76. *Mem:* AAAS; Genetics Soc Am. *Res:* Genes and the control of their replication and expression. *Mailing Add:* McArdle Lab Univ of Wis Madison WI 53706

DOVEL, WILLIAM LAWRENCE, b Harrisonburg, Va, May 23, 33; m 54; c 1. FISH BIOLOGY. *Educ:* Bridgewater Col, BA, 54. *Prof Exp:* Assoc scientist zool, Nat Resources Inst, Univ Md, 60-71; asst scientist estuarine ecol, Boyce Thompson Inst, 71-78; MGR ESTUARINE & MARINE PROGS, WAPORA, INC, 78-; SR SCIENTIST, MOTE MARINE LAB, 81- *Concurrent Pos:* Staff scientist, Oceanic Soc, 79. *Mem:* Am Fisheries Soc. *Res:* Population dynamics of estuarine dependent fishes; attempts to document through illustrations a conceptual characterization of fresh water, estuarine and marine fish populations that utilize the estuarine ecosystem as a nursery; population dynamics of Hudson estuary (New York) sturgeons; comparison of mid-Atlantic and South Atlantic fish fauna. *Mailing Add:* Mote Marine Lab 1600 City Island Park Sarasota FL 33577

DOVENMUEHLE, ROBERT HENRY, b St Louis, Mo, July 10, 24; div; c 5. PSYCHIATRY. *Educ:* St Louis Univ, MD, 48; Am Bd Psychiat & Neurol, dipl psychiat, 63. *Prof Exp:* Resident physician, Hastings State Hosp, 49-51; chief open sect psychiat, William Beaumont Army Hosp, 51-53; resident & chief resident psychiat, Duke Hosp, 54-55, chief in-patient serv, 55-57, from asst prof to assoc prof psychiat, Sch Med, Duke Univ, 57-65, res coordr, Ctr Study Aging, 57-65; dir ment health progs, Western Interstate Comn Higher Educ, 65-66; prof psychiat, Univ Mo-Kansas City, 66-69; dir geriat progs, Kansas City Gen Hosp & Med Ctr, 66-69; exec dir, Dallas County Ment Health & Ment Retardation Ctr, 69-75; clin dir, Guilford County Ment Health Ctr, 75-76. *Concurrent Pos:* Consult, Keeley Inst, 54-65; attend, Vet Admin Hosp, Durham, NC, 55-65 & Roanoke, Va, 59-64; clin prof psychiat, Univ Tex Southwestern Med Sch, 69-75; adj prof, NTex State Univ, 69-75; spec lectr occup ther, Tex Woman's Univ, 70-75; adj prof child develop, Univ NC, Greensboro, 76-; pvt practice, 76- *Mem:* Geront Soc; fel Am Psychiat Asn; AMA. *Res:* Psychiatric problems of older people; criteria of effective psychiatric nursing therapy. *Mailing Add:* 2901G Cottage Pl Greensboro NC 27405

DOVER, CARL BELLMAN, b Milwaukee, Wis, Feb 10, 41; m 69; c 2. THEORETICAL NUCLEAR PHYSICS. *Educ:* Mass Inst Technol, BS, 63; PhD(physics), 67. *Prof Exp:* Scientific asst, Inst Theoret Phys, Univ Heidelberg, 67-70; asst res, Inst Nuclear Physics, Univ Paris, 70-71; STAFF PHYSICIST, BROOKHAVEN NAT LAB, 71- *Mem:* Fel Am Phys Soc. *Res:* Nuclear reaction theory; heavy ion physics; intermediate energy nuclear theory. *Mailing Add:* Dept of Physics Brookhaven Nat Lab Upton NY 11973

DOVERMANN, KARL HEINZ, b Bonn, WGer, Aug 31,48. MATHEMATICS. *Educ:* Univ Bonn, Dipl, 75; Rutgers Univ, PhD(math), 78. *Prof Exp:* L E Dickson instr, Univ Chicago, 78-80; ASST PROF MATH, PURDUE UNIV, 80- *Mem:* Am Math Soc. *Res:* Algebraic topology with emphasis on finite transformation groups on smooth manifolds and on equivariant surgery; existence and classification of actions. *Mailing Add:* Dept Math Purdue Univ West Lafayette IN 47907

DOVERSPIKE, LYNN D, b Cumberland, Okla, Mar 1, 34; m 54; c 3. ATOMIC & MOLECULAR PHYSICS. *Educ:* Okla State Univ, BS, 58; Univ Calif, Los Angeles, MS, 60; Univ Fla, PhD(physics), 66. *Prof Exp:* Asst prof, 67-74, ASSOC PROF PHYSICS, COL WILLIAM & MARY, 74- *Mem:* Am Phys Soc. *Res:* Experimental low energy atomic and molecular physics. *Mailing Add:* Dept of Physics Col of William & Mary Williamsburg VA 23185

DOVIAK, RICHARD J, b Passaic, NJ, Dec 24, 33; m 57; c 3. ATMOSPHERIC SCIENCE. *Educ:* Rensselaer Polytech Inst, BSEE, 56; Univ Pa, MSEE, 59, PhD(elec eng), 63. *Prof Exp:* Instr elec eng, Moore Sch Elec Eng, Univ Pa, 60-61, from assoc lectr to asst prof, 62-70, supvr, Acad Labs, 67-71; SCIENTIST, NAT SEVERE STORMS LAB, NAT OCEANIC & ATMOSPHERIC AGENCY, 71- *Concurrent Pos:* Prin investr, NSF res grant, 69-71; consult, Raytheon, 63-70 & A R K Electronics Corp, 70-71. *Mem:* AAAS; Am Geophys Union; Inst Elec & Electronics Engrs; Am Meteorol Soc. *Res:* Radar meteorology-antennas, propagation and scattering; electromagnetic interference; nonionizing radiation of biological tissues; atmospheric probing. *Mailing Add:* 4016 Oxford Way Norman OK 73069

DOW, BRUCE MACGREGOR, b Newton, Mass, Oct 30, 38. NEUROPHYSIOLOGY, VISION. *Educ:* Wesleyan Univ, AB; Univ Strasbourg, Cert; Univ Rochester, MD. *Prof Exp:* Intern med, Baltimore City Hosp, 66-67; res assoc neurophysiol, Nat Inst Dent Res, 67-70; staff fel, Nat Eye Inst, 70-75; vis scientist neurophysiol, Nat Inst Mental Health, 75-76; res assoc prof, 76-78, ASSOC PROF PHYSIOL, SCH MED, STATE UNIV NY, BUFFALO, 78- *Mem:* Soc Neurosci; Asn Res Vision & Ophthalmol. *Res:* Studies of color vision and mechanisms of fixation/localization in foveal cortical centers of trained monkeys, utilizing single cell neurophsiology, psychophysics, and histological reconstruction. *Mailing Add:* Neurobiol Lab State State Univ NY 4234 Ridge Lea Rd Buffalo NY 14226

DOW, DANIEL G(OULD), b Ann Arbor, Mich, Apr 26, 30; m 54; c 4. ELECTRICAL ENGINEERING. *Educ:* Univ Mich, BSE, 52, MSE, 53; Stanford Univ, PhD(elec eng), 58. *Prof Exp:* Asst prof, Calif Inst Technol, 58-61; dir, Res Tube Div, Varian Assocs, 62-65, mgr microwave semiconductor task force, Cent Res Labs, 65-68; chmn, Dept Elec Eng, 68-77, assoc dir, Appl Physics Lab, 77-79, PROF ELEC ENG, UNIV WASH, 68- *Concurrent Pos:* Mem bd dir, Wash Res Found; dir, Wash Energy Res Ctr, 79-81. *Mem:* AAAS; Inst Elec & Electronics Engrs; Am Soc Engr Educ. *Res:* Microwaves; solid state devices; plasma physics; physical electronics; education. *Mailing Add:* Dept Elec Eng Univ Wash Seattle WA 98195

DOW, JAMES W, b Worcester, Mass, Sept 8, 17; m 67; c 2. MEDICINE, BIOMEDICAL ENGINEERING. *Educ:* Harvard Univ, BS, 41; Tufts Univ, MD, 44. *Prof Exp:* Instr med, Med Sch, Harvard Univ, 49-51; asst prof, Med Sch, Tufts Univ, 53-58; adj prof med sci, Drexel Inst, 60-62; exec secy, bioeng, Training Br, Nat Inst Gen Med Sci, 63-65, head biophys sci sect, 65-66; prof med, Univ Ill Med Ctr, 66-70; prof biomed eng & chmn dept, 70-75, PROF MED, RUSH-PRESBY-ST LUKE'S MED CTR, CHICAGO, 70-; PROF BIOENG & BIOENG PROG, COL ENG, UNIV ILL, CHICAGO CIRCLE, 66- *Concurrent Pos:* Res fel, Nat Heart Inst, 47-49; consult biomed eng training comt, Training Br, Nat Inst Gen Med Sci, 62-63 & training comt on eng in biol & med, 69-; spec consult, Bur Health Serv, 67-68; actg chmn biomed eng, Presby St Luke's Hosp, 68- *Res:* Cardiovascular control systems; analysis of health service systems. *Mailing Add:* 1000 Grand Canyon Pkwy Hoffman Estates IL 60195

DOW, JOHN DAVIS, b Paterson, NJ. THEORETICAL PHYSICS. *Educ:* Univ Notre Dame, BS, 63; Univ Rochester, PhD(physics), 67. *Prof Exp:* From instr to asst prof physics, Princeton Univ, 67-72; assoc prof, 72-75, PROF PHYSICS, UNIV ILL, URBANA-CHAMPAIGN, 75-, RES PROF, COORD SCI LAB, 79- *Concurrent Pos:* NSF fel, 67-68; consult, Western Elec Co, 68-70; vis scientist, RCA Labs, 68 & Argonne Nat Lab, 69 & 75; assoc, Ctr Advan Study, Univ Ill. *Mem:* Fel Am Phys Soc. *Res:* Theory of solids, optical, electronic and transport properites. *Mailing Add:* Dept Physics Univ Ill Urbana IL 61801

DOW, PAUL C(ROWTHER), JR, b Melrose, Mass, Mar 31, 27; m 50; c 4. GUIDANCE & CONTROL, AERONAUTICAL ENGINEERING. *Educ:* US Mil Acad, BS, 49; Univ Mich, MSE(aeronaut eng) & MSE(instrumentation eng), 54, PhD(aeronaut eng), 57. *Prof Exp:* Mgr guid, Control & Commun Dept, Avco Systs Div, Avco Corp, 60-68, prog dir, 68-75; ASSOC DEPT HEAD & FBM PROG MGR, CHARLES STARK DRAPER LAB, INC, 75- *Concurrent Pos:* Lectr, Northeastern Univ, 73-81. *Mem:* Assoc fel Am Inst Aeronaut & Astronaut. *Res:* Project management. *Mailing Add:* C S Draper Lab 555 Technology Square Cambridge MA 02139

DOW, ROBERT STONE, b Wray, Colo, Jan 4, 08; m 34; c 2. ANATOMY, PHYSIOLOGY. *Educ:* Linfield Col, BS, 29; Univ Ore, AM & MD, 34, PhD(anat), 35. *Hon Degrees:* DSc, Linfield Col, 63. *Prof Exp:* Asst anat, Med Sch, Univ Ore, 30-35; intern, Wis Gen Hosp, Madison, 35-36; clin instr neurol, 39-42, from asst prof to assoc prof anat, 39-46, from asst clin prof to assoc clin prof med, 46-69, CLIN PROF MED, DIV NEUROL, MED SCH, UNIV ORE, 69- *Concurrent Pos:* Nat Res Coun fel physiol, Sch Med, Yale Univ, 36-37; Belg-Am Educ Found fel, Brussels & Nat Hosp, London, 37-38; fel, Rockefeller Inst, 38-39; Fulbright scholar, Pisa, Italy, 53-54; dir lab neurophysiol, Good Samaritan Hosp, Portland, Ore, 66-74. *Mem:* Am Physiol Soc; fel Am Col Physicians; Am Asn Neurol Surg; Am Electroencephalog Soc (pres, 57-58); Am Epilepsy Soc (pres, 64). *Res:*

Neurological anatomy and physiology; innefvation of the lung; comparative anatomy of the cerebellum; anatomy and physiology of the cerebellum and vestibular systems; pathology of multiple sclerosis; action potentials in central nervous system. *Mailing Add:* Lab of Neurophysiol Good Samaritan Hosp Portland OR 97210

DOW, W(ILLIAM) G(OULD), b Faribault, Minn, Sept 30, 95; m 24, 68; c 5. CONTROLLED NUCLEAR FUSION. *Educ:* Univ Minn, BS, 16, EE, 17; Univ Mich, MSE, 29. *Hon Degrees:* DSc, Univ Colo, 80. *Prof Exp:* Diversified eng & bus experience, 19-26; from instr to prof elec eng, 26-66, chmn dept, 58-65, sr res space geophysicist, 66-71, EMER PROF ELEC ENG, UNIV MICH ANN ARBOR, 66- *Concurrent Pos:* Res engr, Radio Res Lab, Nat Defense Res Comt Proj, Harvard Univ, 43-45; electronics eng consult, Nat Bur Standards, 45-55; mem bd trustees & consult, Environ Res Inst Mich, 72- *Mem:* AAAS; Inst Elec & Electronics Engrs; Am Soc Eng Educ; Am Geophys Union; Am Phys Soc. *Res:* Remote sensing for earth observations; physical electronics; controlled nuclear fusion; space research and exploration; microwave devices; radar and radar countermeasures; plasmas of all kinds. *Mailing Add:* 915 Heatherway Ann Arbor MI 48104

DOWALIBY, MARGARET SUSANNE, b Dover, NH, Mar 5, 24. OPTOMETRY. *Educ:* Los Angeles Col Optom, DOptom, 50. *Prof Exp:* Clin supvr, Los Angeles Col Optom, 48-53, from assoc prof clin optom to prof optom, 53-65; PROF OPTOM, SOUTHERN CALIF COL OPTOM, 65- *Mem:* Am Acad Optom. *Res:* Cosmetic effect of lenses and frames; optics of lenses. *Mailing Add:* Southern Calif Col of Optom 2001 Associated Rd Fullerton CA 92631

DOWBEN, ROBERT MORRIS, b Philadelphia, Pa, Apr 6, 27; m 50; c 3. BIOPHYSICS, PHYSIOLOGY. *Educ:* Haverford Col, AB, 46; Univ Chicago, MS, 47, MD, 49. *Hon Degrees:* AM, Brown Univ, 49. *Prof Exp:* Instr, Univ Pa, 52-53; dir radioisotope unit, Vet Admin Hosp, Philadelphia, Pa, 53-55; asst prof med, Northwestern Univ, 56-62; assoc prof biol, Mass Inst Technol, 62-68; prof med sci, Brown Univ, 68-72; prof physiol & dir biophys grad prog, Univ Tex Health Sci Ctr, Dallas, 72-80. *Concurrent Pos:* Fel, Inst Atomenergi, Oslo, 50-51; fel, Dept Med, Johns Hopkins Univ, 51-52; Lalor fel, 60; lectr, Harvard Univ, 63-68; mem, Marine Biol Lab; adj prof physiol, Univ Tex Health Sci Ctr, Dallas, 80- *Mem:* Am Chem Soc; Soc Exp Biol & Med; Am Physiol Soc; Am Soc Biol Chem; Biophys Soc. *Res:* Muscle; biological membranes; protein structure; contractile proteins; general medicine. *Mailing Add:* 5459 La Sierra Dr Suite 107 Dallas TX 75231

DOWBENKO, ROSTYSLAW, b Ukraine, Jan 8, 27; nat US:; m 51; c 1. ORGANIC CHEMISTRY. *Educ:* Northwestern Univ, PhB, 54, PhD(org chem), 57. *Prof Exp:* Res chemist, Wrigley Co, 54; sr res chemist, Pittsburgh Plate Glass Co, 57-64, res assoc, 64-67, sr res assoc, 67-69, asst dir resin res, 69-73, scientist, 73-75, mgr radiation cure, 75-77, MGR POLYMER RES & DEVELOP, PPG INDUSTS, INC, 77- *Mem:* Am Chem Soc; Am Inst Chemists; The Chem Soc. *Res:* Organic polymer chemistry. *Mailing Add:* PPG Industs Inc PO Box 9 Allison Park PA 15101

DOWD, JOHN P, b New Bedford, Mass, Feb 1, 38; m 61; c 2. HIGH ENERGY PHYSICS. *Educ:* Mass Inst Technol, SB, 59, PhD(physics), 66. *Prof Exp:* Res asst physics, Mass Inst Technol, 59-66; vis scientist, Ger Electron Synchrotron, Hamburg, 66-67; asst prof, 67-73, assoc prof physics, 73-78, PROF PHYSICS, SOUTHEASTERN MASS UNIV, 78- *Concurrent Pos:* Vis scientist, Univ Bonn, 78-79. *Mem:* Am Phys Soc; Am Asn Physics Teachers. *Res:* Experimental high energy physics. *Mailing Add:* Dept of Physics Southeastern Mass Univ North Dartmouth MA 02747

DOWD, PAUL, b Brockton, Mass, Apr 11, 36; m 60; c 3. ORGANIC CHEMISTRY. *Educ:* Harvard Univ, AB, 58; Columbia Univ, MA, 59, PhD(chem), 62. *Prof Exp:* Lectr chem, Harvard Univ, 63-64, instr, 64-66, lectr, 66-67, asst prof, 67-70; assoc prof, 70-77, PROF CHEM, UNIV PITTSBURGH, 77- *Concurrent Pos:* Alfred P Sloan Found fel, 70-72. *Mem:* Am Chem Soc. *Res:* Reactive intermediates in organic chemistry; mechanism of action of vitamin B12. *Mailing Add:* Dept of Chem Univ of Pittsburgh Pittsburgh PA 15260

DOWD, SUSAN RAMSEYER, b Chicago, Ill, Oct 14, 36. BIOCHEMISTRY, ORGANIC CHEMISTRY. *Prof Exp:* Fel, Mass Inst Technol, 62-63; res asst biol sci, Harvard Med Sch, 64-66, res assoc, 66-69; res assoc, Protein Res Inst, Univ Pittsburgh, 74-78; SR RES BIOLOGIST, DEPT BIOL SCI, CARNEGIE-MELLON UNIV, 79- *Res:* Nuclear magnetic resonance studies of labelled phospholipids. *Mailing Add:* Dept Biol Sci Carnegie Mellon Univ 4400 Fifth Ave Pittsburgh PA 15213

DOWDELL, RODGER B(IRTWELL), b Portsmouth, NH, Mar 18, 25; m 46; c 8. ENGINEERING, FLUID MECHANICS. *Educ:* Yale Univ, BE, 45; Brown Univ, MS, 52; Colo State Univ, PhD, 66. *Prof Exp:* Fluid mech engr, B-I-F Industs, RI, 52-59; assoc prof mech eng & chmn dept, Univ Bridgeport, 59-66; assoc prof mech eng & appl mech, 66-71, PROF MECH ENG & APPL MECH, UNIV RI, 71- *Concurrent Pos:* Mem & deleg, Int Stand Orgn, 59- *Mem:* Am Soc Mech Engrs. *Res:* Flow measurement and control; hydrodynamics; aerodynamics; heat transfer; propulsion. *Mailing Add:* Dept of Mech Eng & Appl Mech Univ of RI Kingston RI 02881

DOWDLE, JOSEPH C(LYDE), b July 3, 27; US citizen; m 56; c 3. ELECTRICAL ENGINEERING. *Educ:* Ala Polytech Inst, BEE, 52, MEE, 58; NC State Col, PhD(elec eng), 62. *Prof Exp:* Instr elec eng, Ala Polytech Inst, 53-57; asst proj engr, Radiation, Inc, 57-58; instr elec eng, NC State Col, 58-62; assoc prof, 62-65, dir grad prog, 62-63, chmn dept eng, 66-69, exec asst to vpres, Huntsville Affairs, 69-77, PROF ELEC ENG, UNIV ALA, HUNTSVILLE, 65-, VPRES ADMIN, 77- *Concurrent Pos:* Consult, Troxler Elec Labs, 58-63; vis scholar, Univ Mich, 68-69. *Mem:* Am Soc Eng Educ; Inst Elec & Electronics Engrs; Am Math Soc. *Res:* High frequency electromagnetics wave phenomena; dielectric materials; powdered dielectrics at millimeter frequencies; magnetic field effect of gyros. *Mailing Add:* Dept of Eng Univ of Ala Huntsville AL 35899

DOWDLE, WALTER R, b Irvington, Ala, Dec 11, 30; m 53; c 2. VIROLOGY. *Educ:* Univ Ala, BS, 55, MS, 57; Univ Md, PhD(microbiol), 60. *Prof Exp:* Asst dir science, 77, dir, Ctr Infections Dis, 80, MEM RES STAFF, VIROL SECT, CTR DIS CONTROL, 60-, DIR VIROL DIV, 70- *Concurrent Pos:* Vis prof, Univ NC; dir, Regional Reference Ctr Respiratory Dis & Int Influenza Ctr, WHO. *Mem:* Am Soc Microbiol; Soc Exp Biol & Med. *Res:* Bacteriophage; human respiratory disease viruses; mycoplasma agents of man. *Mailing Add:* 1708 Mason Mill Rane Atlanta GA 30324

DOWDS, RICHARD E, b Cuyahoga Falls, Ohio, Feb 25, 30; m 50; c 2. MATHEMATICS. *Educ:* Kent State Univ, BS, 51; Purdue Univ, MS, 54, PhD(math), 59. *Prof Exp:* Asst prof, Purdue Univ, 58-59; assoc prof, Butler Univ, 59-64, prof, 64-65; ASSOC PROF MATH, STATE UNIV NY COL FREDONIA, 65- *Mem:* Am Math Soc; Math Asn Am. *Res:* Functional analysis; topological vector spaces; measure theory. *Mailing Add:* Dept of Math State Univ of NY Fredonia NY 14063

DOWDY, EDWARD JOSEPH, b San Antonio, Tex, Sept 25, 39. NUCLEAR STRUCTURE. *Educ:* St Mary's Univ, BS & BA, 61; Tex A&M Univ, MEng, 63, PhD(nuclear eng), 65. *Prof Exp:* Asst prof nuclear eng, Univ Mo-Columbia, 65-67; from asst prof to assoc prof, Tex A&M Univ, 67-73; staff mem nuclear safeguards, 72-77, alt group leader, 77-79, tech adv to dir, Off Safeguards & Security, US Dept Energy, 79-80, GROUP LEADER, DETECTION & VERIFICATION, LOS ALAMOS NAT LAB, UNIV CALIF, 80- *Mem:* Am Phys Soc; Am Nuclear Soc. *Res:* Low energy nuclear physics; nuclear radiation detector design and development. *Mailing Add:* Group Q-2 MS 562 Los Alamos Nat Lab PO Box 1663 Los Alamos NM 87544

DOWDY, ROBERT H, b Union, WVa, June 28, 37; m 58; c 1. SOIL SCIENCE. *Educ:* Berea Col, BS, 59; Univ Ky, MS, 62; Mich State Univ, PhD(soil sci), 66. *Prof Exp:* RES SOIL SCIENTIST, SOIL & WATER CONSERV RES DIV, SCI & EDUC ADMIN-AGR RES, USDA, UNIV MINN, ST PAUL, 66-, ASSOC PROF SOIL SCI, 77- *Concurrent Pos:* Asst prof, Univ Minn, St Paul, 66- *Mem:* Am Soc Agron; Soil Sci Soc Am; Clay Minerals Soc. *Res:* Clay-chemical phenomena; clay-organic interactions and the significance of such associations on the binding together of soil masses. *Mailing Add:* Soil Sci Bldg Univ of Minn St Paul MN 55101

DOWE, THOMAS WHITFIELD, b Eagle Pass, Tex, Jan 26, 19; m 43; c 3. ANIMAL HUSBANDRY. *Educ:* Agr & Mech Col Tex, BS, 42; Kans State Col, MS, 47, PhD(animal nutrit, biochem), 52. *Prof Exp:* Animal husbandman, SDak State Col, 47-48; asst prof animal husb, Col Anr, Univ Nebr, 48-57; DIR AGR EXP STA, UNIV VT, 57-, DEAN, COL AGR, 65-, PROF ANIMAL SCI, 80- *Concurrent Pos:* Dir, Univ Nebr Agr Mission, USAID, Columbia, SAm, 70-72. *Mem:* Am Soc Animal Sci; Am Soc Range Mgt. *Res:* Ruminant nutrition; non-protein nitrogen utilization; roughage utilization; nutrient requirements of ruminants. *Mailing Add:* Col of Agr Univ of Vt Burlington VT 05405

DOWELL, CLIFTON ENDERS, b McKinney, Tex, Dec 12, 32; c 2. MICROBIOLOGY. *Educ:* Tex Christian Univ, BA, 55, MA, 57; Univ Tex Southwestern Med Sch Dallas, PhD(microbiol), 62. *Prof Exp:* NIH res fel biophys, Calif Inst Technol, 62-64; asst prof microbiol, Sch Med, Tulane Univ, 64-66; asst prof bact, Univ Calif, Davis, 66-69; ASSOC PROF MICROBIOL, UNIV MASS, AMHERST, 69- *Concurrent Pos:* Sr int fel, John Fogarty Ctr, NIH, 79-80. *Mem:* Sigma Xi; Am Soc Microbiol. *Res:* Bacteriophage; microbial genetics. *Mailing Add:* Dept of Microbiol Univ of Mass Amherst MA 01003

DOWELL, DOUGLAS C, b Tacoma, Wash, May 31, 24; m 45, 75; c 4. ENGINEERING MECHANICS, NUCLEAR ENGINEERING. *Educ:* Univ Iowa, BS, 49; US Air Force Inst Technol, MS, 56; Iowa State Univ, PhD(eng mech), 64. *Prof Exp:* Proj engr, Armed Forces Spec Weapons Proj, US Air Force, Sandia Base & Los Alamos Sci Lab, 50-54 & US Atomic Energy Comn, Idaho, 56-60, instr physics & math, US Air Force Acad, 60-62, from asst prof to assoc prof eng mech & dep head dept, 64-68; assoc dean, Sch Eng, 68-70, dir educ serv, 70-77, PROF MECH ENG, CALIF STATE POLYTECH UNIV, 77- *Mem:* AAAS; Am Acad Mech; Am Soc Eng Educ; Soc Am Mil Engrs; Asn Energy Engrs. *Res:* Engineering education; effect of shock waves on buried structures. *Mailing Add:* Mech Eng Calif State Polytech Univ 3801 W Temple Ave Pomona CA 91768

DOWELL, EARL HUGH, b Macomb, Ill, Nov 16, 37; m 81; c 3. MECHANICAL ENGINEERING. *Educ:* Univ Ill, BS, 59; Mass Inst Technol, SM, 61, ScD(aeronaut eng), 64. *Prof Exp:* Res engr aerospace div, Boeing Co, 62-63; res asst aeronaut & astronaut, Mass Inst Technol, 63-64, asst prof, 64-65; from asst prof to assoc prof aerospace & mech sci, 65-72, assoc chmn dept, 75-77, PROF AEROSPACE & MECH SCI, PRINCETON UNIV, 72- *Honors & Awards:* Structural Dynamics & Materials Award, Am Inst Aeronaut & Astronaut Structures, 80. *Mem:* Am Inst Aeronaut & Astronaut; Am Soc Mech Eng; Acoust Soc Am; Am Acad Mech; Am Helicoptor Soc. *Res:* Structural dynamics; aeroelasticity; unsteady aerodynamics; acoustics. *Mailing Add:* Dept of Mech & Aerospace Eng Princeton Univ Eng Quadrangle Princeton NJ 08544

DOWELL, FLONNIE, b Marietta, Ga, Feb 7, 47. STATISTICAL PHYSICS, LIQUID CRYSTAL THEORY. *Educ:* Univ SFla, BA, 69; Tex Womans Univ, MS, 74; Georgetown Univ, PhD(phys chem), 77. *Prof Exp:* Phys scientist polymer physics, Nat Bur Standards, 77-79; phys scientist chem physics, Oak Ridge Nat Lab, 79-81; PHYS SCIENTIST THEORET PHYSICS, LOS ALAMOS NAT LAB, 81- *Mem:* Am Phys Soc; Royal Soc Chem; Sigma Xi; AAAS. *Res:* Statistical mechanics of chain molecule systems (liquids, liquid crystals, crystals, glasses and polymers); equation of state calculations. *Mailing Add:* T-4 MS-212 Los Alamos Nat Lab PO Box 1663 Los Alamos NM 87545

DOWELL, FRANK HERBERT, b Birmingham, Ala, Aug 27, 26; m 51; c 3. PARASITOLOGY, MEDICAL ENTOMOLOGY. *Educ:* Birmingham-Southern Col, AB, 48; Univ Tenn, MS, 49, PhD(parasitol, entom), 64. *Prof Exp:* Instr, Univ of the South, 50; instr, US Air Force Sch Aviation Med, 51-55, entomologist & parasitologist 5th epidemiol flight, 55-58, chief environ res br, Entom Div, US Army Biol Labs, 58-59, entomologist spec aerial spray flight, 59-62, chief entomologist 5th epidemiol flight, 64-66; sr res entomologist, Olin Res Ctr, 66-67, mgr pesticides, 67-68; MGR PLANT SCI RES, DOW CHEM CO, 68- *Concurrent Pos:* Mem, Armed Forces Pest Control Bd, 58-62, vchmn, 61-62; adj assoc prof, Southern Conn State Col, 67-68. *Mem:* Entom Soc Am; Sigma Xi. *Res:* Experimental parasitology; experimental entomology. *Mailing Add:* Dow Chem Co 2800 Mitchell Cr Walnut Creek CA 94598

DOWELL, JERRY TRAY, b Yreka, Calif, Feb 12, 38; m 68; c 3. PHYSICS. *Educ:* Univ Calif, Berkeley, AB, 59, PhD(physics), 66. *Prof Exp:* Res scientist physics, Lockheed Palo Alto Res Lab, 66-70; asst prof physics, Univ Mo, Rolla, 70-75; PHYSICIST, IRT CORP, 74- *Mem:* Am Physical Soc. *Res:* Atomic and molecular physics, molecular beams, electron beams, microwave spectroscopy, quantum electronics, physical optics, astronomy, astrophysics, and electromagnetics. *Mailing Add:* IRT Corp PO Box 80817 San Diego CA 92138

DOWELL, MICHAEL BRENDAN, b Bronx, NY, Nov 18, 42; m 68; c 2. HIGH TEMPERATURE CHEMISTRY. *Educ:* Fordham Univ, BS, 63; Pa State Univ, PhD(inorg chem), 67. *Prof Exp:* Physicist, Pitman-Dunn Res Labs, US Army Frankford Arsenal, 67-69; res scientist, 69-74, develop mgr, 74-80, SR GROUP LEADER, PARMA TECH CTR, UNION CARBIDE CORP, 80- *Mem:* AAAS; Am Chem Soc; Am Phys Soc; Am Carbon Soc. *Res:* Kinetics and thermodynamics of phase transformations in solids; vaporization of solids; carbon fibers; intercalation of graphite; electrochemical devices. *Mailing Add:* 368 N Main St Hudson OH 44236

DOWELL, ROBERT VERNON, b San Francisco, Calif, Sept 13, 47; m 74. INSECT ECOLOGY. *Educ:* Univ Calif, Irvine, BS, 69; Calif State Univ, Hayward, MS, 72; Ohio State Univ, PhD(entom), 76. *Prof Exp:* Asst res scientist entom, Univ Fla, 77-80; PEST MGT SPECIALIST III, DIV PEST MGT, DEPT FOOD & AGR, 80- *Mem:* Entom Soc Am; Ecol Soc Am; AAAS; Can Entom Soc; Soc Pop Ecol. *Res:* Plant-insect interrelationships and evolution; insect population biology and evolution of insect-host parasitoid systems. *Mailing Add:* Dept Food & Agr-Div Pest Mgt 1220 N St Sacramento CA 95814

DOWELL, RUSSELL THOMAS, b Cameron, Mo, Sept 23, 41; m 63; c 4. PHYSIOLOGY, PHYSIOLOGICAL CHEMISTRY. *Educ:* Kans State Univ, BS, 64; Univ Ariz, MEd, 65; Univ Iowa, PhD(physiol), 71. *Prof Exp:* Fel med, Univ Chicago, 71-73; asst prof, Univ Tex Med Br, Galveston, 73-77; ASSOC PROF PHYSIOL, UNIV OKLA HEALTH SCI CTR, 77- *Concurrent Pos:* Fel, Chicago & Ill Heart Asn, 71-73; mem, Marine Biomed Inst, Galveston, 73-77. *Honors & Awards:* Jerome Frankel Found Bahr Res Award, Univ Okla, 78. *Mem:* Am Physiol Soc; Int Soc Heart Res; Am Col Sports Med; Soc Exp Biol & Med; Aerospace Med Asn. *Res:* Heart adaptation to stress; exercise physiology. *Mailing Add:* Dept of Physiol & Biophysics PO Box 26901 Oklahoma City OK 73190

DOWELL, VIRGIL EUGENE, b Melver, Kans, June 3, 26; m 61; c 4. FISH BIOLOGY. *Educ:* Kans State Teachers Col, BS, 51, MS, 52; Univ Okla, PhD(zool), 57. *Prof Exp:* Asst, Kans State Teachers Col, 50-52; asst, Univ Okla, 52-53; asst, Okla Biol Surv, 53-56; from asst prof to assoc prof, 56-68, PROF BIOL, UNIV NORTHERN IOWA, 68- *Mem:* Am Inst Biol Sci; Am Fisheries Soc; Am Soc Ichthyologists & Herpetologists. *Res:* Aquatic biology. *Mailing Add:* 1609 Grandview Ct Cedar Falls IA 50613

DOWELL, VULUS RAYMOND, JR, b Mt Vernon, Ky, July 27, 27; m 48; c 4. MICROBIOLOGY, BACTERIOLOGY. *Educ:* Univ Ky, BS, 61; Univ Cincinnati, MS, 62, PhD(microbiol), 66. *Prof Exp:* Instr microbiol & res surg, Univ Cincinnati, 65-66; res microbiologist in chg, Anaerobis Bact Lab, 66-71, chief enterobact br, 71-81, ASST DIR LAB SCI, HOSP INFECTIONS PROG, CTR DIS CONTROL, 81-; ASST PROF, SCH MED, EMORY UNIV, ATLANTA, 77- *Concurrent Pos:* Asst prof, Ga State Univ, 71-; assoc prof, Sch Pub Health, Univ NC; mem ed bd, Appl Microbiol, 73-75; mem ed bd, J Clin Microbiol, 75- *Mem:* Am Soc Microbiol; Sigma Xi; Brit Soc Gen Microbiol; NY Acad Sci; Am Pub Health Asn. *Res:* Hospital acquired infections; clinical anaerobic bacteriology; polymicrobic infections; factors predisposing to microbiol infections; characterization of unusual bacteria, botulism, and foodborne diseases. *Mailing Add:* Hosp Infections Prog Ctr Dis Control Atlanta GA 30333

DOWER, GORDON EWBANK, b Brit, Nov 16, 23; m 47; c 4. ELECTROCARDIOLOGY. *Educ:* St Bartholomew's Hosp Med Col, MB, BS, 49. *Prof Exp:* From instr to asst prof, 54-64, ASSOC PROF PHARMACOL, UNIV BC, 64- *Concurrent Pos:* Can Life Ins Co fel, 54-57; Heart Found Can fel, 57-; consult, Shaughnessy Hosp; res consult, Vancouver Gen Hosp. *Mem:* fel Am Col Cardiol. *Res:* Polarcardiography; computer techniques in electrocardiographic diagnosis. *Mailing Add:* Polarcardiography G 372 Shanghnessy Hosp 4500 Oak St Vancouver BC V6T 1W5 Can

DOWER, JOHN CHARLES, b New York, NY, Mar 4, 24; m 55; c 4. PEDIATRICS, GASTROENTEROLOGY. *Educ:* Johns Hopkins Univ, AB, 50, MD, 54. *Prof Exp:* From intern to resident pediat, Children's Hosp Med Ctr, Boston, 54-56; resident, Babies Hosp, Columbia-Presby Med Ctr, New York, 56-58; consult, Mayo Clin, Rochester, Minn, 60-65; chmn dept, Hosp St Raphael, New Haven, Conn, 65-68; prof, State Univ NY Buffalo, 68-73; PROF PEDIAT, UNIV CALIF, SAN FRANCISCO, 73- *Concurrent Pos:* Consult, Erie County Health Dept, Buffalo, NY, 68-73, Dept Community Health, Eval Unit, Yeshiva Univ, 68-, Community Health Serv, Dept Health, Educ & Welfare, 70-73, Eval Unit, Charles Drew Post-Grad Sch Med, Univ Calif, Los Angeles, 72- & Comprehensive Health Planning Agency, Buffalo, 73. *Mem:* Am Pub Health Asn; Am Pediat Soc; Am Acad Pediat. *Res:* Health services delivery; evaluation of quality of care; organization of health services for teaching. *Mailing Add:* Dept of Pediat Univ of Calif San Francisco CA 94143

DOWLER, CLYDE CECIL, b Moundsville, WVa, Jan 12, 33; m 56; c 4. WEED SCIENCE, IRRIGATION. *Educ:* Univ WVa, BS, 54, MS, 56; Ohio State Univ, PhD(agron), 58. *Prof Exp:* Res agronomist, NC, 59-63, res agronomist, PR, 63-67, RES AGRONOMIST, GA COASTAL PLAIN EXP STA, AGR RES SERV, USDA, 67- *Mem:* Weed Sci Soc Am; Coun Agr Sci & Technol; Am Soybean Asn. *Res:* Effect of cultural and herbicide practices on control and ecology of weeds in agronomic row crops and integrated pest management programs on intensive cropping sequences of agronomic and horticultural crops under irrigation. *Mailing Add:* Ga Coastal Plain Exp Sta Tifton GA 31793

DOWLER, LLOYD, b Chugwater, Wyo, Nov 1, 11; m 35. AGRICULTURE. *Educ:* Univ Wyo, BS, 35, MS, 41. *Prof Exp:* Instr voc agr, high sch, Wyo, 35-43; teacher trainer agr educ, Univ Nev, 46-48; asst prof poultry husb, 48-51, dean sch agr, 51-69, prof, 69-80, EMER PROF AGR EDUC, CALIF STATE UNIV, FRESNO, 80- *Concurrent Pos:* State supvr agr educ, Carson City, Nev, 46-48; mem Calif State Bd Agr, 64-67 & Stanford Res Inst-US Dept Agr-AID Educ Task Force Team, Chile, 65. *Res:* Secondary agricultural education, including careers in agribusiness, curriculum, advisory committees, school farm laboratories; administration of college agricultural programs. *Mailing Add:* Sch of Agr Sci Calif State Univ Fresno CA 93710

DOWLER, WILLIAM MINOR, b Birch Tree, Mo, Nov 10, 32; m 58; c 3. PHYTOPATHOLOGY. *Educ:* Univ Mo, BS, 54, MS, 58; Univ Ill, PhD(plant path), 61. *Prof Exp:* Res plant pathologist, Crops Res Div, 61-75, mem, Nat Prog Staff, 75-81, RES LEADER, PLANT DIS RES LAB, AGR RES SERV, USDA, 81- *Mem:* Am Phytopath Soc; Am Soc Hort Sci; Int Soc Plant Path; Soc Nematologists. *Res:* Diseases of all crops; nematodes; physiology of pathogens and etiology of diseases. *Mailing Add:* 8700 Briarcroft Ln Laurel MD 20708

DOWLING, EDMUND AUGUSTINE, b Waterford, Ireland, July 26, 27; US citizen; m 53; c 4. PATHOLOGY. *Educ:* Nat Univ Ireland, MB, BCh & BAO, 51; Am Bd Path, dipl, 59. *Prof Exp:* From instr to prof path, Sch Med, Univ Ala, Birmingham, 54-74; PROF PATH, SCH MED, UNIV S ALA, 74- *Concurrent Pos:* Consult, Birmingham Baptist Hosps, 62-74. *Mem:* AMA Brit Med Asn; Int Acad Path; Am Soc Cytol. *Res:* Neoplastic diseases; exfoliative cytology. *Mailing Add:* 2451 Fillingim St Mobile AL 36617

DOWLING, HERNDON GLENN, (JR), b Cullman, Ala, Apr 2, 21; m 43, 67; c 4. HERPETOLOGY. *Educ:* Univ Ala, BS, 42; Univ Fla, MS, 48; Univ Mich, PhD(zool), 51. *Prof Exp:* Instr biol, Univ Fla, 47-48; mus asst, Univ Mich, 48-51; instr biol, Haverford Col, 51-52; from asst prof to assoc prof zool, Univ Ark, 52-59; from assoc cur to cur reptiles, NY Zool Park, 59-67; dir herpet info search systs, Am Mus Natural Hist, 68-73; assoc prof, 73-75, PROF BIOL, NY UNIV, 75- *Concurrent Pos:* Fel, Univ Fla, 56-57; res assoc, Dept Amphibians & Reptiles, Am Mus Natural Hist, 57-; adj prof, Univ RI, 64- & NY Univ, 65-73; gen ed, Catalogue Am Amphibians & Reptiles, 66-73; ed, Amphibian & Reptile Sect, Biol Abstr, 68-73 & Herpet Rev, 69-72; ed, Yearbook of Herpet, 74-; vis prof zool, Univ Md, College Park, 80-81. *Mem:* Fel AAAS; Am Inst Biol Sci; Am Soc Ichthyologists & Herpetologists; Am Soc Zoologists; Soc Study Evolution. *Res:* Systematic herpetology; taxonomic studies of colubrid snake genera; higher categories of Serpentes; zoogeographic studies of amphibians and reptiles. *Mailing Add:* Dept Biol 26 Washington Pl New York NY 10003

DOWLING, JEROME M, b Chicago, Ill, July 9, 31; m 56; c 4. INFRARED PHENOMENOLGY, REMOTE SENSING. *Educ:* Ill Inst Technol, BS, 53, MS, 55, PhD(physics), 57. *Prof Exp:* From asst prof to assoc prof physics, Ariz State Univ, 59-63; mem tech staff, 63-69, staff scientist, 69-79, SR SCIENTIST, AEROSPACE CORP, 79- *Concurrent Pos:* Fel pure physics, Nat Res Coun Can, 57-59. *Mem:* Fel Am Phys Soc; Am Asn Physics Teachers; Optical Soc Am. *Res:* Upper atmospheric physics and chemistry; molecular structure and dynamics; interferometry; sensor technology. *Mailing Add:* PO Box 92957 Los Angeles CA 90009

DOWLING, JOHN, b Ashland, Ky, Sept 12, 38; m 63; c 2. PHYSICS. *Educ:* Univ Dayton, BS, 60; Ariz State Univ, MS, 62, PhD(physics), 64. *Prof Exp:* Res assoc molecular spectros, Ariz State Univ, 64; res assoc atmospheric & space physics, Univ Fla, 64-66; asst prof, Univ NH, 66-70; PROF PHYSICS, MANSFIELD STATE COL, 76-, CHMN, PHYSICS DEPT, 81- *Concurrent Pos:* Film ed, Am J Physics, 70- & Bulletin Atomic Sci, 79-; ed, Newsletter Forum, 80- *Mem:* Am Phys Soc; Am Asn Physics Teachers. *Mailing Add:* Dept of Physics Mansfield State Col Mansfield PA 16933

DOWLING, JOHN ELLIOTT, b Pawtucket, RI, Aug 31, 35; m 75; c 3. NEUROBIOLOGY. *Educ:* Harvard Univ, AB, 57, PhD(biol), 61. *Prof Exp:* From instr to asst prof biol, Harvard Univ, 60-64; assoc prof ophthal & biophys, Sch Med, Johns Hopkins Univ, 64-71; PROF BIOL, HARVARD UNIV, 71-, ASSOC DEAN, 80-, MASTER, LEVERETT HOUSE, 81- *Concurrent Pos:* Trustee, Marine Biol Lab, 70-77. *Honors & Awards:* Friedenwald Award, Asn Res Vision & Ophthal, 70. *Mem:* Nat Acad Sci; AAAS; Asn Res Vision & Ophthal; Soc Gen Physiol; Am Acad Arts & Sci. *Res:* Visual physiology; chemistry and anatomy; nervous system, fine structure and function. *Mailing Add:* Biol Labs Harvard Univ 16 Divinity Ave Cambridge MA 02138

DOWLING, JOHN J, b Webster Groves, Mo, Dec 8, 34; m 58; c 5. GEOPHYSICS. *Educ:* St Louis Univ, BS, 57, PhD(geophys), 64; Univ Tulsa, MS, 60. *Prof Exp:* Res engr, Jersey Prod Res Inc, 57-60; asst to dean, Inst Technol, St Louis Univ, 60-63, instr eng, 60-64, res asst geophys, 63-64; res assoc geosci, Southwest Ctr Advan Studies, 64-67; asst prof geophys, Tex

Tech Col, 67-68; MEM MARINE SCI INST, SOUTHEAST BR, UNIV CONN, 68-, ASSOC PROF GEOPHYSICS, 80- *Mem:* AAAS; Am Geophys Union; Seismol Soc Am; Soc Explor Geophys; Am Soc Eng Educ. *Res:* Interior of the earth from elastic waves; marine geophysics; crustal structure in deep oceans and at continental margins. *Mailing Add:* Marine Sci Inst SE Br Univ of Conn Groton CT 06340

DOWLING, JOSEPH FRANCIS, b New York, NY, June 19, 33; m 58; c 2. FOOD CHEMISTRY. *Educ:* Adelphi Univ, BA, 55, MS, 66. *Prof Exp:* From asst chief chemist to chief chemist, 64-69, labs mgr, 69-73, tech serv mgr, Corn Prod, 73-76, TECH MGR, REFINED SUGARS INC, CPC INT INC, 76- *Concurrent Pos:* Secy, Cane Sugar Ref Res Proj, 65-76; vchmn, US Nat Comt Uniform Methods Sugar Anal, 70-74. *Honors & Awards:* George & Eleanor Meade Award, Sugar Indust Tech, 68. *Mem:* Sugar Indust Tech; Am Chem Soc; Am Soc Sugar Beet Technol; Inst Food Technol. *Res:* Sugar chemistry, development of analytical methods and improved means of refining sugar; applications of sugars in the food industry; gas liquid chromatography of sugar and related sugar impurities. *Mailing Add:* Refined Sugars Inc 1 Federal St Yonkers NY 10702

DOWLING, MARIE AUGUSTINE, b Baltimore, Md, Aug 19, 24. MATHEMATICS. *Educ:* Col Notre Dame, Md, BA, 45; Catholic Univ Am, MS, 58. *Prof Exp:* Teacher, St Marys High Sch, Md, 46-48; teacher, Notre Dame Prep Sch, 48-59; chmn dept, 65-80, dir, Winterim, 72-78, ASSOC PROF MATH, COL NOTRE DAME, MD, 59- *Mem:* Am Math Soc; Math Asn Am. *Res:* Teaching mathematics on the undergraduate level; history of mathematics. *Mailing Add:* Dept of Math Col of Notre Dame Baltimore MD 21210

DOWLING, PATRICK J, physics, see previous edition

DOWNER, DONALD NEWSON, b Lexington, Miss, July 2, 44; m 72. MICROBIOLOGY. *Educ:* Univ Miss, BS, 66, PhD(microbiol), 71. *Prof Exp:* Fel microbiol, Med Ctr Univ Miss, 71-72; Killiam fel biochem, Univ Alta, 72-74, prof asst, 74-78; ASST PROF MICROBIOL, MISS STATE UNIV, 78- *Mem:* Am Soc Microbiol; Sigma Xi. *Res:* Virology. *Mailing Add:* 113 Seville Pl Starkville MS 39762

DOWNER, JANE BOS, b Evanston, Ill, Aug 22, 50. NEUROANATOMY. *Educ:* Hope Col, BA, 72; Univ Ill, PhD(anat), 75. *Prof Exp:* asst neuroanatomist, Yerkes Regional Primate Res Ctr, Emory Univ, 75-79; instr, 76-77, ASST PROF ANAT, DEPT ANAT, SCH MED, MOREHOUSE COL, 77- *Mem:* Soc Neurosci; Am Asn Anatomists. *Mailing Add:* Dept Anat Sale Hall Rm 313 Morehouse Col Atlanta GA 30314

DOWNER, NANCY WUERTH, b Washington, DC, Sept 2, 43. PHYSICAL BIOCHEMISTRY. *Educ:* Mt Holyoke Col, AB, 65; Univ Pa, PhD(biochem), 74. *Prof Exp:* Fel molecular biol, Univ Ore, 74-76; fel biophysics, Johns Hopkins Univ, 76-78; ASST PROF BIOCHEM, UNIV ARIZ, 79- *Concurrent Pos:* Fel, Fight for Sight, Inc, 77-78. *Mem:* Biophys Soc; AAAS; NY Acad Sci. *Res:* Mechanism of visual transduction, membrane structure and function, membrane proteins. *Mailing Add:* Dept of Biochem Univ of Ariz Tucson AZ 85721

DOWNER, ROGER GEORGE HAMILL, b Belfast, Northern Ireland, Dec 21, 42; m 66; c 3. INSECT PHYSIOLOGY, NEUROENDOCRINOLOGY. *Educ:* Queen's Univ Belfast, 64, MS, 67; Univ Western Ont, PhD(zool), 70. *Prof Exp:* Asst prof, 70-76, assoc prof, 76-81, PROF BIOL, UNIV WATERLOO, 81- *Concurrent Pos:* Dept Univ Affairs, Prov Ont res grant, 70; Nat Res Coun Can grant, 70-; Japan-Can sr fel, 76. *Mem:* Entom Soc Can; Can Soc Zool. *Res:* Regulation of lipid and carbohydrate metabolism in insects; cyclic nucleotides and prostaglandins; lipid absorption and transport; biogenic amines; biochemistry; insecticide toxicity and vertebrate nervous system. *Mailing Add:* Dept of Biol Univ of Waterloo Waterloo ON N2L 3G1 Can

DOWNES, JOHN ANTONY, b Wimbledon, Eng, Feb 14, 14; m 53; c 5. ENTOMOLOGY. *Educ:* Univ London, BSc, 35. *Prof Exp:* Demonstr zool, Univ London, 39-40; from lectr to sr lectr entom, Glasgow Univ, 40-53; entomologist, Sci Serv, Can Dept Agr, 53-58, head vet & med entom, 58-59, sr entomologist, Res Br, 59-78; RES ASSOC, BIOSYSTEMATICS RES INST, OTTAWA, 79-; RES ASSOC, LYMAN MUS, MCGILL UNIV, MONTREAL, 80- *Concurrent Pos:* Sr sci inspector, Ministry Food, Gt Brit, 41-45; hon sci inspector, Dept Agr, Scotland, 45-47; deleg, Med Res Coun Can, 50; secy, Int Cong Entom, 56; chmn, Sci Comt Terrestrial Anthropods, Biol Surv Can, 79-81. *Honors & Awards:* Gold Medal, Entom Soc Can, 77. *Mem:* Entom Soc Am; Soc Study Evolution; Entom Soc Can; Royal Entom Soc London; Brit Soc Exp Biol. *Res:* Systematics, behavior and physiology of insects, especially diptera and lepidoptera; arctic insects. *Mailing Add:* 877 Riddell Ave Ottawa ON K2A 2V9 Can

DOWNES, JOHN D, b Buckhannon, WVa, Feb 27, 19; m 40; c 2. HORTICULTURE. *Educ:* WVa Univ, BS, 42, MS, 51; Mich State Univ, PhD(hort), 55. *Prof Exp:* Instr & asst hort, WVa Univ, 43-51; asst, Mich State Univ, 51-54; asst horticulturist, Malheur Br Exp Sta, Ore State Col, 54-55; from asst prof to prof hort, Mich State Univ, 55-70; PROF HORT & DIR VEG RES PROG, TEX TECH UNIV, 70- *Concurrent Pos:* Crop specialist, IRI Res Inst, Brazil, 67-68; tech consult veg prod, transport & mkt, Mich State Univ-Inst Nat Tech Agropecuaria, Argentina, 69-70; tech consult, IRI Res Inst, Brazil, 73 & CID, Swaziland, SAfrica, 81. *Mem:* AAAS; Sigma Xi; Am Soc Hort Sci. *Res:* Plant physiology, nutrition, breeding, and genetics; biometry; vegetable production efficiency and economics; wind and windblown soil injury on vegetables and their control. *Mailing Add:* Dept of Plant & Soil Sci Tex Tech Univ Lubbock TX 79409

DOWNES, RONALD ALAN, b Detroit, Mich, Oct 2, 56; m 82. ASTRONOMY. *Educ:* Univ Mich, BS, 78; Univ Calif, Los Angeles, MA, 79. *Prof Exp:* MEM STAFF, DEPT ASTRON, UNIV CALIF, LOS ANGELES, 79- *Mem:* Am Astron Soc. *Res:* Cataclysmic variables; optical identification of x-ray sources. *Mailing Add:* Dept Astron Univ Calif Los Angeles CA 90024

DOWNES, THERON WINSHIP, food science, see previous edition

DOWNES, WILLIAM A(RTHUR), b Providence, RI, Nov 15, 11; m 39. ELECTRONICS. *Educ:* Univ RI, BS, 33; RI Col, BEd, 37. *Prof Exp:* Teacher pub sch, RI, 38-42; proj engr radar, Radiation Lab, Mass Inst Tech, 42-45; electronic engr sonar, US Navy Underwater Sound Lab, 46-48, sect head sonar develop, 48-51, br head, 51-61, div head anti-submarine warfare sonar div, 61-70, head surface ship & surveillance sonar dept, New London Lab, Naval Underwater Systs Ctr, 70-71; RETIRED. *Res:* Radar beacons; sonar equipment and systems. *Mailing Add:* 987 River Rd Mystic CT 06355

DOWNEY, BERNARD JOSEPH, b Philadelphia, Pa, Jan 18, 17; m 55; c 1. PHYSICAL CHEMISTRY. *Educ:* Cath Univ, BA, 38, MS, 45, PhD(phys chem), 52. *Prof Exp:* Instr chem, De La Salle Col, 44-49; from asst prof to assoc prof, La Salle Col, 49-54; asst prof, Seton Hall Univ, 54-59; assoc prof, 59-61, chmn dept, 60-69, assoc dean grad studies, 70-74, PROF CHEM, VILLANOVA UNIV, 61-, DEAN GRAD SCH, 74-, DIR RES, 79- *Concurrent Pos:* Vis res prof, Imp Col, Univ London, 69-70. *Mem:* Am Chem Soc; Sigma Xi. *Res:* Kinetics of metallic film oxidation; diffusion in ionic crystals. *Mailing Add:* Dept of Chem Villanova Univ Villanova PA 19085

DOWNEY, HARRY FRED, b Hagerstown, Md, Aug 6, 39; m 65; c 2. PHYSIOLOGY, BIOPHYSICS. *Educ:* Univ Md, College Park, BS, 61, MS, 64; Univ Ill, Urbana, PhD(biophys), 68. *Prof Exp:* Asst prof vet physiol & pharmacol, Univ Ill, Urbana, 68-71, asst prof physiol & biophys, 70-71; asst prof, 72-77, RES ASSOC PROF PHYSIOL, SOUTHWESTERN MED SCH, UNIV TEX HEALTH SCI CTR, DALLAS, 78-; DIR CARDIOVASC RES, CARDIOPULMONARY INST, METHODIST HOSP, 72- *Concurrent Pos:* Prin investr, Res Coronary Circulation, NIH, 77-; Coun Circulation fel, Am Heart Asn. *Mem:* Am Physiol Soc; Soc Exp Biol & Med. *Res:* Coronary circulation, especially control of coronary blood flow; transcapillary exchange; mammary blood flow, especially its control and relationship to lactation; cardiovascular effects of nicotine. *Mailing Add:* Dept Physiol Univ Tex Health Sci Ctr Dallas TX 75235

DOWNEY, JAMES MERRITT, b Wabash, Ind, Nov 1, 44; m 67; c 2. CORONARY PHYSIOLOGYY, CARDIAC PHARMACOLOGY. *Educ:* Manchester Col, Ind, BS, 67; Univ Ill, Urbana, MS, 69, PhD(physiol), 71. *Prof Exp:* Res asst, Marine Biol Lab, Woods Hole, 70; res fel, Peter Bent Brigham Hosp, Boston, 71-72; asst prof physiol, Univ SFla, 72-75; assoc prof, 75-80, PROF PHYSIOL, UNIV SOUTH ALA, 80- *Concurrent Pos:* Vis asst prof, Southwestern Med Sch, Dallas, 75; vis scientist, Rayne Inst, St Thomas Hosp, London, 81; fel, Am Heart Asn. *Mem:* fel Am Physiol Soc. *Res:* Coronary artery hemodynamics and controlers of blood flow; drug and other interventions which might protect ischemic myocardium. *Mailing Add:* 3024 MSB Univ SAla Mobile AL 36688

DOWNEY, JOHN A, b Regina, Sask, Sept 16, 30; m 53; c 4. MEDICINE, PHYSIOLOGY. *Educ:* Univ Man, BSc & MD, 54; Oxford Univ, PhD(physiol), 62; Am Bd Phys Med & Rehab, dipl. *Prof Exp:* Intern, Vancouver Gen Hosp, BC, 53-54; resident phys med & rehab, Presby Hosp, New York, 54-56, 57-58, res assoc, 58-59; resident internal med, Peter Bent Brigham Hosp, Boston, Mass, 56-57, 59-60; vis worker Christ Church Col, Oxford Univ, 60-62; asst prof med & from asst prof to assoc prof phys med & rehab, 63-70, PROF REHAB MED, COL PHYSICIANS & SURGEONS, COLUMBIA UNIV, 70-; CHMN & DIR REHAB MED, COLUMBIA-PRESBY MED CTR, 74- *Concurrent Pos:* Attend physiatrist, Blythedale Children's Hosp, Valhalla, 62; asst attend physician, Presby Hosp, 62, Assoc attend physician, 64-; Life Inst Med Res Fund fel, 61-62; vis fel phys med, Col Physicians & Surgeons, Columbia Univ, 62-63. *Mem:* Asn Acad Physiatrist; Am Physiol Soc; Am Rheumatism Asn; Am Acad Phys Med & Rehab; Am Cong Rehab Med. *Res:* Physiology of temperature regulation; control of respiration; peripheral circulation; clinical care of patients with chronic disabling illness. *Mailing Add:* Dept of Rehab Med Col Phys & Surg Columbia Univ New York NY 10032

DOWNEY, JOHN CHARLES, b Eureka, Utah, Apr 12, 26; m 49; c 5. ENTOMOLOGY. *Educ:* Univ Utah, BS, 49, MS, 50; Univ Calif, PhD(entom), 57. *Prof Exp:* Instr biol, Univ Utah, 50-52; assoc zool, Univ Calif, 52-56; from asst prof to prof, Southern Ill Univ, 56-68; prof biol & head dept, 68-81, DEAN, GRAD COL, UNIV NORTHERN IOWA, 81- *Mem:* Entom Soc Am; Soc Syst Zool; Am Soc Zoologists. *Res:* General variation and evolution; taxonomy and morphology Lycaenidae; ecology and behavior of insects; ultrastructure, sound and chemical communication in Lepidoptera; eggs and immature stages of butterflies. *Mailing Add:* Grad Col Univ of Northern Iowa Cedar Falls IA 50614

DOWNEY, JOHN FRANCIS, JR, b Somerville, Mass, Aug 3, 33; m 56; c 3. PHOTOGRAPHIC CHEMISTRY. *Educ:* Tufts Univ, BS, 55; Canisius Col, MS, 59. *Prof Exp:* Res chemist, Nat Aniline Div, Allied Chem Corp, 55-59; from asst scientist to scientist chem, 59-63, res group leader, 63-69, dept mgr, 69-73, SR SCIENTIST CHEM, RES DIV, POLAROID CORP, 73- *Res:* Dye chemistry; materials that mordant dyes in photographic systems. *Mailing Add:* 24 Hancock St Lexington MA 02173

DOWNEY, JOSEPH ROBERT, JR, b Charleston, WVa, Nov 27, 41; m 63; c 2. PHYSICAL INORGANIC CHEMISTRY. *Educ:* Western Md Col, BA, 63; Fla State Univ, PhD(inorg chem), 72. *Prof Exp:* Instr chem, Fla State Univ, 72-73; assoc chem, Rensselaer Polytech Inst, 73-76; SR RES CHEMIST, DOW CHEM USA, 76- *Mem:* Am Chem Soc; Sigma Xi. *Res:* Solution interactions and structural determinations via vibrational spectroscopy; hydrogen bonding, ion pairing, complex formation; application of computerized methods to handling of spectroscopic data; curve resolution, interfacing; thermodynamics; thermochemistry; calorimetry; critical evaluation of thermodynamic and physical property data. *Mailing Add:* Midland Res Ctr 1707 Bldg Dow Chem Co Midland MI 48640

DOWNEY, RICHARD KEITH, b Saskatoon, Sask, Jan 26, 27; m 52; c 5. PLANT BREEDING. *Educ:* Univ Sask, BSA, 50, MSc, 52; Cornell Univ, PhD, 61. *Prof Exp:* Res scientist, Exp Farm, Lethbridge, Alta, 52-57; res scientist, Crops Sect, 57-73, ASST DIR, AGR CAN RES STA, 73- *Concurrent Pos:* Nat dir, Agr Inst Can. *Honors & Awards:* Bond Medal, Am Oil Chemists' Soc, 63; Merit Award, Pub Serv Can, 68; Royal Bank Can Award, 75; Grindley Medal, Agr Inst Can, 73; Officer Order Can, 76; Queen's Jubilee Medal, 77. *Mem:* Fel Agr Inst Can; Can Soc Agron (past pres); fel Royal Soc Can. *Res:* Oil seed and forage crop improvement. *Mailing Add:* Agr Can Res Sta 107 Sci Crescent Saskatoon SK S7N 0X2 Can

DOWNEY, RONALD J, b Manitowoc, Wis, Apr 8, 33; m 57; c 5. CELL PHYSIOLOGY. *Educ:* Regis Col, Colo, BS, 55; Creighton Univ, MS, 58; Univ Nebr, PhD(microbiol), 61. *Prof Exp:* Res assoc cell metab, USDA, 61-62; asst prof biol, Univ Notre Dame, 62-66; from assoc prof to prof microbiol, 66-72; PROF ZOOL & MICROBIOL & CHMN DEPT, OHIO UNIV, 72- *Concurrent Pos:* USPHS career develop award. *Mem:* Am Soc Microbiol; Soc Exp Biol & Med; Am Soc Cell Biol; Am Soc Exp Path. *Res:* Oxidative metabolism; synthesis of respiratory enzymes; differentiation in the lower eucaryotes. *Mailing Add:* Dept of Zool & Microbiol Ohio Univ Athens OH 45701

DOWNEY, RONALD STUART, b Smithfalls, Ont, Nov 9, 38; m 62; c 3. VETERINARY MEDICINE. *Educ:* Ont Vet Med Col, DVM, 61, MS, 68. *Prof Exp:* Res asst vet med, Univ Calif, Davis, 61-65; assoc prof, 65-80, CHIEF STAFF SMALL ANIMAL MED & SURG, ONT VET COL, UNIV GUELPH, 70-, PROF VET MED, 80- *Res:* Clinical medicine; cardiovascular physiology. *Mailing Add:* Dept of Clin Studies Ont Vet Col Univ of Guelph Guelph ON N1G 2W1 Can

DOWNEY, VINCENT M, b Kansas City, Kans, Mar 22, 12; m 42. AEROSPACE MEDICINE. *Educ:* Stanford Univ, AB, 33, MD, 38. *Prof Exp:* Staff scientist, 63-66, CONSULT AEROSPACE MED, LOCKHEED MISSILES & SPACE CO, 66- *Concurrent Pos:* Lectr, Sch Med, Stanford Univ, 63-77; mem comt hyperbaric oxygenation, Nat Acad Sci-Nat Res Coun, 65-67; emer clin prof, Sch Med Stanford Univ, 77- *Honors & Awards:* Tuttle Award, Aerospace Med Asn, 64. *Mem:* Aerospace Med Asn; Am Col Physicians. *Res:* Decompression sickness. *Mailing Add:* 2066 Byron St Palo Alto CA 94301

DOWNHOWER, JERRY F, b Indianapolis, Ind, Oct 25, 40; m 64; c 2. BEHAVIORAL ECOLOGY. *Educ:* Occidental Col, BA, 62; Univ Kans, MA, 64, PhD(zool), 68. *Prof Exp:* Res asst, Kans State Biol Surv, 62-64; res asst zool, Univ Kans, 64-68; lectr biol, Cornell Univ, 68-70; asst prof, 70-76, ASSOC PROF ZOOL, OHIO STATE UNIV, 76- *Concurrent Pos:* Mem fac of organ for trop studies, 71; mem steering comt, Biol Sci Curric Studies, 71; mem bd dirs, 71-72; consult, Battelle Columbus Labs, 74-75; prog dir, Pop Biol & Physiol Ecol, NSF, 80-81. *Mem:* Soc Syst Zool; Am Soc Mammalogists; Am Soc Naturalists. *Res:* Behavior; adaptive significance of vertebrate social organization. *Mailing Add:* Dept of Zool Ohio State Univ Columbus OH 43210

DOWNIE, CURRIE STEVENSON, b Detroit, Mich, May 10, 22; m 47; c 2. METEOROLOGY, INFORMATION SCIENCE. *Educ:* Detroit Inst Technol, BS, 42; Univ Chicago, MS, 50, MBA, 60. *Prof Exp:* US Air Force, 42-70, weather officer, Air Weather Serv, 43-52, dep dir high altitude weather res proj, 52-55, chief cloud physics div, Air Force Cambridge Res Labs, 55-59, geophys planning div, off aerospace res, 60-61, resources planning div, 61-63, chief phys sci div Europ off, 63-66, dir Air Force sci & tech info, 66-69, dir plans, 69-70; consult meteorol, air pollution & info sci, 70-72; pres, CJLM, Inc, 73-74; prog mgr weather modification, 74-78, PROG COORDR, NAT CTR ATMOSPHERIC RES, NSF, 78- *Concurrent Pos:* Chmn task group dissemination info comt sci & tech info, Fed Coun Sci & Technol, 67-70. *Mem:* AAAS; Am Meteorol Soc; Air Pollution Control Asn; Am Soc Info Sci. *Res:* Cloud physics; weather modification; atmospheric sciences. *Mailing Add:* NSF 1800 G St NW Washington DC 20006

DOWNIE, DAVID ERNEST, bioengineering, cardiopulmonary physiology, see previous edition

DOWNIE, HARRY G, b Toronto, Ont, June 11, 26; m 50; c 4. PHYSIOLOGY, EXPERIMENTAL SURGERY. *Educ:* Ont Vet Col, DVM, 48, MVSc, 52; Cornell Univ, MS, 51; Univ Western Ont, PhD(physiol), 59. *Prof Exp:* Lectr physiol, 48-49, asst prof, 51-52, assoc prof, 55-56, head dept res, 56-58, head dept physiol sci, 58-69, chmn, Dept Biomed Sci, 69-80, PROF PHYSIOL, ONT VET COL, UNIV GUELPH, 56-, PROF PHYSIOL, DEPT BIOMED SCI, 81- *Concurrent Pos:* Fel coun arteriosclerosis, Am Heart Asn. *Mem:* Fel AAAS; Can Vet Med Asn; Am Soc Res Workers Animal Dis; Am Soc Vet Physiol & Pharmacol; Am Physiol Soc. *Res:* Animal physiology, especially cardiovascular physiology; cardiovascular surgery; blood coagulation; blood flow and vascular disease in man and animals. *Mailing Add:* Dept of Biomed Sci Ont Vet Col Univ of Guelph Guelph ON N1G 2W1 Can

DOWNIE, JOHN, b Glasgow, Scotland, Dec 12, 31; Can citizen; m 59; c 3. CHEMICAL ENGINEERING. *Educ:* Univ Glasgow, BSc, 53; Univ Toronto, MASc, 56, PhD(chem eng), 59. *Prof Exp:* Res engr, Reservoir Mech, Gulf Res & Develop Co, 59-62; from asst prof to assoc prof, 62-71, head chem eng dept, 72-77, PROF CHEM ENG, QUEEN'S UNIV, ONT, 71- *Mem:* Chem Inst Can; Can Soc Chem Engrs. *Res:* Kinetics of gas/solid catalytic oxidation reaction networks using statistical analysis and design of experiments; mathematical modeling of wood gasifiers as a basis for technical assessment. *Mailing Add:* Dept of Chem Eng Queen's Univ Kingston Can

DOWNIE, JOHN WILLIAM, b Winnipeg, Man, May 11, 45. PHARMACOLOGY, UROLOGY. *Educ:* Univ Man, BSc Hons, 67, PhD(pharmacol), 72. *Prof Exp:* Res asst urol, Queen's Univ, Ont, 72-73; lectr urol & pharmacol, 73-75, asst prof urol & pharmacol, 75-80; ASSOC PROF PHARMACOL, DALHOUSIE UNIV, NS, 80- *Concurrent Pos:* Med Res Coun Can scholar, 75-80. *Honors & Awards:* Mihran & Mary Basmajian Med Res Award, Queen's Univ, Ont, 79. *Mem:* Pharmacol Soc Can; Am Soc Pharmacol & Exp Therapeut; Int Continence Soc; Urodynamic Soc. *Res:* Neurotransmission in urinary tract; lower urinary tract dynamics in spinal injury. *Mailing Add:* Dept Pharmacol Dalhousie Univ Halifax NS Can

DOWNING, DARRYL JON, mathematical statistics, see previous edition

DOWNING, DONALD LEONARD, b Willoughby, Ohio, Apr 2, 31; m 59; c 2. FOOD SCIENCE. *Educ:* Univ Ga, BSA, 57, PhD(food sci), 63. *Prof Exp:* Instr food sci, Univ Ga, 61-63; food scientist, Beech-Nut Life Savers, Inc, 63-67; asst prof, NY State Agr Sta, 67-73, mem fac, Dept Food Sci, 77-80, PROF FOOD SCI, CORNELL UNIV, 80- *Mem:* Inst Food Technologists; Int Asn Milk, Food & Environ Sanit. *Res:* Science and technology related to food preservation and environmental quality. *Mailing Add:* Dept Food Sci Cornell Univ Ithaca NY 14853

DOWNING, DONALD TALBOT, b Perth, Western Australia, Mar 11, 29; m 52; c 6. BIOCHEMISTRY OF LIPIDS. *Educ:* Univ Western Australia, BSc, 51, PhD(org chem), 55. *Prof Exp:* Res chemist, Kiwi Polish Co Ltd, Australia, 54-55; res officer wax chem, Commonwealth Sci & Indust Res Orgn, 55-63, sr res officer, 63-64; sr res scientist, 64-66; asst res prof dermat & biochem, 66-69, from assoc prof to prof biochem & assoc res prof to res prof dermat, Sch Med, Boston Univ, 69-78; PROF DERMAT, SCH MED, UNIV IOWA, 78- *Concurrent Pos:* NIH res career develop award, 69-73. *Mem:* Am Chem Soc; Am Oil Chemists Soc; Soc Invest Dermat; AAAS; Am Soc Biol Chemists. *Res:* Chemical composition and biosynthesis of lipids from sebaceous glands, epidermis and other kenotivizing tissues. *Mailing Add:* Dept of Dermat Univ of Iowa Col of Med Iowa City IA 52242

DOWNING, GEORGE V, JR, b Salem, Va, July 29, 23; m 51, 81; c 5. PHYSICAL CHEMISTRY. *Educ:* Haverford Col, BA, 47; Cornell Univ, PhD(phys chem), 52. *Prof Exp:* Chemist, Off Sci Res & Develop Malaria Res Proj, NY Univ, 44-46; res chemist natural prod develop group, 51-56, group leader anal methods develop, 56-62, mgr in-process controls res, 62-65, dir phys & anal res, 65-77, SR DIR ANAL RES, MERCK & CO, INC, 77- *Mem:* AAAS; Am Chem Soc; NY Acad Sci. *Res:* Purity characterization of organic compounds; analytical methods development; trace methods in biological materials; chromatographic methods. *Mailing Add:* 26 Skyline Dr Warren NJ 07060

DOWNING, JOHN SCOTT, b Philadelphia, Pa, July 31, 40. MATHEMATICS, TOPOLOGY. *Educ:* Princeton Univ, AB, 62; Mich State Univ, MS, 66, PhD(math), 69. *Prof Exp:* High sch teacher, Venezuela, 62-65; from asst prof to assoc prof, 69-75, PROF MATH, UNIV NEBR, OMAHA, 75- *Concurrent Pos:* Mem fac, Univ de Oriente, 74-75. *Mem:* Am Math Soc; Math Asn Am. *Res:* Topology of manifolds. *Mailing Add:* Dept of Math & Comp Sci Univ of Nebr Omaha NE 68182

DOWNING, KENTON BENSON, b Montrose, Colo, Nov 5, 40; m 58; c 4. FORESTRY, RECREATION RESOURCE MANAGEMENT. *Educ:* Colo State Univ, BS, 62, MS, 66; Univ Mo, PhD(forestry), 73. *Prof Exp:* Dist forester, Colo State Forest Serv, Colo State Univ, 64-67; instr, Univ Mo, 67-73; asst prof, Ore State Univ, 73-77; ASSOC PROF, DEPT FOREST RESOURCES, UTAH STATE UNIV, 77- *Concurrent Pos:* Prin investr res proj, Ore State Univ & Utah State Univ, 73-; dir, Nat Outdoor Recreation Shortcourse Training Prog, Utah State Univ & US Forest Serv, 79- *Mem:* Sigma Xi. *Res:* Social aspects of natural resource management; conflicts between outdoor recreation and other natural resource uses and outdoor recreation users and natural resource managers. *Mailing Add:* Dept Forest Resources Utah State Univ Logan UT 84322

DOWNING, MANCOURT, b Denver, Colo, May 25, 25; m 48; c 4. BIOCHEMISTRY. *Educ:* Univ Chicago, SB, 52, PhD(biochem), 55. *Prof Exp:* Res assoc, Am Meat Inst Found, 52-55; from instr to asst prof, 55-64, ASSOC PROF CHEM, UNIV COLO, BOULDER, 64- *Concurrent Pos:* NIH fel, Inst Molecular Biol, Univ Wis, 68-69. *Mem:* Fel AAAS; Am Soc Biol Chemists. *Res:* Thermodynamic properties of biological macromolecules; biological and physical properties of vitamin B12 and DNA; intermediary metabolism of nucleic acids; cytokinins. *Mailing Add:* Dept of Chem Univ of Colo Boulder CO 80302

DOWNING, MICHAEL RICHARD, b North Platte, Nebr, Nov 19, 47; m 70; c 1. CLINICAL RESEARCH, HEMATOLOGY. *Educ:* Chadron State Col, Nebr, BA, 70; Okla State Univ, PhD(biochem), 74. *Prof Exp:* Hemat researcher, Mayo Clinic, 74-77, res assoc biochem, 77-79, asst prof, Mayo Med Sch, 78-79; sr scientist, 79-80, mgr clin proj, 80-82, DIR CLIN RES, ALPHA THERAPEUT CORP, 82- *Mem:* Am Hematol Asn; AAAS; Am Chem Soc. *Res:* Research interests include protein structural functional relationships, plasma derived proteins and lipoproteins and proteins involved in coagulation and the inhibition of coagulation. *Mailing Add:* 306 San Antonio Rd Arcadia CA 91006

DOWNING, REGINALD HORTON, b New Ger, NS, Nov 19, 08; nat US; m 49; c 1. MATHEMATICS. *Educ:* Acadia Univ, BA, 30; Univ WVa, MS, 32, PhD(math), 34. *Prof Exp:* Asst math, Univ WVa, 30-34, instr, 34-38; res assoc, Bur Govt Res, WVa, 34-38; instr math, Purdue Univ, 38-42; eng mathematician, Kaiser Fleetwings, Inc, 42-47; assoc prof math, 47-49, prof & head dept, 49-51, dean resident col, 51-56, dir resident instruction, 56-58, dean faculty, 58-61, dean eng, 61-69, dir acad affairs, 69-74, EMER DEAN, AIR FORCE INST, 74- *Honors & Awards:* Sigma Xi Award, 34. *Mem:* AAAS; Am Math Soc; Am Soc Eng Educ; Math Asn Am; Am Inst Aeronaut & Astronaut. *Res:* Engineering education. *Mailing Add:* 432 Avon Way Dayton OH 46429

DOWNING, ROBERT LEE, b Wichita Falls, Tex, Mar 28, 31; m 66. WILDLIFE RESEARCH, RARE SPECIES SURVEYS. *Educ:* Tex A&M Univ, BS, 52; Okla State Univ, MS, 57. *Prof Exp:* Wildlife biologist, Tex Game & Fish Comn, 54-55; proj leader deer res, Ga Game & Fish Comn, 57-64; proj leader deer res, US Fish & Wildlife Serv, 64-75, proj leader strip mine res, 75-77, PROJ LEADER EASTERN COUGAR SURVEY, US FISH & WILDLIFE SERV, 77- *Mem:* Wildlife Soc; Nat Audubon Soc. *Res:* Research on deer population dynamics and population analysis methods and on declining wildlife species, especially the eastern cougar. *Mailing Add:* Dept of Forestry Clemson Univ Clemson SC 29631

DOWNING, SHIRLEY EVANS, b Meredith, NH, June 29, 30; m 55; c 2. PATHOLOGY. *Educ:* Univ NH, BS, 52; Yale Univ, MD, 56. *Prof Exp:* Intern path, Yale-New Haven Hosp, 56-57; USPHS fel, 57-58, Life Ins Med Res Fund fel, 59-60; scientist, Nat Heart Inst, 60-62; assoc physiol, George Washington Univ, 62; from asst prof to assoc prof, 62-74, PROF PATH, SCH MED, YALE UNIV, 74- *Concurrent Pos:* Keese Prize, Sch Med, Yale Univ, 56, fel, Nuffield Inst Med Res, Eng, 58-59; USPHS res career develop award, 62-72; consult, Nat Heart Lung & Blood Inst, NIH, 72-; prin investr res grants, NIH. *Mem:* Am Asn Path; Soc Pediat Res; NY Acad Sci; Int Acad Path; Am Physiol Soc. *Res:* Cardiovascular physiology; pathophysiology. *Mailing Add:* Dept Path 310 Cedar St New Haven CT 06510

DOWNING, STEPHEN WARD, b Philadelphia, Pa, July 27, 43; m 66; c 4. CELL BIOLOGY. *Educ:* Col Wooster, BA, 65; Northwestern Univ, PhD(zool), 69. *Prof Exp:* Res assoc path, Mass Gen Hosp, Harvard Med Sch, 69-72; asst prof anat, Chicago Med Sch-Univ of Health Sci, 72-76; asst prof, 76-79, ASSOC PROF BIOMED ANAT, SCH MED, UNIV MINN, DULUTH, 79- *Mem:* Am Soc Cell Biol; Am Asn Anatomists; Sigma Xi. *Res:* Investigations of epidermal differentiation and morphogenesis in selected vertebrate models, particularly reptilian, agnathan and mammalian epidermal tissues; biology of mucus and the formation and interactions of mucins and fibrous proteins. *Mailing Add:* Dept of Biomed Anat Univ of Minn Sch of Med Duluth MN 55812

DOWNING, WILLIAM LAWRENCE, b Des Moines, Iowa, Oct 2, 21; m 46; c 3. PROTOZOOLOGY. *Educ:* Univ Iowa, BA, 43, MS, 48, PhD(zool), 51. *Prof Exp:* Instr biol, Univ Iowa, 49-51; prof & head dept, Jamestown Col, 51-63; PROF BIOL, HAMLINE UNIV, 63- *Concurrent Pos:* Adv pre-med, Hamline Univ; supvr, Soil & Water Conserv Dist. *Mem:* AAAS; Am Soc Zoologists; Soc Protozoologists; Am Inst Biol Sci. *Res:* Morphogenesis of ciliates; undergraduate biological curricula; soil and water conservation. *Mailing Add:* Dept of Biol Hamline Univ St Paul MN 55104

DOWNS, BERTRAM WILSON, JR, b St Paul, Minn, Dec 11, 25; m 56; c 3. STRONG ELEMENTARY PARTICLE INTERACTIONS. *Educ:* Calif Inst Technol, BS, 46; Univ Minn, MS, 49; Stanford Univ, PhD(physics), 56. *Prof Exp:* Res fel, Univ Birmingham, 55-56; res assoc, Lab Nuclear Studies, Cornell Univ, 56-59; from asst prof to assoc prof physics, 59-65, assoc dean grad sch & actg dir comput ctr, 65-67, PROF PHYSICS, UNIV COLO, BOULDER, 65- *Concurrent Pos:* Consult, Atomic Power Develop Assocs, Mich, 57-58; vacation consult, Atomic Energy Res Estab, Eng, 63-64; mem staff, Oxford Univ, 63-64. *Mem:* Fel Am Phys Soc. *Res:* Hyperon-nucleon interactions and hypernuclei. *Mailing Add:* Dept Physics Univ of Colo Boulder CO 80309

DOWNS, DAVID S, b Woodbury, NJ, Jan 4, 41; m 67. SOLID STATE PHYSICS. *Educ:* Gettysburg Col, BA, 62; Univ Del, MS, 64, PhD(physics), 69. *Prof Exp:* Nat Res Coun res assoc physics, Picatinny Arsenal, 68-69, res physicist, Feltman Res Lab, Solid State Br, 69-77, actg chief, Energy Conversion Sect, 74-75; CHIEF, IGNITION & COMBUSTION SECT, APPL SCI DIV, ARMAMENT RES & DEVELOP COMMAND, US ARMY, 77- *Mem:* Am Phys Soc; Am Asn Physics Teachers. *Res:* Electron spin resonance of transition metals in II-VI compounds; electrical and optical properties of metallic azides; optical and electrical properties of energetic materials. *Mailing Add:* Army Armament Res & Develop Command Appl Sci Div B382 Dover NJ 07801

DOWNS, FREDERICK JON, b New York, NY, Oct 22, 39; m 63; c 2. BIOCHEMISTRY. *Educ:* Hunter Col, BA, 61; NY Med Col, MS, 65, PhD(biochem), 68. *Prof Exp:* Res scientist biochem, Union Carbide Res Inst, 68-69; teacher biol, NY City Bd Educ, 69-70; from lectr to asst prof, 70-74, assoc prof, 74-80, PROF CHEM, HERBERT LEHMAN COL, 80- *Concurrent Pos:* Res assoc, NY Med Col, 68-71, adj asst prof, 71- *Mem:* Am Chem Soc; AAAS; Soc Complex Carbohydrates. *Res:* Isolation and characterization of glycoproteins and glycolipids and their biological significance. *Mailing Add:* 213 45 29th Ave Bayside NY 11360

DOWNS, GEORGE SAMUEL, b San Antonio, Tex, Oct 4, 39; c 1. RADIO ASTRONOMY, RADAR ASTRONOMY. *Educ:* Cornell Univ, BS, 62; Stanford Univ, MS, 64, PhD(elec eng), 68. *Prof Exp:* MEM TECH STAFF ASTRON, JET PROPULSION LAB, 68- *Mem:* Am Astron Soc. *Res:* Timing measurements and analysis of pulsating radio sources including pulsars; radar probes of the terrestrial planets, particularly Mars. *Mailing Add:* Jet Propulsion Lab 4800 Oak Grove Pasadena CA 91103

DOWNS, JAMES JOSEPH, b St Joseph, Mo, Jan 31, 28. PHYSICAL CHEMISTRY, ORGANIC CHEMISTRY. *Educ:* St Benedicts Col, BS, 49; Univ Notre Dame, MS, 52; Fla State Univ, PhD(chem), 54. *Prof Exp:* Prin chemist, Midwest Res Inst, 56-77; dir, 78-79, SR FEL, CHEM PHYSICS CTR, CARNEGIE-MELLON INST RES, 79- *Mem:* AAAS; Am Chem Soc; Am Statist Asn. *Res:* Computer data processing; mass spectroscopy; electron paramagnetic resonance spectroscopy; nuclear magnetic resonance spectroscopy; kinetics; structural chemistry; fiberoptics. *Mailing Add:* 5700 Bunkerhill St Pittsburgh PA 15206

DOWNS, MARTIN LUTHER, b Reading, Pa, March 12, 10; m; c 2. CHEMISTRY. *Educ:* Pa State Univ, BS, 31; Lawrence Col, MS, 32, PhD(pulp, paper making), 34. *Prof Exp:* Develop dept, Mead Corp, 34-37; from chief chemist to tech dir, Thilmany Pulp & Paper Co, 37-70, vpres, 64-70; OWNER & MGR, PAPER CONCEPTS CONSULT, 70- *Mem:* Am Chem Soc; Tech Asn Pulp & Paper Indust. *Res:* Paper chemistry; paper sizing; stock processing; specialty and technical papers; paper recycling. *Mailing Add:* Paper Concepts 1000 Greengrove Rd Appleton WI 54911

DOWNS, ROBERT JACK, b Sapulpa, Okla, June 25, 23; m 45; c 1. BOTANY. *Educ:* George Washington Univ, BS, 50, MS, 51, PhD(bot), 54. *Prof Exp:* Student asst physics & bot, George Washington Univ, 49-50, asst bot, 50-51; phys sci aide, Astrophys Observ, Smithsonian Inst, 51-52; plant physiologist photoperiod proj, Plant Indust Sta, Agr Res Serv, USDA, 52-59, mem pioneering res group, Plant Physiol Lab, Agr Res Serv, Plant Indust Sta, 59-65; PROF BOT & HORT SCI & DIR PHYTOTRON, NC STATE UNIV, 65- *Honors & Awards:* Alex Laurie Award, Am Soc Hort Sci; Henry Allan Gleason Award, NY Bot Garden. *Mem:* Am Soc Hort Sci; Bot Soc Am; Int Soc Biometeorol; Am Soc Agr Engrs; Am Soc Plant Physiologists. *Res:* Phytochrome and the regulatory effects of light on plants; taxonomy of South American plants, especially Xyridaceae and Bromeliaceae; bioengineering and environmental physiology. *Mailing Add:* Southeastern Plant Environ Labs NC State Univ Raleigh NC 27607

DOWNS, THEODORE, b Chicago, Ill, July 1, 19; wid; c 2. VERTEBRATE PALEONTOLOGY. *Educ:* Kans State Teachers Col, BS, 41; Univ Calif, MA, 48, PhD(vert paleont), 51. *Prof Exp:* Cur vert paleont, 52-61, chief cur, 61-80, EMER CHIEF CUR, EARTH SCI DIV, LOS ANGELES COUNTY MUS, 80- *Concurrent Pos:* Nat Res Coun fel, 51-52. *Mem:* AAAS; Geol Soc Am; Soc Vert Paleont; Am Soc Mammalogists; Soc Study Evolution; Soc Syst Zool; Paleont Soc. *Res:* Paleomammalogy; evolution; paleoecology; paleogeographic distribution of middle to late Cenozoic vertebrates; field operations in Nevada, Oregon, California and Mexico. *Mailing Add:* Los Angeles Co Mus Natural Hist 900 Exposition Blvd Los Angeles CA 90007

DOWNS, THOMAS D, b Kalamazoo, Mich, Aug 28, 33; m 62; c 1. BIOSTATISTICS. *Educ:* Western Mich Univ, BS, 60; Univ Mich, MPH, 62, PhD(biostatist), 65. *Prof Exp:* Asst prof, Case Western Reserve Univ, 65-70, assoc prof biomet, Sch Pub Health, 70-77, PROF, UNIV TEX HOUSTON, 77- *Mem:* Math Asn Am; Am Statist Asn; Am Pub Health Asn; Biomet Soc. *Res:* Applied statistics and mathematics in public health. *Mailing Add:* Univ of Tex PO Box 20186 Houston TX 77025

DOWNS, WILBUR GEORGE, b Perth Amboy, NJ, Aug 7, 13; m 40, 72; c 4. VIROLOGY. *Educ:* Cornell Univ, AB, 35, MD, 38; Johns Hopkins Univ, MPH, 41. *Prof Exp:* Mem, State Biol Surv, NY, 35-37; intern & resident med, New York Hosp, 38-40; mem field staff, Div Med & Pub Health, Rockefeller Found, 41-62, assoc dir div biomed sci, 62-71; prof epidemiol, Sch Med & dir arbovirus res unit, 64-71, MEM STAFF, ARBOVIRUS RES UNIT & CLIN PROF EPIDEMIOL, SCH MED, YALE UNIV, 71- *Concurrent Pos:* Mem expert adv panel malaria, WHO, 50-57 & virus dis, 57-; mem standing adv comt med res, Brit WI, 56-71; mem bd virus reference reagents & panel arthropod-borne virus reference reagents, NIH, 63-68; mem comn on malaria, Armed Forces Epidemiol Bd, 65-71; mem, Corp Gongas Mem Lab, 81. *Mem:* Am Soc Trop Med & Hyg; Am Soc Parasitol; Entom Soc Am; Am Soc Viruses; Royal Soc Trop Med & Hyg. *Res:* Malaria; insecticides; arthropod transmitted virus disease. *Mailing Add:* 10 Halstead Lane Branford CT 06405

DOWNS, WILLIAM FREDRICK, b Santa Maria, Calif, Aug 4, 42; m 67. ORE DEPOSIT GEOCHEMISTRY, ROCK WATER INTERACTIONS. *Educ:* Univ Colo, BA, 65, MS, 74; Pa State Univ, PhD(geochem), 77. *Prof Exp:* Res asst, Pa State Univ, 71-74, proj assoc, 74-77; SR SCIENTIST, ENG LAB, EG&G IDAHO, INC, 77- *Concurrent Pos:* Explor geologist, Duval Mining Co, 71; consult & lectr, Univ Idaho, 79- *Mem:* Geochem Soc; Geol Soc Am; AAAS; Am Chem Soc. *Res:* Investigation of the solubility of scale forming minerals in synthetic geothermal brines; experimental calibration of both stable isotope, and chemical specie geothermometers. *Mailing Add:* Rte 7 Box 18 Idaho Falls ID 83401

DOWS, DAVID ALAN, b San Francisco, Calif, July 25, 28; m 50; c 3. LASER CHEMISTRY. *Educ:* Univ Calif, BS, 52, PhD(chem), 54. *Prof Exp:* Instr chem, Cornell Univ, 54-56; from instr to assoc prof, 56-63, chmn dept, 66-72, PROF CHEM, UNIV SOUTHERN CALIF, 63- *Concurrent Pos:* NSF sr res fel, Oxford Univ, 62-63; NATO vis prof, Univ Florence, 70. *Mem:* Am Chem Soc; Am Phys Soc. *Res:* Molecular electronic and vibrational spectroscopy; laser photochemistry; crystal spectroscopy and intermolecular forces in crystals; laser driving of chemical reactions. *Mailing Add:* Dept of Chem Univ of Southern Calif Los Angeles CA 90007

DOWTY, EARL LEONARD, b Webb City, Mo, Apr 14, 39. MECHANICAL ENGINEERING. *Educ:* Okla State Univ, BS, 60, PhD(mech eng), 64; Calif Inst Technol, MS, 61. *Prof Exp:* Lectr fluid mech, Univ Nottingham, 64-65; res engr, Propulsion Res Sect, Martin Co, 65-67; asst prof mech eng, Okla State Univ, 67-69; br mgr, T&FM, Systs Anal & Design, Gen Atomic Co, 69-76; proj engr & proj mgr, Black & Veatch Consult Engrs, 76-77; mgr spec prog, Solar Energy Res Inst, 77-81; RES SCIENTIST II, GETTY RES CTR, 81- *Mem:* Am Soc Mech Engrs. *Res:* Boundary layer flows; thermal conduction and convection; solar technologies; operations and organization management; systems analysis and design. *Mailing Add:* Getty Oil Co PO Box 42214 Houston TX 77042

DOWTY, ERIC, b Pasadena, Calif, July 4, 45. MINERALOGY. *Educ:* Pomona Col, BA, 66; Stanford Univ, PhD(mineral), 70. *Prof Exp:* Res assoc mineral, US Geol Surv, 69-71 & petrol, Inst Meteoritics, Univ NMex, 71-74; ASST PROF MINERAL & CRYSTALLOG, DEPT GEOL & GEOPHYS SCI, PRINCETON UNIV, 74- *Mem:* Mineral Soc Am; Geol Soc Am; Am Crystallog Asn. *Res:* General crystallography and crystal chemistry; spectral techniques in mineralogy; lunar petrology; crystal growth and sector zoning. *Mailing Add:* Dept Geol & Geophys Sci Princeton Univ Princeton NJ 08540

DOXTADER, KENNETH GUY, b San Francisco, Calif, June 22, 38; m 62; c 2. SOIL MICROBIOLOGY. *Educ:* Univ Calif, Berkeley, BS, 61; Cornell Univ, MS, 63, PhD(agron), 65. *Prof Exp:* Res asst soil microbiol, Cornell Univ, 61-65; asst prof, 65-69, ASSOC PROF AGRON, COLO STATE UNIV, 69- *Mem:* AAAS; Am Soc Microbiol; Am Soc Agron; Int Soc Soil Sci. *Res:* Physiology and ecology of soil microorganisms; microbial biogeochemistry; microbial transformations of pesticides and minerals. *Mailing Add:* Dept of Agron Colo State Univ Ft Collins CO 80521

DOYLE, DARRELL JOSEPH, b Allentown, Pa, July 26, 39; m 64; c 2. BIOCHEMISTRY. *Educ:* Lehigh Univ, BA, 61, MS, 63; Johns Hopkins Univ, PhD(biochem), 67. *Prof Exp:* NIH fel, Stanford Univ, 67-69; asst prof anat & cell biol, Med Sch, Univ Pittsburgh, 69-72; assoc cancer res scientist, 72-80, DIR, DEPT CELL & TUMOR BIOL, ROSWELL PARK MEM INST, 80- *Concurrent Pos:* Vis prof, Univ Chile, 71. *Mem:* Am Soc Biol Chemists; AAAS. *Res:* Developmental biology; biochemical genetics; regulatory mechanisms in eukaryotic cells. *Mailing Add:* Dept Cell & Tumor Biol Roswell Park Mem Inst Buffalo NY 14263

DOYLE, EUGENIE F, b New York, NY, Oct 19, 21; m 44; c 5. PEDIATRIC CARDIOLOGY. *Educ:* Johns Hopkins Univ, MD, 46. *Prof Exp:* Intern pediat, Johns Hopkins Hosp, 46-47; resident, Bellevue Hosp, 47-49; from asst prof to assoc prof, 53-70, PROF PEDIAT, SCH MED, NY UNIV, 70-, DIR DEPT PEDIAT CARDIOL, MED CTR, 59- *Concurrent Pos:* Fel pediat cardiol, Med Ctr, NY Univ, 49-53. *Mem:* Am Pediat Soc; Am Heart Asn; fel Am Col Cardiol; fel Am Acad Pediat. *Res:* Treatment of acute rheumatic fever and rheumatic heart disease; natural history of congenital heart disease, especially aortic stenosis and the management of congestive heart failure. *Mailing Add:* Dept Pediat Cardiol New York Univ Med Ctr New York NY 10016

DOYLE, FRANK LAWRENCE, b San Antonio, Tex, Oct 16, 26; m 62; c 1. HYDROLOGY, GEOLOGY. *Educ:* Univ Tex, BS, 50; La State Univ, MS, 55; Univ Ill, PhD(geol), 58. *Prof Exp:* Instr geol, St Mary's Univ, San Antonio, 50-53; asst geologist, Ill State Geol Surv, 56-58; asst prof geol, St Mary's Univ, San Antonio, 58-60, assoc prof, 60-62, chmn dept, 61-62; geologist, Water Resources Div, US Geol Surv, Colo & Ariz, 62-63; assoc prof geol, Univ Conn, 63-65; consult hydrogeologist, 65-78; chief hydrogeologist, Metcalf & Eddy, Inc, 78-79; SR HYDROLOGIST, US NUCLEAR REGULATORY COMN, 79- *Concurrent Pos:* Petrol geologist, Seeligson Eng Comt, 52-53 & Fuels Br, US Geol Surv, Mont, 55; res asst, Ill State Geol Surv, 55-56, assoc geologist, 58-62; consult, Int Resources & Geotech, Inc, 65-68, Tex Instruments Inc, 68-70, Int Ctr Arid & Semi-Arid Land Studies, Tex Tech Univ, 70-71, Ala Geol Surv, 71-77; consult, Johnson Environ & Energy Ctr & adj prof, Div Natural Sci & Math, Univ Ala, Huntsville, 71-77. *Mem:* Fel Geol Soc Am; Am Inst Prof Geologists; Int Asn Hydrogeologists (secy-treas, 80-); Am Asn Petrol Geologists. *Res:* Groundwater; geomorphology; environmental geology and hydrology; Quaternary, areal and subsurface geology; applications of remotely-sensed data; hydrology and geology of volcanic, glacial and limestone terranes, tropics, deserts and semi-arid areas; geomorphology and glaciology. *Mailing Add:* US Nuclear Regulatory Comn Mail Stop 1130-SS Boston MA 20555

DOYLE, FREDERICK JOSEPH, b Oak Park, Ill, Apr 3, 20; m 55; c 4. PHOTOGRAMMETRY, REMOTE SENSING. *Educ:* Syracuse Univ, BCE, 51. *Hon Degrees:* Dr Eng, Hannover Tech Univ, 76. *Prof Exp:* With Inter-Am Geod Surv, S Am, 46-47; from instr to assoc prof photogramm, Syracuse Univ, 52-59; chmn, Dept Geod Sci, Ohio State Univ, 59-60; dir intel systs, Broadview Res Corp, 60-61; res engr, Raytheon-Autometric, 61-67, chief scientist, 67-69; RES SCIENTIST, US GEOL SURV, 69- *Concurrent Pos:* Chmn, Apollo Orbital Sci Photo Team, NASA, 69-74; mem exec comt, Div Earth Sci, Nat Acad Sci, 73-74; actg dir, Earth Resources Observ Satellite, US Dept Interior, 78-80. *Honors & Awards:* Photogram Award, Am Soc Photogram, 68; Exceptional Sci Achievement Award, NASA, 71; Meritorious Serv Award, US Dept Interior, 77. *Mem:* Fel AAAS; Am Cong Surv & Mapping; Am Geophys Union; Am Soc Photogram (pres, 69-70); Int Soc Photogram (secy gen, 76-80, pres, 80-84). *Res:* Aerial and space photogrammetric system design and analysis; science policy. *Mailing Add:* US Geol Surv 516 Reston VA 22092

DOYLE, JOHN ROBERT, b Norwood, Mass, Dec 18, 24; m 56; c 4. ORGANOMETALLIC CHEMISTRY. *Educ:* Mass Inst Technol, BS, 49, MS, 52; Tulane Univ, PhD, 55. *Prof Exp:* Chemist, Mass Inst Technol, 49-52; from instr to assoc prof, 55-65, PROF INORG CHEM, UNIV IOWA, 65- *Mem:* AAAS; Am Chem Soc; Am Crystallog Asn. *Res:* Organometallic compounds with catalytic activity; structures of metaloefin compounds. *Mailing Add:* Dept of Chem Univ of Iowa Iowa City IA 52240

DOYLE, JOSEPH THEOBALD, b Providence, RI, June 11, 18; m 44; c 2. CARDIOLOGY. *Educ:* Harvard Univ, AB, 39, MD, 43; Am Bd Internal Med, dipl, 52 & Am Bd Cardiovasc Dis, dipl, 59. *Prof Exp:* Asst med, Harvard Med Sch, 48-49; asst physiol, Sch Med, Emory Univ, 49-50; instr physiol & asst med, Grady Mem Hosp, Atlanta, Ga, 50-51, dir electrocardiographic lab, 50-52, instr med & physiol & asst coord cardiovasc training prog, 51-52; assoc med, Sch Med, Duke Univ, 52; from asst prof to assoc prof, 52-61, PROF MED, ALBANY MED COL, 61-, HEAD DIV CARDIOL, 60-, DIR CARDIOVASC HEALTH CTR, 52- *Concurrent Pos:* Whitehead res fel, Sch Med, Emory Univ, 49-50; consult, US Vet Admin Regional Off, Atlanta, 51-52; dir pvt diag clin, 57-; cardiac catheterization unit, 57-63; attend staff, Albany Med Ctr Hosp & Albany Vet Admin Hosp, 53-; fel coun arteriosclerosis, coun clin cardiol & coun epidemiol, Am Heart Asn. *Mem:* Am Fedn Clin Res; fel Am Col Physicians; fel Am Col Cardiol; Asn Univ Cardiologists. *Res:* Cardiovascular physiology and epidemiology. *Mailing Add:* Div of Cardiol Albany Med Col Albany NY 12208

DOYLE, LARRY JAMES, b Denver, Colo, Jan 27, 43; m 72. MARINE GEOLOGY. *Educ:* Duke Univ, BA, 65, MA, 67; Univ Southern Calif, PhD(geol), 73. *Prof Exp:* Econ geologist, Global Marine Inc, 69; explor geologist, Gen Oceanog, 70; from asst prof to assoc prof, 72-80, PROF GEOL, DEPT MARINE SCI, UNIV SOUTH FLA, 80- *Mem:* Geol Soc Am; Soc Econ Paleontologists & Mineralogists; Int Asn Sedimentologists; Am Geol Inst; Am Asn Petrol Geologists. *Res:* Marine geology of continental margins, specifically sediments and sedimentary processes of the continental slope of eastern North America and of the continental margin of the Gulf of Mexico. *Mailing Add:* Dept Marine Sci Univ SFla 140 7th Ave St Petersburg FL 33701

DOYLE, LAWRENCE EDWARD, b Cincinnati, Ohio, Mar 12, 09; m 39; c 3. MECHANICAL & INDUSTRIAL ENGINEERING. *Educ:* Yale Univ, BSME, 30; Univ Ill, ME, 50. *Prof Exp:* Engr, Cincinnati Milling Mach Co, 35-40; supvr mfg eng, Allison Div, Gen Motors Corp, 41-43; mech engr, Norman E Miller & Assoc, 43-45; from asst prof to prof mech eng, 46-75, EMER PROF MECH ENG, UNIV ILL, URBANA, 75- *Honors & Awards:* Nat Educ Award, Soc Mfg Engrs, 61. *Mem:* Am Soc Metals; Am Soc Eng Educ; Soc Mfg Engrs. *Res:* Establishment and development of a scientific basis for process design in manufacturing. *Mailing Add:* Mech Eng Bldg Univ of Ill Urbana IL 61801

DOYLE, LEE LEE, b Sacramento, Calif, Sept 22, 32; m 72. REPRODUCTIVE PHYSIOLOGY, ENDOCRINOLOGY. *Educ:* Dominican Col San Rafael, BA, 54; Stanford Univ, MA, 61; Tulane Univ, PhD(reprod physiol), 71. *Prof Exp:* Res assoc obstet & gynec, Med Sch, Stanford Univ, 58-61; asst specialist, Med Sch, Univ Calif, 61-67; from instr to asst prof, Sch Med, Tulane Univ, 67-72; assoc prof, 72-77, PROF OBSTET & GYNEC, MED SCH, UNIV ARK, LITTLE ROCK, 77- *Concurrent Pos:* NIH & inst grant, Tulane Univ & Delta Regional Primate Ctr, 68-72; NIH & Pop Coun grants, Med Sch, Univ Ark & Delta Regional Primate Ctr, 72-; adj scientist reproductive physiol, Delta Regional Primate Ctr, 68- *Honors & Awards:* Rubin Award, Am Fertil Soc, 62; Squibb Prize Paper Award, Pac Coast Fertil Soc, 64. *Mem:* Am Fertil Soc; Asn Planned Parenthood Physicians; Am Primatological Soc; Soc Study Reproduction; Soc Sci Study Sex. *Res:* Improved methods of contraception and delivery of services; primate reproductive physiology and endocrinology. *Mailing Add:* Dept of Obstet & Gynec Univ of Ark Med Ctr Little Rock AR 72201

DOYLE, MARGARET DAVIS, b Chelsea, Okla, Sept 23, 14; m 47; c 1. NUTRITION. *Educ:* Univ Ark, BSc, 34; Univ Chicago, SM, 38, PhD(nutrit), 45; Am Bd Nutrit, dipl. *Prof Exp:* Instr foods, Univ Minn, 38-40; instr foods & nutrit, Conn Col, 40-42; from instr to asst prof, Univ Chicago, 45-53; from asst prof to assoc prof, 60-70, PROF NUTRIT, UNIV MINN, ST PAUL, 70- *Mem:* Fel AAAS; Am Inst Nutrit; Am Dietetic Asn; Am Home Econ Asn. *Res:* Protein-calorie interrelation in young adults; food habits and dietary intake patterns of obese women and of young adults. *Mailing Add:* Dept of Food Sci & Nutrit Col Home Econ Univ Minn 1334 Eckles Ave St Paul MN 55108

DOYLE, MICHAEL P, b Minneapolis, Minn, Oct 31, 42; m 64; c 2. PHYSICAL ORGANIC CHEMISTRY. *Educ:* Col St Thomas, BS, 64; Iowa State Univ, PhD(org chem), 68. *Prof Exp:* Instr org chem, Univ Ill, Chicago Circle, 68; from asst prof to assoc prof, 68-74, PROF ORG CHEM, HOPE COL, 74- *Concurrent Pos:* Camille & Henry Dreyfus Found teacher-scholar award, 73-78; assoc mem, Int Union Pure & Appl Chem Comn on Physical Org Chem, 79- *Mem:* Am Chem Soc; AAAS; Sigma Xi; Coun Undergrad Res. *Res:* Transition metal catalysis in carbenoid transformations; biochemical effects of nitrogen oxides and nitrosyls; electron transfer reactions; synthetic methods in Lewis acid and transition metal catalyzed processes; mechanisms of organic reactions. *Mailing Add:* Dept of Chem Hope Col Holland MI 49423

DOYLE, MICHAEL PATRICK, b Madison, Wis, Oct 3, 49; m 71; c 2. FOOD MICROBIOLOGY. *Educ:* Univ Wis-Madison, BS, 73, MS, 75, PhD(food microbiol), 77. *Prof Exp:* Sr proj leader microbiol, Ralston Purina Co, 77-80; ASST PROF FOOD MICROBIOL, FOOD RES INST, UNIV WIS-MADISON, 80- *Concurrent Pos:* Assoc ed, J of Food Protection, 81- *Mem:* Am Soc Microbiol; Int Asn Milk, Food & Environ Sci; Inst Food Technologists; Soc Indust Microbiol; Sigma Xi. *Res:* Gram-negative foodborne bacterial pathogens; mechanisms of virulence, association with foods, methods of control, methods for their isolation. *Mailing Add:* Food Res Inst 1925 Willow Dr Univ Wis Madison WI 53706

DOYLE, MILES LAWRENCE, b Ashland, Ohio, July 14, 27; m 55; c 2. BIOCHEMISTRY. *Educ:* Ashland Col, AB, 49; St Louis Univ, PhD(biochem), 55. *Prof Exp:* Instr biochem, Vanderbilt Univ, 55-58; asst prof chem, Quincy Col, 58-61; asst res biochemist, Univ Calif, Davis, 61-62; assoc prof chem, Wis State Col, Eau Claire, 62-64; assoc prof chem, Col St Teresa, Minn, 64-66; ASSOC PROF CHEM, ARK STATE UNIV, 66- *Concurrent Pos:* Res biochemist, Thayer Vet Admin Hosp, Tenn, 55-58. *Mem:* Fel AAAS; Am Chem Soc; Brit Biochem Soc. *Res:* Enzymology. *Mailing Add:* Dept Chem Ark State Univ State University AR 72467

DOYLE, PATRICK H, topology, deceased

DOYLE, RICHARD ROBERT, b Camden, NJ, July 29, 37; m 63; c 2. ORGANIC CHEMISTRY, BIOCHEMISTRY. *Educ:* Drexel Univ, BS, 60; Univ Mich, MS, 63, PhD(org chem), 65. *Prof Exp:* NIH fel & res assoc biochem, Univ Mich, 65-67; asst prof, 67-74, ASSOC PROF ORG CHEM, DENISON UNIV, 74- *Mem:* AAAS; Am Chem Soc. *Res:* Amino acid synthesis; mushroom chemistry. *Mailing Add:* 14 Sunset Hill Granville OH 43023

DOYLE, ROGER WHITNEY, b Halifax, NS, Mar 7, 41; m 64. ECOLOGY, GENETICS. *Educ:* Dalhousie Univ, BS, 62, MS, 63; Yale Univ, PhD(biol), 67. *Prof Exp:* Asst prof zool & NIH biol sci support grant, Duke Univ, 67-71; assoc prof, 71-80, PROF BIOL, DALHOUSIE UNIV, 80- *Mem:* Am Soc Limnol & Oceanog; Am Soc Naturalists; Ecol Soc Am; Soc Study Evolution; World Mariculture Soc. *Res:* Population ecology and ecological genetics of marine animals; aquaculture genetics. *Mailing Add:* Dept of Biol Dalhousie Univ Halifax NS B3H 3J5 Can

DOYLE, TERRENCE WILLIAM, b Montreal, Quebec, Aug 8, 42; m 68; c 3. CANCER RESEARCH, ANTIBIOTIC RESEARCH. *Educ:* Loyola Col, BSc, 63; Univ Notre Dame, PhD(chem), 66. *Prof Exp:* NIH fel, Cornell Univ, 66-67; sr res scientist, 67-75, ASST DIR MED CHEM, BRISTOL LABS CAN, DIV BRISTOL MEYERS CO, 75- *Mem:* Am Chem Soc; Chem Inst Can. *Res:* Natural product isolation, structural characterization, biochemistry and organic synthesis primarily in the area of antitumor antibiotics. *Mailing Add:* Bristol Labs PO Box 657 Syracuse NY 13201

DOYLE, THOMAS DANIEL, pharmaceutical chemistry, organic chemistry, see previous edition

DOYLE, WALTER M, b Utica, NY, Sept 26, 37; m 62. ATOMIC PHYSICS. *Educ:* Syracuse Univ, BA, 59; Univ Calif, PhD(physics), 63. *Prof Exp:* Physicist, Hughes Aircraft Co, 63-64; sr scientist, Philco Corp, Ford Motor Co, 64-66, prin scientist, Aeronutronic Div, 66-69; vpres & dir res & develop, 69-78, PRES, LASER PRECISION CORP, 78- *Mem:* Am Phys Soc. *Res:* Solid state physics; optics; quantum electronics; development of optical measuring instruments and electrooptic devices. *Mailing Add:* 2875 Bernard Ct Laguna Beach CA 92651

DOYLE, WILLIAM CARTER, JR, pesticide chemistry, see previous edition

DOYLE, WILLIAM DAVID, b Boston, Mass, June 5, 35; m 58; c 3. SOLID STATE PHYSICS. *Educ:* Boston Col, BS, 57, MS, 59; Temple Univ, PhD(physics), 64. *Prof Exp:* Sr physicist magnetics, Franklin Inst Res & Develop, 59-64; proj leader, UNIVAC Div, Sperry Rand Corp, 64-67, mgr physics sect, 67-70, sr staff scientist, 71-80; MGR BUBBLE MEMORY RES & DEVELOP, MOTOROLA INC, 80- *Concurrent Pos:* Mem adv comt magnetism, Am Inst Physics, 64-; sr res fel, Univ York, Eng, 70-71. *Mem:* Sr mem Inst Elec & Electronics Engrs; Am Phys Soc. *Res:* Magnetic properties of thin films and fine particles; magnetization processes; domain theory; bubble devices. *Mailing Add:* Bubble Memory Res & Develop Motorola Inc 2200 West Broadway Mesa AZ 85202

DOYLE, WILLIAM LEWIS, b Brooklyn, NY, May 19, 10; m 37; c 1. CELL BIOLOGY. *Educ:* Johns Hopkins Univ, AM, 32, PhD(zool), 34. *Prof Exp:* Bruce fel, Johns Hopkins Univ, 34-35; Rockefeller fel, Cambridge Univ, 35-36; Rockefeller fel, Carlsberg Lab, Copenhagen 36-37; asst prof biol, Bryn Mawr Col, 37-42; res assoc & asst prof pharmacol, 42-44, assoc prof, 44-45, from assoc prof to prof anat, 45-76, dir toxicity lab, 45-56, assoc dean div biol sci, 58-61, coordr basic med sci curric, 69-71, EMER PROF ANAT, UNIV CHICAGO, 76- *Concurrent Pos:* Consult, Chem Corps, US Army, 46-59; reserve officer & sci attache, US For Serv, Stockholm, 51-52; from dir to vpres, Mt Desert Island Biol Lab, 64-68, pres, 70-75. *Mem:* Am Asn Anat; Histochem Soc (pres, 61-62); Am Physiol Soc; Am Soc Zoologists; Am Soc Cell Biol. *Res:* Cellular fine structure. *Mailing Add:* Dept Anat 1025 E 57th St Chicago IL 60637

DOYLE, WILLIAM T, b Coalinga, Calif, June 1, 29; m 53; c 4. BRYOLOGY. *Educ:* Univ Calif, Berkeley, BA, 57, PhD(bot), 60. *Prof Exp:* From instr to asst prof biol, Northwestern Univ, 60-65; from asst prof to assoc prof, 65-72, PROF BIOL, UNIV CALIF, SANTA CRUZ, 72-, DIR, CTR COASTAL MARINE STUDIES, 76-, DEAN, DIV NAT SCI, 80- *Mem:* AAAS; Am Bryol & Lichenological Soc; Brit Bryol Soc; Bot Soc Am; Am Soc Plant Physiologists. *Res:* Development, morphology and cytology of bryophytes; development and evolution of land plants; algae. *Mailing Add:* Dept of Biol Sci Appl Sci Bldg Univ of Calif Santa Cruz CA 95064

DOYLE, WILLIAM THOMAS, b New Britain, Conn, Dec 5, 25; m 51; c 2. PHYSICS. *Educ:* Brown Univ, BSc, 51; Yale Univ, MSc, 52, PhD(physics), 55. *Prof Exp:* From instr to assoc prof, 55-64, chmn dept, 66-70, PROF PHYSICS, DARTMOUTH COL, 64- *Concurrent Pos:* NSF fel, 58-59. *Mem:* Am Phys Soc; Am Asn Physics Teachers. *Res:* Experimental nuclear physics; nuclear reactions; solid state physics; optical and magnetic properties of defects in solids; magnetic resonance; high pressure physics. *Mailing Add:* Dept of Physics Dartmouth Col Hanover NH 03755

DOYLE, WORTHIE LEFLER, JR, b Philadelphia, Pa, Feb22. MATHEMATICS. *Educ:* Univ Wash, BA, 43; Calif Inst Technol, PhD, 50. *Prof Exp:* Res engr, Radar Systs Anal, Hughes Aircraft Co, 51-58; res engr, Lincoln Lab, Mass Inst Technol, 58-60; res engr, Aeronutronic Div, Ford Motor Co, 60-61 & Rand Corp, 61-64; COMMUN CONSULT, 64- *Res:* Algebra; noise theory; digital simulations. *Mailing Add:* 1120 Bethel Ave Port Orchard WA 98366

DOYNE, THOMAS HARRY, b Pottsville, Pa, Sept 21, 27; m 55; c 1. BIOCHEMISTRY. *Educ:* Pa State Univ, BS, 50, MS, 53, PhD(biochem), 57. *Prof Exp:* Asst x-ray crystallog & chem, Pa State Univ, 50-57; from asst prof to assoc prof, 57-65, PROF CHEM, VILLANOVA UNIV, 65-, CHMN DEPT, 70- *Mem:* Am Chem Soc; Am Crystallog Asn; The Chem Soc; Royal Soc Chem. *Res:* Determination of the absolute configuration of molecules by means of x-ray analysis; structure of divalent cation salts of amino acids and peptides. *Mailing Add:* Dept of Chem Villanova Univ Villanova PA 19085

DOYON, DOMINIQUE, b Sts Anges, Que, Apr 22, 32; c 3. PLANT ECOLOGY. *Educ:* Laval Univ, BSc, 53, DSc(ecol), 74; Univ Montreal, MSc, 57. *Prof Exp:* Asst botanist plant taxon, 53-55, PLANT ECOLOGIST, RES SERV, MINISTRY AGR, QUE, 56- *Mailing Add:* Complexe Scientifique 2700 rue Einstein Ste-Foy PQ G1P 3W8 Can

DOZSA, LESLIE, b Budapest, Hungary, May 25, 24; m; c 2. VETERINARY MEDICINE. *Educ:* Univ Budapest, Hungary, DVM, 46. *Prof Exp:* Asst prof obstet sterility & clinic obstet, Vet Col, Hungary, 47-51; field veterinarian sterility, Artificial Insemination Ctr, 51-56; from assoc prof to prof animal husb & path, 57-74, PROF VET SCI & ANIMAL PATHOLOGIST, DIV ANIMAL INDUST & VET SCI, W VA UNIV, 74- *Res:* Sterility of cattle, particularly histopathology. *Mailing Add:* Dept of Animal Vet Sci WVa Univ Morgantown WV 26506

DRABEK, CHARLES MARTIN, b Chicago, Ill, July 24, 42; m 65; c 2. ZOOLOGY. *Educ:* Univ Denver, BS, 64; Univ Ariz, MS, 67, PhD(zool), 70. *Prof Exp:* Asst prof biol, Cent State Univ, Okla, 70-75; asst prof, 75-78, ASSOC BIOL, WHITMAN COL, 78- *Concurrent Pos:* vis assoc prof biol, Harvard Univ, 80 & 81. *Mem:* Sigma Xi; AAAS; Am Soc Zoologists; Am Soc Mammalogists. *Res:* Cardiovascular and respiratory morphology adaptations of diving birds and mammals. *Mailing Add:* Dept Biol Whitman Col Walla Walla WA 99362

DRACH, JOHN CHARLES, b Cincinnati, Ohio, Sept 25, 39; m 64; c 2. BIOCHEMICAL PHARMACOLOGY. *Educ:* Univ Cincinnati, BS, 61, MS, 63, PhD(biochem), 66. *Prof Exp:* Assoc res biochemist, Parke, Davis & Co, 66-68, res biochemist, 69-70; from asst prof to assoc prof dent, 70-80, assoc prof med chem, 78-80, PROF DENT, SCH DENT & PROF MED CHEM, COL PHARM, UNIV MICH, 80- *Concurrent Pos:* Mem prof educ comt, Mich Div, Am Cancer Soc, 73-77. *Mem:* Am Soc Microbiol; AAAS; Am Chem Soc. *Res:* mechanism of action and metabolism of antiviral antineoplastic and drugs; function and metabolism of nucleic acids. *Mailing Add:* Dept of Oral Biol Sch of Dent Univ of Mich Ann Arbor MI 48109

DRACHMAN, DANIEL BRUCE, b New York, NY, July 18, 32; m 60; c 3. NEUROLOGY, MUSCULAR PHYSIOLOGY. *Educ:* Columbia Univ, AB, 52; NY Univ, MD, 56. *Prof Exp:* Intern med, Beth Israel Hosp, Boston, Mass, 56-57; asst resident, Neurol Unit, Harvard Univ, 57-58; resident neurol, Boston City Hosp, 58-59, resident neuropath, 59-60; clin assoc neurol, NIH, 60-62, res assoc neuroembryol, 62-63; asst prof neurol, Tufts-New Eng Med Ctr, 63-69; assoc prof, 69-73, PROF NEUROL, SCH MED, JOHNS HOPKINS UNIV, 74- *Concurrent Pos:* Teaching fel, Harvard Univ, 57-60; clin instr, Georgetown Univ, 61-63. *Mem:* AAAS; fel Am Acad Neurol; fel Am Neurol Asn; NY Acad Sci; Royal Soc Med. *Res:* Neuroembryology; congenital neuromuscular defects; diseases of muscle; development and trophic relationship of nerve and muscle; histopathology; physiology; neuroimmunology; myasthenia gravis. *Mailing Add:* Dept of Neurol Johns Hopkins Univ Sch of Med Baltimore MD 21205

DRACHMAN, DAVID A, b New York, NY, July 18, 32; m 59; c 3. NEUROLOGY, PHYSIOLOGICAL PSYCHOLOGY. *Educ:* Columbia Col, AB, 52; NY Univ, MD, 56. *Prof Exp:* Intern med, Duke Univ Hosp, 56-57; resident neurol, Harvard Med Sch, 57-60; clin assoc neurol, Nat Inst Neurol Dis & Stroke, 60-63; from asst prof to prof neurol, Med Sch, Northwestern Univ, 63-77; PROF NEUROL & CHMN DEPT, MED SCH, UNIV MASS, WORCESTER, 77- *Concurrent Pos:* Teaching fel, Harvard Med Sch, 57-60; instr, Sch Med, Georgetown Univ, 61-63; consult, Vet Admin Hosp, Hines, Ill, 63-70; vis scientist, Med Sch, Georgetown Univ, 66-; lectr, Food & Drug Admin, 68- *Mem:* AAAS; fel Am Acad Neurol; Am Neurol Asn; NY Acad Sci. *Res:* Neurology of memory; neuroophthalmology; human spatial orientation; computer diagnosis; neurobiology of aging. *Mailing Add:* Dept of Neurol Univ of Mass Med Sch Worcester MA 01605

DRACHMAN, RICHARD JONAS, b New York, NY, June 2, 30; m 64; c 2. THEORETICAL PHYSICS, ATOMIC PHYSICS. *Educ:* Columbia Col, AB, 51; Columbia Univ, AM, 54, PhD(physics), 58. *Prof Exp:* Asst physics, Columbia Univ, 51-53; physicist, Naval Res Lab, 56-58, Nat Res Coun res assoc, 58-59, physicist, 59-63; asst prof physics, Brandeis Univ, 59-63; MEM STAFF, GODDARD SPACE FLIGHT CTR, NASA, 63- *Concurrent Pos:* Consult, United Aircraft Res Labs, 61-62; mem fac, USDA Grad Sch, 66-73. *Mem:* Fel Am Phys Soc; AAAS. *Res:* Quantum theory; positron systems; atomic scattering. *Mailing Add:* Lab Astron & Solar Physics Code 680 Goddard Space Flight Ctr Greenbelt MD 20771

DRACUP, JOHN ALBERT, b Seattle, Wash, July 14, 34; m 72; c 5. CIVIL ENGINEERING, SYSTEMS ANALYSIS. *Educ:* Univ Wash, BS, 56; Mass Inst Technol, MS, 60; Univ Calif, Berkeley, PhD(civil eng), 66. *Prof Exp:* Engr, Shell Oil Co, Tex, 56-57 & Boeing Aircraft Co, Wash, 58-59; res asst eng, Mass Inst Technol, 59-60; asst prof eng, Ore State Univ, 60-62; teaching fel, Univ Calif, Berkeley, 62-65; PROF ENG SYSTS, UNIV CALIF, LOS ANGELES, 65- *Concurrent Pos:* Univ Calif & US Govt grants, 66-; consult, US Govt Water Resources Coun, 66-67, Lockheed Calif, 67, Rocketdyne, Inc, 67, TRW Systs, Inc, 67- & Environ Dynamics, Inc, 67-; mem US deleg, Int Conf Water for Peace, 67; NSF grant, 77- *Mem:* Fel Am Soc Civil Engrs; Am Water Resources Asn; Am Geophys Union; Int Water Resource Asn. *Res:* Water resources, hydrology. *Mailing Add:* Sch Eng & Appl Sci Univ Calif 7619 Boelter Hall Los Angeles CA 90024

DRACUP, KATHLEEN A, b Santa Monica, Calif, Sept 28, 42; m 72; c 1. CARDIOLOGY. *Educ:* St Xaviers Col, BS, 67; Univ Calif, Los Angeles, MN, 74; Univ Calif, San Francisco, DNSc, 82. *Prof Exp:* Admin nurse, Little County Mary Hosp, 67-70; clin nurse, 71-74, asst prof cardiovasc nursing, 74-78, res assoc, 79-81, ASST PROF CARDIOVASC NURSING, UNIV CALIF, LOS ANGELES, 81- *Concurrent Pos:* Ed, Heart & Lung, J Critical Care, 81-; mem, Am Heart Asn. *Mem:* Am Nurses Asn; Western Coun Nurse Researchers; Am Asn Critical Care Nurses. *Res:* Psychosocial adaptation of patients and their families to cardiovascular disease. *Mailing Add:* 1315 Georgina Ave Santa Monica CA 90402

DRACY, ARTHUR E, b Virgil, SDak, May 12, 17; m 43; c 1. DAIRY HUSBANDRY. *Educ:* Univ Minn, BS, 43, MS, 46, PhD, 49. *Prof Exp:* Herdsman, Univ Minn, 45, asst dairy husb, 46-48; prof dairy husb, 48-67, PROF ANIMAL HUSB, SDAK STATE UNIV, 67- *Concurrent Pos:* UN

Spec Fund, Costa Rica, 66-67; teacher physiol lactation, Univ Coahuila, Mexico, 76. *Mem:* Am Dairy Sci Asn. *Res:* Ova transfer in cattle; bloat in ruminants; immunized milk; bioengineering and physiological monitoring. *Mailing Add:* Dept of Animal Husb SDak State Univ Brookings SD 57006

DRAEGER, WILLIAM CHARLES, b San Francisco, Calif, Apr 7, 42; m 66; c 2. NATURAL RESOURCES, REMOTE SENSING. *Educ:* Univ Calif, Berkeley, BS, 64, MS, 65, PhD(wildland resource sci), 70. *Prof Exp:* Asst res forester, Univ Calif, Berkeley, 70-74; prin appln scientist, Agr & Soils, 74-78, CHIEF TRAINING & ASSISTANCE SECT, EARTH RESOURCE OBSERVATION SYST DATA CTR, US GEOL SURV, 78- *Mem:* Soc Am Foresters; Am Soc Photogram; AAAS. *Res:* Applications of remote sensing techniques to natural resource management problems; specifically concerned with transfer of technology from the research community to potential operational users. *Mailing Add:* Earth Resource Observ Syst Data Ctr Sioux Falls SD 57198

DRAGO, RUSSELL STEPHEN, b Turners Falls, Mass, Nov 5, 28; m 50; c 3. INORGANIC CHEMISTRY. *Educ:* Univ Mass, BS, 50; Ohio State Univ, PhD(chem), 54. *Prof Exp:* Fel, Ohio State Univ, 54-55; from instr to assoc prof, 55-65, PROF INORG CHEM, UNIV ILL, URBANA-CHAMPAIGN, 65- *Concurrent Pos:* Guggenheim fel, 73-74. *Honors & Awards:* Award for Res Inorg Chem, Am Chem Soc, 69. *Mem:* Am Chem Soc; Royal Soc Chem. *Res:* Lewis acid-base interactions; physical inorganic chemistry; spectroscopy; transition metals; non-aqueous solvents; binding of small molecules; catalysis. *Mailing Add:* 3306 Lakeshore Dr Champaign IL 61820

DRAGOIN, WILLIAM BAILEY, b Dothan, Ala, Sept 15, 39; m 61; c 2. EXPERIMENTAL PSYCHOLOGY, DEVELOPMENTAL PSYCHOLOGY. *Educ:* Troy State Col, BS, 63; Auburn Univ, MS, 65; George Peabody Col, PhD(psychol), 69. *Prof Exp:* Instr psychol, Auburn Univ, 65-67, asst prof, 70-72; PROF & CHMN PSYCHOL, GA SOUTHWESTERN COL, 72-, RES DIR, CHARLES MIX MEM FOUND, 72- *Concurrent Pos:* NIH fel, Dept Philos, Stanford Univ, 79. *Mem:* Am Psychol Asn; Sigma Xi. *Res:* Biological and genetic processes which influence animal conditioning; experimental psychology; sociobiology. *Mailing Add:* Charles Mix Found Ga Southwestern Col Americus GA 31709

DRAGON, ELIZABETH ALICE OOSTEROM, b Mineola, NY, June 12, 48; m 72; c 1. VIROLOGY. *Educ:* Univ NH, BS, 70; Yeshiva Univ, PhD(virol & cell biol), 80. *Prof Exp:* Fel, Biol Dept, Brookhaven Nat Lab, 80-82; STAFF SCIENTIST, CODON GENETIC ENG LAB, 82- *Mem:* Am Soc Microbiol; AAAS; NY Acad Sci. *Res:* Regulation of expression of viral genes; cell free translation systems; genetics of adenovirus. *Mailing Add:* Codon 430 Valley Dr Brisbane CA 94005

DRAGOO, ALAN LEWIS, b Grayling, Mich, Aug 29, 38; m 62; c 2. SOLID STATE PHYSICS. *Educ:* Univ Mich, BS, 61, MS, 63; Univ Md, PhD(physics), 75. *Prof Exp:* RES CHEMIST, NAT BUR STANDARDS, 63- *Mem:* Am Chem Soc; Am Ceramic Soc. *Res:* Crystal binding in oxides; diffusion and ionic conductivity; determination of elastic moduli; point defects. *Mailing Add:* Div 565 Rm A221 Bldg 223 Nat Bur Standards US Dept Com Washington DC 20234

DRAGOUN, FRANK J, b Omaha, Nebr, Sept 21, 29; m 54; c 3. HYDROLOGY, CIVIL ENGINEERING. *Educ:* Univ Nebr, BS, 53; Colo State Univ, MS, 66. *Prof Exp:* Civil engr, Soil Conserv Serv, USDA, 53-55, hydraul engr, Agr Res Serv, 55-62, res hydraul engr, 62-70; ASST GEN MGR, CENT NEBR PUB POWER & IRRIG DIST, 70- *Mem:* Am Soc Civil Eng; Nat Soc Prof Eng; Soil Conserv Soc Am; Int Asn Sci Hydrol; Am Geophys Union. *Res:* Removal and transport of sediment from small agricultural watersheds; hydrologic systems of small agricultural watersheds; automated irrigation systems. *Mailing Add:* PO Box 356 Holdrege NE 68949

DRAGOVICH, ALEXANDER, b Podgorica, Yugoslavia, Feb 26, 24; US citizen; m; c 1. MARINE ECOLOGY. *Educ:* Munich Tech Univ, BS, 47; Miss State Col, MS, 50. *Prof Exp:* Lab instr aquatic biol, Miss State Col, 50 & zool, Univ Hawaii, 50-51; res asst dis pineapples, Calif Packing Corp, 51; res asst tuna ecol, Calif Fish & Game Dept, 54-55; FISHERY RES BIOLOGIST, SOUTHEAST FISHERIES CTR-MIAMI LAB, NAT MARINE FISHERIES SERV, 55- *Concurrent Pos:* Consult, Fla Bd Conserv & Fla Univs; mem adj staff fac, Fla Atlantic Univ. *Mem:* Gulf & Caribbean Fisheries Inst. *Res:* Ecology and taxonomy of marine phytoplankton and invertebrates; ecology of tunas and penaeid shrimp; study of Guiana shrimp; fishery-biology, ecology and population dynamics of shrimp stocks. *Mailing Add:* Southeast Fisheries Ctr NMFS 75 Virginia Beach Dr Miami FL 33149

DRAGSDORF, RUSSELL DEAN, b Detroit, Mich, Nov 21, 22; m 48; c 2. SOLID STATE PHYSICS. *Educ:* Mass Inst Technol, SB, 44, PhD(physics), 48. *Prof Exp:* Asst prof, 48-51, assoc prof, 51-56, assoc dean & actg dean grad sch, 65-66, PROF PHYSICS, KANS STATE UNIV, 56- *Concurrent Pos:* Res physicist, Metals Res Lab, Union Carbide Corp, 56-57 & Lawrence Radiation Lab, 68. *Mem:* Am Phys Soc; Am Crystallog Asn; Fr Soc Mineral & Crystallog. *Res:* X-ray diffraction; small angle x-ray scattering; small particle properties; crystal imperfections. *Mailing Add:* Dept of Physics Kans State Univ Manhattan KS 66506

DRAGT, ALEXANDER JAMES, b Lafayette, Ind, Apr 7, 36; m 57; c 3. THEORETICAL HIGH ENERGY PHYSICS, CLASSICAL MECHANICS. *Educ:* Calvin Col, AB, 58; Univ Calif, Berkeley, PhD(physics), 64. *Prof Exp:* Sr scientist, Lockheed Missiles & Space Co, 61-62; staff scientist, Aerospace Corp, 63; mem dept physics, Inst Advan Study, 63-65; from asst prof to assoc prof, 65-69, chmn dept physics & astron, 75-78, PROF PHYSICS, UNIV MD, COLLEGE PARK, 69- *Concurrent Pos:* Vis staff mem, Los Alamos Sci Lab, 78-79. *Mem:* Am Phys Soc; Am Geophys Union. *Res:* Theoretical elementary particle physics; space physics; accelerator design; plasma physics; optics; mathematical physics. *Mailing Add:* Dept of Physics & Astron Univ of Md College Park MD 20742

DRAGUN, HENRY L, b Philadelphia, Pa, Feb 24, 32; m 59. PHYSICAL & ORGANIC CHEMISTRY. *Educ:* Univ Pa, AB, 53; Rutgers Univ, PhD(phys chem), 60. *Prof Exp:* Res phys chemist mech res lab, E I du Pont de Nemours & Co, 59-62; sr chemist, Elkton Div, Thiokol Chem Corp, 62-65; PROF CHEM, ANNE ARUNDEL COMMUNITY COL, 65-, CHMN DIV SCI, 69- *Mem:* AAAS; Am Chem Soc; Am Ord Asn. *Res:* High energy propellant development; investigation of relationship between microstructure of polymeric materials and their macroscopic electrical and mechanical properties. *Mailing Add:* Div of Sci Anne Arundel Community Col Arnold MD

DRAGUN, JAMES, b Detroit, Mich. EARTH SCIENCES. *Educ:* Wayne State Univ, BS, 71; Pa State Univ, MS, 75, PhD(soil chem), 77. *Prof Exp:* Soil chemist, US Environ Protection Agency, 78-80, sr soil chemist, 80-82; MGR, PAC ENVIRON LAB, KENNEDY/JENKS ENGRS, 82- *Concurrent Pos:* Consult, 77-; lectr, 77- *Mem:* Am Chem Soc; Am Soc Agron; Soil Sci Soc Am; Am Soc Agron; Sigma Xi. *Res:* Test protocols to measure the adsorption and chemical reactions of organic and inorganic chemicals in sediments and soils; create estimation techniques to predict the occurrence and extent of these processes; assess the extent of human exposure and environmental fate of toxic substances. *Mailing Add:* 657 Howard St San Francisco CA 94105

DRAHOS, DAVID JOSEPH, b Oceanside, NY, Dec 28, 51; m 78. RECOMBINANT DNA, DNA CHEMICAL SYNTHESIS. *Educ:* Manhattan Col, BS, 73; Univ Pittsburgh, PhD(molecular biol), 79. *Prof Exp:* FEL, MCARDLE LAB, UNIV WIS-MADISON, 79- *Res:* Analysis of genetic control mechanisms at the molecular level using chemically synthesized DNA designed to alter specific nucleotide bases suspected of being directly involved in transcriptional regulation. *Mailing Add:* McArdle Lab Univ Wis 450 N Randall Ave Madison WI 53706

DRAHOVZAL, JAMES ALAN, b Cedar Rapids, Iowa, Feb 13, 39; m 63; c 3. GEOLOGY. *Educ:* Univ Iowa, BA, 61, MS, 63, PhD(geol), 66. *Prof Exp:* Explor geologist resources, Pan Am Petrol Corp, 65-66; res geologist & asst chief, Geol Div, Geol Surv Ala, 66-77, asst state geologist & dir tech opers, 77-78; SR RES GEOLOGIST, GULF SCI & TECHNOL CO, 78- *Concurrent Pos:* NSF travelling grant, Czech, 68; lectr, Dept Geol, Univ Ala, 70; consult geologist, 74- *Mem:* Fel Geol Soc Am; Soc Econ Paleontologists & Mineralogists; Sigma Xi; Am Asn Petrol Geologists; Systematics Asn. *Res:* Applications of remote sensing technology to regional structural geology and stratigraphy; Paleozoic invertebrate paleontology; southern Appalachian geology; geology of thrust belts. *Mailing Add:* 725 12th St Oakmont PA 15139

DRAINE, BRUCE T, b Calcutta, India, Nov 19, 47; US citizen. THEORETICAL ASTROPHYSICS. *Educ:* Swarthmore Col, BA, 69; Cornell Univ, MS, 75, PhD(theoret physics), 78. *Prof Exp:* Ctr res fel astrophysics, Smithsonian Astrophys Observ, 77-80; WITH INST ADVAN STUDY, PRINCETON, 80- *Mem:* Am Astron Soc. *Res:* Theory of the interstellar medium, including physics of interstellar dust. *Mailing Add:* Inst Advan Study Princeton NJ 08540

DRAKE, ALBERT ESTERN, b Stamping Ground, Ky, June 12, 27; m 52; c 4. STATISTICS, AGRICULTURAL ECONOMICS. *Educ:* Univ Ky, BS, 50, MS, 51; Univ Ill, PhD(agr econ), 58. *Prof Exp:* Res asst agr, Univ Ill, 53-55, res assoc food technol, 55-59; from assoc prof to prof biometrics, Auburn Univ, 59-63; dir comput ctr statist & comput, WVa Univ, 63-66; PROF STATIST, UNIV ALA, 66- *Concurrent Pos:* NSF grants, 59-63, Ford Found grants, 75 & 81. *Mem:* Am Inst Decision Sci (secy, 73-74); Biomet Soc; Am Statist Asn; Am Agr Econ Asn. *Res:* Computer assisted instruction in statistics; application of statistical techniques to management decision making. *Mailing Add:* Dept of Statist Univ of Ala PO Box J University AL 35486

DRAKE, ALVIN WILLIAM, b Bayonne, NJ, Sept 21, 35; m 57. OPERATIONS RESEARCH. *Educ:* Mass Inst Technol, SB & SM, 58, EE, 61, ScD(elec eng), 62. *Prof Exp:* From asst prof to assoc prof, 64-73, assoc dir, Opers Res Ctr, 66-77, PROF ELEC ENG, MASS INST TECHNOL, 73- *Concurrent Pos:* Ford fel, Mass Inst Technol, 64-66. *Mem:* Opers Res Soc Am; Inst Elec & Electronics Engrs; Am Asn Blood Banks. *Res:* Probilistic applications in the delivery of public services; blood, organ, and tissue banking; decision analysis and risk assessment. *Mailing Add:* Dept Elec Eng & Comput Sci Mass Inst Technol Cambridge MA 02139

DRAKE, ARTHUR EDWIN, b Elmwood Place, Ohio, Sept 17, 18; m 41; c 3. ELECTROCHEMISTRY. *Educ:* Miami Univ, AB, 40; Western Reserve Univ, MS, 42, PhD(electrochem), 43. *Prof Exp:* Res chemist, Hercules, Inc, 43-45, from sales rep to sales supvr, 45-55, sales mgr, 55-61, dir develop, 61-66, PRES, DRACO, INC, GREENVILLE, 66- *Res:* Electromotive force measurements on molten binary alloys. *Mailing Add:* 2 Swallow Hill Rd Wilmington DE

DRAKE, AVERY ALA, JR, b Kansas City, Mo, Jan 17, 27; m 63; c 2. GEOLOGY. *Educ:* Mo Sch Mines, BS, 50, MS, 52. *Prof Exp:* Asst, Mo Sch Mines, 50-52; geologist, 52-79, ASST CHIEF GEOLOGIST, US GEOL SURV, 79- *Concurrent Pos:* Geologist, Nat Lead Co, 51; mem, NSF-US Navy Exped, Bellingshausen Sea, Antarctica, 61; assoc ed for geol, Am Geophys Union, Antarctic Res Series, 71-; dir advan geol field methods course, Brazilian Dept Mines & Energy, 73-75; vis prof struct geol, Howard Univ, 74. *Mem:* Geol Soc Am; Soc Econ Geol; Geochem Soc. *Res:* Structural geology of central Appalachians; Precambrian geology; Antarctic geology. *Mailing Add:* US Geol Surv Mailstop 953 Reston VA 22092

DRAKE, BILLY BLANDIN, b Warsaw, Mo, Dec 18, 17; m 41; c 3. BIOCHEMISTRY, ENZYMOLOGY. *Educ:* Cent Methodist Col, Mo, AB, 39; Univ Pittsburgh, MS, 41, PhD(biochem), 43. *Prof Exp:* Sr scientist, Rohm and Haas, 43-68, head enzyme technol serv lab, 68-71, head enzyme lab, 71-76, enzymes prod mgr, 75-76; CONSULT, 76- *Mem:* Am Chem Soc. *Res:* Production and properties of enzymes; separation and oxidation of amino acids; microbial fermentations. *Mailing Add:* 711 Pecan Dr Philadelphia PA 19115

DRAKE, CHARLES HADLEY, b Waterloo, Iowa, Feb 8, 16; m 42; c 2. BACTERIOLOGY. *Educ:* Univ Minn, BA, 37, MS, 39, PhD(bact), 42. *Prof Exp:* Teaching asst bact, Univ Minn, 36-42, instr med bact, Exten Div, 42; instr, Sch Lib Arts & Sch Med, Univ Kans, 42-44; from asst prof to prof bact, Wash State Univ, 44-80; RETIRED. *Concurrent Pos:* Agent, Bur Biol Surv & Bur Plant Indust, USDA, 36-42. *Mem:* Am Soc Microbiol. *Res:* Medical mycology and bacteriology; immunology; public health; pathogenicity and allergic properties of Nocardia asteroides; Pseudomonas aeruginose; bacterial limnology. *Mailing Add:* 1310 Orion Dr Pullman WA 99163

DRAKE, CHARLES LUM, b Ridgewood, NJ, July 13, 24; m 50; c 3. GEOPHYSICS. *Educ:* Princeton Univ, BSE, 48; Columbia Univ, PhD(geol), 58. *Prof Exp:* Lectr, Columbia Univ, 53-55, instr, 58-59, from asst prof to assoc prof, 59-67, actg asst dir, Lamont Geol Observ, 63-65; prof & chmn dept, 67-69; dean, Grad Studies, 78-81, assoc dean, Sci Div, 78-81, PROF GEOL, DARTMOUTH COL, 69- *Concurrent Pos:* NSF sr fel, Cambridge Univ, 65-66; Condon lectr, Univ Ore, 69; pres, inter-union comt on geodynamics, Int Coun Sci Unions, 70-75; chmn comt on geodynamics, Nat Acad Sci, 70-79; comt adv to Environ Sci Serv Admin, 70-; chmn, Off Earth Sci, 72-75, mem, Geophys Res Bd; chmn, Geophys Study Comn, 79- *Mem:* Seismol Soc Am; Am Asn Petrol Geol; Geol Soc Am (pres, 75-76); Royal Astron Soc; Soc Explor Geophys. *Res:* Marine geology and geophysics; tectonics; structural geology; seismology. *Mailing Add:* RD 1 East Thetford VT 05043

DRAKE, CHARLES ROY, b Cromwell, Ky, Apr 27, 18; m 49; c 2. PLANT PATHOLOGY. *Educ:* Western Ky State Col, BS, 52; Univ Wis, PhD(plant path), 56. *Prof Exp:* Asst, Univ Wis, 52-56; plant pathologist, Crops Res Div, Va Agr Exp Sta, Agr Res Serv, USDA, 56-62; assoc prof, 62-76, PROF PLANT PATH, VA POLYTECH INST & STATE UNIV, 76- *Concurrent Pos:* Dept coordr, Grad Plant Protection Prog; col div coordr, Develop Innovative Capstone Course for Undergrad Plant Protection Curric; adv, Univ Acad Career; mem, SE Regional Peach Tree Short-Life Comt. *Mem:* Am Phytopath Soc. *Res:* Diseases of fruit, with special interest in apple rots, fire blight, powdery mildew, apple scab and peach brown rot; plant pathological histochemistry; delineated the cause of Golden Delicious leaf blotch as a transpirational stress. *Mailing Add:* Dept Plant Path & Physiol Va Polytech Inst & State Univ Blacksburg VA 24061

DRAKE, CHARLES WHITNEY, b South Portland, Maine, Mar 8, 26; m 52; c 3. ATOMIC PHYSICS. *Educ:* Univ Maine, BS, 50; Wesleyan Univ, MA, 52; Yale Univ, PhD, 58. *Prof Exp:* Intermediate scientist, Westinghouse Elec Corp, 52-53; from instr to asst prof physics, Yale Univ, 57-66; assoc prof, 66-75, actg chmn dept, 76-77, PROF PHYSICS, ORE STATE UNIV, 75-, CHMN DEPT, 77- *Mem:* Am Phys Soc. *Res:* Atomic and molecular beams; polarized particles for nuclear reactions; beam foil spectroscopy. *Mailing Add:* Dept of Physics Ore State Univ Corvallis OR 97331

DRAKE, DARRELL MELVIN, b Stillwater, Okla, Sept 5, 32; m 55; c 4. NUCLEAR PHYSICS. *Educ:* Univ Okla, BS, 54, MS, 56; Univ Wash, PhD(physics), 61. *Prof Exp:* Asst physics, Univ Ill, 62-65; STAFF MEM PHYSICS, LOS ALAMOS SCI LAB, 65- *Concurrent Pos:* Vis staff mem physics, Bruyeres le Chatel Ctr Study, Comn Atomic Energy, France, 75-76. *Res:* Radiative capture of neutrons and protons with energies of 5 to 20 MeV; pion interactions with complex nuclei; fast neutron induced gamma ray production and fast neutron scattering. *Mailing Add:* Los Alamos Sci Lab PO Box 1663 Los Alamos NM 87545

DRAKE, DAVID ALLYN, b Lorain, Ohio, Sept 29, 37; m 59; c 2. MATHEMATICS. *Educ:* Harvard Univ, AB, 59; Syracuse Univ, PhD(math), 67. *Prof Exp:* Systs programmer, Int Bus Mach, 60-62; instr math, Syracuse Univ, 66-67; fel, 67-68, asst prof, 68-73, assoc prof, 73-80, PROF MATH, UNIV FLA, 80- *Concurrent Pos:* Alexander von Humboldt fel, 74-75; vis prof math, Free Univ, Berlin, 79; assoc ed, J Statist Planning & Inference, 79- *Mem:* Am Math Soc; Math Asn Am. *Res:* Combinatorics and finite geometries, particularly Hjelmslev geometries, projective planes and Latin squares. *Mailing Add:* Dept of Math Univ of Fla Gainesville FL 32611

DRAKE, EDGAR NATHANIEL, II, b Springfield, Mo, May 18, 37; m 59; c 3. PHYSICAL CHEMISTRY, ANALYTICAL CHEMISTRY. *Educ:* Univ Houston, BS, 60; Univ Colo, MS, 62; Tex A&M Univ, PhD(chem), 69. *Prof Exp:* Instr, Tex A&I Univ, 62-63; asst prof, Howard Payne Col, 63-65; assoc prof, 65-80, PROF CHEM, ANGELO STATE UNIV, 80- *Mem:* Am Chem Soc. *Res:* Chemistry of coordination compounds; stability of complexes; mechanisms of complex ion reactions. *Mailing Add:* Dept of Chem Angelo State Univ San Angelo TX 76909

DRAKE, EDWARD LAWSON, b Charlottetown, PEI, Apr 9, 30; m 56; c 2. INVERTEBRATE PATHOLOGY, ENTOMOLOGY. *Educ:* McGill Univ, BSc, 50; Cornell Univ, MS, 59; Dalhousie Univ, PhD(biol), 69. *Prof Exp:* Entomologist, Govt of Nyasaland, 52-56; experimentalist, Cornell Univ, 56-57; from lectr to asst prof, 59-69, chmn dept, 69-76, ASSOC PROF BIOL, UNIV PRINCE EDWARD ISLAND, 69- *Concurrent Pos:* Mem, Sci Coun Can, 78- *Res:* Virus diseases of insects; insect fine structure; insect taxonomy. *Mailing Add:* Dept of Biol Univ of Prince Edward Island Charlottetown Can

DRAKE, ELISABETH MERTZ, b New York, NY, Dec 20, 36; m 57. CHEMICAL ENGINEERING. *Educ:* Mass Inst Technol, SB, 58, ScD(chem eng), 66. *Prof Exp:* Staff consult cryog, 58-64, sr engr, 66-70, sr engr safety & fire technol, 71-77, mgr risk assessment group, 77-78, dep head safety & fire technol sect, 78-80, VPRES TECHNOL RISK MGT, A D LITTLE INC, 80- *Concurrent Pos:* Lectr, Univ Calif, Berkeley, 70-71; vis prof, Mass Inst Technol, 73-74; Sci Adv Bd, Environ Protection Agency, 76-77. *Mem:* Am Inst Chem Engrs; Am Chem Soc; AAAS; Sigma Xi. *Res:* Risk assessment and control of hazardous materials, liquefied natural gas technology and safety, cryogenic engineering, risk management. *Mailing Add:* A D Little Inc 20 Acorn Park Cambridge MA 02140

DRAKE, FRANK DONALD, b Chicago, Ill, May 28, 30; m 78; c 5. RADIO ASTRONOMY. *Educ:* Cornell Univ, BEP, 52; Harvard Univ, MA, 56, PhD(astron), 58. *Prof Exp:* Dir astron res group, Ewen Knight Corp, 57-58; from asst astronr to assoc astronr, Nat Radio Astron Observ, WVa, 58-63; chief lunar & planetary sci sect, Jet Propulsion Lab, Univ Calif, 63-64; assoc prof astron, Cornell Univ, 64-66; dir, Arecibo Ionospheric Observ, PR, 66-68; prof astron, 68-76, chmn dept, 69-71, dir, Nat Astron & Ionosphere Ctr, 71-81, GOLDWIN SMITH PROF ASTRON, CORNELL UNIV, 76- *Mem:* Nat Acad Sci; fel Am Acad Arts & Sci; Int Astron Union; Int Sci Radio Union; Am Astron Soc. *Res:* Solar system; 21 centimeter line research; search for extraterrestrial intelligence; radio telescope development. *Mailing Add:* Nat Astron & Ionosphere Ctr Space Sci Bldg Cornell Univ Ithaca NY 14853

DRAKE, GEORGE M(ARSHALL), JR, b Goodlettsville, Tenn, July 25, 32; m 58; c 4. CHEMICAL ENGINEERING. *Educ:* Univ Tenn, BS, 55, MS, 57, PhD(chem eng), 61. *Prof Exp:* Res engr, Spruance Film Res & Develop Lab, 61-74, staff engr, 74-75, sr engr, Tech Sect, Tecumseh, Kans, 76-80, SR ENGR, KAPTON-TEFLON TECH, E I DU PONT DE NEMOURS & CO, INC, CIRCLEVILLE, OH, 80- *Mem:* Am Chem Soc; Am Inst Chem Engrs. *Res:* Film extrusion, process development and improvement. *Mailing Add:* E I DuPont de Nemours & Co Inc PPD Dept PO Box 89 Circleville OH 43113

DRAKE, GORDON WILLIAM FREDERIC, b Regina, Sask, Aug 20, 43; m 66; c 1. ATOMIC PHYSICS. *Educ:* McGill Univ, BSc, 64; Univ Western Ont, MSc, 65; York Univ, Ont, PhD(physics), 67. *Prof Exp:* Nat Acad Sci res fel physics, Smithsonian Astrophys Observ, Mass, 67-69; from asst prof to assoc prof, 69-75, PROF PHYSICS, UNIV WINDSOR, 75- *Concurrent Pos:* Fel, Alfred P Sloan Found, 73. *Mem:* Am Phys Soc; Can Asn Physicists; Inst Physics. *Res:* Theory of atomic processes, including relativistic effects, radiative transitions, electron-atom and atom-atom scattering; precision calculations for two-electron systems and applications to astrophysical problems. *Mailing Add:* Dept of Physics Univ of Windsor Windsor Can

DRAKE, JOHN EDWARD, b Simla, India, Apr 20, 36; m 60; c 4. INORGANIC CHEMISTRY, SPECTROSCOPY. *Educ:* Univ Southampton, BSc, 57, PhD(chem), 60. *Hon Degrees:* DSc, Univ Southampton, 78. *Prof Exp:* Chemist, Lawrence Radiation Lab, Univ Calif, Berkeley, 60-62; asst lectr chem, Univ Hull, 62-63; lectr, Univ Southampton, 63-69; assoc prof, 69-71, PROF CHEM, UNIV WINDSOR, 71- *Concurrent Pos:* Ed adv bd, Can J Chem, 75-78; vis prof, Univ Calif, Berkeley, 79 & Univ Wuppertal, 81. *Mem:* The Chem Soc; fel Chem Inst Can (secy-treas, 81-83); Am Chem Soc. *Res:* Spectroscopic and synthetic studies of main group organometalloids and hydrides; application of electrical discharges to preparative problems; vibrational, nuclear magnetic resonance, and photo-electron spectroscopy. *Mailing Add:* Dept of Chem Univ of Windsor Windsor ON N9B 3P4 Can

DRAKE, JOHN W, b Detroit, Mich, Feb 10, 32; m 60; c 2. GENETICS. *Educ:* Yale Univ, BS, 54; Calif Inst Technol, PhD(biol), 58. *Prof Exp:* Res assoc bact, Univ Ill, Urbana-Champaign, 58-59, from instr to prof microbiol, 59-78; CHIEF, LAB MOLECULAR GENETICS, NAT INST ENVIRON HEALTH SCI, 78- *Concurrent Pos:* Fulbright fel, Weizmann Inst, 57-58; Guggenheim fel, 64-65; USPHS spec res fel & chmn biol sect, Grad Fel Panel, NSF-Nat Res Coun, 71-72; mem, Int Comn Protection Against Environ Mutagens & Carcinogens. *Mem:* Genetics Soc Am; Environ Mutagen Soc. *Res:* Replication and genetics of bacterial viruses; molecular mechanisms of mutation. *Mailing Add:* Lab of Molecular Genetics Nat Inst Environ Health Sci Research Triangle Park NC 27709

DRAKE, LON DAVID, b North Tonawanda, NY, Nov 30, 39; c 4. GEOLOGY. *Educ:* Univ Buffalo, BA, 61; Univ Calif, Los Angeles, MA, 65; Ohio State Univ, PhD(geol), 68. *Prof Exp:* Asst prof, 68-73, assoc prof, 73-79, PROF GEOL, UNIV IOWA, 79- *Mem:* Geol Soc Am; Am Asn Quaternary Res; Am Coun Reclamation Res. *Res:* Processes of glacial till production and deposition; strip mine reclamation; economic pleistocene geology; engineering and low-technology applications. *Mailing Add:* Dept of Geol Univ of Iowa Iowa City IA 52242

DRAKE, MICHAEL JULIAN, b Bristol, Eng, July 8, 46. GEOCHEMISTRY. *Educ:* Univ Manchester, BSc, 67; Univ Ore, PhD(geol), 72. *Prof Exp:* Res assoc lunar sci, Smithsonian Astrophys Observ, 72-73; asst prof planetary sci, 73-78, assoc dir, Lunar & Planetary Lab, 78-80, ASSOC PROF PLANETARY SCI, DEPT PLANETARY SCI & LUNAR & PLANETARY LAB, UNIV ARIZ, 78- *Concurrent Pos:* Assoc ed, Proc Lunar Sci Confs, 75-78. *Mem:* Am Geophys Union; Meteoritical Soc. *Res:* Petrology and geochemistry of lunar samples and meteorites; model calculations of evolution of planetary bodies; experimental investigations of mineral-melt equilibria. *Mailing Add:* Planet Sci & Lunar & Planet Lab Univ of Ariz Tucson AZ 85721

DRAKE, RICHARD LEE, b Columbus, Ohio, Feb 25, 50; m 72; c 2. ANATOMY, CELL BIOLOGY. *Educ:* Mt Union Col, BS, 72; Ind Univ, Bloomington, PhD(anat), 75. *Prof Exp:* Fel cell biol, Dept Nutrit & Food Sci, Mass Inst Technol, 75-77; asst prof anat, Med Col Wis, 77-81; ASST PROF ANAT, COL MED, UNIV CINCINNATI, 81- *Mem:* AAAS; Am Soc Cell Biol; Am Asn Anatomists; Am Diabetes Asn; Sigma Xi. *Res:* Cell and molecular biology; the ability of insulin to alter the structure and function of the liver cell. *Mailing Add:* Univ Cincinnati Col Med 231 Bethesda Ave Milwaukee OH 45267

DRAKE, ROBERT E, b Los Angeles, Calif, Dec 4, 43; m 67; c 2. GEOCHRONOLOGY, ISOTOPE GEOCHEMISTRY. *Educ:* Pomona Col, BA, 65; Univ Calif, Riverside, MA, 67; Univ Calif, Berkeley, PhD(geol), 74. *Prof Exp:* Fel, 74-76, ASST RES GEOLOGIST, UNIV CALIF, BERKELEY, 76- *Res:* Geochronology in the central Chilean Andes; calibration of vertebrate; hominid fossils in East Africa. *Mailing Add:* Dept Geol & Geophys Univ Calif Berkeley CA 94720

DRAKE, ROBERT FIRTH, b Providence, RI, July 4, 47. INORGANIC CHEMISTRY, CHEMICAL EDUCATION. *Educ:* Providence Col, BS, 69; Univ NC, Chapel Hill, PhD(inorg chem), 73. *Prof Exp:* Asst prof inorg & phys chem, Wash Col, 73-75, Metrop State Col, 75-76, Kans State Univ, 76-77 & Whitman Col, 77-78; asst prof gen inorg & phys chem, Colo Sch Mines, 78-80; ASST PROF INORG & PHYS CHEM, MOORHEAD STATE UNIV, 80- *Concurrent Pos:* Res assoc, Univ NC, Chapel Hill, 74 & Wash State Univ, Pullman, 75; res chemist, Geochem & Environ Chem Res, Inc, Rapid City, SDak, 81. *Mem:* Am Chem Soc; Royal Soc Chem; Sigma Xi; Am Soc Eng Educ. *Res:* Magnetic interactions in condensed systems of transition metal ions; advances in chemical education; geochemistry; applied chemistry. *Mailing Add:* 3948 Doral Dr Rapid City SD 57701

DRAKE, ROBERT L, b Bradford, Pa, June 24, 26; m 50; c 4. ELECTRICAL ENGINEERING. *Educ:* Tulane Univ, BSEE, 50, MSEE, 57; Miss State Univ, PhD(elec eng), 65. *Prof Exp:* Plant engr, Buckeye Cellulose Corp Div, Procter & Gamble Co, 50-54; from instr to asst prof elec eng, Tulane Univ, 54-59; mem tech staff, Space Technol Labs, Inc Div, Thompson-Ramo-Wooldridge, Inc, 59-61, proj engr, 61-62; from asst prof to assoc prof elec eng, 62-70, PROF ELEC ENG, TULANE UNIV, 70- *Concurrent Pos:* NSF sci fac fel, 63-64; partner, Systs Technol Inst. *Res:* Control, information and adaptive control systems; engineering applications of information theory. *Mailing Add:* Dept of Elec Eng Tulane Univ New Orleans LA 70118

DRAKE, ROBERT M, JR, b Eagle Cliff, Ga, Dec 13, 20; m 44; c 2. MECHANICAL ENGINEERING. *Educ:* Univ Ky, BSME, 42; Univ Calif, Berkeley, MSME, 46, PhD(eng), 50. *Prof Exp:* From instr to assoc prof heat transfer, fluid mech & thermodyn, Univ Calif, Berkeley, 47-55; prof mech eng & chmn dept, Princeton Univ, 56-63; prof, Univ Ky, 64-71, dean Col Eng, 66-71, chmn, Dept Mech Eng, 66-67; vpres res & develop, Combustion Eng, Inc, 71-75; spec asst to pres, Univ Ky, 75-77; vpres technol, Studebaker Worthington Inc, NY, 77-78; exec vpres, Univ Investment Co Inc, Ky, 78-79, pres, 79-80; CONSULT ENGR, 80- *Concurrent Pos:* Engine design specialist & supvr turbine air design, Gen Elec Co, 54-56, consult, 56-57; consult, McGraw-Hill Book Co, 58-68, Rand Corp, 60-63, Air Preheater Co, 62, NSF, 62-63, Arthur D Little, Inc, 63 & Gen Tel Elec Serv Corp, 80-; consult & dir, Intertech Corp, 62-72; sr staff consult, Arthur D Little, Inc, 63-64; dir, Magnetic Corp Am Inc, Waltham, Mass, 74-; dir & secy-treas, Projectron, Inc, Lexington, Ky, 81- *Mem:* Nat Acad Eng; fel Am Soc Mech Engrs. *Res:* Heat transfer; thermodynamics; fluid mechanics. *Mailing Add:* 648 Tally Rd Lexington KY 40502

DRAKE, STEPHEN RALPH, b Detroit, Mich, June 4, 41; m 65; c 2. FOOD SCIENCE. *Educ:* Miss State Univ, BS, 64, MS, 71, PhD(food sci), 73. *Prof Exp:* Food scientist meat, US Army Natick Res Command, 73-75; food scientist fruit & veg, Wash State Univ, 75-76; RES FOOD TECHNOLOGIST, IRRIGATED AGR RES & EXTEN CTR, AGR RES SERV, USDA, 76- *Honors & Awards:* Nat Food Processors Award, Am Soc Hort Sci, 79. *Mem:* Inst Food Technologists; Am Soc Hort Sci; Am Diet Asn; Sigma Xi. *Res:* Process calculation and varietal evaluations for fruits and vegetables; effect of orchard and field management practises on the nutritional quality of fruits and vegetables. *Mailing Add:* Irrigated Agr & Res Exten Ctr USDA Agr Res Serv Prosser WA 99350

DRAKE, STEVENS STEWART, b Seattle, Wash, Mar 30, 17; m 41; c 1. POLYMER CHEMISTRY. *Educ:* Northwestern Univ, BS, 39, MS, 41; Univ Ill, PhD(org chem), 43. *Prof Exp:* Instr chem, Northwestern Univ, 39-41; instr, Univ Ill, 41-43; from chemist to asst lab dir, Dow Chem Co, 43-51, lab dir, 53-56, dept personnel adminstr, 56-58, lab dir, 58-64, dept patent coordr, 64-69, sr res chemist, 69-74, res specialist, 74-80; CONSULT, 81- *Mem:* AAAS; Am Chem Soc. *Res:* Product development; plastics copolymerization; asymmetric polymerization; synthetic rubber; pigmentation of plastics; personnel administration; patent coordination; applied research. *Mailing Add:* 10727 Camelot Circle Sun City AZ 85351

DRAKONTIDES, ANNA BARBARA, b New York, NY, Aug 21, 33. ELECTRON MICROSCOPY. *Educ:* Hunter Col, BS, 55, MA, 60; Cornell Univ, MS, 68, PhD(anat & pharmacol), 71. *Prof Exp:* Instr physiol, Hunter Col, 62-66, lectr physiol & biol, Sch Gen Studies, 67-69, asst prof anat & physiol, 69-73; instr pharmacol, Med Col, Cornell Univ, 71-73; asst prof, 73-80, ASSOC PROF ANAT, NY MED COL, 80- *Concurrent Pos:* Instr anat & physiol, Sch Nursing, Cornell Univ, 67-68, assoc prof, 74-76; NIH fel, 71-72; fel, Pharmacol Mfrs Asn, 72-74. *Mem:* NY Acad Sci; Am Asn Anatomists; Soc Neurosci. *Res:* Correlated study of the physiologic, pharmacologic and morphologic aspects of the mammalian neuromuscular junction; chemicals and diseases that cause neuropathology. *Mailing Add:* Dept Anat NY Med Col Valhalla NY 10595

DRALEY, JOSEPH EDWARD, b Washington, DC, Jan 26, 19; m 43; c 2. CHEMISTRY, ENGINEERING. *Educ:* Cath Univ, BAppChem, 39, PhD(phys chem), 47. *Prof Exp:* Chemist & group leader, Metall Lab, Univ Chicago, 42-45; engr, Kellex Corp, 45-46; proj engr, Appl Physics Lab, Johns Hopkins Univ, 46-47; sr chemist & sect chief, Oak Ridge Nat Lab, 47-48; sr chemist & group leader, Argonne Nat Lab, 48-71, asst dir, 74-78, mgr ocean thermal energy conversion proj, 78-81; TECH CONSULT, 81- *Honors & Awards:* Whitney Award, Nat Asn Corrosion Engrs, 61. *Mem:* Am Chem Soc; Electrochem Soc; Sigma Xi; Am Nuclear Soc; Am Inst Mining, Metall & Petrol Engrs. *Res:* Aqueous corrosion; aqueous complex ions; gas-metal reactions; liquid sodium-metal reactions; sodium technology; environmental impact assessment; chlorine defouling; ocean thermal energy conversion; program planning; project management; research management. *Mailing Add:* 814 S Bruner St Hinsdale IL 60521

DRANCE, S M, b Bielsko, Poland, May 22, 25; Can citizen; m 52; c 3. OPHTHALMOLOGY. *Educ:* Univ Edinburgh, MB, ChB, 48; Royal Col Surg, dipl ophthal, 53, fel, 56. *Prof Exp:* Res assoc ophthal, Oxford Univ, 55-57; assoc prof ophthal & dir glaucoma clin, Univ Sask, 57-63; assoc prof, 63-68, PROF OPHTHAL, UNIV BC, 68-, HEAD DEPT, 74-, DIR GLAUCOMA SERV, 63- *Concurrent Pos:* Mem subcomt ophthal, Can Dept Health & Welfare Res Grants, 64 & Med Res Coun Can, 67-; ed, Can J Ophthal. *Mem:* Asn Res Vision & Ophthal; Can Med Asn; Can Ophthal Soc; Brit Med Asn; Ophthal Soc UK. *Res:* Behavior of visual function under conditions of raised intraocular pressure; pharmacology of glaucoma medication; natural history of glaucoma. *Mailing Add:* Dept of Ophthal Univ of BC Vancouver BC V6T 1W5 Can

DRANCHUK, PETER MICHAEL, b Poland, Sept 4, 28; Can citizen. PETROLEUM ENGINEERING. *Educ:* Univ Alta, BSc, 52, MSc, 59. *Prof Exp:* Sessional instr petrol eng, 52-53, lectr, 53-59, from asst prof to assoc prof, 59-77, PROF PETROL ENG, UNIV ALTA, 77- *Mem:* AAAS; Am Inst Mining, Metall & Petrol Engrs; Can Inst Mining & Metall; Sigma Xi; NY Acad Sci. *Res:* Petroleum production and reservoir mechanics. *Mailing Add:* Dept of Mineral Eng Univ of Alta Edmonton AB T6G 2E1 Can

DRANE, CHARLES JOSEPH, JR, b Boston, Mass, Nov 21, 27; m 71; c 2. ELECTROMAGNETISM. *Educ:* Boston Col, BS, 50; Mass Inst Technol, SM, 53, MS, 66; Harvard Univ, PhD(appl physics), 75. *Prof Exp:* Physicist, Nat Bur Standards, 52; physicist, Air Force Cambridge Res Labs, 55-76; PHYSICIST, ROME AIR DEVELOP CTR, 76- *Concurrent Pos:* Lectr elec eng, Northeastern Univ, 78- *Honors & Awards:* Lord Brabazon Award, Inst Electron & Radio Engr, 71. *Mem:* Inst Elec & Electronics Engr; assoc mem Int Sci Radio Union; Sigma Xi. *Res:* Electromagnetic theory; applied mathematics; communication theory; antenna theory; array theory; electromagnetic scattering. *Mailing Add:* Electromagnetic Sci Div Rome Air Develop Ctr Hanscom AFB MA 01731

DRANE, JOHN WANZER, b Forest, La, June 26, 33; m 55; c 3. STATISTICS, BIOMETRY. *Educ:* Northwestern State Col, La, BS, 55; Univ Fla, MS, 57; Emory Univ, PhD(biomet), 67. *Prof Exp:* Nuclear engr, Newport News Shipbuildg & Dry Dock Co Va, 56-61; assoc prof math, Randolph-Macon Col, 60-64; instr & spec fel statist & biomet, Emory Univ, 63-65, assoc prof, 65-68; assoc prof, 68-79, PROF STATIST, SOUTHERN METHODIST UNIV, 79- *Concurrent Pos:* Asst prof, chmn div biomath & biostatist, Univ Tex Southwestern Med Sch, 70-73; asst prof med comput sci, Univ Tex Health Sci Ctr, 73-76, adj assoc prof, 76-; sr statist consult, Criterion Anal, Inc, 78-80; pres, Wanzer, Inc, 81- *Mem:* Econometric Soc; Am Statist Asn; Sigma Xi; Biometric Soc; Math Asn Am. *Res:* Application of statistics and mathematics to problems of society, law, biology and the health sciences; modeling, nonlinear regression, contingency tables, EEOC compliance, employment practice analysis. *Mailing Add:* Dept of Statist Southern Methodist Univ Dallas TX 75275

DRANOFF, JOSHUA S(IMON), b Bridgeport, Conn, June 30, 32; m 53; c 3. CHEMICAL ENGINEERING. *Educ:* Yale Univ, BE, 54; Princeton Univ, MSE, 56, PhD(chem eng), 60. *Prof Exp:* Asst prof chem eng, Yale Univ, 57-58 & Northwestern Univ, 58-62; assoc prof, Columbia Univ, 62-63; assoc prof, 63-67, chmn dept, 71-76, PROF CHEM ENG, NORTHWESTERN UNIV, 67-, CHMN DEPT, 79- *Mem:* Am Chem Soc; Am Inst Chem Engrs; Am Soc Eng Educ. *Res:* Chemical reactor analysis; heterogeneous catalysis; photoreaction engineering; chromatographic separations; ion exchange; adsorption on molecular sieves. *Mailing Add:* Dept of Chem Eng Northwestern Univ Evanston IL 60201

DRAPALIK, DONALD JOSEPH, b Chicago, Ill, Dec 10, 34. PLANT TAXONOMY. *Educ:* Southern Ill Univ, Carbondale, BA, 59, MA, 62; Univ NC, Chapel Hill, PhD(bot), 70. *Prof Exp:* Asst prof, 68-73, ASSOC PROF BIOL, GA SOUTHERN COL, 73-, MEM GRAD FAC, 71- *Concurrent Pos:* Fac res grant, Ga Southern Col, 70-71 & 79-80. *Mem:* Int Asn Plant Taxon; Am Soc Plant Taxon; Bot Soc Am; Wilderness Soc. *Res:* Taxonomy, morphology and evolution of the North American milkweeds; floristics of vascular plants in Georgia; reproductive biology of Elliottia. *Mailing Add:* Dept Biol Ga Southern Col Statesboro GA 30458

DRAPER, ARTHUR LINCOLN, b Philadelphia, Pa, Feb 20, 23; m 46; c 3. PHYSICAL CHEMISTRY. *Educ:* Rice Univ, BA, 48, MA, 49, PhD(chem), 51. *Prof Exp:* Res chemist, Jersey Prod Res Co, 51-57; res assoc dept chem, Rice Univ, 58-59; asst prof, 59-61, ASSOC PROF CHEM, TEX TECH UNIV, 61-, ASSOC DEAN, COL ARTS & SCI, 76- *Mem:* Fel AAAS; Geochem Soc; Am Chem Soc. *Res:* Physical and colloid chemistry; thermodynamics; kinetics; solid state; structure; surface chemistry; oxides and mixed oxides; adsorption; catalysis. *Mailing Add:* Dept of Chem Tex Tech Univ Lubbock TX 79409

DRAPER, BRUCE, b Tampa, Fla, July 10, 28; m 56; c 3. PSYCHIATRY. *Educ:* Yale Univ, BS, 50, MD, 54. *Prof Exp:* Intern med, Duke Univ, 54-55, Capt USMC Psychiat, US Army 55-58; res psychiatrist, Univ Mich, 58-61; pvt pract, Ann Arbor, 61-77; ASST PROF, UNIV SFLA, 77- *Concurrent Pos:* Consult, Univ Mich Health Serv, 71-76; pvt pract, Tampa, 78- *Mailing Add:* 911 Barnett Bank Bldg Tampa FL 33620

DRAPER, CARROLL ISAAC, b Maroni, Utah, Sept 27, 14; m 39; c 6. POULTRY NUTRITION. *Educ:* Utah State Univ, BS, 39; Iowa State Col, PhD, 42. *Prof Exp:* Asst prof poultry husb, State Col Wash, 41-43; head poultry dept, Univ Hawaii, 43-45; assoc prof poultry husb, 45-48, head poultry dept, 48-70, PROF ANIMAL SCI, UTAH STATE UNIV, 70-, PROF DAIRY & VET SCI & POULTRY SPECIALIST, EXTEN, 77- *Mem:* Poultry Sci Asn. *Res:* Value of protein feeds in poultry diets. *Mailing Add:* Dept of Animal Sci Utah State Univ Logan UT

DRAPER, E(RNEST) LINN, JR, physics, nuclear engineering, see previous edition

DRAPER, HAROLD HUGH, b Manitoba, Can, Apr 11, 24; nat US; m 47; c 2. NUTRITION. *Educ:* Univ Manitoba, BSA, 45; Univ Alta, MSc, 48; Univ Ill, PhD(nutrit), 52. *Prof Exp:* Lectr animal nutrit, Univ Manitoba, 45-46; lectr, Univ Alta, 48-49; asst, Univ Ill, 49-51; nutritionist, Vet Res Dept, Merck

& Co, Inc, 52-54; asst prof animal nutrit, Univ Ill, Urbana, 54-58, from assoc prof to prof nutrit biochem, 58-75; PROF NUTRIT & CHMN DEPT, UNIV GUELPH, 75- Concurrent Pos: Orgn European Econ Coop fel, Univ Liverpool, 61. Mem: AAAS; Am Inst Nutrit; Can Soc Nutrit Sci. Res: Nutritional and hormonal factors in aging bone loss. Mailing Add: Dept Nutrit Col Biol Sci Univ Guelph Guelph ON N1G 2W1 Can

DRAPER, JAMES EDWARD, b Kansas City, Mo, Sept 14, 24; m 48; c 4. NUCLEAR PHYSICS. Educ: Williams Col, BA, 44; Cornell Univ, PhD(physics), 52. Prof Exp: Instr & asst physics, Williams Col, 46-47; asst, Cornell Univ, 47-52, res assoc, 52; assoc physicist, Brookhaven Nat Lab, 52-56; from asst prof to assoc prof, Yale Univ, 56-62, sr res assoc, 62-63; chmn dept, 66-71, PROF PHYSICS, UNIV CALIF, DAVIS, 64- Concurrent Pos: Res assoc, Nuclear Physics Div, Atomic Energy Res Estab, Harwell, Eng, 71 & 79; consult nuclear physics, Lawrence Berkeley Lab, 80- Mem: Fel Am Phys Soc. Res: Experimental neutron physics; neutron spectroscopy; photonuclear and particle reactions; in-beam gamma and electron spectroscopy. Mailing Add: Dept of Physics Univ of Calif Davis CA 95616

DRAPER, JOHN DANIEL, b Hagerstown, Md, June 13, 19; m 46; c 4. ORGANIC CHEMISTRY. Educ: Franklin & Marshall Col, BS, 41; Univ Md, PhD(org chem), 48. Prof Exp: Asst gen chem, Univ Md, 41-43, res chemist, Comt Med Res Contract, 43-45, asst inorg quant anal, Univ, 45-46; sr res chemist, Phillips Petrol Co, 47-49; res chemist, J T Baker Chem Co, 49-51; from asst prof to assoc prof, 51-54, PROF CHEM & HEAD DEPT, BETHANY COL, 54- Concurrent Pos: Consult, Stoner-Mudge Corp, Pa, 54-63. Mem: Am Chem Soc. Res: Synthesis and analysis of antimalarials; synthetic lubricating oil additives; kinetics of organic reactions. Mailing Add: Dept Chem Bethany Col Bethany WV 26032

DRAPER, LAURENCE RENE, b New York, NY, Apr 14, 30; m 54; c 2. IMMUNOLOGY. Educ: Middlebury Col, AB, 52; Univ Chicago, PhD(microbiol), 56. Prof Exp: Res assoc microbiol, Univ Chicago, 56-57, asst prof, 59-60; res assoc immunol, Argonne Nat Lab, 57-59; res biologist, Physiol Lab, Nat Cancer Inst, 60-68; assoc prof, 68-73, PROF MICROBIOL, UNIV KANS, 73- Concurrent Pos: Logan fel microbiol, Univ Chicago, 60. Mem: Am Asn Immunol; Radiation Res Soc; Am Soc Microbiol. Res: Cellular immunology. Mailing Add: Dept Microbiol Univ Kans Lawrence KS 66044

DRAPER, NORMAN RICHARD, b Southampton, Eng, Mar 20, 31. STATISTICS. Educ: Cambridge Univ, BA, 54, MA, 58; Univ NC, PhD(math statist), 58. Prof Exp: Statistician, Plastics Div, Imp Chem Indust, Eng, 58-60, mem, Math Res Ctr, 60-61; from asst prof to assoc prof, 61-66, chmn dept, 67-73, vis prof, Math Res Ctr, 73-74, PROF STATIST, UNIV WIS, MADISON, 66- Concurrent Pos: Res asst statist tech res group, Princeton Univ, 57. Mem: Fel Inst Math Statist; fel Am Statist Asn; Biomet Soc; fel Royal Statist Soc; fel Am Soc Qual Control. Res: Experimental statistics; design and analysis of experiments; statistical theory; regression analysis; nonlinear estimation; response surface methodology. Mailing Add: Dept of Statist Univ of Wis 1210 W Dayton St Madison WI 53706

DRAPER, RICHARD WILLIAM, b London, Eng, Dec 12, 42; m 72. STEROID CHEMISTRY. Educ: Univ London, BSc, 65, ARIC, 67, PhD(org chem), 68. Prof Exp: Fel, Dept Chem, Univ Rochester, 68-71; prin scientist, Natural Prod Dept, 71-80, PRIN SCIENTIST, PROCESS DEVELOP DEPT, SCHERING CORP, 81- Mem: The Chem Soc; Am Chem Soc. Res: Synthesis and reaction mechanisms, particularly modification of corticosteroids. Mailing Add: Schering Corp Bloomfield NJ 07003

DRAPER, ROY DOUGLAS, b Fresno, Calif, May 30, 33; m 60; c 2. BIOCHEMISTRY. Educ: Sacramento State Col, BS, 55, BA, 59; Univ Calif, Davis, PhD(biochem), 64. Prof Exp: Clin technician, Suttar Hosp, Sacramento, 55-56; clin technician, Hotel Dieu Hosp, El Paso, Tex, 57; PROF CHEM, CALIF STATE UNIV, SACRAMENTO, 64- Concurrent Pos: Danforth Assoc, 72- Res: Enzyme mechanism and general biochemistry. Mailing Add: Dept Chem Calif State Univ Sacramento CA 95819

DRASIN, DAVID, b Philadelphia, Pa, Nov 3, 40; m 63; c 3. MATHEMATICAL ANALYSIS. Educ: Temple Univ, AB, 62; Cornell Univ, PhD(math), 66. Prof Exp: Instr math, Rutgers Univ, 62; from asst prof to assoc prof, 66-74, PROF MATH, PURDUE UNIV, 74- Mem: Math Asn Am; Am Math Soc. Res: Functions of a complex variable; Tauberian theorems. Mailing Add: Dept of Math Purdue Univ West Lafayette IN 47907

DRATZ, ARTHUR FREDERICK, nuclear medicine, see previous edition

DRATZ, EDWARD ALEXANDER, b Minneapolis, Minn, July 2, 40. BIOCHEMISTRY, VISION. Educ: Carleton Col, BA, 61; Univ Calif, Berkeley, PhD(chem), 66. Prof Exp: Helen Hay Whitney fel, Lab Chem Biodynamics, Univ Calif, Berkeley, 66-67 & Dept of Biol, Mass Inst Technol, 67-69; asst prof, 69-77, assoc prof chem, 77-80, ASSOC PROF BIOCHEM, UNIV CALIF, SANTA CRUZ, 77- Mem: Am Soc Photobiol; Asn Res Vision & Ophthal; Biophys Soc; AAAS. Res: Structures and mechanisms of action of biological membranes with emphasis on visual photoreceptors; preservation of membranes in vitro and the mechanisms which prevent degeneration of membranes in vivo. Mailing Add: Natural Sci II Univ of Calif Santa Cruz CA 95064

DRAUGHON, FRANCES ANN, b Tazewell, Va, April 30, 52; m 73. MYCOTOXINS, FOOD BORNE DISEASES. Educ: Univ Tenn, BS, 73, MS, 76; Univ Ga, PhD(food sci), 79. Prof Exp: Grad res asst food sci, Univ Ga, 76-79; ASST PROF FOOD TECHNOL SCI, UNIV TENN, 79- Mem: Am Soc Microbiol; Inst Food Technologists; Int Asn Milk, Food & Environ Sanitarians; AAAS; Sigma Xi. Res: Analysis and reduction control of production of toxic fungal metabolites (mycotoxins) in human food and animal feeds. Mailing Add: Dept Food Technol Sci Univ Tenn Knoxville TN 37916

DRAUGLIS, EDMUND, b Philadelphia, Pa, May 21, 33; m 64; c 3. SURFACE CHEMISTRY, PHYSICS. Educ: Univ Pa, BS, 55; Yale Univ, MS, 59, PhD(phys chem), 61. Prof Exp: Phys chemist, Semiconductor Prod Dept, Gen Elec Co, 61; res scientist, United Aircraft Res Lab, 62-63; PRIN CHEMIST, BATTELLE MEM INST, 64- Mem: Am Chem Soc. Res: Theory of liquid crystals; boundary lubrication; solid-liquid interface; liquid films; ellipsometry; high pressure studies of organic materials; adhesion; plasma polymerization. Mailing Add: Battelle Mem Inst 505 King Ave Columbus OH 43201

DRAUS, FRANK JOHN, b Dupont, Pa, Oct 30, 29; m 56; c 4. BIOCHEMISTRY. Educ: Alliance Col, BS, 51; Duquesne Univ, MS, 53, PhD(biochem), 57. Prof Exp: From asst to assoc prof, 56-65, PROF BIOCHEM, SCH DENT MED, UNIV PITTSBURGH, 65-, HEAD DEPT, 67-, DIR ADMIS, 81- Concurrent Pos: Temporary adv, WHO, 69; indust consult. Mem: AAAS; assoc Am Dent Asn; fel Am Inst Chem; Int Asn Dent Res; NY Acad Sci. Res: Mechanism for the formation of synthetic calculus; isolation and characterization of mucoproteins and mycopolysaccharides from salivary glands. Mailing Add: 1024 Dale Dr Pittsburgh PA 15220

DRAWE, D LYNN, b Mercedes, Tex, Nov 3, 42; m 64; c 2. RANGE MANAGEMENT, WILDLIFE RESEARCH. Educ: Tex A&I Univ, BS, 64; Tex Tech Univ, MS, 67; Utah State Univ, PhD(range ecol), 70. Prof Exp: From asst prof to assoc prof range & wildlife mgt, Tex A&I Univ, 70-74; ASST DIR RANGE & LIVESTOCK MGT & RES, WELDER WILDLIFE FOUND, 74- Mem: Soc Range Mgt. Res: Range livestock management, grazing systems; range animal nutrition including white-tailed deer; brush control, range plant physiology; range plant ecology; fire ecology. Mailing Add: Welder Wildlife Refuge PO Drawer 1400 Sinton TX 78387

DRAY, SHELDON, b Chicago, Ill, Nov 20, 20; m 53, 68; c 2. MEDICINE, IMMUNOLOGY. Educ: Univ Chicago, BS, 41; Univ Ill, MD, 46, MS, 47; Univ Minn, PhD(phys biochem), 54. Prof Exp: Intern, Univ Ill Hosps, Chicago, 46-47; med officer, Nutrit Sect, Bur State Serv, USPHS, 47-49; med officer, Phys Biol Lab, Nat Inst Arthritis & Metab Dis, 49-54, med officer, Lab Clin Invest & Immunol, Nat Inst Allergy & Infectious Dis, 55-65; head dept, 65-80, PROF MICROBIOL & IMMUNOL, UNIV ILL MED CTR, 80- Concurrent Pos: Coun mem, Int Union Immunol Socs; consult, WHO. Mem: AAAS; Am Chem Soc; Am Soc Microbiol; Am Asn Immunol (secy-treas, 64-70); Soc Exp Biol & Med. Res: Physical chemistry of membranes; serum proteins; immunogenetics; maternal-fetal incompatibility; informational RNA; immunoglobulin allotypes; allotype suppression; lymphocyte biology; tumor immunotherapy; cellular immunity. Mailing Add: 155 N Harbor Dr Apt 3508 Chicago IL 60601

DRAYER, DENNIS EUGENE, b Frankfort, SDak, June 24, 28; m 50; c 2. CHEMICAL ENGINEERING. Educ: SDak Sch Mines & Technol, BS, 52; Kans State Univ, MS, 54; Univ Colo, Boulder, PhD(chem eng), 61. Prof Exp: Instr chem eng, Kans State Univ, 53-54; chem engr, Dow Chem Co, 54-58; chem engr, Cryogenic Eng Lab, Nat Bur Stand, 59-61; res engr, 61-65, advan res engr, 65-68, SR RES ENGR, MARATHON OIL CO, 68- Concurrent Pos: Adj assoc prof, Univ Denver, 66-72. Mem: Am Chem Soc; Am Inst Chem Engrs. Res: Heat transfer in cryogenic systems; liquid phase hydrocarbon oxidations; economic evaluation techniques; project evaluation; flow of fluids and slurries. Mailing Add: Marathon Oil Co Denver Res Ctr PO Box 269 Littleton CO 80160

DRAYSON, SYDNEY ROLAND, b Buckhurst Hill, Eng, Dec 21, 37; m 63; c 2. ATMOSPHERIC PHYSICS. Educ: Univ London, BSc, 60; Univ Chicago, MS, 61; Univ Mich, PhD(meteorol), 67. Prof Exp: Asst res mathematician, 63-66, res assoc, 66-67, lectr meteorol & assoc res engr, 68-69, asst prof meteorol, 70-75, assoc prof, 75-80, PROF ATMOSPHERIC SCI, UNIV MICH, ANN ARBOR, 80- Concurrent Pos: Ed, J Atmospheric Sci. Mem: AAAS; Am Meteorol Soc; Am Geophys Soc. Res: Atmospheric radiative transfer, including radiative heating rates, remote sounding of the atmosphere and molecular spectroscopy; numerical methods and computer applications. Mailing Add: 3750 Tremont Lane Ann Arbor MI 48109

DRAZIN, MICHAEL PETER, b London, Eng, June 5, 29. MATHEMATICS. Educ: Cambridge Univ, BA, 50, MA, 53, PhD(math), 53. Prof Exp: Fel Trinity Col, Cambridge Univ, 52-53; sci off, Admiralty Res Lab, Teddington, Eng, 53-55; fel Trinity Col, Cambridge Univ, 55-57; vis lectr, Northwestern Univ, 57-58; sr scientist, Res Inst Advan Study, 58-62; ASSOC PROF MATH, PURDUE UNIV, 62- Honors & Awards: Smith's Prize of Univ of Cambridge, 52. Mem: Am Math Soc; Soc Indust & Appl Math. Res: Non-commutative ring theory; abstract algebra; combinatorial problems; matrix theory; applied mathematics. Mailing Add: Dept of Math Purdue Univ Lafayette IN 47907

DREA, JOHN JAMES, JR, entomology, see previous edition

DREBY, EDWIN CHRISTIAN, III, b Haddonfield, NJ, Sept 2, 15; m 40; c 5. PHYSICAL CHEMISTRY, ORGANIC CHEMISTRY. Educ: Yale Univ, PhD(phys chem), 39. Prof Exp: Res asst, Am Soc Testing & Mat, 39-41; res chemist, 41-54, DIR LAB, SCHOLLER BROS, INC, 54- Mem: Am Chem Soc; Am Asn Textile Chem & Colorists; Am Soc Test & Mat. Res: Development of chemical products to assist in the scouring and dyeing of textile yarns, fabrics and garments and to alter their hand for ease of manufacture and consumer requirements. Mailing Add: Scholler Bros Inc Collins and Westmoreland Sts Philadelphia PA 19134

DRECHSEL, PAUL DAVID, b Newark, NJ, Oct 24, 25; m 50; c 4. POLYMER CHEMISTRY, TEXTILE PHYSICS. Educ: Rutgers Univ, BS, 46; Cornell Univ, PhD(phys chem), 51. Prof Exp: Sr res chemist, Allegany Ballistics Lab, Hercules, Inc, 51-57, res supvr, 57-58, group supvr, 58-61, asst dept supt, 61-62, dept supt, 62-70, res scientist, Res Ctr, 70-71, res assoc, 71-73, MGR RES DEPT, FIBERS RES & DEVELOP LAB, HERCULES INC, 73- Mem: Am Chem Soc; Am Sci Affil. Res: Physical chemistry and mechanical properties of polymers; diffusion; textile chemistry; heat transfer; fibers technology. Mailing Add: 2490 Fieldstone Dr Conyers GA 30208

DRECKTRAH, HAROLD GENE, b La Crosse, Wis, Nov 1, 38; m 62; c 2. INSECT MORPHOLOGY, AQUATIC ENTOMOLOGY. *Educ:* Wis State Univ, La Crosse, BS, 62; Iowa State Univ, MS, 64, PhD(entom), 66. *Prof Exp:* Res asst, Iowa Dept Agr, 62-66; from asst prof to assoc prof, 66-79, PROF BIOL, UNIV WIS-OSHKOSH, 79- *Mem:* Entom Soc Am; Am Entom Soc; NAm Benthological Soc; Sigma Xi. *Res:* Insect morphology, especially the internal reproductive organs of both sexes; aquatic entomology, especially Trichoptera taxonomy. *Mailing Add:* Dept of Biol Univ of Wis Oshkosh WI 54901

DREEBEN, ARTHUR B, b New York, NY, Feb 15, 22; m 50; c 2. INORGANIC CHEMISTRY. *Educ:* Polytech Inst Brooklyn, BS, 48, MS, 50. *Prof Exp:* Asst chem, Res Lab, Gen Elec Co, 50-52; asst, Knolls Atomic Power Lab, 52-53; assoc res engr, Res Dept Lamp Div, Westinghouse Elec Corp, 53-58; MEM TECH STAFF, DAVID SARNOFF RES CTR, RCA CORP, 58- *Mem:* Am Chem Soc; Electrochem Soc; Am Asn Crystal Growth. *Res:* Solid state chemistry; luminescence; photoconduction; crystal growth and imperfections. *Mailing Add:* 75 Dodds Lane Princeton NJ 08540

DREES, DAVID T, b Dyersville, Iowa, Nov 23, 33; m 56; c 4. VETERINARY PATHOLOGY, TOXICOLOGY. *Educ:* Iowa State Univ, DVM, 57; Mich State Univ, MS, 66, PhD(path), 69. *Prof Exp:* Instr anat, Mich State Univ, 64-68, NIH fel path, 68-69; head animal health & path, Warren-Teed Pharmaceut, Inc, 69-76; proj leader & pathologist, Rohm & Haas Co, 76-77; DIR CORP BIOL AFFAIRS, MARION LABS, INC, 77- *Mem:* Am Vet Med Asn; Sigma Xi; Soc Toxicol; Am Bd Toxicol. *Res:* animal models; preclinical efficacy and safety evaluation of drugs; safety evaluation of chemicals (toxicology and pathology). *Mailing Add:* 10234 Russell Overland Park KS 66212

DREES, JOHN ALLEN, b Chicago, Ill, Feb 6, 43; m 67; c 2. PHYSIOLOGY, BIOPHYSICS. *Educ:* DePauw Univ, BA, 65; Ind Univ, PhD(physiol), 72. *Prof Exp:* Asst prof, 70-76, ASSOC PROF PHYSIOL & BIOPHYS, SCH DENT, TEMPLE UNIV, 76- *Mem:* AAAS; Am Physiol Soc; Am Heart Asn. *Res:* Cardiovascular physiology; control of vascular capacity; blood volume; system response to hemorrhage; biosimulation. *Mailing Add:* Dept of Physiol & Biophys Temple Univ Sch of Dent Philadelphia PA 19140

DREESMAN, GORDON RONALD, b Grundy Center, Iowa, Nov 28, 35; c 3. IMMUNOLOGY, VIROLOGY. *Educ:* Cent Col, BA, 57; Kans Univ, MA, 63; Univ Hawaii, PhD(microbiol), 65. *Prof Exp:* Asst prof molecular virol, Sch Med, St Louis Univ, 67-69; asst prof, 69-73, assoc prof, 73-79, PROF VIROL, BAYLOR COL MED, 79- *Concurrent Pos:* Fel, Baylor Col Med, 65-66; consult immunochemist, St John's Mercy Hosp, St Louis, Mo, 69-70. *Mem:* AAAS; Am Soc Microbiol; Am Asn Immunol. *Res:* Viral immunology; protein chemistry of viruses; humoral and cellular immune response of the host with cancer. *Mailing Add:* Dept Virol Baylor Col Med Houston TX 77030

DREESZEN, VINCENT HAROLD, b Palmyra, Nebr, July 23, 21; m 44; c 3. GEOLOGY, HYDROLOGY. *Educ:* Nebr State Teachers Col, Peru, AB, 42; Univ Nebr, MSc, 50. *Prof Exp:* Geologist, 47-59, asst dir div, 59-67, actg dir, 67-69, DIR CONSERV & SERV DIV, UNIV NEBR, LINCOLN, 69-, PROF GEOL, 70-, MEM GRAD FAC, 76- *Mem:* Am Water Works Asn; Asn Am State Geol; Geol Soc Am. *Res:* Optimum use of water resources; conservation of other natural resources; study and correlation of Pleistocene sediments and their land forms. *Mailing Add:* Conserv & Surv Div 113 Nebr Hall Univ of Nebr Lincoln NE 68588

DREGNE, HAROLD ERNEST, b Ladysmith, Wis, Sept 25, 16; m 43; c 4. SOIL SCIENCE. *Educ:* Wis State Univ, BS, 38; Univ Wis, MS, 40; Ore State Univ, PhD(soil chem), 42. *Prof Exp:* Asst, Ore State Univ, 40-42; jr soil scientist, Soil Conserv Serv, USDA, 42-43 & 46; asst prof agron, Univ Idaho, 46-47; asst soil scientist, Wash State Univ, 47-49; prof agron & agronomist, Exp Sta, NMex State Univ, 49-50, prof soils, 50-69; prof agron & chmn dept, 69-72, chmn dept plant & soil sci, 72-78, HORN PROF SOIL SCI, TEX TECH UNIV, 72-, DIR INT CTR ARID & SEMI-ARID LAND STUDIES, 76- *Concurrent Pos:* Head, Inter Col Exchange Prog, Pakistan, 55-57; mem US soil salinity deleg, Soviet Union, 60; soil fertil expert, Food & Agr Orgn, UN, Chile, 61; consult, UNESCO, Tunisia, 67, UN Environ Prog, 75-80 & Food & Agr Orgn, 79-82. *Mem:* Fel AAAS; fel Am Soc Agron; fel Am Soil Sci Soc. *Res:* Chemistry and fertility of arid region soils; saline and sodium soils; irrigation water quality. *Mailing Add:* Dept of Plant & Soil Sci Tex Tech Univ Lubbock TX 79409

DREICER, HARRY, b Bad Lausick, Ger, Oct 6, 27; US citizen; m 50; c 3. PLASMA PHYSICS. *Educ:* Mass Inst Technol, BS, 51, PhD(physics), 55. *Prof Exp:* Mem staff physics, Los Alamos Sci Lab, Univ Calif, 54-66, group leader, 66-75, asst div leader, 75-76; prof physics, astrophysics & astrogeophysics, Univ Colo, Boulder, 77; LEADER, CONTROLLED THERMONUCLEAR RES DIV, LOS ALAMOS SCI LAB, UNIV CALIF, 77- *Concurrent Pos:* Consult, Boeing Sci Res Labs, 59- & Martin Co, 61; part-time prof, Univ NMex, 60; Europ Atomic Energy Community fel, Lab Gas Ionizzati, Frascati, Italy, 64-65 & Saclay Nuclear Res Ctr, France, 65. *Mem:* Fel Am Phys Soc. *Res:* Effect of coulomb interactions and radiation field on plasma distribution functions; runaway electrons in plasmas; measurement of plasma microwave emission and transmission; anomalous high frequency electrical resistivity of plasmas. *Mailing Add:* Los Alamos Sci Lab PO Box 1663 Los Alamos NM 87544

DREIER, WILLIAM MATTHEWS, JR, b Omaha, Nebr, Mar 20, 37; m 61; c 1. CHEMICAL ENGINEERING. *Educ:* Univ Wis, BS, 59, MS, 60; Univ Minn, PhD(chem eng), 64. *Prof Exp:* Aerospace engr, Lewis Res Ctr, NASA, 63-64; sr res chem engr, 64-68, SECT LEADER, JAMES FORD BELL RES CTR, GEN MILLS, INC, 68- *Mem:* Am Inst Chem Engrs. *Res:* Thermodynamics of cryogenic fuels; microwave heating; dehydration. *Mailing Add:* 2255 Valders Ave Minneapolis MN 55427

DREIFKE, GERALD E(DMOND), b St Louis, Mo, June 21, 18; m 51; c 4. ELECTRICAL ENGINEERING, APPLIED MECHANICS. *Educ:* Washington Univ, BS & MS, 48, DSc, 61. *Prof Exp:* Layout & drafting, Curtiss Wright Corp, 36-39, design engr, 39-44; layout engr, Douglas Aircraft, 39; from instr to assoc prof, St Louis Univ, 48-61, prof elec eng, 61-70, secy dept, 51-54, dir dept, 54-71; mgr res & develop, Union Elec Co, 71-77; CONSULT, 77- *Concurrent Pos:* Consult, Emerson Elec Co, 51 & Monsanto Co, 61-; mem tech staff, Bell Tel Labs, 63; ed-in-chief, Instrument Soc Am, 67-; vis prof physics & consult engr, Univ Mo, St Louis, 79- *Honors & Awards:* Cert merit, US War Prod Bd, 42. *Mem:* Inst Elec & Electronics Engrs; Am Soc Eng Educ; Instrument Soc Am; Nat Soc Prof Engrs. *Res:* Automatic controls; electromechanical systems; system dynamics. *Mailing Add:* 4104 Oreon Dr St Louis MO 63121

DREIFUSS, FRITZ EMANUEL, b Dresden, Ger, Jan 20, 26; US citizen; m 54; c 2. MEDICINE. *Educ:* Univ NZ, MB, ChB, 50. *Prof Exp:* House physician & res neurol officer, Nat Hosp, London, Eng, 54-57; from asst prof to assoc prof, 59-68, PROF NEUROL, SCH MED, UNIV VA, 68-, NEUROLOGIST, UNIV HOSP, 59- *Concurrent Pos:* Neurologist, Commonwealth of Va Child Neurol Prog, 59- *Mem:* AAAS; Am Acad Neurol; Asn Res Nerv & Ment Dis; AMA; NY Acad Sci. *Res:* Neurological sciences, especially pediatric neurology; epilepsy and mental retardation. *Mailing Add:* Dept of Neurol Univ of Va Hosp Charlottesville VA 22903

DREILING, CHARLES ERNEST, b Inglewood, Calif, Apr 6, 41; m 62; c 2. BIOCHEMISTRY, NEUROCHEMISTRY. *Educ:* Univ Wash, BA, 64; NMex State Univ, MS, 68; Ore State Univ, PhD(biochem), 70. *Prof Exp:* Teaching asst, Dept Biol, NMex State Univ, 66-67; res asst, Dept Biochem & Biophysics, Ore State Univ, 68-70; asst prof endocrinol, Dept Biol, 71-75, asst prof, 75-81, ASSOC PROF BIOCHEM, SCH MED, UNIV NEV, RENO, 81- *Mem:* AAAS; Sigma Xi; NY Acad Sci. *Res:* Embryology and enzymology of the myelin sheath of the central and peripheral nervous systems; local and humoral factors which initiate normal myelination and control remyelination following injury and disease. *Mailing Add:* Biochem Div Sch Med Sci Univ Nev Reno NV 89507

DREILING, DAVID A, b New York, NY, June 5, 18; m 46; c 1. SURGERY. *Educ:* Cornell Univ, BA, 38; NY Univ, MD, 42; Am Bd Surg, dipl. *Prof Exp:* Dir dept surg, Greenpoint Hosp, Brooklyn, 62-64; DIR EXP GASTROINTESTINAL SURG & ANIMAL RES FACIL, MT SINAI HOSP, 63-, PROF SURG, MT SINAI SCH MED, 66-, VCHMN DEPT, 74- *Concurrent Pos:* Dazian fel exp surg & anat, NY Med Col, 45-46; Ralph Colp fel exp surg & gastroenterol, 46-47; Guggenheim fel exp gastroenterol, 47-49; dir dept surg, Elmhurst Gen Hosp, 64-74; mem bd trustees, Nat Digestive Dis Found, 70- & Am Fedn Digestive Dis, 70-; ed J, Am Col Gastroenterol, 71-; ed, Mt Sinai J Med, 74. *Honors & Awards:* Corpernicus Medal Award. *Mem:* Fel AMA; fel Am Col Surgeons; Am Col Gastroenterol; fel World Med Asn; fel Int Col Surgeons. *Res:* Gastroenterology physiology; diagnosis of pathophysiologic evaluation of pancreatic inflammation; mechanics of secretion of the pancreas. *Mailing Add:* 171 W 57th St New York NY 10019

DREILING, LESLIE ALLEN, astrophysics, physics, see previous edition

DREILING, MARK JEROME, b Kansas City, Mo, Nov 27, 40; m 68; c 2. PHYSICS. *Educ:* Kans State Univ, BS, 62, MS, 64, PhD(physics), 68. *Prof Exp:* Res physicist, 67-80, SUPVR, SOLAR ENERGY SECT, PHILLIPS PETROL CO, 80- *Mem:* Am Chem Soc; Am Phys Soc. *Res:* Electron spectroscopy; surface science; catalysis; x-ray diffraction; photovoltaics. *Mailing Add:* 1301 Cherokee Hills Dr Bartlesville OK 74003

DREIMANIS, ALEKSIS, b Valmiera, Latvia, Aug 13, 14; Can citizen; m 42; c 2. QUATERNARY GEOLOGY. *Educ:* Latvia Univ, Mag rer nat, 38, habil, 41. *Hon Degrees:* DSc, Univ Waterloo, 69, Univ Western Ont, 80. *Prof Exp:* Asst geol, Inst Geol, Latvia Univ, 38-40, lectr, 41, privat-docent, 42-44; assoc prof, Baltic Univ, 46-48; lectr, 48-51, from asst prof to assoc prof, 51-64, prof, 64-80, EMER PROF GEOL, UNIV WESTERN ONT, 80- *Concurrent Pos:* Consult, Inst Res Mineral Resources of Latvia, 42-44 & Ont Dept Planning & Develop, 50-53; consult various Can & US govt agencies, explor & eng consult co, 50-; Can deleg, Int Geol Cong, 60; Can deleg, Int Union Quaternary Res, 65, 69, 73 & 77, pres, Comn Genesis & Lithology Quaternary Deposits, 73-82; mem, Can Nat Adv Comt Res in Geol Sci & chmn subcomt quaternary geol, 67-71; mem, Baltic Res Inst. *Honors & Awards:* Centennial Medal Can, Can Govt, 67; Latvian Cult Found Hon Award Tech & Natural Sci, 77; Queen Elizabeth II 25th Anniversary Medal, Can, 77; Logan Medal, Geol Asn Can, 78. *Mem:* Am Quaternary Asn; Asn Advan Baltic Studies; Geol Soc Am; Soc Econ Paleont & Mineral; Geol Asn Can. *Res:* Pleistocene and glacial geology; lithology and fabric of glacial deposits; pollen analysis; indicator trains; Late Pleistocene stratigraphy of Northern Hemisphere. *Mailing Add:* Dept of Geol Univ of Western Ont London ON N6A 5B8 Can

DREISBACH, JOSEPH HERMAN, b Northampton, Pa, Nov 6, 49. PROTEIN BIOCHEMISTRY, MICROBIAL BIOCHEMISTRY. *Educ:* LaSalle Col, BA, 71; Lehigh Univ, MS, 74, PhD(chem), 77. *Prof Exp:* ASST PROF CHEM, UNIV SCRANTON, 78- *Mem:* Am Chem Soc; Am Soc Microbiol; Sigma Xi. *Res:* Characterization of the processes involved during bacterial enzyme induction by large extracellular molecules prior to interaction at the gene level. *Mailing Add:* Dept Chem Univ Scranton Scranton PA 18510

DREISBACH, ROBERT HASTINGS, b Baker, Ore, Mar 29, 16; m 41; c 2. ENVIRONMENTAL HEALTH. *Educ:* Stanford Univ, AB, 37; Univ Chicago, PhD(pharmacol) & MD, 42. *Prof Exp:* Asst pharmacol, Univ Chicago, 39-42; intern, St Mary's Hosp, 42-43; from instr to prof pharmacol, Sch Med, Stanford Univ, 43-73; CLIN PROF ENVIRON HEALTH, SCH PUB HEALTH & COMMUNITY MED, UNIV WASH, 73- *Res:* Toxicology; environmental pollution. *Mailing Add:* Sch Pub Health & Community Med Univ of Wash SC-34 Seattle WA 98195

DREISS, GERARD JULIUS, b West New York, NJ, July 11, 28; m 59; c 2. THEORETICAL PHYSICS. *Educ:* Rutgers Univ, BA, 58; Univ Pa, MS, 64, PhD(physics), 68. *Prof Exp:* Mathematician, Avco-Everett Res Lab, 59-63; vis instr physics, Northeastern Univ, 68-69, asst prof, 69-71; asst ed, 71-72, ASSOC ED, PHYS REV, 72- *Mem:* Am Phys Soc. *Res:* Theoretical nuclear physics. *Mailing Add:* The Phys Rev Brookhaven Nat Lab Upton NY 11973

DREIZEN, PAUL, b New York, NY, Oct 23, 29. BIOPHYSICS, MEDICINE. *Educ:* Cornell Univ, AB, 51; NY Univ, MD, 54. *Prof Exp:* Intern med, NY Univ-Bellevue Med Ctr, 54-55, asst resident, 55-56, asst med, 58-59; cardiologist, US Naval Hosp, Nat Naval Med Ctr, 56-58; res assoc biol, Mass Inst Technol, 59-62; from asst prof to assoc prof med, 62-71, PROF MED & BIOPHYS, STATE UNIV NY DOWNSTATE MED CTR, 71-, DEAN SCH GRAD STUDIES, 73- *Concurrent Pos:* Nat Res fel, 59-63; career scientist, NY City Health Res Coun, 63-75. *Mem:* Biophys Soc; Soc Gen Physiol; Am Soc Cell Biol; Asn Am Physicians; Am Soc Clin Invest. *Res:* Physical chemistry of contractile proteins; molecular mechanism of muscular contraction. *Mailing Add:* State Univ NY Downstate Med Ctr 450 Clarkson Ave Brooklyn NY 11203

DREIZEN, SAMUEL, b New York, NY, Sept 12, 18; m 56; c 1. NUTRITION. *Educ:* Brooklyn Col, BA, 41; Western Reserve Univ, DDS, 45; Northwestern Univ, MD, 58. *Prof Exp:* Res assoc, Univ Cincinnati, 45-47; from instr to assoc prof nutrit & metab, Northwestern Univ, 47-66; PROF PATH, INST DENT SCI, DENT BR, UNIV TEX, 66-, PROF DENT ONCOL, 76- *Concurrent Pos:* Asst sci dir, Nutrit Clin, Hillman Hosp, 48-60; Clayton Found fel, 49-54; consult nutrit, Am Dent Asn, 64-; consult, M D Anderson Hosp & Tumor Inst, Univ Tex, 67-, prof, Grad Sch Biomed Sci, 68-; mem ed bd, Postgrad Med, 70- *Honors & Awards:* Edgar Martin Mem Award, Odontographic Soc Chicago, 70. *Mem:* AAAS; Am Asn Phys Anthropologists; Int Asn Dent Res; Soc Res Child Develop; NY Acad Sci. *Res:* Dental caries; nutritional deficiency diseases; child growth and development; cancer chemotherapy; oral medicine. *Mailing Add:* Inst for Dent Sci Univ of Tex Dent Br PO Box 20068 Houston TX 77025

DRELICH, ARTHUR (HERBERT), b Jersey City, NJ, Mar 26, 20; m 49; c 5. TEXTILE CHEMISTRY, MICROSCOPY. *Educ:* NY Univ, BA, 40; Univ Pa, MS, 42. *Prof Exp:* Jr chemist protective agents, Edgewood Arsenal, 42-43; supvr chem res, 43-67, sr scientist, Res Div, 67-74, SR RES ASSOC, RES DIV, CHICOPEE MFG CO, JOHNSON & JOHNSON, 74-, SR TECHNOL COUNR, 74-, CONSULT, 79- *Honors & Awards:* Johnson Medal, 76. *Mem:* Am Chem Soc; fel Royal Micros Soc; Fiber Soc; Sigma Xi. *Res:* Properties of thermoplastic polymers; bonding of non-woven fabrics; absorbency; viscose chemistry; physico-chemical methods to rapidly destabilize polymer latexes; fiber and chemical microscopy and scientific photography. *Mailing Add:* 60 Parkside Rd Plainfield NJ 07060

DRELL, SIDNEY DAVID, b Atlantic City, NJ, Sept 13, 26; m 52; c 3. THEORETICAL HIGH ENERGY PHYSICS. *Educ:* Princeton Univ, AB, 46; Univ Ill, AM, 47, PhD(physics), 49. *Hon Degrees:* DSc, Univ Ill, Chicago, 81. *Prof Exp:* Res assoc physics, Univ Ill, 49-50; instr, Stanford Univ, 50-52; res assoc, Mass Inst Technol, 52-53, asst prof, 53-56; assoc prof, 56-60, PROF PHYSICS, STANFORD UNIV, 60-, DEP DIR LINEAR ACCELERATOR CTR, 69- *Concurrent Pos:* Consult, Los Alamos Sci Labs, 56-64 & 68-, Off Sci & Technol, 60-73, Inst Defense (Jason Div), 60-73, Jason Div, SRI Int, 73-81, US Arms Control & Disarmament Agency, 69-81, Nat Security Coun, 73-, Off Technol Assessment, US Congress, 75-, Off Sci & Technol Policy, 77- & consult, Senate Select Comt, Intelligence, 79-; Loeb lectr & vis prof, Harvard Univ, 62 & 70; mem, President's Sci Adv Comt, 66-70; mem bd gov, Weizmann Inst Sci, 70-; chmn high energy physics adv panel, US Dept Energy, 73-; mem vis comt, Dept Physics, Mass Inst Technol, 74-; mem bd trustees, Inst Advan Study, 74-; vis Schrodinger prof, Univ Vienna, Austria, 75; mem bd dirs, Ann Reviews, Inc, 76-; mem bd dirs, The Arms Control Asn, Washington, DC, 78-; mem coun, Foreign Relations, NY, 80-; Guggenheim fel, 61-62 & 71-72. *Honors & Awards:* Ernest Orlando Lawrence Mem Award, US AEC, 72; Richtmyer Mem lectr, Am Asn Physics Teachers, San Francisco, Calif, 78; Leo Szilard Award, Physics Pub Interest, Am Phys Soc, 80- *Mem:* Nat Acad Sci; fel Am Phys Soc; Am Acad Arts & Sci; Fedn Am Sci. *Res:* Quantum field theory; elementary particle physics; understanding of the structure of hadrons, particularly the quark confinement problem; arms control and national security. *Mailing Add:* Stanford Linear Accelerator Ctr PO Box 4349 Stanford CA 94305

DRELL, WILLIAM, b Chicago, Ill, Jan 26, 22; m 43; c 3. BIOCHEMISTRY. *Educ:* Univ Calif, Los Angeles, AB, 43, MA, 46, PhD(chem), 49. *Prof Exp:* Teaching asst chem, Univ Calif, Los Angeles, 43; chemist, Shell Chem Corp, 44-46; asst chem, Univ Calif, Los Angeles, 46-47; res fel, Calif Inst Technol, 49-51; asst res physiol chemist, Univ Calif, Los Angeles, 51-54; estab investr, Am Heart Asn, 54-59; pres, Calbiochem, 59-77, pres, Calbiochem-Behring Corp, 77-78, PRES, CALBIOCHEM DIV, BEHRING CORP, 81- *Concurrent Pos:* Instr, Los Angeles City Col, 47. *Mem:* Am Chem Soc; Soc Exp Biol & Med; Am Soc Biol Chem; The Chem Soc. *Res:* Amino acid and vitamin microassay; antivitamins; animal nutrition; purine and pyrimidine metabolism; chromatography; catecholamine biosynthesis and metabolism; clinical chemistry. *Mailing Add:* 10933 N Torrey Pines Rd La Jolla CA 92037

DREN, ANTHONY THOMAS, b Chisholm, Minn, Feb 15, 36; m 61; c 4. PHARMACOLOGY, PHARMACY. *Educ:* Duquesne Univ, BS, 59, MS, 61; Univ Mich, PhD(pharmacol), 66. *Prof Exp:* Teaching asst pharm, Duquesne Univ, 59-61; retail pharmacist, Heckler Drug Co, 59-61; sr pharmacologist, Abbott Labs, 66-69, group leader pharmacol, 69-72, assoc res fel, 72-75, sect head neuropharmacol, 75-79; SR CLIN RES SCIENTIST, BURROUGHS WELLCOME CO, 79- *Mem:* Am Chem Soc; AAAS; Soc Pharmacol & Exp Therapeut; Soc Neurosci; Sigma Xi. *Res:* Neuropharmacology; cerebral vascular disease; abuse potential of drugs; electroencephalography; psychopharmacology; neurochemistry; cerebral hypoxia; neurophysiology; clinical research. *Mailing Add:* Burroughs Wellcome Co 3030 Cornwallis Rd Research Triangle Park NC 27709

DRENGLER, KEITH ALLAN, b Fermont, Ohio, Jan 6, 53; m 75; c 2. TERPENE BIOSYNTHESIS. *Educ:* Albion Col, BA, 75; Univ Ill, Urbana-Champaign, PhD(org chem), 80. *Prof Exp:* RES CHEMIST ORG CHEM, INT MINERALS & CHEM CORP, 80- *Mem:* Am Chem Soc. *Res:* Elucidating the mechanisms of enzymatic reactions involved in terpene biosynthesis; synthesis of compounds with novel biological activity for potential use as veterinary drugs. *Mailing Add:* Int Minerals & Chem Corp PO Box 207 Terre Haute IN 47808

DRENICK, RUDOLF F, b Vienna, Austria, Aug 20, 14; nat US; m 46; c 3. APPLIED MATHEMATICS. *Educ:* Vienna Univ, PhD(theoret physics), 39. *Prof Exp:* Asst prof math & physics, Villanova Col, 39-44; engr anal, Gen Elec Co, 46-49; mgr anal group, Radio Corp Am, 49-57; res mathematician, Bell Tel Labs, Inc, 57-61; chmn dept, 66-67, PROF ELEC ENG, POLYTECH INST NEW YORK, 61- *Concurrent Pos:* NSF fel, 64-65; consult mathematician, Mathematica, Princeton & Res Triangle Inst, Durham, 62-65; prog dir, Syst Theory & Appln, NSF, 77-78. *Mem:* Fel Inst Elec & Electronics Engrs; Soc Indust & Appl Math; Inst Math Statist; Inst Mgt Sci; Am Acad Mech. *Res:* Application of mathematical methods to engineering problems. *Mailing Add:* Dept Systs Eng Polytech Inst New York Brooklyn NY 11201

DRENNAN, JAMES ELLIOTT, b Salem, Ohio, Nov 21, 26; m 50; c 2. QUALITY. *Educ:* Ohio Wesleyan Univ, BA, 49. *Prof Exp:* Physicist, Columbus Labs-Battelle Mem Inst, 49-52, prin physicist, 52-56, proj leader reliability eng, 56-62, sr physicist, 62-71; sr quality engr, 71-72, PROG QUAL REP, SPACE & ELECTRONIC SYSTS DIV, MARTIN MARIETTA AEROSPACE, 72- *Mem:* Sr mem Inst Elec & Electronics Engr. *Res:* Gaseous electronics; thermionic emission; reliability engineering; test design; radiation and environmental effects; software quality engineering; product assurance. *Mailing Add:* Martin Marietta Aerospace PO Box 179 Denver CO 80201

DRENNAN, OLLIN JUNIOR, b Kirksville, Mo, Apr 11, 25; m 53; c 3. HISTORY OF SCIENCE. *Educ:* Northeast Mo State Teachers Col, AB, 49; Mo Valley Col, BS, 50; Bradley Univ, MS, 55; Univ Wis, PhD(hist sci), 61. *Prof Exp:* Prog dir & engr, Radio Sta KMMO, 49; teacher, high sch, Mo, 51-52; instr physics & chem, Mo Valley Col, 52-53; asst prof physics, Evansville Col, 53-55; instr, Northeast Mo State Teachers Col, 55-64; assoc prof physics, Western Mich Univ, 64-67, dir, 64-67, prof natural sci, 67-77, assoc dean, Col Gen Studies & Area Chmn, Gen Studies Sci, 71-77; prof physics, 77-80, REIGER-BLACK DISTINGUISHED PROF PHYSICS & NATURAL SCI, NORTHEAST MO STATE UNIV, 80- *Res:* 19th and 20th century physical science; general education science. *Mailing Add:* Dept of Physics Northeast Mo State Univ Kirksville MO 63501

DRESCH, FRANCIS WILLIAM, b Sharon, Pa, Sept 21, 13; m 39. ECONOMIC STATISTICS, OPERATIONS RESEARCH. *Educ:* Stanford Univ, AB, 32, AM, 34; Univ Calif, PhD(math), 37. *Prof Exp:* Asst, Univ Calif, 35-37, Florence Noble traveling fel math, Cambridge Univ & Univ Paris, 37-38; instr math, Univ Calif, 38-41; from asst dir to dir comput & ballistics, US Naval Proving Ground, 46-52; sr statistician, 52-57, mgr indust opers res & electronic data processing, 57-61, sr math economist, 62-79, opers analyst, 79-80, SR MATH ECONOMIST, CTR PLANNING & RES, STANFORD RES INST, 80- *Mem:* AAAS; Am Math Soc; Inst Math Statist; Economet Soc; Brit Oper Res Soc. *Res:* Econometrics; ballistics; statistics; computing techniques; economic impact of environmental regulations; macroeconomics; potential rate of post-attack economic recovery. *Mailing Add:* Stanford Res Inst 333 Ravenswood Menlo Park CA 94025

DRESCHER, ROBERT FREDERICK, b Hibbing, Minn, Apr 24, 25; m 50; c 4. INDUSTRIAL MICROBIOLOGY. *Educ:* Univ Minn, BA, 50, MS, 53, PhD(plant path), 56. *Prof Exp:* Chief microbiologist, Paper Sect, Buckman Labs, Tenn, 56-64; vpres, Sharpley Labs, Va, 64-66; scientist, Rohm and Haas Co, Pa, 66-70; PROD MGR, NOPCO CHEM DIV, DIAMOND SHAMROCK CORP, 70- *Mem:* AAAS; Am Phytopath Soc; Soc Indust Microbiol; Tech Asn Pulp & Paper Indust. *Res:* Microbiology of pulp, paper, paints and petroleum; corrosion of metals by microorganisms, foods and textiles. *Mailing Add:* Diamond Shamrock Corp Process Chem Div 350 Mt Kemble Ave Morristown NJ 07960

DRESCHER, WILLIAM JAMES, b Craig, Colo, Aug 20, 18; m 41; c 2. GROUNDWATER HYDROLOGY, HYDROGEOLOGY. *Educ:* Univ Colo, BSE, 40; Univ Wis, MS, 56. *Prof Exp:* Engr, Am Bridge Co Ind, 40-41; hydraul engr, US Geol Surv, Fla, 41-42, La, 42-44 & Wis, 46-51, dist engr, 51-57, br area chief, 57-62, hydraul res engr, 62-66, res hydrologist, 66-70, regional planning officer, Dept Interior, 70-74; CONSULT HYDROLOGIST, 74- *Concurrent Pos:* Lectr, Univ Wis, 74-75; US chmn steering comt, Int Field Year Great Lakes, Int Hydrol Decade, 66-77. *Mem:* Int Asn Hydrogeol; Am Geophys Union. *Mailing Add:* 322 Robin Pkwy Madison WI 53705

DRESCHHOFF, GISELA AUGUSTE-MARIE, b Monchengladbach, Ger, Sept 13, 38; US citizen. RADIATION PHYSICS, GEOPHYSICS. *Educ:* Tech Univ Braunschweig, BS, 61, MS, 65, PhD(physics), 72. *Prof Exp:* Staff scientist radiation protection, Physikalisch Tech Bundesanstalt Ger, 65-67; res assoc nuclear waste disposal, Kans Geol Surv, 71-72; DEP DIR, RADIATION PHYSICS LAB, SPACE TECHNOL CTR, UNIV KANS, 72- *Concurrent Pos:* Vis asst prof physics, Univ Kans, 72-74, adj asst prof, 74-; assoc prof mgr, Div Polar Prog, NSF, 78- *Mem:* Am Phys Soc; Am Geophys Union; Sigma Xi; Am Polar Soc. *Res:* Remote sensing; nuclear waste disposal; reactor radiation protection. *Mailing Add:* Space Technol Ctr 2291 Irving Hill Rd Lawrence KS 66045

DRESDEN, CARLTON F, b Dodgeville, Wis, Oct 17, 31; m 55; c 3. BIOCHEMISTRY, ORGANIC CHEMISTRY. *Educ:* Wis State Univ, Platteville, BS, 53; Univ Wis, MS, 57, PhD(org chem, biochem), 59. *Prof Exp:* Assoc prof chem, Slippery Rock State Col, 59-61; asst prof biochem, La State Univ, 61-62; chmn sci div, 62-70, actg dean, Sch Natural Sci & Math, 76-80,

PROF CHEM, SLIPPERY ROCK STATE COL, 62- *Mem:* AAAS; Am Chem Soc. *Res:* Biochemistry of the myxomycetes; mechanism of action of bacterial toxins. *Mailing Add:* Dept of Chem Slippery Rock State Col Slippery Rock PA 16057

DRESDEN, MARC HENRI, b Hague, Neth, July 21, 38; US citizen; m 60; c 2. BIOCHEMISTRY, DEVELOPMENTAL BIOLOGY. *Educ:* Yale Univ, BS, 60; Harvard Univ, PhD(bact immunol), 66. *Prof Exp:* Asst prof, 68-75, ASSOC PROF BIOCHEM, BAYLOR COL MED, 76- *Mem:* AAAS; Am Soc Biol Chem; Soc Develop Biol; Am Soc Parasitol. *Res:* Collagen metabolism; biochemistry of parasites; limb regeneration in vertebrates. *Mailing Add:* Dept of Biochem Baylor Col of Med Houston TX 77030

DRESDEN, MAX, b Amsterdam, Netherlands, Apr 23, 18; US citizen; m 48; c 2. THEORETICAL PHYSICS. *Educ:* Univ Mich, PhD(physics), 46. *Prof Exp:* Asst physics, Univ Mich, 41-46; from asst prof to prof, Univ Kans, 46-57; prof & chmn dept, Northwestern Univ, 57-60; prof, Univ Iowa, 60-64; PROF PHYSICS, STATE UNIV NY STONY BROOK, 64-, EXEC OFF, INST THEORET PHYSICS, 66- *Concurrent Pos:* Mem bd dirs, Midwest Univs Res Asn, 56-64; sci bd dirs, Midwest Res Inst, 62-; vis prof, Johns Hopkins Univ, 57-58; vis lectr, Am Inst Physics, 57- *Mem:* Fel Am Phys Soc. *Res:* Statistical mechanics; superconductivity; quantum field theory; behavior of positrons; parastatistics; symmetrics and S matrix theory; particle physics. *Mailing Add:* Dept of Physics State Univ of NY Stony Brook NY 11794

DRESDNER, RICHARD DAVID, b New York, NY, Feb 20, 18; m 50; c 2. CHEMISTRY. *Educ:* NY Univ, BA, 41; Pa State Univ, MS, 44, PhD(phys chem), 47. *Prof Exp:* Res engr, Battelle Mem Inst, 47-50; res engr, Picatinny Arsenal, 50-51; res engr, Micrometallic Corp, 51-53; assoc res prof, 53-59, assoc prof, 59-66, chmn div gen chem, 66-76, PROF CHEM, UNIV FLA, 66- *Mem:* Am Chem Soc. *Res:* Electrolytic fluorinations; viscosity; low temperature air rectification; analytical photochemistry; kinetics; pyrotechnics; plastic filters; synthetic reactions; fluorochemicals; photochemical fluorinations. *Mailing Add:* Dept of Chem Univ of Fla Gainesville FL 32611

DRESEL, PETER E, b Ulm, Ger, Feb 27, 25; nat Can; m 47; c 3. PHARMACOLOGY. *Educ:* Antioch Col, BS, 48; Univ Rochester, PhD(pharmacol), 52. *Prof Exp:* Instr pharmacol, Univ Cincinnati, 52; instr, Emory Univ, 53-54; res pharmacologist, Wm S Merrell Co, 54-56; from asst prof to prof pharmacol & therapeut, Univ Man, 56-76; prof, 76-80, CARNEGIE & ROCKEFELLER PROF PHARMACOL, DALHOUSIE UNIV, 80-, HEAD DEPT, 76- *Concurrent Pos:* Vis scientist, Univ Gothenburg, 63-64 & Univ Col, London, 70-71. *Mem:* AAAS; Cardiac Muscle Soc; Am Soc Pharmacol & Exp Therapeut; Pharmacol Soc Can. *Res:* Heart and circulation. *Mailing Add:* Dept of Pharmacol Dalhousie Univ Halifax NS B3H 3J5 Can

DRESHFIELD, ARTHUR C(HARLES), JR, b Kalamazoo, Mich, Nov 9, 29; m 57; c 3. CHEMICAL ENGINEERING. *Educ:* Univ Ill, BS, 51; Lawrence Col, MS, 53, PhD, 56. *Prof Exp:* Res engr papermaking processes, Scott Paper Co, 55-57; from res group mgr pulping & paperboard to dir res, Fibreboard Paper Prod, 57-68, dir prod develop, 68-72; mgr res & develop, 72-81, MEM STAFF, RES & DEVELOP CTR, POTLATCH CORP, 81- *Concurrent Pos:* Chmn indust adv coun, Forest Prod Lab, Univ Calif, 64-65. *Honors & Awards:* Steele Medal, Inst Paper Chem, 56. *Mem:* Tech Asn Pulp & Paper Indust. *Res:* Alkaline pulping; papermaking; packaging. *Mailing Add:* Res & Develop Ctr Potlatch Corp Cloquet MN 55720

DRESHFIELD, ROBERT LEWIS, b Kalamazoo, Mich, Mar 15, 33; m 56; c 2. PHYSICAL METALLURGY. *Educ:* Univ Ill, BS, 54; Univ Mo, MS, 59; Case Western Reserve Univ, PhD(mat sci), 72. *Prof Exp:* Pratt & Whitney Aircraft Div, United Aircraft Corp, 62-64; METALLURGIST, LEWIS RES CTR, NASA, 64- *Mem:* Am Inst Mining, Metall & Petrol Engrs; Am Soc Metals; Am Soc Testing & Mat. *Res:* Development of alloys for use in aircraft gas turbines, phase relationships in superalloys. *Mailing Add:* Lewis Res Ctr 21000 Brookpark Rd Cleveland OH 44135

DRESKA, NOEL, b Kankakee, Ill, Dec 24, 28. MOLECULAR SPECTROSCOPY. *Educ:* Col St Francis, Ill, AB, 50; Ohio State Univ, PhD(physics), 64. *Prof Exp:* Instr physics, Col St Francis, Ill, 64-66; asst prof, 66-70, chmn dept, 70-77, ASSOC PROF PHYSICS, LEWIS UNIV, 70- *Mem:* Am Asn Physics Teachers. *Res:* High resolution, infrared and molecular spectroscopy. *Mailing Add:* Dept of Physics Lewis Univ Romeoville IL 60441

DRESKIN, SANFORD A, b Newark, NJ, June 30, 36; m 59; c 2. PHYSICS, MATHEMATICS. *Educ:* Muhlenberg Col, BS, 58; Stevens Inst Technol, MS, 61. *Prof Exp:* Jr scientist, Feltman Res Lab, Picatinny Arsenal, NJ, 58-59; res engr, Gulton Industs Inc, 59-61; engr, Astro Electronics Div, RCA, 61-62, mem tech staff, David Sarnoff Res Ctr, 62-65; res scientist, Nat Cash Register Co, 65-66; sr scientist, Am Can Res Labs, 66-74; PROF STAFF MEM, PLASMA PHYSICS LAB, PRINCETON UNIV, 74- *Mem:* Am Phys Soc. *Res:* Piezoelectricity; piezoresistance; photoconductivity; transport phenomena in thin films; holography; information storage and retrieval; thin film deposition; physical optics; plasma physics; magnetic field design; computer simulation. *Mailing Add:* Plasma Physics Lab Princeton Univ Princeton NJ 08540

DRESNER, JOSEPH, b Belg, Feb 11, 27; nat US; m 57. SURFACE PHYSICS, SOLID STATE PHYSICS. *Educ:* Univ Mich, BSE, 49, MS, 50; NY Univ, PhD(physics), 58. *Prof Exp:* Physicist, Hosp Joint Dis, NY, 50-53; asst, NY Univ, 54-58; MEM TECH STAFF, DAVID SARNOFF RES CTR, RCA CORP, 58- *Concurrent Pos:* Consult, Hosp Joint Dis, NY, 53-54; vis prof, Inst Physics Sao Carlos, Univ Sao Paulo, 71-72. *Mem:* Fel Am Phys Soc. *Res:* Luminescence and photoconductivity of solids; electronic properties of organic and amorphous materials; thin films; electron impact phenomena; secondary emission; thermionic emission; television display and pickup devices; medical radiation physics; photovoltaic cells. *Mailing Add:* David Sarnoff Res Ctr RCA Corp Princeton NJ 08540

DRESS, WILLIAM JOHN, b Buffalo, NY, June 9, 18. TAXONOMIC BOTANY. *Educ:* Univ Buffalo, BA, 39; Cornell Univ, PhD(bot), 53. *Prof Exp:* Asst, 47-53, asst prof bot, 53-57, taxonomist, 57-60, assoc prof bot, 60-68, PROF BOT L H BAILEY HORTORIUM, CORNELL UNIV, 68- *Mem:* Am Soc Plant Taxon; Int Asn Plant Taxon. *Res:* Plant taxonomy, especially of cultivated plants; revision of genus Chrysopsis. *Mailing Add:* L H Bailey Hortorium Cornell Univ Ithaca NY 14853

DRESSEL, FRANCIS GEORGE, b Hart, Mich, Sept 22, 04; m 32; c 2. MATHEMATICS. *Educ:* Mich State Col, BS, 28; Univ Mich, MS, 29; Duke Univ, PhD(math), 33. *Prof Exp:* From instr to prof, 29-74, EMER PROF MATH, DUKE UNIV, 74- *Concurrent Pos:* Teacher, Civil Aeronaut Admin, Duke Univ, 42-43; asst, Math Sci Div, Army Res Off, 51- *Mem:* Am Math Soc; Math Asn Am. *Res:* Integral equations; Stieltjes integrals; partial differential equations. *Mailing Add:* 2502 Frances St Durham NC 27707

DRESSEL, HERMAN OTTO, b New York, NY, Jan 15, 26; c 1. ELECTROOPTICS. *Educ:* Dartmouth Col, BS, 47, MS, 48. *Prof Exp:* Jr engr, Physics Lab, Sylvania Elec Prod Inc, 48-54, sr engr, 54-60; res engr, 60-61, advan res engr, 62-65, eng specialist, 65-67, mem tech staff, 67-69, group mgr electron optics, 69-74, MEM TECH STAFF, GTE LABS, INC, 74- *Mem:* Inst Elec & Electronics Eng; Sigma Xi. *Res:* Electron tube research and electron optics of devices for operation at centimeter, millimeter and submillimeter wavelengths; system and propagation studies at millimeter wavelengths; research in electron beam accessed imaging, storage and display devices; semiconductor processing research. *Mailing Add:* GTE Labs Inc 40 Sylvan Rd Waltham MA 02154

DRESSEL, PAUL LEROY, b Youngstown, Ohio, Nov 29, 10; m 32; c 3. STATISTICAL ANALYSIS. *Educ:* Wittenberg Col, AB, 31; Mich State Univ, AM, 34; Univ Mich, PhD(statist), 39. *Hon Degrees:* LLD, Wittenberg Univ, 66. *Prof Exp:* From instr to asst prof math, Mich State Univ, 34-44, prof & head bd exam & dir counseling, 44-54, dir comp study eval, 49-53, prof & dir eval serv, 54-59, dir inst res & asst provost, 59-76, prof univ res, 59-81; RETIRED. *Concurrent Pos:* Gen Educ Bd fel, 39-40. *Mem:* AAAS; fel Am Psychol Asn; Psychomet Soc. *Res:* Educational research; higher education; evaluation in general education. *Mailing Add:* 235 Maplewood Dr East Lansing MI 48823

DRESSEL, RALPH WILLIAM, b Buffalo, NY, Mar 3, 22; m 45; c 4. PHYSICS. *Educ:* Union Col, BS, 44; Univ Ill, PhD(physics), 50. *Prof Exp:* Asst instr, Union Col, 42-44; mem staff, Radiation Lab, Mass Inst Technol, 44-46; asst, Univ Ill, 46-49; from asst prof to prof physics, 50-61, from assoc physicist to physicist, Phys Sci Lab, 52-61, head dept physics, Univ, 57-61, PROF PHYSICS, N MEX STATE UNIV, 56-; PHYSICIST, NUCLEAR EFFECTS BR, WHITE SANDS MISSILE RANGE, 61- *Mem:* AAAS; Am Asn Physics Teachers; Am Phys Soc; Philos Sci Asn. *Res:* Electromagnetic radiation; interaction of high energy quanta, electrons with matter. *Mailing Add:* 1740 Imperial Ridge Las Cruces NM 88001

DRESSELHAUS, GENE FREDERICK, b Ancon, CZ, Nov 7, 29; m 58; c 4. SOLID STATE PHYSICS. *Educ:* Univ Calif, AB, 51, PhD(physics), 55. *Prof Exp:* Instr physics, Univ Chicago, 55-56; asst prof, Cornell Univ, 56-60; mem staff, Lincoln Lab, 60-77, SR SCIENTIST, BITTER NAT MAGNET LAB, MASS INST TECHNOL, 77- *Concurrent Pos:* Consult, Gen Elec Res Lab, 56-60 & Oak Ridge Nat Lab, 58-60. *Mem:* Fel Am Phys Soc. *Res:* Electronic energy bands in solids; surface impedance of metals; excitons in insulators; surface electronic states. *Mailing Add:* Bitter Nat Magnet Lab 170 Albany St Cambridge MA 02139

DRESSELHAUS, MILDRED S, b Brooklyn, NY, Nov 11, 30; m 58; c 4. SOLID STATE PHYSICS. *Educ:* Hunter Col, AB, 51; Radcliffe Col, AM, 53; Univ Chicago, PhD(physics), 58. *Hon Degrees:* DEng, Worcester Polytech Inst, 76; DSc, Smith Col, 80. *Prof Exp:* NSF fel, Cornell Univ, 58-60; mem staff, Lincoln Lab, Mass Inst Technol, 60-67, Abby Rockefeller Mauze vis prof elec eng, Inst, 67-68, prof, 68-73, assoc head dept, 72-74, ABBY ROCKEFELLER MAUZE PROF ELEC ENG, MASS INST TECHNOL, 73-, DIR CTR MAT SCI & ENG, 77- *Concurrent Pos:* Mem adv bd, Mat Res Div & Mat Res Labs, NSF, 74-76; mem exec comt phys & math sci, Nat Acad Sci, 75-78; chmn, Steering Comt Eval Panels, Nat Bur Standards, 78-; mem, Sci Adv Comt, Allied Chem Corp, 80- *Mem:* Nat Acad Eng; Am Acad Arts & Sci; fel Am Phys Soc; fel Inst Elec & Electronics Engrs; Nat Acad Eng. *Res:* Electronic, optical and magneto-optical properties of solids; semimetals, semiconductors, magnetic semiconductors, graphite intercalation compounds. *Mailing Add:* Mass Inst of Technol Rm 13-2090 77 Massachusetts Ave Cambridge MA 02139

DRESSER, HUGH W, b Utica, NY, Jan 31, 30; m 51; c 2. GEOLOGY, PALEONTOLOGY. *Educ:* Univ Cincinnati, BS, 50, MS, 51; Univ Wyo, PhD(geol), 60. *Prof Exp:* Jr geologist, Carter Oil Co, 51-52, field geologist, 52-54; geologist II, Humble Oil & Refining Co, 59-64, res geologist, Esso Prod Res Co, 64-65; from asst prof to assoc prof, 65-75, PROF GEOL, MONT COL MINERAL SCI & TECHNOL, 75- *Mem:* Am Asn Petrol Geol; Geol Soc Am; Asn Prof Geol Scientists; Soc Econ Paleont & Mineral; Int Asn Sedimentologists. *Res:* Palichnology, structural geology, geomorphology, stratigraphy. *Mailing Add:* Dept of Geol Mont Col Mineral Sci & Technol Butte MT 59701

DRESSER, MILES JOEL, b Spokane, Wash, Dec 19, 35; m 59; c 3. SURFACE PHYSICS. *Educ:* Linfield Col, BA, 57; Iowa State Univ, PhD(physics), 64. *Prof Exp:* Asst prof, 63-70, ASSOC PROF PHYSICS, WASH STATE UNIV, 70- *Concurrent Pos:* Physicist, Nat Bur Standards, 72. *Mem:* Am Phys Soc; Am Vacuum Soc; Am Asn Physics Teachers. *Res:* Ultra high vacuum surface physics; surface ionization; thermionic and field emission; mass spectrometry; thin film electroluminescence; surface and solid diffusion; heterogeneous catalysis. *Mailing Add:* Dept of Physics Wash State Univ Pullman WA 99164

DRESSER, THORPE, b Garfield, Utah, Mar 2, 11; m 41; c 3. CHEMICAL ENGINEERING. *Educ:* Mo Sch Mines, BS, 33; Rensselaer Polytech Inst, MS, 34, DChE, 36. *Prof Exp:* Technologist, Sinclair Ref Co, 36-40, process engr, 40-49, asst div dir res labs, 49-69; sr res chem engr, Atlantic Richfield Co, 69-72, res assoc, 72-76; CONSULT CHEM ENGR, 76- *Mem:* AAAS; Am Chem Soc; Am Inst Chem Engrs; fel Am Inst Chem. *Res:* Phase equilibria; distillation calculations; thermodynamics; computerized calculations. *Mailing Add:* 9 E Santa Belia Green Valley AZ 85614

DRESSLER, DAVID, b Cincinnati, Ohio, May 29, 41. BIOCHEMISTRY, MOLECULAR BIOLOGY. *Educ:* Columbia Univ, AB, 63; Harvard Univ, AM, 65, PhD(molecular biol, biochem), 69. *Prof Exp:* Res fel, 69-71, asst prof, 71-75, ASSOC PROF BIOCHEM, HARVARD UNIV, 75- *Concurrent Pos:* NIH career develop award, 72-77. *Res:* DNA replication and recombination; virology. *Mailing Add:* Dept of Biochem Harvard Univ Cambridge MA 02138

DRESSLER, EDWARD THOMAS, b Pittsburgh, Pa, May 29, 43; m 66; c 2. PHOTONUCLEAR REACTIONS. *Educ:* Duquesne Univ, BS, 66; Am Univ, MS, 72, PhD(physics), 74. *Prof Exp:* Res fel, Univ Saskatchewan, 74-76; res assoc, Ctr Radiation Res, Nat Bur Standards, 76-78; ASST PROF PHYSICS, PA STATE UNIV, 78- *Mem:* Am Phys Soc; Am Asn Physics Teachers. *Res:* Theory of photonuclear reactions; photo disintegration of light nuclei; relativistic effects in photonuclear processes; pion photoproduction and electroproduction from nuclei. *Mailing Add:* Pa State Univ Ogontz Campus 1600 Woodland Rd Abington PA 19001

DRESSLER, HANS, b Vienna, Austria, July 21, 26; nat US; m 56; c 1. ORGANIC CHEMISTRY, BIOCHEMISTRY. *Educ:* Columbia Univ, AM, 51, PhD(chem), 54. *Prof Exp:* Asst chem, Columbia Univ, 51-52, asst, 53; fel monomer synthesis, Mellon Inst, 54-56; sr chemist, Verona Res Ctr, 56-62, group mgr, 62-67; SR GROUP MGR, MONROEVILLE RES CTR, KOPPERS CO, INC, 67- *Mem:* Am Chem Soc; NY Acad Sci; Royal Soc Chem. *Res:* Organic synthesis; product and process development. *Mailing Add:* Koppers Co Inc 440 College Park Dr Monroeville PA 15146

DRESSLER, ROBERT EUGENE, b New York, NY, Dec 16, 44; m 67; c 3. NUMBER THEORY. *Educ:* Univ Rochester, AB, 65; Univ Ore, MA, 66, PhD(math), 69. *Prof Exp:* Asst prof math, Southern Ill Univ, Carbondale, 69-70; asst prof, 71-73, assoc prof, 73-78, PROF MATH, KANS STATE UNIV, 78- *Mem:* Am Math Soc; Math Asn Am. *Res:* Density; properties of special number theoretic functions; number theory in harmonic analysis. *Mailing Add:* Dept of Math Kans State Univ Manhattan KS 66506

DRESSLER, ROBERT LOUIS, b Marquette, Kans, Aug 12, 23. ORGANIC CHEMISTRY. *Educ:* Univ Denver, BS, 56, MS, 57; Univ Colo, Boulder, PhD(org chem), 62. *Prof Exp:* Res assoc org chem, Fla State Univ, 62-63; res chemist, Denver Res Inst, Univ Denver, 64-66; res assoc org chem, Univ Colo, 66-67; from asst prof to assoc prof chem, 67-76, PROF CHEM, FT HAYS STATE UNIV, 76- *Concurrent Pos:* NIH fel, 62-63. *Mem:* Am Chem Soc; The Chem Soc. *Res:* Chemistry and synthesis of polynuclear aromatic compounds and heterocyclic compounds; elimination reactions and molecular rearrangements. *Mailing Add:* Dept of Chem Ft Hays State Univ Hays KS 67601

DRETCHEN, KENNETH LEWIS, b New York, NY, Jan 15, 46; m 68; c 2. PHARMACOLOGY. *Educ:* Brooklyn Col Pharm, BS, 68; Univ Iowa, MS, 70, PhD(pharmacol), 72. *Prof Exp:* Res assoc, 72-73, instr, 73-74, asst prof, 74-77, ASSOC PROF PHARMACOL, SCH MED, GEORGETOWN UNIV, 77- *Concurrent Pos:* Fac develop award, Pharmaceut Mfr Asn Found, 73. *Mem:* Am Soc Pharmacol & Exp Therapeut; Soc Neurosci; Am Chem Soc; Soc Exp Biol. *Res:* Role of the cyclic nucleotides in the function of the physiology and pharmacology of the motor nerve terminal. *Mailing Add:* Dept of Pharmacol Sch Med & Dent Georgetown Univ Washington DC 20007

DREVDAHL, ELMER R(ANDOLPH), b Marquette, Mich, Aug 24, 26; m 49; c 2. MINING ENGINEERING, COMPUTER SCIENCE. *Educ:* Mich Col Mining & Technol, BS, 48; Univ Wash, Seattle, MS, 51. *Prof Exp:* Mining engr, Jones & Laughlin Ore Co, Mich, 48-50; asst prof mining eng, SDak Sch Mines & Technol, 51-55; from asst prof to assoc prof, Univ Ariz, 55-63; head div tech, Ariz Western Col, 63-65; dir tech ed, 65-66, dean occup educ, 66-69, assoc prof, 69-75, PROF ENG & HEAD DEPT, CLARK COL, 75- *Concurrent Pos:* Instr & examr, US Bur Mines First Aid Training. *Mem:* Am Inst Mining, Metall & Petrol Engrs; Nat Soc Prof Engrs; Am Soc Civil Engrs; Am Soc Eng Educ. *Res:* Analysis of equipment systems and application of computers to mining operations; engineering geology. *Mailing Add:* Dept of Eng Clark Col Vancouver WA 98663

DREVES, ROBERT G(EORGE), b Brooklyn, NY, Oct 24, 14; m 38; c 2. AERONAUTICAL ENGINEERING. *Prof Exp:* Coordr prod control aircraft prod, Sperry Gyroscope Co, 41-43, asst aircraft flight instruments, 43-44; mil training specialist, US Naval Training Device Ctr, 46-52, head, Aerospace Syst Trainers Dept, 60-65, assoc tech dir maintenance eng, 65-69, dir logistics & field eng, 70-73; CONSULT, 74- *Mem:* AAAS; Soc Logistics Engrs; Am Inst Aeronaut & Astronaut. *Res:* Design, development, test and utilization of air weapon system simulators for training of pilots and air crews; logistics management. *Mailing Add:* 1268 Palos Verde Dr Orlando FL 32817

DREW, BRUCE ARTHUR, b Detroit, Mich, Mar 9, 24; m 48; c 5. APPLIED MATHEMATICS. *Educ:* Wayne State Univ, BS, 50. *Prof Exp:* Jr chem engr, Parke, Davis & Co, Mich, 48-50; formulator surface coatings, Rinshed-Mason Co, 50-53; develop engr, Huron Milling Co, 53-56; sr chemist, Hercules Powder Co, Va, 56-59; statistician, 59-66, dir corp qual assurance, 66-68, sr res assoc appl math, 68-80, RES FEL, PILLSBURY CO, 80- *Mem:* Soc Indust & Appl Math; Math Asn Am; Asn Comput Mach; Am Asn Cereal Chem; Royal Statist Soc. *Res:* Computer models of chemical systems. *Mailing Add:* Pillsbury Co 311 Second St SE Minneapolis MN 55414

DREW, DAN DALE, b Abilene, Tex, Sept 29, 26; m 49; c 5. COMPUTER SCIENCE, MATHEMATICS. *Educ:* NTex State Univ, BS, 50, MS, 51; Tex A&M Univ, PhD(eng), 66. *Prof Exp:* Mathematician, US Naval Ord Test Sta, Calif, 51-53; analyst digital comput, Gen Dynamics/Convair, Tex, 53-56, group engr, 56-59; appl sci rep, Int Bus Mach Corp, Tex, 59-60; comput specialist, 60-62, assoc dir, 62-68, assoc prof, 66-68, prof indust eng, dir, Comput & Info Sci Div, 68-80, PROF COMPUT SCI & DIV HEAD, TEX A&M UNIV, 80- *Mem:* Asn Comput Mach; Soc Indust & Appl Math. *Res:* Digital computing; computer languages. *Mailing Add:* I Eng Dept Tex A&M Univ College Station TX 77843

DREW, DANIEL L, b Hobart Mills, Calif, Mar 18, 24; m 56; c 1. STATISTICS, COMPUTER SCIENCE. *Educ:* Reed Col, BA, 49; Stanford Univ, MS, 63. *Prof Exp:* Gen mgr, Sociedade Int & Indust Lda, Angola, Portuguese, WAfrica, 51-59; assoc scientist, 59-61, math analyst, 61-63, res scientist & group leader interactive info systs, 66-69, mgr info systs prog, Lockheed Info Systs, 69-71, STAFF SCIENTIST, LOCKHEED PALO ALTO RES LABS, 71- *Concurrent Pos:* Lectr, Exten, Univ Calif, 63-66 & Univ Santa Clara, 67; asst prof, San Jose State Col, 64-74; consult, Foreign Technol Div, 67- *Mem:* Asn Comput Mach. *Res:* Intelligent exploitation of digital computers; information retrieval; management systems; step-by-step interactive use to deal with ill-defined problems; ultra-reliable computing in time-limited networks. *Mailing Add:* 16360 Sanborn Rd Saratoga CA 95070

DREW, DAVID A(BBOTT), b Philadelphia, Pa, Sept 19, 16; m 43; c 2. CHEMICAL ENGINEERING. *Educ:* Univ Pa, BS, 37, PhD(chem eng), 44. *Prof Exp:* Mem staff, Elec Storage Battery Co, 37-39; chem engr, Hercules Inc, 43-51, supvr, Pilot Plant Div, 51-55, mgr, Gen Serv Div, 55-76, asst dir admin, 76-79; RETIRED. *Mem:* Inst Chem Engrs. *Mailing Add:* Res Ctr Hercules Inc Wilmington DE 19899

DREW, FRANCES L, b Pittsburgh, Pa, Apr 30, 17; m 36, 49; c 3. PUBLIC HEALTH. *Educ:* McGill Univ, MD, 42; Univ Pittsburgh, MPH, 61. *Prof Exp:* Instr, Dept Med, McGill Univ, 44-48; clin instr, Dept Med, 49-61, clin asst prof prev med, 61-69, clin assoc prof community med, 69-74, CLIN PROF COMMUNITY MED, SCH MED, UNIV PITTSBURGH, 74-, ASSOC DEAN STUDENT AFFAIRS, 75-, CLIN ASSOC PROF COMMUNITY MED, POP DIV, GRAD SCH PUB HEALTH, 73- *Concurrent Pos:* Mem, Senate Univ Press Comt, Univ Pittsburgh, 70-76, chmn, 72-76; mem, Chancellor's Comn Tenure, Univ Pittsburgh, 72-73, adv, Sch Nursing, Regional Med Prog grants, Nurse Practitioner Prog, 72-73, mem, Affirmative Action Comt, Sch Med, 73-, chmn, 74-, mem, Univ Ctr Int Activities, Prog Policy Comt, 73-77, chmn, Fac Asn Med Sch, 74-75, chmn comt guidelines for fac contract renewal, Sch Med, 74-75. *Mem:* AMA; Am Psychosom Soc; Asn Teachers Prev Med; NY Acad Sci. *Res:* Hypertension; epidemiology of chronic diseases; social determinants of disease. *Mailing Add:* Off of Assoc Dean Student Affairs M252 Scaife Hall Univ of Pittsburgh Pittsburgh PA 15261

DREW, HENRY D, b Buffalo, NY, Sept 8, 41; m 66; c 2. ANALYTICAL CHEMISTRY. *Educ:* Canisius Col, BS, 63; Seton Hall Univ, MS, 65, PhD(chem), 67. *Prof Exp:* Res assoc, Seton Hall Univ, 64-66; vis asst prof, Purdue Univ, 66-68; asst prof, 68-72, ASSOC PROF CHEM, SOUTHERN ILL UNIV, EDWARDSVILLE, 72- *Concurrent Pos:* Vis assoc prof, State Univ NY Buffalo, 76-77. *Mem:* Am Chem Soc; Soc Appl Spectros. *Res:* Analytical instrumentation, enzyme kinetics and equilibria; computer assisted instruction. *Mailing Add:* Dept of Chem Southern Ill Univ Edwardsville IL 62025

DREW, HOWARD DENNIS, b Newark, Ohio, June 7, 39; m 65. SOLID STATE PHYSICS. *Educ:* Univ Pittsburgh, BS, 62; Cornell Univ, PhD(physics), 68. *Prof Exp:* Res assoc, 67-70, asst prof, 70-75, ASSOC PROF SOLID STATE PHYSICS, UNIV MD, COLLEGE PARK, 75- *Mem:* Am Phys Soc; Am Optical Soc; AAAS. *Res:* Optical spectroscopy of metals, alloys and surfaces and far infrared spectroscopy of semimetals and semiconductors. *Mailing Add:* Dept Physics Univ Md College Park MD 20740

DREW, HOWARD FELSHAW, b Lyons Falls, NY, Oct 22, 23; m 44; c 2. ORGANIC CHEMISTRY. *Educ:* Amherst Col, BA, 44, MA, 47; Univ Minn, PhD(chem), 51. *Prof Exp:* Res chemist, 51-57, head org synthesis sect, 57-58, head org res dept, 58-59, assoc dir, 59-69, dir res div, 69-71, dir foods & coffee technol div, 71-73, dir prod develop, Coffee Div, 73-76, DIR CORP TECHNOL DIV, PROCTER & GAMBLE CO, 77- *Mem:* AAAS; Am Chem Soc. *Mailing Add:* 69 Reily Rd Cincinnati OH 45215

DREW, JAMES VAN, b Flushing, NY, Sept 21, 30; m 56; c 3. SOIL SCIENCE. *Educ:* Rutgers Univ, BS, 52, PhD(soil sci), 57. *Prof Exp:* Asst arctic soils, Rutgers Univ, 55-57; from asst prof to assoc prof agron, Univ Nebr, Lincoln, 57-76, asst dean grad col, 70-71, assoc dean grad studies, 71-74, dean grad studies, 74-76; PROF AGRON, DEAN SCH AGR & LAND RESOURCES MGT & DIR AGR EXP STA, UNIV ALASKA, FAIRBANKS, 76- *Mem:* AAAS; fel Am Soc Agron; Int Soc Soil Sci; Soil Conservation Soc Am; Sigma Xi. *Res:* Soil genesis, classification, survey and mineralogy; remote sensing of soil resources. *Mailing Add:* 309 O'Neill Resources Bldg Univ of Alaska Fairbanks AK 99701

DREW, JOHN H, b Cleveland, Ohio, Nov 7, 43; m 69. MATHEMATICS. *Educ:* Case Inst Technol, BS, 65; Univ Minn, PhD(math), 70. *Prof Exp:* Asst prof, 70-76, ASSOC PROF MATH, COL WILLIAM & MARY, 76- *Mem:* Math Asn Am. *Res:* Optimal allocation of spare parts, including fixed spares pool set up charges; maximizing the permanent function over the set of doubly stochastic matrices. *Mailing Add:* Dept of Math Col of William & Mary Williamsburg VA 23185

DREW, LAWRENCE JAMES, b Astoria, NY, Dec 18, 40; m; c 1. STATISTICS, GEOLOGY. *Educ:* Univ NH, BS, 62; Pa State Univ, MS, 64, PhD, 66. *Prof Exp:* Fel, Pa State Univ, 66-67; res geologist, US Bur Mines, 67; res scientist, Geotech Div, Teledyne Inc, 67-69; sr res geologist, Cities Serv Oil Co, 69-72; GEOLOGIST, US GEOL SURV, 72- *Mem:* Int Asn Math Geol; Am Statist Asn. *Res:* Statistical and economic analysis of supply of mineral resources; analysis and modeling of the exploration process. *Mailing Add:* US Geol Surv Mail Stop 920 Reston VA 22092

DREW, LELAND OVERBEY, b Charleston, SC, June 13, 23; m 44; c 1. AGRICULTURAL ENGINEERING. *Educ:* Clemson Col, BS, 43; Iowa State Col, MS, 45; Mich State Univ, PhD(agr eng), 63. *Prof Exp:* Instr agr eng, Clemson Col, 43-44; asst agr engr, Edisto Br, SC Agr Exp Sta, 45-47; from asst prof to assoc prof, Univ Ga, 47-56; adv, Int Co-op Admin, Lebanon, 56-59 & Pakistan, 59-60; assoc prof, Clemson Univ, 63-68; assoc prof, 68-77, PROF AGR ENG, OHIO STATE UNIV, 77- *Concurrent Pos:* Adv to dean, Col Technol & Agr Eng, Univ Udaipur, India. *Mem:* Am Soc Agr Engrs; Am Soc Eng Educ. *Res:* Agricultural machinery, including tillage and seedling mechanics; chemical preservation of hay; mechanization of vegetable production; instrumentation. *Mailing Add:* Dept of Agr Eng 2070 Neil Ave Columbus OH 43210

DREW, PHILIP GARFIELD, b Dedham, Mass, Jan 25, 32; m 61; c 2. MEDICAL SCIENCES, HEALTH SCIENCES. *Educ:* Carnegie Inst Technol, BS, 54; Harvard Univ, SM, 59, PhD(eng), 64. *Prof Exp:* Res asst control systs eng, Harvard Univ, 61-64; mem prof staff eng, Arthur D Little, Inc, 64-76, mem sr staff, 76-81; PRES, DREW CONSULTS, INC, 81- *Mem:* Inst Elec & Electronics Engrs; Soc Photo-Optical Instrumentation Engrs; NY Acad Sci. *Res:* Systems analyses; medical imaging equipment design. *Mailing Add:* 101 Bedford Rd Carlisle MA 01741

DREW, ROBERT TAYLOR, b Red Bank, NJ, Apr 22, 36; m 62; c 3. TOXICOLOGY. *Educ:* Rensselaer Polytech Inst, BS, 58; NY Univ, MS, 62, PhD(radiation health), 68; Am Bd Toxicol, dipl. *Prof Exp:* Sanit chem trainee, NY State Dept Health, 58-59; chemist, NJ Dept Health, 60; res asst, Inst Environ Med, NY Univ Med Ctr, 60-67, assoc res scientist, 67-69, instr, 69-70; sr staff fel, Nat Inst Environ Health Sci, 70-74; supvry phys scientist, Nat Inst Environ Health Sci, 70-74; ASSOC PROF, PATH DEPT, STATE UNIV NY STONYBROOK, 79- *Concurrent Pos:* Sr staff fel, Nat Inst Environ Health Sci, 70-74. *Mem:* Soc Toxicol; Health Physics Soc; Am Indust Hyg Asn; Am Conf Govt Indust Hygienists; NY Acad Sci. *Res:* Inhalation toxicology, especially effects of short and long term exposures to environmental agents and combinations of agents; environmental radiation. *Mailing Add:* 24 View Rd Setauket NY 11733

DREW, T JOHN, b Pinjarra, Australia, Oct 23, 41; m 67; c 4. FOREST MANAGEMENT, FOREST GENETICS. *Educ:* BC Inst Technol, dipl forestry, 67; NC State Univ, BSc, 70, PhD(forestry), 73. *Prof Exp:* Sr cruiser & party chief, Forestal Int Ltd, Vancouver, BC, 67-68; res asst forestry, Sch Forest Resources, NC State Univ, 70-72; chief res & develop, Jari Florestal E Agropecuaria Ltd, Brazil, 72-74; scientist, centralia, Wash, 74-79, MANAGER FOREST REGENERATION & RES, WEYERHAEUSER, CAN LTD, 79- *Mem:* Soc Am Foresters; Can Inst Forestry. *Res:* Developing management plans which optimize the returns from the use of genetically improved planting stock, utilizing environmental variation and alternatives for cultural treatment. *Mailing Add:* Weyerhaeuser Ltd Forest Regeneration & Res Ctr RR #3 St Annes Rd Armstrong BC V0E 1B0 Can

DREW, WILLIAM ARTHUR, b Grosse Pointe, Mich, Apr 29, 29; m 57; c 1. ARACHNOLOGY. *Educ:* Marietta Col, AB, 51; Mich State Univ, PhD(entom), 58. *Prof Exp:* From asst prof to assoc prof, 58-68, PROF ENTOM, OKLA STATE UNIV, 68-, CUR, 58- *Mem:* Entom Soc Am; Entom Soc Can; Brit Arachnological Soc; Am Arachnological Soc. *Res:* Curator insect collection Oklahoma; taxonomy of Hemiptera and spiders. *Mailing Add:* Dept of Entom Okla State Univ Stillwater OK 74074

DREWES, HARALD D, b Ger, Nov 22, 27; nat US; m 57; c 2. GEOLOGY. *Educ:* Wash Univ, BA, 51; Yale Univ, MA, 52, PhD, 54. *Prof Exp:* GEOLOGIST, US GEOL SURV, 54- *Mem:* Am Geol Soc; Ger Geol Asn. *Res:* Thrust tectonics of the basin and range geologic province, especially southeastern California, eastern Nevada and southeastern Arizona, related problems of faulting, gneiss dome development, magmatism, sedimentation and mineralization. *Mailing Add:* US Geol Surv Mail Stop 930 Fed Ctr Box 25046 Denver CO 80225

DREWES, LESTER RICHARD, b Deshler, Ohio, Apr 11, 43; m 66; c 2. BIOCHEMISTRY. *Educ:* Capital Univ, BS, 65; Univ Minn, PhD(biochem), 70. *Prof Exp:* Fel biochem, Univ Wis, 70-73; asst scientist, 73-76; ASST PROF BIOCHEM, UNIV MINN, DULUTH, 76- *Mem:* Am Soc Biol Chemists; Am Physiol Soc; Int Soc Neurochem; Am Chem Soc; AAAS. *Res:* Transport and utilization of substrates by cells of the central nervous system in vivo and in vitro, under normal and pathological conditions. *Mailing Add:* Dept of Biochem Univ of Minn Duluth MN 55812

DREWES, PATRICIA ANN, b Chicago, Ill, Jan 12, 32. CLINICAL CHEMISTRY. *Educ:* Immaculate Heart Col, BA, 53; Univ Calif, Los Angeles, PhD(biol chem), 65. *Prof Exp:* Control chemist, Vitaminerals, Calif, 53-59; res biochemist, Dept Neurochem & Neuropharmaceut Res, Vet Admin Hosp, Sepulveda, Calif, 59-60; res fel med, Harvard Med Sch & Beth Israel Hosp, 65-67; res scientist, 67-74, asst dir res, 74-77, DIR GEN CHEM, BIO-SCI LABS, 77- *Mem:* AAAS; Am Chem Soc; NY Acad Sci; Am Asn Clin Chem. *Res:* Pharmaceutical analysis; serotonin metabolism; metabolic response of transplantable murine tumors and leukemia cells to radio- and chemotherapy; enzymology and radioimmunoassay. *Mailing Add:* Bio-Sci Labs 7600 Tyrone Ave Van Nuys CA 91405

DREWES, ROBERT CLIFTON, b San Francisco, Calif, Feb 14, 42; m 64; c 4. FUNCTIONAL MORPHOLOGY, AFRICAN AFFAIRS. *Educ:* San Francisco State Univ, BA, 69; Univ Calif, Los Angeles, PhD(biol), 81. *Prof Exp:* Asst dir, Nairobi Snake Park, Nat Mus Kenya, 69-70; curatorial assoc herpet, Calif Acad Sci, 70-73; teaching fel biol, Univ Calif, Los Angeles, 73-75; ASST CURATOR, DEPT HERPET, CALIF ACAD SCI, 75- *Concurrent Pos:* Res assoc, Nat Mus Kenya, 70-; bd dir, San Francisco Zool Soc, 79-81; mem world checklist comn, Asn Syst Collections, 81- *Mem:* Fel Royal Geog Soc; Am Soc Ichthyologists & Herpetologists; Soc Study Amphibians & Reptiles; Herpet Asn Africa. *Res:* Systematics and ecology of African herpetofauna; comparative physiology of arid-adapted amphibians; evolutionary relationships of ranoid frogs. *Mailing Add:* Dept Herpet Calif Acad Sci Golden Gate Park San Francisco CA 94118

DREWINKO, BENJAMIN, b Buenos Aires, Arg, Feb 10, 40; c 4. CELL KINETICS, CELLULAR PHARMACOLOGY. *Educ:* Nat Col Mitre, BS & BA, 56; Buenos Aires Univ, MD, 61; Univ Tex, PhD(biomed), 70. *Prof Exp:* Intern, Mt Sinai Hosp, Chicago, 63-64; resident, Mt Sinai Hosp, New York, 64-65; fel, 67-69, asst prof, 70-73, assoc prof, 73-79, PROF, M D ANDERSON HOSP, 79-, CHIEF HEMAT, 70- *Concurrent Pos:* Dir, Sch Med Technol & Blood Bank, M D Anderson Hosp, 73-75; mem, Computers & Biomath Study Sect, NIH, 76-77; assoc ed, Cancer Res, 82- *Mem:* Am Soc Hemat; Am Asn Cancer Res; Am Soc Clin Pathologists; Am Asn Pathologists; Cell Kinetics Soc (pres, 77-79). *Res:* Mechanisms regulating the growth of tumors and inhibition of this growth by natural agents or antitumor drugs. *Mailing Add:* Rm C3 019 6723 Bertner Houston TX 77030

DREWRY, WILLIAM ALTON, b Dyess, Ark, Oct 23, 36; m 59; c 3. CIVIL ENGINEERING, ENVIRONMENTAL ENGINEERING. *Educ:* Univ Ark, BS, 59, MS, 61; Stanford Univ, PhD(environ eng), 68. *Prof Exp:* Instr civil eng, Univ Ark, 60-62; res asst environ eng, Stanford Univ, 62-65; asst prof, Univ Ark, 65-68; from assoc prof to prof, Univ Tenn, Knoxville, 68-76; PROF CIVIL ENG & CHMN DEPT, OLD DOMINION UNIV, 76-, GRAD PROG DIR & PROF ENVIRON & SANIT ENG, 80- *Mem:* Water Pollution Control Fedn; Am Soc Eng Educ; Am Soc Civil Eng. *Res:* Water pollution control. *Mailing Add:* 992 Edwin Dr Virginia Beach VA 23462

DREWS, MICHAEL JAMES, b Milwaukee, Wis, Oct 2, 45; m 67; c 1. POLYMER CHEMISTRY, TEXTILE CHEMISTRY. *Educ:* Univ Wis-Madison, BS, 67; NTex State Univ, PhD(phys chem), 71. *Prof Exp:* Res assoc, 71-72, sr res assoc, 73-74, vis asst prof, 74-76, asst prof, 76-79, ASSOC PROF TEXTILES, CLEMSON UNIV, 79- *Honors & Awards:* Educ Serv Award, Plastics Inst Am, 75. *Mem:* Am Asn Textile Chemists and Colorists; Am Chem Soc. *Res:* Flame retardants and the chemistry of flame retardant materials; combustion and chemistry of flame retardant materials; surfactants and interfacial phenomena; spectroscopy as applied to polymeric materials; textile dyeing and finishing processes. *Mailing Add:* Dept Textiles Clemson Univ Clemson SC 29631

DREWS, REINHOLD ELDOR, b Mellowdale, Alta, Can, Sept 23, 32; m 57; c 2. PHYSICS. *Educ:* Univ BC, BA, 55, MSc, 57; Univ Calif, Berkeley, PhD(physics), 62. *Prof Exp:* Sr physicist, Astronautics Div, Gen Dynamics, Calif, 61-63; staff scientist, 63-64; scientist, Res & Eng Div, 64-80, SR SCIENTIST, WEBSTER RES CTR, XEROX CORP, ROCHESTER, 80- *Res:* Optical and electrical properties of semiconductor materials; modulation spectroscopy of solids; optical properties of particulate pigment materials; electroluminescent, photoconductive, laser and positive-negative junction devices; paramagnetic resonance properties of solids; photoelectrothoretic color imaging systems; magnetic video recording technology. *Mailing Add:* Xerox Corp 800 Phillips Rd Webster NY 14580

DREXEL, R(OGER) E(DWARD), b Rochester, NY, Feb 10, 20; m 50; c 1. CHEMICAL ENGINEERING. *Educ:* Univ Rochester, BS, 41; Mass Inst Technol, ScD(chem eng), 46. *Prof Exp:* Res assoc, Mass Inst Technol, 42-44; res assoc, 44-62, mgr planning div, 62-66, dir mfg div, 66-67, asst gen mgr dept, 67-69, gen mgr dept, 69-72, vpres biochem, 72-80, VPRES & GEN MGR, PLASTIC PROD & RESINS DEPT, E I DU PONT DE NEMOURS & CO, INC, 80- *Mem:* Am Inst Chem Engrs; Am Chem Soc. *Mailing Add:* Plastic Prod & Resins Dept E I DuPont de Nemours & Co Inc 1007 Market St Wilmington DE 19898

DREXLER, EDWARD JAMES, b Cincinnati, Ohio, Feb 9, 38; m 63; c 4. ANALYTICAL CHEMISTRY. *Educ:* Xavier Univ, Ohio, BS, 59, MS, 62; Wayne State Univ, PhD(zirconium chem), 65. *Prof Exp:* Asst, Xavier Univ, 59-61; assoc, Wayne State Univ, 61-64; asst prof, 64-68, ASSOC PROF CHEM, UNIV WIS, WHITEWATER, 68- *Mem:* Am Chem Soc. *Res:* Analytical chemistry of zirconium and hafnium; specific ion electrodes. *Mailing Add:* Dept of Chem Univ Wis Whitewater WI 53190

DREXLER, HENRY, b Carnegie, Pa, June 24, 27; m 57; c 2. MICROBIOLOGY. *Educ:* Pa State Univ, BS, 54; Univ Rochester, PhD(microbiol), 60. *Prof Exp:* Technician clin chem, Brookhaven Nat Lab, 54-56; instr microbiol, Sch Med, Univ Southern Calif, 60-62; USPHS fel microbial genetics, Karolinska Inst, Sweden, 62-64; from asst prof to assoc prof, 64-75, PROF MICROBIOL, BOWMAN GRAY SCH MED, 75- *Mem:* Am Soc Microbiol. *Res:* Microbial genetics, especially bacteriophage-host cell relationships and transduction. *Mailing Add:* Dept of Microbiol & Immunol Bowman Gray Sch of Med Winston-Salem NC 27103

DREYER, DAVID, b Snoqualmie Falls, Wash, Dec 22, 30; m 53; c 2. ORGANIC CHEMISTRY. *Educ:* Univ Wash, BS, 54, PhD(org chem), 60. *Prof Exp:* NIH fel, 60-61; chemist, Fruit & Veg Chem Lab, USDA, 61-68; from assoc prof to prof chem, San Francisco State Univ, 68-78; CHEMIST, USDA, 78- *Mem:* The Chem Soc. *Res:* Natural products chemistry; chemotaxonomy; structure determination of natural products. *Mailing Add:* USDA 800 Buchanan St Albany CA 94706

DREYER, DUANE ARTHUR, b Ypsilanti, Mich, May 10, 42; m 65; c 2. NEUROPHYSIOLOGY, NEUROPHARMACOLOGY. *Educ:* Univ Cincinnati, BS, 65; Univ Pittsburgh, PhD(pharmacol), 71. *Prof Exp:* Instr pharmacol, Sch Med, Univ Pittsburgh, 71-72; res assoc physiol, Div Neurosurg, Med Ctr, Duke Univ, 72-75; asst prof physiol, Sch Med & asst prof oral biol, Sch Dent, 75-80, ASSOC PROF PHYSIOL, SCH MED & ASSOC PROF ORAL BIOL, SCH DENT, UNIV NC, CHAPEL HILL, 80- *Concurrent Pos:* Res assoc physiol, Dent Res Ctr, Univ NC, 72-73; Nat Inst Dent Res career develop award, 75-80. *Mem:* Am Physiol Soc; Soc Neurosci. *Res:* Sensory neurophysiology; psychophysics; somatic sensation. *Mailing Add:* Dent Res Ctr 210H Univ of NC Chapel Hill NC 27514

DREYER, KIRT A, b Bemidji, Minn, Aug 10, 39; m 59; c 2. PHYSICAL INORGANIC CHEMISTRY, ANALYTICAL CHEMISTRY. *Educ:* Bemidji State Col, BS, 61; Univ Iowa, PhD(chem), 71. *Prof Exp:* ASSOC PROF CHEM, BEMIDJI STATE UNIV, 65- *Mem:* Am Chem Soc. *Res:* Metal complexes of amino acids; kinetics of rapid exchange processes. *Mailing Add:* Dept of Chem Bemidji State Univ Bemidji MN 56601

DREYER, ROBERT MARX, b Chicago, Ill, Jan 6, 14. ECONOMIC GEOLOGY. *Educ:* Northwestern Univ, BS, 34; Calif Inst Technol, MS, 37, PhD(geol), 39. *Prof Exp:* Asst geol, Northwestern Univ, 34-35; soil survr, US Soil Conserv Serv, 36; geologist, US Geol Surv, 38; instr, Univ Kans, 39-41, from asst prof to prof geol & chmn dept, 41-53; chief geologist, Kaiser Aluminum & Chem Corp, 53-59; asst chief geologist, Reynolds Metals Co, 59-61; pres, Western Mineral Assocs, 62-64; mgr mineral div, Assoc Oil & Gas Co, 64-65; PRES, WESTERN MINERAL ASSOCS, 65- *Mem:* Fel Geol Soc Am; Soc Econ Geol; Am Inst Mining, Metall & Petrol Engrs; fel Mineral Soc Am; Am Asn Petrol Geologists. *Res:* Petrography; geographic geology; mineralogy; geophysics; geochemistry. *Mailing Add:* Suite 605 1255 Post St San Francisco CA 94109

DREYER, WILLIAM J, b Kalamazoo, Mich, Aug 11, 28; m 52; c 3. MOLECULAR BIOLOGY, IMMUNOLOGY. *Educ:* Reed Col, BA, 52; Univ Wash, PhD(biochem), 56. *Prof Exp:* Fel, Polio Found, NIH, 56-57, res biochemist, 57-63; PROF BIOL, CALIF INST TECHNOL, 63- *Concurrent Pos:* Consult automated biomed anal to numerous orgn, 63-; mem adv bd, Hereditary Dis Found, 72- *Mem:* Soc Biol Chemists; Asn Advan Med Instrumentation; Biophys Soc; Genetics Soc Am. *Res:* Genetic and molecular basis of antibody formation and embryogenesis; tumor immunology; protein chemistry; development of automated biomedical instruments. *Mailing Add:* Div of Biol Calif Inst of Technol Pasadena CA 91125

DREYFUS, MARC GEORGE, physics, see previous edition

DREYFUS, PIERRE MARC, b Geneva, Switz, Oct 14, 23; US citizen; m 47; c 3. NEUROCHEMISTRY, NUTRITION. *Educ:* Tufts Col, BS, 47; Columbia Univ, MD, 51; Am Bd Psychiat & Neurol, dipl, 58. *Prof Exp:* Intern & asst resident med, NY Hosp, 51-53; asst & chief resident neurol, Harvard Med Sch, 53-55, asst neurol, 58-59, instr, 59-62, assoc, 62-66, asst prof, 66-68; PROF NEUROL & CHMN DEPT, UNIV CALIF, DAVIS, 68-; DIR, SACRAMENTO MED CTR, 68- *Concurrent Pos:* Res fel neuropath, Harvard Med Sch, 55-58; clin assoc, McLean Hosp, 62-67; adv neurosci, WHO, 74- *Mem:* Am Neurol Asn; Am Soc Clin Nutrit; Am Inst Nutrit; Int Soc Neurochem; Am Soc Neurochem. *Mailing Add:* Dept of Neurol Univ of Calif Sch of Med Davis CA 95616

DREYFUS, RUSSELL WARREN, b Michigan City, Ind, Dec 23, 29; c 2. LASERS. *Educ:* Purdue Univ, BS, 51, MS, 53; Yale Univ, MS, 58, PhD(physics), 60. *Prof Exp:* Tech staff mem semiconductor res, Hughes Aircraft Co, 53-54; guest assoc scientist, Brookhaven Nat Lab, 54-56; PHYSICIST, IBM CORP, 58- *Concurrent Pos:* Guest scientist, Swiss Fed Inst Technol, 64; Kernforschwngsanlage Juelich & Max Planck Plasma Physics, WGer, 81-82. *Mem:* Fel Am Phys Soc; NY Acad Sci. *Res:* Defects in ionic and semiconductor crystals by electrical, optical and mechanical properties; crystal growing; dynamical measurements using lasers; ultraviolet lasers pumped by relativistic electron beams; generation and detection of gas phase ions and atoms using tunable lasers; generation of Lyman-alpha radiation for measuring atomic hydrogen in tokamaks. *Mailing Add:* Thomas J Watson Res Ctr IBM Corp PO Box 218 Yorktown Heights NY 10598

DREYFUS, STUART ERNEST, b Ind, Oct 19, 31. OPERATIONS RESEARCH. *Educ:* Harvard Univ, AB, 53, PhD(appl math), 64. *Prof Exp:* Actuarial clerk, Metrop Life Ins Co, 53-54; numerical analyst, Gen Elec Co, 54-55; mathematician, Rand Corp, 55-67; assoc prof, 67-72, PROF INDUST ENG & OPERS RES, UNIV CALIF, BERKELEY, 72- *Res:* Mathematical methods of optimization; operations research; computational aspects of dynamic programming and variational problems; limits of scientific decision-making. *Mailing Add:* Dept of Indust Eng & Opers Res Univ of Calif Berkeley CA 94720

DREYFUSS, JACQUES, b St Gall, Switz, Jan 20, 37; US citizen; wid; c 2. BIOCHEMISTRY. *Educ:* Beloit Col, BS, 58; Johns Hopkins Univ, PhD(biochem), 63. *Prof Exp:* Fel biochem, Princeton Univ, 63-64; sect head drug metab, 64-77, SR RES FEL, DEPT DRUG SAFETY EVAL, E R SQUIBB & SONS, INC, 77- *Mem:* Am Soc Pharmacol & Exp Therapeut; NY Acad Sci; Am Soc Clin Pharmacol Therapeut. *Res:* Drug metabolism; central nervous system and cardiovascular agents. *Mailing Add:* Squibb Inst for Med Res New Brunswick NJ 08903

DREYFUSS, M(AX) PETER, b Frankfurt, Ger, Sept 24, 32; nat US; m 54; c 2. POLYMER CHEMISTRY. *Educ:* Union Col, BS, 52; Cornell Univ, PhD(chem), 57. *Prof Exp:* From res chemist to sr res chemist, Res Ctr, 56-67, res assoc, 66-72, SR RES ASSOC, CORP RES, B F GOODRICH CO, 72- *Concurrent Pos:* Imp Chem Indust fel, Univ Liverpool, 63-65. *Mem:* Am Chem Soc. *Res:* Polymerization of cyclic ethers; polymer chemistry and synthesis. *Mailing Add:* Corp Res B F Goodrich Co Brecksville OH 44141

DREYFUSS, PATRICIA, b Reading, Pa, Apr 28, 32; m 54; c 2. POLYMER CHEMISTRY. *Educ:* Univ Rochester, BS, 54; Univ Akron, PhD(polymer sci), 64. *Prof Exp:* Am Asn Univ Women Marie Curie int fel, Univ Liverpool, 64-65; res chemist, B F Goodrich Res Ctr, 65-71; res assoc chem, Case Western Reserve Univ, 71-74, NIH spec fel, 72-73; RES ASSOC, INST POLYMER SCI, UNIV AKRON, 74- *Mem:* Adhesion Soc (secy, 81-); Am Chem Soc. *Res:* Mechanisms and kinetics of cationic polymerization of cyclic ethers; synthesis and characterization of related graft copolymers; chemical structure-property relationships of polymers; morphology; adhesion. *Mailing Add:* 506 West Point Dr Akron OH 44313

DREYFUSS, ROBERT GEORGE, b Frankfurt-am-Main, Ger, Sept 6, 31; nat US; m 56. INORGANIC CHEMISTRY, GLASS TECHNOLOGY. *Educ:* Union Col, BS, 52. *Prof Exp:* Mgr res & develop control lab, Thatcher Glass Mfg Co, Inc, 52-61; asst dir res & eng, Glass Containers Corp, 61-65; vpres tech serv, Containers, Kraftco Corp, 66-80; VPRES TECH SERV, METROPAK CONTAINERS CORP, 66-; VPRES ENG, MIDLAND GLASS CO, 80- *Mem:* Am Chem Soc; Am Ceramic Soc; Air Pollution Control Asn; German Soc Glass Technol. *Res:* Glass manufacturing. *Mailing Add:* Midland Glass Co Inc Box 557 Cliffwood NJ 07721

DRIBIN, DANIEL MACCABAEUS, b Chicago, Ill, Dec 10, 13; m 36; c 1. ALGEBRA. *Educ:* Univ Chicago, SB, 33, SM, 34, PhD(math), 36. *Prof Exp:* Nat Res fel, Inst Advan Study & Yale Univ, 36-38; instr math, Univ Nebr, 38-42; jr res analyst, US War Dept, 42; analyst, Nat Security Agency, 46-73; EXEC GRAD COMT, DEPT MATH, UNIV MD, 73- *Concurrent Pos:* lectr math, George Washington Univ, 46-58, assoc prof lectr, 58-60, prof lectr, 60-81. *Mem:* Am Math Soc; Math Asn Am. *Res:* Algebraic number fields; algebraic number theory; projective geometry; history of modern mathematics. *Mailing Add:* 1016 Kathryn Rd Silver Spring MD 20904

DRICKAMER, HARRY GEORGE, b Cleveland, Ohio, Nov 19, 18; m 42; c 5. CHEMISTRY, CHEMICAL ENGINEERING. *Educ:* Univ Mich, BSE, 4 'S, 42, PhD(chem eng), 46. *Prof Exp:* Res group leader, Pan Am Refining Co, Tex, 42-46; from asst prof to assoc prof, 46-53, PROF CHEM ENG & PHYS CHEM, UNIV ILL, URBANA, 53- *Honors & Awards:* Colburn Award, Am Inst Chem Eng, 47, Alpha Chi Sigma Award, 66, Walker Award, 72; Ipatieff Prize, Am Chem Soc, 56, Langmuir Award in chem physics, 74; Buckley Solid State Physics Prize, Am Phys Soc, 67; Bendix Res Award, Am Soc Eng Educ, 68; P W Bridgman Award, AIRAPT, 77; Michelson-Morley Award, Case Western Reserve Univ, 78. *Mem:* Nat Acad Sci; Am Chem Soc; Am Inst Chem Eng; Am Phys Soc; Am Soc Eng Educ. *Res:* Physical chemistry; properties of matter at high pressure. *Mailing Add:* Sch of Chem Sci Univ of Ill Urbana IL 61801

DRICKAMER, LEE CHARLES, b Ann Arbor, Mich, May 25, 46; m 68. ANIMAL BEHAVIOR, ECOLOGY. *Educ:* Oberlin Col, BA, 67; Mich State Univ, PhD(zool), 70. *Prof Exp:* Res scientist primatology, NC Found Ment Health Res, 71-72; asst prof biol, 72-78, ASSOC PROF BIOL, WILLIAMS COL, 78- *Concurrent Pos:* NSF fel, NC State Univ & NC Dept Ment Health, 70-71; NIMH res grant, 73; assoc ed, Am Midland Naturalist, 74-; NIH res grant, Nat Inst Child Health & Develop, 75- *Mem:* Sigma Xi; Animal Behav Soc; Ecol Soc Am; Brit Ecol Soc; Int Primatol Soc. *Res:* Laboratory studies of factors affecting sexual maturation in rodents and field investigation of behavioral ecology and bioenergetics of populations of forest rodents. *Mailing Add:* Dept of Biol Williams Col Williamstown MA 01267

DRIES, WILLIAM CHARLES, b Milwaukee, Wis, Nov 4, 30; m 57; c 3. MECHANICAL & METALLURGICAL ENGINEERING. *Educ:* Univ Wis, BS, 53, MS, 56, PhD(metall eng), 62. *Prof Exp:* Consult mech engr, Lofte & Fredericksen, 56-59; res asst metall eng, 60-62, PROJ ASSOC MECH ENG, UNIV WIS, MADISON, 62-; PRES, DRIES JACQUES ASSOCS, INC, 62- *Mem:* Am Soc Mech Engrs; Nat Soc Prof Engrs; Am Soc Heat, Refrig & Air Conditioning Engrs; Am Soc Metals; Brit Inst Metals. *Res:* Physical metallurgy of iron; protective construction for nuclear weapons; project management using network methods; computer applications to engineering problems. *Mailing Add:* 1600 Verona St Middleton WI 53562

DRIESCH, ALBERT JOHN, b Pittsburgh, Pa, Sept 2, 20. ORGANIC CHEMISTRY. *Educ:* St Francis Col, Pa, BA, 43; Univ Notre Dame, MS, 51. *Prof Exp:* Asst prof, 56-63, PROF CHEM, ST FRANCIS COL, PA, 63-, HEAD DEPT, 52- *Mem:* Am Chem Soc. *Res:* General organic chemistry. *Mailing Add:* Dept of Chem St Francis Col Loretta PA 15940

DRIESENS, ROBERT JAMES, b Redford, Mich, Jan 12, 18; m 53; c 3. BACTERIOLOGY. *Educ:* Calvin Col, AB, 39; Mich State Univ, MS, 49, PhD(bact), 52. *Prof Exp:* Bacteriologist, Labs, Mich Dept Health, 52-60; head bact prod develop dept, Corvel, Inc, Omaha, 60-64, develop assoc, 64-65; sr bacteriologist, 65-69, sr microbiologist, 69-75, MEM TECH SERV, BIOCHEM PROD, ELI LILLY & CO, 75- *Mem:* Am Soc Microbiol; AAAS; Sigma Xi. *Res:* Mass culture of microbes; microbial conversions of chemicals; microbial nutrition. *Mailing Add:* Dept MC 413 PO Box 618 Indianapolis IN 46206

DRIEVER, CARL WILLIAM, b Chicago, Ill, Mar 4, 38; m 64; c 1. CLINICAL PHARMACOLOGY. *Educ:* Purdue Univ, BS, 61, MS, 63, PhD(pharmacol), 65. *Prof Exp:* Teaching asst pharm, Sch Pharm, Purdue Univ, 61-62; asst prof pharmacol, Sch Pharm, Univ Md, 65-67; asst prof, 67-68, assoc prof pharmaceut, 68-73, ASSOC PROF CLIN PHARMACY, COL PHARM, UNIV HOUSTON, 73-, MEM GRAD FAC, 80- *Mem:* Am Pharmaceut Asn; Am Soc Hosp Pharmacists; Am Asn Cols Pharm. *Res:* Drug dependence and tolerance; utilization review; drug interactions; pharmacokinetics. *Mailing Add:* Col of Pharm Univ of Houston Houston TX 77004

DRIGGERS, FRANK EDGAR, b El Paso, Tex, Dec 14, 19; m 45; c 2. REACTOR PHYSICS. *Educ:* Univ Calif, AB, 40; Univ Mich, AM, 48, PhD(physics), 51. *Prof Exp:* Jr astronr, Naval Observ, Washington, DC, 40-41; res physicist, Eng Res Inst, Univ Mich, 46-50; reactor physicist, 51-64, MEM STAFF ADV OPER PLANNING, E I DU PONT DE NEMOURS & CO, INC, 64- *Mem:* Fel Am Nuclear Soc; AAAS. *Res:* Isotope technology; nuclear power analysis. *Mailing Add:* Savannah River Lab E I du Pont de Nemours & Co Aiken SC 29801

DRILL, VICTOR ALEXANDER, b Sunderland, Eng, June 10, 16; nat US; 25; m 40; c 3. PHARMACOLOGY. *Educ:* Long Island Univ, BS, 38; Princeton Univ, PhD(physiol), 41; Yale Univ, MD, 48. *Prof Exp:* Asst chemist, Fleischmann Labs, NY, 37-38; instr pharmacol, Col Physicians & Surg, Columbia Univ, 43-44; from instr to asst prof, Med Sch, Yale Univ, 44-48; prof, Med Sch, Wayne Univ, 48-53; dir biol res, G D Searle & Co, 53-70, dir sci & prof affairs, 70-74; PROF PHARMACOL, COL MED, UNIV ILL, CHICAGO, 75- *Concurrent Pos:* Jacobus fel, Princeton Univ, 41-42; Nat Res Coun fel, Northwestern Univ, 42-43; dir educ & assoc physician, Detroit Receiving Hosp, 49-53; prof lectr pharmacol, Col Med, Univ Ill, 54-74; lectr pharmacol, Med Sch, Northwestern Univ, 54-67; mem endocrine panel, Cancer Chemother Nat Serv Ctr, 58-62; consult, Nat Cancer Inst, 65-67; mem US Comn, World Med Asn; mem, Drug Res Bd, Nat Res Coun, 71-76; mem sci adv bd, Nat Ctr Toxicol Res, Fed Drug Admin, Dept Health, Educ & Welfare, 75-76. *Mem:* Soc Toxicol (pres, 72-73); fel NY Acad Sci; fel Royal Soc Med; Am Physiol Soc; Int Family Planning Res Asn (vpres, 72-74). *Res:* Endocrinology, endocrinology, oral contraceptives. *Mailing Add:* Dept of Pharmacol Univ of Ill Col of Med Chicago IL 60680

DRINKARD, WILLIAM CHARLES, JR, b Eufaula, Ala, May 11, 29. INORGANIC CHEMISTRY. *Educ:* Huntingdon Col, BA, 50; Ala Polytech Inst, MS, 52; Univ Ill, PhD(inorg chem), 56. *Prof Exp:* Chemist, Food Mach & Chem Corp, 52-53; chemist, E I du Pont de Nemours & Co, 55; asst prof chem, Univ Calif, Los Angeles, 56-60; mem staff, Exp Sta, 60-70, res supvr, Plastics Dept, 70-72, lab dir, Sabine River Lab, 72-74, ASSOC DIR, CENT RES & DEVELOP DEPT, EXP STA, E I DU PONT DE NEMOURS & CO, INC, 74- *Mem:* Am Chem Soc. *Res:* Complex inorganic compounds; ligand reactivity; homogeneous catalysis by metal ions; organometallic chemistry. *Mailing Add:* 104 Center Ct E I DuPont De Nemours & Co Inc Wilmington DE 19898

DRINKER, PHILIP ALDRICH, b Brookline, Mass, Apr 7, 32; m 53. BIOENGINEERING. *Educ:* Yale Univ, BS, 54; Mass Inst Technol, PhD(hydrodyn), 61. *Prof Exp:* Asst prof civil eng, Mass Inst Technol, 61-65; from res assoc to prin assoc surg & chief bioeng div, 65-73, SR ASSOC SURG, HARVARD MED SCH, 73-; MEM STAFF, DEPT BIOMED ENG, BRIGHAM & WOMEN'S HOSP, 80- *Concurrent Pos:* Consult surg & dir clin eng serv, Peter Bent Brigham Hosp, 65-80; from lectr to sr lectr, Mass Inst Technol, 65-; mem, Cardiol Adv Comt, Nat Heart, Lung & Blood Inst, 75-77; consult bioeng, New England Sinai Hosp, 78- *Mem:* Biomed Eng Soc; Am Soc Artificial Internal Organs; Rehab Eng Soc NAm. *Res:* Rehabilitation engineering; blood oxygenation; equipment design for respiratory care. *Mailing Add:* Dept Biomed Eng Brigham & Women's Hosp Boston MA 02115

DRINKWATER, WILLIAM ORTMO, b Providence, RI, Sept 29, 19; m 49; c 2. HORTICULTURE. *Educ:* Univ Mass, BVA, 47, MS, 49; Rutgers Univ, PhD(hort), 54. *Prof Exp:* Asst veg crops, Rutgers Univ, 51-52; instr, Univ Conn, 49-52, asst prof, 52-56; from asst prof to assoc prof, 56-63, PROF HORT & FORESTRY, RUTGERS UNIV, 63- *Mem:* Am Soc Hort Sci; Am Inst Biol Sci; Sigma Xi. *Res:* Variety evaluation; undergraduate teaching. *Mailing Add:* Blake Hall Cook Col PO Box 231 Rutgers Univ New Brunswick NJ 08903

DRINNAN, ALAN JOHN, b Bristol, Eng, Apr 6, 32; US citizen; m 56; c 2. ORAL PATHOLOGY. *Educ:* Univ Bristol, BDS, 54, MB, ChB, 62; FDSRCS, 62; State Univ NY Buffalo, DDS, 64. *Prof Exp:* Tutor oral surg, Univ Bristol, 57-58; vis asst prof oral path, 62-65, assoc prof, 65-70, PROF ORAL MED & CHMN DEPT, SCH DENT, STATE UNIV NY BUFFALO, 70- *Concurrent Pos:* Consult dentist & chief dent serv, Buffalo Gen Hosp, 66-; WHO consult, Port Moresby Dent Col, Papua, New Guinea, 71; Fulbright prof, Univ Melbourne, 81. *Mem:* Int Asn Dent Res; fel Am Acad Oral Path; Am Dent Asn. *Res:* Experimental carcinogenesis; dental education; medical-dental relationships. *Mailing Add:* 3435 Main St Buffalo NY 14214

DRISCOLL, DENNIS MICHAEL, b Warren, Pa, July 10, 34; m 69. METEOROLOGY. *Educ:* Pa State Univ, BS, 59, MS, 61; Univ Wis, PhD(meteorol), 71. *Prof Exp:* Res assoc meteorol, Travelers Res Ctr, 61-62; instr geog, Univ Wis-Milwaukee, 62-64, teaching asst meteorol, 65-66, instr geog, Univ Wis Ctr Syst, 64-65; ASST PROF METEOROL, TEX A&M UNIV, 69- *Mem:* Am Meteorol Soc; Int Soc Biometeorol. *Res:* Human biometeorology; statistical meteorology-climatology; hydrometeorology. *Mailing Add:* Dept Meteorol Tex A&M Univ College Station TX 77843

DRISCOLL, DOROTHY H, b Boston, Mass, May 30, 24. MEDICAL BIOPHYSICS. *Educ:* Radcliffe Col, SB, 46; Smith Col, MA, 49. *Prof Exp:* Instr sci, Northampton Sch Girls, 46-47; from asst biol sci to instr zool, Smith Col, 48-50; technician, Biophys Lab, Harvard Med Sch, 51-53, res asst clin isotopes, 53-55; res assoc & health safety officer, Atomic Bomb Casualty Comn, Nat Acad Sci, 54-56; jr tech specialist, Med Physics Div, Brookhaven Nat Lab, 56-61; res assoc radiol, 61-67, asst prof, 67-71, assoc prof med physics, 71-76, ASSOC PROF RADIOL, MED COL, THOMAS JEFFERSON UNIV, 76- *Concurrent Pos:* Investr, Marine Biol Labs, Woods Hole, 49-50; adj lectr radiol health prog, Physics Div, Manhattan Col, 65-69; consult clin radioisotopes, Sacred Heart Hosp, Allentown, 66-68, dept oncol, Children's Hosp, Philadelphia, 71- & Am Found New Affairs-New Access Routes to Med Careers, 72-; affil staff, Dept Obstet & Gynec, St Barnabas Hosp, NJ, 74- *Mem:* Am Asn Physicists in Med; Radiol Soc NAm; Radiation Res Soc; Soc Nuclear Med; Int Soc Magnetic Resonance. *Res:* Clinical isotopes; electron paramatic resonance applied to oncology. *Mailing Add:* Dept of Physics Thomas Jefferson Univ Philadelphia PA 19107

DRISCOLL, EGBERT GOTZIAN, b Indianapolis, Ind, Nov 10, 29. INVERTEBRATE ECOLOGY, INVERTEBRATE PALEONTOLOGY. *Educ:* Oberlin Col, BA, 52; Univ Nebr, MS, 56; Univ Mich, PhD(geol), 62. *Prof Exp:* Asst geol, Univ Nebr, 55-56; asst, Mus Paleont, Univ Mich, 57-58, instr geol, Univ & asst cur mus, 60-63; from asst prof to assoc prof, 63-71, PROF GEOL, WAYNE STATE UNIV, 71- *Concurrent Pos:* Fulbright res fel, Finland, 75. *Mem:* Soc Econ Paleont & Mineral; Brit Palaeont Asn; Australian Geol Soc; Am Soc Limnol & Oceanog; Marine Biol Asn UK. *Res:* Benthic ecology of recent marine invertebrates, emphasis upon animal-sediment-water interactions; applications to paleoecologic interpretations; destruction of invertebrate skeletons and its geologic significance. *Mailing Add:* Dept of Geol Wayne State Univ Detroit MI 48202

DRISCOLL, GARY LEE, b Campbellsville, Pa, Mar 30, 40; m 59; c 3. ORGANIC CHEMISTRY. *Educ:* Pa State Univ, BS, 62; Univ Del, PhD(org chem), 68. *Prof Exp:* Res chemist, Res & Develop, 64-70, SR RES CHEMIST, CORP RES, SUN OIL CO, 70- *Mem:* Am Chem Soc; Soc Coatings Technol. *Res:* Development of synthetic lubricants; synthesis and characterization of polymers and oligomers; organic syntheses via photochemistry and electrochemistry; organic synthesis and reaction mechanisms. *Mailing Add:* Sun Tech Box 1135 Marcus Hook PA 19061

DRISCOLL, GEORGE C(LARENCE), JR, b Mineola, NY, Jan 26, 27; div; c 2. CIVIL ENGINEERING. *Educ:* Rutgers Univ, BS, 50; Lehigh Univ, MS, 52, PhD(civil eng), 58. *Prof Exp:* Asst civil eng, 50-52, asst engr tests, Fritz Eng Lab, 52-57, from res instr to res assoc prof, 57-65, PROF CIVIL ENG, LEHIGH UNIV, 65-, ASSOC DIR, FRITZ ENG LAB, 69- *Honors & Awards:* Huber Res Prize, Am Soc Civil Engrs, 66; Davis Silver Medal Award, Am Welding Soc, 58, Adams Mem Award, 70. *Mem:* Am Welding Soc; Nat Soc Prof Engrs; Am Soc Civil Engrs. *Res:* Plastic analysis and design of welded continuous frames and their components; plastic design of multistory steel frames; computer-aided design. *Mailing Add:* Dept of Civil Eng Lehigh Univ Bethlehem PA 18015

DRISCOLL, JOHN G, b New York, NY, Apr 17, 33. MATHEMATICS. *Educ:* Iona Col, BS, 54; St Johns Univ, MS, 57; Columbia Univ, PhD(math), 69. *Prof Exp:* Teacher, St Joseph's Acad, WI, 57-61 & Power Mem Acad, NY, 61-65; asst prof math, 65-71, asst to pres, 69-71, prof math, 71-77, PRES, IONA COL, 71- *Concurrent Pos:* Vchmn, Bd Trustees, Comn Independent Col & Univs State NY; dir, Retional Adv Bd, Nat Bank Westchester; dir, Drexel Burnham Educ Fund. *Mem:* Math Asn Am. *Res:* Algebraic integration theory; mathematical education; mathematical analysis for the behavioral sciences. *Mailing Add:* Off of the Pres Iona Col New Rochelle NY 10801

DRISCOLL, JOHN STANFORD, b Olean, NY, May 31, 34; m 62; c 3. MEDICINAL CHEMISTRY. *Educ:* Mich State Univ, BS, 56; Princeton Univ, MA, 58, PhD(org chem), 60. *Prof Exp:* Sr res chemist, Boston Lab, Monsanto Res Corp, 60-64, res group leader, 64-68; res chemist, 68-74, HEAD, DRUG DESIGN & CHEM SECT, NAT CANCER INST, 74-, DEP CHIEF, LAB MED CHEM & BIOL, 77-, ACTG ASSOC DIR, DEVELOP THERAPEUTICS PROG, 80- *Mem:* Am Chem Soc; Am Asn Cancer Res. *Res:* Drug design; structure-activity relationships; anticancer drugs. *Mailing Add:* Nat Cancer Inst Bldg 37 Rm 6D-22 Bethesda MD 20014

DRISCOLL, MICHAEL JOHN, b Peekskill, NY, Sept 8, 34; wid; c 1. NUCLEAR ENGINEERING. *Educ:* Carnegie Inst Technol, BS, 55; Univ Fla, MS, 62; Mass Inst Technol, NuclE, 64, ScD(nuclear eng), 66. *Prof Exp:* Eng analyst, Phillips Petrol Co, 55-56; nuclear propulsion engr, naval reactor br, Atomic Energy Comn & nuclear propulsion div, bur ships, US Navy, 57-60; from asst prof to assoc prof, 69-80, PROF NUCLEAR ENG, MASS INST TECHNOL, 80- *Honors & Awards:* Outstanding Teacher Award, Am Soc Eng Educ, 75. *Mem:* Am Nuclear Soc; Am Soc Eng Educ. *Res:* Fast and thermal reactor physics and design; engineering economics and fuel management. *Mailing Add:* Dept of Nuclear Eng Mass Inst Technol 138 Albany St Cambridge MA 02139

DRISCOLL, RICHARD CORNELIUS, b Worcester, Mass, July 17, 41; m 65; c 2. CLINICAL CHEMISTRY, PHARMACEUTICAL CHEMISTRY. *Educ:* Northeastern Univ, BS, 64, MS, 66; Univ Conn, PhD(pharmaceut chem), 71. *Prof Exp:* Sr res scientist biochem, Beecham Labs, 70-72, mgr, 72-74; sect head clin chem, Dade Div, 74-76, dir sci planning, 76-79, DIR CLIN SYSTS RES & DEVELOP, AM DADE DIV, AM HOSP SUPPLY CORP, 79- *Mem:* Am Asn Clin Chem; Asn Clin Scientists; NY Acad Sci; Am Pharmaceut Asn. *Mailing Add:* Am Dade Div Am Hosp Supply Corp PO Box 520672 Miami FL 33152

DRISCOLL, RICHARD JAMES, b Chicago, Ill, Aug 14, 28. ANALYTICAL MATHEMATICS. *Educ:* Loyola Univ, Ill, BS, 50, AM, 51; Northwestern Univ, PhD(math), 59. *Prof Exp:* Instr, Northwestern Univ, 57-58; from instr to asst prof, 58-66, ASSOC PROF, LOYOLA UNIV, CHICAGO, 66- *Mem:* Am Math Soc; Math Asn Am. *Res:* Ordinary differential equations; calculus of variations. *Mailing Add:* Dept Math Loyola Univ 820 N Michigan Ave Chicago IL 60611

DRISCOLL, RICHARD STARK, b Denver, Colo, Sept 16, 28; m 54; c 2. RANGE MANAGEMENT, REMOTE SENSING. *Educ:* Colo State Univ, BS, 51, MS, 57; Ore State Univ, PhD(range ecol & soils), 62. *Prof Exp:* Range conservationist, Pac NW Forest & Range Exp Sta, 52-56, proj leader range mgt & wildlife habitat res, 56-60, wildlife habitat res, 60-62, range mgt res, Div Watershed, Recreation & Range Res, 62-65, prin range ecologist, 65-75, MGR RESOURCES EVAL TECH PROG, ROCKY MOUNTAIN FOREST & RANGE EXP STA, US FOREST SERV, 75- *Concurrent Pos:* Lectr, Ore State Univ, 58-60; fac affil, Colo State Univ, 65-; spec instr, Univ Denver, 71. *Mem:* Ecol Soc Am; Am Soc Range Mgt; Am Inst Biol Sci; Am Soc Photogram. *Res:* Range ecology including ecosystem classification; remote sensing of range, wildlife habitat and watershed resources. *Mailing Add:* Rocky Mt Forest & Range Exp Sta US Forest Serv Ft Collins CO 80526

DRISCOLL, WILLIAM THORVALD, b Pagoda, Colo, Jan 5, 20; m 46; c 2. ZOOLOGY. *Educ:* Univ Denver, BA, 42, MS, 48; Univ Calif, PhD(zool), 54. *Prof Exp:* Teacher, High Sch, Colo, 43-44; instr zool, Univ Denver, 44-48; asst, Univ Calif, 48-50, assoc, 50-51; from asst prof to assoc prof, 51-64, chmn dept biol sci, 58-68, PROF BIOL SCI, UNIV DENVER, 64-, ASSOC DEAN COL ARTS & SCI, 68- *Concurrent Pos:* Mem comt exam, Natural Sci Test Col Level Exam Prog, Educ Testing Serv, 71. *Mem:* Fel AAAS; Am Soc Zool; Nat Asn Biol Teachers; Asn Am Med Cols. *Res:* Experimental embryology; amphibian hypophysis and thyroid; teaching by closed circuit television. *Mailing Add:* Dept of Biol Univ of Denver Denver CO 80210

DRISKELL, JUDY ANNE, b Detroit, Mich, Sept 29, 43. NUTRITION. *Educ:* Univ Southern Miss, BS, 65; Purdue Univ, MS, 67, PhD(nutrit), 70. *Prof Exp:* Asst prof nutrit & foods, Auburn Univ, 70-72 & Fla State Univ, 72-74; assoc prof, 74-78, PROF HUMAN NUTRIT & FOODS, VA POLYTECH INST & STATE UNIV, 78- *Mem:* Am Inst Nutrit; Inst Food Technologists; Am Home Econ Asn; Soc Nutrit Educ. *Res:* Vitamin B6 requirements and status; effects of massive ingestion of ascorbic acid; malnutrition and behavior and cellular alterations. *Mailing Add:* Dept Human Nutrit & Foods Va Polytech Inst & State Univ Blacksburg VA 24060

DRISKILL, WILLIAM DAVID, b Sharon Grove, Ky, Dec 5, 38; m 61; c 2. ATOMIC PHYSICS, SCIENCE EDUCATION. *Educ:* Murray State Univ, Ky, BS, 61; Univ of the South, MA, 66; George Peabody Col, PhD(physics educ), 75. *Prof Exp:* Teacher physics, Murray High Sch, Ky, 62-66; PROF PHYSICS, BELMONT COL, 66-, PROF SCI EDUC, 77-, COORDR PHYSICS, DEPT CHEM & PHYSICS, 80- *Concurrent Pos:* Shell merit fel, Shell Oil Co, 66. *Mem:* Am Asn Physics Teachers. *Res:* Establishing priorities in physics education at both the college level and secondary school level; use of Delphi forecasting technique. *Mailing Add:* Dept of Physics Belmont Col Nashville TN 37203

DRISKO, RICHARD WARREN, b San Mateo, Calif, Nov 16, 25; m 75; c 2. ORGANIC CHEMISTRY. *Educ:* Stanford Univ, BS, 47, MS, 48, PhD(chem), 50. *Prof Exp:* sr proj scientist chem, 50-78, DIR, MAT SCI DIV, CIVIL ENG LAB, 78- *Honors & Awards:* Meritorious Civilian Serv Award, US Navy, 53. *Mem:* Am Chem Soc; Nat Asn Corrosion Eng. *Res:* Isolation and identification of alkaloids; determination of amino acid sequence in proteins; analysis of creosote; paints, protective coatings and corrosion control; pollution; ecology. *Mailing Add:* Code L52 Civil Eng Lab Port Hueneme CA 93043

DRISTY, FORREST E, b Eakin, SDak, Oct 23, 31; m 58; c 2. TOPOLOGY. *Educ:* SDak Sch Mines & Technol, BS, 53, MS, 59; Fla State Univ, PhD(math), 62. *Prof Exp:* Indust engr, Eastman Kodak Co, 54; instr math, SDak Sch Mines & Technol, 57-59; from asst prof to assoc prof, Fla Presby Col, 62-66; assoc prof, Clarkson Col Technol, 66-68; PROF MATH, STATE UNIV NY COL OSWEGO, 68- *Concurrent Pos:* Vis fel, Princeton Univ, 67-68. *Mem:* Am Math Soc; Math Asn Am. *Res:* Applications of linear algebra to geometry and topology; history of mathematics. *Mailing Add:* Dept of Math State Univ of NY Col Oswego NY 13126

DRITSCHILO, WILLIAM, b Villach, Austria, Nov 11, 46; m 70; c 2. ENVIRONMENTAL SCIENCE. *Educ:* Univ Pa, BA & BS, 70; Cornell Univ, PhD(ecol), 78. *Prof Exp:* Res assoc, Washington Univ, St Louis, 77-78; ASST PROF ENVIRON SCI, UNIV CALIF, LOS ANGELES, 78- *Mem:* Ecol Soc Am; Entom Soc Am; AAAS. *Res:* Effects of energy supplies and sources on agriculture and environment; environmental indices; community structure in carbid beetles. *Mailing Add:* 3677 Geol Bldg Univ Calif Los Angeles CA 90024

DRIVER, CHARLES HENRY, b Orlando, Fla, Oct, 12, 21; m 43; c 3. FOREST PATHOLOGY, RANGE MANAGEMENT. *Educ:* Univ Ga, BS, 47, MS, 50; La State Univ, PhD, 54. *Prof Exp:* Res technician forest path, USDA, 46-47; instr biol, Emory Univ, 49-52; res botanist, Int Paper Co, 54-57, dir forest res, 57-65; PROF FOREST PATH, COL FOREST RESOURCES, UNIV WASH, 65- *Mem:* Mycol Soc Am; Soc Am Foresters; Soc Range Mgt. *Res:* Pathology of intensely managed forest; forest products pathology; management of wildlands range resources. *Mailing Add:* Col of Forest Resources Univ of Wash Seattle WA 98195

DRIVER, EDGAR STEWARD, b Pittsburgh, Pa, July 12, 21. GEOPHYSICS. *Educ:* Dartmouth Col, AB, 43; Univ Pittsburgh, MLitt, 59. *Prof Exp:* Geophysicist, Gulf Res Develop Co, 45-51; seismic party chief, Mene Grande Oil Co, Venezuela, 51-52; geophysicist, Gulf Res & Develop Co, 52; chief geophysicist, Mene Grande Oil Co, 53-56; res geophysicist, Gulf Res & Develop Co, 56-61, supvr seismic interpretation & develop sect, 61-67, mgr marine explor proj, 67-70, geophys adv explor & prod dept, Gulf Oil Corp, 70-73, chief geophysicst, Gulf Global Explor Co, 73-75, chief geophysicist, Gulf Energy & Minerals Co, Int, 75-76, mgr geophys, 76-77, mgr geol sci dept, 77-79, GEN MGR EXPLOR RES, GULF SCI & TECHNOL CO, 79-82. *Concurrent Pos:* Mem, Joint Oceanog Insts Deep Earth Sampling Site Surv Panel for Deep Sea Drilling Proj, 74-77. *Honors & Awards:* Mem, Order of Brit Empire. *Mem:* Soc Explor Geophys; Am Asn Petrol Geol; Geol Soc Am. *Res:* Geological research; seismic systems; marine geology; geology of continental margins; seismic noise analysis. *Mailing Add:* 2630 Glenchester Rd Wexford PA 15090

DRIVER, GARTH EDWARD, b Waterville, Wash, Aug 18, 23; m 48; c 5. CONTROL ENGINEERING. *Educ:* Univ Kans, BS, 47, MS, 48. *Prof Exp:* Engr, Hanford Labs, 49-59, sr engr, 59-65; res assoc control systs, 65, mgr digital systs sect, 65-68, mgr, Control & Instrumentation Dept, 68-70, mgr, Comput & Control Dept, 70-80, LEADER TECH OPERATIONS, PAC NORTHWEST DIV, BATTELLE MEM INST, 80- *Mem:* Inst Elec & Electronics Engrs. *Res:* Transistor circuits; radiation telemetry; nuclear reactor instrumentation; computer process control; process simulation. *Mailing Add:* 8108 Sunset Lane Pasco WA 99301

DRIVER, RICHARD D, b Aberaeron, Wales, June 23, 48. ATOMIC PHYSICS. *Educ:* Univ London, BSc, 70, DIC & PhD(spectros), 74. *Prof Exp:* Res fel astrophys, Harvard Col Observ, 74-76; res fel physics, Mass Inst Technol, 76-78; RES PHYSICIST, FOXBORO ANAL CO, 78- *Mem:* Am Phys Soc. *Res:* Ultraviolet spectroscopy, laser spectroscopy, combustion research and fiber optics. *Mailing Add:* Foxboro Anal Co 78 Blanchard Rd Burlington MA 01803

DRIVER, RODNEY DAVID, b London, Eng, July 1, 32; US citizen; m 55; c 3. MATHEMATICAL ANALYSIS, ELECTRODYNAMICS. *Educ:* Univ Minn, BS, 53, MS, 55, PhD(math), 60. *Prof Exp:* Fel math, Univ Minn, 56-60; fel, Res Inst Advan Study, 60-61; staff mem, Math Res Ctr, US Army, Univ Wis, 61-62 & Sandia Corp, 62-69; assoc prof, 69-74, PROF MATH, UNIV RI, 74- *Mem:* Am Math Soc. *Res:* Functional-differential equations; two-body problem of classical electrodynamics. *Mailing Add:* Dept of Math Univ of RI Kingston RI 02881

DRLICA, KARL, b Portland, Ore, June 28, 43; m 67. MOLECULAR BIOLOGY. *Educ:* Ore State Univ, BA, 64; Univ Calif, Berkeley, PhD(molecular biol), 71. *Prof Exp:* Fel plant path, Univ Calif, Davis, 71-73; fel biochem, Princeton Univ, 73-76; ASST PROF BIOL, UNIV ROCHESTER, 77- *Concurrent Pos:* Mem, Molecular Biol Study Sect, NIH, 79. *Res:* Bacterial chromosome structure, DNA supercoiling, and gene expression. *Mailing Add:* Dept Biol Univ Rochester Rochester NY 14627

DRNEVICH, VINCENT PAUL, b Wilkinsburg, Pa, Aug 6, 40; m 66. CIVIL ENGINEERING. *Educ:* Univ Notre Dame, BSCE, 62, MSCE, 64; Univ Mich, PhD(civil eng), 67. *Prof Exp:* Res asst soil dynamics, Univ Notre Dame, 62-64 & Univ Mich, 64-65 & 65-67; from asst prof to assoc prof, 67-77, PROF CIVIL ENG, UNIV KY, 77- *Concurrent Pos:* NSF eng res initiation grant, 68-69; mem, Int Soc Soil Mech & Found Eng, 64-, mem soil dynamics comt & preconf pub subcomt, 68-69. *Honors & Awards:* Award, Am Soc Testing & Mat, 66. *Mem:* Am Soc Civil Engrs; Am Soc Testing & Mat. *Res:* Behavior of soils due to dynamic loading, such as caused by machines and earthquakes; improvement of soil testing techniques and equipment. *Mailing Add:* Dept of Civil Eng Univ of Ky Lexington KY 40506

DROBECK, HANS PETER, b Bavaria, Ger, Oct 3, 23; nat US; m 48; c 4. TOXICOLOGY, EXPERIMENTAL PATHOLOGY. *Educ:* Univ Del, BS, 48; Syracuse Univ, MS, 51, PhD(zool), 53. *Prof Exp:* Asst, Syracuse Univ, 48-51; assoc res pathologist, Parke, Davis & Co, 53-56; res pathologist, 56-63, DIR TOXICOL DEPT, STERLING WINTHROP RES INST, NY, 63- *Mem:* AAAS; Soc Toxicol; Am Soc Parasitol. *Res:* Toxicology. *Mailing Add:* Pine Ave RD 1 Rensselaer NY 12144

DROBNEY, RONALD DELOSS, b Ft Dodge, Iowa, Oct 13, 42. WATERFOWL ECOLOGY. *Educ:* Univ Northern Iowa, BA, 65; Univ Mo, MA, 73, PhD(wildlife ecol), 77. *Prof Exp:* Actg dir, Gaylord Mem Lab, Univ Mo, 76-77; ASST PROF WILDLIFE MGT, UNIV MICH, ANN ARBOR, 78- *Honors & Awards:* Citation of Merit, Am Ornithologists Union, 77. *Mem:* Wildlife Soc. *Res:* Feeding ecology, nutrition and reproductive bioenergetics of waterfowl; wetland ecology. *Mailing Add:* Natural Resources Samuel Trask Dana Bldg of Mich Ann Arbor MI 48197

DROBNIES, SAUL ISAAC, b New York, NY, June 8, 33; div; c 1. MATHEMATICS, OPERATIONS RESEARCH. *Educ:* Univ Tex, BS, 55, MA, 58, PhD(math), 61. *Prof Exp:* Fel math, Rice Univ, 61-62; sr opers analyst, Gen Dynamics Corp, 62-63; from asst prof to assoc prof math, 63-70, PROF MATH, SAN DIEGO STATE UNIV, 70- *Mem:* Am Math Soc; Math Asn Am; Soc Indust & Appl Math. *Res:* Mathematical analysis; continued fractions. *Mailing Add:* Dept of Math San Diego State Univ San Diego CA 92182

DROBNYK, JOHN WENDEL, b Trenton, NJ, Sept 30, 35; m 61; c 2. GEOLOGY. *Educ:* Amherst Col, BA, 57; Rutgers Univ, MS, 59, PhD(geol), 62. *Prof Exp:* Asst instr geol, Rutgers Univ, 57-61; res asst, 61-62; geologist, Pan-Am Petrol Corp, 62-64; from instr to assoc prof, 65-71, PROF GEOL, SOUTHERN CONN STATE COL, 71-, CHMN DEPT EARTH SCI, 67- *Mem:* Am Asn Petrol Geol; Soc Econ Paleont & Mineral; Sigma Xi. *Res:* Geology of modern clastic sediments; interpretation of ancient depositional environments. *Mailing Add:* Tuttles Point Guilford CT 06437

DROBOT, STEFAN, b Cracow, Poland, Aug 7, 13; US citizen; m 41; c 3. MATHEMATICS. *Educ:* Univ Jagiellonian, MA, 37; Univ Wroclaw, PhD(math), 47. *Prof Exp:* Asst theoret mech, Lwow Polytech Inst, Poland, 39-40; lectr, Siberian Metall Inst USSR, 41-46; from asst prof to assoc prof math, Wroclaw Univ & Polytech Inst, 46-59; res assoc prof, Univ Chicago, 59-60; from assoc prof to prof, Univ Notre Dame, 60-63; PROF MATH, OHIO STATE UNIV, 63- *Concurrent Pos:* Head dept appl math, Math Inst, Polish Acad Sci, 49-58. *Mem:* Am Math Soc; Math Asn Am. *Res:* Mechanics of continua; dimensional analysis; operational calculus; variational principles. *Mailing Add:* Dept of Math Ohio State Univ Columbus OH 43210

DROBOT, VLADIMIR, UNIFORM DISTRIBUTION OF SEQUENCES. *Educ:* Univ Notre Dame, BS, 63; Univ Ill, PhD(math), 67. *Prof Exp:* Asst prof math, State Univ NY, Buffalo, 67-73; ASSOC PROF MATH, UNIV SANTA CLARA, 73- *Concurrent Pos:* Ed, Problems Sect, Math Asn Am, 79- *Mem:* Am Math Soc; Math Asn Am; Sigma Xi. *Res:* Mathematical analysis. *Mailing Add:* Dept Math Univ Canta Clara Santa Clara CA 95053

DROEGE, JOHN WALTER, b Seymour, Ind, Sept 7, 21. FUEL SCIENCE, THERMOPHYSICAL PROPERTIES. *Educ:* Ind Univ, AB, 42; Ohio State Univ, PhD(chem), 53. *Prof Exp:* CHEMIST, BATTELLE MEM INST, 53- *Mem:* Am Chem Soc. *Res:* Thermodynamics; calorimetry; physical properties of materials; high temperature chemistry; coal chemistry; coal liquefaction; thermophysical and transport properties at elevated pressure and temperature. *Mailing Add:* Battelle Mem Inst 505 King Ave Columbus OH 43201

DROESSLER, EARL GEORGE, b Dubuque, Iowa, Jan 14, 20; m 44, 57; c 5. METEOROLOGY. *Educ:* Loras Col, AB, 42. *Hon Degrees:* ScD, Loras Col, 58. *Prof Exp:* Meteorologist, Off of Naval Res, 46-50, head geophys br, 50; exec dir comt geophys & geog, Res & Develop Bd, 52-53; exec secy, Coord Comt Gen Sci, Off of Asst Secy Defense for Res & Develop, 54-58; prog dir atmospheric sci, NSF, 58-66; prof atmospheric sci & vpres res, State Univ NY Albany, 66-71; prof geosci & dean res, 71-79, DIR UNIV AFFAIRS, NAT OCEANIC & ATMOSPHERIC ADMIN, NC STATE UNIV, 79- *Concurrent Pos:* Mem, Adv Comt Weather Control, 53-57 & US Nat Comt for Int Geophys Year, 55-64; vis res fel, Commonwealth Sci & Indust Res Orgn, Australia, 63-64; chmn bd trustees, Univ Corp Atmospheric Res, 69-73; co-chmn, NSF Adv Panel Weather Modification, 75-77; mem, NC Comn Sci & Technol, 71-79; mem, Mineral Resources Comt, Nat Asn State Univs & Land-Grant Cols, 73-76; mem bd govs, Research Triangle Inst, NC, 73-79, mem exec comt, 75-79; mem, Oak Ridge Assoc Univs Coun, 74-79, mem bd dirs, 75-79, mem exec comt, 78-79; mem bd trustees, Triangle Univs Ctr Advan Studies, Inc, 76-79; exec ed, Weatherwise, Helen Dwight Reid Found, 78- *Mem:* Fel AAAS; fel Am Geophys Union; fel Am Meteorol Soc; Weather Modification Asn. *Res:* Cloud physics; weather modification. *Mailing Add:* 1305 Glenn Eden Dr Raleigh NC 27612

DROLL, HENRY ANDREW, b New York, NY, Sept 2, 26; m 52; c 5. INORGANIC CHEMISTRY. *Educ:* George Washington Univ, BS, 52, MS, 53; Pa State Univ, PhD(chem), 56. *Prof Exp:* AEC asst, George Washington Univ, 52-53 & Pa State Univ, 54-55; sr scientist, Atomic Power Div, Westinghouse Elec Corp, Pa, 55-56; from asst prof to assoc prof, 56-71, PROF CHEM, UNIV MO-KANSAS CITY, 71- *Mem:* Am Chem Soc. *Res:* Chemistry of less familiar elements; chemical equilibrium, especially study of complex ions in aqueous systems; preparation of coordination compounds. *Mailing Add:* Dept of Chem Univ of Mo Kansas City MO 64110

DROLSOM, PAUL NEWELL, b Martell, Wis, July 15, 25; m 50; c 2. AGRONOMY. *Educ:* Univ Wis, BS, 49, MS, 50, PhD(agron, plant path), 53. *Prof Exp:* Asst agron, Univ Wis, 49-52; pathologist, Agr Res Serv, USDA & NC State Univ, 53-58; from asst prof to assoc prof, 58-66, PROF AGRON, UNIV WIS-MADISON, 66- *Concurrent Pos:* Mem, US AID Prog, Brazil, 64-66. *Mem:* AAAS; Am Soc Agron; Am Genetic Asn. *Res:* Corn breeding with major emphasis on development of lines with earliness, cold tolerance and disease resistance. *Mailing Add:* Dept of Agron Univ of Wis Madison WI 53706

DROMGOLD, LUTHER D, b Newport, Pa, Apr 20, 25; m 50; c 4. LUBRICATION, ANALYTICAL CHEMISTRY. *Educ:* Pa State Univ, BS, 49. *Prof Exp:* Engr, 49-54, sales engr, 55-62, MGR NEW PROD DEVELOP, KENDALL/AMALIE DIV, WITCO CHEM CORP, 62- *Mem:* Am Chem Soc; fel Am Soc Lubrication Engrs. *Res:* Petroleum, especially specialized and process lubricants, automotive underbody coatings; rust preventives; petroleum resins; adhesives; emulsions; hydraulic fluids. *Mailing Add:* 21 McKune Ave Bradford PA 16701

DROMMOND, FRED GEORGE, pharmacy, pharmaceutical chemistry, deceased

DRONAMRAJU, KRISHNA RAO, b Pithapuram, India, Jan 14, 37; m 62; c 1. EVOLUTIONARY BIOLOGY, GENETICS. *Educ:* Andhra Univ, BSc, 55; Agra Univ, MSc, 57, PhD(human genetics), 64. *Prof Exp:* Consult, Univ Grants Comn, Govt India, 59-61; res fel, Glasgow Univ, 61-62; asst prof genetics, State Univ NY Buffalo, 65-66; vis fel, Univ Alta, 66-68; vis prof med genetics, Univ Sask, 68-69; chief geneticist, Lancaster Cleft Palate Clin, Pa, 69-72; vis assoc prof genetics, Hershey Med Ctr, Pa State Univ, 72-73; res coordr, Md Comn Afro-Am & Indian Hist & Cult, 74-82; NRSA SR FEL, CTR DEMOGAPHIC & POP GENETICS, UNIV TEX HEALTH SCI CTR, 82- *Mem:* AAAS; Am Soc Human Genetics; NY Acad Sci; Am Asn Phys Anthrop. *Res:* Speciation and theory of evolution; human genetics and evolution; population genetics and polymorphic systems. *Mailing Add:* Univ Tex Health Sci Ctr PO Box 20334 Houston TX 77025

DRONEN, NORMAN OBERT, JR, b Shelton, Wash, Oct 9, 45; m 67; c 3. PARASITOLOGY. *Educ:* Eastern Wash Univ, BA, 68, MS, 70; NMex State Univ, PhD(biol), 73. *Prof Exp:* ASST PROF BIOL, TEX A&M UNIV, 74- *Concurrent Pos:* Co-investr res grant, Environ Protection Agency, 74-75; prin investr, NIH biomed supports grants, Tex A&M Univ, 75-76; co-investr, NSF res proj estab primate colony, Col Vet Med, Tex A&M Univ, 75-76. *Mem:* Sigma Xi; Am Soc Parasitologists. *Res:* Parasites, especially the host-parasite; population dynamics of natural populations of helminths; trophic structure utilization by parasites; experimental manipulation of host-parasite systems. *Mailing Add:* Dept of Biol Col of Sci Tex A&M Univ College Station TX 77843

DROOZ, ARNOLD T, b Albany, NY, Nov 17, 21; m 55; c 2. FOREST ENTOMOLOGY. *Educ:* NY State Col Forestry, BS, 48, MS, 49. *Prof Exp:* Entomologist, Bur Entom & Plant Quarantine, USDA, 49-53, US Forest Serv, 53-57 & Pa State Dept Forests & Waters, 57-60; entomologist, 60-68, proj leader biol control, 68-73, PRIN RES ENTOMOLOGIST, SOUTHEASTERN FOREST EXP STA, US FOREST SERV, 73- *Mem:* Soc Am Foresters; Entom Soc Am; Entom Soc Can; Int Orgn Biol Control. *Res:* Forest insect parasites; ecology of forest insects. *Mailing Add:* Forestry Sci Lab US Forest Serv PO Box 12254 Research Triangle Park NC 27709

DROPESKY, BRUCE JOSEPH, b Philadelphia, Pa, Apr 29, 24; m 48; c 2. NUCLEAR CHEMISTRY. *Educ:* Rensselaer Polytech Inst, BS, 49; Univ Rochester, PhD(phys chem), 53. *Prof Exp:* Mem Staff, 53-70, ASSOC GROUP LEADER, LOS ALAMOS NAT LAB, 70- *Mem:* Am Chem Soc (chmn, Div Nuclear Chem & Technol, 78); Am Phys Soc; Sigma Xi. *Res:* High energy nuclear reactions; nuclear decay scheme studies; nuclear spectroscopy; electromagnetic isotope separation; pi meson induced nuclear reactions. *Mailing Add:* Los Alamos Nat Lab MS-824 PO Box 1663 Los Alamos NM 87545

DROPKIN, JOHN JOSEPH, b Bobruisk, Russia, Feb 22, 10; US citizen; m 33, 57; c 4. SOLID STATE PHYSICS. *Educ:* Columbia Univ, AB, 30; Polytech Inst Brooklyn, MS, 47, PhD(physics), 48. *Prof Exp:* Asst physics, Columbia Univ, 30-35; teacher high sch, NY, 36-48; from asst prof to assoc prof, 48-55, head dept, 57-65, prof physics, 55-78, COORDR, FRESHMAN LEARNING CTR, POLYTECH INST NEW YORK, 78- *Mem:* AAAS; Am Asn Physics Teachers. *Res:* Stimulated phosphorescence and photoconduction in infrared sensitive phosphors; infrared photoconduction in zinc sulfide; solid state physics, especially conduction, photoconduction and luminescence. *Mailing Add:* Freshman Learning Ctr Polytech Inst of New York Brooklyn NY 11201

DROPKIN, VICTOR HARRY, b New York, NY, Mar 21, 16; m 41; c 1. ZOOLOGY. *Educ:* Cornell Univ, BA, 36; Univ Chicago, PhD(zool), 40. *Prof Exp:* Instr, Univ Chicago, 40-41 & US Air Force, 41-45; from instr to assoc prof biol, Roosevelt Univ, 46-51; fel, Naval Med Res Inst, 51-53; nematologist, plant indust sta, USDA, 53-69; PROF PLANT PATH, UNIV MO-COLUMBIA, 69-, CHMN PLANT PATH, 80- *Concurrent Pos:* Vis prof, Univ Wis, 66-67. *Mem:* Soc Nematol (treas, 62-63, vpres, 64-65, pres, 65-66); Am Phytopath Soc; Europ Soc Nematol. *Res:* Nematodes parasitic on plants. *Mailing Add:* Dept of Plant Path Univ of Mo Columbia MO 65201

DROPP, JOHN JEROME, b Monessen, Pa, Dec 2, 40; m 62; c 2. BIOLOGY, HISTOLOGY. *Educ:* Washington & Jefferson Col, BA, 62; Ohio Univ, MS, 64; Ore State Univ, PhD(zool), 69. *Prof Exp:* Neurophysiologist, Walter Reed Army Inst Res, Washington, DC, 68-70; asst prof biol, Wilson Col, 70-76; asst prof, 76-80, ASSOC PROF BIOL, MT ST MARY'S COL, 80- *Mem:* AAAS; Am Soc Zoologists; Am Asn Anatomists; Soc Neurosci. *Res:* Behavioral stress and its effects on various organ systems of the body-effects at the histological level; trophic effects of neurons; mast cells in the vertebrate brain. *Mailing Add:* Dept of Sci & Math Mt St Mary's Col Emmitsburg MD 21727

DROPPO, JAMES GARNET, JR, b Ottawa, Ont, July 24, 43; m 69; c 2. MICROMETEOROLOGY. *Educ:* Cornell Univ, BS, 65; State Univ NY Albany, MS, 68, PhD(atmospheric sci), 72. *Prof Exp:* Res assoc, Atmospheric Sci Res Ctr, Albany, 70-72; SR RES SCIENTIST ATMOSPHERIC SCI, PAC NORTHWEST LABS, BATTELLE MEM INST, 72- *Concurrent Pos:* Lectr, Joint Ctr Grad Study-Continuing Educ Prog, Richland, 75- *Mem:* Inst Elec & Electronics Engrs; Am Meteorol Soc; Can Meteorol & Oceanog Soc. *Res:* Micrometeorological processes influencing energy and pollutant fluxes in the atmospheric surface boundary layer over natural surfaces. *Mailing Add:* Battelle Pac Northwest Labs PO Box 999 Richland WA 99352

DROSDOFF, MATTHEW, b Chicago, Ill, Dec 15, 08; m 35; c 2. SOIL SCIENCE. *Educ:* Univ Ill, BS, 30; Univ Wis, MS, 32, PhD(soil chem), 34. *Prof Exp:* Asst soils, Univ Wis, 30-35; jr soil survr, Soil Chem Div, USDA, 38-40, assoc soil technologist, Tung Lab, Bur Plant Indust, 40-42, Bur Plant Indust, Soil & Agr Eng, 42-53, soil technologist, 45-50, sr soil scientist, 50-53, Hort Crops Res Br, Agr Res Serv, 53-55, soils adv, Int Coop Admin, Peru, 55-60; food & agr officer, AID, Vietnam, 60-64; adminr, Int Agr Develop Serv, USDA, 64-66; PROF SOIL SCI, CORNELL UNIV, 66- *Concurrent Pos:* Adv, Point IV Agr Mission to Colombia, 51-53, Bolivia, 54; consult, Korea & Nigeria, 79, Colombia, Indonesia, Thailand, India, 80. *Honors & Awards:* Int Agron Award, Am Soc Agron, 74. *Mem:* AAAS; Am Soc Agron; Soil Sci Soc Am; Am Agr Econ Asn. *Res:* Chemical studies of colloidal clays; field and laboratory research on genesis and morphology of soils; soil chemistry and fertility related to mineral nutrition of tung trees, including minor elements; soil survey; agricultural development; tropical soils; soil fertility research in the tropics. *Mailing Add:* 115 Randolph Rd Ithaca NY 14850

DROSSMAN, MELVYN MILES, b Brooklyn, NY, June 30, 37; m 58; c 3. COMPUTER SCIENCES, ELECTRONICS ENGINEERING. *Educ:* Polytech Inst Brooklyn, BEE, 57, MEE, 59, PhD(elec eng), 67. *Prof Exp:* Instr elec eng, Polytech Inst Brooklyn, 58-66; res assoc psychophysiol, State Univ NY Downstate Med Ctr, 66-68; assoc prof, 68-70, chmn, Dept Elec Technol, 68-78, PROF ELEC ENG TECHNOL & COMPUT SCI, NY INST TECHNOL, 70- *Concurrent Pos:* Consult, Res Ctr, Rockland State Hosp, 63-66 & HZI Res Co, 74-76, NASA, 76-81, US Army, 78-81. *Mem:* Inst Elec & Electronics Eng; Asn Comput Mach. *Res:* Computer analysis of averaged evoked EEG responses in human subjects using visual and auditory stimuli to determine relationship between EEG and cerebral information processing. *Mailing Add:* Dept of Elec Eng Technol NY Inst of Technol Old Westbury NY 11568

DROSTE, JOHN BROWN, b Hillsboro, Ill, Nov 23, 27; m 51; c 2. SEDIMENTOLOGY. *Educ:* Univ Ill, BS, 51, MS, 53, PhD(geol), 56. *Prof Exp:* Instr geol & dir gen studies, Univ Ill, 56-57; from asst prof to assoc prof, 57-68, PROF GEOL, IND UNIV, BLOOMINGTON, 68- *Mem:* Geol Soc Am; Soc Econ Paleont & Mineral; Clay Minerals Soc. *Res:* Clay mineralogy; sedimentation; sedimentary petrography, particularly the origin and distribution of clay minerla in sedimentary rock, including origin and occurrence of clay minerals in soils and clay mineral diagenesis. *Mailing Add:* Dept Geol Ind Univ Bloomington IN 47401

DROST-HANSEN, WALTER, b Chicago, Ill, Sept 29, 25; m 50; c 2. CHEMICAL PHYSICS. *Educ:* Univ Copenhagen, Magister scientiarum, 50. *Prof Exp:* Asst mass spectros invest, Inst Theoret Physics, Copenhagen, 46-50; Carlsberg Found fel, Inst Phys Chem, 50; spec asst, Ill Inst Technol, 50-51; res phys chemist, Bjorksten Res Labs, 51-52; assoc prof chem physics & sr chem physicist, NMex Inst Mining & Technol, 53-56; sr res engr, Pan-Am Petrol Corp, 56-61; sr res chemist, Jersey Prod Res Co, 61-64; from assoc prof to prof chem physics, Inst Marine Sci, 64-70, chmn div chem oceanog, 67-70, PROF CHEM & DIR LAB WATER RES, UNIV MIAMI, 70- *Mem:* AAAS; Am Chem Soc; NY Acad Sci. *Res:* Structure and properties of water and aqueous solutions; surface and colloid phenomena; physical chemistry of biological systems; thermal pollution. *Mailing Add:* Lab for Water Res Dept of Chem Univ of Miami Coral Gables FL 33124

DROUET, FRANCIS, b Philadelphia, Pa, Mar 1, 07. BOTANY. *Educ:* Univ Mo, AB, 28, AM, 29, PhD(bot), 31. *Prof Exp:* Asst bot, Univ Mo, 26-31, herbarium, 31-35; botanist, Comn Tech Piscicult, Brazil, 35; Seessel fel bot, Yale Univ, 36-38; cur cryptogamic herbarium, Chicago Natural Hist Mus, 38-58; res assoc, NMex Highlands Univ, 58-59; res prof bot, Univ Ariz, 59-61; res fel, 61-75, CUR EMER, ACAD NATURAL SCI PHILADELPHIA, 75- *Concurrent Pos:* Tech consult, Bur Fisheries, 30-31; asst to Mo State Plant Pathologist, 31-35; instr, Marine Biol Lab, Woods Hole, 34, 36-38; res assoc, Northwestern Univ, 46-49; instr, Lake Itasca Biol Sta, 54 & 62; consult algae, Acad Natural Sci, Philadelphia, 75- *Mem:* Torrey Bot Club. Bot Soc Am; Am Micros Soc; Bot Soc Am. *Res:* Systematics and floristics of Myxophyceae; revision of the classification of Myxophyceae. *Mailing Add:* Acad of Natural Sci 1900 Parkway Philadelphia PA 19103

DROUET, MICHEL GEORGES, plasma physics, electrical engineering, see previous edition

DROUGAS, JOHN, b Boston, Mass, Aug 7, 30; m 59; c 2. ORGANIC CHEMISTRY, POLYMER CHEMISTRY. *Educ:* Northeastern Univ, BS, 53, MS, 55; Mich State Univ, PhD(org chem), 59. *Prof Exp:* Chemist res & develop, Arthur D Little, Inc, 59-61; res chemist textile fibers, 61-66, supvr textile fibers dept, 66-78, SR MKT REP, FIBERS DEPT, E I DU PONT DE NEMOURS & CO, INC, 78- *Mem:* AAAS. *Res:* Fiber properties; high polymers. *Mailing Add:* Textile Fiber Dept Centre Rd Bldg E I du Pont de Nemours & Co Inc Wilmington DE 19898

DROZDOWICZ, ZBIGNIEW MARIAN, b Warsaw, Poland, Apr 9, 49. LASERS. *Educ:* Univ Calif, Los Angeles, BS, 72; Mass Inst Technol, PhD(physics), 78. *Prof Exp:* SR SCIENTIST LASERS, RES DIV, RAYTHEON CO, 78- *Mem:* Am Phys Soc; Inst Elec & Electronic Engrs; Optical Soc Am. *Res:* Laser pumped infrared and submillimeter lasers; electrical discharge and chemical infrared lasers. *Mailing Add:* Res Div Raytheon Co 28 Seyon St Waltham MA 02254

DÜRSCH, FRIEDRICH, b Dresden, Ger, June 10, 30; m 51. ORGANIC CHEMISTRY. *Educ:* Dresden Tech Univ, BS, 52; Darmstadt Tech Univ, MS, 55, PhD(org chem), 56. *Prof Exp:* Res assoc natural prod, Univ Va, 57-60; sr chemist pharmaceut, Wallace Labs Div, Carter Prod NJ, 60-62, asst dir, 62-63; SR SCIENTIST, SQUIBB INST MED RES, 64-, SR RES FEL, E R SQUIBB & SONS, 81- *Mem:* Am Chem Soc; AAAS. *Res:* Synthetic organic chemistry; derivatives of hydroxylamine; alkaloids; pharmaceuticals; antibiotics; process development. *Mailing Add:* E R Squibb & Sons New Brunswick NJ 08903

DRUCKER, ARNOLD, b Brooklyn, NY, Mar 18, 32; m 57; c 2. POLYMER CHEMISTRY, ORGANIC CHEMISTRY. *Educ:* City Col New York, BS, 53; Polytech Inst Brooklyn, MS, 56, PhD(polymer & org chem), 64. *Prof Exp:* Res chemist, Merck & Co, 56-58 & Am Cyanamid Co, Conn, 58-71; teacher gen chem, Ridgefield High Sch, 71-77; ASSOC PROF CHEM, UNIV CONN, 77- *Concurrent Pos:* Lectr org chem, City Col New York, 66-74 & Univ Conn, Stamford, 75- *Mem:* AAAS; Am Chem Soc. *Res:* Keratin chemistry; stereospecific polymerization; epoxy resins; triazine polymers; steroids; water soluble polymers; paper chemistry; polymeric flocculants for water treatment. *Mailing Add:* 110 Saw Mill Rd Stamford CT 06903

DRUCKER, DANIEL CHARLES, b New York, NY, June 3, 18; m 39; c 2. APPLIED MECHANICS, MATERIALS ENGINEERING. *Educ:* Columbia Univ, BS, 37, CE, 38, PhD(eng), 40. *Hon Degrees:* DEng, Lehigh Univ, 76. *Prof Exp:* Eng asst, Tunnel Authority, New York, 37; asst, Columbia Univ, 38-39; instr mech eng, Cornell Univ, 40-43; supvr mech solids, Armour Res Found, Ill Inst Technol, 43-45, asst prof mech, 46-47; from assoc prof to prof eng, Brown Univ, 47-64, chmn, Div Eng, 53-59, Ballou prof, 64-68, chmn phys sci coun, 61-63; DEAN, COL ENG, UNIV ILL, URBANA, 68- *Concurrent Pos:* Guggenheim fel, 60-61; NATO sr sci fel, 68; Fulbright travel grant, 68; mem gen comt, Int Coun Sci Unions, 76- *Honors & Awards:* von Karman Medal, Am Soc Civil Engrs, 66; Lamme Medal, Am Soc Eng Educ, 67; M M Frocht Award, Soc Exp Stress Anal, 71; Thomas Egleston Medal, Columbia Univ Sch Eng & Appl Sci, 78. *Mem:* Nat Acad Eng; Polish Acad Sci; fel Am Acad Arts & Sci; Int Union Theoret & Appl Mech (pres, 80-84); Am Soc Eng Educ (pres, 81). *Res:* Photoelasticity; plasticity; mechanics of metal cutting and deformation processing; stress analysis; soil mechanics; materials engineering. *Mailing Add:* 106 Eng Hall Col Eng Univ Ill 1308 W Green St Urbana IL 61801

DRUCKER, E(UGENE) E(LIAS), b New York, NY, Dec 11, 24; m 46; c 3. MECHANICAL ENGINEERING. *Educ:* Mass Inst Technol, BS, 49, MS, 50. *Prof Exp:* Asst mech eng, Mass Inst Technol, 49-50; from instr to assoc prof, US Naval Postgrad Sch, 50-56; assoc prof, 56-62, PROF MECH ENG, SYRACUSE UNIV, 62- *Concurrent Pos:* Engr, Babcock & Wilcox Co, 51 & Westinghouse Atomic Power Div, 54; consult, Mat Adv Bd, Nat Acad Sci, 57-58 & Int Bus Mach, 58; Fulbright lectr, Delft Univ Technol, 65-66. *Mem:* Am Soc Mech Engrs; Am Soc Eng Educ; Am Nuclear Soc; Am Soc Heating, Refrig & Air Conditioning Engrs. *Res:* Thermodynamics, heat transfer, fluid mechanics, applications of these to nuclear power. *Mailing Add:* Dept Mech Eng Syracuse Univ Syracuse NY 13210

DRUCKER, HARRIS, b Brooklyn, NY, July 28, 43; m 66; c 2. ELECTRICAL ENGINEERING. *Educ:* Pa State Univ, BSEE, 64, MSE, 66, PhD(elec eng), 67. *Prof Exp:* Jr engr, Philco Corp, Ford Motor Co, Pa, 64-67; engr, Radio Corp Am, NJ, 67-68; PROF ELECTRONIC ENG, MONMOUTH COL, NJ, 68- *Concurrent Pos:* Consult, Control Data Corp, 81- & Perkin-Elmer, 81- *Mem:* Inst Elec & Electronics Engrs; Am Soc Eng Educ; Acoust Soc Am. *Res:* Speech recognition and speech processing for the hearing impaired; microcomputer software and hardware. *Mailing Add:* Dept Electronic Eng Monmouth Col West Long Branch NJ 07764

DRUCKER, HARVEY, b Chicago, Ill, Jan 1, 41; m 65; c 2. MICROBIOLOGY, BIOCHEMISTRY. *Educ:* Univ Ill, BS, 63, PhD(microbiol), 67. *Prof Exp:* Sr res investr biochem, 69-73, sect mgr molecular biol, 73-79, MGT BIOL DEPT, PAC NORTHWEST LABS, BATTELLE MEM INST, 79- *Concurrent Pos:* Cardiovasc Res Inst fel, Med Ctr, Univ Calif, San Francisco, 67-69; adj prof, Grad Ctr, Richland, Wash, 72- *Mem:* AAAS; Am Soc Microbiol; Am Chem Soc; Fedn Am Soc Exp Biol. *Res:* Regulation of exocellular enzymes affecting degradation of macromolecules; chemistry of proteolytic enzymes. *Mailing Add:* Pac NW Labs-Battelle Mem Inst PO Box 999 Richland WA 99352

DRUCKER, WILLIAM D, b New York, NY, Mar 30, 29; m 56; c 2. INTERNAL MEDICINE, ENDOCRINOLOGY. *Educ:* NY Univ, BA, 50, MD, 54; Am Bd Internal Med, dipl, 73. *Prof Exp:* From instr to assoc prof med, Sch Med, NY Univ, 62-76; PROF MED, MED COL WIS, MILWAUKEE, 76-, PROF ENDOCRINOL, METAB SECT & PROF GEN INTERNAL MED SECT, 80-; ACAD CHIEF MED, ST JOSEPH'S HOSP, 76- *Concurrent Pos:* NIH fel, 59-62; career scientist, Health Res Coun City of New York, 62-73. *Mem:* AAAS; Endocrine Soc; fel Am Col Physicians; Am Fedn Clin Res. *Res:* Spontaneous canine Cushing's syndrome; biologic action and physiologic regulation of the adrenal androgens in man; biology of the adrenal androgens in primates; testis and adrenal in myotonic muscular dystrophy. *Mailing Add:* St Joseph's Hosp 5000 W Chambers St Milwaukee WI 53210

DRUCKER, WILLIAM RICHARD, b Chicago, Ill, Apr 5, 22; m 47; c 4. MEDICINE. *Educ:* Harvard Univ, BS, 43; Johns Hopkins Univ, MD, 46; FRCS(C). *Prof Exp:* From instr to prof surg, Western Reserve Univ, 54-66; prof surg & chmn dept, Univ Toronto, 66-72, surgeon-in-chief, Toronto Gen Hosp, 66-72; prof surg & dean, Sch Med, Univ Va, 72-77; PROF SURG & CHMN DEPT, SCH MED & DENT, UNIV ROCHESTER, 77- *Concurrent Pos:* Charles O Finley scholar, 54-57; Markle scholar, 58-63. *Mem:* Am Surg Asn; Fedn Am Socs Exp Biol; Can Soc Clin Invest; fel Am Col Surg. *Res:* Nutrition and intermediary metabolism in surgical patients; hemorrhagic shock. *Mailing Add:* Dept of Surg Sch of Med & Dent 601 Elmwood Ave Rochester NY 14642

DRUDGE, J HAROLD, b Bremen, Ind, Feb 7, 22; m 46; c 1. VETERINARY PARASITOLOGY. *Educ:* Mich State Univ, DVM, 43; Johns Hopkins Univ, ScD(parasitol), 50. *Prof Exp:* Vet parasitologist, Agr Exp Sta, Miss State Col, 50-51; actg chmn dept, 63-68, chmn dept, 68-73, parasitologist, Agr Exp Sta, 51-63, PROF VET SCI, UNIV KY, 63- *Mem:* Am Vet Med Asn; Am Soc Parasitol. *Res:* Nematode parasites of cattle, sheep and horses. *Mailing Add:* Dept of Vet Sci Univ of Ky Lexington KY 40546

DRUEHL, LOUIS D, b San Francisco, Calif, Oct 9, 36; m 64; c 2. MARINE ECOLOGY, PHYCOLOGY. *Educ:* Wash State Univ, BSc, 59; Univ Wash, MSc, 61; Univ BC, PhD(bot, oceanog), 65. *Prof Exp:* Lectr bot, Univ BC, 65-66; asst prof, 66-71, ASSOC PROF BIOL, SIMON FRASER UNIV, 71- *Concurrent Pos:* Nat Res Coun Can grants, 66-; vis assoc prof, Hokkaido Univ, Japan, 72; adv mariculture, Ministerio da Marinha, Brazil, 75-77, Sci Coun grant, 81-; exchange scientist, Nat Res Coun & Conselho Nacional de Pesquinas; consult & researcher, Marine Biomass Prog, Gen Elec Gas Res Inst, 81-; Environ Can grants, 77-79; Marine Resources Br, BC grants, 79- *Res:* Marine algal distribution ecology; biology of the Laminariales; mariculture of seaweeds. *Mailing Add:* Dept of Biol Sci Simon Fraser Univ Burnaby BC V5A 1S6 Can

DRUELINGER, MELVIN L, b South Bend, Ind, Dec 7, 40; m 59; c 2. HETEROCYCLIC CHEMISTRY, PHOTOCHEMISTRY. *Educ:* Ind Univ, Bloomington, BS, 62; Univ Wis-Madison, PhD(org chem), 67. *Prof Exp:* NIH res fel org chem, Iowa State Univ, 67-68; assoc prof org chem, Ind State Univ, Terre Haute, 68-81; PROF ORG CHEM, UNIV COLO, COLORADO SPRINGS, 81- *Concurrent Pos:* Sabbatical leave, Colo State Univ, 74-75; Air Force Systs Command-URRP fel, US Air Force Acad, 78-79; distinguished vis prof, US Air Force Acad, 80-82. *Mem:* Sigma Xi; Am Chem Soc; Royal Soc Chem; Int Soc Heterocyclic Chem. *Res:* Organic photochemistry; highly reactive organic species; organic reaction mechanisms; cycloadditions, energetic materials synthesis and heterocyclic compounds, especially small strained poly-heterocyclic systems; organo-fluorine compounds. *Mailing Add:* Dept of Chem Ind State Univ Terre Haute IN 47809

DRUFENBROCK, DIANE, b Evansville, Ind, Oct 7, 29. MATHEMATICS. *Educ:* Alverno Col, BA, 53; Marquette Univ, MS, 59; Univ Ill, PhD(math), 61. *Prof Exp:* From asst to prof math, Alverno Col, 61-74; PROF MATH, ST MARY-OF-THE-WOODS COL, IND, 74- *Concurrent Pos:* Lectr, Grad Sch, Marquette Univ; lectr, Univ Wis-Parkside. *Mem:* Am Math Soc; Math Asn Am. *Res:* Theory of prime power metabelian groups. *Mailing Add:* St Mary-of-the-Woods Col St Mary-of-the-Woods IN 47876

DRUGAN, JAMES RICHARD, b Detroit, Mich, May 5, 38; m 57; c 3. SYSTEMS ENGINEERING, STATISTICS. *Educ:* Univ Calif, Los Angeles, BS, 60, MS, 63, PhD(eng), 69. *Prof Exp:* Engr kinematics, Singer-Librascope, 58-62; consult engr, 62-63; sr engr systs dynamics, Singer-Librascope, 63-64; res group supvr, Jet Propulsion Lab, 64-66; staff eng systs anal, Singer Librascope, 66-70, supvr appl anal, 70-74, mgr syst engr, 74-79; PRES, MEASUREMENT ANAL CORP, 80-; PRES, DRUGAN ASSOC, INC, 80- *Res:* Systems analysis; pattern recognition; detection theory; experimental design; computer software systems; information theory; estimation theory; controls; kinematics; systems simulation; dynamic programming; human factors; signal processing; involutometry; dynamics and acoustics. *Mailing Add:* 522 Kenneth Rd Glendale CA 91202

DRUGER, MARVIN, b Brooklyn, NY, Feb 21, 34; m 57; c 3. GENETICS. *Educ:* Brooklyn Col, BS, 55; Columbia Univ, MA, 57, PhD(genetics), 61. *Prof Exp:* From asst prof to assoc prof zool & sci teaching, 61-71, PROF BIOL & SCI EDUC, SYRACUSE UNIV, 71- *Concurrent Pos:* NIH fel, Sydney, Australia, 61-62; NIH res grant, 62-66; Fulbright lectr, Sydney, Australia,

69-70; vis fel, Western Austrailian Inst Technol, 80; Danforth Assoc, 80- *Mem:* AAAS; Genetics Soc Am; Soc Study Evolution; Am Asn Biol Teachers; Nat Sci Teachers Asn. *Res:* Evolutionary genetics; individualized instruction; genetic basis for selection. *Mailing Add:* Dept of Biol Syracuse Univ Syracuse NY 13210

DRUGER, STEPHEN DAVID, b Brooklyn, NY, May 1, 42. MOLECULAR PHYSICS, SOLID STATE PHYSICS. *Educ:* Brooklyn Col, BS, 63; Univ Rochester, MA, 66, PhD(physics), 69. *Prof Exp:* Res assoc physics, Col William & Mary, 69-70; assoc res scientist, NY Univ, 70-72; asst prof, State Univ NY, Binghamton, 72-73; res assoc physics & chem, Univ Rochester, 73-77; res assoc physics, Clarkson Col, 77-79. *Concurrent Pos:* Adj asst prof physics, Clarkson Col, 79- *Mem:* Am Phys Soc. *Res:* Charge transport, defects, and cohesive energies in molecular solids, photoionization, radiationless processes, and adsorption line shapes in large molecules. *Mailing Add:* Clarkson Col Potsdam NY 13676

DRUGG, WARREN SOWLE, b Sitka, Alaska, Jan 29, 29; m 58; c 3. GEOLOGY, PALYNOLOGY. *Educ:* Univ Wash, BS, 52, MS, 58; Claremont Grad Sch, PhD(bot), 66. *Prof Exp:* Geologist, Calif Explor Co, 58-60, assoc res geologist, Calif Res Corp, 60-66, res geologist, Chevron Res Co, 66-68, sr res geologist, 68-77, SR RES ASSOC, CHEVRON OIL FIELD RES CO, STAND OIL CO CALIF, 77- *Mem:* Soc Econ Paleont & Mineral; Am Asn Stratig Palynologists; Am Asn Petrol Geologists; Paleont Soc. *Res:* Fossil dinoflagellates, spores and pollen of Mesozoic and Tertiary Age. *Mailing Add:* Chevron Oil Field Res Co PO Box 446 La Habra CA 90631

DRUI, ALBERT BURNELL, b St Louis, Mo, Aug 31, 26; m 49; c 2. INDUSTRIAL & MECHANICAL ENGINEERING. *Educ:* Univ Washington, St Louis, BS, 49, MS, 57. *Prof Exp:* Planning & design engr, McDonnell Aircraft Corp, 49-53; prod engr, Army Ord Corps, 53; tech economist, Olin Mathieson Chem Corp, 54; plant indust engr, Metals Div, Dow Chem Co, 55-58; sr supvr Div Planning Staff, Boeing Co, 58-60; asst prof mech eng, 60-70, ASSOC PROF MECH ENG, UNIV WASH, 70- *Concurrent Pos:* Consult indust & mech engr, 60-; US Dept HEW res grant radiol opers efficiency, 67-70, co-investr, res grant Medex doctors' asst prog, 69-71; dir, Study Pilot Prog Food Serv, US Army, Natick Labs, 71; auditor & rep in bargaining, Boeing Aerospace Co, 72; consult, Gen Tel NW Systs Anal, 73, Secy State UN, 73 & John Fluke Mfg Co, 75; rep, Teamsters Local 344, 73; supvr, eval Boeing Aerospace Co mfg plans, 74; consult, Boeing Commercial Airplane Co, 76, supvr training manual, 78; auditor, Weyerhaeuser Co, all USA plants. *Mem:* Am Inst Indust Engrs; Inst Mgt Sci. *Res:* Industrial engineering to improve operational systems; work measurement and plant layout; effective delivery of health care by examining radiologists, anesthesiologists, general practitioners and mid medical care professions. *Mailing Add:* Dept of Mech Eng Univ of Wash Seattle WA 98195

DRULLINGER, ROBERT EUGENE, b Lansing, Mich, Dec 23, 44; m 67. CHEMICAL PHYSICS. *Educ:* Mich State Univ, BS, 67; Columbia Univ, PhD(chem), 72. *Prof Exp:* PHYSICIST, NAT BUR STAND, 72- *Concurrent Pos:* Nat Res Coun fel, Nat Bur Stand, 73-74. *Mem:* Am Phys Soc; AAAS. *Res:* Development of new spectroscopic techniques for the elucidation of molecular structure and kinetics; primarily concerned with the excited states of molecules with repulsive ground states. *Mailing Add:* Nat Bur of Stand Div 277-05 Boulder CO 80302

DRUM, CHARLES MONROE, b Richmond, Va, Sept 17, 34; m 58; c 3. SOLID STATE PHYSICS. *Educ:* Washington & Lee Univ, BS, 57; Univ Va, PhD(physics), 63. *Prof Exp:* NSF fel, Atomic Energy Res Estab, Eng, 63-64; MEM TECH STAFF, BELL TEL LABS, INC, 64- *Mem:* Am Phys Soc. *Res:* Imperfections in crystals; electron diffraction; crystal growth. *Mailing Add:* 2604 Gordon St Allentown PA 18104

DRUM, I(AN) M(ONDELET), b Ottawa, Ont, Oct 22, 13; m 44; c 2. CHEMICAL ENGINEERING. *Educ:* Royal Mil Col Can, dipl, 35; Queen's Univ, Ont, BSc, 37. *Prof Exp:* Exec vpres, Dye & Chem Co Can, Ltd, 48-51; mgr special projs, Home Oil Co, Ltd, 51-66, vpres spec projs, 66-76; PRES, DRUM CONSULT LTD, 76- *Concurrent Pos:* Consult, Chem Inst Can, 76- *Mem:* Fel Chem Inst Can. *Res:* Processing, transporting and marketing of natural gas and crude oil. *Mailing Add:* 10-310 Brookmere Rd SW Calgary AB T2N 1N4 Can

DRUM, RYAN WILLIAM, b Milwaukee, Wis, Sept 25, 39; c 3. BIOLOGY, HEALTH SCIENCES. *Educ:* Iowa State Univ, BSc, 61, PhD(phycol), 64. *Prof Exp:* NATO fel, Univs Bonn & Leeds, 64-65; asst prof bot, Univ Ark, 66; asst prof, Univ Mass, Amherst, 66-70; asst prof bot, Fairhaven Col, 70-76; PRIVATE CONSULT, 76- *Concurrent Pos:* Vis asst prof, Univ Calif, Los Angeles, 69-70; lectr, Dominion Herbal Col, 77- *Mem:* AAAS; Am Forestry Asn. *Res:* Cytoplasmic ultrastructure of diatoms; biogenesis of silica in diatoms; grasses and sponges; single-cell ecology; synthetic petrification; silica replication of cell lumens; pre-Columbian technology; herbal medicine; applied kinesiology. *Mailing Add:* Waldron Island WA 98297

DRUMHELLER, DOUGLAS SCHAEFFER, b Bechtelsville, Pa, Dec 31, 42; m 65; c 2. ENGINEERING. *Educ:* Univ Southern Calif, BSME, 64, MSME, 65; Lehigh Univ, PhD(appl mech), 69. *Prof Exp:* Mem tech staff optics, Bell Tel Labs, 65-67; teaching & res asst shell theory, Lehigh Univ, 67-69; MEM TECH STAFF SOLID MECH, SANDIA NAT LABS, 69- *Mem:* Soc Natural Philos; Am Acad Mech. *Res:* Theoretical work in mixture mechanics including bubbly liquids, fluid saturated porous solids, and composite materials. *Mailing Add:* Sandia Nat Labs Kirtland AFB E Albuquerque NM 87185

DRUMHELLER, JOHN EARL, b Walla Walla, Wash, Dec 19, 31; m 56; c 3. MAGNETIC RESONANCE, MAGNETIC SUSCEPTIBILITY. *Educ:* Wash State Univ, BS, 53; Univ Colo, MS, 58, PhD(physics), 62. *Prof Exp:* Engr, Douglas Aircraft Co, Calif, 53-54 & Kaiser Aluminum Co, Wash, 54;

res assoc, Univ Zurich, 62-64; from asst prof to assoc prof, 64-72, PROF PHYSICS, MONT STATE UNIV, 72- *Mem:* Am Phys Soc; Am Asn Physics Teachers. *Res:* Electron paramagnetic resonance in dilute impurity crystals and in lower dimensional magnetic compounds; dielectric and magnetic susceptibility studies; studies of the exchange interaction in magnetic materials; structural and magnetic phase transitions. *Mailing Add:* Dept of Physics Mont State Univ Bozeman MT 59717

DRUMHELLER, KIRK, b Walla Walla, Wash, Jan 14, 25; m 50; c 4. SOLAR ENERGY, MECHANICAL ENGINEERING. *Educ:* Mass Inst Technol, SB, 45. *Prof Exp:* Instr math, Whitman Col, 46-47; engr, Gen Elec Co, 51-53, supvr fuel element prod, 53-55, supvr tool & equip eng, 56-57; mgr design & projs, 58-62, adv fuel develop, 62-65; adv ceramic mat develop, 65-66, mgr mat develop, 66-68, mgr, Jersey nuclear prog, 69-70; prog mgr energy-fusion, 71-73, MEM STAFF SOLAR ENERGY PROGS, PAC NORTHWEST LABS, BATTELLE MEM INST, 74- *Mem:* Int Solar Energy Soc. *Res:* Heliostat manufacturing technology. *Mailing Add:* 2336 Camas Richland WA 99352

DRUMM, MANUEL FELIX, b St Louis, Mo, June 21, 22; m 42; c 6. ORGANIC CHEMISTRY. *Educ:* Monmouth Col, BS, 45; Univ Nev, MS, 48; Univ Mo, PhD(org chem), 51. *Prof Exp:* Res chemist, Plastics Div, 50-52, res group leader, 52-58, res sect leader, 58-60, MGR RES, RESIN PROD DIV, MONSANTO CO, 60- *Mem:* Am Chem Soc. *Res:* Thermosetting polymers; compounding and processing polyvinylchloride; polymer foams; coatings. *Mailing Add:* 730 Worcester St Indian Orchard MA 01151

DRUMMETER, LOUIS FRANKLIN, JR, b Minersville, Pa, Dec 27, 21; m 44; c 4. OPTICS. *Educ:* Johns Hopkins Univ, BA, 43, PhD(physics), 49. *Prof Exp:* Jr instr physics, Johns Hopkins Univ, 42-44, instr, 44, asst, 44-48; physicist, US Naval Res Lab, 48-52, supvr physicist, 52-78, assoc dir res, 78-80; INSTR, UNIV VA, 81- *Mem:* Optical Soc Am. *Res:* Research administration; atmospheric optics; radiative heat transfer; infrared. *Mailing Add:* 2011 Belfast Dr Fort Washington MD 20744

DRUMMOND, BOYCE ALEXANDER, III, b Denison, Tex, Feb 28, 46; m 79; c 1. ECOLOGY, ENTOMOLOGY. *Educ:* Henderson State Col, BS, 67; Univ Tex, Austin, MA, 71; Univ Fla, PhD(zool), 76. *Prof Exp:* Vis asst prof zool, Univ Fla, 76-78; ASST PROF ECOL, ILL STATE UNIV, 78- *Concurrent Pos:* Res assoc, Fla State Collection Arthropods, 74- *Mem:* AAAS; Soc Study Evolution; Ecol Soc Am; Asn Trop Biol; Lepidopterists Soc. *Res:* Evolutionary ecology, population biology and ethology of invertebrates, especially tropical ecology, coevolution of plant-animal interactions, reproductive biology and life history evolution of insects. *Mailing Add:* Dept of Biol Sci Ill State Univ Normal IL 61761

DRUMMOND, CHARLES HENRY, III, b Greensboro, NC, Aug 24, 44. CERAMIC ENGINEERING, GLASS SCIENCE & TECHNOLOGY. *Educ:* Ohio State Univ, BSc, 68, MS, 68; Harvard Univ, SM, 70, PhD(appl physics), 74. *Prof Exp:* asst prof, 74-80, ASSOC PROF CERAMIC ENG, OHIO STATE UNIV, 80- *Concurrent Pos:* NSF grant, 75-77; dir, Am Conf Glass Probs, 76- *Mem:* Am Chem Soc; Soc Glass Technol. *Res:* Structure and properties of glass; X-ray diffraction; phase transformation; physical properties. *Mailing Add:* Dept of Ceramic Eng Ohio Univ 2041 College Rd Columbus OH 43210

DRUMMOND, GEORGE I, b Alta, Jan 19, 25; m 50; c 3. BIOCHEMISTRY, PHARMACOLOGY. *Educ:* Univ Alta, BSc, 49, MSc, 51; Univ Wis, PhD, 55. *Prof Exp:* From asst prof to prof pharmacol, Univ BC, 58-74; PROF BIOCHEM, UNIV CALGARY, 74- *Concurrent Pos:* Fel biochem, Univ Wis, 55; fel pharmacol, Western Reserve Univ, 55-57. *Mem:* AAAS; Am Soc Biol Chem; Am Soc Pharmacol; Am Chem Soc. *Res:* Enzymes; carbohydrate, fat and nucleotide metabolism. *Mailing Add:* Div Biochem Dept Chem Univ Calgary Calgary AB T2N 1N4 Can

DRUMMOND, JAMES, b Warm Springs, Mont, Feb 9, 21; m 50; c 3. ANIMAL SCIENCE. *Educ:* Mont State Col, BS, 48; Univ Wyo, MS, 56. *Prof Exp:* From instr to asst prof animal sci, 48-62, prof & sheep specialist, 62-74, PROF ANIMAL SCI, MONT STATE UNIV, 74-, SUPT WOOL LAB, 51- *Concurrent Pos:* Mem, Nat Lamb & Wool Indust Comt, 64- *Res:* Wool growth; physical characteristics. *Mailing Add:* Wool Lab Mont State Univ Bozeman MT 59715

DRUMMOND, JOHN WENDELL, aeronomy, chemical physics, see previous edition

DRUMMOND, KENNETH HERBERT, b Riverside, Calif, Jan 19, 22; m 55; c 3. OCEANOGRAPHY. *Educ:* Univ Ariz, BS, 49. *Prof Exp:* Marine res technician, Scripps Inst, Univ Calif, 49-50; asst oceanog & chief technician, Res Found, Tex A&M Univ, 50-52, assoc oceanog & proj dir, 53-57; oceanogr, US Navy Oceanog Off, 52-53; res officer, Satellite Tracking Prog, Smithsonian Astrophys Observ, 57-58; asst dir mgt, 59-60; asst to chancellor admin, Univ Calif, San Diego, 60-62; Washington rep, Sci Serv Div, Tex Instruments Inc, 62-69; dir prog develop, Teledyne Inc, 69-70, assoc dir, Alexandria Labs, Teledyne Geotech Corp, 71-72; asst to pres, Ensco, Inc, Springfield, 72-76; prog dir, Marine Resources Ctrs, State of NC, 76-77; ASST TO THE DEAN & DIR SPEC PROJS, CTR WETLAND RESOURCES, LA STATE UNIV, BATON ROUGE, 77- *Concurrent Pos:* Consult, Smithsonian Inst, 60-61; partic scientist, Int Indian Ocean Exped, 62; instr, Naval Reserve Officers Sch, 63-67; exec secy indust investment panel, Comn Marine Resources & Eng Develop, Exec Off of President, 67-68; mem sci adv staff, Nat Planning Asn, 62-69; mem marine adv coun, La State Univ, 69- *Mem:* Fel AAAS; Nat Ocean Industs Asn (treas, 72-76); Marine Technol Soc (treas, 65-68); Explorers Club. *Res:* Scientific administration in the earth sciences; satellite tracking. *Mailing Add:* Ctr for Wetland Resources La State Univ Baton Rouge LA 70803

DRUMMOND, MARGARET CRAWFORD, b Tulsa, Okla, Dec 4, 22. BIOCHEMISTRY. *Educ:* Agnes Scott Col, AB, 44; Emory Univ, MS, 46, PhD(bact), 57. *Prof Exp:* Instr biochem, Nursing Sch Emory Univ, 46; biochemist, USPHS, 47-49; res biochemist tuberc res, Vet Admin Hosp, 49-53; chief res & clin biochem labs, Gravely Sanatorium, 53-54; instr bact, Med Sch & res assoc Div Basic Health Sci, 57-60, asst prof, 60-66, ASSOC PROF MICROBIOL, EMORY UNIV, 66- *Mem:* AAAS; Am Soc Microbiol. *Res:* Host-parasite interrelationships; host resistance factors in tuberculosis; purification and study of mechanism of action of staphylococcal coagulase. *Mailing Add:* Dept of Microbiol Emory Univ Atlanta GA 30322

DRUMMOND, PAUL LINWOOD, b Woodbridge, NJ. Aug 20, 26. GEOLOGY, MINERALOGY. *Educ:* Waynesburg Col, BA, 49; Columbia Univ, PhD(geol), 55. *Prof Exp:* Petrol geologist, Texaco Inc, Tex, 55-57, Tex Co, Inc, 57-62; prof geol, Waynesburg Col, 62-72; MEM STAFF, HARRIS R FENDER CO, 72- *Mem:* Geol Soc Am; Mineral Soc Am; Am Asn Petrol Geologists. *Mailing Add:* Harris R Fender Co 1111 Arlington Dr Tyler TX 75701

DRUMMOND, ROBERT ROLAND, b Martinsville, Ill, Dec 12, 16; m 53; c 3. URBAN GEOGRAPHY, PHYSICAL GEOGRAPHY. *Educ:* Ind State Univ, BS, 39; Univ Ill, MS, 40; Northwestern Univ, PhD(geog), 53. *Prof Exp:* Instr geog, Anderson High Sch, Ind, 40-41; from instr to assoc prof geog & geol, 46-57, PROF GEOG, IND STATE UNIV, TERRE HAUTE, 57- *Concurrent Pos:* Res assoc geog, Am Geog Soc, 52-54; Fulbright teaching fel geog, Univ Mandalay, 57-58; res geogr & chief terrain sect, Proj DUTY, Univ Denver, 64-66; NSF instnl grant for sci, Ind State Univ, 71. *Mem:* AAAS; Asn Am Geogr; Nat Coun Geog Educ. *Res:* Development of terrestrial visibility limitation methods and mapping. *Mailing Add:* Dept of Geog Ind State Univ Terre Haute IN 47809

DRUMMOND, ROGER OTTO, b Peoria, Ill, Aug 11, 31; m 53; c 2. ACAROLOGY. *Educ:* Wabash Col, AB, 53; Univ Md, PhD, 56. *Prof Exp:* Med entomologist, 56-70, invests leader, 70-72, location leader & res leader, 72-77, DIR, US LIVESTOCK INSECTS LAB, AGR RES SERV, USDA, 77- *Mem:* Fel AAAS; Am Entom Soc; Am Acarol Soc; Sigma Xi; Am Soc Parasitol. *Res:* Animal systemic insecticides; livestock parasites, expecially ticks and cattle grubs. *Mailing Add:* US Livestock Insects Lab USDA PO Box 232 Kerrville TX 78028

DRUMMOND, WILLIAM ECKEL, b Portland, Ore, Sept 18, 27; m 53; c 3. THEORETICAL PHYSICS. *Educ:* Stanford Univ, BS, 51, PhD(physics), 58. *Prof Exp:* Physicist, Hanford Labs, Gen Elec Co, 51-52, Calif Res & Develop, 52-54, Radiation Lab, Univ Calif, 54 & Stanford Res Inst, 55-58; prin scientist, Res Lab, Avco Mfg Co, 58-59; physicist, Gen Atomic Div, Gen Dynamics Corp, 59-65; PROF PHYSICS, UNIV TEX, AUSTIN, 65-, DIR, CTR PLASMA PHYSICS & THERMONUCLEAR RES, 66- *Concurrent Pos:* Lectr, Stanford Univ, 55. *Mem:* AAAS; fel Am Phys Soc. *Res:* Plasma physics; collective accelerators; supersonic flow and shock waves; shock waves in solids; nuclear reactor theory. *Mailing Add:* Dept of Physics Univ of Tex Austin TX 78712

DRUMWRIGHT, THOMAS FRANKLIN, JR, b Danville, Va, Sept 8, 28; m 58; c 2. NONDESTRUCTIVE TESTING, ELECTRICAL ENGINEERING. *Educ:* Va Mil Inst, BS, 51; Ohio State Univ, MS, 57. *Prof Exp:* Engr welding, Newport News Shipbuilding & Dry Dock Co, 53-55; engr, 57-70, sr engr, 70-73, group leader non-destructive testing, 73-78, eng assoc, 78-82, SR TECH SPECIALIST, ALCOA RES LABS, 82- *Mem:* Am Soc Testing Mat; fel Am Soc Nondestructive Soc Nondestructuve Testing; Sigma Xi. *Res:* Development of improved methods, instrumentation, and procedures for company-wide nondestructive testing programs; consultation regarding nondestructive testing, process instrumentation and inspection use in all Alcoa plants. *Mailing Add:* 790 Kennedy Ave New Kensington PA 15068

DRURY, LISTON NATHANIEL, b Jacksonville, Fla, Oct 5, 24; m 52; c 2. AGRICULTURAL ENGINEERING. *Educ:* Univ Ga, BSAE, 50, MS, 61. *Prof Exp:* Electrification adv, Suwannee Valley Elec Coop, 50-51 & Talquin Elec Coop, 51-53; instr, Univ TEnn, 53-54; RES AGR ENGR, AGR RES SERV, USDA, 55- *Mem:* Am Soc Agr Engrs. *Res:* Poultry environmental research. *Mailing Add:* 1745 Robert Hardeman Rd Winterville GA 30683

DRURY, MALCOLM JOHN, b Eng, Oct 61, 48; UK/Can citizen. GEOTHERMICS, TECTONOPHYSICS. *Educ:* Univ Wales, BSc, 70; Dalhousie Univ, PhD(geophysics), 77. *Prof Exp:* Fel, 71-79, RES SCIENTIST GEOPHYSICS, SEARTH PHYSICS BR, ENERGY MINES & RESOURCES CAN, 79- *Mem:* Am Geophys Union; Geol Asn Can; Can Geophys Union; Can Geothermal Resources Coun. *Res:* Geothermics; geothermal energy; tectonic evolution of precambrian shields; tectonic evolution of sedimentary basins; role of hydrology in geophysics research. *Mailing Add:* Div Gravity Geothermics & Geodynamics Earth Physics Br Observ Crescent Ottawa ON Can

DRURY, WILLIAM HOLLAND, b Newport, RI, Mar 18, 21; m 51; c 4. ECOLOGY. *Educ:* Harvard Univ, BA, 42, MA, 48, PhD, 52. *Prof Exp:* Asst prof biol & gen educ, Harvard Univ, 52-56; dir res, Mass Audubon Soc, 56-75; MEM FAC BIOL, COL OF THE ATLANTIC, 75- *Concurrent Pos:* Lectr biol, Harvard Univ, 56-75. *Mem:* Ecol Soc Am; Am Ornith Union; Wilson Ornith Soc; Arctic Inst NAm; Cooper Ornith Soc. *Res:* Bird ecology and behavior; plant ecology relative to geological processes. *Mailing Add:* 10 High St Bar Harbor ME 04609

DRUSE-MANTEUFFEL, MARY JEANNE, b Racine, Wis, Oct 17, 46; m 73; c 2. BIOCHEMISTRY, NEUROCHEMISTRY. *Educ:* Duke Univ, AB, 68; Univ NC, Chapel Hill, PhD(biochem), 72. *Prof Exp:* Fel neurobiol, Univ NC, Chapel Hill, 72; fel neurochem, Develop Metab Neurol Br, NIH, 72-73; asst prof, 73-79, ASSOC PROF BIOCHEM, STRITCH SCH MED, LOYOLA UNIV CHICAGO, 79- *Concurrent Pos:* NIMH fel, Univ NC, 69-72; Sloan-Neurobiol fel, Univ NC, 72; NIH fel, Nat Inst Neurol Commun Dis Stroke, 72-73; prin investr, Nat Found March of Dimes, 75-78, Nat Coun Alcoholism, 78-79, Nat Inst Alcohol Abuse & Alcholism, 80-; Alcohol Biomed Rev Comt; Schweppe Found career develop award, 78-81. *Mem:* AAAS; Am Soc Neurochem; Soc Neurosci; Sigma Xi. *Res:* Developmental neurochemistry; development and chemical structure of CNS myelin and synaptic plasma membranes in yound undernourished animals and in an animal model of the fetal alcohol syndrome. *Mailing Add:* Dept of Biochem & Biophys 2160 S First Ave Maywood IL 60153

DRUSHEL, HARRY (VERNON), b Evans City, Pa, Feb 2, 25; m 46; c 3. ANALYTICAL CHEMISTRY. *Educ:* Univ Pittsburgh, BS, 49, PhD, 56. *Prof Exp:* Chemist, 58-66, res assoc, 66-68, sr res assoc, 68-82, SCI ADV, EXXON RES & DEVELOP LABS, 82- *Honors & Awards:* Coates Award, Am Chem Soc. *Mem:* Am Chem Soc. *Res:* Absorption spectroscopy, ultraviolet, visible, infrared; polarography; instrumental analyses; sulfur and nitrogen compounds in petroleum; luminescence spectroscopy; gas and liquid chromatography; microcoulometry; electron spectroscopy for chemical analysis. *Mailing Add:* Exxon Res & Develop Labs Box 2226 Exxon Co USA Baton Rouge LA 70821

DRUSIN, LEWIS MARTIN, b New York, NY, Sept 25, 39. PREVENTIVE MEDICINE, INFECTIOUS DISEASES. *Educ:* Union Col, BS, 60; Cornell Univ, MD, 64; Columbia Univ, MPH, 74. *Prof Exp:* Instr med, 69-70, asst prof, Pub Health, 70-77, asst prof med, 72-79, ASSOC PROF PUB HEALTH, MED COL, CORNELL UNIV, 77-, ASSOC PROF MED, 79-; asst attend physician, 72-79, HEAD DEPT EPIDEMIOL, NEW YORK HOSP, 70-, ASSOC ATTENDING PHYSICIAN, 79- *Concurrent Pos:* Asst attend physician, Mem Hosp Cancer & Allied Dis, 73-81; vis assoc physician, The Rockefeller Univ, 77-; assoc attend physician, Cancer & Allied Dis, Memorial Hosp, New York, 81- *Mem:* Fel Am Col Physicians; fel Am Col Prev Med; Am Fedn Clin Res; Am Pub Health Asn; Med Soc Study Venereal Dis. *Res:* Epidemiology and clinical aspects of hospital acquired infections and sexually transmitted diseases. *Mailing Add:* New York Hosp Cornell Med Ctr 525 E 68th St New York NY 10021

DRUY, MARK ARNOLD, b Jan 11, 55. ORGANIC SOLID STATE CHEMISTRY. *Educ:* Brown Univ, BA, 77; Univ Pa, PhD(chem), 81. *Prof Exp:* MEM TECH STAFF, GTE LABS, 81- *Mem:* Am Chem Soc; Electrochem Soc. *Res:* Conducting polymers, specifically synthesis; characterization of polymers using traditional polymer techniques and electrochemical techniques. *Mailing Add:* GTE Labs Inc 40 Sylvan Rd Waltham MA 02254

DRUYAN, MARY ELLEN, b Washington, DC, July 14, 38; m 81; c 2. BIOCHEMISTRY, PHYSICAL CHEMISTRY. *Educ:* Wellesley Col, BA, 60; Tufts Univ, MS, 62; Univ Chicago, PhD(biochem), 72. *Prof Exp:* Mem staff, Argonne Nat Lab, 72-74; ASST PROF BIOCHEM, LOYOLA UNIV, 74- *Concurrent Pos:* Res chemist, Hines Vet Admin Hosp, Ill, 74-76, consult, 76-; mem study sect oral biol & med, NIH, 80- *Mem:* Am Chem Soc; Am Crystallog Asn; Biophys Soc; Am Asn Women Sci; Am Asn Dent Schs. *Res:* Structural chemistry of molecules of biological interest; small and large molecule crystallography; small angle scattering; spectroscopy. *Mailing Add:* Loyola Univ Sch Dent 2160 S First Ave Maywood IL 60153

DRYDEN, RICHARD LEE, b Pittsburgh, Pa, July 2, 45; m 68; c 2. MICROBIOLOGY, IMMUNOLOGY. *Educ:* Allegheny Col, BS, 67; Univ SC, MS, 69; NC State Univ, PhD(microbiol), 74. *Prof Exp:* ASST PROF BIOL, WASHINGTON & JEFFERSON COL, 73- *Mem:* Am Soc Microbiol. *Res:* Immunotherapy of spontaneous leukemia, lymphoma in mice; Azotobacter vinelandii. *Mailing Add:* Dept of Biol Washington & Jefferson Col Washington PA 15301

DRYDEN, WARREN ARNOLD, b Brooklyn, NY, Dec 29, 26; m 58; c 2. COMPUTER SCIENCES. *Educ:* NY Univ, BS, 52, MS, 53, PhD, 56. *Prof Exp:* Asst meteorologist, NY Univ, 52-55; asst prof meteorol, Fla State Univ, 55-59; data reduction analyst, 59-62, sr engr, 62-68, mgr satellite orbital anal, 68-69, data reduction, 69-71 & data systs processing, 71-73, MGR MATH SERV, MISSILE TEST PROJ, RCA INT SERV CORP, 73- *Res:* Atmospheric turbulence and refraction and their effects on optic and microwave propagation; astrodynamics and orbit determination of earth satellites and space probes; computer programs for scientific and engineering applications of missile and satellite tracking data, business applications and sociological applications. *Mailing Add:* RCA Int Serv Corp Bldg 989 MU811 Patrick Air Force Base FL 32925

DRYER, MURRAY, b Bridgeport, Conn, Nov 4, 25; m 55; c 2. SPACE PHYSICS, FLUID MECHANICS. *Educ:* Stanford Univ, BS, 49, MS, 50; Tel-Aviv Univ, PhD(physics), 70. *Prof Exp:* Res scientist aerodyn, NASA, 50-59; assoc res scientist, Martin-Marietta Corp, 59-65; lectr gasdyn, Univ Colo, Denver, 63-76; CHIEF INTERPLANETARY STUDIES SPACE PHYSICS, NAT OCEANIC & ATMOSPHERIC ADMIN, 65-; LECTR, UNIV COLO, DENVER, 78- *Concurrent Pos:* Vis assoc prof magnetohydrodyn, Colo State Univ, 66-67; mem comt solar-terrestrial res, Nat Acad Sci, 76-79. *Honors & Awards:* Space Sci Award, Am Inst Aeronaut & Astronaut, 75. *Mem:* Am Phys Soc; Am Astron Soc; Am Geophys Union; Am Inst Aeronaut & Astronaut; AAAS. *Res:* Theoretical research concerned with the solar wind and its interactions, under both quiet and disturbed conditions, with obstacles in the solar system. *Mailing Add:* Space Environ Lab Nat Oceanic & Atmospheric Admin Boulder CO 80303

DRYER, ROBERT LEONARD, b New York, NY, July 30, 21; m 44; c 3. BIOCHEMISTRY. *Educ:* Univ Iowa, BS, 43, MS, 47, PhD(biochem), 49; Am Bd Clin Chem, dipl. *Prof Exp:* Anal chemist, Harvard Univ, 43-45; from instr to asst prof biochem, Med Sch, Ind Univ, 49-54; from asst prof to assoc prof, 55-68, PROF BIOCHEM, UNIV IOWA, 68- *Concurrent Pos:* Consult, Camp Atterbury Hosp, 51-53, Thornton-Haymond Labs, Ind, 53-54 & Mattox & Moore, Inc, 54-58; mem comt clin chem, Nat Res Coun, 69-74; dir, Am Bd Clin Chem, 69-; vis prof, Wenner-Gren Inst, 70-71. *Mem:* Am Chem Soc; Soc Exp Biol & Med; Am Asn Clin Chem; Am Soc Biol Chem; Am Oil Chemists Asn. *Res:* Lipid and clinical biochemistry; chemistry of brown adipose tissue. *Mailing Add:* Dept of Biochem Univ of Iowa Iowa City IA 52242

DRYNAN, W(ALTER) RONALD, environmental health engineering, see previous edition

DRYSDALE, JAMES WALLACE, b Edinburgh, Scotland, May 11, 37; div; c 2. BIOCHEMISTRY, MOLECULAR BIOLOGY. *Educ:* Univ Edinburgh, BSc, 60, MSc, 63; Univ Glasgow, PhD(biochem), 65. *Prof Exp:* Asst lectr biochem, Univ Edinburgh, 60-63; asst lectr, Univ Glasgow, 63-66; asst prof, Mass Inst Technol, 66-68; vis lectr molecular biol, Univ Edinburgh, 68-69; prin res assoc biochem, Harvard Med Sch, 69-72; ASSOC PROF BIOCHEM, SCH MED, TUFTS UNIV, 72- *Concurrent Pos:* Consult med res apparatus, 72-; res grants, NIH, NSF & Am Cancer Soc, 69-77. *Mem:* Brit Biochem Soc; Am Soc Biol Chemists; AAAS; Am Soc Cell Biol; Am Soc Hemat. *Res:* Mammalian protein synthesis, gene expression in normal and malignant cells, iron metabolism, structure, function and metabolism of isoferritins. *Mailing Add:* Dept of Biochem & Pharmacol Sch of Med Tufts Univ Boston MA 02111

DRZEWIECKI, TADEUSZ MARIA, b London, Eng, Sept 16, 43; US citizen; m 67; c 2. FLUIDICS, CONTROL SYSTEMS. *Educ:* City Col New York, BE, 66, ME, 68; Naval Postgrad Sch, DrEng, 80. *Prof Exp:* Instr mech eng, City Col New York, 66-68; res engr, 67-73, actg res & develop supvr, 73-77, res & develop supvr fluidics, 77-78, PROJ OFFICER, FLUID CONTROL BR, HARRY DIAMOND LABS, US ARMY, 78- *Concurrent Pos:* David B Steinman mem fel, City Col New York, 66-67; dir, Tadeusz M Drzewiecki, Consult Engr, 75-; assoc ed, J Dynamic Systs, Measurement & Control. *Honors & Awards:* Cert Achievement, US Army, Harry Diamond Labs, 67, Hinman Award, 73, Sustained Super Performance, 75; Army Commendation Medal, US Army Corps Engrs, 71; Res & Develop Award, US Army, 77. *Mem:* Am Soc Mech Engrs; Am Inst Aeronaut & Astronaut; Instrument Soc Am; Sigma Xi. *Res:* Fluidics; fluid mechanics; heat transfer; control and automatic control. *Mailing Add:* Harry Diamond Labs 2800 Powder Mill Rd Adelphi MD 20783

D'SILVA, THEMISTOCLES DAMASCENO JOAQUIM, b Lira, Uganda, July 18, 32; Indian citizen; m 65; c 4. SYNTHETIC ORGANIC CHEMISTRY, STEROID CHEMISTRY. *Educ:* Univ Bombay, BS, 54; Catholic Univ Am, PhD(org chem), 64. *Prof Exp:* Fel, Worcester Found Exper Biol, 64-66; SR RES SCIENTIST PESTICIDE CHEM, UNION CARBIDE CORP, 67- *Mem:* Am Chem Soc. *Res:* Synthesis and structure-activity studies of pest control agents; modifications to impart selectivity to pests and safety to mammals and the environment. *Mailing Add:* Res & Deveop Agr Prod PO Box 8361 Res Triangle Park NC 27709

D'SOUZA, ANTHONY FRANK, b Bombay, India, May 9, 29; US citizen. MECHANICS, MECHANICAL & AEROSPACE ENGINEERING. *Educ:* Univ Poona, India, BE, 54; Univ Notre Dame, MS, 60; Purdue Univ, PhD(eng), 63. *Prof Exp:* Jr engr design, Mahindra & Mahindra Ltd, India, 54-55; asst supt, Air-India Int Corp, 55; consult indust mgt, Ibcon Ltd, 55-57; trainee, Ransomes & Rapier Ltd, Eng, 57-58; asst, Univ Notre Dame, 58-60 & Purdue Univ, 60-63; from asst prof to assoc prof dynamical systs & control, 63-77, ASSOC PROF MECH ENG, ILL INST TECHNOL, 77- *Concurrent Pos:* NSF res grant, 63-65, lab develop grant, 64-66; consult, Argonne Nat Lab, 78-; Dept Energy res grant, 79-81; Dept Transp res grant, 79-81. *Mem:* Am Soc Mech Engrs. *Res:* Vehicle dynamics, handling and stability; self-excited vibrations; stability theory; railroad engineering. *Mailing Add:* Dept Mech Eng Ill Inst Technol Chicago IL 60616

DU, JULIE (YI-FANG) TSAI, b Tsingtao, China; m 64. BIOCHEMISTRY. *Educ:* Nat Taiwan Univ, BS, 59; Tex Tech Univ, MS, 63; Ohio State Univ, PhD(phys chem), 70. *Prof Exp:* NIH fel path, Univ Louisville, 70-71, res assoc biochem, 71-74, res assoc med & vinyl chloride proj, 74-80; RES ASSOC, PROSTAGLANDIN RES, DEPT PHYSIOL & BIOPHYS, GEORGETOWN UNIV, 81- *Mem:* Am Chem Soc; AAAS; Sigma Xi. *Res:* Chemical carcinogenesis, aging, and prostglandin. *Mailing Add:* 1408 Colleen Lane McLean VA 22101

DU, LI-JEN, b Harbin, China, Sept 27, 35; m 64. ELECTRICAL ENGINEERING. *Educ:* Nat Taiwan Univ, BS, 58; Ohio State Univ, MS, 62, PhD(elec eng), 65. *Prof Exp:* Res engr, Electro Sci Lab, Ohio State Univ, 62-68; asst prof, 68-72, ASSOC PROF ELEC ENG, UNIV LOUISVILLE, 72- *Mem:* AAAS; Inst Elec & Electronics Engrs; Optical Soc Am; Sigma Xi; Am Soc Eng Educ. *Res:* Applied electromagnetics; microwave electronics; laser technology. *Mailing Add:* Speed Sci Sch Belknap Campus Univ of Louisville Louisville KY 40292

DUA, PREM NATH, b Bhera, India, Nov 15, 35; m 61; c 2. VETERINARY MEDICINE, PATHOLOGY. *Educ:* Punjab Univ, DVM, 56; Miss State Univ, MS, 63, PhD(nutrit, biochem), 67. *Prof Exp:* Vet surgeon, Punjab Vet Dept, India, 56-59; instr vet med, Punjab Vet Col, 59-61; res asst poultry sci, Miss State Univ, 61-67; res assoc nutrit & biochem, Vanderbilt Univ, 67-69, assoc vet, 69-70; vet, State Lab, Va Dept Agr, 70-77; VET MED OFFICER, FOOD & DRUG ADMIN, 77- *Concurrent Pos:* Ralston Purina Co res fel, 66. *Mem:* Am Inst Nutrit; Am Vet Med Asn. *Res:* Vitamins A and K; carotenoid and lipid metabolism; thiamine metabolism. *Mailing Add:* Food & Drug Admin HFF-134 200 C St SW Washington DC 20204

DUANE, DAVID BIERLEIN, b Port Jervis, NY, June 4, 34; m 57; c 2. MARINE GEOLOGY, COASTAL ENGINEERING. *Educ:* Dartmouth Col, AB, 57; Univ Kans, MS, 59, PhD(geol), 63. *Prof Exp:* Explor geologist, Magnolia Petrol Co, 57 & Mobil Oil Co, 62-64; res phys scientist, US Lake Surv, Corps Engrs, US Army, 64-65, supvry res phys scientist, 65-66, chief geol br, Coastal Eng Res Ctr, 66-75; ASSOC DIR GRANT MGT, NAT SEA GRANT PROG, NAT OCEANOG & ATMOSPHERIC AGENCY, 75- *Concurrent Pos:* Instr, Bur Corresp Study, Univ Kans, 60-68. *Mem:* Fel Geol Soc Am; Soc Econ Paleont & Mineral. *Res:* Geologic processes and history as related to coastal engineering, marine mineral exploration and exploitation; impact of ocean waste disposal on the environment; shore processes, sediment transport, coastal geomorphology, regional geology. *Mailing Add:* US Dept Commerce Nat Oceanic & Atmospheric Admin Rockville MD 20852

DUANE, JOSANN WATKINS, surface physics, see previous edition

DUANE, THOMAS DAVID, b Peoria, Ill, Oct 10, 17; m 44; c 4. OPHTHALMOLOGY. *Educ:* Harvard Univ, BS, 39; Northwestern Univ, MD, 43, MS, 44; Univ Iowa, PhD(physiol), 48. *Prof Exp:* PROF OPHTHAL & CHMN DEPT, JEFFERSON MED COL, THOMAS JEFFERSON UNIV, 62- *Mem:* Am Ophthal Soc; Am Acad Ophthal & Otolaryngol; Am Asn Res Vision & Ophthal; AMA. *Res:* Biophysics of the eye, especially retinal circulation. *Mailing Add:* Dept Ophthal Jefferson Med Col Thomas Jefferson Univ Philadelphia PA 19107

DUANY, LUIS F, JR, b Santiago de Cuba, Cuba, Dec 26, 19; m 48; c 1. DENTAL EPIDEMIOLOGY, PREVENTIVE DENTISTRY. *Educ:* Univ Havana, DDS, 44; Univ NC, Chapel Hill, MPH, 65, DrPH(epidemiol), 70. *Prof Exp:* Pvt pract, Cuba, 44-61; asst prof oral cancer, Sch Dent, Univ Havana, 45-46; scientist adminr res grants, Nat Inst Dent Res, 61-63; asst prof epidemiol & prev dent, Sch Dent, Univ PR, San Juan, 66-67; ASST PROF ORAL BIOL & CHIEF EPIDEMIOL SECT, INST ORAL BIOL, UNIV MIAMI, 67- *Concurrent Pos:* Nat Inst Dent Res fel, Univ Miami & Univ NC, 63-66; consult, Div Oral Biol, Univ Miami, 65-67, Div Family Med, 68-69; consult, Pan-Am Health Orgn, WHO, 68-; lectr, Sch Dent, Univ Antioquia, Colombia, 68-, Sch Dent, Univ El Salvador, 70- & Nat Inst Dent Res, 71- *Honors & Awards:* Dipl, Asn Oral Surgeons Cuba, 47 & PR Pub Health Dept, 67. *Mem:* Am Dent Asn; Int Asn Dent Res; Am Pub Health Asn. *Res:* Epidemiology of dental caries, especially microbiology, dietary regimes, dental plaque extent, oral hygiene, fluoride exposure and their relationship to caries status; studies of caries, particularly free and carie active students. *Mailing Add:* 1475 NW 12th Ave Miami FL 33152

DUAX, WILLIAM LEO, b Chicago, Ill, Apr 18, 39; m 65; c 4. X-RAY CRYSTALLOGRAPHY, MOLECULAR BIOPHYSICS. *Educ:* St Ambrose Col, BA, 61; Univ Iowa, PhD(phys chem), 67. *Prof Exp:* Res fel inorg x-ray crystallog, Ohio Univ, 67-68; res assoc steroid struct & x-ray crystallog, 68-69, head crystallog lab, 69-72, HEAD MOLECULAR BIOPHYS DEPT, MED FOUND BUFFALO, 72- *Concurrent Pos:* Co-prin investr, Nat Cancer Inst grant, 71-; prin investr, Gen Med Sci Inst grant, 73-; adj assoc prof med chem, Sch Pharm, State Univ NY Buffalo, 73-; mem, Nat Comt Crystallog, 81-83; assoc res prof, Roswell Park Div, Dept Biochem, State Univ New York, Buffalo, 81- *Mem:* AAAS; Biophys Soc; Am Crystallog Asn; Am Chem Soc; Am Asn Cancer Res. *Res:* Conformational analysis of crystal structure data for steroids polypeptide hormones, ion transport antibiotics and proteins; elucidation of structural-functional relationships among steroid and ion transport antibiotics; development and application of direct methods of crystal structure determination of large biologically import molecules. *Mailing Add:* Med Found of Buffalo 73 High St Buffalo NY 14203

DUB, MICHAEL, b Opaka, Ukraine, Mar 11, 17; US citizen; m 49; c 1. ORGANOMETALLIC CHEMISTRY, ORGANIC CHEMISTRY. *Educ:* Univ Vienna, MS, 44; City Col New York, BS, 55. *Prof Exp:* Res chemist, NY Quinine & Chem Works, 52-55 & Monsanto Chem Co, 55-60, SR RES CHEMIST, MONSANTO CO, 61- *Mem:* Am Chem Soc. *Res:* Organic synthesis; animal nutrition. *Mailing Add:* 1060 Orchard Lakes Dr St Louis MO 63141

DUBACH, HAROLD WILLIAM, b St Joseph, Mo, Nov 25, 20; m 46; c 4. PHYSICAL OCEANOGRAPHY, METEOROLOGY. *Educ:* Baker Univ, AB, 42; Univ Chicago, cert meteorol, 43. *Prof Exp:* Weather officer upper air, US Air Force Weather Serv, 42-46; res meteorologist cloud physics, Thunderstorm Proj, US Weather Bur, 46-48; phys oceanog res, US Naval Oceanog Off, 48-60, staff tech asst, 68-69; actg dir & dep oceanogr info sci, Nat Oceanog Data Ctr, 60-68; asst dir oceanog & meteorol, Coastal Plains Ctr Marine Develop Serv, 69-73, chmn marine industs dept, Beaufort Tech Educ Ctr, 73-75; oceanogr & consult, Savannah River Lab, ERDA, 75-76; dir, Marine Res Ctr, NC Off Marine Affairs, 77-78; ADMINR, SOUTHEAST UNDERSEA RES FACIL, UNIV NC, WILMINGTON, 80- *Concurrent Pos:* Forecaster & Geophysicist, US Air Force Reserves Air Weather Serv, 46-62; mem, Oceanogr Exam Panel, US Civil Serv Comn, 54-61, Meteorologist Exam Panel, 57-60; mem, Fed Adv Comn Water Pollution, US Dept Interior, 66-69; consult oceanog, Pepperdine Univ, Beaufort, 76; coordr, Ocean Outfall Proj, NC Off Marine Affairs, 76- *Honors & Awards:* Super Accomplishment Award, US Navy Oceanog Off, 62, Patent Award, 67. *Mem:* Am Meteorol Soc; Marine Technol Soc; Int Oceanog Found; Smithsonian Assocs; Nat Geog Soc. *Res:* Marine science documentation, information processing and dissemination; coastal environment and air-sea interaction; oceanographic instrumentation design; marine climatology; cloud physics, thunderstorms and culumni forms. *Mailing Add:* 4609 Dean Dr Wilmington NC 28405

DUBACH, LELAND L, b St Joseph, Mo, Apr 15, 23; m 45; c 3. METEOROLOGY, AERONOMY. *Educ:* Univ Colo, BA, 49; Univ Calif, Los Angeles, MEd, 51, MA, 65. *Prof Exp:* Meteorologist, US Army Air Corps, 43-47; teacher math & sci, Sec Schs, Calif, 49-52; meteorologist, US Air Force, 52-53, mem fac meteorol, Forecaster Supt Sch, Ill, 54-57, consult, USAF-SAC, Omaha, 59-61, chief forecaster, Lajes Field, Azores Islands, 61-63, dep sta comdr & consult, Space Systs Div, Air Force Serv Ctr, El Segundo, 63-67, coord scientist aeron, ionospheric physics & meteorol, Nat Space Sci Data Ctr, Goddard Space Flight Ctr, 67-77, meteorologist, Meteorol Prog Off, 78-79, DEP BR HEAD, SEVERE STORMS BR, GODDARD SPACE FLIGHT CTR, NASA, 80- *Mem:* Am Meteorol Soc. *Res:* Climate; severe storms, Mesometeorology. *Mailing Add:* Goddard Space Flight Ctr NASA Greenbelt MD 20771

DUBAR, JULES R, b Canton, Ohio, June 30, 23; m 64; c 2. INVERTEBRATE PALEONTOLOGY. *Educ:* Kent State Univ, BS, 49; Ore State Univ, MS, 50; Univ Kans, PhD, 57. *Prof Exp:* Asst geol, Ore State Univ, 49-50 & Univ Ill, 50-51; instr, Southern Ill Univ, 51-53 & Univ Kans, 53-54; from instr to asst prof, Southern Ill Univ, 54-57; from asst prof to assoc prof, Univ Houston, 57-62; assoc prof, Duke Univ, 62-64; sr geologist, Res Lab, Esso Prod Res Co, 64-67; from assoc prof to prof geosci & chmn dept, Morehead State Univ, 67-81; DIR EXPLOR, INT RESOURCE DEVELOP

CORP, USA, 81- *Concurrent Pos:* Consult, Fla Geol Surv, 53-59 & Int Minerals & Chem Corp, 63-64; NSF grants, 59-64, 68-70. *Mem:* AAAS; Am Asn Petrol Geol; Geol Soc Am; Am Soc Oceanog; Am Malacol Union. *Res:* Stratigraphy; paleontology and paleoecology of Neogene of eastern seaboard and gulf coastal region; Neogene mollusca. *Mailing Add:* Dept Geosci Morehead State Univ Morehead KY 40351

DUBARD, JAMES LEROY, nuclear physics, see previous edition

DUBAS, LAWRENCE FRANCIS, b Evanston, Ill, Nov 28, 52; m 76. ORGANIC CHEMISTRY. *Educ:* Univ Ill, BS, 74; Stanford Univ, PhD(org chem), 78. *Prof Exp:* RES CHEMIST ORG CHEM, E I DU PONT DE NEMOURS & CO INC, 78- *Mem:* Am Chem Soc. *Res:* Agricultural chemistry. *Mailing Add:* Dept of Biochem Exp Sta B-324 E I du Pont de Nemours & Co Inc Wilmington DE 03470

DUBAY, DENIS THOMAS, b Baltimore, Md, Mar 18, 52; m 77; c 1. ANGIOSPERM SEXUAL REPRODUCTION. *Educ:* Univ Notre Dame, BS, 74; Emory Univ, MS, 79, PhD(biol), 81. *Prof Exp:* RES ASSOC ECOL RES, DEPT BIOL, EMORY UNIV, 81-, ASST PROF, DEPT BIOL, 82- *Mem:* Sigma Xi; Ecol Soc Am; Am Inst Biol Sci; AAAS. *Res:* Interspecific differences in the effects of natural and human-generated stress factors on the sexual reproduction of flowering plants. *Mailing Add:* Dept Biol Emory Univ Atlanta GA 30322

DUBAY, GEORGE HENRY, b Chicago, Ill, May 26, 14; m 46; c 5. MATHEMATICS. *Educ:* Loyola Univ, Ill, BS, 36, MA, 38. *Prof Exp:* Salesman, Midcontinent Chem Corp, 38-39; purchase agent, McKesson & Robbins, Inc, 39-40; teacher pub schs, Ill, 46, 47-48; instr, Marquette Univ, 46-47; from asst prof to assoc prof, 48-69, chmn dept, 52-76, PROF MATH, UNIV ST THOMAS, 69- *Concurrent Pos:* Tech ed, J Data Mgt, Data Processing Mgt Asn. *Honors & Awards:* Minnie Piper Prof award, 58; cert, Data Processing, 64. *Mem:* Asn Comput Mach; Math Asn Am; Soc Indust & Appl Math; Data Processing Mgt Asn; Asn Educ Data Systs. *Res:* Computing. *Mailing Add:* Dept of Math Univ St Thomas 3812 Montrose Blvd Houston TX 77006

DUBBE, RICHARD F, b Minneapolis, Minn, Jan 9, 29; m 50; c 4. ELECTRONICS. *Educ:* Univ Minn, BEE, 53. *Prof Exp:* Tech serv engr, Minn Mining & Mfg Co, 53-58, res engr, 58-63, proj supvr electron beam recording, 63-65, proj mgr, 65-66, res mgr, 66-76, TECH DIR, MINCOM DIV, 3M CO, 76- *Mem:* Soc Motion Picture & TV Engrs; Inst Elec & Electronics Engrs; Soc Photog, Scientists & Engrs. *Res:* Electron beam, magnetic and sound recording; television; motion picture technology. *Mailing Add:* Mincom Div Mincom 3M Ctr St Paul MN 55101

DUBBELDAY, PIETER STEVEN, b Surakarta, Indonesia, Dec 23, 28; nat US; m 58; c 2. HYDROACOUSTICS. *Educ:* Free Univ, Amsterdam, Candidatus, 50, Drs, 53, PhD(nuclear physics), 59. *Prof Exp:* Asst physics, Free Univ, Amsterdam, 51-53 & 54-56, chief asst, 56-59; proj assoc & instr, Nuclear Physics Lab, Univ Wis, 59-61; instr physics, Fla Inst Technol, 60-66, assoc prof, 66-70, prof physics & oceanog, 70-81; RES PHYSICIST, UNDERWATER SOUND REF DIV, NAVAL RES LAB, ORLANDO, 81- *Concurrent Pos:* Engr, Missile Test Proj, RCA Serv Co, 61-63, sr engr, 63-66. *Mem:* Acoust Soc Am; Am Asn Physics Teachers; Am Phys Soc. *Res:* Neutron physics, especially polarization of neutrons; problems in missile tracking; survey and error analyses of atmospheric refraction; physical oceanography; hydroacoustics; shallow water circulation. *Mailing Add:* Dept Oceanog & Ocean Eng Fla Inst of Technol Melbourne FL 32901

DUBBS, DEL ROSE M, b Vesta, Minn, Feb 10, 28. VIROLOGY, BIOCHEMISTRY. *Prof Exp:* Univ Minn, BA, 50, MS, 57, PhD(bact), 61. *Prof Exp:* Res asst bact, Univ Minn, 53-60; res assoc biochem, Univ Tex M D Anderson Hosp & Tumor Inst, 60-62; from asst prof to assoc prof, 62-74; PROF VIROL, BAYLOR COL MED, 74- *Concurrent Pos:* USPHS res career develop award, 65-70. *Mem:* Am Soc Microbiol. *Res:* Studies of the biochemical alterations in virus infected cells and to relate these changes to transformation of normal cells to malignant cells. *Mailing Add:* Dept of Biochem Virol Baylor Col of Med Houston TX 77030

DUBE, DAVID GREGORY, b Cincinnati, Ohio, Aug 28, 48; m 74; c 1. ANALYTICAL CHEMISTRY. *Educ:* Xavier Univ, BS, 70; Pa State Univ, PhD(chem), 79. *Prof Exp:* Res Engr, Chem & Metall Div, Gen Telephone & Electronics, 78-81; MGR METHODS DEVELOP & PHARMACEUT QUALITY CONTROL, MEAD JOHNSON & CO, SUBSID BRISTOL MYERS CORP, 81- *Mem:* Am Chem Soc. *Res:* Methods for the routine analysis of pharmaceuticals; computer-aided experimentation. *Mailing Add:* Mead Johnson & Co 2404 Pa Ave Evansville IN 47721

DUBE, HARVEY ALBERT, b Chicopee, Mass, April 19, 18; m 43; c 3. CHEMISTRY. *Educ:* Niagara Univ, BS, 41; Univ Detroit, MS, 43; Iowa State Col, PhD(plant chem), 47. *Prof Exp:* Asst, Iowa State Col, 43-45; instr, 47-48, from asst prof to assoc prof, 48-59, PROF CHEM, XAVIER UNIV, OHIO, 59-, CHMN DEPT, 75- *Mem:* Am Chem Soc. *Res:* Thermodynamic properties of organic compounds; electro chemistry of molten salts; high polymers; atomic and molecular structure. *Mailing Add:* Dept of Chem Xavier Univ Cincinnati OH 45207

DUBE, MAURICE ANDREW, BOTANY. *Educ:* Wash State Univ, BS, 50; Ore State Univ, MS, 58, PhD(bot), 63. *Prof Exp:* Asst prof bot, 63-68, ASSOC PROF BIOL, WESTERN WASH STATE COL, 68- *Res:* Life history of marine algae. *Mailing Add:* Dept Biol Western Wash State Col Bellingham WA 98225

DUBE, PIERRE ANDRE, b St Jean Port Joli, Que, May 18, 41; m 66; c 3. AGRONOMY, CROP PHYSIOLOGY. *Educ:* Laval Univ, BSc, 67, MSc, 69; Univ Guelph, PhD(ecophysiol), 73. *Prof Exp:* PROF AGRON, DEPT PLANT SCI, FAC AGR, LAVAL UNIV, 72- *Concurrent Pos:* Mem, Que

Comt Agrometerol, 73-, chmn, 75-; mem, Can Comt Agrometeorol, 74- *Mem:* Agr Inst Can; Can Soc Agron. *Res:* Climatic zonation as related to agricultural productivity; lighting related to greenhouse productions. *Mailing Add:* Dept Phytol Fac Agr Laval Univ Ste-Foy Quebec PQ C1K 7P4 Can

DUBE, ROGER RAYMOND, b Portland, Maine, Nov 24, 49; m 72; c 2. PHYSICS. *Educ:* Cornell Univ, AB, 72; Princeton Univ, MA, 74, PhD(physics), 76. *Prof Exp:* Astronomer, Kitt Peak Nat Observ, 76-77; sr staff mem physics, Jet Propulsion Lab, 77-78; asst prof physics, Univ Mich, Dearborne, 78-80; ASST RES PROF, UNIV ARIZ, 80- *Concurrent Pos:* mem, Proposal Rev Comt, NSF, 78-80. *Mem:* AAAS; Am Astron Soc; Soc Advan Chicanos & Native Am in Sci. *Res:* Experimental relativity; cosmology; astrophysics; detector development. *Mailing Add:* Dept Physics Bldg 81 Univ Ariz Tuscon AZ 85721

DUBECK, LEROY W, b Orange, NJ, Mar 1, 39. SOLID STATE PHYSICS. *Educ:* Rutgers Univ, BA, 60, MA, 62, PhD(physics), 65. *Prof Exp:* Teaching asst physics, Rutgers Univ, 60-62; asst prof, 65-69, assoc prof, 69-76, PROF PHYSICS, TEMPLE UNIV, 76- *Mem:* Am Phys Soc; Am Asn Physics Teachers (secy-treas, 78-80). *Res:* Thermal conductivity; magnetization and flux motion properties of superconductors; nuclear magnetic resonance of superconductors; superconducting tunneling; science education. *Mailing Add:* Dept of Physics Temple Univ Philadelphia PA 19122

DUBERG, JOHN E(DWARD), b New York, NY, Nov 30, 17; m 43; c 2. AERONAUTICAL ENGINEERING. *Educ:* Manhattan Col, BS, 38; Va Polytech Inst, MS, 40; Univ Ill, PhD(struct eng), 48. *Prof Exp:* Field engr, Caldwell Wingate Builders, 38-39; asst, Talbot Lab, Univ Ill, 40-43; aeronaut res scientist, Nat Adv Comt Aeronaut, Va, 43-46; asst chief res engr, Standard Oil Co Ind, 46-48; aeronaut res scientist, Nat Adv Comt Aeronaut, 48-52, chief, struct res div, 52-56; res engr, Aeroneutronics Syst, Inc, 56-57; prof struct eng, Univ Ill, 57-59; tech asst to chief, 59-61, tech asst to assoc dir, 61-64, asst dir, 64-68, assoc dir, Theoret Mech Div, 68-80, RES PROF, GEORGE WASH UNIV, JOINT INST FOR ADVAN FLIGHT SCI, LANGLEY RES CTR, NASA, 80- *Concurrent Pos:* Mem panel guided missiles mat, minerals & metals adv bd, Nat Acad Sci. *Honors & Awards:* DeFlorez Training Award, Am Inst Aeronaut & Astronaut, 76. *Mem:* Am Inst Aeronaut & Astronaut; AAAS; Sigma Xi; Soc Indust & Appl Math; Am Soc Eng Educ. *Res:* Fatigue of joints in steel structures; stress analysis of stiffened shells; space environmental effects. *Mailing Add:* George Washington Univ Joint Inst Advan Flight Sci MS 169 Langley Res Ctr NASA Hampton VA 23665

DUBES, GEORGE RICHARD, b Sioux City, Iowa, Oct 12, 26; m 64; c 6. GENETICS. *Educ:* Iowa State Univ, BS, 49; Calif Inst Technol, PhD(genetics), 53. *Prof Exp:* Res assoc inst coop res, McCollum-Pratt Inst, Johns Hopkins Univ, 53-54; res assoc, Sect Virus Res, Med Ctr, Univ Kans, 54-56, from asst prof to assoc prof, 56-64; head viral genetic sect, Eugene C Eppley Inst Res Cancer & Allied Dis, 64-68; assoc prof, 64-81, PROF MICROBIOL, COL MED, UNIV NEBR, OMAHA, 81- *Mem:* Genetics Soc Am; Am Genetic Asn; Am Soc Microbiol; Am Asn Cancer Res; NY Acad Sci. *Res:* Genetics of animal viruses; transfection; amoebic cysts; copper-mediated inactivation of ribonucleic acid. *Mailing Add:* Dept Med Microbiol Col Med Univ Nebr Omaha NE 68105

DUBES, RICHARD C, b Chicago, Ill, Oct 7, 34; m 59; c 1. COMPUTER SCIENCE. *Educ:* Univ Ill, BSEE, 56; Mich State Univ, MS, 58, PhD(elec eng), 62. *Prof Exp:* Mem tech staff, Hughes Aircraft Co, 56-57; asst elec eng, 57-58, asst instr, 58-61, from asst prof to assoc prof, 62-70, PROF ELEC ENG & COMPUT SCI, MICH STATE UNIV, 70- *Mem:* Sigma Xi; Inst Elec & Electronics Engrs; Pattern Recognition Soc. *Res:* Pattern recognition; exploratory data analysis; image processing; signal processing; statistical computing. *Mailing Add:* Dept of Comput Sci Mich State Univ East Lansing MI 48824

DUBEY, JITENDER PRAKASH, b Farrukharbad, India, July 15, 38; US citizen; m 64; c 2. PARASITOLOGY. *Educ:* MP Vet Col, India, BVSc & AH, 60; UP Vet Col, MVSc, 63; Univ Sheffield, Eng, PhD(parasitol), 66. *Prof Exp:* Res assoc path, Dept Path, Univ Kans Med Ctr, 68-73; asst prof, Dept Vet Pathobiol, Ohio State Univ, 73-76, assoc prof, 76-78; PROF VET PARASITOL, DEPT VET SCI, MONT STATE UNIV, 78- *Mem:* Am Soc Parasitologists; Soc Protozool; Am Vet Med Asn; Indian Soc Parasitologists. *Res:* Toxoplasmosis, sarcocystosis, pathogenesis of parasitic diseases. *Mailing Add:* Dept Vet Sci Mont State Univ Bozeman MT 59717

DUBEY, RAJENDRA NARAIN, b Bihar, India, Nov 2, 38; m 67; c 3. MECHANICAL ENGINEERING, APPLIED MATHEMATICS. *Educ:* Patna Univ, BSc, 57; Ranchi Univ, BSc, 61; Univ Waterloo, PhD(civil eng), 66. *Prof Exp:* Asst lectr civil eng, Regional Inst Tech, Jamshedpur, India, 61-62; asst engr, M M Bilaney & Co, India, 63-64; fel civil eng, 66-67, from asst prof to assoc prof mech eng, 67-80, PROF DEPT ENG, UNIV WATERLOO, 80- *Mem:* Assoc Am Soc Mech Engrs. *Res:* Plastic instabilities in solids; convective instabilities in fluids; boundary layer flow; dynamic instabilities. *Mailing Add:* Solid Mech Div Univ of Waterloo Waterloo ON N2L 3G1 Can

DUBEY, SATYA D(EVA), b Sakara Bajid, India, Feb 10, 30; US citizen; m 60; c 1. STATISTICS, MATHEMATICS. *Educ:* Patna Univ, BSc, 51; Indian Statist Inst Calcutta, dipl, 53; Mich State Univ, PhD(statist), 60. *Prof Exp:* Tech asst statist, Indian Inst Technol, 53-56; res asst math, Carnegie Inst Technol, 56-57; instr statist & res asst, Mich State Univ, 57-60; sr math statistician, Procter & Gamble, Co, Ohio, 60-65; head statist sect, 65-66; prin statistician & group leader statist & opers res, Ford Motor Co, Mich 66-68; assoc prof indust eng & opers res, NY Univ, 68-73; actg dir, Div Biometrics, 75-76, CHIEF & STATIST EVAL BR, BUR DRUGS, FOOD AND DRUG ADMIN, HEW, 73- *Concurrent Pos:* Consult, Mich State Budget Div, 58, HEW, 63-66, Dept Defense, 68-70; del, Int Statist Inst, 71; prin investr & dir res contract on statist, Procedures In Reliability Eng, Dept Army, 71- *Honors*

& Awards: Commendable Serv award, Food & Drug Admin, 77. *Mem:* AAAS; fel Royal Statist Asn; NY Acad Sci. *Res:* Statistical inference procedures applicable to engineering, physical, social, biomedical, mathematical and computer sciences. *Mailing Add:* Bur of Drugs 5600 Fishers Lane Rockville MD 20857

DUBIN, ALVIN, b Russia, Jan 23, 14; nat US; m 38; c 2. BIOCHEMISTRY. *Educ:* Brooklyn Col, BA, 40, MS, 42. *Prof Exp:* Asst dir labs, Beth-El Hosp, 38-46; chief biochemist, 47-53, DIR DEPT BIOCHEM, HOKTOEN INST MED RES, COOK COUNTY HOSP, 53-; ASSOC PROF BIOCHEM, RUSH SCH MED, 70- *Concurrent Pos:* Consult, Oak Forest Hosp, 56-, Woodlawn Hosp, 56 & MacNeal Mem Hosp, 58-; asst prof biochem, Univ Ill Col Med, 60-70 & Cook County Grad Sch, 60- *Mem:* Am Asn Clin Chem; Soc Exp Biol & Med; Am Chem Soc; Am Inst Chemists. *Res:* Biochemistry and its relationship to liver and kidney disease; synthesis and degradation of proteins and the excretion of proteins as related to renal damage; relationship of uric acid and calcium metabolism to such diseases as gout and parathyroid diseases. *Mailing Add:* Apt 33C 6101 N Sheridan Rd E Chicago IL 60620

DUBIN, DONALD T, b Brooklyn, NY, Mar 23, 32; m 65; c 6. BIOCHEMISTRY, CELL BIOLOGY. *Educ:* Harvard Univ, AB, 53; Columbia Univ, MD, 56. *Prof Exp:* Intern med, Bronx Munic Hosp, NY, 56-57, resident, 59-60; sr asst surgeon biochem, NIH, 57-59; instr, Harvard Med Sch, 62-63, assoc, 63-66, asst prof, 66-67; assoc prof, 67-71, PROF MICROBIOL, RUTGERS MED SCH, COL MED & DENT, NJ, 71- *Concurrent Pos:* Res fel bact, Harvard Med Sch, 60-62. *Mem:* Am Soc Cell Biol; Am Soc Microbiol; Am Soc Biol Chem. *Res:* Nucleic acid metabolism; mitochondrial biogenesis. *Mailing Add:* Dept Microbiol Rutgers Med Sch Col of Med & Dent of NJ Piscataway NJ 08854

DUBIN, HENRY CHARLES, b Paterson, NJ, Sept 7, 43; m 66; c 2. ELECTROMAGNETICS. *Educ:* St Lawrence Univ, NY, BSc, 65; Ind Univ, Bloomington, MA, 68, PhD(chem physics), 73. *Prof Exp:* Res physicist ballistics, US Army Ballistic Res Labs, 72-75; PHYSICIST ELECTROMAGNETICS, US ARMY SYSTS ANAL ACTIV, 75- *Res:* Computer simulations of antenna radiation patterns and electromagnetic signal propagation. *Mailing Add:* 1619 Chestnut St Cardiff MD 21024

DUBIN, ISADORE NATHAN, pathology, deceased

DUBIN, MARK WILLIAM, b New York, NY, Aug 30, 42; m 64; c 2. NEUROBIOLOGY. *Educ:* Amherst Col, BA, 64; Johns Hopkins Univ, PhD(biophys), 69. *Prof Exp:* Res fel sensory physiol, John Curtin Sch Med Res, Australian Nat Univ, 69-71; ASSOC PROF NEUROBIOL, DEPT MOLECULAR, CELLULAR & DEVELOP BIOL, UNIV COLO, BOULDER, 71- *Concurrent Pos:* Psychiat Inst grant, 72-, Nat Eye Inst grant, 72-, NIH grant, 72-, NSF grant, 77- *Mem:* AAAS; Soc Neurosci; Asn Res Vision & Ophthal. *Res:* Information processing and structure-function relationships in the vertebrate visual system; development of neural connections between levels of the visual system; anatomy of the vertebrate retina. *Mailing Add:* Dept MCD Biol Box 347 Univ Colo Boulder CO 80309

DUBIN, MAURICE, b Boston, Mass, Dec 29, 26; m 60; c 3. PHYSICS, ASTROPHYSICS. *Educ:* Univ Mich, BS, 48; Harvard Univ, AM, 49. *Prof Exp:* Physicist, Cornell Aeronaut Res Lab, 48-50; geophys res directorate, Air Force Cambridge Res Labs, Mass, 50-59 & Goddard Space Flight Ctr, NASA, Md, 59, head aeronomy prof, Off Space Sci, Washington, DC, 59-64, CHIEF INTERPLANETARY DUST & COMETARY PHYSICS, 64- *Concurrent Pos:* Mem synoptic rocket panel working group II, Cmt Exten to Standard Atmos, 60-; mem tech panel on satellites, Int Geophys Year. *Mem:* Am Phys Soc; Sci Res Soc Am; Am Inst Aeronaut & astronaut; Am Geophys Union. *Res:* Space research in atmospheric physics, astrophysical research on interplanetary dust and comets; experimental research with sounding rockets and satellites for investigations of the airglow, the upper atmosphere comads and micrometeorites. *Mailing Add:* NASA Goddard Space Flight Ctr Code 963 Greenbelt MD 20771

DUBIN, NORMAN H, b Paterson, NJ, Feb 13, 42; m 64; c 1. REPRODUCTIVE ENDOCRINOLOGY. *Educ:* Univ Rochester, BA, 63; Rutgers Univ, PhD(zool), 70. *Prof Exp:* Fel, Ohio State Univ, 69-71; asst prof obstet-gynec, Univ Md, 71-75; ASST PROF OBSTET-GYNEC, JOHNS HOPKINS UNIV, 75- *Concurrent Pos:* Lalor Found award, 72. *Mem:* Soc Study Reproduction; AAAS; Endocrine Soc. *Res:* Factors affecting steroid and prostaglandin production during pregnancy; fertility control. *Mailing Add:* Dept of Gynec-Obstet Johns Hopkins Univ Sch of Med Baltimore MD 21205

DUBIN, ROBERT REVEL, chemical physics, recording technology, see previous edition

DUBINS, LESTER ELI, b Washington, DC, Apr 27, 20. MATHEMATICS. *Educ:* City Col New York, BS, 42; Univ Chicago, MS, 50, PhD(math), 55. *Prof Exp:* Mathematician, Inst Air Weapons Res, Chicago, 51-55; asst prof math, Carnegie Inst Technol, 55-57; NSF fel, Inst Adv Study, 57-59; NSF fel, 59-60, from asst prof to assoc prof, 60-65, PROF MATH & STATIST, UNIV CALIF, BERKELEY, 65- *Concurrent Pos:* Consult, Inst Air Weapons Res, Chicago, 55-60. *Mem:* Am Math Soc; Math Asn Am. *Res:* Probability theory; differential geometry; game theory; functional analysis. *Mailing Add:* Dept of Math & Statist Univ of Calif 970 Evans Hall Berkeley CA 94720

DUBINS, MORTIMER IRA, b Boston, Mass, Mar 24, 19; m 51; c 1. GEOLOGY, METEOROLOGY. *Educ:* Tufts Col, BS, 40; Univ Kans, MS, 48; Boston Univ, EdM, 49, EdD(sci educ), 53. *Prof Exp:* Instr chem & sci, Boston Univ, 48-49; teacher & head dept sci, High Sch, Foxboro, 49-53, teacher, 53-54; instr sci educ, Castleton Teachers Col, 54-55; asst prof, Northwestern Univ, 55-57; PROF GEOL & METEOROL, STATE UNIV NY COL ONEONTA, 57- *Concurrent Pos:* Instr, Boston Univ, 50-51; dir, NSF Earth Sci Inst, 61-63. *Mem:* Fel AAAS; Am Meteorol Soc; Mineral Soc Am. *Res:* Meteorology; economic geology; earth science; mineralogy; crystallography. *Mailing Add:* Dept of Earth Sci State Univ of NY Col Oneonta NY 13820

DUBINSKY, BARRY, b Philadelphia, Pa. PHARMACOLOGY. *Educ:* Temple Univ, BS, 62; Univ Pittsburgh, MS, 65, PhD(pharmacol), 68. *Prof Exp:* Asst pharmacol, Univ Pittsburgh, 62-66; sr scientist, Dept Pharmacodyn, Warner-Lambert Res Inst, Morris Plains, 68-77; SR SCIENTIST, DIV PHARMACOL, ORTHO PHARMACEUT CORP, RARITAN, 77-, RES FEL, DIV BIOL RES, 80- *Mem:* Am Soc Pharmacol & Exp Therapeut; AAAS. *Res:* Neuropharmacology; psychopharmacology. *Mailing Add:* Ortho Pharmaceut Corp US Hwy 202 Raritan NJ 08869

DUBISCH, ROY, b Chicago, Ill, Feb 5, 17; m 39; c 3. MATHEMATICS. *Educ:* Univ Chicago, BS, 38, MS, 40, PhD(math), 43. *Prof Exp:* Asst physics, Wilson Jr Col, 38-40; instr math, Ill Inst Technol, 40-41 & Univ Mont, 42-46; asst prof & chmn dept, Triple Cities Col, 46-48; assoc prof, Fresno State Col, 48-54, prof & chmn dept, 55-61; PROF MATH, UNIV WASH, 61- *Mem:* Am Math Soc; Math Asn Am; Nat Coun Teachers Math. *Res:* Mathematical education. *Mailing Add:* 3881 S Skagit Hwy Sedro Woolley WA 98284

DUBISCH, RUSSELL JOHN, b Missoula, Mont, May 15, 45; m 66; c 2. GRAVITATION THEORY, PHILOSOPHY OF SPACETIME. *Educ:* Reed Col, BA, 67; Univ Wash, MS, 69; Univ Pittsburgh, PhD(physics), 78. *Prof Exp:* Vis asst prof, Univ Colo, Colorado Springs, 79-80; ASST PROF PHYSICS, SIENA COL, 80- *Mem:* Am Asn Physics Teachers. *Res:* Mathematical theory of gravitational radiation; classical-background approaches to quantization in general relativity; back-reaction problem in general relativity; philosophy of spacetime; formation of stars. *Mailing Add:* Dept Physics Siena Col Loudonville NY 12211

DUBISKI, STANISLAW, b Warsaw, Poland, Aug 21, 29; Can citizen; m 55; c 1. IMMUNOCHEMISTRY, IMMUNOGENETICS. *Educ:* Wroclaw Univ, MD, 53; Silesian Med Acad, MD(microbiol), 57. *Prof Exp:* Res asst microbiol, Med Sch, Wroclaw Univ, 51-54; res asst, Silesian Med Acad, 54-57, asst prof, 57-59; head dept serol, Inst Hemat, Poland, 59-61; res assoc & clin teacher, 63-67, head immunol res lab, Toronto Western Hosp, 63-78, asst prof path chem & med, 67-70, assoc prof, 70-76, PROF CLIN BIOCHEM, UNIV TORONTO, 76-, PROF MED GENETICS, 78-, MEM INST IMMUNOL, SCH GRAD STUDIES, 71- *Concurrent Pos:* Training scholar, Cambridge Univ & Lister Inst, Eng, 58; vis scientist, Basel Inst for Immunol, Switz, 73-74. *Mem:* Brit Soc Immunol; NY Acad Sci; Am Asn Immunol; Can Soc Immunol (secy, 67-68, vpres, 71-72, pres, 73-75). *Res:* Polymorphism of serum proteins; mechanism and regulation of antibody formation; genetics and immunochemistry of rabbit immunoglobulin allotypes. *Mailing Add:* 4368 Med Sci Bldg Univ Toronto Toronto ON M5S 2R8 Can

DUBLE, RICHARD LEE, b Galveston, Tex, May 31, 40; m 69. AGRONOMY, PLANT PHYSIOLOGY. *Educ:* Tex A&M Univ, BS, 62, MS, 65, PhD(plant & soil sci), 67. *Prof Exp:* Asst prof forage physiol, Agr Res & Exten Ctr, Overton, 67-70, asst prof turf res, 70-73, assoc prof agron, 73-74, TURFGRASS SPECIALIST, TEX AGR EXTEN SERV, TEX A&M UNIV, 75- *Mem:* Am Soc Agron. *Mailing Add:* Tex Agr Exten Serv Tex A&M Univ College Station TX 77843

DUBLIN, THOMAS DAVID, b New York, NY, Jan 18, 12; m 39; c 2. HEALTH CARE ADMINISTRATION. *Educ:* Dartmouth Col, AB, 32; Harvard Univ, MD, 36; Johns Hopkins Univ, MPH, 40, DrPH, 41; Am Bd Prev Med, dipl, 49. *Prof Exp:* Intern, Boston City Hosp, 36-38; asst res physician, Rockefeller Inst Hosp, 38-39; epidemiologist-in-training, State Dept Health, NY, 39-40, asst dist state health officer, 40, epidemiologist, 41-42; assoc prof prev med & community health, Long Island Col Med, 42-43, prof & exec officer dept, 43-48; exec dir, Nat Health Coun, 48-53, med consult, Nat Found Infantile Paralysis, 53-55; med dir community serv prog, Off Dir, NIH, 55-60, actg chief, Geog Dis Studies, 60, chief epidemiol & biomet br, Off Tech Coop & Res, AID, 66-67, Off War Hunger, 67-68; dir, Off Health Manpower, HEW, 68-72; mem staff, Bur Health Manpower Educ, NIH, 72-76; CONSULT, 76- *Concurrent Pos:* Mem, Bd Dirs, Am Bd Prev Med, 61-71, vchmn prev med, 65-71. *Mem:* AAAS; fel Am Pub Health Asn; AMA; Am Epidemiol Soc; fel NY Acad Med. *Res:* Epidemiology; health policy development with special emphasis on health manpower resources. *Mailing Add:* 2938 Garfield St NW Washington DC 20008

DUBLIN, WILLIAM BROOKS, b Little Rock, Ark, Dec 10, 09; m 42; c 1. PATHOLOGY. *Educ:* Univ Calif, Los Angeles, AB, 29; Univ Southern Calif, 29-31; Univ Calif, MA, 33, MD, 36. *Prof Exp:* Pathologist, Western State Hosp, Wash, 40-44; pathologist, Emory Clin, 44-45; pathologist, Indianapolis Gen Hosp, 45-49; pathologist, Vet Admin Hosp, Ft Logan, Colo, 49-54; pathologist, Daniel Freeman Mem Hosp, Inglewood, Calif, 54-65; pathologist, Laurel Grove Hosp, 65-70; chief neuropath, lab serv & dir, Lab Auditory Path, Vet Admin Hosp Martinez, 70-82; CONSULT NEUROPATHOL, HOUSE EAR INST, LOS ANGELES, 82- *Concurrent Pos:* Fel path, Mayo Found, Univ Minn, 37-40; assoc clin prof path, Univ Calif, Davis; emer clin assoc prof otolaryngol, Sch Med, Stanford Univ, 67- *Mem:* Assoc Am Acad Ophthal & Otolaryngol; fel Am Col Physicians; fel Am Soc Clin Pathologists. *Res:* Neuropathology; otologic pathology; histology; anatomy. *Mailing Add:* Lab Serv Vet Admin Hosp Martinez CA 94553

DUBNAU, DAVID, molecular biology, see previous edition

DUBNER, RONALD, b New York, NY, Oct 12, 34; m 58; c 3. NEUROBIOLOGY. *Educ:* Columbia Univ, BA, 55, DDS, 58; Univ Mich, Ann Arbor, PhD(physiol), 64. *Prof Exp:* Intern clin dent, Pub Health Serv Hosp, Baltimore, Md, 58-59, staff dentist, Clin Ctr, NIH, 59-61, investr physiol, 61-64, investr neurophysiol, 65-68, chief neurol mechanisms sect, 68-73, CHIEF NEUROBIOL & ANESTHESIOL BR, NAT INST DENT RES, 73- *Concurrent Pos:* Vis assoc prof, Sch Dent, Howard Univ, 68-80; co-chmn, Conf Oral-Facial Mechanisms, Honolulu, 70; vis scientist, Dept Anat, Univ Col, Univ London, 70-71; sect ed, Pain, 74-; coun mem, Int Asn for the Study of Pain, 75-81; mem, Fed Interagency Comt on New Therapies for Pain and Discomfort, 78-81; assoc-ed, J Neurosci, 80-; bd dir, Am Pain Soc, 80-82. *Honors & Awards:* Meritorious Serv Medal, USPHS, 75. *Mem:* AAAS; Am

Physiol Soc; Int Asn Dent Res (pres, Neurosci Group, 76-77); Soc Neurosci; Int Asn Study Pain (vpres, 81-). *Res:* Mechanisms of oral facial sensation, especially mechanisms of pain, touch and temperature sensation; cortical and subcortical mechanisms of sensation. *Mailing Add:* Neurobiol & Anesthesiol Br Nat Inst Dent Res Bldg 30 Rm B-18 Bethesda MD 20014

DUBNICK, BERNARD, b Brooklyn, NY, May 29, 28; m 52, 66; c 2. PHARMACOLOGY. *Educ:* City Col New York, BS, 49; Univ Ill, PhD(chem), 53. *Prof Exp:* Dir dept pharmacodyn, Warner-Lambert Res Inst, 53-77; DIR CARDIOVASC-CENT NERVOUS SYST RES SECT, MED RES DIV, AM CYANAMID CO, 77- *Mem:* Fel AAAS; Am Chem Soc; fel NY Acad Sci; Am Soc Pharmacol. *Res:* Biochemical pharmacology; central nervous system; cardiovascular; allergy; drug metabolism. *Mailing Add:* Am Cyanamid Co Med Res Div Pearl River NY 10965

DUBOIS, ARTHUR BROOKS, b New York, NY, Nov 21, 23; m 50; c 3. PHYSIOLOGY. *Educ:* Cornell Univ, MD, 46. *Prof Exp:* Intern med, New York Hosp, 46-47; asst resident med, Peter Bent Brigham Hosp, 51-52; from asst prof to prof physiol, Sch Med, Univ Pa, 52-75, from assoc prof to prof med, 57-75; PROF EPIDEMIOL & PHYSIOL, MED SCH, YALE UNIV, 74-; DIR, JOHN B PIERCE FOUND LAB, 74- *Concurrent Pos:* Life Ins med res fel physiol, Sch Med, Univ Rochester, 49-51; NIH res career award, 63-74; investr, Am Heart Asn, 55-63; Bowditch lectr, Am Physiol Soc, 58; consult, US Naval Hosp, Philadelphia, 58-74; mem, Nat Res Coun panel rev NSF fel appln, 59-62; mem Am Inst Biol Sci adv comt physiol, Off Naval Res, 61-64; consult, Philadelphia Gen Hosp, 62-74; chmn comt gaseous environ manned spacecraft, Space Sci Bd, Nat Acad Sci, 62-63; Jackson lectr, Am Col Chest Physicians; mem cardiovasc study sect, NIH, 64-68; Nathanson lectr, Univ Southern Calif, 64; mem comt on toxicol, Nat Res Coun, 66-76, vchmn, 71-76, chmn comt on biol effects atmospheric pollutants, 68-72; chmn panel for selection of lung ctr, Nat Heart & Lung Inst, 71; mem lectr, Sch Med, Yamagata Univ, Japan, 79- *Mem:* Am Physiol Soc; Am Soc Clin Invest; Asn Am Physicians. *Res:* Physiology of respiration and pulmonary circulation; normal and clinical function of the lungs. *Mailing Add:* 370 Livingston St New Haven CT 06511

DU BOIS, DONALD FRANK, b Little Falls, NY, Jan 4, 32; m 55; c 3. THEORETICAL PHYSICS. *Educ:* Cornell Univ, BA, 54; Calif Inst Technol, PhD(physics, math), 59. *Prof Exp:* Instr physics, Calif Inst Technol, 58-59; res physicist, Rand Corp, Calif, 59-62; sr staff physicist, Hughes Aircraft Co, 62-70, sr scientist, Hughes Res Labs, Malibu, Calif, 70-72; vis prof, Univ Colo, Boulder, 72-73; GROUP LEADER STATIST & MAT PHYSICS, LOS ALAMOS SCI LAB, 73- *Concurrent Pos:* Consult, Rand Corp, 58-59 & 70-75, Lawrence Livermore Lab, 72-73 & Univ Colo, Boulder, 73-; adj prof, Univ Colo, Boulder, 79-; J S Guggenheim fel, 81-82. *Mem:* Am Phys Soc. *Res:* Many-particle theory; quantum and statistical mechanics; plasma and solid state physics; electron correlations in metals; transport in semiconductors; nonlinear interaction of radiation with plasmas and plasma turbulence. *Mailing Add:* Group T-11 Los Alamos Sci Lab Los Alamos NM 87545

DUBOIS, DONALD WARD, b Oklahoma City, Okla, Jan 31, 23; div. MATHEMATICS, SCIENCE EDUCATION. *Educ:* Univ Okla, MA, 50, PhD(math), 53. *Prof Exp:* Instr math, Univ Okla, 52-53 & Ohio State Univ, 53-55; from asst prof to assoc prof, 63-68, PROF MATH, UNIV NMEX, 68- *Res:* Real fields and varieties; origins, history and learning of mathematical concepts. *Mailing Add:* Dept of Math Humanities Bldg 419 Univ of NMex Albuquerque NM 87131

DUBOIS, FREDERICK WILLIAMSON, b Newburgh, NY, Nov 6, 23; m 46; c 3. INORGANIC CHEMISTRY. *Educ:* St Lawrence Univ, BS, 46; Univ Mich, MS, 49, PhD(chem), 52. *Prof Exp:* Instr chem, Univ Idaho, 46-47; instr qual anal, Univ Mich, 51; asst group leader, 52-80, ASSOC GROUP LEADER & PROJ LEADER, LOS ALAMOS NAT LAB, 80- *Mem:* Am Chem Soc. *Res:* Complex ions in solution; military high explosives; detonation theory; plastics and elastomers. *Mailing Add:* WX-3 Los Alamos Nat Lab Los Alamos NM 87545

DUBOIS, GRANT EDWIN, b Niagara Falls, NY, May 31, 46; m 79. ORGANIC CHEMISTRY. *Educ:* Capital Univ, Columbus, BS, 67; State Univ NY, Buffalo, PhD(chem), 72. *Prof Exp:* Fel, Stanford Univ, 72-73; res chemist org chem, Dynapol, Palo Alto, 73-81; SR RES CHEMIST ORG CHEM, SYVA CO, PALO ALTO, 81- *Mem:* Am Chem Soc. *Res:* Synthetic organic chemistry; design and synthesis of biologically active molecules especially in the area of non-nutritive sweetener development; immunochemistry, as relates to the development of immunoassay methods for the quantitation of drugs, hormone and other biologically important compounds. *Mailing Add:* Syva Co 900 Arastradero Rd Palo Alto CA 94303

DUBOIS, JOHN R(OGER), b Eau Claire, Wis, Aug 16, 34; m 54; c 3. ELECTRICAL ENGINEERING. *Educ:* Univ Wis, BS, 57, MS, 59, PhD(elec eng), 63. *Prof Exp:* Supvr transmitter eng, TV Wis, Inc, 57-63; sr electronics engr, North Star Res & Develop Inst, 63-65, dir electronics res, 65-71; DIR COMMUN, HENNEPIN COUNTY, MINN, 71- *Concurrent Pos:* Instr elec eng, Univ Wis, 57-63; commun consult, 71- *Mem:* Inst Elec & Electronics Engrs; Int Asn Chiefs Police; Asn Pub Safety Commun Officers; Sigma Xi. *Res:* Solid state devices and applications; electronics technology in law enforcement; very high frequency and ultra-high frequency communications systems; computer aided dispatch design. *Mailing Add:* Commun Div A2309 Hennepin Co Govt Ctr Minneapolis MN 55487

DUBOIS, PAUL FRED, b Oakland, Calif, June 19, 45; m 66. NUMERICAL ANALYSIS, HIGH SPEED COMPUTATION. *Educ:* Univ Calif, Berkeley, BA, 66; Univ Calif, Davis, MA, 68, PhD(math), 70. *Prof Exp:* Fel, Univ Alta, 70-73; asst prof math, NMex Highlands Univ, 73-76; MATHEMATICIAN, LAWRENCE LIVERMORE NAT LAB, UNIV CALIF, 76- *Concurrent Pos:* Vis staff mem, Los Alamos Nat Lab, Univ Calif, 75-76. *Res:* Abelian groups; applied mathematics; algorithms for large scale scientific computation on vector/parallel architecture machines. *Mailing Add:* Box 2081 Livermore CA 94550

DU BOIS, ROBERT LEE, b Omaha, Nebr, Jan 25, 24; m 47. GEOPHYSICS. *Educ:* Univ Wash, BS, 49, MS, 50, PhD(geol), 54. *Prof Exp:* From asst prof to prof geol, Univ Ariz, 52-67; dir, Earth Sci Observ, 67-77, KERR MCGEE PROF GEOL & GEOPHYS, UNIV OKLA, 67-, DIR, LEONARD EARTH SCI OBSERV, 67- *Concurrent Pos:* Consult econ geol, 53- *Mem:* AAAS; Am Geophys Union; fel Geol Soc Am. *Res:* Archeomagnetism; paleomagnetism; rock magnetism. *Mailing Add:* Sch of Geol & Geophys Univ of Okla Norman OK 73019

DUBOIS, RONALD JOSEPH, b Lawrence, Mass, Jan 3, 42. ORGANIC CHEMISTRY. *Educ:* Lowell Inst Technol, BS, 64; Clarkson Tech Univ, PhD(org chem), 69. *Prof Exp:* Res chemist, E I du Pont de Nemours & Co, Inc, 68-71; mem staff, Cancer Res, Microbiol Assocs, Inc, 71-75; MEM STAFF, HERCULES, INC, 75- *Mem:* Am Chem Soc. *Res:* Synthesis of agricultural chemicals for use as herbicides, fungicides and insecticides. *Mailing Add:* Hercules Inc Magna UT 84044

DUBOIS, THOMAS DAVID, b Mexico, Ind, Nov 15, 40; m; c 1. INORGANIC CHEMISTRY. *Educ:* McMurry Col, BS, 62; Ohio State Univ, MS, 65, PhD(inorg chem), 67. *Prof Exp:* Assoc prof, 67-80, PROF CHEM, UNIV NC, CHARLOTTE, 80-, MEM GRAD FAC, 80- *Mem:* Am Chem Soc. *Res:* Coordination compounds; magnetochemistry; coordinated ligand reactions. *Mailing Add:* Dept of Chem Univ of NC Charlotte NC 28223

DUBOS, RENE JULES, pathology, deceased

DUBOSE, LEO EDWIN, b Gonzales, Tex, Apr 22, 31; m 51; c 3. ANIMAL SCIENCE. *Educ:* Abilene Christian Univ, BS, 52; SDak State Col, MS, 54; Tex A&M Univ, PhD(animal breeding), 65. *Prof Exp:* Asst prof animal sci, SDak State Col, 54-57; teacher, San Angelo Col, 57-63; prof animal sci, 65-80, GRAD FAC PROF AGR, ABILENE CHRISTIAN UNIV, 80- *Mem:* Am Soc Animal Sci; Am Soc Range Mgt. *Res:* Digestability of feeds by ruminants; heritability estimates of carcass traits and production traits in beef cattle; correlations between traits in beef cattle. *Mailing Add:* Dept of Agr Abilene Christian Univ Box 8108 Abilene TX 79699

DUBOSE, ROBERT TRAFTON, b Dallas, Tex, Oct 17, 19; m 44; c 3. VETERINARY MEDICINE, VIROLOGY. *Educ:* Tex A&M Univ, BS & 13 DVM, 56, MS, 58. *Prof Exp:* Instr, Tex A&M Univ, 56-59; prof vet microbiol, 59-80, PROF AGR & URBAN PRACTICE, VA POLYTECH INST & STATE UNIV, 80- *Mem:* Am Vet Med Asn; Am Asn Avian Path; Am Soc Microbiol; Wildlife Dis Asn. *Res:* of turkey hemorrhagic enteritis virus in cell cultures; pathogenicity of quail bronchitis virus and chicken embryo lethal orphan virus in birds and cells; modification of infectious bronchitis virus. *Mailing Add:* Dept of Vet Sci Va Polytech Inst & State Univ Blacksburg VA 24060

DUBOW, MICHAEL SCOTT, b Brooklyn, NY, May 29, 50. BIOTECHNOLOGY, GENETIC ENGINEERING. *Educ:* State Univ NY, BSc, 72; Ind Univ, MA, 75, PhD(microbiol), 77. *Prof Exp:* Instr biol, State Univ NY, 71-72; res trainee, Ind Univ, 72-77; fel, Cold Spring Harbor Lab, 77-80; ASST PROF MOLECULAR BIOL, MCGILL UNIV, 80- *Concurrent Pos:* Consult, Rutgers Univ, 77. *Honors & Awards:* Garner Award, Am Soc Microbiol, 75. *Mem:* Am Soc Microbiol; Can Genetics Soc; Can Soc Microbiol. *Res:* Mechanisms, regulation and manipulation of the transposition of bacteriophages Mu and D108 DNAs; isolation of cellular moveable genetic elements and characterizing their functions and use in gene cloning. *Mailing Add:* Dept Microbiol & Immunol McGill Univ 3775 Univ St Montreal PQ H3A 2B4 Can

DUBOWSKI, KURT M(AX), b Berlin, Ger, Nov 21, 21. CLINICAL BIOCHEMISTRY, TOXICOLOGY. *Educ:* NY Univ, AB, 46; Ohio State Univ, MSc, 47, PhD(chem, toxicol), 49; Am Bd Clin Chem, dipl; Am Bd Forensic Toxicol, dipl. *Prof Exp:* Biochemist & asst dir labs, Norwalk Hosp, 50-53; dir chem, Iowa Methodist Hosp, 53-58; assoc prof clin chem & dir clin labs, hosp & clins, Univ Fla, 58-61; assoc prof clin chem & toxicol, 61-64, dir clin chem, 61-65, PROF BIOCHEM, CLIN CHEM, TOXICOL, MED, AND PATH, COL MED, UNIV OKLA, 64-, DIR TOXICOL LABS, HEALTH SCI CTR, 61-,GEORGE LYNN CROSS RES PROF MED, 81- *Concurrent Pos:* Toxicologist to coroner, Fairfield County, Conn, 50-53; lectr, NY Univ & Northwestern Univ, 50-56; mem comt alcohol & drugs, Nat Safety Coun, 50-, chmn, 69-71; chief dep coroner & toxicologist, Polk County, Iowa, 53-58; state criminalist, Iowa Dept Pub Safety, 53-58; lectr, Univ Iowa, 54-58; spec consult, USPHS, 57-62; secy-treas, Am Bd Clin Chem, 58-73, pres, 73-78; vis prof, Ind Univ, 58-; consult, US Vet Admin, 59-, Oklahoma City Police Dept, 61-, Okla State Bur Invest, 66-, Okla Med Res Found, 67-, NIH, 67-75, US Dept Transportation, 68-80, Okla Dept Pub Safety, 69-, NIMH, 71-73, Okla Bur Narcotics & Dangerous Drugs Control, 71-, Exec Off of the President, 72-75, Nat Bur Standards, US Dept Com, 72-, Ctr Dis Control, US Dept Health, Educ & Welfare, 72- & Chem Indust Inst Toxicol, 80-; dir chem tests for alcoholic influence, State of Okla, 70-; Pres, Am Bd Forensic Toxicol, 75-78; George Lynn Cross res prof med, 81. *Honors & Awards:* Outstanding Clin Chemist Award, Tex Sect, Am Asn Clin Chem, 81. *Mem:* Fel NY Acad Sci; fel 75-78. Am Asn Clin Chem; fel Am Acad Forensic Sci (pres, 78-79); fel Asn Clin Sci; life fel Am Inst Chem. *Res:* Effects and determination of alcohol, cannabinoids in biologic materials; clinical chemical and toxicological methodology; clinical pharmacology; evaluation of trace evidence in criminal investigations; forensic chemistry & toxicology. *Mailing Add:* Toxicol Labs Rm 38-R Univ Okla Col Med PO Box 26901 Oklahoma City OK 73190

DUBOWSKY, STEVEN, b New York, NY, Jan 14, 42; m 64; c 3. MECHANICAL ENGINEERING, CONTROL SYSTEM ENGINEERING. *Educ:* Rensselaer Polytech Inst, BME, 63; Columbia Univ, MS, 64, ScD(eng), 71. *Prof Exp:* Engr, Gen Dynamics Corp, 63-64; sr engr, Optical Technol Div, Perkin Elmer Corp, 64-71; assoc prof, 71-80, PROF ENG & APPL SCI, UNIV CALIF, LOS ANGELES, 80- *Concurrent Pos:* NSF grant & consult, 71-; assoc ed, Mechanism & Mach Theory, 74-; assoc,

Danford Found, 77-; vis fac mem, Dept Eng & vis scholar, Queen's Col, Cambridge Univ, 77-78. *Mem:* Am Soc Mech Engrs; Inst Elec & Electronics Engrs; Sigma Xi. *Res:* Dynamics and control of mechanical and electromechanical systems, noise and vibrations in these systems; application of robotic manipulators to the industrial environment; use of microprocessor computers. *Mailing Add:* 4731 Boelter Hall Univ Calif Los Angeles CA 90024

DUBRAVCIC, MILAN FRANE, b Gospic, Croatia, July 25, 22; m 53; c 4. ANALYTICAL CHEMISTRY, FOOD SCIENCE. *Educ:* Univ Zagreb, BS, 48; Univ Mass, Amherst, PhD(food sci), 68. *Prof Exp:* Chemist, Dept Health, Cent Inst Hyg, Zagreb, Yugoslavia, 48-53; chief chemist, Lifeguard Milk Prod Ltd, Australia, 54-56; res chemist, Imp Chem Industs, 56-61 & Commonwealth Sci & Indust Res Orgn, 62-63; from asst prof to assoc prof, 68-79, PROF CHEM TECHNOL, UNIV AKRON, 79-, COORDR CHEM TECHNOL, 72- *Concurrent Pos:* Dir NSF grant for instructional sci equip, Univ Akron, 69-71; vis scientist, Chenoweth Lab, Univ Mass, Amherst, 78-79. *Mem:* Am Chem Soc; Croatian Chem Soc; Inst Food Technol; Sigma Xi. *Res:* Food technology; methodology for analysis of foods and plastics; mechanisms of enzymatic, oxidative, thermal and radiolytic degradation of organic materials. *Mailing Add:* Dept Chem Technol Univ Akron Akron OH 44325

DU BREUIL, FELIX L(EMAIGRE), b Paris, France, Feb 11, 21; nat US; m 49; c 7. MINERAL ENGINEERING. *Educ:* Nat Sch Mines, Paris, IngcMines, 45; Pa State Univ, MS, 47, PhD(elec eng), 49. *Prof Exp:* From instr to assoc prof mineral eng, Pa State Univ, 49-56; field engr, Jeffrey Mfg Co, 56-58; proj engr, 58-70, ASST MGR MINING, BITUMINOUS COAL RES, INC, 70- *Mem:* Inst Elec Engrs; Fr Soc Mineral Indust; Instrument Soc Am. *Res:* Coal mining; health and safety; communications; automation. *Mailing Add:* 1365 Foxwood Rd Monroeville PA 15146

DUBREUIL, ROBERT, b Montreal, Que, Sept 18, 26; m 53; c 4. VIROLOGY, CANCER. *Educ:* Univ Montreal, BSc, 50, MSc, 52, PhD(virol), 70. *Prof Exp:* Res asst, 54-63, res assoc, 63-70, RES MEM VIROL, INST MICROBIOL & HYG MONTREAL, 71- *Mem:* AAAS; Can Soc Microbiol. *Res:* Human and animal virus vaccines; SV40 virus tumors. *Mailing Add:* Dept of Virol Inst of Microbiol PO Box 100 Laval-des-Rapides Can

DUBRIDGE, LEE ALVIN, b Terre Haute, Ind, Sept 21, 01; m 25, 74; c 2. EXPERIMENTAL PHYSICS. *Educ:* Cornell Col, Iowa, AB, 22; Univ Wis, AM, 24, PhD(physics), 26. *Hon Degrees:* Twenty-eight from US cols & univs, 40-70. *Prof Exp:* Instr physics, Univ Wis, 25-26; Nat Res Coun fel, Calif Inst Technol, 26-28; from asst prof to assoc prof, Wash Univ, 28-34; prof & chmn dept, Univ Rochester, 34-46, dean fac arts & sci, 38-42; pres, 46-69, EMER PRES, CALIF INST TECHNOL, 69- *Concurrent Pos:* Assoc ed, Am Physics Teacher, 35-38, Phys Rev, 36-39 & Rev Sci Instruments, 36-42; with phys sci div, Nat Res Coun, 36-42; dir radiation lab, Mass Inst Technol, 40-45; mem gen adv comt, AEC, 46-52; trustee, Rand Corp, 48-61, Rockefeller Found, 56-67 & Mellon Inst, 58-66; mem sci adv comt, Off Defense Mobilization, 51-56, Nat Sci Bd, 52-56, 58-64, Nat Merit Scholar Corp, 63-69, Distinguished Civilian Serv Awards Bd, 63-67 & Gen Motors Corp, 70-76; mem bd dirs, Nat Educ TV, 64-69; sci adv to President, 69-70; mem, Presidents' Sci Adv Comt, 69-72. *Honors & Awards:* Brit Royal Medal, 46; Medal for Merit, 46; Res Corp Award, 47; Lehman Award, NY Acad Sci, 69; Golden Plate Award, Am Acad Achievement, 74. *Mem:* Nat Acad Sci; AAAS; fel Am Phys Soc (vpres, 46, pres, 47); Am Philos Soc. *Res:* Biophysics; nuclear disintegration; photoelectric and thermionic emission; direct current amplification; energy distribution of photoelectrons; theory of photoelectric effect; radar. *Mailing Add:* 1730 Homet Rd Pasadena CA 91106

DUBROFF, LEWIS MICHAEL, b Brooklyn, NY, Jan 22, 47; m 71; c 3. NUCLEIC ACID, NUCLEIC ACID ANTIBODIES. *Educ:* Univ Pa, MD, 71, PhD(molecular biol), 75. *Prof Exp:* Assoc fel, nucleic acid, Inst Cancer Res, 72-75; fel dermat, Mayo Clin, 75-76; res asst prof, Hahnemann Med Col, 76-78; asst prof med, 78-80, RES ASST PROF PHARMACOL, UPSTATE MED CTR, STATE UNIV NY, 80- *Res:* Drug nucleic acid interactions and antibody nucleic acid interactions. *Mailing Add:* Dept Pharmacol Upstate Med Ctr State Univ NY Syracuse NY 13210

DUBROFF, WILLIAM, b Johannesburg, SAfrica, Oct 1, 37; US citizen; m 60; c 1. MATERIALS SCIENCE, METALLURGY. *Educ:* Columbia Univ, BA, 61, MS, 63, PhD(metall), 67. *Prof Exp:* Dir NASA proj metall, Columbia Univ, 65-67; res engr, 67, sr res engr, 67-72, supv res engr, 72-76, asst dir res, 76-80, ASSOC DIR RES, INLAND STEEL CO, 80- *Concurrent Pos:* Ed, Ironmaking & Steelmaking, 78-81. *Mem:* Am Inst Mining, Metall & Petrol Engrs; Am Soc Metals; Sigma Xi. *Res:* Magnetic and mechanical properties, phase transformations, and recrystallization in metals; microstructure-property-processing correlations for nonmetallic materials. *Mailing Add:* Inland Steel Res Labs 3001 E Columbus Dr East Chicago IN 46312

DUBROVIN, KENNETH P, b Chicago, Ill, Oct 24, 31; m 54; c 5. SOIL CHEMISTRY, PLANT PHYSIOLOGY. *Educ:* Univ Ill, BS, 53; Univ Wis, PhD(soil chem), 56; Univ Mo, MBA, 66. *Prof Exp:* Res biologist, Spencer Chem Div, Gulf Oil Corp, 56-66, sr res biologist, Gulf Res & Develop Co, 66-69, sect supvr pesticide res & develop, 69-71; dir res, 71-76, VPRES, GREAT WESTERN SUGAR CO, 76- *Concurrent Pos:* Fulbright scholar, Netherlands, 53-54. *Mem:* Am Chem Soc; Am Soc Agron; Soil Sci Soc Am; Int Soc Soil Sci. *Res:* Improved fertilizers; development of new and unique herbicides, fungicides, insecticides and nematicides; mechanism of action of herbicides. *Mailing Add:* 1901 Arapahoe Dr Longmont CO 80501

DUBRUL, E LLOYD, b New York, NY, Apr 5, 09; m 56. PHYSICAL ANTHROPOLOGY. *Educ:* NY Univ, DDS, 37; Univ Ill, MS, 49, PhD, 55. *Prof Exp:* From instr to asst prof oral & maxillofacial surg, 46-55, from asst prof to prof chg oral anat, Col Dent, 47-64, asst prof post grad studies, 48-51, actg head dept oral anat, 64-66, assoc prof anat, Col Med, 58-59, PROF ORAL ANAT, COL DENT, UNIV ILL MED CTR, 64-, HEAD DEPT, 66-, PROF ANAT, COL MED, 59- *Mem:* Fel AAAS; Am Asn Phys Anthrop; NY Acad Sci. *Res:* Comparative anatomy; neuroanatomy; anthropology. *Mailing Add:* Dept Oral Anat Col Dent Univ of Ill at the Med Ctr Chicago IL 60612

DUBRUL, ERNEST, b Wooster, Ohio, Mar 2, 43; m 66; c 2. BIOCHEMISTRY, DEVELOPMENTAL BIOLOGY. *Educ:* Xavier Univ, Ohio, HAB, 64; Wash Univ, PhD(biol), 69. *Prof Exp:* Fel biol, Oak Ridge Nat Lab, 69-72; res assoc, Mem Res Ctr, Univ Tenn, 72-74; ASST PROF BIOL, UNIV TOLEDO, 74- *Mem:* Soc Develop Biol; Am Soc Cell Biol. *Res:* Nucleic acids and protein synthesis in development. *Mailing Add:* Dept of Biol Univ of Toledo Toledo OH 43606

DUBUC, SERGE, b Montreal, Que, Apr 16, 39; m 62; c 3. MATHEMATICS. *Educ:* Univ Montreal, BSc, 62, MSc, 63; Cornell Univ, PhD(math), 66. *Prof Exp:* Asst math, Cornell Univ, 64-66; asst prof, Univ Montreal, 66-71; assoc prof, Univ Sherbrooke, 71-73; assoc prof, 73-76, PROF MATH, UNIV MONTREAL, 76- . *Concurrent Pos:* Ford Motor Co fel, 68-69. *Mem:* Can Math Cong. *Res:* Functional analysis, especially extreme points theory; mathematical analysis, especially iteration of functions; probability theory, especially branching processes; plane geometry. *Mailing Add:* Dept of Math Univ Montreal Montreal PQ H3C 3J7 Can

DUBY, JOHN, b Alta, Can, June 10, 30; m 60; c 2. ENGINEERING. *Educ:* Univ Alta, BSc, 52; Oxford Univ, BA, MA & PhD, 56. *Prof Exp:* Inspection & field engr equip, Brown & Roote, 52; tutor, Sch Eng Sci, Oxford Univ, 55-56; spec lectr elec eng, Univ Alta, 56-57, assoc prof civil eng, 57-59 & mech eng, 59-64; pres, Digital Anal & Tech Assistance, Ltd, 64-70; partner, Blain Binnie Assoc Eng Ltd, 70-74; AESL Proj coordr, Dubai, United Arab Emirates, 75; pres, Engineered Proj Mgr Ltd, 76-80; pres, 80, EXEC VPRES, CORP PLANNING, UNITED CANSO OIL & GAS, LTD, 81- *Concurrent Pos:* Spec lectr civil eng, Univ Alta, 64-65; spec consult, Dept Pub Works, Govt Alta, 71-72. *Mem:* Eng Inst Can. *Mailing Add:* 2919 Parklane SW Calgary AB T2N 1N4 Can

DUBY, PAUL F(RANCOIS), b Brussels, Belg, Dec 16, 33; m 59; c 3. METALLURGY. *Educ:* Univ Brussels, Mech & Elec E, 56; Columbia Univ, EngScD(mineral eng), 62. *Prof Exp:* Temp res assoc, Ctr Nuclear Sci, Royal Mil Sch, Brussels, 57-58; res assoc mineral eng, Henry Krumb Sch Mines, Columbia Univ, 61-63; asst prof metall eng, Sch Metall Eng, Univ Pa, 63-65; from asst prof to assoc prof, 65-76, PROF MINERAL ENG, HENRY KRUMB SCH MINES, COLUMBIA UNIV, 76- *Mem:* Am Inst Mining, Metall & Petrol Engrs; Electrochem Soc. *Res:* Extractive metallurgy; transport properties of fused salts; applied electrochemistry; hydrometallurgy; surface chemistry; corrosion. *Mailing Add:* Henry Krumb Sch of Mines Columbia Univ New York NY 10027

DUBY, ROBERT T, b Ludlow, Mass, July 10, 40; m 61; c 2. ANIMAL PHYSIOLOGY, REPRODUCTIVE PHYSIOLOGY. *Educ:* Univ Mass, BS, 62, MS, 65, PhD(animal physiol), 67. *Prof Exp:* NIH fel, 67-68; asst prof reproductive physiol, Cornell Univ, 68-70; asst prof, 70-77, ASSOC PROF VET & ANIMAL SCI, UNIV MASS, AMHERST, 77-, ASST PROF GRAD FAC, ANIMAL SCI, 80- *Mem:* Soc Study Reproduction. *Res:* Utero ovarian relationships in domestic animals; separation of X and Y bearing sperm and ovum transfer techniques; sex differentiation in the ovine embryo. *Mailing Add:* Grad Sch Univ of Mass Grad Res Ctr Amherst MA 01003

DUCE, ROBERT ARTHUR, b Midland, Ont, Apr 9, 35; US citizen. ATMOSPHERIC CHEMISTRY. *Educ:* Baylor Univ, BA, 57; Mass Inst Technol, PhD(inorg & nuclear chem), 64. *Prof Exp:* Res assoc geochem, Mass Inst Technol, 64-65; asst prof chem & asst meteorologist, Inst Geophys, Univ Hawaii, 65-68, assoc prof & assoc geochemist, 68-70; assoc prof, 70-73, PROF OCEANOG & DIR CTR ATMOSPHERIC CHEM STUDIES, UNIV RI, 73- *Concurrent Pos:* Mem ocean sci comt, Nat Acad Sci, 73-75, sci adv bd, Environ Protection Agency, 76-79, Int Asn Meteorol & Atmospheric Physics Comn on Atmospheric Chem and Global Pollution, 75-, World Meteorol Orgn Working Group on the interchange of pollutants between the atmosphere and the oceans, 77-; mem adv comt, Ocean Sci Div, NSF. *Mem:* Am Meteorol Soc; Am Chem Soc; Geochem Soc; Am Geophys Union. *Res:* Atmospheric chemistry of the halogens, heavy metals, boron, organic carbon, phosphorus; chemical oceanography; chemical fractionation at the air-sea interface; global transport of atmospheric particulate matter and trace gases; chemistry of the air/sea interface; neutron activation analysis. *Mailing Add:* Grad Sch of Oceanog Univ of RI Kingston RI 02881

DUCHAMP, DAVID JAMES, b St Martinville, La, Oct 15, 39; m 64; c 3. PHYSICAL CHEMISTRY, X-RAY CRYSTALLOGRAPHY. *Educ:* Univ Southwestern La, BS, 61; Calif Inst Technol, PhD(phys chem), 65. *Prof Exp:* RES SCIENTIST, UPJOHN CO, 65- *Mem:* AAAS; Am Chem Soc; Am Crystallog Asn; Am Asn Comput Mach; NY Acad Sci. *Res:* Molecular structure studies by x-ray diffraction; application of mathematics and computers to chemical problems; data acquisition and control, via computer, of physical measurement instruments. *Mailing Add:* Phys & Anal Div Upjohn Co Kalamazoo MI 49001

DUCHAMP, THOMAS EUGENE, b St Martinville, La, Nov 12, 47; m 70. MATHEMATICS. *Educ:* Univ Ill, Urbana, BS, 69, MS, 69, PhD(math), 76. *Prof Exp:* instr math, Univ Utah, 76-79; ASST PROF MATH, UNIV WASH, 79- *Mem:* Am Math Soc; AAAS. *Res:* Differential geometry; foliations; calculus of variations; several complex variables. *Mailing Add:* Univ Wash Seattle WA 98195

DUCHARME, DONALD WALTER, b Saginaw, Mich, June 14, 37; m 58; c 3. PHARMACOLOGY. *Educ:* Cent Mich Univ, AB, 59; Univ Mich, PhD(pharmacol), 65. *Prof Exp:* Sr scientist, 65-80, RES HEAD, CARDIOVASC DIS, UPJOHN CO, 80- *Concurrent Pos:* Adj assoc prof pharmacol, Med Col of Ohio, 77-; mem med adv bd, Coun High Blood Pressure Res, Am Heart Asn; chmn, NCent Region, Res Adv Comt, Am

Heart Asn, 82-83, mem subcomt regional & nat res. *Mem:* Am Heart Asn; Am Soc Pharmacol & Exp Therapeut. *Res:* Cardiovascular physiology and pharmacology, particularly the autonomic control of the capacity vessels and the role of these vessels in the etiology of arterial hypertension. *Mailing Add:* Cardiovasc Dis Res Upjohn Co Kalamazoo MI 49001

DUCHARME, ERNEST PETER, b St Paul, Minn, July 15, 16; m 47; c 1. PLANT PATHOLOGY. *Educ:* St Mary's Col, Minn, BSc, 38; DePaul Univ, MS, 43; Univ Minn, PhD(plant path), 49. *Prof Exp:* Instr, high sch, 38-43; asst plant path, Univ Minn, 43-46; plant pathologist, Agr Res & Educ Ctr, 46-81, EMER PROF PATH, UNIV FLA, 81- *Mem:* Am Phytopath Soc; Bot Soc Am; Int Orgn Citrus Virologists. *Res:* Root diseases of citrus; soil microbiology in relation to the citrus root disease complex; root parasitizing nematodes; soil ecology. *Mailing Add:* 1835 Nicaragua Way Winter Haven FL 33880

DUCHARME, JACQUES R, b Montreal, Que, Jan 1, 28; m 55; c 5. PEDIATRIC ENDOCRINOLOGY, BIOCHEMISTRY. *Prof Exp:* Univ Montreal, BA, 48, MD, 54; Univ Pa, MSc, 61. Prof Exp: Resident pediat, Children's Hosp Philadelphia, 55-57; lectr, Columbia Univ, 57-59; from lectr to assoc prof, 59-69, chmn dept, 69-75, PROF PEDIAT, UNIV MONTREAL, 69- *Concurrent Pos:* Res fel, Babies' Hosp, Columbia-Presby Med Ctr, New York, 57-59; Dept Nat Health & Welfare Can, NATO & Found J L Beaubien grants, 60-; dir pediat res centre, L'Hopital Ste-Justine, 75-77. *Mem:* Am Pediat Soc; Europ Soc Pediat Endocrine; Endocrine Soc; Soc Pediat Res; NY Acad Sci. *Res:* Steroid biochemistry; steroid metabolism in newborn infants, infancy and childhood; regulation of Ley dig cell function; mechanisms of pubertal development. *Mailing Add:* Dept Pediat Univ Montreal Montreal PQ H3C 3J7 Can

DUCHEK, JOHN ROBERT, b St Louis, Mo, Dec 6, 48; m 72; c 1. ORGANIC CHEMISTRY. *Educ:* St Louis Univ, BS, 70, PhD(chem), 75. *Prof Exp:* Teaching asst, St Louis Univ, 70-74; res assoc, Univ Ariz, 74-76; from asst prof to assoc prof org chem, 76-80, PROF NAT SCI, UNIV NFLA, 80- *Concurrent Pos:* Co-investr, NIH grant, 77- *Mem:* Am Chem Soc; Sigma Xi. *Res:* Dye synthesis; lipid bilayer membranes; prebiotic chemistry. *Mailing Add:* Dept of Natural Sci PO Box 17074 Jacksonville FL 32216

DUCIBELLA, TOM, b New Rochelle, NY, Nov 5, 47. TISSUE CULTURE. *Educ:* Princeton Univ, PhD(biol), 73. *Prof Exp:* Fel histol, Harvard Med Sch, 73-76, instr, 76-77; asst prof histol, Univ Tenn, 77-79; asst prof histol, Sch Med, Tufts Univ, 79-82; PROJ MGR, MILLIPORE CORP, 82- *Concurrent Pos:* NIH grant, Sch Med, Univ Tenn, 77-79; prin investr, Sch Med, Tufts Univ, 79-82. *Mem:* Am Soc Cell Biol. *Res:* Role of the cell surface in early development and organization of tumor cells; tissue culture growth systems. *Mailing Add:* Millipore Corp Bedford MA 01730

DUCK, BOBBY NEAL, b Reagan, Tenn, Sept 6, 39; m 62; c 1. CYTOGENETICS. *Educ:* Univ Tenn, BS, 61; Auburn Univ, MS, 63, PhD(agron), 64. *Prof Exp:* Asst agronomist, Agr Exp Sta, Univ Fla, 64-66; from asst prof to assoc prof, 66-73, asst dean sch agr, 70-78, PROF AGRON, UNIV TENN, MARTIN, 73- *Concurrent Pos:* Mem, Coun Agr Sci & Technol. *Mem:* Am Soc Agron; Crop Sci Soc Am; Soil Conserv Soc Am; Wildlife Soc; Coun Agr Sci & Technol. *Res:* Instruction in plant sciences; breeding and management of forage crops. *Mailing Add:* Sch of Agr Univ of Tenn Martin TN 38238

DUCK, IAN MORLEY, b Kamloops, BC, Can, Oct 4, 33; m 63; c 2. NUCLEAR PHYSICS. *Educ:* Queen's Univ, Ont, BSc, 55; Calif Inst Technol, PhD(theoret nuclear physics), 61. *Prof Exp:* Res assoc, Univ Southern Calif, 61-63; res assoc, 63-65, from asst prof to assoc prof, 65-69, PROF PHYSICS, RICE UNIV, 69- *Res:* Weak interactions; nuclear reaction mechanisms; few nucleon problems. *Mailing Add:* Dept of Physics Rice Univ Houston TX 77005

DUCK, WILLIAM N, JR, b Millheim, Pa, Feb 9, 20; m 44; c 2. BIOCHEMISTRY, PHYSICAL CHEMISTRY. *Educ:* Pa State Univ, BS, 42; Drexel Inst, dipl chem eng, 44; Franklin & Marshall Col, MS, 64. *Prof Exp:* Qual control supvr, Nat Dairy Prod, Inc, 42-50; res & develop chemist, Am Stores Co, Inc, 50-54; res dir, Pa Mfrs Confectioners Asn, 54-64; RES CHEMIST, GEN CIGAR CO, 64- *Concurrent Pos:* Consult, flavor & confectionary indust. *Mem:* Am Chem Soc. *Res:* Studies of moisture relations of sugar glasses and fat crystallization of chocolate and other fats. *Mailing Add:* 607 Capri Rd Lancaster PA 17603

DUCKER, THOMAS BARBEE, b Huntington, WVa, Dec 20, 37; m 65; c 3. MEDICAL SCIENCES, HEALTH SCIENCES. *Educ:* Univ Va, BA, 59, MD, 63. *Prof Exp:* Res asst, Univ Va, 62-63; intern surg, Univ Mich, 63-64, asst resident gen surg, 64-65, asst resident neurosurg, 65-66; fel neurosurg & res assoc, Walter Reed Army Med Ctr, 66-68; resident neurosurg, Univ Mich, 68-70; from asst prof to assoc prof surg & neurosurg, Col Med, Med Univ SC, 70-75, mem grad fac, Col Grad Studies, 73-75, asst dean, Col Med, 74-75; PROF SURG & NEUROSURG & HEAD DIV NEUROL SURG, SCH MED, UNIV MD, 75- *Concurrent Pos:* Attend neurosurgeon, Univ Hosp, Charleston, SC, 70-75, mem prof staff, 70-75, secy, 73-75; consult neurosurg, Roper Hosp, Vet Admin Hosp & US Naval Hosp, Charleston, 70-75; mem admis comt, Col Med, Med Univ SC, 70-75, chmn, 74-75, mem curriculum planning comt, Univ, 73-75; attend neurosurgeon, mem sch med coun & mem med staff, Univ Md Hosp, 75-; consult neurosurgeon, Mercy Hosp, Baltimore, Md, 75- *Mem:* Am Asn Neurol Surgeons; Am Col Surgeons; AMA; Am Asn Surg Trauma; Cong Neurol Surgeons. *Res:* Spinal cord injury. *Mailing Add:* Div of Neurol Surg Univ of Md Hosp 22 S Greene St Baltimore MD 21201

DUCKETT, KERMIT EARL, b Asheville, NC, Mar 27, 36; m 65; c 2. PHYSICS. *Educ:* Ga Inst Technol, BS, 58; Univ Colo, MS, 61; Univ Tenn, PhD(physics), 64. *Prof Exp:* Res assoc fiber physics, Am Enka Corp, 58-59; asst prof physics, 65-72, ASSOC PROF PHYSICS, UNIV TENN, KNOXVILLE, 72- *Concurrent Pos:* NSF res assoc, USDA, 65-66. *Mem:* Brit Textile Inst; Am Asn Physics Teachers; NY Acad Sci; fel Textile Inst Eng. *Res:* Infrared spectroscopy; physical properties of cellulosic fibers; yarn mechanics. *Mailing Add:* Dept of Physics Univ of Tenn Knoxville TN 37996

DUCKLES, SUE PIPER, b Oakland, Calif, Mar 1, 46; m 68; c 2. NEUROSCIENCES, CARDIOVASCULAR PHYSIOLOGY. *Educ:* Univ Calif, Berkeley, BA, 68; Univ Calif, San Francisco, PhD(pharmacol), 73. *Prof Exp:* Asst prof resident pharmacol, Sch Med, Univ Calif, Los Angeles, 76-79; ASST PROF PHARMACOL, UNIV ARIZ, TUCSON, 79- *Concurrent Pos:* Fac develop award, Pharmaceut Mfrs Asn Found, 76; estab investr, Am Heart Asn, 82; assoc ed, Life Sci, 80- *Mem:* Am Soc Pharmacol & Exp Therapeut; Soc Neurosci. *Res:* Pharmacology and physiology of vascular smooth muscle; neurogenic control of the cerebral circulation; autonomic and cardiovascular pharmacology; polypeptide transmitters and their actions on vascular smooth muscle; alterations in vascular smooth muscle responsiveness and innervation during development and aging. *Mailing Add:* Dept Pharmacol Col Med Univ Ariz Tucson AZ 85724

DUCKSTEIN, LUCIEN, b Paris, France, Aug 25, 32; US citizen; m 58; c 3. OPERATIONS RESEARCH. *Educ:* Univ Toulouse, MSc, 55, MSc, 56; Nat Polytech Inst Elec Eng & Hydraul, dipl, 56, PhD(fluid mech), 62. *Prof Exp:* Engr, Regie Nat Renault, France & Ger, 58-60; jr civil engr aerodyn, Colo State Univ, 61-62; PROF SYSTS & INDUST ENG & HYDROL & WATER RESOURCES, UNIV ARIZ, 62- *Concurrent Pos:* Sci adv, Metra-Int. *Mem:* Inst Mgt Sci; Opers Res Soc Am. *Res:* Systems engineering; mathematical models of traffic flow; optimization techniques; economic calculus; hydrology and water resources. *Mailing Add:* Dept of Systs & Indust Eng Univ of Ariz Tucson AZ 85721

DUCKWORTH, DONNA HARDY, biochemistry, genetics, see previous edition

DUCKWORTH, HENRY EDMISON, b Brandon, Man, Nov 1, 15; m 42; c 2. ATOMIC PHYSICS. *Educ:* Univ Man, BA, 35, BSc, 36; Univ Chicago, PhD(physics), 42. *Hon Degrees:* DSc, Univ Ottawa, 66, McMaster Univ, 69, Laval Univ, 71, Mt Allison Univ, 71 & Univ NB, 72; Univ Man, LLD, 78. *Prof Exp:* Lectr physics, United Col, 38-40; jr physicist, Nat Res Coun Can, 42-44, asst res chemist, 44-45; asst prof physics, Univ Man, 45-46; assoc prof, Wesleyan Univ, 46-51; prof, McMaster Univ, 51-65, chmn dept, 56-61, dean grad studies, 61-65; vpres develop, Univ Man, 65-66, acad vpres, 66-71; PRES, UNIV WINNIPEG, 71- *Concurrent Pos:* Nuffield fel, 55; ed, Can J Physics, 56-62; mem comn atomic masses, Int Union Pure & Appl Physics, secy, 60-66, chmn, 66-69; mem, Nat Res Coun Can, 61-67 & Defence Res Bd, 65-71; hon fel, United Col, 66; mem, Sci Coun Can, 73-77; mem, Can Environ Adv Coun, 73-76; mem, Nat Libr Adv Bd, 74; chmn, Coun Asn Commonwealth Univs, 77-78; mem, Natural Sci & Eng Res Coun, 78-; dir, Inst Res on Pub Policy, 78- *Honors & Awards:* Medal, Can Asn Physicists, 64; Tory Medal, Royal Soc Can, 65; Officer, Order of Can, 76. *Mem:* Fel Am Phys Soc; Royal Soc Can (pres, 71); Can Asn Physicists (pres, 60). *Res:* Mass spectroscopy; precise determination of atomic masses using mass spectrographic techniques. *Mailing Add:* 49 Oak St Winnipeg MB R3B 2E9 Can

DUCKWORTH, HENRY WILLIAM (HARRY), b Ottawa, Ont, Oct 11, 43; m 73. BIOCHEMISTRY. *Educ:* McMaster Univ, BSc, 65; Yale Univ, PhD(biochem), 70. *Prof Exp:* Asst prof, 72-76, ASSOC PROF CHEM, UNIV MAN, 76- *Concurrent Pos:* Assoc ed, Can J Biochem, 74-80 & 81-; mem adv comt, Atomic Energy Control Bd, 76-78. *Mem:* Can Biochem Soc. *Res:* Structure and function of allosteric proteins; evolution of regulatory properties, with specific reference to bacterial citrate synthases. *Mailing Add:* Dept Chem Univ Man Winnipeg MB R3T 2N2 Can

DUCKWORTH, WALTER DONALD, b Athens, Tenn, July 19, 35; m 55; c 3. SYSTEMATIC ENTOMOLOGY. *Educ:* Middle Tenn State Univ, BSc, 57, NC State Univ, MSc, 60, PhD(entom), 62. *Prof Exp:* Assoc curator, 62-74, CURATOR ENTOM, SMITHSONIAN INST, 74- *Concurrent Pos:* Spec asst, Off Dir, Nat Mus Natural Hist, Smithsonian Inst, 75-78, spec asst, Off Asst Sec Mus Progs, 78- *Mem:* Asn Trop Biol (secy-treas, 67-71); Entom Soc Am; Soc Syst Zool; Am Inst Biol Sci (secy-treas, 78-); Orgn Trop Studies. *Res:* Biosystematics of the Microlepidoptera, particularly tropical groups. *Mailing Add:* Dept of Entom Smithsonian Inst Washington DC 20560

DUCKWORTH, WILLIAM C(APELL), b Jackson, Tenn, Oct 31, 19; m 51; c 3. CHEMICAL ENGINEERING. *Educ:* Univ of the South, BS, 40; Ga Inst Technol, MS, 54; Memphis State Univ, MA, 73. *Prof Exp:* Chem engr, Am Cyanamid Co, 46-47; chem technologist, Tenn Corp, 47-61; mkt res engr, Enjay Chem Co, 61-63; sr chem economist, Southern Res Inst, 63-66; sr proj engr, Gulf Res & Develop Co, 66-71; sr engr, Velsicol Chem Corp, 71-74; SR PROJ ENGR, GULF SCI & TECHNOL CO, 74- *Mem:* Nat Soc Prof Engrs; Am Inst Chem Engrs; Chem Mkt Res Asn. *Res:* Chemical economics; chemical technology and economics; history of technology. *Mailing Add:* Gulf Sci & Technol Co PO Drawer 2038 Pittsburgh PA 15230

DUCKWORTH, WILLIAM CLIFFORD, b Athens, Tenn, Oct 21, 41. ENDOCRINOLOGY, DIABETES. *Educ:* Univ Tenn, BS, 62; Univ Tenn, MD, 66. *Prof Exp:* Intern & resident med, City Memphis Hosps, 66-69; NIH spec fel endocrinol, Med Units, Univ Tenn, 69-71; res assoc, Vet Admin Hosp, Memphis, 71-73, clin investr, 73-76, NIH res career develop award endocrinol, 76-80; PROF MED, SCH MED, IND UNIV, 80- *Concurrent Pos:* Asst prof med, Med Units, Univ Tenn, 72-75; assoc prof med, Ctr Health Sci, Univ Tenn, 75-; vis prof, Univ Geneva, Switz, 79; med sci adv bd, Juv Diabetes Found, 80- *Mem:* Am Fedn Clin Res; Am Diabetes Asn; Soc Clin Invest; Endocrine Soc. *Res:* Diabetes and carbohydrate metabolism; mechanisms of hormonal action and hormonal metabolism. *Mailing Add:* Vet Admin Hosp 1481 W 10th St Indianapolis IN 46202

DUCKWORTH, WINSTON H(OWARD), b Greenfield, Ohio, Oct 15, 18; m 41; c 2. CERAMIC ENGINEERING. *Educ:* Ohio State Univ, BChE, 40, MS, 41. *Prof Exp:* Asst supvr, 46-52, chief ceramic div, 52-66, founding dir, Defense Ceramic Info Ctr, 67-71, FEL, BATTELLE MEM INST, 66-, MEM RES COUN, 79- *Concurrent Pos:* With Atomic Energy Comn, USN, 44; dir, Engrs Joint Coun, 75. *Mem:* AAAS; fel Am Ceramic Soc (vpres, 76); Nat Inst

Ceramic Engrs (pres & permanent secy); Am Soc Testing & Mat; Can Ceramic Soc. *Res:* Processing and behavior of ceramic materials; brittle behavior; aircraft and nuclear ceramics; research management. *Mailing Add:* Battelle Mem Inst 505 King Ave Columbus OH 43201

DUCLOS, LEO ALBERT, plant breeding, see previous edition

DUCOFFE, ARNOLD L, b Montreal, Que, Mar 22, 21; US citizen; m 43; c 4. AEROSPACE ENGINEERING. *Educ:* Ga Inst Technol, BAero Eng, 43, MS, 47; Univ Mich, PhD(gas dyn), 52. *Prof Exp:* Asst prof aerodyn, 45-48, assoc prof, 51-55, actg dir aerospace eng, 63-64, PROF AEROSPACE ENG, GA INST TECHNOL, 55-, DIR AEROSPACE ENG, 64- *Concurrent Pos:* Consult, Aerodyn Div, Sandia Corp, NMex, 54-63; dir, Universal Co Ltd, Que, Rich's Inc, Ga & Unitron Int Systs, Inc, Calif. *Mem:* Am Inst Aeronaut & Astronaut. *Res:* Low speed aerodynamics of helicopters; high speed gas dynamics and heat transfer; laminar and turbulent viscous boundary layer flow; slip flow; stability and control. *Mailing Add:* 1240 Regency Rd NW Atlanta GA 30327

DUCSAY, CHARLES ANDREW, b Pittsburgh, Pa, Apr 5, 53; m 78. PERINATAL BIOLOGY. *Educ:* Fla State Univ, BS, 75; Univ Fla, MS, 77, PhD(reproductive physiol), 80. *Prof Exp:* FEL, ORE REGIONAL PRIMATE RES CTR, 80- *Mem:* Sigma Xi; Soc Study Reproduction; Am Soc Animal Sci. *Res:* Study of uterine and endocrine factors involved in the regulation of gestational length; intiation of parturition in non-human primates. *Mailing Add:* Ore Regional Primate Res Ctr 505 NW 185th Ave Beaverton OR 97006

DUCZEK, LORNE, b Oct 12, 46; Can citizen. PLANT PATHOLOGY, CROP SCIENCE. *Educ:* Univ Sask, BSA, 69, MSc, 71; Univ Toronto, PhD(plant path), 74. *Prof Exp:* Plant path specialist, Sask Dept Agr, 74-77; PLANT PATHOLOGIST, AGR CAN RES STA, 77- *Mem:* Am Phytopath Soc; Can Phytopath Soc. *Res:* Cereal diseases, particularly those of barley and wheat; root diseases. *Mailing Add:* 30 Birch Pl Saskatoon SK S7N 2P6 Can

DUDA, EDWARD JOHN, entomology, see previous edition

DUDA, EDWIN, b Donora, Pa, Oct 15, 28; m 55; c 5. MATHEMATICS. *Educ:* Washington & Jefferson Col, BA, 51; WVa Univ, MS, 53; Univ Va, PhD(math), 61. *Prof Exp:* Instr math, WVa Univ, 53, 55-57 & Univ Va, 60-61; from asst prof to assoc prof, 61-72, actg chmn dept, 67-70 & 76-78, PROF MATH, UNIV MIAMI, 72- *Mem:* Am Math Soc; Math Asn Am; Polish Math Soc. *Res:* Transformations; topological analysis. *Mailing Add:* Dept of Math Univ of Miami Coral Gables FL 33124

DUDA, EUGENE EDWARD, b Chicago, Ill, Apr 3, 40; m 73; c 1. RADIOLOGY. *Educ:* Loyola Univ, BS, 61, MD, 66. *Prof Exp:* Instr, 72-73, asst prof, 73-80, ASSOC PROF RADIOL, PRITZKER SCH MED, UNIV CHICAGO, 80-, DIR, NEURORADIOL LAB, UNIV CHICAGO HOSP & CLIN, 73- *Mem:* Radiol Soc NAm; Am Soc Neuroradiol; AMA; Am Col Radiol; Asn Univ Radiologists. *Res:* Application of computed axial tomography to various diseases of the brain. *Mailing Add:* Dept of Radiol Univ of Chicago Chicago IL 60637

DUDA, J(OHN) L(ARRY), b Donora, Pa, May 11, 36; m 62; c 4. CHEMICAL ENGINEERING. *Educ:* Case Inst Technol, BS, 58; Univ Del, MChE, 61, PhD(chem eng), 63. *Prof Exp:* Res engr, process fundamentals lab, Dow Chem Co, 63-71; PROF CHEM ENG, PA STATE UNIV, 71- *Honors & Awards:* William H Walker Award, Am Inst Chem Engrs. *Mem:* Am Inst Chem Engrs; Am Chem Soc. *Res:* Transport phenomena; molecular diffusion; fluid mechanics; polymer processing; enhanced oil recovery. *Mailing Add:* Dept of Chem Eng Pa State Univ University Park PA 16802

DUDA, JOHN J, b Herbert, Pa, Jan 25, 31; m 57; c 2. MEDICAL MICROBIOLOGY, ELECTRON MICROSCOPY. *Educ:* Washington & Jefferson Col, BA, 61; WVa Univ, MS, 65, PhD(med microbiol), 68. *Prof Exp:* CLIN LAB DIR, BROWNSVILLE GEN HOSP, 57- *Mem:* Am Soc Microbiol; NY Acad Sci; Am Acad Microbiol; Am Asn Clin Chemists. *Res:* Ultrastructure studies of Clostridium botulinum and actinomyces utilizing immuno-cytochemical methods, specifically immuno-ferritin methods. *Mailing Add:* Brownsville Hosp 125 Simpson Rd Brownsville PA 15417

DUDA, RICHARD OSWALD, b Evanston, Ill, Apr 27, 36; m 68; c 2. ELECTRICAL ENGINEERING. *Educ:* Univ Calif, Los Angeles, BS, 58, MS, 59; Mass Inst Technol, PhD(elec eng), 62. *Prof Exp:* SR RES ENGR, INFO SCI LAB, STANFORD RES INST, 62- *Mem:* AAAS; Asn Comput Mach; fel Inst Elec & Electronics Engrs. *Res:* Electronic computers and artificial intelligence, especially pattern recognition and machine learning; information, control and network theory. *Mailing Add:* Fairchild Res & Develop 4001 Miranda Ave Palo Alto CA 94304

DUDAR, JOHN DOUGLAS, b Calgary, Alta, Aug 15, 40; m 62; c 2. NEUROPHYSIOLOGY. *Educ:* Univ Alta, BSc, 62, MSc, 65; Dalhousie Univ, PhD(neurophysiol), 69. *Prof Exp:* Lectr pharm, Univ Alta, 65-66; asst prof, 70-77, ASSOC PROF PHYSIOL, DALHOUSIE UNIV, 77, ACTG ASST DEAN, FAC GRAD STUDIES, 81- *Concurrent Pos:* Med Res Coun Can, Univ BC, 69-70; Dalhousie Univ fel, Inst Neurophysiol, Oslo, Norway, 71-72; vis prof, Med Res Coun, 79. *Mem:* Can Physiol Soc. *Res:* Synaptic transmission; cholinergic systems; septal-hippocampal relationships. *Mailing Add:* Dept of Physiol & Biophys Dalhousie Univ Halifax NS B3H 4H7 Can

DUDAS, MARVIN JOSEPH, b Lethbridge, Alta, Mar 17, 43. SOIL MORPHOLOGY. *Educ:* Univ Alta, BSc, 66, MSc, 68; Ore State Univ, PhD(pedology), 72. *Prof Exp:* Fel, 72-74, res assoc, 72-75, asst prof, 75-78, ASSOC PROF PEDOLOGY, UNIV ALTA, 78- *Mem:* Am Soc Agron; Clay Minerals Soc; Sigma Xi. *Res:* Investigations on the nature of trace elements in the terrestrial ecosystem with emphasis on soils; mineralogical and chemical attributes of natural and disturbed soil bodies. *Mailing Add:* 6808 21st Ave Edmonton AB T6K 2H3 Can

DUDDEY, JAMES E, b Dayton, Ky, Aug 11, 41; m 65; c 2. ORGANIC CHEMISTRY, POLYMER CHEMISTRY. *Educ:* Thomas More Col, AB, 61; St Louis Univ, MS, 65, PhD(org chem), 67. *Prof Exp:* Chemist, Appl Res Lab, US Steel Corp, 66-68; sr res chemist polyester res & develop, 68-77, SR DEVELOP ENGR CHEM MAT PROCESSES DEVELOP, GOODYEAR TIRE & RUBBER CO, 77- *Mem:* Am Chem Soc. *Res:* Reactions of trifluoroacetic acid with alkynes, substituted alkynes and substituted alkyl tosylates; reactions of carbon monoxide; modifications of polyesters. *Mailing Add:* 4548 Pineview Akron OH 44321

DUDECK, ALBERT EUGENE, b West Hazleton, Pa, Oct 16, 36; m 59; c 3. AGRONOMY. *Educ:* Pa State Univ, BS, 58, PhD(agron), 64. *Prof Exp:* Assoc prof turf res, Univ Nebr, 64-70; ASSOC PROF ORNAMENTAL HORT, INST FOOD & AGR SCI, UNIV FLA, 70- *Mem:* Am Soc Agron; Crop Sci Soc Am. *Res:* Turfgrass phase of highway and fine turf research and teaching; grass breeding; turfgrass breeding and genetics. *Mailing Add:* Dept of Ornamental Hort Univ of Fla Gainesville FL 32611

DUDEK, F EDWARD, b Columbus, Nebr, Sept 12, 47; m 78. ELECTROPHYSIOLOGY. *Educ:* Univ Calif, Irvine, BSc, 69, PhD(physiol), 73. *Prof Exp:* Fel sensory physiol, Dept Ophthal Res, Col Physicians & Surgeons, Columbia Univ, 73-74; res assoc neurophysiol, Dept Psychobiol, Univ Calif, Irvine, 74; res assoc neurophysiol, Marine Biomed Inst, Med Br, Univ Tex, Galveston, 74-75; asst prof neurophysiol, Dept Zool, Erindale Col, Univ Toronto, 75-80; ASSOC PROF NEUROPHYSIOL, DEPT PHYSIOL, SCH MED, TULANE UNIV, 80- *Mem:* Am Soc Zoologists; AAAS; Soc Neurosci; Am Physiol Soc. *Res:* Local synaptic circuits in mammalian hippocampus and hypothalamus; mechanisms of synchronization of epileptiform discharges; electrophysiology of neuroendocrine cells; electrotonic coupling in mammalian brain. *Mailing Add:* Dept Physiol Sch Med Tulane Univ 1430 Tulane Ave New Orleans LA 70112

DUDEK, R(ICHARD) A(LBERT), b Clarkson, Nebr, Sept 3, 26; m 54; c 2. INDUSTRIAL ENGINEERING. *Educ:* Univ Nebr, BS, 50; Univ Iowa, MS, 51, PhD(indust eng, mgt), 56. *Prof Exp:* Plant indust engr, Fairmont Foods Co, Sioux City, Iowa, 51-52, div indust engr, Nebr, 52-53; asst instr, Univ Iowa, 53-54; asst prof mech eng, Univ Nebr, 54-56; assoc prof indust eng & res assoc schs health professions, Univ Pittsburgh, 56-58; dir Ctr Biotechnol & Human Performance, 69-71, PROF INDUST ENG & CHMN DEPT, TEX TECH UNIV, 58-, HORN PROF, 70- *Honors & Awards:* Spec Serv award, 62 & appreciation award, 71, Am Inst Indust Engrs. *Mem:* Am Soc Eng Educ; Am Soc Mech Engrs; Am Inst Indust Engrs; Inst Mgt Sci; Nat Soc Prof Engrs. *Res:* Application of operations research; sequencing/scheduling; systems analysis; technology assessment; work analysis and design; biotechnology. *Mailing Add:* Dept of Indust Eng Tex Tech Univ Lubbock TX 79409

DUDEK, THOMAS JOSEPH, b Akron, Ohio, Nov 27, 34; m 56; c 6. POLYMER SCIENCE. *Educ:* Univ Akron, BS, 56, PhD(polymer chem), 61. *Prof Exp:* Proj officer elastomers, US Air Force Mat Lab, Dayton, Ohio, 59-62; mem tech staff chem, Aerospace Corp, Calif, 62-63; aerospace technologist, Ames Res Ctr, NASA, 63-64; mgr mat res dept chem & physics, Lord Corp, Pa, 64-69; section head polymer physics, 69-75, MGR ENG MATH & PHYSICS, RES DIV, GEN TIRE & RUBBER CO, 75- *Mem:* Am Chem Soc; Am Phys Soc. *Res:* Polymer structure-mechanical property relationships; failure properties of elastomers and plastics; dynamic mechanical and damping properties of polymers and polymer composites; cord/rubber composites; tire mechanics. *Mailing Add:* Res Div Gen Tire & Rubber Co Akron OH 44329

DUDERSTADT, EDWARD C(HARLES), b Kansas City, Kans, Dec 20, 28; m 50; c 2. CERAMIC ENGINEERING. *Educ:* Univ Mo-Rolla, BS, 58, MS, 59. *Prof Exp:* Tech engr, aircraft nuclear propulsion dept, 59-61, sr engr, nuclear mat & propulsion oper, 61-66, prin engr, nuclear systs progs, 66-70, engr, advan energy progs, 70-78, SR ENGR, AIRCRAFT ENGINE GROUP, GEN ELEC CO, 78- *Mem:* Am Ceramic Soc. *Res:* Physical and mechanical properties of ceramics, refractory metals and cermets; ceramic materials fabrication processes; rates and mechanisms of gas transport in solids; development of thermal barrier coatings. *Mailing Add:* 5327 Dee Alva Dr Fairfield OH 45014

DUDERSTADT, JAMES, b Ft Madison, Iowa, Dec 5, 42; m 64; c 2. APPLIED PHYSICS. *Educ:* Yale Univ, BEng, 64; Calif Inst Technol, MS, 65, PhD(eng sci, physics), 67. *Prof Exp:* From asst prof to prof nuclear eng, 69-81, DEAN, COL ENG, UNIV MICH, ANN ARBOR, 81- *Mem:* Am Nuclear Soc; Am Phys Soc. *Res:* Nuclear reactor physics; statistical physics; plasma physics; applied mathematics; computer simulation. *Mailing Add:* Col Eng Univ Mich Ann Arbor MI 48109

DUDEWICZ, EDWARD JOHN, b Jamaica, NY, Apr 24, 42; m 63; c 3. STATISTICS. *Educ:* Mass Inst Technol, SB, 63; Cornell Univ, MS, 66, PhD(statist), 69. *Prof Exp:* Res asst statist, Cornell Univ, 65-66; asst prof, Univ Rochester, 67-72; assoc prof, 72-77, grad comt chmn dept, 73-75 & 78-80, math analyst, Comput Ctr, 74-81, PROF STATIST, OHIO STATE UNIV, 77- *Concurrent Pos:* Reviewer, Math Rev, 66- & Zentralblatt für Mathematik, 70-; prin investr grants, Off Naval Res-Ctr Naval Anal, 67-72, 79 & Army Res Off-Durham, 72-74, Nat Cancer Inst, 79, NATO, 78-; consult, Graflex Inc, Singer Co, 69, Gleason Works, 69, Myocardial Infarction Res Unit, Strong Mem Hosp, 70-72, O M Scott & Sons Co, 76- & Ohio Dept Pub Welfare, 78; abstractor, Int Lit Dig Serv, 75-78; ed, Basic Ref on Statist Tech in Qual Control, 75-80, ed, Am J Math & Mgt Sci, 79-; vis assoc prof & vis scholar statist, Stanford Univ, 76; vis prof, Katholieke Univ, Leven, Belgium, 79. *Honors & Awards:* Res Award, Sigma Xi, 77; Jack Youden Prize, Am Soc Qual Control, 81. *Mem:* Am Soc Qual Control; fel NY Acad Sci; fel Inst Math Statist; fel Am Statist Asn; Math Asn Am. *Res:* Statistical selection and ranking procedures; estimation of ordered parameters; statistical inference with unknown and unequal variances; nonparametric techniques; simulation and Monte Carlo techniques; sequential analysis; statistical computation. *Mailing Add:* 1958 Neil Ave Dept Statist Ohio State Univ Columbus OH 43210

DUDEY, NORMAN, b Wichita, Kans, May 18, 37; m 63; c 2. NUCLEAR CHEMISTRY. *Educ:* Univ Kans, AB, 59; Clark Univ, PhD(nuclear chem), 64; Univ Chicago, MBA, 75. *Prof Exp:* Fel, Columbia Univ, 64-65; head nuclear detector sect, Isotopes, Inc Div, Teledyne Inc, 65-67; from asst chemist to assoc chemist, 67-74, mgr anal chem, Argonne Nat Lab, 74-75; ANAL SPECIALIST, EXXON NUCLEAR CO, INC, 75- *Mem:* Am Nuclear Soc. *Res:* Development and radio-assay techniques of neutron detection and neutron dosimetry; studies of fission yields, neutron cross sections and radiation damage analysis; performance of LWR fuels. *Mailing Add:* Quadrex Corp 1700 Dell Ave Campbell CA 95008

DUDKIEWICZ, ALAN BERNARD, b Green Bay, Wis. IMMUNOREPRODUCTION, DEVELOPMENTAL BIOLOGY. *Educ:* Univ Wis, Stevens Point, BS, 65; Univ Mass, Amherst, MA, 68; Univ Tenn, Knoxville, PhD(zool), 73. *Prof Exp:* Instr zool, Univ Tenn, Knoxville, 71-72; res assoc biochem, Reproduction Res Lab, Univ Ga, Athens, 73-76; ASST PROF BIOL, UNIV HOUSTON, 76- *Mem:* AAAS; Am Soc Zoologists; Soc Study Reproduction; Sigma Xi. *Res:* Immunoreproductive and biochemical aspects of unique gamete and embryo proteins which mediate sperm-egg interaction and early embryogenesis in mammals. *Mailing Add:* Dept Biol Univ Houston 4800 Calhoun Houston TX 77004

DUDLEY, ALDEN WOODBURY, JR, b Lynn, Mass, May 15, 37; m 59; c 3. NEUROPATHOLOGY. *Educ:* Duke Univ, AB, 58, MD, 62. *Prof Exp:* Asst prof med & path, Duke Univ, 67-68; asst prof, Univ Wis-Madison, 68-71, assoc dir independent study prog, 73-75, assoc prof path, Univ Wis-Madison, 71-76, dir neuropath training prog, 68-76; chmn dept path, 76-77, PROF PATH, UNIV S ALA, 76- *Concurrent Pos:* NIH training fel neuropath, Duke Univ, 65-67; res assoc, Lab Exp Neuropath, Nat Inst Neurol Dis & Stroke, 63-65; neuropathologist, Ctr for Cerebrovasc Res, Durham, NC, 67-68; consult, Nat Biomed Res Found, Silver Spring, Md & Vet Admin Hosps, Madison & Tomah, Wis, 68-76; consult, Mendota & Cent Colony State Hosps, Madison, 69-76; mem adv bd, Group Res Path Educ, 74-; mem comt prof affairs, Am Asn Neuropathologists, 74-76, mem continuing educ comt, 75-77, chmn awards comt, 75-; mem, World Fedn Neurol Res Coun, 78. *Mem:* Am Asn Path & Bact; Am Soc Exp Path; NY Acad Sci; Am Asn Neuropath; Group Res Path Educ (pres, 75-77). *Res:* Computer analysis of histologic sections of brain; drug, heavy metal and herbicide toxicology; diseases of muscle; mechanism of strokes and related diagnostic procedures; neuropathology of mental retardation, alcoholism and related areas. *Mailing Add:* 3190 Med Sch Bldg Path Univ of S Ala Mobile AL 36688

DUDLEY, DARLE W, b Salem, Ore, Apr 8, 17; m 41; c 2. MECHANICAL ENGINEERING. *Educ:* Ore State Univ, BS, 40. *Prof Exp:* Engr, Gen Elec Co, 40-48, sect head gear develop, 48-57, mgr advan gear eng, 57-64; mgr mech transmissions, Mech Tech Inc, 64-65, tech dir, 65-67; chief gear technol, Solar Turbines Inc, 67-78; GEAR CONSULT, DUDLEY ENG CO, 78- *Honors & Awards:* Edward P Connell Award, 58; Golden Gear Award, Power Transmission Design, 66; Medaille d'Argent, French Inst Gears & Gear Transmissions, 77; Worcester Reed Warner Medal, Am Soc Mech Engrs, 79. *Mem:* Am Soc Mech Engrs; Am Gear Mfrs Asn; Int Fedn Theory of Machines & Mechanisms. *Res:* Fatigue strength; friction and wear; gear arrangements. *Mailing Add:* 17777 Camino Murrillo San Diego CA 92128

DUDLEY, DONALD LARRY, b Spokane, Wash, Sept 12, 36; m 59. PSYCHOPHYSIOLOGY, PSYCHOBIOLOGY. *Educ:* Univ Puget Sound, BS, 58; Univ Wash, MD, 64. *Prof Exp:* Instr psychiat, Univ Wash, 69; chief serv psychiat, US Navy, Bremerton, Wash, 69-71; assoc prof psychiat, Univ Utah, 71-72; assoc prof, 72-77, prof, 77-81, CLIN PROF NEUROL SURG, UNIV WASH, 81- *Concurrent Pos:* Cardiovasc res trainee, Univ Wash, 66-67; dir alcohol drug rehab ctr, Vet Admin Hosp, Salt Lake City, 71-72; staff psychiatrist, Vet Admin Hosp, Seattle, 72-75; chief behav med psychiat, Harborview Med Ctr, Seattle, 75-81. *Mem:* Fel Int Col Psychosom Med; Am Psychosom Soc; Am Psychiat Asn; Am Fedn Clin Res; NY Acad Sci. *Res:* Psychphysiology of pulmonary function and pulmonary diseases; development of physiologic test procedures for diagnosis of depression and mania; studies of psychobiologic factors that initiate and perpetuate chronic disease. *Mailing Add:* Cabrini Towers Suite 1020 901 Boren Seattle WA 98104

DUDLEY, EUGENE F, ecology, see previous edition

DUDLEY, FRANK MAYO, b Umatilla, Fla, Dec 27, 20; m 41; c 2. CHEMICAL EDUCATION. *Educ:* Oglethorpe Univ, AB, 44; Univ Ga, BS, 47; Ohio State Univ, MA, 50, PhD(sci educ), 62. *Prof Exp:* Clin chemist, Downey Hosp, Gainesville, Ga, 46-47 & Theresa-Holland Clin, Leesburg, Fla, 47-48; instr high sch, Ohio, 50-53, head dept sci, 53-55; asst sci educ, Ohio State Univ, 56-57; instr chem, Palm Beach Jr Col, 57-60; eval serv phys sci, Univ SFla, 60-61; clin lab off, US Army Hosp, Fort Polk, La, 61-62; asst prof, 62-69, ASSOC PROF CHEM EDUC, UNIV S FLA, 69- *Honors & Awards:* Dept Army Nat Defense Medal, 69. *Mem:* AAAS. *Res:* Improvised equipment in teaching the biological sciences; relationship of preparation and professional status to the decisions of science teachers; selected electrolytes and chromatography methods for colloidal components with various electrolytes; probable sources of ion complexes of geodes at ballast point; improvisation of materials and equipment for teaching chemistry. *Mailing Add:* Dept of Chem Univ of SFla Tampa FL 33620

DUDLEY, HORACE CHESTER, b St Louis, Mo, June 28, 09; m 35, 54; c 4. PHYSICS, RADIOBIOLOGY. *Educ:* Mo State Teachers Col, AB, 31; Georgetown Univ, PhD, 41; Am Bd Health Physics, dipl, 60. *Prof Exp:* Lab asst, US Bur Stand, 31-32; jr chemist, Bur Chem, USDA, 33-34 & Med Res Div, Chem Warfare Serv, 34-36; biochemist, USPHS, 36-42; explosives specialist, US Navy, 42-47, head allied sci sect, Med Serv Corps, 49-52, head biochem div, Naval Med Res Inst, 47-52, head radioisotope lab, Naval Hosp, St Albans, NY, 52-62, prof physics & chmn dept, Univ Southern Miss, 62-69; prof radiation physics, Univ Ill Med Ctr, 69-77; RETIRED. *Concurrent Pos:* Res collabr, Brookhaven Nat Labs, 52-57; consult, Oak Ridge Inst Nuclear Studies, 48-57, Long Island Jewish Hosp, 57-61 & Vet Hosp, Hines, 70-77. *Mem:* Fel AAAS; Health Physics Soc; Am Phys Soc; Am Asn Physics Teachers; Am Asn Physicists in Med. *Res:* Biochemistry; radioactive isotopes; nuclear theory; theory of neutrinoflux as generalized sub-quantic medium. *Mailing Add:* 405 W 8th Pl Hinsdale IL 61257

DUDLEY, JAMES DUANE, b Twin Falls, Idaho, Sept 8, 28; m 50; c 5. PHYSICS. *Educ:* Brigham Young Univ, BS, 52; Rice Inst, MA, 53; Univ Utah, PhD(physics), 59. *Prof Exp:* Instr physics, Idaho State Col, 53-54; physicist, Hughes Aircraft Co, 54-55; instr physics, 56-58, asst prof, 58-59, from asst prof to assoc prof, 61-69, PROF PHYSICS, BRIGHAM YOUNG UNIV, 69- *Concurrent Pos:* Physicist, Sandia Corp, 59-61 & Kaman Nuclear Corp, 65-66. *Mem:* Am Asn Physics Teachers. *Res:* Musical acoustics. *Mailing Add:* Dept of Physics Brigham Young Univ Provo UT 84602

DUDLEY, JOHN MINOT, b Boston, Mass, July 17, 26; m 60; c 3. PHYSICS. *Educ:* Mass Inst Technol, SB, 46; Univ Calif, Berkeley, PhD(physics), 60. *Prof Exp:* Instr physics, Pomona Col, 55-56; prin physicist, Aerojet-Gen Nucleonics Div, Gen Tire & Rubber Co, 60-63, staff specialist, 63-64; ASSOC PROF PHYSICS, COLBY COL, 64- *Concurrent Pos:* Consult, Thermonuclear Div, Oak Ridge Nat Lab, 70-71; res assoc, Univ Calif, Berkeley, 77-78. *Mem:* Am Phys Soc; Am Asn Physics Teachers. *Res:* Plasma and nuclear physics; history and philosophy of science. *Mailing Add:* Dept of Physics Colby Col Waterville ME 04901

DUDLEY, JOHN WESLEY, b Huntsville, Ind, Sept 29, 31; m 51; c 4. PLANT BREEDING, GENETICS. *Educ:* Purdue Univ, BS, 53; Iowa State Univ, MS, 55, PhD(crop breeding), 56. *Prof Exp:* Plant geneticist, Sugar Beet Sect, Agr Res Serv, USDA, 57-59; plant geneticist, Alfalfa Sect, Crop Sci Dept, NC State Univ, 59-65; assoc prof agron, 65-69, PROF AGRON, UNIV ILL, URBANA, 69- *Concurrent Pos:* Ed, Crop Sci, 71. *Mem:* Biomet Soc; Am Soc Agron; Crop Sci Soc Am. *Res:* Quantitative genetics; plant breeding methods. *Mailing Add:* 1802 Augusta Dr Champaign IL 61820

DUDLEY, KENNETH HARRISON, b Hagerstown, Md, Nov 12, 37; wid; c 2. PHARMACOLOGY, ORGANIC CHEMISTRY. *Educ:* Elon Col, BS, 59; Univ NC, Chapel Hill, PhD(org chem), 63. *Prof Exp:* Chemist, Chem & Life Sci Lab, Res Triangle Inst, 64-67; asst prof, Ctr Res Pharmacol & Toxicol, 67-73, assoc prof, 73-80, PROF PHARMACOL, SCH MED, UNIV NC, CHAPEL HILL, 80- *Concurrent Pos:* NSF fel, Univ Basel, 63-64. *Mem:* Am Chem Soc; Am Soc Exp Therapeut & Pharmacol. *Res:* Drug metabolism; chemical basis of the penicillin hypersensitivity reaction; organic syntheses; analytical chemistry, drug assays. *Mailing Add:* Dept Pharmacol Med Bldg B Univ NC Sch of Med Chapel Hill NC 27514

DUDLEY, PATRICIA, b Denver, Colo, May 22, 29. INVERTEBRATE ZOOLOGY. *Educ:* Univ Colo, BA, 51, MA, 53; Univ Wash, PhD(zool), 57. *Prof Exp:* Res assoc zool, Univ Wash, 57-59, actg instr, 59; instr, 59-62, from asst prof to assoc prof, 62-72, prof zool, 73-80, PROF BIOL, BARNARD COL, COLUMBIA UNIV, 80- *Concurrent Pos:* NSF fel, Univ Wash, 65-66; mem, Corp Marine Biol Lab, Woods Hole, Mass. *Mem:* Am Soc Zool; Marine Biol Asn UK; AAAS; Am Micros Soc; Environ Defense Fund. *Res:* Systematics, development and histology of copepods symbiotic in marine animals; electron microscopy of Crustacea Mesozoa. *Mailing Add:* Dept of Biol Sci Barnard Col of Columbia Univ New York NY 10027

DUDLEY, PETER ANTHONY, b New York, NY, July 27, 38. BIOCHEMISTRY, VISION. *Educ:* Rutgers Univ, BS, 63; Tex A&M Univ, MS, 69; Baylor Col Med, PhD(biochem), 75. *Prof Exp:* Fel, 75-77, res assoc, 77-78, RES INSTR RETINA BIOCHEM, BAYLOR COL MED, 78- *Mem:* Am Chem Soc; NY Acad Sci; Sigma Xi. *Res:* Visual cell biochemistry. *Mailing Add:* NIH Bldg 6 Rm B1A02 Bethesda MD 20014

DUDLEY, RICHARD H(ARRISON), b Los Angeles, Calif, Mar 31, 31; m 55; c 2. PHYSICAL METALLURGY. *Educ:* Columbia Univ, BS, 54, MS, 55; Rensselaer Polytech Inst, PhD(phys metall), 62. *Prof Exp:* Res asst welding, Rensselaer Polytech Inst, 58-62; mem tech staff, 62-68, supvr silicon device technol, 68-70, supvr metals group, 70-73, supvr metals & insulators group, 73-76, SUPVR PACKAGING MAT & PROCESSES GROUP, BELL TEL LABS, INC, 76- *Mem:* Inst Elec & Electronic Engrs; Int Soc Hybrid Microelectronics. *Res:* Materials and processes for packaging of silicon integrated circuits. *Mailing Add:* Bell Labs 555 Union Blvd Allentown PA 18103

DUDLEY, RICHARD MANSFIELD, b East Cleveland, Ohio, July 28, 38; div. EMPIRICAL PROCESSES, GAUSSIAN PROCESSES. *Educ:* Harvard Univ, AB, 59; Princeton Univ, PhD(math), 62. *Prof Exp:* From instr to asst prof math, Univ Calif, Berkeley, 62-66; assoc prof, 67-73, PROF MATH, MASS INST TECHNOL, 73- *Concurrent Pos:* A P Sloan fel, 66-68; assoc ed, Ann of Probability, Inst Math Statist, 72-78, ed, 79-81. *Mem:* Am Math Soc; Inst Math Statist. *Res:* Probability theory; mathematical statistics; analysis; convergence of empirical frequencies to underlying probability laws uniformly over classes of events (sets) or variables (functions); computation of probabilities; other areas of probability, measure theory, and mathematical statistics. *Mailing Add:* Dept Math Mass Inst Technol Cambridge MA 02139

DUDLEY, SUSAN D, b Norfolk, Va, April 8, 49. BEHAVIORAL ENDOCRINOLOGY. *Educ:* Old Dominion Univ, BS, 73; Col William & Mary, MA, 76; Univ Mass, Amherst, PhD(biopsychol), 80. *Prof Exp:* Instr psychol, Wheaton Col, Mass, 79-80; FEL REPROD BIOL, COL MED, M S HERSHEY MED CTR, PA STATE UNIV, 80- *Mem:* Sigma Xi; Soc Neurosci; Am Psychol Asn; AAAS. *Res:* Sexual differentiation and development of central nervous system; reproductive and parental behaviors; interactions of estradiol and insulin in reproduction; feeding and body weight maintenance; actions of estradiol in brain and pituitary cell nuclear-and cytosolic fractions. *Mailing Add:* Dept Obstet & Gynec M S Hershey Med Ctr Pa State Univ Hershey PA 17033

DUDLEY, THEODORE, b Boston, Mass, Dec 31, 36; m 60; c 2. PLANT TAXONOMY. *Educ:* Univ Mass, BS, 58; Univ Edinburgh, PhD(plant taxon), 63. *Prof Exp:* Asst taxonomist, Arnold Arboretum, Harvard Univ, 59-60, hort taxonomist, 63-66; RES BOTANIST, US NAT ARBORETUM, 66- *Mem:* Int Asn Plant Taxonomists; Am Soc Plant Taxon; Am Asn Bot Gardens & Arboretum. *Res:* Generic and specific limits of groups in the Cruciferae; monographic and revisionary studies of the aquifoliaceaei and caprifoliaceae including cultivated representatives; plant exploration in Turkey, the Peruvian Andes, Tierra del Fuego, People's Republic of China and Greece. *Mailing Add:* Herbarium US Nat Arboretum Washington DC 20002

DUDLEY, UNDERWOOD, b New York, NY, Jan 6, 37; m; c 2. MATHEMATICS, HISTORY OF SCIENCE. *Educ:* Carnegie Inst Technol, BS, 57, MS, 58; Univ Mich, PhD(math), 65. *Prof Exp:* Asst prof math, Ohio State Univ, 65-67; from asst prof, to assoc prof, 67-77, PROF MATH, DePAUW UNIV, 77- *Mem:* Am Math Soc; Math Asn Am; Soc Indust & Appl Math. *Res:* Attempts to trisect the angle. *Mailing Add:* Dept Math DePauw Univ Greencastle IN 46135

DUDNEY, CHARLES SHERMAN, b Knoxville, Tenn, June 5, 49; m 77. HEALTH RISK ANALYSIS. *Educ:* Va Polytech Inst, BS, 72; Mass Inst Technol, PhD(biophysics), 78. *Prof Exp:* Instr, Mass Inst Technol, 78-79; MEM RES STAFF, OAK RIDGE NAT LAB, 79- *Concurrent Pos:* Mem, Fed Ad Hoc Task Force, Indoor Air Pollution. *Mem:* Genetics Soc Am; AAAS; Am Soc Microbiol. *Res:* Molecular biology of toxicants; impact on human health of environmental pollutants; DNA metabolism and genetic recombination. *Mailing Add:* Health & Safety Res Div PO Box X Oak Ridge TN 37830

DUDNEY, NANCY JOHNSTON, b Pittsburgh, Pa, Aug 14, 54; m 77. DEFECT CHEMISTRY, CHARGE & MASS TRANSPORT. *Educ:* Col William & Mary, BS, 75; Mass Inst Technol, PhD(ceramics), 79. *Prof Exp:* E P Wigner, fel, 79-81, RES STAFF, OAK RIDGE NAT LAB, 81- *Mem:* Am Ceramics Soc; Am Chem Soc; Sigma Xi. *Res:* Solid state chemistry: defect chemistry, nonstoichiometry, electrical conductivity and diffusion; properties of solid electrolytes and mixed ionic-electronic conductors; fabrication and characterization of ceramic materials; solid state spectroscopy. *Mailing Add:* Solid State Div Oak Ridge Nat Lab PO Box X Oak Ridge TN 37830

DUDOCK, BERNARD S, b New York, NY, Nov 17, 39; m 64; c 3. BIOCHEMISTRY. *Educ:* City Col New York, BS, 61; Pa State Univ, PhD(org chem), 66. *Prof Exp:* NIH fel biochem, Cornell Univ, 66-68; from asst prof to assoc prof, 68-81, PROF BIOCHEM, STATE UNIV NY STONY BROOK, 81- *Concurrent Pos:* Nat Cancer Inst grant, 68- & res career develop award, 73-78. *Mem:* AAAS; Fedn Am Socs Exp Biol. *Res:* Primary structure of nucleic acids; role of nucleic acids in cellular differentiation and development. *Mailing Add:* Dept of Biochem State Univ of NY Stony Brook NY 11794

DUDUKOVIC, MILORAD, b Belgrade, Yugoslavia, Mar 25, 44; m 69; c 2. CHEMICAL ENGINEERING, APPLIED MATHEMATICS. *Educ:* Univ Belgrade, dipl chem eng, 67; Ill Inst Technol, MS, 70, PhD(chem eng), 72. *Prof Exp:* Design engr, Inst Process Design, Belgrade, 67-68; instr, Ill Inst Technol, 70-72; asst prof, Ohio Univ, 72-74; assoc prof, 74-81, PROF CHEM ENG, WASH UNIV, 81- *Concurrent Pos:* Consult, Ill Environ Protection Agency, 71 & Monsanto Com Prods Co, 77-; dir, Chem Reaction Eng Lab, Wash Univ, 74- & Monsanto Prog Prof Develop, 77- *Mem:* Am Inst Chem Engrs; Am Chem Soc; Am Soc Eng Educ; Sigma Xi. *Res:* Chemical reaction engineering; kinetics and diffusion in gas-solid noncatalytic reactions; modelling and tracer studies of multiphase reactors of the trickle-bed and gas lift slurry type. *Mailing Add:* Dept of Chem Eng Wash Univ Box 1198 St Louis MO 63130

DUDZIAK, DONALD JOHN, b Alden, NY, Jan 6, 35; m 59; c 3. NUCLEONICS. *Educ:* US Merchant Marine Acad, BS, 56; Univ Rochester, MS, 57; Univ Pittsburgh, PhD(appl math), 63. *Prof Exp:* From assoc engr to sr engr, Bettis Atomic Power Lab, Westinghouse Elec Corp, 57-65; staff mem, 65-74, alt group leader transport & reactor theory, 75-78, SECT LEADER CTR NEUTRONICS, THEORET DIV, LOS ALAMOS SCI LAB, 74-, GROUP LEADER TRANSPORT & REACTOR THEORY, 79- *Concurrent Pos:* Adj prof, Univ NMex, 66; vis prof, Univ Va, 68-69; mem, Nat Cross Sect Eval Working Group; mem, US Nuclear Data Comt, 73-; guest scientist, Swiss Fed Inst Reactor Res, 81-82. *Mem:* Am Nuclear Soc; Soc Indust & Appl Math; Health Physics Soc. *Res:* Radiation shielding analysis and nuclear hazards evaluation; application of stochastic process theory to nuclear reactor kinetics; nuclear reactor analysis for development of design models; radiological physics and radiation biology; fusion reactor nuclear analysis and methods development. *Mailing Add:* MS 269 Theoret Div Los Alamos Sci Lab Los Alamos NM 87545

DUDZIAK, WALTER FRANCIS, b Adams, Mass, Jan 7, 23; m 54; c 4. COMPUTER SCIENCE, NUCLEAR SCIENCE. *Educ:* Rensselaer Polytech, BS & MS, 48; Univ Calif, Berkeley, PhD(math, physics), 54. *Prof Exp:* Engr, Manhattan Dist Proj, Oak Ridge Nat Lab, 44-46; instr physics, Rensselaer Polytech, 47-48; aeronaut res scientist, Nat Adv Comt Aeronaut, Ohio Univ, 48-49; mem res staff, Lawrence Radiation Lab, Univ Calif, 49-58; tech mil planning oper, Gen Elec Co, 58-60, mgr comput sci oper, 60-64, tech mil planning oper, 64-65; dir info sci inst & exec vpres res & develop, 65-68, CONSULT & MEM BD, PAN-FAX, INC, 65-; PRES, INFO SCI, INC, 68- *Concurrent Pos:* Lectr, Univ Calif, Santa Barbara, 58-59; consult nuclear weapons simulation, Shock Physics. *Mem:* Am Phys Soc; Am Asn Comput Mach; Am Geophys Union; Sigma Xi. *Res:* Leads; application of computer sciences to various scientific disciplines; effects of nuclear detonations; propagation of electromagnetic radiation; optical scanning; digitizing techniques as applied to rapid data transmission; electro-optic systems. *Mailing Add:* Info Sci Inc 123 W Padre Santa Barbara CA 93105

DUDZINSKI, DIANE MARIE, b Erie, Pa, July 23, 46. BIOLOGY. *Educ:* Villa Maria Col, BS, 68; Fordham Univ, MS, 70, PhD(phycol, limnol, biol oceanog), 74. *Prof Exp:* Fel gen biol & limnol, Fordham Univ, 70-73; asst prof gen biol, liminol, marine biol & estuarine ecol, Manhattan Col, 73-78; assoc prof, 78-81, chairperson sci & math, 80-81, PROF BIOL, COL SANTA FE, 81- *Concurrent Pos:* Fel, Fordham Univ, 74-75; mem US-USSR joint oceanog exped to Bering Sea, US Dept Interior, Fish & Wildlife Serv, 77; NIH grant, 80-83. *Mem:* Am Soc Limnol & Oceanog; Am Soc Protozoologists; Am Soc Phycologists; Ecol Soc Am; Am Inst Biol Sci. *Res:* Morphology, physiology and nutrition of the marine symbiotic alga, Symbiodinium microadriaticum; bacterial enumeration of coliforms and pathogens at selected sample sites in the New York harbor; behavior genetics in inbred mouse strains. *Mailing Add:* Dept of Math & Sci Col of Santa Fe Santa Fe NM 87501

DUECK, JOHN, b Altona, Man, Aug 11, 41; m 62; c 3. PLANT PATHOLOGY. *Educ:* Univ Man, BSA, 64; Univ Minn, MSc, 66, PhD(plant path), 71. *Prof Exp:* Agronomist, Soils & Crops Br, Man Dept Agr, 66-68; pathologist bact dis, Harrow, Ont, 71-73, pathologist plant quarantine, Ottawa, 73-74, plant pathologist, Saskatoon, 74-81, DIR, AGR CAN RES STA, REGINA, SASK, 81- . *Mem:* Can Phytopath Soc; Agr Inst Can; Am Phytopath Soc. *Res:* Diseases of rapeseed and sunflower with emphasis on biology and control of Sclerotinia sclerotiorum. *Mailing Add:* Agr Can Res Sta PO Box 440 Regina Saskatoon SK S4P 3A2 Can

DUECKER, HEYMAN CLARKE, b Seville, Ohio, July 18, 29; m 49; c 4. INORGANIC CHEMISTRY. *Educ:* Marion Col, BS, 50; Univ Toledo, MS, 56, Univ Md, PhD, 64. *Prof Exp:* Res chemist, Radio Corp Am, 51-54; res chemist, Sci Lab, Ford Motor Co, 55-58; phys chemist, Nat Bur Standards, 58-66; inorg chemist, W R Grace & Co, 66-67; mgr inorg res, 67-69, dir inorg res, 69-71, VPRES RES, CONSTRUCTION PROD DIV, W R GRACE & CO, 71- *Mem:* AAAS; Am Chem Soc; Am Ceramic Soc. *Res:* Inorganic oxides, preparation, properties and identification; silicates, zeolites; catalytic materials and processes; surface and colloid chemistry; inorganic construction materials. *Mailing Add:* W R Grace & Co 62 Whittemore Ave Cambridge MA 02140

DUEDALL, IVER WARREN, b Albany, Ore, Jan 16, 39; m 61; c 2. OCEANOGRAPHY, PHYSICAL CHEMISTRY. *Educ:* Ore State Univ, BS, 63, MS, 66; Dalhousie Univ, PhD(chem oceanog), 73. *Prof Exp:* Scientist chem oceanog, Marine Ecol Lab, Bedford Inst Oceanog, Dartmouth, NS, 66-72; asst prof, 72-77, ASSOC PROF CHEM OCEANOG, MARINE SCI RES CTR, STATE UNIV NY STONY BROOK, 77- *Mem:* AAAS; Am Geophys Union; Sigma Xi; Am Soc Limnol & Oceanog. *Res:* Physical chemistry of electrolyte systems; partial molal properties; coastal and estuary processes; chemical inputs to the ocean from rivers; deep sea distribution of properties; nutrient dynamics; man's impact on the ocean; international programs in marine sciences; wastes in the ocean. *Mailing Add:* Marine Sci Res Ctr State Univ of NY Stony Brook NY 11794

DUEKER, DAVID KENNETH, b Kansas City, Kans, Nov 4, 44. OPHTHALMOLOGY. *Educ:* Pomona Col, BA, 66; Yale Univ, MD, 70. *Prof Exp:* Intern, Pac Med Ctr, 70-71; resident ophthal, Yale Univ, New Haven Hosp, 71-74; fel glaucoma, Harvard Med Sch, 74-76; clin fel, 74-76, ASST DIR GLAUCOMA SERV & ASST OPHTHAL, MASS EYE & EAR INFIRMARY, 76- *Concurrent Pos:* Prin investr, NIH grant, 77-; instr ophthal, Harvard Med Sch, 76-79, asst prof, 80- *Mem:* AAAS; Am Acad Ophthal & Otolaryngol; Asn Res Vision Ophthal. *Res:* Glaucoma; neovascular glaucoma; angiogenesis in the eye; fluorescein angiography. *Mailing Add:* Mass Eye & Ear Infirmary 243 Charles St Boston MA 02114

DUELAND, RUDOLF (TASS), b Staten Island, NY, Feb 16, 33. VETERINARY MEDICINE. *Educ:* Cornell Univ, DVM, 56; Univ Minn & Mayo Grad Sch Med, MS, 70. *Prof Exp:* Assoc prof & dir small animal clin, Orthop Surg, Western Col Vet Med, Univ Saskatchewan, 71-72; guest lectr surg, Col Engr, Cornell Univ, 72-80; vis scientist, Univ Washington & Swiss Res Inst, Switz, 78-79; assoc prof, NY State Col Vet Med, Cornell Univ, 72-80; PROF & CHMN, DEPT SURG SCI, SCH VET MED, UNIV WIS, MADISON, 80- *Concurrent Pos:* Surgeon & clinician, Henry Bergh Mem Hosp, NY, 59-60; vet, NY City Dept Health, 61-67; dir, DuelandAnimal Clin, Inc, Staten Island, 60-73. *Mem:* Am Vet Med Asn; Am Animal Hosp Asn; Vet Orthop Soc (vpres 75, pres, 77); Orthop Res Soc; Bioelect Repair & Growth Soc. *Res:* Research in vascular and morphological effects of internal fixation of bone; biomechanical and vascular considerations of various cruciate repairs. *Mailing Add:* Dept Surg Sci Sch Vet Med Univ Wis 333 N Randall Ave Madison WI 53715

DUELL, ELIZABETH ANN, b Dayton, Ohio, Jan 9, 36. BIOCHEMISTRY, MOLECULAR BIOLOGY. *Educ:* Univ Dayton, BS, 58; Western Reserve Univ, PhD(biochem), 67. *Prof Exp:* Instr, 70-72, ASST PROF BIOCHEM & DERMAT, UNIV MICH, ANN ARBOR, 72- *Honors & Awards:* Taub Mem Award Psoriasis Res, 73. *Mem:* AAAS; Soc Invest Dermat; NY Acad Sci; Am Fedn Clin Res. *Res:* Role of cyclic nucleotides in control of cell proliferation and differentiation with special emphasis on the epidermis. *Mailing Add:* Univ of Mich Med Sch R 6558 Kresge Med Res Bldg Ann Arbor MI 48104

DUELL, PAUL M, b Goodland, Kans, Dec 11, 24; m 48; c 4. INORGANIC CHEMISTRY. *Educ:* Ft Hays Kans State Col, BA, 50, MS, 51; Kans State Univ, PhD(chem), 58. *Prof Exp:* Instr phys sci, Garden City Jr Col, 51-52; instr chem, Washburn Univ, 52-53 & Kans State Univ, 53-57; from asst prof to prof chem & chmn dept, 57-73, dean col lib arts, 73-77, PROF CHEM, WILLAMETTE UNIV, 77- *Mem:* AAAS; Am Chem Soc. *Res:* Physical properties of mixed aqueous salt solutions, including magnetic susceptibilities, conductivities, partial molal volumes; physical properties of binary aqueous salt solutions; ligand field effects on complex ions in aqueous and nonaqueous solutions. *Mailing Add:* Dept of Chem Willamette Univ Salem OR 97301

DUELL, ROBERT WILLIAM, agronomy, crops, see previous edition

DUELLMAN, WILLIAM EDWARD, b Dayton, Ohio, Sept 6, 30; m 53; c 3. HERPETOLOGY. *Educ:* Univ Mich, MS, 53. *Prof Exp:* Asst herpet, Mus Zool, Univ Mich, 52-56, teaching fel zool, 54-56; instr, Dept Biol, Wayne State Univ, 56-59; from asst prof to assoc prof zool, 59-68, prof, 68-70, asst curator herpet, 59-63, assoc curator, 63-70, PROF SYSTS & ECOL, UNIV KANS, 70-, CURATOR, MUS NATURAL HIST, 70-, ASSOC DIR, 71- *Mem:* Am Soc Ichthyol & Herpet; Soc Study Evolution; Am Soc Syst Zool; Ecol Soc Am; Brit Herpet Soc. *Res:* Systematics; zoogeographic patterns; evolution; zoogeography of New World herpetofauna; evolutionary biology of reptiles and amphibians. *Mailing Add:* Mus of Nat Hist Univ of Kans Lawrence KS 66045

DUELTGEN, RONALD REX, b Salem, Ore, Sept 21, 40; m 62; c 2. INFORMATION SCIENCE. *Educ:* Ore State Univ, BA, 62; Univ Mich, PhD(org chem), 67. *Prof Exp:* Res investr, 67-72, supvr chem doc, 72-74, mgr sci info, G D Searle & Co, 74-77; mgr, Tech Info Serv, 77-81, DIR, INFO & ADMIN SERV, HENKEL CORP, 81- *Mem:* AAAS; Am Chem Soc; Sigma Xi; Am Soc Info Sci. *Res:* Synthetic organic chemistry; information transfer; computer manipulation of scientific and technical information. *Mailing Add:* Henkel Corp 2010 E Hennepin Ave Minneapolis MN 55413

DUERKSEN, JACOB DIETRICH, b Alta, Can, Nov 29, 29; Can citizen; div; c 2. MOLECULAR BIOLOGY, CELLULAR BIOLOGY. *Educ:* Univ BC, BS, 53, MS, 55; Univ Wis, PhD(bact), 58. *Prof Exp:* Asst microbiol, Univ BC, 53-55 & Univ Mich, 55-56; asst bact, Univ Wis, 56-58; asst prof microbiol, Univ Kans, 60-64, assoc prof, Sch Med, 64-70; Alberta Hertiage med res professorship in residence, 81-82, PROF BIOL, UNIV CALGARY, 70- *Concurrent Pos:* NIH res grant, 61-67, spec res fel, 69-70; Kans Cancer Inst res grant, 67-69; Can Nat Res Coun grant, 70-79. *Mem:* Am Soc Cell Biol; Can Soc Cell Biol; Can Biochem Soc. *Res:* Genetic regulatory mechanisms in biosynthesis, growth and development in encaryotic cells; chromosome structure and function especially concerning the transcribed regions of specific gene systems utilized during mammalian development (alpha-fetoprotein) and stress situations (metallothienlin). *Mailing Add:* Dept of Biol Univ of Calgary Calgary AB T2N 1N4 Can

DUERR, FREDERICK G, b St Paul, Minn, May 17, 35; m 54; c 3. ZOOLOGY, COMPARATIVE PHYSIOLOGY. *Educ:* Univ Minn, BA, 56, PhD(zool), 65. *Prof Exp:* Assoc prof zool, Univ SDak, 61-67; assoc prof biol, Univ Sask, Regina, 67-68; assoc prof, 68-77, ADJ ASSOC PROF BIOL, UNIV NDAK, 77- *Mem:* AAAS; Am Soc Zool; Am Soc Parasitol. *Res:* Comparative physiology of digenetic trematode parasitism; physiology of respiration and nitrogen excretion. *Mailing Add:* Dept of Biol Univ of N Dak Grand Forks ND 58201

DUERR, J STEPHEN, b Erie, Pa, Apr 8, 43; m 64; c 3. ELECTRON MICROSCOPY, FAILURE ANALYSIS. *Educ:* Mass Inst Technol, BS, 65, MS, 67, PhD(metall), 71. *Prof Exp:* Metallurgist, Battelle Mem Inst, 65-66; sr metallurgist, Bettis Atomic Power Lab, 71-74; dir anal serv, PhotoMetrics Inc, 74-77; TECH DIR, STRUCT PROBE, INC, 77-; PRES, METUCHEN ANAL, INC, 78- *Concurrent Pos:* course dir, Ctr Prof Advan, 80- *Mem:* Am Soc Metals; Microbeam Anal Soc; Am Vacuum Soc; Am Soc Testing & Mat; Sigma Xi. *Res:* Failure analysis and problem solving investigations in most materials systems including metals; microelectronics devices, catalysts and adhesives; claims substantiation in advertising, litigation and patent development; electron microscopy/microanalysis and surface analysis studies. *Mailing Add:* Struct Probe Inc 230 Forrest St Metuchen NJ 08840

DUERRE, JOHN A, b Webster, SDak, Aug 21, 30; m 57; c 3. MICROBIAL PHYSIOLOGY, BIOCHEMISTRY. *Educ:* SDak State Col, BS, 52, MS, 56; Univ Minn, PhD(bact), 60. *Prof Exp:* Res bacteriologist, Rocky Mt Lab, Nat Inst Allergy & Infectious Dis, 61-63; from asst prof to assoc prof, 63-71, PROF MICROBIOL, SCH MED, UNIV N DAK, 71- *Concurrent Pos:* AEC fel, Argonne Nat Lab, 60-61; NSF reg grant, 63-71; NIH career develop award, 65-75, NIH res grant, 71-; vis scientist, Neuropsychiat Res Unit, Med Res Coun Labs, Eng, 69-70. *Mem:* Am Soc Microbiol; NY Acad Sci; Am Soc Biol Chemists; Sigma Xi. *Res:* Sulfur amino acid metabolism in mammalian and microbial systems; methylation of chromosomal proteins. *Mailing Add:* Dept of Microbiol Univ of NDak Grand Forks ND 58201

DUERSCH, RALPH R, b Berlin, Ger, Feb 28, 26; m 57; c 2. DECISION SUPPORT SYSTEMS, SIMULATION. *Educ:* Newark Col Eng, BS, 57; Rensselaer Polytech Inst, MS, 65; Union Col, MS, 72, PhD(eng & admin), 73. *Prof Exp:* Jr engr, Kearfott Co, Paterson, NJ, 56; elec engr, Switchgear & Control Div, 57, Light Military Electronics Dept, 57-58, Heavy military Electronics Dept, 58-59, Light Military Electronics Dept, 59-60, syst anal engr, Advan Technol Lab, 60-70, INFO SYST ENGR CORP RES & DEVELOP, GEN ELEC CO, 70- *Concurrent Pos:* Adj assoc prof, Inst Admin & Mgt, Union Col, 75- *Mem:* Inst Elec & Electronics Engrs. *Res:* Improved techniques of decision support for management, factory control and scheduling using methods from artificial intelligence, optimization, simulation and computer science. *Mailing Add:* Rm 573 Bldg 37 Gen Elec Co 1 River Rd Schenectady NY 12345

DUERST, RICHARD WILLIAM, b Rice Lake, Wis, Aug 18, 40; m 64; c 3. PHYSICAL CHEMISTRY, ANALYTICAL CHEMISTRY. *Educ:* St Olaf Col, BA, 62; Univ Calif, Berkeley, PhD(chem), 66. *Prof Exp:* Fel phys chem, Lawrence Radiation Lab, Univ Calif, 66-67; Nat Res Coun-Nat Bur Stand res fel, Nat Bur Stand, Md, 67-69; asst prof, 69-74, ASSOC PROF CHEM, UNIV WIS-EAU CLAIRE, 74- *Concurrent Pos:* NSF vis prof & res assoc, Harvard Univ, 74, 75, 76 & 78. *Mem:* Am Chem Soc; Royal Soc Chem; Am Phys Soc; Sigma Xi. *Res:* characterization of hydrogen-bonded systems by spectroscopy (microwave and infrared); dissociation of strong acids; hydration of ionic species in aqueous solution; metal-metal pair interactions; effect of isotopic substitution on physical properties. *Mailing Add:* Dept of Chem Univ of Wis Eau Claire WI 54701

DUESBERY, MICHAEL SERGE, b Hull, UK, May 20, 42; m 64; c 4. SOLID STATE PHYSICS, MATERIALS SCIENCE. *Educ:* Cambridge Univ, BA, 64, PhD(physics), 67. *Prof Exp:* Res fel metals, Dept Metall, Oxford Univ, 66-68; RES OFFICER DEFECTS, DIV PHYSICS, NAT RES COUN CAN, OTTAWA, 68- *Res:* Defects, particularly dislocations, in the solid state. *Mailing Add:* Div of Physics Nat Res Coun Can Ottawa Can

DUESTERHOEFT, WILLIAM CHARLES, JR, b Austin, Tex, Dec 10, 21; m 49; c 1. ELECTRICAL ENGINEERING. *Educ:* Univ Tex, BS, 43, MS, 49; Calif Inst Technol, PhD(elec eng), 53. *Prof Exp:* Elec engr, Gen Elec Co, 43-46; from instr to asst prof elec eng, Univ Tex, 46-49; instr, Calif Inst Technol, 49-52; aerophysics engr, Gen Dynamics/Convair, 52-54; assoc prof, 54-60, PROF ELEC ENG, UNIV TEX, AUSTIN, 60- *Concurrent Pos:* Corp consult, 54- *Mem:* Inst Elec & Electronics Engrs; Am Soc Eng Educ; Am Phys Soc. *Res:* Plasma dynamics; geophysics; power and energy conversion systems. *Mailing Add:* Dept of Elec Eng Univ of Tex Austin TX 78712

DUEWER, ELIZABETH ANN, b Champaign, Ill, June 21, 37; m 63; c 3. LICHENOLOGY. *Educ:* Univ Ill, BS, 60, MS, 62; Univ Ariz, PhD(bot), 71. *Prof Exp:* Teaching asst bot, Univ Ill, 60-62 & Duke Univ, 63; from teaching asst to teaching assoc, Univ Ariz, 63-69; consult floricult, Cushman Nurseries, 75-76 & 78; consult, Univ Wis-Platteville, 79 & 81-82. *Mem:* Am Bryol & Lichenological Soc; Brit Lichen Soc. *Res:* The taxonomy and morphology of the lichen genus Acarospora and its phycobiont Trebouxia. *Mailing Add:* RR 2 Box 376 Platteville WI 53818

DUEWER, RAYMOND GEORGE, b Auburn, Ill, Mar 28, 26; m 63; c 3. HORTICULTURE, AGRICULTURE. *Educ:* Univ Ill, BS, 61, MS, 62; Univ Ariz, PhD(hort), 69. *Prof Exp:* Asst prof, 69-76, ASSOC PROF HORT, UNIV WIS, 77- *Mem:* Am Asn Hort Sci; Am Hort Soc; Am Genetic Asn. *Res:* Microsporogenesis in diploid, triploid, and tetraploid Cucumis melo L on the cytological level; breeding strawberries; germination study of lettuce; embryo culture in muskmelons. *Mailing Add:* Dept of Agr Sci Univ of Wis Platteville WI 53818

DUFAU, MARIA LUISA, b Argentina, Sept 22, 38; US citizen; m 69; c 1. ENDOCRINOLOGY, BIOCHEMISTRY. *Educ:* Nat Univ Cuyo, MD, 62, PhD(med sci), 68. *Prof Exp:* Res assoc, Clin Res Inst Montreal, 67-68; lectr, Dept Med, Monash Univ, Australia, 68-70; sr investr endocrinol, 70-78, CHIEF SECT MOLECULAR ENDOCRINOL, ENDOCRINOL & REPROD RES BR, NAT INST CHILD HEALTH & HUMAN DEVELOP, NIH, 78- *Mem:* Am Endocrine Soc; Am Soc Clin Res; Am Soc Clin Invest; Am Soc Biol Chem. *Res:* Peptide hormone receptors and control of steroidogenesis in testis, ovary and adrenal; properties and biological activity of circulating gonadotropins in physiological regulation and clincial disorders of pituitary and gonadal function. *Mailing Add:* 5673 Bent Branch Rd Bethesda MD 20014

DUFF, DALE THOMAS, b Ross Co, Ohio, Dec 26, 30; m 58; c 1. CROP PHYSIOLOGY. *Educ:* Ohio State Univ, BS, 57, MS, 64; Mich State Univ, PhD(crop sci), 67. *Prof Exp:* Trainee, Soil Conserv Serv, USDA, 55-57; agronomist, Clinton County Farm Bur Coop Asn, Ohio, 58-61; asst instr agron, Ohio State Univ, 61-64; teaching asst crop sci, Mich State Univ, 64-67; asst prof, 67-75, ASSOC PROF PLANT & SOIL SCI, UNIV RI, 75- *Mem:* AAAS; Am Soc Agron; Crop Sci Soc Am; Sigma Xi; Int Turfgrass Soc. *Res:* Stress physiology of turf grasses, especially high temperature and low temperature effects upon growth. *Mailing Add:* Dept of Plant & Soil Sci Univ of RI Kingston RI 02881

DUFF, FRATIS L, b Randlett, Okla, July 7, 10; m 37; c 2. MEDICINE. *Educ:* Univ Okla, BS, 33, MD, 39; Johns Hopkins Univ, MPH, 50, DPH, 53. *Prof Exp:* Dir training & chief trop med dept, Sch Aerospace Med, US Air Force, 43-47, wing surgeon & chief prof serv br, Far East Air Force, Japan, 47-49, prof mil sci & tactics, Johns Hopkins Univ, 49-51, mem staff, Hq, Surgeon Gen Off, 51-53, commandant, US Air Force Sch Aerospace Med, 53-59, dep surgeon, Ger, 59-62, command surgeon, Air Force Systs Command, 62-64, command surgeon, Tactical Air Command, 64-68; dep comnr, 68-75, STATE COMNR HEALTH, TEX DEPT HEALTH, 75- *Mem:* AMA; Am Pub Health Asn; fel Am Col Physicians; Am Col Prev Med; Aerospace Med Asn. *Res:* Military preventive and aviation medicine. *Mailing Add:* Off of Commissioner Tex Dept Health Austin TX 78756

DUFF, GEORGE FRANCIS DENTON, b Toronto, Ont, July 28, 26; m 51; c 5. MATHEMATICS. *Educ:* Univ Toronto, BA, 48, MA, 49; Princeton Univ, PhD(math), 51. *Prof Exp:* Moore instr, Mass Inst Technol, 51-52; from asst prof to assoc prof, 52-61, chmn dept, 68-75, PROF MATH, UNIV TORONTO, 61- *Concurrent Pos:* Ed, Can J Math, 57-61 & 78-81. *Mem:* Am Math Soc; Can Math Cong (pres, 71-73). *Res:* Differential equations. *Mailing Add:* 20 Buckingham Ave Toronto ON M5S 2R8 Can

DUFF, IVAN FRANCIS, b Pendleton, Ore, July 20, 15; m; c 2. INTERNAL MEDICINE. *Educ:* Univ Ore, AB, 38; Univ Mich, MD, 40. *Prof Exp:* Intern, Univ Hosp, 40-41, from asst resident to resident internal med, 41-46, asst physician, 48-53, from instr to assoc prof, 46-60, prof internal med charge, Rockham Arthritis Res Unit, Arthritis Div, 60-69, PROF INTERNAL MED CHARGE ARTHRITIS DIV, UNIV HOSP, 69- *Concurrent Pos:* Dir, Regional Arthritis Control Prog, Mich, 69-71. *Mem:* Am Fedn Clin Res; Am Rheumatism Asn; fel Am Col Physicians. *Res:* Rheumatic and thromboembolic diseases. *Mailing Add:* Arthritis Div Bldg 9 Rm 920 Univ Hosp Ann Arbor MI 48104

DUFF, J(ACK) E(RROL), b Baltimore, Md, May 17, 18; m 47. ELECTRONICS. *Educ:* Case Inst Technol, BS, 39. *Prof Exp:* Jr engr, 39-41, sr engr, 41-45, dir elec sect, 45-54, res coordr, 54-55, DIR RES, HOOVER CO, 55- *Mem:* Inst Elec & Electronics Engrs. *Res:* Small series motor design; industrial electronic control and inspection equipment design; analysis of multivibrator circuits; electrostatic heating-thermal control; frequency multiplier. *Mailing Add:* 645 Glenwood SW Canton OH 44720

DUFF, JAMES MCCONNELL, b Aviemore, Scotland, Sept 24, 40; Can citizen; m 63; c 3. ORGANIC CHEMISTRY, ORGANOMETALLIC CHEMISTRY. *Educ:* Univ Toronto, BSc, 65, PhD(org chem), 70. *Prof Exp:* Fel inorg chem, Univ Leeds, 70-72; res assoc org chem, Univ Toronto, 72-74; mem sci staff pigments, 74-79, group leader inks, 78-80, MGR POLYMER SYNTHESIS, XEROX RES CTR CAN, 80- *Mem:* Am Chem Soc. *Res:* Synthesis and characterization of materials used in copying and duplicating technologies; polymer chemistry. *Mailing Add:* Xerox Res Ctr of Can 2480 Dunwin Dr Mississauga ON L5L 1J9 Can

DUFF, JAMES THOMAS, b Sandusky, Ohio, Jan 23, 25. MICROBIOLOGY. *Educ:* Ohio State Univ, BS, 47, MS, 49; Univ Tex, PhD, 60. *Prof Exp:* Microbiologist, Immunol Br, Med Invest Div, US Army Biol Lab, Ft Detrick, 49-56; res scientist, Dept Bact, Univ Tex, 57-59; microbiologist, Immunol Br, Med Invest Div, US Army Biol Lab, 59-65; microbiologist, 65-66, assoc chief, Viral Carcinogenesis Br, 66-75 & Collab Res Br, 75-76, chief, 76-78, CHIEF, BIOL CARCINOGENESIS BR, NAT CANCER INST, 78- *Mem:* AAAS; Int Asn Comp Res On Leukemia & Related Dis; Tissue Cult Asn; Am Soc Microbiol; Sigma Xi. *Res:* Azotobacter bacteriophage; Clostridium botulinum toxins and toxoids; tissue culture; psittacosis group vaccines; viral oncology. *Mailing Add:* Ladlow Bldg 9A22 7910 Woodmont Ave Bethesda MD 20205

DUFF, RAYMOND STANLEY, b Hodgdon, Maine, Nov 2, 23; m 45; c 3. PEDIATRICS, SOCIOLOGY. *Educ:* Univ Maine, BA, 48; Yale Univ, MD, 52, MPH, 59. *Prof Exp:* Intern & resident pediat, Yale-New Haven Hosp, 52-55; dir bur med serv, New Haven Health Dept, 55-56; instr pediat & pub health, 56-59, asst prof pediat & sociol, 59-67, assoc prof, 67-78, PROF PEDIAT, SCH MED, YALE UNIV, 78- *Concurrent Pos:* Asst dir ambulatory serv, Yale-New Haven Hosp, 56-59. *Mem:* AAAS; fel Am Pub Health Asn; fel Am Acad Pediat; Am Sociol Asn. *Res:* Behavioral aspects of health, especially health or illness care in large hospitals as influenced by patients, families, physicians, nurses, administrators and others. *Mailing Add:* Dept of Pediat Yale Univ Sch of Med New Haven CT 06520

DUFF, ROBERT HODGE, b Durand, Mich, Oct 21, 29; m 58; c 3. ELECTRON MICROSCOPY, CHEMISTRY. *Educ:* Mich State Univ, BS, 51; Ind Univ, PhD(inorg chem), 61. *Prof Exp:* Control chemist, Am Agr Chem Co, Mich, 51-53; asst, Ind Univ, 53-59; electron microscopist & phys chemist, Nat Bur Standards, 59-61; staff scientist electron micros, Avco Corp, Wilmington, 61-66; res assoc, Ledgemont Lab, Kennecott Copper Corp, Lexington, 66-70, anal chemist, 70-72; consult chemist, Technol Inc, 72-73; sr physicist, Systs Res Lab, Dayton, 73-75; sr res chemist, 75-78, ANAL PROJ LECTR, STANDARD OIL OF OHIO, CLEVELAND, 78- *Mem:* AAAS; Am Chem Soc; fel Am Inst Chemists; Electron Micros Soc Am; Int Soc Stereology. *Res:* Use of electron microscopy in all phases of material science; use of x-rays for elemental analysis with the electron microscope. *Mailing Add:* 2201 S Overlook Cleveland Heights OH 44106

DUFF, RUSSELL EARL, b Grand Rapids, Mich, Nov 28, 26; div; c 5. FLUID DYNAMICS, CHEMICAL PHYSICS. *Educ:* Univ Mich, BSE, 47, MS, 48, PhD(physics), 51. *Prof Exp:* Res assoc, Eng Res Inst, Univ Mich, 47-51; mem staff, Los Alamos Sci Lab, 51-61 & Inst Defense Anal, 61-62; proj leader, Lawrence Radiation Lab, 62-64, div leader, 64-67; VPRES & DIV MGR, SYSTS, SCI & SOFTWARE, 67- *Mem:* Am Nuclear Soc; Am Phys Soc. *Res:* Research on safety of underground nuclear testing, shock and detonation hydrodynamics, high pressure material properties; high temperature chemistry. *Mailing Add:* 453 Bay Meadows Way Solana Beach CA 92075

DUFFER, WILLIAM RILEY, aquatic biology, see previous edition

DUFFEY, DICK, b Wabash County, Ind, Aug 26, 17. NUCLEAR ENGINEERING. *Educ:* Purdue Univ, BS, 39; Univ Iowa, MS, 40; Univ Md, PhD(nuclear eng), 56. *Prof Exp:* Engr nuclear proj, Union Carbide, 40-42; nuclear engr, US Atomic Energy Comn, 47-54; head nuclear eng prog, 54-65, assoc prof, 56-59, nuclear reactor dir, 58-68, PROF NUCLEAR ENG, UNIV MD, 59- *Concurrent Pos:* Tech sect adv comt on reactor safeguards, Atomic Energy Comn, 59-66. *Mem:* Am Nuclear Soc; Am Phys Soc; Am Geophys Union; Am Inst Chem Engrs; Am Chem Soc. *Res:* Nuclear reactor design and operation; nuclear reactor safety; neutron uses; californium 252 uses. *Mailing Add:* Nuclear Eng Dept Univ of Md College Park MD 20742

DUFFEY, DONALD CREAGH, b Winchester, Va, Feb 9, 31. PHYSICAL CHEMISTRY, ORGANIC CHEMISTRY. *Educ:* Va Polytech Inst, BS, 53; Rice Inst, MA, 55; Ga Inst Technol, PhD(chem), 59. *Prof Exp:* Res fel, Pa State Univ, 59-60; asst prof, 60-61, assoc prof, 62-67, PROF CHEM, MISS STATE UNIV, 67- *Concurrent Pos:* Johnson Res Found fel, Univ Pa, 64-65; vis prof, Univ Cincinnati, 68, Univ Utah, 79 & Univ Va, 80; fac res partic, Morgantown Energy Technol, 78. *Mem:* Am Chem Soc. *Res:* Reaction mechanisms; chemical spectroscopy. *Mailing Add:* Dept Chem Miss State Univ Mississippi State MS 39762

DUFFEY, GEORGE HENRY, b Manchester, Iowa, Dec 24, 20; m 45; c 3. THEORETICAL PHYSICS. *Educ:* Cornell Col, BA, 42; Princeton Univ, AM, 44, PhD(chem physics), 45. *Prof Exp:* Asst, Princeton Univ, 42-45; from asst prof to prof chem, SDak State Col, 45-58; prof chem & physics, Univ Miss, 58-59; PROF PHYSICS, SDAK STATE UNIV, 59- *Mem:* Am Phys Soc; Am Chem Soc; Ital Soc Physics. *Res:* Alpha-particle nuclear models; symmetry arguments; polarographic theory; valence theory; molecular-orbital calculations; detonation-wave theory. *Mailing Add:* Dept of Physics SDak State Univ Brookings SD 57007

DUFFEY, MICHAEL EUGENE, b Iowa City, Iowa, Nov 15, 45. EPITHELIAL TRANSPORT, ELECTROPHYSIOLOGY. *Educ:* Univ Iowa, BS, 68; Carnegie-Mellon Univ, MS, 69, PhD(bioeng), 77. *Prof Exp:* Biomed engr, Wilford Hall, US Air Force Med Ctr, 70-73; fel, Univ Pittsburgh, 77-79; ASST PROF PHYSIOL, STATE UNIV NY AT BUFFALO, 79- *Concurrent Pos:* Vis asst prof chem eng, Carnegie-Mellon Univ, 79. *Mem:* Am Physiol Soc; Biophys Soc; Am Inst Chem Engrs; Soc Gen Physiologists. *Res:* Investigation of cellular mechanisms by which gastrointestinal epithelia transport ions by determining the electrochemical driving forces and resulting ion fluxes across cell membranes. *Mailing Add:* Dept Physiol Sch Med 120 Sherman Hall State Univ NY Buffalo NY 14214

DUFFEY, SEAN STEPHEN, b Toronto, Ont, Nov 28, 43; m 71; c 2. BIOCHEMICAL ECOLOGY, TOXICOLOGY. *Educ:* Univ BC, Vancouver, BSc, 68, MSc, 70, PhD(bot), 74. *Prof Exp:* fel entom, Univ Ga, Athens, 74-76; ASST PROF ENTOM, UNIV CALIF, DAVIS, 76- *Mem:* Entom Soc Am. *Res:* Mechanisms of resistance of plants against insects with emphasis on biochemical interactions between plants and insects. *Mailing Add:* Dept Entom Univ Calif Davis CA 95616

DUFFIE, JOHN A(TWATER), b White Plains, NY, Mar 31, 25; m 47; c 3. CHEMICAL ENGINEERING. *Educ:* Rensselaer Polytech Inst, BChE, 45, MChE, 48; Univ Wis, PhD(chem eng), 51. *Prof Exp:* Res engr, electrochem dept, E I du Pont de Nemours & Co, 51-52; sci liaison officer, Off Naval Res, 52-53; asst dir eng exp sta, 57-65, dir univ-indust res prog & assoc dean grad sch, 65-76, PROF CHEM ENG, UNIV WIS, MADISON, 69-, DIR SOLAR ENERGY LAB, 54- *Concurrent Pos:* Fulbright fel, Australia, 64 & 76. *Honors & Awards:* Charles G Abbot award, Int Solar Energy Soc. 76. *Mem:* Am Inst Chem Engrs; Am Soc Eng Educ; Int Solar Energy Soc. *Res:* Solar energy research; solar energy thermal processes. *Mailing Add:* 5710 Dorsett Dr Madison WI 53711

DUFFIELD, DEBORAH ANN, b Boston, Mass, Nov 12, 41; m 76; c 2. CYTOGENETICS, POPULATION GENETICS. *Educ:* Pomona Col, BA, 63; Stanford Univ, MA, 66; Univ Calif, Los Angeles, PhD(genetics), 77. *Prof Exp:* Instr biol, Old Dominion Col, 68-70; teaching assoc biol, Univ Calif, Los Angeles, 72-75, lectr, genetics/marine mammal, 75-77; ASST PROF GENETICS/MARINE MAMMAL, BIOL DEPT, PORTLAND STATE UNIV, 77- *Mem:* Am Soc Mammalogists; Int Asn Aquatic Animal Med. *Res:* Genetic variability in natural populations, specifically-comparative cytogenetic and electrophoretic evaluation of cetacean species, emphasizing evolutionary implications and population structure and dynamics; species comparisons of hemoglobin and various red blood cell parameters as they relate to diving capabilities and habitat in cetaceans. *Mailing Add:* Dept Biol Portland State Univ Portland OR 97201

DUFFIELD, ROGER C, b Kansas City, Kans, Apr 7, 37; m; c. MECHANICAL & AEROSPACE ENGINEERING. *Educ:* Univ Kans, BSME, 60, MSME, 64, PhD, 68. *Prof Exp:* Design engr, LFM Mfg Co Div, Rockwell Mfg Co, 60-62; asst instr eng mech, Univ Kans, 64-66; asst prof, 66-70, ASSOC PROF MECH & AEROSPACE ENG, UNIV MO-COLUMBIA, 70- *Mem:* Am Soc Mech Engrs. *Res:* Structural dynamics. *Mailing Add:* Dept of Mech & Aerospace Eng PO Box 188 Columbia MO 65201

DUFFIELD, WENDELL ARTHUR, b Sisseton, SDak, May 10, 41; m 64. STRUCTURAL GEOLOGY. *Educ:* Carleton Col, BA, 63; Stanford Univ, MS, 65, PhD(geol). 67. *Prof Exp:* GEOLOGIST, US GEOL SURV, 66- *Mem:* Geol Soc Am; Am Geophys Union; Geothermal Resources Coun. *Res:* Volcanology and related geothermal resources; igneous and metamorphic petrology; mineralogy. *Mailing Add:* US Geol Surv 345 Middlefield Rd Menlo Park CA 94025

DUFFIN, JOHN H, b Easton, Pa, June 18, 19; m 54. CHEMICAL ENGINEERING. *Educ:* Lehigh Univ, BS, 40; Univ Calif, Berkeley, PhD(chem eng), 59. *Prof Exp:* Lab analyst & chief chemist, Hercules Powder Co, NJ & Utah, 40-44; tech adv & prod foreman uranium isotope prod, Tenn Eastman Corp, 44-45; res engr, Allied Chem & Dye Corp, NY 45-53; res scientist, Battelle Mem Inst, 53-54; instr chem eng, Univ Calif, Berkeley, 54-59; asst prof chem eng & dir comput ctr, San Jose State Col, 59-62; assoc prof, 62-76, chmn, Dept Mat Sci & Chem, 69-76, PROF CHEM ENG, US NAVAL POSTGRAD SCH, 76- *Concurrent Pos:* Consult, Kaiser Aluminum & Chem Co, 57-58 & Int Bus Mach Corp, 60- *Mem:* Fel Am Inst Chemists; Am Inst Chem Engrs; Sigma Xi; NY Acad Sci. *Res:* Mathematical modeling of chemical engineering processes and use of models to investigate control problems for purposes of obtaining optimum control and designing equipment based on dynamic behavior. *Mailing Add:* Dept Elec Eng Code L2DN US Naval Postgrad Sch Monterey CA 93940

DUFFIN, RICHARD JAMES, b Chicago, Ill, Oct 13, 09; m 47; c 2. MATHEMATICS, PHYSICS. *Educ:* Univ Ill, BS, 32, PhD(physics), 35. *Prof Exp:* Instr math, Purdue Univ, 36-40; assoc, Univ Ill, 40-42; physicist, Carnegie Inst, 42-46; prof math, 46-70, UNIV PROF MATH SCI, CARNEGIE-MELLON UNIV, 70- *Concurrent Pos:* Vis prof, Purdue Univ, 49-50 & Dublin Inst Advan Studies, 59-60; consult, Westinghouse Res Labs, 56-; dir appl math res, Duke Univ, 58-59; distinguished vis prof, State Univ NY Stony Brook, 67 & Tex A&M Univ, 68. *Mem:* Nat Acad Sci; Am Acad Arts & Sci; Am Math Soc; Soc Natural Philos; Soc Indust & Appl Math. *Res:* Thermal and magnetic effects in conductors; quantum theory; Fourier type integrals and series; functional inequalities; navigational devices; partial difference equations; elasticity; electrical network theory; linear and non-linear programming. *Mailing Add:* Dept of Math Carnegie-Mellon Univ Pittsburgh PA 15213

DUFFUS, HENRY JOHN, b Vancouver, BC, Aug 27, 25; m 48. PHYSICS. *Educ:* Univ BC, BApSci, 48, BA, 49; Oxford Univ, DPhil(physics), 53. *Prof Exp:* Lectr physics, Carleton Col, 48-51; Nat Res Coun Can spec overseas scholar, 52-53; physicist & defence sci serv officer, Defence Res Bd, 54-59; prof physics & head dept, 59-79, DEAN SCI & ENG, ROYAL ROADS MIL COL, 79- *Res:* Paramagnetism at low temperatures; microwave spectroscopy; geomagnetism; infrared sensing; acoustics. *Mailing Add:* Dept of Physics Royal Rds Mil Col Victoria BC V0S 1B0 Can

DUFFUS, JAMES EDWARD, b Detroit, Mich, Feb 11, 29; m 52; c 3. PLANT PATHOLOGY, PLANT VIROLOGY. *Educ:* Mich State Col, BS, 51; Univ Wis, PhD(plant path), 55. *Prof Exp:* Actg supt, Agr Res Sta, 69-70, PLANT PATHOLOGIST, USDA, 55- *Concurrent Pos:* Assoc, Exp Sta, Univ Calif, Davis & Berkeley, 62-; vis scientist, Tasmanian Dept Agr, Hobart, Tasmania, Australia, 80-81. *Honors & Awards:* Superior Serv Award, Sugarbeet Invests Unit, USDA. *Mem:* Am Soc Sugar Beet Technol; Am Phytopath Soc; Int Soc Plant Path; Int Soc Hort Sci. *Res:* Virus diseases of surgarbeets and vegetable crops; interrelationships of yellowing type virus diseases; virus-vector relations; insect feeding through membranes, infectivity neutralization; role of wild hosts in virus epidemiology. *Mailing Add:* US Agr Res Sta PO Box 5098 Salinas CA 93915

DUFFY, CLARENCE JOHN, b Pasco, Wash, Feb 5, 47; c 1. GEOLOGY, PHYSICAL CHEMISTRY. *Educ:* Mass Inst Technol, BS, 69; Univ BS, PhD(geol), 77. *Prof Exp:* STAFF MEM GEOL, LOS ALAMOS SCI LAB, 77- *Mem:* Mineral Soc Am. *Res:* Chemical aspects of nuclear waste storage; hydrologic parameters of low permeability porosity rocks. *Mailing Add:* CNC-17 Mail Stop 514 Los Alamos Sci Lab Box 1663 Los Alamos NM 87545

DUFFY, FRANK HOPKINS, b Honolulu, Hawaii, Jan 22, 37; m 64; c 4. NEUROPHYSIOLOGY, NEUROLOGY. *Educ:* Univ Mich, BSE(elec eng) & BSE(math), 58; Harvard Univ, MD, 63. *Prof Exp:* Internship, Yale-New Haven Hosp, 63-64; resident neurol surg, Mass Gen Hosp, 64-66; resident neurol, Peter Bent Brigham Hosp & Children's Hosp Med Ctr, Boston, 66-68; instr, 70-71, asst prof neurol, 71-79, ASSOC PROF NEUROL, HARVARD MED SCH, 79-; DIR EXP NEUROPHYSIOL, CHILDREN'S HOSP, BOSTON, 74- *Concurrent Pos:* Res fel neurol, Harvard Med Sch, 66-68; mem comt on vision, Nat Acad Sci-Nat Res Coun, 69-70; neurologist, Peter Bent Brigham Hosp, 70-75, Beth Israel Hosp, 70- & Children's Hosp, Boston, 70- *Res:* Computer analysis of the EEG and evoked potentials; single cell microelectrode studies of visual and somatosensory systems of cats and primates. *Mailing Add:* 49 Harrison St Brookline MA 02146

DUFFY, JACQUES WAYNE, b Nimes, France, July 1, 22; m 50; c 3. MECHANICAL ENGINEERING. *Educ:* Columbia Univ, BA, 47, BSc, 48, MS, 49, PhD(appl mech), 57. *Hon Degrees:* DSc, Univ Nantes, France, 80. *Prof Exp:* Res engr dynamics of aircraft, Grumman Aircraft Eng Corp, 49-51; from asst prof to assoc prof eng, 53-65, chmn Ctr Biophys Sci & Biomed Eng, 69-72, PROF ENG, BROWN UNIV, 65- *Concurrent Pos:* Guggenheim fel, 64-65; Eng Found fel, 78. *Mem:* Soc Exp Stress Anal; fel Am Soc Mech Engrs; Am Soc Testing & Mat; Sigma Xi. *Res:* Dynamic plasticity; dynamic fracture. *Mailing Add:* Dept of Eng Brown Univ Providence RI 02912

DUFFY, NORMAN VINCENT, JR, b Washington. DC, Nov 1, 38; m 62; c 5. INORGANIC CHEMISTRY. *Educ:* Georgetown Univ, BS, 61, PhD(chem), 66. *Prof Exp:* NATO fel, 65-66; vis asst prof chem, 66-67, asst prof, 67-70, asst dean col arts & sci, 73-75, assoc dean, 75-76, assoc prof, 70-80, PROF CHEM, KENT STATE UNIV, 70-, CHMN CHEM, 81- *Mem:* Am Chem Soc; Sigma Xi. *Res:* Dithiocarbamate complexes; metal carbonyls. *Mailing Add:* Dept of Chem Kent State Univ Kent OH 44242

DUFFY, PHILIP, b Nimes, France, July 22, 23; US citizen; m 49; c 2. NEUROLOGY, NEUROPATHOLOGY. *Educ:* Columbia Univ, BA, 43, MD, 47. *Prof Exp:* Instr neuropath, Columbia Univ, 54-55; asst prof neurol, State Univ NY, 55-64; assoc prof, 64-68, PROF NEUROPATH & DIR DIV, COL PHYSICIANS & SURGEONS, COLUMBIA UNIV, 68- *Mem:* Am Acad Neurol; Am Asn Neuropath; Asn Res Nerv & Ment Dis. *Res:* Central nervous system tumors. *Mailing Add:* Div Neuropath Col of Physicians & Surgeons Columbia Univ New York NY 10032

DUFFY, REGINA MAURICE, b Jersey City, NJ. PLANT MORPHOLOGY. *Educ:* Col of New Rochelle, BA, 41; Fordham Univ, MS, 44; Columbia Univ, PhD(bot), 50. *Prof Exp:* Instr biol, NJ State Teachers' Col, 41-42 & 43-44; teacher, Pub Sch, 45-46; instr biol, NJ State Teachers' Col, 46; teaching asst bot, Columbia Univ, 47-50, res assoc, 50-55; asst prof biol, Long Island Univ, 51-52 & 53-55; asst prof, Jersey City State Col, 55-59; lectr, Hunter Col, 59; chmn dept sci, Nanuet Schs, NY, 59-67; admin head, 67-68, PRES, NORTHWESTERN CONN COMMUNITY COL, 68- *Mem:* Sigma Xi; Torrey Bot Club. *Res:* Cellular morphology; liverworts. *Mailing Add:* Northwestern Conn Community Col Winsted CT 06098

DUFFY, ROBERT A, b Buck Run, Pa, Sept 9, 21; m 45; c 5. GUIDANCE, NAVIGATION. *Educ:* Ga Inst Technol, BS, 51. *Prof Exp:* Dir, Guidance & Control, Air Force Ballistic Missile Div, US Air Force, 58-63; staff officer, Dirs Staff Group, Off Secy Defense, 63-67, prog mgr, Dep Reentry Syst, Space & Missile Systs Orgn, 67-70, comdr, 70-71; vpres & dir, Draper Lab Div, Mass Inst Technol, 71-73, PRES, CHIEF EXEC OFFICER & DIR, CHAS STARK DRAPER LAB, INC, 73- *Concurrent Pos:* Dir & trustee, Von Karman Mem Found, Inc, 79-83; chmn, Comt Automation for Combat, Nat Acad Eng, 81- *Honors & Awards:* Thurlow Award, Inst Navig, 64; Thomas D White Award, Nat Geog Soc, 70. *Mem:* Nat Acad Eng; Inst Navig (pres, 76-77); fel Am Inst Aeronaut & Astronaut. *Res:* Development and practical application of guidance and control systems to aircraft, missles and space craft. *Mailing Add:* C S Draper Lab Inc 555 Technology Sq Cambridge MA 02139

DUFFY, ROBERT E(DWARD), b Scranton, Pa, May 27, 30; m 53; c 3. AERONAUTICAL ENGINEERING. *Educ:* Rensselaer Polytech Inst, BAE, 51, MAE, 54, PhD, 65. *Prof Exp:* Aeronaut engr, US Govt, 51-52; from instr to asst prof, 53-65, ASSOC PROF AERONAUT ENG, RENSSELAER POLYTECH INST, 65-, CHMN DEPT, 68- *Concurrent Pos:* Consult, Grumman Aircraft Eng Corp, 58-; Gen Elec Co; Xerox Corp & NY State Bur Educ; dir, Panaflight Corp & Burden Lake Holding Corp. *Mem:* Assoc fel Am Inst Aeronaut & Astronaut. *Res:* Flight mechanisms; experimental aerodynamics. *Mailing Add:* Dept Aeronaut Eng Rensselaer Polytech Inst Troy NY 12181

DUFFY, THOMAS EDWARD, b Baltimore, Md, July 10, 40; m 66; c 3. NEUROCHEMISTRY. *Educ:* Loyola Col, Md, BS, 62; Univ Md, PhD(pharmacol), 67. *Prof Exp:* Asst prof, 70-75, assoc prof, 76-80, PROF BIOCHEM NEUROL, MED COL, CORNELL UNIV, 81- *Concurrent Pos:* USPHS fel, Univ Gothenburg, 67-68 & Sch Med, Wash Univ, 68-70; estab investr, Am Heart Asn, 75-80; mem cardiovasc res study comt, Am Heart Asn, 78-80; mem neurol study sect, NIH, 79-; vis scientist, Lab Cerebral Metab, NIMH, 81-82. *Honors & Awards:* Teacher-Scientist Award, Andrew W Mellon Found, 74-75. *Mem:* Am Soc Biol Chemists; Int Soc Cerebral Blood Flow & Metab; Soc Neurosci; Am Soc Neurochem; Int Soc Neurochem. *Res:* Carbohydrate and energy metabolism in brain; biochemistry of the developing nervous system; hepatic, hyperammonemic, and hypoxic-ischemic encepalo-pathies. *Mailing Add:* Dept of Neurol Cornell Univ Med Col New York NY 10021

DUFFY, THOMAS J, b Philadelphia, Pa, June 16, 41; m 66; c 5. SYSTEMS DESIGN. *Educ:* Villanova Univ, BS, 63; Univ Pa, MS, 65, PhD(systs eng), 75. *Prof Exp:* Consult, Advan Guidance & Control Systs, 75-78, MGR SYSTS ENG, RE-ENTRY SYSTS DIV, GEN ELEC, CO, 78- *Mem:* Inst Elec & Electronics Engrs; Am Inst Aeronaut & Astronaut. *Res:* Navigation and guidance. *Mailing Add:* 20 Vanderveer Ave Holland PA 18966

DUFFY, WILLIAM THOMAS, JR, b San Francisco, Calif, June 30, 30; m 59; c 3. SOLID STATE PHYSICS. *Educ:* Univ Santa Clara, BEE, 53; Stanford Univ, MS, 54, PhD(physics), 59. *Prof Exp:* From asst prof to assoc prof, 59-68, PROF PHYSICS, UNIV SANTA CLARA, 68-, CHMN DEPT, 74- *Concurrent Pos:* NSF fel, State Univ Leiden, 61-62; res assoc & vis scientist, Stanford Univ, 68-69. *Mem:* Am Phys Soc; Sigma Xi. *Res:* Magnetism of organic crystals; linear magnetic chains in crystal solids; nuclear magnetic resonance; antiferromagnetism; superconductivity; electronics in science. *Mailing Add:* Dept of Physics Univ of Santa Clara Santa Clara CA 95053

DUFLOT, LEO SCOTT, b Mayfield, Ky, June 24, 19; m 51; c 5. ANESTHESIOLOGY. *Educ:* Univ Tex, BA, 39, MD, 43; Am Bd Anesthesiol, dipl, 54. *Prof Exp:* From instr to assoc prof, 51-72, PROF ANESTHESIOL, UNIV TEX MED BR GALVESTON, 72-; DIR ANESTHESIOL, DRISCOLL FOUND CHILDRENS HOSP, 81- *Concurrent Pos:* Res assoc, Univ Pa, 51. *Mem:* AMA; Am Soc Anesthesiologists; Am Col Anesthesiologists; Int Anesthesia Res Soc. *Mailing Add:* Dept of Anesthesiol Driscoll Childrens Hosp Corpus Christi TX 78411

DUFOUR, DIDIER, b Baie St-Paul, Que, Feb 7, 26; m 54; c 4. BIOLOGY, EXPERIMENTAL MEDICINE. *Educ:* Laval Univ, BA, 47, PhD, 56; Univ Montreal, VMD, 52. *Prof Exp:* Res asst, Inst Exp Med & Surg, Univ Montreal, 52-53; res asst, Inst Human Biol, Laval Univ, 53-56; asst prof biol, Univ Ottawa, 56-57; from asst prof to assoc prof, 57-67, PROF BIOCHEM, FAC MED, LAVAL UNIV, 67-, DIR BIOMED CTR, 64- *Concurrent Pos:* Res consult, Ministry Health, Prov Que, 63-, mem, Med Res Coun Cancer, 64-; mem, Sanit Comt Can, 63-; mem, Colloquium on Protides of Biol Fluids, Belg, 63-; dir, Health Res Inst, Univ Que, 71- *Mem:* Col Vet Med Can; Can Biochem Soc; Can Fedn Biol Soc; Int Asn Documentalists. *Res:* Immunopathology; immunochemistry of experimental carcinogenesis. *Mailing Add:* Fac Med Laval Univ Quebec PQ G6W 7P4 Can

DUFOUR, JACQUES JOHN, b Baie St-Paul, Que, June 10, 39; m 67; c 2. REPRODUCTIVE PHYSIOLOGY, AGRICULTURE. *Educ:* Laval Univ, BS, 64; Guelph Univ, MSc, 67; Univ Wis, PhD(reproductive physiol), 71. *Prof Exp:* Res officer physiol, 67-68, RES SCIENTIST, RES STA AGR CAN, 71- *Concurrent Pos:* Mem, Prov Eval Comt Res Subvention, 74-78 & Res Comt on Que Orientation Dairy Beef Cattle, 75-76; head, Can Mission Surv Reproductive Physiol in USSR, 76-; researcher, Folliculogenesis in sheep, France, 77-78. *Mem:* AAAS; Can Soc Animal Sci; Soc Can Zootech; Soc Study Reproduction. *Res:* Folliculogenesis in sheep and cattle to achieve twinning. *Mailing Add:* Res Sta Agr Can Lennoxville CP 90 Can

DUFOUR, REGINALD JAMES, b Simmesport, La, July 29, 48. ASTRONOMY. *Educ:* La State Univ, Baton Rouge, BS, 70; Univ Wis, Madison, MS, 71, PhD(astron), 74. *Prof Exp:* Nat Acad Sci-Nat Res Coun res assoc astron, L B Johnson Space Ctr, NASA, 74-75; ASST PROF SPACE PHYSICS & ASTRON, RICE UNIV, 75- *Mem:* AAAS; Royal Astron Soc; Am Astron Soc. *Res:* Observational astronomy and instrumentation; gaseous nebulae; structure and evolution of galaxies; magellanic clouds, ultraviolet spectra of stars. *Mailing Add:* Dept of Space Physics & Astron Rice Univ Houston TX 77001

DUFRAIN, RUSSELL JEROME, b Chicago, Ill, Oct 4, 44; m 67; c 3. REPRODUCTIVE BIOLOGY, RADIOBIOLOGY. *Educ:* Western Ill Univ, BSEd, 67, MS, 68; Cornell Univ, PhD(physiol), 74. *Prof Exp:* From instr to asst prof biol, Moraine Valley Community Col, 69-71; from res asst to res assoc phys biol, NY State Vet Col, Cornell Univ, 72-75; assoc scientist, 75-77, SCIENTIST CYTOGENETICS, MED & HEALTH SCI DIV, OAK RIDGE ASSOC UNIVS, 77- *Mem:* AAAS; Am Inst Biol Sci; NY Acad Sci; Environ Mutagen Soc; Radiation Res Soc; Sigma Xi. *Res:* Use of numerical analysis of cytogenetic and morphological damage to quantify physical and/or chemical effects on mammalian somatic cells, reproductive cells and early embryos. *Mailing Add:* Med & Health Sci Div Oak Ridge Assoc Univs PO Box 117 Oak Ridge TN 37830

DUFRESNE, RICHARD FREDERICK, b Holyoke, Mass, Aug 4, 43. FLAVOR CHEMISTRY, TOBACCO CHEMISTRY. *Educ:* Univ Rochester, BS, 65; Carnegie-Mellon Univ, PhD(org chem), 73. *Prof Exp:* Fel, Med Sch, Johns Hopkins Univ, 72-74, Brandeis Univ, 75-77 & Univ Mass, Amherst, 79-80; MEM STAFF, LORILLARD RES CTR, 80- *Mem:* Am Chem Soc; Sigma Xi. *Res:* Synthesis of heterocycles including indoles and pyrrolidines; vinca alkaloids; benzoazanorbornadienes; flavorants; radioactively-labeled securinega and cephalotax alkaloid precursors. *Mailing Add:* 4407 Williams Dairy Rd Greensboro NC 27406

DUFTY, JAMES W, b Freeport, NY, May 5, 40; m 64. STATISTICAL MECHANICS. *Educ:* Williams Col, AB, 62; Lehigh Univ, MS, 64, PhD(physics), 67. *Prof Exp:* Fel physics, Lehigh Univ, 67-68; fel, 68-70, from asst prof to assoc prof, 71-78, PROF PHYSICS, UNIV FLA, 78- *Concurrent Pos:* Vis scientist, Joint Inst Lab Astrophys, Univ Colo, 79-80. *Mem:* AAAS; Am Phys Soc. *Res:* Problems in classical and quantum mechanical non-equilibrium statistical mechanics. *Mailing Add:* Dept of Physics Univ of Fla Gainesville FL 32601

DUGA, JULES JOSEPH, b Bellaire, Ohio, Mar 21, 32; m 55; c 2. RESEARCH ADMINISTRATION, SCIENCE POLICY. *Educ:* Ohio State Univ, BSc, 53, MSc, 55, PhD, 60. *Prof Exp:* From prin physicist phys chem div to sr res physicist solid state res div, Battelle Mem Inst, 56-70; tech & sci consult, 70-76; TECH & SCI CONSULT, ECON, PLANNING & POLICY ANAL SECT, BATTELLE MEM INST, 76- *Mem:* AAAS; Am Phys Soc; Am Inst Mining, Metall & Petrol Eng; Am Ceramic Soc. *Res:* Technology utilization by state and local governments; science policy in state governments; energy policy planning; technology assessment and transfer; res and development forecasting; economic input-output analysis; macroeconomic impacts of new technologies. *Mailing Add:* 2605 Bryden Rd Bexley OH 43209

DUGAICZYK, ACHILLES, b Kosztowy, Poland, Sept 9, 30; US citizen. CELL BIOLOGY. *Educ:* Jagiellonian Univ, Cracow, Poland, MSc, 55; Univ Calif, San Francisco, PhD(biochem), 63. *Prof Exp:* Res adj biochem, Med Sch, Wroclaw, Poland, 62-66; res asst, Univ Calif, San Francisco, 66-67 & 72-76; vis prof, Nat Polytech, Mexico City, 67-72; ASST PROF BIOCHEM, BAYLOR COL MED, HOUSTON, 76- *Concurrent Pos:* Vis scientist, City of Hope Res Inst, 81. *Mem:* Am Chem Soc; Am Soc Biol Chemists; AAAS. *Res:* Analysis of the human genome using recombinant DNA technologies; molecular basis of the function, control of expression and evolution of human genes. *Mailing Add:* Dept Cell Biol Baylor Col Med Houston TX 77030

DUGAL, HARDEV SINGH, b Bareilly, India, Feb 1, 37; m 68. PAPER CHEMISTRY. *Educ:* Agra Univ, BSc, 55; Harcourt Butler Technol Inst, India, MS, 58; Darmstadt Tech Univ, Dr Ing(cellulose chem), 63. *Prof Exp:* Student apprentice, Distillery Dept, Daurala Sugar Works, India, 55-66; pool officer, Coun Sci & Indust Res, New Delhi, 66-68; dir new projs, Punj Sons Ltd, 68; res fel phys chem, 68-69, res fel phys chem & proj leader, 69-70, dir div indust & environ systs, 74-81, ASST PROF CHEM, INST PAPER CHEM, 70-, DIR, INFO SERV DIV, 81-, HEAD FAC, DEPT SPECIAL STUDIES, 81- *Concurrent Pos:* Chemist, Gwalior Rayon Silk Mfg Co Ltd, Nagda, India, 58-59; student apprentice, Adam Opal, Russelsheim am Main, WGer, 60; fel, Inst Paper Chem, 64-66; mem del, Tech Asn Pulp & Paper Indust Conf on Air & Water Environ, Jacksonville, Fla, 69, Minneapolis, 70 & Boston, 71; consult, Pulp & Paper Indust; mem assessment citizens adv coun, Upper Miss River Basin Comn, 75-; Int Environ Comt Meeting, Helsinki, 75, Montreal, 76, Seattle, 77 & Stockholm, 78. *Mem:* Tech Asn Pulp & Paper Indust; Am Chem Soc; Zellcheming; Cellulose Chemikar Club Darmstadt; Indian Tech Asn Pulp & Paper Indust. *Res:* Pulping, bleaching and paper making; wet-end additives; carbohydrate chemistry; physical and chemical aspects of aqueous environment in pulp and paper industry. *Mailing Add:* Inst Paper Chem PO Box 1048 Appleton WI 54911

DUGAL, LOUIS PAUL, b Quebec, Que, Oct 1, 11; m 37; c 3. PHYSIOLOGY. *Educ:* Laval Univ, BA, 31, MSc, 34; Univ Pa, PhD(biol), 39. *Hon Degrees:* LLD, Univ Toronto, 65, Concordia Univ, 75, Ottawa Univ, 78. *Prof Exp:* From asst prof to prof biol, Univ Montreal, 35-45; prof exp physiol, Laval Univ, 45-55; prof biol, Univ Ottawa, 55-65, chmn dept, 55-62, dean fac pure & appl sci, 62-65; dep dir, Sci Secretariat, Privy Coun Can, 65-66; vdean, Med Sch, Univ Sherbrooke, 66-67, vrector, 67-72; chmn, Comt Approval Univ Prog, 70-74; CONSULT RES, QUE PROV GOVT, 74- *Concurrent Pos:* Mem, Nat Res Coun Can, 44-50; assoc dir, Inst Hyg & Human Biol, 45-55; mem adv comt & chmn arctic med res, Defense Res Bd Can, 47-58; consult, Royal Can Air Force, 48; Guggenheim fel, Columbia Univ, 54-55. *Honors & Awards:* Officer, Order Brit Empire, 46; Laureate, Fr Acad Sci, Montyon Prize, 52. *Mem:* Can Physiol Soc (pres, 51-52); fel Royal Soc Can; Am Physiol Soc; Soc Fr Speaking Physiologists. *Res:* Resistance and acclimatization of mammal to cold environment; respiration at high altitudes. *Mailing Add:* 340 de la Corniche St Nicolas PQ G0S 2Z0 Can

DUGAN, CHARLES HAMMOND, b Baltimore, Md, Apr 2, 31; m 54; c 5. CHEMICAL PHYSICS. *Educ:* Univ Ky, BS, 51; Univ Calif, Los Angeles, MA, 54; Harvard Univ, PhD(appl physics), 63. *Prof Exp:* Physicist, US Navy Electronics Lab, 51-52 & Smithsonian Astrophys Observ, 61-67; from asst prof to assoc prof, 67-75, assoc dean fac grad studies, 78-79, PROF PHYSICS, YORK UNIV, 75- *Concurrent Pos:* Vis fel appl optics, Imperial Col, 73-74; mem staff, Physics Dept, Univ Bielefeld, 80-81 & Dept Elec Eng, Cornell Univ, 81. *Mem:* AAAS; Am Phys Soc; Can Asn Physicists. *Res:* Atomic and molecular processes; laser studies of molecules. *Mailing Add:* Dept of Physics York Univ Downsview ON M3J 1P3 Can

DUGAN, GARY EDWIN, b Batavia, NY, Dec 9, 41; m 69; c 2. PHARMACEUTICAL CHEMISTRY. *Educ:* Rochester Inst Technol, BS, 64; Univ Conn, PhD(med & pharmaceut chem), 69. *Prof Exp:* Sr group leader over the counter drugs, Block Drug Co, 68-74; div clearance officer med liaison, 74-77, asst for chem sci, 77-80, EXEC ASST TO CORP VPRES, RES & DEVELOP, GILLETTE CO, 80- *Mem:* Am Pharmaceut Asn; Soc Cosmetic Chemists. *Res:* Research into skin and its appendages to provide more effective personal care products; applications of biotechnologies to personal care product development. *Mailing Add:* 37 Cushing Hill Rd Norwell MA 02061

DUGAN, JOHN PHILIP, b Darby, Pa, Apr 23, 42; m 64; c 4. PHYSICAL OCEANOGRAPHY. *Educ:* Pa Mil Col, BS, 64; Northwestern Univ, MS, 66, PhD(theoret & appl mech), 67. *Prof Exp:* NSF & Off Naval Res Funds fel mech, Johns Hopkins Univ, 67-69; asst prof mech eng, UniV Toronto, 69-71; RES PHYSICIST, ENVIRON SCI DIV, NAVAL RES LAB, 71- *Concurrent*

Pos: Mem, Int Oceanog Found, 66- *Mem:* Am Soc Mech Engrs; Am Geophys Union; Sigma Xi. *Res:* Theoretical modelling of internal waves; observations of fine and mesoscale upper ocean structure. *Mailing Add:* Environ Sci Div Naval Res Lab Washington DC 20375

DUGAN, KIMIKO HATTA, b Kyoto City, Japan, Oct 21, 24; nat US; wid. MICROSCOPIC ANATOMY. *Educ:* Okla Col Women, BA, 61; Univ Okla, MS, 65, PhD(med sci), 70. *Prof Exp:* Teaching asst human histol & embryol, 64-69, from instr to asst prof, 69-78, ASSOC PROF ANAT SCI, COL MED & GRAD COL, UNIV OKLA HEALTH SCI CTR, 78- *Mem:* Am Asn Anatomists; NY Acad Sci; Electron Micros Soc Am; Am Soc Zoologists; Am Chem Soc. *Res:* Light and electron microscopies; histochemistry and cytochemistry of skin, pancreas and heart; stereological study of cardiac enlargement. *Mailing Add:* Dept Anat Sci Univ Okla Health Sci Ctr Oklahoma City OK 73190

DUGAN, LEROY, JR, b Petersburgh, Ind, Aug 18, 15; m 38; c 3. ORGANIC CHEMISTRY. *Educ:* Ind Univ, BS, 37; Univ Wash, PhD(org chem), 42. *Prof Exp:* Assoc org chem, Am Meat Inst Found, 46-49; chief div org chem, 49-61; assoc prof food sci, 61-66, PROF FOOD SCI & HUMAN NUTRIT, MICH STATE UNIV, 66-, ASST DEAN GRAD SCH, 71- *Mem:* Am Chem Soc; Am Oil Chem Soc; Soc Chem Indust; Inst Food Technol; Sigma Xi. *Res:* Autoxidation of fats; antioxidants for fats and foods; lipid composition, phospholipid studies; lipid-protein interactions; lipid browning; pesticide distribution in foods; lipid nutrition; food chemistry. *Mailing Add:* Dept Food Sci & Human Nutrit Mich State Univ East Lansing MI 48824

DUGAN, PATRICK R, b Syracuse, NY, Dec 14, 31; m 56; c 4. MICROBIOLOGY, BIOCHEMISTRY. *Educ:* Syracuse Univ, BS, 56, MS, 59, PhD(microbiol), 64. *Prof Exp:* Res asst microbiol & biochem, Syracuse Univ Res Corp, 56-58, res assoc, 58-61, assoc res scientist, 61-63; from asst prof to assoc prof, 64-70, chmn dept, 70-73, actg dean, Col Biol Sci, 78, PROF MICROBIOL, OHIO STATE UNIV, 70-, DEAN, COL BIOL SCI, 79- *Mem:* AAAS; Am Soc Microbiol; Soc Indust Microbiol; Water Pollution Control Fedn; fel Am Acad Microbiol. *Res:* Microbial physiology, particularly aquatic organisms; microbial metabolism of inorganic compounds; analytical chemistry; microbiology and biochemistry of coal mine drainage; methane and hydrocarbon oxidation; waste treatment; eutrophication. *Mailing Add:* Dept of Microbiol Ohio State Univ 484 W 12th Ave Columbus OH 43210

DUGAS, HERMANN, b Baie-Comeau, Que, Nov 21, 42; m 66. BIOPHYSICS, ORGANIC CHEMISTRY. *Educ:* Univ Montreal, BSc, 64; Univ NB, PhD(org synthesis), 67. *Prof Exp:* Fel org synthesis, Univ NB, 67-68; fel protein chem, Biochem Lab, Nat Res Coun Can, 68-69 & biophys, 69-70; asst prof, 70-75, ASSOC PROF CHEM, UNIV MONTREAL, 75- *Mem:* Am Chem Soc; Chem Inst Can; Can Biochem Soc. *Res:* Mechanism of enzyme action; utilization of electron spin resonance and nuclear magnetic resonance for the study of biological systems. *Mailing Add:* Dept of Chem Univ of Montreal Montreal Can

DUGDALE, MARION, b Bellavista, Callao, Peru, Oct 7, 28; US citizen; m 55; c 2. INTERNAL MEDICINE, HEMATOLOGY. *Educ:* Bryn Mawr Col, AB, 50; Harvard Med Sch, MD, 54. *Prof Exp:* Intern & resident med, Univ NC, Chapel Hill, 54-57; resident, 58-59, from instr to assoc prof, 59-74, PROF MED, UNIV TENN, MEMPHIS, 74- *Concurrent Pos:* Fel hemat, Duke Hosp, NC, 57-58; mem coun on cerebrovasc dis & mem coun on thrombosis, Am Heart Asn; mem, Nat Heart & Lung Adv Coun, 75-79. *Mem:* Int Soc Thrombosis & Hemostasis; AMA; Am Soc Hemat. *Res:* Hemostasis. *Mailing Add:* 800 Madison Ave Memphis TN 38163

DUGDALE, RICHARD COOPER, b Madison, Wis, Feb 6, 28; m 53, 66; c 3. BIOLOGICAL OCEANOGRAPHY, LIMNOLOGY. *Educ:* Univ Wis, BS, 50, MS, 51, PhD(zool), 55. *Prof Exp:* Fel, Univ Ga, 56; instr zool, Univ Ky, 57; from instr to asst prof zool, Univ Pittsburgh, 58-62; from assoc prof to prof marine sci, Univ Alaska, 62-67; res prof oceanog, Univ Wash, 67-75; res scientist, Bigelow Lab Ocean Sci, West Boothbay Harbor, Maine, 75-80; PROF BIOL SCI & ASSOC DIR, INST MARINE COASTAL STUDIES, UNIV SOUTHERN CALIF, 80- *Concurrent Pos:* Fulbright res fel, Inst Oceanog & Fisheries Res, Athens, Greece, 72-73. *Mem:* AAAS; Am Soc Limnol & Oceanog (vpres, 74, pres, 75); Am Geophys Union. *Res:* Nitrogen cycle in the sea; biological nitrogen fixation in sea and lakes; vitamins and microorganic constituents; mechanisms of nutrient limitation; upwelling ecosystems. *Mailing Add:* Bigelow Lab Ocean Sci West Boothbay Harbor ME 04575

DUGGAL, SHAKTI PRAKASH, b New Delhi, India, Oct 1, 31; m 64; c 2. COSMIC RAY PHYSICS, SPACE PHYSICS. *Educ:* Univ Delhi, BSc, 51, MSc, 53; Gujrat Univ, India, PhD(physics), 59. *Prof Exp:* Res asst space physics, Phys Res Lab, India, 53-58; sr res fel, 58-60; from asst prof to assoc prof, 60-77, PROF COSMIC RAY, BARTOL RES FOUND, FRANKLIN INST, UNIV DEL, 78- *Mem:* Fel Am Phys Soc; life mem Am Geophys Union; AAAS. *Res:* Astrophysics; geophysics; solar-terrestrial physics. *Mailing Add:* Bartol Res Found Univ Del Newark DE 19711

DUGGAN, DANIEL EDWARD, b New York, NY, June 29, 26; m 56; c 3. BIOCHEMICAL PHARMACOLOGY. *Educ:* St Johns Univ, BS, 51; Univ Md, MS, 53; Georgetown Univ, PhD(biochem), 55. *Prof Exp:* Asst, Univ Md, 51-53; biochemist, Nat Heart Inst, 56-62; res assoc, 62-70, sr res fel, 70-73, DIR, BIOCHEM PHARMACOL, MERCK INST THERAPEUT RES, 73- *Concurrent Pos:* Am Instrument Co fel, Nat Heart Inst, 55-56. *Mem:* Am Chem Soc; Am Soc Pharmacol & Exp Therapeut. *Res:* Drug metabolism; pharmacokinetics; biochemistry of active transport; inflammation. *Mailing Add:* Merck Inst Therapeut Res West Point PA 19486

DUGGAN, DENNIS E, b Calgary, Alta, July 13, 30; m 54; c 4. BACTERIAL GENETICS. *Educ:* Univ Alta, BSc, 53; Ore State Univ, MSc, 57, PhD(bact), 61. *Prof Exp:* Sr res bacteriologist, H J Heinz Co, 58-61 & Midwest Res Inst, 61-62; fel bact, Sch Med, Univ Kans, 62; fel genetics, Oak Ridge Nat Lab, 63-64; fel, Sch Med, Yale Univ, 64-67; assoc prof bact, 67-77, ASSOC PROF MICROBIOL & CELL SCI & ASSOC MICROBIOLOGIST, UNIV FLA, 77- *Mem:* Am Soc Microbiol. *Res:* Freezing preservation of bacteria; mass culture and concentration of lactobacilli; radiation and thermal preservation of foods; radiation resistant bacteria; mechanisms of radiation resistance; gene action; transduction; mega plasmids/minichromosomes. *Mailing Add:* Dept of Microbiol McCarty Hall Univ of Fla Gainesville FL 32611

DUGGAN, HELEN ANN, b Essex, Ont, Jan 11, 21; US citizen. CHEMISTRY. *Educ:* Siena Heights Col, BS, 41; Cath Univ Am, PhD(chem), 48. *Prof Exp:* Teacher, Cath Schs, Ill, 41-43; instr chem, Barry Col, 47-53, asst prof, 53-54; teacher, Cath Schs, Mich, 54-56; asst prof chem & physics, Siena Heights Col, 56-62, assoc prof chem & biol, 62-63; prof chem & biol & chmn div natural sci, St Dominic Col, 63-68; prof chem, Barry Col, 68-70; PROF CHEM, SIENA HEIGHTS COL, 75- *Concurrent Pos:* Mem, Cath Round Table Sci, 49. *Mem:* Am Soc Microbiol; Am Chem Soc; Am Inst Chem. *Res:* Chemical genetics; thermal decomposition of hydrocarbons. *Mailing Add:* 1257 E Siena Heights Dr Adrian MI 49221

DUGGAN, JEROME LEWIS, b Columbus, Ohio, Aug 4, 33; m 51; c 3. PHYSICS. *Educ:* NTex State Univ, MS, 56; La State Univ, PhD(physics), 61. *Prof Exp:* Asst prof physics, Univ Ga, 61-63; mem sr staff, Spec Training Div, Oak Ridge Assoc Univs, 63-74; PROF PHYSICS, NTEX STATE UNIV, 74- *Mem:* Am Phys Soc. *Res:* Low energy nuclear physics. *Mailing Add:* Dept of Physics NTex State Univ Denton TX 76203

DUGGAN, MICHAEL J, b Boulder, Colo, May 21, 31; m 58; c 2. PHYSICS. *Educ:* Mass Inst Technol, SB, 52; Ohio State Univ, MS, 53; Stanford Univ, PhD(physics), 64. *Prof Exp:* Asst prof, 64-73, ASSOC PROF PHYSICS, SAN JOSE STATE UNIV, 73- *Res:* Theoretical physics. *Mailing Add:* Dept of Physics San Jose State Univ San Jose CA 95192

DUGGAR, BENJAMIN CHARLES, b Madison, Wis, July 13, 33; m 57; c 3. PUBLIC HEALTH. *Educ:* Yale Univ, BS, 55; Univ Pittsburgh, MS, 56; Harvard Univ, ScD(biotechnol), 63. *Prof Exp:* Res fel, Sch Pub Health, Harvard Univ, 59-62; scientist, Mitre Corp, 62-63; vpres, Bio-Dynamics, Inc, 63-68, pres, 68-70, pres, Res Div, 70-73; dir, Off Anal Health Serv Admin, Dept Health, Educ & Welfare, 73-76; PRES, JRB ASSOCS, 76- *Concurrent Pos:* Gen Motors res fel biotechnol, Sch Pub Health, Harvard Univ, 59-61, Guggenheim fel aviation health & safety, 61-62; dir, Carroll Rehab Ctr Visually Impaired, 69-74; preceptorial prof, Human Ecol Ctr, Antioch Col, 75-77; trustee, Howard County Gen Hosp, 78- *Mem:* AAAS; Human Factors Soc; Brit Ergonomics Res Soc. *Res:* Health services delivery systems; quality assurance; evaluation methodology for social welfare programs. *Mailing Add:* 5511 High Tor Hill Columbia MD 21045

DUGGER, G(ORDON) L(ESLIE), b Winter Haven, Fla, Nov 13, 23; m 45; c 3. CHEMICAL ENGINEERING. *Educ:* Univ Fla, BChE, 44, MSE, 47; Case Inst Technol, PhD(chem eng), 53. *Prof Exp:* Aeronaut res scientist flame res, Nat Adv Comt for Aeronaut, 47-54; supvr chem process develop res div, Int Minerals & Chem Corp, 54-57; proj supvr, 57-63, supvr hypersonic propulsion group, 63-72, asst supvr aeronaut div, 73-77, SUPVR AERONAUT DIV, APPL PHYSICS LAB, JOHNS HOPKINS UNIV, 78- *Concurrent Pos:* Tech ed, Astronaut & Aerospace Engrs, 63, ed-in-chief, J Spacecraft & Rockets, 64-71. *Honors & Awards:* Award eng sci, Wash Acad Sci, 64. *Mem:* Fel AAAS; Combustion Inst; fel Am Inst Aeronaut & Astronaut; Int Solar Energy Soc. *Res:* Flame propagation; flame stability; fuels and propellants; supersonic aerodynamics; heat transfer; supersonic combustion; ramjet and other advanced air breathing engine cycles; ocean thermal energy conversion. *Mailing Add:* 1023 Kathryn Rd Silver Spring MD 20904

DUGGER, GORDON SHELTON, neurosurgery, deceased

DUGGER, HARRY A, b Oklahoma City, Okla, June 28, 36; m 65; c 1. MEDICAL SCIENCE, PHARMACOLOGY. *Educ:* Oklahoma Baptist Univ, AB, 58; Univ Mich, MS, 60, PhD(chem), 62. *Prof Exp:* NIH Fel, Univ Zurich, 62-64; sr chemist, Sandoz Pharmaceut, Inc, 64-69, group leader, 70-75, assoc sect head, 75-81; VPRES RES & DEVELOP, BAURS KREY ASSOCS INC, 81-; VPRES RES & DEVELOP, BCD PROD INC, 81- *Mem:* AAAS; Am Chem Soc; Am Inst Chem; NY Acad Sci. *Res:* Organic synthesis; reaction mechanisms; drug metabolism; synthesis with isotopic labels; drug development; clinical research; government registration of drugs and medical devices. *Mailing Add:* E Lake Tr Mount Kemble Lake NJ 07046

DUGGER, WILLIE MACK, JR, b Adel, Ga, July 28, 19; m 46; c 2. PLANT PHYSIOLOGY. *Educ:* Univ Ga, BSA, 41; Univ Wis, MS, 42; NC State Col, PhD, 50. *Prof Exp:* Asst, Univ Wis, 41-42; asst prof bot, Univ Ga, 46; asst, NC State Univ, 46-50; asst prof plant physiol, Univ Md, 50-55; assoc plant physiologist, Agr Exp Sta, Univ Fla, 55-60; res plant physiologist, Agr Air Res Ctr, 60-63, chmn dept life sci, 64-68, dean, Col Natural & Agr Sci, 68-81, assoc dir, Agr Exp Sta, 70-81, PROF BOT, UNIV CALIF, RIVERSIDE, 63- *Mem:* AAAS; Am Soc Plant Physiol. *Res:* Organic transport and minor element nutrition in plants; desert plant physiology. *Mailing Add:* Dept Bot & Plant Sci Univ Calif Riverside CA 92502

DUGGINS, WILLIAM EDGAR, b Philadelphia, Pa, Aug 3, 20; m 47; c 2. ORGANIC CHEMISTRY. *Educ:* LaSalle Col, AB, 43; Mass Inst Technol, PhD, 49. *Prof Exp:* Res chemist, Gen Aniline & Film Corp, 49-52, sr develop engr, 52-59, supvr new prod develop, 59-60, proj mgr, 61; asst to vpres res & develop, Collier Carbon & Chem Corp, 61-62, mgr mkt res & develop, 62-70, tech mgr, 70-81; TECH MGR, CHEM DIV, UNION OIL CALIF, 81- *Mem:* Am Chem Soc; Com Develop Asn; Chem Mkt Res Asn; Am Carbon Soc. *Res:* Dyes; intermediates; resins; amino acids; high-pressure acetylene chemicals; petrochemicals; fertilizers; pesticides; petroleum coke; carbon; graphite. *Mailing Add:* 3427 Corinna Dr Palos Verdes Peninsula CA 90274

DUGLE, DAVID L, radiation biology, radiation chemistry, see previous edition

DUGLE, JANET MARY ROGGE, b Pierre, SDak, June 7, 34; div. PLANT TAXONOMY. *Educ:* Carleton Col, BA, 56; Univ SDak, MA, 60; Univ Alta, PhD(bot), 64. *Prof Exp:* Secy, Hotpoint Co, Chicago, 56; teacher high sch, SDak, 57-58; instr bot, Univ SDak, 59-60, curator, 58-60; instr, Univ Alta, 64-65; lectr biol, Yale Univ, 65-67, secy biophys, 66-67; RES OFFICER BOT, ATOMIC ENERGY CAN LTD, WHITESHELL NUCLEAR RES ESTAB, 67- *Concurrent Pos:* Univ res fel biol, Yale Univ, 65-66; res assoc, 67, lectr, Univ Man, 68. *Mem:* AAAS; Int Asn Plant Taxon; Am Soc Plant Taxon; Can Bot Asn (secy, 76-78); Ecol Soc Am. *Res:* Plant systematics and ecology; radiation ecology; evolutionary biology. *Mailing Add:* Whiteshell Nuclear Res Estab Pinawa MB R0E 1L0 Can

DUGLISS, CHARLES H(OSEA), b Staatsburg, NY, Oct 12, 21; m 46; c 2. CHEMICAL ENGINEERING. *Educ:* Pratt Inst, BChE, 43. *Prof Exp:* Chem engr, 43-64, sr res scientist, Resins Res Group, 64-68, SR RES SCIENTIST, CHEM ENG DIV, STAMFORD RES LABS, AM CYANAMID CO, 68- *Mem:* Am Inst Chem Engrs; Am Chem Soc. *Res:* Thermosetting and thermoplastic polymers and processes; reinforced plastics; polymer processing. *Mailing Add:* Stamford Res Labs 1937 W Main St Stamford CT 10598

DUGOFF, HOWARD, b Yonkers, NY, Nov 23, 36; m 58; c 3. MECHANICAL ENGINEERING, PHYSICS. *Educ:* Stevens Inst Technol, ME, 58, MS, 60. *Prof Exp:* Res asst underwater weapons, Davidson Lab, Stevens Inst Technol, 59-60, assoc res engr, 60-63, res engr, 63-65, chief vehicle res, 65-67, asst head phys factors, Hwy Safety Res Inst, Univ Mich, 67-71; chief, Anal & Simulation Br, Mobility Systs Lab, US Army Tank-Automotive Command, 71-74; chief, Handling & Stability Div, 74-75, assoc adminr planning & eval, 75-76, assoc adminr res & develop, 76-77, dep adminr, Nat Hwy Traffic Safety Admin, 77-79, ADMINR, RES & SPEC PROG ADMIN, US DEPT TRANSP, 79- *Concurrent Pos:* Mem driving simulation comt, Hwy Res Bd, Nat Acad Sci-Nat Res Coun, 68-; mem comt F-9 on tires, Am Soc Testing & Mat; mem, fed coord comt sci, eng & technol, 79-80; mem, Exec Policy Bd, Alaska Natural Gas Pipeline Syst, 79-; mem, US Radiation Policy Coun, 79-80. *Honors & Awards:* Dept Army Res & Develop Award, 73. *Mem:* Am Soc Mech Engrs; Soc Automotive Engrs; Int Soc Terrain-Vehicle Systs. *Res:* Hydrodynamics and mechanics of submerged vehicles; hydrodynamics performance of amphibious craft; mechanics of off-road vehicles; stability and control of pneumatic tired vehicles; analysis of driver-vehicle highway systems. *Mailing Add:* 11404 Grundy Court Potomac MD 20854

DUGRE, ROBERT, b Montreal, Que, Sept 10, 49. VIROLOGY, BIOLOGY. *Educ:* Univ Montreal, BSc, 73, MSc, 76; Univ Quebec, PhD(virol), 78. *Prof Exp:* FEL VIROL, DEPT MICROBIOL & IMMUNOL, UNIV WESTERN ONT, 78- *Res:* Study of the different hypothesis involved in the establishment of persistent infections by viruses such as measles, using in vitro and in vivo models. *Mailing Add:* Armand-Frappier Inst Ville de Laval Laval-des-Rapides Can

DUGUAY, MICHEL ALBERT, b Montreal, Que, Sept 12, 39; m 63; c 2. PHYSICS. *Educ:* Univ Montreal, BS, 61; Yale Univ, PhD(physics), 66. *Prof Exp:* MEM TECH STAFF LASERS, BELL TEL LABS, 66- *Concurrent Pos:* Mem staff, Sandia Labs, 74-77. *Mem:* Optical Soc Am; Am Phys Soc; Inst Elec & Electronics Engrs; Sigma Xi. *Res:* Laser frequency shifting; laser pulse compression; x-ray lasers; ultrashort laser pulse displays; optical sampling; ultrafast Kerr cells; picosecond lifetime measurements; ultrahigh-speed photography; solar lighting. *Mailing Add:* Bell Labs 4B-423 Holmdel NJ 07733

DUGUID, JAMES OTTO, b Lusk, Wyo, May 22, 40; m 70; c 2. GEOHYDROLOGY, GEOLOGICAL ENGINEERING. *Educ:* Univ Wyo, BS, 63, MS, 64, BS, 66, ME & MA, 70, PhD(geol, civil & geol eng), 73. *Prof Exp:* Res scientist earth sci, Oak Ridge Nat Lab, 72-76, sect head, 76-77; res leader geohydrol, 77-78, STAFF SCIENTIST EARTH SCI, BATTELLE MEM INST, 78- *Mem:* Am Soc Geol Engrs. *Res:* Ground water transport of radionuclides from both low-level radioactive waste disposal sites and deep geologic repositories. *Mailing Add:* Battelle Proj Mgt Div 505 King Ave Columbus OH 43201

DUGUNDJI, JAMES, b New York, NY, Aug 30, 19; m 44. MATHEMATICS. *Educ:* NY Univ, BA, 40; Mass Inst Technol, MS, 47, PhD(math), 48. *Prof Exp:* From asst prof to assoc prof, 48-58, PROF MATH, UNIV SOUTHERN CALIF, 58- *Concurrent Pos:* Res assoc, Mass Inst Technol, 47-48; mem, Inst Advan Study, 51-53; ed, Pac J Math, 63-; vis prof, Univ Frankfurt, 64-65, Univ Pisa, 65; Rice Univ, 66-67, Univ Tübingen, 74, Univ Frankfurt, 75 & Tech Univ Munich, 78; Alexander von Humboldt Found US sr scientist award, 77. *Mem:* Am Math Soc. *Res:* Deformation topology; information theory. *Mailing Add:* Dept of Math Univ of Southern Calif Los Angeles CA 90007

DUGUNDJI, JOHN, b New York, NY, Oct 25, 25; m 65; c 2. AERONAUTICAL ENGINEERING. *Educ:* NY Univ, BAE, 44; Mass Inst Technol, ScD(aeronaut eng), 51. *Prof Exp:* Res engr aerodyn, Grumman Aircraft Eng Corp, 48-49; asst aeroelasticity, Mass Inst Technol, 50-51; prin dynamics engr, Repub Aviation Corp, 51-56; from asst prof to assoc prof, 57-70, PROF AERONAUT & ASTRONAUT, MASS INST TECHNOL, 70- *Mem:* Am Inst Aeronaut & Astronaut. *Res:* Aeroelasticity; structural dynamics. *Mailing Add:* Dept of Aeronaut & Astronaut Mass Inst of Technol Cambridge MA 02139

DUHL, DAVID N, b Staten Island, NY, Apr 20, 39; m 63; c 2. METALLURGY. *Educ:* Rensselaer Polytech Inst, BMetE, 60; Mass Inst Technol, SM, 63, PhD(metall), 64. *Prof Exp:* Res asst metall, Mass Inst Technol, 60-64; res assoc, adv mat res & develop lab, 64-70, sr asst mat proj engr, 70-81, SR PROJ ENGR, MAT ENG & RES LAB, PRATT & WHITNEY AIRCRAFT, COM PROD DIV, UNITED TECHNOL CORP, 81- *Honors & Awards:* George W Mead Award. *Mem:* Am Soc Metals. *Res:* High temperature alloy development and evaluation; phase stability and equilibra. *Mailing Add:* Pratt & Whitney Aircraft 400 Main St East Hartford CT 06118

DUHL, LEONARD J, b New York, NY, May 24, 26; m 51, 80; c 5. PSYCHIATRY, PUBLIC HEALTH. *Educ:* Columbia Univ, AB, 45; Albany Med Col, MD, 48; Am Bd Psychiat & Neurol, dipl psychiat, 56. *Prof Exp:* Intern, Jewish Hosp, Brooklyn, NY, 48-49; resident psychiat, Winter Vet Admin Hosp, Topeka, Kans, 49-54; psychiatrist, Prof Serv Br, NIMH, 54-64, chief off planning, 65-66; spec asst to secy, US Dept Housing & Urban Develop, 66-68; dir dual degree prog health sci & med educ, 73-77, PROF CITY & REGIONAL PLANNING, COL ENVIRON DESIGN & PROF PUB HEALTH, SCH PUB HEALTH, UNIV CALIF, BERKELEY, 68-; PROF PSYCHIAT, MED CTR, UNIV CALIF, SAN FRANCISCO, 68- *Concurrent Pos:* Fel, Sch Psychiat, Menninger Found, 49-54; asst health officer, Contra Costa County Health Dept, Calif, 51-53; clin instr, George Washington Univ, 58-61, assoc, 61-63, asst clin prof, 63-68; mem res adv comt, Off Educ, 56-57, mem joint task force health & housing, 61-, mem comn subcomt cult deprivation-poverty, 63, liaison to asst secy health, 65-66; consult, Peace Corps, 61-65, Model Cities Prog, 66-68; mem bd trustees, Park Forest Col, 65-68 & Robert F Kennedy Found; mem sci & technol adv comt, Calif State Legis, 70-75; mem sci adv coun, House Rep Comt Pub Works, 73; adj prof, Union Grad Sch, Ohio; consult, Assembly Off Res, Calif State Legis, Sacramento, 81-; consult, Assembly Off Res, Calif State Legis, Sacramento, Calif, 81-; bd trustees, Calif Sch Prof Psychol, 78. *Mem:* Fel Am Orthopsychiat Asn; fel Am Psychiat Asn; fel Am Pub Health Asn; Group Advan Psychiat; Int Asn Child Psychiat (asst secy gen, 62-66). *Res:* Humanistic and health science education; public health; medical and health care; holistic health; community development and organization; urban planning; psychotherapy; mental health aspects of education; psychoanalytic concepts, planning and policy. *Mailing Add:* Dept City Planning Wurster Hall Univ of Calif Berkeley CA 94720

DUHL-EMSWILER, BARBARA ANN, b Ft Knox, Ky, Oct 13, 52. PEPTIDE CHEMISTRY. *Educ:* Mich State Univ, Bs, 74, PhD(org chem), 79. *Prof Exp:* Fel, McNeil Pharmaceut, 79-81, SCIENTIST, ORTHO PHARMACEUT CORP, JOHNSON & JOHNSON, 81- *Mem:* Am Chem Soc; AAAS. *Res:* Process development and the synthesis of small peptides; stereocontrolled organic synthesis, especially as relating to Wittig reactions; insect pheromones; leukotrenes and other natural products. *Mailing Add:* Div Immunobiol Ortho Pharmaceut Corp Raritan NJ 08869

DUHRING, JOHN LEWIS, b Plainfield, NJ, May 7, 33; c 3. OBSTETRICS & GYNECOLOGY. *Educ:* McGill Univ, BS, 55; Univ Pa, MD, 59. *Prof Exp:* Investr, Harrison Dept Surg Res, Univ Pa, 56-60; from asst prof to prof obstet & gynec, Med Ctr, Univ Ky, 63-78, dir obstet, 73-78; PROF & CHMN DEPT OBSTET & GYNEC, MED COL OHIO, TOLEDO, 78- *Concurrent Pos:* Asst clin prof obstet & gynec, Univ Hawaii, 67-70; attend staff, Obstet & Gynec Serv, Tripler Gen Hosp, Honolulu, 67-70; vis prof, Letterman Army Med Ctr, 73 & Tripler Army Med Ctr, 74. *Mem:* Am Col Obstetricians & Gynecologists; AMA. *Res:* Continuing effort to reduce perinatal morbidity and mortality in high risk pregnancy through biochemical and biophysical means. *Mailing Add:* Dept of Obstet & Gynec Med Col of Ohio CJ 10008 Toledo OH 43699

DUHRKOPF, RICHARD EDWARD, b Chicago, Ill, Oct 11, 49. GENETICS, ENTOMOLOGY. *Educ:* Ohio State Univ, BS, 71, MSc, 73, PhD(genetics), 77. *Prof Exp:* Vis asst prof biol, Bucknell Univ, 77-78; fel med entom, Johns Hopkins Univ, 78-80; ASST PROF, GRINNELL COL, 80- *Mem:* AAAS; Am Inst Biol Sci; Genetics Soc Am; Animal Behav Soc; Soc Study Evolution. *Res:* Mosquito, behavioral, evolutionary and quantitative genetics. *Mailing Add:* Dept Biol Grinnell Col Grinnell IA 50112

DUICH, JOSEPH M, b Farrell, Pa, June 7, 28; m 53; c 3. AGRONOMY. *Educ:* Pa State Univ, BS, 52, PhD(agron), 57. *Prof Exp:* Instr, 54, from asst prof to assoc prof, 56-67, prof agron, 67-75, PROF TURFGRASS SCI, DEPT AGRON, PA STATE UNIV, 75- *Mem:* Fel AAAS; Am Soc Agron; Crop Sci Soc Am; Weed Sci Soc Am. *Res:* Agronomic research in turfgrass field; breeding, weed control and fertility research. *Mailing Add:* Col of Agr Dept of Agron Pa State Univ University Park PA 16802

DUIGNAN, MICHAEL THOMAS, b Flushing NY, June 14, 50. MULTIPHOTON IONIZATION SPECTROSCOPY, INFRARED MULTIPHOTON EXCITATION. *Educ:* Rutgers Univ, BS, 76; Brandeis Univ, PhD(chem), 81. *Prof Exp:* NAT RES COUN FEL, NAVAL RES LAB, 81- *Mem:* AAAS; Am Phys Soc. *Res:* Infrared multiphoton absorption and decomposition in the gas phase; multiphoton ionization spectroscopy especially for free radicals. *Mailing Add:* Code 6110 Naval Res Lab Washington DC 20375

DUISMAN, JACK ARNOLD, b Ft Knox, Ky, Mar 14, 37; m 61; c 2. PHYSICAL CHEMISTRY. *Educ:* Augustana Col, BA, 59; Univ Calif, Berkeley, PhD(phys chem), 66. *Prof Exp:* NSF fel phys chem, Univ Kans, 66-67; res chemist, Union Carbide Corp, 67-70, proj scientist, 70-71, group leader, 71-73, res supvr, Linde Div, 73-76; SR RES ASSOC, CHEVRON RES CO, 76- *Mem:* Am Chem Soc. *Res:* Chemical thermodynamics; photovoltaic; solid state chemistry; zeolite catalysis; environmental control; solar energy; oxygen chemistry. *Mailing Add:* 576 Standard Ave Richmond CA 94802

DUJOVNE, CARLOS A, b Resistencia, Arg, July 9, 37; m 63; c 1. CLINICAL PHARMACOLOGY, INTERNAL MEDICINE. *Educ:* Univ Buenos Aires, MD, 61. *Prof Exp:* Instr pharmacol & med, Univ Buenos Aires, 62-63; intern, Mt Sinai Hosp, Chicago, 63-64, resident internal med, 64-66; resident, Vet Admin Hosp, Washington, DC, 66-67; asst prof, 70-74, assoc prof, 74-78, PROF MED & PHARMACOL, SCH MED, UNIV KANS, 79- *Concurrent Pos:* NIH fel liver & metab, George Washington Univ, 67-68; fel clin pharmacol, Johns Hopkins Hosp, 68-70; instr, Sch Med, Loyola Univ, Ill, 65; clin asst, Chicago Med Sch, 65-66. *Res:* Treatment and prevention of arteriosclerosis and lipid disorders; hepatotoxicity; drug toxicity and adverse reactions; clinical therapeutic trial. *Mailing Add:* Clin Pharmacol & Toxicol Ctr Univ of Kans Med Ctr Kansas City KS 66103

DUKE, C MARTIN, b Wellsville, NY, Oct 25, 17; m 42; c 1. CIVIL ENGINEERING. *Educ:* Univ Calif, Berkeley, BS, 39, MS, 41. *Prof Exp:* Asst eng aid, US Bur Pub Rd, Calif, 39; assoc civil eng, Univ Calif, Berkeley, 39-41, instr, 41-45, res engr, 44; struct designer, Austin Co, 45-46; sr testing engr, Pac Islands Engrs, Guam, 46-47; from asst prof to assoc prof eng, 47-56, PROF ENG, UNIV CALIF, LOS ANGELES, 56- *Concurrent Pos:* Fulbright res award, Japan, 56-57; bd dam consult, Los Angeles Dept Water & Power, 63-; vis prof, Univ Chile, 67; pres, Earthquake Eng Res Inst, 70-74; mem, Calif strong motion instrumentation prog, 71-77; mem adv panel, earthquake res, US Geol Surv, 73-77; liaison mem, Nat Acad Sci panel on pub policy implications of earthquake prediction, 74-75; mem, Nat Acad Sci comt int disasters, 78-81. *Honors & Awards:* Ernest E Howard Award, Am Soc Civil Engrs, 73. *Mem:* Am Soc Civil Engrs; Seismol Soc Am; Am Soc Eng Educ; Soc Explor Geophys. *Res:* Earthquake engineering; soil mechanics, structures; effects of site conditions on seismic intensity. *Mailing Add:* Dept of Mech & Struct Univ of Calif Los Angeles CA 90024

DUKE, CHARLES BRYAN, b Richmond, Va, Mar 13, 38; m 61; c 2. THEORETICAL SOLID STATE PHYSICS, RESEARCH ADMINISTRATION. *Educ:* Duke Univ, BS, 59; Princeton Univ, PhD(physics), 63. *Prof Exp:* Staff mem physics, Gen Elec Co, 63-69; prof physics, Univ Ill, Urbana, 69-72, res prof, Coord Sci Lab, 69-72, prin scientist res fel, 72-73, MGR MOLECULAR & ORG MAT RES, XEROX CORP, 73- *Concurrent Pos:* Chmn steering comt, Int Conf Solid Surfaces, 71; consult, Gen Elec Co, 69-72; adj prof physics, Dept Physics & Astron, Univ of Rochester, 72-; bd dirs, Am Vacuum Soc, 72-76; sr res fel, Xerox Corp, 73-; bd gov, Am Inst Physics, 76- *Mem:* Fel Am Phys Soc; Am Chem Soc; Sigma Xi; Am Vacuum Soc (pres, 79-81); sr mem Inst Elec & Electronics Engrs. *Res:* Scattering theory; many-body theory; electron tunneling in solids; low-energy electron-solid-scattering; surface crystallography; chemisorption; catalysis; theory of electronic structure of polymers and molecular solids. *Mailing Add:* Xerox Corp Xerox Sq-114 Rochester NY 14644

DUKE, CHARLES LEWIS, b Asheville, NC, Sept 7, 40; m 65; c 2. NUCLEAR PHYSICS. *Educ:* NC State Univ, BS, 62; Iowa State Univ, PhD(physics), 67. *Prof Exp:* AEC fel physics, Ames Lab, Iowa State Univ, 67-68; instr, Inst Physics, Aarhus Univ, 68-69; asst prof, 69-73, ASSOC PROF PHYSICS, GRINNELL COL, 73- *Mem:* Am Phys Soc. *Res:* Production and study of nuclei far from stability through on-line isotope separator techniques; beta-strength function and delayed neutron measurements. *Mailing Add:* Dept of Physics Grinnell Col Grinnell IA 50112

DUKE, DAVID ALLEN, b Salt Lake City, Utah, Nov 26, 35; m 55; c 4. MATERIALS SCIENCE. *Educ:* Univ Utah, BS, 57, MS, 59, PhD(geol eng, ceramics), 62. *Prof Exp:* Jr scientist, Kennecott Copper Res Ctr, 60-61; res mineralogist, 62-67, mgr adv mat res, 67-70, mgr bus develop, 70-74, gen mgr, Indust Prods Div, 75-76, bus mgr, Telecommun, 76-80, VPRES & GEN MGR TELECOMMUN PRODS, CORNING GLASS WORKS, 80- *Mem:* Mineral Soc Am; Am Ceramic Soc; fel Am Inst Chemists. *Res:* Geochemical and instrumental analysis of rocks and minerals; crystal chemistry; crystallization of glass and the properties of glass-ceramic materials; chemical strengthening of glass-ceramics; fiber optics. *Mailing Add:* 7 Theresa Dr Corning NY 14830

DUKE, DOUGLAS, b Philadelphia, Pa, Aug 7, 23; m 44; c 2. ASTRONOMY, ASTROPHYSICS. *Educ:* Univ Calif, AB, 47; Univ Chicago, PhD(astron), 50. *Prof Exp:* Asst, Yerkes Observ, Univ Wis, 47-50; asst prof astron, Univ NC, 50-51; from asst prof to assoc prof astron & phys sci, Univ Fla, 51-54; head visibility br, US Naval Electronics Lab, 54-55; res engr, Convair Astronaut, 55-57; sr engr, Atlantic Missile Range, Radio Corp Am, 57-59; mem tech staff, Inst Defense Anal, DC, 59-62; staff scientist to vpres res, Autonetics Div, NAm Aviation, Inc, 62-64; dir aerospace prog, Data Dynamics, Inc, 64-65; PROF ASTRON, UNIV MIAMI, 66- *Concurrent Pos:* Asst dir, Morehead Planetarium, Chapel Hill, NC, 50-51; consult, Cmndg Gen, NAm Air Defense Command, 61-62. *Mem:* Fel AAAS; Am Astron Soc; Optical Soc Am. *Res:* Observational astrophysics; astrometry; missile and satellite tracking instrumentation; data reduction; satellite and interplanetary orbits; celestial navigation; atmospheric optics; planetarium operation. *Mailing Add:* Dept of Physics Univ of Miami Box 8046 Coral Gables FL 33124

DUKE, ELEANOR LYON, b Marfa, Tex, Apr 12, 18; m 39. PROTOZOOLOGY. *Educ:* Tex Western Col, BA, 39; Univ Tex, Austin, MA, 45, PhD, 67. *Prof Exp:* Technician, Turner's Clin Lab, 38 & El Paso Med & Surg Clin, 39; assoc prof & instr biol sci, Tex Western Col, 40-41, 43 & 45; res technician endocrinol, Ochsner Clin, La, 46; assoc prof, 47-76, PROF BIOL SCI, UNIV TEX, EL PASO, 76- *Mem:* Fel AAAS; NY Acad Sci; Soc Protozool; Am Micros Soc; Ecol Soc Am. *Res:* Electron microscopy of diatoms; biological deposition of silicon compounds. *Mailing Add:* Dept of Biol Sci Univ of Tex El Paso TX 79968

DUKE, EVERETTE LORANZA, b Goochland Co, Va, June 28, 29; m 53; c 2. SOIL SCIENCE. *Educ:* Va State Col, BS, 49; Mich State Univ, MS, 50, PhD(soil sci), 55. *Prof Exp:* Instr hort, Va State Col, 50-51; assoc prof sci, Norfolk State Col, 55-63; prof biol, Norfolk State Col, 63-71, ASST VPRES ACAD AFFAIRS, NORFOLK STATE UNIV, 71- *Concurrent Pos:* Dir, Thirteen-College Curric Prog, Norfolk State Col, 67-71. *Res:* Land use planning; land utilization in relation to land character in rural-urban fringe areas in Southern Michigan. *Mailing Add:* Norfolk State Univ 2401 Corprew Ave Norfolk VA 23504

DUKE, GARY EARL, b Galesburg, Ill, Dec 16, 37; m 61. AVIAN PHYSIOLOGY, ECOLOGY. *Educ:* Knox Col, Ill, BA, 59; Mich State Univ, MS, 64, PhD, 67. *Prof Exp:* From asst prof to assoc prof, 68-76, PROF AVIAN & VET PHYSIOL, UNIV MINN, ST PAUL, 76- *Concurrent Pos:* NSF & Agr Exp Sta res grants, 67-82, 73-80. *Mem:* Am Ornith Union; Poultry Sci Asn; Am Soc Vet Physiologists & Pharmacologists; Am Physiol Soc; Comp Gastroenterol Soc. *Res:* Study of gastrointestinal motility and absorption in turkeys and birds of prey; regulation of motility in turkeys and pellet egestion in birds of prey. *Mailing Add:* Dept of Vet Biol Univ of Minn St Paul MN 55108

DUKE, JAMES A, b Birmingham, Ala, Apr 4, 29; m 50; c 1. BOTANY. *Educ:* Univ NC, AB, 52, MA, 55, PhD(bot), 59. *Prof Exp:* Lab asst bot, Univ NC, 54-59; Chem Corps, USDA, 55-57; res asst, Mo Bot Garden, 59-61, asst cur, 61-63; asst prof bot, Univ Wash, 61-62; res botanist, USDA, 63-65; ecologist, Battelle Mem Inst, 65-71; supvy botanist, New Crops Res Br, 71-72, chief, Plant Taxon Lab, 72-77, CHIEF, ECON BOT LAB, AGR RES SERV, USDA, 77- *Mem:* Asn Trop Biol; Weed Sci Soc; Int Soc Plant Taxon; Soc Econ Botanists; Int Soc Trop Ecol. *Res:* Taxonomy and ecology in Latin America; ecological amplitudes of crops and weeds; crop diversification; medicinal plants; computerized catalog of ecological, ethnomedicinal and nutritional attributes of economic plants. *Mailing Add:* Bldg 265 BARC-E USDA Beltsville MD 20705

DUKE, JODIE LEE, JR, b Kennett, Mo, Aug 3, 45; m 67; c 2. CARBOHYDRATE CHEMISTRY. *Educ:* Univ Mo-St Louis, BS, 67; Univ Mich, Ann Arbor, MA, 69, PhD(biochem), 74. *Prof Exp:* Res assoc immunol, Women's Hosp, Univ Mich, 74; res chemist, A E Staley Mfg Co, 74-77; sr res scientist, R J Reynolds Foods Inc, 77-78; SR RES BIOCHEMIST, LEE SCI INC, 79- *Mem:* Am Chem Soc; Sigma Xi. *Res:* Applied research for the food industry. *Mailing Add:* 1280 Bardat Creve Coeur MO 63141

DUKE, JOHN CHRISTIAN, JR, b Baltimore, Md, May 27, 51; m 78; c 2. NONDESTRUCTIVE EVALUATION, COMPOSITE MATERIAL. *Educ:* Johns Hopkins Univ, BES, 73, MSE, 76, PhD(mat sci eng), 78. *Prof Exp:* Physicist, Nat Bur Standards, 75-77; asst prof mech eng, US Naval Acad, 77-78; fel, Johns Hopkins Univ, 78; asst prof, 78-82, ASSOC PROF ENG MECH, VA POLYTECH INST & STATE UNIV, 82- *Honors & Awards:* Teetor Award, Soc Automotive Engrs, 79. *Mem:* Am Soc Nondestructive Testing; Am Soc Testing & Mat; Am Soc Metals; Sigma Xi. *Res:* Research and development of nondestructive methods of evaluation for understanding deformation mechanism in metal alloys, advanced composites and biomaterials. *Mailing Add:* Rt 4 Box 587 Christiansburg VA 24073

DUKE, JOHN MURRAY, b Montreal, Que, Jan 3, 47; m 75; c 1. MAGMATIC ORES, STRATEGIC MINERALS. *Educ:* McGill Univ, BSc, 68, MSc, 71; Univ Conn, PhD(geol), 74. *Prof Exp:* Fel, Univ Toronto, 74-76; ECON MINERALOGIST, GEOL SURV CAN, 76- *Concurrent Pos:* Mem, Can Geosci Coun Comt on Int Sci Relations. *Mem:* Geol Asn Can; Mineral Asn Can (secy, 78-). *Res:* The genesis of magmatic sulfide and oxide ores of nickel, copper, platinum metals and chromium and the appraisal of their resources. *Mailing Add:* Geol Surv Can 601 Booth St Ottawa ON K1A 0E8 Can

DUKE, JOHN WALTER, b Ballinger, Tex, Oct 30, 37; m 57; c 3. MATHEMATICS. *Educ:* North Tex State Univ, BA, 59; Tex Tech Univ, MS, 61; Univ Colo, PhD(math), 68. *Prof Exp:* Instr, Tex Tech Univ, 61-64, asst prof, 66-68; assoc prof, 68-77, PROF MATH, ANGELO STATE UNIV, 77- *Mem:* Am Math Soc; Math Asn Am. *Res:* Matrices over division algebras; general ring theory. *Mailing Add:* Dept of Math Angelo State Univ San Angelo TX 76901

DUKE, JUNE TEMPLE, b Cambridge, Ohio, June 18, 22. ORGANIC CHEMISTRY, POLYMER CHEMISTRY. *Prof Exp:* Technician, Off Rubber Reserve, Govt Labs, Univ Akron, 44-45, lab supvr rubber res, 45-50, chemist supvr, 50-56; res chemist, Energy Div, Olin Mathieson Chem Corp, 56-59; sr chemist, 59-60, sr res chemist & proj leader polymer res, 60-68, RES ASSOC, STANDARD OIL CO OF OHIO, 68- *Mem:* AAAS; Am Chem Soc; Fedn Socs Paint Technol. *Res:* Polymerization and structure of synthetic rubber; organo-boron polymers; synthetic coatings; emulsion polymerization; resins and plastics. *Mailing Add:* 28649 Jackson Rd Chagrin Falls OH 44022

DUKE, KENNETH LINDSAY, b Heber City, Utah, Feb 22, 12; m 34; c 3. ANATOMY. *Educ:* Brigham Young Univ, AB, 36; Duke Univ, PhD(cytol), 40. *Prof Exp:* Asst zool, Brigham Young Univ, 36-37; asst, 37-39, instr, 40-43, assoc, 43-46, asst prof, 46-51, assoc prof anat, 51-81, EMER PROF, SCH MED, DUKE UNIV, 81- *Concurrent Pos:* China Med Bd NY traveling fel, Malaya, 61; vis instr, Sch Med, Univ Mo, 44; vis instr, Sch Med, Univ NC, 46, vis assoc prof, 55; vis asst prof, Sch Med, Univ Tenn, 49. *Mem:* Am Asn Anat; Am Soc Mammal. *Res:* Histology; cytology; mammalian reproductive tract; germ cells of mammals. *Mailing Add:* Dept of Anat Duke Univ Med Ctr Durham NC 27710

DUKE, MICHAEL SN, b Los Angeles, Calif, Dec 1, 35; m 58; c 4. GEOLOGY, COSMOCHEMISTRY. *Educ:* Calif Inst Technol, BS, 57, MS, 61, PhD(geochem), 63. *Prof Exp:* Geologist, Astrogeol Br, US Geol Surv, 63-70; lunar sample cur, 70-77, CHIEF LUNAR & PLANETARY SCI DIV, JOHNSON SPACE CTR, NASA, 77- *Concurrent Pos:* Adj prof, Rice Univ, 79- *Honors & Awards:* Nininger Meteorite Award, Ariz State Univ, 63; NASA Except Sci Achievement Medal, 73. *Mem:* AAAS; Sigma Xi; Meteoritical Soc; Am Geophys Union. *Res:* Mineralogy, petrology, chemical composition of extraterrestrial material, including lunar rocks, soils, meteorites, and cosmic dust; origin of solar system; development of mineralogical, chemical techniques for laboratory; automated spacecraft applications. *Mailing Add:* Johnson Space Ctr Houston TX 77058

DUKE, RICHARD ALTER, b Geneva, Ohio, Aug 23, 37. MATHEMATICS. *Educ:* Kenyon Col, AB, 59; Dartmouth Col, MA, 61; Univ Va, PhD(math), 65. *Prof Exp:* Instr math, Univ Wash, 65-66, asst prof, 66-72; asst prof, 72-75, asst dir math, 72-79, ASSOC PROF MATH, GA INST TECHNOL, 75- *Concurrent Pos:* Exam leader, Advan Placement Prog Math, Col Bd-Educ Testing Serv, 73-80. *Mem:* Am Math Soc; Math Asn Am. *Res:* Graph theory and combinatorics with an emphasis on the combinatorial properties of finite complexes, Ramsey theorems and the connections with block designs. *Mailing Add:* Sch Math Ga Inst Technol Atlanta GA 30332

DUKE, ROY BURT, JR, b Houston, Tex, Sept 20, 32; m 50; c 3. PETROLEUM CHEMISTRY. *Educ:* Univ Houston, BS, 56, MS, 60; Ga Inst Technol, PhD(chem), 67. *Prof Exp:* Res chemist, Am Oil Co, 56-60 & Tex Eastman Co, 60-62; instr, Ga Inst Technol, 62-65; adv res chemist, 66-74, SR RES CHEMIST, MARATHON OIL CO, 74- *Mem:* Am Chem Soc. *Res:* Catalysis; dehydrogenation; mechanism of the Grignard reaction; kinetics and mechanism of the reaction of alkoxides with methylene halides; aldol and related condensations; pyrolysis and extraction of oil shale; identification of components in oil shale and related mineral deposits; enhanced oil recovery; surfactant flooding, emulsions and demulsification. *Mailing Add:* Marathon Oil Co Box 269 Littleton CO 80160

DUKE, STANLEY HOUSTEN, b Battle Creek, Mich, Oct 9, 44; m 78. PLANT PHYSIOLOGY, PLANT BIOCHEMISTRY. *Educ:* Henderson State Univ, BS, 66; Univ Ark, MS, 69; Univ Minn, PhD(bot), 75. *Prof Exp:* Mem staff, US Army Chem Corps, 68-70; fel, 76-78, ASST PROF PLANT PHYSIOL, UNIV WIS-MADISON, 78- *Concurrent Pos:* Fel, Linnean Soc London, 75. *Mem:* Am Soc Plant Physiologists; Japanese Soc Plant Physiologists; Am Soc Agron; Bot Soc Am; Sigma Xi. *Res:* Plant nitrogen metabolism; enzyme kinetics; low temperature effects on physiology and biochemistry; chronobiology; photomorphogenesis; plant physiological ecology; agronomy. *Mailing Add:* Dept of Agron 1575 Linden Dr Madison WI 53706

DUKE, STEPHEN OSCAR, b Battle Creek, Mich, Oct 9, 44; m 67; c 2. PLANT PHYSIOLOGY. *Educ:* Henderson State Univ, BS, 66; Univ Ark, MS, 69; Duke Univ, PhD(bot), 75. *Prof Exp:* Instr biol, Duke Univ, 74-75; nat res coun assoc, Plant Physiol, 75-76, PLANT PHYSIOLOGIST, SOUTHERN WEED SCI LAB, AGR RES SERV, USDA, 76- *Concurrent Pos:* Assoc ed, Weed Sci, 80- *Mem:* Am Soc Plant Physiologists; Sigma Xi; AAAS; Bot Soc Am; Am Inst Biol Sci. *Res:* Photobiology of plants, including higher plant photomorphogenesis; seed photophysiology, in vivo phytochrome measurement, and photocontrol of enzyme activities; secondary plant metabolism, particularly plant phenolics; greening and photosynthesis; herbicide mechanism of action. *Mailing Add:* Southern Weed Sci Lab Stoneville MS 38776

DUKE, VICTOR HAL, b Kamas, Utah, Jan 15, 25; m 49; c 3. PHARMACOLOGY, PHARMACOGNOSY. *Educ:* Idaho State Univ, BS, 49, BS, 50; Univ Utah, PhD(pharm), 61. *Prof Exp:* Asst prof pharmacol, Univ NMex, 61-65; assoc prof, Col Pharm, Univ Wyo, 65-68; from assoc prof to prof, Univ Mont, 68-72; DEAN, SCH HEALTH SCI, BOISE STATE UNIV, 72- *Concurrent Pos:* Dir drug abuse seminar educators, Univ Mont, 69-71; mem, Nat Adv Coun Health Manpower Educ, 71-72. *Mem:* Am Pharmaceut Asn; Am Public Health Asn; Am Soc Allied Health Prof. *Res:* Effect of drugs on analgesic threshold in animals; drug action in obesity and the evaluation of anorexigenics; research in neuro and behavioral pharmacology of psychotogens. *Mailing Add:* Sch of Health Sci Boise State Univ Boise ID 83725

DUKELOW, DONALD ALLEN, b Ellwood City, Pa, June 13, 32; m 56; c 3. METALLURGY. *Educ:* Geneva Col, BS, 54; Carnegie Inst Technol, MS, 56, PhD(metall), 57. *Prof Exp:* Res engr, Jones & Laughlin Steel Corp, 57-64; asst prof metall eng, Univ Pittsburgh, 64-67; sr res engr, US Steel Corp, Monroeville, 67-80; SR RES ENGR, NAT STEEL CORP, WEIRTON, 80- *Mem:* Am Inst Mining, Metall & Petrol Engrs. *Res:* Physical chemistry of metallurgy. *Mailing Add:* 719 Pinetree Rd Pittsburgh PA 15243

DUKELOW, W RICHARD, b Princeton, Minn, Oct 23, 36; m 58; c 3. REPRODUCTIVE PHYSIOLOGY. *Educ:* Univ Minn, BS, 57, MS, 58, PhD(physiol), 62. *Prof Exp:* Instr, Univ Minn, Grand Rapids, 60-62, asst prof, 62-64; res assoc biochem, Univ Ga, 64-65, asst res prof, 65-69; assoc prof, Endocrine Res Unit, Ctr Lab Animal Resources, 69-74, PROF PHYSIOL & ANIMAL HUSB & DIR ENDOCRINE RES UNIT, MICH STATE UNIV, 74- *Concurrent Pos:* NIH biomed grant, 66-67 & spec fel, 67-68; Lalor Found res grant & Pop Coun grant, 67-68; vis scientist, Ore Regional Primate Res Ctr, 67-68; NIH res career develop award, 70. *Mem:* Am Fertil Soc; Soc Study Fertil; Am Physiol Soc; Soc for Study Reproduction; Am Soc Pharmacol & Exp Therapeut. *Res:* Biochemistry and physiology of reproduction, especially spermatozoa capacitation, intrauterine devices and embryonic mortality; primatology. *Mailing Add:* Endocrine Res Unit Mich State Univ East Lansing MI 48824

DUKEPOO, FRANK CHARLES, b Parker, Ariz, Jan 29, 43; c 1. HUMAN GENETICS. *Educ:* Ariz State Univ, BS, 66, MS, 68, PhD(zool), 73. *Prof Exp:* Instr genetics, Mesa Community Col, Ariz, 71-72; teacher gen sci, Phoenix Indian Sch, Ariz, 72-73; asst prof biol genetics, San Diego State Univ, 73-77; PROG MGR, MINORITY INSTS SCI IMPROVEMENT PROG, NSF, 77- *Concurrent Pos:* Consult, Ctr on Aging, Inst Minority Aging, San Diego, 73-, sec sci prog, Bur Indian Affairs, 73-75 & elderly Indian nutrit res proj, 74; mem ad hoc comt, Minority Sci Prog, NIH, 74-75. *Mem:* AAAS; Soc Advan Chicanos & Native Americans Sci. *Res:* Albinism and inbreeding among the Hopi Indians of Arizona; inter-racial variant biological response to alcohol; cross-cultural study on the minority aged. *Mailing Add:* Minority Insts Sci NSF Washington DC 20550

DUKES, GARY RINEHART, b Lafayette, Ind, Feb 24, 39; m 65; c 3. ANALYTICAL CHEMISTRY. *Educ:* US Naval Acad, BS, 62; Purdue Univ, PhD(chem), 72. *Prof Exp:* NIH fel, Mass Inst Technol, 72-74; asst prof chem, Univ Ala, 74-78; scientist, 78-79, RES HEAD, THE UPJOHN CO, 79- *Mem:* Sigma Xi; Am Chem Soc. *Res:* Laboratory computerization; kinetics and mechanisms of ligand exchange reactions; analytical methods development. *Mailing Add:* The Upjohn Co 7171 Portage Rd Kalamazoo MI 49001

DUKES, JOHN R, b Findlay, Ohio, Oct 9, 30; m 53; c 2. APPLIED PHYSICS, PHYSICS ENGINEERING. *Educ:* Ohio State Univ, BS(physics) & BEE, 54, MBA, 71; Bowling Green State Univ, BS(lib arts), 54. *Prof Exp:* Elec engr, 56-57, physicist, 57-58, physics supvr, 58-61, radiol safety officer, 60-69, mgr appl physics, 61-77, MGR RADIOL REGULATIONS & OPERS, ACCURAY CORP, 77-, HEALTH PHYSICS OFFICER, 69- *Concurrent Pos:* Mem fac, Franklin Univ, 57-65; instr, Ohio State Univ, 68-70; mem comt N43.3, Am Nat Standards Inst, 62-, chmn N43 3.2, 73-, US rep, Int Electrotech Comn TC45, 73- & Int Standards Orgn TC 85, 74- *Mem:* Health Physics Soc; Am Nuclear Soc. *Res:* Development of peaceful uses of atomic and nuclear energy directed toward measurement of material properties for industrial applications. *Mailing Add:* AccuRay Corp 650 Ackerman Rd Columbus OH 43202

DUKES, MICHAEL DENNIS, b Winter Haven, Fla, Nov 4, 52; m 73; c 1. INORGANIC CHEMISTRY. *Educ:* Univ SFla, Tampa, BA, 73; Univ SC, Columbia, PhD(inorg chem), 77. *Prof Exp:* RES CHEMIST RADIOACTIVE WASTE MGT, SAVANNAH RIVER LAB, E I DU PONT DE NEMOURS & CO, INC, 77- *Mem:* Am Chem Soc. *Res:* Selection and testing of solid forms for the immobilization of radioactive wastes. *Mailing Add:* Savannah River Lab E I du Pont de Nemours & Co Inc Aiken SC 29801

DUKES, PETER PAUL, b Vienna, Austria, June 27, 30; US citizen; m 61; c 2. BIOCHEMISTRY, HEMATOLOGY. *Educ:* Univ Chicago, PhD(biochem), 58. *Prof Exp:* Res asst biochem, Univ Chicago, 54-55, from instr to asst prof, 58-67; asst prof, 67-71, ASSOC PROF BIOCHEM & PEDIAT, SCH MED, UNIV SOUTHERN CALIF, 71- *Concurrent Pos:* USPHS spec fel, Physiol Chem Inst, Univ Marburg, 64-65; res assoc, Argonne Cancer Res Hosp, 58-67; mem erythropoietin comt, Nat Heart, Lung & Blood Inst, 70-74. *Mem:* Int Soc Exp Hemat; AAAS; Am Soc Biol Chemists; Am Soc Hemat; Ger Soc Biol Chemists. *Res:* Erythropoietin; regulation of hematopoiesis; control of cell differentiation by hormones; megakaryocytopoiesis. *Mailing Add:* Hemat Res Labs Childrens Hosp 4650 Sunset Blvd Los Angeles CA 90027

DUKES, PHILIP DUSKIN, b Reevesville, SC, Jan 16, 31; m 56; c 2. PLANT PATHOLOGY, PLANT BREEDING. *Educ:* Clemson Univ, BS, 53; NC State Univ, MS, 60, PhD(plant path), 63. *Prof Exp:* Plant chief clerk, Davison Chem Corp, W R Grace & Co, 53-54; asst county agent, SC Exten Serv, 56-58; asst plant pathologist & asst prof plant path, Coastal Plain Exp Sta, Univ Ga, 62-67, assoc prof plant path, 67-70; RES PLANT PATHOLOGIST, US VEG LAB, AGR RES SERV, USDA, 70- *Concurrent Pos:* Adj prof, Clemson Univ, 80- *Honors & Awards:* L M Ware Res Award. *Mem:* Am Phytopath Soc; Int Soc Plant Path; Int Soc Trop Root Crops. *Res:* Physiology of phytopathogenic fungi; physiology of parasitism of root and stem pathogens; breeding disease resistant vegetables; sweet potato diseases; southern peas diseases; physiology and genetics of Fusarium oxysporum batatas; control of vegetable diseases by breeding and other means. *Mailing Add:* US Veg Lab Agr Res Serv USDA 2875 Savannah Hwy Charleston SC 29407

DUKES, THEODOR A, b Vienna, Austria, May 28, 23; US citizen; m 50. MECHANICAL ENGINEERING, BIOENGINEERING. *Educ:* Tech Univ, Budapest, Dipl, 51. *Prof Exp:* Fel Hungarian Acad Sci, 52-55; res engr elec eng, Res Inst Elec Indust, Budapest, 55-56; SR RES SCIENTIST & LECTR, DEPT MECH & AEROSPACE ENG, PRINCETON UNIV, 57- *Mem:* Inst Elec & Electronics Engrs; Am Helicopter Soc; Am Inst Aeronaut & Astronaut. *Res:* Automatic control and man-machine systems applied to helicopters and vertical take-off and landing aircraft; display systems; biomechanics; analysis of human motion. *Mailing Add:* Dept of Mech & Aerospace Eng Princeton Univ Forrestal Campus Princeton NJ 08540

DUKES-DOBOS, FRANCIS N, b Budapest, Hungary, June 7, 20; US citizen; m 47; c 1. EXERCISE PHYSIOLOGY, OCCUPATIONAL HEALTH. *Educ:* Eotvos Lorand Univ, Budapest, MD, 51. *Prof Exp:* Res assoc environ physiol, Nat Inst Occup Health, Budapest, 49-56 & pathophysiol allergy, Johns Hopkins univ, 57-61; SCI ADV, DIV BIOMED & BEHAVIORAL SCI, NAT INST OCCUP SAFETY & HEALTH, 61- *Concurrent Pos:* Asst clin prof, Grad Sch Environ Health, Univ Cincinnati, 66-; environ physiologist, WHO, Geneva, Switz, 67-69. *Mem:* AAAS; Am Indust Hyg Asn; Am Conf Govt Indust Hygienists; Am Physiol Soc; Brit Ergonomics Res Soc. *Res:* Environmental physiology; measurement of workers' industrial heat exposure, analysis of their physiological responses to heat stress and physical work; physiological assessment of fatigue; effect of food on autonomic nervous reactivity; human factors. *Mailing Add:* Robt A Taft Labs NIOSH 4676 Columbia Pkwy Cincinnati OH 45226

DUKLER, A(BRAHAM) E(MANUEL), b Newark, NJ, Jan 5, 25; m 48; c 3. CHEMICAL ENGINEERING. *Educ:* Yale Univ, BE, 45; Univ Del, MS, 50, PhD, 51. *Prof Exp:* Develop engr, Rohm and Haas Co, 45-48; res engr, Shell Oil Co, 50-52; from asst prof to assoc prof chem eng, 52-60, chmn dept, 65-73, PROF CHEM ENG, UNIV HOUSTON, 60-, DEAN ENG, 76- *Concurrent Pos:* Vis prof, Univ Brazil, 63; exec dir, State Tex Energy Coun, 73-75; Lady Davis vis prof, Technion, Israel, 76; consult, US Nuclear Regulatory Comn, Brookhaven Lab & various indust companies. *Mem:* Nat Acad Eng; Am Chem Soc; fel Am Inst Chem Engrs; Am Soc Eng Educ. *Res:* Fluid mechanics; multiphase flow; boundary layer; heat and mass transfer; turbulence. *Mailing Add:* Col of Eng Univ of Houston Houston TX 77004

DULAK, NORMAN CHARLES, b Stevens Point, Wis, Oct 20, 40; m 66; c 2. BIOCHEMISTRY. *Educ:* Univ Wis-Madison, BS, 66, PhD(physiol chem), 71. *Prof Exp:* Fel oncol, Univ Wis-Madison, 70-72; asst prof biochem, Univ Kans Med Ctr, 72-74; asst prof biol, State Univ NY Albany, 74-78; ASST PROF ENVIRON MED, NY UNIV MED CTR, 78- *Mem:* Sigma Xi; Am Chem Soc; NY Acad Sci; AAAS; Tissue Cult Asn. *Res:* Factors which initiate or impede respiratory tract carcinogenesis. *Mailing Add:* Dept of Environ Med 550 First Ave New York NY 10016

DULANEY, EUGENE LAMBERT, b Garbor, Okla, June 2, 19; m 62; c 1. MICROBIOLOGY. *Educ:* Tex Tech Col, BS, 41; Univ Tex, MA, 43; Univ Wis, PhD(bot), 46. *Prof Exp:* Asst biol, Tex Tech Col, 39-41; tutor bot, Univ Tex, 41-43; res, Off Prod Res & Develop proj, 44-45; sr microbiologist, 46-60, res assoc, 60-65, sr res fel, 65-74, sr investr, 74-79, SR SCIENTIST, MICROBIOL RES LABS, MERCK & CO, 79- *Concurrent Pos:* Can Nat Res Coun fel, 55-56. *Mem:* Fel AAAS; Bot Soc Am; Mycol Soc Am; Am Soc Microbiol; Torrey Bot Club. *Res:* Genetics and physiology of microorganisms; biology of streptomyces; mycology; industrial microbiology, cell biology. *Mailing Add:* Merck Inst for Therapeutic Res PO Box 2000 Rahway NJ 07901

DULANEY, JOHN THORNTON, b Sutton, WVa, Sept 28, 37. BIOCHEMISTRY. *Educ:* WVa Wesleyan Col, BS, 58; Univ Chicago, MS, 62; Univ Ill, PhD(biochem), 67. *Prof Exp:* Asst biochemist, Eunice Kennedy Shriver Ctr, 71-76; investr, John F Kennedy Inst, Baltimore, 76-79; ASST PROF, DIV NEPHROL, DEPT MED, CTR HEALTH SCI, UNIV TENN, 79- *Concurrent Pos:* Asst biochem, Dept Neurol, Mass Gen Hosp, 72-76; res assoc neurol, Dept Neurol, Harvard Univ, 75-76; biochemist, Walter E Fernald State Sch, 75-76; asst prof, Dept Pediat, Johns Hopkins Univ, 76-79. *Mem:* Am Soc Neurochem; Soc Complex Carbohydrates; Am Asn Clin Chemists. *Res:* Lysosomal enzymes and storage diseases; structure and function of enzymes of mammalian plasma membranes; erythropoiesis; chronic renal failure. *Mailing Add:* Dept of Med Univ of Tenn Ctr Health Sci Memphis TN 38163

DULBECCO, RENATO, b Catanzaro, Italy, Feb 22, 14; nat US; m 40, 63; c 3. VIROLOGY. *Educ:* Univ Turin, MD, 36. *Hon Degrees:* DSc, Yale Univ, 68; LLD, Univ Glasgow, 70; DM, Vrije Univ, Brussels, 78. *Prof Exp:* Asst path, Univ Turin, 40-45, asst histol & embryol, 45-47; res assoc bact, Univ Ind, 47-49; from assoc prof to prof, Calif Inst Technol, 52-63; sr fel biol, Salk Inst Biol Studies, 63-72; asst dir, Imp Cancer Res Fund, London, 72-74, dep dir res, 74-77; DISTINGUISHED RES PROF, SALK INST, 77- *Concurrent Pos:* Harvey Lectr, Harvey Soc, 67; Prather Lectr, Harvard Univ, 69; distinguished vis lectr, Nat Polytech Inst, Mexico City, Mex, 70; Dunham Lectr, Harvard Univ, 72; Harden Lectr, Wye, Eng, 73; 11th Marjory Stephenson Mem Lect, Imp Col, 73; prof dept path & med, Med Sch, Univ Calif, San Diego, 77-81. *Honors & Awards:* Nobel Prize in Med/Physiol, 75; Albert & Mary Lasker Basic Med Res Award, 64; Howard Taylor Ricketts Award, 65; Paul Ehrlich-Ludwig Darmstaedter Adj Prize, 67; Louisa Gross Horwitz Prize, Columbia Univ, 73; Selman A Waksman Award Microbiol, Nat Acad Sci, 74; Targa d'oro Villa San Giovanni, 78. *Mem:* Nat Acad Sci; AAAS; Am Acad Arts & Sci; foreign mem Royal Soc; foreign mem Ital Acad Sci. *Res:* Cell physiology; oncology. *Mailing Add:* Salk Inst PO Box 1809 San Diego CA 92112

DULGEROFF, CARL RICHARD, b Wood River, Ill, Dec 26, 29; m 57; c 2. PLASMA PHYSICS. *Educ:* Cent Methodist Col, AB, 53; Wash Univ, PhD(physics), 59. *Prof Exp:* Asst physics, Wash Univ, 53-58, res assoc, 58-59; sr physicist, Rocketdyne Div, NAm Aviation, Inc, 59-60, prin scientist, 60-63, sr tech specialist physics, 63-67; sect head, 67-71, SR STAFF PHYSICIST, HUGHES RES LABS, DIV OF HUGHES AIRCRAFT CO, 71- *Mem:* Am Phys Soc; Sigma Xi. *Res:* Beta and gamma ray spectroscopy; positron annihilation; electron polarization; ion propulsion; ultra high vacuum; thermal radiation. *Mailing Add:* 23110 Erwin St Woodland Hills CA 91367

DULIN, WILLIAM E, b Md, Jan 25, 25; m 48; c 2. ZOOLOGY. *Educ:* Wash Col, Md, BS, 47; Univ Ind, PhD, 52. *Prof Exp:* Res scientist, 52-57, head res sect, 57-68, MGR DIABETES & ATHEROSCLEROSIS RES, UPJOHN CO, 68- *Mem:* Am Diabetes Asn; Am Physiol Soc; Endocrine Soc; Soc Exp Biol & Med. *Res:* Carbohydrate metabolism; mechanism of action of hypoglycemic agents and exercise; fat metabolism; physiology of fat deposition and mobilization; steroid and protein hormone assays; studies on experimental diabetes. *Mailing Add:* Upjohn Co Kalamazoo MI 49001

DULING, BRIAN R, b Pueblo, Colo, May 27, 37; m 56; c 3. CARDIOVASCULAR PHYSIOLOGY. *Educ:* Univ Colo, Boulder, AB, 62; Univ Iowa, PhD(cardiovasc physiol), 67. *Prof Exp:* From instr to assoc prof, 68-77, PROF PHYSIOL, SCH MED, UNIV VA, 77- *Concurrent Pos:* USPHS fel physiol, 67-68; Va Heart Asn jr physiol, 68-69; estab investr, Am Heart Asn, 74- *Mem:* AAAS; Biophys Soc; Microcirculatory Soc; Am Physiol Soc. *Res:* Investigation of the mechanisms active in controlling blood flow to tissues, especially relation between blood flow and tissue metabolic activity; delivery of oxygen to tissues. *Mailing Add:* Dept of Physiol Univ of Va Sch of Med Charlottesville VA 22901

DULIS, EDWARD J(OHN), b Brooklyn, NY, Oct 30, 19; m 45; c 3. PHYSICAL METALLURGY. *Educ:* Univ Ala, BS, 42; Stevens Inst Technol, MS, 50. *Prof Exp:* Asst metallurgist, US Naval Air Sta, 42-45; res metallurgist, US Steel Res Lab, NJ, 45-52, supv technologist, appl res lab, Pa, 52-55; res supvr, Crucible Steel Co Am, 55-59, mgr prod res, 59-64, dir prod res & develop, 64-65, dir res, 65-69, managing dir, 69-71, PRES, CRUCIBLE RES CTR, COLT INDUST, 71- *Mem:* Am Soc Metals; Am Iron & Steel Inst. *Res:* Development of new stainless steels, valve steels, high temperature alloys, powder metallurgy products and processes; technical management toward commercial application of scientific developments. *Mailing Add:* Crucible Res Ctr PO Box 88 Pittsburgh PA 15230

DULK, GEORGE A, b Denver, Colo, May 21, 30; m 58; c 1. RADIO ASTRONOMY, ASTROPHYSICS. *Educ:* US Mil Acad, BS, 55; Purdue Univ, MS, 59; Univ Colo, PhD(astro-geophys), 65. *Prof Exp:* Res assoc, 65-66, from asst prof to assoc prof, 66-77, chmn dept, 75-78, PROF ASTROGEOPHYS, UNIV COLO, BOULDER, 77- *Concurrent Pos:* Vis fel, Commonwealth Sci & Indust Res Orgn, Australia, 69-70, 72-73 & 78-79. *Mem:* Am Geophys Union; Am Astron Soc; Int Astron Union; Astron Asn Australia; Int Sci Radio Union. *Res:* Solar-stellar physics; radio astronomy; Jupiter's radio emission; solar radiophysics; coronal structure. *Mailing Add:* Dept of Astro-Geophys Univ of Colo Boulder CO 80302

DULKA, JOSEPH JOHN, b Cleveland, Ohio, Jan 12, 51; m 78. METABOLISM CHEMISTRY, ANALYTICAL CHEMISTRY. *Educ:* Miami Univ, BS, 72; Pa State Univ, PhD(chem), 78. *Prof Exp:* RES CHEMIST PESTICIDES, E I DU PONT DE NEMOURS & CO INC, 77- *Concurrent Pos:* Res fel, Miami Univ, 70-72. *Mem:* Sigma Xi; Am Chem Soc. *Mailing Add:* E I du Pont de Nemours & Co Inc Biochem Dept Bldg 324 Wilmington DE 19898

DULKIN, SOL I, b Chicago, Ill, Dec 17, 15; m 36, 70; c 2. CLINICAL CHEMISTRY. *Educ:* Lewis Inst, BS, 40; Univ Ill, MS, 47; Northwestern Univ, PhD(biochem), 51; Am Bd Clin Chem, dipl, 57. *Prof Exp:* Biochemist, Cook County Hosp, Ill, 39-41; consult chemist, Dr F Hartman & Assocs, 41-44; nutrit chemist, US Army Qm Food & Container Inst, 44-51; tech dir, Chem-Tech Labs, 52-74; CONSULT, 74- *Mem:* AAAS; Am Chem Soc; Am Asn Clin Chemists; Inst Food Technologists; Am Asn Bioanalysts. *Res:* Vitamins; assay procedures, stability studies and requirements; foods and nutrition; Browning reaction; army rations, analytical and adequacy; clinical methodology; metabolism; cancer research. *Mailing Add:* 18033 Sunburst St Northridge CA 91324

DULL, GERALD G, b Laurel, Mont, Aug 20, 30; m 53; c 2. PLANT BIOCHEMISTRY. *Educ:* Mont State Col, BS, 52; Mich State Univ, PhD(chem), 56. *Prof Exp:* Head biochem dept, Pineapple Res Inst, Hawaii, 56-66; plant prod qual invest leader, Human Nutrit Res Div, 66-69, CHIEF, FRUIT & VEG LAB, RICHARD B RUSSELL AGR RES CTR, AGR RES SERV, USDA, 69- *Mem:* AAAS; Am Chem Soc; Am Soc Hort Sci; Inst Food Technol. *Res:* Plant composition; post harvest fruit physiology; fruit and vegetable processing. *Mailing Add:* Richard B Russell Agr Res Ctr USDA Box 5677 Athens GA 30604

DULL, MARTIN HONER, mathematics, deceased

DULLAGHAN, MATTHEW EDWARD, b New York, NY, Feb 4, 24; m 55; c 3. ORGANIC CHEMISTRY, ANALYTICAL CHEMISTRY. *Educ:* Fordham Univ, BS, 47, MS, 49, PhD(synthetic org chem), 53. *Prof Exp:* Proj leader, Evans Res & Develop Corp, 52-54; res chemist, Textile Fibers Dept, E I du Pont de Nemours & Co, Del, 54-60, sr res chemist, Benger Lab, 60-76, SR RES CHEMIST, TEXTILE RES LAB, E I DU PONT DE NEMOURS & CO, 76- *Concurrent Pos:* Asst prof, Sch Educ, Fordham Univ, 53-55. *Res:* Thiophene chemistry; explosives; natural products; textile fibers, polymerization, preparation and evaluation; dyeing and finishing of textiles. *Mailing Add:* E I du Pont de Nemours & Co Chestnut Run Wilmington DE 19898

DULLER, NELSON M, JR, b Houston, Tex, Mar 6, 23; m 55; c 1. NUCLEAR PHYSICS. *Educ:* Tex A&M Univ, BS, 48; Rice Univ, MA, 51, PhD, 53. *Prof Exp:* Asst prof physics, Tex A&M Univ, 53-54; from asst prof to assoc prof, Univ Mo, 54-62; assoc prof, 62-72, PROF PHYSICS, TEX A&M UNIV, 72- *Concurrent Pos:* Sloan Found fel, 56-58. *Mem:* Am Phys Soc; Am Asn Physics Teachers; Ital Phys Soc. *Res:* High energy nuclear and cosmic ray physics. *Mailing Add:* Dept of Physics Tex A&M Univ College Station TX 77843

DULLIEN, FRANCIS A L, b Budapest, Hungary, Dec 14, 25. CHEMICAL ENGINEERING, PHYSICAL CHEMISTRY. *Educ:* Budapest Tech Univ, ChemE, 50; Univ BC, MApplSci, 58, PhD(chem eng), 60. *Prof Exp:* Asst prof phys chem, Budapest Tech Univ, 50-56; asst prof chem eng, Okla State Univ, 60-62; sr res engr, Jersey Prod Res Co, 62-65 & Esso Prod Res Co, 65-66; PROF CHEM ENG, UNIV WATERLOO, 66- *Concurrent Pos:* Vis prof, Purdue Univ, 71-72. *Mem:* Am Inst Chem Engrs; Am Chem Soc; Soc Petrol Engrs; Chem Inst Can; Can Soc Chem NY Acad Sci. *Res:* Diffusion and flow through porous media; determination of structure of porous media; mixing of liquids; air cleaning; diffusion in gaseous and liquid systems; surface chemistry. *Mailing Add:* Dept of Chem Eng Univ of Waterloo Waterloo ON N2L 3G1 Can

DULMAGE, HOWARD TAYLOR, b Bridgeport, Conn, July 13, 23; m 53; c 2. INSECT PATHOLOGY, MICROBIOLOGY. *Educ:* Univ Ill, BS, 47; Rutgers Univ, PhD(microbiol), 51. *Prof Exp:* Res microbiologist, Abbott Labs, Ill, 50-62; res microbiologist, Nutrilite Prod, Calif, 62-63, dir biol res & develop, 63-67; RES MICROBIOLOGIST, COTTON INSECT RES BR, USDA, 67, LOCATION/RES LEADER, 77- *Honors & Awards:* Outstanding Res Award, USDA, 70, Distinguished Serv Medal, 78. *Mem:* Am Chem Soc; Am Soc Microbiol; Soc Invert Path; Entom Soc Am; Am Inst Chem. *Res:* Bacillus thuringiensis; production insecticidal agents by microorganisms; nutrition and strain studies actinomycetes; microbiological insect control; microbial fermentations; production insect viruses. *Mailing Add:* Agr Res SEA USDA PO Box 1033 Brownsville TX 78520

DULMAGE, WILLIAM JAMES, b Winnipeg, Man, June 9, 19; nat US; m 42; c 3. PHYSICAL CHEMISTRY. *Educ:* Univ Man, BSc, 46; Univ Minn, PhD(chem), 51. *Prof Exp:* Lectr chem, Univ Man, 46-47; res & develop chemist, Elec Reduction Co, Can, Ltd, 51-52; res assoc, 52-70, ASST HEAD PHOTOMAT DIV, EASTMAN KODAK CO RES LABS, 70- *Mem:* Am Chem Soc. *Res:* X-ray crystallography; molecular structure; structure and properties of high polymers; phase rule studies; unconventional photoreduction systems. *Mailing Add:* 14 Holmes Rd Rochester NY 14626

DULOCK, VICTOR A, JR, b Waco, Tex, Feb 26, 39; m 59; c 5. APPLIED PHYSICS. *Educ:* Univ St Thomas, BA, 60; Univ Fla, PhD(physics), 64. *Prof Exp:* Res assoc physics, Univ Fla, 64-65; asst prof, La State Univ, New Orleans, 65-67; mem prof staff, TRW Inc, Tex, 67-69, sect head, 69-70, staff engr, 70-72, proj mgr, Fla, 72-74, SR STAFF ENGR, TRW INC, CALIF, 74- *Mem:* Am Phys Soc; Am Asn Physics Teachers. *Res:* Applied mechanics; aerospace sciences; space physics; systems analysis; systems engineering; dynamics. *Mailing Add:* TRW Inc PO Box 1310 San Bernardino CA 92406

DUMAN, JOHN GIRARD, b Spangler, Pa, Aug 25, 46; m 71; c 3. ENVIRONMENTAL PHYSIOLOGY. *Educ:* Pa State Univ, BS, 68; Scripps Inst Oceanog, Univ Calif, San Diego, PhD(marine biol), 74. *Prof Exp:* Asst prof, 74-80, ASSOC PROF BIOL, UNIV NOTRE DAME, 80- *Mem:* AAAS; Am Physiol Soc; Am Soc Zoologists; Soc Cryobiol; Sigma Xi. *Res:* Role of macromolecular antifreeze in freezing resistance of fishes; role of macromolecular solutes in insect frost tolerance. *Mailing Add:* Dept of Biol Univ of Notre Dame Notre Dame IN 46556

DUMAN, MAXIMILIAN GEORGE, b Nicktown, Pa, Feb 21, 06. SYSTEMATIC BOTANY. *Educ:* St Vincent Col, AB, 32; Cath Univ Am, MS, 37, PhD(bot), 41. *Prof Exp:* Instr biol, St Vincent Col, 32-36 & 37-39, assoc prof, 41-56; assoc prof, Cath Univ Am, 57-61; pres col, 62-63, PROF BIOL, ST VINCENT COL, 61- *Concurrent Pos:* Mem, Cath Univ Arctic Exped, 39, Hudson Bay, 38 & 39, North Quebec, 50, Ungava, 51, James Bay, 52, 53, 54, 55 & 56, Yukon, 70 & NW Territories, 71; instr, Latrobe Hosp, 46-58; Arctic field trip, Int Bot Cong, 59; spec grad fac mem, Colo State Univ, 73- *Mem:* AAAS; assoc Bot Soc Am; assoc Am Soc Plant Taxon; Int Asn Plant Taxon. *Res:* Taxonomic and distributional studies of arctic and subarctic carices. *Mailing Add:* Dept of Biol St Vincent Col Latrobe PA 15650

DUMAS, HERBERT M, JR, b El Dorado, Ark, Dec 16, 27; m 53; c 1. SPACE PHYSICS, OPTICAL PHYSICS. *Educ:* Univ Ark, AB, 54, BS, 55, MS, 56. *Prof Exp:* Tech staff mem physics, 56-60, supvr tech sect, 60-65, seismic systs div, 65-69 & satellite sensors div, 69-72, supvr, Sensors Develop Div, 72-76, MGR SPACE SYSTS DEPT, SANDIA LAB, SANDIA CORP, 76- *Mem:* Optical Soc Am. *Res:* Detection instrumentation and diagnostic measurements of atomic detonations; seismic systems development; energy conversion devices; optical sensors for satellite applications. *Mailing Add:* 1304 Florida N E Albuquerque NM 87110

DUMAS, JEAN, b Montreal, Que, June 4, 25; m 53; c 5. ELECTRICAL ENGINEERING. *Educ:* McGill Univ, BEng, 48; Mass Inst Technol, SB, 51, SM, 52. *Prof Exp:* Res scientist, Can Armament Res & Develop Estab, 52-55; from asst prof to assoc prof, 55-68, asst head dept, 66-69, PROF ELEC ENG, LAVAL UNIV, 68- *Concurrent Pos:* Ford fel, Carnegie Inst Technol, 61-62. *Mem:* Inst Elec & Electronics Engrs. *Res:* Measurements; circuits; standards; lines; musical acoustics. *Mailing Add:* Dept of Elec Eng Laval Univ Quebec PQ G1K 7P4 Can

DUMAS, KENNETH J, b New York, NY, Oct 26, 26; m 52; c 3. MEDICINE. *Educ:* Drew Univ, AB, 48; NY Med Col, MD, 52. *Prof Exp:* Assoc dir clin res, Chas Pfizer & Co, Inc, 54-59, dir, 59-61; dir clin res, Syntex Labs, Inc, 61-62, med dir, 62-64, med dir, Syntex Res, 64-66, vpres & dir, Inst Clin Med, 66-73, dir med affairs, 77-80, SR VPRES RES, SYNTEX RES CORP, 73-, SR VPRES & DIR INT DEVELOP & RES, 80-; PRES & DIR GEN RECHERCHE, LAROCHE, NAVARRON, 80- *Res:* International clinical studies; international research and product development; data processing and analysis; pharmaceutical product acquisition and licensing. *Mailing Add:* Syntex Corp Res Div Stanford Indust Park Palo Alto CA 94304

DUMAS, LAWRENCE BERNARD, b Plainwell, Mich, Mar 2, 41; m 65; c 2. MOLECULAR BIOLOGY, BIOCHEMISTRY. *Educ:* Mich State Univ, BS, 63; Univ Wis, Madison, MS, 65, PhD(biochem), 68. *Prof Exp:* USPHS res fel biol, Calif Inst Technol, 68-70; from asst prof to assoc prof, 70-80, PROF BIOCHEM & MOLECULAR BIOL, NORTHWESTERN UNIV, 80- *Concurrent Pos:* Career develop award, USPHS, 74-79. *Mem:* AAAS; Am Soc Biol Chemists; Am Soc Microbiol. *Mailing Add:* Dept of Biochem & Molecular Biol Northwestern Univ Evanston IL 60201

DUMAS, PHILIP CONRAD, b Wash, Apr 9, 23; m 64; c 3. VERTEBRATE ZOOLOGY. *Educ:* Ore State Univ, BS, 48, MA, 49, PhD(zool), 53. *Prof Exp:* From instr to asst prof, Univ Idaho, 53-65; from assoc prof to prof zool, 65-77, PROF BIOL, CENT WASH UNIV, 77- CHMN DEPT BIOL, 66- *Res:* Zoogeography; herpetology; ecology. *Mailing Add:* Dept of Biol Sci Cent Wash Univ Ellensburg WA 98926

DUMBAUGH, WILLIAM HENRY, JR, b Butler, Pa, Dec 12, 29. GLASS CHEMISTRY. *Educ:* Univ Rochester, BS, 51; Pa State Univ, PhD(chem), 59. *Prof Exp:* Sr chemist, 58-66, MGR GLASS CHEM RES, CORNING GLASS WORKS, 66- *Mem:* Am Chem Soc; Brit Soc Glass Technol; Am Ceramic Soc. *Res:* Glass composition; high temperature chemistry. *Mailing Add:* Corning Glass Works Sullivan Park FR51 Corning NY 14831

DUMBROFF, ERWIN BERNARD, b Newark, NJ, Mar 20, 32; m 51; c 3. PLANT PHYSIOLOGY, BIOSTATISTICS. *Educ:* Univ Ga, BSF, 56, MF, 58, PhD(bot, plant physiol), 64. *Prof Exp:* Res forester, US Forest Serv, Fla, 57-60 & Ga, 60-64, plant physiologist, 64-65; asst prof biol, 65-68, ASSOC PROF BIOL, UNIV WATERLOO, 68- *Mem:* AAAS; Am Soc Plant Physiol; Can Soc Plant Physiol; Am Inst Biol Sci. *Res:* Seed physiology; dormancy mechanisms in plants; plant hormones; mechanisms of salt tolerance. *Mailing Add:* Dept of Biol Univ of Waterloo Waterloo ON N2L 3G1 Can

DUMENIL, LLOYD C, b Argyle, Iowa, July 23, 20; m 44; c 1. SOIL FERTILITY. *Educ:* Iowa State Univ, BS, 42, MS, 51, PhD(soil fertil), 58. *Prof Exp:* Res assoc, 46-50, asst prof, 50-58, ASSOC PROF SOILS, IOWA STATE UNIV, 58- *Mem:* Am Soc Agron; Soil Sci Soc Am. *Res:* Influence of soil, management and climatic variables on corn yields in Iowa. *Mailing Add:* Dept of Agron Iowa State Univ Ames IA 50011

DUMIN, DAVID JOSEPH, b Westfield, Mass, Oct 6, 35; m 64; c 2. MICROELECTRONICS. *Educ:* Johns Hopkins Univ, BSEE, 57; Purdue Univ, MSEE, 61; Stanford Univ, PhD(elec eng), 64. *Prof Exp:* Engr solid state electronics, IBM, 57-61; mgr tech support microelectronics, RCA, 64-70; vpres, Inselek, 70-75; pres, DJD Sci, 75-77; tech dir, Allied Corp, 76-77; SAMUEL B RHODES PROF ELEC ENG, CLEMSON UNIV, 77- *Concurrent Pos:* Consult various orgn including, US Navy, Union Carbide, Allied Chem, Siemens, Kyoto Ceramics and others, 75- *Mem:* Am Phys Soc; Inst Elec & Electronics Engrs. *Res:* Microelectronic device material interactions including cryogenics, cryotrons, silicon-on-sapphire, silicon vidicons, epitaxial growth, radiation properties and submicron devices. *Mailing Add:* Clemson Univ Col Eng Clemson SC 29631

DUMKE, WARREN LLOYD, b Milwaukee, Wis, Oct 26, 28; m 63. CHEMICAL PHYSICS, PHYSICAL CHEMISTRY. *Educ:* Univ Wis, BS, 51; Iowa State Univ, MS, 56; Univ Nebr, PhD(phys chem), 65. *Prof Exp:* Res asst phys chem, AEC-Iowa State Univ, 53-56; instr chem physics & sci, Mankato State Col, 56-58; asst chem, Univ Nebr, 58-64; asst prof, Kent State Univ, 64-65, NASA res assoc neutron diffraction, 65-67; asst prof physics, 67-71, ASSOC PROF PHYSICS, MARSHALL UNIV, 71- *Mem:* Am Chem Soc; Am Crystallog Asn. *Res:* X-ray and neutron diffraction; quantum mechanical calculations; x-ray crystal studies of hydrazine-metal complexes. *Mailing Add:* Dept of Physics Marshall Univ Huntington WV 25701

DUMM, MARY ELIZABETH, b Newark, NJ, Dec 9, 16. NUTRITION. *Educ:* Swarthmore Col, AB, 38; Bryn Mawr Col, MA, 40, PhD(biochem), 43. *Prof Exp:* Instr biol, Bryn Mawr Col, 42-44; instr chem, Col Med, NY Univ, 44-47, asst med, 47-50, from adj asst prof to asst prof, 50-59; lectr biochem, Christian Med Col, Vellore, India, 59-60, from assoc prof to prof, 60-71; asst prof, 71-73, ASSOC PROF PATH, COL MED & DENT NJ, RUTGERS MED SCH, 73- *Concurrent Pos:* Vis assoc prof, Teachers Col, Columbia Univ, 71. *Mem:* Am Physiol Soc; Endocrine Soc; Soc Exp Biol & Med; NY Acad Sci. *Res:* Endocrinology and metabolism; medical, clinical and nutritional biochemistry. *Mailing Add:* 13 Samson Ave Madison NJ 07940

DUMMETT, CLIFTON ORRIN, b Georgetown, Brit Guiana, May 20, 19; nat US; m 43; c 1. PERIODONTOLOGY. *Educ:* Roosevelt Col, BS, 41; Northwestern Univ, DDS, 41, MSD, 42; Univ Mich, MPH, 47; Am Bd Periodont & Am Bd Oral Med, dipl. *Prof Exp:* Prof periodont, oral path & pub health, dean & dir dent educ, Sch Dent, Meharry Med Col, 45-49; chief dent serv & exec secy res & educ, Vet Admin Hosp, Tuskegee, 49-64; prof dent, Sch Vet Med, Tuskegee Inst, 64-66; assoc prof periodont, Sch Dent, Univ Ala, 65-66; assoc prof dent, Northwestern Univ, 66; chief dent serv, Vet Admin Res Hosp & chmn res study group oral dis, 66; prof community dent & chmn dept & dent dir multipurpose health serv ctr, 66-68, health ctr dir, 68, assoc dean extramural affairs, 68-75, PROF DENT, UNIV SOUTHERN CALIF, 75- *Concurrent Pos:* Mem comt pub health surv dent, Am Coun Educ; deleg, Nat Citizen Comt, WHO, 53; ed, Nat Dent Asn Bull, 53-75; mem, Inst Med, Nat Acad Sci, 72. *Honors &. Honors & Awards:* Nat Dent Asn Award, 52; Alfred Fones Award, 76; Pierre Fauchard Gold Medalist, 80. *Mem:* AAAS; fel Am Pub Health Asn; hon mem Am Dent Asn; Nat Dent Asn; Int Asn Dent Res (vpres, 67, pres-elect, 68, pres, 69). *Res:* Oral pathology; public health dentistry; dental education; oral diagnosis. *Mailing Add:* Sch of Dent Univ of Southern Calif Los Angeles CA 90007

DUMONT, ALLAN E, b New York, NY, Oct 8, 24; m 49; c 3. SURGERY, PHYSIOLOGY. *Educ:* Hobart Col, BA, 45; NY Univ, MD, 48. *Prof Exp:* From instr to prof, 55-73, J L WHITEHILL PROF SURG, MED SCH, NY UNIV MED CTR, 73- *Concurrent Pos:* A A Berg fel exp surg, 55-59; USPHS fel, 61-62, res career develop award, 61-71; investr, NY Health Res Coun, 59-61; assoc dir surg, Bellevue Hosp, New York, 75- *Honors & Awards:* Porkinge Medal, Czech Med Soc. *Mem:* AAAS; Am Physiol Soc; Soc Exp Biol & Med; Soc Univ Surgeons; Am Surg Asn. *Res:* Function of the lymphatic system; wound healing. *Mailing Add:* Dept of Surg Med Sch NY Univ Med Ctr 550 First Ave New York NY 10016

DUMONT, JAMES NICHOLAS, b Sigourney, Iowa, Sept 19, 35; m 61; c 2. ZOOLOGY, CYTOLOGY. *Educ:* State Univ Iowa, BS, 57, MS, 60; Univ Mass, PhD(zool), 64. *Prof Exp:* Instr biol, Rockford Col, 61-62; res assoc zool, Univ Mass, 64-65, lectr electron micros, 65-66; RES BIOLOGIST, OAK RIDGE NAT LAB, 66- *Concurrent Pos:* Prof, Univ Tenn-Oak Ridge Grad Sch Biomed Sci, 71- *Mem:* Electron Micros Soc Am; Am Soc Cell Biol. *Res:* Cell and developmental biology; reproductive biology; teratology; abnormal embryological development (teratology) in response to teratogens from environmental sources. *Mailing Add:* Biol Div Oak Ridge Nat Lab Oak Ridge TN 37830

DUMONT, KENT P, b Newburyport, Mass, July 10, 41; m; c 3. BOTANY. *Educ:* Gettysburg Col, AB, 63; Cornell Univ, MS, 65, PhD, 70. *Prof Exp:* Assoc cur, 69-77, CUR FUNGI, NY BOT GARDEN, 77- *Concurrent Pos:* Adj asst prof, Lehman Col, City Univ New York; mem prog comt, Second Int Mycol Cong, 75-77; mem adv comt, Proj Flora Amazonica & sci dir cryptogams, Orgn Flora Neotropica, 76-78. *Mem:* Mycol Soc Am; Sigma Xi. *Res:* Taxonomic studies in the fungal family Sclerotiniaceae and related genera of Discomycetes. *Mailing Add:* NY Bot Garden Bronx NY 10458

DUMONTELLE, PAUL BERTRAND, b Kankakee, Ill, June 22, 33; m 55; c 5. GEOLOGY. *Educ:* DePauw Univ, BA, 55; Lehigh Univ, MS, 57. *Prof Exp:* Geologist, Homestake Mining Co, 57-63; geologist, 63-74, coordr, Environ Geol, 74-79, geologist in chg, Earth Mat Technol Sect, Environ Geol, 79, GEOLOGIST & HEAD, ENG GEOL SECT, ILL STATE GEOL SURV, 79- *Mem:* Fel Geol Soc Am; Am Inst Prof Geologists; Asn Engr Geologists; Am Cong Surv & Mapping. *Res:* Engineering and environmental geology; topographic and computer mapping. *Mailing Add:* 2020 Burlison Dr Urbana IL 61801

DUNAGAN, TOMMY TOLSON, b Hamilton, Tex, Oct 17, 31; m 56; c 2. PHYSIOLOGY. *Educ:* Tex A&M Univ, BS, 53, MS, 55; Purdue Univ, PhD(zool), 60. *Prof Exp:* Parasitologist, Arctic Aeromed Lab, 55-57; NIH res fel, Purdue Univ, 58-62; from asst prof to assoc prof, 62-71, PROF PHYSIOL, SOUTHERN ILL UNIV, 71- *Mem:* Am Soc Parasitol; NY Acad Sci. *Res:* Physiological parasitology; biochemistry; tissue culture of helminths. *Mailing Add:* Dept of Physiol Southern Ill Univ Carbondale IL 62901

DUNAVIN, LEONARD SYPRET, JR, b Algood, Tenn, Dec 17, 30; m 62; c 2. AGRONOMY. *Educ:* Tenn Polytech Inst, BS, 52; Univ Fla, MSA, 54, PhD(agron), 59. *Prof Exp:* Asst agronomist, 59-67, ASSOC AGRONOMIST, AGR RES CTR, UNIV FLA, JAY, 67- *Mem:* Am Soc Agron; Crop Sci Soc Am. *Res:* Production and management of pasture and forage crops. *Mailing Add:* Agr Res Ctr Rte 3 Box 575 Jay FL 32565

DUNAWAY, GEORGE ALTON, JR, b Ironton, Mo, June 6, 41; m 67; c 2. BIOCHEMISTRY, ENZYMOLOGY. *Educ:* Cent State Univ, Okla, BS, 65; Univ Okla, PhD(biochem), 70. *Prof Exp:* Res assoc pharmacol, Ind Univ Sch Med, 70-73; sr res assoc cell & molecular biol, State Univ NY, Buffalo, 73-75; asst prof biochem, 75-79, PROF PHARMACOL & BIOCHEM, SCH MED, SOUTHERN ILL UNIV, 79- *Concurrent Pos:* Prin investr, Am Cancer Soc grant, 76-78 & Am Diabetes Asn grant, 76-77; Am Heart grant, 79-81; Nat Inst Arthritis, Metabolism & Digestive Dis grant, 79-82. *Mem:* AAAS; Sigma Xi; Am Soc Biol Chemists; Am Asn Cancer Res. *Res:* Enzymological changes associated with diabetes, nutrition, cancer and development. *Mailing Add:* Dept Pharmacol PO Box 3926 Springfield IL 62708

DUNBAR, BONNIE SUE, b Sterling, Colo, Feb 14, 48. REPRODUCTIVE BIOLOGY, ZOOLOGY. *Educ:* Univ Colo, BA, 70, MA, 71; Univ Tenn, PhD(zool), 77. *Prof Exp:* Scientist, Oceanog Mariculture Industs, 71-72; sr technician marine biol, Harbor Br Found, Smithsonian Inst Ft Pierce Bur, 72-74; res asst reproductive biol, Inst Molecular & Cellular Evolution, Univ Miami, 75; fel, Univ Calif, Davis, 77-78; staff scientist reproductive biol, Pop Coun, Rockefeller Univ, 78-81; ASST PROF, DEPT CELL BIOL, BAYLOR COL MED, HOUSTON, 81- *Mem:* AAAS; Soc Study Reproduction. *Res:* Reproductive biology with particular interest in problems associated with fertilization. *Mailing Add:* Baylor Col Med 1200 Moursund Ave Houston TX 77030

DUNBAR, BURDETT SHERIDAN, b Kewanee, Ill, Dec 6, 38; m 71. MEDICINE, ANESTHESIOLOGY. *Educ:* Univ Ill, Urbana, BS, 60, MD, 63. *Prof Exp:* Intern, Springfield City Hosp, Ohio, 63-64; resident anesthesiol, Hosp Univ Pa, 64-66; clin asst prof, Med Sch, Univ Tex, San Antonio, 68-69; asst prof, Univ Chicago, 69-71; asst prof to assoc prof, 71-74, PROF ANESTHESIOL/CHILD HEALTH & DEVELOP, GEORGE WASHINGTON UNIV & SR ATTEND ANESTHESIOLOGIST, CHILDREN'S HOSP NAT MED CTR, 74- *Concurrent Pos:* NIH res fel, Dept Physiol, Grad Sch Med, Univ Pa, 66-67; attend staff physician, Michael Reese Hosp & Med Ctr, 69-71; staff anesthesiologist, George Washington Univ Hosp, 71-74. *Mem:* AAAS; AMA; Am Soc Anesthesiologists. *Res:* Respiratory physiology. *Mailing Add:* Dept Anesthesiol Children's Hosp Nat Med Ctr Washington DC 20010

DUNBAR, CARL OWEN, paleontology, deceased

DUNBAR, DENNIS MONROE, b Porterville, Calif, May 30, 45; m 67; c 1. ENTOMOLOGY. *Educ:* Fresno State Col, BA, 67; Univ Calif, Davis, PhD(entom), 71. *Prof Exp:* NSF trainee entom, Univ Calif, Davis, 68-70; assoc entomologist urban entom, Conn Agr Exp Sta, New Haven, 70-76; ENTOMOLOGIST, AGR CHEM DIV, FMC CORP, RIVERSIDE, 76- *Mem:* Entom Soc Am; Am Regist Prof Entomologists; Sigma Xi. *Res:* Biology and control of insect pests that attack turf, ornamentals, Christmas trees and shade trees; cotton insect control. *Mailing Add:* FMC Corp Agr Chem Div 612 Parker Dr Clinton MS 39056

DUNBAR, HOWARD STANFORD, b Jersey City, NJ, Sept 30, 19; m 44; c 3. NEUROSURGERY. *Educ:* Cornell Univ, AB, 41, MD, 44. *Prof Exp:* Asst prof neurosurg, 52-64, assoc prof neurol surg, 64-74, prof, 74-79, EMER PROF NEUROL SURG, MED COL, CORNELL UNIV, 79- *Concurrent Pos:* Ledyard fel, Med Col, Cornell Univ, 51-52; dir neurosurg, Roosevelt Hosp; consult, Montrose Vet Hosp. *Mem:* Fel Am Col Surg; Harvey Soc. *Res:* Radioisotopes in localization of brain lesions; stereotaxic surgery. *Mailing Add:* 20 Turret Shell Lane Hilton Head SC 29928

DUNBAR, JOHN SCOTT, b Toronto, Ont, Aug 16, 21; m 49; c 3. RADIOLOGY. *Educ:* Univ Toronto, MD, 45. *Prof Exp:* Dir radiol dept, Montreal Children's Hosp, 52-71, assoc prof med, McGill Univ, 63-71, prof diag radiol & chmn dept, 68-71; prof diag radiol & chmn dept, Univ BC & dir dept diag radiol, Vancouver Gen Hosp, 71-75; DIR, DIV ROENTGENOL, CHILDREN'S HOSP MED CTR & PROF RADIOL & PEDIAT, COL MED, UNIV CINCINNATI, 75- *Mem:* Am Roentgen Ray Soc; Soc Pediat Radiol; Asn Univ Radiologists; Am Col Radiol; Radiol Soc NAm. *Res:* Diagnostic radiology. *Mailing Add:* Div of Roentgenol Children's Hosp Med Ctr Cincinnati OH 45229

DUNBAR, JOSEPH EDWARD, b Bristol, Conn, Feb 9, 24; m 51; c 5. PHARMACEUTICS. *Educ:* Rensselaer Polytech Inst, BS, 49; Univ Ill, MS, 52, PhD(chem), 56. *Prof Exp:* Asst org res chemist, Ill Geol Surv, 49-53; org res chemist, 55-62, sr res chemist, 62-66, group leader, E C Britton Res Lab, 66-73, sr res specialist, Pharmaceut Res & Develop, 73-76, sr res specialist, Biochem Processes Lab, 76-79, RES ASSOC, BIOPROD RES LAB, DOW CHEM USA, 79- *Mem:* AAAS; Am Chem Soc; Am Inst Chem; Sigma Xi. *Res:* Correlation of chemical structure with biological activity; chemistry of organic sulfur compounds; bioalkylating agents; cardiovascular research; design and synthesis of antithrombotic and hypolipidemic drugs; urinary tract antimicrobial research; plant growth regulators; animal growth promoters. *Mailing Add:* 5813 Sturgeon Creek Pkwy Midland MI 48640

DUNBAR, MAXWELL JOHN, b Edinburgh, Scotland, Sept 19, 14; m 45. OCEANOGRAPHY. *Educ:* Oxford Univ, BA, 37, MA, 39; McGill Univ, PhD(zool), 41. *Hon Degrees:* DSc, Mem Univ Nfld, 79. *Prof Exp:* Can Consul, Dept External Affairs, Greenland, 41-46; from asst prof to assoc prof, 46-59, chmn, Marine Sci Centre, 63-77, PROF ZOOL, MCGILL UNIV, 59- *Concurrent Pos:* Guggenheim fel, Denmark, 52-53; convenor, Int Biol Prog, 70-; fel, Arctic Inst NAm, 73. *Honors & Awards:* Bruce Medal for Polar Explor, Royal Soc Edinburgh; Fry Medal, Can Soc Zoologists, 79. *Mem:* Fel AAAS; hon fel Am Geog Soc; fel Royal Soc Can; fel Royal Geog Soc; fel Linnean Soc. *Res:* Marine biology and oceanography; arctic regions; breeding cycles in the arctic plankton; production in arctic water; development of arctic marine resources; history of biology; evolutionary mechanisms in the ecosystem. *Mailing Add:* Marine Sci Centre McGill Univ PO Box 6070 Montreal PQ H3A 2T5 Can

DUNBAR, PHYLLIS MARGUERITE, b Bronxville, NY. PHYSICAL CHEMISTRY. *Educ:* Columbia Univ, BA, 45, MA, 47, PhD(chem), 49. *Prof Exp:* Asst chem, Barnard Col, Columbia Univ, 43-45, lectr, 45-46; fel, Med Col, Cornell Univ, 49-50; ASSOC PROF CHEM, DOUGLASS COL, RUTGERS UNIV, 50- *Concurrent Pos:* Asst, Babies Hosp, Col Physicians & Surgeons, Columbia Univ. *Mem:* Am Chem Soc. *Res:* Reaction mechanisms; structure and reactivity. *Mailing Add:* Dept of Chem Douglass Col Rutgers Univ New Brunswick NJ 08901

DUNBAR, RICHARD ALAN, b Buffalo, NY, Sept 22, 40; m 64; c 3. POLYMER CHEMISTRY. *Educ:* St Bonaventure Univ, BS, 62; Univ Del, PhD(org chem), 67. *Prof Exp:* Res chemist, E I du Pont de Nemours & Co, Inc, 67-68; res specialist, 68-80, SPECIALIST PROCESS CHEM, MONSANTO CHEM INTERMEDIATES DIV, MONSANTO CO, PENSACOLA, FLA, 80- *Mem:* Am Chem Soc; Sigma Xi. *Res:* Polymer preparation; melt spinning; fabric construction; end-use testing; economic evaluation and scale-up studies. *Mailing Add:* Pensacola Tech Ctr PO Box 12830 Pensacola FL 32575

DUNBAR, ROBERT COPELAND, b Boston, Mass, June 26, 43; m 69; c 2. PHYSICAL CHEMISTRY. *Educ:* Harvard Univ, AB, 65; Stanford Univ, PhD(chem physics), 70. *Prof Exp:* Res assoc chem, Stanford Univ, 70; asst prof, 70-75, assoc prof chem, 75-78, PROF CHEM, CASE WESTERN RESERVE UNIV, 78- *Concurrent Pos:* Sloan fel, 73-75; Guggenheim fel, 78-79. *Mem:* Am Phys Soc; Am Chem Soc; Am Soc Mass Spectrometry; Inter-Am Photochem Soc. *Res:* Ion-molecule reaction processes in gas phase; properties of gas-phase ions; ion cyclotron resonance spectroscopy. *Mailing Add:* Dept of Chem Case Western Reserve Univ Cleveland OH 44106

DUNBAR, ROBERT STANDISH, JR, b Providence, RI, Nov 30, 21; m 41; c 2. ANIMAL BREEDING. *Educ:* Univ RI, BS, 49; Cornell Univ, MS, 50, PhD(animal breeding), 52. *Prof Exp:* Assoc prof dairy husb, 52-57, assoc statistician, 57-62, chmn dept animal indust & vet sci, 62-64, dean, Col Agr & Forestry, 64-74, dir, Agr Exp Sta, 71-74, PROF ANIMAL SCI, WVA UNIV, 74- *Mem:* Am Soc Animal Sci; Am Genetic Asn. *Res:* Breeding systems and methods of selection in beef cattle; statistical analysis; biological experiments. *Mailing Add:* Col of Agr & Forestry WVa Univ Morgantown WV 26506

DUNCALF, DERYCK, b York, Eng, Nov 14, 26; US citizen; m 50, 75; c 1. MEDICINE, ANESTHESIOLOGY. *Educ:* Univ Leeds, MB & ChB, 50; Royal Col Physicians London, dipl anesthetics, 53; Royal Col Surgeons Eng, dipl, 53; fel fac anaesthetists; Am Bd Anesthesiol, dipl, 60. *Prof Exp:* House physician, St James Hosp, Leeds, Eng, 50, jr anesthetic officer, 50-51; anesthetic officer, Gen Infirmary, 51-52; res surg officer, Clayton Hosp, Wakefield, 52-53; registr anesthetist, United Leeds Hosp, 53-54; sr registr dept anesthetics, Welsh Nat Sch Med, Univ Wales, 54-56; asst prof anesthesiol, State Univ NY Downstate Med Ctr, 58-61; asst clin prof, Col Physicians & Surgeons, Columbia Univ, 62-64; assoc prof clin anesthesiol, 65-67, assoc prof anesthesiol, 67-71, PROF ANESTHESIOL, ALBERT EINSTEIN COL MED, 71- *Concurrent Pos:* Exchange fel anesthesiol, Mercy Hosp, Pittsburgh, 56-57, assoc dir anesthesia res, 61-62; clin fel anesthesia, Montreal Children's Hosp, 57-58; vis instr, Sch Med, Univ Pittsburgh, 56-57; assoc attend anesthesiologist, Kings County Hosp, Brooklyn, NY, 59-61; actg chief dept anesthesia, Vet Admin Hosp, 61-62; assoc attend anesthesiologist, Montefiore Hosp & Med Ctr, Bronx, NY, 62-64, attend anesthesiologist, 64-, dir anesthesiol residency training prog, 70-75, chmn dept anesthesiol, 75-; assoc vis anesthesiologist, Morrisania City Hosp, 63-75, consult anesthesiologist, 75-; assoc vis anesthesiologist, Bronx Munic Hosp Ctr, 65-69; consult, Wyckoff Heights Hosp, Brooklyn, 66- *Mem:* AAAS; NY Acad Med; Am Soc Anesthesiologists; NY Acad Sci; Asn Anaesthetists Gt Brit & Ireland. *Res:* Pharmacology of muscle relaxants and narcotics; anesthesia in ophthalmology; physiology of respiratory insufficiency; mechanical ventilation. *Mailing Add:* Dept of Anesthesiol Montefiore Hosp & Med Ctr Bronx NY 10461

DUNCAN, ACHESON JOHNSTON, b Leonia, NJ, Sept 24, 04; m 59. APPLIED STATISTICS. *Educ:* Princeton Univ, BS, 25, MA, 27, PhD(econ), 36. *Prof Exp:* From instr to asst prof econ & statist, Princeton Univ, 29-45; from assoc prof to prof statist, 46-71, EMER PROF STATIST, JOHNS HOPKINS UNIV, 71- *Honors & Awards:* Shewhart Medal, Am Soc Qual Control, 64; Dodge Award, Am Soc Testing & Mat, 76. *Mem:* Am Statist Asn; Inst Math Statist; Am Soc Qual Control; Am Soc Testing & Mat; Biomet Soc. *Res:* Economic design of control charts; sampling of bulk material. *Mailing Add:* 4406 Rolnd Ave Baltimore MD 21210

DUNCAN, ANDREW A, b Pencaitland, Scotland, Mar 13, 21; US citizen; m 44, 76; c 4. HORTICULTURE. *Educ:* Univ Md, BS, 50, MS, 52, PhD(physiol), 56. *Prof Exp:* Exten specialist veg crops, Univ Md, 52-58 & Ore State Univ, 58-70; prof hort sci & head dept, Univ Minn, St Paul, 70-75; PROF & DIR AGR RES & EDUC CTR, UNIV FLA, HOMESTEAD, 75- *Mem:* Am Soc Hort Sci. *Res:* Subtropical commercial vegetable production. *Mailing Add:* Agr Res & Educ Ctr 18905 SW 280th St Homestead FL 33030

DUNCAN, BETTIE, b Ashland, Miss, June 21, 33. MICROBIOLOGY. *Educ:* Judson Col, AB, 55; Birmingham-Southern Col, MS, 61; Univ Ark, PhD(microbiol), 66. *Prof Exp:* Assoc biologist, Southern Res Inst, Ala, 57-62; from asst prof to assoc prof, 66-72, PROF MICROBIOL, KANS STATE COL PITTSBURG, 72- *Mem:* Am Soc Microbiol; NY Acad Sci. *Res:* Rare earth metal effects on microorganisms; pigment production in fungi; microbial ecology of the strip pits of southeastern Kansas; nutrition and fat production in fungi. *Mailing Add:* Dept of Biol Kans State Col Pittsburg KS 66762

DUNCAN, BRYAN LEE, b Kansas City, Kans, July 23, 42; m 66; c 2. FISHERIES. *Educ:* Kans State Univ, Pittsburg, BA, 64; Wayne State Univ, PhD(biol), 72. *Prof Exp:* Asst prof biol, Houghton Col, 70-72; US Peace Corps vol aquacult, 72-75; ASST PROF FISHERIES, AUBURN UNIV, 75- *Concurrent Pos:* Fel, Auburn Univ, 75; leader brackish water pond cult proj, Indonesia, 76-81. *Mem:* Am Fisheries Soc; World Maricult Soc. *Res:* Warm-water fish culture; parasites and diseases of cultured fish; pond construction; aquaculture information systems. *Mailing Add:* Dept of Fish & Allied Aquacult Auburn Univ Auburn AL 36830

DUNCAN, BUDD LEE, b Thief River Falls, Minn, Nov 15, 36; m 58; c 3. PHYSICAL CHEMISTRY. *Educ:* Macalester Col, BA, 58; SDak State Univ, MS, 60; Univ Tenn, PhD, 70. *Prof Exp:* Assoc prof chem, Tenn Wesleyan Col, 61-70, chmn dept, 76-79; sr res assoc, Olin Chem, 79-81; PROF CHEM, TENN WESLEYAN COL, 70-; GROUP LEADER, OLIN CHEM, 82- *Mem:* Am Chem Soc; Coblentz Soc. *Res:* Kinetics of Diels-Alder reactions; infra-red spectroscopy. *Mailing Add:* 1207 Towanda Trail Athins TN 37303

DUNCAN, CHARLES DONALD, b Houston, Tex, Oct 7, 48. PHYSICAL ORGANIC CHEMISTRY, THEORETICAL CHEMISTRY. *Educ:* Rice Univ, BA, 70; Yale Univ, PhD(org chem), 74. *Prof Exp:* Instr chem, Univ Va, 74-76; ASST PROF CHEM, UNIV ALA, BIRMINGHAM, 76- *Mem:* Sigma Xi; Am Chem Soc. *Res:* Forbidden organic reactions; kinetics of unimolecular decompositions; singlet|triplet interconversions; chemistry of organic biradicals. *Mailing Add:* Dept of Chem Univ of Ala Birmingham AL 35294

DUNCAN, CHARLES LEE, b Waynesboro, Tenn, Oct 10, 39; m 68. BACTERIOLOGY. *Educ:* Univ Tenn, BS, 61; La State Univ, Baton Rouge, MS, 63; Univ Wis, Madison, PhD(bact), 67. *Prof Exp:* From asst prof to prof bact & food microbiol, Univ Wis-Madison, 68-76; DIR FOOD SAFETY & NUTRITION, CAMPBELL INST FOOD RES, 77-, VPRES, FOOD SCI & TECHNOL, CAMPBELL INST RES & TECHNOL, 79- *Concurrent Pos:* Res Develop Award, Nat Inst Allergy & Infectious Dis, 74. *Mem:* Am Soc Microbiol; Inst Food Technologists. *Res:* Clostridium perfringens food poisoning; sporulation of anaerobic bacteria and germination of their spores; clostridial plasmids; foods and food ingredients. *Mailing Add:* Campbell Inst Res & Technol Camden NJ 08101

DUNCAN, DENNIS ANDREW, b Edinburgh, Scotland, Sept 24, 29; US citizen; m 60; c 2. CHEMICAL ENGINEERING. *Educ:* Univ BC, BA, 49, BASc, 57. *Prof Exp:* Res & process engr oil-gas, Portland Gas & Coke Co, 57-58; sr res engr ethylene, Monsanto Co, 58-64; supvr process develop pyrolysis petrochem, Stone & Webster Eng Corp, 64-72; prof mgr coal gasification res, Am Gas Asn, 72-74; assoc dir hydrocarbon processing res, Inst Gas Technol, 74-81; PROG MGR, PROCESS DEVELOP, STONE & WEBSTER ENG CORP, 81- *Mem:* Am Inst Chem Engrs; Am Chem Soc. *Res:* High temperature, short residence time pyrolysis of hydrocarbons, including steam-cracking to ethylene and other petrochemicals; high pressure hydropyrolysis of coal to liquid and gaseous fuels. *Mailing Add:* Stone & Webster Eng Corp 1 Pen Plaza New York NY 10119

DUNCAN, DON DARRYL, b Mayfield, Ky, Sept 9, 39; m 58; c 2. PHYSICS. *Educ:* Murray State Univ, BS, 61; Univ Ky, MS, 63, PhD(physics), 68. *Prof Exp:* Asst prof, 67-70, ASSOC PROF PHYSICS, MURRAY STATE UNIV, 70- *Mem:* Am Phys Soc. *Res:* Angular correlation studies in nuclear physics. *Mailing Add:* Dept of Physics Murray State Univ Murray KY 42071

DUNCAN, DONALD, b Marietta, Minn, Jan 31, 03; m 24; c 3. ANATOMY. *Educ:* Carleton Col, AB, 23; Univ Minn, AM, 27, PhD(anat), 29. *Prof Exp:* Asst prof anat, Univ Utah, 29-30 & Univ Buffalo, 30-32; from assoc prof to prof, Sch Med, Univ Tex, 32-42; prof & head dept, Sch Med, Univ Buffalo, 42-43; prof, Sch Med, La State Univ, 43-46; prof & chmn dept, 46-68, assoc dean grad sch, 52-69, ASHBEL SMITH PROF ANAT, UNIV TEX MED BR GALVESTON, 68- *Concurrent Pos:* Managing ed jour, Am Asn Anatomists, 60-68; vis prof anat, Stanford Univ, 75, 76 & 78. *Honors & Awards:* Henry Gray Award, Am Asn Anatomists, 71. *Mem:* Am Asn Anatomists (1st vpres, 61, pres, 67); Soc Exp Biol & Med; Am Asn Phys Anthropologists; Am Acad Neurol. *Res:* Degeneration and regeneration of nerve fibers; myelination; structure of spinal nerve roots; action of oil anesthetics; pathology of the spinal cord and cerebellum; history of anatomy; electron microscopy of nervous system. *Mailing Add:* Dept of Anat Univ of Tex Med Br Galveston TX 77550

DUNCAN, DONALD GORDON, b Lincoln, Nebr, Apr 21, 20. MATHEMATICS. *Educ:* Univ BC, BA, 42, MS, 44; Univ Mich, PhD(math), 51. *Prof Exp:* Res engr, Nat Res Coun Can, 43-44; lectr physics, McGill Univ, 44-45; lectr math, Univ BC, 45-47; asst prof, Univ Ariz, 50-54; from asst prof to assoc prof, San Jose State Col, 54-60, prof, 60-63; PROF MATH, CALIF STATE COL SONOMA, 63- *Concurrent Pos:* Consult, Off Naval Res, 57- *Mem:* Am Math Soc; Math Asn Am; London Math Soc. *Res:* Theory of groups; lattice theory; aerodynamics; numerical analysis. *Mailing Add:* Calif State Col Sonoma Rohnert Park CA 94828

DUNCAN, DONALD LEE, b Farmington, Mo, June 7, 30; m 55. MATHEMATICS. *Educ:* Univ Mo-Rolla, BS, 52; Univ Mo-Columbia, MS, 57; Univ Fla, PhD(math), 62. *Prof Exp:* Chem engr design & develop, Union Carbide Nuclear Co, Tenn, 52-53; technician sales & serv, Enjay Chem Co Div, Standard Oil Co NJ, NY, 57-59; assoc prof math, Ga State Univ, 62-67; assoc prof, 67-74, head dept, 67-77, PROF MATH, VALDOSTA STATE

COL, 74- *Concurrent Pos:* Sr res scientist, Ga Inst Technol, 66- *Mem:* Am Math Soc; Math Asn Am. *Res:* Ordinary and partial differential equations; orthogonal polynomials; complex variables; applied mathematics; biomathematics. *Mailing Add:* 2410 Georgia Ave Valdosta GA 31601

DUNCAN, DONALD PENDLETON, b Joliet, Ill, Feb 24, 16; m 56; c 3. FORESTRY. *Educ:* Univ Mich, BSF, 37, MS, 39; Univ Minn, PhD(forestry, bot), 51. *Prof Exp:* Shelterbelt supvr, US Forest Serv, Kans, 39-40; jr forester, Southern Forest Exp Sta, La, 40-41; instr forestry & forester, Exp Sta, Kans State Col, 41-42, asst prof exten, 45-47; from instr to prof forestry, Univ Minn, 47-65, asst dir sch forestry, 64-65; PROF FORESTRY & DIR SCH FORESTRY, FISHERIES & WILDLIFE, UNIV MO-COLUMBIA, 65- *Concurrent Pos:* Consult, Minn Natural Resources Coun, 61-63; vis scientist, Nat Sci Found, 64-65, 68, 69 & 72; consult, Ford Found Latin-Am Fel Prog, 68 & 70, Coop State Res Serv, USDA, 69, 74 & 75 & Coun Grad Schs, 70, forest ecologist, 80-81. *Mem:* AAAS; Soc Am Foresters; Ecol Soc Am; Wildlife Soc; Sigma Xi. *Res:* Forest ecology; forest influences; forest recreation. *Mailing Add:* Sch Forest Fisheries & Wildlife Univ of Mo Columbia MO 65201

DUNCAN, DOUGLAS WALLACE, b Vancouver, BC, Sept 7, 34; m 58; c 2. APPLIED MICROBIOLOGY, RESEARCH ADMINISTRATION. *Educ:* Univ BC, BSA, 57; Mass Inst Technol, PhD(food technol), 61. *Prof Exp:* Mem res staff, Knorr Forschungs Inst, Corn Prod Co, Switz, 61-62; sr microbiologist, 62-65, prog leader microbiol, 65-72, assoc head div appl biol, 72-76, HEAD, DIV CHEM TECHNOL, BS RES COUN, 76-, ASSOC DIR, 82- *Mem:* Brit Soc Gen Microbiol; Forest Prod Res Soc. *Res:* Microbiological leaching of sulfide minerals; gasification of wood waste; TRS compounds in pulp mill emissions; coal liquefaction; fluid bed technology; alternate fuelling of motor vehicles; electro chemistry; wood chemistry; analytical chemistry; industrial chemistry. *Mailing Add:* Chem Tech BC Res 3650 Wesbrook Mall Vancouver BC V6S 2L2 Can

DUNCAN, GEORGE COMER, b Durham, NC, Dec 23, 41; m 67; c 2. PHYSICS. *Educ:* NC State Univ, BS, 64, MS, 66; Brandeis Univ, PhD(physics), 71. *Prof Exp:* From asst prof to assoc prof, 70-80, PROF PHYSICS, BOWLING GREEN STATE UNIV, 80- *Concurrent Pos:* Prin investr, NSF grant, 77. *Mem:* Am Phys Soc; Sigma Xi. *Res:* General relativity and gravitation; mathematical physics; quantum optics; biophysics; light scattering. *Mailing Add:* Dept of Physics Bowling Green State Univ Bowling Green OH 43403

DUNCAN, GEORGE THOMAS, b Chicago, Ill, Aug 7, 42. STATISTICS. *Educ:* Univ Chicago, BS, 63, MS, 64; Univ Minn, PhD(statist), 70. *Prof Exp:* Statistician, Texaco Res Labs, 64-65; vol, US Peace Corps, Philippines, 65-67; asst prof math, Univ Calif, Davis, 70-74; ASSOC PROF STATIST, CARNEGIE-MELLON UNIV, 74- *Mem:* Inst Math Statist; fel Am Statist Asn; Opers Res Soc. *Res:* Applied statistics and decision theory. *Mailing Add:* Dept of Statist Carnegie-Mellon Univ Pittsburgh PA 15213

DUNCAN, GERALD R, pharmacy, see previous edition

DUNCAN, GORDON DUKE, b Clayton, NC, May 25, 26; m 51, 81; c 3. BIOCHEMISTRY. *Educ:* NC State Col, BS, 49, PhD(biochem), 53. *Prof Exp:* Asst, US Plant, Soil & Nutrit Lab, Cornell Univ, 49-53; biochemist, Biochem Res Lab, Elgin State Hosp, 53-57; biochemist, Charlotte Mem Hosp, 57-67; PROF CHEM, QUEENS COL, NC, 67- *Concurrent Pos:* Chmn bd dirs, AquAir Labs Inc; consult biochemist, Cabarrus Mem Hosp, 74- *Res:* Clinical biochemistry. *Mailing Add:* 568 Wakefield Dr Charlotte NC 28209

DUNCAN, GORDON W, b Weehawken, NJ, July 3, 32; m 55; c 4. ENDOCRINOLOGY. *Educ:* Cornell Univ, BS, 54; Iowa State Univ, MS, 55, PhD(reprod physiol), 60. *Prof Exp:* Res assoc & asst prof animal physiol, Iowa State Univ, 59-60; sr res scientist, Upjohn Co, 60-71; sr res scientist, Seattle Res Ctr, Univ Wash, 71-74, asst prof, Endocrinol, 73-80, DIR, POP STUDY CTR, BATTELLE MEM INST, 74-; MGR, UPJOHN CO, KALAMAZOO, MICH, 80- *Concurrent Pos:* Lectr, Western Mich Univ, 60-71. *Mem:* Soc Study Reprod; Am Soc Animal Sci; Endocrine Soc; Am Physiol Soc; Brit Soc Study Fertil. *Res:* Basic and applied research in physiology of reproduction. *Mailing Add:* Upjohn Co Kalamazoo MI 49001

DUNCAN, HARRY ERNEST, b Hartford, WVa, Nov 20, 36; m 58; c 3. PLANT PATHOLOGY. *Educ:* Univ WVa, BS, 59, MS, 61, PhD(plant path), 66. *Prof Exp:* From exten instr to exten assoc prof plant path, 66-77, PROF PLANT PATH & SPECIALIST IN CHARGE, PLANT PATH EXTEN, NC STATE UNIV, 77- *Mem:* Am Phytopath Soc. *Res:* Diseases of vegetable crops and corn; pesticides in plant disease control; extension plant pathology. *Mailing Add:* 1409 Gardner Hall NC State Univ Raleigh NC 27607

DUNCAN, I B R, b Kilmarnock, Scotland, Oct 10, 26; Can citizen; m 57; c 2. MEDICAL MICROBIOLOGY. *Educ:* Glasgow Univ, MB & ChB, 51, MD, 62; FRCP(C). *Prof Exp:* Asst lectr bact, Glasgow Univ, 52-55, lectr, 57-60; res bacteriologist, Hosp Sick Children, Toronto, Ont, 55-57; from asst prof to assoc prof bact, Univ Western Ont, 60-67; PROF MED MICROBIOL, UNIV TORONTO & DIR MICROBIOL, SUNNYBROOK MED CENTRE, 67- *Concurrent Pos:* Dir microbiol, St Joseph's Hosp, London, Ont, 60-67. *Mem:* Fel Col Path Eng; fel Infectious Dis Soc Am; Can Soc Microbiol (vpres, 69-70); Can Asn Med Microbiol (secy-treas, 62-67, pres, 75-76); Path Soc Gt Brit & Ireland. *Res:* Echoviruses; staphylococcal epidemiology; antibiotics and gramnegative bacilli; plasmid epidemiology. *Mailing Add:* Dept of Microbiol Sunnybrook Med Centre Toronto ON M4N 1E2 Can

DUNCAN, IRMA W, b Buffalo, NY, Jan 30, 12; m 37; c 2. CLINICAL CHEMISTRY. *Educ:* Univ Buffalo, BA, 33; Univ Chicago, MA, 35, PhD(biochem), 50. *Prof Exp:* Prof sci, Colo Woman's Col, Denver, 44-48; asst prof chem, Univ Denver, 51-59; res chemist, Arctic Health Res Ctr, Dept Health, Educ & Welfare, Anchorage, Alaska, 60-67, Fairbanks, 67-74; RES CHEMIST, CTR DIS CONTROL, DEPT HEALTH & HUMAN SERV, 74- *Concurrent Pos:* Public Health Serv grant, NIH, 56-57; adj prof chem, Alaska Methodist Univ, Anchorage, 60-62; mem Anchorage Area Subcomt Gov Planning Comt Mental Retardation Prog, 65-66, Gov Adv Comt Mental Retardation, Alaska, 66-72, chmn, 66-67. *Mem:* Am Asn Univ Women; Am Chem Soc; fel AAAS; Am Asn Clin Chemists; Am Pub Health Asn. *Res:* Genetic differences in enzymes of various human populations, methods and quality control for lipids, screening methods for human abnormlities. *Mailing Add:* 2438 Melinda Dr NE Atlanta GA 30345

DUNCAN, JAMES ALAN, b Osage, Iowa, Aug 14, 45. PHYSICAL ORGANIC CHEMISTRY. *Educ:* Luther Col, BA, 67; Univ Ore, PhD(org chem), 71. *Prof Exp:* Sub asst prof chem, Morgan State Col, 71-72; asst prof, Univ Notre Dame, 72-74 & Boston Univ, 74-75; vis asst prof chem, Reed Col, 75-77; vis asst prof, 77-78, ASST PROF CHEM, LEWIS & CLARK COL, 78- *Concurrent Pos:* Res Corp res grant, 73- *Mem:* Am Chem Soc. *Res:* Cycloaddition mechanisms and effects of molecular geometry on pericyclic reactions. *Mailing Add:* Dept of Chem Lewis & Clark Col Portland OR 97219

DUNCAN, JAMES LOWELL, b West Plains, Mo, Dec 14, 37; m 63; c 3. MEDICAL MICROBIOLOGY. *Educ:* Drury Col, AB, 59; St Louis Univ, DDS, 63; Univ Wash, PhD(microbiol), 67. *Prof Exp:* Asst prof, 67-74, ASSOC PROF MICROBIOL, MED & DENT SCHS, NORTHWESTERN UNIV, 74- *Mem:* AAAS; Am Soc Microbiol. *Res:* Bacterial toxins and their effects on mammalian tissues. *Mailing Add:* Dept of Microbiol Northwestern Univ Chicago IL 60611

DUNCAN, JAMES M(OYER), systems & process engineering, see previous edition

DUNCAN, JAMES PLAYFORD, b Adelaide, SAustralia, Nov 10, 19; m 42; c 4. MECHANICAL ENGINEERING. *Educ:* Univ Adelaide, BE, 41, ME, 54; Univ Manchester, DSc(sci publ), 64. *Prof Exp:* Develop engr, Richards Industs Ltd, 41-47; lectr mech eng, Univ Adelaide, 47-51, sr lectr, 53-54; turbine engr, Metrop Vickers Elec Co, Manchester, 52; prof mech eng & head dept, Univ Sheffield, 57-66; head dept, 66-80, PROF MECH ENG, UNIV BC, 66- *Concurrent Pos:* Consult, Firth Brown Tools Ltd, Eng, 61-66, Perkin-Elmer Corp, 66-68 & Caterpillar Tractor Co, 67-; vchmn adv comt, Royal Engrs Eng, 62-66. *Mem:* Soc Exp Stress Anal; assoc Inst Engrs, Australia; Brit Inst Mech Engrs; Brit Inst Prod Engrs; Brit Inst Physics & Phys Soc. *Res:* Design and production of automobile and aircraft sheet metal; stress analysis by optical means of steam power plant components; surface generation by numerical control. *Mailing Add:* Dept of Mech Eng Univ of BC Vancouver BC V6T 1W5 Can

DUNCAN, JAMES THAYER, b Chicago, Ill, Apr 15, 32; div; c 1. DEVELOPMENTAL BIOLOGY. *Educ:* Wabash Col, AB, 54; Stanford Univ, PhD(biol), 60. *Prof Exp:* Asst prof zool, Univ Calif, Riverside, 60-62; from asst prof to assoc prof biol, 62-72, PROF BIOL, SAN FRANCISCO STATE UNIV, 72- *Concurrent Pos:* Am Cancer Soc res grant, 61-63; NSF res grants, 63-65, 68-71; NSF sci fac fel, 65-66. *Mem:* AAAS; Am Soc Zool; Soc Develop Biol. *Res:* Embryonic induction and the developmental control of cellular differentiation in Amphibians. *Mailing Add:* Dept of Biol San Francisco State Univ San Francisco CA 94132

DUNCAN, JOHN L(EASK), b Adelaide, SAustralia, Dec 20, 32; m 61; c 3. MECHANICAL ENGINEERING. *Educ:* Univ Melbourne, BME, 55; Univ Manchester, MST, 63, PhD(eng), 68. *Prof Exp:* Trainee, Caterpillar Tractor Co, 56-58; planning supvr, Caterpillar of Australia Proprietary Ltd, 58-60; asst field engr, Vacuum Oil Co, 60-61; asst lectr eng educ, Inst Sci & Technol, Univ Manchester, 62-63, lectr, 63-68, sr lectr, 68-70; PROF ENG EDUC, McMASTER UNIV, 70- *Mem:* Am Soc Metals. *Res:* Engineering plasticity; sheet metal technology; manufacturing and production processes; metal forming; alloy development. *Mailing Add:* Dept of Mech Eng McMaster Univ Hamilton ON L8S 4L8 Can

DUNCAN, JOHN ROBERT, b Morden, Man, July 17, 37; m 63; c 3. IMMUNOPATHOLOGY. *Educ:* Univ Man, BSA, 59; Univ Toronto, DVM, 63; Univ Guelph, MS, 68; Cornell Univ, PhD(vet immunol), 73; Am Col Vet Pathologists, dipl, 73. *Prof Exp:* Pvt pract, Dauphin Vet Clin, 63-66; asst prof vet path, Ont Vet Col, 66-67; asst vet immunol, Cornell Univ, 68-71, asst prof vet immunol, 71-76; RES SCIENTIST, ANIMAL DISEASES RES INST, 76- *Mem:* Am Vet Med Asn; Am Col Vet Pathologists. *Res:* Immunopathology of infectious diseases of domestic animals, particularly Johne's Disease, venereal vibriosis, characterization of bovine immunoglobulins. *Mailing Add:* Animal Dis Res Inst 801 Fallowfield Rd Nepean ON K2H 8P9 Can

DUNCAN, KATHERINE, b Tamaroa, Ill, Oct 14, 13; m 39; c 2. INTERNAL MEDICINE. *Educ:* Univ Ill, BS, 35, MD, 38. *Prof Exp:* Intern, Hurley Hosp, Flint, Mich, 37-38; pvt pract, Ill, 38-41; staff physician, Crab Orchard Defense Plant, Ill, 43; asst med dir, Nutrit Res Lab, 43-45; attend physician pediat & maternity, Montgomery County Health Dept, Md, 52-53; med officer pharmacol, Bur Biol & Phys Sci, Food & Drug Admin, 60-61, admin med officer, Career Develop Rev Br, 61-70, ADMIN MED OFFICER, OFF PROTECTION FROM RISKS, OFF DIR, NIH, 70- *Res:* Rheumatoid diseases; allergy; medical administration. *Mailing Add:* Off Protection from Res Risks NIH Off of Dir Bethesda MD 20205

DUNCAN, LEONARD CLINTON, b Owensboro, Ky, Dec 28, 36; m 63; c 2. INORGANIC CHEMISTRY, ENVIRONMENTAL CHEMISTRY. *Educ:* Wabash Col, AB, 58; Wesleyan Univ, MA, 61; Univ Wash, PhD(chem), 64. *Prof Exp:* Fel inorg chem, Purdue Univ, 64-65; from asst prof to assoc prof, 65-72, chmn, Dept Chem, 66-68, PROF CHEM, CENT WASH UNIV, 72- *Concurrent Pos:* Res Corp & NSF res grants, 69; res grant, Wash Water Res Ctr, 80. *Mem:* Am Chem Soc. *Res:* Synthesis of highly fluorinated compounds of the lighter elements; environmental chemistry; acid precipitation studies; lake susceptibility studies. *Mailing Add:* Dept of Chem Cent Wash Univ Ellensburg WA 98926

DUNCAN, LEROY EDWARD, JR, b Norfolk, Va, July 30, 17; m 42; c 2. INTERNAL MEDICINE. *Educ:* Duke Univ, AB, 39; Johns Hopkins Univ, MD, 42; Am Bd Internal Med, dipl. *Prof Exp:* Intern, Johns Hopkins Hosp, 42-43, asst resident, 43-44; from asst resident to resident, Vanderbilt Hosp, 47-49; sr investr, Nat Heart Inst, 49-65; chief adult develop & aging br, Nat Inst Child Health & Human Develop, 65-74, spec proj officer, Nat Inst Aging, 74-78; RETIRED. *Concurrent Pos:* Mem coun on arteriosclerosis, Am Heart Asn. *Mem:* Fel Am Col Prev Med; AMA; Am Heart Asn; Am Fedn Clin Res; fel Am Col Physicians. *Res:* Heart failure; atherosclerosis; aging. *Mailing Add:* 400 W Montgomery Ave Rockville MD 20850

DUNCAN, LEWIS MANNAN, b Charleston, WVa, July 11, 51; m 75. NONLINEAR RADIO WAVE PROPAGATION. *Educ:* Rice Univ, BA, 73, MS, 76, PhD(space physics), 77. *Prof Exp:* MEM STAFF, LOS ALAMOS NAT LAB, 77- *Concurrent Pos:* NSF fel, Rice Univ, 77; mem, Arecibo SciAdv Comt, Nat Astron & Ionosphere Ctr, 80- *Mem:* Am Geophys Union; AAAS; Int Radio Sci Union; Sigma Xi. *Res:* High-power radio wave propagation and associated nonlinear wave-plasma interactions; ionospheric modification and active space plasma physics experiments; applications of the ionosphere as a large, natural plasma laboratory-without-walls. *Mailing Add:* Los Alamos Nat Lab Atmospheric Sci Group MS 466 Los Alamos NM 87545

DUNCAN, MARGARET CAROLINE, b Salt Lake City, Utah, June 9, 30; m 58; c 4. PEDIATRIC NEUROLOGY. *Educ:* Univ Tex, BA, 52, MD, 55; Am Bd Pediat, dipl, 62; Am Bd Psychiat & Neurol, cert neurol, 65, cert child neurol, 69. *Prof Exp:* From instr to assoc prof, 61-74, PROF PEDIAT NEUROL, SCH MED, LA STATE UNIV MED CTR, NEW ORLEANS, 74- *Concurrent Pos:* Fel pediat neurol, Johns Hopkins Univ, 60-61; consult, Handicapped Children's Prog, La State Bd Health, 64- *Mem:* Am Acad Neurol; Am Epilepsy Soc. *Res:* Reflex epilepsy; infantile neuroaxonal dystrophy; cerebral edema in infants and children. *Mailing Add:* Dept of Neurol La State Univ Med Ctr New Orleans LA 70112

DUNCAN, MARION M, JR, b Bloomfield, Mo, June 24, 27; m 48; c 2. THEORETICAL PHYSICS. *Educ:* Ala Polytech Inst, BS, 49, MS, 53; Duke Univ, PhD(physics), 56. *Prof Exp:* Instr, Univ NC, 56; vis asst prof, Duke Univ, 56-60; asst prof, Tex A&M Univ, 60-61; assoc prof, 61-66, PROF PHYSICS, UNIV GA, 66-, HEAD DEPT PHYSICS & ASTRON, 68- *Mem:* Am Phys Soc. *Res:* Low energy nuclear physics. *Mailing Add:* Dept of Physics & Astron Univ of Ga Athens GA 30601

DUNCAN, MICHAEL ROBERT, b Frederick, Okla, Oct 11, 47; m 71. CELL BIOLOGY, BIOCHEMISTRY. *Educ:* Okla Christian Col, BS, 69; Okla Univ, PhD(virol), 75. *Prof Exp:* Res assoc, 75-80, ASST SCIENTIST CELL BIOL, SAMUEL ROBERTS NOBLE FOUND, INC, 80- *Mem:* Tissue Cult Asn; Sigma Xi. *Res:* Studies of the basic molecular mechanisms of aging using human diploid fibroblasts cultured in vitro as a model system. *Mailing Add:* Samuel Roberts Noble Found Inc RR 1 Ardmore OK 73401

DUNCAN, RICHARD DALE, b Alhambra, Calif, Apr 1, 41; m 70; c 1. MATHEMATICS. *Educ:* Univ Calif, Berkeley, BSc, 63, MA, 65; Univ Calif, San Diego, PhD, 70. *Prof Exp:* Asst math, Univ Calif, Berkeley, 63-65 & Univ Calif, San Diego, 65-70; asst prof, 70-75, ASSOC PROF MATH, UNIV MONTREAL, 75- *Mem:* Am Math Soc; Can Math Soc. *Res:* Probability; functional analysis; Markov processes and potential theory; probability theory. *Mailing Add:* Dept of Math Univ of Montreal Montreal PQ H3C 3S7 Can

DUNCAN, RICHARD H(ENRY), b St Louis, Mo, Aug 13, 22; m; c 2. PHYSICS, ELECTRICAL ENGINEERING. *Educ:* Univ Mo, BSEE, 49, MS, 51, PhD(physics), 54. *Prof Exp:* Prof elec eng & physicist, phys sci lab, NMex State Univ, 54-65, vpres res, 65-69; TECH DIR & CHIEF SCIENTIST, WHITE SANDS MISSILE RANGE, 69- *Mem:* Inst Elec & Electronics Engrs. *Res:* Integral equations occurring in electromagnetic radiation problems; antenna engineering. *Mailing Add:* STEWS-SC White Sands Missile Range NM 88002

DUNCAN, ROBERT LEON, JR, b Ayer, Mass, Nov 1, 51; m 75; c 1. CELLULAR IMMUNOLOGY, MYCOLOGY. *Educ:* Bloomsburg State Col, BA, 74; Univ Pa, MA, 77, PhD(immunol), 80. *Prof Exp:* Instr immunol, Sch Allied Med Professions, Univ Pa, 78, path, 79-80; ASSOC DERMATOL, SCH MED, EMORY UNIV, 80- *Mem:* Am Soc Microbiol; NY Acad Sci; AAAS. *Res:* Mechanisms involved in transferrin mediated and T-lymphocyte mediated host defense against a variety of opportunistic fungi. *Mailing Add:* Dept Dermatol 215 Woodruff Mem Bldg Sch Med Emory Univ Atlanta GA 30322

DUNCAN, RONALD IAN, biophysics, see previous edition

DUNCAN, RONNY RUSH, b Hereford, Tex, May 21, 46; m 71; c 2. PLANT BREEDING, PLANT PHYSIOLOGY. *Educ:* Tex Technol Univ, BS, 69; Tex A&M Univ, MS, 74, PhD(plant breeding), 77. *Prof Exp:* ASST PROF SORGHUM PLANT BREEDING/PHYSIOL, UNIV GA, 77- *Mem:* Crop Sci Soc Am; Am Soc Agron; Sigma Xi. *Res:* Sorghum plant breeding and development of improved types for environmental stress situations such as: acid soil tolerance, micronutrient imbalances; pest problems, anthracnose resistance and insect pressure; and multiple cropping, minimum tillage practices. *Mailing Add:* Dept of Agron Ga Exp Sta Griffin GA 30212

DUNCAN, STEWART, b Danvers, Mass, Apr 18, 26; m 54; c 2. ZOOLOGY, PARASITOLOGY. *Educ:* Boston Univ, AB, 49, AM, 50, PhD(parasitol), 57. *Prof Exp:* From instr to assoc prof, 50-67, PROF BIOL, BOSTON UNIV, 67- *Concurrent Pos:* Vis prof, Univ Ceylon, 65. *Mem:* Am Soc Parasitol; Am Ornith Union; AAAS; Soc Protozool; Wildlife Dis Asn. *Res:* Parasitology, ornithology; parasites of birds and mammals, with emphasis on coccidia; morphology, taxonomy, histopathology. *Mailing Add:* Dept of Biol Boston Univ Boston MA 02215

DUNCAN, THOMAS O, b Washington, DC, June 5, 28; m 56; c 4. FISH BIOLOGY. *Educ:* Okla State Univ, BS, 53. *Prof Exp:* Fishery aide, Biol Lab, US Fish & Wildlife Serv, Wash, 53-54, fishery biologist, Bur Com Fisheries, 54-60, exec secy, Am Fisheries Adv Comt, DC, 60-62, chief cent reservoir invests fishery biol, Bur Sport Fisheries & Wildlife, 62-74, PROJ LEADER MULTI-OUTLET RESERVOIR STUDY, US FISH & WILDLIFE SERV, 74- *Res:* Sport fishery research on multi-outlet type reservoirs. *Mailing Add:* Multi-Outlet Reservoir Study Box 705 Ouachita Baptist Univ Arkadelphia AR 71923

DUNCAN, THOMAS OSLER, b Cambridge, Ohio, Jan 15, 48; m 74. BOTANY, SYSTEMATICS. *Educ:* Ohio State Univ, BS, 70; Univ Mich, MS, 75, PhD(bot), 76. *Prof Exp:* ASST PROF BOT, UNIV CALIF, BERKELEY, 76- *Concurrent Pos:* Asst curator seed plants, Univ Calif, 77- *Mem:* Am Soc Plant Taxonomists; Int Asn Plant Taxonomy; Classification Soc. *Res:* Classification and evolution of the genus Ranunculus with emphasis on the application of quantitative methods to systematic problems. *Mailing Add:* Dept Bot Univ Calif Berkeley CA 94720

DUNCAN, WALTER E(DWIN), b Red Lodge, Mont, Apr 30, 10; m 39; c 3. CHEMICAL ENGINEERING. *Educ:* Mont State Col, BS, 33; Mont Sch Mines, MS, 34, Min Dr E, 60. *Prof Exp:* Asst to A M Gaudin, Mont, 34-35; mill man, Mont Coal & Iron Co, 35; res metallurgist, Mo Sch Mines, 37-39; metallurgist, Mahoning Mining Co, Ill, 39-46 & Ozark-Mahoning Co, 46-49; assoc prof chem eng, 49-60, asst dir, 60-65, prof, 60-76, dir inst, 71-80, assoc dir, 65-71, EMER PROF CHEM ENG, NAT RESOURCES RES INST, UNIV WYO, 76-; CONSULT, 76- *Concurrent Pos:* Consult, Peruvian Govt, 50. *Mem:* Am Chem Soc; Am Inst Mining, Metall & Petrol Engrs. *Res:* Mineral and chemical processing; testing and beneficiation; mineral treatment and processing; submerged combustion. *Mailing Add:* 810 Flint St Laramie WY 82070

DUNCAN, WILBUR HOWARD, b Buffalo, NY, Oct 15, 10; m 41; c 3. TAXONOMY. *Educ:* Univ Ind, AB, 32, MA, 33; Duke Univ, PhD(bot), 38. *Prof Exp:* Instr, 38-40, from asst prof to prof, 40-78, EMER PROF BOT, UNIV GA, 78- *Mem:* Bot Soc Am; Am Soc Plant Taxon; Asn Trop Biol; Int Asn Plant Taxon. *Res:* Plant taxonomy; floristics; plant identification. *Mailing Add:* 2600 Lexington Rd Athens GA 30605

DUNCAN, WILLIAM PERRY, b Chetopa, Kans, Mar 31, 43; m 65; c 3. SYNTHETIC ORGANIC CHEMISTRY, RADIOCHEMISTRY. *Educ:* Kans State Col, BS, 65, MS, 66; Okla State Univ, PhD(org chem), 72. *Prof Exp:* Asst prof org chem, Panhandle State Univ, 66-70 & 72-73; sr chemist org radiosynthesis, Radiochem Dept, Sci Prod Div, Mallinckrodt Chem Works, 73-74; sr radiochemist org radiosynthesis, 74-79, HEAD ORG & RADIOCHEM SYNTHESIS SECT, MIDWEST RES INST, 79- *Concurrent Pos:* Lectr, Dept Chem, St Mary Col, Leavenworth, Kans, 79- *Mem:* Am Chem Soc; AAAS. *Res:* Synthesis and analysis of isotopically labeled toxic compounds or otherwise biologically active agents; catalytic hydrogenation, hydrogenolysis and dehydrogenation; metal-amine reactions; reactions of polynuclear aromatic hydrocarbons and organophosphorus and organochlorine pesticides. *Mailing Add:* Midwest Res Inst 425 Volker Blvd Kansas City MO 64110

DUNCAN, WILLIAM RAYMOND, b Harlingen, Tex, Aug 14, 49; m 70; c 2. IMMUNOGENETICS. *Educ:* Univ Tex, Austin, BA, 71; Univ Tex Health Sci Ctr, Dallas, PhD(cell biol), 76. *Prof Exp:* ASST PROF CELL BIOL, UNIV TEX HEALTH SCI CTR, DALLAS, 78- *Mem:* Transplantation Soc; Am Asn Immunologists; NY Acad Sci; Am Genetics Asn. *Res:* immunogenetics of the major histocompatibility complex in natural populations. *Mailing Add:* Dept Cell Biol Univ Tex Health Sci Ctr 5323 Harry Hines Blvd Dallas TX 75235

DUNCKHORST, F(AUSTINO) T, b Mogollon, NMex, July 1, 31. CHEMICAL ENGINEERING. *Educ:* NMex State Univ, BS, 57; Univ Pittsburgh, MS, 59, PhD(adsorption chromatography), 64. *Prof Exp:* Jr engr, 57-58, assoc engr, 58-61, engr, 61-64, sr engr, 64-70, fel engr, 70-78, ADV ENGR, BETTIS ATOMIC POWERLAB, WESTINGHOUSE ELEC CORP, 78- *Mem:* NY Acad Sci; Am Inst Chem Engrs; Am Soc Mech Engrs; Am Inst Aeronaut & Astronaut. *Res:* Heat transfer and fluid flow problems in nuclear reactor design. *Mailing Add:* Westinghouse Elec Corp PO Box 79 West Mifflin PA 15122

DUNCOMBE, E(LIOT), b Bahamas, May 30, 16; nat US; m 44; c 3. ENGINEERING MECHANICS. *Educ:* Cambridge Univ, BA, 37, MA, 42; Univ Del, MEE, 56; Univ Pittsburgh, PhD(controls), 65. *Prof Exp:* Prod engr, J Lucas Ltd, Eng, 37-46; sr scientist, Nat Gas Turbine Estab, 46-47; res engr, Nat Res Coun Can, 47-51; sect engr, aircraft power plants, 51-57, ENGR, BETTIS ATOMIC POWER LAB, WESTINGHOUSE ELEC CORP, 57- *Mem:* Am Nuclear Soc. *Res:* Gas dynamics; aviation gas turbines; nuclear power plants; fuel elements; control theory. *Mailing Add:* Westinghouse Elec Corp PO Box 79 West Mifflin PA 15122

DUNCOMBE, RAYNOR LOCKWOOD, b Mt Vernon, NY, Mar 3, 17; m 48; c 1. ASTRONOMY. *Educ:* Wesleyan Univ, BA, 40; Univ Iowa, MA, 41; Yale Univ, PhD, 56. *Prof Exp:* From jr astronr to assoc astronr, US Naval Observ, 42-48; res assoc, Yale Observ, 48-49; astronr, US Naval Observ, 49-63, dir nautical almanac off, 63-75; PROF AEROSPACE SCIENCE, UNIV TEX, AUSTIN, 76- *Mem:* AAAS; Am Inst Aeronaut & Astronaut; Am Astron Soc; Asn Comput Mach; Am Inst Navig. *Res:* Elements of Venus; variable stars; dynamical astronomy; computing machinery. *Mailing Add:* 1804 Vance Circle Austin TX 78701

DUNDEE, DOLORES SAUNDERS, invertebrate ecology, see previous edition

DUNDEE, HAROLD A, b Tulsa, Okla, Aug 23, 24; m 51. HERPETOLOGY. *Educ:* Univ Okla, BS, 48; Univ Mich, MS, 57, PhD, 58. *Prof Exp:* Asst prof, Montclair State Teachers Col, 56-57; from instr to assoc prof zool, 58-74, PROF BIOL, TULANE UNIV, LA, 74- *Concurrent Pos:* Ed, Tulane Studies Zool, 63-68 & 76-; dir Meade Natural Hist Libr, 65-68. *Mem:* Am Soc Ichthyologists & Herpetologists; Soc Study Amphibians & Reptiles; Deut Ges Herpetol; Herpetologists League. *Res:* Aggregative behavior and habitat selection by snakes; ecology and endocrinology of neotenic salamanders. *Mailing Add:* Dept of Biol Tulane Univ of La New Orleans LA 70118

DUNDURS, J(OHN), b Riga, Latvia, Sept 13, 22; m 52; c 3. MECHANICS. *Educ:* Northwestern Univ, BSME, 51, MS, 55, PhD, 58. *Prof Exp:* Designer diesel engines, Int Harvester Co, 52-53; res engr hydraul lab, 53-54, from instr to assoc prof, 55-66, PROF CIVIL ENG, NORTHWESTERN UNIV, 66- *Mem:* Am Soc Mech Engrs; Am Soc Civil Engrs; Am Acad Mech. *Res:* Mechanics of solids. *Mailing Add:* Dept of Civil Eng Northwestern Univ Evanston IL 60201

DUNEER, ARTHUR GUSTAV, JR, b Brooklyn, NY, Aug 29, 24; m 51; c 3. RADIATION PHYSICS. *Educ:* Rensselaer Polytech Inst, BS, 49, MS, 54, PhD(physics), 59. *Prof Exp:* Scientist, Assoc Nucleonics, 56-59; prin physicist, Repub Aviation Corp, 59-64; sr tech specialist, Space & Info Div, NAm Aviation, Inc, 64-66, MEM TECH STAFF, AUTONETICS DIV, ROCKWELL INT CORP, 66- *Mem:* Am Phys Soc. *Res:* Analysis of response of systems to EMP, system generated EMP, nuclear radiation; electromagnetic theory applied to antennae and shielding; application of computers to these analyses; infrared sensors. *Mailing Add:* 519 E Las Palmas Dr Fullerton CA 92635

DUNELL, BASIL ANDERSON, b Vancouver, BC, Apr 5, 23. NUCLEAR MAGNETIC RESONANCE. *Educ:* Univ BC, BASc, 45, MASc, 46; Princeton Univ, MA, 48, PhD(chem), 49. *Prof Exp:* Asst chem, 45-46, from asst prof to assoc prof, 49-65, PROF CHEM, UNIV BC, 65- *Concurrent Pos:* Univ fel, Physics Dept, Univ Nottingham, UK, 78-79. *Mem:* Fel Chem Inst Can; Royal Soc Chem. *Res:* Solid state nuclear magnetic resonance. *Mailing Add:* Dept of Chem Univ of BC Vancouver BC V6T 1Y6 Can

DUNFORD, HUGH BRIAN, b Oyen, Alta, Oct 25, 27; m 52; c 4. PHYSICAL BIOCHEMISTRY. *Educ:* Univ Alta, MSc, 52; McGill Univ, PhD(chem), 54. *Prof Exp:* Fel chem, McMaster Univ, 54-55; asst prof, Dalhousie Univ, 55-57; from asst prof to assoc prof, 57-68, PROF CHEM, UNIV ALTA, 68- *Mem:* Am Chem Soc; fel Chem Inst Can. *Res:* Transient state kinetics; mechanisms of enzyme reactions. *Mailing Add:* Dept Chem Univ Alta Edmonton AB T6G 2E8 Can

DUNFORD, JAMES MARSHALL, b Seattle, Wash, Oct 13, 15; m 41; c 8. NUCLEAR & MARINE ENGINEERING. *Educ:* US Naval Acad, BS, 39; Mass Inst Technol, SM, 44. *Prof Exp:* Design supt marine eng, Norfolk Naval Shipyard, 54-55, dep asst chief nuclear power, Bur Ships, Dept Navy, Washington, DC, 55-61; vpres naval nuclear power, NY Shipbuilding Corp, 61-65; prof mech eng, Univ Pa, 65-67; tech dir, Naval Air Eng Ctr, 67-73; VPRES, CDI MARINE CO, 74- *Concurrent Pos:* Chmn, Comt Requirements & Opportunities Develop Ocean Resources, Maritime Transp Res Bd, Nat Acad Sci. *Mem:* Soc Naval Architects & Marine Engrs; Am Soc Naval Engrs; Am Soc Mech Engrs. *Res:* Nuclear power plants for naval submarine and surface vessels; application of nuclear power of undersea research vessels. *Mailing Add:* CDI Marine Co 9951 Atlantic Blvd Suite 200 Jacksonville FL 32211

DUNFORD, MAX PATTERSON, b Bloomington, Idaho, June 17, 30; m 54; c 6. PLANT CYTOGENETICS, BIOSYSTEMATICS. *Educ:* Brigham Young Univ, BS, 54, MS, 58; Univ Calif, Davis, PhD(genetics), 62. *Prof Exp:* Asst prof biol, Mills Col, 62-63; PROF BIOL, NMEX STATE UNIV, 63- *Mem:* AAAS; Bot Soc Am; Am Genetic Asn. *Res:* Cytogenetics and biosystematics of the genus Grindelia of the family Compositae; somatic crossing over in cotton. *Mailing Add:* Dept of Biol Box 3AF NMex State Univ Las Cruces NM 88003

DUNFORD, RAYMOND A, b Bristol, Eng, June 19, 14; Can citizen; m 40. ANALYTICAL CHEMISTRY, TECHNICAL MANAGEMENT. *Educ:* Univ London, BSc, 37. *Prof Exp:* Chemist, Brit Drug Houses Ltd, 37-39, chief chemist, Can, 39-53, prod mgr, 53-58, plant mgr, 58-64, dir, 64-69; vpres prod, Glaxo Can Ltd, 70-77; CONSULT, PHARMACEUT MFG, 78- *Mem:* Fel Royal Soc Chem; fel Chem Inst Can; Parenteral Drug Asn. *Res:* Determination of steroid hormones and vitamin E. *Mailing Add:* 403 Morrison Rd Oakville ON L6J 4K3 Can

DUNFORD, ROBERT WALTER, b New York, NY, July 9, 46; m 77. PHYSICS. *Educ:* Univ Mich, BSE, 69, MS, 74, PhD(physics), 78. *Prof Exp:* Instr, 78-80, ASST PROF PHYSICS, PRINCETON UNIV, 80- *Mem:* Am Phys Soc. *Res:* Basic symmetries in low energy experiments; parity violation in atoms; time reversal invariance in beta decay; particular interest in testing predictions of gauge theories. *Mailing Add:* Dept of Physics Princeton Univ Princeton NJ 08540

DUNGAN, KENDRICK WEBB, b Science Hill, Ky, Jan 7, 28; m 51; c 3. PHARMACOLOGY, PHYSIOLOGY. *Educ:* Univ Ky, BS, 51. *Prof Exp:* Assoc pharmacologist, William S Merrell Co, Ohio, 51-54; PRIN INVESTR PHARMACOL, MEAD JOHNSON & CO, 54- *Mem:* AAAS; NY Acad Sci; Am Soc Pharmacol & Exp Therapeut; Soc Exp Biol & Med. *Res:* Respiration; uterus; gut; autonomic nervous system. *Mailing Add:* Mead Johnson & Co 2404 Pennsylvania St Evansville IN 47721

DUNGAN, WILLIAM THOMPSON, b Little Rock, Ark, June 12, 30; c 2. PEDIATRIC CARDIOLOGY. *Educ:* Vanderbilt Univ, AB, 51, MD, 54; Am Bd Pediat, dipl & cert cardiol. *Prof Exp:* Asst prof, 60-61 & 65-69, assoc prof, 69-73, PROF PEDIAT, MED CTR, UNIV ARK, LITTLE ROCK, 73- *Concurrent Pos:* Fel pediat cardiol, Univ Chicago Clin, 56-57 & Med Ctr, Univ Ark, Little Rock, 59-60. *Mem:* Am Acad Pediat; Am Col Cardiol. *Mailing Add:* Dept of Pediat Cardiol Univ of Ark Med Ctr Little Rock AR 72201

DUNGWORTH, DONALD L, b Hathersage, Eng, July 16, 31; nat; m 62; c 2. VETERINARY PATHOLOGY. *Educ:* Univ Liverpool, BVSc, 56; Univ Calif, Davis, PhD(vet path), 61; Am Col Vet Pathologists, dipl. *Prof Exp:* Lectr vet path, Univ Calif, Davis, 59-61 & Univ Bristol, 61-62; from asst prof to assoc prof, 62-70, assoc dean res & grad educ, 73-77, PROF VET PATH & CHMN DEPT, SCH VET MED, UNIV CALIF, DAVIS, 70- *Concurrent Pos:* WHO fel, Inst Dis of Chest, Brompton, London, Eng, 68-69; Fulbright fel, Wallaceville Res Ctr, NZ, 77-78. *Mem:* Royal Col Vet Surg; Int Acad Path; Am Asn Path; Am Thoracic Soc. *Res:* Pulmonary pathology, especially effects of air pollution; neoplasia, especially lymphoma/leukemias and myeloprofliferative disorders. *Mailing Add:* Dept of Path Sch of Vet Med Univ of Calif Davis CA 95616

DUNHAM, CHARLES BURTON, b Port Alberni, BC, Jan 25, 38. MATHEMATICS. *Educ:* Univ BC, BA, 59, MA, 63; Univ Western Ont, PhD(math), 68. *Prof Exp:* Res asst comput sci, 64-65, lectr, 65-69, asst prof, 69-74, ASSOC PROF COMPUT SCI, UNIV WESTERN ONT, 74- *Mem:* Asn Comput Mach. *Res:* Approximation theory; numerical analysis; best approximation, with emphasis on Chebyshev approximation; subroutines for mathematical functions; computational arithmetic. *Mailing Add:* Dept of Comput Sci Univ of Western Ont London ON N6A 5B8 Can

DUNHAM, CHARLES W, b Norwich, Vt, May 9, 22; m; c 3. HORTICULTURE. *Educ:* Univ Mass, BS, 46; Univ Wis, MS, 48; Mich State Univ, PhD(hort), 54. *Prof Exp:* Asst hort, Univ Wis, 46-48; instr floricult, Univ Mass, 48-52; asst hort, Mich State Univ, 52-54; from asst prof to assoc prof, 54-71, PROF PLANT SCI, UNIV DEL, 71- *Concurrent Pos:* Ext specialist ornamental hort, Dept Plant Sci, Univ Del, 74- *Honors & Awards:* Alex Laurie Award, 57. *Mem:* Am Soc Hort Sci; Am Hort Soc; Sigma Xi. *Res:* Plant nutrition, especially ornamental plants; plant propagation and physiology applied to growth of ornamental plants. *Mailing Add:* Dept of Plant Sci Univ of Del Newark DE 19711

DUNHAM, DAVID WARING, b Pasadena, Calif, Sept 25, 42; m 70. ASTRONOMY, CELESTIAL MECHANICS. *Educ:* Univ Calif, Berkeley, BA, 64; Yale Univ, PhD(astron), 71. *Prof Exp:* Astronaut engr, Aeronaut Chart & Info Ctr, Mo, 69-72; sci res assoc, Dept Astron, Univ Tex, Austin, 72-75; res asst astron, Cincinnati Observ, Univ Cincinnati, 75-76; ASTRONAUT ENGR, COMPUT SCI CORP, MD, 76- *Mem:* Am Astron Soc; AAAS; Int Occultation Timing Asn (pres); fel Royal Astron Soc; Fedn Am Scientists. *Res:* Astrographic catalog plate constants; total and grazing lunar occultations of stars and solar system objects for diameters, stellar duplicity and astrometry; outer planet satellite orbits; solar eclipse astrometry; spacecraft orbital studies for geomagnetic investigations; asteroid ephemerides, occultations and satellites; astronautical engineering. *Mailing Add:* Comput Sci Corp 8728 Colesville Rd Silver Spring MD 20910

DUNHAM, JAMES GEORGE, b Akron, Ohio, Sept 10, 50; m 79. INFORMATION THEORY, COMMUNICATION THEORY. *Educ:* Stanford Univ, BS & MS, 73, PhD(elec eng), 78. *Prof Exp:* Asst prof, 78-81, ASSOC PROF ELEC ENG, WASHINGTON UNIV, 81- *Concurrent Pos:* Res assoc, Biomed Comput Lab, 79- *Mem:* Inst Elec & Electronics Engrs. *Res:* Information theory, in particular by data compression, channel coding, cryptography and applications of information theory to genetics. *Mailing Add:* Dept Elec Eng Washington Univ St Louis MO 63130

DUNHAM, JEWETT, b Anaheim, Calif, Feb 6, 24; m 51; c 3. ZOOLOGY, PHYSIOLOGY. *Educ:* Univ Iowa, BA, 48, MS, 52, PhD(zool), 57. *Prof Exp:* Instr biol chem, Chadwick Sch, Calif, 50-53; from asst prof to assoc prof, 57-69, PROF ZOOL, IOWA STATE UNIV, 70- *Mem:* AAAS; Am Soc Zool. *Res:* Biological barriers; electrogenesis. *Mailing Add:* Dept Zool Iowa State Univ Ames IA 50010

DUNHAM, JOHN MALCOLM, b San Jose, Calif, June 27, 23; m 51; c 4. ANALYTICAL CHEMISTRY. *Educ:* Univ Calif, Los Angeles, BS, 48, PhD(anal chem), 57. *Prof Exp:* Chemist agr res, Dow Chem Co, Calif, 48-51; asst, Univ Calif, Los Angeles, 52-56; from instr to asst prof chem, Occidental Col, 56-58; res chemist, Sterling-Winthrop Res Inst, NY, 58-62; sr anal chemist, Pitman-Moore Div, Dow Chem Co, 62-66, proj leader, Dow Human Health Res & Develop, 66-67; SECT HEAD ANAL CHEM, SQUIBB INST MED RES, 68- *Mem:* Am Chem Soc. *Res:* Determination of drugs in pharmaceutical dosage forms and biological systems; coulometric titrations; separations; nonaqueous titrations; identity and purity of organic compounds. *Mailing Add:* Squibb Inst for Med Res New Brunswick NJ 08903

DUNHAM, KENNETH ROYAL, b Rochester, NY, Feb 5, 23; m 48, 79; c 2. APPLIED CHEMISTRY. *Educ:* Hobart Col, BA, 43. *Prof Exp:* Chemist, Eastman Kodak Co, 45-47 & Genesee Res Corp, 48-50; res chemist, 50-64, res assoc photoresists, 64-75, RES ASSOC XEROGRAPHY, EASTMAN KODAK CO, 75- *Mem:* Soc Photog Eng & Sci. *Res:* Polycarbonates; polyesters; photoresists; metal organics; stereoregular polymers; organic synthesis; photoconductors. *Mailing Add:* 221 Westminister Rd Rochester NY 14607

DUNHAM, MILTON L(EON), JR, b Philadelphia, Pa, May 19, 22; m 44; c 2. CHEMICAL ENGINEERING. *Educ:* Carnegie Inst Technol, BS, 42. *Prof Exp:* Res & develop engr, Linde Air Prod Co Div, 45-46, supvr prod develop, Silicones Div, 56-63, prod mgr, 63-64, mgr tech serv, 64-67, tech mgr chem & plastics, 67-70, int mgr, 70-77; res assoc, 77-81, CONSULT, UNION CARBIDE CORP, 81- *Mem:* AAAS; Am Inst Chem Engrs. *Res:* Silicone rubber technology and fluids. *Mailing Add:* Union Carbide Corp 10 Rising Rock Rd Stamford CT 06903

DUNHAM, PHILIP BIGELOW, b Columbus, Ohio, Apr 26, 37. PHYSIOLOGY. *Educ:* Swarthmore Col, BA, 58; Univ Chicago, PhD(zool), 62. *Prof Exp:* USPHS fel, 62-63; from asst prof to assoc prof zool, 63-71, PROF BIOL, SYRACUSE UNIV, 71- *Concurrent Pos:* Vis assoc prof, Sch Med, Yale Univ, 68-70; USPHS fel, 69; vis scientist, Physiol Lab, Univ Cambridge, Eng, 79. *Mem:* Soc Gen Physiol; Am Physiol Soc; Biophys Soc. *Res:* Transport of sodium and potassium in mammalian red blood cells. *Mailing Add:* Dept of Biol Syracuse Univ Syracuse NY 13210

DUNHAM, ROBERT JACOB, geology, see previous edition

DUNHAM, THEODORE, JR, b New York, NY, Dec 17, 97; m 26; c 2. ASTROPHYSICS, BIOPHYSICS. *Educ:* Harvard Univ, AB, 21; Cornell Univ, MD, 25; Princeton Univ, PhD, 27. *Prof Exp:* Nat Res Coun fel physics, Mt Wilson Observ, Carnegie Inst, 27-28, asst astronr, 28-36, astronr, 36-47; SCI DIR, FUND ASTROPHYS RES, 36-, PRES, 71-; CONSULT PHYSICS, 66-; HON ASSOC, HARVARD OBSERV, 71- *Concurrent Pos:* Assoc prof, Princeton Univ, 34-36; mem, Nat Geog Soc-US Navy Eclipse Exped, Canton Island, 37; res assoc, Oxford Univ, 38-39; mem sect instruments, Nat Defense Res Comt, 40-42; chief sect optical instruments, Off Sci Res & Develop, 42-46; mem comt vision, Armed Forces-Nat Res Coun, 43-47; Henry E Warren fel, Harvard Med Sch & assoc, Peter Bent Brigham Hosp, 46-48; res assoc, Mass Inst Technol, 47-48 & Harvard Observ, 47-52; res assoc, Inst Optics & fel med, Univ Rochester, 48-57; reader, Australian Nat Univ, 57-61, personal prof, 61-64; sr res fel, Tasmania, 65-70; sr fel, NSF, 67-68; fac assoc, Col of the Atlantic, 71- *Mem:* Am Phys Soc; Am Astron Soc; Optical Soc Am; Royal Astron Soc; Explorers Club. *Res:* Development of telescopes and spectrographs for astronomical spectroscopy; planetary atmospheres; uv spectrophotometry of biological cells; abundances of elements in stars; concentration of atoms and electrons in interstellar space. *Mailing Add:* PO Box D Chocorua NH 03817

DUNHAM, VALGENE LOREN, b Jamestown, NY, Oct 6, 40; m 62. PLANT PHYSIOLOGY, PLANT BIOCHEMISTRY. *Educ:* Houghton Col, BS, 62; Syracuse Univ, MS, 65, PhD(bot), 69. *Prof Exp:* Teacher, Pub Sch, NY, 62-63, head dept biol, 63-64; teaching asst bot, Syracuse Univ, 68-69; res assoc hort, Purdue Univ, 69-73; asst prof, 73-79, ASSOC PROF BIOL, STATE UNIV NY COL FREDONIA, 79- *Concurrent Pos:* Hon lectr plant biochem, Univ Col, Cardiff, UK, 80-81. *Mem:* AAAS; Soc Exp Biol; Am Soc Plant Physiol. *Res:* Multiple DNA polymerases in plants; effects of iron on nitrogen metabolism in bluegreen algae; control of multiple glutamine synthetases in soyben. *Mailing Add:* Dept Biol State Univ NY Col Fredonia NY 14063

DUNHAM, WILLIAM WADE, b Pittsburgh, Pa, Dec 8, 47; m 70; c 2. HISTORY OF MATHEMATICS, STATISTICS. *Educ:* Univ Pittsburgh, BS, 69; Ohio State Univ, MS, 70, PhD(math), 74. *Prof Exp:* Lectr math, Ohio State Univ, 75; asst prof, 75-80, ASSOC PROF MATH, HANOVER COL, 80- *Mem:* Math Asn Am. *Res:* Weak separation properties of general topological spaces; history of analysis in the late nineteenth and early twentieth centuries. *Mailing Add:* Dept of Math Hanover Col Hanover IN 47243

DUNHAM, WOLCOTT BALESTIER, b Boston, Mass, June 15, 00; m 40; c 2. ONCOLOGY. *Educ:* Columbia Univ, AB, 24, MD, 28; Am Bd Microbiol, dipl. *Prof Exp:* Asst bacteriologist, NY Post-Grad Med Sch Hosp, Columbia Univ, 36-46; res biologist, Vet Admin Hosp, 46-61, dir gen med res lab, 49-56, asst dir prof serv res, 56-61, assoc chief of staff, 61-68; vis investr, Jackson Lab, 68-74; ASSOC RES PROF, LINUS PAULING INST SCI & MED, 78- *Concurrent Pos:* Res fel, NY Post-Grad Med Sch Hosp, Columbia Univ, 39-40; assoc, Squibb Inst Med Res, 42-46; assoc prof, Med Col, Univ Tenn, 52-68. *Mem:* AAAS; Am Acad Microbiol; Am Asn Immunologists; Am Col Physicians; NY Acad Med. *Res:* Penicillin therapy in experimental syphilis; infectious hepatitis; virus hemagglutination; granuloma inguinale antigens; tissue cultures; immunological surveillance. *Mailing Add:* 440 Page Mill Rd Palo Alto CA 94306

DUNICZ, BOLESLAW LUDWIK, b Lwow, Poland, Feb 13, 12; nat. PHYSICAL CHEMISTRY. *Educ:* King John Casimir Univ, Poland, MSc,35; King's Col, London, PhD(phys chem), 47. *Prof Exp:* Asst to prof qual anal chem, Univ Lwow, 34-39; asst lectr, Polish Univ Col, London, 47; asst photochem, Univ Colo, 48; res fel, Univ Minn, 49; asst chem thermodyn, Univ Chicago, 50-52; instr phys chem, Chicago Undergrad Div, Univ Ill, 52-53; res assoc chem thermodyn, Col Eng, NY Univ, 53-55; from instr to asst prof phys & gen chem, Univ Long Island, 55-59; asst prof inorg qual anal & phys chem, The Citadel, 59-60; phys chemist, US Naval Radiol Defense Lab, 60-68; lectr physics, Col Notre Dame, Calif, 69-71; DIR CHEM LABS, UNIV SAN FRANCISCO, 70- *Mem:* Fel AAAS; Am Chem Soc; fel Am Inst Chem. *Res:* Photochemistry; kinetics; thermodynamics; fused salts; surface phenomena. *Mailing Add:* Apt 1H Sunset Towers 8 Locksley Ave San Francisco CA 94122

DUNIFER, GERALD LEROY, b Silverton, Ore, Oct 21, 41; m 63. EXPERIMENTAL SOLID STATE PHYSICS. *Educ:* Walla Walla Col, BS, 63; Univ Calif, San Diego, MS, 66, PhD(physics), 68. *Prof Exp:* Asst res physicist, Univ Calif, San Diego, 68-69; mem tech staff, Bell Tel Labs, 69-71; asst prof, 71-77, ASSOC PROF PHYSICS, WAYNE STATE UNIV, 77- *Mem:* Am Phys Soc; Sigma Xi. *Res:* Millimeter microwave transmission spectroscopy of high purity metals at cryogenic temperatures. *Mailing Add:* Dept Physics Wayne State Univ Detroit MI 48202

DUNIGAN, EDWARD P, b Marshfield, Wis, June 16, 34; m 61; c 2. SOIL MICROBIOLOGY. *Educ:* Wis State Univ, Stevens Point, BS, 58; Mich State Univ, MS, 61; Univ Ariz, PhD(agr chem, soils), 67. *Prof Exp:* Res chemist, US Rubber Co & Gen Motors Res Labs, 62-64; res assoc herbicides, Univ Ariz, 64-67; assoc prof soil microbiol, 67-74, assoc prof agron, 74-78, PROF AGRON, LA STATE UNIV, BATON ROUGE, 78- *Mem:* Am Soc Agron; Soil Sci Soc Am; Crop Sci Soc Am. *Res:* Soil organic matter; soybean nodulation; increasing nitrogen fixation in legumes; non-symbiotic nitrogen fixation in grasses and rice; microbial-insect damage and subsequent effects on nitrogen fixation in soybeans. *Mailing Add:* Dept of Agron La State Univ Baton Rouge LA 70803

DUNIKOSKI, LEONARD KAROL, JR, b Newark, NJ, Nov 5, 45; m 72. CLINICAL CHEMISTRY. *Educ:* Rutgers Univ, AB, 66; Pa State Univ, PhD(chem), 71; Am Bd Clin Chem, dipl, 76; Am Bd Bioanal, dipl, 79. *Prof Exp:* Fel clin chem, Georgetown Univ Hosp, 71-73; DIR CLIN CHEM, PERTH AMBOY GEN HOSP, 73-; DIR CLIN CHEM, OLD BRIDGE REGIONAL HOSP, 79- *Concurrent Pos:* Adj asst prof path, Rutgers Med Sch, 74-; adj prof med technol, Middlesex County Col, 75-; consult, NJ Dept Health, 77- & Col Am Pathologists, 77- *Mem:* Am Asn Clin Chem (secy-treas, 81-); Acad Clin Lab Physicians & Scientists. *Res:* Chemistry of blood coagulation including applications of artificial substrates and advanced instrumental analysis techniques; high pressure liquid chromatography techniques for therapeutic drug level analysis in serum. *Mailing Add:* 185 Kemp Ave Fair Haven NJ 07701

DUNIPACE, DONALD WILLIAM, b Bowling Green, Ohio, May 24, 07; m 28; c 2. PHYSICS. *Educ:* Ohio State Univ, BA, 29, MA, 30. *Prof Exp:* Asst physics, Ohio State Univ, 29-32, fel, 32-33; physicist, Libbey-Owens-Ford Glass Co, 35-62; staff scientist, Ball Bros Res Corp, 62-69; sr scientist, Libby-Owens-Ford Co, 69-76; RETIRED. *Mem:* AAAS; Sigma Xi; Am Phys Soc; Optical Soc Am. *Res:* Investigation of glass and glass production problems; optical instrumentation; radiative heat transfer phenomena. *Mailing Add:* 2525 Clearview Dr Carson City NV 89701

DUNIPACE, KENNETH ROBERT, b Bowling Green, Ohio, Sept 26, 29; m 63; c 2. CONTROL SYSTEMS. *Educ:* Ohio State Univ, BS, 51; Mass Inst Technol, SB, 56; Univ Fla, ME, 65; Clemson Univ, PhD(elec eng), 68. *Prof Exp:* Staff engr, Perma-glass, Inc, 53-54; exec officer aerophys res, Mass Inst Technol, 56-58, staff engr Polaris guid, 58-60, test mgr, 60-63, sr rep Apollo guid & navig, 63-65; res asst elec eng, Univ Fla, 66 & Clemson Univ, 66-68; assoc prof, 68-76, PROF ELEC ENG, UNIV MO-ROLLA, 76-, RES ASSOC, TRANSP INST, 68- *Concurrent Pos:* Consult, Instrumentation Lab, Mass Inst Technol, 68-71. *Mem:* Inst Elec & Electronics Eng; Simulation Coun. *Res:* Development of guidance and navigation systems for aerospace and highway application; application of contemporary control theory to transportation problems. *Mailing Add:* Dept of Elec Eng Univ of Mo Rolla MO 65401

DUNIWAY, JOHN MASON, b San Francisco, Calif, Nov 6, 42; m 65; c 2. PLANT PATHOLOGY. *Educ:* Carleton Col, BA, 64; Univ Wis-Madison, PhD(plant path), 69. *Prof Exp:* NSF fel plant physiol, Res Sch Biol Sci, Australian Nat Univ, 69-70; lectr plant path & asst plant pathologist, 70-77, ASSOC PROF PLANT PATH, UNIV CALIF, DAVIS, 77- *Mem:* Am Phytopath Soc; Am Soc Plant Physiol. *Res:* Water relations and photosynthesis in diseased plants; water relations of soil microorganisms. *Mailing Add:* Dept Plant Path Univ Calif Davis CA 95616

DUNKEL, MORRIS, b Brooklyn, NY, Dec 4, 27; m 57; c 3. ORGANIC CHEMISTRY. *Educ:* Long Island Univ, BS, 50; Brooklyn Col, MS, 54; Univ Ark, PhD(org chem), 56. *Prof Exp:* Res chemist, Norda Essential Oil & Chem Co, 51-53, group leader, 56-58; res chemist, Nopco Chem Co, 58-59, head org fine chem res, 59-61; group leader, UOP Chem Div, Universal Oil Prod Co, 61-66, dir appl res, Chem Div, 66-75; mgr, 76-81, DIR ORG RES & DEVELOP, TENNECO CHEM, INC, 81- *Mem:* Am Chem Soc; The Chem Soc. *Res:* Organic synthesis; aroma and flavor chemistry; natural products; vitamins; catalytic hydrogenation; stereochemistry; reactions at elevated temperatures and pressures; flame retardancy; polymer stabilization. *Mailing Add:* Tenneco Chem Inc PO Box 365 Piscataway NJ 08854

DUNKEL, VIRGINIA CATHERINE, b New York, NY, July 15, 34. VIROLOGY, ONCOLOGY. *Educ:* Col New Rochelle, BA, 56; Rutgers Univ, MS, 59, PhD(microbiol), 64. *Prof Exp:* Res scientist virol, E R Squibb & Sons, 59-61; cancer res scientist, Roswell Park Mem Inst, 64-69, asst res prof microbiol, Roswell Park Div, Grad Sch, State Univ NY Buffalo, 67-69; sr staff fel viral oncol, Nat Cancer Inst, 69-72, sr staff fel immunochem, 72-73, mgr biol & immunol segment, 73-76, coordr in vitro carcinogenesis prog, 74-79; CHIEF, GENETIC TOXICOL BR, DIV TOXICOL, BUR FOODS, FOOD & DRUG ADMIN, 80- *Mem:* Am Asn Cancer Res; Sigma Xi; AAAS; Environ Mutagen Soc; Asn Official Anal Chemists. *Res:* Evaluation and development of mutagenicity assays for use in determining the carceogenic/mutagenic potential of chemical compounds. *Mailing Add:* Bur Foods HFF-166 Food & Drug Admin 200 C St SW Washington DC 20024

DUNKELBERGER, TOBIAS HENRY, b Paxinos, Pa, Nov 4, 09; m 41; c 2. PHYSICAL CHEMISTRY, MICROCHEMISTRY. *Educ:* Dickinson Col, ScB, 30; Univ Pittsburgh, PhD(phys chem), 37. *Prof Exp:* Teacher high sch, Pa, 30-31; asst chem, Univ Pittsburgh, 31-36; asst prof, NTex Agr Col, 36-37, Univ Idaho, 37-38, Duquesne Univ, 38-41 & NY State Col Ceramics, Alfred Univ, 41-44; prof & head dept, Duquesne Univ, 44-52; prof chem, 52-76, assoc dean, Col Arts & Sci, 69-75, EMER PROF CHEM, UNIV PITTSBURGH, 76- *Concurrent Pos:* Prof, Univ Pittsburgh Faculties in Ecuador, Agency Int Develop Contract, 63-67; chief-of-party, Faculties in Guatemala, 67-69. *Honors & Awards:* Pittsburgh Award, Am Chem Soc, 70. *Mem:* AAAS; Am Chem Soc. *Res:* Thermodynamics of solutions; microchemistry; chemical education. *Mailing Add:* 5132 Beeler St Pittsburgh PA 15217

DUNKELMAN, LAWRENCE, b Paterson, NJ, June 28, 17; m 50; c 2. PHYSICS, ASTRONOMY. *Educ:* Cooper Union, BEE, 38, EE, 49. *Prof Exp:* Jr marine engr, US Naval Shipyard, NH, 39-41; elec engr, US Bur Ships, US Dept Navy, 41-43, electronics engr, 43-48; physicist, US Naval Res Lab, 48-58; aeronautics & space scientist & head ultraviolet detection systs & planetary optics, Goddard Space Flight Ctr, NASA, Md, 59-64; mem sr staff, Inst Defense Anal, Arlington, Va, 64-65; head planetary optics, Goddard Space Flight Ctr, NASA, 65-69, head astron systs br, 69-74; MEM STAFF, LUNAR & PLANETARY LAB, UNIV ARIZ, 74- *Concurrent Pos:* Consult var univ & indust labs; staff specialist, Astron Orbiting Observ, NASA, 59-61, mem, Comt Astronaut Training & Exp, 62-64; proj scientist, UK-US Ariel II satellite, 61-64; mem, Eclipse Exped, US Navy, Sweden, 54, Peru, 65; mem staff, Goddard Space Flight Ctr, NASA. *Mem:* AAAS; fel Optical Soc Am; Int Astron Union; Sigma Xi. *Res:* Atmospheric attenuation of ultraviolet, visible and near infrared; ultraviolet technology; electrooptics; low light level photography; spectrophotometric instrumentation for space research; planetary atmospheres; solar research; manned space sciences. *Mailing Add:* 1606 Tilton Dr Silver Spring MD 20902

DUNKER, ALAN KEITH, b New Orleans, La, Mar 16, 43; m 65. BIOPHYSICS. *Educ:* Univ Calif, Berkeley, BS, 65; Univ Wis-Madison, MS, 67, PhD(biophys), 69. *Prof Exp:* Fel biophys, Yale Univ, 69-70, NIH fel molecular biophys & biochem, 70-72; res asst, Sloan-Kettering Cancer Res Inst, 72-75; asst prof chem, 75-79, ASSOC PROF, WASH STATE UNIV, 79- *Concurrent Pos:* Investr, Am Heart Asn, 78- *Mem:* Biophys Soc; Am Chem Soc; Am Soc Microbiol; Sigma Xi. *Res:* Structure of alpha-helical protein bundles and their applicability to membrane proteins such as bacteriorhodopsin and the adenosine triphosphatase from sarcoplasmic reticulum; proton hole in alpha-helices containing proline and the role of this proton hole as a proton motive force transducer. *Mailing Add:* Prog Biochem & Biophys Wash State Univ Pullman WA 99163

DUNKER, MELVIN FREDERICK WILLIAM, b Baltimore, Md, June 12, 13; m 41; c 3. PHARMACEUTICAL CHEMISTRY. *Educ:* Univ Md, PhG, 33, BS, 34, MS, 36, PhD(pharmaceut chem), 39. *Prof Exp:* Asst, Sch Pharm, Univ Md, 34-39, Warner fel, 39-40; Rockefeller Found assoc, Northwestern Univ, 40-41; from instr to asst prof pharm, Univ Wis, 41-45; assoc prof, Col Pharm, Wayne State Univ, 45-49, prof pharmaceut chem, 49-81; RETIRED. *Mem:* AAAS; Am Chem Soc; Am Pharmaceut Asn. *Res:* Replacement of diazonium boro-fluoride by mercury; aliphatic amines; steroids; the i-ethers of 3-hydroxy-5-cholenic acid; fluorine substituted phenols; phenobarbital. *Mailing Add:* Col of Pharm Wayne State Univ Detroit MI 48202

DUNKIN, JOHN WILLIAM, b Fayette Co, Ind, Dec 2, 27; m 49; c 5. ENGINEERING. *Educ:* Purdue Univ, BS, 53, MS, 54, PhD(eng sci), 61. *Prof Exp:* Instr eng mech, Purdue Univ, 54-61; sr res engr, Jersey Prod Res Co, Standard Oil Co NJ, 61-64; SR RES ADV, EXXON PROD RES CO, 64- *Mem:* Soc Explor Geophys; Am Geophys Union; Soc Eng Sci. *Res:* Elastodynamics; transient response of layered elastic media; wave propagation in electromagnetic elastic media and in randomly inhomogeneous media; exploration seismology. *Mailing Add:* Exxon Prod Res Co PO Box 2189 Houston TX 77001

DUNKL, CHARLES FRANCIS, b Vienna, Austria, Sept 16, 41; US citizen; m 65. MATHEMATICS. *Educ:* Univ Toronto, BSc, 62, MA, 63; Univ Wis, PhD(math), 65. *Prof Exp:* Instr math, Princeton Univ, 65-67; from asst prof to assoc prof, 67-80, PROF MATH, UNIV VA, 80- *Concurrent Pos:* Vis assoc prof, Ga Inst Technol, 77-78. *Mem:* Am Math Soc; Soc Indust & Appl Math. *Res:* Harmonic analysis; special functions. *Mailing Add:* Dept Math Math Astron Bldg Univ of Va Charlottesville VA 22903

DUNKLE, LARRY D, b Helena, Okla, Feb 19, 43; m 65; c 4. PHYTOPATHOLOGY. *Educ:* Colo State Col, BA, 65; Univ Wis, MS, 68, PhD(bot), 70. *Prof Exp:* From asst prof to assoc prof plant path, Univ Nebr, 71-78; USDA PLANT PATHOLOGIST, PURDUE UNIV, WEST LAFAYETTE, 78- *Concurrent Pos:* NIH fel, Univ Nebr, 71. *Mem:* Am Phytopath Soc; Am Soc Plant Physiol. *Res:* Fungal physiology; biochemistry of host-parasite interaction and the role of microbial toxins in plant diseases. *Mailing Add:* Dept of Bot & Plant Path Purdue Univ West Lafayette IN 47907

DUNKLE, MICHAEL PATRICK, b Dover, NJ, Oct 15, 32; m 61; c 3. PHYSICAL CHEMISTRY, ANALYTICAL CHEMISTRY. *Educ:* Fordham Univ, BS, 54; Purdue Univ, PhD(phys chem), 64. *Prof Exp:* Res chemist, Photo Prods Res Lab, E I du Pont de Nemours & Co, Inc, 63-66, process chemist, 66-75, process supvr, 75-77, sr process chemist, Control Lab, 78-80; RETIRED. *Mem:* Am Chem Soc; Am Inst Chem; Soc Photog Scientists & Engr. *Res:* Silver halide and polymer photosensitive systems; instrumental analysis; environmental control; industrial hygiene. *Mailing Add:* RD 1 Box 77 Towanda PA 18848

DUNKLEY, WALTER LEWIS, b Olds, Alta, Feb 15, 18; nat US; m 43; c 3. FOOD SCIENCE. *Educ:* Univ Alta, BSc, 39, MSc, 41; Univ Wis, PhD(dairy indust, biochem), 43. *Prof Exp:* Lectr & asst prof dairying, Univ Alta, 43-46; res chemist, Golden State Co, Ltd, Calif, 46-48; from asst prof to assoc prof food sci & technol, 48-58, PROF FOOD SCI & TECHNOL, UNIV CALIF, DAVIS, 58- *Concurrent Pos:* Fulbright awards, Fats Res Lab, New Zealand, 56-57 & Agr Inst Ireland, 63-64; mem fac chem eng, Univ Guayaquil, 69. *Honors & Awards:* Borden Award, Am Dairy Sci Asn. *Mem:* Am Dairy Sci Asn; Inst Food Technol; Int Asn Milk, Food & Environ Sanit; Am Inst Nutrit; Am Oil Chemists Soc. *Res:* Chemistry and processing of dairy products; oxidative and hydrolytic rancidity; polyunsaturated meat and dairy products from ruminants. *Mailing Add:* Dept of Food Sci & Technol Univ of Calif Davis CA 95616

DUNKS, GARY BURR, organometallic chemistry, see previous edition

DUNLAP, BOBBY DAVID, b Post, Tex, Mar 21, 38; m 65; c 2. EXPERIMENTAL SOLID STATE PHYSICS. *Educ:* Tex Tech Col, BS, 59; Univ Wash, PhD(physics), 66. *Prof Exp:* Assoc mem tech staff physics, Bell Tel Labs, Inc, 62-63; resident res assoc, 66-70, physicist, 70-79, SR PHYSICIST, ARGONNE NAT LAB, 79-, ASST DIV DIR, SOLID STATE SCI DIV, 79- *Res:* Solid state physics by application of the Mossbauer effect. *Mailing Add:* Dept of Solid State Argonne Nat Lab Argonne IL 60439

DUNLAP, BRETT IRVING, b Oakland, Calif, Apr 24, 47; c 2. PHYSICS. *Educ:* Univ Iowa, BA, 69; Johns Hopkins Univ, MA, 72, PhD(physics), 76. *Prof Exp:* Assoc physics, Univ Fla, 75-77; assoc surface sci, Nat Bur Standards, 77-79; assoc chem, George Washington Univ, 79-80; RES PHYSICIST, NAVAL RES LAB, 80- *Mem:* Am Phys Soc; Sigma Xi. *Res:* Theoretical surface science. *Mailing Add:* Code 6171 Naval Res Lab Washington DC 20375

DUNLAP, CHARLES EDWARD, b New York, NY, June 8, 08; m 37; c 4. PATHOLOGY. *Educ:* Harvard Univ, AB, 30, MD, 34. *Prof Exp:* Intern, Univ Chicago, 34-35, asst resident path, 36-37, resident & asst, 37; asst, Harvard Med Sch, 39-40, instr, 40-43; from asst prof to prof, 43-78, chmn dept, 45-75, EMER PROF PATH, SCH MED, TULANE UNIV, 78- *Concurrent Pos:* Littauer fel path, Harvard Cancer Comn, 37-39; res fel, Collis P Huntington Hosp, 39-43; asst res, Presby Hosp, Chicago, 35; vis pathologist, Charity Hosp, New Orleans, 43-46; sr vis pathologist, 46-; consult, Armed Forces Inst Path, 52-; consult path study sect, USPHS, 54-57, consult training grants comt, 57-58, mem path training comt, 58-62, mem cancer training comt, 62-64; mem clin cancer training comt, 65-67 & mem radiation biol effects adv comt, 66-70; mem comt on path effects of radiation, Nat Res Coun, 55-58; mem bd dirs, Oak Ridge Inst Nuclear Studies, 55-62 & Urban Maes Res Found, 57-61; mem adv comt, President's Comn Heart Dis & Cancer, 64. *Mem:* Am Asn Cancer Res; Am Soc Exp Path (vpres, 62-63, pres, 63-64); Soc Exp Biol & Med; Am Asn Pathologists & Bacteriologists; fel Col Am Pathologists. *Res:* Carcinogenic hydrocarbons; biologic effects of radiation; human cancer. *Mailing Add:* Tulane Univ Sch of Med 1430 Tulane Ave New Orleans LA 70112

DUNLAP, CLAUD EVANS, III, b Camp Atterbury, Ind, Aug 13, 46; m 67; c 3. OPIATE PHARMACOLOGY, RECEPTOROLOGY. *Educ:* Univ Fla, BS, 71, PhD(pharmacol), 75. *Prof Exp:* NIH fel, Addiction Res Found, 76-79; ASST PROF PHARMACOL, BOWMAN GRAY SCH MED, WAKE FOREST UNIV, 79- *Mem:* AAAS; NY Acad Sci; Sigma Xi. *Res:* Mechanisms of pharmacologic receptor activity and regulation; opiate neuropharmacology; neurobiology of opioid peptides, with particular emphasis on their roles in neuroendocrine regulation. *Mailing Add:* 417 Burkewood Dr Winston-Salem NC 27104

DUNLAP, DONALD GENE, b Bend, Ore, Sept 21, 26; m 56; c 1. VERTEBRATE ZOOLOGY, ANIMAL ECOLOGY. *Educ:* Ore State Univ, BS, 49, MA, 51; Wash State Univ, PhD(zool), 55. *Prof Exp:* Asst zool, Ore State Univ, 49-51; asst, Wash State Univ, 51-55, jr physiologist, Col Vet Med, 55-56; asst prof biol, Ripon Col, 56-59; from asst prof to assoc prof zool, 59-63, actg chmn dept zool, 65-66, actg chmn dept biol, 74-75, PROF ZOOL, UNIV SDAK, VERMILLION, 64- *Concurrent Pos:* Vis prof, Coe Col, 57. *Mem:* Fel AAAS; Am Soc Ichthyol & Herpet; Am Soc Zool; Ecol Soc Am; Am Inst Biol Sci. *Res:* Biology of the amphibians and reptiles; animal systematics; physiological ecology. *Mailing Add:* Dept of Biol Univ of SDak Vermillion SD 57069

DUNLAP, G(EORGE) WESLEY, b Gardnerville, Nev, Apr 13, 11; m 35; 68; c 5. ELECTRICAL ENGINEERING. *Educ:* Stanford Univ, AB, 31, PhD(elec eng), 36. *Prof Exp:* Student engr, Gen Elec Co, 35-36, develop engr high voltage & impulse sect, Gen Eng Lab, 36-45, asst div engr, High Voltage & Nucleonics Div, Gen Eng & Consult Lab, 45-51, div engr, 51-53, mgr, Instrument & Nuclear Radiation Eng Servs Dept, 53-55, mgr, Eng Physics & Anal Lab, 55-61, sr engr, Adv Technol Labs, 61-66, consult engr, Res & Develop Ctr, 66-76; CONSULT ENGR, 76- *Concurrent Pos:* Vis Webster prof, Mass Inst Technol, 55-56. *Honors & Awards:* Alfred Noble Prize, 42. *Mem:* Nat Soc Prof Engrs; fel Inst Elec & Electronics Engrs; Am Nuclear Soc. *Res:* High voltage phenomenon; circuit interruption; particle accelerators; radiation and electronic instruments; electrical measurements; nuclear engineering; energy conversion; electron physics; oceanology. *Mailing Add:* 1970 Village Rd Schenectady NY 12309

DUNLAP, HENRY FRANCIS, b Ennis, Tex, Oct 4, 16; m 42; c 3. GEOPHYSICS, PETROLEUM ENGINEERING. *Educ:* Rice Inst, BA, 38, MA, 39, PhD(physics), 41. *Prof Exp:* Asst physicist, Dept Terrestrial Magnetism, Carnegie Inst, 41-42; physicist, Univ NMex, 42-45, lectr physics, 43-44; maj physicist, Atlantic Ref Co, 45-66, head long range res sect, 66-69, res scientist, Atlantic Richfield Co, 69-76; CONSULT, 76- *Concurrent Pos:* Adj prof, Petrol Eng Dept, Univ Tex, Austin, 76-81. *Mem:* Am Phys Soc; Soc Prof Well Log Analysts; Soc Explor Geophys (vpres, 64-65); Am Asn Petrol Geol; Am Inst Min, Metall & Petrol Eng. *Res:* Nuclear physics; internal and external ballistics; geophysics; instrumentation in supersonic aerodynamics; meteorites; well logging; geothermal energy; economics. *Mailing Add:* PO Box 98 Wimberley TX 78676

DUNLAP, JULIAN LEE, b LaGrange, Ga, Jan 27, 32; m 60; c 2. PHYSICS. *Educ:* Ga Inst Technol, BEE, 54; Vanderbilt Univ, PhD(physics), 59. *Prof Exp:* PHYSICIST, FUSION ENERGY DIV, OAK RIDGE NAT LAB, 59- *Mem:* Am Phys Soc. *Res:* Plasma physics and controlled thermonuclear research. *Mailing Add:* Fusion Energy Div Oak Ridge Nat Lab PO Box Y Oak Ridge TN 37830

DUNLAP, PAUL R, b Chungsha, China, Nov 21, 25; US citizen; m 47; c 3. STATISTICS. *Educ:* Pa State Univ, BA, 48, MEd, 50; Am Univ, PhD(statist), 68. *Prof Exp:* Teacher high schs, Pa, 48-53; group leader, Ralph M Parsons Co, Md, 53-55; sr engr, Martin Marietta Co, 55-56; sr statistician, Res & Develop Div, Avco, Mass, 56-60; mem tech staff, Mitre Corp, Mass, 60-67; assoc prof quant methods, Col Bus Admin, Ohio Univ, 67-80; SR STATIST ENVIRON PROTECTION AGENCY, INDUST ENVIRON RES LAB, 81-82. *Mem:* Inst Math Statist; Am Statist Asn; Am Inst Decision Sci. *Res:* Biometrics, equipment reliability and quality control; systems engineering and information management; multidisciplinary approach to problem solving through applications of statistical methods, for example, communication, price theory, urban blight and teaching effectiveness. *Mailing Add:* 4-F Booker Creek Apts Chapel Hill NC 27514

DUNLAP, RICHARD M(ORRIS), b Columbia, Mo, Sept 5, 17; m 46, 69; c 5. MECHANICAL ENGINEERING. *Educ:* Mass Inst Technol, BS & MS, 41. *Prof Exp:* Trainee engr, United Shoe Mach Corp, 38-39; jr engr, Sperry Prod Co, 41; proj engr, Res Construct Co, 41-45; teacher, Robert Col, 45-48; mech engr, US Naval Underwater Ord Sta, 48-59, head appl sci dept, 59-61; assoc dir res, US Naval Underwater Weapons Res & Eng Sta, 61-71; assoc dir long range planning, US Naval Underwater Systs Ctr, Dept Defense, 71-76, dir planning & prog, 76-78; CONSULT, NAT CTR ATMOSPHERIC RES, 79- *Concurrent Pos:* Adj prof mech eng & appl mech, Univ RI, 78- *Mem:* Am Inst Aeronaut & Astronaut; Inst Elec & Electronics Engrs. *Res:* Underwater weapons systems. *Mailing Add:* 452 Mitchell Lane Middletown RI 02840

DUNLAP, ROBERT BRUCE, b Elgin, Ill, Oct 14, 42; m 64; c 2. ENZYMOLOGY. *Educ:* Beloit Col, BS, 64; Ind Univ, PhD(biochem), 68. *Prof Exp:* NIH fel biochem, Scripps Clin & Res Found, 68-71; from asst prof to assoc prof, 71-78, PROF CHEM, UNIV SC, 78- *Mem:* Am Chem Soc; Am Soc Biol Chemists; AAAS; Am Asn Cancer Res. *Res:* Enzyme mechanisms, coenzyme chemistry, nucleotide metabolism, application of multinuclear magnetic resonance spectroscopy to biochemical systems, model systems for enzyme catalyzed reactions. *Mailing Add:* Dept of Chem Univ of SC Columbia SC 29208

DUNLAP, ROBERT D, b Carbondale, Pa, Apr 5, 22; m 53; c 3. PHYSICAL CHEMISTRY. *Educ:* Colgate Univ, BA, 43; Pa State Univ, MS, 44, PhD(chem), 49. *Prof Exp:* Asst chem, Pa State Univ, 43-49; from instr to assoc prof, 49-59, PROF CHEM, UNIV MAINE, ORONO, 59-, CHMN DEPT, 77- *Mem:* Am Chem Soc. *Res:* Physical chemistry; fluorocarbon of solutions. *Mailing Add:* Dept of Chem Aubert Hall Univ of Maine Orono ME 04473

DUNLAP, WILLIAM CRAWFORD, b Denver, Colo, July 21, 18; m 40; c 1. PHYSICS. *Educ:* Univ NMex, BS, 38; Univ Calif, PhD(physics), 43. *Prof Exp:* Asst physics, Univ Calif, 38-42; res physicist, USDA, 42-45; res assoc, Gen Elec Res Lab, 45-55; consult semiconductors, Gen Elec Electronics Lab, 55-56; supvr solid state res, Bendix Res Labs, 56-58; dir semiconductors res & solid state electronic res, Raytheon Res Div, 58-64; asst dir electronic components res, Electronics Res Ctr, NASA, 64-68; dir res, 68-70; sci adv, Transport Systs Ctr, US Dept Transp, Cambridge, 70-74; PRES, W C DUNLAP & CO, 74- *Concurrent Pos:* Assoc prof, Evening Session, Siena Col, 52-54; ed-in-chief, Solid State Electronics, 59- *Mem:* Fel Am Phys Soc; fel Inst Elec & Electronics Engrs. *Res:* Cosmic rays; dielectrics; color and spectrophotometry; semiconductors; solid state physics. *Mailing Add:* 126 Prince St West Newton MA 02165

DUNLAP, WILLIAM JOE, b Wichita Falls, Tex, Oct 9, 29; m 57; c 1. GROUND WATER POLLUTION, ENVIRONMENTAL CHEMISTRY. *Educ:* Tex A&M Univ, BS, 52; Univ Okla, PhD(chem), 61. *Prof Exp:* Food technologist, Mrs Tuckers Foods, Tex, 52-55; res assoc chem, Univ Okla, 60-62; biochemist, Kerr-McGee Oil Indust, Inc, Okla, 62-63; res chemist, Res Inst, Univ Okla, 63-67; RES CHEMIST, ROBERT S KERR ENVIRON RES LAB, ENVIRON PROTECTION AGENCY, 67- *Mem:* Am Chem Soc. *Res:* Chemistry of water pollution; sub-surface biochemistry; anaerobic degradation of organic compounds; chromatography; movement and fate of pollutants in ground water; soil biochemistry. *Mailing Add:* Robert S Kerr Environ Res Lab Environ Protect Agcy Box 1198 Ada OK 74820

DUNLEAVY, JOHN M, b Omaha, Nebr, June 6, 23; m 47; c 4. PLANT PATHOLOGY. *Educ:* Univ Nebr, PhD(plant path), 53. *Prof Exp:* From asst prof to assoc prof, Iowa State Univ, 53-61; plant pathologist, USDA, 53-59; PROF PLANT PATH, IOWA STATE UNIV, 61-; SOYBEAN DIS RES COORDR, USDA, 59- *Concurrent Pos:* Leader, Iowa Fed Soybean Proj, 72- *Mem:* AAAS; Am Phytopath Soc; Am Soc Microbiol; Am Soybean Asn; Brit Soc Gen Microbiol. *Res:* Diseases of soybeans. *Mailing Add:* Dept of Plant Path Iowa State Univ Ames IA 50011

DUNLOP, D L, b Medicine Hat, Alta, Feb 15, 25; m 52; c 5. OBSTETRICS & GYNECOLOGY. *Educ:* Univ Man, BSc & MD, 52; Univ Nebr, MS, 66; FRCPS(C), 63. *Prof Exp:* Asst instr, Univ Nebr, 65-66; assoc prof, 67-70, PROF OBSTET & GYNEC, FAC MED, UNIV ALTA, 70- *Concurrent Pos:* Teaching fel obstet & gynec, Univ Man, 62; NIH fel, 65-66. *Mem:* Can Med Asn; fel Am Col Obstetricians & Gynecologists. *Res:* Vasopressor substances in amniotic fluid and serum. *Mailing Add:* Dept of Obstet & Gynec Univ of Alta Edmonton AB T6G 2E8 Cán

DUNLOP, DOUGLAS WAYNE, b Milwaukee, Wis, Jan 27, 15; m 38; c 1. BOTANY. *Educ:* Univ Wis, PhB, 37, PhM, 38, PhD(bot), 40. *Prof Exp:* Asst instr bot, Univ Wis, 37-40; instr biol, Brooklyn Col, 40-46; from asst prof to prof, 46-77, chmn dept, 69-73, EMER PROF BOT, UNIV WIS-MILWAUKEE, 77- *Mem:* AAAS; Bot Soc Am; Am Fern Soc; Soc Econ Botanists; Int Soc Plant Morphol. *Res:* Biomagnetics; cytology; morphology; biological effects of high gravity. *Mailing Add:* Rte 1 Box 363 Mukonago WI 53149

DUNLOP, EDWARD CLARENCE, b Center, Mo, Jan 18, 16; m 45; c 2. CHEMISTRY. *Educ:* Westminster Col, Mo, AB, 36; Univ Ill, MS, 38, PhD(chem), 42. *Prof Exp:* Instr chem, Westminster Col, Mo, 36-37; asst, Buswell & Rodebush, Ill, 38-41; asst water anal, State of Ill, 41-42; chemist, E I du Pont de Nemours & Co, Del, 42-43 & Wash, 43-45, asst head, 46-63, head phys & anal div, 63-80; RETIRED. *Mem:* Am Chem Soc; Optical Soc Am; Soc Appl Spectros; Am Inst Chemists. *Res:* Analytical chemistry. *Mailing Add:* 504 Cranebrook Rd Wilmington DE 19803

DUNLOP, ROBERT HUGH, veterinary pharmacology, veterinary physiology, see previous edition

DUNLOP, WILLIAM HENRY, b Salt Lake City, Utah, June 14, 43; m 71; c 3. NUCLEAR PHYSICS. *Educ:* Univ Pa, BA, 67; Univ Calif, Los Angeles, MS, 69, PhD(physics), 71. *Prof Exp:* Fel physics, Univ Calif, Los Angeles, 71-72; RES PHYSICIST, LAWRENCE LIVERMORE LAB, 72- *Concurrent Pos:* Mem, US Deleg Conf Disarmament, Geneva, Switz, 79. *Mailing Add:* Lawrence Livermore Lab Livermore CA 94550

DUNLOP, WILLIAM ROBERT, b Mt Pleasant, Ont, Aug 2, 16. AVIAN PATHOLOGY, CELL BIOLOGY. *Educ:* Univ Toronto, DVM, 38. *Prof Exp:* Dir, D&B Labs, 38-48; lectr histol & embryol, Ont Vet Col, Univ Toronto, 48, poultry pathologist, 49-50; asst poultry pathologist, 50-51, prof poultry sci & res pathologist, 51-77, PROF ANIMAL SCI, UNIV NH, 77- *Mem:* AAAS; Am Vet Med Asn; Poultry Sci Asn; Am Soc Microbiol; Am Pub Health Asn. *Res:* Avian virology; cancer research. *Mailing Add:* Dept of Animal Sci Univ of NH Durham NH 03824

DUNN, ADRIAN JOHN, b London, Eng, June 16, 43; m 73. NEUROCHEMISTRY, BIOCHEMISTRY. *Educ:* Univ Cambridge, BA, 65; MA & PhD(biochem), 68. *Prof Exp:* From instr to asst prof biochem, Univ NC, Chapel Hill, 71-73; ASSOC PROF NEUROSCI, UNIV FLA, 78- *Concurrent Pos:* Nat Res Coun Italy fel, Int Lab Genetics & Biophys, Naples, 68-69; NIMH fel biochem, Univ NC, Chapel Hill, 70-71. *Mem:* AAAS; Am Soc Neurochem; Soc Neurosci; Biochem Soc; Int Soc Neurochem. *Res:* Protein and nucleic acid synthesis in nervous tissue; biochemical changes in nervous tissue due to stimulation; the molecular basis of learning and memory; the interaction of hormones with the brain in behavior. *Mailing Add:* Dept Neurosci Univ of Fla Col of Med Gainesville FL 32610

DUNN, ANDREW FLETCHER, b Sydney, NS, Jan 17, 22; m 43; c 2. EXPERIMENTAL PHYSICS. *Educ:* Dalhousie Univ, BSc, 42, MSc, 47; Univ Toronto, PhD(physics), 50. *Prof Exp:* Jr res officer physics, Atlantic Fisheries Exp Sta, 46-47; asst res officer, 50-54, assoc res officer, 54-63, SR RES OFFICER, NAT RES COUN, CAN, 63-, HEAD ELEC SECT, 71- *Mem:* Fel Inst Elec & Electronics Eng; Can Asn Physicists. *Res:* Precision electrical measurements; national primary standards; absolute determination of electrical quantities. *Mailing Add:* Div of Physics Nat Res Coun of Can Montreal Rd Ottawa Can

DUNN, ARNOLD SAMUEL, b Rochester, NY, Jan 31, 29; m 52; c 2. PHYSIOLOGY, ENDOCRINOLOGY. *Educ:* George Washington Univ, BS, 50; Univ Pa, PhD(physiol), 55. *Prof Exp:* Res assoc metab & endocrinol, Michael Reese Hosp Res Inst, 55-56; from instr to asst prof pharmacol, Sch Med, NY Univ, 56-62; from asst prof to assoc prof, 62-70, PROF MOLECULAR BIOL, UNIV SOUTHERN CALIF, 70- *Concurrent Pos:* Vis prof, Hebrew Univ Jerusalem & vis scientist & prof, Dept of Biophys, Weizmann Inst Sci, Rehovat, Israel, 72-73; USPHS res fel, 72-73. *Mem:* Endocrine Soc; Am Physiol Soc; Fedn Am Socs Exp Biol; Am Soc Biol Chem. *Res:* Physiology of cell division; biochemistry; endocrine control of metabolism; carbohydrate metabolism; development of isotope techniques for metabolism; hormone mechanisms. *Mailing Add:* Dept Molecular Biol Univ Southern Calif Los Angeles CA 90007

DUNN, BEN MONROE, b Neptune, NJ, Mar 22, 45; m 67; c 2. BIO-ORGANIC CHEMISTRY, PHYSICAL BIOCHEMISTRY. *Educ:* Univ Del, BS, 67; Univ Calif, PhD(bio-org chem), 71. *Prof Exp:* Staff fel protein chem, Chem Biol Lab, NIH, 73-74; asst prof biochem, 74-80, asst prof molecular biol, 77-80, ASSOC PROF BIOCHEM & MOLECULAR BIOL, UNIV FLA, 80- *Mem:* Am Chem Soc; Am Soc Biol Chemists; Biophys Soc. *Res:* The relationship between the structure and functionality of enzyme active sites and the catalytic activity studied by peptide synthesis, enzyme kinetics and model systems. *Mailing Add:* Dept of Biochem Univ of Fla Gainesville FL 32611

DUNN, BENJAMIN ALLEN, b Etowah, Tenn, Aug 3, 41; m 65; c 3. FOREST MANAGEMENT, FORESTRY. *Educ:* Univ Ga, BSF, 65, MF, 68, PhD(forestry), 71. *Prof Exp:* Res asst forestry, Univ Ga, 69-71; biologist, Tenn Valley Authority, 71-72, environ scientist, 72-73; asst prof, 73-76, ASSOC PROF FORESTRY, CLEMSON UNIV, 76- *Mem:* Soc Am Foresters; Sigma Xi; Am Forest Asn. *Res:* Taxonomic, biological and ecological investigations of endangered and threatened forest plant species; edaphic and vegetative relationships on forest sites impacted by recreation; socioeconomic aspects of forest management. *Mailing Add:* Dept of Forestry Clemson Univ Clemson SC 29631

DUNN, BRUCE PARTRIDGE, cancer, pollution chemistry, see previous edition

DUNN, CHARLES NORD, b Elk River, Minn, Oct 25, 36; m 58; c 4. SOLID STATE PHYSICS. *Educ:* Univ Minn, BS, 58, MSEE, 60, PhD(elec eng), 64. *Prof Exp:* MEM TECH STAFF, BELL LABS, INC, 64- *Mem:* Inst Elec & Electronic Eng; Am Phys Soc. *Res:* Integrated circuit device development; development of microwave diodes; oxide-coated-cathode; charge transport in non-ionized gases. *Mailing Add:* Bell Labs Inc 2525 N 12th St Reading PA 19604

DUNN, CHRISTOPHER DAVID REGINALD, b Berkeley, Eng, Nov 13, 45; m 75; c 1. PHARMACOLOGY, HEMATOLOGY. *Educ:* Univ Bradford, BPharm Hons, 67; Univ London, PhD(pharmacol), 70. *Prof Exp:* Lectr biophysics, Inst Cancer Res, London, 70-72; sr sci officer, hemat, Welsh Nat Sch Med, Univ Wales, Cardiff, 72-75; asst prof med biol, Mem Res Ctr, Univ Tenn, 76-79, assoc prof, 79-80; SR SCIENTIST, NORTHROP SERV INC, 80-; RES ASSOC PROF, BAYLOR COL MED, 80- *Concurrent Pos:* Sr sci officer, Univ Hosp Wales, Cardiff, 72-75; fel, Brit Coun Younger Scientist Interchange Scheme, 73; consult, NASA, 78- *Mem:* Int Soc Exp Hemat; Am Soc Hemat; Brit Soc Hemat; Soc Exp Biol & Med; Aerospace Med Asn. *Res:* Hormonal control of hemopoiesis; hemopoietic stem cell regulation; cell kinetics and anti-tumor therapy; erythropoietic effects of space flight. *Mailing Add:* Northrop Serv Inc PO Box 34416 Houston TX 77034

DUNN, CLARK A(LLAN), b Stickney, SDak, Sept 9, 01; m 28; c 2. CIVIL ENGINEERING. *Educ:* Univ Wis, BS, 23; Okla State Univ, CE, 34, MS, 37; Cornell Univ, PhD, 41. *Prof Exp:* Engr, Bridge Div, SDak State Hwy Comn, 23-27; assoc with J E Kirkham, Consult Engr, 27; construct engr, Bridge Div, Ark State Hwy Dept, 27-29; from asst prof to prof civil eng, Okla State Univ, 29-66, head gen eng, 41-66, dir eng res & head sch gen eng, 45-66, assoc dean, Col Eng, 66-67, EMER PROF CIVIL ENG, OKLA STATE UNIV, 67- *Concurrent Pos:* Observer, Task Force Frigid Opers, Alaska. *Mem:* Fel AAAS; Am Soc civil Engrs; Am Soc Eng Educ; Nat Soc Prof Engrs (vpres, 55-57, pres, 58-59). *Res:* Electric welding inspection. *Mailing Add:* 2119 W University Ave Stillwater OK 74075

DUNN, DANNY LEROY, b Wichita, Kans, July 12, 46; m 67; c 2. ANALYTICAL CHEMISTRY, ORGANIC CHEMISTRY. *Educ:* Wichita State Univ, BS, 68, MS, 70; NTex State Univ, PhD(org chem), 76. *Prof Exp:* Fel bio-org, Health Sci Ctr, Univ Tex, 76-78; sr scientist, 78-81, HEAD HIGH PERFORMANCE LIQUID CHROMATOGRAPHY CHEM, ALCON LABS, 81- *Mem:* Am Chem Soc. *Res:* applications of high performance liquid chromatography to drug analysis; optimization of analytical methods; resolution of optically active compounds using chromatography. *Mailing Add:* Alcon Labs PO Box 1959 Ft Worth TX 76101

DUNN, DAPHNE FAUTIN, b Urbana, Ill, May 25, 46; m 69. MARINE INVERTEBRATE ZOOLOGY. *Educ:* Beloit Col, BS, 66; Univ Calif, Berkeley, PhD(zool), 72. *Prof Exp:* NIH fel marine pharmacol, Univ Hawaii Sch Med, 72-73; res assoc zool, Univ Malaya, 73-75; RES BIOLOGIST INVERT ZOOL, CALIF ACAD SCI, 75- *Concurrent Pos:* NSF grant, Calif Acad Sci, 77- *Mem:* Soc Syst Zool; Sigma Xi; Malaysian Soc Marine Sci; Int Oceanog Found. *Res:* Marine invertebrate reproduction particularly brooding and biogeography; systematics of coelenterates, especially anthozoa; marine symbiology; tropical marine ecosystems. *Mailing Add:* Dept of Invert Zool Golden Gate Park San Francisco CA 94118

DUNN, DARREL EUGENE, b Clay Center, Kans, July 15, 32; m 65; c 2. HYDROGEOLOGY. *Educ:* Univ Ill, Urbana, BS, 55, PhD(geol), 67. *Prof Exp:* Geologist, Pure Oil Co, 57-61; groundwater geologist, Alta Res Coun, Edmonton, Can, 66-67; asst prof geol, Mont State Univ, 67-71; assoc prof geol, Univ Toledo, 71-74, HYDROGEOLOGIST, EARTH SCI SERV, INC, 74- *Mem:* Geol Soc Am; Am Water Resources Asn; Am Asn Petrol Geol; Nat Waterwell Asn. *Res:* Computer modeling of ground water systems and watershed systems. *Mailing Add:* Earth Sci Serv Inc PO Box 1985 Bozeman MT 59715

DUNN, DAVID BAXTER, b Mustang, Okla, Jan 10, 17; m 42; c 6. BOTANY. *Educ:* Univ Calif, Los Angeles, BA, 40, MA, 43, PhD(bot), 48. *Prof Exp:* Asst bot, Univ Calif, Los Angeles, 40-42 & 46-47; instr bot & genetics, Calif State Polytech Col, 47-48; asst bot, Atomic Energy Proj, Univ Calif, Los Angeles, 48-50; asst biol, NMex Agr & Mech Col, 50-53; vis lectr, Univ Minn, 54; vis botanist, Rancho Santa Ana Bot Garden, 53-55 & Occidental Col, 55-56; from asst prof to assoc prof, 56-70, PROF BOT & CUR HERBARIUM, UNIV MO, 70- *Concurrent Pos:* Ed, Trans, Mo Acad Sci, 66- & Mus Contrib Monographic Series, 70- *Mem:* Fel AAAS; Soc Study Evolution; Am Soc Plant Taxon; Bot Soc Am; Ecol Soc Am. *Res:* Lupinus, the taxonomy, breeding systems, genetics, ecological races, intersterility and interfertility between colonies as well as races; desert ecology. *Mailing Add:* 1306 Hinkson Columbia MO 65201

DUNN, DAVID EVAN, b Dallas, Tex, Oct 13, 35; m 58; c 2. ROCK MECHANICS, STRUCTURAL GEOLOGY. *Educ:* Southern Methodist Univ, BS, 57, MS, 59; Univ Tex, PhD(geol), 64. *Prof Exp:* Asst prof struct geol, Tex Tech Col, 62-63; vis asst prof, Univ NC, Chapel Hill, 63-64, from asst prof to assoc prof, 64-73, actg chmn dept geol, 67, asst chmn, 66-69, prof struct geol, 73-79; PROF EARTH SCI & DEAN, COL SCI, UNIV NEW ORLEANS, 79- *Concurrent Pos:* Consult geologist, 60, 61; first vchmn, Struct Geol & Tectonics Div, Geol Soc Am, 80-e; counr, La Univs Marine Consortium, 79-, chmn, 81-82. *Mem:* AAAS; Am Geophys Union; Asn Prof Geol Scientists; Geol Soc Am; Nat Asn Geol Teachers. *Res:* Deformation in orogenic belts; rock mechanics. *Mailing Add:* Dept of Geol Lake Front New Orleans LA 70148

DUNN, DEAN ALAN, b Groton, Conn, Nov 11, 54. PALEOCLIMATOLOGY, BIOSTRATIGRAPHY. *Educ:* Univ Southern Calif, BS, 76 & 77; Univ RI, PhD(oceanog), 82. *Prof Exp:* Geophys asst, Western Region Explor Off, Union Oil Co, Calif, 76; lab tech II, Dept Geol Sci, Univ Southern Calif, 76-77; teaching asst, phys geol lab, Dept Geol, Fla State Univ, 77-78; RES ASST IV, GRAD SCH OCEANOG, UNIV RI, 78- *Concurrent Pos:* Shipboard sedimentologist, Deep Sea Drilling Proj Leg 85-Equatorial Pac Paleoenvirons, 82. *Mem:* Geol Soc Am; Am Asn Petrol Geologists; NAm Micropaleontol Sect, Soc Econ Mineralogists & Paleontologists. *Res:* Paleoclimatology of the Miocene Equatorial Pacific Ocean by the study of spectral analysis of deep-sea carbonate sediments; potential for using carbonate oscillations for correlative lithostratigraphy. *Mailing Add:* Grad Sch Oceanog Univ RI Narragansett RI 02882

DUNN, DONALD A(LLEN), b Los Angeles, Calif, Dec 31, 25; m 48; c 2. COMMUNICATIONS. *Educ:* Calif Inst Technol, BS, 46; Stanford Univ, MS, 47, LLB, 51, PhD(elec eng), 56. *Prof Exp:* Res assoc elec eng, Stanford Univ, 51-59; dir res, Eitel-McCullough, Inc, 59-61; assoc prof & dir plasma physics lab elec eng, 61-68, assoc prof, 69-72, PROF ENG ECON SYSTS, STANFORD UNIV, 72- *Concurrent Pos:* Mem 20th Century Fund task force on int satellite commun; consult, Nat Acad Eng comt on telecommun; consult, Fed Commun Comn, Senate subcomt on commun & Dept Justice Antitrust Div; mem rev panels, Off Sci & Technol, NSF & Nat Acad Sci. *Mem:* Fel Inst Elec & Electronics Engrs; Asn Pub Policy & Mgt; AAAS. *Res:* Telecommunications systems; public policy analysis. *Mailing Add:* Dept of Eng-Econ Systs Stanford Univ Stanford CA 94305

DUNN, DONALD WILLIAM, b Kingston, Ont, Apr 10, 23. FLUID MECHANICS, ASYMPTOTIC ANALYSIS. *Educ:* Queen's Univ, Ont, BA, 48; Mass Inst Technol, PhD(math), 53. *Prof Exp:* Asst math, Mass Inst Technol, 52-53, res assoc, 53-54; res fel aeronaut, Johns Hopkins Univ, 54-57; asst res officer, Nat Res Coun Can, 57-65; MATH CONSULT, 65- *Mem:* Am Math Soc; Soc Indust & Appl Math; Can Math Soc. *Res:* Laminar flow stability; turbulence; applications in engineering, geophysics and astrophysics. *Mailing Add:* PO Box 244 280 Laurier Ave E Kingston ON K7L 4V8 Can

DUNN, DORIS FRANKEL, b New York, NY, July 9, 27; m 52; c 2. BIOCHEMISTRY. *Educ:* Brooklyn Col, BS, 47; Univ Rochester, MS, 52; Temple Univ, PhD(biochem), 56. *Prof Exp:* Asst biochem, Sch Hyg, Johns Hopkins Univ, 49-50; AEC asst, Univ Rochester, 50-52; res assoc metab & endocrinol, Res Inst, Michael Reese Hosp, 55-56; res fel, Sloan-Kettering Inst Cancer Res, 56-57; res biochemist, Sch Med, Univ Southern Calif, 63-66; info analyst, Brain Info Serv, Brain Res Inst, Univ Calif, Los Angeles, 70-76; res assoc, 77-78, asst prof, Sch Libr Sci, 78-81, ASST PROF, SCH MED, UNIV SOUTHERN CALIF, 81- *Mailing Add:* 1272 Monument St Pacific Palisades CA

DUNN, FLOYD, b Kansas City, Mo, Apr 14, 24; m 50; c 2. BIOPHYSICS, BIOENGINEERING. *Educ:* Univ Ill, BS, 49, MS, 51, PhD(elec eng), 56. *Prof Exp:* From asst to res asst prof elec eng, 49-57, from res asst prof to prof elec eng & biophys, 57-65, PROF BIOPHYS, ELEC ENG & BIOENG, UNIV ILL, URBANA, 65-, DIR, BIOACOUST RES LAB, 76-, CHMN, BIOENG FAC, 78- *Concurrent Pos:* NIH spec res fel microbiol, Univ Col S Wales, 68-69; Am Cancer Soc-Eleanor Roosevelt int fel, Inst Cancer Res, Sutton, Eng, 75-76; assoc ed, Bioacoustics, Acoust Soc Am; mem, Tech Electronic Prod Radiation Standards Comt, Food & Drug Admin, 74-76; mem, Radiation Study Sect, NIH, 76- *Mem:* Biophys Soc; fel Acoust Soc Am (vpres, 81-82); AAAS; fel Inst Elec & Electronics Engrs; fel Am Inst Ultrasound in Med. *Res:* Ultrasonics; ultrasonic biophysics; ultrasonic absorption microscopy and spectroscopy; physical mechanism of the action of ultrasound on biological systems; ultrasonic toxicity; ultrasonic dosimetry; bioacoustics; infrasonics. *Mailing Add:* Bioacoust Res Lab Univ Ill Urbana IL 61801

DUNN, FLOYD WARREN, b Huntington, Ark, Dec 15, 20; m 44; c 3. BIOCHEMISTRY. *Educ:* Abilene Christian Univ, BS, 44; Univ Colo, MS, 46, PhD(biochem), 50. *Prof Exp:* Prof chem, Abilene Christian Univ, 46-60; assoc prof biochem, Med Units, Univ Tenn, 60-63, prof, 63-65; prof biochem, Col Med, Univ Ill, assigned to fac med, Chiengmai Univ, Thailand, 65-68; PROF BIOCHEM, DEPT CHEM, ABILENE CHRISTIAN UNIV, 68-, DEAN GRAD SCH, 74- *Concurrent Pos:* Tech adv chem, US Int Co-op Admin at Chulalongkorn Univ, Bangkok, Thailand, 58-59. *Mem:* Am Chem Soc; Am Soc Biol Chem; Soc Exp Biol & Med. *Res:* Synthesis of amino acids and peptides; amino acid antagonists; proteolytic enzymes; microbiological assay. *Mailing Add:* Dept Chem Abilene Christian Univ Abilene TX 79601

DUNN, FREDERICK LESTER, b Seneca Falls, NY, Dec 24, 28; m 69; c 2. EPIDEMIOLOGY, ANTHROPOLOGY. *Educ:* Harvard Univ, AB, 51, MD, 56; Univ London, DTM&H, 60; Univ Malaya, PhD, 73. *Prof Exp:* Intern, King County Hosp, Seattle, Wash, 56-57; from asst chief to chief influenza surveillance unit, Commun Dis Ctr, USPHS, Ga, 57-59; from asst res epidemiologist & asst clin prof trop med to assoc res epidemiologist & assoc clin prof, 60-67, assoc prof epidemiol, 67-69, chmn grad group in anthrop, 71-72, PROF EPIDEMIOL & MED ANTHROP, UNIV CALIF, SAN FRANCISCO, 69- *Concurrent Pos:* Lectr, Sch Pub Health, Univ Calif, Berkeley, 65- *Mem:* AAAS; Am Pub Health Asn; Soc Epidemiol Res; Am Soc Trop Med & Hyg; Soc Med Anthrop. *Res:* Communicable disease epidemiology and control; international health; medical anthropology; comparative medical systems. *Mailing Add:* Dept of Epidemiol & Int Health Univ of Calif San Francisco CA 94143

DUNN, GARY RAYMOND, b Boston, Mass, June 14, 45; m 66; c 2. GENETICS. *Educ:* Gettysburg Col, BA, 66; Univ Maine, MS, 68; Univ Tenn, PhD(biomed sci), 71. *Prof Exp:* Res fel genetics, Univ Edinburgh, Scotland, 71-72; staff fel genetics, Human Develop, Nat Inst Child Health, 72-74; ASSOC GENETICS, HARVARD MED SCH, 74- *Concurrent Pos:* Instr embryol, Georgetown Univ, 73-74. *Mem:* Genetics Soc Am. *Res:* Histocompatibility genetics. *Mailing Add:* Dept of Radiation Ther Harvard Med Sch Boston MA 02115

DUNN, GEORGE LAWRENCE, b Groton, Conn, May 5, 36; m 59; c 3. ORGANIC CHEMISTRY. *Educ:* Univ Conn, BA, 58; Univ Maine, MS, 60, PhD(org chem), 62. *Prof Exp:* Sr med chemist, 62-69, sr investr, 69-75, ASST DIR CHEM, SMITH KLINE & FRENCH LABS, 75- *Mem:* Am Chem Soc; Sigma Xi. *Res:* Steroid synthesis; heterocyclic and polycyclic cage compounds; antibiotics; semisynthetic penicillins and cephalosporins. *Mailing Add:* Smith Kline & French Labs PO Box 7929 Philadelphia PA 19101

DUNN, GERALD EMERY, b Hampton, NS, May 12, 19; m 45; c 3. PHYSICAL ORGANIC CHEMISTRY. *Educ:* Acadia Univ, BS, 43; Univ Toronto, MA, 46; Iowa State Col, PhD(chem), 50. *Prof Exp:* From asst prof to assoc prof, 51-60, head dept, 75-80, PROF CHEM, UNIV MAN, 60- *Concurrent Pos:* Corp fel, Harvard Univ, 50-51. *Mem:* Am Chem Soc; Chem Inst Can. *Res:* Mechanisms; isotope effects. *Mailing Add:* Dept of Chem Univ of Man Winnipeg Can

DUNN, GERALD MARVIN, b Canfield, WVa, Sept 4, 19; m 55; c 4. PLANT BREEDING, GENETICS. *Educ:* Univ WVa, BS, 48; Purdue Univ, MS, 50, PhD(plant breeding & genetics), 51. *Prof Exp:* Asst plant breeding, Purdue Univ, 48-51; from asst prof to assoc prof agron, 51-62; prof agron, 62-74, PROF PLANT SCI, UNIV NH, 74- *Mem:* Am Soc Agron; Am Genetic Asn. *Res:* Genetic studies on chemical composition and diseases of corn; breeding and genetics of perennial grasses and legumes; minimum tillage of forage crops. *Mailing Add:* 35 Bagdad Rd Durham NH 03824

DUNN, GORDON HAROLD, b Montpelier, Idaho, Oct 11, 32; m 52; c 8. ATOMIC PHYSICS, MOLECULAR PHYSICS. *Educ:* Univ Wash, BS, 55, PhD(physics), 61. *Prof Exp:* Nat Bur Standards-Nat Res Coun fel atomic collisions, 61-62, PHYSICIST, JOINT INST FOR LAB ASTROPHYS, NAT BUR STANDARDS, 62- *Concurrent Pos:* Lectr physics & astrophys, Univ Colo, 62-74, adj prof, 74-; mem gen comt, Int Conf Physics of Electronic & Atomic Collisons, 69-73; chmn, Gaseous Electronics Conf, 71 & 72; fel, Comt Sci & Technol, US House Rep, 75-76. *Honors & Awards:* Gold Medal, Dept Com, 70. *Mem:* Fel Am Phys Soc. *Res:* Investigation of collisions of electrons and photons with ions and with other simple atomic and molecular systems. *Mailing Add:* Joint Inst Lab Astrophys Univ of Colo Boulder CO 80302

DUNN, HENRY GEORGE, b Leipzig, Ger, Apr 18, 17; m 54; c 2. PEDIATRIC NEUROLOGY. *Educ:* Univ Cambridge, MB & BCh, 42, MA, 43; DCH, 50; FRCP(C), 72; FRCP, 73. *Prof Exp:* Registr, Children's Dept, London Hosp, Eng, 49-51 & Hosp Sick Children, London, 51-52; asst pathologist, Babies Hosp, Columbia-Presby Med Ctr, 52-53; chief resident pediat, Vancouver Gen Hosp, 53-54; from asst prof to assoc prof, 56-68, PROF PEDIAT, UNIV BC, 68- *Concurrent Pos:* Holt fel, Columbia Univ, 52-53; fel pediat, Univ BC, 54-55; R S McLaughlin travelling fel, 66-67; res assoc, Harvard Med Sch, 59 & Children's Med Ctr, 59; consult, Woodlands Sch Retarded. *Mem:* Am Asn Ment Deficiency; Can Med Asn; Can Pediat Soc; Can Neurol Soc; Royal Soc Med. *Res:* Mental retardation; nerve conduction studies in children; metabolic disorders in children; child neurology. *Mailing Add:* 4088 Maple Crescent Vancouver BC V6J 4B2 Can

DUNN, HOWARD EUGENE, b Kansas City, Mo, Apr 14, 38; m 61; c 2. ORGANIC CHEMISTRY. *Educ:* William Jewell Col, AB, 60; Univ Ill, PhD(org chem), 65. *Prof Exp:* Res chemist, Res Ctr, Phillips Petrol Co, 65-69; asst prof, 69-74, assoc prof, 74-78, PROF CHEM, IND STATE UNIV, EVANSVILLE, 78- *Concurrent Pos:* Res grant, Southern Ill Univ, 71. *Mem:* Am Chem Soc. *Res:* Organoboron, sulfoxide and sulfone chemistry; homogeneous catalysis; trace analysis; environmental chemistry. *Mailing Add:* Dept of Chem Ind State Univ Evansville IN 47712

DUNN, IRVING JOHN, b Berkeley, Calif, Dec 15, 38; m 62; c 3. FERMENTATION TECHNOLOGY, BIOCHEMICAL ENGINEERING. *Educ:* Univ Wash, BS, 60; Princeton Univ, PhD(chem eng), 63. *Prof Exp:* Asst prof chem eng, Univ Idaho, 64-68; assoc prof, Robert Col, 68-70; DOZENT CHEM ENG, SWISS FED INST TECHNOL, 71- *Mem:* Am Chem Soc. *Res:* Biochemical engineering including fermentation technology and biological waste water treatment; design of gas-liquid biological reactors and biological film reactors; modelling and simulation of biological processes; instrumentation and control. *Mailing Add:* Chem Eng Lab Swiss Fed Inst Technol 8092 Zurich Switzerland

DUNN, J(OHN) HOWARD, b Omaha, Nebr, Aug 29, 09; m 35; c 3. MECHANICAL ENGINEERING. *Educ:* Iowa State Univ, BS, 31. *Prof Exp:* Asst mgr, Dunn Mfg Co, 31-34; develop engr, Aluminum Co Am, 34-41, asst to mgr prod planning, 41-44, automotive develop mgr, 44-49, asst mgr, Develop Div, 49-53, mgr, 53-59, mgr, Process Develop Labs, 59-67, dir develop, 67-70, vpres res & develop, 70-74; RETIRED. *Honors & Awards:* Prof Achievement Award in Eng, Iowa State Univ, 71. *Mem:* Soc Automotive Engrs; Sigma Xi. *Res:* Applications of aluminum alloys and products, especially in the automotive field. *Mailing Add:* 1078 Wade Lane Oakmont PA 15139

DUNN, JAMES ELDON, b Fairbury, Nebr, Jan 8, 36; m 64; c 2. MATHEMATICAL STATISTICS. *Educ:* Univ Nebr, BSc, 57, MSc, 61; Va Polytech Inst, PhD(statist), 63. *Prof Exp:* From asst prof to assoc prof, 63-76, PROF MATH, UNIV ARK, FAYETTEVILLE, 76- *Concurrent Pos:* Statist consult, Ark State Judiciary Comn, 63-65, Bur Sport Fisheries & Wildlife, 65-71 & Sport Fishing Inst, 68-71; NSF sci fac fel, Stanford Univ, 71-72. *Mem:* Am Statist Asn; Biomet Soc. *Res:* Statistical applications in biology. *Mailing Add:* Dept of Math Univ of Ark Fayetteville AR 72701

DUNN, JAMES ROBERT, b Sacramento, Calif, Oct 18, 21; m 70; c 5. GEOLOGY. *Educ:* Univ Calif, AB, 43, PhD(geol), 50. *Prof Exp:* Asst, Univ Calif, 46-50; from assoc prof to prof, 50-73, ADJ PROF GEOL, RENSSELAER POLYTECH INST, 73- *Concurrent Pos:* Geologist, New Idria Quicksilver Mining Co, 46 & Iron Ore Co, Can, 51; indust & govt consult, 53-; pres, Dunn Geosci Corp, 60-71, chmn bd, 71-; pres, Am Inst Prof Geol Found, 81. *Mem:* Am Inst Prof Geologists (vpres, 79, pres, 80); Asn Eng Geol; Soc Econ Geol; Am Inst Planners; Am Soc Testing & Mat. *Res:* Physical and chemical characteristics of available materials for filling subsurface coal mines; potential alkali reactivity of chert in portland cement concrete; socio-economic applications of geology, including environmental geology, conservation and planning; utilization of geothermal heat; computer simulation techniques in planning for mineral resource development. *Mailing Add:* Dunn Geosci Corp 5 Northway Lane N Latham NY 12110

DUNN, JOHN FREDERICK, JR, b Passaic, NJ, May 13, 30; m 53; c 5. MECHANICAL ENGINEERING. *Educ:* Mass Inst Technol, SB, 51, SM, 53, ScD(mech eng), 57. *Prof Exp:* Proj engr, Dynamic Anal & Control Lab, Mass Inst Technol, 51-57; proj engr, Res Div, Walworth Co, 57-58, asst dir valve res, 58-59, chief engr design & prod control res, 59-62; assoc prof mech eng, 62-63, PROF MECH ENG, NORTHEASTERN UNIV, 63- *Concurrent Pos:* Mem exec comt, Mfrs Standardization Soc Valve & Fitting Indust, 61-62. *Mem:* Am Soc Mech Engrs; Am Soc Eng Educ. *Res:* Components for high-performance electro-hydraulic and electro-pneumatic control systems. *Mailing Add:* Dept of Mech Eng Rm 47OUR Northeastern Univ Boston MA 02115

DUNN, JOHN MICHAEL, b Lynn, Mass, Nov 25, 48; m 70. PHYSICAL BIOCHEMISTRY, NUTRITIONAL BIOCHEMISTRY. *Educ:* Univ SFla, BS & BA, 71; Univ Kans, PhD(biochem), 77. *Prof Exp:* Fel phys biochem, Univ Kans, 77-78; ASST PROF BIOCHEM, NAT COL NATUROPATHIC MED, 78- *Res:* Ribosome assembly; nutritional biochemistry; protein folding; antimutagenic screening. *Mailing Add:* Nat Col Naturopathic Med 11231 Southeast Market St Portland OR 97213

DUNN, JOHN PATRICK JAMES, b Pottsville, Pa, May 29, 44; m 66; c 2. MOLECULAR BIOLOGY. *Educ:* West Chester State Col, AB, 66; Rutgers Univ, New Brunswick, PhD(microbiol), 70. *Prof Exp:* Fel molecular genetics, Univ Heidelberg, 70-72; asst microbiologist, 72-74, assoc microbiologist, 74-77, MICROBIOLOGIST, BROOKHAVEN NAT LAB, 77- *Concurrent Pos:* Adj asst prof microbiol, State Univ NY Stonybrook, 75-80, adj prof, 80- *Mem:* AAAS; Am Soc Biol Chemists. *Res:* Transcription of DNA, processing of mRNA and translation of mRNA. *Mailing Add:* Dept of Biol Brookhaven Nat Lab Upton NY 11973

DUNN, JOHN ROBERT, b Andover, Eng, May 12, 30; m 55; c 4. PHYSICAL ORGANIC CHEMISTRY, RUBBER TECHNOLOGY. *Educ:* Univ London, BSc, 51, DPhil(phys org chem), 53. *Prof Exp:* Nat Res Coun Can fel, 53-55; sr chemist, Natural Rubber Producers' Res Asn, 55-62; sr res chemist, 62-66, supvr compounding res, Polymer Corp, Ltd, 66-71, SCI ADV, POLYSAR, LTD, 71- *Mem:* Fel Chem Inst Can; Am Chem Soc; Int Orgn Standardization. *Res:* Rubber technology; oxidation and antioxidants in rubber and aldehydes; vulcanization of rubber; physical properties of polymers; photolysis of ketones; flame retardancy; polymer blends; modification of polymers. *Mailing Add:* Polysar Ltd Vidal St Sarnia ON N7T 7M2 Can

DUNN, JOHN THORNTON, b Washington, DC, Oct 27, 32; m 62; c 3. ENDOCRINOLOGY. *Educ:* Princeton Univ, AB, 54; Duke Univ, MD, 58. *Prof Exp:* Intern med, NY Hosp-Cornell Univ, 58-59; resident, Univ Utah Hosps, 59-61; asst prof, 66-70, assoc prof, 70-76, PROF MED, SCH MED, UNIV VA, 76- *Concurrent Pos:* Fel thyroid, Mass Gen Hosp-Harvard Univ, 61-62 & 63-64; fel, Presby Hosp-Columbia Univ, 62-63; fel biochem, Harvard Med Sch, 64-66; Nat Inst Arthritis & Metab Dis res grant, 66-; USPHS res career develop award, 71-76; consult, Pan Am Health Orgn. *Honors & Awards:* Van Meter Prize, Am Thyroid Asn, 68. *Mem:* Am Soc Biol Chemists; Am Thyroid Asn; Endocrine Soc; Am Fedn Clin Res. *Res:* Thyroglobulin structure; endemic goiter; thyroid disease; thyroid physiology. *Mailing Add:* Univ Va Sch Med Box 511 Charlottesville VA 22908

DUNN, JON D, b La Junta, Colo, June 12, 37; m 63; c 3. NEUROENDOCRINOLOGY. *Educ:* Col of Idaho, BS, 62; Univ Kans, PhD(anat), 67. *Prof Exp:* From instr to assoc prof neuroanat, La State Univ Med Ctr, 68-74, res assoc, 74-75; assoc prof neuroanat, Stritch Sch Med, Loyola Univ Chicago, 75-78; PROF NEUROANAT, SCH MED, ORAL ROBERTS UNIV, 78- *Honors & Awards:* W B Peck Sci Res Award, Interstate Postgrad Med Asn NAm, 71. *Mem:* Soc Neurosci; Am Asn Anatomists; Am Physiol Soc; Endocrine Soc; Int Soc Neuroendocrinol. *Res:* Influence of various environmental factors on pituitary-adrenal and pituitary-gonadal function and the neural substrate involved in producing changes in these systems. *Mailing Add:* Dept of Anat 7777 S Lewis Tulsa OK 74171

DUNN, JOSEPH CHARLES, b New York, NY. APPLIED MATHEMATICS, OPTIMIZATION THEORY. *Educ:* Polytech Inst Brooklyn, BAeroE, 59, MS, 63; Adelphi Univ, PhD(math), 67. *Prof Exp:* Dynamics engr, Grumman Aerospace Corp, 59-61, res engr, 61-67, staff scientist, 67-69; asst prof theoret & appl mech, Cornell Univ, 69-76; assoc prof, 76-79, PROF MATH, NC STATE UNIV, 79- *Concurrent Pos:* Adj asst prof, Adelphi Univ, 68-69; NSF res initiation grant, 70, res grants, 78-80 & 80-83. *Mem:* Am Math Soc; Soc Indust & Appl Math. *Res:* Nonlinear functional analysis and optimization theory; singular optimal control problems; fixed point theory; computational methods for optimization and fixed point problems; group averaging and fuzzy partitioning techniques in pattern classification. *Mailing Add:* Dept Math NC State Univ Raleigh NC 27650

DUNN, MARVIN I, b Topeka, Kans, Dec 21, 27; m 56; c 2. INTERNAL MEDICINE, CARDIOLOGY. *Educ:* Univ Kans, BA, 50, MD, 54; Am Bd Internal Med, dipl, 63, Am Bd Cardiovasc Dis, dipl, 65. *Prof Exp:* From instr to assoc prof, 58-71, PROF MED, UNIV KANS, 71-, DIR, CARDIOVASC LAB, 63-, FRANKLIN E MURPHY DISTINGUISHED PROFESSORSHIP CARDIOL, 78-, DEAN, SCH MED, 80- *Concurrent Pos:* Fel cardiovasc dis, Univ Kans, 58-60; consult, Vet Admin Hosp, Kansas City, Mo, 60-, Menorah Hosp, 61-, Bethany & Providence Hosps, Kansas City, Kans, 65- & US Air Force; fel coun clin cardiol, Am Heart Asn, 66- *Mem:* AMA; fel Am Col Cardiol; fel Am Col Physicians; Asn Univ Cardiologists; NY Acad Sci. *Res:* Clinical cardiovascular problems and hemodynamics. *Mailing Add:* Cardiovasc Lab Univ of Kans Med Ctr Kansas City KS 66103

DUNN, MARY CATHERINE, b Iva, SC, Apr 29, 24. ZOOLOGY. *Educ:* Winthrop Col, BS, 45; Univ Mich, MS, 47; Univ Ga, PhD(zool), 57. *Prof Exp:* Analyst chem, Tenn Eastman Corp, 45-46; instr biol, Culver-Stockton Col, 47-48; asst res parasitologist, Parke Davis & Co, 48-51; asst prof zool, Philadelphia Col Pharm, 57-58; res assoc parasitol, Columbia Univ, 58-63; assoc prof biol, Shorter col, 63-65; assoc prof biol, 65-71, PROF BIOL, MIDDLE TENN STATE UNIV, 71- *Mem:* AAAS; Am Soc Parasitol; Am Soc Trop Med & Hyg; Am Micros Soc. *Res:* General zoology; cytology of trematodes; general parasitology. *Mailing Add:* Dept Biol Mid Tenn State Univ Murfreesboro TN 37132

DUNN, MICHAEL F, b Greeley, Colo, July 11, 39; m 58; c 4. BIOCHEMISTRY, ENZYMOLOGY. *Educ:* Colo Sch Mines, PRE, 61; Ga Inst Technol, MS, 63, PhD(phys org chem), 66. *Prof Exp:* Res assoc enzym, Inst Molecular Biol, Univ Ore, 66-69; res assoc physics & chem inst, Tech Univ Denmark, 69-70; asst prof biochem, 70-76, PROF BIOCHEM, UNIV CALIF, RIVERSIDE, 76- *Concurrent Pos:* NIH fel, 66-67; USPHS trainee, 67-69; NATO fel, 69-70; Am Cancer Soc grant, 71-72; NSF res grant, 75-78; Am Cancer Soc res grant, 73-75. *Mem:* Am Chem Soc; Am Soc Biol Chemists. *Res:* Enzyme structure, function and catalytic mechanism via rapid kinetic techniques; dehydrogenases; aldolases; growth factor proteins. *Mailing Add:* Dept of Biochem Univ of Calif Riverside CA 92521

DUNN, OLIVE JEAN, b Winnipeg, Can, Sept 1, 15; US citizen; c 3. BIOSTATISTICS. *Educ:* Univ Calif, Los Angeles, AB, 36, MA, 51, PhD(math), 56. *Prof Exp:* From asst prof biostatist, Sch Pub Health & asst prof prev med & pub health, Sch Med to assoc prof biostatist, Sch Pub Health & assoc prof prev med & pub health, Sch Med, 57-70, asst dean sch pub health, 70-72, PROF BIOSTATIST, SCH PUB HEALTH & PROF BIOMATH, SCH MED, UNIV CALIF, LOS ANGELES, 70- *Mem:* Fel AAAS; fel Am Statist Asn; Biomet Soc; fel Am Pub Health Asn; Inst Math Statist. *Res:* Statistical methods; discriminant analysis; confidence intervals; dependent correlation coefficients. *Mailing Add:* Sch Pub Health Div Biostatist Univ Calif Los Angeles CA 90024

DUNN, PETER EDWARD, b St Petersburg, Fla, May 26, 46; m 81; c 1. INSECT PATHOLOGY, DEVELOPMENTAL BIOLOGY. *Educ:* Fordham Univ, BS, 68; Purdue Univ, PhD(biochem), 73. *Prof Exp:* Res asst biochem, Dept Biochem, Purdue Univ, 68-73; res assoc, Dept Biochem, Univ Chicago, 73-77; ASST PROF ENTOM, DEPT ENTOM, PURDUE UNIV, 77- *Mem:* AAAS; Entom Soc Am; Soc Invert Path. *Res:* Insect biochemistry; immune responses of insects; hormonal control of insect development. *Mailing Add:* Dept Entom Purdue Univ West Lafayette IN 47907

DUNN, RICHARD B, b Baltimore, Md, Dec 14, 27; m 51. ASTRONOMY, MECHANICAL ENGINEERING. *Educ:* Univ Minn, BME, 49, MS, 50; Harvard Univ, PhD, 61. *Prof Exp:* PHYSICIST SOLAR ASTRON, SACRAMENTO PEAK OBSERV, 53- *Mem:* Am Astron Soc. *Res:* Solar astronomy; instrumentation. *Mailing Add:* Sacramento Peak Observ Sunspot NM 88349

DUNN, RICHARD HUDSON, b Lancaster, Ky, Apr 7, 20; m 43; c 2. BIOLOGY, BOTANY. *Educ:* Wilberforce Univ, BS, 42; Ohio State Univ, MS, 45, PhD(bot, hort), 53. *Prof Exp:* Instr biol, Fla Agr & Mech Univ, 45-46; instr hort, 46-48, asst prof, 48-52, assoc prof biol & plant sci, 52-62, PROF BIOL, VA STATE COL, 62-, DIR SCH ARTS & SCI, 67- *Concurrent Pos:* Consult, Va Teachers Asn, 57- & State Dept Educ, Va, 58; assoc prog dir, Inst Sect, NSF; dir, Acad Year Inst High Sch Teachers Biol, 65-66. *Mem:* AAAS; Nat Asn Biol Teachers; Nat Sci Teachers Asn. *Res:* Plant nutrition; science teaching; biological science. *Mailing Add:* Sch of Arts & Sci Va State Col Petersburg VA 23803

DUNN, RICHARD LEE, b Pitt County, NC, Nov 28, 40; m 59; c 2. BIOMATERIALS, CONTROLLED RELEASE. *Educ:* Univ NC, Chapel Hill, BS, 63; Univ Fla, PhD(org chem), 67. *Prof Exp:* Res chemist, Beaunit Corp, El Paso Prod, 67-72, develop supt, 72-74, dir fiber develop, 74-77, dir viscose develop, 77-78, dir viscose tech serv, 78-79; sr chemist, 79-80, head, Biomat Sect, 80-82, HEAD, POLYMER DIV, SOUTHERN RES INST, 82- *Mem:* Am Chem Soc; Controlled Release Soc. *Res:* Synthesis and characterization monomers and polymers for maxillofacial prostheses, biodegradable implants, and controlled-release drug delivery systems; fabrication of biomaterials by molding, casting, and melt-extrusion processes; preparation of fibers and films from synthetic polymers and ceramic precursors. *Mailing Add:* 3412 Sagewood Trail Birmingham AL 35243

DUNN, ROBERT FOWLER, b Mt Vernon, NY, June 22, 32; m 60; c 1. ZOOLOGY, ELECTRON MICROSCOPY. *Educ:* Univ Calif, Los Angeles, AB, 60, PhD(zool), 65. *Prof Exp:* Asst res zoologist, Univ Calif, Los Angeles, 65-69, from asst prof to assoc prof surg, 69-76; ASSOC PROF OTOLARYNGOL & ASSOC PROF, DEPT ANAT & CELL BIOL, UNIV PITTSBURGH, 76- *Mem:* Electron Micros Soc Am; Am Asn Anatomists; Am Soc Cell Biol; Soc Neurosci; Asn Res Otolaryngol. *Res:* Functional anatomical interrelationships of the receptor cells and neurons in the vestibular system of the inner ear. *Mailing Add:* Dept of Otolaryngol Rm 925 230 Lothrop St Pittsburgh PA 15213

DUNN, ROBERT GARVIN, b Lake Village, Ark, July 30, 17; m 50; c 3. ALTERNATE ENERGY SOURCES, ALTERNATE FUELS. *Educ:* La State Univ, BS, 42; Ohio State Univ, MS, 49, PhD(chem eng), 64. *Prof Exp:* Chem analyst, Esso Labs, Standard Oil Co La, 40-43; proj engr, Power Plant Lab, US Air Force, Ohio, 44-49, unit chief, 49-51, res engr, Propulsion Res Br, Aeronaut Res Lab, 51-54, res group chief, Fluid Dynamics Facilities Res Lab, Aerospace Res Labs, 54-61, proj scientist, Wright-Patterson AFB, 61-65, br chief, 65-67, dep lab dir, 67-74, lab dir, 74-75, exp eng br chief, Air Force Flight Dynamics Lab, 75-79; CONSULT ALTERNATE ENERGY SOURCES RES, 79- *Concurrent Pos:* Chmn combustion group, Coord Comt Sci, Dept Defense, 59-60. *Honors & Awards:* Sci Achievement Award, US Air Force, 72, Meritorious Civilian Serv Medal, 74. *Mem:* Combustion Inst; Am Inst Aeronaut & Astronaut; Am Chem Soc; fel Am Inst Chemists. *Res:* Fluid dynamics; propulsion; supersonic combustion; aeromechanics simulation techniques; gaseous detonation; aircraft engine testing at extreme temperatures; aerospace wind tunnel and arc tunnel testing. *Mailing Add:* 121 Redder Ave Dayton OH 45405

DUNN, SAMUEL L, b Tipton, Ind, Apr 17, 40; m 63; c 2. MATHEMATICS. *Educ:* Olivet Nazarene Col, BA, 61, BS, 62; Univ Wis-Milwaukee, MS, 64, PhD(math), 69. *Prof Exp:* Teacher high sch, Ill, 61-62; asst prof, 68-71, assoc prof, 71-77, PROF MATH, SEATTLE PAC UNIV, 77-, DIR, SCH NATURAL & MATH SCI, 78- *Mem:* World Future Soc; Math Asn Am. *Res:* Ring theory, particularly quasi-Frobenius quotient rings; quotient rings and their topologies; mathematical modeling, mathematics-economics; futurism. *Mailing Add:* Dept of Math Seattle Pac Univ Seattle WA 98119

DUNN, STANLEY AUSTIN, b Long Beach, Calif, Nov 13, 21; m 44, 57, 75; c 4. CHEMISTRY. *Educ:* Calif Inst Technol, BS, 43; Johns Hopkins Univ, MA, 48, PhD(chem), 51. *Prof Exp:* Chemist, Jackson Lab, E I du Pont de Nemours & Co, 50-54; from res assoc to head anal dept, Rhodia, Inc, 54-59; from proj leader to assoc dir, 59-73, dir inorg & high temperature div, 73-76, TECH DIR & MEM BD DIRS, BJORKSTEN RES LABS, INC, 76- *Mem:* Am Ceramic Soc; Am Chem Soc; Am Inst Chem Engrs; Am Inst Chemists; Sigma Xi. *Res:* Materials science; reaction kinetics; equilibria; thermodynamics; rheology; surface chemistry; statistical design. *Mailing Add:* Bjorksten Res Labs Inc Box 9444 Madison WI 53715

DUNN, THOMAS GUY, b Livingston, Mont, Jan 31, 35; m 60; c 2. REPRODUCTIVE PHYSIOLOGY, ENDOCRINOLOGY. *Educ:* Mont State Univ, BS, 62; Univ Nebr, Lincoln, MS, 65; Colo State Univ, PhD(physiol), 69. *Prof Exp:* Asst prof animal sci, Purdue Univ, 68-70; asst prof animal physiol, 70-74, assoc prof, 74-78, PROF ANIMAL PHYSIOL, UNIV WYO, 78- *Mem:* AAAS; Am Soc Animal Sci; Soc Study Reproduction. *Res:* Influence of nutrition on reproductive performance and endocrinology of beef cattle; influence of maternal malnutrition on growth, development and endocrinology of the ovine and bovine fetus; control of ovine fetal pituitary secretions. *Mailing Add:* Div of Animal Sci Univ of Wyo Box 3354 Univ Sta Laramie WY 82071

DUNN, THOMAS M, b Sydney, Australia, Apr 25, 29; m 53; c 3. PHYSICAL CHEMISTRY. *Educ:* Univ Sydney, BSc, 49, MSc, 51; Univ London, PhD(phys chem), 57. *Prof Exp:* Teaching fel chem, Univ Sydney, 50-52; from asst lectr to lectr phys chem, Univ Col, Univ London, 54-63; PROF PHYS CHEM, UNIV MICH, ANN ARBOR, 63-, HEAD DEPT, 74- *Concurrent Pos:* Plenary lectr, Int Conf Co-ord Chem, Stockholm, Sweden, 62. *Mem:* Am Chem Soc; fel The Chem Soc. *Res:* High resolution vapour phase spectra of organic and inorganic molecules in the visible and ultraviolet regions; electronic spectra at 4 degrees Kalvin of both organic and inorganic crystals. *Mailing Add:* Dept of Chem Univ of Mich Ann Arbor MI 48109

DUNN, WILLIAM HOWARD, Americus, Ga, July 16, 42; m 65; c 2. ANALYTICAL ABSORPTION SPECTROSCOPY. *Educ:* John Jay Col, City Univ NY, BS, 74; Long Island Univ, MS, 78; Polytech Inst NY, PhD(phys chem), 81. *Prof Exp:* Detective chemist, Forensic Sect, New York City Police Dept, 63-73; instr chem, Mount Moriah High Sch, New York, 74-78; SR SCIENTIST, BEECHAM PRODUCTS, 78- *Concurrent Pos:* Special investr, Bur Narcotics & Dangerous Drugs, US Dept Justice, 70-74; lectr chem, Brooklyn Col, 81- *Mem:* Am Chem Soc; Am Phys Soc; AAAS; fel Am Inst Chemists; NY Acad Sci. *Res:* Application of reaction kinetics and spectroscopy to the elucidation of atomic structure and chemical bonding; determination of the reaction mechanisms responsible for drug stability-instability; determination of molecular structures and conformations; characterization of reaction intermediates. *Mailing Add:* Beecham Prod Western Hemisphere Res 1500 Littleton Rd Parsippany NJ 07054

DUNN, WILLIAM JOSEPH, b Shreveport, La, Feb 17, 41; m 65; c 1. MEDICINAL CHEMISTRY. *Educ:* ETex Baptist Col, BS, 63; Okla State Univ, MS, 65, PhD(chem), 70. *Prof Exp:* NIH res asst, Pomona Col, 70-71; assoc prof, 71-80, PROF MED CHEM, COL PHARM, MED CTR, UNIV, 80- *Concurrent Pos:* Lectr, Am Found Pharmaceut Educ, 72. *Mem:* Am Chem Soc. *Res:* Quantitative structure-activity relationships; drug design. *Mailing Add:* Dept of Med Chem Col of Pharm Univ of Ill at the Med Ctr Chicago IL 60680

DUNN, WILLIAM LAWRIE, b London, Ont, Oct 23, 27; m 56; c 3. PATHOLOGY. *Educ:* Univ Western Ont, BSc, 50, MD, 54; Univ London, PhD(exp path), 63; Royal Col Physicians & Surgeons Can, cert path, 64, FRCP(C), 72. *Prof Exp:* From asst prof to assoc prof path, Univ BC, 63-69, head dept, 69-76; dir labs, 70-76, MEM STAFF ANAT PATH, VANCOUVER GEN HOSP, 76-; PROF PATH, UNIV BC, 69- *Concurrent Pos:* Teaching fel path, Univ Western Ont, 57-59; teaching fel, Harvard Univ, 59-60; examr gen surg, Royal Col Physicians & Surgeons Can, 70-73 & mem credentials & anat path comts; consult, Can Tumor Reference Ctr, 71-74 & Liver Path Reference Ctr, 75-; mem med adv bd, Can Hepatic Found, 71- *Mem:* AAAS; NY Acad Sci; Int Acad Path; Can Asn Pathologists. *Res:* Liver disease; tumor biology; diagnostic pathology. *Mailing Add:* Dept of Path Univ of BC Vancouver BC V6T 1W5 Can

DUNN, WILLIAM W(ILEY), materials science, metallurgy, see previous edition

DUNNAM, FRANCIS EUGENE, JR, b Alexandria, La, Jan 29, 31; m 65; c 2. NUCLEAR PHYSICS. *Educ:* La State Univ, BS, 52, MS, 54, PhD(physics), 58. *Prof Exp:* Asst physics, La State Univ, 54-56, instr, 56-57; from asst prof to assoc prof, 58-74, dep chmn dept physics, 72-74, actg chmn dept physics & astron, 74-75, chmn dept, 75-79, PROF PHYSICS, UNIV FLA, 75-, ASSOC DEAN, COL LIBERAL ARTS & SCI, 79- *Concurrent Pos:* Consult, Oak Ridge Nat Lab, 61-63. *Mem:* AAAS; Am Phys Soc; Am Asn Physics Teachers. *Res:* Experimental nuclear physics; musical acoustics; pedagogy. *Mailing Add:* Dept Physics Univ of Fla Gainesville FL 32611

DUNNE, THOMAS, b Prestbury, Eng, Apr 21, 43. GEOMORPHOLOGY, HYDROLOGY. *Educ:* Cambridge Univ, BA, 64; Johns Hopkins Univ, PhD(geog), 69. *Prof Exp:* Asst prof geog, McGill Univ, 69-73; from asst prof to assoc prof, 73-79, PROF GEOL SCI, UNIV WASH, 79- *Concurrent Pos:* Vis Rockefeller prof, Univ Nairobi, 69-71; mem, Int Environ Progs Comt, Nat Res Coun, 79-82. *Mem:* Am Geophys Union; Japanese Geomorphol Union; British Geomorphol Res Group; AAAS; Sigma Xi. *Res:* Study of hillslope processes in geomorphology and hydrology with particular reference to accelerated soil erosion in tropical regions; erosion and sedimentation of forested regions; mudflow mechanics and erosion of tephra on Mt St Helens. *Mailing Add:* Dept of Geol Sci Univ of Wash Seattle WA 98195

DUNNE, THOMAS GREGORY, b Los Angeles, Calif, Oct 10, 30. PHYSICAL INORGANIC CHEMISTRY. *Educ:* Univ Calif, Los Angeles, BS, 52; Univ Wash, PhD(chem), 57. *Prof Exp:* Assoc chemist, Int Bus Mach Corp, 57-61; res assoc, Mass Inst Technol, 61-63; from asst prof to assoc prof, 63-81, PROF CHEM, REED COL, 81- *Res:* Coordination complex studies; oxidation-reduction mechanisms. *Mailing Add:* Dept Chem Reed Col Portland OR 97202

DUNNEBACKE-DIXON, THELMA HUDSON, embryology, zoology, see previous edition

DUNNETT, CHARLES WILLIAM, b Windsor, Ont, Aug 24, 21; m 47; c 3. STATISTICS. *Educ:* McMaster Univ, BA, 42; Univ Toronto, MA, 46; Aberdeen Univ, DSc, 60. *Prof Exp:* Instr math, Columbia Univ, 46-48 & Maritime Col, 48-49; biometrician, Can Dept Nat Health & Welfare, 49-52; res assoc statist, Cornell Univ, 52-53; statistician, Lederle Labs, Am Cyanamid Co, 53-74; prof appl math & chmn dept, 77-79, PROF CLIN EPIDEMIOL & BIOSTATIST, HEALTH SCI CTR, MCMASTER UNIV, 74-, PROF MATH SCI, 79- *Honors & Awards:* Mem, Order Brit Empire. *Mem:* Fel Am Statist Asn; Biomet Soc; Royal Statist Soc; Int Statist Inst. *Res:* Application of statistics to design and analysis of experiments in medical and biological sciences; statistical methodology; categorical data analysis in medical statistics. *Mailing Add:* Health Sci Ctr McMaster Univ Hamilton ON L8S 3Z5 Can

DUNNICK, JUNE K, b New York, NY. TOXICOLOGY. *Educ:* Cornell Univ, BS, 65; Cornell Med Col, PhD(med sci), 69. *Prof Exp:* Res assoc biochem, Univ Rochester, 69-71; hepatitis prog officer, NIH, 71-73; life sci res assoc, Med Sch, Stanford Univ, 73-76; antiviral prog officer, NIH, 76-80; CHEMIST & MGR, NAT TOXICOL PROG, NAT INST ENVIRON HEALTH SCI, 80- *Concurrent Pos:* Fel, NIH, 69-71. *Mem:* Sigma Xi; Soc Toxicol; AAAS. *Res:* Toxicology; drug development; treatment of infectious diseases; antiviral drug development; use and clinical trials in interferon and antiviral drugs. *Mailing Add:* Nat Toxicol Prog PO Box 12233 Nat Inst Environ Health Sci Res Triangle Park NC 27709

DUNNIGAN, JACQUES, b St Jerome, Que, May 1, 35; m 63; c 4. PHYSIOLOGY. *Educ:* St Laurent Col, BA, 56; Univ Ottawa, BSc, 60, PhD, 63. *Prof Exp:* Res asst med, Laval Univ, 63-64; adj prof sci, 64-68, assoc prof, 68-73, vdean res, 74-75, assoc vrector res, 75-79, dir prog res, Asbestos, 79-80, PROF SCI, UNIV SHERBROOKE, 73-, DIR GEN, INST RES & DEVELOP, ASBESTOS, 80- *Res:* Asbestos technology. *Mailing Add:* Inst Res & Develop Asbestos Univ of Sherbrooke Sherbrooke PQ J1K 2R1 Can

DUNNING, DOROTHY COVALT, b Washington, DC, Jan 1, 37; m 60. ANIMAL BEHAVIOR. *Educ:* Middlebury Col, BA, 58; Mt Holyoke Col, MA, 60; Tufts Univ, PhD(biol), 66. *Prof Exp:* Teaching fel biol, Tufts Univ, 66-67; scholar animal behav, Max Planck Inst Physiol of Behav, 67; instr zool, Duke Univ, 68-69; asst prof biol, 69-75, ASSOC PROF BIOL, WVA UNIV, 75- *Mem:* AAAS; Am Soc Zoologists; Am Soc Mammal. *Res:* Physiological mechanisms of animal behavior. *Mailing Add:* Dept of Biol WVa Univ Morgantown WV 26506

DUNNING, ERNEST LEON, b Ky, Nov 13, 20; c 2. MECHANICAL ENGINEERING. *Educ:* Univ Rochester, BSME, 46; Univ Ky, MSME, 50; Univ Houston, PhD, 67. *Prof Exp:* Instr physics & math, Pikeville Col, 47-49; assoc prof mech eng, Evansville Col, 50-54 & La Polytech Inst, 55-57; assoc prof, 57-77, PROF ELEC SCI & SYSTS ENG, SOUTHERN ILL UNIV, CARBONDALE, 77- *Concurrent Pos:* Consult, Schnacks Refrig Co, 53-54 & Christopher Unitemp Heating Co, 46-57; res engr, Sch Indust Prog, Hughes Aircraft Co, 59. *Mem:* Nat Soc Prof Engrs; Am Soc Mech Engrs; Am Soc Eng Educ. *Res:* Thermodynamics; heat transfer; refrigeration and air conditioning. *Mailing Add:* Sch of Eng & Technol Southern Ill Univ Carbondale IL 62901

DUNNING, FRANK BARRYMORE, b Tadcaster, Eng, Apr 10, 45; m 68. ATOMIC PHYSICS, SURFACE PHYSICS. *Educ:* Univ Col, Univ London, BSc, 66, PhD(atomic physics), 69. *Prof Exp:* Imp Chem Industs fel exp atomic physics, Univ Col, Univ London, 69-71; res assoc exp atomic & laser physics, 71-74, asst prof space physics & astron, 74-78, ASSOC PROF SPACE PHYSICS & ASTRON, RICE UNIV, 78- *Mem:* Am Phys Soc; Inst Physics; Optical Soc Am. *Res:* Atomic collision studies; development of tunable ultraviolet lasers and their applications to studies of photon interaction processes important in aeronomy and astrophysics; application of electron spin plurisation measurements; study of surface geometric and electronic structure. *Mailing Add:* Dept of Space Physics & Astron Rice Univ Houston TX 77001

DUNNING, GORDON MERRILL, b Cortland, NY, Sept 11, 10; m 36; c 2. HEALTH PHYSICS, SCIENCE EDUCATION. *Educ:* Syracuse Univ, MS, 41, EdD(sci educ), 48; Am Bd Health Physics, cert, 60. *Prof Exp:* Pub sch teacher, NY, 32-41; teacher physics, NY State Agr & Tech Inst, 47-48 & Pa State Teachers Col, 48-51; biophys res analyst, Div Biol & Med, AEC, 51-57, chief radiation effects weapons br, 57-59; sci adv, Div Radiol Health, USPHS, 59-60; asst dir off health & safety, AEC, 60-61, dept dir div oper safety, 61-68, tech adv, 68-70, sr scientist, Off Environ Affairs, 70-72; Comnr, Ariz Atomic Energy Comn, 75-79. *Concurrent Pos:* Mem US deleg, Int Conf Peaceful Uses Atomic Energy, Switz, 55; fac affil, Colo State Univ, 67-68. *Mem:* Fel AAAS; Health Physics Soc; Am Asn Physics Teachers; Am Nuclear Soc; Nat Sci Teachers Asn. *Res:* Developing criteria for radiation protection. *Mailing Add:* PO Box 1153 Green Valley AZ 85614

DUNNING, JAMES MORSE, b New York, NY, Oct 16, 04; m 35, 75; c 2. DENTISTRY, PUBLIC HEALTH. *Educ:* Harvard Univ, AB, 26, MPH, 47; Columbia Univ, DDS, 30. *Prof Exp:* Asst oper dent, Dent Sch, Columbia Univ, 30-35; dent dir, Metrop Life Ins Co, 35-45; dean sch dent med, 47-52, lectr pub health dent, 52-60, from asst clin prof to clin prof, 60-65, prof, 65-72, EMER PROF ECOL DENT, SCH DENT MED, HARVARD UNIV, 72- *Concurrent Pos:* Pvt pract, 30-42 & 52-65; pres, Dent Health Serv, Inc, 41-45; mem comn dent, Nat Res Coun, 47-51; dir dent health serv, Univ Health Serv, Harvard-Radcliffe, 55-65; consult, USPHS Hosp, Brighton, Mass, 60-80. *Honors & Awards:* Lemuel Shattuck Award, Mass Pub Health Asn, 62; Ruth E Boynton Award, Am Col Health Asn, 74. *Mem:* Sr mem Inst Med-Nat Acad Sci; fel Am Col Dent; fel Am Pub Health Asn; Am Dent Asn. *Res:* Principles of dental public health; epidemiology of dental caries; dental education; industrial dental service. *Mailing Add:* 81 Gloucester St Arlington MA 02174

DUNNING, JEREMY DAVID, b Washington, DC, Feb 15, 41; m 72. ROCK MECHANICS. *Educ:* Colgate Univ, BA, 73; Rutgers Univ, MS, 75; Univ NC, PhD(geol), 78. *Prof Exp:* Res asst geol, Univ NC, 75-78; asst prof geol, Ore State Univ, 78-79; ASST PROF GEOL, IND UNIV, 79- *Mem:* Am Geophys Union; Geol Soc Am. *Res:* Low temperature rock mechanics; microseismic monitoring of crack propagation and brittle failure; microseismic modeling of fault behavior. *Mailing Add:* Dept Geol Ind Univ Bloomington IN 47405

DUNNING, JOHN RAY, JR, b New York, NY, Nov 26, 37. PHYSICS. *Educ:* Yale Univ, BS, 60, MS, 61; Harvard Univ, PhD(physics), 65. *Prof Exp:* Lectr physics, Harvard, 65-66, instr, 66-68, res fel & lectr, 68-69; from asst prof to assoc prof, 69-80, PROF PHYSICS, CALIF STATE COL, SONOMA, 80- *Mem:* AAAS; Am Phys Soc. *Res:* High energy experimental physics, especially the electromagnetic structure of nucleons and mesons. *Mailing Add:* Dept of Physics Calif State Col Sonoma Rohnert Park CA 94928

DUNNING, JOHN WALCOTT, b Ottumwa, Iowa, Dec 20, 12; m 39; c 3. ORGANIC CHEMISTRY. *Educ:* Iowa State Col, BS, 35, PhD(biophys chem), 38. *Prof Exp:* Lab & pilot plant dir, Anderson Clayton & Co, 37-42; chemist, Northern Regional Res Lab, Bur Agr & Indust Chem, USDA, 42-44, in chg synthetic liquid fuels proj, 44-48; dir res, Anderson IBEC, 48-53, vpres, 53-64, pres, 64-75, chmn, 75-77; RES CONSULT, 78- *Mem:* Am Chem Soc; Am Oil Chem Soc. *Res:* Saccharification; industrial fermentation; pyrolysis; esterification; pulping; pilot plant developments; bacterial oxydations; vitamin C synthesis; vegetable oils; vegetable seed processing; finish drying of synthetic rubber. *Mailing Add:* Anderson IBEC 19699 Progress Dr Strongsville OH 44136

DUNNING, KENNETH LAVERNE, b Yale, Iowa, Sept 24, 14; m 41; c 4. NUCLEAR PHYSICS. *Educ:* Univ Minn, BEE, 38, Univ Md, MS, 50; Cath Univ Am, PhD, 68. *Prof Exp:* Commun engr, Western Union Tel Co, 38-41; electron scientist, Naval Res Lab, 45-50, physicist, 50-51, head Van de Graaff Br, Nuclear Sci Div, 51-74, consult radiation technol div, 75-80; CONSULT, 80- *Mem:* Am Phys Soc; Inst Elec & Electronics Engrs; Sigma Xi. *Res:* Centimeter and millimeter wave guide components; Cockroft-Walton accelerators; nuclear weapons tests; Van de Graaff accelerators; nuclear interactions; ion-induced x-rays; charged particle energy loss; surface analysis; computer programming; nuclear instrumentation. *Mailing Add:* 502 Highland Ct Port Ludlow WA 98365

DUNNING, RANALD G(ARDNER), b Lyndon, Ohio, Oct 6, 02; m 37; c 2. CHEMICAL ENGINEERING. *Educ:* Princeton Univ, BS, 24, AM, 25; Mass Inst Technol, SM, 27. *Prof Exp:* Chem engr, Roessler & Hasslacher Chem Co, NJ, 26-31; develop engr, Barber Asphalt Co, 31-38; chem engr, Merck & Co, Inc, 38-40, process develop head, 40-45, res proj analyst, 45-49, tech asst, off of sci dir, 49-53, tech asst, sci admin div, 53-57; mgr res & develop, Metalwash Mach Co, NJ, 57; chief engr, Chemirad Corp, 59-66; consult chem engr, 66-72; RETIRED. *Mem:* Am Chem Soc; Am Inst Chem Engrs; Chem Mkt Res Asn. *Res:* Equilibrium in the synthesis and decomposition of methanol; sulfuric acid recovery; synthesis of ethylene imine. *Mailing Add:* 227 Tuttle Pkwy Westfield NJ 07090

DUNNING, THOMAS HAROLD, JR, b Jeffersonville, Ind, Aug 3, 43; m 61; c 3. THEORETICAL CHEMISTRY. *Educ:* Univ Mo-Rolla, BS, 65; Calif Inst Technol, PhD(chem), 70. *Prof Exp:* Fel, Battelle Mem Inst, 70-71; res fel, A A Noyes Lab Chem Physics, Calif Inst Technol, 71-74; mem staff, Los Alamos Sci Lab, Univ Calif, 74-78; GROUP LEADER, THEORET CHEM GROUP, ARGONNE NAT LAB, 78- *Mem:* Am Phys Soc; Am Chem Soc. *Res:* electronic structure of atoms and molecules; theoretical chemical kinetics (molecular potential energy surfaces). *Mailing Add:* Theoret Chem Group Chem Div Argonne Nat Lab Argonne IL 60439

DUNNING, VIRGINIA ALEXANDRIA, b Perth Amboy, NJ, June 14, 43; m 66; c 3. SPECTROCHEMISTRY. *Educ:* Lebanon Valley Col, BS, 65; Univ Mich, MS, 67, PhD(chem), 72. *Prof Exp:* Sr res chemist, PPG Industs, 75-78; res assoc, Univ RI, 78-80; group leader, Am Cyanamid, 79-80; CO-OWNER & VPRES, COMPUTERLAND, ATLANTA, 80- *Mem:* Am Chem Soc; Soc Appl Spectros. *Res:* Application of infrared spectroscopy to chemical problems. *Mailing Add:* PO Box 723115 2423 Cobb Parkway Atlanta GA 30339

DUNNING, WILHELMINA FRANCES, b Topsham, Maine, Sept 12, 04. PATHOLOGY. *Educ:* Univ Maine, AB, 26; Columbia Univ, MA, 28, PhD(zool), 32. *Hon Degrees:* DSc, Univ Maine, 60. *Prof Exp:* Asst, Inst Cancer Res, Columbia Univ, 26-30, assoc, 30-41; instr path, Col Med, Wayne Univ, 41-48, asst prof oncol, 48-50, res assoc, 45-50; res assoc, Detroit Inst Cancer Res, 46-50; prof zool, Univ Miami, 50-52, res prof exp path, 52-65, res prof dept med, 65-75; res assoc, Papanicolaou Cancer Res Inst, 71-78. *Mem:* AAAS; Am Asn Cancer Res; Genetics Soc Am; Am Soc Zoologists; NY Acad Sci. *Res:* Mammalian genetics; experimental pathology; nutrition and cancer; endocrinology and genetics in experimental cancer. *Mailing Add:* 2850 Coconut Ave Miami FL 33942

DUNNY, STANLEY, b Northampton, Mass, Aug 2, 39. ORGANOMETALLIC CHEMISTRY. *Educ:* Univ Mass, BS, 61; Univ Wis, MS, 63; Purdue Univ, PhD(chem), 67. *Prof Exp:* Asst prof, 69-70, assoc prof, 70-75, PROF CHEM, HOLYOKE COMMUNITY COL, 75- *Mem:* Am Chem Soc. *Res:* Hydrosilylation of acetylenes via amine catalysis; organosilicon chemistry; synthesis of rings containing silicon atoms. *Mailing Add:* Dept Chem Holyoke Commun Col 303 Homestead Ave Holyoke MA 01040

DUNPHY, DONAL, b Northampton, Mass, Feb 24, 17; m 44; c 3. PEDIATRICS. *Educ:* Col Holy Cross, BA, 39; Yale Univ, MD, 44. *Prof Exp:* Instr pediat, Sch Med, Yale Univ, 47-50; attend pediatrician, Bridgeport Gen Hosp, 50-53; assoc pediatrician, Sch Med, Univ Buffalo, 55-56, from asst prof to assoc prof pediat, Buffalo Children's Hosp, 56-61; prof & head dept, Col Med, Univ Iowa, 61-73; PROF PEDIAT, UNIV NC, CHAPEL HILL, 73- *Concurrent Pos:* Fel cardiol, Dept Pediat, Sch Med, Yale Univ, 50-52; dir pediat out-clin, Buffalo Children's Hosp, 55-61, dir child develop study, 55-59, dir, NIH Collab Proj, 58-61; pediat consult, Nat Insts Neurol Dis & Blindness, 60-61. *Mem:* AAAS; Am Pediat Soc; NY Acad Sci; Am Acad Pediat; Asn Am Med Cols. *Res:* Cord blood gas analysis in twins; factors affecting neurological status of children and methods for early recognition; plasmin in the therapy of hyaline membrane disease. *Mailing Add:* Dept of Pediat Univ of NC Chapel Hill NC 27514

DUNPHY, J ENGLEBERT, medicine, surgery, deceased

DUNPHY, JAMES FRANCIS, b Boston, Mass, May 16, 30; m 61; c 3. POLYMER CHEMISTRY. *Educ:* Boston Col, BS, 51; Univ Ill, PhD(org chem), 60. *Prof Exp:* Chemist, Nat Starch & Chem Corp, 52-57; res chemist, Film Dept, Yerkes Res & Develop Lab, 59-70, staff scientist, Tecumseh Film Plant, Topeka, Kans, 70-78, SR RES CHEMIST, WASHINGTON LAB, E

I DU PONT DE NEMOURS & CO, INC, 78- *Mem:* Am Chem Soc. *Res:* Organic chemistry of high polymers; preparation and characterization of addition and condensation polymers; chemistry of cellulose and the viscose process; development of high performance polymer blends and grafts. *Mailing Add:* E I du Pont Washington Lab PO Box 1217 Parkersburg WV 26101

DUNSHEE, BRYANT R, b Des Moines, Iowa, Mar 13, 21; m 49; c 3. BIOCHEMISTRY. *Educ:* Univ Mich, BS, 42; Univ Wis, PhD(biochem), 49. *Prof Exp:* Supvr prod, Hercules Powder Co, 42-45; instr physiol chem, Univ Minn, 49-52; sr biochemist food res, Cent Res Lab, 52-57, sect leader food develop dept, 57-62, RES ASSOC FOOD DEVELOP ACTIVITY, JAMES FORD BELL RES CTR, GEN MILLS, INC, 62- *Mem:* Am Chem Soc; Inst Food Technologists; Sigma Xi. *Res:* Use of dairy and vegetable proteins in food fortification. *Mailing Add:* Gen Mills Inc Bell Res Ctr 9000 Plymouth Ave N Minneapolis MN 55427

DUNSING, MARILYN MAGDALENE, b Chicago, Ill, Feb 19, 26. HUMAN ECOLOGY. *Educ:* Univ Chicago, MBA, 48, PhD(family & consumption econ), 54. *Prof Exp:* Instr econ, Bowling Green State Univ, 48-49; asst, Univ Ill, Urbana, 49-50; instr econ & social sci, Wilson Jr Col, Chicago, 50-53; from instr to assoc prof family econ, Univ Calif, Davis, 54-62; assoc prof, 62-65, head dept, 78-79, PROF FAMILY & CONSUMPTIONS ECON, UNIV ILL, 66-, DIR, SCH HUMAN RESOURCES & FAMILY STUDIES, 79- *Mem:* Am Econ Asn; Am Home Econ Asn; Sigma Xi. *Res:* Environmental influences; quality of life; standards and levels of living; employment status of wives; volunteer work. *Mailing Add:* 161 Bevier Hall Univ of Ill Urbana IL 61801

DUNSON, WILLIAM ALBERT, b Cedartown, Ga, Dec 17, 41; m 63; c 3. ZOOLOGY, PHYSIOLOGY. *Educ:* Yale Univ, BS, 62; Univ Mich, MS, 64, PhD(zool), 65. *Prof Exp:* PROF BIOL, PA STATE UNIV, UNIVERSITY PARK, 65- *Concurrent Pos:* Sr scientist, Stanford Univ, 68; NSF grants, 68-; chief scientist Res/Vessel Alpha Helix, Scripps Inst Oceanog, 70, 72 & 75; sci collabr, Everglades Nat Park, 79-81; mem, Great Barrier Reef Cruise, 81. *Mem:* AAAS; Am Physiol Soc; Am Soc Zool; Am Inst Biol Sci; Am Soc Ichthylogists & Herpetologists. Am Soc Limnol & Oceanog; Ecol Soc Am. *Res:* Physiological ecology and environmental physiology, particularly in relation to ionic and osmotic regulation and ion transport; salt glands; reptilian skin permeability, behavioral osmoregulation; tolerance to low pH; physiological ecology of reptiles; biology of sea snakes. *Mailing Add:* Dept of Biol 208 Mueller Bldg Pa State Univ University Park PA 16802

DUNSTAN, WILLIAM MORGAN, b Greenville, NJ, Nov 4, 35; m 59; c 5. BIOLOGICAL OCEANOGRAPHY. *Educ:* Yale Univ, BS, 56; Fla State Univ, MS, 67, PhD(biol), 69. *Prof Exp:* Loan analyst, Int Div, Chase Manhattan Bank, 60-62; prod develop engr, Celanese Corp Am, 62-65; NSF fel, Fla State Univ, 65-69; asst scientist, Woods Hole Oceanog Inst, Mass, 69-72; assoc prof biol oceanog, Skidaway Inst Oceanog, 72-77; SCI PROG MGR, INTERSTATE ELECTRONICS CORP, 77- *Concurrent Pos:* Adj assoc prof biol oceanog, Univ Ga, 73-77. *Mem:* Marine Biol Asn UK; Phycol Soc Am; Am Soc Limnol & Oceanog. *Res:* Physiological ecology of marine plants involving the influence of pollutants on nearshore and continental shelf organisms. *Mailing Add:* Interstate Electronics Corp 1745 Jefferson Davis Hwy Suite 601 Arlington VA 22202

DUNSWORTH, FRANCIS ALFRED, b Halifax, NS, Feb 27, 20; m 44; c 10. PSYCHIATRY. *Educ:* Dalhousie Univ, MD, 43. *Prof Exp:* Asst prof, 48-63, ASSOC PROF PSYCHIAT, DALHOUSIE UNIV, 63-, HEAD DEPT, HALIFAX INFIRMARY, 61- *Concurrent Pos:* Fel, Menninger Sch Psychiat, Topeka, Kans, 47-48. *Mem:* Can Med Asn; Am Psychiat Asn; Can Psychiat Asn (pres, 61-62); Med Soc NS (pres, 70). *Mailing Add:* 961 S Bland St Suite 204 Halifax NS B3H 2S6 Can

DUNTLEY, SEIBERT QUIMBY, b Bushnell, Ill, Oct 2, 11; m 37; c 3. PHYSICS. *Educ:* Mass Inst Technol, BS, 33, ScD(physics), 39; Calif Inst Technol, MS, 35. *Prof Exp:* Asst physics, Calif Inst Technol, 33-34; teaching fel, Mass Inst Technol, 37-39, from instr to asst prof, 39-52; assoc res physicist & dir, Visibility Lab, Univ Calif, 52-54, prof physics, Scripps Inst Oceanog, 66-77, EMER PROF PHYSICS, SCRIPPS INST OCEANOG, 77-, RES PHYSICIST & DIR, VISIBILITY LAB, UNIV CALIF, 54- *Concurrent Pos:* Consult & physicist, Work Projs Admin, 40-42; consult, Gen Elec Co, 46-51, Bur Ships, US Dept Navy, 49-68 & US Air Force, 42; tech aide, Nat Defense Res Comt & Off Sci Res & Develop, 42-46. *Honors & Awards:* Army-Navy Cert Appreciation; Ives Medalist, Optical Soc Am, 61. *Mem:* Illum Eng Soc; fel Optical Soc Am (pres, 65 & 66); Soc Photo Optical Instrumentation Engrs. *Res:* Design of optical instruments; spectrophotometry; goniophotometry; colorimetry; photometry; optical properties of diffusing materials; spectrophotometry of living human skin; atmospheric optics; visibility; hydrologic optics; vision in space; remote sensing. *Mailing Add:* Scripps Inst of Oceanog Univ of Calif La Jolla CA 92093

DUNTON, MARGUERITE ELIZABETH, mathematics, deceased

DUNWORTH, WILLIAM PAUL, b New York, NY, Jan 19, 25; m 47; c 3. ORGANIC CHEMISTRY. *Educ:* Fordham Univ, BS, 47, MS, 49, PhD(phys chem), 52. *Prof Exp:* Fel, Mellon Inst, 52-54; chemist, 54-70, SR RES CHEMIST, E I DU PONT DE NEMOURS & CO, INC, 70- *Res:* Dyes; petroleum additives. *Mailing Add:* 1416 Drake Rd Wilmington DE 19803

DUPONT, ANDRE GUY, b Port-Alfred, Que. MOLECULAR NEUROENDOCRINOLOGY. *Educ:* Laval Univ, MD, 65, PhD, 72. *Prof Exp:* Res assoc & fel, Tulane Univ, 73-75; resident surg, 66-69 & 72-73, asst prof endocrinol, Ctr Hosp & asst prof physiol, Laval Univ, 75-80, ASSOC PROF MOLECULAR ENDOCRINOL, LAVAL UNIV, 80- *Concurrent Pos:* Instr anat, Laval Univ, 67-68, fel physiol, 72-73; Med Res Coun Can fel, 73-75; Health Res Coun Que res scholar, 75-78. *Mem:* Can Soc Clin Invest; Int Soc Neuroendocrinol; Endocrine Soc; Am Physiol Soc. *Res:* Relationship of brain endorphins and neuroendocrine functions; isolation or characterisation of prolactine inhibiting factor and prolactin releasing factor; inactivation of neuropeptides by rat plasma and tissues. *Mailing Add:* Lab of Molecular Endocrinol 2705 Blvd Laurier Quebec PQ G1V 4G2 Can

DUPONT, CLAIRE HAMMEL, b Washington, DC, Apr 27, 33; m 66; c 2. BIOCHEMISTRY, PEDIATRICS. *Educ:* George Washington Univ, MD, 58; Univ Md, PhD(biochem), 64. *Prof Exp:* Intern, Philadelphia Gen Hosp, 58-59; resident pediat, Children's Hosp DC, 59-61; asst prof pediat res, Sch Med, Univ Md, 64-66; asst prof biochem, Fac Med, Univ Montreal, 66-71; asst dir biochem, Montreal Children's Hosp, 71-76; asst prof pediat, 72-78, ASSOC PROF, MCGILL UNIV, 78- *Concurrent Pos:* Nat Inst Neurol Dis & Blindness spec fel extra-mural prog, Sch Med, Univ Md, 61-64; asst, Sch Med, George Washington Univ, 60-61; dir biochem, Montreal Children's Hosp, 77- *Mem:* Can Soc Clin Investr; fel Am Acad Pediat; Can Biochem Soc; Can Soc Clin Chem (secy, 80-83); Am Asn Clin Chem. *Res:* Development of pediatric clinical chemistry methodology; medical decision-making and utilization of diagnostic tests. *Mailing Add:* One Haverstock Rd Hamstead Montreal PQ H3X 1P1 Can

DUPONT, HERBERT LANCASHIRE, b Toledo, Ohio, Nov 12, 38; m 63; c 2. INTERNAL MEDICINE, INFECTIOUS DISEASES. *Educ:* Ohio Wesleyan Univ, BA, 61; Emory Univ, MD, 65. *Prof Exp:* From intern to resident internal med, Univ Minn, 65-67; from asst prof to assoc prof med, Div Infectious Dis, Univ Md, 70-73; PROF MED & DIR PROG INFECTIOUS DIS & CLIN MICROBIOL, UNIV TEX MED SCH HOUSTON, 73- *Concurrent Pos:* Fel infectious dis, Univ Md, 67-69; consult, Ctr Dis Control, Atlanta, Ga, 69-, WHO, Geneva, Switz, 71, US Dept Army, 72-74 & 77-81, Pan Am Health Orgn, 74 & Am Bd Internal Med; assoc ed, Am Journal Epidemiol, 77-81; chmn ad hoc comt bact dis, US Dept Army, 79-81. *Mem:* Fel Am Col Physicians; Am Fedn Clin Res; Am Soc Microbiol; Infectious Dis Soc Am; Am Soc Clin Invest. *Res:* Enteric diseases, particularly diarrheal disease, pathogenesis, diagnosis, treatment and vaccine development. *Mailing Add:* Prog Infect Dis & Clin Microbiol Univ Tex Med Sch Houston TX 77030

DUPONT, JACQUELINE (LOUISE), b Plant City, Fla, Mar 4, 34. NUTRITION. *Educ:* Fla State Univ, BS, 55, PhD(nutrit), 62; Iowa State Univ, MS, 59. *Prof Exp:* Home economist, Human Nutrit Res Div, USDA, 55-56, nutrit specialist, 56-62, res nutrit specialist, 62-64; asst prof biochem, Col Med, Howard Univ, 64-66; from asst prof to assoc prof food sci & nutrit, Colo State Univ, 66-73, prof, 73-78; PROF FOOD & NUTRIT & CHMN DEPT, IOWA STATE UNIV, 78- *Concurrent Pos:* Consult nutrit study sect, USPHS, 72-76; res career develop award, NIH, 72-77; vis prof, Dept Pediat, Univ Colo Med Ctr, 77-78. mem coun arteriosclerosis, Am Heart Asn. *Mem:* Am Dietetic Asn; Am Oil Chem Soc; Am Inst Nutrit; NY Acad Sci; Am Aging Asn. *Res:* Effects of dietary fat upon metabolism of cholesterol and fatty acids, prostaglandins, atherosclerosis and aging. *Mailing Add:* Dept of Food & Nutrit Iowa State Univ Ames IA 50011

DUPONT, PAUL EMILE, b Chicopee, Mass, Aug 21, 41; m 63; c 2. ORGANIC CHEMISTRY. *Educ:* Univ Mass, BS, 63; Rensselaer Polytech Inst, PhD(chem), 68. *Prof Exp:* Asst res chemist, 63-68, assoc res chemist, 68-74, PATENT AGENT, STERLING-WINTHROP RES INST, 74- *Mem:* Am Chem Soc. *Mailing Add:* 5 Greenbrier Way E Greenbush NY 12061

DUPONT, ROBERT L, JR, b Toledo, Ohio, Mar 25, 36; m 63; c 2. PSYCHIATRY. *Educ:* Emory Univ, BA, 58; Harvard Med Sch, MD, 63. *Prof Exp:* Res psychiatrist & actg assoc dir community serv, DC Dept Corrections, 68-70; adminr, Narcotic Treatment Admin, Dept Human Resources, DC, 70-73; dir, Spec Action Off Drug Abuse Prev, Exec Off of President, 73-75; dir, Nat Inst Drug Abuse, 73-78; PRES, INST BEHAV & HEALTH, 78- *Concurrent Pos:* Consult res & develop, DC Dept Corrections, 67-68, Child Res Br, NIH, 68-71 & Spec Comt Crime Prev & Control, Am Bar Asn, 71-72; mem Nat Adv Coun Drug Abuse Prev, 72-73; mem drug abuse task force, Nat Adv Comn Criminal Justice Standards & Goals, Dept Justice, 72-73, mem, Coord Coun Juv Justice & Delinq Prev, 74-78; actg adminr, Alcohol, Drug Abuse & Ment Health Admin, Dept Health, Educ & Welfare, 74. *Mem:* Fel Am Psychiat Asn; World Psychiat Asn; Pan Am Med Asn; Am Pub Health Asn; Phobia Soc Am (pres, 80-). *Res:* Behavioral health and related policy. *Mailing Add:* 8708 Susanna Lane Chevy Chase MD 20015

DUPONT, TODD, b Houston, Tex, Aug 29, 42; m 64; c 2. NUMERICAL ANALYSIS. *Educ:* Rice Univ, BA, 63, PhD(math), 69. *Prof Exp:* Res mathematician, Esso Prod Res Co, 67-68; from instr to asst prof math, 68-74, assoc prof, 74-76, PROF MATH, UNIV CHICAGO, 76- *Mem:* Am Math Soc; Soc Indust & Appl Math. *Res:* Numerical solution of partial differential equations; nonlinear boundary-value problems. *Mailing Add:* Dept of Math Univ of Chicago Chicago IL 60637

DUPONT, WILLIAM DUDLEY, b Montreal, Que, Nov 6, 46; m 74. BIOSTATISTICS, EPIDEMIOLOGY. *Educ:* McGill Univ, BSc, 69, MSc, 71; Johns Hopkins Univ, PhD(biostatist), 76. *Prof Exp:* ASST PROF BIOSTATIST, VANDERBILT UNIV, 76- *Mem:* Am Statist Asn; Biomet Soc; Sigma Xi. *Res:* Statistical inference in medicine; data management; design, analysis and management of clinical trials and observational longitudinal studies; ecological statistics; estimation of animal abundance. *Mailing Add:* Dept of Prev Med Vanderbilt Univ Sch of Med Nashville TN 37232

DU PRE, DONALD BATES, b Houston, Tex, Mar 17, 42; m 64; c 1. CHEMICAL PHYSICS. *Educ:* Rice Univ, BA, 64; Princeton Univ, MA, 66, PhD(chem), 68. *Prof Exp:* Fel chem physics, Sci Ctr, N Am Rockwell Corp, 68-69; asst prof chem, 69-72, assoc prof, 72-76, PROF CHEM, UNIV LOUISVILLE, 76- *Concurrent Pos:* Grants, Res Corp, Petrol Res Fund, Nat Sci Found & NIH. *Mem:* Am Phys Soc; Biophys Soc; AAAS. *Res:* Laser light scattering spectroscopy; chemical physics of polymers and liquid crystals. *Mailing Add:* Dept of Chem Univ of Louisville Louisville KY 40208

DUPRE, EDMUND J, b New Bedford, Mass, Aug 13, 12; m 60. TEXTILE CHEMISTRY, ORGANIC POLYMER CHEMISTRY. *Educ:* NC State Col, BS, 48; Univ Boston, MEd, 59. *Prof Exp:* Colorist, Jeandors Dye & Print Works, 34-36; asst dyer, US Finishing Co, 36-38; textile chemist, Fruit of the Loom, Inc, 38-42; instr textile chem, New Bedford Inst Technol, 42; chemist, Better Fabrics Testing Bur, 43-45; from instr to assoc prof chem, 45-75, ASSOC PROF TEXTILE SCI, SOUTHEASTERN MASS UNIV, 75- *Mem:* Am Asn Textile Chemists & Colorists; Am Soc Eng Educ; fel Am Inst Chem. *Res:* Practical uses of synthetic polymeric hydrophilic colloids in the paper and textile industries; *Mailing Add:* Southeastern Mass Univ North Dartmouth MA 02747

DUPREE, ANDREA K, b Boston, Mass, Sept 17, 39; m 61; c 2. ASTROPHYSICS. *Educ:* Wellesley Col, BA, 60; Harvard Univ, PhD(astron), 68. *Prof Exp:* Res fel, 68-74, res assoc, 74-75, sr res assoc astron & astrophys, 75-79, LECTR, DEPT ASTRON, HARVARD COL OBSERV, HARVARD UNIV, 70-, ASTROPHYSICIST, SMTIHSONIAN ASTROPHYS OBSERV, 79-, ASSOC DIR SOLAR & STELLAR, CTR ASTROPHYS, 80- *Concurrent Pos:* Phillips lectr, Haverford Col, 72. *Honors & Awards:* Bart J Bok Prize, Harvard Col Observ, 73. *Mem:* Am Astron Soc; Int Astron Union. *Res:* Stellar and solar atmospheres; H II regions and the interstellar medium; high resolution spectroscopy. *Mailing Add:* Ctr for Astrophys 60 Garden St Cambridge MA 02138

DUPREE, DANIEL EDWARD, b Coushatta, La, Dec 1, 32; m 54; c 1. MATHEMATICS. *Educ:* La Polytech Inst, BS, 54; Auburn Univ, MS, 59, PhD(math), 60. *Prof Exp:* Asst prof math, Auburn Univ, 60-61; chmn dept, 61-64, PROF MATH & DEAN COL PURE & APPL SCI, NORTHEAST LA UNIV, 64- *Concurrent Pos:* Res grants, NSF, 63-64 & Sigma Xi, 64-65; consult, Marshall Space Flight Ctr, 61-62. *Mem:* Am Math Soc; Math Asn Am. *Res:* Interpolation theory and multivariable approximation. *Mailing Add:* Col of Pure & Appl Sci Northeast La Univ Monroe LA 71201

DUPUIS, GILLES, b St Jacques, Que, Mar 11, 43; c 3. BIOCHEMISTRY. *Educ:* Univ Montreal, BSc, 64, MSc, 65; Univ Pittsburgh, PhD(biochem), 69. *Prof Exp:* Fel allergy, Univ BC, 69-72; ASSOC PROF BIOCHEM, UNIV SHERBROOKE, 72- *Mem:* Am Biochem Soc; Can Soc Immunol; NY Acad Sci; Nutrit Soc. *Res:* Study of the structure of lectins and the nature of their receptor sites; study of the mechanism of contact dermatitis using the in vitro test of lymphocytes transformation. *Mailing Add:* Biochem Dept CxH C H U Univ of Sherbrooke Sch of Med Sherbrooke Can

DUPUY, DAVID LORRAINE, b Asheville, NC, Mar 7, 41; m 69. ASTRONOMY. *Educ:* King Col, AB, 63; Wesleyan Univ, MA, 67; Univ Toronto, PhD(astron), 72. *Prof Exp:* ASSOC PROF ASTRON & OBSERV DIR, ST MARY'S UNIV, 72-, CHMN, DEPT ASTRON, 80- *Concurrent Pos:* Mem, Nat Res Coun Can Assoc Comt Astron & chmn subcomt, 74-77; mem nat comt, Hist Astron in Can, 75-76. *Mem:* Can Astron Soc; Am Astron Soc; Royal Astron Soc Can; fel Royal Astron Soc Eng; Int Astron Union. *Res:* Observational studies of variable stars, especially RV Tauri stars; studies of young star clusters and resulting structure of galactic associations; previous research in peculiar galaxies; development of astronomical instrumentation. *Mailing Add:* Burke Gaffney Observ Dept Astron St Mary's Univ Halifax Can

DUPUY, HAROLD PAUL, b Lockport, La, Sept 10, 22. BIOCHEMISTRY. *Educ:* La State Univ, BS, 50, MS, 53, PhD(biochem), 56. *Prof Exp:* Res chemist, 56-75, SUPVRY RES CHEMIST, FOOD FLAVOR RES, OILSEED & FOOD LAB, SOUTHERN REGIONAL RES CTR, USDA, 75- *Honors & Awards:* Super Serv Award, USDA, 67 & 77; Fed Bus Asn Sci Award, 76; Gulf Coast Sect IFT Award, 77. *Mem:* Am Chem Soc; Am Oil Chemists' Soc; Inst Food Technol; Am Inst Chem. *Res:* Lathyrism; fats and oils; surface coatings; unconventional instrumental techniques for flavor analysis. *Mailing Add:* Southern Regional Res Ctr 1100 Robert E Lee Blvd New Orleans LA 70179

DUPUY, HARSTRY JOSEPH, immunology, see previous edition

DUQUESNOY, RENE J, b The Hague, Neth, May 24, 38; US citizen; m 68; c 2. IMMUNOLOGY. *Educ:* Delft Technol Univ, Ingenieur, 63; Univ Tenn, Memphis, PhD(exp path), 67. *Prof Exp:* Res assoc path, Med Units, Univ Tenn, Memphis, 63-67; asst clin prof microbiol, Med Col Wis, 70-76; assoc prof, 76-80, CLIN PROF HEALTH SCI, UNIV WIS, 80-; DIR RES & DEVELOP, MILWAUKEE BLOOD CTR, 74- *Concurrent Pos:* Fel pediat, Univ Minn, 68-70; assoc adj prof microbiol, Med Col Wis, 76-; adj prof biol, Marquette Univ, 80- *Mem:* Am Asn Clin Histocompatibility Testing (treas); Am Asn Blood Banks; Am Asn Immunologists; Soc Exp Biol & Med; Int Soc Exp Hemat. *Res:* Histocompatibility testing. *Mailing Add:* Milwaukee Blood Ctr 701 W Wisconsin Ave Box 10G Milwaukee WI 53201

DUQUETTE, ALFRED L, b Troy, Vt, Oct 14, 23; div. MATHEMATICS. *Educ:* Univ Mass, BS, 48; Columbia Univ, AM, 50; Univ Colo, PhD, 60. *Prof Exp:* Instr math, Mont State Univ, 52-54; asst prof, St John's Univ, 52-54; instr, Univ Colo, 54-55; off naval res asst, Univ Ill, 58-60; asst prof, Univ Ky, 60-61; sr scientist, Jet Propulsion Lab, 61-62; sr mem tech staff, ITT Fed Labs, Calif, 62-64; adv engr, Future Comput Technol, IBM Space Guidance Ctr, 64-66; PROF MATH, W GA COL, 66- *Mem:* Am Math Soc; Math Asn Am. *Res:* Advanced computer development. *Mailing Add:* Dept of Math WGa Col Carrollton GA 30118

DUQUETTE, DAVID J(OSEPH), b Springfield, Mass, Nov 4, 39; m 61; c 2. METALLURGY, MATERIALS SCIENCE. *Educ:* US Coast Guard Acad, BS, 61; Mass Inst Technol, PhD(metall), 68. *Prof Exp:* Res asst metall, corrosion lab, Mass Inst Technol, 65-68; res assoc, adv mat res & develop lab, Pratt & Whitney Div, United Aircraft Corp, 68-70; from asst prof to assoc prof metall eng, 70-76, PROF METALL ENG, RENSSELAER POLYTECH INST, 76- *Concurrent Pos:* Alcoa Found Res Award, 79 & 80. *Mem:* Am Soc Metals; Am Inst Mining, Metall & Petrol Engrs; Nat Asn Corrosion Engrs.

Res: Corrosion science and engineering including the effect of environment on mechanical properties of crystalline materials; mechanical properties of metals and alloys; fatigue. *Mailing Add:* Dept of Mat Eng Rensselaer Polytech Inst Troy NY 12181

DURACHTA, CHESTER WILLIAM, b Chicago, Ill, Dec 22, 25; m 55; c 5. MICROBIOLOGY. *Educ:* Northwestern Univ, BS, 50, MS, 53, PhD(parasitol), 57. *Prof Exp:* Lab instr biol, Northwestern, 54-56; technician toxicol, cardiovasc physiol & hemat, G D Searle & Co, 52-57; sr scientist res & develop, Smith Kline & French, Philadelphia, 57-61; DIR RES ADMIN & ADMIN ASST TO VPRES RES & DEVELOP, MEAD JOHNSON & CO, 61- *Mem:* AAAS; Am Soc Info Sci. *Res:* Electronic data processing, especially pharmacology, medicine, nutrition; develop and maintain computer applications for processing, correlating and retrieving biomedical and chemical data. *Mailing Add:* 115 Nunning Rd Evansville IN 47712

DURACK, DONALD LEE, b Oaklandon, Ind, July 8, 49. APPLIED MATHEMATICS. *Educ:* Mich State Univ, BS, 71; State Univ NY, Stony Brook, MA, 72, PhD(appl math), 76. *Prof Exp:* STAFF MEM, LOS ALAMOS NAT LAB, 76- *Mem:* Soc Indust & Appl Math. *Res:* Numerical solution of differential equations. *Mailing Add:* T-7 MS 233 Los Alamos Nat Lab Los Alamos NM 87545

DURAI-SWAMY, KANDASWAMY, b Thondipatti, India, Sept 28, 45; US citizen; m 71; c 1. FUEL ENGINEERING, CHEMICAL ENGINEERING. *Educ:* Annamalai Univ, India, BChE, 67; Bucknell Univ, MSChE, 70; Univ Utah, MEA, 71, PhD(fuels eng), 73. *Prof Exp:* Teaching assoc chem eng, Indian Inst Technol, 67-68; res engr fuels eng, Garrett Res & Develop Co, Occidental Petrol Corp, 73-75; mem tech staff, TRW Energy Systs, 75-77; sr res engr fuels eng, 77-81, PRINC RES ENGR & GROUP LEADER, OCCIDENTAL RES CORP, IRVINE, CALIF, 81- *Mem:* Am Chem Soc; Am Inst Chem Engrs. *Res:* Synthetic fuels from coal; pyrolysis; gasification and liquefaction of coal, oil shale, tar sand, and other carbonaceous materials; hydrotreating coal derived liquids. *Mailing Add:* Occidental Res Corp 2100 SE Main St Irvine CA 92714

DURAN, BENJAMIN S, b Tularosa, NMex, Nov 25, 39; m 59; c 4. MATHEMATICS, STATISTICS. *Educ:* Albuquerque Univ, BS, 61; Colo State Univ, MS, 64, PhD(statist), 66. *Prof Exp:* Asst prof math, Eastern NMex Univ, 66-69; asst prof, Baylor Med Sch, 69-71; asst prof, 71-75, ASSOC PROF MATH & STATIST, TEX TECH UNIV, 75- *Concurrent Pos:* Asst prof, Div Biomath, Tex Inst Rehab & Res, 70-71; adj asst prof math sci, Rice Univ, 70-71. *Mem:* Inst Math Statist; Am Statist Asn; Math Asn Am. *Res:* Nonparametric statistics; statistical computing; mathematical statistics. *Mailing Add:* Dept of Math Tex Tech Univ Lubbock TX 79409

DURAN, RUBEN, b Calif, Sept 30, 24; m 43; c 5. PLANT PATHOLOGY. *Educ:* Calif State Polytech Univ, San Luis Obispo, BS, 54; Wash State Univ, PhD(plant path), 58. *Prof Exp:* Res asst plant path, Wash State Univ, 54-58; jr instr plant path, 58-59; plant pathologist, Agr Mkt Serv, USDA, 59-61; from asst prof to assoc prof, 61-64, PROF PLANT PATH, WASH STATE UNIV, 71- *Mem:* Am Phytopath Soc; Mycol Soc Am. *Res:* Taxonomy and biology of the Ustilaginales; teaching mycology and plant pathology at the postgraduate level. *Mailing Add:* Dept of Plant Path Wash State Univ Pullman WA 99163

DURAN, SERVET A(HMET), b Kutahya, Turkey, Jan 2, 20; nat US; m 46; c 3. PHYSICAL METALLURGY, MATERIALS SCIENCE. *Educ:* Mo Sch Mines, BS, 43; Stanford Univ, AM, 45, PhD(mat sci), 63. *Prof Exp:* Asst metallog, Stanford Univ, 46; from instr to assoc prof, 47-61, chmn dept, 59-70, PROF PHYS METALL, WASH STATE UNIV, 61- *Concurrent Pos:* Vis assoc prof, Stanford Univ, 56-58; consult, Mid E Tech Univ, Turkey, 69. *Mem:* Am Soc Metals; assoc Am Inst Mining, Metall & Petrol Engrs; Am Soc Eng Educ. *Res:* Solid-state reactions; creep of metals; engineering education. *Mailing Add:* Dept of Mat Sci & Eng Wash State Univ Pullman WA 99163

DURAN, WALTER NUNEZ, b Maria Elena, Chile, Nov 1, 42; m 69; c 4. CARDIOVASCULAR PHYSIOLOGY, MICROCIRCULATION. *Educ:* Catholic Univ Chile, PhD(biol), 65; Duke Univ, PhD(physiol & pharmacol), 74. *Prof Exp:* Asst prof physiol, Catholic Univ Chile, 66-69; res assoc physiol & pharmacol, Duke Univ Med Ctr, 70-74; asst med res prof physiol & surg, 74-77; asst prof, 77-79, ASSOC PROF PHYSIOL & GRAD SCH BIOMED SCI, NJ MED SCH, UNIV MED & DENT NJ, 79- *Concurrent Pos:* Res assoc biophysics, Univ Chile, 67-69; vis prof Inst Biol Sci, Catholic Univ Chile, 80-81; pharm travel award, Microcirculatory Soc Inc, 78; mem coun, Am Heart Asn. *Mem:* Am Physiol Soc; Microcirculatory Soc. *Res:* Regulation of microvascular transport of solutes and blood flow in the heart and skeletal muscle; multiple tracer methods, intravital microscopy, computer-aided data acquisition and analysis; elucidation of a microvascular reserve for transport in the myocardium. *Mailing Add:* Dept Physiol Univ Med & Dent NJ 100 Bergen St Newark NJ 07103

DURANA, JEAN FREDERICKA, physical chemistry, see previous edition

DURAND, BERNICE BLACK, b Clarion, Iowa, Dec 28, 42; m 70. THEORETICAL PHYSICS. *Educ:* Iowa State Univ, BS, 65, PhD(physics), 71. *Prof Exp:* Lectr physics, 70-77, ASST PROF PHYSICS, UNIV WIS-MADISON, 77- *Concurrent Pos:* Vis staff mem, Los Alamos Nat Lab, 75, consult, 77-; mem, Inst Advan Study, 75-76; trustee, Aspen Ctr for Physics, 80- *Mem:* Am Phys Soc; AAAS; Sigma Xi. *Res:* Use of algebra in theoretical physics; position operators in quantum field theory; high energy scattering theory; gauge field theories; supersymmetry. *Mailing Add:* Dept of Physics Univ of Wis Madison WI 53706

DURAND, DONALD P, b New York, NY, Oct 18, 29; m 51; c 4. MICROBIOLOGY, VIROLOGY. *Educ:* Guilford Col, AB, 55; Kans State Univ, MS, 57, PhD(microbiol), 60. *Prof Exp:* Asst prof microbiol, Sch Med, Univ Mo, 59-64, assoc prof, 64-68; assoc prof bact, 68-72, prof bact, 72-80,

PROF MICROBIOL, IOWA STATE UNIV, 80- *Concurrent Pos:* NIH grant, 60-66 & spec fel, Cambridge Univ, 66-67. *Mem:* AAAS; Am Soc Microbiol; Brit Soc Gen Microbiol. *Res:* Animal viruses in conjunction with their physical and biochemical properties as they relate to virus-host cell interaction. *Mailing Add:* Dept of Bact Iowa State Univ Ames IA 50011

DURAND, EDWARD ALLEN, b Duluth, Minn, Dec 20, 19; m 49; c 5. METAL FINISHING, CORROSION PROTECTION. *Educ:* St Mary's Col Col, Minn, BS, 41; Creighton Univ, MS, 43; Univ Wis, PhD(chem), 50. *Prof Exp:* Chemist, Martin-Nebr Aircraft Co, 43-45; assoc inorg chemist, Armour Res Found, 45-46; res engr, Res Labs, Aluminum Co Am, 50; sr res chemist, Ekco Prod Co, Ill, 51-61; staff chemist, IBM Corp, 62-66; assoc ed, Metals Handbook, Am Soc Metals, 66-70, sr ed, 70-76; eng mgr, Tech Serv Co, Solon, Ohio, 76-77; MGR, COATINGS RES & DEVELOP, EMPIRE PLATING CO, CLEVELAND, 77- *Mem:* AAAS; Am Chem Soc; Nat Asn Corrosion Engineers; Am Electroplaters Soc. *Res:* Chemical and electrochemical surface treatment of metals; corrosion; selection, processing and fabrication of metals; writing and editing. *Mailing Add:* 7002 Fox Hill Dr Solon OH 44139

DURAND, JAMES BLANCHARD, b Cranford, NJ, June 13, 29; m 52; c 3. BIOLOGY. *Educ:* Rutgers Univ, BSc, 51; Harvard Univ, MA, 54, PhD(biol), 55. *Prof Exp:* From instr to assoc prof, 55-67, PROF ZOOL, RUTGERS UNIV, 67- *Mem:* Am Soc Zool. *Res:* Arthropods and molluscs; field work in marine biology. *Mailing Add:* Dept of Zool Rutgers Univ Camden NJ 08102

DURAND, LOYAL, III, b Madison, Wis, May 19, 31; m 54, 70; c 3. THEORETICAL PHYSICS. *Educ:* Yale Univ, BS, 53, MS, 54, PhD(physics), 57. *Prof Exp:* Vis mem physics, Inst Advan Study, 57-59; res assoc, Brookhaven Nat Lab, NY, 59-61; asst prof, Yale Univ, 61-65; chmn dept, 69-71, PROF PHYSICS, UNIV WIS-MADISON, 65- *Concurrent Pos:* NSF fel, 57-59; mem physics adv comt, Nat trustee, Aspen Ctr Physics, Colo, 68-, chmn exec comt, 68-72, pres, 72-76; mem long range planning comt, Fermi Nat Accelerator Lab, 72-75; assoc ed, J Math Physics, 73-75; consult theory div, Los Alamos Sci Lab, 75-, vis staff mem, Theory Div, 76; vis mem, Inst Advan Study, 75; mem, ZGS Prog Comt, Argonne Nat Lab, 77-79. *Mem:* Am Phys Soc; AAAS; Am Math Soc; Am Asn Univ Prof. *Res:* Theoretical physics, mainly high energy particle physics; astrophysics; radiation phenomena; applied mathematics; theory of special functions. *Mailing Add:* Dept of Physics Univ of Wis Madison WI 53706

DURAND, MARC L, b Ware, Mass, Sept 24, 40; m 63; c 3. ORGANIC CHEMISTRY. *Educ:* Holy Cross Col, BS, 62; Univ NH, PhD(chem), 67. *Prof Exp:* Asst prof chem, Alliance Col, 66-68; assoc prof, 68-71, chmn dept, 74-77, PROF CHEM, WEST CHESTER STATE COL, 71-, DEAN ARTS & SCI, 81- *Mem:* Am Chem Soc. *Res:* Synthetic organic chemistry; natural products with experience in infrared, ultraviolet, nuclear magnetic resonance spectroscopy and optical rotatory dispersion. *Mailing Add:* Dept Chem West Chester State Col West Chester PA 19380

DURAND, RALPH EDWARD, b Calgary, Alta, June 16, 47; m 74. RADIOBIOLOGY. *Educ:* Univ Calgary, BSc, 69; Univ Western Ont, PhD(biophys), 73. *Prof Exp:* Asst prof radiol, Univ Wis-Madison, 73-77, from asst prof to assoc prof human oncol & radiol, 75-77; ASSOC PROF ONCOL & ENVIRON HEALTH SCI, JOHNS HOPKINS UNIV, 77- *Mem:* Radiation Res Soc; Biophys Soc; Can Asn Physicists; Am Asn Cancer Res. *Res:* Cellular radiobiology; tumor radiobiology; tumor cell kinetics; radiation-drug interactions. *Mailing Add:* Radiobiol Sect 601 N Broadway Baltimore MD 21205

DURANT, FREDERICK C(LARK), III, b Ardmore, Pa, Dec 31, 16; m 47; c 3. ASTRONAUTICS. *Educ:* Lehigh Univ, BS, 39. *Prof Exp:* Asst area engr, E I du Pont de Nemours & Co, NJ, 39-41; rocket engr, Bell Aircraft Corp, NY, 47-48; div eng, US Naval Air Rocket Test Sta, 48-51; consult, Washington, DC, 51-54; sr staff mem, Arthur D Little, Inc, Mass, 54-57; exec asst to dir, Avco-Everett Res Lab, 57-59; dir pub & govt rels, res & develop div, Avco Corp, 59-61; sr rep aerospace-rockets, Bell Aerosysts Co, Washington, DC, 61-64; consult astronaut, 64-65; asst dir astronaut, Nat Air & Space Mus, Smithsonian Inst, 65-81; CONSULT, ASTRO ASSOCS, 81- *Concurrent Pos:* Consult, US Dept Defense Res & Develop Bd, 53-54; pres, Int Astronaut Fedn, 53-56. *Mem:* Fel Am Inst Aeronaut & Astronaut; Am Astronaut Soc; Brit Interplanetary Soc; Deut Ges Luft & Raumfahrt. *Res:* History of rockets and spaceflight; rocket engineering; national and international astronautical societies; public communications of astronautics. *Mailing Add:* Nat Air & Space Mus Smithsonian Inst Washington DC 20560

DURANT, JOHN ALEXANDER, III, b Lynchburg, SC, Jan 20, 39; m 58, 76; c 1. ENTOMOLOGY. *Educ:* Clemson Univ, BS, 61, MS, 63; Auburn Univ, PhD(entom), 66. *Prof Exp:* Assoc prof, 65-80, PROF ENTOM, CLEMSON UNIV, 80- *Mem:* Entom Soc Am. *Res:* Corn and cotton insects ecology and control. *Mailing Add:* Pee Dee Exp Sta Clemson Univ Florence SC 29503

DURANT, JOHN RIDGWAY, b Ann Arbor, Mich, July 29, 30; m 54; c 3. INTERNAL MEDICINE, ONCOLOGY. *Educ:* Swarthmore Col, BA, 52; Temple Univ, MD, 56; Am Bd Internal Med, dipl, 63. *Prof Exp:* From instr to asst prof med, Sch Med, Temple Univ, 63-67; assoc prof, 68-70, dir div hemat & oncol, 69-74, PROF MED, SCH MED, UNIV ALA, BIRMINGHAM, 70-, DIR COMPREHENSIVE CANCER CTR, 70-, PROF RADIATION ONCOL, 80- *Concurrent Pos:* Spec fel med neoplasia, Mem Hosp, New York, 62-63; Am Cancer Soc adv clin fel, 64-67; mem prof educ comt, Am Cancer Soc, 70-; consult, Vet Admin Hosp, Tuskegee, 70-; chmn, Southeastern Cancer Study Group, 75- *Mem:* AAAS; Am Col Physicians; Am Fedn Clin Res; Am Asn Cancer Educ; Am Asn Cancer Res. *Res:* Cancer chemotherapy; cytogenetics; immunology. *Mailing Add:* Univ of Ala Sch of Med University Sta Birmingham AL 35294

DURANT, THOMAS MORTON, clinical medicine, deceased

DURANTE, ANTHONY JOSEPH, b New York, NY, Apr 8, 43. ORGANIC CHEMISTRY. *Educ:* Iona Col, BS, 64; Fordham Univ, PhD(org chem), 71. *Prof Exp:* Res & develop chemist, 68-75, proj scientist, 75-78, GROUP LEADER, UNION CARBIDE CORP, TARRYTOWN, 78- *Mem:* Am Chem Soc; Am Asn Textile Colorists & Chemists. *Res:* Synthesis of natural products; synthesis of pesticide synergists; silicone chemistry, especially synthesis and evaluation of silicone resins in high performance protective coatings; urethane coatings for carpets and textiles; silicone surfactants for urethane foam. *Mailing Add:* RD 3 Shamrock Dr 14 Putnam Valley NY 10579

DURANTE, RAYMOND W, nuclear engineering, see previous edition

DURANTE, VINCENT ANTHONY, b Plainfield, NJ, Aug 27, 50; m 73; c 1. CATALYSIS, PHOTOCHEMISTRY. *Educ:* Rutgers Univ, BA, 72; Univ Calif, Santa Barbara, PhD(inorg chem), 77. *Prof Exp:* SR RES CHEMIST, MINERALS & CHEM DIV, ENGELHARD CORP, 77- *Mem:* Am Chem Soc. *Res:* Study of heterogeneous catalytic mechanisms and reaction kinetics especially over zeolites and clay mineral supports; inorganic photchemistry especially photoinduced reactions of supported systems; surface anchored homogeneous catalysts. *Mailing Add:* Minerals & Chem Div Engelhard Corp Edison NJ 08818

DURAY, JOHN R, b Whiting, Ind, Jan 28, 40; m 66; c 2. EXPERIMENTAL NUCLEAR PHYSICS. *Educ:* St Procopius Col, BS, 62; Univ Notre Dame, PhD(physics), 68. *Prof Exp:* From res assoc to asst prof physics, Ohio State Univ, 68-70; instr, Princeton Univ, 70-74; mem staff, 74-75, SR PHYSICIST & MGR SUBSURFACE SYSTS DEPT, BENDIX FIELD ENG CORP, 75- *Concurrent Pos:* Asst prof, Ind Univ Northwest, 75. *Mem:* Am Phys Soc; Sigma Xi; Soc Prof Well Log Analysts. *Res:* Nuclear physics as applied to subsurface uranium exploration and assessment. *Mailing Add:* Bendix Field Eng Corp Box 1569 Grand Junction CO 81502

DURBECK, ROBERT C(HARLES), b Poughkeepsie, NY, Apr 26, 35; m 63; c 2. CONTROL SYSTEMS, MECHANICAL ENGINEERING. *Educ:* Union Col, NY, BSME, 56; Cornell Univ, MS, 58; Case Inst Technol, PhD(control systs), 65. *Prof Exp:* Assoc design engr, data systs div, 58-61, res staff mem control systs, res div, 64-68, mgr power systs studies, 68-69, mgr mech technol, 69-71, mgr appl technol, 71-73, MGR, EXPLORATORY TECHNOL, RES DIV, IBM CORP, 73- *Honors & Awards:* Outstanding contribution award, IBM Corp, 68. *Mem:* Am Soc Mech Engrs; Inst Elec & Electronics Engrs; Soc Info Display. *Res:* Design and control of large scale physical and information systems; high performance mechanical and electro-mechanical systems; display and printing technologies; magnetic recording systems. *Mailing Add:* IBM Res Lab 5600 Cottle Rd San Jose CA 95193

DURBETAKI, PANDELI, b Istanbul, Turkey, May 31, 28; nat US; m 54; c 3. MECHANICAL ENGINEERING. *Educ:* Robert Col, Turkey, BS, 51; Univ Rochester, MS, 54; Mich State Univ, PhD(mech eng), 64. *Prof Exp:* Asst mech eng, Univ Rochester, 51-52; asst drafting & design, Anstice Co & Rochester Button Co, NY, 52-53; from instr to asst prof mech eng, Univ Rochester, 53-60; instr, Mich State Univ, 60-61, NSF sci fac fel, 61-63, instr, 63-64; assoc prof, 64-77, coordr grad studies, 68-74, PROF MECH ENG, GA INST TECHNOL, 77- *Mem:* Am Soc Mech Engrs; Combustion Inst; AAUP; Sigma Xi. *Res:* Classical, statistical and non-equilibrium thermodynamics; combustion; particle combustion; combustion in stratified charge mixtures; stratified charge operation of spark ignition engines; flammability and fire hazard; coal and biomas pyrolysis and combustion. *Mailing Add:* Sch Mech Eng Ga Inst Technol Atlanta GA 30332

DURBIN, ENOCH JOB, b New York, NY, Sept 6, 22; m 45; c 3. AEROSPACE & MECHANICAL SCIENCES. *Educ:* City Col New York, BS, 43; Rensselaer Polytech Inst, MS, 47. *Prof Exp:* Mem res staff, Appl Physics Lab, Johns Hopkins Univ, 44-45 & A D Cardwell Mfg Co, 46; lectr transient anal linear syst, Univ Va, 47-48; head appl physics sect, Aerophys Lab, NAm Aviation, Inc, 51-53; DIR INSTRUMENT & CONTROL LAB, PRINCETON UNIV, 53-, PROF MECH & AEROSPACE ENG, 65- *Concurrent Pos:* Consult various US Corp, 50-, NATO, 53- & SUD Aviation, France, 59-65; dir res & labs, US Army, Washington, DC, 66-67; electronics command, Ft Monmouth, 66-; mem exec bd, Found Instrumentation, Educ & Res; mem, Army Sci Adv Panel & Sci Adv Group for Aviation Systs; founder & dir, Alternate Fuels Lab, Univ BC. *Mem:* Fel AAAS. *Res:* Analysis of dynamic engineering data and physical transducer principles; alternate fueling of the internal combustion engine; fuel economy pollution control in the internal combustion engine. *Mailing Add:* Dept of Mech & Aerospace Eng Princeton Univ Princeton NJ 08540

DURBIN, JOHN RILEY, b Elk City, Kans, Nov 18, 35; m 58; c 3. ALGEBRA. *Educ:* Univ Wichita, BA, 56, MA, 58; Univ Kans, PhD(math), 64. *Prof Exp:* Asst prof, 64-69, assoc prof, 69-79, PROF MATH, UNIV TEX, AUSTIN, 79- *Concurrent Pos:* On leave, Cambridge Univ, 66-67. *Mem:* Am Math Soc; Math Asn Am. *Res:* Group theory; representations and applications of groups. *Mailing Add:* Dept of Math Univ of Tex Austin TX 78712

DURBIN, LEONEL DAMIEN, b Riviera, Tex, Nov 13, 35; m 63; c 1. CHEMICAL ENGINEERING. *Educ:* Tex Col Arts & Indust, BS, 57; Rice Univ, PhD(chem eng), 61. *Prof Exp:* Asst prof, 61-69, PROF CHEM ENG, TEX A&M UNIV, 69- *Mem:* Am Inst Chem Engrs; Am Chem Soc. *Res:* Chemical process dynamics; analog and digital simulation with feedback, adaptive, and optimal control; dynamics of distributed flow systems; optimal design methods. *Mailing Add:* Dept of Chem Eng Tex A&M Univ College Station TX 77840

DURBIN, PATRICIA WALLACE (MRS JAMES T HEAVEY), b Oakland, Calif, Apr 7, 27; m 58; c 1. BIOPHYSICS. *Educ:* Univ Calif, BS, 48, PhD(biophys), 53. *Prof Exp:* Asst, Univ Calif, 50, asst, Lawrence Berkeley Lab, 52, res fel, 54-56, lectr, 57-59, physiologist, 51-77, MEM STAFF,

LAWRENCE BERKELEY LAB, UNIV CALIF, 77- *Concurrent Pos:* Mem comt, II, Nat Coun Radiation Protection, 57, comts 30 & 34, 69-, coun mem, 75- *Mem:* AAAS; Radiation Res Soc; Health Physics Soc. *Res:* Biological effects of radiation; radioactive tracers; bone metabolism; biology of the transuranic elements. *Mailing Add:* Bldg 74B Lawrence Berkeley Lab Univ of Calif Berkeley CA 94720

DURBIN, PAUL THOMAS, b Louisville, Ky, July 6, 33. PHILOSOPHY OF TECHNOLOGY. *Educ:* Providence Col, BA, 57; Cath Univ Am, MA, 62; Aquinas Inst Philos, PhD(philos sci), 66. *Prof Exp:* Lectr, St Stephen's Col, 62-64, asst prof, 66-68; asst prof, Lincoln Univ, 68-69; asst prof, 69-72, ASSOC PROF PHILOS, UNIV DEL, 72- *Concurrent Pos:* Vis lectr, Lowell Technol Inst, 68. *Mem:* Philos Sci Asn; Soc for Philos & Technol; Am Philos Asn; Humanities & Technol Asn. *Res:* Place of science and technology in contemporary society; ethics of science and technology. *Mailing Add:* Philos Dept Ctr Sci & Cult Univ Delaware Newark DE 19711

DURBIN, RICHARD DUANE, b Santa Ana, Calif, Sept 6, 30; m 54; c 3. PLANT PATHOLOGY. *Educ:* Univ Calif, BS, 52, PhD, 58. *Prof Exp:* Res asst, Univ Calif, 53-54, sr lab tech, 54-57; NSF res fel, 57-58, asst prof plant path, Univ Minn, 58-62; assoc prof, 62-67, PROF PLANT PATH, UNIV WIS-MADISON, 67-; LAB CHIEF, PIONEERING RES LAB, USDA, 65- *Concurrent Pos:* Plant pathologist, Oat Invests, Pioneering Res Lab, USDA, 62-65. *Mem:* Am Phytopath Soc; Am Soc Plant Physiol. *Res:* Physiology of plant parasitism; mode of action and structure toxins; hypersensitivity. *Mailing Add:* Dept of Plant Path Univ of Wis Madison WI 53706

DURBIN, RICHARD PAUL, b Columbus, Ohio, June 3, 23; m 44; c 4. PHYSIOLOGY, BIOPHYSICS. *Educ:* Ohio State Univ, BSc, 43; Columbia Univ, PhD(physics), 53. *Hon Degrees:* MD, Royal Univ Umea, Sweden, 75. *Prof Exp:* Instr physics, Columbia Univ, 52-53; assoc biophys, Biophys Lab, Harvard Med Sch, 55-58; vis res assoc, Univ Col, Univ London, 58-59; asst prof, Harvard Med Sch, 59-61; from assoc res biophysicist to res biophysicist, 61-70, ADJ PROF PHYSIOL, CARDIOVASC RES INST, UNIV CALIF, SAN FRANCISCO, 70- *Concurrent Pos:* Nat Found fel biophys, Biophys Lab, Harvard Med Sch, 53-55; Am Heart Asn estab investr, Univ Col, Univ London, 58-59, Harvard Med Sch, 59-61 & Univ Calif, San Francisco, 61-63; vis scientist fel, Swed Med Res Coun, 75. *Mem:* Am Physiol Soc; Am Gastroenterol Asn. *Res:* Transport of water and acid by gastric mucosa. *Mailing Add:* Cardiovasc Res Inst Univ of Calif San Francisco CA 94143

DURBIN, RONALD PRIESTLEY, b Bement, Ill, Jan 23, 39; m 61; c 2. ANALYTICAL CHEMISTRY. *Educ:* MacMurray Col, BA, 61; Univ Ill, Urbana, PhD(anal chem), 66. *Prof Exp:* Res chemist, 65-70, sr res chemist, 70-77, res supvr, 77-78, MGR, ANAL DIV, HERCULES, INC, 78- *Mem:* Am Chem Soc. *Res:* Chromatography; thermodynamics of solute-solvent interactions; solvent effects in organic chemistry; spectrochemical methods of analysis; organic analysis via functional groups. *Mailing Add:* Res Ctr Hercules Inc Wilmington DE 19899

DURDEN, CHRISTOPHER JOHN, b London, Eng, Feb 25, 40; Can citizen; div; c 2. PALEONTOLOGY, SYSTEMATIC ENTOMOLOGY. *Educ:* McGill Univ, BSc, 61; Yale Univ, MS, 68, PhD(geol, biol), 72. *Prof Exp:* Asst park naturalist, Algonquin Park Nature Mus, Ont Dept Lands & Forests, 55-56; asst entom, Entom Res Inst, Res Br, Can Dept Agr, 57-58; geol asst, Sudbury Basin Proj, Int Nickel Co, 59; asst reconnaissance mapping, Geol Surv Can, 60; asst party chief, Bedrock Stratig Mapping, Geol Serv, Ministry Natural Resources, Que, 61; teaching asst geol, Yale Univ, 62-64, teaching asst biol, 64-65; res asst invert paleont, Carnegie Mus, Pa, 66-68; CUR GEOL, TEX MEM MUS, 68-, CUR ENTOM, 72- *Concurrent Pos:* Curatorial asst invert paleont & entom, Peabody Mus Natural Hist, 62-66; dir, Tex Arch Geol Res, 70- *Mem:* Fel AAAS; Paleont Soc; Lepidop Soc; fel Geol Asn Can. *Res:* Paleozoic insect evolution; speciation ecology in modern and fossil Lepidoptera, Orthoptera, Collembola, corals and woody plants; Paleozic coral evolution; Carboniferous and Silurian biostratigraphic correlation; biotic provinciality; ecosystem dynamics evolution; natural selection; micropaleoehtomology. *Mailing Add:* Tex Mem Mus 2400 Trinity St Austin TX 78712

DURDEN, DAVID ALAN, b Manchester, Eng, June 25, 43. ANALYTICAL CHEMISTRY, PHYSICAL CHEMISTRY. *Educ:* Univ BC, BSc, 63; Univ Alta, PhD(phys chem), 69. *Prof Exp:* Res fel, gas kinetics, Univ Essex, 69-71; res assoc, Dept Psychiat & Biochem, 71-78, RES CHEMIST, DEPT HEALTH, SASK, CAN, 78- *Mem:* Am Soc Mass Spectrometry; Can Biochem Soc. *Res:* Use of high resolution mass spectrometry for the quantitation of metabolites and drugs in tissue and physiological fluids; study of metabolites implicated in psychiatric disorders. *Mailing Add:* Psychiat Res Div 508A Univ Hosp Saskatoon SK S7N 0X0 Can

DURDEN, JOHN APLING, JR, b Phoenix, Ariz, July 7, 28; m 55; c 5. PHARMACEUTICAL CHEMISTRY, ORGANIC CHEMISTRY. *Educ:* Ariz State Univ, BS, 50; Univ Miss, MS, 52; Univ Kans, PhD(pharm & org chem), 57. *Prof Exp:* Instr org & phys chem, Midwestern Univ, 54-56; res chemist, 57-67, res scientist, 67-73, sr res scientist, Chem & Plastics Operating Div, 73-76, assoc dir res & develop, Agr Prod Div, Union Carbide Corp, WVa, 76-80, ASSOC DIR RES & DEVELOP, UNION CARBIDE AGR PROD CO, INC, NC, 80- *Mem:* Am Chem Soc. *Res:* Organic synthesis; reaction mechanisms; agricultural chemistry; structure-activity correlations. *Mailing Add:* Union Carbide Agr Prod Co Inc TW Alexander Dr Res Triangle Park NC 27709

DURE, LEON S, III, b Macon, Ga, Jan 19, 31; m 58; c 4. BIOCHEMISTRY. *Educ:* Univ Va, BA, 53, MA, 57; Univ Tex, PhD(biol), 60. *Prof Exp:* Fel biochem, 60-62, from asst prof to assoc prof, 62-69, PROF BIOCHEM, UNIV GA, 69- *Concurrent Pos:* NSF grant, 63-; AEC contract, 64-; USPHS career develop award, 67-72; consult, Biol Div, Oak Ridge Nat Lab, 63- *Mem:* Am Soc Biol Chem; Am Soc Plant Physiol. *Res:* Developmental biochemistry; nucleic acid and protein biosynthesis. *Mailing Add:* Dept of Biochem Univ of Ga Athens GA 30601

DUREN, PETER LARKIN, b New Orleans, La, Apr 30, 35; m 57; c 2. MATHEMATICS. *Educ:* Harvard Univ, AB, 56; Mass Inst Technol, PhD(math), 60. *Prof Exp:* Instr math, Stanford Univ, 60-62; from asst prof to assoc prof, 62-69, PROF MATH, UNIV MICH, ANN ARBOR, 69- *Concurrent Pos:* Sloan Found fel, 64-66; mem, Inst Advan Study, Princeton, NJ, 68-69; res assoc eval panel, Nat Res Coun, 71; assoc ed, Proc Am Math Soc, 73-75; managing ed, Mich Math J, 76-77; prin lectr, LMS/NATO conf on complex anal, Eng, 79; vis prof, Univ Md, 82. *Mem:* Am Math Soc; Math Asn Am; London Math Soc. *Res:* Complex analysis; univalent functions; linear spaces of analytic functions; harmonic analysis. *Mailing Add:* Dept of Math Univ of Mich Ann Arbor MI 48109

DURET, MAURICE FRANCIS, b Gainsborough, Sask, Jan 27, 22; m 53; c 2. MATHEMATICS, PHYSICS. *Educ:* Queens Univ, Ont, BSc, 49, MSc, 50; Univ Toronto, PhD(math, physics), 53. *Prof Exp:* Res officer, 53-61, BR HEAD APPL MATH, ATOMIC ENERGY OF CAN, LTD, 61- *Res:* Reactor design and operation. *Mailing Add:* Atomic Energy Can Ltd Chalk River ON K0J 1J0 Can

DURETTE, PHILIPPE LIONEL, b Manchester, NH, Aug 17, 44; m 67; c 2. ORGANIC CHEMISTRY, CARBOHYDRATE CHEMISTRY. *Educ:* Marquette Univ, BS, 66; Ohio State Univ, PhD(org chem), 71. *Prof Exp:* Sci Res Coun fel, Dept Chem, Queen Elizabeth Col, Univ London, 71-72; Alexander von Humboldt Found fel, Org Chem & Biochem Inst, Univ Hamburg, Ger, 72-73; sr res chemist, 73-78, RES FEL, MERCK SHARP & DOHME RES LAB, 78- *Mem:* Am Chem Soc; The Chem Soc; Sigma Xi. *Res:* Synthetic organic chemistry; synthetic and mechanistic carbohydrate chemistry; cell membrane structure and membrane effectors; conformational analysis; nuclear magnetic resonance spectroscopy; arachidonic acid metabolism. *Mailing Add:* Merck Sharp & Dohme Res Lab PO Box 2000 Rahway NJ 07065

DURFEE, RAPHAEL B, b Bisbee, Ariz, Apr 7, 18; m 43; c 2. OBSTETRICS & GYNECOLOGY. *Educ:* Stanford Univ, AB, 39, MD, 44. *Prof Exp:* From asst prof to assoc prof, 57-66, prof obstet & gynec, 66-76, CLIN PROF, MED SCH, UNIV ORE, 76- *Concurrent Pos:* Regent for State of Ore, Int Col Surgeons. *Mem:* Fel Am Col Surg; fel Am Col Obstet & Gynec; fel Am Soc Abdominal Surg; fel Int Col Surg; fel Pan-Am Med Asn. *Res:* Clinical research and investigation in gynecologic surgery. *Mailing Add:* Dept of Obstet & Gynec Univ of Ore Med Sch Portland OR 97201

DURFEE, ROBERT LEWIS, b Farmville, Va, May 15, 36; m 60; c 2. CHEMICAL ENGINEERING. *Educ:* Va Polytech Inst, BS, 57, MS, 59, PhD(chem eng), 61. *Prof Exp:* Res engr chem systs, Atlantic Res Corp, 61-69; dir life sci, 69-71, V PRES OPERS & CHIEF RES EXEC, VERSAR INC, 71- *Res:* Solid state radiation chemistry; projects on advanced fuels, non-Newtonian flow, cryogenic systems, and boiling heat transfer; life sciences and environmental systems; new product development. *Mailing Add:* Versar Inc 6621 Electronic Dr Springfield VA 22151

DURFEE, WAYNE KING, b North Scituate, RI, Oct 1, 24; m 51. AVIAN PHYSIOLOGY, AQUACULTURE. *Educ:* Univ RI, BS, 50, MS, 53; Rutgers Univ, PhD, 63. *Prof Exp:* prof animal sci, 51-81, PROF AQUACULT SCI & PATH, UNIV RI, 81- *Concurrent Pos:* Ombudsman, Univ RI, 74-76; res proj mgr, RI Agr Exp Sta, 76-, prin investr oyster res. *Mem:* AAAS; Poultry Sci Asn; Sigma Xi; World's Poultry Sci Asn; World Maricult Soc. *Res:* Embryology; behavior; poultry management; aquaculture; closed system culture and formulated rations for American oyster, Crassostrea virginica. *Mailing Add:* Dept Aquacult Sci & Path Univ of RI Kingston RI 02881

DURFEE, WILLIAM HETHERINGTON, b Montague, Mass, Apr 12, 15; m 39; c 4. MATHEMATICS. *Educ:* Harvard Univ, AB, 36, MA, 40; Cornell Univ, PhD(math), 43. *Prof Exp:* Instr math, Cornell Univ, 40-43 & Yale Univ, 43-45; math physicist, Nat Defense Res Coun, Northwestern Univ, 45-46; from instr to asst prof math, Dartmouth Col, 46-51; mathematician, Nat Bur Stand, 51-53 & Opers Res Off, 53-55; from assoc prof to prof, 61-80, EMER PROF MATH, MT HOLYOKE COL, 80- *Mem:* Am Math Soc; Math Asn Am. *Res:* Algebra. *Mailing Add:* Dept Math Mt Holyoke Col South Hadley MA 01075

DURFLINGER, ELIZABETH WARD, b Ft Wayne, Ind, July 8, 13; m 49. INVERTEBRATE ZOOLOGY. *Educ:* Western Col, BA, 33; Univ Cincinnati, MA, 34, PhD(zool), 39. *Prof Exp:* From instr to prof, 40-75, dean women, 40-65, EMER PROF ZOOL, BUTLER UNIV, 75- *Concurrent Pos:* Consult & sci writer, George F Cram Co, Indianapolis, 75- *Mem:* Sigma Xi. *Res:* Ecology of entomostraca; aquatic invertebrates. *Mailing Add:* 1010 Oakwood Trail Indianapolis IN 46260

DURGIN, WILLIAM W, b Framingham, Mass, Apr 26, 42; m 64; c 3. FLUID MECHANICS. *Educ:* Brown Univ, BS, 64, PhD(fluid dynamics), 70; Univ RI, MS, 66. *Prof Exp:* Asst prof eng sci & mech, Univ Fla, 70-71; asst prof mech eng & res eng, 71-75, assoc prof mech eng & head res & develop, 75-81, PROF MECH & LEAD RES ENG, WORCESTER POLYTECH INST, 81- *Mem:* Am Soc Mech Engrs; Sigma Xi. *Res:* Turbulence; flow induced vibration; physical and analytic modeling. *Mailing Add:* Alden Res Labs Worcester Polytech Inst Worcester MA 01609

DURHAM, CLARENCE ORSON, JR, b Victoria, Tex, Oct 20, 20; m 59; c 2. GEOLOGY. *Educ:* Univ Tex, BS, 42; Univ Chicago, cert meteorol, 43; Columbia Univ, PhD(geol), 57. *Prof Exp:* From lab asst to lab instr geol, Univ Tex, 46-48; asst, Bur Econ Geol, Univ Tex, 48-49 & Columbia Univ, 49-50; instr struct geol, 51-53, from asst prof to assoc prof geol, La State Univ, 53-63, prof geol, 63-77, chmn dept, 65-77, dir sch geol, 66-77, MEM STAFF, DURHAM GEOL ASSOCS, 77- *Concurrent Pos:* Res geologist, La Geol Surv, 55-57, dir res, 57-63. *Mem:* AAAS; Am Asn Petrol Geol; Soc Econ Paleont & Mineral; Am Geophys Union. *Res:* Mesozoic and Cenozoic stratigraphy; structural geology; geology of Gulf of Mexico region; sedimentary iron ores. *Mailing Add:* Durham Geol Assocs 8312 Florida Blvd Baton Rouge LA 70806

DURHAM, FRANK EDINGTON, b Jonesboro, La, July 12, 35; m 56, 77; c 3. NUCLEAR PHYSICS. *Educ:* La Polytech Inst, BS, 56; Rice Univ, MA, 58, PhD(physics), 60. *Prof Exp:* From asst prof to assoc prof physics, 60-67, arts & science head, Dept Physics, 72-74, PROF PHYSICS, TULANE UNIV, 67-, UNIV CHMN, 74- *Concurrent Pos:* Mem La Nuclear & Space Auth, 68-74; consult, Gulf S Res Inst, 70-76; dir res & develop, Ultra Prod Syst, Inc, 75- *Mem:* Am Phys Soc; AAAS; Sigma Xi. *Res:* Experimental studies of nuclear structure at low energies. *Mailing Add:* Dept of Physics Tulane Univ New Orleans LA 70118

DURHAM, FRANKLIN P(ATTON), b Wiley, Colo, Dec 22, 21; m 43; c 3. AERONAUTICAL ENGINEERING. *Educ:* Univ Colo, BS, 43, MS, 49, AeroEng, 53. *Prof Exp:* Exp test engr, Pratt & Whitney Aircraft, 43-47; from instr to prof aeronaut eng, Univ Colo, 47-55, head dept, 56; group leader, 57-61, alternate div leader, 61-76, assoc div leader, 76-78, PROG MGR, LOS ALAMOS NAT LAB, 78- *Mem:* Assoc fel Am Inst Aeronaut & Astronaut. *Res:* Thermodynamics; heat transfer; laser fusion. *Mailing Add:* 3100 Arizona Ave Los Alamos NM 87544

DURHAM, GEORGE STONE, b Portland, Ore, Dec 26, 12; m 35, 58; c 2. PHYSICAL CHEMISTRY. *Educ:* Reed Col, BA, 35; NY Univ, PhD(phys chem), 39. *Prof Exp:* Asst chem, NY Univ, 35-39; res chemist, Weyerhaeuser Timber Co, Wash, 39-40; instr chem, Ore State Col, 40-41; instr, Univ Ill, 41-43; from instr to prof, 43-77, chmn dept, 58-66 & 72-75, EMER PROF CHEM, SMITH COL, 77- *Concurrent Pos:* Vis asst prof, Univ Mass, 44-45, vis lectr, 57-62, mem grad faculty, 61-; vis asst prof, NY Univ, 45 & 46; res grants & res contracts, Sigma Xi, NSF, Off Naval Res, Air Force Off Sci Res, Off Ord Res & Army Res Off. *Mem:* Am Chem Soc. *Res:* Solid solutions of inorganic salts; solid state theory of the alkali halides. *Mailing Add:* Arch Cape OR 97102

DURHAM, HARVEY RALPH, b Perry, Fla, Feb 25, 38; m 63; c 3. TOPOLOGY. *Educ:* Wake Forest Univ, BS, 59; Univ Ga, MA, 62, PhD(math), 65. *Prof Exp:* Assoc prof math, 65-73, chmn dept, 67-71, assoc dean fac, 71-73, PROF MATH, APPALACHIAN STATE UNIV, 73-, ASSOC VCHANCELLOR ACAD AFFAIRS, 73- *Concurrent Pos:* Partic, Am Coun Educ Acad Admin Internship Prog, 69-70. *Mem:* Math Asn Am. *Res:* Combinatorial topology. *Mailing Add:* Off of Acad Affairs Appalachian State Univ Boone NC 28608

DURHAM, JAMES IVEY, b Alpine, Tex, Nov 6, 33; m 68; c 2. PLANT PHYSIOLOGY. *Educ:* Tex A&M Univ, BS, 55, MS, 61, PhD(biochem), 71. *Prof Exp:* plant physiologist, US Sugar Corp, 75-80; MEM FAC, DEPT PLANT SCI, TEX A&M UNIV, 80- *Mem:* Am Chem Soc; Am Soc Plant Physiologists. *Res:* Growth and development of sugarcane and forage crops. *Mailing Add:* Dept Plant Sci Tex A&M Univ College Station TX 77843

DURHAM, JOHN WYATT, b Okanogan, Wash, Aug 22, 07; m 35, 72; c 1. INVERTEBRATE PALEONTOLOGY. *Educ:* Univ Wash, BSc, 33; Univ Calif, MA, 36, PhD(paleont), 41. *Prof Exp:* Asst geol, Univ Calif, 35-36; geologist, Stand Oil Co Calif, 36-39; asst, Mus Paleont, Univ Calif, 41-42; geologist & chief paleontologist, Tropical Oil Co, Colombia, 43-46; assoc prof paleont, Calif Inst Technol, 46-47; from assoc prof to prof, 47-75, chmn dept, 56-58, EMER PROF PALEONT, UNIV CALIF, BERKELEY, 75- *Concurrent Pos:* Guggenheim fel, 54-55 & 65-66; mem, Paleont Res Inst & US Nat Comt Geol, 66-70. *Mem:* AAAS; Am Soc Syst Zool; fel Paleont Soc (vpres, 52-53, pres, 65-66); Soc Econ Paleontologists & Mineralogists; fel Geol Soc Am. *Res:* Tertiary Molluscan paleontology; tertiary stratigraphy; recent corals and echinoids; cretaceous ammonites; paleoclimates; paleobiogeography; lower Cambrian, Pre-Cambrian fossils. *Mailing Add:* Dept of Paleontology Univ of Calif Berkeley CA 94720

DURHAM, LEONARD, b Glen Carbon, Ill, Aug 27, 25; m 48; c 4. AQUATIC ECOLOGY, FISHERIES MANAGEMENT. *Educ:* Univ Ill, BS, 49, MS, 50, PhD(zool), 55. *Prof Exp:* Lab & field asst, Ill Natural Hist Surv, 47-49, tech asst, 49-50; fishery biologist, Ill Dept Conserv, 50-55; PROF ZOOL, EASTERN ILL UNIV, 55-, DIR DIV LIFE SCI, 67-, DIR ENVIRON BIOL, 69-, CHMN DEPT ZOOL, 75- *Concurrent Pos:* Mem, Ill Nature Preserves Comn, 70-73, mem adv bd. *Mem:* AAAS; Am Soc Ichthyologists & Herpetologists; Am Fisheries Soc; Am Inst Fisheries Res Biologists. *Res:* Fishery biology; ecology of fishes and fish management; conservation; water pollution; thermal studies. *Mailing Add:* Div of Life Sci Eastern Ill Univ Charleston IL 61920

DURHAM, LOIS JEAN, b Oakland, Calif, Dec 21, 31. ORGANIC CHEMISTRY. *Educ:* Univ Calif, BS, 54; Stanford Univ, PhD(org chem), 59. *Prof Exp:* Instr org chem, Stanford Univ, 59-60; sr res chemist, Stanford Res Inst, 60-61; NUCLEAR MAGNETIC RESONANCE SPECTROSCOPIST, STANFORD UNIV, 61- *Mem:* Am Chem Soc; Soc Appl Spectros. *Res:* Application of nuclear magnetic resonance spectroscopy in determination of organic structural analysis; organic reaction mechanisms, organic peroxides. *Mailing Add:* 180 El Dorado Ave Palo Alto CA 94306

DURHAM, MICHAEL DEAN, b Key West, Fla, Dec 11, 49; m 77. AEROSOL PHYSICS, AIR POLLUTION CONTROL. *Educ:* Pa State Univ, BS, 71; Univ Fla, MS, 75, PhD(environ eng), 78. *Prof Exp:* Info analyst, Nat Acad Sci, 72-73 & Am Psychol Asn, 73-74; res asst, Univ Fla, 75-78; RES ENGR, DENVER RES ENG, 78- *Concurrent Pos:* Consult, Environ Eng Consult, 75-78. *Mem:* Sigma Xi; Air Pollution Control. *Res:* Sampling and analysis of particulate matter and works in the design, development and evaluation of air pollution control equipment. *Mailing Add:* Electronics Div Denver Res Inst PO Box 10127 Denver CO 80208

DURHAM, NORMAN NEVILL, b Ranger, Tex, Feb 14, 27; m 52; c 4. BACTERIOLOGY. *Educ:* North Tex State Univ, BS, 49, MS, 51; Univ Tex, PhD(bact), 54. *Prof Exp:* Lab asst bot & bact, NTex State Univ, 46-49, student instr, 49-51; res scientist, Univ Tex, 52-54; from asst prof to assoc prof bact, 54-60; dir, Environ Inst & Community Develop Inst, 73-77, PROF BACT, OKLA STATE UNIV, 60-, DEAN, GRAD COL, 68-, DIR, WATER RES INST, 77- *Concurrent Pos:* Vis lectr, Sch Med, Univ Okla, 63 & Kans State Univ, 65; consult biol sci, NASA, 63-69; with div biol & med, AEC, 66-68; mem coun manpower planning, US Off Educ, 70-; mem eval team, Nat Coun Accreditation Teacher Educ, 68-; Sigma Xi regional lectr, 73-74. *Honors & Awards:* Outstanding Scientist Award, Okla, 77. *Mem:* AAAS; Am Acad Microbiol; Am Soc Microbiol; Brit Soc Gen Microbiol; Biochem Soc. *Res:* Radiations; bacterial metabolism and metabolic pathways; genetics; agricultural bacteriology; protein and enzyme synthesis; mechanism of antibiotic action; metabolic regulations, cell growth and reproduction; genetic transformation; chemotherapy, molecular interactions; cell structure, composition and conformation. *Mailing Add:* Grad Col Okla State Univ Stillwater OK 74074

DURHAM, RALPH MARION, b Bristol, Colo, Dec 20, 23; m 46; c 8. GENETICS, ANIMAL HUSBANDRY. *Educ:* Colo Agr & Mech Col, BS, 48; Univ Wis, MS, 49, PhD, 51. *Prof Exp:* Asst animal breeding, Univ Wis, 48-51; asst prof genetics & animal breeding, NMex Col, 51-53; animal husbandman, Swine Sect, Animal & Poultry Husb Res Br, Agr Res Serv, USDA, 54-55; exten animal breeding specialist & assoc prof, Iowa State Col, 55-59; prof animal husb, 59-74, head dept, 59-65, prof, 74-80, EMER PROF ANIMAL SCI, TEX TECH UNIV, 80- *Mem:* AAAS; Am Soc Animal Sci; Poultry Sci Asn. *Res:* Genetics of growth and reproduction in cattle, sheep and swine; heterosis and carcass improvement in swine; performance testing methods in beef and swine. *Mailing Add:* Dept of Animal Sci Tex Tech Univ Lubbock TX 79409

DURHAM, ROSS M, b Toronto, Ont, Sept 19, 30; US citizen; m 55; c 3. NEUROPHYSIOLOGY, SPACE BIOLOGY. *Educ:* Univ Calif, Los Angeles, AB, 62, PhD(zool), 68. *Prof Exp:* Proj biologist, Space Biol Labs, Brain Res Inst, Univ Calif, Los Angeles, 68-70, asst res psychologist, 70-71; asst prof biol, 71-73, ASSOC PROF BIOL, UNIV TENN, CHATTANOOGA, 73- *Concurrent Pos:* Vis prof, Univ Southern Calif, 70-71; consult, Vet Admin Hosp, Sepulveda, Calif, 70-71. *Res:* Water balance in vertebrates; thirst, its cause and control; renal physiology; physiological psychology; electrophysiological recording from units in subcortical nuclei. *Mailing Add:* Dept of Biol Univ of Tenn Chattanooga TN 37402

DURHAM, WILLIAM BRYAN, b Ithaca, NY, May 20, 47. EXPERIMENTAL ROCK MECHANICS, MATERIALS SCIENCE. *Educ:* Cornell Univ, BS, 69; Mass Inst Technol, PhD(geophys), 75. *Prof Exp:* Res assoc earth sci, Univ Paris, 75-77; PHYSICIST EARTH SCI, LAWRENCE LIVERMORE LAB, UNIV CALIF, 77- *Mem:* Am Geophys Union. *Res:* Rheology of upper mantle rocks and minerals; physical properties of rocks at high pressure and temperature; microstructure such as dislocations, subgrains and microcracks of rocks and minerals. *Mailing Add:* Lawrence Livermore I ab Univ of Calif Livermore CA 94550

DURHAM, WILLIAM FAY, b Cedartown, Ga, Apr 19, 22; m 47; c 3. BIOCHEMISTRY. *Educ:* Emory Univ, AB, 43, MS, 48, PhD(biochem), 50. *Prof Exp:* Biochemist, Toxicol Sect, Technol Br, Commun Dis Ctr, USPHS, 50-57, chief, Wenatchee Field Sta, 57-67, Pesticide Res Lab, 67-70, Perrine Primate Lab, 70-75, dir, Environ Toxicol Div, 75-80, SR RES SCIENTIST, ENVIRON PROTECTION AGENCY, 80- *Mem:* Fel AAAS; Soc Toxicol; Am Soc Pharmacol & Exp Therapeut; Sigma Xi; Am Chem Soc. *Res:* Toxicology of pesticides. *Mailing Add:* Environ Toxicol Div Nat Environ Res Ctr Research Triangle Park NC 27711

DURICA, THOMAS EDWARD, b Cleveland, Ohio, Oct 25, 42; m 76. DEVELOPMENTAL NEUROBIOLOGY, ANATOMY. *Educ:* John Carroll Univ, BS, 66; Loyola Univ Chicago, PhD(anat), 77. *Prof Exp:* ASST PROF ANAT, RUSH MED COL, 77- *Mem:* AAAS; Sigma Xi; Soc Neuroscience. *Res:* Development of the nervous system, specifically the axon reaction of the pyramidal cells of the cerebral cortex of the developing hamster. *Mailing Add:* Dept Anat 1753 W Congress Pkwy Chicago IL 60612

DURIEUX, CHARLES W(OGAN), b Havana, Cuba, Dec 26, 20; US citizen; m 51; c 2. INFORMATION SCIENCES, MATHEMATICS. *Educ:* La State Univ, BS, 42; Stanford Univ, MS, 50. *Prof Exp:* Physicist, Nat Bur Standards, 50-53; Diamond Ord Fuze Lab, 53-56; assoc mathematician, Rand Corp, 56-57; dept mgr, Syst Develop Corp, 57-68; br mgr, Comput Sci Corp, 68-69; sr ADP res & develop specialist, Defense Commun Agency, 69-70; mem exec staff, East Region Systs Div, Comput Sci Corp, 70-74; sr consult, prog mgr, Optimum Systs Inc, 74-76; MATHEMATICIAN COMMAND CONTROL TECHNOL CTR, DEFENSE COMMUN AGENCY, 76- *Mem:* Inst Elec & Electronics Eng. *Res:* Development of computer based information processing systems; automatic data processing. *Mailing Add:* Command Control Technol Ctr Defense Commun Agency Washington DC 20301

DURIG, JAMES ROBERT, b Washington Co, Pa, Apr 30, 35; m 55; c 3. PHYSICAL CHEMISTRY. *Educ:* Washington & Jefferson Col, BA, 58; Mass Inst Technol, PhD(phys chem), 62. *Prof Exp:* From asst prof to prof chem, Univ SC, 62-70, Educ Found prof, 70-73, DEAN, COL SCI & MATH, UNIV SC, 73- *Honors & Awards:* Russel Award for res, 68; Coblentz Soc Award, 70; Charles A Stone Award, Am Chem Soc, 75, Southern Chemist Award, 76; Alexander von Humbolt Sr Scientist Award, WGer, 76. *Mem:* Fel Am Phys Soc; Am Chem Soc; Soc Appl Spectros; Coblentz Soc (pres, 74-76). *Res:* Infrared, Raman and microwave spectra of polyatomic molecules, especially molecules having low frequency vibrations; torsional barriers; molecular structure of organometallic molecules. *Mailing Add:* Col of Sci & Math Univ of SC Columbia SC 29208

DURIO, WALTER O'NEAL, b Arnaudville, La, Jan 17, 38. PARASITOLOGY. *Educ:* Southwestern La Univ, BSc, 59, MS, 60; Univ Nebr, Lincoln, PhD(zool, physiol), 66. *Prof Exp:* Asst prof, 66-74, ASSOC PROF BIOL, UNIV SOUTHWESTERN LA, 74- *Mem:* Am Soc Parasitol; Am Micros Soc. *Res:* Helminthology; taxonomy of digenetic trematodes. *Mailing Add:* Dept of Biol Univ of Southwestern La Lafayette LA 70504

DURISEN, RICHARD H, b Brooklyn, NY, Nov 24, 46. ASTROPHYSICAL FLUID DYNAMICS, STELLAR EVOLUTION. *Educ:* Fordham Col, Bronx, NY, BS, 67; Princeton Univ, PhD(astron), 72. *Prof Exp:* Fel, Lick Observ, 71-73; res assoc, Ames Res Ctr, NASA, 74-76; asst prof, 76-81, ASSOC PROF ASTRON, DEPT ASTRON, IND UNIV, 81- *Mem:* Am Astron Soc; AAAS; Int Astron Union. *Res:* Theoretical astrophysics involving fluid or particle dynamics; rotationally driven instabilities in stars and gas disks; globular cluster winds; white dwarf accretion and planetary ring dynamics. *Mailing Add:* Dept Astron Swain West 319 Ind Univ Bloomington IN 47405

DURKAN, JAMES P, b Baltimore, Md, Jan 13, 34; m 58; c 4. MEDICINE, OBSTETRICS & GYNECOLOGY. *Educ:* Loyola Col, Md, AB, 55; Univ Md, MD, 59; Am Bd Obstet & Gynec, dipl, 67. *Prof Exp:* Intern, Mercy Hosp, Baltimore, Md, 59-60; resident, 60-64, asst prof, 64-71, ASSOC PROF OBSTET & GYNEC, UNIV MD, BALTIMORE CITY, 71-; HEAD DEPT OBSTET & GYNEC, MERCY HOSP, 68- *Mem:* Fel Am Col Obstet & Gynec. *Res:* Neurologic influence on menstrual function; clinical oncology; clinical family planning. *Mailing Add:* Dept of Obstet & Gynec Univ of Md Sch of Med Baltimore MD 21201

DURKEE, LAVERNE H, b Darien, NY, June 23, 27; m 56; c 2. PLANT TAXONOMY. *Educ:* Syracuse Univ, BS, 51, MS, 54, PhD, 60. *Prof Exp:* Asst prof biol, Grove City Col, 58-61; asst prof, Parsons Col, 61; from asst prof to assoc prof, 62-70, PROF BIOL, GRINNELL COL, 70- *Mem:* Am Inst Biol Sci; Bot Soc Am; Am Soc Plant Taxonomists; Int Asn Plant Taxonomists. *Res:* Taxonomy of Acanthaceae. *Mailing Add:* Dept of Biol Grinnell Col Grinnell LA 50112

DURKEE, LENORE T, b Utica, NY, Nov 26, 32; m 56; c 2. BOTANY. *Educ:* Syracuse Univ, AB, 54, MS, 58; Univ Iowa, PhD(bot), 77. *Prof Exp:* ASST PROF BIOL, GRINNELL COL, 77- *Mem:* Bot Soc Am; Electron Micros Soc Am. *Res:* Ultrastructure, physiology, and adaptiveness of floral and extra-floral nectaries in Passiflora. *Mailing Add:* Dept of Biol Grinnell Col Grinnell IA 50112

DURKIN, DOMINIC J, b St Johnsbury, Vt, Dec 24, 30; m 58; c 4. HORTICULTURE, PLANT PHYSIOLOGY. *Educ:* Univ NH, BS, 52; Ohio State Univ, MS, 58, PhD(hort), 60. *Prof Exp:* From asst prof to assoc prof hort, Purdue Univ, 60-69; chmn dept hort & forestry, 71-77, PROF FLORICULT, RUTGERS UNIV, 69- *Mem:* Am Soc Hort Sci. *Res:* Bud dormancy in the rose; florist crop physiology; post harvest physiology; cut flowers. *Mailing Add:* Dept of Hort Rutgers Univ New Brunswick NJ 08903

DURKOVIC, RUSSELL GEORGE, b Cheyenne, Wyo, Jan 22, 40. NEUROPHYSIOLOGY. *Educ:* Va Polytech Inst, BS, 62; Case Western Reserve Univ, PhD(physiol), 68. *Prof Exp:* Fel, 68-70, asst prof, 70-76, ASSOC PROF PHYSIOL, STATE UNIV NY UPSTATE MED CTR, 76- *Concurrent Pos:* Consult, Neurobiol Panel, Nat Sci Found, 78-81. *Mem:* Soc Neurosci; Int Brain Res Orgn; AAAS; NY Acad Sci. *Res:* Use of a simplified model approach to identify neurophysiological mechanisms of learning, including analysis of sensory, integrative and motor systems of the cat spinal cord. *Mailing Add:* Dept Physiol State Univ NY Upstate Med Ctr Syracuse NY 13210

DURLAND, JOHN R(OYDEN), b Chicago, Ill, Mar 7, 14; m 36; c 4. CHEMICAL ENGINEERING. *Educ:* Mich Col Mining & Technol, BS, 35; Univ Wis, PhD(org chem), 39. *Prof Exp:* Res chemist, 39-40, res chemist & leader group, Nitro, 41-45, develop supt, 46; plant mgr, Monsanto Co, 47-52, asst prod mgr, org chem div, 52-53, plant mgr, J F Queeny, 53-55, tech prod mgr, org chem div, 55-60, prod dir, 60-65, mgr int & interdivisional mfg, 65-67, vpres, Mitsubishi Monsanto Chem Co, 67-79; RETIRED. *Mem:* Am Chem Soc; Am Inst Chem Engrs. *Res:* Hydrogenation; process research in production of organic chemicals. *Mailing Add:* 3176 Cumberland Court Westlake Village CA 91362

DURLEY, RICHARD CHARLES, b Hertford, Eng, Mar 11, 43; m 73. PLANT BIOCHEMISTRY. *Educ:* Bristol Univ, BSc, 65, PhD(org chem), 68. *Prof Exp:* Fel plant growth regulators, Dept Biol, 69-71, res assoc, 71-74, PROF RES ASSOC, DEPT CROP SCI, UNIV SASK, 74- *Mem:* Int Plant Growth Substances Asn; fel The Chem Soc; Royal Soc Chem; Am Soc Plant Physiologists. *Res:* Chemical analysis; biosynthesis and function of the plant growth regulators, auxins, gibberellins, cytokinins, and abscisins; function of these regulators during environmental stress. *Mailing Add:* Dept of Crop Sci Univ of Sask Saskatoon SK S7N 0W0 Can

DURLING, ALLEN E(DGAR), b Summit, NJ, Dec 21, 34; m 60; c 3. COMMUNICATIONS. *Educ:* Lafayette Col, BS, 60; Syracuse Univ, MEE, 62, PhD(elec eng), 64; Univ Fla, MFA, 80. *Prof Exp:* Elec engr, prod develop lab, Int Bus Mach Corp, 60-61; asst elec eng, Syracuse Univ, 61-62, instr, 62-64; from asst prof to prof, Univ Fla, 64-77; sr assoc, 77-80, PRIN, BOOZ, ALLEN & HAMILTON, MGT CONSULTS, 80- *Mem:* Inst Elec & Electronics Engrs. *Res:* Communications systems; digital signal processing; analog/digital and hardware/software interactions. *Mailing Add:* Booz Allen & Hamilton 4330 East West Hwy Bethesda MD 20014

DURLING, FREDERICK CHARLES, b Detroit, Mich, July 31, 31. MATHEMATICAL STATISTICS, MATHEMATICS. *Educ:* Arlington State Col, BA, 65; Southern Methodist Univ, MS, 67, PhD(statist), 69. *Prof Exp:* Asst prof math statist, Med Univ SC, 69-71; from lectr to sr lectr, Univ Waikato, NZ, 71-76; sr lectr math statist, Western Australian Inst Technol, 76-79; STATISTICIAN/DEMOGRAPHER, DEPT LANDS, NORTHERN TERRITORY, 79- *Mem:* AAAS; Inst Math Statist; Am Statist Asn; Am Acad Arts & Sci; Am Math Soc. *Res:* Multivariate distributional theory; bivariate Burr distribution-development and investigation of theoretical and empirical properties; multivariate statistical analysis; cluster analysis; factor analysis; multidimensional scaling. *Mailing Add:* PO Box 1239 Darwin Northern Territory 5794 Australia

DURNEY, CARL H(ODSON), b Blackfoot, Idaho, Apr 22, 31; m 53; c 6. ELECTRICAL ENGINEERING. *Educ:* Utah State Univ, BS, 58; Univ Utah, MS, 61, PhD(elec eng), 64. *Prof Exp:* Assoc res engr control systs, Boeing Airplane Co, Wash, 58-59; asst res prof elec eng, 63-68, assoc prof, 68-75, chmn, Dept Elec Eng, 77-82, PROF ELEC ENG & RES PROF BIOENG, UNIV UTAH, 75- *Concurrent Pos:* On leave, mem tech staff, Crawford Hill Lab, Bell Tel Labs, NJ, 65-66; comt mem, Am Nat Standards Inst, C95 subcomt III on radiation safety levels and/or tolerances with respect to personnel, 73- *Mem:* Inst Elec & Electronics Engrs; Am Soc Eng Educ; Int Union Radio Sci; Bioelectromatgnetics Soc (vpres, 80-81, pres, 81-82). *Res:* Electromagnetic field theory; microwave theory and devices; engineering pedagogy; interaction of electromagnetic fields and living systems. *Mailing Add:* Dept of Elec Eng Univ of Utah Salt Lake City UT 84112

DURNFORD, ROBERT F(RED), b Carlton, Mont, June 29, 22; m; c 2. ELECTRICAL ENGINEERING. *Educ:* Mont State Col, BS, 44, MS, 49; Ohio State Univ, PhD, 65. *Prof Exp:* Assoc prof, 47-66, PROF ELEC ENG, MONT STATE UNIV, 66- *Mem:* Am Soc Eng Educ; Inst Elec & Electronics Engrs. *Res:* Industrial electronics; control; energy conversion. *Mailing Add:* Dept of Elec Eng Mont State Univ Bozeman MT 59717

DURNICK, THOMAS JACKSON, b Ft Leavenworth, Kans, Mar 1, 46. ANALYTICAL CHEMISTRY, SPECTROSCOPY. *Educ:* Rensselaer Polytech Inst, BS, 67, PhD(phys chem), 71. *Prof Exp:* Res assoc, Res Found, State Univ NY Binghamton, 71-72; fel, Univ Alta, 72-74; sr res chemist, Eastern Res Ctr, Stauffer Chem Co, 74-80; MGR ANAL CHEM, AM STERILIZER CO, 80- *Mem:* Am Chem Soc; Soc Appl Spectros. *Res:* Application of infrared, Raman and ultraviolet spectroscopy to problems of structure elucidation and identification; sample handling techniques for compounds of industrial interest; general industrial analytical chemistry. *Mailing Add:* Eastern Res Ctr Stauffer Chem Co Dobbs Ferry NY 10522

DURNO, WILLIAM HENRY, b Pittsburgh, Pa, Aug 28, 14; m 43. CHEMISTRY. *Educ:* Univ Pittsburgh, BS, 37. *Prof Exp:* Chemist, Fed Labs, Inc, 37-39, plant supt, 39-44, chief chemist, 44-60, asst sales mgr, 60-64, qual control mgr, 64-74, govt sales engr, 74-81; RETIRED. *Mem:* Fel Am Inst Chemists; Am Chem Soc. *Res:* Chemical explosives; electrochemistry; pyrotechnics. *Mailing Add:* 135 Ben Franklin Rd N Indiana PA

DUROCHER, DONALD FRANCIS, b Springfield, Mass, June 19, 47; m 68; c 3. PHYSICAL CHEMISTRY. *Educ:* Union Col, NY, BS, 69; Brandeis Univ, PhD(phys & inorg chem), 74. *Prof Exp:* Asst prof chem, Brandeis Univ, 74-75; sr scientist, GCA Corp, Technol Div, 75-76; res scientist, 76-78, MGR TECH SERV, SPOTSWOOD MILL, SCHWEITZER DIV, KIMBERLY CLARK CORP, 78- *Res:* Cellulose chemistry, improvement in process control on paper machines. *Mailing Add:* Spotswood Mill Schweitzer Div Kimberly Clark Corp Spotswood NJ 08816

DURR, ALBERT MATTHEW, JR, b Nebraska City, Nebr, May 22, 23; m 45; c 2. ORGANIC CHEMISTRY. *Educ:* Okla State Univ, BS, 50, MS, 51. *Prof Exp:* Res chemist, Chem Dept, Beacon Res Labs, Tex Co, 51-55; lubricants group, 55-56, sr res chemist, 56-58, from actg res group leader to res group leader, 58-73, sr res scientist, 73-80, RES ASSOC, RES & DEVELOP DEPT, CONOCO INC, 80- *Mem:* Am Chem Soc; AAAS; Sigma Xi; Am Soc Lubrication Eng; Int Soc Gen Semantics. *Res:* Fundamental organic chemistry; petroleum lubricants. *Mailing Add:* 111 Glenside Ave Ponca City OK 74601

DURR, FRIEDRICH (E), b Poughkeepsie, NY, July 28, 33; m 57; c 4. INFECTIOUS DISEASES, THERAPEUTICS. *Educ:* St Johns Univ, BS, 55; Univ Wis, MS, 58, PhD(med microbiol), 60. *Prof Exp:* Instr microbiol, Col Med & Dent, Seton Hall Univ, 60-63; res virologist, J L Smith Mem Cancer Res, Pfizer, Inc, 63-71; group leader, 71-76, DEPT HEAD CHEMOTHER RES, LEDERLE LABS, 76- *Mem:* Am Soc Microbiol; NY Acad Sci; AAAS; Am Asn Cancer Res. *Res:* Effect of viruses on transplantable mouse tumors; bioassay of murine leukemia viruses; studies on the infectivity of EBV for human lymphoblastoid cells; anticancer chemotherapy, including studies with immunomodulating agents; viral chemotherapy, particularly effect of drugs on influenza virus and herpesvirus infections in vivo and in vitro; effect of drugs on viral antigen synthesis as determined by immunofluorescence; cancer chemotherapy; immunopharmacology. *Mailing Add:* Lederle Labs Pearl River NY 10965

DURRANI, SAJJAD H(AIDAR), b Jalalpur, Pakistan, Aug 27, 28; US citizen; m 59; c 3. ELECTRICAL ENGINEERING. *Educ:* Govt Col, Lahore, Pakistan, BA, 46; Eng Col, Lahore, BScEng, 49; Univ Manchester, MScTech, 53; Univ NMex, ScD(elec eng), 62. *Prof Exp:* Lectr elec eng, Eng Col, Lahore, 49-56, asst prof, 56-59; instr & res assoc, Univ NMex, 59-62; sr engr commun prod dept, Gen Elec Co, Va, 62-64; prof elec eng & chmn dept & dir res, Eng Univ, Lahore, 64-65; assoc prof elec eng, Kans State Univ, 65-66; sr engr, Space Ctr, RCA Corp, 66-68; mem tech staff, Commun Satellite Corp, 68-69; br mgr, Systs Anal Lab, 69-71; staff scientist, Adv Studies Lab, 71-73; sr scientist, Opers Res Inc, Md, 73-74; sr engr, Goddard Space Flight Ctr, 74-79, SR COMMUN SCIENTIST, HQ, NASA, 79- *Concurrent Pos:* Pres, Teaching Staff Asn, Eng Univ, Pakistan, 64-65; mem, US Comns C & F, Int Sci Radio Union; consult, Off Telecommun Policy, Exec Off of President, 75-77 & Nat Telecommun & Info Admin, Dept Com, 78-79. *Honors & Awards:* Spec Achievement Awards, NASA, 77, 78. *Mem:* Fel Inst Elec & Electronics Engrs; assoc fel Am Inst Aeronaut & Astronaut. *Res:* Communications systems; antennas and propagation; adaptive multibeam phased array experiment for Spacelab. *Mailing Add:* 17513 Lafayette Dr Olney MD 20832

DURRANT, BARBARA SUSAN, b Lansing, Mich, Aug 22, 49. ANIMAL PHYSIOLOGY. *Educ:* NC State Univ, BS, 72, MS, 75, PhD(physiol), 79. *Prof Exp:* Fel, 79-81, STAFF SCIENTIST REPRODUCTIVE PHYSIOL, ZOOL SOC SAN DIEGO, 81- *Concurrent Pos:* Lectr, Univ Calif San Diego Exten Course, 81 & Zool Soc San Diego Zoo Inst Course, 82; lectr, Zoo Work

Explor Student Training Prog, 79-; consult, Gifted & Talented Educ Prog, San Diego City Sch, 81- *Mem:* Int Embryo Transfer Soc; Sigma Xi; Am Asn Zool Parks & Aquariums. *Res:* Estrus synchronization of various hoofed-stock species; artificial insemination; semen collection and freezing; interspecies embryo transfer; embryo freezing and in vitro fertilization. *Mailing Add:* Zool Soc San Diego PO Box 551 San Diego CA 92112

DURRELL, CORDELL, b San Francisco, Calif, Aug 7, 08; m 37. GEOLOGY. *Educ:* Univ Calif, AB, 31, PhD(geol), 36. *Prof Exp:* Instr geol, Univ Calif, 36-37; field geologist, 37-38; instr geol, Univ Calif, Los Angeles, 38-41, from asst prof to prof, 41-53; prof, 63-76, EMER PROF GEOL, UNIV CALIF, DAVIS, 76- *Concurrent Pos:* Assoc geologist, US Geol Surv, 43-47; prof, Petroleo Brasileiro, Salvador, Brazil, 58 & 59. *Mem:* Am Asn Petrol Geologists; fel Geol Soc Am. *Res:* Geologic structure; ore deposits; stratigraphy; metamorphism; petrology. *Mailing Add:* Dept of Geol Univ of Calif Davis CA 95616

DURRELL, WILLIAM S, b Miami, Fla, Oct 14, 31; m 53; c 5. ORGANIC CHEMISTRY, POLYMER CHEMISTRY. *Educ:* Univ Fla, BS, 53, PhD(org chem), 61. *Prof Exp:* Chemist, Peninsular Chem Res, Fla, 53-55, coordr res & develop, 61-64; res chemist, Ethyl Corp, La, 55-56; res assoc, Burke Res Co, 64-65; group leader, Geigy Chem Corp, Ala, 65-68, asst develop mgr, 68-69, develop mgr, RI, 69-70, dir res & vpres, Plastics & Additives Div, Ciba-Geigy Corp, Ardsley, 70-77; vpres technol, E F Houghton & Co, 77-79; vpres res & develop, J M Walter Corp, 79-82; DIR RES & DEVELOP, AGR & PERFORMANCE CHEM DIV, PPG INDUST INC, 82- *Mem:* Am Chem Soc. *Res:* Fluorine compounds, plastics, lubricants and additives. *Mailing Add:* c/o Jim Walter Corp PO Box 22601 Tampa FL 33622

DURRENBERGER, JOHN A, b Perham, Minn, Aug 22, 20; m 46; c 3. AERONAUTICAL ENGINEERING, OPERATIONS ANALYSIS. *Educ:* Univ Minn, BAeroE. *Prof Exp:* Supvry physicist, Hq Air Proving Ground Command, Eglin Air Force Base, Fla, 54-58; supvry opers analyst, Hq Air Defense Command, Ent Air Force Base, Colo, 58-61; dep dir opers anal, Hq US Air Forces Europe, Ger, 61-64; chief scientist & chief opers anal, US Air Force Tactical Air Warfare Ctr, Eglin Air Force Base, 64-67, dir opers anal, Hq US Air Forces Europe, 67-72, chief scientist, Hq Tactical Air Warfare Ctr, 72-75, MEM RES STAFF, INST DEFENSE ANAL, 75- *Honors & Awards:* Presidential citation, 65. *Mem:* Opers Res Soc Am; Mil Opers Res Soc. *Res:* Operational test and evaluation of electronic warfare in close air support; operational field tests of cruise missile vulnerability. *Mailing Add:* IDA-SED 400 Army-Navy Dr Arlington VA 22202

DURRILL, PRESTON LEE, b Ft Madison, Iowa, Apr 4, 36; m 66. CHEMISTRY. *Educ:* Mass Inst Technol, SB, 57, SM, 59; Va Polytech Inst, PhD(chem eng), 66. *Prof Exp:* Chem engr, Esso Res Labs, La, 59-60; assoc prof, 65-70, PROF CHEM, RADFORD COL, 70- *Mem:* AAAS; Am Chem Soc; Am Inst Chem Eng; Soc Plastics Engr. *Res:* Diffusion of gases in solids and molten polymers. *Mailing Add:* Radford Col Station PO Box 639 Radford VA 24142

DURRUM, EMMETT LEIGH, b Spokane, Wash, May 4, 16; m 41; c 3. BIOCHEMISTRY. *Educ:* Harvard Univ, BS, 39; Stanford Univ, MD, 46. *Prof Exp:* Engr, Shell Develop Co, San Francisco, 39-42; med officer, Field Res Lab, Med Dept, US Dept Army, 46-51, chief biochem sect, Cardiorespiratory Dis Dept, Army Med Serv Grad Sch, 51-52, chief biochem sect, Dept Pharmacol, 52-54; assoc dir res, Spinco Div, Beckman Instruments, Inc, 55-62; chmn bd & res dir, Durrum Instrument Corp, 62-72, PRES, ELDEX LABS INC, 72- *Concurrent Pos:* Assoc clin prof, Sch Med, Stanford Univ, 54-60. *Mem:* AAAS; Am Chem Soc; Am Soc Biol Chemists; NY Acad Sci. *Res:* Electrophoresis, separations by physical methods for proteins; amino acid; atherosclerosis; computerized amino acid analyzers; automated laboratory equipment; synthetic peptides. *Mailing Add:* 170 Buckthorn Way Menlo Park CA 94025

DURSO, DONALD FRANCIS, b Youngstown, Ohio, Jan 30, 25; m 48; c 5. CELLULOSE CHEMISTRY. *Educ:* Case Inst Technol, BS, 47; Purdue Univ, MS, 49, PhD(biochem), 51. *Prof Exp:* Asst, Purdue Univ, 47-51; res chemist, Buckeye Cellulose Corp, Tenn, 51-53, org group leader, 53-56, mgr res dept, 56-71; prof forest sci, Tex A&M Univ, 71-75; DIR ABSORBENT TECHNOL, JOHNSON & JOHNSON, 75- *Mem:* Am Chem Soc; Tech Asn Pulp & Paper Indust; Forest Prod Res Soc. *Res:* Enzyme degradation and synthesis of cellulose; sorption of body fluids; carbon column chromatography of sugars; structure of polysaccharides; cellulose composition; structure and preparation of cellulose derivatives; chemistry of pulping and bleaching. *Mailing Add:* Johnson & Johnson Absorbent Technol 21 Lake Dr East Windsor NJ 08520

DURSO, JOHN WILLIAM, b Brooklyn, NY, Feb 1, 38; m 59; c 4. THEORETICAL PHYSICS. *Educ:* Cornell Univ, AB, 59; Pa State Univ, PhD(theoret physics), 64. *Prof Exp:* Res asst physics, Pa State Univ, 60-64; res assoc, Inst Theoret Physics, Naples, 64-65; res assoc theoret physics, Mich State Univ, 65-67; from asst prof to assoc prof physics & comput studies, 67-78, PROF PHYSICS & COMPUT STUDIES, MT HOLYOKE COL, 78- *Concurrent Pos:* Vis prof, Nordisk Inst Theoret Atomic Physics, 74-75 & NY State Univ, Stony Brook, 81-82. *Mem:* Sigma Xi; Am Phys Soc. *Res:* Nuclear theory; many-body problems; scattering theory. *Mailing Add:* Dept of Physics Mt Holyoke Col South Hadley MA 01075

DURST, HAROLD EVERETT, b Morrowville, Kans, Feb 18, 24; m 49; c 1. ENVIRONMENTAL BIOLOGY. *Educ:* Kans State Univ, BS, 48; Univ Colo, MEd, 53; Ore State Univ, PhD(sci educ), 67. *Prof Exp:* Teacher, Ness City Pub Schs, Kans, 48-54, prin, 53-54; off mgr, Firestone Tire & Rubber Co, 54-57; buyer, Boeing Airplane Co, 57-58; teacher, Wichita Pub Schs, Kans, 58-61 & 62-63; consult writer, Biol-Sci Curriculum Study, 61-62; from instr to assoc prof, 63-75, PROF BIOL, EMPORIA STATE UNIV, 75-, DEAN, GRAD SCH, 74- *Concurrent Pos:* Area consult, Biol Sci Curriculum Study, 62-65; dir, Sci Workshop, Peace Corps, India, 68 & NSF In-Serv Insts for Sec Teachers of Sci & Math, 68-73. *Mem:* Fel AAAS; Am Inst Biol Sci. *Res:* Curriculum evaluation; college biology; affective behavior and assessment of postgraduate needs of high school biology teachers. *Mailing Add:* Div of Biol Emporia State Univ Emporia KS 66801

DURST, JACK ROWLAND, b Stow, Ohio, June 22, 26; m 48, 67; c 5. BIOCHEMISTRY, FOOD SCIENCE. *Educ:* Ohio Univ, BS, 48; Ohio State Univ, MS, 53; Purdue Univ, PhD(biochem), 56. *Prof Exp:* Chemist, Goodyear Tire & Rubber Co; res asst, Kettering Res Found, Ohio State Univ, 49-53, res assoc, 53; res chemist, Swift & Co, 56-57; sr res chemist, 57-60, sr scientist, 60-66, tech mgr, 66-68, res assoc appl res, 68-74, sr res assoc, 74-79, RES FEL, PILLSBURY CO, 79- *Mem:* Am Chem Soc; Inst Food Technol; Nutrit Today Soc; Am Asn Cereal Chemists; Sigma Xi. *Res:* Natural products research; invention of new food forms through control of structure and nutritional makeup; formulation and fabrication of foods for astronauts; source, function and nutrition of proteins; dietary studies; ions in foods; water activity in foods. *Mailing Add:* 12152 Miss Dr Champlin MN 55316

DURST, LINCOLN KEARNEY, b Santa Monica, Calif, Aug 5, 24; m 56; c 3. NUMBER THEORY. *Educ:* Univ Calif, Los Angeles, BA, 45; Calif Inst Technol, BS, 46, PhD(math), 52. *Prof Exp:* Instr math, Rice Univ, 51-55, from asst prof to assoc prof, 55-67; prof, Claremont Men's Col & Claremont Grad Sch, 67-70; DEP EXEC DIR, AM MATH SOC, 70- *Concurrent Pos:* Exec dir, Comt on Undergrad Prog in Math, Math Asn Am, 66-67; mem bd dirs, Nat Fedn Sci Abstracting & Indexing Serv, 71-74. *Mem:* AAAS; Am Math Soc; Math Asn Am; Can Math Cong; Soc Indust & Appl Math. *Mailing Add:* Am Math Soc PO Box 6248 Providence RI 02940

DURST, RICHARD ALLEN, b New Rochelle, NY, Dec 27, 37; m 64; c 3. ANALYTICAL CHEMISTRY. *Educ:* Univ RI, BS, 60; Mass Inst Technol, PhD(anal chem), 63. *Prof Exp:* Nat Acad Sci-Nat Res Coun res assoc chem, Nat Bur Stand, 63-64; vis asst prof, Pomona Col, 64-65; asst prof, Boston Col, 65-66; res chemist, Anal Chem Div, Nat Bur Stand, 66-70, chief, Electrochem Anal Sect, 70-73; group leader clin chem, Radiometer A/S, Copenhagen, Denmark, 73-74; asst chief, Air & Water Pollution Anal Sect, 74-78, sci asst to dir, Ctr Anal Chem, 78-79, GROUP LEADER, ORG ELECTROCHEM, NAT BUR STANDARDS, 79- *Concurrent Pos:* Assoc mem comn electrochem, Int Union Pure & Appl Chem, 71-79; vis prof chem, Univ Md, 76-80; assoc mem comt electroanal chem, Int Union Pure & Appl Chem, 80- *Mem:* AAAS; Am Chem Soc; Am Asn Clin Chemists; Sigma Xi; Bioelectrochem Soc. *Res:* Electroanalytical chemistry; organic electrochemistry; spectroelectrochemistry; voltammetry; ion-selective electrodes. *Mailing Add:* Ctr for Anal Chem Bldg Rm A113 Nat Bur of Standards Washington DC 20234

DURST, TONY, b San Martin, Romania, Jan 21, 38; Can citizen; m 64; c 2. ORGANIC CHEMISTRY. *Educ:* Univ Western Ont, BSc, 61, PhD(chem), 64. *Prof Exp:* From asst prof to assoc prof, 67-77, PROF CHEM, UNIV OTTAWA, 77- *Mem:* Am Chem Soc; Chem Inst Can. *Mailing Add:* Dept of Chem Univ of Ottawa Ottawa Can

DURSTON, COLIN, b Bristol, Eng, Sept 7, 35; m 60; c 3. NUCLEAR ENGINEERING, COMPUTER SCIENCE. *Educ:* Bristol Univ, BSc, 57. *Prof Exp:* Performance engr gas turbines, Rolls Royce Aero Eng, 57-61; exp officer fast reactor physics, UK Atomic Energy Authority, 61-69; prin engr nuclear design, Advan Reactor Div, Westinghouse Elec Corp, 69-74; nuclear engr advan fuels prog, Argonne Nat Lab, 74-76; nuclear engr eng & advan reactor safety, 76-81, SR CONSULT PHYSICIST, COMBUSTION ENG, POWER SYSTS DIV, 81- *Res:* Application of computers and numerical methods to advanced nuclear reactor safety problems; evaluation of nuclear data, especially heavy element resonances. *Mailing Add:* 43 Liso Dr Mt Sinai NY 11766

DURY, GEORGE H, b Hellidon, Eng, Sept 11, 16. GEOMORPHOLOGY. *Educ:* Univ London, BA, 37, MA, 44, PhD(geomorphol), 51, DSc, 71. *Prof Exp:* Lectr in chg geog & geol, Enfield Tech Col, Middlesex, Eng, 46-48; lectr geog, Birkbeck Col, Univ London, 49-62; McCaughey prof, Univ Sydney, 62-69, dean fac sci, 67-68; prof geog & geol, Univ Wis-Madision, 69-79, chmn, Dept Geog, 71-74. *Concurrent Pos:* Div staff scientist, Water Resources Div, US Geol Surv, 60-61; vis prof dept geol, Fla State Univ, 67; Fenneman professorship, Univ Wis-Madison & mem staff, Sidney Sussex Col, Univ Cambridge, Eng, 78. *Honors & Awards:* Meritorious Contribution Award, Asn Am Geographers, 75. *Mem:* Royal Geog Soc: Geol Soc London; Am Geog Soc; Inst Brit. Geographers. *Res:* General theory of meandering valleys; deep weathering and duricrusting; glacial diversions of surface drainage; pedimentation; paleoclimatology. *Mailing Add:* 46 Woodland Close Risby IP28 6QN 53706 England

DURYEA, WILLIAM R, b Port Jervis, NY, July 29, 38; m 61; c 5. ENVIRONMENTAL BIOLOGY, SOIL MICROBIOLOGY. *Educ:* St Bernardine Siena Col, BS, 62; St Bonaventure Univ, PhD(biol), 67. *Prof Exp:* PROF BIOL, ST FRANCIS COL (PA), 66- *Mem:* AAAS; Am Inst Biol Sci. *Res:* Relationship of low available-water and soil microbial activity; botanical ecology and taxonomy. *Mailing Add:* Dept of Biol St Francis Col Loretto PA 15940

DURZAN, DONALD JOHN, b Hamilton, Ont, Aug 4, 36; m 59; c 2. PLANT PHYSIOLOGY, BIOCHEMISTRY. *Educ:* McMaster Univ, BSc, 59; Cornell Univ, PhD(plant physiol), 64. *Prof Exp:* Res officer physiol, Can Dept Forestry, 59-68, res scientist & head biochem sect, Forest Ecol Res Inst, Dept Environ, 68-75, sr adv policy planning & assessment, Environ Mgt Serv, Environ Can, 75-77; prof biochem, sr res assoc & head biochem unit, Inst Paper Chem, 77-81; CHMN, DEPT POMOL, UNIV CALIF, DAVIS, 81- *Concurrent Pos:* Res asst, Cornell Univ, 60-63; Can Soc Plant Physiologists rep, Biol Coun Can, 75-78. *Mem:* AAAS; Am Soc Plant Physiol; Can Soc Plant Physiol (exec secy, 75-77); Royal Soc Chem; Soc Am Foresters. *Res:* Metabolism of nitrogenous compounds in relation to growth and development of forest trees. *Mailing Add:* Dept Pomol Univ Calif Davis CA 95616

DUS, KARL M, b Vienna, Austria, Jan 2, 32; m 71; c 2. BIOCHEMISTRY, BIOCHEMICAL PHARMACOLOGY. *Educ:* Univ Vienna, Staatsexamen, 54, PhD(chem, biochem), 58. *Prof Exp:* Res assoc biochem, Brandeis Univ, 60-61; asst res chemist, Univ Calif, San Diego, 61-65, assoc res chem I & II, 65-67; instr biochem, Inst Genetics-Physiol, Nat Ctr Sci Res, Gif-sur-Yvette, France, 65-66; asst prof, Univ Ill, Urbana-Champaign, 68-73; ASSOC PROF BIOCHEM, MED SCH, ST LOUIS UNIV, 74- *Concurrent Pos:* Res fel med, Harvard Med Sch-Mass Gen Hosp, 58-59; NIH trainee chem, Univ Calif, San Diego, 62-65; co-prin investr, NASA Contract Feasibility of Miniaturizing Automatic Amino Acid Analyzer for Apollo & Mars Voyager, 66-68; invited speaker var conf, cong, symp & orgn, 67- *Mem:* Am Chem Soc; Am Soc Biol Chemists; NY Acad Sci; Instrument Soc Am; Am Soc Photobiol. *Res:* Protein structure and evolution; intermolecular electron transfer, photosynthesis; biological oxygen fixation, biotransformation, drug detoxification, biochemical and molecular pharmacology; protein sequence determinations. *Mailing Add:* Dept of Biochem St Louis Univ Med Sch St Louis MO 63103

DUSANIC, DONALD G, b Chicago, Ill, Dec 15, 34; m 71; c 5. PARASITOLOGY. *Educ:* Univ Chicago, SB, 57, SM, 59, PhD(microbiol), 63. *Prof Exp:* Instr microbiol, Univ Chicago, 63-64; from asst prof to prof, Univ Kans, 64-72; PROF LIFE SCI, IND STATE UNIV, TERRE HAUTE, 72-, ADJ PROF MICROBIOL, SCH MED, 72- *Concurrent Pos:* Vis asst prof parasitol, Univ Philippines, 64 & Nat Taiwan Univ, 71; consult med ecol, Naval Med Res Unit 2, 76; guest, Univ Catolica dePelotas, Brazil, 80. *Mem:* Am Soc Parasitol; Soc Protozool; Am Soc Trop Med & Hyg; NY Acad Sci; Sigma Xi. *Res:* Immunology and physiology of animal parasites, trypanosomes. *Mailing Add:* Dept of Life Sci Ind State Univ Terre Haute IN 47809

DUSCHINSKY, ROBERT, b Vienna, Austria, Oct 25, 00; nat US; wid. MEDICINAL CHEMISTRY. *Educ:* Univ Vienna, PhD(chem), 26. *Prof Exp:* Chemist, Soc Indust Res & Develop, France, 27-28; Mfrs Pure Chem Prod, Paris, 28-29; res fel, Hoffmann-La Roche, Inc, 30-65; assoc scientist, Sloan-Kettering Inst Cancer Res, New York & Inst Chem Natural Substances, Gif-sur-Yvette, France, 65-67; CHEMIST & HEAD ORG CHEM, SWISS INST EXP CANCER RES, 67- *Mem:* Am Chem Soc; NY Acad Sci; Am Asn Cancer Res; Asn Swiss Chemists. *Res:* Amino acids in particular resolutions; synthesis of biotin analogs; synthesis of 0-nitronucleosides; nitrosated and fluorinated amino acid derivatives; fluorinated pyrimidines and 2-nitroimidazoles used as cytostatics, antimicrobials and radio-sensibilizers. *Mailing Add:* Swiss Inst for Exp Cancer Res 1066 Epalinges s/Lausanne Switzerland

DUSEL-BACON, CYNTHIA, b San Jose, Calif, Aug 16, 46; m 77. GEOLOGY. *Educ:* Univ Calif, Santa Barbara, BA, 68; San Jose State Univ, BA, 75. *Prof Exp:* Teacher Span, Healdsburg High Sch Dist, 70-74; phys sci technician geol, 75-80, GEOLOGIST, US GEOL SURV, 80- *Honors & Awards:* Spec Achievement Award, US Geol Surv, 78. *Mem:* AAAS. *Res:* Geology of east central Alaska; metamorphic petrology and petrography; metamorphic textures; petrology of ortho-augen gneiss and a sillimanite gneiss dome in east central Alaska; metamorphic facies map of Alaska; geochemistry of meta-igneous rocks. *Mailing Add:* Br of Alaskan Geol 345 Middlefield Rd Menlo Park CA 94025

DUSENBERRY, WILLIAM EARL, b Oxford, Nebr, June 11, 43; m 65; c 3. STATISTICS. *Educ:* Univ Wyo, BA, 64, MS, 66; Va Polytech Inst & State Univ, MS, 71, PhD(statist), 73. *Prof Exp:* Statistician air pollution res, USPHS, Cincinnati, 66-70; sr statistician, Eli Lilly & Co, 73-77; statistician, Div Biostatist, Univ Utah Med Ctr, 77; SUPVRY STATISTICIAN & CHIEF SECT TECH SERV, DENVER WILDLIFE RES CTR, US FISH & WILDLIFE SERV, 77- *Concurrent Pos:* Instr statist, Butler Univ, 73-77. *Mem:* Am Statist Asn; Biomet Soc. *Res:* Sampling moments of moments; moment and ratio estimators; percentage points; statistical aspects of wildlife research. *Mailing Add:* Denver Wildlife Res Ctr Bldg 16 Denver Fed Ctr Denver CO 80225

DUSENBERY, DAVID BROCK, b Portland, Ore, Apr 30, 42; m 65. NEMATODE BEHAVIOR, GENETICS. *Educ:* Reed Col, BA, 64; Univ Chicago, PhD(biophys), 70. *Prof Exp:* Asst prof, 73-78, ASSOC PROF BIOL & PHYSICS, GA INST TECHNOL, 78- *Concurrent Pos:* USPHS fel, Calif Inst Technol, 70-73. *Mem:* Biophys Soc; Genetics Soc Am; Soc Nematologists; Soc Neurosci. *Res:* Studies of behavior especially sensory responses, neurogenetics, thermal acclimation and aging in the nematode; Caenorhabditis elegans using techniques such as laser microbeam ablation, genetic dissection, fluorescence polarization measurements of membrane viscosity and fluorescence spectroscopy of age pigment. *Mailing Add:* Sch of Biol Ga Inst of Technol Atlanta GA 30332

DUSENBERY, RUTH LILLIAN, b Chicago, Ill, May 30, 44; m 65. MOLECULAR BIOLOGY. *Educ:* Univ Chicago, BS, 66, PhD(chem), 70. *Prof Exp:* Res assoc, 75-78, SR RES ASSOC BIOL, EMORY UNIV, 78- *Mem:* Am Chem Soc; Genetics Soc Am; Environ Mutagen Soc. *Res:* Investigation of DNA repair pathways in the eukaryotic organism Drosophila melanogaster, using a number of repair deficient strains; correlation of unrepaired or misrepaired damage to mutagenesis and carcinogenesis. *Mailing Add:* Dept Biol Emory Univ Atlanta GA 30322

DUSENBURY, JOSEPH HOOKER, b Troy, NY, Nov 18, 23; m 47. PHYSICAL CHEMISTRY. *Educ:* Union Col, BS, 47; Univ Calif, Berkeley, PhD(chem), 50. *Prof Exp:* Res chemist, Am Cyanamid Co, 47; asst chem, Univ Calif, 47-50; res chemist, Am Cyanamid Co, 50-53; from head phys org chem sect to assoc res dir, Textile Res Inst, NJ, 53-61; sect leader, 61-64, DEPT MGR, CHEM DEPT, MILLIKEN RES CORP, 64- *Concurrent Pos:* Mem, Textile Res Inst. *Honors & Awards:* Harold Dewitt Smith Mem Award, Am Soc Testing Mat, 80. *Mem:* Fel AAAS; Am Chem Soc; Fiber Soc; Soc Rheol; fel Am Inst Chemists. *Res:* Reactions of nitrous acid; dyeing and finishing of textiles; polymerization; physical properties and chemical modification of fibers. *Mailing Add:* 413 Overland Dr Spartanburg SC 29302

DU SHANE, JAMES WILLIAM, b Madison, Ind, Apr 17, 12; m 39; c 2. PEDIATRICS, CARDIOLOGY. *Educ:* DePauw Univ, AB, 33; Yale Univ, MD, 37; Am Bd Pediat, dipl. *Prof Exp:* From instr to prof, 47-79, EMER PROF PEDIAT, MAYO GRAD SCH MED, UNIV MINN, 79- *Concurrent Pos:* Head pediat sect, Mayo Clin, 57-69, mem bd gov, 60-72, head pediat cardiol sect, 69-73; chmn coun rheumatic fever & congenital heart dis, Am Heart Asn, 59-61; chmn sub-bd cardiol, Am Bd Pediat, 60-65; mem bd trustees, Mayo Found, 65-73. *Mem:* Am Pediat Soc; Am Heart Asn; Am Col Chest Physicians. *Res:* Congenital heart disease; pathology; symptomatology; electrocardiology. *Mailing Add:* Mayo Clin Rochester MN 55901

DUSI, JULIAN LUIGI, b Columbus, Ohio, Nov 10, 20; m 47. VERTEBRATE ZOOLOGY, ENVIRONMENTAL BIOLOGY. *Educ:* Ohio State Univ, BS, 43, MS, 46, PhD(zool), 49. *Prof Exp:* Asst, Ohio State Univ, 46-49; PROF ZOOL-ENTOM, AUBURN UNIV, 49- *Concurrent Pos:* Environ consult, Ala Power Co, 72-, Southern Eng Ga, 74, Bechtel Corp, 74-, Army Corps Engrs, 75, TVA, 77- & Burns & McDonnell, 80. *Mem:* AAAS; Am Soc Mammal; Wilson Ornith Soc; Am Ornith Union; Am Inst Biol Sci. *Res:* Bird and mammal behavior and ecology; wading bird biology; environmental impacts on birds and mammals. *Mailing Add:* Dept of Zool-Entom Auburn Univ Auburn AL 36830

DUSKY, JOAN AGATHA, b Tacoma, Wash, Aug 13, 51. WEED SCIENCE, PLANT PHYSIOLOGY. *Educ:* Baldwin-Wallace Col, BS, 73; NDak State Univ, MS, 75, PhD(bot), 78. *Prof Exp:* res assoc plant physiol, Metab & Radiation Res Lab, Sci & Educ Admin, USDA, 78-80; ASST PROF WEED SCI, AGR RES & EDUC CTR, UNIV FLA, 80- *Mem:* Am Soc Plant Physiologists; Weed Sci Soc Am; AAAS; Am Soc Hort Sci. *Res:* Weed control management practices in vegetables crops, sugarcane, rice; weed biology; herbicide selectivity, mode of action and metabolism; allelopathy; plant growth regulation; herbicide metabolism in relation to the environment; allelopathy and biological weed control. *Mailing Add:* Univ Fla PO Drawer A Belle Glade FL 33430

DUSSEAU, JERRY WILLIAM, b Toledo, Ohio, July 30, 41; m 66. CARDIOVASCULAR PHYSIOLOGY. *Educ:* Earlham Col, BA, 63; La State Univ, Baton Rouge, MS, 66, PhD(vert physiol), 69. *Prof Exp:* Asst prof biol, Earlham Col, 69-70; asst prof biol, Hope Col, 70-76; res assoc, 76-79, ASST PROF RES, BOWMAN GRAY MED SCH, 79- *Mem:* AAAS; Soc Chronobiol; Am Soc Physiol. *Res:* Biological rhythms; hypertension; regulation of microvessel density; endocrine basis for biological clock mechanisms. *Mailing Add:* Dept of Physiol & Pharmacol Bowman Gray Sch of Med Winston-Salem NC 27103

DUSTAN, HARRIET PEARSON, b Craftsbury Common, Vt, Sept 16, 20. INTERNAL MEDICINE. *Educ:* Univ Vt, BS, 42, MD, 44; Am Bd Internal Med, dipl. *Hon Degrees:* DSc, Univ Vt, 77; Cleveland State Univ, 78; DHL, St Michaels Col, 81. *Prof Exp:* Intern, Mary Fletcher Hosp, Burlington, Vt, 44-45; resident internal med, Royale Victoria Hosp, Montreal, 45; res fel & mem asst staff, Res Div, Cleveland Clin, 55-77, vchmn, 71-77; DIR, CARDIOVASC RES & TRAINING CTR, MED CTR, UNIV ALA, 77- *Concurrent Pos:* Mem adv coun, Nat Heart & Lung Inst, 72-76; mem residency rev comt internal med, Am Bd Internal Med. *Mem:* Am Col Physicians; Am Heart Asn (pres, 76-77); Am Soc Clin Invests; Asn Am Physicians. *Mailing Add:* Cardiovasc Res & Training Ctr Univ Ala Med Col Birmingham AL 35294

DUSTMAN, JOHN HENRY, b Buffalo, NY, Apr 18, 40; m 63; c 2. ZOOLOGY, ENDOCRINOLOGY. *Educ:* Canisius Col, BS, 61; Ind Univ, PhD(zool), 66. *Prof Exp:* Asst prof zool & asst chmn dept, 66-70, chmn, Dept Biol, 70-80, ASSOC PROF ZOOL, IND UNIV NORTHWEST, 70-, DIR NORTHWEST CTR MED EDUC, IND UNIV SCH MED, 70-, ASSOC PROF PHYSIOL, 74- *Concurrent Pos:* Consult water pollution, Boise Cascade Corp, 70- *Mem:* Biol Photog Asn; Am Soc Zool; Soc Study Reproduction; Nat Asn Biol Teachers; Am Inst Biol Sci. *Res:* Chemical nature and biological activity of synthetic steroids on the reproductive system of fowl. *Mailing Add:* 5570 Marcella Rd Merrillville IN 46410

DUSTO, ARTHUR RONALD, b Libertyville, Ill, Oct 22, 29; m 54; c 3. ENGINEERING MECHANICS. *Educ:* Purdue Univ, BS, 52; Univ Wash, MS, 62, PhD(aeronaut & astronaut), 63. *Prof Exp:* Stress analyst, Northrop Aircraft Inc, 52-53; jr officer, Civil Engrs Corp, US Navy, 53-58; res engr, Boeing Co, 58-60; instr aeronaut & astronaut, Univ Wash, 60-63; res specialist gas dynamics, Boeing Co, 63-64; assoc prof aerospace eng, Univ Ariz, 64-65; res specialist aerodynamics, Boeing Commerical Airplane Co, 65-80, PRIN ENGR, BOEING MILITARY AIRPLANE CO, 80- *Concurrent Pos:* Lectr fluid mech, Dept Aeronaut & Astronaut, Univ Wash, 68 & 70. *Mem:* Am Inst Astronaut & Aeronaut; Sigma Xi. *Res:* Developing analytical models and computational methods for predicting aerodynamics of flexible airplanes. *Mailing Add:* Boeing Military Airplane Co PO Box 3707 Seattle WA 98124

DUSWALT, ALLEN AINSWORTH, JR, b New York, NY, Nov 18, 32; m 54; c 2. ANALYTICAL CHEMISTRY. *Educ:* Queens Col, NY, BS, 54; Purdue Univ, MS, 56, PhD(anal chem), 59. *Prof Exp:* Asst, Purdue Univ, West Lafayette, 54-57; res chemist, 58-74, SR RES CHEMIST, HERCULES, INC, 74- *Mem:* Am Chem Soc. *Res:* Differential thermal analysis; thermal gravimetric analysis; analytical instrumental design; general methods development; catalyst characterization; thermal analysis of polymers; kinetics; hazards evaluation; solution calorimetry; special polymers. *Mailing Add:* Hercules Res Ctr Lancester Pike Wilmington DE 19899

DUSZYNSKI, DONALD WALTER, b Chicago, Ill, July 28, 43. PARASITOLOGY, ECOLOGY. *Educ:* Wis State Univ, River Falls, BS, 66; Colo State Univ, MS, 68, PhD(zool), 70. *Prof Exp:* From asst prof to assoc prof, 70-79, PROF BIOL, UNIV NMEX, 79- *Mem:* Am Inst Biol Sci; Am Soc Parasitol; Soc Protozool; Wildlife Dis Asn; Am Micros Soc. *Res:* The coccidia of wild animals; host-parasite/parasite-parasite competition and interactions; gastrointestinal pathophysiology; parasite ecology. *Mailing Add:* Dept Biol Univ NMex 87131

DUTARY, BEDSY ELSIRA, b Panama, May 9, 39. ARBOVIROLOGY. *Educ:* Univ Autonoma, Mex, BS, 64; Univ Tex, MS, 77, PhD(ecol), 81. *Prof Exp:* Res asst tissue culture, 64-68, res asst virol, 68-76, FEL VIROL, GORGAS MEM LAB, 79- *Concurrent Pos:* Fel, Pan Am Health Orgn, 77-78. *Mem:* Am Soc Trop Med & Hyg. *Res:* Role of vectorial capacity in the long-term maintenance of arboviruses in tropical ecosystem, using mosquitoes, identified as vectors of jungle yellow fever and the yellow fever virus as a model. *Mailing Add:* Gorgas Mem Lab PO Box 935 APO Miami FL 34002

DUTCH, STEVEN IAN, b Milford, Conn, May 10, 47; m 75; c 2. STRUCTURAL GEOLOGY. *Educ:* Univ Calif, Berkeley, BA, 69; Columbia Univ, MPhil, 74, PhD(geol), 76. *Prof Exp:* ASST PROF GEOL, UNIV WIS, GREEN BAY, 76- *Mem:* Geol Soc Am. *Res:* Tectonics; Precambrian geology. *Mailing Add:* Sci & Environ Change Univ of Wis Green Bay WI 54302

DUTCHER, CLINTON HARVEY, JR, b Vallejo, Calif, Apr 28, 32. PHYSICS, ELECTRICAL ENGINEERING. *Educ:* Univ Fla, BS, 59, MS, 61, PhD(physics), 68. *Prof Exp:* Mem tech staff, Bell Tel Labs, 61-63; instr physics, Univ Fla, 63-68; group leader appl res, Electronic Commun, Inc, 68-70; consult, 71-74; sect mgr, Schlumberger Well Serv, 74-80, SR PROJ ENGR, SCHLUMBERGER TECH CORP, 80- *Mem:* sr mem Inst Elec & Electronics Engrs. *Res:* Communications theory; electromagnetics; physical geology. *Mailing Add:* Schlumberger Tech Corp PO Box 2175 Houston TX 77001

DUTCHER, JAMES DWIGHT, b Highland Park, Mich, Aug 4, 50; m 72; c 2. ENTOMOLOGY. *Educ:* Mich State Univ, BS, 72, BS, 74, MS, 75; Univ Ga, PhD(entom), 78. *Prof Exp:* ASST PROF ENTOM, UNIV GA, 78- *Mem:* Entom Soc Am. *Res:* Bionomics and control of insect pests in fruit and nut crops, specifically apples, grapes and pecans; ecological energetics of phytophagous insects. *Mailing Add:* Dept of Entom & Fisheries Univ of Ga Tifton GA 31793

DUTCHER, RUSSELL RICHARDSON, b Brooklyn, NY, Oct 28, 27; m 52; c 2. GEOLOGY. *Educ:* Univ Conn, BA, 51; Univ Mass, MS, 53; Pa State Univ, PhD(geol), 60. *Prof Exp:* Instr geol, Univ Mass, 52-53; res asst, Pa State Univ, 56-60, res assoc, 60-63, from asst prof to assoc prof, 63-70, asst dir coal res sect, 60-70; PROF GEOL & CHMN DEPT, SOUTHERN ILL UNIV, 70- *Mem:* Geol Soc Am; Am Asn Petrol Geologists; Am Inst Mining, Metall & Petrol Engineers; Am Inst Prof Geologists. *Res:* Coal petrology, petrography and stratigraphy; alteration of coals by igneous intrusives. *Mailing Add:* Dept of Geol Southern Ill Univ Carbondale IL 62901

DUTE, JOHN C, instrumentation, engineering, see previous edition

DUTEMPLE, OCTAVE J, b Hubbell, Mich, Dec 10, 20; m 51; c 2. NUCLEAR & CHEMICAL ENGINEERING. *Educ:* Mich Technol Univ, BS, 48, MS, 49; Northwestern Univ, MBA, 55. *Prof Exp:* Assoc chem engr fuel reprocessing, Argonne Nat Lab, 49-58; EXEC DIR, AM NUCLEAR SOC, 58- *Honors & Awards:* Distinguished Service Award, Am Nuclear Soc, 78. *Mem:* AAAS; Am Nuclear Soc; Am Inst Chem Engrs; Am Chem Soc; Coun Eng & Sci Soc Execs (pres, 75-76). *Res:* Administration of scientific society; economics of nuclear industry; archeology, prehistoric copper; agriculture. *Mailing Add:* Am Nuclear Soc Inc 555 N Kensington Ave La Grange Park IL 60525

DUTHIE, HAMISH, b Aberdeen, Scotland, Aug 30, 38; m 62; c 4. FRESH WATER BIOLOGY, PHYCOLOGY. *Educ:* Univ Col NWales, BSc, 60, PhD(biol), 64. *Prof Exp:* From lectr to asst prof, 63-68, ASSOC PROF BIOL, UNIV WATERLOO, 68- *Mem:* Phycol Soc Am; Am Soc Limnol & Oceanog; Can Bot Asn. *Res:* Primary production of phytoplankton and relation to physical and chemical factors; biology of reservoirs; algal ecology and taxonomy. *Mailing Add:* 241 Park Lawn Pl Waterloo Can

DUTKA, BERNARD J, b Ft William, Ont, Oct 5, 32; m 57; c 2. MICROBIOLOGY. *Educ:* Queen's Univ, Ont, BA, 55, Hons, 56, MSc(microbiol & immunol), 64. *Prof Exp:* Lab supvr, Kingston Gen Hosp, Ont, 57-66; head bact labs, Pub Health Eng Div, Dept Nat Health & Welfare, 66-71; HEAD MICROBIOL SECT, CAN CTR INLAND WATERS, DEPT ENVIRON, 71- *Concurrent Pos:* Can chmn, Sub-Comt SC4, Int Standards Orgn, Sub-Comt SC5 & Sub-Comt SC6; mem chlorine objectives task force, Int Joint Comn, mem standing comt health aspects, chmn group IV biol hazards, Standing comt Res Needs; mem steering comt workshop on water qual & health significance bact indicators of pollution, NSF; chmn, Can Adv Comt, Int Standards Orgn. *Mem:* Am Soc Microbiol; Am Water Works Asn. *Res:* Development of microbiol water pollution methodology; role of microorganisms in recycling of nutrients from sediment; evaluation of microbiol methods for assessment of toxicity and mutagen content of water and sewage; distribution of Legionaella Pneurophila in water bodies. *Mailing Add:* PO Box 5050 Burlington ON L7R 4A6 Can

DUTKA, JACQUES, b New York, NY, Dec 29, 19; m 45; c 2. MATHEMATICS. *Educ:* City Col New York, BS, 39; Columbia Univ, AM, 40, PhD(math), 43. *Prof Exp:* Asst statistician, US War Dept, 42; asst res mathematician, Appl Math Panel, Columbia Univ, 43; instr math, Princeton Univ, 46-47; asst prof, Rutgers Univ, 47-53; mathematician, Norden-Ketay Corp, 53-56; sr engr, Radio Corp Am, 56-59, leader, 59-61, mgr, 61-63; staff scientist, Ford Instrument Co, 64-66, systs analyst & eval mgr, 66-67; staff scientist, Sperry-Rand Corp, 67, Riverside Res Inst, 67-70 & Am Tel & Tel Co, 71-73; CONSULT, AUDITS & SURVS CO, INC, 73- *Concurrent Pos:* Adj assoc prof elec eng, Columbia Univ, 54-59, adj prof, 59-72; consult, Opers Res Group, US Dept Navy, 44-45; consult, Off Naval Res, 46-47. *Mem:* Am Math Soc; Inst Math Statist; Sigma Xi. *Res:* Probability; statistics; systems analysis; communication theory; numerical analysis and computer applications; history of mathematics. *Mailing Add:* 39 Claremont Ave New York NY 10027

DUTRA, FRANK ROBERT, b Sacramento, Calif, Jan 7, 16; m 46. PATHOLOGY. *Educ:* Northwestern Univ, AB, 40, MS, 41, MD, 42. *Prof Exp:* Intern, City Hosp, Cleveland, Ohio, 41-42; res pathologist, Hosp, Western Reserve Univ, 42-43; from asst prof to assoc prof indust & forensic path, Kettering Lab, Cincinnati, 47-52; asst clin prof, 53-62, ASSOC CLIN PROF PATH, MED SCH, UNIV CALIF, SAN FRANCISCO, 62-, ASST CLIN PROF DERMAT, 77-; PATHOLOGIST, PATH LABS, LOS GATOS, 77- *Concurrent Pos:* Rocke Legal Med fel, Harvard Univ, 43-44; pathologist, Sutter Hosp, Sacramento, 53-54; pathologist & dir labs, Eden Hosp, 54-77; consult, San Francisco Vet Admin Hosp, 53-, Martinez Vet Admin Hosp, Oakland, 59-, US Naval Hosp, 63- & Santa Clara County Med Ctr, 63- *Mem:* Fel AMA; Am Soc Clin Pathologists; affil Am Acad Dermat; Am Soc Dermatopath. *Res:* Pathogenic aspects of certain metals; carcinogenesis; physiologic aspects of heat; pathology of the skin; toxicology of some industrial substances; surgical and clinical pathology. *Mailing Add:* Path Labs 464 Monterey Ave Los Gatos CA 95030

DUTRA, GERARD ANTHONY, b Paterson, NJ, Oct 23, 45; m 68. ORGANIC CHEMISTRY, AGRICULTURAL CHEMISTRY. *Educ:* St Louis Univ, BS, 67; Wayne State Univ, PhD(org chem), 72. *Prof Exp:* res specialist, 72-80, SR RES GROUP LEADER, AGR RES, MONSANTO CO, 80- *Mem:* Am Chem Soc; Sigma Xi. *Res:* Development of manufacturing processes for agricultural chemicals, environmental chemistry and synthesis of biologically active compounds; organo phosphorous and heterocyclic compounds. *Mailing Add:* Monsanto Co T4G 800 N Lindbergh Blvd St Louis MO 63166

DUTRA, RAMIRO CARVALHO, b Ponta Delgada, Portugal, Sept 27, 31; US citizen; m 58; c 2. ORGANIC CHEMISTRY, FOOD CHEMISTRY. *Educ:* Univ Calif, Davis, BS, 54, MS, 56, PhD(agr chem), 59. *Prof Exp:* Jr specialist dairy indust, Calif Agr Exp Sta, 54-57, asst specialist food chem, 57-59; from asst prof to assoc prof chem, 59-69, PROF FOODS & NUTRIT & CHMN DEPT, CALIF STATE POLYTECH UNIV, 69- *Mem:* Inst Food Technol; Soc Nutrit Educ. *Res:* Isolation and identification of organoleptic compounds; nonenzymatic browning of foods; fortification of cereal proteins; technology of proteins from unconventional sources. *Mailing Add:* Dept of Foods & Nutrit Calif State Polytech Univ Pomona CA 91766

DUTRO, JOHN THOMAS, JR, b Columbus, Ohio, May 20, 23; m 48; c 3. GEOLOGY, PALEONTOLOGY. *Educ:* Oberlin Col, AB, 48; Yale Univ, MS, 50, PhD(geol), 53. *Prof Exp:* GEOLOGIST, US GEOL SURV, 48-; RES ASSOC, SMITHSONIAN INST, 62- *Concurrent Pos:* Mem geol panel, Bd Civil Serv Exam, 58-65; chief paleont & stratig br, US Geol Surv, 62-68, mem geol names comt, 62-68, 70-; assoc ed, Geol Soc Am, 74-; bd dir & field trip chmn, 9th Int Carboniferous Cong, Paleont Res Int & Assoc Earth Sci Eds. *Mem:* AAAS; Geol Soc Am; Arctic Inst NAm; Palaeont Asn; Am Geol Inst (secy-treas, 66-71). *Res:* Devonian, Carboniferous and Permian brachiopods; late Paleozoic stratigraphy; paleogeography of Alaskan Paleozoic. *Mailing Add:* Rm E-316 US Mus of Natural Hist Washington DC 20560

DUTSON, THAYNE R, b Idaho Falls, Idaho, Oct 3, 42; m 62, 81; c 1. MEAT SCIENCE. *Educ:* Utah State Univ, BS, 66; Mich State Univ, MS, 69, PhD(food sci), 71. *Prof Exp:* Res asst meat sci, Mich State Univ, 66-71; fel, Univ Nottingham, 71-72; asst prof, 72-77, ASSOC PROF MEAT CHEM, TEX A&M UNIV, 77- *Honors & Awards:* Meat Res Award, Am Soc Animal Sci, 81. *Mem:* Am Soc Animal Sci; Inst Food Technologists; Am Meat Sci Asn. *Res:* Elucidation of the biochemical factors responsible for differences in meat tenderness and studies on the mechanisms responsible for biosynthesis and net accumulation of muscle tissue. *Mailing Add:* Dept Animal Sci Tex A&M Univ College Station TX 77843

DUTT, GAUTAM SHANKAR, b Calcutta, India, Oct 24, 49. THERMAL PHYSICS, MECHANICAL ENGINEERING. *Educ:* Univ London, BSc, 70; Princeton Univ, MA, 75, PhD(aerospace), 77. *Prof Exp:* Res assoc, 76-77, MEM RES STAFF ENERGY RES, CTR ENVIRON STUDIES, PRINCETON UNIV, 77- *Res:* Thermal performance of buildings and energy conservation strategies; development of diagnostic techniques for monitoring the energy performance of buildings; energy conservation and development in the third world; efficient wood-burning cook stoves for less developed countries. *Mailing Add:* Ctr for Environ Studies Princeton Univ Princeton NJ 08544

DUTT, GORDON RICHARD, b Choteau, Mont, Oct 25, 29; m 54; c 2. SOIL CHEMISTRY, WATER CHEMISTRY. *Educ:* Mont State Col, BS, 56; Purdue Univ, West Lafayette, MS, 59, PhD(soil chem), 60. *Prof Exp:* Asst res irrigationist, Univ Calif, 60-64; assoc prof, 64-68, PROF SOIL & WATER SCI, UNIV ARIZ, 68- *Mem:* Am Soc Enologists; Soil Sci Soc Am. *Res:* Physical chemistry of soil and water systems. water quality and ground water hydrology; run off farming; grape and wine production. *Mailing Add:* Dept of Soils Water & Eng Univ of Ariz Tucson AZ 85721

DUTT, RAY HORN, b Bangor, Pa, Aug 26, 13; m 46; c 2. ANIMAL SCIENCE. *Educ:* Pa State Univ, BS, 41; Univ Wis, MS, 42, PhD(genetics), 48. *Prof Exp:* From asst to assoc animal husbandman, 48-58, PROF ANIMAL SCI, UNIV KY, 58- *Concurrent Pos:* Ed, J Animal Sci, 64-66. *Mem:* Fel AAAS; Am Soc Animal Sci (pres, 67-68); Biomet Soc; Genetics Soc Am; Am Dairy Sci Asn. *Res:* Physiology of reproduction. *Mailing Add:* 437 Bristol Rd Lexington KY 40502

DUTTA, PULAK, b Calcutta, India, Oct 1, 51. PHYSICS. *Educ:* Presidency Col, Univ Calcutta, BSc, Hons, 70; Univ Delhi, MSc, 73; Univ Chicago, PhD(physics), 80. *Prof Exp:* Res fel, Argonne Nat Lab, 79-81; ASST PROF PHYSICS, NORTHWESTERN UNIV, 81- *Concurrent Pos:* Vis assoc, Argonne Nat Lab & Brookhaven Nat Lab, 81- *Mem:* Am Phys Soc. *Res:* Studies of structures of condensed matter phases and transitions between them, especially structures and transitions in surfaces and overlayers; x-ray and neutron diffraction; microcalorimetry. *Mailing Add:* Dept Physics & Astron Northwestern Univ Evanston IL 60201

DUTTA, PURNENDU, b Calcutta, India, Nov 10, 37; US citizen; m 63; c 2. GENERAL SURGERY, CRYOSURGERY. *Educ:* Univ Calcutta, MBBS, 60, MS, 64; FRCS, 66, FACS, 74. *Prof Exp:* Sr house surgeon, Manchester Northern Hosp, UK, 66; registrar surg, Royal Postgrad Med Sch, Hammersmith Hosp, London, 66-68; consult surgeon, BC Royal Mem Hosp Children, Calcutta India, 68-70; surg res fel, Univ Minn, 70-71; ASST PROF SURG, STATE UNIV NY & VET ADMIN MED CTR, BUFFALO, 71- *Mem:* Asn Vet Admin Surgeons; Soc Cryobiol; fel Am Col Cryosurg; fel Am Col Surgeons. *Res:* Gastrointestinal physiology and surgery; endocrine surgery with particular interest in thyroid, parathyroid and adrenal diseases. *Mailing Add:* 3495 Bailey Ave Buffalo NY 14215

DUTTA, SARADINDU, b Dacca, Bangladesh, Jan 28, 31; m 62; c 3. PHARMACOLOGY, VETERINARY MEDICINE. *Educ:* Univ Calcutta, BSc, 52, GVSc, 53; Univ Wis, MS, 59; Ohio State Univ, PhD(pharmacol), 62. *Prof Exp:* Res asst animal physiol, Indian Vet Res Inst, 54-57; res assoc, 63-64, from instr to assoc prof pharmacol, Ohio State Univ, 70-74; PROF PHARMACOL, WAYNE STATE UNIV, 74- *Concurrent Pos:* Res grants, Nat Heart Inst, 65-68 & Cent Ohio Heart Asn, 66-68. *Mem:* AAAS; Am Soc Pharmacol & Exp Therapeut. *Res:* Isolation and characterization of digitalis receptors from the cardiac cell. *Mailing Add:* Dept of Pharmacol Wayne State Univ Sch of Med Detroit MI 48202

DUTTA, SHIB PRASAD, b Calcutta, India, Nov 27, 35; m 69. ORGANIC CHEMISTRY, MEDICINAL CHEMISTRY. *Educ:* Univ Calcutta, BSc, 55, MSc, 58, PhD(org chem), 67. *Prof Exp:* Chemist, Alkali & Chem Corp India, Ltd, 57-60; sr chemist, Union Carbide India, Ltd, 60-62; res chemist, Jadavpur Univ, 62-64; res fel, Bose Inst, Calcutta, 65-67; res assoc med chem, Sch Pharm, State Univ NY Buffalo, 67-69; CANCER RES SCIENTIST, ROSWELL PARK MEM INST, 69- *Mem:* Am Chem Soc. *Res:* Chemistry and synthesis of modified nucleosides and nucleotides in transfer RNA; isolation and identification of nucleic acid metabolites in human biological fluids; toxicologic and metabolic studies on biologically active nucleoside derivatives; mass spectrometry of biological compounds. *Mailing Add:* Dept Biophysics Roswell Park Mem Inst 666 Elm St Buffalo NY 14263

DUTTA, SISIR KAMAL, b Bengal, India, Aug 28, 28; m 55; c 1. MOLECULAR GENETICS. *Educ:* Univ Dacca, BS, 49; Kans State Univ, MS, 58, PhD(genetics), 60. *Prof Exp:* Lectr biol, K N Col, Calcutta Univ, 49-50; asst plant sci, Agr Res Inst, Calcutta, 50-56; asst, Exp Sta, Kans State Univ, 56-59; res assoc bot, Chicago & Columbia Univ, 59-61; dir & chief res officer, Pineapple Res Sta, Malaya, 61-64; res assoc biol, Rice Univ, 64-65; asst prof, Tex Southern Univ, 65-66; chmn div sci & math, Jarvis Christian Col, 66-67; PROF MOLECULAR GENETICS, HOWARD UNIV, 67- *Concurrent Pos:* Res grants, US Dept Naval Res, US Environ Protection Agency, US Dept Energy, Res Corp, Anna Fuller Fund, NSF & NIH, 67- *Mem:* AAAS; Genetics Soc Am; Am Soc Microbiol; Sigma Xi; NY Acad Sci. *Res:* Molecular biology; microbial genetics; gene isolation; regulation; mutagenic tests; radiation genetics. *Mailing Add:* Dept Bot Howard Univ Washington DC 20059

DUTTA, SUNIL, b Naihati, India, Nov 2, 37. CERAMICS ENGINEERING. *Educ:* Univ Calcutta, BSc, 57, MScTech, 60; Univ Sheffield, MS, 62, PhD(ceramics), 65; Babson Col, MBA, 74. *Prof Exp:* Sr sci officer ceramics & refractories, Nat Metall Lab, India, 66-67; sr res ceramic engr, US Army Mat & Mech Res Ctr, 68-76; SR MAT ENGR, LEWIS RES CTR, NASA, 76- *Concurrent Pos:* Fel mat res ctr, Lehigh Univ, 67-68; tech supvr, US-Can Defense Develop Sharing Proj, 68-70, Avco Corp, 70-73 & Ceradyne, Inc, 72-73; proj mgr, Ford Motor Co. *Mem:* Fel Am Ceramic Soc; Nat Inst Ceramic Engrs; Ceramic Educ Coun; Sigma Xi; fel Brit Inst Ceramics. *Res:* Correlations among processing, microstructures and physical, mechanical, ballistic properties of carbide, oxide, and nitride ceramics; thermal shock, oxidation and phase relationships in gas turbine and nuclear ceramics; ceramic materials development for gas turbine, diesel and stirling engine and other structural applications. *Mailing Add:* Lewis Res Ctr MS49-3 NASA Cleveland OH 44135

DUTTAAHMED, A, b India, Apr 3, 35; m 57; c 2. PHYSICAL INORGANIC CHEMISTRY, THEORETICAL CHEMISTRY. *Educ:* Univ Calcutta, BSc, 54, MSc, 57, DPhil, 63; La State Univ, New Orleans, PhD, 72. *Prof Exp:* Lectr chem, Univ Calcutta, 58-63; res officer inorg chem, Indian Asn Cultivation Sci, 63-70; fel chem, La State Univ, New Orleans, 68-72 & 72-74; prof collabr, State Univ Campinas, 74; res assoc inorg chem, Tex Christian Univ, 75-76; asst prof, SDak State Univ, 76-77; assoc prof, 77-80, PROF INORG CHEM, BUCKS COUNTY COMMUNITY COL, 81- *Mem:* Am Chem Soc; Sigma Xi. *Res:* Inorganic and bioinorganic syntheses-linkage isomers, complexes of DNA bases and organic and inorganic acid hydrazides; spectroscopy-inorganic molecular complexes, metal-metal bond, experimental electronic structure; molecular orbital methods and calculations-theoretical electronic structure; cobalt, rhodium, iridium, macrocycle chemistry. *Mailing Add:*Sci Dept Bucks County Col Newton PA 18940

DUTTON, ARTHUR MORLAN, b Des Moines, Iowa, July 28, 23; m 45; c 2. APPLIED STATISTICS. *Educ:* Iowa State Univ, BS, 45, PhD(statist), 51. *Prof Exp:* Instr & res assoc statist, Iowa State Univ, 47-51; instr radiation biol, Univ Rochester, 51-53, from asst prof to assoc prof, 53-68, lectr math, 51-57; chmn dept math sci, 68-74, prof, 68-76, PROF STATIST, UNIV CENT FLA, 76- *Mem:* AAAS; Am Statist Asn; Biomet Soc; Inst Math Statist; Am Math Soc. *Res:* Statistical techniques; mathematics and statistics education; application of statistical methods. *Mailing Add:* Univ Cent Fla Orlando FL 32816

DUTTON, CYNTHIA BALDWIN, b Albany, NY, July 17, 29; m 58; c 2. INTERNAL MEDICINE. *Educ:* Cornell Univ, BA, 52; Univ Rochester, MD, 56; Harvard Univ, MPH, 79. *Prof Exp:* Intern internal med, State Univ NY Upstate Med Ctr, 56-57, asst resident, 57-58, resident, 58-59; fel, Sch Med, Johns Hopkins Univ, 59-63, instr, 63-69; asst prof, 69-72, ASSOC PROF MED, ALBANY MED COL, 72- *Mem:* Am Fedn Clin Res; fel Am Col Physicians. *Res:* Methods of health care delivery; measurement of quality of health care; physician extenders, evaluation of their clinical performance. *Mailing Add:* Dept of Med Albany Med Col New Scotland Ave Albany NY 12208

DUTTON, DAVID B, physics, see previous edition

DUTTON, GARY ROGER, b Spokane, Wash, June 27, 38; m 62; c 2. NEUROBIOLOGY, CELL CULTURE. *Educ:* Univ Wash, BSc, 61; Ind Univ, MSc, 64, PhD(biochem), 67. *Prof Exp:* Nat Inst Mental Health fel psychiat, Albert Einstein Col Med, 68-70; asst res biochemist, Univ Calif, San Diego, 70-72; sr res fel, Open Univ, UK, 72-80; asst prof, 80-81, ASSOC PROF PHARMACOL, UNIV IOWA, 81- *Concurrent Pos:* Vis fel, Australian Nat Univ, Canberra, 76; vis scientist, Inst Physiol, Czechoslovak Acad Sci Prague, 77. *Mem:* Am Soc Neurochem; Soc Neurosci; Sigma Xi; Int Soc Neurochem; Am Soc Pharmacol & Exp Therapeut. *Res:* Developmental neurobiology: central nervous system cultures as models for brain development; receptor, neurotransmitter interaction and cell surface (monclonal antibodies) studies; cerebral microvasculature: properties of cell line so derived. *Mailing Add:* Dept Pharmacol Col Med Univ Iowa Iowa City IA 52242

DUTTON, GUY GORDON STUDDY, b London, Eng, Feb 26, 23; m 51; c 3. ORGANIC CHEMISTRY. *Educ:* Cambridge Univ, BA, 43, MA, 46; Univ London, MSc, 52; Univ Minn, PhD(agr biochem), 55. *Prof Exp:* Jr sci officer, UK Govt, 43-45; lectr org & inorg chem, Sir John Cass Col, 45-49; from asst prof to assoc prof, 49-64, PROF ORG CHEM, UNIV BC, 64- *Concurrent Pos:* Vis prof, Univ Grenoble, 65-66, 74-75, Rhodes Univ, 80, Univ Cape Town, 80, Tech Univ Chile, 80; NATO lectr, Tech Univ Denmark, 68 & Max Planck Inst, Freiburg, 68 & 74; chmn, 62nd Can Chem Conf, Vancouver, 79, 28th Cong, Int Union Pure & Appl Chem, Vancouver, 81 & 11th Int Carbohydrate Symp, Vancouver, 82. *Mem:* Fel Royal Soc Chem; fel Chem Inst Can; Am Chem Soc. *Res:* Carbohydrate chemistry, particularly structures of polysaccharides. *Mailing Add:* Dept Chem Univ BC Vancouver BC V6T 1Y6 Can

DUTTON, HERBERT JASPER, b Evansville, Wis, May 30, 14; m 37; c 3. CHEMISTRY. *Educ:* Univ Wis, BA, 36, MA, 38, PhD(plant physiol), 40. *Prof Exp:* Asst bot & chem, Univ Wis, 39-41; assoc chemist, Western Regional Res Lab, Bur Agr & Indust Chem, USDA, 41-45, head chem & phys properties invests, Northern Utilization Res & Develop Div, 53-74, chief, Oilseed Crops Lab, Northern Regional Res Lab, 74-81; HON FEL, HORMEL INST, UNIV MINN, 81- *Honors & Awards:* Super Serv Award, USDA, 56, Res Award, 57; Can Res Award, 61; Lewkowitsch Mem lectr, London, 81. *Mem:* Am Chem Soc; Am Oil Chemists' Soc; AAAS. *Res:* Quantum efficiency of carotenoid-sensitized photosynthesis; instrumental methods of lipid analysis; kinetics and mechanism of heterogeneous and homogeneous catalytic hydrogenation; computer simulation; fatty acid metabolism in humans; energy transfer in photosynthesis. *Mailing Add:* PO Box 205 Cable WI 54821

DUTTON, JOHN ALTNOW, b Detroit, Mich, Sept 11, 36; m 62; c 3. METEOROLOGY. *Educ:* Univ Wis, BS, 58, MS, 59, PhD(meteorol), 62. *Prof Exp:* From asst prof to assoc prof, 65-71, PROF METEOROL, PA STATE UNIV, UNIVERSITY PARK, 71-, HEAD, DEPT METEOROL, 81- *Concurrent Pos:* Expert, Systs Eng Group, Res & Tech Div, Air Force Systs Command, 65-71; vis scientist, Nat Lab Riso, Denmark, 72 & 78-79; trustee, Univ Corp Atmospheric Res, 74-81, secy, 77-78, treas, 78-79, vchmn, 79-80; vis prof, Tech Univ Denmark, 78-79; ed, Meteorol Monographs, Am Meteorol Soc, 80-; mem, Comt Atmospheric Sci, Nat Acad Sci, 81- *Mem:* Fel Am Meteorol Soc; Math Asn Am; Soc Indust & Appl Math. *Res:* Theoretical meteorology; dynamics of atmospheric motion; global thermodynamics and energetics of the general circulation. *Mailing Add:* Dept Meteorol 503 Walker Bldg Pa State Univ University Park PA 16802

DUTTON, JONATHAN JOSEPH, b New York, NY, Oct 2, 42; m 73; c 1. BIOMEDICAL OPHTHALMOLOGY. *Educ:* Queens Col, NY, BA, 65; Harvard Univ, MS, 67, PhD(biol), 70; Rutgers Med Sch, MMS, 75; Wash Univ, MD, 77. *Prof Exp:* Asst prof paleobiol, Princeton Univ, 70-73; mem med staff, Univ Wash Hosp, 77-78; MEM RES STAFF OPHTHAL, MED SCH, WASH UNIV, 78- *Concurrent Pos:* NSF fel, 70-71; Fight for Sight Found fel, 78-79. *Res:* Glaucoma; biology of vision; diabetic retinopathy. *Mailing Add:* Dept of Ophthal Wash Univ Sch of Med St Louis MO 63110

DUTTON, RICHARD W, b London, Eng, May 16, 30; US citizen; m 77; c 3. CELL BIOLOGY, IMMUNOLOGY. *Educ:* Cambridge Univ, BA, 52, MA, 55; Univ London, PhD(biochem), 55. *Prof Exp:* Fel, Med Sch, Univ London, 55-56; vis lectr biochem, Med Col Va, 57-58; res instr biochem & med, Sch Med & Dent, Rochester Univ, 58-59; asst lectr chem path, Med Sch, Univ London, 59-62; assoc exp path, Scripps Clin & Res Found, 62-68; assoc prof, 68-70, PROF BIOL, SCH MED, UNIV CALIF, SAN DIEGO, 70- *Concurrent Pos:* Am Cancer Soc Dernham fel, 63-68. *Mem:* Am Soc Immunol; Fedn Am Socs Exp Biol. *Res:* Cellular immunology; molecular basis of antigen stimulation. *Mailing Add:* Dept Biol M001 Univ Calif at San Diego PO Box 109 La Jolla CA 92093

DUTTON, ROBERT EDWARD, JR, b Milford, NH, Aug 11, 24; m 58; c 2. PHYSIOLOGY, MEDICINE. *Educ:* Med Col Va, MD, 49. *Prof Exp:* Instr med, State Univ NY Upstate Med Ctr, 56-59; from instr to asst prof environ med, Sch Hyg & Pub Health & Med, Johns Hopkins Univ, 61-68; assoc prof physiol, 68-74, assoc prof, 70-77, PROF MED, ALBANY MED COL, UNION UNIV, 77-, PROF PHYSIOL, 74- *Concurrent Pos:* Nat Heart Inst fel environ med, Sch Hyg & Pub Health & Med, Sch Med, Johns Hopkins Univ, 59-61; clin investr, US Vet Admin, 61-64; asst chief phys med & rehab, Baltimore City Hosp, Md, 64-68; consult pulmonary dis, Vet Admin Hosp, Baltimore, 67-68; attend physician, Albany Med Ctr Hosp & Vet Admin Hosp, Albany, 70-; prof biomed eng, Rensselaer Polytech Inst, 71-; vis prof med, Harvard Univ, Boston, 78-79. *Mem:* Am Fedn Clin Res; Am Thoracic Soc; Am Physiol Soc; Biomed Eng Soc. *Res:* Pulmonary physiology, particularly control of respiration; pulmonary diseases; internal medicine. *Mailing Add:* Dept of Physiol Albany Med Col Albany NY 12208

DUTTON, ROGER, b Tonyrefail, Gamorgan, UK, Sept 8, 41; Can citizen; m 65; c 2. MATERIALS SCIENCE, METALLURGY. *Educ:* Univ Wales, BSc, 63, PhD(metall), 66. *Prof Exp:* Res officer, 67-71, HEAD MAT SCI BR, ATOMIC ENERGY CAN LTD, 71- *Concurrent Pos:* Mem task force Can Prog Controlled Thermonuclear Fusion, Ministry State Sci & Technol, 73-74. *Res:* Underlying materials science research in support of the Canadian nuclear reactor system; irradiation damage, creep deformation and fracture. *Mailing Add:* Atomic Energy of Can Ltd Whiteshell Nuclear Res Estab Pinawa MB R0E 1L0 Can

DUTTWEILER, DAVID W(ILLIAM), b Buffalo, NY, Sept 15, 27; m 53; c 5. SANITARY ENGINEERING. *Educ:* Univ Mich, BSE, 48; Johns Hopkins Univ, MSE, 57 PhD(sanit eng), 63; Am Acad Environ Eng, dipl, 66. *Prof Exp:* Designer struct eng, T H McKaig, Consult Engr, NY, 48-49; sanit eng off, US Army Med Serv Corp, 49-69; DIR, ENVIRON RES LAB, US ENVIRON PROTECTION AGENCY, ATHENS, GA, 69- *Concurrent Pos:* Res assoc, Univ Ga, 69-; mem comn environ health, Armed Forces Epidemiol Bd, 70-74; adj prof, Clemson Univ, 71- *Mem:* Am Soc Civil Engrs; Water Pollution Control Fedn; Conf Fed Environ Engrs; Sigma Xi; Int Asn Water Pollution Res. *Res:* Mathematical models in sanitary engineering; research management; water quality control; heat exchange in natural waters; environmental health. *Mailing Add:* Environ Res Lab College Station Rd Athens GA 30613

DUTY, ROBERT C, b Morrison, Ill, Sept 28, 31; m 58; c 2. ORGANIC CHEMISTRY, COAL CHEMISTRY. *Educ:* Univ Ill, BS, 53; St Louis Univ, cert meteorol, 54; Midwestern Univ, MEd, 56; Univ Iowa, PhD(org chem), 61. *Prof Exp:* Sr chemist, Petrol Prod Lab, Humble Oil & Refining Co, La, 60-61; assoc prof chem, Western State Col Colo, 61-63; assoc prof, 63-67, PROF CHEM, ILL STATE UNIV, 67- *Mem:* AAAS; Am Chem Soc. *Res:* Organic polarography; chromatography; coal chemistry. *Mailing Add:* Dept Chem Ill State Univ Normal IL 61761

DUTZ, WERNER, b Vienna, Austria, June 7, 28; m; c 2. PATHOLOGY. *Educ:* Univ Vienna, MD, 53; Am Bd Path, cert anat path, 59; FRCPath, 62; FRCPath(C), 72. *Prof Exp:* Prof path & chmn dept, Pahlavi Univ, Iran, 60-73; prof surg path, Med Col Va, 74-81; DIR, GEN HOSP PLANNING CORP, VIENNA, AUSTRIA, 81- *Concurrent Pos:* Consult, WHO, 70 & 74. *Mem:* Int Acad Path; Am Soc Clin Pathologists; Int Soc Geog Path; Int Soc Lymphol. *Mailing Add:* Dir AKPE Postfach 2 A 1097 Wien Vienna Austria

DUVAL, CLAIBORNE ALEXANDER, JR, b Austin, Tex, Jan 12, 19; m 39; c 2. CHEMICAL ENGINEERING. *Educ:* Univ Tex, BS, 42. *Prof Exp:* Process engr, Beaumont Tech Dept, Mobil Oil Corp, 41-48, supvr res & develop, Beaumont Labs, 49-55, chief process engr, 56-58, sr technologist, 58-59, mgr process res & develop, Mobil Chem Co, Tex, 60-66, tech dir res & develop, NY, 66-67, asst mgr res & develop, NJ, 67-68, MGR, RES & DEVELOP LABS, MOBIL CHEM CO, TEX, 68- *Mem:* Am Chem Soc; Am Inst Chem Engrs. *Res:* Research management and organization; process development; petrochemicals. *Mailing Add:* Mobil Chem Co 1710 Madison Beaumont TX 77701

DU VAL, MERLIN KEARFOTT, b Montclair, NJ, Oct 12, 22; m 44; c 3. SURGERY. *Educ:* Dartmouth Col, AB, 43; Cornell Univ, MD, 46; Nat Bd Med Exam, dipl, 47; Am Bd Surg, dipl. *Prof Exp:* From instr to asst prof surg, Sch Med, State Univ NY, 54-56; assoc prof, Sch Med, Univ Okla, 57-60, prof & asst dir med ctr, 61-63; dean col med, Univ Ariz, 64-71; asst secy health & sci affairs, Dept Health, Educ & Welfare, Washington, DC, 71-74; dean med & prof surg, Univ Ariz, 74-79, vpres health sci, 74-79; PRES, NAT CTR HEALTH EDUC, 79-82. *Concurrent Pos:* Asst attend surgeon, US Vet Admin Hosp, NY, 55-56 & US Naval Hosp, NY, 55-56; Markle scholar, 56-61. *Mem:* Inst Med-Nat Acad Sci; Soc Univ Surg; Am Med Asn; Am Col Surg; Am Surg Asn. *Mailing Add:* Nat Ctr Health Educ 211 Sutter St San Francisco CA 94108

DUVALL, ARNDT JOHN, III, b St Paul, Minn, Jan 14, 31; m 56; c 4. OTOLOGY, OTOLARYNGOLOGY. *Educ:* Univ Minn, BA, 52, MD, 55, MS, 62. *Prof Exp:* From asst prof to assoc prof, 63-70, PROF OTOLARYNGOL, UNIV MINN, MINNEAPOLIS, 70- *Concurrent Pos:* Fel, Karolinska Hosp & Karolinska Inst, Sweden, 62-63; res asst, Minn Vet Hosps, 63- *Mem:* AAAS; Soc Head & Neck Surgeons; Am Laryngol, Rhinol & Otol Sco; Am Acad Ophthal & Otolaryngol; Am Acad Facial Plastic & Reconstruct Surg. *Res:* Anatomy, pathology and physiology of the ear, particularly the use of electron microscopy. *Mailing Add:* Dept of Otolaryngol Univ of Minn Minneapolis MN 55455

DUVALL, GEORGE EVERED, b Leesville, La, Feb 6, 20; m 41; c 2. PHYSICS. *Educ:* Ore State Col, BS, 46; Mass Inst Technol, PhD(physics), 48. *Prof Exp:* Assoc physicist, underwater sound, Div War Res, Univ Calif, 41-46; res assoc, Res Lab Electron, Mass Inst Technol, 46-48; physicist, Gen Elec Co, 48-50, head theoret group, 50-54; sr physicist, Poulter Labs, Stanford Res Inst, 54-57, sci dir, 57-62, dir, 62-64; PROF PHYSICS, WASH STATE UNIV, 64- *Mem:* AAAS; Am Phys Soc; Am Asn Physics Teachers; Combustion Inst. *Res:* Underwater sound; stochastic processes; reactor physics; shock and detonation phenomena; equations of state of solids; finite amplitude wave propagation; dislocations; kinetics of polymorphic transitions; shockwave chemistry. *Mailing Add:* Dept of Physics Wash State Univ Pullman WA 99164

DUVALL, HARRY MAREAN, b Lanham, Md, Oct 27, 10. ORGANIC CHEMISTRY. *Educ:* Univ Md, BS, 32, PhD(org chem), 36. *Prof Exp:* E R Squibb & Sons fel, Univ Va, 36-38; res chemist, Jackson Lab, E I du Pont de Nemours & Co, Inc, 38-50, Thiokol Chem Corp, 50-53 & Masonite Corp, 54-58; prof chem & head dept, 58-78, EMER PROF CHEM, VALDOSTA STATE COL, 79- *Mem:* Am Chem Soc. *Res:* Process development of dyestuffs; rubber chemicals; organic chemicals; synthetic rubber; liquid polymers; wood products. *Mailing Add:* Box 36 Rte 6 Valdosta GA 31601

DUVALL, JACQUE L, b Rensselaer, Ind, July 17, 24; m 48; c 7. PHYSICAL CHEMISTRY, ORGANIC CHEMISTRY. *Educ:* Univ Calif, BS, 50. *Prof Exp:* Asst chief engr, Excello Mfg Co, 51-53; res staff mem, Indust & Aircraft Labs, J B Ford Div, Wyandotte Chem Corp, 53-57; supvr specification develop, Turco Prod Co, 57; supvr, Los Nietos Res Labs, J B Ford Div, Wyandotte Chem Corp, 57-63, dir res, 63-66, res assoc, 66-70, res assoc, Chem Specialties Div, 70-77, tech mgr, chem specialties div, BASF-Wyandotte Corp, 77-80, SUPVR PULP & PAPER LAB, DIVERSEY WYANDOTTE CORP, 80. *Mem:* Am Chem Soc; Am Oil Chemists' Soc; Am Soc Testing & Mat; Chem Specialties Mfrs Asn; Tech Asn Pulp & Paper Indust. *Res:* Colloidal and surface chemistry; detergency. *Mailing Add:* Diversey Wyandotte Corp PO Box 2369 Los Nietos CA 90610

DUVALL, JOHN JOSEPH, b Sedro-Woolley, Wash, Oct 20, 36; m 56; c 6. PHYSICAL ORGANIC CHEMISTRY. *Educ:* Brigham Young Univ, BS, 58, PhD(org chem), 63. *Prof Exp:* Teaching assoc, Brigham Young Univ, 59-60; RES CHEMIST, LARAMIE ENERGY TECH CTR, US DEPT ENERGY, 63- *Concurrent Pos:* Guest chemist, Brookhaven Nat Lab, 69-70. *Mem:* Am Chem Soc; Sigma Xi. *Res:* Radiation chemistry of shale oil components; shale oil analysis; in situ oil shale retorting. *Mailing Add:* Box 3331 Univ Sta Laramie WY 82071

DUVALL, PAUL FRAZIER, JR, b Atlanta, Ga, Aug 19, 41; m 63; c 1. TOPOLOGY. *Educ:* Davidson Col, BS, 63; Univ Ga, MA, 65, PhD(math), 67. *Prof Exp:* Asst prof math, Univ Ga, 67-68; asst prof, Va Polytech Inst & State Univ, 70-71; assoc prof, 71-78, PROF MATH, OKLA STATE UNIV, 78- *Concurrent Pos:* Consult, Dept Defense, 70- *Mem:* Am Math Soc; Math Asn Am. *Res:* Geometric topology; mappings between manifolds; actions of discrete groups on manifolds; embedding of complexes in manifolds. *Mailing Add:* Dept of Math Okla State Univ Stillwater OK 74078

DUVALL, RONALD NASH, b Needham, Mass, June 17, 24; m 53; c 3. PHARMACEUTICAL CHEMISTRY. *Educ:* Mass Col Pharm, BS, 49, MS, 51, PhD(pharmaceut chem), 57. *Prof Exp:* Asst pharmaceut chem, Mass Col Pharm, 52-54, instr, 54-57, asst prof, 57-62; sect head corp pharmaceut res lab, 62-63, actg dir, 63-64, dir, 64-70, asst dir pharmaceut res & develop lab, 70-72, DIR APPL PHARMACEUT LAB, MILES LABS, INC, 72- *Concurrent Pos:* Consult, Muro Pharmacal Labs, Mass, Chester A Baker, Inc & Hoyt Pharmaceut Co, 59-62. *Mem:* Am Pharmaceut Asn; Am Chem Soc; Acad Pharmaceut Sci. *Res:* Pharmaceutical analysis; metal chelates of medicinal agents; antiradiation compounds; drug dosage form stability; carbohydrate browning mechanisms; salicylamide metabolism; industrial pharmacy. *Mailing Add:* Miles Labs Pharmaceut R&D Lab 1127 Myrtle St Elkhart IN 46514

DUVALL, THOMAS LEE, JR, b Pittsburgh, Penn, Oct 30, 50; m 72. SOLAR PHYSICS. *Educ:* Johns Hopkins Univ, BA, 72; Stanford Univ, MS, 75, PhD(appl physics), 78. *Prof Exp:* Res asst, Stanford Univ, 72-78; res assoc solar physics, Kitt Peak Nat Observ, 77-79; ASTRONOMER, GODDARD SPACE FLIGHT CTR, NASA, 79- *Concurrent Pos:* Fel, Kitt Peak Nat Observ, 78- *Res:* Large-scale solar magnetic fields and velocity fields. *Mailing Add:* Goddard Space Flight Ctr NASA Greenbelt MD 20770

DUVALL, WILBUR IRVING, b Gaithersburg, Md, Jan 3, 15; m 45; c 4. PHYSICS. *Educ:* Univ Md, BS, 36, MS, 38. *Prof Exp:* Instr high sch, Md, 36-37; lab instr, Amherst Col, 38-39; jr phys sci aide, US Bur Mines, 39-40, from jr physicist to supvry physicist, 40-52, supvry physicist, Blasting Res, Md, 52-65, supvry res physicist, Rock Mech, 65-72; RETIRED. *Concurrent Pos:* Adj prof rock mech, Colo Sch Mines, 69-74, sr sci adv, 74-; consult rock mech, 72- *Mem:* Am Inst Mining, Metall & Petrol Engrs. *Res:* Experimental stress analysis; stresses in underground mining structures; generation and propagation of explosive waves; electronics; rock mechanics. *Mailing Add:* 8820 W Dover Circle Denver CO 80226

DUVARNEY, RAYMOND CHARLES, b Clinton, Mass, Oct 11, 40; m 63; c 4. SOLID STATE PHYSICS. *Educ:* Clark Univ, BA, 62, PhD(physics), 68; Univ NH, MS, 64. *Prof Exp:* Asst prof, 68-74, ASSOC PROF PHYSICS, EMORY UNIV, 74- *Concurrent Pos:* Vis prof physics, Univ Gesamthochschole-Paderborn, Fed Repub Ger, 78-79. *Mem:* Am Phys Soc; Sigma Xi; AAAS. *Res:* Investigations of the pyroelectric and ferroelectric properties of solids using the techniques of magnetic resonance; defects and impurities in insulating solids; radiation damage. *Mailing Add:* Dept Physics Emory Univ Atlanta GA 30322

DUVICK, DONALD NELSON, b Sandwich, Ill, Dec 18, 24; m 50; c 3. GENETICS, PLANT BREEDING. *Educ:* Univ Ill, BS, 48; Wash Univ, PhD(bot), 51. *Prof Exp:* Corn breeder maize genetics & physiol, 51-71, dir dept corn breeding, 71-75, DIR DIV PLANT BREEDING, PIONEER HI-BRED INT, INC, 75- *Mem:* AAAS; Genetics Soc Am; Am Soc Plant Physiol; Bot Soc Am; Am Soc Agron. *Res:* Cytoplasmic inheritance of pollen sterility in maize; immunological identification of plant proteins; developmental morphology and anatomy of maize endosperm; measurement of genetic contributions to long-term yield gains in hybrid maize. *Mailing Add:* Plant Breeding Div Pioneer Hi-Bred Int Inc Johnston IA 50131

DUVIVIER, JEAN FERNAND, b Rio de Janeiro, Brazil, Dec 17, 26; US citizen; m 56; c 5. AERONAUTICAL ENGINEERING. *Educ:* Boston Univ, BSc, 55; Mass Inst Technol, SM, 58, EAA, 66. *Prof Exp:* Teaching asst aircraft design, Tech Inst Aeronaut, Sao Paulo, Brazil, 51-53; res staff aeroelasticity, Mass Inst Technol, 55-58, proj leader aerodynamics, 58-61; sci staff opers res, Ctr Naval Anal, 61-66; sr res engr, Elec Boat Div, Gen Dynamics Corp, 66-68; mgr systs eval, 68-72, mgr res & develop, 72-73, MGR INT MKT S AM, VERTOL DIV, BOEING CO, 73- *Concurrent Pos:* Consult, Res Anal Corp, 66. *Mem:* Assoc fel Am Inst Aeronaut & Astronaut; Am Helicopter Soc; Inst Strategic Studies; assoc mem US Naval Inst. *Res:* Aerodynamics; aeroelasticity; structural dynamics; operations research; systems analysis; transportation systems; risk analysis. *Mailing Add:* PO Box 16858 Philadelphia PA 19142

DUVOISIN, ROGER C, b Towaco, NJ, July 27, 27; m 48; c 4. NEUROLOGY. *Educ:* New York Med Col, MD, 54. *Prof Exp:* Intern, Lenox Hill Hosp, New York, 54-55, resident neurol, 55-56; resident, Presby Hosp, Columbia Presby Med Ctr, New York, 56-58; res assoc, Col Physicians & Surgeons, Columbia Univ, 62-65, from asst prof to prof neurol, 65-73; prof neurol, Mt Sinai Sch Med, City Univ New York, 73-79; CHMN & PROF NEUROL, RUTGERS MED SCH, UNIV MED & DENT, NJ, 79- *Concurrent Pos:* Parkinson's Dis Found Clin res fel, 63-64; mem, NIH Study Group Encephalitis, 63; consult, New York Bd Educ, 63-; consult adminr, Fed Aviation Admin, 65-73; mem res adv bd, Parkinson's Dis Found, 65-; mem extrapyramidal dis comn, World Fedn Neurol, 72-; vis prof, King's Col Hosp & Inst Psychiat, London, 73; mem adv panel on neurol dis ther, US Pharmacopeia. *Mem:* AAAS; Am Soc Clin Pharmacol & Therapeut; AMA; fel Am Col Physicians; Am Neurol Asn. *Res:* Neurological complications of achondroplastic dwarfs; cerebral vascular disease; syncopal mechanisms; convulsive syncope; infectious polyneuritis; clinical features, natural history, epidemiology, pathology, clinical pharmacology and treatment of Parkinson's disease and postencephalitic Parkinsonism; development of L-dopa therapy of Parkinsonism; clinical features olivoponocerebellar atrophy due to deficiency of glutamate dehydrogenase. *Mailing Add:* Rutgers Med Sch Hoe's Ln Piscataway NJ 08854

DUWE, ARTHUR EDWARD, b Saginaw, Mich, July 17, 22; wid; c 3. IMMUNOLOGY, EMBRYOLOGY. *Educ:* Alma Col, BS, 49; Ohio State Univ, MS, 50, PhD(zool), 53. *Prof Exp:* Asst instr zool, Ohio State Univ, 52; asst prof, North State Teachers Col, 53-54; asst prof, Wis State Col, Superior, 54-59, assoc prof 59-64; prof biol, Waynesburg Col, 64-68; PROF BIOL, LAKE SUPERIOR STATE COL, 68- *Concurrent Pos:* Sigma Xi grant, 59; NIH grants, 60-65. *Mem:* AAAS; Am Soc Ichthyol & Herpet; Am Soc Parasitol. *Res:* Comparative immunology. *Mailing Add:* Dept of Biol Lake Superior State Col Sault Ste Marie MI 49783

DUWELL, ERNEST JOHN, b Chicago, Ill, Mar 12, 29; m 50; c 4. PHYSICAL CHEMISTRY. *Educ:* Univ Iowa, BS, 50, PhD(chem), 54; Purdue Univ, West Lafayette, MS, 52. *Prof Exp:* Asst, Purdue Univ, West Lafayette, 50-52; sr res chemist, Jones & Laughlin Steel Corp, 54-56; res specialist, 56-66, RES MGR ABRASIVES DIV, MINN MINING & MFG CO, 66- *Mem:* Am Chem Soc. *Res:* Metal cutting and finishing; corrosion; ceramics. *Mailing Add:* 904 Seventh St Hudson WI 54016

DUWEZ, POL EDGARD, b Mons, Belg, Dec 11, 07; nat US; m 35; c 1. METALLURGY, PHYSICS. *Educ:* Polytech Fac Mons, Belg, MetE, 32; Free Univ Brussels, ScD (physics & math), 33. *Prof Exp:* Prof, Sch of Mines, Polytech Fac Mons, 38-40; res engr, 41-47, from assoc prof to prof mech eng, 47-66, PROF APPL PHYSICS & MAT SCI, CALIF INST TECHNOL, 66- *Concurrent Pos:* Mem sci adv bd to Chief of Staff, USAF, 45-55. *Honors & Awards:* Dudley Award, Am Soc Test & Mat, 51; Mathiewson Gold Medal, Am Inst Mining, Metall & Petrol Engrs, 64; Francis J Clamer Medal, Franklin Inst, 68; Prix Gouverneur Cornez, Belg Govt, 73; Albert Sauveur Mem Award, Am Soc Metal, 73; Lebau Medal, Fr Soc Hygh Temperatures, 74; Int Prize New Mat, Am Phys Soc; W Hume-Rothery Award, Am Soc Metall Engrs. *Mem:* Nat Acad Sci; Nat Acad Eng; fel AAAS; Am Inst Mining, Metall & Petrol Engrs; fel Am Acad Arts & Sci. *Res:* Physics of metals; high temperature materials; powder metallurgy. *Mailing Add:* Keck Lab of Eng Mat Calif Inst of Technol Pasadena CA 91125

DUX, JAMES PHILIP, b New York, NY, July 15, 21; m 48; c 2. PHYSICAL CHEMISTRY. *Educ:* Queens Col, NY, BS, 42; Columbia Univ, MA, 47; Polytech Inst Brooklyn, PhD(phys chem), 55. *Prof Exp:* Anal chem, Gen Chem Co, 42-44; res chemist, Phys & Anal Chem, Merck & Co, Inc, 47-50; group leader phys chem, Cellulose Sect, Am Viscose Div, FMC Corp, 54-59, group head anal chem, 59-61, sect leader, Acetate Fibers, 61-70 & Synthetic Staple & Indust Yarns, 70-75, sect leader polyester, acetate & vinyon sect, Fibers Div, 75-76; SR TECH ASSOC & MKT MGR, LANCASTER LABS, INC, 77- *Mem:* Am Mgt Asn; Am Chem Soc. *Res:* Analytical and physical chemistry in polymers; polyelectrolytes; reaction kinetics; cellulose chemistry; statistics; radiochemistry; diffusion problems; fiber physics and chemistry. *Mailing Add:* Lancaster Labs Inc 2425 New Holland Pike Lancaster PA 17601

DUXBURY, ALYN CRANDALL, b Olympia, Wash, Dec 1, 32; m 56:; c 3. OCEANOGRAPHY. *Educ:* Univ Wash, BS, 55, MS, 56; Tex A&M Univ, PhD(phys oceanog), 63. *Prof Exp:* Res assoc & lectr phys oceanog, Bingham Oceanog Lab, Yale Univ, 60-64; RES ASSOC PROF PHYS OCEANOG, UNIV WASH, 64- *Mem:* AAAS; Am Soc Limnol & Oceanog; Am Geophys Union. *Res:* Descriptive physical oceanography, hydrographic survey work. *Mailing Add:* Dept Oceanog Univ Wash Seattle WA 98195

DUXBURY, DEAN DAVID, b Tripoli, Wis, Dec 20, 34; m 60; c 3. FOOD SCIENCE. *Educ:* Univ Wis-Madison, BS, 56, MS, 57. *Prof Exp:* Res asst, Univ Wis-Madison, 56-57; food technologist, Swift & Co, 59-61, sect head canned meats, 61-65, group leader, 65-69, res mgr, Res & Develop Ctr, 69-78; V PRES TECH OPERS, AM POUCH FOOD CO, 78- *Concurrent Pos:* Adv comt mem, Comt on Food Irradiation, Nat Res Coun, 75- *Mem:* Am Soc Testing & Mat; Inst Food Technol. *Res:* Storage life studies for fresh packaged cranberries; irradiated canned beef studies for sterility and flavor acceptance; canned foods new product development; development of flexible packaged foods; food sterilization and safety. *Mailing Add:* Am Pouch Food Co Inc 695 Executive Dr Willowbrook IL 60521

DUXBURY, THOMAS CARL, b Ft Wayne, Ind. GEODESY, ASTRONOMY. *Educ:* Purdue Univ, BS, 65, MS, 66. *Prof Exp:* TECH GROUP SUPVR, JET PROPULSION LAB, CALIF INST TECHNOL, 66- *Concurrent Pos:* Arecibo prin investr, NSF & Cornell Univ, 76-77; Viking team mem, NASA, 76-, prin investr, 77- *Honors & Awards:* Except Sci Achievement Medal, NASA, 73; Samuel Burka Award, Inst Navigation, 74. *Mem:* Am Astron Soc; Am Inst Aeronaut & Astronaut; Am Geophys Union. *Res:* Geodesy and cartography analysis of the Earth, Mars and its two moons Phobos and Deimos, Jovian moons and Saturnian moons from spacecraft synthetic aperture radar and television imaging as well as analysis of astrometric observations of outer planet satellites from earth. *Mailing Add:* Jet Propulsion Lab Calif Inst of Technol Pasadena CA 91103

DUYKERS, LUDWIG RICHARD BENJAMIN, b Surabaia, Indonesia, Oct 2, 29; US citizen; m 73; c 1. PHYSICS. *Educ:* Delft Univ Technol, ME, 57. *Prof Exp:* Engr arrays, Physics Lab, Rijks Verdedigings Organisatie- Dutch Inst Appl Sci Res, Neth, 57-59; sr scientist undersea acoust, Saclant Acoust Surface Wave Res Ctr, Italy, 59-66; PHYSICIST UNDERWATER ACOUST, NAVAL OCEAN SYSTS CTR, 66- *Mem:* Acoust Soc Am. *Res:* Linear arrays, underwater acoustics, resonance of gas-filled cavities, including mammals; systems engineering. *Mailing Add:* 6657 Alcala Knoll Dr San Diego CA 92111

DUYSEN, MURRAY E, b Henderson, Iowa, July 27, 36; m 56; c 2. PLANT PHYSIOLOGY. *Educ:* Univ Omaha, BA, 59; Univ Nebr, MSc, 62, PhD(bot), 66. *Prof Exp:* From asst prof to assoc prof bot, 65-75, PROF BOT, NDAK STATE UNIV, 75- *Mem:* AAAS; Am Soc Plant Physiol; Bot Soc Am; Sigma Xi. *Res:* Chloroplast development and activity; water relations and plant development. *Mailing Add:* Dept of Bot NDak State Univ Fargo ND 58102

DVONCH, WILLIAM, b Chicago, Ill, June 22, 15; m 52; c 4. BIO-ORGANIC CHEMISTRY. *Educ:* Univ Ill, BS, 39; Purdue Univ, MS, 48, PhD(biochem), 50. *Prof Exp:* Asst, Wright Jr Col, Chicago, 39-40; chemist, Starch & Dextrose Sect, Northern Regional Res Lab, Bur Agr & Indust Chem, USDA, 41-46, biochemist, Fermentation Sect, Northern Utilization Res Br, Agr Res Serv, 50-54; BIOCHEMIST, RES DIV, WYETH LABS, 54- *Mem:* Am Chem Soc. *Res:* Carbohydrate chemistry; isolation of antibiotics; enzymes; antitumor compounds; penicillins and cephalosporins. *Mailing Add:* 75 Ivywood Lane Radnor PA 19087

DVORACEK, L(OUIS) M(ARTIN), b Grant Co, NDak, Dec 1, 27; m 53; c 2. CHEMICAL ENGINEERING. *Educ:* Univ Wash, BS, 50, MS, 51, PhD, 53. *Prof Exp:* SR DESIGN ENGR, UNION OIL CO CALIF, 54- *Mem:* Nat Asn Corrosion Engrs; Am Inst Chem Engrs; Am Inst Mech Engrs. *Res:* Corrosion and metallurgy. *Mailing Add:* 610 Linden Way Brea CA 92621

DVORACEK, MARVIN JOHN, b Penelope, Tex, July 16, 32; m 57; c 2. AGRICULTURAL ENGINEERING. *Educ:* Texas A&M Univ, BS, 53 & 59; Univ Calif, Davis, MS, 62. *Prof Exp:* Soil conservationist, Soil Conserv Serv, USDA, 53 & 56; instr eng graphics, Texas A&M Univ, 57-59, instr agr eng, 59; lectr & jr specialist, Univ Calif, Davis, 60-62; asst prof, 62-67, ASSOC PROF AGR ENG, TEX TECH UNIV, 67-, CHMN AGR ENG & TECHNOL DEPT, 77- *Concurrent Pos:* NSF fac fel, Dept Hydrol & Water Resources, Univ Ariz, 70-71, lectr, 71-72; Nat Asn Col Teachers Agr fel, 76- *Mem:* Am Soc Agr Engrs; Am Soc Civil Engrs; Nat Soc Prof Engrs; Am Soc Eng Educ; Nat Asn Col Teachers Agr. *Res:* Ground water recharge; irrigation; water conservation; evaporation; ground water pollution; runoff; hydrologic cycle. *Mailing Add:* Dept of Agr Eng & Technol Texas Tech Univ Lubbock TX 79409

DVORAK, ANN MARIE-TOMPKINS, b Bangor, Maine, May 19, 38; m 62; c 3. IMMUNOPATHOLOGY. *Educ:* Univ Maine, AB, 59; Univ Vt, MD, 63. *Prof Exp:* From intern to resident pediat, Boston Floating Hosp, 63-65; resident pediat path, Children's Hosp of DC, 65-66; resident path, Georgetown Univ Sch Med & Peter Bent Brigham Hosp, 66-69; res fel, Harvard Med Sch, 69-71; from asst prof to assoc prof path, Tuft Med Sch, 71-75; ASSOC PROF PATH, HARVARD MED SCH, 75-; PATHOLOGIST, BETH ISRAEL HOSP, 79- *Concurrent Pos:* Assoc pathologist, Mass Gen Hosp, 75-79. *Mem:* Am Asn Immunologists; Am Asn Cell Biologist; Am Asn Pathologists & Bacteriologists; Am Soc Exp Path; Int Acad Path. *Res:* Immunopathologic reactions in which basophils predominate in order to elucidate the functions of this cell in order to understand their roles in tumors and graft rejection as well as in other disease. *Mailing Add:* Dept Path Harvard Med Sch Boston MA 02114

DVORAK, FRANK ARTHUR, b Kerrobert, Sask, Aug 8, 39; US citizen; m 63. AERONAUTICAL ENGINEERING, FLUID DYNAMICS. *Educ:* Royal Mil Col Can, BASc, 62; Univ BC, MASc, 64; Cambridge Univ, PhD(aeronaut eng), 67. *Prof Exp:* Sr engr aeronaut res, Boeing Co, 67-72; div mgr comput simulation, Flow Indust Inc, 72-74; PRES ANAL METHODS INC, 74- *Concurrent Pos:* Athlone Fel, Cambridge Univ, 64-66. *Honors & Awards:* Tech Award, NASA, 76. *Mem:* Am Helicopter Soc; Can Aeronaut & Space Inst. *Res:* High lift subsonic and transonic aerodynamics; stalled flight, especially massive flow separation; boundary layer control. *Mailing Add:* 100 116th Ave S E Bellevue WA 98004

DVORAK, HAROLD FISHER, b Milwaukee, Wis, June 20, 37; m 62; c 3. PATHOLOGY. *Educ:* Princeton Univ, AB, 58; Harvard Med Sch, MD, 63. *Prof Exp:* Instr path, Harvard Med Sch, 67-69; from asst pathologist to pathologist, Mass Gen Hosp, 69-79; CHIEF, DEPT PATH, BETH ISRAEL HOSP, BOSTON, 79- *Concurrent Pos:* From asst prof to assoc prof path, Harvard Med Sch, 69-77, prof, 77-79, Mallinckrodt prof, 79-; NIH career develop awardee, 70-75. *Mem:* Am Asn Immunol; Am Asn Path & Bact; NY Acad Sci; Am Soc Exp Path; Int Acad Path. *Res:* Role of basophilic leukocytes and tissue mast cells in cell-mediated immune reactions in man and animals; tumor secreted mediators and the tumor micro environment. *Mailing Add:* Dept Path Beth Israel Hosp 330 Brookline Ave Boston MA 02215

DVORAK, JAN, b Jindrichuv Hradec, Czech, Dec 13, 44; Can citizen. CYTOGENETICS. *Educ:* Agr Univ, Czech, ING, 66; Univ Sask, PhD(crop sci), 72. *Prof Exp:* Fel, Dept Crop Sci, Univ Sask, 72-73; res assoc, 73-76; asst prof cytogenetics, 76-80, ASSOC PROF AGRON & RANGE SCI, DEPT AGRON, UNIV CALIF, DAVIS, 80- *Mem:* Am Soc Genetics; Crop Sci Soc Am; Can Soc Genetics. *Res:* Chromosomal evolution and homoeology in related species; evolution of polyploids; evolution of diploidizing genetic systems; interspecific transfer of chromosomes; interspecific transfer of genes. *Mailing Add:* Dept of Agron & Range Sci Univ of Calif Davis CA 95616

DVORCHIK, BARRY HOWARD, b Bridgeport, Conn, Feb 29, 44; m 66; c 3. DEVELOPMENTAL PHARMACOLOGY, DEVELOPMENTAL TOXICOLOGY. *Educ:* Univ Conn, BS, 66; Univ Fla, PhD(pharmacol), 72. *Prof Exp:* Instr, 72-74, asst prof, 74-79, ASSOC PROF OBSTET & GYNEC & PHARMACOL, HERSHEY MED CTR, PA STATE UNIV, 79- *Concurrent Pos:* USPHS grant fetal pharmacol, Hershey Med Ctr, Pa State Univ, 75-81, Nat Found-March of Dimes grant, 75-78; USPHS grant, Hershey Med Ctr, Pa State Univ, 79-82; consult, Div Biopharaceutics, Fed Drug Admin, Dept Health, commonwealth Pa. *Mem:* NY Acad Sci; Am Col Pharmacol; Am Soc Clin Pharmacol & Therapueut; AAAS; Am Soc Pharmacol & Exp Therapeut. *Res:* Fetal and neonatal pharmacology; pharmacokinetics. *Mailing Add:* Dept Obstet & Gynec Pa State Univ Hershey Med Ctr Hershey PA 17033

DVORNIK, DUSHAN MICHAEL, b Mezica, Yugoslavia, Oct 23, 23; Can citizen; m 51; c 1. BIOCHEMISTRY, ORGANIC CHEMISTRY. *Educ:* Univ Zagreb, Chem Eng, 48, DSc(chem), 54. *Prof Exp:* Res chemist, Pliva Chem Works, Yugoslavia, 46-49, head dept synthetic chem, 50-52, res scientist, 52-54; fel natural prod, Lab Org Chem, Swiss Fed Inst Tech, 54-55; fel alkaloids, Nat Res Coun Can, 55-58, synthetic chem, Univ Ottawa, 58-59; res chemist, 59-64, ASSOC DIR RES, AYERST RES LABS, 64-, DIR BIOCHEM DEPT, 64- *Concurrent Pos:* Fel coun arteriosclerosis, Am Heart Asn, 63- *Mem:* Am Chem Soc; Am Soc Biol Chemists; Soc Exp Biol & Med; fel Chem Inst Can; Can Biochem Soc. *Res:* Lipid metabolism; drug metabolism; biochemical pharmacology. *Mailing Add:* Ayerst Res Labs Biochem Dept PO Box 6115 Montreal PQ H3C 3J1 Can

DWARAKANATH, MANCHAGONDANAHALLI H, b Bangalore, India, May 15, 43; US citizen; m 69; c 1. ELECTRICAL ENGINEERING, CONTROL SYSTEMS. *Educ:* Univ Mysore, BS, 64; Worcester Polytech Inst, MS, 67; Polytech Inst Brooklyn, PhD(elec eng), 77. *Prof Exp:* Jr engr, Mysore State Elec Bd, 64; lectr, Nat Inst Eng, Univ Mysore, 64-65; sr engr, Am Elec Power, 66-78, sr specialist engr elec eng, 78-80, PRIN ENGR ELEC ENG, BOEING COMPUT SERV DIV, BOEING CO, 80- *Concurrent Pos:* Vis scientist, Indian Inst Sci, India, 79; tech consult, Govt of India, 81. *Mem:* Sigma Xi; sr mem, Inst Elec & Electronics Engrs. *Res:* Application of digital computers, modern control theory and system identification techniques for real time monitoring and control of power system; power systems. *Mailing Add:* Boeing Comp Serv MS 9C-02 565 Andover Park West Tukwila WA 98188

DWASS, MEYER, b New Haven, Conn, Apr 9, 23; m 49; c 4. MATHEMATICAL STATISTICS. *Educ:* George Washington Univ, AB, 48; Columbia Univ, AM, 49; Univ NC, PhD(math statist), 52. *Prof Exp:* Math statistician, Bur Census, 49-52; from asst prof to assoc prof math, Northwestern Univ, 52-61; prof, Univ Minn, 61-62; PROF MATH, NORTHWESTERN UNIV, 62-, DIR, CTR STATISTICS & PROBABILITY, 80- *Concurrent Pos:* Prof math, Hebrew Univ Jerusalem, 71-72. *Mem:* Am Math Soc; fel Inst Math Statist; Am Statist Asn. *Res:* Nonparametric statistics; renewal theory; probability theory; computers and teaching. *Mailing Add:* Dept of Math Northwestern Univ Evanston IL 60201

DWELLE, ROBERT BRUCE, b Neenah, Wis; m 70; c 2. PLANT PHYSIOLOGY. *Educ:* Carleton Col, AB, 70; Univ Mont, PhD(bot), 74. *Prof Exp:* NDEA Title IV fel plant physiol, Univ Mont, 70-73, teaching asst bot, 73-74; res assoc, 74-76, asst prof, 76-81, ASSOC PROF PLANT PHYSIOL, UNIV IDAHO, 81- *Concurrent Pos:* Lectr crop physiol, Univ Idaho, 79; prin investr, USDA Competitive Res grant, 81-84. *Mem:* Am Soc Plant Physiologists; Crop Sci Soc Am; AAAS; Potato Asn Am; Europ Asn Potato Res. *Res:* Varied rates and mechanisms of photosynthesis, partitioning of photosynthates, and the influence of plant growth regulators on sink-source relationships of potatoe clones. *Mailing Add:* Res & Extension Ctr Univ Idaho Aberdeen ID 83210

DWIGGINS, CLAUDIUS WILLIAM, JR, b Amity, Ark, May 11, 33. PHYSICAL CHEMISTRY. *Educ:* Univ Ark, BS, 54, MS, 56, PhD(chem), 58. *Prof Exp:* proj leader petrol composition res, US Bur Mines & Energy Res & Develop Admin, 58-79, RES CHEMIST, THERMODYNAMICS, US DEPT ENERGY, 79- *Mem:* AAAS; NY Acad Sci; Am Chem Soc; Am Crystallog Asn. *Res:* X-ray diffraction and structure determination; small angle x-ray scattering; colloid physics. *Mailing Add:* Energy Technol Ctr US Dept of Energy Bartlesville OK 74005

DWINELL, LEW DAVID, b Albuquerque, NMex, Mar 24, 38; m 61; c 3. PLANT PATHOLOGY. *Educ:* Colo State Univ, BS, 61; Univ Denver, MS, 63; Cornell Univ, PhD(plant path), 67. *Prof Exp:* PLANT PATHOLOGIST, FORESTRY SCI LAB, US FOREST SERV, 66- *Mem:* Soc Am Foresters; Am Phytopath Soc. *Res:* Forest tree diseases, particularly rust and canker diseases. *Mailing Add:* Forestry Sci Lab US Forest Serv Carlton St Athens GA 30601

DWINGER, PHILIP, b The Hague, Netherlands, Sept 25, 14. PURE MATHEMATICS. *Educ:* Univ Leiden, PhD(math), 38. *Prof Exp:* Prof math & head dept, Univ Indonesia, 53-56; from asst prof to prof, Purdue Univ, West Lafayette, 56-62; prof, Univ Delft, 62-65; head dept, 75-79, PROF MATH, UNIV ILL, CHICAGO CIRCLE, 65-, DEAN, COL LIB ARTS SCI, 79- *Mem:* Am Math Soc; corresp mem Royal Netherlands Acad Sci; Netherlands Math Soc. *Res:* Algebra, particularly ordered sets and lattices; Boolean algebras. *Mailing Add:* Dept of Math Box 4348 Univ of Ill Chicago IL 60680

DWIVEDY, RAMESH C, b Etawah, India, Mar 15, 43; m 67; c 1. BIOENGINEERING, AGRICULTURAL ENGINEERING. *Educ:* Univ Allahabad, BS, 63; Univ Guelph, MS, 65; Univ Mass, Amherst, PhD(agr eng), 70. *Prof Exp:* Lectr agr eng, Univ Udaipur, India, 63-64; asst prof agr eng, Univ Del, 70-74; resources engr, Dept Natural Resources & Environ Control, State of Del, 74-78; PROJ ENGR, DELMARVA POWER & LIGHT CO, 78- *Mem:* Assoc Am Soc Agr Engrs; Water Pollution Control Fedn. *Res:* Stress analysis in grain mass inside a bin; electrophysiological research to develop a non-chemical device of insect control; aquacultural engineering. *Mailing Add:* 14 Kenwich Ct Charter Oaks Hockessin DE 19707

DWORETZKY, MURRAY, b New York, NY, Aug 18, 17; m 43; c 2. ALLERGY, IMMUNOLOGY. *Educ:* Univ Pa, BA, 38; Long Island Col Med, MD, 42; Univ Minn, MS, 50; Am Bd Internal Med, dipl, 52, cert allergy, 54; Am Bd Allergy & Immunol, dipl, 72. *Prof Exp:* Intern, City Hosp, New York, 42-43, asst resident path, 43, fel, 46-47; resident, Univ Chicago, 47-48; fel med, Mayo Found, 48-50; asst med, 51-52, instr, 52-56, clin asst prof, 56-61, clin asst prof pub health, 57-62, clin assoc prof med, 61-66, CLIN PROF MED, MED COL, CORNELL UNIV, 66- *Concurrent Pos:* Asst physician, Outpatient Dept, New York Hosp, 51, physician, 51-56, asst attend physician, 56-61, assoc attend physician, 61-66, attend physician, 66-, physician-in-chg, Allergy Clin, 61-; attend physician, Manhattan Eye, Ear & Throat Hosp, 52-62; med dir-at-large asthma, Allergy Found Am, 63-78, mem med coun, 78-; examr allergy subspecialty, Am Bd Internal Med, 69-72; mem bd gov, Am Bd Allergy & Immunol, 71-74; consult med (allergy), Mem Hosp, 72. *Mem:* Fel AAAS; AMA; fel Am Acad Allergy (treas, 66, pres elect, 67); fel Am Col Physicians. *Res:* Anaphylaxis; toxic and allergic reactions to staphylococcal fractions; management of asthma. *Mailing Add:* 115 E 61st St New York NY 10021

DWORJANYN, LEE O(LEH), b Lviv, Ukraine, Feb 18, 34; m 58; c 4. CHEMICAL ENGINEERING. *Educ:* Univ Sydney, BSc, 55, BE, 57; Univ London, PhD(diffusion), 62. *Prof Exp:* Leverhulme scholar, Univ London, 60-62; chem engr, Imp Chem Indust, Australia & NZ, 57-59; res engr prod develop, 62-69, sr res engr, Orlon-Lycra Tech Div, 70-72, res supvr, 72-76, PROCESS SUPVR, CHRISTINA LAB, I E DU PONT DE NEMOURS & CO, INC, 76- *Mem:* Am Chem Soc; Royal Australian Chem Inst. *Res:* Dyed and pigmented fibers; simulated furs; thermodynamic equilibria; waste incineration; electrochemistry; electrochemical cell design. *Mailing Add:* 1570 Citation Dr Aiken SC 29801

DWORKEN, HARVEY J, b Cleveland, Ohio, Aug 1, 20; m 49; c 2. INTERNAL MEDICINE, GASTROENTEROLOGY. *Educ:* Dartmouth Col, BA, 41; Case Western Reserve Univ, MD, 44. *Prof Exp:* Intern, Michael Reese Hosp, Chicago, Ill, 44-45; resident psychiat, New Eng Med Ctr, Boston, 47-48; asst resident med, Mt Sinai Hosp, Cleveland, Ohio, 48-49, chief resident, 49-50; from clin instr to asst clin prof, 52-62, physician-in-chg, Gastrointestinal Labs, 62-81, asst prof, 62-65, dir, Div Gastroenterol, Dept Med, 73-81, ASSOC PROF MED, CASE WESTERN RESERVE UNIV, 66- *Concurrent Pos:* Fel gastroenterol, Univ Hosp Pa, 50-52; chmn curric revision comt, Case Western Reserve Univ, 66-70, coordr, Phase 2 Curric, 72-75. *Mem:* Am Col Physicians; Am Gastroenterol Asn; AMA. *Res:* Curriculum planning; clinical investigation on gastric secretion and inflammatory diseases of the intestinal tract; medical education research. *Mailing Add:* 2074 Abington Rd Cleveland OH 44106

DWORKIN, JUDITH MARCIA, b Worcester, Mass, July 14, 49; m 74. WATER RESOURCES. *Educ:* Clark Univ, MA, 75, PhD(geog), 78. *Prof Exp:* Geographer, US Army Corp Engrs, 75-76; instr geography, Univ Toronto, 76-78; ASST PROF WATER RESOURCES, UNIV ARIZ, 78- *Concurrent Pos:* Consult, Indianapolis Water Co, 76-77, US Water Resources Coun, 78 & US Agency Int Develop, 78- *Mem:* Am Asn Geographers; AAAS; Am Geophys Union. *Res:* Institutional arrangements for efficient and equitable groundwater management; impacts of water supply projects in developing countries; community attitudes in resource decision-making. *Mailing Add:* 4250 N Bear Claw Way Tucson AZ 85715

DWORKIN, MARTIN, b New York, NY, Dec 3, 27; m 57; c 2. MICROBIOLOGY. *Educ:* Ind Univ, AB, 51; Univ Tex, PhD(bact), 55. *Prof Exp:* Res scientist bact, Univ Tex, 52-53; from asst prof to assoc prof microbiol, Med Ctr, Ind Univ, 57-62; assoc prof, 62-69, PROF MICROBIOL, UNIV MINN, MINNEAPOLIS, 69- *Concurrent Pos:* Res fel, Univ Calif, 55-57; NIH fels, 55-57, NIH career develop award, 64 & 69; vis prof, Oxford Univ, 70-71 & Stanford Univ, 78-79; Found for Microbiol lectr, 74, 77 & 81; Guggenheim fel, 78-79. *Mem:* Am Soc Microbiol; Brit Soc Gen Microbiol. *Res:* Microbial physiology; myxobacteria; developmental microbiology. *Mailing Add:* Dept of Microbiol Univ of Minn Minneapolis MN 55455

DWORNIK, EDWARD JOHN, b Buffalo, NY, Mar 23, 20; m 46; c 3. MINERALOGY. *Educ:* Univ Buffalo, BA, 41, MA, 48. *Prof Exp:* Researcher mineral, 48-55, adminr, Geochem & Petrol Br, 56-61, RESEARCHER MINERAL, ANAL LABS, US GEOL SURV, 61- *Concurrent Pos:* Co-investr, Lunar Apollo Prog NASA, 70-75. *Honors & Awards:* Super Performance Awards, US Dept Interior, 63 & US Geol Surv, 75. *Mem:* Fel Geol Soc Am; Mineral Soc Am; Electron Micros Soc Am. *Res:* Application of electron and X-ray optics in research on fine-grained minerals, lunar and other geological materials. *Mailing Add:* US Geol Surv 12201 Sunrise Valley Dr Herndon VA 22092

DWORNIK, JULIAN JONATHAN, b Colonsay, Sask, Mar 11, 38; m 63; c 1. ANATOMY. *Educ:* Andrews Univ, BA, 61; Univ Man, MSc, 64, PhD(anat, neuroanat), 69. *Prof Exp:* Demonstr microanat, Univ Man, 63-64, teaching asst anat, 65-66; from instr to asst prof, Univ Louisville, 67-70; asst prof, 70-73, asst dean admis, 72-75, ASSOC PROF ANAT, COL MED, UNIV S FLA, 73-, ASSOC DEAN ADMIS, 75- *Mem:* Pan Am Asn Anatomists; Can Asn Anatomists. *Res:* Gross anatomy and teratology. *Mailing Add:* Col of Med Box 3 12901 N 30th St Tampa FL 33612

DWORSCHACK, ROBERT GEORGE, b Milwaukee, Wis, Feb 26, 20; m 45; c 4. INDUSTRIAL MICROBIOLOGY. *Educ:* Univ Wis, BS, 42; Bradley Univ, MS, 49. *Prof Exp:* Chemist, Kurth Malting Co, 41; chemist, Northern Regional Res Lab, Bur Agr & Indust Chem, USDA, 42-44 & 45-51, chemist, Northern Utilization Res Div, Agr Res Serv, 51-60; chemist, Columbia Malting Co, 60-64; CHEMIST, CLINTON CORN PROCESSING CO, 64- *Mem:* Am Soc Microbiol. *Res:* Process and product development in microbiology; starch chemistry; enzymology. *Mailing Add:* Clinton Corn Processing Co 1251 Beaver Channel Pkwy Clinton IA 52732

DWORZECKA, MARIA, b Warsaw, Poland. NUCLEAR PHYSICS. *Educ:* Warsaw Univ, MSc, 64, PhD(physics), 69. *Prof Exp:* Asst physics, Warsaw Univ, 64-66, jr fac mem, 66-69; res assoc, Mich State Univ, 70-72; asst prof, Univ Mass, Amherst, 72-73, adj asst prof, 73-74; vis asst prof, 74-80, ASST PROF PHYSICS, UNIV MD, COLLEGE PARK, 80- *Res:* Nuclear structure--Hartree-Fock theory, Strutinsky approach, semiclassical approach; nuclear dynamics--heavy ions scattering, fluid dynamical descriptions, time-dependent Hartree-Fock theory, dynamical extended Thomas-Fermi approximation. *Mailing Add:* Dept Physics & Astron Univ Md College Park MD 20742

DWYER, DENNIS MICHAEL, b Passaic, NJ, Feb 26, 45; m 69; c 2. PARASITOLOGY, PROTOZOOLOGY. *Educ:* Montclair State Col, BA, 67; Univ Mass, Amherst, MS, 70, PhD(zool), 71. *Prof Exp:* Nat Inst Allergic & Infectious Dis fel parasitol, Rockefeller Univ, 71-73, asst prof parasitol, 73-76; res microbiologist, Lab Parasitic Dis, 76-80, SUPVRY RES MICROBIOLOGIST, CELL BIOL & IMMUNOL SECT, LAB PARASITIC DIS, NAT INST ALLERGIC & INFECTIOUS DIS, 80- *Concurrent Pos:* Adj assoc prof parasitol, Rockefeller Univ, 76-; adj assoc prof zool, Univ Mass, Amherst, 77-; ad hoc grant reviewer, Spec Prog Res Training Trop Dis, WHO & Cellular Biol Sect, NSF; grant revr, Trop Med Parasitol Study Sect, & Microbiol Infectious Dis Study Sect, Nat Inst Allergic & Infectious Diss, Nat Inst Health. *Honors & Awards:* Henry Baldwin Ward Medal, Am Soc Parasitol, 80. *Mem:* Soc Protozool; Am Soc Parasitol; Am Soc Trop Med Hyg; Am Soc Cell Biol; AAAS. *Res:* Chemical and immunochemical characterization of parasite cell surfaces; intracellular parisitism; aspects of pathogenicity and immunology of various parasitic protozoan groups; mechanisms and etiology of protozoan diseases. *Mailing Add:* Bldg 5 Room 112 NIH Bethesda MD 20014

DWYER, DON D, b Hugoton, Kans, Dec 28, 34; m 56; c 2. RANGE MANAGEMENT. *Educ:* Ft Hays Kans State Col, BS, 56, MS, 58; Tex A&M Univ, PhD(range mgt), 60. *Prof Exp:* Asst prof forestry, Ariz State Col, 59-60; asst prof agron & bot, Okla State Univ, 60-64; from assoc prof to prof range mgt, NMex State Univ, 64-71; PROF RANGE SCI & HEAD DEPT, UTAH STATE UNIV, 71- *Concurrent Pos:* Extensive Int experience, Africa & Latin Am. *Mem:* Soc Range Mgt; Ecol Soc Am; Am Soc Agron. *Res:* Grazing management on native rangeland; ecology of native range plants. *Mailing Add:* Dept Range Sci Utah State Univ Logan UT 84322

DWYER, FRANCIS GERARD, b Philadelphia, Pa, June 13, 31; m 61; c 5. CHEMICAL ENGINEERING. *Educ:* Villanova Univ, BChE, 53; Univ Pa, MS, 63, PhD(chem eng), 66. *Prof Exp:* Jr engr, 53-54, chem engr, 56-62, sr chem engr, 62-69, engr assoc, 69-78, sr res assoc, 78-80, MGR, CATALYST SYNTHESIS & DEVELOP, MOBIL RES & DEVELOP CORP, 80- *Mem:* Am Inst Chem Engrs; Am Chem Soc; Catalysis Soc. *Res:* Catalyst and process development in petroleum processing; zeolite catalysis; petrochemical processing and auto exhaust catalysis; catalytic kinetics and reaction mechanisms of complex chemical reactions. *Mailing Add:* Mobil Res & Develop Corp Paulsboro NJ 08066

DWYER, JAMES MICHAEL, b Paterson, NJ, Nov 16, 31. PHYSICAL CHEMISTRY, FORENSIC SCIENCE. *Educ:* Princeton Univ, AB, 53; Univ Rochester, PhD(nuclear chem), 63. *Prof Exp:* Res assoc radiochem, Brookhaven Nat Lab, 62-63; asst prof chem, Adelphi Univ, 63-67; ASSOC PROF CHEM, C W POST COL, LONG ISLAND UNIV, 67- *Concurrent Pos:* Res assoc, Biomech Lab, NY Univ, 74-75. *Mem:* Am Chem Soc; The Chem Soc; Am Asn Univ Prof. *Res:* Design and use of digital instruments in chemical, biological and forensic applications; study of rates of cyclic reactions; dynamics of social processes. *Mailing Add:* Dept of Chem C W Post Col Greenvale NY 11548

DWYER, JOHN B, chemical engineering, deceased

DWYER, JOHN DUNCAN, b Newark, NJ, Apr 26, 15; m 42; c 4. SYSTEMATIC BOTANY. *Educ:* St Peter's Col, AB, 36; Fordham Univ, MS, 38, PhD(bot), 41. *Prof Exp:* Instr biol, St Francis Col, NY, 42; prof, Albany Col Pharm, 42-47 & Siena Col, 47-53; assoc prof, 53-59, head dept, 53-63, PROF BIOL, ST LOUIS UNIV, 59- *Concurrent Pos:* Nat Acad Sci res grant, Mus Natural Hist, Paris, 52; cur trop SAm Phanerogams, Mo Bot Gardens, 64-; consult, US Army Tropic Test Ctr, Panama, 65; consult, Ciba Pharm Co; consult, Am Inst Res & Indust Technol, Guatemala, 70- *Mem:* AAAS; Torrey Bot Club; Am Soc Plant Taxon; Asn Taxon Study Trop African Flora. *Res:* American species of Ochnaceae and Leguminosae; general flora of Central America and Peru. *Mailing Add:* Dept of Biol St Louis Univ St Louis MO 63103

DWYER, LAWRENCE ARTHUR, b Minneapolis, Minn, Aug 1, 47. ENZYMOLOGY, LIPID BIOCHEMISTRY. *Educ:* Univ Nev, Reno, BA, 72, PhD(biochem), 80. *Prof Exp:* Microbiol tech & lab supvr, Cetus Corp, 73-75; res fel, Univ Nev, Reno, 75-80; FEL, BIOCHEM DEPT, MED SCH, NORTHWESTERN UNIV, 80- *Mem:* Am Chem Soc; AAAS; Sigma Xi. *Res:* Mechanism of action of xenobiotic detoxication and activation reactions catalyzed by purified isozymes of rabbit liver cytochrome P-450; cuticular lipid biosynthesis in the American cockroach. *Mailing Add:* Biochem Dept Northwestern Univ Med Sch 303 E Chicago Ave Chicago IL 60611

DWYER, MICHAEL J, b Brooklyn, NY, Mar 22, 48; m 76; c 2. ORIGINS OF LIFE, FUNDAMENTAL RESEARCH. *Educ:* Boston Col, BS, 70; Univ Pa, PhD(molecular biol), 79. *Prof Exp:* Pres, Controlled Bio-Syst, Inc, 75-77; group mgr, Franklin Inst, 77-78; consult, Pathfinder, Inc, 78-82; PRES, MIMARK INST, 82- *Concurrent Pos:* Guest researcher, Ames Res Ctr, NASA, 70 & 71; fel, Res Inst Natural Sci, 72; instr sci, Harcum Jr Col, 77; founder, Mimark Inst, 79. *Mem:* Int Soc Study Origins Life; Soc Gen Syst Res; AAAS. *Res:* long term fundamental experimental and theoretical research in areas which have potential for significant contributions to scientific thought technological advancement and man's view of himself and the world. *Mailing Add:* 22 Eastwood Dr West Berlin NJ 08091

DWYER, ROBERT FRANCIS, b Utica, NY, Feb 20, 30; m 53; c 2. ANALYTICAL CHEMISTRY, PHYSICAL CHEMISTRY. *Educ:* Syracuse Univ, BS, 51; Pa State Univ, MS, 53. *Prof Exp:* Res chemist, Linde Div, 53-61, sr res chemist, 61-62, group leader, Low Temperature Measurement & Radiation Serv, 62-66, supvr anal servs, 66-69, mgr anal serv, Realty Div, 69-73, mgr sci serv, Gen Serv, 73-80, DIR ADMIN, UNION CARBIDE CORP, 80- *Concurrent Pos:* Mem sampling & anal panel, Group on Composition Exhaust Gases, Coord Res Coun, 61-67. *Mem:* Am Chem Soc. *Res:* Instrumental methods of analysis; research applications of radioisotopes; radiation chemistry; blood preservation; low-temperature measurements of physical properties; rheologic and thermodynamics properties of slush and solid hydrogen. *Mailing Add:* Union Carbide Corp Tarrytown Tech Ctr Tarrytown NY 10591

DWYER, ROWLAND WILLIAM, JR, b Teaneck, NJ, Dec 14, 46. QUANTUM CHEMISTRY. *Educ:* Richmond Prof Inst, BS, 68; Va Commonwealth Univ, PhD(chem), 76. *Prof Exp:* SCIENTIST CHEM, PHILIP MORRIS, INC, 68- *Res:* Involved in studies of mechanisms and kinetics of heterogeneous catalysis; physico-chemical chromatography; theoretical spectroscopy. *Mailing Add:* 1518 W Laburnum Ave Richmond VA 23227

DWYER, SAMUEL J, III, b San Antonio, Tex, June 8, 32; m 53; c 6. ELECTRICAL ENGINEERING, RADIOLOGY. *Educ:* Univ Tex, BS, 57, MS, 59, PhD(elec eng), 63. *Prof Exp:* Instr elec eng, Univ Tex, 57-63; from asst prof to assoc prof, 63-70, PROF ELEC ENG, UNIV MO-COLUMBIA, 70-, DIR BIOENG, 76- *Concurrent Pos:* Res engr, Defense Res Lab, 60-61; NIMH res grant, 65- *Mem:* Inst Elec & Electronics Engrs; Asn Comput Mach; Inst Math Statist; Am Statist Asn. *Res:* Application of statistics and information theory to radiology; statistical communication theory. *Mailing Add:* Univ Kans Med Ctr 39th & Rainbow Kansas City KS 66103

DWYER, SEAN G, b New York, NY, Mar 12, 45; m 68; c 3. PHYSICAL ORGANIC CHEMISTRY, POLYMER CHEMISTRY. *Educ:* Univ NDak, BS, 66, PhD(org chem), 70. *Prof Exp:* sr chemist product res, 70-76, res & develop mgr business develop, 77-78, MGR, PROD RES SECT, S C JOHNSON & SONS, INC, 78- *Mem:* Am Chem Soc; Sigma Xi. *Res:* Arsonium ylides and imines; attempted synthesis of stable carbenes; product development in floor care, cleaners and sanitizers; personal care products, industrial cleaners. *Mailing Add:* 1709 Four Mile Rd Racine WI 53402

DWYER, THOMAS A, b New York, NY, Nov 18, 23. COMPUTER SCIENCE, APPLIED MATHEMATICS. *Educ:* Dayton Univ, BS, 45; Case Western Reserve Univ, MS, 51, PhD(math), 60. *Prof Exp:* Chmn math dept, Cathedral Latin Sch, 47-57; assoc prof comput sci, Dayton Univ, 60-67; assoc prof, 68-76, PROF COMPUT SCI, UNIV PITTSBURGH, 76- *Concurrent Pos:* NSF fel, Case Western Reserve Univ; prin investr, Proj SOLO, 69-71. *Mem:* Am Math Soc; Soc Indust & Appl Math; Asn Comput Mach. *Res:* Nonlinear networks and boundary value problems; optimization; computers in education; computer assisted instruction; man-machine systems. *Mailing Add:* Dept Comput Sci Univ Pittsburgh 4200 5th Ave Pittsburgh PA 15260

DWYER, THOMAS ALOYSIUS WALSH, III, b Rio de Janeiro, Brazil, Oct 19, 40; US & Brazil citizen. MATHEMATICS. *Educ:* Inst Pure & Appl Math, Rio de Janeiro, MSc, 65; Univ Md, College Park, MA, 69, PhD(math), 71. *Prof Exp:* Librn & res asst math, Inst Pure & Appl Math, Rio de Janeiro, 64-65; asst prof, 70-76, ASSOC PROF MATH, NORTHERN ILL UNIV, 76- *Concurrent Pos:* Vis lectr math, Nat Univ Ireland, 72-73; guest lectr, Univ Trier-Kaiserslautern, WGer, 73. *Mem:* Am Math Soc; Control Systs Soc; Soc Indust & Appl Math; Inst Elec & Electronics Engrs. *Res:* Nonlinear functional analysis, partial differential equations in infinite dimensions; mathematical systems theory. *Mailing Add:* Dept of Math Sci Northern Ill Univ De Kalb IL 60115

DY, KIAN SENG, b Philippines, June 28, 40; m 67. SOLID STATE PHYSICS. *Educ:* Ohio State Univ, BSc, 61; Cornell Univ, PhD(physics), 67. *Prof Exp:* Res assoc physics, Univ Ill, Urbana, 67-68; asst prof, 68-74, ASSOC PROF PHYSICS, UNIV NC, CHAPEL HILL, 74- *Res:* Quantum statistical mechanics; transport properties of fluids; lattice dynamics. *Mailing Add:* Dept of Physics Univ of NC Chapel Hill NC 27514

DYAL, PALMER, b Odon, Ind, Oct 27, 33; m 55; c 2. PHYSICS, ASTROPHYSICS. *Educ:* Coe Col, BA, 55; Univ Ill, Urbana-Champaign, PhD(chem physics), 59. *Hon Degrees:* DSc, Coe Col, 78. *Prof Exp:* Proj scientist, US Air Force, Kirtland AFB, 61-66; RES SCIENTIST, AMES RES CTR, NASA, 66- *Concurrent Pos:* Fel physics, Univ Calif, Berkeley, 73-74. *Honors & Awards:* Sci Achievement Award, Air Force Systs Command, 62; Apollo Achievement Award, NASA, 69, Medal for Exceptional Sci Achievement, 72. *Mem:* AAAS; Am Phys Soc; Am Geophys Union; Am Astron Soc; Explorers Club. *Res:* Magnetic field research on the moon in the Apollo Program; magnetic field and particle experiments on high altitude nuclear bursts; photo production of pions from complex nuclei. *Mailing Add:* 26405 Ascension Dr Los Altos Hills CA 94022

DYAR, JAMES JOSEPH, b Marietta, Ohio, Nov 1, 31; m 58; c 3. PLANT PHYSIOLOGY. *Educ:* Univ WVa, AB, 54, MS, 57; Ohio State Univ, PhD(bot), 60. *Prof Exp:* Asst prof biol, Univ WVa, 60-61; researcher tobacco, Brown & Williamson Tobacco Corp, 61-62; from asst prof to assoc prof, 62-70, PROF & AREA COORDR BIOL, BELLARMINE COL, 70-, CHMN DEPT, 69- *Concurrent Pos:* Tobacco Indust Res Comt grant, 63-64; NSF res grant, 64-65. *Mem:* AAAS; Am Soc Plant Physiol; Am Inst Biol Sci. *Res:* Organic translocation in plants; molecular research in tobacco. *Mailing Add:* Dept of Biol Bellarmine Col 2000 Norris Pl Louisville KY 40205

DYBALL, CHRISTOPHER JOHN, b Melksham, Eng, Apr 3, 51; m 75. POLYMER CHEMISTRY. *Educ:* Lancaster Univ, PhD(polymer chem), 75. *Prof Exp:* Trainee technician, Avon Rubber Co, Eng, 68-69; assoc, Nat Res Coun Can, 75-76; group leader polymer chem, Lucidol Div, Pennwalt Co,

76-79; MGR RES & DEVELOP SPECIALTY POLYMERS, DUOLITE INT, DIAMOND SHAMROCK CORP, 79- *Mem:* Plastics & Rubber Inst; Am Chem Soc; Soc Photog Scientists & Engrs. *Res:* Polymerisation kinetics-structure, property relationships of polymers. *Mailing Add:* Duolite Int Diamond Shamrock Corp 800 Chestnut St Redwood City CA 94064

DYBALSKI, JACK NORBERT, b Chicago, Ill, Oct 19, 24; m 51; c 3. INDUSTRIAL ORGANIC CHEMISTRY, HIGHWAY ENGINEERING. *Educ:* Univ Chicago, PhB, 51. *Prof Exp:* Chemist, Armour Indust Chem Co, 53-54, res chemist, 54-60, sect leader asphalt res, 60-64, proj mgr water conserv, 62-71, res mgr, Hwy Chem Div, 71-78, MGR, HWY CHEM DEPT, ARMAK CO, 78-, COMMERCIAL DEVELOP, 64- *Concurrent Pos:* Mem hwy res bd, Nat Acad Sci-Nat Res Coun, 60- *Mem:* Am Chem Soc; Asn Asphalt Paving Technol; Am Soc Testing & Mat; Am Soc Civil Eng. *Res:* Bituminous research and development based on cationic concept pertaining to hydrological uses for water conservation and industrial uses in building, paving and hazardous waste containment. *Mailing Add:* 4754 S Wood St Chicago IL 60609

DYBAS, LINDA KATHRYN, b Chicago, Ill, Oct 15, 42. ELECTRON MICROSCOPY, INVERTEBRATES. *Educ:* Knox Col, BA, 64; Calif State Univ, San Francisco, MA, 73; Univ Ulm, WGer, Dr rer(human biol), 76. *Prof Exp:* Res asst otolaryngol, Mass Eye & Ear Infirmary, 66, path, Med Ctr, Univ Calif, San Francisco, 67-74; asst, Univ Ulm, WGer, 67-74; ASST PROF BIOL, KNOX COL, GALESBURG, ILL, 77- *Mem:* AAAS; Int Soc Develop & Comp Immunol; Sigma Xi; Am Soc Zoologists. *Res:* Cell morphology, specifically, the structure and function, including cellular defense reactions, of marine invertebrate blood cells; spermatogenesis; oogenesis in insects and marine invertebrates. *Mailing Add:* Knox Col Galesburg IL 61401

DYBBS, ALEXANDER, heat transfer, fluid mechanics, see previous edition

DYBCZAK, Z(BIGNIEW) W(LADYSLAW), b Zaleszczyki, Poland, June 27, 24; US citizen; m 57; c 2. MECHANICAL & NUCLEAR ENGINEERING. *Educ:* Univ London, BSc, 50; Univ Toronto, PhD(mech eng), 59. *Prof Exp:* Indust design engr, Eng, 49-51; grad instr & res asst mech eng, Univ Toronto, 52-54, instr, 54-56, lectr, 56-59; assoc mech engr res & develop, Argonne Nat Lab, 60; PROF & DEAN ENG, TUSKEGEE INST, 60- *Concurrent Pos:* Consult, Can & US Govt, Industs & Founds. *Honors & Awards:* Bendix Award, Am Soc Eng Educ, 81. *Mem:* Am Soc Mech Engrs; Am Nuclear Soc; Am Soc Eng Educ. *Res:* Photoelastic stress analysis; design and vibration analysis; nuclear reactor shielding; experimental reactor physics; solar energy. *Mailing Add:* 129 Arrowhead Dr Montgomery AL 36117

DYBING, CLIFFORD DEAN, b Deadwood, SDak, Nov 6, 31; m 53; c 4. PLANT PHYSIOLOGY. *Educ:* Colo Agr & Mech Col, BS, 53, MS, 55; Univ Calif, Davis, PhD(plant physiol), 59. *Prof Exp:* Asst bot & plant path, Colo Agr & Mech Col, 53-55; asst bot, Univ Calif, Davis, 55-58; PLANT PHYSIOLOGIST, NORTH CENT REGION, AGR RES SERV, SCI & EDUC ADMIN, USDA, 60- *Concurrent Pos:* Vis scientist, Prairie Regional Lab, Nat Res Coun Can, Sask, 67-68; prof, SDak State Univ, 71-; ed-in-chief, Crop Sci Soc Am & ed, Crop Sci J, 77-79. *Mem:* Am Soc Plant Physiol; Am Soc Agron; Weed Sci Soc Am; Crop Sci Soc Am; Soc Econ Bot. *Res:* Lipid metabolism; plant growth regulators; environmental influences on plant growth; fruit and seed development. *Mailing Add:* Plant Sci Dept Box 2109 SDak State Univ Brookings SD 51096

DYBOWSKI, CECIL RAY, b Yorktown, Tex, Sept 23, 46. PHYSICAL CHEMISTRY. *Educ:* Univ Tex, Austin, BS, 69, PhD(chem, physics), 73. *Prof Exp:* Res fel chem eng, Calif Inst Technol, 73-76; asst prof, 76-81, ASSOC PROF CHEM, UNIV DEL, 81- *Mem:* Am Chem Soc; Sigma Xi; Am Phys Soc. *Res:* Pulsed nuclear magnetic resonance; surface studies; dynamics in ordered fluids. *Mailing Add:* Dept Chem Univ Del Newark DE 19711

DYBVIG, DOUGLAS HOWARD, b Bemidji, Minn, Feb 14, 35; m 57; c 5. ORGANIC CHEMISTRY. *Educ:* St Olaf Col, BA, 57; Univ Ill, PhD(org chem), 61. *Prof Exp:* Sr res chemist, 60-70, mgr lab, 70-73, res dir, Cent Res, 73-77, TECH DIR, INDUST GRAPHICS DIV, 3M CO, 77- *Concurrent Pos:* Asst prof chem, St Olaf Col, 64-65. *Mem:* Am Chem Soc; The Chem Soc. *Res:* Organic reaction mechanisms; synthesis and chemistry of fluorine compounds; chemistry of rocket fuels; printing; color reproduction. *Mailing Add:* 3M Co Bldg 234-1W 3M Ctr St Paul MN 55144

DYCE, ROLF BUCHANAN, b Guelph, Ont, Oct 12, 29; US citizen; m 59; c 2. PLANETARY SCIENCES. *Educ:* Cornell Univ, BS, 51, PhD(elec eng), 55. *Prof Exp:* Res engr radio propagation, Stanford Res Inst, 57-63, staff scientist, 63-64; res assoc planetary radar, Arecibo Observ, Cornell Univ, 64-65, assoc dir, 65-79; CHIEF SCIENTIST, EQUATORIAL COMMUN CO, 79- *Concurrent Pos:* Mem comn III, IV, US Nat Comt, Int Sci Radio Union, 53-; propagation ed, Trans Group Antennas & Propagation, 64-69; res assoc, radiosci Lab, Stanford Univ, 66-68. *Mem:* Inst Elec & Electronics Engineers. *Res:* Experimental studies of the ionosphere employing low frequency radar, satellite or cosmic signals; radar exploration of the moon and planets. *Mailing Add:* Arecibo Observ Box 995 Arecibo PR 00612

DYCK, GERALD WAYNE, b Borden, Sask, July 11, 38; m 66; c 3. REPRODUCTIVE PHYSIOLOGY. *Educ:* Univ Sask, BSA, 60; Univ Man, MSc, 63; Iowa State Univ, PhD(reproductive physiol), 66. *Prof Exp:* Res scientist, 66-71, RES SCIENTIST II, AGR CAN, 71- *Concurrent Pos:* Adj prof, Univ Man, 69- *Mem:* Agr Inst Can; Brit Soc Study Fertil; Soc Study Reproduction; Am Soc Animal Sci; Can Soc Animal Sci (pres, 77-78). *Res:* Reproductive physiology, especially female swine embryonic survival and litter size, nutritional and environmental effects, ovulation rate and uterine function; nature of estrus-post weaning and puberty. *Mailing Add:* Agr Can Res Sta Box 610 Brandon MB R7A 5Z7 Can

DYCK, PETER LEONARD, b Manitoba, Mar 31, 29; m 58; c 2. GENETICS. *Educ:* Univ Man, BSA, 56, MSc, 57; Univ Calif, Davis, PhD(genetics), 60. *Prof Exp:* RES SCIENTIST, CAN DEPT AGR, 60- *Mem:* Genetics Soc Can; Am Soc Agron. *Res:* Genetics of wheat, particularly leaf and stem rust resistance. *Mailing Add:* Can Dept of Agr Res Sta 195 Dafoe Rd Winnipeg MB R3T 2M9 Can

DYCK, RUDOLPH HENRY, b Pasadena, Calif, Apr 17, 31; m 55; c 3. PHYSICAL CHEMISTRY. *Educ:* Univ Calif, BS, 52, PhD(chem), 56. *Prof Exp:* Mem tech staff, RCA Labs, 55-62; mem tech staff, 62-67, SECT MGR, OPTOELECTRONICS, FAIRCHILD RES & DEVELOP LAB, FAIRCHILD SEMICONDUCTOR, 67- *Mem:* AAAS; Am Phys Soc; Soc Photo-Optical Instrumentational Engrs. *Res:* Photosensitive devices, arrays and subsystems; light emitting diodes, arrays and subsystems. *Mailing Add:* 4001 Miranda Ave Palo Alto CA 94304

DYCK, WALTER PETER, b Winkler, Man, Dec 7, 35; m 65; c 4. INTERNAL MEDICINE, GASTROENTEROLOGY. *Educ:* Bethel Col, Kans, BA, 57; Univ Kans, MD, 61. *Prof Exp:* Intern & resident med, Henry Ford Hosp, Detroit, 61-63 & 65-66; INVESTR EXP PHYSIOL, SCOTT & WHITE MEM HOSP, 68-, SR STAFF CONSULT GASTROENTEROL, SCOTT & WHITE CLIN, 68-, DIR, DIV GASTROENTEROL, 73- *Concurrent Pos:* Res fel gastroenterol, Univ Zurich, 63-64; res fel gastrointestinal enzyme, Univ Toronto & Hosp for Sick Children, Toronto, 64-65; NIH trauma fel gastroenterol, Mt Sinai Sch Med, 66-68; consult, Vet Admin Ctr, Temple, Tex, 68- & Gen Med A Study Sect, NIH, 73-77; chmn dept res, Scott & White Clin, 70-73; clin instr internal med, Southwestern Med Sch, Univ Tex, 70- *Mem:* AMA; Am Fedn Clin Res; Am Gastroenterol Asn; Am Col Physicians; Soc Exp Biol & Med. *Res:* Hormonal control of pancreatic secretion; intestinal enzyme secretion; gastric secretion; peptic ulcer disease. *Mailing Add:* Dept Med Scott & White Clin 2401 S 31st St Temple TX 76501

DYCKES, DOUGLAS FRANZ, b New Haven, Conn, May 13, 42; m 67; c 2. BIOLOGICAL CHEMISTRY. *Educ:* Yale Univ, AB, 63; Case Western Reserve Univ, PhD(chem), 70. *Prof Exp:* Res assoc chem, Cornell Univ, 70-72; sci officer, MRC Lab Molecular Biol, 72-74; ASST PROF CHEM, UNIV HOUSTON, 74- *Mem:* AAAS; Am Chem Soc; Brit Chem Soc. *Res:* The synthesis, structure and basis of biological activity in naturally occurring peptides and proteins and their analogs. *Mailing Add:* Dept of Chem Univ of Houston Houston TX 77004

DYE, DAVID L, b Seattle, Wash, Aug 5, 25; m 52; c 3. PHYSICS. *Educ:* Univ Wash, BS, 45, PhD(physics), 52. *Prof Exp:* Res assoc, Radiol Lab, Med Ctr, Univ Calif, 54-55; chmn physics, Gordon Col, Rawalpindi, 55-58; res assoc, Radiol Lab, Med Ctr, Univ Calif, 58-59; res specialist, Aero-Space Div, Boeing Co, 59-62, chief radiation effects lab, 62-64, chief radiation effects unit, 64-68; sr scientist, Air Force Spec Weapons Ctr, 68-70; mem staff, Minuteman Physics Technol, 70-72, mgr, Minuteman Hardness Data Prog, 72-74, mgr energy systs, 74-77, NUCLEAR SCI, BOEING COMPUT SERV, 77- *Mem:* AAAS; Am Phys Soc; Inst Elec & Electronics Eng. *Res:* Radiation dosimetry and health physics; radiation effects on electronics components and systems; space radiation and nuclear physics; system survivability; nuclear reactor physics; fuel cycle technology; phyilosophy of science. *Mailing Add:* 12825 SE 45th Pl Bellevue WA 98006

DYE, FRANK J, b Bronx, NY, Jan 12, 42; m 67; c 2. DEVELOPMENTAL BIOLOGY. *Educ:* Danbury State Col, BS, 63; Fordham Univ, MS, 66, PhD(cytol), 69. *Prof Exp:* From instr to assoc prof, 67-78, PROF BIOL, WESTERN CONN STATE COL, 78- *Concurrent Pos:* Res assoc, New Eng Inst, 68-70, adj prof, 73; fel, Univ Conn Health Ctr, 75-76, vis assoc prof, 76-78. *Mem:* AAAS; Tissue Cult Asn; Am Inst Biol Scientists; Am Soc Zool; Sigma Xi. *Res:* Origin of tissue culture populations; morphogenesis; gene activation; in vitro movement of epithelial cells; tooth germ morphogenesis; purine metabolism. *Mailing Add:* Dept of Biol Western Conn State Col Danbury CT 06810

DYE, HENRY ABEL, b Dunkirk, NY, Feb 14, 26; m 78; c 2. MATHEMATICS. *Educ:* Univ Chicago, MS, 47, PhD(math), 50. *Prof Exp:* Bateman fel, Calif Inst Technol, 50-52; instr math, Calif Inst Technol, 52-53; mem sch math, Inst Adv Study, 53-54; asst prof math, Univ Iowa, 54-56; assoc prof, Univ Southern Calif, 56-59; assoc prof, Univ Iowa, 59-60; chmn dept, 75-78, PROF MATH, UNIV CALIF, LOS ANGELES, 60- *Mem:* Am Math Soc; Sigma Xi. *Res:* Functional analysis. *Mailing Add:* 7917 Math Sci Bldg Univ of Calif Los Angeles CA 90024

DYE, JAMES EUGENE, b Rock Springs, Wyo, Oct 17, 39. CLOUD PHYSICS, ATMOSPHERIC SCIENCES. *Educ:* Univ Wash, BS, 62, PhD(atmospheric sci), 67. *Prof Exp:* Res assoc, Dept Atmospheric Sci, Univ Wash, 62-67; res assoc, Inst Meteorol, Univ Stockholm, 67-68; asst prof, Atmospheric Simulation Lab, Dept Mech Eng, Colo State Univ, 69-70; SCIENTIST, NAT CTR ATMOSPHERIC RES, 70- *Concurrent Pos:* Fulbright travel grant, Comt Int Exchange Persons, Fulbright-Hays prog with Sweden, 67-68; affil prof, Colo State Univ, 72- *Mem:* Am Meteorol Soc. *Res:* Cloud and precipitation physics including weather modification; aerosol physics; meteorological instrumentation. *Mailing Add:* Nat Ctr for Atmospheric Res Box 3000 Boulder CO 80303

DYE, JAMES LOUIS, b Soudan, Minn, July 18, 27; m 48; c 3. PHYSICAL CHEMISTRY. *Educ:* Gustavus Adolphus Col, AB, 49; Iowa State Col, PhD(chem), 53. *Prof Exp:* Asst phys chem, Inst Atomic Res & Dept Chem, Iowa State Col, 49-53; PROF PHYS CHEM, MICH STATE UNIV, 53- *Concurrent Pos:* NSF sci fac fel, Max Planck Inst, Gottingen, Ger, 61-62; vis scientist, Ohio State Univ, 68-69; Fulbright res scholar & Guggenheim fel, 75-76. *Mem:* AAAS; Am Chem Soc. *Res:* Electrochemistry spectra rates of metal-amine solutions; kinetics of fast electron and proton transfers and enzymic transients; solvated electron and alkali metal anion properties in pure and mixed solvents. *Mailing Add:* Dept of Chem Mich State Univ East Lansing MI 48824

DYE, ROBERT F(ULTON), b Gloster, Miss, Oct 18, 20; m 47; c 3. CHEMICAL ENGINEERING. *Educ:* Miss State Univ, BS, 43; Ga Inst Tech, MS, 51, PhD(chem eng), 53. *Prof Exp:* Chem engr, Inorg & Org Res, Monsanto Chem Co, 46-49; asst, Chem Eng Dept, Ga Inst Technol, 50-51 & 52-53; sr process & design proj engr, Process Develop Div, Phillips Petrol Co, 53-62; dir, Miss Indust & Technol Res Comn, 62-65; STAFF ENGR, SHELL OIL CO, 65- *Mem:* AAAS; Am Chem Soc; Am Inst Chem Engrs; NY Acad Sci. *Res:* Gas diffusion; diffusional processes; chemical technology; applied economics. *Mailing Add:* Shell Oil Co PO Box 3105 Houston TX 77001

DYE, WILLIAM THOMSON, JR, b Chattanooga, Tenn, July 8, 18; m 44; c 2. ORGANIC CHEMISTRY. *Educ:* Univ NC, BS, 40, PhD(org chem), 44. *Prof Exp:* Res chemist, Naval Res Lab, DC, 44-46; res chemist, Monsanto Chem Co, 47-52; res chemist, Chemstrand Corp, 52-58, group leader, 58-60; group leader, Chemstrand Res Ctr, Inc, Monsanto Co, 60-70; MGR PATENT LIAISON, BURLINGTON INDUSTS CORP RES & DEVELOP, 70- *Mem:* Am Chem Soc; Am Asn Textile Chemists & Colorists. *Res:* Organic phosphorus compounds; synthetic fibers; textiles; patent liaison. *Mailing Add:* Burlington Indust Corp R&D PO Box 21327 Greensboro NC 27420

DYER, ALAN RICHARD, b Seattle, Wash, Aug 19, 45. BIOSTATISTICS. *Educ:* Stanford Univ, BS, 67; Univ Chicago, MS, 68, PhD(statist), 72. *Prof Exp:* Asst prof, 72-77, ASSOC PROF COMMUNITY HEALTH & PREV MED, MED SCH, NORTHWESTERN UNIV, 77- *Mem:* Am Statist Asn; Biomet Soc; Am Heart Asn. *Res:* Epidemiology; cardiovascular disease. *Mailing Add:* Dept Community Health & Prev Med Northwestern Univ Med Sch Chicago IL 60611

DYER, ALLAN EDWIN, b Toronto, Ont, Aug 23, 23; m 44; c 4. PHARMACOLOGY. *Educ:* Univ Toronto, PhmB, 49, PhD(pharmacol), 55, MD, 67; Univ Buffalo, BSc, 51. *Prof Exp:* Res assoc & head bioassay dept, Connaught Med Res Labs, 56-67; intern, Toronto Western Hosp, 67-68; chief drugs & biol, 68-75, dir drugs & therapeut, 75-77, exec chmn, Area Planning Coordr, 77-78, ASST DEP MINISTER, INSTNL HEALTH SERV, ONT MINISTRY OF HEALTH, 74- *Concurrent Pos:* Can Life Ins Off Asn fel, Univ Toronto, 54-56, univ fel, 55-56. *Mem:* Pharmacol Soc Can; Can Fedn Biol Soc. *Res:* Methodology for screening and assessing pharmacological and toxicological activity. *Mailing Add:* W-980 Hepburn Block Ministry of Health Toronto Can

DYER, CHARLES CHESTER, b Sutton, Que, June 8, 46. COSMOLOGY. *Educ:* Bishop's Univ, Que, BSc, 68; Univ Toronto, MSc, 69, PhD(astron), 73. *Prof Exp:* Vis astron, Kitt Peak Nat Observ, 71-72; sr visitor, Inst Astron, Univ Cambridge, Eng, 73-75; instr & res assoc, 75-78, ASST PROF DEPT ASTRON, UNIV TORONTO, 78- *Concurrent Pos:* Univ res fel, 80- *Mem:* Can Astron Soc; Int Soc Gen Relativity & Gravitation; Royal Astron Soc. *Res:* Optics in general relativity and its application to problems in observational cosmology; gravitational lenses and applications. *Mailing Add:* Div Phys Sci Scarborough Col Univ Toronto West Hill Can

DYER, CHARLES ROBERT, b Gilroy, Calif, Mar 14, 51; m 79. IMAGE PROCESSING, COMPUTER VISION. *Educ:* Stanford Univ, BS, 73; Univ Calif, Los Angeles, MS, 74; Univ Md, PhD(comput sci), 79. *Prof Exp:* Grad res asst, Univ Calif, Los Angeles, 74; grad res asst, Comput Sci Ctr, Univ Md, 75-76, fac res asst, 76-79, fac res assoc, 79; ASST PROF COMPUT SCI, DEPT INFO ENG, UNIV ILL, CHICAGO, 79- *Concurrent Pos:* Consult, Imtech, Inc, 76-79, NIH, 79-81 & Int Harvester, 81- *Mem:* Asn Comput Mach; Am Asn Artificial Intel; Inst Elec & Electronics Engrs; Asn Comput Mach. *Res:* Parallel algorithms and computer architectures for image processing and scene analysis; hierarchial representation techniques for computer vision; texture analysis; very large scale integration systems for computer vision applications. *Mailing Add:* Dept Info Eng Univ Ill Chicago Circle Box 4348 Chicago IL 60680

DYER, DENZEL LEROY, b McCool Jct, Nebr, Oct 12, 29; m 52; c 3. CHEMISTRY. *Educ:* York Col, BS, 50; Univ Nebr, MS, 53, PhD(chem), 55. *Prof Exp:* Chemist, Dow Chem Co, 55-59; assoc res scientist, Life Sci Dept, Martin Marietta Corp, 59-64; prin scientist, Life Sci Dept, Northrop Corp Labs, 64-69; OWNER, DYER LABS, 69- *Mem:* Am Chem Soc; Am Soc Microbiol; Soc Indust Microbiol; Consult Chemists Asn (pres, 70-75); Soc Photo-optical Instrumentation Engineers. *Res:* Microbiology; microbial physiology and chemistry. *Mailing Add:* Suite 311 2675 Skypark Dr Torrance CA 90505

DYER, DONALD CHESTER, b Great Bend, Kans, July 8, 39; m 59; c 2. PHARMACOLOGY. *Educ:* Univ Kans, BS, 61, PhD(pharmacol), 65. *Prof Exp:* Asst prof pharmacol, Ore State Univ, 67-68; from asst prof to assoc prof, Sch Med, Univ Wash, 68-7S; assoc prof, 75-80, PROF VET PHYSIOL & PHARMACOL & CHMN DEPT, IOWA STATE UNIV, 80- *Concurrent Pos:* Fel pharmacol, Univ Man, 65-67. *Mem:* AAAS; Am Soc Pharmacol & Exp Therapeut; Western Pharmacol Soc. *Res:* Polypeptides; smooth muscle stimulating lipids; hallucinogens; autonomic drugs; fetal pharmacology. *Mailing Add:* Dept Vel Physiol & Pharmacol Iowa State Univ Col of Vet Med Ames IA 50011

DYER, ELDON, mathematics, see previous edition

DYER, ELIZABETH, b Haverhill, Mass, May 10, 06. ORGANIC CHEMISTRY. *Educ:* Mt Holyoke Col, AB, 27, AM, 29; Yale Univ, PhD(chem), 31. *Prof Exp:* Asst chem, Mt Holyoke Col, 27-29; asst chem, Yale Univ, 29-31, Chem Found fel, 31-33; from instr to prof chem, 33-71, EMER PROF CHEM, UNIV DEL, 71- *Mem:* Am Chem Soc. *Res:* Polymers; isocyanates; pyrimidines and purines. *Mailing Add:* 232 Cheltenham Rd Newark DE 19711

DYER, FRANK FALKONER, b Webbers Falls, Okla, Nov 18, 31; m 57; c 2. ANALYTICAL CHEMISTRY, NUCLEONICS. *Educ:* Okla State Univ, BS, 53, MS, 55; Univ Tenn, PhD(chem), 58. *Prof Exp:* Chemist, Pan Am Petrol Corp, 58-60; CHEMIST, OAK RIDGE NAT LAB, 60- *Mem:* Am Chem Soc. *Res:* Gamma-ray spectroscopy; evaluation of condition and performance of nuclear reactor fuel; radiochemistry; activation analysis; diffusion processes; fission product behavior; nuclear safety. *Mailing Add:* 4417 Crestfield Rd Knoxville TN 37921

DYER, HUBERT JEROME, b Daylesford, Australia, June 4, 14; US citizen; m 41; c 2. BOTANY. *Educ:* Univ Chicago, SB, 39, SM, 40, PhD(plant physiol), 46. *Prof Exp:* Qual control res, Libby, McNeill & Libby, Ill, 43-47, head res dept, 47-48; from instr to assoc prof bot, 48-72; prof, 72-79, EMER PROF BIOL, BROWN UNIV, 79- *Mem:* AAAS; Am Soc Plant Physiol; Bot Soc Am. *Res:* Effects of ultrasound. *Mailing Add:* Div of Biol & Med Sci Brown Univ Providence RI 02912

DYER, IRA, b Brooklyn, NY, June 14, 25; m 49; c 2. ACOUSTICS. *Educ:* Mass Inst Technol, SB, 49, SM, 51, PhD(acoustics), 54. *Prof Exp:* Asst physics, Mass Inst Technol, 49-51; acoust scientist, Bolt Beranek & Newman Inc, 51-61, vpres & dir phys sci, 61-71, dir prog advan study, 64-67; dept head, 71-81 PROF OCEAN ENG, MASS INST TECHNOL, 71- *Concurrent Pos:* Assoc dir and dir sea grant prog, Mass Inst Technol, 72-75; chmn, res adv comt, US Coast Guard, 75-79; mem, Bd Visitors, Maine Maritime Acad, 73-81, mem, Marine Bd, Nat Res Coun, 78-81. *Honors & Awards:* Acoust Soc Am Biennial Award, 60. *Mem:* Nat Acad Eng; fel Acoust Soc Am; Soc Naval Architects & Marine Engineers; fel AAAS; fel Inst Elec & Electronics Engrs. *Res:* Acoustic waves and vibrations; acoustic scattering and diffraction; noise of aerodynamic origin; structure-borne sound; underwater acoustics; Arctic Ocean acoustics; oceanographic engineering; ocean environmental acoustics; sonar engineering. *Mailing Add:* 26 Valleyspring Rd Newton MA 02158

DYER, IRWIN ALLEN, animal science, see previous edition

DYER, JAMES ARTHUR, b San Antonio, Tex, Feb 10, 32; m 53. MATHEMATICS. *Educ:* Univ Tex, BS, 52, MA, 54, PhD(math), 60. *Prof Exp:* Res scientist physics, Defense Res Lab, Univ Tex, 54-58, asst prof math, Univ, 60-61; asst prof, Univ Ariz, 61-62; from asst prof to assoc prof, Southern Methodist Univ, 62-65; assoc prof, 66-70, PROF MATH, IOWA STATE UNIV, 70- *Mem:* Math Asn Am; Soc Indust & Appl Math; Inst Elec & Electronics Engineers. *Res:* Integration; functional analysis; integral equations; signal processing. *Mailing Add:* Dept of Math Iowa State Univ Ames IA 50010

DYER, JAMES LEE, b Long Beach, Calif, Sept 2, 34; m 60. ENGINEERING. *Educ:* Univ Calif, Los Angeles, BS, 57, MS, 60, PhD(eng), 65. *Prof Exp:* Teaching fel eng, Univ Calif, Los Angeles, 65; mem tech staff, TRW Systs, 65-66; from asst prof to assoc prof, 66-76, chmn dept, 70-74, PROF MECH ENG, CALIF STATE UNIV, LONG BEACH, 76- *Mem:* AAAS. *Res:* Thermodynamics of phase changes and irreversible processes. *Mailing Add:* Dept of Mech Eng 1250 Bellflower Blvd Long Beach CA 90840

DYER, JOAN L, b Brooklyn, NY, Aug 4, 41; m 67. MATHEMATICS. *Educ:* Barnard Col, Columbia Univ, AB, 61; NY Univ, PhD(math), 65. *Prof Exp:* Vis lectr, Sch Gen Studies, Australian Nat Univ, 65; Ritt instr math, Columbia Univ, 65-67; asst prof, 67-71, assoc prof, 71-77, PROF, MATH, LEHMAN COL & GRAD CTR, CITY UNIV NEW YORK, 78- *Mem:* Am Math Soc. *Res:* Residual properties of polycyclic groups and generalized free products with amalgamations; automorphisms of groups. *Mailing Add:* Dept Math Herbert H Leman Col Bedford Park Blvd W Bronx NY 10468

DYER, JOHN, b Beckenham, Eng, June 8, 35; nat US; m 64; c 2. POLYMER CHEMISTRY. *Educ:* ARIC, 59; Univ Manchester, PhD(chem), 64. *Prof Exp:* Lab asst, Brit Nylon Spinners, 52-57, res asst, 57-58, asst tech officer, 59; res chemist, Am Viscose Div, FMC Corp, 64-68, sr res chemist, 68-74, res assoc, Fiber Div, 74-76; res assoc, 77, Eastern Res Div, ITT Rayonier Inc, 77, mgr appl res, 78-81; STAFF SCIENTIST, JOHNSON & JOHNSON PROD, INC, 82- *Honors & Awards:* Fiber Soc Award, 73. *Mem:* Am Chem Soc; Fiber Soc. *Res:* Cellulose and viscose rayon; thiocarbonates, reaction mechanisms and kinetics; fibers, polymers, characterization and applications; technical-economic investigations of process and product development projects; pollution chemistry; nonwovens, personal care and wound dressings. *Mailing Add:* 57 Meadowbrook Rd Randolph NJ 07869

DYER, JOHN H, b Kent, England, Feb 12, 29; m 54; c 1. PHYSICAL CHEMISTRY, FIRE EXTINGUISHMENT. *Educ:* Univ Manchester, BS, 61, MS, 65; Univ London, PhD(phys sci), 67. *Prof Exp:* Group coord chemist formulation, Indestructible Paints Ltd, 51-58; tech mgr fire sci, Timber Fireproofing Co, 58-66; consult, Fire Protection Indust, 66-72; head fire technol, Graviner Ltd, subsid Wilkinson Match, 72-75; DIR CORP RES & DEVELOP, FIRE SCI, ANSUL CO, 75-, CORP DIR, CENT TECH SERV, 80- *Concurrent Pos:* UK deleg, Eur Econ Community Tech Comt Fire Standards, 70-75; USA deleg, Int Stand Orgn Comts, 71. *Honors & Awards:* Gold Medallist, Royal Soc Humanities, 71. *Mem:* Nat Fire Protection Asn; fel Inst Fire Engrs. *Res:* Detection and extinguishment of fires and explosions; professional research and development management; product safety research and evaluations. *Mailing Add:* Ansul Co One Stanton St Marinette WI 54143

DYER, JOHN KAYE, b Portland, Maine, Jan 25, 35; m 63; c 2. MICROBIOLOGY, IMMUNOLOGY. *Educ:* Eastern NMex Univ, BS, 63; Ore State Univ, MS, 65, PhD(microbiol), 67; Registry Med Technol, cert, 59; Nat Registry Microbiologists, cert pub health & med lab microbiol, 74. *Prof Exp:* Med technologist, Borgess Hosp, Kalamazoo, Mich, 59-63; res assoc microbiol, Mich State Univ, 67-69; ASSOC PROF MICROBIOL, DEPT ORAL BIOL, COL DENT, UNIV NEBR-LINCOLN, 69- *Concurrent Pos:* Nat Inst Dent Res spec dent res award grant, Col Dent, Univ Nebr-Lincoln, 73-76; consult, Vet Admin Hosp, Lincoln, Nebr, 72- *Mem:* Am Soc Microbiol; Am Soc Clin Pathologists; Int Asn Dent Res. *Res:* Metabolism in anaerobic bacteria; identification of anaerobic bacteria; hypersensitivity immune responses against bacterial antigens as associated with periodontal disease. *Mailing Add:* Dept of Oral Biol Univ of Nebr Col of Dent Lincoln NE 68583

DYER, JOHN NORVELL, b Norfolk, Va, July 19, 30; m 51; c 2. NUCLEAR PHYSICS. *Educ:* Univ Calif, Berkeley, AB, 56, PhD(physics), 61. *Prof Exp:* From asst prof to assoc prof, 61-69, PROF PHYSICS, NAVAL POSTGRAD SCH, 69-, CHMN DEPT, 79- *Concurrent Pos:* Consult, Lawrence Radiation lab, Univ Calif, 61-65 & Aerospace Corp, Calif, 63-64. *Mem:* Am Phys Soc; Sigma Xi. *Res:* Electron scattering; linear accelerators; nuclear resonances; electron energy loss in matter; radiation effects. *Mailing Add:* Dept Physics & Chem Naval Postgrad Sch Monterey CA 93940

DYER, JUDITH GRETCHEN, b New York, NY, Apr 27, 37; m 62; c 1. ENTOMOLOGY. *Educ:* Bethany Col, WVa, BA, 58; William Paterson Col NJ, MS, 71; Rutgers Univ, PhD, 75. *Prof Exp:* Ed, Int Tel & Tel, 60-62; asst prof biol, St Peter's Col, NJ, 74-78; AGR TECH ED/WRITER, AM CYANAMID CO, 79- *Mem:* Entom Soc Am. *Res:* Arrhenotokous reproduction in Phytoseiid mites; environmental effects on mite populations; distribution and abundance of predatory mites. *Mailing Add:* 123 Lakeshore Dr Oakland NJ 07436

DYER, LAWRENCE D, b Los Angeles, Calif, Sept 3, 30; m 52; c 3. PHYSICAL CHEMISTRY. *Educ:* Calif Inst Technol, BS, 51; Univ Va, PhD(phys chem), 57. *Prof Exp:* Eng asst, Helipot Corp, 49-50; chem asst org chem, US Naval Ord Test Sta, Calif, 51; jr chemist fused hydroxide corrosion, Oak Ridge Nat Lab, 51-53; sr res phys chemist, Res Labs, Gen Motors Corp, 57-66; MEM TECH STAFF, TEX INSTRUMENTS INC, 66- *Mem:* Electrochem Soc; Am Asn Crystal Growth; Am Chem Soc. *Res:* Surface physics and chemistry; friction and wear; fused salts and hydroxides; crystal growth of copper and silicon; silicon epitaxial growth; plastic deformation in copper and silicon. *Mailing Add:* 905 Waterview Circle Dallas TX 75218

DYER, MELVIN I, zoology, see previous edition

DYER, PEGGY LYNN, b Bryan, Tex, Sept 13, 46. NUCLEAR PHYSICS. *Educ:* Univ Tex, Austin, BS, 68; Calif Inst Technol, PhD(physics), 73. *Prof Exp:* Res fel, Kellogg Radiation Lab, Calif Inst Technol, 73-74; res assoc, Nuclear Physics Lab, Univ Wash, 74-77; asst prof physics, Cyclotron Lab, Mich State Univ, 77-81; STAFF MEM, LOS ALAMOS NAT LAB,, 81- *Concurrent Pos:* Mem comt nuclear sci, Nat Res Coun, 74-77. *Mem:* Am Phys Soc. *Res:* Experimental nuclear astrophysics, heavy ion physics, weak interaction physics; laser spectroscopy. *Mailing Add:* MS-442 Los Alamos Nat Lab Los Alamos NM 87545

DYER, RANDOLPH H, b Ft Smith, Ark, Oct 31, 40; m 64; c 2. BIOCHEMISTRY. *Educ:* Transylvania Col, AB, 62. *Prof Exp:* Chemist, Melpar Inc, Va, 63-66; CHEMIST, ALCOHOL, TOBACCO & FIREARMS LAB, US TREASURY DEPT, 66- *Mem:* Asn Off Anal Chemists; Am Soc Brewing Chemists; Am Soc Enol; Int Food Technol. *Res:* Analytical chemistry and biochemistry, especially enzymes and fermentation processes and products. *Mailing Add:* 8504 Georgan Place Annandale VA 22003

DYER, ROBERT FRANK, b Sewickley, Pa, Apr 21, 37; m 60; c 3. ANATOMY, CELL BIOLOGY. *Educ:* Geneva Col, BS, 59; Univ Pittsburgh, PhD(anat, cell biol), 66. *Prof Exp:* From instr to asst prof, 66-73, assoc prof, 73-77, PROF ANAT, SCH MED, LA STATE UNIV, 77- *Concurrent Pos:* Edward G Schlieder Educ Found grant, 70-76; HEW Fogarty Int Sr Fel, MRC Group Peridont Physiol, Fac of Dent, Univ Toronto, 78-79; consult cell biol, USPHS Hosp, Carville. *Mem:* Am Asn Anatomists; Electron Micros Soc Am; Pan-Am Asn Anatomists. *Res:* Morphology of female reproductive systems; morphology of connective tissue cells and fibers; effect of sex hormones on rat peridontium and gingiva. *Mailing Add:* Dept of Anat La State Univ Med Ctr New Orleans LA 70112

DYER, ROLLA MCINTYRE, JR, b Elizabethtown, Ky, Dec 30, 22; m 47; c 3. ANALYTICAL CHEMISTRY. *Educ:* Univ Louisville, PhD, 63. *Prof Exp:* Instr chem, Campbellsville Col, 59-60; vis instr, Univ Louisville, 60-63; asst prof, Northeast La Univ, 63-67; from asst prof to assoc prof, 67-71, PROF CHEM, IND STATE UNIV, EVANSVILLE, 71- *Res:* Separation and identification of components of complex mixtures; design and preparation of instructional models especially three dimensional magnetic field maps. *Mailing Add:* Div of Sci & Math Ind State Univ Evansville IN 47712

DYER, WILLIAM GERALD, b Boston, Mass, Oct 27, 29; m 65; c 2. HELMINTHOLOGY. *Educ:* Boston Univ, AB, 57, AM, 58; Colo State Univ, PhD(parasitol), 65. *Prof Exp:* Res asst endocrinol, Worcester Found Exp Biol, 58-60; res asst biochem, Harvard Med Sch, 60-62; asst prof, Minot State Col, 65-66, assoc prof, 66-67, prof zool & head, Dept Biol, 67-69; asst prof, 69-72, assoc prof, 72-75, asst dean, Col Sci, 75-76, PROF ZOOL & ASSOC DEAN, SOUTHERN ILL UNIV, 76- *Mem:* Am Soc Parasitol; Wildlife Dis Asn; Am Inst Biol Sci. *Res:* Taxonomy; ecology. *Mailing Add:* Dept of Zool Southern Ill Univ Carbondale IL 62901

DYER, WILLIAM JOHN, b Antigonish, NS, Oct 30, 13; m 44; c 4. BIOCHEMISTRY. *Educ:* St Francis Xavier Univ, BSc, 34; McGill Univ, MSc, 37, PhD, 40. *Prof Exp:* Analyst soil surv & soil anal, NS Agr Col, 34-35; asst soil res, Nat Res Coun Can, Macdonald Col, McGill Univ, 36-39, analyst gen res, 39-40; jr biochemist, Forest Prod Lab, Dept Mines & Forests, Ottawa, 40; biochemist, Fisheries Res Bd Can, 40-64, prin biochemist, 64-75, prog mgr, 72-74, consult, Halifax Lab, 75-78; RETIRED. *Honors & Awards:* Merit Award, Pub Serv Can, 74. *Mem:* Fel Chem Inst Can; mem emeritus, Can Inst Food Sci & Technol. *Res:* Quality changes in frozen fish; antemortem and postmortem biochemical changes relating to product quality; minced fish products utilization. *Mailing Add:* Halifax Lab Dartmouth NS B2Y 3A2 Can

DYER-BENNET, JOHN, b Leicester, Eng, Apr 17, 15; nat US; m 51; c 2. ALGEBRA. *Educ:* Univ Calif, AB, 36; Harvard Univ, MA, 39, PhD(math), 40. *Prof Exp:* Asst math, Univ Calif, 36-37; instr, Vanderbilt Univ, 40-41 & 45-46; from instr to assoc prof, Purdue Univ, 46-60; assoc prof, 60-65, chmn dept math & astron, 64-66, prof, 65-80, EMER PROF MATH, CARLETON COL, 80- *Concurrent Pos:* NSF faculty fel, Switz, 58-59. *Mem:* Am Math Soc; Math Asn Am. *Res:* Abstract algebra. *Mailing Add:* Dept Math Carleton Col Northfield MN 55057

DYKE, ARTHUR SILAS, b Eastport, Nfld, Nov 26, 50. GEOMORPHOLOGY. *Educ:* Mem Univ Nfld, BSc, 72; Univ Colo, MA, 74, PhD(geomorphol), 77. *Prof Exp:* PHYS SCIENTIST SURFICIAL GEOL, GEOL SURV OF CAN, 75- *Mem:* Am Quaternary Asn. *Res:* Glacial, sea-level, and climatic history of Arctic Canada, and application of surficial geological mapping to land use and resource development problems. *Mailing Add:* Terrain Sci Div 601 Booth St Ottawa Can

DYKE, BENNETT, US citizen. BIOLOGICAL ANTHROPOLOGY, HUMAN GENETICS. *Educ:* Trinity Col, BA, 55; Univ Mich, PhD, 68. *Prof Exp:* Instr anthrop, Bucknell Univ, 64-70; asst prof anthrop, Pa State Univ, 70-74, assoc prof, 74-81; ASSOC SCIENTIST, SOUTHWEST FOUND RES & EDUC, SAN ANTONIO, 81- *Concurrent Pos:* Pop Coun fel, 69-70. *Mem:* AAAS; Am Soc Human Genetics; Am Asn Phys Anthrop; Soc Study Human Biol. *Res:* Genetic demography; computer simulation of human populations; population genetics. *Mailing Add:* SW Found Res & Educ PO Box 28147 San Antonio TX 78284

DYKE, MAURICE ARTHUR, b Winfield, Kans, Oct 15, 37. INDUSTRIAL HYGIENE CHEMISTRY. *Educ:* NTex State Univ, BS, 61, MS, 62; Rice Univ, PhD(phys chem), 66. *Prof Exp:* Asst prof chem, Sam Houston State Univ, 66-70; chemist, Anal Lab, Occupational Safety & Health Admin, 71-79, indust hygienist, 79-81; OCCUPATIONAL HEALTH LAB MGR, CONTINENTAL NAT AM INSURANCE CO, 81- *Mem:* Am Acad Indust Hyg; Am Indust Hyg Asn; Soc Appl Spectroscopy; Am Crystallog Asn. *Res:* Determination of crystal and molecular structures by x-ray crystallography; development of analytical procedures for chemical health hazards; development of computer programs and interfaces for chemical calculations and acquiring data from analytical instrumentation. *Mailing Add:* PO Box A3687 Chicago IL 60690

DYKE, RICHARD WARREN, b Chicago, Ill, Oct 22, 22; m 47; c 6. MEDICINE, HEMATOLOGY. *Educ:* Ind Univ, AB, 44, MD, 46; Am Bd Internal Med, dipl, 55. *Prof Exp:* Intern, Marion County Gen Hosp, Indianapolis, Ind, 46-47, resident, 49-53, dir med educ, 53-59; from instr to assoc prof, 53-72, PROF MED, SCH MED, IND UNIV, INDIANAPOLIS, 72-; CICLIN PHARMACOLOGIST, LILLY LABS CLIN RES, ELI LILLY & CO, WISHARD MEM HOSP, 69- *Concurrent Pos:* Dir poison control ctr, 55-69, clin dir internal med, Marion County Gen Hosp, 59-69, chmn formulary comn, 63-68. *Mem:* Fel Am Col Physicians; AMA; Am Soc Hemat. *Res:* Clinical research in cancer chemotherapy. *Mailing Add:* 542 W 83rd St Indianapolis IN 46260

DYKE, THOMAS ROBERT, b Akron, Ohio, Dec 16, 44; m 70; c 1. PHYSICAL CHEMISTRY. *Educ:* Col Wooster, BA, 66; Harvard Univ, MA & PhD(chem), 72. *Prof Exp:* Fel chem, Univ Rochester, 71-74; asst prof, 74-80, ASSOC PROF CHEM, UNIV ORE, 80- *Mem:* Am Chem Soc; Am Phys Soc. *Res:* Molecular beam spectroscopy; electric resonance spectroscopy and electric deflection studies of hydrogen-bonded molecules and of excited vibrational states of small molecules; energy transfer in molecular beam solid-surface interactions. *Mailing Add:* Dept of Chem Univ of Ore Eugene OR 97403

DYKEN, MARK LEWIS, b Laramie, Wyo, Aug 26, 28; m 51; c 6. MEDICINE, NEUROLOGY. *Educ:* Ind Univ, BS, 51, MD, 54. *Prof Exp:* Resident neurol, Med Ctr, Ind Univ, 55-58; clin dir & dir res, New Castle State Hosp, 58-61; from asst to assoc prof, 61-69, prin investr & dir, Cerebral Vascular Clin Res Ctr, 66-74, PROF NEUROL, SCH MED, IND UNIV, INDIANAPOLIS, 69-, CHMN DEPT, 71- *Concurrent Pos:* Med dir, Ind Mult Sclerosis Soc Clin, 61-; asst dir, Multicategorical Clin Res Facil, Ind, 62-66; consult, Cerebral Palsy Clin, 61-70; mem adv comt, Neurol Sensory Dis Serv Prog, Bur State Serv, USPHS, 64-67; mem bd dirs, Ind Neuromuscular Res Lab, 65-; dir, Ind Regional Med Stroke Prog, 68; mem clin mgt study group & mem epidemiol study group, Joint Comt Stroke Facil, 70-73. *Mem:* AMA; fel Am Acad Neurol; Asn Res Nerv & Ment Dis. *Res:* Cerebrovascular disease; epilepsy; muscle disease; changes in brain and vasculature following injury early in life; demyelinating diseases. *Mailing Add:* Dept Neurol Ind Univ Sch Med Indianapolis IN 46223

DYKEN, PAUL RICHARD, b Casper, Wyo, Mar 14, 34; c 3. PEDIATRICS, NEUROLOGY. *Educ:* Ind Univ, BA, 56, MD, 59; Am Bd Psychiat & Neurol, dipl, 66. *Prof Exp:* Intern, Philadelphia Gen Hosp, Pa, 59-60; resident neurol, Ind Univ & Affiliated Hosps, 60-63; from asst prof to assoc prof pediat neurol, Med Ctr, Ind Univ, Indianapolis, 65-69; from assoc prof to prof neurol & pediat, Med Col Wis, 69-72, dir pediat neurol, 69-72, head dept neurol, 71-72; PROF & CHIEF PEDIAT NEUROL, MED COL TALMADGE HOSP, 72- *Concurrent Pos:* Fel neurophysiol, Barnes Hosp, Washington Univ, 63-64; fel pediat neurol, Univ Chicago, 64-65; chief neurologist, Milwaukee Children's Hosp, 69-72; consult, Southern Wis Colony, 69-72, Milwaukee County Gen Hosp, 69-72 & Woods Vet Hosp, 71-72; asst examr, Study Sect Develop Behav Sci, 74- *Mem:* AAAS; Asn Res Nerv & Ment Dis; Am Neurol Asn; fel Am Acad Neurol; Child Neurol Soc. *Res:* Central nervous system degenerative disease; child neurology; cerebral spinal fluid; electroencephalography. *Mailing Add:* Sect Pediat Neurol Med Col Ga Augusta GA 30912

DYKES, ROBERT WILLIAM, b Portland, Ore, Apr 5, 43; m 66; c 3. NEUROPHYSIOLOGY. *Educ:* Univ Calif, Berkeley, BA, 65; Johns Hopkins Univ, PhD(physiol), 70. *Prof Exp:* Asst prof, 71-76, assoc prof sensory neurophysiol, Dalhousie Univ, 76-78; ASSOC PROF SURG & PHYSIOL, NEUROL & NEUROSURG, MCGILL UNIV & MONTREAL NEUROL INST, 78- *Concurrent Pos:* NIH fel, New York Med Col, 70-71; assoc dir of microsurg Res Labs, Royal Victoria Hosp, 78-; Killiam res scholar, 78-80. *Mem:* Can Physiol Soc; Soc Neurosci; Can Philos Soc. *Res:* Somatosensory neurophysiology, especially peripheral nerve injuries, and cortical somatotopic organization. *Mailing Add:* Dept Neurol & Neurosurg McGill Univ Montreal PQ H3A 2T5 Can

DYKHUIZEN, DANIEL EDWARD, b Muskegon, Mich, Oct 31, 42; m 68; c 3. GENETICS, EVOLUTION. *Educ:* Stanford Univ, BS, 65; Univ Chicago, PhD(biol), 71. *Prof Exp:* Fel bact genetics, Stanford Univ, 71-72; res fel genetics, Australian Nat Univ, 72-76; res scientist pop genetics, Purdue Univ, 76-81; ASSOC RES PROF, WASH UNIV, 81- *Mem:* Genetics Soc Am; Soc Study Evolution; Am Soc Microbiol; AAAS. *Res:* Experimental study of natural selection using laboratory strains of E Coli. *Mailing Add:* Dept Genetics Box 8031 Wash Univ Med Sch St Louis MO 63110

DYKLA, JOHN J, b Chicago, Ill, July 15, 44; m 81. THEORETICAL ASTROPHYSICS. *Educ:* Loyola Univ Chicago, BS, 66; Calif Inst Technol, PhD(physics), 72. *Prof Exp:* Res assoc physics, Univ Tex, Austin, 71-73; asst prof, 73-77, ASSOC PROF PHYSICS, LOYOLA UNIV CHICAGO, 77- *Concurrent Pos:* Regional sci adv, Univ Tex, Austin, 71-73; res grant, Loyola Univ Chicago, 78. *Mem:* Am Asn Physics Teachers; AAAS; Sigma Xi. *Res:* General relativistic astrophysics, especially black holes in space and cosmology; interpretation of exact solutions of Einstein's gravitational field equations; astrophysical implications of alternate relativistic gravitational theories. *Mailing Add:* Dept Physics 6525 N Sheridan Rd Chicago IL 60626

DYKMAN, ROSCOE A, b Pocatello, Idaho, Mar 20, 20; m 44, 80; c 4. PSYCHOPHYSIOLOGY. *Educ:* PhD(human develop), 49. *Prof Exp:* Instr psychol, Ill Inst Technol, 47-50; USPHS fel, Johns Hopkins Hosp, 50-52, instr psychiat, 52-53; asst dir studies, Asn Am Med Cols, 53-55; assoc prof psychol, 55-61, PROF PSYCHOL, MED CTR, UNIV ARK, 61-, PROF & HEAD, DIV BEHAV SCI, 75- *Mem:* Am Psychol Asn; Soc Psychophysiol Res. *Res:* Clinical child psychology; learning. *Mailing Add:* Slot 588 Dept Psychiat Univ Ark Med Sci Little Rock AR 72201

DYKSTERHUIS, EDSKO JERRY, b Hospers, Iowa, Dec 27, 08; m 33; c 3. RANGE ECOLOGY. *Educ:* Iowa State Col, BS, 32; Univ Nebr, PhD(bot), 45. *Prof Exp:* Field asst, Powell Nat Forest, Utah, 30; jr forester, Nat Forests, NMex, 33-34 & Southwestern Forest & Range Exp Sta, US Forest Serv, 34; jr range exam & sr forest ranger, Crook Nat Forest, Ariz, 34-35; asst range exam, Carson Nat Forest, NMex, 35-38; assoc range exam, Southern Forest Exp Sta, Tex, 38-39; sr flood control rep, US Forest Serv, Kans & Ozarks, 39-41; range conservationist, US Soil Conserv Serv, Tex, Okla, La & Ark, 43-49, head range conservationist, Mont, Wyo, NDak, SDak & Nebr, 49-64; prof range ecol, 64-70, EMER PROF RANGE ECOL, TEX A&M UNIV, 71-; CONSULT NATURAL FORAGES, AID, US DEPT STATE, 71- *Concurrent Pos:* Vis prof, Mont State, 50; mem Nat Resources Coun, 51-52; bot assoc ed, Ecol Monogr, 59-61; vis prof, Kans State Univ, 62; exten range specialist, SDak State Univ, 64. *Honors & Awards:* Mercer Award, Ecol Soc Am, 49; Authorship Award, USDA, 57, Merit Award, 58; Merit Award Superior Leadership, US Soil Conserv Serv, 64; Outstanding achievement award, Am Soc Range Mgt, 67; Prof Conservationist Award, Am Motors Corp, 72. *Mem:* Fel AAAS; Am Inst Biol Sci; Soil Conserv Soc Am; Ecol Soc Am; fel, Am Soc Range Mgt (pres, 68). *Res:* Prairie and savanna rangelands in relation to soils, climate, fire and grazing. *Mailing Add:* 3807 Oaklawn Bryan TX 77801

DYKSTRA, CLIFFORD ELLIOT, b Chicago, Ill, Oct 30, 52. PHYSICAL CHEMISTRY, THEORETICAL CHEMISTRY. *Educ:* Univ Ill, Urbana-Champaign, BS, 73; Univ Calif, Berkeley, PhD(chem), 76. *Prof Exp:* Res assoc, Univ Calif, Berkeley, 76-77; ASST PROF CHEM, UNIV ILL, URBANA-CHAMPAIGN, 77- *Concurrent Pos:* Consult, Theoret Chem Group, Chem Div, Argonne Nat Lab, 78-80. *Mem:* Am Chem Soc: Am Phys Soc. *Res:* Theoretical molecular electronic structure; electron pair theories; electron correlation effects in chemical systems: rearrangement reactions, organic anions, instellar molecules, and small molecular clusters. *Mailing Add:* Sch of Chem Sci Univ Ill Urbana IL 61801

DYKSTRA, DEWEY IRWIN, JR, b Baltimore, Md, June 13, 47; m 69; c 1. PHYSICS EDUCATION, SOLID STATE PHYSICS. *Educ:* Case Western Reserve Univ, BS, 69; Univ Tex, Austin, PhD(physics), 78. *Prof Exp:* Instr physics, Cleveland Pub Sch, 69-72, Frederick County Bd of Educ, 72-73; asst prof physics, Okla State Univ, 78-81; ASST PROF PHYSICS, BOISE STATE UNIV, 81- *Mem:* Am Asn Physics Teachers; Nat Sci Teachers Asn; Nat Asn Res Sci Teaching; Asn Educ Teachers Sci; Jean Piaget Soc. *Res:* Application of theories of cognitive development to physics education; pulsed calorimetric studies of solid-solid structural phase transition. *Mailing Add:* Dept Physics/Eng Boise State Univ Boise ID 83725

DYKSTRA, MARK ALLAN, b Hull, Iowa, Oct 17, 46; m 71; c 2. MEDICAL MYCOLOGY, DIAGNOSTIC MICROBIOLOGY. *Educ:* Cent Col, Pella, Iowa, BA, 69; Northern Ill Univ, MS, 71; Tulane Univ, PhD(microbiol), 76. *Prof Exp:* Resident pub health & med microbiol, Hartford Hosp, 76-78; ASST PROF, DEPT MED MICROBIOL, CREIGHTON UNIV, 78-; DIR, DIAG MICROS LAB, ST JOSEPH HOSP, OMAHA, 78- *Mem:* Am Soc Microbiol; Am Fedn Clin Res; Med Mycol Soc Am. *Res:* Pathogenesis of cryptococcosis, especially nonspecific resistance mechanisms in murine model. *Mailing Add:* 2319 S 113th Ave Omaha NE 68144

DYKSTRA, MICHAEL JACK, mycology, cell biology, see previous edition

DYKSTRA, RICHARD LYNN, b Des Moines, Iowa, Oct 19, 42; m 64; c 3. ANALYTICAL STATISTICS. *Educ:* Cent Col, Iowa, BA, 65; Univ Iowa, PhD(statist), 68. *Prof Exp:* From asst prof to assoc prof, 68-81, PROF STATIST, UNIV MO-COLUMBIA, 81- *Mem:* Am Statist Asn; Inst Math Statist. *Res:* Probability theory; stochastic processes; multivariate analysis; mathematical statistics. *Mailing Add:* Dept of Statist Univ of Mo Columbia MO 65201

DYKSTRA, STANLEY JOHN, b Eddyville, Iowa, Apr 27, 24; m 49; c 2. ORGANIC CHEMISTRY. *Educ:* Calvin Col, AB, 49; Wayne Univ, PhD(chem), 53. *Prof Exp:* Asst, Wayne Univ, 52; res assoc, Stanford Univ, 53-54; sr res chemist, 54-61, group leader, 61-68, sect leader, 68-70, DIR CHEM DEVELOP, MEAD JOHNSON RES CTR, MEAD JOHNSON & CO, 70- *Mem:* Am Chem Soc; Sigma Xi. *Res:* Epoxyethers; primary aliphatic hydroperoxides; medicinals. *Mailing Add:* Mead Johnson Res Ctr 2404 Pennsylvania Evansville IN 47721

DYKSTRA, THOMAS KARL, b Grand Rapids, Mich, May 9, 35; m 59; c 3. ORGANIC CHEMISTRY, POLYMER CHEMISTRY. *Educ:* Calvin Col, BA, 57; Univ Ill, PhD(org chem), 61. *Prof Exp:* Res chemist, 61-65, lab head, 71-81, RES ASSOC CHEM, EASTMAN KODAK CO, 66-, PROG DIR, 81- *Mem:* Am Chem Soc. *Res:* Application of organic and polymer chemistry to electrophotography. *Mailing Add:* Bldg 59 Kodak Park Rochester NY 14650

DYLLA, HENRY FREDERICK, b Atlanta, Ga, Mar 17, 49. PHYSICS. *Educ:* Mass Inst Technol, BS & MS, 71, PhD(physics), 75. *Prof Exp:* Res asst atomic physics, Mass Inst Technol, 70-75; RES STAFF MEM PLASMA PHYSICS, PRINCETON UNIV, 75- *Mem:* Am Phys Soc; Am Vacuum Soc. *Res:* Plasma-wall interactions in controlled fusion devices; surface physics; mass spectrometry; electron spectroscopy; vacuum technology. *Mailing Add:* Plasma Physics Lab PO Box 451 Princeton NJ 08544

DYM, CLIVE L, b Leeds, Eng, July 15, 42; US citizen; c 2. STRUCTURAL DYNAMICS, BUCKLING & STABILITY. *Educ:* Cooper Union BCE, 62; Polytech Inst Brooklyn, MS, 64; Stanford Univ, PhD(aeronaut), 67. *Prof Exp:* Asst prof, State Univ NY, Buffalo, 66-69; mem res staff, Inst Defense Anal, 69-70; assoc prof, Dept Civil Eng, Carnegie-Mellon Univ, 70-74; sr scientist, Bolt Beranek & Newman, Inc, Cambridge, 74-77; PROF & DEPT HEAD, DEPT CIVIL ENG, UNIV MASS, AMHERST, 77- *Concurrent Pos:* Vis assoc prof, Dept Aeronaut Eng, Israel Inst Technol, Haifa, 71; vis sr res fel, Inst Sound & Vibration Res, Univ Southampton, Eng, 73; consult, Bell Aerospace Co, 67-69, Dravo Corp, 70-71, Salem Corp, 72, Gen Anal, Inc, 72, ORI, Inc, 79, Bolt Beranek & Newman, Inc, 79-, AVCO-AERL, Inc, 81- *Mem:* fel Am Soc Civil Engrs; fel Am Soc Mech Engrs; fel Acoustical Soc Am; AAAS; Inst Noise Control Eng. *Res:* Vibration and stability of structures; interaction of structures and acoustic media; shell structures; applied mathematics, especially variational methods; mathematical modeling; systems analysis. *Mailing Add:* Dept Civil Eng Univ Mass Amherst MA 01003

DYMENT, JOHN CAMERON, b Hamilton, Ont, June 7, 38; m 63; c 3. SOLID STATE PHYSICS, OPTOELECTRONIC DEVICES. *Educ:* McMaster Univ, BSc, 60; Univ BC, MSc, 62; McGill Univ, PhD(physics), 65. *Prof Exp:* Mem tech staff, Bell Labs, Murray Hill, 65-73, MEM STAFF, BELL-NORTHERN RES, 73- *Concurrent Pos:* Lectr fiber optics, Carleton Univ, Ottawa, 77-81; guest ed, J Quantum Electronics, Inst Elec & Electronics Engrs, 79; Can deleg, Standards for Fiber Optic Terminals, Indust Electrification Coun, 80-81. *Mem:* Am Inst Physics. *Res:* Paramagnetic resonance; optoelectronic device research; lasers, light emiting diodes, detectors, modulators; management of crystal growth, processing, device characterization and packaging. *Mailing Add:* Bell-Northern Res PO Box 3511 Sta C Ottawa ON K1Y 4H7 Can

DYMERSKI, PAUL PETER, b Pittsburgh, Pa, June 12, 47. PHYSICAL CHEMISTRY. *Educ:* Duquesne Univ, BS, 69; Univ Idaho, MS, 71; Case Western Reserve Univ, PhD(phys chem), 74. *Prof Exp:* Fel, Cornell Univ, 74-75; fel chem, Univ Toronto, 75-76, DIR MASS SPECTROMETRY, NY STATE HEALTH DEPT, 76- *Mem:* Sigma Xi; Am Soc Mass Spectrometry & Allied Topics; Am Chem Soc. *Res:* Applications of mass spectrometry to environmental and health chemistry. *Mailing Add:* NY State Health Dept D250 Empire State Plaza Albany NY 12201

DYMICKY, MICHAEL, b Ukraine, Oct 1, 20; nat US; m 43; c 2. ORGANIC CHEMISTRY, PHYSICAL CHEMISTRY. *Educ:* Polytech Lwiw, Ukraine, Chem Tech, 43; Innsbruck Univ, dipl chem, 47, Doctorandum, 49; Temple Univ, PhD(org chem), 60. *Prof Exp:* Fel, Univ Pa, 52-53; res chemist, Wyeth Inst, 53-56, US Agr Res Serv, 56-59 & Wyeth Inst, 59-62; assoc prof chem, Kutztown State Col, 62-65; assoc prof, Gwynedd-Mercy Col, 65-66; mem staff, Smoke Invests Tobacco Lab, Eastern Utilization Res & Develop Div, Agr Res Serv, 66-72, SR RES CHEMIST, MEAT, HIDES & LEATHER, EASTERN REGIONAL RES CTR, USDA, 72- *Concurrent Pos:* Adv bd Manor Jr Col, Philadelphia. *Mem:* Am Chem Soc; Sigma Xi. Soc. *Res:* Chemistry of plants; physiological compounds occurring in nature; organic syntheses; spectroscopy; chemistry of the pigments of the meat. *Mailing Add:* 9653 Dungan Rd Philadelphia PA 19115

DYMSZA, HENRY A, b Newton, NH, Jan 14, 22; m 56; c 4. NUTRITIONAL BIOCHEMISTRY, FOOD SCIENCE. *Educ:* Pa State Univ, BS, 43, PhD(agr & biochem), 54; Univ Wis, MS, 50. *Prof Exp:* Res nutritionist, Gen Foods Corp, 54-59; sr res assoc nutrit, Mass Inst Technol, 59-64; head metab sect, Food Div, US Army Natick Labs, 64-66; assoc prof, 66-70, chmn dept, 66-77, PROF FOOD & NUTRIT SCI, UNIV RI, 70- *Concurrent Pos:* Chief, Clin Nutrit Br, Bur Foods, Food & Drug Admin, Washington, DC, 79-80. *Honors & Awards:* Commendation for Research, US Army, 66. *Mem:* AAAS; Am Chem Soc; Am Inst Nutrit; Am Dietetic Asn; Inst Food Technol; Am Asn Lab Animal Sci. *Res:* Nutritional biochemistry; synthetic and unusual nutrients and diets; energy metabolism; food preservation and safety; fish nutrition; hyper-vitaminosis and over-nutrition; nutritional status evaluation; nutrition education and behavior. *Mailing Add:* Dept Food & Nutrit Sci Nutrit & Dietetics Quinn Hall Univ of RI Kingston RI 02881

DYNE, PETER JOHN, b London, Eng, Sept 14, 26; Can citizen; m 53; c 2. RADIATION CHEMISTRY. *Educ:* Univ London, BSc, 46, PhD(phys chem), 49. *Prof Exp:* Asst lectr phys chem, King's Col, Univ London, 49, lectr, Imp Col, 49-50; fel physics, Nat Res Coun Can, 50-52; fel chem, Jet Propulsion Lab, Calif Inst Technol, 52-53; sci officer, Atomic Energy Can, Ltd, 53-65, head mat sci br, Whiteshell Nuclear Res Estab, 65-71, dir Chem & Mat Sci Div, 71-76; DIR GEN, OFF ENERGY RES & DEVELOP, DEPT ENERGY, MINES & RESOURCES, 76- *Mem:* Fel Chem Inst Can; The Chem Soc. *Res:* Photochemistry; molecular spectroscopy; problems in pure and applied chemistry and in materials relevant to reactor technology; sciences technology of storing radioactive wastes. *Mailing Add:* Energy Res & Develop Energy Mines & Resources Ottawa ON K1A 0E4 Can

DYNES, J ROBERT, b Miller, SDak, Oct 18, 22; m 47; c 2. ANIMAL SCIENCE. *Educ:* SDak State Col, BS, 47, MS, 49; Tex A&M Univ, PhD, 68. *Prof Exp:* Instr, High Sch, 50-51; instr, 51-56, asst prof, 56-62, ASSOC PROF MEATS, MONT STATE UNIV, 62- *Mem:* Am Soc Animal Sci; Am Meat Sci Asn; Inst Food Tech. *Res:* Meats research; carcass and red meat development in live animals. *Mailing Add:* Dept of Animal & Range Sci Mont State Univ Bozeman MT 59717

DYNES, ROBERT CARR, b London, Ont, Nov 8, 42; m 67; c 1. SOLID STATE PHYSICS. *Educ:* Univ Western Ont, BSc, 64; McMaster Univ, MSc, 65, PhD(physics), 68. *Prof Exp:* Mem tech staff physics, 68-75, HEAD DEPT PHYSICS, BELL LABS, 75- *Mem:* Am Phys Soc. *Res:* Low temperature solid state physics; details of phonons and electron transport and the phenomena of superconductivity and superfluidity. *Mailing Add:* Bell Labs Rm 1 d 4320 Murray Hill NJ 07974

DYOTT, THOMAS MICHAEL, b Rochester, NY, Aug 9, 47; m 69. RESEARCH MANAGEMENT, AGRICULTURAL CHEMICALS. *Educ:* Gettysburg Col, BA, 69; Princeton Univ, MA, 71, PhD(chem), 73. *Prof Exp:* sr scientist chem, 73-79, proj leader, 80-81, DEPT MGR, ROHM AND HAAS CO, 81- *Mem:* Am Chem Soc; Asn Comput Mach. *Res:* Environmental fate, formulation, experiment station and computer research related to agricultural research. *Mailing Add:* Rohm and Haas Co Norristown Rd Spring House PA 19477

DYRKACZ, W WILLIAM, b Arnold, Pa, Apr 17, 19; m 43. METALLURGICAL ENGINEERING. *Educ:* Carnegie Inst Technol, BSc, 42. *Prof Exp:* Mat engr jet engines, Gen Elec Co, 42-46; chief metallurgist forgings, Cameron Mfg Co, 46-49; assoc dir res, chief metallurgist & mgr prod develop specialty steels, Allegheny Ludlum Steel Corp, 49-66; vpres opers titanium, Teledyne Titanium, 66-68; INDUST CONSULT METALL MFG FACIL PLANNING, METALL ENG & FAILURE ANAL, 68- *Concurrent Pos:* Consult, Mat Adv Bd, Nat Acad Sci, 56-73 & Aerospace Struct Mat Handbk, Mech Properties Data Ctr, 69-79. *Honors & Awards:* F B Lounsberry Award, 55. *Mem:* Am Soc Metals; Am Inst Mining & Metall Engrs; Am Vacuum Soc; Am Powder Metall Inst; fel Am Soc Metals. *Res:* Advanced melting and metal working processes for the production of superalloys, specialty steels, titanium, zirconium, and refractory-base alloys. *Mailing Add:* Lochaven Rd Rte 3 Waxhaw NC 28173

DYRNESS, CHRISTEN THEODORE, b Chicago, Ill, June 4, 33; m 62; c 3. FOREST SOILS. *Educ:* Wheaton Col, Ill, BS, 54; Ore State Univ, MS, 56, PhD(soil sci), 60. *Prof Exp:* Soil scientist, 59-74, PRIN SOIL SCIENTIST WATERSHED MGT RES, PAC NORTHWEST FOREST & RANGE EXP STA, US FOREST SERV, 74-; ASSOC PROF SOIL SCI, ORE STATE UNIV, CORVALLIS, 59- *Concurrent Pos:* Prog leader, Inst Northern Forestry, Fairbanks, Alaska, Pac Northwest Forest & Range Exp Sta, US Forest Serv, 74-, affil prof forestry, Univ Alaska, Fairbanks, 74- *Mem:* AAAS; Soil Sci Soc Am; Am Soc Agron. *Res:* Physical and morphological properties of soil and plant soil relationships; physical properties of forest soils as affected by management practices; plant-soil relationships on pumice soils; plant-soil relationships in the taiga of interior Alaska. *Mailing Add:* Inst of Northern Forestry US Forest Serv 308 Tanana Dr Fairbanks AK 99701

DYROFF, DAVID RAY, b St Louis, Mo, Feb 16, 40; m 61; c 3. INDUSTRIAL CHEMISTRY. *Educ:* Univ Ill, BS, 62; Calif Inst Technol, PhD(chem), 65. *Prof Exp:* Sr res chemist, 65-67, res group leader, 67-79, RES GROUP LEADER, DETERGENTS & PHOSPHATES DIV, MONSANTO, CO, 79- *Res:* Phosphate chemistry; industrial process research and development; detergent ingredients; toothpaste ingredients. *Mailing Add:* Monsanto Co 800 N Lindbergh Blvd St Louis MO 63166

DYRUD, JARL EDVARD, b Maddock, NDak, Oct 20, 21; m 52; c 3. PSYCHIATRY. *Educ:* Concordia Col, Moorhead, Minn, AB, 42; Johns Hopkins Univ, MD, 45. *Prof Exp:* Intern, Johns Hopkins Univ, 45-46; intern, Vet Admin Ment Hyg Clin, DC, 48-49; resident psychiat, Chestnut Lodge, Inc, 49-51, staff psychiatrist, 51-56; pvt pract, 56-68; assoc chmn dept psychiat, Univ Hosp, 68-78; PROF PSYCHIAT, SCH MED, UNIV CHICAGO 68-; ASSOC DEAN FAC AFFAIRS, DIV OF BIOL SCI & PRITZKER SCH OF MED, UNIV OF CHICAGO, 78- *Concurrent Pos:* USPHS fel & resident, Spring Grove State Hosp, 52-53; consult, Md State Hosp, 56-68; prin investr behav anal, Inst Behav Res, 63-68; dir psychiat, Chestnut Lodge Res Inst, 67-68; consult, Lab Adult Psychiat, NIMH, 67-68, mem clin projs res rev comt, 70-74. *Honors & Awards:* John Nuveen lectr, Univ Chicago, 78. *Mem:* AAAS; Am Psychiat Asn; Am Psychoanal Asn; Acad Psychoanal. *Res:* Ego psychology; operant analyses of behavior; psychobiology of schizophrenia; minimal brain dysfunction; normal and abnormal child development. *Mailing Add:* Dept Psychiat Univ Chicago Hosp Chicago IL 60637

DYSART, BENJAMIN CLAY, III, b Columbia, Tenn, Feb 12, 40; m 60. ENVIRONMENTAL ENGINEERING. *Educ:* Vanderbilt Univ, BEng, 61, MS, 64; Georgia Inst Technol, PhD(civil eng), 69. *Prof Exp:* Staff engr, Union Carbide Corp, 61-62 & 64-65; sci adv to asst secy Army Civil Works, Dept Army, 75-76; asst prof environ & water resources, 68-70, assoc prof eng & dir water resources eng grad prog, 70-75, prof environ eng, 76-82, MCQUEEN QUATTLEBAUM PROF ENG, CLEMSON UNIV, 82- *Concurrent Pos:* Mem, Civil Works Adv Comt, Dept Army, 75-76, Nonpoint Source Pollutant Task Force, US Environ Protection Agency, 79-81, Outer Continental Shelf Adv Bd, US Dept Interior, 79-82, Sci Comt, 79-82, Nuclear Energy Ctr Environ Task Force, US Dept Energy, 79-81; consult, major energy related corp. *Mem:* Asn Environ Eng Prof (pres, 81-82); Am Geophys Union; Am Soc Civil Engrs; Water Pollution Control Fedn; Nat Wildlife Fedn (vpres, 78-). *Res:* Environmental aspects of energy production; environmental impact assessment; national water resources policy; mathematical modeling; simulation of water quality and water resources. *Mailing Add:* Rhodes Eng Res Ctr Clemson Univ Clemson SC 29631

DYSART, GORDON, b Dallas, Tex, Nov 20, 27; m 51; c 2. PETROLEUM ENGINEERING. *Educ:* Univ Tex, BS, 61. *Prof Exp:* Plant mgr, Dysart Mfg Co, Tex, 49-57; res asst, Tex Petrol Res Comt, 57-61; petrol engr, Standard Oil Co Tex, 61-66; res engr, West Co, 66-70; CONSULT PETROL ENGR, INT DIV, DEGOLYER & MACNAUGHTON, 70- *Mem:* Soc Petrol Engrs; Am Petrol Inst. *Res:* Heat exchange in oilwell tubing and fractured formations; hydraulic and explosive fracturing of rock to stimulate oil and gas production. *Mailing Add:* 400 One Energy Sq Dallas TX 75206

DYSART, RICHARD JAMES, b Chicago, Ill, May 6, 32. ENTOMOLOGY. *Educ:* Univ Ill, BS, 54, PhD(entom), 61. *Prof Exp:* From asst entomologist to assoc entomologist, Ill Natural Hist Surv, 60-65; res entomologist, European Parasite Lab, USDA, Sevres, France, 65-71, DIR, BENEFICIAL INSECTS RES LAB, USDA, NEWARK, 71- *Mem:* Entom Soc Am; Int Orgn Biol Control. *Res:* Ecology of insect pests of forage and pasture crops; biological control of insects. *Mailing Add:* Beneficial Insects Res Lab USDA 501 S Chapel St Newark DE 19711

DYSINGER, PAUL WILLIAM, b Burns, Tenn, May 24, 27; m 58; c 4. TROPICAL PUBLIC HEALTH, PUBLIC HEALTH. *Educ:* Southern Missionary Col, BA, 51; Loma Linda Univ, MD, 55; Harvard Univ, MPH, 62. *Prof Exp:* Med attache, Am Embassy, Phnom Penh, Cambodia, 58-60; res assoc prev med, Sch Med, Loma Linda Univ, 61; dir pub health & trop med, Field Sta, Tanganyika, EAfrica, 62-64; asst prof pub health, 64-67, chmn, Dept Trop Health, 67-71, assoc dean acad affairs & int health, 71-78, PROF INT HEALTH, LOMA LINDA UNIV, 71- *Concurrent Pos:* WHO traveling fel, 69; consult, New Guinea, 64-, TRW, Inc, 67- & Voc Rehab, Calif, 67-; pub health adv, Ministry Health, Dor es Salaam, Tanzania, 78-80 & Rural Health Educ Ctr, Chuhar Kana Mandi, Sheikhupura, Pakistan, 80-81. *Mem:* AAAS; fel Am Pub Health Asn; Am Soc Trop Med & Hyg; Am Geog Soc; fel Royal Soc Trop Med & Hyg. *Res:* Statistical epidemiology, especially mortality studies in emphysema and accidents; manpower studies in Southeast Asia and East Africa. *Mailing Add:* Sch Health Loma Linda Univ Loma Linda CA 92350

DYSON, DEREK C(HARLESWORTH), b San Eduardo, Arg, Dec 23, 32; m 61; c 2. CHEMICAL ENGINEERING. *Educ:* Cambridge Univ, BA, 55; Univ London, PhD(chem eng), 66. *Prof Exp:* Develop engr, Du Pont of Can, 58-60; res engr, Pennsalt Chem Corp, 60-62; res asst chem eng, Imp Col, London, 62-65; from asst prof to assoc prof, 66-77, PROF CHEM ENG, RICE UNIV, 77- *Mem:* Am Inst Chem Engrs; Sigma Xi. *Res:* Optimization of chemical processes; theory of interfacial stability in the capillary regime; computer control of chemical processes. *Mailing Add:* Dept of Chem Eng Rice Univ Box 1892 Houston TX 77001

DYSON, FREEMAN JOHN, b Crowthorne, Eng, Dec 15, 23; nat US; m 50; c 6. MATHEMATICAL PHYSICS, ASTROPHYSICS. *Educ:* Cambridge Univ, BA, 45. *Prof Exp:* Res fel, Trinity Col, Cambridge Univ, 46-49 & Univ Birmingham, 49-51; prof physics, Cornell Univ, 51-53; PROF PHYSICS, INST ADVAN STUDY, 53- *Honors & Awards:* Heineman Prize, Am Inst Physics, 65; Lorentz Medal, Royal Netherlands Acad, 66; Hughes Medal, Royal Soc, 68; Max Planck Medal, Ger Phys Soc, 69; J Robert Oppenheimer Mem Prize, Ctr Theoret Studies, 70; Harvey Prize, Israel Inst of Technol, 77; Wolf Prize, Israel, 81. *Mem:* Nat Acad Sci; fel Royal Soc; Am Phys Soc. *Mailing Add:* Inst for Advan Study Princeton NJ 08540

DYSON, IAN FRASER, b Leeds, Eng, Apr 5, 40; m 63; c 2. ORGANIC CHEMISTRY. *Educ:* Univ Leeds, BSc, 60, PhD(org chem), 63. *Prof Exp:* Res chemist, Org Chem Dept, 63-68, supvr, 68-69, div head, 69-72, tech mgr, 72-75, res mgr, Petrochem Dept, 75-77, mgr bus anal, 77-79, PRIN CONSULT CORP PLANS & MKT MGR, ADVAN ELECTRONIC SYSTS, ORG E I DU PONT DE NEMOURS & CO INC, 81- *Res:* Natural products; petroleum chemistry; synthetic organic chemistry; chemistry applied to electronics. *Mailing Add:* Photo Prod Dept E I du Pont de Nemours & Co Inc Wilmington DE 19898

DYSON, JOHN DOUGLAS, b Lemmon, SDak, Auug 9, 18; m 40; c 4. ANTENNA THEORY, COMPUTER CONTROL MEASUREMENTS. *Educ:* SDak State Univ, BS, 40, BS (elec eng), 49; Univ Ill, MS, 50, PhD(elec eng), 57. *Prof Exp:* Statistician, SDak Hwy Planning Surv, 40-41; officer, US Army Separated as Lt Colonel, 41-46; engr, Res Staff, Sandia Corp, 51-52; res asst, 52-57, asst prof, 58-60, assoc prof, 60-66, PROF ELEC ENG, UNIV ILL, 66- *Mem:* Antennas & Propagation Soc; fel Inst Elec & Electronics Engrs; Int Sci Radio Union; Microwave Theory & Techniques Soc. *Res:* Log spiral frequency independent antennas; design of antenna systems; direction finding systems; measurement techniques. *Mailing Add:* 1004 S Western Ave Champaign IL 61820

DYSON, ROBERT DUANE, b Minneapolis, Minn, May 18, 39; m 61; c 3. CELL PHYSIOLOGY. *Educ:* Univ Ore, BS, 61, MD, 77; Univ Ill, Urbana, MS, 63, PhD(biophys chem), 65, Ore Health Sci Univ, MD, 77. *Prof Exp:* NIH fel & res assoc molecular biol, Univ Calif, Berkeley, 65-67; asst prof biophysics, Ore State Univ, 67-71, assoc prof biochem & biophysics, 71-73; CLIN INSTR OBSTET & GYNEC, ORE HEALTH SCI UNIV, 81- *Concurrent Pos:* Courtesy appointment, Ore State Univ, 74-76; resident obstet & gynec, Univ Ore Health Sci Ctr, 78-81. *Mem:* AAAS; Am Soc Biol Chemists; Am Soc Cell Biol; Am Col Obstet & Gynec; Am Fertil Soc. *Res:* Human reproduction, comparative enzymology of developing, mature and malignant cells. *Mailing Add:* 3822 NE 142 Ave Portland OR 97230

DYSON-HUDSON, V RADA, b Huntington, NY, July 8, 30; m 53; c 3. BIOLOGICAL ANTHROPOLOGY. *Educ:* Swarthmore Col, BA, 51; Oxford Univ, DPhil(ecol), 54. *Prof Exp:* Researcher human ecol, Karamoja, Uganda, 57-59; lectr zool, Univ Khartoum, 61-63; res assoc human ecol, Dept Social Rels, Johns Hopkins Univ, 65-71, assoc prof human ecol & res scientist, Dept Pathobiol & Dept Social Rels, 71-73; assoc prof, State Univ Ny Col Environ Sci & Forestry, 73-74; ASSOC PROF ANTHROP, CORNELL UNIV, 74- *Concurrent Pos:* J S Guggenheim & Fulbright res fels, Uganda, 54-55, Penrose Fund grants, 54-56 & Permanent Sci Found grant, 56-57; Sigma Xi grants, Uganda, 56-57, Univ Khartoum, 61-63 & Johns Hopkins Univ, 66-67; Marion Talbot fel, Oxford Univ, 58-59; NSF grant-in-aid, Johns Hopkins Univ, 65-68 & res grant, 72, Kendall Fund grant, 67 & Wenner-Gren Found Anthrop Res grant, 67-68; NSF grant-in-aid, 80-81. *Mem:* AAAS; fel Am Anthrop Asn. *Res:* Study of Drosophila ecology in England; study of low-energy agricultural tribe of East Africa; a general synthesis of human ecology as an integration of many disciplines; ecology of nomadic pastoralists in East Africa. *Mailing Add:* Dept of Anthrop Cornell Univ Col of Arts & Sci Ithaca NY 14853

DZIADYK, BOHDAN, b Aschaffenburg, WGer, Mar 26, 48; US citizen; m 74; c 2. ECOLOGY OF TALLGRASS PRAIRIE. *Educ:* Southern Ill Univ, BA, 70, MS, 80; NDak State Univ, PhD(bot), 82. *Prof Exp:* ASST PROF BIOL, AUGUSTANA COL, 80- *Mem:* Ecol Soc Am; Soc Range Mgt; Sigma Xi. *Res:* Analysis of structure and function in terrestrial, especially grassland, ecosystems; dynamics of primary production. *Mailing Add:* Dept Biol Augustana Col Rock Island IL 61201

DZIAK, ROSE MARY, b Pittston, Pa, Apr 11, 46. CELL PHYSIOLOGY. *Educ:* Col Misericordia, BS, 67; Univ Rochester, MS, 70, PhD(radiation biol), 74. *Prof Exp:* Instr biol, Col Misericordia, 69-70; NIH fel, Med Sch, Northwestern Univ, 74-75; instr physiol, Med Ctr, La State Univ, 75-76; asst res prof, 76-77, ASST PROF ORAL BIOL, STATE UNIV NY BUFFALO, 77- *Concurrent Pos:* George S Clarke Mem fel, Arthritis Found, 76. *Mem:* AAAS; Endocrine Soc; Am Soc Bone & Min Res; NY Acad Sci. *Res:* Calcium regulation in isolated bone cells in an attempt to understand the mechanism of action of agents that influence bone resorption and formation. *Mailing Add:* Dept of Oral Biol State Univ NY 4510 Main St Buffalo NY 14226

DZIDIC, ISMET, b Derventa, Yugoslavia, June 14, 39. PHYSICAL CHEMISTRY, ANALYTICAL BIOCHEMISTRY. *Educ:* Univ Zagreb, dipl eng, 63; Univ Alta, PhD(phys chem), 70. *Prof Exp:* Res chemist, Res Inst Org Chem Industs, 63-64; teaching asst phys chem, Univ Alta, 65-70; fel, Inst Lipid Res, Baylor Col Med, 71-74, res asst prof chem, 74-81; SR RES CHEM, SHELL DEVELOP CO, 81- *Mem:* Am Chem Soc; Am Soc Mass Spectrometry. *Res:* Mass spectrometric study of gaseous ion-molecule reactions, solvation of ions in the gas phase; proton affinities of organic molecules; application of the chemical ionization mass spectrometry for structural studies of biological compounds. *Mailing Add:* Shell Develop Co PO Box 1380 Houston TX 77001

DZIECIUCH, MATTHEW ANDREW, b Edmonton, Alta, Oct 11, 31; m 58; c 3. ENVIRONMENTAL CHEMISTRY, ELECTROCHEMISTRY. *Educ:* Univ Alta, BSc, 57, MSc, 58; Univ Ottawa, PhD(electrochem), 62. *Prof Exp:* RES SCIENTIST ELECTROCHEM, FORD MOTOR CO, 61- *Mem:* AAAS; Sigma Xi; Electrochem Soc. *Res:* Batteries; electrochemical kinetics; deposition and oxidation kinetics; pollution chemistry, particularly treatment and disposal of pollutants in water. *Mailing Add:* Ford Motor Co Sci Lab PO Box 2053 Dearborn MI 48121

DZIERZANOWSKI, FRANK JOHN, b Plains, Pa, Aug 28, 29; m 54; c 2. PHYSICAL CHEMISTRY. *Educ:* Rutgers Univ, BS, 56. *Prof Exp:* Jr res chemist, Minerals & Chem Corp Am, 56-60, from res chemist to sr res chemist, Minerals & Chem Phillipp Corp, 60-66; res supvr fundamental res, 66-74, group leader fundamental res, 74-76, GROUP LEADER PHYS MEASUREMENTS, ENGELHARD CORP, 76- *Mem:* Catalysis Soc; Am Chem Soc; Clay Minerals Soc; Am Soc Testing & Mat. *Res:* Synthesis and properties of inorganic compounds; hydothermal synthesis of minerals; clay mineralogy; adsorption and catalysis; xray diffraction; characterization of materials. *Mailing Add:* 8 Norfolk Rd Somerset NJ 08873

DZIEWIATKOWSKI, DOMINIC DONALD, b Chicago, Ill, Feb 20, 15; m 42; c 1. BIOCHEMISTRY. *Educ:* Western State Teachers Col, Mich, AB, 39; Univ Mich, MS, 41, PhD(biol chem), 43. *Prof Exp:* Instr biochem, Sch Med, Vanderbilt Univ, 43-46; asst prof, Johns Hopkins Univ, 46-48; assoc, Rockefeller Inst Hosp, 48-57, assoc prof, Rockefeller Univ, 57-67; chmn dept oral biol, Sch Dent & dir dent res inst, Sch Med, 67-77, PROF BIOCHEM & DENT, SCH MED & DENT, UNIV MICH, ANN ARBOR, 67- *Mem:* Harvey Soc; Am Soc Biol Chem; Am Chem Soc. *Res:* Physiology of connective tissues. *Mailing Add:* Dept of Oral Biol Univ of Mich Sch of Dent Ann Arbor MI 48104

DZIEWONSKI, ADAM MARIAN, b Lwow, Poland, Nov 15, 36; m 67. SEISMOLOGY, GEOMAGNETISM. *Educ:* Univ Warsaw, MS, 60; Acad Mining & Metall, Cracow, DrTechSci(appl geol), 65. *Prof Exp:* Res asst seismol, Inst Geophys, Polish Acad Sci, 61-65, res assoc, 65; res assoc, Southwest Ctr Advan Studies, 65-69, asst prof Geophysics, Univ Tex, Dallas, 69-71; assoc prof geophys & assoc, Ctr Earth & Planetary Physics, 72-76, PROF GEOL & MEM, CTR EARTH & PLANETARY PHYSICS, HARVARD UNIV, 76- *Concurrent Pos:* Mem, Polish Sci Exped to NVietnam, Int Geophys Year, 58-59. *Mem:* Seismol Soc Am; Am Geophys Union; Soc Explor Geophys; AAAS. *Res:* Physical properties of the earth's interior from observations of seismic wave propagation; earthquake mechanism; electrical and thermal properties of the crust and upper mantle from geomagnetic deep soundings. *Mailing Add:* Holyoke Ctr 831 350 Mass Ave Cambridge MA 02138

DZIMIANSKI, JOHN W(ILLIAM), b Baltimore, Md, Dec 13, 24; m 52; c 3. ELECTRICAL ENGINEERING. *Educ:* Johns Hopkins Univ, BE, 47, Dr Eng, 52. *Prof Exp:* Asst high frequency insulation, Johns Hopkins Univ, 47-52; group leader, Elec Res Sect, Allis-Chalmers Mfg Co, 52-56; ADV ENGR, SYSTS DEVELOP DIV, WESTINGHOUSE ELEC CORP, 56- *Mem:* Inst Elec & Electronics Eng; Electrochem Soc. *Res:* Molecular electronics; semiconductor reliability physics; MNOS semiconductor memonics; charged coupled devices. *Mailing Add:* 412 Forest Lane Catonsville MD 21228

DZIUK, HAROLD EDMUND, b Foley, Minn, Apr 27, 30; m 52; c 5. ANIMAL PHYSIOLOGY. *Educ:* Univ Minn, BS, 51, DVM, 54, MS, 55, PhD(vet physiol), 60. *Prof Exp:* Instr vet physiol, Col Vet Med, Univ Minn, 51-54 & 57-60; scientist, Hanford Prod Oper, Gen Elec Co, Wash, 60-61; assoc prof, Iowa State Univ, 61; from asst prof to assoc prof, 61-69, chmn dept vet biol, 72-75, PROF VET PHYSIOL, COL VET MED, UNIV MINN, ST PAUL, 69-, CHMN DEPT VET BIOL, 76- *Mem:* Conf Res Workers Animal Dis; Am Vet Med Asn; Am Physiol Soc. *Res:* Comparative gastrointestinal physiology; pathogenesis of diseases of the gastrointestinal tract. *Mailing Add:* Dept of Vet Biol Col of Vet Med Univ of Minn St Paul MN 55101

DZIUK, PHILIP J, b Foley, Minn, Mar 24, 26; m 51; c 7. REPRODUCTIVE PHYSIOLOGY, ENDOCRINOLOGY. *Educ:* Univ Minn, BS, 50, MS, 52, PhD(dairy husb), 55. *Prof Exp:* From asst prof to assoc prof animal physiol, 55-67, PROF ANIMAL PHYSIOL, UNIV ILL, URBANA, 67- *Concurrent Pos:* Lalor fel, 58-59; vis investr, R B Jackson Lab, 59; Pig Indust Develop Auth & Lalor fels, Cambridge, Eng, 61-62; mem comt on hormones, Nat Acad Sci-Nat Res Coun, 62-; indust consult; Alexander von Humboldt sr US scientist award, 80. *Honors & Awards:* Upjohn Award, Am Fertil Soc, 70; Physiol & Endocrinol Award, Am Soc Animal Sci, 71. *Mem:* AAAS; Am Asn Anat; Am Soc Animal Sci; Brit Soc Study Fertil; Soc Study Reproduction. *Res:* Egg transfer in cattle and swine; control of ovulation in cattle, sheep and swine; superovulation; artificial insemination; early stages of fertilization of eggs; embryonal mortality; sperm transport in male and female. *Mailing Add:* Dept of Animal Sci 111 Genetics Univ of Ill 1301 W Taft Dr Urbana IL 61801

DZOMBAK, WILLIAM CHARLES, b McKeesport, Pa, Dec 4, 21; m 53. PHYSICAL CHEMISTRY. *Educ:* Univ Pittsburgh, BSc, 43; Purdue Univ, PhD(chem), 50. *Prof Exp:* Assoc prof, Providence Col, 50-52; assoc chemist, Argonne Nat Lab, 52-53; assoc prof, 53-64, PROF PHYS CHEM, ST VINCENT COL, 64- *Mailing Add:* Dept of Phys Chem St Vincent Col Latrobe PA 15650

E

EACHUS, ALAN CAMPBELL, b Champaign, Ill, July 11, 39; m 61; c 2. SANITARY CHEMISTRY. *Educ:* Syracuse Univ, BS, 60; State Univ NY Col Forestry, Syracuse Univ, PhD(org chem), 64; Northwestern Univ, MM, 75. *Prof Exp:* Fel abstraction kinetics, State Univ NY Col Forestry, Syracuse Univ, 64; res chemist, Dow Chem Co, 66-67, develop specialist, 67-69, res chemist, 69-70; sr res chemist, Alberto-Culver Corp, Melrose Park, 70-72, group leader, 72; mkt develop specialist, Com Solvents Corp, 72-76; prod mgr, 76-80, MKT MGR, INT MINERALS & CHEM, 80- *Mem:* Am Chem Soc; NY Acad Sci; fel Am Inst Chemists; Soc Indust Microbiol. *Res:* Disinfectant/detergent formulations; flame fuels; chemical specialty items; antimicrobial agents. *Mailing Add:* 644 S Michigan Ave Villa Park IL 60181

EACHUS, JOSEPH JACKSON, b Anderson, Ind, Nov 5, 11; m 45; c 2. MATHEMATICS. *Educ:* Miami Univ, AB, 33; Syracuse Univ, AM, 36; Univ Ill, PhD(math, physics), 39. *Prof Exp:* Asst math, Syracuse Univ, 34-36; asst, Univ Ill, 36-39; instr, Purdue Univ, 39-42; elec engr, US Dept Defense, 46-55; systs dir, DatAmatic Corp, Minneapolis-Honeywell Regulator Corp, 55-62, prin staff scientist, Electronic Data Processing Div, Honeywell Inc, 62-70, group dir, Appl Res Div, Honeywell Info Systs, 70-75, prin staff scientist, Electronic Data Processing Div, 75-76; prin engr, Equip Div, Raytheon Co, 77-81; CONSULT, 82- *Concurrent Pos:* Mem info systs panel, Comput Sci & Eng Bd, Nat Acad Sci, 70-; consult, Inst for Defense Analyses, 75- *Mem:* Am Math Soc; Asn Comput Mach; fel Inst Elec & Electronics Engrs; fel AAAS. *Res:* Differential equations; q-difference equations; orthogonal functions; computing machinery; communications, electronics. *Mailing Add:* 85 Washington Ave Cambridge MA 02140

EACHUS, RAYMOND STANLEY, b Bowdon, Eng, June 11, 44; m 66. PHYSICAL INORGANIC CHEMISTRY. *Educ:* Univ Salford, BS, 66; Univ Leicester, PhD(chem), 69. *Prof Exp:* Teaching fel phys chem, Univ BC, 69-70; res assoc, 70-80, HEAD CHEM PHYS LAB, EASTMAN KODAK CO, 80- *Mem:* Sigma Xi; Royal Inst Chem; The Chem Soc; Am Chem Soc. *Res:* Study of the kinetics and mechanisms of photochemical events in inorganic solids using physical techniques, especially electron spin resonance spectroscopy. *Mailing Add:* Chem Physics Lab Bldg 81 Eastman Kodak Co Kodak Park Rochester NY 14650

EACHUS, SPENCER WILLIAM, b Plainfield, NJ, Mar 11, 44; m 66. WOOD CHEMISTRY. *Educ:* Clarkson Col Technol, BS, 65; Syracuse Univ, PhD(org chem), 72. *Prof Exp:* Res assoc wood chem, Empire State Paper Res Inst, 71-73; res scientist pulping, 73-77, GROUP LEADER, UNION CAMP CORP, 77- *Mem:* Tech Asn Pulp & Paper Indust; Am Chem Soc. *Res:* Methods and equipment for the pulping and bleaching of wood fibers. *Mailing Add:* Union Camp Corp Res & Develop Box 412 Princeton NJ 08540

EADE, KENNETH EDGAR, b Ft William, Ont, Jan 16, 26; m 56; c 2. REGIONAL GEOLOGY. *Educ:* Queen's Univ, Ont, BSc, 48; McGill Univ, MSc, 50, PhD(geol), 55. *Prof Exp:* Geologist, Geol Surv Can, 51-53 & Port WAfrica Proj, 53-54; GEOLOGIST, GEOL SURV CAN, 55- *Mem:* Geol Soc Am; Soc Econ Geologists; Arctic Inst NAm; Can Geol Soc; Can Inst Mining & Metall. *Res:* Precambrian geology in northern Canada. *Mailing Add:* Geol Surv of Can 601 Booth St Ottawa Can

EADES, CHARLES HUBERT, JR, b Dallas, Tex, July 19, 16; m 42; c 3. BIOCHEMISTRY. *Educ:* Southern Methodist Univ, BS, 38; Univ Tex, MA, 40; Univ Ill, PhD(biochem), 48. *Prof Exp:* Instr sci, Paris Jr Col, Tex, 40-42; supvr sect anal lab, Pan Am Refining Corp, 42-45; spec res asst, Univ Ill, 45-48; from instr to asst prof biochem, Univ Tenn, 48-55; sr chemist, Mead Johnson & Co, 55-56, group leader, 56-57, sect leader, 57-59; sr scientist, Warner Lambert Res Inst, 59-64, sr res assoc, 64-70, sr clin res assoc, 70-77, asst dir med res, 77-81; CONSULT MED RES, 81- *Concurrent Pos:* Consult, Dept Path, Booth Mem Hosp, Flushing, NY, 63-70; fel coun arteriosclerosis, Am Heart Asn, mem coun clin cardiol & mem coun high blood pressure res. *Mem:* NY Acad Sci; Soc Exp Biol & Med; Am Soc Biol Chemists; Am Inst Nutrit; Am Med Writers Asn. *Res:* Amino acid requirements of man; nutrition of lactic acid bacteria; amino acid metabolism in stress; health and disease; automatic instrumentation; human nutrition; lipid and cholesterol metabolism; clinical investigation of cardiovascular agents in angina, hypertension and allied diseases; arteriosclerosis and cardiovascular disease; use of radioisotopes in metabolic and biochemical studies. *Mailing Add:* Consult/Med Res 50 Hillcrest Rd Mountain Lakes NJ 07046

EADES, JAMES B(EVERLY), JR, b Bluefield, WVa, July 22, 23; m 50; c 3. AEROSPACE ENGINEERING, ENGINEERING MECHANICS. *Educ:* Va Polytech Inst, BS, 44, MS, 49, PhD(eng mech), 58. *Prof Exp:* Instr aeronaut eng, Va Polytech Inst, 47-48, asst prof, 48-51, 53-57, prof aerospace eng, 57-69, head dept, 61-69; sr analyst, Anal Mech Assoc, Inc, Seabrook, 69-75, sr scientist, 75-77; prin scientist, Bus & Technol Systs, Inc, 77-81; VPRES & PRIN SCIENTIST, MAR ASSOCS, INC, 81- *Concurrent Pos:* Dir, Conf Lunar Explor, Blacksburg, Va, 62; aeronaut res specialist, Naval Ord Lab, White Oak, Md, 63-75; Nat Acad Sci sr fel, Goddard Space Flight Ctr, 67-69; vpres, Celestial Mech Inst, Inc; consult, US Army Transp Corps, Naval Ord Lab & Res Anal Corp, Naval Ship Res & Develop Ctr. *Mem:* Sr mem Am Astron Soc; assoc fel Am Inst Aeronaut & Astronaut. *Res:* Transonic flow phenomenon; high speed aerodynamics, flight and control; wind-tunnel testing of structures and vehicles; space flight, space mechanics and celestial mechanics; hydrodynamics and underwater systems. *Mailing Add:* MAR Assocs Inc 1335 Rockville Pike Rockville MD 20852

EADES, JAMES L, b Charlottesville, Va, Apr 21, 21; m 41; c 2. MINERALOGY. *Educ:* Univ Va, BA, 50, MA, 53; Univ Ill, PhD(geol), 62. *Prof Exp:* Soils res engr, Va Coun Hwy Invest & Res, 52-58; res asst, Univ Ill, Urbana, 58-62, res asst prof geol, 62-70; chmn dept, 73-80, ASSOC PROF GEOL, UNIV FLA, 70- *Concurrent Pos:* Mem hwy res bd, Nat Acad Sci-Nat Res Coun; consult, Lime Indust & Hwy Depts; mem staff, USAID Projs, Africa; Nat Lime Asn res grant, 58-; mem staff, USAID Proj, SAm, 72-75. *Mem:* Am Soc Testing & Mat; Clay Minerals Soc; Geol Soc Am; Am Inst Prof Geologists (pres). *Res:* Clay mineralogy; calcium silicate reactions at ambient and elevated temperatures; sulfur dioxide reactions; toxic elements in limestones. *Mailing Add:* Dept of Geol GPA 1112 Univ of Fla Gainesville FL 32601

EADIE, GEORGE ROBERT, b Eldorado, Ill, Sept 24, 23; m 43; c 2. MINING ENGINEERING. *Educ:* Univ Ill, BS, 49, MS, 56, EM, 57. *Prof Exp:* From asst prof to assoc prof mining eng, Univ Ill, 54-63; mem staff, Freeman Coal Mining Corp, 63-65; assoc ed, Coal Mining & Processing, 65-68; admin engr, Ill State Geol Surv, 68-76; PROF MINING ENG TECHNOL, IND STATE UNIV, EVANSVILLE, 76- *Concurrent Pos:* Prof, Univ Ill, Urbana; mining consult, 76- *Mem:* Soc Mining Engrs (secy, 72-79); Am Soc Eng Educ. *Res:* Mine safety; education in minerals industry. *Mailing Add:* Technol Div Ind State Univ Evansville IN 47712

EADON, GEORGE ALBERT, b Islip, NY, Oct 2, 45; m 73. ORGANIC CHEMISTRY, TOXICOLOGY. *Educ:* Mass Inst Technol, BS, 67; Stanford Univ, PhD(chem), 71. *Prof Exp:* asst prof, 71-76, assoc prof chem, 76-79, res scientist, 79-81, DIR, TOXICOLOGY INST, STATE UNIV NY, ALBANY, 81- *Mem:* Am Chem Soc; AAAS; Sigma Xi. *Res:* Mechanisms of electron-impact induced, photochemical and thermal reactions especially those involving hydrogen-atom transfer; application of mass spectrometry to stereochemical biochemical and analytical problems; chemistry of environmental contaminants. *Mailing Add:* Div Lab & Res NY State Health Dept Albany NY 12020

EADS, EWIN ALFRED, b Rockdale, Tex, Jan 24, 15; m 42; c 2. INORGANIC CHEMISTRY. *Educ:* NTex State Univ, BS, 40, MS, 42; Tulane Univ, PhD(inorg chem), 62. *Prof Exp:* Instr sci, NTex State Univ, 44-46; PROF CHEM, LAMAR UNIV, 46-, DIR ENVIRON STUDIES, 69- *Concurrent Pos:* Instr, Tulane Univ, 58-62; State of Tex res grant boron nitrogen heterocycles, 61-64. *Mem:* AAAS; Am Chem Soc. *Res:* Boron nitrogen heterocycles; flame reactions of organohalogens in presence of methane, air and copper oxide. *Mailing Add:* Dept of Chem Lamar Univ Beaumont TX 77710

EAGAN, ROBERT JOHN, b Rochester, NY, Aug 25, 44; m 76. GLASS SCIENCE, CERAMICS ENGINEERING. *Educ:* Alfred Univ, BS, 66; Univ Ill, MS, 68, PhD(ceramic eng), 71. *Prof Exp:* Mem tech staff ceramic eng, 71-77, SUPVR CERAMIC DEVELOP DIV I, SANDIA LABS, 77- *Concurrent Pos:* Mem subcomt 7, Int Comn Glass, 77-; trustee & mem exec comt, Int Glass Cong XII, Inc. 78- *Mem:* Am Ceramic Soc; Nat Inst Ceramic Engrs. *Res:* Development and characterization of new glass and glass ceramic materials; glass and glass ceramic to metal seal technology. *Mailing Add:* Div 5845 Sandia Labs Albuquerque NM 87158

EAGAR, ROBERT GOULDMAN, JR, b Richmond, Va, Feb 12, 47; m 73. BIO-ORGANIC CHEMISTRY, MICROBIOLOGY. *Educ:* Va Polytech Inst & State Univ, BSc, 69; Calif Inst Technol, PhD(chem), 74. *Prof Exp:* RES CHEMIST, UNION CARBIDE CORP, 75- *Mem:* Am Chem Soc; AAAS; Am Soc Microbiol. *Res:* Industrial microbiocides. *Mailing Add:* Specialty Chem & Plastics Div Union Carbide Corp Tarrytown NY 10591

EAGEN, CHARLES FREDERICK, b Detroit, Mich, Apr 13, 46; m 70; c 1. SOLID STATE PHYSICS. *Educ:* Oakland Univ, BA, 67; Iowa State Univ, PhD(physics), 72. *Prof Exp:* Presidential intern, Naval Res Lab, 72-73; RES SCIENTIST PHYSICS, FORD MOTOR CO RES LABS, 73- *Mem:* Am Vacuum Soc; Am Phys Soc. *Res:* Electronic and magnetic properties of metals. *Mailing Add:* Sci Res Staff Ford Motor Co Dearborn MI 48121

EAGER, GEORGE S, JR, b Baltimore, Md, Sept 5, 15; m 45; c 3. ELECTRICAL ENGINEERING. *Educ:* Johns Hopkins Univ, BE, 36, Dr Eng(elec eng), 41. *Prof Exp:* Physicist, Armstrong Cork Co, Pa, 45-47; asst dir res, Gen Cable Corp, 48-70, assoc dir res, 70-80; PRES, GRJ CORP, 80- *Mem:* Fel Inst Elec & Electronics Eng; Int Conf Large Elec Systs. *Res:* Electrical wires and cables; dielectrics; electrical transmission; high voltage testing. *Mailing Add:* 14 Bellegrove Dr Montclair NJ 07043

EAGER, RICHARD LIVINGSTON, b Kenaston, Sask, Aug 27, 17; m 49; c 2. PHYSICAL CHEMISTRY. *Educ:* Univ Sask, BE, 43, MSc, 45; McGill Univ, PhD(chem), 49. *Prof Exp:* From asst prof to assoc prof chem, 47-65, PROF CHEM, UNIV SASK, 65- *Concurrent Pos:* Vis lectr, Univ Leeds, 64-65. *Mem:* Chem Inst Can. *Res:* Use of biomass as a source of energy. *Mailing Add:* Dept of Chem & Chem Eng Univ of Sask Saskatoon SK S7N 0W0 Can

EAGLE, DONALD FROHLICHSTEIN, b St Louis, Mo, Jan 30, 33; m 61; c 2. MEDICAL PHYSICS. *Educ:* Yale Univ, BS, 54; Ga Inst Technol, MS, 56, PhD(physics), 62. *Prof Exp:* Asst res physicist, Eng Exp Sta, Ga Inst Technol, 56-61; sr physicist, Magnetic Tape Lab, Ampex Corp, 62-67; sr res physicist, Dikewood Corp, 67-69; mem tech staff, Sandia Labs, 69-73; fel med physics, Univ Tex M D Anderson Hosp & Tumor Inst, 73-74; med physicist, St Joseph Hosp & X-Ray Assocs, Albuquerque, 74-77; CHIEF PHYSICIST, BOCA RATON COMMUNITY HOSP, BOCA RATON, FLA, 77- *Concurrent Pos:* Adj prof radiol technol, Univ Albuquerque, 74-77. *Mem:* Am Asn Physicists in Med; Health Physics Soc; Am Phys Soc. *Res:* Microwave spectroscopy and molecular structure; magnetic materials and magnetism; systems analysis; radiological physics; physics of radiation therapy. *Mailing Add:* Dept of Radiation Oncol 800 Meadows Rd Boca Raton FL 33432

EAGLE, EDWARD, b Baltimore, Md, Nov 27, 08; m 42; c 4. PHYSIOLOGY, TOXICOLOGY. *Educ:* Johns Hopkins Univ, AB, 29; Univ Va, MS, 31; Univ Chicago, PhD(physiol), 40. *Prof Exp:* Asst physiol, Univ Chicago, 36-38, res asst, 38-42; res physiologist, Res Labs, Swift & Co, 46-49, head div toxicol & physiol, Res & Develop Ctr, 49-73; CONSULT TOXICOL, 73- *Concurrent Pos:* Mem coun arteriosclerosis, Am Heart Asn. *Mem:* Am Physiol Soc; Am Soc Pharmacol & Exp Therapeut; Soc Exp Biol & Med; Soc Toxicol. *Res:* Adrenal extracts; conditioned reflexes; choline; metabolism; cottonseed physiology; nutrition; chemicals in foods; toxicological evaluations. *Mailing Add:* 2230 Asbury Ave Evanston IL 60201

EAGLE, HARRY, b New York, NY, July 13, 05; m 28; c 1. MEDICINE. *Educ:* Johns Hopkins Univ, AB, 23, MD, 27. *Hon Degrees:* MS, Yale Univ, 48; DSc, Wayne State Univ, 65; DSc, Duke Univ, 81. *Prof Exp:* Intern, Hosp, Johns Hopkins Univ, 27-28, asst, Med Sch, 29-30, instr, 30-32; assoc bact, Sch Med, Univ Pa, 33-35, asst prof, 35-36; dir lab exp therapeut, Johns Hopkins Univ & USPHS, 36-46; sci dir res br, Nat Cancer Inst, 47-49, chief lab exp therapeut, Microbiol Inst, NIH, 49-58, chief exp ther, Nat Inst Allergy & Infectious Dis, 58-59, chief lab cell biol, 59-61; chmn dept cell biol, 61-70, PROF CELL BIOL, ALBERT EINSTEIN COL MED, 61-, ASSOC DEAN SCI AFFAIRS, 70-, DIR CANCER RES CTR, 75- *Concurrent Pos:* Fel, Johns Hopkins Univ, 28-29; res fel, Harvard Med Sch, 32-33; lectr, Sch Med, Johns Hopkins Univ, 36-47; trustee, Microbiol Found, Rutgers Univ. *Honors & Awards:* Lilly Bronze Medal, 36; Alvarenga Prize, Col Physicians Philadelphia, 36; Borden Award, Asn Am Med Col, 64; Einstein Commemorative Award, 69; NY Acad Med Award, 70; Louisa Gross Horowitz Award, 73; Sidney Farber Med Res Award, 74. *Mem:* Nat Acad Sci; Am Acad Arts & Sci; Am Soc Biol Chemists; Am Soc Clin Invest; Asn Am Physicians. *Res:* Immunochemistry; antigen-antibody reaction; serodiagnosis and chemotherapy of syphilis; blood coagulation; trypanosomiasis and tropical diseases; detoxification of metal poisoning; mode of action of antibiotics; cell and tissue culture. *Mailing Add:* Cancer Res Ctr Albert Einstein Col of Med Bronx NY 10461

EAGLE, SAM, b St Anthony, Idaho, July 11, 12; m 41; c 6. CHEMICAL ENGINEERING. *Educ:* Mont State Col, BS, 34; Carnegie Inst Technol, MS, 35, DSc(chem), 38. *Prof Exp:* Night sch instr, Carnegie Inst Technol, 37-38; res chemist, Res & Develop Sect, Chevron Res Co, Richmond, 38-41, asst foreman, Cracking Div, Richmond Refinery, 41-43, foreman, 43-45, res chemist, Calif Res Corp, 46-49, sr res chemist, 49-56, tech asst chem, 56-61, res engr, 62-72; RETIRED. *Mem:* Am Inst Chem Engrs; Am Chem Soc. *Res:* Process development in oil refining; adsorption; petrochemicals; catalyst research. *Mailing Add:* 7769 Baron Ct El Cerrito CA 94530

EAGLEMAN, JOE R, b Howell Co, Mo, Oct 9, 36; m 60; c 3. METEOROLOGY, SOIL PHYSICS. *Educ:* Univ Mo, BS, 59, MS, 61, PhD(meteorol), 63. *Prof Exp:* From asst prof to assoc prof meteorol, 63-75, PROF METEOROL, UNIV KANS, 75- *Mem:* Am Meteorol Soc; Am Soc Agron; Sigma Xi; Air Pollution Control Soc. *Res:* Methods of measuring and calculating evapotranspiration; surface energy budget and water balance; soil moisture movement and methods of measurement; microclimatology; structure of thunderstorms and tornadoes; tornado damage to buildings. *Mailing Add:* Dept of Geog & Meteorol Univ of Kans Lawrence KS 66044

EAGLES, DOUGLAS ALAN, b New Britain, Conn, Feb 22, 43; m 67; c 2. NEUROPHYSIOLOGY. *Educ:* Lake Forest Col, BA, 65; Univ Mass, MA, 68, PhD(zool), 72. *Prof Exp:* NIH fel neurobiol, Univ Iowa, 71-73; ASST PROF BIOL, GEORGETOWN UNIV, 73- *Mem:* AAAS; Am Soc Zoologists; Sigma Xi. *Res:* Physiology of mechanoreception, organization of motor systems and the roles of sensory feedback in the coordination of movement. *Mailing Add:* Dept of Biol Georgetown Univ 37th & O Sts NW Washington DC 20057

EAGLES, ELDON LEWIS, b Moncton, NB, Mar 9, 11; US citizen; m 57. MEDICINE, PUBLIC HEALTH ADMINISTRATION. *Educ:* Dalhousie Univ, MD & CM, 36; Univ Toronto, dipl, 40; Johns Hopkins Univ, DrPH, 58; FRCPS(C), 72. *Prof Exp:* Gen pract med & surg, NS, Can, 36-39; div med health officer, Dept Pub Health, NS, 40-54, dir child & maternal health, 54-56; assoc res prof, Grad Sch Pub Health, Univ Pittsburgh, 57-64; asst dir, Nat Inst Neurol Dis & Stroke, 64-70, dep dir admin & res, 70-79; RETIRED. *Concurrent Pos:* Res fel, Sch Hyg & Pub Health, Johns Hopkins Univ, 56-57; mem adv comt neurol & sensory dis serv, USPHS, 62-63, mem grants rev panel & commun dis res training comt, Nat Inst Neurol Dis & Blindness, 62-64. *Mem:* Fel AAAS; fel Am Speech & Hearing Asn; fel Am Pub Health Asn. *Res:* Neurological and sensory diseases, especially hearing. *Mailing Add:* 3703 Bloodsbury Ct Silver Springs MD 20907

EAGLES, JAN, histology, anatomy, see previous edition

EAGLESHAM, ALLAN ROBERT JAMES, b Rutherglen, Scotland, Apr 2, 45; Brit citizen. PLANT PHYSIOLOGY. *Educ:* Univ Glasgow, BSc, 68; Univ Bristol, PhD(biochem), 72. *Prof Exp:* Higher scientific officer, soil microbiol, Rothamsted Exp Sta, 73-76; asst plant physiologist, 76-82, ASSOC PLANT PHYSIOLOGIST, BOYCE THOMPSON INST PLANT RES, 82- *Concurrent Pos:* Vis scientist, Int Inst Trop Agr, 78. *Mem:* Soc Exp Biol; Am Soc Agron; Am Soc Plant Physiol; Am Soc Microbiol. *Res:* All aspects of nitrogen metabolism of plants with particular emphasis on the root nodule symbiosis of legumes, from both the fundamental and agronomical viewpoints. *Mailing Add:* Boyce Thompson Inst Tower Rd Ithaca NY 14853

EAGLESON, GERALD WAYNE, b Sioux City, Iowa, Apr 24, 47; m 74; c 1. ENDOCRINOLOGY, DEVELOPMENTAL BIOLOGY. *Educ:* Univ Calif, Riverside, BA, 68; Calif State Univ, Fullerton, MA, 73; Simon Fraser Univ, Burnaby, PhD(biol), 78. *Prof Exp:* Instr biol, Toloa Col, Tonga, 70-72; teaching asst molecular biol, Calif State Univ, Fullerton, 69-70, 72-73; teaching asst biol, Simon Fraser Univ, 74-77; instr, Univ Tex, Austin, 77-78, fel develop biol, 78-79; ASST PROF, LORAS COL, IOWA, 79- *Mem:* Am Soc Zoologists; Herpetologist's League; Am Asn Scientists. *Res:* Development and maturation of the pituitary, thyroids and gonads; timing of hypothalamic control of the hypothalamo-pituitary-thyroid (and gonad) axes. *Mailing Add:* Dept Biol Loras Col Dubuque IA 52001

EAGLESON, HALSON VASHON, b Bloomington, Ind, Mar 14, 03; m 32, 41; c 3. PHYSICS. *Educ:* Ind Univ, AB, 26, AM, 31, PhD(physics), 39. *Prof Exp:* Prof math & physics, Morehouse Col, 27-35, head dept physics, 35-47; PROF PHYSICS, HOWARD UNIV, 47- *Concurrent Pos:* Head dept, Clark Col, 40-47. *Mem:* Acoust Soc Am; Am Asn Physics Teachers; Nat Inst Sci (pres, 48). *Res:* Architectural acoustics; sound transmission; design of optical instruments; musical acoustics; ultrasonics; shock waves. *Mailing Add:* 3818-20th St NE Washington DC 20018

EAGLESON, PETER STURGES, b Philadelphia, Pa, Feb 27, 28; m 49, 74; c 3. HYDROLOGY. *Educ:* Lehigh Univ, BS, 49, MS, 52; Mass Inst Technol, ScD(civil eng), 56. *Prof Exp:* Asst fluid mech, Lehigh Univ, 50-51; asst fluid mech, 52-54, instr, 54-55, asst prof hydraul eng, 55-61, assoc prof civil eng, 61-65, head dept, 70-75, PROF CIVIL ENG, MASS INST TECHNOL, 65- *Honors & Awards:* Res Prize, Am Soc Civil Eng, 63; Horton Award, Am Geophys Union, 80. *Mem:* Am Soc Civil Eng; fel Am geophys Union; Int Asn Hydraul Res; Int Asn Sci Hydrol. *Res:* Hydrologic systems. *Mailing Add:* Dept of Civil Eng Rm 48-335 Mass Inst of Technol Cambridge MA 02139

EAGLETON, LEE C(HANDLER), b Vallejo, Calif, July 27, 23; m 53; c 3. CHEMICAL ENGINEERING. *Educ:* Mass Inst Technol, SB, 47, SM, 48; Yale Univ, DEng, 51. *Prof Exp:* Res assoc chem eng, Columbia Univ, 50-51; develop engr, Rohm and Haas Co, 51-56; from assoc prof to prof chem eng, Univ Pa, 56-70; PROF CHEM ENG & HEAD DEPT, PA STATE UNIV, 70- *Concurrent Pos:* Consult, Rohm and Haas Co, 56-74. *Mem:* Am Chem Soc; Am Soc Eng Educ; Am Inst Chem Engrs. *Res:* Heat and mass transfer to packed beds; adsorption; thermodynamics; kinetics; process optimization; mixing in liquid phase reactors; evaporation. *Mailing Add:* Dept of Chem Eng Fenske Lab Pa State Univ University Park PA 16802

EAGLETON, ROBERT DON, b Ladonia, TEx, Aug 19, 37; m 63; c 4. SOLID STATE PHYSICS. *Educ:* Okla State Univ, 59, MS, 62, PhD(physics), 69. *Prof Exp:* Instr physics, US Naval Nuclear Power Sch, Calif, 62-65; asst prof, 68-80, PROF PHYSICS, CALIF STATE POLYTECH UNIV, POMONA, 80- *Mem:* Am Asn Physics Teachers; Sigma Xi. *Res:* Temperature dependence of positronium annihilation in solids; thermally stimulated luminescence in stannic oxide single crystals and ceramics. *Mailing Add:* Dept of Physics Calif State Polytech Univ Pomona CA 91768

EAGON, JOHN ALONZO, b Portsmouth, NH, May 5, 32; m 57; c 2. MATHEMATICS. *Educ:* Princeton Univ, BA, 54; Univ Chicago, MS, 58, PhD(math), 61. *Prof Exp:* NATO fel math, Univ Sheffield, 61-62; asst prof, Univ Ill, Urbana, 62-67; assoc prof, 67-74, PROF MATH, UNIV MINN, MINNEAPOLIS, 74- *Mem:* Am Math Soc. *Res:* Commutative rings; linear graphs. *Mailing Add:* Dept Math Grad Sch Univ Minn Minneapolis MN 55455

EAGON, ROBERT GARFIELD, b Salesville, Ohio, Oct 29, 27; m 52; c 1. MICROBIOLOGY. *Educ:* Ohio State Univ, BSc, 51, MSc, 52, PhD(bact), 54. *Prof Exp:* Fulbright scholar, Pasteur Inst, Paris, 54-55; asst prof bact, 55-59, assoc prof microbiol, 59-66, PROF MICROBIOL, UNIV GA, 66- *Mem:* AAAS; Am Soc Microbiol; fel Am Acad Microbiol. *Res:* Bacterial metabolism; physiology. *Mailing Add:* Dept of Microbiol Univ of Ga Athens GA 30602

EAKER, CHARLES MAYFIELD, b Bonne Terre, Mo, Aug 3, 19; m 43; c 3. CHEMISTRY. *Educ:* Cent Col, AB, 41; Univ Md, PhD(org chem), 46. *Prof Exp:* Asst, Off Sci Res & Develop, Md, 43-45; res chemist, 46-52, res group leader, 52-69, RES SPECIALIST, MONSANTO CO, 69- *Mem:* Am Chem Soc. *Res:* Synthetic organic chemistry; rubber antioxidants and vulcanization agents; agricultural chemicals. *Mailing Add:* 241 Grayling Dr Akron OH 44313

EAKER, CHARLES WILLIAM, b St Louis, Mo, May 25, 49; m 74. CHEMICAL PHYSICS. *Educ:* Mich State Univ, BS, 71; Univ Chicago, PhD(chem), 74. *Prof Exp:* R A Welch fel chem, Univ Tex, Dallas, 74-76; instr, 76-78, asst prof, 78-81, ASSOC PROF CHEM, UNIV DALLAS, 81- *Mem:* Am Chem Soc. *Res:* Calculation of potential energy surfaces of small molecular systems using ab initio and semiempirical techniques; determination of dynamical properties of reacting systems on calculated potential surfaces; use of microcomputer graphics to simulate potential energy surfaces and to animate chemical reactions. *Mailing Add:* Univ of Dallas Station Irving TX 75061

EAKIN, BERTRAM E, b Jerome, Idaho, Oct 9, 28; m 52; c 3. CHEMICAL ENGINEERING, PETROLEUM ENGINEERING. *Educ:* Mass Inst Technol, BS, 51; Ill Inst Technol, MS, 57, PhD(gas technol), 62. *Prof Exp:* Lab technician, Chem & Geol Labs, Casper, Wyo, 51-53; lab technician, Inst Gas Technol, Ill Inst Technol, 53-54, asst chem engr, 54-57, assoc chem engr, 57-62, chem engr, 62-64, sr chem engr, 64-71; dir res, P-V-T Inc, 71-75; SR RES SCIENTIST, GETTY OIL CO, 76- *Concurrent Pos:* From adj instr to adj asst prof, Ill Inst Technol, 53-71. *Mem:* Am Inst Chem Engrs. *Res:* Experimental measurement of thermodynamic and transport properties of gases and liquids at cryogenic temperatures and elevated pressures, enhanced oil recovery processes, rock-fluid properties. *Mailing Add:* 2714 Morning View Dr Houston TX 77080

EAKIN, RICHARD MARSHALL, b Florence, Colo, May 5, 10; m 35; c 2. ZOOLOGY. *Educ:* Univ Calif, AB, 31, PhD(zool), 35. *Hon Degrees:* LLD, Univ Calif, Berkeley, 77. *Prof Exp:* Asst zool, Univ Calif, 31-34; Nat Res Coun fel, Univ Erlangen & Univ Freiburg, 35-36; from instr to assoc prof zool, 36-49, asst dean, Col Letters & Sci, 39-42, chmn dept, 42-48 & 52-57, chmn Miller inst basic res sci, 61-67, Miller res prof, 61-62 & 69-70, prof zool, 49-77, EMER PROF ZOOL, UNIV CALIF, BERKELEY, 77- *Concurrent Pos:* Guggenheim fel, Stanford Univ, 53; NSF fel, Univ Berne, 57; assoc ed, J Exp Zool, 67-71, J Ultrastruct Res, 73- & Zoomorphology, 77-; nat lectr, Sigma Xi, 74; distinguished vis prof biol, Tougaloo Col, 78; vis prof biol, Taladega Col, 79 & Fisk Univ, 81; trustee, Talladega Col, 81- *Honors & Awards:* Walker Prize, Boston Mus Sci, 76. *Mem:* Am Soc Zoologists (pres, 75); Sigma Xi; Soc Develop Biol; Int Soc Develop Biol; Electron Micros Soc Am. *Res:* Determination and regulation in amphibian development; fine structure of photoreceptors and of amphibian embryo. *Mailing Add:* Dept of Zool Univ of Calif Berkeley CA 94720

EAKIN, RICHARD R, b New Castle, Pa, Aug 6, 38; m 60. MATHEMATICS. *Educ:* Geneva Col, BA, 60; Wash State Univ, MA, 62, PhD(math), 64. *Prof Exp:* From asst prof to assoc prof math, 64-72, asst dean, Grad Sch, 69-72, vprovost student affairs, 72-78, vice provost, Instnl Planning & Student Affairs, 78-80, EXEC VICE PROVOST PLANNING & BUDGETING, BOWLING GREEN STATE UNIV, 80- *Mem:* Math Asn Am. *Res:* Combinatorial mathematics. *Mailing Add:* McFall Ctr Bowling Green State Univ Bowling Green OH 43403

EAKIN, RICHARD TIMOTHY, b Birmingham, Ala, May 25, 42. BIOPHYSICAL CHEMISTRY. *Educ:* Univ Tex, Austin, BS, 63; Calif Inst Technol, PhD(biochem), 68. *Prof Exp:* NIH fel, Stanford Univ, 68-71; RES ASSOC CHEM, UNIV TEX, AUSTIN, 71- *Concurrent Pos:* Vis staff mem, Los Alamos Sci Lab, 72- *Mem:* Am Chem Soc. *Res:* Respiratory-deficient cytoplasmic mutants of Neurospora; structure and function of cytochromes; biochemical applications of carbon-13 nuclear magnetic resonance spectroscopy. *Mailing Add:* Dept of Chem Univ of Tex Austin TX 78712

EAKINS, KENNETH E, b London, Eng, July 17, 35; m 61; c 2. PHARMACOLOGY, OPHTHALMOLOGY. *Educ:* Univ London, BPharm, 58, PhD(pharmacol), 62. *Prof Exp:* From asst prof to assoc prof ophthal, Col Physicians & Surgeons, Columbia Univ, 65-72, assoc prof, 72-76, prof pharmacol, 76-80; HEAD, PHARMACOL DEPT, WELLCOME RES LABS, UK, 80- *Concurrent Pos:* Nat Coun to Combat Blindness fel, Wilmer Inst, Med Sch, Johns Hopkins Univ, 62-63; USPHS grants, Nat Eye Inst, 66-; vis prof, Inst Ophthal, Univ London, 71-72; consult, NIH, 73-80; ed, Exp Eye Res, 75- *Mem:* Am Soc Pharmacol & Exp Therapeut; Brit Pharmacol Soc; Asn Res Vision & Ophthal; Int Soc Eye Res; Brit Res Asn. *Res:* Ocular inflammation; glaucoma; prostaglandin antagonists. *Mailing Add:* Wellcome Res Labs Langley Court Beckenham England

EAKINS, PETER RUSSELL, b Montreal, Que, May 17, 27; m 50, 62; c 3. GEOLOGY. *Educ:* McGill Univ, BSc, 48, MSc, 49, PhD(geol), 52. *Prof Exp:* Geochemist, Cerro de Pasco Corp, 52-55; explor geologist, Malartic Gold Fields, Ltd, 55-57; chief geologist, Mineral Mgt Ltd, 57-58; lectr geol, 58-59, asst prof, 59-64, ASSOC PROF GEOL, McGILL UNIV, 64- *Concurrent Pos:* Prof officer & geosci consult, Expo 65; consult geologist, Mkuski Copper Mines, Zambia, Africa, 67-68; chmn exhibits comt, Georama, 72, Int Geol Cong Montreal, 72; ed, Mineral Explor Res Inst, Montreal, 77- *Mem:* Geol Soc Am; Geochem Soc fel Royal Geog Soc; fel Geol Asn Can; Can Inst Min & Metall. *Res:* Structural geology; mineral exploration; Malartic gold deposits, Quebec; structures in the Quebec Appalachians; volcanic rock types of Northwestern Quebec; geochemical prospecting techniques for copper deposits in Peru. *Mailing Add:* Dept Geol Sci McGill Univ Montreal PQ H3A 2T5 Can

EAKS, IRVING LESLIE, b Sawtelle, Calif, May 24, 23; m 48; c 3. PLANT PHYSIOLOGY, BIOCHEMISTRY. *Educ:* Colo Agr & Mech Col, BS, 48; Univ Calif, Davis, MS, 50, PhD(plant physiol), 53. *Prof Exp:* Asst, Univ Calif, Davis, 48-52; from jr plant physiologist to assoc plant physiologist, Citrus Exp Sta, 52-62, PLANT PHYSIOLOGIST, UNIV CALIF, RIVERSIDE, 62-, LECTR BIOCHEM, 73- *Mem:* Am Soc Plant Physiol; Am Soc Hort Sci. *Res:* Post-harvest physiology, handling and chemical composition of fruits; chilling injury; biogenesis of and responses to ethylene. *Mailing Add:* Dept of Biochem Univ of Calif Riverside CA 92502

EALES, JOHN GEOFFREY, b Wolverhampton, Eng, Sept 9, 37; m 63; c 1. ANIMAL PHYSIOLOGY, ENDOCRINOLOGY. *Educ:* Oxford Univ, BA, 59; Univ BC, MSc, 61, PhD(zool), 63. *Prof Exp:* Asst prof biol, Univ NB, 63-67; from asst prof to assoc prof zool, 67-73, PROF ZOOL, UNIV MAN, 73- *Mem:* Can Soc Zoologists; Am Soc Zoologists. *Res:* Thyroid function in fish. *Mailing Add:* Dept of Zool Univ of Man Winnipeg MB R3B 2E9 Can

EALY, ROBERT PHILLIP, b Kay Co, Okla, July 6, 14; m 39. ORNAMENTAL HORTICULTURE, ECOLOGY. *Educ:* Okla State Univ, BS, 41; Kans State Col, MS, 46; La State Univ, PhD, 55. *Prof Exp:* Asst hort, Kans State Col, 41-42; from asst prof to prof, Okla State Univ, 46-61; prof hort & head dept, 61-63, prof hort & landscape archit & head dept, 63-66, dir landscape archit, 66-69, assoc dean, Col Archit & Design, 67-74, head dept, 69-79, PROF LANDSCAPE ARCHIT, KANS STATE UNIV, 66- *Mem:* Fel Am Soc Landscape Archit. *Res:* Landscape architecture; outdoor recreation; plant ecology; environmental planning; ornamental landscape plant materials; dwarfing rootstocks; herbaceous perennial flowers; chlorosis of ornamentals; graft unions; container grown nursery stock; radioactive tracers. *Mailing Add:* 1925 Vermont St Manhattan KS 66502

EAMES, ARNOLD C, b West Paris, Maine, Feb 10, 30; m 54; c 3. PAPER CHEMISTRY. *Educ:* Rensselaer Polytech Inst, BME, 51; Inst Paper Chem, Lawrence, MS, 57, PhD(paper chem), 59. *Prof Exp:* Res engr, S D Warren Co, 53-54; proj engr, Container Corp Am, 57; res engr, 59-61, asst res dir new prod develop, 62-74, prod develop mgr, 74-77, ASST RES DIR, GRAPHIC ARTS & REPROGRAPHIC PROD, S D WARREN CO, 77- *Mem:* Tech Asn Pulp & Paper Indust. *Res:* Coated paper technology for printing and other special uses. *Mailing Add:* S D Warren Co Westbrook ME 04092

EAMES, M(ICHAEL) C(URTIS), b Birmingham, Eng, Feb 6, 31; m 56; c 2. NAVAL ARCHITECTURE. *Educ:* Univ Durham, BSc, 50 & 51; NS Tech Col, ME, 57. *Prof Exp:* Shipbldg apprentice, R & W Hawthorn-Leslie & Co, Ltd, Eng, 47-52; sci officer hydrodyn, 52-58, group leader appl math, 58-60, head spec studies team, 60-63, head fluid mech sect, 63-74, SR SCIENTIST, CAN DEFENCE RES ESTAB ATLANTIC, 74- *Concurrent Pos:* Adj prof, Naval Archit, Tech Univ NS, 79- *Mem:* Soc Naval Archit & Marine Engrs; Am Soc Naval Engrs; Can Aeronaut & Space Inst; Royal Inst Naval Architects; Royal Aeronaut Soc. *Res:* Applied hydrodynamics and aerodynamics; naval architecture; aeronautical engineering; ocean engineering. *Mailing Add:* 49 Murray Hill Dr Dartmouth NS B2Y 3B2 Can

EAMES, WILLIAM, b Minnedosa, Man, Sept 21, 29; m 62; c 4. MATHEMATICAL ANALYSIS. *Educ:* Brandon Univ, BSc, 50; Univ Man, BSc, 52, MSc, 53; Queen's Univ, Ont, PhD(math), 56. *Prof Exp:* Nat Res Coun fel, Univ Col, Univ London, 56-57; asst prof math, Univ NB, 57-58; from lectr to sr lectr, Sir John Cass Col, Eng, 58-66; assoc prof, 66-78, PROF MATH, LAKEHEAD UNIV, 66- CHMN DEPT, 78- *Mem:* Am Math Soc; Can Math Cong; London Math Soc. *Res:* Measure theory. *Mailing Add:* Dept of Math Lakehead Univ Thunder Bay Can

EAMES, WILMER B, b Kansas City, Mo, May 8, 14; m 39; c 2. DENTISTRY. *Educ:* Kansas City-Western Dent Col, DDS, 39. *Prof Exp:* Prof oper dent, Dent Sch, Northwestern Univ, Chicago, 61-67, assoc dean, 64-67; prof, 67-79, EMER PROF OPER DENT, SCH DENT, EMORY UNIV, 79- *Concurrent Pos:* Vis prof, Sch Dent, Colo Univ, 80- *Honors & Awards:* Hallenback Mem Prize, 78. *Mem:* Am Dent Asn; Int Asn Dent Res; Am Acad Restorative Dent. *Res:* Dental materials and operative techniques; clinical studies comparing dental materials. *Mailing Add:* Apt 501 14390 E Marina Dr Aurora CO 80014

EANES, EDWARD DAVID, b Rochester, NY, Sept 2, 34; m 61; c 2. BIOPHYSICAL CHEMISTRY. *Educ:* Col William & Mary, BS, 57; Johns Hopkins Univ, MA, 59, PhD(crystal struct), 61. *Prof Exp:* Phys chemist, Nat Bur Standards, 60-61; asst prof phys chem, Med Col, Cornell Univ, 63-67; chief molecular struct sect, 67-80, CHIEF MINERAL CHEM & STRUCT SECT, LAB BIOL STRUCT, NAT INST DENT RES, 80- *Mem:* AAAS; Am Chem Soc; Am Crystallog Asn; Int Asn Dent Res; Sigma Xi. *Res:* Calcium phosphate chemistry; biological calcification. *Mailing Add:* Lab of Biol Struct Nat Inst of Dent Res Bethesda MD 20205

EARECKSON, WILLIAM MILTON, III, b Philadelphia, Pa, Oct 10, 22; m 48; c 4. ORGANIC POLYMER CHEMISTRY. *Educ:* Univ Md, BS, 43, PhD(chem), 50. *Prof Exp:* Asst phys chem, Univ Md, 46-48; res chemist, Textile Fibers Dept, Pioneering Res Lab, Del, 50-56, res supvr, 56-61, sr res chemist, Spruance Res & Develop Lab, 61-79, develop assoc, 79-81, CONSULT, E I DU PONT DE NEMOURS & CO, INC, 81- *Concurrent Pos:* Guest lectr chem, Grad Sch, Univ Richmond, 68. *Mem:* AAAS; Am Chem Soc; Sigma Xi. *Res:* Synthetic fiber and cellulosic papers; spun bonded fabric products; polymer synthesis, stabilization and characterization; high temperature polymers; polymer ingredients; high strength fibers. *Mailing Add:* 8409 Freestone Ave Richmond VA 23229

EARGLE, GEORGE MARVIN, b Salisbury, NC, Sept 29, 39. APPLIED MATHEMATICS. *Educ:* Univ NC, Chapel Hill, BS, 61, NC State Univ, MA, 63, PhD(math), 68. *Prof Exp:* Asst prof math, NC State Univ, 66-69; from asst prof to assoc prof, 69-79, PROF MATH SCI, APPALACHIAN STATE UNIV, 79- *Mem:* Soc Indust & Appl Math; Math Asn Am. *Res:* Applications of mathematics; elasticity theory. *Mailing Add:* Dept of Math Appalachian State Univ Boone NC 28608

EARHART, CHARLES FRANKLIN, JR, b Melrose Park, Ill, Oct 26, 41. MOLECULAR BIOLOGY, MICROBIAL PHYSIOLOGY. *Educ:* Knox Col, Ill, AB, 62; Purdue Univ, PhD(molecular biol), 67. *Prof Exp:* NIH fel, Sch Med, Tufts Univ, 67-68; fac assoc microbiol, 68-70, asst prof, 70-77, ASSOC PROF MICROBIOL, UNIV TEX, AUSTIN, 77- *Mem:* AAAS; Am Soc Microbiol; Genetics Soc Am; Sigma Xi. *Res:* Bacterial cell envelopes; genetics and physiology of iron assimilation in microbial systems. *Mailing Add:* Dept of Microbiol Univ of Tex Austin TX 78712

EARHART, J RONALD, b Hershey, Pa, July 29, 41; m 63; c 2. PHYSICS. *Educ:* Lebanon Valley Col, BS, 63; Univ NH, MS, 66, PhD(physics), 69. *Prof Exp:* Sr physicist, high frequency radar-propagation, Int Tel & Tel Electro Physics Labs, 68-73; SR PHYSICIST SONAR-SYSTS ANAL, APPL PHYSICS LAB, JOHNS HOPKINS UNIV, 73- *Mem:* Am Geophys Union; Sigma Xi. *Res:* Ionospheric propagation; radar; system analysis; space physics (particles); sonar; doppler navigation. *Mailing Add:* Appl Physics Lab Johns Hopkins Rd Laurel MD 20707

EARHART, RICHARD WILMOT, b Columbus, Ohio, Jan 19, 40; m 73. PHYSICS. *Educ:* Middlebury Col, AB, 60; Ohio State Univ, BSc, 61, MSc, 66. *Prof Exp:* Staff asst planning, Off Dir Defense Res & Eng, 66-69; RES SCIENTIST PLANNING & ANAL, COLUMBUS DIV, BATTELLE MEM INST, 71- *Mem:* AAAS; Soc Am Mil Engrs. *Res:* Economic analyses and planning of civil space systems. *Mailing Add:* Univ Sta PO Box 3161 Columbus OH 43210

EARING, MASON HUMPHRY, b Albany, NY, Oct 23, 21; m 49; c 4. ORGANIC POLYMER CHEMISTRY. *Educ:* Rensselaer Polytech Inst, PhD(chem), 50. *Prof Exp:* Mem staff org res, Wyandotte Chem Corp, 50-60, sr res chemist, 60-63 & Ballast Dept, Gen Elec Co, 63-75; RES SUPVR, SPENCER KELLOGG DIV, TEXTRON INC, 75- *Mem:* Fel AAAS; Am Chem Soc; fel Am Inst Chemists. *Res:* Industrial and polymer chemistry; polyethers and urethane polymers; dielectric and acoustic properties of polymers. *Mailing Add:* Spencer Kellogg Res 4201 Genesee Buffalo NY 14225

EARL, ALFRED ELLSWORTH, b Mt Vernon, NY, June 8, 19; m 41; c 4. TOXICOLOGY. *Educ:* Cornell Univ, DVM, 41. *Prof Exp:* Pvt pract, 41-48; sr res vet, Admin Comt Macrobiol Res, Ciba Pharmaceut Co, 48-54, dir vet res, 54-62, dir toxicol & path res, 62-69; head vet res, Animal Health Div, Ayerst Res Labs, 69-74; state vet, NY Dept Agr & Health, 74-77; DIR OTISVILLE BR, BUR LABS, NEW YORK DEPT HEALTH, 77- *Concurrent Pos:* Mem sci adv comt, Animal Health Inst. *Mem:* Am Vet Med Asn; Soc Toxicol; Pharmaceut Mfrs Asn; Pan-Am Med Asn; Am Asn Lab Animal Sci. *Res:* Pathology; experimental surgery; lab animal care; biologic quality control; pharmacology. *Mailing Add:* Otisville Br New York Dept of Health Otisville NY 10963

EARL, ALLAN EDWIN, b Kingston, Ont, Sept 19, 39; m 61; c 3. FOOD SCIENCE. *Educ:* Queens Univ, BS, 61, MS, 63; Univ Alta, PhD(carbohydrate chem), 68. *Prof Exp:* Sr scientist, Labatt Breweries Can Ltd, 68-74; food prod develop engr, 74-75, dir, Can Food Prod Develop Ctr, Man Res Coun, 75-77; res coordr, Rapeseed Asn Can, 77-79; EXEC DIR, CANOLA COUNCIL CAN, 79- *Mem:* Can Inst Food Sci & Technol; Inst Food Technologists; Am Asn Cereal Chemists; Chem Inst Can. *Res:* Food processing, new and improved. *Mailing Add:* 863 Beaverhill Bl Winnipeg Can

EARL, BOYD L, b Pa, July 20, 27; m 49; c 4. MATHEMATICS. *Educ:* Wilkes Col, BS, 52; Bucknell Univ, MS, 57. *Prof Exp:* Teacher high sch, Pa, 52-56; instr math, Bucknell Univ, 56-61; ASSOC PROF MATH, WILKES COL, 61- *Mem:* Math Asn Am; Am Math Soc. *Res:* Topology; algebra. *Mailing Add:* Dept of Math Wilkes Col Wilkes-Barre PA 18703

EARL, CHARLES RILEY, b San Diego, Calif, Oct 27, 33; m 60; c 2. POLYMER CHEMISTRY, PHYSICAL CHEMISTRY. *Educ:* Whittier Col, AB, 55; Polytech Inst Brooklyn, PhD(polymer chem), 70. *Prof Exp:* Chemist, US Food & Drug Admin, 55-56 & Aerojet-Gen Corp, 56-59; res fel, Jewish Hosp Brooklyn, 59-61; sr res fel, Polytech Inst Brooklyn, 62-68; sr res chemist, Deering Milliken Res Corp, 68-72; head dept chem & textiles, Spartanburg Tech Col, 72-81. *Concurrent Pos:* vis assoc prof, Clemson Univ, 81-82. *Mem:* Am Chem Soc. *Res:* Adsorption, adhesion of polymers to textile fibers; relationship of polymer structure and properties; polyelectrolytes. *Mailing Add:* 440 Harrell Dr Spartanburg SC 29302

EARL, FRANCIS LEE, b Jasper, Mo, Dec 12, 24; m 50; c 2. VETERINARY TOXICOLOGY. *Educ:* Mich State Col, DVM, 47. *Prof Exp:* Vet, State Vet Off, State Mo, 47-48; sta vet, Animal Husb Div, Bur Animal Indust, USDA, Md, 48-52, vet, Path Div, 52-61; vet, Div Toxicol, Food & Drug Admin, 61-63, vet med officer, Bur Foods, 64-75, facil mgr, Spec Pharmacol Animal Lab, 75-80; VET CONSULT, 80- *Mem:* Am Vet Med Asn; Am Col Vet Toxicol; Am Asn Lab Animal Sci; Teratology Soc. *Res:* Atrophic rhinitis in swine; swine erysipelas; use of swine on drug toxicity research; comparative toxicology of dogs and swine; diseases and housing of miniature swine; clinical laboratory values of dogs and swine; ocular toxicity in dogs; teratogenic effects of compounds in dogs and miniature swine; perinatal toxicology. *Mailing Add:* 2613 Hughes Rd Adelphi MD 20783

EARL, JAMES ARTHUR, b Omaha, Nebr, Aug 14, 32; m 55; c 4. PHYSICS. *Educ:* Mass Inst Technol, BS, 53, PhD(physics), 57. *Prof Exp:* Physicist, Ft Monmouth, 58; from lectr to asst prof physics, Univ Minn, 58-65; assoc prof, 65-75, PROF PHYSICS, UNIV MD, 75- *Concurrent Pos:* Sr scientist award, Alexander von Humboldt Found, 77-78. *Mem:* Fel Am Phys Soc; Am Geophys Union; Am Astron Soc. *Res:* Cosmic ray extensive air showers; solar cosmic rays; primary cosmic ray electrons; charged particle transport theory. *Mailing Add:* Dept Physics & Astron Univ of Md College Park MD 20742

EARL, ALVIN MATHEWS, b Topeka, Kans, Mar 20, 31; m 54; c 3. ANATOMY. *Educ:* Loyola Univ, Ill, BS, 54; Univ Colo, MS, 58, PhD(zool), 62. *Prof Exp:* Assoc prof biol & chmn dept, Regis Col, Colo, 60-66; ASSOC PROF ANAT, UNIV NEBR MED CTR, OMAHA, 68- *Concurrent Pos:* NIH spec res fel, Med Ctr, Univ Kans, 66-68. *Mem:* AAAS; Am Asn Anatomists; Sigma Xi. *Res:* Comparative anatomy; vertebrate embryology; comparative neuroanatomy. *Mailing Add:* Dept Anat Univ Nebr Med Ctr Omaha NE 68105

EARLE, CLIFFORD JOHN, JR, b Racine, Wis, Nov 3, 35; m 60; c 2. MATHEMATICS. *Educ:* Swarthmore Col, BA, 57; Harvard Univ, MA, 58, PhD(math), 62. *Prof Exp:* Instr & res fel math, Harvard Univ, 62-63; mem, Inst Advan Study, 63-65; from asst prof to assoc prof, 65-69, chmn dept, 76-79, PROF MATH, CORNELL UNIV, 69- *Mem:* AAAS; Am Math Soc. *Res:* Functions of a complex variable; Riemann surfaces; quasiconformal mappings; automorphic forms. *Mailing Add:* Dept of Math Cornell Univ Ithaca NY 14853

EARLE, DAVID PRINCE, JR, b Englewood, NJ, May 23, 10; m 36; c 4. MEDICINE. *Educ:* Princeton Univ, AB, 33; Columbia Univ, MD, 37, MedScD(int med), 42. *Prof Exp:* Intern, St Luke's Hosp, New York, 37-39; resident, Columbia Univ & res serv, Goldwater Hosp, 39-41; from instr to assoc prof, Sch Med, NY Univ, 41-54; chmn dept, 65-73, prof med, 54-78, EMER PROF MED, SCH MED, NORTHWESTERN UNIV, CHICAGO, 78- *Concurrent Pos:* Res assoc, NY Univ Res Serv, Goldwater Hosp, 41-46, dir, 46-47; consult, Surgeon Gen, 52-56; mem cardiovasc study sect, USPHS, 58-62; mem metab training grants comt, Nat Inst Arthritis & Metab Dis, 64-67, chmn, 66-67, mem urol res training grants comt, 67-69, chmn, 68-69, mem, Nat Adv Arthritis & Metab Dis Coun, 70-74. *Mem:* Am Soc Clin Invest; Am Clin & Climat Asn; Am Physiol Soc; master Am Col Physicians; Asn Am Physicians. *Res:* Clinical and experimental renal disease; chemotherapy of human malaria; streptococcal infections; hemorrhagic fever. *Mailing Add:* Northwestern Univ Med Sch Chicago IL 60611

EARLE, ELIZABETH DEUTSCH, b Vienna, Austria, Oct 6, 37; US citizen; m 60; c 2. PLANT TISSUE CULTURE, CELL BIOLOGY. *Educ:* Swarthmore Col, BA, 59; Radcliffe Col, MA, 60; Harvard Univ, PhD(biol), 64. *Prof Exp:* Res assoc biol, Harvard Univ, 68-69; res assoc & lectr floricult, Cornell Univ, 70-74; vis res assoc biol, Stanford Univ, 74-75; res assoc plant breeding, 75-78, sr res assoc, 78-79, ASSOC PROF PLANT BREEDING, CORNELL UNIV, 79- *Concurrent Pos:* NIH fel, 64-65; NSF grants 77-81. *Mem:* Am Soc Plant Physiologists; Int Asn Plant Tissue Cult. *Res:* Culture of plant cells and protoplasts; genetic manipulations with plant cells; effects of phytopathogenic toxins on ultrastructure and physiology of plants and cells. *Mailing Add:* Dept of Plant Breeding & Biomet Cornell Univ Ithaca NY 14853

EARLE, ERIC DAVIS, b Carbonear, Nfld, Nov 26, 37; c 3. NUCLEAR PHYSICS. *Educ:* Memorial Univ Nfld, BSc, 58; Univ BC, MSc, 60; Oxford Univ, DPhil, 64. *Prof Exp:* RES SCIENTIST NUCLEAR PHYSICS, ATOMIC ENERGY CAN, 64- *Mem:* Can Asn Physicists; Am Phys Soc. *Mailing Add:* Chalk River Nuclear Lab Atomic Energy Can Ltd Chalk River Can

EARLE, ERNEST L, JR, b Cambridge, Mass, May 24, 22; m 56; c 2. CHEMICAL ENGINEERING. *Educ:* Northeastern Univ, BSChE, 47. *Prof Exp:* Jr technologist, Corp Res Dept, Gen Foods, Inc, 47-48, asst technologist, 48-50, assoc technologist, 50-52, proj leader, 52-54, sect head, 54-60, lab mgr, 60-77, cent res mgr, 77-81, PRIN SCIENTIST, GEN FOODS CORP, 81- *Mem:* Inst Food Technologists; Am Inst Chem Engrs. *Mailing Add:* 3 Prides Crossing New City NY 10956

EARLE, NORMAN WILLISTON, entomology, see previous edition

EARLE, RALPH HERVEY, JR, b Cranston, RI, Apr 15, 28. SCIENCE ADMINISTRATION, INDUSTRIAL CHEMISTRY. *Educ:* Brown Univ, ScB, 49; Ga Inst Tech, MS, 50; Purdue Univ, PhD(org chem), 57. *Prof Exp:* Chemist, Hercules Powder Co, 50, 52-54, res chemist, 57-68, supvr com develop adv planning, Pine & Paper Chem Dept, Hercules Inc, 68-71, venture mgr, new enterprise dept, 71-74, CORP MGR NEW TECHNOL, HERCULES INC, 74- *Concurrent Pos:* Fel chem, Univ Canterbury, 66-67. *Mem:* Am Chem Soc; The Chem Soc; Soc Chem Indust; World Future Soc. *Res:* Chemistry of wet strength resins; nitrogen-containing heterocycles; amine-epichlorhydrin reactions, retention and flocculation. *Mailing Add:* Hercules Inc 910 Market St Wilmington DE 19899

EARLE, ROBERT WALLACE, pharmacology, deceased

EARLEY, JAMES WILLIAM, b Adelaide Twp, Ont, July 6, 22; US citizen; m 46; c 3. GEOCHEMISTRY. *Educ:* Univ Western Ont, BSc, 45; Queen's Univ, Ont, 47; Univ Toronto, PhD(mineral), 50. *Prof Exp:* Mineralogist, Gulf Res & Develop Co, 49-50, head, Chem Mineral Sect, 50-57, asst dir, Div Geol & Geochem, 57-62, supvr, Geochem Sect, 62-66, training mgr, Gulf Res & Develop Co, 66-67, mgr explor, Nuclear Fuels Div, Gulf Oil Corp, 67-68, vpres, 68-74, SR VPRES, GULF MINERAL RESOURCES CO, 74- *Mem:* Fel Mineral Soc Am; Geochem Soc; Geol Soc Am; Am Asn Petrol Geol; Can Mineral Asn. *Res:* Geochemical and mineralogical processes involved in deposition of sediments; formation of rocks; origin, migration and accumulation of oil. *Mailing Add:* Gulf Mineral Resources Co 1720 S Bellaire St Denver CO 80222

EARLEY, JOSEPH EMMET, b Providence, RI, Apr 6, 32; m 56; c 3. PHYSICAL INORGANIC CHEMISTRY. *Educ:* Providence Col, BS, 54; Brown Univ, PhD(phys chem), 57. *Prof Exp:* Res assoc inorg chem, Univ Chicago, 57-58; from asst prof to assoc prof chem, 58-69, PROF CHEM, GEORGETOWN UNIV, 69- *Concurrent Pos:* Consult & coordr chem res eval, US Air Force Off Sci Res, 61-; vis assoc, Calif Inst Technol, 67-68; guest researcher, Free Univ Brussels, 76. *Honors & Awards:* Potter Prize, Brown Univ, 57. *Mem:* AAAS; Am Chem Soc; Soc Study Process Philos. *Res:* Mechanisms of inorganic oxidation reactions in aqueous solution; process philosophy. *Mailing Add:* Dept of Chem Georgetown Univ Washington DC 20057

EARLEY, LAURENCE E, b Ahoskie, NC, Jan 23, 31; m; c 2. INTERNAL MEDICINE. *Educ:* Univ NC, BS, 53, MD, 56. *Prof Exp:* From instr to asst prof, Harvard Med Sch, 63-68; from assoc prof to prof med, Univ Calif, San Francisco, 68-73; prof med & chmn dept, Univ Tex Health Sci Ctr San Antonio, 73-77; PROF MED & CHMN DEPT, UNIV PA, 77- *Concurrent Pos:* Boston Med Found grant, 61-63; NIH career develop award, 67-68; mem drug efficacy study, Nat Res Coun-Nat Acad Sci, 67-68; mem training grants comt, Nat Inst Arthritis & Metab Dis, 68-72; mem sci adv coun, Nat Kidney Found, 68, mem fel comt, 69-72; mem exec comt renal sect, Am Heart Asn, 68. *Mem:* Am Fedn Clin Res; Am Soc Clin Invest (pres, 75-76); Asn Am Physicians; Am Physiol Soc; Am Soc Nephrology (pres, 77-78). *Res:* Physiology and pathophysiology of renal function and electrolyte physiology; physio-pharmacology of diuretic agents; physiology and pathophysiology of regulation of extracellular fluid volume; clinical renal diseases. *Mailing Add:* Dept of Med 3400 Spruce St Philadelphia PA 19104

EARLL, FRED NELSON, b Berkeley, Calif, Mar 5, 24; m 46; c 3. GEOLOGY. *Educ:* Univ Southern Calif, BS, 54; Univ Utah, PhD(geol), 57. *Prof Exp:* Geologist, Western Consult Serv, Utah, 54-57; from asst prof to assoc prof, 57-64, HEAD DEPT GEOL, MONT COL MINERAL SCI & TECHNOL, 58-, PROF, 64- *Mem:* Am Inst Mining, Metall & Petrol Engrs; Am Inst Prof Geologists; Soc Econ Geol. *Res:* Base and precious metal mining districts; geochemical prospecting; ore mineralogy. *Mailing Add:* Dept Geol Eng Mont Col Mineral Sci & Technol Butte MT 59701

EARLOUGHER, ROBERT CHARLES, JR, b Tulsa, Okla, June 26, 41; m 70. PETROLEUM ENGINEERING. *Educ:* Stanford Univ, BS, 63, MS, 64, PhD(petrol eng), 66. *Prof Exp:* Res engr, Marathon Oil Co, 66-69, adv res engr, 69-71; sr consult, Sci Software Corp, 72; advan res engr, 72-74; sr res engr, 74-77, mgr engr, Dept Res Div, 77-81, DIV RESERVOIR ENGR, MARATHON OIL CO, 81- *Honors & Awards:* Lester C Uren Award, Asn Inst Mining Engrs Soc Petrol Engrs, 79. *Mem:* Sci Res Soc Am; Soc Petrol Engrs; Am Inst Mining, Metall & Petrol Engrs. *Res:* Thermal and miscible water flooding methods of petroleum recovery; reservoir engineering; transient testing methods; reservoir simulation technique. *Mailing Add:* Marathon Oil Co Box 120 Casper WY 82602

EARLY, ALAN CLAIR, agricultural engineering, see previous edition

EARLY, JAMES G(ARLAND), b Washington, DC, Nov 8, 37; m 61; c 3. METALLURGY. *Educ:* Lehigh Univ, BS, 59; Rensselaer Polytech Inst, PhD(metall), 63. *Prof Exp:* METALLURGIST, NAT BUR STANDARDS, 63- *Mem:* Am Soc Metals; Am Inst Mining, Metall & Petrol Engrs; Am Soc Testing & Mat; Planseeberichte für Pulvermetallurgie. *Res:* Characterization of perfect metal crystals and origin of defects in metal crystals; hydrogen embrittlement of steels; fracture toughness testing; powder metallurgy; resource recovery. *Mailing Add:* Fracture & Deformation Div Nat Bur Standards Washington DC 20234

EARLY, JAMES M, b Syracuse, NY, July 25, 22; m 48; c 8. PHYSICS. *Educ:* NY State Col Forestry, Syracuse, BSc, 43; Ohio State Univ, MSc, 48, PhD(elec eng), 51. *Prof Exp:* Instr & res assoc elec eng, Ohio State Univ, 46-51; mem tech staff, Bell Tel Labs, 51-56, dept head, 56-62, dir, 62-69; div vpres, Fairchild Res & Develop Div, 69-80, MGR, VERY LARGE SCALE INTEGRATION ADVAND RES & DEVELOP LAB, FAIRCHILD CAMERA & INSTRUMENT CORP, 80- *Mem:* AAAS; Am Phys Soc; Inst Elec & Electronics Engrs. *Res:* Electron devices, particularly semiconductor; technology and engineering. *Mailing Add:* Fairchild Camera & Instrument Corp 4001 Miranda Ave M/S 30-200 Palo Alto CA 94304

EARLY, JOSEPH E, b Williamsburg, Ky, Jan 14, 40; m 63; c 1. MATHEMATICS EDUCATION. *Educ:* Cumberland Col, Ky, BS, 63; Univ Tenn, Knoxville, MMath, 66, EdD(math educ), 69. *Prof Exp:* Teacher elem sch, Ohio, 59-60 & high sch, Ky, 63-65; prof math, 69-77, PROF MATH & PHYSICS, CUMBERLAND COL, KY, 77-, CHMN DEPT MATH, 69- *Mem:* Math Asn Am. *Res:* Grade level teaching preferences of prospective elementary teachers with respect to their attitudes toward arithmetic and achievements in mathematics. *Mailing Add:* Dept of Math Cumberland Col Williamsburg KY 40769

EARNEST, ANDREW GEORGE, b York, Pa, July 14, 49; m 74. QUADRATIC FORMS. *Educ:* Elizabethtown Col, BS, 70; Ohio State Univ, MS, 72, PhD(math), 75. *Prof Exp:* Instr math, Ohio State Univ, 76; asst prof math, Univ Southern Calif, 76-81; ASST PROF MATH, SOUTHERN ILL UNIV, 81- *Mem:* Am Math Soc; Sigma Xi. *Res:* Arithmetic theory of integral quadratic forms; class numbers of genera and spinor genera of such forms, especially binary forms, and with the integers represented by ternary forms. *Mailing Add:* Dept Math Southern Ill Univ Carbondale IL 62901

EARNEST, SUE W, b Grand Forks, NDak, Sept 19, 07; m 28; c 2. SPEECH PATHOLOGY. *Educ:* San Diego State Col, BA, 29; Univ Southern Calif, MA, 37, PhD, 47. *Prof Exp:* Instr eng, Univ Louisville, 45-46; asst prof, 47-48, assoc prof speech, 48-54, chmn dept speech path & audiol, 54-61, prof, 54-77, EMER PROF SPEECH PATH & AUDIOL, SAN DIEGO STATE UNIV, 77- *Concurrent Pos:* Mem western regional educ comn, United Cerebral Asn, 63-66. *Mem:* Fel Am Speech & Hearing Asn; Int Soc Rehab Disabled. *Res:* Aphasia; cerebral palsy; geriatrics and speech. *Mailing Add:* Dept of Speech Path & Audiol San Diego State Univ San Diego CA 92115

EARNSHAW, JOHN W, b Toronto, Ont, July 22, 39; m 65. ELECTRON PHYSICS. *Educ:* Univ Toronto, BASc, 61; Cambridge Univ, PhD(electron physics), 65. *Prof Exp:* Asst sci res officer electron physics, Nat Res Coun Can, 65-67; asst prof, 67-70, ASSOC PROF PHYSICS, TRENT UNIV, 70-, HEAD DEPT, 76- *Mem:* Am Vacuum Soc. *Res:* Ultra high vacuum electron optics. *Mailing Add:* Dept of Physics Trent Univ Peterborough Can

EARTLY, DAVID PAUL, b Hammond, Ind, Mar 16, 42. EXPERIMENTAL HIGH ENERGY PHYSICS. *Educ:* Univ Notre Dame, BS, 63; Univ Chicago, MS, 65, PhD(physics), 69. *Prof Exp:* PHYSICIST, FERMI NAT ACCELERATOR LAB, UNIVS RES ASN, ENERGY RES & DEVELOP ADMIN, 69- *Mem:* Am Phys Soc. *Res:* Strong interaction physics via the study of fundamental nucleon-nucleon and meson-nucleon interactions. *Mailing Add:* 43W 920 Red Oaks Dr Elburn IL 60119

EASH, JOHN T(RIMBLE), b Albany, Ind, Sept 1, 06; m 27; c 2. METALLURGY. *Educ:* Purdue Univ, BS, 28; Univ Mich, MS, 29, PhD(metall), 32. *Prof Exp:* Asst, Univ Mich, 29-31; res metallurgist, Res Lab, Int Nickel Co, 31-35, sect supvr, 35-50, metall supvr, 50-54, from asst mgr to mgr, 54-70, mgr res, 70-73; METALL CONSULT, 73- *Mem:* Am Soc Metals; Am Foundrymen's Soc. *Res:* Copper-nickel-tin alloys constitution and properties; platinum and palladium dental alloys; cast iron melting; high strength low alloy steels; elevated temperature alloys; maraging steels. *Mailing Add:* 43 Bradrick Lane Allendale NJ 07401

EASLEY, JAMES W, b Los Angeles, Calif, Nov 17, 22; m 46; c 2. PHYSICS. *Educ:* Univ Calif, Berkeley, BA, 50, PhD(physics), 55. *Prof Exp:* Mem tech staff, Bell Tel Labs, 54-60, mgr radiation effects dept, Sandia Lab, 60-62, dir radiation physics res orgn, 62-64, dir, Mil Digital Systs Lab, 64-70, DIR, OCEAN SYSTS DEVELOP LAB, BELL LABS, 70- *Concurrent Pos:* Consult, Off Dir of Defense Res & Eng, 66-72. *Mem:* Sr mem Inst Elec & Electronics Engrs. *Res:* High energy nucleon-nucleon scattering; semiconductor device physics; radiation damage in semiconductors; ocean acoustics; information processing. *Mailing Add:* Ocean Systs Develop Lab Bell Labs Whippany NJ 07981

EASLEY, WARREN C, b Monterey Park, Calif, June 18, 41; m 67; c 1. PHYSICAL CHEMISTRY. *Educ:* Univ Calif, Riverside, BA, 63; Univ Calif, Berkeley, PhD(chem), 67. *Prof Exp:* Fel chem, Univ Fla, 67-69; res chemist, 69-75, res supvr, Exp Sta, 75-76, RES SUPVR, SPRUANCE RES LAB, E I DU PONT DE NEMOURS & CO, INC, 76- *Mem:* AAAS; Am Chem Soc. *Res:* Electron spin resonance of matrix isolated molecules; bonding in ground and excited states of small, reactive molecules; solid state chemistry; matrix-molecule interactions. *Mailing Add:* 3606 Seminary Ave Richmond VA 23227

EASON, ROBERT GASTON, b Bells, Tenn, May 15, 24; m 50; c 2. NEUROPSYCHOLOGY, PSYCHOPHYSIOLOGY. *Educ:* Univ Mo, BA, 50, MA, 52, PhD(psychol), 56. *Prof Exp:* Res assoc electrophysiol, Univ Calif, Los Angeles, 56-57; res psychologist, US Navy Electronics Lab, 57-60; from asst prof to prof psychol, San Diego State Col, 60-67; prof psychol & head dept, 67-80, ROSENTHAL PROF PSYCHOL, UNIV NC, GREENSBORO, 80- *Mem:* AAAS; Am Psychol Asn; Psychonomic Soc; Soc Psychophysiol Res; Soc Neurosci. *Res:* Electrophysiological correlates of arousal, motivation, emotion, attention and perception. *Mailing Add:* Dept Psychol Univ NC Greensboro NC 27412

EASSON, IAN WHITEMAN, b Ocean Falls, BC, Apr 9, 48; m 70. THEORETICAL ASTROPHYSICS. *Educ:* Univ BC, BSc, 69, MSc, 71, PhD(physics), 74. *Prof Exp:* Res assoc astrophys, Univ Ill, 75-77; RES ASSOC ASTROPHYS, MCMASTER UNIV, 77- *Res:* Neutron stars, pulsars, plasmas, superfluidity, superconductivity. *Mailing Add:* Dept of Physics SSC-318 McMaster Univ Hamilton Can

EASSON, WILLIAM MCALPINE, b Evanston, Ill, July 3, 31; m 58; c 4. PSYCHIATRY. *Educ:* Aberdeen Univ, MB & ChB, 54, MD, 67; FRCP. *Prof Exp:* Instr psychiat, Univ Sask, 59-61; staff psychiatrist, Menninger Found, 63-67; prof psychiat & chmn dept, Med Col Ohio, 67-72; prof & dir div child & adolescent psychiat, Med Sch, Univ Minn, 73-74; PROF PSYCHIAT & BEHAV SCI & HEAD DEPT, LA STATE UNIV MED CTR, NEW ORLEANS, 74- *Concurrent Pos:* Ed, J Clin Psychiat, 77-80. *Mem:* Fel Am Psychiat Asn; fel Am Orthopsychiat Asn. *Res:* Adolescent psychiatry; childhood psychosis. *Mailing Add:* Dept of Psychiat & Behav Sci La State Univ Med Ctr New Orleans LA 70112

EAST, CONRAD, meteorology, atmospheric physics, see previous edition

EAST, JAMES LINDSAY, b Senatobia, Miss, Nov 5, 36; m 63; c 1. VIROLOGY. *Educ:* Memphis State Univ, BS, 63, MS, 67; Univ Tenn, PhD(microbiol), 70. *Prof Exp:* Spec technologist virol, St Jude Childrens Res Hosp, 63-67; proj investr, 70-71, asst virol, 71-79, ASSOC VIROLOGIST, UNIV TEX SYST CANCER CTR, M D ANDERSON HOSP & TUMOR INST, 79- *Concurrent Pos:* USPHS trainee, St Jude Childrens Res Hosp, 67-70. *Mem:* Am Soc Microbiol; Int Asn Comp Res on Leukemia & Related Diseases; Am Asn Cancer Res. *Res:* Relatedness of retroviruses and human cancer. *Mailing Add:* Dept Tumor Virol M D Anderson Hosp & Tumor Inst Houston TX 77030

EAST, LARRY VERNE, b Apr 16, 37; US citizen; m 59; c 1. PHYSICS. *Educ:* Univ Wichita, BS, 58, MS, 60; Case Inst Technol, PhD(physics), 65. *Prof Exp:* Part-time instr, Case Inst Technol, 62-65; staff mem physics, Los Alamos Sci Lab, Univ Calif, 67-75; systs eng mgr, 75-80, MGR SOFTWARE DEVELOP, CANBERRA INDUSTS, 80- *Concurrent Pos:* Mem staff, Int Atomic Energy Agency, 82-83. *Mem:* Am Nuclear Soc; Am Phys Soc; Inst Nuclear Mat Mgt; AAAS. *Res:* Gamma-ray and x-ray spectroscopy; fission neutrons; nuclear physics instrumentation; software systems; nuclear safeguards. *Mailing Add:* Canberra Industs Inc 70 Gracey Ave Meriden CT 06450

EASTER, ROBERT ARNOLD, b San Antonio, Tex, Oct 10, 47; m 72; c 3. SWINE. *Educ:* Tex A&M Univ, BS, 70, MS, 72; Univ Ill, PhD(animal sci), 76. *Prof Exp:* Lectr, 76, asst prof, 76-80, ASSOC PROF ANIMAL NUTRIT, UNIV ILL, 80- *Mem:* Am Soc Animal Sci. *Res:* Nutrition of the pig with particular interests in amino acid and B-vitamin nutrition of the reproducing female and young suckling piglet. *Mailing Add:* 318 Mumford Hall 1301 WGregory Dr Urbana IL 61801

EASTER, STEPHEN SHERMAN, (JR), b New Orleans, La, Feb 12, 38; m 63; c 2. PHYSIOLOGY, ANATOMY. *Educ:* Yale Univ, BS, 60; Johns Hopkins Univ, PhD(biophys), 67. *Prof Exp:* USPHS fel physiol, Cambridge Univ, 67-68, Miller Inst Basic Res, Univ Calif, Berkeley, 68-69 & Wilmer Ophthal Inst, Johns Hopkins Univ, 69; asst prof zool, 70-74, chmn dept zool, 78-80, 81-82, assoc prof, 74-78, PROF BIOL, UNIV MICH, ANN ARBOR, 78- *Concurrent Pos:* Mem & chmn, Visual Sci B Study Sect, NIH, 78-82. *Mem:* Asn Res Vision & Ophthal; Biophys Soc; Soc Neurosci; Am Physiol Soc; Int Brain Res Orgn. *Res:* Development and plasticity of nervous systems, particularly visual; neurobiology. *Mailing Add:* Div Biol Sci Univ Mich Ann Arbor MI 48109

EASTER, WILLIAM TAYLOR, b Winston-Salem, NC, Dec 19, 31; m 61; c 2. ENGINEERING. *Educ:* NC State Univ, BS, 59; Carnegie Inst Tech, Carnegie-Mellon Univ, MS, 60. *Prof Exp:* Instr, 63-66, asst prof, 66-75, ASSOC PROF ELEC ENG, NC STATE UNIV, 75-, ASSOC DEPT HEAD, 80- *Concurrent Pos:* Dir, Eng Oper Prog, NC State Univ, 70-80. *Mem:* Inst Elec & Electronics Engrs; Am Soc Eng Educ; Am Soc Eng Mgt. *Mailing Add:* Elec Eng Dept NC State Univ PO Box 5275 Raleigh NC 27650

EASTERBROOK, DON J, b Sumas, Wash, Jan 29, 35; m 57. GLACIAL GEOLOGY. *Educ:* Univ Wash, Seattle, BS, 58, MS, 59, PhD(geol), 62. *Prof Exp:* From instr to assoc prof, 59-66, chmn dept, 65-77, PROF GEOL, WESTERN WASH UNIV, 68- *Concurrent Pos:* NSF res grants, 62-64, 64-66, 66-68, 80-81 & 80-82. *Mem:* Am Geophys Union; Geol Soc Am; Am Quarternary Asn; Int Quarternary Asn. *Res:* Glacial geology; geomorphology; sedimentation; environmental geology; quaternary glacial chronology; paleomagnetism of sediments; genesis of sediments; depositional environments; use of remanent magnetism of sediments in Pleistocene chronology; glaciation of the Puget lowland and Columbia plateau and correlations with European countries. *Mailing Add:* Dept of Geol Western Wash State Col Bellingham WA 98225

EASTERBROOK, ELIOT KNIGHTS, b Dudley, Mass, Oct 28, 27; m 57; c 2. POLYMER CHEMISTRY, ORGANIC CHEMISTRY. *Educ:* Univ NH, BS, 48, MS, 50; Ohio State Univ, PhD(phys org chem), 53. *Prof Exp:* Sr res chemist, Chem Div, US Rubber Co, 52-62, group leader stereo polymer res, 62-67, res scientist, Uniroyal Inc, 67-74, SR RES SCIENTIST, CHEM DIV, UNIROYAL INC, 74- *Mem:* Am Chem Soc. *Res:* Polymerization of butadiene and acrylonitrile; nonaqueous polymerization of ethylene and propylene elastomers. *Mailing Add:* Chem Div Uniroyal Inc Naugatuck CT 06770

EASTERBROOK, KENNETH BRIAN, b Ilford, Eng, June 4, 35. MICROBIOLOGY. *Educ:* Bristol Univ, BSc, 56; Australian Nat Univ, PhD(virol), 62. *Prof Exp:* Lectr virol, Univ Western Australia, 62-64; assoc prof, 67-74, PROF MICROBIOL, DALHOUSIE UNIV, 74- *Concurrent Pos:* Fel, Australian Nat Univ, 64-65; USPHS int fel, Calif Inst Technol, 65-66; fel, Ont Cancer Inst, 66-67. *Mem:* Can Soc Microbiol; Am Soc Microbiol; Electron Micros Soc Am; Can Soc Cell Biol; Micros Soc Can. *Res:* Structure and morphogenesis of viruses; microbial ultrastructure; structure, production and function of bacterial spinae. *Mailing Add:* Dept of Microbiol Dalhousie Univ Halifax Can

EASTERDAY, BERNARD CARLYLE, b Hillsdale, Mich, Sept 16, 29. COMPARATIVE MEDICINE. *Educ:* Mich State Univ, DVM, 52; Univ Wis, MS, 58, PhD(vet microbiol, path), 61. *Prof Exp:* Gen practice, Mich, 52, veterinarian, Ft Detrick, Md, 55-56, 58-61; asst, 56-58, assoc prof vet sci, 61-66, chmn dept, 68-74, prof vet sci, 66-79, DEAN SCH VET MED, UNIV WIS-MADISON, 79- *Concurrent Pos:* Mem expert panel on zoonoses, WHO; mem, Comt Animal Health, Nat Res Coun-Nat Acad Sci. *Mem:* Am Col Vet Microbiol; Asn Am Vet Med Cols (pres, 75-76); Am Vet Med Asn; Conf Res Workers Animal Dis. *Res:* Infectious diseases, viral; pathogenesis; influenza; epidemiology; herpesvirus latent infections. *Mailing Add:* Dept of Vet Sci Univ of Wis Madison WI 53706

EASTERDAY, HARRY TYSON, b Sault Ste Marie, Mich, Oct 6, 22; m 47; c 2. NUCLEAR PHYSICS. *Educ:* Univ Calif, AB, 47, PhD, 53. *Prof Exp:* Physicist, Radiation Lab, Univ Calif, 53-55; asst prof physics, Univ Ore, 55-60; assoc prof, 60-67, PROF PHYSICS, ORE STATE UNIV, 67- *Concurrent Pos:* Mem staff, Lawrence Radiation Lab, Univ Calif, Berkeley, 63-64. *Mem:* Am Phys Soc. *Res:* Low energy experimental nuclear physics. *Mailing Add:* Dept of Physics Ore State Univ Corvallis OR 97331

EASTERDAY, JACK L(EROY), b Crestline, Ohio, Mar 24, 28; m 50; c 2. ELECTRONICS ENGINEERING. *Educ:* Univ Toledo, BS, 52. *Prof Exp:* Assoc engr, Sperry Rand Corp, 52-55; elec engr, Reliability Eng Div, 57-60, proj leader, 60-62, sr engr, 62-64, asst dir adv electronics group, 64, assoc chief adv, Electronics Div, 65-73, assoc sect mgr, Eng Physics & Electronics Sect, 73-80, QUAL ASSURANCE SPECIALIST, OFF NUCLEAR WASTE ISOLATION, BATTELLE PROJ MGT DIV, BATTELLE MEM INST, 80- *Concurrent Pos:* Mem, Nat Eng Consortium, Microcomput Archit Interfaces, Testing, Reliability and Systs Design, 78. *Mem:* Inst Elec & Electronics Eng. *Res:* Reliability, system modeling, analysis and prediction of availability; maintainability, dependability, safety, microprocessors applications; electronic packaging; design review for production improvement including computerized circuit analyses; reliability and nuclear quality assurance; interpretation, development, implementation, specification, monitoring and auditing of nuclear quality assurance programs. *Mailing Add:* Off Nuclear Waste Isolation Battelle Mem Inst 505 King Ave Columbus OH 43201

EASTERDAY, KENNETH E, b Kirksville, Ind, June 27, 33; m 59; c 1. MATHEMATICS. *Educ:* Ind Univ, BS, 55, MA, 60; Western Reserve Univ, EdD, 63. *Prof Exp:* Teacher pub sch, Ohio, 57, 59-63 & Ind, 57-59; assoc prof math, State Univ NY, 63-64; from asst prof to assoc prof math in sec educ, 64-72, PROF MATH IN SEC EDUC, AUBURN UNIV, 72- *Res:* Construction of mathematics programs in grades seven through twelve; methods of teaching mathematics at all levels; modern algebra. *Mailing Add:* Dept of Math Educ 5064 Haley Ctr Auburn Univ Auburn AL 36830

EASTERDAY, OTHO DUNREATH, b Allen Co, Ind, Oct 3, 24; m 49; c 4. PHARMACOLOGY, RADIOBIOLOGY. *Educ:* Ball State Univ, BA, 48; Univ Iowa, MS, 50, PhD(pharmacol), 53. *Prof Exp:* Res asst pharmacol, Univ Iowa, 48-51; assoc pharmacologist, Brookhaven Nat Lab, 53-62;

pharmacologist & radiobiologist, Hazleton Labs, Inc, 62-66; dir dept pharmacol & radiation, Gulf S Res Inst, La, 66-68; head toxicol & pharmacol res, Res & Develop Ctr, 68-77, VPRES & CHIEF TOXICOLOGIST, INT FLAVORS & FRAGRANCES, INC, 77- *Mem:* Fel AAAS; fel NY Acad Sci; Am Soc Pharmacol & Exp Therapeut; Soc Toxicol; Biomet Soc. *Res:* Chemical structure and activity; pharmacodynamics; toxicology; biometry; radiation; radioactive tracers; spectroscopy; chemical synthesis; boron and lithium pharmacology and toxicology; natural products; radio respirom, and pharmacology. *Mailing Add:* Int Flavors & Fragrances Inc 521 W 57th New York NY 10019

EASTERDAY, RICHARD LEE, b Green Bay, Wis, Apr 2, 38; m 76. BIOCHEMISTRY. *Educ:* N Cent Col, BA, 60; Va Poly Tech Inst & State Univ, MA, 62, PhD(biochem & nutrit), 67. *Prof Exp:* Res assoc biochem, NY Univ Med Sch, 64-65; supvr tech serv, Pharmacia Fine Chem, 65-67, mgr, tech serv, 67-68, mgr res tech serv & qual control, Pharmacia Inc, 68-70, dir res, 71-76, dir res & develop & mkt, 77, gen mgr, 78-79, VPRES, PHARMACIA FINE CHEM, 79- *Mem:* Am Chem Soc; AAAS; NY Acad Sci. *Res:* Separation science; liquid chromatography; gel filtration. *Mailing Add:* 1729 Merriam Dr Martinsville NJ 08836

EASTERLING, GEORGE RILEY, b Guernsey Co, Ohio, Oct 15, 05; m 39; c 3. ZOOLOGY. *Educ:* Ohio Univ, AB, 27, MA, 33; Case Western Reserve Univ, MS, 65. *Prof Exp:* Teacher rural sch, Ohio, 24-26, teacher high sch, 27-40; from asst prof to assoc prof, 46-67, EMER PROF BIOL, KENT STATE UNIV, 67- *Concurrent Pos:* Teaching fel biol, Ohio Univ, 31-33. *Mem:* Sigma Xi; Am Asn Univ Profs. *Res:* Human heredity. *Mailing Add:* 223 Highland Ave Kent OH 44240

EASTERLING, RONALD E, b Benton Harbor, Mich, Apr 14, 32; m 54; c 5. INTERNAL MEDICINE, NEPHROLOGY. *Educ:* Univ Mich, Ann Arbor, MD, 57. *Prof Exp:* From instr to asst prof internal med, Univ Mich, Ann Arbor, 66-68; chief hemodialysis unit, Vet Admin Hosp, Ann Arbor, 68-70; from assoc prof to prof internal med, Univ Mich, Ann Arbor, 70-77; DIR, RENAL DIALYSIS & TRANSPLANT SERV, HURLEY MED CTR, MICH, 78- *Concurrent Pos:* Mem sci adv bd, Kidney Found Mich, 67-; consult, Nat Inst Arthritis, Metab & Digestive Dis, 74-; clin prof med, Mich State Univ, 78- *Mem:* Fel Am Col Physicians; Am Soc Artificial Internal Organs; Am Fedn Clin Res; Am Soc Nephrology; Asn Advan Med Instrumentation. *Res:* Treatment of renal failure by dialysis methods; in vivo evaluation of hemodialyzers; pathophysiology of renal failure. *Mailing Add:* Suite 310 Park Plaza G 1071 Ballenger Hwy Flint MI 48504

EASTERLING, WILLIAM EWART, JR, b Raleigh, NC, Oct 8, 30. OBSTETRICS & GYNECOLOGY. *Educ:* Duke Univ, AB, 52; Univ NC, MD, 56. *Prof Exp:* From intern med to resident obstet & gynec, NC Mem Hosp, 56-61, instr, 60-61; from asst prof to assoc prof, 64-72, assoc dean, Sch Med, 74-76, vice dean, Sch Med, 76-81, PROF OBSTET & GYNEC, NC MEM HOSP, UNIV NC, 67-, CHIEF-OF-STAFF, 74-, ASSOC DEAN CLIN AFFAIRS, SCH MED, 81- *Concurrent Pos:* Fordham Award, 61; fel reprod physiol, Univ Calif, 63-64. *Mem:* AAAS; AMA; Am Col Obstetricians & Gynecologists; Endocrine Soc; Soc Gynec Invest. *Res:* Endocrinology of obstetrics and gynecology. *Mailing Add:* Dept of Obstet & Gynec Univ of NC Sch of Med Chapel Hill NC 27514

EASTERLY, NATHAN WILLIAM, b Lewisburg, WVa, Sept 9, 27; m 52; c 3. TAXONOMIC BOTANY, BIOLOGY. *Educ:* WVa Univ, AB, 49, PhD(plant taxon), 57; State Univ Iowa, MS, 51. *Prof Exp:* Instr, 57-60, asst prof biol, 60-64, assoc prof, 64-75, PROF BOT SCI & CUR HERBARIUM, BOWLING GREEN STATE UNIV, 76- *Concurrent Pos:* Res fel, Ohio Acad Sci, Columbus, 60. *Mem:* Am Soc Plant Taxonomists; Sigma Xi. *Res:* A comparitive study of flora of northwestern Ohio. *Mailing Add:* Dept of Biol Sci Bowling Green State Univ Bowling Green OH 43403

EASTES, FRANK ELISHA, b Wilson Co, Tenn, July 31, 24; m 53; c 6. ORGANIC CHEMISTRY. *Educ:* Tenn Polytech Inst, BS, 49; Vanderbilt Univ, MS, 51, PhD, 55. *Prof Exp:* Staff scientist, E I du Pont de Nemours & Co, 53-62; sr proj leader, 62-66, SECT HEAD FILM COATINGS, CRY-O-VAC DIV, W R GRACE & CO, 66- *Mem:* AAAS; Am Chem Soc. *Res:* Reactions of thiophthalic anhydride; resolutions of racemic amines; cellulose chemistry; film coating and adhesion. *Mailing Add:* 729 Otis Blvd Spartanburg SC 29302

EASTHAM, ARTHUR MIDDLETON, b Vancouver, BC, Feb 15, 17; m 46; c 3. ORGANIC CHEMISTRY. *Educ:* Univ BC, BA, 37, MA, 39; McGill Univ, PhD(chem), 42. *Prof Exp:* Res chemist, Nat Res Coun Can, 42-45; res chemist, Polymer Corp, 45-48; res chemist, Nat Res Coun Can, 48-80; RETIRED. *Mem:* Am Chem Soc; Chem Inst Can; Royal Soc Chem. *Res:* Physical organic chemistry; catalysis by Friedel-Crafts reagents. *Mailing Add:* 265 Crestview Montreal Rd Ottawa ON K1H 5G4 Can

EASTHAM, JAMES NORMAN, b Cumberland, RI, Dec 10, 03; wid; c 3. MATHEMATICS. *Educ:* Providence Col, BS, 26; Catholic Univ, MA, 28, PhD(math), 31. *Prof Exp:* Instr math, Providence Col, 30-31; head dept math & physics, Nazareth Col, NY, 31-46; from asst prof to prof math, Cooper Union, 46-61; prof, 61-74, chmn dept, 61-69, dean open admissions serv, 71-74, EMER PROF MATH, QUEENSBOROUGH COMMUNITY COL, CITY UNIV NEW YORK, 74- *Concurrent Pos:* Instr, Univ Rochester, 40-42; consult, Rheem Mfg Co, 50-52. *Mem:* Math Asn Am; Am Soc Eng Educ. *Res:* Quartic curves; vibration theory. *Mailing Add:* 149-41 Hawthorn Ave Flushing NY 11355

EASTHAM, JEROME FIELDS, b Daytona Beach, Fla, Sept 22, 24; m 49; c 3. ORGANIC CHEMISTRY. *Educ:* Univ Ky, BS, 48; Univ Calif, PhD(chem), 51. *Prof Exp:* Asst, Univ Calif, 48-51; US AEC fel, London Univ, 51-52 & Univ Wis, 52-53; from asst prof to assoc prof, 53-62, PROF CHEM, UNIV TENN, KNOXVILLE, 62- *Mem:* AAAS; Am Chem Soc; The Chem Soc. *Res:* Chemistry of steroids and related natural products; mechanisms of organic reactions; organometallic chemistry. *Mailing Add:* Dept of Chem Univ of Tenn Knoxville TN 37916

EASTIN, EMORY FORD, b Picayune, Miss, Nov 27, 40; m 61; c 4. WEED SCIENCE, PLANT PHYSIOLOGY. *Educ:* Miss State Univ, BS, 62, MS, 63; Auburn Univ, PhD(bot, plant physiol), 66. *Prof Exp:* Asst prof weed sci, Miss State Univ, 66-67; from asst prof to assoc prof, 67-78, PROF AGRON, TEX A&M UNIV, 78- *Mem:* Weed Sci Soc Am; Am Soc Agron; Crop Sci Soc Am; Int Plant Growth Substances Asn; Int Weed Sci Soc. *Res:* Mode of action of herbicides in plants; absorption, translocation and metabolism of herbicides by plants; plant growth regulators. *Mailing Add:* Tex Agr Exp Sta Rte 7 Box 999 Beaumont TX 77706

EASTIN, JERRY DEAN, b Madrid, Nebr, Jan 18, 31; m 57; c 3. AGRONOMY. *Educ:* Univ Nebr, BSc, 53, MSc, 55; Purdue Univ, PhD(crop physiol), 60. *Prof Exp:* Nat Acad Sci-Nat Res Coun res assoc, Army Biol Labs, Ft Detrick, Md, 60-61; asst prof agron, Univ Nebr, 61-64; res plant physiologist, Crops Res Div, Agr Res Serv, USDA, 64-70; assoc prof agron, 70-72, PROF AGRON, UNIV NEBR, 72- *Concurrent Pos:* Fel, NZ Nat Climate Lab, 73. *Mem:* AAAS; fel Am Soc Agron; Crop Sci Soc Am; Am Soc Plant Physiol. *Res:* Carbon dioxide fixation in Bacillus anthracis; characterization of wheat gluten proteins by chemical and physical methods; physiology of the grain sorghum plant. *Mailing Add:* 205 KCRL Univ of Nebr Lincoln NE 68503

EASTIN, JOHN A, b Grant, Nebr, June 13, 34; m 61. AGRONOMY. *Educ:* Univ Nebr, BS, 58; Purdue Univ, MS, 61, PhD(crop physiol, biochem), 63. *Prof Exp:* Res asst crop physiol, Purdue Univ, 58-63; asst prof agron, Univ Wis, 63-68; res agronomist, DeKalb Agr Res Inc, 68-73; AGRONOMIC CONSULT, 73- *Mem:* AAAS; Crop Sci Soc Am; Am Soc Agron; Am Soc Plant Physiol; Soil Sci Soc Am. *Res:* Crop physiology and production; seed production technique improvement; manufacture of nitrogen fertilizer. *Mailing Add:* PO Box 389 Grant NE 69140

EASTIN, WILLIAM CLARENCE, JR, b Lorain, Ohio, Oct 22, 40; m 66; c 2. PHYSIOLOGIST, ZOOLOGY. *Educ:* Kent State Univ, BA, 67, MS, 70; Univ Iowa, PhD(physiol), 76. *Prof Exp:* Res scientist physiol, Univ Iowa Hosp, 76-77; res physiologist, Dept Interior, US Fish & Wildlife Serv, 77-81; PHYSIOLOGIST, DEPT HEALTH HUMAN SERV, NAT INST ENVIRON HEALTH SCI, 81- *Concurrent Pos:* Proj leader physiol, Dept Interior, US Fish & Wildlife Serv, 77-81, oil team res leader, 77-79. *Mem:* Soc Environ Toxicol Chem. *Res:* Animal physiology (membrane transport, biochemistry, and toxicology); carcinogenesis and toxicologic evaluation. *Mailing Add:* Progress Ctr NIEHS PO Box 12233 Res Triangle Park NC 27709

EASTLAND, DAVID MEADE, b Meridian, Miss, Nov 27, 22; m 44. THERMODYNAMICS, AIR CONDITIONING. *Educ:* Miss State Univ, BS, 44, MS, 50. *Prof Exp:* From instr to assoc prof, 46-58, PROF MECH ENG, MISS STATE UNIV, 58- *Mem:* Am Soc Mech Engrs; Nat Soc Prof Engrs; Am Soc Eng Educ. *Res:* Thermodynamics; fluid flow; instruments. *Mailing Add:* Dept of Mech Eng Drawer ME Miss State Univ Mississippi State MS 39762

EASTLAND, GEORGE WARREN, JR, b Omaha, Nebr, Sept 5, 39; m 67; c 2. INORGANIC CHEMISTRY, PHYSICAL CHEMISTRY. *Educ:* Wittenberg Univ, BS, 61; SDak State Univ, PhD(inorg chem), 69. *Prof Exp:* Teacher high sch, Ohio, 61-63; lab asst chem, Wittenberg Univ, 63-64; asst, SDak State Univ, 64-69; from asst prof to assoc prof, 69-78, PROF CHEM, SAGINAW VALLEY STATE COL, 78- *Concurrent Pos:* Vis scientist, Univ Leicester, 75-76. *Mem:* Am Chem Soc; Royal Soc Chem; NY Acad Sci. *Res:* Preparation and investigation of properties of novel coordination compounds of transition metals, such as rhenium and rhodium; synthesis of antitumor agents; electron spin resonance of chemical systems. *Mailing Add:* Saginaw Valley State Col 2250 Pierce Rd University Center MI 48710

EASTLER, THOMAS EDWARD, b Boston, Mass, Oct 10, 44; m 65; c 1. ENVIRONMENTAL GEOLOGY. *Educ:* Brown Univ, ScB, 66; Columbia Univ, MA, 68, PhD(geol), 71. *Prof Exp:* Asst prof geophys, US Air Force Inst Technol, 70-72; sr res geologist, US Army Engr Topog Labs, Washington, DC, 72-74; ASSOC PROF ENVIRON GEOL, UNIV MAINE, FARMINGTON, 74- *Concurrent Pos:* Vis lectr, Univ Dayton, & Wittenberg Col, Ohio, 70-72; fac assoc, Western Maine Energy Ctr, 77-; mem, New Eng Cong Caucus, 78. *Mem:* AAAS; Am Geophys Union; Geol Soc Am; Nat Asn Geol Teachers; Am Soc Photogram. *Res:* Environmental impact of engineering endeavors; remote sensing and environmental studies; ecosystems analysis; resources, energy and society; human ecology. *Mailing Add:* Dept of Geol Univ of Maine Farmington ME 04938

EASTLICK, HERBERT LEONARD, b Platteville, Wis, Apr 24, 08; m 35. ZOOLOGY. *Educ:* Univ Mont, AB, 30; Wash Univ, MS, 32, PhD(zool), 36. *Prof Exp:* Asst, Wash Univ, 31-34, instr zool, 34-35, asst, 35-36, instr, Univ Col, 35-36; instr, Stephens Col, 36-37 & Univ Mo, 37-39; Nat Res Coun fel, Univ Chicago, 39-40; from asst prof to prof zool, 40-73, chmn dept, 47-64, EMER PROF ZOOL, WASH STATE UNIV, 73- *Mem:* AAAS; fel Am Soc Naturalists; Soc Develop Biol; Am Asn Anat; Am Soc Zool. *Res:* Experimental embryology and carcinogenesis; cytology; histology; interspecies incompatibility; feather character and pathology in transplanted limbs; cytology of invertebrate and vertebrate muscle and adipose tissue; origin of avian melanoblasts. *Mailing Add:* Northeast 600 Garfield Pullman WA 99163

EASTMAN, ALAN D, b San Francisco, Calif, Oct 10, 46; m 70; c 4. INORGANIC CHEMISTRY. *Educ:* Univ Utah, BA, 71, PhD(chem), 75. *Prof Exp:* chemist, 75-81, MKT RES SPECIALIST, PHILLIPS PETROL CO, 81- *Mem:* Am Chem Soc; Sigma Xi. *Res:* Catalysis, especially the role of lattice oxygen in oxidation catalysts involving transition-metal mixed oxides. *Mailing Add:* Res & Develop Phillips Petrol Co Bartlesville OK 74004

EASTMAN, CAROLINE MERRIAM, b Columbus, Ohio, Dec 25, 46; m 68. INFORMATION RETRIEVAL, DATA BASE MANAGEMENT SYSTEMS. *Educ:* Radcliffe Col, BA, 68; Univ NC, Chapel Hill, MS, 74, PhD(comput sci), 77. *Prof Exp:* ASST PROF MATH & COMPUT SCI, FLA STATE UNIV, 77- *Mem:* Asn Comput Mach; Inst Elec & Electronic Engrs; Am Soc Info Sci; Asn Women Comput; Asn Women Math. *Res:* Information retrieval; data base management systems. *Mailing Add:* Dept Math & Comput Sci Fla State Univ Tallahassee FL 32306

EASTMAN, DANIEL ROBERT PEDEN, b Semans, Sask, Jan 23, 33; m 55; c 2. PHYSICS. *Educ:* Houghton Col, BS, 55; Pa State Univ, MS, 57, PhD(physics), 61. *Prof Exp:* Optical engr, Plummer & Kershaw, Pa, 61-62; from asst prof to prof physics, Houghton Col, 62-65; asst prof, 65-69, ASSOC PROF PHYSICS, PA STATE UNIV, 69- *Mem:* Optical Soc Am; Am Asn Physics Teachers. *Res:* Vibration rotation spectra; high precision spectroscopy; brillouin spectroscopy. *Mailing Add:* Dept of Physics Pa State Univ University Park PA 16802

EASTMAN, DAVID WILLARD, b Angela, NY, April 30, 39; c 6. GRAFT POLYMERIZATION, FREE RADICAL CHEMISTRY. *Educ:* Erie Co Tech Inst, AAS, 58; Canisius Col, BS, 61; State Univ NY, Buffalo, PhD(org chem), 70. *Prof Exp:* Group leader spectros, 61-66, sr chemist, 69-76, res mgr, PVC Prod, 76-80, tech dir, Ruco Div, 80-81, DIR TECHNOL, PVC FABRICATED PROD DIV, HOOKER CHEM & PLASTICS CO, 81- *Mem:* Soc Plastics Engrs. *Res:* Polyvinyl chloride polymers; compounds and processing of vinyl polymers; graft reactions; free radical chemistry; polymer rheology; polymer alloys. *Mailing Add:* PO Box 699 Pottstown PA 19464

EASTMAN, JOHN W, b Charleston, Ill, May 10, 35; m 66; c 2. CLINICAL CHEMISTRY. *Educ:* Pa State Univ, BS, 57; Univ Calif, Berkeley, PhD(chem), 61. *Prof Exp:* Teaching asst chem, Univ Calif, Berkeley, 57-58; NSF fel, 61-62; res asst quantum chem, Univ Uppsala, 62-63; chemist, Shell Develop Co, 63-71; chemist, Med Sch, Univ Calif, 71-73; asst prof, Med Sch, George Washington Univ, 73-74; CHEMIST, US FOOD & DRUG ADMIN, 74- *Concurrent Pos:* Alexander Von Humboldt res fel phys chem, Univ Mainz, 68-69. *Mem:* AAAS; Am Chem Soc; Am Asn Clin Chemists. *Res:* Electronic structure of molecules; photochemistry; medical analysis of calcium, calcium binding, lipids; medical lab data systems. *Mailing Add:* Western Path Labs 2945 Webster St Oakland CA 94609

EASTMAN, JOSEPH THORNTON, b Minneapolis, Minn, Nov 2, 44; m 70; c 2. COMPARATIVE ANATOMY, HUMAN ANATOMY. *Educ:* Univ Minn, Minneapolis, BA, 66, MS, 68, PhD(zool), 70. *Prof Exp:* From instr to asst prof anat sci, Med Ctr, Univ Okla, 70-73; asst prof anat, Sch Med, Brown Univ, 73-79; ASSOC PROFESSOR ANAT, OHIO UNIV, 79- *Mem:* AAAS; Am Asn Anat; Am Soc Zoologists; Am Soc Ichthyologists & Herpetologists. *Res:* Gross anatomical histological and ultrastructural studies of fishes (especially antarctic fishes) with emphasis on morphology as related to physiology, ecology and evolution. *Mailing Add:* Dept Anat Irvine Hall Brown Univ Providence RI 02912

EASTMAN, LESTER F(UESS), b Utica, NY, May 21, 28; m 48; c 3. ELECTRICAL ENGINEERING. *Educ:* Cornell Univ, BEE, 53, MS, 55, PhD(elec eng), 57. *Prof Exp:* From instr to assoc prof, 54-66, PROF ELEC ENG, CORNELL UNIV, 66-, FOUNDER & DIR, JOINT SERV ELECTRONIC PROG, 80- *Concurrent Pos:* Consult, Westinghouse Elec Co, 55-64, Sylvania Elec Co, 56, Cornell Aero Lab, 57-64, Int Bus Mach Corp, 61-64 & Raytheon Mfg Co, 61-64; vis assoc prof electronics, Chalmers Tech Inst, Sweden, 60-61; vis mem tech staff, RCA Res Labs, Princeton, 64-65; cofounder & consult, Cayuga Assoc, 67-, pres, 70- *Mem:* Fel Inst Elec & Electronics Engrs. *Res:* Compound semiconductor materials, microwave device technology and physical electronics. *Mailing Add:* 425 Phillips Hall Cornell Univ Ithaca NY 14853

EASTMAN, MICHAEL PAUL, b Lancaster, Wis, Apr 14, 41; m 80; c 2. PHYSICAL CHEMISTRY. *Educ:* Carleton Col, BA, 63; Cornell Univ, PhD(phys chem), 68. *Prof Exp:* Fel, Los Alamos Sci Lab, 68-70; from asst prof to assoc prof, 68-80, PROF CHEM, UNIV TEX, EL PASO, 80- *Mem:* Am Chem Soc; Int Soc Magnetic Resonance. *Res:* Magnetic resonance; ion pairing; geochemistry. *Mailing Add:* Dept Chem Univ Tex El Paso TX 79968

EASTMAN, PHILIP CLIFFORD, b Port Hope, Ont, May 28, 32; m 56; c 2. SOLID STATE PHYSICS. *Educ:* Univ McMaster, BSc, 55, MSc, 56; Univ BC, PhD(physics), 60. *Prof Exp:* NATO fel & Rutherford Mem Award, Univ Bristol, 60-61; sr sci officer, Defence Res Telecommun Estab, Ottawa, 61-63; asst prof, 63-65, ASSOC PROF PHYSICS, UNIV WATERLOO, 65- *Mem:* Can Asn Physicists. *Res:* Galvanomagnetic and optical properties of metals; semimetals, semiconductors and insulators in single crystal, polycrystal and thin film forms. *Mailing Add:* Dept of Physics Univ of Waterloo Waterloo ON N2L 3G1 Can

EASTMAN, RICHARD HALLENBECK, b Erie, Pa, Oct 30, 18; m 42; c 3. ORGANIC CHEMISTRY. *Educ:* Princeton Univ, AB, 41; Harvard Univ, AM, 43, PhD(org chem), 44. *Prof Exp:* Asst, Harvard Univ, 44-46; from instr to assoc prof org chem, 46-58, PROF ORG CHEM, STANFORD UNIV, 59- *Concurrent Pos:* NSF fel, 58-59. *Mem:* Am Chem Soc. *Res:* Chemistry of natural products; ultraviolet and infrared spectroscopy; organic photochemistry. *Mailing Add:* Dept of Chem Stanford Univ Stanford CA 94305

EASTMAN, ROBERT M(ERRIAM), b Dayton, Ohio, Apr 17, 18; m; c 3. INDUSTRIAL ENGINEERING. *Educ:* Antioch Col, AB, 40; Ohio State Univ, MS, 48; Pa State Univ, PhD, 55. *Prof Exp:* Asst instr eng drawing, Ohio State Univ, 47-48; instr indust eng, Pa State Univ, 48-51; assoc prof & res assoc, Eng Exp Sta, Ga Inst Technol, 51-55; chmn indust eng dept, 55-68, PROF INDUST ENG, UNIV MO-COLUMBIA, 55- *Concurrent Pos:* Fulbright lectr, Indust Univ Santander, 62-63; consult area redevelop admin, US Dept Com, 62-65; consult, US Off Educ, 68-69; vis prof, Mid East Tech Univ, Ankara, 69-71; consult, Dept Health, Educ & Welfare, 71, mem steering comt, Nat Ctr Health Serv Res & Develop, Health Serv & Ment Health Admin, 71- *Mem:* Am Soc Eng Educ; fel AAAS. *Res:* Engineering economy; technical aid to developing countries; operations research; regional development and planning; resource recovery from solid waste; robotics. *Mailing Add:* 600 S Glenwood Ave Columbia MO 65201

EASTMAN, WILLARD L, applied mathematics, see previous edition

EASTMOND, ELBERT JOHN, b San Francisco, Calif, July 6, 15; m 37; c 4. PHYSICS. *Educ:* Brigham Young Univ, AB, 37; Univ Calif, PhD(physics), 43. *Prof Exp:* Physicist, Western Regional Res Lab, Bur Agr & Indust Chem, USDA, 42-50; from asst prof to assoc prof, 51-57, PROF PHYSICS, BRIGHAM YOUNG UNIV, 57- *Concurrent Pos:* Mem tech staff, Space Technol Labs, Los Angeles, 58 & Aerospace Corp, 63-64. *Mem:* Am Asn Physics Teachers; Optical Soc Am. *Res:* Diatomic molecular spectroscopy; spectrochemical analysis; spectrophotometry and colorimetry; rotational analysis of a band system attributed to ionized nitric oxide. *Mailing Add:* Dept of Physics Brigham Young Univ Provo UT 84602

EASTON, ALAN MICHAEL, b Geneva, NY, June 3, 53. MOLECULAR BIOLOGY. *Educ:* Rensselaer Polytech Inst, BS, 74; Univ Wis-Madison, PhD(biochem), 81. *Prof Exp:* FEL, UNIV GA, ATHENS, 81- *Mem:* Sigma Xi. *Res:* Mechanisms of incompatibility and control of replication of bacterial plasmids; control of gene expression in lower eukaryotes. *Mailing Add:* Dept Molecular & Pop Genetics Univ Ga Athens GA 30602

EASTON, DEXTER MORGAN, b Rockport, Mass, Sept 13, 21; m 53; c 4. NEUROPHYSIOLOGY. *Educ:* Clark Univ, BA, 43; Harvard Univ, MA, 44, PhD(biol), 47. *Prof Exp:* Asst, Clark Univ, 42-43 & Harvard Univ, 45; instr zool, Univ Wash, 47-50; res physiologist, Med Sch, 52-55; asst prof physiol, 55-58, assoc prof biol sci, 58-78, PROF BIOL SCI, FLA STATE UNIV, 78- *Concurrent Pos:* Fulbright scholar, Otago Med Sch, NZ, 50-51. *Mem:* Fel AAAS; Am Soc Zoologists; Soc Gen Physiol; Am Physiol Soc; Soc Neurosci. *Res:* Neuromuscular transmission; analysis of cell potentials and excitability; electrical activity of peripheral nerve; axonology; mathematical modelling. *Mailing Add:* Dept of Biol Sci Fla State Univ Tallahassee FL 32306

EASTON, ELMER C(HARLES), b Newark, NJ, Dec 23, 09. ELECTRICAL ENGINEERING. *Educ:* Lehigh Univ, BS, 31, MS, 33; Lehigh Univ, ScD(elec eng), 42. *Hon Degrees:* DEng, Lehigh Univ, 65. *Prof Exp:* Mem fac, Newark Col Eng, 35-42; mem fac, Grad Sch Eng, Harvard Univ, 42-48, asst dean, 46-48; dean col eng, 48-74, EMER DEAN COL ENG, RUTGERS UNIV, 74- *Mem:* Am Soc Eng Educ (pres, 64-65); Nat Soc Prof Engrs; Inst Elec & Electronics Eng. *Res:* Conduction of electricity through gases. *Mailing Add:* 4 Orchard Rd Piscataway NJ 08854

EASTON, GENE DOUGLAS, plant pathology, see previous edition

EASTON, IVAN G(EORGE), b Sweden, Nov 20, 16; nat US; m 41; c 4. ELECTRICAL ENGINEERING. *Educ:* Northeastern Univ, BS, 38; Harvard Univ, MS, 39. *Prof Exp:* Instr physics, Harvard Univ, 39-40; mgr eng, Gen Radio Co, 40-64, vpres, 64-68, sr vpres, 68-72; consult dir standards, Inst Elec & Electronics Engrs, 76-80; PRES, US NAT COMT, INT ELECTROTECH COMN, 80- *Mem:* Am Soc Testing & Mat; fel Inst Elec & Electronics Engrs. *Res:* National and international voluntary standards. *Mailing Add:* 16 Winthrop Rd Lexington MA 02173

EASTON, NELSON ROY, b Craftsbury, Vt, Oct 8, 19; m 44; c 3. ORGANIC CHEMISTRY. *Educ:* Middlebury Col, AB, 41; Univ Ill, PhD(org chem), 46. *Prof Exp:* Chemist, Merck & Co, NJ, 41-43; asst org chem, Univ Ill, 43-44; asst 44-46; sr chemist, J T Baker Chem Co, NJ, 46-47; asst prof org chem, Lehigh Univ, 47-53; res chemist, Labs, Eli Lilly & Co, 53-62, res assoc, 62-64, asst dir chem res, 64-66, dir, 66-69, assoc dir res, 69-72, exec dir res, 72-74, VPRES LILLY RES LABS, ELI LILLY & CO, 74- *Mem:* Am Chem Soc. *Res:* Hypotensive agents; reactions of acetylenes; heterocyclic compounds from acetylenic amines. *Mailing Add:* Eli Lilly & Co Indianapolis IN 46285

EASTON, RICHARD J, b Beaver, Utah, July 12, 38; m 62; c 3. COMPUTER SCIENCES. *Educ:* Univ Utah, BS, 60, MS, 63, PhD(math), 66. *Prof Exp:* Asst prof math, Weber State Col, 65-67; from asst prof to assoc prof, 67-75, PROF MATH, IND STATE UNIV, 75- *Concurrent Pos:* Lectr, Hill Air Force Base, 66-67. *Mem:* Am Math Soc; Am Asn Univ Prof; Am Fedn Teachers; Math Asn Am. *Res:* Vector measures; integration theory; applications software. *Mailing Add:* Dept Math & Comput Sci Ind State Univ Terre Haute IN 47809

EASTON, ROBERT WALTER, b Chicago, Ill, Dec 8, 41; m 65. MATHEMATICS. *Educ:* Univ Wis, BS, 63, MS, 65, PhD(math), 67. *Prof Exp:* Asst prof appl math, Brown Univ, 67-72; assoc prof, 72-80, PROF MATH, UNIV COLO, BOULDER, 80- *Mem:* Am Math Soc. *Res:* Differential equations; celestial mechanics. *Mailing Add:* Dept of Math Univ of Colo Boulder CO 80309

EASTON, THOMAS W, b Bridgton, Maine, Oct 6, 21; m 43; c 4. CYTOLOGY, EVOLUTION. *Educ:* Univ Maine, BA, 43, MA, 48; Brown Univ, PhD(cytol), 51. *Prof Exp:* Instr anat, Sch Med, Johns Hopkins Univ, 51-52; Brown Univ pres fels, France, 53-54; res coordr, US Dept Defense, 55-60; asst prof biol, 60-63, ASSOC PROF BIOL, COLBY COL, 64- *Mem:* AAAS. *Res:* Developmental anatomy and consequences of defects; origin and function of mammalian macrophages; structure of antarctic fishes. *Mailing Add:* Dept Biol Colby Col Waterville ME 04901

EASTON, WILLIAM HEYDEN, b Bedford, Ind, Jan 14, 16; m 40; c 2. PALEONTOLOGY. *Educ:* George Washington Univ, BS, 37, AM, 38; Univ Chicago, PhD(geol), 40. *Prof Exp:* Asst, US Nat Mus, 36-38; asst, Univ Chicago, 39-40; from asst geologist to assoc geologist, Ill Geol Surv, 40-44; from asst prof to assoc prof, 44-51, chmn dept, 63-67, prof, 51-81, EMER

PROF GEOL, UNIV SOUTHERN CALIF, 81-; CONSULT GEOLOGIST, 81- *Concurrent Pos:* Asst, George Washington Univ, 37-38; asst, US Geol Surv, 52-53; Guggenheim fel, 59-60; actg chmn, Dept French & Italian, Univ Southern Calif, 75-76. *Mem:* Paleont Soc; fel Geol Soc Am; Soc Econ Paleont & Mineral; Am Asn Petrol Geol. *Res:* Paleozoic paleontology and stratigraphy; oil and gas exploration; Carboniferous corals; radioisotopic dating coral reefs and raised shore lines. *Mailing Add:* Dept of Geol Sci Univ of Southern Calif Los Angeles CA 90007

EASTWOOD, ABRAHAM BAGOT, b Philadelphia, Pa, Nov 8, 43; m 68; c 1. CYTOPATHOLOGY, ELECTRON MICROSCOPY. *Educ:* Muhlenberg Col, BS, 65; Lehigh Univ, MS, 67, PhD(biol), 71. *Prof Exp:* Fel physiol & ultrastruct, Lab Neurophysiol, 71-75, DIR, LAB OF MUSCLE MORPHOL, COL PHYSICIANS & SURGEONS, COLUMBIA UNIV, 75-, ASST PROF, DEPT ANAT, 78- *Mem:* AAAS; Biophys Soc; Sigma Xi. *Res:* Structural and functional substrates of excitation-contraction coupling in muscle; ultrastructural manifestations of disease in human muscle. *Mailing Add:* Lab of Muscle Morphol Col Phys & Surg Columbia Univ New York NY 10032

EASTWOOD, BASIL R, b Argyle, Wis, Dec 17, 36; m 63; c 2. ANIMAL GENETICS, DAIRY SCIENCE. *Educ:* Wis State Univ, Platteville, BS, 58; SDak State Univ, MS, 60; Mich State Univ, PhD(dairy cattle breeding), 67. *Prof Exp:* Exten dairyman, Univ Mass, 63-65; asst prof animal sci, Iowa State univ, 65-71, assoc prof, 71-75, exten dairyman, 65-80, prof animal sci, 75-80; PROG LEADER DAIRY PROD, EXTEN SERV, USDA, 80- *Mem:* Am Dairy Sci Asn. *Res:* Use of records in genetic improvement of dairy cattle. *Mailing Add:* Dairy Prod Exten Serv USDA 5525 S Bldg Washington DC 20250

EASTWOOD, DELYLE, b Upper Darby, Pa, Nov 19, 32. PHYSICAL CHEMISTRY, SPECTROSCOPY. *Educ:* Univ Chicago, MS, 55, PhD(phys chem), 64. *Prof Exp:* Res asst chem res insts, Univ Chicago, 54-56, teaching asst, 57-59, phys chemist, 59-60, res asst, Inst Study Metals, 61-64; res fel phys chem & spectros, Harvard Univ, 64-66; res assoc, Univ Wash, 66-69; res assoc, Northeastern Univ, 70-71; sr chemist, Baird-Atomic, Inc, 71-72; proj chemist, Bendix Res Labs, 72-73; res chemist, US Coast Guard Res & Develop Ctr, 74-81; CHEMIST, DEPT NUCLEAR ENERGY, BROOKHAVEN NAT LAB, 81- *Mem:* AAAS; Am Phys Soc; Am Chem Soc; Am Soc Testing & Mat; Soc Appl Spectros. *Res:* Molecular spectroscopy applied to environmental pollution, especially fluorescence and luminescence for oil identification and to porphyrins, chlorophyll, dyes and aromatics; DC argon plasma emission and photoelectron spectroscopy; low temperature magnetism of transition metal halides. *Mailing Add:* Dept Nuclear Energy Brookhaven Nat Lab Upton Long Island NY 11973

EASTWOOD, DOUGLAS WILLIAM, b Ellsworth, Wis, Sept 17, 18; m 43; c 4. ANESTHESIOLOGY. *Educ:* Coe Col, AB, 40; Univ Iowa, MD, 43, MS, 49. *Prof Exp:* From intern to asst resident, Receiving Hosp, Detroit, Mich, 44-45; from asst resident to resident anesthesiol, Univ Hosps, Univ Iowa, 47-49, from instr to assoc prof, Col Med, 49-55; asst prof & chief, Sch Med, Wash Univ, 50-54; prof, Sch Med, Univ Va, 55-72, chmn dept, 55-71; assoc prof med educ, 72-75, PROF ANESTHESIOL, CASE WESTERN RESERVE UNIV, 72-; DIR OBSTET ANESTHESIOL, UNIV HOSP CLEVELAND, 75- *Concurrent Pos:* Instr internal med, Wayne State Univ, 44-45; dir anesthesiol prog, Vet Admin Hosp, Cleveland, 72-75. *Mem:* Am Soc Anesthesiologists; Int Anesthesia Res Soc. *Res:* Educational resources; evaluation of educational methods; obstetric anesthesia. *Mailing Add:* Dept of Anesthesiol Case Western Reserve Univ Cleveland OH 44106

EASTWOOD, RAYMOND L, b Pawnee City, Nebr, Aug 27, 40; m 80. GEOCHEMISTRY, PETROLOGY. *Educ:* Kans State Univ, BS, 62, MS, 65; Univ Ariz, PhD(geol), 70. *Prof Exp:* Res asst geol, Univ Ariz, 64-68; res mineralogist geochem, Res & Develop Dept, Phillips Petrol Co, Okla, 68-70; asst prof geol, Northern Ariz Univ, 70-79; SR RES GEOLOGIST, RES & DEVELOP, ARCO OIL & GAS CO, PLANO, TEX, 79- *Mem:* Am Geophys Union; Geochem Soc; Geol Soc Am. *Res:* Isotope geology; strontium isotope ratios; igneous and metamorphic petrology; bore hole geophysics; geochronology; mineralogy; geochemistry and petrology of volcanic rocks; volcanology. *Mailing Add:* Rte 7 Box 475 McKinney TX 75069

EASTWOOD, THOMAS ALEXANDER, b London, Ont, Nov 27, 20; m 49; c 4. NUCLEAR CHEMISTRY, CHEMICAL KINETICS. *Educ:* Univ Western Ont, BA, 42, MA, 43; McGill Univ, PhD(chem), 46; Oxford Univ, DPhil(chem), 51. *Prof Exp:* Control chemist, Imperial Oil Ltd, 43-44; res officer chem, Atomic Energy Proj, Nat Res Coun Can, 47-49; res officer chem, 51-69, DIR CHEM & MAT DIV, CHALK RIVER NUCLEAR LABS, ATOMIC ENERGY CAN LTD, 69- *Concurrent Pos:* Hon lectr, McGill Univ, 46-47; Nat Res Coun Can fel, Oxford Univ, 49-50, Carnegie Res Award, 50-51; chemist, UK Atomic Energy Authority, Eng, 64-65. *Mem:* Am Phys Soc; sr mem Am Chem Soc; Can Asn Physicists; fel Chem Inst Can. *Res:* Radio chemistry; nuclear physics; kinetics of chemical reactions. *Mailing Add:* Atomic Energy of Can Ltd Chalk River Nuclear Labs Chalk River Can

EASTY, DWIGHT BUCHANAN, b Lakewood, Ohio, Mar 8, 34; m 58; c 3. ANALYTICAL CHEMISTRY. *Educ:* Ohio Wesleyan Univ, BA, 56; Lawrence Col, MS, 58, PhD(paper chem), 61. *Prof Exp:* Develop engr, Paper Sect, Res & Develop Lab, Nat Vulcanized Fibre Co, 61-62, group leader, 62-66; vis asst prof chem, Ohio Wesleyan Univ, 66-67; res assoc, Univ Wis-Madison, 67-68, lectr, 68-69; asst prof chem, 69-72, ASSOC PROF CHEM, INST PAPER CHEM, 72- *Mem:* AAAS; Am Chem Soc. *Res:* Determination of trace elements and compounds in the environment; analysis of paper. *Mailing Add:* 2101 Clover Lane Appleton WI 54911

EATHERLY, WALTER PASOLD, b Washington, DC, June 23, 23; m 44; c 3. PHYSICS. *Educ:* Calif Inst Technol, BS, 48, MS, 49. *Prof Exp:* Jr physicist gas kinetics, Carbide & Carbon Chem Co, 44-46; engr vacuum eng, Consol Eng Corp, 47-49; supvr solid state physics, Atomics Int, 49-54; asst dir res, Carbon Prod Div, Union Carbide Corp, 57-62, gen mgr, Nuclear Fuels Dept, 63-67; consult, 67-70, HEAD, CARBON DEVELOP LAB, OAK RIDGE NAT LAB, 70- *Mem:* AAAS; Am Phys Soc; Am Nuclear Soc; Am Carbon Soc. *Res:* Nuclear materials engineering; solid state physics. *Mailing Add:* Carbon Develop Lab Oak Ridge Nat Lab PO Box X Oak Ridge TN 37830

EATON, ALVIN RALPH, b Toledo, Ohio, Mar 13, 20; m 70; c 2. RESEARCH & DEVELOPMENT ADMINISTRATION, SYSTEMS ENGINEERING. *Educ:* Oberlin Col, AB, 41; Calif Inst Technol, MS, 43. *Prof Exp:* Asst aeronaut eng, Calif Inst Technol, 41-42, res supersonic aerodyn, 42-43, engr, Southern Calif Coop Wind Tunnel, 44-45; engr & supvr guided missile prog, 45-65, supvr, Missile Systs Div, 65-73, asst dir tactical systs, 73-79, SUPVR, FLEET SYSTS DEPT, APPL PHYSICS LAB, JOHNS HOPKINS UNIV, 73-, ASST DIR, 79- *Concurrent Pos:* Consult to Under Secy Defense, Dept Defense, 76-, chmn, Task Force on US Army Patriot Syst, Off Under Secy Defense, Defense Sci Bd, 76-78; consult, Asst Secy Army, 80-; mem, Defense Sci Bd Task Force Countermeasures, 79-81 & Army Sci Bd, 80- *Honors & Awards:* Distinguished Pub Serv Award, US Navy, 75. *Mem:* Cosmos Club; fel Explorers Club. *Res:* Defense related applied physics. *Mailing Add:* 6701 Surrey Lane Clarksville MD 21029

EATON, BRYAN THOMAS, b Belfast, Ireland, Nov 10, 43; Can citizen; m 70; c 2. VIROLOGY. *Educ:* Queen's Univ Belfast, BSc, 65 & 67; McGill Univ, MSc, 69; Queen's Univ, Ont, PhD(virol), 73. *Prof Exp:* Med Res Coun Can res fel virol, John Curtin Sch Med Res, Canberra, Australia, 73-75; asst prof, 75-81, ASSOC PROF MICROBIOL, QUEEN'S UNIV, ONT, 81- *Concurrent Pos:* Med Res Coun Can scholar, 75-80. *Mem:* Am Soc Microbiol. *Res:* Replication of togaviruses in vertebrate and invertebrate cells; mechanisms of virus persistence in invertebrate cells. *Mailing Add:* Dept Microbiol & Immunol Queen's Univ Kingston ON K7L 3N6 Can

EATON, DAVID FIELDER, b Peterborough, NH, Oct 4, 46; m 74. PHYSICAL ORGANIC CHEMISTRY. *Educ:* Wesleyan Univ, BA, 68; Calif Inst Technol, PhD(org chem), 72. *Prof Exp:* Res chemist org chem, Univ Calif, San Diego, 72-73; res chemist, Cent Res & Develop Dept, 73-79, sr res chemist, Photo Prod Dept, 79-80, group leader, 80-81, RES SUPVR, CENT RES & DEVELOP DEPT, E I DU PONT DE NEMOURS & CO INC, 81- *Mem:* InterAm Photochem Soc; Am Chem Soc. *Res:* Photochemistry and electron transfer reactions of organic and organometallic compounds; photoimaging systems. *Mailing Add:* Cent Res & Develop Dept Exp Sta E I du Pont de Nemours & Co Inc Wilmington DE 19898

EATON, DAVID J, b Detroit, Mich, Dec 18, 49. ENVIRONMENTAL ENGINEERING, SYSTEMS ANALYSIS. *Educ:* Oberlin Col, BA, 71; Unit Pittsburgh, MSc, 72; Johns Hopkins Univ, PhD(environ eng), 77. *Prof Exp:* Asst prof pub policy, Lyndon B Johnson Sch Pub Affairs, 76-80, ASSOC PROF PUB POLICY & GEOG, UNIV TEX, AUSTIN, 80- *Concurrent Pos:* Consult, NSF, 74-75; prin investr grants, USDA, 75-76, US Agency Int Develop, 76-79 & US Environ Protection Agency, 77-79; Fulbright res scholar, 81-82. *Mem:* AAAS; Inst Mgt Sci; Coun Foreign Rel; Am Pub Health Asn; Am Waterworks Asn. *Res:* Delivery of health services; design of grain reserves; rural water supply and waste treatment; air and water pollution; appropriate technology. *Mailing Add:* LBJ Sch of Pub Affairs Univ of Tex Austin TX 78712

EATON, DAVID LEO, b Minneapolis, Minn, Jan 11, 32; m 54; c 5. INORGANIC CHEMISTRY, MATERIALS ENGINEERING. *Educ:* St Thomas Col, BS, 54. *Prof Exp:* Jr chemist ext metall, Ames, Lab, 54-56; sr design engr nuclear fuel elements, Martin Aircraft Co, 56-60; proj engr thermoelec, Gen Instruments Corp, 60-61; DEVELOP ASSOC CHEM MAT ENG, CORNING GLASS WORKS, 61- *Mem:* Am Chem Soc; Am Ceramics Soc. *Res:* Separation sciences; immobilized biological composites and their applications; material engineering. *Mailing Add:* Corning Glass Works Sullivan Sci Park Corning NY 14830

EATON, DONALD REX, b Leicester, Eng, July 20, 32; m 59; c 4. PHYSICAL CHEMISTRY. *Educ:* Oxford Univ, BA, 55, MA, 59, DPhil(chem), 58. *Prof Exp:* Fel div pure physics, Nat Res Coun Can, 58-60; res chemist, Cent Res Dept, E I Du Pont de Nemours & Co, 60-64, res supvr, 64-68; assoc prof chem, 68-71, PROF CHEM, MCMASTER UNIV, 71- *Mem:* Am Chem Soc; Can Inst Chem; Royal Soc Chem. *Res:* Transition metal chemistry; magnetic resonance. *Mailing Add:* Dept of Chem McMaster Univ Hamilton Can

EATON, DOUGLAS CHARLES, b Sioux Falls, SDak, Jan 31, 45. NEUROPHYSIOLOGY, TRANSPORT. *Educ:* Calif Inst Technol, BS, 67; Scripps Inst Oceanog, MS, 69, Univ Calif, San Diego, PhD(neurosci), 71. *Prof Exp:* Res assoc neurophysiol, Med Sch, Univ Calif, Los Angeles, 71-73; vis assoc neurophysiol, Dept Biol, Calif Inst Technol, 73; ASSOC PROF PHYSIOL, DEPT PHYSIOL & BIOPHYS, UNIV TEX MED BR GALVESTON, 73- *Mem:* Biophys Soc; Soc Gen Physiologists; Am Physiol Soc. *Res:* Electrophysiology of excitable membranes and ephithelial tissue. *Mailing Add:* Dept of Physiol & Biophys Univ of Tex Med Br Galveston TX 77560

EATON, GARETH RICHARD, b Lockport, NY, Nov 3, 40; m 69. INORGANIC CHEMISTRY. *Educ:* Harvard Univ, BA, 62; Mass Inst Technol, PhD(chem), 72. *Prof Exp:* From asst prof to assoc prof, 72-80, PROF CHEM, UNIV DENVER, 80- *Mem:* Am Chem Soc; Royal Soc Chem; AAAS; Soc Appl Spectros; Int Soc Magnetic Resonance. *Res:* Synthesis and spectroscopy of inorganic complexes and organic free radicals, with emphasis on nuclear magnetic resonance and electron paramagnetic resonance. *Mailing Add:* Dept of Chem Univ of Denver Denver CO 80208

EATON, GEORGE T(HOMAS), b Edmonton, Alta, Apr 18, 10; nat US; m 36; c 3. CHEMICAL ENGINEERING. *Educ:* McMaster Univ, BA, 31, MA, 33; Acadia Univ, BS, 33. *Prof Exp:* Chemist, Photog Chem, Kodak Res Labs, 37-43, staff asst, 43-46, supvr indust sales studio, Sales Div, 46-51, ed, Sales Serv Div, 51-53, staff asst, Applied Photog Div, 53-56, asst div head, 57-75, head,

Photog Chem Dept, 56-75; RETIRED. *Concurrent Pos:* Lectr, Rochester Inst Technol, 52-75. *Mem:* Fel Photog Soc Am; Soc Photog Sci & Engrs (pres, 57-61); Soc Motion Picture & TV Engrs. *Res:* Chemistry of photographic processing; photoreproduction; engineering drawings; microfilming; editorial work on photographic yearbooks and encyclopedia; teaching. *Mailing Add:* 699 Heritage Rd Rochester NY 14615

EATON, GEORGE WALTER, b Upper Canard, NS, Sept 4, 33; m 56; c 2. HORTICULTURE. *Educ:* Univ Toronto, BSA, 55; Ohio State Univ, PhD(pomol), 59. *Prof Exp:* Exten specialist pomol, Ont Dept Agr, 55-58, res scientist, 58-64; from asst prof to assoc prof, 64-74, PROF POMOL, UNIV BC, 74- *Honors & Awards:* G M Darrow Award, Am Soc Hort Sci. *Mem:* Am Soc Hort Sci; Can Soc Hort Sci; Am Statist Asn. *Res:* Reproductive physiology and morphology of fruit crops; mineral nutrition; biometrics. *Mailing Add:* Dept Plant Sci Univ BC Vancouver BC V6T 1W5 Can

EATON, GORDON GRAY, b Carmangay, Alta, June 5, 41; m 75; c 1. ANIMAL BEHAVIOR. *Educ:* Univ Victoria, BA, 64; Univ Calif, PhD(psychol), 70. *Prof Exp:* Asst scientist primate behav, Ore Regional Primate Res Ctr, 70-73; asst prof, 71-75, ASSOC PROF PSYCHOL, SCH MED, UNIV ORE HEALTH SCI CTR, 75-, ASSOC SCIENTIST PRIMATE BEHAV, ORE REGIONAL PRIMATE RES CTR, 73- *Mem:* AAAS; Am Psychol Asn; Animal Behav Soc; Int Primatological Soc; Sigma Xi. *Res:* Environmental and endocrine control of primate behavior. *Mailing Add:* Ore Regional Primate Res Ctr 505 NW 185th Ave Beaverton OR 97006

EATON, GORDON PRYOR, b Dayton, Ohio, Mar 9, 29; m 51; c 2. PHYSICAL GEOLOGY. *Educ:* Wesleyan Univ, BA, 51; Calif Inst Technol, MS, 53, PhD(geol, geophys), 57. *Prof Exp:* From instr to asst prof geol, Wesleyan Univ, 55-59; from asst prof to assoc prof, Univ Calif, Riverside, 59-67; geologist, US Geol Surv, 67-72 & 74-76, dep chief, Off Geochem & Geophys, 72-74, scientist-in-chg, Hawaiian Volcano Observ, 76-78, assoc chief geologist, 78-81; DEAN, COL GEOSCI, TEX A&M UNIV, 81- *Concurrent Pos:* Res geologist, US Geol Surv, 63-65; chmn dept geol sci, Univ Calif, Riverside, 66-67. *Mem:* Geol Soc Am; Am Geophys Union; Soc Explor Geophys. *Res:* Physical geology; regional geophysics. *Mailing Add:* Col Geosci Tex A&M Univ College Station TX 77843

EATON, HAMILTON DEAN, b Elmhurst, NY, Nov 24, 16; m 46; c 3. ANIMAL NUTRITION. *Educ:* Iowa State Univ, BS, 39; Rutgers Univ, MS, 41; Cornell Univ, PhD(animal husb), 47. *Prof Exp:* Asst dairy husb, Rutgers Univ, 39-41; asst animal husb, Cornell Univ, 41-42 & 46-47; from asst prof to prof animal nutrit, 47-70, prof nutrit sci, 70-77, EMER PROF NUTRIT SCI, UNIV CONN, 77- *Honors & Awards:* Am Dairy Sci Asn Awards, 52 & 62. *Mem:* AAAS; Am Soc Animal Sci; Am Dairy Sci Asn; Am Inst Nutrit. *Res:* Nutrition; vitamin A metabolism; hypo- and hypervitaminosis A. *Mailing Add:* 40 Storrs Heights Rd Storrs CT 06269

EATON, J(AMES) H(OWARD), b Woodland, Calif, Nov 28, 33; m 56; c 3. ELECTRICAL ENGINEERING. *Educ:* Univ Calif, Berkeley, BS, 58, MS, 60, PhD(elec eng), 62. *Prof Exp:* Asst prof systs theory, Univ Calif, Berkeley, 62-64; mgr systs dept, IBM Res Lab, 64-71, DIR TECH PLANNING, IBM CORP, 71-, LAB DIR, 76- *Concurrent Pos:* Consult, IBM Res, 63-64. *Mem:* Inst Elec & Electronics Engrs. *Res:* Theory of optimal control; systems theory and its application to the design and analysis of computer systems. *Mailing Add:* IBM Corp Old Orchard Rd Armonk NY 10504

EATON, JEROME F, b Newark, NJ, Jan 7, 41; m 64; c 2. GEOPHYSICS. *Educ:* Lehigh Univ, BS, 63; Princeton Univ, MA, 65, PhD(geophys), 68. *Prof Exp:* Res geophysicist, Gulf Res & Develop Co, 68-73, sr staff geophysicist, Gulf Oil Co-Eastern Hemisphere, 73-76, EASTERN HEMISPHERE INTERPRETATION COORDR, GULF EXPLOR & PROD CO-INT, 76- *Mem:* Soc Explor Geophysicists. *Res:* Steady and transient states of strain in igneous rocks at high temperature; relationships between continental margins and ocean basins; seismic response of trapped fluids; exploration seismology; marine and land field data acquisition; seismic data processing and interpretation. *Mailing Add:* Gulf Explor & Prod Co-Int PO Box 2100 Houston TX 77001

EATON, JERRY PAUL, b Fresno Co, Calif, Dec 11, 26; m 47; c 4. SEISMOLOGY. *Educ:* Univ Calif, AB, 49, PhD(geophys), 53. *Prof Exp:* Asst seismol, Univ Calif, 50-53; geophysicist, Hawaiian Volcano Observ, 53-61 & crustal studies br, 61-65, res geophysicist, Off Earthquake Res & Crustal Studies, 65-70, chief, 70-75, RES GEOPHYSICIST, OFF EARTHQUAKE RES & CRUSTAL STUDIES, US GEOL SURV, 75- *Concurrent Pos:* Lectr, Univ Calif, Berkeley, 60-61. *Mem:* Geol Soc Am; Am Geophys Union. *Res:* Mechanics of earthquake generation; detailed studies of seismicity; geophysics of volcanoes; structure of the continental crust. *Mailing Add:* Off Earthquake Res US Geol Surv 345 Middlefield Rd Menlo Park CA 94025

EATON, JOEL A, b Paducah Ky, Jan 2, 48. STELLAR ASTRONOMY. *Educ:* Auburn Univ, BS, 70; Vanderbilt Univ, MS, 71; Univ Wis, PhD(astron), 75. *Prof Exp:* Vis asst prof astronomy, Univ Ala, Tuscaloosa, 75-76; res asst, Nat Res Coun, Goddard Space Flight Ctr, NASA, 76-78; asst prof, Pa State Univ, 78-79; ASST PROF ASTRONOMY, VANDERBILT UNIV, 80- *Concurrent Pos:* Vis astronomer, Copernicus Astron Ctr, Warsaw, 79. *Mem:* Am Astro Soc; Int Astro Union; Astron Soc Pac; Soc Mfg Engrs. *Res:* Stellar photometry and spectroscopy; untraviolet observations from spacecraft; analysis of eclipsing binary light curves; Wolf-Rayet and stars with expanding atmospheres; stellar limb and gravity darkening; stellar chromospheres and surface activity. *Mailing Add:* Vanderbilt Univ Box 1807 Sta B Nashville TN 37235

EATON, JOHN LEROY, b Decatur, Ill, Sept 21, 39; m 61; c 2. INSECT PHYSIOLOGY. *Educ:* Univ Ill, BS, 62, PhD(entom), 66. *Prof Exp:* Kettering Found teaching intern biol, Kalamazoo Col, 66-67, asst prof, 67-69; asst prof entom, 69-75, ASSOC PROF ENTOM, VA POLYTECH INST & STATE UNIV, 75- *Mem:* AAAS; Entom Soc Am; Sigma Xi. *Res:* Insect neurophysiology, morphology and behavior. *Mailing Add:* Dept of Entom Va Polytech Inst & State Univ Blacksburg VA 24061

EATON, JOHN WALLACE, b Ann Arbor, Mich, Mar 13, 41; m 63. HEMATOLOGY, PHYSIOLOGY. *Educ:* Fla State Univ, BA, 63; Univ Fla, MA, 64; Univ Mich, PhD(biol anthrop), 69. *Prof Exp:* Res asst biochem, Univ Fla, 64-65; instr anthrop, Fla State Univ, 65-66; res assoc human genetics, Univ Mich, Ann Arbor, 69-70; asst prof anthrop, Wash Univ, 70-72; from asst prof to assoc prof, 72-79, PROF MED, LAB MED & PATHOL & DIR MED GENETICS, UNIV MINN, MINNEAPOLIS, 79- *Concurrent Pos:* Consult, NIH, 73- & NSF, 74- *Mem:* Am Asn Phys Anthrop; Am Fedn Clin Res; Am Soc Hemat. *Res:* Red cell metabolism and function; hemolytic anemia; oxygen transport; physiological adaptation. *Mailing Add:* Sect Hemat Dept Med Univ Minn Minneapolis MN 55455

EATON, LARRY RODNEY, b Garden City, Kans, Aug 11, 38; m 63; c 4. ATMOSPHERIC PHYSICS, CLOUD PHYSICS. *Educ:* Colo State Univ, BS, 61, MS, 63; Univ Nev, Reno, PhD(atmospheric physics), 71. *Prof Exp:* Res asst atmospheric physics, Desert Res Inst, Univ Nev, Reno, 63-71; sr scientist atmospheric physics, McDonnell Douglas Astronaut Co, 71-75; ENVIRON PHYSICIST & GROUP LEADER, SPACE DIV, GEN ELEC CO, 75- *Honors & Awards:* Lett Commendation, NASA, 74. *Mem:* Am Meteorol Soc; Am Inst Physics. *Res:* Large chamber simulation of atmospheric physics problems relating to pollution, energy and precipitation processes; implementation of an atmospheric cloud microphysics laboratory shuttle-spacelab payload. *Mailing Add:* Space Div Gen Elec Co 9900 Global Rd Philadelphia PA 19115

EATON, MERRILL THOMAS, JR, b Howard Co, Ind, June 25, 20; m 42; c 3. PSYCHIATRY. *Educ:* Ind Univ, AB, 41, MD, 44; Am Bd Psychiat & Neurol, dipl. *Prof Exp:* Intern, St Elizabeth's Hosp, 44-45; resident physician, Colo State Hosp, 47-48 & Sheppard-Pratt Hosp, 48-49; assoc psychiat, Sch Med, Univ Kans, 49-51, from asst prof to assoc prof, 51-60; assoc prof, 60-62, PROF PSYCHIAT, UNIV NEBR MED CTR, OMAHA, 62-, CHMN DEPT, 68-; DIR, NEBR PSYCHIAT INST, 68- *Mem:* Am Psychiat Asn; Asn Am Med Cols; Group Advan Psychiat; Am Col Physicians. *Res:* Psychotherapy; medical education. *Mailing Add:* 602 S 45th St Omaha NE 68105

EATON, MONROE DAVIS, b Stockton, Calif, Dec 2, 04; m 33; c 4. IMMUNOLOGY, ONCOLOGY. *Educ:* Stanford Univ, AB, 27, AM, 28; Harvard Univ, MD, 30. *Prof Exp:* Asst bact, Harvard Med Sch & instr biochem sci, Harvard Univ, 30-33, res tutor, 31-33; instr bact, Sch Med, Yale Univ, 33-36; asst prof bact & immunol, Wash Univ, 36-37; mem staff, Int Health Div, Rockefeller Found, 37-47; from assoc prof to prof bact & immunol, 47-71, EMER PROF BACT & IMMUNOL, HARVARD MED SCH, 71- *Concurrent Pos:* Dir res lab, State Dept Pub Health, Calif, 39-47; sr scientist, Dept Med Microbiol, Med Sch, Stanford Univ, 71-74, adj prof, 75-78, emer adj prof, 78- *Mem:* AAAS; Am Soc Microbiol; Am Asn Immunol; Soc Exp Biol & Med; Am Acad Arts & Sci. *Res:* Bacterial variation; bacterial toxins; immunology of malaria; influenza and virus pneumonia; chemotherapy of virus diseases; tumor immunity; autoimmunity. *Mailing Add:* 1965 Byron St Palo Alto CA 94301

EATON, MORRIS LEROY, b Sacramento, Calif, Aug 10, 39; m 64; c 1. MATHEMATICAL STATISTICS. *Educ:* Univ Wash, BS, 61; Stanford Univ, MS, 63, PhD(statist), 66. *Prof Exp:* Res assoc statist, Stanford Univ, 66; from asst prof to assoc prof, Univ Chicago, 66-71; prof, Univ Copenhagen, 71-72; from assoc prof to prof statist, 72-77, PROF THEORET STATIST & CHMN DEPT, UNIV MINN, 77- *Mem:* Fel Am Statist Asn; fel Inst Math Statist; Int Statist Inst. *Res:* Multivariate analysis; decision theory ranking procedures; invariance in statistical problems. *Mailing Add:* Dept Theoret Statist Univ Minn Minneapolis MN 55455

EATON, NORMAN RAY, b Turlock, Calif, June 30, 26; m 51; c 2. MICROBIOLOGY. *Educ:* Univ Calif, BA, 51; Univ Wash, Seattle, MS, 53, PhD, 55. *Prof Exp:* Instr bact, Univ Calif, 55-57; res instr med & microbiol, Univ Wash, Seattle, 57-63; from asst prof to assoc prof, 63-70, PROF BIOL, BROOKLYN COL, 70-; RES BIOCHEMIST, VET ADMIN HOSP, 57- *Mem:* AAAS; Am Soc Microbiol; Genetics Soc Am. *Res:* Catabolic processes of microbial metabolism; microbial biosynthesis of lipids. *Mailing Add:* Dept of Biol Brooklyn Col Brooklyn NY 11210

EATON, PAUL BERNARD, b Elkhart, Ind, May 21, 17. INDUSTRIAL & METALLURGICAL ENGINEERING. *Educ:* Univ Notre Dame, BS, 48; Purdue Univ, MS, 52. *Prof Exp:* Instr gen eng, 48-52, asst prof metals processing, 52-62, ASSOC PROF METALS PROCESSING, PURDUE UNIV, 62- *Concurrent Pos:* Consult, indust orgns, 55-; mem, Foundry Educ Found, 60- *Mem:* Am Soc Metals; Am Inst Mining, Metall & Petrol Engrs; Am Soc Eng Educ; Am Foundrymen's Soc. *Res:* Physical and process metallurgy of ferrous metals. *Mailing Add:* Sch of Metall Eng Purdue Univ Lafayette IN 47907

EATON, PAUL WENTLAND, b Minneapolis, Minn, Sept 30, 27; m 50; c 2. STATISTICS, ECONOMICS. *Educ:* Univ Minn, BA, 49, MA, 54, PhD(econ), 65. *Prof Exp:* Mkt analyst, Munsingwear, 53-54; instr statist, Univ Minn, 55-59; asst prof statist & econ, Mich Technol Univ, 59-75, assoc prof, 65-69, head quant anal sect, 67-69; ASSOC PROF STATIST, NORTHERN ILL UNIV, 69- *Concurrent Pos:* Consult, MacKinac Bridge Surv, 62 & Western Upper Peninsula Health Coun, 67-69; actg dir, Copper Country Health Surv, 68. *Mem:* Economet Soc; Am Statist Asn. *Res:* Statistical and economic theory. *Mailing Add:* Dept of Finance Northern Ill Univ DeKalb IL 60115

EATON, PHILIP EUGENE, b Brooklyn, NY, June 2, 36. ORGANIC CHEMISTRY. *Educ:* Princeton Univ, AB, 57; Harvard Univ, MA, 60, PhD(chem), 61. *Prof Exp:* Asst prof chem, Univ Calif, Berkeley, 60-62; from asst prof to assoc prof 62-72, PROF CHEM, UNIV CHICAGO, 72- *Concurrent Pos:* Alfred P Sloan Found res fel, 63-69; consult, E I du Pont de Nemours & Co, Inc, 65-77, NIH, 68-72 & US Army, 81- *Honors & Awards:* Res Award, Rohm and Haas, 75. *Res:* Chemistry of small ring compounds cubane and dodecahedrane; photochemistry; highfield nuclear magnetic resonance; synthesis. *Mailing Add:* Dept of Chem Univ of Chicago Chicago IL 60637

EATON, ROBERT CHARLES, b Los Angeles, Calif, Aug 14, 46. NEUROBIOLOGY. *Educ:* Univ Calif, Riverside, BA, 68, PhD(biol), 74; Univ Ore, MS, 70. *Prof Exp:* Asst res neuroscientist, Sch Med & Scripps Inst Oceanog, Univ Calif, San Diego, 74-77; ASST PROF BIOL, UNIV COLO, 78- *Concurrent Pos:* NIH fel, Univ Calif, San Diego, 74-77; INSERM fel, C H U Pitie-Salpetriere, Paris, France, 77. *Honors & Awards:* Res Serv Award, NIH, 74. *Mem:* Soc Neurosci. *Res:* The neurobiological bases of behavior, neuronal plasticity and development. *Mailing Add:* Dept of Environ Pop & Org Biol Univ of Colo Boulder CO 80309

EATON, SANDRA SHAW, b Boston, Mass, Jan 23, 46; m 69. INORGANIC CHEMISTRY, MAGNETIC RESONANCE. *Educ:* Wellesley Col, BA, 68; Mass Inst Technol, PhD(chem), 72. *Prof Exp:* Asst prof, 73-79, ASSOC PROF CHEM, UNIV COLO, DENVER, 79- *Mem:* Sigma Xi. *Res:* Dynamic processes in metallorporphyrins; synthesis and spectroscopy of inorganic compounds; electron paramagnetic resonance. *Mailing Add:* Dept of Chem 1100 14th St Denver CO 80202

EATON, STEPHEN WOODMAN, b Geneva, NY, Dec 22, 18; m 46. ORNITHOLOGY. *Educ:* Cornell Univ, PhD(zool), 49. *Prof Exp:* From asst prof to assoc prof biol, 49-57, PROF BIOL, ST BONAVENTURE UNIV, 57- *Concurrent Pos:* Ed, Sci Studies, 66-78. *Mem:* AAAS; Am Ornith Union; Wilson Ornith Soc; Am Soc Mammalogists; Ecol Soc Am. *Res:* Vertebrate zoology; faunal studies; biology of Parulidae and of the wild turkey; Canandaigua Lake as an ecosystem. *Mailing Add:* Dept of Biol St Bonaventure Univ St Bonaventure NY 14778

EATON, WILLIAM ALLEN, b Philadelphia, Pa, June 4, 38; m 62; c 2. BIOPHYSICS, PHYSICAL BIOCHEMISTRY. *Educ:* Univ Pa, AB, 59, MD, 64, PhD(molecular biol), 67. *Prof Exp:* Surgeon, Lab Phys Biol, 68-70, sr staff fel biophys & phys biochem, 70-72, sr surgeon, 72-78, MED DIR, LAB CHEM PHYSICS, NAT INST ARTHRITIS, METAB & DIGESTIVE DIS, USPHS, 79-, CHIEF, SECT MACROMOLECULAR BIOPHYSICS, 79- *Concurrent Pos:* Vis prof, Dept Biochem & Molecular Biol, Harvard Univ, 76. *Mem:* Biophys Soc; Found Advan Educ Sci; Am Soc Biol Chemists; Am Chem Soc. *Res:* physical chemistry of protein polymerization; molecular pathophysiology and pharmacology of sickle cell disease; time resolved optical spectroscopy of macromolecules. *Mailing Add:* Lab Chem Physics Bldg 2 Rm B1-04 NIAMDD NIH Bethesda MD 20014

EATON, WILLIAM THOMAS, b Long Beach, Calif, Feb 22, 38; m 61; c 2. MATHEMATICS. *Educ:* Univ Utah, BS, 61, MS, 63, PhD(math), 67. *Prof Exp:* Asst prof math, Univ Tenn, Knoxville, 67-70; assoc prof, 70-77, PROF MATH, UNIV TEX, AUSTIN, 77- *Concurrent Pos:* Mem, Inst Advan Study, 69-70; Alfred P Sloan fel, 69-71. *Mem:* Am Math Soc. *Res:* Topology of manifolds, particularly embeddings of manifolds in three-manifolds; piecewise linear topology and combinatories; statistics and probability theory. *Mailing Add:* Dept of Math Univ of Tex Austin TX 78712

EATOUGH, DELBERT J, b Provo, Utah, Sept 15, 40; m 64; c 7. CALORIMETRY. *Educ:* Brigham Young Univ, BS, 64, PhD(phys chem), 67. *Prof Exp:* Res chemist, Shell Develop Co, 67-70; DIR, THERMOCHEM INST, BRIGHAM YOUNG UNIV, 70- *Honors & Awards:* Sunner Award, Calorimetry Conf, 80. *Mem:* Am Chem Soc; AAAS; Sigma Xi; Calorimetry Conf. *Res:* Development of solution calorimetric instrumentation and application to study of surfactant, biochemical and surface chemistry; chemical characterization of atmospheric particulate matter resulting from anthropogenic activities. *Mailing Add:* Thermochem Inst 267 FB Brigham Young Univ Provo UT 84602

EATOUGH, NORMAN L, b Bingham Canyon, Utah, Oct 18, 33; m 56; c 5. PHYSICAL CHEMISTRY, ATMOSPHERIC SULFUR CHEMISTRY. *Educ:* Brigham Young Univ, BS, 57, BES, 58, MS, 59, PhD(phys chem), 68; Univ Wash, MSChE, 60. *Prof Exp:* Sr develop engr, Hercules Powder Co, 60-64; asst prof chem, Dixie Jr Col, 64-65; instr chem eng, Brigham Young Univ, 65-66; from asst prof to assoc prof, 68-80, PROF CHEM, CALIF STATE POLYTECH COL, 80- *Concurrent Pos:* Consult, Hercules Powder Co, 64-65. *Mem:* Am Chem Soc; Sigma Xi. *Res:* Atmospheric chemistry; high pressure chemistry. *Mailing Add:* 1508 Gulf St San Luis Obispo CA 93401

EAVES, BURCHET CURTIS, b Shreveport, La, Nov 25, 38; div; c 2. OPERATIONS RESEARCH, NUMERICAL ANALYSIS. *Educ:* Carnegie Inst Technol, BS, 61; Tulane Univ, MBA, 65; Stanford Univ, MS & PhD(oper res), 69. *Prof Exp:* Asst prof bus admin & oper res, Univ Calif, Berkeley, 68-70; from asst prof to assoc prof oper res, Stanford Univ, 70-75; vis assoc prof econ & org mgt, Yale Univ, 74-75; PROF OPER RES, STANFORD UNIV, 75- *Mem:* Inst Mgt Sci; Oper Res Soc Am; Soc Indust Appl Math; Am Math Soc; Math Asn Am. *Res:* Solving equations arising in optimization, economics and game theory. *Mailing Add:* Dept of Opers Res Stanford Univ Stanford CA 94305

EAVES, DAVID MAGILL, b New York, NY, Dec 7, 33; m 57, 66; c 3. MATHEMATICS. *Educ:* Mass Inst Technol, BSc, 56; Univ Wash, Seattle, MSc, 63, PhD(math), 66. *Prof Exp:* Instr, 65-66, ASST PROF MATH, SIMON FRASER UNIV, 66- *Mem:* Am Math Soc; Math Asn Am; Am Stat Asn. *Res:* Math Stat Inference. *Mailing Add:* Dept of Math Simon Fraser Univ Burnaby BC V5A 1S6 Can

EAVES, GEORGE NEWTON, b Athens, Tenn, Mar 12, 35. MEDICAL MICROBIOLOGY. *Educ:* Univ Chattanooga, BA, 57; Univ Tenn, MS, 59; Wayne State Univ, PhD(med microbiol), 62. *Prof Exp:* Asst prof biol, Washington & Jefferson Col, 62-63; grants assoc, Div Res Grants, NIH, 65-66, health scientist adminr, Div Res Facil & Resources, 66-67, exec secy molecular biol study sect, Div Res Grants, 67-73, exec secy adv coun, Nat Heart & Lung Inst, 73-74; staff mem, President's Biomed Res Panel, 74-76; asst to dir, 76-80, DEPUTY DIR, DIV BLOOD DIS & RESOURCES, NAT HEART, LUNG & BLOOD INST, NIH, 80- *Concurrent Pos:* Fel microbiol, Bryn Mawr Col, 63-65; guest investr, Rockefeller Univ, 70-71. *Res:* Exocellular enzymes of bacteria; metabolic effects of bacterial endotoxins. *Mailing Add:* Fed Bldg Rm 516A Nat Insts Health Bethesda MD 20014

EAVES, JAMES CLIFTON, b Hillside, Ky, June 26, 12; m 38; c 2. ALGEBRA. *Educ:* Univ Ky, AB, 35, MA, 41; Univ NC, PhD(matrix algebra), 49. *Prof Exp:* Asst prof math, Univ Ala, 49-50; assoc prof, Ala Polytech Inst, 50-51, res assoc prof, 51-52; prof math & res assoc, Auburn Res Found, 52-53; prof math & admin asst, Ala Polytech Inst, 53-54; prof math & astron, Univ Ky, 54-67, head dept, 54-63; chmn dept, 67-72, CENTENNIAL PROF MATH, W VA UNIV, 67- *Honors & Awards:* C C MacDuffee Distinguished Serv Award for meritorious contrib to math. *Mem:* Am Math Soc; Math Asn Am; Soc Indust & Appl Math. *Res:* Matrices; simultaneous reductions; inverse approximations; computer analysis; patents and patent law; space trajectories and transformations; higher dimensional matrices. *Mailing Add:* Dept of Math West Va Univ Morgantown WV 26506

EAVES, REUBEN ELCO, JR, b Baltimore, Md, Jan 20, 44. ELECTRICAL ENGINEERING. *Educ:* Johns Hopkins Univ, BES, 64; Brown Univ, ScM, 66, PhD(elec eng), 69. *Prof Exp:* Electronics engr, NASA Electronics Res Ctr, 68-70; US Dept Transp Transp Systs Ctr, 70-76; staff mem, Lincoln Lab, Mass Inst Technol, 76-81; MGR SATELLITE DESIGN, COMMUN SATELLITE CORP, 81- *Concurrent Pos:* Vis asst prof, Div Eng, Brown Univ, 73-76, sr res assoc, 76-77. *Mem:* Sigma Xi; Inst Elec & Electronics Engrs; Soc Indust & Appl Math; Am Phys Soc; Am Inst Aeronaut & Astronaut. *Res:* Satellite communications, communications systems, electromagnetic theory, applied mathematics. *Mailing Add:* Commun Satellite Corp 950 L'Enfant Plaza SW Washington DC 20024

EBACH, EARL A, b Saginaw, Mich, May 13, 28; m 53; c 4. CHEMICAL ENGINEERING. *Educ:* Univ Mich, BS, 51, MS, 52, PhD(chem eng), 57. *Prof Exp:* Proj leader, 57-69, CHEM ENGR, DOW CHEM CO, 57-, GROUP LEADER, 69-, PROCESS ENGR, 77- *Mem:* Am Inst Chem Engrs. *Res:* Research and development in organic chemicals. *Mailing Add:* 4610 Andre Midland MI 48640

EBADI, MANUCHAIR, b Shahmirzad, Iran, Sept 6, 35; m 59; c 3. NEUROPHARMACOLOGY, NEUROCHEMISTRY. *Educ:* Park Col, BS, 60; Univ Mo-Kansas City, MS, 62; Univ Mo-Columbia, PhD(pharmacol), 66. *Prof Exp:* Res asst pediat, Sch Med, Univ Mo-Columbia, 64-66, res assoc pediat & instr pharmacol, 66-67; asst prof pediat, 67-68, from asst prof to assoc prof pharmacol, 68-71, actg chmn dept, 70-71, PROF PHARMACOL & CHMN DEPT, UNIV NEBR MED CTR, 71- *Concurrent Pos:* NIMH int prof fel, 69-70; mem, US Pharmacopoeial Conv, 70. *Honors & Awards:* AMA Golden Apple Award, 71, 72 & 75; Univ Nebr Best Basic Sci Award, 73 & 74. *Mem:* AAAS; Am Chem Soc; Am Soc Pharmacol & Exp Therapeut; Am Soc Neurochem; fel Am Soc Clin Pharmacol. *Res:* Neurochemical pharmacological aspects of central nervous system drugs. *Mailing Add:* Dept of Pharmacol Univ of Nebr Med Ctr Omaha NE 68105

EBAUGH, FRANKLIN G, JR, b Philadelphia, Pa, Dec 25, 21; m 71; c 4. MEDICAL ADMINISTRATION, HEMATOLOGY. *Educ:* Dartmouth Col, BA, 44; Cornell Univ, MD, 46. *Prof Exp:* From intern med to resident hemat, NY Hosp, 46-50; asst med, Sch Med, Boston Univ, 50-53, instr, 53; surgeon, NIH, 53-55; asst prof hemat, Dartmouth Med Sch, 55-58, assoc prof clin path, 58-64; dean med sch, Boston Univ, 64-69; prof med & dean med sch, Med Ctr, Univ Utah, 69-72; PROF CLIN MED & ASSOC DEAN MED SCH, STANFORD UNIV, 72-; CHIEF OF STAFF, VET ADMIN HOSP, PALO ALTO, 72- *Concurrent Pos:* Asst, Med Sch, Cornell Univ, 48-50; res assoc, Mass Mem Hosp, 50-53. *Mem:* AAAS; Am Soc Clin Invest; fel Am Col Physicians; Col Am Pathologists; Am Soc Hemat. *Res:* Measurement of red cell survival in vivo; nature of interaction of hemoglobin and red cells with the chromate ion. *Mailing Add:* 3801 Miranda Ave Palo Alto CA 94305

EBBERT, ARTHUR, JR, b Wheeling, WVa, Aug 25, 22. INTERNAL MEDICINE. *Educ:* Univ Va, BA, 44, MD, 46. *Prof Exp:* Instr & asst to dean sch med, Univ Va, 52-53; instr & asst dean med, 53-54, asst prof & asst dean, 54-63, assoc dean, 60-74, assoc prof, 63-71, PROF MED, SCH MED, YALE UNIV, 71-, DEP DEAN, 74- *Concurrent Pos:* Physician, Univ Va Hosp, 52-53; assoc physician, Grace-New Haven Hosp, 53-60, asst attend physician, 60-68; consult, Waterbury Hosp, 57-; attend physician, Yale-New Haven Hosp, 68- *Mem:* Asn Am Med Cols. *Res:* Medical education. *Mailing Add:* Yale Univ Sch of Med 333 Cedar St PO Box 3333 New Haven CT 06510

EBBESEN, LYNN ROYCE, b Rapid City, SDak, Jan 27, 48; m 72; c 1. MECHANICAL ENGINEERING. *Educ:* SDak Sch Mines & Technol, BS, 70; Okla State Univ, MS, 72, PhD(mech eng), 76. *Prof Exp:* From asst prof to assoc prof, Sch Mech & Aerospace Eng, Okla State Univ, 77-81; SR ENG, SCI SIMULATION INC, ALBUQUERQUE, NMEX, 81- *Mem:* Am Soc Mech Engrs; Nat Soc Prof Engrs. *Res:* Automatic control; digital simulation of large scale systems. *Mailing Add:* Sci Simulation Inc Box 9331 Albuquerque NM 87119

EBBESMEYER, CURTIS CHARLES, b Los Angeles, Calif, Apr 24, 43; m 65; c 2. OCEANOGRAPHY. *Educ:* Calif State Univ, Northridge, BS, 66; Univ Wash, MS, 68, PhD(oceanog), 73. *Prof Exp:* Sr res engr & oceanogr, Mobil Res & Develop Corp, 69-72, assoc res engr & oceanogr, 72-74; MGR PHYS OCEANOG, EVANS-HAMILTON, INC, 74- *Concurrent Pos:* Asst adj prof, Marine Sci Res Ctr, State Univ NY Stony Brook, 74-; consult, Univ Wash, Univ BC, Mobil Oil Can, Ltd, Bethlehem Steel Corp & City of Seattle, 74-75. *Mem:* Sigma Xi; Am Geophys Union. *Res:* Physical oceanographic studies of waves, tides, currents, icebergs, and advection-diffusion processes, and phytoplankton dynamics using theoretical and field approaches. *Mailing Add:* Evans Hamilton Inc 6306 21st Ave NE Seattle WA 98115

EBBESSON, SVEN O E, b Backaby, Sweden, Oct 14, 37; US citizen; m 62; c 3. NEUROANATOMY. *Educ:* Southwestern Col, Kans, BA, 57; Univ Md, PhD(anat), 64. *Prof Exp:* Asst anat, Tulane Univ, 58-60; neuroanatomist, Walter Reed Army Med Ctr, 62-65; asst neuroanat, Sch Med, Univ Md, 63-64, instr, 64-65; neuroanatomist, Lab Perinatal Physiol, Nat Inst Neurol Dis & Blindness, 65-69; from assoc prof to prof neurosurg & anat, Sch Med, Univ Va, 69-77; ASSOC DEAN BIOMED SCI, MED SCI CAMPUS, UNIV PR,

SAN JUAN, 77- *Concurrent Pos:* Vis asst prof, Sch Med, Univ PR & hon mem, Inst Marine Biol, 66-70. *Mem:* AAAS; Am Asn Anat; Int Soc Stereol. *Res:* Comparative neurology; stereology. *Mailing Add:* Med Sci Campus PO Box 5067 San Juan PR 00936

EBBIGHAUSEN, EDWIN G, b Crookston, Minn, June 28, 11; m 37; c 2. ASTRONOMY. *Educ:* Univ Minn, BA, 36; Univ Chicago, PhD(astron), 40. *Prof Exp:* Instr math & astron, Wilson Col, 39-41; asst prof, Allegheny Observ, Pittsburgh, 41-44; res engr, Westinghouse Res Labs, 44-45; assoc prof, 46-58, prof, 58-76, EMER PROF PHYSICS, UNIV ORE, 76- *Concurrent Pos:* Lectr, Buhl Planetarium, Pa, 42-44; Carnegie intern fel, Harvard Univ, 55-56, Dom Astrophys Observ, 58-59 & Kitt Peak Nat Observ, 65-66; coordr, Ore Ctr Sci Teaching Improv Prog, AAAS, 56-58. *Mem:* AAAS; Am Astron Soc; Astron Soc Pac. *Res:* Spectroscopic binaries; eclipsing binary photometry. *Mailing Add:* 3150 Onyx Eugene OR 97405

EBBIN, ALLAN J, b New York, NY, May 2, 38; m; c 3. PEDIATRICS. *Educ:* NY Univ, BA, 60; State Univ NY Upstate Med Ctr, MD, 64; Univ Calif, Los Angeles, MPH, 76; Am Bd Pediat, cert, 69; Am Bd Prev Med, cert, 77. *Prof Exp:* Instr pediat, Emory Univ, 67-69; asst prof, 69-73, ASSOC PROF PEDIAT, SCH MED, UNIV SOUTHERN CALIF, 73-, ASST DIR GENETICS DIV, LOS ANGELES COUNTY-MED CTR, UNIV SOUTHERN CALIF, 69- *Concurrent Pos:* Actg chief, Congenital Malformations Unit, Leukemia Sect, Ctr Dis Control, Atlanta, Ga, 67-69; proj officer sequelae of rubella & birth defects, Nat Ctr Dis Control, 69-73; asst proj dir, Cytogenetics Lab, Child Develop & Ment Retardation Ctr, Maternal & Child Health Serv, 69-, actg dir, 77; partic, Crippled Children's Serv Panel, 70-; prin investr, Am Acad Pediat, Nat Inst Environ Health Sci, 72-75; mem adv comt, Sickle Cell Coun, Los Angeles County Health Dept, 72-; asst prog dir fetal diag high risk pregnancies, Nat Found-March Dimes, 72-, actg dir, 77; mem, Calif Tay-Sachs Dis Prev Prog, 74-; Nat Cancer Inst fel, Univ Calif, Los Angeles, 75-76; consult to var hosps. *Mem:* Am Soc Human Genetics; Soc Pediat Res; Am Acad Pediat. *Res:* Preventive medicine and genetics; epidemiology as applied to clinical genetics. *Mailing Add:* Los Angeles County-USC Med Ctr 1200 N State St Rm 1G-24 Los Angeles CA 90033

EBBING, DARRELL DELMAR, b Peoria, Ill, July 1, 33; m 55; c 3. PHYSICAL CHEMISTRY. *Educ:* Bradley Univ, BS, 55; Ind Univ, PhD(phys chem), 60. *Prof Exp:* Res assoc chem, Ind Univ, 60-62; from asst prof to assoc prof, 62-69, PROF CHEM, WAYNE STATE UNIV, 69- *Mem:* Am Chem Soc; Am Phys Soc; AAAS; Sigma Xi. *Res:* Quantum mechanical study of molecular properties and chemical binding. *Mailing Add:* Dept of Chem Wayne State Univ Detroit MI 48202

EBBS, JANE COTTON, b Newport, RI, May 11, 12. PHYSIOLOGY, NUTRITION. *Educ:* Univ RI, BS, 35, MS, 37. *Prof Exp:* Asst instr nutrit, Univ RI, 38-39; asst home econ, USDA, 42; nutrit adv, Off Qm Gen, Dept Army, 42-49, spec feeding & nutrit adv, 49-62; spec asst to dir, Defense Supply Agency, 62-65; adv, 65-70, CHIEF PROG PLANNING & EVAL, NUTRIT DIV, FOOD & AGR ORGN, UN, 70- *Mem:* Am Chem Soc; Am Inst Nutrit; assoc fel Am Astronaut Soc; fel Am Pub Health Asn; Am Dietetic Asn. *Res:* Vitamin A requirement of young adults; space nutrition; food processing methods; world food problems and new foods; feeding the armed forces. *Mailing Add:* PO Box S3731 Old San Juan PR 00904

EBDON, DAVID WILLIAM, b Detroit, Mich, Apr 9, 39; m 67; c 3. PHYSICAL CHEMISTRY. *Educ:* Univ Mich, Ann Arbor, BS, 61; Univ Md, PhD(phys chem), 67. *Prof Exp:* Lectr chem, Univ Md, 67-68; asst prof phys chem, 68-73, assoc prof phys chem, 73-80, PROF PHYS CHEM, EASTERN ILL UNIV, 80-, CHMN, DEPT CHEM, 77- *Concurrent Pos:* Sr res scientist, Nat Biomed Res Found, 67-68; res scientist, Univ Texas, Austin, 78-79. *Mem:* Am Chem Soc; Royal Soc Chem. *Res:* Thermodynamic and kinetic properties of electrolyte solutions; chemical oceanography; measurement of ionic association constants; computer modeling of natural water systems; ionic activity in multicomponent electrolyte solutions; divalent ion interactions with surfactants used in enhanced oil recovery; surfactant ion-selective electrodes. *Mailing Add:* Dept of Chem Eastern Ill Univ Charleston IL 61920

EBEL, MARVIN EMERSON, b Waterloo, Iowa, Sept 23, 30; m 60; c 4. THEORETICAL HIGH ENERGY PHYSICS, SOLID STATE PHYSICS. *Educ:* Iowa State Univ, BS, 50, MS, 52, PhD(physics), 53. *Prof Exp:* NSF fel, Inst Theoret Physics, Copenhagen, 53-54; from instr to asst prof, Yale Univ, 54-57; from asst prof to assoc prof physics, 57-64, PROF PHYSICS, UNIV WIS-MADISON, 64-, ASSOC DEAN GRAD SCH, 76- *Concurrent Pos:* Sloan Found fel, 57-62. *Mem:* Fel Am Phys Soc. *Res:* High energy physics. *Mailing Add:* Dept of Physics Univ of Wis Madison WI 53706

EBELING, ALFRED W, b Anaheim, Calif, Mar 30, 31; m 56; c 2. ZOOLOGY. *Educ:* Univ Calif, Los Angeles, BS, 54, PhD(zool), 60. *Prof Exp:* Asst prof biol, Yale Univ, 60-63; from asst prof to assoc prof zool, 63-72, contracts & grants officer, 66-67, PROF ZOOL, UNIV CALIF, SANTA BARBARA, 72- *Concurrent Pos:* NSF grants, 61-65, 66-68, 73-75 & 76-78; assoc, Los Angeles County Mus Natural Hist. *Mem:* AAAS; Am Soc Zoologists; fel Am Soc Fisheries Biologists; Am Soc Ichthyologists & Herpetologists; Am Soc Limnol & Oceanog; Am Soc Naturalists. *Res:* Ichthyology; marine ecology. *Mailing Add:* Dept of Biol Sci Univ of Calif Santa Barbara CA 93106

EBELING, DOLPH G, b New York, NY, Aug 1, 20; m 42; c 2. METALLURGY. *Educ:* Rensselaer Polytech Inst, BS, 40, MS, 48, PhD(metal), 50. *Prof Exp:* Metal asst, Carnegie Il Steel Corp, 40-41; ord specialist, US Naval Proving Ground, 41-46; develop metallurgist, Chem Dept, Gen Elec Co, 46-51, res assoc, Res Lab, 51-53, mgr metal unit, Turbine Div, 53-60, consult, Knolls Atomic Power Lab, 60-61, mat eng serv, 61-66, mgr eng educ, 66-70; PRES, EBELING ASSOC, INC, 70- *Mem:* Am Soc Metals; Am Soc Mech Engrs; NY Acad Sci; Am Inst Mining, Metall & Petrol Engrs; Brit Iron & Steel Inst. *Res:* Permanent magnets; high temperature alloys; fracture of metals and alloy embrittlement; structure-property relationships; alloy design and process development. *Mailing Add:* 2063 Coolidge Pl Schenectady NY 12309

EBERHARD, ANATOL, b Istanbul, Turkey, Nov 13, 38; US citizen; m 64. ORGANIC CHEMISTRY, BIOCHEMISTRY. *Educ:* Univ Calif, Berkeley, BA, 59; Harvard Univ, MA, 60, PhD(chem), 64. *Prof Exp:* NIH fel, Univ Calif, Berkeley, 64-66; asst prof biol, Harvard Univ, 66-71; assoc prof chem, Fairleigh Dickinson Univ, 71-72; ASSOC PROF CHEM, ITHACA COL, 72- *Mem:* AAAS; Am Chem Soc. *Res:* Biochemistry of bacterial bioluminescence. *Mailing Add:* Dept of Chem Ithaca Col Ithaca NY 14850

EBERHARD, EVERETT, b Topeka, Kans, Mar 15, 15; m 41; c 2. ELECTRICAL ENGINEERING. *Educ:* Univ Kans, BS, 36; Yale Univ, ME, 38. *Prof Exp:* Instr elec eng, SDak State Col, 39-40; elec engr, Hobart Bros Co, 40; instr, US Air Force Radio & Radar Schs, 40-42; sr engr, Victor Div, Radio Corp Am, 46-50; sect head in chg integrated circuits, Motorola Inc, 60-67, sr engr & proj leader systs develop, Western Mil Electronic Ctr, 50-80, sr elec engr, Tactical Electronics Dept, 67-80; RETIRED. *Mem:* Sr mem Inst Elec & Electronics Engrs. *Res:* Automation in field of test equipment; design of transistor oscillator circuits; application of all types of integrated circuits to military equipment. *Mailing Add:* Rt 2 Box 1711 Lakeside AZ 85929

EBERHARD, JEFFREY WAYNE, b New Braunfels, Tex, Feb 21, 50; m 79. SOLID STATE PHYSICS. *Educ:* Univ Tex, Austin, BA, 72; Univ Chicago, SM, 74, PhD(physics), PhD(physics), 78. *Prof Exp:* PHYSICIST ULTRASONICS, GEN ELEC RES & DEVELOP CTR, 77- *Mem:* Am Phys Soc. *Res:* Ultrasonic imaging; 1/f noise in solids. *Mailing Add:* Gen Elec Co Res & Develop Ctr PO Box 8 Bldg K-1 Rm 3A42 Schenectady NY 12301

EBERHARD, PHILIPPE HENRI, b Lausanne, Switz, July 8, 29; m 54; c 2. PARTICLE PHYSICS. *Educ:* Polytech Sch, Univ Lausanne, Dipl, 52; Univ Paris, PhD(sci), 57. *Prof Exp:* Researcher physics, Nat Ctr Sci Res & Col France, 55-63; physicist, Lawrence Berkeley Lab, 63-71; vis scientist particle physics, Europ Orgn Nuclear Res, Geneva, Switz, 71-72; PHYSICIST, LAWRENCE BERKELEY LAB, 72- *Mem:* Am Phys Soc. *Res:* Search for magnetic monopoles; foundations of quantum theory; electron-positron physics; superconducting magnets. *Mailing Add:* 772 Colusa Ave El Cerrito CA 94530

EBERHARD, WILLIAM GRANVILLE, behavioral biology, arachnology, see previous edition

EBERHARDT, KEITH RANDALL, b Los Angeles, Calif, July 10, 47; m 78; c 2. SURVEY SAMPLING THEORY. *Educ:* Case Western Reserve Univ, BS, 69; Johns Hopkins Univ, PHD(statist), 75. *Prof Exp:* Instr statist, Ohio State Univ, 73-75, asst prof, 75-78; MATH STATISTICIAN, NAT BUR STANDARDS, 78- *Mem:* Am Statist Asn; Inst Math Statist; Int Asn Survey Statisticians. *Res:* Prediction approach to survey sampling theory using linear regression models; linear models; propagation of error; general statistical inference. *Mailing Add:* Rm A337 Admin Bldg Statist Eng Div Nat Bur Standards Washington DC 20234

EBERHARDT, LESTER LEE, biology, see previous edition

EBERHARDT, MANFRED KARL, b Heidenheim, Ger; Dec 5, 30. ORGANIC CHEMISTRY. *Educ:* Univ Tübingen, PhD(org chem), 57. *Prof Exp:* Res assoc, Univ Chicago, 57-59, Univ Ark, 59-60 & Univ Notre Dame, 60-62; fel radiation chem & org chem, Mellon Inst, 62-64; scientist, Munich Tech Univ, 65-67; scientist, PR Nuclear Ctr, 67-76; assoc prof, Sch Med, Univ PR, Cayey, 76-78; ASSOC PROF, SCH MED CANCER CTR, UNIV PR, SAN JUAN, 78- *Concurrent Pos:* Consult, PR Dept Health, 78-79. *Mem:* Am Chem Soc; NY Acad Sci. *Res:* Mechanism of organic reactions, free radicals, quantum chemistry; environmental carcinogenesis; radiation chemistry. *Mailing Add:* Univ PR Med Sci Campus Cancer Ctr GPO Box 5067 San Juan PR 00936

EBERHARDT, NIKOLAI, b Rakvere, Estonia, July 2, 30; m 56; c 4. MICROWAVE ELECTRONICS, ELECTROMAGNETICS. *Educ:* Univ Munich, dipl physics, 57; Munich Inst Technol, PhD(physics), 62. *Prof Exp:* Res engr, Siemens und Halske A G, Ger, 56-62; assoc prof, 62-70, PROF ELEC ENG, LEHIGH UNIV, 70- *Concurrent Pos:* Consult, Bell Tel Labs, 63- *Res:* Physics of magnetically confined electron beams; color display tubes; theoretical and experimental investigations in the area of passive microwave devices, especially ferrite devices and filters. *Mailing Add:* Dept of Elec Eng Lehigh Univ Bethlehem PA 18015

EBERHARDT, WILLIAM HENRY, b Montclair, NJ, Feb 11, 20; m 46; c 3. PHYSICAL CHEMISTRY. *Educ:* Johns Hopkins Univ, AB, 41; Calif Inst Technol, PhD(phys chem), 45. *Prof Exp:* Asst, Calif Inst Technol, 41-44, instr, 44-46; assoc dean, Col Sci & Lib Studies, 70-77, from asst prof to assoc prof, 46-55, PROF CHEM, GA INST TECHNOL, 55- *Concurrent Pos:* Hon fel, Univ Minn, 53; vis prof, Harvard Univ, 64. *Mem:* AAAS; Am Chem Soc; Am Phys Soc. *Res:* Visible and ultraviolet spectroscopy; molecular structure. *Mailing Add:* Sch of Chem Ga Inst of Technol Atlanta GA 30332

EBERHART, BRUCE MACLEAN, b San Jose, Calif, Oct 14, 27; m 51; c 3. BIOCHEMICAL GENETICS. *Educ:* San Jose State Col, AB, 50; Stanford Univ, PhD, 56. *Prof Exp:* From instr to asst prof genetics, Princeton Univ, 56-63; head dept, 63-80, PROF BIOL, UNIV NC, GREENSBORO, 63- *Mem:* Genetics Soc Am. *Res:* Genetic control of enzyme synthesis in microbes, particularly Neurospora; role of enzymes in cellular metabolism and differentiation. *Mailing Add:* Dept of Biol Univ of NC Greensboro NC 27412

EBERHART, H(OWARD) D(AVIS), b Lima, Ohio, Aug 16, 06; m 61; c 2. CIVIL ENGINEERING, ENGINEERING EDUCATION. *Educ:* Univ Ore, BS, 29; Ore State Col, MS, 35. *Prof Exp:* Coach & instr, high sch, 29-33; jr topog engr, US Geol Surv, 34; mem staff, US Eng Off, Bonneville Dam, 35-36; from instr to prof civil eng, Univ Calif, Berkeley, 36-74, chmn dept, 59-63 & 71-74; res engr & vchmn biomech lab, Univ Hosp, San Francisco, 70-76; EMER PROF CIVIL ENG, UNIV CALIF, BERKELEY, 74-; CHMN

CIVIL ENG DEPT, KING ABDULAZIZ UNIV, SAUDI ARABIA, 76- *Concurrent Pos:* Consult, Consol Vultee Aircraft Corp, 43-44; in-charge res concrete pavement invests, Hamilton Field, 44; consult res proj, Comt Prosthetic Res & Develop, Nat Res Coun, 45-76, mem-at-large, Div Eng & Indust Res, 60-66; Fulbright lectr, Univ Assiut, 64-65. *Mem:* Fel Am Soc Civil Engrs; Nat Acad Eng; Am Soc Eng Educ; Am Concrete Inst; Soc Exp Stress Analysis. *Res:* Structural engineering; biomechanics; experimental stress analysis; prosthetic devices; engineering education development and evaluation. *Mailing Add:* Dept of Civil Engineering Univ of Calif Berkeley CA 94720

EBERHART, JAMES GETTINS, b Columbus, Ohio, Feb 6, 36; c 2. PHYSICAL CHEMISTRY, SURFACE CHEMISTRY. *Educ:* Ohio State Univ, BSc, 57, PhD(chem), 63. *Prof Exp:* Tech staff mem mat sci, Sandia Labs, Albuquerque, NMex, 63-68; chemist, Argonne Nat Lab, Ill, 68-78; assoc prof, 78-81, PROF CHEM, AURORA COL, 81- *Concurrent Pos:* Consult, Argonne Nat Lab, 78-79. *Mem:* Am Chem Soc. *Res:* Wetting behavior of liquids; limit of superheat of liquids; equations of state; surface tension of liquids and solids; surface diffusion; critical properties of fluids. *Mailing Add:* Dept Chem 347 S Gladstone Ave Aurora IL 60507

EBERHART, PAUL, b Douglas Co, Kans, May 21, 06; m 40; c 2. MATHEMATICS. *Educ:* Washburn Univ, BS, 28; Univ Kans, MA, 29; Brown Univ, PhD(math), 43. *Hon Degrees:* DSc, Washburn Univ, 80. *Prof Exp:* Asst instr math, Univ Kans, 29-30; instr, Brown Univ, 30-37; from instr to prof, 37-71, head dept, 42-66, EMER PROF MATH & EMER HEAD DEPT, WASHBURN UNIV, 71- *Mem:* Math Asn Am. *Res:* Fourier series; summability; summability of derived and conjugate derived Fourier series. *Mailing Add:* 2068 Lane St Topeka KS 66604

EBERHART, ROBERT CLYDE, b Oakland, Calif, Apr 17, 37; m 63; c 3. BIOMATERIALS, HEAT & MASS TRANSFER. *Educ:* Harvard Univ, AB, 58; Univ Calif, Berkeley, MS, 60, PhD(mech eng), 65. *Prof Exp:* Sr scientist biomed eng, Inst Med Sci, 64-75; assoc prof mech eng, Univ Tex, Austin, 75-76; ASSOC PROF ENG SURG, SOUTHWESTERN MED SCH, 76- *Concurrent Pos:* Adj prof biomed eng, Univ Tex, Austin, 76-, Southern Methodist Univ, 78- & Univ Tex, Arlington, 79- *Mem:* Am Soc Mech Eng; Am Soc Artificial Internal Organs; Soc Critical Care Med; Inst Elec & Electronics Engrs; Am Soc Eng Educ. *Res:* Biomaterials; cardiopulmonary assist devices; ion sensing field effect transistors; computers in critical care medicine; heat and mass transfer analysis in medicine. *Mailing Add:* Dept Surg Southwestern Med Sch 5323 Harry Hines Blvd Dallas TX 75235

EBERHART, ROBERT J, b Lock Haven, Pa, Sept 9, 30; m 53; c 4. VETERINARY MEDICINE. *Educ:* Cornell Univ, AB, 52; Univ Pa, VMD, 59; Pa State Univ, PhD(physiol), 66. *Prof Exp:* Instr vet sci, Pa State Univ, 59-63; fel, Am Vet Med Asn, 63-65; from asst prof to assoc prof, 66-78, PROF VET SCI, PA STATE UNIV, 78- *Mem:* AAAS; Am Vet Med Asn. *Res:* Bovine mastitis. *Mailing Add:* Dept of Vet Sci Pa State Univ University Park PA 16802

EBERHART, STEVE A, b Keya Paha, SDak, Nov 11, 31; m 53; c 4. GENETICS, STATISTICS. *Educ:* Univ Nebr, BSc, 52, MSc, 58; NC State Univ, PhD(genetics, statist), 61. *Prof Exp:* Res geneticist, Iowa State Univ, USDA, 61-64, Nat Agr Res Sta, Kenya, 64-68 & Agr Res Serv, 68-74, prof agron, Agr Res Serv, Iowa State Univ, USDA, 74-75; assoc dir res, 75-77, VPRES RES, FUNK SEEDS INT, 78- *Honors & Awards:* Arthur S Flemming Award, 70. *Mem:* Am Soc Agron; Biomet Soc. *Res:* Statistical genetics of maize, including estimation of additive, dominance and epistatic variances; development of a model to study the gene action in diallels of fixed varieties and to predict variety and variety cross performance. *Mailing Add:* Funk Seeds Int 1300 W Washington Bloomington IL 61701

EBERLE, HELEN I, b Oakland, Calif, Mar 2, 32; m 58; c 3. MOLECULAR BIOLOGY, BIOPHYSICS. *Educ:* Calif State Col, Los Angeles, BS, 56; Univ Calif, Los Angeles, PhD(microbiol), 65. *Prof Exp:* Pub Health microbiologist, Los Angeles County Health Dept, 56-60; NIH fels, Kans State Univ, 65-67, Univ Rochester, 67-68; instr, 68-69, asst prof, 69-76, ASSOC PROF RADIATION BIOL & BIOPHYS, UNIV ROCHESTER, 76- *Concurrent Pos:* Am Cancer Soc grant, 70-72; dir educ, Dept Radiation Biol & Biophys, Sch Med, Univ Rochester, 76-; res contract with Energy Res & Develop Admin-Dept Energy, 70-; mem, Nat Res Coun Comt on Pure & Appl Biophysics, 78-; consult, Chevron Corp, 80-; NIH grant, 81-84. *Honors & Awards:* Faculty Res Award, Am Cancer Soc, 69. *Mem:* AAAS; Am Soc Microbiol; Biophys Soc. *Res:* Mechanism and regulation of DNA replication in Escherichia coli with emphasis on the characterization proteins involved in the initiation process; molecular genetics. *Mailing Add:* Dept Radiation Biol & Biophys Univ of Rochester Rochester NY 14620

EBERLE, JON WILLIAM, b Chillicothe, Ohio, Aug 28, 34; m 56; c 4. BIOMEDICAL ENGINEERING, ELECTROMAGNETICS. *Educ:* Ohio State Univ, BS, 57, MS, 60, PhD(elec eng), 64. *Prof Exp:* Res assoc phased arrays, Antenna Lab, Ohio State Univ, 57-61, assoc supvr, 61-65; mem tech staff, Tex Instruments Inc, 65-66, mgr advan radar develop br, 66, mgr surface systs dept, 66-68, mgr corp mkt, 68-69; vpres biomed, Intermed Corp, 69-70; consult to dean biomed & elec eng, 70-71, assoc prof biomed & elec eng, 71-76, ADJ PROF ELEC ENG, SOUTHERN METHODIST UNIV, 76- *Concurrent Pos:* Fel, Dept Bus Admin, Ohio State Univ, 64-65; res scientist, Div Thoracic & Cardiovasc Surg, Med Sch, Univ Tex, 70-; mem subpanel on elec safety, Am Nat Stand Inst, 70-; elec engr, Vet Hosp, Dallas, 71- *Mem:* Inst Elec & Electronics Eng; Asn Advan Med Instrumentation. *Res:* Membrane oxygenators having heparin ionically bound to their surfaces; continuous monitoring of pH of blood and partial pressures of O_2 and CO_2 in blood; computerized medical records; x-ray holography. *Mailing Add:* Dept of Elec Eng Southern Methodist Univ Dallas TX 75275

EBERLEIN, GEORGE DONALD, b New Brunswick, NJ, Nov 21, 20; m 69; c 1. GEOLOGY. *Educ:* Yale Univ, BS, 42. *Prof Exp:* Geologist, Big Sandy Mine, Inc, Ariz, 41; geologist metals sect, US Geol Surv, 42-47, Br Alaskan Mineral Resources, 47-53, staff geologist mineral deposits, 53-57, asst br chief, 57-59, br chief, 59-63, RES GEOLOGIST, BR ALASKAN GEOL, US GEOL SURV, 63- *Concurrent Pos:* Teaching fel & asst, Stanford Univ; Binney fel & Penfield Prize, Yale Univ. *Mem:* Fel Geol Soc Am; Mineral Soc Am; Soc Econ Geol; Mineral Asn Can; Int Union Geol Sci. *Res:* Petrology of igneous and metamorphic rocks; mineral resources of Alaska; optical crystallography; Precambrian rocks of Alaska. *Mailing Add:* Br of Alaskan Geol US Geol Surv 345 Middlefield Rd Menlo Park CA 94025

EBERLEIN, PATRICIA JAMES, b Washington, DC, July 15, 25; m 46, 56; c 7. NUMERICAL ANALYSIS, COMPUTER SCIENCE. *Educ:* Univ Chicago, BS, 44; Mich State Univ, PhD(math), 55. *Prof Exp:* Instr math, Wayne Univ, 55-56; mathematician, Inst Advan Study, 56-57; res assoc, Comput Ctr, Univ Rochester, 57-61, asst dir anal, 61-68; assoc prof math & comput sci, 68-74, PROF COMPUT SCI, STATE UNIV NY BUFFALO, 74-, CHMN, 81- *Mem:* Am Math Soc; Soc Indust & Appl Math; Asn Comput Mach; AAAS; Math Asn Am. *Res:* Applied mathematics; linear algebra; complexity and analysis of algorithms. *Mailing Add:* Dept Comput Sci State Univ NY Buffalo 4226 Ridge Lea Rd Amherst NY 14226

EBERLEIN, PATRICK BARRY, b San Francisco, Calif, March 3, 44; m 68; c 2. DIFFERENTIAL GEOMETRY. *Educ:* Harvard Col, AB, 65; Univ Calif, Los Angeles, MA, 67, PhD(math), 70. *Prof Exp:* Instr & lectr math, Univ Calif, Los Angeles, 70; lectr, Univ Calif, Berkeley, 70-71; vis researcher, Univ Bonn, WGer, 71-72; lectr, Univ Calif, Berkeley, 72-73; from asst prof to assoc prof, 73-81, PROF MATH, UNIV NC, CHAPEL HILL, 81- *Concurrent Pos:* Mem, Sch Math, Inst Advan Study, 78-79; prin investr, NSF Grant, 74-78, 79- *Res:* Differential geometric properties of Riemanmian manifolds of nonpositive sectional curvature; geodesic flows, isometry groups, end structure of noncompact manifolds of finite volume and geometric properties of compact manifolds that are homotopy invariants. *Mailing Add:* Dept Math Univ NC Chapel Hill NC 27514

EBERLEIN, WILLIAM FREDERICK, b Shawano, Wis, June 25, 17; m 43, 56; c 7. MATHEMATICS. *Educ:* Harvard Univ, AB, 38, PhD(math), 42; Univ Wis, MA, 39. *Prof Exp:* Propeller res analyst, Bur Ships, 41-42, instr math, Purdue Univ, 46; instr math, Univ Mich, 46-47; mem, Inst Advan Study, 47-48; from asst prof to assoc prof math, Univ Wis, 48-55; vis prof, Wayne State Univ, 55-56; mem, Inst Math Sci, NY Univ, 56-57; PROF MATH, UNIV ROCHESTER, 57- *Concurrent Pos:* Mem ergodic theory panel, Int Cong Mathematicians, 50. *Mem:* Am Math Soc; Math Asn Am. *Res:* Functional analysis; mathematical physics. *Mailing Add:* Dept of Math Univ of Rochester Rochester NY 14627

EBERLY, JOSEPH HENRY, b Carlisle, Pa, Oct 19, 35; m 60; c 3. THEORETICAL PHYSICS, QUANTUM OPTICS. *Educ:* Pa State Univ, BS, 57; Stanford Univ, MS, 59, PhD(physics), 62. *Prof Exp:* Res physicist, Stanford Linear Accelerator Ctr, 62; resident res assoc, Nuclear Physics Div, US Naval Ord Lab, Md, 62-65; res assoc, 65-67, asst prof, 67-69, assoc prof, 69-76, prof physics, 76-78, PROF PHYSICS & OPTICS, UNIV ROCHESTER, 79- *Concurrent Pos:* Nat Acad Sci-Nat Res Coun resident res associateship, 62-64; lectr, Univ Md, 64-65; Nat Acad Sci vis lectr, eastern Europe, 70-; consult, Dept Energy, Dept Defense; vis fel, Joint Inst Lab Astrophys, Univ Colo & Nat Bur Standards, 77-78. *Honors & Awards:* Civilian Serv Award, US Navy, 64. *Mem:* Fel Am Phys Soc; fel Optical Soc Am. *Res:* Multiphoton interactions of electrons, atoms, molecules; quantum electrodynamics; quantum optics. *Mailing Add:* Dept of Physics & Astron Univ of Rochester Rochester NY 14627

EBERLY, WILLIAM ROBERT, b North Manchester, Ind, Oct 4, 26; m 46; c 3. ZOOLOGY, LIMNOLOGY. *Educ:* Manchester Col, AB, 48; Ind Univ, MA, 55, PhD(zool), 58. *Prof Exp:* Sci instr pub schs, Ind, 47-52; asst zool, Ind Univ, 52-55; from asst prof to assoc prof biol, 55-67, PROF BIOL MANCHESTER COL, 67-, DIR ENVIRON STUDIES, 72- *Concurrent Pos:* Vis scientist, Univ Uppsala, 63-64. *Mem:* Am Soc Limnol & Oceanog; Int Asn Theoret & Appl Limnol. *Res:* Oxygen producation in lakes and lake typology; ecology and taxonomy of blue-green algae; eutrophication in lakes. *Mailing Add:* 304 Sunset Ct North Manchester IN 46962

EBERSOLE, A(LVIN) J(AMES), b Filer, Idaho, Apr 10, 21; m 47; c 3. CHEMICAL ENGINEERING. *Educ:* Univ Wis, BS, 44. *Prof Exp:* Res engr, Calif Res Corp, 44-50; sr res engr, 50-57, comput engr, 57-66, chief comput engr, 66-70, DIR TELECOMMUN, FLUOR CORP, 70- *Res:* Treating of gasoline and refining oils; investigation of bubble cap performance; gas treating; sulfur dioxide recovery; application of digital computer to engineering problems; design, installation, and operation of national and international voice and data communications facilities. *Mailing Add:* Fluor Corp 3333 Michelson Dr Irvine CA 92730

EBERSOLE, JEFFREY LEE, immunology, microbiology, see previous edition

EBERSOLE, JOHN FRANKLIN, b Boston, Mass, Feb 21, 46; m 68; c 2. OPTICAL PHYSICS. *Educ:* Col Holy Cross, AB, 68; Univ Fla, MS, 71, PhD(physics), 74. *Prof Exp:* Teaching asst optics, Dept Physics & Astron, Univ Fla, 68-72, instr, 71-72; from optical engr to sr optical engr, Itek Corp, 72-75, res & develop mgr optics, 74-75; SR RES SCIENTIST, APPL SCI DIV, AERODYNE RES, INC, 75- *Mem:* Optical Soc Am; Inst Elec & Electronics Engrs; Sigma Xi; Soc Photo-Optical Instrumentation Engrs. *Res:* Optical physics, including electro-optics, laser scattering by aerosols, optical information processing, holography, acousto-optics, integrated optics and optical materials. *Mailing Add:* Appl Sci Div Aerodyne Res Inc Bedford Res Park Bedford MA 01730

EBERSTEIN, ARTHUR, b Chicago, Ill, Apr 23, 28; m 61; c 2. BIOPHYSICS. *Educ:* Ill Inst Technol, BS, 50; Univ Ill, MS, 51; Ohio State Univ, PhD(biophys), 57. *Prof Exp:* NSF fel, Copenhagen Univ, 57-58, NIH fel, 58-59; res scientist biophys, Inst Muscle Dis, 59-61; res scientist physics, Am Bosch Arma Corp, 61-63; head med electronics dept, Lundy Electronics & Systs, Inc, 63-64; assoc prof rehab med, 70-72, ASST PROF BIOPHYS, SCH MED, NY UNIV, 64-, PROF REHAB MED, 72- *Mem:* Biophys Soc; Am Physiol Soc. *Res:* Muscle physiology. *Mailing Add:* Inst of Rehab Med NY Univ Med Ctr New York NY 10016

EBERT, ANDREW GABRIEL, b Brooklyn, NY, Jan 5, 36; m 61; c 3. PHARMACOLOGY, FOOD SCIENCE. *Educ:* Long Island Univ, BS, 57; Purdue Univ, MS, 61, PhD(pharmacol), 62. *Prof Exp:* Sr res scientist, Squibb Inst Med Res, 61-65; supvr pharmacol, Int Minerals & Chem Corp, 65-68, mgr pharmacol & govt registrn, 68-70, mgr prod safety eval, 70-72; dir prod safety & regulatory affairs, 72-75, VPRES SCI & TECH AFFAIRS, WILLIAM UNDERWOOD CO, 76- *Concurrent Pos:* Guest lectr, Mass Inst Tech, 78. *Mem:* Am Pharmaceut Asn; Am Soc Pharmacol & Exp Therapeut; Soc Toxicol; Inst Food Technologists; Sigma Xi. *Res:* Quality control; product development; national and international regulation of foods; metabolic fate of foods; drugs; food additives; agricultural chemicals. *Mailing Add:* William Underwood Co 1 Red Devil Lane Westwood MA 02090

EBERT, CHARLES DEWEY, b Las Vegas, Nev, Nov 20, 53. PHARMACEUTICAL CHEMISTRY. *Educ:* Univ Utah, BS, 77, PhD(pharmaceut), 81. *Prof Exp:* Res physiologist, Hosp Res Ctr, 77-78; res asst, Dept Pharmaceut, Univ Utah, 78-81, res assoc, 81-82; RES SCIENTIST, PFIZER CENT RES, 82- *Concurrent Pos:* Vis scientist, Netherlands, 81. *Mem:* Am Chem Soc; Am Pharmaceut Asn; NY Acad Sci. *Res:* Design of novelle drug delivery systems utilizing controlled release and/or biodegradable polymers; surface phenomena in general. *Mailing Add:* Pfizer Cent Res Groton CT 06340

EBERT, CHARLES H V, b Ger, June 23, 24; US citizen; m 49; c 1. PHYSICAL GEOGRAPHY. *Educ:* Univ NC, BA, 51, MA, 53, PhD(geog), 57. *Prof Exp:* Instr geog & geol, Univ Buffalo, 54-56, from asst prof to assoc prof, 56-63, actg dean undergrad div, State Univ NY Buffalo, 70-71, dean undergrad div, 71-77, PROF GEOG, STATE UNIV NY BUFFALO, 63- *Concurrent Pos:* Adv, Peruvian Develop Found, 69- *Mem:* Asn Am Geog; Int Oceanog Found; Soil Sci Soc Am; Am Soc Agron; Int Soil Sci Soc. *Res:* Soils geography and soil morphology; environmental problems in land development; physical environmental factors in planning and development; soils field research in connection with archeological excavations at Tel Ifshar, Israel and Old Fort Niagra, New York; research and consulting on leachate diffusion from chemical dumps. *Mailing Add:* Dept Geog State Univ NY Buffalo NY 14260

EBERT, EARL ERNEST, b Oakland, Calif, Sept 28, 31; m 57; c 3. FISH BIOLOGY. *Educ:* San Jose State Col, BA, 59. *Prof Exp:* Aquatic biologist, Marine Resources Lab, 60-63, from asst marine biologist to assoc marine biologist, Menlo Park, 63-70, SR MARINE BIOLOGIST & DIR MARINE CULT LAB, CALIF DEPT FISH & GAME, MONTEREY, 70- *Mem:* Am Inst Fishery Res Biologists; Nat Shellfisheries Asn; World Maricult Soc. *Res:* Mariculture feasibility studies; mariculture feasibility studies of selected shellfish species. *Mailing Add:* Calif Dept Fish & Game Granite Canyon Coast Rte Monterey CA 93940

EBERT, GARY LEE, Beaver Dam, Wis, June 30, 47; m 78; c 3. FINITE GEOMETRIES, COMBINATORIAL DESIGNS. *Educ:* Univ Wis, Madison, BS, 69, MS, 71, PhD(math), 75. *Prof Exp:* Vis lectr math, Tex Tech Univ, 75-77; asst prof, 77-81, ASSOC PROF MATH, UNIV DEL, 81- *Concurrent Pos:* Comput programmer, Chevrolet Eng Ctr, 69-70. *Mem:* Am Math Soc; Math Asn Am. *Res:* Finite geometries (principally affine, projective, and inversive) and their associated combinatorial structures and properties; spreads and packings in finite projective spaces. *Mailing Add:* Dept Math Sci Univ Del Newark DE 19711

EBERT, IAN O, b Mingo, Iowa, Mar 13, 20; m 45; c 2. ELECTRICAL ENGINEERING. *Educ:* Iowa State Col, BS, 42; Univ Ill, MS, 47. *Prof Exp:* Electronic res engr, Naval Res Lab, 43-46 & 47-48; asst, Univ Ill, 46-47; asst prof, 48-54, ASSOC PROF ELEC ENG, MICH STATE UNIV, 54- *Concurrent Pos:* Adv, Eng Col, Univ Poona, 63-64; vis engr, Eng Summer Insts, India, 65, 66 & 70. *Mem:* AAAS; Am Soc Eng Educ; Inst Elec & Electronics Engrs. *Res:* Semiconductor physics and electronics; audio circuits and acoustical systems; electronic circuits; communication system development. *Mailing Add:* Dept of Elec Eng Mich State Univ East Lansing MI 48824

EBERT, JAMES DAVID, b Bentleyville, Pa, Dec 11, 21; m 46; c 3. EMBRYOLOGY. *Educ:* Washington & Jefferson Col, AB, 42; Johns Hopkins Univ, PhD(biol), 50. *Hon Degrees:* ScD, Washington & Jefferson Col, 69; ScD, Yale Univ, 73, Ind Univ, 75; LLD, Moravian Col, 79. *Prof Exp:* Jr instr biol, Johns Hopkins Univ, 46-49; instr, Mass Inst Technol, 50-51; from asst prof to assoc prof zool, Ind Univ, 51-55; dir dept embryol, 56-76, PRES CARNEGIE INST WASHINGTON, 78- *Concurrent Pos:* Vis scientist, Brookhaven Nat Lab, 53-54; mem adv panel, Comt Growth, Nat Res Coun, 53-55, chmn, Assembly Life Sci, 73-77; mem comt basic res aging, Am Inst Biol Sci, 55-60, pres inst, 63; mem comt genetic & develop biol, NSF, 55-56 & div comt biol & med sci, 63-67; mem cell biol study sect, USPHS, 58-62 & Comn Undergrad Educ Biol Sci, 63-67; mem vis comts, Mass Inst Technol, 59-68, Case Western Reserve Univ, 64-68, Univ Pa, 67-69, Columbia Univ, 67-69, Univ Ore, 67-72, Harvard Univ, 69-75, Princeton Univ, 70-76, Univ Chicago, 74- & Boston Univ, 77-; Philips vis prof, Haverford Col, 60-61; Patten vis prof, Ind Univ, 62-63; dir embryol training prof, Marine Biol Lab, Woods Hole, 62-66, trustee, 64-, dir, 70-75 & 77-78, pres, 70-78; with Univ Sci Develop Adv Panel, NSF, 65-70; with comt Inst Progs, 71; mem bd sci coun, Nat Cancer Inst, 67-71 & Nat Inst Child Health & Human Develop, 73-76; bd sci overseers, Jackson Lab, 67-80, bd gov trustees, 74-; bd dirs, Oak Ridge Assoc Univs, 67-71; NIH lectr, 67; Yamagiwa Mem lectr, Univ Tokyo, 68; Tamaki mem lectr, Univ Kyoto, 72; regents' lectr, Univ Calif, 75; Storer lectr, Univ Calif, Davis, 77. *Honors & Awards:* First Distinguished Serv Award, Washington & Jefferson Col, 65; Eminent Scientist Award, Japan Soc Prom Sci, 72; President's Medal, Am Inst Biol Sci, 72. *Mem:* Nat Acad Sci (vpres, 81-); Am Philos Soc; Inst Med; Soc Develop Biol (pres, 57-58); Am Soc Zool (pres, 70). *Res:* Acquisition of biological specificity; protein synthesis and interactions in development; heart development; graft versus host reactions; viruses as tools in developmental biology; melanogenesis; amino acid and vitamin metabolism in development; tumorigenic viruses; viral oncogenic sequences; cell replicating mechanisms; ionic regulation of differentiation. *Mailing Add:* Carnegie Inst of Washington 1530 P St NW Washington DC 20005

EBERT, LAWRENCE BURTON, b Bronxville, NY, Jan 14, 49. PHYSICAL CHEMISTRY, MATERIALS SCIENCE. *Educ:* Univ Chicago, SB, 71; Stanford Univ, MS, 74, PhD(chem), 75. *Prof Exp:* Res chemist, 75-78, sr chemist res, 78-79, STAFF CHEMIST, EXXON CORP, 79- *Mem:* Am Chem Soc; Am Phys Soc; Sigma Xi. *Res:* Solid state chemistry and physics of carbonaceous materials; with emphasis on intercalation compounds of graphite. *Mailing Add:* Exxon Corp Res PO Box 45 Linden NJ 07036

EBERT, LYNN J, b Sandusky, Ohio, Apr 17, 20; m 43; c 4. METALLURGICAL ENGINEERING. *Educ:* Case Western Reserve Univ, BS, 41, MS, 43, PhD (metall), 54. *Prof Exp:* From asst to res assoc, 41-51, sr res assoc, 51-54, from asst prof to assoc prof metall eng, 54-65, PROF METALL ENG, CASE WESTERN RESERVE UNIV, 65- *Mem:* Am Soc Metals; NY Acad Sci; Am Inst Mining, Metall & Petrol Engrs. *Res:* Mechanical and physical behaviors of ferrous and non-ferrous metals and alloys; failure analysis; fiber composite performance. *Mailing Add:* Dept of Metal & Mat Sci University Circle Cleveland OH 44106

EBERT, PATRICIA DOROTHY, b Youngstown, Ohio, June 13, 49; m 77. BEHAVIORAL GENETICS. *Educ:* Miami Univ, BA, 70; Bowling Green State Univ, MA, 72, PhD(psychol), 75. *Prof Exp:* Asst prof psychol, Winthrop Col, 74-77; asst prof, 77-80, ASSOC PROF PSYCHOL & CHMN DEPT, NIAGARA UNIV, 80- *Mem:* AAAS; Behav Genetics Asn; Animal Behav Soc; Int Soc Res Aggression; Sigma Xi. *Res:* Animal behavior genetics; aggressive behavior; comparative, behavioral and physiological sex differences; comparative development of social behavior. *Mailing Add:* Dept of Psychol Niagara Univ Niagara University NY 14109

EBERT, PAUL ALLEN, b Columbus, Ohio, Aug 11, 32; m 54; c 3. CARDIOVASCULAR SURGERY, PHYSIOLOGY. *Educ:* Ohio State Univ, BS, 54, MD, 58. *Prof Exp:* Intern surg, Johns Hopkins Hosp, 58-59, asst resident, 59-60; sr resident, Clin of Surg, Nat Heart Inst, 60-62; asst resident, Johns Hopkins Hosp, 62-65, chief resident, 65-66; from asst prof to assoc prof, Med Ctr, Duke Univ, 66-71; prof, 71-72, chmn dept, 71-74, surgeon in chief, New York Hosp-Cornell Med Ctr, 71-74, JOHNSON & JOHNSON DISTINGUISHED PROF SURG, MED COL, CORNELL UNIV, 72- *Concurrent Pos:* Nat Cancer Inst fel, 62-63; Mead Johnson scholar, 64; Markle scholar, 67. *Mem:* Asn Acad Surg; Am Heart Asn; Am Col Surg; Soc Univ Surg; Soc Vascular Surg. *Mailing Add:* Dept of Surg Univ of Calif 593M San Francisco CA 94143

EBERT, PAUL JOSEPH, b New Orleans, La, Jan 11, 36; m 57; c 5. PHYSICS. *Educ:* La State Univ, BS, 57, MS, 59, PhD(physics), 62. *Prof Exp:* Nuclear res officer, Sch Aerospace Med, US Air Force, 61-64; sr physicist, L-Div, 64-69, dep group leader, L-Div, Res & Develop Group, 69-72, group leader, 72-77, ASSOC DIV LEADER, L-DIV, LAWRENCE LIVERMORE LAB, UNIV CALIF, 77- *Mem:* Am Phys Soc; Sigma Xi. *Res:* Applied physics. *Mailing Add:* Lawrence Livermore Lab PO Box 808 Livermore CA 94550

EBERT, PHILIP E, b Milwaukee, Wis, Sept 4, 29; m 57; c 2. TEXTILE CHEMISTRY, TEXTILE ENGINEERING. *Educ:* Purdue Univ, BSChE, 51; Univ Pa, PhD(org polymer chem), 60. *Prof Exp:* Chem engr res & develop, Hercules Inc, 51-55; res chemist 60-64, tech serv rep dyeing & finishing, 64-66, tech serv supvr, 66-78, SR RES CHEMIST, TEXTILE FIBERS DEPT, E I DU PONT DE NEMOURS & CO, INC, 78- *Mem:* Am Chem Soc; Sigma Xi. *Res:* Textile technology of manmade fibers. *Mailing Add:* 611 Andover Rd Edenridge Wilmington DE 19803

EBERT, RICHARD VINCENT, b St Paul, Minn, Oct 25, 12; m 47. CLINICAL MEDICINE. *Educ:* Univ Chicago, BS, 33, MD, 37. *Prof Exp:* Intern, Boston City Hosp, Mass, 37-39; asst resident med, Peter Bent Brigham Hosp, Boston, 39-41, jr assoc, 41-42; fel, Harvard Med Sch, 40-42; chief med serv, Vet Admin Hosp, 46-52, 53-54; prof med, Sch Med, Univ Minn, 49-52, Clark prof, 52-53; prof, Northwestern Univ, 53-54; prof & chmn dept, Sch Med, Univ Ark, 54-66; prof med & chmn dept, sch med, Univ Minn, Minneapolis, 66-78; PROF MED, UNIV ARK, 78- *Mem:* AMA; Am Col Physicians; Am Soc Clin Invest (pres, 58); Soc Exp Biol & Med; Asn Am Physicians. *Res:* Pulmonary and cardiovascular physiology; cardiac catheterization in humans; blood volume and peripheral circulation in humans; pulmonary pathology. *Mailing Add:* Vet Admin Hosp Little Rock AR 72206

EBERT, ROBERT H, b Minneapolis, Minn, Sept 10, 14; m 39; c 3. INTERNAL MEDICINE, MEDICAL ADMINISTRATION. *Educ:* Univ Chicago, BS, 36, MD, 42; Oxford Univ, DPhil, 39; Am Bd Internal Med, dipl, 52. *Hon Degrees:* AM, Harvard Univ, DSc, Northeastern Univ, 68, Univ Md, 70, LLD, Univ Toronto, 70; LHD, Rush Univ, 74. *Prof Exp:* Dir med, Univ Hosps, Cleveland, 56-64; mem spec adv group, Vet Admin, Washington, DC, 59-63; chief med serv, Mass Gen Hosp, 64-65; dean, Harvard Med Sch & Fac Med & pres, Harvard Med Ctr, 65-77; pres, Harvard Community Health Plan, 68-74, chmn, 74-; trustee, Pop Coun, Rockefeller Found & Dermat Found; dir, Milbank Mem Fund; mem inst med, Nat Acad Sci. *Honors & Awards:* Distinguished Serv Award, Univ Chicago, 62. *Mem:* Am Soc Clin Invest; Asn

Am Physicians (vpres-pres, 71-73); Am Clin & Climat Asn; Am Col Physicians; Am Acad Arts & Sci. *Res:* Tuberculosis and mechanisms of inflammation. *Mailing Add:* Milbank Mem Fund 1 E 75th St New York NY 10021

EBERT, THOMAS A, b Appleton, Wis, July 10, 38; m 60; c 2. ECOLOGY. *Educ:* Univ Wis-Madison, BS, 61; Univ Ore, MS, 63, PhD(biol), 66. *Prof Exp:* Instr biol, Univ Ore, 66-67; asst prof zool, Univ Hawaii, 67-69; asst prof, 69-72, assoc prof, 72-75, PROF BIOL, SAN DIEGO STATE UNIV, 75- *Mem:* AAAS; Ecol Soc Am; Am Soc Limnol & Oceanog; Am Soc Naturalists. *Res:* Population biology; marine ecology; population ecology of echinoderms. *Mailing Add:* Dept of Biol San Diego State Univ San Diego CA 92182

EBERT, WESLEY W, b Maple Grove Twp, Minn, Mar 22, 26; m 54; c 5. GENETICS, BOTANY. *Educ:* Univ Minn, BS, 61; Univ Calif, Davis, MS, 63, PhD(genetics), 64. *Prof Exp:* From asst prof to assoc prof, 64-71, chmn dept, 69-74, PROF BIOL, SONOMA STATE UNIV, 71- *Mem:* Bot Soc Am; Am Genetic Asn; Am Soc Agron. *Res:* Genetics and anatomical development of Carthamus tinctorius. *Mailing Add:* Dept of Biol Sonoma State Univ 1801 E Cotati Ave Rohnert Park CA 94928

EBERT, WILLIAM R, b Philadelphia, Pa, Aug 2, 22; m 54; c 3. QUALITY CONTROL, DRUG DELIVERY SYSTEMS. *Educ:* Univ Mich, BS, 52, MS, 54, PhD(pharm chem), 56. *Prof Exp:* Res assoc, Sterling-Winthrop Res Inst, 56-58; dir res & develop, Lemmon Pharmacal Co, 59-60; dir res & develop, Philips Roxane Lab, 60-68, vpres, 68-73; VPRES RES & DEVELOP, R P SCHERER CORP, 73- *Concurrent Pos:* Chmn, Eino Nelson Mem Conf, 77-; comt mem, US Pharmacopeia Rev Comt, 80- *Mem:* Sigma Xi; Am Pharmaceut Asn; Am Chem Soc; NY Acad Sci. *Res:* Pharmaceutical technology, mainly in the area of drug delivery systems, improving drug absorption, bioavailability studies and drug stability improvement. *Mailing Add:* R P Scherer Corp 2725 Scherer Dr-Roosevelt Blvd St Petersburg FL 33702

EBERT, WILLIAM ROBLEY, b Philadelphia, Pa, Aug 2, 22; m 54; c 3. PHARMACEUTICAL CHEMISTRY. *Educ:* Univ Mich, BS, 52, MS, 54, PhD(pharmaceut chem), 56. *Prof Exp:* Res fel pharmaceut, Sterling-Winthrop Res Inst, 56-58; chief chemist, Vick Chem Co, 58-59; dir pharmaceut res & develop, Lemmon Pharmacal Co, 59-60; sci dir pharmaceut res, Philips Roxane Labs, 60-61, dir, 61-62, from asst dir to dir res & develop, 62-68, vpres pharmaceut res, 68-73; VPRES RES & DEVELOP, R P SCHERER CORP, 73- *Mem:* Am Pharmaceut Asn; Am Soc Hosp Pharmacists; fel Am Inst Chemists; Am Chem Soc; Drug Info Asn. *Res:* Technology of soft gelatin capsule dosage forms. *Mailing Add:* 4935 62nd Ave S St Petersburg FL 33715

EBERTS, ROBERT EUGENE, b Columbus, Ohio, May 30, 31; m 53; c 5. INORGANIC CHEMISTRY, PHYSICAL CHEMISTRY. *Educ:* Univ Dayton, BS, 53; Iowa State Univ, PhD(phys chem), 57. *Prof Exp:* Res asst phys chem, Ames Lab, USAEC, 53-57; res chemist inorg chem, Wyandotte Chem Corp, 57-62; res chemist prod develop, Nat Res Corp, 62-63, sr chemist, 63-65, sr chemist, Metals Div, Norton Co, 65-69; staff mem metall eng, Arthur D Little Inc, 69-70; SR CHEMIST, MEARL CORP, PEEKSKILL, 71- *Mem:* Am Chem Soc. *Res:* Process development; pigments; product development; extractive metallurgy. *Mailing Add:* 6 Locust Hill Rd Mahopac NY 10541

EBETINO, FRANK FREDERICK, b Rye, NY, Jan 12, 27; m 50; c 2. ORGANIC CHEMISTRY. *Educ:* Ohio Univ, BS, 49; Lehigh Univ, MS, 53; Tohoku Univ, Japan, PhD(org chem), 74. *Prof Exp:* Res chemist, Eaton Labs Div, Norwich Pharmacal Co, 49-51 & Johns-Manville Corp, 53-55; sr res chemist, Chem Res Div, 55-60, unit leader, 60-61, chief chem sect, 61-68, asst dir chem div, 68-69, DIR CHEM RES DIV, NORWICH-EATON PHARMACEUT, DIV MORTON-NORWICH PROD INC, 69- *Mem:* Pharm Soc Japan; NY Acad Sci; Am Chem Soc; Sigma Xi. *Res:* Organic synthesis in field of heterocyclic chemistry; chemical structure-biological activity relationships. *Mailing Add:* Chem Res Div Norwich-Eaton Pharmaceut PO Box 191 Norwich NY 13815

EBIN, DAVID G, b Los Angeles, Calif, Oct 24, 42; m 71. MATHEMATICS. *Educ:* Harvard Univ, AB, 64; Mass Inst Technol, PhD(math), 67. *Prof Exp:* NSF fel, 67-68; lectr math, Univ Calif, Berkeley, 68-69; assoc prof, 69-78, PROF MATH, STATE UNIV NY STONY BROOK, 78- *Mem:* Am Math Soc. *Res:* Differential geometry; infinite dimensional manifolds; nonlinear partial differential equations; mathematical theory of fluid mechanics; mathematical theory of motion of slightly compressible fluids. *Mailing Add:* Dept of Math State Univ of NY Stony Brook NY 11794

EBINGER, JOHN EDWIN, botany, taxonomy, see previous edition

EBLE, JOHN NELSON, b St Louis, Mo, May 19, 27; m 50; c 3. BIOCHEMISTRY. *Educ:* Univ Mo, BS, 49; Univ Wis, MS, 52, PhD(biochem), 54. *Prof Exp:* From instr to asst prof pharmacol & physiol, Kirksville Col, 54-60; pharmacologist, 60-64, assoc scientist, 64-66, ASSOC SCIENTIST, HUMAN HEALTH RES LAB, DOW CHEM CO, 66- *Mem:* AAAS; Am Physiol Soc; Soc Exp Biol & Med; Am Soc Pharmacol & Exp Therapeut; Brit Pharmacol Soc. *Res:* Warfarin; blood coagulation; interchange between somatic and autonomic nervous systems; autonomic and central nerous system pharmacology. *Mailing Add:* Human Health Res Lab Dow Chem Co PO Box 68511 Indianapolis IN 46268

EBLE, THOMAS EUGENE, b Toledo, Ohio, Sept 15, 23; m 45; c 6. BIOCHEMISTRY. *Educ:* Loyola Univ, Ill, BSc, 44; Georgetown Univ, MS, 46, PhD(biochem), 48. *Prof Exp:* Chemist, Bur Standards, 45, Food & Drug Admin, 45-48 & Haris Res Labs, 48; res chemist, 48-59, SECT HEAD, UPJOHN CO, 59- *Mem:* AAAS; Am Chem Soc; Am Oil Chemists Soc. *Res:* Antibiotics; chromatographic separation methods; isolation, characterization and identification of antibiotics; biosynthesis of antibiotics; structure of antibiotics; chemical and biochemical modification of antibiotics. *Mailing Add:* Upjohn Co Kalamazoo MI 49001

EBNER, CHARLES ARTHUR, low temperature physics, see previous edition

EBNER, FORD FRANCIS, b Colfax, Wash, Feb 10, 34; m 60; c 2. NEUROSCIENCES. *Educ:* Wash State Univ, BS, 54, DVM, 58; Univ Md, PhD(neuroanat), 65. *Hon Degrees:* MS, Brown Univ, 69. *Prof Exp:* Asst prof anat & physiol, Univ Md, 65-66; from asst prof to assoc prof biol & med, 66-73, PROF BIOL & MED, BROWN UNIV, 73- *Concurrent Pos:* NIH fel physiol, Johns Hopkins Univ, 60-63; spec fel anat, Univ Md, 63-65. *Mem:* AAAS; Am Asn Anat; Am Asn Neuropath; Neurosci Soc. *Res:* Anatomy and physiology of thalamus and cortex. *Mailing Add:* Neurosci Sect Div of Biol & Med Brown Univ Providence RI 02912

EBNER, HERMAN GEORGE, b Chicago, Ill, Apr 1, 31. POLYMER CHEMISTRY, ORGANIC CHEMISTRY. *Educ:* Loyola Univ, Ill, BS, 53, MS, 55; Carnegie-Mellon Univ, PhD(org chem), 59. *Prof Exp:* Asst proj chemist, Standard Oil Co, Ind, 59-61, proj chemist, Am Oil Co, 61-63; sr proj chemist, 63-69, RES SUPVR, AMOCO CHEM CORP, 69- *Mem:* Soc Petrol Engrs; Am Chem Soc. *Res:* Condensation polymers; polymer characterization; polymer products; petroleum additives. *Mailing Add:* Amoco Chem Corp PO Box 400 Naperville IL 60566

EBNER, JERRY RUDOLPH, b LaCrosse, Wis, Nov 11, 47; m 69; c 1. INORGANIC CHEMISTRY, HETEROGENEOUS CATALYSIS. *Educ:* Univ Wis-LaCrosse, BS, 69; Purdue Univ, PhD(inorg chem), 75. *Prof Exp:* Res asst chem, AEC, Ames, Iowa, 69; instr chem, Purdue Univ, 69-75; res prof chem, 75-78, res specialist, 78-81, SR RES SPECIALIST, MONSANTO CO, 81- *Mem:* Am Chem Soc. *Res:* Chemistry of metal-metal bonded complexes, their properties and reactions, and application of electron spectroscopic chemical analysis and Raman spectroscopic techniques for the study of heterogeneous catalysts; synthesis of heterogeneous catalysts. *Mailing Add:* 233 Bentwood Lane St Charles MO 63301

EBNER, KURT E, b New Westminster, BC, Mar 30, 31; m 57; c 3. BIOCHEMISTRY. *Educ:* Univ BC, BSA, 55, MSA, 57; Univ Ill, PhD(dairy biochem), 60. *Prof Exp:* Can Overseas Nat Res Coun fel, Nat Inst Res Dairying, Reading, Eng, 60-61; instr physiol chem & fel, Univ Minn, 61-62; from asst prof to prof biochem, Okla State Univ, 62-74; CHMN DEPT BIOCHEM, UNIV KANS MED CTR, 74- *Concurrent Pos:* NIH career develop award, 69; Sigma Xi lectr, 70. *Honors & Awards:* Borden Award, Am Chem Soc, 69. *Mem:* Am Chem Soc; Am Soc Biol Chemists; AAAS; Soc Complex Carbohydrates. *Res:* Mechanism of hormone action at the enzyme level; enzyme mechanisms. *Mailing Add:* Dept Biochem Univ Kans Med Ctr Kansas City KS 66103

EBNER, STANLEY GADD, b Lincoln, Nebr, Oct 29, 33; m 56; c 2. ENGINEERING MECHANICS, AEROSPACE ENGINEERING. *Educ:* Univ Nebr, Lincoln, BS, 55; Univ Colo, Boulder, BS, 63, MS, 64, PhD(eng mech), 68. *Prof Exp:* From instr to assoc prof eng mech, US Air Force Acad, 64-70, dep head dept, 70-71, div chief, Space & Missile Systs Orgn, 71-76; DEAN TECHNOL, DOWNTOWN COL, UNIV HOUSTON, 76- *Concurrent Pos:* Chmn, Gulf Coast Alliance Minorities in Eng, 77-81. *Mem:* Am Soc Eng Educ; Am Soc Civil Engrs. *Res:* Dynamics and vibrations. *Mailing Add:* Univ Houston Downtown Col 1 Main St Houston TX 77002

EBY, CHARLES J, b Detroit, Mich, May 29, 29; m 51; c 4. ORGANIC CHEMISTRY. *Educ:* Univ Mich, BS, 51; Dartmouth Col, MA, 53; Duke Univ, PhD(org chem), 56. *Prof Exp:* Res chemist, Monsanto Chem Co, 56-63, mem staff govt rels, Monsanto Res Corp, 63-66, MGR RES & DEVELOP MKT, MONSANTO RES CORP, 66- *Mem:* Am Chem Soc; AAAS. *Res:* Materials and systems; condensations; eliminations; substitutions; rearrangements; cyclizations. *Mailing Add:* 1101 17th St NW Washington DC 20006

EBY, DAVID EUGENE, b Harrisburg, Pa, Sept 26, 47; m 68; c 2. SEDIMENTOLOGY, SEDIMENTARY PETROLOGY. *Educ:* Franklin & Marshall Col, AB, 69; Brown Univ, MS, 72; State Univ NY Stony Brook, PhD(sedimentology), 77. *Prof Exp:* Adj asst prof geol, Southampton Col, Long Island Univ, 73 & Franklin & Marshall Col, 73-74; instr geosci, Univ Tex, Dallas, 75-77, asst prof, 77-79; RES GEOLOGIST, MOBIL OIL FIELD RES LAB, 79- *Concurrent Pos:* Explor geologist, Standard Oil Tex, Chevron Oil Co, 69. *Mem:* Geol Soc Am; Soc Econ Paleontologists & Mineralogists; Am Asn Petrol Geologist; Nat Asn Geol Teachers. *Res:* Carbonate sedimentology and diagenesis; sedimentary petrology; depositional systems; Precambrian sedimentation of North America; evaporite diagenesis. *Mailing Add:* 522 Johnson Dr Duncanville TX 75116

EBY, DENISE, b Baltimore, Md, Dec 8, 17. CHEMISTRY. *Educ:* St Joseph Col, Md, BS, 39; Cath Univ Am, MS, 53; Univ Md, PhD, 70. *Prof Exp:* Teacher high schs, Md, 39-41, 46-50, NY, 42-45 & WVa, 45-46; from asst prof to prof chem, St Joseph Col, Md, 50-73; RES ASSOC, SCH MED, UNIV MD BALTIMORE, 74-; ADJ ASSOC PROF CHEM, LOYOLA COL, 75- *Concurrent Pos:* Consult sci educ, Sisters of Charity pvt schs, 73- *Mem:* Am Soc Biol Chemists; Nat Sci Teachers Asn; Am Chem Soc. *Res:* Chemical education; enzyme kinetics and studies of glyceraldehyde-3-phosphate dehydrogenase, including the interaction of nicotinamide adenine dinucleotide. *Mailing Add:* 2800 N Charles St Baltimore MD 21218

EBY, EDWARD STUART, SR, b Chicago, Ill, Oct 3, 34; m 65. MATHEMATICS. *Educ:* Univ Ill, BS, 56, MS, 57, PhD(math), 64. *Prof Exp:* Mathematician, US Navy Underwater Sound Lab, 57-64, res mathematician & res assoc, 64-70; RES MATHEMATICIAN, DIR INDEPENDENT RES & INDEPENDENT EXPLOR DEVELOP PROG & DIR INDUST INDEPENDENT RES & DEVELOP REVIEWS, US NAVAL UNDERWATER SYSTS CTR, 70- *Concurrent Pos:* Lectr, Dept Elec Eng, Univ Conn, 65-68. *Mem:* AAAS; Am Math Soc; Math Asn Am; Acoust Soc Am. *Res:* Underwater acoustics; signal processing. *Mailing Add:* 20 Colonial Dr Waterford CT 06385

EBY, FRANK SHILLING, b Kansas City, Mo, Apr 6, 24; m 58; c 3. NUCLEAR PHYSICS. *Educ:* Univ Ill, BS, 49, MS, 50, PhD(physics), 54. *Prof Exp:* Res assoc physics, Univ Ill, 54; mem proj, Sherwood Res, 54-58 & Atomic Weapons Design, 58-67, div leader device design, 67-72, SR SCIENTIST, LAWRENCE LIVERMORE LAB, UNIV CALIF, 72- *Mem:* AAAS; Am Phys Soc. *Res:* Nuclear reactions; scintillation crystals; plasma physics; high explosives; weapons design. *Mailing Add:* Lawrence Livermore Lab Bldg 111 Livermore CA 94550

EBY, HAROLD HILDENBRANDT, b Platteville, Colo, Mar 3, 18; m 42; c 3. ORGANIC CHEMISTRY. *Educ:* Colo State Col, BS, 40; Univ Nebr, MA, 47, PhD(org chem), 49. *Prof Exp:* Asst, Univ Nebr, 40-42 & 46-48; res chemist, Continental Oil Co, 48-52, sr res chemist & actg group leader, 52-54, res group leader, 54-58, supvry res chemist, 58-69, supvr, 69-72, dir tech info serv, 72-79, DIR CORP SERV SECT, RES & DEVELOP DEPT, CONOCO, INC, 79- *Mem:* AAAS; Am Soc Info Sci; Am Chem Soc. *Res:* Lubricants; fuels; waxes; specialty petroleum products; technical information; radiochemistry; environmental science. *Mailing Add:* Corp Serv Sect Res Develop Dept Conoco Inc Ponca City OK 74601

EBY, JOHN EDSON, b Wabash, Ind, Mar 18, 33; m 53; c 5. SOLID STATE PHYSICS, OPTICS. *Educ:* Col Wooster, BA, 54; Univ Rochester, PhD(physics), 59. *Prof Exp:* Engr physics, Sylvania Elec Prod, Inc, 59-69, ENGR PHYSICS, GTE SYLVANIA, INC, GEN TEL & ELECTRONICS CORP, 69- *Mem:* Optical Soc Am; Am Phys Soc; Electrochem Soc. *Res:* Optical properties of solids; radiometry; high temperature interactions of gases with refractory metals. *Mailing Add:* GTE Sylvania Inc 100 Endicott St Danvers MA 01923

EBY, JOHN MARTIN, b Reading, Pa, Dec 8, 39; m 62; c 3. ORGANIC CHEMISTRY. *Educ:* Goshen Col, BA, 60; Univ Del, PhD(org chem), 65. *Prof Exp:* Res chemist, Res & Develop Ctr, Armstrong Cork Co, 65-75; PROJ CHEMIST, MANNINGTON MILLS, INC, 75- *Mem:* Royal Soc Chem. *Res:* Organic synthesis; vinyl degradation reactions; vinyl plastics applications. *Mailing Add:* 32 Canterbury Dr Pennsville NJ 08070

EBY, LAWRENCE THORNTON, b South Bend, Ind, May 3, 16; m 41; c 2. ORGANIC CHEMISTRY. *Educ:* Univ Notre Dame, BS, 38, MS, 39, PhD(org chem), 41. *Prof Exp:* Res chemist, Standard Oil Develop Co, 41-55; res chemist, Esso Res & Eng Co, 55-57; sr mkt develop eng, Enjay Co, Inc, 57-58, asst mgr, Mkt Develop Div, 58-64; pres, Protective Treatments, Inc, Aeroplast Corp & Dellrose Industs, Helene Curtis Industs, Inc, 64-65; res dir, Chem Div, Chrysler Corp, Mich, 65-67; mgr, Polymer Div, 67-73, ASSOC DIR RES, US GYPSUM CO, 73- *Honors & Awards:* Honor Scroll, Am Inst Chemists, 61. *Mem:* AAAS; Chem Mkt Res Asn; Am Chem Soc; Soc Plastics Eng; fel Am Inst Chemists. *Res:* Adhesives; sealants; lubricating oil additives; antioxidants for synthetic rubber; vulcanization of butyl rubber; toxicity of petroleum products; synthesis of petrochemicals; polymerization; diesel fuel additives; chemicals for paper and textiles; market development of petrochemicals; paints, coatings and building materia ls. *Mailing Add:* US Gypsum Co Res Dept 1000 E Northwest Hwy Des Plaines IL 60016

EBY, PETER BYERLY, b Lancaster, Pa, Dec 14, 42. PHYSICS. *Educ:* Brown Univ, ScB, 64; Univ NC, PhD(physics), 68. *Prof Exp:* STAFF SCIENTIST PHYSICS, SPACE SCI LAB, MARSHALL SPACE FLIGHT CTR, 68- *Mem:* Sigma Xi. *Res:* Experimental relativity; Mach's principle; heavy charged particle interactions. *Mailing Add:* Marshall Space Flight Ctr ES63 Huntsville AL 35812

EBY, ROBERT NEWCOMER, b Pittsburgh, Pa, July 17, 31; m 55; c 2. CHEMICAL ENGINEERING. *Educ:* Princeton Univ, BSE, 52; Univ Ill, PhD(chem eng), 58. *Prof Exp:* Res engr, Plastics Div, Union Carbide Corp, 55-56, group leader, 56-62, prod supvr, Mfg Dept, 62-64, area supvr eng & qual control, 64-66, prod supt, 66-67, prod supt & mgr, Vinyl Fabrics Dept, 67-69; prod mgr film mfg, 69-71, sr prod mgr, 71-78, PLANT MGR, POLAROID CORP, NORWOOD, 78- *Mem:* Am Chem Soc; Am Inst Chem Engrs. *Res:* Non-Newtonian flow; heat and mass transfer from high viscosity fluids; optimization of capital expenditures for process modification and expansion; diffusion transfer photographic films. *Mailing Add:* 20 Baskin Rd Lexington MA 02173

EBY, RONALD KRAFT, b Reading, Pa, May 7, 29; m 52; c 2. PHYSICS. *Educ:* Lafayette Col, BSc, 52; Brown Univ, MS, 55, PhD(physics), 58. *Prof Exp:* Asst, Brown Univ, 52-57; physicist, Polychems Dept, Exp Sta, E I du Pont de Nemours & Co, 57-63; physicist, Polymers Div, 63-67, chief polymer crystal physics sect, 67-68, chief polymers div, 68-78, CHIEF POLYMER SCI & STANDARDS DIV, NAT BUR STANDARDS, 78- *Concurrent Pos:* Lectr, Johns Hopkins Univ, 80- *Mem:* Acoustical Soc Am; Am Phys Soc; Electron Micros Soc Am; Soc Plastics Engrs; Am Soc Testing & Mat. *Res:* Polymer physics; physical acoustics; ultrasonic propagation. *Mailing Add:* Polymer Div Nat Bur of Standards Washington DC 20234

ECANOW, BERNARD, b Chicago, Ill, Nov 22, 23; m 65; c 2. PHARMACEUTICAL SCIENCES. *Educ:* Univ Minn, BChE, 47, BS, 51, PhD(pharmaceut chem), 55. *Prof Exp:* From asst prof to assoc prof mfg pharm, Butler Univ, 56-58; from asst prof to assoc prof, 58-69, PROF PHARMACEUT SCI, UNIV ILL, 70- *Concurrent Pos:* Consult, McGraw Hill-Air Force Proj, 59-60, Presby-St Lukes Hosp, 67- & Rush Med Col 70-; consult sr scientist anesthesiol, Hines Vet Admin Hosp, 73-77; consult, Ecanow & Assoc Consults Health Sci. *Mem:* Am Pharmaceut Asn. *Res:* The coacervate model of biology and theories of cancer, anesthesia, lung gas transfer, psychological states and the emergent mind; surfactants of biological interests; physical-chemical and biological aspects of pharmaceutical formulation; toxic effects of environmental pollutants. *Mailing Add:* Univ of Ill Col of Pharm 833 S Wood St Chicago IL 60612

ECCLES, SAMUEL FRANKLIN, b Reno, Nev, Sept 19, 30; m 53; c 2. NUCLEAR PHYSICS. *Educ:* Univ Nev, BS, 52; La State Univ, MS, 54; Univ Wash, Seattle, PhD(physics), 58. *Prof Exp:* Res physicist, Inst Nuclear Physics, Amsterdam, Holland, 58-59; asst prof gen physics, Univ Nev, 59-62; RES PHYSICIST, LAWRENCE LIVERMORE LAB, UNIV CALIF, 62- *Mem:* Am Inst Physics; Am Phys Soc. *Res:* Medium energy nuclear physics including scattering and reaction experiments; nuclear structure physics; reactor and neutron physics; reactor fuel cycles; transuranium heavy element production in nuclear devices; fission processes; astrophysics. *Mailing Add:* Lawrence Livermore Lab Univ Calif PO Box 808 Livermore CA 94550

ECCLES, WILLIAM J, b Owatonna, Minn, Apr 18, 32; m 67. ELECTRICAL ENGINEERING, COMPUTER SCIENCE. *Educ:* Mass Inst Technol, SB, 54, SM, 57; Purdue Univ, PhD(elec eng), 65. *Prof Exp:* Instr elec eng, Purdue Univ, 59-65; asst prof elec eng & dir comput ctr, 65-72, assoc prof comput sci, 72-79, ASSOC PROF ENG, UNIV SC, 79- *Mem:* Asn Comput Mach; Inst Elec & Electronics Eng; Am Soc Eng Educ. *Mailing Add:* Col Eng Univ of South Carolina Columbia SC 29208

ECCLESHALL, DONALD, b Warrington, UK, July 8, 27; m 57; c 2. RESEARCH ADMINISTRATION, APPLIED PHYSICS. *Educ:* Univ Liverpool, BSc, 52, PhD(physics), 56. *Prof Exp:* Prin sci officer, UK Atomic Energy Authority, Atomic Weapons Res Estab, 56-68; res physicist radiation physics, US Army Ballistics Res Lab, 68-72, PHYS SCI ADMINR, APPL PHYSICS BR, US ARMY BALLISTICS RES LABS, 72- *Concurrent Pos:* Res fel nuclear physics, Univ Pa, 66-67. *Mem:* Am Phys Soc; Sigma Xi. *Res:* Mathematical modeling of physical processes; radiation and accelerator physics; EM propulsion. *Mailing Add:* Ballistics Res Lab US Army ARRADCOM Aberdeen Proving Ground MD 21005

ECHANDI, EDDIE, b San Jose, Costa Rica, Nov 21, 27; m 52; c 2. PLANT PATHOLOGY. *Educ:* Univ Costa Rica, IngAgr, 51; Univ Wis, PhD(plant path), 55. *Prof Exp:* Prof plant path, Univ Costa Rica, 55-61; head plant, Indust & Soils Dept, Inter-Am Inst Agr Sci, 62-64, basic food crops prog, 64-67; PROF PLANT PATH, NC STATE UNIV, 67- *Concurrent Pos:* Vis scientist, Univ Calif, Berkeley, 65; co-leader, Nat Bean Prog, NC State Univ Agr Mission to Peru, Lima, 67-; vis prof, Agrarian Univ, Peru, 68- *Honors & Awards:* Award of Merit, Am Phytopathological Soc, 73. *Mem:* Am Phytopath Soc; Latin Am Asn Phytopath. *Res:* Diseases of tropical plants; host-parasite relations; ecology of plant disease and plant pathogens; cultivation and production of beans and pulses; bacterial diseases of vegetable crops; bacteriocins and bacteriophages as they relate to bacterial plant pathogens. *Mailing Add:* Dept of Plant Path NC State Univ Raleigh NC 27607

ECHELBERGER, HERBERT EUGENE, b Buffalo, NY, Jan 6, 38; m 64; c 2. FOREST RECREATION. *Educ:* Southern Ill Univ, BS, 65, MS, 66; State Univ NY Col Environ Sci & Forestry, PhD(resource mgt), 76. *Prof Exp:* RES SOCIAL SCIENTIST, FOREST RECREATION RES, FOREST SERV, USDA, 66- *Concurrent Pos:* Adj instr, State Univ NY Col Environ Sci & Forestry, 66-69, adj asst prof, 69-77, adj assoc prof, 77-78; adj assoc prof, Univ NH, 81- *Mem:* Sigma Xi; Soc Am Foresters; Am Forestry Asn. *Res:* Identify the changing characteristics of major forest recreation trends, including participant numbers, participation styles, geographic and size distribution trends, and costs of providing forest recreation opportunities. *Mailing Add:* Forest Serv USDA PO Box 640 Durham NH 03824

ECHELBERGER, WAYNE F, JR, b Pierre, SDak, Oct 23, 34; m 60; c 2. ENVIRONMENTAL HEALTH ENGINEERING. *Educ:* SDak Sch Mines & Technol, BS, 56; Univ Mich, MS, 59, MPH, 60, PhD(civil eng), 64. *Prof Exp:* Civil engr, City of Milwaukee, Wis, 56; pub health engr, State of SDak, 56-60; res asst civil eng, Univ Mich, 60 & 61, teaching fel, 60-61, instr, 64-65; asst prof, Univ Notre Dame, 65-67, assoc prof environ health eng, 67-73; PROF, SCH PUB & ENVIRON AFFAIRS, IND UNIV, 73- *Concurrent Pos:* NSF res grant, 66-67 & res equip grant, 67-68; Fed Water Pollution Control Admin demonstration grant, 66-69; consult & secy-treas, TenEch, Inc, 69-77; Environ Protection Agency Water Qual Off res & demonstration grant, 71-72; prin investr, HUD-Nat League of Cities, Urban Observ, 75-77, Ind Higher Educ Comn, Ind State Bd Health, Ind Dept Natural Resources, 78-79, US Environ Protection Agency Munic Environ Res Lab, 80-83 & US Environ Protection Agency Clean Lakes Prog, 81-82. *Honors & Awards:* Harrison Prescott Eddy Medal, Water Pollution Control Fedn, 73; Engr of the Year Award, Soc Prof Engrs, 76. *Mem:* Am Soc Civil Engrs; Water Pollution Control Fedn; Asn Environ Eng Prof (secy-treas, 71-73); Nat Soc Prof Engrs; Am Pub Works Asn. *Res:* Solid waste management; environmental quality planning and management; biological and chemical treatment of water and wastewater; industrial waste treatment; studies and control of freshwater eutrophication. *Mailing Add:* Sch of Pub & Environ Affairs Ind Univ Indianapolis IN 46223

ECHELLE, ANTHONY ALLAN, ichthyology, see previous edition

ECHOLS, CHARLES E(RNEST), b Alderson, WVa, Dec 5, 24; m 60, 77; c 4. CIVIL ENGINEERING, FINANCE. *Educ:* Univ Va, BCE, 49, MCE, 55, LLB, 54. *Prof Exp:* Instr civil eng, Mich State Univ, 55-57; ASST PROF CIVIL & APPL MECH, UNIV VA, 57- *Concurrent Pos:* Vpres construction & eng, A B Torrence & Co, Inc, 50-; vpres, Willson Finance Serv Inc, Staunton; dir, Monticello Bank, Charlottesville; mem, Hwy Res Bd, Nat Acad Sci-Nat Res Coun. *Mem:* Am Soc Civil Engrs. *Res:* Economics and construction. *Mailing Add:* 1650 W Pines Dr Charlottesville VA 22906

ECHOLS, DOROTHY JUNG, b New York, NY, Sept 9, 16; m 41; c 4. GEOLOGY. *Educ:* NY Univ, BA, 36; Columbia Univ, MA, 38. *Prof Exp:* Subsurface geologist & micropaleontologist, Am Republics Corp, 38-41; gen geologist, Foreign Div, Tex Co, 41-42; consult, Pond Fork Oil & Gas Co, 46-51; assoc prof, 51-82, EMER PROF GEOL, WASH UNIV, 82- *Concurrent Pos:* Partner, Curtis & Echols Consult Geologists. *Mem:* AAAS; Paleont Soc; fel Geol Soc Am; Am Asn Petrol Geol; Soc Econ Paleont &

Mineral. *Res:* Micropaleontology; biological and morphological studies of microorganisms; some emphasis on Forminifera and Ostracoda; biostratigraphy; subsurface geology; paleoclimatelogy. *Mailing Add:* Dept Earth & Planetary Sci Wash Univ Box 1169 St Louis MO 63130

ECHOLS, JOAN, b Dayton, Ohio, Jan 31, 32. VERTEBRATE PALEONTOLOGY. *Educ:* Ohio State Univ, BSc, 55; Univ Tex, Austin, MA, 59; Univ Okla, PhD(geol), 72. *Prof Exp:* Instr earth sci, 64-66 & 68-73, ASST PROF EARTH SCI, E TEX STATE UNIV, 73- *Mem:* Soc Vert Paleontology; Soc Econ Paleontologists & Mineralogists; Am Asn Petrol Geologists; Nat Asn Geol Teachers. *Res:* Cretaceous reptiles, invertebrates and fishes of Taylor Group, northeast Texas. *Mailing Add:* Dept of Earth Sci ETex State Univ Commerce TX 75428

ECHOLS, JOSEPH TODD, JR, b Raleigh, NC, July 5, 36; m 63. PHYSICAL CHEMISTRY. *Educ:* Belhaven Col, BA, 59; Univ Miss, PhD(phys chem), 63. *Prof Exp:* Assoc prof chem, ECarolina Col, 63-64; vis asst prof & fel, La State Univ, 64-65; prof, Belhaven Col, Miss, 65-67; assoc prof, 67-80, PROF CHEM, PFEIFFER COL, 80-, HEAD DEPT, 70- *Mem:* Am Chem Soc. *Res:* Kinetics; free radical reactions. *Mailing Add:* Dept of Chem Pfeiffer Col Misenheimer NC 28109

ECHTERNACHT, ARTHUR CHARLES, b Indianapolis, Ind, Sept 3, 39; m 62; c 2. VERTEBRATE ZOOLOGY, ECOLOGY. *Educ:* Univ Iowa, BA, 61; Ariz State Univ, MS, 64; Univ Kans, PhD(zool), 70. *Prof Exp:* Asst prof biol, Boston Univ, 68-75; asst prof, 75-78, ASSOC PROF, DEPT ZOOL & GRAD PROG ECOL, UNIV TENN, KNOXVILLE, 78-, ASSOC DEPT HEAD, ZOOL, 78- *Mem:* Am Soc Ichthyologists & Herpetologists; Soc Study Amphibians & Reptiles; Soc Syst Zool; Asn Trop Biol; Ecol Soc Am. *Res:* Systematics and ecology of macroteiid lizards of the genera Ameiva and Cnemidophorus; systematics and ecology of tropical reptiles and amphibians. *Mailing Add:* Dept Zool Univ of Tenn Knoxville TN 37996

ECK, DAVID LOWELL, b Bagely, Minn, Nov 21, 41; c 1. ORGANIC CHEMISTRY. *Educ:* Univ Mont, BA, 63; Wash State Univ, PhD(chem), 67. *Prof Exp:* Anal chemist, Anaconda Co, 63; Petrol Res Fund res fel, Univ Calif, Santa Cruz, 67-69; Sloan Found vis asst prof chem, Reed Col, 69-70; asst prof, 70-74, ASSOC PROF CHEM, CALIF STATE COL, SONOMA, 74- *Concurrent Pos:* Cong fel, Am Chem Soc, 80-81. *Res:* Elucidation of mechanisms in biomolecular elimination reactions involving weak bases; mechanistic considerations involving the formation of small ring oxygen and sulfur heterocycles. *Mailing Add:* Dept of Chem Calif State Col Sonoma Rohnert Park CA 94928

ECK, GERALD GILBERT, b Marinette, Wis, Mar 8, 42. PHYSICAL ANTHROPOLOGY, PRIMATE PALEONTOLOGY. *Educ:* Univ Chicago, BA, 64; Univ Calif, Berkeley, MA, 74, PhD(anthrop), 77. *Prof Exp:* ASST PROF ANTHROP, UNIV WASH, 75- *Mem:* AAAS; Am Asn Phys Anthropologists. *Res:* Primate paleontology and toxonomy, especially that of hominids and cercopithecoids. *Mailing Add:* Dept of Antrhop Univ of Wash Seattle WA 98195

ECK, HAROLD VICTOR, b Newkirk, Okla, Nov 14, 24; m 47; c 5. SOIL FERTILITY. *Educ:* Okla Agr & Mech Col, BS, 48; Ohio State Univ, PhD(agron), 50. *Prof Exp:* Asst prof agron, Okla Agr & Mech Col, 51-57; SOIL SCIENTIST, AGR RES SERV, USDA, 51- *Concurrent Pos:* Assoc ed, Soil Sci Soc Am J, 80- *Mem:* Am Soc Agron; Soil Sci Soc Am; Soil Conserv Soc Am; Am Soc Plant Physiol. *Res:* Soil management; soil fertility; plant physiology. *Mailing Add:* USDA Conserv & Prod Res Lab Bushland TX 79012

ECK, JOHN CLIFFORD, b Livingston, Mont, Dec 2, 09; m 35; c 3. ORGANIC CHEMISTRY, CHEMICAL ENGINEERING. *Educ:* Mont State Col, BS, 31; Univ Ill, MS, 32, PhD(org chem), 35. *Prof Exp:* Res assoc, Iowa State Univ, 35-41; res chemist, Air Reduction Co, 41-45; res engr, Allied Chem Corp, 45-72; CONSTRUCT CONSULT, WILPUTTE CORP, MURRAY HILL, 72- *Mem:* Fel Am Inst Chemists; Am Inst Chem Engrs; Am Chem Soc; NY Acad Sci. *Res:* Basic organic chemicals; coal gasification; oil gasification; water pollution control; incineration. *Mailing Add:* 27 Kitchell Rd Covent NJ 07961

ECK, JOHN STARK, b West Hempstead, NY, Mar 18, 41; m 64; c 3. NUCLEAR PHYSICS, SOLID STATE PHYSICS. *Educ:* Polytech Inst Brooklyn, BS, 62; Johns Hopkins Univ, PhD(physics), 67. *Prof Exp:* Jr instr physics, Johns Hopkins Univ, 62-65, res asst, 65-67; res assoc, Fla State Univ, 67-69; from asst prof to assoc prof, 69-79, PROF PHYSICS, KANS STATE UNIV, 79-, DEPT HEAD, 81- *Mem:* Am Phys Soc. *Res:* Nuclear and solid state properties from coulomb excitation Mossbauer studies; nuclear heavy ion interactions from elastic and inelastic scattering of 0-16 and He-4 from medium weight nuclei; optical model interpretation of nuclear scattering of protons, alphas and heavy ions; nuclear instrumentation; nuclear interactions of the light heavy ions lithium-7 and beryllium-9. *Mailing Add:* Dept of Physics Kans State Univ Manhattan KS 66502

ECK, PAUL, b Elizabeth, NJ, Sept 3, 31; m 55; c 4. HORTICULTURE, SOILS. *Educ:* Rutgers Univ, BS, 53; Univ Mass, MS, 55; Univ Wis, PhD(soils), 57. *Prof Exp:* Asst prof floricult, Univ Mass, 57-60; assoc prof, 60-70, PROF POMOL, RUTGERS UNIV, 70- *Mem:* Am Soc Hort Sci. *Res:* Physiology and nutrition of fruit crops, especially apple, blueberry and cranberry. *Mailing Add:* Dept of Hort Rutgers Univ New Brunswick NJ 08903

ECK, ROBERT EDWIN, b Ames, Iowa, Nov 28, 38; m 74; c 1. PHYSICS. *Educ:* Rutgers Univ, BA, 60; Univ Pa, MS, 62, PhD(physics), 66; Univ Calif, Santa Barbara, MA, 74. *Prof Exp:* Sr scientist, Ford Sci Lab, Ford Motor Co, 66-69; mem tech staff, 69-75, mgr, IR Components Res & Develop Lab, 76-78, ASST MGR IR COMPONENTS, SANTA BARBARA RES CTR, 78- *Mem:* AAAS. *Res:* New technology in infrared detectors, including new detector materials, focal plane design concepts and computer-controlled display readout of infrared detectors. *Mailing Add:* Santa Barbara Res Ctr 75 Coromar Dr Goleta CA 93117

ECK, THOMAS G, b Genoa, NY, Oct 19, 29; m 59. PHYSICS. *Educ:* Univ Buffalo, BA, 51; Columbia Univ, PhD(physics), 58. *Prof Exp:* From asst prof to assoc prof, 62-69, PROF PHYSICS, CASE WESTERN RESERVE UNIV, 69- *Mem:* Am Phys Soc. *Res:* Low temperature physics; solid state physics; atomic spectroscopy. *Mailing Add:* Dept of Physics Case Western Reserve Univ Cleveland OH 44106

ECKARDT, MICHAEL JON, b Glendale, Calif, Apr 3, 43; m 68; c 2. MEDICAL PSYCHOLOGY, ALCOHOLISM. *Educ:* Calif State Univ, Northridge, BA 66; Univ Southern Calif, MS, 67; Univ Mich, MS, 70; Univ Ore Health Sci Ctr, PhD(psychol), 75. *Prof Exp:* Lectr, Dept Zool, Univ Mich, 70; res psychobiologist, Psychobiol Sect, Vet Admin Hosp, 75-76; fel, Dept Psychiat, Col Med, Univ Calif, Irvine, 76; res psychologist, clin & biobehav res, 76-78, RES PSYCHOLOGIST, LAB PRECLIN STUDIES, DIV INTRAMURAL RES, NAT INST ALCOHOL ABUSE & ALCOHOLISM, 78- *Mem:* AAAS; Soc Neurosci; Am Psychol Asn. *Res:* Investigating the acute and chronic effects of alcohol and other addictive substances on various anatomic and physiologic systems; studying the diagnostic utility of automated batteries of clinical laboratory tests. *Mailing Add:* Lab Preclin Studies NIAAA 12501 Washington Ave Rockville MD 20852

ECKARDT, ROBERT E, b Fanwood, NJ, May 1, 16; m 65; c 4. BIOCHEMISTRY, TOXICOLOGY. *Educ:* Antioch Col, BS, 37; Western Reserve Univ, MS, 39, PhD(biochem), 40, MD, 43; Am Bd Internal Med, dipl, 50; Am Bd Prev Med, dipl, 55. *Prof Exp:* Intern, NY Hosp, 43-44, asst resident med, 44, 47-48; spec res physician, Standard Oil Co, NJ, 48-50, asst dir med res sect, 50; dir med res div, Esso Res & Eng Co, 51-74, assoc med dir, Exxon Corp, 74-78; RETIRED. *Concurrent Pos:* Asst attend physician, Outpatient Dept, NY Hosp, 48-70, physician to outpatients, 70-78; instr med, Med Col, Cornell Univ, 43-70, assoc clin prof, 70-78; assoc clin prof, Postgrad Med Sch, NY Univ-Bellevue Med Ctr, 53-78. *Mem:* Fel Am Col Physicians; AMA; Am Indust Hyg Asn; Am Occup Med Asn (vpres, 57-59, pres, 60); NY Acad Med. *Res:* Medicine; industrial hygiene. *Mailing Add:* 7355 E Claremont St Scottsdale AZ 85253

ECKBLAD, JAMES WILBUR, b Minneapolis, Minn, May 13, 41; m 65; c 2. AQUATIC ECOLOGY. *Educ:* Univ Minn, BS, 64; Cornell Univ, PhD(limnol), 71. *Prof Exp:* ASSOC PROF BIOL, LUTHER COL, 71- *Concurrent Pos:* Proj dir, NSF Undergrad Res Participation, 73-; consult, Interstate Power Co, 73-74; mem citizen's adv comt, Upper Miss Basin Planning Comn, 75- *Mem:* Sigma Xi; AAAS; Ecol Soc Am; Am Soc Limnol & Oceanog. *Res:* Ecology and productivity of backwater lakes of the upper Mississippi River. *Mailing Add:* Dept of Biol Luther Col Decorah IA 52101

ECKE, GEORGE GRAFF, b Pittsburgh, Pa, May 11, 21. ORGANIC CHEMISTRY. *Educ:* Carnegie Inst Technol, BS, 42; Pa State Col, MS, 47, PhD(chem), 49. *Prof Exp:* Jr chemist, Shell Develop Co, 43-46; chemist, Ethyl Corp, 49-58; group mgr, Koppers Co, 58-62; fel, Wayne State Univ, 62-63; RES ASSOC PPG INDUSTS, INC, 64- *Mem:* Am Chem Soc. *Res:* Pesticides, particularly synthesis, mechanism and metabolite identification. *Mailing Add:* PPG Indust Inc 95 Columbia Ct Akron OH 44310

ECKEL, EDWIN BUTT, b Washington, DC, Jan 27, 06; m 31; c 3. GEOLOGY. *Educ:* Lafayette Col, BS, 28; Univ Ariz, MS, 30. *Prof Exp:* Geologist, US Geol Surv, 30-42, in charge invests domestic quicksilver deposits, 42-43, asst chief mil geol unit, 44-45, chief eng geol br, 45-61, chief spec proj br, 62-65, res geologist, 65-68; ed, 68-71, exec secy, Geol Soc Am, 70-74; RES GEOLOGIST, US GEOLOGICAL SURV, 74- *Concurrent Pos:* Chmn, Comt Landslide Invest, Hwy Res Bd, 51-62; mem comt Alaska earthquake, Nat Acad Sci, 64-71. *Honors & Awards:* Merit Award, Univ Ariz, 60; Distinguished Serv Award, US Dept Interior, 65. *Mem:* Fel Geol Soc Am; fel Mineral Soc Am; Asn Eng Geol (pres, 65); hon mem Geol Soc London. *Res:* Engineering geology; ore deposits; German underground factories; Italian quicksilver industry; geology of Paraguay; geology of underground nuclear explosions; geology of Alaska earthquake; technical writing. *Mailing Add:* 1109 S High St Denver CO 80210

ECKEL, FREDERICK MONROE, b Philadelphia, Pa, Mar 25, 39; m 63; c 2. PHARMACY. *Educ:* Philadelphia Col Pharm, BSc, 61; Ohio State Univ, MSc, 63. *Prof Exp:* Resident pharm, Ohio State Univ, 61-63, supvr pharmacists, Ohio State Univ Hosp, 63-65, asst dir pharm, 63-66; from instr to assoc prof, 66-77, PROF HOSP PHARM, UNIV NC, CHAPEL HILL, 77-, CHMN DEPT PHARM PRACT, 75- *Concurrent Pos:* Pharm consult, St Ann's Hosp for Women, 64-66; dir, Plan Pharm Assistance, 66-72, Duke Endowment & Reynolds Found Plan of Pharm Assistance grant, 66-70; dir pharm serv, NC Mem Hosp, 68-73. *Mem:* Am Soc Hosp Pharmacists (pres, 74-75); fel AAAS; Am Asn Col Pharm; Am Pharmaceut Asn. Mem: Development, improvement and implementation of professional pharmaceutical services; drug utilization review; pharmacy practice issues; pharmacy service to small hospitals and nursing homes. *Mailing Add:* 713 Churchill Dr Chapel Hill NC 27514

ECKEL, ROBERT EDWARD, b Buffalo, NY, Mar 17, 18; m 47; c 3. MEDICINE. *Educ:* Dartmouth Col, BA, 38; Harvard Univ, MD, 42. *Prof Exp:* Fel med, Sch Med, Case Western Reserve Univ, 48-49, Am Cancer Soc fel biochem, 49-51, Nat Found Infantile Paralysis fel, 51-53; asst prof, 53-63, ASSOC PROF MED, SCH MED, CASE WESTERN RESERVE UNIV, 63- *Res:* Mechanism of ion transport; renal disease. *Mailing Add:* Sch of Med Case Western Reserve Univ Cleveland OH 44106

ECKELBARGER, KEVIN JAY, b Goshen, Ind, May 27, 44; m 68. INVERTEBRATE ZOOLOGY. *Educ:* Calif State Univ, Long Beach, BA, 67, MA, 69; Northeastern Univ, PhD(biol), 74. *Prof Exp:* Teaching asst biol, Calif State Univ, Long Beach, 67-69, Northeastern Univ, 69-73; asst res scientist, 73-79, assoc res scientist, 79-81, SR RES SCIENTIST, HARBOR BR FOUND, INC, 81- *Mem:* Am Soc Zoologists; Sigma Xi. *Res:* Reproductive biology and development Polychaetous annelids; gametogenesis, spawning behavior, larval settlement behavior of marine invertebrates. *Mailing Add:* Harbor Br Found Inc RFD 1 Box 196 Ft Pierce FL 33450

ECKELMAN, CARL A, b Columbus, Ind, Feb 14, 33; m 61; c 3. WOOD SCIENCE, STRUCTURAL ENGINEERING. *Educ:* Purdue Univ, BS, 59, MS, 62, PhD(wood sci), 68. *Prof Exp:* Asst, 59-63, from instr to assoc prof, 63-79, PROF WOOD SCI, PURDUE UNIV, 79- *Res:* Furniture engineering; wood moisture relations; basic fiber science. *Mailing Add:* Dept of Forestry Purdue Univ West Lafayette IN 47907

ECKELMANN, FRANK DONALD, b Englewood, NJ, May 25, 29; m 53; c 2. GEOLOGY. *Educ:* Wheaton Col, Ill, BS, 51; Columbia Univ, MS, 54, PhD, 56. *Prof Exp:* Res asst geochem, Lamont-Doherty Geol Observ, Columbia Univ, 51-52, teaching asst geol, 52-55, res assoc geochem, 56-57; from asst prof to prof geol sci, Brown Univ, 57-78, chmn dept, 61-68, dean col, 68-71; prof & head dept geol, Univ Ga, 78-81; DEAN, COL ARTS & SCI, GEORGE MASON UNIV, 81- *Mem:* Geol Soc Am; Geochem Soc; Mineral Soc Am; Am Geophys Union. *Res:* Nature, accurrence and geologic significance of zircon in igneous and metamorphic rocks. *Mailing Add:* Dept Geol Univ Ga Athens GA 30602

ECKELMANN, WALTER R, b Englewood, May 25, 29; m 51; c 3. GEOCHEMISTRY. *Educ:* Wheaton Col, Ill, BS, 51; Columbia Univ, MA, 54, PhD(geochem), 56. *Prof Exp:* Res asst geochem, Columbia Univ, 51-55, res assoc, 55-57; res chemist, Jersey Prod Res Co, 57-59, sr res chemist, 59-62, sect head, 62-64, res mgr, European Lab, Esso Prod Res Co, Standard Oil Co, NJ, 64-66, dist prod geologist, Okla & oper mgr, New Orleans, Humble Oil & Refining Co, 66-70, gen mgr, Geol Res, 70-72, pres, 72-75, opers mgr, Explor Dept, Exxon Co USA, Houston, 75-76, dir, Esso Australia, Sydney, 76-78, DEP MGR, SCI & TECHNOL DEPT, EXXON CORP, FLORHAM PARK, NEW YORK, 78- *Mem:* AAAS; Geol Soc Am; Am Geochem Soc; Am Chem Soc; Am Asn Petrol Geologists. *Res:* Isotope geochemistry; mass spectrometry; low level radiation; research and operations. *Mailing Add:* Exxon Corp 220 Park Ave Florham Park NJ 07932

ECKELMEYER, KENNETH HALL, b Philadelphia, Pa, June 20, 43; m 65; c 2. PHYSICAL METALLURGY. *Educ:* Lafayette Col, BS, 65; Lehigh Univ, MS, 67, PhD(metall), 71. *Prof Exp:* Mem tech staff metall, 71-79, DIV SUPVR, ELECTRON OPTICS & X-RAY ANAL, SANDIA LBAS, 79- *Mem:* Am Soc Metals; Inst Metallog Soc. *Res:* Phase transformations; microstructural characterization; microstructure-mechanical property relations in metals, especially uranium alloys. *Mailing Add:* Electron Optics & X-ray Anal Div Sandia Labs Org 5822 Albuquerque NM 87185

ECKELS, ARTHUR R(AYMOND), b New Haven, Conn, Nov 16, 19; m 44; c 4. ELECTRICAL ENGINEERING. *Educ:* Univ Conn, BS, 41; Harvard Univ, MS, 42; Yale Univ, DEng, 50. *Prof Exp:* Elec engr, Bur Ships, US Navy, 42-43; from marine engr to chief engr, US Merchant Marine, 43-46; instr elec eng, Yale Univ, 47-49; prof, NC State Col, 49-56; prof & chmn dept, Univ Vt, 56-61; PROF ELEC ENG, NC STATE UNIV, 61- *Concurrent Pos:* Res partic, Oak Ridge Inst Nuclear Studies, 53; opers analyst, US Air Force, 54-; Fulbright lectr, Chiao Tung Univ, 60; consult, NASA, 63-64; vis prof, Japan Nat Defense Col, 64; sr elec engr adv, Environ Protection Agency, 78-82; prog coordr, NC Cent Univ, 80-82. *Mem:* Am Soc Eng Educ; Inst Elec & Electronics Engrs. *Res:* Electrical instrumentation and control. *Mailing Add:* Dept Elec Eng NC State Univ Raleigh NC 27607

ECKELS, KENNETH HENRY, b Baltimore, Md, Oct 11, 42; m 65. VIROLOGY, VACCINE DEVELOPMENT. *Educ:* Univ Md, BS, 65, MS, 69, PhD(microbiol), 73. *Prof Exp:* Biol lab technician, Dept Hazardous Microorganisms, 65-66, microbiologist, 66-81 & ASST CHIEF, DEPT BIOL RES, WALTER REED ARMY INST RES, 81- *Concurrent Pos:* Adj assoc prof, Univ Md, 80- *Mem:* Am Soc Microbiol; AAAS; Sigma Xi. *Res:* Viral vaccine development including the development of live attenuated dengue virus vaccines. *Mailing Add:* Bldg 501 Forest Glen Sect Walter Reed Army Inst Res Washington DC 20012

ECKENFELDER, WILLIAM WESLEY, JR, b New York, NY, Nov 15, 26; m 50; c 2. SANITARY ENGINEERING. *Educ:* Manhattan Col, BCE, 46; Pa State Univ, MS, 48; NY Univ, MCE, 56. *Prof Exp:* Sanit engr, Atlantic Refining Co, 48-49; res assoc, NY Univ, 49-50; from asst prof to assoc prof civil eng, Manhattan Col, 55-65; prof environ health eng, Univ Tex, 65-70; DISTINGUISHED PROF ENVIRON & WATER RESOURCES ENG, VANDERBILT UNIV, 70- *Concurrent Pos:* Vpres, Weston, Eckenfelder & Assocs, 52-56; consult, 56-; pres, Hydrosci Inc; Assoc Water & Air Resources Engrs, Tenn. *Honors & Awards:* Allen Mem Award, NY State Sewage & Indust Wastes Asn, 59; Gold Medal, Synthetic Organic Chem Mgrs Asn, 74; Camp Medal, Water Pollution Control Fed, 81. *Mem:* Am Soc Civil Engrs; Am Chem Soc; Am Inst Chem Engrs; Water Pollution Control Fedn; Am Soc Eng Educ. *Res:* Biological treatment of sewage and industrial wastes; mass transfer and aeration in waste treatment; process design of industrial waste treatment plants; water quality management. *Mailing Add:* Dept of Environ & Water Resources Eng Vanderbilt Univ Nashville TN 37240

ECKENHOFF, JAMES BENJAMIN, b Durham, NC, Mar 4, 43. BIOENGINEERING. *Educ:* Univ Pa, AB, 66; Northwestern Univ, MS, 73. *Prof Exp:* Jr bioengr, 73-74, sr bioengr & asst proj leader, 74-78, PROJ LEADER DEVELOP ENGR & AREA DIR BIOTECHNOL GROUP & PROG DIR RES, OSMOTIC SYSTS, ALZA RES, ALZA CORP, 78- *Mem:* Biomed Eng Soc. *Res:* Transport phenomena, reverse osmosis, optics, and instrumentation in the design of drug delivery systems. *Mailing Add:* Alza Res 950 Page Mill Rd Palo Alto CA 94304

ECKENHOFF, JAMES EDWARD, b Easton, Md, Apr 2, 15; m 38, 73; c 4. ANESTHESIOLOGY. *Educ:* Univ Ky, BS, 37; Univ Pa, MD, 41; Am Bd Anesthesiol, dipl. *Hon Degrees:* DSc, Transylvania Univ, 70. *Prof Exp:* Harrison fel anesthesiol, Sch Med, Univ Pa, 45-47; asst instr pharmacol, Sch Med, Univ Pa, 45-47, from asst instr to asst prof surg, 44-52, from assoc prof to prof anesthesiol in surg, 52-65, asst dir dept, 53-65, assoc clin pharmacol, 48-65; chmn dept anesthesia, 66-70, PROF ANESTHESIA, MED SCH, NORTHWESTERN UNIV, 66-, DEAN, MED SCH, 70-, PRES, MCGAW MED CTR, 80- *Concurrent Pos:* Asst surgeon, Children's Hosp, Pa, 49-53, consult, 53-65; consult, Valley Forge Army Hosp, Pa, 49-58, Anesthesiol Ctr, WHO, Denmark, 52, Vet Admin Hosp, Pa, 53-65 & US Naval Hosp, Pa; assoc ed, Anesthesiol, Am Soc Anesthesiol, 55-58, ed, 58-62; consult to surgeon gen, US Navy; mem surg study sect, NIH, 62-66, mem anesthesia training grants comt, 66-70; Hunterian prof, Royal Col Surg, 65; dir, Am Bd Anesthesiol, 65-73, pres, 72-73. *Mem:* Am Soc Anesthesiol; Am Physiol Soc; AMA; fel Am Col Anesthesiol; Am Col Physicians. *Res:* Physiological and pharmacological problems pertaining to coronary circulation; effects of opiates and antagonists upon normal and anesthetized man and the effect of changing carbon dioxide tensions upon the heart and circulation; deliberate hypotension; clinical anesthesiological problems. *Mailing Add:* Northwestern Univ Med Sch Chicago IL 60611

ECKENWALDER, JAMES EMORY, b Neuilly-sur-Seine, France, Oct 30, 49; US citizen; m 71. SYSTEMATIC BOTANY. *Educ:* Reed Col, BA, 71; Univ Calif, Berkeley, PhD(bot), 77. *Prof Exp:* Asst taxonomist, Fairchild Trop Garden, Fla, 77-78; ASST PROF BOT, UNIV TORONTO, 78- *Mem:* Am Soc Plant Taxonomists; Bot Soc Am; Inst Asn Plant Taxon; Soc Study Evolution; Soc Systematic Zool. *Res:* Systematics and phylogeny of gymnosperms, Salicaceae and miscellaneous woody dicotyledons; taxonomy of cultivated plants. *Mailing Add:* Dept of Bot Univ of Toronto Toronto ON M5S 1A1 Can

ECKER, EDWIN D, b Grovertown, Ind, Mar 26, 34; m 55; c 3. MATHEMATICS. *Educ:* Ball State Univ, BS, 56; Univ Ill, Urbana, MS, 59; Iowa State Univ, PhD(math), 66. *Prof Exp:* From instr to assoc prof, 59-73, PROF MATH, MacMURRAY COL, 73- *Concurrent Pos:* Vis lectr, Univ Ill, Urbana, 70-71. *Mem:* Math Asn Am; Nat Coun Teachers Math; Asn Comput Mach. *Res:* Group theory. *Mailing Add:* Dept Math MacMurray Col Jacksonville IL 62650

ECKER, HARRY ALLEN, b Athens, Ga, Oct 22, 35; m 59; c 3. ELECTRICAL ENGINEERING. *Educ:* Ga Inst Technol, BEE, 57, MSEE, 59; Ohio State Univ, PhD(elec eng), 65. *Prof Exp:* Res asst, Ga Inst Technol, 57-59; proj engr, Navig & Guid Lab, Wright-Patterson AFB, US Air Force, 59-60, syst prog officer, 60-61, electronic engr opers anal br, Synthesis & Anal Div, 61-62, actg chief, 62-63, aerospace engr, directorate of synthesis, dep for studies & anal, 63-65, chief opers anal group, 65-66; sr res engr, Radar Lab, Eng Exp Sta, Ga Inst Technol, 66-69, head radar br, Electronics Div, 69-76; gen mgr, Electro-Prod Div, 77-79, vpres res & develop, 79, DIR RES, SCI-ATLANTA, INC, 76-, VPRES TELECOMMUN, 79- *Mem:* Fel Inst Elec & Electronics Engrs; Sigma Xi. *Res:* Antennas; radar; systems analyses; bio-engineering. *Mailing Add:* Sci-Atlanta Inc 3845 Pleasantdale Rd Atlanta GA 30340

ECKER, RICHARD EUGENE, b Waverly, Iowa, Mar 13, 30; m 53; c 5. PHYSIOLOGY. *Educ:* Iowa State Univ, BS, 58, PhD(bact), 61. *Prof Exp:* Instr bact, Iowa State Univ, 60-61; instr microbiol, Col Med, Univ Fla, 62-64; from asst biologist to assoc biologist, Argonne Nat Lab, 64-73; pres, Vitose Corp, 73-81; CONSULT PHYSIOLOGIST, 81- *Concurrent Pos:* Nat Cancer Inst fel, 61-62; NIH res grant, 62-64; distinguished vis prof, Morehouse Col, 69-70; instr physiol, Marine Biol Lab, 72. *Res:* Regulation of biological function. *Mailing Add:* Box 211 Clarendon Hills IL 60514

ECKERLE, KENNETH LEE, b Jasper, Ind, Oct 18, 36. APPLIED PHYSICS. *Educ:* Ind State Univ, BS, 58; Univ Md, MS, 62. *Prof Exp:* Asst physics, Univ Md, 58-60, asst solid state physics, 60-62; atomic physicist, 62-67, PHYSICIST, NAT BUR STANDARDS, 67- *Mem:* Optical Soc Am. *Res:* Standards and measurements of transmittance and reflectance in the ultraviolet, visible and infrared spectral regions; spectrophotometry, instrument development. *Mailing Add:* Rm A321 Metrol Bldg Nat Bur Standards Washington DC 20234

ECKERLIN, HERBERT MARTIN, b New York, NY, Oct 23, 35; m 57; c 4. ENERGY CONSERVATION, SOLAR ENERGY. *Educ:* Va Polytech Inst, BS, 58; NC State Univ, MS, 68, PhD(eng sci), 72. *Prof Exp:* Test eng, Norfolk Naval Shipyard, 58-59; efficiency engr, Va Elec & Power Co, 59-60; design engr, Combustion Eng, 60-65; sr res engr, Corning Glass Works, 65-68; exten specialist mech, 68-73, asst prof, 73-76, ASSOC PROF MECH ENG, NC STATE UNIV, 76- *Concurrent Pos:* Energy consult, Indust Com Cos, 75-; dir, NC State Univ Walk-through Prog, 77-; pres, Energy Conserve Limited, 78-; prin investr, NC State Univ Solar House, 79-; seminar leader, McGraw-Hill, 79- *Mem:* Am Soc Mech Engrs; Sigma Xi. *Res:* Evaluation of the energy conservation potential of all types of industrial processes and systems; passive and active solar thermal systems. *Mailing Add:* Dept Mech & Aerospace Eng Box 5246 NC State Univ Raleigh NC 27612

ECKERMAN, JEROME, b Brooklyn, NY, Nov 18, 25; m 48; c 2. PHYSICS, ELECTRICAL ENGINEERING. *Educ:* Worcester Polytech Inst, BS, 48; Cath Univ, MS, 56, PhD(physics), 58. *Prof Exp:* Res scientist, Nat Adv Comt Aeronaut, 48-51; physicist & br chief, US Naval Ord Lab, 51-59; sr staff scientist, Avco, 59-65, assoc sect chief appl physics, Avco Corp, 65-68; physicist, NASA Electronics Res Ctr, Mass, 68-70, physicist/br chief, Microwave Sensor Br, Goddard Flight Ctr, 70-81; RES STAFF, SYST PLANNING CORP, ARLINGTON, VA, 81- *Mem:* Am Phys Soc; sr mem Inst Elec & Electronics Engrs; Am Meteorol Soc; Sigma Xi. *Res:* Ballistics range research; chemical kinetics in air and alkali metal plasmas; laminar wake transition behind hypervelocity models; turbulent wake growth; laboratory studies of flow field observables; flow analysis by interferometry; experimental and analytical development in microwave radars and radiometers for space applications; light gas gun development. *Mailing Add:* 11817 Hunting Ridge Ct Potomac MD 20854

ECKERSLEY, ALFRED, b Manchester, Eng, Dec 2, 28; nat US; m 57; c 2. ELECTRICAL ENGINEERING. *Educ:* Col Tech, Eng, BSc, 49; Univ Pa, MSEE, 54. *Prof Exp:* Assoc elec eng, Univ Pa, 49-57; lectr & res assoc, Univ NMex, 57-59; elec engr, Ark Electronics Corp, 59-61; res engr, United

Control Corp, 61-64; RES ENGR, AEROSPACE GROUP, BOEING CO, 64- *Concurrent Pos:* US deleg, Spec Int Comt Radioelec Perturbations. *Mem:* Sr mem Inst Elec & Electronics Eng; assoc mem Sigma Xi. *Res:* Electronics; avionics; radio noise; interference measurement; electromagnetic compatibility. *Mailing Add:* 16745 Maplewild SW Seattle WA 98166

ECKERT, ALFRED CARL, JR, b Newark, NJ, June 12, 20; m 44; c 4. ANALYTICAL CHEMISTRY. *Educ:* Wheaton Col, BS, 41; Univ Ill, PhD(anal chem), 45. *Prof Exp:* Lab asst chem, Wheaton Col, 39-41; asst, Univ Ill, 41-44; jr chemist, Univ Chicago, 44-45; res chemist, Chem Div, Union Carbide Corp, Tenn, 45-48; res engr, Battelle Mem Inst, 48-52; tech personnel off rep, Chem Div, Union Carbide Corp, Tenn, 53-56, tech serv group coordr chem & spectros, Speedway Labs, 56-58; sr exp res chemist, Allison Div, Gen Motors Corp, 58-65; mgr, Appl Res Group, Globe-Union Inc, 65-78, MGR, MAT TESTING LAB, APPL RES GROUP, JOHNSON CONTROLS INC, 78- *Concurrent Pos:* Lectr, Univ Tenn, 47-48. *Mem:* Am Chem Soc; Soc Appl Spectros; fel Am Sci Affil; fel Am Inst Chem. *Res:* Mesomorphic state with special reference to carbon blacks; effects of magnetism on dislocation movements in nickel foil; quantative analysis of lead alloys by x-ray fluorescence; significance of blood lead analyses; working reference materials for analytical quality evaluation; trends in requirements for lead acid battery materials. *Mailing Add:* 4605 N 107th St Wauwatosa WI 53225

ECKERT, BARRY S, b Binghamton, NY, Dec 16, 49; m 71; c 1. CELL BIOLOGY, ANATOMY. *Educ:* State Univ NY Albany, BS, 71, MS, 73; Univ Miami, PhD(anat), 76. *Prof Exp:* Res assoc cell biol, Univ Colo, 76-77; ASST PROF ANAT, STATE UNIV NY BUFFALO, 77- *Concurrent Pos:* Prin investr, NIH basic Sci res grants, State Univ NY Buffalo, 77-78, NSF grant, 78-79 & 81-84. *Mem:* Am Soc Cell Biol; Sigma Xi; Soc Develop Biol; Am Asn Anatomists; Electron Micros Soc Am. *Res:* Studying the role of microtubules, intermediate filaments and microfilaments in motility of cultured mammalian cells. *Mailing Add:* Dept Anat Sch Med Univ NY Buffalo NY 14214

ECKERT, CHARLES, b Denver, Colo, Nov, 22, 14; m 43; c 2. SURGERY. *Educ:* Wash Univ, MD, 39; Am Bd Surg, dipl, 45. *Prof Exp:* Asst, Wash Univ, 41-44, from instr to assoc prof, 44-56; chmn dept, 56-74, PROF SURG, ALBANY MED COL, 56- *Concurrent Pos:* Asst surgeon, Barnes & St Louis Children's Hosps, 44-56; attend surgeon, St Louis - City Hosp, 45-56; surgeon-in-chief, Albany Med Ctr Hosp, 56-74, attend surgeon, 74-; consult, Albany Vet Admin Hosp, Vassar Bros Hosp, Poughkeepsie, NY & Mary McClellan Hosp, Cambridge; mem bd visitors, Roswell Park Mem Inst, Buffalo, NY; mem, Am Bd Surg, 64-70, vchmn, 68-69, chmn, 69-70. *Mem:* AAAS; fel Am Col Surg; AMA; Soc Univ Surg; Am Surg Asn. *Res:* Cancer; surgical research. *Mailing Add:* Dept of Surg Albany Med Ctr Albany NY 12208

ECKERT, CHARLES ALAN, b St Louis, Mo, Dec 13, 38; m 61; c 2. CHEMICAL ENGINEERING. *Educ:* Mass Inst Technol, SB, 60, SM, 61; Univ Calif, Berkeley, PhD(chem eng), 65. *Prof Exp:* NATO fel high pressure physics, High Pressure Lab, Nat Ctr Sci Res, Bellevue, France, 64-65; from asst prof to assoc prof, 65-73, PROF CHEM ENG, UNIV ILL, URBANA, 73-, HEAD, DEPT CHEM ENG, 80- *Concurrent Pos:* NATO fel, 64-65; consult various companies; Guggenheim fel, 71; vis prof, Stanford Univ, 71-72. *Honors & Awards:* Allan Colburn Award, Am Inst Chem Engrs, 73; Ipatieff Prize, Am Chem Soc, 77. *Mem:* Am Inst Mining, Metall & Petrol Engrs; Am Chem Soc; Am Inst Chem Engrs; Am Soc Eng Educ; Chem Soc London. *Res:* Molecular thermodynamics and applied chemical kinetics; effects of high pressure on reactions in solution; phase equilibria at high pressure and temperature. *Mailing Add:* Dept of Chem Eng 213 E Chem Bldg Univ Ill Urbana IL 61801

ECKERT, DONALD JAMES, b Akron, Ohio, Aug 30, 49; m 78. SOIL FERTILITY, CONSERVATION TILLAGE. *Educ:* Mich State Univ, BS, 71; Ohio State Univ, MA, 74, PhD(agron), 78. *Prof Exp:* ASST PROF AGRON, OHIO STATE UNIV, 78- *Mem:* Am Soc Agron; Soil Sci Soc Am; Crop Sci Soc Am; Soil Conserv Soc Am; Sigma Xi. *Res:* Energy conservation in crop production systems; conservation tillage systems, particularly fertility and weed control; crop rotations to reduce nitrogen fertilizer requirements. *Mailing Add:* Dept Agron Ohio Agr Res Develop Ctr Wooster OH 44691

ECKERT, EDWARD ARTHUR, b New York, NY, July 2, 20; m 59. VIROLOGY. *Educ:* Brooklyn Col, BA, 40; Mass Inst Technol, MS, 47; Duke Univ, PhD(biol), 51. *Prof Exp:* Res assoc surg, Duke Univ, 51-55, Am Cancer Soc res scholar, 52-55, instr bact, 53-55; assoc prof, State Univ NY Med Ctr, 55-64; assoc prof, 64-70, PROF EPIDEMIOL, SCH PUB HEALTH, UNIV MICH, ANN ARBOR, 70- *Mem:* Soc Exp Biol & Med; Am Asn Immunol. *Res:* Properties of animal viruses; electron microscopy; immunology; biometry. *Mailing Add:* 2200 Fuller Rd Ann Arbor MI 48105

ECKERT, ERNST R(UDOLF) G(EORG), b Prague, Czech, Sept 13, 04; nat US; m 31; c 4. THERMODYNAMICS. *Educ:* German Inst Technol, Prague, Dipl Ing, 27, Dr Ing, 31; Inst Technol, Danzig, Dr habil, 38; Munich Tech Univ, Dr Ing E H, 68. *Hon Degrees:* Dr Eng, Purdue Univ, 68; DSc, Univ Manchester, 68, Univ Notre Dame, 72 & Polytech Inst, Romania, 73. *Prof Exp:* Asst, German Inst Technol, Prague, 28-34; lectr, Inst Technol, Danzig, 35-38; sect chief, Aeronaut Res Inst, Braunscheig; consult power plant lab, USAF, Wright-Patterson AFB, 45-49; consult turbine & compressor div, Lewis Res Ctr, NASA, 49-51; prof mech eng, Univ Minn, Minneapolis, 51-73, dir, Thermodyn & Heat Transfer Div & Heat Transfer Lab, 55-73, regents prof, 66-73, EMER PROF, UNIV MINN, MINNEAPOLIS, 73- *Concurrent Pos:* Docent, Inst Technol, Braunschweig, 39-40; prof & dir inst thermodyn, German Inst Technol, Prague, 43-45; Fulbright Award, 62-63; vis prof, Purdue Univ, 55-65; US rep aerodyn panel, Int Comt Flame Radiation; chmn, Am Div, Commonwealth & Int Libr Sci; past pres sci coun, Int Ctr Heat & Mass Transfer, Yugoslavia; US rep, Int Heat Transfer Conf; mem, Nat Comn Fire Prev & Control, 70-72; Humboldt award, 80. *Honors & Awards:* Max Jakob Award, 61; Gold Medal, Fr Inst Energy & Fuel, 67; Vincent Bendix Award, Am Soc Eng Educ, 72; Adams Memorial Mem Award, Am Welding Soc, 73. *Mem:* Fel Am Inst Aeronaut & Astronaut; hon mem Am Soc Mech Engrs; fel NY Acad Sci; Sigma Xi; German Soc Aeronaut & Astronaut. *Res:* Heat transfer; thermodynamics; gas turbines; jet propulsion; energy conservation. *Mailing Add:* 60 W Wentworth Ave West St Paul MN 55118

ECKERT, GEORGE FRANK, b Akron, Ohio, Feb 21, 24; m 48; c 3. CHEMICAL EDUCATION. *Educ:* Akron Univ, BS, 44; Ohio State Univ, PhD(chem), 50. *Prof Exp:* Instr phys chem, Captial Univ, 47-48; res chemist, E I du Pont de Nemours & Co, Inc, 51-54; assoc prof, 54-60, PROF CHEM, CAPITAL UNIV, 60- *Mem:* Am Chem Soc. *Mailing Add:* 867 Pleasant Ridge Ave Columbus OH 43209

ECKERT, HANS ULRICH, b Danzig, Ger, Apr 20, 16; nat US; m 46; c 2. PHYSICS. *Educ:* Danzig Tech Univ, Cand Phys, 38; Tech Univ, Berlin, DiplEng, 41. *Prof Exp:* Test group leader, Aerodyn Inst Ger Army Ord, 43-45; task scientist, Aeronaut Res Lab, Wright Air Develop Ctr, Ohio, 46-54; sr aerodyn engr, Convair, 54-56, staff scientist, sci res lab, 56-62; staff scientist, Phys & Life Sci Lab, Lockheed-Calif Co, 62-63, head plasma physics lab, 63-67; mem tech staff chem & physics lab, 67-78, CONSULT, AEROSPACE CORP ANALYTICA, STOCKHOLM, 79- *Mem:* AAAS; Am Inst Aeronaut & Astronaut; Am Phys Soc; Soc Appl Spectroscopy. *Res:* Electrical discharges in gases; plasma flow; plasma chemistry; spectrochemical analysis. *Mailing Add:* 3901 Via Pavion Palos Verdes Estates CA 90274

ECKERT, JOHN ANDREW, electrochemistry, see previous edition

ECKERT, JOHN S, b Delta, Ohio, June 29, 10; m; c 1. PHYSICAL & BIOLOGICAL SCIENCES. *Educ:* Ohio State Univ, BChE, 33. *Prof Exp:* Jr chem engr, Goodyear Tire & Rubber Co, 33-37; area supvr, E I du Pont de Nemours & Co, 37-42; plant processing engr, B F Goodrich Co, 42-44; plant mgr, US Stoneware Co, 44-50, dir eng, Norton Co, 50-77; CONSULT ENGR, 77- *Concurrent Pos:* Adj assoc prof, Ohio State Univ, 63-75. *Mem:* Am Inst Chem Engrs; Am Soc Metals; Instrument Soc Am; Nat Asn Corrosion Engrs; Nat Soc Prof Engrs. *Res:* Mass transfer and performance of packed beds for distillation; absorption and stripping processes. *Mailing Add:* 216 Hollywood Ave Akron OH 44313

ECKERT, JOSEPH WEBSTER, b St Louis, Mo, Mar 27, 31; m 57; c 3. PLANT PATHOLOGY. *Educ:* Univ Calif, Los Angeles, BS, 52; Rutgers Univ, MS, 53; Univ Calif, Davis, PhD(plant path), 57. *Prof Exp:* Res asst, Univ Calif, Davis, 55-57, jr plant pathologist, 57-58, asst plant pathologist, 58-62, from asst prof to assoc prof, 62-70, PROF PLANT PATH, UNIV CALIF, RIVERSIDE, 70- *Concurrent Pos:* Fulbright Res Scholar, Netherlands-Am (Fulbright) Comn for Educ Exchange, 74-75; sr res fel, Agr Univ, Netherlands, 74-75. *Mem:* Am Phytopath Soc. *Res:* Post harvest fruit and vegetable diseases; physiology of fungi, fungicides. *Mailing Add:* Dept of Plant Path Univ of Calif Riverside CA 92521

ECKERT, JUERGEN, b Heilbronn, WGer, June 14, 47; m 79. SOLID STATE PHYSICS, MATERIALS SCIENCE. *Educ:* Yale Univ, BS, 70; Princeton Univ, MA, 72, PhD(mat sci), 75. *Prof Exp:* Res assoc physics, 75-77, asst physicist, Brookhaven Nat Lab, 77-79; STAFF MEM, LOS ALAMOS NAT LAB, 79- *Mem:* AAAS. *Res:* Neutron scattering studies at high pressures and low temperatures, molecular solids, lattice dynamics and molecular rotations; structural and magnetic phase transitions; vibrational spectroscopy on metal hybrids and molecular crystals. *Mailing Add:* MS 805 p-8 Los Alamos Nat Lab Los Alamos NM 87545

ECKERT, RICHARD EDGAR, JR, b Kansas City, Mo, July 24, 29; m 51; c 6. RANGE SCIENCE. *Educ:* Univ Calif, BS, 52; Univ Nev, MS, 54; Ore State Univ, PhD(farm crops), 57. *Prof Exp:* Range scientist, Agr Res Serv, Western Region, USDA, 57-78; MEM STAFF, RENEWABLE RESOURCE CTR, UNIV NEV, RENO, 70- *Mem:* Soc Range Mgt; Sigma Xi. *Res:* Range weed control and seeding; plant competition; ecological resource inventory; grazing management systems. *Mailing Add:* Renew Resource Ctr Univ of Nev 920 Valley Rd Reno NV 89502

ECKERT, RICHARD RAYMOND, b Youngstown, Ohio, July 15, 42; m 74; c 2. MICROCOMPUTERS APPLICATIONS. *Educ:* Case Inst Technol, BS, 64; Univ Kans, MS, 66, PhD(physics), 71. *Prof Exp:* Prof physics, Universidad de Oriente, Venezuela, 66-68; PROF PHYSICS & COMPUT SCI, CATH UNIV, PR, 71- *Concurrent Pos:* Prin investr, Cath Univ Biomed Res Prog, Minority Biomed Support Prog, NIH, 78- *Mem:* Am Asn Physics Teachers. *Res:* Effects of airborne pollutants on public health; microcomputers and their application to various academic tasks. *Mailing Add:* Box 145 Sta 6 Ponce PR #00732

ECKERT, ROGER E(ARL), b Lakewood, Ohio, Aug 8, 26; c 3. CHEMICAL ENGINEERING. *Educ:* Princeton Univ, BSE, 48; Univ Ill, MS, 49, PhD(chem eng), 51. *Prof Exp:* Sr engr, E I du Pont de Nemours & Co, 51-64; assoc prof chem, 64-73, asst head, Chem Eng Sch, 70-75, PROF CHEM ENG, PURDUE UNIV, 73- *Concurrent Pos:* Consult, Glidden Co, 64-71, Packaging Corp of Am, 65-71 & Mobil Chem Co, 81- *Mem:* Am Inst Chem Engrs; Soc Rheol. *Res:* Design and statistical analysis of experiments; stocastic modeling of processes; rheology of viscoelastic polymer melts; organic and inorganic process development; diffusion in solids; mechanochemistry; biomedical engineering; scientific data processing and information retrieval. *Mailing Add:* 153 Indian Rock Dr West Lafayette IN 47906

ECKERT, ROGER OTTO, b New York, NY, Dec 12, 34; div; c 4. NEUROPHYSIOLOGY, NEUROBIOLOGY. *Educ:* Atlantic Union Col, BA, 56; Columbia Univ, MA, 57, PhD(zool), 60. *Prof Exp:* Univ res fel & NIH fel, Harvard Univ, 61-62; from asst prof to assoc prof zool, Syracuse Univ, 62-68; PROF BIOL, UNIV CALIF, LOS ANGELES, 68- *Concurrent Pos:* NIH spec fel, Univ Saarlandes, 66-67; mem, Corp of Marine Biol Lab; mem neurobiol panel, NSF, 78-80. *Honors & Awards:* Sr Award, Alexander Von Humboldt Found, 73. *Mem:* Soc Gen Physiol; Am Physiol Soc; Am Soc Cell Biol; Biophys Soc; Soc Neurosci. *Res:* Cellular neurobiology; membrane calcium mechanisms; regulatory functions of calcium; bioelectric phenomena and behavior in protozoa; membrane channel mechanisms; synaptic transmission; molluscan neurons; marine neurobiology; membrane biophysics. *Mailing Add:* Dept of Biol Univ of Calif Los Angeles CA 90024

ECKHARDT, CRAIG JON, b Rapid City, SDak, June 26, 40. PHYSICAL CHEMISTRY. *Educ:* Univ Colo, BA, 62; Yale Univ, MS, 64, PhD(chem), 67. *Prof Exp:* From asst prof to assoc prof, 67-78, PROF PHYS CHEM, UNIV NEBR, LINCOLN, 78- *Concurrent Pos:* Consult, Appl Sci Knowledge, Inc, Nebr, 68-72; adv, Nebr State Dept Ed Phys Sci Proj, 68-69; mem, NSF Mat Res Lab Adv Panel, 76-79 & NSF Adv Panel for Sect Condensed Matter, 77-78; John Simon Guggenheim fel, 79-80. *Mem:* Am Inst Physics; Faraday Soc; Am Asn Physics Teachers; Sigma Xi; Soc Photog Scientists & Engrs. *Res:* Experimental and theoretical study of the electronic structure of molecules and crystals, molecular complexes and molecules of biological importance; applications of specular reflection of light; piezomodulation spectroscopy; electronic structure and spectra of dyes; electronic energy transfer in condensed phases; optical properties of materials; magnetic and natural dichroism; non-linear laser spectroscopy; Roman and Brillouin scattering. *Mailing Add:* Dept Chem Univ Nebr Lincoln NE 68588

ECKHARDT, DONALD HENRY, b Flushing, NY, Dec 20, 32; m 55; c 4. GEOPHYSICS. *Educ:* Mass Inst Technol, BS, 55, PhD(geophys), 61. *Prof Exp:* Geologist, Magnolia Petrol Co, Socony Mobil Oil Co, 55-56, seismic interpreter, Socony Mobil Oil Co, Venezuela, 56-58; res assoc, Ohio State Univ Res Found, 60-61, res assoc lunar & planetary lab, Univ Ariz, 61-63; res physicist, 63-75, CHIEF GEODESY & GRAVITY BR, AIR FORCE GEOPHYS LAB, 75- *Concurrent Pos:* Res assoc, Div Sponsored Res, Mass Inst Technol, 61-62. *Mem:* Am Geophys Union. *Res:* Geomagnetic induction; geodesy; selenodesy; planetary physics; lunar librations; gravity. *Mailing Add:* Air Force Geophysics Lab Hanscom AFB MA 01731

ECKHARDT, EILEEN THERESA, b Passaic, NJ, May 17, 28. PHARMACOLOGY. *Educ:* Caldwell Col, BA, 49; Tulane Univ, MS, 60, PhD(pharmacol), 62. *Prof Exp:* From asst pharmacologist to assoc pharmacologist, Schering Corp, NJ, 49-58; teaching asst pharmacol, Tulane Univ, 58-62; from instr to asst prof, Univ Vt, 62-67; ASST PROF PHARMACOL, NJ COL MED, 67- *Res:* Liver hemodynamics; liver function; bromsulphalein excretion; role of the liver in drug metabolism. *Mailing Add:* Dept of Pharmacol NJ Col of Med Newark NJ 07103

ECKHARDT, GISELA (MARION), b Frankfurt, Ger; m 57. PHYSICS. *Educ:* Univ Frankfurt, Ger, dipl, 52, Dr Phil nat(physics), 58. *Prof Exp:* Engr adv mat group, Semiconductor & Mat Div, Radio Corp Am, 58-60; mem tech staff, Quantum Electronics Dept, 60-66, mem plasma physics dept, 71, high voltage systems, 71-78, Optical Physics Dept, 78-80, SR MEM TECH STAFF, QUANTUM ELECTRONICS DEPT, HUGHES RES LABS, 69-, MEM TECH STAFF, CHEM PHYSICS DEPT, 80- *Concurrent Pos:* Mem, Adv Coun, Dept Physics/Astron, Calif State Univ, Long Beach. *Mem:* Am Phys Soc. *Res:* Lasers and nonlinear optics; solid state physics; plasma and gas discharge physics. *Mailing Add:* Hughes Res Labs 3011 Malibu Canyon Rd Malibu CA 90265

ECKHARDT, RICHARD DALE, b Dekalb, Ill, June 24, 18; m 46; c 4. INTERNAL MEDICINE. *Educ:* Univ Ill, AB, 40; Harvard Univ, MD, 43; Am Bd Internal Med, dipl, 50. *Prof Exp:* Intern & resident, Harvard Med Serv, Boston City Hosp, 44-46, assoc, Thorndike Mem Lab, 46-49; assoc internal med, Col Med, Univ Iowa, 49-52; res assoc, Harvard Med Sch, 52; from clin asst prof to clin assoc prof, 52-60, prof, 60-80, EMER PROF INTERNAL MED, COL MED, UNIV IOWA, 80-; from asst chief to chief med Serv, Vet Admin Hosp, Chief of staff, 68-80, asst dean vet hosp affairs, 68-80. *Concurrent Pos:* Fel, Harvard Med Sch, 44-45, res fel, 46-49; dir, Hepatitis Surv Group, Kyoto, Japan, 52; from clin asst prof to clin assoc prof internal med, Col Med, Univ Iowa, 52-60, clin prof, 60-, asst dean vet hosp affairs, 68-; chief med serv, West Side Hosp & attend physician, med serv, Res & Educ Hosps, Chicago, Ill, 57-58; assoc prof int med, Col Med, Univ Ill, 57-58. *Mem:* AAAS; Am Fedn Clin Res; fel AMA; Am Asn Study Liver Dis; Soc Exp Biol & Med. *Res:* Liver disease; protein and amino acid metabolism; nutrition. *Mailing Add:* 1675 Ridge Rd Iowa City IA 52240

ECKHARDT, ROBERT BARRY, b Jersey City, NJ, July 14, 42; m 64; c 4. BIOLOGICAL ANTHROPOLOGY, POPULATION GENETICS. *Educ:* Rutgers Univ, New Brunswick, BS, 64; Univ Mich, MS, 66, MA, 67, PhD(anthrop, human genetics), 71. *Prof Exp:* Instr anthrop, Univ Mich, 68-69, lectr, 69-71; asst prof anthrop, 71-80, ASSOC PROF ANTHROP, PA STATE UNIV, UNIVERSITY PARK, 81- *Concurrent Pos:* Dir lab phys anthrop, Univ Mich, 68-71; cur phys anthrop, Pa State Univ, University Park, 71-; dir, Mus Non-Western Man, 71-74; NSF grant, Pa State Univ, 72-73; book rev ed, J Human Evolution; co-ed, J Gen Educ; NIH grant, 78-79; Harry Frank Guggenheim Found grant, 81- *Mem:* AAAS; Am Asn Phys Anthropologists; Am Asn Human Biologists; Am Anthrop Asn; NY Acad Sci. *Res:* Non-human primate and human evolution; population genetics; inheritance of quantitative characteristics and rates of evolution, particularly in polygenic systems. *Mailing Add:* Dept Anthrop 409 Carpenter Sci Bldg Pa State Univ University Park PA 16802

ECKHARDT, ROBERT CAMPBELL, ecology, evolution, see previous edition

ECKHARDT, RONALD A, b Baltimore, Md, Nov 18, 42. CELL BIOLOGY. *Educ:* Loyola Col, Md, BS, 64; Cath Univ Am, PhD(biol), 69. *Prof Exp:* Teaching asst biol, Cath Univ Am, 65-67; instr biol, Gallaudet Col, 64-65 & Xaverian Col, 66-67; vis investr, Oak Ridge Nat Lab, 67-69; fel biol, Yale Univ, 69-71; assoc prof, 71-80, PROF BIOL, BROOKLYN COL, CITY UNIV NEW YORK, 80- *Mem:* Am Soc Cell Biol; Soc Develop Biol; Sigma Xi. *Res:* Studies of the molecular organization of the eukaryotic genome, including studies of repetitive nucleotide sequences and nuclear proteins. *Mailing Add:* Dept of Biol Brooklyn Col Bedford Ave & Ave H Brooklyn NY 11210

ECKHARDT, WILFRIED OTTO, b Frankfurt, Ger, Mar 30, 28; m 57. PHYSICS. *Educ:* Univ Frankfurt, dipl, 52, Dr phil nat(physics), 58. *Prof Exp:* Asst, Phys Inst, Univ Frankfurt, 53-57; mem staff, Microwave & Plasma Electronics Group, Radio Corp Am, 58-60; mem tech staff, Plasma Physics Dept, 60-63, sr staff physicist & sect head, 63-68, sr scientist & head LM cathode devices proj, 68-78, SR SCIENTIST, EXPLOR STUDIES DEPT, HUGHES RES LABS, 78- *Mem:* Am Phys Soc; assoc fel Am Inst Aeronaut & Astronaut; Ger Phys Soc. *Res:* Artificial intelligence; plasma and gas discharge physics; high voltage and high power technology; electric propulsion; direct energy conversion; microwave and infrared physics. *Mailing Add:* Hughes Res Labs 3011 Malibu Canyon Rd Malibu CA 90265

ECKHART, WALTER, b Yonkers, NY, May 22, 38; m 65. MOLECULAR BIOLOGY, VIROLOGY. *Educ:* Yale Univ, BS, 60; Univ Calif, Berkeley, PhD(molecular biol), 65. *Prof Exp:* Res assoc, 65-69, mem staff, 70-73, assoc prof, 73-79, PROF, SALK INST, 79-, CHMN, TUMOR VIROL LAB, 73-, DIR, ARMAND HAMMER CTR CANCER BIOL, 76- *Concurrent Pos:* NSF fel, Salk Inst, 65-67, Am Cancer Soc fel, 67-70; assoc adj prof, Univ Calif, San Diego, 72-79, adj prof, 79-; mem rev comt, NIH Cancer Ctr, 80- *Mem:* AAAS; Am Soc Microbiol. *Res:* Mechanisms of malignant cell transformation by tumor viruses; organization and expression of viral and cellular genes; growth regulation in mammalian cells. *Mailing Add:* Salk Inst PO Box 85800 San Diego CA 92138

ECKHAUSE, MORTON, b New York, NY, May 17, 35; m 68; c 3. HIGH ENERGY PHYSICS. *Educ:* NY Univ, AB, 57; Carnegie Inst Technol, MS, 61, PhD(physics), 62. *Prof Exp:* Res assoc physics, Carnegie Inst Technol, 62; instr, Yale Univ, 62-64; from asst prof to assoc prof, 64-73, PROF PHYSICS, COL WILLIAM & MARY, 73- *Concurrent Pos:* Res visitor, Rutherford Lab, Eng, 73-74. *Mem:* Am Phys Soc. *Res:* Experimental high-energy nuclear physics; muon lifetimes; structure of muonium; kaonic, sigma hyperonic and antiprotonic x-rays. *Mailing Add:* Dept of Physics Col of William & Mary Williamsburg VA 23185

ECKHOFF, NORMAN DEAN, b Meade, Kans, Apr 10, 38; m 59; c 2. NUCLEAR & INDUSTRIAL ENGINEERING. *Educ:* Kans State Univ, BS, 61, MS, 63, PhD(nuclear eng), 68. *Prof Exp:* Res engr, Boeing Co, Kans, 62-63; process engr, Litwin Eng Corp, 63; reactor engr, AEC, Tenn, 63-64; instr, 64-68, asst prof, 68-72, assoc prof, 72-76, PROF NUCLEAR ENG, KANS STATE UNIV, 76-, DEPT HEAD, 77- *Concurrent Pos:* Consult, Econ Res Serv, USDA, 69, Systs Res Co, Kans, 68-73, Comet Rice Mills, Tex, 68-69, Kemin Indust, Iowa, 71-, McNally-Pittsburg, Kans, 72, Kansas Gas & Elec, 73 & 81, US Atomic Energy Comn, Washington, DC, 73 & Off Tech Assistance, Washington, DC, 80. *Mem:* Am Nuclear Soc; AAAS; Am Soc Eng Educ. *Res:* Neutron activation analysis; nuclear fuel management and economics; statistical models; systems analysis. *Mailing Add:* Dept of Nuclear Eng Kans State Univ Manhattan KS 66502

ECKLER, ALBERT ROSS, b Boston, Mass, Aug 29, 27; m 51; c 3. STATISTICS, OPERATIONS RESEARCH. *Educ:* Swarthmore Col, BA, 50; Princeton Univ, PhD(math statist), 54. *Prof Exp:* Res asst statist & opers res, James Forrestal Res Lab, Princeton Univ, 53-54; mem tech staff, Bell Tel Labs, Whippany, 54-58, supvr, 58-62, head, Mil Statist Dept, 62-72, head, Appl Math & Statist Dept, Holmdel, 72-74, head, Common Systs Anal Dept, Whippany, 74-80, HEAD, ELECTRONICS TECHNOL ANAL DEPT, BELL LABS, MURRAY HILL, 80- *Honors & Awards:* Best Surv Paper Award, Technometrics, 70. *Mem:* Am Statist Asn; Sigma Xi. *Res:* Probability models of target coverage and missile allocation; mathematical models of telephone operations; optimal resource usage; statistical and historical evaluation of claims of extreme longevity in humans. *Mailing Add:* Spring Valley Rd Morristown NJ 07960

ECKLER, PAUL EUGENE, b Mexico, Mo, May 17, 46. SYNTHETIC ORGANIC CHEMISTRY. *Educ:* Univ Mo, Rolla, BS, 69; Univ Ore, MA, 70, PhD(chem), 75. *Prof Exp:* Clin chemist, Walter Reed Army Med Ctr, 70-72; teaching asst org chem, Univ Ore, 69-70, 73-74; res & develop chemist, 75-80, SR RES SCIENTIST, TECH SERV DEPT, INT MINERALS & CHEM CORP, 80- *Mem:* Am Chem Soc. *Res:* Organic synthesis and analysis, clinical chemistry; Diels-Alder reactions, natural products, monosaccharides, polyols, nitroparaffin derivatives, and heterocycles; instrumental analysis; coatings and resins. *Mailing Add:* Cent Res & Develop Div PO Box 207 Terre Haute IN 47808

ECKLUND, EARL FRANK, JR, b Seattle, Wash, Apr 19, 45; m 76; c 1. NUMBER THEORY, OPERATING SYSTEMS. *Educ:* Pac Lutheran Univ, BS, 66; Western Wash State Col, MA, 68; Wash State Univ, PhD(math), 72. *Prof Exp:* Instr math, Northern Ill Univ, 71-72, asst prof comput sci, 72-73; fel comput sci, Univ Man, 73-74; asst prof comput sci, Ill State Univ, 74-77; ASST PROF, DEPT COMPUT SCI, ORE STATE UNIV, 77- *Concurrent Pos:* Consult, 78- *Mem:* Am Math Soc; Math Asn Am; Soc Indust & Appl Math; Asn Comput Mach; Inst Elec & Electronics Engrs. *Res:* Computer science, especially database operating systems, information systems, operating systems; computational and combinatorial number theory, especially factorization and primality, distribution of residues and non-residues; computer science, especially factorization and primality testing, distribution of residues and nonresidues, factors of integers in progressions, programming methodologies and languages. *Mailing Add:* Dept of Comput Sci Ore State Univ Corvallis OR 97331

ECKLUND, O(SCAR) F(REDERICK), b Newton, Iowa, May 18, 13; m 37; c 2. FOOD TECHNOLOGY. *Educ:* Iowa State Col, BS, 35. *Prof Exp:* Chemist, Wis Steel Works, 35-38; technologist res dept, Am Can Co, 38-57, group leader plastics & paper, 57-64, supvr blow molding & thermoforming plastics res, 65-68, mgr plastics tech serv, 68-69; proprietor, O F Ecklund, Custom Thermocouples, 47-74; PRES, O F ECKLUND, INC, 74- *Mem:* Inst Food Technol; Soc Plastic Eng. *Res:* Food processing including process determination; aseptic canning; container development; plastics. *Mailing Add:* O F Ecklund Inc PO Box 279 Cape Coral FL 33904

ECKLUND, PAUL RICHARD, b Denver, Colo, June 20, 41; m 62; c 2. PLANT PHYSIOLOGY. *Educ:* Western State Col Colo, BA, 64; Ore State Univ, PhD(plant physiol), 68. *Prof Exp:* Asst prof biol, Vassar Col, 68-74; MEM FAC BIOL, CORNELL UNIV, 74- *Mem:* Am Soc Plant Physiol; Sigma Xi; Am Inst Biol Sci. *Res:* Hormonal control of plant growth, development and senescence; biochemical and physiological changes associated with plant senescence. *Mailing Add:* Dept of Biol Cornell Univ Ithaca NY 14850

ECKLUND, STANLEY DUANE, b Minneapolis, Minn, Mar 18, 39; m 64; c 3. EXPERIMENTAL HIGH ENERGY PHYSICS. *Educ:* Univ Minn, BS, 61; Calif Inst Technol, PhD(physics), 67. *Prof Exp:* Res assoc photoprod, Stanford Linear Accelerator Ctr, 66-71; sr res assoc hyperons, Nat Accelerator Lab, Fermilab, 71-74, staff physicist elastic scattering, 74-77, head, Colliding Beams Group, 77-80; WITH STANFORD LINEAR ACCELERATOR LAB, 80- *Mem:* Am Phys Soc; AAAS. *Res:* Experimental high energy particle physics research, specializing in: photoproduction, elastic and inelastic scattering, meson form factors, hyperon decays and hyperon interactions and colliding beam physics. *Mailing Add:* Stanford Linear Accelerator Lab PO Box 4349 Stanford CA 94305

ECKMAN, MICHAEL KENT, b Denver, Colo, May 18, 42; m 63; c 2. ANIMAL PARASITOLOGY. *Educ:* Univ Northern Colo, BA, 65, MA, 66; Auburn Univ, PhD(avian dis), 70. *Prof Exp:* Sr res parasitologist, Morton-Norwich Prod, Inc, 66-68, 70-71; res specialist avian coccidiosis, Dow Chem Co, 71-77; POULTRY PATHOLOGIST, ALA COOP EXTEN SERV, AUBURN UNIV, 77- *Mem:* Am Soc Parasitologists; Poultry Sci Asn; Soc Protozoologists. *Res:* Avian diseases, prevention, diagnosis and treatment; conduct educational clinics and short courses for poultry and allied industries. *Mailing Add:* Ala Coop Exten Serv Auburn Univ Auburn AL 36830

ECKNER, FRIEDRICH AUGUST OTTO, b Plauen, Ger, Aug 26, 26; US citizen; m 56; c 3. PATHOLOGY. *Educ:* Univ Cologne, 49-55, Dr med, 57. *Prof Exp:* Asst med, Univ Cologne, 55, 56-57, asst path, 56, 57-58; resident path, Salem Hosp, Mass, 58-60 & Univ Chicago, 60-62; pathologist in training, Congenital Heart Dis Res Ctr, Hektoen Inst Med Res, 62-64, head sect histochem, 64-70, assoc pathologist, 67-70; ASSOC PROF PATH, UNIV ILL COL MED, 70- *Concurrent Pos:* Res assoc path, Univ Chicago & lectr, Univ Ill, 62-70. *Res:* Pathology of congenital and acquired cardiac disease by qualitative and quantitative methods at the gross and microscopic level; experimental study of extracorporal circulation, elective cardiac arrest and cardiac transplantation by its tissue reactions. *Mailing Add:* Dept Path Univ Ill Col Med PO Box 6998 Chicago IL 60680

ECKROAT, LARRY RAYMOND, b Bloomsburg, Pa, July 18, 41; m 71. GENETICS, FISH BIOLOGY. *Educ:* Bloomsburg State Col, BS, 64; Pa State Univ, MS, 66, PhD(zool), 69. *Prof Exp:* Asst prof, 69-75, ASSOC PROF BIOL, BEHREND COL, PA STATE UNIV, 75- *Mem:* AAAS; Am Fisheries Soc; Genetics Soc Am; Am Genetics Asn. *Res:* Genetics of soluble protein polymorphisms in natural and hatchery populations of fishes and salamanders; chromosome polymorphism in natural populations of the house mouse. *Mailing Add:* Dept Biol Col Sci Behrend Col Pa State Univ Erie PA 16510

ECKROTH, CHARLES ANGELO, b Mandan, NDak, May 10, 34; m 62; c 2. PHYSICS. *Educ:* St John's Univ, Minn, BA, 56; Iowa State Univ, PhD(physics), 66. *Prof Exp:* From instr to asst prof physics, Univ Mo-Columbia, 65-69; from asst prof to assoc prof, 69-75, PROF PHYSICS, ST CLOUD STATE UNIV, 75- *Mem:* Am Asn Physics Teachers. *Res:* Point symmetry groups; optics. *Mailing Add:* Dept of Physics St Cloud State Univ St Cloud MN 56301

ECKROTH, DAVID RAYMOND, b Orwigsburg, Pa, Nov 20, 39; m 66. ORGANIC CHEMISTRY. *Educ:* Franklin & Marshall Col, AB, 61; Princeton Univ, MA, 63, PhD(org chem), 66. *Prof Exp:* Assoc res chemist, Sterling-Winthrop Res Inst, 65-66; asst prof chem, Wake Forest Univ, 66-69; vis asst prof, Iowa State Univ, 69-70; asst prof chem, York Col, NY, 70-75; ASSOC ED, KIRK-OTHMER ENCYCL CHEM TECHNOL, JOHN WILEY & SONS, 75- *Mem:* AAAS; Am Chem Soc; The Chem Soc; NY Acad Sci; assoc Comn Nomenclature Organic Chem. *Res:* Nomenclature of organic chemistry. *Mailing Add:* John Wiley & Sons 605 Third Ave New York NY 10158

ECKSTEIN, BERNARD HANS, b Ulm, Ger, Dec 19, 23; nat US; m 58. PHYSICAL CHEMISTRY. *Educ:* Princeton Univ, AB, 48; Cornell Univ, PhD(phys chem), 53. *Prof Exp:* Res assoc chem, Cornell Univ, 52-54; res chemist, Textile Fibers Dept, E I du Pont de Nemours & Co, 54-57; res chemist, 57-77, RES SCIENTIST, PARMA TECH CTR, UNION CARBIDE CORP, 77- *Mem:* Am Chem Soc; Soc Plastics Engrs; Sigma Xi; NAm Thermal Soc. *Res:* Carbon fibers; composite and high performance materials; reaction mechanisms; high temperature density. *Mailing Add:* 8930 Albion Rd North Royalton OH 44133

ECKSTEIN, EUGENE CHARLES, b Bucyrus, Ohio, Oct 31, 46; m 68; c 3. RHEOLOGY, ARTIFICIAL ORGANS. *Educ:* Mass Inst Technol, SB & SM, 70, PhD(mech eng), 75. *Prof Exp:* Assoc med biomed eng, Peter Bent Brigham Hosp, Harvard Sch Med, 74-75; asst prof, 75-79, ASSOC PROF BIOMED ENG, UNIV MIAMI, 79- *Concurrent Pos:* NIH prin investr, 78-84. *Mem:* Am Soc Mech Engrs; Am Soc Artificial Internal Organs; Int Soc Artificial Organs. *Res:* Biomechanical engineering; rheological effects in thrombus formation and development of an artificial urinary bladder. *Mailing Add:* Sch Eng & Arch Univ Miami PO Box 248294 Coral Gables FL 33124

ECKSTEIN, JOHN WILLIAM, b Central City, Iowa, Nov 23, 23; m 47; c 5. INTERNAL MEDICINE. *Educ:* Loras Col, BS, 46; Univ Iowa, MD, 50. *Prof Exp:* Intern, Letterman Gen Hosp, 50-51; from asst resident to resident, 51-53, asst, 53-55, from instr to assoc prof, 54-65, PROF INTERNAL MED, UNIV IOWA, 65-, DEAN COL MED, 70-, ESTAB INVESTR, CARDIOVASC LAB, UNIV HOSPS, 58- *Concurrent Pos:* Am Heart Asn res fel, Univ Hosps, Univ Iowa, 54-55, Rockefeller Found fel, 53-54; Nat Heart Inst res fel, Evans Mem Hosp & Mass Mem Hosps, 55-56. *Mem:* AMA; Am Soc Clin Invest; Asn Am Physicians; Am Physiol Soc; Cent Soc Clin Res. *Res:* Internal medicine and cardiovascular physiology. *Mailing Add:* Univ of Iowa Col of Med Iowa City IA 52242

ECKSTEIN, RICHARD WALDO, b Tiro, Ohio, Oct 9, 11; m 37; c 3. MEDICINE. *Educ:* Heidelberg Col, BS, 33; Western Reserve Univ, MA, 36, MD, 38. *Prof Exp:* From intern to asst resident med, Lakeside Hosp, 39-41, sr instr physiol, Sch Med, 45-46, sr instr med, 46-49, asst prof, 49-53, asst prof physiol & med, 53-60, ASSOC PROF PHYSIOL & MED, SCH MED, CASE WESTERN RESERVE UNIV, 60- *Concurrent Pos:* Estab investr, Am Heart Asn, 54. *Mem:* AAAS; Am Physiol Soc; Soc Exp Biol & Med; Am Heart Asn; Am Psychiat Asn. *Res:* Coronary artery blood flow; cardiovascular; limb blood flow in dogs during shock; coronary collateral circulation; coronary blood supply of chemoreceptors. *Mailing Add:* Univ Hosps Cleveland OH 44106

ECKSTEIN, YONA, b Mankent, USSR, Dec 20, 41; Israel citizen; m 64; c 3. PHYSICAL CHEMISTRY, ANALYTICAL CHEMISTRY. *Educ:* Hebrew Univ, BSc, 66, MSc, 70, PhD(chem), 77. *Prof Exp:* Res asst, Hebrew Univ, 67-74; fel polymers, Inst Polymer Sci, Akron Univ, 78-81; ADVAN SCIENTIST, OWENS CORNING FIBERGLAS TECH CTR, GRANVILLE, OHIO, 81- *Mem:* Adhesion Soc. *Res:* Chemical and physical properties of polymers and graft-copolymers; absorption and emission spectroscopy of doped inorganic glasses; characteristics of glasses as possible semiconductors; mechanism of adhesion of elastomers and thermosets to inorganic substances. *Mailing Add:* 266 Sherwood Downs S Newark OH 43055

ECKSTEIN, YORAM, b Krakow, Poland, Jan 24, 38; Israel citizen; m 64; c 3. GEOTHERMICS & HYDROGEOLOGY. *Educ:* Hebrew Univ, BSc, 59, MSc, 65, PhD(geol), 77. *Prof Exp:* Hydrogeologist, 62-63; sr hydrogeologist, Geol Surv Israel, 63-74; vis scientist geol, Mass Inst Technol, 74-75; sr hydrogeologist geothermics, Hydro-Search Inc, Reno, 75-76; assoc prof, 76-81, PROF GEOL, KENT STATE UNIV, 81- *Concurrent Pos:* Sr consult, Ministry of Agr, Repub of Korea, 66-67; sr hydrogeologist, Geol Surv Israel, 74-78; sr consult, Hydro-Search Inc, 76-, Geonomics Inc, 77-78 & Int Eng Co, Inc, 78-; vis staff mem, Los Alamos Sci Lab, 77-80. *Mem:* Geol Soc Am; Am Inst Prof Geologists; Am Geophys Union; Nat Water Well Asn; Geothermal Resources Coun. *Res:* Geothermal exploration; hydro-geochemistry; terrestrial heat flow; geotectonics. *Mailing Add:* Dept of Geol Kent State Univ Kent OH 44242

ECKSTROM, DONALD JAMES, b St James, Minn. CHEMICAL PHYSICS, LASERS. *Educ:* Univ Minn, BS, 61, MS, 62; Stanford Univ, PhD(aerophysics), 71. *Prof Exp:* Aerodynamics engr, Lockheed Missiles & Space Co, 62-68; CHEM PHYSICIST, SRI INT, 70- *Mem:* Combustion Inst. *Res:* Laser development; visible chemical lasers; energy transfer; vibrational relaxation of small molecules; gas-phase reactions. *Mailing Add:* 331 Grove Dr Portola Valley CA 94025

ECOBICHON, DONALD JOHN, b Lindsay, Ont, June 21, 37; m 60; c 2. BIOCHEMICAL PHARMACOLOGY. *Educ:* Univ Toronto, BScPhm, 60, MA, 62, PhD(pharmacol), 64. *Prof Exp:* Demonstr pharmacol, Fac Med, Univ Toronto, 60-64; from asst prof to assoc prof, Ont Vet Col, Univ Guelph, 65-66, assoc prof pharmacol, Dalhousie Univ, 69-77; PROF PHARMACOL, McGILL UNIV, 77- *Concurrent Pos:* Nat Res Coun Can fel protein chem, 64-65. *Mem:* Soc Toxicol Can; Pharmacol Soc Can; NY Acad Sci; Soc Toxicol. *Res:* Study of drug hydrolysis by tissue esterases of various mammalian species; pharmacodynamics; mechanism of action; toxicology of chlorinated hydrocarbon and organophosphorus insecticides. *Mailing Add:* Dept of Pharmacol & Therapeut McGill Univ Montreal Can

ECONOMIDES, MICHAEL JOHN, b Famagusta, Cyprus, Sept 6, 49; m 76; c 2. PETROLEUM ENGINEERING. *Educ:* Univ Kans, BS, 74, MS, 76; Univ Calif, Berkeley, Stanford Univ, PhD(petrol eng), 81. *Prof Exp:* Process engr, Celanese Chem Co, 74-75; res asst, Univ Kans, 75-76; res assoc chem eng, Univ Calif, Berkeley, 76-78; res, Stanford Univ, 78-80; ASST PROF PETROL ENG, UNIV ALASKA, FAIRBANKS, 80- *Concurrent Pos:* Reservoir engr, Shell Oil Co, 72; chem engr, Black & Veatch Consult Eng, 76; wall testing, Ente Nazionale per l Enargia Eletrica, 78; reservoir engr, Hughes Aircraft Co & Shell Oil Co, 79. *Mem:* Soc Petrol Engrs. *Res:* Wall test analysis; petroleum and geothermal reservoir engineering; separation process and cold temperature rheology. *Mailing Add:* Dept Petrol Eng 107 Brooks Bldg Univ Alaska Fairbanks AK 99701

ECONOMOS, GEO(RGE), b Haverhill, Mass, Aug 22, 19; m 47; c 2. METALLURGY, CERAMICS. *Educ:* Northeastern Univ, BS, 49; Mass Inst Technol, SM, 51, ScD(ceramics), 54. *Prof Exp:* Asst prof metall, Mass Inst Technol, 54-61; electronics consult res admin, Allen-Bradley Co, Milwaukee, 61-71, mgr, Mat Dept, Sprague Elec Co, Grafton, Wis, 72-77; SR STAFF OFFICER, NAT ACAD SCI, NAT MAT ADV BD, WASHINGTON, 77- *Concurrent Pos:* Vis prof, Sch Appl Sci & Eng, Univ Wis, Milwaukee, 71. *Mem:* Fel AAAS; Am Chem Soc; fel Am Ceramic Soc; Am Soc Metals. *Res:* Ceramic dielectrics, ferroelectrics and ferromagnetics; powder metallurgy; polymers. *Mailing Add:* 6204 Bradley Blvd Bethesda MD 20817

ECONOMOU, ELEFTHERIOS NICKOLAS, b Athens, Greece, Feb 7, 40; m 66. SOLID STATE PHYSICS, SURFACE PHYSICS. *Educ:* Polytech Inst Athens, dipl, 63; Univ Chicago, MS, 67, PhD(solid state physics), 69. *Prof Exp:* Res asst physics, Univ Chicago, 66-69, res assoc, 69-70; asst prof, 70-73, assoc prof, 73-80, PROF PHYSICS, UNIV VA, 80- *Concurrent Pos:* Expert/consult, Naval Res Lab, 74-; vis assoc prof physics, Univ Chicago, 75-76. *Mem:* Am Phys Soc; Greek Soc Engrs; Sigma Xi. *Res:* Properties of disordered systems, mainly transport; surface plasmons in various geometries; electron-electron correlations and magnetic properties; amorphous and crystalline semiconductors. *Mailing Add:* Dept of Physics Univ of Va Charlottesville VA 22901

ECONOMOU, STEVEN GEORGE, b Chicago, Ill, July 4, 22; m 50; c 3. SURGICAL ONCOLOGY. *Educ:* Hahnemann Med Col, MD, 47. *Prof Exp:* From intern med to resident orthop, St Francis Hosp, Evanston, Ill, 47-50; resident surg, Presby Hosp, Chicago, 50-52 & 54; asst prof, 54-62, assoc prof, 62-68, CLIN PROF SURG, UNIV ILL COL MED, 68-; prof surg, 71-81, JACK FRASER PROF SURG, RUSH MED COL, 81- *Concurrent Pos:* Fel path, Cook County Hosp, Chicago, 49; from asst attend surgeon to assoc attend surgeon, Presby-St Luke's Hosp, 57-65, attend surgeon, 65-, dir lab surg res, 65-69. *Mem:* AMA; Am Asn Cancer Res; Am Surg Asn; Soc Head & Neck Surgeons; Soc Surg Oncol. *Res:* Cancer surgery. *Mailing Add:* 3118 Melrose Ct Wilmette IL 60091

ECONOMY, GEORGE, b Detroit, Mich, Jan 7, 27; m 59; c 4. METALLURGY, CORROSION. *Educ:* Wayne State Univ, BS, 56; Ohio State Univ, PhD(metall eng), 60. *Prof Exp:* Engr finishes, Alcoa Res Lab, 60-64; engr corrosion, Inco Res Lab, 64-68; SR ENGR PHYS CHEM, WESTINGHOUSE RES & DEVELOP CTR, 68- *Mem:* Am Soc Metals; Nat Asn Corrosion Engrs. *Res:* High temperature corrosion of power plant materials; high temperature chemistry relevant to power plants. *Mailing Add:* Westinghouse Res & Develop Ctr Beulah Rd Pittsburgh PA 15235

ECONOMY, JAMES, b Detroit, Mich, Mar 28, 29; m 61; c 4. ORGANIC CHEMISTRY. *Educ:* Wayne State Univ, BS, 50; Univ Md, PhD(chem), 54. *Prof Exp:* Res assoc polymer res & Marvel fel, Univ Ill, 54-56; gen res leader in charge res Semet-Solvay Petrochem Div, Allied Chem Corp, 56-60; mgr chem dept, Res Develop Div, Carborundum Co, 60-70, mgr res br, 70-74, corp scientist, 74-75; MGR ORG & POLYMER RES, IBM, CORP, 75- *Concurrent Pos:* Lectr, Canisius Col, 61-62; adj prof, State Univ NY Buffalo, 74- *Honors & Awards:* Schoellkopf Gold Medal, Am Chem Soc, 72; fourteen IR 100 Awards, Indust Res Mag, 66-75. *Mem:* AAAS; Am Chem Soc; fel Am Inst Chem; NY Acad Sci. *Res:* New polymers-high temperature, ionic, thermosetting and photoconductive; new fibers-reinforcing, flame resistant, superconducting, refractory and for pollution control; ceramic composites; carbon film hyperfilter; polymer characterization; structure property relationships. *Mailing Add:* IBM Corp K42-282 Monterey & Cottle Rd San Jose CA 95114

EDAMURA, FRED Y, b Vancouver, BC, Jan 25, 39; m 62; c 4. ORGANIC CHEMISTRY, ANALYTICAL CHEMISTRY. *Educ:* Univ Alta, BS, 60; Johns Hopkins Univ, MA, 62, PhD(org chem), 65. *Prof Exp:* Res chemist, Halogens Res Lab, Midland, Mich, 65-72; sr res chemist, 72, res specialist, Ag-Org Res, Walnut Creek, Calif, 72-74, res specialist & proj mgr, 74-79, group leader, 79-82, RES MGR, WESTERN DIV RES, DOW CHEM CO, PITTSBURG, CALIF, 82- *Mem:* Am Chem Soc; Sigma Xi. *Res:* Organic synthesis; terpene, carbene and organic fluorine chemistry; synthesis of biologically active compounds; organic process research; analytical chemistry. *Mailing Add:* Western Div Res Lab Dow Chem Co PO Box 1398 Pittsburg CA 94565

EDBERG, STEPHEN CHARLES, b New York, NY, Mar 13, 45; m 69; c 2. MICROBIOLOGY, IMMUNOLOGY. *Educ:* Lehigh Univ, BA, 67; Hofstra Univ, MA, 68; State Univ NY Buffalo, NIH fel & PhD(microbiol), 71; Am Acad Microbiol, dipl, 74. *Prof Exp:* Asst prof microbiol & immunol, 71-75, ASST PROF MICROBIOL & IMMUNOL & PATH, ALBERT EINSTEIN COL MED, 75-; ASSOC DIR MICROBIOL, MONTEFIORE HOSP MED CTR, 71- *Concurrent Pos:* Montefiore Hosp Med Ctr fel, Univ Wash, 72; adj assoc prof, City Univ New York, 74- *Mem:* Am Soc Microbiol; Soc Exp Biol Med; NY Acad Sci. *Res:* Theoretical and applied microbiology; immunology of tumors, transplants and dextran. *Mailing Add:* 111 E 210th St New York NY 10467

EDDE, HOWARD JASPER, b Page City, Kans, Dec 14, 37; m 61; c 3. CIVIL ENGINEERING. *Educ:* Kans State Univ, BS, 59; Univ Kans, MS, 61; Univ Tex, Austin, PhD(civil eng), 67. *Prof Exp:* Regional engr, Nat Coun Paper Indust Air & Stream Improvement, 62-64; mem staff, La State Univ, Baton Rouge, 64-66; proj engr, Roy F Weston, West Chester, Pa, 66-67; regional mgr, Nat Coun Paper Indust Air & Stream Improvement, 67-70; vpres, Eko No, Inc Consult Engrs, 70-74; AFFIL PROF, UNIV WASH, SEATTLE, 72-; PRES, HOWARD EDDE, INC ENGRS, 74- *Concurrent Pos:* Lectr, Johns Hopkins Univ, Baltimore, 67-70. *Mem:* Tech Asn Pulp & Paper Asn; Water Pollution Control Asn; Am Soc Civil Engrs. *Res:* Research, design and operation of aerated stabilization basin to treat domestic sewage; development of pulp mill in-plant pollution control techniques. *Mailing Add:* 1402 140th Place NE Bellevue WA 98007

EDDINGER, CHARLES ROBERT, b Emlenton, Pa, Feb 21, 39. ORNITHOLOGY, ECOLOGY. *Educ:* Clarion State Col, BSc, 61; Univ Hawaii, MS, 67, PhD(zool), 70. *Prof Exp:* Instr biol, Kingswood Sch, Kalaw, Burma, 61-64; teacher sci, Mt Pleasant Sch Syst, Mich, 64-65; INSTR ZOOL, HONOLULU COMMUNITY COL, 71- *Concurrent Pos:* Res consult, Res Comt Environ Ctr, Univ Hawaii, 72-74; environ consult, Parsons-Brinckerhoff-Hirota Assocs; wildlife biologist, Bur Fisheries & Wildlife, US Dept Interior; researcher, Chapman Mem Fund grant & Eastern Bird-Banding Asn grant. *Mem:* Am Ornithologists' Union; Cooper Ornith Soc; Wilson Ornith Soc; Am Fedn Avicult; Avicult Soc. *Res:* Breeding biology of Hawaii's endemic birds. *Mailing Add:* 156 Forest Ridge Way Honolulu HI 96822

EDDINGER, RALPH TRACY, b Wilkes-Barre, Pa, Feb 5, 22; m 45, 72; c 4. CHEMICAL ENGINEERING, FUEL TECHNOLOGY. *Educ:* Pa State Univ, BS, 42; Ohio State Univ, MS, 47, PhD(metall), 48. *Prof Exp:* Operating engr, Koppers Co, Inc, 42-46; res engr, Consolidation Coal Co, 48-51; mgr res lab, Eastern Gas & Fuel Assocs, 51-61; sr res engr, FMC Corp, 61-66, mgr proj coed, 66-72; tech/eng mgr, Cogas Develop Co, 72-81; MGR PILOT FACIL, FMC CORP, 81- *Concurrent Pos:* Chmn, Gordon Res Conf on Coal Sci, 69. *Honors & Awards:* Storch Award, Am Chem Soc, 74. *Mem:* Am Chem Soc; Am Inst Chem Engrs; Brit Inst Fuel; Am Inst Mining, Metall & Petrol Engrs. *Res:* Industrial high-temperature and fluidized-bed low-temperature carbonization of coal; coal processing and utilization; chemical process research and development. *Mailing Add:* FMC Corp PO Box 8 Princeton NJ 08540

EDDINGTON, CARL LEE, b Tulsa, Okla, Dec 26, 32; m 58; c 3. BIOCHEMISTRY, SCIENCE EDUCATION. *Educ:* Univ Tulsa, BS, 55; St Louis Univ, PhD(biochem), 68. *Prof Exp:* Chemist, Indust Serv Div, Dow Chem Co, 58-62; res chemist, Samuel Roberts Noble Found, 66-71; ASSOC PROF CHEM, E CENT OKLA STATE UNIV, 71- *Mem:* Sigma Xi; Am Chem Soc. *Res:* Tumor-host relationships, particularly leukocyte production of humoral factors, acute phase globulins, fever, iron metabolism, enzymes, endotoxins and immunology; biochemistry of lactation, particularly hormones, nucleic acid and protein biosynthesis. *Mailing Add:* Dept of Chem ECent Univ Ada OK 74820

EDDLEMAN, ELVIA ETHERIDGE, JR, b Birmingham, Ala, Oct 20, 22; c 1. INTERNAL MEDICINE, CARDIOLOGY. *Educ:* Howard Col, BS, 44; Emory Univ, MD, 48; Am Bd Internal Med, dipl, 56. *Prof Exp:* Intern, Grady Mem Hosp, Atlanta, Ga, 48-49; resident, Parkland Hosp, Dallas, Tex, 49-50; from instr to assoc prof, 53-62, prof, 62-81, EMER PROF MED, SCH MED, UNIV ALA, 81- *Concurrent Pos:* Fel, Sch Med, Univ Ala & res fel, Med Col Ala, 52-53; asst chief med & chief cardiovasc sect, Vet Admin Hosp, 54-57, assoc chief of staff res, 54-, actg chief cardiovasc sect & chief med serv, 57-62. *Mem:* Fel Am Col Cardiol; fel Am Col Physicians; Am Fedn Clin Res; Am Heart Asn; Ballistocardiographic Res Soc. *Res:* Cardiovascular research. *Mailing Add:* Dept of Med Univ of Ala Sch of Med Birmingham AL 35233

EDDLEMAN, LEE E, b Broadus, Mont, May 8, 37; m 58; c 3. RANGE ECOLOGY. *Educ:* Colo State Univ, BS, 60, MS, 62, PhD(plant ecol), 67. *Prof Exp:* Assoc prof, 63-77, PROF RANGE SCI, SCH FORESTRY, UNIV MONT, 77- *Mem:* Soc Range Mgt. *Res:* Evaluation of native plant species for reclamation of coal mine spoils; northern Rocky Mountain shrub ecology. *Mailing Add:* Sch of Forestry Univ of Mont Missoula MT 59801

EDDLEMON, GERALD KIRK, b Washington, DC, Sept 16, 45; m 74; c 2. ENVIRONMENTAL IMPACT ANALYSIS. *Educ:* Univ Tenn, Knoxville, BS, 70, MS, 74. *Prof Exp:* Grad teaching asst zool & biol, Univ Tenn, 71-74; RES ASSOC, OAK RIDGE NAT LAB, 74- *Mem:* Ecol Soc Am; Am Fisheries Soc. *Res:* Risk analyses and environmental impact assessment of unconventional energy technologies (coal conversion, oil shale, and geothermal development); transport, fate and effects of trace contaminants in aquatic ecosystems. *Mailing Add:* Bldg 1505 Oak Ridge Nat Lab PO Box X Oak Ridge TN 37830

EDDS, GEORGE TYSON, b Heidenheimer, Tex, Jan 9, 13; m 31; c 3. PHARMACOLOGY, VETERINARY MEDICINE. *Educ:* Tex A&M Univ, BS & DVM, 36, MS, 38; Univ Minn, PhD(pharmacol), 52. *Prof Exp:* From instr to prof physiol & pharmacol, Tex A&M Univ, 35-50; vpres, Ft Dodge Labs, Iowa, 50-62; PROF VET SCI, UNIV FLA, 62-, VETERINARIAN, INST FOOD & AGR SCI. *Mem:* Am Vet Med Asn; US Animal Health Asn. *Res:* Pharmacology-toxicology drug actions on animals; chemotherapy; anthelmintics; heavy metals; poisonous plants as hazards to animals; residues as hazards for mankind; aflatoxins as carcinogens. *Mailing Add:* Dept of Prev Med Univ of Fla Gainesville FL 32601

EDDS, LOUISE LUCKENBILL, b Lebanon, Pa, Nov 19, 36; m 71. DEVELOPMENTAL BIOLOGY, NEUROBIOLOGY. *Educ:* Oberlin Col, BA, 58; Brown Univ, PhD(biol), 64. *Prof Exp:* Arthritis Found res fel arthritis & connective tissue dis, Sch Med, Boston Univ, 65-66; instr res dermat, 66-68; sci fel, Hubrecht Lab, Royal Netherlands Acad Sci & Letters, 68-69; asst prof biol sci, Smith Col, 69-75; instr, Dept Neuropath, Harvard Med Sch, 75-77; ASSOC PROF ZOOL & BIOMED SCI, OHIO UNIV, ATHENS, 77- *Mem:* AAAS; Am Soc Zool; Soc Develop Biol; Soc Neurosci. *Res:* development of flat fish optic tectum; histogenesis of sympathetic neurons; migration and differentiation of neural crestcells. *Mailing Add:* Col Osteop Med Ohio Univ Athens OH 45701

EDDY, CARLTON ANTHONY, b Boston, Mass, July 12, 42; m 68; c 2. REPRODUCTIVE PHYSIOLOGY. *Educ:* Merrimack Col, BA, 67; Univ Mass, MS, 70, PhD(animal sci), 73. *Prof Exp:* Instr obstet & gynec, 73-75, instr physiol, 74-75, asst prof obstet & gynec & asst prof physiol, 75-79, ASSOC PROF OBSTET & GYNEC, UNIV TEX HEALTH SCI CTR, SAN ANTONIO, 79- *Concurrent Pos:* Surg consult, Bexar Co Med Dist, 77- & Audey Murphy Vet Admin Hosp, 80- *Mem:* Soc Study Reproduction; Soc Gynec Invest; Am Fertil Soc; Soc Study Fertil. *Res:* Investigation of mechanisms concerned with the control of fertility; reproductive physiology and endocrinology of the non-human primate; tubal physiology; tuboplastic microsurgery. *Mailing Add:* Dept of Obstet & Gynec Univ of Tex Health Sci Ctr San Antonio TX 78284

EDDY, DENNIS EUGENE, b Pawnee City, Nebr, Jan 12, 35; m 59; c 1. BIOCHEMISTRY. *Educ:* Univ Omaha, BA, 66; Univ Nebr-Omaha, PhD(biochem), 73. *Prof Exp:* Asst instr chem, Univ Omaha, 66-68; res assoc biochem, Med Ctr, Univ Nebr, Omaha, 73-77; ASSOC STAFF BIOCHEMIST, QUAKER OATS-JOHN STUART RES LABS, 77- *Concurrent Pos:* Instr anal chem, Col St Mary, Omaha, 73-74, adv undergrad res proj, 73-; co-adv grad-undergrad res proj, Dept Psychol, Univ Nebr-Omaha, 74-77; instr gen chem, Metrop Tech Community Col, Omaha, 75-77.

Mem: Am Chem Soc; Am Oil Chemists' Soc; Geront Soc; Am Aging Asn. *Res:* Aging, with emphasis on antioxidants and other dietary components as they affect biological systems. *Mailing Add:* 614 Pamela Ct Wauconda IL 60084

EDDY, EDWARD MITCHELL, b Parsons, Kans, Feb 9, 40; m 63; c 2. CELL BIOLOGY, DEVELOPMENTAL BIOLOGY. *Educ:* Kans State Univ, BS, 62, MS, 64; Univ Tex, PhD(anat), 67. *Prof Exp:* Fel anat, Harvard Med Sch, 67-69, instr, 69-70; asst prof, 70-76, vchmn, 75-78, actg chmn, 78-81, ASSOC PROF BIOL STRUCT, UNIV WASH, 76- *Concurrent Pos:* Prin investr, NSF & NIH res grants; fel, NSF & NIH. *Mem:* Am Soc Cell Biol; Am Asn Anat; Soc Develop Biol; Am Soc Zool; Int Soc Develop Biologists. *Res:* Origin and potential of germ cell line, fertilization and initiation of development. *Mailing Add:* Dept Biol Struct Univ Wash Seattle WA 98195

EDDY, GEORGE AMOS, b Unity, Sask, June 8, 28; m 50; c 5. METEOROLOGY, CLIMATOLOGY. *Educ:* Univ BC, BASc, 50; Univ Toronto, MA, 51; McGill Univ, PhD(meteorol), 63. *Prof Exp:* From asst prof to assoc prof atmospheric sci, Univ Tex, Austin, 63-68; PROF METEOROL & ENVIRONMENTAL DESIGN, UNIV OKLA, 68-; DIR, OKLA CLIMATOL SURV & STATE CLIMATOLOGIST, 78- *Concurrent Pos:* Vis assoc prof, Mass Inst Technol, 67-68; pres, Amos Eddy, Inc, 81- *Mem:* Am Asn State Climatologists; Royal Meteorol Soc. *Res:* Operational weather modification evaluation; statistical climatology; urban-rural ecosystem modeling; resource management modeling; applied climatology. *Mailing Add:* Dept Meteorol Univ Okla Norman OK 73069

EDDY, GERALD ARTHUR, b Durand, Mich, Oct 11, 31; m 64; c 2. VIROLOGY. *Educ:* Mich State Univ, BS, 53, DVM, 55; Univ Notre Dame, PhD(microbiol), 68. *Prof Exp:* US Army, 57-, vet officer pub health, 57-62, lab officer virol, Walter Reed Army Inst Res, Univ Notre Dame, 62-68, virologist, Med Res Univ, Panama, 68-72, CHIEF VIROL DIV, MED RES INST INFECTIOUS DIS, US ARMY, 72- *Concurrent Pos:* Am Soc Microbiol, Latin Am vis prof, Med Col, Univ Buenos Aires, 78; consult, WHO, 81- *Mem:* Am Soc Microbiol; Am Vet Med Asn; Am Soc Trop Med & Hyg; Am Asn Pathologists; Arg Soc Virol. *Res:* Viral pathogenesis and immunity; vaccine development against hazardous viruses; epidemiology of zoonotic viruses; viral hemorrhage fevers. *Mailing Add:* US Army Med Res Inst of Infectious Dis Frederick MD 21701

EDDY, HUBERT ALLEN, b Boston, Mass, June 2, 30; m 59; c 2. RADIOBIOLOGY, PATHOLOGY. *Educ:* Boston Univ, BA, 52, MA, 54; Univ Rochester, PhD(radiation biol), 64. *Prof Exp:* Instr human ecol, Boston Univ, 53-54; from res asst to res assoc radiation biol, 57-63, instr, 64-68, ASST PROF RADIOL, SCH MED & DENT, UNIV ROCHESTER, 68- *Concurrent Pos:* Mem, Late Effects Group NAm. *Mem:* AAAS; Sigma Xi; Radiation Res Soc; Am Asn Univ Prof; Int Soc Oxygen Transport to Tissue. *Res:* Study of mechanisms of effect of ionizing radiations of mammaliam tissue and organ systems; tumor angiogenesis and the effect of ionizing radiations on tumor vasculature; comparative radiation oncology; radiation pathology. *Mailing Add:* Sch of Med & Dent Univ of Rochester Rochester NY 14642

EDDY, JERRY KENNETH, b Wheeling, WVa, Aug 17, 40; m 62; c 3. NUCLEAR PHYSICS. *Educ:* WLiberty State Col, AB, 62; WVa Univ, MS, 64, PhD(physics), 67. *Prof Exp:* Asst prof, 67-74, assoc prof, 74-78, PROF PHYSICS, INDIANA UNIV PA, 79- *Res:* Van de Graaff accelerators; nuclear spectroscopy; neutron induced charged particle reactions using the deuteron tritium reaction; activation analysis; charged particle induced x-ray analysis. *Mailing Add:* RD 5 Box 25 Indiana PA 15701

EDDY, JOHN ALLEN, b Pawnee City, Nebr, Mar 25, 31; m 53; c 4. ASTROPHYSICS, SOLAR PHYSICS. *Educ:* US Naval Acad, BS, 53; Univ Colo, PhD(astrogeophys), 62. *Prof Exp:* Physicist, Nat Bur Standards, 62-63, SR SCIENTIST, HIGH ALTITUDE OBSERV, 63- *Concurrent Pos:* Prof Adjoint, Univ Colo, 63-, res assoc, Harvard-Smithsonian Ctr Astrophys, 77-79. 67-70. *Honors & Awards:* Boulder Scientist Award, 65. *Mem:* Am Astron Soc; AAAS; Am Geophys Union; Sigma Xi; Int Astron Union. *Res:* Infrared astronomy; history of astronomy; archaeo-astronomy. *Mailing Add:* High Altitude Observ Box 3000 Boulder CO 80307

EDDY, LOWELL PERRY, b Portland, Ore, Nov 25, 20; m 46; c 3. INORGANIC CHEMISTRY. *Educ:* Ore State Col, BS, 42, MS, 48; Purdue Univ, PhD(chem), 52. *Prof Exp:* Instr chem, Univ Wyo, 50-51; res assoc & instr, Reed Col, 52-53; res chemist cellulose, Puget Sound Pulp & Timber Co, 53-57; asst prof, 57-64, ASSOC PROF CHEM, WESTERN WASH STATE COL, 64- *Concurrent Pos:* Am Chem Soc, Petrol Res Fund int faculty award & hon res asst, Univ Col, Univ London, 64; res assoc, Sch Chem, Univ New South Wales, 69-70 & vis UNESCO lectr, 75. *Mem:* Am Chem Soc. *Res:* Analytical methods in the sulfite pulp industry; coordination compounds of transition elements. *Mailing Add:* 206 N Garden St Bellingham WA 98225

EDDY, NELSON WALLACE, b Burford, Ont, Jan, 15, 39; m 66; c 2. NUCLEAR PHYSICS. *Educ:* McMaster Univ, BA, 61; Univ Mass, Amherst, MS, 63; Ariz State Univ, PhD(nuclear physics), 69. *Prof Exp:* Asst prof, 68-74, ASSOC PROF PHYSICS, CONCORDIA UNIV, SIR GEORGE WILLIAMS CAMPUS, MONTREAL, 74- *Concurrent Pos:* Vis prof, Foster Radiation Lab, McGill Univ, Montreal, 75-76. *Mem:* Can Radiation Protection Asn; Am Phys Soc; Am Inst Physics. *Res:* Nuclear spectroscopy of (p,xn) reactions, fission products, fast neutron reactions and microdosimetry; Monte Carlo applications to shielding and radiation effects in biological materials. *Mailing Add:* Dept of Physics Sir George Williams Campus Montreal PQ H3G 1M8 Can

EDDY, ROBERT DEVEREUX, b Providence, RI, Oct 15, 14; m 39; c 3. INORGANIC CHEMISTRY. *Educ:* Brown Univ, AB, 35; Princeton Univ, AM & PhD(chem), 38. *Prof Exp:* Asst chem, Princeton Univ, 37-39; instr, Dartmouth Col, 39; from instr to assoc prof, 39-53, prof, 53-80, EMER PROF

CHEM, TUFTS UNIV, 80- *Concurrent Pos:* Consult, Educ Testing Serv, 54-75. *Res:* Phase rule studies; vapor pressure of water above solutions or salt hydrate systems; solubilities in ordinary water and deuterium water. *Mailing Add:* 4 Fairview Terrace Winchester MA 01890

EDDY, THOMAS A, b Parsons, Kans, Dec 31, 34; m 64; c 1. ENTOMOLOGY, WILDLIFE MANAGEMENT. *Educ:* Kans State Univ, BS, 57, PhD(entom), 70; Univ Ariz, MS, 59. *Prof Exp:* From instr to asst prof, 60-71, ASSOC PROF BIOL, EMPORIA STATE UNIV, 71- *Mem:* Wildlife Soc; Conserv Educ Asn. *Res:* Hymenoptera ecology and behavior. *Mailing Add:* R R 1 Emporia KS 66801

EDDY, WILLIAM FROST, b Boston, Mass, Sept 18, 44; m 78. STATISTICS. *Educ:* Princeton Univ, AB, 71; Yale Univ, MA, 72, MPhil, 73, PhD(statist), 76. *Prof Exp:* asst prof, 76-80, ASSOC PROF STATIST, CARNEGIE-MELLON UNIV, 80- *Concurrent Pos:* NSF grant, 78-80. *Mem:* Am Statist Asn; INst Math Statist; Am Math Soc; fel Royal Statist Soc; AAAS. *Res:* Data analysis; statistical computation; applied and mathematical statistics. *Mailing Add:* Dept of Statist Schenley Park Pittsburgh PA 15213

EDE, ALAN WINTHROP, b Stamford, Conn, Jan 16, 33; m 57; c 3. MICROELECTRONICS. *Educ:* Worcester Polytech Inst, BS, 55; Univ Maine, Orono, MS, 63; Ore State Univ, PhD(elec eng), 68. *Prof Exp:* Engr, Raytheon Mfg Co, 55-60; from instr to assoc prof elec eng, Univ Maine, Orono, 60-71; ASSOC PROF INDUST EDUC, ORE STATE UNIV, 74- *Concurrent Pos:* Pres, Dirigo Electronics Eng, 71- *Mem:* Inst Elec & Electronics Engrs; Am Soc Eng Educ. *Res:* Electrofishing. *Mailing Add:* 1307 NW Buchanan Corvallis OR 97331

EDEIKEN, JACK, b Philadelphia, Pa, May 25, 23; m 42; c 5. RADIOLOGY. *Educ:* Univ Pa, MD, 47; Am Bd Radiol, dipl, 51. *Prof Exp:* Asst prof, Sch Med, Univ Pa, 51-58; assoc prof, 58-67, PROF RADIOL, THOMAS JEFFERSON UNIV, 67-; CHIEF DIAG DIV, UNIV HOSP, 69-, CHMN DEPT RADIOL, 71- *Concurrent Pos:* Consult, Vet Admin Hosps, Wilmington, Del, 55- & Philadelphia, Pa, 63-, consult, US Air Force. *Res:* Radiol Soc NAm; fel Am Col Radiol; AMA. *Mailing Add:* Dept of Radiol Thomas Jefferson Univ Hosp Philadelphia PA 19107

EDELBERG, ROBERT, b NJ, Aug 2, 21; m 44; c 4. PSYCHOPHYSIOLOGY. *Educ:* Rutgers Univ, BS, 42; Univ Pa, PhD(physiol), 49. *Prof Exp:* asst prof physiol, Long Island Univ, 49-51; from asst prof to assoc prof, Col Med, Baylor Univ, 56-63; prof psychophysiol & physiol, Med Ctr, Univ Okla, 63-70; PROF PSYCHIAT, RUTGERS MED SCH & PROF PSYCHOL, GRAD SCH, RUTGERS UNIV, 70- *Concurrent Pos:* Res & develop officer, Aero Med Lab, Wright Air Develop Ctr, 51-55; Sr res fel, USPHS, 58-62; assoc ed, Psychophysiol 65-; mem, Exp Psychol Study Sect, NIH, 66-69; consult ed, J Comp & Physiol Psychol, 66-70. *Honors & Awards:* Distinguished Contrib Psychophysiol Award, Soc Psychophysiol Res, 74. *Mem:* Am Physiol Soc; Soc Psychophysiol Res (pres, 65-66); fel Am Psychol Soc; Am Psychosom Soc. *Res:* Psychophysiological adaptation; electrodermal physiology and measurement; cardiovascular processes and behavior. *Mailing Add:* Dept of Psychiat CMDNJ Rutgers Med Sch Piscataway NJ 08854

EDELBERG, SEYMOUR, b Brooklyn, NY, Nov 21, 23; m 51; c 2. OPTICAL PHYSICS. *Educ:* City Col New York, BEE, 44; Polytech Inst Brooklyn, MEE, 47, DEE, 53. *Prof Exp:* Res engr, Haskins Labs, 44-47; proj engr, Sperry Gyroscope Co, 49-52; head, Electronic Div, Balco Res Labs, 52-55; assoc group leader, 55-69, GROUP LEADER ADVAN TECH & SYSTS, LINCOLN LAB, MASS INST TECHNOL, 69- *Mem:* AAAS; Am Phys Soc; Inst Elec & Electronics Engrs. *Res:* Antennas; radar scattering; reentry technology; electromagnetic and microwave theory; optics and lasers. *Mailing Add:* Lincoln Lab Mass Inst Technol Lexington MA 02173

EDELEN, DOMINIC GARDINER BOWLING, b Washington, DC, Jan 3, 33; m 54; c 6. APPLIED MATHEMATICS. *Educ:* Johns Hopkins Univ, BES, 54, MSE, 56, PhD, 65. *Prof Exp:* Jr instr math & mech, Johns Hopkins Univ, 54-56; engr, Martin Co, Md, 56-59; mem tech staff, Hughes Aircraft Co, Calif, 59-60; mem res staff, Rand Corp, 60-66; prof math, Purdue Univ, 66-69; PROF MATH & ASTRON, CTR APPLN MATH, LEHIGH UNIV, 69- *Mem:* Soc Eng Sci; Soc Natural Philos. *Res:* Theory and applications of Lie groups and exterior differential forms to problems in nonlinear partial differential equations and in mechanics; axiomatization of theoretical physics and the use of continuum mechanics and thermodynamics in relativity; non-local variational mechanics. *Mailing Add:* Ctr for Appln of Math Lehigh Univ Bethlehem PA 18015

EDELHAUSER, HENRY F, b Dover, NJ, Sept 9, 37; m 61; c 2. PHYSIOLOGY, OPHTHALMOLOGY. *Educ:* Paterson State Col, BA, 62; Mich State Univ, MS, 64, PhD(physiol), 66. *Prof Exp:* Lab technician, Warner Lambert Pharmaceut Res Inst, 62; asst physiol, Mich State Univ, 62-65; from instr to asst prof physiol & ophthal, 66-71, res assoc ophthal, 67-68, assoc prof physiol & ophthal, 71-75, PROF PHYSIOL & OPHTHAL, MED COL WIS, 75- *Concurrent Pos:* Fel physiol, Med Col Wis, 66-67; Nat Eye Inst grant, 69-81; prin investr, Wis Dept Nat Res grant, 69-71. *Mem:* Am Soc Biol Sci; Am Soc Zool; Asn Res Vision & Ophthal; Am Physiol Soc. *Mem:* Membrane physiology; physiology and biochemistry of the eye; pathophysiology of the eye; fish physiology and eye disease; ocular toxicology; physiological effects of vitrectomy; cellular toxicology of ophthalmic drugs. *Mailing Add:* Dept of Physiol & Ophthal Med Col of Wis Milwaukee WI 53226

EDELHEIT, LEWIS S, b Chicago, Ill, Aug 24, 42; m 65; c 2. SOLID STATE PHYSICS, GENERAL MEDICAL SCIENCE. *Educ:* Univ Ill, BS, 64, MS, 65, PhD(physics), 69. *Prof Exp:* Physicist, Gen Elec Corp Res & Develop, 69-77, MGR COMPUTERIZED TOMOGRAPHY PROD ENG, GEN ELEC MED SYSTS DIV, GEN ELEC CORP, 77- *Mem:* Sigma Xi; Am Phys Soc. *Res:* Medical imaging systems; computerized imaging systems. *Mailing Add:* Gen Elec Med Systs Div PO Box 414 Milwaukee WI 53201

EDELMAN, DAVID ANTHONY, biostatistics, see previous edition

EDELMAN, GERALD MAURICE, b New York, NY, July 1, 29; m 50; c 3. BIOCHEMISTRY. *Educ:* Ursinus Col, BS, 50; Univ Pa, MD, 54; Rockefeller Inst, PhD(biochem), 60. *Hon Degrees:* DSc, Univ Pa, 73; ScD, Ursinus Col, 74 & Williams Col, 79; MD, Univ Sienna, Italy, 74; DSc, Gustavus Adolphus Col, Minn, 75. *Prof Exp:* Med house officer, Mass Gen Hosp, 54-55; served to capt, M C AUS, 55-57; asst physician, Hosp of Rockefeller Inst, 57-60, mem fac, 60-, assoc dean grad studies, 63-66, prof, 66-74, VINCENT ASTOR DISTINGUISHED PROF, HOSP ROCKEFELLER UNIV, 74- *Concurrent Pos:* Chmn adv bd, Basel Inst Immunol, 70-, bd govs, Weizmann Inst Sci, 71-, bd trustees, Salk Inst Biol Studies; trustee, Rockefeller Br Fund, 72-; mem bd overseers, Fac Arts & Sci, Univ Pa; mem adv comt, Carnegie Inst Washington; mem bd sci overseers, Jackson Lab; assoc sci chmn, Neurosci Res Prog, 80, dir, Neurosci Inst, 81. *Honors & Awards:* Nobel Prize physiol or med, 72; recipient Spencer Morris Award, Univ Pa, 54; Alumni Award Ursinus Col, 69; Albert Einstein Commemorative Award Yeshiva Univ, 74; Buchman Mem Award, Cal Inst Technol, 75; Eli Lilly award biol chem, 65. *Mem:* Fel NY Acad Sci; Am Acad Art & Sci; Nat Acad Sci; Am Soc Cell Biol; Genetics Soc. *Res:* Research structure antibodies. *Mailing Add:* 35 E 85 St New York NY 10028

EDELMAN, ISIDORE SAMUEL, b New York, NY, July 23, 20; m 42; c 4. MEDICINE. *Educ:* Ind Univ, BA, 41, MD, 44. *Prof Exp:* Intern, Greenpoint Hosp, 44-45; resident physician, Montefiore Hosp, 47-48; from asst prof med to prof med & physiol, Sch Med, Univ Calif, San Francisco, 52-67, fac res lectr, 66-67, Samuel Neider res prof med, 67-78, prof biophys, 69-78; ROBERT WOOD JOHNSON JR PROF BIOCHEM & CHMN DEPT, COLUMBIA UNIV, 78- PROF MED, SCH MED, UNIV CALIF, SAN FRANCISCO, 67-, PROF BIOPHYS, 69- *Concurrent Pos:* Dazian Found fel, Montefiore Hosp, 48-49; AEC fel, Harvard Med Sch & Peter Bent Brigham Hosp, 49-50, Am Heart Asn fel, 50-52; sr res fel chem, Calif Inst Technol, 58-59; estab investr, Am Heart Asn, 52-57; chief med serv, San Francisco Gen Hosp, Univ Calif, 56-58; John Punnett Peters mem lectr, Sch Med, Yale Univ, 64; mem NIH study comt, Off Sci & Technol, 64; vis scientist, Weizmann Inst Sci, 65-66; res career awards comt, Nat Inst Gen Med Sci, 69-73; Harry T Dozor vis prof biochem, Ben-Gurion Univ, Israel, 80. *Honors & Awards:* Eli Lilly Award, Endocrine Soc, 69; Gregory Pincus Mem lectr, Worcester Found Exp Biol, 79; Mayo Soley Award, Western Soc Clin Res, 80; Homer W Smith Award, NY Heart Asn, 80. *Mem:* Nat Acad Sci; Am Fedn Clin Res; Endocrine Soc; Am Physiol Soc; Am Soc Clin Invest. *Res:* Body water and electrolyte metabolism; molecular biology of sodium/potassium transport; active transport across biological membranes; mechanism of action of steroid hormones, thyroid hormone and antidiuretic hormone. *Mailing Add:* Dept of Biochem 630 W 168th St New York NY 10032

EDELMAN, JULIAN, b New York, NY; m 55; c 4. QUALITY CONTROL. *Educ:* City Col New York, BBA, 51; Columbia Univ, MSIE, 61. *Prof Exp:* Supvr reliability eng, Loral Electronics, 53-57; dir reliability eng, Perkin Elmer Corp, 59-63; SR ENG SPECIALIST LOGISTICS & ECON ANAL, GTE SYLVANIA INC, 63- *Concurrent Pos:* Master lectr mgt, Boston Univ, 63-74 & Suffolk Univ, 68-; asst secy TC-56 & sr ed, Int Electrotech Comn. *Mem:* Fel Am Soc Qual Control; Soc Logistics Engrs; sr mem Inst Elec & Electronics Engrs. *Mailing Add:* GTE Sylvania Inc 77 A St Needham MA 02194

EDELMAN, LEONARD EDWARD, b Scranton, Pa, July 16, 13; m 43. POLYMER CHEMISTRY. *Educ:* Hobart Col, BA, 36; Univ Cincinnati, MA, 39, PhD(chem), 41. *Prof Exp:* Chemist, Eastman Kodak Co, NY, 36; chemist, Lake Erie Chem Co, Ohio, 37-38; chemist, Eastman Kodak Co, 39 & Amecco Chem Co, 40; res dir & vpres, Lake Erie Chem Co, 41-44; dir tech serv, Johnson & Johnson Co, NJ, 44; fel, Mellon Inst, 46-49; res dir, Medaseal Co & Med Iodine Labs, 49-51; eng mgr, Micarta Div, Westinghouse Elec Corp, 51-67, mgr polymer chem, Res & Develop Ctr, 67-77; RETIRED. *Concurrent Pos:* Consult elec indust, 77- CHEM, RES & DEVELOP CTR, WESTINGHOUSE ELEC CORP, 67- *Mem:* AAAS. *Res:* Polymers; coatings; laminates; electrical insulation; foams. *Mailing Add:* 718 MacFarlane Dr Pittsburgh PA 15235

EDELMAN, MARVIN, b New York, NY, Aug 22, 39; US & Israeli citizen; m 61; c 5. MOLECULAR BIOLOGY, MOLECULAR GENETICS. *Educ:* Yeshiva Univ, BA & BHL, 61; Brandeis Univ, PhD(biol), 65. *Prof Exp:* Res assoc & fel, Harvard Med Sch, 66-67; res assoc & fel biochem, 67-69, intermediate scientist plant genetics, 69-71, sr scientist plant genetics, Weizmann Inst Sci, 71-80, dir grad teaching labs biol, Feinberg Grad Sch, 72-81, ASSOC PROF PLANT GENETICS, WEIZMANN INST SCI, 81- *Concurrent Pos:* Vis scientist biol, Biol Labs, Harvard Univ, 76. *Mem:* Israel Bot Soc; Israel Biochem Soc; Am Asn Plant Physiologists; Europ Molecular Biol Orgn. *Res:* Assembly, processing and decay of chloroplast proteins and structure, function and photocontrol of proteins in the chloroplast membrane; cell-free translation of chloroplast messenger and analysis of chloroplast and mitochondrial DNA from plant cell cultures by restriction endonucleases; construction of cloned chloroplast DNA to analyze specific protein-coding sequences and restructuring of chloroplast DNA by genetic engineering. *Mailing Add:* Dept of Plant Genetics PO Box 26 Rehovot Israel

EDELMAN, ROBERT, b Brooklyn, NY, Apr 30, 42. ORGANIC CHEMISTRY, POLYMER CHEMISTRY. *Educ:* Brooklyn Col, BS, 63; Rutgers Univ, PhD(org chem), 69. *Prof Exp:* Fel, Univ Fla, 68-69; res chemist, 69-74, sr res chemist, Celanese Res Co, 74-79, RES ASSOC, CELANESE PLASTICS & SPECIALTIES CO, 79- *Mem:* Am Chem Soc; Soc Plastics Engrs. *Res:* Resin matrix materials for carbon fibers; polyacetals and polyesters; synthesis and evaluation. synthesis and evaluation. *Mailing Add:* Graphite Appl & Prod Develop 86 Morris Ave Summit NJ 07901

EDELMAN, SEYMOUR, b Jersey City, NJ, May 12, 14; m 48; c 4. MECHANICS, METEOROLOGY. *Educ:* NY Univ, BS, 46. *Prof Exp:* Observer meteorol, US Weather Bur, 37-43, meteorologist, 44-46; physicist acoust, Nat Bur Standards, 46-64, chief, Vibration Measurements Sect, 64-67, physicist, Instrumentation Appln Sect, 68-70, act chief, 70-71; RETIRED. *Mem:* Acoust Soc Am. *Res:* Use of optical methods to measure vibration; measurement of sound absorption and sound transmission; piezoelectric and pyroelectric effects in polymers. *Mailing Add:* 9115 Glenridge Rd Silver Spring MD 20910

EDELMAN, WALTER E(UGENE), JR, b Oregon, Ill, July 15, 33. MECHANICAL ENGINEERING. *Educ:* Univ Minn, BME, 56, MSME, 58; Ore State Univ, PhD(mech eng), 67. *Prof Exp:* Engr, Minneapolis Honeywell, Inc, 53-56; instr mech eng, Univ Minn, 57-58; mem tech staff, Hughes Aircraft Co, 58-61; instr mech eng, Ore State Univ, 61-66; from asst prof to assoc prof, 67-75, PROF MECH ENG, CALIF STATE UNIV, LONG BEACH, 75- *Honors & Awards:* Ralph R Teetor Ed Award, Soc Automotive Engrs, 68. *Mem:* Am Soc Mech Engrs; Am Soc Eng Educ. *Res:* Design in mechanical engineering; automotive engineering. *Mailing Add:* 20822 Woodlea Lane Huntington Beach CA 92646

EDELMANN, CHESTER M, JR, b New York, NY, Dec 26, 30; m 53; c 3. PEDIATRICS. *Educ:* Columbia Univ, AB, 51; Cornell Univ, MD, 55; Am Bd Pediat, dipl & cert pediat nephrology. *Prof Exp:* From asst instr to assoc prof, 57-70, chmn dept, 73-80, PROF PEDIAT, ALBERT EINSTEIN COL MED, 70-, ASSOC DEAN, 80- *Concurrent Pos:* Res fel renal physiol, Albert Einstein Col Med, 58-59, 61-63; NIH res career develop award, 63-68; mem med adv bd, Kidney Found NY, 69-; mem sci adv bd, Nat Kidney Found, 69-75, vchmn, 73-74, chmn, 74-76; mem kidney dis & nephrology index adv comt, NIH, 70-, gen med study sect B, 71-75, chmn, 73-75; mem sub-bd pediat nephrology, Am Bd Pediat, 73-77; mem coun on circulation, Am Heart Asn; mem ed bd, Pediat Res, Pediatrics, Kidney Int & The Kidney. *Mem:* AAAS; Am Acad Pediat; Am Soc Clin Invests; Am Physiol Soc; Soc Pediat Res. *Res:* Developmental renal physiology; renal disease in infants and children. *Mailing Add:* Dept of Pediat Albert Einstein Col of Med Bronx NY 10461

EDELSACK, EDGAR ALLEN, b New York, NY, June 14, 24. PHYSICS. *Educ:* Univ Southern Calif, BS, 48. *Prof Exp:* Asst, Univ Southern Calif, 48-49; physicist, Emery Tumor Group, 49-53; head, Van de Graaff Accelerator Sect, US Naval Radio Defense Lab, 53-56; physicist, San Francisco Br, 56-57 & Physics Prog, Wash, 67-72, liaison scientist, London, 72-73, PHYSICIST ELECTRONIC & SOLID STATE SCI PROG, OFF NAVAL RES, WASHINGTON, DC, 73- *Concurrent Pos:* Consult, Dept Radiation Ther, Univ Md Hosp, Baltimore, 68-77. *Mem:* AAAS; Am Phys Soc; Am Asn Physicists Med; Royal Inst Gt Brit. *Res:* Superconductivity and applications; radiation therapy; accelerators and radioisotopes; biophysics; hyperthermia; microwave biological effects. *Mailing Add:* Off Naval Res Code 414 800 N Quincy St Arlington VA 22217

EDELSON, ALLAN L, b Los Angeles, Calif, Jan 1, 40. MATHEMATICS. *Educ:* Univ Calif, Berkeley, BSc, 62; State Univ NY Stony Brook, PhD, 68. *Prof Exp:* Instr math, State Univ NY Stony Brook, 68-69; asst prof, 69-77, ASSOC PROF, UNIV CALIF, DAVIS, 77- *Mem:* AAAS; Am Math Soc. *Res:* Algebraic topology, differential equations; brain research instrumentation. *Mailing Add:* Dept of Math Univ of Calif Davis CA 95616

EDELSON, BURTON IRVING, b New York, NY, July 31, 26; m 52; c 3. SATELLITE COMMUNICATIONS, SPACE TECHNOLOGY. *Educ:* US Naval Acad, BS, 47; Yale Univ, MS, 54, PhD(metall), 60. *Prof Exp:* Mem staff, Naval Bur Ships, 59-62, Nat Aeronaut & Space Coun, 62-65 & Off Naval Res, London, 65-67; dir, 68-80, SR VPRES COMSAT LABS, COMMUN SATELLITE CORP, 80- *Concurrent Pos:* Consult satellite commun, NASA, 78- *Honors & Awards:* Henry M Howe Award, Am Soc Metals, 63; Legion of Merit, 65. *Mem:* Fel AAAS; fel Am Inst Aeronaut & Astronaut; Am Soc Metals; fel Inst Elec & Electronics Eng; fel Brit Interplanetary Soc. *Res:* Communications satellite systems. *Mailing Add:* Comsat Labs Clarksburg MD 20734

EDELSON, DAVID, b Brooklyn, NY, Nov 27, 27; m 53, 62; c 4. CHEMICAL KINETICS. *Educ:* Polytech Inst Brooklyn, BS, 46; Yale Univ, PhD(chem), 49. *Prof Exp:* Asst chem, Yale Univ, 46-49, Sterling res fel, 49-50; MEM TECH STAFF, BELL LABS, 50- *Mem:* Am Chem Soc; Am Phys Soc; Combustion Inst. *Res:* Chemical kinetics; aeronomy; modeling and simulation by computer of complex chemical systems. *Mailing Add:* Chem Kinetics Res Dept Bell Labs 600 Mountain Ave Murray Hill NJ 07974

EDELSON, EDWARD HAROLD, b New York, NY, Jan 28, 47; m 70; c 1. ORGANIC CHEMISTRY, ANALYTICAL CHEMISTRY. *Educ:* Lehman Col, BS, 73; Rensselaer Polytech Inst, PhD(org chem), 77. *Prof Exp:* Res assoc bio-org chem, NASA-Ames Res Ctr, 77-79; res assoc & lectr, org chem, Univ Southern Calif, 79-80; SR RES CHEMIST, SYNTHETIC FUELS CHEM, EXXON RES & ENG CO, BAYTOWN, TEX, 80- *Mem:* AAAS; Am Chem Soc; Clay Minerals Soc; Int Soc Study Origin Life; Sigma Xi. *Res:* Organic chemistry of coal and synthetic fuels; coal conversion processes, particularly coal liquefactions; chemical evolution and prebiotic formation of biomacromolecules; catalysis and catalyst synthesis; clay chemistry and clay-organic reactions. *Mailing Add:* 4115 Bayou Grove Dr Seabrook TX 77586

EDELSON, JEROME, b New York, NY, Nov 17, 32; m 56; c 3. BIOLOGICAL CHEMISTRY, DRUG METABOLISM. *Educ:* Brooklyn Col, BS, 54; Univ Tex, MA, 57, PhD(biol chem), 60. *Prof Exp:* Asst prof chem, Univ Southwestern La, 60-63; sr biochemist, Wallace Labs, Carter-Wallace, Inc, 63-74; DIR DEPT DRUG METAB & DISPOSITION, STERLING-WINTHROP RES INST, 74- *Mem:* AAAS; Am Chem Soc; Am Soc Pharmacol & Exp Therapeut. *Res:* Synthesis and biological activity of amino acid analogues; biochemical pharmacology; pharmacokinetics and biopharmaceutics; models for human drug metabolism. *Mailing Add:* Dept of Drug Metab & Disposition Sterling-Winthrop Res Inst Rensselaer NY 12144

EDELSON, ROBERT ELLIS, b Camden, Tenn, Jan 20, 43; m 67; c 4. COMMUNICATIONS SYSTEMS. *Educ:* Mass Inst Technol, SB, SM, 63; Univ Calif, Los Angeles, MBA, 70. *Prof Exp:* Mem tech staff, Hughes Aircraft Co, 69-70; sr engr, 67-69, 71-73, group supvr, 73-75, tech mgr, 75-78, SECT MGR, JET PROPULSION LAB, 78- *Concurrent Pos:* Proj mgr, Search for Extraterrestrial Intel, Int Astronaut Asn, 78- *Mem:* Inst Elec & Electron Engrs. *Res:* Telecommunications systems. *Mailing Add:* 4800 Oak Grove Dr Pasadena CA 91103

EDELSON, SIDNEY, b New York, NY, Aug 24, 16; m 47. MATHEMATICS, PHYSICS. *Educ:* Brooklyn Col, BA, 38; NY Univ, MA, 49; Georgetown Univ, MA, 53, PhD(solar radiation), 61. *Prof Exp:* Captain, China Waterways Transport, Shanghai, 46-47; mathematician, US Naval Observ, DC, 48-50, astronomer, 50-56; astronomer, US Naval Res Lab, 56-62, res astronomer proj leader, 62-64; res scientist, Solar Studies, Ames Res Ctr, NASA, 64-66, res scientist optical physics & planetary atmospheres, 66-71, res scientist solar magnetic fields & non-thermal radiative processes, 71-72; consult solar physics, Ministry Sci & Res, Univ Graz, Austria, 72-74; consult staff scientist, Techno-Econ Opportunity Inst, Calif, 74-75; SOLAR ENERGY CONSULT, 75- *Concurrent Pos:* Vol sci adv, 19th Cong Dist, 78-81. *Honors & Awards:* Apollo Achievement Award, NASA, 69. *Mem:* Am Astron Soc; Sigma Xi; Math Asn Am; NY Acad Sci. *Res:* Optical physics; planetary atmospheres; radio astronomy; solar physics; space physics; astronomy. *Mailing Add:* PO Box 1264 Main PO Santa Barbara CA 93102

EDELSTEIN, ALAN SHANE, b St Louis, Mo, June 27, 36; m 63; c 2. SOLID STATE PHYSICS. *Educ:* Wash Univ, BS, 58; Stanford Univ, MS, 59, PhD(physics), 63. *Prof Exp:* Res assoc physics, Stanford Univ, 63-64; NSF fel, Univ Leiden, 64-65; res assoc, IBM Corp, NY, 65-68; assoc prof physics, Univ Ill, Chicago Circle, 68-80; physicist, Energy Conversion Devices, Troy, MI, 80-81; PHYSICIST, CONDENSED MAT & RADIATION SCI DIV, NAVAL RES LAB, WASHINGTON, DC, 81- *Concurrent Pos:* Consult, Solid State Sci Div, Argonne Nat Lab, 69-77. *Mem:* Am Phys Soc. *Res:* Superconducting and normal state properties of Kondo alloys, compounds and valence fluctuation systems containing cerium or ytterbium as the magnetic impurity; modes of investigation including electron tunneling, resistivity, specific heat, susceptibility, sound velocity and neutron scattering measurements; transport properties of amorphous materials. *Mailing Add:* Condensed Mat & Radiation Sci Div Naval Res Lab Washington DC 20375

EDELSTEIN, PAUL HERBERT, b Los Angeles, Calif, Jan 30, 48. INFECTIOUS DISEASES. *Educ:* Univ Calif, Los Angeles, MD, 73. *Prof Exp:* Intern med, Vet Admin Wadsworth Med Ctr, 73-74, resident, 74-76, fel infectious dis, 76-78; ASST PROF, SCH MED, UNIV CALIF, LOS ANGELES, 78- *Concurrent Pos:* Assoc investr, Vet Admin Wadworth Med Ctr, 78-80, dir, Legionnaires Dis Lab, 78-, res assoc, 80- *Mem:* Am Col Physicians; Am Soc Microbiol; Infectious Dis Soc Am; Am Thoracic Soc; Am Fedn Clin Res. *Res:* Laboratory diagnosis of Legionnaires diesease; environmental ecology of Legionella. *Mailing Add:* Vet Admin Wadsworth Med Ctr Wilshire & Sawtell Blvds Los Angeles CA 90073

EDELSTEIN, RICHARD MALVIN, b Los Angeles, Calif, May 28, 30; m 55; c 3. PHYSICS. *Educ:* Pomona Col, BA, 51; Columbia Univ, PhD(particle physics), 60. *Prof Exp:* Res physicist, 60-62, from asst prof to assoc prof, 62-69, assoc dean, Mellon Col Sci, 78-81, PROF PHYSICS, CARNEGIE-MELLON UNIV, 69- *Concurrent Pos:* Weizmann Inst fel, 70-71. *Mem:* Fel Am Phys Soc. *Res:* Mu meson physics; high energy proton and pi meson scattering; charmed particle production and decay. *Mailing Add:* Dept of Physics Carnegie-Mellon Univ Schenley Park Pittsburgh PA 15213

EDELSTEIN, STUART J, b Perth Amboy, NJ, Sept 6, 41; m 64; c 2. BIOCHEMISTRY. *Educ:* Tufts Univ, BS, 63; Univ Calif, Berkeley, PhD(biochem), 67. *Prof Exp:* Nat Res Coun fel cellular biochem, Pasteur Inst, Paris, 67-68; asst prof biochem & molecular biol, 68-74, assoc prof biochem, molecular & cell biol, 74-77, chmn dept, 78-80, PROF BIOCHEM, MOLECULAR & CELL BIOL, CORNELL UNIV, 77- . *Concurrent Pos:* Alfred P Sloan Found res fel, 73-75; vis scientist, Weizmann Inst Sci, 74 & Inst Pasteur, 80-81; vis prof, Univ Paris, 80-81; Eleanor Roosevelt Int Cancer fel, 80-81. *Mem:* Am Soc Biol Chemists; Am Soc Cellular Biol. *Res:* Structure of fibers of sickle cell hemoglobin and microtubules; electron microscopy, optical diffraction and image reconstruction. *Mailing Add:* Wing Hall Cornell Univ Ithaca NY 14853

EDELSTEIN, WARREN STANLEY, b Baltimore, Md, June 11, 37; m 65; c 1. APPLIED MATHEMATICS, SOLID MECHANICS. *Educ:* Lehigh Univ, BA, 58; Duke Univ, MA, 61; Brown Univ, PhD(appl math), 64. *Prof Exp:* Fel mech, Johns Hopkins Univ, 64-65; asst prof to assoc prof, 65-80, PROF MATH, ILL INST TECHNOL, 80- *Mem:* Soc Indust & Appl Math; Soc Eng Sci; Am Acad Mech. *Res:* Boundary value problems of heat conduction, viscoelasticity and nonlinear creep in metals. *Mailing Add:* Dept of Math Ill Inst of Technol Chicago IL 60616

EDEN, FRANCINE CLAIRE, b Oakland, Calif, Sept 6, 45. BIOCHEMISTRY, MOLECULAR BIOLOGY. *Educ:* Occidental Col, BA, 67; Univ Wash, PhD(microbiol), 73. *Prof Exp:* Res assoc biol, Calif Inst Technol, 74-76; res assoc zool, Ind Univ, 76-77; STAFF FEL BIOCHEM, NAT CANCER INST, NIH, 77- *Mem:* Am Soc Biol Chemists. *Res:* DNA sequence organization; evolution of genome organization; structure and expression of repetitive sequences in DNA, methylation of DNA. *Mailing Add:* Lab Biochem NIH Nat Cancer Inst Bldg 37 Rm 4A15 Bethesda MD 20014

EDEN, HENRY FRANCIS, b Newcastle on Tyne, Eng, Dec 23, 34; US citizen; m 79. GEOSCIENCES. *Educ:* Durham Univ, BSc, 56, PhD(physics), 59. *Prof Exp:* Sci officer, Nat Phys Lab, Eng, 59-60; sr res assoc physics, King's Col, Durham Univ, 60-62; res assoc geophys, Mass Inst Technol, 62-64; physicist, Arthur D Little, Inc, Mass, 64-70; prog dir meteorol, 70-76, head atmospheric res sect, 76-79, sr staff scientist, Off Mgt & Budget, Exec Off Pres, 79-80, SR SCI ASSOC, ASTRON, ATMOSPHERIC, EARTH & OCEAN SCI DIRECTORATE, NSF, 80- *Mem:* Am Geophys Union; Am Meteorol Soc; fel Royal Meteorol Soc. *Res:* Propagation of sound in air and water; model experiments in geophysical fluid dynamics relating to the atmosphere and oceans; atmospheric electricity. *Mailing Add:* NSF 1800 G St NW Washington DC 20550

EDEN, JAMES GARY, b Washington, DC, Oct 11, 50; m 72; c 2. LASER PHYSICS, QUANTUM ELECTRONICS. *Educ:* Univ Md, BSEE, 72; Univ Ill, MS, 73, PhD(elec eng), 76. *Prof Exp:* Res asst gas discharge physics, Elec Eng Dept, Univ Ill, 72-75; res assoc laser physics, Nat Res Coun, Washington, DC, 75-76; res staff physicist laser physics, Naval Res Lab, 76-79; asst prof, 79-81, ASSOC PROF ENG, UNIV ILL, URBANA-CHAMPAIGN, 81- *Concurrent Pos:* Naval Res Lab publ award, 79- *Mem:* Am Phys Soc; Am Soc Eng Educ; Inst Elec & Electronics Engrs. *Res:* Collisional and optical behavior of atoms and molecules suitable for laser action in the visible or ultraviolet; non-linear optics (photoionization of the rare gases); laser-induced deposition of thin semiconductor films. *Mailing Add:* Univ Ill Dept Elec Eng 1406 W Green St Urbana IL 61801

EDEN, MURRAY, b Brooklyn, NY, Aug 17, 20; m 45, 62; c 5. INSTRUMENTATION. *Educ:* City Col New York, BS, 39; Univ Md, MS, 44, PhD(phys chem), 51. *Prof Exp:* Phys chemist, Nat Bur Standards, 43-49; biophysicist, Nat Cancer Inst, 49-53; spec fel math biol, USPHS, Princeton Univ, 53-55; biophysicist, Nat Heart Inst, 55-59; prof, 59-69, EMER PROF ELEC ENG, MASS INST TECHNOL, 69- *Concurrent Pos:* Lectr, Am Univ, 47-48 & Harvard Med Sch, 60-73; consult to dir-gen, WHO, 63-75; chmn, US Nat Comt on Eng in Med & Biol, 67-72; ed-in-chief, Info & Control, 67-; chief, Biomed Eng & Instrumentation Br, Div Res Serv, NIH, 76- *Mem:* Am Physiol Soc; Biophys Soc; Inst Elec & Electronics Engrs; Soc Photo-Optical Instrumentation Engrs; Asn Advan Med Instrumentation. *Res:* Physiological measurements; mathematical models for biology; pattern recognition; human cognitive processes. *Mailing Add:* Div Res Serv Bldg 13 Rm 3W13 NIH Bethesda MD 20205

EDEN, RICHARD CARL, b Anamosa, Iowa, July 10, 39; m 64. SOLID STATE PHYSICS. *Educ:* Iowa State Univ, BS, 61; Calif Inst Technol, MS, 62; Stanford Univ, PhD(solid state physics), 67. *Prof Exp:* Res asst elec eng, Calif Inst Technol, 61-62; res asst elec eng, Stanford Univ, 62-67, res assoc, 67-68; mem tech staff, NAm Rockwell Corp, 68-74; PRIN SCIENTIST SOLID STATE ELECTRONICS, SCI CTR, ROCKWELL INT, 74- *Mem:* Am Phys Soc; Inst Elec & Electronics Eng. *Res:* Investigation of the electronic structure of solids by means of such experimental techniques as photoemission and measurements of optical properties; solid state optical detector and other semiconductor device research. *Mailing Add:* 1817 Colgate Dr Thousand Oaks CA 91360

EDEN, WILLIAM GIBBS, b Talledega, Ala, May 3, 18; m 40; c 2. ECONOMIC ENTOMOLOGY. *Educ:* Auburn Univ, BS, 40, MS, 47; Univ Ill, PhD, 50. *Prof Exp:* Asst county agr agent, Geneva, Ala, 40-43 & 46; asst entomologist & asst prof entom, Auburn Univ, 48-50, assoc entomologist & assoc prof, 50-53, entomologist & prof, 53-65; chmn dept, 65-75, EMER PROF ENTOM, UNIV FLA, 75-; PROF ENTOM, LAWSON STATE COMMUNITY COL, ALA, 75- *Concurrent Pos:* Prof entom, Lawson State Community Col, Ala, 75-80. *Mem:* AAAS; Entom Soc Am (pres, 72). *Res:* Biology and control of insects of corn, cotton, peanuts, vegetables, fruits; toxicology; teach insect toxicology; immature insects. *Mailing Add:* R-4 Box 70 Pell City AL 35125

EDENBERG, HOWARD JOSEPH, b New York, NY, Jan 29, 48; m 78; c 1. MOLECULAR BIOLOGY, BIOCHEMISTRY. *Educ:* Queens Col, BA, 68; Stanford Univ, AM, 70, PhD(biol sci), 73. *Prof Exp:* Fel biol, Mass Inst Technol, 73-76; fel biol chem, Harvard Med Sch, 76-77; ASST PROF BIOCHEM, SCH MED, IND UNIV, 77- *Concurrent Pos:* Fel, Damon Runyon-Walter Winchell Cancer Fund, 73-75; fel, NIH, 75-77; prin investr, NIH grant, 78- *Mem:* Biophys Soc; AAAS; Am Soc Microbiol; NY Acad Sci. *Res:* Mammalian DNA replication in vivo and in vitro; SV40 DNA replication; enzymology of replication; DNA repair. *Mailing Add:* Dept of Biochem Sch Med Ind Univ Indianapolis IN 46223

EDENS, FRANK WESLEY, b Big Stone Gap, Va, Dec 18, 46. POULTRY PHYSIOLOGY, AVIAN PHYSIOLOGY. *Educ:* Va Polytech Inst, BS, 69; Va Polytech Inst & State Univ, MS, 71; Univ Ga, PhD(physiol), 74. *Prof Exp:* asst prof physiol, 73-80, ASSOC PROF POULTRY SCI, NC STATE UNIV, 80- *Mem:* Poultry Sci Asn; Sigma Xi; AAAS; Animal Behav Soc; NY Acad Sci. *Res:* Body temperature regulation in birds; interactions between heavy metals and pesticides in birds; physiological behavior in domestic fowl; male reproductive physiology in fowl. *Mailing Add:* Dept of Poultry Sci Box 5307 NC State Univ Raleigh NC 27650

EDENS, WALTER W(ILLIAM), b West Allis, Wis, Jan 7, 10; m 36; c 2. METALLURGY. *Educ:* Marquette Univ, BS, 34; Univ Wis, MS, 37. *Prof Exp:* Mech engr, Heil Co, 35-36; chief metallurgist, Ampco Metal, Inc, 37-45, tech dir, 45-47; vpres & works mgr, Badger Brass & Aluminum Foundry Co, 47-51; assoc proj dir, Alloy Eng & Casting Co, Ill, 51-52; res supvr, Allis-Chalmers Mfg Co, 52-60, asst dir res, 60-69; dir prod planning, Ampco Metal, Inc, 69-71, mgr res & develop, 71-80; RETIRED. *Mem:* Am Soc Metals; Am Inst Mining, Metall & Petrol Engrs; Am Soc Testing & Mat; Am Foundrymen's Soc. *Res:* Physical and chemical metallurgy; alloying; melting; casting; extrusion; welding; fabrication. *Mailing Add:* W315 N7677 Hwy 83 N Lk Hartland WI 53029

EDER, DOUGLAS JULES, b Milwaukee, Wis, Apr 26, 44; m 68; c 3. PHYSIOLOGY, BIOPHYSICS. *Educ:* Col Wooster, AB, 66; Fla State Univ, MS, 69, PhD(biophys), 73. *Prof Exp:* Res asst biophys, Fla State Univ, 70-71, psychobiol fel, 71-73; postdoc fels, Fight for Sight, 74, NIH, 74-75; asst prof, 75-80, ASSOC PROF BIOL SCI, SOUTHERN ILL UNIV, EDWARDSVILLE, 80- *Concurrent Pos:* Res grant-in-aid, Sigma Xi,

Southern Ill Univ, Edwardsville, 76-77. *Mem:* Asn Res Vision & Ophthal; Soc Neurosci; Am Soc Zoologists; Sigma Xi. *Res:* Investigating molecular mechanisms whereby photoreceptor cells in retina transform light energy into neural signal, also investigating light-evoked neural activity in neuroendocrine brain centers such as pituitary, pineal, hypothalamus. *Mailing Add:* Dept of Biol Sci Box 65 Southern Ill Univ Edwardsville IL 62025

EDER, HOWARD ABRAM, b Milwaukee, Wis, Sept 23, 17; m 54; c 3. MEDICAL RESEARCH. *Educ:* Univ Wis, BA, 38; Harvard Univ, MD, 42, MPH, 45. *Prof Exp:* From intern to asst resident physician, Peter Bent Brigham Hosp, Boston, 42-44; asst physician, Rockefeller Inst Hosp, 46-50; asst prof med, Med Col, Cornell Univ, 50-54; investr, Nat Heart Inst, 54-55; assoc prof, Col Med, State Univ NY, Brooklyn, 55-57; assoc prof, 57-60, PROF MED, ALBERT EINSTEIN COL MED, 60-; ADJ PROF, ROCKEFELLER UNIV, 75- *Concurrent Pos:* Chmn lipid metab adv comt, Nat Heart, Lung & Blood Inst, 78-80; mem res comt, Am Heart Asn. *Mem:* Am Soc Clin Invest; Am Soc Biol Chem; Asn Am Physicians; Am Physiol Soc; Brit Biochem Soc. *Res:* Lipid metabolism and atherosclerosis. *Mailing Add:* Albert Einstein Col of Med New York NY 10461

EDERER, FRED, b Vienna, Austria, Mar 5, 26; US citizen; m 58; c 3. EPIDEMIOLOGY, CLINICAL TRIALS. *Educ:* City Col New York, BS, 49; Am Univ, MA, 59. *Prof Exp:* Mem staff, NY City Employees' Retirement Syst, 49-50 & NY City Health Dept, 50-52; statistician, Bur Labor Statist, 55-57, Nat Cancer Inst, 57-64, Nat Heart & Lung Inst, 64-71, head, Clin Trials Sect, Nat Eye Inst, 71-74, CHIEF, OFF BIOMET & EPIDEMIOL, NAT EYE INST, 74- *Concurrent Pos:* Lectr, Am Univ, 65-68; Johns Hopkins Univ, 77-78 & London Sch Hyg & Trop Med, 80; dir, Statist Ctr, Nat Diet-Heart Study, 64-67; dir, Coord Ctr, Urokinase-Pulmonary Embolism Trial, 68-71; mem, Exec Comt & Data Monitoring Comt, Collab Diabetic Retinopathy Study, 71-79. *Mem:* Fel Am Col Epidemiol; Soc Clin Trials; fel Am Statist Asn; Biomet Soc; Soc Epidemiol Res. *Res:* Biometry; epidemiology; evaluation of therapeutic efficacy. *Mailing Add:* Nat Eye Inst 9000 Rockville Pike Bethesda MD 20014

EDERER, GRACE MARY, b Morton, Minn, June 27, 19. CLINICAL MICROBIOLOGY, MEDICAL TECHNOLOGY. *Educ:* Col St Catherine, BA, 41; Univ Minn, MPH, 62. *Prof Exp:* Staff technologist chem, Henry Ford Hosp, 45-52; asst to dir clin lab & asst prof, Univ Minn Hosps, 52-67, assoc prof, 67-76, PROF CLIN MICROBIOL, LAB MED & PATH, UNIV MINN, MINNEAPOLIS, 76- *Concurrent Pos:* Consult new micro prod, Minn Mining & Mfg Co, 73- *Mem:* Am Soc Microbiol; Am Soc Med Technol; AAAS; Acad Clin Lab Physicists & Scientists. *Res:* Development of rapid test methods and media which expedite the identification of microorganisms of importance in the diagnosis of infectious disease. *Mailing Add:* Dept Lab Med & Path Univ Minn Box 198 Mayo Bldg Minneapolis MN 55455

EDERSTROM, HELGE ELLIS, b Torsas, Sweden, Feb 28, 08; nat US. PHYSIOLOGY. *Educ:* Beloit Col, BS, 37; Northwestern Univ, MS, 39, PhD(zool), 41. *Prof Exp:* Asst, Northwestern Univ, 37-41; asst prof physiol & pharmacol, Sch Med, Univ Mo, 42-47; assoc prof physiol, Sch Med, St Louis Univ, 47-52; prof, 52-77, EMER PROF PHYSIOL, SCH MED, UNIV N DAK, 77- *Mem:* AAAS; Am Physiol Soc; Soc Exp Biol & Med; Aerospace Med Asn; Am Soc Zool. *Res:* Temperature regulation; cardiovascular physiology. *Mailing Add:* Dept Physiol Univ NDak Grand Forks ND 58202

EDESKUTY, F(REDERICK) J(AMES), b Minneapolis, Minn, Sept 29, 23; m 47; c 4. CHEMICAL ENGINEERING. *Educ:* Univ Minn, BChE, 44, PhD(chem eng), 50. *Prof Exp:* Mem res staff, Los Alamos Sci Lab, Univ Calif, 50-53; consult engr air conditioning, J V Edeskuty & Assocs, 53-54; MEM RES STAFF, LOS ALAMOS SCI LAB, UNIV CALIF, 54- *Mem:* Int Inst Refrig. *Res:* Cryogenic engineering, cryogenics, hydrogen energy systems; adsorption kinetics; high pressure. *Mailing Add:* Los Alamos Sci Lab PO Box 1663 Los Alamos NM 87545

EDGAR, ALAN D, b Glasgow, Scotland, July 5, 35; Can citizen; m 75. GEOCHEMISTRY, PETROLOGY. *Educ:* McMaster Univ, BA, 58; Univ Manchester, MSc, 61, PhD(geol), 63. *Prof Exp:* Lectr, 63-64, from asst prof to assoc prof, 64-78, PROF GEOL, UNIV WESTERN ONT, 78- *Concurrent Pos:* Res grants, Nat Res Coun, 63-81; Ont Res Found, 64-65; Geol Surv Can, 65-71, NATO, 66-67, 73-74 & 81-82 & Ont Geol Sci Res Group, 80-81; vis prof, Imp Col, Univ London, 71; vis fel, Australian Nat Univ, 74. *Mem:* Fel Mineral Soc Am; Mineral Soc Gt Brit & Ireland; fel Geol Asn Can. *Res:* Mineralogy and crystallography of feldspathoids; experimental studies of silicate systems pertinent to alkaline igneous rocks; petrology of alkaline undersaturated rocks; geochemistry and petrology of ultrapotassis igneous rocks. *Mailing Add:* Dept Geol Univ Western Ont London ON N6A 5B8 Can

EDGAR, ALBERT CORTLAND, b Anadarko, Okla, Dec 27, 08; m 35; c 2. CHEMICAL ENGINEERING. *Educ:* Iowa State Col, BS, 33. *Prof Exp:* Res chemist, Wilson & Co, Inc, 34-47; asst dir res & technol div, 47-69, dir food res, 69-71, mgr New Prod Div, Wilson Cert Foods, Inc, 72-73; RETIRED. *Mem:* Am Chem Soc; Inst Food Technol; Am Meat Asn. *Res:* Food research, principally meat; food technology and chemistry. *Mailing Add:* 3217 Rock Hollow Rd Oklahoma City OK 73120

EDGAR, ARLAN LEE, b Gratiot Co, Mich, June 3, 26; m 52; c 3. ZOOLOGY. *Educ:* Univ Mich, MA, 50, MS, 57, PhD, 60. *Prof Exp:* From instr to assoc prof, 50-64, chmn dept, 71-77, PROF BIOL, ALMA COL, 65- *Concurrent Pos:* Vis prof biol sta, Univ Mich, 65- *Mem:* Am Micros Soc; Am Soc Zool; Am Archeol Soc; NAm Benthol Soc. *Res:* Proprioceptive organs of phalangids; physiological ecology and behavior of phalangids; taxonomy of phalangids in the Great Lakes region; effects of car exhaust on litter invertebrates; terrestrial litter ecology. *Mailing Add:* Dept Biol Alma Col Alma MI 48801

EDGAR, NORMAN TERENCE, b Bristol, Eng, Oct 22, 33; m 60; c 2. MARINE GEOLOGY, GEOPHYSICS. *Educ:* Middlebury Col, BA, 57; Fla State Univ, MSc, 60; Columbia Univ, PhD(marine geol), 68. *Prof Exp:* Geologist, Shell Oil Co Can Ltd, 59-63; geophysicist, Lamont Geol Observ, 63-68; coord staff geologist, Deep Sea Drilling Proj, Scripps Inst Oceanog, Univ Calif, San Diego, 68-70, chief scientist, 70-75; dep chief, 75-79, CHIEF, OFF MARINE GEOL, US GEOL SURV, 79- *Mem:* AAAS; Geol Soc Am. *Res:* Sedimentology; stratigraphy; structural geology; marine seismology. *Mailing Add:* US Geol Surv Nat Ctr Mail Stop 915 Reston VA 22092

EDGAR, ROBERT KENT, b New York, NY, Dec 29, 43. SYSTEMATIC BOTANY, ECOLOGY. *Educ:* Univ Va, BA, 65; Rutgers Univ, MS, 68, PhD(bot), 70. *Prof Exp:* From instr to assoc prof, 68-79, PROF BIOL, SOUTHEASTERN MASS UNIV, 79- *Concurrent Pos:* Consult, Westinghouse Environ Systs, 72-76; res assoc, Farlow Herbarium & Library Harvard Univ, 76- *Res:* Systematics of marine benthic diatoms; historical development of microbiology. *Mailing Add:* Hellerman Diatom Herbarium Southeastern Mass Univ North Dartmouth MA 02747

EDGAR, ROBERT STUART, b Calgary, Alta, Sept 15, 30; m 57. MOLECULAR GENETICS. *Educ:* McGill Univ, BSc, 53; Univ Rochester, PhD(biol), 57. *Prof Exp:* Gosney & res fels, Biol Div, Calif Inst Technol, 57; fel med sci, Nat Res Coun, 57-59; from asst prof to prof biol, Calif Inst Technol, 60-70; PROF BIOL, UNIV CALIF, SANTA CRUZ, 70- *Mem:* Genetics Soc. *Mailing Add:* Thimann Labs Univ of Calif Santa Cruz CA 95064

EDGAR, SAMUEL ALLEN, b Stafford, Kans, Feb 6, 16; m 39; c 2. MICROBIOLOGY, PATHOLOGY. *Educ:* Sterling Col, AB, 37; Kans State Univ, MS, 39; Univ Wis, PhD(zool), 44. *Hon Degrees:* ScD, Sterling Col, 62. *Prof Exp:* Asst zool, Kans State Univ, 37-38, instr, 38-41; asst, Univ Wis, 41-44; PROF POULTRY SCI & POULTRY PATHOLOGIST, AUBURN UNIV, 47- *Concurrent Pos:* Sr scientist, USPHS, Tahiti, 49-50. *Mem:* Fel AAAS; Am Soc Parasitol; Am Micros Soc; fel Poultry Sci Asn; fel NY Acad Sci. *Res:* Resistance of animals to parasitic infections; virus, bacterial and parasitic diseases of poultry; development of the protozoan parasites Eimeria in domestic poultry; immunity of poultry to coccidial infections. *Mailing Add:* Dept Poultry Sci Auburn Univ Auburn AL 36849

EDGE, ORLYN P, b Platteville, Wis, Mar 29, 39; m 61; c 3. MATHEMATICAL STATISTICS. *Educ:* Wis State Univ, Platteville, BS, 61, Univ Iowa, MS, 63, PhD(math), 66. *Prof Exp:* ASSOC PROF MATH, ILL STATE UNIV, 66- *Mem:* Inst Math Statist; Am Statist Asn; Math Asn Am. *Mailing Add:* Dept of Math Stevenson Hall Ill State Univ Normal IL 61761

EDGE, RONALD (DOVASTON), b Bolton, Eng, Feb 3, 29; m 56; c 2. NUCLEAR PHYSICS, SOLID STATE PHYSICS. *Educ:* Cambridge Univ, MA, 52, PhD, 56. *Prof Exp:* Res fel nuclear physics, Australian Nat Univ, 54-58; asst prof, Univ SC, 58-62; res fel, Yale Univ, 63; PROF PHYSICS, UNIV SC, 64- *Honors & Awards:* Russell Award; Pegram Award. *Mem:* Fel Am Phys Soc; Am Asn Physics Teachers; Sigma Xi. *Res:* Pion physics at intermediate energies; channeling in crystals; ion-solid interactions. *Mailing Add:* Dept of Physics Univ of SC Columbia SC 29208

EDGELL, MARSHALL HALL, b San Jose, Calif, Apr 17, 39. MOLECULAR BIOLOGY, GENETICS. *Educ:* Mass Inst Technol, BS, 61; Pa State Univ, MS, 64, PhD(biophys), 65. *Prof Exp:* From asst prof to assoc prof, 68-78, PROF BACT, MED SCH, UNIV NC, CHAPEL HILL, 78- *Concurrent Pos:* NDEA Title IV grant, Calif Inst Technol, 65; vis scientist, NIH, 76-77; ed, J Biol Chem. *Mem:* Am Chem Soc; Am Soc Microbiol. *Res:* Organization expression and regulation of eukaryotic genomes; mouse beta hemoglobin genes; DNA sequence evolution; DNA mediated transformation; genetic disease and gene therapy. *Mailing Add:* Dept of Bact & Immunol Univ of NC Sch of Med Chapel Hill NC 27514

EDGELL, WALTER FRANCIS, b Logansport, Ind, July 26, 16; m 37; c 4. CHEMISTRY. *Educ:* Univ Calif, BS, 39; Univ Iowa, MS, 41; Harvard Univ, PhD(phys chem), 44. *Prof Exp:* Chemist, Div Eight, Nat Defense Res Comt, Harvard Univ, 43; instr phys chem, Univ Iowa, 43-46, assoc prof, 46-49; PROF PHYS CHEM, PURDUE UNIV, 49- *Concurrent Pos:* Guggenheim fel, 56-57. *Mem:* Am Chem Soc; Soc Appl Spectros; Coblentz Soc. *Res:* Infrared and Raman spectroscopy; dynamics, structure and chemistry in electrolytic solutions; theory of symmetry in molecules and spectroscopic selection rules; metal carbonyls. *Mailing Add:* Dept of Chem Purdue Univ West Lafayette IN 47907

EDGERLEY, DENNIS A, b Chicago, Ill, Aug 23, 48; m 81. MASS SPECTROMETRY. *Educ:* Tex A&M Univ, BS, 70, PhD(chem), 77. *Prof Exp:* STAFF SCIENTIST CHEM, ROCKWELL INT, 79- *Mem:* Sigma Xi. *Res:* Chemical analysis of liquid and gaseous synthetic fuel mixtures derived from coal and petroleum with emphasis on mass spectrometric characterization of isotopically labeled compounds produced in mechanistic studies. *Mailing Add:* 1286 Alessandro Dr Newbury Park CA 91320

EDGERLEY, EDWARD, JR, b Lancaster, Pa, Mar 8, 31; m 54; c 4. CIVIL & SANITARY ENGINEERING. *Educ:* Pa State Univ, BS, 52; Mass Inst Technol, SM, 54; Univ Calif, Berkeley, PhD(sanit eng), 68. *Prof Exp:* From asst prof to assoc prof sanit eng, Wash Univ, 57-72, asst dean eng, 68-69; sr vpres, Envirodyne Engrs, 77-79; PRES, ENVIRON & ENERGY CONSULT, 79- *Concurrent Pos:* From vpres to pres, Ryckman Edgerley Tomlinson & Assocs, Consult Engrs, 57-77; mem rev comt environ health, NIH, 69-71. *Mem:* Am Soc Civil Engrs; Am Soc Eng Educ; Air Pollution Control Asn; Am Indust Hyg Asn; Am Chem Soc. *Res:* Industrial waste water treatment; water treatment; trace organics in water; air pollution abatement; noise control; ion exchange treatment of liquid and solids waste. *Mailing Add:* Environ & Energy Consult Inc 2350 Seventh Blvd St Louis MO 63104

EDGERLY, CHARLES GEORGE MORGAN, b Gilmanton, NH, Nov 29, 18; m 44; c 7. DAIRY HUSBANDRY. *Educ:* Univ NH, BS, 48; Rutgers Univ, MS, 50. *Prof Exp:* Asst prof animal husb & asst animal husbandman, Agr Exp Sta, Univ Maine, 50-55; asst prof, 55-65, ASSOC PROF DAIRY HUSB, N DAK STATE UNIV & ASSOC ANIMAL HUSBANDMAN, AGR EXP STA, 65- *Mem:* Am Dairy Sci Asn; Am Fedn Mineral Socs. *Res:* Calf feeding; dairy cattle management; dairy herd waste disposal. *Mailing Add:* 1317 Eighth Ave S Fargo ND 58102

EDGERTON, H(AROLD) E(UGENE), b Fremont, Nebr, Apr 6, 03; m 28; c 3. ELECTRICAL ENGINEERING. *Educ:* Univ Nebr, EE, 25; Mass Inst Technol, MS, 27, DSc(elec eng), 31. *Hon Degrees:* DEng, Univ Nebr, 48; LLD, Doane Col & Univ SC, 69; DSc, Washington Univ, St Louis, 79. *Prof Exp:* Mem test lab, Gen Elec Co, 25-26; from instr to prof elec eng, 26-66, INST EMER PROF & EMER PROF ELEC ENG, MASS INST TECHNOL, 66- *Honors & Awards:* Nat Medal Sci, 73; Lockheed Award Marine Sci & Eng, Marine Technol Soc, 78. *Mem:* Nat Acad Sci; Nat Acad Eng; Am Acad Arts & Sci; fel Inst Elec & Electronics Engrs; fel Photog Soc Am. *Res:* Electrical methods of producing flash lighting; angular transients of synchronous machines; stroboscopic motion pictures of rapidly moving mechanisms; sonar devices for instrumentation and exploration in the sub-bottom of the sea; underwater photography devices. *Mailing Add:* 100 Memorial Dr Cambridge MA 02142

EDGERTON, LOUIS JAMES, b Adena, Ohio, Jan 28, 14; m 46; c 3. HORTICULTURE, PLANT PHYSIOLOGY. *Educ:* Ohio State Univ, BS, 37; Cornell Univ, PhD(pomol), 41. *Prof Exp:* Asst pomol, Cornell Univ, 37-41, instr, 41; res assoc, Rutgers Univ, 42-45; head dept, 70-75, PROF POMOL, CORNELL UNIV, 46- *Concurrent Pos:* Fulbright grant, Cairo Univ, 66. *Mem:* Am Soc Plant Physiol; fel Am Soc Hort Sci. *Res:* Studies on cold hardiness of fruit plants; chemical thinning and control of preharvest apple drop with plant growth regulators; absorption, translocation and metabolism of plant growth regulators by apple and peach trees. *Mailing Add:* Dept of Pomol Cornell Univ Ithaca NY 14853

EDGERTON, MILTON THOMAS, JR, b Atlanta, Ga, July 14, 21; m 45; c 4. PLASTIC SURGERY. *Educ:* Emory Univ, AB, 41; Johns Hopkins Univ, MD, 44; Am Bd Surg, dipl, 51; Am Bd Plastic Surg, dipl, 51. *Prof Exp:* Intern surg, Barnes Hosp, St Louis, Mo, 44-45; asst resident, Johns Hopkins Hosp, 47-49, from instr to prof plastic surg, Sch Med, Johns Hopkins Univ, 49-70; prof, 70-80, CHMN DEPT, SCH MED, UNIV VA, 70-, ALUMNI PROF PLASTIC SURG, 80- *Concurrent Pos:* Surgeon in chg, Johns Hopkins Univ Hosp, 52-70; vchmn, Am Bd Plastic Surg, 69-70; trustee, Cell Sci Ctr, NY, 70-; consult, USPHS, Vet Admin, Baltimore City & Children's Hosps, Baltimore, Nat Clin Ctr, NIH & Walter Reed Hosp, Bethesda & Vet Admin Hosp, Salem, Va; chmn, Coord Comt Acad Policies in Plastic Surg, 76-79. *Honors & Awards:* Dow Corning Award, Am Soc Plastic & Reconstruct Surg, 74. *Mem:* AMA; fel Am Col Surg; Am Asn Plastic Surg (vpres, 72, pres, 74-75); Am Soc Plastic & Reconstruct Surg; Am Soc Maxillofacial Surgeons. *Res:* Head and neck cancer surgery; reconstructive surgery; congenital defects; hand surgery; tissue transplantation research. *Mailing Add:* Dept of Plastic Surg Univ of Va Med Ctr Charlottesville VA 22908

EDGERTON, ROBERT FLINT, b Rochester, NY, Oct 16, 17; m 42; c 2. CHEMISTRY. *Educ:* Univ Rochester, BA, 40; Univ Mich, MS, 41, PhD(org chem), 44. *Prof Exp:* Fel Army specialized training prog, Univ Mich, 41-44; res chemist, Gen Elec Co, Mass, 44-45; tech sales, 46-47; tech staff, Paper Serv Div, Eastman Kodak Co, 47-53, group leader, Prof Papers, 50-52, group leader prod improv, 52-53, tech asst, Europ & Overseas Orgn, 53-55, tech asst, Int Div, 55-57, tech asst, Paris Off, France, 57-59, prod mgr graphic arts, 59-65, dir int advert planning, Int Mkt Div, 65-69, mgr advert & customer serv, Int Photog Div, 69-75, MGR INSTRUCTIONAL OPERS, US & CAN MKTS DIV, EASTMAN KODAK CO, 75- *Mem:* Photog Soc Am. *Res:* Synthesis of perhydrophenanthrene derivatives and antimalarials; dehydrogenation; emulsion polymerization; purification of phenolic materials; photographic paper fixation, toning and washing. *Mailing Add:* Eastman Kodak Co MEC Riverwood 343 State Rochester NY 14650

EDGERTON, ROBERT HOWARD, b Canton, Conn, Dec 27, 33; m 55; c 2. MECHANICAL ENGINEERING. *Educ:* Univ Conn, BS, 55, MS, 57; Cornell Univ, PhD(mech eng), 61. *Prof Exp:* Asst prof eng, Dartmouth Col, 62-67; ASSOC PROF ENG, OAKLAND UNIV, 67- *Concurrent Pos:* NIH grant, 64-66; Ford Found fel, Indust Prog, IBM Corp, 66-67. *Mem:* Am Soc Mech Engrs; Am Soc Eng Educ; Am Inst Aeronaut & Astronaut. *Res:* Heat transfer, fluid mechanics and transport theory; flow and temperature measurements and instrumentation; biomedical engineering; blood flow; infra-red technology. *Mailing Add:* Dept of Eng Oakland Univ Rochester MI 48063

EDGINGTON, DAVID NORMAN, b Oxford, Eng, Dec 18, 33. CHEMICAL LIMNOLOGY, OCEANOGRAPHY. *Educ:* Univ Oxford, Eng, BA, 57, BSc, 58, DPhil, 60. *Hon Degrees:* MA, Univ Oxford, 60. *Prof Exp:* Fel chem, Northwestern Univ, 61-62; fel, 61-62 & Radiol & Environ Res Div, Argonne Nat Lab, 62-63; staff scientist environ studies, 63-79; DIR, CTR GREAT LAKES STUDIES, UNIV WIS-MILWAUKEE, 79-, PROF GEOL SCI, 80- *Concurrent Pos:* Lectr, Northwestern Univ, 62-67. *Mem:* Royal Soc Chem; Am Soc Limnol & Oceanog; Int Asn Great Lakes Res. *Res:* Use of natural and artificial radionuclides for studying chemical and biological processes in natural waters and sediments; long term behavior of persistent pollutants in aquatic environments. *Mailing Add:* Ctr for Great Lakes Res Univ of Wis Milwaukee WI 53201

EDGINGTON, THOMAS S, b Los Angeles, Calif, Feb 10, 32; m 57; c 2. PATHOLOGY, IMMUNOLOGY. *Educ:* Stanford Univ, AB, 53, MD, 57. *Prof Exp:* Intern, Hosp Univ Pa, 57-58; resident path, Univ Calif, Los Angeles, 58-60; pathologist, Atomic Bomb Casualty Comn, Japan, 60-62; asst prof path, Univ Calif, Los Angeles, 62-65; assoc mem, 68-80, PROF DEPT PATH, SCRIPPS CLIN & RES FOUND, 80- *Concurrent Pos:* Sr res fel, Dept Exp Path, Scripps Clin & Res Found, 65-68; assoc adj prof path, Univ Calif, San Diego, 68- *Mem:* AAAS; Am Asn Immunol; Am Soc Exp Pathologists; Col Am Path. *Res:* Mechanisms of autoimmunity and the character of cell surfaces. *Mailing Add:* Dept Molecular Immunol Scripps Clin & Res Found 10666 N Torrey Pines Rd La Jolla CA 92037

EDGREN, JAMES W, b Iowa Falls, Iowa, Aug 17, 29; m 53; c 2. FOREST ECOLOGY. *Educ:* Iowa State Univ, BS, 57, MS, 59. *Prof Exp:* Plant pathologist, Pac Northwest Forest & Range Sta, 59-77, REFORESTATION SPECIALIST, REGION 6 TIMBER MGT, US FOREST SERV, 77- *Res:* Regeneration of forest stands; seedling morphology as influenced by nursery practices; seedling survival and growth as influenced by planting site characteristics. *Mailing Add:* Region 6 Timber Mgt US Forest Serv PO Box 3623 Portland OR 97208

EDGREN, RICHARD ARTHUR, b Chicago, Ill, May 28, 25; m 52; c 2. ENDOCRINOLOGY. *Educ:* Northwestern Univ, PhD(biol), 52. *Prof Exp:* Asst biol, Northwestern Univ, 49-52; sr investr, G D Searle & Co, 52-60; asst mgr, Nutrit & Endocrinol Sect, Wyeth Labs, 60-68, mgr endocrinol sect, 68-71; assoc dir clin res, Warner-Lambert Co, 71-72, dir endocrinol, 72-75; sect dir endocrinol, Parke, Davis Co, 75-78; assoc med dir, 78-81, DIR SCI AFFAIRS, SYNTEX LABS, 81- *Concurrent Pos:* Mem, Coun on Arteriosclerosis, Am Heart Asn. *Mem:* Ecol Soc Am; Am Soc Zool; Am Soc Pharmacol & Exp Therapeut; Endocrine Soc; Royal Soc Med. *Res:* Endocrine pharmacology of steroidal and peptide hormones with special reference to reproductive physiology. *Mailing Add:* Syntex Labs Div of Med Affairs 3401 Hillview Ave Palo Alto CA 94304

EDIDIN, MICHAEL AARON, b Chicago, Ill, Mar 31, 39; m 64; c 2. EMBRYOLOGY, IMMUNOLOGY. *Educ:* Univ Chicago, BS, 60; Univ London, PhD, 63. *Prof Exp:* Asst prof, 66-71, assoc prof, 71-75, PROF BIOL, JOHNS HOPKINS UNIV, 75- *Concurrent Pos:* NSF fel cell biol, Weizmann Inst, 63-64; Am Heart Asn res fel immunol, Harvard Med Sch, 64-66. *Honors & Awards:* Cole Medal, Am Biophys Soc. *Mem:* AAAS; Am Asn Immunol; Am Soc Cell Biol. *Res:* Membrane structure differentiation and chemistry of transplantation antigens. *Mailing Add:* Dept of Biol Johns Hopkins Univ Baltimore MD 21218

EDIGER, ROBERT I, b Hutchinson, Kans, Apr 2, 37; m 58, 81; c 1. PLANT TAXONOMY, ECOLOGY. *Educ:* Bethel Col, AB, 59; Kans State Teachers Col, MS, 64; Kans State Univ, PhD(bot), 67. *Prof Exp:* Teacher, Ford Pub Schs, 59-62; teacher, Hays Pub Schs, 62-63; from asst prof to assoc prof, 67-75, chmn dept biol sci, 74-77, PROF BOT, CALIF STATE UNIV, CHICO, 75- *Concurrent Pos:* Dir biol, Eagle Lake Biol Sta, 68-74. *Mem:* Bot Soc Am; Am Soc Plant Taxon; Int Asn Plant Taxon; Orgn Biol Field Sta (pres, 75-76). *Res:* Taxonomy of higher plants, especially the genus Senecio and Arnica in the family Compositae. *Mailing Add:* Dept of Biol Sci Calif State Univ Chico CA 95929

EDINGER, HENRY MILTON, b New York, NY, Feb 28, 43; m 67; c 3. PHYSIOLOGY, NEUROPHYSIOLOGY. *Educ:* City Col New York, BS, 64; Univ Pa, PhD(physiol), 69. *Prof Exp:* Asst prof physiol, 71-75, asst prof neurosci, 72-75, ASSOC PROF PHYSIOL & NEUROSCI, COL MED & DENT NJ, NJ MED SCH, 75- *Concurrent Pos:* NIH fel, Rockefeller Univ, 69-71; consult, Vet Admin Hosp, East Orange, NJ, 72- *Mem:* Soc Neurosci; Am Physiol Soc; NY Acad Sci. *Res:* Limbic system-neuroanatomy and neurophysiology. *Mailing Add:* Dept of Physiol NJ Med Sch Newark NJ 07103

EDINGER, JAMES (G), b Van Nuys, Calif, June 16, 18; m 46; c 2. METEOROLOGY. *Educ:* Univ Calif, Los Angeles, AB, 40, MA, 48, PhD(meteorol), 54. *Prof Exp:* Res asst, 46-53, from asst prof to assoc prof, 53-73, PROF METEOROL, UNIV CALIF, LOS ANGELES, 73- *Mem:* Am Meteorol Soc. *Res:* Air pollution; atmospheric diffusion. *Mailing Add:* Dept of Atmospheric Sci Univ of Calif Los Angeles CA 90024

EDINGER, STANLEY EVAN, ANALYTICAL CHEMISTRY, MATERIAL PROPERTIES. *Educ:* Brooklyn Col, BS, 64; NY Univ, MS, 69, PhD(phys chem), 70. *Prof Exp:* Teaching fel phys chem, NY Univ, 64-66, res asst, 66-70; tech translr & ed solid state chem, 70-71; clin asst chemist, tech supvr, Mt Sinai Hosp & Med Ctr, 71-76; USPHS sr scientist clin lab sci & regulations, Bur Qual Assurance, 76-77; SR SCIENTIST, CLIN LAB SCI & REGULATIONS, HEALTH CARE FINANCING ADMIN, HEALTH STANDARDS & QUAL BUR, DEPT HEALTH & HUMAN SERV, 77- *Concurrent Pos:* Consult, Prof Exam Serv, 75-76; sr scientist comdr, USPHS Comn Corps, 76-; mem, Nat Coun Health Lab Serv, 76-; USPHS Task Force on Clin Labs, 78-; proj officer, Dept Health & Human Serv Clin Lab Proficiency Exam Prog; mem nat comt, Clin Lab Studies, 80- *Mem:* Fel Am Inst Chemists; Am Chem Soc; Am Asn Clin Chem; Am Pub Health Asn; AAAS. *Res:* Gypsum chemistry; laboratory automation and computerization; educational testing in laboratory sciences; development, writing, interpretation and implementation of regulations for clinical laboratories; quality control and proficiency testing. *Mailing Add:* 12000 Old Georgetown Rd Apt 404N Rockville MD 20852

EDINGTON, CHARLES W, b Knoxville, Tenn, Feb 26, 25; m 46, 81; c 2. GENETICS. *Educ:* Univ Tenn, AB, 48, MS, 49, PhD, 55. *Prof Exp:* Asst biol div, Oak Ridge Nat Lab, 52-54, assoc biologist, 55-57; from asst prof to assoc prof zool, Fla State Univ, 57-65; geneticist, USAEC, 63-67, chief biol br, Div Biol & Med, 67-73; assoc dir, Res & Develop Progs, Div Biomed & Environ Res, 73-79, dep dir, Off Health & Environ Res, 79-80, actg dir, 80-81, ASSOC DIR, OFF HEALTH & ENVIRON RES, OFF ENERGY RES, US DEPT OF ENERGY, 81- *Res:* Radiation biology, genetics. *Mailing Add:* Off Health & Environ Res ER-70 US Dept of Energy Washington DC 20545

EDINGTON, JEFFREY WILLIAM, b Newcastle upon Tyne, Eng, May 28, 39. MATERIALS SCIENCE. *Educ:* Univ Birmingham, BSc, 60, PhD(metall), 63, DSc(metall), 75; Cambridge Univ, MA, 67. *Prof Exp:* Sr scientist metal sci, Battelle Mem Inst, 64-67; asst dir res mat, Cambridge Univ, 67-76; CHPERSON METALL & MAT & DIR MAT DURABILITY DIV, UNIV DEL, 76- *Concurrent Pos:* Vis prof, Univ Brisbane, Australia, 74; vis prof & consult, Brown Boverie & Co, Switz, 75-76. *Mem:* Am Soc Metals; fel Inst Metallurgists. *Res:* Materials durability; erosion; stress corrosion; corrosion fatigue; electron microscopy; analytical microscopy; superplasticity. *Mailing Add:* Col of Eng Univ of Del Newark DE 19711

EDISON, ALLEN RAY, b Plainview, Nebr, Sept 21, 26; m 49; c 2. ELECTRICAL ENGINEERING. *Educ:* Univ Nebr, BSc, 50, MSc, 57; Univ NMex, DSc(elec eng), 62. *Prof Exp:* Elec engr, Silas Mason Co, 50-53; from instr to assoc prof, 53-64, PROF ELEC ENG, UNIV NEBR-LINCOLN, 70- *Concurrent Pos:* Res assoc, Univ NMex, 57-61; engr, Inst Telecommun, Dept of Com, 65. *Mem:* Inst Elec & Electonics Engrs; Am Asn Eng Educ. *Res:* Electronic instrumentation. *Mailing Add:* 194 W Nebraska Hall Univ Nebr Lincoln NE 68588

EDISON, LARRY ALVIN, b Aberdeen, Wash, Nov 8, 36; m 60; c 4. MATHEMATICS. *Educ:* Whitman Col, BA, 58; Stanford Univ, PhD(math), 65. *Prof Exp:* Asst prof math, Reed Col, 64-70; assoc prof, 70-80, PROF MATH, ALMA COL, 80-, CHMN DEPT, 70- *Mem:* Am Math Soc; Math Asn Am. *Res:* Harmonic analysis; almost periodic functions; functional analysis. *Mailing Add:* Dept of Math Alma Col Alma MI 48801

EDLICH, RICHARD FRENCH, b New York, NY, Jan 19, 39; m 61; c 3. PLASTIC SURGERY. *Educ:* Sch Med, NY Univ, MD, 62. *Prof Exp:* From instr to assoc prof, 71-76, PROF PLASTIC SURG & BIOMED ENG, SCH MED, UNIV VA, 76-, DIR EMERGENCY MED SERV & BURN CTR, 74- *Concurrent Pos:* Physician tech adv, Bur Emergency Serv, HEW, 74-; consult, Div Health Manpower & Nat Ctr Health Serv Res, 77- *Mem:* Soc Univ Surgeons; Am Asn Surg Trauma; Am Burn Asn; Am Spinal Cord Injury Asn; Univ Asn Emergency Med. *Res:* Biology of wound repair and infection. *Mailing Add:* Sch Med Univ Va Charlottesville VA 22908

EDLIN, FRANK E, b Eskridge, Kans, Aug 25, 09; m 36; c 2. SOLAR ENERGY, ENGINEERING. *Educ:* Kans State Univ, BS, 31. *Prof Exp:* Field engr, Indust Eng Div, E I du Pont de Nemours & Co, 37-39, field supvr, 39-40, process engr, Design Div, 40-51, consult engr, Eng Serv Div, 51-60, engr, Develop Dept, 60-62, sr res engr, Eng Res Div, 62-65, lectr eng, Ariz State Univ, 65-71; pres, Water Appln, Inc, 71-73; CONSULT ENGR, 75- *Concurrent Pos:* Vpres, Int Plastics, Inc, Colwich, Kans, 67-75. *Mem:* AAAS; Am Inst Chem Engrs; Solar Energy Soc (exec secy, 65-67); Am Soc Mech Engrs; Nat Soc Prof Engrs. *Res:* Atomic energy; fusion; subsoil irrigation; chemical engineering unit operations. *Mailing Add:* 17826 Palo Verde Dr Sun City AZ 85373

EDLIN, JOHN CHARLES, b Wilmington, Del, June 16, 43; m 69; c 3. PEDIATRICS. *Educ:* Duke Univ, BS, 65; Univ Tenn, Memphis, MD, 68. *Prof Exp:* From intern to resident pediat, Duke Univ Med Ctr, 69-71; fel growth & develop, Univ London, 71-72; fel adolescent med, Harvard Med Sch, 72-73; ASST PROF PEDIAT & INTERNAL MED, SOUTHWESTERN MED SCH, UNIV TEX, 73- *Concurrent Pos:* Dir adolescent med prog, Dept Pediat, Univ Tex, 73-81; consult, Baylor Col Dent, 78; Timberlawn Psychiat Hosp, 78 & Western State Col, Colo; private practice adolescent med, 81- *Mem:* Am Soc Adolescent Psychiat; Soc Adolescent Med; fel Am Acad Pediat. *Res:* Growth and development; physiological changes which occur at puberty. *Mailing Add:* Dept Pediat Southwestern Med Sch Univ Tex 5323 Harry Hines Dallas TX 75235

EDLUND, MILTON CARL, b Jamestown, NY, Dec 13, 24; m 45; c 2. PHYSICS. *Educ:* Univ Mich, MS, 48, PhD, 66. *Prof Exp:* Physicist reactor physics, Gaseous Diffusion Plant, Oak Ridge Nat Lab, 48-50, physicist & lectr, Sch Reactor Tech, 50-51, sr physicist & sect chief, 53-55; mgr physics & math dept, Babcock & Wilcox Co, 55-60, develop dept, 60-62, appln develop dept, 62-65, asst div mgr, 65-66; prof nuclear eng, Univ Mich, 66-67; consult, Union Carbide Corp, 67-70; PROF MECH ENG, VA POLYTECH INST & STATE UNIV, 70- *Concurrent Pos:* Vis lectr, Swedish Atomic Energy Comn, 53. *Honors & Awards:* Ernest Orlando Lawrence Award, 65. *Mem:* Nat Acad Eng; Am Soc Mech Engrs; Am Phys Soc; Sigma Xi; Am Nuclear Soc. *Res:* Neutron diffusion; nuclear reactor design. *Mailing Add:* Dept of Mech Eng Va Polytech & State Univ Blacksburg VA 24060

EDMAN, JAMES RICHARD, b Kandiyohi Co, Minn, June 6, 36; m 58; c 3. ORGANIC CHEMISTRY, RESEARCH ADMINISTRATION. *Educ:* Gustavus Adolphus Col, BS, 58; Univ Nebr, MS, 60, PhD(chem), 63. *Prof Exp:* Res chemist, 63-69, RES SUPVR PHOTOCHEM CATALYSIS, E I DU PONT DE NEMOURS & CO, 69- *Mem:* Am Chem Soc. *Mailing Add:* Plastic Prod & Resins Dept E I du Pont de Nemours & Co Circleville OH 43113

EDMAN, JOHN DAVID, b Jan 20, 38; US citizen; m 59; c 3. MEDICAL ENTOMOLOGY. *Educ:* Gustavus Adolphus Col, BSc, 59; Univ Minn, MSc, 61; Kans State Univ, PhD(entom), 64. *Prof Exp:* Sr scientist & asst dir, Fla Med Entom Lab, Fla State Div Health, 64-75; assoc prof entom, 75-81, PROF & ACTG HEAD, UNIV MASS, AMHERST, 81- *Concurrent Pos:* NIH res grant, 65-; WHO travel-study fel, 75; consult, Res Resources Br, Nat Inst Allergy & Infectious Dis, 67- & Vector Biol Br, WHO, 70-; ad hoc mem trop med & parasitol study sect, NIH, 78. *Mem:* AAAS; Entom Soc Am; Am Mosquito Control Asn. *Res:* General biology, physiology and behavior of mosquitoes; immunological techniques. *Mailing Add:* Dept of Entom Univ of Mass Amherst MA 01003

EDMINSTER, TALCOTT W(HITE), agricultural engineering, deceased

EDMISON, MARVIN TIPTON, b Lincoln, Nebr, July 21, 12; m 39; c 2. ACADEMIC ADMINISTRATION, ORGANIC CHEMISTRY. *Educ:* Univ Nebr, AB, 33, MSc, 47; Okla Agr & Mech Col, PhD(chem), 52. *Prof Exp:* Teacher, Shattuck Mil Acad, 38-41; teacher, Wentworth Mil Acad, 47-48; from asst prof to assoc prof chem, Univ Ark, 51-55, asst to vpres & provost, 55; dir res found & prof chem, 55-78, asst vpres acad affairs, 68-78, exec dir, Okla State Univ Educ & Res Found, Inc, 72-78, EMER PROF & EMER RES COORDR, OKLA STATE UNIV, 78- *Concurrent Pos:* Proj dir, Ordark Res Proj, Univ Ark, 52-53; res adminr, Inst Sci & Technol, 54; mem Nat Coun Univ Res Adminrs & Nat Conf Advan Res; dir, Okla Water Resources Res Inst, 65-78. *Mem:* AAAS; Am Inst Chem; Nat Wildlife Fedn. *Res:* Radical substitution of aromatic nuclei; thermal decomposition of organic azides and inorganic oxidants; classified governmental research. *Mailing Add:* Res Found Okla State Univ Stillwater OK 74074

EDMISTON, CLYDE, b Greeley, Colo, June 4, 37; m 58. PHYSICAL CHEMISTRY. *Educ:* Colo State Col, BA, 58; Iowa State Univ, PhD(chem), 63. *Prof Exp:* Nat Res Coun res assoc phys chem, Nat Bur Standards, 63-64; from asst prof to assoc prof, 64-73, PROF CHEM, UNIV WYO, 73- *Concurrent Pos:* Am Chem Soc Petrol Res Fund grant, 64-65; NSF res grant, 65-72 & NSF sr fel, Univ Fla, 70-71. *Mem:* Am Chem Soc; Am Phys Soc. *Res:* Quantum chemistry; molecular structure. *Mailing Add:* Dept of Chem Univ of Wyo Laramie WY 82071

EDMONDS, DEAN STOCKETT, JR, b Brooklyn, NY, Dec 24, 24; m 51; c 4. ATOMIC PHYSICS. *Educ:* Mass Inst Technol, BS, 50, PhD(physics), 58; Princeton Univ, MA, 52. *Prof Exp:* Res asst physics, Mass Inst Technol, 52-56, guest physicist & res fel, Cambridge Electron Accelerator, Mass Inst Technol & Harvard Univ, 59-61; asst prof, 61-67, ASSOC PROF PHYSICS, BOSTON UNIV, 67- *Concurrent Pos:* Dir, Tachisto, Inc, 71- & Gen Ionex, Inc, 75- *Mem:* Am Phys Soc; Am Asn Physics Teachers; Inst Elec & Electronic Engrs. *Res:* High energy accelerators; mass spectroscopy; molecular beam investigations; laser technology; communication techniques; physical electronics. *Mailing Add:* Dept Physics Boston Univ Boston MA 02215

EDMONDS, FRANK NORMAN, JR, b Minneapolis, Minn, Sept 2, 19; m 45; c 2. ASTROPHYSICS. *Educ:* Princeton Univ, AB, 41; Univ Chicago, PhD(astron & astrophys), 50. *Prof Exp:* Asst prof astron, Univ Mo, 50-52; asst prof math & astron, 52-58, assoc prof astron, 58-65, PROF ASTRON, UNIV TEX, AUSTIN, 65- *Concurrent Pos:* Guggenheim fel, 62-63. *Mem:* Am Astron Soc; Royal Astron Soc; Int Astron Union; Astron Soc Pac. *Res:* Solar and stellar atmospheres; solar photospheric inhomogeneities; stellar spectroscopy; astronomical physics. *Mailing Add:* Dept of Astron Univ of Tex Austin TX 78712

EDMONDS, HARVEY LEE, JR, b Leavenworth, Kans, Sept 23, 42; m 70. NEUROPHARMACOLOGY. *Educ:* Univ Kans, Lawrence, BA, 64, BS, 67; Univ Calif, Davis, PhD(pharmacol), 74. *Prof Exp:* Instr pharmacol, US Army Med Field Serv Sch, Ft Sam Houston, 68-70; asst prof pharmacol, Wash State Univ, 74-77; ASSOC PROF ANESTHESIOL, UNIV LOUISVILLE, 77- *Concurrent Pos:* Consult toxicol, 78- *Mem:* Res Soc Alcoholism; Am Epilepsy Soc; Soc Neurosci; AAAS; Sigma Xi. *Res:* Investigation of the etiology and treatment of convulsive disorders associated with idiopathic epilepsy and alcohol withdrawal. *Mailing Add:* Dept of Anesthesiol Univ of Louisville Sch of Med Louisville KY 40232

EDMONDS, JAMES D, JR, b Texarkana, Tex, July 28, 39; m 57; c 4. PHYSICS. *Educ:* San Diego State Univ, BA, 62; Cornell Univ, PhD(appl physics), 67. *Prof Exp:* Asst appl physics, Cornell Univ, 63-67, res assoc electron micros, 67; mem tech staff, Hughes Res Labs, 67-69; asst prof physics, Calif Western Col, 69-72; vis asst prof physics, Ore State Univ, 72-73; lectr physics, San Diego State Univ, 73-75; vis asst prof physics, Joint Sci Prog, Claremont Cols, 75-76; vis asst prof physics, Bucknell Univ, 76-78; ASSOC PROF & CHMN PHYSICS, MERCER UNIV, 78- *Concurrent Pos:* Lectr, Los Angeles Valley Col, 68; lectr, Calif Luth Col, 68-69. *Mem:* Am Asn Physics Teachers. *Res:* Thin film vacuum nucleation; x-ray diffractometry and structure analysis; transmission and scanning electron microscopy; ultrahigh vacuum; liberal arts-physics teaching; foundations of field theory and origins of mass. *Mailing Add:* Dept of Physics Mercer Univ Macon GA 31207

EDMONDS, JAMES WILLIAM, b Long Beach, Calif, Oct 14, 43; m 66; c 3. CRYSTALLOGRAPHY. *Educ:* Harvey Mudd Col, Calif, BS, 65; Rice Univ, Houston, PhD(chem), 68. *Prof Exp:* Res assoc, Brookhaven Nat Lab, AEC, 68-70; sr fel, State Univ NY Buffalo, 70-71; asst res scientist, Med Found Buffalo, 71-74; res specialist, 74-78, res leader, 78-80, SR RES CHEMIST, DOW CHEM CO, MIDLAND, 80- *Concurrent Pos:* Crystallog consult, State Univ NY Buffalo, 71-74; mem bd dir, Joint Comt on Powder Diffraction Standards, 81- *Mem:* Am Crystallog Asn; Am Chem Soc. *Res:* X-ray and neutron powder and single crystal diffraction; optical emission spectroscopy; high resolution Gurnier camera/monochruator; computer automatization; aromatic moner process development. *Mailing Add:* 2020 Ashman St Midland MI 48640

EDMONDS, MARY P, b Racine, Wis, May 7, 22. BIOCHEMISTRY. *Educ:* Milwaukee-Downer Col, BA, 43; Wellesley Col, MA, 45; Univ Pa, PhD(biochem), 51. *Prof Exp:* Instr chem, Wellesley Col, 45-46; fel, Univ Ill, 50-52; res assoc, Cancer Res Inst, Univ Wis, 52-55 & Montefiore Hosp Res Inst, 55-65; asst prof, Grad Sch Pub Health, 65-67, assoc res prof, 67-71, assoc prof biochem, 71-75, PROF BIOL SCI, UNIV PITTSBURGH, 76- *Res:* Molecular biology; structure and biosynthesis of nucleic acids; chemistry and enzymology of nucleic acids and nucleotides. *Mailing Add:* Dept of Biol Sci A527 Langley Hall Univ Pittsburgh Pittsburgh PA 15260

EDMONDS, PETER DEREK, b Tunbridge Wells, Eng, Mar 29, 29; m 63. BIOMEDICAL ENGINEERING, BIOCHEMICAL PHYSICS. *Educ:* Univ London, BSc, 52, dipl, PhD(physics), 59. *Prof Exp:* Asst physics, Phys Inst, Stuttgart Tech Inst, 55-56; physicist, Mullard Res Labs, Eng, 56-58, Akers

Res Labs, Imp Chem Industs, Ltd, 58-61 & Plastics Div Res Labs, 61-62; res fel chem eng, Calif Inst Tech, 62-63; asst prof, 63-68, assoc prof elec eng & biomed eng, Univ Pa, 68-70; adminr tech serv, Inst Elec & Electronics Engrs, 70-76; SR RES PHYSICIST, BIOENG RES CTR, STANFORD RES INST INT, 76- Concurrent Pos: Sr res fel biomed eng, Univ Wash, 69-70; mem task group 1, Assessment of Ultrasonic Diagnostic Instrumentation, NSF-Alliance for Eng in Med & Biol, 73-74; mem, Ultrasonics Tissue Signature Comt, NSF-Carnegie-Mellon Univ, 77-78 & Bioeffects Comt, Am Inst Ultrasound Med, 79-81. Mem: Fel Acoust Soc Am; sr mem Inst Elec & Electronics Engrs; fel Brit Phys Soc. Res: Ultrasonic measurements of absorption and velocity in liquids and liquid mixtures; kinetics of fast reactions; relaxation mechanisms; mesomorphic liquid states; aqueous solutions of proteins; biomaterials; bioeffects of ultrasound; ultrasonics phantoms. Mailing Add: Stanford Res Inst Int 333 Ravenswood Ave Menlo Park CA 94025

EDMONDS, RICHARD H, b Carbondale, Pa, May 10, 33; m 53; c 3. ANATOMY. Educ: State Univ NY Buffalo, BS, 59, PhD(anat), 65. Prof Exp: From asst prof to assoc prof, 65-76, PROF ANAT, ALBANY MED COL, 76-, DIR, ANATOMICAL GIFT PROG, 76-, ASST DEAN, 80- Mem: Am Asn Anat; Am Soc Cell Biol. Res: Cell biology; developmental hematology; electron microscopy. Mailing Add: Dept of Anat Albany Med Col Albany NY 12208

EDMONDS, ROBERT L, b Sydney, Australia, May 6, 43; m 69; c 2. FOREST PATHOLOGY, SOIL MICROBIOLOGY. Educ: Univ Sydney, BS, 64; Univ Wash, MS, 68, PhD(forest path), 71. Prof Exp: Res forestry officer, Forest Res Inst, Australia, 64-65; res asst, Dept Forestry, Australian Nat Univ, 65-66; from res asst to res assoc, Col Forest Resources, Univ Wash, 66-71; prog coordr, Bot Dept, Univ Mich, 71-73; res asst prof, 73-76, asst prof, 76-79, ASSOC PROF, COL FOREST RESOURCES, UNIV WASH, 79- Concurrent Pos: Mem nat comt, Nat Res Coun/Nat Acad Sci, 72-74, chmn, Aerobiol Comt, 77-80. Mem: Sigma Xi; Soc Am Foresters; Am Phytopath Soc; Ecol Soc Am; Am Meteor Soc. Res: Forest pathology, root diseases; soil microbiology, litter decomposition, microbiology of sewage sludge; aerobiology, aerial dispersal of bacteria, fungus spores and insects. Mailing Add: Col of Forest Resources Univ of Wash Seattle WA 98195

EDMONDS, SYLVAN MILTON, chemistry, deceased

EDMONDS-CREPS, ELAINE SUE, b Toledo, Ohio, July 14, 46; m 70, 78; c 1. NEUROANATOMY, NEUROENDOCRINOLOGY. Educ: Ohio Univ, AB, 68; Univ Mich, MS, 69; Univ Ariz, PhD(anat), 73. Prof Exp: Fel physiol, Univ Ariz, 73-74; asst prof anat, Univ NMex, 74-76; ASST PROF ANAT, IND UNIV, 77- Mem: Soc Neurosci; AAAS; Am Asn Anatomists. Res: Hypothalamic regulation of the endocrine system, especially reproductive system of the genetically obese rat. Mailing Add: Northwest Ctr for Med Educ Ind Univ Gary IN 46408

EDMONDSON, ANDREW JOSEPH, b Leavenworth, Kans, May 11, 35; m 56; c 2. MECHANICAL ENGINEERING. Educ: Tex Tech Col, BS, 57; Pa State Univ, MS, 61; Tex A&M Univ, PhD(mech eng), 64. Prof Exp: Instr mech eng, Tex Tech Col, 57-59 & 60-61; from asst prof to assoc prof mech & aero eng, 64-76, PROF MECH & AERO ENG, UNIV TENN, KNOXVILLE, 76- Concurrent Pos: Consult, Oak Ridge Nat Lab, 67- Mem: Am Soc Eng Educ. Res: Theoretical and experimental studies of shell problems; experimental investigations concerning the sealing mechanisms of mechanical face seals. Mailing Add: Dept of Mech & Aerospace Eng Univ of Tenn Knoxville TN 37916

EDMONDSON, DALE EDWARD, b Morris, Ill, Oct 13, 42; m 72. BIOCHEMISTRY. Educ: Northern Ill Univ, BS, 64; Univ Ariz, PhD(chem), 70. Prof Exp: NIH fel biochem, Univ Mich, 70-72; from asst res biochemist to assoc res biochemist, Univ Calif, San Francisco, 72-80; ASSOC PROF BIOCHEM, EMORY UNIV, 80- Mem: Am Chem Soc; Am Soc Biol Chemists; Sigma Xi. Res: Structure and function of oxidation-reduction enzymes. Mailing Add: Dept Biochem Emory Univ Atlanta GA 30322

EDMONDSON, FRANK KELLEY, b Milwaukee, Wis, Aug 1, 12; m 34; c 2. ASTRONOMY. Educ: Ind Univ, AB, 33, MA, 34; Harvard Univ, PhD(astron), 37. Prof Exp: Asst, Ind Univ, 29-33, Lowell Observ, 34-35 & Harvard Univ, 36-37; from instr to assoc prof astron, 37-49, dir, Kirkwood Observ, 45-48, chmn dept astron, 44-78, dir, Goethe Link Observ, 48-78, PROF ASTRON, IND UNIV, BLOOMINGTON, 49-, RES ASSOC, MCDONALD OBSERV, 41- Concurrent Pos: Prog dir astron, NSF, 56-57; mem bd, Asn Univs Res Astron, from vpres to pres, 57-65; cor mem, Am Mus Natural Hist, 58-; mem, Int Astron Union, chmn US Nat Comt, 62-64, from vpres to pres Comn 20, 67-73. Honors & Awards: Order of Merit, Govt of Chile, 64. Mem: AAAS (vpres, 62); Am Astron Soc (treas, 54-75). Res: Stellar motions and distribution; radial velocities of faint stars; rediscovery and observation of asteroids on the critical list. Mailing Add: Dept of Astron 319 Swain Hall W Ind Univ Bloomington IN 47405

EDMONDSON, HUGH ALLEN, b Maysville, Ark, Jan 3, 06; m 30; c 4. PATHOLOGY. Educ: Univ Okla, AB, 26; Univ Chicago, MD, 31. Hon Degrees: LLD, Univ Southern Calif, 77. Prof Exp: From instr to assoc prof, 38-48, chmn dept, 51-72, PROF PATH, SCH MED, UNIV SOUTHERN CALIF, 48- Concurrent Pos: Asst pathologist, Los Angeles County Gen Hosp, 38-39, attend pathologist, 39-, dir labs & chief pathologist, Los Angeles County-Univ Southern Calif Med Ctr, 68-72; asst pathologist, St Luke Hosp, Pasadena, 40-42, pathologist, 42-43; mem bd trustees, Estelle Doheny Eye Found, 71-, mem bd dir, 74-; mem bd trustees, Eisenhower Med Ctr, 74- Mem: AMA; Am Asn Path & Bact; fel Am Col Physicians; Am Soc Clin Path; Am Gastroenterol Asn. Res: Diseases of the liver, gallbladder and bile ducts; tumors of the liver, gallbladder and extrahepatic bile duct. Mailing Add: Dept of Path Univ of Southern Calif Sch Med Los Angeles CA 90033

EDMONDSON, MORRIS STEPHEN, b San Antonia, Tex, Sept 9, 41; m 62; c 2. ORGANIC CHEMISTRY, ORGANOMETALIC CHEMISTRY. Educ: Southwest Tex State Univ, BS, 63; Univ Tex Austin, MA, 66, PhD(org chem), 70. Prof Exp: Res chemist, Jefferson Chem Co, 65-67; res chemist, Petro-Tex Chem Corp, 70-72, sr res chemist, 72-74, res group head, 74-77; RES ASSOC, DOW CHEM, USA, 77- Concurrent Pos: Welch Found fel, 69-70. Mem: Am Chem Soc. Res: Permanent press fabric treating agents and surfactants; liquid phase chlorination of dienes; heterogeneous catalysis; emulsian polymerization; elastomers; organometallic and Ziegler catalysis. Mailing Add: Rte 7 130 Mohawk Dr Alvin TX 77511

EDMONDSON, W THOMAS, b Milwaukee, Wis, Apr 24, 16; m 41. LIMNOLOGY. Educ: Yale Univ, BS, 38, PhD(zool), 42. Prof Exp: Asst zool, Univ Wis, 39; asst biol, Yale Univ, 39-41; asst phys oceanog, Am Mus Natural Hist, 42-43; res assoc, Oceanog Inst, Woods Hole, 43-46; lectr biol, Harvard Univ, 46-49; from asst prof to assoc prof zool, 49-57, PROF ZOOL, UNIV WASH, 57- Concurrent Pos: NSF fel, 59-60; mem environ studies bd, Nat Acad Sci-Nat Res Coun, 74-76. Honors & Awards: Cottrell Award Environ Qual, Nat Acad Sci, 73; Einar Naumann-August Thienemann Medal, Int Asn Theoret & Appl Limnol, 80. Mem: Nat Acad Sci; Freshwater Biol Asn; Am Soc Limnol & Oceanog; Ecol Soc Am; Int Asn Theoret & Appl Limnol. Res: Ecology and taxonomy of Rotifera; population dynamics of plankton; lake productivity. Mailing Add: Dept of Zool NJ-15 Univ of Wash Seattle WA 98195

EDMONSON, DON ELTON, b Dallas, Tex, Sept 6, 25; m 51; c 3. MATHEMATICS. Educ: Southern Methodist Univ, BS, 45, MS, 48; Calif Inst Technol, PhD(math), 54. Prof Exp: Res instr math, Tulane Univ, 54-55; from asst prof to assoc prof, Southern Methodist Univ, 55-60; assoc prof, 60-64, vchmn dept, 69-70, PROF MATH, UNIV TEX, AUSTIN, 64-, PROF EDUC, 76- Concurrent Pos: Consult, Tex Instruments, Inc, 58-59 & Tex Ed Agency, 62-64. Mem: Am Math Soc; Soc Indust & Appl Math; Math Asn Am. Res: Abstract algebra, lattice theory; topological lattices; real and complex analysis. Mailing Add: Dept Math Univ of Tex Austin TX 78712

EDMUND, ALEXANDER GORDON, b Toronto, Ont, Aug 11, 24; m 51; c 4. VERTEBRATE PALEONTOLOGY. Educ: Univ Toronto, BA, 51, MA, 52; Harvard Univ, PhD, 57. Prof Exp: Asst cur, 54-64, CUR, DEPT VERT PALEONT, ROYAL ONT MUS, 64- Concurrent Pos: Assoc prof, Dept Geol, Univ Toronto, 71. Mem: Soc Vert Paleont; Lepidopterists Soc. Res: Morphology; evolution; systematics and zoogeography of Pleistocene edentate mammals from North and South America. Mailing Add: Royal Ont Mus 100 Queens Park Toronto ON M5S 2C6 Can

EDMUND, RUDOLPH WILLIAM, b Lockridge, Iowa, Mar 9, 10; m 39; c 3. GEOLOGY. Educ: Augustana Col, AB, 34; Univ Iowa, MS, 38, PhD(struct geol), 40. Hon Degrees: DSc, Calif Lutheran Col, 80. Prof Exp: Instr geol, Coe Col, 39-40; geologist, Shell Oil Co, Inc, 40-45; asst div geologist, Globe Oil & Refining Co, Okla, 45-48; regional geologist, 51-53; from assoc prof to prof geol, Augustana Col, 48-51; vpres & gen mgr, Sohio Petrol Co, Okla, 53-60; prof geol & chmn div sci, Augustana Col, 60-69; vpres acad affairs, 69-74, prof, 74-80, EMER PROF GEOL, CALIF LUTHERAN COL, 80- Mem: Fel AAAS; fel Geol Soc Am; Nat Asn Geol Teachers; Soc Explor Geophys; Soc Econ Paleontologists & Mineralogists. Res: Structural geology; regional stratigraphy; stratigraphic oil traps; paleogeologic maps. Mailing Add: Dept of Geol Calif Lutheran Col Thousand Oaks CA 91360

EDMUNDOWICZ, JOHN MICHAEL, b Nanticoke, Pa, May 18, 38; m 60; c 2. BIOCHEMISTRY. Educ: Philadelphia Col Pharm & Sci, BS, 60; Univ Del, MS, 63, PhD(chem), 66. Prof Exp: SR BIOCHEMIST, ANTIBIOTIC MFG & DEVELOP DIV, ELI LILLY & CO, 66- Mem: Am Chem Soc. Res: Isolation, purification and chemistry of the beta-lactam antibiotics, polyethers and macrolides. Mailing Add: Dept K418 Eli Lilly & Co Kentucky Ave Indianapolis IN 46206

EDMUNDS, GEORGE FRANCIS, JR, b Salt Lake City, Utah, Apr 28, 20. ENTOMOLOGY, EVOLUTION. Educ: Univ Utah, BS, 43, MS, 46; Univ Mass, PhD(entom), 52. Prof Exp: Instr biol, 45-52, from asst prof to assoc prof, 52-65, actg chmn dept biol, 69-70, dept environ biol, 68-69, PROF ZOOL & ENTOM, UNIV UTAH, 65- Concurrent Pos: Consult air pollution agr & forestry. Honors & Awards: Distinguished Res Award, Univ Utah, 74. Mem: Entom Soc Am; Soc Syst Zool. Res: Evolution; biogeography; taxonomy and biology of Ephemeroptera; ecology of insect outbreaks in relation to air pollution; coevolution of insects and forest trees. Mailing Add: 201 Biol Bldg Univ Utah Salt Lake City UT 84112

EDMUNDS, LAFE REES, b Salt Lake City, Utah, June 22, 24; m 47; c 3. ENTOMOLOGY. Educ: Univ Utah, BS, 47, MS, 49; Ohio State Univ, PhD, 52. Prof Exp: Asst, Univ Utah, 47-48; asst, Ohio State Univ, 50-52; sr asst scientist, USPHS, 52-54; asst prof zool & entom, Miss State Univ, 54-56; prin entomologist, Res & Develop Lab, Ft Belvoir, Va, 56-59; prof asst, NSF, 59-61, assoc prog dir, 61-64; int adv to Mex, Pan Am Health Orgn, WHO, 65-68; prof assoc & prog coordr, 69-71, exp projs coordr educ, 71-74, PROG DIR, STUDENT-ORIENTED PROGS GROUP, NSF, 74- Mem: Entom Soc Am. Res: Culicidae; mosquitoes; Hymenoptera; Evaniidae; cockroach biology and parasites; insect ecology; science education. Mailing Add: Nat Sci Found 1800 G St Washington DC 20550

EDMUNDS, LELAND NICHOLAS, JR, b Aiken, SC, Apr 21, 39; m 64, 81; c 3. BIOLOGICAL RHYTHMS, CELL BIOLOGY. Educ: Davidson Col, BS, 60; Princeton Univ, MA, 62, PhD(biol), 64. Prof Exp: NSF-Orgn Trop Studies fel, Univ Costa Rica, 64; instr & res asst biol, Princeton Univ, 64-65; from asst prof to assoc prof, 65-76, actg provost & head div biol sci, 75-76, prof biol, 76-81, PROF ANAT SCI, HEALTH SCI CTR, STATE UNIV NY STONY BROOK, 81- Concurrent Pos: Student trainee & biol aide, Insect Physiol Lab, Agr Res Ctr, USDA, Md, 56-60; vis investr, Carnegie Inst, Dept Terrestrial Magnetism, 62; NSF res grants, 65-82; vis investr, Carlsberg Found, Biol Inst, Copenhagen, 72; vis investr, Ctr Nat Res Sci, Le Phytotron,

Gif-sur-Yvette, 78-79; vis prof, Lab Biol Cellulair Veg, Univ Paris VII, 81. *Mem:* Am Soc Plant Physiol; Am Soc Photobiol; Soc Protozoologists; Int Soc Chronobiol; Am Soc Microbiol. *Res:* Circadian rhythms; synchrony in cell division and growth; control and regulation of the cell cycle; oscillatory enzyme systems; cellular communication. *Mailing Add:* Div Biol Sci State Univ NY Stony Brook NY 11794

EDMUNDS, LEON K, b Madison, Wis, Mar 25, 29; m 50; c 9. PLANT PATHOLOGY. *Educ:* Univ Wis, BS, 53, PhD(plant path), 58. *Prof Exp:* Res assoc plant path, Univ Wis, 58-60; RES PLANT PATHOLOGIST, USDA, AGR RES SERV, KANS STATE UNIV, 60- *Mem:* Am Phytopath Soc. *Res:* Diseases of grain sorghum in semihumid to semiarid areas of central United States. *Mailing Add:* Dickins Hall Kansas State Univ Manhattan KS 66504

EDMUNDS, LOUIS HENRY, JR, b Seattle, Wash, Aug 12, 31; c 3. THORACIC SURGERY. *Educ:* Univ Wash, BS, 53; Harvard Med Sch, MD, 56; Am Bd Surg, dipl, 64; Am Bd Thoracic Surg, dipl, 65. *Prof Exp:* From intern to resident, Mass Gen Hosp, 56-63; clin asst, Mass Gen Hosp, 64; sr registrar, Leeds Gen Infirmary, Eng, 64-65; assoc, Mason Clin, Seattle, Wash, 65-66; from asst prof to assoc prof surg, Med Ctr, Univ Calif, San Francisco, 66-73, assoc, Cardiovasc Res Inst, 66-73, dir, Exp Surg Labs, 67-73; WILLIAM M MEASEY PROF SURG & CHIEF CARDIOTHORACIC SURG, UNIV PA, 73-, INSTR SURG, 80- *Concurrent Pos:* Teaching fel, Harvard Med Sch, 63-64; res fel thoracic surg, Leeds Univ, 64; investr, Va Mason Res Ctr, Seattle, Wash, 65. *Mem:* AAAS; Am Heart Asn; Am Col Cardiol; Am Soc Artificial Internal Organs; Am Asn Thoracic Surg. *Mailing Add:* Dept of Surg Univ of Pa Philadelphia PA 19104

EDMUNDSON, ALLEN B, b Flat River, Mo, June 16, 32; m 55; c 3. BIOCHEMISTRY. *Educ:* Dartmouth Col, AB, 54; Rockefeller Univ, PhD(biochem), 61. *Prof Exp:* Sr biochemist, Div Biol & Med Res, Argonne Nat Lab, 64-76; PROF BIOCHEM & BIOL, UNIV UTAH, 76- *Concurrent Pos:* USPHS fel biochem, Unit Molecular Biol, Med Res Coun, Eng, 60-64. *Res:* Protein chemistry; determinations of structures and genetically controlled variations of proteins; correlation of structure and functions; protein crystallography and chemistry. *Mailing Add:* Dept Biol Univ Utah Salt Lake City UT 84108

EDMUNDSON, HAROLD PARKINS, b Los Angeles, Calif, Dec 13, 21; m 63. MATHEMATICS. *Educ:* Univ Calif, Los Angeles, BA, 46, MA, 48, PhD(math), 53. *Prof Exp:* Asst math, Univ Calif, Los Angeles, 49-50, 51-52; mathematician, Indust Logistics Res Proj, 53, US Dept Defense, 53-54 & Rand Corp, 54-59; sr assoc, Planning Res Corp, 59-61; mem sr staff, Thompson-Ramo-Wooldridge, Inc, 61-64; sr scientist, Syst Develop Corp, 64-67; PROF COMPUT SCI & MATH, UNIV MD, 67- *Concurrent Pos:* Lectr, George Washington Univ, 53-54, Univ Southern Calif, 54-56 & Univ Calif, Los Angeles, 57-63, assoc res mathematician, 64-67. *Mem:* Am Math Soc; Math Asn Am; Am Soc Info Sci; Inst Math Statist; Asn Comput Mach. *Res:* Computability theory and automata theory; mathematical statistics and logic; probability, matrix and information theories; stochastic processes; automatic translation; mathematical and computational linguistics. *Mailing Add:* Dept Comput Sci Univ Md College Park MD 20742

EDNEY, NORRIS ALLEN, b Natchez, Miss, July 17, 36; m 59; c 3. BIOLOGY. *Educ:* Tougaloo Southern Christian Col, BSc, 57; Antioch Col, MSc, 62; Mich State Univ, PhD(conserv), 69. *Prof Exp:* Prof biol, Natchez Jr Col, 57-62; from instr to asst prof, Alcorn Agr & Mech Col, 63-66; teaching asst, Mich State Univ, 66-69; PROF BIOL, ALCORN STATE UNIV, 69-, CHMN DEPT BIOL & DIR ARTS & SCI DIV, 73-, DIR GRAD STUDIES, 75- *Concurrent Pos:* Res conserv aide, Dept Natural Resources, State of Mich, 68-69; dir, Coop Col-Sch Sci Prog; dir, Microbial Conversion Proj, USDA, 73-77, dir, Pesticide Residue Res Proj, 76-, dir, Biodegradation Animal Waste Proj, 78-; dir, Instruct Implementation Improv Prog, NSF, 74-75 & 75-76, dir, Pre-Col Teacher Develop Sci Prog, 78-79, 79-80 & 80-81; dir, NIH Allied Health Grant, 75-78; mem comt, Effects of Alanap Proj, USDA Cucurbits Proj, 81. *Mem:* AAAS; Soc Protozool; Mycol Soc Am; Soc Econ Bot; Bot Soc Am. *Res:* Ecological succession of protozoa in pond and sewage water; histochemical study of certain enzyme systems in Trichomonas vaginalis; study of infections of fish by certain saprolegniaceous fungi. *Mailing Add:* Dept of Biol Alcorn State Univ Box 870 Lorman MS 39096

EDNIE, NORMAN A(LEX), b Leven, Scotland, July 5, 20; nat US; m 45; c 4. CHEMICAL ENGINEERING. *Educ:* Univ Wis, PhD(chem eng), 51. *Prof Exp:* Res mgr, Spunbonded Prod Res Div, E I Du Pont De Nemours & Co, 50-67, res mgr, Nylon End-Use Apparel, 67-77, develop assoc, Multifiber Res, 77-80; RETIRED. *Mem:* Am Inst Chem Eng; Am Chem Soc; Sigma Xi. *Res:* Synthetic fibers; synthetic fiber papers and non-woven fabrics; research and development management. *Mailing Add:* 22 Watergreen Ln Berlin MD 21811

EDOZIEN, JOSEPH CHIKE, b Asaba, Nigeria, July 28, 25; m 55; c 6. NUTRITION, PATHOLOGY. *Educ:* Univ London, BSc, 48; Nat Univ Ireland, BSc & MSc, 48, MD, 54; MRCP(E), 54, FRCP(E), 63; FRCPath(L), 67. *Hon Degrees:* DSc, Univ Rio de Janeiro, 63. *Prof Exp:* Prof chem path & head dept, Univ Ibadan, 61-66, dean fac med, 62-66; vis prof clin nutrit, Mass Inst Technol, 67-71, dir, Mass Nutrit Prog, 69-71; PROF NUTRIT & CHMN DEPT, SCH PUB HEALTH, UNIV NC, CHAPEL HILL, 71- *Concurrent Pos:* Leader Nigerian deleg & vpres conf, UN Con Appl Sci & Technol to Probs Less-Develop Countries, 63; mem, Expert Panel Res Immunol, WHO, 63-, chmn, Expert Comt Immunol & Parasitic Dis, 64, mem, Expert Comt Nutrit in Pregnancy & Lactation, 65 & Adv Comt Med Res, 65-70. *Mem:* Am Inst Nutrit; Am Soc Clin Nutrit; Asn Clin Pathologists. *Res:* Nutritional assessment, diet-hormone interactions and metabolic adaptation. *Mailing Add:* Dept of Nutrit Univ of NC Sch Pub Health Chapel Hill NC 27514

EDSALL, GEOFFREY, immunology, medicine, deceased

EDSALL, JOHN TILESTON, b Philadelphia, Pa, Nov 3, 02; m 29; c 3. PROTEIN BIOCHEMISTRY, HISTORY OF BIOCHEMISTRY. *Educ:* Harvard Univ, AB, 23, MD, 28. *Hon Degrees:* DSc, Univ Chicago, 67, Case Western Reserve Univ, 67, New York Med Col, 67 & Univ Mich, 68; DPhil, Univ Goteborg, Sweden, 72. *Prof Exp:* Tutor biochem sci, 28, instr, 28-32, from asst prof to prof biochem, 32-73, EMER PROF BIOCHEM, HARVARD UNIV, 73- *Concurrent Pos:* Chmn, Bd Tutors Biochem Sci, 31-57; Guggenheim Mem Found fels, Calif Inst Technol, 40-41 & Harvard Univ, 54-56; mem, US Nat Comn for UNESCO, 50-56; Fulbright vis lectr, Cambridge Univ, 52 & Univ Tokyo, 64; vis prof, Col France, 55-56; ed in chief, J Biol Chem, 58-67; pres, Int Cong Biochem, NY, 64; vis fel, Australian Nat Univ, 70; scholar, Fogarty Int Ctr, NIH, 70-71; vis prof, Univ Calif, Los Angeles, 77; dir, Surv Sources Hist Biochem & Molecular Biol, 75-79; vis prof, Univ Calif, Riverside, 80. *Honors & Awards:* Passano Found Award, 66; Willard Gibbs Medal, Am Chem Soc, 72. *Mem:* Nat Acad Sci; AAAS; Am Soc Biol Chemists (pres, 57-58); Am Philos Soc; Hist Sci Soc. *Res:* Physical chemistry of amino acids and proteins; proteins of blood and muscle; flow birefringence; Raman spectroscopy; light scattering; carbonic anhydrase; history of biochemistry. *Mailing Add:* Dept Biochem & Molecular Biol Harvard Univ 7 Divinity Ave Cambridge MA 02138

EDSBERG, ROBERT LESLIE, b Seattle, Wash, Feb 7, 22; m 48; c 3. ANALYTICAL CHEMISTRY. *Educ:* Univ Minn, BChem, 44; Univ Pa, MS, 52. *Prof Exp:* Res chemist, Gen Aniline & Film Co, 44-52; mgr chem sect, Burroughs Cent Res Labs, 52-55; mgr chem res, 55-66, dir res & eng, Todd Co Div, 66-77, staff engr, 77-79, MGR PROD SPECIF, OFF SUPPLIES DIV, BURROUGHS CORP, ROCHESTER, 79- *Mem:* Am Chem Soc. *Res:* Graphic arts research as related to business machines, supplies. *Mailing Add:* 141 Butler Dr Pittsford NY 14534

EDSE, RUDOLPH, b Hamburg, Ger, Dec 14, 13; nat US; m 39; c 2. AERONAUTICAL ENGINEERING. *Educ:* Univ Hamburg, Dipl Chem, 37, Dr rer nat(phys chem), 39. *Prof Exp:* Res phys chemist, Inst Aeronaut Sci, Ger, 39-44, dep head chem dept, 44-46; sci consult, Wright-Patterson AFB, US Air Force, 45-51; from asst prof to assoc prof aeronaut eng, 51-57, dir rocket res lab, 51-80, PROF AERONAUT & ASTRONAUT ENG, OHIO STATE UNIV, 57- *Concurrent Pos:* Consult, Allegany Ballistics Lab, Md, 57-63. *Mem:* Am Inst Aeronaut & Astronaut. *Res:* Propulsion; thermodynamics, combustion and high speed aerodynamics. *Mailing Add:* Dept of Aeronaut & Astronaut Eng Ohio State Univ Columbus OH 43210

EDSON, CHARLES GRANT, b West Springfield, Mass, Dec 16, 16; m 42; c 1. HYDRAULICS, MECHANICS. *Educ:* Univ Mass, BS, 38; Univ Fla, MSE, 50. *Prof Exp:* Engr, Corps Engrs, RI, 38-40, Fla, 40-42 & 46; asst prof, 46-51, ASSOC PROF HYDRAUL & MECH, UNIV FLA, 51- *Concurrent Pos:* Consult, Corps Engrs, Jacksonville, Fla, 48-49, DC, 50-52 & Brevard Eng Co, 70. *Mem:* Fel Am Soc Civil Engrs. *Res:* Open channel hydraulics; empirical relations in hydrology; three-body problem of mechanics; geometry; nomography and crystallography. *Mailing Add:* 2212 NW 15th Ave Gainesville FL 32601

EDSON, JAMES EDWARD, JR, b Fort Smith, Ark, May 26, 42. PALYNOLOGISTS. *Educ:* Ark Tech Univ, BS, 65; Univ Ark, Fayetteville, MS, 71; Tulane Univ, PhD(paleont), 76. *Prof Exp:* Sr palentologist, Mobil Oil Corp, 73-74; paleontologist, Shell Oil Co, 74-75; geologist, 75-77; ASST PROF GEOL, UNIV ARK, MONTICELLO, 77- *Mem:* Geol Soc Am; Am Asn Stratigraphic Palynologists; Nat Asn Geol Teachers. *Res:* Palyno-stratigraphy of Paleozoic and Mesozoic strata. *Mailing Add:* Box 2451 Univ Ark Monticello AR 71655

EDSON, QUENTIN A, b Burton, Wash, July 12, 26; m 50; c 2. ENVIRONMENTAL ASSESSMENT, FISHERIES MANAGEMENT. *Educ:* Univ Wash, BS, 51. *Prof Exp:* Biol aide, Wash Dept Fisheries, 44-51, biologist, 51; from jr biologist to biologist, Alaska Dept Fisheries, 51-55; fisheries biologist, Wash Dept Fisheries, 55-64; fisheries biologist, City of Tacoma, 64-70; head, Unit Conserv, 70-75, chief, Environ Anal Br, 75-80, DIR, DIV ENVIRON ANAL, FED ENERGY REGULATORY COMN, 80- *Mem:* Am Fisheries Soc. *Res:* Research and management of Pacific Salmon; research and development of fish passage facilities at hydroelectric projects. *Mailing Add:* Fed Energy Regulatory Comn 825 N Capitol St N E Washington DC 20426

EDSON, WILLIAM A(LDEN), b Burchard, Nebr, Oct 30, 12; m 42; c 3. ELECTRICAL ENGINEERING. *Educ:* Univ Kans, BS, 34, MS, 35; Harvard Univ, ScD(commun eng), 37. *Prof Exp:* Mem tech staff, Bell Tel Labs, 37-41, 43-44, supvr, 44-45; asst prof elec eng, Ill Inst Tech, 41-43; prof physics, Ga Inst Tech, 45-46, prof elec eng, 46-52, dir sch elec eng, 51-52; vis prof & res assoc, Stanford Univ, 52-54; consult engr, Microwave Lab, Gen Elec Co, 55-59, mgr klystron subsect, 59-61; dir, Electromagnetic Technol Corp, 61-62, pres, 62-70; sr scientist, Vidar Corp, 70-71; dir, Wescon, 75-79, SR RES ENGR, SRI INTERNATIONAL, 71-, STAFF SCIENTIST, 77- *Concurrent Pos:* Consult, Nat Bur Standards, 51-64. *Mem:* Fel Inst Elec & Electronics Eng; Am Phys Soc. *Res:* Communication and radar systems; filters; electronic oscillators; cavity and quartz crystal resonators; broad band and microwave amplifiers. *Mailing Add:* SRI Int 333 Ravenswood Ave Menlo Park CA 94025

EDSTROM, RONALD DWIGHT, b Oakland, Calif, Mar 21, 36; m 59; c 3. BIOCHEMISTRY. *Educ:* Univ Calif, Berkeley, AB, 58; Univ Calif, Davis, PhD(biochem), 62. *Prof Exp:* Res assoc, Univ Mich, 62-63; asst prof, 65-71, ASSOC PROF BIOCHEM, MED SCH, UNIV MINN, MINNEAPOLIS, 71- *Concurrent Pos:* USPHS fel physiol chem, Sch Med, Johns Hopkins Univ, 63-65. *Mem:* AAAS; Am Soc Biol Chem. *Res:* Structure, degradation and biosynthesis of carbohydrate containing polymers; biochemistry of carbohydrate polymers on mammalian cell surfaces and their role in the response of cells to external stimuli; regulation of glycogen metabolism. *Mailing Add:* Dept of Biochem Univ Minn Sch of Med Minneapolis MN 55455

EDWARD, COSMAS, b Baltimore, Md, Apr 5, 26. GENETICS. *Educ:* Manhattan Col, BA, 51; Fordham Univ, MS, 57, PhD(biol), 62. *Prof Exp:* Teacher, La Salle Acad, RI, 47-49, St Peter's High Sch, NY, 49-50 & 54-58, Christian Bros Acad, 50-54 & Manhattan Col High Sch, 58-59; from instr to asst prof, 59-68, ASSOC PROF BIOL, MANHATTAN COL, 68- *Mem:* AAAS; Am Soc Zoologists; Sigma Xi. *Res:* Regeneration in amphibians; antigenicity and homograft reactions in newts and other salamanders. *Mailing Add:* Dept Biol Manhattan Col Bronx NY 10471

EDWARD, DEIRDRE WALDRON, b Detroit, Mich, June 23, 23; Can citizen; m 53; c 3. BIOCHEMISTRY. *Educ:* Univ Birmingham, BSc, 44, PhD(path chem), 54. *Prof Exp:* Staff res off, Bakelite Corp, 44-46; clin biochemist, Children's Hosp, Birmingham, Eng, 46-49; res assoc, 60-65, asst prof, 65-67, ASSOC PROF EXP SURG, McGILL UNIV, 67- *Concurrent Pos:* Lasdon res fel, Trinity Col, Dublin, 54-57. *Mem:* Can Biochem Soc; Brit Biochem Soc; NY Acad Sci. *Res:* Structure and metabolism of polysaccharides, glycoproteins; absorption of metal ions and radionuclides by gastrointestinal tract; biosynthesis of glycoproteins; acid glycosidases. *Mailing Add:* Dept of Exp Surg Donner Bldg McGill Univ Docteur Penfield Ave Montreal PQ H3A 1A4 Can

EDWARD, JOHN THOMAS, b London, Eng, Mar 23, 19; Can citizen; m 53; c 3. PHYSICAL ORGANIC CHEMISTRY. *Educ:* McGill Univ, BSc, 39, PhD(org chem), 42; Oxford Univ, DPhil, 49; Trinity Col Dublin, MA, 55, ScD, 71. *Prof Exp:* Asst res scientist, Nat Res Coun Can, 43-45 & Can Armaments Res & Develop Estab, Que, 45-46; lectr, Univ Manitoba, 46-47; Imp Chem Industs res fel, Birmingham, 49-52; lectr, Trinity Col, Dublin, 52-56; lectr, 56-57, from asst prof to assoc prof, 57-66, PROF CHEM, McGILL UNIV, 66- *Concurrent Pos:* Exhib of 1851 sci scholar, 46-49. *Mem:* Am Chem Soc; fel Royal Soc Can; fel Chem Inst Can. *Res:* Explosives; heterocyclic compounds; strychnine; terpenes; steroids; paper electrophoresis; amino acids; reaction mechanisms and stereochemistry; acidity functions; substituent and solvation effects on reactivities of organic molecules. *Mailing Add:* Dept of Chem McGill Univ Montreal PQ H3A 2T5 Can

EDWARDS, ALAN KENT, b Wichita, Kans, Apr 29, 40; m 62; c 2. EXPERIMENTAL ATOMIC PHYSICS. *Educ:* Cent Methodist Col, AB, 62; Univ Nebr, Lincoln, MS, 64, PhD(physics), 68. *Prof Exp:* Res assoc physics, Univ Wash, 67-70; asst prof, 70-76, ASSOC PROF PHYSICS, UNIV GA, 76- *Concurrent Pos:* Vis scientist, Argonne Nat Lab, 80. *Mem:* Am Phys Soc. *Res:* Atomic and molecular physics. *Mailing Add:* Dept of Physics Univ of Ga Athens GA 30602

EDWARDS, ALAN M, b Denver, Colo, Oct 8, 33; m 55; c 3. AERONAUTICS, ASTRONAUTICS. *Educ:* US Mil Acad, BS, 55; Mass Inst Technol, SM, 61; Stanford Univ, PhD(aeronaut, astronaut), 65. *Prof Exp:* From asst prof to assoc prof eng mech, US Air Force Acad, 61-68, dep dir academics, Aerospace Res Pilot Sch, 68-69, dir, 69-70, dir, 614th Tactical Fighter Squadron, 70-71, aerospace asst, Nat Aeronaut & Space Coun, 71-73, mil asst int progs, Off Secy Defense, 73-75; MGR SYSTS ANAL, FIGGIE INT, INC, ARLINGTON, 75- *Concurrent Pos:* Consult, Air Force Flight Test Sch, 66. *Mem:* Am Defense Preparedness Asn; Aviation Hist Soc. *Res:* Shell structures; aeroelasticity; flight dynamics. *Mailing Add:* 7207 Masonville Dr Annandale VA 22003

EDWARDS, ARTHUR L, b Sacramento, Calif, Feb 24, 33; m 53; c 4. CHEMICAL ENGINEERING, APPLIED MATHEMATICS. *Educ:* Univ Wash, SEattle, BS, 54; Univ Ill, MS, 59, PhD(chem eng), 61. *Prof Exp:* PHYSICS ENGR, APPL MATH & COMPUT, LAWRENCE RADIATION LAB, UNIV CALIF, 60- *Mem:* Am Inst Chem Eng; Am Chem Soc; AAAS. *Res:* High pressure solid state physics; application of computers to transient transport phenomena such as heat conduction, fluid flow and other potential flow problems; hydrodynamics. *Mailing Add:* 4265 Davis Way Livermore CA 94550

EDWARDS, BEN E, b Ross, Calif, Oct 14, 35; m 57, 66, 77; c 9. INDUSTRIAL ORGANIC CHEMISTRY. *Educ:* Mass Inst Technol, SB, 57; Ind Univ, PhD(org chem), 62. *Prof Exp:* NIH fel org chem, Columbia Univ, 62-63; res assoc, Southwest Found Res & Educ, 63-67; res chemist, Chem Sci Div, Res Inst, Ill Inst Technol, 67-68; asst prof, Dept Chem, Univ NC, Greensboro, 68-73; CHIEF CHEMIST, OLD-NORTH MFG CO, INC, 73- *Concurrent Pos:* Part-time prof, Appalachian State Univ, 81. *Mem:* AAAS; Am Chem Soc; The Chem Soc. *Res:* Concrete curing membranes; accessory chemicals for concrete construction; organic synthesis; steroids; sulfur compounds; medicinal chemistry. *Mailing Add:* Old-North Mfg Co Inc Box 598 Lenoir NC 28645

EDWARDS, BENJAMIN FRANK, b Everett, Wash, Jan 20, 47; m 71. DEVELOPMENTAL BIOLOGY. *Educ:* Univ Calif, Davis, BS, 69, PhD(zool), 75. *Prof Exp:* RES ASST EMBRYOL, DEPT BIOL, REED COL, 74- *Concurrent Pos:* Sigma Xi res grant in aid, 71; A Sloan fel, Reed Col, 74-75. *Mem:* AAAS; Am Soc Zoologists; Soc Develop Biol; Sigma Xi. *Res:* Biochemistry of early development; surface macromolecules in cell-cell recognition and interaction. *Mailing Add:* Dept of Biol Reed Col Portland OR 97202

EDWARDS, BETTY F, b Athens, Ga, Mar 13, 15; m 36; c 2. ANATOMY. *Educ:* Agnes Scott Col, AB, 35; Emory Univ, MA, 51, PhD(anat), 63. *Prof Exp:* Instr biol, Emory Univ, 43-45, instr anat, 51-55; instr biol, Ga State Col, 49-50 & 55-61; instr anat, 63-66, asst prof histol & embryol, 66-81, EMER PROF ANAT, EMORY UNIV, 81- *Mem:* Am Soc Zool; Am Inst Biol Sci; Am Asn Anat; Tissue Cult Asn; Sigma Xi. *Res:* Muscle and plant tissue culture; responses of animal and plant tissues to gravity; effects of weightlessness on growth. *Mailing Add:* Dept of Anat Emory Univ Atlanta GA 30322

EDWARDS, BRENDA KAY, b Paducah, Ky, Oct 17, 46. BIOSTATISTICS. *Educ:* Murray State Univ, BS, 68; Vanderbilt Univ, MS, 70; Univ NC, Chapel Hill, PhD(biostatist), 75. *Prof Exp:* Asst prof biostatist, Col Med, Univ Cincinnati, 75-78; BIOSTATISTICIAN, NAT CANCER INST, 78- *Mem:* Am Statist Asn; Biomet Soc. *Res:* Analysis of survival data and other statistical methods applicable to epidemiological research. *Mailing Add:* Apt 1 10524 Weymouth St Bethesda MD 20814

EDWARDS, BRIAN RONALD, b Norwich, UK, Nov 20, 44; m 68; c 2. MEDICAL PHYSIOLOGY, RENAL PHYSIOLOGY. *Educ:* Sheffield Univ, BSc, 66, PhD(endocrinol), 69. *Prof Exp:* asst prof, 73-80, ASSOC PROF PHYSIOL, DARTMOUTH MED SCH, 73-80. *Concurrent Pos:* Can Med Res Coun res fel, McGill Univ, 69-73. *Mem:* Am Physiol Soc; Am Soc Nephrol. *Res:* Clearance studies in unanesthetized rats, emphasizing hormonal control of renal function in normal and diabetes insipidus rats. *Mailing Add:* Dept of Physiol Dartmouth Med Sch Hanover NH 03755

EDWARDS, BYRON N, b Trinidad, Colo, Sept 16, 32; m 56; c 3. APPLIED PHYSICS, ELECTRICAL ENGINEERING. *Educ:* Univ Calif, Berkeley, BS, 55, MS, 57, PhD(elec eng), 60. *Prof Exp:* Assoc elec eng, Univ Calif, Berkeley, 56-58; res scientist appl physics, Aeronutronics Div, 59-62, res scientist appl physics, Philco Res Labs, 62-80, SUPVR FORD AEROSPACE & COMS AERONUTRONIC, FORD MOTOR CO, 80- *Concurrent Pos:* Lectr, Univ Calif, Irvine, 70- *Mem:* Inst Elec & Electronics Engrs. *Res:* Microwave engineering and applications of gas discharges; infrared engineering and physics, communication and tracking systems; electro-optical devices. *Mailing Add:* 847 S Cedarwood Ave Orange CA 92669

EDWARDS, CAROL ABE, b Hilo, Hawaii; c 1. APPLIED MATHEMATICS. *Educ:* Univ Calif, Berkeley, AB, 60; Univ Ill, Urbana, AM, 62, PhD(math), 73. *Prof Exp:* From instr to asst prof math, Hilo Col, Univ Hawaii, 62-71; asst prof, St Louis Univ, 73-75; assoc prof, 75-77, PROF MATH, ST LOUIS COMMUNITY COL, FLORISSANT VALLEY, 77- *Concurrent Pos:* Adj assoc prof math, St Louis Univ, 75, adj prof math, 80. *Mem:* Math Asn Am; Nat Coun Teachers Math. *Res:* Subgroups of the group of permutations and complementations of the independent variables of a Boolean function; the teaching of mathematics at the undergraduate level, especially the lower division. *Mailing Add:* Math Dept St Louis Community Col 3400 Pershall Rd St Louis MO 63135

EDWARDS, CECILE HOOVER, b East St Louis, Ill, Oct 20, 26; m 51; c 3. NUTRITION, BIOCHEMISTRY. *Educ:* Tuskegee Inst, BS, 46, MS, 47; Iowa State Univ, PhD(nutrit), 50; Am Bd Nutrit, dipl human nutrit, 63. *Prof Exp:* Res assoc nutrit, Iowa State Univ, 49-50; asst prof & res assoc foods & nutrit, Tuskegee Inst, 50-56; prof nutrit, NC A&T State Univ, 56-71, chmn dept home econ, 68-71; chmn dept home econ, 71-74, PROF NUTRIT, HOWARD UNIV, 71-, DEAN SCH HUMAN ECOL, 74- *Concurrent Pos:* Head dept foods & nutrit, Tuskegee Inst, 52-56; collabr, Bur Human Nutrit & Home Econ, Agr Res Serv, USDA, 52-55; guest scientist, Cent Food Technol Res Inst, Mysore, India, 67-68; partic distinguished scientists lect series, Bennett Col, 70; adj prof, Univ NC, Chapel Hill, 71; mem exec bd, Asn Adminrs Home Econ, mem nat adv comt long range res in home econ; mem comt interpretation of recommended dietary allowances, Nat Res Coun; pres, Southeastern Col Conf Teachers of Food & Nutrit; chmn panel community nutrit educ, White House Conf Food, Nutrit & Health, 69; vpres opers, Am Home Econ Asn, 75-77; mem, Expert Panel Nitrates, Nitrites & Nitrosamines, 75-79; mem adv comt dir, NIH, 76-78; consult, Nat Inst Cancer, 72-74. *Honors & Awards:* Plaque for Contributions to Sci, Nat Coun Negro Women, 63; Scroll & Key Outstand Contribution to Sci & Educ, City East St Louis, Ill. *Mem:* Am Inst Nutrit; Am Home Econ Asn; Soc Nutrit Educ; Am Dietetic Asn; Nat Inst Sci. *Res:* Amino acid composition of foods; utilization of protein from vegetable sources; utilization of wheat by adult man; utilization of the amino acid methionine; utilization of amino acids in protein deficiency; pica; wheat-soy-beef mixtures; adaptation to protein deficiency; plant protein supplement from locally grown grains in Nigeria. *Mailing Add:* Sch Human Ecol Howard Univ Washington DC 20059

EDWARDS, CHARLES, b Washington, DC, Sept 22, 25; m 51; c 4. PHYSIOLOGY, BIOPHYSICS. *Educ:* Johns Hopkins Univ, AB, 45, MA, 48, PhD(biophys), 53. *Prof Exp:* Hon res asst biophys, Univ Col, London, 53-54, asst lectr, 54-55; from instr to asst prof physiol optics, Johns Hopkins Univ, 55-58; asst res prof physiol, Univ Utah, 58-60; from assoc prof to prof, Univ Minn, 60-67; PROF BIOL SCI, STATE UNIV NY ALBANY, 67-, DIR NEUROBIOL RES CTR, 70- *Concurrent Pos:* Nat Found Infantile Paralysis fel, 53-54; Lalor fel, Marine Biol Lab, 57; Lederle fel, 59-60; Japan Soc Prom Sci fel; mem physiol study sect, NIH, 71-75; vis prof physiol, Czech Acad Sci, US Nat Acad & Czech Acad Exchange, 80. *Mem:* Soc Gen Physiol (secy, 71-73); Am Physiol Soc; Biophys Soc. *Res:* Membrane phenomena in excitable tissue; muscle contraction. *Mailing Add:* Dept of Biol Sci State Univ of NY Albany NY 12222

EDWARDS, CHARLES HENRY, JR, b Pleasant Hill, Tenn, Sept 27, 37; m 58; c 3. MATHEMATICS. *Educ:* Univ Tenn, BS, 58, PhD(math), 60. *Prof Exp:* Asst prof math, Univ Tenn, 61; from instr to asst prof, Univ Wis, 61-64; assoc prof, 64-69, dir, Inst Res Planning, 74-76, PROF MATH, UNIV GA, 69- *Concurrent Pos:* Sloan res fel, 64-66; mem, Inst Advan Study, 65-66. *Mem:* Am Math Soc; Math Asn Am. *Res:* Topology and geometry of manifolds and applications; history of mathematics. *Mailing Add:* Dept of Math Univ of Ga Athens GA 30602

EDWARDS, CHARLES RICHARD, b Lubbock, Tex, Jan 22, 45; m 66; c 2. INTEGRATED PEST MANAGEMENT. *Educ:* Tex Tech Univ, BS, 68; Iowa State Univ, MS, 70, PhD(entom), 72. *Prof Exp:* PROF ENTOM, DEPT ENTOM, PURDUE UNIV, 72- *Concurrent Pos:* Chmn res soybean arthropods, Coop State Res Serv, USDA, 81-82; mem task force, Exten Comt Orgn & Policy, Integrated Pest Mgt, 77-82 & Coun Agr Sci Technol, Integrated Pest Mgt, 78-82; consult, Agri-PACE Inc, 80- *Mem:* Entom Soc Am; Am Registry Prof Entom. *Res:* Development of management tactics for arthropod pests of soybeans, especially development of economic injury levels; host plant resistance; effect of cropping systems on arthropod pests and chemical control with emphasis on pest species targeting. *Mailing Add:* Dept Entom Hall Entom Purdue Univ West Lafayette IN 47907

EDWARDS, CONSTANCE CARVER, b Baltimore, Md, June 8, 49. PURE MATHEMATICS. *Educ:* Col Notre Dame, Md, BA, 68; Univ Wis-Milwaukee, MA, 70, PhD(math), 75. *Prof Exp:* Teaching asst math, Univ Wis-Milwaukee, 68-75, instr, Univ Wis-Parkside, 74; asst prof, 75-81, ASSOC PROF MATH, IND UNIV-PURDUE UNIV, FT WAYNE, 81- *Concurrent Pos:* Res grant, Ind Univ-Purdue Univ, Ft Wayne, 78. *Mem:* Am Math Soc; Math Asn Am. *Res:* Regular semigroups and ordered semigroups. *Mailing Add:* Dept of Math Ind Univ-Purdue Univ Ft Wayne IN 46805

EDWARDS, DALE IVAN, b Mattoon, Ill, Jan 12, 30; m 55; c 4. NEMATOLOGY, PLANT PATHOLOGY. *Educ:* Eastern Ill Univ, BS, 56; Univ Ill, MS, 60, PhD(plant path), 62. *Prof Exp:* Asst plant path, Univ Ill, 56-62; assoc pathologist, Tela Railroad Co, 62-65; asst prof plant path, 73-77, NEMATOLOGIST, SCI & EDUC ADMIN-AGR RES, USDA, UNIV ILL, URBANA, 65-, ASSOC PROF PLANT PATH, 77- *Mem:* Soc Nematol; Europ Soc Nematol; Org Trop Nematol. *Res:* Host-parasite relationships and control of plant parasitic nematodes affecting soybean. *Mailing Add:* Univ Ill Dept Plant Path 1102 S Goodwin Urbana IL 61801

EDWARDS, DALLAS CRAIG, b Clearfield, Pa, Sept 9, 39; m 64. POPULATION ECOLOGY, COMMUNITY ECOLOGY. *Educ:* Swarthmore Col, BA, 61; Univ Chicago, PhD(zool), 65. *Prof Exp:* NSF fel, Scripps Inst, Univ Calif, 65-66; asst prof zool, 66-72, ASSOC PROF ZOOL, UNIV MASS, AMHERST, 72- *Concurrent Pos:* Vis investr systematics-ecol prog, Woods Hole Marine Biol Lab, 70-72. *Mem:* Ecol Soc Am; Brit Ecol Soc; Am Soc Naturalists; Estuarine Res Soc. *Res:* Population and community ecology of benthic marine invertebrates, especially the molluscs of intertidal sedimentary habitats. *Mailing Add:* Dept of Zool Univ of Mass Amherst MA 01003

EDWARDS, DAVID FRANKLIN, b Ironton, Ohio, Mar 2, 28; m 54; c 2. SOLID STATE PHYSICS, LIGHT SCATTERING SPECTROSCOPY. *Educ:* Miami Univ, Ohio, AB, 49; Univ Cincinnati, MS, 53, PhD(nuclear shell struct), 53. *Prof Exp:* Solid state physicist, Battelle Mem Inst, 53-55, Willow Run Lab, Univ Mich, 55-61 & Lincoln Lab, Mass Inst Technol, 61-65; prof physics, Colo State Univ, 65-69, prof physics & elec eng, 69-74; PHYSICIST, LOS ALAMOS NAT LAB, NMEX, 74- *Concurrent Pos:* Fulbright prof physics, Univ Rio Grande do Sul, Brazil, 70-71; Nat Acad Sci & USSR Acad Sci vis scientist to USSR, Lebedev Physics Inst, 75-76. *Mem:* Am Phys Soc. *Res:* Solid state spectroscopy; nonlinear optical effects; second harmonic generation; mixing at optical frequencies; laser induced damage; laser-matter interaction; laser isotope separation; procurement of kilohertz carbon lasers for operation in uranium isotope separation plant; laser interaction with window and mirror materials. *Mailing Add:* Los Alamos Nat Lab MS 564 Los Alamos NM 87545

EDWARDS, DAVID OLAF, b Liverpool, Eng, Apr 27, 32. PHYSICS. *Educ:* Oxford Univ, BA, 53, MA, PhD(physics), 57. *Prof Exp:* Pressed Steel Co res fel, Clarendon Lab, Oxford Univ, 57-58; vis asst prof, 58-60, from asst prof to assoc prof, 60-65, PROF PHYSICS, OHIO STATE UNIV, 65- *Concurrent Pos:* Vis prof, Univ Sussex, 68, Israel Inst Technol, 71 & Univ Paris, 78, 82; consult, Brookhaven Nat Lab, 75-77 & Los Alamos Nat Lab, 79- *Mem:* fel Am Phys Soc. *Res:* Liquid and solid He3 and He4; superfluidity; cryogenics. *Mailing Add:* Dept Physics Ohio State Univ 174 W 18th Ave Columbus OH 43210

EDWARDS, DAVID OWEN, b Buffalo, NY, Dec 15, 30; m 53; c 3. FINANCIAL CONTROL. *Educ:* Univ Mich, BS, 53; Univ Wis, PhD(chem eng), 61. *Prof Exp:* Instr chem eng, Univ Wis, 57-58; res engr, Film Dept, 60-69, consult, Cent Systs & Serv Dept, Systs & Comput Div, 69-74, auditor, Finance Dept, 74-77, planning specialist, Cent Res & Develop, 77-80, SR CONSULT, FINANCE DEPT, E I DU PONT DE NEMOURS & CO, INC, 80- *Res:* Plastic film manufacture and processing; applications of computer techniques; venture modeling and computer applications. *Mailing Add:* Cent Res & Develop Dept E I du Pont de Nemours & Co Wilmington DE 19898

EDWARDS, DONALD K, b Richmond, Calif, Oct 11, 32; m 55; c 2. THERMODYNAMICS. *Educ:* Univ Calif, Berkeley, BS, 54, MS, 56, PhD(mech eng), 59. *Prof Exp:* Thermodyn engr, Lockheed Missile & Space Div, Calif, 58-59; from asst prof to prof eng, Univ Calif, Los Angeles, 59-81, chmn, Chem Nuclear & Thermal Eng Dept, 75-78. *Concurrent Pos:* Fac investr, NSF grants, 59-81; consult, TRW Systs, 62-81; pres & chmn bd, Gier Dunkle Instruments, Inc, Santa Monica, 63-66; assoc ed, J Heat Transfer, 75-81. *Honors & Awards:* Am Soc Mech Engrs Mem Award, 73; First Thermophysics Award, Am Inst Aeronautics & Astronautics, 76. *Mem:* Am Soc Mech Engrs; Optical Soc Am; Solar Energy Soc; Am Inst Aeronaut & Astronaut. *Res:* Heat and mass transfer; thermal radiation; radiant energy transfer between solids and through absorbing, emitting, scattering media; molecular gas radiation; thermal radiation instrumentation; natural convection; radiation and convection. *Mailing Add:* Dept Chem Nuclear & Thermal Eng Sch of Eng Univ of Calif Los Angeles CA 90024

EDWARDS, DONALD M(ERVIN), b Tracy, Minn, Apr 16, 38; m 64; c 3. AGRICULTURAL ENGINEERING. *Educ:* SDak State Univ, BS, 60, MS, 61; Purdue Univ, PhD(agr & civil eng), 66. *Prof Exp:* Mem coop educ prog, Soil Conserv Serv, USDA, 56-61; asst agr eng, SDak State Univ, 60-61 & Purdue Univ, 62-66; assoc prof, 66-70, asst dean, 70-73, dir, Eng Res Ctr, 73-76, PROF AGR ENG, UNIV NEBR, LINCOLN, 70-, ASSOC DEAN COL ENG & TECHNOL, 73-, DIR ENERGY RES & DEVELOP CTR, 76- *Concurrent Pos:* Consult & collabr to several state & fed agencies & industs. *Honors & Awards:* Outstanding Educr Award, Am Soc Agr Engrs, 76. *Mem:* AAAS; Am Soc Agr Engrs; Sigma Xi; Am Soc Eng Educ; Nat Soc Prof Engrs. *Res:* Water resources engineering, particularly irrigation; porous media; water pollution; engineering education as related to new teaching techniques and engineering educational programs; energy. *Mailing Add:* Off of the Dean Univ of Nebr Lincoln NE 68588

EDWARDS, DOUGLAS CAMERON, b Ottawa, Ont, Oct 21, 25; m 49; c 5. RUBBER CHEMISTRY. *Educ:* Queen's Univ, Ont, BSc, 47. *Prof Exp:* Res chemist, 49-64, res assoc, 64-69, SCI ADV RUBBER CHEM, POLYSAR LTD, 69- *Mem:* Am Chem Soc; Chem Inst Can. *Res:* Rubber science and technology. *Mailing Add:* Tech Develop Div Polysar Ltd Sarnia Can

EDWARDS, DOYLE RAY, b Dexter, Mo, Dec 22, 38; m 59; c 4. NUCLEAR ENGINEERING. *Educ:* Mo Sch Mines, BS, 59; Mass Inst Technol, SM, 61, ScD(nuclear eng), 63. *Prof Exp:* From asst prof to assoc prof, 63-73, PROF NUCLEAR ENG, UNIV MO-ROLLA, 73- *Concurrent Pos:* NSF res grant, 64-66; AEC equip grant, 65, 66 & 68, traineeship grant, 65-71; consult, Assoc Elec Coop, Inc, 75-; Elec Power Res Inst grant, 80- *Mem:* Am Nuclear Soc; Nat Soc Prof Engrs. *Res:* Computer methods in nuclear engineering; computer simulation of radiation damage; economical recovery of waste heat; heat transfer in fuel bundles. *Mailing Add:* Nuclear Eng Univ Mo Rolla MO 65401

EDWARDS, ERNEST PRESTON, b Landour, India, Sept 25, 19; US citizen; m 55. ORNITHOLOGY. *Educ:* Univ Va, BA, 40; Cornell Univ, MA, 41, PhD(ornith), 49. *Prof Exp:* Instr biol, Univ Ky, 49-50; civilian biologist, US Army Chem Corps, 52-54; asst prof biol, Hanover Col, 55-56; assoc dir, Mus Natural Hist Houston, 57-60; prof biol, Univ of the Pac, 60-65; PROF BIOL, SWEET BRIAR COL, 65- *Mem:* Cooper Ornith Soc; Wilson Ornith Soc; Am Ornith Union; Sigma Xi. *Res:* Ecology, distribution and taxonomy of tropical birds; ecology of the Blue Ridge Mountains; nomenclature and distribution of birds of the world. *Mailing Add:* Dept Biol Sweet Briar Col Sweet Briar VA 24595

EDWARDS, FREDERICK H(ORTON), b Can, June 23, 15; US citizen; m 51; c 2. ELECTRICAL ENGINEERING. *Educ:* Univ BC, BASc, 49; NS Tech Col, MSc, 55. *Prof Exp:* Design engr, Apparatus Div, Can Westinghouse, 49-55; ASSOC PROF ELEC ENG, UNIV MASS, AMHERST, 55- *Concurrent Pos:* NSF fel, Cambridge Math Lab, 65-66. *Mem:* Inst Elec & Electronics Engrs. *Res:* Switching circuit theory and digital system design; energy conversion. *Mailing Add:* Dept of Elec Eng Univ of Mass Amherst MA 01003

EDWARDS, GAYLE DAMERON, b Alexandria, La, Mar 8, 27; m 55. PETROLEUM CHEMISTRY. *Educ:* La Col, BA, 47; Univ Tex, MA, 48, PhD(chem), 51. *Prof Exp:* Res chemist, Pan Am Refining Corp, 51-53; supvr, 53-66, mgr tech serv, Neches Plant, 66-77, COORDR ENVIRON CONTROL, TEXACO CHEM CO, 77- *Mem:* Am Chem Soc. *Res:* Petrochemicals; surface active agents; organometallic compounds. *Mailing Add:* Texaco Chem Co 4800 Fournace Pl Bellaire TX 77401

EDWARDS, GEORGE, b Glasgow, Scotland, June 28, 18; nat US; m 44; c 3. CHEMISTRY. *Educ:* Glasgow Univ, BSc, 41, PhD(chem), 46. *Prof Exp:* Exp officer chem eng, S W Scotland Br, Woolwich Arsenal, 41-46; lectr, Royal Col Sci & Technol, Scotland, 46-52; res assoc chem, Enrico Fermi Inst Nuclear Studies, Univ Chicago, 52-55; group leader geol age measurement, 55-64, mgr anal chem, 64-81, RES ASSOC, SHELL DEVELOP CO, 81- *Honors & Awards:* Sir James Bielby Prize, 43. *Mem:* Brit Inst Chem Eng. *Res:* Stable isotope absolute geologic age measurement; cosmic abundance of elements; analytical chemistry. *Mailing Add:* 3100 Mid Lane Houston TX 77027

EDWARDS, GERALD ALONZO, b Henderson, NC, Nov 22, 21; m 51; c 3. PHYSICAL CHEMISTRY. *Educ:* NC Col, BS, 41; Univ Buffalo, PhD(chem), 51. *Prof Exp:* Chemist, Lake Ont Ord Works, 42-43; chem operator, Hooker Electrochem Co, 43-45; chemist, Bell Aircraft Corp, 45-47; asst, Univ Buffalo, 64-66, teacher, Dept Chem, NC Col, 50-51; res assoc, Carver Found & asst prof chem, Tuskegee Inst, 51-55, assoc prof, 55-56; prof chem & chmn dept, NC A&T State Univ, 56-70 & chmn div nat sci & math, 68-70; prog mgr, Africa & Asia Sects, 74-81, PROG MGR, LATIN AM & PAC SECTS, DIV INT PROGS, NSF, 81- *Concurrent Pos:* Consult Chem, Columbia Univ-Agency Int Develop & Ohio State Univ-Agency Int Develop Proj, Regional Col Educ, Mysore, India, 66-68; assoc prog dir, Sci Educ, NSF, 70-74. *Mem:* Sigma Xi; Am Soc Pub Admin; Am Chem Soc. *Res:* Physical chemistry of polymers; copolymerization; electrical conductance; utilization and transport of amino acids. *Mailing Add:* Nat Sci Found 1800 G St NW Washington DC 20550

EDWARDS, GERALD ELMO, b Gretna, Va, Sept 17, 42; m 69. PLANT SCIENCE, PHYSIOLOGY. *Educ:* Va Polytech Inst, BS, 65; Univ Ill, MS, 66; Univ Calif, Riverside, PhD(plant sci), 69. *Prof Exp:* Fel biochem, Univ Ga, 69-71; from asst prof to assoc prof, 71-78, PROF & CHMN, BOTANY DEPT, WASH STATE UNIV, PULLMAN, 81- *Concurrent Pos:* Vis prof bot, Univ Sheffield, 77-78. *Mem:* Am Soc Plant Physiol; Japanese Soc Plant Physiol. *Res:* Photosynthesis; biological energetics. *Mailing Add:* Botany Dept Wash State Univ Pullman WA 99164

EDWARDS, GLEN ROBERT, b Monte Vista, Colo, July 21, 39; m 59; c 2. PHYSICAL METALLURGY, METALLURGY. *Educ:* Colo Sch Mines, BS, 61; Univ NMex, MS, 67; Stanford Univ, PhD(mat sci), 71. *Prof Exp:* Staff mem plutonium metall, Los Alamos Sci Lab, 63-67; asst mat sci, Stanford Univ, 67-71; asst & assoc prof, Naval Postgrad Sch, 71-76; assoc prof, 76-79, PROF METALL ENG, COLO SCH MINES, 79- *Honors & Awards:* Pres Award, Am Soc Metals, 80; Adams Mem Membership Award, Am Welding Soc, 81-85. *Mem:* Am Soc Metals; Am Inst Minimg & Metall Engrs; Sigma Xi; Am Welding Soc. *Res:* Mechanical metallurgy; deformation processes; reactive metals; welding metallurgy. *Mailing Add:* Dept Metall Eng Colo Sch Mines Golden CO 80401

EDWARDS, GORDON STUART, b Old Greenwich, Conn, Feb 11, 38; c 2. TOXICOLOGY. *Educ:* Amherst Col, BA, 59; Harvard Univ, MA, 63; Mass Inst Technol, ScD(nutrit biochem), 70; Am Bd Toxicol, dipl. *Prof Exp:* Prof fel cell biol, Rockefeller Univ, 70-72; chief biol sect, Cancer Res Div, Thermo Electron Corp, 77-81; asst prof, 72-77, ASSOC PROF PHARMACOL & GENETICS, GEORGE WASHINGTON UNIV, 77-; CONSULT

TOXICOL, 81- *Concurrent Pos:* Consult, Food & Drug Admin, 74-76 & Environ Protection Agency, 77; staff mem, Med Col Va Cancer Ctr, 75-77 & Howard Univ Cancer Ctr, 75-77. *Mem:* Am Asn Cancer Res; Soc Toxicol; Environ Mutagen Soc; Genetic Toxicol Asn. *Res:* Mechanisms of chemical carcinogenesis; DNA repair; genetic toxicology; carcinogen metabolism; occupational toxicology. *Mailing Add:* 34 Everett St 45 First Ave Natick MA 01760

EDWARDS, H(ERBERT) M(ARTELL), b Brockville, Ont, Dec 16, 21; m 45; c 3. CIVIL ENGINEERING. *Educ:* Queen's Univ, Ont, BSc, 44; Purdue Univ, MSCE, 54. *Prof Exp:* Design engr aircraft, Can Ltd, 44 & Douglas Aircraft, Inc, Calif, 44-45; stress analyst & designer, Can Ltd, 45-46; lectr, 46-53, from asst prof to assoc prof, 54-67, assoc dean, Fac Appl Sci, 71-75, PROF CIVIL ENG, QUEEN'S UNIV, ONT, 67-, HEAD DEPT, 75- *Concurrent Pos:* Consult, 55- *Mem:* Fel Inst Transp Engrs; Eng Inst Can. *Res:* Traffic planning; mathematical explorations for traffic movements; soils engineering; highway pavement design. *Mailing Add:* Ellis Hall Queen's Univ Kingston ON K7L 3N6 Can

EDWARDS, HARDY MALCOLM, JR, b Ruston, La, Nov 16, 29; m 54; c 1. NUTRITIONAL BIOCHEMISTRY. *Educ:* Southwestern La Inst, BSA, 49; Univ Fla, MSA, 50; Cornell Univ, PhD(nutrit biochem), 53. *Prof Exp:* Res fel animal nutrit, Univ Fla, 49-50; res asst & nutrit chemist, Cornell Univ, 50-53; from res biochemist to sr res biochemist, Int Minerals & Chem Corp, 55-57; from asst prof to assoc, 57-66, dean, Grad Sch, 72-79, PROF NUTRIT BIOCHEM, UNIV GA, 66- *Concurrent Pos:* Res career develop award, NIH, 63-72; res assoc, Dept Physiol Chem, Univ Lund, 64-65; Guggenheim Mem fel & vis prof, Tours, France & Cambridge, Eng. *Honors & Awards:* Poultry Nutrit Res Award, Am Feed Mfg Asn, 62. *Mem:* Am Soc Animal Sci; Poultry Sci Asn; Am Inst Nutrit; Soc Exp Biol & Med. *Res:* Lipid nutrition of aves; mechanism of divalent ion adsorption. *Mailing Add:* Dept of Poultry Sci Univ of Ga Athens GA 30601

EDWARDS, HAROLD HENRY, b Andes, NY, July 14, 32; m 62; c 3. BIOPHYSICS. *Educ:* Cornell Univ, BEP, 55; Rensselaer Polytech Inst, PhD(biophys), 69. *Prof Exp:* Electronic engr, Res & Develop Ctr, Gen Elec Co, 55-65; asst, Rensselaer Polytech Inst, 65-69; res assoc anat, Med Ctr, Duke Univ, 69-71; asst mem biochem dept, 71-75, DIR ELECTRON MICROSCOPE FACIL, ST JUDE CHILDREN'S RES HOSP, 75- *Concurrent Pos:* Adj prof biol, Memphis State Univ, 75- *Mem:* Biophys Soc; Inst Elec & Electronic Engrs; Electron Microscope Soc Am; NY Acad Sci. *Res:* Membrane structure and function; interaction of cytoskeleton with membranes; electron microscopy. *Mailing Add:* Biochem-St Jude Child Res Hosp 332 N Lauderdale Memphis TN 38101

EDWARDS, HAROLD HERBERT, b Milford, Mich, Oct 31, 37; m 62; c 2. PLANT PHYSIOLOGY, BIOCHEMISTRY. *Educ:* Albion Col, BA, 60; Univ Wis, MS, 62, PhD(bot), 65. *Prof Exp:* Wis Alumni res fel, Univ Wis, 65; NIH fel, Univ Nebr, 65-67; asst prof, 67-72, assoc prof, 72-77, PROF BIOL SCI, WESTERN ILL UNIV, 77- *Res:* Plant physiology, ultrastructure and biochemistry of the obligate parasite-host complex of powdery mildewed barley and brown spot disease of soybeans. *Mailing Add:* Dept of Biol Western Ill Univ Macomb IL 61455

EDWARDS, HAROLD M, b Champaign, Ill, Aug, 6, 36; m 79. NUMBER THEORY. *Educ:* Univ Wis, BA, 56; Columbia Univ, MA, 57; Harvard Univ, PhD(math), 61. *Prof Exp:* Instr math, Harvard Univ, 61-62; res assoc math, Columbia Univ, 62-63, asst prof math, 63-66; asst prof, 66-70, assoc prof, 70-79, PROF MATH, NY UNIV, 79- *Concurrent Pos:* Vis sr lectr, Australian Nat Univ, 71; fel, John Simon Guggenheim Mem Fdn, 81. *Honors & Awards:* Steele Prize, Am Math Soc, 80. *Mem:* Fel NY Acad Sci; Am Math Soc; Math Asn Am. *Res:* History of mathematics and the history of number theory, particularly in the latter part of the 19th century. *Mailing Add:* Courant Inst NY Univ New York NY 10012

EDWARDS, HARRY WALLACE, b Syracuse, NY, Oct 6, 39; m 66; c 2. PHYSICAL CHEMISTRY, ENVIRONMENTAL SCIENCE & ENGINEERING. *Educ:* Univ Nev, BS, 62; Univ Ariz, PhD(phys chem), 66. *Prof Exp:* Asst prof, 66-70, assoc prof, 70-76, PROF MECH ENG, COLO STATE UNIV, 76- *Concurrent Pos:* Res grants, NSF, 67-77, Pub Serv Co Colo, 67-70 & Environ Protection Agency, 70-73; consult, NSF, 71-72, NASA, 76-77 & Solar Energy Res Inst, 79-; alt mem, Comt Motor Vehicle Emissions, Colo Air Pollution Control Comn, 74-76; res, NASA, 75-78; sr vis fel, Univ Lancaster, 77-78; regional ed, Environ Technol Letters, 79- *Mem:* Am Chem Soc; AAAS; Air Pollution Control Asn; NY Acad Sci. *Res:* Surface chemistry; air pollution; environmental effects of trace substances; air pollution control, especially oxides of nitrogen; aerosol behavior; identification of pollution sources. *Mailing Add:* Dept of Mech Eng Colo State Univ Ft Collins CO 80523

EDWARDS, HOWARD D(AWSON), b Athens, Ga, Dec 11, 23; m 46; c 4. AEROSPACE ENGINEERING. *Educ:* Univ Ga, BS, 44; Duke Univ, PhD(physics), 50. *Prof Exp:* Atmospheric physicist & chief, Atmospheric Composition Sect, Air Force Cambridge Res Labs, 49-51 & Atmospheric Energy Br, 51-56; opers res scientist, Lockheed Aircraft, 56-59; res assoc prof physics, Ga Inst Technol, 59-64, assoc prof aerospace eng, 64-65, prof aerospace eng, 65-81; PRES, SIR-ATLANTA, INC, 63- *Res:* Upper atmosphere research; automatic test equipment design and manufacture. *Mailing Add:* SIR-Atlanta Inc 331 Luckie St Atlanta GA 30313

EDWARDS, J GORDON, b Wilmington, Ohio, Aug 24, 19; m 46; c 1. ENTOMOLOGY, SYSTEMATIC ZOOLOGY. *Educ:* Butler Univ, BS, 42; Ohio State Univ, MSc, 46, PhD(entomol), 49. *Prof Exp:* Instr entomol & zool, 49-52, from asst prof to assoc prof, 52-59, PROF ENTOMOL, SAN JOSE STATE COL, 59- *Concurrent Pos:* Bd mem, Coun Environ Balance. *Mem:* Sierra Club; Entom Soc Am; Nat Audubon Soc; Am Coun Sci & Health; Coun Agr Sci & Technol. *Res:* Coleoptera biology and taxonomy; high altitude biology; medical entomology; tropical biology; chemical pesticides and the environment. *Mailing Add:* Dept of Biol San Jose State Univ San Jose CA 95192

EDWARDS, JAMES WESLEY, b Evansville, Ind, Sept 1, 38; m 61; c 1. ZOOLOGY, GENETICS. *Educ:* Evansville Col, AB, 60; Utah State Univ, MS, 62, PhD(zool), 64. *Prof Exp:* Asst prof biol, St Francis Col, Pa, 64-65; assoc prof, 65-69, chmn dept, 65-80, PROF BIOL, SALEM COL, 69- *Mem:* AAAS. *Res:* Genetics of abnormal head development in Drosophila melanogaster, with special reference to eyelessness. *Mailing Add:* 3432 Kinnamon Rd Winston-Salem NC 27104

EDWARDS, JESSE EFREM, b Hyde Park, Mass, July 14, 11; m 52; c 2. PATHOLOGY. *Educ:* Tufts Col, BS, 32, MD, 35. *Prof Exp:* Intern, Albany Hosp, NY, 36-37; resident path, Mallory Inst Path, Boston City Hosp, 35-36, asst, 37-40, assoc pathologist, 41-53; from asst prof to prof path anat, Mayo Found, 46-60, CLIN PROF PATH, SCH MED & PROF GRAD SCH, UNIV MINN, ST PAUL, 60-; DIR LABS, CHARLES T MILLER HOSP, 60- *Concurrent Pos:* Fel, Nat Cancer Inst, 40-42; instr, Sch Med, Boston Univ, 38 & Tufts Col, 39-40; consult, Wash Home Incurables, 40-42, Mayo Clin, 46-60, Surgeon Gen, Dept Army, Hennepin County Hosp, Minneapolis, 64-, Dept Med, Minneapolis Vet Hosp, 66- & St Paul Ramsey Hosp, 69- *Honors & Awards:* Distinguished Serv Award, Mod Med, 64; Distinguished Teacher Award, Minn Med Found, 74. *Mem:* Am Acad Pediat; fel AMA; Am Asn Path & Bact; Am Heart Asn (pres, 67-68); Int Acad Path (pres). *Res:* Congenital anomalies of heart and great vessels; pathology of cardiovascular diseases, congenital and acquired; induction of carcinoma in experimental animals; pathology of experimental and human cancer. *Mailing Add:* United Hosps Miller Div St Paul MN 55102

EDWARDS, JIMMIE GARVIN, b Boswell, Okla, July 27, 34; m 56; c 3. HIGH TEMPERATURE CHEMISTRY, MASS SPECTROMETRY. *Educ:* Cent State Col, Okla, BS, 56; Okla State Univ, PhD(chem), 64. *Prof Exp:* Instr chem, Univ Nev, Reno, 60-61; chemist, Radiochem, Inc, 61-62; res assoc chem, Univ Kans, 64-65; asst prof chem, Univ Mo-Rolla, 65-66; res assoc chem, Univ Kans, 66-67; asst prof, 67-71, assoc prof, 71-76, PROF CHEM, UNIV TOLEDO, 76- *Mem:* Am Chem Soc; AAAS; Am Soc Spectrometry; Sigma Xi; Electrochem Soc. *Res:* High temperature physical and inorganic chemistry; materials research: mass spectrometry; thioboric acids; binary and ternary metal sulfides; rarefied gas dynamics. *Mailing Add:* Dept Chem Univ Toledo Toledo OH 43606

EDWARDS, JOHN ANTHONY, b Chester, Eng, Nov 9, 35; US citizen; c 2. MEDICAL GENETICS. *Educ:* Liverpool Univ, MB & ChB, 59, MD, 72. *Prof Exp:* From res asst prof to res assoc prof, 69-74, assoc prof med & clin assoc prof pharmacol, 74-79, PROF MED, STATE UNIV NY, BUFFALO, 79-; CHIEF MED, SISTERS CHARITY HOSP, 78- *Concurrent Pos:* Vis consult med genetics, West Seneca Develop Ctr, 74-; assoc attend physician, Childrens Hosp Buffalo, 75-; asst physician, Buffalo Gen Hosp, 75-; NIH career res develop award, 72; mem staff, Sisters of Charity Hosp, 78-; consult physicians, Buffalo Gen Hosp & Childrens Hosp, Buffalo, 80- *Mem:* Am Soc Human Genetics; Am Soc Hemat; Am Fedn Clin Res; Am Soc Clinical Invest. *Res:* Genetic heterogeneity in human Mendelian traits; familial hyperlipoproteinemia; inherited anemias in laboratory animals. *Mailing Add:* Dept Med Sisters Charity Hosp 2157 Main St Buffalo NY 14214

EDWARDS, JOHN AUERT, b Middletown, NY, July 2, 30; m 51; c 2. HEAT TRANSFER, FLUID MECHANICS. *Educ:* NC State Univ, BSME, 55, MS, 57; Purdue Univ, PhD(mech eng), 62. *Prof Exp:* Engr, Texaco, Inc, 57-58; res assoc heat transfer, Purdue Univ, 58-61; assoc prof eng mech, 62-70, prof eng mech & marine sci, 70-76, PROF MECH & AEROSPACE ENG, NC STATE UNIV, 76- *Concurrent Pos:* NSF grants, 64-66; consult, Oak Ridge Nat Lab, 66-68; Atomic Energy Comn res contract, 69- *Mem:* Am Soc Eng Educ; Am Soc Mech Engrs. *Res:* Liquid metals lubrication; heat transfer with boiling alkali metals and dropwise condensation; fuels research; free convection and radiative heat transfer; turbulent lubrication; secondary turbulent flows; turbulent jets; fluidics. *Mailing Add:* Dept of Mech & Aero Eng NC State Univ Raleigh NC 27650

EDWARDS, JOHN C, b Petersburg, Va, Nov 10, 13; m 40; c 4. ANALYTICAL CHEMISTRY, ENVIRONMENTAL SCIENCE. *Educ:* Univ Richmond, BS, 36. *Prof Exp:* Asst chemist, Solvay Process Co, Va, 36-41; assoc chemist, Navy Dept, US Govt, 41-46; anal res chemist, E I du Pont de Nemours & Co, Inc, 47-50, supvr process control labs, May Plant, 50-57, anal res dir, 57-66, dir environ control, 66-78; RETIRED. *Concurrent Pos:* Co-analyst, Nat Bur Standards; mem, SC Water Resources Comn, 69-; consult, 78- *Mem:* Am Chem Soc. *Res:* Analytical research development of methods and techniques to identify, characterize and process acrylic fibers and related materials; application of instrumentation for analytical research; coordinator programs air and water pollution abatement. *Mailing Add:* 2000 Forest Dr Camden SC 29020

EDWARDS, JOHN D, b Hackensack, NJ, June 17, 25; m 46; c 5. PETROLEUM GEOLOGY. *Educ:* Cornell Univ, BS, 46; Columbia Univ, PhD(geol), 52. *Prof Exp:* Field geologist, US Geol Surv, 49-50; geologist spec invests, Shell Oil Co, 50-55, dist geologist, 55-62, staff geologist, 62, div explor mgr, 62-64, area explor mgr, 64-67, chief geologist, 67-68, asst to vpres explor, 68-71, struct geol teacher, 71-73, MGR EXPLOR TRAINING, SHELL DEVELOPMENT CO, 74- *Concurrent Pos:* Lectr, Columbia Univ, 50. *Mem:* AAAS; Geol Soc Am; Am Inst Mining, Metall & Petrol Engrs; Am Asn Petrol Geologists. *Res:* Structural geology; petroleum exploration. *Mailing Add:* Shell-Bellaire Res Ctr Box 481 Houston TX 77002

EDWARDS, JOHN OELHAF, b Sewickley, Pa, July 21, 22; m 50; c 2. INORGANIC CHEMISTRY. *Educ:* Colgate Univ, AB, 47; Univ Wis, PhD(chem), 51. *Prof Exp:* Res assoc chem, Cornell Univ, 50-51; chemist, E I du Pont de Nemours & Co, 52; from instr to assoc prof, 52-63, PROF CHEM, BROWN UNIV, 63- *Concurrent Pos:* Consult, FMC Corp, 64-; fel, John Simon Guggenheim Mem Found, 67-68. *Mem:* AAAS; Am Chem Soc. *Res:* Chemistry of oxoanions and peroxides; kinetics and mechanisms of reactions. *Mailing Add:* Dept of Chem Brown Univ Providence RI 02912

EDWARDS, JOHN R, b Streator, Ill, Feb 27, 37; m 61; c 3. BIOCHEMISTRY. *Educ:* Ill Wesleyan Univ, BS, 59; Univ Ill, PhD(biochem), 64. *Prof Exp:* NIH fel microbiol, Sch Med, Tufts Univ, 64-66; from asst prof to assoc prof, 66-79, PROF CHEM, VILLANOVA UNIV, 79-, CHMN DEPT, 80- *Mem:* Am Chem Soc; Am Soc Microbiol; Sigma Xi; AAAS; Am Soc Biol Chemists. *Res:* Structure and synthesis of dextran from cariogenic Streptococcus; characterization of the capsular polysaccharides from Actinomyces viscosus. *Mailing Add:* Dept of Chem Villanova Univ Villanova PA 19085

EDWARDS, JOHN S, b Auckland, NZ, Nov 25, 31; m 57; c 4. ZOOLOGY, NEUROBIOLOGY. *Educ:* Univ Auckland, BSc, 54, MSc, 56; Cambridge Univ, PhD(entom), 60. *Prof Exp:* Sci officer insect physiol, Sch Agr, Cambridge Univ, 60-61; res assoc, Western Reserve Univ, 61-62, asst prof biol, 62-67; assoc prof, 67-70, PROF ZOOL, UNIV WASH, 70- *Mem:* Am Soc Zool; Soc Develop Biol; Brit Soc Exp Biol; Royal Entom Soc; Soc Neurosci. *Res:* Neurobiology; insect nervous system, development, aging and regeneration; alpine ecology. *Mailing Add:* Dept of Zool Univ of Wash Seattle WA 98195

EDWARDS, JONATHAN, JR, b Richmond, Va, Jan 19, 33; m 59; c 4. STRUCTURAL GEOLOGY. *Educ:* Va Polytech Inst & State Univ, 55, MS, 60; Colo Sch Mines, DSc(geol), 66. *Prof Exp:* Field geologist, Va Dept Hwys, 59-61; GEOLOGIST, MD GEOL SURV, 66- *Mem:* Geol Soc Am. *Res:* Field investigation in the western Piedmont of Maryland to determine the stratigraphy, structure and geologic history. *Mailing Add:* Md Geol Surv Rm 214 Latrobe Hall Johns Hopkins Univ Baltimore MD 21218

EDWARDS, JOSEPH D, JR, b Alexandria, La, Nov 25, 24; m 60. ORGANIC CHEMISTRY. *Educ:* La Col, BS, 44; Univ Tex, MA, 48, PhD(chem), 50. *Prof Exp:* Chemist, Oak Ridge, Tenn, 44; chemist, US Naval Res Lab, 45; fel, Univ Tex, 46-50; asst prof chem, Col Med, Baylor Univ, 51-58; assoc prof, Clemson Univ, 59; sr res chemist, Monsanto Chem Co, Tex, 59-60; from assoc prof to prof chem, Lamar State Col, 60-67; head dept, 67-72, PROF CHEM, UNIV SOUTHWESTERN LA, 67- *Concurrent Pos:* Fel, Univ Ill, 50-51; prin scientist, Res Div, US Vet Admin Hosp, Houston, 51-58. *Mem:* Am Chem Soc; Royal Soc Chem. *Res:* Alkaloids; plant pigments; synthetic organic chemistry. *Mailing Add:* Dept of Chem Univ of Southwestern La Lafayette LA 70504

EDWARDS, JOSHUA LEROY, b Jasper, Fla, Aug 9, 18; m 53; c 3. PATHOLOGY, IMMUNOLOGY. *Educ:* Univ Fla, BS, 39; Tulane Univ, MD, 49. *Prof Exp:* Intern, Baptist Host, New Orleans, La, 43-44; resident, Touro Infirmary, 48-49; from resident to chief resident path, NE Deaconess Hosp, Boston, Mass, 49-51; instr, Duke Univ, 51-52, assoc, 52-53; asst prof, Rockefeller Inst, 53-54; prof path & chmn dept, Med Col, Univ Fla, 55-67; prof path & chmn dept, Med Col, Univ Fla, 55-67; prof path & dir combined degree prog med sci, Ind Univ, Bloomington, 67-69; prof path & chmn dept, Med Ctr, 69-80, PROF PATH, SCH MED, IND UNIV, 80- *Concurrent Pos:* Instr, Harvard Univ, 49-51. *Res:* Radiation pathology; cellular distribution of antigens; growth and development of cells and tissues; dynamics of antibody formation; cytology; immunopathology. *Mailing Add:* Ind Univ Sch Med Indianapolis IN 46223

EDWARDS, KATHRYN LOUISE, b Washington, Pa, May 8, 47. PLANT PHYSIOLOGY. *Educ:* Oberlin Col, AB, 69; Univ NC, PhD(bot), 74. *Prof Exp:* Assoc plant physiol, Yale Univ, 74-76; asst prof biol, Rollins Col, 76-78; PHYSIOL, ASST PROF BIOL, KENYON COL, 78- *Mem:* Sigma Xi; Am Soc Plant Physiologists; AAAS. *Res:* Mechanism of auxin and abscesic acid uptake in root cells; investigation of the distribution, translocation, and metabolism of abscesic acid, auxin, gibberrellin, and ethylene to determine theor roles in the geo response of roots. *Mailing Add:* Dept of Biol Kenyon Col Gambier OH 43022

EDWARDS, KENNETH WARD, b Ann Arbor, Mich, Jan 18, 33; m 56; c 2. ANALYTICAL CHEMISTRY, PHYSICAL CHEMISTRY. *Educ:* Univ Mich, BS, 54; Dartmouth Col, MA, 56; Univ Colo, PhD(kinetics, calorimetry), 63. *Prof Exp:* Instr phys chem, Colo Sch Mines, 57-60; res chemist, US Geol Surv, 61-66; asst prof, 66-72, ASSOC PROF ANAL & PHYS CHEM, COLO SCH MINES, 72- *Concurrent Pos:* Chmn bd dirs, Nat Resources Lab, Inc. *Mem:* Am Chem Soc. *Res:* Analysis of trace concentrations of radionuclides in water and the physical chemistry and geochemistry of natural radionuclides and other trace elements in water; analytical and physical chemistry of trace metals and metalloids in the environment, especially problems in geochemical and pollution analysis and pollution abatement. *Mailing Add:* Dept Chem & Geochem Colo Sch of Mines Golden CO 80401

EDWARDS, KENNETH WESTBROOK, b Lansing, Mich, July 22, 34; m 60, 76; c 2. ELEMENTARY PARTICLE PHYSICS. *Educ:* Univ Mich, BSE, 56; Princeton Univ, PhD(physics), 61. *Prof Exp:* Asst physics, Eng Res Inst, Univ Mich, 54-56; asst, Princeton Univ, 56-61, instr, 61; res assoc, Univ Iowa, 61-63, asst prof, 63-67; assoc prof, 67-78, PROF PHYSICS, CARLETON UNIV, 78- *Concurrent Pos:* Mem coun, Inst Particle Physics, Can, 73-76. *Mem:* Am Phys Soc. *Res:* Scattering theory; experimental elementary particle physics, particularly measurement of strong interaction cross sections. *Mailing Add:* Dept of Physics Carleton Univ Ottawa ON K1S 5B6 Can

EDWARDS, KIAH, III, developmental biology, see previous edition

EDWARDS, LAWRENCE JAY, b Cornwall, NY, July 13, 40; m 62; c 3. PHYSIOLOGY, BIOCHEMISTRY. *Educ:* State Univ NY Albany, 62; Cornell Univ, MS, 65, PhD(insect physiol), 67. *Prof Exp:* Res asst insect physiol, Cornell Univ, 63-67; res entomologist, USDA, Ga, 67-68; res assoc biochem, O'Donnell Res Lab, NY, 68; asst prof insect physiol, toxicol & apicult, Univ Mass, Amherst, 68-73; textbook publ, C V Mosby & John Wiley & Sons, 74-78; PRES, BIO-CONTROL, 79- *Mem:* NY Acad Sci; Entom Soc Am. *Res:* Urban entomology; pest control; biological consulting; inspection services; integrated pest control; quality control. *Mailing Add:* Bio-Control 639 Bridge St Suffield CT 06078

EDWARDS, LAWRENCE K(NIGHT), b Delaware, Ohio, July 10, 19; m 45, 76; c 2. AEROSPACE ENGINEERING, MASS TRANSIT. *Educ:* Miami Univ, AB, 40. *Prof Exp:* Supvr eng, Curtiss-Wright Corp, NY, 40-43; mgr airplane & missile eng, McDonnell Aircraft Corp, Mo, 43-56; mgr systs eng, Polaris Prog, Lockheed Aircraft Corp, Calif, 56-59, mgr vehicle develop, Agena Prog, 59-62, asst dir eng, 62-65, mgr adv spacecraft progs, 66; pres, Tube Transit Corp, 67-70; sr staff engr, Space Systs Div, Lockheed Missiles & Space Co, 70-72; mgr, Transit Innovations, Palo Alto, Calif, 73-76; MGR ADVANCE SPACE TRANSP, OFF SPACE TRANSP SYSTS, NASA HQ, WASHINGTON, DC, 76- *Concurrent Pos:* Leader, Skylab re-entry team, NASA, 79. *Mem:* Assoc fel Am Inst Aeronaut & Astronaut. *Res:* Systems engineering; satellites; spacecraft; large structures; guidance and controls; dynamics; urban transportation and planning; design of Project 21 transit system. *Mailing Add:* Off Space & Transp Systs NASA Washington DC 20546

EDWARDS, LEILA, b San Juan, PR, Apr 9, 37; US citizen; m 68; c 2. CLINICAL CHEMISTRY. *Educ:* Univ PR, BS, 58; Kans State Univ, MS, 61; State Univ NY Buffalo, PhD(biochem), 66; Am Bd Clin Chem, dipl, 77. *Prof Exp:* Instr chem, Col Agr & Mech Arts, Univ PR, 58-59, res assoc cancer res, Sch Med, 61-62; fel biochem, Ore State Univ, 66-67; res assoc biochem, State Univ NY Buffalo, 67-69; supvr clin chem, 69-70, ASST DIR CLIN CHEM, ERIE COUNTY LAB, 70- *Concurrent Pos:* Clin asst prof biochem, State Univ NY Buffalo, 70-, clin asst prof med chem & pathol, 71-; consult clin chem, Buffalo Children's Hosp, 74-76; mem, Comn Radionuclides & Radioassay Clin Chem, Am Asn Clin Chem, 74-, Nat Educ Comt, 75-77; head study group, Thyroxine Standards, 78-80. *Honors & Awards:* Distinguished Serv Award, Soc Appl Spectros & Amer Chem Soc, 78. *Mem:* Am Asn Clin Chem; Am Chem Soc; NY Acad Sci; Am Asn Clin Lab Physicians & Scientists. *Res:* Lipoproteins; lipid methodology; clinical endocrinology. *Mailing Add:* 20 Parkwood Dr Buffalo NY 14226

EDWARDS, LEON ROGER, b New Ulm, Minn, May 2, 40; m 62; c 2. SOLID STATE PHYSICS. *Educ:* Univ Minn, BPhys, 62; Iowa State Univ, PhD(physics), 67. *Prof Exp:* Staff mem, orgn, 5131, 67-69, STAFF MEM, PHYSICS SOLIDS RES DIV, 5132, SANDIA CORP, 69- *Mem:* Am Phys Soc. *Res:* Low temperature physics; transport properties of rare earth metals and dilute alloys; equation of state. *Mailing Add:* Div 5132 PO Box 5800 Albuquerque NM 87115

EDWARDS, LESLIE ERROLL, b Montesano, Wash, Dec 26, 14; m 46; c 3. PHYSIOLOGY. *Educ:* State Col Wash, BS, 37, MS, 39; Univ Rochester, PhD(physiol), 44. *Prof Exp:* Instr, Univ Rochester, 43-46 & Fels Res Found, 46-47; assoc, 47-49, from asst prof to assoc prof, 49-64, prof, 64-79, EMER PROF PHYSIOL, MED COL VA, 79- *Mem:* AAAS; Am Physiol Soc; Soc Gen Physiol; Am Chem Soc. *Res:* Lowering of ionic barriers in tissue; intermediary metabolism of carbohydrate and fat; biological value of proteins; gastric secretion; gastrointestinal hormones, insulin; glucagon; pancreatic function; muscle metabolism. *Mailing Add:* Rte 1 Box 521 Sandston VA 23150

EDWARDS, LEWIS HIRAM, b Frederick, Okla, Nov 6, 38; m 60; c 2. AGRONOMY, GENETICS. *Educ:* Okla State Univ, BS, 61; NDak State Univ, PhD(agron), 65. *Prof Exp:* Res geneticist, Agr Res Serv, USDA, 65-67; asst prof, 67-70, assoc prof, 70-73, PROF GENETICS, OKLA STATE UNIV, 73- GENETICIST-PLANT BREEDER, 67- *Mem:* Am Soc Agron; Crop Sci Soc Am. *Res:* Genetic research in soybeans, including mutation studies, quantitative genetic studies; soybean and mungbean. *Mailing Add:* Dept of Agron Okla State Univ Stillwater OK 74074

EDWARDS, LOIS ADELE, b Kansas City, Mo, Oct 14, 40. PROTEIN CHEMISTRY. *Educ:* Northwest Nazarene Col, BA, 62; Univ Mich, PhD(biophysics), 79. *Prof Exp:* Physicist, Atomic Energy Comn, 63-65; asst prof, 71-78, ASSOC PROF BIOCHEM & PHYSICS, SPRING ARBOR COL, 78- *Concurrent Pos:* Vis prof, Mich State Univ, 81- *Res:* Mapping the sulfhydryl groups of rat brain hexokinase with respect to their interaction with substrate and other ligands. *Mailing Add:* 4415 Hull Rd # 19 Leslie MI 49251

EDWARDS, LOUIS LAIRD, JR, b Bozeman, Mont, June 20, 36; m 58; c 2. CHEMICAL ENGINEERING. *Educ:* Rensselaer Polytech Inst, BChE, 58; Univ Del, MChE, 60; Univ Idaho, PhD(chem eng), 66. *Prof Exp:* From instr to asst prof chem eng, Univ Idaho, 61-66; Ford Found resident, Union Carbide Corp, 66-67; assoc prof chem eng, 67-71, PROF CHEM ENG, UNIV IDAHO, 71- *Concurrent Pos:* Guest researcher, Swedish Forest Prod Lab, 71-72; consult, Pulp & Paper Indust, 74- *Mem:* Am Inst Chem Engrs; Am Soc Eng Educ; Tech Asn of Pulp & Paper Indust. *Res:* Application of chemical engineering principles to pulp and paper processes; process design and economics; mathematical modeling; optimization and computer applications; ozone technology. *Mailing Add:* Dept of Chem Eng Univ of Idaho Moscow ID 83843

EDWARDS, LUCY ELAINE, b Richmond, Va, Feb 28, 52. PALEONTOLOGY, BIOSTRATIGRAPHY. *Educ:* Univ Ore, BA, 72; Univ Calif, Riverside, PhD(geol sci), 77. *Prof Exp:* GEOLOGIST PALEONT, US GEOL SURV, 77- *Mem:* Am Asn Stratig Palynologists; Geol Soc Am; Paleont Soc. *Res:* Cenozoic and Mesozoic dinoflagellates; techniques of biostratigraphic correlation. *Mailing Add:* US Geol Surv 971 Nat Ctr Reston VA 22092

EDWARDS, MCIVER WILLIAMSON, JR, b Darlington, SC, Aug 24, 35; m 63; c 2. PHYSIOLOGY, ANESTHESIOLOGY. *Educ:* Mass Inst Technol, BS, 56; Univ Pa, MD, 62, Am Bd Anesthesiol, cert, 73. *Prof Exp:* Intern & instr med, Johns Hopkins Hosp, 62-63; instr physiol, 63-64, assoc, 64-65, 67-68, resident, 69-71, ASST PROF PHYSIOL, MED SCH, UNIV PA, 68-, ASST PROF ANESTHESIA, 71-; CHIEF, ANESTHESIA SECT, VET ADMIN MED CTR, 80- *Concurrent Pos:* Pa Plan fel, Univ Pa, 63-65, 67-68; USPHS fel, Middlesex Hosp Med Sch, Eng, 65-67; vis res fel physiol, Oxford Univ, 77-78. *Mem:* AAAS; Am Heart Asn; Coun Cardiopulmonary Dis; fel Am Col Anesthesiologists; Am Soc Anesthesiol. *Res:* Respiratory physiology; neurophysiology; control of breathing; effects of anesthesia on respiration. *Mailing Add:* Anesthesia Sect Vet Admin Med Ctr Philadelphia PA 19104

EDWARDS, MARC BENJAMIN, b New York, NY, Dec 19, 46; m 76. SEDIMENTARY GEOLOGY. *Educ:* City Col New York, BS, 68; Oxford Univ, DPhil(geol), 72. *Prof Exp:* Sr res scientist sedimentology, Continental Shelf Inst Norway, 72-78; res scientist, Bur Econ Geol, Univ Tex, Austin, 78-81; EXPLOR GEOLOGIST, KERR, JAIN & ASSOC, HOUSTON, TEX, 81- *Mem:* Soc Econ & Paleont Mineralogists; Int Asn Sedimentologists; Am Asn Petrol Geologists. *Res:* Facies analysis and reconstruction of depositional environments in ancient sedimentary rocks; interpretation of basin history, paleogeography and paleoclimatology; Spitzbergen, Arctic Norway and Texas; growth faulting and sedimentation, northern Gulf Basin. *Mailing Add:* Kerr Jain & Assoc 16825 Northchase Houston TX 77060

EDWARDS, MARTIN HASSALL, b St Annes-on-Sea, Eng, Nov 10, 27; nat Can; m 49; c 2. PHYSICS. *Educ:* Univ BC, BA, 49, MA, 51; Univ Toronto, PhD(physics), 53. *Prof Exp:* Res assoc, Univ Toronto, 53-54; from asst prof to assoc prof, 54-61, PROF PHYSICS, ROYAL MIL COL, CAN, 61, CHMN DEPT, 78- *Concurrent Pos:* Res assoc, Stanford Univ, 64-65; Ont Royal Comnr ducks & pesticides, 69-70; mem, Environ Assessment Bd Ont, 77- *Mem:* Fel Am Phys Soc; Can Nature Fedn (vpres, 74-77; pres, 77-79); Int Union Conserv Nature & Natural Resources. Can Asn Physicists; Asn Sci, Eng & Technol Community Can. *Res:* Low temperature physics; low temperature properties of helium liquid and vapor; expansion coefficient; refractive index and density; lambda point and critical point; environmental impact of technology. *Mailing Add:* 19 Jane Royal Mil Col Kingston ON K7M 3G6 Can

EDWARDS, MERRILL ARTHUR, b Amherst, NS, May 12, 32; m 56; c 2. PHYSICS, BIOPHYSICS. *Educ:* Univ NB, BSc, 53; Univ Western Ont, MSc, 56, PhD, 60. *Prof Exp:* Assoc prof, 59-74, asst dean grad studies, 74-78, PROF PHYSICS, UNIV NB, 74-, CHMN PHYSICS DEPT, 77-, ACTG ASSOC DEAN GRAD STUDIES, 78- *Concurrent Pos:* Nat Res Coun Overseas fel, 66-67. *Mem:* Biophys Soc; Can Asn Physicists. *Res:* Geophysics; peripheral circulation; use of radioactive clearance methods in determining the circulation; spectroscopy; surface physics of microspheres. *Mailing Add:* Dept of Physics PO Box 4400 Fredericton NB E3B 5A3 Can

EDWARDS, MILES JOHN, b Portland, Ore, 1929; m 56; c 4. MEDICINE. *Educ:* Willamette Univ, BA, 51; Univ Ore, MS & MD, 56; Am Bd Internal Med, dipl, 64; Am Bd Pulmonary Dis, dipl, 69. *Prof Exp:* From asst prof to assoc prof, 64-70, PROF MED & CHIEF DIV CHEST DIS, SCH MED, UNIV ORE, 70- *Concurrent Pos:* NIH fel, Cardiovasc Res Inst, Med Ctr, Univ Calif, San Francisco, 63-64. *Mem:* AAAS; Am Thoracic Soc. *Res:* Respiratory physiology, alterations in blood and oxygen affinity with various types of hypoxia. *Mailing Add:* Dept of Med Univ of Ore Med Sch Portland OR 97201

EDWARDS, NANCY CLAIRE, b Montgomery, Ala, Oct 16, 36. EMBRYOLOGY, DEVELOPMENTAL BIOLOGY. *Educ:* Agnes Scott Col, BA, 58; Univ NC, Chapel Hill, MA, 66, PhD(zool), 71. *Prof Exp:* Asst dir pub rels & develop, Agnes Scott Col, 58-59, dir publicity, 59-61; from instr to asst prof, 68-75, ASSOC PROF BIOL, UNIV NC, CHARLOTTE, 75- *Mem:* AAAS; Am Soc Zool; Soc Develop Biol; Sigma Xi. *Res:* Macromolecular patterns in coelenterate development; amphibian regeneration. *Mailing Add:* Dept of Biol Univ of NC Charlotte NC 28223

EDWARDS, OGDEN FRAZELLE, b Leslie, Mich, Apr 26, 09; m 32; c 2. MICROBIOLOGY. *Educ:* Mich State Col, BS, 31, MS, 33; Yale Univ, PhD(bact), 36. *Prof Exp:* Asst bact, Mich State Col, 31-33; asst bacteriologist, Yale Univ, 33-36; instr, Univ Ill, 36-42; asst prof, 46-47, assoc prof, 47-74, ASSOC EMER PROF BACT, UNIV KY, 74- *Res:* Electron microscopy of viruses; bacterial enzymes; actinomycetes. *Mailing Add:* Thomas H Morgan Sch of Biol Sci Univ of Ky Lexington KY 40506

EDWARDS, OLIVER EDWARD, b Wales, Jan 8, 20; Can citizen; m 45; c 2. ORGANIC CHEMISTRY. *Educ:* Univ Alta, BSc, 41; Northwestern Univ, MS, 43, PhD(chem), 48. *Prof Exp:* CHEMIST, ORG CHEM & ALKALOIDS, NAT RES COUN CAN, 48- *Mem:* Am Chem Soc; Can Inst Chem; fel Royal Soc Can. *Res:* Reactions of dihydropyran and tetrahydropyran derivatives, electron deficient carbon and nitrogen; studies on the constitution of the Aconite alkaloids, chemistry of diterpenes; n-heterocyclics. *Mailing Add:* Nat Res Coun Sussex St Rm 2093 Ottawa ON K1A 0R6 Can

EDWARDS, OSCAR WENDELL, b Marion, Ala, Jan 2, 16; m 43; c 1. PHYSICAL CHEMISTRY. *Educ:* Birmingham-Southern Col, BS, 36; Univ Ala, MS, 41; Emory Univ, 59. *Prof Exp:* Teacher pub schs, 36-41, 43-44; chem aide, Tenn Valley Authority, 41-42, jr anal chemist, 42-45, asst anal chemist, 45-46, res chemist III, 46-56, res chemist IV, 56-81; RETIRED. *Concurrent Pos:* Researcher ion-selective electrodes, Univ North Ala, Florence. *Mem:* Am Chem Soc. *Res:* Determination of phosphorus in phosphatic materials; microdetermination of phosphorus by an organic reagent; diffusion of phosphates and phosphoric acid by conductimetric and optical methods; measurement of dissociation and stability constants; calculation of composition and activities in multicomponent solutions by iterative methods using computer. *Mailing Add:* Riverview Dr Florence AL 35630

EDWARDS, PALMER LOWELL, b Enterprise, Ala, Mar 9, 23; m 64. PHYSICS. *Educ:* La State Univ, BS, 44; Harvard Univ, SM, 47; Univ Md, PhD, 58. *Prof Exp:* Physicist, Naval Ord Lab, 44-48, res assoc, 49-55, solid state physicist, 55-60; from assoc prof to prof, Tex Christian Univ, 60-67; chmn physics fac, 67-76, PROF PHYSICS, UNIV W FLA, 67- *Mem:* Am Phys Soc; Acoust Soc Am. *Res:* Magnetism; properties of materials; acoustics. *Mailing Add:* 8866 Burning Tree Rd Pensacola FL 32504

EDWARDS, RICHARD ARCHER, b Niagara Falls, NY, Apr 24, 08; m 31. PALEONTOLOGY. *Educ:* Univ Mich, BS, 31; Univ Cincinnati, MA, 33; Univ NC, PhD(paleont), 38. *Prof Exp:* Asst geol, Univ Mich, 29-31; asst, Univ Cincinnati, 31-34; fel, Univ NC, 34-35, instr, 35-38 & 39-40; jr geologist, US Geol Surv, 38-39; from asst prof to prof phys sci, 40-47, prof geol, 47-74, actg chmn dept, 66-69, EMER PROF GEOL, UNIV FLA, 74- *Concurrent Pos:* Head dept geol, Univ Fla, 51-58; head Ford Found prog from Univ Fla to Univ Mandalay, Burma, 58-62. *Mem:* Soc Vert Paleont; Paleont Soc; Asn Prof Geol Scientists; Am Inst Prof Geologists. *Res:* Micropaleontology of ostracods; physiography of land forms in Florida. *Mailing Add:* 1608 SW 35th Pl Gainesville FL 32608

EDWARDS, RICHARD GLENN, b Harlan, Ky, Mar 30, 40; m 66; c 1. ENVIRONMENTAL ENGINEERING. *Educ:* Univ Ky, BS, 62, MS, 64, PhD(bioeng), 70. *Prof Exp:* Res asst, Wenner-Gren Lab, Univ Ky, 62-64 & 66-74; develop engr, Tenn Eastman Corp, 65-66; vpres AME Technol, Inc, 74-75; PRIN ENGR, WATKINS & ASSOC, INC, 75- *Mem:* Sigma Xi; Am Soc Mech Engrs; Biomed Eng Soc; Inst Environ Sci. *Res:* Response of man and animals to noise, vibration and acceleration; mobile health screening systems; audiometry, energy and environmental engineering. *Mailing Add:* Watkins & Assoc Inc 446 E High Lexington KY 40508

EDWARDS, RICHARD M(ODLIN), b Wilmington, Del, Sept 6, 20; m 43; c 2. CHEMICAL ENGINEERING. *Educ:* Purdue Univ, BS, 41; Univ Wash, MS, 48; Univ Ariz, PhD(chem eng), 64, EChem, 74. *Prof Exp:* Chem supvr, E I du Pont de Nemours & Co, 42-44; chem engr, Mallinckrodt Chem Works, 48-52, asst to tech dir, 52-54, from asst mgr to mgr process develop, 54-59; from instr to assoc prof chem eng, 59-64, asst to dean, 64-67, from asst dean to actg dean, 67-71, PROF CHEM ENG, UNIV ARIZ, 64-, VPRES STUDENT RELS, 71- *Concurrent Pos:* Consult, Am Potash & Chem Co, 66-71; assoc dean, Col Mines, Univ Ariz, 71. *Mem:* Am Inst Chem Engrs; Am Soc Eng Educ; Am Inst Mining, Metall & Petrol Engrs; Am Chem Soc. *Res:* Technology of uranium production; fluidized bed heat transfer; chemical separation processes; liquid-liquid extraction. *Mailing Add:* Admin 610 Univ of Ariz Tucson AZ 85721

EDWARDS, ROBERT LEE, b Barnardsville, NC, Jan 21, 22; m 51; c 1. ANIMAL NUTRITION. *Educ:* Berea Col, BS, 46; NC State Col, MS, 54, PhD(animal Indust), 58. *Prof Exp:* Teacher pub schs, NC, 46-52; asst agr ed, NC State Col, 52-53 & animal indust, 54-58; asst prof & asst animal husbandman, Clemson Col, 58-64, assoc prof, 64-79, PROF, CLEMSON UNIV, 79- *Mem:* AAAS; Am Soc Animal Sci; Am Inst Biol Sci; Am Forage and Grassland Coun; Coun Agr Sci & Technol. *Res:* Nutrition of large animals; utilization of dietary lipids in ruminants; forage utilization by cattle and sheep; agricultural waste utilization; nitrogen requirements of equines. *Mailing Add:* Dept Animal Sci Clemson Univ Clemson SC 29631

EDWARDS, ROBERT LOMAS, b Philadelphia, Pa, Aug 24, 20; m 42; c 4. ECOLOGY. *Educ:* Colgate Univ, BA, 47; Harvard Univ, AM, 49, PhD(biol), 51. *Prof Exp:* Instr, Tufts Univ, 49-50; in charge, Arctic Res Prog, 50, 53 & 54; instr, Air Staff & Command Col, Maxwell Field, Ala, 54; chief indust fishery invests, Fish & Wildlife Serv, 55-59; asst dir, Woods Hole Fisheries Res Lab, 59-69, asst dir plans & progs, Bur Com Fisheries, Washington, DC, 70-72; DIR, NORTHEAST FISHERIES CTR HQS, WOODS HOLE, 72- *Concurrent Pos:* Mem & coordr, Working Group US-USSR Studies Biol Productivity & Biochem World Ocean, 74-; deleg, Int Coun Exlor Seas, 75-; sci adv fishery negotiations USSR, Poland, Int Comn Northwest Atlantic Fisheries. *Honors & Awards:* Gold Medal, Dept of Com, 77. *Mem:* Soc Am Archaeol; Am Soc Mammal; Wilson Ornith Soc. *Res:* Vertebrate ecology, especially marine; ecology of arctic fishes and mammals; systematics and evolution of bird parasites; growth of fish. *Mailing Add:* Box 505 Woods Hole MA 02543

EDWARDS, ROBERT V(ALENTINO), b Baltimore, Md, Dec 15, 40; m 62; c 2. CHEMICAL ENGINEERING. *Educ:* Johns Hopkins Univ, AB, 62, MS, 64, PhD(chem eng), 68. *Prof Exp:* From res assoc to sr res assoc, 68-70, from asst prof to assoc prof, 70-79, PROF CHEM ENG, CASE WESTERN RESERVE UNIV, 79- *Mem:* AAAS; Am Inst Chem Engrs; Am Chem Soc; Am Optic Soc; Am Phys Soc. *Res:* Gas phase photochemistry; measurement of the scalar transport properties of moving fluids and velocity measurements by light scattering; complex transport phenomena, mixing and chemical reaction. *Mailing Add:* Dept of Chem Eng Case Western Reserve Univ Cleveland OH 44106

EDWARDS, ROY LAWRENCE, b Southampton, Eng, Dec 2, 22; Can citizen; m 49; c 3. ECOLOGY. *Educ:* Oxford Univ, BA, 50, MA & PhD(entom), 52. *Prof Exp:* Lectr entomol, Univ Hull, Eng, 52-57; Nat Res Coun Can fel, 57-58; res officer, Can Agr Res Lab, 58-61; asst prof biol, Univ Sask, 61-64; assoc prof, 64-66, chmn dept, 66-69, PROF BIOL, TRENT UNIV, 66- *Mem:* Ecol Soc Am; Entom Soc Am; Am Soc Limnol & Oceanog; Entom Soc Can; fel Royal Entom Soc. *Res:* Ecology and behavior of invertebrates. *Mailing Add:* Dept of Biol Trent Univ Peterborough ON K9J 7B8 Can

EDWARDS, STEVE, b Quincy, Fla, June 16, 30; m 64; c 2. THEORETICAL NUCLEAR PHYSICS. *Educ:* Fla State Univ, BS, 52, MS, 54; Johns Hopkins Univ, PhD(theoret physics), 60. *Prof Exp:* From asst prof to assoc prof, 60-69, assoc chmn dept, 65-73, chmn dept physics, 73-79, PROF PHYSICS, FLA STATE UNIV, 69- *Concurrent Pos:* Mem adv comt, Intermediate Sci Curric Study. *Mem:* Am Asn Physics Teachers; Am Phys Soc. *Res:* Group theoretic analysis of vibration problems; direct nuclear reaction theories, especially stripping and pick-up reactions of all types in low-energy nuclear physics. *Mailing Add:* Dept of Physics Fla State Univ Tallahassee FL 32306

EDWARDS, SUZAN, b Columbia, Mo, June 15, 51; m 73. ASTRONOMY. *Educ:* Dartmouth Col, BA, 73; Univ Hawaii, MS, 75, PhD(astron), 80. *Prof Exp:* ASST PROF ASTRON, SMITH COL, 80- *Mem:* Am Astron Soc; Sigma Xi; Astron Soc Pac. *Res:* Star formation. *Mailing Add:* Five Col Astron Dept Smith Col Northampton MA 01063

EDWARDS, TERRY WINSLOW, b Sheboygan, Wis, Nov 2, 35; m 58; c 1. ASTRONOMY. *Educ:* Univ Wis, BS, 58, MS, 61, PhD(astron), 68. *Prof Exp:* Satellite observer, Astrophys Observ, Smithsonian Inst, 58-59; res asst physics, Midwestern Univs Res Asn, 64-66; from instr to asst prof, 66-71, ASSOC PROF PHYSICS & ASTRON, UNIV MO, 71- *Concurrent Pos:* NASA res grant, Space Sci Res Ctr, Univ Mo, 66-69; vis assoc prof, Univ Rochester, 81. *Mem:* AAAS; Am Astron Soc; Asn Comput Mach; Astron Soc Pac; Sigma Xi. *Res:* Astrophysics; stellar thermodynamics; stellar structure; nucleosynthesis; celestial mechanics; binary and variable stars; digital computing; dense stars theory. *Mailing Add:* Dept of Physics & Astron Univ of Mo Columbia MO 65201

EDWARDS, THOMAS CLAUDE, b San Antonio, Tex, July 10, 43; m 66; c 4. THERMODYNAMICS, MACHINE DESIGN. *Educ:* NMex State Univ, BSME, 66, MSME, 67; Purdue Univ, PhD(mech eng), 70. *Prof Exp:* Reactor engr, US AEC, 66-67; instr eng, Purdue Univ, 67-70; asst prof eng, Fla Technol Univ, 70-72; pres, 72-78, CHMN BD RES & DEVELOP MGT, ROVAC CORP, 78- *Mem:* Am Soc Heating, Refrig & Air Conditioning Engrs; Am Soc Metals. *Res:* Thermodynamic cycles; invented the Edwards air vapor air conditioning cycle; positive displacement totaling compression-expansion machinery. *Mailing Add:* The ROVAC Corp 100 Rovac Pkwy Rockledge FL 32955

EDWARDS, THOMAS F, b Pittsfield, Ill, July 17, 27; m 50; c 3. SCIENCE EDUCATION. *Educ:* Ill State Univ, BS, 51; Ariz State Univ, MA, 57; Mich State Univ, EdD(sci educ), 66. *Prof Exp:* Teacher high schs, Ill, 51-57; from instr to assoc prof chem, 57-70, prof sci educ, 72-77, PROF ELEM EDUC, ILL STATE UNIV, 70- *Concurrent Pos:* Instr, Mich State Univ, 65-66; dir NSF Insts, Ill State Univ, 71-; sci consult, Ill State Dept Educ, 71-74, Lincoln High Sch, Ill, 72-75, Ottawa Pub Schs, Ill, 75 & Rand McNally Publ Co; US Dept Educ Title III Elem & Secondary Educ Act Proj validator, 73. *Mem:* Nat Sci Teachers Asn; Nat Asn Res Sci Teaching. *Mailing Add:* 300 Edwards Hall Ill State Univ Normal IL 61761

EDWARDS, THOMAS HARVEY, b Chilliwack, BC, Feb 12, 24; nat US; m 46; c 4. PHYSICS. *Educ:* Univ BC, BA, 47, MA, 48; Univ Mich, PhD(physics), 55. *Prof Exp:* Instr, Univ Mich, 51-53, res assoc, 53-54; from asst prof to assoc prof, 54-65, PROF PHYSICS, MICH STATE UNIV, 65- *Mem:* Optical Soc Am; Am Phys Soc. *Res:* High-resolution infrared spectroscopy; molecular structure of asymmetric and symmetric top molecules. *Mailing Add:* Dept of Physics Mich State Univ East Lansing MI 48824

EDWARDS, THOMAS REINACH, b Kenosha, Wis, Mar 25, 36; m; c 1. SPECTROSCOPY, COMPUTER SCIENCE. *Educ:* Pa State Univ, BS, 58; State Univ NY Buffalo, PhD(physics), 66. *Prof Exp:* Jr physicist transistors, Philco Corp, 58-59 & Gen Elec Co, 59-60; PHYSICIST SPECTROS, NASA, 68- *Concurrent Pos:* Nat Acad Sci electron micros fel, 66-68. *Mem:* Am Soc Mass Spectrometry. *Res:* Statistics; mathematical modeling in linear spaces. *Mailing Add:* ES64 NASA Marshall Space Flight Ctr Huntsville AL 35812

EDWARDS, VICTOR HENRY, b Galveston, Tex, Oct 17, 40; m 63; c 2. CHEMICAL ENGINEERING, MOLECULAR BIOLOGY. *Educ:* Rice Univ, BA, 62; Univ Calif, Berkeley, PhD(chem eng), 67. *Prof Exp:* Asst prof chem eng, Cornell Univ, 67-73; res fel, Merck & Co, Inc, 73-76; supv res eng, United Energy Resources, Inc, 76-78; CONSULT, EDWARDS & ASSOCS, 79- *Concurrent Pos:* Assoc prog dir eng chem prog, Nat Sci Found, 71, prog mgr advan technol appln, 71-73; UNESCO lectr, Japan, 72; vis prof environ eng, Rice Univ, 79-80; prin processing engr, Fluor Engrs & Constructors, 80- *Honors & Awards:* Robert L Churchwell Award, Am Inst Chem Engrs, 81. *Mem:* Am Chem Soc; Am Inst Chem Engrs; NY Acad Sci; AAAS. *Res:* Manufacturing and environmental processes involving enzymes, microorganisms and plants; separation and purification technology; biomass resources; pollution control technology. *Mailing Add:* PO Box 7544 The Woodlands TX 77380

EDWARDS, W FARRELL, b Logan, Utah, Oct 5, 31; m 55. ELECTROMAGNETISM, PLASMA PHYSICS. *Educ:* Univ Utah, BS, 55; Calif Inst Technol, MS, 57, PhD(physics), 60. *Prof Exp:* From asst prof to assoc prof, 59-66, head dept, 66-72, PROF PHYSICS, UTAH STATE UNIV, 66- *Mem:* Am Phys Soc. *Res:* Foundations of electromagnetism; studies of the equations of electromagnetism in Eulerian form using the action-integral approach and standard Langrangian densities; the equations of motion have in certain plasmas, important observational consequences. *Mailing Add:* Dept of Physics Utah State Univ Logan UT 84321

EDWARDS, W STERLING, b Birmingham, Ala, July 23, 20; m 46; c 4. SURGERY. *Educ:* Va Mil Inst, BS, 42; Univ Pa, MD, 45; Am Bd Surg, dipl, 54; Am Bd Thoracic Surg, dipl, 59. *Prof Exp:* From intern to resident surg, Mass Gen Hosp, Boston, 45-52; instr, Med Col Ala, 52-53, from asst prof to prof, 53-69; chmn cardiothoracic div, 69-74, PROF SURG, SCH MED, UNIV N MEX 69-, CHMN DEPT. *Concurrent Pos:* USPHS res fel, Western Reserve Univ, 50-51; consult, Vet Admin Hosp, Albuquerque. *Mem:* Soc Vascular Surg; AMA; Am Col Surg. *Res:* Cardiovascular surgery and physiology; development of arterial and heart valve substitutes. *Mailing Add:* Dept of Surg Univ of NMex Sch of Med Albuquerque NM 87107

EDWARDS, WALTER MURRAY, b Jacksonville, Fla, Sept 29, 22; m 42; c 3. POLYMER CHEMISTRY. *Educ:* Univ Ga, BS, 44, MS, 48; Ohio State Univ, PhD(org chem), 52. *Prof Exp:* Chemist, Tenn Eastman Co, 44; chemist, Battelle Mem Inst, 48-52; chemist, Sales Tech Lab, E I Du Pont de Nemours & Co, 52-70, res assoc, Exp Sta, 70-72, tech rep, Exp Sta, 72-81; CONSULT POLYMER CHEM, 81- *Mem:* Am Chem Soc; Am Soc Testing & Mat; Fedn Socs Paint Technol. *Res:* Condensation and vinyl polymers; polymeric binders; processing of thermoplastics; polymer structure and relation to performance in coatings, specifically in acrylics, polyamides, and nylons; methacrylate polymer concrete; polymer concretes general. *Mailing Add:* 203 Stoney Run Rd Wilmington DE 19809

EDWARDS, WILLIAM BRUNDIGE, III, b Philadelphia, Pa, Oct 10, 42. FLAVOR CHEMISTRY, NATURAL PRODUCT CHEMISTRY. *Educ:* Lehigh Univ, BA, 64; Univ Pa, PhD(org chem), 69. *Prof Exp:* Res asst org chem, Wyeth Labs, Inc, 64-65; res chemist, Ravdin Inst, 65-66 & Arco Chem Corp, Atlantic Richfield Co, 66; spectroscopist, Univ Pa, 66-68; fel, Synvar Res Inst, 69-70; assoc prof org res, 71-73, res scientist, 73-80, ASSOC SR SCIENTIST & PROJ LEADER, RES CTR, PHILIP MORRIS INC, 80- *Concurrent Pos:* Teaching asst, Univ Pa, 65-67. *Mem:* AAAS; Am Chem Soc; The Chem Soc; Sigma Xi; Asn Chemoreception Sci. *Res:* Synthesis and study of perfume and flavor compounds; synthesis of terpenoid flavorants and in the factors governing structure-flavor relationships. *Mailing Add:* Res Ctr Philip Morris Inc PO Box 26583 Richmond VA 23261

EDWARDS, WILLIAM CHARLES, b Waukegan, Ill, May 17, 34; m 61; c 2. ECOLOGY, ENERGY. *Educ:* Carleton Col, BA, 56; Univ Wyo, MS, 58; Univ Nebr, PhD(bot), 66. *Prof Exp:* Teacher high sch, Wyo, 58-63; from asst prof to assoc prof biol, Mankato State Col, 66-70; INSTR BIOL, LARAMIE COUNTY COMMUNITY COL, 70- *Concurrent Pos:* Wyo state legislator, 74-82; mem nat adv bd, Energy Exten Serv, Dept Energy. *Mem:* Sigma Xi; Audubon Soc. *Res:* Reproduction in antelope; growth pattern in birch. *Mailing Add:* Dept of Biol Laramie County Community Col Cheyenne WY 82001

EDWARDS, WILLIAM DEAN, b Wichita, Kans, Nov 12, 48; m 69. CARDIOVASCULAR PATHOLOGY. *Educ:* Univ Kans, BA, 70, MD, 74; Am Bd Path, dipl, 78. *Prof Exp:* Assoc consult path, 78-80, CONSULT ANAT PATH, MAYO CLIN & FOUND, 80- *Mem:* AMA: Am Heart Asn; Am Col Cardiol. *Res:* Congenital heart disease; pulmonary hypertension; acquired heart disease. *Mailing Add:* Dept Anat Path Mayo Clin Rochester MN 55901

EDWARDSON, JOHN RICHARD, b Kansas City, Mo, Apr 17, 23; m 48; c 3. GENETICS. *Educ:* Agr & Mech Col Tex, BS, 48, MS, 49; Harvard Univ, PhD(biol), 54. *Prof Exp:* From asst agronomist to assoc agronomist, 53-66, AGRONOMIST, UNIV FLA, 66- *Mem:* AAAS; Genetics Soc Am; Am Bot Soc; Am Genetic Asn; NY Acad Sci. *Res:* Cytology and genetics of cytoplasmic characters in plants; cytology of plant virus induced inclusions. *Mailing Add:* Dept of Agron Univ of Fla Gainesville FL 32607

EELLS, JAMES, JR, b Cleveland, Ohio, Oct 25, 26; m 50; c 4. MATHEMATICS. *Educ:* Bowdoin Col, BA, 47; Harvard Univ, AM, 51, PhD(math), 54. *Prof Exp:* Instr math, Robert Col, Turkey, 47-48; instr, Amherst Col, 48-50; teaching fel, Harvard Univ, 51-53; instr, Tufts Col, 53-54; mem, Inst Adv Study, 54-56, 62-63, 72 & 77; asst prof, Univ Calif, Berkeley, 56-58 & Columbia Univ, 58-60, assoc prof, 60-63; overseas fel, Cambridge Univ, 63-64 & 66-67; prof math, Cornell Univ, 64-69; PROF MATH, UNIV WARWICK, 69- *Concurrent Pos:* Mem, Inst Adv Study, 62-63, 72 & 77. *Mem:* Am Math Soc; Soc Math France. *Res:* Global topological and differential geometric properties of analysis; calculus of variations. *Mailing Add:* Math Inst Univ Warwick Coventry England

EER NISSE, ERROL P(ETER), b Rapid City, SDak, Feb 15, 40. ELECTRICAL ENGINEERING, PHYSICS. *Educ:* SDak State Univ, BSEE, 62; Purdue Univ, MSEE, 63, PhD(elec eng), 65. *Prof Exp:* Staff mem res, Sandia Labs, 65-68, div supvr, Device Physics Res Div, 68-79; PRES, QUARTEX, INC, UTAH, 79- *Mem:* Fel Inst Elec & Electronics Engrs; fel Am Phys Soc. *Res:* Ferroelectric, piezoelectric and semiconductor devices. *Mailing Add:* Quartex Inc 1020 Atherton Dr C-202 Salt Lake City UT 84107

EESLEY, GARY, b Grove City, Ohio, May 6, 50; m 76. QUANTUM ELECTRONICS, ELECTRICAL ENGINEERING. *Educ:* Case Western Reserve Univ, BSEE, 72; Univ Southern Calif, MSEE, 76, PhD(elec eng), 78. *Prof Exp:* Engr res, Westinghouse Elec Corp, 72-74; assoc sr res scientist, 78-80, SR RES SCIENTIST, GEN MOTORS CORP, 80- *Honors & Awards:* Phys Sci Res Award, Sigma, Xi, 78. *Mem:* Sigma Xi; Inst Elect & Electronic Engrs; Optical Soc Am. *Res:* Quantum electronics; nonlinear optics; nonlinear spectroscopy; spontaneous and coherent Raman spectroscopy; laser applications. *Mailing Add:* Dept of Physics Gen Motors Res Lab Warren MI 48090

EFFER, W R, b Warrington, Eng, Jan 1, 27; Can citizen; m 53; c 2. PLANT PHYSIOLOGY. *Educ:* Univ Durham, BSc, 51; Univ Newcastle, PhD(plant physiol), 66. *Prof Exp:* Res chemist, Horlicks Ltd, Slough, Eng, 51-54; res scientist, Ont Res Found, Univ Toronto, 54-63, 66-67; biologist, 67-70, supvr environ studies, 70-75, head, 75-79, MGR, ENVIRON STUDIES & ASSESSMENTS SECT, ONT HYDRO, 80- *Mem:* Air Pollution Control Asn; NY Acad Sci. *Res:* Biological changes associated with heat polution, acid rain. *Mailing Add:* Design & Develop Div Ont Hydro 700 Univ Ave Toronto ON M5G 1X6 Can

EFFORD, IAN ECOTT, b London, Eng, Jan 4, 36; Can citizen; m 59; c 4. ENVIRONMENTAL MANAGEMENT. *Educ:* Univ London, BSc, 57; Oxford Univ, DPhil(pop ecol), 60. *Prof Exp:* Royal Soc Murray traveling studentship marine ecol, Scripps Inst Oceanog, Univ Calif, San Diego, 60-61; demonstr zool & ecol, Bur Animal Pop, Oxford Univ, 61-62; from asst prof to assoc prof, 62-71, prof ecol, Univ BC, 71-75; res dir, 75-78, dir-gen, Conserv & Renewable Energy Br, 78-81, SPECIAL ADVISOR, ENERGY POLICY, MINISTRY ENERGY MINES & RESOURCES, GOVT CAN, 81- *Concurrent Pos:* Mem, Can Med Exped Easter Island, 64-65; mem freshwater comt, Can Int Biol Prog, 67-72 & Marion Lake proj, 67-73; sr consult, Envirocon Ltd, 74-75. *Res:* Energy policy and decision making in ecological and environmental problems, especially those relating to energy. *Mailing Add:* Conserv & Renewable Energy Br MEMR 580 Booth St Ottawa ON K1A 0E4 Can

EFFRON, EDWARD, b Cincinnati, Ohio, Feb 23, 30; m 55; c 2. CHEMICAL ENGINEERING. *Educ:* Univ Cincinnati, ChE, 53; Johns Hopkins Univ, DSc(chem eng), 62. *Prof Exp:* Engr, 53-57 & 62-65, SR ENGR, EXXON RES & ENG CO, 65- *Res:* Reactor design; kinetics; transport phenomena; unit operations; fluid mechanics; catalysis; physical chemistry. *Mailing Add:* 45 Fernhill Rd Springfield NJ 07081

EFFROS, EDWARD GEORGE, b New York, NY, Dec 10, 35. MATHEMATICS. *Educ:* Mass Inst Technol, SB, 56; Harvard Univ, AM, 58, PhD(math), 62. *Prof Exp:* Instr math, Columbia Univ, 61-64; from asst prof to prof math, Univ Pa, 64-76, grad group chmn, 73-76, Thomas A Scott prof, 76-80; PROF MATH, UNIV CALIF-LOS ANGELES, 80- *Mem:* Am Math Soc. *Res:* Abstract analysis; representation theory of topological groups. *Mailing Add:* Dept Math Univ Calif Los Angeles CA 90024

EFNER, HOWARD F, b Ann Arbor, Mich, Sept 23, 44; m 70; c 1. PRODUCT DEVELOPMENT, PROCESS OPTIMIZATION. *Educ:* Eastern Mich Univ, BS, 67; Univ Iowa, MS, 71; Univ NDak, PhD(chem), 75. *Prof Exp:* Nat Res Coun resident res assoc, Naval Res Lab, 75-77; res chemist, 77-82, SR RES CHEMIST, PHILLIPS PETROL CO, 82- *Mem:* Am Chem Soc; Am Inst Chemists; Soc Automotive Engrs; Sigma Xi. *Res:* Additives for fuels and lubricants; petroleum processing. *Mailing Add:* 2100 Jefferson Rd Bartlesville OK 74003

EFRON, HERMAN YALE, b Brooklyn, NY, Apr 30, 26; m 47; c 3. HEALTH SCIENCES, RESEARCH ADMINISTRATION. *Educ:* City Col New York, BS, 47; Columbia Univ, MA, 49; NY Univ, PhD(psychol), 53. *Prof Exp:* Psychologist, Riverside Hosp, 53-54; res psychologist, Vet Hosp, Louisville, 54-56; asst chief psychol serv, Vet Hosp, Lyons, NJ, 56-68; vis fel psychometrics, Princeton Univ, 68-69; proj dir patient care eval, 69-77, HEALTH SCI SPECIALIST, VET ADMIN CENT OFF, 77- *Concurrent Pos:* James McKeen Cattell fel, 68. *Mem:* Am Psychol Asn; Am Statist Asn; Psychometric Soc. *Res:* Development of methodologies for assessment of quality of health care delivery; consumer satisfaction and its relationships to health care system characteristics; effectiveness of evaluation methodologies as causal agents for improvement. *Mailing Add:* 909 Brentwood Lane Silver Spring MD 20902

EFRON, ROBERT, b New York, NY, Dec 22, 27; m 67; c 3. NEUROPSYCHOLOGY, NEUROPHYSIOLOGY. *Educ:* Columbia Col, BA, 48; Harvard Univ, MD, 52. *Prof Exp:* Med house off, Peter Bent Brigham Hosp, Boston, Mass, 52-53; chief neurophysiol-biophys res unit, Vet Admin Hosp, Boston, 60-70; PROF NEUROL, MED SCH, UNIV CALIF, DAVIS, 70-; CHIEF NEUROPHYSIOLBIOPHYS RES LAB, 70-, ASSOC CHIEF STAFF RES & DEVELOP, VET ADMIN HOSP, MARTINEZ, 75- *Concurrent Pos:* Moseley traveling fel, Harvard Univ, 53-54; Nat Found Infantile Paralysis fel, Nat Hosp, Queens Sq, London, Eng, 56-60; mem adv bd, Int Soc Study Time, 66- *Mem:* Am Acad Aphasia; AAAS; NY Acad Sci; Am Acad Neurol; Acoustics Soc Am. *Res:* Neurophysiology and neuropsychology of perception. *Mailing Add:* 2955 Pierce St San Francisco CA 94123

EFTHYMIOU, CONSTANTINE JOHN, b Athens, Greece, Apr 21, 30; m 64; c 3. MEDICAL MICROBIOLOGY, BACTERIOLOGY. *Educ:* Athens Agr Col, BS, 52; Univ Md, MS, 58, PhD(microbiol), 61. *Prof Exp:* Asst dairy tech, Univ Md, 55-58, asst microbiol, 58-61; asst prof, Carnegie Inst Technol, 61-64; asst prof, 64-68, assoc prof, 68-81, PROF MICROBIOL, GRAD SCH, ST JOHNS UNIV, NY, 81- *Concurrent Pos:* Res assoc, Queens Hosp Ctr Affiliation, 68-76. *Mem:* AAAS; Am Soc Microbiol. *Res:* Microbiology and biochemistry of cheese ripening; microbial physiology and immunochemistry; immunology. *Mailing Add:* Dept of Biol Sci St Johns Univ Jamaica NY 11439

EFTINK, MAURICE R, b Cape Girardeau, Mo, July 26, 51; m 72; c 2. BIOCHEMISTRY, BIOPHYSICS. *Educ:* Univ Mo-Columbia, BS, 73, PhD(biochem), 76. *Prof Exp:* Res assoc biochem, Univ Va, 76-78; ASST PROF CHEM, UNIV MISS, 78- *Concurrent Pos:* NIH fel, Univ Va, 77-78. *Mem:* Am Chem Soc; Biophys Soc. *Res:* Thermodynamics of protein, ligand interactions; protein dynamics; energetics of enzyme catalyzed reactions. *Mailing Add:* Dept of Chem Univ of Miss University MS 38677

EGAMI, TAKESHI, b Fukuoka, Japan, July 15, 45; m 69; c 3. MATERIALS SCIENCE, SOLID STATE PHYSICS. *Educ:* Univ Tokyo, BEng, 68; Univ Pa, PhD(metall & mat sci), 71. *Prof Exp:* Fel appl sci, Univ Sussex, 71-72; vis scientist physics, Max Planck Inst Metal Res, 72-73 & 79-80; asst prof, 73-76, ASSOC PROF METALL & MAT SCI, 76-80, PROF MAT SCI ENG, UNIV PA, 80- *Honors & Awards:* R L Hardy Gold Medal, Am Inst Mining, Metall & Petrol Engrs. *Mem:* Am Inst Mining, Metall & Petrol Engrs; Am Phys Soc; Am Soc Metals. *Res:* Magnetic, mechanical and structural properties of metallic glasses; energy dispersive x-ray diffraction; crystal field effect. *Mailing Add:* Dept Mat Sci & Eng Univ of Pa Philadelphia PA 19104

EGAN, EDMUND ALFRED, b Chicago, Ill, Apr 24, 41; m 64; c 6. NEONATAL MEDICINE, PERINATAL MEDICINE. *Educ:* Emory Univ, Atlanta, Ga, MD, 67. *Prof Exp:* Resident pediat, Col Med, Univ Fla, 67-70; chief neonatology pediat, Madigan Gen Hosp, US Army, 70-72; investr physiol, Med Sch, Univ Col Hosp, London, 72-73; asst prof pediat, Col Med, Univ Fla, 73-76, assoc prof pediat, 76-77; assoc prof pediat, 77-82, ASST PROF PHYSIOL, SCH MED, STATE UNIV NY, BUFFALO, 78-, PROF PEDIAT, 82-; CHIEF NEONATOLOGY, CHILDREN'S HOSP, BUFFALO, NY, 77- *Concurrent Pos:* NIH prin investr, Alveolar Permeability & Lung Dis, 74-83; mem NIH Pulmonary Technol Task Force, 80-81. *Mem:* Am Physiol Soc; Am Acad Pediat; Soc Pediat Res; Perinatal Res Soc; Am Thoracic Soc. *Res:* Mechanisms of water and solute balance in adult and perinatal lungs; surfactant replacement in animals; clinical research in newborn infants. *Mailing Add:* Children's Hosp 219 Bryant St Buffalo NY 14222

EGAN, FRANCIS P, b New York, NY, Oct 17, 17; m 40. MATHEMATICS. *Educ:* Manhattan Col, BA, 37; Univ Notre Dame, MS, 51, PhD(math educ), 60. *Prof Exp:* From instr to prof math, Niagra Univ, 37-55; lectr, State Univ NY Buffalo, 55-59; chmn dept, 62-73, PROF MATH, STATE UNIV NY COL ONEONTA, 59- *Mem:* Math Asn Am. *Res:* Logic; metamathematics; teacher education. *Mailing Add:* Dept of Math State Univ of NY Oneonta NY 13820

EGAN, HOWARD L, b St Louis, Mo, May 2, 38. MATHEMATICS. *Educ:* Wash Univ, AB, 60, AM, 62, PhD(group theory), 65. *Prof Exp:* Asst prof math, Univ Md, 65-71; ASSOC PROF MATH, GALLAUDET COL, 71- *Mem:* Am Math Soc. *Res:* Infinite group theory; algebraic coding theory. *Mailing Add:* Dept of Math Gallaudet Col Washington DC 20002

EGAN, JAMES JOHN, b Oak Park, Ill, May 22, 27. PHYSICAL CHEMISTRY. *Educ:* Northwestern Univ, BS, 49; Univ Ind, PhD(phys chem), 54. *Prof Exp:* Assoc phys chemist, 53-60, chemist, 60-81, SR CHEMIST, BROOKHAVEN NAT LAB, 81- *Mem:* Am Chem Soc; Electrochem Soc; Bunsengesellschaft. *Res:* High temperature chemistry; molten salt chemistry; solid state chemistry; light scattering in aerosols. *Mailing Add:* Brookhaven Nat Lab Upton NY 11973

EGAN, JAMES JOSEPH, b Covington, Ky, Nov 7, 41; m 64; c 3. EXPERIMENTAL NUCLEAR PHYSICS. *Educ:* Thomas More Col, BA, 63; Univ Ky, MS, 66, PhD(physics), 69. *Prof Exp:* Asst prof, 69-76, ASSOC PROF PHYSICS, UNIV LOWELL, 76- *Mem:* AAAS; Am Phys Soc; Sigma Xi; NY Acad Sci. *Res:* Low energy experimental nuclear structure physics; neutron scattering cross section measurements. *Mailing Add:* Dept Physics Univ Lowell Lowell MA 01854

EGAN, MARIANNE LOUISE, b Jersey City, NJ, June 9, 42; m 75; c 1. IMMUNOCHEMISTRY, IMMUNOBIOLOGY. *Educ:* Col St Elizabeth, AB, 64; Jefferson Med Col, PhD(biochem), 69. *Prof Exp:* Instr biochem, Jefferson Med Col, 69-70; from jr res scientist to asst res scientist, 70-72, assoc res scientist immunochem, City of Hope Nat Med Ctr, 72-76; RES ASST PROF MICROBIOL, UNIV ALA, BIRMINGHAM, 77- *Concurrent Pos:* Assoc scientist, Multipurpose Arthritis Ctr, Comprehensive Cancer Ctr; chairperson, Diagnosis Working Group Breast Cancer Task Force. *Mem:* Am Asn Immunologists; Am Asn Cancer Res; Sigma Xi. *Res:* Mouse-mouse and human-human hybridomas; lymphocyte surface antigens; human immune response. *Mailing Add:* Dept of Microbiol Univ Ala Birmingham AL 35294

EGAN, MERRITT H, b Bountiful, Utah, Oct 20, 18; m 41; c 11. PSYCHIATRY. *Educ:* Univ Utah, BA, 41; Hahnemann Med Col, MD, 46; Am Bd Pediat, dipl, 53; Am Bd Psychiat & Neurol, dipl & cert psychiat, 62, cert child psychiat, 63. *Prof Exp:* Intern med, LDS Hosp, Salt Lake City, 46-47; resident pediat, Salt Lake City Gen Hosp, Univ Utah, 48-50; instr pediat, Univ Utah, 50, clin instr, 51-64, asst prof psychiat, Col Med, 64-69, ASSOC PROF PSYCHIAT, COL MED, UNIV UTAH, 69-, ASST PROF PEDIAT, 64-; DIR DIV CHILD & ADOLESCENT PSYCHIAT, DEPT PSYCHIAT, 62- *Concurrent Pos:* Gen practr med, 47-48; mem staff, LDS Hosp, Salt Lake City, 47-62; pediat resident, Dept Psychiat, Univ Utah, 49-50; pvt practr pediat, Utah, 50-53 & 55-59; chief resident pediat, Salt Lake City Gen Hosp, 49, resident psychiat, 59-50, chief resident, 60; pres med staff, Primary Children's Hosp, 57-58; fel child psychiat, Univ Utah, 60-62; mem adv coun, Salt Lake City-Community Ment Health Ctr & chmn prog & planning comt & workshop comt, 62-65; chmn, Leonard H Taboroff Lectureship Comt & prog chmn, Ann Workshop Child Psychiat, Univ Utah, 62-67; consult, Jordan Sch Dist, 63-66; mem adv comt children's serv, State Div Ment Health, 68-72; mem adv coun, Region Three A, Comprehensive Community Ment Health Ctr, 70-73; mem comt relig & psychiat, Am Psychiat Asn, 70-73; mem comt family ther, Am Acad Child Psychiat, 75- *Mem:* AMA; Am Psychiat Asn; fel Am Orthopsychiat Asn; Am Acad Pediat; fel Am Acad Child Psychiat. *Res:* New methods of teaching pediatric residents in using psychiatric knowledge; new tools in the outpatient treatment of severely disturbed children; evaluation of activity group therapy in treatment of children. *Mailing Add:* Suite 201A 4525 S 23rd East Salt Lake City UT 84117

EGAN, MICHAEL EUGENE, b Denver, Colo, Oct 24, 45; m 73; c 1. DIAGNOSTIC IMAGING. *Educ:* Univ Pa, BA, 67; Univ Tex, Austin, PhD(zool), 73. *Prof Exp:* Res asst steroid chem, Roosevelt Hosp Labs, 67-68; res asst, Univ Tex, Austin, 68-71; instr zool, St Edwards Univ, 72; instr physiol, Univ Tex, Austin, 73-74; NIH res fel biol, Princeton Univ, 74-76; asst prof biol, Lawrence Univ, 76-72; CONSULT, 79- *Mem:* Am Soc Zoologists; AAAS; Am Asn Physicist Med. *Res:* Computerized fluoroscopy and video tomography as primary non-invasive diagnostic tools. *Mailing Add:* 2326 Woodglen Richardson TX 75081

EGAN, RAYMOND D(AVIS), b Honolulu, Hawaii, Aug 22, 31; m 55; c 4. ELECTRICAL ENGINEERING. *Educ:* Stanford Univ, BS, 55, MS, 56, PhD(elec eng), 60. *Prof Exp:* Res assoc, Stanford Univ, 59-61; mgr appl res, 62-68, VPRES, GRANGER ASSOCS, 68- *Concurrent Pos:* Mem, US Comn 3, Int Sci Radio Union, 61- *Mem:* Inst Elec & Electronics Engrs; Am Geophys Union. *Res:* Radio propagation; ionospheric physics; ionosphere sounding; telecommunication systems. *Mailing Add:* Granger Assocs 3101 Scott Blvd Santa Clara CA 95051

EGAN, RICHARD L, b Omaha, Nebr, Dec 27, 17; m 43; c 2. MEDICINE. *Educ:* Creighton Univ, BSM, 38, MD, 40. *Prof Exp:* From instr to prof med, Sch Med, Creighton Univ, 41-71, from asst dean to dean, 54-70, asst to pres health sci, 70-71; asst dir dept undergrad med educ, AMA, 71-75, dir dept undergrad med educ & secy, Liaison Comt Med Educ, 75-76, DIR DIV EDUC STAND & EVAL & SECY COUN MED EDUC, AMA, 76- *Concurrent Pos:* Consult, Vet Admin Hosps, Omaha & Lincoln, Nebr, 59-70. *Mem:* AMA; Asn Am Med Cols; Am Asn Hist Med. *Res:* Internal medicine; medical education. *Mailing Add:* Coun on Med Educ AMA 535 N Dearborn St Chicago IL 60610

EGAN, RICHARD STEPHEN, b Chicago, Ill, Aug 16, 41; m 64; c 3. ANALYTICAL CHEMISTRY, SPECTROSCOPY. *Educ:* Univ Ill Med Ctr, BS, 63, PhD(pharmaceut chem), 71. *Prof Exp:* Sect head chem, Abbott Labs, 66-79; DIR, MCNEIL PHARMACEUT, 79- *Mem:* Am Chem Soc. *Res:* Analytical development of new drug substance and dosage forms including methods development and assay and stability studies. *Mailing Add:* McNeil Pharmaceut Anal Develop Spring House PA 19477

EGAN, ROBERT L, b Morrilton, Ark, May 9, 20; m 50; c 5. RADIOLOGY. *Educ:* Univ Pittsburgh, MD, 50; Am Bd Radiol, dipl, 56. *Prof Exp:* Asst radiologist, Univ Tex M D Anderson Hosp & Tumor Inst, 56-61, assoc prof radiol, Postgrad Sch Med, Univ Tex, 61-62; radiologist, Methodist Hosp Ind, 62-65; assoc prof, 65-68, PROF RADIOL, SCH MED, EMORY UNIV, 68-, CHIEF MAMMOGRAPHY SECT, 65- *Concurrent Pos:* Chief sect exp diag radiol & assoc radiologist, Univ Tex M D Anderson Hosp & Tumor Inst, 61-62; spec consult, cancer control prog, div chronic dis, Bur State Serv, USPHS, 61-; consult, Health Ins Plan of NY Mammography Surv Prog, 62- *Mem:* Am Cancer Soc; Radiol Soc NAm; Roentgen Ray Soc; fel Am Col Radiol; AMA. *Res:* Cancer of the breast; teaching, evaluating and accumulating data on mammography and related procedures. *Mailing Add:* Mammography Sect Emory Univ Clin Atlanta GA 30322

EGAN, ROBERT SHAW, b Buffalo, NY, Apr 21, 45; m 66; c 2. LICHENOLOGY. *Educ:* Univ Colo, Boulder, BA, 67, MA, 69, PhD(biol), 71. *Prof Exp:* Asst prof biol, Castleton State Col, 71-75; asst prof biol, Tex A&M Univ, 75-79; ASSOC PROF & CHMN, DEPT BIOL, UNIV NEBR, OMAHA, 79- *Mem:* Am Bryol & Lichenological Soc; Bot Soc Am; Brit Lichen Soc; Mycol Soc Am; Am Soc Plant Taxon. *Res:* Taxonomy, ecology and phytogeography of lichens; chemosystematics; scanning electron microscopy. *Mailing Add:* Dept Biol Univ Nebr Omaha NE 68182

EGAN, ROBERT WHEELER, b Mineola, NY, Apr 15, 43; m 66; c 2. BIOCHEMISTRY. *Educ:* Brown Univ, BSc, 65; McGill Univ, PhD(chem), 72. *Prof Exp:* Chemist, Rohm & Haas Co, 65-67; NIH fel, Johns Hopkins Univ, 72-74; sr res biochemist, 74-81, ASSOC DIR, MERCK & CO, INC, RAHWAY, 81- *Mem:* Am Chem Soc. *Res:* Enzymology of prostaglandin, leukotriac, biosynthesis, and the generation and utilization of free radicals by peroxidases; physical studies of membrane structure; biochemical basis for inflammatory and immediate hypersensitivity disorders. *Mailing Add:* 45 Virginia Ave Manasquan NJ 08736

EGAN, THOMAS J, b Winnipeg, Man, Sept 13, 25; m 53; c 3. MEDICINE, PEDIATRICS. *Educ:* Univ BC, BA, 48; McGill Univ, MD, CM, 52. *Prof Exp:* Asst instr pediat, Univ Pittsburgh, 57-59; instr, Western Reserve Univ, 59-62; dir res lab, Children's Hosp Akron, 59-62; asst prof pediat, Sch Med, Univ Pittsburgh & dir res ctr, Children's Hosp Pittsburgh, 62-65; assoc prof pediat, Sch Med, Northwestern Univ, 65-71; prof pediat & prev & community med, 71-74; PROF PEDIAT, UNIV TORONTO, 74-; DIR AMBULATORY SERV, HOSP SICK CHILDREN, 74- *Concurrent Pos:* Fel res med, Univ Pittsburgh, 54-55; dir clin res ctr, Children's Mem Hosp, Chicago, 65-70, med dir ambulatory serv, 70-74. *Mem:* Soc Pediat Res; Am Acad Pediat; Can Pediat Soc. *Res:* Health care organization. *Mailing Add:* Hosp for Sick Children 555 University Ave Toronto ON M5G 1X8 Can

EGAN, WALTER GEORGE, b New York, NY, Oct 12, 23; m 63. SOLID STATE PHYSICS, ELECTRICAL ENGINEERING. *Educ:* City Col New York, BEE, 49; Columbia Univ, MA, 51; Polytech Inst Brooklyn, PhD(solid state physics), 60. *Prof Exp:* Engr, Egan Lab, NY, 44-50; nuclear physicist, Nucleonics Sect, Naval Mat Lab, 50-56; prof elec eng, City Col New York, 56-57; prin res engr, Ford Instrument Co Div, Sperry-Rand Corp, 57-58, eng proj supvr, 58-60, asst dir res, 60-62, exec asst to vpres res, 62-63; STAFF SCIENTIST, GRUMMAN AEROSPACE CORP, 63- *Concurrent Pos:* Mem airlines electronic eng comt, Air Lines Commun Admin Coun, 58-; adv group aeronaut res & develop, NATO, 61- *Mem:* Am Phys Soc; Inst Elec & Electronics Eng; Sigma Xi. *Res:* Thin films; infrared; cryogenics; magnetics; microwaves and millimeter waves; lasers; masers; high vacuum; military and space sciences including guidance, navigation, oceanography, communications, countermeasures and antisubmarine warfare; astronomy; polarization properties of terrestrial and planetary surfaces. *Mailing Add:* 84-26 86th St Wood Haven NY 11421

EGAN, WILLIAM MICHAEL, b New York, NY, Aug 22, 44. PHYSICAL CHEMISTRY, BIOCHEMISTRY. *Educ:* Manhattan Col, BS, 66; Princeton Univ, PhD(chem), 71. *Prof Exp:* Res assoc chem, Lund Inst Technol, 71-75; staff fel, Nat Inst Child Health & Human Develop, NIH, 75-76; RES CHEMIST, BUR BIOLOGICS, FOOD & DRUG ADMIN, 76- *Concurrent Pos:* Adj assoc prof, Cath Univ Am. *Mem:* Am Chem Soc; Int Soc Magnetic Resonance; AAAS. *Res:* Nuclear magnetic resonance spectroscopy; bacterial capsular polysaccharide structure. *Mailing Add:* Bur of Biologics Bldg 29 Rm 432 8800 Rockville Pike Bethesda MD 20014

EGAR, JOSEPH MICHAEL, b Jacksonville, Fla, Feb 2, 30; m 61; c 4. MATHEMATICS. *Educ:* Univ Okla, BS, 52; Tex A&M Univ, PhD(geol, geophys, math), 59. *Prof Exp:* Eng trainee, Savannah River Proj, E I du Pont de Nemours & Co, 52; instr geol, Marietta Col, 55; asst prof geol & math, Tex A&M Univ, 57-59, NSF sci fac fel math, 59-60; assoc prof, Ball State Teachers Col, 60-63 & Univ Akron, 63-66; ASSOC PROF MATH, CLEVELAND STATE UNIV, 66- *Concurrent Pos:* Sr lectr math, Hatfield Polytech, Hertfordshire, Eng, 74-75; hon res fel, Dept Math & Physics, Birmingham Univ, Eng, 80. *Mem:* AAAS; Math Asn Am. *Res:* Seismology, especially surface wave phenomena and underwater acoustics; applied mathematics; numerical analysis. *Mailing Add:* Dept of Math Cleveland State Univ Cleveland OH 44115

EGAR, MARGARET WELLS, b Princeton, WVa, July 25, 34; m 61; c 4. ANATOMY, ELECTRON MICROSCOPY. *Educ:* Concord Col, BS, 56; Emory Univ, MS, 58, PhD(biol), 60. *Prof Exp:* Asst prof biol, Ball State Univ, 60-62; res assoc regeneration, 65-73, lectr anat, 73-77, ASST PROF ANAT, SCH MED, CASE WESTERN RESERVE UNIV, 77- *Mem:* Sigma Xi; AAAS; Am Asn Anat. *Res:* Ependymal scaffolding in regeneration and development; electron microscopy of peripheral nervous system. *Mailing Add:* Dept of Anat Sch of Med Case Western Reserve Univ Cleveland OH 44106

EGBERG, DAVID CURTIS, b Minneapolis, Minn, Oct 13, 42; m 70; c 1. ORGANIC CHEMISTRY. *Educ:* Macalester Col, BA, 64; Univ Minn, PhD(org chem), 72. *Prof Exp:* RES CHEMIST ANAL CHEM, GEN MILLS, INC, 72- *Concurrent Pos:* Chmn vitamin methods comt, Am Asn Cereal Chemists, 74- *Res:* Development of analytical methods for the food industry; continuous flow automation and high pressure liquid chromatography. *Mailing Add:* James Ford Bell Res Ctr Gen Mills Inc 9000 Plymouth N Minneapolis MN 55427

EGBERT, GARY TRENT, US citizen. MOLECULAR SPECTROSCOPY. *Educ:* Western Ill Univ, BS, 63; Univ SDak, MS, 67; Univ Nebr, PhD(physics), 74. *Prof Exp:* Teacher physics, Burlington High Sch, Iowa, 63-66; asst prof, 67-69 & 72-77, ASSOC PROF PHYSICS & CHMN DEPT, UNIV WIS-LA CROSSE, 77- *Mailing Add:* Cowley Hall of Sci 1707 Pine St Univ of Wis La Crosse WI 54601

EGBERT, ROBERT B(ALDWIN), b Chosica, Peru, SAm, Dec 13, 16; US citizen; m 41; c 5. CHEMICAL ENGINEERING. *Educ:* Cooper Union, BChE, 38; Mass Inst Technol, MSc, 40, DSc(chem eng), 41. *Prof Exp:* Asst, Mass Inst Technol, 39-41; prod & design engr, Carbon & Carbide Chem Corp, 41-47; chief engr & vpres, Sci Design Co, Inc, 47-58; pres, Chem Process Corp, 58-69; INDEPENDENT CONSULT ENGR, 69- *Honors & Awards:* Walker Award, Am Inst Chem Engrs. *Mem:* AAAS; Am Inst Chem Engrs; NY Acad Sci. *Res:* Heat transmission by radiation from gases; development of commercial processes for the manufacture of ethylene oxide, maleic anhydride, phthalic anhydride; iso and terephthalic acids. *Mailing Add:* 8 Rip Rd Hanover NH 03755

EGDAHL, RICHARD H, b Eau Claire, Wis, Dec 13, 26; m 53; c 4. SURGERY. *Educ:* Harvard Univ, MD, 50; Univ Minn, PhD, 57. *Prof Exp:* Instr surg, Univ Minn, 57-58; dir surg res labs, Med Col Va, 58-64; PROF SURG & CHMN DEPT, SCH MED, BOSTON UNIV, 64-, DIR, MED CTR & ACAD VPRES HEALTH AFFAIRS, 73-, DIR, HEALTH POLICY INST, 75-, DIR, CTR INDUST & HEALTH CARE, 76- *Concurrent Pos:* USPHS spec res fel, Univ Minn, 57-58; Markle scholar, 58-; consult, Boston & Providence Vet Hosps. *Honors & Awards:* Ciba Award, Endocrine Soc, 62. *Mem:* Inst Med-Nat Acad Sci; Am Col Surgeons; Am Surg Asn; Am Soc Clin Invest; Int Asn Endocrine Surgeons (pres, 81-83). *Res:* Experimental and clinical endocrinology; trauma; shock; pancreatitis. *Mailing Add:* Univ Hosp 750 Harrison Ave Boston MA 02118

EGE, SEYHAN NURETTIN, b Ankara, Turkey, Jan 11, 31. ORGANIC CHEMISTRY. *Educ:* Am Col for Girls, Istanbul, BS, 49; Smith Col, MA, 52; Univ Mich, PhD(org chem), 56. *Prof Exp:* Instr chem, Univ Mich, 56-57 & Am Col for Girls, Istanbul, 57-59; res assoc, Boston Univ, 59-61; asst prof, Mt Holyoke Col, 61-62; res assoc & part time lectr, Univ Toronto, 62-65; lectr, 65-67, from asst prof to assoc prof, 67-80, PROF CHEM, UNIV MICH, 80- *Mem:* AAAS; Am Chem Soc; The Chem Soc. *Res:* Molecular rearrangements; organic nitrogen compounds; organic photochemistry of heterocycles. *Mailing Add:* Dept Chem 3301 Chem Bldg Univ Mich Ann Arbor MI 48104

EGEBERG, ROGER O, b Chicago, Ill, Nov 13, 03; m 29; c 4. INTERNAL MEDICINE, MEDICAL ADMINISTRATION. *Educ:* Cornell Univ, BA, 25; Northwestern Univ, MD, 29. *Prof Exp:* Chief med & prof serv, Vet Admin Hosp, 46-56; med dir, Los Angeles County Hosp, 56-58; med dir, Los Angeles County Dept Charities, 58-64; prof med & dean sch med, Univ Southern Calif, 64-69; asst secy health & sci affairs, 69-71, SPEC ASST TO SECY FOR HEALTH POLICY & CONSULT TO PRESIDENT ON HEALTH AFFAIRS, DEPT HEALTH, EDUC & WELFARE, 71- *Concurrent Pos:* Med consult, Armed Forces, 46; physician-in-residence, Vet Admin Hosps, 56-; chmn, Gov Comt Study Med Aid & Health, Calif, 60; mem, President's Panel Spec Study Narcotics, 62 & Presidential Adv Comn Narcotics & Drug 63; mem & past pres, Calif State Bd Health, 63-68; mem nat adv cancer coun, Nat Cancer Inst, 64-68; mem & chmn spec med adv group, Vet Admin, 65-69; chief med officer, Medicare Bur & dir off prof & sci activ, Health Care Financing Admin, HEW, 77- *Mem:* Fel Am Col Physicians. *Res:* Ecology of Coccidioides immitis, especially the reasons for spotty distribution in the soil of endemic areas; identification of antagonists and their susceptibility to high temperatures and high salinity. *Mailing Add:* Dept of Health & Human Serv Washington DC 20201

EGELHOFF, WILLIAM FREDERICK, (JR), b Norfolk, Va, July 8, 49; m 76; c 1. CHEMICAL PHYSICS, SOLID STATE PHYSICS. *Educ:* Hampden-Sydney Col, BS, 71; Cambridge Univ, PhD(phys chem), 75. *Prof Exp:* Fel chem eng, Calif Inst Technol, 75-76; res physicist, Gen Motors Res Labs, Warren, 76-79; RES PHYSICIST, SURFACE SCI DIV, NAT BUR STANDARDS, 79- *Mem:* Am Phys Soc; Am Vacuum Soc. *Res:* Photoelectron spectroscopy; chemical reaction dynamics; surface physics; surface chemistry. *Mailing Add:* Surface Sci Div Nat Bur Standards Washington DC 20234

EGER, F MARTIN, b Lwow, Poland, May 31, 36; US citizen. THEORETICAL PHYSICS. *Educ:* Mass Inst Technol, BS, 58; Brandeis Univ, PhD(physics), 63. *Prof Exp:* Res assoc theoret physics, Brandeis, 63-64; fel, Lawrence Radiation Lab, Univ Calif, 65-67; asst prof physics, 67-72, ASSOC PROF PHYSICS, COL STATEN ISLAND, CITY UNIV NEW YORK, 72- *Mem:* AAAS; Am Phys Soc; NY Acad Sci. *Res:* Statistical mechanics and the many-body-problem; history and philosophy of science; education. *Mailing Add:* Dept Physics Col Staten Island City Univ New York Staten Island NY 10301

EGERMEIER, EDWARD R, b Oklahoma City, Okla, Aug 17, 31; m 53; c 2. DAIRY SCIENCE, BACTERIOLOGY. *Educ:* Okla State Univ, BS, 53, MS, 56. *Prof Exp:* Instr dairy bact, Okla State Univ, 56-57; chemist, Res Labs, Carnation Co, Van Nuys, 57-60, group leader dairy res, 60-67; sr scientist, Robert A Johnston Co, 67; dairy res mgr, 67-70, dir prod develop, Chicago, 70-77, opers mgr & tech dir, Sanna Div, 77-79, VPRES OPER, SANNA INC,

BEATRICE FOODS C0, 79- *Mem:* Am Dairy Sci Asn; Int Food Tech Soc; Am Dry Milk Inst. *Res:* Product development in dairy and imitation dairy products as well as other food items in the dehydrated and frozen areas; bacteriophage in cheese cultures; aseptic and dry dairy foods. *Mailing Add:* Oper Sanna Inc Box 8046 Subsid Beatrice Foods Co Menomonie WI 54751

EGERMEIER, R(OBERT) P(AUL), b Oklahoma City, Okla, Dec 25, 27; m 52; c 2. SYSTEM ENGINEERING. *Educ:* Univ Okla, BS, 51; NMex State Univ, MS, 57; Lasalle Inst, LLB, 76. *Prof Exp:* Asst physicist, Phys Sci Lab, NMex State Univ, 53-57, asst prof mech eng, 57-62; staff engr & sect mgr, Aerospace Corp, Calif, 62-67; staff eng scientist & mgr ord systs, Radio Corp Am, 67-69; sr scientist, 69-79, SR SCIENTIST, HUGHES AIRCRAFT CO, 81- *Concurrent Pos:* Consult, 69- *Mem:* AAAS; Am Inst Aeronaut & Astronaut; Am Soc Mech Engrs; Inst Elec & Electronics Engrs; Am Bar Asn. *Res:* Analog systems; thermodynamics; product liability and safety; microprocessor applications. *Mailing Add:* Hughes Aircraft Co 8433 Fallbrook Ave Canoga Park CA 91304

EGERTON, JOHN RICHARD, b Boulder, Colo, Dec 3, 27; m 51; c 3. PARASITOLOGY. *Educ:* Colo Agr & Mech Col, BS, 51; Kans State Col, MS, 51, PhD(parasitol), 53. *Prof Exp:* Res asst parasitol, Kans State Col, 50-53; from instr to asst prof zool, Okla Agr & Mech Col, 53-55; res assoc, 55-65, res fel, 65-71, sr res fel, 71-78, SR INVESTR PARASITOL, MERCK INST THERAPEUT RES, 78- *Mem:* Am Soc Parasitol; Biomet Soc; World Asn Adv Vet Parasitol; Am Heartworm Soc. *Res:* Nematode immunology; chemotherapy of helminth diseases; biometrics. *Mailing Add:* Merck Inst Therapeut Res MSDRL PO Box 2000 Rahway NJ 07065

EGGAN, LAWRENCE CARL, b Fargo, NDak, Jan 10, 35; m 71; c 5. NUMBER THEORY, COMBINATORICS. *Educ:* Pac Lutheran Univ, BA, 56; Univ Ore, MS, 58, PhD(number theory), 60. *Prof Exp:* Teaching fel math, Univ Ore, 56-59; from instr to asst prof, Univ Mich, 60-65; assoc prof & chmn dept, Pac Lutheran Univ, 65-68; assoc prof, 68-73, PROF MATH, ILL STATE UNIV, 73- *Concurrent Pos:* Sigma Xi res grant, Univ Ore, 60; lectr, Imp Col, London, 63-64; vis prof, Royal Holloway Col, London, 76-77; assoc ed, Math Reviews, 79-81. *Mem:* Am Math Soc; Math Asn Am; London Math Soc; Sigma Xi. *Res:* Number theory, especially Diophantine approximations; logic, especially automata and finite automata; combinatorics, especially graph theory. *Mailing Add:* Dept of Math Ill State Univ Normal IL 61761

EGGE, ALFRED SEVERIN, b Long Beach, Calif, Apr 30, 33; m 53; c 3. ZOOLOGY. *Educ:* Long Beach State Col, BA, 57; Univ Ariz, MS, 59, PhD(zool, biochem), 62. *Prof Exp:* Asst zool, Univ Ariz, 57-61; asst prof physiol, Long Beach State Col, 61-64; asst res physiologist, Sch Med, Univ Calif, San Francisco, 64-66; assoc prof, 66-70, chmn dept, 68-74, PROF BIOL, CALIF STATE COL, SAN BERNARDINO, 70- *Mem:* Am Physiol Soc. *Res:* Neuroendocrinology; mechanism for aldosterone secretion. *Mailing Add:* Dept of Biol Calif State Col 5500 College Pkwy San Bernardino CA 92376

EGGEN, DONALD T(RIPP), b Hemet, Calif, Feb 11, 22; m 42; c 4. NUCLEAR ENGINEERING. *Educ:* Whittier Col, BA, 43; Ohio State Univ, PhD(physics), 48. *Prof Exp:* Res physicist mass separation of uranium, Tenn Eastman Corp, 44-45; res asst physics, Ohio State Univ, 45-48; res engr, Exp Physics, NAm Aviation, Inc, 49-53, group engr, Component Develop, 53-57, res specialist, Exp Physics, 57-58, proj mgr, Adv Epithermal Thorium Reactor, 59-63, proj mgr fast reactor & sodium components, 63-66; prog mgr fast reactor core design, Argonne Nat Lab, 66-68; PROF NUCLEAR ENG, TECHNOL INST, NORTHWESTERN UNIV, 68- *Concurrent Pos:* Deleg, US Nuclear Regulatory Comn, Cabri Proj, Cadarache Centre E'tudes Nucleaire, France, 78-79. *Mem:* AAAS; Am Phys Soc; fel Am Nuclear Soc. *Res:* Fast reactor core design; safety; liquid metal technology and heat transfer. *Mailing Add:* Dept of Eng Sci & Appl Math Technol Inst Northwestern Univ Evanston IL 60201

EGGEN, DOUGLAS AMBROSE, b Rushford, Minn, Apr 30, 25; m 50; c 3. PATHOLOGY. *Educ:* Univ Chicago, PhB, 47, SB, 55, PhD(biophys), 57. *Prof Exp:* Res assoc biophys, Res Insts, Univ Chicago, 55-58; res assoc path, 58-61, from instr to assoc prof path, 61-70, assoc prof path & biomet, 70-72, dir, Biomed Comput Ctr, 72-75, actg head, Dept Biomet, 76, 78-79, PROF PATH & BIOMET, LA STATE UNIV MED CTR, NEW ORLEANS, 72- *Concurrent Pos:* Mem coun on arteriosclerosis, Am Heart Asn. *Mem:* AAAS; Am Asn Path; Biophys Soc; Sigma Xi. *Res:* Experimental atherosclerosis and cholesterol metabolism in non-human primates; geographic pathology of atherosclerosis. *Mailing Add:* Dept of Path La State Univ Med Ctr New Orleans LA 70112

EGGEN, OLIN JEUCK, astrophysics, see previous edition

EGGENA, PATRICK, b London, Eng, Feb 1, 38; US citizen; m 65; c 2. PHYSIOLOGY. *Educ:* Univ Cincinnati, MD, 66. *Prof Exp:* ASSOC PROF PHYSIOL, MT SINAI MED SCH, 73-, ASSOC PROF BIOPHYS, 77- *Concurrent Pos:* NIH fel, 67-70; estab investr, Am Heart Asn, 71-76, mem renal coun. *Mem:* Am Physiol Soc; Tissue Cult Soc. *Res:* Mechanism of secretion and action of the antidiuretic hormone, Vasopressin. *Mailing Add:* Dept of Physiol Mt Sinai Med Sch New York NY 10029

EGGENBERGER, ANDREW JON, b Harlowton, Mont, May 8, 38. EARTHQUAKE ENGINEERING, APPLIED MECHANICS. *Educ:* Carnegie Inst Technol, BS, 61, PhD(magnetohydrodyn), 67; Ohio State Univ, ScM, 63. *Prof Exp:* Assoc res engr, Boeing Co, 61-63; fac fel magnetohydrodyn, Advan Res Inst, Lewis Res Ctr, NASA, 67-68; asst prof eng, Univ SC, 67-72; NUCLEAR PROJS MGR, D'APPOLONIA CONSULT ENGRS, INC, 72- *Concurrent Pos:* Fac fel fluid turbulence, Aero-Astrodyn Lab, George C Marshall Space Flight Ctr, NASA, 69. *Mem:* Am Inst Aeronaut & Astronaut; Am Soc Eng Educ; Am Nuclear Soc. *Res:* Fluid mechanics; magnetohydrodynamics. *Mailing Add:* D'Appolonia Consult Engrs Inc 10 Duff Rd Pittsburgh PA 15235

EGGENBERGER, DELBERT NORGAARD, applied physics, deceased

EGGENS, CECILE J, b New York, NY. PLASMA PHYSICS, COMPUTATIONAL PHYSICS. *Educ:* Univ Calif, Davis, PhD(physics), 76. *Prof Exp:* Physicist, Nuclear Assocs, 68-78; PHYSICIST, LAWRENCE LIVERMORE LAB, UNIV CALIF, 70- *Res:* Controlled thermonuclear fusion. *Mailing Add:* Lawrence Livermore Lab PO Box 808 Livermore CA 94550

EGGER, CARL THOMAS, b Monticello, Iowa, Feb 5, 37; m 57; c 5. PROCESS PLANT ENGINEERING, ALCOHOL PRODUCTION. *Educ:* Univ Iowa, BSChE, 59, MS, 60, PhD(chem eng), 62. *Prof Exp:* Reservoir engr, Shell Develop Co, Tex, 62; mgr process develop, 64-66, dir develop, 66-73, protein mgr, 73-76, dir eng, 76-80, VPRES, GRAIN PROCESSING CORP, 80- *Honors & Awards:* Citizen Chem Eng, Iowa Sect Am Inst Chem Engrs, 77. *Mem:* Am Inst Chem Engrs. *Res:* Secondary recovery; cryogenics; computer simulation; aerospace; fermentation technology; wet milling; distillation; waste treatment; enzymes; process control; solvent extraction; centrifugation; membrane separations; protein extraction and modification; energy conservation. *Mailing Add:* 1304 Houser Muscatine IA 52761

EGGER, M(AURICE) DAVID, b Bakersfield, Calif, June 21, 36; m 58; c 3. NEUROPHYSIOLOGY, NEUROANATOMY. *Educ:* Stanford Univ, BS, 58; Yale Univ, MS, 60, PhD(physiol psychol), 62. *Prof Exp:* From instr to assoc prof anat, Sch Med, Yale Univ, 65-74; assoc prof, 74-78, PROF ANAT, RUTGERS MED SCH-COL MED & DENT NJ, 78- *Concurrent Pos:* USPHS fel psychiat, Sch Med, Yale Univ, 62-63; vis scientist, Med Res Coun Cerebral Function Res Group, Univ London, 69-70; NIMH res scientist develop award, 69-74, mem res scientist rev comt, 75-79. *Mem:* Am Psychol Asn; Am Asn Anat; Am Physiol Soc; Soc Neurosci; fel AAAS. *Res:* Neural basis of learning; organization of spinal reflexes; anatomy of spinal cord. *Mailing Add:* Dept of Anat Col Med & Dent NJ Rutgers Med Sch Piscataway NJ 08854

EGGERS, A(LFRED) J(OHN), JR, b Omaha, Nebr, June 24, 22; m 50; c 2. AERODYNAMICS. *Educ:* Univ Omaha, AB, 44; Stanford Univ, MS, 49, PhD(eng mech), 56. *Prof Exp:* With NASA & predecessor, 44-71, chief vehicle environ div, Ames Res Ctr, 59-63, asst dir res & dir res & develop anal & planning, 63-64, dep assoc adminr advan res & technol, NASA Hq, 64-68, asst adminr policy, 68-71; asst dir res appln, NSF, 71-77; dir, Lockheed Palo Alto Res Lab, 77-79; PRES, RANN INC, 79- *Concurrent Pos:* Mem sci adv bd, US Air Force, 58-72. *Honors & Awards:* Arthur S Flemming Award, 56; H Julian Allen Award, NASA, 69. *Mem:* Nat Acad Eng; fel Am Inst Aeronaut & Astronaut; fel Am Astron Soc; AAAS. *Res:* Supersonic and hypersonic aerodynamics; aerodynamic heating, aerospace vehicles; aerospace research and development management, planning, and policy analysis and development; energy research and development management. *Mailing Add:* Rann Inc Suite 414 Courthouse Plaza 260 Sheridan Ave Washington DC 20550

EGGERS, DAVID FRANK, JR, b Oak Park, Ill, July 8, 22; m 45; c 3. PHYSICAL CHEMISTRY. *Educ:* Univ Ill, BS, 43; Univ Minn, PhD(chem), 51. *Prof Exp:* Asst, Univ Minn, 43-44; chemist, Tenn Eastman Corp, 44-47; instr, 50-52, from asst prof to assoc prof, 52-63, PROF CHEM, UNIV WASH, 63- *Mem:* Am Chem Soc; Optical Soc Am. *Res:* Vibrational spectra and molecular structure; infrared and Raman spectra of solids, liquids and gases; vibrational spectra and molecular structure. *Mailing Add:* Dept of Chem BG-10 Univ of Wash Seattle WA 98195

EGGERS, GEORGE W NORDHOLTZ, JR, b Galveston, Tex, Feb 22, 29; m 55; c 2. MEDICINE, ANESTHESIOLOGY. *Educ:* Rice Inst, BA, 49; Univ Tex, MD, 53; Am Bd Anesthesiol, dipl, 59. *Prof Exp:* From instr to asst prof, Med Br, Univ Tex, 56-61; assoc prof, 61-67, PROF ANESTHESIOL, SCH MED, UNIV MO-COLUMBIA, 67-, CHMN DEPT, 70- *Concurrent Pos:* Grants, Med Res Found Tex & Galveston Heart Asn, 59-60, Tex Heart Asn, 60-61, NIH, 61-68; vis res prof, Med Sch, Northwestern Univ, 68. *Mem:* AAAS; fel Am Col Anesthesiol; AMA; Am Soc Anesthesiol; Asn Am Med Cols. *Res:* Human pharmacology and physiology; cardiovascular dynamics; pulmonary circulation. *Mailing Add:* Univ of Mo Med Ctr Columbia MO 65201

EGGERS, RICHARD CARL, nuclear chemistry, deceased

EGGERT, ARTHUR ARNOLD, b Shawano, Wis, Sept 9, 44; m 66; c 3. ANALYTICAL CHEMISTRY, COMPUTER SCIENCE. *Educ:* Univ Wis-Madison, BS, 66, PhD(anal chem), 70. *Prof Exp:* Asst prof chem, Duke Univ, 70-71; asst prof, 71-78, ASSOC PROF PATH & ASSOC DIR CLIN LABS, UNIV WIS-MADISON, 78-; DIR SPECIMEN & DATA PROCESSING, CLIN LABS, 72- *Concurrent Pos:* Dir comput programming, Lab Computing, Inc, 75-76. *Mem:* Am Chem Soc; Asn Comput Mach; Asn Clin Chemists; Inst Elec & Electronics Engrs. *Res:* Computer applications in quality control; clinical laboratory information systems. *Mailing Add:* Clin Labs Univ Hosp 600 Highland Ave Madison WI 53792

EGGERT, DONALD A, b Cleveland, Ohio, May 13, 34. PALEOBOTANY. *Educ:* Western Reserve Univ, BA, 56; Yale Univ, MS, 58, PhD(bot), 60. *Prof Exp:* NSF fel, Univ Ill, 60-61; asst prof bot, Southern Ill Univ, 61-65 & Univ Iowa, 65-69; assoc prof, 69-74, PROF BIOL SCI, UNIV ILL, CHICAGO CIRCLE, 74- *Concurrent Pos:* Sigma Xi grant, 62-63; NSF grants, Southern Ill Univ, 63-65 & Univ Iowa, 65-68; vis lectr, Yale Univ, 64-65. *Res:* Morphology; anatomy; evolution of vascular land plants with emphasis upon the fossil forms of the late Paleozoic. *Mailing Add:* Dept of Biol Sci Univ of Ill at Chicago Circle Chicago IL 60680

EGGERT, FRANKLIN PAUL, b Buffalo, NY, May 13, 20; m 45; c 4. HORTICULTURE. *Educ:* Cornell Univ, PhD(pomol), 49. *Prof Exp:* Head dept, 49-63, dean grad sch, 62-75, PROF HORT, UNIV MAINE, ORONO, 49- *Concurrent Pos:* Dir res, Univ Maine, Orono, 63-69, actg dir res, 70-71. *Mem:* AAAS; Am Soc Hort Sci; Bot Soc Am; Am Pomol Soc. *Res:* Research administration. *Mailing Add:* Box 262C Verona ME 04416

EGGERT, ROBERT GLENN, b Bennet, Nebr, Feb 27, 27; m 52; c 2. ANIMAL SCIENCE. *Educ:* Univ Nebr, BS, 50, MS, 52; Cornell Univ, PhD(animal nutrit), 54. *Prof Exp:* Asst, Nebr Exp Substa, 50; assoc, Animal Husb Dept, Univ Nebr, 50-52 & Cornell Univ, 52-54; animal nutritionist, Res Div, 54-59, group leader, Agr Div, 59-68, swine prog mgr, 68-72, livestock prog mgr, 72-77, group leader, 77-80, RUMINANT PROG MGR, AGR RES DIV, AM CYANAMID CO, 80- *Mem:* Am Soc Animal Sci. *Res:* Amino acid and trace mineral requirements of swine; non-protein nitrogen utilization by ruminants; antibiotics; hormones for growth and reproduction; anthelmintics for swine and cattle. *Mailing Add:* Am Cyanamid Co PO Box 400 Princeton NJ 08540

EGGIMANN, WILHELM HANS, b Zurich, Switz, Apr 18, 29; m 61; c 2. ELECTRICAL ENGINEERING, SOLID STATE PHYSICS. *Educ:* Swiss Fed Inst Technol, dipl, 54; Case Inst Technol, MS, 59, PhD(elec eng), 61. *Prof Exp:* Asst microwave tech, Swiss Fed Inst Technol, 54-56; electromagnetic theory, Case Inst Technol, 56-61, asst prof elec eng, 61-64; ASSOC PROF ELEC ENG, WORCESTER POLYTECH INST, 64- *Mem:* AAAS; Inst Elec & Electronics Engrs. *Res:* Electromagnetic theory; problems in diffraction theory; wave propagation and microwave techniques; plasma physics; collective interaction in solids; quantum electronics. *Mailing Add:* Dept of Elec Eng Worcester Polytech Inst Worcester MA 01609

EGGLER, DAVID HEWITT, b Ashland, Wis, May 15, 40; m 74; c 2. MINERALOGY, PETROLOGY. *Educ:* Oberlin Col, AB, 62; Univ Colo, PhD(geol), 67. *Prof Exp:* Asst prof geol, Tex A&M Univ, 70-72; mem staff geochem, Geophys Lab, Carnegie Inst Wash, 72-77; res assoc, 67-70, ASSOC PROF, DEPT GEOCHEM, PA STATE UNIV, 77- *Concurrent Pos:* Assoc ed, Am Mineralogist, 79. *Honors & Awards:* L R Wager Prize, Int Asn Volcanology & Geochem of Earth's Interior, 79. *Mem:* Am Geophys Union; Geol Soc Am; Mineral Soc Am; Geochem Soc. *Res:* Geology and petrology of Kimberlites; experimental high-pressure, high temperature phase equilibria of magmatic arc rocks, mantle, carbonated melts, redox equilibria, super critical fluids. *Mailing Add:* Dept Geosci Pa State Univ University Park PA 16802

EGGLER, WILLIS ALEXANDER, b La Crosse, Wis, Mar 28, 04; m 29; c 2. BOTANY. *Educ:* Northland Col, AB, 27; Univ Minn, MS, 36, PhD(bot), 39. *Prof Exp:* Instr high sch, Wis, 27-34; asst bot, Univ Minn, 35-39; instr bot, zool & geol, Gogebic Jr Col, 39-42; prof biol & head dept, Alma Col, 42-45; assoc prof, Cent Mich Col, 45-47; from asst to assoc prof, 47-69, emer prof bot, Newcomb Col, Tulane Univ, 69-70; assoc prof biol, Warren Wilson Col, 70-81; RETIRED. *Mem:* AAAS; Ecol Soc Am. *Res:* Ecology of deciduous forests; revegetation of volcanic areas; hardwoods of Mississippi river flood plains; Gulf Coast marshes; pinelands. *Mailing Add:* Daisy Hill Rd Rte 2 Box 171 Asheville NC 28805

EGGLESTON, FORREST CARY, b New York, NY, Sept 28, 20; m 46; c 2. MEDICINE, SURGERY. *Educ:* Princeton Univ, AB, 42; Cornell Univ, MD, 45; Am Bd Surg & Am Bd Thoracic Surg, dipl. *Prof Exp:* Jr attend surgeon, First Surg Div & Thoracic Surg Dept, Bellevue Hosp, NY, 53; THORACIC SURGEON, CHRISTIAN MED COL, INDIA, 54-, PROF SURG, 55-, HEAD DEPT, 80- *Concurrent Pos:* Med supt & thoracic surgeon, Lady Irwin Sanatorium, 54-74. *Mem:* Fel Am Col Surg; Asn Surgeons India. *Mailing Add:* Dept of Surg Christian Med Col Ludhiana Punjab India

EGGLESTON, GLEN E, b Salt Lake City, Utah, Aug 20, 23; m 44; c 3. THERMODYNAMICS. *Educ:* Univ Utah, BS, 44; Univ Wash, MS, 49; Purdue Univ, PhD(mech eng), 53. *Prof Exp:* Supvry serv engr, Westinghouse Elec & Mfg Co, 46-48; instr mech eng, Univ Utah, 49-51; design engr, Douglas Aircraft Co, 53-58, rep air conditioning sect, Aircraft Div, 58-59, asst chief mech sect, Missiles & Space Systs Div, 59-62, sect chief, 62, asst chief vehicle design br, 62-64, br chief mech sect, 64-67, asst chief engr crew systs, Manned Orbiting Lab Prog, 67-69, ASST CHIEF ENGR ENVIRON ENG, McDONNELL DOUGLAS CORP, 69- *Concurrent Pos:* Instr, night sch, Carnegie Inst Technol, 46-47; lectr, Univ Calif, Los Angeles, 54-55. *Mem:* Am Soc Mech Engrs. *Res:* Heat transfer in the specific areas of aerodynamic heating. *Mailing Add:* 27161 Fond du Lac Rd Palos Verdes Peninsula CA 90274

EGGLESTON, JOHN M, b San Francisco, Calif, June 26, 26; m 50; c 4. AERONAUTICAL ENGINEERING. *Educ:* Va Polytech Inst, BS, 49; Univ Va, MS, 54; Princeton Univ, MS, 58; Mass Inst Technol, MS, 66. *Prof Exp:* Aeronaut engr, High Speed Flight Res Ctr, Nat Adv Comt Aeronaut, Edwards AFB, 49-51, aeronaut res scientist, Stability & Control Br, Langley Res Ctr, 51-59, asst head flight mech, NASA, 59-62, tech asst, Spacecraft Tech Div, 62, asst chief space environ div, 62-64, sect chief, Space Sci Div, 66-67, dep chief, Lunar & Earth Sci Div, 67-69, asst to dir eng & develop, Manned Spacecraft Ctr, 70-80. *Concurrent Pos:* Instr univ exten, Univ Va, 58-61; instr, Clear Lake Ctr, Univ Houston, 81. *Res:* Engineering management; scientific experiments in space; mission planning; space mechanics; guidance; navigation; stability and control; atmospheric turbulence. *Mailing Add:* 1006 Falling Leaf Friendswood TX 77546

EGGLESTON, PATRICK MYRON, b Panama, Apr 20, 41; US citizen; m 66; c 1. PHYCOLOGY, LIMNOLOGY. *Educ:* Mich State Univ, BS, 63; Cornell Univ, MS, 66; Ohio State Univ, PhD(zool), 75. *Prof Exp:* Teacher sci, Chenango Valley Jr High Sch, 65-67; teacher biol, Voorheesville High Sch, 67-70; teaching assoc zool, Ohio State Univ, 70-75; asst prof, 75-81, ASSOC PROF BIOL, KEENE STATE COL, 81- *Mem:* Phycol Soc Am; Crustacean Soc. *Res:* Ecology of fresh water algae and crustacea. *Mailing Add:* 22 Clark Circle Keene NH 03431

EGGLETON, REGINALD CHARLES, b Hillsdale, Mich, July 6, 20; m 44; c 3. ULTRASOUND, MEDICAL SCIENCE. *Educ:* Eastern Mich Univ, BS, 61; Univ Ill, MS, 66. *Prof Exp:* Engr, Physicists Res Co, 41-47; gen mgr, Haller, Raymond & Brown, Inc, 47-50; head eng develop, Alden Prod Co, 50-53; res assoc elec eng, Univ Ill, 53-57; pres & sr res scientist, Intersci Res Inst, 57-72; assoc prof, 72-78, PROF SURG RES, SCH MED, IND UNIV, INDIANAPOLIS, 78-; DIR, FORTUNE-FRY RES LAB, INDIANAPOLIS CTR ADVAN RES, 72- *Concurrent Pos:* Res assoc, Bioacoust Res Lab, Univ Ill, 57-69; sr res scientist, Ultrasound Res Labs, 78- *Mem:* AAAS; Instrument Soc Am; Am Soc Echocardiography; Am Inst Ultrasound Med; Asn Advan Med Instrumentation. *Res:* Medical applications of ultrasound, both as diagnostic and therapeutic modalities; acoustic microscopy of viable mouse embryo hearts, ultrasonic surgery, acoustic diffraction, spectroscopy and real-time cross-sectional echocardiography. *Mailing Add:* Indianapolis Ctr for Advan Res 410 Beauty Ave Room 149 Indianapolis IN 46202

EGLE, DAVIS MAX, b New Orleans, La, Jan 31, 39; m 63; c 2. MECHANICAL ENGINEERING, MECHANICS. *Educ:* La State Univ, BS, 60; Tulane Univ, MS, 62, PhD(mech eng), 65. *Prof Exp:* From asst prof to assoc prof, 65-73, prof, 73-81, DIR, AEROSPACE, MECH & NUCLEAR ENG, UNIV OKLA, 81- *Honors & Awards:* Okla Regents Teaching Award, 68. *Mem:* Am Soc Mech Engrs; Acoust Soc Am; Am Soc Nondestructive Testing; Am Acad Mech. *Res:* Theoretical and experimental dynamics of solids; nondestructive evaluation. *Mailing Add:* Sch of Aerospace & Mech Eng Univ of Okla Norman OK 73019

EGLE, JOHN LEE, JR, b Martinsburg, WVa, July 13, 39; m 61; c 2. PHARMACOLOGY, PHYSIOLOGY. *Educ:* Shepherd Col, BS, 61; Univ WVa, MS, 63, PhD(pharmacol), 64. *Prof Exp:* Asst, Univ WVa, 61-64; cardiovasc training, Bowman Gray Sch Med, 64-66; asst prof pharmacol, 68-74, ASSOC PROF PHARMACOL, MED COL VA, VA COMMONWEALTH UNIV, 74- *Mem:* Am Col Pharmacists; Am Soc Pharmacol Exp Therapeut; Soc Toxicol; Sigma Xi. *Res:* Effects of antibiotics on the flora and fauna of the rat cecum; cardiovascular and respiratory pharmacology and toxicology; mechanisms of the effects of hypoxia on the cardiovascular system and their alteration by drugs. *Mailing Add:* Med Col of Va Va Commonwealth Univ Richmond VA 23298

EGLER, FRANK EDWIN, b New York, NY, Apr 26, 11; m 68. PLANT ECOLOGY. *Educ:* Univ Chicago, BS, 32; Univ Minn, MS, 34; Yale Univ, PhD(plant ecol), 36. *Prof Exp:* Res fel, Yale & Bishop Mus, 36-37; asst prof forest bot, NY State Col Forestry, Syracuse Univ, 37-44; dir exp sta, Chicle Develop Co, 41-44; IN CHARGE ATON FOREST, 45- *Concurrent Pos:* Assoc prof, Univ Conn, 47-48; tech adv, R/W Maintenance Corp, 50-54; res assoc, Dept Conserv, Am Mus Natural Hist, 51-55; Guggenheim fel, 56-58; consult vegetationist, 49-; vis prof, Wesleyan Univ, 62 & Yale Univ, 65; adv, Elec Power Res Inst, 80- *Honors & Awards:* Distinguished Serv Citation, Ecol Soc Am, 78. *Mem:* Fel AAAS; Ecol Soc Am; fel Am Geog Soc; fel Am Mus Natural Hist. *Res:* Vegetation science and management; general ecology. *Mailing Add:* Aton Forest Norfolk CT 06058

EGLI, DENNIS B, b Ft Dodge, Iowa, Sept 4, 42. AGRONOMY, CROP PHYSIOLOGY. *Educ:* Pa State Univ, BS, 65; Univ Ill, MS, 67, PhD(agron), 69. *Prof Exp:* Asst prof, 69-74, assoc prof, 74-79, PROF AGRON, UNIV KY, 79- *Mem:* Am Soc Agron; Crop Sci Soc Am; Am Asn Plant Physiologists. *Res:* Crop production, ecology and physiology; soybean production; seed physiology, quality. *Mailing Add:* Dept of Agron Univ of Ky Lexington KY 40546

EGLITIS, IRMA, b Riga, Latvia, Oct 13, 07; nat US; m 38. ANATOMY, DERMATOLOGY. *Educ:* State Univ Latvia, MD, 31; State Univ NY Buffalo, cert, 68. *Prof Exp:* From asst instr to instr gross anat, histol, embryol, State Univ Latvia, 31-44; instr gross anat, Ernst Moritz Arndt Univ, Ger, 44-45; from instr to prof, 52-78, EMER PROF ANAT, COL MED, OHIO STATE UNIV, 78- *Mem:* Am Asn Anat; Am Med Womens Asn; Sigma Xi. *Res:* Integument; visual apparatus; blood vessels. *Mailing Add:* Dept of Anat Ohio State Univ Col of Med Columbus OH 43210

EGLITIS, JOHN ARNOLD, b Latvia, Dec 16, 02; nat US; m 38. ANATOMY, OTORHINOLARYNGOLOGY. *Educ:* State Univ Latvia, MD, 31; DSc(med), 40, DrHabil, 42; Univ Hamburg, dipl, 47; State Univ NY Buffalo, cert, 68. *Prof Exp:* From asst to assoc prof histol & embryol & chmn dept histol, State Univ Latvia, 27-44; assoc prof histol, Fac Med, Ernst Moritz Arndt Univ, Griefswald, Ger, 44-45; chmn dept histol, Fac Med, Baltic Univ, Hamburg, Ger, 46-49; from instr to assoc prof, Dept Anat, 51-61, prof, Col Med, Col Dent & Grad Sch, 61-73, EMER PROF, OHIO STATE UNIV, 73- *Honors & Awards:* Latvia Cult Fund Prize, 40; Man of Year, State Univ Col Med, 65; Golden Key & Certificate, Ohio State Univ Col Dent, 67. *Mem:* Am Asn Anat; Sigma Xi. *Res:* Glandular division; tissue cultures; blood vessels; metaplasia; spinal cord. *Mailing Add:* Dept Anat Col Med Ohio State Univ 333 W 10th Ave Columbus OH 43210

EGLITIS, MARTIN ALEXANDRIS, b Washington, DC, June 12, 55. MAMMALIAN DEVELOPMENTAL BIOLOGY. *Educ:* Univ Va, BA, 76, PhD(anat), 80. *Prof Exp:* Fel, Roche Inst Molecular Biol, 80-82; STAFF FEL, LAB MOLECULAR HEMAT, NAT HEART, LUNG & BLOOD INST, 82- *Mem:* Soc Develop Biol; AAAS. *Res:* Gene function in early development, its role in control of differentiation and timing of developmental events; interaction of the cytoplasm/cell surface with the nucleus; mechanism of induction of differentiation in embryonal carcinoma cells. *Mailing Add:* Lab Molecular Hemat Bldg 10 Rm 7018 NIH Bethesda MD 20205

EGLOFF, DAVID ALLEN, b Mason City, Iowa, Apr 13, 35; m 59; c 2. ECOLOGY. *Educ:* Amherst Col, BA, 57; Yale Univ, MS, 59; Stanford Univ, PhD(biol), 67. *Prof Exp:* Asst prof, 66-74, assoc prof, 74-81, PROF BIOL, OBERLIN COL, 81-, DIR, ENVIRON STUDIES PROG, 79- *Mem:* Ecol Soc Am; Am Soc Limnol & Oceanog; Freshwater Biol Asn; Int Soc Limnol. *Res:* Cyclomorphosis; sex ratio and population dynamics of copepods; aquaculture. *Mailing Add:* Dept of Biol Oberlin Col Oberlin OH 44074

EGLOFF, JULIUS, JR, b Washington, DC, Sept 19, 46. MARINE GEOLOGY, MARINE GEOPHYSICS. *Educ:* Univ Miami, BS, 69. *Prof Exp:* Oceanogr marine geol, Naval Oceanogr Off, 65-76; OCEANOGR MARINE GEOL, SEA FLOOR DIV, NAVAL OCEAN RES & DEVELOP ACTIV, 76- *Concurrent Pos:* Chmn, Ocean Study Group Am, 78-; Pres, Re-Evaluations Co, 80- *Mem:* Am Asn Petrol Geologists. *Res:* Submarine mapping; geologic sampling, photography. *Mailing Add:* PO Box C Pass Christian MS 39571

EGLY, RICHARD S(AMUEL), b Grabill, Ind, July 6, 14; m 49; c 4. CHEMICAL ENGINEERING. *Educ:* Purdue Univ, BS, 36; Univ Ill, MS, 38, PhD(chem eng), 40. *Prof Exp:* Asst chem, Univ Ill, 36-40; chem engr, Commercial Solvents Corp, 40-43, chief chem eng group, 43-50, dir chem res, 50-55, dir nitroparaffin develop, 55-57, assoc sci dir, 58-61, dir process develop, 62-76; CONSULT, 76- *Concurrent Pos:* With Off Sci Res & Develop, 44. *Mem:* Am Chem Soc; Soc Indust Chem; Nat Asn Corrosion Engrs; Am Inst Chem Engrs; Am Soc Test & Mat. *Res:* High pressure properties and techniques; heat transfer; manufacture of aliphatic amines; nitration of hydrocarbons and reactions of nitroparaffins; explosives; propellants; hazard potential of chemicals. *Mailing Add:* Box 304 RR 15 West Terre Haute IN 47885

EGNER, DONALD OTTO, b Cleveland, Ohio, Apr 18, 28; m 50; c 4. ATMOSPHERIC PHYSICS, OPERATIONS RESEARCH. *Educ:* Western Md Col, BA, 49. *Prof Exp:* Chief surv sect, Health Physics Group, Chem Center, 49-51, physicist, Spec Projs Div, Chem Res & Develop Lab, 51 & Nuclear Defense Lab, 53-55, chief, Theoret Physics Sect, 55-62, phys scientist, Land War Lab, 62-74, opers res analyst & head, law enforcement technol team, 74-80, DIRECTORATE CHIEF, HUMAN ENG LAB, US ARMY, 80- *Concurrent Pos:* Tech dir, Tech Assocs, Inc, 68-74. *Mem:* Soc Rheol; NY Acad Sci. *Res:* Atmospheric physics; micrometeorology; air pollution; biomedical research; human engineering; technical management. *Mailing Add:* 5806 Pine Hill Dr White Marsh MD 21162

EHLE, BYRON LEONARD, b Seattle, Wash, Jan 18, 37; m 58; c 4. NUMERICAL ANALYSIS, COMPUTER SCIENCE. *Educ:* Whitman Col, BA, 59; Stanford Univ, MSc, 61; Univ Waterloo, PhD(comput sci), 69. *Prof Exp:* Teaching asst, Stanford Univ, 59-61; from instr to asst prof, 61-77, ASSOC PROF MATH & COMPUT SCI, UNIV VICTORIA, BC, 77- *Concurrent Pos:* Lectr, Univ Waterloo, 66-69; res assoc, 68-69. *Mem:* Asn Comput Mach; Am Math Soc; Math Asn Am; Can Info Processing Soc. *Res:* Numerical methods for the solution of ordinary differential equations, particularly stiff equations; development of effective teaching tools for computer software. *Mailing Add:* Dept of Math Univ of Victoria Victoria BC V8W 2Y2 Can

EHLE, FRED ROBERT, b Bayside, NY, Feb 17, 52. ANIMAL SCIENCE, NUTRITION. *Educ:* Cornell Univ, BS, 74, MS, 77, PhD(animal nutrit), 80. *Prof Exp:* Res assoc dairy nutrit, Univ Ill, 79-80; RES ANIMAL SCIENTIST, AGR RES SERV, USDA, 80- *Concurrent Pos:* Adj asst prof, Dept Animal Sci, Univ Minn, 80- *Mem:* Am Soc Animal Sci; Am Dairy Sci Asn; Am Forage & Grassland Coun; Coun for Agr Sci & Technol. *Res:* Maximize the intake and efficiency of utilization of forages in ruminant diets. *Mailing Add:* 130 H Haecker Hall Dept Animal Sci 1364 Eckles Ave Univ Minn St Paul MN 55108

EHLER, ARTHUR WAYNE, b Los Angeles, Calif, May 21, 22; m 57; c 2. PLASMA PHYSICS. *Educ:* Univ Southern Calif, BE, 47, BA, 48, MS, 50, PhD(physics), 55. *Prof Exp:* Proj engr, Aerophys Develop Corp, 54-56; asst chief res sect plasma physics, Douglas Aircraft Co, 56-60; mem tech staff, Hughes Res Labs, 60-70; mem tech staff, Ames Res Ctr, 70-72; STAFF MEM, LOS ALAMOS SCI LAB, 72- *Mem:* AAAS; Am Phys Soc; Sigma Xi. *Res:* Absorption of radiation by plasma; production of plasma by lasers magnetically driven shocks; electric field dissociation of molecular ions; analysis of proposed methods of producing hot, dense plasma; molecular laser research. *Mailing Add:* 450 Navajo Los Alamos NM 87544

EHLER, KENNETH WALTER, bio-organic chemistry, see previous edition

EHLERINGER, JAMES RUSSELL, b Portland, Ore, July 2, 49. PHYSIOLOGICAL ECOLOGY, PHOTOSYNTHESIS. *Educ:* San Diego State Univ, BS, 72, MS, 73; Stanford Univ, PhD(biol), 77. *Prof Exp:* ASSOC PROF BIOL, UNIV UTAH, 77- *Honors & Awards:* Murray Bell Award, Ecol Soc Am, 77. *Mem:* Ecol Soc Am; Am Soc Plant Physiologists. *Res:* Physiology and ecology of arid land plants, with an emphasis on photosynthesis, water relations, and energy balance. *Mailing Add:* Biol Dept Univ Utah Salt Lake City UT 84112

EHLERS, ERNEST GEORGE, b New York, NY, Jan 17, 27; m 51; c 2. MINERALOGY. *Educ:* Univ Chicago, MS, 50, PhD(geol), 52. *Prof Exp:* Asst geol, Univ Chicago, 50-51; geologist, NJ Zinc Co, 52-54; from asst prof to prof mineral, 54-72, PROF GEOL & MINERAL, OHIO STATE UNIV, 72- *Concurrent Pos:* Fulbright sr lectr awards, State Univ Utrecht, 66-67 & Univs Athens, Patras & Thessaloniki, 71-72. *Mem:* Fel Mineral Soc Am; fel Geol Soc Am; Sigma Xi. *Res:* Hydrothermal and high pressure equilibria; petrology; optical mineralogy. *Mailing Add:* Dept of Geol & Mineral Ohio State Univ Columbus OH 43210

EHLERS, FRANCIS EDWARD, b Portland, Ore, Nov 5, 16; m 44; c 4. APPLIED MECHANICS, AERODYNAMICS. *Educ:* Ore State Col, BS, 41; Brown Univ, MS, 47, PhD(appl math), 49. *Prof Exp:* Asst math, Ore State Col, 41-42; staff mem, Radiation Lab, Mass Inst Technol, 42-45; from intern to assoc grad div appl math, Brown 47-50; instr math, Ore State Col, 50-51; aerodynamicist, Boeing Co, 51-54, res specialist, Math Serv Unit, Phys Res Staff, 54-58 & Math Lab, Sci Res Labs, 58-72, res specialist, Aerodyn Res Group, Boeing Com Airplane Co, 72-78, RES SPECIALIST, APPL MATH GROUP, BOEING COMPUTER SERVS, 78- *Mem:* Am Math Soc; Soc Indust & Appl Math; assoc fel Am Inst Aeronaut & Astronaut. *Res:* Fluid mechanics; linearized theory; hodograph method; gas dynamics; mechanics; elasticity; transonic unsteady flow; supersonic flow. *Mailing Add:* 2685 SW 172nd St Seattle WA 98166

EHLERS, KENNETH WARREN, b Dix, Nebr, Aug 3, 22; m 47; c 1. PLASMA PHYSICS, ATOMIC PHYSICS. *Educ:* Mass Inst Technol, Elec Eng, 46. *Prof Exp:* Radar technician, US Navy, 42-46; head electronic landing aids dept, Landing Aids Exp Sta, Calif, 46-50; staff physicist, 50-78, SR PHYSICIST, LAWRENCE BERKELEY LAB, UNIV CALIF, 78- *Concurrent Pos:* Consult, Appl Radiation Corp, Thompson Ramo Wooldridge, Inc, Avco Corp & Brobeck Assoc. *Mem:* AAAS: Am Phys Soc; Am Vacuum Soc. *Res:* Ion beams and sources; particle accelerators; controlled thermonuclear research. *Mailing Add:* Lawrence Berkeley Lab Bldg 4 Rm 214 Univ of Calif Berkeley CA 94720

EHLERS, MELVIN H, b Twin Falls, Idaho, June 7, 18; m 44; c 2. ANIMAL PHYSIOLOGY. *Educ:* Univ Idaho, BS, 43; State Col Wash, MS, 50, PhD(animal sci), 54. *Prof Exp:* Instr & jr dairy scientist, Wash State Univ, 52-55, from asst prof to assoc prof, 59-67, prof dairy sci, 67-81; RETIRED. *Mem:* Am Soc Animal Sci; Am Dairy Sci Asn. *Res:* Physiological and environmental influences on milk production. *Mailing Add:* Dept of Animal Sci Wash State Univ Pullman WA 99164

EHLERS, VERNON JAMES, b Pipestone, Minn, Feb 6, 34; m 58; c 4. ATOMIC PHYSICS. *Educ:* Univ Calif, Berkeley, AB, 56, PhD(physics), 60. *Prof Exp:* Res physicist, Lawrence Radiation Lab, Univ Calif, 60-61; NATO fel, Univ Heidelberg, 61-62; res physicist, Lawrence Radiation Lab, Univ Calif, 62-66; assoc prof, 66-68, chmn dept, 77-80, PROF PHYSICS, CALVIN COL, 68- *Concurrent Pos:* Lectr, Univ Calif, Berkeley, 61-66; consult, Lawrence Radiation Lab, Univ Calif, 66-; NSF vis sci faculty fel, Joint Inst Lab Astrophys, Univ Colo, Boulder, 71-72; non-resident mem, Joint Inst Lab Astrophys, Boulder, Colo, 73-; mem IBS Eval Panel, Nat Bur Standards, 74- *Mem:* AAAS; Am Phys Soc; Nat Sci Teachers Asn; Am Asn Physics Teachers; Am Sci Affiliation. *Res:* Atomic-beam, magnetic-resonance measurements of the spins and nuclear moments of radioactive nuclei and hyperfine structure; electron excitation of atoms; laser research and development. *Mailing Add:* Dept of Physics Calvin Col Grand Rapids MI 49506

EHLERT, THOMAS CLARENCE, b Milwaukee, Wis, July 1, 31; m 63; c 4. PHYSICAL CHEMISTRY. *Educ:* Univ Wis, BS, 57, MS, 58, PhD(chem), 63. *Prof Exp:* Instr chem, Univ Wis, Milwaukee, 57-60, US Dept Defense fel, 63-64; asst prof, 64-69, assoc prof, 69-78, PROF CHEM, MARQUETTE UNIV, 78- *Mem:* Am Chem Soc. *Res:* High temperature chemistry; mass spectroscopy; thermodynamics. *Mailing Add:* Dept of Chem Marquette Univ Milwaukee WI 53233

EHLIG, CARL F, b Los Angeles, Calif, Apr 2, 24; c 5. PLANT PHYSIOLOGY, BIOCHEMISTRY. *Educ:* Univ Calif, BS, 49, MS, 50, PhD(plant physiol), 54. *Prof Exp:* Sr lab technician, Univ Calif, 54-55; plant physiologist, US Salinity Lab, 55-64; res plant physiologist, US Plant, Soil & Nutrit Lab, NY, 64-67; PLANT PHYSIOLOGIST, IMPERIAL VALLEY CONSERV RES CTR, 67- *Mem:* Am Soc Agron; Soil Sci Soc Am; Crop Sci Soc Am. *Res:* Plant and soil water relations; plant response to saline and alkaline conditions; mineral nutrition; cotton physiology. *Mailing Add:* Imperial Valley Conserv Res Ctr 4151 Hwy 86 Brawley CA 92227

EHLIG, PERRY LAWRENCE, b San Gabriel, Calif, May 23, 27; m 51; c 5. PETROLOGY, GEOLOGY. *Educ:* Univ Calif, Los Angeles, BA, 52, PhD(geol), 58. *Prof Exp:* Assoc prof, 56-67, PROF GEOL, CALIF STATE UNIV, LOS ANGELES, 67- *Mem:* Geol Soc Am; Mineral Soc Am; Am Asn Petrol Geol; Nat Asn Geol Teachers. *Res:* Metamorphic petrology, particularly the evolution of Pelona and similar schists in California; structural geology; history of the San Andreas fault. *Mailing Add:* Dept of Geol Calif State Univ Los Angeles CA 90032

EHLIG-ECONOMIDES, CHRISTINE ANNA, b Pasadena, Tex, June 8, 49; m 76; c 1. GEOTHERMAL RESERVOIR ENGINEERING. *Educ:* Rice Univ, BA, 71; Univ Kans, MAT, 74, MS, 76; Stanford Univ, PhD(petrol eng), 79. *Prof Exp:* Res asst petrol eng, Stanford Univ, 76-78, prog mgr Geothermal Prog, 78-80, actg asst prof petrol eng, 79-80; asst prof, 80-81, DEPT HEAD PETROL ENG, UNIV ALASKA, FAIRBANKS, 81- *Concurrent Pos:* Engr, Shell Develop Co, 77, 79 & 81. *Mem:* Soc Petrol Engrs; Sigma Xi. *Res:* Pressure transient testing of petroleum and geothermal wells; well testing; reservoir simulation; petrophysics; simulation of groundwater formations. *Mailing Add:* Univ Alaska 702A Tanana Dr Fairbanks AK 99701

EHLMANN, ARTHUR J, b St Charles, Mo, May 18, 28; m 56; c 2. MINERALOGY. *Educ:* Univ Mo, BS, 52, MA, 54; Univ Utah, PhD(mineral), 58. *Prof Exp:* Subsurface geologist, Shell Oil Co, 54-56; from asst prof to assoc prof, 58-70, PROF GEOL, TEX CHRISTIAN UNIV, 76-, CHMN DEPT, 76- *Mem:* Mineral Soc Am; Soc Econ Paleont & Mineral. *Res:* Mineralogy; genesis of clays; hydrothermal synthesis; trace studies; x-ray diffraction studies. *Mailing Add:* Dept of Geol Tex Christian Univ Ft Worth TX 76129

EHMANN, EDWARD PAUL, b Rochester, NY, June 6, 40; m 67; c 3. FOOD SCIENCE, FOOD CHEMISTRY. *Educ:* Univ Toronto, BA, 63, MA, 65; Univ Mass, PhD(food sci & technol), 72. *Prof Exp:* Lectr, Univ Toronto, 65-68; engr, Westinghouse Res Labs, 72-74; sr food scientist, H J Heinz Co, 74-76; MGR, RES & TECH SERVS, PEPSICO, INC, 77- *Mem:* Inst Food Technologists; Sigma Xi. *Res:* Food colorimetry/appearance measurement; research management, administrative & technical; technical training & development for R & D personnel; technical corporate quality assurance. *Mailing Add:* Pepsico Inc Tech Ctr Valhalla NY 10595

EHMANN, WILLIAM DONALD, b Madison, Wis, Feb 7, 31; m 55; c 4. RADIOCHEMISTRY, GEOCHEMISTRY. *Educ:* Univ Wis, BS, 52, MS, 54; Carnegie Inst Technol, PhD(radiochem), 57. *Prof Exp:* Asst, Univ Wis, 52-54; AEC proj chemist, Carnegie Inst Technol, 54-57, res assoc, 57; Nat Res Coun-Nat Acad Sci res assoc, Argonne Nat Lab, 57-58; from asst prof to assoc prof, 58-66, distinguished prof, Col Arts & Sci, 68-69, chmn & dir grad studies, Dept Chem, 72-76, PROF CHEM, UNIV KY, 66-, ASSOC DEAN RES, GRAD SCH, 80-- *Concurrent Pos:* Consult, Argonne Nat Lab, 59-67; proj dir, US AEC, Univ Ky, 60-71, NASA, 68-77 & NIH, 77-80; alumni res award, 64, univ res prof, 77-78; Fulbright res scholar & hon res fel, Inst Advan Studies, Australian Nat Univ, 64-65; vis prof, Ariz State Univ, 69; invited lectr, Advan Study Inst, NATO, Oslo, 70; vis prof, Fla State Univ, 72. *Mem:* Fel AAAS; fel Meteoritical Soc; Am Chem Soc; Soc Environ Geochem & Health; Int Asn Geochem & Cosmochem. *Res:* Nuclear chemistry; geochemistry; cosmochemistry; chemistry of the human brain; activation analysis; lunar chemistry; trace elements in environmental health; coal chemistry. *Mailing Add:* Dept Chem Univ of Ky Lexington KY 40506

EHNI, GEORGE (JOHN), b Pekin, Ill, Feb 18, 14; m 39; c 6. NEUROSURGERY. *Educ:* Northwestern Univ, BS, 38, MD, 40; Univ Minn, MS, 43. *Prof Exp:* Mem sect neurosurg, Mayo Clin, 43-44; neurosurgeon, Scott & White Clin, Temple, Tex, 44-49; assoc prof neurol surg, Postgrad Med Sch, Univ Tex, 49-59; PROF NEUROL SURG & HEAD DEPT, BAYLOR COL MED, 59- *Concurrent Pos:* Fel, Mayo Clin, Univ Minn, 40-43; asst prof, M D Anderson Hosp Cancer Res, 49-59. *Mem:* AMA; Am Col Surgeons; Am Asn Neurol Surg; Am Neurol Asn. *Mailing Add:* Dept of Neurol Surg Baylor Col of Med Houston TX 77030

EHRENBECK, RAYMOND, b Hackensack, NJ, Oct 13, 30; m 58; c 1. MECHANICAL ENGINEERING. *Educ:* Stevens Inst Technol, BS, 53; Northeastern Univ, MS, 60. *Prof Exp:* Design engr, E I du Pont de Nemours & Co, 53; consult mech engr, Air Force Cambridge Res Labs, 55-66; mech engr, NASA Electronics Res Ctr, 66-70; STAFF MECH ENGR, TRANSP SYSTS CTR, DEPT TRANSP, 70- *Mem:* Am Soc Mech Engrs. *Res:* Development and evaluation of ground transportation systems. *Mailing Add:* Transp Systs Ctr (DTS-731) Dept of Transp 55 Broadway Cambridge MA 02142

EHRENFELD, DAVID W, b New York, NY, Jan 15, 38; m 70. ECOLOGY, CONSERVATION. *Educ:* Harvard Univ, BA, 59, MD, 63; Univ Fla, PhD(zool), 66. *Prof Exp:* Interim asst prof biol sci, Univ Fla, 67; from asst prof to assoc prof, Barnard Col, Columbia Univ, 67-74; PROF BIOL, COOK COL, RUTGERS UNIV, NEW BRUNSWICK, 74- *Mem:* Ecol Soc Am; AAAS. *Res:* Orientation and navigation of sea turtles; supporting studies of visual and olfactory physiology of sea turtles; biological conservation; endangered species; philosophy of conservation, fiction. *Mailing Add:* Dept of Hort & Forestry Blake H Cook Col Rutgers Univ PO Box 231 New Brunswick NJ 08903

EHRENFELD, ELVERA, b Philadelphia, Pa, Mar 1, 42. CELL BIOLOGY, VIROLOGY. *Educ:* Brandeis Univ, BA, 62; Univ Fla, PhD(biochem), 67. *Prof Exp:* From asst prof to assoc prof cell biol, Albert Einstein Col Med, 69-74; assoc prof biochem & microbiol, 74-79, PROF BIOCHEM, CELL, VIRAL & MOLECULAR BIOL, MED CTR, UNIV UTAH, 79- *Concurrent Pos:* Fel, Albert Einstein Col Med, 67-69; NSF res grant, 70-; USPHS career develop award, 71-76; NIH res grant. *Res:* RNA virus replication and inhibition of host-cell function; regulation of gene expression in animal cells. *Mailing Add:* Dept of Biochem Univ of Utah Med Ctr Salt Lake City UT 84112

EHRENFELD, JOHN R(OOS), b Chicago, Ill, May 16, 31; m 56; c 3. CHEMICAL ENGINEERING, ENVIRONMENT & RESOURCES POLICY. *Educ:* Mass Inst Technol, BS, 53, ScD, 57. *Prof Exp:* Proj leader, Arthur D Little Inc, 57-61; staff engr, Prototech, Inc, 61-62; dep dir, appl sci lab, GCA Tech Div, GCA Corp, 62-65, dir, 65-66, dir appl res opers, 66-68; pres, Walden Res Corp, 68-75; vpres & tech dir, Energy Resources Co, 75-78; chmn, New England River Basin Comn, 78-81; SR STAFF MEM, ARTHUR D LITTLE INC, 81- *Mem:* AAAS; Am Chem Soc (chmn, Indust & Eng Chem Div, 77); Am Inst Chem Engrs. *Res:* Environmental resources policy; applied mathematics; air pollution control. *Mailing Add:* 24 Percy Rd Lexington MA 02173

EHRENFELD, ROBERT LOUIS, b New York, NY, Sept 18, 21; m 55; c 3. ORGANIC CHEMISTRY. *Educ:* Cornell Univ, AB, 42, PhD(org chem), 48. *Prof Exp:* Asst, Cornell Univ, 42-43; res chemist, Off Sci Res & Develop & Manhattan Proj, Columbia Univ, 43-46; res assoc, Mass Inst Technol, 48-49; PRES, HALOCARBON PRODS CORP, 50- *Mem:* Am Chem Soc. *Res:* Preparation, polymerization and depolymerization of organic fluorine compounds; reactions of free fluorine; photochemical chlorination of chlorofluoro ethylenes as related to their fluroination with elementary fluorine. *Mailing Add:* Halocarbon Prods Corp 82 Burlews Ct Hackensack NJ 07601

EHRENFELD, SYLVAIN, b Antwerp, Belgium, June 4, 29; nat US; m 55; c 2. MATHEMATICAL STATISTICS. *Educ:* City Col New York, BS, 50; Columbia Univ, MS, 51, PhD(math statist), 56. *Prof Exp:* Res assoc statist, Res Div, NY Univ, 57-58, assoc prof indust eng & opers res, 58-61; indust eng, Columbia Univ, 61-66; prof opers res, Sch Eng & Sci, NY Univ, 66-73; PROF STATIST, BARUCH COL, CITY UNIV NEW YORK, 73- *Mem:* Fel Am Statist Asn; Inst Math Statist; Inst Mgt Sci; Opers Res Soc Am. *Res:* Statistical methods in experimental design; sequential decision making; utility inference. *Mailing Add:* Baruch Col Dept of Statist 17 Lexington Ave New York NY 10010

EHRENFRIED, CHARLES E, b Tiffin, Ohio, Mar 11, 35; m 56; c 4. PHYSICS, AEROSPACE ENGINEERING. *Educ:* Bowling Green State Univ, BS, 57; Univ Ill, MS, 62; Air Force Inst Technol, PhD(aerospace eng), 73. *Prof Exp:* Proj officer physics, US Air Force, 57-78; TECH DIR RELIABILITY, IIT RES INST, 78- *Res:* Reliability of electronic equipment and components. *Mailing Add:* 1170 N George Rome NY 31140

EHRENHAFT, JOHANN L, b Vienna, Austria, Oct 10, 15; nat US; c 1. SURGERY. *Educ:* Univ Iowa, MD, 38. *Prof Exp:* Intern surg, Hopkins Hosp, 38-39; resident, 40-42, 45-47, from instr to assoc prof, 47-53, PROF GEN SURG, COL MED, UNIV IOWA, 53-, CHMN DIV THORACIC SURG, 49- *Concurrent Pos:* Halsted fel, Johns Hopkins Hosp, 39-40; fel, Barnes Hosp, St Louis, Mo, 48-49. *Mem:* Am Surg Asn; AMA; fel Am Col Surg; Asn Thoracic Surg; Am Col Chest Physicians. *Res:* Thoracic and cardiac disease; subjects in cardiovascular surgery. *Mailing Add:* 325 Beldon Ave Iowa City IA 52240

EHRENPREIS, LEON, b Brooklyn, NY, May 22, 30; m 61; c 2. MATHEMATICS. *Educ:* City Col, BS, 50; Columbia Univ, MA, 51, PhD(math), 53. *Prof Exp:* Instr math, Johns Hopkins Univ, 53-54; mem, Inst Adv Study, 54-57; assoc prof, Brandeis Univ, 57-59 & Yeshiva Univ, 59-61; prof, Courant Inst Math Sci, NY Univ, 62-68; PROF, YESHIVA UNIV, 68- *Mem:* Am Math Soc. *Res:* Partial differential equations; lie groups; several complex variables; automorphic functions; theory of distributions; methodology in learning for students and researchers. *Mailing Add:* Dept of Math Yeshiva Univ Washington Heights New York NY 10033

EHRENPREIS, SEYMOUR, b Brooklyn, NY, June 20, 27; m 54; c 3. BIOCHEMISTRY, PHARMACOLOGY. *Educ:* City Col New York, BS, ; PhD, 54. *Prof Exp:* Res assoc biochem, Sch Med, Univ Pittsburgh, 53-55; res assoc & instr chem, Cornell Univ, 55-57; res assoc & asst prof biochem, Col Physicians & Surgeons, Columbia Univ, 57-61; assoc prof pharmacol, Sch Med, Georgetown Univ, 61-68; assoc prof pharmacol & head lab molecular pharmacol, New York Med Col, 68-70; chief pharmacol, NY State Res Inst Neurochem & Drug Addiction, 71-76; PROF & CHMN DEPT PHARMACOL, CHICAGO MED SCH, 76- *Concurrent Pos:* Burger lectr, Univ Va, 65; mem vis sci prog, Am Pharmaceut Asn, 68-72; ed, Neurosci Res, 69-73 & Rev Neurosci, 74-; adj prof pharmacol, Sch Pharmaceut Sci, Columbia Univ, 72-75. *Mem:* Fel AAAS; fel Am Inst Chem; Am Soc Biol Chem; Am Soc Pharmacol & Exp Therapeut; Am Chem Soc. *Res:* Protein interactions and modifications; kinetics and equilibria in the fibrogen-thrombin system; mechanism of quaternary ammonium-macromolecular interactions; molecular mechanisms of nerve activity and neurotropic drug action; mechanism of opiate action; isolation of drug receptors; cholinesterase; endorphins; smooth muscle pharmacology. *Mailing Add:* Dept of Pharm 2020 W Ogden Ave Chicago IL 60664

EHRENREICH, HENRY, b Frankfurt, Ger, May 11, 28; nat US; m 53; c 3. THEORETICAL PHYSICS. *Educ:* Cornell Univ, AB, 50, PhD(physics), 55. *Hon Degrees:* AM, Harvard Univ, 63. *Prof Exp:* Theoret physicist, Res Lab, Gen Elec Co, 55-63; GORDON MCKAY PROF APPL PHYSICS, HARVARD UNIV, 63- *Concurrent Pos:* Vis lectr, Harvard Univ, 60-61; vis prof, Brandeis Univ & Univ Paris, 69; mem solid state comn, Int Union Pure and Appl Physics, 72- *Mem:* Fel Am Acad Arts & Sci; fel Am Phys Soc; Int Union Pure and Appl Physics. *Res:* Solid state physics; optical properties of solids; transport and many particle theory; semiconductors; theory of metals; electronic properties of disordered systems. *Mailing Add:* Div of Eng & Appl Physics Harvard Univ Cambridge MA 02138

EHRENREICH, JOHN HELMUTH, b New London, Wis, Feb 17, 29; m 54; c 2. FORESTRY, RANGE MANAGEMENT. *Educ:* Colo State Univ, BS, 51, MS, 54; Iowa State Univ, PhD(plant ecol), 57. *Prof Exp:* Res aide, Colo State Univ, 53-54; from asst to instr gen bot, Iowa State Univ, 55-57; proj leader range & wildlife res, US Forest Serv, 57; res assoc forestry, Univ Mo, 57-60, assoc prof, 60-64; prof range mgt, Univ Ariz, 64-65; prof watershed mgt & head dept, 65-71; prof forestry, 71-77, PROF RANGE RESOURCES, UNIV IDAHO, 77-, DEAN COL FORESTRY, WILDLIFE & RANGE SCI, 71- & DIR FORESTRY, WILDLIFE & RANGE EXP STA, 74- *Mem:* Ecol Soc Am; Am Soc Range Mgt; Soc Am Foresters; Wildlife Soc. *Res:* Ecological research in soil-plant relations. *Mailing Add:* Col of Forestry Wildlife & Range Sci Univ of Idaho Moscow ID 83843

EHRENREICH, THEODORE, b New York, NY, July 30, 13. PATHOLOGY. *Educ:* Univ Paris, MD, 39; Am Bd Path, dipl. *Prof Exp:* Pathologist, Bronx Vet Admin Hosp, 48-58; dir labs, St Francis Hosp, 58-66; DIR LABS, LUTHERAN MED CTR, 68-; ASSOC CLIN PROF, COMMUNITY & ENVIRON MED, MOUNT SINAI SCH MED, 69- *Concurrent Pos:* Littauer fel path, Harvard Univ, 42-44; assoc prof path, NY Med Col, 56-66, clin prof path, 66-; consult cancer res, Bronx Vet Admin Hosp; lectr forensic med, Sch Med, NY Univ, 67-74, asst prof, 74-; attend pathologist, Metrop Hosp 68-; dir labs, Lutheran Med Ctr, 68-81. *Mem:* Am Soc Clin Path; fel Col Am Path; AMA; Am Asn Path; NY Acad Med. *Res:* Pathologic anatomy; cancer; nephropathology; environmental sciences. *Mailing Add:* 400 E 57th St New York NY 10022

EHRENSON, STANTON JAY, b New York, NY, Oct 13, 31; m 60; c 2. THEORETICAL CHEMISTRY, PHYSICAL ORGANIC CHEMISTRY. *Educ:* Long Island Univ, BS, 52; Univ Wis, MS, 54; Ga Inst Technol, PhD(chem), 57. *Prof Exp:* Fel chem, Pa State Univ, 57-58, instr, 58-59; res assoc, Univ Chicago, 59-62; assoc chemist, 63-66, chemist, 66-77, SR CHEMIST, BROOKHAVEN NAT LAB, 77- *Concurrent Pos:* Vis scientist, Dept of Chem, Univ Calif, Irvine, 68; mem adv ed bd, Jour Org Chem, 73-78. *Mem:* Fel AAAS; Am Chem Soc; Fedn Am Scientists. *Res:* Molecular structure; quantum chemistry; reaction mechanisms; structure-activity relationships. *Mailing Add:* Dept of Chem Brookhaven Nat Lab Upton NY 11973

EHRENSTEIN, GERALD, b New York, NY, Sept 27, 31; m 60; c 3. BIOPHYSICS. *Educ:* Cooper Union, BEE, 52; Columbia Univ, MA, 58, PhD(physics), 62. *Prof Exp:* Asst microwave spectros, Columbia Univ Radiation Lab, 57-62; PHYSICIST, NIH, 62- *Concurrent Pos:* Mem, Sci Technol Adv Comt, Wash Tech Inst; mem corp, Marine Biol Lab, Woods Hole, Mass; vis prof, Sch Med, Israel Inst Technol Sch Med, 72-73. *Mem:* Am Phys Soc; Biophys Soc. *Res:* Mechanism of nervous excitation; membrane phenomena; molecular structure. *Mailing Add:* Lab of Biophysics NIH Bethesda MD 20205

EHRENSTORFER, SIEGLINDE K M, b Regensburg, Ger, Oct 24, 27; div; c 2. INORGANIC CHEMISTRY, PHYSICAL CHEMISTRY. *Educ:* Univ Munich, BS, 54, MS, 57, PhD(phys chem), 60. *Prof Exp:* Res chemist, Allied Chem Corp, 60-66 & Stauffer Chem Corp, 66-68; sr res chemist, Armour Pharmaceut Co, 68-70; vpres, 70-78, PRES, RING-APOCH, INC, 78-, OWNER, 79-; PRES, S E RES INC, 79- *Mem:* Am Chem Soc; Soc German Chem. *Res:* Physical and medicinal chemistry; reactions in the solid state; zeolitic phosphates; gas hydrates; catalysis; colloids; antiperspirants; emulsions; purines; antiemetics geriatric agents. *Mailing Add:* 1162 Tuxedo Sq Teaneck NJ 07666

EHRENTHAL, IRVING, b New York, NY, Sept 22, 18; m 46; c 3. BIOCHEMISTRY. *Educ:* Yeshiva Univ, BA, 39; Univ Mich, MS, 40; Univ Minn, PhD(agr biochem), 50. *Prof Exp:* Org chemist, Org Med Res, Wm R Warner & Co, 46-47; sr biochemist, Maimonides Hosp, 51; sr chemist vitamins, Nopco Chem Co, 51-53; group leader carbohydrates, 54-76, RES ASSOC, CORN PROD RES DEPT, ANHEUSER-BUSCH, INC, 76- *Mem:* Am Chem Soc. *Res:* Carbohydrates; starch and starch hydrolyzates; polysaccharide structure. *Mailing Add:* Corn Prod Res Dept 110 Wyoming St St Louis MO 63118

EHRET, ANNE, b Belleville, Ill, Oct 10, 37. ORGANIC CHEMISTRY. *Educ:* Univ Ill, Urbana, BS, 59; Univ Calif, Los Angeles, MS, 63, PhD(org chem), 67. *Prof Exp:* Asst prof chem, Drake Univ, 66-71; fel, Harvard Univ, 71-74, Brandeis Univ, 74-78; SCIENTIST, POLAROID CORP, 78- *Mem:* Am Chem Soc. *Res:* Investigation of mechanisms of organic reactions. *Mailing Add:* 234 Lakeview Ave #B Cambridge MA 02138

EHRET, CHARLES FREDERICK, b New York, NY, Mar 9, 23; m 45; c 8. CHRONOBIOLOGY, CIRCADIAN REGULATION. *Educ:* City Col New York, BS, 45; Univ Notre Dame, MS, 48, PhD(zool), 51. *Prof Exp:* Teaching fel zool, Univ Notre Dame, 46-48; biologist, 48-66, SR BIOLOGIST, DIV BIOL & MED RES, ARGONNE NAT LAB, 66- *Concurrent Pos:* USPHS fel, Biophys Lab, Univ Geneva, 60-61; vis prof life sci, Ind Univ, 63 & McArdle Lab, Univ Wis, 71-72; chmn, Biotron Nat Adv Comt, Univ Wis/NSF, 75-77; consult shift work, Commonwealth Edison, Ont Hydro, Detroit Edison & Philadelphia Elec, 80-; vchmn, Gordon Res Conf Chronobiol, 81; mem adv comt, Ctr Indust Schedules, Cambridge, 81. *Mem:* Int Soc Chronobiol (vpres, 81); Int Soc Study Time; Bioelectromagnetics Soc. *Res:* Chronobiology and circadian regulation; molecular-genetic strategies in the control of the biological clock in higher organisms including man; shift-work rotation schedules and chronohygiene; biological effects of electric fields. *Mailing Add:* Div Biol & Med Res Argonne Nat Lab 9700 S Cass Ave Argonne IL 60439

EHRHART, INA C, b Yoe, Pa, Aug 30, 41; m 61; c 1. MEDICAL PHYSIOLOGY. *Educ:* Ohio State Univ, BS, 68, PhD(physiol), 72. *Prof Exp:* Res asst physiol, Ohio State Univ, 69, NIH spec nurse res fel, 69-72; NIH fel physiol, Mich State Univ, 72-74; asst prof, 74-81, ASSOC PROF PHYSIOL, MED COL GA, 81- *Mem:* Am Physiol Soc; Sigma Xi; AAAS. *Res:* Lung microvessel permeability following injury and the affects of varying the composition of blood components in the solution perfusing the isolated, ventilated canine lung lobe. *Mailing Add:* Dept of Physiol Sch of Med Med Col Ga Augusta GA 30902

EHRHART, LLEWELLYN MCDOWELL, b Dallastown, Pa, Apr 22, 42; m 64; c 2. MAMMALOGY, MARINE TURTLE BIOLOGY. *Educ:* Franklin & Marshall Col, BA, 64; Cornell Univ, PhD, 71. *Prof Exp:* Instr vertebrate zool, Cornell Univ, 67; asst prof, 69-74, ASSOC PROF BIOL SCI, UNIV CENT FLA, 74-, GORDON J BARNETT PROF ENVIRON SCI, 76- *Mem:* Am Soc Mammal; Ecol Soc Am; Soc Study Evolution; Herepetologists' League; Animal Behav Soc. *Res:* Behavioral ecology of the cricetine rodent genus, Peromyscus; population ecology of Florida rodents and carnivores; biology of loggerhead turtles and green turtles. *Mailing Add:* Dept of Biol Sci Univ Cent Fla Orlando FL 32816

EHRHART, WENDELL A, b Dallastown, Pa, Nov 12, 34; m 58; c 2. POLYMER CHEMISTRY. *Educ:* Franklin & Marshall Col, 56; Princeton Univ, MA, 58, PhD(org chem), 61. *Prof Exp:* Chemist floor div, 60-64, chemist, 64-74, RES ASSOC, CHEM DIV, ARMSTRONG CORK CO, 74- *Mem:* Am Chem Soc; Sigma Xi. *Res:* Synthesis and property studies of amidines, pyrimidines, pyrimido (4,5-d) pyrimidines, polyesters and polyurethanes; formulation and processing of polymers. *Mailing Add:* 160 Sch House Lane Hillam PA 17406

EHRICH, FELIX FREDERICK, b New York, NY, Oct 19, 19; m 53; c 3. ORGANIC CHEMISTRY. *Educ:* City Univ New York, BS, 39; Univ Iowa, MS, 40; Univ Md, PhD(org chem), 42. *Prof Exp:* Asst chem, Univ Md, 40-42; org res chemist, Corn Prods Refining Co, 42; org res chemist, E I Du Pont de Nemours & Co, 46-58, res supvr, 58-70, tech dir, Pigments Dept, Colorquim SA de CV, 70-72, tech mgr pigment colors, Int Develop Div, 73-75, tech mgr pigment colors, Mkt Div, Pigments Dept, 75-78, TECH CONSULT, E I DU PONT DE NEMOURS & CO, 78- *Mem:* Am Chem Soc; Sigma Xi. *Res:* Synthetic pigments; barbituric acids; molecular rearrangements; spiropyrimidine and heterocyclic syntheses; phthalocyanine and quinacridone pigments. *Mailing Add:* E I Du Pont de Nemours & Co Chem Dyes & Pigments Dept Wilmington DE 19898

EHRICH, FREDRIC F(RANKLIN), b New York, NY, Dec 17, 28; m 55; c 3. MECHANICAL ENGINEERING. *Educ:* Mass Inst Technol, BS, 47, ME, 50, ScD(mech eng), 51. *Prof Exp:* Supvr anal & mech develop & tech rep, Rolls Royce, Eng, Westinghouse Elec Corp, 51-57; mgr preliminary design, Turbomach Eng Oper & T64 Engine Design, 57-66, mgr preliminary design, Turbomach & Mech Syst Eng Oper, Aircraft Engine Group, 66-68, mgr design tech oper, 68-70, MGR TECH PLANS, AIRCRAFT ENGINE GROUP, GEN ELEC CO, 70- *Mem:* Am Soc Mech Engrs; Am Inst Aeronaut & Astronaut; Sigma Xi; fel Am Soc Mech Engrs. *Res:* Aerodynamics; applied mechanics; mechanical design. *Mailing Add:* Aircraft Engine Group Gen Elec Co 1000 Western Ave Lynn MA 01910

EHRICKE, KRAFFT ARNOLD, b Berlin, Ger, Mar 24, 17; US citizen; m 45; c 3. AEROSPACE & ENERGY TECHNOLOGY. *Educ:* Tech Univ, Berlin, MS, 42; Nat Col Educ, Evanston, LHD, 61. *Prof Exp:* Rocket develop engr, Ger, 42-45; jet propulsion engr, Dept Army, Ft Bliss, 47-50, chief gasdynamics sect, Army Ballistic Missile Ctr, Redstone Arsenal, 50-52; systs engr, Bell Aircraft Corp, 52-54; design specialist, Convair Div, Gen Dynamics Corp, 54-55, chief design & systs anal, 56-57, asst to tech dir, Convair-Astronaut, 57-58; originator & prog dir, Centaur Space Vehicle, 58-62, dir, Advan Studies Dept, 62-65; asst div dir, Astrionics Div, NAm Aviation, 65-68; chief sci adv space systs & appln, Space Div, NAm Rockwell Corp, 68-77; PRES, SPACE GLOBAL CO, 77- *Concurrent Pos:* Consult, Dept Defense-US Air Force, 58-61; chmn adv comt elec energy systs, NASA, 59-62. *Honors & Awards:* Guenther Loeser Medal, Int Astronaut Fedn, 56; Astronaut Award, Am Inst Aeronaut & Astronaut, 57 & G Edward Pendray Award, 61. *Mem:* Fel Am Astron Soc; Am Inst Aeronaut & Astronaut; Brit Interplanetary Soc; Int Acad Astronaut; Ger Soc Space Res (pres, 42-43). *Res:* Space technology, spacecraft, space habitats; space-lunar industries, production-service facilities; econometrics, energy technology space and earth, especially solar, fission and fusion. *Mailing Add:* 845 Lamplight Dr La Jolla CA 92038

EHRIG, RAYMOND JOHN, b Jersey City, NJ, Dec 31, 28; m 50; c 5. POLYMER CHEMISTRY. *Educ:* Seton Hall Univ, BS, 50; Polytech Inst Brooklyn, MS, 53, PhD(chem), 57. *Prof Exp:* Anal chemist, US Testing Co, 50-52; from res chemist to sr res chemist, Shell Chem Corp, 57-62; res supvr, W R Grace & Co, 62-66; mgr polymerization res, Chemplex Co, 66-69; CHIEF DIV POLYMERS, RES LAB, US STEEL CORP, 69- *Concurrent Pos:* Lectr, Univ Calif, Long Beach, 57-59, Col Immaculate Conception, 60-62, Col Notre Dame, Md, 63-65, Elmhurst Col, 66-69 & Duquesne Univ, 81- *Mem:* AAAS; Am Chem Soc; Soc Plastics Engrs; Soc Plastic Industs. *Res:* Ionic and radical polymerization and copolymerization; polymer kinetics and thermal decomposition studies; polystyrene; polyethylene. *Mailing Add:* 2360 Milgrove Rd Pittsburgh PA 15241

EHRILICH, KARL FORREST, physiological ecology, behavioral biology, see previous edition

EHRLICH, ANNE HOWLAND, b Des Moines, Iowa, Nov 17, 33; m 54; c 1. ENVIRONMENTAL SCIENCES. *Prof Exp:* Res Asst, 59-72, res assoc, 72-75, SR RES ASSOC BIOL SCI, STANFORD UNIV, 75- *Concurrent Pos:* Consult, Coun Environ Qual, 77-80; lectr, Human Biol Prog, Stanford Univ, 81. *Res:* Comparative morphology of Papillionoidea; reproductive strategies of Papillionoidea; world population, environmental, and resource problems and their interrelationships. *Mailing Add:* Dept Biol Sci Stanford Univ Stanford CA 94305

EHRLICH, EDWARD NORMAN, b Detroit, Mich, Sept 20, 28; m 61; c 3. INTERNAL MEDICINE. *Educ:* Univ Mich, BS, 48, MD, 52. *Prof Exp:* From intern to resident, Wayne County Gen Hosp, 52-54; resident, 57-60, from instr to prof med, Univ Chicago, 60-74; PROF MED, ASSOC CHMN DEPT MED & HEAD SECT ENDOCRINOL, UNIV WIS-MADISON, 74-; CHMN MED, MADISON GEN HOSP, 74- *Mem:* AAAS; Am Fedn Clin Res; Endocrine Soc; Cent Soc Clin Res; Soc Gynecol Invest. *Res:* Adrenocortical regulation of salt metabolism in humans. *Mailing Add:* Clin Sci Ctr Univ Wis 600 Highland Ave Madison WI 53792

EHRLICH, GEORGE EDWARD, b Vienna, Austria, July 18, 28; US citizen; m 68; c 1. RHEUMATOLOGY, INTERNAL MEDICINE. *Educ:* Harvard Univ, AB, 48; Chicago Med Sch, MB, MD, 52. *Prof Exp:* Intern, Michael Reese Hosp, Chicago, Ill, 52-53; asst resident surg & path, Francis Delafield Hosp, New York, 55-56; asst resident med, Beth Israel Hosp, Boston, Mass, 56-57; resident, New Eng Ctr Hosp, 57-58; trainee, Nat Inst Arthritis & Metab Dis, Bethesda, Md, 58-59; instr med, Med Col, Cornell Univ, 59-64; asst prof med & phys med & rehab, Temple Univ, 64-66, assoc prof phys med & rehab, 66-74, assoc prof med, 67-72, prof med, sch med, 72-80, prof rehab med, 74-80; dir arthritis ctr & sect rheumatology, Albert Einstein Med Ctr & Moss Rehab Hosp, 64-80, sr attend physician, 64-80; PROF MED, DIR DIV RHEUMATOLOGY, HAHNEMANN MED COL & HOSP, 80- *Concurrent Pos:* Fel, Hosp Spec Surg NY, 59-60; fel, Sloan Kettering Inst, 60-61; spec fel, Arthritis & Rheumatism Found, 64; Squibb-Olin fel, Mem Ctr Cancer & Allied Dis, 68; consult, US Naval Hosp, Philadelphia, 64-78 & Food & Drug Admin; ed, J Albert Einstein Med Ctr, 68-72; ed, Arthritis & Rheumatic Dis Abstr, 68-70. *Honors & Awards:* Distinguished Alumnus Award, Chicago Med Sch, 69; Philip Hench Award, 71; Citation, City of Philadelphia, 69, 74; Distinguished Serv Award, Arthritis Found, 71, 72; Cavaliere, Order Star Italian Solidarity, 74. *Mem:* Fel Am Col Physicians; Am Rheumatism Asn; AMA; fel Am Col Clin Pharmacol; Am Fedn Clin Res. *Res:* Rheumatology; investigations of osteoarthritis; clinical and genetic pharmacology; pathogenesis of arthritis manifestations; Behcet's syndrome. *Mailing Add:* 230 N Broad St Hahemenn Med Col/Hosp Philadelphia PA 19102

EHRLICH, GERT, b Vienna, Austria, June 22, 26, nat US; m 57. SURFACE PHYSICS. *Educ:* Columbia Univ, AB, 48; Harvard Univ, AM, 50, PhD(chem), 52. *Prof Exp:* Res assoc physics, Univ Mich, 52-53; res assoc physics, Metal Res Dept, Gen Elec Res Lab, 53-68; PROF PHYS METALL & RES PROF, COORD SCI LAB & MAT RES LAB, UNIV ILL, URBANA, 68- *Honors & Awards:* Medard W Welch Award, Am Vacuum Soc, 79; Kendall Award, Am Chem Soc, 82. *Mem:* Am Chem Soc; fel Am Phys Soc; Am Vacuum Soc. *Res:* Crystal surfaces; atomic motion and interactions; surface reactions. *Mailing Add:* Univ Ill Coord Sci Lab 1101 W Springfield Ave Urbana IL 61801

EHRLICH, GERTRUDE, b Vienna, Austria, Jan 7, 23; nat US. MATHEMATICS. *Educ:* Ga State Col Women, BS, 43; Univ NC, MA, 45; Univ Tenn, PhD(math), 53. *Prof Exp:* Instr math, Oglethorpe Univ, 46-50; asst, Univ Tenn, 50-52, instr, 52-53; from instr to assoc prof, 53-69, PROF MATH, UNIV MD, COLLEGE PARK, 69- *Concurrent Pos:* Chmn math competition, Univ Md, 79- *Mem:* Math Asn Am; Am Math Soc; Sigma Xi. *Res:* Continuous geometry; ring theory. *Mailing Add:* 6702 Wells Pkwy University Park MD 20782

EHRLICH, H PAUL, b Honolulu, Hawaii, Aug 17, 41; m 66; c 2. BIOCHEMISTRY, BIOLOGY. *Educ:* Univ Calif, Berkeley, BS, 64; Univ Calif, San Francisco, PhD(biochem), 71. *Prof Exp:* Fel biochem, Univ Wash, 71-73 & Strangeways Res Lab, Cambridge, Eng, 73-75; ASST PROF PATH & BIOCHEM, HARVARD MED SCH, MASS GEN HOSP & SHRINERS BURNS HOSP, 75- *Concurrent Pos:* NIH grants, 78-81 & 80-83. *Honors & Awards:* Brit Am Heart Award, Am Heart Asn, 73. *Mem:* Am Soc Cell Biol; Am Heart Asn; AAAS. *Res:* Collagen metabolism in biology and pathology; would healing and scar metabolism. *Mailing Add:* Shriners Burns Hosp 51 Blossom St Boston MA 02114

EHRLICH, HENRY LUTZ, b Stettin, Ger, Aug 31, 25; nat US. MICROBIOLOGY. *Educ:* Harvard Univ, BS, 48; Univ Wis, MS, 49, PhD(agr bact), 51. *Prof Exp:* Alumni Res Found asst, Univ Wis, 48-50, asst, 50-51; from asst prof to assoc prof, 51-64, PROF BIOL, RENSSELAER POLYTECH INST, 64- *Mem:* AAAS; fel Am Acad Microbiol; Am Soc Microbiol; Am Inst Biol Sci; Sigma Xi. *Res:* Investigations of geomicrobially important transformations, including oxidation of manganese, metal sulfides, arsenic; reduction of manganese, chromium; microbial role in ferromanganese nodule genesis; manganese oxidation by bacteria from deep-sea hydrothermal vents; bacterial leaching of ores. *Mailing Add:* Dept of Biol Rensselaer Polytech Inst Troy NY 12181

EHRLICH, HOWARD GEORGE, b Milwaukee, Wis, Nov 9, 24; m 55; c 2. CYTOLOGY. *Educ:* Marquette Univ, BS, 48; Univ Minn, PhD(cytol), 56. *Prof Exp:* Asst bot, Marquette Univ, 46-48; res asst plant path, Univ Minn, 50-52, asst bot, 52-54, 55-56, res fel, Cancer Soc, 56-58, Dight Inst, 58, instr bot, 59; from asst prof to assoc prof, 59-68, actg chmn, 70-71, PROF BIOL, DUQUESNE UNIV, 68-, CHMN DEPT BIOL SCI, 71- *Mem:* AAAS; Bot Soc Am; Mycol Soc Am. *Res:* Mycology; electron microscopy; growth. *Mailing Add:* Dept of Biol Sci Duquesne Univ Pittsburgh PA 15219

EHRLICH, I(RA) ROBERT, b Washington, DC, Sept 1, 26; m 50; c 2. MECHANICAL ENGINEERING. *Educ:* US Mil Acad, BS, 50; Purdue Univ, MS, 56; Univ Mich, PhD(eng), 60. *Prof Exp:* Supvr prog, Int Elec Corp, 60-62; mgr transp res group, 62-74, DEAN RES, STEVENS INST TECHNOL, 74- *Concurrent Pos:* Consult, Grumman Aircraft Corp, 60-69, Midwest Appl Sci Corp, 62-65 & Chrysler Corp, 65; guest lectr, US Mil Acad, 63-73. *Mem:* Int Soc Terrain-Vehicle Systs (secy, 63-78, vpres, 78-81, pres, 81-); Sigma Xi; Am Soc Testing & Mat; Nat Soc Prof Engrs; Am Defense Preparedness Asn. *Res:* Transportation research; highway safety; accident reconstruction. *Mailing Add:* Stevens Inst of Technol Castle Point Sta Hoboken NJ 07030

EHRLICH, JULIAN, b New York, NY. BIOPHYSICAL CHEMISTRY, BIOCHEMISTRY. *Educ:* City Col New York, BS, 42; NY Univ, DDS, 45; Stevens Inst Technol, MS, 63, PhD(chem), 71. *Prof Exp:* Private practice, New York, 47-60; head anal div, Schwarz Bio-Res Corp, NY, 60-62; res chemist, M&T Chem, Inc, Div Am Can Co, NJ, 62-65; fel, USPHS, 65-70; res assoc, Stevens Inst Technol, 70-71, res scientist, 71-73; asst prof, 73-76, ASSOC PROF, COL MED & DENT NJ, 76- *Concurrent Pos:* Lectr, Plastics Inst Am, 66-69; consult, Stevens Inst Technol, 73-75; adj assoc prof, Stevens Inst Technol, 77- *Mem:* Am Chem Soc; fel Royal Soc Chem; Biophys Soc; fel Am Inst Chemists; fel Plastics & Rubber Inst, London. *Res:* Polysaccharide chemistry; biochemistry; analytical ultracentrifugation; characterization of biopolymers and synthetic polymers; polyphosphate chemistry. *Mailing Add:* Col of Med & Dent 100 Bergen St Newark NJ 07103

EHRLICH, LOUIS WILLIAM, b Baltimore, Md, Oct 4, 27; m 59; c 3. NUMERICAL ANALYSIS. *Educ:* Univ Md, BS, 51, MA, 56; Univ Tex, PhD, 63. *Prof Exp:* Proj engr, Hercules Powder Co, 51-54; asst math, Univ Md, 54-56; numerical analyst, Space Tech Labs, Ramo-Wooldridge Corp, 56-59; res scientist, Univ Tex, 59-62; NUMERICAL ANALYST, APPL PHYSICS LAB, JOHNS HOPKINS UNIV, 62- *Mem:* Am Math Soc; Asn Comput Mach; Soc Indust & Appl Math. *Res:* Linear algebraic systems, finite difference approximations to elliptic partial differential equations and nonlinear systems. *Mailing Add:* Appl Physics Lab Johns Hopkins Rd Laurel MD 20707

EHRLICH, MARGARETE, b Vienna, Austria, Sept 28, 15; nat US. RADIATION PHYSICS. *Educ:* Cath Univ Am, PhD(physics), 55. *Prof Exp:* PHYSICIST, NAT BUR STANDARDS, 48- *Concurrent Pos:* Consult, Int Atomic Energy Agency, 60-61; partic meetings concerned with ionizing radiation, Int Atomic Energy Agency & Int Standards Orgn. *Honors & Awards:* Meritorious Serv Award, US Dept Commerce, 62, Distinguished Serv Award, 77. *Mem:* Am Asn Physicists in Med; Health Physics Soc. *Res:* Dosimetry and spectrometry of ionizing radiation in applications to medicine and radiation protection. *Mailing Add:* C-210 Radiation Physics Bldg Nat Bur Standards Washington DC 20234

EHRLICH, MARY ANN, b Buffalo, NY, July 12, 26; m 55; c 2. BOTANY, PLANT PATHOLOGY. *Educ:* Marquette Univ, PhB, 47; Univ Minn, PhD(plant Minneapolis, PhD(plant path), 55. *Prof Exp:* Instr biol, Marquette Univ, 53-57; ed asst, J Plant Physiol, 57-59; RES ASSOC BIOL, DUQUESNE UNIV, 59- *Mem:* AAAS; Bot Soc Am; Am Phytopath Soc. *Res:* Electron microscopy of plant fungal parasitism. *Mailing Add:* Dept of Biol Duquesne Univ Pittsburgh PA 15219

EHRLICH, MELANIE, b New York, NY, June 12, 45; m 66; c 2. BIOCHEMISTRY, MICROBIOLOGY. *Educ:* Barnard Col, AB, 66; State Univ NY Stony Brook, PhD(biochem), 70. *Prof Exp:* asst prof, 72-80, ASSOC PROF BIOCHEM, SCH MED, TULANE UNIV, 80- *Concurrent Pos:* Jane Coffin Childs fel, Albert Einstein Col Med, 70-71; Jane Coffin Childs grant, Sch Med, Tulane Univ, 72-74, USPHS grant, 74- *Mem:* Am Soc Microbiol; Am Soc Photochem. *Res:* Biochemistry of nucleic acids; bacteriophage with unusually modified DNA; uptake of DNA by cultured mammalian cells; photochemistry of DNA. *Mailing Add:* Dept Biochem Tulane Univ Sch of Med New Orleans LA 70112

EHRLICH, MORRIS JOSEPH, physical optics, see previous edition

EHRLICH, PAUL, b Vienna, Austria, Feb 26, 23; nat US; m 49; c 5. PHYSICAL CHEMISTRY. *Educ:* Queens Col, NY, BS, 44; Univ Wis, MS, 48, PhD, 51. *Prof Exp:* Phys chemist, Nat Bur Standards, 51-53; fel chem, Harvard Univ, 53-54; res chemist, Monsanto Co, 55-59, res specialist, 59-60, group leader, 60-61, scientist, 61-67; assoc prof, 67-70, PROF CHEM ENG, STATE UNIV NY, BUFFALO, 70- *Mem:* AAAS; Am Phys Soc; Am Chem Soc; Am Inst Chem Engrs. *Res:* Thermodynamic interactions of polymers; electronic structure and electron transport in polymers; polymerization processes. *Mailing Add:* Dept of Chem Eng State Univ of NY Buffalo NY 14214

EHRLICH, PAUL EWING, b Schenectady, NY, Aug 8, 48. MATHEMATICS. *Educ:* Harvad Col, BA, 70; State Univ NY Stony Brook, MA, 71, PhD(math), 74. *Prof Exp:* Vis scientist, Math Inst, Univ Bonn, 74-76; asst prof, 76-79, ASSOC PROF MATH, UNIV MO-COLUMBIA, 79- *Concurrent Pos:* Vis scholar, Sch Math, Inst Adv Study, 80. *Mem:* Am Math Soc; Math Asn Am. *Res:* Differential geometry and general relativity. *Mailing Add:* Dept of Math Univ Of Mo-Columbia Columbia MO 65211

EHRLICH, PAUL RALPH, b Philadelphia, Pa, May 29, 32; m 54; c 1. BIOLOGY. *Educ:* Univ Pa, AB, 53; Univ Kans, MA, 55, PhD(entom), 57. *Hon Degrees:* DHA, Univ Pac, 70. *Prof Exp:* Asst entom, Univ Kans, 53-54, assoc, 58-59; res assoc, Chicago Acad Sci, 57-58; from asst prof to assoc prof, 59-66, PROF BIOL, STANFORD UNIV, 66-, BING PROF POP STUDIES, 76- *Honors & Awards:* John Muir Award, Sierra Club, 80. *Mem:* Soc Syst Zool; Ecol Soc Am; Am Soc Naturalists; Soc Study Evolution; Lepidop Soc (secy, 57-63). *Res:* Population biology. *Mailing Add:* Dept Biol Sci Stanford Univ Stanford CA 94305

EHRLICH, RICHARD, b New York, NY, Dec 25, 21; m 45; c 2. REACTOR PHYSICS. *Educ:* Harvard Univ, BA, 41; Cornell Univ, PhD(theoret physics), 47. *Prof Exp:* Asst physics, Cornell Univ, 41-43 & nat res fel, 46; jr scientist, Los Alamos Sci Lab, Univ Calif, 43-46; res assoc physics, 47-54, supvr theoret physics, 54, mgr, 54-55, mgr math anal, 55-58, mgr advan develop, Schenectady, NY, 58-76, MGR NUCLEAR SAFETY & SAFEGUARDS, GEN ELEC CO, 76- *Concurrent Pos:* Mem adv comt reactor physics, US AEC, 60-75 & Energy Res & Develop Admin, 75-76; chmn adv comt, Nat Nuclear Data Sect Ctr, Brookhaven Nat Lab, 67- *Mem:* Fel AAAS; Am Phys Soc; fel Am Nuclear Soc. *Res:* Theoretical physics work in atomic energy field; nuclear reactor design and analysis; digital computations; technical management; nuclear safety and safeguards. *Mailing Add:* 175 Curtner Ave MC306 San Jose CA 95125

EHRLICH, RICHARD, b Bedzin, Poland, Jan 19, 24; nat US; m 50; c 2. ENVIRONMENTAL HEALTH. *Educ:* Munich Tech Univ, MS, 48, PhD(dairy bact), 49. *Prof Exp:* Res asst, Munich Tech Univ, 47-49; lab dir, Am Butter Inst, 49-52; assoc bacteriologist, 52-53, res bacteriologist, 53-57, supvr biol res, 57-60, asst dir, 60-62, assoc dir, 62-63, dir life sci, 63-77, V PRES RES OPERS, IIT RES INST, 77- *Concurrent Pos:* Mem subcomt nitrogen oxides, Div Med Sci, Nat Res Coun, Nat Acad Sci, 73- *Mem:* AAAS; Am Soc Microbiol; Pub Health Asn; foreign assoc mem French Soc Tuberculosis & Respiratory Dis. Soc Occup Environ Health. *Res:* Public health bacteriology; respiratory infections; bacterial aerosols; infectious aerobiology; health effects of air pollution. *Mailing Add:* Life Sci Res Div IIT Res Inst 10 W 35th St Chicago IL 60616

EHRLICH, ROBERT, b St Paul, Minn, Mar 4, 36. GEOLOGY, SEDIMENTOLOGY. *Educ:* Univ Minn, BA, 58; La State Univ, MS, 61, Mobil fel & PhD(geol), 65. *Prof Exp:* From asst prof to assoc prof geol, Mich State Univ, 65-74; PROF GEOL, UNIV SC, 74- *Mem:* Geol Soc Am; Int Asn Sedimentol; Am Asn Petrol Geologists; Meteorit Soc. *Res:* Detrital sedimentology; geometrics; crustal dynamics as expressed in sediments; geology of North Africa; shape analysis. *Mailing Add:* Dept of Geol Univ of SC Columbia SC 29208

EHRLICH, ROBERT STARK, b New York, NY, Aug 30, 40; m 67; c 1. BIOPHYSICAL CHEMISTRY. *Educ:* Columbia Col, AB, 62; Rutgers Univ, MS, 64, PhD(physics), 69. *Prof Exp:* Asst prof physics, Muskingum Col, 69-70; instr, City Col New York, 70-71; res assoc biochem, Rutgers Med Sch, 71-73; RES ASSOC BIOCHEM, DEPT CHEM, UNIV DEL, 73- *Mem:* Am Phys Soc; AAAS; Biophys Soc. *Res:* Structure and function of enzymes using techniques of fluorescence, nuclear magnetic resonance, binding and chemical modification. *Mailing Add:* 1424 Carson Rd Wilmington DE 19803

EHRLICH, S PAUL, JR, b Minneapolis, Minn, May 4, 32; m 59; c 2. EPIDEMIOLOGY, PUBLIC HEALTH. *Educ:* Univ Minn, BA, 53, BS, 55, MD, 57; Univ Calif, MPH, 61; Am Bd Prev Med, dipl. *Prof Exp:* Intern, USPHS, Staten Island, NY, 57-58, med officer, Coast Guard, 58-59, med officer, Nat Heart Inst, 59-60, chief heart dis control prog, Field & Training Sta, 61-66, asst chief prog develop, Heart Dis Control Prog, Div Chronic Dis, 66-67, chief tech resources, Off Int Health, 67-70, dep dir off int health, 69-70, asst surgeon gen, 70-73, actg surgeon gen, 73-77, dir off int health, Off of Secy, US Dept Health, Educ & Welfare, 70-77; vpres, Am Inst Res, 78-79; DEP DIR, PAN AM HEALTH ORGN, WHO, 79- *Concurrent Pos:* Resident, Sch Pub Health, Univ Calif, 61-63; rep to exec bd, WHO, 69-76; assoc prof, Georgetown Univ, 69-; adj prof, Sch Pub Health, Univ Tex, Houston, 70-; fel coun epidemiol, Am Heart Asn. *Mem:* AAAS; fel Am Col Prev Med; AMA; fel Am Pub Health Asn; Am Geriat Soc. *Res:* Epidemiology of cardiovascular diseases; chronic disease in geriatric groups. *Mailing Add:* Pan Am Health Orgn 525 23rd St NW Washington DC 20037

EHRLICH, SANFORD HOWARD, b New York, NY, June 11, 31; m 55; c 2. CHEMICAL PHYSICS. *Educ:* NY Univ, BS, 53, MS, 59; Adelphi Univ, PhD(chem physics), 63. *Prof Exp:* Chem physicist, Air Prod & Chem, Inc, 63-65; sr scientist, Am Optical Co, Mass, 65-70; MEM STAFF, RES LABS, EASTMAN KODAK CO, 70- *Mem:* Am Chem Soc; Am Vacuum Soc; Am Phys Soc. *Res:* Energy transfer in gases and solids; spectroscopy of surface adsorbed molecules; photochemistry; thermodynamics of nonaqueous solutions; transference phenomena in nonaqueous media; luminescence and energy transfer in organic molecules. *Mailing Add:* 12 Courtenay Circle Pittsford NY 14534

EHRLICH, STANLEY L(EONARD), b Newark, NJ, Jan 7, 25; m 49; c 3. ACOUSTICS, SYSTEMS ENGINEERING. *Educ:* Brown Univ, ScB, 44, ScM, 45. *Prof Exp:* Physicist, US Navy Underwater Sound Lab, 48-53; sr engr transducer develop, 53-57, sr engr, Sonar Systs Develop, 57-59, sect mgr, 59-62, prin engr, 62-70, CONSULT ENGR, SONAR SYSTS DEVELOP, SUBMARINE SIGNAL DIV, RAYTHEON CO, 70- *Concurrent Pos:* Deleg, Am Nat Standards Inst, Inst Elec & Electronics Engrs, 71; assoc ed, J Oceanic Eng, 75- *Honors & Awards:* Freeman Award for Eng Achievement, Providence Eng Soc, 76. *Mem:* AAAS; Am Phys Soc; fel Acoust Soc Am; sr mem Inst Elec & Electronics Engrs; Nat Security Indust Asn. *Res:* Magnetostriction; electrostriction; electroacoustics; design of transducers; development of sonar systems; normal modes in solids, especially cylinders. *Mailing Add:* One Acacia Dr Middletown RI 02840

EHRLICH, WALTER, b Bosicany, Bohemia, Sept 22, 15; US citizen; m 40; c 3. CARDIOVASCULAR PHYSIOLOGY. *Educ:* Charles Univ, Prague, MD, 47; Czech Acad Sci, CSc, 61. *Prof Exp:* Secundar path, Sch Hyg, Charles Univ, Prague, 47-48, secundar internal med, 48-51; chief res group clin & exp res, Inst Cardiovasc Res, Prague, 51-63; chief physiol labor, Inst Hyg, Prague, 63-66; asst prof, 67-70, ASSOC PROF, DEPT ENVIRON PHYSIOL, SCH HYG, JOHNS HOPKINS UNIV, 70-, ASSOC PROF, DEPT PSYCHIAT & BEHAV, SCH MED, 70- *Mem:* Am Physiol Soc; Am Heart Asn; Fedn Am Scientists. *Res:* Intrinsic and reflectory regulation of circulation. *Mailing Add:* Sch of Hyg Rm 7014 615 N Wolfe St Baltimore MD 21205

EHRLINGER, HENRY P, III, b Kellogg, Idaho, Aug 5, 25; m; c 4. METALLURGICAL ENGINEERING. *Educ:* Colo Sch Mines, EM, 50; Univ Nev, MS, 57. *Prof Exp:* Metall engr, Mex Mining Dept, Am Smelting & Refining Co, 50-53; metall engr, Atomic Energy Comn res proj, Univ Nev, 53-57; metall engr, Mex Mining Dept, Am Smelting & Refining Co, 57-59, mill supt, Charcas Unit, 60-64; mill engr, Pima Mining Co, 64-66; minerals engr, Minerals Eng Sect, Ill State Geol Surv, 66-73; mgr, Calcilox Prod, Dravo Lime Co, 73-79, SR DEVELOP ENGR, DRAVO CORP, 79- *Mem:* Am Inst Mining, Metall & Petrol Engrs; Mining & Metall Soc Am; Sigma Xi. *Mailing Add:* Dravo Res Ctr Neville Island Pittsburgh PA 15225

EHRMAN, JOACHIM BENEDICT, b Nuremberg, Ger, Nov 12, 29; nat US; m 61; c 1. PLASMA PHYSICS. *Educ:* Univ Pa, AB, 48; Princeton Univ, AM, 49, PhD(physics), 54. *Prof Exp:* Mem dept physics, Atomic Energy Res Dept, NAm Aviation, Inc, 51-53; instr, Sloane Physics Lab, Yale Univ, 54-55; physicist nucleonics div, US Naval Research Lab, 55-66 & plasma physics div, 66-68; PROF APPL MATH, UNIV WESTERN ONT, 68- *Concurrent Pos:* Assoc prof lectr physics, George Washington Univ, 56-57; lectr, Univ Md, 63-64; consult plasma physics div, US Naval Res Lab, 69-70; vis mem res staff, Plasma Physics Lab, Princeton Univ, 75-76. *Mem:* Am Phys Soc. *Res:* Fusion, tokamak; saturation of resistive tearing mode in toroidal plasma; electron ring accelerator; electron beams; magnetohydrodynamics; electron penetration through matter; nuclear reactors; nuclear physics. *Mailing Add:* Dept of Appl Math Univ of Western Ont London ON N6A 3K7 Can

EHRMAN, LEE, b New York, NY, May 25, 35; m 55; c 2. POPULATION GENETICS. *Educ:* Queens Col, NY, BS, 56; Columbia Univ, MA, 57, PhD(genetics), 59. *Prof Exp:* Lectr zool, Barnard Col, Columbia Univ, 56-58, USPHS fels genetics, Univ, 59-62; res assoc pop genetics, Rockefeller Univ, 62-64, asst prof, 64-71; assoc prof natural sci, 71-74, PROF NATURAL SCI, STATE UNIV NY COL PURCHASE, 74-, CHMN DEPT BIOL, 78- *Concurrent Pos:* Am Asn Univ Women Shirley Farr fel, 62-63; Sigma Xi grant-in-aid, 63; Nat Inst Child Health & Human Develop res career develop award, 64-74; lectr, State Univ NY Col Purchase, 70-71; from adj assoc prof to adj prof, Rockefeller Univ, 71-75; res assoc animal behav, Am Mus Natural Hist, 73, res assoc mammology, 81-; State Univ NY fac exchange scholar, 74-81; assoc ed, Am Naturalist, 75-79. *Mem:* Fel AAAS; Behav Genetics Asn (pres); Am Soc Human Genetics; Sigma Xi; Soc Study Social Biol. *Res:* Reproductive isolating mechanisms, especially hybrid sterility and sexual behavioral isolation; cytoplasmic inheritance; frequency-dependent selection. *Mailing Add:* Div Natural Sci State Univ NY Col Purchase NY 10577

EHRMAN, LEONARD, b New York, NY, Jan 24, 32; m 57; c 1. ELECTRICAL ENGINEERING. *Educ:* Mass Inst Technol, BS, 53, MS, 55; Northeastern Univ, PhD(elec eng), 67. *Prof Exp:* Mem tech staff, Sandia Corp, NMex, 58-61; group leader, Res & Adv Develop Div, Avco Corp, Mass, 61-63; res scientist, 63-80, SR CONSULT SCIENTIST, SIGNATRON, INC, 80- *Mem:* Sr mem Inst Elec & Electronics Engrs. *Res:* Digital communications; radar analysis; signal processing; computer usage; data processing; bandwidth compression; channel characterization. *Mailing Add:* 83 Bertwell Rd Lexington MA 02173

EHRMANN, RITA MAE, b Jersey City, NJ, Aug 27, 28. GEOMETRY. *Educ:* Univ Dayton, BS, 51; Villanova Univ, AM, 57; St Louis Univ, PhD(math), 69. *Prof Exp:* Teacher math-sci, Mt St Michael High Sch, 51-65; teacher math, 69-80, ASSOC PROF MATH, VILLANOVA UNIV, 80- *Concurrent Pos:* Dir, NSF In-Serv Inst, Villanova Univ, 71-73. *Mem:* Am Math Soc; Math Asn Am; Sigma Xi. *Res:* Geometric properties, especially convexity, of metric spaces; finite geometrics from a foundations standpoint; sensory aids for math students, especially the blind; educational movies for college mathematics. *Mailing Add:* Dept of Math Villanova Univ Villanova PA 19085

EHRMANTRAUT, HARRY CHARLES, b Washington, DC, Nov 25, 21; m 48; c 1. INSTRUMENTATION. *Educ:* George Washington Univ, BS, 47; Georgetown Univ, MS, 48; Univ Ill, PhD(biophys), 50. *Prof Exp:* Asst photosynthesis proj, Univ Ill, 48-50; exec secy panel med aspects atomic warfare, Res & Develop Bd, Off Secy Defense, 50-51; asst to dir res, Toni Co, 51-52; res biophysicist, Armour Res Found, 52-54; sr biophysicist, Stanford Res Inst, 54-55; dir applns res dept, Spinco Div, Beckman Instruments, Inc, 56-59; pres, Mechrolab, Inc, 59-66; sci adv, Found for Nutrit & Stress Res, 66-68; pres, Gymnas Corp, 68-70; chmn, Improved Commun Inc, 70-71; partner, Bus Anal Assocs, 72-78, Pres, Cal/Quest Corp, 75-76; PRES, AVM ASSOCS, 78- *Concurrent Pos:* Pres & dir, Altos Ctr, Inc, 70-71; pres, Quercine Corp, 73-74; mem, Int Oceanog Found. *Mem:* AAAS; Am Chem Soc; NY Acad Sci; Inst Elec & Electronics Engrs; Biophys Soc. *Res:* Medical and biophysical instrumentation. *Mailing Add:* 1090 Bay Oaks Dr Los Osos CA 93402

EHRREICH, ALBERT LEROY, b Pipestone, Minn, June 11, 23; m 51; c 2. GEOLOGY. *Educ:* Univ Calif, Los Angeles, BA, 50, MA, 55, PhD(geol), 65. *Prof Exp:* Geologist, US Bur Reclamation, 51-53; from asst prof to assoc prof, 57-74, PROF GEOL, CALIF STATE UNIV LONG BEACH, 74- *Mem:* Geol Soc Am; Geochem Soc; Mineral Soc Am; Nat Asn Geol Teachers. *Res:* Igneous and metamorphic petrology. *Mailing Add:* Dept of Geol Calif State Univ Long Beach CA 90840

EHRREICH, STEWART JOEL, b Brooklyn, NY, Mar 24, 36; m 60; c 2. PHARMACOLOGY. *Educ:* Queens Col, NY, BS, 57; State Univ NY Downstate Med Ctr, MS, 61, PhD(pharmacol), 63. *Prof Exp:* Asst pharmacol, Downstate Med Ctr, 58-63; sr pharmacologist, Smith Kline & French Labs, 65-67, sr investr, 67-69; sect head, Geigy Pharmaceut Div, Ciba-Geigy Ltd, 69-71; sect leader, 72-75, sect leader, Scheringplough Corp, 75-77; group leader antihypertensive drugs, 78-79, DEP DIR, CARDIO-RENAL DIV, FOOD & DRUG ADMIN, 80- *Concurrent Pos:* USPHS fel, Med Col, Cornell Univ, 63-65; lectr biol, Queens Col, NY, 63-65 & Brooklyn Col, 64-65. *Mem:* Am Soc Pharmacol & Exp Therapeut; Am Soc Clin Pharmacol. *Res:* Pharmacology, physiology and electro-physiology of smooth and cardiac muscle; autonomic pharmacology. *Mailing Add:* 9513 Ash Hollow Pl Gaithersburg MD 20760

EHRSTEIN, JAMES ROBERT, solid state physics, see previous edition

EIAN, GILBERT LEE, b Fergus Falls, Minn, Apr 15, 43; m 66; c 2. ORGANIC CHEMISTRY. *Educ:* Univ Minn, Minneapolis, BChem, 65; Iowa State Univ, MS, 67, PhD(chem), 69. *Prof Exp:* Sr chemist, 69-73, RES SPECIALIST, 3M CO, 73- *Mem:* Am Chem Soc. *Res:* Organic synthesis; organic photochemistry and imaging systems; free radical chemistry; nitrogen chemistry, product development, and specialty filters. *Mailing Add:* Occup Health & Safety Prod 230-BE 3M Ctr St Paul MN 55144

EIB, WILHELM ERNST-HELMUT, solid state physics, see previous edition

EIBECK, RICHARD ELMER, b Cincinnati, Ohio, Feb 17, 35; m 62; c 2. INORGANIC CHEMISTRY. *Educ:* Univ Cincinnati, BS, 57; Univ Ill, MS, 59, PhD(chem), 61. *Prof Exp:* Res chemist, Gen Chem Div, Allied Chem Corp, 60-64, sr res chemist, 64-67, tech supvr, Indust Chem Div, 67, tech supvr, Specialty Chem Div, 67-81, MGR RES & DEVELOP, ALLIED CHEM CO, 81- *Res:* Chemistry of nonmetals; fluorine compounds, including sulfur fluorides; nitrogen fluorides; fluorocarbons; dielectric materials; alkali metal polysulfidies. *Mailing Add:* 23 Pine Terrace Orchard Park NY 14127

EIBEN, GALEN J, b Monticello, Iowa, May 23, 36; m 56; c 3. ENTOMOLOGY. *Educ:* Wartburg Col, BA, 60; Iowa State Univ, MS, 62, PhD(entom), 67. *Prof Exp:* Instr biol, Tex Lutheran Col, 62-64; res assoc entom, Iowa State Univ, 64-66; asst prof biol, 67-74, ASSOC PROF BIOL, WARTBURG COL, 74- *Mem:* Am Entom Soc. *Res:* Methodology involved in screening corn for resistance to corn rootworms; corn root development and its relation to rootworm populations. *Mailing Add:* Dept of Biol Wartburg Col Waverly IA 50677

EIBEN, ROBERT MICHAEL, b Cleveland, Ohio, July 12, 22; m 46; c 6. MEDICINE. *Educ:* Western Reserve Univ, BS, 44, MD, 46. *Prof Exp:* From instr to asst prof pediat, 49-65, asst prof neurol, 63-72, assoc prof pediat, 65-75, PROF PEDIAT, CASE WESTERN RESERVE UNIV, 75-, ASSOC PROF NEUROL, 72- *Concurrent Pos:* Fel, Univ Wash, 60-63; asst med dir, Dept Contagious Dis, Cleveland City Hosp, 49-50, actg dir, 50-52, asst dir dept pediat & contagious dis, 54-60, med dir, Respirator Care & Rehab Ctr, 54-60; asst pediatrist, Univ Hosps, 49-51, assoc pediatrist, 51-; pediat neurologist, Cleveland Metrop Gen Hosp, 63- *Mem:* Am Acad Neurol; Am Soc Human Genetics; Am Acad Pediat; Child Neurol Soc; Am Pediat Soc. *Res:* Biochemical studies of heredofamilial disorders of the nervous system. *Mailing Add:* 2 Oakshore Dr Bratenahl OH 44108

EIBERT, JOHN, JR, b St Louis, Mo, Sept 18, 18; m; c 4. PHARMACEUTICAL CHEMISTRY. *Educ:* Washington Univ, BS, 40, MS, 42, PhD(chem), 44. *Prof Exp:* Chemist, Scullin Steel Co, St Louis, 42-43; lectr physics, Washington Univ, 43-44; res chemist, Pan Am Refining Corp, Tex, 44-45 & Anheuser-Busch, Inc, Mo, 45-46; consult chemist & secy-treas, 46-61, PRES, SCI ASSOCS, 61- *Mem:* AAAS; Am Chem Soc; NY Acad Sci; Am Inst Chemists; assoc Inst Food Technol. *Res:* Calorimetry; measurement of vapor pressure; catalysis; protein hydrolysis; thermodynamic properties of certain aromatic hydrocarbons. *Mailing Add:* Sci Assocs 6200 S Lindbergh Blvd St Louis MO 63123

EIBLING, JAMES A(LEXANDER), b Marion, Ohio, Nov 22, 17; m 40; c 2. MECHANICAL ENGINEERING, SOLAR ENERGY. *Educ:* Ohio State Univ, BME, 39. *Prof Exp:* Mech engr, B F Goodrich Co, Akron, 40-42; res engr, 46-56, asst div chief, 56-60, chief, Thermal Systs Div, 60-73, prog mgr solar energy res, Battelle Mem Inst, 73-79; HEAD CONSULT, EIBLING THERMAL SYSTS TECHNOL, 79- *Honors & Awards:* Award, Am Soc Heat, Refrig & Air-Conditioning Engrs, 74. *Mem:* Fel Am Soc Mech Engrs; Am Soc Heat, Refrig & Air-Conditioning Engrs; Int Solar Energy Soc (pres, Am Sect, 73-74, int vpres, 75-78); Int Inst Refrig. *Res:* Refrigeration; air conditioning; thermal systems; sea water conversion; energy conversion devices; heat transfer; thermal and flow models. *Mailing Add:* Eibling Thermal Systs 1380 Camelot Dr Columbus OH 43220

EICH, ROBERT, b Ann Arbor, Mich, Oct 4, 23; m 51; c 3. MEDICINE, CARDIOLOGY. *Educ:* Univ Mich, AB, 47, MD, 51. *Prof Exp:* From asst prof to assoc prof, 57-71, PROF MED, STATE UNIV NY UPSTATE MED CTR, 71- *Res:* Cardiovascular disease; internal medicine. *Mailing Add:* State Univ of NY Upstate Med Ctr Syracuse NY 13210

EICH, STEPHEN JOSEPH, b New York, NY, Aug 31, 24; m 46; c 2. BIOCHEMISTRY. *Educ:* Queens Col, BS, 48; Fordham Univ, MS, 50, PhD(biochem), 55. *Prof Exp:* Asst, Fordham Univ, 52-54; res assoc, Cornell Univ Med Col, 54-56, instr, 56-57; res investr, 57-68, sr res investr, 68-71, asst dir biochem res, 71-73, asst dir biol res, 73-76, assoc dir biol res, 76-80, SR RES SCIENTIST, G D SEARLE & CO, 80- *Mem:* AAAS; Am Chem Soc; NY Acad Sci. *Res:* Mode of action of thiamine antagonists; ergothioneine; polysaccharides; peptides; biochemistry of mammalian reproduction; protein chemistry. *Mailing Add:* G D Searle & Co Box 5110 Chicago IL 60680

EICHBAUM, BARLANE RONALD, b New Brunswick, NJ, Sept 1, 26; m 50; c 3. SOLID STATE PHYSICS, MATERIAL SCIENCE ENGINEERING. *Educ:* Rutgers Univ, BS, 51, PhD(ceramic eng), 56; Univ Tex, MS, 53; Temple Univ, BA, 65. *Prof Exp:* Prod & control engr, Hercules Powder Co, 50-52; res & develop engr, Am Rock Wool Corp, 52; Tex State scholar & Edward Orton Jr fel, 52-53; proj engr, US Signal Corps, Rutgers Univ, 53-56; res engr, Int Bus Mach Corp, 56-57, develop engr & tech consult, Prod Develop Labs, 57-59; mgr magnetic tech, Aeronutronic Comput Div, Ford Motor Co, 59-60, mgr solid state devices, Aeronutronic Res Labs, 60, mgr molecular eng, 60-62, asst dir, Philco Res Labs, 62-63, dir phys electronics, Philco Corp, 63-65; dir corp develop & tech asst to vpres eng & res, AMP, Inc, Pa, 65-67; dir res & asst to vpres eng, Gulton Industs, Inc, NJ, 67-68; dir res & develop & staff scientist, Lear Motors Corp, 68-70; consult engr, P & S Domestique, 72-73; TECH CONSULT, 71-; CHEM ENGR, US BUR MINES, 75- *Mem:* Electrochem Soc; Am Ceramic Soc; sr mem Inst Elec & Electronics Eng; Sigma Xi; fel Am Inst Chemists. *Res:* Chemistry; ceramics; crystallography; metallurgy; mineral processing; general, electronic and mechanical engineering; materials in advanced equipment; electronic systems technology. *Mailing Add:* 12065 Stoney Brook Dr Reno NV 89511

EICHBERG, JORG WILHELM, b Stuttgart, Ger, Nov, 14, 39; m 63; c 2. VETERINARY MEDICINE, IMMUNOLOGY. *Educ:* Univ Munich, DVM, 67; Univ Tex, San Antonio, PhD, 74. *Prof Exp:* Asst prof, Free Univ Berlin, 67-70; ASSOC FOUND SCIENTIST, SOUTHWEST FOUND RES & EDUC, 74- *Concurrent Pos:* Adj asst prof pediat & lab animal sci, Univ Tex Health Sci Ctr, San Antonio, 76-; prin investr, Nat Cancer Inst grant, 76-78. *Mem:* Am Soc Microbiol; AAAS; Asn Gnotobiotics; Am Asn Lab Animal Sci; Am Asn Immunologists. *Res:* Primatoloty; virology; immunology. *Mailing Add:* Southwest Found for Res & Educ PO Box 28147 San Antonio TX 78284

EICHBERG, JOSEPH, b Oct 5, 35; US Citizen; m 64; c 3. BIOCHEMISTRY. *Educ:* Mass Inst Technol, BS, 57; Harvard Univ, PhD(biochem), 62. *Prof Exp:* Res assoc, Harvard Med Sch, 64-68, assoc, 68-69, from asst prof to assoc prof biol chem, 69-75; assoc prof biophys sci, 75-80, PROF BIOCHEM & BIOPHYS SCI, UNIV HOUSTON,, 80- *Concurrent Pos:* USPHS fel, 62-65; estab investr, Am Heart Asn, 68-73; tutor biochem sci, Harvard Univ, 69-74. *Mem:* Am Soc Neurochem; Int Soc Neurochem; Brit Biochem Soc; Soc Neurosci; Am Soc Biol Chem. *Res:* Lipid biochemistry and metabolism; neurochemistry; membrane biochemistry. *Mailing Add:* Dept Biochem & Biophys Sci Univ Houston Houston TX 77004

EICHBERGER, LE ROY CARL, b Chicago, Ill, Oct 26, 27; m 55; c 3. MECHANICAL ENGINEERING. *Educ:* Univ Ill, BS, 51, MS, 55, PhD(theoret & appl mech), 59. *Prof Exp:* Layout draftsman, McCormick Works, Int Harvester Corp, 51-53; res asst theot & appl mech, Univ Ill, 53-55, res assoc, 55-57, instr, 57-59; asst prof mech eng, 59-63, ASSOC PROF MECH ENG, UNIV HOUSTON, 63- *Concurrent Pos:* Tech consult, Reed Roller Bit Co, Houston, 59-61, Houston Eng Res Co, 61-62 & Humble Oil & Refining Co, 68-; vis prof, Univ Mich, 61-62. *Mem:* Soc Exp Stress Anal; Am Soc Mech Engrs; Sigma Xi (secy-treas, 64-65, pres-elect, 65-67). *Res:* Applied mechanics, specifically in areas of elasticity, shell analysis, vibration, dynamics, mechanics of materials, photoelasticity and experimental stress analysis. *Mailing Add:* Dept of Mech Eng 3801 Collen Blvd Houston TX 77004

EICHEL, HERBERT JOSEPH, biochemistry, enzymology, see previous edition

EICHEL, HERMAN JOSEPH, b Toledo, Ohio, Aug 2, 24; m 49; c 5. BIOCHEMISTRY, ORGANIC CHEMISTRY. *Educ:* Univ Dayton, BS, 48; DePaul Univ, MS, 56; Univ Cincinnati, PhD(biochem), 66. *Prof Exp:* Res chemist, Abbott Labs, 48-53 & C F Kettering Found, 53-57; sr res chemist, Diamond Labs, 57-58; proj leader microencapsulation, Nat Cash Register Co, 58-62; asst to dir res, 62-63, asst res dir, 63-64, dir pharmaceut res, 64-66, vpres pharmaceut res & prod, 66-68, exec vpres, Hoechst Pharmaceut Co, 68-74; PRES, ADRIA LABS INC, 74- *Mem:* Am Chem Soc; Am Inst Chem; NY Acad Sci. *Res:* Synthesis of photosynthetic intermediates, coacervation studies; molecular heterogeniety of D-amino acid oxidase; synthetic studies of pyran chemistry; research in areas of tropical disease, tuberculosis, thyroid disease, CNS and cardiovascular agents; diagnostics and veterinary products. *Mailing Add:* Adria Labs Inc PO Box 16529 Columbus OH 43216

EICHELBERGER, JOHN CHARLES, b Syracuse, NY, Oct 3, 48; m 69; c 1. PETROLOGY, VOLCANOLOGY. *Educ:* Mass Inst Technol, BS & MS, 71; Stanford Univ, PhD(geol), 74. *Prof Exp:* staff mem geol, Los Alamos Sci Lab, 74-79; STAFF MEM, SANDIA NAT LABS, 79- *Mem:* Am Geophys Union; Geol Soc Am. *Res:* Origin and evolution of intermediate and silicic magmas; volatiles in magmas; eruption processes. *Mailing Add:* Geophysics Res Div 5541 Sandia Nat Labs Albuquerque NM 87185

EICHELBERGER, ROBERT JOHN, b Washington, Pa, Apr 10, 21; m 43; c 4. PHYSICS. *Educ:* Washington & Jefferson Col, AB, 42; Carnegie Inst Technol, MS, 48, PhD(physics), 54. *Prof Exp:* Instr physics, Washington & Jefferson Col, 42; res physicist, Carnegie Inst Technol, 43-45, res supvr, 45-55; supvry physicist, 55-62, assoc tech dir, 62-67, assoc tech dir res & technol, US Armament Res & Develop Command, 77-81, DIR, US ARMY BALLISTIC RES LABS, 67- *Mem:* AAAS; Am Phys Soc; Am Inst Aeronaut & Astronaut. *Res:* Effects of extremely high temperatures and pressures on solids; non-steady fluid dynamics at extreme pressures; hypervelocity ballistics; shock phenomena; brittle fracture in metals. *Mailing Add:* 409 Catherine Bel Air MD 21014

EICHELBERGER, ROBERT LESLIE, b Wichita, Kans, Jan 18, 26; m 47; c 3. PHYSICAL CHEMISTRY. *Educ:* Univ Calif, Los Angeles, BS, 48, MS, 49; Univ Wy, PhD(chem), 57. *Prof Exp:* Supvr anal chem, Truesdail Labs, Calif, 49-52; instr col eng, Univ Wy, 52-54; res chemist liquid metals, NAm Aviation, Inc, 54-57, supvr liquid metal chem, 57-66, sr tech specialist, Atomics Int Div, NAm Rockwell Corp, 66-73, SR STAFF SCIENTIST, ENERGY TECHNOL ENG CTR, ROCKWELL INT, 73- *Mem:* Am Chem Soc. *Res:* Liquid metal chemistry; metal-gas reactions; analytical methods; chemical engineering. *Mailing Add:* 937 Sandpiper Cir Westlake Village CA 91361

EICHELBERGER, W(ILLIAM) H, b Wichita, Kans, Dec 5, 21; m 43; c 4. ELECTRICAL ENGINEERING. *Educ:* Univ Colo, BS, 43. *Prof Exp:* Elec design engr, Radio Corp Am, 43-46; asst chief engr, Hathaway Instrument Co, 46-52; res engr, Res Inst, 52-62, MGR COMPUT CTR, UNIV DENVER, 62-, DIR SYSTS DEVELOP, 70-, SR SYSTS ANALYST, 76- *Mem:* Sr mem Inst Elec & Electronics Engrs; Asn Comput Mach. *Res:* Applications of digital computers; digital computer logic and circuit design; pulse and digital instrumentation; audio engineering; radio receivers; electronic instrumentation. *Mailing Add:* Comput Ctr BA469 Univ Denver Denver CO 80210

EICHELMAN, BURR S, JR, b Hinsdale, Ill, Mar 20, 43. BEHAVIORAL NEUROCHEMISTRY, AGGRESSION. *Educ:* Univ Chicago, MD, 68, PhD(biopsychol), 70. *Prof Exp:* Intern pediat, Univ Calif Med Ctr, San Francisco, 69-70; staff assoc biopsychol, NIH & USPHS, Bethesda, 70-72; resident fel psychiat, Stanford Univ Med Ctr, 72-75, Kennedy fel med, law & ethics, 75-76; asst prof, Univ Wis, 76-79; CHIEF PSYCHIAT SERV, WILLIAM S MIDDLETON MEM VET ADMIN HOSP, 76-; ASSOC PROF, UNIV WIS-MADISON, 79- *Concurrent Pos:* Prin investr, Vet Admin grant, 77-84 & NSF grant; dir, Lab behav Neurochem, Waisman Ctr, Univ Wis, 76- *Honors & Awards:* A B Bennett Award, Soc Biol Psychiat, 72. *Mem:* Am Psychiat Asn; fel Am Psychol Asn; Soc Neurosci; Am Col Neuropsychopharmacol; Int Soc Res Aggression. *Res:* Behavioral neurochemistry and pharmacology focusing on animal models of aggression and human violent behavior; concerned with ethical issues in aggression research. *Mailing Add:* Wm S Middleton Mem Vet Admin Hosp Psychiat Serv 2500 Overlook Terr Madison WI 53705

EICHEN, ERWIN, physical metallurgy, see previous edition

EICHENBERGER, HANS P, b Fribourg, Switz, Dec 29, 21; US citizen; m 66; c 5. ENGINEERING SCIENCE, FLUID MECHANICS. *Educ:* Swiss Fed Inst Technol, Dipl, 46; Pa State Univ, MS, 49; Mass Inst Technol, ScD(mech eng), 51. *Prof Exp:* Asst internal combustion eng, Swiss Fed Inst Technol, 46-48; res asst diesel eng, Pa State Univ, 48-49; instr gas turbines fluid flow, Mass Inst Technol, 50-52; asst chief aerodyn, Garret Corp, Calif & Ariz, 52-56; chief eng sci, TRW Inc, 57-62; dir res, Res Ctr, Ingersoll Rand Co, 63-68; dir res lab, IBM, Switz, 68-71, asst to corp dir res, 71-76; SCI REP EUROP, GEN ELEC CTR RES & DEVELOP, 76- *Concurrent Pos:* Lectr, Case Inst Technol, 57-59. *Mem:* Inst Elec & Electronics Engrs. *Res:* Internal flow in machinery; external flow of bodies; drag reduction. *Mailing Add:* Gen Elec Ctr for Res & Develop Pelikanstr 37 Zurich Ch 8001 Switzerland

EICHENHOLZ, ALFRED, b Dabrowa, Poland, Apr 5, 27; US citizen; m 52; c 1. INTERNAL MEDICINE, METABOLISM. *Educ:* Univ Munich, MD, 51; Univ Minn, Minneapolis, MSc, 64; Am Bd Internal Med, dipl, 60. *Prof Exp:* Staff physician pulmonary dis serv, Vet Admin Hosp, Minneapolis, 57-59, asst chief, 59-61, chief clin radioisotope sect, 61-67; chief radioisotope serv, 67-70, CHIEF MED SERV, VET ADMIN HOSP, 70-; ASSOC PROF MED, SCH MED, UNIV PITTSBURGH, 67- *Concurrent Pos:* Instr, Univ Minn, Minneapolis, 57-64, asst prof, 64-67. *Mem:* AMA; Am Fedn Clin Res; NY Acad Sci; Soc Nuclear Med. *Res:* Acid Base, fluid and electrolyte balance; renal physiology; pulmonary disease. *Mailing Add:* Med Serv Vet Admin Hosp Pittsburgh PA 15240

EICHENWALD, HEINZ FELIX, b Ger, Mar 3, 26; nat US; m 51; c 3. PEDIATRICS, MICROBIOLOGY. *Educ:* Harvard Univ, AB, 46, Cornell Univ, MD, 50. *Prof Exp:* From instr to prof, Cornell Univ, 55-64; PROF PEDIAT & CHMN DEPT, UNIV TEX HEALTH SCI CTR DALLAS, 64- *Concurrent Pos:* USPHS career res investr award, 63; consult, USPHS, 55-; chmn antibiotics panel I, Nat Drug Study, Nat Res Coun-Nat Acad Sci, 67-70; vis prof, Fac Med, Univ Saigon, 69-; dir pediat prog, AMA-Vietnam Med Sch Proj, 69-; mem nat adv coun, Nat Inst Child Health & Human Develop, 69-; consult, Food & Drug Admin, 70-; mem res comt, United Cerebral Palsy Found, 70-; mem, Bd Maternal, Child & Family Health, Nat Res Coun-Nat Acad Sci, 73- & Bd Dir, Lamplighter Sch, Winston Sch, Children's Develop Ctr; chief of staff, Children's Med Ctr, Dallas; pediatrician in chief, Parkland Hosp, Dallas; consult, various hosps. *Honors & Awards:* USPHS career res investr award, 63; Markle Award, 53; von Humboldt Prize, 78; Weinstein-Goldensen Award, Fed Repub Ger, 79; Med Res Award, United Cerebral Palsy Res Found, 79. *Mem:* Am Pediat Soc; Infectious Dis Soc Am; Harvey Soc; Soc Pediat Res; Sci Res Soc Am. *Res:* Infectious diseases of children; host-parasite interaction. *Mailing Add:* Dept of Pediat Univ Tex Health Sci Ctr Dallas TX 75235

EICHER, DON LAUREN, b Lincoln, Nebr, Dec 12, 30; m 54. GEOLOGY. *Educ:* Univ Colo, BA, 54, MS, 55; Yale Univ, PhD(geol), 58. *Prof Exp:* From asst prof to assoc prof, 58-70, PROF GEOL, UNIV COLO, BOULDER, 70- *Mem:* Geol Soc Am; Paleont Soc. *Res:* Cretaceous micropaleontology; stratigraphy; marine paleocology. *Mailing Add:* Dept of Geol Sci Univ of Colo Boulder CO 80302

EICHER, EVA MAE, b Kalamazoo, Mich, Sept 26, 39. GENETICS. *Educ:* Kalamazoo Col, BA, 61; Univ Rochester, MS, 63, PhD(genetics), 67. *Prof Exp:* Res assoc, Univ Rochester, 67-70; assoc staff scientist, 71-73, STAFF SCIENTIST, JACKSON LAB, 73- *Concurrent Pos:* Lectr, Univ Rochester, 68; investr, Oak Ridge Nat Lab, 70-71. *Honors & Awards:* Donald R Charles Mem Award, Univ Rochester, 64. *Mem:* AAAS; Genetics Soc Am; Soc Develop Biol. *Res:* Mammalian genetics; mouse cytogenetics; mammalian x-chromosome; neurological mutations. *Mailing Add:* Jackson Lab Bar Harbor ME 04609

EICHER, GEORGE J, b Bremerton, Wash, Aug 27, 16; m 51; c 2. FISH BIOLOGY. *Educ:* Ore State Univ, BS, 41. *Prof Exp:* Field party leader, US Bur Fisheries, 39-41; free lance writer, 41-43; chief fisheries biologist, Ariz Game & Wildlife Comn, 43-47; proj leader, US Fish & Wildlife Serv, 47-56; aquatic biologist, Portland Gen Elec Co, 56-71, mgr dept environ serv, 71-78; PRES, EICHER ASSOCS, INC, 78- *Concurrent Pos:* Consult indust & govt orgn, US & Can, 57- *Mem:* Am Fisheries Soc (1st & 2nd vpres, 62-64, pres, 64); Wildlife Soc; Am Soc Limnol & Oceanog; Am Inst Fishery Res Biol; fel Int Acad Fishery Sci. *Res:* Fish behavior; fish passage at dams; red salmon in Alaska; aquatic weed control. *Mailing Add:* 8787 SW Becker Dr Portland OR 97223

EICHER, JOHN HAROLD, b Dayton, Ohio, Mar 30, 21; m 57; c 2. ORGANIC CHEMISTRY. *Educ:* Purdue Univ, BS, 42, PhD(chem), 52. *Prof Exp:* Asst mineral, Purdue Univ, 42, org chem, 45-48 & asst instr, 48-51; Am Petrol Inst asst, Ohio State Univ, 43; chemist, Manhattan Proj, Carbide & Carbon Chem Corp, SAM Labs, Columbia Univ, 43-45; res consult, Tungston Plantation, Newport Ships, 51-52; from asst prof to assoc prof, 52-78, PROF CHEM, MIAMI UNIV, 78- *Concurrent Pos:* Faculty res fel, Miami Univ, 58. *Mem:* AAAS; Am Chem Soc. *Res:* Gas viscosities; natural products; organic nitrogen compounds; stereochemistry. *Mailing Add:* Dept of Chem 216 Hughes Labs Miami Univ Oxford OH 45056

EICHHOLZ, ALEXANDER, b Zagreb, Yugoslavia, Dec 12, 27; US citizen; m 55. BIOCHEMISTRY. *Educ:* Blackburn Col, BA, 54; Univ Ill, MS, 60, PhD(biochem), 62. *Prof Exp:* From instr to asst prof biochem, Chicago Med Sch, 62-66; from asst prof to assoc prof physiol, 66-78, PROF PHYSIOL & BIOPHYS, RUTGERS MED SCH, 78- *Concurrent Pos:* Schweppe Found fel, 63-; Chicago Med Sch bd trustees res award, 65. *Mem:* AAAS; Fedn Am Soc Exp Biol; Am Soc Cell Biol; Brit Biochem Soc. *Res:* Membrane structure and transport; intestinal transport. *Mailing Add:* 3 Wimple Way Bridgewater NJ 08876

EICHHOLZ, GEOFFREY G(UNTHER), b Hamburg, Ger, June 29, 20; US citizen. PHYSICS, NUCLEAR ENGINEERING. *Educ:* Univ Leeds, BSc, 42, PhD(physics), 47, DSc, 79. *Prof Exp:* Exp officer radar develop, Brit Admiralty, 42-46; demonstr physics, Univ Leeds, 46-47; asst prof, Univ BC, 47-51; head radiation lab & physics & radiotracer subdiv, Can Bur Mines, 51-63; REGENTS PROF NUCLEAR ENG, GA INST TECHNOL, 63- *Concurrent Pos:* Lectr, Univ Ottawa, 56-58; Int Atomic Energy Agency regional adv, Southeast Asia, 68, 78; vis prof, Mex, 72, 74 & Iran, 78. *Mem:* Am Phys Soc; Health Physics Soc; fel Am Nuclear Soc; Can Asn Physicists; fel Brit Phys Soc. *Res:* Industrial applications of radioisotopes; radiation effects; activation analysis; semiconductors; nuclear radiation detectors; environmental aspects of nuclear technology; architectural acoustics; radioactive waste management. *Mailing Add:* 1784 Noble Dr NE Atlanta GA 30306

EICHHORN, EDGAR LEO, chemical physics, see previous edition

EICHHORN, GUNTHER LOUIS, b Frankfurt am Main, Ger, Feb 8, 27; nat US; m 64; c 2. INORGANIC BIOCHEMISTRY. *Educ:* Univ Louisville, AB, 47; Univ Ill, MS, 48, PhD(chem), 50. *Prof Exp:* Asst inorg chem, Univ Ill, 47-49, asst, General Aniline stipend, 49-50; asst prof inorg chem, Univ La, 50-54, assoc prof, 54-57; assoc prof, Georgetown Univ, 57-58; chief, Sect Molecular Biol, Gerontol Res Ctr, Nat Heart Inst, Md, 58-66; chief, Sect Molecular Biol, 66-78, CHIEF, LAB CELLULAR MOLECULAR BIOL & HEAD, SECT INORG BIOCHEM, GERONTOL RES CTR, NAT INST ON AGING, NIH, 78- *Concurrent Pos:* Sr asst scientist, Nat Inst Mental Health, USPHS, 54-57; distinguished lectr, Mich State Univ, 71; mem, Panel on Nickel, Nat Res Coun, 73-75; co-ed, Advan Inorg & Biochem, 79- *Mem:* Fel AAAS; fel Geront Soc; Am Inst Chem; Am Chem Soc; Am Soc Biol Chem. *Res:* Function of metals in biological processes; hemoproteins; metal ion catalysis; coordination chemistry; nucleic acids; gerontology; metal ions and the transfer of genetic information; metal ions and aging. *Mailing Add:* Ger Res Ctr Nat Inst Aging NIH Baltimore City Hosp Baltimore MD 21224

EICHHORN, HEINRICH KARL, b Vienna, Austria, Nov 30, 27; nat US; m 52, 77; c 4. ASTRONOMY, STATISTICAL ANALYSIS. *Educ:* Univ Vienna, PhD(astron), 49. *Prof Exp:* From instr to asst prof, Univ Vienna, 50-56; asst prof astron, Georgetown Univ, 56-69; assoc prof, Wesleyan Univ, 59-64; prof & chmn, Dept Astron, Univ South Fla, 64-79; PROF & CHMN, DEPT ASTRON, UNIV FLA, 75- *Concurrent Pos:* Brit Coun scholar, Univ Glasgow, 51-52; Int Coop Admin fel, McCormick Observ, 54-56; sr consult, Geonautics, Inc, 57-70; consult, Radio Corp Am Serv Co, 59, Perkin-Elmer Co, 62, Smithsonian Astrophys Observ, 61-63, Yale Univ Observ, 63-64 & 74-75, Minneapolis Honeywell Regulator Co, 64, Geo-Space Co, 65, US Army Map Serv, 65-70 & Lockheed Missiles & Space Co, 80-; vis prof, Univ Vienna, 71, Univ Graz, 71 & 76 & Yale Univ, 76; grants, NSF, NASA, US Army, US Air Force & US Naval Res Lab; partic & lectr, nat & int conf astron; hon prof, Univ Graz, Austria, 76- *Mem:* Am Astron Soc; Int Astron Union (vpres, 76-79). *Res:* Photographic astrometry; positional astronomy; celestial mechanics; stellar dynamics; statistical adjustment of data. *Mailing Add:* Dept Astron Univ Fla Gainesville FL 32611

EICHHORN, J(ACOB), b Sheboygan, Wis, Sept 14, 24; m 59; c 3. CHEMICAL ENGINEERING. *Educ:* Univ Mich, BS, 46, MS, 47, PhD(chem eng), 50. *Prof Exp:* Mem staff, 50-56, div leader, 56-61, mgr spec proj, Plastics Dept, 61-62, develop mgr, Packaging Dept, 62-66, mgr spec proj, 66-68, exec asst, 68-71, ventures mgr, Plastics Dept, 71-79, LAB DIR, DOW CHEM CO, 79- *Concurrent Pos:* Instr, Univ Mich, 52-54; mem prog mgt develop, Harvard Univ, 68. *Mem:* Am Chem Soc; Am Inst Chem Engrs. *Res:* Research, development and venture operations. *Mailing Add:* 4501 Arbor Dr Midland MI 48640

EICHHORN, ROGER, b Slayton, Minn, Apr 1, 31; m 52; c 5. HEAT TRANSFER, FLUID MECHANICS. *Educ:* Univ Minn, BEE, 53, MSME, 55, PhD(mech eng), 59. *Prof Exp:* Instr mech eng, Univ Minn, 55-59; from asst prof to assoc prof, Princeton Univ, 59-63, assoc prof aerospace & mech sci, 63-67; prof mech eng & chmn dept, 67-75, actg dean, Col Eng, 75-76, assoc dean res, Grad Sch, 76-78, DEAN, COL ENG, UNIV KY, 79- *Concurrent Pos:* Nat Sci Found fel, Imp Col, Univ London, 63-64. *Mem:* AAAS; fel Am Soc Mech Engrs; Am Inst Aeronaut & Astronaut; Am Soc Eng Educ; Nat Soc Prof Engrs. *Res:* Heat Transfer in natural convection; channel and boundary layer flows; multiphase flows. *Mailing Add:* Col Eng 2117 Anderson Hall Univ of Ky Lexington KY 40506

EICHINGER, BRUCE EDWARD, b Canby, Minn, Oct 25, 41; m 62; c 3. POLYMER CHEMISTRY. *Educ:* Univ Minn, BCh, 63; Stanford Univ, PhD(polymer solutions), 67. *Prof Exp:* Fel chem, Yale Univ, 67-68; from asst prof to assoc prof, 68-80, PROF PHYS CHEM, UNIV WASH, 80- *Mem:* Am Chem Soc. *Res:* Thermodynamics of polymer solutions; theory of elasticity. *Mailing Add:* Dept of Chem Univ of Wash Seattle WA 98195

EICHINGER, JACK WALDO, JR, b Ottumwa, Iowa, Sept 11, 04; m 26; c 2. INORGANIC CHEMISTRY. *Educ:* Iowa State Col, BS, 26, PhD(chem), 31. *Prof Exp:* From asst to instr, Iowa State Col, 31-34; asst prof chem, Univ Detroit, 34-37, assoc prof, 37-41; assoc prof, Williams Col, 46-47; prof & coordr nuclear sci prog, Fla State Univ, 48-62; prof, Univ Baghdad, 62-64; prof chem, 64-72, EMER PROF CHEM, FLA STATE UNIV, 72- *Concurrent Pos:* Asst dir chem, US Mil Acad, 44-46. *Mem:* Am Chem Soc. *Res:* Levulose sugar; corrosion of metals; caramels; sour taste of acids; phosphorescence spectroscopy; electron configurations; electron chart. *Mailing Add:* 3284 Longleaf Rd Tallahassee FL 32304

EICHLER, VICTOR B, b Dixon, Ill, July 13, 41; m 65; c 2. EXPERIMENTAL EMBRYOLOGY. *Educ:* Univ Ill, BS, 63, MS, 64; Univ Iowa, PhD(zool, embryol), 69. *Prof Exp:* NIH fels anat, Univ Chicago, 69-71; asst prof biol sci, 71-77, ASSOC PROF BIOL SCI, WICHITA STATE UNIV, 77- *Concurrent Pos:* Danforth tutorship, 70; NASA Am Soc Eng Educ Fel, 75, 76; Danforth Assoc, 78-; guest investr & vis scholar, Mus Comparative Zool, Univ Calif, Berkeley, 79; vis res assoc prof, Dept Biol Sci, Dartmouth Col, 80. *Mem:* AAAS; Am Soc Zoologists; Soc Study Amphibians & Reptiles; Am Asn Anatomists; Soc Neurosci. *Res:* Development, morphology, physiology of vertebrate visual systems and epithalamic structures; influence of environmental lighting on body growth and development; evolution of pineal structures and role in body functions. *Mailing Add:* Dept Biol Sci Box 26 Wichita State Univ Wichita KS 67208

EICHLING, JOHN O, radiation biophysics, see previous edition

EICHMAN, PETER L, b Philadelphia, Pa, Nov 18, 25; m; c 4. NEUROLOGY, MEDICINE. *Educ:* St Joseph's Col, BS, 45; Jefferson Med Col, MD, 49. *Prof Exp:* Intern, Fitzgerald-Mercy Hosp, 49-50; resident, Walter Reed Army Hosp, 50-51; Jefferson Med Col, 51-52, Mayo Found, 52-54 & Univ Wis, 54-55; from instr neuropsychiat to prof neurol & med, Univ Wis-Madison, 55-71, dir student health, 62-65, asst dean clin affairs, 65, dean med sch & dir med ctr, 65-71; dep dir, Bur Health Manpower Educ, NIH, 72-73; PROF NEUROL, UNIV WIS-MADISON, 73- *Concurrent Pos:* Fel, Walter Reed Army Hosp, 50-51, Jefferson Med Col, 51-52, Mayo Found, 52-54 & Univ Wis, 54-55; consult, Vet Admin Hosp, 60-65; State Dept Pub Welfare, 60-65. *Mem:* Am Acad Neurol; Am Col Physicians; AMA; Am Col Health Asn. *Res:* Relationship of perinatal injury and central nervous system defects; trace mineral excretion in porphyria; immunological responses in liver disease; development of a university health service. *Mailing Add:* Dept Neurol Univ Wis Med Sch Madison WI 53706

EICHMANN, GEORGE, b Budapest, Hungary, Nov 3, 36; US citizen; m 62; c 1. ELECTRICAL ENGINEERING. *Educ:* City Col New York, BEE, 61, MEE, 63; City Univ New York, PhD(eng), 68. *Prof Exp:* Jr engr elec eng, Data Syst Div, IBM, 61-62; lectr, 63-68, from asst prof to assoc prof, 68-79, PROF ELEC ENG, CITY COL NEW YORK, 79- *Concurrent Pos:* Nat Sci Found grant, 69-71; City Univ New York Res Found grant, 71-72 & 77-78; Air Force Off Sci Res grant, 77-; consult, Naval Res Lab, Washington, DC, 78-80 & NAm Philips, NY, 79-80. *Mem:* Am Soc Eng Educ; Inst Elec & Electronics Engrs; Optical Soc Am; Soc Photog Instrumentation Engrs. *Res:* Electromagnetic theory; quantum electronics; fiber optics and image processing. *Mailing Add:* Dept Elec Eng City Col New York New York NY 10031

EICHNA, LUDWIG WALDEMAR, b Tallin, Estonia, May 9, 08; nat US. MEDICINE. *Educ:* Univ Pa, AB, 29, MD, 32. *Prof Exp:* Asst instr, Sch Med, Univ Pa, 34-35; instr med, Sch Med, Johns Hopkins Univ, 36-40; instr med, Col Med, NY Univ, 40; from asst prof to prof, 41-60; prof med & chmn dept, State Univ NY Downstate Med Ctr, 60-74; RETIRED. *Concurrent Pos:* Fel, Sch Med, Johns Hopkins Univ, 36-40, Commonwealth fel & asst physician, Hosp, 36-40, asst vis physician, 47-; vis physician & dir med serv, Kings County Hosp, Brooklyn, 60-74; mem fel sect, Comt on Growth, Nat Res Coun, 53, Comt Cardiovasc Syst, 54, chmn, 57, med fel bd, 56; mem res coun, Pub Health Res Inst, 57; mem comt clin invest, Nat Found, 58; med scientist training comt, NIH, 63; panel & review comt, Health Res Coun, NY City. *Mem:* Am Soc Clin Invest; Am Physiol Soc; Soc Exp Biol & Med; Asn Prof Med (pres, 69-70); Asn Am Physicians (pres, 70-71). *Res:* Cardiovascular investigation involving hemodynamics of congestive heart failure. *Mailing Add:* 210 Columbia Heights Brooklyn NY 11203

EICHNER, EDUARD, b Cleveland, Ohio, Nov 11, 05; m 31; c 2. OBSTETRICS, GYNECOLOGY. *Educ:* Western Reserve Univ, AB, 25, MD, 29; Am Bd Obstet & Gynec, dipl. *Prof Exp:* Jr vis obstetrician & gynecologist, 36-41, dir, Family Planning Clin, 69-78, ASSOC, MT SINAI HOSP, 41-; ASSOC CLIN PROF REPRODUCTIVE BIOL, SCH MED, CASE WESTERN RESERVE UNIV, 73- *Concurrent Pos:* Dir educ, St Ann Hosp, 49-56; consult, Cleveland State Hosp, 49-74; asst clin prof obstet & gynec, Sch Med, Case Western Reserve Univ, 54-73; dir res obstet & gynec, Mt Sinai Hosp, 58-, asst dir, Div Obstet-Gynec, 69-73; med dir, Preterm-Cleveland, 73-78, consult, 78- *Honors & Awards:* Gold Award, Ohio State Med Asn, 55. *Mem:* AAAS; Endocrine Soc; Soc Exp Biol & Med; Am Col Surg; Am Col Obstet & Gynec. *Res:* Medicine; anatomy; pathology; physiology; pharmacology; gynecic lymphatics; physiology fertility, pregnancy and labor; internal and external genitalia; effects of drugs on mother and fetus in pregnancy, labor and the neonatal period. *Mailing Add:* Severance Med Art Bldg Suite 712 5 Severance Circle Cleveland OH 44118

EICHNER, EDWARD RANDOLPH, b Fort Wayne, Ind, Mar 7, 38; m 62; c 3. HEMATOLOGY. *Educ:* Baylor Univ, BA, 59; Johns Hopkins Univ, MD, 63. *Prof Exp:* Fel hematol, Univ Wash, 68-70, instr med, 70-71; from asst prof to prof med, Sch Med, La State Univ, Shreveport, 71-76, chief hematol & oncol, 71-76; PROF MED & CLIN PROF PATH, UNIV OKLA SCH MED, 77-, CHIEF HEMATOL & ONCOL, 77- *Mem:* Am Fedn Clin Res; Am Soc Hematol; Soc Exp Biol & Med. *Res:* Effect of ethanol on hematologic and nutritional status of man; effect of ethanol and other drugs on human folate and other vitamin metabolism. *Mailing Add:* Sect Hematol & Oncol Univ Okla Health Sci Ctr Oklahoma City OK 73190

EICHORN, PAUL ANTHONY, b Boston, Mass, Aug 8, 16; m 47; c 4. CYTOLOGY, RESEARCH ADMINISTRATION. *Educ:* Boston Col, AB, 41, MA, 42; Weston Col, PhL, 42; Fordham Univ, PhD(biol), 46. *Prof Exp:* Lab asst biol, Fordham Univ, 42-44; prof, Seton Hall Col, 46-47; dir clin invest, Lederle Labs, 47-49; cytologist & biologist, Lederle Labs, 49-55; consult, 55-56, tech dir vet div, Warner-Chilcott Labs, 56-57; dir new prod coord, Warner-Lambert Res Inst, 57-66; mgr, Tech Planning & Info Div, 66-75, ASST TO DIR ADMIN & TECH SERV, PHILIP MORIS RES CTR, 75- *Concurrent Pos:* Mem adv bd, Adlephi Univ, 60-62. *Mem:* AAAS; NY Acad Sci; Inst Mgt Sci; Planning Exec Inst; Nat Conf Advan Res. *Res:* Research, organization and administration; technical planning and assessment; psychology; physiology; management information systems; patents; tobacco agriculture technology. *Mailing Add:* Philip Morris Res Ctr Box 26583 Richmond VA 23261

EICHTEN, ESTIA JOSEPH, b Stillwater, Minn, Oct 12, 46. FIELD THEORY. *Educ:* Mass Inst Technol, BS, 68, PhD(physics), 72. *Prof Exp:* Res asst, Stanford Linear Accelerator Ctr, 72-74 & 74-77; asst prof physics, Harvard Univ, 77-81; ASSOC SCIENTIST, FERMI NAT ACCELERATOR CTR, 81- *Concurrent Pos:* vis scientist, Enrico Fermi Inst, Univ Chicago, 81- *Res:* Theoretical high energy particle physics; dynamical symmetry; breaking; lattice gauge theories; phenomenology. *Mailing Add:* Theory Group Fermi Nat Accelerator Lab PO Box 500 Batavia IL 60510

EICHWALD, ERNEST J, b Ger, Dec 13, 13; nat US; m 41; c 3. PATHOLOGY. *Educ:* Univ Freiburg, MD, 38; Univ Utah, MD, 53. *Prof Exp:* Instr path, Med Sch, Harvard Univ, 46-48; from asst prof to assoc prof, Univ Utah, 48-54; dir lab exp med, Mont Deaconess Hosp, 54-66; prof microbiol, Mont State Univ, 66-70; PROF PATH & SURG & CHMN DEPT PATH, COL MED, UNIV UTAH, 70- *Concurrent Pos:* Ed, Transplantation Bull, 53-61; ed adv, Cancer Res, 54-57; chmn comt tissue transplantation, Nat Acad Sci-Nat Res Coun, 57-69; ed, Transplantation, 61-; dir, McLaughlin Res Inst, Great Falls, Mont, 66-70. *Mem:* Am Soc Exp Path; Soc Exp Biol & Med; Am Asn Cancer Res; Am Asn Path & Bact. *Res:* Transplantation immunity. *Mailing Add:* Dept of Path Col of Med Univ of Utah Med Ctr Salt Lake City UT 84112

EICK, HARRY ARTHUR, b Rock Island, Ill, Dec 9, 29; m 54; c 8. SOLID STATE CHEMISTRY, RARE EARTH CHEMISTRY. *Educ:* St Ambrose Col, BS, 50; Univ Iowa, PhD(chem), 56. *Prof Exp:* Asst prof chem, Univ Ky, 56-57; res assoc, Univ Kans, 57-58; from asst prof to assoc prof, 58-67, assoc chmn dept, 70-71, interim dir comput lab, 71-72, PROF CHEM, MICH STATE UNIV, 67-, ASSOC DEAN, COL NATURAL SCI, 74- *Mem:* Am Chem Soc; Am Crystallog Asn. *Res:* Solid state preparatory and x-ray diffraction studies on lanthanide halide compounds. *Mailing Add:* Col of Natural Sci Mich State Univ East Lansing MI 48824

EICKELBERG, W WARREN B, b New York, NY, Jan 19, 25; m 52; c 4. BIOMECHANICS. *Educ:* Hope Col, AB, 49; Wesleyan Univ, MA, 51. *Prof Exp:* Assoc prof, 52-69, PROF BIOL, ADELPHI UNIV, 69- *Concurrent Pos:* Dir develop, Adelphi Univ, 58-60, vpres, 60-66; res consult, Human Resources Ctr; mem biochem consult group, President's Comt Employ the Handicapped, 70-71; chmn premed curriculum, Adelphi Univ, 70. *Mem:* AAAS; Int Soc Biomech; Sigma Xi; NY Acad Sci. *Res:* Cell physiology; protein metabolism; neurophysiology; industrial physiology and ergonomics. *Mailing Add:* Dept of Biol Adelphi Univ Garden City NY 11530

EICKHOFF, THEODORE C, b Cleveland, Ohio, Sept 13, 31; m 52; c 3. MEDICINE. *Educ:* Valparaiso Univ, AB, 53; Western Reserve Univ, MD, 57; Am Bd Internal Med, dipl, 66. *Prof Exp:* Dept chief invests sect, Epidemiol Br, Commun Dis Ctr, USPHS, 64-66, chief bact dis sect, 66-67; asst prof med, 67-68, assoc prof med, 68-75, head div infectious dis, 69-80, PROF MED, MED CTR, UNIV COLO, 75-, V CHMN DEPT MED, 76- *Concurrent Pos:* Mem comt meningococcal infections, Armed Forces Epidemiol Bd, 64-73, assoc mem comn acute respiratory dis, 65-73; assoc mem comn influenza, 69-73; clin asst prof prev med, Sch Med, Emory Univ, 64-67; consult, Fitzsimons Army Hosp, 68-; consult to med dir, NASA, 69-72; mem adv comt immunization practices, USPHS, 70-74; mem infectious dis test comt, Am Bd Internal Med, 73-80; mem ed bd, Antimicrobial Agents & Chemother, 74-; consult, Bur Biologies, Food & Drug

Admin Centers for Dis Control; mem comt on infections within hosps, Am Hosp Asn; dir, Dept Med, Denver Gen Hosp, 78-81. *Mem:* AAAS; Infectious Dis Soc Am; NY Acad Sci; Am Soc Microbiol; Am Fedn Clin Res. *Res:* Internal medicine; infectious diseases. *Mailing Add:* Dept Med Box B168 Univ Colo Med Ctr Denver CO 80220

EICKHOLT, THEODORE HENRY, b Springfield, Minn, July 17, 32. PHARMACOLOGY. *Educ:* Univ Minn, BS, 55, PhD(pharmacol), 62. *Prof Exp:* Asst prof pharmacol, 63-66, assoc prof, 66-72, PROF PHARMACOL, NORTHEAST LA UNIV, 72- *Mem:* Soc Toxicol. *Res:* Iron absorption and its mechanisms of control; gastrointestinal activity of cathartics; activity studies in laboratory animals; analgesic studies of the phenothiazine compounds. *Mailing Add:* Sch of Pharm Northeast La Univ Monroe LA 71209

EICKSTAEDT, LAWRENCE LEE, b Davenport, Iowa, July 20, 39; m 60; c 2. ECOLOGY, MARINE BIOLOGY. *Educ:* Buena Vista Col, BS, 61; Univ Iowa, MS, 64; Stanford Univ, PhD(biol), 69. *Prof Exp:* Asst prof biol, Calif State Col, Hayward & Moss Landing Marine Labs, 68-69; asst prof, State Univ NY Col Old Westbury, 69-70; MEM FAC BIOL, EVERGREEN STATE COL, 70- *Mem:* AAAS. *Res:* Ecological physiology; reproductive biology of marine invertebrates; environmental design. *Mailing Add:* Dept of Biol Evergreen State Col Olympia WA 98505

EICKWORT, GEORGE CAMPBELL, b New York, NY, June 8, 40; m 65; c 3. SYSTEMATICS. *Educ:* Mich State Univ, BS, 62, MS, 63; Univ Kans, PhD(entom), 67. *Prof Exp:* From asst prof to assoc prof, 67-78, PROF ENTOM, STATE UNIV NY COL AGR & LIFE SCI, CORNELL UNIV, 78- *Concurrent Pos:* Consult, Harvard Univ Mus Comp Zool, 70 & Time-Life Books, 74-; res assoc entom div, Univ Calif, Berkeley, 75-76; vis prof entom, Univ Calif, Davis, 79. *Mem:* AAAS; Asn Trop Biol; Entom Soc Am; Int Union Study Social Insects. *Res:* Systematics, morphology, behavior and ecology of wild bees; systematics and biology of mites associated with insects. *Mailing Add:* Dept of Entom St U NY Col Agr Life Sci Cornell Ithaca NY 14853

EIDELBERG, EDUARDO, b Lima, Peru, Apr 30, 30; m 56; c 2. PHYSIOLOGY. *Educ:* San Marcos Univ, Lima, MD, 55. *Prof Exp:* Assoc res prof anat, Univ Calif, Los Angeles, 57-61; res prof neurophysiol, Ariz State Univ, 61-69; chmn div neurobiol, Barrow Neurol Inst, 61-77; adj prof neurol, Col Med, Univ Ariz, 71-77; PROF NEUROSURG & PHYSIOL, UNIV TEX HEALTH SCI CTR, SAN ANTONIO, 77- *Concurrent Pos:* Med investr, Vet Admin. *Res:* Physiology of the nervous system; physiology of movement control; spinal cord injury. *Mailing Add:* Vet Admin Hosp 112-D 7400 Merton Minter Blvd San Antonio TX 78284

EIDELS, LEON, b Jersey City, NJ, May 25, 42; m 73; c 2. BIOCHEMISTRY. *Educ:* Univ Calif, Davis, BS, 64, MS, 66, PhD(biochem), 69. *Prof Exp:* Teaching asst biochem, Univ Calif, Davis, 66-69; res assoc microbiol, Health Ctr, Univ Conn, 70-74; asst prof microbiol, 74-80, ASSOC PROF MICROBIOL, UNIV TEX HEALTH SCI CTR, DALLAS, 80- *Concurrent Pos:* Arthritis Found fel, 70-73. *Mem:* AAAS; Am Soc Microbiol; Sigma Xi; Am Soc Biol Chemists; Am Asn Immunologists. *Res:* Biochemistry of cell-surface immunoglobulins, biosynthesis and translocation; biochemistry of diphtheria toxin and its receptor. *Mailing Add:* Dept of Microbiol Univ Tex Southwestern Med Sch Dallas TX 75235

EIDER, NORMAN GEORGE, b Brooklyn, NY, May 3, 30; m 54; c 4. ANALYTICAL CHEMISTRY. *Educ:* City Univ NY, BS, 52. *Prof Exp:* Jr chemist, Ames Lab, US AEC, Iowa State Univ, 52-54; sr chemist, Uniroyal Chem Div, US Rubber Co, 56-67; group leader anal chem, 67-76, LAB MGR CHEM ANAL, TENNECO CHEM INC, 76- *Mem:* Am Chem Soc; Am Soc Testing Mat. *Res:* Analytical method research and development in wet chemical analysis; atomic absorption spectrophotometry, gas chromatography and infrared analysis. *Mailing Add:* Tenneco Chem Inc PO Box 365 Piscataway NJ 08854

EIDINGER, DAVID, b Montreal, Que, Jan 4, 31; m 57; c 2. MICROBIOLOGY, IMMUNOLOGY. *Educ:* McGill Univ, BSc, 52, PhD(anat), 58; Columbia Univ, MD, 59. *Prof Exp:* Demonstr anat, Columbia Univ, 55-56; res assoc allergy, Royal Victoria Hosp, Montreal, Que, 61-64; from asst prof to prof microbiol, 73-77; head dept, 77-80, PROF MICROBIOL, UNIV SASKATCHEWAN, 77- *Concurrent Pos:* Fel, Banting Res Found, Can, 53-54; Ont Heart Found grant, 64-; Nat Cancer Inst grant, 67-; Med Res Coun grant, 67-; res assoc, Can Heart Found, 61-64; dir, Clin Microbiol & Immunol Labs, Univ Hosp, 77- *Mem:* Brit Soc Immunol; Can Soc Immunol; Can Soc Microbiol. *Res:* Mechanism of antigenic competition; cell cooperation in delayed hypersensitivity; effect of hormonal changes on immune response. *Mailing Add:* Dept of Microbiol Univ of Saskatchewan Saskatoon SK S7H 0W0 Can

EIDINOFF, MAXWELL LEIGH, b New York, NY, Feb 16, 15; m 38; c 2. PHYSICAL CHEMISTRY, BIOCHEMISTRY. *Educ:* Brooklyn Col, BA, 34; Pa State Col, PhD(phys chem), 38. *Prof Exp:* Asst phys chem, Pa State Col, 34-38; instr chem, Queens Col (NY), 38-42; res supvr div war res, Columbia Univ, 42-43; res group leader, Metall Lab, Univ Chicago, 43-44; from asst prof to assoc prof, 45-59, PROF CHEM, QUEENS COL (NY), 59- *Concurrent Pos:* Assoc mem, Sloan-Kettering Inst Cancer Res, NY, 49-66, assoc scientist, 66-70. *Mem:* Am Chem Soc; Am Asn Cancer Res; Am Asn Biol Chem. *Res:* Biochemistry of viruses; low temperature calorimetry; statistical mechanics; isotope exchange and separation; isotope mass effects in chemical reaction rates; radiochemical measurements; application of radioactive tracers in medical research; intermediary metabolism studies. *Mailing Add:* Dept of Chem Queens Col Flushing NY 11367

EIDMAN, RICHARD AUGUST LOUIS, b Belleville, Ill, Sept 19, 36; m 59; c 3. CHEMICAL ENGINEERING. *Educ:* Washington Univ, St Louis, BS, 58, ScD(chem eng), 63. *Prof Exp:* Engr polyolefins res, Sabine River Works, 63-66, tech rep, Polyolefins Div, Plastics Dept, 66-77, PROD SPECIALIST, CHESTNUT RUN LABS, E I DU PONT DE NEMOURS & CO, 77- *Mem:* Tech Asn Pulp & Paper Indust. *Res:* Physical and chemical treatment of surfaces of high polymers; physical properties of polymers and relationships with molecular parameters; extrusion coatings. *Mailing Add:* Plastics Dept Chestnut Run Labs E I du Pont de Nemours & Co Wilmington DE 19898

EIDSON, WILLIAM WHELAN, b Indianapolis, Ind, July 22, 35; m 60; c 3. NUCLEAR PHYSICS, ATOMIC PHYSICS. *Educ:* Tulane Univ, BS, 57; Ind Univ, MS, 59, PhD(physics), 61. *Prof Exp:* Teaching asst physics, Ind Univ, 57-59, from instr to assoc prof, 61-67; prof & chmn dept, Univ Mo-St Louis, 67-72; PROF PHYSICS & ATMOSPHERIC SCI & HEAD DEPT, DREXEL UNIV, 72- *Mem:* AAAS; Am Asn Physics Teachers; Am Physics Soc; Inst Elec & Electronic Engrs; NY Acad Sci. *Res:* Accelerator studies of nuclear structure and reaction mechanisms; nuclear instrumentation; solid state detectors; ion-electron recombination; corona discharge signature analysis; world energy impact studies. *Mailing Add:* Dept of Physics & Atmos Sci Drexel Univ Philadelphia PA 19104

EIDT, DOUGLAS CONRAD, b Fergus, Ont, July 2, 28; m 51; c 5. ECOLOGY, TOXICOLOGY. *Educ:* Univ Guelph, BSA, 50; Univ Toronto, MSA, 52; Univ Sask, PhD(biol), 56. *Prof Exp:* Res officer entom, Agr Can, 51-56; RES SCIENTIST ENTOM, CAN FORESTRY SERV, 56- *Concurrent Pos:* Forest entom, Food & Agr Org of UN, 61-63; sci ed, Entom Soc Can, 78- *Mem:* Entom Soc Can; Can Soc Environ Biologists; Freshwater Biol Asn; NAm Benthological Soc. *Res:* Effects of forest harvesting and forest spraying on aquatic invertebrates. *Mailing Add:* Maritimes Forest Res Ctr PO Box 4000 Fredericton NB E3B 5A7 Can

EIDT, ROBERT C, b Mt Pleasant, Mich, Jan 20, 23; m 56; c 2. SOILS ANALYSIS. *Educ:* Univ Calif, Los Angeles, AB, 47, MA, 51, PhD(geog), 54. *Prof Exp:* Instr geog, Univ Minn, 54-56; from asst prof to prof, Calif State Univ, Los Angeles, 56-67; prof geog, 67-81, DIR, STATE SOILS LAB, UNIV WIS-MILWAUKEE, 81- *Concurrent Pos:* Consult, Fulbright Prog, US Dept State, 60-65 & Lockheed Int, 65; NSF sr res grants, Europe & Latin Am, 64-66, 69-70 & 74-; corresp mem, Pan Am Inst Regional Geog & Hist, Orgn Am States, 66-74; assoc ed, Geoforum, 68-; ed geosci, Pergamon Press, Braunschweig, Ger, 72-73; consult ed, Encycl Britannica, 74-; mem adv bd, Ctr Latin Am, Univ Wis-Milwaukee, 75- *Mem:* Am Meteorol Soc; Asn Am Geogrs; Soil Sci Soc Am; Sigma Xi. *Res:* Position, form, structure and distribution of settlements according to genesis, function, and evolution; phosphate soil analysis for interpreting abandoned settlement sites. *Mailing Add:* Soils Lab Univ of Wis-Milwaukee Milwaukee WI 53201

EIDUSON, SAMUEL, b Buffalo, NY, Dec 15, 18; c 1. NEUROCHEMISTRY. *Educ:* Univ Calif, Los Angeles, BS, 47, PhD(biochem), 52. *Prof Exp:* Res asst chem, Univ Calif, Los Angeles, 48-50, res asst physiol chem, 51-52; res biochemist, Vet Admin Ctr, Los Angeles, 52-54; asst clin prof physiol chem, 57-63, assoc prof psychiat & biol chem, 63-73, PROF BIOL CHEM & PSYCHIATRY, UNIV CALIF, LOS ANGELES, 73- *Concurrent Pos:* USPHS grant, Brain Res Inst, Univ Calif, Los Angeles, 74-75, Ralph L Smith Found grant, 74-; Prin scientist & chief neurobiochem res, Brentwood Neuro-psychiat Hosp Los Angeles, Vet Admin Ctr, 52-61; consult neurobiochem lab, 61-; chief res biochemist, Neuropsychiat Inst, Univ Calif, Los Angeles, 62-70, dep dir training & educ, Brain Res Inst, 74-; consult, Career Res Scientist Develop Award Prog, NIMH, 67-71, Biol Sci Training Rev Comt, 74-78. *Mem:* AAAS; Am Soc Biol Chem; Am Soc Neurochem; Int Soc Neurochem; Int Soc Develop Psychobiol (treas, 70-71, pres, 73-74). *Res:* Investigation of monoamine oxidase; also and forms in blood platelets of human schizophrenic and control subjects. *Mailing Add:* Dept of Biol Chem Sch of Med Univ of Calif Ctr for Health Sci Los Angeles CA 90024

EIFRIG, DAVID ERIC, b Oak Park, Ill, Jan 4, 35; m 57; c 4. OPHTHALMOLOGY. *Educ:* Carleton Col, BA, 56; Johns Hopkins Univ, MD, 60; Am Bd Ophthal, dipl. *Prof Exp:* Asst prof ophthal, Univ Ky, 68-70; assoc prof ophthal, Univ Minn, Minneapolis, 70-77; PROF & CHMN DEPT OPHTHAL, UNIV NC, CHAPEL HILL, 77- *Mem:* Retina Soc; Am Acad Ophthal; Am Col Surgeons. *Res:* Intraocular lenses; choriocapillaris. *Mailing Add:* Dept of Ophthal Univ of NC Chapel Hill NC 27514

EIGEL, EDWIN GEORGE, JR, b St Louis, Mo, June 4, 32; m 59; c 2. MATHEMATICS. *Educ:* Mass Inst Technol, BS, 54; St Louis Univ, PhD(math), 61. *Prof Exp:* From asst prof to prof math, St Louis Univ, 69-79, acad vpres, 72-79; PROF MATH, PROVOST & ACAD VPRES, UNIV BRIDGEPORT, 79- *Concurrent Pos:* Asst to dean grad sch, St Louis Univ, 65-67, actg dean, 67-68, dean, 68-71, assoc acad vpres, 71-72; Danforth assoc, 64-; comnr, McDonnell Planetarium, St Louis, 72-79. *Mem:* Am Math Soc; Sigma Xi; Math Asn Am. *Res:* Numerical applications of functional analysis; theory of approximation; analytic theory of numbers. *Mailing Add:* Univ Bridgeport Park & Univ Aves Bridgeport CT 06602

EIGEN, EDWARD, b New York, NY, June 29, 23; m 45; c 2. CHEMISTRY, MICROBIOLOGY. *Educ:* Brooklyn Col, BA, 44, MA, 55. *Prof Exp:* Bacteriologist, Food Res Labs, 44-46, microbiologist, 47-52; microbiologist, US Vitamin & Pharmaceut Corp, 52-53, asst supvr anal labs, 53-59; sr res biochemist, 59-62, sect head biochem, 62-70, sect head household prod res, 70-75, sr res assoc, 75-79, SR SCIENTIST, COLGATE PALMOLIVE CO, 79- *Mem:* Am Chem Soc; Int Asn Dent Res; NY Acad Sci. *Res:* Isolation of materials from natural products; microbiology; chromatography; oral health and skin research. *Mailing Add:* Colgate Palmolive Co 909 River Rd Piscataway NJ 08854

EIGHME, LLOYD ELWYN, b Wenatchee, Wash, Jan 15, 27; m 51. ENTOMOLOGY, HORTICULTURE. *Educ:* Pac Union Col, BA, 51, MA, 53; Ore State Univ, PhD(entom), 65. *Prof Exp:* Instr biol, Pac Union Col, 58-62; res asst entom, Ore State Univ, 62-65; from asst prof to assoc prof, 65-73, PROF BIOL & AGR, PAC UNION COL, 73- *Mem:* Entom Soc Am; Am Registry Prof Entomologists; Am Hort Soc. *Res:* Applied entomology; insects in stored grain; taxonomy of Hymenoptera, Sphecidae; plant propagation-Ericaceous shrubs. *Mailing Add:* Dept of Biol Pac Union Col Angwin CA 94508

EIGNER, JOSEPH, b Swampscott, Mass, Dec 13, 33; m 63; c 2. ENVIRONMENTAL MANAGEMENT, HAZARDOUS WASTES. *Educ:* Dartmouth Col, AB, 55; Harvard Univ, AM, 58, PhD(phys chem), 60. *Prof Exp:* Netherlands Orgn Health Res fel, State Univ Leiden, 60-62; NSF fel biol chem, Univ Mich, 62-64; asst prof microbiol, Sch Med, Wash Univ, 64-74; chief, Hazardous Waste Proj, Mo Dept Natural Resources, 75-77; dir solid waste proj mgt, Bi-State Develop Agency, 78-80; PRES, JOSEPH EIGNER & CO INC, 81- *Mem:* AAAS. *Res:* Solid waste resource recovery; hazardous waste management. *Mailing Add:* 6802 Waterman Ave St Louis MO 63130

EIKENBARY, RAYMOND DARRELL, b Quay, Okla, Nov 2, 29; m 53; c 5. ENTOMOLOGY, FORESTRY. *Educ:* Okla State Univ, BA, 57; Clemson Univ, MS, 63, PhD(entom), 64. *Prof Exp:* Dist forester, Bur Land Mgt, 57-59; exten agent educ, 59-61, from asst prof to assoc prof, 64-73, PROF ENTOM, OKLA STATE UNIV, 73- *Mem:* Entom Soc Am. *Res:* Ecology; biological control of insects. *Mailing Add:* Dept of Entom Okla State Univ Stillwater OK 74074

EIKENBERRY, JON NATHAN, b Oelwein, Iowa, Jan 15, 42; m 63; c 2. PHYSICAL ORGANIC CHEMISTRY. *Educ:* Iowa State Univ, BS, 63; Tex A&M Univ, MS, 66; Univ Wis, PhD(org chem), 72. *Prof Exp:* Fel bio-org chem, Mass Inst Technol, 72-73; SR RES CHEMIST PHYS ORG CHEM, EASTMAN KODAK CO RES LABS, 73- *Mem:* AAAS; Am Chem Soc; Am Asn Clin Chem. *Res:* Coating of chemical reagents in thin films for quantitative analysis. *Mailing Add:* 168 Pinecrest Dr Rochester NY 14617

EIKREM, LYNWOOD OLAF, b Lansing, Mich, June 11, 19; m 46; c 4. SPECTROCHEMISTRY, INSTRUMENTATION. *Educ:* Mich State Col, BS, 41; Mass Inst Technol, SM, 48. *Prof Exp:* Spectrochemist, Diamond Alkali Co, 41-42; chief spectrochemist, Chrysler Evansville Ord Plant, 42-44; field engr spectros, Harry Dietert Co, 44; assoc prof chem, La Polytech Inst, 46-47; adv fel, Mass Inst Technol, 47-49; tech dir spectros, Jarrell-Ash Co, 49-53; proj engr emission spectros, Baird-Atomic Inc, 53-59; staff engr, Geophys Corp Am, Inc, 59-60; prod develop mgr, David W Mann Co, 60-63, dir mkt, 64-65; vpres, Appl Res Labs, Inc, 65-72; vpres & dir res progs, 73-79, PRES, DARLING, PATERSON & SALZER MGT CONSULTS, 80- *Concurrent Pos:* Chmn, Strategic Directions Int, 81- *Mem:* Optical Soc Am; Am Soc Testing & Mat; NY Acad Sci; fel, Am Inst Chemists; Soc Appl Spectros. *Res:* Design, testing and applications of spectroscopic analytical instrumentation; interferometry; meteorological instrumentation; x-ray; microprocessor applications to analytical instruments. *Mailing Add:* 4902 Alta Canyada Rd La Canada CA 91011

EILBER, FREDERICK RICHARD, b Detroit, Mich, Aug 17, 40; m 65; c 4. SURGERY, ONCOLOGIC SURGERY. *Educ:* Univ Mich Med Sch, MD, 65. *Prof Exp:* Clin assoc surg br, Nat Cancer Inst, NIH, 67-70; asst & chief surg resident, Univ Md Hosp, 71-72; M D Anderson Hosp & Tumor Inst, 72-73; assoc prof, 75-79, PROF SURG, DIV ONCOL, SCH MED, UNIV CALIF, LOS ANGELES, 79- *Concurrent Pos:* Staff surgeon, Vet Admin Hosp, Sepulveda, 73- *Honors & Awards:* Ewing Award, Soc Surg Oncol, 70. *Mem:* Soc Head & Neck Surg; Soc Surg Oncol; Soc Univ Surg; Am Col Surg; Pac Coast Surg Asn. *Res:* Tumor immunology; viral oncology; cancer chemotherapy. *Mailing Add:* 9th Floor Factor Bldg Sch Med John Wayne Cancer Clin Univ Calif Los Angeles CA 90024

EILENBERG, SAMUEL, b Warsaw, Poland, Sept 30, 13; nat US. MATHEMATICS. *Educ:* Univ Warsaw, MA, 34, PhD(math), 36. *Prof Exp:* From instr to assoc prof math, Univ Mich, 40-46; prof, Ind Univ, 46-47; prof, 47-74, UNIV PROF MATH, COLUMBIA UNIV, 74- *Concurrent Pos:* Vis lectr, Princeton Univ, 45-46; vis prof, Fulbright & Guggenheim fel, Paris, 50-51; vis prof, Tata Inst, Bombay, 53-54, 56-57, Hebrew Univ, 54 & Univ Paris, 66-67. *Mem:* Nat Acad Sci; Am Acad Arts & Sci; Am Math Soc; Math Asn Am. *Res:* Topology, algebra and computer mathematics. *Mailing Add:* Dept of Math 522 Math Bldg Columbia Univ New York NY 10027

EILER, HUGO, b Santiago, Chile, Nov 4, 35; m 62; c 3. ENDOCRINOLOGY, REPRODUCTION. *Educ:* Univ Chile, DVM, 60; Univ Ga, MS, 74; Univ Ill, PhD(physiol), 76. *Prof Exp:* Asst prof physiol, Col Vet Med, Univ Chile, 62-66, assoc prof, 67-71, asst prof, Sch Human Med, 63-67, prof, Sch Nursing, 64-71; res assoc endocrinol, Dept Animal Sci, Univ Ill, 71-73, teaching assoc physiol, Col Vet Med, 73-76; ASSOC PROF PHYSIOL, COL VET MED, UNIV TENN, 76- *Mem:* Soc Study Reproduction. *Res:* Development of endocrine testing procedures in animals; endocrine factors affecting the physiology of the uterus. *Mailing Add:* Col Vet Med Univ Tenn PO Box 1071 Knoxville TN 37901

EILER, JOHN JOSEPH, b Jacksonville, Fla, Jan 25, 10; m 44; c 1. BIOCHEMISTRY. *Educ:* Univ Calif, AB, 33, PhD(biochem), 37. *Prof Exp:* Mem enzymes res staff, Cutter Labs, 37-38; from instr to assoc prof biochem & pharm, 38-51, prof, 51-72, prof biochem & biophys, 72-76, asst dean, Col Pharm, 48-56, assoc dean, 56-72, chmn, Dept Pharmaceut Chem, 58-72, EMER PROF BIOCHEM & BIOPHYS, SCH MED, UNIV CALIF, SAN FRANCISCO, 76- *Concurrent Pos:* Consult, USPHS, 47 & US Army, 47-; mem, Int Union Physiol Sci. *Mem:* Am Chem Soc; Soc Exp Biol & Med; Am Pharmaceut Asn; Am Soc Biol Chemists; NY Acad Sci. *Res:* Chemistry and metabolism of purines and nucleic acids; metabolism of carbohydrates; thyroid hormone and renal and intestinal functions; action of drugs on aerobic phosphorylation; biological action of narcotics and stimulants; mode of action of antimitotic agents. *Mailing Add:* 4315 Paradise Dr Tiburon CA 94920

EILERS, FREDERICK IRVING, b Milwaukee, Wis, July 5, 38; m 61; c 2. GENETICS, MYCOLOGY. *Educ:* Univ Wis, Milwaukee, BS, 61; Univ Mich, MS, 63, PhD(bot), 68. *Prof Exp:* Res asst, Univ Mich, 61-64, teaching fel bot, 64-66; instr microbiol, Ohio Wesleyan Univ, 66-67; instr gen biol & plant physiol, Oberlin Col, 67-68; ASSOC PROF MICROBIOL, GENETICS & MYCOL, UNIV SOUTH FLA, 68-, ASST CHMN DEPT, 79- *Concurrent Pos:* Vis prof, Carnegie-Mellon Univ, 75-76. *Res:* Physiology involving fungi such as: mushroom growth, spore germination, mushroom toxins and mushroom cap digestion in the genus Coprinus. *Mailing Add:* Dept Biol Univ S Fla Tampa FL 33612

EILERS, LAWRENCE JOHN, b Ireton, Iowa, May 21, 27; m 49; c 4. PLANT TAXONOMY, PHYTOGEOGRAPHY. *Educ:* State Col Iowa, BS, 49, MA, 60; Univ Iowa, PhD(bot), 64. *Prof Exp:* Instr high schs, Iowa, 49-51; elec engr, Collins Radio Co, 52-56, environ engr, 56-57; environ engr, Admiral Radio Corp, Ill, 57-58; instr sci, Charles City Consol Schs, Iowa, 58-59; instr forest bot, State Univ NY Col Forestry, Syracuse, 64-65; asst prof life sci, Ind State Univ, 65-68; assoc prof, 68-77, PROF BIOL, UNIV NORTHERN IOWA, 77- AAAS; Soc Study Evol; Am Soc Plant Taxon; Bot Soc Am; Am Inst Biol Sci. *Res:* Biosystematics of the genus Sullivantia; flora and phytogeography of the Midwest. *Mailing Add:* Dept of Biol Univ of Northern Iowa Cedar Falls IA 50613

EILERS, RUSSELL JAY, b St Paul, Minn, May 20, 25. CLINICAL PATHOLOGY. *Educ:* Univ Minn, BA, 49, BS, 50, BM, 52, MD, 53. *Prof Exp:* Assoc path, Med Ctr, Univ Kans, 57-58, from asst prof to prof, 61-75, dir clin labs, 58-72, consult to exec vchancellor, 72-75; dir, 75-76, MED DIR, BIO-SCI ENTERPRISES, BIOSCI LABS, 76- *Concurrent Pos:* Mem, Int Comt Standardization Hemat, 64-, pres, 74-76; mem bd dirs & pres, Nat Comt Clin Lab Stand, 68-71. *Mem:* AAAS; AMA; Am Soc Clin Path; Col Am Path; Int Acad Path. *Res:* Creatin metabolism; renal function; quality control programs in clinical laboratories; clinical laboratory methodology. *Mailing Add:* BioSci Labs 7600 Tyrone Ave Van Nuys CA 91405

EILERTS, CHARLES KENNETH, b Charleston, Okla, Nov 7, 04; m 25; c 3. NUMERICAL ANALYSIS, PETROLEUM ENGINEERING. *Educ:* Okla Agr & Mech Col, BS, 26; Univ Tulsa, MS, 63. *Prof Exp:* Mem staff, Indust Process Co, Calif, 27-29; res supvr, Apache Powder Co, Ariz, 29-30; res supvr, 30-49 & 58-63, prin phys chemist, 49-58, res scientist, 63-73, GAS CONSULTANT, US BUR MINES, 73- *Concurrent Pos:* Lectr, French Inst Petrol, 58, Okla State Univ, 59, Univ Tex, 61, Miss State Univ, 62 & Alta Univ, 64. *Honors & Awards:* Hanlon Award, Natural Gas Producers Asn, 69. *Mem:* Am Gas Asn; Am Chem Soc; Am Inst Mining, Metall & Petrol Engrs; Soc Petrol Engrs; Am Inst Mech Engrs. *Res:* Cracking and polymerization of natural hydrocarbon mixtures; properties of nitroglycerine explosives; inhibitors and corrosion resistance of metals; phase relations of gas-condensate fluids; transient flow of natural gas, helium and condensate fluids in reservoirs; pressure-, saturation-, and velocity-dependence of mobility of gas-condensate fluids; transient flow in pipeline networks and fluids in petroleum structures. *Mailing Add:* 811 SE Crown Dr Bartlesville OK 74003

EIME, LESTER OSCAR, b Sappington, Mo, June 22, 22; div. INDUSTRIAL CHEMISTRY. *Educ:* Univ Mo, AB, 44, AM, 47; Ohio State Univ, cert, 69. *Prof Exp:* Instr chem, Christian Col, 44-47; res chemist, Aluminum Co Am res labs, 47-57; Petreco Div, Petrolite Corp, 57-62; sr res chemist, Space & Electronics Div, Emerson Elec Co, 62-65; engr, McDonnell Aircraft Div, McDonnell-Douglas Corp, 65-73; res chemist, Brown Shoe Co, Brown Group, Inc, 73-75; RES CHEMIST, WESTERN LITHOPLATE & SUPPLY CO, DIV BEMIS CO, 76- *Concurrent Pos:* Asst chem, Univ Mo, 46-47. *Mem:* Am Chem Soc. *Res:* Purification of hydrocarbons and other chemicals through electrical and catalytic processes; aluminum organic compounds; pigments for paint, plastics, rubber and paper coating industries; petroleum catalyst preparations; ablative materials and high temperature polymers; electrochemical corrosion studies of metals; printed circuits; urethane adhesives; long wearing lithographic coatings, lithographic developers and chemicals. *Mailing Add:* 111 Pebble Acres Ct St Louis MO 63141

EIMERL, DAVID, b Eng. PHYSICS. *Educ:* Oxford Univ, Eng, BA, 69; Northwestern Univ, PhD(physics), 73. *Prof Exp:* Res physicist physics, Univ Calif, San Diego, 73-75; staff scientist, Phys Dynamics, Inc, 75-76; STAFF SCIENTIST LASER FUSION, LAWRENCE LIVERMORE LAB, UNIV CALIF, 76- *Concurrent Pos:* Consult, Phys Dynamics, Inc, 76-77. *Mem:* Am Phys Soc. *Res:* Raman scattering; Raman compressors; amplified spontaneous emission and parasitics control in large lasers; laser system design for laser fusion applications; theoretical physics. *Mailing Add:* Lawrence Livermore Lab L-472 PO Box 5508 Livermore CA 94550

EINARSSON, ALFRED W, b Berkeley, Calif, Apr 13, 15; m 47; c 2. PHYSICS. *Educ:* Univ Calif, PhD(physics), 46. *Prof Exp:* Asst prof physics, Univ Southern Calif, 46-50; asst prof, 50-57, PROF PHYSICS, SAN JOSE STATE COL, 57- *Mem:* Am Phys Soc; Int Soc Solar Energy. *Res:* General physics; physical optics; electrical conduction in gases. *Mailing Add:* Dept of Physics San Jose State Univ San Jose CA 95192

EINAUDI, FRANCO, b Turin, Italy, Oct 31, 37; m 66; c 2. ATMOSPHERIC PHYSICS. *Educ:* Turin Polytech Inst, BSc, 61; Cornell Univ, MSc, 65, PhD(atmospheric & plasma physics), 67. *Prof Exp:* Instr elec eng, Turin Polytech Inst, 61-62; res asst microwaves, Cornell Univ, 62-64, res asst plasma & atmospheric physics, 64-67; fel atmospheric physics, Univ Toronto, 67-69; vis fel, Univ Colo, Nat Oceanic Atmospheric Admin, 69-71, fel, 71-74, physicist aeronomy lab, 75-76, physicist, Wave Propagation Lab, 76-79; PROF GEOPHYS, SCH GEOPHYS SCI, GA INST TECHNOL, 79- *Mem:* Am Meteorol Soc; Am Geophys Union; Royal Meterol Soc. *Res:* Atmospheric physics; atmospheric dynamics. *Mailing Add:* Sch Geophys Sci Ga Inst Technol Atlanta GA 30332

EINAUDI, MARCO TULLIO, b New York, NY, Dec 24, 39; c 3. ECONOMIC GEOLOGY. *Educ:* Cornell Univ, BA, 61; Harvard Univ, MA, 65, PhD(geol), 69. *Prof Exp:* Geologist, Anaconda Co, 69-75; asst prof, 75-77, assoc prof, 77-80, PROF APPL EARTH SCI & GEOL, STANFORD UNIV, 80-, CHMN, DEPT APPL EARTH SCI, 82- *Concurrent Pos:* Geol consult, Anaconda Co, 75-76, SRI Int, 76- & Conoco Minerals, 78-; chmn, Gordon Res Conf Geochem, 81; vis investr, Washington Geophys Lab, Carnegie Inst, 81-82. *Mem:* Geol Soc Am; Soc Econ Geologists. *Res:* Genesis of porphyry copper molybdenum deposits, cordilleran base and precious metal vein deposits and skarn deposits; development of empirical and theoretical ore deposit models for use in exploration. *Mailing Add:* Dept of Appl Earth Sci Stanford Univ Stanford CA 94305

EINBINDER, SEYMOUR KENNETH, b Brooklyn, NY, Jan 15, 25; m 48; c 5. SYSTEM ENGINEERING, SYSTEMS ANALYSIS. *Educ:* NY Univ, BME, 49, MME, 51; Stevens Inst Technol, MS, 57; Polytech Inst, Brooklyn, PhD(syst eng), 73. *Prof Exp:* Mech engr, Picatinny Arsenal, 50-56, supv phys scientist, 56-77; SUPV ARMAMENT ENGR, US ARMY ARMAMENT RES & DEVELOP COMMAND, 77- *Concurrent Pos:* Adj prof mgt sci, Fla Inst Technol, 80- *Mem:* Sigma Xi. *Res:* Operations research; reliability; systems analysis. *Mailing Add:* US Army ARRADCOM Attention DRDAR-LCS-E Dover NJ 07801

EINERT, ALFRED ERWIN, b Kearney, NJ, Feb 6, 39; m 67; c 1. ORNAMENTAL HORTICULTURE, PLANT PHYSIOLOGY. *Educ:* Ark State Univ, BSA, 64; Miss State Univ, MS, 65, PhD(ornamental hort), 69. *Prof Exp:* Res assoc, Mich State Univ, 69-70; from asst prof to assoc prof, 70-78, PROF ORNAMENTAL HORT, UNIV ARK, FAYETTEVILLE, 78- *Concurrent Pos:* Netherlands Flower-Bulb Inst trainee, Mich State Univ, 68-70. *Mem:* Am Soc Hort Sci; Am Soc Plant Physiol; Am Soc Landscape Archit. *Res:* Growth and development of bulb flower crops; role of environmental factors and growth regulators on lilies, tulips, irises. *Mailing Add:* Dept of Hort Univ of Ark Fayetteville AR 72701

EINHELLIG, FRANK ARNOLD, b Independence, Mo, July 7, 38; m 61; c 2. BOTANY, PHYSIOLOGICAL ECOLOGY. *Educ:* Kans State Univ, BS, 60; Univ Kans, BS, 61; Univ Okla, MS, 64, PhD(bot), 69. *Prof Exp:* Sci teacher, Shawnee Mission High Sch Dist, Kans, 61-67; from asst prof to assoc prof biol, 69-78, PROF BIOL, UNIV S DAK, 78- *Concurrent Pos:* Prin investr, eight sci educ and res grants, 72-82. *Mem:* Am Soc Plant Physiologists; Sigma Xi; Plant Growth Regulator Soc Am. *Res:* Allelopathy; mechanism of inhibition caused by weedy species and specific inhibitors such as effects on photosynthesis, stomatal aperture, plant water status and repiration; plant inhibitors affecting animal growth and metabolism. *Mailing Add:* Dept of Biol Univ SDak Vermillion SD 57069

FINHORN, MARTIN B, b Dayton, Ohio, Aug 14, 42; m 67; c 1. THEORETICAL HIGH ENERGY PHYSICS, ELEMENTARY PARTICLE PHYSICS. *Educ:* Calif Inst Technol, BS, 65; Princeton Univ, PhD(physics), 68. *Prof Exp:* Res physicist, Stanford Linear Accelerator Ctr, 68-70 & Lawrence Berkeley Lab, 70-72; res physicist, Fermi Nat Accelerator Lab, 72-76; assoc res scientist, 76-79, ASSOC PROF, DEPT PHYSICS, UNIV MICH, 79- *Mem:* Am Phys Soc. *Res:* Quantum chromodynamics, solitons in unified gauge field theories; grand unification and cosmology. *Mailing Add:* Randall Lab Univ of Mich Ann Arbor MI 48109

EINOLF, WILLIAM NOEL, b Baltimore, Md, July 5, 43; m 65; c 2. ANALYTICAL CHEMISTRY, ORGANIC CHEMISTRY. *Educ:* Johns Hopkins Univ, BA, 64; Univ Del, PhD(chem), 71. *Prof Exp:* Teacher chem, Great Valley High Sch, 64-66; chemist, Wyeth Labs, 66-67; instr chem, Lincoln Univ, 67-68; chemist, Johns Hopkins Univ Sch Med, 71-72; CHEMIST, PHILIP MORRIS RES CTR, 72- *Mem:* Am Chem Soc; Am Soc Mass Spectrometry. *Res:* Tobacco and smoke chemistry; natural products; mass spectrometry. *Mailing Add:* Philip Morris Res Ctr PO Box 26583 Richmond VA 23261

EINSET, EYSTEIN, b Geneva, NY, Mar 19, 25; m 54; c 3. FOOD SCIENCE. *Educ:* Cornell Univ, BS, 50, MS, 51, PhD(biochem), 56. *Prof Exp:* Chemist, Bur Com Fisheries, US Fish & Wildlife Serv, 55-57, lab dir, 57-60; asst prof biochem, Agr Exp Sta, Cornell Univ, 60-62; mgr food res, Tectrol Div, 62-64, sr res biochemist, res & eng div, 64-69, STAFF SCIENTIST, RES & ENG DIV, WHIRLPOOL CORP, 69- *Mem:* Am Chem Soc; Inst Food Technol; Sigma Xi; Int Inst Refrig. *Res:* Food chemistry and processing; biochemistry of storage life extension of fresh plant, animal and fishery food products by control of environmental variables. *Mailing Add:* Whirlpool Corp Res & Eng Ctr Monte Rd Benton Harbor MI 49022

EINSET, JOHN, pomology, deceased

EINSET, JOHN WILLIAM, b Waterloo, NY, Nov 14, 47; m 81. PLANT PHYSIOLOGY. *Educ:* Cornell Univ, BS, 69; Univ Wis, PhD(bot), 74. *Prof Exp:* Res assoc plant physiol, Univ Wis, 74-77; ASST PROF PLANT PHYSIOL, UNIV CALIF, 77- *Concurrent Pos:* Lectr plant physiol, Univ Wis, 74. *Mem:* Sigma Xi; Am Soc Plant Physiologists; Tissue Culture Asn; Am Soc Hort Sci; Int Asn Plant Tissue Culture. *Res:* Regulation of plant growth and development by hormones in tissue cultures. *Mailing Add:* Bot & Plant Sci Univ Calif Riverside CA 92521

EINSPAHR, DEAN WILLIAM, b Sioux City, Iowa, May 24, 23; m 46; c 2. FOREST GENETICS. *Educ:* Iowa State Univ, BS, 49, MS, 50, PhD(soils, silvicult), 55. *Prof Exp:* Asst wood technol, Gamble Bros, Inc, Ky, 50-51; res assoc soils & silvicult, Iowa Agr Exp Sta, 52-55; res asst forest genetics, 55-58, res aide, 59-62, res assoc & chief genetics & physiol group, 63-70, sr res assoc forest genetics & group coordr, Div Natural Mat & Systs, 70-77, SR RES ASSOC & DIR, FOREST BIOL SECT, LAWRENCE UNIV, 77-, HEAD DEPT ADVAN STUDIES, INST PAPER CHEM, 80- *Mem:* Tech Asn Pulp & Paper Industs; Soil Sci Soc Am; Soc Am Foresters. *Res:* Forest soils; silviculture; wood quality-paper quality relationship. *Mailing Add:* Forest Biol Sect Inst Pap Chem Lawrence Univ Appleton WI 54912

EINSPAHR, HOWARD MARTIN, b Beaumont, Tex, Feb 7, 43; m 75; c 1. PROTEIN CRYSTALLOGRAPHY. *Educ:* Rice Univ, BA, 64; Univ Pa, PhD(chem), 70. *Prof Exp:* Res fel, Calif Inst Technol, 70-72; res assoc, Inst Dent Res, 72-77; INSTR, DEPT BIOCHEM & ASSOC SCIENTIST, COMPREHENSIVE CANCER CTR, UNIV ALA, BIRMINGHAM, 77- *Concurrent Pos:* Investr, Inst Dent Res, 77-; res career develop award, USPHS, 81- *Mem:* AAAS; Am Crystallog Asn; Sigma Xi. *Res:* Structural studies of macromolecules by X-ray diffraction; the geometry of calcium binding by organic ligands. *Mailing Add:* Rm 244 LHR SDB Box 13 Univ Ala Birmingham AL 35294

EINSPRUCH, NORMAN G(ERALD), b Brooklyn, NY, June 27, 32; m 53; c 3. SOLID STATE SCIENCE. *Educ:* Rice Inst, BA, 53; Univ Colo, MS, 55; Brown Univ, PhD(appl math), 59. *Prof Exp:* Asst, Univ Colo, 53-54; asst, Metals Res Lab, Brown Univ, 56-59, res assoc, 59; mem tech staff, Tex Instruments Inc, 59-62, head, Electron Transport Physics Br, Physics Res Lab, 62-68, actg head, Thin Film Physics Br, 64-65, dir advan technol lab, Corp Res & Eng, 68-69, dir chem mat div, Tech Ctr, 69-72, dir, Cent Res Labs, 72-75, asst vpres, 75-77; DEAN, SCH ENG & ARCHIT, UNIV MIAMI, 77- *Concurrent Pos:* chmn panel film microstructure sci & technol, Nat Res Ctr, 78-79; dir, Ogden Corp. *Mem:* AAAS; fel Am Phys Soc; fel Acoust Soc Am; fel Inst Elec & Electronics Engrs; Am Inst Indust Engrs. *Res:* Transport in solids; physical acoustics; ultrasonic wave propagation in solids; management technology; microstructure science. *Mailing Add:* Sch of Eng & Archit PO Box 248294 Coral Gables FL 33124

EINSTEIN, ELIZABETH ROBOZ, b Szaszvaros, Hungary; nat US; m 59. NEUROCHEMISTRY. *Educ:* Univ Budapest, PHD(biochem), 38. *Prof Exp:* Res asst bioorg chem, Calif Inst Technol, 41-45; assoc prof chem, Univ Wyo, 45-48; res assoc enzyme & carbohydrate res, Stanford Univ, 48-52; assoc prof biochem, Sch Med, Georgetown Univ, 52-58; assoc prof, neurochem, Sch Med, Stanford Univ, 58-59; PROF NEUROCHEM & LECTR BIOCHEM, SCH MED, UNIV CALIF, SAN FRANCISCO, 59- *Concurrent Pos:* NIH, Multiple Sclerosis Soc & Hartford Found grants; SEATO scholar, Univ Bangkok, 61-62; res consult, Sugar Res Found NY, 45-48; lectr orient & advan researcher, Univ Bangkok, 61-62. *Honors & Awards:* Raskob Award, Georgetown Univ, 56; Medaglia d'oro di Milano, Int Cong Neurochem, Milan, Italy, 69; mem, Inst Human Develop, Univ Calif, Berkeley. *Mem:* Am Chem Soc; Soc Exp Biol & Med; Am Acad Neurol. *Res:* Neurochemical investigations; chemistry of demyelinating diseases; developing brain; cerebrospinal fluid; author or coauthor of over ninety publications. *Mailing Add:* 1090 Creston Rd Berkeley CA 94708

EINSTEIN, FREDERICK W B, b Auckland, NZ, Nov 7, 40; m 65; c 2. INORGANIC CHEMISTRY. *Educ:* Univ NZ, BSc, 62; Univ Canterbury, MSc, 63, PhD(chem), 65. *Prof Exp:* Fel chem, Univ BC, 65-67; from asst prof to assoc prof, 67-75, PROF CHEM, SIMON FRASER UNIV, 75- *Mem:* Am Crystallog Asn; Chem Inst Can. *Res:* Inorganic structural chemistry; crystal structure analysis; computing. *Mailing Add:* Dept of Chem Simon Fraser Univ Burnaby Can

EINSTEIN, J RALPH, b Providence, RI, Oct 17, 25; m 60; c 3. CRYSTALLOGRAPHY, BIOPHYSICS. *Educ:* Yale Univ, BS, 44, BMus, 47, MMus, 48; Harvard Univ, PhD(biochem), 59. *Prof Exp:* NSF fel, 59-60; res assoc x-ray crystallog, Col Physicians & Surgeons, Columbia Univ, 60-65; BIOPHYSICIST BIOL DIV, OAK RIDGE NAT LAB, 65- *Mem:* Am Crystallog Asn. *Res:* X-ray crystallography; molecular and crystal structures of molecules of biological interest. *Mailing Add:* Biol Div Oak Ridge Nat Lab PO Box Y Oak Ridge TN 37830

EINSTEIN, THEODORE LEE, b Cleveland, Ohio, Jan 20, 47. THEORETICAL SOLID STATE PHYSICS, SURFACE PHYSICS. *Educ:* Harvard Univ, BA, MA, 69; Univ Pa, PhD(physics), 73. *Prof Exp:* Res investr physics, Univ Pa, 73-74; vis asst prof, 75-77, asst prof, 77-80, ASSOC PROF PHYSICS, UNIV MD, 80- *Mem:* Am Phys Soc. *Res:* Theory of gas adsorption onto and absorption into metals: energetics, electronic distributions, experimental probes, order-disorder transitions, multi-adatom effects and mechanical changes; extended appearance of potential fine structure. *Mailing Add:* Dept Physics & Astron Univ Md College Park MD 20742

EINWICH, ANNA MARIA, b Baltimore, Md, Feb 7, 17; c 4. OCEANOGRAPHY, MARINE GEOLOGY. *Educ:* Johns Hopkins Univ, BA, 67. *Prof Exp:* Civil eng technologist mapping, Forest Serv, USDA, 67-68; oceanogr magnetics, US Naval Oceanog Off, 69-76; OCEANOGR MARINE GEOL, SEA FLOOR DIV, NAVAL OCEAN RES & DEVELOP ACTIV, 76- *Res:* Histories of ocean basins, especially in the Caribbean, Western Atlantic and Gulf of Mexico; velocities in sediments. *Mailing Add:* 112 Palm Ave Pass Christian MS 39571

EINZIGER, ROBERT EMANUEL, materials science, see previous edition

EIPPER, ALFRED WARD, b Montague, Mass, Nov 16, 19; m 42; c 3. FISH BIOLOGY, CONSERVATION. *Educ:* Reed Col, BA, 41; Univ Maine, BS, 49; Cornell Univ, PhD(fishery biol), 53. *Prof Exp:* Asst fish biol, Univ Maine, 48-49; res asst, Cornell Univ, 49-51, res assoc, 52-63, assoc prof, 63-75; leader, NY Coop Fisheries Unit, US Fish & Wildlife Serv, 63-75; activ leader, Northeast Power Plant, 75-80; CONSULT, 80- *Mem:* AAAS; Am Fisheries Soc. *Res:* Biology and management of fish populations and water resources; environmental problems and policies; environmental effects of power plants. *Mailing Add:* US Fish & Wildlife Serv Suite 700 One Gateway Ctr Newton Corner MA 02158

EIPPER, BETTY ANNE, b Elmira, NY, Nov 11, 45; m 68; c 2. ENDOCRINOLOGY, PEPTIDES. *Educ:* Brown Univ, ScB & MS, 68; Harvard Univ, PhD(biophys), 73. *Prof Exp:* Am Cancer Soc fel, Anna Fuller Fund, Univ Ore, 73-75; asst prof, 76-79, ASSOC PROF PHYSIOL, UNIV COLO HEALTH SCI CTR, 79- *Concurrent Pos:* Prin investr, NIH, 76- *Mem:* Endocrine Soc; Am Soc Biol Chemists. *Res:* Biosynthesis of bioactive peptides (especially ACTH and endorphin); post-translational processing of peptide hormones (proteolysis, glycosylation, acetylation, amidation, phosphorylation); tissue culture of peptide synthesizing endocrine and neural tissues. *Mailing Add:* Physiol Dept C-240 Health Sci Ctr Univ Colo 4200 E 9th Denver CO 80262

EIPPER, EUGENE B(RETHERTON), b Heyburn, Idaho, Aug 10, 12; m 37; c 3. MECHANICAL ENGINEERING. *Educ:* Univ Colo, BS, 34; Chrysler Inst Eng, MME, 37. *Prof Exp:* Draftsman, Gen Motors Truck Co, Pontiac, Mich, 34-35, exp engr, Detroit Diesel Eng Div, Corp, Detroit, 35-37; plant engr, DeSoto-Chrysler Corp, 37; asst chief engr, Andover Motors Corp, NY, 42-45; asst chief engr, Wilkening Mfg Co, Pa, 45-47; automotive supvr, Petrol Lab, E I du Pont de Nemours & Co, Inc, 47-53, supt petrol lab, 53-57, lab engr, 57-62, engr, 62-65, patent engr, Jackson Lab, 65-71; test engr automotive exhaust catalysts, Air Prod & Chem, Inc, 74-77; CONSULT AUTOMOTIVE EXHAUST CATALYSTS, 78- *Mem:* Soc Automotive Engrs. *Res:* Development of lubricating oil and gasoline additives. *Mailing Add:* 605 Vassar Ave Pitman NJ 08071

EIRICH, FREDERICK ROLAND, b Vienna, Austria, May 23, 05; m 36; c 2. CHEMISTRY. *Educ:* Univ Vienna, PhD(phys chem), 29, DSc(phys chem), 38. *Hon Degrees:* MA, Cambridge Univ, 39. *Prof Exp:* Res & assoc colloid chem, Univ Vienna, 28-32, first chem inst, 33-38; res assoc colloid sci, Cambridge Univ, 38-40, res assoc & lectr phys chem, 44-46; sr res officer, Univ Melbourne, 41-43; from assoc prof to prof polymer chem, 47-69, dean res, 67-70, DISTINGUISHED PROF POLYMER CHEM, POLYTECH INST BROOKLYN, 69- *Concurrent Pos:* Vis prof, Bristol Univ, 64-65; consult, major chem companies; ed, J Soc Rheol, 52-56. *Mem:* Fel NY Acad Sci; Am Chem Soc; Soc Rheol (from vpres to pres, 70-73). *Res:* Constitution of colloid gold; colloidal metals; colloidal solutions; serum proteins; rheology; ultracentrifuge; liquid explosives; polymer chemistry. *Mailing Add:* Polytech Inst of Brooklyn 333 Jay St Brooklyn NY 11201

EISA, HAMDY MAHMOUD, b Hihia, Egypt, Aug 4, 38; m 64; c 1. PLANT BREEDING, VEGETABLE CROPS. *Educ:* Cairo Univ, BSc, 59; Cornell Univ, MSc, 66, PhD(plant breeding), 69. *Prof Exp:* Asst prof hort, Univ Nebr, Lincoln, 69-70; plant breeder, Environ Res Lab, Univ Ariz, 70-71, res assoc, 71-75; HORTICULTURIST, WORLD BANK, WASHINGTON, DC, 75- *Concurrent Pos:* Plant breeder, Univ Ariz team, Arid Lands Res Ctr, Abu Dhabi, Arabian Gulf, 71- *Honors & Awards:* Asgrow Award, Am Soc Hort Sci, 69. *Mem:* Am Soc Hort Sci. *Res:* Breeding of vegetable crops adapted to warm, humid conditions. *Mailing Add:* World Bank D-741 1818 H St NW Washington DC 20433

EISBERG, ROBERT MARTIN, b Kansas City, Mo, July 1, 28; m 51. NUCLEAR PHYSICS. *Educ:* Univ Ill, BS, 49; Univ Calif, PhD(physics), 53. *Prof Exp:* Res asst physics, Univ Calif Radiation Lab, 51-53; res assoc, Brookhaven Nat Labs, 53-55 & Univ Minn, 55-56; physicist, Cavendish Lab, Eng, 56-57; from asst prof to assoc prof physics, Univ Minn, 57-60; Fulbright-Guggenheim fel, Univ Tokyo, 60-61; assoc prof, 61-62, PROF PHYSICS, UNIV CALIF, SANTA BARBARA, 63- *Concurrent Pos:* Physicist, Cyclotron Lab, Arg, 62 & Rutherford Lab, Eng, 65; visitor, Europ Coun Nuclear Res, Switz, 69; Fulbright-Hays fel, Univ Peireira, Colombia, 70; vis prof, Flinders Univ, Australia, 72 & Univ Surrey, Eng, 78. *Mem:* Fel Am Phys Soc; Am Asn Physics Teachers; Fedn Am Sci. *Res:* Experimental research in nuclear scattering and reactions; passage of particles through matter; textbook writing and computer assisted instruction. *Mailing Add:* Dept of Physics Univ of Calif Santa Barbara CA 93106

EISCH, JOHN JOSEPH, b Milwaukee, Wis, Nov 5, 30; m 53; c 5. ORGANIC CHEMISTRY. *Educ:* Marquette Univ, BS, 52; Iowa State Univ, PhD(chem), 56. *Prof Exp:* Union Carbide Corp fel, Ger, 56-57; res assoc, Europ Res Assocs, Belg, 57; asst prof chem, St Louis Univ, 57-59 & Univ Mich, 59-63; from assoc prof to prof & chmn dept, Cath Univ Am, 63-72; PROF CHEM, STATE UNIV NY BINGHAMTON, 72- *Concurrent Pos:* Consult, var corp. *Mem:* Am Chem Soc; Am Inst Chem. *Res:* Synthesis and properties of organometallic compounds; reactive intermediates, particularly anions, radical-anions and charge transfer complexes; mechanisms of organic reactions; stereoselectivity and regioselectivity of carbon-metal and hydrogen-metal bond additions; non-benzenoid aromatic rings. *Mailing Add:* Dept Chem State Univ NY Binghamton Binghamton NY 13901

EISDORFER, CARL, b Bronx, NY, June 20, 30; c 3. PSYCHIATRY, PSYCHOPHYSIOLOGY. *Educ:* NY Univ, BA, 51, MA, 53, PhD(psychol), 59; Duke Univ, MD, 64; Am Bd Psychiat & Neurol, dipl, 74. *Prof Exp:* Social investr, Children's Placement Serv, Bur Child Welfare, City of New York, 52-53, psychologist-in-training, Bur Child Guid, Bd Educ Intern Prog, 53-54; clin psychol specialist, Ment Hyg Consult Serv, US Army, Ft Dix, NJ, 54-55, neuropsychiat serv, Ryukyus Army Hosp, Okinawa, Japan, 55-56; res asst, Duke Univ, 56-58, from instr to prof med psychol & head div, 58-72, from assoc prof to prof psychiat, 68-72; prof psychiat & chmn, Dept Psychiat & Behav Sci, Sch Med, Univ Wash, Seattle, 72-81; PRES, MONTEFIORE HOSP & MED CTR, 81-; PROF, DEPT PSYCHIAT & NEUROSCI, ALBERT EINSTEIN COL MED, BRONX, NY, 81- *Concurrent Pos:* Lectr, Dept Psychol, Duke Univ, 59-72, intern, Med Ctr, 65, dir training & res coordr, Ctr Study Aging & Human Develop, 65-70, dir ctr, 70-72, dir med studies year III, Dept Psychiat, 68-71, dir behav sci prof, Sch Med, 68-72; coordr community ment health serv, Halifax County Health Dept, NC, 59-69, prog dir, 69-71, prin consult, 71-72; vis prof, Dept Archit, Sch Environ Design, Univ Calif, Berkeley, 69-70, vis fac, Univ, 70-; vis prof psychiat, Langley Porter Neuropsychiat Inst, Univ Calif Med Ctr, San Francisco, 69-70; adj prof psychol, Univ Wash, 72-81; spec consult, White House Comt Aging, 61, mem, 71-73; NIMH spec fel, 62-64; consult adult develop & aging, Res & Training Rev Comt, Nat Inst Child Health & Human Develop, 69-71; mem primary care study comt, Coun Acad Socs & Asn Am Med Cols, 71; mem panel death with dignity, Inst Med of Nat Acad Sci, 71-72; mem adv comt older Americans, Dept Health, Educ & Welfare, 71-73; consult,

Psychiat Educ Br, NIMH, 71, 72 & 74-; mem, Fed Coun Aging & chmn, Res & Manpower Subcomt, 74-; soc sci award & Kesten award, Ethel Percy Andrus Geront Ctr, Univ Southern Calif, 75-76; consult, Vet Admin Health Care Resources Comt, Div Med Sci, Nat Res Coun, 75-; H T Dozor Distinguished Vis Prof Geriat & Psychiat, Ben Gurion Univ, Negev, 80. *Honors & Awards:* Robert W Kleemeier Award, Geront Soc, 69; Edward B Allen Award, Am Geriat Soc, 74; Kesten Award, Univ Southern Calif, 76, Social Sci Award, 76; Billings lectr, Mt Airy Hosp, Denver, 78; Joseph Freeman Award, Geront Soc, 79; Distinguished Prof Contrib Knowledge Award, Am Psychol Asn, 81. *Mem:* Inst of Med of Nat Acad Sci; fel Am Psychiat Asn; fel Am Psychol Asn; fel Geront Soc (pres, 71-72); fel Am Geriat Soc. *Res:* Psychophysiology of aging, learning, adaptation and human capacity. *Mailing Add:* Montefiore Hosp & Med Ctr 111 E 210 St Bronx NY 10467

EISELE, CAROLYN, b New York, NY. MATHEMATICS. *Educ:* Hunter Col, AB, 23; Columbia Univ, AM, 25. *Hon Degrees:* Dr humanities, Tex Tech Univ, 80. *Prof Exp:* From instr to prof, 23-72, EMER PROF MATH, HUNTER COL, 72- *Concurrent Pos:* Res grants, Am Philos Soc, 52-54 & 64-67 & NSF, 64-67 & 78-81; Hunter Col deleg, Int Cong Math, Hist of Sci, Logic, Methodology & Philos of Sci Semiotics, 54-; Am Coun Learned Socs travel grants, 58, 59; chmn adv screening comt, Fulbright & Smith-Mundt Awards, 60-68; John Dewey Found publ grants, 72 & 79; mem staff, Inst Studies in Pragmaticism, Tex Tech Univ, 76-; NSF travel grant, 76; Am Res Coun grants, 77 & 78. *Mem:* Fel AAAS; fel NY Acad Sci; Charles S Peirce Soc (pres, 73-75); Am Math Soc; Math Asn Am. *Res:* History and philosophy of mathematics and science of the late nineteenth century; the thought of Charles S Peirce; new elements of mathematics. *Mailing Add:* 215 E 68th St New York NY 10021

EISELE, CHARLES WESLEY, b New Albany, Ind, Apr 6, 06; m 33, 63; c 2. MEDICINE. *Educ:* NCent Col, BA, 28; Northwestern Univ, MS, 31, MB, 32, MD, 33. *Prof Exp:* Asst med, Univ Chicago, 34-35, from instr to assoc prof, 35-51, secy dept med, 41-47, chief gen med clin, 41-51; asst dean, 51-55, assoc prof med, 51-67, assoc dean, Postgrad Med Educ, 55-72, prof med, 67-74, prof prev med & comprehensive health care, 69-74, EMER PROF MED, SCH MED, UNIV COLO, DENVER, 81- *Concurrent Pos:* Mem staff & consult, various hosps; consult surgeon gen, USPHS, 60-; prog dir, Estes Park Inst, 74- *Mem:* Fel Am Col Physicians; fel AMA; Soc Exp Biol & Med; hon fel Am Col Hosp Adminr. *Res:* Brucellosis; toxoplasmosis; salmonellosis; evaluation and control of quality of medical care. *Mailing Add:* Estes Park Inst PO Box 400 Englewood CO 80151

EISELSTEIN, HERBERT LOUIS, b Pomeroy, Ohio, Mar 15, 19; c 3. METALLURGY. *Educ:* Univ Cincinnati, ChemE, 41. *Prof Exp:* Coop student metall, 37-41, metallurgist, 41-54, chief testing engr lab, 54-55, sect head metall lab, Res & Develop Lab, 55-67, prod develop mgr, 67-71, asst vpres & res & develop mgr, 71-76, VPRES, TECHNOL, HUNTINGTON ALLOYS INC, 76- *Mem:* Am Inst Mining Metall & Petrol Engrs; fel Am Soc Metals; Am Soc Testing & Mat. *Mailing Add:* Huntington Alloys Inc PO Box 1958 Huntington WV 25720

EISEMAN, BEN, b St Louis, Mo, Nov 2, 17; m 46; c 4. SURGERY. *Educ:* Yale Univ, BA, 39; Harvard Univ, MD, 43; Am Bd Surg, dipl, 51, Am Bd Thoracic Surg, dipl, 58. *Prof Exp:* Instr & asst prof surg, Sch Med, Wash Univ, 50-53, asst dean, 50-52; assoc prof & prof, Sch Med, Univ Colo, 53-61; prof surg & chmn dept, Col Med, Univ Ky, 61-67; PROF SURGERY, UNIV COLO MED CTR & DIR DEPT SURGERY, DENVER GEN HOSP, 67- *Concurrent Pos:* Chief surg serv, Vet Admin Hosp, Denver, 53-61; chief surg, Denver Gen Hosp, 67-71; mem comt trauma, Nat Res Coun, 60-69; surg study sect, NIH, 61-65; exec coun cardiovasc surg, Am Heart Asn, 62-68; mem bd, Am Bd Surg, 64-70; chief surgery, Rose Med Ctr, 77- *Mem:* Am Col Surg; Am Surg Asn; Soc Clin Surg; Soc Univ Surg (pres, 62); Soc Vascular Surg. *Res:* General surgery; tracheostomy and trauma; experimental coronary arterial surgery; peptic ulcer; histamine metabolism; gastric hypersecretion; role of ammonia in production of hepatic coma; treatment of hepatic coma with extracorporeal liver. *Mailing Add:* Dept of Surg Univ of Colo Med Ctr Denver CO 80220

EISEMAN, FRED S, organic chemistry, see previous edition

EISEMANN, KURT, b Nuremberg, Ger, June 22, 23; US citizen; m 69; c 2. APPLIED MATHEMATICS, OPERATIONS RESEARCH. *Educ:* Yeshiva Univ, BA, 50; Mass Inst Technol, MS, 52; Harvard Univ, PhD(appl math), 62. *Prof Exp:* Sr mathematician, Int Bus Mach Corp, NY, 52-56, res mathematician, NY & Mass, 56-61; mgr math res, Univac Div, Sperry Rand Corp, DC, 61-63; assoc prof, Sch Eng & dir comput ctr, Cath Univ Am, 63-66; tech dir, Comput Usage Develop Corp, Mass, 66-68; dir acad comput serv & prof comput sci, Northeastern Univ, 68-74; DIR COMPUT SERV & PROF MATH & COMPUT SCI, UNIV MO-KANSAS CITY, 74- *Concurrent Pos:* Lectr, Yeshiva Univ, 53-55 & Cath Univ Am, 62-63. *Mem:* Soc Indust & Appl Math. *Res:* Applications of mathematics to concrete problems; linear programming; numerical analysis; effective use of computers; physical and engineering problems; general computer sciences; educational administration. *Mailing Add:* Dept of Comput Serv Univ of Mo Kansas City MO 64110

EISEN, EDWIN OTTO, chemical & nuclear engineering, see previous edition

EISEN, EUGENE J, b New York, NY, May 14, 38; m 60; c 3. GENETICS, STATISTICS. *Educ:* Univ Ga, BSA, 59; Purdue Univ, MS, 62, PhD(genetics), 65. *Prof Exp:* From asst prof to assoc prof, 64-73, PROF ANIMAL GENETICS, NC STATE UNIV, 73- *Concurrent Pos:* Vis prof, Univ Edinburgh, 79-80. *Mem:* AAAS; Genetics Soc Am; Biomet Soc; Am Soc Animal Sci. *Res:* Experimental quantitative genetical studies with mice, involving genetical aspects of dynamics of growth and maternal influences on quantitative traits, and effects on inbreeding and selection on these traits. *Mailing Add:* Dept of Animal Sci NC State Univ Raleigh NC 27650

EISEN, FRED HENRY, b Tulsa, Okla, June 2, 29; m 54; c 3. PHYSICS. *Educ:* Calif Inst Technol, BS, 51; Princeton Univ, MA, 53, PhD(physics), 56. *Prof Exp:* Asst, Princeton Univ, 51-56; from sr physicist to res specialist, Atomics Int Div, 56-65, mem tech staff, 65-78, group leader, 78-80, DIR GALLIUM ARSENIDE ELECTRONIC DEVELOP RES, SCI CTR, ROCKWELL INT CORP, INC, 80- *Concurrent Pos:* Vis scientist, Inst Physics, Aarhus Univ, 70-71. *Mem:* Am Phys Soc; Sigma Xi; Inst Elec & Electronics Engrs. *Res:* Diffusion in solids; semiconductors; radiation damage; ion implantation in semiconductors; channeling. *Mailing Add:* Rockwell Int Sci Ctr PO Box 1085 Thousand Oaks CA 91360

EISEN, HENRY, b Brooklyn, NY, Dec 18, 21. PHARMACEUTICAL CHEMISTRY. *Educ:* St John's Univ (NY), BS, 49; Rutgers Univ, MS, 51; Univ Conn, PhD(pharmaceut chem), 54. *Prof Exp:* From asst prof to assoc prof pharm, 54-61, chmn dept, 61-76, PROF PHARMACEUT, ST JOHN'S UNIV, NY, 61-, CHMN DEPT, 79- *Mem:* Am Pharmaceut Asn; Acad Pharmaceut Sci. *Res:* Pharmacy research and development; dosage form design and evaluation. *Mailing Add:* Col Pharm & Allied Hlth Profns St John's Univ Jamaica NY 11439

EISEN, HERMAN NATHANIEL, b Brooklyn, NY, Oct 15, 18; m 48; c 5. IMMUNOLOGY. *Educ:* NY Univ, AB, 39, MD, 43. *Prof Exp:* Asst path, Col Physicians & Surgeons, Columbia Univ, 44-46; NIH fel, Col Med, NY Univ, 47-48, fel chem, 48-49, asst prof indust med, 49-53, assoc prof, 53-55; prof med, 55-61, prof microbiol & head dept, Sch Med, Wash Univ, St Louis, 61-73; PROF IMMUNOL, CTR CANCER RES & DEPT BIOL, MASS INST TECHNOL, 73- *Concurrent Pos:* Consult to Surgeon Gen, USPHS & US Army; mem comn immunization, Armed Forces Epidemiol Bd, 60; mem allergy & immunol study sect, NIH, 56-60, 61-66, chmn, 63-66; mem bd sci adv, Howard Hughes Med Inst, Mass Gen Hosp, Children's Hosp, Boston, Merck Sharp & Dohme Res Labs & other orgn. *Mem:* Nat Acad Sci; Am Soc Clin Invest (vpres, 65); Am Asn Immunol (pres, 68-69); Am Soc Biol Chem; Am Acad Arts & Sci. *Res:* Antigen recognition; antibody formation; tumor immunology. *Mailing Add:* Ctr Cancer Res Dept of Biol Mass Inst Of Technol Cambridge MA 02139

EISEN, JAMES DAVID, b Chicago, Ill, July 27, 32; m 59, 78; c 2. HUMAN GENETICS, CYTOGENETICS. *Educ:* Univ Ill, BS, 53; Emory Univ, MS, 54, PhD(cytol), 60. *Prof Exp:* prof human genetics, Univ Nebr Med Ctr, Omaha, 62-81, dir genetic serv, 68-81, dir genetic & birth defects prev progs, 72-81, dir, Genetic Semen Bank & dir, Ctr Human Genetics, 74-81; PRES, VIVIGEN INC, 81- *Concurrent Pos:* NIH fel, Univ Uppsala, 60-61 & Univ Lund, 61-62. *Mem:* AAAS; Tissue Cult Asn; Am Soc Human Genetics; Am Asn Mental Deficiency; Soc Cryobiol. *Res:* Human cytogenetics; cytogenetic basis for forms of mental retardation and congenital malformations; in utero detection of genetic abnormalities. *Mailing Add:* 550 St Michael's Dr Santa Fe NE 87501

EISEN, MARTIN, mathematics, see previous edition

EISENBARTH, GEORGE STEPHEN, b Brooklyn, NY, Sept 17, 47; m 69; c 2. ENDOCRINOLOGY, CELLULAR BIOLOGY. *Educ:* Columbia Col, NY, BA, 69; Duke Univ, PhD(physiol, pharmacol) & MD, 74. *Prof Exp:* Intern, Duke Univ, 75, jr resident med, 76; fel endocrinol, Lab Biochem Genetics, Nat Heart, Lung & Blood Inst, 77, res assoc cellular biol, 77-79; ASST PROF MED, DUKE UNIV, 79- *Mem:* Endocrine Soc; Am Fedn Clin Res; assoc Am Col Physicians. *Res:* Immunoendocrinology and developmental cellular biology; studies of the immunogenetics of polyglandular failure and cell surface membrane antigens using immunologic hybridoma techniques. *Mailing Add:* Duke Univ Hosp PO Box 3021 Durham NC 27710

EISENBERG, ADI, b Breslau, Ger, Feb 18, 35; US citizen; m 57; c 1. PHYSICAL CHEMISTRY. *Educ:* Worcester Polytech Inst, BS, 57; Princeton Univ, MA, 59, PhD(phys chem), 60. *Prof Exp:* Res assoc polymer chem, Princeton Univ, 60-61; NATO fel, Univ Basel, 61-62; asst prof chem, Univ Calif, Los Angeles, 62-67; assoc prof, 67-75, PROF CHEM, MCGILL UNIV, 75- *Concurrent Pos:* Consult, jet Propulsion Lab, 62-67, Owens-Ill, 64-68 & Energy Conversion Devices, 70- *Mem:* Am Chem Soc; Soc Rheol; fel Am Phys Soc; Sigma Xi; Chem Inst Can. *Res:* Viscoelastic properties and relaxation mechanisms in organic and inorganic polymers and glasses; polymer equilibria; glass transition phenomena in amorphous materials; properties of ionic polymers; polymer chemistry. *Mailing Add:* Dept of Chem Otto Maass Bldg 801 Sherbrooke St W Montreal PQ H3A 2K6 Can

EISENBERG, BENNETT, b Washington, DC, Oct 9, 42; m 70; c 1. SEQUENTIAL ANALYSIS, STOCHASTIC PROCESSES. *Educ:* Dartmouth Col, AB, 64; Mass Inst Technol, PhD(math), 68. *Prof Exp:* Instr math, Cornell Univ, 67-70; vis asst prof, Univ NMex, 70-72; ASSOC PROF MATH, LEHIGH UNIV, 72- *Concurrent Pos:* Assoc ed, Commun Statist, 81- *Mem:* Indust Math Soc; Math Asn Am. *Res:* Properties of sequential statistical tests. *Mailing Add:* Dept Math Lehigh Univ Bethlehem PA 18015

EISENBERG, CAROLA, b Buenos Aires, Arg; US citizen. PSYCHIATRY. *Educ:* Univ Buenos Aires, MD, 43. *Prof Exp:* Psychiat resident, Mercedes Hosp, Buenos Aires, 43-45; fel child psychiat, Johns Hopkins Hosp, 45-47, psychiatrist outpatient dept, 47-50; consult psychiat, Dept Educ, City of Baltimore, 51-53; instr, Univ Md, 55-59; instr psychiat & pediat, Johns Hopkins Univ, 58-66, asst prof, 66-67; staff psychiatrist, Mass Inst Technol, 68-72, dean student affairs, 72-78; DEAN STUDENT AFFAIRS, HARVARD MED SCH, 78- *Concurrent Pos:* Pvt pract child & adolescent psychiat, Balitmore, 55-67; consult psychiat, Park Sch Baltimore, 57-67, Sheppard Pratt Hosp, 60-67, Mass Gen Hosp, 68- & McLean Hosp, 69-; lectr, Harvard Med Sch, 68- *Mem:* Fel Am Psychiat Asn; fel Am Orthopsychiat Asn; Asn Adolescent Psychiat; Am Asn Univ Prof; Am Women's Med Soc. *Res:* Psychiatric disturbances in adolescence; pediatric psychiatry; psychotherapy. *Mailing Add:* Dean Student Affairs Harvard Med Sch Boston MA 02115

EISENBERG, DAVID, b Chicago, Ill, Mar 15, 39; m 63; c 2. BIOPHYSICAL CHEMISTRY. *Educ:* Harvard Univ, AB, 61; Oxford Univ, DPhil(theoret chem), 64. *Prof Exp:* NSF fel chem, Princeton Univ, 64-66; res fel, Calif Inst Technol, 66-68; asst prof, 68-71, assoc prof, 71-76, PROF CHEM, UNIV CALIF, LOS ANGELES, 76- *Concurrent Pos:* USPHS Career Develop Award, 72-77; mem biophys chem study sect, NIH, 74-77; Alfred P Sloan fel. *Res:* Study of biological macromolecules by x-ray diffraction; structure and properties of water. *Mailing Add:* Dept of Chem Univ of Calif Los Angeles CA 90024

EISENBERG, FRANK, JR, b Philadelphia, Pa, Apr 14, 20; m 48; c 4. BIOCHEMISTRY. *Educ:* Univ Pa, BS, 41, PhD, 51. *Prof Exp:* Chemist, Synthetic Fiber Res, Celanese Corp Am, 41-42; chemist org chem, Gen Foods Corp, 43-44; instr biochem, Univ Pa, 50-51; biochemist, Gen Med Res, Vet Admin, 51-52; asst intermediary metab, Pub Health Res Inst NY, 52-54; BIOCHEMIST, NAT INSTS HEALTH, 54- *Mem:* Sigma Xi; NY Acad Sci; Am Soc Biol Chemists. *Res:* Mechanism of action of dextransucrase and levansucrase; biosynthesis of inositol; metabolism of glucuronic acid; biosynthesis of glucuronic acid; gas chromatography of sugars and sugar phosphates; glucuronic acid pathway. *Mailing Add:* 6028 Avon Dr Bethesda MD 20814

EISENBERG, JOHN FREDERICK, b Everett, Wash, June 20, 35; m 57; c 2. ETHOLOGY. *Educ:* Wash State Univ, BS, 57; Univ Calif, Berkeley, MA, 59, PhD(zool), 62. *Prof Exp:* Asst prof zool, Univ BC, 62-64; asst prof, 64-65, res assoc prof, 65-72, RES PROF, UNIV MD, COLLEGE PARK, 72-; resident scientist, 65-79, ASST DIR, NAT ZOOL PARK, SMITHSONIAN INST, 79- *Concurrent Pos:* Adj prof zool, Univ Md, 72-; assoc dept ment hyg, Johns Hopkins Univ, 73-78. *Honors & Awards:* C Hart Merriam Award, Am Soc Mammal, 81. *Mem:* Am Soc Zoologists; Am Soc Mammal; Animal Behav Soc (pres, 73); Ecol Soc Am. *Res:* Mammalian social behavior; analysis of social structure; determination of factors responsible for limiting population growth; philosophy of science. *Mailing Add:* Nat Zool Park Smithsonian Inst Washington DC 20008

EISENBERG, JOHN MEYER, b Atlanta, Ga, Sept 24, 46; c 1. INTERNAL MEDICINE, HEALTH CARE ADMINISTRATION. *Educ:* Princeton Univ, AB, 68; Wash Univ, MD, 72; Univ Pa, MBA, 76. *Prof Exp:* Jol Katz asst prof, 78-81, JOL KATZ ASSOC PROF GEN MED, UNIV PA, 81-, ASSOC DIR, NAT HEALTH CARE MGT CTR, 76-, CHIEF GEN MED, 78- *Concurrent Pos:* Consult, Nat Prof Standard Rev Orgn, 78- & Bur Radiol Health, 79- *Mem:* Soc Res & Educ in Primary Care Internal Med (secy-treas, 78-80, pres-elect, 81-82); Am Fedn Clin Res; Soc Med Decision Making (vpres, 80-81); Am Col Physicians. *Res:* Cost containment by physicians; use of diagnostic tests. *Mailing Add:* Silverstein Pavilion 3 3400 Spruce St Philadelphia PA 19104

EISENBERG, JUDAH MOSHE, b Cincinnati, Ohio, Dec 17, 38; m 61; c 3. THEORETICAL PHYSICS. *Educ:* Columbia Univ, AB, 58; Mass Inst Technol, PhD(physics), 63. *Prof Exp:* From asst prof to prof physics, Univ Va, 62-75, chmn dept, 70-74, Francis H Smith prof, 75-76; PROF, TEL-AVIV UNIV, 75- *Concurrent Pos:* Mem prog adv comt, Los Alamos Meson Physics Facil, 72-75; Giulio Racah vis prof physics, Hebrew Univ Jerusalem, 74-75. *Mem:* Am Phys Soc; Israel Phys Soc. *Res:* Meson nuclear structure theory; medium-energy physics; pion-nucleus interactions; nuclear reaction theory. *Mailing Add:* Dept Physics & Astron Tel-Aviv Univ Ramat-Aviv 69978 Tel-Aviv Israel

EISENBERG, LAWRENCE, b New York, NY, June 9, 33; m 58; c 3. SYSTEMS ENGINEERING, CONTROL SYSTEMS. *Educ:* Fairleigh Dickinson U Univ, BSEE, 60; NY Univ, MS, 61; Newark Col Eng, DEngSc, 66; Univ Pa, MA, 73. *Prof Exp:* Elec engr, Syst Develop Corp, 60-61; from instr to assoc prof elec eng, Newark Col Eng, 61-68; from asst prof to assoc prof, 68-76, dir, Energy Ctr, Univ, 75, PROF SYSTS ENG, MOORE SCH ELEC ENG, UNIV PA, 76-, ASSOC DEAN, 80- *Concurrent Pos:* Deleg, Am Automatic Control Coun, 69-78; consult, Elec Safety Comt, Univ Pa Hosp, 70; mem, Energy Div, City Philadelphia, 73- & Energy Adv Coun, Camden, NJ, 78-80. *Mem:* Inst Elec & Electronics Engrs; Instrument Soc Am; Am Soc Eng Educ; Franklin Inst; AAUP. *Res:* Linear and nonlinear automatic controls; lumped and distributed circuit theory; system theory applied to transportation problems; power system analysis; energy system analysis; environmental impact of energy. *Mailing Add:* 143 Thornhill Rd Cherry Hill NJ 08003

EISENBERG, LAWRENCE, b New York, NY, Dec 21, 19; m 50; c 2. ELECTRONIC ENGINEERING. *Educ:* City Col New York, BS, 40, BEE, 44; Polytech Inst Brooklyn, MEE, 52, PhD(elec eng), 66. *Prof Exp:* Sr instr electronics, Sch Indust Technol, 50-52; proj engr, Polytech Res & Develop Corp, 52-56; sr logician, Digitronics Corp, LI, 56-58; lectr elec eng, City Col New York, 58; res assoc electronics, 58-66, ASST PROF, ROCKEFELLER UNIV, 66-, CO-HEAD DEPTS ELECTRONICS & COMPUT SCI & SR RES ASSOC, 70- *Concurrent Pos:* Instr in charge, Grad Dept Elec Eng, Polytech Inst Brooklyn, 56- *Mem:* Inst Elec & Electronics Engrs. *Res:* Electrical stimulation of tissue by radiofrequency methods, particularly the heart, bladder and phrenic nerve; control of scholiosis by electronic bioconditioning. *Mailing Add:* Depts of Electronics & Comput Sci Rockefeller Univ New York NY 10021

EISENBERG, LEON, b Philadelphia, Pa, Aug 8, 22; m 47; c 2. PSYCHIATRY. *Educ:* Univ Pa, AB, 44, MD, 46. *Hon Degrees:* AM, Harvard Univ, 67; ScD, Univ Manchester. *Prof Exp:* Instr physiol, Med Sch, Univ Pa, 47-48; asst instr neurophysiol, Basic Sci Course, Army Med Dept Res & Grad Sch, 48-50; res physician psychiat, Sheppard Pratt Hosp, Md, 50-52; asst psychiatrist, Children's Psychiat Serv, Johns Hopkins Hosp, 52-53, from instr psychiat & pediat to prof child psychiat, 53-67; prof psychiat, 67-74; Pressley prof psychiat, 74-80, PRESSLEY PROF & CHMN SOCIAL MED, HARVARD MED SCH, 80-; SR ASSOC PSYCHIAT, CHILDRENS HOSP, 74- *Concurrent Pos:* Dir, Glen Burnie Ment Hyg Clin, 53-54; psychiat ed, Crownsville State Hosp, 53-57; psychiatrist, Johns Hopkins Hosp, 54-57, asst psychiatrist-in-chg, 57-59, psychiatrist, Johns Hopkins Hosp, 54-57, asst psychiatrist-in-chg, Children's Psychiat Serv, 59-; consult, Rosewood State Training Sch, 56-58, Baltimore City Hosp, 58 & Sinai Hosp, 64-67; psychiatrist-in-chief, Mass Gen Hosp, 67-74; ed, J Orthopsychiat, 62-73; consult ed, Social Psychiat, J Pediat & J Child Psychol & Psychiat. *Honors & Awards:* Morris prize, Med Sch Univ Pa, 46; Aldrich Award, Am Acad Pediat, 80; Orton Award, Orton Soc, 80. *Mem:* Inst Med, Nat Acad Sci; Am Pediat Soc; Am Acad Pediat; Am Psychiat Asn; Asn Res Nerv & Ment Dis. *Res:* Child psychiatry, especially early infantile autism, school phobia, psychopharmacology and studies in the development of cognition; learning disorders. *Mailing Add:* Dept Social Med Harvard Med Sch Boston MA 02115

EISENBERG, M MICHAEL, b New York, NY, Jan 27, 31; m 53; c 3. SURGERY, GASTROENTEROLOGY. *Educ:* NY Univ, AB, 52; Harvard Univ, MD, 56. *Prof Exp:* From instr exp surg to assoc prof surg, Col Med Univ Fla, 62-68; prof surg, Col Med, Univ Minn, Minneapolis, 68-81; PROF SURG & VCHMN DEPT, STATE UNIV NY DOWNSTATE MED CTR, 81- *Concurrent Pos:* Res fel, Col Med, Univ Fla, 62-63 & Univ Calif, 65-66; sr investr, NIH res projs, 66-; chief surg, Mt Sinai Hosp, Minneapolis, 68-75; attend surgeon, Univ Minn Hosps, 68-; consult, Minneapolis Vet Admin Hosp, 69-; dir surg, Long Island Col Hosp, 81- *Mem:* Am Col Surg; Soc Univ Surg; Am Gastroenterol Asn; Soc Exp Biol & Med; Am Physiol Soc. *Res:* Physiology of secretory and motor mechanisms in the pancreas, biliary tract and stomach and duodenum. *Mailing Add:* Dept Surg Univ Minn Minneapolis MN 55455

EISENBERG, MARTIN A(LLAN), b Brooklyn, NY, Mar 8, 40; m 60. SOLID MECHANICS. *Educ:* NY Univ, BAeroE, 60, MS, 62; Yale Univ, ME, 64, DEng(solid mech), 67. *Prof Exp:* Asst res scientist, Eng Res Div, NY Univ, 60-61; struct engr, Sikorsky Aircraft Div, United Aircraft Corp, 61-64; asst instr eng & appl sci, Yale Univ, 65-66; from asst prof to assoc prof, 66-75, PROF ENG SCI, UNIV FLA, 75-, ASSOC CHMN ENG SCI, 80- *Mem:* Am Soc Mech Engrs; Am Acad Mech; Am Soc Eng Educ; Soc Eng Sci. *Res:* Theory of plasticity; stress wave propagation in solids; continuum mechanics. *Mailing Add:* Dept of Eng Sci Univ of Fla Gainesville FL 32611

EISENBERG, MAX, b Oct 29, 41; US citizen; c 2. INORGANIC CHEMISTRY, PHYSICAL CHEMISTRY. *Educ:* City Col NY, BS, 65; Univ Mass, MS, 68; Northeastern Univ, PhD(inorg chem), 71. *Prof Exp:* Teaching asst chem, Univ Mass, 65-67; res asst, Northeastern Univ, 67-71; lab liaison, 71-74; ASST DIR, ENVIRON HEALTH ADMIN, MD DEPT HEALTH, 74-; ASSOC PROF CHEM, TOWSON STATE UNIV, 75- *Concurrent Pos:* Mem, Gov Md Hazardous Substances Adv Coun, Comn Atomic Energy, 78-, Gov Toxic Substances Adv Coun; teaching asst, Univ Mass, 65-67. *Mem:* Sigma Xi: Am Chem Soc. *Res:* Behavior of paramagnetic metal ions, such as chronium (III), in solution utilizing nuclear magnetic resonance relaxation techniques; utilizing vacuum line techniques; chemistry of certain environmental pollutants; new phosphates. *Mailing Add:* 3114 Bonnie Rd Baltimore MD 21208

EISENBERG, MURRAY, b Philadelphia, Pa, May 23, 39; m 61; c 2. TOPOLOGY, ASSEMBLY PROGRAMMING LANGUAGE. *Educ:* Univ Pa, BA, 60, MA, 62; Wesleyan Univ, PhD(math), 65. *Prof Exp:* From asst prof to assoc prof, 65-80, PROF MATH, UNIV MASS, AMHERST, 81- *Concurrent Pos:* Prin investr, NSF Instrnl Sci Equip Prog grant, 80-81 & Logarithmic Comput Instrument grant, 81- *Mem:* Am Math Soc; Math Asn Am; Sigma Xi; Asn Develop Comput-Based Instr Systs. *Res:* Dynamical systems; uses of assembly programming language in teaching mathematics and statistics. *Mailing Add:* Dept Math & Statist Univ Mass Amherst MA 01003

EISENBERG, PHILLIP, b Detroit, Mich, Nov 6, 19; m 42; c 2. MECHANICS. *Educ:* Wayne State Univ, BS, 41; Calif Inst Technol, CE, 48. *Prof Exp:* Instr civil eng, Univ Iowa, 42; physicist hydrodyn, David Taylor Model Basin, 42-44, head, Fluid Phenomena Br, 45-53 & Mech Br, Off Naval Res, 53-59; pres, 59-76, CHMN EXEC COMT, HYDRONAUTICS, INC, 76- *Concurrent Pos:* Guest lectr, Univ Hamburg, 53; ed, J Ship Res, Soc Naval Architects & Marine Engrs, 61-71; mem cavitation comt, Int Towing Tank Conf, 63. *Honors & Awards:* Meritorious Civilian Award, US Navy, 44, Superior Accomplishment Award, 58; First Tech Award, Am Soc Mech Engrs, 59. *Mem:* AAAS; Am Inst Aeronaut & Astronaut; Acoust Soc Am; fel Am Soc Mech Engrs; Soc Naval Architects & Marine Engrs (vpres, 70 70-72). *Res:* Hydrodynamics, especially cavitation; structural mechanics. *Mailing Add:* Hydronautics, Inc 7210 Peindell Sch Rd Laurel MD 20810

EISENBERG, RICHARD, b New York, NY, Feb 12, 43; m 66; c 2. INORGANIC CHEMISTRY. *Educ:* Columbia Col, AB, 63; Columbia Univ, MA, 64, PhD(chem), 67. *Prof Exp:* From asst prof to assoc prof chem, Brown Univ, 67-73; assoc prof, 73-76; PROF CHEM, UNIV ROCHESTER, 76- *Concurrent Pos:* Alfred P Sloan fel, Brown Univ, 72; Guggenheim fel, 77-78; vis scientist, Caltech, 77; vis prof, Cambridge Univ, 78. *Mem:* Am Chem Soc; Am Crystallog Asn; The Chem Soc. *Res:* Synthetic and structural studies of transition metal complexes; organo-transition metal chemistry; systems of catalytic interest; nitrosyls; x-ray diffraction. *Mailing Add:* Dept of Chem Univ of Rochester Rochester NY 14627

EISENBERG, RICHARD MARTIN, b Weehawken, NJ, May 15, 42; m 66; c 3. PHARMACOLOGY, NEUROENDOCRINOLOGY. *Educ:* Univ Calif, Los Angeles, BA, 63, MS, 67, PhD(pharmacol), 70. *Prof Exp:* Res fel anat, Univ Rochester, 70-71; asst prof, 71-76, ASSOC PROF PHARMACOL, UNIV MINN, DULUTH, 76-, ACTG CHMN DEPT, 77-, DEPT HEAD, 80- *Mem:* Endocrine Soc; Am Soc Pharmacol. *Res:* Mechanisms underlying development of tolerance and physical dependence to narcotics; effects of drugs of abuse on ACTH release; influence of neurotransmitter systems on the adenohypophysis; pituitary-adrenal feedback relationships. *Mailing Add:* Dept of Pharmacol Univ Minn Sch Med Duluth MN 55812

EISENBERG, RITA B, b Chicago, Ill, Mar 25, 21. AUDIOLOGY, ENVIRONMENTAL MEDICINE. *Educ:* Brooklyn Col, BA, 41; Columbia Univ, MA, 46; Johns Hopkins Univ, ScD(audiol), 57. *Prof Exp:* Audiologist, San Francisco Speech & Hearing Ctr, Calif, 56-58; chief audiol serv, Cincinnati Speech & Hearing Ctr, Ohio, 58-61; DIR BIOACOUSTIC LAB, ST JOSEPH HOSP, 61- *Concurrent Pos:* Nat Inst Neurol Dis & Blindness spec res fel, 61-64; consult, Hamilton County Diag Clin, Cincinnati Gen Hosp, 58-61 & Child Guid Clin, Cincinnati, 58-61; instr, Sch Med & Kettering Inst, Univ Cincinnati, 59-61; consult, Lancaster Cleft Plate Clin, 61-70, Lancaster County Dept Spec Serv, 61-, consult subcomt commun & its disorders, Nat Adv Comt, Nat Inst Neurol Dis & Stroke, 66; mem, Panel Rev ENT Devices, Food & Drug Admin, 74-78 & consult, 78-; consult ed, Child Develop, 68-71, Jour Learning Disabilities, 73- & Audiol & Hearing Educ, 75- *Mem:* AAAS; Int Soc Develop Psychobiol; fel Am Psychol Asn; fel Am Speech & Hearing Asn; Psychonomic Soc. *Res:* Ontogeny of communicative functions, normal and aberrant; biochemical and bioelectrical correlates of behavior; predictive potential of neonatal measures. *Mailing Add:* St Joseph Hosp Bioacoustic Lab 250 College Ave Lancaster PA 17603

EISENBERG, ROBERT C, b Denison, Tex, Aug 5, 38; m 56; c 2. MICROBIOLOGY. *Educ:* Northwest Mo State Col, BS, 60; NC State Univ, MS, 62, PhD(microbiol), 66. *Prof Exp:* Res assoc dairy sci, Univ Ill, Urbana, 66-67; from asst prof to assoc prof, 67-80, PROF BIOMED SCI, WESTERN MICH UNIV, 80- *Mem:* AAAS; Am Soc Microbiol; NY Acad Sci. *Res:* Bacterial membranes and electron transport complexes; carbohydrate transport, metabolism and regulation processes in Pseudomonas. *Mailing Add:* Dept Biomed Sci Western Mich Univ Kalamazoo MI 49008

EISENBERG, ROBERT MICHAEL, b Chicago, Ill, Mar 11, 38; m 62; c 3. ECOLOGY. *Educ:* Univ Chattanooga, BA, 61; Univ Mich, MS, 64, PhD(zool), 65. *Prof Exp:* Asst prof biol, Rice Univ, 65-73; asst prof, 73-77, ASSOC PROF BIOL, UNIV DEL, 77- *Mem:* Ecol Soc Am. *Res:* Factors determining population size and structure. *Mailing Add:* Sch of Life & Health Sci Univ of Del Newark DE 19711

EISENBERG, ROBERT S, b New York, NY, Apr 25, 42; m 64; c 1. ELECTROPHYSIOLOGY, BIOPHYSICS. *Educ:* Harvard Univ, AB, 62; Univ London, PhD(biophys), 65. *Prof Exp:* Assoc physiol, Duke Univ, 65-68; from asst prof to assoc prof, 68-74, from assoc prof to prof physiol & biomath, Univ Calif, Los Angeles, 74-76; CHMN PHYSIOL, RUSH UNIV, 76- *Concurrent Pos:* Chmn, Physiol Study Sect, NIH. *Mem:* Am Physiol Soc; Biophys Soc; Soc Gen Physiol; Am Soc Cell Biol; Inst Elec & Electronics Eng. *Res:* Electrophysiology of muscle and lens; impedance measurements; properties of the sarcotublar system; three dimensional electrical field problems. *Mailing Add:* Dept Physiol Rush Med Col 1750 W Harrison Chicago IL 60612

EISENBERG, ROSELYN JANE, microbiology, biochemistry, see previous edition

EISENBERG, SHELDON MERVEN, b Philadelphia, Pa, May 14, 42; m 71. MATHEMATICS. *Educ:* Temple Univ, AB, 63; Lehigh Univ, MS, 65, PhD(math), 68. *Prof Exp:* Instr math, Temple Univ, 65-68; from asst prof to assoc prof, 68-78, PROF MATH, UNIV HARTFORD, 78- *Mem:* Am Math Soc; Math Asn Am. *Res:* Approximation theory. *Mailing Add:* Dept of Math Univ of Hartford West Hartford CT 06117

EISENBERG, SIDNEY EDWIN, b New Britain, Conn, Jan 15, 13; m 46; c 2. MEDICINE. *Educ:* Wesleyan Univ, AB, 35; Univ Rochester, MD, 39; certified, Am Bd Internal Med, 50. *Prof Exp:* Clin instr internal med, Sch Med, Yale Univ, 45-54, asst clin prof, 54-60; dep chief med, 64-67, ASSOC CHIEF MED, NEW BRITAIN GEN HOSP, 67- *Concurrent Pos:* Sr attend physician & cardiologist, Hosps, 45- *Mem:* Fel Am Col Physicians. *Res:* Anemia, cardiology. *Mailing Add:* 41 Brookside Rd New Britain CT 06052

EISENBERG, SYLVAN, b New York, NY, Aug 30, 13; div; c 3. THERMODYNAMICS. *Educ:* Univ Pa, BA, 34, MS, 35; Stanford Univ, PhD(chem), 43. *Prof Exp:* Dir lab & corp consult, West Foods Lab, Lactol Corp, Calif, 36-41; DIR & OWNER, ANRESCO, 41-; PRES, MICRO TRACERS, INC, 61- *Concurrent Pos:* Consult, Vacudry Corp, 43-44; tech dir & co-owner, Desiccated Foods Co, NY, 43-47; asst prof, Univ Santa Clara, 46-48; lectr, Univ San Francisco, 50-56. *Mem:* Am Chem Soc; Am Asn Cereal Chemists; Inst Food Technol; Nat Soc Prof Engrs; Am Soc Testing & Mat. *Res:* Mixing of solids; foods; cleaning materials; corrosion. *Mailing Add:* Anresco, Inc 1370 Van Dye Ave San Francisco CA 94124

EISENBERGER, PETER MICHAEL, b New York, NY, July 20, 41; m 65; c 1. X-RAY PHYSICS. *Educ:* Princeton Univ, BA, 63; Harvard Univ, MA, 65, PhD(appl physics), 67. *Prof Exp:* Fel, Harvard Univ, 67-68; mem staff, Bell Labs, 68-76, dept head, 76-81; DIR, EXXON RES & ENG CO, 81- *Concurrent Pos:* Adj prof appl physics, Stanford Univ, 76. *Mem:* Am Phys Soc; AAAS; Optical Soc Am; Am Chem Soc. *Res:* X-ray techniques which use the capabilities presented by synchrotron radiation to determine microscopic properties of materials of interest to the physicist, chemist and biologist. *Mailing Add:* Exxon Res & Eng Co PO Box 46 Linden NJ 07036

EISENBRANDT, DAVID LEE, b Kansas City, Mo, July 14, 45; m 65; c 2. COMPARATIVE PATHOLOGY, TOXICOLOGY. *Educ:* Kans State Univ, BS, 67, DVM, 69, MS, 73; Colo State Univ, PhD(path), 76; Am Col Vet Pathologists, dipl, 80. *Prof Exp:* Chief vet serv, pub health, Grand Forks AFB, 69-71; instr path, Kans State Univ, 71-73; chief vet serv, pub health, Edwards AFB, 73-74; head comp path, Naval Med Res Inst, 76-79; head anat path, Sch Aerospace Med, Brooks AFB, Tex, 79-81; RES LEADER, DOW CHEM USA, MIDLAND, MICH, 81- *Concurrent Pos:* Lectr & contribr, Armed Forces Inst Path, 78- *Mem:* Int Acad Path; Am Asn Lab Animal Sci; Sigma Xi; Am Col Vet Pathologists; Electron Micros Soc Am. *Res:* Mechanisms an,d pathogenesis of disease, especially renal pathology and laboratory animal pathology; applications of transmission and scanning electron microscopy to pathology; utilization of morphometry and stereology in pathology; toxicology. *Mailing Add:* Toxicol Res Lab Health & Environ Sci Dow Chem USA 1803 Bldg Midland MI 48640

EISENBRANDT, LESLIE LEE, b Chanute, Kans, June 23, 08; m 36, 52; c 4. PHARMACOLOGY. *Educ:* Col Emporia, AB, 32; Kans State Univ, MS, 34; Rutgers Univ, PhD(zool), 36. *Prof Exp:* Asst, Kans State Univ, 32-34; asst, Rutgers Univ, 34-36; from instr to asst prof biol, Univ Mo-Kansas City, 36-42, from asst prof to assoc prof physiol, Sch Dent, 42-47, from assoc prof to prof pharmacol, Sch Pharm, 47-66, dean sch, 53-66; prof, 67-73, chmn, 72-73, EMER PROF PHARMACOL, SCH MED UNIV MOCOLUMBIA, 73- *Concurrent Pos:* Res assoc, Sch Med Univ Calif, 48-49; consult, Midwest Res Inst, 55-62; mem bd trustees, US Pharmacopeia, 70-75. *Mem:* Am Soc Pharmacol & Exp Therapeut; Am Asn Hist Med; Am Soc Clin Pharmacol & Therapeut; Am Soc Trop Med & Hyg; Sigma Xi. *Res:* Drug metabolism and biliary excretion. *Mailing Add:* 8359 Somerset Dr Prairie Village KS 66207

EISENBRAUN, ALLAN ALFRED, b Lodz, Poland, Nov 7, 28; m 57; c 2. ORGANIC CHEMISTRY. *Educ:* Univ Innsbruck, BSc, 52; McGill Univ, PhD(org chem), 59. *Prof Exp:* Res chemist, Ogilvie Flour Mills Co, Ltd, 52-59, res assoc, Diamond Labs, 59-60; sr res chemist, Nitrogen Div, Allied Chem Corp, 60-66; from polymer chemist to sr polymer chemist, 66-72, RES ASSOC, ETHYL CORP, 72- *Mem:* Am Chem Soc. *Res:* Carbohydrates; amino acids; heterocyclic chemistry; polymerization kinetics; polymer stabilization; new polymers for packaging applications; syntheses of new polymers. *Mailing Add:* Ethyl Corp Res & Develop Dept Gulfstate Rd POB 341 Baton Rouge LA 70821

EISENBRAUN, EDMUND JULIUS, b Wewela, SDak, Dec 10, 20; m 49; c 3. ORGANIC CHEMISTRY. *Educ:* Univ Wis, BS, 50, MS, 51, PhD, 55. *Prof Exp:* Res chemist, Monsanto Chem Co, Ohio, 55-56; res fel, Wayne State Univ, 56-59; sr res assoc chem, Stanford Univ, 59-61; res dir, Aldrich Chem Co, Wis, 61-62; assoc prof, 62-68, prof chem, 68-75, REGENTS PROF CHEM, OKLA STATE UNIV, 75- *Concurrent Pos:* Dir res proj 58A, Am Petrol Inst, 62-68; Sigma Xi lectr, Okla State Univ, 80. *Mem:* Am Chem Soc; The Chem Soc. *Res:* Synthesis structure proof and reaction of hydrocarbons and methylcyclopentane monoterpenoids, metal-amine reactions; Favorskii reaction; catalytic hydrogenation, hydrogenolysis and dehydrogenation. *Mailing Add:* Dept of Chem Okla State Univ Stillwater OK 74074

EISENBUD, DAVID, b New York, NY, Apr 8, 47. ALGEBRA. *Educ:* Univ Chicago, BS, 66, MS, 67, PhD(math), 70. *Prof Exp:* Lectr & res assoc math, 70-72, asst prof, 72-77, assoc prof, 77-80, PROF MATH, BRANDEIS UNIV, 80- *Concurrent Pos:* Fel, Alfred P Sloan Found, 74-76. *Mem:* Am Math Soc; Math Asn Am. *Res:* Commutative algebra; algebraic geometry; singularities of differentiable maps. *Mailing Add:* Dept of Math Brandeis Univ Waltham MA 02154

EISENBUD, LEONARD, b Elizabeth, NJ, Aug 3, 13; m 46; c 1. THEORETICAL PHYSICS. *Educ:* Union Univ, NY, BS, 35; Princeton Univ, PhD(theoret physics), 48. *Prof Exp:* Physicist, Bartol Res Found, Pa, 48-58; chmn dept, 58-62 & 68-69, PROF PHYSICS, STATE UNIV NY STONY BROOK, 58- *Concurrent Pos:* Mem, Inst Adv Study, 41. *Mem:* Fel Am Phys Soc. *Res:* Nuclear physics; quantum mechanics. *Mailing Add:* Dept of Physics State Univ of NY Stony Brook NY 11790

EISENBUD, MERRIL, b New York, NY, Mar 18, 15; m 39; c 3. ENVIRONMENTAL HEALTH. *Educ:* NY Univ, BSEE, 36. *Hon Degrees:* ScD, Fairleigh Dickinson Univ, 60; DHC, Cath Univ Rio de Janeiro, 70. *Prof Exp:* Indust hygienist, Liberty Mutual Ins Co, 36-47; assoc prof, 45-55, adj prof, 55-59, PROF ENVIRON MED, NY UNIV MED CTR, 59- *Concurrent Pos:* Dir health & safety lab, US AEC, 47-57, mgr, NY Opers Off, 54-59; mem bd on radioactive waste mgt, Nat Acad Sci, 56-; mem expert adv panel radiation, WHO, 57-; mem, Nat Coun Radiation Protection, 64-; adminr, Environ Protection Admin, New York, 68-70; mem, NY State Health Adv Coun, 69-81; mem, Nat Adv Coun, Electric Power Res Inst. *Honors & Awards:* Arthur Holly Compton Award, Am Nuclear Soc; Power-Life Award, Inst Elec & Electronics Engrs. *Mem:* Nat Acad Eng; fel AAAS; Radiation Soc; fel Am Nuclear Soc; Health Physics Soc (pres, 64-66). *Res:* Environmental radioactivity; urban pollution; environmental effects of power generation; human ecology. *Mailing Add:* PO Box 837 Tuxedo NY 10987

EISENFELD, ARNOLD JOEL, b Pittsburgh, Pa, July 26, 36; m 60; c 2. PHARMACOLOGY, INTERNAL MEDICINE. *Educ:* Washington & Jefferson Col, AB, 58; Yale Univ, MD, 62. *Prof Exp:* Intern & resident med, Yale-New Haven Hosp Ctr, Conn, 62-64; res assoc, NIH, 64-66; from asst prof to assoc prof pharmacol & internal med, 67-77, SR RES SCIENTIST OBSTET & GYNEC, YALE UNIV, 77- *Concurrent Pos:* Fel pharmacol, Sch Med, Yale Univ, 66-67. *Mem:* Am Soc Pharmacol & Exp Therapeut. *Res:* Interaction of estrogens, androgens and progestins with target organs; birth control; clinical pharmacology; hypertension. *Mailing Add:* Dept of Pharmacol Yale Univ Sch of Med New Haven CT 06510

EISENFELD, JEROME, b New York, NY, Oct 13, 38; m 62; c 1. APPLIED MATHEMATICS. *Educ:* City Col New York, BS, 60; Univ Chicago, MS, 64, PhD, 66. *Prof Exp:* Res assoc math, Univ Chicago, 66; asst prof, Rensselaer Polytech Inst, 66-72; assoc prof, 72-76, PROF MATH, UNIV TEX, ARLINGTON, 76- *Concurrent Pos:* Vis prof, Univ Tex Health Sci Ctr, Dallas, 75-81, adj prof, 73- *Mem:* Am Math Soc. *Res:* System identification; mathematic modeling in medicine; differential equations; linear algebra. *Mailing Add:* Dept Math Univ Tex Arlington TX 76010

EISENHARDT, RUDOLPH HERMANN, b Berlin, Ger, Aug 10, 24; m 53; c 3. PHYSICAL BIOCHEMISTRY. *Educ:* Univ Calif, Berkeley, BA, 52; Univ Chicago, MS, 54, PhD(phys & anal chem), 62. *Prof Exp:* Engr, Westminster Co, Bolivia, 45-47, chief engr, 47-49; instr chem, Univ Ill, 55-56; RES ASSOC PHYS BIOCHEM, HARRISON DEPT SURG RES, SCH MED, UNIV PA, 57- *Concurrent Pos:* Vis prof, Wenner-Gren Inst, Univ Stockholm, 67-68; vis scholar, Dept Chem, Molecular Biol Inst, Univ Calif, Los Angeles, 74-75; mem, Franklin Inst. *Mem:* AAAS; Biophys Soc; Soc Gen Chem. *Res:* Bioenergetics; metabolic transients; stable and radioactive isotopes; isotope methodology; instrumentation; rapid mixing and sampling techniques. *Mailing Add:* Duval Manor Apts 6350 Greene St Philadelphia PA 19144

EISENHARDT, WILLIAM ANTHONY, JR, b Lorain, Ohio, Nov 15, 42; m 69; c 1. FOOD CHEMISTRY, BIOPHYSICS. *Educ:* Western Reserve Univ, AB, 65; State Univ NY Buffalo, PhD(chem), 70. *Prof Exp:* Res assoc chem, Univ Chicago, 70-71; res scientist chem, Union Carbide Corp, 71-76, group leader, 76-78, sr group leader immunochem & clin chem, 78-79; mgr, Phys Chem Lab, Gen Foods Corp, 79-81; DIR, ANAL RES & DEVELOP, ROSS LABS, DIV ABBOTT LABS, 81- *Mem:* Am Chem Soc; Sigma Xi. *Res:* Organic and bio-organic chemistry related to novel analytical and diagnostic reagents; analytical biochemistry related to design of new clinical analytical systems; surface chemistry/physics and chemistry/physics of water at low temperatures; synthesis of bioactive and radioisotopically-labeled molecules. *Mailing Add:* Ross Labs 625 Cleveland Ave Columbus OH 43216

EISENHART, CHURCHILL, b Rochester, NY, Mar 11, 13; m 39; c 2. MATHEMATICAL STATISTICS. *Educ:* Princeton Univ, AB, 34, AM, 35; Univ London, PhD(math statist), 37. *Prof Exp:* Instr math, Univ Wis, 37-40, from asst prof to assoc prof, 40-47, statistician & biometrician, Exp Sta, 37-47; chief, Statist Eng Lab, 46-63, SR RES FEL, NAT BUR STANDARDS, 63- Prof Exp: Res assoc, Tufts Col, 43; res mathematician, Appl Math Group, Columbia Univ, 43-44, prin math statisticain, Statist Res Group, 44-45. *Honors & Awards:* Naval Ord Develop award, 46; US Dept of Commerce exceptional serv award, 57; Rockefeller Pub Serv award, 58. *Mem:* Fel AAAS; Hist Sci Soc; fel Inst Math Statist (vpres, 48); Math Asn Am; Fel Am Statist Asn (vpres, 58-59, pres, 71). *Res:* Mathematical statistics and its applications in the biological and physical sciences and in engineering and industry; history of statistical methodology. *Mailing Add:* Nat Bur of Standards MET B-268 Washington DC 20234

EISENHAUER, CHARLES MARTIN, b New York, NY, Feb 6, 30; m 58; c 2. RADIATION SHIELDING, NEUTRON STANDARDS. *Educ:* Queens Col, NY, BS, 51. *Prof Exp:* Jr mathematician reactor physics, Brookhaven Nat Lab, 51-52; nuclear physicist radiation penetration, Armed Forces Spec Weapons Proj, 53-54; vis scientist cold neutron exp, Brookhaven Nat Lab, 56-57; RADIATION PHYSICIST, NAT BUR STANDARDS, 58- *Concurrent Pos:* Consult, Oak Ridge Nat Lab, 64; adj prof, Cath Univ Am, 68-72; president's comn on accident at Three Mile Island, 79. *Honors & Awards:* Silver Medal, US Dept Commerce, 62. *Mem:* Fel Am Nuclear Soc; Health Physics Soc. *Res:* Penetration of nuclear radiation; experimental use of cold neutrons to study the dynamics of solids and liquids; neutron spectra and detector responses in reactors; energy deposition by charged particles; calibration of neutron personnel monitors. *Mailing Add:* Nat Bur Standards Gaithersburg MD 20760

EISENHAUER, HUGH ROSS, b Lethbridge, Alta, Oct 11, 27; m 71; c 5. ENVIRONMENTAL SCIENCES. *Educ:* Univ Saskatchewan, BA, 49, MA, 50; Univ Wis, PhD(org chem), 53. *Prof Exp:* Res chemist, Can Indust Ltd, 53-54; res chemist, Du Pont Co Can, 54-62, sr res chemist, 62-66; res scientist, Pub Health Eng Div, 66-70, head water sci subdiv, Hydrol Sci Div, 70-72, chief, Water Quality Res Div, 72-74, sr res adv, 74-78, CHIEF RES PLANNING & COORD, INLAND WATERS DIRECTORATE, DEPT ENVIRONMENT, GOVT CAN, 78- *Mem:* Fel Chem Inst Can; Water Pollution Control Fedn; Int Asn Water Pollution Res. *Res:* Water chemistry, limnology, hydrology, glaciology, hydraulics. *Mailing Add:* Inland Waters Dir Dept Environ Place Vincent Massey Ottawa ON K1A 0E7 Can

EISENLOHR, W(ILLIAM) S(TEWART), JR, b Philadelphia, Pa, Nov 16, 07; m 32; c 3. ENGINEERING. *Educ:* Univ Pa, BS in CE, 28. *Prof Exp:* Hydraul engr, US Geol Surv, Mass, 28, Va, 28-29, Ala, 29-31, Ariz, 31-33, Washington, DC, 33-61, Colo, 61-70; RETIRED. *Mem:* Fel Am Soc Civil Engrs; Am Geophys Union. *Res:* Hydraulics of natural channels; coefficients for velocity distribution in open channel flow; effect of water temperature on flow of natural streams; floods of North Central Pennsylvania; hydrology of prairie potholes. *Mailing Add:* 2550 Queen St Lakewood CO 80215

EISENMAN, GEORGE, b New York, NY, May 6, 29; m 52; c 2. BIOPHYSICS. *Educ:* Harvard Univ, AB, 49, MD, 53. *Prof Exp:* Res assoc, Harvard Univ, 54-55; sr staff scientist, Dept Basic Res, Eastern Pa Psychiat Inst, 56-62; assoc prof physiol, Col Med, Univ Utah, 62-65; prof physiol, Univ Chicago, 65-69, prof biophys, 67-69; PROF PHYSIOL, SCH MED, UNIV CALIF, LOS ANGELES, 69- *Concurrent Pos:* Res fel, Harvard Univ, 53-54; consult, Corning Glass Works, 62-72; mem biophys & biophys chem study sect, NIH, 67-71; mem ed bd, Biophys J, Biophys Soc, 68-, J Membrane Biol, 69-, Physiol Reviews, 74- *Mem:* Am Physiol Soc; Biophys Soc; fel Royal Soc Arts. *Res:* Membrane biophysics; molecular biology; physical chemistry. *Mailing Add:* Dept of Physiol Univ of Calif Med Ctr Los Angeles CA 90024

EISENMAN, JOSEPH SOL, physiology, neurophysiology, see previous edition

EISENMAN, LEONARD MAX, b Brooklyn, NY, July 7, 42; m 66; c 2. NEUROSCIENCES. *Educ:* Brooklyn Col, BA, 64; Miami Univ, MA, 65; Duke Univ, PhD(physiol psychol), 74. *Prof Exp:* Fel anat, Col Physicians & Surgeons, Columbia Univ, 73-76; ASST PROF ANAT, THOMAS JEFFERSON MED COL, 76- *Concurrent Pos:* Individual res fel, Nat Inst Neurol Dis & Stroke, 74. *Mem:* Soc Neurosci; Acoust Soc Am; Sigma Xi; Am Asn Anatomists. *Res:* Neural coding in the sensory systems, especially the auditory system; relationships between the auditory system and the cerebellum and the functional implications of these relationships. *Mailing Add:* Dept of Anat Thomas Jefferson Med Col Philadelphia PA 19107

EISENMAN, RICHARD L, b Bridgeport, Conn, July 12, 28; m 52; c 3. SYSTEMS ANALYSIS. *Educ:* Col Holy Cross, AB, 49; Univ Conn, MA, 50; Univ Mich, PhD(math), 64. *Prof Exp:* Instr math, Fairfield Univ, 49, Univ Md, 50-52 & US Air Force, 52-72; res mathematician, Wright Patterson AFB, 53-56, US Air Force Acad, 58-68; chief tactical anal, Tan Son Nhut AFB, Vietnam, 68-69; chief systems anal personnel plans, Hq, US Air Force, DC, 69-72; prog dir, Human Resources Res Orgn, 72-76; specialist in nat defense, Libr of Cong, 77-78; LECTR, UNIV MARYLAND, 78- *Concurrent Pos:* Consult, Air Battle Anal Hq, US Air Force, 65, Kaman Nuclear Corp, 65-66 & Holly Sugar Corp, 68; staff asst systs anal, Off Secy Defense, DC, 66-67; prof, George Washington Univ, 69-70 & Univ Md, 70-; vpres, Ferry Landing Woods, Inc, 74- & Chaney Station, Inc, 78- *Mem:* Math Asn Am; Sigma Xi; Am Statist Asn. *Res:* Theory and application of mathematical models. *Mailing Add:* White Hall Dunkirk MD 20754

EISENMANN, EUGENE, ornithology, deceased

EISENREICH, STEVEN JOHN, b Eau Clarie, Wis,Sept 9, 47. AQUATIC & ENVIRONMENTAL CHEMISTRY. *Educ:* Univ Wis-Eau Claire, BS, 69; Univ Wis-Milwaukee, MS, 73; Univ Wis-Madison, PhD(water chem), 75. *Prof Exp:* Asst prof, 75-79, ASSOC PROF ENVIRON ENG, DEPT CIVIL & MINERAL ENG, UNIV MINN, MINNEAPOLIS, 79- *Concurrent Pos:* Consult, Environ Protection Agency & Minn State Planning Agency, 76-78. *Mem:* Am Chem Soc; Int Asn Great Lakes Res; Am Soc Limnol & Oceanog. *Mailing Add:* Environ Eng Prog Univ of Minn Minneapolis MN 55455

EISENSON, JON, b New York, NY, Dec 17, 07; m 31; c 2. SPEECH & HEARING SCIENCES. *Educ:* City Col New York, BSS, 28; Columbia Univ, MA, 30, PhD(educ psychol), 35; Am Bd Prof Psychol, dipl. *Prof Exp:* Instr, NY Schs, 28-35; instr speech, Brooklyn Col, 35-42; from asst prof to prof & dir speech clin, Queens Col, NY, 46-62; prof hearing & speech sci & dir, Inst Childhood Aphasia, 62-73, EMER PROF HEARING & SPEECH SCI, SCH MED, STANFORD UNIV, 73- *Concurrent Pos:* Consult, US Vet Admin Hosps, Calif, 62-; chmn spec educ adv comt & mem med & sci comt, United Cerebral Palsy Asn, 64-69; lectr, Col Physicians & Surgeons, Columbia Univ; distinguished prof spec educ, San Francisco State Univ, 75-81. *Mem:* Fel AAAS; fel Am Speech & Hearing Asn (pres, 58-59); fel Am Psychol Asn; Speech Commun Asn. *Res:* Language; speech pathology with emphasis on stuttering and aphasia; psychology of speech; communication; psycholinguistics; child language and language delay; confirmation and information in rewards and punishments. *Mailing Add:* 82 Pearce Mitchell Place Stanford CA 94305

EISENSTADT, ARTHUR A, b New York, NY, Jan 23, 18; m 42; c 3. SPEECH PATHOLOGY. *Educ:* Brooklyn Col, AB, 38, MA, 46; NY Univ, PhD(speech path), 54. *Prof Exp:* Instr speech, Brooklyn Col, 45-46; asst, Cornell Univ, 46-48; asst prof, Rutgers Univ, 48-55; speech pathologist, Newark Div Speech Educ, 55-63; PROF SPEECH & DIR SPEECH EDUC, ST JOHN'S UNIV, NY, 63- *Honors & Awards:* Fulbright award, US Dept HEW, 59-60; Shell Oil Co res grant, 72. *Mem:* Fel Am Speech & Hearing Asn; Am Asn Univ Prof. *Res:* Geriatric speech pathology; pediatric speech pathology; language acquisition disorders. *Mailing Add:* Dept of Speech Commun & Theatre St John's Univ Jamaica NY 11432

EISENSTADT, BERTRAM JOSEPH, b New York, NY, Mar 28, 23; m 58; c 1. MATHEMATICS. *Educ:* City Col New York, BS, 43; Brown Univ ScM, 46; Univ Mich, PhD(math), 51. *Prof Exp:* Res assoc physics, Nat Adv Comt Aeronaut, 44-46; from asst prof to assoc prof, 49-61, PROF MATH, WAYNE STATE UNIV, 61-, CHMN DEPT, 75- *Mem:* Am Math Soc; Math Asn Am. *Res:* Functional analysis. *Mailing Add:* Dept of Math Wayne State Univ Detroit MI 48202

EISENSTADT, JEROME MELVIN, b Chicago, Ill, June 11, 26; m 60. BIOCHEMISTRY, HUMAN GENETICS. *Educ:* Roosevelt Univ, BS, 52; Brandeis Univ, MA, 59, PhD(biol), 60. *Prof Exp:* From asst prof to assoc prof microbiol, 62-74, assoc prof, 74-77, PROF HUMAN GENETICS, SCH MED, YALE UNIV, 77- *Concurrent Pos:* Fel biochem, Oak Ridge Nat Labs, 60-62; NIH fel, 61-62; consult, Oak Ridge Nat Labs, 60-61, 62- *Mem:* Am Soc Cell Biol; Am Soc Biol Chem; Am Soc Microbiol. *Res:* genetics of mitochondria; control mechanisms of protein and nucleic acid synthesis; somatic cell genetics. *Mailing Add:* Dept of Human Genetics Yale Univ Sch of Med New Haven CT 06510

EISENSTADT, MAURICE, b New York, NY, June 10, 31; m 61. PHYSICS. *Educ:* City Col New York, BCE, 52; Columbia Univ, AM, 53, PhD(physics), 58. *Prof Exp:* Asst physics, Columbia Univ, 54-58; physicist, Watson Labs, Int Bus Mach Corp, 58-63; physicist, Hudson Labs, Columbia Univ, 63-69; asst prof, 69-80, PHYSICIST, ALBERT EINSTEIN COL MED, 69-, ASSOC PROF MED, 80- *Mem:* Am Phys Soc. *Res:* Nuclear magnetic resonance; dielectric studies of macromolecules. *Mailing Add:* Albert Einstein Col Med 1300 Morris Park Ave Bronx NY 10461

EISENSTADT, RAYMOND, b Brooklyn, NY, May 13, 21; m 57; c 4. MECHANICAL ENGINEERING. *Educ:* City Col New York, BSME, 41; Columbia Univ, MSME, 43, PhD(mech eng), 53. *Prof Exp:* Construct engr, Mediter Theater, US Govt War Dept, 46; tech consult war surplus mat, Italy, 46-47; design engr heat, vent & air conditioning, P M Gussow, 48 & Corgett-Tinghir, 48-49; engr res lubrication, Atomic Energy Comn, Columbia Univ, 52-53; engr wind tunnel proj inst res, Lehigh Univ, 53-54, asst prof mech eng, 53-54; assoc prof, 54-69, PROF MECH ENG, UNION COL, NY, 69-, DIR, TECH INST, 70- *Concurrent Pos:* NSF fac fels, Mass Inst Technol & Univ Mich, 60-61, Inst Mech & Dynamics, Yale Univ, 63 & Smith Inst Solid State Sci Res, 64; NASA Lewis Struct Div res grant, 68-69; Gen Elec Co res fel, 69-78; mem subcomt plastic fatigue strength, pressure vessel res comt, Welding Res Coun. *Mem:* Fel Am Soc Mech Engrs; Am Soc Eng Educ; Am Soc Metals; Soc Exp Stress Anal; Am Soc Testing & Mat. *Res:* Mechanical behavior of materials; fatigue of metals. *Mailing Add:* Dept Mech Eng Union Col Schenectady NY 12308

EISENSTARK, ABRAHAM, b Warsaw, Poland, Sept 5, 19; nat US; m 48; c 3. BACTERIOLOGY. *Educ:* Univ Ill, AB, 41, AM, 42, PhD(bact), 48. *Prof Exp:* Electron microscopist, Univ Ill, 46-48; asst prof bact, Okla Agr & Mech Col, 48-51; from assoc prof to prof, Kans State Univ, 51-71; DIR & PROF DIV BIOL SCI, UNIV MO-COLUMBIA, 71- *Concurrent Pos:* Guggenheim fel, Inst Microbiol, Copenhagen, Denmark, 59; NSF sr fel, Univ Leicester, 66; sect head & prog dir molecular biol sect, NSF, Washington, DC, 69-70. *Mem:* AAAS; Am Soc Microbiol; Am Soc Photobiol. *Res:* Microbial genetics and photobiology. *Mailing Add:* 2002 Valley View Rd Columbia MO 65201

EISENSTATT, PHILLIP, b Omaha, Nebr, Oct 16, 22; m 52; c 3. GEOLOGY. *Educ:* Univ Nebr, BSc, 43. *Prof Exp:* Geologist, 43-50, div geologist, 50-62, STAFF GEOLOGIST, EXPLOR DEPT, SHELL OIL CO, 62- *Mem:* Fel Geol Soc Am; Am Asn Petrol Geologists. *Res:* Subsurface and field geology assignments which could result in the discovery of oil and gas reserves; geological data processing applications. *Mailing Add:* Explor Dept Shell Oil Co PO Box 60193 New Orleans LA 70160

EISENSTEIN, ALBERT BERNARD, b Doniphan, Mo, Nov 9, 20; m 41; c 5. INTERNAL MEDICINE, ENDOCRINOLOGY. *Educ:* Univ Mo, AB, 41; Wash Univ, MD, 44. *Prof Exp:* From instr to assoc prof prev med & med, Wash Univ, 52-66; chief endocrinol, Med Serv, John Cochran Vet Hosp, 66-68; dir dept med, Cumberland Hosp, 68-72; chief dept med, Gouverneur Hosp, 72-76; ASSOC CHIEF STAFF/RES, VET ADMIN MED CTR, BROOKLYN, 76-; PROF MED, STATE UNIV NY, DOWNSTATE MED CTR, 76- *Concurrent Pos:* Res fel nutrit, Sch Med, Wash Univ, 50-52; dir div med, Jewish Hosp St Louis, 58-63, mem dept med, 63-66. *Mem:* AAAS; Am Soc Clin Invest; Am Soc Clin Nutrit; Soc Exp Biol & Med; Endocrine Soc. *Res:* Adrenal cortical physiology and biochemistry; relationship of nutritional factors to endocrine function. *Mailing Add:* Vet Admin Med Ctr 800 Poly Pl Brooklyn NY 11209

EISENSTEIN, BOB I, b New York, NY, Feb 4, 39; m 64. HIGH ENERGY PHYSICS. *Educ:* Columbia Univ, AB, 59, AM, 61, PhD(physics), 64. *Prof Exp:* Res assoc physics, Columbia Univ, 64; res fel, Harvard Univ, 64-67; asst prof, 67-70, assoc prof, 70-78, PROF PHYSICS, UNIV ILL, URBANA, 78- *Mem:* Am Phys Soc. *Res:* Electron position annihilation; charm particles; data analysis. *Mailing Add:* Dept of Physics Univ of Ill Urbana IL 61801

EISENSTEIN, BRUCE A, b Philadelphia, Pa; m 63; c 3. PATTERN RECOGNITION. *Educ:* Mass Inst Technol, BSEE, 63; Drexel Inst Tech, MSEE, 65; Univ Pa, PhD(elec eng), 70. *Prof Exp:* HEAD, DEPT ELEC ENG, DREXEL UNIV, 80- *Concurrent Pos:* Vis prof, Princeton Univ, 70-71. *Mem:* Sr mem Inst Elec & Electron Engrs (secy-treas, 80-81). *Res:* Pattern recognition by digital signal processing to achieve compaction of feature set. *Mailing Add:* Elec Eng Dept Col Eng Drexel Univ Philadelphia PA 19104

EISENSTEIN, JULIAN (CALVERT), b Warrenton, Mo, Apr 3, 21; m 48; c 3. THEORETICAL PHYSICS. *Educ:* Harvard Univ, BS, 41, PhD(physics), 48. *Prof Exp:* Res assoc acoust, Harvard Univ, 42-45; instr physics, Univ Wis, 48-52; from asst prof to assoc prof, Pa State Univ, 53-57; physicist, Nat Bur Standards, 57-66; PROF PHYSICS, GEORGE WASHINGTON UNIV, 66- *Concurrent Pos:* Nat Res fel, 52-53. *Mem:* Am Phys Soc; Brit Inst Physics. *Res:* Low temperature physics; paramagnetism; absorption spectra of complex ions. *Mailing Add:* 82 Kalorama Circle NW Washington DC 20008

EISENSTEIN, ROBERT ALAN, b St Louis, Mo, July 17, 42; m 67; c 2. NUCLEAR PHYSICS, PARTICLE PHYSICS. *Educ:* Oberlin Col, AB, 64; Yale Univ, MS, 66, PhD(physics), 68. *Prof Exp:* Res fel physics, Weizmann Inst Sci, Israel, 68-70; from asst prof to assoc prof, 70-80, PROF PHYSICS, CARNEGIE-MELLON UNIV, 80- *Concurrent Pos:* Mem prog adv comt, Los Alamos Meson Physics Facil, 73-75. *Mem:* Am Phys Soc. *Res:* Experimental studies of the interaction of elementary particles with nuclei. *Mailing Add:* Dept of Physics Carnegie-Mellon Univ Pittsburgh PA 15213

EISENSTEIN, TOBY K, b Philadelphia, Pa, Sept 15, 42; m 63; c 3. MICROBIOLOGY, IMMUNOLOGY. *Educ:* Wellesley Col, BA, 64; Bryn Mawr Col, PhD(microbiol), 69. *Prof Exp:* Instr microbiol, 69-71, asst prof, 71-77, ASSOC PROF MICROBIOL & IMMUNOL, SCH MED, TEMPLE UNIV, 77- *Concurrent Pos:* USPHS res grants & contracts bact & mycol, 76-80. *Mem:* AAAS; Am Soc Microbiol; Sigma Xi; Reticuloendothelial Soc. *Res:* Immunity to bacterial infections, salmonella, group B streptococci, Legionella; vaccines; macrophages and cellular immunity. *Mailing Add:* Dept of Microbiol & Immunol Temple Univ Sch of Med Philadelphia PA 19140

EISENTRAUT, KENT JAMES, b Troy, NY, July 31, 38; m 64; c 2. ANALYTICAL CHEMISTRY. *Educ:* St Michael's Col, AB, 60; Rensselaer Polytech Inst, PhD(anal chem), 64. *Prof Exp:* Res scientist, Aerospace Res Labs, 64-75, res chemist, Air Force Mat Lab, Wright-Patterson AFB, 75-79, RES CHEMIST, AIR FORCE WRIGHT AERONAUT LABS, 79- *Concurrent Pos:* US Air Force Res & Develop award, 66. *Mem:* Am Chem Soc; fel Am Inst Chemists; NY Acad Sci. *Res:* Metal coordination chemistry; gas chromatography of volatile rare earth, transition and alkali metal chelates; atomic absorption spectroscopy; synthesis of volatile chelates; infrared and nuclear magnetic resonance spectroscopy; differential thermal and thermal gravimetric analysis; metal analysis of Apollo 11, 12, 14, 15 & 16 lunar samples; research support of Air Force Oil Analysis Program; fluids, lubricants and lubrication technology research and development. *Mailing Add:* 1827 Trebein Rd Xenia OH 45385

EISER, ARTHUR L, b Geneva, Ill, Apr 16, 28; m 55; c 3. PLANT TAXONOMY, PLANT ECOLOGY. *Educ:* Univ Denver, BA, 50; Iowa State Univ, MS, 52; Va Polytech Inst, PhD(plant taxon, ecol), 61. *Prof Exp:* Asst biol, Univ Denver, 47-50; asst bot, Iowa State Univ, 50-52; instr hort, Va Polytech Inst, 54-56, asst, 56-58; asst prof sci, 58-63, assoc prof biol, 63-69, PROF BIOL, BALL STATE UNIV, 69- *Mem:* Ecol Soc Am; Sigma Xi. *Res:* Plant taxonomy of flowering and ornamental plants; uses in landscaping. *Mailing Add:* Dept of Biol Ball State Univ Muncie IN 47306

EISERLING, FREDERICK A, b San Diego, Calif, May 8, 38. MICROBIOLOGY. *Educ:* Univ Calif, Los Angeles, BA, 59, PhD(microbiol), 64. *Prof Exp:* USPHS fel biophys, Univ Geneva, 64-66; from asst prof to assoc prof, 66-74, chmn dept, 81, PROF MICROBIOL, UNIV CALIF, LOS ANGELES, 74- *Concurrent Pos:* Ed, J Ultrastruct Res; prog dir, Res Training Molecular Biol. *Mem:* Am Soc Microbiol; AAAS; Soc Gen Microbiol. *Res:* Structure of bacteria and bacterial viruses; light harvesting structures. *Mailing Add:* Dept Microbiol Univ Calif Los Angeles CA 90024

EISINGER, JOSEF, b Vienna, Austria, Mar 19, 24; US citizen; m 63; c 2. BIOPHYSICS, FUORESCENCE SPECTROSCOPY. *Educ:* Univ Toronto, BA, 47, MA, 48; Mass Inst Technol, PhD(physics), 51. *Prof Exp:* Res assoc, Mass Inst Technol, 51-52, Nat Res Coun Can, 52-53 & Rice Univ, 53-54; MEM TECH STAFF, BELL LABS, 54- *Concurrent Pos:* Adj assoc prof physics, NY Univ, 60-63; Guggenheim fels, Switz, 63-64 & Eng, 78-79. *Mem:* Fel Am Phys Soc; Biophys Soc; Am Soc Biol Chemists; Am Soc Photobiol. *Res:* Excited states of biological molecules; energy transfer and emission spectroscopy; diagnostic screening tests in environmental medicine; history of medicine; membrane biology. *Mailing Add:* Bell Labs Murray Hill NJ 07974

EISLER, RONALD, b Brooklyn, NY, Feb 23, 32; m 63; c 2. MARINE BIOLOGY, POLLUTION BIOLOGY. *Educ:* NY Univ, BA, 52; Univ Wash, MS, 57, PhD(fisheries biol), 61. *Prof Exp:* Asst marine lab, Univ Miami, 52-53; biol aide, US Army Med Nutrit Lab, Colo, 53-55; asst, Col Fisheries, Univ Wash, 56; aquatic biologist, NY State Conserv Dept, 57-58; asst, Lab Radiation Biol, Univ Wash, 58-61; fishery res biologist, Sandy Hook Marine Lab, US Fish & Wildlife Serv, 61-66; res aquatic biologist, Nat Marine Water Qual Lab, US Environ Protection Agency, 66-79; BIOSCI ADV, FISH & WILDLIFE SERV, US DEPT INTERIOR, 79- *Concurrent Pos:* Adj prof, Grad Sch Oceanog, Univ RI, 70-; vis prof, Hebrew Univ Jerusalem, Israel & resident dir, Marine Biol Lab, Israel, 72-73; adj prof, Biol Dept, American Univ, 80- *Mem:* Am Fish Soc; Marine Biol Asn UK; Israel Ecol Soc; Nat Shellfish Asn. *Res:* Ecological aspects of coastal pollution; physiological ichthyology; aquatic toxicology; environmental contaminants evaluation. *Mailing Add:* Fish & Wildlife Serv US Dept Interior Washington DC 20240

EISLEY, JOE G(RIFFIN), b Auglaize Co, Ohio, Apr 7, 28; m 56; c 2. AEROSPACE ENGINEERING. *Educ:* St Louis Univ, BS, 51; Calif Inst Technol, MS, 52, PhD(aeronaut, physics), 56. *Prof Exp:* From asst prof to assoc prof, 56-65, PROF AERONAUT & ASTRONAUT ENG, UNIV MICH, 65-, ASSOC DEAN COL ENG, 67- *Concurrent Pos:* Consult, Bendix Systs Div, 59-60, Boeing Co, 61 & Conductron Corp, 64; NSF fac fel, 62-63. *Mem:* Am Inst Aeronaut & Astronaut; Am Soc Eng Educ; Am Soc Mech Engrs; Soc Hist Technol. *Res:* Structural dynamics; nonlinear vibrations; aeroelasticity; stress analysis; engineering curriculum development; history of technology; graduate and continuing education. *Mailing Add:* Col of Eng Univ of Mich Ann Arbor MI 48103

EISNER, ALAN MARK, b Brooklyn, NY, June 3, 43. EXPERIMENTAL HIGH ENERGY PHYSICS. *Educ:* Harvard Univ, BA, 64, MA, 65, PhD(physics), 71. *Prof Exp:* Asst res physicist, 71-73, asst prof physics, 73-80, ASSOC RES PHYSICIST, UNIV CALIF, SANTA BARBARA, 80- *Concurrent Pos:* Adj assoc prof physics, Univ Calif, San Diego, 81- *Mem:* Am Phys Soc. *Res:* Studies of hadronic structure using electromagnetic probes; interactions of high energy photons with matter and with each other. *Mailing Add:* Dept Physics B019 Univ Calif San Diego La Jolla CA 92093

EISNER, ELMER, b Poughkeepsie, NY, Mar 8, 19; m 43; c 3. EXPLORATION PHYSICS. *Educ:* Brooklyn Col, BA, 39; Johns Hopkins Univ, PhD(physics), 44. *Prof Exp:* Asst physicist, Nat Bur Standards, 43-44; asst prof physics, Rutgers Univ, 44-47; physicist, Argonne Nat Lab, 47-50; physicist, 51-60, res assoc, 60-69, SR RES ASSOC, TEXACO INC, 69- *Mem:* AAAS; Am Phys Soc; Am Math Soc; Soc Explor Geophysicists. *Res:* Analysis of nuclear scattering; design of electronic proximity fuses; analysis of pile behavior; geophysical exploration methods; numerical analysis; inverse problems in wave equation. *Mailing Add:* Texaco Inc Bellaire Lab PO Box 425 Bellaire TX 77401

EISNER, HOWARD, b New York, NY, Aug 8, 35; m 57; c 3. ELECTRICAL ENGINEERING, OPERATIONS RESEARCH. *Educ:* City Col New York, BEE, 57; Columbia Univ, MS, 58; George Washington Univ, DSc(eng appl sci), 66. *Prof Exp:* Teaching asst elec eng, Columbia Univ, 57; substitute teacher physics, Brooklyn Col, 57-59; res engr, 59-63, prog dir eng & opers res, 64-66, assoc dir eng anal div, 66-68, vpres, 68-71, EXEC V PRES, OPERS RES INC, SILVER SPRING, 71- *Concurrent Pos:* Lectr physics, Sch Gen Studies, Brooklyn Col, 58-59; lectr, Sch Eng & Appl Sci, George Washington, 60-64; asst prof lectr, 64-66, Col Gen Studies, 66-67. *Mem:* Inst Elec & Electronics Engrs; Am Inst Aeronaut & Astronaut; Opers Res Soc Am; Inst Mgt Sci; fel NY Acad Sci. *Res:* Communications; information theory; systems. *Mailing Add:* ORI Inc 1400 Spring St Silver Spring MD 20910

EISNER, MARK JOSEPH, b Poughkeepsie, NY, July 18, 38; m 62; c 2. OPERATIONS RESEARCH. *Educ:* Harvard Univ, BA, 60; Cornell Univ, PhD(opers res), 70. *Prof Exp:* Opers analyst, Res Analysis Corp, 60-65; asst prof opers res, Cornell Univ, 69-75; sect head, Math, Computers & Systs Dept, 75-79, SECT HEAD, EXXON RES & ENG DEPT, EXXON CORP, 79- *Concurrent Pos:* NSF grant, 71-74; assoc ed, Transactions, 75 & Opers Res, 78. *Mem:* Opers Res Soc Am; Inst Mgt Sci; Am Inst Indust Engrs. *Res:* Computer project management; game theory; traffic control theory; military operations research; mathematical programming. *Mailing Add:* Exxon Corp Box 153 Florham Park NJ 07932

EISNER, MELVIN, physics, see previous edition

EISNER, PHILIP NATHAN, b Springfield, Mass, Mar 7, 34; m 60; c 1. PHYSICS. *Educ:* Mass Inst Technol, BS, 55; NY Univ, PhD(physics), 69. *Prof Exp:* Sr engr, ITT Labs, 57-61; res assoc, Dewey Electronics Corp, 61-65, assoc dir, Physics Res Lab, 68-72; proj mgr laser isotope separation, Corp Res Labs, 72-80, PROJ MGR, RES & DEVELOP STRATEGIC PLANNING & TECHNOL DEPT, EXXON RES & ENG CO, 81- *Concurrent Pos:* Instr, NY Univ, 69-70. *Mem:* AAAS; Am Phys Soc. *Res:* Ionospheric physics; ion-molecule interactions; atomic and molecular scattering of electrons; laser isotope separation; sub-micron particles; chemistry of the upper atmosphere; decision analysis, probability. *Mailing Add:* 25 Newcomb Dr New Providence NJ 07974

EISNER, ROBERT LAWRENCE, experimental high energy physics, see previous edition

EISNER, ROBERT LINDEN, b Brooklyn, NY, June 21, 27; m 53; c 3. APPLIED PHYSICS, FORENSIC SCIENCE. *Educ:* Brooklyn Col, BA, 48; Univ Iowa, PhD(physics), 54. *Prof Exp:* Asst physics, Univ Iowa, 48-51, res asst, 51-53; res engr, Westinghouse Res Labs, 53-61, sr engr, 61-66, semiconductor div, 66-67, sr reliability engr, Westinghouse Astronuclear Lab, 67-71 & Westinghouse Transportation Div, 71-72; MGR TECH CONSULT, BASIC TECHNOL, INC, 73-, MGR PROD ASSURANCE SERV, 75- *Mem:* Am Inst Mining, Metall & Petrol Engrs; Am Phys Soc; Electrochem Soc. *Res:* Reliability physics in special materials applications; systems safety and reliability analyses; physics of failure; accident reconstruction; failure analysis; hazards anticipation; nondestructive testing. *Mailing Add:* Basic Technol Inc 7125 Saltsburg Rd Pittsburgh PA 15235

EISNER, THOMAS, b Berlin, Ger, June 25, 29; nat US; m 52; c 3. ZOOLOGY. *Educ:* Harvard Univ, BA, 51, PhD, 55. *Prof Exp:* Res fel, Harvard Univ, 55-57; from asst prof to prof, 57-76, SCHURMAN PROF BIOL, CORNELL UNIV, 76- *Concurrent Pos:* USPHS & NSF grants, 55-; Guggenheim fels, 64 & 72; mem bd dirs, Zero Pop Growth, 69-70 & Nat Audubon Soc, 70-75; mem nat coun, Nature Conservancy, 69-74. *Honors & Awards:* Newcomb-Cleveland Prize, AAAS, 67; Founder's Mem Award, Entom Soc Am, 69. *Mem:* Nat Acad Sci; Am Acad Arts & Sci; Royal Soc Arts; AAAS. *Res:* Insect physiology; chemical ecology; comparative behavior; biocommunication; pheromones; defensive secretions. *Mailing Add:* NB&B Langmuir Lab Cornell Univ Ithaca NY 14853

EISS, ABRAHAM L(OUIS), b New York, NY, Dec 28, 34; m 57; c 2. MATERIALS ENGINEERING, NUCLEAR ENGINEERING. *Educ:* Purdue Univ, BS, 55, MS, 56; Drexel Inst Technol, MS, 64. *Prof Exp:* Engr, Sylcor Div, Sylvania Elec Co, 56-59; eng specialist, Nuclear Div, Martin Co, 59-63; proj engr, Hittman Assocs, Inc, 63-65, chief mat eng & anal, 65-70; vpres eng, Mat Resources, Inc, Cockeysville, 70-72; sr mat engr, US Atomic Energy Comn, 72-76; TECH ASST TO DIR OF ENG TECHNOL, OFF RES, US NUCLEAR REGULATORY COMN, 76- *Mem:* Sci Res Soc Am; Am Inst Mining, Metall & Petrol Engrs; Am Soc Metals; Am Soc Testing & Mat. *Res:* Powder metallurgy; thermoelectrics; thermionics; nuclear power plant engineering; nuclear materials including structural, fuels, radioisotopes. *Mailing Add:* 6800 Hunt Ct Baltimore MD 21209

EISS, ALBERT FRANK, b La Fargeville, NY, Feb 2, 10; m 34; c 3. SCIENCE EDUCATION. *Educ:* Houghton Col, AB, 33; St Lawrence Univ, MA, 42; NY Univ, PhD(sci educ), 54. *Prof Exp:* Teacher pub schs, NY, 34-46; instr chem, Clarkson Col Technol, 46-49; head physics dept, Paul Smith's Col, 49-57; prof sci educ, Indiana State Col, Pa, 57-59; sci educ specialist, bur curric serv, Dept Pub Instr, 59-64; assoc exec secy, Nat Sci Teachers Asn, 64-71; educ systs specialist, WGa Educ Serv Ctr, 71-74; PRES, INNOVATIONS, INC, 74- *Mem:* AAAS; Nat Sci Teachers Asn; Nat Asn Res Sci Teaching. *Res:* Improvement in the teaching of science. *Mailing Add:* 118 Alice Lane Carrollton GA 30117

EISS, NORMAN SMITH, JR, b Buffalo, NY, Mar 13, 31; m 75; c 3. MECHANICAL ENGINEERING. *Educ:* Rensselaer Polytech Inst, BME, 53; Cornell Univ, MS, 59, PhD(mech eng), 61. *Prof Exp:* Process engr, E I du Pont de Nemours & Co, 53-54; res engr, Cornell Aeronaut Lab, Inc, 56-66; assoc prof, 66-77, PROF MECH ENG, VA POLYTECH INST & STATE UNIV, 77- *Concurrent Pos:* Nat Sci Found sci fac fel, Imp Col, London, 70-71. *Mem:* Am Soc Mech Engrs; Am Soc Lubrication Eng; Am Soc Eng Educ; Am Soc Testing & Mat. *Res:* Friction; wear; lubrication; grinding with abrasives; surface topography characterization. *Mailing Add:* Dept Mech Eng Va Polytech Inst & State Univ Blacksburg VA 24061

EISSENBURG, DAVID M(ARTIN), b Brooklyn, NY, Aug 5, 29; m 53; c 5. ENGINEERING. *Educ:* Col William & Mary, BS, 50; Mass Inst Technol, BS, 52; Univ Tenn, MS, 63, PhD(chem eng), 72. *Prof Exp:* Mem staff reactor opers, Homogeneous Reactor Exp, 52-53, mem staff eng res & develop, 53-72 & long-range planning, 72-76, SR DEVELOP ENGR PROG MGT, OAK RIDGE NAT LAB, 76- *Res:* Fluid mechanics and heat transfer of non-Newtonian suspensions; boiling heat transfer; condensation heat transfer; seawater desalination technology; energy technology management. *Mailing Add:* Oak Ridge Nat Lab PO Box Y Oak Ridge TN 37830

EISSLER, ROBERT L, b Evansville, Ind, Feb 8, 21; m 48; c 4. PHYSICAL CHEMISTRY. *Educ:* Evansville Col, BS, 49; Univ Ill, MS, 56, PhD(chem), 60. *Prof Exp:* Asst chem engr, Ill State Geol Surv, 52-60, assoc chemist, 60-61; mgr graphic arts res, Ball Bros Res Corp, 61-65; PRIN CHEMIST, NORTHERN REGIONAL LAB, AGR RES SERV, USDA, 65- *Concurrent Pos:* Vis prof, Ball State Teachers Col, 62-63. *Mem:* Am Chem Soc. *Res:* Surface chemistry; coal and petroleum; photoengraving and lithographing processes; organic and inorganic coatings; emulsions. *Mailing Add:* Northern Regional Lab Agr Res Serv USDA 1815 N University Peoria IL 61604

EISSNER, ROBERT M, b Newark, Del, Nov 10, 26; m 57; c 3. STATISTICS. *Educ:* Univ Del, BA, 48, MA, 53. *Prof Exp:* Mathematician, Comput Lab, 48-50, supvry math statistician, Surveillance & Reliability Lab, 50-70, SUPVRY PHYS SCIENTIST, US ARMY MAT SYSTS ANAL ACTIVITY, ABERDEEN PROVING GROUND, MD, 70- *Mem:* Inst Math Statist; Am Statist Asn. *Res:* Design and evaluation of experiments to study the reliability, availability and maintainability characteristics of developmental and fielded US Army weapons, munitions, communications and electronic equipment. *Mailing Add:* 49 Kells Ave Newark DE 19711

EISTER, W(ARREN) K(ENNETH), b Sunbury, Pa, Mar 22, 19; m 42; c 2. CHEMICAL ENGINEERING. *Educ:* Bucknell Univ, BS, 40. *Prof Exp:* Engr smokeless powder mfg, E I du Pont de Nemours & Co, Inc, 40-43; engr atomic energy, radiochem process develop, Oak Ridge Nat Lab, 43-61; chief radioisotope prod & mat, Atomic Energy Comn, 61-71, licensing eng, Reactor Effluent Systs, 71-78, SYSTS ENGR WASTE MGT, DEPT ENERGY, 73- *Concurrent Pos:* Lectr, Oak Ridge Sch Reactor Technol, 49-52, Inst Nuclear Studies, 48-54. *Mem:* Am Chem Soc; Am Inst Chem Engrs. *Res:* Radiochemical process development; radioactive waste disposal. *Mailing Add:* 4 Holly Dr Gaithersburg MD 20760

EISZNER, JAMES RICHARD, b Chicago, Ill, Aug 12, 27; m 50; c 2. CHEMISTRY. *Educ:* Univ Ill, BS, 50; PhD(org Univ Chicago, PhD(org chem), 52. *Prof Exp:* Res chemist, Standard Oil Co, Ind, 52-54; mkt analyst, Indoil Chem, 54-57; supvr mkt res & develop, Amoco Chem Corp, Standard Oil Co, Ind, 57-58, dir mkt develop, 58-63; vpres mkt, Ott Chem Co, Mich, 63-65, exec vpres, 65-67; vpres, CPC Develop Co, 68-70, vpres, CPC Int, Inc, 71-76, pres, Indust Div, 71-76, exec vpres & chief admin officer, 77-79, DIR, CPC INT INC, 75-, PRES & CHIEF OPER OFFICER, 79- *Concurrent Pos:* Chmn bd, Ott Chem Co, Mich, 69-70. *Mem:* Am Chem Soc; Corn Refiners Asn (dir). *Res:* New product development; petrochemicals; pharmaceuticals; agricultural chemicals. *Mailing Add:* CPC Int Inc Int Plaza Englewood Cliffs NJ 07632

EITEN, GEORGE, b Morristown, NJ, Nov 20, 23; wid. VEGETATION SCIENCE, ANGIOSPERM TAXONOMY. *Educ:* Cornell Univ, AB, 49; Columbia Univ, MS, 58, PhD(bot), 59. *Prof Exp:* Prof biol, Willimantic Teachers Col, 57-58; prof bot genetics, Hofstra Col, 58-59; botanist, Inst de Bot, Sao Paulo, 59-75; PROF TITULAR BOT & ECOL, UNIV DE BRASILIA, 75- *Mem:* Asn Trop Biol; Soc Bot do Brasil. *Res:* Description of vegetation of the world; phytosociology of Brazilian vegetation, principally the cerrado; phytosociological concepts; taxonomy of the genus Oxalis. *Mailing Add:* Univ de Brasilia VEG-IB Caixa Postal 153081 70910 Brasilia DF Brazil

EITENMILLER, RONALD RAY, b Pekin, Ill, Nov 23, 44; m 66; c 2. FOOD SCIENCE. *Educ:* Univ Ill, BS, 66; Univ Nebr, MS, 68, PhD(food sci), 71. *Prof Exp:* Asst prof, 71-76, ASSOC PROF FOOD SCI, UNIV GA, 76- *Honors & Awards:* Young Scientist Travel Award, Inst Food Technologists, 74. *Mem:* Inst Food Technologists; Am Dairy Sci Asn; Sigma Xi. *Res:* Role of enzymes in quality, storage stability and safety of foods; nutritional evaluation of foods; vitamin assay methodology. *Mailing Add:* Dept of Food Sci Univ of Ga Athens GA 30602

EITZEN, DONALD GENE, b Hillsboro, Kans, Oct 21, 42; m 64; c 2. ENGINEERING MECHANICS, ACOUSTICS. *Educ:* Univ NMex, BS, 64, MSc, 66; Univ Wash, PhD(eng mech), 71. *Prof Exp:* Staff mem shock testing, Sandia Labs, 64-67; mech engr, 71-75, LEADER ULTRASONICS, NAT BUR STANDARDS, 75- *Concurrent Pos:* Teaching assoc, Univ Wash, 70-71. *Mem:* Am Soc Mech Engrs; Am Soc Testing & Mat. *Res:* Research on methods for characterizing ultrasonic transducers and on reference artifacts for ultrasonic measurement; basic research on acoustic emission. *Mailing Add:* Ultrasonics A147 Nat Bur Standards Washington DC 20234

EITZMAN, DONALD V, b Madison, Wis, June 6, 27; m 54; c 5. MEDICINE, PHYSIOLOGY. *Educ:* Northeastern Univ Ill, BS, 50; Univ Iowa, MD, 54. *Prof Exp:* Instr pediat, Univ Minn, 56-57; instr, Univ Tex Health Sci Ctr, Dallas, 57-58; from asst to assoc prof, 58-68, PROF PEDIAT, UNIV FLA, 68- *Concurrent Pos:* NIH trainee immunol, 57-58, fel, 58-60; Daland fel clin med, 60-64; spec fel with Dr K Cross, 67-68. *Mem:* Soc Pediat Res; Am Pediat Soc; Am Physiol Soc. *Res:* Newborn physiology; ontogeny of the immune response in infants; comparative immunology in primates; perinatal physiology; acid base control; control of pulmonary blood flow. *Mailing Add:* Col of Med Univ of Fla Gainesville FL 32601

EK, ALAN R, b Minneapolis, Minn, Sept 5, 42; m 64; c 2. FORESTRY, RESOURCE MANAGEMENT. *Educ:* Univ Minn, BS, 64, MS, 65; Ore State Univ, PhD(forestry), 69. *Prof Exp:* Res off, Can Dept Forestry & Rural Develop, 66-69; from asst prof to assoc prof forestry, Univ Wis-Madison, 75-77; assoc prof, 77-79, PROF, COL FORESTRY, UNIV MINN, ST PAUL, 79- *Concurrent Pos:* Consult, forest indust & govt agencies; prin, Forestronics, Inc. *Mem:* Biomet Soc; Soc Am Foresters; Am Soc Photogram; Int Union Forest Res Orgn. *Res:* Mensuration; sampling; forest inventory and survey design; biomathematical modeling; quantitative silviculture; forest growth and yield projection. *Mailing Add:* Col of Forestry Univ of Minn St Paul MN 55108

EKBERG, CARL E(DWIN), JR, b Minneapolis, Minn, Oct 28, 20; m 44; c 4. CIVIL ENGINEERING. *Educ:* Univ Minn, BCE, 43, MS, 47, PhD, 54. *Prof Exp:* Instr math & mech, Univ Minn, 46-51; asst prof civil eng, NDak Agr Col, 51-53; from asst prof to assoc prof, Lehigh Univ, 53-59; PROF & HEAD DEPT CIVIL ENG, IOWA STATE UNIV, 59- *Mem:* Fel Am Soc Civil Engrs; fel Am Concrete Inst; Am Soc Eng Educ; Am Rwy Eng Asn; Am Soc Prof Engrs. *Res:* Structural engineering with particular emphasis on structural concrete; continuing study of composite floor system utilizing light-gage steel. *Mailing Add:* Dept of Civil Eng Iowa State Univ Ames IA 50010

EKBERG, DONALD ROY, b Hinsdale, Ill, Dec 23, 28; m 61; c 2. ENVIRONMENTAL PHYSIOLOGY. *Educ:* Univ Ill, BS, 50, PhD(physiol), 57; Univ Chicago, MS, 52. *Prof Exp:* Instr physiol, Univ Ill, 55-58; physiologist, Gen Elec Co, 58-65, mgr life sci, 65-71, mgr appl sci, 71-76; CHIEF ENVIRON & TECH SERV DIV, SOUTHEASTERN REGION, NAT MARINE FISHERIES SERV, NAT OCEANIC & ATMOSPHERIC ADMIN, 76- *Concurrent Pos:* Fel, US Pub Health, Ger, 59-60; adj prof, Drexel Univ, 69-71. *Mem:* Am Physiol Soc; Soc Gen Physiol; Am Soc Zool; Sigma Xi. *Res:* Marine environmental biology; environmental assessment; aviation and space physiology. *Mailing Add:* Duval Bldg 9450 Koger Blvd St Petersburg FL 33702

EKDALE, ALLAN ANTON, b Burlington, Iowa, Aug 30, 46; m 69; c 2. PALEOECOLOGY. *Educ:* Augustana Col, BA, 68; Rice Univ, MA, 72, PhD(geol), 74. *Prof Exp:* Asst prof, 74-78, ASSOC PROF GEOL, UNIV UTAH, 78- *Mem:* Soc Econ Paleontologists & Mineralogists; Paleont Soc; AAAS. *Res:* Deep-sea trace fossils; ecology and paleoecology of marine mollusks. *Mailing Add:* Dept of Geol & Geophys Univ of Utah Salt Lake City UT 84112

EKERN, PAUL CHESTER, b Ardmore, Okla, July 2, 20; m 50, 56; c 4. SOIL PHYSICS, HYDROLOGY. *Educ:* Westminster Col, Mo, BA, 42; Univ Wis, PhD, 50. *Prof Exp:* Instr soils & meteorol, Univ Wis, 50-52, asst prof, 52-55; soil physicist, Pineapple Res Inst, 55-63; PROF SOILS & AGRON, UNIV HAWAII & HYDROLOGIST, WATER RESOURCES RES CTR, 64- *Mem:* AAAS; Soil Sci Soc Am; Am Meteorol Soc; Soil Conserv Soc Am; Am Geophys Union. *Res:* Consumptive use of moisture in evapotranspiration; micrometeorology of mulches and tillage; soil erosion. *Mailing Add:* Dept of Agron & Soil Sci Univ of Hawaii Honolulu HI 96822

EKERN, RONALD JAMES, b Rice Lake, Wis, Dec 22, 38; m 67; c 2. SURFACE PHYSICS, ELECTROCHEMICAL SYSTEMS. *Educ:* Univ Wis-Milwaukee, BS, 68, MS, 70; Clarkson Col Technol, PhD(physics), 75. *Prof Exp:* Fel surface sci, Argonne Nat Lab, 74-76; proj scientist, Gould Labs, 76-79; DEPT MGR, RAYOVAC CORP, 79- *Mem:* Am Phys Soc; Am Vacuum Soc; Sigma Xi. *Res:* Ultra-high vacuum technology; ion accelerators for surface physics research; surface electrochemistry; electrochemical systems research and development; problem definition and analysis for active, inactive and envelope materials; corrosion, compatibility, performance domain of materials for batteries. *Mailing Add:* Ray-O-Vac 630 Forward Dr Madison WI 53711

EKLER, KURT, physical chemistry, see previous edition

EKLOF, PAUL CHRISTIAN, b Brooklyn, NY, Dec 28, 42; m 72. ALGEBRA. *Educ:* Columbia Col, AB, 64; Cornell Univ, PhD(math), 68. *Prof Exp:* J W Gibbs instr math, Yale Univ, 68-70; asst prof, Stanford Univ, 70-73; assoc prof, 73-78, PROF MATH, UNIV CALIF, IRVINE, 78- *Mem:* Am Math Soc; Asn Symbolic Logic; London Math Soc. *Res:* Logic and algebra; model theoretic and set theoretic algebra. *Mailing Add:* Dept Math Univ Calif Irvine CA 92717

EKLUND, CURTIS EINAR, b Austin, Tex, May 23, 31. MICROBIOLOGY. *Educ:* Univ Tex, BA, 53, MA, 55, PhD(microbiol), 63. *Prof Exp:* Instr bact, Med Br, Univ Tex, 54-55; bacteriologist, Imp Sugar Co, Tex, 55-58; instr biol, genetics & bact, Tex Col Arts & Indust, 58-60; asst prof bact, Austin, 60-66, assoc prof, El Paso, 66-71, PROF MICROBIOL, UNIV TEX, EL PASO, 71- *Concurrent Pos:* Dir tech studies, Peace Corps Pub Health Proj, Morocco, 64. *Mem:* Am Soc Microbiol. *Res:* Petroleum microbiology; general and sugar bacteriology; bacteriophage, with emphasis on phage-induced enzymes. *Mailing Add:* Dept of Biol Univ of Tex El Paso TX 79968

EKLUND, DARREL LEE, b Ottawa Co, Kans, July 28, 42; m 65; c 3. APPLIED STATISTICS. *Educ:* Kans State Univ, BS, 64, MS, 66, PhD(statist), 71. *Prof Exp:* Surv statistician, Nat Ctr Health Statist, 66-68; asst prof agron & statist, Univ Mo-Columbia, 72-77; CHIEF RES & ANAL SECT, KANS DEPT HEALTH & ENVIRON, 77- *Mem:* Am Statist Asn; Am Asn Vital Records & Pub Health Statist; Sigma Xi. *Res:* Statistical computation; survey sampling; recreational use surveys; human nutrition; perinatal mortality. *Mailing Add:* 1400 Caledon Topeka KS 66611

EKLUND, KARL E, b New York, NY, July 3, 29; m 67, 81; c 2. APPLIED PHYSICS. *Educ:* Mass Inst Technol, BS, 50; Columbia Univ, MA, 56, PhD(physics), 60. *Prof Exp:* Physicist, Army Nuclear Defense Labs, 51-54; dir res, Radiation Dynamics, Inc, 60-61; res assoc physics, Columbia Univ, 62; asst dir nuclear struct lab, Yale Univ, 63-65; cur phys labs, State Univ NY Stony Brook, 65-66, dir, 66-68, asst to exec vpres systs, 68-69, dir budget, 70-71, asst to exec vpres, 71; PRIN ASSOC, EKLUND ASSOCS, 71- *Concurrent Pos:* Consult, Parameters, Inc, 54-60; lectr, Stratos Div, Fairchild, 56-58; assoc prof, US Merchant Marine Acad, 62; aerospace consult, 62-63; energy coordr, Southeast Mass Regional Planning and Econ Develop Dist, 80- *Res:* Nuclear structure physics; research management and administration; management systems; energy management; educational theory; matrix theory of human behavior with applications to collective behavior; matrix behaviorism. *Mailing Add:* Eklund Assocs 76 Myricks St Assonet MA 02702

EKLUND, MELVIN WESLEY, b Saco, Mont, July 16, 33; m 60; c 2. MICROBIOLOGY, FOOD MICROBIOLOGY. *Educ:* Wash State Univ, BS, 55, MS, 57; Purdue Univ, PhD(food sci & microbiol), 62. *Prof Exp:* SUPVRY RES MICROBIOLOGIST, UTILIZATION DIV, NAT MARINE FISHERIES SERV, US DEPT COMMERCE, 61- *Concurrent Pos:* Dept of Com rep, US-Japan Coop Prog Dev & Utilization of Nat Res, 75-; consult nitrit comt, Nat Acad Sci, 81; affil assoc prof, Univ Wash, 80- *Honors & Awards:* Prof Serv Award, Seattle Fed Exec Bd, 69, Employee of Year, 70. *Mem:* Sigma Xi; Am Acad Microbiol; Am Soc Microbiol; Inst Food Technol; Soc Appl Bact. *Res:* Clostridium botulinum incidence in marine environment; heat destruction and factors affecting toxin production; yeasts in foods; bacteriophages and toxicity of Clostridium botulinum, C Novyi and other Clostridia; fish diseases; Vibrio parahaemolyticus; sudden infant death; infant botulism; botulism as major cause of juvenile fish mortality in US; efficacy of nitrites as inhibitor of c botulinum and search for replacements for nitrites. *Mailing Add:* 18727 35th Ave NE Seattle WA 98155

EKMAN, CARL FREDERICK W, b Caribou, Maine, Feb 13, 32; m 59. INORGANIC CHEMISTRY, SOLID STATE CHEMISTRY. *Educ:* Northeastern Univ, BS, 55; Mass Inst Technol, PhD(inorg chem), 61. *Prof Exp:* Sect head inorg chem res, Itek Corp, 61-65, mgr res lab, 65-66; vpres & dir res & develop, Carter's Ink Co, 66-77; mem staff, 77-80, VPRES & DIR RES, COULTER SYSTS CORP, 80- *Mem:* AAAS; Am Chem Soc; fel Am Inst Chem; Soc Photog Scientists & Engrs; NY Acad Sci. *Res:* Physical inorganic chemistry of divalent silver; solid state photochemistry; chemical and physical consequences of actinic light on solids, particularly related to image forming systems; physics. *Mailing Add:* Coulter Systs Corp 35 Wiggins Ave Bedford MA 01730

EKMAN, FRANK O(SCAR), b London, Eng, Mar 26, 17; US citizen; m 44; c 3. POLLUTION ENGINEERING, CHEMICAL ENGINEERING. *Educ:* Univ BC, BASc, 44, MASc, 46; Univ Ill, PhD(chem eng), 50. *Prof Exp:* Mem staff, MacMillian Indust, Ltd, 44-45; asst, Univ Ill, 46-48; mem staff, Howard Smith Paper Mills, Ltd, 49-51; Nat Lead Co, 51-58; asst mgr res & develop, Glidden Co, 58-59; mem staff, Pittsburgh Plate Glass Co, 59-64; res eng, Babcock & Wilcox Co, 64-66; tech dir, Environeering Inc, 66-74; sr educ consult, Inst Gas Technol, 74-77; sr develop eng, Barber-Greene Co, 77-79; consult, 79-81; REGIONAL PARTIC & SULFER DIOXIDE EXPERT, US ENVIRON PROTECTION AGENCY, 81- *Mem:* Am Chem Soc; Air Pollution Control Asn. *Res:* Industrial air pollution abatement. *Mailing Add:* RR3 Tamarack Lane Barrington IL 60010

EKNOYAN, OHANNES, b Jan 15, 44; US citizen. SEMICONDUCTOR DEVICES, ELECTROMAGNETIC FIELDS & WAVES. *Educ:* Tex A&M Univ, BS, 69, MS, 70, Columbia Univ, MPhil & PhD(elec eng), 75. *Prof Exp:* Mem tech staff, Microwave Semiconductor Devices, Bell Telephone Lab, Murray Hill, NJ, 72-73; fac res high temperature semiconductor, Saudia Nat Lab, 79-80; asst prof, 75-79, ASSOC PROF ELEC ENG, TEX A&M UNIV, 80- *Mem:* Inst Elec & Electronic Engrs; Sigma Xi. *Res:* Semiconductor devices, fabrication and characterization; all phases of processes from initial material preparation to the final characterization of packaged devices. *Mailing Add:* Elec Eng Dept Tex A&M Univ College Station TX 77840

EKSTEDT, RICHARD DEAN, b East St Louis, Ill, Nov 13, 25; m 55; c 2. MICROBIOLOGY, IMMUNOLOGY. *Educ:* Wash Univ, AB, 49; Univ Mich, MS, 51, PhD(bact), 55. *Prof Exp:* Res assoc biochem, Sch Med, Univ Ill, 54-55; res assoc med, 55-56, from instr to assoc prof, 56-71, PROF MICROBIOL, MED SCH, NORTHWESTERN UNIV, 71- *Concurrent Pos:* Helen Hay Whitney Found fel, 58-61. *Mem:* Am Soc Microbiol; Am Asn Immunol; Brit Soc Gen Microbiol; Reticuloendothelial Soc. *Res:* Mechanisms of microbial pathogenicity; nonspecific host defense mechanisms; bacteriocidal activity of blood; immunity to staphylococci; lectins in tumor and immunobiology; host parasite relationships. *Mailing Add:* Dept of Microbiol-Immunol Northwestern Univ Med Sch Chicago IL 60611

EKSTRAND, KENNETH ERIC, b Chicopee, Mass, Sept 3, 42; m 70. MEDICAL PHYSICS. *Educ:* Mass Inst Technol, BS, 64; Cornell Univ, PhD(physics), 71; Am Bd Radiol, dipl, 76. *Prof Exp:* Res assoc physics, Nat Comn Nuclear Energy, Frascati, Italy, 71-72; res assoc, 72-73, from instr to asst prof, 73-78, ASSOC PROF RADIOL, BOWMAN GRAY SCH MED, WAKE FOREST UNIV, 78- *Mem:* Am Asn Physicists Med; Am Col Radiol; Am Soc Therapeut Radiol. *Res:* Radiological physics; use of computers in radiology and radiation therapy; medical applications of nuclear magnetic resonance. *Mailing Add:* Bowman Gray Sch Med Wake Forest Univ Winston-Salem NC 27103

EKSTROM, LINCOLN, b Providence, RI, Aug 21, 32; m 57. PHYSICAL CHEMISTRY. *Educ:* Brown Univ, ScB, 53; Mass Inst Technol, PhD(chem), 57. *Prof Exp:* MEM TECH STAFF, LABS, RCA CORP, 57- *Honors & Awards:* David Sarnoff Outstanding Achievement Award, 63. *Mem:* AAAS; Am Chem Soc; Am Phys Soc; fel Am Inst Chem. *Res:* Thermoelectric materials; compound semiconductors; physical chemistry of compound semiconductors; absorption spectrophotometry of ionic solutions; magnetic recording materials. *Mailing Add:* RCA Labs Princeton NJ 08540

EL-AASSER, MOHAMED S, b Shobrakhit, Egypt, Feb 10, 43; m 72; c 2. EMULSION POLYMERS. *Educ:* Alexandria Univ, BSc, 62, MSc, 66; McGill Univ, PhD(chem), 72. *Prof Exp:* Asst prof, 74-78, assoc prof, 78-82, PROF CHEM ENG, LEHIGH UNIV & CO-DIR, EMULSION POLYMERS INST, 82- *Concurrent Pos:* Consult, Rohm & Haas Co, 79-81 & IBM, 80- *Mem:* Am Chem Soc; Am Inst Chem Engrs; Sigma Xi; AAAS. *Res:* Emulsion polymers and latex technology; preparation of homo and co-polymer latexes; colloidal stability; surface characterization; kinetics of emulsion polymerization; emulsions; film formation and drying of latexes; electrodeposition. *Mailing Add:* Emulsion Polymers Inst Bldg #7 Lehigh Univ Bethlehem PA 18015

EL-ABIAD, AHMED H(ANAFI), b Mersa Matruh, Egypt, May 24, 26; US citizen; m 52; c 2. ELECTRICAL ENGINEERING. *Educ:* Univ Cairo, BSc, 48; Purdue Univ, MSEE, 53, PhD(elec eng), 56. *Prof Exp:* Asst engr, Egyptian State Tel & Tel, 48-49; asst elec eng, Univ Cairo, 49-52; from instr to assoc prof elec eng, Purdue Univ, 53-65, prof, 65-80; MEM FAC, UNIV PETROL & MINERALS, SAUDI ARABIA, 80- *Concurrent Pos:* Consult, EBASCO Serv, NY, 56, Egyptian Electrification Comt, 56-58, Am Elec Power Serv Corp, 59-64, Edison Elec Inst, 63-64 & Consumers Power Co, 66-68; lectr, Cairo Univ, 56-58; vis asst prof, Mass Inst Technol, 61-62; partic, Int Conf-Large High Tension Elec Systs, France; mem adv comt, Elec Power Res & Develop Ctr; vis prof, Kuwait Univ, 79-80. *Mem:* Fel Inst Elec & Electronics Engrs. *Res:* Computer methods for power systems; power system security control; optimization and dynamics; large scale systems. *Mailing Add:* PO Box 144 Univ Petrol & Minerals Box 1937 Dhahran Saudi Arabia

ELAKOVICH, STELLA DAISY, b Texarkana, Tex, Jan 15, 45. ORGANIC CHEMISTRY. *Educ:* Tex Christian Univ, BS, 66; La State Univ, PhD(chem), 71. *Prof Exp:* Instr chem, La State Univ, 71; fel, Univ Saarland, Ger, 71-72 & Univ Tex Med Br, Galveston, 72-74; asst prof, 74-78, ASSOC PROF CHEM, UNIV SOUTHERN MISS, 78- *Mem:* Am Chem Soc; Sigma Xi. *Res:* Chemical education; organic natural products. *Mailing Add:* Dept Chem Univ Southern Miss Box 5043 Hattiesburg MS 39406

ELAM, EDWARD UNDERWOOD, b Pamplin, Va, Aug 14, 22; m 46; c 4. ORGANIC CHEMISTRY. *Educ:* Va Polytech Inst, BS, 42. *Prof Exp:* From asst res chemist to sr res chemist, 46-67, RES ASSOC, 67- *Mem:* Am Chem Soc; Sigma Xi; Res Soc NAm. *Res:* Oxo and related reactions; catalytic hydrogenation; ketene chemistry. *Mailing Add:* 702 Yadkin St Kingsport TN 37660

ELAM, JACK GORDON, b Glendale, Calif, Aug 25, 21; m 74; c 4. GEOLOGY. *Educ:* Univ Calif, Los Angeles, AB, 43, MA, 48; Rensselaer Polytech Inst, PhD(geol), 60. *Prof Exp:* Geologist, Stanley & Stolz, Calif, 46-47, Richfield Oil Corp, 47-49 & Cameron Oil Co, Calif & Tex, 49-51; consult geologist, 51-56; asst prof petrol geol, Rensselaer Polytech Inst, 56-60; CONSULT GEOLOGIST, 60- *Concurrent Pos:* Independent oil producer, 64-; pres, Permian Basin Grad Ctr, 70-79, chmn bd, 79-; gen partner, Explor Ltd, 73-78; dir & vpres, Keba Oil & Gas Co, 75-81; adj prof, Univ Tex, Arlington, 78-80. *Mem:* Am Asn Petrol Geologists; Geol Soc Am. *Res:* Petroleum geology; sedimentology, particularly carbonate sedimentology; structural geology and global tectonics; tectonic evolution of the Permian Basin. *Mailing Add:* 219 N Main St PO Box 195 Midland TX 79702

ELAM, LLOYD CHARLES, b Little Rock, Ark, Oct 27, 28; m 57; c 2. PSYCHIATRY. *Educ:* Roosevelt Univ, BS, 50; Univ Wash, MD, 57; Am Bd Neurol & Psychiat, dipl, 65. *Hon Degrees:* DSc, St Lawrence Univ, 74; LHD, Roosevelt Univ, 74; LLD, Harvard Univ, 76. *Prof Exp:* Intern, Univ Ill, 57-58; resident psychiat, Univ Chicago, 58-61; prof psychiat & chmn dept, 61-68, interim dean, Sch Med, 67-68, PRES, MEHARRY MED COL, 68- *Concurrent Pos:* NIMH fel, Riverside Hosp, Nashville, 58-61, consult, 62-67; lectr, Univ Tenn, 63-67. *Mem:* Nat Inst Med-Nat Acad Sci; Nat Med Asn; Am Col Psychiatrists; AMA; Am Psychiat Asn. *Res:* Comprehensive health care. *Mailing Add:* Meharry Med Col 1005 18th Ave N Nashville TN 37208

ELAM, WILLIAM WARREN, b Alamo, Ga, May 1, 29; m 54; c 3. FOREST PHYSIOLOGY. *Educ:* Univ Ga, BS, 61, PhD(plant sci), 65. *Prof Exp:* Asst prof bot & forestry, 65-70, ASSOC PROF FORESTRY, MISS STATE UNIV, 70- *Mem:* Soc Am Foresters; Bot Soc Am. *Res:* Tree physiology, especially growth and development in Southern conifers; hardwood regeneration; prescribed burning; physiology of seeds and seedlings of Southern Red Oaks. *Mailing Add:* Dept Forestry Miss State Univ PO Drawer FD Mississippi State MS 39762

ELAND, JOHN HUGH DAVID, b Salop, Eng, Aug 6, 41; m 67; c 3. PHYSICAL CHEMISTRY, PHYSICS. *Prof Exp:* Res lectr chem, Christ Church, 68-73; fel, Univ Freiburg, Ger, 73-74; assoc prof, Univ Paris, 74-76; physics, Argonne Nat Lab, 76-80; LECTR, QUEEN'S COL, OXFORD, ENGLAND, 80- *Mem:* Am Phys Soc; Am Soc Mass Spectrometry. *Mailing Add:* Phys Chem Lab S Parks Rd Oxford 0X1 5EZ England

ELANDER, RICHARD PAUL, b Worcester, Mass, Sept 17, 32; m 58; c 3. MICROBIOLOGY. *Educ:* Univ Detroit, BS, 55, MS, 56; Univ Wis, PhD(bot, bacteriol), 60. *Prof Exp:* Asst bot, Univ Wis, 56-60; sr microbiologist, Antibiotic Mfg & Develop Div, Eli Lilly & Co, 60-65, res scientist, Res Labs, 65-67; mgr process develop, Wyeth Antibiotic Labs, 67-68, mgr bulk antibiotic prod & process develop, Wyeth Labs, Inc, 68-71, assoc dir prod & process develop, Bulk Prod, 71-73; assoc dir microbiol res, Smith Kline & French Labs, 73-75; dir fermentation develop, 75-79, SR DIR FERMENTATION RES & DEVELOP, INDUST DIV, BRISTOL-MYERS CO, 79- *Concurrent Pos:* Fel, Univ Minn, 66. *Mem:* Mycol Soc Am; Am Chem Soc; Soc Indust Microbiol (secy, 66-67, pres, 74-75); Am Soc Microbiol; NY Acad Sci. *Res:* Genetics of industrial microorganisms; antibiotic fermentation process development; screening for microbial metabolites; genetic engineering. *Mailing Add:* Indust Div Bristol-Myers Co PO Box 657 Syracuse NY 13201

ELANDT-JOHNSON, REGINA C, b Nowogrod, Poland, Nov 22, 18; m 64. MATHEMATICS, STATISTICS. *Educ:* Univ Poznan, Poland, PhM, 46; Poznan Univ Agr, PhD(statist), 55. *Prof Exp:* Asst exp statist, Poznan Univ Agr, 46-53, lectr, 53-57, assoc prof, 57-63, head dept statist, 63-64; assoc prof, 64-71, PROF BIOSTATIST, UNIV NC, CHAPEL HILL, 71- *Concurrent Pos:* Polish Acad Sci scholar, Univ Col, London, 58-59; fel, Case Inst Technol, 60-61. *Res:* Statistics applied to agricultural experiments; statistical genetics; statistics in medical research. *Mailing Add:* Dept of Biostatist Univ of NC Chapel Hill NC 27514

ELASHOFF, JANET DIXON, b Princeton, NJ, Mar 22, 42; div; c 2. APPLIED STATISTICS. *Educ:* Stanford Univ, BS, 62; Harvard Univ, PhD(statist), 66. *Prof Exp:* Asst prof statist, Sch Educ, Stanford Univ, 67-74; statist adv, Ctr Advan Study Behav Sci, 74-75; assoc res statistician, Ctr Ulcer Res, Univ Calif, Los Angeles, 75-77, res statistician, 78-81. *Concurrent Pos:* Consult, Nat Assessment of Educ Progress, 73-; mem biomet & epidemiol contract rev comt, Nat Cancer Inst, 73-76; assoc ed, Am Statist Asn, 76-79; adj prof, Dept Biomath, Ctr Ulcer Res, Univ Calif, Los Angeles, 81- *Honors & Awards:* Palmer O Johnson Mem Award, Am Educ Res Asn, 71. *Mem:* Fel Am Statist Asn; Soc Clin Trials; Biomet Soc; fel AAAS. *Res:* Improvement of design and data analysis techniques for problems in the biological and behavioral sciences, specifically robustness of statistical methods to violation of assumptions, and analysis of repeated measures designs. *Mailing Add:* Ctr for Ulcer Res Bldg 115 Rm 115 Vet Admin Los Angeles CA 90073

ELASHOFF, ROBERT M, statistics, see previous edition

EL-ASHRY, MOHAMED T, b Cairo, Egypt, Jan 21, 40; m; c 2. GEOLOGY. *Educ:* Cairo Univ, BS, 59; Univ Ill, MS, 63, PhD(geol), 66. *Prof Exp:* Teaching asst geol, Cairo Univ, 59-61, asst prof, 66-69; from asst prof to prof environ sci, Wilkes Col, 69-75, chmn dept environ sci, 72-75; staff scientist & co-chmn water & land resources prog, Environ Defense Fund, 75-79; ASST MGR NATURAL RESOURCES, TENN VALLEY AUTHORITY, 79- *Mem:* Fel Geol Soc Am; fel AAAS; Am Asn Petrol Geologists; Sigma Xi. *Res:* Coastal erosion and sedimentation including origin of coastal landforms; environmental geology including energy development and water resources in arid regions; environmental impact assessment; remote sensing. *Mailing Add:* Tenn Valley Authority Knoxville TN 37902

ELATTAR, TAWFIK MOHAMMED ALI, b Cairo, Egypt, Nov 6, 25; m 56; c 1. BIOCHEMISTRY, ENDOCRINOLOGY. *Educ:* Cairo Univ, BSc, 47, MSc, 55; Univ Mo, PhD(biochem), 57. *Prof Exp:* Biochemist nutrit, Agr Chem Dept, Ministry Agr, Egypt, 47-55; asst prof physiol chem, Univ Bonn, 61-64; asst res biochemist med, Med Sch, Univ Calif, San Francisco, 64-68; assoc prof, 68-70, PROF BIOCHEM & DIR HORMONE RES, SCH DENT & MED, UNIV MO KANSAS CITY, 70- *Concurrent Pos:* Fel biophys, Univ Calif, Berkeley, 57-58; fel biochem, Worcester Found Exp Biol, Mass, 58-59; fel endocrinol, Med Sch, Univ Miami, 59-60; metabolism and mode of action of steroid hormones; biochemistry of steroid hormones. *Mailing Add:* Dept Hormone Res Univ of Mo Sch of Dent Kansas City MO 64108

EL-AWADY, ABBAS ABBAS, b Dakahlia, UAR, Jan 2, 39; m 65; c 1. PHYSICAL INORGANIC CHEMISTRY. *Educ:* Univ Cairo, BSc, 58; Univ Minn, PhD(phys inorg chem), 65. *Prof Exp:* Lab instr chem, fac sci, Univ Cairo, 58-59; res assoc, Univ Calif, Los Angeles, 65-66; from asst prof to assoc prof, 66-76, PROF CHEM, WESTERN ILL UNIV, 76- *Concurrent Pos:* With Environ Protection Agency, 74-75. *Mem:* Am Chem Soc. *Res:* Applications of physical methods to the study of inorganic reactions in solution; kinetics and mechanisms of transition metal complexes; photochemistry; environmental chemistry. *Mailing Add:* Dept of Chem Western Ill Univ Macomb IL 61455

ELBAUM, CHARLES, b May 15, 26; US citizen; m 56; c 3. SOLID STATE SCIENCE, NEUROSCIENCES. *Educ:* Univ Toronto, MASc, 51, PhD(appl sci), 54. *Hon Degrees:* MA, Brown Univ, 61. *Prof Exp:* Res fel metal physics, Univ Toronto, 54-57 & Harvard Univ, 57-59; asst prof appl physics, 59-61, assoc prof physics, 61-63, PROF PHYSICS, BROWN UNIV, 63-, CHMN, DEPT PHYSICS, 80- *Concurrent Pos:* Indust consult. *Mem:* Fel Am Phys Soc; Am Inst Mining, Metall & Petrol Engrs; Soc Neurosci; AAAS. *Res:* Crystal defects; mechanical properties of solids; ultrasonic wave propagation; phonon and electron transport and interactions; phase transitions; biophysics; solid helium. *Mailing Add:* Dept of Physics Brown Univ Providence RI 02912

ELBAUM, DANEK, b Poland, Mar 24, 48; US citizen; m 70; c 2. BIOPHYSICS. *Educ:* Columbia Univ, MS, 71; Fordham Univ, PhD(chem), 74. *Prof Exp:* ASST PROF MED, ALBERT EINSTEIN COL MED, 77- *Res:* Biophysical and biochemical properties of hemoglobin and red cell membrane proteins; the structure and function of the red cell membrane. *Mailing Add:* 1300 Morris Park Ave Dept Med Albert Einstein Col Med Bronx NY 10461

ELBAUM, MAREK, b Kovel, USSR, May 8, 41; US citizen; m 68; c 1. ELECTRICAL ENGINEERING, QUANTUM ELECTRONICS. *Educ:* Warsaw Tech Univ, MSc, 66; Columbia Univ, PhD(elec eng), 77. *Prof Exp:* Res assoc, Microwave Lab, Polish Acad Sci, 66-68; mem res staff, Electro-Optics Lab, 69-79, MGR, ELECTRO-OPTICAL SENSOR SYST, RIVERSIDE RES INST, 80- *Concurrent Pos:* Adj prof, Columbia Univ, 78- *Mem:* Optical Soc Am. *Res:* Optical communications; statistical communication; application of lasers; theory of coherence; author or coauthor of over thirty technical papers. *Mailing Add:* Riverside Res Inst 80 West End Ave New York NY 10023

EL-BAYOUMI, MOHAMED ASHRAF, b Cairo, Egypt, Dec 7, 34; m 56; c 3. PHYSICAL CHEMISTRY, ELECTRONIC SPECTROSCOPY. *Educ:* Univ Alexandria, BSc, 54; Fla State Univ, MSc, 57, PhD(phys chem), 61. *Prof Exp:* Res assoc electronic spectra, Fla State Univ, 61 & Mass Inst Technol, 61-62; lectr phys chem, fac sci, Univ Alexandria, 62-67; res assoc electronic spectra, Fla State Univ, 67-68; assoc prof, 68-72, PROF ELECTRONIC SPECTRA, MICH STATE UNIV, 72- *Mem:* AAAS; Am Phys Soc; Biophys Soc; Am Chem Soc; NY Acad Sci. *Res:* Relaxation processes in excited molecular systems; nanosecond time resolved spectroscopy; fluorescence probes of biomolecular conformation; electronic spectra of organic and biological molecules. *Mailing Add:* Dept of Biophys & Chem Mich State State Univ East Lansing MI 48824

EL-BAZ, FAROUK, b Zagazig, Egypt, Jan 1, 38; US citizen; m 63; c 4. GEOLOGY, SPACE SCIENCE. *Educ:* Ain Shams Univ, Cairo, BSc, 58; Mo Sch Mines, MS, 61; Univ Mo, PhD(geol), 64. *Prof Exp:* Demonstr micropaleontol, Assiut Univ, 58-60; lectr econ geol, Univ Heidelberg, 64-65; explor geologist petrol, Pan Am UAR Oil Co, Egypt, 65-66; supvr, lunar sci planning geol, Bellcomm Inc, 67-72 & lunar explor syst eng, Bell Tell Labs, 72-73; RES DIR, EARTH & PLANET STUDIES, NAT AIR & SPACE MUSEUM, SMITHSONIAN INST, 73- *Concurrent Pos:* Mem NASA, Apollo Orbital Sci Photographic Team, 70-72, Crew Training Group, 70-72, Lunar Sci Review Panel, 74-75; mem, US/USSR joint lunar cartographic activ, 73-75 & Int Astron Union, 74-78; prin investr, Earth Observ Apollo-Soyuz Mission, 74-78; adj prof geol & geophys, Univ Utah, 74-76; adj prof geol, Ain Shams Univ, 76-78. *Honors & Awards:* Exceptional Sci Achievement Medal, NASA, 71; Cert Spec Commendation, Geol Soc Am, 73. *Mem:* AAAS; fel Geol Soc Am; Am Soc Photogrammetry; Am Geophys Union; Meteorol Soc. *Res:* Comparative planetology with emphasis on interpretation of space-born photographs of surface features of planets and their moons and applications of space technology to desert studies. *Mailing Add:* Nat Air & Space Museum Smithsonian Inst Washington DC 20560

ELBEIN, ALAN D, b Lynn, Mass, Mar 20, 33; m 54; c 3. MICROBIOLOGY, BIOCHEMISTRY. *Educ:* Clark Univ, AB, 54; Univ Ariz, MS, 56; Purdue Univ, PhD(microbiol), 60. *Prof Exp:* Res assoc microbiol, Purdue Univ, 60-61 & Univ Mich, 61-63; asst res biochemist, Univ Calif, Berkeley, 63-64; from asst prof to assoc prof biol, Rice Univ, 64-69; assoc prof, 69-70, PROF BIOCHEM, UNIV TEX HEALTH SCI CTR, SAN ANTONIO, 70- *Mem:* Am Soc Biol Chem; Am Soc Plant Physiol; Am Chem Soc; Am Soc Microbiol; Am Acad Microbiol. *Res:* Biosynthesis of microbial and plant cell walls; trehalose metabolism and biosynthesis; glycoprotein biosynthesis in aorta tissue; effects of polyelectrolytes on enzymes. *Mailing Add:* Dept of Biochem Univ of Tex Health Sci Ctr San Antonio TX 78284

ELBEL, ROBERT E, b Hannibal, Mo, July 8, 25; m 60; c 3. ENTOMOLOGY. *Educ:* Univ Kans, BA, 48, MA, 50; Univ Okla, PhD(zool), 64. *Prof Exp:* Med biol technician typhus invests, Commun Dis Ctr, USPHS, 50, dysentary studies, 50-51, typhus studies, 51; plague control adv, US Opers Mission Thailand, 51-53, malaria control adv, 53-55; asst zool, Norman & Willis Biol Sta, Univ Okla, 56-59; trainee malaria eradication, career develop div, AID, Jamaica & Mex, 60, malaria specialist, US Opers Mission Thailand, 61-63; med zoologist & entomologist ecol & epidemiol br, Dugway Proving Ground, 63-75; res assoc, Entom Lab, Univ Utah, Salt Lake City, 74-80; RES ASSOC PROF BIOL, UNIV WASH, 80- *Concurrent Pos:* Consult mosquito-arbovirus prog, Dugway Proving Ground, 75-77; consult fleas of NAm, Brigham Young Univ, Provo, 76; consult malaria-parasite surv, Multinat Agribus Systs, Inc, 76- *Mem:* Siam Soc; Am Mosquito Control Asn; Soc Syst Zool. *Res:* Bird Mallophaga; flea larvae; arboviruses. *Mailing Add:* 1518 Evergreen Salt Lake City UT 84106

ELBERG, SANFORD SAMUEL, b San Francisco, Calif, Dec 1, 13; m 43; c 2. MEDICAL MICROBIOLOGY. *Educ:* Univ Calif, AB, 34, PhD(microbiol), 38. *Hon Degrees:* LHD, Hebrew Union Col, 67. *Prof Exp:* Asst bact, Hooper Found, 36-38, lectr pub health pract, 38-40, from instr to prof bact, 41-78, chmn dept bact, 52-57, dean, Grad Div, 61-78, EMER PROF BACT & EMER DEAN, GRAD DIV, UNIV CALIF, BERKELEY, 78- *Prof Exp:* Instr, State Col Wash, 40 & San Francisco City Col, 40-41. *Concurrent Pos:* Instr, State Col Wash, 40 & San Francisco City Col, 40-41; consult, Naval Radiol Defense Lab, 51-62; actg dir & mem adv panel, Naval Biol Lab, 56-57; consult, WHO; Guggenheim Found fel, 57-58; Navy lectr, Univ Mich, 64; mem comt animal health, Nat Res Coun, 78-80. *Mem:* AAAS; Am Soc Microbiol; Am Asn Immunol. *Res:* Cellular immunity; immunity in Brucella infections; biochemistry and physiology of Clostridia; air-borne respiratory infections; physiology and biochemistry of infection; bacteriology and immunity. *Mailing Add:* Dept Biomed & Environ Health Sci Sch Pub Health Univ of Calif Berkeley CA 94720

ELBERGER, ANDREA JUNE, b New York, NY, Feb 11, 52; m 78. DEVELOPMENTAL NEUROBIOLOGY, NEUROSCIENCES. *Educ:* State Univ NY, Albany, BA, 72; State Univ, Stony Brook, PhD(psychobiol), 77. *Prof Exp:* Teaching asst psychol, State Univ NY, Stony Brook, 73-74, res asst, 74, res asst psychiat, Med Sch, 75-76; trainee anat, Sch Med, Univ Pa, 77-80; ASST PROF ANAT, MED SCH, UNIV TEX, HOUSTON, 80- *Mem:* Soc Neurosci; Int Soc Develop Neurosci. *Res:* Developmental neurobiology of the corpus callosum and the visual system; using the behavioral anatomical and electrophysiological techniques to investigate the functional interactions of interhemispheric communication and visual development. *Mailing Add:* Dept Neurobiol & Anat Med Sch Univ Tex PO Box 20708 Houston TX 77025

EL-BERMANI, AL-WALID I, b Baghdad, Iraq, Jan 30, 37; US citizen; m 70; c 2. ANATOMY. *Educ:* Adhamia, Iraq, BA, 54; Sch Med, Baghdad Univ, MBChB, 60; Boston Univ, PhD(anat), 69. *Prof Exp:* Resident chest surg, Mirgan Hosp Chest Dis, Iraq, 60-63; instr anat, Sch Med, Baghdad Univ, 63-65; from instr to asst prof anat, Sch Med, Boston Univ, 66-76; asst prof, 76-79, ASSOC PROF ANAT, SCH MED, TUFTS UNIV, 79- *Concurrent Pos:* Consult, Hewlett Packard Corp, 76-80 & Codman & Shurtleff Corp, 79-81. *Mem:* Am Asn Anatomist; NY Acad Sci. *Res:* Innervation of the lung; toxicological effect of acid rain on the lung. *Mailing Add:* Dept Anat & Cellular Biol 136 Harrison Ave Boston MA 02111

ELBERTY, WILLIAM TURNER, JR, b East Orange, NJ, Mar 8, 30; m 52; c 3. GEOLOGY. *Educ:* St Lawrence Univ, BS, 52; Dartmouth Col, MA, 55; Ind Univ, PhD(geol), 60. *Prof Exp:* Instr geol, 58-60, from asst prof to assoc prof geol & geog, 60-74, PROF GEOL, ST LAWRENCE UNIV, 74- *Concurrent Pos:* Dir prof in Nairobi, St Lawrence Univ, 77-78. *Mem:* AAAS; Geochem Soc. *Res:* Mineralogy of Pleistocene sands and gravels; conservation and property zoning; mineralogy; geochemistry; economic geology. *Mailing Add:* Dept of Geol & Geog St Lawrence Univ Canton NY 13617

ELBLE, RODGER JACOB, b Alton, Ill, Aug 10, 48; m 71; c 2. NEUROLOGY, NEUROPHYSIOLOGY. *Educ:* Purdue Univ, BSAE, 71; Ind Univ, PhD(physiol), 75, MD, 77. *Prof Exp:* Intern med, Ind Univ Med Ctr, 77-78; resident neurol, Barnes Hosp, Wash Univ, 78-81; ASST PROF NEUROL, SCH MED, SOUTHERN ILL UNIV, 81- *Mem:* Am Acad Neurol; Soc Neurosci; Am Physiol Soc; AMA; NY Acad Sci. *Res:* Neuromuscular control in man and the mechanisms of physiologic and pathologic tremors. *Mailing Add:* 800 N Rutledge Springfield IL 62708

ELBLING, IRVING NELSON, b Salem, Mass, July 30, 20; m 46; c 2. ORGANIC CHEMISTRY. *Educ:* Northeastern Univ, BSc, 43. *Prof Exp:* From lab asst to instr, Northeastern Univ, 40-43; student & engr, 43-44, res chemist plastics & resins, res lab, 44-50, chemist, org coatings, paint & varnish dept, 50-52, res chemist, res lab, 52-53, supvr insulation dept, 53-66, mgr specialty coatings, 66-78, OPERS MGR, CHEM SCI DIV, RES LABS, WESTINGHOUSE ELEC CO, 78- *Honors & Awards:* Roon Award Winner, 59. *Mem:* Am Chem Soc; Fedn Socs Paint Technol. *Res:* Organic coatings; phenolic alkyd and epoxy resins; electrical insulating varnishes; insulating tapes; adhesives; fluidized bed powders; financial management. *Mailing Add:* Westinghouse Res Labs Pittsburgh PA 15235

ELCHLEPP, JANE G, b St Louis, Mo, May 26, 21. PATHOLOGY. *Educ:* Harris Teachers Col, BA, 43; Univ Iowa, MS, 46, PhD(zool), 48; Univ Chicago, MD, 55. *Prof Exp:* Teacher, Pub Sch, Mo, 43-44; asst zool, Univ Iowa, 45-48; instr biol, Roosevelt Univ, 48-51; asst anat, Univ Chicago, 51-53; asst pharmacol, Wash Univ, 54; asst med, Univ Chicago, 54-55; field investr, Nat Cancer Inst, 55-62; asst prof path, 62-67, asst to vpres health affairs, 69-71, assoc prof path, 67-80, ASST VPRES HEALTH AFFAIRS, PLANNING & ANAL, DUKE UNIV, 71- *Mailing Add:* Box 2901 Duke Hosp Durham NC 27706

ELCRAT, ALAN ROSS, b Chicago, Ill, Jan 13, 42; m 69. APPLIED MATHEMATICS. *Educ:* Univ NMex, BS, 64; Ind Univ, MA, 65, PhD, 67. *Prof Exp:* Asst prof, 67-70, assoc prof, 70-77, PROF MATH, WICHITA STATE UNIV, 77- *Mailing Add:* Dept of Math Wichita State Univ Wichita KS 67208

ELDE, ROBERT PHILIP, b Mt Vernon, Wash, March 7, 47; m 69; c 2. NEUROSCIENCE, NEUROHISTOLOGY. *Educ:* NPark Col, Chicago, BA, 69; Univ Minn, PhD(anat), 74. *Prof Exp:* Instr anat, Univ Minn, Minneapolis, 74-75; guest scientist histol, Karolinska Inst, Stockholm, 75-76; asst prof, 77-79, ASSOC PROF ANAT, UNIV MINN, MINNEAPOLIS, 80- *Mem:* Soc Neurosci; Am Asn Anatomists; Histochem Soc. *Res:* Distribution and function of transmitter-coded circuits in the mammalian central nervous system, including opioid peptides and neuropepetide hormones. *Mailing Add:* Dept Anat Univ Minn 321 Church St Southeast Minneapolis MN 55455

ELDEFRAWI, AMIRA T, b Giza, Egypt, Feb 10, 37; US citizen; m 57; c 3. NEURO-PHARMACOLOGY, TOXICOLOGY. *Educ:* Univ Alexandria, BSc, 57; Univ Calif, Berkeley, PhD(toxicol PhD(toxicol), 60. *Prof Exp:* Asst prof toxicol, Univ Alexandria, 63-68; res assoc neurobiol, Cornell Univ, 68-72; sr res assoc, 72-76; assoc res prof, 76-79, RES PROF PHARMACOL, SCH MED, UNIV MD, BALTIMORE, 79- *Concurrent Pos:* Consult, Lab Neuromuscular Physiol, Dept Neurol, Sch Med, Univ Va, 77-79; NIH grants. *Mem:* Am Soc Pharmacol & Exp Therapeut; Entom Soc Am; Soc Neurosci. *Res:* Neuropharmacology; acetylcholine receptors; ionic channels. *Mailing Add:* Dept of Pharmacol & Exp Therapeut 660 W Redwood St Baltimore MD 21201

ELDEFRAWI, MOHYEE E, b Egypt, Oct 15, 32; US citizen; m 57; c 3. NEUROPHARMACOLOGY, TOXICOLOGY. *Educ:* Univ Alexandria, BSc, 53; Univ Calif, Berkeley, PhD(entom), 60. *Prof Exp:* From asst prof to assoc prof toxicol, Univ Alexandria, 60-68; sr res assoc neurobiol, Cornell Univ, 69-71, assoc prof, 71-76; PROF PHARMACOL, SCH MED, UNIV MD, BALTIMORE, 76- *Concurrent Pos:* Grants, NSF, NIH, Muscular Dystrophy Asn Am & US Army. *Mem:* Am Soc Pharmacol & Exp Therapeut; Am Chem Soc; NY Acad Sci; Entom Soc Am; Int Soc Neurochem. *Res:* Molecular neurobiology; acetylcholine receptors; ionic channels. *Mailing Add:* Dept of Pharmacol & Exp Therapeut 660 W Redwood St Baltimore MD 21201

ELDEN, RICHARD EDWARD, b Seneca Falls, NY, Feb 25, 23; m 55; c 4. INDUSTRIAL CHEMISTRY. *Educ:* Mass Inst Technol, SB, 44; Univ Wash, MS, 52, Seton Hall Univ, JD, 81. *Prof Exp:* Chemist, Carbide & Carbon Chem Co, Columbia, 44; from chemist to chief chemist, inorg chem div, 44-56, prod mgr, 56-59, resident mgr, Vancouver Plant, 59-63, mgr spec res proj, 63-66, asst to dir, Indust Chem Div, 67-77, patent liaison, 77-81, PATENT AGENT & LAWYER, FMC CORP, 81- *Mem:* Am Chem Soc. *Res:* Analytic instrumentation; administration. *Mailing Add:* FMC Corp PO Box 8 Princeton NJ 08540

ELDER, ALEXANDER STOWELL, b Medford, Mass, July 29, 15; m 47; c 2. MATHEMATICS. *Educ:* Harvard Univ, BA, 38; Boston Univ, MEd, 40; Univ Del, MA, 56. *Prof Exp:* Elec technician, Niagara, Lockport & Ont Power Co, NY, 40-41; physicist, Watertown Arsenal, Mass, 46-49: from mech engr to chief, Dynamics Sect, 50-59, chief, Solid Properties Group, 69-76, DEP CHIEF, MECH & STRUCTURES BR, PROPULSION DIV, ARMY BALLISTIC RES LAB, 76- *Concurrent Pos:* Eve instr math, Harford Jr Col, 59-61. *Honors & Awards:* Meritorious Civilian Serv Award, 73. *Mem:* Am Acad Mech; AAAS; Math Asn Am; Am Math Soc; Soc Rheol. *Res:* Mechanics of solids, including vibration theory, elasticity and viscoelasticity; mechanical design of specialized apparatus and components. *Mailing Add:* US Army Armament Res & Develop Comd Ballistic Res Lab DRDAR-BLP Aberdeen Proving Ground MD 21005

ELDER, FRED A, b Carrollton, Ohio, Dec 4, 29; m 55; c 4. PHYSICAL CHEMISTRY. *Educ:* Muskingum Col, BS, 51; Univ Chicago, MS, 62, PhD(chem phys), 68. *Prof Exp:* Chemist, Nat Bur Standards, 54-55; lab researcher, Calif Res Corp, 57-59; res asst mass spectros, Univ Chicago, 62-69; asst prof chem, Rochester Inst Technol, 69-72; scientist, 72-80, SR TECH SPECIALIST, XEROX CORP, 80- *Res:* Mass spectroscopy. *Mailing Add:* Xerox Corp 800 Phillips Rd Webster NY 14580

ELDER, FRED KINGSLEY, JR, b Coronado, Calif, Oct 19, 21; m 47; c 8. PHYSICS. *Educ:* Univ NC, SB, 41; Yale Univ, MS, 43, PhD(physics), 47. *Prof Exp:* Student asst, Nat Bur Standards, 41; lab asst physics, Yale Univ, 41-43, res asst, 43, instr, 43-44, asst instruction, 46-47; physicist, Naval Res Lab, Washington, DC, 44-46; instr physics, Univ Pa, 47-49; asst prof, Univ Wy, 49-50; sr physicist, Appl Physics Lab, Johns Hopkins Univ, 50-53; assoc prof, Wabash Col, 53-55; prof & chmn dept, Belhaven Col, 55-59; physicist, Antisubmarine Warfare Lab, Naval Air Develop Ctr, 59-60, head res br, 60-65; chmn dept, 65-72, PROF PHYSICS, ROCHESTER INST TECHNOL, 65- *Concurrent Pos:* Lectr, Vis Sci Prog, 58-59; physicist, Naval Ord Lab, Md, 57-59. *Mem:* Am Phys Soc; Am Asn Physics Teachers; Netherlands Phys Soc; Am Geophys Union. *Res:* Isotope separation by thermal diffusion; nuclear and atomic physics; separation and transmutation of neon isotopes; fluid dynamics; physics and geophysics of submarine detection. *Mailing Add:* Dept of Physics Col of Sci Rochester Inst of Technol Rochester NY 14623

ELDER, H E, b Eldorado, Ill, Nov 5, 24; m 48; c 2. ELECTRONIC ENGINEERING. *Educ:* Univ Ill, BS, 48; Newark Col Eng, MS, 54. *Prof Exp:* Engr, 48-51, mem tech staff, Bell Tel Labs, Inc, 51-57, SUPVR, BELL TEL LABS, INC, AM TEL & TEL CO, 57- *Res:* Microwave device development; magnetrons, traveling wave tubes, mixer and detector diodes, masers, klystrons and varactor diodes; solid state light-emitting diode and laser development. *Mailing Add:* Bell Tel Labs Inc 2525 N 11th St Reading PA 19604

ELDER, JAMES FRANKLIN, JR, b Mount Airy, NC, Aug 10, 49; m 71; c 2. MASS SPECTROMETRY, LABORATORY DATA SYSTEMS. *Educ:* Univ NC, Chapel Hill, 71; Purdue Univ, PhD(anal chem), 76. *Prof Exp:* Sr anal chemist, Dow Chem Co, 76-77; sr res chemist, 77-80, RES & DEVELOP PROG MGR, R J REYNOLDS TOBACCO CO, 80- *Mem:* Am Soc Mass Spectrometry. *Res:* Applications of mass spectrometry to chemical and physical properties of gaseous ions; applications of analytical chemistry to production problems, especially to applications of computers to spectrometry. *Mailing Add:* Res Dept R J Reynolds Tobacco Co Winston-Salem NC 27102

ELDER, JAMES TAIT, b Baltimore, Md, Mar 9, 25; m 47; c 5. PHYSICS. *Educ:* Univ NC, AB, 47; Johns Hopkins Univ, PhD(physics), 52. *Prof Exp:* Jr instr physics, Johns Hopkins Univ, 47-50, res asst, 50-52; investr, Res Dept, NJ Zinc Co, 52-59; sr res physicist, Cent Res Labs, 59-62, head physics phenomena group, 62-64; mgr gen physics res, Minn Mining & Mfg Co, 64-67, tech mkt analyst, New Bus Ventures Div, 67-70, mgr Detection Prod, 71-73, gen mgr, New Bus Ventures Div, 73-80, asst vpres, Res & Develop, 80-81; PRES NEW VENTURES GROUP, ALLIED CORP, 81- *Concurrent Pos:* Adj prof mkt & indust eng, Univ Minn, 80-81. *Mem:* AAAS; Inst Elec & Electronics Eng; Am Phys Soc; Am Asn Physics Teachers. *Res:* Infrared spectroscopy; mining geophysics; electrophotography; solid state physics; magnetic materials and measurements; security devices and techniques; research management; product and market development; general business management. *Mailing Add:* 100 Upper Mountain Ave Montclair NJ 07042

ELDER, JOHN THOMPSON, JR, b Fall River, Mass, June 30, 27; m 58; c 2. PHARMACOLOGY. *Educ:* Mass Col Pharm, BS, 53, MS, 55; Univ Wash, PhD(pharmacol), 59. *Prof Exp:* From instr to asst prof pharmacol, Univ Wash, 57-65; from asst prof to assoc prof, 65-74, PROF PHARMACOL, CREIGHTON UNIV, 74- *Mem:* Am Soc Pharmacol & Exp Therapeut. *Res:* Psychopharmacology and autonomic pharmacology, especially as it applies to central nervous system function. *Mailing Add:* Dept of Pharmacol Creighton Univ Omaha NE 68178

ELDER, JOHN WILLIAM, b Ann Arobr, Mich, June 27, 33. ORGANIC CHEMISTRY. *Educ:* Spring Hill Col, BS, 58; Loyola Univ, Ill, MS, 60, PhD(org chem), 62. *Prof Exp:* Asst prof chem, Regis Col, Colo, 67-69; from asst prof to assoc prof, 69-78, PROF CHEM, FAIRFIELD UNIV, 78- *Mem:* Am Chem Soc. *Res:* Organic chemistry of natural products. *Mailing Add:* Dept of Chem Fairfield Univ Fairfield CT 06430

ELDER, RICHARD CHARLES, b Ann Arbor, Mich, June 9, 39; div. INORGANIC CHEMISTRY. *Educ:* St Louis Univ, BS, 61; Mass Inst Technol, PhD(chem), 64. *Prof Exp:* Res assoc chem, Mass Inst Technol, 64-65; from instr to asst prof, Univ Chicago, 65-70; assoc prof, 70-78, PROF CHEM, UNIV CINCINNATI, 78- *Mem:* Am Crystallog Asn; Am Chem Soc. *Res:* Structural chemistry of transition metal complexes; structural trans effects; single crystal x-ray diffraction; technetium complexes; gold-based anti-arthritic drugs; x-ray absorption spectroscopy. *Mailing Add:* Dept Chem 172 Univ of Cincinnati Cincinnati OH 45221

ELDER, ROBERT LEE, b Louisville, Ky, Apr 5, 31; m 55; c 2. RADIOLOGICAL PHYSICS. *Educ:* Ind Univ, BS, 53; Univ NC, MS, 55; Ore State Univ, BS, 58; Johns Hopkins Univ, ScD(biophys), 64. *Prof Exp:* Asst sanit eng, Univ NC, 53-55; engr, USPHS, Nev, 58-60, sr engr, 60-61, sr scientist, Ala, 64-65, sr scientist, Div Radiol Health, 65-67, assoc dir, Bur Radiol Health, 67-70, dir div electronic prod, 70-72, dep dir, Bur Radiol Health, 72-76, dep assoc comnr sci, 76-79, DIR COSMETIC INGREDIENT REV, FOOD & DRUG ADMIN, USPHS, 79- *Concurrent Pos:* Res lectr, Auburn Univ, 64-65; assoc prof, Ore State Univ, 65-68; asst surgeon gen, USPHS. *Mem:* AAAS; Am Soc Civil Eng; Am Soc Microbiol. *Res:* Response of cells and organ systems to toxic substances. *Mailing Add:* 8610 Buckhnon Dr Potomac MD 20854

ELDER, SAMUEL ADAMS, b Baltimore, Md, July 13, 29; m 55; c 5. PHYSICS. *Educ:* Hampden-Sydney Col, BS, 50; Brown Univ, ScM, 53, PhD(physics), 56. *Prof Exp:* Asst physics, Brown Univ, 50-55; physicist assoc staff, appl physics lab, Johns Hopkins Univ, 56, sr staff, 56-64; assoc prof physics, 64-68, PROF PHYSICS, US NAVAL ACAD, 68- *Mem:* Acoust Soc Am; Catgut Acoust Soc; Am Asn Physics Teachers; Sigma Xi. *Res:* Nonlinear acoustics; fluid dynamics; computer science; musical acoustics. *Mailing Add:* Dept Physics US Naval Acad Annapolis MD 21402

ELDER, VINCENT ALLEN, b Yankton, SDak, May 3, 48. ANALYTICAL CHEMISTRY, ENVIRONMENTAL CHEMISTRY. *Educ:* Mich State Univ, BS, 70; Univ Hawaii, MS, 75, PhD(soil sci), 78. *Prof Exp:* Volunteer qual control anal, Am Peace Corps, India, 70-72; fel chem eng, Mass Inst Technol, 78-79; res assoc, Sch Pub & Environ Affairs, Ind Univ, 79-80; GROUP LEADER TECH SERVS, MARY KAY COSMETICS, 80- *Mem:* Am Chem Soc; Soil Sci Soc Am; Soc Cosmetic Chemists; Coun Agr Sci & Technol; Am Soc Mass Spectroscopists. *Res:* Analysis of cosmetics; organic mass spectroscopy; environmental chemistry; gas and liquid chromatography; soil science. *Mailing Add:* Dept of Chem Eng Mass Inst of Technol Cambridge MA 02139

ELDER, WILLIAM HANNA, b Oak Park, Ill, Dec 24, 13; m 41; c 2. WILDLIFE CONSERVATION. *Educ:* Univ Wis, BS, 36, PhM, 38, PhD(zool), 42. *Prof Exp:* Asst zool, Univ Wis, 36-41; game technician, Nat Hist Surv, Ill, 41-43; asst pharmacol, Univ Chicago, 43-45; from asst prof to prof zool, 45-54, RUCKER PROF FISHERIES & WILDLIFE, UNIV MO-COLUMBIA, 54- *Concurrent Pos:* Mem staff, toxicol lab, Univ Chicago, 43-45; Guggenheim fel, 56-57; Fulbright fel, 65-66; NSF grant, Africa, 67-68. *Mem:* Am Soc Mammalogists; Wildlife Soc; Wilson Ornith Soc; Wilderness Soc. *Res:* Physiology of reproduction; biology of the Canada goose; measures of productivity in wild populations; lead poisoning; biology of bats; avian chemosterilants; African elephant; natural area inventories. *Mailing Add:* 108 Stephens Hall Univ of Mo Columbia MO 65201

ELDERFIELD, ROBERT COOLEY, organic chemistry, deceased

ELDERKIN, CHARLES EDWIN, b Seattle, Wash, Aug 6, 30; m 59; c 1. ATMOSPHERIC SCIENCES. *Educ:* Univ Wash, BS, 53, PhD(atmospheric sci), 66. *Prof Exp:* Sr res scientist atmospheric sci, 65-66, sect mgr atmospheric physics, 66-72, assoc mgr dept atmospheric sci, 72-79, proj mgr wind characteristics prog element, Fed Wind Energy Prog, 76-79, MGR DEPT ATMOSPHERIC SCI, PAC NORTHWEST LAB, BATTELLE MEM INST, 79- *Concurrent Pos:* Mem, Field Observ Fac Adv Panel, Nat Ctr Atmospheric Res, 72-75. *Honors & Awards:* Ernest Orlando Lawrence Mem, US Dept Energy, 76. *Mem:* Am Meteorol; Sigma Xi. *Res:* Air pollution; physics and chemistry of clouds and precipitation; atmospheric turbulence and its effects on structures and siting of facilities; wind and solar energy; climatic effects from energy developments; evaluation of air sampling methodologies and pollution control techniques; astronomy and weather forecasting services. *Mailing Add:* Richland WA

ELDERKIN, RICHARD HOWARD, b Butte, Mont, May 4, 45; m 70. MATHEMATICAL ANALYSIS. *Educ:* Whitman Col, BA, 67; Univ Colo, Boulder, MA, 68, PhD(math), 71. *Prof Exp:* Asst prof math, State Univ NY, Albany, 72-73; asst prof & res fel appl math, Brown Univ, 73-74; asst prof, 74-80, ASSOC PROF MATH, POMONA COL, 80- *Mem:* Am Math Soc; Soc Indust & Appl Math. *Res:* Qualitative theory of ordinary differential equations; application of differential equations to epidemiology. *Mailing Add:* Dept of Math Pomona Col Claremont CA 91711

ELDERS, MINNIE JOYCELYN, b Schaal, Ark, Aug 13, 33; m 60; c 2. PEDIATRICS, ENDOCRINOLOGY. *Educ:* Philander Smith Col, BA, 52; Brooke Army Med Sch, cert phys ther, 54; Univ Ark, Little Rock, MD, 60; Am Bd Pediat, dipl, 64. *Prof Exp:* Intern pediat, Univ Minn Hosp, 60-61; resident, 61-64, from instr to asst prof, 64-71, assoc prof, 71-74, PROF PEDIAT, MED CTR, UNIV ARK, LITTLE ROCK, 74- *Concurrent Pos:* Nat Inst Child Health & Human Develop res fel, Med Ctr, Univ Ark, Little Rock, 64-67, career develop award, 67- *Mem:* Soc Pediat Res; Endocrinol Soc; Am Fedn Clin Res. *Res:* Metabolism; effect of glucocorticoids on growth and maturation; control of mucopolysaccharide synthesis and degradation; growth hormone and somatomedin in acute leukemia. *Mailing Add:* Dept of Pediat Univ of Ark Med Ctr Little Rock AR 72201

ELDERS, WILFRED ALLAN, b Sunderland, Eng, Mar 25, 33; m 61. GEOLOGY. *Educ:* Univ Durham, BSc, 57, PhD(geol), 61. *Prof Exp:* Demonstr petrol, Univ Durham, 59-61; from instr to asst prof geol, Univ Chicago, 61-68, assoc prof, Univ Ill, Chicago Circle, 68-69; assoc prof, 69-73, PROF GEOL, UNIV CALIF, RIVERSIDE, 73- *Concurrent Pos:* Louis Block Fund res grant, Univ Chicago, 62-63; NSF grants, 64-69 & 72-78; res geologist, Inst of Geophys & Planetary Physics, 73- *Mem:* AAAS; fel Brit Geol Soc; Am Mineral Soc; Am Geophys Union; Geol Soc Am. *Res:* Geology, geochemistry and geophysics of geothermal areas; water/rock interaction in geothermal reservoirs; geology of Salton Trough. *Mailing Add:* Dept of Earth Sci Univ of Calif Riverside CA 92521

ELDIN, HAMED KAMAL, b Cairo, Egypt, Dec 31, 24; US citizen; m 51; c 3. INDUSTRIAL ENGINEERING, ENGINEERING MANAGEMENT. *Educ:* Cairo Univ, BSc, 45; Calif Inst Technol, MSc, 48; Univ Iowa, PhD(indust eng), 51. *Prof Exp:* Asst prof indust eng, Cairo Univ, 51-52; employee & pub rels mgr, Esso Standard Near East Inc, 52-57; admin mgr, Mobil Oil Egypt, 57-61; mem bd dirs, Nat Inst Mgr Develop, 61-63; consult comput systs, Mobil Oil Corp, 63-65 & Mobil Int, 65-66, rels dept, 66-67; PROF INDUST ENG & MGT, OKLA STATE UNIV, 68- *Concurrent Pos:* Vis prof, Cairo Univ, 52-63; gen mgr, Ras Mallab Gypsum Co, 57-60; lectr, Am Univ Cairo, 58-60; vis prof, Army Engr Corps, 58-62. *Honors & Awards:* Arab Petrol Conf Award, 61. *Mem:* Sr mem Am Inst Indust Engrs; Am Soc Eng Educ; Inst Mgt Sci; Opers Res Soc Am. *Res:* Management science; software package library; computer oriented management information systems; simulation utility programs for production facilites design. *Mailing Add:* Dept of Indust Eng & Mgt Okla State Univ Stillwater OK 74074

ELDIS, GEORGE THOMAS, b Detroit, Mich, Apr 19, 44. METALLURGY. *Educ:* Mass Inst Technol, BS, 66, PhD(metall), 71. *Prof Exp:* Vis scientist, Max-Planck Int Metall, 71-73; sr res assoc, 73-77, res supvr, 77-79, RES MGR, CLIMAX MOLYBDENUM CO OF MICH, DIV OF AMAX, INC, 79- *Mem:* Am Inst Mining, Metall & Petrol Eng; Am Soc Metals; Am Foundrymen's Soc; Soc Automotive Engrs. *Res:* Development of wrought and cast ferrous alloys: rail steels, carburizing steels, low-alloy constructional and abrasion resistant steels in the wrought category; various graphitic and abrasion-resistant white irons in the cast category. *Mailing Add:* 1931 Sheffield Dr Ypsilanti MI 48197

ELDRED, EARL, b Tacoma, Wash, Feb 27, 19; m 44; c 3. NEUROPHYSIOLOGY. *Educ:* Univ Wash, BS, 39; Northwestern Univ, MD & MS, 50. *Prof Exp:* Intern, Va Mason Hosp, Seattle, Wash, 50-51; from instr to assoc prof, 51-62, PROF ANAT, MED SCH, UNIV CALIF, LOS ANGELES, 62- *Concurrent Pos:* Mem staff, Karolinska Inst, Sweden, 52-53; Markle fel, 51-56. *Mem:* Inst Brain Res Orgn; Soc Neurosci; Am Asn Anat. *Res:* Sensory receptors in muscle; motor control. *Mailing Add:* Dept Anat Univ Calif Los Angeles CA 90024

ELDRED, KENNETH M, b Springfield, Mass, Nov 25, 29; m 57; c 1. ACOUSTICS, ENVIRONMENTAL ENGINEERING. *Educ:* Mass Inst Technol, BS, 50. *Prof Exp:* Supvry engr, Boston Naval Shipyard, 51-54; supvry physicist & chief phys acoust sect, US Air Force, Wright Field, Ohio, 56-57; vpres & consult acoust, Western-Electro Acoust Labs, Los Angeles, 57-63; tech dir sci serv & systs group, Wyle Labs, El Segundo, Calif, 63-73; vpres & dir archit technol & noise control div, Bolt Beranek & Newman Inc, 73-77, prin consult, 77-81; DIR, KEN ELDRED ENG, 81- *Concurrent Pos:* Chmn peer group gen eng, Nat Acad Eng, 77-78; mem comt hearing, bioacoust & diomedics, Nat Res Coun, 63-; mem comt aircraft noise, Soc Automotive Engrs, 62- *Mem:* Nat Acad Eng; Inst Noise Control Eng (pres, 76); fel Acoust Soc Am; Soc Naval Architects & Marine Engrs; Am Nat Standards Inst. *Res:* Aircraft acoustics; response of humans to noise; modeling of national noise impact relative to sources. *Mailing Add:* Bolt Beranek & Newman Inc 50 Moulton St Cambridge MA 02138

ELDRED, NELSON RICHARDS, b Oberlin, Ohio, Mar 6, 21; m 45; c 5. ORGANIC CHEMISTRY. *Educ:* Oberlin Col, AB, 43; Wayne Univ, MS, 47; Pa State Col, PhD(chem), 51. *Prof Exp:* Asst, Parke Davis & Co, 43-46; res chemist, Union Carbide Co, 50-68; asst mgr develop, Buckman Labs, Inc, 69; supvr chem div, 70-75, MGR TECHNO-ECON FORECASTING, GRAPHIC ARTS TECH FOUND, 75- *Mem:* AAAS; Tech Asn Pulp & Paper Indust; Am Chem Soc; fel Am Inst Chemists. *Res:* Synthetic resins and fibers; chemistry of papermaking; chemistry of paper and ink; technological forecasting; graphic arts industries. *Mailing Add:* Graphic Arts Tech Found 4615 Forbes Ave Pittsburgh PA 15213

ELDREDGE, DONALD HERBERT, b South Bend, Ind, July 5, 21; m 47; c 4. PHYSIOLOGY, BIOPHYSICS. *Educ:* Harvard Univ, SB, 43; Harvard Med Sch, MD, 46. *Prof Exp:* Intern, Boston City Hosp, 46-47; asst resident, Barnes Hosp, St Louis, 52-53; res asst, 54-58, res instr, 58-60, res asst prof, 60-61, res assoc prof, 61-64, RES PROF OTOLARYNGOL, SCH MED, WASH UNIV, 64-; res assoc, 53-70, asst dir, 70-78, ASSOC DIR RES, CENT INST DEAF, 78- *Concurrent Pos:* Mem, Comt Hearing & Bioacoustics, Armed Forces-Nat Res Coun, 53-70. *Mem:* Acoust Soc Am; Soc Neurosci; Asn Res Otolaryngol. *Res:* Normal and pathologic physiology and mechanical function of the ear. *Mailing Add:* Cent Inst for the Deaf 818 S Euclid St Louis MO 63110

ELDREDGE, KELLY HUSBANDS, b Salt Lake City, Utah, Apr 5, 21; m 45, 54; c 4. VIROLOGY. *Educ:* Univ Utah, BS, 43, MS, 45; Stanford Univ, PhD(virol), 49. *Prof Exp:* Asst, Univ Utah, 42-45; instr life sci, San Francisco State Col, 48-49; asst prof bact, Ariz State Univ, 49-52; lab technologist, Mem Med Ctr, 53-54; teacher, Pub Sch, 54-55; from asst prof to assoc prof life sci, 55-70, PROF BIOL SCI, CALIF STATE UNIV, SACRAMENTO, 70- *Concurrent Pos:* Consult, Friedlanders Labs, Sacramento County Hosp, Eskaton Health Care Ctr & Am River Hosp. *Mem:* Am Soc Microbiol; Am Pub Health Asn. *Res:* Effect of certain compounds on bacteriophage production; pathogenic fungi. *Mailing Add:* 2904 Crescent Ct Sacramento CA 95825

ELDREDGE, LUCIUS G, b East Greenwich, RI, Mar 1, 38; m 58; c 4. MARINE BIOLOGY. *Educ:* Univ RI, BS, 59; Univ Hawaii, PhD(zool), 65. *Prof Exp:* Assoc prof biol, 65-67, prof & chmn dept, 67-71, dir marine lab, 71-73, PROF BIOL, MARINE LAB, UNIV GUAM, 73-; RES ASSOC MARINE ZOOL, BERNICE P BISHOP MUS, UNIV HAWAII, 64- *Mem:* Am Soc Zool; Soc Syst Zool; Crustacean Soc; Pac Sci Asn; Brit Soc Bibliog Natural Hist. *Res:* Taxonomy and ecology of ascidians; taxonomy of Indo-Pacific intertidal gastropods, crustaceans and lancelets; Indo-Pacific marine invertebrates; zoogeography; taxonomy; ecology. *Mailing Add:* Marine Lab UOG Sta Univ Guam Mangilao GU 96913

ELDREDGE, NILES, b Brooklyn, NY, Aug 25, 43; m 64. PALEOBIOLOGY. *Educ:* Columbia Univ, AB, 65, PhD(geol), 69. *Prof Exp:* Asst cur, 69-74, assoc cur invert paleont, 74-79, CUR INVERTEBRATES, AM MUS NATURAL HIST, 79- *Concurrent Pos:* Adj prof biol, City Univ NY, 72-80; adj assoc prof geol, Columbia Univ, 75-; co-ed, Syst Zool, 74-77. *Honors & Awards:* Schuchert Award, Paleont Soc, 79. *Mem:* Paleont Soc; Brit Palaeont Asn; Soc Study Evolution; Soc Syst Zool. *Res:* Trilobite systematics and evolutionary theory. *Mailing Add:* Dept Invert Am Mus Natural Hist New York NY 10024

ELDRIDGE, BRUCE FREDERICK, b San Jose, Calif, Mar 26, 33; m 57; c 3. MEDICAL ENTOMOLOGY. *Educ:* San Jose State Univ, AB, 54; Wash State Univ, MS, 56; Purdue Univ, PhD(entom), 65. *Prof Exp:* US Army, 56-77, instr, Army Med Serv Sch, Tex, 57-58, med entomologist, Walter Reed Army Inst Res, Washington, DC, 58-60 & 61-63, instr med entom, Med Field Serv Sch, 65-66, med entomologist, Atlantic-Pac Interoceanic Canal Study Comn, 68-69, entomologist, 68-69, chief dept entom, Walter Reed Army Inst Res, US Army, 69-77; consult med entom, US Army Surg Gen, 77; PROF ENTOM & CHMN DEPT, ORE STATE UNIV, 78- *Concurrent Pos:* Actg chief entom res br, US Army Med Res & Develop Command, 69-70; chmn, Armed Forces Pest Control Bd, 71-73. *Mem:* Entom Soc Am; AAAS; Am Mosquito Control Asn; Am Soc Trop Med & Hyg. *Res:* Ecology and physiology of mosquitos. *Mailing Add:* Dept Entom Ore State Univ Corvallis OR 97331

ELDRIDGE, DAVID WYATT, b Chattanooga, Tenn, Oct 31, 40; m 62; c 2. MICROBIAL PHYSIOLOGY. *Educ:* Tenn Polytech Inst, BS, 62; Auburn Univ, MS, 64, PhD(bot), 69. *Prof Exp:* Instr bot, Auburn Univ, 64-66, res asst, 66-68; ASSOC PROF BIOL, BAYLOR UNIV, 68- *Mem:* Am Soc Microbiol. *Res:* Biochemistry and physiology of microbial toxins, especially aflatoxins produced by Aspergillus flavus. *Mailing Add:* Dept of Biol Baylor Univ Col of Arts & Sci Waco TX 76703

ELDRIDGE, FRANKLIN ELMER, b Fruitland, Idaho, June 14, 18; m 41; c 3. ANIMAL GENETICS, CYTOGENETICS. *Educ:* Univ Idaho, BS, 41; Kans State Col, MS, 42; Cornell Univ, PhD(animal breeding), 48. *Prof Exp:* Asst dairy husb, Kans State Col, 41-42 & Cornell Univ, 42-43; animal res investr, Nat Resources Sect, Agr Div, Gen Hq, Supreme Command Allied Powers, Japan, 46; asst animal husb, Cornell Univ, 46-48; assoc prof, Kans State Col, 48-54, prof, 54; assoc dir resident instr, 54-61, dir, 61-72, assoc dean col agr, 68-72, PROF ANIMAL SCI, UNIV NEBR, 54- *Concurrent Pos:* Res assoc, Inst Animal Genetics, Univ Edinburgh, 72-73. *Mem:* AAAS; Am Dairy Sci Asn; Am Genetic Asn; Am Soc Animal Sci. *Res:* Cytogenetics of cattle; genetics of conformation and production of dairy cattle; chromosome studies of cattle and other livestock. *Mailing Add:* Inst Agr & Nat Resources Univ of Nebr Lincoln NE 68583

ELDRIDGE, FREDERIC L, b Kansas City, Mo, July 8, 24; m 51; c 2. RESPIRATORY PHYSIOLOGY. *Educ:* Stanford Univ, AB, 45, MD, 48. *Prof Exp:* Intern med, Stanford Univ Hosps, 47-48; resident pediat, Univ Tex Med Br, 48-50; resident med, hosps, 50-51, from instr to prof, Sch Med, Stanford Univ, 54-73, head div respiratory med, 64-73; PROF MED & PHYSIOL, SCH MED, UNIV NC, CHAPEL HILL, 73- *Concurrent Pos:* Chief med serv, Palo Alto Vet Hosp, 60-68; Irving fel, Sch Med, Stanford Univ, 53, Neizer fel, 53-54; USPHS spec res fel pulmonary physiol, St Bartholomews Hosp, Univ London, 54-55 & neurophysiol, Col Med, Univ Utah, 68-69; Bank of Am-Giannini Found fel, 55-56; Markle Found scholar med sci, 56-61. *Mem:* Am Fedn Clin Res; Am Soc Clin Invest; Soc Neurosci; Am Physiol Soc; Am Thoracic Soc. *Res:* Cardiopulmonary physiology; mechanics of respiration; metabolism of lactic acid; respiratory control mechanisms. *Mailing Add:* Dept of Physiol Univ of NC Chapel Hill NC 27514

ELDRIDGE, JEROME MICHAEL, b Youngstown, Ohio, May 21, 32; m 59; c 3. SURFACE CHEMISTRY, SOLID STATE PHYSICS. *Educ:* Case Western Reserve Univ, BS, 55; NY Univ, MS, 60, PhD(metall & mat sci), 67. *Prof Exp:* Proj engr metall, Reactive Metals Corp, 55-58; scientist surface chem, US Steel Corp, 60-63; res staff mem surface chem & solid state physics, 66-70, MGR SURFACE CHEM GROUP, RES DIV, IBM CORP, 70-, MGR CORROSION STUDIES, 75- *Mem:* Am Vacuum Soc. *Res:* Semiconductor devices for computer memory and logic. *Mailing Add:* 20568 Lomita Ave Saratoga CA 95070

ELDRIDGE, JOHN CHARLES, b Chicago, Ill, June 7, 42. REPRODUCTIVE PHYSIOLOGY, ENDOCRINOLOGY. *Educ:* NCent Col, BA, 65; Northern Ill Univ, MS, 67; Med Col Ga, PhD(endocrinol), 72. *Prof Exp:* Instr, Dept Biol & Health Sci, Orange County Comn Col, NY, 67-68; fel, NIH & Med Res, Bordeaux, France, 71-72; res assoc, Dept Endocrinol, Med Col Ga, 73; asst prof lab med, Med Univ SC, 73-78; ASST PROF PHYSIOL & PHARMACOL & MEM GRAD FAC, BOWMAN GRAY SCH MED, WAKE FOREST UNIV, 78- *Concurrent Pos:* Consult non-med prof staff, Med Univ Hosp & mem joint fac, Col Allied Health & Col Grad Studies, Med Univ SC, 74-78. *Mem:* Endocrine Soc; Soc Study Reprod; AAAS; Am Fertility Soc; Am Soc Androl. *Res:* Interaction between steroid and gonadotropic hormones; clinical and animal reproductive physiology; hormone receptor activity; pathophysiology of stress. *Mailing Add:* Dept Physiol Pharmacol Bowman Gray Sch Med Winston-Salem NC 27103

ELDRIDGE, JOHN W(ILLIAM), b Nashua, NH, Aug 22, 21; m 42; c 3. CHEMICAL ENGINEERING. *Educ:* Univ Maine, BS, 42; Syracuse Univ, MS, 45; Univ Minn, PhD(chem eng), 49. *Prof Exp:* Chem engr, Semet-Solvay Co, 42-46 & Barrett Div, Allied Chem & Dye Corp, 49-50; from asst prof to assoc prof chem eng, Univ Va, 50-62; head dept, 62-76, PROF CHEM ENG, UNIV MASS, AMHERST, 76- *Concurrent Pos:* Consult, Albemarle Paper Mfg Co, 51-63 & Holyoke Water Power Co, 62-64; vpres, Gen Aerosols Corp, 55- *Mem:* Am Chem Soc; Am Inst Chem Engrs; Am Soc Eng Educ. *Res:* Continuous flow chemical reactor systems; thermodynamics; kinetics; polymerization. *Mailing Add:* Dept of Chem Eng Univ of Mass Amherst MA 01002

ELDRIDGE, KLAUS EMIL, b Breslau, Ger, June 5, 38; US citizen; m 60; c 2. MATHEMATICS. *Educ:* Hardin-Simmons Univ, BA, 60; Okla State Univ, MS, 62; Univ Colo, PhD(math), 65. *Prof Exp:* Instr math & physics, Hardin-Simmons Univ, 62; asst prof math, 65-70, ASSOC PROF MATH, OHIO UNIV, 70- *Mem:* Nat Coun Teachers Math; Am Asn Univ Prof; Math Asn Am; Am Math Soc. *Res:* Structures of fields, rings and algebras and their relations to the structure of groups. *Mailing Add:* Dept of Math Ohio Univ Athens OH 45701

ELDRIDGE, MARIE DELANEY, b Baltimore, Md, June 1, 26; m 61; c 2. STATISTICS. *Educ:* Col Notre Dame, Md, AB, 48; Johns Hopkins Univ, ScM, 53. *Prof Exp:* Methods statistician, Revere Copper & Brass, 48-50; asst, Sch Hyg, Johns Hopkins Univ, 50-53; sr statistician, Ralph M Parsons Co, Md, 53-54; anal statistician, US Dept Army, 54-55; asst chief statist br, Soc Security Admin, 55-60; chief statist opers, US Off Educ, 60-61, adv & develop servs, 61-62; statistician, NIMH, 62-65; dep dir, Off Statist Progs & Stands, US Postal Serv, 65-68, dir, 68-72; dir math anal div, Res Inst, Nat Hwy Traffic Safety Admin, Dept Transp, 72-73, actg dir, Off Accident Investigation & Data Anal, 73-74, dir, Off Statist & Anal, Res & Develop, 74-75; ADMINR, NAT CTR EDUC STATIST, OFF ASST SECY EDUC, DEPT HEALTH, EDUC & WELFARE, 76- *Concurrent Pos:* Lectr, Univ Baltimore, 57-59; comnr, Educ Comn of the States, 76- *Mem:* Fel Am Statist Asn; Am Educ Res Asn; Int Asn Surv Statisticians. *Res:* Sample survey methodology; theory of sampling and quality checks on mass data; new analytical techniques. *Mailing Add:* 3610 East West Hwy Chevy Chase MD 20015

ELDRIDGE, MAXWELL BRUCE, b Chicago, Ill, Dec 15, 42; m 65; c 2. FISH BIOLOGY, ECOLOGICAL PHYSIOLOGY. *Educ:* Univ Calif, Santa Barbara, BA, 65; Humboldt State Univ, MS, 70. *Prof Exp:* Marine biologist aquacult, Inmont Corp, 70; fishery biologist res, Bur Sport Fisheries, US Fish & Wildlife Serv, 70-71; SUPVR FISHERY BIOLOGIST POLLUTION PHYSIOL, NAT MARINE FISHERIES SERV, DEPT COMM, 71- *Mem:* Am Fisheries Soc; Am Inst Fishery Res Biologists. *Res:* Physiological ecology of marine aquatic organisms with special interest in physiology of early life stages of fishes; pollution physiology and pollutant effects on bioenergetic processes. *Mailing Add:* Southwest Fisheries Ctr 3150 Paradise Dr Tiburon CA 94920

ELDRIDGE, ROSWELL, b Great Neck, NY, Jan 1, 34; m 68; c 5. MEDICAL GENETICS, NEUROLOGY. *Educ:* Haverford Col, BS, 55; Univ Rochester, MD, 60. *Prof Exp:* Sr surg genetics, Epidemiol Br, Nat Inst Neurol & Dis, NIH, 66-68, head sect genetics & epidemiol, 68-75; head sect neurogenetics, 75-76, HEAD SECT GENETICS IN EPIDEMIOL, INFECT DIS BR, INTRAMURAL PROG, NAT INST NEUROL & COMMUNICATIVE DIS & STROKE, NIH, 76- *Concurrent Pos:* Mem med adv bd, Dystonia Found, 74- & Nat Found Jewish Genetic Dis, 75- *Mem:* Am Soc Human Genetics; Am Fedn Clin Res. *Res:* Application of Mendelian genetics to study of general neurological syndromes in effort to define discreet hereditary disease; role of genetic predisposition in disorders of immune response such as multiple sclerosis. *Mailing Add:* Sect on Genetics in Epidemiol NINCDS Nat Inst Health Bethesda MD 20014

ELDUMIATI, ISMAIL IBRAHIM, b Damanhour, Egypt, Jan 19, 40; m 64; c 2. ELECTRICAL ENGINEERING. *Educ:* Univ Alexandria, BScEE, 62; Univ Mich, Ann Arbor, MS, 66 & 68, PhD(elec eng), 70. *Prof Exp:* Instr elec eng, Univ Alexandria, 62-65; assoc dir biophys, Sensors Inc, 70-72; MEM TECH STAFF, BELL LABS, 72- *Mem:* AAAS; Inst Elec & Electronics Engrs. *Res:* Solid state materials and devices; integrated circuits; digital communications; signal processing; microcomputer design. *Mailing Add:* Bell Labs Crawford Corner Holmdel NJ 07733

ELEDER, JOHN PHILIP, b London, Eng, Jan 30, 31; m 75; c 2. THERMAL ANALYSIS, ELECTROCHEMISTRY. *Educ:* Liverpool Univ, BSc, 54, MSc, 56, PhD(electrochem), 61. *Prof Exp:* Fel, Royal Inst Technol, Stockholm, Sweden, 61-63; Argonne Nat Lab, 63-65; sr electrochemist, Metals Control Div, Tex Instruments, Inc, 65-69; sr scientist, Tech Ctr, ESB, Inc, 70-72; mgr, Mellter Instrument Corp, 72-79; SR CHEMIST, INST MINING & MINERALS RES, UNIV KY, 79- *Mem:* Electrochem Soc; Am Chem Soc; NAm Thermal Anal Soc; Am Soc Testing & Mat. *Res:* Thermal analytical studies of fossil fuels; thermogravimetry and differential scanning calormetry are elmployed for studying the kinetics of the degradation of coals and oil shales. *Mailing Add:* Inst Mining & Minerals Res Iron Works Pike PO Box 13015 Lexington KY 40512

ELEFTHERIOU, BASIL E, endocrinology, biochemistry, see previous edition

ELESPURU, ROSALIE K, b Memphis, Tenn, May 3, 44; m 73; c 1. CANCER RESEARCH. *Educ:* Univ Rochester, AB, 66; Univ Tenn, Oak Ridge, PhD(biomed sci), 76. *Prof Exp:* Fel, Cancer Biol Prog, 76-78, scientist, Biol Carcinogenesis Prog, 79-81, GROUP LEADER, FERMENTATION PROG, FREDERICK CANCER RES CTR, 81- *Mem:* Environ Mutagen Soc. *Res:* Bacterial assays for use in the screening of chemical carcinogens and in the search for new cancer treatment drugs. *Mailing Add:* Frederick Cancer Res Ctr Nat Cancer Inst Bldg 434 PO Box B Frederick MD 21701

ELEUTERIO, HERBERT SOUSA, b New Bedford, Mass, Nov 23, 27; m 51; c 6. ORGANIC CHEMISTRY. *Educ:* Tufts Col, BS, 49; Mich State Univ, PhD(chem), 53. *Prof Exp:* Res chemist, Polychem Dept, Exp Sta, 54-58, supvr, 58-59, supvr, Indust & Biochem Dept, 59-62, res sect head, Eastern Lab, 62-64 & Exp Sta Lab, 64-68, dir, 68-70, dir, Eastern Lab, Explosives Dept, 70-72 & Exp Sta Lab, 72, asst dir, Res & Develop Div, Explosives Dept, 72-76, prod mgr, Nylon Intermediates Div, Polymer Intermediates Dept, 76-77, res dir, Polymer Intermediates Dept, 77-78, RES DIR, PETROCHEM DEPT, E I DU PONT DE NEMOURS & CO, 78- *Mem:* Am Chem Soc. *Res:* Reaction mechanisms; stereochemistry; polymer chemistry. *Mailing Add:* E I du Pont de Nemours & Co Petrochem Dept Wilmington DE 19898

ELEUTERIUS, LIONEL NUMA, b Biloxi, Miss, Dec 25, 36; m 69; c 2. MARINE BOTANY. *Educ:* Univ Southern Miss, BS, 66, MS, 68; Miss State Univ, PhD(bot), 74. *Prof Exp:* Biol technician plant path, US Forest Serv, 61-65; res asst bot, Univ Southern Miss, 65-68; botanist marine bot, 68-70, HEAD BOT SECT, GULF COAST RES LABS, 70- *Concurrent Pos:* Instr night classes bot & gen biol, Univ Southern Miss, 68-72; adj prof, Univ Miss, Miss State Univ & Univ Southern Miss; mem, Nat Wetland Tech Coun, Washington, DC. *Mem:* Am Bot Soc; Estuarine Res Fedn; Torrey Bot Club; Ecol Soc; Am Soc Naturalists. *Res:* Botanical aspects of marine communities to include ecology of salt marshes, sea grass beds and algal habitats, especially the rush, Juncus Roemerianus. *Mailing Add:* Gulf Coast Res Lab Ocean Springs MS 39564

ELEY, JAMES H, b Montgomery, Ala, July 16, 40; m 62; c 2. BIOCHEMISTRY, PLANT PHYSIOLOGY. *Educ:* Univ Tex, Austin, BA, 62, MA, 64, PhD(physiol), 67. *Prof Exp:* NIH fel biochem of photosynthesis, Brandeis Univ, 67-68; asst prof bot, Univ Ky, 68-74; ASSOC PROF BIOL, UNIV COLO, 74- *Mem:* AAAS; Am Soc Plant Physiol; Am Inst Biol Sci; Japanese Soc Plant Physiol. *Res:* AAAS; Am Soc Plant Physiol; Am Inst Biol Sci; Japanese Soc Plant Physiol. Res: Photosynthesis; plant physiology. *Mailing Add:* Dept of Biol Univ of Colo Colorado Springs CO 80907

ELFBAUM, STANLEY GOODMAN, b Boston, Mass, Sept 24, 38; m 70; c 3. CLINICAL CHEMISTRY. *Educ:* Northeastern Univ, BS, 61; Northwestern Univ, 64-65, PhD(biochem), 66. *Prof Exp:* Clin chemist, Boston Med Lab, Mass, 57-61; sr biochemist, Gillette Med Res Inst, 65-67, proj supvr biomed div, 67-70; dept supvr, 70-73, tech dir, Boston Med Lab, Inc, 73-77; PRES & TECH DIR, CLIN SCI LAB, INC, 77- *Concurrent Pos:* Clin chem instr, Northeastern Univ, 73- *Mem:* Am Chem Soc; Am Asn Clin Chem. *Res:* Radioimmunoassay of thyroid hormones; detection of abnormal hemoglobins; physical biochemistry of proteins. *Mailing Add:* 48 Williams Rd Sharon MA 02067

ELFNER, LLOYD F, b Manitowoc, Wis, Sept 13, 23; m 63; c 3. PSYCHOACOUSTICS, EXPERIMENTAL PSYCHOLOGY. *Educ:* Univ Wis, BS, 58, MS, 60, PhD(exp psychol), 62. *Prof Exp:* From asst prof to assoc prof psychol, Kent State Univ, 62-67; assoc prof, 67-70, PROF PSYCHOL, FLA STATE UNIV, 70- *Concurrent Pos:* Grants, NSF, 64-66 & 67-69, NIH, 64-66 & 69-72; mem, Evoked Audiometry Study Group. *Mem:* Am Psychol Asn; Acoust Soc Am; Psychonomic Soc. *Res:* Temporal, intensive and spectral resolving powers of the human auditory system; auditory evoked potentials; effects of noise on behavior. *Mailing Add:* Dept of Psychol Fla State Univ Tallahassee FL 32306

ELFNER, LYNN EDWARD, b Springfield, Ohio, Aug 29, 44; m 68; c 3. PLANT ECOLOGY, ZOOLOGY. *Educ:* Ohio State Univ, BS, 67, MS, 71. *Prof Exp:* Sci teacher, Mount Orab Local Schs, 67-70; teaching asst botany, Ohio State Univ, 70-71; executive dir admin, Ohio Environ Coun, 71-73; budget mgt analyst admin, Ohio Off Budget & Mgt, 73-74; EXEC OFFICER ADMIN, OHIO ACAD SCI, 75- *Mem:* AAAS; Asn Academies Sci; Sigma Xi. *Res:* Plant ecology; post glacial plant migration; history of science; science policy. *Mailing Add:* 445 King Ave Columbus OH 43201

ELFORD, HOWARD LEE, b Chicago, Ill, Sept 2, 35; m 62; c 2. BIOCHEMISTRY, CANCER. *Educ:* Univ Ill, BS, 58; Cornell Univ, PhD(biochem), 62. *Prof Exp:* Res asst biochem, Cornell Univ, 62; asst prof, Med Sch, Univ Mich, Ann Arbor, 64-69; asst prof exp med & pharmacol, Med Sch, Duke Univ, 69-75; assoc prof biochem, Med Col Va, Va Commonwealth Univ, 75-80; SR BIOCHEMIST, VA ASSOC RES CAMPUS, COL WILLIAM & MARY, 80- *Concurrent Pos:* NIH fel, Mass Inst Technol, 62-64. *Mem:* Am Soc Biol Chem; AAAS; Am Asn Cancer Res; Am Chem Soc; Sigma Xi. *Res:* Deoxyribonucleotide and DNA biosynthesis; biochemistry and pharmacology of cancer and cancer drug development; mechanisms of vitamin B-12 and its role in mammalian metabolism. *Mailing Add:* Va Assoc Res Campus 12070 Jefferson Ave Newport News VA 23606

ELFSTROM, GARY MACDONALD, b Vancouver, BC, Aug 14, 44; m 69; c 2. AERONAUTICAL ENGINEERING. *Educ:* Univ BC, BASc, 68; Univ London, PhD(aeronaut eng), 71. *Prof Exp:* Asst prof aeronaut eng, Space Inst, Univ Tenn, 71-73; assoc res officer aeronaut eng, Nat Res Coun Can, 73-81; SR ENGR AERODYN, DEFENSE SUPPLY MAT AGENCY INTERNATIONAL, INC, TORONTO, ONT, 81- *Concurrent Pos:* Res fel, Space Inst, Univ Tenn, 71-72; sessional lectr aeronaut eng, Carleton Univ, Ottowa, Ont, 79-81. *Mem:* Am Inst Aeronaut & Astronaut; assoc fel Can Aeronaut & Space Inst; Sigma Xi. *Res:* Fluid mechanics, specifically turbulent boundary layer flow at high speeds; experimental facility development. *Mailing Add:* Defense Supply Mgt Agency Int Inc 4195 Dundas St W Toronto ON M8X 1Y4 Can

ELFTMAN, ALICE G, b Byron, NY, Mar 27, 04; m 30; c 2. ANATOMY. *Educ:* NY State Col Teachers, Albany, BA, 26; Cornell Univ, MA, 29, PhD(anat), 39. *Prof Exp:* Instr biol, NY State Col Teachers, Albany, 26-28; from instr to prof biol sci, Hunter Col, 29-62, chmn dept, 55-62; prof, 62-71, EMER PROF BIOL SCI, LEHMAN COL, 72- *Mem:* Am Asn Anat. *Res:* Histology of mammalian respiratory system; developmental anatomy of hypobranchial muscles; histochemistry of gold excretion; comparative anatomy of vertebrates. *Mailing Add:* 305 Cape Ct Mill Valley CA 94941

ELFTMAN, HERBERT (OLIVER), b Minneapolis, Minn, Oct 31, 02; m 30; c 2. ANATOMY. *Educ:* Univ Calif, AB, 23, AM, 25; Columbia Univ, PhD(zool), 29. *Prof Exp:* Asst paleont & geol, Univ Calif, 23-25; asst zool, 26-28, lectr, Seth Low Jr Col, 28-29, asst prof, 29-40, from instr to prof anat, 40-71, EMER PROF ANAT, COL PHYSICIANS & SURGEONS, COLUMBIA UNIV, 71- *Mem:* AAAS; Am Asn Anat; Am Physiol Soc; Histochem Soc; Soc Exp Biol & Med; NY Acad Sci. *Res:* Biomechanics of human locomotion; histochemistry of phospholipids; cytochemistry of endocrine glands. *Mailing Add:* 305 Cape Ct Mill Valley CA 94941

ELFVIN, MYRA L, b Los Angeles, Calif, Oct 23, 38. CELL BIOLOGY. *Educ:* Univ Calif, Los Angeles, BA, 59, MA, 61, PhD(ultrastruct res), 65. *Prof Exp:* Res assoc muscle res, Univ Ore, 68-70; res assoc, Med Sch, Univ Pa, 70-71; res assoc prof med, 75-80, ASST PROF ANAT, MED COL PA, 71- *Concurrent Pos:* USPHS fel zool, Univ Calif, Los Angeles, 65-66; USPHS fel, Wenner Grens Inst, Univ Stockholm, 66-68. *Mem:* Am Soc Cell Biol; Electron Micros Soc Am; Histochem Soc; Biophys Soc. *Res:* Muscle research, especially comparative ultrastructure and protein chemistry, ATP-ase histochemistry, immunohistochemistry, regulatory proteins. *Mailing Add:* Dept of Anat Med Col Pa Philadelphia PA 19129

ELFVING, DONALD CARL, b Albany, Calif, June 20, 41. APPLE PRODUCTION, APPLE PHYSIOLOGY. *Educ:* Univ Calif, Davis, BS, 64, MS, 66; Univ Calif, Riverside, PhD(plant physiol), 71. *Prof Exp:* Asst prof pomol, Cornell Univ, 72-77, assoc prof, 77-79; SR RES POMOLOGIST, MINISTRY AGR & FOOD, HORT EXP STA, SIMCOE, ONT, 79- *Concurrent Pos:* Consult, US Agency for Int Develop, 77, Int Agr Develop Serv, NY, 81- & Mountain Agr Proj, Cornell Univ, 78; vis prof, Dept Entom, Mich State Univ, 78. *Mem:* Am Soc Hort Sci; Int Dwarf Fruit Tree Asn; Sigma Xi. *Res:* Integration of cultivar-rootstock interactions, pruning and training, growth regulators, irrigation and soil management into orchard-management systems for improved apple production; relevant tree-physiology problems. *Mailing Add:* Hort Exp Sta Box 587 Simcoe ON N3Y 4N5 Can

ELGERD, O(LLE) I(NGEMAR), b Oxberg, Sweden, Mar 31, 25; nat US; m 48; c 3. ELECTRICAL ENGINEERING. *Educ:* Orebro Tech Col, Sweden, 45; Royal Inst Technol, Sweden, Dipl, 50; Washington Univ, St Louis, DSc(elec eng), 56. *Prof Exp:* Designer relay & control of hydroplants, Swed Elec Co, Sweden, 48-51; asst chief engr, Utility Co, 51-52; designer control windtunnels & steamplants, Sverdrup & Parcel, Consult Engrs, Mo, 52-53; instr elec eng, Washington Univ, St Louis, 53-56; PROF ELEC ENG, UNIV FLA, 56- *Concurrent Pos:* Vis prof, Univ Colo, 64-65; consult, Maloney Transformer Co, Gen Elec Co, Va, Hughes Aircraft Co, Calif, Martin Co, Fla, St Regis Paper Co & Aerospace Corp. *Mem:* Sr mem Inst Elec & Electronics Engrs; Swed Soc Eng & Archit. *Res:* Electromechanical componentry; general control theory with computer applications; electric energy conversion and automatic control. *Mailing Add:* Dept of Elec Eng Univ of Fla Gainesville FL 32603

ELGERT, KLAUS DIETER, b Schwarmstedt, Ger, Mar 5, 48; US citizen; m 69; c 2. CELLULAR IMMUNOLOGY, TUMOR IMMUNOLOGY. *Educ:* Evangel Col, BS, 70; Univ Mo-Columbia, PhD(immunol), 73. *Prof Exp:* Teaching asst med microbiol, Med Sch, Univ Mo-Columbia, 71-72, from res asst to res assoc immunol, 73-74; asst prof, 74-80, ASSOC PROF MICROBIOL, VA POLYTECH INST & STATE UNIV, 80- *Concurrent Pos:* Prin investr, Nat Cancer Inst, NIH, 81-84. *Mem:* Reticuloendothelial Soc; AAAS; Am Soc Microbiol; Am Asn Immunologists. *Res:* Cell-mediated immunity during tumor growth; specifically, the effect on immune capabilities of lymphoid cells, their cellular interactions, tumor-induced suppressor cells, kinetics of interleukin activity, and how these relate to cellular immune competence. *Mailing Add:* Dept of Biol Va Polytech Inst & State Univ Blacksburg VA 24061

ELGIN, JOSEPH C(LIFTON), b Nashville, Tenn, Feb 11, 04; m 29, 60; c 4. CHEMICAL ENGINEERING. *Educ:* Univ Va, ChemE, 24, MS, 26; Princeton Univ, PhD(phys chem), 29. *Prof Exp:* Actg asst prof phys chem, Univ Va, 26-27; from instr to prof, 29-72, chmn dept chem eng, 36-54, assoc dean eng, 50-54, dean eng, 54-71, EMER PROF CHEM ENG, PRINCETON UNIV, 72- *Concurrent Pos:* Am Petrol Inst fel, Princeton Univ, 29-31, Brooks fel, Eng Sch, 31; consult, indust firms, 31-, Nat Defense Res Comt, 40-44 & Atomic Energy Comn, NY, 46-50; chief copolymer & copolymer equip develop br, Off Rubber Dir, 42-44; chem engr & div head, Substitute Alloy Mat Lab, Columbia Univ, 44-45; mem div chem & chem tech, Nat Res Coun, 47-58; mem grants comt, Res Corp, 50-64, dir, 64-; trustee, Princeton, Assoc Univs, Inc, 50-62 & 68-71, chmn bd, 57-58; trustee, Procter Found, 62-66; mem, Textile Res Inst, 65-71. *Honors & Awards:* Walker Award, Am Inst Chem Engrs, 57; Lamme Award, Am Soc Eng Educ, 69; Warren K Lewis Award, Am Inst Chem Engrs, 75. *Mem:* Am Inst Chem Engrs; Am Chem Soc; Am Soc Eng Educ. *Res:* Solvent extraction; mechanics of countercurrent contacting towers and fluidized systems; chemical engineering separation methods; phase equilibria in nonideal systems; rubber reclaiming; hydrocarbon separation; polymerization. *Mailing Add:* 226 Prospect Ave Princeton NJ 08540

ELGIN, SARAH CARLISLE ROBERTS, b Washington, DC, July 16, 45; m 67; c 1. MOLECULAR GENETICS. *Educ:* Pomona Col, BA, 67; Calif Inst Technol, PhD(biochem), 71. *Prof Exp:* Teaching asst biochem, Calif Inst Technol, 67-71, Jane Coffin Childs Mem Fund res fel, 71-73; asst prof, 73-77, assoc prof biochem & molecular biol, Harvard Univ, 77-81; ASSOC PROF BIOL, WASHINGTON UNIV, 81- *Mem:* Am Chem Soc; Biophys Soc; Am Soc Cell Biol; AAAS; Am Soc Biol Chem. *Res:* Chromosomal proteins; chromatin structure and mechanisms of gene activation in eukaryotes, particularly Drosophila. *Mailing Add:* Dept Biol Box 1137 Washington Univ St Louis MO 63130

EL GUINDY, MAHMOUD ISMAIL, b Cairo, Egypt. CHEMICAL METALLURGY. *Educ:* Ain Shams Univ, Cairo, BSc, 60; Rensselaer Polytech Inst, MSc, 66, PhD(inorg chem), 68. *Prof Exp:* Instr chem, Assiut Univ, Egypt, 60-63; lectr, Siena Col, NY, 66-67; res assoc metall, McGill Univ, 67-70; res group leader, Refinery Dept, Engelhard Industs, 70-72, mgr refining develop, Minerals & Chem 72-74, tech mgr refining, Engelhard Minerals & Chem Corp, Newark, 74-78; VPRES, SABIN METALS & PRES, PLATINUM GROUP REFINERY INC, 78- *Mem:* Am Inst Mining & Metall Eng; Int Precious Metals Inst; Am Chem Soc; Sigma Xi. *Res:* Recovery and purification of precious metals from ores; solvent extraction of metals, hydrometallurgy; electrochemistry; inorganic compounds of Pt metals; recovery of metals from spent catalyst; pyrometallurgical refining of Pt metals and Re chemistry and metallurgy. *Mailing Add:* Sabin Metals Box F Scottsville NY 14546

EL-HAWARY, MOHAMED EL-AREF, b Sohag, Egypt, Feb 3, 43; Can citizen; m 66; c 3. SYSTEMS ENGINEERING. *Educ:* Univ Alexandria, Egypt, BSc, 65; Univ Alberta, Can, PhD(elec eng), 72. *Prof Exp:* Instr elec eng, Dept Elec Eng, Univ Alexandria, 65-68; teaching & res asst, Dept Elec Eng, Univ Alberta, 68-72, res assoc, 72; assoc prof, Grad Sch, Fed Univ Rio de Janeiro, 72-73; asst prof, Mem Univ, Newfoundland, 74-76, assoc prof, 76-81, chmn dept, 76-81, prof, 81; PROF ELEC ENG, TECH UNIV, NOVA SCOTIA, 81- *Concurrent Pos:* Consult, Newfoundland & Labrador Hydro, 74-; mem, Natural Sci(s) & Eng Res Coun Can, Grant Selection Comt Elec Eng, 81-; assoc ed, Can Elec Eng J, 81- *Mem:* Inst Elec & Electronics Engrs; Can Soc Elec Eng; Can Elec Asn. *Res:* Modeling, simulation and optimization in electric power systems; planning, operation and control. *Mailing Add:* Dept Elec Eng Tech Univ Nova Scotia Halifax NS B3J 2X4 CAN

ELHILALI, MOSTAFA M, b Minia, UAR, Nov 3, 37; m 69; c 5. CANCER. *Educ:* Univ Cairo, MD, 59, DS, 62, DU, 63, MCh, 64; McGill Univ, PhD(exp surg), 69; FRCS(C), 69. *Prof Exp:* Intern med, Univ Cairo Hosp, 60-61, resident urol, 61-63, clin demonstr, 63-65; resident surg, Royal Victoria Hosp, Montreal, 67-68, resident, Ottawa Civic Hosp, 69; from asst prof to assoc prof, 69-80, PROF UROL, FAC MED, SHERBROOKE UNIV, 80-, CHMN DEPT, 75- *Concurrent Pos:* Clin fel, Royal Victoria Hosp, Montreal, 65-67, clin fel urol, 68-69; Nat Cancer Inst Can fel, 66-68 & grant, 72-77; Med Res Coun Can grant, 69-72. *Mem:* Can Med Asn; Am Urol Asn; Can Urol Asn; Can Soc Immunol. *Res:* Isoenzyme changes in prostatic cancer and of lactate dehydrogenase in bladder cancer; urodynamics; immunological aspects of genitourinary cancer. *Mailing Add:* Dept of Urol Sherbrooke Univ Sherbrooke Can

EL-HOSSEINY, FAROUK, b Sherbin, Egypt, Dec 12, 38; Can citizen; m 63; c 3. FIBER SCIENCE. *Educ:* Alexandria Univ, Egypt, BSc, 60; NC State Univ, MS, 66; Leeds Univ, PhD(textile physics), 69. *Prof Exp:* Scientist, Pulp & Paper Res Inst Can, 69-76; SCI SPECIALIST RES & DEVELOP, WEYERHAEUSER CO, 76- *Mem:* Tech Asn Pulp & Paper Indust; Fiber Soc. *Res:* Optical and mechanical properties of natural and man-made fibers, the relation between paper and fiber properties; hydrodynamics of pulp suspensions; paper forming; pressing and drying. *Mailing Add:* Weyerhaeuser Technol Ctr Tacoma WA 98413

ELIA, RAYMOND J, b Farrell, Pa, Feb 20, 25; m 56; c 4. ORGANIC CHEMISTRY. *Educ:* Duquesne Univ, BS, 50, MS, 52; Mich State Univ, PhD(phys org chem), 56. *Prof Exp:* Sr res chemist, 56-67, tech serv supvr, Int Dept, Geneva, Switz, 67-70, RES SUPVR TEXTILE RES LAB, E I DU PONT DE NEMOURS & CO, INC, 70- *Res:* Fiber/fabric responses and correlation of properties. *Mailing Add:* Textile Res Labs E I du Pont de Nemours & Co Inc Wilmington DE 19803

ELIA, VICTOR JOHN, b Portland, Ore, May 11, 42; m 66; c 3. ENVIRONMENTAL HEALTH, ANALYTICAL CHEMISTRY. *Educ:* Portland State Univ, BS, 65; Univ Nebr, Lincoln, PhD(chem), 70. *Prof Exp:* Fel mech org chem, Notre Dame Univ, 69-71; fel environ res, Kettering Lab, Sch Med, Univ Cincinnati, 71-73; asst prof, Defiance Col, 73-74; res assoc, Kettering Lab, Dept Environ Health, Univ Cincinnati, 76-81; RES CHEMIST & INDUST HYGIENIST, NAT COUN PAPER INDUST FOR AIR & STREAM IMPROV, CORVALLIS, 81- *Honors & Awards:* Merck, Sharp & Dohme, Inc Outstanding Res Award, 69. *Mem:* Am Chem Soc; Am Indust Hyg Asn; Am Acad Indust Hyg. *Res:* Synthesis, reaction and mechanistic studies of organic nitrogen compounds; alkaline decomposition of organic disulfides; trace metals; isolation and biological studies of potential toxic environmental pollutants; development and evaluation of air sampling and analysis methods; analysis of organics in air, water, wastewater and biological samples. *Mailing Add:* Nat Coun Air Stream Improv Univ of Cincinnati Col of Med Corvallis OR 97333

ELIAS, HANS GEORG, b Bochum, Ger, Mar 29, 28; m 56; c 2. POLYMER CHEMISTRY. *Educ:* Tech Univ Hannover, dipl-chem, 54; Tech Univ Munich, Dr rer nat, 57; Swiss Fed Inst Technol, Zurich, privatdozent, 61. *Prof Exp:* Sci asst chem technol, Tech Univ Munich, 56-59; from sci head asst chem technol to assoc prof polymer chem, Swiss Fed Inst Technol, Zurich, 60-71; PRES, MICH MOLECULAR INST, MIDLAND, 71- *Concurrent Pos:* Adj prof, Mich Technol Univ, 72-, Case Western Reserve Univ, 78- & Cent Mich Univ, 81-; exec dir, Mich Found Advan Res, 74-79. *Mem:* Am Chem Soc; Am Phys Soc; Sigma Xi; Soc Ger Chem; Swiss Chem Asn. *Res:* Synthesis and solution properties of polymers. *Mailing Add:* Mich Molecular Inst 1910 W St Andrews Dr Midland MI 48640

ELIAS, JOEL JESSE, zoology, anatomy, see previous edition

ELIAS, LORNE, b Ottawa, Ont, Feb 2, 30; m 57; c 4. PHYSICAL CHEMISTRY. *Educ:* Carleton Univ, BSc, 52; McGill Univ, PhD(chem), 56. *Prof Exp:* Res assoc chem, McGill Univ, 56-60; RES OFFICER CHEM, NAT AERONAUT ESTAB, NAT RES COUN CAN, 60- *Res:* Trace vapour detection; detection of explosives vapours; atmospheric monitoring of pesticides ; trace vapour calibration sources. *Mailing Add:* Nat Aeronaut Estab Nat Res Coun of Can Ottawa Can

ELIAS, MICHAEL HANS, b Darmstadt, Ger, June 28, 07; nat US; m 36; c 2. MICROSCOPIC ANATOMY. *Educ:* Univ Giessen, PhD(biol math), 31. *Prof Exp:* Teacher schs, Ger, 31-34; res fel, Fed Polytechnicum, Univ Zürich, 35 & Univ Padua, 36; chief, Histol Lab & Sci Cinematography, Italian Nat Res Coun, 37-38; Athenaeum Pontificium Lateranense, Rome, 39; biol labs, Harvard Univ, 39; prof histol & embryol, Middlesex Vet Col, 39-45; proj supvr prod med films, USPHS, 45-50; asst prof micros anat, 50-53, from assoc prof to prof anat, 53-72, EMER PROF ANAT, CHICAGO MED SCH, 72- *Concurrent Pos:* Consult, Inst Ed Cinematography, Rome; vis prof anat, Univ Heidelberg, 73-75; prof anat, City Col, San Francisco, 75-; res assoc, Univ Calif, San Francisco, 75- *Honors & Awards:* Awards, AMA, 50, 55, 58. *Mem:* Fel AAAS; Am Asn Anat; Am Soc Zoologists (hon pres); Int Soc Stereology. *Res:* Histology; embryology; surgical anatomy; cosmology; geometry of sectioning; four dimensional geometry; education; art; oncology. *Mailing Add:* 463 Marietta Dr San Francisco CA 94127

ELIAS, PETER, b New Brunswick, NJ, Nov 26, 23; m 50; c 3. INFORMATION THEORY. *Educ:* Mass Inst Technol, SB, 44; Harvard Univ, MA, 48, ME, 49, PhD(appl sci), 50. *Prof Exp:* Asst appl sci, Harvard Univ, 48 & 49; from asst prof to prof elec eng, 53-69, head dept, 60-66, Cecil H Green Prof, Elec Eng, 70-72, EDWIN S WEBSTER PROF ELEC ENG, MASS INST TECHNOL, 74-, ASSOC HEAD, DEPT ELEC ENG & COMP SCI, 81- *Concurrent Pos:* Lowell fel, Harvard Univ, 50-53; consult, Baird Atomic, 53, E I du Pont de Nemours & Co, 53-57, Polaroid, 58 & Biophys Study Sect, NIH, 58; vis lectr, Univ Calif, 58. *Mem:* Nat Acad Sci; Nat Acad Eng; fel Inst Elec & Electronics Engrs; Am Acad Arts & Sci; AAAS. *Res:* Information theory; reliable communication over unreliable channels; reliable computation with unreliable components; data compression; economical storage and retrieval of information; complexity of data processing. *Mailing Add:* Dept of Elec Eng Mass Inst of Technol Cambridge MA 02139

ELIAS, ROBERT WILLIAM, b Canton, Ill, Apr 18, 42; m 65; c 2. PHYSIOLOGICAL ECOLOGY. *Educ:* Univ Ill, Urbana, BS, 64, MS, 70; Univ Tex, Austin, PhD(bot), 73. *Prof Exp:* Res fel geochem, Calif Inst Technol, 73-76; ASST PROF BOT, VA POLYTECH INST & STATE UNIV, 76- *Mem:* Am Inst Biol Sci; Ecol Soc Am; AAAS; Soc Environ Geochem & Health. *Res:* Biogeochemistry of trace metals in natural ecosystems. *Mailing Add:* Dept of Biol Va Polytech Inst & State Univ Blacksburg VA 24061

ELIAS, THOMAS S, b Cairo, Ill, Dec 30, 42; m 64; c 1. SYSTEMATIC BOTANY, MORPHOLOGY. *Educ:* Southern Ill Univ, BA, 64, MA, 66; St Louis Univ, PhD(biol), 69. *Prof Exp:* Teaching asst, Southern Ill Univ, 64-66; asst curator bot, Arnold Arboretum, Harvard Univ, 69-72; adminr & dendrologist, 72-74, ASST DIR, CARY ARBORETUM, NEW YORK BOT GARDEN, 74- *Mem:* Am Soc Plant Taxon; Int Asn Plant Taxon; AAAS; Bot Soc Am. *Res:* Trees of North America; floristics and phytogeography of woody plants of temperate Asia and Eastern Europe; morphology and biology of nectaries and other secretory structures; urban tree research. *Mailing Add:* Fowler Rd Millbrook NY 12545

ELIAS, VICTOR W, high energy physics, see previous edition

ELIASON, MORTON A, b Fargo, NDak, Apr 26, 32; m 56; c 4. PHYSICAL CHEMISTRY. *Educ:* Concordia Col, Moorhead, Minn, BA, 54; Univ Wis, PhD(phys chem), 59. *Prof Exp:* From asst prof to assoc prof chem, 58-69, chmn div natural sci, 71-76, PROF CHEM, AUGUSTANA COL, ILL, 69-, CHMN, CHEM DEPT, 80- *Concurrent Pos:* Vis assoc prof chem, Theoret Chem Inst, Univ Wis, 66-67. *Mem:* Am Chem Soc. *Res:* Quantum theory of small molecules; theory of reaction rates, liquids; solubility of inert gases in fused salts; collision processes and energy transfer in gases; theory of charge transfer complexes; oscillating chemical reactions. *Mailing Add:* Dept of Chem Augustana Col Rock Island IL 61201

ELIASON, STANLEY B, b McVille, NDak, Aug 31, 39; m 64. MATHEMATICAL ANALYSIS. *Educ:* Concordia Col, Moorhead, Minn, BA, 61; Univ Nebr, Lincoln, MA, 63, PhD(math), 67. *Prof Exp:* Instr math, Univ Nebr, Lincoln, 63-67; asst prof, 67-71, ASSOC PROF MATH, UNIV OKLA, 71-, ASSOC CHMN, MATH DEPT, 81- *Concurrent Pos:* US Air Force res grants, 70-71, 72-73; Danforth Assoc, 78-84. *Mem:* Am Math Soc; Sigma Xi; Math Asn Am. *Res:* Mathematical analysis; ordinary differential equations; distance between zeros; comparison theorems; second order linear and nonlinear differential equations; differential equations with deviating arguments; second order elliptic linear partial differential equations. *Mailing Add:* Dept of Math 601 Elm Ave Rm 423 Univ of Okla Norman OK 73019

ELIASSEN, ROLF, b New York, NY, Feb 22, 11; m 41; c 2. SANITARY ENGINEERING. *Educ:* Mass Inst Technol, BS, 32, MS, 33, ScD(sanit eng), 35. *Prof Exp:* Sanit engr, Dorr Co, Inc, Chicago & Los Angeles, 36-40; prof sanit eng, NY Univ, 40-49 & Mass Inst Technol, 49-61; prof, 61-73, EMER PROF ENVIRON ENG, STANFORD UNIV, 73-; partner & sr vpres, 61-73, CHMN BD, METCALF & EDDY, 73- *Concurrent Pos:* Dir, Millipore Filter Corp, Mass, 58-62; partner & sr vpres, Metcalf & Eddy, 61-73, chmn bd, 73-; consult, Int Atomic Energy Agency, 57-62, Off Sci & Tech, Exec Off President, 61 & Calif Dept Water Resources, 64-; mem gen adv comt, AEC, 70-75. *Honors & Awards:* George Westinghouse Award, 50. *Mem:* Nat Acad Eng; Am Soc Eng Educ; hon mem Am Soc Civil Engrs; Am Water Works Asn; Water Pollution Control Fedn. *Res:* Methods of water and sewage treatment; industrial and radioactive waste treatment processes. *Mailing Add:* Metcalf & Eddy, Inc 1029 Corporation Way Box 10-046 Palo Alto CA 94303

ELIASSON, SVEN GUSTAV, b Malmo, Sweden, Apr 16, 28; m 51; c 3. NEUROLOGY. *Educ:* Univ Lund, PhD(physiol), 52; Royal Carolina Univ, Lund, MD, 54. *Prof Exp:* From asst prof to assoc prof physiol, Univ Lund, 49-52, instr neurol, 53; jr res anatomist, Univ Calif, Los Angeles, 54-55, asst res anatomist, 55-56; asst prof neurol, Univ Tex Health Sci Ctr, Dallas, 56-63; assoc prof, 63-67, PROF NEUROL, SCH MED, WASH UNIV, 67- *Concurrent Pos:* Rotary Int fel, 54-55. *Mem:* Am Physiol Soc; Am Acad Neurol; Am Neurol Asn; Am Soc Clin Invest; Am Fedn Clin Res. *Res:* Gastrointestinal physiology; neurochemical and nuerophysiological disturbances in peripheral nerves. *Mailing Add:* Dept of Neurol Wash Univ Sch of Med St Louis MO 63110

EL-IBIARY, MOHAMED YOUSIF, b Alexandria, Egypt, Sept 9, 28; m; c 2. ELECTRICAL ENGINEERING, NUCLEAR ENGINEERING. *Educ:* Cairo Univ, BSc, 49; Univ London, PhD(elec eng), 54. *Prof Exp:* Lectr elec eng, Cairo Univ, 55-61, prof, 61-73; vis prof, 73-80, PROF ELEC ENG, UNIV OKLA, 80- *Concurrent Pos:* Res assoc, Joint Estab Nuclear Energy Res, Norway, 55-56; res assoc nuclear eng, Atomic Energy Can, 60-61; consult, Intertrade Corp, 61-67; vis prof elec eng, Univ Mosul, 68-69 & Univ Tripoli, 70-71. *Honors & Awards:* State Merit Award, Egyptian Acad Sci, 59; Merit Medal Sci & Arts, President of Egypt, 59. *Mem:* Sr mem Inst Elec & Electronics Engrs; Am Soc Eng Educ. *Res:* Nuclear electronics, especially semiconductor detectors; microwaves, particularly communications; fiber optics. *Mailing Add:* Sch Elec Eng Univ Okla Norman OK 73019

ELICEIRI, GEORGE LOUIS, b Buenos Aires, Arg, Oct 27, 39; US citizen; m 66; c 3. MOLECULAR CELL BIOLOGY, BIOCHEMISTRY. *Educ:* Univ Buenos Aires, MD, 60; Univ Okla, PhD(biochem), 65. *Prof Exp:* Instr cell biol, Sch Med, NY Univ, 68-69; asst prof, 69-73, assoc prof, 73-76, PROF PATH, SCH MED, ST LOUIS UNIV, 76- *Concurrent Pos:* Damon Runyon Mem Fund fel, Univ Chicago, 65-67; USPHS spec fel, Sch Med, NY Univ, 67-69, USPHS career develop award, Sch Med, St Louis Univ, 72-77. *Mem:* Am Soc Cell Biol; Am Soc Biol Chem; Am Asn Pathologists. *Res:* Mammalian cell gene expression; function, biosynthesis and metabolism of mammalian small nuclear ribonucleic acids and their ribonucleoprotein particles. *Mailing Add:* Dept Path St Louis Univ Sch Med St Louis MO 63104

ELICH, JOE, b Tooele, Utah, Sept 28, 18. MATHEMATICS. *Educ:* Utah State Agr Col, BS, 40; Univ Calif, MA, 42. *Prof Exp:* Asst prof math, 46-58, PROF MATH, UTAH STATE UNIV, 58-, ASST HEAD DEPT, 77- *Mem:* Am Math Soc; Math Asn Am. *Mailing Add:* Dept of Math Utah State Univ Logan UT 84322

ELIEL, ERNEST LUDWIG, b Cologne, Ger, Dec 28, 21; US citizen; m 49; c 2. ORGANIC CHEMISTRY. *Educ:* Univ Havana, Dr phys-chem Sci, 46; Univ Ill, PhD(org chem), 48. *Prof Exp:* From instr to prof chem, Univ Notre Dame, 48-72, head dept, 64-66; W R KENAN, JR PROF CHEM, UNIV NC, CHAPEL HILL, 72- *Concurrent Pos:* NSF sr fels, 58-59, 67-68; Guggenheim fel, Stanford & Princeton Univs, 75-76; Benjamin Rush lectr, Univ Pa, 78; Sir C V Raman vis prof, Univ Madras, India, 81. *Honors & Awards:* Teaching Award, Mfg Chem Asn, 65; Morley Medal, 65; Laurent Lavoisier Medal, 68. *Mem:* Nat Acad Sci; Am Acad Arts & Sci; Am Chem Soc; Royal Soc Chem; AAAS. *Res:* Stereochemistry; conformational analysis; asymmetric synthesis; heterocyclic chemistry; organosulfur chemistry; carbanion chemistry; nuclear magnetic resonance. *Mailing Add:* Dept of Chem Univ of NC Chapel Hill NC 27514

ELIEL, LEONARD PAUL, b Los Angeles, Calif, Sept 14, 14; m 43; c 2. ENDOCRINOLOGY. *Educ:* Harvard Univ, BS, 36, MD, 40. *Prof Exp:* From instr to asst prof med, Cornell Univ, 49-51; from assoc prof to prof med, Med Sch, Univ Okla, 51-74, prof res med, 56-66, exec vpres med ctr affairs & dir med ctr, 71-73, head endocrinol sect, 73-74; ASSOC CHIEF STAFF FOR RES, VET ADMIN HOSP, AM LAKE, 74-; PROF MED, UNIV WASH, 77- *Concurrent Pos:* Clin asst physician, Med Serv, Mem Hosp, 48; asst, Sloan-Kettering Inst, 48-49, assoc, 49-51; head cancer res sect, Okla Med Res Found, 51-64, exec dir, 59-65, vpres & dir res, 65-70; res fel pediat, Harvard Med Sch & Children's Hosp, 46-47, Milton fel, Harvard Med Sch, 47-48; Damon Runyon sr clin res fel, 49-51; clin prof med, Univ Wash, 74-77. *Mem:* Am Soc Clin Invest; AMA; Am Fedn Clin Res; Endocrine Soc; fel Am Col Physicians. *Res:* Metabolic bone disease. *Mailing Add:* Vet Admin Hosp American Lake WA 98493

ELIEZER, ZWY, b Buhusi, Romania, Sept 21, 33; US citizen; m 66; c 1. METALLURGY. *Educ:* Univ Bucharest, dipl physics, 59; Israel Inst Technol, MS, 69, DSc 72. *Prof Exp:* Engr operator, Geophys & Geol Prospecting Co, Bucharest, 58-63; res assoc mat eng, 72-74, asst prof, 74-79, ASSOC PROF MECH ENG, UNIV TEX, AUSTIN, 79- *Mem:* Am Inst Mining, Metall & Petrol Engrs; Am Soc Metals; Am Soc Testing & Mat; Sigma Xi. *Res:* Tribological properties of metals and graphite fiber-metal matrix composites; corrosion of metals in geothermal environments; sensitization of welded austenitic stainless steels. *Mailing Add:* Dept of Mech Eng Univ of Tex Austin TX 78712

ELIN, RONALD JOHN, b Minneapolis, Minn, Apr 14, 39; m 69; c 3. PATHOLOGY, MICROBIOLOGY. *Educ:* Univ Minn, BA, 60, BS, 62, MD, 66, PhD(biochem), 69. *Prof Exp:* Resident anat path, Univ Minn, 66-69; intern, Univ Hosp, San Diego County, 69-70; res assoc infectious dis, Nat Inst Allergy & Infectious Dis, 70-73; resident clin path, 73-74, CHIEF, DEPT CLIN PATH, NIH, 75-, CHIEF CLIN CHEM SERV, 77- *Concurrent Pos:* Clin prof, Uniformed Serv Univ Health Sci, 78- *Mem:* Col Am Pathologists; Am Soc Clin Pathologists; Am Asn Clin Chem; Nat Comt Clin Lab Standards; Am Col Nutrit. *Res:* Magnesium metabolism; host defense mechanisms; endotoxin; development of better and new laboratory tests for the diagnosis of disease; factors which affect the production of acute phase reactants in humans; clinical chemistry. *Mailing Add:* Clin Path Dept Bldg 10 Rm 2C-306 NIH 9000 Rockville Pike Bethesda MD 20205

ELING, THOMAS EDWARD, b Cincinnati, Ohio, Oct 26, 41. PHARMACOLOGY, BIOCHEMISTRY. *Educ:* Univ Cincinnati, MS, 64; Univ Ala, PhD(biochem), 68. *Prof Exp:* RES CHEMIST, NAT INST ENVIRON HEALTH SCI, 69- *Concurrent Pos:* Fel drug metab, Univ Iowa, 68-69. *Mem:* Am Soc Pharmacol & Exp Therapeut. *Res:* Synthesis and metabolism of labeled drugs; effect of drugs on microsomal drug metabolizing enzymes, factors controlling the development of these enzymes in newborn animals and man; pharmacokinetics of environment agents; non-respiratory lung function; prostaglandin biosynthesis and metabolism; oxidation of chemicals by prostaglandin synthetase by lungs; mechanism of chemical uptake processes of the lung. *Mailing Add:* Nat Inst Environ Health Sci PO Box 12233 Research Triangle Park NC 27709

ELINGS, VIRGIL BRUCE, b Des Moines, Iowa, May 9, 39; m 62; c 1. PHYSICS, INSTRUMENTATION. *Educ:* Iowa State Univ, SB, 61; Mass Inst Technol, PhD(physics), 65. *Prof Exp:* Res assoc, Mass Inst Technol, 66; asst prof, 66-72, ASSOC PROF PHYSICS, UNIV CALIF, SANTA BARBARA, 72- *Concurrent Pos:* AEC grant, 66- *Mem:* Am Phys Soc. *Res:* Elementary particle physics; cardiac modeling; medical instrumentation. *Mailing Add:* Physics Dept Univ of Calif Santa Barbara CA 93106

ELINS, HERBERT SAMUEL, photographic chemistry, see previous edition

ELIOFF, THOMAS, b Monroe, La, Dec 11, 33; m 56; c 1. HIGH ENERGY PHYSICS. *Educ:* La Polytech Inst, BS, 54; Univ Calif, Berkeley, PhD(physics), 60. *Prof Exp:* PHYSICIST, LAWRENCE BERKELEY LAB, UNIV CALIF, 60- *Mem:* Am Phys Soc. *Res:* Experimental high energy physics concerning interactions of elementary particles; accelerator development. *Mailing Add:* Bldg 50 Lawrence Berkeley Lab Univ of Calif Berkeley CA 94720

ELION, GERTRUDE BELLE, b New York, NY, Jan 23, 18. BIOCHEMISTRY, PHARMACOLOGY. *Educ:* Hunter Col, AB, 37; NY Univ, MS, 41. *Hon Degrees:* DSc, George Washington Univ & DMS, Brown Univ, 69. *Prof Exp:* Lab asst biochem, sch nursing, NY Hosp, 37; asst org chem, Denver Chem Co, 38-39; teacher chem & physics, New York, 41-42; analyst food chem, Quaker Maid Co, 42-43; res chemist org chem, Johnson & Johnson, 43-44; sr res chemist, Wellcome Res Labs, 44-67, asst to dir, chemother div, 63-67, HEAD EXP THER, BURROUGHS WELLCOME CO, 67- *Concurrent Pos:* Consult, chemother study sect, USPHS, 60-64; adj prof pharmacol & exp med, Duke Univ, 71-, adj prof pharmacol, Univ NC, 73- *Honors & Awards:* Garvan Medal, Am Chem Soc, 68. *Mem:* AAAS; Am Asn Cancer Res; Am Chem Soc; NY Acad Sci; The Chem Soc. *Res:* Chemistry of Purines, Pyrimidines and Pteridines; bacterial metabolism; metabolism of radioactive purines in bacteria and animals; chemotherapy; immunosuppression. *Mailing Add:* Burroughs Wellcome Co 3030 Cornwallis Rd Research Triangle Park NC 27709

ELION, HERBERT AARON, physics, see previous edition

ELIOT, ROBERT S, b Oak Park, Ill, Mar 8, 29; m 57; c 2. CARDIOLOGY, CHEMISTRY. *Educ:* Univ NMex, BS, 51; Univ Colo, MD, 55. *Prof Exp:* Intern, Evanston Hosp, Ill, 55-56; resident internal med, Univ Colo, 56-58; from instr to asst prof med, Med Ctr, Univ Minn, 63-67; assoc prof med & cardiologist, Sch Med, Univ Fla, 67-69, prof med, 69-72; PROF MED, DIR DIV CARDIOVASC MED & DIR CARDIOVASC CTR, UNIV NEBR MED CTR, OMAHA, 72- *Concurrent Pos:* Actg chief cardiol, Vet Admin Hosps, Denver, Colo, 59, consult physician, Minneapolis, Minn, 65-67 &actg chief med serv, Gainesville, Fla, 69-70, chief cardiol sect, 69-72; contribr prof jour; mem ed bd, Heart & Lung; creator educ TV ser heart dis prev, Heartline to Health; res fel cardiol, Sch Med, Univ Colo, 58-60, med fel specialist cardiac path, Univ Minn, 62-63; Nat Heart Inst fel & res trainee cardiovasc path, Charles T Miller Hosp, St Paul, Minn, 62-63; pres elect, Interstate Postgrad Med Assembly, 81; chmn, Bethesda Conf Comt on Prevention of Coronary Dis in Occupational Setting, 80-81; consult central nervous system & sudden death, Nat Acad Sci, 80-; bd dir, Am Inst Stress, 80-; mem adv bd, Stress & Cardiovascular Res Ctr, Eckerd Col, St Petersburg, 80- *Honors & Awards:* Kent award, 56. *Mem:* Am Med Asn; fel Am Col Physicians; Am Heart Asn; Biophys Soc; fel Am Col Cardiol. *Res:* Abnormal hemoglobin oxygen affinity in smokers and patients having signs of coronary insufficiency; myocardial proteins; cardiac pathology; effects of changes in blood-oxygen transport and their role in producing or in treating heart disease; mechanisms causing heart attacks; role of stress in heart disease; vectorcardiography; electrocardiography. *Mailing Add:* 405 Ridgewood Dr Bellevue NE 68005

ELISBERG, BENNETT LA DOLCE, b New York, NY, Nov 11, 25; m 64. INFECTIOUS DISEASES, INTERNAL MEDICINE. *Educ:* NY Univ, BA, 44; Tulane Univ, MS, 48, MD, 50; Am Bd Med Microbiol, dipl. *Prof Exp:* Intern, St Joseph's Mercy Hosp, 50-51; from jr to sr resident internal med, Kern Co Gen Hosp, 51-52, chief resident, 54-55; sr med officer res infectious dis, US Army Med Res Unit, Malaya, 55-58, dep dir, 59-61; med officer res, Dept Virus Dis, Walter Reed Army Inst Res, 61-62, med officer res, Dept Rickettsial Dis, 62-63, chief, 63-72; dir div path, 73-80, DIR DIV PROD QUAL CONTROL, BUR BIOLOGICS, FOOD & DRUG ADMIN, 80- *Mem:* AAAS; Am Soc Microbiol; Am Soc Trop Med & Hyg; Infectious Dis Soc Am; Am Asn Immunol. *Res:* Virus and rickettsial diseases of man. *Mailing Add:* Div Prod Qual Control Bur of Biologics FDA Bethesda MD 20205

ELITZUR, MOSHE, b Borzchow, Poland, April 29, 44; Israeli citizen; m 70; c 3. ASTROPHYSICS. *Educ:* Hebrew Univ, Jerusalem, BSc, 64; Weizmann Inst, Israel, MSc, 66, PhD(physics), 71. *Prof Exp:* Res assoc physics, Rockefeller Univ, 70-72; res fel physics, Calif State Technol Univ, Pasadena, 72-74; scientist physics, Weizman Inst, Israel, 74-75, sr scientist, 75-79; ASSOC PROF PHYSICS, UNIV KY, LEXINGTON, 80- *Concurrent Pos:* Vis res asst prof physics, Univ Ill, Urbana, 77-80. *Res:* Theoretical astrophysics, mainly problems related to the interstellar medium. *Mailing Add:* Dept Physics & Astron Univ Ky Lexington KY 40506

ELIZAN, TERESITA S, b Naga City, Philippines, Dec 12, 31. NEUROLOGY, NEUROVIROLOGY. *Educ:* Univ Philippines, MD, 55; Am Bd Psychiat & Neurol, dipl, 63 & 75. *Prof Exp:* Asst resident gen path, St Mary's Hosp, Waterbury, Conn, 55-56, asst resident neurol, Sch Med, Yale Univ & Grace-New Haven Hosp, Conn, 56-58; clin fel neurol & neuropath, Inst Neurol, Nat Hosp, Univ London, 58-59; chief resident neurol, Montreal Neurol Inst, McGill Univ, 59-60; res asst, Mt Sinai Hosp, New York, 60-61, res assoc, 61-62; asst prof & head neurol sect, Col Med, Univ Philippines, 62; vis scientist & officer-in-chg, Res Ctr, Nat Inst Neurol Dis & Blindness, Guam, 63-65, vis scientist, Epidemiol Br, Md, 65-66, res neurologist & neuropathologist, Sect Infectious Dis, Nat Inst Neurol & Commun Dis & Stroke, 66-68; asst prof neurol & asst attend neurologist, 68-71, assoc prof neurol & assoc attend neurologist, 71-77, PROF NEUROL & ATTEND NEUROLOGIST, MT SINAI SCH MED, 77- HEAD LAB NEUROVIROL, 68- *Concurrent Pos:* Clin asst prof, Sch Med, Georgetown Univ, 65-; USPHS clin fel neurol, Sch Med, Yale, 56-58; Dazian Found Med Res fel, Mt Sinai Hosp, New York, 60-62; consult neurologist, Bronx Vet Admin Hosp, 75- *Mem:* Fel Am Acad Neurol; Am Asn Neuropath; Am Neurol Asn; Am Soc Microbiol; Soc Neurosci. *Res:* Virological and immunological aspects of central nervous system degenerations and infections; clinical neurology; epidemiology of chronic, degenerative neurological diseases; neurovirology; parkinsonism; pre-senile and senile dementias. *Mailing Add:* Dept of Neurol Mt Sinai Sch of Med New York NY 10029

ELIZER, ISAAC, b Sofia, Bulgaria; m; c 3. PHYSICAL CHEMISTRY, INORGANIC CHEMISTRY. *Educ:* Hebrew Univ Jerusalem, MSc, 56, PhD(phys & inorg chem), 60; FRIC. *Prof Exp:* Instr anal, inorg & phys chem, Hebrew Univ Jerusalem, 54-60; sr scientist dept inorg radiochem, Atomic Energy Comn Labs, 60-65; res assoc theoret chem, Univ Southern Calif, 65-67; assoc prof chem, Tel Aviv Univ, 67-72; dir, Col Pract Engrs, 72-74; adj prof chem & mgr, MHD Energy Res, Mont State Univ, 75-80; ASSOC DEAN, COL ARTS & SCI, OAKLAND UNIV, 80- *Concurrent Pos:* Mem, Comt Data Sci & Technol, Int Coun Sci Unions, 71-; ed, Israel Jour Chem, 71-75; mem, Gen Comt, Int Conf Physics Electronic & Atomic Collisions, 71-75; vis prof, Weizmann Inst Sci, 72-75; mem, Subcommission Solubility, Comn Equilibria, Anal Div, Int Union Pure & Appl Chem, 74-; mem, Adv Comt, Mont Energy Res & Develop Inst, 76- *Mem:* Am Chem Soc; Sigma Xi; AAAS; fel London Chem Soc. *Res:* Physical inorganic and analytical chemistry; theoret chemistry; high-temperature inorganic materials; ion exchange; thermodynamics; solution chemistry; energy and the environment. *Mailing Add:* Dean Col Arts & Sci Oakland Univ Rochester MI 48063

ELKAN, GERALD HUGH, b Berlin, Ger, Aug 3, 29. BACTERIOLOGY. *Educ:* Brigham Young Univ, AB, 51; Pa State Univ, MS, 55; Va Polytech Inst & State Univ, PhD(bact), 59. *Prof Exp:* From asst prof to assoc prof, 58-70, asst univ dean res, 77-79, PROF MICROBIOL, NC STATE UNIV, 70- *Concurrent Pos:* Fulbright res fel, Inst Microbiol, Sweden, 63-64; mem, State of NC Water Control Comn, 70-76; Fulbright res fel, Nat Univ East Monagas, Venezuela, 80-81; res grants, NSF, NIH, AID, USDA & Nat Soybean Asn. *Mem:* AAAS; Am Soc Microbiol; fel Am Acad Microbiol; Can Soc Microbiol; Sigma Xi. *Res:* Microbial physiology and metabolism; function and physiology of symbiotic nitrogen fixing bacteria. *Mailing Add:* Dept Microbiol NC State Univ Raleigh NC 27650

EL-KAREH, AUGUSTE BADIH, b Baabda, Lebanon, July 9, 32; US citizen; m 58; c 2. ELECTRICAL ENGINEERING, APPLIED PHYSICS. *Educ:* Delft Univ Technol, DipIng, 56, DSc, 62. *Prof Exp:* Asst, res labs, Europe, 53-55; asst engr, Delft Univ Technol, 55-58; instr elec eng, Univ NMex, 58-59; instr, Univ Pa, 59-60; mem tech staff, RCA Labs, NJ, 60-63; assoc prof elec eng & head electron physics lab, Pa State Univ, 63-66; prof elec eng, Clarkson Col Technol, 66-67; prof, Syracuse Univ, 67-71; prof elec eng & dir, Electron Beam Lab, 71-81, ASSOC DEAN GRAD PROGS & RES, COL ENG, UNIV HOUSTON, 76-; PRES, ABEK, INC, COLORADO SPRINGS, 81- *Concurrent Pos:* Chmn, Int Electron Beam Symp, 64-65. *Mem:* Sr mem Inst Elec & Electronics Engrs. *Res:* High power microwave tubes; electron beam techniques; millimeter wave generation; electron optics; electron physics. *Mailing Add:* Dept of Elec Eng Univ of Houston Houston TX 77004

ELKES, JOEL, b Germany, Nov 12, 13; m 43; c 1. PSYCHIATRY, PSYCHOPHARMACOLOGY. *Educ:* Univ Birmingham, MB, ChB, 47, MD, 49. *Prof Exp:* Lectr, Univ Birmingham, 45-48, sr lectr & actg dir dept pharmacol, 48-50, prof exp psychiat & chmn dept, 51-57; clin prof psychiat, Sch Med, George Washington Univ, 57-63; Henry Phipps prof, 63-76, DISTINGUISHED SERV PROF PSYCHIAT & DIR DEPT, JOHNS HOPKINS UNIV, 76-; PSYCHIATRIST-IN-CHIEF, JOHNS HOPKINS HOSP, 63- *Concurrent Pos:* Consult psychiatrist, Birmingham United Hosp & Birmingham Regional Hosp Bd, 53-57; sci dir, Birmingham Regional Psychiat Early Treat Ctr, 53- 57; examr, Univ London, 53-56; chief clin neuropharmacol res ctr, NIMH, DC, 57-63, mem psychopharmacol study sect, 57-64; dir behav & clin studies ctr, St Elizabeths Hosp, DC, 57-63; mem adv comt biol sci, Air Force Off Sci Res, 64; dir, Found Fund for Res in Psychiat, 67-; Distinguished Serv Prog, Johns Hopkins Univ, 74; Samuel McLaughlin Prof-in-Residence, McMaster Univ, Hamilton, Ont, 75. *Mem:* Fel Am Psychiat Asn; Am Soc Pharmacol & Exp Therapeut; fel Am Psychopath Asn (pres, 69); Am Col Neuropsychopharmacol (1st pres, 61); NY Acad Sci. *Mailing Add:* Dept of Psychiat & Behav Sci Johns Hopkins Hosp Baltimore MD 21205

EL KHADEM, HASSAN S, b Cairo, Egypt, Mar 24, 23; m 51; c 2. ORGANIC & CARBOHYDRATE CHEMISTRY. *Educ:* Cairo Univ, BSc, 46; Swiss Fed Inst Technol, DScTech, 49; Univ London, PhD(org chem) & DIC, 52; Univ Alexandria, DSc, 63; Univ London, DSc, 67. *Prof Exp:* From lectr to prof chem, Univ Alexandria, 52-71; prof chem, 71-81, head, Dept Chem & Chem Eng, 75-80, PRESIDENTIAL PROF CHEM, MICH TECHNOL UNIV, 81-; HEAD DEPT CHEM & CHEM ENG, 75- *Concurrent Pos:* Fulbright scholar, Ohio State Univ, 63-67. *Honors & Awards:* Nat Sci Award, Egypt, 61. *Res:* Carbohydrates; nitrogen heterocycles; metal chelates; polysaccharides; glycosides; natural product chemistry. *Mailing Add:* Dept of Chem & Chem Eng Mich Technol Univ Houghton MI 49931

ELKHOLY, HUSSEIN A, b Elmansoura, Egypt, Oct 30, 33; m 61; c 3. PHYSICS. *Educ:* Cairo Univ, BSc, 57; Hungarian Acad Sci, Kandidat, 61; Eotvos Lorand Univ, Budapest, Dr rer nat(physics), 61. *Prof Exp:* Fel, Eotvos Lorand Univ, Budapest, 61-62; asst prof physics, Cairo Univ, 62-63 & Univ Khartoum, 63-64; asst prof physics, 64-65, chmn dept, 65-67, CHMN DEPT MATH & PHYSICS, FAIRLEIGH DICKINSON UNIV, 67- *Mem:* AAAS; Am Phys Soc; Am Asn Physics Teachers; Am Math Soc; Math Asn Am. *Res:* Phase transformation; lattice defects; radiation effects in solids; microelectronics. *Mailing Add:* Dept Math Fairleigh Dickinson Univ Madison NJ 07940

ELKIN, LYNNE OSMAN, b New York, NY, June 10, 46; m 67. PLANT PHYSIOLOGY, PHOTOMICROSCOPY. *Educ:* Univ Rochester, AB, 67; Univ Calif, Berkeley, PhD(bot), 73. *Prof Exp:* Lectr, 71-72, asst prof, 72-76, ASSOC PROF BIOL SCI, CALIF STATE UNIV, HAYWARD, 76- *Concurrent Pos:* Asst specialist instrnl biol, Univ Calif, Berkeley, 75-78; grant-in-aid res, Sigma Xi, 75. *Mem:* Am Soc Plant Physiol; Sigma Xi; Bot Soc Am. *Res:* Light reactions of photosynthesis; C4 pathway of photosynthesis; fluorescence photomicroscopy; scientific photography; photorespiration; crassulacean acid metabolism. *Mailing Add:* Dept of Biol Sci Calif State Univ Hayward CA 94542

ELKIN, MILTON, b Boston, Mass, Feb 24, 16; m 43; c 3. RADIOLOGY. *Educ:* Harvard Univ, AB, 37, MD, 41. *Prof Exp:* Assoc radiologist, Peter Bent Brigham Hosp, Boston, 51-52; asst radiologist, New Eng Med Ctr, Boston, 52-53; PROF RADIOL & CHMN DEPT, ALBERT EINSTEIN COL MED, YESHIVA UNIV, 54- DIR RADIOL, BRONX MUNIC HOSP CTR, 54- *Concurrent Pos:* Assoc radiologist, Cedars of Lebanon Hosp, Los Angeles, 53-54; Knox lectr, London, Eng & Holmes lectr, Boston, Mass, 70; Rigler lectr, Tel Aviv, Israel, 71; prog dir, Nat Inst Gen Med Sci training grant diag radiol; prin investr, Nat Inst Gen Med Sci res grant; spec consult, USPHS-Nat Inst Gen Med Sci Res Prog-Proj Comt. *Honors & Awards:* Gold Medal, Am Col Radiol, 77. *Mem:* Fel Am Col Radiol; Radiol Soc NAm (pres elect, 79-80, pres, 80-81); Am Roentgen Ray Soc; AMA; Asn Univ Radiol. *Res:* Renal physiology; effects of radiation on tissue. *Mailing Add:* Albert Einstein Col of Med Yeshiva Univ Bronx NY 10461

ELKIN, ROBERT GLENN, b Passaic, NJ, May 7, 53; m 81. AMINO ACID NUTRITION, AMINO ACID METABOLISM. *Educ:* Pa State Univ, BS, 75; Purdue Univ, MS, 77, PhD(animal nutrit), 81. *Prof Exp:* ASST PROF ANIMAL SCI, PURDUE UNIV, 81- *Mem:* Poultry Sci Asn; AAAS; World's Poultry Sci Asn. *Res:* Amino acid nutrition; amino acid metabolism in poultry. *Mailing Add:* Dept Animal Sci Lilly Hall Purdue Univ West Lafayette IN 47907

ELKIN, WILLIAM FUTTER, b Atlantic City, NJ, May 5, 16; m 44; c 1. BIOSTATISTICS, PUBLIC HEALTH. *Educ:* Harvard Univ, BS, 37; Univ Mich, MS, 41, MSPH, 42. *Prof Exp:* Asst statistician, Res Div, Off Price Admin, 42-43; res secy, Philadelphia Tuberc & Health Asn, 43-45; statistician, Oak Ridge Dept Health, Tenn, 45-48 & Health Physics Div, Oak Ridge Nat Lab, 48-49; res staff mem, Dept Biostatist, Sch Pub Health, Univ NC, 50-54; biostatist consult, Fife-Hamill Mem Health Ctr, 54-58; biostatistician, Periodontal Res Proj, Sch Dent, Temple Univ, 58-60; res assoc, Henry Phipps Inst, Sch Med, Univ Pa, 60-62, guest lectr, Sch Nursing, 59-62; STATISTICIAN & STATIST CONSULT, US DEPT HEALTH & HUMAN SERV, 62- *Mem:* Fel AAAS; fel Am Pub Health Asn; Am Statist Asn. *Res:* Public health. *Mailing Add:* 6005 McKinley St Bethesda MD 20817

ELKIND, JEROME I, b New York, NY, Aug 30, 29; m 59; c 3. COMPUTER SCIENCES. *Educ:* Mass Inst Technol, SB & SM, 52, ScD(elec eng), 56. *Prof Exp:* Staff mem psychol, Lincoln Lab, 54-56; head human eng, Airborne Systs Lab, Radio Corp Am, 56-58; sr scientist eng psychol, Bolt Beranek & Newman, 58-61, dept head, 61-64, vpres info sci, 64-66, sr vpres, 66-70; vis prof mgt, Mass Inst Technol, 70-71; mgr comput sci lab, 71-76, vpres advan systs dept, 76-79, VPRES, INFO SYSTS, XEROX PALO ALTO RES CTR, 79- *Concurrent Pos:* Ed, Trans Inst Elec & Electronics Engrs, 59-63; mem res adv comt guid, control & navig, NASA, 60-65. *Honors & Awards:* Franklin Taylor Award, Inst Elec & Electronics Engrs, 68. *Mem:* Inst Elec & Electronics Engrs; Asn Comput Mach; fel Human Factors Soc. *Res:* Interactive man-computer systems; manual control; office information systems. *Mailing Add:* Xerox Palo Alto Res Ctr 3333 Coyote Hill Rd Palo Alto CA 94304

ELKIND, MICHAEL JOHN, b Detroit, Mich, July 23, 22; m 52; c 4. INORGANIC CHEMISTRY. *Educ:* Univ Detroit, BS, 43, MS, 48; Wayne Univ, PhD(chem), 51. *Prof Exp:* Develop chemist pharmaceut prods, R P Scherer Corp, 43-44; fel chem, Univ Detroit, 46-48 & Wayne Univ, 48-50, instr, 50-51; sr res & develop chemist photo prods dept, E I du Pont de Nemours & Co, 51-52, Wyandotte Chem Corp, 52-53 & J T Baker Chem Co, 53-56; mem tech staff, 56-80, SUPVR, BELL TEL LABS, 80- *Mem:* Am Chem Soc; Sigma Xi. *Res:* Inorganic fine and heavy chemicals; photographic chemistry; phase studies in non-aqueous media; chemistry of electron device materials and processing. *Mailing Add:* Bell Tel Labs Reading PA 19604

ELKIND, MORTIMER M, b Brooklyn, NY, Oct 25, 22; m 60; c 3. BIOPHYSICS, RADIOBIOLOGY. *Educ:* Cooper Union, BME, 43; Polytech Inst Brooklyn, MME, 49; Mass Inst Technol, MS, 51, PhD, 53. *Prof Exp:* Asst proj engr, Wyssmont Co, 43-44; proj engr, Safe Flight Instrument Corp, 46-47; head instrumentation, Sloan-Kettering Inst Cancer Res, 47-49; biophysicist, Nat Cancer Inst, 49-69, sr scientist biol dept, Brookhaven Nat Lab, 69-73; mem staff, Exp Radiopath Res Unit, Med Res Coun, Hammersmith Hosp, London, Eng, 71-73; SR BIOPHYSICIST, DIV BIOL & MED RES, ARGONNE NAT LAB, 73-; PROF RADIOL, UNIV CHICAGO, 73-, CHMN, DEPT RADIOL & RADIATION BIOL, 81- *Concurrent Pos:* Mem radiation study sect, NIH, 61-65 & molecular biol study sect, 69-71; sr fel, Nat Cancer Inst, 71-73. *Honors & Awards:* E O Lawrence Award, US AEC, 67; Superior Serv Award, Dept Health, Educ & Welfare, 69; L H Gray Award, Int Comn on Radiation Units & Measurements, 77; E W Bertner Award, M D Anderson Hosp & Tumor Inst, 79; Arthur W Erskine Award, Radiol Soc NAm, 80. *Mem:* Biophys Soc; Radiation Res Soc (pres, 81-). *Res:* Radiobiology of microorganisms and mammalian cells in tissue culture; DNA damage and repair. *Mailing Add:* Div Biol & Med Res Argonne Nat Lab Argonne IL 60439

ELKINS, DONALD MARCUM, b Woodville, Ala, Sept 15, 40; m 63; c 2. AGRONOMY. *Educ:* Tenn Polytech Inst, BS, 62; Auburn Univ, MS, 64, PhD(agron), 67. *Prof Exp:* From asst prof to assoc prof agron, 67-74, PROF AGRON, SOUTHERN ILL UNIV, 74- *Mem:* Am Soc Agron; Crop Sci Soc Am. *Res:* No-tillage or conservation tillage methods; intercropping; row cropping in living or suppressed forage sods; herbicides; growth regulators. *Mailing Add:* Dept of Plant & Soil Sci Southern Ill Univ Carbondale IL 62901

ELKINS, EARLEEN FELDMAN, b South Bend, Ind, Mar 20, 33; m 54; c 3. AUDIOLOGY. *Educ:* Univ Md, BA, 54, MA, 56, PhD(audiol), 67. *Prof Exp:* Instr speech, Univ Md, 54-56; rehab audiologist, Walter Reed Army Med Ctr, 56-57; res assoc, Electronic Teaching Labs, DC, 60-61; asst speech & hearing, Univ Md, College Park, 63-67, res assoc, Biocommun Lab, 67-70, res asst prof, 70-76; res audiologist, Vet Admin Hosp, Washington, DC, 67-76; AUDIOLOGIST, NAT INST NEUROL & COMMUN DISORDERS & STROKE, HHS, BETHESDA, MD, 76- *Concurrent Pos:* Res asst, Nat Inst Child Health & Human Develop, 64. *Mem:* Am Speech & Hearing Asn; Acoust Soc Am; Am Auditory Soc; AAAS; Asn Res Otolaryngol. *Res:* Speech intelligibility and perception. *Mailing Add:* 5821 Edson Lane No 104 Rockville MD 20852

ELKINS, JOHN RUSH, b Beckley, WVa, Nov 16, 41; m 63; c 2. ORGANIC CHEMISTRY. *Educ:* WVa Inst Technol, BS, 63; WVa Univ, PhD(org chem), 66. *Prof Exp:* Instr chem, WVa Inst Technol, 66-67; fel, Univ Ky, 67-68; asst prof chem, Bluefield State Col, 68-70, assoc prof, 70-74 & 75-78, chmn dept, 69-74; assoc prof, 75-78, PROF CHEM, CONCORD COL, 78- *Concurrent Pos:* Vis prof plant path, Va Polytech Inst & State Univ, 74-75, adj prof, 75-78 & 78- *Mem:* Am Phytopath Soc; Sigma Xi; Phytochem Soc NAm; Am Chem Soc. *Res:* Chestnut blight-chemical basis for host-parasite interaction between the American chestnut tree and the blight fungus with emphasis on developing a method for screening chestnut progeny for blight resistance. *Mailing Add:* Dept of Chem Concord Col Athens WV 24712

ELKINS, JUDITH MOLINAR, b Stamford, Conn, Apr 20, 35. APPLIED MATHEMATICS. *Educ:* Wellesley Col, BA, 56; Harvard Univ, MA, 59; Univ Wis-Madison, PhD(math), 66. *Prof Exp:* Instr math, Mt Holyoke Col, 60-63; asst prof, Calif State Univ, San Diego, 66-67, Rutgers Univ, 67-68 & Ohio State Univ, 68-75; assoc prof, 75-79, PROF MATH, SWEET BRIAR COL, 79- *Concurrent Pos:* NSF-sci fac prof develop, Comput Sci, Univ Md, 81-82. *Mem:* Am Math Soc; Math Asn Am; Asn Women in Math; Soc Indust Appl Math. *Res:* Best approximation real-valued functions on the positive real axis. *Mailing Add:* Dept of Math Sweet Briar Col Sweet Briar VA 24595

ELKINS, L(LOYD) E(DWIN), b Golden, Colo, Apr 1, 12; m 34; c 3. PETROLEUM ENGINEERING. *Educ:* Colo Sch Mines, PPE, 34. *Hon Degrees:* ScD, Col of Ozarks, 62. *Prof Exp:* From roustabout to prod res dir, Pan Am Petrol Corp, 34-71; prod res dir, Amoco Prod Co, 71-77; RETIRED. *Concurrent Pos:* Petrol consult, 77- *Honors & Awards:* Citizens Award, Tulsa, 61; Distinguished Achievement Medal, Colo Sch Mines, 61; Engr Hall Fame, Okla State Univ, 61; Lucas Gold Medal, Am Inst Mining, Metall & Petrol Engrs, 66. *Mem:* Nat Acad Eng; Am Petro Inst; hon mem Am Inst Mining, Metall & Petrol Engrs (pres, 62); Am Asn Petrol Geol. *Res:* Oil field reservoir engineering; oil field drilling and well completion; oil field appraisals. *Mailing Add:* PO Box 4758 Tulsa OK 74104

ELKINS, ROBERT HIATT, b Marion, Ind, Oct 2, 18; m 50; c 5. CHEMISTRY. *Educ:* DePauw Univ, AB, 40; Western Reserve Univ, PhD(chem), 45. *Prof Exp:* Res chemist, Standard Oil Co, Ohio, 40-43, res chemist, Great Lakes Carbon Corp, 44-49; res chemist, Sinclair Res Lab, Inc, 49-56; mgr, Org & Polymer Chem, Borg Warner Res Ctr, 56-58, assoc dir, Chem Dept, 58-60; tech mgr com develop & cent res, Nalco Chem Co, 60-66; SR PROG ADV, INST GAS TECHNOL, ILL INST TECHNOL, 66- *Mem:* AAAS; Am Chem Soc; Sigma Xi. *Res:* Polymer chemistry; water soluble polymer applications; hydrocarbon processes; plastics; catalysis; petrochemicals; sulfur recovery from hydrogen sulfide; reactive carbon; indoor environmental control: air quality, energy conservation. *Mailing Add:* 119 N Grant St Hinsdale IL 60521

ELKINS, WILLIAM L, b Boston, Mass, Aug 2, 32. TRANSPLANTATION IMMUNOLOGY. *Educ:* Princeton Univ, AB, 54; Harvard Univ, MD, 58. *Prof Exp:* Intern surg, St Vincents Hosp, New York, 58-59; resident, Univ Hosp, 59-61, from instr to asst prof, 66-71, ASSOC PROF PATH, SCH MED, UNIV PA, 71- *Concurrent Pos:* Fel Wistar Inst, Univ Pa & fel path, Sch Med, 65-66. *Mem:* AAAS; Am Soc Exp Path; Am Asn Immunologists; Transplantation Soc. *Res:* Immunobiology of bone marrow and lymphocyte transplantation. *Mailing Add:* Dept of Path Sch of Med Univ of Pa Philadelphia PA 19174

ELKINTON, J(OSEPH) RUSSELL, b Pa, Oct 12, 10; m 40; c 2. MEDICINE. *Educ:* Haverford Col, AB, 32; Harvard Univ, MD, 37; Am Bd Internal Med, dipl, 45. *Prof Exp:* Intern, Pa Hosp, 37-39, resident physician, 39-40, asst instr, Sch Med, 39-40; from instr to asst prof med, Yale Univ, 42-48; assoc physician, New Haven Hosp, 42-48; ward physician, Univ Hosp, 48-72, from asst prof to prof, 48-72, EMER PROF MED, UNIV PA, 72-; HON SR RES FEL, UNIV BIRMINGHAM, 73- *Concurrent Pos:* Fel med, Univ Pa, 39-40; Nat Res Coun fel electrolyte physiol, Sch Med, Yale Univ, 40-42; estab investr, Am Heart Asn, 49-59; consult surg gen, USPHS, 54-58; ed, Ann Internal Med, Am Col Physicians, 60-71, consult ed, 71-72, emer ed, 72- *Mem:* Am Soc Clin Invest; Am Physiol Soc; fel & master Am Col Physicians; Asn Am Physicians; fel Royal Col Physicians London. *Res:* Electrolyte physiology; cardiovascular science; metabolic and renal diseases. *Mailing Add:* Fairfield Old Church Rd Colwall Malvern WR13 6EZ England United Kingdom

ELLE, GEORGE O, b Falls City, Ore, May 22, 14; m 42; c 4. HORTICULTURE, VEGETABLE CROPS. *Educ:* Ore State Col, BS, 38; Tex Tech Col, MS, 41; Cornell Univ, PhD(veg crops), 51. *Prof Exp:* Agr census, US Dept Interior, 40; agr mkt admin, USDA, 42; asst prof hort, Tex Tech Col, 46-48; res asst, Cornell Univ, 48-51; prof, 51-54, asst dean sch agr, 54-69, prof agr sci, 69-80, EMER PROF HORT, TEX TECH UNIV, 80- *Mem:* AAAS; Am Soc Hort Soc. *Res:* Physiology and breeding of vegetable crops. *Mailing Add:* Col of Agr Sci Tex Tech Univ Lubbock TX 79409

ELLEFSEN, PAUL, b Oak Park, Ill, June 20, 39; m 62; c 4. ANALYTICAL CHEMISTRY. *Educ:* Monmouth Col, BA, 61; Case Inst Technol, PhD(chem), 65. *Prof Exp:* ASSOC PROF CHEM, HANOVER COL, 65- *Mem:* Am Chem Soc. *Res:* Reaction mechanisms and analytical chemistry in nonaqueous solvents. *Mailing Add:* Dept of Chem Hanover Col Hanover IN 47243

ELLEFSON, RALPH DONALD, b Glenwood, Minn, Jan 25, 31; m 55; c 3. ORGANIC CHEMISTRY. *Educ:* Luther Col, Iowa, BA, 53; Univ Iowa, MS, 56, PhD(chem), 58. *Prof Exp:* Asst chem, Luther Col, Iowa, 52-53; asst, Univ Iowa, 53-57; asst, Vet Admin Hosp, Iowa City, 57; instr org chem, Iowa Wesleyan Col, 57-58; instr biochem, 63-68, asst prof, 68-76, ASSOC PROF BIOCHEM & LAB MED, MAYO GRAD SCH MED, UNIV MINN, 76-, MEM STAFF, MAYO CLIN, 63-, DIR LIPIDS & LIPOPROTEINS LAB, 76- *Concurrent Pos:* Res fel biochem, Mayo Clin & Found, 58-60, res assoc, 60, asst to staff, 60-63; consult in clin chem, NIH. *Mem:* AAAS; Am Chem Soc. *Res:* Nitrogen heterocycles; lipid chemistry and metabolism; lipoproteins. *Mailing Add:* Dept of Biochem Mayo Grad Sch of Med Univ of Minn Rochester MN 55901

ELLEMAN, DANIEL DRAUDT, b Lancaster, Ohio, Sept 6, 31; m 54; c 3. PHYSICS. *Educ:* Ohio State Univ, BSc & MSc, 55, PhD(physics), 59. *Prof Exp:* Res specialist, 59-66, group supvr, 66-74, sect mgr physics, 74-76, MEM TECH STAFF, JET PROPULSION LAB, 76- *Mem:* Am Phys Soc. *Res:* Low temperature physics with special emphasis in high field superconductivity; high resolution nuclear magnetic resonance and multiple irradiation experiments. *Mailing Add:* Jet Propulsion Lab 4800 Oak Grove Dr Pasadena CA 91103

ELLEMAN, THOMAS SMITH, b Dayton, Ohio, June 19, 31; m 54; c 3. PHYSICAL CHEMISTRY. *Educ:* Denison Univ, BS, 53; Iowa State Col, PhD(chem), 57. *Prof Exp:* Chemist inst atomic res, Ames Lab, 53-57; radiochemist, Battelle Mem Inst, 57-64; assoc prof, 64-67, head dept, 74-79, PROF NUCLEAR ENG, NC STATE UNIV, 67-; VPRES, NUCLEAR SAFETY & RES DEPT, CAROLINA POWER & LIGHT CO, 79- *Mem:* Am Chem Soc; Am Nuclear Soc. *Res:* Radioisotopes applications; radiation effects; reactor chemistry. *Mailing Add:* Dept Nuclear Eng NC State Univ Raleigh NC 27607

ELLENBERG, JONAS HAROLD, b Long Beach, NY, Apr 26, 42; m 69; c 2. BIOSTATISTICS. *Educ:* Univ Pa, BSc, 63; Harvard Univ, AM, 64, PhD(statist), 70. *Prof Exp:* Consult biostatist, Tufts Univ Med Sch, 66-69; HEAD SECT MATH STATIST, NAT INST NEUROL & COMMUNICATIVE DIS & STROKE, NIH, 69- *Concurrent Pos:* Assoc ed, Am Statistician. *Mem:* Am Statist Asn; Inst Math Statist; Biometrics Soc; Int Biomet Soc (treas). *Res:* Applied: comprehensive statistical analysis of collaborative perinatal project, the prospective study of 60,000 pregnant women and their offspring; theoretical: general linear model, outlier theory. *Mailing Add:* NINCDS Nat Inst Health 7550 Wisconsin Ave Rm 7C10A Bethesda MD 20205

ELLENBERGER, HERMAN ALBERT, b Annville, Pa, Mar 24, 16; m 50; c 3. TOXICOLOGY, OCCUPATIONAL HEALTH. *Educ:* Lebanon Valley Col, BS, 38; Pa State Univ, MS, 46, PhD(biochem, org chem), 48. *Prof Exp:* Technician, Pa Dept Agr, 39-41; chemist, Whitmoyer Labs, Inc, 41-43; res asst, Pa State Univ, 43-48; biochemist, Limestone Prod Corp, 48-63; toxicologist, Conn State Dept Health, 63-68; toxicologist, NS Dept Pub Health, 68-75; TOXICOLOGIST, VICTORIA GEN HOSP, HALIFAX, NS, 75-; ASST PROF PATH, DALHOUSIE UNIV, 69- *Mem:* Can Soc Clin Chem; Chem Inst Can; Am Asn Clin Chem; Can Soc Forensic Sci; Am Chem Soc. *Res:* Analytical methodology related to fields of toxicology; analysis of street drugs received through medical sources. *Mailing Add:* Victoria Gen Hosp Dept of Path 5788 University Ave Halifax NS B3H 1J8 Can

ELLENBOGEN, LEON, b Brooklyn, NY, May 3, 27; m 51; c 3. NUTRITION, HEMATOLOGY. *Educ:* City Col, BS, 49; NY Univ, MS, 51; Ind Univ, PhD(chem), 54. *Prof Exp:* Anal chemist, Novocol Chem Co, 45; res technician 1st res div, Columbia, Goldwater Mem Hosp, 49-51; from asst to res asst, Ind Univ, 51-53; chemist, 53-59, sr res chemist & group leader, Lederle Labs Div, 59-77, ASSOC DIR PROF SERV, MED RES DIV, CHIEF NUTRIT SCI & ASSOC DIR PROF PHARMACEUT SERV, LEDERLE LABS DIV, AM CYANAMID CO, 77- *Concurrent Pos:* Adj prof nutrit med, Cornell Univ Med Col, 78-; adj prof community & preventive med, NY Med Col, 81- *Mem:* Am Chem Soc; Am Inst Nutrit; Am Soc Hemat; Am Soc Clin Nutrit; Am Soc Biol Chemists. *Res:* Cardiovascular biochemistry; thrombosis; vitamin B-12 and intrinsic factor; brain biochemistry; protein fractionation; absorption and metabolism of vitamin B-12 and iron; gastrointestinal absorption; nutrition; vitamins; biochemical pharmacology; biogenic amines; catecholamine metabolism; coenzymes. *Mailing Add:* Lederle Labs Am Cyanamid Co Pearl River NY 10965

ELLENBOGEN, WILLIAM CROMWELL, b Danville, Pa, Oct 20, 17; m 43. ANALYTICAL CHEMISTRY, RESEARCH ADMINISTRATION. *Educ:* Ursinus Col, BS, 39; St Joseph's Col, Pa, MS, 56. *Prof Exp:* Res chemist, leather tanning & anal chem, Wm Amer Co, 40-43; sr res chemist, anal chem & refrig, York Corp, 43-47, sr anal chemist, pharmaceut anal, res & develop anal sect, Smith, Kline & French Labs, 47-48, head sect, 48-62, gen lab dept mgr, 62-68; progs mgr, 68-78, CONTRACT ADMINR, UNIV CITY SCI CTR, 78- *Mem:* Am Chem Soc. *Res:* Laboratory administration; analytical chemistry; pharmaceutical research and development; general project management. *Mailing Add:* Univ City Sci Ctr 3624 Sci Ctr Philadelphia PA 19104

ELLENBURG, JANUS YENTSCH, b Linthicum, Md, Jan 14, 22; m 43. SPECTROCHEMISTRY. *Educ:* Western Md Col, BS, 42, ScD(chem), 68. *Prof Exp:* Asst dir res, Crown Cork & Seal Co, Md, 44-47; spectroscopist, Fairchild Engine & Aircraft Corp, Tenn, 49-52; sr chemist, Oak Ridge Nat Lab, 52-57; chemist, Southern Res Inst, Ala, 57-58; spectroscopist, Hayes Int Corp, 58-60 & McWane Cast Iron Pipe Co, 60-61; sr chemist, 61-68, SR SCIENTIST, HAYES INT CORP, 68- *Concurrent Pos:* Adv, Bessemer State Technol Inst, Ala, 71-72. *Honors & Awards:* Merit Award, Inventions & Contrib Bd, NASA, 70. *Mem:* Am Inst Aeronaut & Astronaut; Am Chem Soc; Optical Soc Am; Am Inst Phys; Soc Appl Spectros. *Res:* Trace elements in matrices by emission spectroscopy; laminar sublayer effects in circulating fluids; dust particle blocking mechanisms; surface cleanliness of aerospace fluid systems; additives for dispersing fine particle clouds. *Mailing Add:* 1133 Lido Dr Birmingham AL 35226

ELLENSON, JAMES L, b Fort Dodge, Iowa, Apr 25, 46; m 78; c 1. PLANT STRESS PHYSIOLOGY. *Educ:* Oberlin Col, BA, 68; Univ Calif, Berkeley, PhD(chem), 73. *Prof Exp:* Res fel, Harvard Univ, 73-79; RES ASSOC, BOYCE THOMPSON INST PLANT RES, 79- *Mem:* Biophys Soc; AAAS. *Res:* Biophysicsl aspects of photosynthesis; plant stress physiology; air pollution effects on plants. *Mailing Add:* Boyce Thompson Inst Tower Rd Ithaca NY 14853

ELLENTUCK, ERIK, b New York, NY, May 13, 34. MATHEMATICAL LOGIC. *Educ:* NY Univ, AB, 56; Univ Calif, Berkeley, PhD(math), 62. *Prof Exp:* Res assoc logic, Stanford Univ, 61-62; mathematician, Shell Develop Co, 62-63; staff mem, Inst Advan Study, 63-65, fel, 63-64; from asst prof to prof math, 65-76, RES ASSOC, UNIV CALIF, BERKELEY, 77-; PROF MATH, UNIV CALIF, BERKELEY, 76- *Concurrent Pos:* NSF fel, 64-65; NJ Res Coun fac fel, 68-69 & 71-72; res assoc, Kyoto Univ, 68-69; staff mem & inst fel, Inst Advan Study, 71-72. *Mem:* Am Math Soc; Asn Symbolic Logic. *Res:* Theory of Dedekind finite cardinals and Isols. *Mailing Add:* Dept of Math Univ Calif Berkeley CA 94720

ELLER, ARTHUR L, JR, b Chilhowie, Va, Nov 5, 33; m 60; c 4. ANIMAL SCIENCE. *Educ:* Va Polytech Inst & State Univ, BS, 55, MS, 66; Univ Tenn, PhD(animal sci), 72. *Prof Exp:* Asst county agent agr, Coop Exten Serv, 55-56, county exten agent, 56-60; asst prof, 60-61, exten specialist, 61-80, ASSOC PROF ANIMAL SCI, VA POLYTECH INST & STATE UNIV, 80- *Mem:* Am Soc Animal Sci. *Res:* Beef cattle breeding and genetics. *Mailing Add:* Dept of Animal Sci Va Polytech Inst & State Univ Blacksburg VA 24061

ELLER, CHARLES HOWE, b Bloomington, Ind, June 5, 04; m 33; c 2. EPIDEMIOLOGY, PUBLIC HEALTH ADMINISTRATION. *Educ:* Stanford Univ, AB, 27; Univ Colo, MD, 30; Johns Hopkins Univ, DrPH, 34. *Prof Exp:* Health officer, NMex & Va, 32-36; assoc prof prev med, Sch Med, Univ Va, 35-36; dir rural health, State Dept Health, Va, 36-37; dir eastern health dist, Baltimore, 37-46; assoc prof pub health, Med Col Va, 46-49; prof community health, Med Sch, Univ Louisville, 49-59; prof, 59-73, EMER PROF PUB HEALTH, SCH MED, WASH UNIV, 73- *Concurrent Pos:* Assoc prof, Sch Hyg & Pub Health & lectr, Sch Med, Johns Hopkins Univ, 37-40; dir pub health, Univ Richmond, 46 & Louisville & Jefferson County Health Dept, Ky, 49-55; consult, Community Res Assoc, NY, 55- & USPHS; comnr health, St Louis County, 59-73; exec dir, Health Delivery Systs, Inc, 73-75. *Mem:* Fel Am Pub Health Asn. *Res:* Diphtheria; medical care. *Mailing Add:* Apt 515 250 E Alameda Santa Fe NM 87501

ELLER, DEAN JAMES GERALD, b Robbinsville, NC, Jan 30, 21; m 43; c 3. ECOLOGY. *Educ:* Western Carolina Univ, BS, 43; Univ NC, Chapel Hill, PhD(zool), 63. *Prof Exp:* From instr to assoc prof, 47-63, chmn dept biol, 64-67, dean arts & sci, 67-73, PROF BIOL, WESTERN CAROLINA UNIV, 63- *Honors & Awards:* Coker Award, 63. *Mem:* Am Conf Acad Deans; AAAS; Sigma Xi. *Res:* Higher education; ecology of aquatic insects; seasonal regulation in Odonata and Ephemeroptera. *Mailing Add:* Sch of Arts & Sci Western Carolina Univ Cullowhee NC 28723

ELLER, PHILLIP GARY, b New Martinsville, WVa, Aug 18, 47. CHEMISTRY. *Educ:* WVa Univ, BS, 67; Ohio State Univ, PhD(chem), 71. *Prof Exp:* Fel inorg chem, Ga Inst Technol, 71-73; MEM STAFF, LOS ALAMOS SCI LAB, 73- *Mem:* Sigma Xi; Am Chem Soc; Am Crystallog Soc. *Res:* Structure and bonding in transition metal andactinide compounds. *Mailing Add:* Los Alamos Sci Lab PO Box 1663 Los Alamos NM 87545

ELLERS, ERICH WERNER, b Berlin, Ger, Sept 11, 28; m 56; c 2. PURE MATHEMATICS. *Educ:* Univ Hamburg, Staatsexamen, 56, Dr rer nat, 59. *Prof Exp:* Asst prof math, Univ Hamburg, 58-63 & Univ Braunschweig, 63-64; Reader, Flinders Univ SAustralia, 66-68; assoc prof, Univ NB, 68-69; assoc prof, 69-75, PROF MATH, UNIV TORONTO, 75- *Mem:* Ger Math Asn; Am Math Soc; Can Math Cong. *Res:* Classical groups; geometry; factorization of members of classical groups into simple isometries or involutions; length problem; geometric and algebraic characterizations of classical groups. *Mailing Add:* Dept of Math Univ of Toronto Toronto ON M5S 1A1 Can

ELLERSICK, FRED W(ILLIAM), b Jersey City, NJ, May 12, 33; m 58; c 4. ELECTRICAL ENGINEERING. *Educ:* Rensselaer Polytech Inst, BEE, 54; Syracuse Univ, MEE, 61; Univ Md, PhD(elec eng), 67. *Prof Exp:* Engr, Int Bus Mach Corp, 54-56, assoc engr, Mil Prods Div, 56-58, staff engr, Fed Systs Div, 58-63, develop engr, 63-69, sr engr, 69; mem tech staff, 69-70, group leader, 70-76, ASSOC DEPT HEAD, COMMUN SYSTS DIV, MITRE CORP, BEDFORD, 76- *Concurrent Pos:* Ed, Inst Elec & Electronics Engrs Trans on Commun, 81, ed-in-chief, Commun Mag, 82- *Mem:* AAAS; sr mem Inst Elec & Electronics Engrs. *Res:* System engineering for computer-communications systems; communication theory; operations research. *Mailing Add:* 29 Fairland St Lexington MA 02173

ELLERT, MARTHA SCHWANDT, b Jersey City, NJ, Nov 27, 40; m 62, 72; c 2. PHYSIOLOGY. *Educ:* Barry Col, BS, 62; Univ Miami, PhD(physiol), 67. *Prof Exp:* Lab technician physiol, Sch Med, Univ Miami, 64-66; instr, 67-70, asst prof physiol & dir summer refresher prog, Sch Med, St Louis Univ, 70-75; ASSOC PROF PHYSIOL, SCH MED, SOUTHERN ILL UNIV, 75-, RES GRANT, 68-, ASST DEAN CURRIC, SCH MED, 81- *Res:* Intestinal transport, particularly of sugars; effects of intestinal resection and dietary glucose on transport rates; mechanism of gastric acid secretion; effects of drugs. *Mailing Add:* Sch of Med Southern Ill Univ Carbondale IL 62901

ELLESTAD, GEORGE A, b Coalinga, Calif, Dec 8, 34; m 60; c 3. ORGANIC CHEMISTRY. *Educ:* Ore State Univ, BS, 56 & 57, MS, 58; Univ Calif, Los Angeles, PhD(chem), 62. *Prof Exp:* NIH fel with Prof W B Whalley, Sch Pharm, Univ London, 62-64; CHEMIST, LEDERLE LABS, AM CYANAMID CO, 64- *Mem:* Am Chem Soc; Roayl Soc Chem. *Res:* Organic chemistry of natural products. *Mailing Add:* Med Res Div Am Cyanamid Co Pearl River NY 10965

ELLESTAD, REUBEN B, b Lanesboro, Minn, May 10, 00; m 34; c 3. CHEMISTRY. *Educ:* Univ Minn, BS, 22, MS, 24, PhD(anal chem), 29. *Prof Exp:* instr chem, Tufts Col, 28-29 & Univ Minn, 29-42; res dir, Lithium Corp Am, 42-67, sr scientist, 67-74, vpres, 56-74; RETIRED. *Concurrent Pos:* Chemist, Rock Anal Lab, 29-42. *Mem:* Am Chem Soc. *Res:* Inorganic and analytical chemistry. *Mailing Add:* 620 Holiday Rd Gastonia NC 28052

ELLETT, CLAYTON WAYNE, b Northfield, Ohio, Nov 12, 16; m 54; c 1. PLANT PATHOLOGY. *Educ:* Kent State Univ, BS, 38; Ohio State Univ, MS, 40, PhD, 55. *Prof Exp:* Asst bot, 39-42, asst plant path, 42-44, instr bot & plant path, 46-55, from asst prof to assoc prof, 56-67, prof, 67-81, EMER PROF PLANT PATH, OHIO STATE UNIV, 81-; CONSULT, CHEM LAWN CORP, 81- *Concurrent Pos:* Res asst, Univ Minn, 48; dir, Plant Dis Clin, Col Agr, Ohio State Univ. *Mem:* Am Phytopath Soc; Mycol Soc Am. *Res:* Diseases of ornamentals and corn; parasitic fungi of Ohio; teaching; mycology. *Mailing Add:* Dept Plant Path Ohio State Univ 1735 Neil Ave Columbus OH 43210

ELLETT, D MAXWELL, b Richmond, Va, July 1, 22; m 58; c 2. MECHANICAL ENGINEERING, APPLIED MECHANICS. *Educ:* Univ Va, BME, 43; Yale Univ, MEng, 50, DEng, 52. *Prof Exp:* Mem staff mech eng, Sandia Lab, 46-49; asst, Yale Univ, 49-52; MEM ENG STAFF, SANDIA CORP, 52- *Mem:* Am Nuclear Soc; Soc Am Mil Engrs. *Res:* Vibration and shock theory and analysis; operation of steady state and pulsed reactors; weapon system vulnerability and associated test methods; ground motion and building response from underground nuclear explosions. *Mailing Add:* PO Box 5062 Kirkland AFB NM 87115

ELLETT, EDWIN WILLARD, b Midlothian, Va, May 21, 25; m 49; c 1. VETERINARY MEDICINE & VETERINARY SURGERY. *Educ:* Univ Ga, DVM, 53; Va Polytech Inst, BSc, 54; Tex A&M Col, MS, 61. *Prof Exp:* Vet in pvt pract, 53-56; asst prof vet med & surg, Okla State Univ, 56-58; assoc prof, 58-61, chief small animal clin, 61-76, PROF VET MED & SURG, TEX A&M UNIV, 61-, PROJ COORDR CLIN FACIL BLDG PROG, 76- *Concurrent Pos:* Consult, M D Anderson Hosp & Tumor Inst, 61-71 & Alcon Labs, 64-68; trainee comp ophthal, Sch Med, Stanford Univ, 70; develop coordr, Col Vet Med, Tex A&M Univ, 80- *Mem:* Am Vet Med Asn; Am Asn Vet Clinicians; Am Soc Vet Ophthal. *Res:* Surgery, especially ophthalmic and nonsuture techniques; cataracts; evaluation of new drugs; ocular diseases of animals and their comparison with diseases of man. *Mailing Add:* Dept of Vet Med & Surg Tex A&M Univ College Station TX 77843

ELLETT, WILLIAM H, b Alliance, Ohio, Oct 10, 29; m 65; c 3. RADIOLOGICAL HEALTH. *Educ:* Rensselaer Polytech Inst, BS, 53; NY Univ, MS, 58; Univ London, PhD(radiation physics), 68. *Prof Exp:* Res asst radiol physics, Sloan-Kettering Inst, 53-55; physicist, Hosp for Joint Dis, 55-57; asst physicist, Biophys, Mass Gen Hosp, Boston, 57-64; phys sci adminr, US Naval Radiol Defense Lab, 64-66; hon res asst, Royal Post Grad Med Sch, Univ London, 66-68; assoc prof radiation biophys, Radiation Ctr, Ore State Univ, 68-71; sr scientist, Off Res & Monitoring, 71-74, CHIEF BIOEFFECTS ANAL BR, OFF OF RADIATION PROGS, US ENVIRON PROTECTION AGENCY, 74- *Concurrent Pos:* Attend physicist, Manhattan Vet Admin Hosp, 56-57; fel, Harvard Med Sch, 59-61, res assoc, 61-64. *Mem:* AAAS; Am Asn Physicists in Med; Radiation Res Soc; Soc Risk Anal. *Res:* Radiation physics; radiation dosimetry; environmental health physics and hazard analysis. *Mailing Add:* Off of Radiation Progs (ANR-460) US Environ Protection Agency Washington DC 20460

ELLGAARD, ERIK G, b Des Moines, Iowa, June 5, 39; m 62; c 3. GENETICS, DEVELOPMENTAL BIOLOGY. *Educ:* Drake Univ, BA, 61; Univ Iowa, PhD(zool, genetics), 68. *Prof Exp:* USPHS fel, Purdue Univ, 68-70; asst prof, 70-76, ASSOC PROF BIOL, TULANE UNIV, 76- *Mem:* AAAS; Genetics Soc Am. *Res:* Chromosomal puffing and its relationship to RNA and protein metabolism; developmental control of gene action; effects of aquatic pollutants on locomotor activities of fish; fisheries biology; effects of acid precipitation on the environment. *Mailing Add:* Dept Biol Tulane Univ New Orleans LA 70118

ELLGEN, PAUL CLIFFORD, catalysis, organometallic chemistry, see previous edition

ELLIAS, LORETTA CHRISTINE, b Jacksonville, Fla, Sept 3, 19. BACTERIAL METABOLISM. *Educ:* Fla State Col Women, BS, 43; Univ Ky, MS, 46; Univ Mich, PhD(bact), 58. *Prof Exp:* From instr to asst prof, 46-63, ASSOC PROF BACT, FLA STATE UNIV, 63- *Concurrent Pos:* Dir, Tallahassee Regional Lab, State Bd Health, 48-49. *Mem:* AAAS; Am Soc Microbiol. *Res:* Terminal oxidation and redox potential; development of audio and video learning tools for courses in microbiology; purification of the streptococcus cyclic adenosine monophosphate factor. *Mailing Add:* Dept of Biol Sci Fla State Univ Tallahassee FL 32306

ELLIKER, PAUL R, b La Crosse, Wis, Feb 12, 11; div; c 3. MICROBIOLOGY. *Educ:* Univ Wis, BS, 34, MS, 35, PhD(dairy bact), 37. *Prof Exp:* Asst, Univ Wis, 34-37, instr dairy & food bact, 37-38; Nat Elec Mfrs Asn fel, Univ Md, 38-39; instr agr bact, Univ Wis, 39-40; asst prof dairy bact, Purdue Univ, 40-42, assoc prof, 42-43, 45-47; prof microbiol & microbiologist in charge, Agr Exp Sta, 47-76, chmn, Dept Microbiol, 52-76, EMER PROF MICROBIOL, ORE STATE UNIV, 76- *Concurrent Pos:* Tech dir, Dairy Soc Int-US exhibit, Madrid Int Trade Fair, 59; US State Dept off deleg, Int Dairy Cong, Denmark, 62, Munich, 66; consult to food indust on sanit. *Honors & Awards:* Borden Award, Am Dairy Sci Asn, 54, Kraftco Award, 74. *Mem:* Int Asn Milk, Food & Environ Sanit (pres, 66-67); Am Soc Microbiol; Am Dairy Sci Asn; Am Acad Microbiol; Inst Food Technol. *Res:* Microbiology of dairy products; dairy farm and plant sanitation; germicides used in the food industries. *Mailing Add:* Dept of Microbiol Ore State Univ Corvallis OR 97331

ELLIN, ROBERT ISADORE, b Poland, Nov 25, 25; nat US; m 50; c 2. PHARMACEUTICAL CHEMISTRY. *Educ:* Johns Hopkins Univ, AB, 46; Univ Md, PhD(pharmaceut chem), 50. *Prof Exp:* Asst chem, Col Pharm, Univ Md, 48-50; pharmaceut chemist, Med Div, Army Chem Ctr, 50-51; prof pharmaceut chem & chmn dept chem, RI Col Pharm, 51-56; med dir pharmaceut chem, Clin Lab Br, Med Res Lab, Edgewood Arsenal, 56-65, supvry res chemist, Clin Res Dept, 65-66, chief, Clin Lab Br, 66-77; RES CHEMIST, BIOSCI DIV, ABERDEEN PROVING GROUND, 77- *Honors & Awards:* Res & Develop Tech Achievement Award, Dept Army, 73. *Mem:* AAAS; Am Asn Clin Chem; Am Pharmaceut Asn; Am Chem Soc. *Res:* Organophosphorus and pesticide toxicology and chemistry; pesticide and nerve gas antidotes; dimercaprol toxicology; skin protection; pharmacokinetics and bioavailability; trace drug analysis; human effluent detection; gas and liquid chromatography and mass spectrometry. *Mailing Add:* Pathobiol Br Biomed Lab Aberdeen Proving Ground MD 21010

ELLING, LADDIE JOE, b Lawton, Okla, June 18, 17; m 42, 76; c 3. PLANT BREEDING. *Educ:* Okla Agr & Mech Col, BS, 41; Univ Minn, MS, 48, PhD(plant genetics), 50. *Prof Exp:* Res assoc alfalfa breeding & seed prod, 50-53, from asst prof to assoc prof, 53-68, PROF AGRON & PLANT GENETICS, UNIV MINN, ST PAUL, 68- *Mem:* Am Soc Agron; Crop Sci Soc Am. *Res:* Forage grass and legume seed production; undergraduate teaching. *Mailing Add:* Dept of Agron & Plant Genetics Univ of Minn St Paul MN 55108

ELLINGBOE, ALBERT HARLAN, b Lakeville, Minn, Apr 3, 31; m 58; c 4. PLANT PATHOLOGY, GENETICS. *Educ:* Univ Minn, BS, 53, MS, 55, PhD(plant path), 57. *Prof Exp:* Asst plant path, Univ Minn, 54-57, res fel, 57-58; res fel biol, Harvard Univ, 58-60; frrom asst prof to assoc prof bot & plant path, Mich State Univ, 60-70, prof biol, Bot& Plant Path, 70-80, dir, Genetics Prog, 73-80; RES DIR, INT PLANT RES INST, SAN CARLOS, CA, 80- *Concurrent Pos:* NIH spec fel & vis assoc prof genetics, Univ Wash, 66-67; vis prof, Univ Sydney, 75. *Mem:* AAAS; Genetics Soc Am; Bot Soc Am; fel Am Phytopath Soc. *Res:* Genetics of host-parasite relationships; recombination in somatic tissues in fungi. *Mailing Add:* Int Plant Res Inst San Carlos CA 94070

ELLINGBOE, J(ULES) K, b Tucson, Ariz, Mar 18, 27; m 48; c 2. ELECTRICAL ENGINEERING. *Educ:* Univ Ariz, BSEE, 50. *Prof Exp:* Electronics engr, Radio Corp Am, 50-52; mem tech staff, Hughes Aircraft Co, 52-55; sr proj engr, Am Electronics, 55-56; mem tech staff, Space Tech Labs, 56-66; proj mgr, Defense Space Systs Div, 66-71, mgr orbital opers, Space Vehicles Div, 71-74, asst mgr mat, 74-77, PROJ MGR TDRSS GROUND STA, TRW SYSTS GROUP, 77- *Mem:* Inst Elec & Electronics Engrs. *Res:* Ballistic missile ground support equipment systems engineering; aerospace support equipment; spacecraft and ground station systems engineering; project management; spacecraft orbital operations. *Mailing Add:* 1420 E Sycamore Ave El Segundo CA 90245

ELLINGBOE, JAMES, b Wilmington, Del, June 10, 37; m 67; c 2. BIOCHEMISTRY, PHARMACOLOGY. *Educ:* Oberlin Col, AB, 59; Harvard Univ, PhD(biochem), 66. *Prof Exp:* Fel biochem, Karolinska Inst, Stockholm, 66-68; asst res biochemist, Sch Med, Univ Calif, San Diego, 68-70; assoc in psychiat, 70-72, PRIN RES ASSOC PSYCHIAT, HARVARD MED SCH, 72-; ASSOC BIOCHEMIST, McLEAN HOSP, BELMONT, MASS, 73-; CHIEF BIOCHEM LAB, ALCOHOL & DRUG ABUSE RES CTR, McLEAN HOSP & HARVARD MED SCH, 73- *Concurrent Pos:* NIH fel, 66-67; dir biochem, Drug Surveillance & Biochem Lab, Boston City Hosp, 70-73. *Mem:* Am Chem Soc; Int Narcotic Res Assoc; Int Soc Psychoneuroendocrinol; Am Soc Pharmacol Exp Therapeuts; Soc Neurosci. *Res:* Neuroendocrine regulatory mechanisms; biochemical pharmacology; lipid biochemistry; analytical biochemistry; endocrinology. *Mailing Add:* Biochem Lab Alcohol & Drug Abuse McLean Hosp 115 Mill St Belmont MA 02178

ELLINGER, MARK STEPHEN, b Crookston, Minn, Apr 12, 49; m 71. DEVELOPMENTAL BIOLOGY, EMBRYOLOGY. *Educ:* Augsburg Col, BA, 71; Univ Minn, Minneapolis, PhD(zool), 76. *Prof Exp:* Vis asst prof biol, Eastern Wash Univ, 76-77; asst prof, 77-81, ASSOC PROF ZOOL, SOUTHERN ILL UNIV, CARBONDALE, 81- *Concurrent Pos:* Am Cancer Soc res grant, 79. *Mem:* Am Soc Zoologists; AAAS; Int Soc Differentiation; Sigma Xi; Soc Develop Biol. *Res:* Nucleo-cytoplasmic interactions in amphibian development; chemical carcinogenesis and developmental potentials of embryonic nuclei, as revealed by egg microinjection and nuclear transplantation; cellular interactions in haploid embryos; mode of action of tumor promoters. *Mailing Add:* Dept Zool Southern Ill Univ Carbondale IL 62901

ELLINGER, RUDOLPH H, b Grand Rapids, Mich, Aug 18, 20; m 50; c 2. FOOD SCIENCE, FOOD MICROBIOLOGY. *Educ:* Mich State Univ, BS, 50; Iowa State Univ, MS, 53, PhD(biochem), 54. *Prof Exp:* Biochemist cent res labs, Pillsbury Co, Minn, 54-57, tech mgr prod improv, Refrig Prod Res & Develop Labs, Ky, 57-59; dir res prod develop, J D Jewell, Inc, Ga, 59-61; supvr tech serv labs, Durkee Famous Foods, Ill, 61-64; mgr food prod develop, Stauffer Chem Co, NY, 64-69; dir tech serv, Stouffer Foods Corp, 70-71; mgr regulatory compliance, Kraft Foods Div, 71-76; corp dir qual assurance & regulatory compliance, 76-79, dir, Quality Assurance-Int, Kraft, Inc, 79-81; CONSULT FOOD INDUST, 81- *Concurrent Pos:* Mem, Tech Comt, Grocery Mfrs Am & Coun Indust Liaison Panel, Food & Nutrit Bd, Nat Acad Sci-Nat Res Coun. *Mem:* Am Soc Qual Control; Am Soc Prof Consults; Am Coun Sci & Health; Inst Food Technol. *Res:* Baking and food technology; microbiology. *Mailing Add:* 500 Peshtigo Ct Chicago IL 60690

ELLINGHAUSEN, HERMAN CHARLES, JR, b Annapolis, Md, Nov 3, 26; m 51; c 3. BACTERIOLOGY. *Educ:* Univ Md, BS, 50, PhD(bact), 55; Univ NC, MSc, 52. *Prof Exp:* Asst bact, Univ Md, 52-55; PRIN RES MICROBIOLOGIST, PROJ LEADER LEPTOSPIROSIS RES, AGR RES SERV, ANIMAL DIS & PARASITE RES DIV, BACTERIAL & MYCOTIC DIS INVESTS, NAT ANIMAL DIS LAB, 55- *Concurrent Pos:* Mem staff, Grad Sch, USDA & lectr, NIH, 55-60; adv to grad studies, Univ NC & Colo State Univ; mem staff, Dept Biol, Drake Univ. *Mem:* Am Soc Microbiol; Am Acad Microbiol; Conf Res Workers Animal Dis; Am Asn Vet Lab Diag; US Animal Health Asn. *Res:* Mammalian nutrition; bacterial metabolism; enzymes of pathogenic bacteria, visible and infrared spectrophotometry; electron microscopy; pathogenesis and immunological aspect of leptospirosis; serolgical characteristics of leptospires. *Mailing Add:* USDA Nat Animal Dis Lab PO Box 70 Ames IA 50010

ELLINGSON, HAROLD VICTOR, aerospace medicine, preventive medicine, deceased

ELLINGSON, JOHN S, b Rockford, Ill, Mar 25, 40. BIOCHEMISTRY. *Educ:* Univ Ill, Urbana, BS, 62; Univ Mich, Ann Arbor, MS, 64, PhD(biochem), 68. *Prof Exp:* Asst prof, 70-77, ASSOC PROF BIOCHEM, MED SCH, WVA UNIV, 77- *Concurrent Pos:* Trainee, Brandeis Univ, 67-70. *Res:* Phospholipids and membranes; regulation of development in cellular slime molds. *Mailing Add:* Dept of Biochem Sch of Med WVa Univ Morgantown WV 26506

ELLINGSON, ROBERT GEORGE, b Chicago, Ill, Dec 30, 45; m 69; c 1. ATMOSPHERIC RADIATION, CLIMATE MODELING. *Educ:* Fla State Univ, BS, 67, MS, 68, PhD(meteorol), 72. *Prof Exp:* Comput programmer, Nat Ctr Atmospheric Res, 67; res asst, Fla State Univ, 68-72; fel, Nat Ctr Atmospheric Res, 72-73; asst prof, 73-78, ASSOC PROF METEOROL, UNIV MD, 78- *Concurrent Pos:* aircraft scientist, Atlantic Trop Exp, Global Atmospheric Res Prog, 74, Monsoon Exp, 77-79; consult, Lawrence Livermore Lab, 78- *Mem:* Am Meteorol Soc. *Res:* Theoretical and computer modeling of atmospheric radiative transfer, airborne observations of electromagnetic radiation; remote sensing of climate parameters and testing of numerical weather/climate prediction models. *Mailing Add:* Dept Meteorol Univ Md College Park MD 20742

ELLINGSON, ROBERT JAMES, b Chicago, Ill, June 7, 23; m 48; c 2. ELECTROENCEPHALOGRAPHY, CLINICAL NEUROPHYSIOLOGY. *Educ:* Northwestern Univ, BS, 47, MA, 49, PhD(psychol), 50; Univ Nebr, MD, 63. *Prof Exp:* Res assoc psychol, Mooseheart Lab Child Res, 48-50; assoc, 50-51, from asst prof to assoc prof, 51-64, prof physiol, 68-70, PROF MED PSYCHOL, COL MED, UNIV NEBR, OMAHA, 64-, PROF NEUROL, 70-; ASSOC DIR, NEBR PSYCHIAT INST, 63- *Concurrent Pos:* Chief electroencephalog tech, Nebr Psychiat Inst, 50-76; mem adv comt prog sci, technol & human values, Nat Endowment for the Humanities, 74-76. *Mem:* Fel AAAS; Int Soc Develop Psychobiol; Am Electroencephalog Soc (secy, 64-67; pres, 68-69); Int Fedn Soc Electroencephalog & Clin Neurophysiol (secy, 69-81). *Mailing Add:* Res Div Nebr Psychiat Inst 602 S 44th Ave Omaha NE 68105

ELLINGSON, RUDOLPH CONRAD, b Madison, Wis, Mar 8, 11; m 39; c 2. ORGANIC CHEMISTRY. *Educ:* St Olaf Col, BA, 33; Johns Hopkins Univ, PhD(org chem), 38. *Prof Exp:* Lab technician, Mass Inst Technol, 33-34; asst chem, Johns Hopkins Univ, 34-38, instr, 38-39; res chemist, Mead Johnson & Co, 39-50, chief res div, 50-53, asst dir res, 53-54, dir nutrit res & prod develop, 54-59, sr res scientist, Prod Develop, 59-60, dir sci admin, 60-65, exec dir admin, 65-66, dir clin & med res admin, 66-68, dir planning & coord, Res Ctr, 68-75; RETIRED. *Mem:* Am Chem Soc; Am Inst Chem; NY Acad Sci. *Res:* Vitamins; pyrrole and porphyrin chemistry; pyrazine chemistry; chemotherapeutics; carbohydrates; nutrition. *Mailing Add:* 6921 Arcadian Hwy Evansville IN 47715

ELLINGTON, EARL FRANKLIN, b Salt Lick, Ky, Nov 15, 33; m 53; c 2. ANIMAL PHYSIOLOGY. *Educ:* Univ Ky, BS, 55, MS, 56; Univ Calif, PhD(animal physiol), 62. *Prof Exp:* Asst prof, Ore State Univ, 62-68; assoc prof, 68-75, prof animal physiol, 75-78, ASST DEAN, COL AGR, UNIV NEBR, LINCOLN, 78- *Mem:* Am Dairy Sci Asn; Am Soc Animal Sci; Soc Study Reproduction; Nat Asn Col & Teachers Agr. *Res:* Endocrinology and reproduction. *Mailing Add:* 101 Agr Hall Univ of Nebr Lincoln NE 68583

ELLINGTON, JOE J, b Yuma, Ariz, Dec 3, 34. ENTOMOLOGY. *Educ:* Univ Ariz, BS, 56; Cornell Univ, MS, 58, PhD(entom), 63. *Prof Exp:* Field res specialist, Calif Chem Co, 63-65; from asst prof to assoc prof, 65-76, PROF ENTOM, N MEX STATE UNIV, 76- *Mem:* Entom Soc Am; Sigma Xi. *Res:* Insects of economic importance, specifically alfalfa and cotton insects; beneficial insects; short plant resistance; sampling. *Mailing Add:* Dept of Bot & Entomol NMex State Univ University Park NM 88003

ELLINGTON, REX T(RUESDALE), JR, chemical engineering, synthetic fuels, see previous edition

ELLINGTON, WILLIAM ROSS, b Asheville, NC, July 2, 49; m 71; c 2. COMPARATIVE PHYSIOLOGY. *Educ:* Univ Fla, BS, 71; Univ SFla, MA, 71; Univ RI, PhD(biol sci), 76. *Prof Exp:* Fel biochem dept chem, Pomona Col, 76-77; vis asst prof zool, Univ Vt, 77-78; asst prof biol, Univ Southwestern La, 78-81; ASST PROF BIOL SCI, FLA STATE UNIV, 81- *Mem:* Am Soc Zoologists; AAAS; Sigma Xi; Am Physiol Soc. *Res:* Physiological and biochemical adaptions of invertebrates to life in extreme environments; comparative and evolutionary biochemistry. *Mailing Add:* Dept Biol Sci Fla State Univ Tallahassee FL 32306

ELLINWOOD, EVERETT HEWS, JR, b Wilmington, NC, June 27, 34; c 3. PSYCHIATRY, NEUROPHARMACOLOGY. *Educ:* Univ NC, BS, 56, MD, 59. *Prof Exp:* Clin instr psychiat, Univ Ky, 64-65; assoc, 66-67, from asst prof to assoc prof, 67-72, PROF, BEHAV NEUROPHARMACOL SECT & DIR PSYCHIAT, MED CTR, DUKE UNIV, 72- *Concurrent Pos:* Res fel, Med Ctr, Duke Univ, 65-66. *Mem:* AAAS; AMA; Am Psychiat Asn; Am Psychopath Asn; Soc Biol Psychiat. *Res:* Analysis in rats, cats and monkeys of the neuropharmacological and behavioral concomitants of chronic stimulant intoxication which in humans is often associated with a psychosis; examination of behavioral, neuropsychological and neuropharmacological measures in man that predict therapeutic and side effects of psychopharmacologic agents. *Mailing Add:* Dept of Psychiat Box 3870 Duke Univ Med Ctr Durham NC 27710

ELLINWOOD, HOWARD LYMAN, b Davenport, Iowa, Feb 25, 26; m 51; c 5. GEOLOGY. *Educ:* Univ Minn, BA, 49, PhD(geol), 53. *Prof Exp:* Geologist, Bur Econ Geol, Tex, 49-50 & Calif Co, 52-58, dist geologist, 58-61, div geologist, 61-68, div supt, 68-70, chief geologist, 70-73, geol consult, 73-74, CHIEF GEOLOGIST, STANDARD OIL CO CALIF, 74- *Mem:* Geol Soc Am; Am Asn Petrol Geol. *Res:* Petroleum geology. *Mailing Add:* Standard Oil Co Calif Box 3495 San Francisco CA 94104

ELLINWOOD, WILLIAM EDWARD, b Chicago, Ill, Aug 7, 50; m 73; c 2. REPRODUCTIVE BIOLOGY, ENDOCRINOLOGY. *Educ:* Univ Colo, BA, 72; Colo State Univ, PhD(physiol), 78. *Prof Exp:* Fel, Colo State Univ, 73-78; fel, 78-80, ASST SCIENTIST, ORE REGIONAL PRIMATE RES CTR, 80- *Mem:* Endocrine Soc; Soc Study Reproduction; AAAS. *Res:* Endocrine function of the nonhuman primate ovary; nonhuman primate fetal endocrinology; relationships between gonadal secretions and pituitary-hypothalamic function. *Mailing Add:* 505 NW 185th Avenue Beaverton OR 97006

ELLION, M EDMUND, b Boston, Mass, Jan 20, 23; m 54; c 2. MECHANICAL ENGINEERING, PHYSICS. *Educ:* Northeastern Univ, BS, 44; Harvard Univ, MS, 47; Calif Inst Technol, PhD(physics, mech eng), 53. *Prof Exp:* Res engr, Bell Aerospace Corp, 47-50, consult aerospace indust, 53-60; exec dir appl mech & aerodyn, Nat Eng Sci Co, 60-62; pres, Dynamic Sci Corp, 62-65; mgr propulsion & elec power systs, 65-78, ASST DIV MGR SPACE & COMMUN & MGR TECHNOL DEVELOP, HUGHES AIRCRAFT CO, LOS ANGELES, 78- *Concurrent Pos:* Lectr, Univ Calif, Los Angeles, 55-56 & Calif Inst Technol, 75-78. *Mem:* Am Inst Aeronaut & Astronaut. *Res:* Propulsion, flight control, structures and thermal control of missile and space craft systems; seven patents in communication satellites and propulsion. *Mailing Add:* 2152 Highland Oaks Dr Arcadia CA 91006

ELLIOT, ALFRED JOHNSTON, b Calgary, Alta, Aug 16, 11; m 42; c 4. OPHTHALMOLOGY. *Educ:* Univ BC, BA, 32; Univ Toronto, MD, 37; Columbia Univ, MedScD, 41; Am Bd Ophthal, dipl, 41; Royal Col Physicians & Surgeons, Univ London, dipl ophthalmic med & surg, 45; FRCP(C), 57. *Prof Exp:* Clin teacher ophthal, Univ Toronto, 45-46, prof & head dept, 46-61; prof ophthal & head dept, 61-73, EMER PROF OPHTHAL, UNIV BC, 78- *Concurrent Pos:* Chief serv, Toronto Gen Hosp & Sunnybrook Vet Admin Hosp, 46-61; consult, Hosp for Sick Children, 46-61; guest lectr, Univ Mich, 55; head ophthal, Vancouver Gen Hosp, 61-73 & Shaughnessy Hosp, 61-73; adv to dir gen, Can Dept Vet Affairs, 66-78; chmn med adv bd, Shaugnessy Hosp DVA, 68-70 & Vancouver Gen Hosp, 69-72; sen active, Vancouver Gen Hosp; hon consult, Shaughnessy, Vancouver & Toronto Gen Hosps. *Honors & Awards:* Golden Jubilee Award, Can Nat Inst Blind, 68. *Mem:* Am Acad Ophthal & Otolaryngol; Am Ophthal Soc; sr mem Can Med Asn; Can Ophthal Soc; Ophthal Soc UK. *Res:* Recurrent intraocular hemorrhage; carotid-cavernous fistulae; keratoconjunctivitis sicca. *Mailing Add:* 750 W Broadway Vancouver Can

ELLIOT, ARTHUR MCAULEY, b Minneaplis, Minn, May 13, 28; m 54; c 4. PHYTOPATHOLOGY, MYCOLOGY. *Educ:* Univ Minn, BSc, 53, MSc, 60, PhD(plant path), 61. *Prof Exp:* Asst prof, 61-66, ASSOC PROF BIOL, TEX TECH UNIV, 66- *Mem:* AAAS; Am Phytopath Soc; Mycol Soc Am; Am Inst Biol Sci; Int Soc Plant Path. *Res:* Field and vegetable crop diseases; ornamental tree diseases; vector transmission of plant pathogens; plant and insect phenology. *Mailing Add:* Dept of Biol Sci Tex Tech Univ Lubbock TX 79409

ELLIOT, DAVID HAWKSLEY, b Eng, May 22, 36. GEOLOGY, PETROLOGY. *Educ:* Cambridge Univ, BA, 59; Univ London, DIC, 60; Univ Birmingham, PhD(geol), 65. *Prof Exp:* Geologist, Brit Antarctic Surv, 60-66; fel, 66-67, res assoc, 67-69, from asst prof to assoc prof, 69-79, PROF, DEPT GEOL & MINERAL, OHIO STATE UNIV, 79-, DIR, INST POLAR STUDIES, 73- *Mem:* Geol Soc London; Geol Soc Am. *Res:* Antarctic geology, including Beacon stratigraphy; petrology and geochemistry of Jurassic igneous rocks of the Transantarctic Mountains; stratigraphy and petrology of Mesozoic and Cenozoic strata and evolution of the Antarctic Peninsula. *Mailing Add:* Inst Polar Studies Ohio State Univ 125 S Oval Mall Columbus OH 43210

ELLIOT, ERIC CHARLES, b Blenheim, Ont, Aug 27, 23; US citizen; m 49; c 3. CARDIOVASCULAR PHYSIOLOGY. *Educ:* Univ Toronto, MD, 47; Univ Alta, BSc, 57, MSc, 61, PhD(physiol), 68. *Prof Exp:* Intern, 47-49; gen pract, Can, 49-55; lectr exp surg, Univ Alta, 58-61, sessional demonstr physiol, 61-64; med officer res, Walter Reed Army Inst Res, 64-76; MED OFFICER, ADMIN, GEN CLIN RES CTRS BR, DIV RES RESOURCES, NIH, 76- *Concurrent Pos:* Can Life Ins med fel, 56-59; Can Heart Found fel, 59-64. *Mem:* Am Physiol Soc. *Res:* Coronary circulation; cardiovascular. *Mailing Add:* Div Res Resources Gen Clin Res Centers Br Bldg 31 Rm 5B-51 NIH Bethesda MD 20014

ELLIOT, JAMES I, b Toronto, Ont, Aug 21, 38; c 2. ANIMAL NUTRITION, ANIMAL MANAGEMENT. *Educ:* Univ Toronto, BSA, 62; Univ Alta, MSc, 65, PhD(animal nutrit), 69. *Prof Exp:* Lectr animal sci, Univ Alta, 68-69; asst prof, Macdonald Col, McGill Univ, 69-72; RES SCIENTIST, AGR CAN ANIMAL RES INST, 72- *Concurrent Pos:* Dir, Mgt Accountability, Agr Can. *Mem:* Agr Inst Can; Can Soc Animal Sci; Am Soc Animal Sci. *Res:* Investigation of copper as a growth promotant in swine rations and its involvement in the synthesis of unsaturated fatty acids in the pig; neonatal and prenatal metabolism of methionine in the pig; survival of colostrum-deprived neonatal piglets reared artificially; nutrient requirements of the neonatal pig; nutrition of the breeding female. *Mailing Add:* 400 Island Park Dr Animal Res Inst CEF Ottawa ON K1Y 0A9 Can

ELLIOT, JAMES LUDLOW, b Columbus, Ohio, June 17, 43; m 67; c 2. ASTRONOMY. *Educ:* Mass Inst Technol, SB & SM, 65; Harvard Univ, AM, 67, PhD(astron), 72. *Prof Exp:* Fel astron, Smithsonian Astrophys Observ, 72; res assoc, Cornell Univ, 72-74, sr res assoc, 74-77, asst prof astron, 77-78; ASSOC PROF ASTRON & PHYSICS & DIR, WALLACE ASTROPHYS OBSERV, MASS INST TECHNOL, 78- *Mem:* Am Astron Soc; Int Astron Union; Astron Soc Pac; Am Asn Variable Star Observers. *Res:* Astronomical instrumentation; optical observations of planets, satellites and quasars; lunar and planetary occulation observations. *Mailing Add:* Bldg 422A Mass Inst Technol Cambridge MA 02139

ELLIOT, JOE OLIVER, b Ames, Iowa, Feb 8, 23; m 50; c 2. OCEANOGRAPHY. *Educ:* Iowa State Col, BS, 43; Columbia Univ, AM, 47; Univ Md, PhD(physics), 55. *Prof Exp:* Res physicist, Div of War Res, Iowa State Univ, 44; dept terrestrial magnetism, Carnegie Inst, 45; lectr & asst, Columbia Univ, 46-49; res nuclear physicist, 49-65, PHYS SCI ADMINR, NAVAL RES LAB, 65- *Concurrent Pos:* Sabbatical fel, Inst Oceanog, Univ BC, 68-69. *Mem:* AAAS; Am Phys Soc; Am Geophys Union. *Res:* Parameters of excited states of nuclei; neutron scattering; decay time of luminescence of phosphors; scintillation spectrometry; reactor technology; physical oceanography. *Mailing Add:* Naval Res Lab Washington DC 20390

ELLIOT, JOHN MURRAY, b Can, Nov 6, 27; nat US; m 51; c 2. ANIMAL NUTRITION. *Educ:* McGill Univ, BSc, 49; Univ Vt, MS, 50; Cornell Univ, PhD(animal nutrit), 58. *Prof Exp:* Instr animal husb, Univ Mass, 50-53, asst prof dairy & animal sci, 53-60; from asst prof to assoc prof, 60-71, PROF ANIMAL SCI, CORNELL UNIV, 71- *Mem:* Am Soc Animal Sci; Am Dairy Sci Asn; Am Inst Nutrit. *Res:* Dairy cattle nutrition; vitamin B12 production and absorption. *Mailing Add:* Dept of Animal Sci 262 Morrison Hall Cornell Univ Ithaca NY 14853

ELLIOTT, ALFRED MARLYN, b Humboldt, SDak, June 19, 05; m 28; c 2. ZOOLOGY. *Educ:* Yankton Col, BA, 28; NY Univ, MS, 31, PhD(protozool), 34. *Prof Exp:* Instr high sch, SDak, 28-30; teaching fel, NY Univ, 30-34; instr biol, Minn State Col, Bemidji, 34-38, prof & chmn sci div, 38-47; from asst prof to prof zool, 47-71, EMER PROF ZOOL, UNIV MICH, 71- *Concurrent Pos:* Trustee, Am Type Cult Collection, 60-66; dir, Acad Year Inst, NSF, 62-65; mem corp, Marine Biol Lab, Woods Hole. *Mem:* Fel AAAS; Am Micros Soc (vpres, 56, pres, 60); hon mem Soc Protozool (vpres, 56, pres, 60); fel NY Acad Sci; Am Soc Zool. *Res:* Physiology of protozoa; protein, fat and carbohydrate utilization; intermediate metabolism; biochemical genetics; protozoan distribution; electron microscopy. *Mailing Add:* 2345 Tarpon Rd Naples FL 33940

ELLIOTT, ALICE, b Reece, Kans, Oct 7, 19. ZOOLOGY, PARASITOLOGY. *Educ:* Kans State Teachers Col, Emporia, BS, 42; Kans State Univ, MS, 47, PhD(parasitol), 50. *Prof Exp:* Asst zool, Kans State Univ, 46-47, instr, 47-50; asst prof biol, Kans State Teachers Col, Pittsburg, 50-51 & Hope Col, 52-54, assoc prof, 54-55; asst prof sci, Ball State Teachers Col, 55-59; prof biol, Hope Col, 59-62; from assoc prof to prof biol, Cent Mo State Col, 62-81; RETIRED. *Concurrent Pos:* Res assoc, inst cellular res, Univ Nebr, 58-59. *Mem:* AAAS; Am Soc Cell Biol; Am Soc Parasitol; Am Micros Soc. *Res:* Taxonomy and ecology of fishes; helminthology; physiology of parasites; tissue culture. *Mailing Add:* Rte 1 BOx 167 Louisville TN 37777

ELLIOTT, ARTHUR YORK, b Tyler, Tex, Feb 8, 36; m 56; c 2. MICROBIOLOGY, VIROLOGY. *Educ:* NTex State Univ, BA, 57, MS, 58; Purdue Univ, PhD(virol), 69. *Prof Exp:* Res assoc virol, M D Anderson Tumor Inst, 60-61; res assoc, Baylor Col Med, 61-62; sr res staff & sr virologist, Pitman Moore Div Dow Chem Co, 62-70; asst prof microbiol, Med Sch, Univ Minn, Minneapolis, 70-72, assoc prof microbiol & urol surg, 72-78; MGR BIOL MFG, MERCK SHARP & DOHME, WEST POINT, PA, 78- *Mem:* Am Soc Microbiol; Tissue Cult Asn. *Res:* Human urologic tumors; tissue cultrue and virology. *Mailing Add:* Biol Mfg Merck Sharp & Dohme West Point PA 19486

ELLIOTT, BERNARD BURTON, b Ottawa, Ont, Can, Nov 10, 21; US citizen; m 45; c 4. ENZYMOLOGY. *Educ:* McGill Univ, BS, 49, MS, 50; Purdue Univ, PhD, 52. *Prof Exp:* Demonstr plant physiol, McGill Univ, 49-50; enzymologist, R J Reynolds Tobacco Co, 52-59; asst dir res & develop, Froedtert Malt Corp, 59-62; pres & managing dir, Brewing & Malting Res Inst, 62-64; DIR RES & DEVELOP, FROEDTERT MALT CORP, 64- *Mem:* AAAS; Am Chem Soc; Am Soc Brewing Chem; Master Brewers Asn Am; Am Asn Cereal Chem. *Res:* Fermentations; isolation of natural products. *Mailing Add:* Froedtert Malt Corp 3830 W Grant Milwaukee WI 53201

ELLIOTT, CECIL MICHAEL, b Ga, Aug 1, 49. ANALYTICAL CHEMISTRY, BIO-INORGANIC CHEMISTRY. *Educ:* Davidson Col, BS, 71; Univ NC, Chapel Hill, PhD(anal chem), 75. *Prof Exp:* asst prof, 77-80, ASSOC PROF CHEM, UNIV VT, 80- *Mem:* Am Chem Soc. *Res:* Electrochemistry. *Mailing Add:* Dept of Chem Univ of Vt Burlington VT 05401

ELLIOTT, DAN WHITACRE, b Greenville, Ohio, Aug 5, 22; m 62; c 2. SURGERY. *Educ:* Yale Univ, MD, 49; Ohio State Univ, MSc, 56. *Prof Exp:* From asst prof to prof surg, Ohio State Univ, 57-64; prof surg, Univ Pittsburgh, 64-76; PROF & CHMN DEPT SURG, WRIGHT STATE UNIV, 76- *Concurrent Pos:* Consult, Vet Admin Hosps, Dayton, Ohio, 57-64, 76- & Pittsburgh, Pa, 64-70, chief surg, 70-76. *Mem:* Am Surg Asn; Soc Univ Surg; Am Gastroenterol Asn; Am Burn Asn; Int Soc Surg. *Res:* Diseases of the pancreas; gastric acid secretion; biliary tract surgery and infection. *Mailing Add:* 701 Murrell Dr Kettering OH 45429

ELLIOTT, DANA EDGAR, nondestructive testing, electrical engineering, see previous edition

ELLIOTT, DANA RAY, b Grain Valley, Mo, Feb 7, 45; m 78; c 2. BIOLOGY. *Educ:* William Jewell Col, Liberty, Mo, BA, 67; Cent Mo State Univ, MS, 71; Univ Mo, Columbia, PhD(entom), 81. *Prof Exp:* ASST PROF BIOL, CENT METHODIST COL, FAYETTE, MO, 74- *Mem:* Ecol Soc Am; Entom Soc Am; Nat Sci Teachers Am. *Res:* Correlation of the species diversity of leafhoppers and vascular plants as indicators of the stage development of old-field succession in central Missouri. *Mailing Add:* Dept Biol Cent Methodist Col Fayette MO 65248

ELLIOTT, DAVID, b Montreal, Que, Mar 25, 38; m 67; c 1. STRUCTURAL GEOLOGY, TECTONICS. *Educ:* McGill Univ, BSc, 60; Glasgow Univ, PhD(geol), 64. *Prof Exp:* Asst lectr struct geol, Imp Col, Univ London, 65-67; from asst prof to assoc prof struct geol, 67-75, PROF EARTH & PLANETARY SCI, JOHNS HOPKINS UNIV, 75- *Mem:* Am Geophys Union; Geol Soc Am; Can Soc Petrol Geologists. *Res:* Structures and mechanical properties in naturally deformed rocks. *Mailing Add:* Dept of Earth & Planetary Sci Johns Hopkins Univ Baltimore MD 21218

ELLIOTT, DAVID DUNCAN, b Los Angeles, Calif, Aug 4, 30; m 62; c 1. RESEARCH MANAGEMENT. *Educ:* Stanford Univ, BS, 51; Calif Inst Technol, MS, 53, PhD(physics), 59. *Prof Exp:* Res scientist space physics, Lockheed Missiles & Space Co, 59-61; mem tech staff, Aerospace Corp, 61-66, staff scientist, 66-67, head, Space Radiation & Atmospheric Dept, 67-70, sci adv, Nat Aeronaut & Space Coun, 70-72; sr staff mem for sci affairs, Nat Security Coun, 72-77; exec dir, 77-81, VPRES & DIR RES & ANAL DIV, SRI INT, 81- *Concurrent Pos:* Consult, Off Sci & Tech Policy, Exec Off of the President, Cent Intel Agency. *Mem:* AAAS; Am Phys Soc; Am Geophys Union; Am Inst of Aeronaut & Astronaut; Armed Forces Commun & Electronics Asn. *Res:* Scientific aspects of national security and foreign policy. *Mailing Add:* SRI Int 333 Ravenswood Ave Menlo Park CA 94025

ELLIOTT, DAVID LEROY, b Cleveland, Ohio, May 29, 32; div; c 2. SYSTEMS THEORY, APPLIED MATHEMATICS. *Educ:* Pomona Col, BA, 53; Univ Southern Calif, MA, 59; Univ Calif, Los Angeles, PhD(systs sci), 69. *Prof Exp:* Trainee, R H Hodgson, Patent Agent, 54-55; mathematician, US Naval Ord Test Sta, 55-69; instr & lectr systs sci, Univ Calif, Los Angeles, 68-71; from asst prof to assoc prof, 71-80, PROF MATH THEORY SYSTS, WASHINGTON UNIV, 80- *Concurrent Pos:* Consult, Electro-Optical Systs, Inc, 60-69; NSF grants, 71-75, 77-81 & 81-; Nat Inst Heart, Lung & Blood Dis grant, 76-81; assoc ed, Math Systs Theory, 76- & Soc Indust & Appl Math Rev, 79- *Mem:* Soc Indust & Appl Math; Am Math Soc; Inst Elec & Electronics Engrs; Math Asn Am. *Res:* Control systems on manifolds; bilinear systems; enzyme kinetics of blood coagulation. *Mailing Add:* Dept Systs Sci & Math Wash Univ St Louis MO 63130

ELLIOTT, DENIS ANTHONY, b Los Angeles, Calif, Dec 2, 46. IMAGE PROCESSING, ASTRONOMY. *Educ:* Calif Inst Technol, BS, 68; Univ Calif, Los Angeles, MA, 70, PhD(astron), 74. *Prof Exp:* MEM TECH STAFF IMAGE PROCESSING, JET PROPULSION LAB, CALIF INST TECHNOL, 73- *Mem:* Am Astron Soc; AAAS; Soc Photoptical Indust Engrs. *Res:* Image processing, especially analysis of multispectral images, galactic structure and evolution; behavior of infrared detectors; infrared detector calibration. *Mailing Add:* Jet Propulsion Lab 68-427 4800 Oak Grove Ave Pasadena CA 91103

ELLIOTT, DOUGLAS FLOYD, b Rapid City, SDak, May 21, 32; m 56; c 3. ELECTRICAL ENGINEERING. *Educ:* Univ Hawaii, BA, 54; Univ Wash, MS, 56; Univ Southern Calif, PhD(elec eng), 69. *Prof Exp:* Elec engr, Pac Tel & Tel, 56-59; MEM TECH STAFF ELEC ENG, ROCKWELL INT, 59- *Concurrent Pos:* Instr, Rockwell Int, 74-, Univ Southern Calif, 75-76 & Inst Elec & Electronics Engrs, Orange County, 76-78. *Mem:* Sigma Xi; sr mem Inst Elec & Electronics Engrs. *Res:* Digital signal processing, including digital filters, fast transforms and sample-data control systems; continuous control systems; sonar and radar system design and analysis. *Mailing Add:* Dept 521 BB85 3370 Miraloma Ave Anaheim CA 92803

ELLIOTT, EUGENE WILLIS, b Longmont, Colo, May 29, 16; m 46; c 2. INORGANIC CHEMISTRY, BOTANY. *Educ:* Univ Mont, BA, 41; Univ Iowa, MS, 47, PhD(mycol), 48. *Prof Exp:* Res asst plant physiol, Univ Wis, 41-42; dir microbiol res lab, Monsanto Chem Co, Mo, 48-51; eng draftsman, US Bur Reclamation, 51-52; sr draftsman, Shell Oil Co, Mont, 52-58; from instr to asst prof chem & bot, 58-62, assoc prof chem & plant physiol, 62-66, prof chem & bot, 66-81, EMER PROF CHEM, EASTERN MONT COL, 81- *Concurrent Pos:* Consult, Nat Parks Asn, 62- Effects of paradichlorobenzene on fungi; swarm cells of Myxomycetes. *Mailing Add:* Dept Phys Sci Eastern Mont Col Billings MT 59101

ELLIOTT, FRED IRVINE, b New Concord, Ohio, Oct 16, 15; m 41:; c 3. REPRODUCTIVE PHYSIOLOGY. *Educ:* Ohio State Univ, BS, 38; Cornell Univ, PhD(animal husb), 44. *Prof Exp:* Exten instr, Cornell Univ, 41-44; dir livestock work, Near East Found, 44-46; assoc prof dairy husb, NC State Col, 47-49; prof dairy husb & head depbt animal industs, Univ Conn, 49-52; mgr, Am Breeders Serv, NC, 52-53; dir res, Am Breeders Serv, Wis, 53-65, prod mgr, 56-65, dir labs & res, 65-78, dir, Prod Div, 79-81; RETIRED. *Honors & Awards:* Spallanzani Award, Milan, Italy, 72. *Mem:* AAAS; Am Soc Animal Sci; Am Dairy Sci Ans; Soc Study Reproduction; Soc Cryobiol. *Res:* Factors affecting reproductive processes; methods of evaluating fertility of bull semen samples; factors affecting functional sterility; extenders, freezing and thawing rates; processing techniques for frozen bovine semen. *Mailing Add:* Am Breeders Serv 4005 Monona Dr Monona WI 53716

ELLIOTT, GEORGE ALGIMON, b Trappe, Md, June 6, 25; m 49; c 3. PATHOLOGY. *Educ:* Va Mil Inst, 47-48; Univ Md, 48-49; Univ Ga, DVM, 53; Univ Pa, MS, 57; Am Col Vet Path, dipl. *Prof Exp:* Instr vet path, Vet Sch, Univ Pa, 55-58, assoc, 58-59, asst prof, 59-60; asst prof, Sch Med, Vanderbilt Univ, 60-62; res assoc path & toxicol res, 62-79, SR RES VET PATHOLOGIST & TOXICOLOGIST, UPJOHN CO, 79- *Mem:* Int Acad Path; NY Acad Sci. *Res:* Neuropathology; toxicology; immunopathology. *Mailing Add:* Path & Toxicol Res Upjohn Co Kalamazoo MI 49001

ELLIOTT, H(ELEN) MARGARET, b Galveston, Tex, Aug 16, 25; m 70. MATHEMATICAL ANALYSIS. *Educ:* Rice Inst, BA, 45; Univ Calif, MA, 46; Radcliffe Col, PhD(math), 48. *Prof Exp:* Asst, Univ Calif, 46; Am Asn Univ Women Hill fel, Harvard Univ, 48-49; instr, Washington Univ, St Louis, 49-51, from asst prof to assoc prof, 51-64; actg prof, Col William & Mary, 64-65; PROF MATH, UNIV BRIDGEPORT, 68-, CHMN DPET, 69- *Concurrent Pos:* NSF faculty fel, Mass Inst Technol & Harvard Univ, 57-58. *Mem:* Am Math Soc; Math Asn Am; Nat Coun Teachers Math. *Res:* Analysis; approximation theory. *Mailing Add:* Dept of Math Univ of Bridgeport Bridgeport CT 06601

ELLIOTT, HOWARD CLYDE, b Birmingham, Ala, Sept 21, 24; m 58; c 5. BIOCHEMISTRY. *Educ:* Birmingham-Southern Col, BS, 48; Univ Ala, MS, 51, PhD(biochem), 56. *Prof Exp:* Chemist, Cancer Res Dept, 49-50, from asst instr biochem to prof chem, 51-69, RES PROF CHEM, MED COL, UNIV ALA, BIRMINGHAM, 70-; ASST PROF BIOCHEM MED, 66-; BIOCHEMIST, BAPTIST MED CTR, 70- *Mem:* Soc Exp Biol & Med; Am Chem Soc; fel Nat Acad Clin Biochem; Am Asn Clin Chem. *Res:* Biochemistry of benzoate congeners; renal transport mechanisms; electrolyte metabolism; cholesterol metabolism in man. *Mailing Add:* Chem Lab Baptist Med Ctr 800 Montclair Rd Birmingham AL 35213

ELLIOTT, IRVIN WESLEY, b Newton, Kans, Oct 21, 25; m 52; c 2. ORGANIC CHEMISTRY. *Educ:* Univ Kans, BS, 47, MS, 49, PhD(chem), 52. *Prof Exp:* Instr chem, Southern Univ, 49-50; assoc prof, Fla Agr & Mech Col, 52-53, prof, 53-57; fel, Harvard Univ, 57-58; PROF CHEM, FISK UNIV, 58- *Concurrent Pos:* Vis prof, Howard Univ, 64-65; fel, Orsted Inst, Univ Copenhagen, 74. *Mem:* Am Chem Soc; Nat Inst Sci; Royal Soc Chem; Sigma Xi. *Res:* Synthetic organic chemistry; alkaloids. *Mailing Add:* Dept of Chem Fisk Univ Nashville TN 37203

ELLIOTT, J(ACK) G(RESHAM), b Detroit, Mich, June 16, 23; m 45; c 3. SYSTEMS ENGINEERING, MATHEMATICAL ANALYSIS. *Educ:* Mich State Univ, BS, 48, MA, 49, PhD(math), 58. *Prof Exp:* Instr math, Ohio Univ, 53-54; mgr dept, 54-77, sr dept consult, 77-80, HEAD BENDIX APPL STATIST MATH METHODS CTR, SYSTS SYNTHESIS DEPT, BENDIX RES LABS, 80- *Concurrent Pos:* Instr, Appl Mgt & Technol Ctr, Wayne State Univ, 66-70 & Lawrence Inst Technol, 70- *Mem:* Math Asn Am; Inst Elec & Electronics Engrs; Indust Math Soc. *Res:* Statistical and reliability analysis; dynamic analysis of aerospace and automotive systems. *Mailing Add:* Bendix Appl Statist Math Methods Ctr 9140 Old Annapolis Rd Md 108 Columbia MD 21045

ELLIOTT, J LELL, b Warrensburg, Mo, Dec 8, 08; m 35. PHYSICAL ORGANIC CHEMISTRY. *Educ:* Univ Colo, AB, 30, AM, 32, PhD(chem), 35. *Prof Exp:* Instr chem, 35-46, head, Div Sci & Math, 46-52, dir, Sci Div, 52-65, dir res, 56-65, head dept, 65-74, prof, 46-79, emer head dept, 74-79, EMER PROF, PAN AM COL, 79- *Mem:* Fel AAAS; fel Am Inst Chemists; Am Chem Soc. *Res:* Instrumentation and computer applications. *Mailing Add:* 930 W Ebony Dr Edinburg TX 78539

ELLIOTT, JAMES ANGUS, b Wawota, Sask, Feb 4, 23; m 52. FOOD MICROBIOLOGY. *Educ:* Univ Sask, BSA, 51; Univ Wis, MS, 52, PhD(dairy indust), 55. *Prof Exp:* Res officer, Dairy Res Inst, Can Dept Agr, 54-62, head microbiol sect, Food Res Inst, 62-80; RETIRED. *Honors & Awards:* Pfizer Award, Am Dairy Sci Asn, 73. *Mem:* Am Dairy Sci Asn; Can Soc Microbiol; Can Inst Food Technol. *Res:* Microbiology of food products; role of bacteria in flavor development of cheese. *Mailing Add:* Food Res Inst CEF Can Dept of Agr Ottawa ON K1A 0C6 Can

ELLIOTT, JAMES GARY, b Atlanta, Ga, Mar 23, 45; m 72; c 2. NUTRITION, FOOD SCIENCE. *Educ:* Univ Ga, BS, 68, MS, 71; Rutgers Univ, PhD(nutrit), 77. *Prof Exp:* Food technologist, Great Western United Corp, 69-70; food chemist, Res Ctr, Hercules, Inc, 70-71; res scientist,

Thomas J Lipton, Inc, 71-74; res asst, Rutgers Univ, 74-77; mgr nutrit sci, Campbell Soup Co, 77-80; ASSOC SCIENTIST, RALSTON PURINA CO, 80- Mem: Am Inst Nutrit; Inst Food Technologists; Am Chem Soc; Nutrit Today Soc; NY Acad Sci. Res: Protein quality methodology; dietary fiber and cholesterol metabolism; bioavailability of essential nutrients and toxic elements; effects of food processing on nutrient retention; nutritional toxicology of intentional and non-intentional food additives. Mailing Add: Biochem Lab Cent Res Ralston Purina Co Checkerboard Square St Louis MO 63188

ELLIOTT, JAMES H, b Hastings, Nebr, Jan 15, 27; m 78. OPHTHALMOLOGY. Educ: Phillips Univ, BA, 49; Univ Okla, MD, 52. Prof Exp: Intern, Mercy Hosp, Oklahoma City, Okla, 52-53; res ophthal, Med Ctr, Univ Okla, 60-62; instr, Harvard Med Sch, 65-66; assoc prof, 66-68, PROF OPHTHAL & CHMN DEPT, SCH MED, VANDERBILT UNIV, 68-, OPHTHALMOLOGIST-IN-CHIEF, UNIV HOSP, 72- Concurrent Pos: Consult, Vet Admin Hosp, Nashville, 66-; res fel, Harvard Med Sch, 62-65. Mem: Asn Res Vision & Ophthal (vpres, 78); Am Acad Ophthal & Larcyncol; AMA; fel Am Col Surg; assoc mem Am Ophthal Soc. Res: Immunology as applied to ophthamology, specifically immunosuppression of experimental corneal hypersensitivity and corneal graft rejection reactions. Mailing Add: Dept Ophthal Vanderbilt Hosp Nashville TN 37232

ELLIOTT, JAMES MCFARLAND, science education, deceased

ELLIOTT, JAMES PARKER, fluid mechanics, gas dynamics, see previous edition

ELLIOTT, JANE ELIZABETH INCH, b Kalamazoo, Mich, Apr 20, 11; m 32; c 3. MICROPALEONTOLOGY. Educ: Univ Mich, BS, 32, PhD(geol), 59; Mich State Col, MS, 49. Prof Exp: From instr to prof geol, 49-78, asst dean, 70-77, EMER PROF GEOL, MICH STATE UNIV, 78- DIR ACAD ADVISING, LYMAN BRIGGS COL, 69- Mem: Sigma Xi. Res: Invertebrate paleontology and micropaleontology. Mailing Add: 545 Elizabeth St East Lansing MI 48823

ELLIOTT, JARRELL RICHARD, b Little Rock, Ark, June 3, 29; m 58; c 4. AERODYNAMICS, APPLIED MATHEMATICS. Educ: Auburn Univ, BS, 51, MS, 56. Prof Exp: Aerodyn design engr aircraft, Chance Vought Aircraft, Inc, 53-55; aerospace engr, 56-63, SUPVRY AEROSPACE ENGR AIRCRAFT STABILITY, CONTROL & DYNAMICS, NASA, 63- Honors & Awards: Apollo Achievement Award, NASA, 69. Mem: Am Inst Aeronaut & Astronaut. Res: Atmospheric and orbital flight mechanics, stability and control theory and applications, optimization and identification procedures, aerodynamics, applied mathematics. Mailing Add: NASA Langley Res Ctr Theoret Mech Br Hampton VA 23665

ELLIOTT, JERRY CHRIS, b Oklahoma City, Okla, Feb 6, 43. PHYSICS, SPACE SCIENCES. Educ: Univ Okla, BS, 66. Prof Exp: Guid engr, Gemini Prog, 66-67; guid engr, Apollo Prog, 67-68; trajectory engr, 68-72, optics sensor engr earth resources, 72-74, prog engr, Apollo-Soyuz, 74-75, PROJ ENGR SPACE SHUTTLE, NASA, 75- Honors & Awards: Bausch & Lomb Nat Sci Award, 61; Presidential Medal Freedom, 70; Nat Sci & Eng Achievement Award, Am Indian Art & Cult Exchange, 76; Achievement Award, NASA Lewis Res Ctr, 78. Mem: Am Indian Sci & Eng Soc; AAAS. Res: Slow-scan televideo applications; wide and narrow-band telecommunications; general technology transfer; energy technology. Mailing Add: PO Box 58182 Houston TX 77058

ELLIOTT, JOANNE, b Providence, RI, Dec 5, 25. MATHEMATICS. Educ: Brown Univ, BA, 47; Cornell Univ, MA, 49, PhD(math), 50. Prof Exp: Asst, Cornell Univ, 47-50; instr math, Swarthmore Col, 50-52; asst prof, Mt Holyoke Col, 52-55; from asst prof to assoc prof, Barnard Col, Columbia Univ, 55-64; PROF MATH, RUTGERS UNIV, 64- Concurrent Pos: Vis asst prof, Brown Univ, 54-55; NSF sr fel, 61-62. Mem: Am Math Soc; Math Asn Am. Res: Integral equations; applications of semigroups to integro-differential equations; differential equations. Mailing Add: Dept of Math Rutgers the State Univ New Brunswick NJ 08903

ELLIOTT, JOHN FRANK, metallurgy, see previous edition

ELLIOTT, JOHN HABERSHAM, b Baltimore, Md, July 20, 13; m 41; c 2. RHEOLOGY, POLYMER CHEMISTRY. Educ: Haverford Col, AB, 35; Univ Pa, MS, 37, PhD(phys chem), 40. Prof Exp: Res chemist, Philadelphia Lab, E I du Pont de Nemours & Co, 35-37; chief chemist, J E Rhodes & Sons, 37-42; res chemist, Res Ctr, Hercules, Inc, 42-43, supvr, 43-73, res scientist, 73-78; CONSULT, 78- Mem: Am Chem Soc; Soc Rheol. Res: Acid strength studies; polymer rheology; effect of substituents on the acid strength of benzoic acid; rheology of polyelectrolytes in aqueous solution. Mailing Add: 305 Wilson Rd Newark DE 19711

ELLIOTT, JOHN KIEFER, electrical engineering, physical electronics, see previous edition

ELLIOTT, JOHN RAYMOND, b Auburn, Nebr, Jan 4, 16; m 43; c 2. ORGANIC POLYMER CHEMISTRY, ENGINEERING MANAGEMENT. Educ: Iowa State Col, BS, 37; Univ Ill, PhD(org chem), 43. Prof Exp: Chemist, Gen Elec Co, Mass, 37-40, res assoc lab, 43-52, mgr org chem res sect, 52-65 & org chem br, Res & Develop Ctr, 65-68; mgr, Loctite Corp, 69-71; corp vpres res & develop, 71-81; CONSULT MGT INNOVATION & RES DEVELOP, VENTURE CAPITOL INVESTMENTS, 81- Mem: AAAS; Am Chem Soc. Res: Organic reactions; silicones; organic polymers; oxidation chemistry; adhesives; anaerobic and cyanocrylote chemistry. Mailing Add: 19 Hillsboro Ln Avon CT 06001

ELLIOTT, JOSEPH ROBERT, b Kansas City, Kans, Dec 11, 23; m 53; c 2. CLINICAL CHEMISTRY. Educ: Univ Kans, AB, 49; Univ Kans, MS, 51, PhD(biochem), 53. Prof Exp: Fel biochem, Med Sch, Northwestern Univ, 53-55; res assoc biol, Rice Univ, 55-58; instr biochem, Col Med, Baylor Univ, 58-67; assoc prof lab med & dir clin chem lab, Med Sch, Univ Okla, 67-70; CLIN CHEMIST, ST LUKE'S HOSP, 70- Concurrent Pos: Mem staff, Jefferson Davis Hosp, 57-59; biochemist, St Luke's Episcopal Hosp, 59-67. Mem: AAAS; Am Physiol Soc; Am Asn Clin Chemists; Soc Exp Biol & Med. Res: Clinical chemistry; hormone assay. Mailing Add: St Luke's Hosp 44th & Wornall Rd Kansas City MO 64111

ELLIOTT, K(ENNETH) ALLAN C(ALDWELL), b Kimberley, SAfrica, Aug 24, 03; Can citizen; m 36; c 3. BIOCHEMISTRY. Educ: Rhodes Univ, SAfrica, MSc, 24; Cambridge Univ, PhD(biochem), 30, ScD, 50. Prof Exp: Shift chemist, Rhodesia Broken Hill Develop Co, 25; chemist, Modderfontein Dynamite Factory, SAfrica, 25-26; res chemist, Biochem Res Found, Franklin Inst, 33-39; in-chg chem res lab, Inst Pa Hosp, 39-44, asst prof biochem in psychiat, Univ Pa, 39-44; from asst prof to assoc prof biochem, McGill Univ, 44-59, prof & head dept, 59-68, Gilman Cheyney prof, 68-71; Can Univ Serv Overseas vol prof physiol chem, Univ Nigeria, Enugu, 71-73; EMER PROF, McGILL UNIV, 74- Concurrent Pos: Beit Mem fel, 29, 4th yr fel, 32; fel, Cambridge Univ, 33-36; dir, Donner Lab Exp Neurochem, Montreal Neurol Inst, 44-65, ed, Can J Biochem & Physiol, 56-59; Nat Res Coun Can sr res fel, 63; McGill Univ Bethune exchange prof, Peking Chinese Med Coun, 64; overseas vis prof, Can Exec Serv, Univ Jos, Nigeria, 78. Honors & Awards: Centennial Medal, Can, 67. Mem: AAAS; Am Soc Biol Chemists; Can Physiol Soc; Can Biochem Soc; fel Royal Soc Can. Res: Tissue metabolism, neurochemistry. Mailing Add: Dept Biochem McIntyre Med Bldg Montreal PQ H3G 1Y6 Can

ELLIOTT, LARRY P, b Fleming, Mo, Sept 27, 38; m 61; c 3. MEDICAL MICROBIOLOGY. Educ: William Jewell Col, BA, 60; Univ Wis, MS, 62, PhD(bact), 65. Prof Exp: From asst prof to assoc prof, 65-78, PROF BIOL, WESTERN KY UNIV, 78-, MED TECHNOL COORDR, 81- Concurrent Pos: Clin microbiologist, Greenview Hosp, 74- Mem: AAAS; Am Sci Affil; Am Soc Microbiol; Sigma Xi; Asn Southeastern Biologists. Res: Staphylococcal bovine mastitis, especially ecology in the dairy herd and environment; ground water quality and air pollution with emphasis on microbial aspects. Mailing Add: Dept of Biol Western Ky Univ Bowling Green KY 42101

ELLIOTT, LARRY PAUL, b Manhattan, Kans, Oct 16, 31; m 56; c 2. RADIOLOGY. Educ: Univ Fla, BS, 54; Univ Tenn, MD, 57. Prof Exp: Assoc prof radiol, Sch Med, Wash Univ, 65-67; prof radiol, Shands Teaching Hosp, Col Med, Univ Fla, 67-76; PROF RADIOL, ALA MED CTR, 76- Res: Diagnostic radiology; congenital heart disease, especially roentgenographic and pathologic correlation. Mailing Add: 2733 Old Trace Birmingham AL 35243

ELLIOTT, LLOYD FLOREN, b Clear Lake, SDak, July 7, 37; m 58; c 2. SOIL MICROBIOLOGY, SOIL BIOCHEMISTRY. Educ: SDak State Univ, BS, 59; Kansas State Univ, MS, 61; Ore State Univ, PhD(microbiol), 65. Prof Exp: Res microbiologist, Soil & Water Conserv Res Div, Northern Plains Br, Agr Res Serv, 65-75, MICROBIOLOGIST SOIL, WATER & AIR SCI, LAND MGT & WATER CONSERV RES UNIT, USDA-AGR RES SERV, WESTERN REGION, 75- Mem: Am Soc Microbiol; Soil Conserv Soc Am; Am Soc Agron. Res: Soil microbiology; energetics of bacterial oxidations; research on beef feedlot wastes; pollution control; waste disposal; crop residue management for improved crop growth, soil conservation and nitrogen fixation. Mailing Add: USDA-Agr Res Serv 215 Johnson Hall Wash State Univ Pullman WA 99164

ELLIOTT, LOIS LAWRENCE, b Cincinnati, Ohio, July 3, 31; wid. PSYCHOACOUSTICS, AUDIOLOGY. Educ: Bryn Mawr Col, AB, 53; Cornell Univ, PhD, 56. Prof Exp: Res psychologist, Opers Lab, US Air Force Personnel & Training Res Lab, 56-58; res psychologist, Personnel Lab, Lackland AFB, 58-60; res psychologist, Audiol Lab, US Air Force Sch Aerospace Med, 60-63; res psychologist, Cent Inst for Deaf, 63-70, res psychologist, Bur Educ for Handicapped, US Off Educ, 70-73, head directed res in communicative dis, Nat Inst Neurol & Communicative Dis & Stroke, NIH, 73-75; head prog audiol & hearing impairment, 76-78, PROF AUDIOL, NORTHWESTERN UNIV, 76-, PROF OTOLARYNGOL, 77- Concurrent Pos: Assoc prof psychol, Washington Univ, 66-70. Mem: Fel Am Psychol Asn; Int Soc Audiol; fel Acoust Soc Am; Psychonomic Soc; Am Speech & Hearing Asn. Res: Psychoacoustics; audiology and experimental design; speech perception; auditory development. Mailing Add: Frances Searle Bldg Northwestern Univ Evanston IL 60201

ELLIOTT, MARTIN A(NDERSON), b Baltimore, Md, Feb 21, 09; m 34; c 2. ENGINEERING. Educ: Johns Hopkins Univ, BE, 30, PhD(gas eng), 33. Prof Exp: Instr, Johns Hopkins Univ, 30-34; gas engr, Consol Gas, Elec Light & Power Co, Md, 34-38; gas engr, US Bur Mines, 38-41, chem engr, 41-46, asst chief res & develop br, 46-51, chief, 51-52; res prof mech eng, Ill Inst Technol, 52-56, dir inst gas technol, 56-61, acad vpres, 61-67; sci adv, Tex Eastern Transmission Corp, 67-74; RETIRED. Concurrent Pos: Consult, 74- Honors & Awards: Distinguished Serv Medal, US Bur Mines, 52; Percy Nicholls Award, Am Soc Mech Engrs & Am Inst Mining, Metall & Petrol Engrs, 67; Gas Indust Res Award, 75. Mem: Nat Acad Eng; Am Inst Chem Engrs; Am Gas Asn; Am Chem Soc; fel Am Soc Mech Engrs. Res: Performance of diesel engines; stability and sensitivity of explosives; coal hydrogenation and gasification; Fischer-Tropsch process; catalysis of steam-carbon reactions; combustion; long range energy supply. Mailing Add: 13623 Alchester Lane Houston TX 77079

ELLIOTT, PAUL M, b Kingsville, Tex, Oct 20, 22; m 46; c 3. PHYSICS. Educ: US Naval Acad, BS, 44; Tex Col Arts & Indust, MS, 60; Tex A&M Univ, PhD(physics), 64. Prof Exp: From instr to assoc prof physics, 60-69, PROF PHYSICS, TEX A&I UNIV, 69- Mem: AAAS; Am Phys Soc; Am Asn Physics Teachers. Res: Atmospheric physics. Mailing Add: Dept of Physics Tex A&I Univ Kingsville TX 78363

ELLIOTT, PAUL RUSSELL, b Pueblo, Colo, Aug 26, 33; div; c 2. BIOCHEMISTRY, MEDICAL EDUCATION. *Educ:* Phillips Univ, BA, 55; Univ Mich, MS, 57, PhD(zool), 60. *Prof Exp:* From asst prof to assoc prof zool, Univ Fla, 63-71, asst dean preprof educ, Cols Arts & Sci, Dent & Med, 69-71, asst dean Tallahassee progs, Col Med, 71-78; dir prog med sci, Fla State Univ, Fla A&M Univ & Univ Fla, 71-78; asst vpres, 78-80, ASSOC VPRES ACAD AFFAIRS, FLA STATE UNIV, 80-, PROF BIOL SCI, 71- *Concurrent Pos:* NIH fel biochem, Johns Hopkins Univ, 60-63; NIH res grant, 64-67. *Res:* Cytochemistry and physiology of the epididymis; bioluminescence in bacteria and ctenophorans; medical education research; minority student access to graduate and professional education. *Mailing Add:* 313 Westcott Hall Fla State Univ Tallahassee FL 32306

ELLIOTT, RALPH BENJAMIN, b Buffalo, NY, July 4, 07; m 37; c 2. PHYSICAL CHEMISTRY. *Educ:* Univ Buffalo, AB, 29; Princeton Univ, MA, 32, PhD(chem), 34. *Prof Exp:* Asst dir res lab, Williams Gold Ref Co, NY, 29-31; res & develop chemist, Electrochem Dept, E I du Pont de Nemours & Co, Inc, 33-39, sales develop peroxygens, 39-41, prod supvr, 41-46, sales mgr, Sodium Prod, 46-47, prod supt peroxygens, 48-50, res supvr, 52, plant supt, Dresden Plant, 53-59, Wash rep, 60-63, mem staff, Mkt Res, 64-66, air-water pollution specialist, 66-70; TECH CONSULT AIR-WATER POLLUTION, UNIV DEL, 70- *Concurrent Pos:* With Air Pollution Study, Taiwan, 72-73, Columbia, 75-76 & Brazil, 77. *Mem:* Am Chem Soc. *Res:* Physical and inorganic chemistry; electrochemical units of measurement; standard cells; peroxides. *Mailing Add:* 526 Ruxton Dr Wilmington DE 19809

ELLIOTT, RICHARD AMOS, b Lowbanks, Ont, May 17, 37; m 58; c 2. OPTICS, THEORETICAL PHYSICS. *Educ:* Queen's Univ, Ont, BA, 60, BSc, 61, MSc, 63; Univ BC, PhD(physics), 66. *Prof Exp:* Res assoc physics, Inst Fundamental Studies, Univ Rochester, 66-69; asst prof, 69-77, ASSOC PROF PHYSICS, ORE GRAD CTR, 77- *Mem:* Optical Soc Am; Can Asn Physicists. *Res:* Statistical mechanics; kinetic theory; random walk; exciton mobility; small scale turbulence; optical propagation in turbulent media; atmospheric physics; laser pulse shaping; pulse propagation through optically thick media; effects of turbulence on non-linear optical phenomena. *Mailing Add:* Ore Grad Ctr 19600 NW Walker Rd Beaverton OR 97005

ELLIOTT, ROBERT A, b Darke Co, Ohio, Dec 29, 24; m 46; c 4. BACTERIOLOGY. *Educ:* Miami Univ, AB, 49; Ohio State Univ, MS, 51, PhD(bact), 53. *Prof Exp:* Asst & fel dairy sci, Ohio State Univ, 54-55; bacteriologist, Biol Develop Dept, 55-64, sr bacteriologist, Biol Assay Develop Dept, 64-69, sr bacteriologist, biol tech serv & qual control, 69-76, sr mirobiologist, 76-78, RES SCIENTIST, VET RES, ELI LILLY & CO, GREENFIELD, 78- *Mem:* Am Soc Microbiol; NY Acad Sci. *Res:* Bacterial resistance. *Mailing Add:* 9817 E Michigan St Indianapolis IN 46229

ELLIOTT, ROBERT DARYL, b Nashville, Tenn, June 4, 35; m 68; c 4. ORGANIC CHEMISTRY. *Educ:* Vanderbilt Univ, BA, 57; Wayne State Univ, PhD(org chem), 61. *Prof Exp:* Sr asst scientist, Tech Develop Labs, USPHS, Ga, 60-63; SR CHEMIST, SOUTHERN RES INST, 63- *Mem:* Am Chem Soc. *Res:* Synthesis of folic acid analogs and nucleocides as anticancer drugs. *Mailing Add:* Southern Res Inst PO Box 3307-8 Birmingham AL 35205

ELLIOTT, ROBERT DUNSHEE, b Yonkers, NY, Dec 30, 14; m 41; c 5. METEOROLOGY. *Educ:* Calif Inst Technol, BS, 36, MS, 37. *Prof Exp:* Meteorologist, Eastern Airlines, Ga, 37-39 & Krick Weather Serv, Calif, 39-42; instr meteorol, Calif Inst Technol, 40-42, asst prof, 46-47; dir res, Am Inst Aerological Res, Pasadena, 47-50; vpres, NAm Weather Consult, 50-57, pres, 57-78; pres, Aerometric Res, Inc, 56-78. *Concurrent Pos:* Mem adv comt weather serv, US Dept Com. *Honors & Awards:* Appl Meteorol Award, Am Meteorol Soc, 68. *Mem:* AAAS; Am Meteorol Soc (co-ed, J Appl Meteorol, 60-67); Am Soc Civil Engrs. *Res:* Synoptic meteorology and weather modification. *Mailing Add:* North Am Weather Consult 1141E 3900 S Suite A-130 Salt Lake City UT 84117

ELLIOTT, ROBERT S(TRATMAN), b New York, NY, Mar 9, 21; m 51; c 4. ELECTRICAL ENGINEERING, ENGINEERING ECONOMICS. *Educ:* Columbia Univ, AB, 42, BS, 43; Univ Ill, MS, 47, PhD(elec eng), 52; Univ Calif, Santa Barbara, MA, 71. *Prof Exp:* Jr engr radar, Appl Physics Lab, 43-46; asst prof elec eng, Univ Ill, 46-52; res physicist electromagnetic probs, Hughes Aircraft Co, 53-56; tech dir & vpres, Rantec Corp, 56-59; asst dean grad studies eng, 66-69, PROF ENG, UNIV CALIF, LOS ANGELES, 59-, CHMN DEPT, 69- *Mem:* Fel Inst Elec & Electronics Engrs. *Res:* Electromagnetics; microwave tubes and antennas; electrical properties of materials; engineering economics. *Mailing Add:* Sch of Eng & Appl Sci 7400 Boelter Hall Univ of Calif Los Angeles CA 90024

ELLIOTT, ROSEMARY WAITE, b Great Yarmouth, Eng, June 16, 34; wid; c 6. MOLECULAR GENETICS, BIOCHEMISTRY. *Educ:* Univ Birmingham, BSc, 55; Univ Buffalo, MA, 52; State Univ NY Buffalo, PhD(biochem), 64. *Prof Exp:* Cancer res scientist, 64-66, sr cancer res scientist, 66-79, CANCER RES SCIENTIST IV, ROSWELL PARK MEM INST, 79- *Mem:* AAAS; Genetic Soc Am; Am Soc Microbiol. *Res:* Regulation of levels of lysomal enzymes in mice; host-controlled variation in bacteriophages; lysogenic association between bacteriophages and host cells; genetic determination of processing of lysosomal proteins; detection and mapping mouse polymorphisms detectable by 2D-electrophoresis; detection and mapping of mouse DNA polymorphisms. *Mailing Add:* Dept of Molecular Biol Roswell Park Mem Inst Buffalo NY 14263

ELLIOTT, SHELDEN DOUGLESS, JR, b Anaheim, Calif, Feb 3, 31; m 54; c 2. PHYSICS, SOLAR ENERGY. *Educ:* Yale Univ, BS, 53, MS, 54, PhD, 59. *Prof Exp:* Physicist, US Naval Weapons Ctr, 58-77; PHYSICIST, US DEPT ENERGY, 77- *Mem:* Am Phys Soc; Int Solar Energy Soc; Weather Modification Asn (pres, 74). *Res:* Low temperature physics; second sound in liquid helium isotope mixtures; atmospheric physics; astronomy; meteor physics; weather modification; solar energy. *Mailing Add:* 1952 Oak Grove Rd Walnut Creek CA 94598

ELLIOTT, SHELDON ELLWOOD, b Asuncion, Paraguay, July 9, 25; US citizen; m 48; c 3. EXPLORATION GEOPHYSICS, APPLIED MATHEMATICS. *Educ:* Phillips Univ, AB, 48; Univ Mich, MA, 49. *Prof Exp:* Fel, Univ Mich, 50-51 & 55-56, jr instr, 56-57; mathematician, 51-55 & 57-64, MGR GEOPHYS RES, PHILLIPS PETROL CO, 64-, MATH GEOPHYSICIST, 69- *Mem:* Am Math Soc; Soc Explor Geophysicists; Inst Elec & Electronics Engrs; Sigma Xi. *Res:* Seismology; operational calculus; differential equations; numerical methods; topology. *Mailing Add:* 1512 Macklyn Lane Bartlesville OK 74003

ELLIOTT, STUART BRUCE, b Oakland, Calif, July 11, 27; m 53; c 2. PHYSICS. *Educ:* Stanford Univ, BS, 49, MS, 51, PhD(physics), 60. *Prof Exp:* Asst prof physics, Kenyon Col, 55-60; asst prof, 60-67, chmn dept, 71-74, ASSOC PROF PHYSICS, OCCIDENTAL COL, 67- *Concurrent Pos:* Sci ed, Optics & Spectros, Optical Soc Am, 68- *Mem:* Am Asn Physics Teachers; Optical Soc Am. *Res:* Holography; holographic contouring. *Mailing Add:* Dept of Physics Occidental Col Los Angeles CA 90041

ELLIOTT, WILLARD BUFORD, biochemistry, immunochemistry, deceased

ELLIOTT, WILLIAM H, b St Louis, Mo, June 4, 18; m 49; c 4. BIOCHEMISTRY, ORGANIC CHEMISTRY. *Educ:* St Louis Univ, BSChem, 39, MS, 41, PhD(org chem), 44. *Prof Exp:* From instr to assoc prof, 44-59, actg chmn dept, 70-71, PROF BIOCHEM, SCH MED, ST LOUIS UNIV, 59-, PROF CHEM, 77- *Concurrent Pos:* Consult radioisotopes, Vet Admin, 55-58, consult biochem, 69-71 & 72-79; consult, Res Career Award Comt, Nat Inst Gen Med Sci, 62-65; mem ed bd, J of Lipid Res, 76-; Nat Defense Res Comt fel, Ind Univ, Bloomington, 44; St Louis Univ-NIH-Med Res Coun fel & vis prof, Dept Biochem, Univ Edinburgh, 74. *Mem:* Fel AAAS; Am Chem Soc; Am Soc Biol Chem; Am Soc Mass Spectrometry; Soc Exp Biol & Med. *Res:* Chemistry and metabolism of sterols, bile acids and fat-soluble vitamins; mass spectrometry. *Mailing Add:* Dept of Biochem St Louis Univ Sch of Med St Louis MO 63104

ELLIOTT, WILLIAM PAUL, b Geneva, Ill, June 16, 28; m 52; c 2. METEOROLOGY, CLIMATOLOGY. *Educ:* St John's Col, Md, AB, 47; Univ Chicago, MS, 52; Tex A&M Univ, PhD(phys oceanog), 58. *Prof Exp:* Res assoc meteorol, Tex A&M Univ, 52-57, from instr to asst prof, 53-56; atmospheric physicist micrometeorol, US Air Force Cambridge Res Lab, 57-68; res assoc prof, Sch of Oceanog, Ore State Univ, 68-74, RES METEOROLOGIST, AIR RESOURCES LAB, NAT OCEANIC & ATMOSPHERIC ADMIN, 74- *Mem:* AAAS; Am Meteorol Soc; Royal Meteorol Soc; Wilson Ornith Soc. *Res:* Micrometeorology; climatology; long-range transport of pollutants, ornithology. *Mailing Add:* Air Resources Labs 8060 13th St Silver Spring MD 20918

ELLIS, ALAN F, organic chemistry, see previous edition

ELLIS, ALBERT TROMLY, b Atwater, Calif, Apr 22, 17; m 54. APPLIED MECHANICS. *Educ:* Calif Inst Technol, BS, 43, MS, 47, PhD(mech eng, physics), 53. *Prof Exp:* Asst physiol, Calif Inst Technol, 42-43; res engr electronics & instrumentation, Columbia Univ, 44-46; electronics engr & asst head electronics hydrodyn lab, Calif Inst Technol, 46-47; physicist, Theory Controls & Servomechanisms, US Naval Ord Test Sta, 47-49; res engr hydrodyn, Calif Inst Technol, 49-54, sr res fel eng, 54-57, assoc prof appl mech, 58-67; PROF APPL MECH, UNIV CALIF, SAN DIEGO, 67- *Concurrent Pos:* Consult, Space Technol Labs, 56- & Naval Undersea Ctr, San Diego; sr vis, Dept Appl Math & Theoret Physics, Cambridge Univ, 64-65. *Mem:* AAAS; Inst Elec & Electronics Eng; Am Soc Mech Eng; Am Phys Soc; Acoust Soc Am. *Res:* Cavitation and drag reduction in dilute polymer flows; laser radiation interactions with solids and liquids; wave propagation in composite materials; high speed holography. *Mailing Add:* Dept of Appl Mech 6226 Urey Hall Univ of Calif La Jolla CA 92037

ELLIS, BERNARD, b Chicago, Ill, Dec 25, 20; m 42; c 2. ENGINEERING. *Educ:* Ill Inst Technol, BS, 42. *Prof Exp:* Eng trainee, Lockheed Aircraft Corp, 42; chief foreign engine anal br, Air Tech Intel Ctr, 45-46; purchasing agent, Rocket Div, Gen Tire & Rubber Co, 46; thermodyn analyst, Consol Vultee Aircraft Corp, 47; sr engr, Heating & Vent Sect, NAm Aviation, Inc, 47-48; head rocket br, Naval Air Missile Test Ctr, 48-53; proj engr, Reaction Motors, Inc, 53-55; engr, Flight Sci Div, Missile Systs Div, 55-57, mgr propulsion dept, 57-62 & Prod Assurance, 62-63, consult engr systs eng, 63-69, mgr eastern tech off, 69-72, eng mkt, 69-77, STAFF ENGR, ACQUISITION MGT, LOCKHEED MISSILES & SPACE CO, LOCKHEED AIRCRAFT CORP, 77- *Mem:* Assoc fel Am Inst Aeronaut & Astronaut. *Res:* Physical chemistry; propulsion physics; preliminary design and general performance; systems engineering. *Mailing Add:* Lockheed Aircraft Corp PO Box 504 Sunnyvale CA 94088

ELLIS, BOYD G, b Havensville, Kans, Nov 3, 32; m 55; c 3. SOIL CHEMISTRY. *Educ:* Kans State Univ, BS, 54, MS, 55; Mich State Univ, PhD(soil chem), 61. *Prof Exp:* From asst prof to assoc prof soil sci, 61-68, PROF SOIL SCI, MICH STATE UNIV, 68- *Mem:* Fel Am Soc Agron; Clay Minerals Soc; fel Soil Sci Soc Am; Int Soil Sci Soc. *Res:* Soil fertility; chemistry of nutrients in the soil and their effect on plant growth; factors affecting availability of potassium, phosphorus, magnesium and zinc; Soil chemistry related to environmental quality. *Mailing Add:* Dept of Crop & Soil Sci Mich State Univ East Lansing MI 48824

ELLIS, CHARLES HOWARD, b Milwaukee, Wis, May 17, 29; m 52; c 2. PALEONTOLOGY. *Educ:* Beloit Col, BS, 51; Univ Colo, MS, 58. *Prof Exp:* Geologist paleont, Humble Oil & Ref Co, 58-59; geologist paleont, Denver Res Ctr, Marathon Oil Co, 59-69, advan res paleontologist, 69-81; STAFF GEOLOGIST & SUPVR MICROPALEONTOL, SOHIO PETROL CO, 81- *Concurrent Pos:* Nannoplankton paleontologist, Deep Sea Drilling proj, 73 & 78. *Mem:* Soc Econ Paleontologists & Mineralogists; Paleont Soc. *Res:* Invertebrate paleontology, primarily micropaleontology dealing with stratigraphic and paleontologic zonation, correlation and paleoecology; calcareous nannofossils of Cretaceous and tertiary sediments. *Mailing Add:* Sohio Petrol Co 100 Pine St San Francisco CA 94111

ELLIS, CLIFFORD ROY, b Yarmouth, NS, Jan 7, 41; c 2. ECONOMIC ENTOMOLOGY. *Educ:* McGill Univ, BS, 63, MS, 65; Univ Alta, PhD(entom), 70. *Prof Exp:* Exten entomologist, NS Dept Agr & Mkt, 65-67; asst prof, 70-76, ASSOC PROF ECON ENTOM, DEPT ENVIRON BIOL, UNIV GUELPH, 76- *Mem:* Entom Soc Can; Entom Soc Am. *Res:* Pests of forage and field crops with particular emphasis on the biology, control and economic thresholds of various pests. *Mailing Add:* Dept Environ Biol Univ Guelph Guelph ON N1G 2W1 Can

ELLIS, DANIEL B(ENSON), b Rochdale, Eng, May 15, 37; US citizen; m 63; c 2. BIOCHEMISTRY, BIOCHEMICAL PHARMACOLOGY. *Educ:* Univ Sheffield, BSc, 58; McGill Univ, PhD(biochem), 61. *Prof Exp:* Res assoc microbiol, Wistar Inst, Univ Pa, 62-64; biochemist cancer res, Stanford Res Inst, 64-65; sr res biochemist, Smith Kline & French Labs, 65-70, sr investr, 70-74; sect head biochem, Betz Labs, 74-76; mgr biochem, 76-78, ASSOC DIR BIOL SCI, HOECHST-ROUSSEL PHARMACEUT INC, 78- *Concurrent Pos:* Radiation safety officer, Hoechst-Roussel Pharmaceut Inc, 77- *Mem:* Am Soc Biol Chemists; AAAS; Am Chem Soc; Biochem Soc; Soc Complex Carbohydrates. *Res:* Drug research and development; neurochemistry; regulatory control mechanisms; drug metabolism; influence of drugs on central nervous system; psychotropic and anti-hypertensive agents; biosynthesis of glycoproteins; cancer chemotherapy. *Mailing Add:* Hoechst-Roussel Pharmaceut Inc Rte 202/206 N Somerville NJ 08876

ELLIS, DAVID ALLEN, b Seattle, Wash, Mar 25, 17; m 43; c 1. PHYSICAL CHEMISTRY, INORGANIC CHEMISTRY. *Educ:* Univ Wash, BS, 39; Univ Southern Calif, MS, 48, PhD(chem), 50. *Prof Exp:* Chemist, Puget Sound Pulp & Timber Co, 40; observer, US Weather Bur, 40-41; asst, Univ Southern Calif, 45-48; res chemist, Dow Chem Co, 49-67; prof chem, 67-82, chmn, Div Sci & Math, 71-78, EMER PROF CHEM, AZUSA PAC COL, 82- *Mem:* Am Chem Soc. *Res:* Solvent extraction; inorganic chemicals; ion exchange. *Mailing Add:* 735 Sequoia Lane Azusa CA 91702

ELLIS, DAVID GREENHILL, b Marietta, Ohio, Mar 9, 36. THEORETICAL PHYSICS. *Educ:* Marietta Col, AB, 58; Cornell Univ, PhD(theoret physics), 64. *Prof Exp:* Res assoc theoret physics, Ind Univ, 63-65; from asst prof to assoc prof physics & astron, 65-75, chmn dept, 74-79, PROF PHYSICS & ASTRON, UNIV TOLEDO, 75- *Concurrent Pos:* vis prof, Univ Lund, Sweden, 76-77. *Mem:* Am Phys Soc. *Res:* Theoretical atomic physics; quantum mechanics; beam-foil spectroscopy; astrophysics. *Mailing Add:* Dept Physics & Astron Univ Toledo Toledo OH 43606

ELLIS, DAVID M, b Ithaca, NY, Nov 15, 37; m 63; c 2. ELECTRICAL ENGINEERING, SOLID STATE PHYSICS. *Educ:* Pa State Univ, BS, 59; Univ Wash, MS, 65, PhD(elec eng), 68. *Prof Exp:* Res engr, Burroughs Corp, Pa, 59-63; asst prof elec eng, Univ Vt, 68-77; develop engr, 77-80, PROJ LEADER, HEWLETT-PACKARD CO, 80- *Concurrent Pos:* Consult components div, IBM Corp, Vt, 68-70 & Vertek Inc, 70- *Mem:* Inst Elec & Electronics Engrs. *Res:* Theory and applications of thin magnetic films; semiconductor electronics; nuclear magnetic resonance. *Mailing Add:* Hewlett-Packard Co 175 Wyman St Waltham MA 02254

ELLIS, DAVID WERTZ, b Huntingdon, Pa, Feb 8, 36; m 61; c 3. ANALYTICAL CHEMISTRY. *Educ:* Haverford Col, AB, 58; Mass Inst Technol, PhD(anal chem), 62. *Prof Exp:* Asst prof, 62-67, asst dean, Col Technol, 67-68, assoc off acad vpres, 68-69, actg acad vpres, 69, assoc acad vpres, 70-71, assoc prof chem, Univ NH, 67-68, vice provost acad affairs, 71-77, vpres, 77-78; PRES, LAFAYETTE COL, EASTON, PA, 78- *Mem:* AAAS; Am Chem Soc; Sigma Xi. *Res:* Excited-state chemical reactions using fluorescence and phosphorescence; development of new methods of chemical analysis; analysis of water pollutants. *Mailing Add:* Markle Mall Lafayette Col Easton PA 18042

ELLIS, DEREK V, b Windsor, Eng, July 26, 30; Can citizen; m 57; c 3. BIOLOGY. *Educ:* Univ Edinburgh, BSc, 51, Hons, 52; McGill Univ, MSc, 54, PhD(zool), 57. *Prof Exp:* From asst scientist to assoc scientist, Fisheries Res Bd Can, 57-63; asst prof zool, Univ Man, 63-64; assoc prof biol, 64-81, PROF BIOL, UNIV VICTORIA, BC, 81- *Res:* Ethology and ecology of aquatic animals; marine environmental impact assessment. *Mailing Add:* Dept Biol Univ Victoria Victoria BC B8W 2Y2 Can

ELLIS, DON EDWIN, b Ames, Iowa, Apr 8, 08; m 29; c 1. PLANT PATHOLOGY. *Educ:* Nebr Cent Col, AB, 28, BS, 29; La State Univ, MS, 32; Univ NC, PhD(plant path), 45. *Prof Exp:* Teacher high sch, Juniata, Nebr, 29-31; asst plant path, Exp Sta, La State Univ, 31-33; supv technician forest path, State Emergency Conserv Work, Iowa State Col, 33; asst pathologist, Div Forest Path, Bur Plant Indust, USDA, 34-40; asst plant pathologist, Exp Sta, 40-44, from assoc prof to prof, 44-73, EMER PROF PLANT PATH, NC STATE UNIV, 73-, HEAD DEPT, 54- *Honors & Awards:* Distinguished Serv Trop Plant Path, Am Phytopathol Soc, 73. *Mem:* Am Phytopath Soc; Mycol Soc Am; Asn Trop Biol; Am Inst Biol Sci; AAAS. *Res:* Diseases of vegetable crops. *Mailing Add:* Dept Plant Path NC State Univ Raleigh NC 27650

ELLIS, DONALD EDWIN, b San Diego, Calif, Feb 20, 39; m 65. SOLID STATE PHYSICS, MOLECULAR PHYSICS. *Educ:* Mass Inst Technol, SB, 61, MS, 64, PhD(physics), 66. *Prof Exp:* Asst prof physics, Univ Fla, 66-68; from asst prof to assoc prof, 68-78, PROF PHYSICS & CHEM, NORTHWESTERN UNIV, EVANSTON, 78- *Mem:* Am Phys Soc; Am Chem Soc. *Res:* Electronic structure of molecules; transition metal, rare earth, and actinide complexes; band structure of solids. *Mailing Add:* Dept of Physics Northwestern Univ Evansville IL 60201

ELLIS, EDWIN M, b Watertown, SDak, Mar 11, 14; m 42; c 3. MICROBIOLOGY. *Educ:* Adrian Col, BS; Wayne State Univ, MS; Mich State Univ, PhD(microbiol & DVM. *Prof Exp:* Asst microbiol, Mich State Univ, 51-53; animal pathologist, Ft Detrick, Md, 53-54; asst microbiol, Mich State Univ, 54-56; immunologist, Ga Coastal Plain Exp Sta, Dept Animal Dis,

USDA, 56-59; bacteriologist, Fla State Dept Agr, 59-60; CHIEF MICROBIOL, LAB SERV, NAT ANIMAL DIS CTR AGR RES SERV, USDA, 60- *Mem:* Am Soc Microbiol; Am Vet Med Asn; fel Am Acad Microbiol. *Res:* Fluorescent antibody techniques applied to animal viruses; animal disease; tuberculosis; isolation and immunology. *Mailing Add:* 6912 South Shore Dr South Pasadena FL 33707

ELLIS, EFFIE O'NEAL, b Hawkinsville, Ga, June 15, 13; m 53; c 1. PUBLIC HEALTH. *Educ:* Spelman Col, AB, 33; Atlanta Univ, MS, 35; Univ Ill, MD, 50. *Prof Exp:* Dir med educ, Provident Hosp, Baltimore, Md, 53-61; pediat consult & dir maternal & child health, Ohio Dept Health, Columbus, 61-65; regional med dir, US Children's Bur, HEW, Chicago, 61-67, regional comnr, Social & Rehab Serv, Chicago, 67-70; SPEC ASST FOR HEALTH SERV, AMA, 70- *Concurrent Pos:* Lectr, 53-; consult & co-dir, Quality of Life Ctr, Chicago; consult community health progs; mem, Ohio Planning Comt Health Educ, 61-65 & Ohio Comn Ment Health & Ment Retardation Planning, 63-65; chmn panel group, White House Conf Food & Nutrit, 69; vchmn panel group, White House Conf on Children, 70. *Honors & Awards:* Outstanding Serv Award, Am Asn Maternal & Child Health, 65; Golden Plate Award, Am Acad Achievement, 70; Distinguished Serv Award, Nat Med Asn. *Mem:* Inst Med-Nat Acad Sci; hon fel Am Sch Health Asn; Am Pub Health Asn; Am Pub Welfare Asn; Am Asn Ment Deficiency. *Mailing Add:* 300 N State St Chicago IL 60610

ELLIS, ELIZABETH CAROL, b Columbus, Ga. ATMOSPHERIC GAS MEASUREMENT. *Educ:* Auburn Univ, BS, 68; Duke Univ, PhD(phys chem), 75. *Prof Exp:* Res chemist, US Environ Protection Agency, 73-77; SUPVR RES SCIENTIST, SOUTHERN CALIF EDISON CO, 77- *Concurrent Pos:* Lectr, Univ Calif, Los Angeles, 79- *Mem:* Am Chem Soc; Sigma Xi; Am Asn Aerosol Res. *Res:* Environmental effects from gaseous, particulate and thermal emission from fossil-fueled electric power generating stations on the properties of the atmosphere; ambient air quality; long range transport; deposition; visibility. *Mailing Add:* Southern Calif Edison Co Res & Develop PO Box 800 Rosemead CA 91770

ELLIS, ELLIOT F, b Englewood, NJ, Apr 7, 29; m 55; c 4. PEDIATRICS, ALLERGY. *Educ:* Kenyon Col, AB, 50; Case Western Reserv Univ, MD, 54; Am Bd Pediat, dipl; Am Bd Pediat Allergy, dipl; Am Bd Allergy & Immunol, dipl. *Prof Exp:* Intern, Lenox Hill Hosp, New York, 54-55, resident, Babies Hosp, Columbia-Presby Med Ctr, 57-59, instr pediat, Col Med, Univ Fla, 63-66, from asst prof to assoc prof pediat, Univ Colo, Denver, 66-74, PROF PEDIAT, STATE UNIV NY, BUFFALO, 74- *Concurrent Pos:* Chief pediat, Nat Jewish Hosp & Res Ctr, Denver, 70-74; dir div allergy & immunol, Children's Hosp Buffalo, 74-75; chmn pediat dept, State Univ NY Buffalo, 75; fel, Children's Asthma Res Inst & Hosp, Denver, Colo, 62-63; fel allergy & immunol, Col Med, Univ Fla, 63-66. *Honors & Awards:* Bela Schick Award, Am Col Allergists, 64. *Mem:* Am Acad Pediat; Am Acad Allergy; Am Col Physicians; Am Asn Immunologists. *Res:* Pediatric allergy and clinical immunology. *Mailing Add:* 219 Bryant St Buffalo NY 14222

ELLIS, ERIC HANS, b Mannheim, Ger, Aug 25, 35; US citizen; m 58; c 3. PHYSICS. *Educ:* Syracuse Univ, BS, 56, PhD(physics), 65. *Prof Exp:* Asst physics, Syracuse Univ, 56-64; from instr to assoc prof, 64-80, PROF PHYSICS, UNIV OF THE SOUTH, 80- *Mem:* Am Asn Physics Teachers. *Res:* Infrared background radiation; atmospheric optical noise; fluorescence and spectroscopic analysis of bone. *Mailing Add:* Dept of Physics Univ of the South Sewanee TN 37375

ELLIS, EVERETT LINCOLN, b Kent, Wash, May 13, 19; m 43; c 4. WOOD SCIENCE & TECHNOLOGY. *Educ:* Univ Wash, BS, 41, PhD(wood prod), 56; Mich State Univ, MS, 43. *Prof Exp:* Asst, Mich State Univ, 41-42; res wood technologist, Chem Div, Borden Co, 43-46; from asst to assoc prof wood utilization, Univ Idaho, 46-56; assoc prof wood technol, Univ Mich, 56-65; prof forest prod, Forest Res Lab, Ore State Univ, 65-71, head dept, 65-70; NZ FOREST PROD LTD PROF WOOD SCI, SCH FORESTRY, UNIV CANTERBURY, 71- *Concurrent Pos:* Vis prof, Univ Ariz, 81 & Univ Wash, 82. *Mem:* Forest Prod Res Soc; Brit Inst Wood Sci; Soc Wood Sci & Technol; Tech Asn Pulp & Paper Indust. *Res:* Wood and fiber anatomy and structure, including chemistry and mineral composition; factors of growth as related to wood structure and properties; education in wood science and technology; energy and forest biomass; forest products marketing. *Mailing Add:* Sch of Forestry Univ of Canterbury Christchurch New Zealand

ELLIS, FORREST ALBERT, b Central City, Nebr, Nov 28, 11; m 38. HUMAN PHYSIOLOGY. *Educ:* Whittier Col, AB, 34, MS, 36; Stanford Univ, PhD(physiol), 49. *Prof Exp:* Prof biol, William Penn Col, 37-42; teacher high sch, Calif, 42-46; prof, 46-76, EMER PHYSIOL, SAN JOSE STATE UNIV, 76- *Concurrent Pos:* Res asst, Stanford Univ, 48-49. *Mem:* AAAS. *Res:* Body temperature and respiratory physiology. *Mailing Add:* 1109 Steinway Campbell CA 95008

ELLIS, FRANK RUSSELL, b Celina, Ohio, Oct 19, 15; m 41; c 4. CLINICAL PATHOLOGY. *Educ:* Univ Mich, MD, 43; Am Bd Path, dipl, 53. *Prof Exp:* Resident asst path, Sch Med, Univ Utah, 47-49; pathologist, St Anthony Hosp, Wenatchee, Wash, 50-52; instr path, Sch Med, Univ Colo, 53-54; clin pathologist, Wayne Co Gen Hosp, Eloise, Mich, 54-66; dir, Southeastern Mich Red Cross Blood Ctr, 66-72; assoc med dir, Am Nat Red Cross Blood Prog, 73-76; MED DIR, MO-ILL REGIONAL RED CROSS BLOOD SERV, 76- *Concurrent Pos:* Pathologist, DePaul Hosp, Wyo, 52-54; consult, Warren AFB, Wyo, 54; tech adv blood transfusion res div, Army Med Res Lab, Ky, 65-74; res fel, Univ Wash, 49-50. *Mem:* Fel AAAS; Am Acad Forensic Sci; fel Am Soc Clin Path; AMA; Int Soc Blood Transfusion. *Res:* Detection and surveillance of the healthy carrier of hepatitis among volunteer blood donors. *Mailing Add:* Mo-Ill Regional Red Cross 4050 Lindell Blvd St Louis MO 63108

ELLIS, FRANKLIN HENRY, JR, b Washington, DC, Sept 20, 20. THORACIC & CARDIOVASCULAR SURGERY. *Educ:* Yale Univ, AB, 41; Columbia Univ, MD, 44; Univ Minn, PhD(surg), 51; Am Bd Surg, dipl, 53; Am Bd Thoracic Surg, dipl, 54. *Prof Exp:* Instr surg, Mayo Grad Sch Med, Univ Minn, 52-56, from asst prof to prof, 56-70; CHMN, DEPT THORACIC & CARDIOVASC SURG, LAHEY CLIN FOUND & NEW ENGLAND DEACONESS HOSP, 71- *Concurrent Pos:* Lectr surg, Harvard Med Sch, 70-74, assoc clin prof, 74-80, clin prof, 80- *Honors & Awards:* Billings Gold Medal, Esophagitis, AMA, 55. *Mem:* Am Asn Thoracic Surg; Int Soc Surg; Int Cardiovasc Soc: Am Surg Asn; Am Heart Asn. *Res:* Thoracic and cardiovascular surgery. *Mailing Add:* Lahey Clin Med Ctr 41 Mall Rd Box 541 Burlington MA 01805

ELLIS, FRED E, b Hutchinson, Kans, Apr 22, 26; m 58; c 2. PHYSICS, ASTRONOMY. *Educ:* ETex State Col, BS, 54, MS, 55; La State Univ, PhD(physics), 65. *Prof Exp:* Instr physics, ETex State Col, 55-58; asst prof, Southern Miss Univ, 64-65; res collabr, Nat Radio Astron Observ, 65; assoc prof physics, 66-80, PROF ASTRON, PAN AM UNIV, 80- *Res:* Astrometry of extended radio sources; radio galactic spur. *Mailing Add:* Dept of Astron Pan Am Univ Edinburg TX 78539

ELLIS, FRED WILSON, b Heath Springs, SC, Apr 24, 14; m 40; c 4. PHARMACOLOGY, BIOCHEMISTRY. *Educ:* Univ SC, BS, 36; Univ Fla, MS, 38; Univ Md, PhD(pharmacol), 41; Duke Univ, MD, 51. *Prof Exp:* Supt biochem lab, Univ Md Hosp, 41-42; assoc pharmacol, Jefferson Med Col, 42-43; from asst prof to assoc prof, 43-67, PROF PHARMACOL, SCH MED, UNIV NC, CHAPEL HILL, 67-; CONSULT, 80- *Concurrent Pos:* Mem sci adv coun, Distilled Spirits Coun US, 73-; mem res grants rev bd, Nat Coun Alcoholism, 73-; mem, NC Alcoholism Res Authority, 74-, vchmn & mem exec comt, 78; res fel pharmacol, Univ Md, 41-42. *Mem:* AAAS; AMA; Am Soc Pharmacol; Res Soc Alcoholism; Soc Exp Biol & Med. *Res:* Adrenal function in experimental alcoholism; experimentally-induced physical dependence on ethanol in animals; development of animal models of alcoholism in monkeys and dogs; development of Beagle model of the fetal alcohol syndrome. *Mailing Add:* Sch Med Univ NC Chapel Hill NC 27514

ELLIS, HAROLD BERNARD, b Havre, Mont, Dec 31, 17; m 44; c 4. CIVIL ENGINEERING. *Educ:* Washington State Univ, BS, 41; Mass Inst Technol, MS, 47; Iowa State Univ, PhD(civil eng), 63. *Prof Exp:* Chief of schs & training sect, Engr Off, Hq Cent Pac Area, US Army, Hawaii, 44, commandant, Hq Amphibious Training Ctr, 44-45, instr & chief, Opers & Construct Sect, Engrs S Ft Belvoir, Va, 45-46, unit instr, 118th Engr Combat Battalion, Nat Guard, RI, 47-50, asst dist engr, Dist Engr Off, Washington, DC, 50-52; exec off & commander, Hq 931st Engr Group, 52-53, staff off, Aviation Engr Force, Wolters AFB Tex, 53-55, assoc prof mil sci & tactics, Army ROTC, Iowa State Univ, 55-59, dep comdr depot oper, Army Gen Depot, France, 59-62; from asst prof to prof civil eng, Iowa State Univ, 62-73, head tech inst, 62-73; DIR PERSONNEL DEVELOP, BLACK & VEATCH CONSULT ENGRS, KANSAS CITY, 73- *Mem:* Am Soc Civil Engrs; Am Soc Eng Educ. *Mailing Add:* Black & Veatch Consult Engrs PO n Box 8405 Kansas City MO 64114

ELLIS, HOMER GODSEY, b Paris, Tex, Sept 29, 33; m 57; c 2. MATHEMATICS, PHYSICS. *Educ:* Univ Tex, BA, 55, MA, 58, PhD(math), 61. *Prof Exp:* Asst prof math, Univ Utah, 61-62 & Univ Wash, 62-65; vis asst prof appl math, 65-67, asst prof, 67-68, ASSOC PROF MATH, UNIV COLO, BOULDER, 68- *Concurrent Pos:* Fac fel, Univ Colo, 74-75; guest scientist, Int Ctr Theoret Physics, Italy, 74-75. *Mem:* Am Math Soc; Math Asn Am; Int Soc Gen Relativity & Gravitation. *Res:* Relativity theory; differential geometry; mathematical physics. *Mailing Add:* 771 Crescent Dr Boulder CO 80303

ELLIS, J S, b Kingston, Ont, Jan 10, 27; m 64. CIVIL ENGINEERING. *Educ:* Queen's Univ, Ont, BSc, 49; McGill Univ, MEng, 49; Cambridge Univ, PhD(civil eng), 57. *Prof Exp:* Design engr, H G Acres & Co Ltd, 49-54; struct engr, J D Lee & Co Ltd, 57-59; prof struct eng, 59-80, PROF CIVIL ENG, ROYAL MIL COL CAN, 80-, HEAD DEPT, 69- *Concurrent Pos:* Defence Res Bd Can res grants, 62-64 & 65; chmn task group III, US Column Res Coun; trustee, Rd Safety Res Fund, Eng Inst Can; vis prof, Royal Mil Col 71. *Honors & Awards:* Duggan Medal, Eng Inst Can, 65. *Mem:* Eng Inst Can. *Res:* Ultimate capacity of steel columns; automation and traffic control. *Mailing Add:* Dept of Civil Eng Royal Mil Col Kingston Can

ELLIS, JACK BARRY, b Toronto, Ont, Jan 4, 36; m 61; c 2. ELECTRICAL ENGINEERING. *Educ:* Univ Toronto, BASc, 58; Univ London, MSc & 61; Mich State Univ, PhD(elec eng), 65. *Prof Exp:* Lectr elec eng, Univ Waterloo, 61-62; asst, Mich State Univ, 62-63, asst instr resource develop, 64-65; asst prof elec eng, Univ Waterloo, 65-66, assoc prof, 66-70, dir continuing res prog probs urbanization, 68-70; PROF FAC ENVIRON STUDIES, YORK UNIV, 70- *Concurrent Pos:* Consult, res contract, Dept Conserv, Mich, 65-66; Nat Res Coun Can oper grant, 65-; Dept Hwy, Ont res grant, 65- *Mem:* Inst Elec & Electronics Engrs. *Res:* Nonlinear control systems; optimal control and systems theories; applications of systems theory and control theory to transportation networks, planning, economic and sociological systems. *Mailing Add:* Fac Environ Studies York Univ Downsview ON M3J 2R3 Can

ELLIS, JAMES EDGAR, animal ecology, animal behavior, see previous edition

ELLIS, JAMES EUGENE, b Warren, Ohio. CLINICAL CHEMISTRY. *Educ:* Ohio State Univ, BS, 70, MS, 72. *Prof Exp:* Jr res chemist, New England Nuclear Corp, 72-75; mgr res & develop RIA, Nuclear Int Corp, 75-77; SR SCIENTIST RIA DEVELOP, CORNING GLASS WORKS, 77- *Mem:* Am Asn Clin Chem. *Res:* Commercial production of radioimmunoassay kits for clinical diagnosis. *Mailing Add:* Corning Med & Sci 333 Coney St East Walpole MA 02081

ELLIS, JAMES PERCY, JR, b Palacios, Tex, Oct 21, 27; m 49; c 5. BIOCHEMISTRY. *Educ:* Southwest Tex State Univ, BS, 48, MS, 49; Tex A&M Univ, PhD(biochem), 67. *Prof Exp:* Asst biochem, Univ Tex Med Br, 50-52; RES BIOCHEMIST, US AIR FORCE SCH AEROSPACE MED, 52- *Res:* Development and use of biochemical methods for the assessment of physiologic function. *Mailing Add:* Crew Technol Div US Air Force Sch Aerospace Med Brooks AFB TX 78235

ELLIS, JAMES WATSON, b Uruguaiana, Brazil, Aug 16, 27; US citizen; m 51; c 3. PURE MATHEMATICS. *Educ:* Wofford Col, AB, 48; Tulane Univ, MS, 51, PhD(math), 55. *Prof Exp:* Asst prof math, Fla State Univ, 52-57, assoc prof, 57-58; assoc prof, 58-61, prof & chmn dept, 61-64, DEAN, JR DIV, UNIV NEW ORLEANS, 64- *Mem:* Am Math Soc; Math Asn Am. *Res:* Linear topological spaces and topological algebras. *Mailing Add:* 2328 Lark St New Orleans LA 70122

ELLIS, JASON ARUNDEL, b Newell, SDak, Dec 22, 18; m 52; c 1. PHYSICS. *Educ:* SDak Sch Mines & Technol, BS, 42; Univ Iowa, MS, 52, PhD(physics), 62. *Prof Exp:* Engr, Gen Elec Co, 42-45; physicist, US Bur Standards, 47 & Radiation Res Lab, Univ Iowa, 51-53; asst prof physics, North Tex State Univ, 58-63; asst prof, 63-69, ASSOC PROF PHYSICS, UNIV TEX, ARLINGTON, 69- *Concurrent Pos:* Co-ed, Spacetime. *Mem:* AAAS; Am Phys Soc; Am Asn Physics Teachers; Optical Soc Am; Int Soc Gen Semantics. *Res:* Theoretical physics; mathematical biophysics. *Mailing Add:* Dept of Physics Univ of Tex Arlington TX 76019

ELLIS, JERRY WILLIAM, b Pittsburg, Kans, Aug 22, 37; m 58; c 2. ORGANIC CHEMISTRY. *Educ:* Kans State Col, BS, 59, MS, 61; Okla State Univ, PhD(org chem), 65. *Prof Exp:* Instr chem, Kans State Col Pittsburg, 61 & Okla State Univ, 61-62; asst prof org chem, Wis State, Whitewater, 65-66; asst prof, 66-69, assoc prof, 69-76, PROF ORG CHEM, EASTERN ILL UNIV, 76- *Concurrent Pos:* Vis prof chem, Johns Hopkins Univ, 79-80. *Mem:* Am Chem Soc; Royal Soc Chem. *Res:* Total synthesis of terpenes; reactions of lead tetraacetate. *Mailing Add:* Dept of Chem Eastern Ill Univ Charleston IL 61920

ELLIS, JOHN EMMETT, b San Pedro, Calif, May 26, 43; m 66. ORGANOMETALLIC CHEMISTRY, INORGANIC CHEMISTRY. *Educ:* Univ Southern Calif, BSc, 66; Mass Inst Technol, PhD(chem), 71. *Prof Exp:* Res fel inorg chem, Mass Inst Technol, 66-71; asst prof, 71-76, ASSOC PROF CHEM, UNIV MINN, MINNEAPOLIS, 76- *Concurrent Pos:* Dir, Inst Organometallic Chem, Univ Minn, 72- & NSF Undergrad Res Partic Prog, 74-; DuPont Young fac award, 76. *Mem:* Am Chem Soc; The Chem Soc; Sigma Xi. *Res:* Synthesis and characterization of fundamentally important organometallic compounds of the transitional and main group elements, which may function as useful stoichiometric and/or catalytic reagents in organometallic and organic synthesis. *Mailing Add:* Dept of Chem 207 Pleasant St SE Univ Minn Minneapolis MN 55455

ELLIS, JOHN FLETCHER, b Laurel, Del, Apr 26, 37; m 59; c 2. WEED SCIENCE. *Educ:* Univ Del, BS, 59; Rutgers Univ, MS, 61, PhD(weed sci), 64. *Prof Exp:* Res rep, 66-67, res specialist herbicides, 67-69, group leader, 69-71, prod planner all prod, 71-74, mgr biol res herbicides & plant growth regulators, Agr Div, 74-78, dir, Regist & Toxicol, 78-80, DIR BIOL RES, AGR DIV, CIBA-GEIGY CORP, 80- *Mem:* Am Soc Agron; Weed Sci Soc Am; Sigma Xi; AAAS. *Res:* Evaluation of chemical products for herbicidal plant growth regulator insecticidal and fungicidal properties that might lead to valuable tools for food production. *Mailing Add:* Greensboro NC 27410

ELLIS, JOHN FRANCIS, b Torrington, Conn, July 29, 22; m 46; c 3. BIOLOGY. *Educ:* Amherst Col, BA, 48, MA, 50; Univ Edinburgh, PhD(animal genetics), 55. *Prof Exp:* Teaching asst, Amherst Col, 48-50, from instr to asst prof biol, 58-59; from asst prof to assoc prof, 59-68, PROF BIOL, HAMILTON COL, 68- *Concurrent Pos:* USPHS trainee, State Univ NY Upstate Med Ctr, 66-67; consult, NY State Dept Ment Health, Marcy State Hosp. *Mem:* Fel AAAS; Genetics Soc Am; Am Inst Biol Sci. *Res:* Human cytogenetics; genetics of mental retardation and mental illness; tissue culture and cell hybridization; Drosophila biochemical genetics. *Mailing Add:* Dept of Biol Hamilton Col Clinton NY 13323

ELLIS, JOHN OGBORN, b Ithaca, NY, Dec 25, 30; m 53; c 4. METEOROLOGY. *Educ:* Amherst Col, AB, 52; Univ Chicago, SM, 54. *Prof Exp:* From res meteorologist to gen meteorologist, US Weather Bur, 55-66, gen meteorologist, Environ Sci Serv Admin, 66-70; PHYS SCIENTIST, ENVIRON SCI INFO CTR, NAT OCEANIC & ATMOSPHERIC ADMIN, 70- *Mem:* AAAS; Am Meteorol Soc; Am Geophys Union. *Res:* Application of statistical methods and dynamical procedures to development of short range weather forecasting techniques; scientific publication review. *Mailing Add:* Environ Sci Info Ctr D81 Environ Data Serv NOAA Rockville MD 20852

ELLIS, JOHN TAYLOR, b Lufkin, Tex, Dec 27, 20; m 42; c 3. PATHOLOGY. *Educ:* Univ Tex, BA, 42; Northwestern Univ, MD, 45; Am Bd Path, dipl, 51. *Prof Exp:* Rotating intern, St Luke's Hosp, 45-46; asst, William Buchanan Blood Ctr, Baylor Hosp, 48; asst path, Col Med, Cornell Univ, 48-59, from instr to assoc prof, 49-62; prof path & chmn dept, Sch Med, Emory Univ, 62-68; PROF PATH & CHMN DEPT, COL MED, CORNELL UNIV, 68- *Concurrent Pos:* From asst resident pathologist to asst attend pathologist, New York Hosp, 50-55, assoc attend pathologist, 55-; mem comt blood, health resources adv comt, Off Emergency Planning, Exec Off Pres, 64-71; mem path study sect, NIH, 65-69, chmn, 69-70; mem bd ed, Am J Path, 65-; mem sci adv bd consult, Armed Forces Inst Path, 70-75; chmn histopath comt, Polycythemia Vera Study Group, 72-; attend pathologist, Mem Hosp Cancer & Allied Dis, 73- *Mem:* Am Soc Exp Path; Soc Exp Biol & Med; Am Asn Path & Bact; Col Am Path; Int Acad Path. *Res:* Nephrosis and experimental proteinuria; muscular dystrophy and experimentally induced diseases of muscle; iron metabolism; polycythemia vera. *Mailing Add:* Dept of Path Cornell Univ Med Col New York NY 10021

ELLIS, KEITH OSBORNE, b Albany, NY, Oct 18, 41; m 63; c 2. PHARMACOLOGY, PHYSIOLOGY. *Educ:* Heidelberg Col, BA, 63; Univ Cincinnati, PhD(pharmacol), 69. *Prof Exp:* High sch teacher biol, chem & physics, Ohio Bd Educ, North Baltimore, 63-64; sr res pharmacologist, 70-73, unit leader pharmacol, 74-77, proj mgr, 78-81, SECT CHIEF PHARMACOL, NORWICH-EATON PHARMACEUT, 77- *Concurrent Pos:* Fel neurophysiol, Grass Found, Woods Hole, Mass, 69; fel, Baylor Col Med, 69-70; adj instr, State Univ NY Agr & Tech Col Morrisville, 73-78, Upper Div Col, State Univ NY Utica-Rome, 75-77, Sch Gen Studies, State Univ NY Binghamton, 77-79 & Dept Pharmacol, Upstate Med Ctr, State Univ NY, 79- *Mem:* NY Acad Sci; Soc Exp Biol & Med; Am Soc Pharmacol & Therapeut. *Res:* Skeletal muscle pharmacology; central nervous system pharmacology; cardiovascular pharmacology. *Mailing Add:* 23 Aurora Hills Dr RD 1 Norwich NY 13815

ELLIS, KENNETH JOSEPH, b Terre Haute, Ind, July 14, 44; m 71; c 2. MEDICAL PHYSICS, HEALTH PHYSICS. *Educ:* Univ Tex-El Paso, BS, 66; Vanderbilt Univ, PhD(physics), 72. *Prof Exp:* Med assoc physics, 72-73, res assoc, 73-74, asst scientist, 74-76, assoc scientist, 76-79, SCIENTIST, MED DEPT, BROOKHAVEN NAT LAB, 79- *Concurrent Pos:* AEC Health Physics fel, 80. *Mem:* Health Physics Soc. *Res:* Medical physics; in vivo neutron activation; whole body counting; tracer kinetics; compartmental modeling; photon absorptionetry; neutron shielding; health physics. *Mailing Add:* Dept of Med Brookhaven Nat Lab Upton NY 11973

ELLIS, LARRY EDWARD, organic chemistry, pharmaceutical chemistry, see previous edition

ELLIS, LEGRANDE CLARK, b Farmington, Utah, June 20, 32; m 54; c 7. REPRODUCTIVE ENDOCRINOLOGY. *Educ:* Utah State Univ, BS, 54, MS, 56; Okla State Univ, PhD(physiol, endocrinol), 61. *Prof Exp:* From instr to asst prof cellular physiol, Okla State Univ, 57-62; fel quant biol, Univ Utah, 62-64; asst prof physiol & endocrinol, 64-66, assoc prof, 66-71, PROF PHYSIOL & BIOCHEM, UTAH STATE UNIV, 71- *Mem:* Am Physiol Soc; Endocrine Soc; Soc Study Reproduction; Am Soc Zoologists; Sigma Xi. *Res:* Environmental influences on endocrinology and reproduction; synthesis, metabolism and interactions of steroid hormones, biogenic amines, prostaglandins and cyclic nucleotides; pineal gland and radiation. *Mailing Add:* Dept of Biol UMC-53 Utah State Univ Logan UT 84322

ELLIS, LEONARD CULBERTH, b Portsmouth, Va, Dec 13, 34; m 54; c 3. ORGANIC CHEMISTRY. *Educ:* Col William & Mary, BS, 56; Univ Va, PhD(org chem), 62. *Prof Exp:* Res chemist, 61-76, ASSOC DIR RES & DEVELOP, VA CHEM INC, PORTSMOUTH, 76- *Res:* Gas chromatographic analysis of amine mixtures; biogenetic mechanisms by tracer studies; amine derivatives; corrosion inhibitors; conformational analysis; stabilization of dithionites; groundwood pulp bleaching. *Mailing Add:* 2432 Taylorwood Blvd Chesapeake VA 23321

ELLIS, LESLIE LEE, JR, b Norfolk, Va, Sept 13, 25; m 49; c 4. ZOOLOGY. *Educ:* Tulane Univ, BS, 48, MS, 49; Univ Okla, PhD(zool), 52. *Prof Exp:* Asst zool, Tulane Univ, 48; asst, Univ Okla, 49-50, 51-52, spec instr & asst, Univ Biol Sta & State Biol Surv, 50-51; res aide, USPHS, 52; from asst prof to prof zool & entom, Miss State Univ, 52-68, head dept zool, 62-68; prof biol sci, 68, chmn dept, 68-69, dir grad studies & res, 69-70, dean grad studies & res, Fla Technol Univ, 70-74, vpres acad affairs, 79-81, PROVOST & VPRES ACAD AFFAIRS, UNIV CENT FLA, 81- *Concurrent Pos:* NSF panelist; indust consult. *Mem:* Entom Soc Am; Sigma Xi; AAAS. *Res:* Aquatic biology; medical entomology and parasitology; bee diseases. *Mailing Add:* Off of Acad Affairs Univ Cent Fla Orlando FL 32816

ELLIS, LYNDA BETTY, b Los Angeles, Calif, Nov 25, 45; m 66. BIOMEDICAL COMPUTING, BIOCHEMISTRY. *Educ:* Univ Southern Calif, BS, 65; Brandeis Univ, PhD(biochem), 71. *Prof Exp:* Res specialist biochem, 71-73, asst prof, 73-80, ASSOC PROF HEALTH COMPUT SCI, UNIV MINN, 80- *Mem:* Sigma Xi. *Res:* Computer-aided instruction; health information systems; biochemical simulation. *Mailing Add:* Univ Minn 420 SE Delaware St Minneapolis MN 55455

ELLIS, NATHAN KENT, b Maple Rapids, Mich, Jan 14, 09; m 34; c 3. HORTICULTURE. *Educ:* Mich State Col, BS, 32, MS, 35, PhD(hort), 50. *Prof Exp:* Chg muck crops invests, Purdue Univ, 35-41, asst prof hort, 41-47, assoc prof & actg head dept, 47-50, prof & head dept, 50-58, asst dir, Agr Exp Sta, 58-67, assoc dir, 67-72; vpres & opers mgr, Environ Farming of the Pac, 72-74; sr res adv, Develop & Resources Corp, Calif & Iran, 74-76. *Concurrent Pos:* Consult, Hawaiian Agron Int, 78 & 80. *Mem:* Fel AAAS; fel Am Soc Hort Sci. *Res:* Vegetable crop production; production of essential oils from Mentha species; nutriculture systems and controlled environment. *Mailing Add:* 2333 Kapiolani Blvd Marco Polo Apt 3310 Honolulu HI 96826

ELLIS, PATRICIA MENCH, b Rochester, NY, Mar 6, 49. GEOLOGY, EARTH SCIENCES. *Educ:* Univ Rochester, Ba, 71; Duke Univ, MA, 73. *Prof Exp:* Teaching asst geol, Duke Univ, 71-73; teaching asst, Univ Tex, 73-76, res asst, Bur Econ Geol, 76-78; res geologist, Explor Res Div, 78-81, PROJ GEOLOGIST, CONOCO, INC, 81- *Concurrent Pos:* Geologist, Phillip Petrol Co, 74 & Texaco, Inc, 75. *Mem:* Soc Econ Paleontologists & Mineralogists; Geol Soc Am; Am Asn Petrol Geologists; Can Asn Petrol Geologists. *Res:* Geological research in carbonate petrology, diagenesis, depositional environments and geochemistry; exploration geology, Montana and Idaho overthrust belt. *Mailing Add:* Conoco, Inc 555 17th St Denver CO 80202

ELLIS, PAUL JOHN, b Northampton, Eng, May 25, 41; m 73; c 1. NUCLEAR PHYSICS. *Educ:* Bristol Univ, BSc, 62; Univ Manchester, PhD(nuclear physics theory), 66. *Prof Exp:* Res assoc nuclear theory, Univ Mich, 66-68 & Rutgers Univ, 68-70; res officer nuclear theory, Nuclear Physics Lab, Oxford Univ, 70-73; asst prof, 73-77, ASSOC PROF NUCLEAR THEORY, UNIV MINN, 77- *Mem:* Am Phys Soc. *Res:* Theoretical nuclear physics. *Mailing Add:* Sch Physics & Astron Univ Minn Minneapolis MN 55455

ELLIS, PHILIP PAUL, b Saginaw, Mich, Oct 30, 23. OPHTHALMOLOGY. *Educ:* Baylor Univ, MD, 48; Am Bd Ophthal, dipl, 55. *Prof Exp:* From instr to asst prof ophthal, Col Med, Univ Iowa, 54-58; assoc prof & head dept, Sch Med, Univ Ark, 58-60; assoc prof, 60-67, PROF OPHTHAL, SCH MED, UNIV COLO, DENVER, 67-, HEAD DEPT, 60- *Mem:* AMA; Am Acad Ophthal & Otolaryngol; Asn Res Vision & Ophthal; Am Ophthal Soc. *Res:* Ocular pharmacology and toxicology; therapeutics; immunology. *Mailing Add:* Dept of Ophthal Univ of Colo Sch of Med Denver CO 80220

ELLIS, RICHARD AKERS, b Brewster, Mass, May 5, 28. BIOLOGICAL STRUCTURE. *Educ:* Univ Mass, AB, 49; Harvard Univ, AM, 51, PhD, 54; Brown Univ, AM, 62. *Prof Exp:* Instr anat, Sch Med, Harvard Univ, 54; res assoc, Bermuda Biol Sta, 56; from instr to assoc prof, 56-67, PROF BIOL, BROWN UNIV, 67- *Mem:* AAAS; Am Asn Anatomists; Histochem Soc; Am Soc Zoologists; Am Soc Cell Biol. *Res:* Histochemistry and electron microscopy of salt-secreting epithelia and skin; innervation and vascularization of taste buds; histochemistry of the metrial gland in pregnancy and pseudopregnancy. *Mailing Add:* Div Biol & Med Brown Univ Providence RI 02912

ELLIS, RICHARD BASSETT, b Abilene, Tex, May 12, 15; m 40; c 3. PHYSICAL CHEMISTRY. *Educ:* Vanderbilt Univ, BA, 36, MS, 37, PhD(anal & phys chem), 40. *Prof Exp:* Supvr anal div, Res & Develop Dept, Joseph E Seagram & Sons, 40-42; res chemist, Corning Glass Works, 42-46; instr chem, Univ Fla, 46-47; asst prof, Univ Miami, 47-51; from sr chemist to head inorg sect, Southern Res Inst, 51-68; prof physics & head dept, Huntingdon Col, 68-70; prof sci, Troy State Univ, Montgomery, 70-80, head dept sci, 71-76; RETIRED. *Concurrent Pos:* Lectr, Birmingham-Southern Col, 54-66 & Univ Ala, Birmingham, 66-68. *Res:* Analysis distillery products; surface chemistry; electrochemistry; fused salt technology; high-temperature materials. *Mailing Add:* 3115 Partridge Rd Montgomery AL 36111

ELLIS, RICHARD JOHN, b New Castle, Ind, Apr 11, 39; m 62; c 2. PLANT PHYSIOLOGY. *Educ:* Univ Calif, Santa Barbara, BA, 60; Univ Calif, Berkeley, PhD(bot), 67. *Prof Exp:* Asst prof biol, City Col New York, 67-68; from asst prof to assoc prof, 68-81, PROF BIOL, BUCKNELL UNIV, 81- *Concurrent Pos:* NSF fac fel sci, 75. *Mem:* Phycol Soc Am; Am Soc Plant Physiol; Japanese Soc Plant Physiologists. *Res:* Regulation of chlorophyll synthesis; mechanisms of herbicidal toxicity in algae; physiology of reproduction in algae and fungi. *Mailing Add:* Dept of Biol Bucknell Univ Lewisburg PA 17837

ELLIS, RICHARD JOHN, physics, see previous edition

ELLIS, RICHARD STEVEN, b Brookline, Mass, May 15, 47; m 69; c 2. MATHEMATICS. *Educ:* Harvard Univ, BA, 69; NY Univ, MS, 71, PhD(math), 72. *Prof Exp:* Mem tech staff appl probability, Bell Tel Labs, 69-72; asst prof math, Northwestern Univ, 72-75; assoc prof, 75-77, assoc prof math, 77-81, PROF MATH, UNIV MASS, AMHERST, 81- *Concurrent Pos:* Mem, Comn Concerned Scientists; Alfred P Sloan res fel, 77-81; Lady Davis fel, 82. *Mem:* Am Math Soc; Int Asn Math Physics. *Res:* applications of probability theory to statistical mechanics; correlation inequalities and limit theorems for Ising models of ferromagnetism; large deviations and asymptotic problems in probability theory and statistical mechanics. *Mailing Add:* Dept of Math & Statist Univ of Mass Amherst MA 01003

ELLIS, ROBERT ANDERSON, JR, b Kansas City, Mo, Oct 16, 27; m 54; c 4. PHYSICS. *Educ:* Fisk Univ, BA, 48; Yale Univ, MS, 49; Univ Iowa, PhD(physics), 54. *Prof Exp:* From instr to prof physics, Tenn State Univ, 49-56; MEM RES STAFF, PLASMA PHYSICS LAB, PRINCETON UNIV, 56- *Concurrent Pos:* Head, Physics Sect, Int Atomic Energy Agency, 79-81. *Mem:* Fel Am Phys Soc. *Res:* Plasma physics. *Mailing Add:* Plasma Physics Lab Princeton Univ Princeton NJ 08540

ELLIS, ROBERT HOMER, b Madison, Wis, Apr 13, 29; m 52; c 2. MULTIDISCIPLINARY PROGRAM MANAGEMENT. *Educ:* Univ Wis, BA, 51, MS, 53, PhD(microbiol), 57. *Prof Exp:* Teaching asst, Univ Wis, 50-51 & 53; officer, US Army, 51-61; res scientist, Aerospace Div, Boeing Co, 61-62; scientist, Sci & Tech Bur, US Arms Control & Disarmament Agency, 62-64; dir opers res div, Travelers Res Ctr, 64-67, dep dir math sci dept, 67-68, dir resource mgt studies dept & vpres, 68-69, pres, Travelers Res Corp, 69-70; pres, Ctr for Environ & Man Inc, 70-72; asst to pres, Rensselaer Hartford Grad Ctr, 72-77; pres & chief exec dir, NJ Marine Sci Consortium, 77-81; SR CONSULT, ARTHUR D LITTLE INC, 81- *Concurrent Pos:* Consult, US Arms Control & Disarmament Agency, 64-67; chmn mgt comt, Off Res & Planning, Lutheran Church in Am, 72-76; planning & anal consult, Chesapeake Res Consortium Inc, 73-77; mem nat sea grant adv panel, Dept Com, Nat Oceanic & Atmospheric Admin, 74-76. *Mem:* AAAS; Am Soc Microbiol; Sigma Xi. Am Geog Soc. *Res:* General and medical microbiology; human intestinal microbial flora; microbial ecology; environmental science and technology; ecosystems analysis and modeling; environmental resources and coastal zone management; marine resource development. *Mailing Add:* Arthur D Little Inc Acorn Park Camridge MA 02140

ELLIS, ROBERT J, b Washington, DC, May 1, 28; m 57; c 2. BACTERIOLOGY, MICROBIOLOGY. *Educ:* Univ Md, BS, 50; Rutgers Univ, MS, 52; Purdue Univ, PhD(microbiol), 55. *Prof Exp:* mem staff, Lab Br, Bact & Diag Reagents Sect, 54-58, chief reagents eval unit, 58-70, chief immunobiologics, Biol Prod Div, 70-81, CHIEF IMMUNOLOGICS, HOST FACTORS DIV, CTR DIS CONTROL, USPHS, 81- *Mem:* Am Soc Microbiol; Conf Pub Health Lab Dirs. *Res:* Quality control procedures for microbiological laboratories; immunobiologics distributed by Center for Disease Control; collection, handling and shipment of microbiological specimens; standardization and evaluation of microbiological diagnostic reagents and procedures. *Mailing Add:* Ctr for Dis Control USPHS Atlanta GA 30333

ELLIS, ROBERT L, b Richmond, Ind, July 26, 38; m 62; c 1. MATHEMATICS. *Educ:* Miami Univ, AB, 60; Duke Univ, PhD(math), 66. *Prof Exp:* From instr to asst prof math, Duke Univ, 64-66; asst prof, 66-71, ASSOC PROF MATH, UNIV MD, COLLEGE PARK, 71- *Concurrent Pos:* NSF grant, 67-69. *Honors & Awards:* Sr US Scientist Award, WGer Govt-Alexander von Humboldt Found, 72. *Mem:* Am Math Soc. *Res:* Functional analysis and topology, particularly topological vector spaces. *Mailing Add:* Dept of Math Univ of Md Col of Arts & Sci College Park MD 20742

ELLIS, ROBERT MALCOLM, b Meaford, Ont, Mar 16, 36; m 60; c 2. GEOPHYSICS. *Educ:* Univ Western Ont, BA, 57, MSc, 58; Univ Alta, PhD(physics), 64. *Prof Exp:* Instr math, Univ Western Ont, 59-60; from asst prof to assoc prof, 64-74, PROF GEOPHYS, UNIV BC, 74- *Concurrent Pos:* Prin fel, Seismic Proj, Arctic Inst NAm, 66; vis scientist, Univ Alta, 71-72; vis prof, Ahmadu Bello Univ, Nigeria, 74-76; vis res scholar, Macquarie Univ, 81. *Mem:* Am Geophys Union; Geol Asn Can; Can Geophys Union. *Res:* Seismology. *Mailing Add:* Dept Geophys & Astron Univ BC Vancouver BC V6T 1W5 Can

ELLIS, ROBERT WILLIAM, b Wendell, Idaho, Aug 26, 40; m 63; c 2. BIOCHEMISTRY, TOXICOLOGY. *Educ:* Col Idaho, BS, 63; Ore State Univ, MS, 65, PhD(biochem), 70. *Prof Exp:* Fel biochem, Kans State Univ Med Ctr, 69-70; instr chem, Lorado Jr Col, 70-71; PROF BIOCHEM, BOISE STATE UNIV, 71- *Concurrent Pos:* NIH grant, 69-70; consult, Valley Trout Co, 78-79. *Res:* Toxicology of heavy metals; water quality in aquaculture; geothermal aquaculture. *Mailing Add:* Dept of Chem Boise State Univ Boise ID 83725

ELLIS, ROBERT WILLIAM, JR, b Richmond, Va, Oct 16, 39; m 60; c 4. ENGINEERING MECHANICS. *Educ:* Va Polytech Inst, BS, 62, MS, 63, PhD(eng), 66. *Prof Exp:* From asst prof to assoc prof eng, Univ Southern Fla, 65-69, asst dean acad affairs grad studies, 71-72, asst vpres acad affairs & prof eng, 71-72; dean, Sch Technol, Fla Int Univ, 72-78, dean, Sch Bus & Orgn Sci, 72-74, provost, North Miami Campus, 77; exec vpres & chief acad officer, Detroit Inst Technol, 78-80, pres, 80-81; MECH ENGR, US ARMY TANK AUTOMOTIVE COMMAND, WARREN, MICH, 81- *Concurrent Pos:* Metall engr, Polysci Div, Litton Indust, Inc, 62-63; instr, Va Polytech Inst, 64-65; lectr mechanical eng, Lawrence Inst Technol, 81- *Honors & Awards:* Nat Fac Serv Award, Nat Univ Exten Asn, 77. *Mem:* Soc Exp Stress Anal; Nat Soc Prof Engrs; Am Soc Metals; Am Soc Eng Educ. *Res:* Engineering and composite materials; materials. *Mailing Add:* 35945 Fredericksburg Detroit MI 48018

ELLIS, ROSCOE, JR, b Havensville, Kans, Jan 9, 20; m 49; c 4. SOIL CHEMISTRY. *Educ:* Kans State Univ, BS, 48, MS, 50; Univ Wis, PhD(soils), 54. *Prof Exp:* From instr to assoc prof soils, 49-60, res soil chemist, 74-80, PROF AGRON, KANS STATE UNIV, 60- *Concurrent Pos:* Vis prof, Mich State Univ, 61-62. *Mem:* Am Soc Agron; Soil Sci Soc Am. *Res:* Plant nutrition and clay mineralogy. *Mailing Add:* Dept of Agron Waters Hall Col of Agr Kans State Univ Manhattan KS 66502

ELLIS, ROSEMARY, b Berkeley, Calif, July 22, 19. NURSING. *Educ:* Univ Calif, Berkeley, BA, 41, BS, 44; Univ Chicago, MA, 53, PhD(human develop), 64. *Prof Exp:* Asst supt nurses, Univ Calif Hosp, San Fransisco, 49-52; mem fac, Univ Chicago, 53-59; MEM FAC, CASE WESTERN RESERVE UNIV, 64-, PROF NURSING, 68- *Concurrent Pos:* Assoc, dept nursing, Univ Hosp Cleveland, 64- *Mem:* AAAS; Soc Health & Human Values; Midwest Res Nursing Soc; Coun Nurse Researchers-Am Nurses Asn. *Res:* Clinical sensory deprivation or alteration; history of nursing science. *Mailing Add:* Case Western Reserve Univ 2121 Abington Rd Cleveland OH 44106

ELLIS, ROSS COURTLAND, b McKinney, Tex, Feb 23, 29; m 51; c 3. GEOLOGY. *Educ:* Occidental Col, BA, 53; Univ Wash, Seattle, PhD, 59. *Prof Exp:* Asst prof geol, Univ Wash, 57-62; from asst prof to assoc prof, 62-74, PROF GEOL, WESTERN WASH STATE COL, 74- *Res:* Structural geology; geomorphology; petrology. *Mailing Add:* Dept of Geol Western Wash State Col Bellingham WA 98225

ELLIS, ROY, b Ky, June 30, 14; m 43; c 3. OCEANOGRAPHY. *Educ:* Western Ky State Univ, BS, 37; Ind Univ, MA, 39; Agr & Mech Col Tex, PhD, 59. *Prof Exp:* Teacher pub sch, Miss, 39-42; radio instr, US Army Air Force, 42-43; instr math, Vanderbilt Univ, 46; from asst prof to assoc prof, Center Col, KY, 46-67, chmn dept, 67-76, prof, 67-79; RETIRED. *Mem:* Am Meteorol Soc; Am Asn Physics Teachers. *Res:* Gravity induced pressure variations in the presence of a submerged cylinder; physical oceanography. *Mailing Add:* Rte 1 Gravel Switch KY 40328

ELLIS, SAMUEL BENJAMIN, b Reardan, Wash, 04; m 29; c 2. ELECTROANALYTICAL CHEMISTRY. *Educ:* Univ Wash, BS, 26; Lafayette Col, MS, 27; Columbia Univ, PhD(phys inorg chem), 33. *Prof Exp:* Asst, Columbia Univ, 27-30, instr, 30-32; res chemist, US Rubber Prod, Inc, 33-37, Hellige, Inc, 37-49 & New York Lab Supply Co, 49-66; prof chem, Dutchess Community Col, 66-71; mem staff res & develop, Delta Sci Corp, 71-75; RETIRED. *Mem:* Am Chem Soc; Instrument Soc Am. *Res:* Physical chemistry; rheology; electrical measurements; determination of hydrogen-ion concentration; general colorimetric analysis; instruments; laboratory equipment; electrostatics; automatic analyzers, water and sewage; the experimental development of a space field-force hypothesis explaining electrostatic forces solely as attractions, negating any possibility of repulsion. *Mailing Add:* 64 Grove St Lindenhurst NY 11757

ELLIS, STANLEY, b California, Pa, Sept 2, 23; m 43; c 2. ENDOCRINOLOGY, BIOCHEMISTRY. *Educ:* Wayne State Univ, BS, 47, MS, 49, PhD(biochem), 51. *Prof Exp:* Res biochemist hormones, Inst Exp Biol, Univ Calif, Berkeley, 51-55; asst prof biochem, Emory Univ, 56-60; sr protein chemist, Cutter Labs, Berkeley, 60-62; br chief endocrine biochem, 62-76, RES SCIENTIST BIOCHEM, AMES RES CTR, NASA, 77- *Concurrent Pos:* Career Develop Award, NIH, 59-60, mem, Endocrinol Study Sect, 69-73; mem, med adv bd, Nat Pituitary Agency, 77-81. *Honors & Awards:* Except Sci Achievement Award, NASA, 71. *Mem:* AAAS; Am Soc Biol Chemists; Endocrine Soc. *Res:* Anterior pituitary hormones; intracellular peptidases; muscle biochemistry; space biology. *Mailing Add:* NASA Ames Res Ctr Moffett Field CA 94035

ELLIS, STEPHEN DEAN, b Detroit, Mich, June 7, 43; m 66, 81. ELEMENTARY PARTICLE PHYSICS. *Educ:* Univ Mich, Ann Arbor, BSE(eng physics) & BSE(eng math), 65; Calif Inst Technol, PhD(theoret physics), 71. *Prof Exp:* Res physicist, Fermi Nat Accelerator Lab, 71-73; vis scientist, Europ Orgn Nuclear Res, Geneva, Switz, 73-74; res physicist, Fermi Nat Accelerator Lab, 74-75; res asst prof high energy physics, 75-80, ASSOC PROF PHYSICS, UNIV WASH, 80- *Concurrent Pos:* Vis lectr, Dept Appl Math & Theoret Physics, Cambridge Univ, 75. *Mem:* AAAS; Am Phys Soc; Sigma Xi. *Res:* Studies of the theoretical problems of gauage field theories of the strong interactions and phenomenological application of these ideas to hadronic processes, especially large transverse momentum reactions, and lepton induced reactions, especially ete-annihilation. *Mailing Add:* Dept of Physics FM-15 Univ of Wash Seattle WA 98195

ELLIS, SYDNEY, b Boston, Mass, Apr 20, 17; m 42; c 2. PHARMACOLOGY, BIOCHEMISTRY. *Educ:* Boston Univ, SB, 38, AM, 39, PhD(med sci), 41. *Prof Exp:* Asst biochem, Boston Univ, 39-41; Nat Defense Res Comt toxicologist, NY Univ, 42; asst pharmacol, Harvard Med Sch, 42-44; asst prof, Sch MEd, Duke Univ, 46-49; assoc prof, Sch Med, Temple Univ, 49-57; prof pharmacol & chmn dept, Woman's Med Col Pa, 57-67; prof pharmacol & toxicol & dept chmn, Univ Tex Med Br, Galveston, 67-80; DEP DIR, DIV DRUG BIOL, FOOD & DRUG ADMIN, WASHINGTON, DC, 80- *Concurrent Pos:* Consult, Smith Kline & French Labs, 57, NIH Study Sects, Pharmacol & Exp Therapeaut, 60-64 & Med Chem B, 64-68, Nat Bd Med Exam, 64-68 & Astra Pharmaceut Prod, 73; res fel pharmacol, Harvard Med Sch, 41-42; vis investr, Univ Paris, 72; vis scientist, Inst Pub Admin, Food & Drug Admin, Washington, DC, 79-80. *Honors & Awards:* Lindback Found Award, 64. *Mem:* fel, AAAS; Am Soc Pharmacol; Am Chem Soc; Soc Exp Biol & Med; NY Acad Sci. *Res:* Enzymes; effects of enzyme inhibitors on tissues; chemistry and biochemistry of drug decomposition and metabolism; toxins and toxicological mechanisms; biochemical mechanisms of action of autonomic agents; autonomic pharmacology; catecholamines on metabolism. *Mailing Add:* HFD 410 Drug Biol FDA 200 C St, SW Washington DC 20204

ELLIS, WADE, b Chandler, Okla, June 9, 09; m 32; c 2. MATHEMATICS. *Educ:* Wilberforce Col, BS, 28; Univ NMex, MS, 38; Univ Mich, PhD(math), 44. *Prof Exp:* Instr math, Fisk Univ, 38-40 & Univ Mich, 43-45; staff mem radiation lab, Mass Inst Technol, 45-46; physicist, US Air Force Lab, Cambridge, 46-48; from asst prof to prof math, Oberlin Col, 48-67; prof & assoc dean grad sch, 67-77, EMER PROF MATH, UNIV MICH, 77- *Concurrent Pos:* Lectr math, Boston Univ, 47-48; fac fel, India & France, 54-55; mem, Entebbe Workshop, Africa, 62; vis writing panels, Sch Math Study Group, 63 & 65, bd adv, 64-67; vis prof, Nat Univ Eng, Peru, 64; mem bd trustees, Marygrove Col, 69-71, chmn acad affairs comt, 70-71; comt int educ, Asn Grad Schs, 70-72; mem exec bd, Comn Insts Higher Educ, NCent Asn Cols & Sec Schs, 70-75; mem bd trustees, Inst Man & Sci, 70-; chmn deleg, US-Japan Bi-Nat Conf Math Educ, Tokyo, 71; vpres, Col Placement Servs, Inc, 72-81; vchancellor, Acad Affairs, Univ Md, Eastern Shore, 78-79; interim pres, Marygrove Col, Detroit, 79-80; consult mathemetician microcomputers, 80- *Honors & Awards:* Comdr, Orden de las Palmas Magisteriales del Peru, 64. *Mem:* Math Asn Am; Am Math Soc. *Res:* Computer science; analytic mechanics; curriculum development; finite fields. *Mailing Add:* 1141 Chestnut Rd Ann Arbor MI 48104

ELLIS, WALTON P, b Mammoth Spring, Ark, Aug 25, 31; m 56; c 2. SURFACE CHEMISTRY. *Educ:* Univ Calif, Berkeley, BS, 53; Univ Chicago, PhD(chem), 57. *Prof Exp:* STAFF MEM CHEM RES, LOS ALAMOS SCI LAB, 57- *Mem:* AAAS; Am Chem Soc; Am Vacuum Soc. *Res:* Gas-solid reaction kinetics; optical, chemical and physical properties of surfaces and thin films; low energy electron diffraction; high energy electron diffraction; auger, loss and photoelectron spectra; catalysis studies. *Mailing Add:* Los Alamos Sci Lab PO Box 1663 CMB-8 Los Alamos NM 87545

ELLIS, WILLIAM C, b Clay, La, Apr 23, 31; m 55; c 1. ANIMAL NUTRITION. *Educ:* La Polytech Inst, BS, 53; Univ Mo, MS, 55, PhD, 59. *Prof Exp:* Asst, Univ Mo, 53-55, from instr to asst prof animal husb, 55-61; from asst prof to assoc prof, 61-70, PROF ANIMAL SCI, TEX A&M UNIV, 70- *Concurrent Pos:* N Atlantic fel, 59-60. *Mem:* Fed Am Socs Exp Biol; Am Soc Animal Sci. *Res:* Ruminant physiology; nutrition and metabolism; protein and energy metabolism by rumen microorganisms and the ruminants tissues; forage utilization by ruminants. *Mailing Add:* Dept of Animal Sci Tex A&M Univ College Station TX 77843

ELLIS, WILLIAM HAYNES, b Cedar Hill, Tenn, Dec 4, 31; m 52. SYSTEMATIC BOTANY, PLANT ECOLOGY. *Educ:* Austin Peay State Col, BS, 53, MA, 56; Univ Tenn, PhD(bot), 63. *Prof Exp:* Teacher high sch, Tenn, 55-56; from instr to asst prof biol, Austin Peay State Col, 56-60; investr plant taxon, Oak Ridge Inst Nuclear Studies, 61 & Highlands Biol Sta, 62; instr bot, Univ Tenn, 62-63, vis asst prof, 62; assoc prof biol, 63-68, dir grad studies, 66-67, from assoc dean to dean fac, 67-71, vpres acad affairs, 71-72, dir instnl res, 72-77, PROF BIOL, AUSTIN PEAY STATE UNIV, 68-, DEAN GRAD SCH, 77- *Concurrent Pos:* Vis scientist, Tenn Acad Sci, 64-65. *Mem:* AAAS; Am Soc Plant Taxon; Bot Soc Am; Nat Asn Biol Teachers. *Res:* Systematic revision of the genus Acer, section rubra, with emphasis on cytogenetics; pigment studies by chromatography, ecological considerations and morphological study; ecology of the woody flora of Kentucky and Tennessee. *Mailing Add:* Austin Peay State Univ Clarksville TN 37040

ELLIS, WILLIAM HOBERT, b Albany, Ga, Dec 28, 28; m 50; c 4. NUCLEAR CHEMISTRY & ENGINEERING. *Educ:* NGa Col, BS, 57; State Univ, PhD(nuclear & inorg chem), 63. *Prof Exp:* Asst prof, 62-66, ASSOC PROF NUCLEAR ENG & CHEM, UNIV FLA, 66- *Mem:* AAAS; Am Nuclear Soc; Am Chem Soc. *Res:* Nuclear and radio chemistry; nuclear instrumentation and spectrometry; activation analysis and direct energy conversion; inorganic chemistry. *Mailing Add:* Dept of Nuclear Eng Sci Univ of Fla Gainesville FL 32601

ELLIS-AKOVALI, YURDANUR A, b Ankara, Turkey; div; c 2. NUCLEAR PHYSICS. *Educ:* Univ Ankara, BS, 58; Univ Md, PhD(nuclear physics), 67. *Prof Exp:* Lab asst elec, Dept Physics, Sci Fac, Univ Ankara, 58-59; teaching asst physics, Univ Md, 59-61; RES MEM STAFF NUCLEAR DATA, PHYSICS DIV, OAK RIDGE NAT LAB, 67- *Concurrent Pos:* Consult & lectr, 78. *Mem:* Am Phys Soc. *Mailing Add:* Physics Div Oak Ridge Nat Lab X-10 Oak Ridge TN 37830

ELLISON, ALFRED HARRIS, b Quincy, Mass, Dec 23, 23; m 51; c 5. SURFACE CHEMISTRY, AIR POLLUTION. *Educ:* Boston Col, BS, 50; Tufts Univ, MS, 51; Georgetown Univ, PhD(surface chem), 56. *Prof Exp:* Chemist, US Naval Res Lab, 51-56; res chemist, Texaco Res Ctr, 56-65; res chemist, Harris Res Labs, 65; res chemist, Gillette Res Inst, Inc, 65-69; dep dir, 69-79, ACTG DIR, ENVIRON SCI RES LAB, OFF RES & DEVELOP, ENVIRON PROTECTION AGENCY, 79- *Mem:* AAAS; Air Pollution Control Asn; Am Chem Soc. *Res:* Management of chemistry and physics research and development programs on atmospheric processes and on methods and instrumentation for measuring air pollutants in the air and in the emissions from sources. *Mailing Add:* Environ Sci Res Lab Rm Q-304 Tech Ctr Research Triangle Park NC 27711

ELLISON, BART T, b San Diego, Calif, Apr 21, 42; m 65; c 4. CHEMICAL ENGINEERING, CORROSION. *Educ:* Univ Calif, Berkeley, BS, 64, MS, 66, PhD(mech eng), 69. *Prof Exp:* engr, 69-70, RES SUPVR, SHELL DEVELOP CO, 80- *Mem:* Am Soc Chem Engrs; Electrochem Soc; Sigma Xi; Nat Asn Corrosion Engrs. *Res:* Corrosion. *Mailing Add:* Shell Develop Co PO Box 1380 Houston TX 77001

ELLISON, FRANK OSCAR, b Omaha, Nebr, June 18, 26; m 59; c 2. QUANTUM CHEMISTRY. *Educ:* Creighton Univ, BS, 49; Iowa State Univ, PhD(phys chem), 53. *Prof Exp:* Res asst spectros & theoret chem, Inst Atomic Res, Iowa State Univ, 50-53; from instr to asst prof phys chem, Carnegie Inst Technol, 53-65; assoc prof, 65-68, PROF PHYS CHEM, UNIV PITTSBURGH, 68- *Mem:* AAAS; Am Phys Soc; Am Chem Soc. *Res:* Theory of molecular spectra and electronic structure of molecules; chemical physics. *Mailing Add:* Dept of Chem Univ of Pittsburgh Pittsburgh PA 15260

ELLISON, GAYFREE BARNEY, b Brownwood, Tex, Feb 2, 43. CHEMISTRY, ORGANIC CHEMISTRY. *Educ:* Trinity Col, Conn, BS, 65; Yale Univ, PhD(chem), 74. *Prof Exp:* Appointment chem physics, Joint Inst Lab Astrophys, 75-77; ASST PROF CHEM, UNIV COLO, 77- *Mem:* Am Chem Soc; Am Phys Soc; Am Soc Mass Spectrom. *Res:* Chemical physics of organic molecules. *Mailing Add:* Dept of Chem Univ of Colo Boulder CO 80309

ELLISON, JOHN VOGELSANGER, b Cape Girardeau, Mo, Aug 7, 19; m 49; c 4. ELECTRONICS, UNDERWATER ACOUSTICS. *Educ:* Southeast Mo State Col, AB, 39. *Prof Exp:* Instr high sch, 39-41; instr physics, Ill Inst Technol, 41; instr & dean physics & electronics, Am TV Labs, 41-43; staff mem underwater sound, Div War Res, Columbia Univ, 43-45; sect head appl electronics, Sound Div, Naval Res Lab, 45-59; assoc scientist, Res Div, 59-62, proj electronics engr, Electronics Systs Eng Dept, 62-65, mgr, Reconnaissance Lab, 65-73, PRIN STAFF ENGR, ELECTRONIC SYSTS TECHNOL, MCDONNELL AIRCRAFT CO, MCDONNELL DOUGLAS CORP, 73- *Mem:* Acoust Soc Am; Am Soc Photogram. *Res:* Propagation and scattering of electromagnetic waves; remote sensing; electro-optics; underwater sound; communications. *Mailing Add:* 2 Douglass Lane St Louis MO 63122

ELLISON, LOIS TAYLOR, b Ft Valley, Ga, Oct 28, 23; m 45; c 5. MEDICAL & HEALTH SCIENCES. *Educ:* Univ Ga, BS, 43; Med Col Ga, MD, 50. *Prof Exp:* Asst res prof physiol, 51-65, asst res prof surg, 60-65, assoc res prof physiol & surg, 65-68, assoc prof, 68-71, assoc dean curric, 74-75, PROF MED & SURG, MED COL GA, 71-, DIR CARDIOPULMONARY LAB, 56-, PROVOST, 75- *Concurrent Pos:* NIH res career develop award, 63-68. *Mem:* Am Physiol Soc; fel Col Chest Physicians; Am Thoracic Soc; Am Heart Asn; Asn Am Med Col. *Res:* Pulmonary disease; preoperative and postoperative pulmonary function; heart and lung transplantation; lung surfactant; oxygen transport. *Mailing Add:* Dept of Med & Surg Med Col of Ga Augusta GA 30902

ELLISON, MARLON L, b Woodbine, Iowa, Dec 18, 16; m 49. BOTANY. *Educ:* Iowa State Univ, BS, 40; Trinity Univ, MS, 61; Univ Kans, PhD(bot), 64. *Prof Exp:* Instr bot, Stephen F Austin State Col, 63-64; from asst prof to assoc prof, 64-68, PROF BIOL, UNIV TAMPA, 68- *Res:* Marine algae of Tampa Bay. *Mailing Add:* Dept of Biol Univ of Tampa Tampa FL 33606

ELLISON, ROBERT G, b Millen, Ga, Dec 4, 16; m 45; c 5. CARDIOVASCULAR SURGERY, THORACIC SURGERY. *Educ:* Vanderbilt Univ, AB, 39; Med Col Ga, MD, 43; Am Bd Surg, dipl; Am Bd Thoracic Surg, dipl. *Prof Exp:* From instr to assoc prof thoracic surg, 47-59, res assoc physiol & asst res prof, 53, PROF SURG, MED COL GA, 59-, CHIEF DIV THORACIC SURG, 55- *Concurrent Pos:* Mem surg study sect, NIH, 69-73 & Am Bd Thoracic Surg, 71-; consult, Crippled Children Serv, Atlanta, Vet Admin Hosp; chmn, Am Bd Thoracic Surg, 79-81. *Mem:* Am Surg Asn; Soc Univ Surgeons; fel Am Col Chest Physicians; Am Physiol Soc; Am Col Surgeons. *Mailing Add:* Div Thoracic Surg Med Col Ga Augusta GA 30902

ELLISON, ROBERT HARDY, b Temple, Tex, June 22, 50; m 72; c 3. PROCESS CHEMISTRY. *Educ:* Univ Tex, BS, 72, Northwestern Univ, PhD(chem), 76. *Prof Exp:* Fel org chem, Syntex Res, 76-77; staff chemist org chem, Gen Elec Res & Develop Ctr, 77-80; RES CHEMIST, SHELL DEVELOP CO, 80- *Mem:* Am Chem Soc. *Res:* Synthesis of natural products and compounds relating to new monomer-polymer systems; process chemistry. *Mailing Add:* Shell Develop Co PO Box 1380 Houston TX 77001

ELLISON, ROBERT L, b Williamsport, Pa, Jan 14, 30. GEOLOGY. *Educ:* Cornell Univ, AB, 52; Pa State Univ, PhD(geol), 61. *Prof Exp:* Lab asst, Pa State Univ, 55-58, instr geol, 58-59; actg asst prof geol, 59-61, asst prof, 61-67, chmn dept environ sci, 69-70 & 71-72, assoc prof geol, 67-80, ASSOC PROF ENVIRON SCI, UNIV VA, 80- *Concurrent Pos:* Ed, J Foraminiferal Res, 76-; mem, Cushman Found Foraminiferal Res. *Mem:* Geol Soc Am; Am Soc Limnol & Oceanog; Nat Asn Geol Teachers. *Res:* Distribution and ecology of Foraminifera; structure of benthic marine communities; estaurine geology and ecology. *Mailing Add:* Dept of Environ Sci Clark Hall Univ of Va Charlottesville VA 22903

ELLISON, ROSE RUTH, b New York, NY, June 5, 23; m 46; c 2. ONCOLOGY. *Educ:* Columbia Univ, BA, 43, MD, 48. *Prof Exp:* From intern to resident med, Maimonides Hosp, Brooklyn, NY, 48-50; asst, State Univ NY Downstate Med Ctr, 50-51; res fel hemat, Sloan-Kettering Inst, New York, 51-54, spec fel & asst & assoc mem, 51-62; assoc chief med A, Roswell Park Mem Inst, 62-72; from asst res prof to assoc res prof med, State Univ NY Buffalo, 64-72, from assoc prof to prof, 72-78, res prof pharmacol, Roswell Park Div, Grad Sch, 70-78; PROF MED, COL PHYSICIANS & SURGEONS, COLUMBIA UNIV, 78-, AM CANCER SOC ENID A HAUPT PROF CLIN ONCOL, 79- *Concurrent Pos:* Spec fel med, Mem Hosp, New York, 51-53; mem, Pharmacol & Exp Therapeut B Study Sect, NIH, 66-70, exec officer, Acute Leukemia Group B & chmn, Acute Leukemia Comt, 66-76, chmn chemother comt, 77-79; consult, Dept Med A & Dept Exp Therapeut, Roswell Park Mem Inst, 72-79; mem, Cancer Clin Invest Rev Comt, Nat Cancer Inst, 72-76. *Mem:* Am Soc Hemat; Am Fedn Clin Oncol Socs; Am Asn Cancer Res; Am Soc Clin Oncol (secy-treas, 70-73, pres elect, 73-74, pres, 74-75); Leukemia Soc Am (vpres med & sci affairs, 75-79). *Res:* Cancer chemotherapy and natural history of neoplastic diseases. *Mailing Add:* Col of Physicians & Surgeons 630 W 168th St New York NY 10032

ELLISON, SAMUEL PORTER, JR, b Kansas City, Mo, July 1, 14; m 40; c 3. GEOLOGY. *Educ:* Univ Kansas City, AB, 36; Univ Mo, AM, 38, PhD(geol), 40. *Prof Exp:* From instr to asst prof geol, Mo Sch Mines, 39-44; from geologist to dist geologist, Stanolind Oil & Gas Co, 44-48; prof geol sci, 48-71, chmn, Dept Geol, 52-56, actg dean, Col Arts & Sci, 70-71, dean, Col Natural Sci, 71-73, Deussen prof energy resources in geol sci, 73-79, EMER PROF, UNIV TEX, AUSTIN, 79- *Concurrent Pos:* Asst geologist, US Geol Surv, 42-44; consult, Humble Oil & Refining Co, 58-71, Repub Gypsum Co, 78-81, Alpine Resources Ltd, 80-81, Ashton Resources Co, 81 & Dresser Industs, 81; Fulbright sr res fel, Ger, 70. *Honors & Awards:* Conodont Res Medal Award, C H Pander Soc & Distinguished Serv Award, Am Asn Petrol Geologists, 77. *Mem:* Am Inst Prof Geologists; Soc Petrol Engrs; Am Asn Petrol Geologists (vpres, 72-73); hon mem Soc Econ Paleont & Mineral (secy-treas, 53-58, pres, 59-60); Nat Asn Geol Teachers (vpres, 63-64, pres, 64-65). *Res:* Micropaleontology; stratigraphy; petroleum geology; sedimentation; structural geology. *Mailing Add:* Dept of Geol Sci Univ of Tex Austin TX 78712

ELLISON, SOLON ARTHUR, b New York, NY, July 13, 22; m 46; c 2. MICROBIOLOGY. *Educ:* City Col New York, BS, 42; Columbia Univ, DDS, 46, PhD(microbiol), 58. *Prof Exp:* Instr microbiol, Col Physicians & Surgeons, Columbia Univ, 51-52, assoc, 52-58, asst prof, 59-62; assoc prof, Sch Dent & Oral Surg, State Univ NY Buffalo, 62-64, prof oral biol & chmn dept, 64-78; PROF MICROBIOL, COL PHYSICIANS & SURGEONS, COLUMBIA UNIV, 78-, PROF DENT, 80- *Mem:* Am Soc Microbiol; Am Asn Immunol; Int Asn Dent Res. *Res:* Dentistry; immunology; salivary physiology. *Mailing Add:* Sch of Dent & Oral Surg 630 W 168th St New York NY 10032

ELLISON, THEODORE, b Milwaukee, Wis, July 15, 30; m 53; c 3. TOXICOLOGY. *Educ:* Univ Wis, BS, 52, MS, 56, PhD(biochem, pharmacol), 59; Iona Col, MBA, 75. *Prof Exp:* Asst vet sci, Univ Wis, 52-59, sr res biochemist, Smith Kline & French Labs, 59-65; sr biochemist & head drug metab group, Riker Labs, 65, leader pharmacokinetics group, 65-69, sect head pharmacokinetics, 69-71; head bioavailability sect, Vick Divs Res, 71-74; biomed specialist, Gen Foods Corp, 74-76; sr toxicologist, Mobil Oil Corp, 76-79; PRES, T ELLISON ASSOC, INC, 79- *Concurrent Pos:* Assoc prof pharmacol, NY Med Col, 75- & assoc prof toxicol, Drexel Univ, 81- *Mem:* Am Chem Soc; NY Acad Sci; Am Pharmaceut Asn; Am Soc Pharmacol & Exp Therapeut; Soc Toxicol. *Res:* Drug metabolism; radioisotopes; pharmacokinetics; biopharmaceutics; bioanalytical research; biochemical pharmacology; bioavailability; toxicology of industrial chemicals. *Mailing Add:* 1216 Yardley Rd Yardley PA 19067

ELLISON, WILLIAM THEODORE, b Wilmington, NC, Nov 30, 41; m 68; c 2. UNDERWATER ACOUSTICS, NAVAL ARCHITECTURE. *Educ:* US Naval Acad, BS, 63; Mass Inst Technol, MS & NavEng, 68, PhD(acoust), 70. *Prof Exp:* Dep proj mgr & tech dir, AN/SQS-26 Sonar Proj, US Navy, 70-72, exec asst to comdr, Naval Sea Systs Command, 72-73, asst qual assurance officer to supvr of shipbldg, Groton, Conn, 73-74; scientist, 74-76, V PRES & SR SCIENTIST, CAMBRIDGE ACOUST ASSOCS, INC, 76- *Mem:* Acoust Soc Am. *Res:* Underwater acoustics, particularly detection and localization of objects; bioacoustics, spectral analysis of marine mammal vocalizations; arctic underwater acoustics and ice dynamic modeling. *Mailing Add:* Cambridge Acoust Assocs Inc 53 Rindge Ave Ext Cambridge MA 02140

ELLISTON, JOHN E, b Palmerton, Pa, Feb 10, 44; m 68; c 1. PLANT PATHOLOGY. *Educ:* Muhlenberg Col, BS, 67; Purdue Univ, PhD(plant pathol), 75. *Prof Exp:* Anal chemist, Shell Chem Co, 67-69; asst, Purdue Univ, 69-75; ASST PLANT PATHOLOGIST, CONN AGR EXP STA, 75- *Mem:* Am Pathol Soc; AAAS. *Res:* Hypovirulence agents for the biological control of chestnut blight. *Mailing Add:* Dept Plant Pathol & Bot Conn Agr Exp Sta PO Box 1106 New Haven CT 06504

ELLMAN, GEORGE LEON, b Chicago, Ill, Dec 27, 23; m 48; c 1. BIOCHEMISTRY. *Educ:* Univ Ill, BS, 48; State Col Wash, MS, 49; Calif Inst Technol, PhD(chem), 52. *Prof Exp:* Res biochemist, Dow Chem Co, 52-59; chief res biochemist, Langley-Porter Inst, San Francisco, 59-74; ASSOC PROF BIOCHEM, DEPT PSYCHIAT, UNIV CALIF, SAN FRANCISCO, 74-; MEM STAFF, BRAIN BEHAV RES CTR, SONOMA STATE HOSP, ELDRIDGE, 80- *Concurrent Pos:* Res assoc pharmacol & psychiat & lectr biochem, Med Ctr, Univ Calif, 59. *Mem:* Soc Pharmacol & Exp Therapeut. *Res:* Drug action; cell growth; methodology. *Mailing Add:* Brain Behav Res Ctr Sonoma State Hosp Eldridge CA 95431

ELLNER, PAUL DANIEL, b New York, NY, May 2, 25; m 48, 65; c 3. MEDICAL MICROBIOLOGY. *Educ:* Long Island Univ, BS, 49; Univ Southern Calif, MS, 52; Univ Md, PhD(microbiol), 56; Am Bd Med Microbiol, dipl. *Prof Exp:* Res bacteriologist, Elenite Prod, Inc, 47-48; res bacteriologist, Foster D Snell, Inc, 52; asst, Mt Sinai Hosp, 53; asst, Univ Ind, 53-54; instr microbiol, Col Med, Univ Fla, 56-60; asst prof, Col Med, Univ Vt, 60-63; from asst prof to assoc prof, 63-66, staff microbiologist, Presby Hosp, 63-70, PROF MICROBIOL & PATH, COL PHYSICIANS & SURGEONS, COLUMBIA UNIV, 70-, DIR CLIN MICROBIOL SERV, PRESBY HOSP, 70- *Mem:* Am Soc Microbiol; fel Am Acad Microbiol; Acad Clin Lab Physicians & Scientists. *Res:* Clinical bacteriology; infectious diseases; clostridia. *Mailing Add:* Columbia-Presby Med Ctr 622 W 168th St New York NY 10032

ELLS, CHARLES EDWARD, b Canard, NS, Jan 20, 23; m 62; c 2. PHYSICAL METALLURGY. *Educ:* Univ Toronto, BASc, 50, MA, 51; Univ Birmingham, PhD(metall), 57. *Prof Exp:* Res officer metall, Can Dept Mines & Tech Survs, 51-53; engr, Westinghouse Elec Corp, Can, 56-57; RES OFFICER METALL, ATOMIC ENERGY CAN LTD, 57- *Mem:* Am Soc Metals. *Res:* Gases in metals; beryllium metallurgy; metallurgy of zirconium alloys. *Mailing Add:* Atomic Energy of Can Ltd Chalk River Can

ELLS, FREDERICK RICHARD, b Norwalk, Conn, Apr 3, 34; m 68. POLYMER CHEMISTRY. *Educ:* Lehigh Univ, BS, 56; Univ Akron, MS, 60, PhD(polymer chem), 63. *Prof Exp:* Res chemist polymers, Firestone Tire & Rubber Co, 56-58; sr res chemist, Chem Div, PPG Industs, 63-67 & J T Baker Chem Co, Richardson-Merrell, 67-68; develop scientist, B F Goodrich Chem Co, 68-75; SR POLYMER CHEMIST, TREMCO, INC, 76- *Mem:* Am Chem Soc. *Res:* Synthesis, mechanism and kinetics of polymers made by anionic, free radical and Ziegler-Natta polymerizations. *Mailing Add:* Tremco Inc 10701 Shaker Blvd Cleveland OH 44104

ELLS, JAMES E, b Cambridge, Mass, June 15, 31; m 58; c 1. HORTICULTURE. *Educ:* Univ Mass, BS, 57; Mich State Univ, MS, 58, PhD(hort), 61. *Prof Exp:* Asst prof, 61-69, ASSOC PROF HORT, EXP STA, COLO STATE UNIV, 69-, PROCESSING CROPS SPECIALIST, EXTEN SERV, 61- *Res:* Culture and processing of horticultural crops. *Mailing Add:* Dept of Hort Colo State Univ Ft Collins CO 80521

ELLS, VICTOR RAYMOND, b Benton Harbor, Mich, Dec 7, 14. PHYSICAL CHEMISTRY. *Educ:* Kalamazoo Col, AB, 35; Brown Univ, MS, 38; Univ Rochester, PhD(phys chem, photochem), 39. *Prof Exp:* Instr chem & spectros, Univ Mo, 39-43; res phys chemist, Method Develop Res Norwich Pharmacol Co, Eaton Labs Div, 43-53, head, Phys & Anal Res Lab, 53-61, sr phys anal chemist, 61-77; RETIRED. *Mem:* AAAS; Am Phys Soc; Optical Soc; Am Chem Soc; Coblentz Soc. *Res:* Spectrographic analysis; spectrophotometry and absorption spectra; photochemistry; application of physical chemical methods to drug development, characterization and analysis. *Mailing Add:* 119 S Broad St Norwich NY 13815

ELLSON, ROBERT A, b New York, NY, Dec 15, 34; m 58; c 3. MECHANICAL ENGINEERING. *Educ:* City Col New York, BS, 57; Univ Rochester, MS, 63, PhD(mech eng), 66. *Prof Exp:* Mech engr, Gen Elec Co, NY, 57-58; jr engr, New York Authority, 58-59; instr mech eng, Univ Rochester, 59-64; engr, NASA, Lewis Res Ctr, ASSOC PROF MECH ENG, ROCHESTER INST TECHNOL, 68- *Honors & Awards:* Dow Chem Co Award, 70; Award, Am Soc Eng Educ, 70; Centennial Medallion, Am Soc Mech Engrs, 80. *Mem:* Am Soc Mech Engrs; Am Soc Eng Educ. *Res:* Educational television; computer assisted instruction; engineering mechanics and thermodynamics. *Mailing Add:* Dept of Mech Eng One Lomb Memorial Dr Rochester NY 14623

ELLSTRAND, NORMAN CARL, b Elmhurst, Ill, Jan 1, 52. EVOLUTIONARY ECOLOGY, POPULATION GENETICS. *Educ:* Univ Ill, Urbana, BS, 74; Univ Tex, Austin, PhD(biol), 78. *Prof Exp:* Res assoc, Duke Univ, 78-79; ASST PROF PLANT ECOL, UNIV CALIF, RIVERSIDE, 79- *Mem:* Soc Study Evolution; Ecol Soc Am; Am Soc Plant Toxonomists; Genetic Soc Am; Int Soc Plant Pop Biologists. *Res:* Evolutionary genetics; plant breeding systems; effects of population structure; adaptive significance of sexual reproduction. *Mailing Add:* Bot & Plant Sci Univ Calif Riverside CA 92521

ELLSWORTH, LOUIS DANIEL, b Hamler, Ohio, Apr 27, 17; m 41; c 2. PHYSICS. *Educ:* Case Inst Technol, BS, 37; Ohio State Univ, MSc, 38, PhD(physics), 41. *Prof Exp:* Asst physics, Ohio State Univ, 37-40; instr, Haverford Col, 41-42; staff mem nat defense res comt, Radiation Lab, Mass Inst Technol, 42-45; assoc prof, 45-58, PROF PHYSICS, KANS STATE UNIV, 58- *Concurrent Pos:* Res physicist, Rauland Corp, Ill, 45-46. *Mem:* Am Phys Soc; Am Asn Physics Teachers. *Res:* X-ray diffraction analysis; mutations in bacteria by x-rays; electronics; nuclear reactor instrumentation; low energy nuclear physics; interactions of medium energy charged particles with matter. *Mailing Add:* Dept of Physics Kans State Univ Manhattan KS 66502

ELLSWORTH, ROBERT KING, b Plattsburgh, NY, Nov 22, 41; m 63; c 2. PLANT BIOCHEMISTRY. *Educ:* State Univ NY Col Plattsburgh, BS, 63, MS, 66; Iowa State Univ, PhD(biochem), 68. *Prof Exp:* Teacher, Lake Placid Cent Sch, NY, 63-64 & Beekmantown Cent Sch, 64-65; instr chem, State Univ NY Col Plattsburgh, 65-66; from asst prof to assoc prof, 68-73, PROF BIOCHEM, STATE UNIV NY COL PLATTSBURGH, 73- *Mem:* Am Soc Biol Chemists; AAAS; Am Chem Soc; Am Soc Plant Physiol. *Res:* Chlorophyll biosynthesis and enzymology; chloroplast physiology; analytical biochemistry; radio biochemical techniques. *Mailing Add:* Dept Chem State Univ NY Col Plattsburgh NY 12901

ELLSWORTH, ROBERT LOVELL, b Mesa, Ariz, May 8, 30; m 53; c 4. PLANT BREEDING. *Educ:* Ariz State Univ, BS, 58; Kans State Univ, MS, 60; Univ Wis, PhD(plant breeding), 71. *Prof Exp:* Res asst agron, Kans State Univ, 58-60; agronomist plant breeding, Frontier Hybrids, Inc, 60-66; corn breeder, L Teweles Seed Co, 66-72; sorghum breeder, 72-74, RES DIR PLANT BREEDING, RING AROUND PROD, INC, 74- *Mem:* Am Soc Agron; Crop Sci Soc. *Res:* Development of superior breeding multiple eared lines in corn; development of superior insect and disease resistance in sorghum. *Mailing Add:* 1401 Zephyr Plainview TX 79072

ELLWEIN, LEON BURNELL, b Roscoe, SDak, Dec 21, 42; m 65; c 2. OPERATIONS RESEARCH, INDUSTRIAL ENGINEERING. *Educ:* SDak State Univ, BSME, 64, MS, 66; Stanford Univ, PhD(opers res & indust eng), 70. *Prof Exp:* Assoc engr design, Int Bus Mach Corp, 64-65; mech engr, NIH, 66-67, systs anal officer planning, Nat Cancer Inst, 70-72; SR SCIENTIST APPL RES, SCI APPLN, INC, 72- *Concurrent Pos:* Rev comt mem, Diag Res Adv Group, Nat Cancer Inst, 72-74; consult, Nat Bladder Cancer Proj, 73-; working cadre mem, Nat Pancreatic Cancer Proj, 74; consult, Bur Drugs, Food Drug Admin, 74-76 & Sch Pub Health, Univ Calif, Los Angeles, 75-77. *Mem:* Opers Res Soc Am; AAAS; Am Inst Indust Engrs; The Inst Mgt Sci. *Res:* Application of quantitative methodology to management and decision making under uncertainty, operations and process modeling, and risk and cost-benefit assessments. *Mailing Add:* 2521 Ardath Ct La Jolla CA 92037

ELLWOOD, BROOKS B, US citizen; c 3. PALEOMAGNETISM. *Educ:* Fla State Univ, BS, 70; Grad Sch, Univ RI, MS, 74, PhD(oceanog), 76. *Prof Exp:* Res assoc, Ohio State Univ, 76-77; asst prof, 77-80, ASSOC PROF GEOPHYS, UNIV GA, 80- *Res:* Paleomagnetism of igneous, metamorphic, and sedimentary (including deep-sea sediments) rocks. *Mailing Add:* Dept Geol Univ Ga Athens GA 30602

ELLWOOD, ERIC LOUIS, b Melbourne, Australia, Sept 8, 22; US citizen; m 47; c 3. FOREST PRODUCTS. *Educ:* Univ Melbourne, BSc, 44, MSc, 51; Yale Univ, PhD(wood technol), 53. *Prof Exp:* Asst forester, Victorian Forests Comn, Australia, 45-47; res officer wood technol, Commonwealth Sci & Indust Res Orgn, 47-51, prin res officer, 53-57; wood technologist & lectr, Forest Prod Lab, Univ Calif, 57-61; prof wood & paper sci & head dept, 61-71, DEAN SCH FOREST RESOURCES, NC STATE UNIV, 71-, PROF WOOD & PAPER SCI, 80- *Mem:* Forest Prod Res Soc; fel Tech Asn Pulp & Paper Indust; Soc Wood Sci & Technol (pres, 65-66); Australian Inst Foresters (secy-treas, 46); Int Acad Wood Sci. *Res:* Wood physics, especially wood-fluid relations and its application to drying and treating processes; relation between anatomy, wood and fiber properties. *Mailing Add:* Sch of Forest Resources NC State Univ Raleigh NC 27650

ELLWOOD, PAUL M, JR, b San Francisco, Calif, July 16, 26; m 49; c 3. REHABILITATION MEDICINE. *Educ:* Stanford Univ, BA, 49, MD, 53. *Prof Exp:* Dir inpatient serv, Elizabeth Kenny Inst, 53-58, med adminr, Kenny Rehab Inst, 58-62, exec dir, Am Rehab Found, 63-73, PRES, INTERSTUDY, 73- *Concurrent Pos:* Fel pediat, Univ Minn, 53-55, fel neurol, 55-57; consult, Arg Ministry Pub Health, 56 & US Dept State Int Coop Admin, Nicaragua, 58; clin assoc prof neurol & pediat, Univ Minn, 58-, clin prof phys med & rehab, 62-; pres, mem bd dirs & res comt, Asn Rehab Ctrs, 60-62; mem, Surgeon Gen Nat Adv Health Serv Coun, 66; mem sci & prof adv bd, Nat Ctr Health Serv Res & Develop, 68-69; consult, Off Asst Secy Health & Sci Affairs, Dept Health, Educ & Welfare, 69, consult, Off Secy, 69; mem bd dirs, Nat Health Coun, 71-76. *Honors & Awards:* Award, Arg Ministry Pub Health, 57 & Am Acad Neurol, 58; Cert Merit, AMA, 59; President's Citation, President's Comt Employment Handicapped, 62. *Res:* Human resources policy research; health services research; pediatric neurology. *Mailing Add:* InterStudy PO Box S Excelsior MN 55331

ELLYIN, FERNAND, b Urmia, Azerbaijan, Iran, Aug 27, 38; Can citizen; m 66; c 2. STRUCTURAL & SOLID MECHANICS. *Educ:* Univ Tehran, MSc, 62; Univ Waterloo, PhD(civil eng), 66. *Prof Exp:* Engr, Beta Co, Iran, 62-63; res asst civil eng, Univ Waterloo, 63-66; asst prof, 66-69, assoc prof civil eng, 69-73, head struct & solid mech sect, 70-81, PROF CIVIL ENG, UNIV SHERBROOKE, 73- *Concurrent Pos:* Sr res officer, Dept Eng, Oxford Univ, 68-69; vis Div Theoret Studies & Res, Ctr Exp Res Bldg & Pub Works, Paris, France, 69; proj dir, subcomt reinforced openings & external loads, Pressure Vessel Res Comt, New York, 66-76; consult, Ingersoll Rand Co, S W Hooper & Co, Unit Cast Div, Mildland-Ross Can, Lynn & MacLoad Metall; vis prof, Carleton Univ, 77-78; spec consult, Atomic Energy Control Bd, 77-78. *Mem:* Am Soc Civil Engrs; Can Standards Asn; Am Soc Mech Engrs; Eng Inst Can; Am Acad Mech. *Res:* Stress analysis and design of pressure vessels and piping systems; inelastic material behaviour under multiaxial states of stress; stress concentration in plates and shells; reliability of structures and mechanical systems; low cycle fatigue and fracture; dynamic response of mechanical systems including interaction effects; developing models to predict material response under multiaxial states of stress and varying environments. *Mailing Add:* Dept Mech Eng Univ Alberta Edmonton AB T6G 2G8 Can

ELLZEY, JOANNE TONTZ, b Baltimore, Md, Mar 23, 37; m 69. MYCOLOGY, ULTRASTRUCTURE. *Educ:* Randolph-Macon Woman's Col, BA, 59; Univ NC, Chapel Hill, MA, 63; Univ Tex, Austin, PhD(bot), 69. *Prof Exp:* From teaching asst to instr biol, Univ NC, Greensboro, 62-64; asst prof, 69-75, ASSOC PROF BIOL, UNIV TEX, EL PASO, 75-, DIR ULTRASTRUCT LAB, 73- *Mem:* AAAS; Mycol Soc Am; Electronic Micros Soc Am; Am Soc Microbiol; Sigma Xi. *Res:* Utilization of electron microscopy and cytochemistry to study the ultrastructure of gametogenesis and cell wall formation in saprolegniaceous fungi; ultrastructure of diabetic mice and the chestnut blight fungus, endothia parasitica. *Mailing Add:* Dept of Biol Sci Univ of Tex El Paso TX 79968

ELLZEY, MARION LAWRENCE, JR, b Shattuck, Okla, Apr 13, 39; m 69. CHEMISTRY, QUANTUM CHEMISTRY. *Educ:* Rice Univ, BA, 61; Univ Tex, Austin, PhD(physics), 66. *Prof Exp:* R A Welch fel, Univ Tex, Austin, 66-68; asst prof chem, 68-74, chmn fac senate, 79-81, ASSOC PROF CHEM, UNIV TEX, EL PASO, 74- *Concurrent Pos:* Robert A Welch Found grant, Tex, 71-79. *Mem:* Am Phys Soc; Am Chem Soc; Sigma Xi. *Res:* Molecular quantum mechanics with emphasis on complexed transition metal ions and their electronic and magnetic properties; group theory and linear algebra; graph theory applications on chemistry. *Mailing Add:* Dept Chem Univ Tex El Paso TX 79968

ELLZEY, SAMUEL EDWARD, JR, b Mobile, Ala, May 16, 31; m 60; c 3. ORGANIC CHEMISTRY. *Educ:* Spring Hill Col, BS, 54; Tulane Univ, MS, 57, PhD(chem), 59. *Prof Exp:* CHEMIST, SOUTHERN REGIONAL RES CTR, USDA, 59- *Mem:* Am Chem Soc. *Res:* Organic fluorine compounds; chemical modification of cotton; nuclear magnetic resonance; fire-retardant textiles; phosphorus compounds; natural products. *Mailing Add:* 6335 Dwyer Rd New Orleans LA 70126

ELMADJIAN, FRED, b Aleppo, Syria, Oct 5, 15; US nat; m 52. PHYSIOLOGY. *Educ:* Mass Col Pharm, BS, 40, MS, 42; Clark Univ, MA, 47; Tufts Col, PhD(physiol), 49. *Prof Exp:* Staff mem, Worcester Found, 44-62, sr scientist, 55-62, res assoc, Worcester State Hosp, 47-58, dir biol res, 58-62, dir labs, 55-62; chief biol sci sect, Training & Manpower Resources Br, 62-66, chief biol sci sect, Behav Sci Training Br, NIMH, 66-75, ASSOC DIR RES TRAINING, DIV MANPOWER & TRAINING PROGS, NAT INST MENT HEALTH, ALCOHOL, DRUG ABUSE & MENT HEALTH ADMIN, DHEW, 75- *Concurrent Pos:* Asst chemist, Mass State Dept Ment Health, 45; physiologist, Mem Found Neuro-Endocrine Res, 46; res assoc, Med Sch, Tufts Col, 50-51; prof lectr & res assoc, Mass Col Pharm, 50-53; physiologist, field sta, NIMH, Mass, 51-53; neurophysiologist, Mass State Dept Ment Health, 57-62; mem revision comt, US Pharmacopoeia, 55-60; consult, opers res off, Johns Hopkins Univ, 52-61, dept psychiat, New Eng Med Ctr, 59-62 & Worcester Found, 62-63. *Mem:* AAAS; Am Physiol Soc; Am Pharmaceut Asn; Endocrine Soc; NY Acad Sci. *Res:* Stress physiology; adrenal cortical physiology; adrenal medulla; adrenaline and nonadrenaline, in normal and mental diseases. *Mailing Add:* Rm 8-101 5600 Fishers Lane Rockville MD 20857

ELMAGHRABY, SALAH ELDIN, b Fayoum, Egypt, Oct 21, 27; US citizen; m 64; c 3. OPERATIONS RESEARCH, SYSTEMS ENGINEERING. *Educ:* Cairo Univ, BSc, 48; Ohio State Univ, MSc, 55; Cornell Univ, PhD(indust eng), 58. *Prof Exp:* Tutor mech eng, Sch Eng, Cairo, Egypt, 49; engr, Foreign Inspection Off Egyptian State Rwys, London, Brussels & Budapest, 48-54; res asst opers res, Cornell Univ, 55-58; res leader systs anal, Western Elec Co Res Ctr, Princeton, NJ, 58-62; assoc prof opers res, Yale Univ, 62-67; PROF OPERS RES & INDUST ENG & DIR OPERS RES PROG, NC STATE UNIV, 67- *Honors & Awards:* Distinquished Res Award, Am Inst Indust Engrs, 70; Res Div Award, Am Inst Indust Engrs, 80. *Mem:* Opers Res Soc Am; Inst Mgt Sci; Am Inst Indust Engrs. *Res:* Activity networks, scheduling theory, production control and operations research applications in optimal design of energy systems. *Mailing Add:* NC State Univ PO Box 5511 Raleigh NC 27650

EL-MASRY, EZZ ISMAIL, b Alexandria, Egypt; Can citizen. CIRCUIT THEORY & DESIGN. *Educ:* Univ Alexandria, BSc, 67, MSc, 72; Univ Man, PhD(elec eng), 77. *Prof Exp:* Instr & res engr elec eng, Univ Alexandria, 67-72; res & teaching asst, Univ Man, 72-77; res assoc, Nat Res Coun Can, 78; ASST PROF ELEC ENG, ELEC ENG DEPT & RES ASST PROF, COORD SCI LAB, UNIV ILL, URBANA-CHAMPAIGN, 78- *Mem:* Inst Elec & Electronics Engrs; Asn Prof Engrs. *Res:* Analytical and computer aided design of low-sensitivity structures for analog (active), digital and switched-capacitor filters; stastical analysis of the phase-locked loop. *Mailing Add:* 2103 Winchester Dr Champaign IL 61820

ELMEGREEN, BRUCE GORDON, b Milwaukee, Wis, Feb 24, 50; m 76. ASTROPHYSICS. *Educ:* Univ Wis-Madison, BS, 71; Princeton Univ, PhD(astrophys), 75. *Prof Exp:* Jr fel astrophys, Harvard Soc Fels, 75-78; ASST PROF ASTROPHYS, COLUMBIA UNIV, 78- *Concurrent Pos:* Vis prof, Univ Calif, Berkeley, 81, Univ Sussex, Eng, 81 & Inst Astron, Cambridge, Eng, 81. *Mem:* Am Astron Soc; Int Astron Union. *Res:* Study of the interstellar gaseous medium, with application to the formation and structure of star-forming clouds and to large scale properties of spiral galaxies. *Mailing Add:* Dept of Astron Pupin Lab Columbia Univ New York NY 10027

ELMEGREEN, DEBRA MELOY, b South Bend, Ind, Nov 23, 52; m 76. ASTRONOMY. *Educ:* Princeton Univ, AB, 75; Harvard Univ, AM, 77, PhD(astron), 79. *Prof Exp:* Res asst, Thermophysics Div, Goddard Space Flight Ctr, 69, Lab Cosmic Ray Physics, Naval Res Lab, 71-72, Spectros Div, Nat Bur Standards, 73, Kitt Peak Nat Observ, 74, Arecibo Observ, 75; teaching fel, Harvard Univ, 77; Carnegie fel, Mt Wilson & Las Campanas Observ, 79-81; vis astronomer, Royal Greenwich Observ & Inst Astron, Cambridge Univ, Eng, 81; VIS SCIENTIST, T J WATSON RES CTR, IBM CORP, 82- *Mem:* Am Astron Soc; Sigma Xi; Royal Astron Soc; Int Astron Union. *Res:* optical and millimeter observations of external galaxies to study sites of star formation and the orgins of spiral structure. *Mailing Add:* IBM T J Watson Res Ctr PO Box 218 Yorktown Heights NY 10598

ELMENDORF, CHARLES HALSEY, III, b Los Angeles, Calif, July 1, 13; m 45; c 7. ELECTRICAL ENGINEERING. *Educ:* Calif Inst Technol, BS, 35, MS, 36. *Prof Exp:* Mem staff, Bell Tel Labs, 36-55, asst dir, Submarine Cable Systs Dept, Am Tel & Tel Co, 55-59, dir, 59-61, assoc exec domestic systs, Mass, 61-66, asst vpres eng dept, 66-78; RETIRED. *Mem:* Nat Acad Eng; fel Inst Elec & Electronics Engrs. *Mailing Add:* 34 Cross Gate Rd Madison NJ 07940

ELMER, OTTO CHARLES, b Vienna, Austria, Jan 8, 18; nat US; m 45; c 7. ORGANIC CHEMISTRY. *Educ:* Bluffton Col, BA, 43; Univ Minn, PhD(org chem), 48. *Prof Exp:* Asst, Carleton Col, 43-44; asst, Univ Minn, 44-45 & 46-48; chemist, Tex Co, 48-53; chemist, 53-71, group leader, 71-79, RES SCIENTIST, GEN TIRE & RUBBER CO, 79- *Concurrent Pos:* Chemist, Rubber Reserve Co, 44-45, asst scientist, 46. *Mem:* Am Chem Soc; Am Inst Chemists. *Res:* Synthetic glycerides; autoxidation; reaction mechanisms; heterocycles; synthetic lubricants; lubricant additives; polymer chemistry; urethane elastomers and coatings; tire cord adhesives. *Mailing Add:* 720 Hillsdale Ave Akron OH 44303

ELMER, WILLIAM ARTHUR, b Bridgeton, NJ, May 12, 38; m 62; c 2. DEVELOPMENTAL GENETICS. *Educ:* Susquehanna Univ, AB, 60; NMex Highlands Univ, MS, 63; Univ Conn, PhD, 67. *Prof Exp:* Fel biol, Oak Ridge Nat Lab, 67-69; asst prof, 69-75, ASSOC PROF BIOL, EMORY UNIV, 75- *Concurrent Pos:* vis prof, Univ Glasgow, 79; Minna-James Heineman fel, NATO, 79. *Mem:* AAAS; Teratology Soc; Am Soc Zoologists; Int Soc Develop Biol. *Res:* Genetic control of limb development; molecular aspects of hereditary skeletal anomalies; in vitro growth of genetically abnormal chondrocytes. *Mailing Add:* Dept Biol Emory Univ Atlanta GA 30322

ELMES, GREGORY ARTHUR, b Shoreham, Sussex, Eng, Apr 26, 50. QUANTITATIVE SPATIAL ANALYSIS. *Educ:* Univ Newcastle Upon Tyre, BSc, 68; Pa State Univ, MS, 74, PhD(geog), 79. *Prof Exp:* ASST PROF GEOG, WVA UNIV & RES ASSOC, REGIONAL RES INST, 78- *Mem:* Asn Am Geographers; AAAS. *Res:* Energy and transportation modeling; investigation of fly ash as a source of strategic minerals from location and economic perspectives; analysis of United States transportation trends. *Mailing Add:* Regional Res Inst WVa Univ Morgantown WV 26506

ELMORE, CARROLL DENNIS, b Pheba, Miss, Apr 3, 40; m 77. PLANT PHYSIOLOGY. *Educ:* Miss State Univ, BS, 62; Univ Ariz, MS, 66; Univ Ill, PhD(agron), 70. *Prof Exp:* PLANT PHYSIOLOGIST, DELTA STATES AGR RES CTR, USDA, 70- *Mem:* Am Soc Agron; Crop Sci Soc Am; AAAS; Am Inst Biol Sci; Am Soc Plant Physiol. *Res:* Adequacy of carbohydrate and mineral reserves for the developing cotton fruit; translocation patterns of reserve nutrients; genetic aspects of fruiting, fruit retention and fruit development in the cotton plant. *Mailing Add:* Cotton Physiol Lab Agr Res USDA PO Box 225 Stoneville MS 38776

ELMORE, DAVID, b Los Alamos, NMex, Dec 19, 45; m 68; c 2. SOLAR VARIABILITY. *Educ:* Case Inst Technol, BS, 68; Univ Rochester, PhD(physics), 74. *Prof Exp:* Res assoc, 74-80, SR RES ASSOC, NUCLEAR STRUCTURE RES LAB, UNIV ROCHESTER, 80- *Mem:* Am Phys Soc. *Res:* Measure and interpret very low concentration of long lived radioisotopes in natural samples using the new technique of tandem accelerator mass spectrometry. *Mailing Add:* Nuclear Structure Res Lab Univ Rochester Rochester NY 14627

ELMORE, GLENN VAN NESS, b Topeka, Kans, Apr 2, 16; m 48; c 1. ELECTROCHEMISTRY. *Educ:* Washburn Univ, BS, 38; Ga Inst Technol, MS, 40. *Prof Exp:* Instr chem, Ga Inst Technol, 40-41; res chemist, Tenn Valley Auth, 41-47; res chemist, Oak Ridge Nat Labs, 47-48; res chemist, Tenn Valley Auth, 48-53; electrochemist, Kettering Found, 53-62; ELECTROCHEMIST, SYSTS PROD DIV, IBM CORP, 62- *Mem:* Am Chem Soc; Electrochem Soc. *Res:* Chemistry of phosphorus nitrides; radiation chemistry of decomposition of water; endothermic photochemical reactions; electrodeposition; fuel cells; adhesion of electroless metals. *Mailing Add:* 3133 Briarcliff Ave Vestal NY 13850

ELMORE, JAMES LEWIS, b Chattanooga, Tenn, May 28, 48; m 72. AQUATIC ECOLOGY. *Educ:* Univ Tenn at Chattanooga, BA, 71, Knoxville, MS, 73; Univ SFla, PhD(biol), 80. *Prof Exp:* Teaching asst limnol & gen biol, Univ Tenn, 71-73; teaching asst ecol, sex & reproduction, Univ SFla, 74-76; RES ASSOC, ENVIRON SCI DIV, OAK RIDGE NAT LAB, 80- *Concurrent Pos:* Consult, Biol Res Assoc, 74-80, Dames & Moore, 79; prin investr, Dept Health & Rehab Serv, State Fla, 79-80. *Mem:* Am Soc Limnol & Oceanog; Soc Int Limnol; Sigma Xi; Ecol Soc Am. *Res:* Factors regulating distributions of freshwater copepods of the genus Diaptomus; longterm changes in zooplankton community composition; effects of synthetic oils on zooplankton communities in experimental ponds; environmental assessment of US Department of Energy projects. *Mailing Add:* Environ Sci Div Oak Ridge Nat Lab Oak Ridge TN 37830

ELMORE, JOHN JESSE, JR, b Spokane, Wash, Jan 3, 36. PHYSICAL BIOCHEMISTRY, MOLECULAR BIOLOGY. *Educ:* Reed Col, BA, 57; Hofstra Univ, MA, 67; State Univ NY Stony Brook, PhD(biochem), 72. *Prof Exp:* Res assoc, 72-74, asst scientist, 74-76, assoc scientist, 76-78, SCIENTIST, DEPT MED, BROOKHAVEN NAT LAB, 78- *Mem:* AAAS; Am Chem Soc; NY Acad Sci. *Res:* Reaction mechanisms involved in oxidative cytotoxicity and damage to biological membranes, proteins and nucleic acids and in biological actions of antioxidants, drugs, hormones and carcinogens and mutagens. *Mailing Add:* Med Dept Brookhaven Nat Lab Upton NY 11973

ELMORE, STANLEY MCDOWELL, b Raleigh, NC, Dec 17, 33; m 58; c 4. MEDICINE, ORTHOPEDIC SURGERY. *Educ:* Vanderbilt Univ, AB, 55, MD, 58; Am Bd Orthop Surg, dipl, 69. *Prof Exp:* Assoc prof orthop surg & chmn div, Med Col Va, 66-73; ATTEND ORTHOP SURGEON,

CHIPPENHAM HOSP, 73- & JOHNSTON-WILLIS HOSP, 73- *Concurrent Pos:* USPHS grant orthop surg, Sch Med, Vanderbilt Univ, 65-66; consult, McGuire Vet Admin Hosp, Richmond, Va, 66-70. *Honors & Awards:* Borden Award, 57 & 58. *Mem:* Am Acad Orthop Surg; Orthop Res Soc. *Res:* Physical properties of articular cartilage; genetics of orthopedic diseases; bone changes in renal transplant patients; total joint replacement. *Mailing Add:* Chippenham Med Bldg 7135 Jahnke Rd Richmond VA 23225

ELMS, JAMES CORNELIUS, b East Orange, NJ, May 16, 16; m 42; c 4. PHYSICS. *Educ:* Calif Inst Technol, BS, 48; Univ Calif, Los Angeles, MA, 50. *Prof Exp:* Jr stress analyst, Consol Vultee Aircraft Corp, 40-41; chief develop engr, G M Giannani Co, 48; res assoc geophys, Univ Calif, Los Angeles, 49-50; res engr electronics, NAm Aviation Corp, 50-52, proj engr electromech eng, 52, asst sect chief electronics, 53-55, mgr fire control, 55-57; mgr avionics dept, Martin Co, 57-59; vpres electronics systs, Crosley Div, AVCO Corp, 59, exec vpres, 59-60; gen opers mgr, Aeronutronic Div, Ford Motor Co, 60-63; dep dir, Manned Spacecraft Ctr, NASA, Tex, 63-64; vpres & div gen mgr, Space & Info Systs Div, Raytheon Co, Mass, 64-65; dep assoc adminr for Manned Space Flight, Hq, NASA, 65-66, dir, Electronics Res Ctr, 66-70; dir, Transp Systs Ctr, US Dept Transp, 70-74; consult govt & indust, 75-81; ADMINR, NASA, 81- *Concurrent Pos:* Mem space systs comt, Space Prog Adv Coun, NASA, 70-77; mem comt fed labs, 70-76; dep dir, Space Shuttle Oper Mgt Assessment Team, 75; consult to adminr, Energy Res & Develop Admin, 75-77. *Honors & Awards:* NASA Spec Award, 64, Except Serv Medal, 69, Outstanding Leadership Medal, 70; Secretary's Award Meritorious Serv, US Dept Transportation, 74. *Mem:* Nat Acad Eng; Am Phys Soc; assoc fel Am Inst Aeronaut & Astronaut; fel Inst Elec & Electronics Engrs. *Res:* Seismic investigation of earth's crustal structure; ordnance mechanisms; armament control; radar; missile guidance and control; spacecraft design; transportation analysis; energy policy. *Mailing Add:* 112 Kings Pl Newport Beach CA 92663

ELMSLIE, JAMES STEWART, b Quincy, Ill, Dec 30, 30; m 54; c 2. ORGANIC POLYMER CHEMISTRY. *Educ:* Grinnell Col, AB, 52; Univ Del, PhD(org chem), 59. *Prof Exp:* Anal chemist, Hercules Powder Co, 52-53 & 55, sr res chemist, Allegany Ballistics Lab, Hercules, Inc, 58-69, TECH SPECIALIST, HERCULES, INC, MAGNA, 69- *Mem:* Am Chem Soc. *Res:* Encapsulation of solid particles; new ablative insulators; new sprayable insulation material; synthesis of high energy compounds for use in solid propellants; new binders for solid propellants. *Mailing Add:* 3733 Twinbrook St Salt Lake City UT 84109

ELMSTROM, GARY WILLIAM, b Chicago, Ill, Jan 10, 39; m 67; c 3. PLANT BREEDING, PLANT NUTRITION. *Educ:* Southern Ill Univ, BS, 63, MS, 64; Univ Calif, Davis, PhD(plant physiol), 69. *Prof Exp:* From asst prof to assoc prof, 69-81, PROF HORT, UNIV FLA, 81-, CTR DIR, AGR RES CTR, 78- *Mem:* Am Soc Hort Sci; Coun Agr Sci & Technol. *Res:* Development of cultural practices including weed control, nutrition, and growth regulators to maximize cucurbit production; evaluation of cucurbit varieties; cantaloupe breeding. *Mailing Add:* Agr Res Ctr Univ of Fla Box 388 Leesburg FL 32748

EL-NEGOUMY, ABDUL MONEM, b Cairo, Egypt, May 23, 20; US citizen; m 51; c 2. AGRICULTURAL BIOCHEMISTRY. *Educ:* Cairo Univ, BS, 43; Univ Wis, MS, 48, PhD(dairy chem), 51. *Prof Exp:* Instr bot, Univ Alexandria, 43-46, from lectr to assoc prof food biochem, 51-58; res assoc & fel dairy chem, Iowa State Univ, 58-62; from asst prof to assoc prof, 62-69, PROF AGR BIOCHEM, MONT STATE UNIV, 69- *Mem:* AAAS; fel Am Inst Chemists; Am Dairy Sci Asn; Inst Food Technologists; Am Asn Cereal Chemists. *Res:* Dairy and food chemistry; autoxidation of food fats and oils; genetic variants and interactions of food proteins. *Mailing Add:* Dept of Animal & Range Sci 123B Linfield Hall Mont State Univ Bozeman MT 59715

ELOFSON, RICHARD MACLEOD, b Ponoka, Alta, June 14, 19; m 41; c 4. ORGANIC CHEMISTRY. *Educ:* Univ Alta, BSc, 41; Univ Wis, PhD(org chem), 44. *Prof Exp:* Chemist, Defence Indust, Ltd, Can, 41; res chemist, F W Horner, Ltd, 44-45, dir res, 45-46; res chemist, Gen Aniline & Film Corp, 47-49; self employed, 49-53; SR RES CHEMIST, ALTA RES COUN, 53- *Mem:* Fel Can Inst Chem; Am Chem Soc. *Res:* Polarography and oxidation reduction potentials of organic compounds; protein hydrolysates; chemistry of acetylene; coalification; electron spin resonance spectroscopy; nitrogen fixation. *Mailing Add:* Alta Res Coun 11315 87th Ave Edmonton Can

ELOWE, LOUIS N, b Baghdad, Iraq, Apr 2, 22; US citizen; m 53; c 3. PHARMACY, CHEMISTRY. *Educ:* Col Pharm & Chem, Iraq, PhC, 44; Univ Wis, MS, 52, PhD(pharm, chem), 54. *Prof Exp:* Managing dir, Eastern Wholesale Drug Store, Iraq, 46-50; asst, Univ Wis, 51-54; asst prof pharm, Univ Toronto, 54-57; assoc prof, Fordham Univ, 57-59; sr pharmaceut chemist, Schering Corp, 59; develop chemist, Lederle Labs, Am Cyanamid Co, 59-60, group leader, 60-64, mgr pharmaceut prod develop, Cyanamid Int, 64-66; mgr int res & control, Chesebrough-Pond's, Inc, 66-69, dir int res & control, 69-74; dir int res & develop, Consumer Prod, Schering-Plough Inc, 74-79; dir int regulatory affairs, G D Searle Co, 79-81; PROF, UNIV TORONTO, 81- *Mem:* Am Pharmaceut Asn; Am Chem Soc; Can Pharmaceut Asn; Soc Cosmetic Chem. *Res:* Development of analytical methods in drug analysis; development in the field of pharmaceuticals, cosmetics, consumer products, hospital supplies, agriculturals. *Mailing Add:* Faculty Pharm Univ Toronto Toronto ON M5S 2W9 Can

ELRICK, DAVID EMERSON, b Toronto, Ont, Sept 6, 31; m 58; c 4. SOIL PHYSICS. *Educ:* Ont Agr Col, BSA, 53; Univ Wis, MS, 55, PhD(soils), 57. *Prof Exp:* Asst prof physics, Ont Agr Col, 57-60; res officer, Div Plant Indust, Commonwealth Sci & Indust Res Orgn, Australia, 60-62; assoc prof, 62-65, chmn dept, 71-75, actg dean grad studies, 75-76, actg dean res, 78, PROF SOIL SCI, UNIV GUELPH, 65- *Concurrent Pos:* Sr fel, Grenoble, France, 68-69; mem hydrol subcomt, Nat Res Coun Can, 66-73. *Mem:* AAAS; Am Geophys Union; Soil Conserv Soc Am; Am Soc Agron; Agr Inst Can. *Res:* Fluid flow in unsaturated media; miscible displacement. *Mailing Add:* Dept of Land Resource Sci Univ of Guelph Guelph ON N1G 2W1 Can

ELROD, ALVON CREIGHTON, b Walhalla, SC, Dec 28, 28; m 51; c 6. MECHANICAL ENGINEERING. *Educ:* Clemson Univ, BME, 49, MME, 51; Purdue Univ, PhD(mech eng), 59. *Prof Exp:* From instr to asst prof, 53-58, ASSOC PROF MECH ENG, CLEMSON UNIV, 58- *Concurrent Pos:* NSF res grant, 60-62; Ford Found indust residency, Gen Elec Flight Propulsion Div, 67-68. *Mem:* Am Soc Mech Engrs. *Res:* Heat transfer from dissociated gases and in boiling water situations; air and water pollution. *Mailing Add:* Dept of Mech Eng Clemson Univ Clemson SC 29631

ELROD, BRYANT D(ENNIS), b Detroit, Mich, June 9, 34; m 61; c 5. ELECTRICAL ENGINEERING, ASTRONAUTICAL ENGINEERING. *Educ:* Univ Detroit, BEE, 57; Yale Univ, MEng, 59, PhD(elec eng), 62. *Prof Exp:* Fulbright fel math, Univ Gottingen, 61-62; systs scientist command & control systs, Air Force Electronic Systs Div, 62-63; asst prof elec eng, Air Force Inst Technol, 63-65; mem tech staff space technol, Bellcomm Inc, 65-72; mem tech staff, Air Transp Systs, MITRE Corp, 72-77; MEM TECH STAFF & DEPT MGR NAVIG SYSTS ANAL, STANFORD TELECOMMUN, INC, 78- *Concurrent Pos:* Consult, MB Electronics Div, Textron Inc, 62-63. *Mem:* Inst Elec & Electronics Engrs; Inst Navigation. *Res:* Air traffic control and radionavigation systems; navigation; control and guidance theory; space vehicle tracking; satellite communications. *Mailing Add:* Stanford Telecommun Inc 6888 Elm St McLean VA 22101

ELROD, HAROLD G(LENN), JR, b Manchester, NH, Nov 19, 18; m 42; c 3. ENGINEERING. *Educ:* Mass Inst Technol, BSc, 42; Harvard Univ, PhD(eng sci), 49. *Prof Exp:* Instr marine eng, US Naval Acad, 42-45; res engr refrig, Clayton & Lambert Mfg Co, 46; heat transfer & fluid flow, Babcock & Wilcox Co, 49-51; asst prof mech eng, Case Inst Technol, 51-55; from assoc prof to prof, Columbia Univ, 55-62; prof, Mich State Univ, 62-63; PROF MECH ENG, COLUMBIA UNIV, 63- *Concurrent Pos:* Vis prof, Univ Southampton England, 69-70; liaison scientist, US Off Naval Res, London, 74; vis prof, Tech Univ Denmark & Inst Nat des Sci Appl, France, 77-78. *Mem:* Am Soc Mech Engrs; Am Inst Aeronaut & Astronaut; NY Acad Sci. *Res:* Fluid mechanics; heat transfer; lubrication; kinetic theory. *Mailing Add:* Dept of Mech Eng Columbia Univ New York NY 10027

ELROD, LLOYD MELVIN, b Nebraska City, Nebr, Aug 6, 17; m 45; c 1. PHYSIOLOGY, ZOOLOGY. *Educ:* Nebr Wesleyan Univ, AB, 48; Univ Nebr, MS, 50, PhD(zool, physiol), 59. *Prof Exp:* Asst physiol, Univ Nebr, 48-52, instr physiol, 52-53; from asst prof to prof biol, Westminster Col, Mo, 53-63; res biologist path, Med Sch, Northwestern Univ, 63-67; PROF BIOL, DAVIS & ELKINS COL, 67- *Mem:* AAAS; Soc Protozool; Tissue Cult Asn; Am Inst Biol Sci; Am Soc Cell Biol. *Res:* Protozoan respiration and metabolism; metabolism and cell division in tissue culture. *Mailing Add:* Dept of Biol Davis & Elkins Col Elkins WV 26241

ELROD, MCLOWERY, b Atlanta, Ga, July 29, 38; m 69; c 2. APPLIED MATHEMATICS. *Educ:* Univ Tex, BA, 60; Univ Ga, PhD(appl math), 73. *Prof Exp:* Math analyst, Off Comput Activities, Univ Ga, 69-74; tech staff math, Anal Serv, Inc, 74-75; sr staff mem math, Appl Physics Lab, Johns Hopkins Univ, 75-77; MGR ADVAN TECHNOL ANAL GROUP, COLLINS TELECOMMUN SYSTS DIV, ROCKWELL INT, 77- *Mem:* Soc Indust & Appl Math; Inst Math Statist; AAAS; Sigma Xi; NY Acad Sci. *Res:* Development of analytic and numeric methods for the solution of stochastic differential equations, with emphasis on operators with physically realizable stochastic processes. *Mailing Add:* Collins Telecommun Systs Div 1200 N Alma Rd Richardson TX 75080

EL-SADEN, MUNIR RIDHA, b Baghdad, Iraq, Aug a 16, 28; US citizen; m 50; c 3. THERMODYNAMICS. *Educ:* Univ Denver, BSc, 51; Univ Mich, MS, 53, PhD(mech eng), 57. *Prof Exp:* Instr eng mech, Univ Mich, 55-57; unit engr, Daura Ref, Iraq, 57-58; lectr mech eng, Univ Baghdad, 58-59; asst prof, Univ Tex, 59-61; from assoc prof to prof, NC State Uni 61-66; PROF ENG, CALIF STATE UNIV, FULLERTON, 66- *Concurrent Pos:* Lectr, Ga Inst Technol, 62, E I du Pont de Nemours & Co, NC, 64 & Catholic Univ, 65; US Air Force Off Sci Res grant, 65-67. *Mem:* Am Soc Mech Engrs; Am Inst Aeronaut & Astronaut; Am Soc Eng Educ. *Res:* Heat transfer; fluid mechanics; (magneto-hydrodynamics; energy conversion; nonequilibrium thermodynamics; thermomagnetic and galvanomagnetic devices. *Mailing Add:* Div of Eng Calif State Univ 800 N State College Blvd Fullerton CA 92634

EL SAFFAR, ZUHAIR M, b Baghdad, Iraq, Sept 23, 34; m 66; c 5. CHEMICAL PHYSICS. *Educ:* Univ Wales, BS, 57, PhD(physics), 60. *Prof Exp:* Asst prof physics, Mich State Univ, 60-62; from asst prof to assoc prof, Univ Baghdad, 62-67; res assoc solid state physics, Oak Ridge Nat Lab, 65-66; res assoc chem, Johns Hopkins Univ, 67-68; from asst prof to assoc prof physics, 68-76, PROF PHYSICS, DEPAUL UNIV, 76-, CHMN DEPT, 78- *Concurrent Pos:* Consult, Argonne Nat Lab, 69. *Mem:* Am Phys Soc; Am Crystallog Asn; Brit Inst Physics & Phys Soc. *Res:* Nuclear magnetic resonance in nonmetallic solids, especially hydrocarbons, hydrates and ferroelectrics; solar energy. *Mailing Add:* Physics Dept DePaul Univ 2219 N Kenmore Chicago IL 60614

ELSAS, LOUIS JACOB, II, b Atlanta, Ga, Feb 10, 37; m 60; c 3. MEDICAL GENETICS. *Educ:* Harvard Univ, BA, 58; Univ Va, MD, 62; Am Bd Internal Med, dipl, 72. *Prof Exp:* From intern to sr resident, Yale-New Havven Hosp, 62-65; clin fel metab, Sch Med, Yale Univ, 65-66, res fel genetics, 66-68, from instr to asst prof pediat & med, 68-70; from asst prof to prof pediat & biochem, 70-77, dir, Med Sci Prog, 77-80, DIR, GENETICS DIV, SCH MED, EMORY UNIV, 70-; DIR, COMPREHENSIVE GENETIC SYST, STATE OF GA, 74- *Concurrent Pos:* Res career develop award, Nat Inst Child Health & Develop, 73-78; consult, Ga Dept Human Resources, 74-; dir, Tay Sachs Dis Prev Prog, 75-; vis res prof, Japan Soc Prom Sci, 76-77. *Honors & Awards:* John Horsely Mem Award, Sch Med, Univ Va, 72. *Mem:* Sigma Xi; Am Fedn Clin Res; Am Soc Human Genetics; Soc Pediat Res; Endocrine Soc. *Res:* Genetic, biochemical and developmental control of aminoacids and hexose transport by plasma membrane; genetic control of human enzyme complexes and the mechanism of action of active co-factors. *Mailing Add:* Div Med Genetics Box 23344 Sch Med Emory Univ Atlanta GA 30322

ELSASSER, WALTER M, b Mannheim, Ger, Mar 20, 04; nat US; m 37, 64; c 2. PHYSICS, GEOPHYSICS. *Educ:* Univ Gottingen, PhD(physics), 27. *Prof Exp:* Asst, Tech Univ, Berlin, 28-30; instr physics, Univ Frankfurt, 30-33; res fel, Inst Henri Poincare, Sorbonne, 33-36; asst meteorol, Calif Inst Technol, 36-41; res assoc, Blue Hill Meteorol Observ, Harvard Univ, 41-42; war res, Signal Corps Labs, 42-44; mem radio wave propagation comt, Nat Defense Res Comt, 44-45; indust res on electronics labs, Radio Corp of Am, NJ, 45-47; assoc prof physics, Univ Pa, 47-50; prof, Univ Utah, 50-56 & Univ Calif, San Diego, 56-62; prof geophys, Princeton Univ, 62-68; res prof geophys, Inst Fluid Dynamics & Appl Math, Univ Md, College Park, 68-74; ADJ PRO GEOPHYS, JOHNS HOPKINS UNIV, 75- *Concurrent Pos:* Lectr, Sorbonne, 35 & 36; lectr, Mass Inst Technol, 38; actg head dept physics, Univ NMex, 60-61. *Honors & Awards:* German Phys Soc Prize, 32; Bowie Medal, Am Geophys Union, 59, Fleming Medal, 71; Gauss Medal, Ger, 77. *Mem:* Nat Acad Sci; fel Am Phys Soc; Am Geophys Union. *Res:* Theoretical physics; quantum theory; physics of the earth and atmosphere; geomagnetism; theoretical biology. *Mailing Add:* Dept of Earth & Planetary Sci Johns Hopkins Univ Baltimore MD 21218

ELSAYED, ELSAYED ABDELRAZIK, b Egypt, Dec 29, 47; m 75; c 3. INDUSTRIAL ENGINEERING, OPERATIONS RESEARCH. *Educ:* Cairo Univ, BSc, 69, MSc, 73; Univ Windsor, PhD(indust eng), 76. *Prof Exp:* Lectr mech eng, Cairo Univ, 69-73; teaching asst indust eng, Univ Windsor, 73-76; teaching & res assoc, Univ Utah, 76-77; asst prof, 77-81, ASSOC PROF INDUST ENG, RUTGERS UNIV, 81. *Concurrent Pos:* Prin investr, Rutgers Res Coun, 78, Sea-Land Serv Inc res grant, 78-, NSF, 80-81 & Environ Protection Agency, 80- *Mem:* Am Inst Indust Engrs; Am Soc Mech Engrs; Am Soc Eng Educ; Sigma Xi. *Res:* Production planning and control; stochastic processes with specialization in queueing theory and reliability models. *Mailing Add:* Dept Indust Eng PO Box 909 Piscataway NJ 08854

EL-SAYED, MOSTAFA AMR, b Zifta, Egypt, May 8, 33; m 57; c 5. PHYSICAL CHEMISTRY. *Educ:* Ain Shams Univ, Cairo, BSc, 53; Fla State Univ, PhD(phys chem), 59. *Prof Exp:* Instr chem, Ain Shams Univ, Cairo, 53-54; res asst spectros, Fla State Univ, 54-57, res assoc, 58-59; res fel, Harvard Univ, 59-60; res assoc, Calif Inst Technol, 60-61; from asst prof to assoc prof, 61-67, PROF CHEM, UNIV CALIF, LOS ANGELES, 67- *Concurrent Pos:* Alfred P Sloan fel, 65-67; John S Guggenheim fel, 67; vis prof, Am Univ Beirut, 67-68. *Honors & Awards:* Fresenius Award, 67; McCoy Award, 69. *Mem:* Nat Acad Sci; Am Chem Soc; Am Phys Soc; Am Asn Univ Prof; NY Acad Sci. *Res:* Molecular spectroscopy; mechanisms of inter and intramolecular energy transfer; inter and intramolecular interactions, their effects on the spectra; photo-ionization potentials; nonlinear effects and laser spectroscopy; laser multiphoton ionization processes and laser time resolved studies of picosecond intermediates in photobiology; spectral diffusion in disordered systems. *Mailing Add:* Dept of Chem Univ of Calif Los Angeles CA 90024

ELSBACH, PETER, b Zeist, Netherlands, Nov 9, 24; m 59; c 2. MEDICINE, CELL BIOLOGY. *Educ:* Univ Amsterdam, MD, 50; State Univ Leiden, Dr(med sci), 64. *Prof Exp:* Asst resident med, Bellevue Hosp, Sch Med, NY Univ, 53-55, resident, 55-56; res assoc & asst physician, Rockefeller Inst, 56-59; from instr to assoc prof, 59-72, PROF MED, SCH MED, NY UNIV, 72- *Concurrent Pos:* NY Heart Asn sr res fel, 59-64; Health Res Coun career scientist award, NY, 64-75; mem coun atherosclerosis, Am Heart Asn, 63- *Mem:* Soc Exp Biol & Med; Am Physiol Soc; Am Soc Clin Invest; Am Asn Physicans; NY Acad Sci. *Res:* Biochemical and clinical investigation pertaining to leukocyte function and bactericidal mechanisms. *Mailing Add:* Dept of Med NY Univ Sch of Med New York NY 10016

ELSBERND, HELEN, b Calmar, Iowa, Jan 15, 38. INORGANIC CHEMISTRY. *Educ:* Viterbo Col, BA, 65; Univ Ill, Urbana, MA, 67, PhD(chem), 69. *Prof Exp:* ASSOC PROF CHEM, VITERBO COL, 69-, ACAD DEAN, 76- *Mem:* AAAS; Am Chem Soc. *Res:* Electron exchange reaction rates; studies of tris (ethylenediamine) ruthenium complexes; kinetic studies of ligand substitution reactions in complexes. *Mailing Add:* Off Acad Dean Viterbo Col LaCrosse WI 54601

ELSBERRY, RUSSELL LEONARD, b Audubon, Iowa, Sept 26, 41; m 63; c 4. TROPICAL METEOROLOGY, AIR-SEA INTERACTION. *Educ:* Colo State Univ, BS, 63, PhD(atmospheric sci), 68. *Prof Exp:* Jr meteorologist, Colo State Univ, 66-68; from asst prof to assoc prof, 68-79, PROF METEOROL, NAVAL POSTGRAD SCH, 79- *Mem:* Am Meteorol Soc; Sigma Xi. *Res:* Diagnosis and prediction of tropical weather disturbances; large-scale air-sea interaction; coupled atmosphere-ocean modeling. *Mailing Add:* Dept Meteorol Naval Postgrad Sch Monterey CA 93940

ELSDON, WILLIAM LLOYD, physical chemistry, see previous edition

ELSEA, JOHN ROBERT, b Alexandria, Va, Aug 31, 25; m 52; c 4. TOXICOLOGY. *Educ:* Col William & Mary, BS, 47; Cath Univ, MS, 50, PhD(biol), 53. *Prof Exp:* Instr sci, Emerson Inst, 47-53; toxicologist, Hazleton Labs Inc, 53-60; dir toxicol, Hill Top Res Inc, 60-67, admin vpres, 67-68; MGR TOXICOL, RES & DEVELOP DIV, A H ROBINS CO, 68- *Concurrent Pos:* Instr, Cath Univ, 52. *Mem:* Am Soc Parasitol; Soc Toxicol; NY Acad Sci. *Res:* Toxicological techniques. *Mailing Add:* Res Labs A H Robins Co Richmond VA 23220

ELSENBAUMER, RONALD LEE, b Allentown, Pa, July 18, 51; m 73; c 1. ORGANIC CHEMISTRY, CONDUCTING POLYMERS. *Educ:* Purdue Univ, BS, 73; Stanford Univ, PhD(org chem), 77. *Prof Exp:* RES CHEMIST, ALLIED CHEM CO, 77- *Mem:* Am Chem Soc. *Res:* Asymmetric organic reactions; reaction mechanisms; industrial chemistry; electrically conducting polymers; lithium, polymer batteries; organic chemistry. *Mailing Add:* Allied Chem Co PO Box 1021R Morristown NJ 07960

ELSERMANN, EDI, b Schwelm, WGer, May 25, 18; Can citizen; m 49. ANALYTICAL CHEMISTRY. *Educ:* Tech Univ Aachen, Diplom, 48, Dr rer nat, 51. *Prof Exp:* Chemist, Badische, Anilin & Soda Fabrik, 51-53; res fel, Ont Res Found, 54-55; from res chemist to dir lab serv, Res & Develop Div, Columbia Cellulose Co Ltd, 55-68; TEACHING MASTER INSTRUMENTATION CHEM, ST LAWRENCE COL APPL ARTS & TECHNOL, CORNWALL, ONT, 68- *Mem:* Fel Chem Inst Can; Am Chem Soc; Soc Ger Chemists. *Res:* Cellulose chemistry; chemical instrumentation. *Mailing Add:* 509 Shirley Ave Cornwall Can

ELSEVIER, ERNEST, b Amsterdam, Holland, Dec 26, 14; nat US; m 44; c 2. MECHANICAL ENGINEERING. *Educ:* Ala Polytech Inst, BS, 49; Ga Inst Technol, MS, 50. *Prof Exp:* Instr mech eng, Ala Polytech Inst, 49; grad asst mech eng, Ga Inst Technol, 50; from instr to asst prof, 50-57, ASSOC PROF MECH ENG, COL ENG, DUKE UNIV, 57- *Concurrent Pos:* Res assoc, John D Latimre & Assoc, 58-; consult, Pub Serv Co, NC & Burlington Industs, 64-; partner, Gardner, Elsevier & Kline; mem adv bd, Fayetteville Technol Inst; mem adv bd, NC State Bd Prof Engrs & Land Surveyors, 67-70, secy, 70. *Honors & Awards:* Award, Am Soc Mech Engrs, 62; Gov Award, 71. *Mem:* AAAS; Am Soc Mech Engrs. *Res:* Environmental sciences and fuels; thermodynamics; internal combustion; temperature; instantaneous temperature and pressures. *Mailing Add:* Col of Eng Duke Univ Durham NC 27706

ELSEVIER, SUSAN MARIA, b Mobile, Ala, Mar 25, 45; m 72. CELL GENETICS. *Educ:* Vanderbilt Univ, BA, 67; Univ Wis, MS, 70; Yale Univ, PhD(biol), 76. *Prof Exp:* Fel, Inst Molecularbiol II, Univ Zurich, 76-77; ASST PROF BIOL SCI, UNIV PITTSBURGH, 78- *Mem:* AAAS; Sigma Xi. *Res:* Mammalian somatic cell genetics. *Mailing Add:* Dept of Biol Sci Univ of Pittsburgh Pittsburgh PA 15260

ELSEY, JOHN C(HARLES), b Salt Lake City, Utah, May 27, 35; m 55; c 4. ELECTRICAL ENGINEERING. *Educ:* Univ Utah, BS, 56; Mass Inst Technol, MS, 60; Univ Ill, PhD(elec eng), 63. *Prof Exp:* MEM TECH STAFF, ROCKWELL INT CORP, 63- *Mem:* Inst Elec & Electronics Engrs. *Res:* Digital computer technology; digital image processing; switching circuit theory; programing; numerical techniques; guidance and control of aerospace vehicles; computer applications. *Mailing Add:* Rockwell Int Corp 3370 Miraloma Ave Anaheim CA 92803

ELSEY, KENT D, b Seattle, Wash, Sept 20, 41; m 82; c 1. ENTOMOLOGY. *Educ:* Wash State Univ, BS, 63; NC State Univ, MS, 66, PhD(entom), 69. *Prof Exp:* RES ENTOMOLOGIST, US VEGETABLE LAB, SEA, USDA, 69- *Mem:* AAAS; Entom Soc Am. *Res:* Integrated and biological control of vegetable insect pests. *Mailing Add:* US Vegetable Lab USDA 2875 Savannah Hwy Charleston SC 29407

ELSEY, MARGARET GRACE, b St Louis, Mo, Aug 16, 29. MATHEMATICS. *Educ:* Webster Col, AB, 51; Cath Univ, MA, 60, PhD(math), 63. *Prof Exp:* Instr, Loretto High Sch, 54-58; from instr to assoc prof, 62-73, chmn dept, 62-71, PROF MATH & PHYSICS, LORETTO HEIGHTS COL, 73- *Mem:* Am Math Soc; Math Asn Am; Am Asn Physics Teachers; Nat Coun Teachers Math; Asn Educ Data Systs. *Res:* Finitely compact spaces and convergence of normal Ritt series and also computer extended calculus. *Mailing Add:* Dept Math Sci Loretto Heights Col Denver CO 80236

EL-SHARKAWY, TAHER YOUSSEF, b Alexandria, Egypt, May 3, 41; m 78; c 1. GASTROENTEROLOGY, ELECTROPHYSIOLOGY. *Educ:* Univ Alexandria, Egypt, BSc, 61, MSc, 67; Univ Alberta, PhD(pharmacol), 74. *Prof Exp:* Asst researcher pharmacol, Med Res Inst, Alexandria, Egypt, 63-68; res assoc, Univ Alberta, Can, 68-73; asst physiol, Univ Leuven, Belgium, 74-75; res assoc med, Univ Toronto, 75; res fel physiol, Mayo Grad Sch Med, Rochester, 75-76; asst prof physiol & pharmacol, 76-81, ASSOC PROF MED, UNIV TORONTO, 81- *Concurrent Pos:* scholar, Med Res Coun Can, 77-82. *Mem:* Am Motility Soc; Int Asn Study Gastrointestinal Motility. *Res:* Physiology, pathophysiology and pharmacology of gastrointestinal motor functions at both the cellular and live, conscious animal level; electrophysiology of smooth muscles and electrophysiological actions of drugs; autonomic nervous system, hormones and other humoral substances in the control of smooth muscle functions. *Mailing Add:* Dept Physiol Med Sci Bldg Univ Toronto Toronto ON M5S 1A8 Can

EL-SHIEKH, ALY H, b Rahmania, Egypt, Apr 27, 31; m 58; c 2. POLYMER SCIENCE, MECHANICAL ENGINEERING. *Educ:* Univ Alexandria, BSc, 56; Mass Inst Technol, MS, 61, MechE, 64, DSc(mech eng), 65. *Prof Exp:* Instr workshop technol, Univ Alexandria, 56-58, lectr textile technol, 65-68; vis lectr, 68-70, assoc prof, 70-74, PROF TEXTILE TECHNOL, NC STATE UNIV, 74- *Mem:* Fiber Soc; fel Brit Textile Inst. *Res:* Mechanics of textile structures; fiber crimp; processing dynamics; textured yarns; spindle vibration; journal bearings; carpet mechanics; fiber migration; snagging of knitted fabrics; dynamic properties of wool yarns; yarn forming systems. *Mailing Add:* Dept of Textile Technol NC State Univ Raleigh NC 27607

EL-SHIMI, AHMED FAYEZ, b Alexandria, Egypt, May 18, 38. PHYSICAL CHEMISTRY. *Educ:* Univ Alexandria, BSc, 60; Moscow State Univ, PhD(chem), 67. *Prof Exp:* Instr chem, Univ Assiut, 60-62; asst prof, Fac Eng, Cairo Univ, 67-69; sr res chemist, Res Ctr, Lever Bros Co, 69-72, sr res scientist, 72-75; SR CHEMIST, CLOROX CO, 76- *Mem:* Am Chem Soc; Egyptian Chem Soc; D I Mendeleyev All-Union Chem Soc. *Res:* Colloid and surface chemistry, detergents, hair, skin, rheology, foods and bleaches; colloid stability, particularly stability of emulsions and foams; applied aspects of colloid chemistry in detergent, cosmetic and food areas. *Mailing Add:* Clorox Co Tech Ctr 7200 Johnson Dr Pleasanton CA 94566

ELSHOFF, JAMES L(ESTER), b Sidney, Ohio, Jan 3, 44; m 67. COMPUTER SCIENCE. *Educ:* Miami Univ, BA, 66; Pa State Univ, MS, 69, PhD(comput sci) 70. *Prof Exp:* Asst comput sci, Pa State Univ, 66-69, asst elec eng, 69-70; RES SCIENTIST, GEN MOTORS RES LABS, 70- *Concurrent Pos:* Vis prof eng, Oakland Univ, 73-76. *Honors & Awards:* Outstanding Technical Paper, Am Fedn Info Processing Soc, 74; McKuen Award, Gen Motors Corp, 77. *Mem:* Asn Comput Mach; Inst Elec & Electronics Engrs. *Res:* Software engineering; software metrics; text preparation aids. *Mailing Add:* Gen Motors Res Labs 12 Mile & Mound Rd Warren MI 48090

ELSIK, WILLIAM CLINTON, b Snook, Tex, Oct 8, 35; m 57; c 3. PALYNOLOGY. *Educ:* Tex A&M Univ, BS, 57, MS, 60, PhD(geol), 65. *Prof Exp:* GEOLOGIST, EXXON CO, USA, 62- *Mem:* Am Asn Stratig Palynologists (vpres, 74-75, pres, 77-78); Mycol Soc Am; Geol Soc Am. *Res:* Fossil fungal spores and their classification and taxonomy; identification of fossil microscopic angiosperm remains other than pollen. *Mailing Add:* Exxon Co USA PO Box 2189 Houston TX 77001

ELSNER, NORBERT BERNARD, b Queens Village, NY, Oct 25, 33; m 58; c 2. METALLURGICAL ENGINEERING. *Educ:* Va Polytech Inst, BS, 55; Pepperdine Univ, MBA, 76. *Prof Exp:* Res assoc, Solar Div, Int Harvester, 59-61; staff assoc thermionic power conversion, 61-64, MGR THERMOELEC PROG, GEN ATOMIC, INC, 64- *Mem:* Am Soc Metals. *Res:* Thermoelectric materials; alloy development; joining of semiconductors to conductors; high temperature testing; refractory metals; vapor deposition of W; mechanical forming; specialty braze alloys; diffusion bonding and welding; reentry Oxide fuel capsules; behavior of organic insulations in inert atmospheres. *Mailing Add:* 5656 Soledad Rd La Jolla CA 92037

ELSNER, ROBERT, b Boston, Mass, June 3, 20; m 46; c 3. COMPARATIVE PHYSIOLOGY, MARINE BIOLOGY. *Educ:* NY Univ, BA, 50; Univ Wash, MS, 55, PhD(physiol), 59. *Prof Exp:* Res physiologist, Arctic Aeromed Lab, 53-56; physiologist, Inst Andean Biol, Peru, 59-61; assoc res physiologist, Scripps Inst Oceanog, Univ Calif, San Diego, 63-70, assoc prof, 70-73; PROF MARINE PHYSIOL, INST MARINE SCI, UNIV ALASKA, 73- *Concurrent Pos:* USPHS res career develop award, 65-70; mem biol & med sci comt polar res, Nat Acad Sci-Nat Res Coun, 71-74; US deleg mem, US-USSR Marine Mammal Proj, Environ Protection Agreement, 73- *Mem:* AAAS; Am Physiol Soc; Arctic Inst NAm; Microcirculatory Soc; Undersea Med Soc. *Res:* Marine physiology; marine mammal biology and ecology; comparative physiology of diving. *Mailing Add:* Inst of Marine Sci Univ of Alaska Fairbanks AK 99701

ELSOHLY, MAHMOUD AHMED, b Egypt, Dec 31, 45; m 72; c 2. PHARMACOGNOSY. *Educ:* Cairo Univ, BSc, 66, MSc, 71; Univ Pittsburgh, PhD(pharmacog), 75. *Prof Exp:* Teaching asst pharmacog, Cairo Univ, 66-72; teaching fel, Univ Pittsburgh, 72-75; RES ASSOC PHARMACOL, UNIV MISS, 75- *Mem:* Am Soc Pharmacog. *Res:* Isolation and structure elucidation of natural products with particular emphasis on pharmacologically active ones. *Mailing Add:* Res Inst Pharmaceut Sci Univ of Miss University MS 38677

ELSON, CHARLES, b Des Moines, Iowa, July 15, 34; m 71; c 2. NUTRITION. *Educ:* Iowa State Univ, BS, 56, MS, 61; Mich State Univ, PhD(food sci), 64. *Prof Exp:* Res fel nutrit, Sch Pub Health, Harvard Univ, 64-66; from asst prof to assoc prof, 66-77, PROF NUTRIT SCI, UNIV WIS, MADISON, 77- *Mem:* AAAS; Am Inst Nutrit; Am Soc Clin Nutrit. *Res:* Nutrient induced alterations in lipid metabolism. *Mailing Add:* Dept of Nutrit Sci Univ of Wis Madison WI 53706

ELSON, ELLIOT, b St Louis, Mo, June 15, 37; m. BIOCHEMISTRY. *Educ:* Harvard Univ, AB, 59; Stanford Univ, PhD(biochem), 65. *Prof Exp:* Fel chem, Univ Calif, San Diego, 65-68; from asst prof to assoc prof chem, Cornell Univ, 68-78, prof, 78-79; PROF BIOL CHEM, SCH MED, WASHINGTON UNIV, 79- *Res:* Physical chemistry of nucleic acids and proteins; interactions between cell surface and cyloskeleton; cell surface phenomena. *Mailing Add:* Dept Biol Chem Sch Med Washington Univ St Louis MO 63110

ELSON, HANNAH FRIEDMAN, b Poland, July 10, 43; m 73; c 2. CELL BIOLOGY, BIOPHYSICS. *Educ:* Vassar Col, BA, 64; Mass Inst Technol, PhD(biophys), 70, Cambridge Univ, MA, 71. *Prof Exp:* Fel cell biol, MRC Lab Molecular Biol, Cambridge, Eng, 70-72; asst prof biol, Univ Calif, San Diego, 72-77, asst res biologist, 77-79; RES PATHOLOGIST, VET ADMIN MED CTR, LA JOLLA, 79- *Concurrent Pos:* Fel, Arthritis Found, 70-72. *Mem:* Soc Develop Biol; Biophys Soc; Am Chem Soc; Sigma Xi; Am Soc Cell Biol. *Res:* Membrane proteins of differentiating skeletal muscle cells in cell culture; modulation of development by components of the extracellular matrix; identification and isolation of membrane receptors; biosynthesis of membrane proteins; muscular dystrophy; developmental biology. *Mailing Add:* Dept Path V-113 Univ Calif San Diego La Jolla CA 92093

ELSON, JESSE, b Brooklyn, NY, Apr 6, 10; m 40; c 2. PHYSICAL CHEMISTRY. *Educ:* Rutgers Univ, BS, 37, PhD, 53; NC State Col, MS, 39; Va Polytech Inst, BS, 43. *Prof Exp:* Soil surveyor, Soil Conserv Serv, 38-39; soil technologist, Exp Sta, Va Polytech Inst, 39-41; proj supvr, Soil Conserv Serv, USDA, 41-42; soil technologist, Exp Sta, Va Polytech Inst, 42-43; PROF CHEM, DELAWARE VALLEY COL, 46- *Concurrent Pos:* Res fel, NC State Col & Soil Conserv Serv. *Mem:* Fel Am Inst Chem; Am Chem Soc. *Res:* Relationship between atom size and ion size of element and its position in the periodic table, calculation of bonding parameters; derivation of empirical bond energy equations. *Mailing Add:* Dept of Chem Delaware Valley Col of Sci & Agr Doylestown PA 18901

ELSON, JOHN ALBERT, b Kaiting, China, Mar 2, 23; m 57; c 2. QUATERNARY GEOLOGY. *Educ:* Univ Western Ont, BSc, 45; McMaster Univ, MSc, 47; Yale Univ, MS, 50, PhD, 56. *Prof Exp:* Instr geog, McMaster Univ, 45-46; geologist, Geol Surv, Can, 46-56; from asst prof to assoc prof, 56-68, chmn dept, 74-75, PROF GEOL, McGILL UNIV, 68-, DIR GRAD STUDIES, 69- *Concurrent Pos:* Mem assoc comt quaternary res, Nat Res Coun Can, 71-74; mem comn genesis & lithol quaternary deposits, Int Asn Quaternary Res, 74-78. *Mem:* Fel Geol Soc Am; fel Geol Asn Can; Glaciol Soc; Am Quaternary Asn; Am Soc Photogram. *Res:* Surficial geology in Southwestern Manitoba; deposition from glaciers; Quaternary geology; photogeology, regional geomorphology of Canada; Pleistocene stratigraphy; Glacial Lake Agassiz; Champlain Sea; freeze-thaw processes; denudation; climatic significance of talus; glacial lakes. *Mailing Add:* Dept of Geol Sci McGill Univ 3450 University St Montreal Can

ELSON, JOHN MERLE, physics, see previous edition

ELSON, LEE STEPHEN, b Chicago, Ill, June 26, 47; m 72; c 2. ATMOSPHERIC SCIENCES. *Educ:* Univ Calif, Berkeley, BS, 69; Univ Wash, MS, 70, PhD(atmospheric sci), 75. *Prof Exp:* Resident res assoc planetary atmospheres, NASA-Nat Res Coun, 76-78; sr scientist planetary atmospheres, 78-80, MEM TECH STAFF, JET PROPULSION LAB, CALIF INST TECHNOL, 80- *Mem:* Am Meteorol Soc; Am Astron Soc. *Res:* Winds and thermal structure of the upper atmospheres of Mars and Venus from remote sensing; normal modes of planetary atmospheres. *Mailing Add:* 183/301 Jet Propulsion Lab 4800 Oak Grove Dr Pasadena CA 91109

ELSON, ROBERT EMANUEL, b St Louis, Mo, Feb 17, 18; m 43; c 4. INORGANIC CHEMISTRY. *Educ:* Univ Chicago, BS, 39, MS, 42. *Prof Exp:* Res chemist, Pittsburgh Plate Glass Co, 42-46; res chemist, Argonne Nat Lab, 46-52; chmn phys chem sect, 64-68, assoc div leader, 68-72, RES CHEMIST, LAWRENCE LIVERMORE NAT LAB, UNIV CALIF, 52- *Concurrent Pos:* Israel Atomic Energy Comn fel, 61-62. *Mem:* AAAS; Am Chem Soc. *Res:* Solution chemistry; chemistry of actinides and group V A elements. *Mailing Add:* L310 Lawrence Livermore Nat Lab Univ Calif Livermore CA 94550

ELSPAS, B(ERNARD), b New York, NY, July 26, 25; m 51; c 2. ELECTRONIC ENGINEERING. *Educ:* City Col New York, BEE, 46; NY Univ, MEE, 48; Stanford Univ PhD(elec eng), 55. *Prof Exp:* Instr, City Col New York, 46-49; from res asst to res assoc Electronics Lab, Stanford Univ, 51-55; sr res engr, Comput Tech Lab, 56-58, STAFF SCIENTIST, SRI INT, 68- *Mem:* Sigma Xi; fel Inst Elec & Electronics Engrs; Asn Comput Mach. *Res:* Switching theory; logical design of digital computers; information theory; electronic computers. *Mailing Add:* SRI Int 333 Ravenswood Ave Menlo Park CA 94025

ELSTON, CHARLES WILLIAM, b Philadelphia, Pa, Dec 7, 14; m 39; c 2. MECHANICAL ENGINEERING. *Educ:* Drexel Univ, BSME, 37. *Prof Exp:* Mem staff, 37-58, gen mgr gas turbine dept, 58-60, gen mgr large steam turbine-generator dept, 60-65, MGR OPERATIONAL PLANNING TURBINE OPERS, GEN ELEC CO, 66- *Concurrent Pos:* Chmn bd trustees, Schenectady County Community Col, 70-; trustee, Green Mountain Col, 71-; mem bd mgrs, Eliis Hosp, Schenectady, NY, 70- *Honors & Awards:* Westinghouse Gold Medal, 74. *Mem:* Nat Acad Eng; fel Am Soc Mech Engrs; Soc Prof Engrs. *Mailing Add:* 1294 Lenox Rd Schenectady NY 12308

ELSTON, DONALD (PARKER), b Chicago, Ill, June 17, 26; m 47; c 4. PALEOMAGNETISM. *Educ:* Syracuse Univ, AB, 50, MS, 51; Univ Ariz, PhD, 68. *Prof Exp:* Geologist, Mineral Deposits & Fuels Br, 53-62, Br Astrogeol & Br Petrophys & Remote Sensing, 62-73, GEOLOGIST, REGIONAL GEOPHYS, US GEOL SURV, 73- *Concurrent Pos:* Res assoc geol, Univ Ariz, 67-69. *Honors & Awards:* Nininger Meteorite Award, Ctr Meteorite Studies, Ariz State Univ, 68; Antarctica Serv Medal, NSF, 81. *Mem:* AAAS; Geol Soc Am; Am Asn Petrol Geol; Am Geophys Union; Meteoritical Soc. *Res:* Geologic field investigations of salt structures and uranium deposits, Colorado Plateau; lunar geologic mapping; manned lunar exploration studies; Apollo 16 geologic support, Earth Resources Technology Satellite and Skylab studies; paleomagnetism and magnetostratigraphy of Precambrian and Phanerozoic rocks; paleomagnetism of glaciogenic sediment, Dry Valleys and McMurdo Sound, Antarctica; climate change studies. *Mailing Add:* US Geol Surv 2255 N Gemini Dr Flagstaff AZ 86001

ELSTON, STUART B, b Elmira, NY, Mar 11, 46. ATOMIC PHYSICS. *Educ:* Rochester Inst Technol, BS, 68; Univ Mass, MS, 72, PhD(physics), 75. *Prof Exp:* RES ASSOC ATOMIC PHYSICS, UNIV TENN, KNOXVILLE, 75- *Mem:* Am Phys Soc. *Res:* Heavy ion collision studies, emphasis on auger and autoionization electron spectroscopy. *Mailing Add:* 101 Brentway Cir No 5 Knoxville TN 37919

ELSTON, WOLFGANG EUGENE, b Berlin, Ger, Aug 13, 28; nat US; m 52; c 2. VOLCANOLOGY, ECONOMIC GEOLOGY. *Educ:* City Col New York, BS, 49; Columbia Univ, AM & PhD(geol), 53. *Prof Exp:* Lectr geol, City Col New York, 49-51; lectr, Columbia Univ, 51-52; asst prof, Tex Tech Col, 55-57; from asst prof to assoc prof, 57-67, PROF GEOL, UNIV N MEX, 67- *Concurrent Pos:* NASA res grants, 64-; vis scientist, Am Geophys Union, 68 & 71; vis geol scientist, Am Geol Inst, 68; NSF res grants, 78- *Mem:* Fel AAAS; fel Geol Soc Am; Int Astron Union; Asn Prof Geol Scientists; fel Meteoritical Soc. *Res:* Volcanology, economic geology, planetology. *Mailing Add:* Dept of Geol Univ of NMex Albuquerque NM 87131

EL-SWAIFY, SAMIR ALY, b Port Said, UAR, July 14, 37; m 61; c 3. SOIL SCIENCE, SOIL CHEMISTRY. *Educ:* Univ Alexandria, BS, 57; Univ Calif, Davis, PhD(soil sci), 64. *Prof Exp:* Asst researcher, Soil Salinity Lab, Univ Alexandria, UAR, 58-59; fel soil chem, Univ Calif, Riverside, 64-65; from asst prof to assoc prof soil sci, 65-75, PROF SOIL SCI, UNIV HAWAII, 75- *Concurrent Pos:* Vis scientist, Commonwealth Sci & Indust Res Orgn, Australia, 73; adj res fel, E-W-Ctr, Environ & Policy Inst, Honolulu, 80. *Mem:* Am Soc Agron; Soil Sci Soc Am; Int Soc Soil Sci; Soil Conserv Soc Am. *Res:* Soil and water conservation; soil salinity; irrigation water quality; physicochemical properties of tropical soils; clay colloidal properties and rheology; swelling properties of clays; soil structural stability in relation to sesquioxides; soil erosion. *Mailing Add:* Dept of Agron & Soil Sci Univ of Hawaii 3190 Maile Way Honolulu HI 96822

ELTER, JOHN FREDERICK, mechanics, electrophotography, see previous edition

ELTERICH, G JOACHIM, b Dresden, Ger, May 22, 30; US citizen; m 61; c 3. LABOR MARKET ANALYSIS. *Educ:* Rheinische Fredrich-Wilhelms Univ Bonn, dipl sci agr, 56; Univ Ky, MS, 60; Mich State Univ, PhD(agr econ), 64. *Prof Exp:* Res assoc, Rheinische Friedrich-Wilhelms Univ Bonn, 64-67; PROF AGR ECON, UNIV DEL, 67- *Concurrent Pos:* Vis prof, Univ Kiel, Ger, 74; innovative teaching grant comp assisted instr, Univ Del, 75; consult, US Agency Int Develop, 77-, & Minimum Wage Study Comn, 80-81. *Mem:* Am Agr Econ Asn; Am Econ Asn; Northeast Agr Econ Coun; Int Asn Agr Econ. *Res:* Quantitative supply analysis (milk); economic analysis of impact of Manpower programs; unemployment insurance, minimum wage, programming of agricultural production and risk analysis; evaluation and prescription of development projects. *Mailing Add:* 145 Timberline Dr Newark DE 19711

ELTGROTH, PETER GEORGE, b Baltimore, Md, Sept 17, 40; m 67. PLASMA PHYSICS. *Educ:* Calif Inst Technol, BS, 62; Harvard Univ, AM, 63, PhD(physics), 66. *Prof Exp:* Nat Res Coun-Nat Acad Sci res fel astrophysics, NASA, 66-67; PHYSICIST, LAWRENCE LIVERMORE LAB, UNIV CALIF, 67- *Res:* Hydrodynamics; astrophysics; general relativity. *Mailing Add:* 1245 Lillian Livermore CA 94550

ELTHERINGTON, LORNE, b Calgary, Alta, June 2, 33; m 60; c 4. ANESTHESIOLOGY, PHARMACOLOGY. *Educ:* Univ BC, BA, 57; Univ Wash, MSc, 59, PhD(pharmacol), 61; Univ Calif, San Francisco, MD, 67. *Prof Exp:* Instr pharmacol, Univ Wash, 61-62; intern San Francisco Gen Hosp, 67-68; resident, Dept Anesthesiol, Med Ctr, Univ Calif, San Francisco, 68-70; vis prof pharmacol, Mahidol Univ, Bangkok, 70-74; ASSOC PROF ANESTHESIA, STANFORD UNIV, 74- *Concurrent Pos:* NIH grant, 61-63. *Res:* Rational use of drugs, local anesthesia for outpatient surgery; methods of chronic pain relief. *Mailing Add:* Dept of Anesthesia Sch of Med Stanford Univ Stanford CA 94305

ELTIMSAHY, ADEL H, b Damanhoor, Egypt, June 10, 36; m 67. ELECTRICAL ENGINEERING. *Educ:* Cairo Univ, BS, 58; Univ Mich, Ann Arbor, MS, 61, PhD(elec eng), 67. *Prof Exp:* Res asst elec eng, Nat Res Ctr, Egypt, 58-59 & 62; consult temperature control, Maxitrol Co, Mich, 66; asst prof elec eng, Univ Tenn, 67-68; from asst prof to assoc prof, 68-78, PROF ELEC ENG, UNIV TOLEDO, 78-, CHMN, ELEC ENG DEPT, 80- *Concurrent Pos:* Consult, Nat Bur Standards, 73-74 & DANA Corp, 75. *Honors & Awards:* Paper Award, Indust Appln Soc, Inst Elec & Electronics Engrs, 77. *Mem:* Inst Elec & Electronics Engrs; Simulation Coun; Int Solar Energy Soc; Am Soc Eng Educ. *Res:* The optimal control of solar heating and photovoltaic systems; optimization of energy usage in homes; system simulation. *Mailing Add:* Dept of Elec Eng Univ of Toledo Toledo OH 43606

ELTINGE, LAMONT, b Chicago, Ill, May 9, 26; m 53; c 2. RESEARCH ADMINISTRATION, ENGINEERING. *Educ:* Purdue Univ, BS, 47; Ill Inst Technol, MS, 56, PhD(mech eng), 65. *Prof Exp:* Trainee/foreman, Electro-Motive Div, Gen Motors Co, 47-51; sect leader, Am Oil, Standard Oil, Co, Inc, 51-62; res asst, Inst Gas Technol, Ill Inst Technol, 63-64; dir, Automotive Res, Ethyl Corp, 64-68; vpres & technician, Cummins Engine Co, Inc, 68-73; DIR RES, EATON CORP, 73- *Honors & Awards:* Horning Award, Soc Automotive Engrs, 73. *Mem:* Soc Automotive Engrs; Indust Res Inst; Am Soc Mech Engrs; Sigma Xi. *Res:* Energy; engines; fuels and lubricants; identification and application of emerging technology to transporation and industrial systems and components. *Mailing Add:* Eaton Corp PO Box 766 Southfield MI 48037

ELTON, EDWARD FRANCIS, b Teaneck, NJ, Dec 3, 35; m 57; c 5. CHEMICAL ENGINEERING, PULP & PAPER TECHNOLOGY. *Educ:* Stevens Inst Technol, ME, 57; Lawrence Col, MS, 59, PhD(chem kinetics), 62. *Prof Exp:* From asst prof to assoc prof chem eng, Univ Maine, 62-70; supvr pulp processes res & develop, Am Can Co, 70-75; CORP COORDR PULP & PAPER, AIR PROD & CHEM INC, 76- *Concurrent Pos:* NSF eng res initiation grant, 64-66. *Mem:* Tech Asn Pulp & Paper Indust; Am Chem Soc. *Res:* Chemical kinetics; kinetics of delignification reaction; hydrogenolysis of lignin; black liquor oxidation; oxygen bleaching; oxygen pulping; ozone bleaching; chemical reactor design. *Mailing Add:* Air Prod & Chem Inc PO Box 538 Allentown PA 18105

ELTON, RAYMOND CARTER, b Baltimore, Md, May 30, 32; m 53; c 3. ATOMIC PHYSICS, PLASMA PHYSICS. *Educ:* Va Polytech Inst, BS, 53; Univ Md, MS, 56, PhD(physics), 63. *Prof Exp:* Physicist ballistics, US Naval Weapons Ctr, Dahlgren, Va, 51-52; electronic engr radar, Bendix Corp, Md, 53-54; asst upper atmosphere physics, Univ Md, 54-58; PHYSICIST ATOMIC, LASER & PLASMA PHYSICS, NAVAL RES LAB, 58- *Concurrent Pos:* Physicist missile guid, Appl Physics Lab, Johns Hopkins Univ, 55. *Mem:* Fel Am Phys Soc; fel Optical Soc Am; AAAS; Sigma Xi (pres). *Res:* Research on short wavelength lasers; spectroscopy on high temperature plasmas in vacuum ultraviolet region; solar and astrophysical spectroscopy; atomic physics as related to plasmas. *Mailing Add:* Naval Res Lab Code 5504 Washington DC 20375

ELTZ, ROBERT WALTER, b Callicoon, NY, June 22, 32; m 62; c 3. BIOTECHNOLOGY. *Educ:* Rensselaer Polytech Inst, BS, 53; Cornell Univ, PhD(bact), 58. *Prof Exp:* Asst Cornell Univ, 53-57; res microbiologist, Chas Pfizer & Co, Inc, 57-61; res microbiologist, Sun Oil Co, Pa, 61-67; chief appl microbiol sect, 67-68, asst to mgr, basic res div, 69-70, tech planning analyst, 70; TECH DIR, KRAUSE MILLING CO, 80- *Mem:* Am Chem Soc (secy-treas, Microbiol & Biochem Technol Div, 77-80, chmn-elect, 80-81, chmn, 81-82); NY Acad Sci; Am Soc Microbiol. *Res:* Microbial metabolism; biochemical production of antibiotics and organic chemicals; hydrocarbon processing; grain processing. *Mailing Add:* Krause Milling Co 4222 W Burnham St Milwaukee WI 53215

ELTZE, ERVIN MARVIN, b Crete, Nebr, May 9, 38; m 63; c 3. MATHEMATICAL ANALYSIS. *Educ:* Doane Col, BA, 60; Univ SDak, MA, 62; Iowa State Univ, PhD(math), 70. *Prof Exp:* Instr math, Creighton Univ, 62-65 & Iowa State Univ, 68-70; asst prof, 70-75, assoc prof, 75-79, PROF MATH, FT HAYS STATE UNIV, 79- *Mem:* Am Math Soc; Math Asn Am; Soc Indust & Appl Math; Asn Comput Mach. *Res:* Integration. *Mailing Add:* Dept Math Ft Hays State Univ 600 Park St Hays KS 67601

ELVEBACK, LILLIAN ROSE, b Sidney, Mont, Dec 5, 15. BIOSTATISTICS. *Educ:* Univ Minn, BA, 41, PhD(statist), 55; Columbia Univ, MA, 48. *Prof Exp:* Instr math, Univ Minn, Minneapolis, 43-44; tech aide, Nat Defense Res Coun, 44-45; instr biostatist, Sch Pub Health, Columbia Univ, 46-50; lectr, Univ Minn, 55-59; prof statist, Tulane Univ, 59; head sect, Pub Health Res Inst, New York, 60-65; PROF BIOSTATIST, MAYO MED SCH, UNIV MINN & MAYO CLIN, 65- *Concurrent Pos:* Consult epilepsy, Nat Inst Neurol Dis & Stroke, 72-; clin appln & prev adv comt, Nat Heart, Lung & Blood Inst, 75-80. *Mem:* Am Epidemiol Soc; fel Am Pub Health Asn; Biomet Soc; Inst Math Statist; fel Am Statist Asn. *Res:* Statistical methods in the design, execution and evaluation of experimental research in biological science, medicine and public health. *Mailing Add:* Mayo Clin 200 First St SW Rochester MN 55901

ELVING, PHILIP JULIBER, b Brooklyn, NY, Mar 14, 13; m 37; c 2. ANALYTICAL CHEMISTRY. *Educ:* Princeton Univ, AB, 34, AM, 35, PhD(chem), 37. *Prof Exp:* Instr chem, Pa State Col, 37-39; from instr to asst prof anal chem, Purdue Univ, 39-43; asst dir chem res, Publicker Indust, Inc, 43-47; assoc prof chem, Purdue Univ, 47-49; prof anal chem, Pa State Col, 49-52; PROF CHEM, UNIV MICH, ANN ARBOR, 52-, H H WILLARD PROF CHEM, 81- *Concurrent Pos:* Vis lectr, Harvard Univ, 51-52 & Hebrew Univ, Jerusalem, 66, 73 & 81. *Honors & Awards:* Anachem Award, Am Chem Soc, 57, Fisher Award, 60. *Mem:* Am Chem Soc; Electrochem Soc. *Res:* Polarography and electrochemistry of organic compounds; methods of inorganic and organic analysis. *Mailing Add:* Dept of Chem Univ of Mich Ann Arbor MI 48109

ELVIN-LEWIS, MEMORY P F, b Vancouver, BC, May 20, 33; m 57; c 2. VIROLOGY, BACTERIOLOGY. *Educ:* Univ BC, BA, 52; Univ Pa, MSc, 57; Baylor Univ, MSc, 60; Univ Leeds, PhD(microbiol), 66. *Prof Exp:* Med technologist trainee, Shaughnessy Mil Hosp, Vancouver, BC, 52-53; bacteriologist, Pearson Tuberc Hosp, 54-55; med technician, Am Soc Clin Path, 55; from asst prof to assoc prof, 67-81, PROF MICROBIOL, SCH DENT, WASH UNIV, 81- *Concurrent Pos:* Asst clin prof oral path, Sch Dent, St Louis Univ, 68; adj assoc prof biol, Wash Univ, 74-75. *Mem:* Am Asn Dent Socs; Am Soc Microbiol; Int Asn Dent Res. *Res:* Medical botany; oral cavity bacteriology; recurrent aphthous stomatitis; epidemiology, oral virus diseases; epidemiology; chewing sticks; antibiotic and healing potential plants. *Mailing Add:* Dept of Microbiol Sch of Dent Wash Univ St Louis MO 63130

EL-WAKIL, M(OHAMED), b Alexandria, Egypt, Mar 9, 21; m 50; c 2. MECHANICAL & NUCLEAR ENGINEERING. *Educ:* Cairo Univ, BS, 43; Univ Wis, MS, 47, PhD(mech eng), 49. *Prof Exp:* Lectr mech eng, Univ Alexandria, 50-52; res assoc, Univ Wis, 52-54; asst prof, Univ Minn, 54-55; from assoc prof to prof mech eng, 56-64, PROF MECH & NUCLEAR ENG, UNIV WIS-MADISON, 64- *Concurrent Pos:* Fulbright fel, 66 & 78. *Honors & Awards:* Am Soc Mech Engrs Award, 51; Westerm Elec Award, Am Soc Eng Educ, 69, Benjamin Smith Reynolds Award, 70, Nuclear Eng Award, 71; Arthur Holly Compton Award, Am Nuclear Soc, 79. *Mem:* Am Soc Mech Engrs; fel Am Nuclear Soc; Am Soc Eng Educ. *Res:* Heat and mass transfer; fuel vaporization studies; two-phase flow; nuclear power; nuclear heat transport; nuclear energy conversion. *Mailing Add:* Dept Mech Eng Univ Wis Madison WI 53706

EL WARDANI, SAYED ALY, b Alexandria, Egypt, Feb 26, 27; m 56; c 3. OCEANOGRAPHY, ENVIRONMENTAL SCIENCES. *Educ:* Univ Alexandria, BS, 48; Univ Calif, Scripps Inst Oceanog, La Jolla, MS, 52, PhD(chem, oceanog), 56. *Prof Exp:* Sr oceanogr, Univ Wash, 56-57, res asst prof, 57-59; asst prof, Portland State Col, 59-60 & San Jose State Col, 60-63; res oceanogr, US Naval Radiol Defense Lab, 63-64; staff scientist, Lockheed Ocean Lab, San Diego, 64-68, chief scientist, Gen Ocean Sci & Resources, San Diego, 68-73; consult, 73-80. *Concurrent Pos:* Assoc prof, US Int Univ, 64-68; dir, Middle East Prog, Nat Educ Corp, Newport Beach, Calif. *Mem:* AAAS; Am Chem Soc; Geochem Soc. *Res:* Oceanography; marine geochemistry and biogeochemistry; marine environmental pollution; impacts of water resources projects; impacts of municipal and industrial waste disposal; land impacts of wastewater reclamation; planning and management of technical assistance and training programs in developing countries. *Mailing Add:* 1830 Avenida Del Mundo Coronado CA 92118

ELWARD-BERRY, JULIANNE, b Chicago, Ill, Nov 25, 46; m 67; c 2. PHYSICAL CHEMISTRY, COLLOIDAL CLAY CHEMISTRY. *Educ:* Univ Calif, Berkeley, BS, 68, MS, 69; Univ Wis-Madison, PhD(phys chem), 78. *Prof Exp:* Chemist, Allied Chem Corp, 76-78; sr res chemist, Merck & Co, 78-81; SR RES CHEMIST, EXXON PROD RES CO, 81- *Mem:* Am Chem Soc; Am Phys Soc; Clay Minerals Soc. *Res:* Chemistry of clay dispersions; flocculation of colloidal clays; fluorescence probes and spectroscopy; mechanisms of heterogeneous catalysis, especially as probed by infrared spectroscopy; molecular reaction dynamics; Raman spectroscopy; lasers. *Mailing Add:* Exxon Prod Res Co PO Box 2189 Houston TX 77001

ELWELL, DAVID LESLIE, b Newton, NJ, Oct 6, 40; m 65; c 3. LOW TEMPERATURE PHYSICS, SOLAR ENERGY. *Educ:* Amherst Col, BA, 62; Duke Univ, PhD(low temperature physics), 67. *Prof Exp:* Res asst liquid helium, Duke Univ, 62-67; asst prof physics, Col Wooster, 67-76; res assoc, 77-80, RES SCIENTIST, OHIO AGR RES & DEVELOP CTR, 80- *Mem:* Am Phys Soc; Am Asn Physics Teachers. *Res:* Properties of liquid helium and the nature of the superfluid transition; energy conservation; properties of solar ponds. *Mailing Add:* Ohio Agr Res & Develop Ctr Wooster OH 44691

ELWOOD, JAMES KENNETH, b Ladysmith, Wis, Apr 21, 36; m 63; c 2. ORGANIC CHEMISTRY. *Educ:* Wis State Col, Eau Claire, BA, 58; Mich State Univ, PhD(org chem), 63. *Prof Exp:* Chemist, Minn Mining & Mfg Co, 61; sr res chemist, 63-70, RES ASSOC, EASTMAN KODAK CO, 70- *Mem:* Am Chem Soc. *Res:* Heterocyclic chemistry; spectroscopy; organic dyes; reaction mechanisms; relationship between structure and color of dyes. *Mailing Add:* 990 Raccoon Run Victor NY 14564

ELWOOD, JERRY WILLIAM, b Kalispell, Mont, Dec 18, 40. ECOLOGY. *Educ:* Mont State Univ, BS, 63; Univ Minn, PhD(aquatic ecol), 68. *Prof Exp:* Fisheries biologist, Mont Fish & Game Dept, 61-63; res asst, Univ Minn, 63-68; res assoc, 68-72, RES STAFF MEM, OAK RIDGE NAT LAB, 72- *Concurrent Pos:* Prin investr, US Dept Energy res grant, 71-73 & NSF, 78-; adj asst prof, Univ Tenn, 78- *Mem:* Am Soc Limnol & Oceanog; Ecol Soc Am; Int Asn Theoret & Appl Limnol; Sigma Xi; AAAS. *Res:* Nutrient and carbon dynamics in stream ecosystems; production biology of benthic invertebrates and fishes in streams; behavior of toxic materials and radionuclides in aquatic food chains. *Mailing Add:* Bldg 1505 Environ Sci Div Oak Ridge Nat Lab Oak Ridge TN 37830

ELWOOD, JOHN CLINT, b Beatrice, Nebr, Mar 5, 30; m 53; c 2. BIOCHEMISTRY. *Educ:* Willamette Univ, BS, 56; Univ Ore, MS, 58, PhD(biochem), 60. *Prof Exp:* From instr to asst prof, 61-67, ASSOC PROF BIOCHEM, STATE UNIV NY UPSTATE MED CTR, 67-, ACTG CHMN DEPT, 80- *Concurrent Pos:* USPHS res fel, Cancer Res Inst, Philadelphia, Pa, 60-61; USPHS res grants, 62-65. *Mem:* Sigma Xi; AAAS; Am Asn Clin Chemists; Nat Acad Clin Biochemists; Am Col Nutrit. *Res:* Fatty acid and cholesterol biosynthesis in normal and diabetic animals; lipoprotein metabolism in hypenlipidemic and diabetic humans; phospholipid metabolism in relation to plasma membrane; structure and metastasis; fatty livers and hypolipidemic drugs. *Mailing Add:* Dept of Biochem State Univ of NY Upstate Med Ctr Syracuse NY 13210

ELWOOD, WILLIAM K, b Ashtabula, Ohio, Oct 15, 28; m 56; c 3. DENTISTRY. *Educ:* Ohio Wesleyan Univ, BA, 50; Ohio State Univ, MSc, 53, DDS, 57; Wayne State Univ, PhD(anat), 65. *Prof Exp:* Res assoc dent, Henry Ford Hosp, Detroit, 57-65; guest investr, Rockefeller Inst, 65-66; asst prof restorative dent, 66-70, asst prof anat, 66-72, asst prof oral biol, 70-72, ASSOC PROF ORAL BIOL & ANAT, MED CTR, UNIV KY, 72- *Mem:* Am Asn Anat; Am Soc Cell Biol; Int Asn Dent Res; Electron Micros Soc Am; Am Dent Asn. *Res:* Normal and abnormal development of dental tissues; anatomy. *Mailing Add:* Dept Anat Univ Ky Med Ctr Lexington KY 40506

ELWYN, ALEXANDER JOSEPH, b New York, NY, May 14, 27; m 52; c 3. EXPERIMENTAL NUCLEAR PHYSICS. *Educ:* Grinnell Col, AB, 51; Washington Univ, PhD(physics), 57. *Prof Exp:* Res assoc physics, Brookhaven Nat Lab, 56-59; from asst scientist to scientist, 59-79, SR SCIENTIST, PHYSICS DIV, ARGONNNE NAT LAB, 79- *Mem:* Am Phys Soc; Sigma Xi. *Res:* Nuclear reaction mechanisms; neutron scattering and reactions; nuclear spectroscopy; neutron polarization in scattering and reactions; charged particle induced reactions; nuclear astrophysics. *Mailing Add:* Physics Div Argonne Nat Lab 9700 S Cass Ave Argonne IL 60439

ELWYN, DAVID HUNTER, b NY, Jan 9, 20; m 41; c 4. BIOCHEMISTRY. *Educ:* Columbia Univ, AB, 41, PhD(biochem), 50. *Prof Exp:* Instr biochem, Harvard Med Sch, 53-54, assoc, 54-57, asst prof, 57-60; res assoc & asst dir dept surg res, Michael Reese Hosp & Med Ctr, 60-63; assoc dir dept surg res, Hektoen Inst Med Res, Cook County Hosp, 63-68; asst prof biol chem, Med Sch, Univ Ill, 64-68; assoc prof surg, Mt Sinai Sch Med, 68-74; SR RES ASSOC SURG, COL PHYSICIANS & SURGEONS, COLUMBIA UNIV, 75- *Concurrent Pos:* Life Ins Med Res fel, Columbia Univ, 50-53. *Mem:* AAAS; Am Soc Biol Chemists; AAAS. *Res:* Amino acid metabolism; metabolism of trauma and sepsis; parenteral nutrition; in vivo reaction rates. *Mailing Add:* Dept Surg Col Physicians & Surg 630 W 168th St New York NY 10032

ELY, BERTEN E, III, b Newark, NJ, Nov 26, 48; m 70; c 2. MICROBIAL GENETICS. *Educ:* Tufts Univ, BS, 69; Johns Hopkins Univ, PhD(biol), 73. *Prof Exp:* ASST PROF BIOL, UNIV SC, 73- *Mem:* Am Soc Microbiol. *Res:* Genetics of differentiation in Caulobacter crescentus; genetic regulation of Salmonella histidine operon; cloning the Caulobacter crescentus genome. *Mailing Add:* Dept of Biol Univ of SC Columbia SC 29208

ELY, CHARLES A, b Washington, Pa, Dec 11, 13. ANATOMY. *Educ:* Washington & Jefferson Col, AB, 36; Univ Hawaii, MS, 40; Univ Wis, PhD(zool, anat), 48. *Prof Exp:* From instr to assoc prof anat, 48-75, PROF ANAT, COL PHYSICIANS & SURGEONS, COLUMBIA UNIV, 75- *Mem:* AAAS; Am Asn Cancer Res; Endocrine Soc; Soc Exp Biol & Med. *Res:* Endocrinology; antigonadotrophins; experimental tumors of the gonads. *Mailing Add:* Dept Anat Col Physicians & Surg Columbia Univ 630 W 168th St New York NY 10032

ELY, CHARLES ADELBERT, b Wellsboro, Pa, Jan 8, 33; m 57; c 2. VERTEBRATE ZOOLOGY. *Educ:* Pa State Univ, BS, 55; Univ Okla, MS, 57, PhD(zool), 60. *Prof Exp:* From asst prof to assoc prof, 60-67, PROF ZOOL, FT HAYS KANS STATE COL, 67- *Concurrent Pos:* Field dir Pac proj biol res, Div Birds, Smithsonian Inst, 63-66. *Mem:* Am Ornith Union; Cooper Ornith Soc; Wilson Ornith Soc. *Res:* Avian distribution and taxonomy; speciation; birds of Mexico, High Plains area, United States and central Pacific. *Mailing Add:* Dept of Zool Ft Hays Kans State Col Hays KS 67601

ELY, DANIEL LEE, b Dayton, Ohio, Feb 6, 45; m 71; c 2. MEDICAL PHYSIOLOGY, NEUROENDOCRINOLOGY. *Educ:* Univ Southern Calif, BA, 67, MS, 69, PhD(physiol), 71. *Prof Exp:* Res scientist, Univ Southern Calif, 71-74; lectr biol, Univ Calif, Riverside, 74-76; asst prof, 76-80, ASSOC PROF BIOL, UNIV AKRON, 80- *Mem:* Soc Neurosci; Am Physiol Soc; AAAS. *Res:* Etiology of essential hypertension and the involvement of the sympathetic nervous system, neuroendocrine factors and psychosocial factors; development of preventive medicine programs for hypertension. *Mailing Add:* Dept of Biol Univ of Akron Akron OH 44325

ELY, DONALD GENE, b Hastings, Okla, Dec 15, 37; m 60; c 2. ANIMAL SCIENCE. *Educ:* Okla State Univ, BS, 61, MS, 65; Univ Ky, PhD(animal sci), 66. *Prof Exp:* Asst, Okla State Univ, 61-63, res asst, 63-66; asst prof animal sci, Kans State Univ, 66-68; from asst prof to assoc prof, 68-76, PROF ANIMAL SCI, UNIV KY, 76- *Mem:* Am Soc Animal Sci. *Res:* Digestion and metabolism of protein and nonprotein nitrogen sources by ruminant animals. *Mailing Add:* Dept of Animal Sci Univ of Ky Lexington KY 40506

ELY, JAMES FRANK, b Indianapolis, Ind, Dec 25, 45; m 65; c 2. FLUID PROPERTIES, COMPUTER MODELLING. *Educ:* Butler Univ, BS, 68; Ind Univ, PhD(chem physics), 71. *Prof Exp:* Res assoc, Nat Bur Standards, 71-73; res assoc, Dept Chem Eng, Rice Univ, 73-75; sr res chemist, Shell Develop Co, 75-79; CHEMIST, NAT BUR STANDARDS, 79-; ADJ ASSOC PROF CHEM ENG, COLO SCH MINES, 80- *Concurrent Pos:* Mem, Prog Comt, Am Inst Chem Engrs, 81- *Mem:* Am Inst Chem Engrs; Sigma Xi. *Res:* Theoretical and experimental studies of the thermophysical properties of pure fluids and fluid mixtures; phase equilibria and transport phenomena. *Mailing Add:* 3470 Longwood Ave Boulder CO 80303

ELY, JOHN FREDERICK, b Chicago, Ill, Mar 20, 30; m 52; c 5. SOLID MECHANICS. *Educ:* Purdue Univ, BSCE, 54; Northwestern Univ, MS, 58, PhD(mech), 63. *Prof Exp:* Struct draftsman, Am Bridge Div, US Steel Corp, Ind, 47-50; instr civil eng, Northwestern Univ, 56-58, lectr, 58-62, asst prof civil eng & dir truss bridge res proj, 62-63; from asst prof to assoc prof civil eng & eng mech, 63-76, assoc dean acad affairs, 76-80, PROF CIVIL ENG, NC STATE UNIV, 76-, ASST DEAN UNDERGRAD PROG, SCH ENG, 80- *Concurrent Pos:* NSF res grants, & 70-72. *Mem:* Am Soc Civil Engrs. *Res:* Theory of elasticity; optimization of structural systems; nonlinear stability analysis of trussed domes. *Mailing Add:* Dept of Civil Eng NC State Univ Raleigh NC 27607

ELY, JOHN THOMAS ANDERSON, b San Francisco, Calif. COSMIC RADIATION. *Educ:* Eastern Wash State Col, BA, 52; Univ Wash, MS, 59, PhD(physics), 69. *Prof Exp:* Physicist, Cambridge Res Labs, US Air Force, 60-66; SR RES ASSOC PHYSICS, UNIV WASH, 69- *Concurrent Pos:* Lectr physics, Grad Prog, Northeastern Univ, 62-64; consult, space sci, Off Naval Res, 75- *Mem:* Am Phys Soc; Am Physiol Soc; AAAS; Am Geophys Union. *Res:* Theory to explain solar activity influence on weather by cosmic ray modulation of ionization of the atmosphere at 10 kilometer altitude and of stratus cloud cover at high latitudes; contributions of cosmic radiation to aging and cancer; theories of immune response in viral and neoplastic disease, and of metabolic derangement in pathology. *Mailing Add:* Physics Dept Univ Wash Seattle WA 98195

ELY, KATHRYN R, b Omaha, Nebr, Oct 2, 44; m 66; c 1. BIOCHEMISTRY. *Educ:* Clarke Col, Dubuque, Iowa, BA, 66; Univ Utah, Salt Lake City, PhD(biol), 81. *Prof Exp:* Sci asst, Argonne Nat Lab, 66-74, sci assoc, 74-76; res instr biochem, 76-81, RES ASSOC PROF BIOL & ADJ ASST PROF BIOENG, UNIV UTAH, 81- *Mem:* Sigma Xi. *Res:* X-ray crystallographic investigations of the three-dimensional structures of proteins, principally immunoglobulins; crystallization and characterization of proteins; structural analysis using computer graphics. *Mailing Add:* Dept Biol Univ Utah Salt Lake City UT 84112

ELY, RALPH LAWRENCE, JR, b Roney's Point, WVa, Nov 26, 17; m 48; c 4. NUCLEAR PHYSICS. *Educ:* Washington & Jefferson Col, BS, 40; Univ Colo, MS, 44; Univ Pittsburgh, PhD(physics), 51. *Prof Exp:* Asst physics, Univ Colo, 40-42, instr, 42-44; assoc physicist, US Navy Radio & Sound Lab, 44-46; instr physics, Univ Pittsburgh, 46-48; res assoc, Sarah Mellon Scaife Radiation Lab, 48-51; sr scientist, Westinghouse Atomic Power Div, 51-54; tech dir & vpres, Nuclear Sci & Eng Corp, 54-59; dir measurement & controls lab, 59-65, dir off indust serv, 65-69, assoc for res, Off VPres, 69-75, DIR UNIV RELS, RES TRIANGLE INST, 75- *Mem:* Am Phys Soc; Am Nuclear Soc; Am Soc Testing & Mat. *Res:* Application nuclear techniques to industry; nuclear instrumentation; isotope tracing; interdisciplinary research liaison, research administration, university liaison. *Mailing Add:* Res Triangle Inst PO Box 12194 Research Triangle Park NC 27709

ELY, RAYMOND LLOYD, b Warren, Ohio, Sept 12, 19; m 42; c 3. MISSILE SYSTEMS ENGINEERING. *Educ:* Carnegie Inst Technol, BS, 40, DSc(math), 51; Calif Inst Technol, MS, 44. *Prof Exp:* Aeronaut engr, Grumman Aircraft Eng Corp, 40-42 & Aircraft Lab, Wright-Patterson AFB, 46-47; teaching asst mech, Carnegie Inst Technol, 47-50; engr struct res, Pittsburgh-Des Moines Steel Co, 50-51; ENGR MISSILE DESIGN, APPL PHYSICS LAB, JOHNS HOPKINS UNIV, 53- *Mem:* Am Inst Aeronaut & Astronaut; Am Defense Preparedness Asn; Math Asn Am. *Res:* Guided missile system design; warwead and fuze systems; structural dynamics; aerodynamics. *Mailing Add:* Appl Physics Lab Johns Hopkins Rd Laurel MD 20707

ELY, ROBERT P, JR, b Freeport, Ill, Apr 2, 30; m 52; c 4. PHYSICS. *Educ:* Mass Inst Technol, BS, 52, MS, 53, PhD(physics), 60. *Prof Exp:* Res assoc, Lawrence Berkeley Lab, 59-62, from asst prof to assoc prof, 62-75, PROF PHYSICS, UNIV CALIF, BERKELEY, 75- *Mem:* Am Phys Soc. *Res:* Elementary particle physics; bubble chambers in association with proton synchrotron accelerators. *Mailing Add:* Lawrence Berkeley Lab Univ of Calif Berkeley CA 94720

ELY, THOMAS HARRISON, b Roanoke, Va, Mar 24, 42; m 63; c 2. ANIMAL PHYSIOLOGY, CELL PHYSIOLOGY. *Educ:* Emory & Henry Col, BS, 63; Vanderbilt Univ, MS, 65; Univ Ala, PhD(biol), 71. *Prof Exp:* Asst prof biol, Longwood Col, 69-75; asst prof biol, Univ North Ala, 75-79; ASSOC PROF BIOL, CAPITAL UNIV, 79- *Mem:* Sigma Xi; Am Soc Cell Biol; Am Soc Zoologists; Am Inst Biol Sci. *Res:* Genetic controls of the induction of males in Volvox aureus. *Mailing Add:* Dept Biol Capital Univ Columbus OH 43209

ELZAY, RICHARD PAUL, b Lima, Ohio, Dec 6, 31; m 51; c 1. DENTISTRY, ORAL PATHOLOGY. *Educ:* Ind Univ, BS, 57, DDS, 60, MSD, 62. *Prof Exp:* From instr to assoc prof oral path, 62-74, asst dean acad affairs, 70-74, PROF ORAL PATH, MED COL VA, 74-, CHMN DEPT, 66- *Concurrent Pos:* Consult, US Navy Hosp, Portsmouth, Va, 62- & Vet Admin Hosp, Richmond, Va, 62-; USPHS fel, Ind Univ, 60-62. *Mem:* AAAS; Am Acad Oral Path (pres, 74); Am Soc Clin Path; Am Dent Asn; Int Asn Dent Res. *Res:* Radiation effects on oral structure and oral carcinogenesis. *Mailing Add:* Dept of Oral Path Med Col of Va Sch of Dent Richmond VA 23219

ELZERMAN, ALAN WILLIAM, b Ann Arbor, Mich, April 2, 49; m 70; c 2. ENVIRONMENTAL CHEMISTRY. *Educ:* Williams Col, BA, 71; Univ Wis, Madison, PhD(water chem), 76. *Prof Exp:* Res asst water chem, Univ Wis, 73-76; fel scholar, Woods Hole Oceanog Inst, Mass, 76-78; fel, Atomic Energy Res Estab, Eng, 78; asst prof, 78-81, ASSOC PROF ENVIRON CHEM, ENVIRON SYSTS ENG, CLEMSON UNIV, 81- *Mem:* Am Chem Soc; Water Pollution Cent Fedn; Asn Environ Eng Prof; Am Soc Limnol & Oceanog; Am Geophys Union. *Res:* Environmental chemistry; environmental engineering chemistry; analytical chemistry; sources, fate, distribution and control of chemicals in the environment; air-water interfacial processes. *Mailing Add:* Environ Systs Eng Clemson Univ 401 Rhode Clemson SC 29631

ELZINGA, D(ONALD) JACK, b Coupeville, Wash, Jan 16, 39; m 81; c 3. OPERATIONS RESEARCH. *Educ:* Univ Wash, BE, 60; Northwestern Univ, MS, 65, PhD(chem eng), 68. *Prof Exp:* Teaching asst chem eng, Northwestern Univ, 63-65; asst prof chem eng, Johns Hopkins Univ, 67-68, asst prof opers res, 68-73, assoc prof, 73-78, res scientist & assoc prof, Ctr Metrop Planning & Res & Geog & Environ Eng, 78-79; assoc prof, 78-79, PROF & CHMN OPERS RES, INDUST & SYSTS ENG DEPT, UNIV FLA, 79- *Concurrent Pos:* Engr, Shell Develop Co, 60-61; volunteer, Peace Corps, 61-63; mathematician, Bur Health Manpower, Health Educ & Welfare & Grad Med Educ Nat Adv Comt, 77-80. *Mem:* Opers Res Soc Am; Math Prog Soc; Am Inst Indust Engrs; Sigma Xi. *Res:* Mathematical programming-theoretical aspects and its application to real-world problems including facility location and manpower supply. *Mailing Add:* Indust & Systs Eng Dept Univ Fla 303 Weil Hall Gainesville FL 32611

ELZINGA, MARSHALL, b Hudsonville, Mich, Mar 25, 38; m 60; c 3. BIOCHEMISTRY. *Educ:* Hope Col, AB, 60; Univ Ill, Urbana, MS, 63, PhD(physiol), 64. *Prof Exp:* Res assoc biol, Brookhaven Nat Lab, 64-66, asst biochemist, 66-67; res assoc biochem, Retina Found, 67-69; staff scientist, Boston Biomed Res Inst, 69-73, sr scientist biochem, 73-76; BIOCHEMIST DEPT BIOL, BROOKHAVEN NAT LAB, 77- *Concurrent Pos:* Estab investr, Am Heart Asn, 68-73; assoc, Harvard Med Sch, 69-76; vis scientist, Max Planck Inst, Heidelberg, Ger, 72-73. *Mem:* AAAS; Biophys Soc; Am Chem Soc; Am Soc Biol Chemists. *Res:* Structure and function of proteins; amino acid sequence of myosin, actin, digestive enzymes; microtubule protein; chemical modification of proteins; sequence techniques. *Mailing Add:* Dept of Biol Brookhaven Nat Lab Upton NY 11973

ELZINGA, RICHARD JOHN, b Salt Lake City, Utah, Apr 23, 31; m 57; c 5. ENTOMOLOGY. *Educ:* Univ Utah, BS, 55, MS, 56, PhD(entom), 60. *Prof Exp:* Nat Acad Sci resident res assoc, US Army Biol Warfare Lab, Md, 60-61; from asst prof to assoc prof, 61-73, PROF ENTOM, KANS STATE UNIV, 73- *Concurrent Pos:* Vis prof, Univ Minn, 81; lectr, Mid Am State Univs Asn, 78-79. *Mem:* Entom Soc Am; Acarological Soc Am. *Res:* Acarology; ectoparasites of rodents; mites associated with army ants. *Mailing Add:* Dept of Entom Kans State Univ Manhattan KS 66506

EMANUEL, ALEXANDER EIGELES, b Bucuresti, Romania, Mar 8, 37; US citizen; m 60; c 1. ENGINEERING. *Educ:* Israel Inst Technol, BSc, 63, MSc, 65, DSc(elec eng), 69. *Prof Exp:* Instr elec eng, Israel Inst Technol, 63-65, lectr, 68-69; sr res & develop engr, High Voltage Eng Corp, 69-74; asst prof, 74-78, ASSOC PROF ELEC ENG, WORCESTER POLYTECH INST, 78- *Concurrent Pos:* Investr, Elec Power Res Inst, 73-74, consult, 75-77 & Allied Chem Res Div, 74-; prin investr, New England Elec res grant, 75- *Mem:* Inst Elec & Electronics Engrs; Soc Royale Belg Electriciens; Sigma Xi. *Res:* Thyristor applications; dielectrics; electro-mechanical energy conversion; harmonics in power systems. *Mailing Add:* Dept Elec Eng Worcester Polytech Inst Worcester MA 01609

EMANUEL, GEORGE, b New York, NY, Apr 3, 31; m 58; c 2. ENGINEERING, LASERS. *Educ:* Univ Calif, Los Angeles, BA, 52; Univ Southern Calif, MS, 56; Stanford Univ, PhD(gas dynamics), 62. *Prof Exp:* Res assoc gas dynamics, Stanford Univ, 62-63; mem tech staff, Aerospace Corp, 63-72; mem tech staff, TRW, 72-76; mem tech staff, Los Alamos Nat Lab, 76-80; PROF AERO, MECH & NUCLEAR ENG, UNIV OKLA, 80- *Mem:* AAAS; Am Inst Aeronaut & Astronaut; Am Phys Soc. *Res:* Gas dynamics; chemical nonequilibrium; thermal radiation; chemical lasers; photochemistry. *Mailing Add:* 504 Willow Branch Norman OK 73069

EMANUEL, IRVIN, b Baltimore, Md, Oct 9, 26; m 60; c 2. EPIDEMIOLOGY. *Educ:* Rutgers Univ, BS, 51; Univ Ariz, MA, 56; Univ Rochester, MD, 60; Univ Wash, MS, 66. *Prof Exp:* Asst prof anthrop & asst dir, US Air Force Anthrop Proj, Antioch Col, 53-55; phys anthropologist, US Dept Air Force, Aerospace Med Lab, 55-56, consult anthrop, 57-60; intern pediat, Cleveland Metrop Gen Hosp, Ohio, 60-61; asst resident pediat, 61-62, from instr to assoc prof, 64-74, PROF EPIDEMIOL & PEDIAT, UNIV WASH, 74-, DIR, CHILD DEVELOP & MENT RETARDATION CTR, 73- *Concurrent Pos:* Guest investr, US Naval Med Res Univ 2, Taipei, Taiwan, 64-66; mem, Harvard-Peabody Mus, Solomon Islands Exped, 66 & Wash State Develop Disabilities Planning Coun, 75-79; bd dirs, Am Asn Univ Affil Progs for Developmentally Disabled, 77-80; sr fel prev med & pediat, Univ Wash, 62-66; USPHS res career develop award, Nat Inst Child Health & Human Develop, 66-71. *Honors & Awards:* US Dept Air Force award, 61. *Mem:* Am Asn Ment Deficiency; Int Epidemiol Asn; Teratology Soc; Soc Epidemiol Res; Am Epidemiol Soc. *Res:* Epidemiology of abnormal pregnancy outcome; international health; public health; pediatrics. *Mailing Add:* Child Develop & Ment Retard Ctr Univ of Wash WJ-10 Seattle WA 98195

EMANUEL, JACK HOWARD, b Centerville, Iowa, Sept 26, 21; m 46; c 2. STRUCTURAL ENGINEERING, CIVIL ENGINEERING. *Educ:* Iowa State Univ, BS, 43, MS, 60, PhD, 65. *Prof Exp:* Weight control engr, Curtiss-Wright Corp, NY, 43-44; archit designer, Early Lumber Store, Iowa, 47-51; mgr & part-owner, Kingsley Lumber Co, 51-54; asst to pres & owner, H F Phelps, Oltmann and Phelps Bank, 54-58; from instr to asst prof civil eng, Iowa State Univ, 58-65; from asst prof to assoc prof, Univ NDak, 65-68; assoc prof, 68-77, PROF CIVIL ENG, UNIV MO-ROLLA, 77- *Concurrent Pos:* Mem comt A2C01 on general struct, Transp Res Bd, Nat Res Coun. *Mem:* Am Soc Civil Engrs; Am Concrete Inst; Am Soc Eng Educ; Nat Soc Prof Engrs; Prestressed Concrete Inst. *Res:* Temperature distribution and thermal stresses and movements in bridges; bridge inspection, maintenance, repair and upgrading; model analysis of structures; concrete growth; bridge supporting and expansion devices; stability of frames. *Mailing Add:* Dept of Civil Eng Univ of Mo Rolla MO 65401

EMANUEL, WILLIAM ROBERT, b Denver, Colo, Sept 16, 49; m 71; c 2. SYSTEMS ECOLOGY, GLOBAL ELEMENT CYCLING. *Educ:* Okla State Univ, BS, 71, MS, 73, PhD(elec eng), 75. *Prof Exp:* Res asst, Okla State Univ, 73-75; res assoc, 75-80, RES STAFF MEM, ENVIRON SCI DIV, OAK RIDGE NAT LAB, 80- *Mem:* Ecol Soc Am; AAAS; Sigma Xi; Am Geophys Union. *Res:* Application of systems analysis in ecology and geochemistry with particular interest in global carbon cycling. *Mailing Add:* Environ Sci Div PO Box X Oak Ridge TN 37830

EMARA, YEHIA ABDELAZIZ SALEH, genetics, see previous edition

EMBER, GEORGE, b Budapest, Hungary, Jan 6, 30; US citizen; m 56. CHEMICAL ENGINEERING. *Educ:* Budapest Tech Univ, dipl, 53; Univ Del, MChE, 61, PhD(chem eng), 62. *Prof Exp:* Sr proj engr res & develop, Amoco Chem Corp, 62-65; sr res engr, Halcon Int Inc, 65-67; sr process engr, 67-77, mgr chem eng develop, 77-81, DIR CHEM ENG DEVELOP, HOFFMAN LA ROCHE CO, 81- *Mem:* Am Inst Chem Engrs. *Res:* Distillation; combustion; transport properties; chemical reaction engineering. *Mailing Add:* Hoffman La Roche Co Kingsland Rd Nutley NJ 07110

EMBLETON, TOM WILLIAM, b Guthrie, Okla, Jan 3, 18; m 43; c 5. PLANT NUTRITION. *Educ:* Univ Ariz, BS, 41; Cornell Univ, PhD(pomol), 49. *Prof Exp:* Jr sci aide bur plant indust, soils & agr eng, USDA, US Date Garden, Indio, Calif, 42, sci aide to horticulturist P-1, Fruit & Veg Crops & Dis, 46; asst horticulturist irrig exp sta, State Col Wash, 49-50; from asst horticulturist to assoc horticulturist, 50-62, HORTICULTURIST, CITRUS RES CTR, UNIV CALIF, RIVERSIDE, 62-, PROF HORT SCI, 72- *Mem:* Fel AAAS; fel Am Soc Hort Sci; Soil Sci Soc Am; Am Soc Agron. *Res:* Education; nitrogen fertilizer management programs for subtropical fruit trees vs nitrate pollution of ground waters; nitrate pollution of groundwater. *Mailing Add:* Dept Bot & Plant Sci Univ Calif Riverside CA 92521

EMBLETON, TONY FREDERICK WALLACE, b Hornchurch, Eng, Oct 1, 29; m 53; c 1. ACOUSTICS. *Educ:* Univ London, BSc, 50, PhD(physics), 52, DSc, 64. *Prof Exp:* Fel, 52-53, from assoc res officer to sr res officer, 54-74, PRIN RES OFFICER, NAT RES COUN CAN, 74- *Concurrent Pos:* Vis lectr, Univ Ottawa, 59-69 & Mass Inst Technol, 64, 67 & 72; adj prof, Casleton Univ, 78- *Honors & Awards:* Award, Acoust Soc Am, 64 & Soc Automotive Engrs, 74. *Mem:* Acoust Soc Am. *Res:* Acoustic radiation forces, standards; shock and explosion waves; industrial noise control. *Mailing Add:* Div of Physics Nat Res Coun of Can Ottawa Can

EMBLEY, DAVID WAYNE, b Salt Lake City, Utah, Oct 30, 46; m 70; c 8. COMPUTER SCIENCE. *Educ:* Univ Utah, BA, 70, MS, 72; Univ Ill, PhD(comput sci), 76. *Prof Exp:* Asst prof, 76-81, ASSOC PROF COMPUT SCI, UNIV NEBR, 81- *Mem:* Asn Comput Mach. *Res:* Very high level programming languages; interactive computing; database query languages; forms-based programming and query language; behavioral aspects of computer text editors. *Mailing Add:* Dept Comput Sci Univ Nebr Lincoln NE 68588

EMBODEN, WILLIAM ALLEN, JR, b South Bend, Ind, Feb 24, 35. SYSTEMATIC BOTANY, ETHNOBOTANY. *Educ:* Purdue Univ, BA, 57; Ind Univ, MA, 60; Univ Calif, Los Angeles, PhD(bot), 65. *Prof Exp:* From asst prof to assoc prof, 65-74, PROF BIOL, CALIF STATE UNIV, NORTHRIDGE, 74- *Concurrent Pos:* Mem hon fac, Los Angeles County Mus Natural Hist, 67-70. *Mem:* Am Soc Plant Taxon; Sigma Xi; Int Asn Plant Taxon; fel Linnear Soc London. *Res:* Chemotaxonomy; cytogeography and chemogeography; chemical and cytological bases for distribution patterns in populations of Salvia and Bursera. *Mailing Add:* Dept of Biol Calif State Univ Northridge CA 91330

EMBODY, DANIEL ROBERT, b Ithaca, NY, July 10, 14; wid; c 3. STATISTICS. *Educ:* Cornell Univ, BS, 38, MS, 39. *Prof Exp:* Sr math statistician, Arnold Bernhard & Co, Inc, 47-48; res statistician, Washington Water Power Co, 49-52; from head statist sect to coordr electronic data processing, E R Squibb & Sons, Olin Mathieson Chem Corp, 53-65; math statistician, Bur Ships, Dept Navy, 65-67; biometrician, Biomet Serv Staff & Plant Protection Div, 67-72, BIOMETRICIAN, ANIMAL & PLANT HEALTH INSPECTION SERV, USDA, 72- *Concurrent Pos:* Consult, State Dept Fish & Game, Idaho, 49-60, NJ, 55-65 & US Geol Surv, 52-58. *Mem:* Am Statist Asn; Biomet Soc; Entom Soc Am. *Res:* Application of statistical and biometric science to problems of medical research; fishery biology; entomology; pesticide monitoring; dynamics of insect trap operations. *Mailing Add:* 5025 Edgewood Rd College Park MD 20740

EMBREE, EARL OWEN, b Alton, Ill, Feb 17, 24; m 62. MATHEMATICS. *Educ:* Morgan State Col, BS, 50; Univ Ill, MS, 52, PhD(math), 63. *Prof Exp:* Mathematician, Ballistics Res Labs, Md, 53-55; teacher, 55-58, from asst prof to assoc prof, 60-74, PROF MATH, MORGAN STATE COL, 74- *Mem:* Am Math Soc; Math Asn Am. *Res:* Ordinary linear differential equations involving distributions; symbolic logic; algebra. *Mailing Add:* 700 Camberly Circle Apt B-4 Baltimore MD 21204

EMBREE, HARLAND DUMOND, b Monmouth, Ill, May 8, 23; m 47; c 4. ORGANIC CHEMISTRY. *Educ:* Univ Calif, BS, 48; Univ Minn, PhD(chem), 52. *Prof Exp:* Res chemist, Charles Pfizer & Co, 52-53; asst prof chem, Hamline Univ, 53-57; assoc prof, 57-65, PROF CHEM, SAN JOSE STATE UNIV, 65- *Mem:* Am Chem Soc. *Res:* Chemical education; author of college textbooks on general chemistry and oganic chemistry. *Mailing Add:* Dept of Chem San Jose State Univ San Jose CA 95192

EMBREE, JAMES WILLARD, JR, b Tacoma, Wash, June 22, 48. TOXICOLOGY. *Educ:* Univ Wash, BS, 70, MS, 72; Univ Calif-San Francisco, PhD(toxicol), 76; Am Bd Toxicol, dipl. *Prof Exp:* Res toxicologist, Univ Calif, San Francisco, 76-77, asst res toxicologist, 77, instr toxicol, 77-78, asst prof toxicol, 78; EXP TOXICOLOGIST, CHEVRON ENVIRON HEALTH CTR, 78- *Concurrent Pos:* Mgr, Toxicol Res Lab, Univ Calif, San Francisco, 76-77, dir 77-78; lectr, Univ Calif, San Francisco, 78- *Res:* Environmental and industrial toxicology; genetic toxicology. *Mailing Add:* Chevron Environ Health Ctr Standard Oil Calif PO Box 1272 Richmond CA 94802

EMBREE, M(ILTON) L(UTHER), b Marceline, Mo, May 27, 24; m 50; c 2. ELECTRICAL ENGINEERING, ENGINEERING PHYSICS. *Educ:* Univ Ill, BS, 49, MS, 50; Lehigh Univ, MS, 57. *Prof Exp:* Mem res staff, Univ Ill, 59-51; MEM TECH STAFF, SEMICONDUCTOR DEVICE & INTEGRATED CIRCUIT DEVELOP, BELL TEL LABS, INC, 51- *Mem:* Inst Elec & Electronics Engrs. *Mailing Add:* 3225 Eisenbrown Rd Riverview Park Reading PA 19605

EMBREE, NORRIS DEAN, b Kemmerer, Wyo, Nov 29, 11; m 37; c 3. APPLIED CHEMISTRY. *Educ:* Univ Wyo, BA, 31; Yale Univ, PhD(phys chem), 34. *Prof Exp:* Res chemist, Distillation Prod Industs, Eastman Kodak Co, 34-48, dir res, 48-60, vpres in charge tech opers, 60-68, asst dir res, Res Labs, Tenn Eastman Co, 68-74; CONSULT, 75- *Concurrent Pos:* Mem oil & fat sect, Int Union Pure & Appl Chem, 61-; chmn comt fats & oils, Assembly Math & Phys Sci, Nat Res Coun, 68-76. *Mem:* Am Chem Soc; Am Oil Chemists' Soc (pres, 59); Am Inst Chem Engrs; Am Soc Biol Chemists. *Res:* High vacuum equipment and distillation; chemistry and technology of fats and oils; chemical products for use in nutrition and health care. *Mailing Add:* 89 Crown Colony Kingsport TN 37660

EMBREE, ROBERT WILLIAM, b Elliott, Iowa, Dec 9, 32; m 59; c 3. BOTANY. *Educ:* Simpson Col, BA, 54; Univ Nebr, MS, 56; Univ Calif, Berkeley, PhD(bot), 62. *Prof Exp:* NSF fel, Birkbeck Col, London, 61-63; vis lectr bot, Univ Calif, Berkeley, 63-64; asst prof, Brown Univ, 64-68; ASSOC PROF BOT, UNIV IOWA, 68- *Mem:* AAAS; Bot Soc Am; Mycol Soc Am; Phycol Soc Am; Brit Mycol Soc. *Res:* Growth and development of fungi; ecology of coprophilous fungi; biology of mucoraceous fungi. *Mailing Add:* Dept of Bot Univ of Iowa Iowa City IA 52242

EMBRY, BERTIS L(LOYD), b Drummonds, Tenn, Nov 23, 14; m 41; c 5. ELECTRICAL ENGINEERING. *Educ:* Utah State Univ, BS, 41, MS, 49; Stanford Univ, EE, 54; Univ Mo, PhD(elec eng), 66. *Prof Exp:* Jr engr, Rural Electrification Admin, 41-42 & 46; electronics technician, Radiation Lab, Univ Calif, 42-43; from asst prof to assoc prof agr eng, 46-56, prof elec eng, 56-80, EMER PROF ELEC ENG & AGR & IRRIG ENG, UTAH STATE UNIV, 80- *Concurrent Pos:* Adv elec & agr eng, Utah State Contract, Iran, 60-62; consult drainage, Colombia & Cent Am, 71; irrig consult & adv, Guatemala, 77-81. *Mem:* Inst Elec & Electronics Engrs; Am Soc Eng Educ; Nat Soc Prof Engrs. *Res:* Electrical engineering in power and machinery; electronics; agricultural engineering; irrigation and direct energy conversion. *Mailing Add:* 1304 E 1700 North Logan UT 84322

EMBRY, LAWRENCE BRYAN, b Morgantown, Ky, June 25, 18; m 48. ANIMAL HUSBANDRY. *Educ:* Univ Ky, BSA, 42; Cornell Univ, MSA, 48; PhD(animal husb), 50. *Prof Exp:* Assoc prof, 50-54, PROF ANIMAL SCI, SDAK STATE UNIV, 54- *Mem:* AAAS; Am Soc Animal Sci; Am Inst Nutrit; NY Acad Sci. *Res:* Nutritive requirements of livestock; compositon and nutritive value of feeds; feed additives. *Mailing Add:* Dept Animal Sci SDak State Univ Brookings SD 57007

EMBRY-WARDROP, MARY RODRIGUEZ, b Monroe, La, Aug 22, 33. MATHEMATICAL ANALYSIS. *Educ:* Southwestern at Memphis, BS, 55; Univ Va, MA, 58; Univ NC, Chapel Hill, PhD(math), 64. *Prof Exp:* From asst prof to assoc prof math, Univ NC, Charlotte, 64-72, prof math, 72-77; PROF MATH, CENT MICH UNIV, MT PLEASANT, 77- *Concurrent Pos:* Res prof, Cent Mich Univ, 80-81. *Mem:* Am Math Soc; Math Asn Am; Sigma Xi. *Res:* Operators on Hilbert space; semigroups of operators, the numerical range of an operator, invariant subspaces of operators. *Mailing Add:* Dept of Math Cent Mich Univ Mt Pleasant MI 48859

EMBURY, JANON FREDERICK, JR, b Baltimore, Md, Sept, 9, 45; m 69. OPTICS OF AEROSOLS. *Educ:* Johns Hopkins Univ, BA, 67; Drexel Univ, MS, 73, PhD(physics), 77; RES PHYSICIST CHEM SYSTS LAB, US ARMY, 78- *Concurrent Pos:* Lectr, Camden County Col, 74-75; consult, Rohm & Haas Co, 77-78. *Mem:* Optical Soc Am; Am Phys Soc. *Res:* Electromagnetic radiation scattering and absorption by nonspherical particles-theory and experiment; radiotive transfer through aerosol clouds-theory and experiment; refractive index measurements from visible to millimeter wavelengths; powder spectroscopy. *Mailing Add:* DRDAR-CLB-PS/Embury Chem Systs Lab Aberdeen Proving Ground MD 21010

EMBURY, JOHN DAVID, b Grantham, Eng, July 12, 39; m 63. PHYSICAL METALLURGY. *Educ:* Univ Manchester, BSc, 60; Cambridge Univ, PhD(metall), 63. *Prof Exp:* Res scientist, US Steel Res Ctr, Pa, 63-65; sr res assoc metall, Univ Newcastle, 65-66; from asst prof to assoc prof, 66-77, PROF METALL & MAT SCI, McMASTER UNIV, 77- *Concurrent Pos:* Vis fel, Battelle Mem Inst, 71. *Mem:* Am Soc Metals; Am Inst Mining, Metall & Petrol Engrs; Brit Inst Metals. *Res:* Microstructure of deformed materials; mechanisms of deformation and fracture in metals; stress corrosion failure; mechanism of nucleation and growth processes in solids. *Mailing Add:* Dept of Metall & Mat Sci McMaster Univ Hamilton ON L8S 4L8 Can

EMCH, GEORGE FREDERICK, b Washington, DC, June 17, 25; m 50; c 2. PHYSICS. *Educ:* Trinity Col, BS, 47. *Prof Exp:* Assoc physicist, 48-56, PHYSICIST, APPL PHYSICS LAB, JOHNS HOPKINS UNIV, 56- *Mem:* Am Phys Soc; Inst Elec & Electronics Engrs. *Res:* Simulation; search radar and weapon control system design and analysis. *Mailing Add:* Appl Physics Lab Johns Hopkins Rd Laurel MD 20810

EMCH, GERARD G, b Geneva, Switz, July 21, 36; m 59; c 2. MATHEMATICAL PHYSICS. *Educ:* Col Geneva, Switz, Maturite Sci, 55; Univ Geneva, Physics Dipl, 59, PhD(quant mech, spec relativity), 63. *Prof Exp:* Asst exp physics, Exp Physics Res Lab, Univ Geneva, 59-60, asst theoret physics, Univ, 59-63, chief, 63-64; res assoc, Princeton Univ, 64-65 & Univ Md, 65-66; assoc prof math & physics, 71-78, PROF MATH & PHYSICS, UNIV ROCHESTER, 78- *Concurrent Pos:* Vis prof, Roman Cath Univ Nijmegen, 70-71; mem, Ctr Interdisciplinary Res, Univ Bielefeld, 75-76. *Mem:* Am Phys Soc; Math Asn Am. *Mailing Add:* Dept of Math & Physics Univ of Rochester Rochester NY 14627

EMELE, JANE FRANCES, b Phillipsburg, NJ, Nov 14, 25. PHARMACOLOGY. *Educ:* Upsala Col, BS, 47; Univ Ill, MS, 49; Yale Univ, PhD(pharmacol), 54. *Prof Exp:* Res asst, Biol Div, Schering Corp, 47-48; res asst physiol, Univ Ill, 49-50; microanal chemist, Bell Tel Labs, 51; chief sect pharmacodyn, Div Pharmacol, Eaton Labs, Norwich Pharmacol Co, 54-55; sr res assoc, Div Pharmacol, Warner-Lambert Res Inst, 55-65, mgr, Div Proprietary Pharmacol, 65-66, dir dept pharmacol, Consumer Prod Res Div, 66-70, assoc dir biol res, Proprietaries & Toiletries, Warner-Lambert Co, 70-72, dir biol res, Consumer Prod Groups, 72-74, dir biol res, Am Chicle Div, 74-77, DIR BIOL & CLIN AFFAIRS, AM CHICLE DIV, WARNER-LAMBERT CO, 77- *Concurrent Pos:* Nat Heart Inst res fel, 52-54; mem, Morris County Asn Ment Health, 56-69, chmn educ comt, chmn indust adv comt,, vpres, bd dirs, secy-exec comt & bd dirs; mem, Morris County Bd Ment Health, 59-65; mem bd dirs, dirs & educ comt, NJ Asn Ment Health, 62-64; mem, Morris County Asn Health & Welfare Agencies, 64-66; lectr & vis scientist, Rutgers Univ, 64-67; mem bd trustees, Upsala Col, 78-; mem invest subcomt, Morristown Mem Hosp, 78- *Mem:* AAAS; Am Soc Pharmacol & Exp Therapeut; Am Pharmaceut Asn; sr mem Acad Pharmaceut Sci; Am Therapeut Soc. *Res:* Neuropharmacology; analgesia, gastrointestinal and respiratory; cardiovascular neurophysiology; clinical and laboratory evaluation of cough-cold, gastrointestinal, analgesics, breath, skin and shaving products. *Mailing Add:* Am Chicle Div 170 Tabor Dr Rd Morris Plains NJ 07950

EMERICH, DONALD WARREN, b Schuylkill Haven, Pa, July 12, 20; m 43; c 3. ANALYTICAL CHEMISTRY. *Educ:* Pa State Univ, BS, 42; Ohio State Univ, PhD, 51. *Prof Exp:* Chemist, Hercules Powder Co, 42-45; chem engr, Badger Ord Works, 45-47; res chemist, Niacet Chem Div, US Vanadium Corp, 47-49; asst, Ohio State Univ, 49-51; asst prof chem, Kans State Univ, 51-54; prof, Centenary Col, 54-60; actg head dept, 64-66 & 80-81, head dept, 66-76, PROF ANAL CHEM, MISS STATE UNIV, 60- *Mem:* Am Chem Soc; Sigma Xi. *Res:* Electrochemistry; nonaqueous titrimetry. *Mailing Add:* 2007 Pin Oak Dr Starkville MS 39759

EMERICK, ANNE WALES, microbiology, molecular biology, see previous edition

EMERICK, HAROLD B(URTON), b New Brighton, Pa, July 6, 13; m 38; c 2. METALLURGICAL ENGINEERING. *Educ:* Carnegie Inst Technol, 32-38. *Prof Exp:* Supvr, Jones & Laughlin Steel Corp, 35-55, dir tech serv, 55-69, vpres res & technol, 69-72; CONSULT, 72- *Honors & Awards:* McKune Mem Award, Am Inst Mining, Metall & Petrol Engrs, 42. *Mem:* Am Inst Mining, Metall & Petrol Engrs; fel Am Soc Metals; fel Metall Soc (pres, 65). *Res:* Process metallurgy; iron and steel production technology. *Mailing Add:* 479 Salem Dr Pittsburgh PA 15243

EMERICK, ROYCE JASPER, b Tulsa, Okla, Jan 1, 31; m 53; c 3. ANIMAL NUTRITION. *Educ:* Okla State Univ, BS, 52; Univ Wis, MS, 55, PhD(biochem, animal husb), 57. *Prof Exp:* PROF CHEM & ANIMAL SCI, SDAK STATE UNIV, 57- *Concurrent Pos:* Res fel, Univ Wis, 65-66. *Mem:* Am Inst Nutrit; Am Soc Animal Sci. *Res:* Urinary calculi; nitrate and mineral metabolism. *Mailing Add:* Sta Biochem Sect SDak State Univ Brookings SD 57006

EMERMAN, JOANNE TANNIS, b Kenora, Ontario; Can citizen; m 63; c 3. ONCOLOGY, ENDOCRINOLOGY. *Educ:* Hofstra Univ, Hempstead, BA, 65; Univ Calif, Berkeley, MA, 67, PhD(zool), 77. *Prof Exp:* Fel, Lab Chem Biodynamics, Univ Calif, Berkeley, 77-80; ASST PROF OBSTET & GYNEC, FAC MED, UNIV COL, VANCOUVER, 80-, ASSOC MEM, DEPT ANAT, 81- *Concurrent Pos:* Vis prof, Dept Cancer Endocrinol, Cancer Control Agency, 80-; res scholar, Nat Cancer Inst Can, 81-; prin investr, Nat Cancerr Inst Can grant, 81-83. *Mem:* Can Fedn Biol Soc; Can Soc Clin Invest; Am Soc Cell Biol; Tissue Culture Asn; Sigma Xi. *Res:* Effect of hormones on growth; differentiation of normal and malignant mammary epithelial cells; hormone and drug interractions in mammary carcinoma therapy. *Mailing Add:* Dept Obstet & Gynec Fac Med Univ Vancouver Gen Hosp Vancouver BC V5Z 1M9 Can

EMERSON, BEVERLY MARIE, b Eugene, Oregon, Jan 18, 52. EUCARYOTIC GENE EXPRESSION, CHROMATIN STRUCTURE. *Educ:* Univ Calif, San Diego, BA, 75; Washington Univ, Mo, PhD(molecular biol), 81. *Prof Exp:* STAFF FEL, LAB MOLECULAR BIOL, NAT INST ARTHRITIS, DIGESTIVE DISEASE & KIDNEY, NIH, 81- *Res:* The relationship between chromatin structure and specific gene activation in developmental systems; identifying macromolecules which induce developmental events (via chromatin) and understanding the physical basis of their action. *Mailing Add:* Bldg 2 Rm 425 Nat Inst Health Bethesda MD 20205

EMERSON, DAVID EDWIN, b Checotah, Okla, May 15, 32; m 53; c 3. ANALYTICAL CHEMISTRY. *Educ:* Southeastern State Col, BS, 55. *Prof Exp:* From chemist to supvry chemist, 58-63, chief br lab serv, Helium Res Ctr, 63-71, CHIEF SECT RES & ANAL SERV, HELIUM OPERS, BUR MINES, 71- *Mem:* Am Chem Soc. *Res:* Development of gas analysis apparatus, especially helium and the impurities in helium; development methods in isotopic analysis, preparation of primary standards and sample preparation; analysis of helium-3 in natural gas. *Mailing Add:* Helium Opers Bur Mines 1100 S Fillmore St Amarillo TX 79101

EMERSON, DAVID WINTHROP, b Littleton, Mass, Mar 13, 28; m 54; c 3. ORGANIC CHEMISTRY. *Educ:* Dartmouth Col, AB, 52; Univ Mich, MS, 54, PhD(chem), 58. *Prof Exp:* Res chemist, Shell Oil Co, 57-63; from asst prof to assoc prof chem, Univ Mich-Dearborn, 63-69, chmn div lit, sci & arts, 67-69, chmn dept natural sci, 73-75, prof chem, 69-81, dean, Col Arts, Sci & Letters, 79-81; DEAN, COL SCI, MATH & ENG, UNIV NEV, LAS VEGAS, 81- *Mem:* Am Chem Soc; Royal Soc Chem; AAAS. *Res:* Mechanisms of organic reactions; reactive intermediates; organosulfur chemistry; solid phase reagents. *Mailing Add:* Col Sci Math & Eng Univ Nev Las Vegas NV 89154

EMERSON, DONALD ORVILLE, b Long Beach, Calif, July 19, 31; m 57; c 3. GEOLOGY, PETROLOGY. *Educ:* Calif Inst Technol, BS, 53; Pa State Univ, MS, 55, PhD(mineral, petrol), 59. *Prof Exp:* From asst prof to assoc prof geol, Univ Calif, Davis, 57-69; GEOLOGIST, LAWRENCE LIVERMORE LAB, 69- *Mem:* Geol Soc Am; Mineral Soc Am; Am Nuclear Soc. *Res:* Applied geology and petrology. *Mailing Add:* Lawrence Livermore Lab PO Box 808 Livermore CA 94550

EMERSON, ERNEST BENJAMIN, JR, b Bridgewater, Mass, Apr 29, 12; m 38; c 2. SURGERY. *Educ:* Williams Col, AB, 34; Univ Rochester, MD, 38. *Prof Exp:* Instr surg, 41-53, ASST PROF SURG, DIV OTORHINOLARYNGOL, SCH MED & DENT, UNIV ROCHESTER, 53-, BRONCHOSCOPIST, LAB RES DIS OF CHEST, DEPT MED, 41- *Concurrent Pos:* Asst surgeon, Highland Hosp, 41-; jr surgeon, Univ Rochester Hosp, 41-52; asst surgeon, Strong Mem Hosp & Rochester Munic Hosp, 43-; mem courtesy staff, Genesee Hosp, 46-; consult, Canandaigua Vet Admin Hosp, 46-52 & Batavia Vet Admin Hosp, 48-; chief staff, Town Webb Health Ctr, Old Forge. *Res:* Bronchoesophagology; development of new instruments; tonsil surgery; radium treatment of deafness. *Mailing Add:* Gray Lake Old Forge NY 13420

EMERSON, FRANK HENRY, b Kansas City, Mo, June 22, 21; m 44; c 3. HORTICULTURE, PLANT PATHOLOGY. *Educ:* Univ Kans, AB, 47, MA, 48; Cornell Univ, PhD, 51. *Prof Exp:* Asst bot, Univ Kans, 47-48; asst plant path, Cornell Univ, 48-51; asst tech dir agr chem, Stauffer Chem Co, NY, 51-55; asst prof exten horticulturist, 55-58, assoc prof hort res, 58-73, PROF HORT RES, PURDUE UNIV, 73- *Mem:* Am Soc Hort Sci; Am Pomol Soc; Am Phytopath Soc; Sigma Xi. *Res:* Tree fruits; chemical growth regulators; winter hardiness; frost control; population density; training systems; chemical thinning, breeding and selection of new varieties resistant to apple scab. *Mailing Add:* Dept of Hort Purdue Univ West Lafayette IN 47907

EMERSON, FREDERICK BEAUREGARD, JR, b Wellsville, NY, Nov 21, 35; m 58; c 3. MEDICINE. *Educ:* Alfred Univ, BA, 57; Cornell Univ, PhD(wildlife mgt), 61; Vanderbilt Univ, MD, 70. *Prof Exp:* Asst wildlife mgt, Cornell Univ, 57-61; biologist wildlife mgt, Tenn Valley Auth, 62-65; asst prof forestry, Univ Tenn, 65-66; intern, Med Ctr, Univ Colo, Denver, 70-71, resident med, 71-73, instr med, 73-75, asst prof med, 75-77; PHYSICIAN, EMERGENCY DEPT, GOLETA VALLEY COMMUNITY HOSP, 77-; MEM STAFF, UNIV CALIF, SANTA BARBARA, 77- *Concurrent Pos:* Staff physician, Dept Emergency Med Servs, Denver Gen Hosp, 73-77; NIH fel marine biol, Univ Miami, 61-62. *Res:* Emergency medicine; ecology; conservation of natural resources. *Mailing Add:* 4601 Sierra Madre Road Santa Barbara CA 93110

EMERSON, GERALDINE MARIELLEN, US citizen. MEDICAL SCIENCE, BIOCHEMISTRY. *Educ:* Univ Miami, BA, 49; Univ Ala Med Ctr, PhD(physiol, biochem, pharmacol & neuroanat), 60. *Prof Exp:* asst prof, 64-77, ASSOC PROF BIOCHEM, MED CTR, UNIV ALA BIRMINGHAM, 77- *Concurrent Pos:* Partic, Max Planck Inst Brain Res, Frankfort, 77-78. *Mem:* AAAS; Gerontol Soc; Am Physiol Soc; Sigma Xi; Am Inst Chem. *Res:* Endocrine factors in growth; aging in the Long-Evans rat; cancer immunotherapy; comparison of enzyme activities from different organs of the Long-Evans rat; parameters of human longevity; gerontology. *Mailing Add:* Univ Ala Med Ctr Box 442 Univ Sta Birmingham AL 35294

EMERSON, GLADYS ANDERSON, b Caldwell, Kans, July 1, 03. NUTRITION, BIOCHEMISTRY. *Educ:* Univ Sci & Arts, Okla, AB & BS, 25; Stanford Univ, MA, 26; Univ Calif, Berkeley, PhD(nutrit, biochem), 32. *Prof Exp:* Asst, Stanford Univ, 25-26 & Iowa State Col, 30-31; res assoc, Inst Exp Biol, Univ Calif, Berkeley, 33-42; head dept nutrit, Merck Inst Therapeut Res, 42-57; prof nutrit & head div, Sch Pub Health, 57-70, EMER PROF NUTRIT, SCH PUB HEALTH, UNIV CALIF, LOS ANGELES, 71- *Concurrent Pos:* Lectr sch med, Univ Calif, San Francisco, 45; mem adv bd, QM Food & Container Inst, 48-49; res assoc, Sloan-Kettering Inst Cancer Res, 50-53; lectr, Pa State Col, 51; assoc ed, J Nutrit, 52-56; mem US nat comt, Int Union Nutrit Scientists, 58-62; mem food & nutrit bd, Nat Res Coun, 59-64, mem comt dietary allowances, 60-64; mem exec comt, Am Bd Nutrit, 59-68; mem, State Nutrit Comt, 66-71 & Calif Nutrit Coun, 71-; vchmn panel new foods, White House Conf Food Nutrit & Health, 69 & 71; mem bd, Meals for Millions, 70-; mem bd, Southern Calif Comt for WHO, 70-, chmn, 73-75; speaker session chmn & discussion leader, Int Cong Vitamin E, Japan, 70; expert witness, Food & Drug Admin, Fed Trade Comn & Postal Serv, 72-75; mem, Southern Calif Comt Food & Nutrit, 73-76; partic, Int Vitamin E Conf, 73; lectr, Sch Pharm, Kobe Gakuin Univ, 75. *Honors & Awards:* Garvan Medal, Am Chem Soc, 52. *Mem:* Fel AAAS; Fel Am Inst Nutrit; Am Chem Soc; fel NY Acad Sci. *Res:* Amino acids; vitamin E; vitamin B complex; antimetabolites; co-isolator of vitamin E. *Mailing Add:* Sch of Pub Health Univ of Calif Los Angeles CA 90024

EMERSON, JAMES L, b Garrett, Ind, Jan 23, 38; m 62; c 3. VETERINARY PATHOLOGY. *Educ:* Ohio State Univ, DVM, 62; Purdue Univ, MS, 64, PhD, 66. *Prof Exp:* From instr to asst prof path, Sch Vet Sci & Med, Purdue Univ, 62-66; res assoc pathologist, Norwich Pharmacal Co, 66-69; pathologist, Human Health Res & Develop Labs, Dow Chem Co, 69-75, sr res specialist, Health & Consumer Prod Dept, Dow Chem USA, 75-76; mgr dept path, Abbott Labs, North Chicago, 76-79; mgr life sci, 79-80, ASSOC DIR, EXTERNAL TECH AFFAIRS DEPT, THE COCA-COLA CO, 80- *Concurrent Pos:* Assoc mem fac, Ind Univ-Purdue Univ, Indianapolis, 69-; mem path/toxicol expert comt, Int Life Sci Inst. *Mem:* Am Vet Med Asn; Am Col Vet Pathologists; Soc Toxicol; Int Acad Path. *Res:* Drug safety evaluation; carcinogenesis bioassay. *Mailing Add:* 290 Landfall Rd NW Atlanta GA 30328

EMERSON, JOHN DAVID, b Oswego, NY, July 18, 46; m 68; c 2. SURVIVAL THEORY, EXPLORATORY DATA ANALYSIS. *Educ:* Univ Rochester, BA, 68; Cornell Univ, MS, 70, PhD(math), 73, cert statist, 76-77. *Prof Exp:* Teaching fel math, Cornell Univ, 68-73; asst prof, 73-81, ASSOC PROF MATH, MIDDLEBURY COL, 81- *Concurrent Pos:* Appl math, Eastman Kodak, 68; adj prof, Tompkins-Cortland Community Col, 69-70 & Cornell Univ, 73; assoc to dean, Middlebury Col, 76 & asst to acad vpres, 76-77; teaching fel, Univ Minn, 78; vis res fel biostatist, Harvard Univ, 78-79 & res fel, 80-81. *Mem:* Am Statist Asn; Biomet Soc; Math Asn Am. *Res:* Statistics and biostatistics; use of statistical methods in medical research; methods of robust statistics and exploratory data analysis. *Mailing Add:* Dept Math Middlebury Col Middlebury VT 05753

EMERSON, JOHN WILFORD, b Bloomington, Ind, Dec 27, 33; m 59; c 3. GEOLOGY. *Educ:* Univ NMex, BS, 59, MS, 61; Fla State Univ, PhD(geol), 66. *Prof Exp:* Geologist, Pan Am Petrol Corp, Colo, 66-67; from asst prof to assoc prof, 67-76, PROF EARTH SCI, CENT MO STATE UNIV, 76-HEAD DEPT, 68- *Mem:* Geol Soc Am; Am Quaternary Asn. *Res:* Sedimentology; sedimentary petrology; stratigraphy. *Mailing Add:* Dept of Earth Sci Cent Mo State Univ Warrensburg OH 64093

EMERSON, KARY CADMUS, b Sasakwa, Okla, Mar 13, 18; m 39; c 3. MEDICAL ENTOMOLOGY, PARASITOLOGY. *Educ:* Okla State Univ, BS, 39, MS, 40, PhD(entom), 49. *Prof Exp:* US Army, 40-66, med entomologist, Philippines, 40-42, asst prof, Okla State Univ, 46-49, tech liaison, Off Chief Res & Develop, 59-60, spec asst for res, 60-74, dep for sci & technol & actg asst secy army for res & develop, 75-79, MEM ARMY SCI BD, US ARMY, 79- *Concurrent Pos:* Consult, Univs & US Depts Agr & Interior, 49-; res assoc, Smithsonian Inst, 59-; res assoc, Seminole Indian Nation Mus; res assoc, Mus, Okla State Univ & adj prof, 71-; US mem, NATO Long-Term Sci Study Panel; mem, Defense Comt Res, White House Panel Systs & Taxon & White House Comt Environ Qual; res assoc, Fla Dept Agr & Consumer Affairs. *Honors & Awards:* Two Except Civilian Serv Awards, US Army; Award for Meritorious Civilian Serv, US Dept Defense. *Mem:* Soc Syst Zool; fel Entom Soc Am; Am Soc Trop Med & Hyg; Am Soc Parasitol; Wildlife Dis Asn. *Res:* Mallophaga; ectoparasites; arthropod-borne diseases. *Mailing Add:* 560 Boulder Dr Sanibel FL 33957

EMERSON, KENNETH, b Pasadena, Calif, Nov 9, 31; m 56; c 3. PHYSICAL CHEMISTRY, INORGANIC CHEMISTRY. *Educ:* Harvard Univ, BA, 53; Univ Ore, MA, 58; Univ Minn, PhD(chem), 61. *Prof Exp:* Noyes fel chem, Calif Inst Technol, 61-62; from asst prof to assoc prof, 62-70, PROF CHEM, MONT STATE UNIV, 70- *Concurrent Pos:* Fulbright res fel, Univ Canterbury, 68-69; vis prof, Univ of the Andes, Venezuela, 72-73. *Mem:* AAAS; Am Chem Soc; Am Crystallog Asn. *Res:* Inorganic structure and its relation to the theory of the chemical bond; solid state chemistry of low-dimensional structures. *Mailing Add:* Dept of Chem Mont State Univ Bozeman MT 59717

EMERSON, LEWIS COTESWORTH, b Columbia, SC, July 16, 25; m 48; c 3. SURFACE PHYSICS. *Educ:* Ga Inst Technol, BEE, 49; Univ Tenn, PhD(physics), 63. *Prof Exp:* Dept head health physics, Union Carbide Nuclear Co, 50-56; RES STAFF MEM, OAK RIDGE NAT LAB, 57- *Concurrent Pos:* Lectr, WHO, Belg, 57 & India, 58; US AEC advan fel, 59-62. *Mem:* Am Vacuum Soc; Am Phys Soc. *Res:* Health physics; interaction of radiation with matter; radiation physics; optical properties of thin films; ellipsometry; electron spectroscopy; materials science; fusion energy technology. *Mailing Add:* Oak Ridge Nat Lab PO Box X Oak Ridge TN 37830

EMERSON, MARION PRESTON, b Washburn, Mo, Feb 24, 18; m 47; c 3. ALGEBRA. *Educ:* Southwest Mo State Col, BS, 38; Univ Wis, MS, 48; Univ Ill, PhD(math), 52. *Prof Exp:* Asst prof math, Harpur Col, 52-56; assoc prof, Southwest Mo State Col, 56-61; head dept, 61-79, PROF MATH, EMPORIA STATE UNIV, 79- *Mem:* Am Math Soc; Math Asn Am. *Res:* Modular lattices. *Mailing Add:* Dept of Math Emporia State Univ Emporia KS 66801

EMERSON, MERLE T, b Spokane, Wash, Aug 19, 30; m 54; c 2. PHYSICAL CHEMISTRY, ANALYTICAL CHEMISTRY. *Educ:* Whitworth Col, Wash, BS, 52; Wash State Col, MS, 58; Univ Wash, PhD(phys chem), 58. *Prof Exp:* Res assoc chem, Fla State Univ, 58-60, asst, Inst Molecular Biophys, 60-62; asst prof, Wayne State Univ, 62-64; asst prof, Fla State Univ, 64-69; actg dir natural sci & math div, 71, ASSOC PROF CHEM, UNIV ALA, HUNTSVILLE, 69- *Concurrent Pos:* NIH res grant, 64-67; vis assoc prof, Univ Hawaii, Hilo Campus, 68-69, Univ Hawaii, 78-79. *Mem:* Am Crystallog Soc. *Res:* Molecular structure using nuclear magnetic resonance spectroscopy; x-ray determination of crystal and molecular structures and instrumentation. *Mailing Add:* Dept Chem Univ Ala Huntsville AL 35899

EMERSON, RALPH, mycology, deceased

EMERSON, STERLING (HOWARD), b Lincoln, Nebr, Oct 29, 00; m 24; c 2. GENETICS. *Educ:* Cornell Univ, BSc, 22; Univ Mich, AM, 24, PhD(genetics), 28. *Prof Exp:* Instr bot, Univ Mich, 24-28; from asst prof to prof genetics, 28-71, EMER PROF GENETICS, CALIF INST TECHNOL, 71- *Concurrent Pos:* Fulbright fel, Cambridge Univ & Guggenheim fel, Cambridge Univ & Univ Paris, 51-52; geneticist, Div Biol & Med, US AEC, 55-57; vis prof, Univ Wash, 63, Cornell Univ, 65 & Copenhagen Univ, 66. *Mem:* Emer mem Nat Acad Sci; AAAS; Genetics Soc Am. *Mailing Add:* 1207 Morada Place Altadena CA 91001

EMERSON, THOMAS EDWARD, JR, b Wilson, Okla, Feb 3, 35; m 55; c 3. CARDIOVASCULAR PHYSIOLOGY. *Educ:* Univ Okla, BS, 58, PhD(med physiol), 64; Univ Alta, MSc, 61. *Prof Exp:* Res physiologist, Civil Aeromed Res Inst, Okla, 61-65; asst prof physiol & res asst prof med surg, Med Ctr, Univ Okla, 65-66; assoc prof, 66-73, PROF PHYSIOL, MICH STATE UNIV, 73- *Concurrent Pos:* Fel, Coun Circulation, Am Heart Asn, 75- *Mem:* Soc Exp Biol & Med; Am Physiol Soc; Am Fedn Clin Res. *Res:* Cardiovascular physiology; cardiovascular mechanisms during endotoxin and hemorrhagic shock; regulation of vasoactive agents and effects on peripheral blood flow; effects of vasoactive hormones on arteries and veins; metabolic abnormalities in muscle and adipose tissue during circulatory shock; cerebral blood flow regulation. *Mailing Add:* Dept of Physiol Mich State Univ East Lansing MI 48824

EMERSON, WILLIAM KEITH, b San Diego, Calif, May 1, 25. MALACOLOGY. *Educ:* San Diego State Col, AB, 48; Univ Southern Calif, MS, 50; Univ Calif, Berkeley, PhD(paleont), 56. *Prof Exp:* Mus paleontologist, Univ Calif, Berkeley, 51-55; from asst cur to assoc cur invert, 55-66, chmn dept living invert, 60-74, CUR INVERT, AM MUS NATURAL HIST, 66- *Concurrent Pos:* Leader, Puritan-Am Mus Natural Hist Exped, 57 & mem, Belvedere Exped, 62 & Western Mex; res assoc, San Diego Natural Hist Mus, 62- *Honors & Awards:* Dorothy K Palmer Award for Res, Univ Calif, 54. *Mem:* Fel AAAS; Paleont Soc; Am Malacol Union (pres, 62); Soc Syst Zool. *Res:* General invertebrate zoology; systematic malacology of New World marine faunas, especially Gastropoda and Scaphopoda; geographical distribution and ecology of Cenozoic marine mollusks. *Mailing Add:* Am Mus of Natural Hist New York NY 10024

EMERT, JACK ISAAC, b Brooklyn, NY, Oct 22, 48; m 69; c 2. ORGANIC CHEMISTRY. *Educ:* Brooklyn Col, BS, 70; Columbia Univ, MS, 72, PhD(chem), 74. *Prof Exp:* ASST PROF ORG CHEM, POLYTECH INST NEW YORK, 74- *Mem:* Am Chem Soc; Sigma Xi; Royal Chem Soc. *Res:* Rates and mechanism of heme oxidation in aqueous solution in the presence and absence of micelle-forming surfactants; novel intramolecular excimer forming; microviscometric probes of the interior of micelles. *Mailing Add:* Dept of Chem Polytech Inst of NY 333 Jay St Brooklyn NY 11201

EMERY, ALAN ROY, b Feb 21, 21, 39; Canadian citizen; m 62; c 2. ICHTHYOLOGY, MARINE SCIENCES. *Educ:* Univ Toronto, BSc, 62; McGill Univ, MSc, 64; Univ Miami, PhD(marine sci, ichthyol), 68. *Prof Exp:* Scientist in chg resource mgt, Fisheries Res Bd Can, 64-65; res scientist, Ont Ministry Nat Resources, 68-73; cur ichthyol, Royal Ont Mus, 73-80; ASSOC PROF, UNIV TORONTO, 80- *Concurrent Pos:* Sr scientist, Sublimnos Proj, J A MacInnis Found, 69-72; mem, Oil Pollution Working Group, Int Joint Comn, Great Lakes, 71; sci coord, Royal Ont Mus, 75-78. *Mem:* Am Soc Ichthyologists & Herpetologists; Japanese Ichthyol Soc; Am Fisheries Soc; Sigma Xi; Royal Can Inst. *Res:* Systematics of coral reef fishes; field and experimental ethology of fishes, particularly communication; theoretical and applied ecology; particularly as applied to resource management and human society; systematics; behavior. *Mailing Add:* Dept Ichthyol & Herpet 100 Queens Park Toronto ON M5S 2C6 Can

EMERY, ALDEN H(AYES), JR, b Pittsburgh, Pa, May 2, 25; m 52; c 2. CHEMICAL ENGINEERING. *Educ:* Pa State Univ, BS, 47; Mass Inst Technol, SM, 49; Univ Ill, PhD, 55. *Prof Exp:* Chem engr, E I du Pont de Nemours & Co, 49-52; from asst prof to assoc prof, 54-64, PROF CHEM ENG, PURDUE UNIV, 64- *Mem:* AAAS; Am Chem Soc; Am Inst Chem Engrs; Am Soc Microbiol; Soc Indust Microbiol. *Res:* Immobilized enzyme technology; reactor design; biochemical engineering. *Mailing Add:* 815 N Vine West Lafayette IN 47906

EMERY, ARTHUR JAMES, JR, b Middleburg, Pa, Dec 1, 23; m 48. BIOCHEMISTRY. *Educ:* Bucknell Univ, BS, 47; Univ Rochester, PhD(biochem), 54. *Prof Exp:* Res assoc bact, NY State Agr Exp Sta, Cornell Univ, 47-48, asst, 48-49; res chemist biol stain comn, Sch Med & Dent, Univ Rochester, 49-51, from jr scientist biochem, Flash Burn Sect, Atomic Energy Proj, to assoc scientist & instr biochem, 54-57; from asst prof to assoc prof biol chem, Univ Md Sch Med, Baltimore, 57-67; sci analyst, Sci Anal Br, Life Sci Div, Off Chief Res & Develop, Army Res Off, 67-70; prog dir microbiol, Biol Sci Div, Off Naval Res, Arlington, 70-81; RETIRED. *Concurrent Pos:* Actg head dept biol chem, Univ Md Sch Med, Baltimore, 62-63. *Mem:* AAAS; Am Chem Soc; Am Inst Biol Sci; Am Soc Microbiol. *Res:* Nucleic acids and nucleoprotein complexes in protein synthesis; mechanisms of protein synthesis; chemistry and structure of nucleic acids and nucleoprotein complexes. *Mailing Add:* 9921 Evergreen Ave Allview Estates Columbia MD 21046

EMERY, ASHLEY F, b San Francisco, Calif, Oct 16, 34; m 59; c 2. MECHANICAL ENGINEERING. *Educ:* Univ Calif, Berkeley, BS, 56, MS, 58, PhD(mech eng), 61. *Prof Exp:* Res engr, Univ Calif, Berkeley, 55-60; assoc prof, 61-69, PROF MECH ENG, UNIV WASH, 69- *Mem:* Am Soc Mech Engrs. *Res:* Heat transfer; gas dynamics; thermal stresses; fracture mechanics; building energy conservation. *Mailing Add:* Dept Mech Eng Univ Wash Seattle WA 98195

EMERY, DONALD ALLEN, b South Berwick, Maine, Dec 22, 28; m 56; c 2. PLANT BREEDING. *Educ:* Univ NH, BS, 50, MS, 55; Univ Wis, PhD(agron), 58. *Prof Exp:* Asst agron, Univ NH, 53-55 & Univ Wis, 55-58; from asst prof to assoc prof, 58-66, PROF CROP SCI, NC STATE UNIV, 66- *Concurrent Pos:* Vis prof agron, Univ Fla, 75. *Honors & Awards:* Ensminger Award, Nat Asn Col & Teachers Agr, 74; Agron Educ Award, Am Soc Agron, 75; Golden Peanut Res Award, Nat Peanut Coun, 76. *Mem:* Fel Am Soc Agron. *Res:* Radiation genetics; breeding of peanuts; cytoplasmic inheritance and physiological genetics of cultivated peanut. *Mailing Add:* Dept of Crop Sci NC State Univ Raleigh NC 27607

EMERY, DONALD F, b Amboy, Ill, Dec 19, 28; m 52; c 2. FOOD CHEMISTRY. *Educ:* Knox Col, BA, 50; Purdue Univ, MS, 52, PhD(biol chem), 55. *Prof Exp:* Proj leader food res, 55-62, head mix develop dept, 62-68, tech dir qual control, 68-70, DIR TECH & QUAL CONTROL SERV, GEN MILLS, INC, 70- *Mem:* Am Asn Cereal Chemists; Inst Food Technologists. *Res:* Food product analysis; microbiology; cereal product development; food preservation methods; quality control; nutrition. *Mailing Add:* J F Bell Tech Ctr Gen Mills Inc 9000 Plymouth Ave Minneapolis MN 55427

EMERY, EDWARD MORTIMER, b New York, NY, Jan 23, 26; m 49; c 4. PHYSICAL CHEMISTRY. *Educ:* Univ Colo, BS, 48, PhD(chem), 52. *Prof Exp:* From res engr to sr res engr, Res Dept, Servel, Inc, 52-55; res chemist, Org Chem Div, 55-60, res proj leader, 60-64, res group leader, 64-70, SR RES GROUP LEADER, MONSANTO INDUST CHEM CO, 70- *Concurrent Pos:* VChmn comt E-19 on chromatog, Am Soc Testing & Mat, 65-68, chmn, 69-70. *Mem:* Am Chem Soc; Sigma Xi. *Res:* Gas and liquid chromatography; organic spectroscopy; physical analytical chemistry; absorption refrigeration; calorimetry; aliphatic fluorine chemistry; instrument development. *Mailing Add:* Monsanto Indust Chem Co 800 N Lindbergh Blvd St Louis MO 63166

EMERY, GUY TRASK, b Manchester, NH, May 22, 31; m 55; c 2. PHYSICS. *Educ:* Bowdoin Col, AB, 53; Harvard Univ, AM, 54, PhD(physics), 59. *Prof Exp:* Res assoc physics, Brookhaven Nat Lab, 59-61, from asst physicist to assoc physicist, 61-66; assoc prof, 66-69, PROF PHYSICS, IND UNIV, 69- *Concurrent Pos:* Vis assoc prof, State Univ NY Stony Brook, 65-66; guest scientist, Keruphysisch Versueller Inst, Univ Groningen, 78-79. *Mem:* Fel Am Phys Soc; Am Asn Physics Teachers; Nederlandse Natuurdandige Ver. *Res:* Intermediate-energy nuclear physics; radioactive decay; neutron-capture gamma rays; atomic effects on nuclear properties; nuclear structure and spectroscopy. *Mailing Add:* Dept of Physics Ind Univ Bloomington IN 47401

EMERY, JERRELL BEMIS, b Toledo, Ohio, Aug 14, 29; m 51; c 3. BACTERIOLOGY, VIROLOGY. *Educ:* Univ Toledo, BEd, 51, MSc, 52; Purdue Univ, PhD, 60. *Prof Exp:* Asst virologist, Children's Hosp Res Found, 52-53; res assoc, Pitman-Moore Co, 53-60, sr virologist, 60-69, sr res virologist, Human Health Res & Develop Dept, 69, SR RES VIROLOGIST, PITMAN-MOORE INC, DOW CHEM CO, 70- *Mem:* AAAS; Am Soc Microbiol; NY Acad Sci. *Res:* Animal virology; immunology. *Mailing Add:* Pitman Moore Inc PO Box 344 Washington Crossing NJ 08560

EMERY, KENNETH ORRIS, b Swift Current, Sask, June 6, 14; US citizen; m 41; c 2. MARINE GEOLOGY. *Educ:* Univ Ill, BS, 37, MS, 39, PhD(geol), 41. *Prof Exp:* Assoc geologist, Ill State Geol Surv, 41-43; marine geologist, Div War Res, Univ Calif, 43-45; from asst prof to prof geol, Univ Southern Calif, 45-62; MARINE GEOLOGIST, WOODS HOLE OCEANOG INST, 62- *Concurrent Pos:* Geologist, US Geol Surv, 46-60; mem, Navy Res & Develop Bd; mem comt paleoecol, Nat Res Coun Del, Pac Sci Cong, NZ, 49 & Philippines, 53; Guggenheim fel, Mid East, 59; oceanog adv to govts of US, Israel & Rep of China; spec adv comt coord offshore prospecting, Econ Coun Asia & Far East, 66-; mem, Nat Acad Sci Comt Oceanog, 71- *Honors & Awards:* Compass Distinguished Serv Award, Marine Technol Soc, 74. *Mem:* Nat Acad Sci; Am Acad Arts & Sci; fel Geol Soc Am; Soc Econ Paleont & Mineral; Am Asn Petrol Geologists. *Res:* Physiography, sediments and lithology of sea floor off California; general marine geology; marine geology of Bikini and nearby atolls, Guam, Persian Gulf; Dead Sea; eastern Mediterranean Sea; geological history of Atlantic continental shelf and slope; oil regions of continental margin off eastern Asia; structure of continental margin off western Africa. *Mailing Add:* 74 Ranson Rd Falmouth MA 02540

EMERY, PHILIP ANTHONY, b Neodesha, Kans, Oct 20, 34; m 60; c 2. HYDROGEOLOGY, GEOLOGY. *Educ:* Univ Kans, BS, 60, MS, 62. *Prof Exp:* Hydrologist, 62-75, DIST CHIEF, US GEOL SURV, WATER RESOURCES DIV, 75- *Mem:* Geol Soc Am; Int Asn Hydrogeologists; Nat Water Well Asn; Sigma Xi; AAAS. *Res:* Hydrologic modeling, hydrology of limestone terranes; hydrology of valley-fill aquifers. *Mailing Add:* US Geol Surv Rm 572 Fed Bldg 600 Fed Pl Louisville KY 40202

EMERY, RICHARD MEYER, b Toledo, Ohio, Mar 19, 39; c 2. LIMNOLOGY, RADIATION ECOLOGY. *Educ:* Univ Toledo, BEd, 62; Ohio State Univ, MS, 66; Univ Wash, PhD(appl limnol), 72. *Prof Exp:* Teacher biol, Clay Sr High Sch, Ohio, 63-66; biologist, Tenn Valley Authority, 66-69; Environ Protection Agency res fel appl limnol, Univ Wash, 69-72; RES SCIENTIST APPL LIMNOL, BATTELLE NORTHWEST LAB, 72- *Mem:* Am Soc Limnol & Oceanog; NAm Benthological Soc; Int Soc Theoret & Appl Limnol; Sigma Xi. *Res:* Characterization and measurement of the ecological behavior of radionuclides in freshwater ecosystems. *Mailing Add:* Dept Ecosyst Battelle Northwest Lab Richland WA 99352

EMERY, ROY SALTSMAN, b Ill, Sept 22, 28; m 52; c 4. ANIMAL NUTRITION, BIOCHEMISTRY. *Educ:* Colo Agr & Mech Col, BS, 50, MS, 52; Mich State Univ, PhD(nutrit, biochem), 55. *Prof Exp:* Asst, 52-55, from asst prof to assoc prof, 55-67, PROF DAIRY NUTRIT, MICH STATE UNIV, 67- *Mem:* Am Feed Mfrs Award, 61; Sigma Xi Jr Res Award, 69. Mem: Am Soc Microbiol; Am Inst Nutrit; Am Dairy Sci Asn; Am Soc Animal Sci. *Res:* Biochemistry and fermentation; digestion and nutrition in ruminants; intermediate and microbial metabolism. *Mailing Add:* Dept of Dairy Sci Mich State Univ East Lansing MI 48824

EMERY, THOMAS FRED, b Ross, Calif, July 31, 31; m 62. BIOCHEMISTRY. *Educ:* Calif Inst Technol, BS, 53; Univ Calif, Berkeley, PhD(biochem), 60. *Prof Exp:* NSF fel, Nat Ctr Sci Res, France, 60-61; from instr to assoc prof biochem, Sch Med, Yale Univ, 61-70; PROF CHEM, UTAH STATE UNIV, 70- *Concurrent Pos:* Brown Mem grant, 61-62; prin investr, USPHS res grant, 62-81. *Mem:* AAAS; Am Chem Soc; Fedn Am Socs Exp Biol. *Res:* Isolation, structure, function and biosynthesis of naturally occurring iron chelates. *Mailing Add:* Dept Chem & Biochem Utah State Univ Logan UT 84322

EMERY, VICTOR JOHN, b Boston, Eng, May 16, 34; m 59; c 3. THEORETICAL PHYSICS. *Educ:* Univ London, BSc, 54; Univ Manchester, PhD(theoret physics), 57. *Prof Exp:* Res assoc, Cambridge Univ, 57-59; Harkness fel, Commonwealth Fund, Univ Calif, Berkeley, 59-60; lectr, Birmingham Univ, 60-63; vis asst prof, Univ Calif, Berkeley, 63-64; SR PHYSICIST, BROOKHAVEN NAT LAB, 64- *Concurrent Pos:* Vis prof, Nordita, Copenhagen, 71-72 & Univ Paris, France, 76 & 81. *Mem:* Fel Am Phys Soc. *Res:* Theoretical solid state; low temperature and statistical physics. *Mailing Add:* Dept of Physics Brookhaven Nat Lab Upton NY 11973

EMERY, W(ILLIS) L(AURENS), b Salt Lake City, Utah, Nov 23, 15; m 41; c 3. ELECTRICAL ENGINEERING. *Educ:* Univ Utah, BS, 36; Iowa State Col, MS, 40, PhD(elec eng), 47. *Prof Exp:* Instr elec eng, Univ Utah, 36-37; sales engr, Campbell-Elsey Co, 37-38; instr elec eng, Univ Utah, 38-39; instr, Iowa State Col, 41-43; radio engr, Naval Res Lab, Washington, DC, 43-45; asst prof, Iowa State Col, 46-47; assoc prof elec eng, Univ Utah, 47-50; assoc prof, 50-53, PROF ELEC ENG, UNIV ILL, URBANA, 53- *Concurrent Pos:* Vis prof, Indian Inst of Technol, Kharagpur, 60-62. *Mem:* AAAS; Inst Elec & Electronics Engrs; Am Phys Soc; Am Soc Eng Educ. *Res:* Microwaves; electrooptics; displays. *Mailing Add:* Dept of Elec Eng Univ of Ill Urbana IL 61801

EMERY, WILLIAM HENRY PERRY, b Wickford, RI, Feb 10, 24; m 46; c 2. CYTOLOGY, TAXONOMY. *Educ:* RI State Col, BS, 48; Univ Conn, MS, 50; Univ Tex, PhD(cyto-taxon), 56. *Prof Exp:* Fel cyto-taxon, 57, from instr to assoc prof biol, 57-67, PROF BIOL, SOUTHWEST TEX STATE UNIV, 67- *Concurrent Pos:* Plant taxonomist, Espey Huston Assoc & Southwest Res Inst, 74- *Mem:* AAAS; Am Bot Soc. *Res:* Cyto-taxonomy and breeding of aquatic grasses. *Mailing Add:* Dept Biol Southwest Tex State Univ San Marcos TX 78666

EMERY, WILLIAM JACKSON, b Honolulu, Hawaii, Apr 15, 46; m 70; c 3. PHYSICAL OCEANOGRAPHY. *Educ:* Brigham Young Univ, BS, 71; Univ Hawaii, PhD(phys oceanog), 75. *Prof Exp:* Res assoc phys oceanog, Univ Hawaii, 75-76; res assoc phys oceanog, Tex A&M Univ, 76-78; ASST PROF PHYS OCEANOG, UNIV BC, 78- *Mem:* Am Meteorol Soc; Am Geophys Union; Can Meteorol Oceanog Soc. *Res:* Large scale ocean and ocean-atmosphere problems; temperature and salinity structures of the Pacific ocean; mesoscale temperature studies. *Mailing Add:* Inst of Oceanog 2075 Wesbrook Mall Vancouver BC V6T 1W5 Can

EMGE, ROBERT GEORGE, b San Diego, Calif, Sept 13, 18; m 60; c 1. PLANT PATHOLOGY. *Educ:* Univ Ill, BS, 46, PhD(plant path), 50. *Prof Exp:* Exten plant pathologist, Univ Ark, 49-51; plant pathologist, Ft Detrick, Md, 51-57, Taft Sanit Eng Ctr, USDA, Ohio, 57-59 & Ft Detrick, Md, 59-71; plant pathologist, Plant Dis Res Lab, USDA, 71-80, quarantine officer, 77-80; CONSULT, 80- *Mem:* Am Phytopath Soc. *Res:* Diseases of cereal crops; epiphytology of cereal rusts; host-pathogen relationships; biocontrol (pathogenic) of weeds; microclimatology; air pollution. *Mailing Add:* 604 Biggs Ave Frederick MD 21701

EMIGH, CHARLES ROBERT, b Seattle, Wash, Apr 7, 20; m 46; c 3. PHYSICS. *Educ:* Univ Colo, BS, 42; Univ Ill, MS, 48, PhD(physics), 51. *Prof Exp:* Jr engr, Res & Develop, Westinghouse Elec Corp, 42-44; asst physics, Univ Ill, 46-51; mem staff, 51-72, dir intense neutron source facil, 72-78, ASSOC DIV LEADER ENERGY TECHNOL, LOS ALAMOS NAT LAB, 78- *Concurrent Pos:* Ford Found sr fel, Europ Ctr Nuclear Res, Geneva, 57; adj prof physics, Univ NMex, 67-73 & 80- *Mem:* Am Phys Soc; Soc Nondestructive Testing; Inst Elec & Electronics Engrs; Am Nuclear Soc. *Res:* Experimental and theoretical physics; design and development of apparatus used in experimental physics; solid state physics; accelerator physics and engineering. *Mailing Add:* 215 Barranca Rd Los Alamos NM 87544

EMIGH, G DONALD, b Burley, Idaho, Jan 21, 11; m 38; c 2. MINING, METALLURGY. *Educ:* Univ Idaho, BS, 32, MS, 34; Univ Ariz, PhD(geol), 56. *Prof Exp:* Mining engr, Gen Elec Co, 36-37 & US Vanadium Corp, 37-48; dir mining, Monsanto Co, St Louis, 49-76; CONSULT, 76- *Mem:* Distinguished mem Am Inst Mining, Metall & Petrol Engrs; Soc Econ Geol; Geol Soc Am; Am Inst Prof Geologists; Can Inst Mining & Metall. *Res:* Mineral industry and exploration. *Mailing Add:* 202 Churchill Dr Burley ID 83318

EMILIANI, CESARE, b Bologna, Italy, Dec 8, 22; m 51; c 2. CLIMATOLOGY, MARINE GEOLOGY. *Educ:* Univ Bologna, Doctorate, 45; Univ Chicago, PhD(geol), 50. *Prof Exp:* Geologist petrol, Nat Soc Hydrocarbons, Italy, 46-48; res assoc geochem, Univ Chicago, 50-56; assoc prof, 57-63, PROF MARINE GEOL, UNIV MIAMI, 63- *Mem:* Fel AAAS; fel Am Geophys Union. *Res:* Isotope paleoclimatology. *Mailing Add:* Dept Geol Univ Miami Miami FL 33124

EMIN, DAVID, b New York, NY, Oct 2, 41; m 63. SOLID STATE PHYSICS. *Educ:* Fla State Univ, BA, 62; Univ Pittsburgh, PhD(physics), 68. *Prof Exp:* Asst res physicist, Univ Calif, Los Angeles, 68-69; MEM TECH STAFF THEORET PHYSICS, SANDIA NAT LABS, 69- *Mem:* Fel Am Phys Soc. *Res:* Low- mobility electrical transport theory; small-polaron motion; polaron theory; atomic diffusion; amorphous semiconductors. *Mailing Add:* Div 5151 Sandia Nat Labs Albuquerque NM 87185

EMINO, EVERETT RAYMOND, b Milford, Mass, Feb 8, 42; m 67; c 2. HORTICULTURE, FLORICULTURE. *Educ:* Univ Mass, BS, 65; Mich State Univ, MS, 67, PhD(hort), 72. *Prof Exp:* Grad asst hort, Mich State Univ, 65-67, instr, 67-72; asst prof plant sci, Univ Mass, 72-75; ASSOC PROF FLORICULT, TEX A&M UNIV, 75- *Mem:* Am Soc Hort Sci; Am Hort Soc; Bot Soc Am; Int Plant Propagators Soc; Nat Asn Col & Teachers Agr. *Res:* Investigations on the morphology and physiology of floricultural crops with special emphasis on the soil plant relationship and the environmental control of flowering. *Mailing Add:* Dept of Hort Sci Tex A&M Univ College Station TX 77843

EMKEN, EDWARD ALLEN, b Yates City, Ill, Aug 12, 40; m 64; c 2. LIPID CHEMISTRY, ORGANIC BIOCHEMISTRY. *Educ:* Bradley Univ, BS, 63; Univ Iowa, MS, 68, PhD(org chem), 69. *Prof Exp:* Sci trainee, 59-63, asst res chemist, 63-64, assoc res chemist, 64-69, RES LEADER, NORTHERN REGIONAL RES LABS, USDA, 69- *Concurrent Pos:* Teaching asst, Univ Iowa, 66-69; adj prof, Peoria Sch Med. *Honors & Awards:* Bond Award, Am Oil Chemist's Soc, 72. *Mem:* Am Chem Soc; Am Oil Chemist's Soc. *Res:* Enzyme reactions of lipids; synthesis of radioisotope and deuterium-labeled compounds, isomeric fatty acids and pheromones; methods developed for lipid and fatty acid isomer analysis, separation and determination of physical properties; biochemistry and nutrition of dietary fats and oils; clinical studies on lipid related diseases and disorders. *Mailing Add:* USDA Northern Regional Res Ctr 1815 N University St Peoria IL 61604

EMLEN, JOHN MERRITT, b Sacramento, Calif, Jan 15, 38. ECOLOGY. *Educ:* Univ Wis, BA, 61; Univ Wash, PhD(zool), 66. *Prof Exp:* Asst prof biol, Univ Colo, Boulder, 66-68; asst prof, State Univ NY Stony Brook, 68-71; asst prof, 71-78, ASSOC PROF BIOL, IND UNIV, BLOOMINGTON, 78- *Concurrent Pos:* NSF grant, 67-69. *Mem:* AAAS; Ecol Soc Am; Am Soc Naturalists. *Res:* Theoretical and behavioral ecology; natural selection; population biology. *Mailing Add:* Dept of Zool Ind Univ Bloomington IN 47401

EMLEN, JOHN THOMPSON, JR, b Philadelphia, Pa, Dec 28, 08; m 34; c 3. ZOOLOGY. *Educ:* Haverford Col, BS, 31; Cornell Univ, PhD(ornith), 34. *Hon Degrees:* DSc, Haverford Col, 70. *Prof Exp:* Jr biologist, Bur Biol Surv, USDA, 34-35; from instr zool & jr biologist to asst prof zool & asst zoologist, Exp Sta, Univ Calif, 35-43; res assoc, Rockefeller Inst, 43-46; from assoc prof to prof, 46-73, chmn dept, 51-53 & 54-55, EMER PROF ZOOL, UNIV WIS-MADISON, 73- *Concurrent Pos:* Guggenheim fel, Cent Africa, 53-54; NSF res fel, Africa, 59 & Antarctica, 62-64. *Mem:* AAAS; Am Ornith Union (pres, 75); Am Soc Mammalogists; Wilson Ornith Soc (pres, 60); Ecol Soc Am. *Res:* Population and behavior studies of birds and mammals. *Mailing Add:* Dept of Zool Univ of Wis Madison WI 53706

EMLEN, STEPHEN THOMPSON, b Sacramento, Calif, Aug 21, 40; m 73; c 2. ANIMAL BEHAVIOR, ECOLOGY. *Educ:* Swarthmore Col, BA, 62; Univ Mich, MS, 64, PhD(zool), 66. *Prof Exp:* From asst prof to assoc prof, 66-75, PROF ZOOL, CORNELL UNIV, 75- *Mem:* AAAS; Animal Behav Soc; Ecol Soc Am; Am Ornith Union; Cooper Ornith Soc. *Res:* Orientation and navigation behavior; visual and acoustical communication systems; evolution of social organization among vertebrates. *Mailing Add:* Div of Biol Sci Cornell Univ Ithaca NY 14850

EMLET, HARRY ELSWORTH, JR, b New Oxford, Pa, Sept 21, 27; m 51; c 2. SYSTEMS ANALYSIS, HEALTH SCIENCES. *Educ:* Princeton Univ, AB, 52. *Prof Exp:* Systs reviewer automatic data processing, Prudential Ins Co, 55-56; aeronaut engr, Martin Co, 56-57; res analyst weapons systs anal, Melpar, Inc, 57-58; aeronaut engr & proj leader, 58-65, chief plans br, 65-67, chief tactical br, 67-70, mgr tactical div & health serv studies, 70-74, mgr, 74-76, VPRES HEALTH SYSTS, ANAL SERV, INC, 76- *Concurrent Pos:* Mem, US Air Force Keese Comt Air Force Space Plan, 61 & Holzapple Comt Air Force Space Prog, 62; mem adv comt health model develop, Mil Health Care Study, Off Mgt & Budget, 74-75; chmn health appln sect, Opers Res Soc Am, 76-; mem bd dirs, Symp Comput-Appln in Med Care, Inc, 79-, gen chmn, 80- *Mem:* Opers Res Soc Am; Soc Advan Med Systs (vpres, 75-76, pres-elect, 76-77, pres, 77-78); Am Inst Aeronaut & Astronaut. *Res:* Military operational requirements analysis; research and development planning; weapons system analysis; planning techniques; philosophy; health systems analysis and evaluation. *Mailing Add:* 400 Army-Navy Dr Arlington VA 22202

EMLING, BERTIN LEO, b Erie, Pa, July 9, 05. ORGANIC CHEMISTRY. *Educ:* St Vincent Col, AB, 31; Johns Hopkins Univ, MA, 38; Univ Notre Dame, PhD(chem), 41. *Prof Exp:* From instr to prof org chem, 37-80, mem bd dirs, 57-65, EMER PROF ORG CHEM, ST VINCENT COL, 80- *Concurrent Pos:* Proj dir, Nat Coop Undergrad Chem Res Prog, 48-57. *Mem:* AAAS; Am Chem Soc. *Res:* Sulfonic acid esters; furyl amines; acetylenes; olefins; Schiff bases; polyester resins; autoxidation. *Mailing Add:* Dept of Chem St Vincent Col Latrobe PA 15650

EMMANOUILIDES, GEORGE CHRISTOS, b Drama, Greece, Dec 17, 26; US citizen; m 59; c 5. PEDIATRICS, CARDIOLOGY. *Educ:* Univ Thessaloniki, MD, 51; Univ Calif, Los Angeles, MS, 63. *Prof Exp:* From asst prof to assoc prof, 63-73, PROF PEDIAT, SCH MED, UNIV CALIF, LOS ANGELES, 73- *Concurrent Pos:* Chief div pediat cardiol & neonatology, Harbor Gen Hosp, Torrance, Calif, 63-69 & div pediat cardiol, 69-; mem coun cardiovasc dis of young, clin cardiol & cardiopulmonary dis, Am Heart Asn; fel pediat hemat, Children's Hosp of DC, 59-60; Ont Heart Asn fel, Hosp for Sick Children, Toronto, 60-61; USPHS trainee pediat cardiol, Med Ctr, Univ

Calif, Los Angeles, 61-63; chmn exec comt, Sect Cardiol, Am Acad Pediat, 78-80. *Mem:* AAAS; Am Pediat Soc; fel Am Col Cardiol; Am Soc Pathologists; Am Acad Pediat. *Res:* Cardiorespiratory adjustments of the newborn; fetal and neonatal physiology; pediatric cardiology. *Mailing Add:* Harbor-UCLA Med Ctr 1000 W Carson Ave Torrance CA 90509

EMMANUEL, GEORGE, b Tanta, Egypt, Sept 19, 25; US citizen; m 59; c 4. CARDIOPULMONARY PHYSIOLOGY. *Educ:* Nat Univ Athens, MD, 52. *Prof Exp:* Mem fac cardiopulmonary physiol, Belleview Hosp, Columbia Univ, 57-59; from instr to asst prof, 59-67, ASSOC PROF MED, STATE UNIV NY DOWNSTATE MED CTR, 67- *Mem:* Am Physiol Soc; Am Soc Clin Invest; Am Heart Asn; Harvey Soc. *Res:* Cardiopulmonary physiology; teachings of medicine. *Mailing Add:* 193 Clinton Ave Brooklyn NY 11205

EMMATTY, DAVY A, b Trichur, India, Sept 29, 41; m 68; c 1. PHYTOPATHOLOGY. *Educ:* Univ Kerala, BS, 61; Purdue Univ, MS, 66, PhD(plant path), 68. *Prof Exp:* SR RES PLANT PATHOLOGIST, H J HEINZ CO, 68- *Res:* Development of tomatoes resistant to bacterial canker, tobacco mosaic virus, Verticillium, Fusarium race 1 & 2, bacterial spot, bacterial wilt and anthracnose; development of cucumbers resistant to Pseudomonas, cucumber mosaic virus, watermelon mosaic virus, Cladosporium and Mycosphaerella. *Mailing Add:* Agr Res Dept H J Heinz Co 13737 Middleton Pike Bowling Green OH 43402

EMMEL, THOMAS C, b Inglewood, Calif, May 8, 41. POPULATION BIOLOGY, GENETICS. *Educ:* Reed Col, BA, 63; Stanford Univ, PhD(pop biol), 67. *Prof Exp:* Lectr entom, San Jose State Col, 65-66; course coordr, Orgn Trop Studies, Inc, Costa Rica & prof trop biol, Univ Costa Rica, 67-69; asst prof biol sci & zool, 68-73, assoc prof zool, 73-75, PROF ZOOL & CHMN DEPT, UNIV FLA, 75- *Concurrent Pos:* NIH fel genetics, Univ Tex, Austin, 67-68. *Mem:* AAAS; Soc Study Evolution; Asn Trop Biol; Ecol Soc Am; Lepidop Soc. *Res:* Population biology of tropical and Nearctic organisms; ecological genetics of natural populations, especially satyrid and nymphalid butterflies and land snails; territorial behavior. *Mailing Add:* Dept of Zool Univ of Fla Gainesville FL 32611

EMMEL, VICTOR MEYER, b St Louis, Mo, Mar 22, 13; m 43; c 4. HISTOLOGY. *Educ:* Brown Univ, AB, 35, MS, 37, PhD(biol), 39; Univ Rochester, MD, 47. *Prof Exp:* From instr to prof, 40-78, EMER PROF ANAT, SCH MED & DENT, UNIV ROCHESTER, 78- *Concurrent Pos:* Intern, Strong Mem Hosp, Rochester, 47-48; trustee & secy, Biol Stain Comn, 55-80; Nat Res Coun fel med sci, Sch Med, Yale Univ, 39-40; assoc ed, Stain Technol. *Mem:* Am Asn Anat; AAAS; Soc Exp Biol & Med; Nutrit Today Soc; Histochem Soc. *Res:* Chemistry of sea-water; menstruation in the monkey; cytology and cytochemistry of the kidney and intestine; histopathology of kidney and intestine in vitamin E deficiency. *Mailing Add:* 55 Reservoir Ave Rochester NY 14620

EMMERICH, WERNER SIGMUND, b Düsseldorf, Ger, June 3, 21; nat US; m 53; c 3. PLASMA PHYSICS. *Educ:* Ohio State Univ, BS, 49, MS, 50, PhD(physics), 53. *Prof Exp:* Res engr nuclear physics, 53-57, adv physicist, 57-64, mgr arc & plasma res, 64-75, DIR POWER SYSTS RES & DEVELOP, WESTINGHOUSE RES & DEVELOP CTR, 75- *Mem:* NY Acad Sci; AAAS; fel Am Phys Soc; Combustion Inst; Am Nuclear Soc. *Res:* Optical model of atomic nucleus; beta, gamma and neutron spectroscopy; power circuit interruption; research planning. *Mailing Add:* 1883 Beulah Rd Pittsburgh PA 15235

EMMERS, RAIMOND, b Liepaja, Latvia, Apr 19, 24; US citizen; m 56. MEDICAL PHYSIOLOGY, NEUROPHYSIOLOGY. *Educ:* ETex Baptist Col, BA, 53; Univ NC, MA, 55; Syracuse Univ, PhD(neurophysiol), 58. *Prof Exp:* Asst prof, 61-71, ASSOC PROF PHYSIOL, COL PHYSICIANS & SURGEONS, COLUMBIA UNIV, 71- *Concurrent Pos:* Dir, Nat Inst Neurol Dis & Stroke Res Proj, 61; Nat Inst Neurol Dis & Blindness res fel, 58-60; res fel neurophysiol, Univ Wis, 59-61. *Mem:* Am Physiol Soc; Am Asn Anat. *Res:* Neural mechanisms of taste and somesthesia; significance of taste in nutrition; sensory coding in the central nervous systems. *Mailing Add:* Dept of Physiol Columbia Univ Col of Physicians & Surgeons New York NY 10032

EMMERSON, JOHN LYNN, b Princeton, Ind, Nov 21, 33; m 57; c 2. PHARMACOLOGY, TOXICOLOGY. *Educ:* Purdue Univ, BS, 58, MS, 60, PhD(pharmacol), 62. *Prof Exp:* Sr pharmacologist, Eli Lilly & Co, 61-65; assoc prof toxicol, Purdue Univ, 65-66; sr toxicologist, 66-67, head exp toxicol & path, 67-77, DIR TOXICOL STUDIES, ELI LILLY & CO, 77- *Mem:* AAAS; Am Soc Pharmacol & Exp Therapeut; Soc Toxicol. *Res:* Biochemical mechanisms and metabolic aspects of drug toxicity. *Mailing Add:* Lilly Toxicol Labs Eli Lilly & Co Greenfield IN 46140

EMMERT, GILBERT A, b Merced, Calif, June 2, 38; m 64; c 2. PLASMA PHYSICS. *Educ:* Univ Calif, Berkeley, BS, 61; Rensselaer Polytech Inst, MS, 64; Stevens Inst Technol, PhD(physics), 68. *Prof Exp:* Anal engr, Energy Conversion Systs, United Aircraft Corp, 61-64; asst prof, 68-72, assoc prof, 72-79, PROF NUCLEAR ENG, UNIV WIS-MADISON, 79- *Mem:* Am Phys Soc. *Res:* Theoretical plasma physics; waves and instabilities in magnetically confined plasmas; plasma-wall interactions; systems studies of controlled thermonuclear fusion. *Mailing Add:* Dept of Nuclear Eng Eng Res Bldg Univ of Wis Madison WI 53706

EMMERT, R(ICHARD) E(UGENE), b Iowa City, Iowa, Feb 23, 29; m 49; c 3. CHEMICAL ENGINEERING. *Educ:* Univ Iowa, BS, 51; Univ Del, MChE, 52, PhD(chem eng), 54. *Prof Exp:* Res engr chem eng, 54-58, res proj supvr, 58-61, sr res engr, 61, res supvr, 61-63, mgr indust develop, 63-64, area supvr mfg, 64-66, mfg supt, 66-67, asst plant mgr, 67-69, mgr eng technol & mat res, 69-72, dir res & develop, Pigments dept, 72-74, dir instrument prod, 75-76, dir electronic prod, 77-78, gen mgr textile fibers, 79-80, VPRES CORP PLANS, E I DU PONT DE NEMOURS & CO, INC, 81- *Mem:* Am Inst Chem Engrs; Am Chem Soc. *Res:* Reaction kinetics; polymerization technology; mass transfer; gas absorption. *Mailing Add:* E I du Pont de Nemours & Co Inc Wilmington DE 19898

EMMETT, EDWARD ANTHONY, b Sydney, Australia, Feb 29, 40. ENVIRONMENTAL HEALTH, OCCUPATIONAL MEDICINE. *Educ:* Univ Sydney, MB, BS, 64; FRACP, 74; Univ Cincinnati, MS, 75. *Prof Exp:* Med intern, Royal Prince Alfred Hosp, Sydney, 64, resident physician, 65; med resident, Repatriation Gen Hosp, Concord, Australia, 66-69; fel environ health, Univ Cincinnati, 70, asst prof environ health & internal med, 71-75, assoc prof environ health, med, & dermat, 75-78; PROF ENVIRON HEALTH SCI & DIR DIV OCCUP MED, JOHNS HOPKINS UNIV, 78- *Mem:* Am Fedn Clin Res; Soc Investigative Dermat; Am Soc Photobiol; NY Acad Sci; Am Occup Med Asn. *Res:* Epidemiology, pathogenesis and prevention of occupational and environmental disease; photobiology. *Mailing Add:* Dept Environ Health Sci 615 N Wolfe St Baltimore MD 21205

EMMETT, PAUL HUGH, b Portland, Ore, Sept 22, 00; m 30. PHYSICAL CHEMISTRY. *Educ:* Ore State Col, BS, 22; Calif Inst Technol, PhD(phys chem), 25. *Hon Degrees:* DSc, Ore State Col, 39, Clarkson Col, 69, Univ Wis, Milwaukee, 71; Dr, Univ Lyons, 64; LLD, Hokkaido Univ, Japan, 76. *Prof Exp:* Instr, Ore State Col, 25-26; from asst to sr chemist, Fixed Nitrogen Res Lab, Bur Chem & Soils, USDA, 26-37; prof chem eng, Johns Hopkins, 37-44; sr fel, Mellon Inst, 44-55; W R Grace prof chem, Johns Hopkins Univ, 55-71; INDUST, GOVT & ACAD CONSULT & LECTR, 71- *Concurrent Pos:* Lectr, George Washington Univ, 27-29, 31-32, 33-34 & 35-36; mem comt contact catalysis, Nat Res Coun, 37-42; div chief, Manhattan Proj, Columbia Univ, 43-44; mem, Coun Sci Res, Madrid, Spain, 64; vis prof chem, Portland State Univ, 71- *Honors & Awards:* Pittsburgh Award, Am Chem Soc, 53, Kendall Award, 58, Md Award, 70. *Mem:* Nat Acad Sci; Am Chem Soc. *Res:* Contact catalysis; adsorption of gases on solids; heterogeneous gas-solid equilibria. *Mailing Add:* 23 Da Vinci Lake Oswego OR 97034

EMMETT-OGLESBY, MICHAEL WAYNE, b Portland, Ore, Sept 12, 47; m 75. PHARMACOLOGY. *Educ:* Univ Chicago, BA, 69; State Univ NY Buffalo, PhD(pharmacol), 73. *Prof Exp:* NIH fel pharmacol, Univ Chicago, 73-75; asst prof pharmacol, 75-80, ASSOC PROF PHARMACOL, TEX COL OSTEOP MED, 80- *Mem:* AAAS; Soc Neurosci; Am Soc Pharmacol & Exp Therapeut. *Res:* Behavioral and neurochemical studies of mechanisms mediating the effects of drugs on behavior. *Mailing Add:* Dept Pharmacol Tex Col Osteop Med Fort Worth TX 76107

EMMICK, ROBERT D, b Holland, Mich, Aug 13, 20; m 45. ORGANIC CHEMISTRY. *Educ:* Hope Col, AB, 42; Univ Ill, PhD(org chem), 46. *Prof Exp:* Asst, Univ Ill, 42-44 & Nat Defense Res Comt & Off Rubber Res Contracts, 44-46; res chemist, Electrochem Dept, 46-57, patent chemist, 57-59, supvr, Patent Sect, 59-62, patent agt, 62-63, sr patent chemist, Textile Fibers Dept, 63-66, patent supvr, 66-72, patent mgr, 72-77, ASST TO TECH DIR, TEXTILE FIBERS DEPT, E I DU PONT DE NEMOURS & CO, INC, 77- *Res:* Polymerization; nonwoven fabrics. *Mailing Add:* 39 Shellburne Wilmington DE 19803

EMMICK, THOMAS LYNN, b Indianapolis, Ind, Aug 1, 40; m 62; c 2. ORGANIC CHEMISTRY. *Educ:* Wabash Col, AB, 62; Northwestern Univ, PhD(org chem), 67. *Prof Exp:* Sr org chemist res, Eli Lilly & Co, 66-71, head agr prod develop, 71-72, HEAD AGR ORG CHEM, LILLY RES LABS, DIV ELI LILLY & CO, 72- *Mem:* Am Chem Soc. *Res:* Synthetic organic chemicals useful in the agricultural area as pesticides, as agents to stimulate growth in meat producing animals, or as agents effective against diseases in animals. *Mailing Add:* Dept IC212 Bldg 1702 Eli Lilly & Co Indianapolis IN 46285

EMMONS, ARDATH HENRY, b Albert Lea, Minn, Mar 12, 24; m 44; c 5. NUCLEAR ENGINEERING. *Educ:* Univ Dubuque, BS, 48; Univ Mich, MS, 54, PhD(nuclear sci), 60. *Prof Exp:* Jr chemist, Oak Ridge Nat Lab, 49-51; assoc radiation safety officer, Univ Mich, 51-55, lab supvr, Phoenix Lab, 55-60; dir res reactor, 60-70, PROF NUCLEAR ENG, UNIV MO-COLUMBIA, 64-, V PRES RES, 70- *Mem:* AAAS; Health Physics Soc; Am Nuclear Soc; Am Soc Eng Educ. *Res:* Wavelength dependence of radiation effects; radiation and reactor applications; laboratory and reactor design; science and research administration. *Mailing Add:* 309 University Hall Univ of Mo Columbia MO 65201

EMMONS, DOUGLAS BYRON, b Can May 23, 30; m 53; c 5. AGRICULTURE, DAIRY INDUSTRY. *Educ:* Ont Agr Col, BSA, 52; Univ Wis, MS, 53, PhD(dairy indust), 57. *Prof Exp:* From instr to asst prof, Univ Wis, 55-58; PRIN RES SCIENTIST, CAN DEPT AGR, 58- *Honors & Awards:* Pfizer Paul-Lewis Award, Am Dairy Sci Asn, 63; William J Eva Award, Can Inst Food Sci Technol, 81. *Mem:* Am Dairy Sci Asn; Agr Inst Can; Can Inst Food Technol. *Res:* Cottage and cheddar cheese. *Mailing Add:* Food Res Inst Agr Can Ottawa ON K1A 0C6 Can

EMMONS, HAMILTON, b London, Eng, Dec 30, 30; US citizen; m 59; c 3. OPERATIONS RESEARCH. *Educ:* Harvard Col, AB, 52; Univ Minn, MS, 58; NY Univ, MS, 62; Johns Hopkins Univ, PhD(opers res), 68. *Prof Exp:* Mem tech staff, Bell Tel Labs, 58-64; asst prof opers res, Cornell Univ, 68-73; chmn dept, 76-79, ASSOC PROF OPERS RES, CASE WESTERN RESERVE UNIV, 73- *Mem:* AAAS; Inst Mgt Sci; Opers Res Soc Am. *Res:* Management of health care; scheduling theory; stochastic processes; semi-Markov decision processes. *Mailing Add:* Dept Opers Res Sears Libr Bldg Case Western Reserve Univ Cleveland OH 44106

EMMONS, HOWARD W(ILSON), b Morristown, NJ, Aug 30, 12; m 35; c 3. MECHANICAL ENGINEERING. *Educ:* Stevens Inst Technol, ME, 33, MS, 35; Harvard Univ, ScD(eng), 38. *Hon Degrees:* DEng, Stevens Inst Technol, 63. *Prof Exp:* Res engr, Westinghouse Elec Co, 37-39; asst prof mech eng, Univ Pa, 39-40; from asst prof to assoc prof, 40-50, PROF MECH ENG, HARVARD UNIV, 50- *Concurrent Pos:* Fulbright-Guggenheim fel, Eng, 52-53; Hunsaker vis prof, Mass Inst Technol, 57-58; consult, Pratt & Whitney Aircraft, 40-78, Army Ord Ballistics Res Lab, Aberdeen Proving Ground, Md, 40-55 & Naval Ord Lab, 46-52; mem space sci technol panel, Off Sci & Technol, 60-71; mem Govt adv comt on sci & Technol, 65-71; chmn

Mass Sci & Technol Found, 70-74; mem Mass Nuclear Safety Comn, 74-75; with Nat Adv Comt Aeronaut, 44 & Adv Bd Nav Ord Test Sta, 49-55; mem, Fire Res Comt, Nat Acad Sci, 56-73; mem, Gas Centrifuge Theory Consult Group, 79-; chmn, Nat Eng Lab, Nat Bur Statist, 81- *Mem:* Nat Acad Sci; Nat Acad Eng; Am Phys Soc; Am Soc Mech Engrs; Am Acad Arts & Sci. *Res:* Aerodynamics of combustion; supersonic aerodynamics; numerical solution of differential equations; fundamentals of gas dynamics. *Mailing Add:* 308 Pierce Hall Harvard Univ Cambridge MA 02138

EMMONS, LARRIMORE BROWNELLER, b Dover, NJ, Oct 6, 35; m 59; c 2. HOLOGRAPHY, COLORIMETRY. *Educ:* Lehigh Univ, BS, 57; Univ Rochester, PhD(physics), 66. *Prof Exp:* Advan develop engr physics, Lighting Group, GTE-Sylvania, 66-71; instr physics, Salem State Col, 71; RES SCIENTIST, ARMSTRONG WORLD INDUST, 72- *Mem:* Optical Soc Am. *Res:* Optical properties of polymers; light scattering by particles and fibers; analysis and synthesis of images by computer for research and process control; illuminating engineering. *Mailing Add:* 974 Hermosa Ave Lancaster PA 17601

EMMONS, LYMAN RANDLETT, b Lawrence, Mass, June 14, 27; m 71; c 2. BIOLOGY. *Educ:* Trinity Col, Conn, BS, 51; Univ Va, MA, 59, PhD(biol), 61. *Prof Exp:* Master, Episcopal High Sch, Va, 51-57; from asst prof to assoc prof, 61-69, PROF BIOL, WASHINGTON & LEE UNIV, 69- *Mem:* Genetics Soc Am; Am Soc Human Genetics; Am Soc Zool. *Res:* Mammalian cytogenetics; biochemical and microbial genetics. *Mailing Add:* Dept of Biol Washington & Lee Univ Lexington VA 24450

EMMONS, RICHARD CONRAD, b Winnipeg, Man, Aug 28, 98; nat US; m. GEOLOGY. *Educ:* Univ BC, BA, 19, MA, 20; Univ Wis, PhD(geol), 24. *Prof Exp:* Instr geol, Univ Chicago, 24; instr, 25, from asst prof to assoc prof, 26-37, PROF GEOL, UNIV WIS-MADISON, 37- *Concurrent Pos:* Geologist, Geol Surv Can, 20-28. *Mem:* Fel Geol Soc Am (vpres, 45); fel Mineral Soc Am (pres, 44). *Res:* Mineralogy; optical mineralogy; petrology; geology of the original Huronian area; the Ontario Pre-Cambrian; five axis universal stage; optical properties of feldspars; silicosis; geology of central Wisconsin; selected petrogenic aspects of plagioclase; steel penetration in foundry sand; genesis of geosynclinal granites; granites by recrystallization; gem stones. *Mailing Add:* Weeks Hall Univ of Wis Madison WI 53706

EMMONS, RICHARD WILLIAM, b New York, NY, Oct 21, 31; m 59; c 5. PUBLIC HEALTH, VIROLOGY. *Educ:* Earlham Col, BA, 53; Univ Pa, MD, 57; London Sch Hyg & Trop Med, DTM&H, 61; Univ Calif, Berkeley, MPH, 62, PhD(epidemiol), 65; Am Bd Prev Med, cert, 69. *Prof Exp:* Intern, Cincinnati Gen Hosp, 57-58; med officer, Div Indian Health, USPHS, 58-60; PUB HEALTH MED OFFICER, VIRAL & RICKETTSIAL DIS LAB, CALIF STATE DEPT HEALTH, 65- *Concurrent Pos:* Lectr, Sch Pub Health, Univ Calif, Berkeley, 71-; consult arbovirus dis, WHO, 71- *Mem:* Am Soc Trop Med & Hyg; Am Pub Health Asn; Am Soc Microbiol; Wildlife Dis Asn. *Res:* Investigation by laboratory research, field studies, and epidemiological research, of viral, rickettsial, and bacterial zoonotic infectious diseases. *Mailing Add:* Viral & Rickettsial Dis Lab 2151 Berkeley Way Berkeley CA 94704

EMMONS, SCOTT W, b Boston, Mass, July 14, 45. EUKARYOTE GENE EXPRESSION, DEVELOPMENTAL BIOLOGY. *Educ:* Harvard Univ, AB, 67; Stanford Univ, PhD(biochem), 74. *Prof Exp:* Fel molecular biol, Carnegie Inst of Washington, Baltimore, 74-76, Univ Colo, Boulder, 76-79; ASST PROF, ALBERT EINSTEIN COL MED, 79- *Res:* Genome organization and control of gene expression on the nematode caenorhabditis elegans. *Mailing Add:* Dept Molecular Biol Albert Einstein Col Med 1300 Morris Park Ave Bronx NY 10461

EMMONS, WILLIAM DAVID, b Minneapolis, Minn, Nov 18, 24; m 49; c 3. ORGANIC CHEMISTRY. *Educ:* Univ Minn, BS, 47; Univ Ill, PhD(chem), 51. *Prof Exp:* Sr chemist, 51-52, group leader org chem, 52-57, lab head, 57-61, res supvr, 61-72, DIR PIONEERING RES, ROHM AND HAAS CO, 73- *Concurrent Pos:* Ed, Org Syntheses, 61-69. *Mem:* Am Chem Soc. *Res:* Peracids; small ring heterocycles; organophosphorous chemistry; polymers and surface coatings. *Mailing Add:* 1411 Holcomb Rd Huntingdon Valley PA 19006

EMPEN, JOSEPH A, b Ashton, Ill, Mar 6, 40; m 62; c 3. ORGANIC POLYMER CHEMISTRY. *Educ:* Knox Col, Ill, BA, 62; Univ Iowa, MS, 64, PhD(org chem), 66. *Prof Exp:* Fel polymers, Univ Ariz, 66-67; res chemist, Plastics Dept, E I du Pont de Nemours & Co, 67-71; sr res chemist, 71-75, group leader, paper & paper converting, 75-78, group leader, paper, 75-78, lab mgr, New Prod Div, 78-80, MGR, GUNTHER PROD DIV, A E STALEY MFG CO, 80- *Mem:* Am Chem Soc; Tech Asn Pulp & Paper Indust. *Res:* Modification of starches to fit the ever changing bonding needs of the paper industry. *Mailing Add:* A E Staley Mfg Co Decatur IL 62525

EMPTAGE, MICHAEL ROLLINS, b Jersey City, NJ, June 10, 39; m 69. CHEMICAL PHYSICS. *Educ:* Middlebury Col, AB, 60; Harvard Univ, PhD(chem), 65. *Prof Exp:* NATO fel, Free Univ Brussels, 64-65; res assoc chem, Brown Univ, 65-66; asst prof, Univ Md, 66-68; ASST PROF CHEM, SOUTHERN ILL UNIV, 68- *Mem:* AAAS; Am Phys Soc; Am Chem Soc. *Res:* Microwave spectroscopy; statistical mechanics of transport phenomena; chemical reactions in imperfect gases. *Mailing Add:* Dept of Chem Southern Ill Univ Carbondale IL 62901

EMRICH, GROVER HARRY, b Englewood, NJ, Apr 9, 29; m 52; c 6. ENVIRONMENTAL GEOLOGY. *Educ:* Franklin & Marshall Col, BS, 52; Fla State Univ, MS, 57; Univ Ill, PhD(geol), 62. *Prof Exp:* Asst geol, Fla State Univ, 54-56; field surveyor, Fla Geol Surv, 55; asst, Ill Geol Surv, 56-58, asst geologist, 58-63; ground water geologist, State Dept Health, Pa, 63-71; mgr, Environ Resources Dept, 71-74, vpres, A W Martin Assocs, 74-79, PRES, SMC MARTIN INC, 80- *Mem:* Fel Geol Soc Am; Nat Water Well Asn; Am Water Resources Asn; Water Pollution Control Fedn. *Res:* Ground water pollution and geology; stratigraphy and sedimentation; areal and ground water geology of Pennsylvania, Illinois and the Upper Mississippi Valley; development and management of programs for land disposal of wastes; ground water development. *Mailing Add:* SMC Martin Inc PO Box 859 Valley Forge PA 19482

EMRICH, RAYMOND JAY, b Denver, Colo, Nov 30, 17; m 42; c 2. FLUID DYNAMICS. *Educ:* Princeton Univ, AB, 38, AM & PhD(physics), 46. *Prof Exp:* Asst Nat Defense Res Comt, Princeton Univ, 41-45; from asst prof to assoc prof, 46-55, chmn dept, 58-68, PROF PHYSICS, LEHIGH UNIV, 55- *Concurrent Pos:* Vis scientist, Ernst Mach Inst, Ger, 68; Nat Acad Sci exchange vis, Siberia, 70-71 & 79; mem comt sci & arts, Franklin Inst; guest prof, Ruhr Univ, Bochum, WGer, 80. *Mem:* Fel AAAS; fel Am Phys Soc; Am Asn Physics Teachers. *Res:* Small scale and short time fluid motions; fluctuations in non-equilibrium processes; small particle deposit and transport; shock tube. *Mailing Add:* Physics Bldg 16 Lehigh Univ Bethlehem PA 18015

EMRICH, WILLIAM OSCAR, b Pittsburgh, Pa, Jan 30, 42. ORGANIC CHEMISTRY. *Educ:* Bucknell Univ, BS, 63; Carnegie-Mellon Univ, MS, 66, PhD(chem), 68. *Prof Exp:* Mkt mgr, Electrode Corp, 67-77, MEM STAFF ELECTROLYTIC SYSTS DIV, DIAMOND SHAMROCK CORP, 77- *Mem:* Sigma Xi; AAAS; Am Chem Soc. *Res:* Applied electrochemistry; polyelectrolytes; wastewater treatment; flocculation, coagulation and sedimentation; organic synthesis; market research; new products; agricultural and biological chemistry. *Mailing Add:* Electrolytic Systs Div PO Box 229 Chardon OH 44024

EMRICK, DONALD DAY, b Waynesfield, Ohio, Apr 3, 29. ORGANIC CHEMISTRY. *Educ:* Miami Univ, BS, 51; Purdue Univ, MS, 54, PhD(org chem), 56. *Prof Exp:* Asst, Purdue Univ, 51-55; sr chemist, Standard Oil Co of Ohio, 55-56, tech specialist, 56-61, res assoc, 61-64; sr res chemist, Nat Cash Register Co, 65-73; sr res chemist, Monsanto Co, 73-74; CHEM CONSULT, 74- *Mem:* Am Chem Soc; AAAS. *Res:* Organic sulfur chemistry; stereochemistry of ring compounds; lubricants; polymers; electronic absorption spectra; rare earths; polyolefins; borate esters; encapsulation. *Mailing Add:* 4240 Lesher Dr Kettering OH 45429

EMRICK, EDWIN ROY, b Pittsburgh, Pa, Mar 1, 29; m 54; c 2. ANALYTICAL CHEMISTRY. *Educ:* Duquesne Univ, BS, 51; Univ Pittsburgh, PhD(anal chem), 59. *Prof Exp:* Sr chemist, Pratt & Whitney Aircraft Div, United Aircraft Corp, 59-61, proj chemist, 61-63; anal chemist, Nalco Chem Co, 63-77; ANAL SUPVR, C H PATRICK & CO, 78- *Mem:* Am Chem Soc; fel Am Inst Chemists; Am Asn Textile Chemists & Colorists; Sigma Xi. *Res:* Polymer characterization; gel, thin-layer, gas and liquid chromatography; infra-red and nuclear magnetic resonance spectroscopy. *Mailing Add:* C H Patrick & Co PO Box 2526 Greenville SC 29602

EMRICK, ROY M, b Akron, Ohio, May 6, 32; m 58; c 3. SOLID STATE PHYSICS. *Educ:* Cornell Univ, AB, 54; Univ Ill, MS, 58, PhD(physics), 60. *Prof Exp:* Res assoc physics, Univ Ill, 60; assoc prof, 60-72, PROF PHYSICS, UNIV ARIZ, 72- *Mem:* Fel AAAS; Am Phys Soc. *Res:* Study of lattice defects in metals. *Mailing Add:* Dept of Physics Univ of Ariz Tucson AZ 85721

EMRY, ROBERT JOHN, b Ainsworth, Nebr, Nov 4, 40; c 2. VERTEBRATE PALEONTOLOGY, GEOLOGY. *Educ:* Colo State Univ, BS, 66; Columbia Univ, PhD(vert paleont), 70. *Prof Exp:* RES CUR VERT PALEONT, SMITHSONIAN INST, 71- *Mem:* Soc Vert Paleont; Paleont Soc; Am Soc Mammal. *Res:* North American Tertiary fossil mammals and the geology Tertiary deposits of North America; relationships of North American fossil faunas to those of other continents. *Mailing Add:* Dept of Paleobiol Smithsonian Inst Washington DC 20560

EMSHWILLER, MACLELLAN, b Grand Rapids, Mich, Oct 27, 27; m 59. PHYSICS, COMMUNICATIONS ENGINEERING. *Educ:* Univ Mich, BS, 52, MS, 53; Univ Calif, Berkeley, PhD(physics), 59. *Prof Exp:* MEM TECH STAFF PHYSICS, BELL TEL LABS, 69- *Mem:* AAAS; Am Phys Soc; Inst Elec & Electronics Engrs; Sigma Xi; Audio Eng Soc. *Res:* Signal processing techniques using optical techniques; nuclear magnetic resonance. *Mailing Add:* Bell Tel Labs 1600 Osgood St North Andover MA 01845

EMSLEY, JAMES ALAN BURNS, b Oban, Scotland, May 12, 43; Can citizen; m 66; c 3. ANIMAL GENETICS, QUANTITATIVE ANALYSES. *Educ:* Carleton Univ, Ont, BSc, 68; Univ Nebr-Lincoln, PhD(genetics), 73. *Prof Exp:* Res scientist dairy breeding, Agr Can, 73-77, res scientist poultry breeding, 77-78; GENETICIST, H&N INC, 78- *Mem:* Am Soc Animal Sci; Am Genetics Asn; Can Soc Animal Sci; Poultry Sci Asn; Biometric Soc. *Res:* Layer breeding program including primary breeding stock and experimental lines; evaluation of alternative breeding schemes; production systems in poultry. *Mailing Add:* H&N Inc 15305 NE 40th St Redmond WA 98052

EMSLEY, MICHAEL GORDON, b Bedford, Eng, May 2, 30; US citizen; m 72; c 2. ENTOMOLOGY, HERPETOLOGY. *Educ:* Univ London, BS, 53; Royal Col Sci, London, ARCS, 53; Univ London, PhD(zool), 64. *Prof Exp:* Entomologist, Empire Cotton Growing Corp, Nigeria, 54-57; asst lectr zool, Univ West Indies, 57-65; resident dir, William Beebe Tropical Field Sta, NY Zool Soc, Trinidad, 65-66; assoc cur, Acad Natural Sci, Philadelphia, 66-69; chmn dept biol, 69-74, PROF BIOL, GEORGE MASON UNIV, 69- *Concurrent Pos:* Ed, Biotropica, Asn Trop Biol, Inc, 72- *Mem:* Asn Trop Biol; AAAS; Inst Biol London. *Res:* Systematics of the tettigoniidae; taxonomy of the Schizapteridae; Caribbean snakes. *Mailing Add:* Dept of Biol George Mason Univ Fairfax VA 22030

EMSLIE, ALFRED GEORGE, b Aberdeen, Scotland, Nov 28, 07; nat US; m 33; c 2. APPLIED PHYSICS. *Educ:* Aberdeen Univ, MA, 28; Cornell Univ, PhD(physics), 33; Cambridge Univ, PhD(physics), 38. *Prof Exp:* Asst physics, Aberdeen Univ, 28-30; from instr to asst prof, Williams Col, 37-43;

staff mem, Radiation Lab, Mass Inst Technol, 43-46; res lectr electronics, Harvard Univ, 46-47; from assoc prof to prof physics, Williams Col, 47-51; head physics group, Arthur D Little, Inc, 51-61, staff assoc, 61-72; CONSULT IN APPL PHYSICS, 72- *Concurrent Pos:* Consult, Arthur D Little, Inc, 46-50. *Res:* Classical theoretical physics; electromagnetic waves; underwater sound; physical optics; heat radiation and transmission; exotic inertial sensing; hydrodynamics of viscous fluids; infrared radiative transfer. *Mailing Add:* 14 Prospect Ave Scituate MA 02066

EMSLIE, RONALD FRANK, b Winnipeg, Man, Feb 27, 32; m 60; c 3. GEOLOGY, PETROLOGY. *Educ:* Univ Manitoba, BSc, 56, MSc, 58; Northwestern Univ, PhD, 61. *Prof Exp:* Geologist, Geol Surv Can, 60-65; vis asst prof geol, Queen's Univ, Ont, 65-66, geologist, Geol Surv Can, 66-69; guest investr, Geophys Lab, Carnegie Inst of Washington, 69-70; RES SCIENTIST, GEOL SURV CAN, 70- *Mem:* Geol Soc Am; fel Geol Asn Can; Mineral Asn Can. *Res:* Anorthositic and related rocks of the Eastern Canadian shield; high temperature-high pressure mineral equilibria; igneous and metamorphic petrology. *Mailing Add:* Geol Surv of Can 601 Booth St Ottawa ON K1A 0E8 Can

EMSON, HARRY EDMUND, b Swinton, Eng, Nov 16, 27; m 53; c 2. PATHOLOGY. *Educ:* Oxford Univ, BA, 48, BM, BCh, 52, MA, 53; Royal Col Physicians & Surgeons Can, dipl, 58, FRCPS(C), 72; Univ Sask, MD, 59. *Prof Exp:* Intern, Manchester Royal Infirmary, Eng, 52, resident clin pathologist, 52-53; pathologist, Brit Mil Hosp, Ger, 53-55; registr path, Birmingham Accident Hosp, 55-56; resident, St Paul's Hosp, 56-57; asst resident, Univ Hosp, 57-58, asst pathologist, 58-60, dir labs, St Paul's Hosp, Saskatoon, 60-75; PROF & HEAD, DEPT PATH, COL MED, UNIV SASK, 75-; DIR LABS, UNIV HOSP, SASKATOON, 75- *Mem:* Can Med Asn; Can Asn Path (past pres); Can Soc Forensic Sci (past pres); Brit Asn Clin Path; Am Acad Forensic Sci. *Res:* Diagnostic human pathology; forensic pathology. *Mailing Add:* Univ Hosp Saskatoon SK S7N 0X0 Can

EMSWILER, BONNIE SUE, microbiology, see previous edition

EMTAGE, PETER ROESCH, b London, Eng, Jan 1, 35; m 60; c 3. SOLID STATE PHYSICS. *Educ:* Oxford Univ, BA, 56, MA & PhD(physics), 59. *Prof Exp:* Fel physics, Northwestern Univ, Evanston, 59-60; physicist, Electronics Lab, Gen Elec Co, 60-63; PHYSICIST, WESTINGHOUSE RES LAB, WESTINGHOUSE ELEC CO, 63- *Res:* Theoretical solid state physics, including electron structure and transport in solids, properties of interfaces, and magnetic media. *Mailing Add:* Res/Develop Ctr Westinghouse Elec 1310 Beulah Rd Pittsburgh PA 15235

ENDAHL, GERALD LEROY, b Lane, SDak, Dec 16, 24; m 54; c 2. BIOCHEMISTRY. *Educ:* Augustana Col, BA, 49; Univ SDak, MA, 53; Univ Okla, PhD(biochem), 59. *Prof Exp:* Res assoc, Okla Med Res Found, 53-57; res fel, Med Sch, Univ Ala, 57-60; from asst prof to assoc prof physiol chem & surg, Ohio State Univ, 60-70; ASSOC PROF PATH & BIOCHEM, UNIV SOUTHERN CALIF, 70- *Mem:* AAAS; AMA; Am Chem Soc; Am Asn Clin Chemists; NY Acad Sci. *Res:* Enzymes of carbohydrate metabolism; metabolism of steroid hormones; hormones of gastric acid secretion; aminotransferases. *Mailing Add:* Dept of Path 2825 S Hope St Los Angeles CA 90007

ENDAL, ANDREW SAMSON, b Brooklyn, NY, Sept 1, 49; m 73. THEORETICAL ASTROPHYSICS, CLIMATE PHYSICS. *Educ:* Univ Rochester, BS, 71; Univ Fla, PhD(astrophys), 74. *Prof Exp:* Res assoc astrophys, NASA Goddard Space Flight Ctr, 74-76; vis asst prof physics, Kans State Univ, 76-78; from asst prof to assoc prof physics & astron, La State Univ, 78-81; SR SCIENTIST, APPL RES CORP, 82. *Mem:* Am Astron Soc; Int Astron Union; Am Geophys Union. *Res:* Stellar evolution; stellar rotation; nucleosynthesis; climate modeling. *Mailing Add:* Appl Res Corp 8401 Corp Dr Landover MD 20785

ENDE, NORMAN, b Petersburg, Va, Apr 5, 24; m 48; c 1. PATHOLOGY. *Educ:* Univ Richmond, BS, 45; Med Col Va, MD, 47; Am Bd Clin Path, dipl, 53, cert anat path, 54. *Prof Exp:* Intern, Bronx Hosp, NY, 48; resident path & surg, Vet Admin Hosp, New Orleans, La, 49-52, pathologist, Houston, Tex, 54-55, chief path, Fresno, Calif, 55-58; asst clin prof, Vanderbilt Univ, 58-61, from asst prof to assoc prof, 61-67; dir path labs, Grady Mem Hosp, 67-69, chief path, 69-70; actg chmn dept, 74-76, PROF PATH, COL MED & DENT NJ, 70- *Concurrent Pos:* Instr, Col Med, Baylor Univ, 54-55, asst prof, 55; chief lab serv path, Vet Admin Hosp, Nashville, 58-67; prof path, Emory Univ, 67-69; chief clin path, Martland Hosp, 70-74, chief path, 74-77. *Mem:* Fel Am Col Physicians; fel Col Am Path; Am Soc Exp Path; Am Asn Path & Bact; fel Am Soc Clin Path. *Res:* Mast cell, fibrinolysis and the hyper-coagulable state; carcinoma of the prostate and thromboangiitis obliterans; starvation; transplantation; circulating antibodies. *Mailing Add:* Col of Med & Dent NJ 100 Bergen St Newark NJ 07103

ENDERBY, CHARLES ELDRED, b Chicago, Ill, Nov 15, 34; m 57; c 3. PHYSICS. *Educ:* Univ Ill, BS, 57, MS, 58, PhD(elec eng), 61. *Prof Exp:* Asst prof elec eng, Univ Ill, 60-61; mem tech staff, Gen Elec Co, 61-65; from vpres to pres, Electro Optics Assocs, Inc, 66-71; exec vpres, Optics Technol, Inc, 71-76; VPRES, MOLECTRON CORP, 77- *Mem:* Inst Elec & Electronics Engrs; Optical Soc Am; Am Mktg Asn; fel Am Soc Lasers Med. *Res:* Optical modulation; millimeter wave generation; gas laser design. *Mailing Add:* 1852 Edgewood Dr Palo Alto CA 94303

ENDERS, ALLEN COFFIN, b Wooster, Ohio, Aug 5, 28; m 50; c 4. HUMAN ANATOMY, REPRODUCTIVE BIOLOGY. *Educ:* Swarthmore Col, AB, 50; Harvard Univ, AM, 52, PhD, 55. *Prof Exp:* Teaching fel biol, Harvard Univ, 52-53 & Brandeis Univ, 53-54; res assoc, Rice Univ, 54-55, from asst prof to assoc prof, 55-63; from assoc prof to prof anat, Sch Med, Washington Univ, 63-75; chmn dept, 75-80, PROF HUMAN ANAT, UNIV CALIF, DAVIS, 75- *Concurrent Pos:* Consult, NIH, 64-; mem anat test comt, Nat Bd Med Examr. *Mem:* AAAS; Am Asn Anat; Soc Study Reprod; Am Soc Cell Biol; Histochem Soc. *Res:* Fine structure of placenta and female reproductive tract; mechanisms of implantation. *Mailing Add:* Dept of Human Anat Univ of Calif Davis CA 95616

ENDERS, GEORGE LEONHARD, JR, b Glendale, NY, Nov 13, 45; m 69; c 3. CLINICAL MICROBIOLOGY, FERMENTATION MICROBIOLOGY. *Educ:* Rutgers Univ, BA, 67; Immaculate Heart Col, Los Angeles, MA, 71; Univ Kans, PhD(microbiol), 74. *Prof Exp:* Res assoc microbiol, Food Res Inst, Univ Wis, 74-77; res scientist, 77-80, SR RES SCIENTIST MICROBIOL, BIOTECHNOL GROUP, AMES CO, MILES LABS, INC, 80- *Concurrent Pos:* Nat Inst Environ Health Sci fel, Food Res Inst, Univ Wis, 75- *Mem:* Am Soc Microbiol; Sigma Xi; Inst Food Technologists; Am Soc Animal Sci. *Res:* Research and development in food and agricultural microbiology fermentations; characterization of the enterotoxin elaborated by Clostridium perfringens: studies dealing with the structure, biological and serological activities and mechanism of action of this enterotoxin; anaerobes, especially physiological aspects and toxins; effects of bacteriophage infection on the metabolism of Escherichia coli envelope components; lipids, proteins and Lipopolysaccharides; characterization of the lipids of thermophiles. *Mailing Add:* Biotech Group Miles Labs Inc 1127 Myrtle St Elkhart IN 46515

ENDERS, JOHN FRANKLIN, b West Hartford, Conn, Feb 10, 97; m 27, 51; c 2. MICROBIOLOGY. *Educ:* Yale Univ, AB, 19; Harvard Univ, MA, 22, PhD(bact, immunol), 30. *Hon Degrees:* DSc, Yale Univ, 53, Trinity Col, 55, Harvard Univ, 56, Northwestern Univ, 56, Western Reserve Univ, 58, Tufts Univ, 60, Jefferson Med Col, 62, Univ Pa, 64, Univ Ibadan, 68 & Oxford Univ, 75; LLD, Tulane Univ, 58; DLH, Hartford Univ, 60. *Prof Exp:* Asst, Harvard Med Sch, 29-30, from instr to assoc prof, 30-56, prof, Children's Hosp, 56-62, univ prof, 62-67, EMER UNIV PROF BACT & IMMUNOL, HARVARD MED SCH, 67-, CHIEF RES DIV INFECTIOUS DIS, CHILDREN'S MED CTR, 47- *Concurrent Pos:* Mem comn viral infections, Armed Forces Epidemiol Bd; sci adv bd of consult, Armed Forces Inst Path; adv panel on virus dis, WHO; corresp, Acad Sci Inst France, 71; ed, Virology, Soc Exp Biol & Med; ed jour, Am Asn Immunol. *Honors & Awards:* Nobel Prize in Med & Physiol, 54; Passano Award, 53; Kimble Res Award Methodology, 54; Dyer Lectr Award, USPHS, 54; Lasker Award, Am Pub Health Asn, 54; Chapin Medal, 55; Wilson Medal, 55; Bruce Mem Lectr Award, 56; Mod Med Award, 56; Cameron Prize, Univ Edinburgh, 60; Howard T Ricketts Award, Univ Chicago, 62; Diesel Gold Medal & Robert-Koch Medal, Ger, 62; Sci Achievement Award, AMA, 63; Presidential Medal of Freedom, 63; Comdr, Repub Upper Volta, 65. *Mem:* Nat Acad Sci; AAAS; Soc Exp Biol & Med; Am Soc Microbiol; Am Philos Soc. *Res:* Virus disease of man and animal. *Mailing Add:* 64 Colbourne Crescent Brookline MA 02146

ENDERSON, JAMES H, b Sioux City, Iowa, Nov 3, 36; m 57; c 1. ZOOLOGY. *Educ:* Univ Ill, BS & MS, 59; Univ Wyo, PhD(zool), 62. *Prof Exp:* From asst prof to assoc prof, 62-74, PROF BIOL, COLO COL, 74- *Concurrent Pos:* NSF fac fel systs & ecol, Cornell Univ, 69-70. *Mem:* AAAS; Am Inst Biol Sci; Am Ornith Union; Wilson Ornith Soc; Cooper Ornith Soc. *Res:* Raptor ecology. *Mailing Add:* Dept of Biol Colo Col Colorado Springs CO 80903

ENDERTON, HERBERT BRUCE, b Hawaii, Apr 15, 36; m 61; c 2. MATHEMATICAL LOGIC. *Educ:* Stanford Univ, BS, 58; Harvard Univ, MA, 59, PhD(math), 62. *Prof Exp:* Instr math, Mass Inst Technol, 62-64; asst prof, Univ Calif, Berkeley, 64-68; LECTR MATH, UNIV CALIF, LOS ANGELES & ED, J SYMBOLIC LOGIC, 68- *Mem:* Am Math Soc; Asn Symbolic Logic; Asn Comput Mach. *Res:* Recursive function theory; definability theory; models of analysis; computational complexity; history of logic. *Mailing Add:* Dept Math Univ Calif Los Angeles CA 90024

ENDICOTT, JOHN F, b Eugene, Ore, Aug 1, 32. INORGANIC CHEMISTRY. *Educ:* Reed Col, BA, 57; Johns Hopkins Univ, PhD(phys chem), 61. *Prof Exp:* Res assoc inorg chem, Stanford Univ, 61-63; from asst prof to assoc prof, Boston Univ, 63-69; assoc prof, 69-72, PROF CHEM, WAYNE STATE UNIV, 72- *Concurrent Pos:* Res collabr, Dept Chem, Brookhaven Nat Lab, 77-78. *Mem:* Am Chem Soc; Am Phys Soc; AAAS. *Res:* Mechanisms of inorganic reactions; photochemistry of coordination complexes; reactivity of macrocyclic complexes. *Mailing Add:* Dept of Chem Wayne State Univ Detroit MI 48202

ENDICOTT, KENNETH MILO, b Canon City, Colo, June 6, 16; m 39; c 3. PATHOLOGY. *Educ:* Univ Colo, AB, 36, MD, 39. *Prof Exp:* Intern, US Marine Hosp, Wash, 39-40; asst surgeon, USPHS, 40-42, asst surgeon, Div Path, NIH, 42-52, sci dir, Div Res Grants, 52-55; chief cancer chemother, Nat Serv Ctr, 55-58; assoc dir, NIH, 58-60, dir, Nat Cancer Inst, 60-69, dir bur health manpower educ, 69-80, EXEC OFF, AM ASN PATHOLOGISTS, NIH, 80- *Concurrent Pos:* Extern, St Luke's Hosp, Denver, 38 & Mt Airy Sanitarium, 38-39; mem res proj, Med Ctr Fed Prisoners, Mo, 42. *Mem:* AAAS; fel AMA; Am Asn Path & Bact (exec officer, 77); Am Soc Exp Path; Soc Exp Biol & Med. *Res:* Pathologic physiology of blood-forming tissues; pathology of nutritional diseases; application of tracers in pathology; pathology of radiation injury; pathology of toxic substances; research administration. *Mailing Add:* 9650 Rockville Pike Bethesda MD 20014

ENDLER, JOHN ARTHUR, b Montreal, Que, Oct 8, 47; US citizen. EVOLUTIONARY BIOLOGY, POPULATION BIOLOGY. *Educ:* Univ Calif, Berkeley, BA, 69; Univ Edinburgh, PhD(zool), 73. *Prof Exp:* Fel pop biol, Princeton Univ, 72-73, asst prof biol, 73-79; ASSOC PROF BIOL, UNIV UTAH, 79- *Mem:* Am Soc Naturalists; Am Soc Icthyologists & Herpetologists; Ecol Soc Am; Soc Study Evolution; Asn Trop Biol. *Res:* The adaptive nature, causes and mechanisms of geographic variation; the genetic structure of populations and its significance for speciation; ecological genetics and genetical biogeography of Poecilia reticulata and its predators; biogeography. *Mailing Add:* Dept Biol Univ Utah Salt Lake City UT 84112

ENDO, BURTON YOSHIAKI, b Castroville, Calif, Feb 5, 26; m 52; c 2. NEMATOLOGY. *Educ:* Iowa State Univ, BS, 51; NC State Univ, MS, 55, PhD(plant path), 58. *Prof Exp:* Asst hort, NC State Univ, 53-55; asst nematologist, Nematol Sect, 55-58, nematologist, WTenn Exp Sta, 58-63, res nematologist, Beltsville Agr Res Ctr-West, 63-74, chief nematol lab, 74-75,

CHMN, PLANT PROTECTION INST, US DEPT AGR, 74- *Mem:* AAAs; Am Phytopath Soc; Soc Nematol (secy, 68-71, vpres, 72, pres, 73); Am Inst Biol Sci. *Res:* Host-parasite relations of nematode infected plants; plant disease resistance. *Mailing Add:* 9215 Wofford Lane College Park MD 20740

ENDO, ROBERT MINORU, b Mountain View, Calif, Mar 30, 25; m 50; c 3. PLANT PATHOLOGY. *Educ:* Rutgers Univ, BS, 50; Univ Ill, MS, 52, PhD(plant path), 54. *Prof Exp:* Res asst plant path, Dept Hort, Univ Ill, 51-54, agent sect cereal crops & dis, Field Crops Res Br, Agr Res Serv, USDA, 54-56, plant pathologist, 56-58; asst prof plant path & asst plant pathologist, Univ Calif, Los Angeles, 59-61, from asst prof & asst plant pathologist to assoc prof & assoc plant pathologist, 61-71, PROF PLANT PATH & PLANT PATHOLOGIST, UNIV CALIF, RIVERSIDE, 71- *Mem:* Am Phytopath Soc; Mycol Soc Am; Am Inst Biol Scientists. *Res:* Diseases of turf grass and vegetables; yellow dwarf disease of cereals. *Mailing Add:* Dept of Plant Path Univ of Calif Riverside CA 92521

ENDOW, SHARYN ANNE, b Hood River, Ore, May 22, 48. RIBOSOMAL GENE GENETICS. *Educ:* Stanford Univ, BA, 70; Yale Univ, MPhil, 72, PHD(cell & molecular biol), 75. *Prof Exp:* Fel, Cold Spring Harbor Lab, 74-76 & Mammmalian Genome Unit, Med Res Coun, Edinburgh, Scotland, 76-78; ASST PROF, DUKE UNIV, 78- *Concurrent Pos:* Staff scientist, Mammalian Genome Unit, Med Res Coun, Edinburgh, Scotland, 78; NIH res career develop award, 82- *Mem:* Genetics Soc Am; Sigma Xi. *Res:* Eukaryotic gene organization; DNA replicative and recombinative events which result in gene copy number changes. *Mailing Add:* Med Ctr Duke Univ PO Box 3020 Durham NC 27710

ENDRENYI, LASZLO, b Budapest, Hungary, May 6, 33; Can citizen; m 56. PHARMACOKINETICS, MODEL BUILDING. *Educ:* Tech Univ Budapest, Hungary, Dipl Eng, 56; Univ Toronto, PhD(chem), 65. *Prof Exp:* Res assoc, 66-69, from asst prof to assoc prof, 69-76, PROF PHARMACOL & BIOSTAST, DEPT PHARMACOL, PREV MED & BIOSTAT, UNIV TORONTO, 76- *Mem:* Am Statist Asn; Statist Soc Can; Chem Inst Can; Biometric Soc. *Res:* Design and statistical analysis of enzyme and pharmacokinetic experiments and of clinical trials; kinetic modeling; model identification; parameter estimation; robust procedures. *Mailing Add:* Dept Pharmacol Univ Toronto Toronto ON M5S 1A8 Can

ENDRES, JOSEPH GEORGE, b Chicago, Ill, Aug 15, 32; m 59; c 3. FOOD SCIENCE. *Educ:* Univ Ill, BS, 55, PhD(food chem), 61. *Prof Exp:* Res chemist fat & oil chem, Food Res Div, Armour & Co, 61-62, sect head, 62-64, asst mgr, 64-70; vpres res & develop, CFS Continental, 70-72; dir food prod develop, Chicago, 72-78, DIR FOOD RES, CENT SOYA-FOOD RES, 78- *Concurrent Pos:* Asst prof food sci dept, Univ Ill, 74- *Mem:* Am Oil Chemists' Soc; Inst Food Technologists. *Res:* Food product and process development for institutional, food service and retail. *Mailing Add:* 4806 W Hamilton Rd S Ft Wayne IN 46804

ENDRES, LELAND SANDER, b Akron, Ohio, Mar 31, 36; m 59; c 4. ORGANIC CHEMISTRY, PHYSICAL CHEMISTRY. *Educ:* Middlebury Col, AB, 58; Univ Ore, MA, 63; Univ Ariz, PhD(chem), 67. *Prof Exp:* Instr & res assoc chem, Univ Nebr, 66-67; sr res chemist, Minn Mining & Mfg Co, 67-69; asst prof chem, 69-74, assoc prof, 74-78, PROF CHEM, CALIF POLYTECH STATE UNIV, SAN LUIS OBISPO, 79- *Mem:* Am Chem Soc. *Res:* Reaction kinetics; carbonium ions; small ring heterocyclics; fluorocarbons. *Mailing Add:* Dept Chem Calif Polytech State Univ San Luis Obispo CA 93407

ENDRES, PAUL FRANK, b Peoria, Ill, Feb 10, 42. PHYSICAL CHEMISTRY. *Educ:* Bradley Univ, BS, 63; Univ Rochester, PhD(chem), 67. *Prof Exp:* Fel chem, Univ Rochester, 67-69; asst prof, 69-74, ASSOC PROF CHEM, BOWLING GREEN STATE UNIV, 74- *Mem:* Am Phys Soc. *Res:* Energy transfer in molecular collisions; molecular dynamics. *Mailing Add:* Dept of Chem Bowling Green State Univ Bowling Green OH 43403

ENDRIZZI, JOHN EDWIN, b Wilburton, Okla, July 28, 23; m 55; c 5. CYTOGENETICS. *Educ:* Tex A&M Univ, BS, 49, MS, 51; Univ Md, PhD(bot), 55. *Prof Exp:* Asst prof cytogenetics, Tex Agr Exp Sta, 55-63; head dept, 63-71, PROF PLANT GENETICS, UNIV ARIZ, 63- *Honors & Awards:* Cotton Genetics Res Award, Nat Cotton Coun Am, 69. *Mem:* AAAS; Am Genetic Asn; Genetics Soc Am; Genetics Soc Can; Am Inst Biol Sci. *Res:* Cytogenetics of Gossypium. *Mailing Add:* Dept of Plant Sci Col of Agr Univ of Ariz Tucson AZ 85721

ENDSLEY, L(OUIS) E(UGENE), JR, b Lafayette, Ind, May 24, 12; m 40; c 3. MECHANICAL ENGINEERING. *Educ:* Purdue Univ, BS, 34, MS, 36. *Prof Exp:* Asst instr mech eng, Purdue Univ, 34-36; mech engr, 36-54, asst to mgr tech servs, 54-56, dir, 56-58, asst mgr, 58-60, planning dir eng, 60-69, mgr sci planning, 69-75, mgr planning & admin, Res & Technol Dept, Texaco, Inc, 75-77; RETIRED. *Concurrent Pos:* Mech engr, Wright Field, US Army Air Force, 39; consult to Asst Secy Defense, 50-54 & 55-63. *Mem:* Sigma Xi; Soc Automotive Engrs. *Res:* Petroleum fuels and lubricants; research and development. *Mailing Add:* 12 Sheldon Dr Poughkeepsie NY 12603

ENELL, JOHN WARREN, b New York, NY, June 24, 19; m 49; c 4. APPLIED STATISTICS, RESEARCH MANAGEMENT. *Educ:* Univ Pa, BS, 40, ME, 48; NY Univ, MAdmE, 47, DEngSc(indust eng & statist), 49. *Prof Exp:* Exp engr, Curtiss-Wright Corp, 40-46; res assoc human body motion, NY Univ, 46-48, from instr to prof statist & qual control, 47-57; dir surv, 54-61, dir res, 61-67, V PRES RES, AM MGT ASN, 67- *Concurrent Pos:* Consult, Dept Defense, 51; adv, US Mutual Security Agency, Italy, 52-53; mem bd dirs, Engr Coun Prof Develop, 70-78, treas, 72-78; vpres, Am Found Mgt Res, 70-74; adv, AID, Vietnam, 72. *Mem:* Am Statist Asn; Am Soc Qual Control; fel Am Inst Indust Engrs; Am Soc Mech Engrs; Sigma Xi. *Res:* Organization structures; organizational behavior; motivation of executives; organizational objectives and policy formulation. *Mailing Add:* Am Mgt Asn 135 W 50th St New York NY 10020

ENEMARK, JOHN HENRY, b Lamberton, Minn, Aug 24, 40; m 62; c 2. INORGANIC CHEMISTRY. *Educ:* St Olaf Col, BA, 62; Harvard Univ, AM, 64, PhD(chem), 66. *Prof Exp:* Res assoc chem, Northwestern Univ, 66-68; from asst prof to assoc prof, 68-72, PROF CHEM, UNIV ARIZ, 72- *Concurrent Pos:* NSF res fel, Northwestern Univ, 66-67. *Mem:* AAAS; Am Chem Soc; Am Crystallog Asn. *Res:* Transition metal compounds; bioinorganic chemistry; x-ray crystallography. *Mailing Add:* Dept of Chem Univ of Ariz Tucson AZ 85721

ENENSTEIN, NORMAN H(ARRY), b Los Angeles, Calif, Nov 2, 23; m 43; c 2. ELECTRICAL ENGINEERING. *Educ:* Univ Calif, Los Angeles, AB, 46; Calif Inst Technol, MS, 47, PhD(elec eng, physics), 49. *Prof Exp:* Res physicist, Hughes Aircraft Co, 49-54, proj anti-airborne defense tactical data syst, US Army, 54-56; vpres & dir engr, Electro-Pulse, Inc, 56-58; dir tactical systs lab, Litton Industs, 58-62; mgr systs div, 62-70, MGR DATA PROCESSING PRODS DIV, GROUND SYSTS GROUP, HUGHES AIRCRAFT CO, 70- *Mem:* Inst Elec & Electronics Engrs. *Res:* Management of large scale military programs in the fields of data processing, radar, communications and weapon systems. *Mailing Add:* 3009 Milagro Way Fullerton CA 92635

ENESCO, HILDEGARD ESPER, b Seattle, Wash, June 16, 36; m 64. CELL BIOLOGY. *Educ:* Reed Col, BA, 58; Columbia Univ, MA, 59, PhD(zool), 62. *Prof Exp:* USPHS fel anat, McGill Univ, 62-63; Shirley Farr fel biol, Univ Montreal, 63-64; res assoc biochem, Allan Mem Inst, McGill Univ, 64-68; from asst prof to assoc prof, 68-78, actg chmn dept, 74-75, chmn dept, 75-77, PROF BIOL, SIR GEORGE WILLIAMS CAMPUS, CONCORDIA UNIV, 78- *Mem:* Geront Soc; Can Soc Cell Biol; Am Soc Cell Biol; Geront Soc Can; Soc Develop Biol. *Res:* Cell function and aging. *Mailing Add:* Dept of Biol Sci Concordia Univ Montreal PQ H3G 1M5 Can

ENFIELD, CARL GEORGE, b Indianapolis, Ind, Nov 13, 42; m 66; c 3. SOIL PHYSICS. *Educ:* Purdue Univ, BS, 65, MS, 68; Univ Ariz, PhD(agr chem & soils), 73. *Prof Exp:* Enfiron hydrologist instrumentation, Burr Brown Res Corp, 68-69; sr res scientist, Battelle Northwest, Battelle Mem Inst, 69-71; res assoc soil physics, Univ Ariz, 71-72; civil engr, 72-80, SOIL SCIENTIST, ROBERT S KERR ENVIRON RES LAB, US ENVIRON PROTECTION AGENCY, 80- *Mem:* Am Soc Agron; Soil Sci Soc Am; Sigma Xi; Am Soc Agr Eng; Int Soil Sci Soc. *Res:* Kinetics of soil municipal wastewater interactions and the mathematical prediction of the movement of chemical pollutants through soil profiles; primary emphasis on the reactions of phosphorus, nitrogenous and organic compounds. *Mailing Add:* PO Box 1198 Ada OK 74820

ENFIELD, FRANKLIN D, b Woolstock, Iowa, Dec 26, 33; m 55; c 3. GENETICS. *Educ:* Iowa State Univ, BS, 55; Okla State Univ, MS, 57; Univ Minn, Minneapolis, PhD(animal breeding), 60. *Prof Exp:* Asst prof animal breeding, Univ Minn, Minneapolis, 60-65, assoc prof animal sci, 65-66; assoc prof, 66-70, dir grad studies in genetics, 71-75, PROF GENETICS, UNIV MINN, ST PAUL, 70- *Mem:* Genetics Soc Am; Am Soc Animal Sci; AAAS. *Res:* Population and quantitative genetics of Tribolium; biological control in the cotton boll weavil. *Mailing Add:* Dept of Genetics & Cell Biol Col of Biol Sci Univ of Minn St Paul MN 55108

ENG, CHEE PING, immunology, see previous edition

ENG, JOHN F, SYSTEM DESIGN, SYSTEMS SCIENCE. *Educ:* Seton Hall Univ, BS, 72; Purdue Univ, MS, 75, PhD(pesticide/agr chem), 77. *Prof Exp:* TECH STAFF INSTRUMENTATION, DEPT CHEM, PRINCETON UNIV, 77- *Mem:* Inst Elec & Electronics Engrs. *Mailing Add:* Dept Chem Princeton Univ Princeton NJ 08544

ENG, LAWRENCE F, b Spokane, Wash, Feb 19, 31; m 58; c 4. BIOCHEMISTRY. *Educ:* Wash State Univ, BS, 52; Stanford Univ, MS, 54, PhD(chem), 62. *Prof Exp:* Res scientist biochem toxicol, Aero Med Lab, Wright Air Develop Ctr, 54-57; asst biochem, Stanford Univ, 58-61; BIOCHEMIST, PALO ALTO VET ADMIN HOSP, 61- *Concurrent Pos:* Sr scientist path, Sch Med, Stanford Univ, 70-75, adj prof, 75- *Mem:* Am Chem Soc; Int Soc Neurochem; Am Soc Neurochem; AAAS; Am Soc Biol Chemists. *Res:* Clinical chemistry; biochemistry, development, and protein chemistry of the brain; investigation of myelinating diseases of the central nervous system. *Mailing Add:* Lab Serv Vet Admin Hosp Palo Alto CA 94304

ENG, LESLIE, b Baltimore, Md, June 9, 41; m 69; c 1. PHYSICAL ORGANIC CHEMISTRY. *Educ:* Johns Hopkins Univ, BA, 65; Pa State Univ, PhD(chem), 70. *Prof Exp:* Org chemist, 70-73, res chemist, 73-77, CHEMIST, US ARMY TOXIC & HAZARDOUS MAT AGENCY, EDGEWOOD ARSENAL, 77- *Mem:* Am Chem Soc; Sigma Xi. *Res:* Kinetics and mechanisms of organic reactions; thermal decomposition of organic and inorganic salts; decontamination of toxic chemicals; methods of analysis for trace quantities of toxic chemicals; analytical quality assurance and quality control. *Mailing Add:* 1510 Green Rd Edgewood MD 21040

ENG, SVERRE T(HORSTEIN), b Skaanland, Norway, July 30, 28; US citizen; m 57; c 3. SOLID STATE ELECTRONICS, ELECTROOPTICS. *Educ:* Chalmers Univ Technol, Sweden, MS, 53, PhD(appl physics), 67. *Prof Exp:* Res engr, Res Lab Electronics, Chalmers Univ Technol, Sweden, 53-56; mem tech staff, Semiconductor Div, Hughes Aircraft Co, 56-57; asst electronics, Stanford Univ, 57-58; sect head microwave & optical semiconductor physics & electronics, Res Labs, Hughes Aircraft Co, 58-62, dept head, 62-67; staff scientist & mem tech staff, Autonetics Div, N Am Rockwell Corp, 67-71; head, Inst Elec Measurements, 71-80, PROF MICROWAVE & ELECTROOPTIC ELECTRONICS, CHALMERS UNIV TECNOL, SWEDEN, 71-, DIR, INST ELEC MEASUREMENTS, 80- *Mem:* Am Phys Soc; Inst Elec & Electronics Engrs; Sigma Xi; Optical Soc Am. *Res:* Microwave semiconductor devices, especially high frequency transistors, parametric diodes, mixers, tunnel and backward diodes, integrated electronics, measurements and application studies; infrared detection; semiconductor and carbon dioxide lasers; superheterodyne instrumentation; laser radar. *Mailing Add:* Inst Elec Measurements Gibraltargatan 5G 41296 Gothenburg Sweden

ENGBRETSON, GUSTAV ALAN, b Fargo, NDak, Nov 28, 43. SENSORY BIOLOGY, NEUROBIOLOGY. *Educ:* Calif State Univ, Sacramento, BA, 68, MA, 71; Univ Okla, PhD(zool), 76. *Prof Exp:* Lectr anat sci, State Univ NY Stony Brook, Health Sci Ctr, 75-76, fel, 76-77, res asst prof, 78-79; RES ASST PROF SENSORY SCI, INST SENSORY RES, SYRACUSE UNIV, 79- *Concurrent Pos:* Vis res fel, Dept Neurobiol & Behav, Cornell Univ, 78-81; res asst prof, dept anat, State Univ NY, Upstate Med Ctr, 79- *Mem:* Asn Res Vision & Ophthal; AAAS; Am Soc Zoologists; Sigma Xi. *Res:* Role of centrifugal neurons to sensory organs especially in the visual system, using anatomical, electrophysiological and immunological techniques. *Mailing Add:* Inst Sensory Res Syracuse Univ Syracuse NY 13210

ENGBRING, NORMAN H, b Milwaukee, Wis, Mar 30, 25; m 50; c 3. MEDICINE. *Educ:* Marquette Univ, MD, 51. *Prof Exp:* From intern to resident, Milwaukee Co Gen Hosp, 51-55; from instr to asst prof, 55-65, assoc prof med, Sch Med, Marquette Univ, 65-72; asst dean, 72-80, PROF MED, MED COL WIS, 72-, ASSOC DEAN, GRAD MED EDUC, 80- *Concurrent Pos:* Dir radioisotope lab, Milwaukee Co Gen Hosp, 58-67, chief metab serv, 65-74; fel metab, Milwaukee Co Gen Hosp, 55-58. *Mem:* AAAS; Am Fedn Clin Res; Am Diabetes Asn; Endocrine Soc; Am Col Physicians. *Res:* Endocrine and metabolic disorders. *Mailing Add:* 8700 W Wisconsin Ave Milwaukee WI 53226

ENGDAHL, ERIC ROBERT, b Worcester, Mass, June 11, 37; m 57; c 3. GEOPHYSICS. *Educ:* Rensselaer Polytech Inst, BS, 58; St Louis Univ, PhD(geophys), 68. *Prof Exp:* Explor geophysicist, Delta Explor Co, 58-60; res geophysicist, Theoret Studies Group, Environ Res Lab, Nat Oceanic & Atmospheric Admin, 60-77; SUPVRY GEOPHYSICIST, BR GLOBAL SEISMOL, OFF EARTHQUAKE STUDIES, US GEOL SURV, 77- *Concurrent Pos:* Mem Stand Earth Model Interas Comt & Chmn Int Asn Seismol & Physics Earths Interior Working Group Optimization Algorithms Determination Earthquake Parameters, Int Union Geol & Geophys, 71-; Adj assoc prof geophys, Univ Colo, Boulder, 72-, fel geophys, Coop Inst Res Environ Sci, 72-77; assoc ed, J Geophys Res, 74-76; liaison res, Adv Panel Earthquake Progs, US Geol Surv, 74-; mem, Comt Seismol, Nat Res Coun-Nat Acad Sci, 74-77, chmn, Panel Seismog Networks. *Mem:* Fel Am Geophys Union; Seismol Soc Am; AAAS. *Res:* Plate tectonics and earthquake prediction in an active subduction zone; application of seismic ray tracing to the study of plate structure and lateral heterogeneities in the Earth. *Mailing Add:* US Geol Surv Box 25046 Stop 967 Denver CO 80225

ENGDAHL, RICHARD BOTT, b Elgin, Ill, Apr 16, 14; m 40; c 2. MECHANICAL ENGINEERING. *Educ:* Bucknell Univ, BS, 36; Univ Ill, MS, 38; Am Acad Environ Engrs, dipl. *Prof Exp:* Asst, Univ Ill, 36-39, instr mech eng, 39-40; res engr, Battelle Mem Inst, 41-45, asst supvr, 45-46, supvr fuels, 47-50, chief, Fuels & Air Pollution Div, 50-57, chief, Thermal Eng Div, 57-58, staff engr, 58-65, fel environ res, 65-76, RES CONSULT, BATTELLE-COLUMBUS LABS, 76- *Concurrent Pos:* environ consult, Malaysia, WHO, 79-80; combustion consult, Turkey, Int Exec Serv Corps, 80, UN Develop Prog, China, 81. *Mem:* Fel AAAS; Am Indust Hyg Asn; Am Soc Mech Engrs; Am Soc Heat, Refrig & Air-Conditioning Engrs. *Res:* Combustion of pulverized coal; steam ejector performance; gas turbine locomotive; meter for flow of pulverized coal suspended in air; air pollution; heat pump; environmental control; incineration. *Mailing Add:* Battelle-Columbus Labs 505 King Ave Columbus OH 43201

ENGE, HARALD ANTON, b Fauske, Norway, Sept 28, 20; nat US; m 47; c 3. NUCLEAR PHYSICS. *Educ:* Tech Univ Norway, Eng Dipl, 47; Univ Bergen, Dr Philos, 54. *Prof Exp:* Lab engr, Tech Univ Norway, 47; res assoc & lectr, Univ Bergen, 48-55; from instr to assoc prof, 55-63, PROF PHYSICS, MASS INST TECHNOL, 63- *Concurrent Pos:* Co-founder & chmn, Deltaray Corp, 69-73 & Gammaray Corp, 81. *Mem:* Fel Am Phys Soc; Europ Phys Soc; Norweg Phys Soc. *Res:* Low energy nuclear physics; nuclear instrumentation. *Mailing Add:* Rm 58-015 Mass Inst of Technol Cambridge MA 02139

ENGEBRECHT, RONALD HENRY, b Oregon City, Ore, Jan 18, 34; m 54; c 3. PHOTOCHEMISTRY. *Educ:* Ore State Univ, BS, 56, PhD(org chem), 64; Mich State Univ, MA, 59. *Prof Exp:* Instr, Ore High Schs, 56-59; asst prof cancer res, Ore State Univ, 63-65; SR RES CHEMIST, EASTMAN KODAK CO, 65- *Mem:* Am Chem Soc. *Res:* Organic photochemistry; synthesis of light-sensitive polymers; application of light-sensitive polymers for photoresists. *Mailing Add:* Res Lab Eastman Kodak Co Rochester NY 14650

ENGEBRETSON, GORDON ROY, b Milwaukee, Wis, June 15, 36; m 58; c 3. PHYSICAL CHEMISTRY, MEDICAL ADMINISTRATION. *Educ:* Carroll Col, Wis, BS, 58; Iowa State Univ, PhD(phys chem), 62. *Prof Exp:* Asst crystallog res, Ames Lab, 58-62; res chemist, Sinclair Res, Inc, 62-66; asst dir, Dept Environ Health, AMA, 66-69; dep dir, Fla Regional Med Prog, 69-75, dir, 75-76; exec dir, Southern Health Found, 76-78; assoc adj prof, Univ Tampa, 79-80; DIR GOVT PROGS, VITA-STAT SYSTS, INC, 81- *Concurrent Pos:* Adj asst prof, Univ SFla; community prof, Fla Int Univ, 72-75; assoc adj prof, Nova Univ, 78-79; consult, 78-80; vpres, Solarium Prod Fla, Inc, 78-81. *Mem:* AMA. *Res:* Physico-chemical and structural investigations of solid state materials, solid state catalysts, and catalytic processes via modern instrumental techniques; health planning, program development and evaluation; biomedical equipment sales. *Mailing Add:* 3405 McFarland Rd Tampa FL 33618

ENGEL, ADOLPH JAMES, b Erie, Pa, Oct 13, 29; m 52; c 3. ELECTROANALYTICAL CHEMISTRY. *Educ:* Columbia Union Col, BA, 51; Univ Md, MS, 55; Univ Md, PhD, 72. *Prof Exp:* Lab asst, Columbia Union Col, 48-51; asst, Univ Md, 51-54; chemist fertilizer sect, USDA, 54-56; instr chem, Union Col, 56-58 & Wis State Univ, Eau Claire, 58-64; asst prof, Columbia Union Col, 64-74; asst prof, North Adams State Col, 74-75; anal lab supvr, McKee Baking Co, 76-80; ASST PROF, CHATANOOGA STATE TECH COMMUNITY COL, 80- *Mem:* Am Chem Soc. *Res:* Micro methods of determination of metals; instrumental methods, including polarography. *Mailing Add:* PO Box 1025 Collegedale TN 37315

ENGEL, ALBERT EDWARD JOHN, b St Louis, Mo, June 16, 16; m 44; c 2. GEOLOGY, GEOCHEMISTRY. *Educ:* Univ Mo, BA, 38, MA, 39; Princeton Univ, MA, 41, PhD(geol), 42. *Prof Exp:* From instr to asst prof geol, Univ Mo, 38-42; from asst prof to prof, Calif Inst Technol, 48-58; PROF GEOL, UNIV CALIF, SAN DIEGO & SCRIPPS INST OCEANOG, 58-; GEOLOGIST, US GEOL SURV, 42- *Mem:* Nat Acad Sci; fel AAAS; Am Acad Arts & Sci; Geol Soc Am; Am Geophys Union. *Res:* Crustal evolution. *Mailing Add:* Div Geol Res Scripps Inst Oceanog Univ Calif San Diego PO Box 109 La Jolla CA 92093

ENGEL, ALFRED J, b Munich, Ger, Mar 30, 27; US citizen; m 53; c 4. CHEMICAL ENGINEERING. *Educ:* Cornell Univ, BChE, 52; Univ Wis, PhD(chem eng), 61. *Prof Exp:* Engr petrochem, Calif Res Corp, 52-55; instr chem eng, Univ Wis, 57-59; from asst prof to assoc prof, 59-71, PROF CHEM ENG, PA STATE UNIV, 71- *Concurrent Pos:* Consult, Socony Mobil Oil Co, NY, 64; Fulbright sr lectr, Ben Gurion Univ, Israel, 74-75. *Mem:* Am Inst Chem Engrs; Am Chem Soc. *Res:* Chemical reaction kinetics and mass transfer; air pollution control and administration. *Mailing Add:* Dept of Chem Eng Pa State Univ University Park PA 16802

ENGEL, ANDREW G, b Budapest, Hungary, July 12, 30; US citizen; m 58; c 3. NEUROPATHOLOGY, BIOCHEMISTRY. *Educ:* McGill Univ, BS, 53, MD, 55. *Prof Exp:* Resident internal med & neurol, Mayo Clin, 56-57; clin assoc neurol, Nat Inst Neurol Dis & Blindness, 58-59; resident internal med & neurol, Mayo Clin, 60-62; instr neurol, 66-67, assoc prof, 67-73, PROF NEUROL, MAYO MED SCH, 73- *Concurrent Pos:* Consult, Mayo Clin, 65-; spec fel neuropath, Col Physicians & Surgeons, Columbia Univ, 62-65. *Mem:* Am Asn Neuropath; Am Soc Cell Biol. *Res:* Experimental neuropathology; muscle biochemistry; biochemical and ultrastructural studies of mechanisms of weakness in human and experimentally induced myopathies. *Mailing Add:* Dept of Neurol Mayo Clin Rochester MN 55901

ENGEL, BERNARD THEODORE, b Chicago, Ill, Apr 18, 28; m 51; c 3. PHYSIOLOGICAL PSYCHOLOGY. *Educ:* Univ Calif, Los Angeles, BA, 54, PhD(physiol psychol), 56. *Prof Exp:* Jr res psychologist, Univ Calif, Los Angeles, 56; res psychologist, Michael Reese Hosp, Inst Psychosom & Psychiat, 57-58; lectr med psychol & mem sr staff cardiovasc res, Sch Med, Univ Calif, 59-67; CHIEF, LAB BEHAV SCI & PSYCHOPHYSIOL SECT, GERONT RES CTR, NAT INST AGING, NIH, 67-; PROF BEHAV BIOL, SCH MED, JOHNS HOPKINS UNIV, 70- *Honors & Awards:* Pavlovian Soc Award, 79. *Mem:* AAAS; Soc Psychophysiol Res (pres, 70-71); Am Psychosom Soc (secy-treas, 81-); Biofeedback Soc Am (pres, 81-82). *Res:* Psychophysiological mechanisms underlying the learned control of autonomic responses; application of operant conditioning techniques to the clinical control of cardiovascular urinary or gastrointestinal disorders; psychophysiological changes associated with aging. *Mailing Add:* Gerontol Res Ctr Baltimore City Hosp Baltimore MD 21224

ENGEL, CHARLES ROBERT, b Vienna, Austria, Jan 28, 22; m 51; c 4. ORGANIC CHEMISTRY. *Educ:* Univ Grenoble, BS, 41; Swiss Fed Inst Technol, Chem Eng, 47, DSc(org chem), 51; Univ Paris, DSc, 70. *Prof Exp:* From asst prof to assoc prof med res & hon spec lectr, Univ Western Ont, 51-58; PROF CHEM, LAVAL UNIV, 58- *Concurrent Pos:* Can Life Ins Off Asn Med fel, 52-58; ed, Steroids, 63-; vis prof, Inst Natural Chem Substances, Nat Ctr Sci Res, France, 66-67; consult, Royal Soc Chem. *Mem:* Am Chem Soc; NY Acad Sci; Fr Chem Soc; Swiss Chem Soc; Royal Soc Chem. *Res:* Synthetic organic chemistry; steroids and related products; carbanionic rearrangements; chemical endocrinology; biologically active natural products; stereochemistry; chiroptical properties. *Mailing Add:* Dept of Chem Laval Univ Quebec PQ G1K 7P4 Can

ENGEL, ERIC, b Geneva, Switz, Oct 12, 25; m 50; c 3. MEDICINE. *Educ:* Univ Geneva, BS, 47, MD, 51, PhD, 58. *Prof Exp:* Instr internal med, Geneva Univ Hosp, 58-60; instr med, Harvard Med Sch, 60-63; from asst prof to assoc prof, 63-72, PROF MED & HEAD DIV GEN MED, SCH MED, VANDERBILT UNIV, 72- *Concurrent Pos:* Clin & res fel cytogenetics, Mass Gen Hosp, 60-63; Prof Genetics & Dir Genetics Inst, Cantonal Hosp, Univ of Geneva, Switz, 79- *Mem:* Am Soc Clin Invest. *Mailing Add:* Dept of Med Vanderbilt Univ Sch of Med Nashville TN 37203

ENGEL, FRANK AUGUST, JR, b Steubenville, Ohio, July 29, 17; m 40; c 4. COMPUTER SCIENCE. *Educ:* Univ Pittsburgh, BS, 38, MS, 51. *Prof Exp:* Sales & develop engr, Speer Carbon Co, 39-41; design & test engr, Penn Elec Co, 41-42; res physicist, B F Goodrich Co, 42-43, sr physicist, Mine Safety Appliances, 43-51; supvr gen anal & comput sect, Atomic Power Div, Westinghouse Elec Corp, 51-55, adv engr, Anal Dept, Eng & Serv Dept, 55-62; dir comput ctr, Harvard Univ, 62-64; mgr appl sci dept, Electronic Data Processing Div, Honeywell, Inc, 64-66; subdept head, EDP Systs Anal, Mitre Corp, 66-72; CONSULT, 72- *Concurrent Pos:* Pres, SHARE, 56-57, vpres, 60-61, mem exec bd, 57-58; chmn comt FORTRAN prog lang standards, Am Nat Standards Inst, 70-77. *Mem:* AAAS; Am Math Soc; Brit Comput Soc; Am Nuclear Soc; Asn Comput Mach. *Res:* Digital computer design; programming systems development, scientific and business data processing applications; FORTRAN programming language development; EDP system performance evaluation. *Mailing Add:* 179 Lewis Rd Belmont MA 02178

ENGEL, FRED C, b Hamburg, Ger, Mar 12, 18; nat US; m 49; c 3. MECHANICAL ENGINEERING. *Educ:* Ohio State Univ, BME, 43; Univ Pittsburgh, MSc, 54. *Prof Exp:* Test engr, Columbus McKinnon Chain Corp, 43-44; design engr, Cleveland Pneumatic Tool Co, 44-45; design engr x-ray div, 45-46, res engr, res labs, 46-57, SR ENGR, ATOMIC POWER DEPT, WESTINGHOUSE ELEC CORP, 57- *Mem:* Am Nuclear Soc; Am Soc Mech Engrs; Combustion Inst. *Res:* Combustion; fuel atomization; hydraulics; 2 phase flow; liquid metal heat transfer. *Mailing Add:* Advan Reactor Develop Dept PO Box 158 Madison PA 15663

ENGEL, GEORGE LIBMAN, b New York, NY, Dec 10, 13; m 38; c 2. MEDICINE, PSYCHIATRY. *Educ:* Dartmouth Col, BA, 34; Johns Hopkins Univ, MD, 38; Univ Bern, Switzerland, MD. *Prof Exp:* From instr to asst prof med & psychiat, Col Med, Univ Cincinnati, 42-46; from asst prof to assoc prof med, 46-57, PROF MED, SCH MED & DENT, UNIV ROCHESTER, 57-; PSYCHIATRIST & PHYSICIAN, STRONG MEM HOSP, 57- *Concurrent Pos:* Clinician, Med Serv, Cincinnati Gen Hosp, 42-44, asst attend psychiatrist, 43-44; consult, Off Surgeon Gen; consult, Fitzsimons Gen Hosp, 48 & res studies sect, Nat Adv Ment Health Coun, USPHS, 49-53; fel med, Harvard Med Sch, 41-42; USPHS career res award, 62. *Mem:* AAAS; Am Soc Clin Invest; Am Psychosom Soc; Am Psychiat Asn; Am Psychoanal Asn. *Res:* Physiology of respiration and circulation; electroencephalography; syncope; delirium; migranine; decompression sickness; problems of clinical and psychosomatic medicine; psychoanalysis; medical education. *Mailing Add:* Strong Mem Hosp 260 Crittenden Blvd Rochester NY 14642

ENGEL, JAMES DOUGLAS, b Staten Island, NY, Apr 6, 47; m 68; c 2. MOLECULAR BIOLOGY. *Educ:* Univ Calif, San Diego, BA & BS, 70; Univ Ore, PhD(chem), 75. *Prof Exp:* ASST PROF MOLECULAR BIOL, DEPT BIOCHEM & MOLECULAR CELL BIOL, NORTHWESTERN UNIV, 78- *Concurrent Pos:* Consult, Centaur Genetics, 81- *Res:* Eucaryotic gene expression. *Mailing Add:* Dept Biochem 2153 Sheridan Rd Northwestern Univ Evanston IL 60201

ENGEL, JAMES FRANCIS, b Kansas City, Mo, Jan 25, 41; m 61; c 4. SYNTHETIC ORGANIC CHEMISTRY. *Educ:* Rockhurst Col, AB, 61. *Prof Exp:* Instr chem, Rockhurst High Sch, Mo, 63-64; from asst chemist to assoc chemist org synthesis, 64-72, sr chemist, 72-76, head org & radiochem synthesis sect, 76-77, assoc dir Chem Sci Div, 77-79, DIR BIORGANIC CHEM DEPT, MIDWEST RES INST, 79- *Concurrent Pos:* Instr chem, Donnelly Jr Col, 65-68. *Mem:* Am Chem Soc. *Res:* Research and development synthesis and analysis of toxic materials, metabolites and/or degradation products with or without isotopic label, mass or radioactive, especially polynuclear aromatic hydrocarbon derivatives. *Mailing Add:* 425 Volker Blvd Kansas City MO 64110

ENGEL, JAN MARCIN, b Gdansk, Danzig, May 1, 24; US citizen; wid; c 2. SOLID STATE PHYSICS. *Educ:* Univ London, BSc, 46. *Prof Exp:* Res physicist, Socony-Vacuum Oil Co, NJ, 50-51; res physicist, Electronics Lab, Gen Elec Co, NY, 51-53; sr proj engr, Motorola Inc, Ariz, 53-54; res physicist, Pac Semiconductors Inc, 54-57; assoc physicist, Res Lab, 58-59, staff physicist, Adv Systs Div, 59-60, adv physicist thin film devices, Components Lab, NY, 60-63 & electron devices, Gen Prods Div, 64-65, adv physicist electron devices, Systs Develop Div, 65-71, ADV PHYSICIST, DEVELOP LAB, GEN PRODS DIV, IBM CORP, 71- *Concurrent Pos:* Consult, Electro-Optical Systs Inc, Calif, 57-58; lectr, Dept Liberal Arts, Univ Exten, Univ Calif, Los Angeles, 57-58 & Univ Calif, Berkeley, 58-60; voluntary ed progs, IBM Corp, 62-; pres, Genealogical Data Systs, San Jose, Calif, 80- *Mem:* Am Inst Physics; Am Phys Soc; Sigma Xi; fel Brit Inst Physics & Phys Soc; sr mem Inst Elec & Electronics Eng. *Res:* Development of novel devices utilizing physical phenomena that are usually studied in the fields of solid state physics and utilizing semiconductor, thin film and/or electron beam technologies. *Mailing Add:* 2980 Cambridge Dr San Jose CA 95125

ENGEL, JEROME, JR, b Albany, NY, May 11, 38; m 67; c 3. NEUROPHYSIOLOGY, NEUROLOGY. *Educ:* Cornell Univ, BA, 60; Stanford Univ, MD, 65, PhD(physiol), 66; Am Bd Qualification EEG, cert; Am Bd Psychiat & Neurol, cert. *Prof Exp:* Intern med, Ind Univ Med Ctr, 66-67; resident neurol, Albert Einstein Col Med, 67-68; NIH, NINCDS, Lab Perinatal Physiol, 68-69; staff assoc, Lab Neural Control, 69-70; resident neurol, 70-72, asst prof neurol & neurosci, Albert Einstein Col Med, 72-76; assoc prof, 76-79, PROF NEUROL & ANAT, SCH MED, UNIV CALIF, LOS ANGELES, 80- *Concurrent Pos:* Vis asst prof, Sch Med, Univ PR, 68-69; NIH fel, Stanford Univ & Nat Ctr Sci Res, France, 65-66; Fulbright scholar, Inst Neurol & Psychiat, London, 71-72; NIH career develop award, 72-76. *Mem:* Soc Neurosci; Am Neurol Asn; Am Acad Neurol; Am EEG Soc; Am Epilepsy Soc. *Res:* Clinical neurophysiology; pathophysiology of epilepsy; positron computed tomography. *Mailing Add:* Reed Neurol Res Ctr Sch Med Univ Calif Los Angeles Los Angeles CA 90025

ENGEL, JOHN FRANCIS, b Cincinnati, Ohio, Sept 15, 42; m 65; c 2. ORGANIC CHEMISTRY. *Educ:* Univ Cincinnati, BS, 64; Duke Univ, MS, 70, PhD(org chem), 71. *Prof Exp:* Res chemist org chem, Cincinnati Milacron, Inc, 64-67; RES CHEMIST ORG CHEM, AGR CHEM DIV, FMC CORP, 71- *Mem:* Am Chem Soc. *Res:* Organic pesticides. *Mailing Add:* Agr Chem Div FMC Corp 100 Niagara St Middleport NY 14105

ENGEL, JOHN HAL, JR, b Detroit, Mich, Dec 12, 30; m 57; c 3. ORGANIC CHEMISTRY, POLYMER CHEMISTRY. *Educ:* Univ Detroit, BS, 56, MS, 58; Mich State Univ, MBA, 75. *Prof Exp:* Res chemist, Gen Motors Res Labs, 58-62; sr res chemist, R P Scherer Corp, 62-63; from res scientist to sr res scientist, Chrysler Corp Res Labs, Detroit, 63-67, group leader polymer res, 67-70, group leader emissions, 70-74, res staff scientist, 74-75, sr res staff scientist emissions & govt rels & mgr high temperature mat res, 75-79, mgr rubber & plastics eng, 79-81; ASSOC MAT ENGR, FISHER BODY DIV, GEN MOTORS CORP, 81- *Concurrent Pos:* Adj prof chem, Marygrove Col, 68-; Adj prof mat eng, Detroit Inst Technol, 80-81. *Mem:* Am Chem Soc. *Res:* Solventless and aqueous paint and adhesive systems; polymer synthesis; infrared analysis of polymer systems; polyurethanes; conversion of emissions from engines and factories, superalloys, ceramics for structural applications; plastics for automotive application, automotive coatings. *Mailing Add:* 705 Washington Rd Grosse Pointe MI 48230

ENGEL, JOHN JAY, b Milwaukee, Wis, July 27, 41; m 62; c 2. BRYOLOGY. *Educ:* Univ Wis-Milwaukee, BS, 65, MS, 67; Mich State Univ, PhD(bot), 72. *Prof Exp:* Asst cur, 72-77, ASSOC CUR BRYOL, FIELD MUS NATURAL HIST, 77- *Mem:* Am Bryol Soc; Int Asn Bryologists; Int Asn Plant Taxonomists. *Res:* The taxonomy and phytogeography of south temperate and subantarctic liverworts; evolution, relationships, ecology and distribution of several liverwort families. *Mailing Add:* Dept Bot Field Mus Natural Hist Roosevelt Rd at Lake Shore Dr Chicago IL 60605

ENGEL, JOSEPH H(ENRY), b New York, NY, May 15, 22; m 43; c 3. MATHEMATICS, OPERATIONS RESEARCH. *Educ:* City Col New York, BS, 42; Univ Wis, MA, 47, PhD(math), 49. *Prof Exp:* Opers analyst opers eval group, Mass Inst Technol, 49-57, dep dir, 57-62; dir opers eval group, ctr naval anal, Franklin Inst, 62-65, asst chief scientist, 65-67; dir planning res & serv, Commun Satellite Corp, 67-70; head, systs eng dept, 70-76, PROF SYSTS ENG, UNIV ILL, CHICAGO CIRCLE, 70- *Concurrent Pos:* Chmn, adv panel oper res, NATO, 70-73, chmn, spec prog panel systs sci, NATO, 73; prin investr, Chicago Area Transp Study, 73 & Dupage County Regional Planning Comn, 75- *Mem:* Fel AAAS; Am Math Soc; Opers Res Soc Am (secy, pres, 68-69); Int Fedn Opers Res Soc (vpres, 74); Am Inst Indust Engrs. *Res:* Operations research; stochastic processes; decision problems; transportation and land use; equation of combat; safety standards for television receivers; establishment of manufacturing facilities in space; mathematical modelling of complex systems. *Mailing Add:* Dept of Systs Eng Box 4348 Chicago IL 60680

ENGEL, LAWRENCE J, b St Louis, Ill, May 10, 29; m 52; c 4. CHEMICAL ENGINEERING. *Educ:* Ga Inst Technol, BChE, 51, MSChE, 54, PhD(chem eng), 56. *Prof Exp:* Asst instr chem eng, Ga Inst Technol, 53-56; engr, Esso Res & Eng Co, NJ, 56-59, sr engr, Spec Projs Unit, 59-63, mem chem staff, 63-65; staff adv, Enjay Polymer Labs, 65-67, res assoc, Enjay Additives Labs, 67-68, proj coordr, Paramins Div, Enjay Chem Co, NY, 68-70; SR ASSOC, EXXON RES & ENG CO, 70- *Res:* Petroleum and chemical process research from lab bench sales through design and operation of commercial unit; economics and staff planning and analysis of projects. *Mailing Add:* 226 Globe Ave Union NJ 07083

ENGEL, MILTON BAER, b Chicago, Ill, Aug 7, 16; m 42; c 2. DENTISTRY. *Educ:* Univ Ill, DDS, 38, MS, 40. *Prof Exp:* From res assoc to assoc prof, 45-57, PROF HISTOL, COL DENT, UNIV ILL, MED CTR, 57- *Concurrent Pos:* Practicing orthodontist; Carnegie fel orthod, Col Dent, Univ Ill, Med Ctr, 41-42. *Mem:* AAAS; Am Dent Asn; Am Asn Orthodont; Am Soc Exp Path; Int Asn Dent Res. *Res:* Experimental pathology; histochemistry; growth; orthodontics. *Mailing Add:* Univ of Ill Col of Dent Chicago IL 60612

ENGEL, NIELS N(IKOLAJ), b Bern, Switzerland, Nov 21, 04; US citizen; m 34; c 3. METALLURGY, THEORETICAL PHYSICS. *Educ:* Tech Univ, Denmark, BS, 25, MS, 28; Univ Copenhagen, Cand Phil, 26; Aachen Tech Univ, Dr Ing(metall), 31. *Prof Exp:* Assoc prof, Tech Univ, Denmark, 36-51; assoc prof metall eng, Univ Ala, 51-59; prof, Ga Inst Technol, 59-72; PROF METALL ENG, NMEX INST TECHNOL, 73- *Concurrent Pos:* Consult, Oak Ridge Nat Lab, 64-70, Southern Saw, Ga, 66 & Southwire, Ga, 68- *Honors & Awards:* Adolf Martens Medal, Ger, 66. *Mem:* Am Soc Metals; Am Vacuum Soc. *Res:* Basic conception of physical world; bonding between atoms; metallic properties; applied physical metallurgy. *Mailing Add:* 720 Gonzales Rd Santa Fe NM 87501

ENGEL, PAUL SANFORD, b Pittsburgh, Pa, July 19, 42. PHYSICAL ORGANIC CHEMISTRY. *Educ:* Univ Calif, Los Angeles, BS, 64; Harvard Univ, PhD(chem), 68. *Prof Exp:* Sr asst scientist, NIH, 68-70; asst prof, 70-75, assoc prof, 74-80, PROF CHEM, RICE UNIV, 80- *Concurrent Pos:* Alfred P Sloan fel, 75-78. *Mem:* Am Chem Soc. *Res:* Organic photochemistry; azo compounds; extrusion reactions; energy transfer; rearrangements of beta, gamma-unsaturated ketones; free radical chemistry. *Mailing Add:* Dept Chem Rice Univ PO Box 1892 Houston TX 77001

ENGEL, PAULINUS P, industrial microbiology, see previous edition

ENGEL, PETER ANDRAS, b Kassa, Hungary, July 10, 35; US citizen; m 61; c 2. APPLIED MECHANICS, TRIBOLOGY. *Educ:* Vanderbilt Univ, BE, 58; Lehigh Univ, MS, 60; Cornell Univ, PhD(theoret & appl mech), 68. *Prof Exp:* Struct civil engr, Praeger-Kavanagh-Waterbury Engrs, New York, 60-62; res engr, Boeing Co, New Orleans, La, 62-65; RES ENGR MAT SCI, ENDICOTT LAB, IBM CORP, 68- *Mem:* Am Soc Mech Engrs. *Res:* Contact of solids, with applications to sliding, rolling, and impact; wear studies; structural dynamics. *Mailing Add:* IBM Endicott Lab Dept E21 PO Box 6 Endicott NY 13760

ENGEL, ROBERT DAVID, b Los Angeles, Calif, Nov 22, 32; m 57; c 2. COMPUTER SCIENCE. *Educ:* Univ Calif, Los Angeles, BS, 58, MS, 59, PhD(eng), 63. *Prof Exp:* Res engr plasma properties, Univ Calif, Los Angeles, 61-63, asst prof eng, 63-66; mem staff comput, opers dept, Beckman Instrument Corp, 66-67; assoc provost, 67-80, PROF ENG, UNIV REDLANDS, 67-, CHMN DEPT, 80- *Concurrent Pos:* Consult, electronics div, Rand Corp, 60-66. *Mem:* Inst Mgt Sci; Inst Elec & Electronics Engrs. *Res:* Applied electromagnetic theory; microwaves; electronics; computers; simulation; systems. *Mailing Add:* Dept of Eng Univ of Redlands Redlands CA 92373

ENGEL, ROBERT RALPH, b Pittsburgh, Pa, Aug 30, 42; m 66. SYNTHETIC ORGANIC CHEMISTRY. *Educ:* Carnegie Inst Technol, BS, 63; Pa State Univ, PhD(chem), 66. *Prof Exp:* Asst prof chem, 68-71, assoc prof & chmn, Dept Chem, 77-79, PROF CHEM & BIOCHEM, QUEENS COL, CITY UNIV NEW YORK, 76-, DEP EXEC OFFICER PHD PROG BIOCHEM, 77- *Concurrent Pos:* NATO sr res fel, McGill Univ, 75. *Mem:* Am Chem Soc; NY Acad Sci; The Chem Soc. *Res:* Mechanism studies on reactions of organophosphorus compounds; organophosphorus synthesis; preparation of analogues of natural phosphates; hydrogenolysis mechanisms; aromatic substitution reactions. *Mailing Add:* Dept of Chem Queens Col Flushing NY 11367

ENGEL, RUBEN WILLIAM, b Shawano, Wis, July 10, 12; m 39; c 3. BIOCHEMISTRY. *Educ:* Univ Wis, PhB, 36, PhD(biochem), 39. *Prof Exp:* Asst, Univ Wis, 36-39; assoc animal nutritionist, Ala Polytech Inst, 39-43, animal nutritionist, 46-52; head dept, 52-66, assoc dean res, Col Agr, 66-78, prof, 68-78, EMER PROF BIOCHEM & NUTRIT, VA POLYTECH INST & STATE UNIV, 78- *Concurrent Pos:* Mem panel on nutrit, Comt on

Growth, Nat Res Coun, mem food & nutrit bd & mem US nat comt nutrit; nutrit adv, US Agency Int Develop, Manila, Philippines, 68-80. *Honors & Awards:* Conrad A Elvehjem Award, Am Inst Nutrit, 74; Gamma Sigma Delta Int Award for Distinguished Serv to Agr, 78. *Mem:* Am Asn Cancer Res; Am Chem Soc; Am Inst Nutrit (pres, 64); Am Dairy Sci Asn; hon mem Philippine Asn Nutrit. *Res:* Chemical and pathological changes associated with B vitamin deficiencies; choline metabolism; relation of nutrition to cancer; minor elements in animal nutrition. *Mailing Add:* 1726 Donlee Dr Blacksburg VA 24060

ENGEL, RUDOLF, b Bonn, Ger, Aug 28, 04; US nat; m 33; c 4. MEDICINE. *Educ:* Univ Bonn, MD, 29; Univ Berlin, Dr med habil, 35; Univ Minn, MSc & MD, 49. *Prof Exp:* Resident, Univ Berlin Hosp, 29-30; asst pediat, Univ Minn, 31; resident, Univ Heidelberg Hosp, 32-34; resident, Univ Berlin Hosp, 34-36; asst prof, Univ Hamburg, 36-38; assoc prof internal med, Univ Berlin, 38-45; head dept, Luisen Hosp, Aachen, Ger, 46-48; from clin asst prof to assoc prof pediat, Univ Minn, 50-52; clin instr neurol, 52-57, from asst prof to prof pediat, 57-73, EMER PROF PEDIAT, MED SCH, UNIV ORE, 73- *Concurrent Pos:* Fulbright lectr, Univ Ceylon, 55-56, Univ Hamburg, 62 & Univ Munich, 74. *Mem:* AAAS; Am Electroencephalog Soc; Am Acad Cerebral Palsy; fel Am Col Physicians. *Res:* Causes of cerebral palsy; mental retardation and other malformations; biological sciences; neonatal electroencephalography; evoked potentials. *Mailing Add:* Dept of Pediat Univ of Ore Health Sci Ctr Portland OR 97201

ENGEL, STANFORD LOWELL, b Philadelphia, Pa, July 26, 24. PHARMACOLOGY. *Educ:* Philadelphia Col Pharm, BS, 44; Columbia Univ, PhD(pharmacol), 59. *Prof Exp:* Res bacteriologist, McNeil Labs, 46-51; asst prof pharmacol, Rutgers Univ, 56-59; head pharmacol & toxicol, Nopco Labs, 59-62; SR RES SCIENTIST, SQUIBB INST MED RES, 62- *Mem:* AAAS; NY Acad Sci. *Res:* Endocrinology; biochemistry and physiology of the neurophypophysis; pituitary regulation of metabolism; water and electrolyte balance; neuroendocrinology; gastrointestinal hormones. *Mailing Add:* Squibb Inst for Med Res Princeton NJ 08540

ENGEL, THOMAS WALTER, b Yokohama, Japan, Apr 2, 42; US citizen. PHYSICAL CHEMISTRY, SURFACE SCIENCE. *Educ:* Johns Hopkins Univ, BA, 63, MA, 64; Univ Chicago, PhD(chem), 69. *Prof Exp:* Res assoc surface sci, Clausthal Tech Univ, 69-75 & Univ Munich, 75-78; res assoc surface sci, IBM Res Lab Zurich, 78-80; ASSOC PROF CHEM, UNIV WASH, 80- *Res:* Surface physics and chemistry; structure of solid surfaces; oxidation; molecular beam scattering from surfaces. *Mailing Add:* Dept Chem Univ Wash Seattle WA 98195

ENGEL, TOBY ROSS, b New York, NY, Mar 6, 42; m 65; c 3. CARDIOLOGY. *Educ:* Univ Col, NY Univ, BA, 62, Sch Med, MD, 66. *Prof Exp:* Resident, Univ Pa, 66-68; resident, Ohio State Univ, 70-71, fel cardiol, 71-73; from asst prof to assoc prof, 73-78, PROF MED, MED COL PA, 78- *Concurrent Pos:* Assoc ed, Annals of Internal Med, 77- *Mem:* Am Col Physicians; Am Col Cardiol; Am Heart Asn; Am Col Clin Phamacol; Am Soc Clin Pharmacol & Therapeuts. *Res:* Clinical electrophysiology, concentrating on sinus node dysfunction; ventricular tochycardia; atriol fibrillation and flutter; pharmacologic approach to arrthymias. *Mailing Add:* 3300 Henry Ave Philadelphia PA 19129

ENGEL, WILLIAM KING, b St Louis, Mo, Nov 19, 30; m 54; c 3. NEUROLOGY. *Educ:* Johns Hopkins Univ, BA, 51; McGill Univ, MD, 55; Am Bd Neurol & Psychiat, dipl, 62. *Prof Exp:* Intern neurol, Univ Mich Hosp, 55-56; clin assoc, Med Neurol Br, Nat Inst Neurol Dis & Blindness, 56-59; clin clerk, Nat Hosp, London, Eng, 59-60; assoc neurologist, 60-62, actg chief, 62-63, CHIEF MED NEUROL BR, NAT INST NEUROL DIS & STROKE, 63- *Concurrent Pos:* Nat Inst Neurol Dis & Blindness trainee, 59-60; mem med bd, NIH, 68-69; clin prof, Sch Med, George Washington Univ, 69-; mem med adv bd, St Jude's Children's Res Hosp, Memphis, 70-; mem med adv bd, Myasthenia Gravis Found, 70-; mem exec comt, Res Group Neuromuscular Disorders, World Fedn Neurol, 70-; mem adv coun, Amyotrophic Lateral Sclerosis Found, 71-; assoc exam, Am Bd Neurol & Psychiat. *Honors & Awards:* S Weir Mitchell Award, Am Acad Neurol, 62; Meritorious Serv Medal, USPHS, 71. *Mem:* Fel Am Acad Neurol; Histochem Soc; Am Soc Cell Biol; Am Asn Neuropath; AMA. *Res:* Clinical and investigative neurology; neuromuscular diseases. *Mailing Add:* Nat Inst of Health 10-D018 Clin Ctr Bethesda MD 20014

ENGELBART, DOUGLAS C(ARL), b Portland, Ore, Jan 30, 25; m 51; c 4. ELECTRICAL ENGINEERING. *Educ:* Ore State Col, BS, 48; Univ Calif, EE, 53, PhD(elec eng), 55. *Prof Exp:* Elec engr, Nat Adv Comt Aeronaut, Ames Aero Lab, Calif, 48-51; assoc elec eng, Univ Calif, 54-55, asst prof, 55-56; pres & tech dir, Digital Tech, Inc, 56-57; res engr, 57-65, PROG HEAD, MAN-MACH INFO SYSTS, SRI INT, 65- *Concurrent Pos:* Consult, Marchant Res, Inc, Calif, 55-56. *Res:* Digital computers; new device research with gas discharge and magnetics; man-computer on-line problem solving. *Mailing Add:* 89 Catalpa Dr Atherton CA 94025

ENGELBERG, JOSEPH, b Vienna, Austria, June 2, 28; nat US; m 54; c 2. THEORY OF LIVING SYSTEMS. *Educ:* Cooper Union, BME, 50; Univ Pa, MS, 53, PhD(physics), 58. *Prof Exp:* Res engr surg instrumentation, Univ Pa, 50-53; res engr bioeng, Franklin Inst, 53-54; instr biophys, Univ Colo, 58-60; Am Cancer Soc fel, Univ Calif, Berkeley, 60-61; from asst prof to assoc prof, 61-70, PROF PHYSIOL & BIOPHYS, SCH MED, UNIV KY, 70- *Concurrent Pos:* USPHS fel, 58-60. *Honors & Awards:* Lederle Award, 63-66. *Mem:* Biophys Soc; Am Physiol Soc. *Res:* Design of artificial kidney and artificial heart-lung machines; mechanics of pulmonary circulation; mammalian cells, especially physiology and effects of radiation; development of health delivery systems; theory of living systems. *Mailing Add:* Dept of Physiol & Biophys Univ of Ky Med Ctr Lexington KY 40536

ENGELBRECHT, HARLEN J, b Marcus, Iowa, May 26, 20; m 44; c 3. VETERINARY MEDICINE. *Educ:* Iowa State Univ, DVM, 44. *Prof Exp:* Mem res staff, Diag Lab, 47-59, MEM RES STAFF, PROD DEVELOP, FT DODGE LAB DIV, AM HOME PROD CORP, 59- *Mem:* Am Vet Med Asn; Am Soc Parasitol. *Res:* Veterinary parasitology and bacteriology. *Mailing Add:* Ft Dodge Labs Ft Dodge IA 50501

ENGELBRECHT, R(ICHARD) S(TEVENS), b Ft Wayne, Ind, Mar 11, 26; m 48; c 2. SANITARY ENGINEERING, MICROBIOLOGY. *Educ:* Univ Ind, AB, 48; Mass Inst Technol, MS, 52, ScD(sanit sci), 54. *Prof Exp:* Asst microbiol, sch med, Univ Ind, 48-50; asst civil & sanit eng, Mass Inst Technol, 50-52, instr, 52-54; from asst prof to assoc prof sanit eng, 54-59, PROF ENVIRON ENG, UNIV ILL, URBANA, 59- *Concurrent Pos:* Chmn, Ohio River Valley Water Sanit Comn, 80-82. *Honors & Awards:* Harrison P Eddy Medal, 66 & Arthur Sidney Bedell Award, 73, Water Pollution Control Fedn; George W Fuller Award, 74 & publ award, 76, Am Water Works Asn; Ernest Victor Balsam Commemmoration Lecture, Inst Pub Health Engrs, London, 78; Eric H Vick Award, Inst Pub Health Engrs, 79. *Mem:* Nat Acad Eng; Am Soc Microbiol; Am Water Works Asn; Water Pollution Control Fedn (pres, 77-78); AAAS. *Res:* Water quality and stream pollution; water and wastewater treatment; environmental science. *Mailing Add:* Dept Civil Eng Univ Ill Urbana-Champaign 208 N Romine St Urbana IL 61801

ENGELDER, JAMES TERRY, b Oswego, NY, Jan 31, 46; m 70; c 1. TECTONOPHYSICS, ROCK MECHANICS. *Educ:* Pa State Univ, BS, 68; Yale Univ, MS, 72; Tex A&M Univ, PhD(geol), 73. *Prof Exp:* Geologist marine geol, Texaco Inc, 68; RES ASSOC TECTONOPHYSICS, LAMONT DOHERTY GEOL OBSERV, 73- *Concurrent Pos:* Rock mech subcomt mem, Nat Acad Sci. *Mem:* Geol Soc Am; Am Geophys Union; Seismol Soc Am. *Res:* Structural geology; in situ stress; rock friction; laboratory rock mechanics; regional tectonics. *Mailing Add:* Lamont Doherty Geol Observ Palisades NY 10964

ENGELDER, THEODORE CARL, b Detroit, Mich, Aug 31, 27; m 52; c 2. NUCLEONICS. *Educ:* Univ Mich, BS, 49; Yale Univ, MS, 50, PhD(physics), 53. *Prof Exp:* Proj engr, Dow Chem Co, 52-56; physicist, Chrysler Corp, 56; group supvr, Atomic Energy Div, 56-60, chief exp physics sect, Res & Develop Div, 60-67, mgr physics labs, 67-69, asst dir nuclear develop ctr, 69-71, DIR LYNCHBURG RES CTR, BABCOCK & WILCOX CO, 71- *Mem:* Am Phys Soc; Am Nuclear Soc. *Res:* Nuclear reactor design and development. *Mailing Add:* 2236 Taylor Farm Rd Lynchburg VA 24503

ENGELER, WILLIAM E, b Brooklyn, NY, Nov 13, 28; m 55; c 4. SOLID STATE PHYSICS, SEMICONDUCTOR DEVICE PHYSICS. *Educ:* Polytech Inst Brooklyn, BS, 51; Syracuse Univ, MS, 58, PhD(physics), 61. *Prof Exp:* Physicist, 51-52, physicist semiconductor prod dept, 52-55, PHYSICIST, RES LAB, GEN ELEC CO, 61- *Mem:* Inst Elec & Electronics Engrs; Electrochem Soc; Am Phys Soc. *Res:* Semiconductors; infrared optical properties; electronics; metal-oxide semiconductor devices; device physics; integrated circuit electronics. *Mailing Add:* Signal Electronics Lab PO Box 8 Schenectady NY 12301

ENGELHARD, ARTHUR WILLIAM, b Dayton, Ohio, Apr 9, 28; c 3. PHYTOPATHOLOGY, BOTANY. *Educ:* Ohio Univ, BS, 50; Yale Univ, MS, 52; Iowa State Univ, PhD(plant path), 55. *Prof Exp:* Asst plant path, Iowa State Univ, 52-55; asst plant pathologist, Ill State Natural Hist Surv, 55-56; res biologist, E I du Pont de Nemours & Co, 56-64, sr sales res biologist, 64-65, sr res biologist, 66; ASSOC PROF PLANT PATH & ASSOC PLANT PATHOLOGIST, 66-77, PROF & PLANT PATHOLOGIST, RES & EDUC CTR, UNIV FLA, 77- *Concurrent Pos:* Int consult to floral indust, 70- *Mem:* Am Phytopath Soc; Int Soc Plant Path. *Res:* Cause and control of diseases of floral and ornamental crops; foliage and soil fungicides; integrated control of Fusarium wilt; integrated pest management of ornamental crops; disease control of vegetable crops. *Mailing Add:* Agr Res & Educ Ctr 5007 60th St E Bradenton FL 33508

ENGELHARD, ROBERT J, b Milwaukee, Wis, May 16, 27; m 60; c 2. FORESTRY. *Educ:* Utah State Univ, BS, 50; Univ Denver, MS, 52; Mich State Univ, PhD(forestry), 69. *Prof Exp:* Forester, US Forest Serv, 52-56 & Trees for Tomorrow, Inc, 56-65; from instr to assoc prof, 65-77, PROF FORESTRY, UNIV WIS-STEVENS POINT, 77- *Mem:* Soc Am Foresters. *Res:* Resource economics; forest policy; forest products acquisition and marketing. *Mailing Add:* Dept of Forestry Univ of Wis Stevens Point WI 54481

ENGELHARDT, ALBERT GEORGE, b Toronto, Ont, Mar 17, 35; m 60; c 3. PHYSICS, ELECTRICAL ENGINEERING. *Educ:* Univ Toronto, BASc, 58; Univ Ill, MS, 59, PhD(elec eng, math), 61. *Prof Exp:* Asst elec eng, Univ Ill, 60-61; res engr physics & elec eng, Westinghouse Elec Corp, 61-62, sr engr, 62-66, mgr advan plasma concepts, 66-70; sr staff mem, Inst Res Hydro-Que, 70-74; STAFF MEM, LOS ALAMOS SCI LAB, 74- *Concurrent Pos:* Vis prof, Univ Que, 71-77; adj prof elec eng, Tex Tech Univ, 76- *Mem:* Am Phys Soc; Brit Inst Physics & Phys Soc; Inst Elec & Electronics Engrs. *Res:* Plasma physics; collision phenomena in atomic and molecular gases; laser interaction with matter; electromagnetic wave propagation. *Mailing Add:* Los Alamos Sci Lab PO Box 1663 MS 554 Los Alamos NM 87545

ENGELHARDT, DAVID MEYER, b Austria, June 15, 12; nat US; m 52; c 3. PSYCHIATRY. *Educ:* City Col New York, BS, 32; Univ Vienna, MD, 37; Am Bd Psychiat & Neurol, dipl. *Prof Exp:* Assoc, Long Island Col Med & State Univ NY Col Med, 48-49, assoc prof clin psychiat, 49-50, clin prof psychiat, 50-53, assoc prof, 53-62, actg chmn dept, 58-60, exec officer, Dept, 60-64, dir psychopharmacol treat & res unit, 56-80, PROF PSYCHIAT, STATE UNIV NY DOWNSTATE MED CTR, 62- *Concurrent Pos:* Asst dir, assoc dir & actg dir, Kings County Psychiat Hosp, Brooklyn, 47-60, vis psychiatrist hosp ctr, 59-, dir clin servs, 60-64; mem comt clin drug eval, NIMH, 61-65, chmn adv coun childhood ment illness, 62-64, mem psychopharmacol study sect, 65-67, mem clin psychopharmacol res rev comt,

67-69, mem clin projs res rev comt, 70-74, chmn, 72-74; mem bd trustees, Res Fedn, Nat Asn Ment Health, 63-65; mem panel on drugs used in psychiat, Drug Efficacy Study, Nat Res Coun-Nat Acad Sci, 66-68. *Mem:* Fel AAAS; fel Acad Psychoanal; fel Am Col Neuropsychopharmacol; fel Am Psychiat Asn; Am Psychopath Asn. *Res:* Psychopharmacology; psychiatric treatment research. *Mailing Add:* Dept of Psychiat State Univ NY Downstate Med Ctr Brooklyn NY 11203

ENGELHARDT, DEAN LEE, b Oak Park, Ill, Jan 15, 40; m 70. CELL BIOLOGY, MOLECULAR BIOLOGY. *Educ:* Amherst Col, BA, 61, MA, 63; Rockefeller Univ, PhD(molecular biol), 67. *Prof Exp:* Asst prof biol, Univ Conn, 69-73; asst prof microbiol, Col Physicians & Surgeons, Columbia Univ, 73-80, assoc prof, 80-81; VPRES RES, ENZO BIOCHEM INC, 81- *Concurrent Pos:* Am Cancer Soc fels, Salk Inst, La Jolla, Calif, 68 & Albert Einstein Col Med, 68-69; adj assoc prof microbiol, Col Physicians & Surgeons, Columbia Univ. *Res:* Growth controls of cultured animal cells; in vitro protein synthesis; mechanisms in cellular aging; immunology. *Mailing Add:* 173 River Dr New York NY 10024

ENGELHARDT, DONALD WAYNE, b Blue Island, Ill, Feb 25, 35; m 58; c 3. PALEOBOTANY. *Educ:* Wabash Col, AB, 57; Ind Univ, MA, 61, PhD(paleobot), 62. *Prof Exp:* Res scientist palynology, 61-67, staff paleontologist of palynology, 67-78, REGIONAL PALEONTOLOGIST HOUSTON REGION, AMOCO PROD CO RES CTR, 78- *Mem:* Inst Org Paleobot; Soc Econ Paleontologists & Mineralogists; Am Asn Stratig Palynologists (vpres, 71, pres, 73); Am Asn Petrol Geologists. *Res:* Pleistocene geology and palynology; palynology of Gulf Coast Tertiary; Tertiary and Mesozoic sediments of Alaska. *Mailing Add:* Amoco Prod Co PO Box 3092 Houston TX 77001

ENGELHARDT, EDWARD LOUIS, b Paramaribo, Dutch Guiana, Aug 22, 19; m 47; c 1. ORGANIC CHEMISTRY. *Educ:* Haverford Col, BS, 41; Univ Wis, PhD(org chem), 44. *Prof Exp:* Asst org chem, Univ Wis, 42-44; res assoc, Sharp & Dohme, Inc, 44-53, res assoc, Sharp & Dohme Div, Merck & Co, Inc, 53-56, res assoc, 56-60, asst dir, Med Chem Dept, 60-73, dir med chem, 73-75, sr dir med chem, 75-79, DISTINGUISHED SR SCIENTIST, MERCK SHARP & DOHME RES LABS, 79- *Mem:* Fel AAAS; Am Chem Soc; NY Acad Sci; The Chem Soc; Soc Chem Indust. *Res:* Chemistry of synthetic drugs; cardiovascular diseases; nervous and mental disorders; allergy; cancer. *Mailing Add:* Med Chem Dept Merck Sharp & Dohme Res Labs West Point PA 19486

ENGELHARDT, HUGO TRISTRAM, b Houston, Tex, Jan 17, 12; m 39; c 2. INTERNAL MEDICINE. *Educ:* Tulane Univ, MD, 37; Am Bd Internal Med, dipl, 45. *Prof Exp:* Asst internal med, Sch Med, Tulane Univ, 40-41, instr, 41-45; from instr to assoc prof clin med, Col Med, Baylor Univ, 45-64; LECTR, SCH MED, TULANE UNIV, 64- & CLIN PROF PHYSIOL & MED, MED SCH, UNIV TEX HEALTH SCI CTR, SAN ANTONIO, 67- *Concurrent Pos:* Vis physician, Charity Hosp, New Orleans & chief, White Diabetes Clin, Tulane Serv, 43-45; chief internist, Humble Oil & Refinery Co, 45-64; chief diabetes clin, Jefferson Davis Hosp, Houston, 47-57, assoc physician, 48- *Mem:* Fel am Col Physicians; AMA; Am Diabetes Asn. *Res:* Diabetes mellitus. *Mailing Add:* Star Rte 3 Box 1 New Braunfels TX 78130

ENGELHARDT, VAUGHN ARTHUR, b Chicago, Ill, Apr 14, 18; m 47; c 3. ORGANIC CHEMISTRY. *Educ:* Northwestern Univ, BS, 40; Univ Minn, MS, 44, PhD(org chem), 48. *Prof Exp:* Jr res chemist, Com Solvents Corp, Ind, 40, 41; res chemist, Nat Defense Res Comt, Columbia Univ, 42; res chemist, 48-57, ASSOC DIR, E I DU PONT DE NEMOURS & CO, INC, 57- *Mem:* Am Chem Soc. *Res:* Synthesis of organic compounds; cyclopropanes; chloracetone; acetylene; cyanocarbons; agrichemicals. *Mailing Add:* Biochem Dept E I du Pont de Nemours & Co Wilmington DE 19898

ENGELKE, CHARLES EDWARD, b New York, NY, July 26, 30; m 55; c 3. NUCLEAR PHYSICS, ATOMIC PHYSICS. *Educ:* Queens Col, NY, BS, 51; Columbia Univ, MA, 53, PhD(physics), 61. *Prof Exp:* Asst prof, 61-66, ASSOC PROF PHYSICS, LEHMAN COL, 66-, ASSOC PROF ASTRON, 80- *Mem:* Am Phys Soc; Sigma Xi. *Res:* Neutron-proton interaction; COL & GRAD FAC, CITY UNIV NEW YORK, paradox; interference effects involving systems whose wave functions have been reduced by observations on correlated systems; community total energy systems exploiting interseasonal thermal storage. *Mailing Add:* Dept of Physics & Astron Herbert H Lehman Col Bronx NY 10468

ENGELKE, JOHN LELAND, b Ancon, CZ, Sept 5, 30; m 57, 70, 78; c 1. PHYSICAL CHEMISTRY. *Educ:* Mich Col Mining & Technol, BS, 52, MS, 54; Univ Calif, PhD(chem), 59. *Prof Exp:* Resident student assoc, Argonne Nat Lab, 52-54; asst, Univ Calif, 54-55, asst, Radiation Lab, 57-59; solid state chemist, Stanford Res Inst, 59-62; mem staff, Arthur D Little, Inc, 62-68; assoc prof, 68-73, PROF CHEM, SALEM STATE COL, 73- *Mem:* Am Chem Soc; Sigma Xi. *Res:* High temperature chemistry; thermodynamics; molecular spectroscopy; solid state chemistry; refractory materials. *Mailing Add:* Dept of Chem Salem State Col Salem MA 01970

ENGELKE, RAYMOND PIERCE, b New York, NY, June 22, 38. DETONATION PHYSICS, QUANTUM MECHANICS. *Educ:* Long Beach State Col, BS, 60, MA, 62; Univ NMex, PhD(physics), 70. *Prof Exp:* Teacher physics & math, US Peace Corps, Nigeria, 64-66; res assoc ozone distrib, Univ NMex, 70-71; STAFF MEM DETONATION PHYSICS, LOS ALAMOS SCI LAB, 71- *Mem:* Am Phys Soc; Sigma Xi. *Res:* Molecular quantum mechanics. *Mailing Add:* M-3 MS-960 PO Box 1663 Los Alamos NM 87545

ENGELKING, PAUL CRAIG, b Glendale, Calif, May 11, 48; m 75; c 1. PHYSICAL CHEMISTRY. *Educ:* Calif Inst Technol, BS, 71; Yale Univ, MPhil, 74, PhD(chem), 76. *Prof Exp:* Res assoc chem, Joint Inst Lab Astrophys, Univ Colo & Nat Bur Standards, 75-78; ASST PROF CHEM, UNIV ORE, 78- *Mem:* Am Phys Soc; Am Chem Soc. *Res:* Radicals, ions and reaction intermediates; laser spectroscopy; flowing afterglow; photodetachment of negative ions; vibronic mixing and Jahn-Teller effects in molecules; photoionization. *Mailing Add:* Dept of Chem Univ of Ore Eugene OR 97403

ENGELMAN, ARTHUR, b New York, NY, Mar 17, 30; m 55; c 3. ATMOSPHERIC PHYSICS, METEOROLOGY. *Educ:* City Col New York, BS, 50; NY Univ, MS, 51. *Prof Exp:* Asst meteorol, NY Univ, 51-52 & 54-55; physicist, Rome Air Develop Ctr, 55-57; sect head radio propagation, Missile Div, Raytheon Co, 57-59; dept mgr atmospheric physics, 59-70, div vpres & tech dir, Technol Div, 70-74, VPRES & MGR AEROSPACE SCI LAB, TECHNOL DIV, GCA CORP, 74- *Mem:* Am Geophys Union. *Res:* Micrometeorology; tropospheric and ionospheric radio propagation and military defense system analysis; upper atmosphere physics; nuclear weapons effects; physics of detonation-atmosphere interaction. *Mailing Add:* 15 Woodward Rd Framingham MA 01701

ENGELMAN, DONALD MAX, b Los Angeles, Calif, Jan 25, 41; m 63; c 2. BIOPHYSICS, BIOCHEMISTRY. *Educ:* Reed Col, BA, 62; Yale Univ, MS, 64, PhD(biophys), 67. *Prof Exp:* From asst prof to assoc prof, 70-78, PROF MOLECULAR BIOPHYS & BIOCHEM, YALE UNIV, 78- *Concurrent Pos:* Guest asst biophysicist, Brookhaven Nat Lab, 72-74; guest assoc biophysicist, 74-78, guest biophysicist, 78-; Bay area res fel, Cardiovasc Res Inst, Med Ctr, Univ Calif, San Francisco, 67-68; NIH fel, King's Col, Univ London, 68-70, Guggenheim fel, Inst Laue-Langevin, Grenoble, France & Lab Molecular Biol, Med Res Coun, Cambridge, Eng, 78-79. *Mem:* Biophys Soc; Am Soc Biol Chem; Am Chem Soc. *Res:* Studies of the molecular organization of biological membranes, ribosomes, atheroma and mixed lipid systems using x-ray and neutron scattering. *Mailing Add:* Dept of Molecular Biophys & Biochem Yale Univ New Haven CT 06520

ENGELMANN, FRANZ, b Kenzingen, Ger, Dec 19, 28; m 54; c 2. BIOLOGY. *Educ:* Univ Berne, PhD(zool), 57. *Prof Exp:* Mem staff, Albert Einstein Col Med, 58-60; asst zool, Univ Mainz, 60-63; from asst prof to prof zool, 63-69, PROF BIOL, UNIV CALIF, LOS ANGELES, 69- *Concurrent Pos:* Privatdozent, Univ Mainz, 62; Alexander von Humboldt award, 79. *Mem:* Am Soc Zool; Entom Soc Am. *Res:* Endocrinology of invertebrates; reproduction in insects, insect physiology. *Mailing Add:* Dept Biol Univ Calif Los Angeles CA 90024

ENGELMANN, MANFRED DAVID, b Chicago, Ill, June 1, 30; m 54; c 2. ANIMAL ECOLOGY. *Educ:* Northwestern Univ, BS, 53; Univ Ill, MS, 55; Univ Mich, PhD(ecol), 60. *Prof Exp:* Instr zool, Univ Mich, 59-60; from instr to assoc prof natural sci, 60-70, PROF NATURAL SCI, MICH STATE UNIV, 70- *Concurrent Pos:* Res consult, Univ Mich, 61; NSF grants, 63-65. *Mem:* Fel AAAS; Ecol Soc Am; Am Soc Zool. *Res:* Ecology of arthropod fauna found in field or grassland; soils and physiology of soil arthropods, particularly oribatid mites. *Mailing Add:* Dept of Natural Sci Mich State Univ East Lansing MI 48824

ENGELMANN, REINHART WOLFGANG H, b Berlin, Ger, Aug 21, 34; m 67; c 4. ELECTRONIC PHYSICS. *Educ:* Tech Univ, Munich, dipl-physics, 58, Dr rer nat, 61. *Prof Exp:* Mem tech staff semicon devices, CBS Labs, Stamford, Conn, 61-63, Hewlett-Packard Assoc, Palo Alto, Calif, 63-69 & AEG-Telefunken, Ulm, Ger, 67-73; MEM TECH STAFF MICROWAVE & SEMICON DEVICES, HEWLETT-PACKARD LABS, 73- *Mem:* Am Phys Soc. *Res:* Microwave and optical semiconductor device physics, optical waveguides. *Mailing Add:* Hewlett-Packard Labs 1501 Page Mill Rd Palo Alto CA 94304

ENGELMANN, RICHARD H(ENRY), b Cincinnati, Ohio, Jan 6, 23; m 47; c 2. ELECTRICAL ENGINEERING. *Educ:* US Naval Acad, BS, 44; Univ Cincinnati, MS, 49. *Prof Exp:* From instr to assoc prof, 48-61, head dept, 67-79, PROF ELEC ENG, UNIV CINCINNATI, 61-, ASSOC DEAN, 81- *Concurrent Pos:* Guest prof, Bengal Eng Col, India, 63-64; consult, Planet Prod Corp, Midland Discount Co, Binns Mach Prod; Avco Corp, Welco Indust, Inc & Cartridge TV, Inc, 71-73; contract rev, NIH, 71- *Mem:* Am Soc Eng Educ; Inst Elec & Electronics Engrs. *Res:* Electromagnetic devices; feedback control systems. *Mailing Add:* Dept of Elec & Comput Eng Mail Location 30 Cincinnati OH 45221

ENGELS, WILLIAM LOUIS, zoology, deceased

ENGELSTAD, ORVIS P, b Fertile, Minn, Feb 19, 28; m 52; c 3. RESEARCH ADMINISTRATION. *Educ:* Univ Minn, BS, 52, MS, 54; Iowa State Univ, PhD(soils), 60. *Prof Exp:* Res assoc soil fertil, Iowa State Univ, 55-60; agronomist, 60-77, Chief, Soils & Fertilizer Res Br, 78-81, ASST DIR, DIV AGR DEVELOP, TENN VALLEY AUTHORITY, 81- *Mem:* Fel Am Soc Agron; fel Soil Sci Soc Am. *Res:* Agronomic and economic interpretation of crop responses to fertilizer; study of accumulated fertilizer residues in soils; evaluation of fertilizers for temperate and tropical soils. *Mailing Add:* Tenn Valley Authority Muscle Shoals AL 35660

ENGEMANN, JOSEPH GEORGE, b Belding, Mich, Nov 27, 28; m 64; c 3. INVERTEBRATE ZOOLOGY. *Educ:* Aquinas Col, BA, 50; Mich State Univ, MS, 56, PhD(zool), 63. *Prof Exp:* From instr to assoc prof, 60-80, PROF BIOL, WESTERN MICH UNIV, 80- *Concurrent Pos:* Consult freshwater ecol. *Mem:* AAAS; NAm Benthol Soc; Am Micros Soc; Soc Syst Zool; Am Soc Zool. *Res:* Invertebrate zoology; aquatic ecology; evolution; creativity. *Mailing Add:* Dept Biol Western Mich Univ Kalamazoo MI 49008

ENGEN, GLENN FORREST, b Battle Creek, Mich, Apr 26, 25; m 52; c 3. PHYSICS, ELECTRICAL ENGINEERING. *Educ:* Andrews Univ, BA; Univ Colo, PhD, 69. *Prof Exp:* Physicist instrumentation, US Naval Ord Lab, 50-52; electronics engr, Johns Hopkins Univ, 52-54; SR RES SCIENTIST, NAT BUR STANDARDS, 54- *Honors & Awards:* US Dept Com Silver Medal for meritorious serv, 61, Gold Medal, 76. *Mem:* Int Sci Radio Union. *Res:* Microwave circuit theory; microwave measurements; measurements via six-port methods. *Mailing Add:* Boulder Heights Boulder CO 80302

ENGEN, IVAR A, b Everett, Wash, Nov 13, 32; m 53; c 3. GEOTHERMAL ENGINEERING, COMPUTER SCIENCE. *Educ:* Idaho State Col, BS, 62, Univ Idaho, MS, 70. *Prof Exp:* Psychiat technician, Idaho Dept Health, 54-62; teacher math, Blackfoot High Sch, 62; sci asst, Argonne Nat Lab, 63-72; mathematician, 73-77, sr engr, 78-79, PROG SPECIALIST, EG&G IDAHO INC, 81- *Concurrent Pos:* Resource person, AAAS, 78- *Mem:* Inst Elec & Electronics Engrs; Am Nuclear Soc; Geothermal Resource Coun. *Res:* Direct applications, non-electric, of geothermal energy, including feasibility and conceptual design; engineering and scientific computer applications; nuclear applications and geothermal applications and economics. *Mailing Add:* EG&G Idaho Inc WCB-E3 PO Box 1625 Idaho Falls ID 83415

ENGEN, RICHARD LEE, b Irene, SDak, Oct 30, 32; m 55; c 3. PHYSIOLOGY, BIOMEDICAL ENGINEERING. *Educ:* Iowa State Univ, BS, 54, PhD(physiol), 65; Colo State Univ, MS, 58. *Prof Exp:* Res nutritionist, Morris Res Lab, Univ Kans, 58-62; from asst prof to assoc prof, 65-74, PROF PHYSIOL, COL VET MED, IOWA STATE UNIV, 74- *Mem:* Am Physiol Soc; assoc mem Soc Exp Biol & Med; Am Soc Vet Physiol & Pharmacol. *Res:* Pulmonary physiology; cardiopulmonary vascular dynamics. *Mailing Add:* Dept of Anat Pharmacol & Physiol Col of Vet Med Iowa State Univ Ames IA 50010

ENGER, CARL CHRISTIAN, b Chicago, Ill, Oct 26, 29. BIOMEDICAL ENGINEERING. *Prof Exp:* Consult biomed engr, Biol Powered Pacemakers, 60-67; clin instr biophys, Case Western Reserve Univ, 66-67, sr instr, 67-72; asst prof surg bioeng, Med Univ SC, 72-73; prin investr, heart-powered pacemaker proj, Cleveland Clin Found, 74-77; sr res scientist, Electrophysiol Found, 77-80; Pres, Biotelemetrics, Inc, 80- *Mem:* Soc Biomat; Am Soc Artificial Internal Organs; AAAS; Sr mem Instrument Soc Am; Asn Advan Med Instrumentation. *Res:* Principal investigator for the development of a biologically energized cardiac pacemaker utilizing piezoelectric energy converters; research and development of impermeable biomaterials for encapsulated electronic implants; research and development of implantable sub-miniature biotelemetry devices. *Mailing Add:* 12700 Lake Ave Lakewood OH 44107

ENGER, MERLIN DUANE, b Williston, NDak, Dec 8, 37; m 58; c 3. BIOCHEMISTRY. *Educ:* NDak State Univ, BS, 59, MS, 61; Univ Wis-Madison, PhD(biochem), 64. *Prof Exp:* staff mem group H-9, 64-80, GROUP LEADER, GENETICS GROUP, LOS ALAMOS NAT LAB, UNIV CALIF, 80- *Concurrent Pos:* Adj asst prof microbiol, Univ NMex, 74- *Mem:* Fel Am Inst Chemists; fel Am Soc Biol Chemists; Am Chem Soc; AAAS; Am Soc Cell Biol. *Res:* RNA and protein metabolism in cultured animal cells. *Mailing Add:* Group LS-3 MS 886 Los Alamos Sci Lab Los Alamos NM 87545

ENGERMAN, RONALD LESTER, b Chicago, Ill, May 4, 29; m 51; c 5. OPHTHALMOLOGY. *Educ:* Univ Wis, BS, 51, MS, 58, PhD(zool, biochem), 64. *Prof Exp:* Technician, Bjorksten Res Labs, 51; rubber technologist, Army Engr Res & Develop Labs, Va, 53-54; fel, Dept Surg, Univ Wis, 60-61, from instr to asst prof, 61-68, assoc prof, 68-77, PROF OPHTHAL, SCH MED, UNIV WIS-MADISON, 77- *Honors & Awards:* Fight for Sight Citation, Nat Coun Combat Blindness & Asn Res Ophthal, 64. *Mem:* Asn Res Vision & Ophthal; AAAS; Am Diabetes Asn; Soc Exp Biol & Med. *Res:* Diabetic retinopathy and microangiopathy; biology of the microvasculature. *Mailing Add:* Dept of Ophthal Univ of Wis Sch of Med Madison WI 53792

ENGERT, MARTIN, b Chicago, Ill, Nov 6, 38; m 71. MATHEMATICAL ANALYSIS. *Educ:* Carleton Col, BA, 60; Stanford Univ, MS, 62, PhD(math), 65. *Prof Exp:* Asst prof math, Univ NC, Chapel Hill, 65-67; staff mem, Aarhus Univ, 67-69; ASSOC PROF MATH, UNIV WIS-WHITEWATER, 69- *Mailing Add:* Dept of Math Univ of Wis Whitewater WI 53190

ENGH, HELMER A, JR, b Litchfield, Ill, May 21, 35; m 60. GENETICS. *Educ:* Wash Univ, AB, 57; Southern Ill Univ, MS, 59; Univ Md, PhD(poultry sci), 66. *Prof Exp:* Asst prof biol, 66-70, assoc prof, 70-75, PROF BIOL SCI, MANKATO STATE UNIV, 70-75. *Mem:* Genetics Soc Am; Am Genetic Asn; Soc Study Evolution. *Res:* Biochemical genetics of serum enzymes. *Mailing Add:* Dept of Biol Sci Mankato State Univ Box 34 Mankato MN 56001

ENGH, ROBERT OSWALD, b New Rockford, NDak, Jan 11, 24. CRYSTAL GROWTH. *Educ:* Univ Minn, BChem, 48; Univ Ore, MS, 53. *Prof Exp:* Res chemist, Hanford Works, 48-51; from res scientist to sr res scientist, 53-68, PRIN RES SCIENTIST, HONEYWELL RES CTR, 68- *Honors & Awards:* H W Sweat Outstanding Engr-Scientist Award, 68. *Mailing Add:* Honeywell Inc Honeywell Plaza Minneapolis MN 55408

ENGIBOUS, JAMES CHARLES, b Norway, Mich, Aug 12, 23; m 47; c 4. SOIL BIOCHEMISTRY. *Educ:* Northern Mich Col, BS, 47; Ore State Col, MS, 50; Ohio State Univ, PhD(biochem), 52. *Prof Exp:* Res asst, Ore State Col, 48-50 & Ohio State Univ, 50-52; soil biochemist, Monsanto Chem Co, 52-54; group leader agron res, Int Minerals & Chem Corp, 54-55; supvr soils & plant nutrit res, 55-59, mgr agr prod res, 59-62, agr serv, Mat Dept, 62-63, Tech Serv Dept, 63-70; CHMN DEPT AGRON & SOILS, WASH STATE UNIV, 71- *Mem:* fel Am Inst Chem; fel Am Soc Agron; fel Soil Sci Soc Am; Soil Cons Soc Am. *Res:* Soil chemistry, bacteriology and physics. *Mailing Add:* Dept Agron & Soils Wash State Univ Pullman WA 99164

ENGIN, ALI ERKAN, b Samsun, Turkey, Feb 23, 43; US citizen; m 71; c 2. MECHANICS, BIOMECHANICS. *Educ:* Mich State Univ, BS, 65, Univ Mich, MS, 66, PhD(eng mech), 68. *Prof Exp:* Asst prof eng sci, Mid East Tech Univ, Ankara, 69-70; assoc res engr biomech, Hwy Safety Res Inst, Univ Mich, 70-71; from asst prof to assoc prof, 71-77, PROF MECH, OHIO STATE UNIV, 77- *Concurrent Pos:* Consult, UN Environ Prog/Int Referral Syst, 79. *Mem:* Am Acad Mech; Am Soc Eng Educ; Am Soc Biomech; Int Soc Biomech. *Res:* Mechanics, especially fluid-solid interaction problems and analysis of shells; biomechanics, particularly head injury, biological material properties, experimental and theoretical biomechanics of the major human joints and biodynamic modeling of various parts of the human body. *Mailing Add:* Dept Eng Mech 155 W Woodruff Ave Columbus OH 43210

ENGLAND, ALAN COULTER, b Belleville, Ill, Mar 1, 32; c 3. PHYSICS. *Educ:* Univ Ill, BS, 54; Univ Rochester, PhD(physics), 61. *Prof Exp:* PHYSICIST, FUSION ENERGY DIV, OAK RIDGE NAT LAB, 60- *Concurrent Pos:* Vis scientist, Inst Plasma Physics, Munich, Ger, 67-68. *Mem:* Sigma Xi; Am Phys Soc. *Res:* High-energy nuclear physics; tokamak plasmas; hot-electron plasmas. *Mailing Add:* Oak Ridge Nat Lab PO Box Y Oak Ridge TN 37830

ENGLAND, ANTHONY W, b Indianapolis, Ind, May 15, 42; m 62. GEOPHYSICS, ASTROGEOLOGY. *Educ:* Mass Inst Technol, SB & SM, 65, PhD(geophys), 70. *Prof Exp:* Scientist-Astronaut, Manned Spacecraft Ctr, NASA, 67-72; geophysicist, US Geol Surv, 72-79; ASTRONAUT, MANNED SPACECRAFT CTR, NASA, 79- *Honors & Awards:* Outstanding Sci Achievement Medal, NASA, 73. *Mem:* AAAS; Am Geophys Union; Soc Explor Geophys; Int Glaciol Soc; Sigma Xi. *Res:* Remote sensing geophysics; physics of solids; theory and application of microwave technology to remote sensing geophysics. *Mailing Add:* 15802 Craighurst Dr Houston TX 77054

ENGLAND, BARRY GRANT, b Tooele, Utah, Oct 13, 40; m 66; c 3. ENDOCRINOLOGY, REPRODUCTIVE PHYSIOLOGY. *Educ:* Utah State Univ, BS, 65, MS, 67; Univ Wis, PhD(endocrinol, reprod physiol), 71. *Prof Exp:* Instr, 73-74, ASST PROF BIOL REPRODUCTION, UNIV MICH, ANN ARBOR, 74- *Concurrent Pos:* Ford Found, Univ Mich, Ann Arbor, 71-73. *Mem:* AAAS; Soc Study Reprod; Am Soc Animal Sci. *Res:* Study of reproductive endocrinology in the mammalian female; development of new radio-ligand assay techniques. *Mailing Add:* Dept of Path Univ of Mich Ann Arbor MI 48104

ENGLAND, CHARLES BENNETT, watershed management, see previous edition

ENGLAND, DAVID CHARLES, b Myrtle, Mo, Jan 4, 22; m 46, 73; c 5. ANIMAL BREEDING. *Educ:* Wash State Univ, BS, 49; Univ Minn, MS, 50, PhD, 52. *Prof Exp:* Res asst, Univ Minn, 49-51, res fel, 51-52, asst prof animal husb, 52-55; from asst prof to assoc prof, 55-69, PROF ANIMAL HUSB, ORE STATE UNIV, 69- *Concurrent Pos:* Mem coop state res serv, USDA, 68-69; consult, Ore Regional Primate Ctr, 75-, Livestock Indust, 72-, Kroc Found Med Res, 76-, Battelle Labs, 78-, Elec Power Res Inst, 81- & Noti Ranches, 81- *Mem:* Am Soc Animal Sci; Sigma Xi; Am Soc Animal Sci (secy-treas, 77-80, pres-elect, 80-81, pres, 81-82). *Res:* Genetics; swine production. *Mailing Add:* Dept Animal Sci Withycombe 112 Ore State Univ Corvallis OR 97331

ENGLAND, JAMES DONALD, b Liles, Tenn, Feb 4, 37; m 61; c 2. ORGANIC BIOCHEMISTRY. *Educ:* Austin Teay Univ, BS, 58; Univ Ark, MS, 60; Univ Miss, PhD(med chem), 66. *Prof Exp:* Asst prof, 60-63, assoc prof, 66-71, PROF CHEM, HARDING UNIV, 71- *Concurrent Pos:* Fel, Miss Heart Asn, 63. *Mem:* Am Chem Soc; Sigma Xi. *Mailing Add:* Dept of Med Chem Box 903 Harding Univ Searcy AR 72143

ENGLAND, JAMES WALTON, b Newton, Kans, July 20, 38; m 61; c 1. MATHEMATICS. *Educ:* Kans State Col Pittsburg, AB, 60; Univ Mo, MA, 61, PhD(math). 64. *Prof Exp:* Asst prof math, Univ Va, 64-68; assoc prof math, Swarthmore Col, 69-74, prof, 74-81, chmn, Dept Math, 77-81; DEAN FAC & ACAD VPRES, OCCIDENTAL COL, 81- *Mem:* Am Math Soc; Math Asn Am. *Res:* Topological dynamics, ergodic theory. *Mailing Add:* Dean Fac Occidental Col 1600 Campus Rd Los Angeles CA 90041

ENGLAND, MILTON (W), b Shamrock, Tex, Feb 28, 17; m 40; c 2. ANIMAL BREEDING. *Educ:* Panhandle Agr & Mech Col, BS, 42; Okla Agr & Mech Col, MS, 49. *Prof Exp:* Asst prof, 42-44, PROF ANIMAL SCI, PANHANDLE STATE UNIV, 44-, HEAD DEPT, 55- *Mem:* Am Soc Animal Sci. *Res:* Performance testing of beef cattle; high concentrate rations for fattening beef cattle; grain preparation for feedlot cattle. *Mailing Add:* Dept of Animal Sci Panhandle State Univ Goodwell OK 73939

ENGLAND, RICHARD JAY, b Springfield, Ill, Aug 5, 26; m 51; c 3. POLYMER CHEMISTRY, ANALYTICAL CHEMISTRY. *Educ:* Bradley Univ, BS, 51. *Prof Exp:* Chemist, Explosives Dept, NJ, 53-55, process chemist, 55-56, res chemist, WVa, 56-57, Textile Fibers Dept, Va, 57 & NC, 57-59, RES CHEMIST, FILM DEPT, E I DU PONT DE NEMOURS & CO, INC, 59- *Res:* High explosives; polyester films and fibers; supervision; petroleum products. *Mailing Add:* E I du Pont de Nemours & Co Circleville Res Lab Circleville OH 43113

ENGLAND, WALTER BERNARD, b Hallettsville, Tex, Aug 23, 42. COMPUTATIONAL CHEMISTRY, PHYSICAL CHEMISTRY. *Educ:* Purdue Univ, BS, 65; Iowa State Univ, PhD(phys chem), 73. *Prof Exp:* Fel physics, Colo State Univ, 73-74; res assoc chem, Argonne Nat Lab, 74-78; ASST PROF CHEM, UNIV WIS, MILWAUKEE, 78- *Mem:* Am Phys Soc; Am Chem Soc; Am Vacuum Soc; NY Acad Sci. *Res:* Adaptation of ordinary many-body field-theoretic methods to chemical bonds and surfaces; application of computational quantum chemical methods to atoms, molecules and surfaces. *Mailing Add:* Dept Chem Lab Surface Studies Univ Wis Milwaukee WI 53211

ENGLAND, WAYNE H, plant anatomy, mycology, see previous edition

ENGLANDE, ANDREW JOSEPH, b New Orleans, La, July 31, 44; m 66; c 3. ENVIRONMENTAL SCIENCES. *Educ:* Tulane Univ, BS, 67, MS, 69; Vanderbilt Univ, PhD(environ eng), 74. *Prof Exp:* Asst prof, 72-76, ASSOC PROF ENVIRON HEALTH SCI & LAB DIR RIVERSIDE RES LABS, SCH PUB HEALTH, TULANE UNIV, 74- *Concurrent Pos:* Assoc environ div, Gulf SRes Inst, 74- *Honors & Awards:* Delta Omega Key, Pub Health Nat Honor Soc, 74. *Mem:* Int Asn Water Pollution Res; Water Pollution Control Fedn; Am Water Works Asn; Am Chem Soc. *Res:* Biological and physical chemical wastewater treatment methods for industrial wastes; general water quality management techniques; and trace contaminant accumulation and translocation. *Mailing Add:* Dept of Environ Health Sci Sch of Pub Health Tulane Univ New Orleans LA 70112

ENGLANDER, HAROLD ROBERT, b New York, NY, Dec 11, 23; m 49; c 1. DENTISTRY. *Educ:* City Col New York, BS, 45; Columbia Univ, DDS, 48, MPH, 51; Am Bd Dent Pub Health, dipl. *Prof Exp:* Dir, US Naval Dent Inst, Great Lakes, Ill, 53-58; prof dent, Dent Col, Univ Ill, 59-62; mem staff, Nat Inst Dent Res, 62-67, dent dir & chief field trials, Epidemiol & Biomet Br, 67-75; mem fac, Univ Tex Health Sci Ctr, 75; prof dent pub health, Sch Pub Health, Houston, 78; MEM STAFF, DENT SCH, UNIV TEX HEALTH SCI CTR, 79- *Concurrent Pos:* Vis prof, Howard Univ; vis lectr, Johns Hopkins Univ Sch Pub Health & Univ Md; past consult prev dent, Surgeon Gen, US Army. *Mem:* AAAS; Am Dent Asn; fel Am Pub Health Asn; fel Am Col Dent; Sigma Xi. *Res:* Epidemiology; caries research in hamsters; clinical trials of anticaries agents; studies of peridontal disease; studies on waterborne fluoride. *Mailing Add:* 11502 Whisper Bluff San Antonio TX 78230

ENGLANDER, SOL WALTER, b Baltimore, Md, Jan 25, 30; m 54; c 3. BIOPHYSICS. *Educ:* Univ Md, BS, 51; Univ Pittsburgh, MS, 54, PhD(biophys), 59. *Prof Exp:* Biophysicist, NIH, 59-61; from instr to asst prof biochem, Dartmouth Med Sch, 61-67; assoc prof, 67-74, PROF BIOCHEM, SCH MED, UNIV PA, 74-, ASSOC CHMN, DEPT BIOCHEM & BIOPHYSICS, 78- *Concurrent Pos:* Am Cancer Soc fel, 61-63. *Res:* Physical biochemistry; protein and nucleic acid structure and function; hydrogen exchange. *Mailing Add:* 6511 N 11th Philadelphia PA 19123

ENGLARD, SASHA, b Antwerp, Belg, June 28, 29; US nat; m 51; c 3. BIOCHEMISTRY. *Educ:* City Col New York, BS, 49; Western Reserve Univ, PhD, 53. *Prof Exp:* Assoc prof, 61-68, asst dean admis, 69-72, PROF BIOCHEM, ALBERT EINSTEIN COL MED, YESHIVA UNIV, 68- *Concurrent Pos:* NIH fel & vis prof, Hebrew Univ, Israel, 61-62 & 69; Am Heart Asn fel, Pratt Inst, Johns Hopkins Univ, 53-55. *Mem:* Am Soc Biol Chem; Brit Biochem Soc. *Res:* Mechanism of enzyme reaction; stereospecificity of enzymatically catalyzed reactions; carbohydrate metabolism; biochemical aspects of aging. *Mailing Add:* 1234 Pawnee Pl New York NY 10461

ENGLE, A(LLEN) WENDELL, b Sapulpa, Okla, Sept 7, 17; m 41; c 1. ENGINEERING. *Educ:* Okla Agr & Mech Col, BS, 39, MS, 53. *Prof Exp:* Field engr, Well Surv, Okla, & Lane Wells Co, Houston, 41-42; instr electronics, Okla Agr & Mech Col, 42-45; res engr, Well Surv, Inc, Okla, 45-59, proj supvr, 59-61; sr res engr, Lane-Wells Co, 61-68; sr res engr, 68-73, systs mgr, 73-77, MGR ACOUSTIC RES AND DEVELOP, DRESSER ATLAS, 77- *Mem:* Am Geophys Union; Soc Explor Geophys; Acoust Soc Am; Inst Elec & Electronics Engrs. *Res:* Design of nuclear measuring equipment; radioactivity and electrical well logging; acoustic well log systems; digital systems design. *Mailing Add:* Dresser Atlas PO Box 1407 Houston TX 77001

ENGLE, DAMON LAWSON, b Troy, WVa, June 22, 19; m 43; c 4. ANALYTICAL CHEMISTRY. *Educ:* Marshall Univ, BS, 41. *Prof Exp:* Anal chemist, Chem Div, 42-51, group leader synthetic fibers & polymers, 52-59, asst dir res & develop, 59-66, dir, 66-69, asst plant mgr, Chem & Plastics Div, 69-72, PLANT MGR, UNION CARBIDE CORP, 72- *Mem:* Am Chem Soc; Soc Rheology; Am Soc Testing & Mat. *Res:* Synthetic polymer technology. *Mailing Add:* Chem & Plastics Div Union Carbide Corp PO Box 471 Texas City TX 77590

ENGLE, IRENE MAY, b Harrisburg, Pa. THEORETICAL PHYSICS. *Educ:* Pa State Univ, BS, 63, MS, 66, PhD(physics), 70. *Prof Exp:* Instr physics, Ripon Col, 65-66; asst prof physics, Juniata Col, 69-79, chmn dept, 75-77; MEM FAC, US NAVAL ACAD, 79- *Concurrent Pos:* Vis physicist, Argonne Nat Lab, 70; adj fac mem, Univ Kans, 77-79. *Mem:* Am Phys Soc; Am Geophys Union; Am Asn Physics Teachers. *Res:* Electromagnetic structure of the nucleon; symmetries and symmetry breaking; planetary magnetospheric physics; electronic properties of metals, especially thermionic-field emission phenomena; high energy charged particle kinematics in the solar system. *Mailing Add:* Physics Dept US Naval Acad Annapolis MD 21402

ENGLE, JESSIE ANN, b Chicago, Ill, Sept 17, 18; m 51; c 3. ANALYSIS, FUNCTIONAL ANALYSIS. *Educ:* Bennington Col, BA, 40; Ohio State Univ, MS, 64, PhD(math), 71. *Prof Exp:* Teacher music, Black Mountain Col, 40-42; engr, Columbia Broadcasting Corp, 42-44; res assoc, Radio Res Lab, Harvard Univ, 44-46; engr, Airborne Instruments Lab, 46-68; recording engr, Juilliard Sch Music, 49-53; violist, Columbus Symphony, 58-62; vis asst prof, 71-72, asst prof, 72-77, ASSOC PROF MATH, OHIO STATE UNIV, 77- *Mem:* Am Math Soc; Math Asn Am; Asn Women Math; Nat Coun Teachers Math. *Res:* Generalization of hear measure; design and tesing of microwave antennas and components for aircraft. *Mailing Add:* 153 E Lane Ave Columbus OH 43201

ENGLE, JOHN FRANKLIN, b Shoshone, Idaho, Aug 15, 21; m 44; c 5. ELECTRICAL ENGINEERING. *Educ:* Ore State Univ, BS, 47, MS, 51. *Prof Exp:* From instr to assoc prof, 47-69, PROF ELEC ENG, STATE UNIV, 69- *Concurrent Pos:* Consult, hydroelec design br, N Pac Div, US Army Corps Engrs, 62- *Mem:* Asn Comput Mach; Am Soc Eng Educ; Inst Elec & Electronics Engrs. *Res:* Electric power systems; digital simulation; component modeling; on-line digital control. *Mailing Add:* Dept of Elec Ore State Univ Corvallis OR 97331

ENGLE, MARY ALLEN ENGLISH, b Madill, Okla, Jan 26, 22; m 45; c 2. PEDIATRICS, CARDIOLOGY. *Educ:* Baylor Univ, AB, 42; Johns Hopkins Univ, MD, 45; Am Bd Pediat, dipl & cert cardiol. *Prof Exp:* Intern pediat, Johns Hopkins Hosp, 45-46, asst dir outpatient dept, 46-47, asst physician, Cardiac Clin, 47-48, instr Sch Med, 46-48; asst pediat, 48-49, asst pharmacol, 49-50, from instr to assoc prof pediat, 50-69, PROF PEDIAT, MED COL, CORNELL UNIV, 69-; DIR PEDIAT CARDIOL, NEW YORK HOSP, 62-, STAVROS S NIARCHOS PROF PEDIAT CARDIOL, 79- *Concurrent Pos:* Asst resident, Sydenham Hosp, Md, 46; from asst resident to sr asst resident, New York Hosp, 48-49, from asst attend pediatrician to assoc attend pediatrician, 52-62, attend pediatrician, 62-; med dir, Inst Care of Premature Infants, 52-55; mem cardiac surg adv comt, New York City Dept Health; mem, NY State Cardiac Adv Comt; assoc ed, J Cardiol. *Honors & Awards:* Spence-Chapin Award, 58; Pres Panel Heart Dis Award, 72; Cummings Humanitarian Award, 73; 76; Am Heart Asn Award Merit, 75; Helen B Taussig Award, 76; Philoptochos Award of Merit, 78. *Mem:* Am Acad Pediat; Soc Pediat Res; Am Col Chest Physicians; Am Pediat Soc; Am Col Cardiol. *Res:* Pediatric cardiology, especially congenital malformations of heart and great vessels. *Mailing Add:* New York Hosp 525 E 68th St New York NY 10021

ENGLE, PAUL RANDAL, b Newton, Iowa, Oct 16, 19; m 45; c 1. ASTRONOMY, PHYSICS. *Educ:* Pan Am Col, BA, 58; Mich State Univ, MAT, 72. *Prof Exp:* Jr engr & instr astron, Phys Sci Lab, NMex State Univ, 48-51; flight instr & asst to dir, Calif Eastern Aviation, Tex, 51-58; dir observ, Pan Am Univ, 56-74, dir, Geod Satellite Prog, 66-74; dir planetarium, 75-80, ASST PROF PLANETARIUM EDUC ASTRON, UNIV ARK, LITTLE ROCK, 75- *Concurrent Pos:* Prin investr, NSF grants, 62-65; dir, NASA-Goddard Minitrack Optical Tracking Sta, 66- *Mem:* Asn Lunar & Planetary Observers; Am Astronaut Soc; Am Asn Physics Teachers; Pan Am Soc Astrophys Res (pres, 61-); Int Soc Planetarium Educr (pres, 71 & 72). *Res:* Astronomical instrumentation; development of course programs in astro-science and astronomy for college and high school levels. *Mailing Add:* Dept of Physics & Astron Univ of Ark Little Rock AR 72204

ENGLE, RALPH LANDIS, JR, b Philadelphia, Pa, June 11, 20; m 45; c 2. MEDICINE, HEMATOLOGY. *Educ:* Univ Fla, BS, 42; Johns Hopkins Univ, MD, 45; Am Bd Internal Med, dipl. *Prof Exp:* Intern path, New York Hosp, 45-46 & internal med, 48-49, asst resident, 49-51, resident hemat, 50-51; asst, 49-51, from asst prof to assoc prof, 52-69, PROF MED, MED COL, CORNELL UNIV, 69-, PROF PUB HEALTH, 73-, ASSOC DIR OFF RES & SPONSORED PROGS, 75- *Concurrent Pos:* From asst attend physician to assoc attend physician, New York Hosp, 54-69, attend physician, 69-, chief hemat div, Dept Med, 61-67, dir dept med systs & comput serv, 68-72; consult, Vet Admin Hosp, New York, 64-; chief div med systs & comput sci, Dept Med, New York Hosp-Cornell Univ, 67-74; mem, Cancer Clin Invest Rev Comt, Nat Cancer Inst, 68-72 & Comt Sci & Tech Commun, Nat Acad Sci-Nat Acad Eng, 67-70; res fel, Med Col, Cornell Univ, 50; Am Cancer Soc fel, Wash Univ, 51-52; Markle scholar, 52-57. *Mem:* AAAS; Am Soc Hemat; Am Fedn Clin Res; Soc Exp Biol & Med. *Res:* Hematology; pathology; computer applications to medicine; public health. *Mailing Add:* New York Hosp 525 E 68th St New York NY 10021

ENGLE, ROBERT RUFUS, b Sullivan Co, Ind, Jan 29, 30; m 54; c 6. ORGANIC CHEMISTRY. *Educ:* DePauw Univ, BA, 51; Wayne State Univ, MS, 53, PhD(chem), 58. *Prof Exp:* Asst, Wayne State Univ, 51-52, 55; sr res chemist, Riker Labs, Inc, 58-65; head chem & drug procurement sect, 65-76, HEAD CHEM RESOURCES SECT, NAT CANCER INST, 76- *Mem:* Am Chem Soc; Am Asn Cancer Res. *Res:* Synthesis; chemistry of natural products; structure determination; pharmaceuticals; cancer chemotherapy. *Mailing Add:* 8305 Tuckerman Lane Potomac MD 20854

ENGLE, THOMAS WILLIAM, b Southbend, Ind, June 5, 51; m 78; c 2. AGRICULTURAL CHEMISTRY. *Educ:* Rose-Hulman Inst Tech, BS, 73; State Univ NY Buffalo, PhD(med chem), 79. *Prof Exp:* Technician, Pfizer Co, 72, Anaconda Aluminum Co, 73; fel, Catholic Univ, 78-81; MEM STAFF, UNION CARBIDE AGR PRODS CO, INC, 81- *Concurrent Pos:* Lectr, Univ DC, 81. *Mem:* Am Chem Soc. *Res:* Development of systems to measure physical chemical parameters used in quantitative structure activity relationships; investigation of such relationships for insecticides and herbicides. *Mailing Add:* Union Carbide Agr Prods, Co, Inc T W Alexander Dr PO Box 12014 Research Triangle Park NC 27709

ENGLEHART, EDWIN THOMAS, JR, b Johnstown, Pa, Aug 7, 21; m 51; c 1. CHEMICAL METALLURGY. *Educ:* Pa State Univ, BS, 43. *Prof Exp:* Res engr, Corrosion Res Labs, Aluminum Co Am, 43-59, sect head chem metall div, 59-77, SECT HEAD ALLOY TECHNOL DIV, ALCOA LABS, 77- *Mem:* Fel Am Inst Chem; Sigma Xi. *Res:* Solution of fundamental and practical corrosion problems dealing with aluminum, its alloys and other metals. *Mailing Add:* 450 Dakota Dr New Kensington PA 15068

ENGLEHART, RICHARD W(ILSON), b Sept 2, 38; m 64; c 2. NUCLEAR ENGINEERING, ENVIRONMENTAL SCIENCES. *Educ:* Carnegie-Mellon Univ, BS, 60; Pa State Univ, MS, 63, PhD(nuclear eng), 69. *Prof Exp:* Proj engr, US Army reactors group, AEC, 64-66; asst prof nuclear eng, Univ Fla, 68-73; MGR RADIOL PROG DEPT, NUS CORP, 73- *Concurrent Pos:* Reactor supvr, Univ Fla, 69-71; Am Soc Eng Educ-Ford Found resident fel prog consult engr, Gilbert Assocs, Inc, 71-72. *Mem:* Am Nuclear Soc; Sigma Xi. *Res:* Radiological analyses and environmental impact assessments related to the nuclear fuel cycle; safety and environmental assessments for applications of nuclear power in outer space. *Mailing Add:* NUS Corp 4 Research Place Rockville MD 20850

ENGLEMAN, EPHRAIM PHILIP, b San Jose, Calif, Mar 24, 11; m 41; c 3. MEDICINE. *Educ:* Stanford Univ, AB, 33; Columbia Univ, MD, 37. *Prof Exp:* From asst clin prof to assoc clin prof, 48-64, chief rheumatic dis group, Med Ctr, 58-77, PROF MED, SCH MED, UNIV CALIF, SAN FRANCISCO, 64-, DIR, ROSALIND RUSSELL ARTHRITIS CTR, MED

CTR, 77- *Concurrent Pos:* Consult, Regional Off, US Vet Admin, San Francisco, 50-77; San Francisco Army Hosp, 60-77; pres-elect, Int League Against Rheumatism, 61-81, pres, 81-85; chmn, Nat Comn Arthritis, 75-77; mem, Nat Arthritis Adv Bd, 77-80. *Mem:* Am Rheumatism Asn (pres, 62-63); Am Col Physicians; Am Fedn Clin Res. *Res:* Rheumatic diseases. *Mailing Add:* Dept Med Univ Calif Sch Med San Francisco CA 94143

ENGLEMAN, KARL, b New York, NY, June 23, 33; m 56; c 3. MEDICINE, PHARMACOLOGY. *Educ:* Rutgers Univ, BS, 55; Harvard Univ, MD, 59; Univ Pa, MS, 71. *Prof Exp:* Intern & asst resident med, Mass Gen Hosp, Boston, 59-61, sr resident, 64; sr investr, Nat Heart Inst, NIH, Bethesda, Md, 65-70; ASSOC PROF MED & PHARMACOL, SCH MED, UNIV PA, 70- *Concurrent Pos:* Clin assoc, Nat Heart & Lung Inst, NIH, Bethesda, Md, 61-66; consult, Vet Admin Hosp, Philadelphia, 70- & Children's Hosp, Philadelphia, 72-; dir, Clin Res Ctr, Hosp Univ Pa, 72-; mem, Hypertension Res Coun, Am Heart Asn; mem adv panel, US Pharmacopia & Nat Formulary. *Mem:* Fel Am Col Physicians; Am Heart Asn; Am Soc Pharmacol & Exp Therapeut. *Res:* Hypertension; catecholamines and clinical pharmacology. *Mailing Add:* 633 Maloney Bldg 36th & Spruce St Philadelphia PA 19104

ENGLEMAN, ROLF, JR, b Norman, Okla, Mar 16, 34; m 56; c 5. PHYSICAL CHEMISTRY. *Educ:* Univ Okla, BS, 55; Calif Inst Technol, PhD(chem), 59. *Prof Exp:* STAFF MEM CHEMIST, LOS ALAMOS SCI LAB, 59- *Mem:* AAAS; Am Chem Soc; Am Optical Soc. *Res:* Spectroscopy and kinetics of atoms and simple molecules studied by high resolution optical spectroscopy. *Mailing Add:* Los Alamos Sci Lab Group CMB-1 MS 740 Los Alamos NM 87545

ENGLEMAN, VICTOR SOLOMON, b Brooklyn, NY, Dec 31, 40; m 65; c 2. CHEMICAL ENGINEERING. *Educ:* Calif Inst Technol, BS, 62; Univ Calif, MS, 64, PhD(chem eng), 67. *Prof Exp:* Proj engr, Air Force Rocket Propulsion Lab, 67-70; res engr, Exxon Res & Eng Co, 70-77; asst div mgr, 76-80, DIV MGR, SCI APPLN INC, 80- *Concurrent Pos:* Lectr, Golden Gate Col, 69-70. *Mem:* Am Inst Chem Engrs; Combustion Inst; Am Chem Soc. *Res:* fossil fuel conversion and utiliation; combustion; chemical kinetics; air pollution. *Mailing Add:* Sci Appln Inc 6791 Edmonton Ave San Diego CA 92122

ENGLER, ARNOLD, b Czernovitz, Romania, July 19, 27; m 61. PHYSICS. *Educ:* Univ Berne, PhD(physics), 53. *Prof Exp:* Res assoc physics, Univ Berne, 53-54, Bristol Univ, 54-56 & Univ Rochester, 56-58; sr res officer, Oxford Univ, 58-60; res assoc & assoc prof, Duke Univ, 60-61; assoc prof, Northwestern Univ, 61-62; assoc prof, Carnegie Inst Technol, 62-66, PROF PHYSICS, CARNEGIE-MELLON UNIV, 66- *Concurrent Pos:* Fel, St Cross Col, Oxford Univ, 66-67. *Mem:* Fel Am Phys Soc; Italian Phys Soc. *Res:* Elementary particle physics; cosmic ray physics. *Mailing Add:* Dept of Physics Carnegie-Mellon Univ Pittsburgh PA 15213

ENGLER, CADY ROY, b Topeka, Kans, May 13, 47; m 70; c 2. CHEMICAL ENGINEERING. *Educ:* Kans State Univ, BS, 69, MS, 74; Univ Waterloo, PhD(chem eng), 80. *Prof Exp:* Process engr, Exxon, 69-72; res asst chem eng, Kans State Univ, 73-74; teaching asst, Univ Waterloo, 74-78; asst prof bioeng, 78-81, ASST PROF AGR ENG, TEX A&M UNIV, 81- *Concurrent Pos:* Engr res assoc, Food Protein Res & Development Ctr, Tex Eng Exp Sta, 80- *Mem:* Am Inst Chem Engrs; Am Chem Soc; Inst Food Technologists; Am Soc Agr Engrs; AAAS. *Res:* Production of chemicals from biomass via fermentation processes and utilization of plant oils as alternative diesel fuels. *Mailing Add:* Dept Agr Eng Tex A&M Univ College Station TX 77843

ENGLER, EDWARD MARTIN, b Brooklyn, NY, Aug 22, 47; m 67; c 3. PHYSICAL ORGANIC CHEMISTRY, SOLID STATE CHEMISTRY. *Educ:* Providence Col, BS, 69; Princeton Univ, MA, 71, PhD(chem), 73. *Prof Exp:* RES STAFF ORG CHEM, THOMAS J WATSON RES CTR, IBM CORP, 73- *Mem:* Am Chem Soc. *Res:* Design and synthesis of organic molecules with unusual solid state properties; chemistry and properties of organochalogens. *Mailing Add:* Thomas J Watson Res Ctr IBM Corp Yorktown Heights NY 10598

ENGLER, HAROLD S, b Augusta, Ga, Jan 10, 23; m 50; c 5. MEDICINE, SURGERY. *Educ:* Med Col Ga, MD, 50; Am Bd Surg, dipl, 58. *Prof Exp:* From instr to assoc prof, 50-66, PROF SURG, MED COL GA, 66- *Mem:* Am Col Surgeons; James Ewing Soc. *Res:* Cancer and surgical research. *Mailing Add:* Dept Surg Med Col Ga Augusta GA 30902

ENGLER, RETO ARNOLD, b Zurich, Switz, Nov 20, 31; US citizen; m; c 1. ORGANIC CHEMISTRY. *Educ:* Swiss Fed Inst Technol, dipl chem eng, 54; Univ Tübingen, PhD(chem), 58. *Prof Exp:* Asst virol, Max Planck Inst Virus Res, 58-60; lectr pediat, Med Ctr, Univ Kans, 60-61, asst prof, 61-66, asst biochem, 66-68; virologist div microbiol, Fed Food & Drug Admin, 68, res chemist, 68-71; toxicologist & chemist, Hazard Eval Div, 71-79, CHIEF, DISINFECTANTS BR, REGIST DIV, ENVIRON PROTECTION AGENCY, 79- *Concurrent Pos:* Lectr, Univ Mo-Kansas City, 63-67. *Mem:* AAAS; NY Acad Sci; Am Soc Microbiol; Soc Invert Path. *Res:* Biosynthesis of viruses in plants and animals, especially the synthesis of viral nucleic acid; health hazard of viruses in food; virology; microbiological control of pests; toxicology of pesticide chemicals. *Mailing Add:* Hazard Eval Div 401 M St SW Washington DC 20460

ENGLERT, DU WAYNE CLEVELAND, b WaKeeney, Kans, Dec 1, 32; m 53; c 2. GENETICS. *Educ:* Univ Kans, BS, 54; Purdue Univ, MS, 61, PhD(genetics), 64. *Prof Exp:* Asst prof zool, 63-69, assoc prof, 69-77, PROF ZOOL, SOUTHERN ILL UNIV, 77- *Concurrent Pos:* Vis prof dept animal sci, Purdue Univ, 68-69; consult, UN Develop Prog, Food & Agr Orgn, Nat Dairy Res Inst, Karnal, India, 79. *Mem:* Am Genetics Asn; Genetics Soc Am; Biomet Soc; Genetics Soc Can. *Res:* Genotype by environment interactions in Drosophila and Tribolium; selection and interrelationship of growth traits; genetic differences in growth curves; genetic recombination in Tribolium castaneum; population regulatory mechanisms in Tribolium. *Mailing Add:* Dept Zool Southern Ill Univ Carbondale IL 62901

ENGLERT, EDWIN, JR, b Brooklyn, NY, Oct 14, 26; c 2. INTERNAL MEDICINE, GASTROENTEROLOGY. *Educ:* Columbia Univ, BA, 46, MD, 49. *Prof Exp:* From intern to resident internal med, Bellevue Hosp, New York, 49-52; chief resident med, Vet Admin Hosp & Col Med, Univ Utah, 54-55; from instr to assoc prof, Col Med, Univ Utah, 54-72, chmn div gastroenterol, 58-70; from asst chief to chief med serv, 58-70, chief, Gastroenterol Sect, Vet Admin Hosp, 70-80, STAFF PHYSICIAN, GASTROENTEROL SECT, VET ADMIN MED CTR, 81-; PROF MED, COL MED, UNIV UTAH, 72- *Concurrent Pos:* Asst med, Sch Med, Boston Univ, 56-58; prof dir, NIH Training Grant Prog Gastroenterol, Col Med, Univ Utah, 60-70, co-dir, 71; prof dir, Vet Admin Res & Educ Training Grant Prog Gastroenterol, Vet Admin Hosp, Salt Lake City, 68-76; Nat Inst Arthritis & Metab Dis res fels, Col Med, Univ Utah, 55-56 & spec res fel, Sch Med, Boston Univ, 56-58; mem nat adv comt, Vet Admin Res & Educ Training Progs Gastroenterol, 67-72 & nat Vet Admin res merit rev bd gastroenterol, 72-74. *Mem:* Am Asn Univ Professors; Am Fedn Clin Res; Am Asn Study Liver Dis; Am Col Physicians; Am Gastroenterol Asn; Asn Vet Admin Chiefs Med (vpres, 69). *Res:* Physiology of the gallbladder and biliary tract; the cause of gallstones; pigment metabolism in the liver; functional disorders of the digestive system. *Mailing Add:* Gastroent Div Dept Internal Med Univ Utah Med Ctr Salt Lake City UT 84132

ENGLERT, MARY ELIZABETH, b New Orleans, La, July 11, 01. CHEMISTRY. *Educ:* Loyola Univ, La, AB, 23, MA, 25; Univ Wis, MS, 28, PhD(org chem), 33. *Prof Exp:* Instr, 24-28, PROF CHEM, ST MARY'S DOMINICAN COL, 28- *Concurrent Pos:* Assoc res mem, Inst Divi Thomae, 40- *Mem:* AAAS; Am Chem Soc; Am Inst Chemists. *Res:* Local anesthetics; nucleoproteins; growth promoting substances; pyrazolones derived from carbethoxypiperidones. *Mailing Add:* St Mary's Dominican Col 7214 St Charles Ave New Orleans LA 70118

ENGLERT, ROBERT D, b Portland, Ore, Feb 11, 20; m 54. ENVIRONMENTAL SCIENCE, RESEARCH ADMINISTRATION. *Educ:* Univ Portland, BS, 42; Ore State Univ, BS & MS, 44; Univ Colo, PhD(org chem), 49. *Prof Exp:* Asst, Ore State Univ, 43; biochemist, Naval Med Res Inst, 46; sr org chemist, Stanford Res Inst, 49-55, mgr phys sci res, Southern Calif Labs, 55-59, chmn, 59-62, dir, 62-68, exec dir, 68-70; VPRES & GEN MGR, ADVAN TECHNOL CTR, DRESSER INDUST, INC, 70- *Mem:* AAAS; Am Chem Soc; Sigma Xi; Air Pollution Control Asn. *Res:* Fats and oils; chemistry of boron and antimony; herbicides and insecticides; pollution control hardware; new equipment in energy field; new materials. *Mailing Add:* 1312 Sandcastle Dr Cornona Del Mar CA 92625

ENGLESBERG, ELLIS, b New York, NY, Oct 19, 21; c 3. GENETICS. *Educ:* Brooklyn Col, BA, 45; Univ Calif, MA, 48, PhD(bact), 50. *Prof Exp:* Teaching asst bact, Univ Calif, 46-49, res asst, 49-50, asst res bacteriologist, Hooper Found Med Res, 50-54; microbiologist, Long Island Biol Asn, 54-58; prof bact, Univ Pittsburgh, 58-65; chmn dept biol sci, 66-69, PROF MICROBIOL, UNIV CALIF, SANTA BARBARA, 65- *Concurrent Pos:* Mem adv panel genetic biol, NSF, 62-65; Guggenheim fel, 71-72. *Mem:* AAAS; Genetics Soc Am. *Res:* A study of the mechanism of transport of amino acids by mammalian cells in culture using a genetic approach. *Mailing Add:* Dept Biol Sci Univ Calif Santa Barbara CA 93106

ENGLEY, FRANK B, JR, b Wallingford, Conn, Oct 26, 19; m 48; c 4. MICROBIOLOGY. *Educ:* Univ Conn, BS, 41; Univ Pa, MS, 44, PhD(bact), 49; Am Bd Microbiol, dipl. *Prof Exp:* Asst instr bact, Sch Med, Univ Pa, 41-44; bacteriologist, Chem Corps, US Dept Army, Camp Detrick, 46-50; assoc prof bact & parasitol & consult bacteriologist, Med Br Hosps, Univ Tex, 50-55; asst dean sch med, 56-60, prof prev med & chmn dept, 60-61, chmn dept, 55-77, PROF MICROBIOL, SCH MED, UNIV MO-COLUMBIA, 55- *Concurrent Pos:* Consult bacteriologist, Vet Admin Hosp, 54-56; mem, Am Inst Biol Sci Adv Comt to NASA on Sterilization of Spacecraft, 66-68; vis prof, Univ Lagos, 73; mem & consult, Food & Drug Admin OTC Panel on Antimicrobials, 73-81. *Mem:* Fel AAAS; Am Soc Microbiol; Soc Exp Biol & Med; fel Am Pub Health Asn; Asn Am Med Cols. *Res:* Bacterial toxins; antiseptics and disinfectants; plastics in microbiology; ethylene oxide sterilization; survival of microorganisms. *Mailing Add:* Dept of Microbiol Univ of Mo Sch of Med Columbia MO 65212

ENGLISH, ALAN DALE, b San Diego, Calif, June, 8, 47; m 69; c 2. MACROMOLECULAR STRUCTURE, DYNAMICS. *Educ:* Univ Calif, Los Angeles, BS, 69, Santa Barbara, PhD(chem), 73. *Prof Exp:* RES CHEM, CENT RES & DEVELOP DEPT, E I DU PONT DE NEMOURS & CO, INC, 73- *Mem:* Am Phys Soc. *Res:* Modern solid state nuclear magnetic resonance techniques used to illucidate both structure and dynamics of macromolecular systems. *Mailing Add:* Cent Res & Develop Dept Exp Sta E I Du Pont de Nemours & Co Inc Wilmington DE 19898

ENGLISH, ALAN TAYLOUR, b Los Angeles, Calif, Mar 14, 34; m 55; c 4. METALLURGY. *Educ:* Stanford Univ, BS, 56; Mass Inst Technol, MS, 60, PhD(metall), 63. *Prof Exp:* SUPVR, RELIABILITY STUDIES, BELL TEL LABS, MURRAY HILL, 63- *Mem:* Am Vacuum Soc; Electrochem Soc. *Res:* Metal processing; brittle fracture; hot working of metals; crystallographic and mechanical textures in metals; structure-dependant magnetic properties; recrystallization; phase transformations; solid phase welding; thin-film materials; reliability of semiconductor devices; microlithographic processes. *Mailing Add:* 4 Drum Hill Dr Summit NJ 07901

ENGLISH, ARTHUR ROBERT, b Kankakee, Ill, Feb 29, 20; m 52; c 2. BACTERIOLOGY. *Educ:* Univ Ill, BS, 42; Univ Wis, MS, 46, PhD(bact, biochem), 50. *Prof Exp:* Res bacteriologist, 50-74, RES ADV, PFIZER, INC, 74- *Mem:* AAAS; Am Soc Microbiol; Soc Indust Microbiol; Soc Exp Biol & Med; Am Acad Microbiol. *Res:* Infection models; chemotherapeutic evaluation of new antibiotics. *Mailing Add:* Pfizer Inc Bldg 69 Groton CT 06340

ENGLISH, ARTHUR WILLIAM, b Ft Hueneme, Calif, Oct 20, 45. NEUROBIOLOGY, MOTOR SYSTEMS NEUROBIOLOGY. *Educ:* Univ Ore, BS, 67; Univ Ill, BS, 70, PhD(anat), 74. *Prof Exp:* Instr, 74-76, asst prof, 76-81, ASSOC PROF ANAT, COL MED, EMORY UNIV, 81- *Concurrent Pos:* Affil scientist neurobiol, Yerkes Regional Primate Res Ctr, 82- *Mem:* Am Soc Zoologists; Am Asn Anatomists; Soc Neurosci. *Res:* Neural mechanisms used in the control of movement and in particular the structural and functional features of the neural control of locomotion. *Mailing Add:* Dept Anat Emory Univ Atlanta GA 30322

ENGLISH, BRUCE VAUGHAN, b Richmond, Va, Aug 6, 21; m 49. ENVIRONMENTAL PHYSICS, ENVIRONMENTAL SCIENCES. *Educ:* Randolph-Macon Col, BS, 42; Ind Univ, MS, 43; Univ Va, PhD(physics), 58. *Prof Exp:* Asst physics, Ind Univ, 42-43; assoc prof, Randolph-Macon Col, 43-44; physicist, US Naval Res Lab, Washington, DC, 44-45, NJ, 45-46 & Fla, 46-48; assoc prof physics, Randolph-Macon Col, 48-58, prof, 58-64, actg head dept, 52-58, head dept, 58-64; consult physicist, 64-67; pres, Pollution Control Assocs, 67-71; PHYSICIST & CONSULT, 71- *Concurrent Pos:* Ford fel, Pa State Col, 51-52; Herald-Progress columnist, Impact on Environ, 71- *Mem:* AAAS; Am Phys Soc; Brit Soc Clean Air. *Res:* Ultracentrifuge; gravity; clean air; pollution control. *Mailing Add:* PO Box 267 Ashland VA 23005

ENGLISH, DARREL STARR, b Newton, Kans, Sept 6, 36; m 60; c 3. GENETICS. *Educ:* Southwestern Col, BA, 59; La State Univ, Baton Rouge, MS, 61; Iowa State Univ, PhD(genetics), 68. *Prof Exp:* Asst zool, La State Univ, 59-61; instr biol, Millsaps Col, 61-64; from asst to instr genetics, Iowa State Univ, 64-67; asst prof, 67-71, ASSOC PROF GENETICS, NORTHERN ARIZ UNIV, 71- *Concurrent Pos:* Danforth Assoc, 69; NSF partic histochem, Vanderbilt Univ, 71; sabbatical leave, M D Anderson Hosp & Tumor Inst, Houston, Tex, 78-; instr basic methods in tissue cult, Calif State Univ, Long Beach, 81. *Mem:* Am Genetics Asn; Sigma Xi; Somatic Cell Genetics Asn. *Res:* Developmental genetics in Chironomus; biochemical taxonomy and cytogenetics. *Mailing Add:* Box 5640 Dept Biol Northern Ariz Univ Flagstaff AZ 86011

ENGLISH, FLOYD L, b East Nicolaus, Calif, June 10, 34; m 55; c 2. SOLID STATE PHYSICS. *Educ:* Chico State Col, AB, 59; Ariz State Univ, MS, 62, PhD(physics), 65. *Prof Exp:* Staff mem tech, Sandia Lab, 65-69, div supvr microelectronics, 69-73; dir mkt, MOS/Components Div, Collins Radio Group, Rockwell Int, 73-74, gen mgr, 74-75; pres, Darcom Inc, 75-79; vpres US opers, 80-82, PRES US OPERS, ANDREW CORP, 82- *Mem:* Inst Elec & Electronics Engr. *Res:* Electrical characteristics of rectifying junctions; surface effects on ferroelectric and piezoelectric materials. *Mailing Add:* Andrew Corp 10500 W 153rd St Orland Park IL 60460

ENGLISH, GERALD ALAN, b Chester, Pa, Sept 17, 46. NUCLEAR CHEMISTRY, ANALYTICAL CHEMISTRY. *Educ:* LaSalle Col, BA, 68; Purdue Univ, West Lafayette, MS, 72, PhD(nuclear chem), 74. *Prof Exp:* Teaching asst chem, Purdue Univ, 68-70, res asst nuclear chem, 70-74; coal & anal chemist, Energy Systs Group, Rockwell Int, 74-80; NUCLEAR CHEMIST, PACIFIC GAS & ELEC CO, SAN FRANCISCO, CALIF, 81- *Mem:* Am Chem Soc; Am Phys Soc; Sigma Xi. *Res:* Energy-related problems concerned with breeder reactor fuel, advanced reactor fuels, coal gasification and liquefaction, upgrading of fossil fuels, pollution control and radioactive waste treatment; post-accident sampling and analysis (Diablo Canyon). *Mailing Add:* Pacific Gas & Elec Co 245 Market St San Francisco CA 94105

ENGLISH, JACKSON POLLARD, b Richmond, Va, Jan 25, 15; m 39; c 2. ORGANIC CHEMISTRY. *Educ:* Va Mil Inst, BS, 35; Johns Hopkins Univ, PhD(chem), 40. *Prof Exp:* Chemist, Am Cyanamid Co, 39-42; sr group leader, Chemother Div, 42-54, asst to dir, 54-55, unit leader org chem sect, Pearl River Labs, 55-56, asst dir exp therapeut sect, Lederle Labs, 56-60, dir chem res & develop, Agr Div, 60-69; dir res admin, Polaroid Corp, 69-71; ADJ PROF CHEM, DARTMOUTH COL, 75- *Mem:* Fel AAAS; Am Chem Soc; fel NY Acad Sci; The Chem Soc. *Res:* Synthesis of chemotherapeutic agents; natural products; experimental therapeutics; pesticides; agricultural chemicals. *Mailing Add:* Dept of Chem Dartmouth Col Hanover NH 03755

ENGLISH, JAMES ANDREW, b Harrison Valley, Pa, May 14, 10; m 34, 60; c 2. DENTISTRY. *Educ:* Pa State Col, BS, 32; Univ Pa, DDS, 36, MS, 48; Johns Hopkins Univ, PhD, 55. *Prof Exp:* Intern, Hosp, Univ Pa, 35-36; head dent br, Off Naval Res & Res Div, Bur Med Surg, 52-53, res assoc, Dent Dept, Naval Med Res Inst, 52-58, head dent br, 52-55, liaison officer, Off Naval Res, Eng, 56-57, head med & dent br, 58-60; dean, Sch Dent, State Univ NY Buffalo, 60-70, prof oral biol, Sch Dent, 60-75. *Concurrent Pos:* Chmn comn res, Int Dent Fedn, 67-72; mem nat adv dent res coun, NIH, 68-73. *Mem:* AAAS; Int Asn Dent Res (pres, 61); Am Dent Asn; fel Am Col Dent; fel Int Col Dent. *Res:* Pathology; biochemistry; specific emphasis on dental problems; radiobiology. *Mailing Add:* Dept of Oral Biol State Univ NY Sch of Dent Buffalo NY 14226

ENGLISH, JOSEPH T, b Philadelphia, Pa, May 21, 33; m 69. MEDICAL ADMINISTRATION. *Educ:* St Joseph's Col, AB, 54; Jefferson Med Col, MD, 58. *Prof Exp:* Intern, Jefferson Med Col Hosp, Philadelphia, 58-59; resident psychiat, Inst of Pa Hosp, Philadelphia, 59-61 & NIMH, 61-62; psychiatrist, Off of Dir, NIMH, 64-65, asst chief policy & prog coord, 65-66, dept chief off interagency liaison, 66; dep asst dir health affairs, Off Econ Opportunity, 66, actg asst dir, 66-68, asst dir, 69; adminr, Health Serv & Ment Health Admin, HEW, 69-70; PRES, NEW YORK CITY HEALTH & HOSPS CORP, 70-73; DIR DEPT PSYCHIAT, ST VINCENT'S HOSP & MED CTR, 73-; PROF PSYCHIAT, NY MED COL, 80-, ASSOC DEAN, 80- *Concurrent Pos:* Pvt pract psychiat, 62-; chief psychiatrist, Med Prog Div, Peace Corps, 62-66; adj prof psychiat, Cornell Univ; chmn interagency task force emergency food & med prog for US, Off Econ Opportunity-HEW, USDA, 68-69; chmn Alaska subcomt fed health progs, President's Rev Comn Alaska, 69-; chmn adv comt accessible environ for disabled, Bldg Res Adv Bd, 74-; chmn exec comt, Comt Ment Health Serv, Greater NY Hosp Asn, 74-; exec coordr panels on ment health serv delivery, President's Comn Ment Health, 77. *Honors & Awards:* John XXIII Medal, Col New Rochelle, 66; Meritorious Award Exemplary Achievement Pub Admin, William A Jump Mem Found, 66; Flemming Award & Personal Commendation, President of US, 68. *Mem:* Inst of Med of Nat Acad Sci; fel Am Psychiat Asn; NY Acad Med; Am Col Psychiatrists; AMA. *Mailing Add:* St Vincent's Hosp & Med Ctr 203 W 12th St New York NY 10011

ENGLISH, LEONARD STANLEY, b Hull, UK, July 2, 37; m 60; c 3. IMMUNOLOGY. *Educ:* Univ Wales, BSc, 71; Australian Nat Univ, PhD(immunol), 75. *Prof Exp:* Lectr, Mem Univ Nfld, 75-76, asst prof immunol, 76-77; asst prof, 77-81, ASSOC PROF IMMUNOL, SCH MED, EAST CAROLINA UNIV, 81- *Concurrent Pos:* Med Res Coun Can res grant, 75-77; NIH grant, 79-82. *Res:* Examination of the in vivo production of soluble factors by lymphoid cells during the immune response in the sheep. *Mailing Add:* East Carolina Univ Sch Med Greenville NC 27834

ENGLISH, SPOFFORD GRADY, chemistry, research administration, deceased

ENGLISH, THOMAS SAUNDERS, b Washington, DC, Aug 6, 28; m 67; c 2. BIOLOGICAL OCEANOGRAPHY. *Educ:* Iowa State Univ, BS, 50, MS, 51; Univ Wash, PhD(fisheries), 61. *Prof Exp:* Res assoc, Fisheries Res Inst, Univ Wash, 51; lectr fisheries, Univ Alaska, 56-57; sr oceanogr, Arctic Inst NAm, 57-58; instr fisheries, Univ Alaska, 58-59; asst prof, 59-65, ASSOC PROF OCEANOG, UNIV WASH, 65- *Mem:* Am Soc Limnol & Oceanog; Am Fisheries Soc; Am Inst Fishery Res Biol; Ecol Soc Am; Am Soc Ichthylogists & Herpetologists. *Res:* Fisheries biology; plankton sampling; arctic oceanography. *Mailing Add:* Dept of Oceanog Univ of Wash Seattle WA 98195

ENGLISH, WILLIAM HARLEY, b LaCrosse, Wash, Apr 12, 11; m 36; c 3. PLANT PATHOLOGY. *Educ:* State Col Wash, BS, 35, PhD(plant path), 40. *Prof Exp:* Asst plant path, State Col Wash, 35-37, instr, 37-39; jr pathologist, USDA, 39-43, asst pathologist, 43-46; assoc prof plant path, Ore State Col, 46-47; from asst prof to assoc prof, 47-56, PROF PLANT PATH, UNIV CALIF, DAVIS, 56- *Mem:* AAAS; Am Phytopath Soc. *Res:* Bacterial and fungus diseases of deciduous fruit trees; mycology. *Mailing Add:* Dept of Plant Path Univ of Calif Davis CA 95616

ENGLISH, WILLIAM JOSEPH, b Oil City, Pa, Nov 29, 41; m 78; c 1. ANTENNAS & PROPAGATION. *Educ:* St Vincent Col, BA, 63; Carnegie Inst Technol, BSEE, 64, MS, 65; Carnegie-Mellon Univ, PhD(space sci), 69. *Prof Exp:* Mem tech staff, Commun Satellite Corp, 70-77; SECT CHIEF ANTENNAS & PROPAGATION, RES & DEVELOP DEPT, INTELSAT, 77- *Concurrent Pos:* Asst prof & lectr, George Washington Univ, 72-76. *Mem:* Inst Elec & Electronics Engrs; Am Inst Aeronaut & Astronaut. *Res:* Design, development and measurement of communication spacecraft antennas, earth station antennas and research and develop on propagation effects in the 1-30 gugahertz range. *Mailing Add:* Intelsat 490 Lenfant Plaza Southwest Washington DC 20024

ENGLISH, WILLIAM KIRK, b Lexington, Ky, Jan 27, 29. INFORMATION SCIENCE. *Educ:* Univ Ky, BS, 50; Stanford Univ, MS, 64. *Prof Exp:* Staff mem, Sandia Corp, 50-52; staff engr, Univ Chicago, 52-54; sr res mem, Stanford Res Inst, 58-71; prin scientist, 71-80, MGR, INT BUS PLANNING, XEROX PALO ALTO RES CTR, 80- *Mem:* Inst Elec & Electronics Engrs; Soc Info Display. *Res:* Computer-based information processing and information retrieval. *Mailing Add:* 4117 Alpine Rd Portola Valley CA 94025

ENGLUND, CHARLES R, b Oak Park, Ill, Feb 20, 36; m 56; c 3. ORGANIC CHEMISTRY. *Educ:* Wheaton Col, Ill, BS, 58; Southern Ill Univ, MA, 63, PhD(chem), 68. *Prof Exp:* Teacher, High Sch, 58-60; asst chem, Southern Ill Univ, 60-62; from instr to asst prof, Concordia Teachers Col, Ill, 62-65; instr, Southern Ill Univ, 65-67; assoc prof phys sci & math, 68-80, PROF CHEM, BETHANY COL, KANS, 80- *Mem:* Am Chem Soc. *Res:* Preparation and structure determination of steroidal derivatives. *Mailing Add:* Dept of Chem 415 N Chestnut Lindsborg KS 67456

ENGLUND, JOHN ARTHUR, b Omaha, Nebr, June 4, 26; m 52; c 5. OPERATIONS RESEARCH. *Educ:* Creighton Univ, BS, 49; Mass Inst Technol, SM, 51. *Prof Exp:* From instr to asst prof math, Creighton Univ, 51-56; opers analyst, Hq Strategic Air Command, 56-62; mil systs analyst, US Arms Control & Disarmament Agency, 62-63; mathematician, 63-64, chief, Strategic Br, 64-70, mgr, Strategic Div, 70-76, mgr intel studies, 71-80, exec vpres, 76-81, past pres, 80-81, PRES, ANAL SERV INC, 81- *Concurrent Pos:* Vpres admin, Mil Opers Res Soc, 78- *Mem:* Am Math Soc. *Res:* Algebraic and analytic number theory; military systems analysis. *Mailing Add:* ANSER 400 Army Navy Dr Arlington VA 22202

ENGLUND, PAUL THEODORE, b Worcester, Mass, Mar 25, 38; m 61; c 2. BIOCHEMISTRY. *Educ:* Hamilton Col, BA, 60; Rockefeller Univ, PhD(biochem), 66. *Prof Exp:* Asst prof, 68-73, assoc prof, 73-80, PROF PHYSIOL CHEM, SCH MED, JOHNS HOPKINS UNIV, 80- *Concurrent Pos:* Fel, Sch Med, Stanford Univ, 66-68. *Mem:* Am Soc Biol Chem; Am Chem Soc. *Res:* Protein chemistry; enzymology of nucleic acids. *Mailing Add:* Dept Physiol Chem Johns Hopkins Univ Sch of Med Baltimore MD 21205

ENGQUIST, ELMER H(OWARD), b Chicago, Ill, Feb 16, 21; m 47; c 5. CHEMICAL ENGINEERING, NUCLEAR ENGINEERING. *Educ:* Univ Ill, BS, 43; Northwestern Univ, MS, 47; Univ Mich, MS, 58. *Prof Exp:* Res assoc, Chem Warfare Serv Develop Lab, Mass Inst Technol, 43-45; chem & electronic engr, Tech Command Army Chem Ctr, 45-46; res assoc chem, Northwestern Univ, 46-47; asst chief, Radiological Div, Chem & Radiological Labs, Army Chem Ctr, Chem Systs Lab, 47-56, exec asst to chief scientist, Chem Warefare Labs, Edgewood Arsenal, 56-58, dep dir res, Chem Res & Develop Labs, 58-62, dir defensive systs, 62-65, chief, Dissemination Res

Dept, 66-74, chief engr, Develop & Eng Directorate, 74-77, chief, Systs Assessment Off, 77-78, decontamination mgt officer, 78-80; SR RES SCIENTIST, COLUMBUS DIV, BATTELLE MEM INST, 80- *Mem:* Am Chem Soc; Sigma Xi. *Res:* Radiological defense; properties of aerosols; development of aerosol sampling equipment; efficiency of aerosol filtration equipment; chemical warfare; defensive equipment. *Mailing Add:* 616 E Wheel Rd Bel Air MD 21014

ENGSTER, HENRY MARTIN, b Troy, NY, May 6, 49; m 72. NUTRITION, PHYSIOLOGY. *Educ:* St Lawrence Univ, BS, 71; Univ Vt, MS, 74, PhD(nutrit), 77. *Prof Exp:* Res fel nutrit & biochem, Hormel Inst, Univ Minn, Austin, 77; nutritionist, 77-79, sr nutritionist, 79-81, RES MGR, RALSTON PURINA CO, 81- *Concurrent Pos:* Head, Subcomt Determination Biol Availiability Amino Acids Poultry, Animal Nutrit Res Coun, 81- *Mem:* Sigma Xi; Poultry Sci Asn; AAAS; Am Oil Chemists Soc. *Res:* Dietary fats and lipids; effects of fats and essential fatty acids on endocrine physiology; nutritional and management research on pullets, commercial layers, roosters, turkeys, especially energy content of feedstuffs, nutrient requirements and product and program development for poultry. *Mailing Add:* 860 Dielman Rd St Louis MO 63132

ENGSTROM, HERBERT LEONARD, b San Francisco, Calif, Dec 16, 41; m 72. ELECTRONICS ENGINEERING. *Educ:* Univ Calif, Berkeley, AB, 64, PhD(physics), 72. *Prof Exp:* Solid state physicist, Univ Paris, Orsay, 72-74; solid state physicist, Brookhaven Nat Lab, 75-77; solid state physicist, Oak Ridge Nat Lab, 77-81; INSTRUMENTATION ENGR, SPERRY-UNIVAC, SANTA CLARA, 81- *Mem:* Inst Elec & Electronics Engrs. *Res:* Optical properties and light scattering of defects and impurities in semiconductors and insulators. *Mailing Add:* Sperry-Univac 3333 Scott Blvd Santa Clara CA 95051

ENGSTROM, LEE EDWARD, b Rock Island, Ill, Sept 30, 41; m; c 1. DEVELOPMENTAL GENETICS. *Educ:* Iowa Wesleyan Col, BS, 65; Univ Ill, Urbana, MS, 67, PhD(develop genetics), 71. *Prof Exp:* From asst prof to assoc prof, 70-79, PROF BIOL, BALL STATE UNIV, 79-; ASSOC PROF ANAT, IND UNIV, MUNCIE CTR MED EDUC, 75- *Mem:* Genetics Soc Am; Soc Develop Biol. *Res:* Genetic controls and developmental relationships of gonad development in Drosophila melanogaster. *Mailing Add:* Dept Biol Ball State Univ Muncie IN 47306

ENGSTROM, NORMAN ARDELL, b DeKalb, Ill, July 2, 45; m 67. MARINE ECOLOGY, ETHOLOGY. *Educ:* Cornell Col, AB, 67; Univ Miami, MS, 70; Univ Wash, PhD(invert ecol), 74. *Prof Exp:* Asst prof marine sci, Univ PR, 74-77; ASST PROF BIOL, NORTHERN ILL UNIV, 77- *Mem:* AAAS; Ecol Soc Am; Am Soc Zoologists. *Res:* Escape responses of invertebrates to marine gastropod predators; prey-predator relations between cassis tuberosa and sea urchins in seagrass beds; agonistic behavior of brachyuran crabs. *Mailing Add:* Dept of Biol Sci Northern Ill Univ DeKalb IL 60115

ENGSTROM, RALPH WARREN, b Grinnell, Iowa, Oct 24, 14; m 37; c 2. PHYSICS. *Educ:* St Olaf Col, BA, 35; Northwestern Univ, MS, 37, PhD(physics), 39. *Prof Exp:* Instr physics & math, St Cloud State Teachers Col, Minn, 39-41; res physicist, Nat Defense Res Comt, 41; res physicist, RCA Mfg Co, NJ, 41-43, tech adv, Electro-optics Prod, RCA Corp, 43-80; CONSULT, 80- *Mem:* Fel Am Phys Soc; Optical Soc Am; Sigma Xi. *Res:* Multiplier phototubes; television camera tubes; photoconductors; image converter tubes. *Mailing Add:* 62 Orchard Rd Blossom Hill Lancaster PA 17601

ENGVALL, EVA SUSANNA, b Stockholm, Sweden, Mar 11, 40. IMMUNOCHEMISTRY. *Educ:* Univ Stockholm, BSc, 64, PhD(immunol), 75. *Prof Exp:* Res assoc biochem, Res Lab LKB, Stockholm, 65-66 & KABI AB, Stockholm, 66-69; jr res scientist immunol, Univ Stockholm, 69-75; fel immunol, Univ Helsinki, 75-76; fel, City Hope Med Ctr, 76-77, asst res scientist immunol, 77-79; SCIENTIST, LA JOLLA CANCER RES FOUND, 79- *Concurrent Pos:* Fel, Europ Molecular Biol Orgn, 75-77. *Honors & Awards:* Biochem Anal Award, Ger Soc Clin Chem, 76. *Mem:* Am Asn Cancer Res; Am Asn Immunologists. *Res:* Molecular interactions of extracellular matrix components. *Mailing Add:* La Jolla Cancer Res Found 10901 N Torrey Pines Rd La Jolla CA 92037

ENIG, JULIUS WILLIAM, b Brooklyn, NY, Apr 29, 31; m 58; c 3. MATHEMATICS. *Educ:* City Col New York, BS, 52; Univ Md, MA, 60. *Prof Exp:* Res physicist, Chem Res Dept, 52-64; sr scientist, 64-69, chief math anal div, 69-77, HEAD MATH ANAL DIV, US NAVAL ORD LAB, 77- *Concurrent Pos:* Vis staff mem math, Imp Col, Univ London, 62-63. *Honors & Awards:* Meritorious Civilian Serv Award, US Navy, 60. *Mem:* Combustion Inst; Am Math Soc; London Math Soc; Edinburgh Math Soc. *Res:* Detonation and combustion theory of condensed explosives and propellants; explosives initiation phenomena; numerical solutions of compressible flow; high pressure equations of state of solids and liquids; thermal explosions; heat conduction. *Mailing Add:* Math Anal Div US Naval Ord Lab Silver Spring MD 20910

ENKE, CHRISTIE GEORGE, b Minneapolis, Minn, July 8, 33; m 56; c 3. ANALYTICAL CHEMISTRY. *Educ:* Principia Col, BS, 55; Univ Ill, MS, 57, PhD(chem), 59. *Prof Exp:* From instr to asst prof chem, Princeton Univ, 59-66; assoc prof, 66-74, PROF CHEM, MICH STATE UNIV, 74- *Concurrent Pos:* Alfred P Sloan res fel, 64-67. *Mem:* AAAS; Am Chem Soc; Am Soc Mass Spectrometry; Inst Elec & Electronics Engr. *Res:* Electrochemistry, spectrometry, mass spectrometry, chemical instrumentation, the application of mini and micro computers to chemical measurement and control systems. *Mailing Add:* Dept Chem Mich State Univ East Lansing MI 48824

ENKE, GLENN L, b Oakland, Calif, Jan 8, 09; m 34; c 4. CIVIL ENGINEERING. *Educ:* Univ Calif, Berkeley, BS, 28; Utah State Univ, CE, 72. *Prof Exp:* Detailer, Am Bridge Co, Ind, 28-29; designer, Indust Plant, Giffels & Vallet, Inc, Mich, 29-31; engr design, Calif Bridge Dept, 31-41; struct engr, D R Warren Co, 41-42; asst chief engr, Utah-Pomeroy-Morrison, 42-43; dist engr, Morrison-Knudsen, Inc, Idaho, 43-47; struct engr, Caldwell, Richards & Sorensen, Utah, 47-48; dist engr, Utah Construct Co, 48-52; prof civil & mech eng & chmn dept, Brigham Young Univ, 52-53; chief engr, Church Jesus Christ Latter Day Saints, 53-55; gen supvr design eng, US Steel Corp, 55-62; prof civil eng sci, 62-74, EMER PROF CIVIL ENG SCI, BRIGHAM YOUNG UNIV, 74-; OWNER, GLENN L ENKE, CONSULT CIVIL & STRUCT ENGR, 74- *Concurrent Pos:* Consult struct engr, 36-; partner, Enke & Long, Consult Engrs, Calif, 54-; vpres, Van Sickle Assocs, Consult Engrs, Colo, 56-; dir, Western Zone, Nat Coun State Bd Eng Exam, 60-62. *Honors & Awards:* Lincoln Arc Welding Found Award, 37, 42, 47 & 59. *Mem:* Fel Am Soc Civil Engrs. *Res:* Structural analysis methods for indeterminate structures; arc welding design; dynamics of long-span suspension systems; seismic force effects on multi-story buildings; engineering economics and law. *Mailing Add:* 4657 N 265th E Provo UT 84601

ENLOE, LOUIS HENRY, b Eldorado Springs, Mo, Mar 4, 33; m 56; c 3. ELECTRICAL ENGINEERING, COMMUNICATIONS. *Educ:* Univ Ariz, BS, 55, MS, 56, PhD(elec eng), 59. *Prof Exp:* Instr elec eng, Univ Ariz, 56-59; mem tech staff commun res, 59-66, head visual systs res dept, Commun Systs Div, 66-67, HEAD OPTO-ELECTRONICS RES DEPT, COMMUN SYSTS DIV, BELL TEL LABS, 67- *Mem:* Inst Elec & Electronics Engrs. *Res:* Noise and modulation theory, particularly problems associated with space communications; visual systems research. *Mailing Add:* Bell Tel Labs Data Commun Holmdel NJ 07733

ENLOW, DONALD HUGH, b Mosquero, NMex, Jan 22, 27; m 45; c 1. ANATOMY. *Educ:* Univ Houston, BS, 49, MS, 50; Agr & Mech Col, Tex, PhD, 55. *Prof Exp:* Instr zool, Univ Houston, 49-52; asst, Agr & Mech Col, Tex, 52-53; cur natural hist & Anthrop, Witte Mus, 54-55; asst prof biol, WTex State Col, 55-56; instr anat, Med Col, Univ SC, 56-57; from instr to prof anat, Sch Med, Univ Mich, Ann Arbor, 57-72, dir phys growth prog, Ctr Human Growth & Develop, 68-72; prof anat & chmn dept, Sch Med, WVa Univ, 72-77; PROF ORTHOD, CHMN DEPT, ASST DEAN GRAD STUDIES & RES & THOMAS HILL DISTINGUISHED PROF, SCH DENT, CASE WESTERN RESERVE UNIV, 77- *Mem:* Am Asn Anat; Royal Soc Med; Int Asn Dent Res. *Res:* Histology; embryology; gross and comparative anatomy; comparative histology of bone tissue; bone remodeling; facial growth. *Mailing Add:* Dept of Orthod Case Western Reserve Univ Cleveland OH 44106

ENLOWS, HAROLD EUGENE, b Mason City, Ill, June 11, 11; m 40. PETROGRAPHY. *Educ:* Univ Tulsa, BS, 35; Univ Chicago, MS, 36; Univ Ariz, PhD(econ geol), 39; US Naval Acad, cert, 44. *Prof Exp:* Instr geol, Univ Tulsa, 38-43, prof, 46-64; assoc prof, 64-70, prof geol & chmn dept, 70-77, EMER PROF GEOL, ORE STATE UNIV, 77- *Mem:* Fel Mineral Soc Am; Soc Econ Paleont & Mineral; Am Asn Petrol Geol; fel Geol Soc Am. *Res:* Stratigraphy of Great Basin; volcanics of Chiricahua Mountains; sedimentary petrography; volcanic sediments; volcanics of central Oregon. *Mailing Add:* Dept of Geol Ore State Univ Corvallis OR 97331

ENNA, SALVATORE JOSEPH, b Kansas City, Mo, Dec 19, 44; m 69; c 2. PHARMACOLOGY, NEUROBIOLOGY. *Educ:* Rockhurst Col, BA, 65; Univ Mo-Kansas City, MS, 67, PhD(pharmacol), 70. *Prof Exp:* Fel pharmacol, Univ Tex Med Sch, Dallas, 70-72, Hoffmann La Roche & Co, Basel, Switzerland, 73-74, & Sch Med, Johns Hopkins Univ, 74-76; from asst prof to assoc prof, 76-80, PROF PHARMACOL & NEUROBIOL, UNIV TEX MED SCH, HOUSTON, 80-; from asst prof to assoc prof, 76-80, PROF PHARMACOL & NEUROBIOL, UNIV TEX MED SCH HOUSTON, 80- *Concurrent Pos:* Consult pharmacol, ICI-USA, Wilmington, Del, 75-77, Merck Sharp & Dohme Res Lab, West Point, Pa, 76-81 & Mead Johnson Pharmaceut Div, Evansville, Ind, 81-; Nat Inst Neurol & Commun Dis & Stroke res career develop award, Univ Tex Med Sch Houston, 78-83. *Honors & Awards:* John J Abel Award, Am Soc Pharmacol & Exp Therapeut. *Mem:* Soc Neurosci; Am Soc Neurochem; Am Soc Pharmacol & Exp Therapeut; Am Chem Soc; AAAS. *Res:* Central nervous system pharmacology, with particular emphasis on the interaction of drugs with neurotransmitter receptors; neurotransmitter receptors. *Mailing Add:* Dept of Pharmacol Neurobiol & Anat Univ Tex Med Sch PO Box 20708 Houston TX 77025

ENNEKING, EUGENE A, b Idaho Co, Idaho, Jan 17, 40; m 65; c 2. MATHEMATICAL STATISTICS. *Educ:* St Martins Col, BS, 62; Wash State Univ, MA, 64, PhD(math). *Prof Exp:* Asst math, Wash State Univ, 62-66; asst prof, St Louis Univ, 66-68; from asst prof to assoc prof, 68-80, HEAD DEPT MATH, PORTLAND STATE UNIV, 78-, PROF MATH, 80- *Mem:* Am Math Soc; Inst Math Statist; Math Asn Am; Am Statist Asn. *Res:* Combinatorial theory; probability theory. *Mailing Add:* Dept of Math Portland State Univ Portland OR 97207

ENNEKING, MARJORIE, b Eugene, Ore, June 21, 41; m 65; c 2. MATHEMATICS. *Educ:* Willamette Univ, BA, 62; Wash State Univ, MA, 64, PhD(math), 66. *Prof Exp:* Teaching asst math, Wash State Univ, 62-66; asst prof, Univ Mo-St Louis, 66-68; asst prof, 68-75, ASSOC PROF MATH, PORTLAND STATE UNIV, 75- *Mem:* Am Math Soc; Math Asn Am. *Mailing Add:* Dept of Math Portland State Univ Portland OR 97207

ENNEKING, WILLIAM FISHER, b Madison, Wis, May 9, 26; m 47; c 7. MEDICINE. *Educ:* Univ Wis, BS, 45, MD, 49. *Prof Exp:* Intern, Med Ctr, Univ Colo, 49-50; prof orthop surg & dir div, Med Ctr, Univ Miss, 56-59; assoc prof surg & path & dir div orthop surg, 59-62, prof & chief div, 62-74, chmn dept, 74-80, PROF ORTHOP, COL MED, UNIV FLA, 74-, DISTINGUISHED SERV PROF, 80- *Mem:* Orthop Res Soc; AMA; NY Acad Sci. *Res:* Clinical orthopedic pathology; immunological aspects of bone transplantation. *Mailing Add:* Dept of Orthopaed Surg Univ of Fla Med Ctr Gainesville FL 32601

ENNEVER, JOHN JOSEPH, b Ossining, NY, June 7, 20; m 46; c 2. DENTISTRY, MICROBIOLOGY. *Educ:* Wash Univ, DMD, 47; Ohio State Univ, MSc, 50. *Prof Exp:* Res assoc, Ohio State Univ, 47-50; asst prof periodont, Univ Kans City, 50-56; mem res staff, Procter & Gamble Co, 56-68; PROF DENT, DENT SCI INST, UNIV TEX, HOUSTON, 68- *Mem:* Sigma Xi; Soc Exp Biol Med; Int Asn Dent Res. *Res:* microbiologic calcification; biologic calcification model systems. *Mailing Add:* Dent Sci Inst Univ Tex PO Box 20068 Houston TX 77025

ENNIS, ELLA GRAY WILSON, b Sampson Co, NC, May 2, 25; m 62. PHYSIOLOGY. *Educ:* Univ NC, Greensboro, AB, 45, Univ NC, Chapel Hill, MA, 48, PhD(physiol), 64. *Prof Exp:* Teacher high sch, NC, 45-47; dir health & phys educ, St Mary's Jr Col, Md, 48-49; asst prof, Furman Univ, 49-56; res assoc pharmacol, 65, instr physiol, 65-67, asst prof, Sch Med, 67-69, asst prof, Sch Med & Sch Nursing, 69-74, lectr, Dept Med, 74-75, ASSOC PROF, DEPT MED ALLIED HEALTH PROF & LECTR, DEPT PHYSIOL, SCH MED, UNIV NC, CHAPEL HILL, 75- *Res:* Effect of various enzymes on in vitro blood coagulation tests; factor V and thrombin in the intrinsic and extrinsic clotting systems; preparation of self-instructional materials; colloidal aspects of blood clotting; nursing research with physiological implications; development of videotape study guide instructional program on cardiovascular physiology. *Mailing Add:* Dept of Physiol Univ of NC Sch of Med Chapel Hill NC 27514

ENNIS, HERBERT LEO, b Brooklyn, NY, Jan 6, 32; m 60; c 2. MICROBIOLOGY. *Educ:* Brooklyn Col, BS, 53; Northwestern Univ, MS, 54, PhD, 57. *Prof Exp:* USPHS fel, Northwestern Univ, 57-58; res fel bact & immunol & USPHS fel, Harvard Univ, 58-59; fel, Brandeis Univ, 59-60; instr pharmacol, Harvard Med Sch, 60-64; from asst prof to assoc prof biochem, St Jude Hosp & Col Med, Univ Tenn, 64-69; assoc mem, 69-77, MEM, ROCHE INST MOLECULAR BIOL, 77- *Mem:* AAAS; Am Soc Microbiol; Am Soc Biol Chem; NY Acad Sci. *Res:* Microbial physiology; genetics; antibiotics. *Mailing Add:* Roche Inst Molecular Biol Nutley NJ 07110

ENNOR, KENNETH STAFFORD, b Wadebridge, Eng, May 15, 33; m 65; c 2. ORGANIC CHEMISTRY. *Educ:* Univ London, BSc, 54, PhD(org chem), 57. *Prof Exp:* Fels, Ohio State Univ, 57-58 & Boston Univ, 58-59; tech officer plastics res, Imp Chem Industs Ltd, Eng, 59-62; scientist appln res resins, Esso Res Ltd, Eng, 62-65; sr scientist appln res tall oil prod, Brit Oxygen Chem Ltd, 65-68; SUPVR DOC & INFO CONTROL, CHEM DIV, UNION CAMP CORP, 68- *Mem:* Assoc Royal Inst Chem; Brit Oil & Colour Chem Asn; Am Chem Soc; Am Soc Testing & Mat; Adhesives & Sealants Coun. *Res:* Wood-based fatty acids and resins for surface coatings, printing inks, ore flotation and adhesives; tall oil products; dimer acids; polyamide resins. *Mailing Add:* Chem Div Union Camp Corp PO Box 2668 Savannah GA 31402

ENNS, ERNEST GERHARD, b Alta, June 13, 40; m 64, 77. MATHEMATICAL STATISTICS, OPERATIONS RESEARCH. *Educ:* Univ BC, BSc, 61, PhD(statist mech), 65. *Prof Exp:* Mem sci staff appl math, Northern Elec Res & Develop Labs, Ottawa, 65-67; consult teletraffic, Australian PMG, Melbourne, 67; lectr statist, Univ Queensland, 68; mem sci staff teletraffic, Siemens AG, Munich, 69; assoc prof, 69-77, PROF STATIST, UNIV CALGARY, 77- *Res:* Decision theory, queueing theory and geometrical probability. *Mailing Add:* Dept Math & Statist Univ of Calgary Calgary AB T2N 1N4 Can

ENNS, HENRY, plant breeding, genetics, see previous edition

ENNS, JOHN HERMANN, b Schonau, Russia, July 18, 07; nat US; m 38; c 3. PHYSICS. *Educ:* Kans State Col, BS, 32; Univ Mich, AM, 35, PhD(physics), 41. *Prof Exp:* Instr physics, Detroit Inst Technol, 36-39; res physicist, Diamond Chain & Mfg Co, Indianapolis, 41-42; asst prof physics, Mich State Col, 42-44; res physicist, 44-58, from assoc prof to prof eng mech, 58-73, EMER PROF ENG MECH, UNIV MICH, ANN ARBOR, 73- *Mem:* Am Phys Soc; Optical Soc Am. *Res:* Sound and vibrations; emission spectroscopy; air interrupter type stabilized control gap for spark and alternating current arc source spectroscopy; solid state studies of photographic latent image formation; lattice dynamics and micromechanics of solids. *Mailing Add:* 12546 Nacido Dr Rancho Bernardo CA 92128

ENNS, RICHARD HARVEY, b Winnipeg, Man, Nov 5, 38; m 67; c 2. THEORETICAL PHYSICS. *Educ:* Univ Alta, BSc, 60, PhD(theoret physics), 64. *Prof Exp:* Asst prof, 65-70, assoc prof, 70-76, PROF PHYSICS, SIMON FRASER UNIV, 76- *Concurrent Pos:* Nat Res Coun Can fel, Univ Liverpool, 64-65; res grant, 65- *Mem:* Can Asn Physicists. *Res:* Transport theory in solids; absorption and dispersion of sound in gases, nonlinear optics; other nonlinear problems. *Mailing Add:* Dept of Physics Simon Fraser Univ Burnaby BC V5A 1S6 Can

ENNS, THEODORE, b Alexanderkrone, Russia, Jan 10, 16; nat US; m 43; c 3. PHYSICS, OCEANOGRAPHY. *Educ:* Univ Sask, BE, 37; Univ Rochester, PhD(physics), 40. *Prof Exp:* Asst physics, Univ Rochester, 37-40 & Wash Univ, 40-41; res fel radiol, Sch Med & Dent, Univ Rochester, 41-42, res assoc, Dept Radio, 42-43, assoc, Manhattan Dept, 43-46; chief physicist, Biochem Res Found, 46-48; asst prof med, Johns Hopkins Univ, 48-64, assoc prof physiol chem, 57-64; RES PHYSIOLOGIST & LECTR, SCRIPPS INST OCEANOG, UNIV CALIF, SAN DIEGO, 62- *Concurrent Pos:* Fulbright grant & Guggenheim fel, Univ Oslo, 56-57. *Mem:* Am Phys Soc; Am Physiol Soc; Microcirculatory Soc. *Res:* Nuclear physics; cyclotrons; mass spectrometry; radioactive and stable tracers; respiration and renal physiology; biological transport. *Mailing Add:* Scripps Inst of Oceanog Univ of Calif at San Diego La Jolla CA 92093

ENNS, WILBUR RONALD, b Henderson, Nebr, Feb 26, 13; m 46; c 1. ENTOMOLOGY. *Educ:* Univ Mo, BS, 41, AM, 46; Univ Kans, PhD(entom), 55. *Prof Exp:* Asst, 42, from instr to prof, 48-78, dir entom mus, 52-78, EMER PROF ENTOM, UNIV MO-COLUMBIA, 78- *Mem:* Entom Soc Am; Soc Syst Zool; Am Entom Soc; Am Inst Biol Sci; Entom Soc Can. *Res:* Insect taxonomy; control of insects and mites. *Mailing Add:* 1-79 Agr Bldg Dept Entom Univ Mo Columbia MO 65211

ENNULAT, REINHARD D, physics, mathematics, see previous edition

ENO, CHARLES FRANKLIN, b Atwater, Ohio, May 21, 20; m 48; c 2. SOIL SCIENCE. *Educ:* Ohio State Univ, BS, 42, MS, 48; Purdue Univ, PhD(soil microbiol), 51. *Prof Exp:* Soil microbiologist, 50-65, CHMN DEPT SOIL SCI, UNIV FLA, UNIV FLA, 65-, PROF SOIL MICROBIOL, 74- *Mem:* Am Soc Agron; Soil Sci Soc Am. *Res:* Soil microbiology and related research in soil fertility. *Mailing Add:* Dept of Soil Sci Univ of Fla Gainesville FL 32611

ENOCH, JACOB, b Berlin, Ger, Feb 17, 27; nat US; m 55; c 3. PLASMA PHYSICS. *Educ:* Brooklyn Col, BS, 52; Univ Wis, MS, 54, PhD(physics), 56. *Prof Exp:* Asst physics, Univ Wis, 52-56; mem staff, Midwestern Univs Res Asn, 56-57, Los Alamos Sci Lab, Univ Calif, 57-60 & Space Sci Lab, Gen Elec Co, 60-62; asst prof, 62-64, assoc prof physics, 64-80, ASSOC PROF PHYSICS & ASTRON, UNIV KANS, 80- *Concurrent Pos:* Vis staff mem, Los Alamos Sci Lab, 68-70, 73-; guest scientist, Max Plank Inst Plasma Physics, Ger, 70-71; Fulbright sr res fel, 70-71; vis prof, Ben Gurian Univ of the Negev, Israel, 71-73. *Mem:* Am Phys Soc. *Res:* Statistical mechanics; kinetic theory; equilibrium and stability of high temperature plasmas. *Mailing Add:* Dept of Physics Univ of Kans Lawrence KS 66044

ENOCH, JAY MARTIN, physiological optics, vision, see previous edition

ENOCHS, EDGAR EARLE, b McComb, Miss, Sept 13, 32; m 58; c 7. MATHEMATICS, ALGEBRA. *Educ:* La State Univ, BS, 58; Univ Notre Dame, PhD(math), 58. *Prof Exp:* Instr math, Univ Chicago, 58-60; from asst prof to assoc prof, Univ SC, 60-67; PROF MATH, UNIV KY, 67- *Concurrent Pos:* NSF res grant, 63-64. *Res:* Abelian group theory; modules over integral domains; general topology; homological algebra. *Mailing Add:* Dept Math Univ Ky Lexington KY 40506

ENOCHS, NETTIE JEAN, b Jackson, Tenn, Dec 13, 39. DEVELOPMENTAL BIOLOGY, BOTANY. *Educ:* David Lipscomb Col, BS, 61; Purdue Univ, MS, 64, PhD(biol), 67. *Prof Exp:* Staff biologist, Comn Undergrad Educ Biol Sci, NSF, 66-67; asst prof, 67-77, ASSOC PROF BIOL, MICH STATE UNIV, 77- *Mem:* AAAS; Bot Soc Am; Am Inst Biol Sci; Nat Asn Biol Teachers; Nat Sci Teachers Asn. *Res:* Effects of gibberellic acid on plant growth; histological study of disease resistant reaction of plants; autoradiographic study of RNA in plant cell; plant physiology and development; biology education. *Mailing Add:* Sci & Math Teaching Ctr Mich State Univ East Lansing MI 48824

ENOS, HERMAN ISAAC, JR, b Alhambra, Calif, Apr 30, 20; m 48; c 3. ORGANIC CHEMISTRY. *Educ:* Univ Southern Calif, AB, 42; Univ Ill, PhD(org chem), 46. *Prof Exp:* Lilly fel, Columbia Univ, 46; from instr to asst prof org chem, Swarthmore Col, 46-48; res chemist, Res Ctr, Hercules Powder Co, 48-54, res supvr, 54-65, res assoc, 65-67, RES ASSOC, RES CTR, HERCULES INC, 67- *Mem:* Am Oil Chemists Soc; Am Chem Soc; Royal Soc Chem. *Res:* Synthetic organic chemistry; rosin and terpenes; hydrocarbon alkylation and oxidation; hydroperoxides and peroxides; unsaturated fatty acids. *Mailing Add:* Box 3714 Greenville Wilmington DE 19807

ENOS, PAUL (PORTENIER), b Topeka, Kans, July 25, 34; m 58; c 4. GEOLOGY. *Educ:* Univ Kans, BSc, 56; Stanford Univ, MSc, 61; Yale Univ, PhD(geol), 65. *Prof Exp:* Asst instr geol, Yale Univ, 62-64; geologist, Shell Develop Co, 64-65, res geologist, 65-70; assoc prof, 70-76, PROF GEOL, STATE UNIV NY BINGHAMTON, 76- *Concurrent Pos:* consult, Petrol Co. *Mem:* Soc Econ Paleontologists & Mineralogists. *Res:* Sedimentology of flysch deposits; recent carbonates, Florida and Bahamas; Cretaceous carbonates, Mexico; deep sea sediments, Western North Atlantic; carbonate diagenesis. *Mailing Add:* Dept Geol Sci State Univ of NY Binghamton NY 13901

ENQUIST, IRVING FRITIOF, b Superior, Wis, June 25, 20; m 44; c 3. SURGERY. *Educ:* Univ Minn, BS, 42, MD, 44, MS, 51. *Prof Exp:* From instr to assoc prof, 52-60, PROF SURG, STATE UNIV NY DOWNSTATE MED CTR, 60-, ASSOC DEAN, 77-; DIR SURG, METHODIST HOSP BROOKLYN, 65- *Concurrent Pos:* Consult surg, US Vet Hosp, Brooklyn & St John's Episcopal Hosp, Brooklyn. *Mem:* AAAS; Am Col Surg; Am Surg Asn; Soc Surg Alimentary Tract; Int Soc Surg. *Res:* Wound healing; gastrointestinal physiology. *Mailing Add:* Methodist Hosp Brooklyn 506 Sixth St Brooklyn NY 11215

ENQUIST, LYNN WILLIAM, b Denver, Colo, Oct 23, 45; m 68; c 1. MOLECULAR BIOLOGY, MICROBIOLOGY. *Educ:* SDak State Univ, BS, 67; Med Col Va, PhD(microbiol), 71. *Prof Exp:* NSF fel, Med Col Va, 71; fel, Roche Inst Molecular Biol, 71-73; staff fel, Nat Inst Child Health & Human Develop, NIH, 73-77, scientist molecular biol, 77-81; EXEC SCIENTIST, MOLECULAR GENETICS, INC, MINNETONKA, MINN, 81- *Mem:* Am Soc Microbiol; AAAS; Sigma Xi. *Res:* Genetics and biochemistry of temperate bacteriophage replication and recombination; use of microorganisms in recombinant DNA research. *Mailing Add:* 10320 Bren Rd E Minnetonka MN 55343

ENRIETTO, JOSEPH FRANCIS, b Spring Valley, Ill, May 7, 31; m 52; c 4. METALLURGY. *Educ:* Univ Ill, BS, 56, MS, 57, PhD(metall), 60. *Prof Exp:* Sr res engr, Res Lab, Jones & Laughlin Steel Corp, 60-63; supvr physics of metals group, 63-66, asst dir phys metall, 66-71; mgr mat eng, 71-77, mgr metall & nondestructive eval anal, 77-78, MGR MAT TECHNOL, NUCLEAR TECHNOL DIV, WESTINGHOUSE ELEC CORP, 78- *Mem:* Am Inst Mining, Metall & Petrol Engrs; Am Soc Metals; Welding Res Coun. *Res:* Internal friction in ferrous alloys; strain ageing; precipitation in ferrous base alloys; deep drawing; fatigue; nuclear pressure vessel materials; nondestructive examination; welding; stainless steel corrosion; fracture mechanics. *Mailing Add:* Westinghouse Elec Corp Box 855 Pittsburgh PA 15230

ENRIGHT, JAMES THOMAS, b Baker, Ore, Nov 23, 32. ZOOLOGY. *Educ:* Univ Calif, Los Angeles, AB, 57, MA, 59, PhD(zool), 61. *Prof Exp:* NSF fel, Max-Planck-Inst Physiol of Behav, Ger, 61-63; asst prof zool, Univ Calif, Los Angeles, 63-66; from asst prof to assoc prof oceanog, 66-73, PROF BEHAV PHYSIOL, UNIV CALIF, SAN DIEGO, 73- *Mem:* AAAS. *Res:* Behavioral physiology; biological rhythms; orientation; photoperiodism; marine ecology. *Mailing Add:* Dept of Oceanog A-002 Univ of Calif at San Diego La Jolla CA 92093

ENROTH-CUGELL, CHRISTINA, b Helsingfors, Finland, Aug 27, 19; US citizen; m 55. VISION, NEUROPHYSIOLOGY. *Educ:* Karolinska Inst, Sweden, Med lic, 48, Med dr(neurophysiol of vision), 52, Ophthal Specialist Cert, 57. *Prof Exp:* Resident ophthal, Sabbatsberg Hosp, Stockholm, Sweden, 48-49; res fel, Karolinska Inst, Sweden, 50-53, resident, Karolinska Hosp, 53 & 54-56; from asst prof to assoc prof physiol & biol sci, 62-72, assoc prof biol & elec eng, 72-74, PROF BIOL & ELEC ENG, NORTHWESTERN UNIV, EVANSTON, 74- *Concurrent Pos:* NIH res fel biol, Harvard Univ, 53-54; NIH spec trainee, Med Sch, Northwestern Univ, 58-61 & career develop award, 62- *Mem:* Am Physiol Soc; assoc mem Physiol Soc UK. *Res:* Visual physiology, particularly retinal neurophysiology. *Mailing Add:* Bio-Med Eng Ctr Northwestern Univ Technol Inst Evanston IL 60201

ENSIGN, PAUL ROSELLE, b Shantung, China, Aug 27, 06; US citizen; m 39; c 1. PUBLIC HEALTH, PEDIATRICS. *Educ:* Univ Kans, BA, 27; Northwestern Univ, MD, 36; Johns Hopkins Univ, MPH, 42. *Prof Exp:* Pediat consult, Ga State Health Dept, 43-45; div dir maternal & child health, Kans State Bd Health, 45-50, dept state health officer, 50-51; div dir maternal & child health, Mont State Health Dept, 51-55, dep state health officer, 55-57; health officer, City-Co Health Dept, Great Falls, 57-62; dir div ment health, Utah State Health Dept, 62-64; field consult, Ford Found, 64-69; DIR PREV DIS & ENVIRON HEALTH, ACTG STATE DIR HEALTH & DIR CHILD HEALTH, UTAH STATE DIV HEALTH, 69- *Concurrent Pos:* Assoc prof prev med & instr pediat, Univ Kans, 46-51; assoc prof prev med, Univ Utah, 62-64; consult health & family planning, Govt of India, 64-; pres, Asn State Maternal & Child Health Dirs, 54; NIMH grant community ment health, Great Falls, Mont, 60-65. *Mem:* Am Pub Health Asn. *Res:* Maternal and child health, particularly nutrition, prevention of otitis media in Indian children; mental health and hospital nursery infections. *Mailing Add:* 4725 Bron Breck St Salt Lake City UT 84117

ENSIGN, RONALD D, b Cameron, Mo, Apr 10, 22; m 47; c 2. AGRONOMY, CROP BREEDING. *Educ:* Northwestern Mo State Col, BS, 47; Colo State Univ, MS, 49; Cornell Univ, PhD(plant breeding), 52. *Prof Exp:* Asst agron, Colo State Univ, 47-49; asst plant breeding, Cornell Univ, 49-52; supt, 52-55, assoc dir, Agr Exp Sta, 55-71, PROF PLANT SCI, AGR EXP STA, UNIV IDAHO, 71- *Mem:* Am Soc Agron; AAAS; Sigma Xi. *Res:* Improvement of biological performance of Idaho fescue, Kentucky bluegrass and white clover by various plant breeding techniques; studies of various cultural treatments in production of Kentucky bluegrass seed; cultural treatments in turf production. *Mailing Add:* Dept of Plant & Soil Sci Univ of Idaho Moscow ID 83843

ENSIGN, STEWART ELLERY, b Waterloo, Iowa, Nov 25, 25; m 46; c 3. GENETICS. *Educ:* Bob Jones Univ, BA, 50; Univ Wyo, MS, 54; Univ Nebr, PhD(genetics), 59. *Prof Exp:* Instr biol, Bob Jones Univ, 52-55; res fel, Yale Univ, 59-61 & Univ Calif, San Diego, 61-63; asst prof, 63-70, PROF BIOL, WESTMONT COL, 70-, CHMN DEPT, 73- *Mem:* AAAS; Am Sci Affil; Genetics Soc Am; Asn Am Med Cols. *Res:* Reproductive isolation in the Affinis Subgroup of the genus Drosophila; gene-enzyme relations in the tryptophan synthetase system of Neurospora crassa; production of ovarian proteins in Blattella germanica. *Mailing Add:* Dept of Biol Westmont Col 955 La Paz Rd Santa Barbara CA 93103

ENSIGN, THOMAS CHARLES, b Minneapolis, Minn, Mar 6, 41; m 62; c 3. SOLID STATE PHYSICS. *Educ:* Macalester Col, BA, 63; Univ Wyo, MS, 65, PhD(physics), 68. *Prof Exp:* Lab asst physics, Macalester Col, 60-63; teaching asst, Univ Wyo, 63-64, res asst, 64-65, teaching asst, 65-66; Nat Res Coun res assoc, Nat Bur Standards, 68-69; sr res scientist, Res Inst Advan Studies, Martin Marietta Corp, 69-74; res specialist, Cent Res Labs, 74-78, LAB MGR, SOLID STATE PROCESS DEVELOP, 3M, 78- *Mem:* Am Phys Soc. *Res:* Solid state physics; microelectronics; lasers; thin films. *Mailing Add:* Process Technol Lab Cent Res 208-1 3M Ctr St Paul MN 55144

ENSINCK, JOHN WILLIAM, b Montreal, Que, Feb 19, 31; m 60; c 1. ENDOCRINOLOGY. *Educ:* McGill Univ, BSc, 52, MD, 56. *Prof Exp:* Resident med, Royal Victoria Hosp, 56-58; res assoc & asst physician, Rockefeller Inst, 58-60; asst med, Sch Med, Univ Wash, 60-61, instr & asst dir, Clin Res Ctr, Univ Hosp, 61-62; vis lectr, dept med, Univ Newcastle, 62-64; asst dir, Clin Res Ctr, Univ Hosp, 64-72, from asst prof to assoc prof med, Sch Med, 64-72, PROF MED, SCH MED, UNIV WASH, 72-, DIR CLIN RES CTR, UNIV HOSP, 72-, PROG DIR, 70- *Mem:* AAAS; Am Diabetes Asn; Am Fedn Clin Res; Am Soc Clin Invest; Endocrine Soc. *Res:* Endocrinological investigation with application of protein chemistry in relationship of insulin to carbohydrate metabolism. *Mailing Add:* Clin Res Ctr Univ of Wash Hosp Seattle WA 98195

ENSLEY, HARRY EUGENE, b Charleston, SC, Aug 18, 45; m 66; c 2. ORGANIC CHEMISTRY. *Educ:* Vanderbilt Univ, BS, 70; Harvard Univ, PhD(chem), 75. *Prof Exp:* asst prof, 75-80, ASSOC PROF, DEPT CHEM, TULANE UNIV, 81- *Mem:* AAAS; Am Chem Soc; Sigma Xi. *Res:* Mechanism of reactions of singlet oxygen; synthesis of natural products and the development of new synthetic methodology. *Mailing Add:* Dept Chem Tulane Univ New Orleans LA 70118

ENSMINGER, DALE, b Mt Perry, Ohio, Sept 26, 23; m 48; c 6. ULTRASONICS. *Educ:* Ohio State Univ, BME, 50, BEE, 50. *Prof Exp:* Res engr ultrasonics, 50-70, sr elec engr, 70-78, sr res scientist, 78-81, MGR ULTRASONICS RES PROGS, BATTELLE MEM INST, 81- *Mem:* Acoustical Soc Am; Soc Nondestructive Testing. *Res:* Low and high intensity applications of ultrasonics; all applications of ultrasonics. *Mailing Add:* Columbus Labs Battelle Mem Inst 505 King Ave Columbus OH 43201

ENSMINGER, LEONARD ELROY, b Stover, Mo, Sept 25, 12; m 41; c 1. AGRONOMY. *Educ:* Univ Mo, BS, 35; Univ Ill, PhD(soil chem), 40. *Prof Exp:* Asst prof agr chem, Univ Idaho, 39-42; soil chemist, Exp Sta, Univ Fla, 42-44; assoc prof, 44-53, prof, 53-79, head, Dept Agron & Soils, 66-79, EMER PROF AGRON, AUBURN UNIV, 79- *Mem:* Fel Am Soc Agron. *Res:* Factors affecting the availability to plants of native and added phosphorus in soils; identification of clay minerals in soils; sulfur in relation to soil fertility. *Mailing Add:* Dept of Agron & Soils Auburn Univ Auburn AL 36830

ENSMINGER, MARION EUGENE, b Stover, Mo, May 28, 08; m 41; c 1. ANIMAL SCIENCE. *Educ:* Univ Mo, BS, 31, MS, 32; Univ Minn, PhD(animal sci), 41. *Prof Exp:* Asst to supt, US Soil Erosion Sta, 33; soil erosion specialist, US Dept Interior & USDA, Ill, 34; mgr, Dixon Springs Proj, USDA, 34-37; asst prof, Univ Mass, 37-40; teaching asst, Univ Minn, 40-41; prof animal husb & chmn dept, Wash State Univ, 41-62; AGR CONSULT, 62- *Concurrent Pos:* Distinguished prof, Univ Wis-River Falls, 63-; adj prof, Univ Ariz & Calif State Univ, Fresno, 72-; consult, Gen Elec Co; collabr, USDA; mem bd dirs, Am Nat Bank, 73-; pres, Agriserv Found. *Mem:* Fel AAAS; Am Genetic Asn; Am Soc Range Mgt; Am Soc Animal Sci (vpres, 57-58, pres, 58-59); Am Soc Agr Consult (pres, 63-64). *Res:* Animal nutrition; breeding and livestock production. *Mailing Add:* Agriserv Found 648 W Sierra Ave Clovis CA 93612

ENSOR, DAVID SAMUEL, b Spokane, Wash, Aug 22, 41; m 70. AIR POLLUTION. *Educ:* Wash State Univ, BS, 63; Univ Wash, MS, 68, PhD(eng), 72. *Prof Exp:* Chem engr, E I du Pont de Nemours & Co, Inc, 63-65; res scientist aerosols, Meteorol Res Inc, 72-79; HEAD CENT TECHNOL RES, RES TRIANGLE INST, 79- *Concurrent Pos:* Adj prof chem eng, NC State Univ; air pollution special fel. *Mem:* Am Chem Soc; Air Pollution Control Asn; Am Optical Soc; Am Inst Chem Engrs; Sigma Xi. *Res:* Applied aerosol science; light scattering, particle size distribution and chemical composition measurement; control technology; chemical engineering; fabric filtration; economic analysis of gas cleaning equipment; plume opacity and visibility. *Mailing Add:* Energy & Eng Res DIv Res Triangle Inst POB 12194 Research Triangle Park NC 27709

ENSOR, PHYLLIS GAIL, b Baltimore, Md, Nov 11, 38. COMMUNITY HEALTH, MEDICAL ADMINISTRATION. *Educ:* Taylor Univ, BA, 61; Univ Md, MA, 68; NY Univ, PhD(community health), 77. *Prof Exp:* Dir health educ, Nat Found-March Dimes, White Plains, NY, 69-73; ASSOC PROF COMMUNITY HEALTH, TOWSON STATE UNIV, 73- *Concurrent Pos:* Eval grant, Acad Dean's Off, Towson State Univ, 78. *Mem:* Soc Pub Health Educ; Am Pub Health Asn. *Res:* Alcoholism, relationship of drinking patterns husbands, wives and socioeconomic status research in progress. *Mailing Add:* Dept of Health Sci Towson State Univ Baltimore MD 21204

ENSSLIN, NORBERT, nuclear physics, see previous edition

ENSTROM, JAMES EUGENE, b Alhambra, Calif, June 20, 43; m 78. EPIDEMIOLOGY, PHYSICS. *Educ:* Harvey Mudd Col, BS, 65; Stanford Univ, MS, 67, PhD(physics), 70; Univ Calif, Los Angeles, MPH, 76. *Prof Exp:* Res assoc, Stanford Linear Accelerator Ctr, Stanford Univ, 70-71; res physicist & consult, Lawrence Berkeley Lab, Univ Calif, 71-75; C D Rogers cancer res fel, 73-75, Nat Cancer Inst fel, 75-76, cancer epidemiol researcher, 76-81, ASSOC RES PROF, SCH PUB HEALTH, UNIV CALIF, LOS ANGELES, 81-; PROG DIR CANCER CONTROL EPIDEMIOL, JONSSON COMPREHENSIVE CANCER CTR, 78- *Concurrent Pos:* Consult physicist, Rand Corp, Santa Monica, Calif, 69-73 & R & D Assocs, Marina Del Ray, 71-75; consult epidemiologist, Linus Pauling Inst Sci & Med, 76- *Honors & Awards:* Preventive Oncology Academic Award, Nat Cancer Inst, 81- *Mem:* AAAS; Am Pub Health Asn; Am Phys Soc; Soc Epidemiol Res; Am Heart Asn. *Res:* Epidemiology of cancer and other diseases, especially among low-risk populations such as Mormons; experimental nuclear particle physics; applied atomic and fluid physics. *Mailing Add:* Sch of Pub Health Univ Calif Los Angeles CA 90024

ENSTROM, RONALD EDWARD, b New York, NY, Mar 22, 35; m 58; c 2. MATERIALS SCIENCE, SOLID STATE PHYSICS. *Educ:* Mass Inst Technol, SB, 57, SM, 62, ScD, 63. *Prof Exp:* Asst metall, metals res lab, Union Carbide Corp, 57-58; mat engr, Nuclear Metals, Inc, Div, Textron, Inc, 58-60; asst metall, Mass Inst Technol, 60-63; MEM TECH STAFF, DAVID SARNOFF RES CTR, RCA CORP, 63- *Concurrent Pos:* Vis scientist, Swiss Fed Inst Technol, 73-74. *Honors & Awards:* David Sarnoff Outstanding Achievement Award, RCA Corp, 67. *Mem:* Electrochem Soc; Am Phys Soc; Am Inst Mining, Metall & Petrol Engrs; sr mem Inst Elec & Electronics Engrs; Am Soc Crystal Growth. *Res:* Preparation and properties of superconducting materials; vapor phase synthesis and characterization of III-V compounds for microwave, power and opto-electronic applications; finite element modeling; high conductivity polyacetylenes; glass and plastics technology. *Mailing Add:* RCA Labs Princeton NJ 08540

ENTERLINE, HORATIO THEODORE, b Ashland, Pa, Oct 16, 19; m 41; c 3. PATHOLOGY. *Educ:* Univ Mich, BS, 41; Univ Pa, MD, 44. *Prof Exp:* Assoc surg path, 52-54, from asst prof to assoc prof path, 54-64, PROF PATH, SCH MED, UNIV PA, 64-, DIR DIV SURG PATH, 80- *Concurrent Pos:* Consult, Children's Hosp, US Naval Hosp, Philadelphia. *Mem:* Am Soc Clin Path; Col Am Path; Am Soc Cytol; NY Acad Sci; Int Acad Path. *Res:* Neoplasm motility of neoplastic cells; histologic and clinical aspects of various neoplasms; surgical pathology. *Mailing Add:* Dept of Path Div of Path Anat Hosp Univ Pa Philadelphia PA 19104

ENTIN, MARTIN A, b Simferopole, Crimea, Oct 19, 12; Can citizen; m; c 3. PLASTIC SURGERY, RECONSTRUCTIVE SURGERY. *Educ:* Temple Univ, BA, 41; McGill Univ, MSc, 42, MD & CM, 45. *Prof Exp:* Resident surg, Montreal Gen, Royal Victoria & Montreal Children's Hosps, 46-49; clin asst plastic surg, Royal Victoria Hosp, 50-55; asst lectr, McGill Univ, 57-62, asst prof, 64-71; asst surgeon, Royal Victoria Hosp, 63-70, actg surgeon-in-chief, Sub-Dept Plastic Surg, 70-71, surgeon-in-chg, Subdept plastic surg, 71-77, SR SURGEON, DEPT SURG, ROYAL VICTORIA HOSP, 77-; ASSOC PROF SURG, MCGILL UNIV, 71- *Concurrent Pos:* Chmn, Plastic Surg Res Coun, 59; Nat Res Coun Can fel, McGill Univ, 46-47, Med Res Coun Exp Work & Nat Res Coun grants, 58-65; Nat Res Coun Can res fel surg hand, Stanford Univ Hosp, 49-50; Defense Res Bd Can grants, 51-54. *Mem:* Am Soc Plastic & Reconstruct Surg; fel Am Col Surg; Am Soc Surg of Hand (vpres, 71, pres-elect, 72-73, pres, 73-74); Can Soc Plastic Surg; Brit Asn Plastic Surg. *Res:* Experimental and clinical investigation and reconstruction of congenital anomalies of upper extremities; experimental production of rheumatoid arthritis; wound healing evolve toward pathogenesis of thermal injury; investigation of feasibility of autogenous whole joint transplantation. *Mailing Add:* 1538 Sherbrooke St W Montreal PQ H3A 2T5 Can

ENTMAN, MARK LAWRENCE, b New York, NY, Dec 24, 38; m 68; c 2. CELL PHYSIOLOGY. *Educ:* Duke Univ, MD, 63. *Prof Exp:* Res fel cardiol, Med Ctr, Duke Univ, 62-63; intern osler serv, Johns Hopkins Hosp, Baltimore, 63-64; fel, Med Ctr, Duke Univ, 64-65, fel, Res Training Prog, 65-66, from asst resident to assoc, 67-68; res physician & actg chief muscle metab, Armed Forces Inst Path, 68-70; asst prof med & myocardial biol, Baylor Col Med, 70-73, asst prof cell biophys, 72-73, from assoc prof to prof med & cell biophys, 73-77; investr cardiol & biophys, Howard Hughes Med Inst, 72-78; PROF & CHIEF SECT CARDIOVASC SCI, DEPT MED, BAYLOR COL MED, 77-, DIR DIV RES, NHLBI RES & DEMONSTRATION CTR, 77- *Concurrent Pos:* Mem, Pharmacol Study Sect, Div Res Grants, NIH, 75-; mem, Vet Admin Career Develop Prog, 76- *Honors & Awards:* Young Investr Award, Am Col Cardiol, 67. *Mem:* Am Soc Pharmacol & Exp Therapeut; Am Fedn Clin Res; Int Soc Heart Res; Biophys Soc; Am Heart Asn. *Res:* Cardiac and skeletal muscle cell biology, in particular, the role of ion flux, sarcoplasmic reticulum, glycogenolysis and microtubules in excitation-contraction coupling and its link to energy metabolism; basic mechanisms of myocardial ischemic damage. *Mailing Add:* Baylor Col Med 6516 Bertner Dr Houston TX 77030

ENTNER, NATHAN, b Philadelphia, Pa, Oct 1, 20; m 47; c 2. BIOCHEMISTRY. *Educ:* Univ Calif, Los Angeles, BA, 46, MA, 48; Univ Calif, PhD, 52. *Prof Exp:* Res assoc pharmacol, Sch Med, Univ Calif, 52-54 & Sch Med, La State Univ, 54-55; from asst prof to assoc prof prev med, 56-76, ADJ PROF PARASITOL, SCH MED, NY UNIV, 76- *Mem:* Am Soc Microbiol; Am Soc Biol Chem; Soc Trop Med & Hyg; Soc Protozool. *Res:* Biochemical bases of life processes; biochemical processes in the developmental stages of parasites. *Mailing Add:* Dept of Prev Med NY Univ Sch of Med New York NY 10016

ENTREKIN, DURWARD NEAL, b Ga, Nov 25, 26; m 54. PHARMACY. *Educ:* Univ Ga, BS, 50; Univ Fla, MS, 51, PhD(pharm), 53. *Prof Exp:* Res assoc pharm, E R Squibb & Sons, 53-57; from asst prof to assoc prof, 57-65, PROF PHARM, SCH PHARM, UNIV GA, 65-, ASSOC DEAN, 68- *Mem:* Am Pharmaceut Asn. *Res:* Use of imitation flavors for masking distasteful drugs. *Mailing Add:* Sch of Pharm Univ of Ga Athens GA 30602

ENTRINGER, ROGER CHARLES, b Iowa City, Iowa, May 17, 31; m 55; c 4. COMBINATORICS & FINITE MATHEMATICS. *Educ:* Univ Iowa, BS, 52; Univ NMex, MS, 57, PhD(math), 63. *Prof Exp:* From instr to assoc prof, 58-74, PROF MATH, UNIV NMEX, 74- *Mem:* Am Math Soc; Math Asn Am; Soc Indust Appl Math. *Res:* Graph and combinatorial theory. *Mailing Add:* Dept of Math Univ of NMex Albuquerque NM 87131

ENY, DESIRE M(ARC), b Algiers, France, Feb 8, 15; nat US; m 44; c 2. ENVIRONMENT, PUBLIC WORKS. *Educ:* Univ Algiers, BS, 35; Breguet Inst, Paris, MSE, 38; Cornell Univ, PhD(chem, physiol), 48. *Prof Exp:* Mgr electrochem dept, Precision Metal Prod Co, 40-43; res assoc, Univ Calif, 44-46; prof, Univ Fla, 48-49; bio-engr, Firestone Tire & Rubber Co, 49-51; coordr for Latin Am, USDA, 51-53; chief biol warfare br, US Army Chem Ctr, Md, 53-54, chem biol & nuclear protection div, 54-57, dir chem, biol & nuclear protection directorate, 57-62; dir planning, US Naval Exp Sta, 62-63; mgr eng & prod div, chem group, Glidden Co, 63-66; environ opers div, Spindletop Ctr, Ky, 66-67; pres, D Marc Eny Assocs, 67-82; CONSULT WATER & POLLUTION CONTROL, 82- *Concurrent Pos:* Consult, Army Res Off & Off Civil Defense & Mobilization, 56-63, States of KY & Md, US Econ Develop Admin, 66-68, City of Baltimore, 68-71 & US Small Bus Admin, 68-74; mem, State of Ky Sci Comn, 66-68; tech adv, Baltimore Harbor Pollution Comt, 68-; chmn, Harford County Environ Comt, 71-73. *Honors & Awards:* Commendation, US Small Bus Admin, 70; Wisdom Award, 70. *Mem:* Fel Am Inst Chemists; Am Soc Civil Engrs; Am Inst Chem Engrs; Inst Elec & Electronics Engrs; Am Water Works Asn. *Res:* Environmental engineering; water; waste-water; air; solid waste studies; design; master-plans. *Mailing Add:* PO Box 244 Kingsville MD 21087

ENZ, JOHN WALTER, US citizen. AGRICULTURAL CLIMATOLOGY, MICROCLIMATOLOGY. *Educ:* Univ Wis-Stevens Point, BS, 68; Univ Minn, MS, 71, PhD(soil sci), 76. *Prof Exp:* Res asst soil sci, Univ Minn, 69-76; res assoc, 76-77; ASST PROF SOILS, NDAK STATE UNIV, 77- *Mem:* Am Meterol Soc; Am Soc Agron; Sigma Xi. *Res:* Meso and micro climatology and meteorology; solar radiation and energy budget studies; crop or yield modeling. *Mailing Add:* Dept of Soils NDak State Univ Fargo ND 58105

ENZER, NORBERT BEVERLEY, b Milwaukee, Wis, Nov 26, 30; m 56; c 3. CHILD PSYCHIATRY, PEDIATRICS. *Educ:* Yale Univ, BA, 52; McGill Univ, MD, 56. *Prof Exp:* Intern pediat, Med Ctr, Duke Univ, 56-57, resident, 57-58 & 60-61, resident psychiat, 61-64, asst prof psychiat & assoc pediat, 65-68; from assoc prof to prof psychiat & pediat, Sch Med, Univ New Orleans, 68-73, head dept psychiat & biobehav sci, 71-73; chmn dept psychiat, 73-81, PROF PSYCHIAT, COL MED, MICH STATE UNIV, 73-, ASSOC DEAN ACAD AFFAIRS, COL HUMAN MED, 81- *Concurrent Pos:* Fel child psychiat, Duke Univ, 63-65. *Mem:* Am Acad Pediat; Am Psychiat Asn; Am Acad Child Psychiat; Soc Res Child Develop. *Res:* Child psychiatry and development. *Mailing Add:* Dept of Psychiat Mich State Univ Col of Med East Lansing MI 48824

ENZINGER, FRANZ MICHAEL, b Rohrbach, Austria, Feb 17, 23; US citizen; m 62; c 1. PATHOLOGY. *Educ:* Innsbruck Univ, MD, 50. *Prof Exp:* Asst anat & histol, Innsbruck Univ, 50-51, asst forensic med, 53-54; intern, Westchester Hosp, Mt Kisco, NY, 51-52; resident & instr path, Univ Iowa, 52-53, 54-57; assoc pathologist, 57-59, CHIEF SOFT TISSUE DIV, ARMED FORCES INST PATH, 60- *Concurrent Pos:* Chief, Int Ctr Soft Tissue Tumors, WHO; clin prof path, Uniformed Serv Univ, Bethesda, MD. *Mem:* Am Soc Clin Path; Int Acad Path. *Res:* Neoplastic diseases, especially soft tissue tumors; diagnostic pathology. *Mailing Add:* Armed Forces Inst of Path 6825 16th St Washington DC 20305

ENZMANN, ROBERT D, b Peking, China, Nov 5, 30; US citizen; m 58; c 6. GEOLOGY, ELECTRICAL ENGINEERING. *Educ:* Harvard Univ, AB, 49; Univ Witwatersrand, SAfrica, BS & MS, 53; Mass Inst Technol, PhD, 56; Uppsula, Swed, PhD, 78. *Prof Exp:* Consult geol & geophys mining co, Africa, Mediterranean Basin & Greenland, 50-57; consult, Radio Corp Am, 58-59, Convair rep & design specialist, 59-60, sr engr, Alaska & Greenland, 60-62; consult plans & projects, Avco Corp, 62-65; sr engr, Raytheon, 65-73; PRES, NORTHEAST UNIV, 72-; PROF, TRANSKEI INT UNIV, 80- *Concurrent Pos:* Asst, Mass Inst Technol, 54-55; res asst prof, Radiation Lab, Univ Mich, 62; asst prof, Northeastern Univ, 63-; asst prof, Univ Boston. *Mem:* Am Geophys Union; Am Inst Aeronaut & Astronaut; Geol Soc SAfrica; Swedish Geol Soc; fel NY Acad Sci. *Res:* Field geology; weapons systems design; space mission planning and planetology; use of instruments and engineering values in planetary orbital space, electrospheres, atmospheres, hydrospheres and endospheres. *Mailing Add:* 29 Adams St Lexington MA 02173

EOFF, KAY M, b Refugio, Tex, Sept 20, 32; m 65. PHYSICS. *Educ:* Tex Col Arts & Sci, BS, 53, MS, 55; Univ Fla, PhD(physics), 63. *Prof Exp:* Nuclear engr, Convair Div, Gen Dynamics Corp, 54-55; asst prof physics & astron, 56-77, asst prof phys sci, 77-80, ASST PROF PHYS SCI & GEOG, UNIV FLA, 80- *Mem:* Am Phys Soc. *Mailing Add:* Dept of Phys Sci Univ of Fla Gainesville FL 32611

EOLL, JOHN GORDON, astrophysics, see previous edition

EPAND, RICHARD MAYER, b New York, NY, Dec 31, 37; m 65; c 2. BIOPHYSICAL CHEMISTRY. *Educ:* Johns Hopkins Univ, AB, 59; Columbia Univ, PhD(biochem), 64. *Prof Exp:* Fel biophys chem, Cornell Univ, 65-68; vis scientist, Inst Biochem Res, Buenos Aires, Arg, 68-69; asst prof chem, Univ Guelph, 69-74; assoc prof, 74-78, PROF BIOCHEM, MCMASTER UNIV, 78- *Concurrent Pos:* vis prof molecular biochem & biophysics, Yale Univ, 80-81. *Mem:* Am Soc Biol Chemists; AAAS; Am Chem Soc; Can Biochem Soc. *Res:* Structure and mechanism of action of polypeptide hormones and their interaction with plasma membranes; organization of macromolecules in biological membranes. *Mailing Add:* Dept of Biochem McMaster Univ Health Sci Centre Hamilton ON L8N 3Z5 Can

EPEL, DAVID, b Detroit, Mich, Mar 26, 37; m 60; c 3. DEVELOPMENTAL BIOLOGY, CELL BIOLOGY. *Educ:* Wayne State Univ, AB, 58; Univ Calif, Berkeley, PhD(zool), 63. *Prof Exp:* Asst prof biol, Hopkins Marine Sta, Stanford Univ, 65-70; from assoc prof to prof marine biol, Univ Calif, San Diego, 70-77; PROF BIOL SCI, HOPKINS MARINE STA, STANFORD UNIV, 77- *Concurrent Pos:* Johnson Res Found fel, Sch Med, Univ Pa, 63-65; mem adv panel, Develop Biol Sect, NSF, 74-75; co-dir embryol, Marine Biol Lab, Woods Hole, 75-78; Guggenheim fel, 76-77; overseas fel, Churchill Col, Univ Cambridge, 76-77. *Mem:* Fel AAAS; Am Soc Cell Biol; Soc Develop Biol; Int Soc Develop Biol; Soc Gen Physiologists. *Res:* Cell biology; biochemistry of fertilization and early development; comparative embryology. *Mailing Add:* Hopkins Marine Sta Stanford Univ Pacific Grove CA 93950

EPEL, JOSEPH NORMAN, b Mich, Jan 27, 21; m 48; c 5. PHYSICAL CHEMISTRY. *Educ:* Wayne State Univ, BS, 43, PhD(phys chem), 51. *Prof Exp:* Rubber chemist, US Rubber Co, 41-45; chem consult & vpres, Hefco Labs, 45-49; pres, Duralastic Prods Co & Lamp Prod Co, 52-69; DIR PLASTIC RES & DEVELOP CTR, BUDD CO, 69- *Concurrent Pos:* Chem consult, Detroit Test Labs, 51- *Mem:* NY Acad Sci; Am Acad Sci; Soc Automotive Engrs; Nat Mat Adv Bd, Sigma Xi. *Res:* Molecular weight determination by light scattering measurements; reinforced plastics. *Mailing Add:* Budd Plastic Res & Develop Ctr 356 Executive Dr Troy MI 48084

EPHREMIDES, ANTHONY, b Athens, Greece, Sept 19, 43; US citizen; m 74. COMMUNICATION SYSTEMS, COMMUNICATION NETWORKS. *Educ:* Nat Tech Univ, Athens, BS, 67; Princeton Univ, MA, 69, PhD(elec eng), 71. *Prof Exp:* Res asst elec eng, Princeton Univ, 67-71; asst prof, 71-74, assoc prof, 74-81, PROF ELEC ENG, UNIV MD, 81- *Concurrent Pos:* Prin investr res grants, Univ Md, 71-; invited lectr, numerous int agencies & univs, 71-; consult, Naval Res Lab, 77-; ed, Transactions Automatic Control, Inst Elec & Electronics Engrs, 78-80; pres, Pontos Inc, 81- *Mem:* Inst Elec & Electronics Engrs; AAAS. *Res:* Statistical communications; computer communications. *Mailing Add:* Elec Eng Dept Univ Md College Park MD 20742

EPIFANIO, CHARLES EDWARD, b New York, NY, Aug 28, 44; m 66; c 2. MARINE BIOLOGY. *Educ:* Lafayette Col, AB, 66; Duke Univ, PhD(zool), 71. *Prof Exp:* asst prof, 71-81, ASSOC PROF MARINE STUDIES, UNIV DEL, 81- *Mem:* AAAS; Am Soc Zoologists; Nat Shellfisheries Asn. *Res:* Nutritional requirements of bivalve molluscs in maricultural systems; biology of marine invertebrate larvae. *Mailing Add:* Col Marine Studies Univ Del Lewes DE 19958

EPIS, RUDY CHARLES, b Bingham Canyon, Utah, Apr 25, 30; m 57; c 1. GEOLOGY. *Educ:* Univ Calif, Berkeley, AB, 52, PhD(geol), 56. *Prof Exp:* From instr to assoc prof, 56-69, PROF GEOL, COLO SCH MINES, 69- *Concurrent Pos:* Geologist, US Geol Surv, 65-72. *Mem:* AAAS; fel Geol Soc Am. *Res:* Structural and stratigraphic problems of southeastern Arizona; Cenozoic volcanism of southern Rocky Mountains; geological sciences; field geology; petrology; volcanology. *Mailing Add:* Dept of Geol Colo Sch of Mines Golden CO 80401

EPLER, JAMES L, b Lancaster, Pa, Aug 10, 37; m 75; c 5. GENETICS, BIOCHEMISTRY. *Educ:* Millersville State Col, BS, 59; Fla State Univ, MS, 62, PhD(zool), 63. *Prof Exp:* Instr radiation biol, Fla State Univ, 64; USPHS fel, 64-66, GENETICIST, BIOL DIV, OAK RIDGE NAT LAB, 66-; LECTR ZOOL ENTOM, UNIV TENN, 69-, SECT HEAD MUTAGENESIS, 80- *Mem:* Genetics Soc Am; Environ Mutagen Soc; AAAS. *Res:* Human genetics; chemical mutagenesis; nucleic acids. *Mailing Add:* Box Y Biol Div Oak Ridge Nat Lab Oak Ridge TN 37830

EPLEY, DONALD L, electrical engineering, see previous edition

EPLEY, RICHARD JESS, b Pana, Ill, Aug 31, 42. MEAT SCIENCE, FOOD SCIENCE. *Educ:* Univ Ill, Urbana, BS, 65; Univ Mo-Columbia, MS, 67, PhD(animal husb), 70. *Prof Exp:* Instr food sci, Univ Mo-Columbia, 69-70; assoc prof, 70-74, exten specialist, 74-80, PROF ANIMAL SCI, AGR EXTEN, UNIV MINN, ST PAUL, 80- *Mem:* AAAS; Am Soc Animal Sci; Am Meat Sci Asn; Inst Food Technologists. *Res:* Extension meat science. *Mailing Add:* Dept of Animal Sci Univ of Minn St Paul MN 55108

EPLING, GARY ARNOLD, b Elkhorn City, Ky, June 22, 45; m 66. PHYSICAL ORGANIC CHEMISTRY, PHOTOCHEMISTRY. *Educ:* Mass Inst Technol, SB, 67; Univ Wis, PhD(org chem), 72. *Prof Exp:* Res assoc chem, Yale Univ, 72-73; asst prof chem, Fordham Univ, 73-78; asst prof chem, 78-80, ASSOC PROF CHEM, UNIV CONN, 80- *Mem:* Am Chem Soc. *Res:* Mechanistic organic photochemistry and exploratory photochemistry of biologically important compounds; chemical reactions associated with phototoxicity; preparative organic electrochemistry. *Mailing Add:* Dept of Chem Univ of Conn Storrs CT 06268

EPP, CHIROLD DELAIN, b Fairview, Okla, Mar 31, 39; m 61; c 3. NUCLEAR PHYSICS. *Educ:* Northwestern State Col, Okla, BS, 61; Univ Okla, MS, 65; Univ Tex, Austin, PhD(physics), 69. *Prof Exp:* Instr physics, Northwestern State Col, Okla, 63-65; ASST PROF PHYSICS, MIDWESTERN UNIV, 69- *Mem:* Am Phys Soc; Am Asn Physics Teachers. *Res:* High pressure research on pressure, volume and temperature properties of argon to 10 kilobars; high energy nuclear physics with emphasis on quasi-free electron scattering from nuclei; physics teaching. *Mailing Add:* Dept of Physics Midwestern Univ Wichita Falls TX 76308

EPP, DONALD JAMES, b Hastings, Nebr, June 23, 39; m 61; c 2. AGRICULTURAL ECONOMICS, RESOURCE ECONOMICS. *Educ:* Univ Nebr, BS, 61; Mich State Univ, MS, 64, PhD(agr econ), 67. *Prof Exp:* Instr agr econ, Mich State Univ, 65-67; from asst prof to assoc prof, 67-81, PROF AGR ECON & ASST DIR, INST RES LAND & WATER RESOURCES, PA STATE UNIV, 81- *Concurrent Pos:* Consult, Govt Comt Preserv Agr Land, Pa, 68-69; US Congress, 78-79, US Army Corps of Engrs, 80. *Mem:* Am Agr Econ Asn; Am Econ Asn; Asn Environ & Resource Economists. *Res:* Economic aspects of environmental quality and resource policy, especially the effects of land use and water quality policies; interaction between economic growth and environmental quality; hazardous waste management. *Mailing Add:* Dept of Agr Econ & Rural Sociol Pa State Univ University Park PA 16802

EPP, EDWARD RUDOLPH, b Saskatoon, Sask, July 21, 29; m 57. MEDICAL PHYSICS, RADIATION PHYSICS. *Educ:* Univ Sask, BA, 50, MA, 52; McGill Univ, PhD(physics), 55; Am Bd Health Physics, dipl, 61. *Prof Exp:* Asst physics, Nat Res Coun Can, 52-53; physicist radiation physics, Dept Radiol, Montreal Gen Hosp, 55-57; asst biophys, Sloan-Kettering Div, Cornell Univ Med Col, 57-58, assoc, 58-60, from asst prof to prof biophysics, 60-74, chmn dept, 66-74, mem & chief div phys biol, Sloan-Kettering Inst Cancer Res, 68-74; HEAD DIV RADIATION BIOPHYSICS, DEPT RADIATION MED, MASS GEN HOSP, BOSTON & PROF RADIATION THERAPY, HARVARD MED SCH, 74- *Concurrent Pos:* Consult, Reddy Mem Hosp, 55-57 & Montreal Children's Hosp, 56-57; asst, Sloan-Kettering Inst Cancer Res, 57-60, assoc, 60-64, assoc mem, 64-68; mem task group, Int Comn Radiol Units & Measurements, 65-70; assoc attend physicist, Dept Med Physics, Mem Hosp for Cancer & Allied Dis, 67-74; mem radiation study sect, NIH, 71-75; mem ad hoc comt hot particles, Adv Comt Biol Effects Ionizing Radiations, Nat Acad Sci, 74-76 & comt review use ionizing radiations for treatment of benign dis, 75-77; mem, Clin Cancer Prog Proj Rev Comt, Nat Cancer Inst, 77-81; mem, Comt Dept Energy Res Health Effects Ionizing Radiation, Nat Acad Sci, 78-79, Comt Fed Res Biol & Health Effects Ionizing Radiation, 79-; assoc ed, Int J Radiation Oncol Biol Physics, 79- *Mem:* AAAS; Am Phys Soc; Health Physics Soc; Radiation Res Soc (secy-treas, 81-); Am Asn Physicists in Med. *Res:* Radiobiology, especially cellular radiobiology; biophysics; health physics; effects of ionizing radiation of ultra-high intensity on living cells. *Mailing Add:* Mass Gen Hosp Div Radiation Biophysics Boston MA 02114

EPP, LEONARD G, b Neptune, NJ, Aug 14, 44; m 69. DEVELOPMENTAL BIOLOGY. *Educ:* Gettysburg Col, BA, 66; Pa State Univ, MS, 68, PhD(zool), 70. *Prof Exp:* Asst prof, 70-77, ASSOC PROF BIOL, MT UNION COL, 77- *Concurrent Pos:* Vis scientist, Indiana Univ, 77 & 80 & Zool Inst, Univ Zurich, 78-79. *Mem:* AAAS; Soc Develop Biol; Am Soc Zoologists; Sigma Xi. *Res:* Biology of hydra; development of pigmentation in amphibia. *Mailing Add:* Dept of Biol Mt Union Col Alliance OH 44601

EPP, MELVIN DAVID, b Newton, Kans, June 16, 42; m 64; c 2. PLANT TISSUE CULTURE, MUTATION BREEDING. *Educ:* Wheaton Col, BS, 64; Univ Conn, MS, 67; Cornell Univ, PhD(genetics), 72. *Prof Exp:* Damon Runyan fel, Brookhaven Nat Lab, 72-74; sr res biologist, Monsanto Co, 74-77; res supt, 77-82, MGR, PHILIPPINE PACKING CORP, DEL MONTE CORP, 82- *Mem:* Bot Soc Am; Genetics Soc Am; AAAS; Int Plant Tissue Cult Soc. *Res:* Genetic modification and selection of plant cells with improved usefulness, for example, disease resistance, increased yield, and nematode resistance by using tissue culture, mutation breeding and rapid propagation in culture. *Mailing Add:* PO Box 36 San Leandro CA 94577

EPPENSTEIN, WALTER, b Berlin, Ger, Dec 14, 20; nat US; m 44; c 3. EXPERIMENTAL PHYSICS. *Educ:* Robert Col, Istanbul, BS, 42; Rensselaer Polytech Inst, MS, 52. *Prof Exp:* Instr physics, Robert Col, Istanbul, 42-46; from instr to assoc prof, 46-73, exec officer, 69-81, PROF PHYSICS, RENSSELAER POLYTECH INST, 73-, ASSOC CHMN, 81- *Concurrent Pos:* Hon res assoc, Harvard Univ, 64-65. *Mem:* Am Soc Eng Educ; Am Asn Physics Teachers. *Res:* Educational developments in physics including new demonstration and laboratory experiments; uses of microcomputers and microprocessors. *Mailing Add:* Dept of Physics Rensselaer Polytech Inst Troy NY 12181

EPPERSON, EDWARD ROY, b Burnsville, Miss, Oct 14, 32; m 60; c 2. INORGANIC CHEMISTRY. *Educ:* Millsaps Col, BS, 54; Univ NC, MA, 57; Univ of the Pac, PhD, 65. *Prof Exp:* From asst prof to prof chem, Elon Col, 57-66; PROF CHEM & HEAD DEPT PHYS SCI, HIGH POINT COL, 66- *Concurrent Pos:* NSF fac fel, 64-65. *Mem:* Am Chem Soc. *Res:* Synthesis of the anhydrous metal halides; lower oxidation states of molybdenum and tungsten. *Mailing Add:* Dept Chem High Point Col High Point NC 27262

EPPINK, RICHARD THEODORE, b Cleveland, Ohio, May 7, 31; m 75; c 2. STRUCTURAL ENGINEERING, APPLIED MECHANICS. *Educ:* Case Inst Technol, BS, 53; Univ Ill, MS, 56, PhD(civil eng), 60. *Prof Exp:* Struct engr, Glenn L Martin Co, 53; instr, Univ Ill, 59-60; mem tech staff, Nat Eng Sci Co, 60-62; MEM FAC CIVIL ENG, UNIV VA, 62- *Mem:* Am Soc Civil Engrs. *Res:* Structural dynamics and vibrations; blast effects of nuclear weapons; application and accuracy of finite element methods in structural analysis; numerical methods of structural analysis; stress analysis of aortic heart valves. *Mailing Add:* Dept of Civil Eng Univ of Va Charlottesville VA 22903

EPPLE, AUGUST WILHELM, comparative endocrinology, see previous edition

EPPLER, RICHARD A, b Lynn, Mass, Apr 30, 34; m 59; c 5. CERAMICS, INORGANIC CHEMISTRY. *Educ:* Carnegie-Mellon Univ, BS, 56; Univ Ill, MS, 58, PhD(chem eng & physics), 60. *Prof Exp:* Res chemist, Corning Glass Works, 59-65; SR SCIENTIST, PEMCO CERAMICS GROUP, MOBAY CHEM CORP, 65- *Concurrent Pos:* Instr math, Elmira Col, 64. *Honors & Awards:* Dwight Joyce Award, SCM Corp, 67; John Marquis Award, Am Ceramic Soc, 74. *Mem:* Fel Am Ceramic Soc; Nat Soc Prof Engrs; Am Chem Soc; Electrochem Soc; Sigma Xi. *Res:* Crystallization phenomena, particularly from vitreous media; glass; glass-ceramics; glaze and enamel compositions and properties; solid state chemistry, reaction kinetics; high pressure research on solid materials; inorganic pigments; luminescent and photochromic materials. *Mailing Add:* Pemco Ceramics Group Mobay Chem Corp 5601 Eastern Ave Baltimore MD 21224

EPPLEY, RICHARD WAYNE, b Puyallup, Wash, Oct 12, 31; m 53; c 2. BIOLOGICAL OCEANOGRAPHY. *Educ:* State Col Wash, BS, 53; Stanford Univ, PhD(biol), 57. *Prof Exp:* From instr to asst prof biol, Univ Southern Calif, 57-60; plant physiologist, Northrop Corp, 60-63; assoc res biologist, 63-70, LECTR & RES BIOLOGIST, SCRIPPS INST OCEANOG, UNIV CALIF, SAN DIEGO, 70-, ASSOC DIR, INST MARINE RESOURCES, 75- *Concurrent Pos:* Adj assoc prof biol, Univ Southern Calif, 61-63; consult, NSF, 70-74; marine biologist, US AEC, 72-73. *Honors & Awards:* Darbaker Prize Phycol, Bot Soc Am, 71. *Mem:* Am Soc Limnol & Oceanog (pres, 81); fel AAAS; Am Soc Plant Physiol; Phycol Soc Am. *Res:* Physiology of marine phytoplankton. *Mailing Add:* Scripps Inst of Oceanog Univ of Calif at San Diego La Jolla CA 92093

EPPLING, FREDERIC JOHN, b Sheboygan, Wis, Mar 16, 20; m 47; c 4. NUCLEAR PHYSICS. *Educ:* Univ Wis, PhB & PhM, 42, PhD(physics), 53. *Prof Exp:* Mem res staff nuclear physics, Lab Nuclear Sci, 53-58, RES PHYSICIST & LECTR, LAB NUCLEAR SCI, MASS INST TECHNOL, 58-, ASSOC DIR, 64- *Concurrent Pos:* Exec officer, Mass Inst Technol, 62-64. *Mem:* Am Phys Soc. *Res:* Study of energy levels of light nuclei; construction of electrostatic generators for nuclear research; mass spectroscopy. *Mailing Add:* Lab Nuclear Sci Rm 26-505 Mass Inst Technol 77 Massachusetts Ave Lincoln MA 01773

EPPRIGHT, MARGARET, b Manor, Tex, Apr 21, 13. BIOCHEMISTRY, NUTRITION. *Educ:* Univ Tex, BA, 33, MA, 35, PhD(chem), 45. *Prof Exp:* Instr, Pub Sch, Tex, 36-40; asst, Univ Tex, 41-44; assoc prof chem, Sam Houston State Col, 45-46; assoc prof nutrit & res assoc, Iowa State Univ, 46-48; prof chem & head dept, Sam Houston State Col, 48-49; assoc prof home econ, 49-54, head div nutrit, 54-64, chmn dept home econ, 61-71, PROF HOME ECON, UNIV TEX, AUSTIN, 54- *Mem:* Am Dietetic Asn; Am Chem Soc; fel Am Inst Chem; Am Home Econ Asn. *Res:* Synthesis of hydantoins; vitamin assay methods; nutritonal status of population groups; mineral nutrition of microorganisms; metabolic patterns in health and disease. *Mailing Add:* Dept Home Econ Univ Tex Austin TX 78712

EPPS, ANNA CHERRIE, b New Orleans, La, July 8, 30; m 68. IMMUNOLOGY. *Educ:* Howard Univ, BS, 51, PhD(zool), 66; Loyola Univ La, MS, 59. *Prof Exp:* Technologist, Clin Labs, Our Lady of Mercy Hosp, Cincinnati, Ohio, 53-54 & Clin Labs, Flint-Goodridge Hosp, New Orleans, 54-55; asst prof microbiol, Sch Med, Howard Univ, 61-69; USPHS fac fel & asst prof med, 69-71, assoc prof, 71-75, PROF MED, SCH MED, TULANE UNIV, 75-, DIR MED REP, MED CTR, 69-, ASST DEAN STUDENT SERV, 80- *Concurrent Pos:* Technologist, Clin Labs, Mercy Hosp, Hamilton, Ohio, 54 & Sch Med, La State Univ, 59-60; asst prof med technol & actg chmn dept, Xavier Univ La, 54-60. *Mem:* Am Soc Clin Pathologists; Am Soc Med Technologists; Am Soc Bacteriologists; Sigma Xi; Am Soc Trop Med & Hyg. *Res:* Immunological studies in autoimmune diseases; immunological embryology; transplantation immunology; hepatitis immunology. *Mailing Add:* Tulane Univ Med Ctr 1430 Tulane Ave New Orleans LA 70112

EPPS, HARLAND WARREN, b Hawthorne, Calif, July 29, 36; m 76; c 2. ASTRONOMY, OPTICAL DESIGN. *Educ:* Pomona Col, BA, 59; Univ Wis, MS, 61, PhD(astron), 64. *Prof Exp:* Asst prof astron, San Diego State Col, 64-65; from asst prof to assoc prof, 65-75, PROF ASTRON, UNIV CALIF, LOS ANGELES, 75- *Concurrent Pos:* Consult optical design. *Mem:* Int Astron Union; Am Astron Soc; Soc Photo-optical Instrumentation Engr. *Res:* Spectroscopy of peculiar stars and astronomical instrumentation; optical design; spectroscopy of planetary rebulae and quasi stellar sources. *Mailing Add:* Dept of Astron Univ of Calif Los Angeles CA 90024

EPPS, JON ALBERT, b Merced, Calif, April 27, 42; m 64; c 2. PAVEMENT MATERIALS, PAVEMENT DESIGN. *Educ:* Univ Calif, Berkeley, BS, 65, MS, 66, PhD(eng), 68. *Prof Exp:* Asst prof, Tex A&M Univ, 68; prog mgr, 75-81, HEAD, DIV II & MAT ENG DIV, TEX TRANSP INST, TEX A&M UNIV, 81- *Mem:* Am Soc Testing & Mat; Asn Asphalt Paving Technologists; Am Soc Civil Engrs; Nat Soc Prof Engrs. *Res:* Transportation materials and pavement rehabilitation maintenance design. *Mailing Add:* Dept Civil Eng Tex A&M Univ College Station TX 77843

EPPS, WILLIAM MONROE, b Latta, SC, Oct 31, 16; m 42; c 2. PLANT PATHOLOGY. *Educ:* Clemson Univ, BS, 37; Cornell Univ, PhD(plant path), 42. *Prof Exp:* Asst, NY State Col Agr, Cornell, 38-42; assoc plant pathologist, Exp Sta, Clemson Univ, 45-56, head dept bot & bact, 56-69, head dept plant path & physiol, 69-78; RETIRED. *Mem:* Am Phytopath Soc; Soc Nematologists. *Res:* Vegetable diseases and breeding. *Mailing Add:* 211 Wyatt Ave Clemson SC 29631

EPPSTEIN, DEBORAH ANNE, b Kalamazoo, Mich, Oct 16, 48; m 75. VIROLOGY, BIOCHEMISTRY. *Educ:* Grinnell Col, BA, 70; Univ Ark, PhD(biochem), 75. *Prof Exp:* NIH fel virol, Univ Calif, Santa Barbara, 76-78; staff researcher vaccine develop, 78-79, STAFF RESEARCHER, INST BIO-ORG CHEM, SYNTEX RES, 80- *Mem:* Am Soc Microbiol; Am Chem Soc; AAAS; NY Acad Sci. *Res:* Liposome delivery systems; mechanism of interferon action. *Mailing Add:* Syntex Res 3401 Hillview Palo Alto CA 94304

EPREMIAN, E(DWARD), b Schenectady, NY, Sept 3, 21; m 48; c 2. METALLURGY. *Educ:* Mass Inst Technol, BS, 43; Rensselaer Polytech Inst, MS, 47; Carnegie Inst Technol, DSc(metall), 51. *Prof Exp:* Res assoc metall, res lab, Gen Elec Co, 43-46; res assoc, metals res lab, Carnegie Inst Technol, 50-51; sci liaison officer, Off Naval Res, London Br, 51-52, asst sci dir, 52-53, dept sci dir, 53-54; chief metals & mat br, res div, Atomic Energy Comn, 54-57; sr metallurgist, res lab, metals div, Union Carbide Corp, 57-59, tech coordr, tech dept, 60-61, mgr, new prod mkt, 61-63, asst dir res, carbon prod div, 63-65, gen mgr, aerospace mat dept, 65-68, gen mgr, advan mat dept, 68-70, mgr tantalum & columbium prod, mining & metals div, 70-71, mgr, spec prod, 71-72, dir new ventures, 73-76; EXEC DIR, COMN SOCIOTECH SYSTS, NAT ACAD SCI, NAT RES COUN, 76- *Concurrent Pos:* Mem adv bd, Int Symposium High Temperature Technol, 56, 59 & 63; US sci secy, Atoms for Peace Conf, Geneva, 56; mem mat adv bd, Nat Acad Sci, chmn, refractory metals comt, 57-59, mem panel solid propellant rocket motors, 59-60 & mem comt standing rev of Dept Defense Mat Prog, 61-63; mem, adv comt, Univ Pa, Sch Metall & Mat Sci, 69-73; mem bd dir, Acta Metallurgica, 71-73; mem bd trustees, Webb Inst Naval Archit & Marine Eng, 76- *Mem:* Fel Am Soc Metals; Am Inst Mining, Metall & Petrol Engrs; fel AAAS; Sigma Xi. *Res:* Fatigue of metals; refractory metals; nuclear and high temperature metallurgy; physical chemistry; graphite technology. *Mailing Add:* Nat Res Coun 2101 Constitution Ave Washington DC 20418

EPSTEIN, ALAN NEIL, b New York, NY, July 29, 32; m 57; c 3. NEUROPSYCHOLOGY. *Educ:* Johns Hopkins Univ, BA & MA, 54, MD, 58. *Prof Exp:* Nat Found fel, Inst Neurol Sci, Sch Med, 58-61, asst prof zool, 61-64, assoc prof biol, 64-69, prof, 69-77, mem, Inst Neurol Sci, 63-80, PROF NEUROPSYCHOL, UNIV PA, 77- *Concurrent Pos:* Mem neuropsychol res rev comt, NIMH, 69-73, biol sci fel rev comt, 75-; NIMH spec fel, Col of France, Paris, 69-70; Overseas fel, Churchill Col, Univ Cambridge, 75-76. *Mem:* Fel Am Psychol Asn; AAAS; Soc Neurosci; Am Physiol Soc. *Res:* Neurological basis of behavior; feeding and drinking and the specific hungers; behavioral thermoregulation. *Mailing Add:* Leidy Lab Dept of Biol Univ of Pa Philadelphia PA 19174

EPSTEIN, ARTHUR JOSEPH, b Brooklyn, NY, June 2, 45; m 69; c 2. CONDUCTING POLYMERS, QUASI-ONE-DIMENSIONAL SYSTEMS. *Educ:* Polytech Inst Brooklyn, BS, 66; Univ Pa, MS, 67, PhD(physics), 71. *Prof Exp:* Tech staff technol assessment, Mitre Corp, 71-72; sr scientist, 72-80, PRIN SCIENTIST SOLID STATE PHYSICS, WEBSTER RES CTR, XEROX CORP, 80- *Concurrent Pos:* Mem organizing comt, Conf Synthesis & Properties Low-Dimensional Mats, NY Acad Sci, 77; vis physicist, Dept Physics & Mats Res Lab, Penn State Univ, 78, Dept Physics, Univ Md, 79 & City Col, City Univ New York, 80; vis scientist, Dept Physics, Univ Calif, Los Angeles Calif, 77, 78 & 79; guest scientist, Francis Bitter Nat Magnet Lab, Mass Inst Technol, Cambridge, 78; lectr, Advanced Study Inst Physics & Chem Low Dimensional Solids, Tomar, Portugal, 79; vis scientist, Lab Physique Solides, Univ Paris-Sud, Orsay, France, 80; co-chmn, Int Conf Low Dimensional Conductors, Boulder, Colo, 81; co-ed, Proceedings Int Conf Low-Dimensional Conductors, Molecular Crystals & Liquid Crystals. *Mem:* Fel Am Phys Soc. *Res:* Experimental and theoretical studies of charge transport mechanisms electronic structure, crystal binding and applications of anisotropic conducting molecular solids including conducting polymers and organic charge transfer salts. *Mailing Add:* Webster Res Ctr Xerox Corp 800 Phillips Rd Bldg 114 Webster NY 14580

EPSTEIN, ARTHUR WILLIAM, b New York, NY, May 15, 23; m 55; c 4. PSYCHIATRY, NEUROLOGY. *Educ:* Columbia Univ, AB, 44, MD, 47. *Prof Exp:* Intern, Mt Sinai Hosp, NY, 47-48; clin asst psychiat, State Hosp, Norristown, Pa, 48; resident neurol, Mt Sinai Hosp, NY, 49-50; asst, 50-52, instr psychiat & neurol, 52-54, asst prof neurol, 54-58, assoc prof psychiat & neurol, 58-64, PROF PSYCHIAT & NEUROL, SCH MED, TULANE UNIV, 64- *Mem:* AAAS; Am Acad Neurol; Soc Biol Psychiat (asst secy, 73-76, secy-treas, 76-79, pres, 81); Am Psychiat Asn; Am Epilepsy Soc. *Res:* Brain behavior relationships, epileptic and dream mechanisms. *Mailing Add:* 1430 Tulane Ave New Orleans LA 70112

EPSTEIN, AUBREY, b Detroit, Mich, June 4, 23; m 50; c 2. AUDIOLOGY, SPEECH PATHOLOGY. *Educ:* Ind Univ, BA, 46; Western Reserve Univ, MA, 47; Univ Iowa, PhD(speech path, audiol), 53. *Prof Exp:* From asst prof to assoc prof speech path & audiol, Univ Pittsburgh, 53-63; assoc prof speech path & audiol, 63-68, PROF AUDIOL, IND UNIV, BLOOMINGTON, 69- *Concurrent Pos:* Consult, Vet Admin, 55- *Mem:* Fel Am Speech & Hearing Asn; Acoust Soc Am; assoc fel Am Acad Ophthal & Otolaryngol. *Res:* Auditory phenomena relative to aural pathology. *Mailing Add:* Dept Speech & Hearing Sci Ind Univ Bloomington IN 47401

EPSTEIN, BARRY D, b New York, NY, Mar 30, 42; m 66, 81; c 2. ELECTROCHEMISTRY, ANALYTICAL CHEMISTRY. *Educ:* City Col New York, BS, 62; Univ Calif, Riverside, PhD(anal chem), 66. *Prof Exp:* Res fel chem, Calif Inst Technol, 66-67; staff scientist, 67-80, PRIN STAFF SCIENTIST, GEN ATOMIC CO, 80- *Honors & Awards:* Samuel Goldman Award, 62. *Mem:* Am Chem Soc; Electrochem Soc; Am Soc Testing & Mat. *Res:* Instrumentation; pollution analysis; batteries; biomaterials; nuclear fuels; fission product chemistry; gas chromatography. *Mailing Add:* 6954 Beloit Ave San Diego CA 92111

EPSTEIN, BENJAMIN, b Boston, Mass, Mar 5, 18; m 40; c 3. STATISTICS, OPERATIONS RESEARCH. *Educ:* Mass Inst Technol, BS, 37, MS, 38; Univ Ill, PhD(math), 41. *Prof Exp:* From asst to instr math, Univ Ill, 39-42; physicist & mathematician, Frankford Arsenal, 42-44; mem staff, Westinghouse Elec Corp, 44-45; mem staff, Coal Res Lab, Carnegie Inst Technol, 45-48, lectr math, 45-48; from assoc prof to prof, Wayne State Univ, 48-60; statist consult, 60-68; vis prof statist, 68-70, PROF STATIST, ISRAEL INST TECHNOL, 70-, HEAD, STATIST AREA, TECHNION, 73- *Concurrent Pos:* Vis prof, Stanford Univ, 55-56, 57-60 & Univ Calif, Berkeley, 65-66; NSF lectr prog vis lectr statist, 63-65. *Honors & Awards:* Electronics Div Award, Am Soc Qual Control, 75, Shewhart Medal, 75. *Mem:* Fel Am Soc Qual Control; Sigma Xi; fel AAAS; fel Inst Math Statist; fel Am Statist Asn. *Res:* Mathematical statistics and theory of probability, particularly as applied to science, engineering and biomedicine; stochastic processes; theory of extreme values; theory and application of extreme values; statistical theory for the analysis of incomplete life length data; stochastic reliability models; quantile and tail estimation. *Mailing Add:* Fac Indust & Mgt Eng Israel Inst Technol Haifa Israel 32448

EPSTEIN, BERNARD, b Harrison, NJ, Aug 10, 20; m 47; c 6. MATHEMATICS. *Educ:* NY Univ, BA, 40, MS, 42; Brown Univ, PhD(appl math), 47. *Prof Exp:* Jr physicist, Nat Bur Stand, Washington, DC, 41-43; from asst physicist to assoc physicist, Manhattan Proj, 43-45; asst div appl math & instr eng, Brown Univ, 45-46; res assoc aeronaut eng, Grad Sch, Harvard Univ, 46-47; from instr to assoc prof math, Univ Pa, 47-60; prof, Yeshiva Univ, 60-63; PROF MATH, UNIV NMEX, 63- *Concurrent Pos:* Vis res assoc inst math sci, NY Univ, 53; vis assoc prof, Stanford Univ, 57-58; liaison scientist, US Off Naval Res, London, Eng, 64-66; vis prof math, Israel Inst Technol, 71-72. *Mem:* Am Math Soc. *Res:* Study of motion of compressible fluid by hodograph method; conformal mapping; boundary value problems of potential theory; extremal problems relating to analytic functions. *Mailing Add:* Dept of Math Univ of NMex Albuquerque NM 87131

EPSTEIN, CHARLES JOSEPH, b Philadelphia, Pa, Sept 3, 33; m 56; c 4. MEDICAL GENETICS, DEVELOPMENTAL BIOLOGY. *Educ:* Harvard Univ, AB, 55, MD, 59. *Prof Exp:* Intern med, Peter Bent Brigham Hosp, Boston, Mass, 59-60, asst resident, 60-61; res assoc, Nat Heart Inst, 61-63, med officer, Nat Inst Arthritis & Metab Dis, 63-66, chief sect genetics & develop, Lab Chem Biol, 66-67; assoc prof pediat, 67-72, assoc prof biochem, 70-72, PROF PEDIAT & BIOCHEM, SCH MED, UNIV CALIF, SAN FRANCISCO, 72- *Concurrent Pos:* Asst med, Sch Med, Univ Wash, 63-64; res fel med genetics, Sch Med, Univ Wash, 63-64; prof lectr inherited metab dis, Sch Med, George Washington Univ, 65-67; asst med, Johns Hopkins Univ, 65-67. *Mem:* Am Pediat Soc; Asn Am Physicians; Am Soc Biol Chem; Am Soc Clin Invest; Soc Pediat Res. *Res:* Hereditary diseases; biochemistry of early mammalian development; developmental genetics. *Mailing Add:* Dept of Pediat Sch of Med Univ of Calif San Francisco CA 94143

EPSTEIN, DAVID AARON, b Philadelphia, Pa, Dec 30, 42; US & Israeli citizen; m 68; c 2. INTERFERON, GENE EXPRESSION. *Educ:* Univ Calif, Berkeley, BA, 65; Brandeis Univ, MA, 70; Israel Inst Technol, DSc, 76. *Prof Exp:* Staff fel molecular virol, NIH, Nat Inst Neurol & Commun Disorders & Stroke, 76-78; staff fel interferon action, Lab Exp Path, 78-81, SR STAFF FEL MAMMALIAN GENE EXPRESSION, LAB BIOCHEM PHARMACOL, NIH, NAT INST ARTHRITIS, METAB & DIGESTIVE DIS, 81- *Res:* Mechanism of interferon action in the virus infected cell; regulation of biological processes; gene expression. *Mailing Add:* 12508 Village Square Terr Rockville MD 20852

EPSTEIN, DAVID LEE, b Chicago, Ill, June 23, 44; m 68; c 1. OPHTHALMOLOGY. *Educ:* Johns Hopkins Univ, BA, 65, MD, 68. *Prof Exp:* Resident ophthal, 73-75, fel glaucoma, 75-76, instr, 76-77, ASST PROF OPHTHAL, HARVARD MED SCH, 78-; ASST DIR GLAUCOMA SERV, MASS EYE & EAR INFIRMARY, 76- *Mem:* Asn Res Vision & Ophthal; AAAS. *Res:* Glaucoma. *Mailing Add:* 243 Charles St Boston MA 02114

EPSTEIN, EDWARD SELIG, b New York, NY, Apr 29, 31; m 54; c 4. METEOROLOGY. *Educ:* Harvard Univ, AB, 51; Columbia Univ, MBA, 53; Pa State Univ, MS, 54, PhD(meteorol), 60. *Prof Exp:* Res assoc & lectr meteorol, Univ Mich, 59-61, asst prof, 61-63; consult to asst secy com for sci & tech, US Dept Com, 63-64; from assoc prof to prof meteorol, Univ Mich, 63-73, from actg chmn to chmn dept meteorol & oceanog, 69-73; assoc adminr for environ monitoring & prediction, 73-77, dir, US Climate Prog Off, 78-81, DIR, EARTH SCI LAB, NAT EARTH SATELLITE SERV, NAT OCEANIC & ATMOSPHERIC ADMIN, 81- *Concurrent Pos:* NSF grants, 61-64, 65-68, 70-72; vis prof, Int Meteorol Inst, Stockholm, 68-69; Univ Corp Atmospheric Res rep, 69-73; mem goal & eval comt, 69-71; ed, J Appl Meteorol, 71-73; mem adv panel atmospheric sci, NSF, 71-73; fed coordr for meteorol, 75-78. *Mem:* Fel Am Meteorol Soc; Am Geophys Union; fel AAAS. *Res:* Probability and statistics in meteorology; stochastic dynamic prediction. *Mailing Add:* Nat Oceanic & Atmospheric Admin World Weather Bldg Washington DC 20233

EPSTEIN, ELIOT, soil physics, see previous edition

EPSTEIN, EMANUEL, b Detroit, Mich, July 1, 22; m 50; c 3. CLINICAL CHEMISTRY. *Educ:* Wayne State Univ, BS, 45, MS, 53, PhD(biochem), 57. *Prof Exp:* Chemist, Frederick Stearns & Co, 45-46 & Fund Crippling Dis, 46-47; asst, Wayne State Univ, 48-50, res assoc, 50-57; res chemist, St Joseph Mercy Hosp, 57-68; CLIN CHEMIST, WILLIAM BEAUMONT HOSP, 68- *Concurrent Pos:* Asst prof, Wayne State Univ, 63-77, clin assoc prof, 77- *Mem:* Am Asn Clin Chem; Endocrine Soc; Am Chem Soc. *Res:* Steroids; analysis; electrophoretically separated proteins, analysis; chromatography; automation. *Mailing Add:* William Beaumont Hosp 3601 W 13 Mile Rd Royal Oak MI 48072

EPSTEIN, EMANUEL, b Ger, Nov 5, 16; nat US; m 43; c 1. PLANT NUTRITION. *Educ:* Univ Calif, BS, 40, MS, 41, PhD(plant physiol), 50. *Prof Exp:* Asst bot, Univ Calif, 43; asst plant nutrit, 46-49; assoc plant physiologist, USDA, 49-51, plant physiologist, 51-58; lectr plant nutrit & assoc plant physiologist, 58-65, PROF PLANT NUTRIT & PLANT PHYSIOLOGIST, UNIV CALIF, DAVIS, 65- *Concurrent Pos:* Guest investr biophys lab, Carnegie Inst, 50; adv, US Deleg, Conf Peaceful Uses Atomic Energy, 55; Guggenheim fel, Calif Inst Technol, 58; partic, Nat Acad Sci-Nat Res Coun Desalination Res Conf, Mass, 61; Fulbright res grant, Australia, 65-66; Fulbright sr res scholar, Sci & Indust Res, NZ, 74-75. *Honors & Awards:* Cherubim Gold Medal, Univ Pisa, 62. *Mem:* Nat Acad Sci; AAAS; Am Soc Plant Physiol; Am Inst Biol Sci; Scand Soc Plant Physiol. *Res:* Mechanisms of ion transport in plants; salt relations of plants; selection and breeding of salt tolerant crops; genetic and ecological aspects of mineral plant nutrition. *Mailing Add:* Dept Land Air & Water Resources Univ Calif Davis CA 95616

EPSTEIN, ERVIN HAROLD, b Vallejo, Calif, May 17, 09; m 36; c 2. DERMATOLOGY. *Educ:* Univ Calif, AB, 31, MD, 35. *Prof Exp:* ASSOC CLIN PROF DERMAT MED, SCH MED, UNIV CALIF, SAN FRANCISCO, 62- *Concurrent Pos:* Consult var Calif hosps; assoc clin prof dermat med, Sch Med, Stanford Univ, 50-64. *Mem:* Am Dermat Asn; Soc Invest Dermat; Am Acad Dermat; Int Soc Dermat surg; Am Soc Dermat Surg. *Res:* Disease of the skin; skin surgery; regional dermatologic diagnosis; radio-dermatitis; techniques in skin surgery; controversies in dermat. *Mailing Add:* 400 30th St Oakland CA 94609

EPSTEIN, EUGENE ETHAN, b Los Angeles, Calif, Aug 8, 34. ASTRONOMY. *Educ:* Calif Inst Technol, BS, 56; Harvard Univ, MS, 59, PhD(astron), 62. *Prof Exp:* Mem tech staff, 62-72, STAFF SCIENTIST, RADIO ASTRON PROG, AEROSPACE CORP, 72- *Concurrent Pos:* Mem, Comn V, Int Union Radio Sci. *Mem:* Am Astron Soc; Int Astron Union; Astron Soc Pac. *Res:* Millimeter wavelength studies of the thermophysical characteristics of planetary surfaces; intensity and time variability of the millimeter emission of galactic objects, quasars and Seyfert galaxies. *Mailing Add:* Aerospace Corp Box 92957 Los Angeles CA 90009

EPSTEIN, FRANKLIN HAROLD, b Brooklyn, NY, May 5, 24; m 51; c 4. INTERNAL MEDICINE, PHYSIOLOGY. *Educ:* Brooklyn Col, BA, 44; Yale Univ, MD, 47. *Prof Exp:* House officer, Yale Med Ctr, 47-49; res fel, Sch Med, Boston Univ, 49-50; res assoc physiol, Walter Reed Army Med Ctr, 50-52; from asst prof to prof med, Sch Med, Yale Univ, 54-72, chief metab div, 65-72; head dept med, 72-74, PROF MED, HARVARD MED SCH, 72- *Concurrent Pos:* Estab investr, Am Heart Asn, 56-61; consult, Off Surgeon Gen, US Army, 64-69; career investr, USPHS, 64-72; chmn nephrol test comt, Am Bd Internal Med, 70-74; trustee, Mt Desert Island Biol Lab, 70-; dir, Harvard Med Unit, Boston City Hosp & Thorndike Mem Lab, 72-73; Herrman Blumgart prof & physician-in-chief, 73-80, William Applebaum prof med & dir, Renal Div, Beth Israel Hosp, 81- *Mem:* Am Soc Clin Invest (vpres, 69-70); Am Physiol Soc; Asn Am Physicians. *Res:* Renal physiology and disease. *Mailing Add:* Dept of Med Beth Israel Hosp Boston MA 02115

EPSTEIN, GABRIEL LEO, b Manhattan, NY, Apr 8, 41; m 70. SOLAR PHYSICS, ATOMIC PHYSICS. *Educ:* City Col New York, BChE, 62; Univ Calif, Berkeley, PhD(physics), 69. *Prof Exp:* Teaching asst elem physics, Univ Calif, Berkeley, 63-65, res asst atomic physics & spectros, 65-69; Nat Acad Sci-Nat Res Coun Res assoc, Nat Bur Standards, Dept Com, 69-70; STAFF SCIENTIST OPTICAL SYSTS, NASA GODDARD SPACE FLIGHT CTR, 70- *Mem:* AAAS; Optical Soc Am; Am Astron Soc. *Res:* Fabry-Perot interferometry; optical isotope shifts; production and analysis of the spectra of moderately ionized atoms; design of equipment for solar observations; deduction of solar atmospheric conditions from such observations. *Mailing Add:* 1716 Shilling Lane Silver Spring MD 20906

EPSTEIN, GARY MARTIN, b Los Angeles, Calif, Jun 9, 42; m 65; c 2. PARTICLE PHYSICS. *Educ:* Univ Calif, Riverside, BA, 64, PhD(physics), 69. *Prof Exp:* Assoc prof, 69-80, PROF MATH, CALIF POLYTECH STATE UNIV, SAN LUIS OBISPO, 80- *Mem:* Am Phys Soc. *Res:* Construction of dispersion relations for Regge parameters in high energy scattering theory; mathematical modelling of physiological systems at the cellular level. *Mailing Add:* Dept Math Calif Polytech State Univ San Luis Obispo CA 93402

EPSTEIN, GEORGE, b Boston, Mass, Nov 9, 26; m 51; c 2. PLASTICS CHEMISTRY, MATERIALS SCIENCE. *Educ:* Univ Mass, BS, 48; Mass Inst Technol, MS, 51. *Prof Exp:* Asst adhesives lab, Mass Inst Technol, 50-52; res engr, NAm Aviation, Inc, 52-55; prin engr & asst chief engr struct mat div, Aerojet-Gen Corp Div, Gen Tire & Rubber Co, 55-61; prin engr & staff scientist, Aeronutronic Div, Ford Motor Co, 61-63; proj scientist, Aerospace Res Assocs, Inc, 63-66; SR STAFF ENGR, MAT SCI LAB, AEROSPACE CORP, 66- *Concurrent Pos:* Instr, Univ Calif, Los Angeles, 54-74; mem, Fed Steering Comt Adhesives Technol, 71-74; ed, Pac Coast Plastics & Rubber, 75-; pres, Technol Conf Asn, 75- *Honors & Awards:* Meritorious Serv Award, Soc Aerospace Mat & Process Eng, 63; Distinguished Serv Award, Western Sect, Soc Plastics Indust, 74; Willard Lundberg Mem Award, Soc Plastics Engrs, 75. *Mem:* Soc Plastics Engrs; Am Chem Soc; Am Soc Testing & Mat; Soc Plastics Indust; Soc Aerospace Mat & Process Eng (vpres, 63-64). *Res:* Nonmetallic materials, plastics, resins, adhesives, sealants and coatings for high-performance applications; energy absorbing materials; advanced test and inspection methods; major applications to rockets, missiles and space vehicles. *Mailing Add:* 6222 Orange St Los Angeles CA 90048

EPSTEIN, GEORGE, b Bayonne, NJ, July 4, 34; m 56; c 3. MATHEMATICS, COMPUTER SCIENCE. *Educ:* Calif Inst Technol, BS, 55; Univ Ill, MS, 57; Univ Calif, Los Angeles, PhD(math), 59. *Prof Exp:* Mem tech staff comput sci, Hughes Aircraft, Calif, 57-59; sr staff scientist, ITT Gilfillan, Inc, Van Nuys, 59-72; PROF COMP SCI, IND UNIV, BLOOMINGTON, 73- *Mem:* Am Math Soc; Math Asn Am; Asn Symbolic Logic; Asn Comput Mach; Inst Elec & Electronics Engrs. *Res:* Cybernetics; philosophy; psychology; literature; electrical circuits and systems; linguistics and education; decision algebras. *Mailing Add:* Dept of Comp Sci Ind Univ Bloomington IN 47401

EPSTEIN, HARVEY IRWIN, b Brooklyn, NY, Mar 29, 46. SOFTWARE SYSTEMS. *Educ:* Brooklyn Col, BA, 67; Univ Wis, Madison, MA, 69, PhD(math), 75. *Prof Exp:* Instr math, Viterbo Col, 69-71; asst prof math & comput sci, St Cloud State Univ, 74-75; asst prof math, Boston Col, 75-78; sr eng, Raytheon Co, 78-81; TECH STAFF, MITRE CORP, 81- *Mem:* Asn Comput Mach; Am Math Soc; Am Math Assoc; NY Acad Sci. *Res:* Computer security, especially operating system and database. *Mailing Add:* RFD 1 Durham NC 03824

EPSTEIN, HENRY F, b Bronx, NY, 1944; m 69; c 2. MOLECULAR BIOLOGY. *Educ:* Columbia Univ, AB, 64; Stanford Univ, MD, 68; Nat Bd Med Exam, dipl, 70. *Prof Exp:* Res asst biochem, Stanford Univ, 65-67, res fel & res staff molecular biophysicist, 68-69; staff assoc chem biol, NIH, 69-71; Nat Found fel genetics cell biol, Med Res Coun Lab Molecular Biol, Cambridge, Eng, 71-73; asst prof pharmacol, Stanford Univ, 78-79; assoc prof neurol & biochem, 78-79, assoc prof, neurol biochem med, 79-81, PROF NEUROL, BAYLOR COL MED, 81- *Concurrent Pos:* Ed consult biochem, W H Freemen, 78-80; mem, Tech Rev Panel, Nat Inst Aging, NIH, 79, prog comt, Int Muscular Dystrophy Meeting Motor Unit, Key Biscayne, 80, Nat Aging Review Comt, Nat Inst Aging & NIH, 81. *Honors & Awards:* Borden Award, 68. *Mem:* Am Soc Biol Chemists; Neurosci; Am Soc Cell Biol; Am Chem Soc. *Res:* Molecular biology of muscle development; muscle structure, genetics of muscle disease, biochemistry of protein structure, function and regulation. *Mailing Add:* Dept Neurol Baylor Col Med 1200 Mousund Houston TX 77030

EPSTEIN, HERMAN THEODORE, b Portland, Maine, Apr 13, 20; m 47; c 4. BIOPHYSICS. *Educ:* Univ Mich, BA, 41, MA, 43, PhD(physics), 49. *Prof Exp:* Physicist, Nat Adv Comt Aeronaut, 44-46; asst prof biophys & physics, Univ Pittsburgh, 49-53; asst prof physics, 53-55, assoc prof biophys, 55-61, chmn dept biol, 71-74, PROF BIOPHYS, BRANDEIS UNIV, 61- *Concurrent Pos:* NSF sr fel, 59-60; Guggenheim fel, 69-70; vis prof, Tel Aviv Univ, 70-71. *Mem:* Biophys Soc; Soc Neurosci; Int Soc Develop Psychobiol; NY Acad Sci; AAAS. *Res:* Brain and intelligence development in humans and in mice; educational implications of physiological growth stages. *Mailing Add:* Dept of Biol Brandeis Univ Waltham MA 02154

EPSTEIN, IRVING ROBERT, b Brooklyn, NY, Aug 9, 45; m 71; c 2. CHEMICAL PHYSICS, THEORETICAL CHEMISTRY. *Educ:* Harvard Univ, AB, 66; Oxford Univ, dipl math, 67; Harvard Univ, MA, 68, PhD(chem physics), 71. *Prof Exp:* NATO fel, Cavendish Lab, Cambridge Univ, 71; from asst prof to assoc prof, 71-81, PROF CHEM, BRANDEIS UNIV, 81- *Concurrent Pos:* NSF fel, Max Planck Inst, Gottingen, 77-78; mem adv bd, J Phys Chem, 81- *Honors & Awards:* Liebmann Award, Am Chem Soc. *Mem:* Am Chem Soc. *Res:* Experimental and theoretical studies of oscillating chemical reactions, multiple stable states and dynamic instabilities; mathematical modeling of phenomena in biochemical kinetics. *Mailing Add:* Dept of Chem Brandeis Univ Waltham MA 02154

EPSTEIN, ISADORE, b Tallinn, Estonia, Oct 23, 19; nat US; m 64. ASTRONOMY, ASTROPHYSICS. *Educ:* Univ Cincinnati, AB, 41, MS, 47; Princeton Univ, AM & PhD(astron), 50. *Prof Exp:* Assoc, 50-53, from asst prof to assoc prof, 53-71, PROF ASTRON, COLUMBIA UNIV, 71- *Mem:* Am Astron Soc. *Mailing Add:* Dept of Astron Columbia Univ New York NY 10027

EPSTEIN, JACK BURTON, b New York, NY, Dec 27, 35; m 58; c 1. GEOLOGY. *Educ:* Brooklyn Col, BS, 56; Univ Wyo, MA, 58; Ohio State Univ, PhD, 70. *Prof Exp:* Field asst geol, 56, GEOLOGIST, US GEOL SURV, 57, 58-60, 64- *Concurrent Pos:* Instr, Ohio State Univ, 64. *Mem:* Geol Soc Am; Am Asn Petrol Geol; Soc Econ Paleont & Mineral. *Res:* Areal geology of western United States and eastern Pennsylvania; groundwater investigations in Louisiana; principals of environmental geology in United States. *Mailing Add:* US Geol Surv Nat Ctr 12201 Sunrise Valley Dr Reston VA 22092

EPSTEIN, JEANNE ALICE, b NJ, Jan 19, 23; m 60; c 1. MEDICINE. *Educ:* Rutgers Univ, BS, 42; Woman's Med Col Pa, MD, 53. *Prof Exp:* Res technician rheumatic fever, Rockefeller Inst Med Res, 44-49; intern, Beth Israel Hosp, 53-54; asst med, Col Physicians & Surgeons, Columbia Univ, 54-55; fel therapeut & endocrinol, Bellevue Med Ctr, New York, 55-58; ASST PROF CLIN MED, NY UNIV, 58- *Concurrent Pos:* Resident, Columbia Div, Goldwater Hosp, 54-55; asst adj, Beth Israel Hosp, 55-64; endocrinologist, Margaret Sanger Res Bur, 56-64, asst med dir, 64-73; asst attend, Knickerbocker Hosp, 57-64; asst attend, NY Univ Hosp, 57-; asst vis, Bellevue Hosp, 58-; res assoc, Irvington House, 59-62; attend physician, NY Infirmary, 59-; asst attend, French-polyclin Health Ctr, 62-75, assoc attend, 75- *Mem:* Am Soc Microbiol; Endocrine Soc; Am Fertil Soc; AMA; Am Fedn Clin Res. *Res:* Rheumatic fever; etiology and prophylaxis; endocrinology of the gonads; infertility; clinical investigation in general endocrinology. *Mailing Add:* 136 E 36th St New York NY 10016

EPSTEIN, JOSEPH, b Philadelphia, Pa, June 30, 18; m 45; c 4. PHYSICAL CHEMISTRY, ORGANIC CHEMISTRY. *Educ:* Temple Univ, AB, 38; Univ Pa, MS, 40; Univ Del, PhD, 66. *Prof Exp:* Plant chemist, Chem Corps Med Labs, Army Chem Ctr, 40-44, res assoc toxicol, Edgewood Arsenal, 44-45, chief anal sect, Gassing Br, 45-47, Sanit Chem Br, 47-58 & Protection Res Br, 58-62, chief defense res div, Chem Res & Develop Labs, 62-66, chief defense res dept, Res Labs, 66-71, chief defense res br, Chem Labs, 71-73, chief, Environ Res Div, 73-80; CHEM CONSULT, 80- *Concurrent Pos:* Consult, USPHS, 54. *Honors & Awards:* Res & Develop Award, Off Res & Develop, US Army, 74 & 77. *Mem:* AAAS; Sigma Xi; Am Chem Soc; Am Ord Asn; NY Acad Sci. *Res:* Protection against and decontamination, detection and identification of chemical warfare agents; properties of chemical warfare materials in aqueous and nonaqueous media; reaction mechanisms and kinetics of reactions; development of analytical methods, especially micro methods; environmental problems, pollution abatement and control. *Mailing Add:* 4020 Essex Rd Baltimore MD 21207

EPSTEIN, JOSEPH WILLIAM, b Brooklyn, NY, May 9, 38; m 64; c 2. ORGANIC CHEMISTRY. *Educ:* Cooper Union, BChE, 60; NY Univ, MS, 64, PhD(org chem), 65. *Prof Exp:* Fel org chem, Technion-Israel Inst Technol, 65-66; SR RES CHEMIST & GROUP LEADER, LEDERLE LABS, MED RES DIV, AM CYANAMID CO, 66- *Concurrent Pos:* Adj assoc prof, Dept Chem, Hunter Col, City Univ New York, 68-76. *Mem:* Am Chem Soc. *Res:* Synthesis of compounds related to the functions of the central nervous system and the cardiovascular-renal system. *Mailing Add:* Lederle Labs Am Cyanamid Co Pearl River NY 10965

EPSTEIN, L(UDWIG) IVAN, b Duisburg, Ger, Nov 25, 18; US citizen; m 55. BIOPHYSICS. *Educ:* Calif Inst Technol, BS, 40, MS, 41; Ohio State Univ, PhD(physics), 67. *Prof Exp:* Res staff mem rockets, Calif Inst Technol, 43-46; optical engr, Bausch & Lomb Optical Co, 47-54; engr math physics, Martin Co, Baltimore, 54-58; asst prof physics, Lowell Technol Inst, 58-63; assoc prof, Marietta Col, 63-64; assoc prof biophys, Med Col Va, Va Commonwealth Univ, 67-82; RETIRED. *Concurrent Pos:* NIH grants, Va Commonwealth Univ, 73-74 & 79-81; vis prof, Optical Sci Ctr, Univ Ariz, 82. *Mem:* Optical Soc Am; Asn Res Vision & Ophthal. *Res:* Geometrical, physical, and physiological optics; molecular orbital theory; nomography; physics applied to anesthesiology. *Mailing Add:* 8121 E Renaud Lane Tucson AZ 85710

EPSTEIN, LAWRENCE MELVIN, b Brooklyn, NY, Apr 23, 23; m 46; c 4. PHYSICAL CHEMISTRY. *Educ:* Cooper Union, BChE, 43; Polytech Inst Brooklyn, MS, 52, PhD(phys chem), 55. *Prof Exp:* Chemist, Am Aniline Prod, 46-47; instr anal chem, New York Community Col, 47-55; fel polymer properties, Mellon Inst, 55-56; sr scientist radiation res, Westinghouse Res Labs, 56-63, supvry scientist, 63-67; ASSOC PROF CHEM, UNIV PITTSBURGH, 67- *Mem:* Am Chem Soc. *Res:* Radiation chemistry and processing; radiation damage to materials; Mossbauer effect; chemical kinetics; polymer properties. *Mailing Add:* Dept of Chem Univ of Pittsburgh Pittsburgh PA 15260

EPSTEIN, LEO FRANCIS, b New York, NY, Dec 9, 13; m 42; c 2. PHYSICAL CHEMISTRY. *Educ:* Mass Inst Technol, BS, 35, PhD(phys chem), 39. *Prof Exp:* Asst photochem, Solar Energy Res Comt, Mass Inst Technol, 39-41; asst chemist, Nat Defense Res Comt, High Explosives Res Div, US Bur Mines, 41-42; res engr, Crystal Res Labs, Inc, Conn, 45-47; res assoc, Knolls Atomic Power Lab, Gen Elec Co, 47-57, phys chemist, Vallecitos Atomic Lab, 57-68; sr chemist, Proj Mgt Support Div, Argonne Nat Lab, 68-80; RETIRED. *Concurrent Pos:* Sci adv, US Deleg Geneva Conf Peaceful Uses Atomic Energy, 55 & 71. *Mem:* Am Chem Soc; Am Phys Soc; Am Nuclear Soc; Math Asn Am; Sigma Xi. *Res:* Physical chemistry of solutions such as nonaqueous, electrolytes and liquid metals; dyestuff solutions; high explosives; mathematical analysis; ultrasonics; applications of physical chemistry to materials problems in nuclear systems; liquid sodium; fast breeder reactors. *Mailing Add:* 110 Gough St 12A San Francisco CA 94109

EPSTEIN, LEON J, b Jersey City, NJ, June 7, 17; c 2. PSYCHIATRY. *Educ:* Vanderbilt Univ, AB, 37, MA, 38; George Peabody Col, PhD, 41; Univ Tenn, MD, 49. *Prof Exp:* Staff psychiatrist, St Elizabeths Hosp, Washington, DC, 54-56; dep dir res, Calif State Dept Ment Hyg, 56-61; from asst prof to assoc prof, 61-68, PROF PSYCHIAT, SCH MED, UNIV CALIF, SAN FRANCISCO, 68-, VCHMN DEPT, 69- *Concurrent Pos:* Assoc med dir, Langley Porter Neuropsychiat Inst, 61-80. *Mem:* Am Psychiat Asn; Am Col Neuropsychopharmacol; Geront Soc; Am Col Psychiat; The Geriatric Soc. *Res:* Psychopharmacology; emotional disorders in the elderly. *Mailing Add:* Univ of Calif Med Ctr San Francisco CA 94143

EPSTEIN, LOIS BARTH, b Cambridge, Mass, Dec 29, 33; m 56; c 4. MEDICAL SCIENCE, HEALTH SCIENCE. *Educ:* Radcliffe Col, AB, 55; Harvard Med Sch, MD, 59. *Prof Exp:* Resident path, Peter Bent Brigham Hosp, 59-60; intern med, New Eng Ctr Hosp, 60-61; res med officer, Nat Inst Arthritis & Metab Dis, 62-63; res fel, Med Sch, Univ Wash, 63-64; NIH spec res fel, Nat Inst Arthritis & Metab Dis & Nat Inst Allergy & Infectious Dis, 64-66, res med officer, Nat Inst Allergy & Infectious Dis, 66-69; from asst res physician to assoc res physician, 69-74, assoc dir cancer res inst, 74-77, assoc prof pediat, 74-80, PROF PEDIAT, UNIV CALIF, SAN FRANCISCO, 80- . *Concurrent Pos:* Mem allergy & immunol training grants adv comt, Nat Inst Allergy & Infectious Dis, 72-73, mem allergy & immunol res adv comt, 73-76; vis scientist, Univ Col, Univ London, 73-74; Nat Cancer Inst res grant, 73-76; Nat Inst Allergy & Infectious Dis res grant, 74-; mem grad comt immunol, Univ Calif, San Francisco, 75-; mem immunol sci study sect, NIH, 77-81; res assoc, Cancer Res Inst, 77-; March Dimes Birth Defect Found grant, 79- *Mem:* Am Soc Clin Invest; Am Asn Immunologists; Am Soc Hemat; Am Asn Cancer Educ; Am Fedn Clin Res. *Res:* Cellular and tumor immunology and the role of interferon in each; the production, action, genetic control and delivery of interferon. *Mailing Add:* Cancer Res Inst M1282 Univ of Calif San Francisco CA 94143

EPSTEIN, MARTIN EDEN, organic chemistry, see previous edition

EPSTEIN, MARVIN PHELPS, b New York, NY, Sept 28, 20; m 64; c 1. MATHEMATICS. *Educ:* Univ Calif, AB, 47, AM, 48; Columbia Univ, PhD(math), 53. *Prof Exp:* Asst math, Univ Calif, 47-48; lectr, Columbia Univ, 49-51; instr, Univ Calif, 53-55; asst prof, Johns Hopkins, 55-56; SUPVR MATH ANAL & CONSULT GROUP, BELL TEL LABS, 56- *Concurrent Pos:* Mem staff, Stevens Inst Technol, 58-60, Fairleigh Dickinson, 58-67, Drew Univ, 67- & Seton Hall Univ, 70- *Mem:* Math Asn Am; Soc Indust & Appl Math; Am Asn Comput Mach. *Res:* Differential algebra; analysis; numerical analysis; numerical linear algebra. *Mailing Add:* 36 Melrose Pl Montclair NJ 07042

EPSTEIN, MAX, b Lodz, Poland, Feb 5, 25; US citizen; m 63; c 3. ELECTRICAL ENGINEERING, SOLID STATE PHYSICS. *Educ:* Israel Inst Technol, BS, 52; Ill Inst Technol, MS, 55, PhD(elec eng), 63. *Prof Exp:* Instr elec eng, Ill Inst Technol, 54-58, res engr, ITT Res Inst, 58-64, sr res engr, 64-67; PROF ELEC ENG, NORTHWESTERN UNIV, 67- *Concurrent Pos:* Consult, IIT Res Inst Israel Defense Army, 48-49. *Mem:* AAAS; Am Phys Soc; Inst Elec & Electronics Engrs. *Res:* Fiber optics; microacoustics. *Mailing Add:* Dept of Elec Eng & Comput Sci Northwestern Univ Evanston IL 60201

EPSTEIN, MELVIN, engineering, physics, see previous edition

EPSTEIN, MORTON BATLAN, b New York, NY, June 8, 17; m 42; c 2. CLINICAL CHEMISTRY. *Educ:* NY Univ, BS, 37; Univ Ill, PhD(chem), 42. *Prof Exp:* Asst, Univ Ill, 41-42; chemist, Picatinny Arsenal, NJ, 42-45; Am Petrol Inst res assoc, Nat Bur Stand, 46-49; res assoc, Colgate Palmolive Co, 49-54, Onyx Oil & Chem Co, 54-57, Colgate Palmolive Co, 57-63 & div adult health & aging, Chicago Bd Health, 63-69; CLIN CHEMIST, CHRIST HOSP, 69- *Concurrent Pos:* Assoc clin path, Chicago Med Sch, 70-74; asst prof, Med Sch, Northwestern Univ, Chicago, 74- *Mem:* Am Asn Clin Chemists; Am Chem Soc; Am Oil Chem Soc. *Res:* Physical and thermodynamic properties of hydrocarbons; analysis of petroleum; physical chemistry of detergents and foams; atherosclerosis and hypertension. *Mailing Add:* 5039 S Ellis Ave Chicago IL 60615

EPSTEIN, NATHAN BERNIC, b New Waterford, NS, Mar 3, 24; m 51; c 3. PSYCHIATRY. *Educ:* Dalhousie Univ, MD & CM, 48; McGill Univ, dipl psychiat, 52; Columbia Univ, cert psychoanal, 55; Am Bd Psychiat & Neurol, dipl, 53. *Prof Exp:* Sr intern & asst resident psychiat, Allan Mem Inst & Royal Victoria Hosp, Montreal, 48-50; resident & jr physician, Boston State Hosp, Mass, 50-51; vol clin asst child psychiat, Outpatient Dept, Mt Sinai Hosp, New York, 51-53; actg dir, Ment Health Ctr, Paterson, NJ, 53-54; mem staff psychiat, Jewish Gen Hosp, 55-58, head sub-dept child & family psychiat, 58-59, asst psychiatrist, 59-60, psychiatrist-in-chief, 60-67; prof psychiat & chmn dept, McMaster Univ, 67-75; PROF & CHMN, SECT PSYCHIAT & HUMAN BEHAVIOR, BROWN UNIV, 78-; MED DIR, BUTLER HOSP, PROVIDENCE, RI, 78- *Concurrent Pos:* Res assoc, McGill Univ, 55-58, lectr & res asst, 58-61, assoc prof, 61-67, co-dir human develop study, 58, training analyst comt psychoanal, 59; vis prof, McMaster Univ, 78. *Mem:* Fel Acad Psychoanal; fel Am Psychiat Asn; Can Psychiat Asn; Can Med Asn; Can Psychoanal Soc. *Res:* Family structure, organization and transaction dynamics and application to family therapy groups. *Mailing Add:* Butler Hosp 345 Blackstone Blvd Providence RI 02906

EPSTEIN, NORMAN, b Montreal, Can, Dec 6, 23; m 54; c 3. CHEMICAL ENGINEERING. *Educ:* McGill Univ, BE, 45, ME, 46; NY Univ, EngScD(chem eng), 53. *Prof Exp:* Lectr chem eng, McGill Univ, 46-48; instr, NY Univ, 49-51; from instr to assoc prof, 51-65, PROF CHEM ENG, UNIV BC, 65- *Concurrent Pos:* Consult, Heat Transfer Res Inc, 71-; Killiam sr fel, 75-76; hon res fel, Univ Col, London, 76; chmn, Can Nat Comt Heat Transfer, 79-; res assoc, Atomic Energy Res Estab, Harwell, 81. *Mem:* Am Chem Soc; fel Am Inst Chem Engrs; fel Chem Inst Can; Can Soc Chem Eng (vpres, 78-79, pres, 79-80). *Res:* Momentum; heat; mass transfer; fouling of heat exchangers; liquid- and three-phase fluidization; spouted beds; colloid mechanics. *Mailing Add:* Dept of Chem Eng Univ of BC Vancouver BC V6T 1W5 Can

EPSTEIN, PAUL MARK, b Brooklyn, NY, June 24, 46; m 75; c 1. ENZYMOLOGY, PHARMACOLOGY. *Educ:* Columbia Univ, AB, 67; Albert Einstein Col Med, Yeshiva Univ, PhD(molecular biol), 75. *Prof Exp:* Res assoc pharmacol, Univ Tex Med Sch, Houston, 75-78, instr, 78-79; ASST PROF PHARMACOL, UNIV CONN HEALTH CTR, 79- *Concurrent Pos:* Proj investr immunol, Dept Develop Theapeut, M D Anderson Hosp & Tumor Inst, Univ Tex & Syst Cancer Ctr, 75-78. *Mem:* Sigma Xi; AAAS; NY Acad Sci. *Res:* Cyclic nucleotide metabolism, calcium and calmodulin in the control of cell growth and development; purification, characterization and hormonal regulation of cyclic nucleotide phosphodiesterases. *Mailing Add:* Dept Pharmacol Univ Conn Health Ctr Farmington CT 06032

EPSTEIN, ROBERT BERNARD, hematology, see previous edition

EPSTEIN, ROBERT MARVIN, b New York, NY, Mar 10, 28; m 50; c 3. ANESTHESIOLOGY. *Educ:* Univ Mich, BS, 47, MD, 51; FRCS(E), 81. *Prof Exp:* Intern, Univ Mich Hosp, 51-52; asst resident anesthesiol, Presby Hosp, NY, 52-53 & 55-56; from instr to prof, Col Physicians & Surgeons, Columbia Univ, 56-72; PROF ANESTHESIOL & CHMN DEPT, SCH MED, UNIV VA, 72- *Concurrent Pos:* NY Heart Asn fel med, Columbia Univ, 56-57, Nat Inst Gen Med Sci grant, 59-72; asst anesthesiol, Presby Hosp, New York, 56-58, from asst attend anesthesiologist to assoc attend anesthesiologist, 58-70, attend anesthesiologist, 70-72; vis scientist & Guggenheim Mem Found fel, Dept Pharmacol, Oxford Univ, 66-67; mem anesthesiol training comt, Nat Inst Gen Med Sci, 66-69 & comt anesthesia, Nat Res Coun, 70-71; dir, Am Bd Anesthesiol, 72-, pres, 79-80; ed, Anesthesiology, 74-; Am Bd Anesthesiol rep, Am Bd Med Specialties, 74- *Mem:* AAAS; Am Soc Anesthesiol; Asn Univ Anesthetists (secy, 69-72, pres, 74-75); Am Soc Pharmacol & Exp Therapeut; Am Physiol Soc. *Res:* Circulatory physiology; effects of anesthetics on splanchnic circulation and its neural control; effects of anesthetics and neuromuscular blocking agents on neuromuscular transmission and the electromyogram; effects of carbon dioxide; pharmacokinetics of anesthetics. *Mailing Add:* Dept of Anesthesiol Univ of Va Charlottesville VA 22908

EPSTEIN, SAMUEL, b Poland, Dec 9, 19; US citizen; m 46; c 2. GEOCHEMISTRY. *Educ:* Univ Man, BSc, 41, MSc, 42; McGill Univ, PhD(phys chem), 44. *Hon Degrees:* DSc, Univ Manitoba, Winnipeg, Can, 80. *Prof Exp:* Res chemist, Nat Res Coun Can, 44-47; res assoc, Inst Nuclear Studies, Univ Chicago, 48-52; res fel, 52-53, sr res fel, 53-54, assoc prof, 54-59, PROF GEOCHEM, CALIF INST TECHNOL, 59- *Honors & Awards:* Arthur L Day Medal, Geol Soc Am, 78. *Mem:* Nat Acad Sci; fel AAAS; Geol Soc Am; Geochem Soc; Am Geophys Union. *Res:* Stable isotope geochemistry; application of isotope measurments to the problems related meteorology, hydrology, glaciology, petrology, biochemistry, plant physiology, climatology, paleontology, meteoritics, and lunar samples. *Mailing Add:* Div of Geol & Planetary Sci Calif Inst of Technol Pasadena CA 91109

EPSTEIN, SAMUEL DAVID, b Brooklyn, NY, Aug 4, 46; m 68; c 2. COMPUTER SCIENCE, SYSTEMS ENGINEERING. *Educ:* Drexel Univ, BS, 68. *Prof Exp:* Analyst comput sci, Auerbach Corp, 65-68; proj leader, 68-69, dir, Philadelphia Div, 69-70, VPRES, ANALYTICS INC, 70- *Concurrent Pos:* NSF fel, 67-68. *Mem:* Am Inst Physics; Armed Forces Commun & Electronics Asn; Tech Mkt Soc Am. *Res:* Multi-user interactive data storage and retrieval concentrating on free form English and semantic interpretation. *Mailing Add:* Analytics Inc 2500 Maryland Rd Willow Grove PA 19090

EPSTEIN, SAMUEL STANLEY, b Middlesborough, Eng, Apr 13, 26; US citizen; m 59; c 3. PATHOLOGY, ENVIRONMENTAL SCIENCES. *Educ:* Univ London, BSc, 47, MB & BS, 50, dipl trop med & surg, 52, dipl path, 54, MD, 58, dipl microbiol & pub health, 63; Am Bd Microbiol, dipl, 63. *Prof Exp:* Demonstr morbid anat, Guy's Hosp, Univ London, 50; house physician med, St Johns's Hosp, Eng, 51; lectr path & bact, Inst Laryngol & Otol, Eng, 55-58; tumor pathologist & Brit Empire Cancer Campaign fel, Hosp Sick Children & Chester Beatty Cancer Res Inst, Eng, 58-60; consult path, Mem Hosp Peterborough, Eng, 60; chief labs environ toxicol & carcinogenesis, Children's Cancer Res Found, Inc, Boston, Mass, 61-71; prof pharmacol & Swetland Prof environ health & human ecol, Med Sch, Case Western Reserve Univ, 71-76; PROF ENVIRON & OCCUP MED, SCH PUB HEALTH, UNIV ILL MED CTR, 76- *Concurrent Pos:* Res assoc path, Harvard Med Sch, 62-71; consult, US Senate Comt Pub Works, 70-, Ctr Studies Narcotic & Drug Abuse, NIMH, 70- & Environ Health Progs, Inc, 70-; mem panel on polycyclic org matter, Nat Acad Sci, 70-; mem pesticide bd, Commonwealth of Mass, 70-; mem, US Senate Subcomt Exec Reorgn & Govt Res; pres, Rachel Carson Trust, Inc, DC; chairperson, Comn Advan Pub Interest Orgns, DC; dir environ health resource ctr, State Ill, 78- *Honors & Awards:* Montefiore Gold Medal Trop Med, Royal Army Med Corps, 53, Montefiore Prize Trop Hyg, 53, Ranald Martin Prize Mil Surg, 53; Achievement Award, Soc Toxicol, 69. *Mem:* AAAS; Soc Occup & Environ Health (pres); fel Royal Soc Health; Environ Mutagen Soc (secy, 69); Air Pollution Control Asn. *Res:* Toxicology; carcinogenesis; mutagenesis; preventive medicine; bacteriology and protozoology; biological hazards, including carcinogenesis, mutagenesis, due to chemical pollution of the environment, including food additives, pesticides, fertilizers, industrial chemicals and drugs; ecological effects of chemical pollutants. *Mailing Add:* Univ of Ill Med Ctr Sch of Pub Health Chicago IL 60680

EPSTEIN, SAUL THEODORE, b Southampton, NY, June 14, 24; m 48; c 3. THEORETICAL PHYSICS. *Educ:* Mass Inst Technol, SB, 44, PhD(physics), 48. *Prof Exp:* With Inst Advan Study, 47-48; instr physics, Columbia Univ, 48-51 & Boston Univ, 52-53; from asst prof to prof, Univ Nebr, 54-63; PROF PHYSICS & CHEM & MEM THEORET CHEM INST, UNIV WIS-MADISON, 63- *Mem:* Am Phys Soc; Am Asn Physics Teachers. *Res:* Basic quantum theory; atomic and molecular structure. *Mailing Add:* Dept of Physics Univ of Wis Madison WI 53706

EPSTEIN, SEYMOUR, b New York, NY, Mar 19, 21; m 55; c 4. PHYSICS, ENGINEERING. *Educ:* City Col New York, BME, 43; Polytech Inst Brooklyn, MS, 51, PhD(physics), 61. *Prof Exp:* Instr physics & math, Univ Akron, 43-44; physics, Assoc Cols Upper NY, 46-47; descriptive geometry, Brooklyn Col, 47-50; eng writer consult, CBS-Columbia, Inc, 50-51; PHYS SCIENTIST, LASER TECH AREA, COMBAT SURVEILLANCE & TARGET ACQUISITION LAB, US ARMY ELECTRONICS COMMAND, FT MONMOUTH, 52- *Concurrent Pos:* Tool engr, Goodyear Aircraft Corp, 43-44. *Mem:* AAAS; Am Phys Soc. *Res:* Electrooptics; solid state physics. *Mailing Add:* US Army Electronics Command CT|L|C Ft Monmouth NJ 07703

EPSTEIN, STEPHEN EDWARD, b Brooklyn, NY, Dec 23, 35; m 57; c 3. CARDIOLOGY. *Educ:* Columbia Col, BA, 57; Cornell Univ, Med Sch, MD, 61. *Prof Exp:* Intern, New York Hosp, 61-62, resident, 62-63; clin assoc, Nat Heart Inst, 63-66, cardiologist to surg serv, 66-68; clin instr med, Sch Med, Georgetown Univ, 67-68; actg chief, Cardiol Br, Nat Heart Inst, 68-69, CHIEF, SECT CIRCULATORY PHYSIOL, NAT HEART & LUNG INST, 68-, CHIEF, CARDIOL BR, 69- *Concurrent Pos:* Clin assoc prof med, Sch Med, Georgetown Univ, 71-74, clin prof, 74-; mem, Coun Circulation & Coun Basic Sci, Am Heart Asn. *Honors & Awards:* William C Thro Prize; William Mecklenburg Polk Prize; Harold H Bix lectr, 78; James B Herrick Mem lectr, Chicago Heart Asn, 79. *Mem:* Am Fedn Clin Res; Am Physiol Soc; Am Col Cardiol; Am Soc Clin Invest. *Res:* Biological mechanisms controlling cardiac function and those that lead to cardiac dysfunction; to develop new diagnostic and therapeutic approaches to cardiac disease. *Mailing Add:* NIH Wisconsin Ave Bethesda MD 80252

EPSTEIN, WALLACE VICTOR, b New York, NY, Dec 10, 26; m 49; c 3. INTERNAL MEDICINE. *Educ:* City Col New York, BS, 48; Columbia Univ, MD, 52. *Prof Exp:* Res fel internal med, Columbia Univ, 55-56; res fel, 56-58, from asst prof to assoc prof med, 58-73, prof community med, 73-77, PROF MED, UNIV CALIF, SAN FRANCISCO, 77- *Mem:* AMA; Am Rheumatism Asn. *Res:* Arthritis; clinical and experimental immunology. *Mailing Add:* Dept of Med 992 Moffitt Hosp San Francisco CA 94143

EPSTEIN, WILLIAM L, b Cleveland, Ohio, Sept 6, 25; m 54; c 2. MEDICINE, DERMATOLOGY. *Educ:* Univ Calif, Berkeley, AB, 49; Univ Calif, San Francisco, MD, 52. *Prof Exp:* Instr dermat, Univ Pa, 56-57; from asst prof to assoc prof, 57-69, actg chmn div, 66-67, chmn div, 67-70, actg chmn dept, 70-74, PROF DERMAT, UNIV CALIF, SAN FRANCISCO, 69-, DIR DERMAT RES, 57-, CHMN DEPT DERMAT, 74- *Concurrent Pos:* Consult dermatologist, 57- *Honors & Awards:* Dohi lectr, Tokyo, 82. *Mem:* AAAS; AMA; Am Acad Dermat; Soc Invest Dermat; Am Dermat Asn. *Res:* Immunology, especially delayed and granulomatous hypersensitivity and viral and cancer immunology; skin anatomy and epidermal cell turnover. *Mailing Add:* Dept of Dermat Univ of Calif Med Ctr San Francisco CA 94143

EPSTEIN, WILLIAM WARREN, b Kremmling, Colo, Sept 10, 31; m 53, 80; c 3. BIO-ORGANIC CHEMISTRY. *Educ:* Univ Denver, BS, 53; Univ Calif, PhD(chem), 59. *Prof Exp:* Res scientist, Weyerhaeuser Co, 58-60; fel, Univ Ill, 60-61; from asst prof to assoc prof, 61-73, PROF CHEM, UNIV UTAH, 73- *Mem:* Am Chem Soc; Chem Soc London; Sigma Xi. *Res:* Biosynthesis of terpenoids; natural products. *Mailing Add:* Dept Chem Univ Utah Salt Lake City UT 84112

EPSTEIN, WOLFGANG, b Breslau, Ger, May 7, 31; US citizen; m 61; c 3. BIOCHEMISTRY. *Educ:* Swarthmore Col, BA, 51; Univ Minn, MD, 55. *Prof Exp:* Fel biophys, Harvard Med Sch, 61-63; guest investr molecular biol, Pasteur Inst, Paris, 63-65; res assoc biophys, Harvard Med Sch, 65-67; from asst prof to assoc prof, 67-79, PROF BIOCHEM, UNIV CHICAGO, 79- *Concurrent Pos:* Mem, NIH Microbial Chem Study Sect, 73-77. *Mem:* Am Soc Biol Chemists; Am Soc Microbiol; Biophys Soc; AAAS. *Res:* Transport, regulation and genetic mechanisms in bacteria with major reliance on genetic analysis of these processes. *Mailing Add:* Dept of Biochem Univ of Chicago Chicago IL 60637

ERASMUS, BETH DE WET, b Niagara Falls, NY, Oct 19, 35; m 65; c 2. PHYSIOLOGY. *Educ:* Wellesley Col, AB, 57; State Univ NY Buffalo, PhD(physiol), 67. *Prof Exp:* Res asst pharmacol, Chas Pfizer Co Inc, 58-60; from instr to asst prof, 67-72, CLIN ASST PROF PHYSIOL, STATE UNIV NY BUFFALO, 72- *Mem:* Assoc Am Phys Soc. *Res:* Gas exchange and acid-base balance in the avian embryo. *Mailing Add:* Dept of Physiol Sherman Hall State Univ of NY Buffalo NY 14214

ERB, DENNIS J, b Philadelphia, Pa, Apr 19, 52; m 74. MEDICINAL CHEMISTRY. *Educ:* E Stroudsburg State Col, BA, 73; State Univ NY, Buffalo, PhD(med chem), 78. *Prof Exp:* Res asst prof chem, Kalamazoo Col, 78-79; ASST PROF CHEM, EAST STROUDSBURG STATE COL, 79- *Mem:* Am Chem Soc; NY Acad Sci; Sigma Xi. *Res:* Design and synthesis of new compounds whose most profound activity might involve a direct interaction with DNA and elicit biological activities through their interaction. *Mailing Add:* Dept of Chem East Stroudsburg State Col East Stroudsburg PA 18301

ERB, JOHN HOFFMAN, b Harrisburg, Pa, Nov 7, 05; m 33; c 5. DAIRY SCIENCE. *Educ:* Pa State Univ, BS, 27; Ohio State Univ, MSc, 28. *Prof Exp:* Asst supt prod, Reid Ice Cream Co, 28-29; from instr to asst prof dairy technol, Ohio State Univ, 29-43; lab dir, Borden Co, 43-44, dir prod, Midwest Div, 44-53, vpres in-chg, 53-69, vpres res & develop, 69-70; CONSULT, 70- *Concurrent Pos:* Chmn res & develop comt, Borden Fluid Milk & Ice Cream Div, 63- *Mem:* Am Dairy Sci Asn. *Res:* Effect of pasteurization on nutritive value of milk; ingredients for ice cream; effect of light on vitamins and flavor of milk; condensed and dry milk; dairy products manufacturing. *Mailing Add:* 1697 Berkshire Rd Columbus OH 43221

ERB, KENNETH, b Souderton, Pa, Apr 28, 39; m 64. HORTICULTURE. *Educ:* Goshen Col, BA, 61; WVa Univ, MS, 64, PhD(agr microbiol), 66. *Prof Exp:* Lectr biol, Vassar Col, 66-67, asst prof, 67-69; asst prof, 69-77, ASSOC PROF BIOL, HOFSTRA UNIV, 77- *Mem:* Mycol Soc Am; Phycol Soc Am; Bot Soc Am. *Res:* field botany (ecosystem flora determination). *Mailing Add:* Dept of Biol Hofstra Univ Hempstead NY 11550

ERB, RALPH EUGENE, b Dow, Ill, May 28, 17; m 41; c 1. ANIMAL PHYSIOLOGY. *Educ:* Univ Ill, BS, 40; Purdue Univ, MS, 42, PhD(physiol), 47. *Prof Exp:* Asst instr dairy husb, Purdue Univ, 40-43, instr, 46-47; from asst prof to prof, State Col Wash, 47-62; prof, 62-79, EMER PROF ANIMAL SCI, PURDUE UNIV, WEST LAFAYETTE, 79- *Mem:* Am Dairy Sci Asn; Am Soc Animal Sci; Endocrine Soc. *Res:* Endocrine physiology; reproductive physiology; milk secretion. *Mailing Add:* 85 Calypso Ct Olympia WA 98503

ERB, ROBERT ALLAN, b Ridley Park, Pa, Jan 30, 32; m 53; c 3. PHYSICAL CHEMISTRY. *Educ:* Univ Pa, BS, 53; Drexel Inst, MS, 59; Temple Univ, PhD(phys chem), 65. *Prof Exp:* Chemist, Gates Eng Co, Del, 53-54; res asst, 54-56, res engr, 56-61, sr res chemist, 61-65, sr staff chemist, 65-68, prin scientist, 68-81, INST FEL, RES CTR, FRANKLIN INST, 81- *Mem:* AAAS; Am Chem Soc; Soc Plastics Engrs; Int Solar Energy Soc; Sigma Xi. *Res:* Physical chemistry of surfaces; technology of polymeric and colloidal materials; adhesion; rheology; heterogeneous nucleation; desalination; medical applications of physical science; environmental science; waste management; solar energy applications. *Mailing Add:* Franklin Inst Res Ctr 20th & Parkway Philadelphia PA 19103

ERBACHER, JOHN KORNEL, b Washington, DC, Aug 4, 42; m 66; c 3. PHYSICAL INORGANIC CHEMISTRY. *Educ:* Cath Univ Am, BA, 64, MS, 67; Colo State Univ, PhD(phys chem), 73. *Prof Exp:* Res chemist, Directorate Chem Sci, Frank J Seiler Res Lab, 73-75, dep dir, 75-77; chief thermal battery res, 77-78, ASST CHIEF METALS BR, MANTECH DIV, AIR FORCE MAT LAB, WRIGHT-PATTERSON AFB, 78- *Concurrent Pos:* Mem, Subgroup Chromates, Joint Deps Labs Comts Subpanel Thermal Batteries, 75- *Mem:* Electrochem Soc. *Res:* Oxidation-reduction and substitution kinetics of inorganic metal ion systems; physical and electrochemical properties of aluminum chloride based molten salt systems; molten salt primary, secondary, and thermal batteries; aluminum and titanium powder metallurgy; manufacturing methods pertaining to metals fabrication. *Mailing Add:* Air Force Mat Lab AFML/LTM Wright-Patterson AFB OH 45433

ERBAR, JOHN HAROLD, b El Reno, Okla, Nov 23, 31; m 59. CHEMICAL ENGINEERING. *Educ:* Okla State Univ, BS, 54, MS, 59, PhD(chem eng), 60. *Prof Exp:* Res engr, Calif Res Corp, 60-61; plant foreman, Standard Oil Co Calif, 61-62; from asst prof to assoc prof chem eng, 62-69, PROF CHEM ENG, OKLA STATE UNIV, 69- *Concurrent Pos:* Ford Found engr res, Monsanto Co, 66-67. *Mem:* Am Inst Chem Engrs; Am Chem Soc; Nat Soc Prof Engrs. *Res:* Transport properties of liquid mixtures; distillation; reaction kinetics. *Mailing Add:* 1 Fox Ledge Lane RR 4 Stillwater OK 74074

ERBE, LAWRENCE WAYNE, b Ancon, CZ, June 30, 24; m 55; c 5. BOTANY. *Educ:* Univ Vt, BS, 53, MS, 55; Univ Tex, PhD(bot), 60. *Prof Exp:* Asst prof, 60-66, ASSOC PROF BIOL, UNIV SOUTHWESTERN LA, 66- *Mem:* Bot Soc Am. *Res:* Hybridization of Lotus tenuis and Lotus corniculatus; biosystematics of annual phloxes. *Mailing Add:* Dept of Biol Univ of Southwestern La Lafayette LA 70506

ERBER, THOMAS, b Vienna, Austria, Dec 6, 30; nat US; m 57. PHYSICS. *Educ:* Mass Inst Technol, BSc, 51; Univ Chicago, MS, 53, PhD(physics), 57. *Prof Exp:* From asst prof to assoc prof, 57-69, PROF PHYSICS, ILL INST TECHNOL, 69- *Concurrent Pos:* Ill Inst Technol fac fel, 58-59; res fel, Univ Brussels, 63-64; vis scientist, Stanford Linear Accelerator Ctr, 70; vis prof, Graz Univ, 71 & Univ Calif, Los Angeles, 78; vis prof, Univ Grenoble, France, 82 & Neel Lab, 82. *Mem:* Sr mem Inst Elec & Electronics Engrs; fel Am Phys Soc; Am Math Soc; Austrian Phys Soc; Europ Phys Soc. *Res:* Classical and quantum electrodynamics; ultra high magnetic fields; cooperative systems; statistical physics. *Mailing Add:* Dept Physics Ill Inst of Technol Chicago IL 60616

ERBISCH, FREDERIC H, b Sebawaing, Mich, June 24, 37; m 57; c 2. BOTANY, CYTOLOGY. *Educ:* Mich State Univ, BS, 59; Univ Mich, MS, 61, PhD(bot), 66. *Prof Exp:* prof bot, 63-80, ACTG DIR RES, MICH TECHNOL UNIV, 80- *Mem:* Sigma Xi; Biol Photographers Asn; Bot Soc Am; Am Bryol & Lichenological Soc; Mycol Soc Am. *Res:* Cytodevelopment of lichen asci and ascospores; effects of gamma irradiation on lichens and lichen-forming fungi and algae; enzyme systems of wood rotting fungi. *Mailing Add:* Res Off Mich Technol Univ Houghton MI 49931

ERBY, WILLIAM ARTHUR, b Lebanon, Pa, Apr 4, 33; m 57; c 2. ORGANIC CHEMISTRY. *Educ:* Lebanon Valley Col, BS, 55; Bucknell Univ, MS, 57; State Univ NY Col Forestry, PhD(chem), 61. *Prof Exp:* Chemist, Kimberly Clark Corp, 60-63; chemist, Air Prod & Chem Inc, 63-64, group leader, 64-68; mgr res, 68-70, VPRES RES, DAUBERT CHEM CO, 70- *Mem:* Am Chem Soc. *Res:* Wood, polymer and textile chemistry. *Mailing Add:* Daubert Chem Co 4700 Central Ave Chicago IL 60638

ERCK, ANNA, biochemistry, see previous edition

ERDAL, BRUCE ROBERT, b Albuquerque, NMex, June 15, 39; m 70. NUCLEAR CHEMISTRY, RADIOCHEMISTRY. *Educ:* Univ NMex, BS, 61; Washington Univ, St Louis, PhD(nuclear chem), 66. *Prof Exp:* Asst chem, Washington Univ, 61-63, asst nuclear chem, 63-66, res assoc, 66-67; res assoc, Brookhaven Nat Lab, NY, 67-69; NSF fel, Europ Orgn Nuclear Res, 69-70, vis scientist, 70-71; asst physicist, Ames Lab, US AEC, 71-72; staff mem, 72-80, DEP GROUP LEADER, ISOTOPE GEOCHEM GROUP, LOS ALAMOS NAT LAB, 80- *Mem:* Am Chem Soc; Sigma Xi; Am Inst Chemists. *Res:* Nuclear structure, fission and reactions; radiochemistry; electromagnetic isotope separation; nuclear waste management; geochemistry. *Mailing Add:* CNC-11 MS514 Los Alamos Sci Lab Los Alamos NM 87545

ERDELYI, IVAN NICHOLAS, b Timisoara, Romania, Apr 14, 26; US citizen; m 50. MATHEMATICAL ANALYSIS. *Educ:* Univ Cluj, grad, 51; Univ Rome, Docent, 68. *Prof Exp:* Asst prof physics & math, Polytech Inst Timisoara, 51-59; math analyst, Olivetti Gen Elec, Italy, 62-67; assoc prof comput sci, Kans State Univ, 67-69; assoc prof, 69-72, PROF MATH, TEMPLE UNIV, 72- *Mem:* Am Math Soc; NY Acad Sci. *Res:* Abstract and functional analysis. *Mailing Add:* Dept of Math Temple Univ Philadelphia PA 19122

ERDLE, PHILIP J, mechanics, see previous edition

ERDLEY, HAROLD F(REDERICK), b Los Angeles, Calif, Nov 27, 25; m 52; c 5. ELECTRONIC ENGINEERING. *Educ:* Univ Calif, BS, 48, MS, 50. *Prof Exp:* Systs engr, N Am Aviation, Inc, 50-54; electromech sect head, Litton Industs, 54-57, mgr guid & control dept, 57-59, div guid systs lab, 59-60, vpres & dir eng, Litton Systs, Inc, 60-61, electromech eng, 61-63, instrument res, 63-68; dir navig systs progs, 68-70, vpres navig systs progs, 70-80, VPRES DIR ADV SYSTS, TELEDYNE SYSTS CO, 80- *Mem:* Inst Elec & Electronics Engrs; Instrument Soc Am. *Res:* Inertial navigation systems and associated devices. *Mailing Add:* Teledyne Controls Co Adv Systs 12333 Olympic Bl Los Angeles CA 90064

ERDMAN, ANNE MARIE, b Voorburg, Neth, June 10, 16; nat US. NUTRITION. *Educ:* Col Home Econ, Neth, BS, 39, dipl, 42; Fla State Univ, MS, 53, PhD, 56. *Prof Exp:* Instr foods & nutrit, Col Home Econ, Neth, 42-52; res assoc, Inst Rural Home Econ Res, 56-57; assoc prof, 57-71, PROF FOOD & NUTRIT, FLA STATE UNIV, 71- *Concurrent Pos:* Govt dietitian, Pub Health Serv, Indonesia. *Mem:* AAAS; Am Home Econ Asn; Am Dietetic Asn; Inst Food Technol. *Res:* Food consumption patterns, factors affecting them. *Mailing Add:* Dept of Food & Nutrit Fla State Univ Tallahassee FL 32306

ERDMAN, ARTHUR GUY, b Hackensack, NJ, July 7, 45; div; c 2. COMPUTER AIDED DESIGN MECHANISMS. *Educ:* Rutgers Univ, BS, 67; Rensselaer Polytech Inst, MS, 68, PHD(mech eng), 71. *Prof Exp:* Asst prof, 71-75, assoc prof, 75-80, PROF MECH ENG, UNIV MINN, 80- *Concurrent Pos:* Co-prin investr, NIH, 75-79; lectr, Honeywell, Inc, 76-77; consult, Truth Inc, 78-, Proctor & Gamble Co, 79-80, Yamaha Corp, 80- & Zerox, 82-; prin investr, Lawrence Livermore Labs, Dept Energy, 79-81; mem, Mech Syst Adv Comt, NSF, 82- *Honors & Awards:* Ralph R Teetor Eng Educ Award, Soc Automotive Engrs, 77 & 81; Gustus L Larson Mem Award, Am Soc Mech Engrs, 80. *Mem:* Am Soc Mech Engrs; Am Soc Eng Educ; Sigma Xi; Soc Advan Educ. *Res:* Mechanical design; computer aided design; bioengineering; kinematics; dynamical and computer graphics. *Mailing Add:* Dept Mech Eng Univ Minn 111 Church St SE Minneapolis MN 55455

ERDMAN, HOWARD E, b Hazleton, Pa, May 18, 30; m 59; c 2. GENETICS, RADIATION ECOLOGY. *Educ:* Muhlenberg Col, BS, 53; Lehigh Univ, MS, 55; NC State Col, PhD(genetics), 59. *Prof Exp:* Scientist ecol, Gen Elec Co, 59-65, sr res scientist, Battelle Northwest Labs, 65-70; ASSOC PROF BIOL, TEX WOMAN'S UNIV, 71-, RADIATION SAFETY OFFICER, 75- *Concurrent Pos:* Prog officer, Int Atomic Energy Agency, Vienna, Austria, 66-69. *Mem:* AAAS; Ecol Soc Am; Entom Soc Am; Entom Soc Can. *Res:* Genetics, morphology, cytology and histopathology of radiation effects; population ecology. *Mailing Add:* Dept of Biol Tex Woman's Univ Denton TX 76204

ERDMAN, JOHN GORDON, b Baltimore, Md, Apr 12, 19; m 48. PETROLEUM, ORGANIC GEOCHEMISTRY. *Educ:* Johns Hopkins Univ, BA, 40, PhD(org chem), 43. *Prof Exp:* Jr instr org chem, Johns Hopkins Univ, 42-43; res chemist, Nat Defense Res Comt, 43-45; res chemist, Off Sci Res & Develop & fel, Mellon Inst, 45-56, sr fel, 56-65; mgr geochem br, 65-74, SR SCIENTIST EXPLOR & PROD, PHILLIPS PETROL CO, 74- *Mem:* Am Asn Petrol Geologists; Am Chem Soc; Geol Soc Am; Geochem Soc; Am Geophys Union. *Res:* Genesis of petroleum; physics and electrochemistry of primary and secondary migration; applied exploration and production methods; integrated computerized systems utilizing geological, geochemical and geophysical data for evaluation of economic potential of basins; biotechnology, biochemical products. *Mailing Add:* Res & Develop Dept Phillips Petrol Co Bartlesville OK 74004

ERDMAN, JOHN PAUL, b Oak Park, Ill, Oct 2, 42; m 65; c 2. RUBBER CHEMISTRY. *Educ:* Univ Miami, BS, 64; Univ Md, PhD(org chem), 71. *Prof Exp:* RES CHEMIST, ELASTOMER CHEM DEPT, EXP STA, E I DU PONT DE NEMOURS & CO, INC, 69- *Mem:* Am Chem Soc; Sigma Xi. *Res:* Thermodynamics of cyclic dienes; olefinic carbanions; organic fluorine chemistry. *Mailing Add:* Elastomer Chem Dept E I du Pont de Nemours & Co Wilmington DE 19898

ERDMAN, JOHN WILSON, JR, b Hackensack, NJ, July 7, 45; m 74. FOOD SCIENCE. *Educ:* Rutgers Univ, BS, 68, MS, 73, MPhil, 74, PhD(food sci), 75. *Prof Exp:* Flavor chemist prod res, Pepsico Corp Res, 68; from res asst to res intern food sci, Rutgers Univ, 70-75; asst prof, 75-80, ASSOC PROF FOOD SCI, UNIV ILL, 80- *Mem:* Inst Food Technologists; assoc mem Am Inst Nutrit; Soc Nutrit Educ; Sigma Xi; Nutrit Today Soc. *Res:* The effects of food processing upon nutrient retention with emphasis on soybean products; the metabolic role of vitamin A, especially as it relates to lipogenesis; bioavailability of minerals from foods. *Mailing Add:* Dept Food Sci 567 Bevier Hall Univ Ill 905 S Goodwin Ave Urbana IL 61801

ERDMAN, KIMBALL S, b Salt Lake City, Utah, June 13, 37; m 67; c 3. BOTANY. *Educ:* Brigham Young Univ, BA, 59, MS, 61; Iowa State Univ, PhD(bot), 64. *Prof Exp:* Asst prof bot, Weber State Col, 64-67; assoc prof biol, 67-71, PROF BIOL, SLIPPERY ROCK STATE COL, 71- *Concurrent Pos:* Field consult, Natural Nat Landmark Prog, Dept Interior, 72-80. *Mem:* Sigma Xi. *Res:* Distribution of the native trees of Utah; monograph of the genus Spenopholis; natural areas of western Pennsylvania; forest ecology; alternative evolution models; alternative ancient history models. *Mailing Add:* Dept of Biol Slippery Rock State Col Slippery Rock PA 16057

ERDMAN, TIMOTHY ROBERT, b Eau Claire, Wis, July 16, 44; m 68; c 2. ORGANIC CHEMISTRY. *Educ:* Univ Chicago, BS, 66; Stanford Univ, PhD(chem), 71. *Prof Exp:* Nuffield Found fel chem, Univ Aberdeen, 70-71; NIH fel, Univ Hawaii, 71-73; res chemist, 73-80, SR RES CHEMIST, CHEVRON RES CO, STANDARD OIL CO, CALIF, 80- *Mem:* Am Chem Soc. *Res:* Lubricating oil additives; marine natural products. *Mailing Add:* Chevron Res Co PO Box 1627 Richmond CA 94802

ERDMAN, WILLIAM JAMES, II, b Philadelphia, Pa, Apr 8, 21. MEDICINE. *Educ:* Swarthmore Col, BA, 43; Univ Pa, MD, 50, MSc, 52; Am Bd Phys Med & Rehab, dipl. *Prof Exp:* Asst instr phys med & rehab, Sch Med, 51-53, instr, 53-54, assoc & actg chmn dept, Grad Sch Med, 54-55, asst prof, Sch Med, 56-60, asst dean, Sch Med, 68-74, med dir, 68-78, PROF PHYS MED & REHAB, SCH MED & GRAD SCH MED, UNIV PA, 60-, CHMN DEPT, 56-, DIR, DEPT PHYS MED & REHAB, UNIV HOSP, 56- *Concurrent Pos:* Mem spec med adv group, Vet Admin; chief, Philadelphia Gen Hosp; attend physician & consult, Vet Admin Hosp, Philadelphia; consult, Vet Admin Hosps, Lebanon & Wilmington. *Honors & Awards:* Gold Key Award, Am Cong Rehab Med, 66. *Mem:* AAAS; fel Am Col Physicians; Am Cong Rehab Med (pres, 64-65, treas, 70); Int Rehab Med Asn (treas, 70-). *Res:* Neuromuscular disorders. *Mailing Add:* Dept Phys Med & Rehab Univ of Pa Hosp Philadelphia PA 19104

ERDMANN, DAVID E, b St Charles, Minn, July 15, 39; m 69. ANALYTICAL CHEMISTRY, INORGANIC CHEMISTRY. *Educ:* Winona State Col, BS, 60; Univ Nebr, Lincoln, MS, 66, PhD(chem), 68. *Prof Exp:* Chemist, 68-71, res chemist, 71-78, LAB DIR, WATER RESOURCES DIV, US GEOL SURV, 78- *Mem:* Am Chem Soc. *Res:* Investigation of spectroscopic properties of some copper II beta-ketoamine chelates; improvement and development of analytical methods for water analysis; automation of water analysis methods. *Mailing Add:* Water Resources Div 6481-H Peachtree Industrial Blvd Doraville GA 30340

ERDMANN, DUANE JOHN, b Rochester, Minn, Apr 21, 46; m 68. PHOTOGRAPHIC CHEMISTRY. *Educ:* Iowa State Univ, BS, 68; Univ Minn, PhD(chem), 74. *Prof Exp:* res chemist, 74-80, RES SUPVR, PHOTO PROD DEPT, E I DU PONT DE NEMOURS & CO, INC, 80- *Mem:* Am Chem Soc; Soc Photog Scientists & Engrs. *Res:* Research and development of photographic emulsion with emphasis on those having monodisperse grains; products for graphic arts applications; related raw materials testing. *Mailing Add:* Photo Prod Div 666 Driving Park Rochester NY 14613

ERDMANN, JOACHIM CHRISTIAN, b Danzig, Poland, June 5, 28; m 57; c 3. ELECTROOPTICS, SOLID STATE PHYSICS. *Educ:* Tech Univ Braunschweig, Ger, Dipl Phys, 55, Dr rer nat(physics), 58. *Prof Exp:* Res specialist, Boeing Sci Res Labs, 60-72, PRIN ENGR, BOEING COM AIRPLANE CO, 73- *Concurrent Pos:* Vis prof, Max Planck Inst Metal Res, 68-69. *Mem:* Am Phys Soc; Optical Soc Am; Soc Photo-Optical Instrumentation Engrs. *Res:* Low-temperature experimental physics; laser applications; statistical optics. *Mailing Add:* MS 47-06 Boeing Co PO Box 3707 Seattle WA 98124

ERDMANN, ROBERT CHARLES, b Paterson, NJ, Jan 3, 39; m 69; c 4. NUCLEAR ENGINEERING. *Educ:* Newark Col Eng, BS, 60; Univ Calif, Los Angeles, MS, 62; Calif Inst Technol, PhD(appl mech & physics), 65. *Prof Exp:* Mem tech staff, Hughes Aircraft Co, 60-62; from asst prof to prof eng, Univ Calif, Los Angeles, 65-75; MGR, SCI APPLN, INC, 73- *Concurrent Pos:* Consult to industs, labs & comns, 65-; mem, Atomic Indust Forum Comt Reactor Safety & Licensing, 73- *Mem:* Fel Am Nuclear Soc; Am Phys Soc. *Res:* Nuclear reactor safety and reliability analysis; risk analysis in engineering; fast reactor accident physics; chemical industry safety analysis. *Mailing Add:* Sci Appln Inc 5 Palo Alto Sq Suite 200 Palo Alto CA 94304

ERDOGAN, FAZIL, b Kars, Turkey, Feb 5, 25; m 61; c 2. APPLIED MECHANICS. *Educ:* Tech Univ Istanbul, MS, 48; Lehigh Univ, PhD(mech eng), 55. *Prof Exp:* Instr eng, Tech Univ Istanbul, 48-52; asst, 52-55, from asst prof to assoc prof mech eng, 57-63, PROF MECH, LEHIGH UNIV, 63- *Mem:* Am Soc Mech Engr; Soc Eng Sci; Soc Indust & Appl Math; Am Math Soc; Turkish Soc Pure & Appl Math. *Res:* Mechanics of non-homogeneous media; thermoelasticity; viscoelasticity; brittle fracture; metal fatigue; integral equations. *Mailing Add:* Dept of Mech Eng & Mech Lehigh Univ Bethlehem PA 18015

ERDOS, ERVIN GEORGE, b Budapest, Hungary, Oct 16, 22; US citizen; m 52; c 3. PHARMACOLOGY. *Educ:* Univ Munich, MD, 50. *Prof Exp:* Asst, Inst Pathophysiol, Budapest, 47-50; res assoc biochem, Res Lab, Surg Clin, Munich, 52-54; res fel, Sch Med, Univ Pittsburgh, 54-55; res assoc anesthesia, Mercy Hosp, Pa, 55-58; from clin asst prof to clin assoc prof pharmacol, Univ Pittsburgh, 58-63; prof, Sch Med, Univ Okla, 63-70, George Lynn Cross res prof pharmacol, 70-73; PROF PHARMACOL & INTERNAL MED, UNIV TEX HEALTH SCI CTR, DALLAS, 73- *Concurrent Pos:* Fel biochem, Mellon Inst, 58-63; mem, Coun High Blood Pressure Res. *Mem:* AAAS; Am Soc Pharmacol & Exp Therapeut; Am Heart Asn; Int Soc Hypertension. *Res:* Biochemical pharmacology; cardiovascular diseases and hypertension. *Mailing Add:* Dept of Pharmacol Univ of Tex Southwestern Med Sch Dallas TX 75235

ERDOS, GREGORY WILLIAM, b Akron, Ohio, Sept 21, 45. MYCOLOGY. *Educ:* Ohio State Univ, BS, 67; Univ NC, PhD(bot), 71. *Prof Exp:* Res assoc mycol, Univ Wis-Madison, 71-77; MEM FAC MYCOL, UNIV FLA, 77- *Mem:* Mycol Soc Am; Am Soc Microbiol; AAAS; Am Soc Cell Biol. *Res:* Developmental ultrastructure and genetics of cellular slime molds and related organisms. *Mailing Add:* Dept Microbiol & Cell Sci Univ of Fla Gainesville FL 32611

ERDTMANN, BERND DIETRICH, b Breslau, Ger, Aug 17, 39. PALEONTOLOGY, PALEOECOLOGY. *Educ:* Univ Hamburg, MS, 62, DSc(geol), 75; Univ Oslo, PhD(geol), 65. *Prof Exp:* Fel geol, Laval Univ, 66; Can Nat Res Coun fel, Carleton Univ, 66-68; from asst prof to assoc prof, 68-76, chmn dept, 76-80, PROF GEOL, IND UNIV, FT WAYNE, 76- *Concurrent Pos:* Attend, Int Conf Continental Drift, Nfld, 67; consult, Can Geol Surv, 68-71; mem, Cambrian-Ordovician Boundary Comt, Int Union Geol Sci, 74- & Graptolite Res Comt, Int Asn Planetology, 77-; vis prof, Ariz State Univ, 78- *Mem:* Ger Geol Soc; Norweg Geol Soc; Swedish Geol Soc; Geol Soc Am; Soc Econ Paleontologists & Mineralogists. *Res:* Paleontology, biostratigraphy, and numerical taxonomy of Ordovician graptolites; taphonomy and fossilization of recent invertebrate marine biota; paleoichnology (trace fossils); carbonate sedimentary systems analysis. *Mailing Add:* Dept of Geol Ind Univ Ft Wayne IN 46805

ERECINSKA, MARIA, b Warsaw, Poland, Aug 17, 39. MEDICINE, BIOCHEMISTRY. *Educ:* Med Sch, Gdansk, MD, 61; Polish Acad Sci, PhD(biochem), 67. *Prof Exp:* Res assoc biochem, Univ Tex Med Br Galveston, 61-63; res assoc, Polish Acad Sci, 64-67, asst prof, 67-69; fel biophys, Univ Pa, 69-71; asst prof biophys, 71-78, ASSOC PROF PHARMACOL, UNIV PA, 78- *Concurrent Pos:* Travel fel, Nat Ctr Sci Res, France, 68; Pa Plan scholar, 70. *Honors & Awards:* Merck Award, 71. *Mem:* Polish Biochem Soc; Am Soc Biol Chem. *Res:* Mitochondrial structure and function; bioenergetics; hemoproteins. *Mailing Add:* Dept Pharmacol Univ Pa Philadelphia PA 19174

ERENRICH, ERIC HOWARD, b West Palm Beach, Fla, Jan 10, 44; m 67; c 2. ORGANIC COATINGS, RHEOLOGY. *Educ:* Carnegie Inst Technol, BS, 65; Cornell Univ, PhD(phys chem), 71. *Prof Exp:* Res fel, Cornell Univ, 71-72; sr chemist, Rohm and Haas Co, 72-76; group leader, NL Indust, 76-79; appl res, Rheometrics, Inc, 80; INDUST MGR FIBERS & PLASTICS CO, ALLIED CORP, 80- *Mem:* Am Chem Soc; Sigma Xi; Fedn Soc Coating Technol. *Res:* Physical chemistry of polymers and coatings; applied rheology; modification of coatings, adhesive and inks by low moleculer weight polyethylene and waxes. *Mailing Add:* Fibers & Plastics Co Allied Corp Box 2332R Morristown NJ 07960

ERENRICH, EVELYN SCHWARTZ, b New York, NY, Dec 16, 46; m 67; c 2. ENZYMOLOGY, PHYSICAL BIOCHEMISTRY. *Educ:* Cornell Univ, BS, 67, MS, 69, PhD(biophys chem), 71. *Prof Exp:* Lectr chem, Cornell Univ, 71-72; from scientist to prin scientist, Leeds & Northrup Co, 72-78; CHEM CONSULT, 78- *Mem:* Am Chem Soc. *Res:* Structure, function and application of enzymes and biopolymers; analytical applications of biochemicals; enzyme immobilization. *Mailing Add:* 9 Constitution Ct East Brunswick NJ 08816

ERF, ROBERT K, b Cleveland, Ohio, Oct 29, 31; m 54; c 4. LASER METROLOGY. *Educ:* Univ Mich, BSEE, 53; Harvard Univ, MS, 54. *Prof Exp:* Res engr, 54-61, supvr gen instrumentation, 61-68, CHIEF, OPTICS & ACOUST, UNITED TECHNOL RES CTR, 68- *Concurrent Pos:* Ed, Laser Appl Series, Acad Press. *Mem:* Optical Soc Am; Acoust Soc Am; Am Soc Nondestructive Testing. *Res:* Interferometry; ultrasonics; applications of lasers to optical instruments; holographic technology for flow visualization; nondestructive testing; strain measurement and vibration analysis; laser machining systems development; acoustic emission. *Mailing Add:* United Technol Res Ctr East Hartford CT 06108

ERFLE, JAMES DAVID, b Saskatchewan, Can, Aug 15, 33; m 58; c 4. RUMINANT NUTRITION. *Educ:* Univ Sask, BSA, 57, MS, 59; Univ Ill, PhD(nutrit biochem), 63. *Prof Exp:* RES SCIENTIST, ANIMAL RES INST, AGR CAN, 64- *Concurrent Pos:* Vis scientist, Harvard Univ, 70-71. *Mem:* Am Dairy Sci Asn. *Res:* Bovine ketosis, pathway of ketone body synthesis; ruminant nutrition and rumen bacteriology, nitrogen assimilation into amino acids and proteins. *Mailing Add:* 2048 Neatby Bldg CEF Ottawa ON K1A 0C6 Can

ERHARDT, PAUL WILLIAM, b Minneapolis, Minn, Oct 31, 47; m 71; c 5. MEDICINAL CHEMISTRY. *Educ:* Univ Minn, BA, 69, PhD(med chem), 74. *Prof Exp:* Res assoc, Drug Dynamics Inst, Col Pharm, Univ Tex, Austin, 74-75; asst prof med chem, Col Pharm, Northeastern Univ, 75-76; res investr, Med-Organic Chem Dept, 76-79, SR RES INVESTR, AM CRITICAL CARE, MCGAW PARK, ILL, 79- *Mem:* Am Chem Soc; Am Pharmaceut Asn; Acad Pharmaceut Sci. *Res:* Cardiovascular and dopaminergic medicinal chemistry; design of prodrugs and soft drugs. *Mailing Add:* Arnar-Stone Labs 1600 Waukegan Rd McGaw Park IL 60085

ERHARDT, PETER FRANKLIN, b Grand Rapids, Mich, June 26, 33; m 58; c 4. POLYMER PHYSICS. *Educ:* Aquinas Col, BS, 55; Univ Mich, MS, 57; Univ Mass, PhD(phys chem), 68. *Prof Exp:* Instr chem, Aquinas Col, 57-60; res trainee polymer physics, Gen Elec Res Lab, NY, 60-63; res asst, Polymer Res Inst, Univ Mass, Amherst, 63-66; res chemist, Gen Elec Co, 66-67; from scientist to sr scientist, 67-73, prin scientist, 73-80, MGR, MKT MAT AREA, XEROX CORP, 80- *Mem:* Am Chem Soc; Am Phys Soc. *Res:* Rheology; rheo-optics and optical properties of synthetic polymers; mechanical, thermal property measurements on polymers and structure-property correlations; xerographic developer materials; toners and carriers; inks; color. *Mailing Add:* Xerox Corp 800 Phillips Rd Webster NY 14580

ERHART, RAINER R, b Monstab, Ger, June 25, 35; US citizen; m 61; c 2. PHYSICAL GEOGRAPHY. *Educ:* Eastern Mich Univ, BA, 59; Univ Ill, MA, 61, PhD(geog), 67. *Prof Exp:* Asst prof, 65-68, ASSOC PROF GEOG, WESTERN MICH UNIV, 68- *Mem:* AAAS; Asn Am Geogr; Am Geog Soc; Nat Coun Geog Educ; Am Soc Photogram. *Res:* New media development in geography; remote sensing; agricultural geography. *Mailing Add:* Dept of Geog Western Mich Univ Kalamazoo MI 49008

ERHLICH, ROBERT, b Brooklyn, NY, Feb 6, 38; m 61; c 1. PHYSICS. *Educ:* Brooklyn Col, BS, 59; Columbia Univ, PhD(physics), 64. *Prof Exp:* Res investr physics, Univ Pa, 63-66; asst prof, Rutgers Univ, 66-74; assoc prof physics & actg chmn dept, State Univ NY, New Paltz, 74-77; PROF PHYSICS & CHMN DEPT, GEORGE MASON UNIV, FAIRFAX, VA, 77- *Mem:* Am Phys Soc. *Res:* Experimental elementary particle research. *Mailing Add:* Dept Physics George Mason Univ Fairfax VA 22030

ERICH, LEON (DUDLEY), microbiology, biochemistry, see previous edition

ERICKSEN, GEORGE EDWARD, b Butte, Mont, Mar 17, 20; m 48. ECONOMIC GEOLOGY. *Educ:* Mont State Univ, BA, 46; Ind Univ, MA, 49; Columbia Univ, PhD(geol), 54. *Prof Exp:* Geologist, US Geol Surv, 42-45 & 46; geologist, Ind Geol Surv, 47; GEOLOGIST, US GEOL SURV, 48- *Concurrent Pos:* Instr, Ind Univ, 47-49; chief br Latin Am & African geol, US Geol Surv, 71-74; mem US-Japan panel wind & seismic effects, 72-76. *Mem:*

AAAS; Geol Soc Am; Soc Econ Geol; Am Mineral Soc; Geochem Soc. *Res:* Study of metalliferous and saline deposits of the Andes; geology and mineralogy of Chilean nitrate deposits; engineering geology related to earthquakes. *Mailing Add:* US Geol Surv Nat Ctr Reston VA 22092

ERICKSEN, JERALD LAVERNE, b Portland, Ore, Dec 20, 24; m 46; c 2. MECHANICS, MATHEMATICAL PHYSICS. *Educ:* Univ Wash, Seattle, BS, 47; Ore State Univ, MA, 49; Univ Ind, PhD(math), 51. *Prof Exp:* Asst, Univ Wash, Seattle, 46-47; res & asst, Univ Ind, 49-51; mathematician, Naval Res Lab, 51-52 & 53-57; assoc prof theoret mech, 57-60, PROF THEORET MECH, JOHNS HOPKINS UNIV, 60- *Concurrent Pos:* Res assoc, Univ Ind, 52-53; lectr, Univ Md, 51-52 & 53-57. *Honors & Awards:* Bingham Medal, Soc Rheol, 68; Timoshenko Medal, Am Soc Mech Engrs, 79. *Mem:* Soc Natural Philos (treas, 63-64); Soc Rheol; Soc Interaction Mech & Math. *Res:* Nonlinear continuum theories. *Mailing Add:* Dept Mech & Mat Sci Johns Hopkins Univ Baltimore MD 21218

ERICKSEN, MARY FRANCES, b Fortville, Ind, Aug 25, 25; m 48. PHYSICAL ANTHROPOLOGY, HUMAN ANATOMY. *Educ:* Ind Univ, AB, 47; Columbia Univ, MA, 57; George Washington Univ, PhD(anat), 73. *Prof Exp:* Cur paleont, Univ Ky, 47-49; teaching fel, 67-73, spec lectr, 73-78, asst prof, 78-81, ASSOC PROF LECTR ANAT, GEORGE WASHINGTON UNIV, 81- *Concurrent Pos:* Vis prof summer anat prog, Sch Med, Univ Md, 76-80. *Mem:* Am Asn Phys Anthropologists; Am Asn Anatomists; Am Anthrop Asn; Asn Am Archaeol. *Res:* Aging changes in the skeleton; archaeological and contemporary populations; physical anthropology of archaeological populations; paleopathology. *Mailing Add:* Dept of Anat 2300 I St NW Washington DC 20037

ERICKSEN, RICHARD HAROLD, b Seattle, Wash, Aug 17, 38; m 67; c 3. COMPOSITE MATERIALS, FABRICS. *Educ:* Whitman Col, BA, 61; Columbia Univ, BS, 61, MS, 63; Univ Wash, PhD(metall eng), 67. *Prof Exp:* STAFF MEM METALL & MAT ENG, SANDIA NAT LABS, 67- *Mem:* Am Soc Metals; Am Inst Mining Metall & Petrol Engrs; Am Inst Aeronaut & Astronaut. *Res:* Mechanical behavior of composite materials; reinforcing filaments and materials for parachute applications. *Mailing Add:* Div 5814 Sandia Nat Labs Albuquerque NM 87185

ERICKSEN, WILHELM SKJETSTAD, b Green Bay, Wis, May 3, 12; m 39; c 3. MATHEMATICS. *Educ:* St Olaf Col, BA, 36; Univ Wis, MA, 38, PhD(math), 43. *Prof Exp:* Asst prof math, St Olaf Col, 42-43; prof, NDak State Teachers Col, Minot, 43-44; fel mech, Brown Univ, 44; aerodynamicist, Bell Aircraft Corp, Buffalo, 45-46; mathematician, Forest Prod Lab, US Forest Serv, 46-53; PROF MATH, AIR FORCE INST TECHNOL, 53- *Mem:* Am Math Soc; Math Asn Am. *Res:* Sandwich construction for aircraft; stresses in wood structural members. *Mailing Add:* 3598 Eastern Dr Dayton OH 45432

ERICKSON, ALAN ERIC, b Boston, Mass, Feb 6, 28; m 51; c 4. EMBRYOLOGY. *Educ:* Middlebury Col, AB, 49; Boston Univ, MA, 55, PhD(biol), 60; Simmons Col, MLS, 68. *Prof Exp:* Asst inst biol, Boston Univ, 54-55, instr, 55-60; scientist embryol, Worcester Found Exp Biol, 60-66; actg assoc librn for admin, Harvard Col Libr, 70-72; SCI SPECIALIST, HARVARD UNIV LIBR, 66-, LIBRARIAN, GODFREY LOWELL CABOT SCI LIBR, 73- *Mem:* Teratology Soc. *Res:* Hormones in development of the embryonic reproductive system. *Mailing Add:* Cabot Sci Libr Harvard Univ Cambridge MA 02138

ERICKSON, ANTON EARL, b Chicago, Ill, June 5, 19; m 43; c 3. SOIL SCIENCE. *Educ:* Univ Ill, BS, 41, PhD(agron), 48. *Prof Exp:* Asst soil surv, Univ Ill, 41-48; from asst prof to assoc prof soil sci, 48-59, PROF SOIL SCI, MICH STATE UNIV, 59- *Mem:* Fel AAAS; fel Am Soc Agron; fel Soil Sci Soc Am. *Res:* Soil physics; physical soil-plant relations; soil aeration; soil water conservation; land treatment and disposal of waste. *Mailing Add:* 4594 Comanche Okemos MI 48924

ERICKSON, BRUCE WAYNE, b New Haven, Conn, Oct 19, 42; m 69; c 1. BIOCHEMISTRY. *Educ:* Ohio State Univ, BS, 63; Harvard Univ, AM, 65, PhD(org chem), 70. *Prof Exp:* Res assoc, 69-73, asst prof biochem, 73-77, ASSOC PROF BIOCHEM, ROCKEFELLER UNIV, 77- *Mem:* Am Soc Biol Chemists; Am Chem Soc; Am Asn Immunologists; NY Acad Sci; AAAS. *Res:* Solid-phase peptide synthesis; biochemistry of synthetic peptides from complement, antibody and secretory proteins; pattern analysis of nucleic acid and protein sequences. *Mailing Add:* Rockefeller Univ New York NY 10021

ERICKSON, CARL O, b Ames, Iowa, May 21, 24. METEOROLOGY. *Educ:* Guilford Col, AB, 49; Univ Chicago, MS, 55. *Prof Exp:* Meteorologist, US Weather Bur, 49-53 & 55-60, res meteorologist, 60-65, meteorologist, Nat Environ Sattelite Serv, 65-79, RES METEROLOGIST, CLIMATE ANALYSIS CTR, NAT OCEANIC & ATMOSPHERIC ADMIN, 79- *Mem:* Am Geophys Union; Am Meteorol Soc. *Res:* Synoptic meteorology; applications of meteorological satellite data to synoptic weather analysis and interpretation; climate analysis and diagnostics. *Mailing Add:* Climate Analysis Ctr Nat Weather Serv Nat Oceanic & Atmospheric Admin Camp Springs MD 20233

ERICKSON, CARLTON KUEHL, b Manistee, Mich, Apr 6, 39; m 65; c 4. PHARMACOLOGY. *Educ:* Ferris State Col, BS, 61; Purdue Univ, MS, 63, PhD(pharmacol), 65. *Prof Exp:* From asst prof to prof pharmacol, Sch Pharm, Univ Kans, 65-77; PROF PHARMACOL, COL PHARM, UNIV TEX, 78- *Concurrent Pos:* Vis researcher toxicol, Karolinska Inst, Sweden, 73-74. *Mem:* AAAS; Am Soc Pharmacol & Exp Therapeut; Soc Neurosci; Res Soc Alcoholism (vpres, 81-82). *Res:* Effects of ethanol on central neurotransmitters; mechanisms of drugs of abuse; central cholinergic mechanisms; development of sustained release forms of abused drugs. *Mailing Add:* Col of Pharm Univ of Tex Austin TX 78712

ERICKSON, CHARLES EDWARD, inorganic chemistry, deceased

ERICKSON, CYRUS CONRAD, b Alexandria, Minn, Aug 18, 09; m 37; c 3. PATHOLOGY. *Educ:* Univ Minn, BS, 30, BM, 32, MD, 33; Am Bd Path, dipl. *Prof Exp:* Asst resident & res assoc path, Med Sch, Univ Rochester, 35-37; instr, Sch Med, Duke Univ, 37-39, assoc, 39-46, assoc prof, 46-50, assoc pathologist, Univ Hosp, 39-42, 46-50; prof path, 50-77, EMER PROF PATH, MED SCH, UNIV TENN, 77-, HEAD CLIN LAB SCI & DIR SCH MED TECHNOL, 71- *Concurrent Pos:* Fel pediat, Univ Minn, 34-35; consult, US Vet Admin Bur, 55-; actg chmn dept path, Univ Tenn, 68-71. *Honors & Awards:* Award, Am Soc Cytol, 65; Distinguished Serv Award, Am Cancer Soc, 69. *Mem:* AMA; Am Soc Exp Path (secy, 53-56, vpres, 58-59, pres, 59-60); Am Soc Clin Path; Am Soc Cytol (vpres, 57-59, pres, 60-61); fel Col Am Path. *Res:* Choline deficiency and tumor incidence in rats; histogenesis and incidence of intraepithelial carcinoma of cervix in humans; factors influencing development of carcinoma of cervix in mice with prolonged sex steroid administration; investigations on uterine cancer by epidemiological study following genital cytology population screening. *Mailing Add:* 267 Kimbrough St Memphis TN 38104

ERICKSON, DAVID EDWARD, b Grand Island, Nebr, July 15, 31; m 56; c 3. PHYSICAL CHEMISTRY, COLLOID CHEMISTRY. *Educ:* SDak Sch Mines & Technol, BS, 52; Ohio State Univ, PhD(chem), 56. *Prof Exp:* Res chemist, E I du Pont de Nemours & Co, 56-64; sr res chemist, Res Div, Gen Tire Co, 64-66, group leader, 66-69, develop assoc, Chem-Plastics Div, 69-71, res scientist, 71-79, GROUP LEADER, RES & DEVELOP DIV, GEN TIRE & RUBBER CO, 79- *Mem:* Am Chem Soc; Sigma Xi. *Res:* Polymer chemistry; colloids; adhesion; surface science. *Mailing Add:* Gen Tire & Rubber Co Res Div 2990 Gilchrist Rd Akron OH 44305

ERICKSON, DAVID R, b Portland, Ore, Oct 26, 29; m 51; c 3. AGRICULTURAL CHEMISTRY. *Educ:* Ore State Univ, BS, 57, MS, 58; Univ Calif, Davis, PhD(agr chem), 63. *Prof Exp:* Res lipid chemist, Swift & Co, 63-67, head edible fats & margarine res div, 67-70, gen mgr indust prod res, 70-75; dir res, Unitech Chem Inc, 75-78; DIR SOY OIL PROGS, AM SOYBEAN ASN, 78- *Mem:* Sigma Xi; Am Chem Soc; Inst Food Technol; Am Oil Chemists Soc. *Res:* Oxidation of milk and antioxidants in milk and milk products; chemistry of processing edible fats and oils; vegetable proteins, emulsifiers, stabilizers, adhesives. *Mailing Add:* 9059 Monmouth Dr St Louis MO 63117

ERICKSON, DENNIS JOHN, b Minneapolis, Minn, June 9, 42; m 65; c 3. SOLID STATE PHYSICS. *Educ:* Augsberg Col, BA, 64; Univ Tenn, Knoxville, PhD(physics), 71. *Prof Exp:* Res asst physics, Univ NC, Chapel Hill, 68-70, res assoc, 71; Fel physics, 72-73, STAFF MEM, DYNAMIC TESTING DIV, LOS ALAMOS NAT LAB, 74-, DEP GROUP LEADER, SHOCK WAVE PHYSICS, 78- *Mem:* Am Phys Soc. *Res:* Explosive driven pulse power and applications of magnetic flux compression material behavior in ultrahigh magnetic fields, low temperature properties of materials; magnetism, lattice dynamics, super conductivity. *Mailing Add:* Los Alamos Nat Lab MS 970 Los Alamos NM 87545

ERICKSON, DUANE GORDON, b Vinton, Iowa, Jan 30, 31; m 52; c 1. ENTOMOLOGY, BIOCHEMIST. *Educ:* Univ Minn, BA, 53, MS, 57, PhD, 64. *Prof Exp:* US Army, 56-, parasitologist, Sixth Army Med Lab, Calif, 56, parasitologist, Second Army Med Lab, Md, 57-58, chief helminth dept, Army Trop Res Med Lab, PR, 59-61, asst chief dept med zool, Walter Reed Army Inst Res, 64-65, consult parasitol, US Army & chief parasitol br, 9th Med Lab, Vietnam, 66-67, coordr schistosomiasis res & chief schistosomiasis unit, Dept Med Zool, Walter Reed Army Inst Res, 67-71, chief dept med zool, 406th Med Lab, Japan, 71-74, exec secy, Armed Forces Epidemiol Bd, Washington, DC, 74-78, EXEC OFFICER, US ARMY MED BIOENG RES & DEVELOP LAB, FT DETRICK, MD, 78- *Mem:* Am Soc Parasitol; Am Soc Trop Med & Hyg; fel Royal Soc Trop Med & Hyg; Sigma Xi. *Res:* Schistosomatoidea; immunity and pathology of parasitic infections; medical entomology; electron microscopy; immunity and pathology of schistosomiasis; chemotherapy of schistosomiasis; ultrastructural pathology. *Mailing Add:* US Army Med Bioeng Res & Develop Lab Ft Detrick MD 21701

ERICKSON, DUANE OTTO, b Fargo, NDak, Mar 26, 30; m 54; c 3. ANIMAL NUTRITION. *Educ:* NDak State Univ, BS, 57, MS, 60, PhD(animal sci, biochem), 65. *Prof Exp:* Instr & asst animal sci, 59-65, asst prof, 65-67, assoc prof, 67-77, PROF ANIMAL SCI, NDAK STATE UNIV, 77- *Mem:* AAAS; Am Soc Animal Sci. *Res:* Development of methods for forage evaluation; metabolism within the rumen of a ruminant; nutritional requirements of feeder lambs. *Mailing Add:* Dept of Animal Sci NDak State Univ Fargo ND 58102

ERICKSON, EDWARD HERBERT, b Oakland, Calif, Feb 16, 44; m 66; c 3. MEDICINAL CHEMISTRY. *Educ:* Univ Calif, Santa Barbara, BA, 65, PhD(org chem), 68. *Prof Exp:* Res chemist, Riker Labs, Calif, 68-71, res chemist, 71-78, PROJ LEADER PULMONARY-ALLERGY, 3M CO, 78- *Mem:* AAAS; Am Chem Soc. *Res:* Enzyme inhibition and rational drug design; preparation of antiinflammatory and antiallergic drugs. *Mailing Add:* Bldg 270-25 3M Ctr St Paul MN 55101

ERICKSON, EDWIN FRANCIS, b Seattle, Wash, July 13, 34; m 63; c 4. ASTROPHYSICS. *Educ:* Stanford Univ, BS, 57, MS, 59, PhD(physics), 66. *Prof Exp:* Res scientist physics, US Army, 63-65 & NASA, 65-66; res assoc physics, Univ Strasbourg, 66-70; RES SCIENTIST INFRARED ASTRON, AMES RES CTR, NASA, 70- *Concurrent Pos:* Sr res assoc, Nat Res Coun, 70-72. *Mem:* Am Phys Soc; Am Astron Soc; Sigma Xi; AAAS; Am Fedn Scientists. *Res:* Observational infrared astronomy from aircraft and ground-based telescopes; infrared emissions from stars, planets and nebulae. *Mailing Add:* Mail Stop 245-6 NASA-Ames Res Ctr Moffett Field CA 94035

ERICKSON, EDWIN SYLVESTER, JR, b Brooklyn, NY, July 9, 28; m 53; c 4. MINERALOGY, PETROGRAPHY. *Educ:* City Col New York, BS, 51; Pa State Univ, PhD(mineral), 63. *Prof Exp:* Geologist, US Geol Surv, 52-53; res asst geochem & mineral, Pa State Univ, 53-58; RES ENGR, BETHLEHEM STEEL CORP, 58- *Concurrent Pos:* Assoc dept geol, Lehigh Univ, 66- *Res:* Mineralogical investigation of raw materials and refractories for iron and steelmaking; agglomerated iron and manganese ores; mineralogy of refractory clays and bentonites; evaluation of raw materials and interpretation of beneficiation test results. *Mailing Add:* Homer Res Labs Bethlehem Steel Co Bethlehem PA 18016

ERICKSON, EUGENE E, b Fargo, NDak, Sept 15, 23; m 46; c 5. CHEMICAL ENGINEERING. *Educ:* Univ Minn, BChE, 44; NC State Col, PhD(chem eng), 57. *Prof Exp:* Res chem engr, Russell-Miller Milling Co, Minn, 44-50, Minn Mining & Mfg Co, 50-52 & NC State Col, 52-57; res chem engr, Atomic Energy Div, Phillips Petrol Co, 57-60, group leader, 60-62, staff engr reactor safety, 62-63; sr chem engr, N Star Res Inst, 63-64, assoc dir phys sci & eng div, 64-66, dir div, 66-74, mgr environ sci, Midwest Res Inst, 75-77; PRES, FILMTEC CORP, 77- *Mem:* Am Chem Soc; Am Inst Chem Engrs; Am Water Works Asn; Water Supply Improvement Asn. *Res:* Nuclear fuels processing; research administration; environmental systems; water treatment; reverse osmosis. *Mailing Add:* 14125 Prince Pl Minnetonka MN 55343

ERICKSON, GLEN WALTER, b St Paul, Minn, Aug 1, 34; m 55; c 4. THEORETICAL PHYSICS. *Educ:* Univ Minn, BS, 55, PhD(physics), 60. *Prof Exp:* Res assoc, Inst Field Physics, Univ NC, 60-62, vis asst prof physics, 61-62; adj asst prof, NY Univ, 62-64; assoc prof, 64-74, PROF PHYSICS, UNIV CALIF, DAVIS, 74- *Concurrent Pos:* Mem comt fundamental constants, Nat Res Coun-Nat Acad Sci, 69-71; sr res fel, Sci Res Coun Eng, 70-71. *Mem:* Am Phys Soc. *Res:* Quantum field theory, especially quantum electrodynamics. *Mailing Add:* Dept of Physics Univ of Calif Davis CA 95616

ERICKSON, HAROLD PAUL, b Chattanooga, Tenn, Jan 16, 40; div; c 1. BIOPHYSICS, ELECTRON MICROSCOPY. *Educ:* Carnegie-Mellon Univ, BS, 62; Johns Hopkins Univ, PhD(biophys), 68. *Prof Exp:* NIH res fel, Med Res Coun Lab Molecular Biol, Cambridge, Eng, 68-70; from asst prof to assoc prof, 70-81, PROF ANAT, DUKE UNIV, 82- *Concurrent Pos:* NIH res career develop award, 72-76; mem staff biophys chem study sect, NIH, 80-83. *Mem:* Am Soc Cell Biol; Biophys Soc. *Res:* Molecular biology; electron microscopy; image analysis and reconstruction; structure and self-assembly of protein complexes. *Mailing Add:* Dept Anat Duke Univ Med Ctr Durham NC 27710

ERICKSON, HARVEY D, b Belgrade, Minn, Apr 12, 12; m 54; c 1. FOREST PRODUCTS. *Educ:* Univ Minn, BS, 34, MS, 36, PhD(wood technol, biochem), 37. *Prof Exp:* From asst prof to prof forest util, WVa Univ, 37-47; assoc prof, 47-59, prof, 59-77, EMER PROF FOREST PROD, UNIV WASH, 77- *Mem:* AAAS; Am Chem Soc; Soc Wood Sci & Technol; Soc Am Foresters; Tech Asn Pulp & Paper Indust. *Res:* Permeability of wood; effect of chemicals on strength of woods; wood shrinkage; wood-moisture relations; wood quality and growth factors affecting quality; chemical analysis of wood; wood preservation; freeze drying effects on wood. *Mailing Add:* 4186 Galbar Pl Oceanside CA 92056

ERICKSON, HOMER THEODORE, b Pulaski, Wis, Mar 8, 25; m 55; c 4. HORTICULTURE. *Educ:* Univ Wis, BS, 51, MS, 53, PhD(hort, genetics), 54. *Prof Exp:* Asst prof hort, Univ Maine, 54-56; asst prof, 56-64, head dept, 67-75, PROF HORT, PURDUE UNIV, WEST LAFAYETTE, 64- *Concurrent Pos:* With Purdue Univ training team, Agr Univ, Minas Gerais, 59-63, hon prof, 63; UN Develop Prog consult hort, Ghana, WAfrica, 72; res ctr coordr, Spain, 75-76; plant germplasm collections, Brazil, 66-67 & 78. *Mem:* Am Soc Hort Sci; Am Genetic Asn. *Res:* Physiology and genetics of the more important commercial vegetables; tropical horticulture in general. *Mailing Add:* 1409 N Salisbury St West Lafayette IN 47906

ERICKSON, HOWARD HUGH, b Wahoo, Nebr, Mar 16, 36; m 59; c 2. CARDIOPULMONARY PHYSIOLOGY, CARDIOVASCULAR INSTRUMENTATION. *Educ:* Kans State Univ, BS & DVM, 59; Iowa State Univ, PhD(physiol biomed eng), 66. *Prof Exp:* Area vet, 59th Vet Inspection Flight, US Air Force, UK, 60-63, res vet officer, Biodynamics Br, 66-70, vet scientist, Appl Physiol Br, 70-73, asst chief, Biodynamics Br, 73-74, spec asst to dir, Sch Aerospace Med, 75, chief, Tech Plans & Anal Div, 76-79, chief, Mech Forces Div, 79-81; PROF PHYSIOL, DEPT ANAT & PHYSIOL, COL VET MED, KANS STATE UNIV, 81- *Concurrent Pos:* Vis mem grad fac, Tex A&M Univ, 68-; spec mem grad fac, Colo State Univ, 70-; clin asst prof, Health Sci Ctr, Univ Tex, 72-; sci adv, Nat Res Coun-Air Force Systs Command Associateship Prog, 71-73. *Mem:* Fel AAAS; Am Vet Med Asn; Inst Elec & Electronics Eng; assoc fel Aerospace Med Asn; Am Physiol Soc. *Res:* cardiovascular instrumentation and control; coronary circulation; research administration; cardiovascular physiology. *Mailing Add:* 2017 Arthur Dr Manhattan KS 66502

ERICKSON, HOWARD RALPH, b Indiana, Pa, Nov 23, 19; m 55; c 3. VERTEBRATE ZOOLOGY. *Educ:* Indiana Univ Pa, BS, 52; Pa State Univ, MS, 56; Cornell Univ, PhD(vert zool), 59. *Prof Exp:* Res asst zool, Pa State Univ, 54-56; res asst vert zool, Cornell Univ, 56-59; instr biol & zool, 59-62, assoc prof vert zool, 62-66, prof vert zool, 66-77, PROF BIOL, TOWSON STATE UNIV, 77-, CHMN DEPT, 66- *Concurrent Pos:* Annual res grant, Towson State Col, 66-68. *Mem:* AAAS; Am Soc Mammal; Ecol Soc Am; Wildlife Soc. *Res:* Environmental conservation; vertebrate ecology; muskrat growth; reproduction; population dynamics; movements; control methods and procedures; ecology of fresh water piscine species. *Mailing Add:* Dept of Biol Towson State Univ Baltimore MD 21204

ERICKSON, JAMES C, III, b Philadelphia, Pa, Oct 7, 27; m 56; c 1. ANESTHESIOLOGY. *Educ:* Univ Pa, BA, 49; Temple Univ, MD, 53, MSc, 58; Am Bd Anesthesiol, dipl, 60. *Prof Exp:* Instr anesthesiol, Med Sch, Temple Univ, 57-58; assoc, Guthrie Clin, 58-61; assoc, Med Sch, Temple Univ, 61-64, asst prof, 64-67; prof, Woman's Med Col Pa, 67-69; prof anesthesiol, Jefferson Med Col, Thomas Jefferson Univ, 69-80; PROF CLIN ANESTHESIA, NORTHWESTERN UNIV MED SCH, 80- *Concurrent Pos:* Staff, Rehabilitation Inst Chicago, 80-; consult, Lakeside Vet Admin Hosp, 80- *Mem:* AMA; Am Soc Regional Anesthesiol; Am Soc Clin Hypn; Soc Clin & Exp Hypn; Int Soc Hypn. *Res:* Vasopressor effect of indigo carmine; clinical evaluation of local anesthetic drugs; use of hypnosis in anethesia and pain control; pain control and diagnostic evaluation; evaluation of neurolytic agents. *Mailing Add:* Dept Anesthesiol Northwestern Univ Med Sch Chicago IL 60611

ERICKSON, JAMES ELDRED, b Stambaugh, Mich, Dec 1, 49; m 72; c 2. ZOOLOGY. *Educ:* North Park Col, BA, 71; Univ Minn, MS, 74, PhD(zool), 77. *Prof Exp:* ASST PROF ZOOL, WESTERN MICH UNIV, 77- *Mem:* Am Fisheries Soc; Am Soc Ichthyologists & Herpetologists; Sigma Xi. *Res:* Zoogeography and ecological life histories of fresh water fishes, especially minnows and darters; winter ecology of stream fishes; parasites of freshwater fishes. *Mailing Add:* Biol Dept Western Mich Univ Kalamazoo MI 49008

ERICKSON, JAMES GEORGE, b Sioux City, Iowa, May 18, 29; m 50; c 3. ZOOLOGY. *Educ:* Doane Col, BA, 50; Iowa State Univ, MS, 51; Univ Wyo, PhD(zool & physiol), 64. *Prof Exp:* Fisheries biologist, Div Wildlife, Ohio Dept Natural Resources, 53-56; fisheries biologist, Wyo Game & Fish Comn, 56-61; from asst prof to assoc prof biol, 64-74, PROF BIOL, FT LEWIS COL, 74- *Mem:* Am Soc Zoologists. *Res:* Behavior and endocrinology of fishes. *Mailing Add:* Dept of Biol Ft Lewis Col Durango CO 81301

ERICKSON, JOHN (ELMER), b Sioux City, Iowa, June 17, 23; m 46; c 3. CYTOGENETICS. *Educ:* Univ Omaha, BA, 48; Ind Univ, MA, 50; Univ Ore, PhD(genetics), 64. *Prof Exp:* Instr biol, McCook Jr Col, 54-59 & Univ Ore, 59-62; asst prof, 64-66, ASSOC PROF BIOL, WESTERN WASH UNIV, 66- *Mem:* Genetics Soc Am; Am Genetic Asn. *Res:* Cytogenetics of meiotic drive in Drosophila males; fragmentation of Y chromosome; mating, insemination and fertility problems. *Mailing Add:* Dept of Biol Western Wash Univ Bellingham WA 98225

ERICKSON, JOHN GERHARD, b Northfield, Minn, July 14, 17; m 54; c 4. ORGANIC CHEMISTRY. *Educ:* St Olaf Col, BA, 38; NDak State Col, MS, 40; Univ Minn, PhD(org chem), 44. *Prof Exp:* Asst, NDak State Col, 38-40; instr, St Olaf Col, 40-41; chemist, Minn Valley Canning Co, 41; res asst soils, Univ Minn, 41, asst, 42-44; res chemist, Am Cyanamid Co, 44-50; sr res chemist, Gen Mills, Inc, 51-56; sr res chemist, Minn Mining & Mfg Co, 56-59, supvr, 59-64, mgr synthesis res, 64-66, dir sci & tech commun, 66-76, dir technol anal, 76-79. *Concurrent Pos:* Dir & treas, Avochem, Inc, 53-61, pres, 59-61. *Res:* Organic nitrogen compounds; heterocycles; sugar derivatives; acrylic derivatives; hydrogen cyanide; orthoformic esters; glycidyl esters; polymers; fluorine chemistry; textile agents; greases; rocket propellants; birds of the Labrador coast; flight behavior of the Procellariiformes. *Mailing Add:* 1344 S Second St Stillwater MN 55082

ERICKSON, JOHN M, b Curtiss, Wis, Apr 28, 18; m 48; c 4. PHYSICAL CHEMISTRY. *Educ:* Univ Wis, BS, 40; SDak State Col, MS, 53; Iowa State Univ, PhD(phys chem), 56. *Prof Exp:* From prod dept foreman to cost control engr, Procter & Gamble Mfg Co, Ill, 40-43; instr chem & math, SDak State Col, 47-51; asst, Iowa State Univ, 51-56; assoc prof phys chem, SDak State Col, 56-60; assoc prof, 60-66, PROF CHEM, ST CLOUD STATE UNIV, 66- *Mem:* Am Chem Soc. *Res:* Complex ions in mixed solvents; ion-exchange equilibria; water pollution. *Mailing Add:* Dept Chem St Cloud State Univ St Cloud MN 56301

ERICKSON, JOHN MARK, b Orange, NJ, Dec 21, 43. INVERTEBRATE PALEONTOLOGY. *Educ:* Tufts Univ, BS, 65; Univ NDak, MS, 68, PhD, 71. *Prof Exp:* Asst prof, 71-75, ASSOC PROF INVERT PALEONT, ST LAWRENCE UNIV, 75-, CHMN DEPT GEOL & GEOG, 81- *Mem:* Fel AAAS; Geol Soc Am; Paleont Soc; Am Soc Limnol & Oceanog; Brit Palaeont Asn. *Res:* Upper Cretaceous gastropod taxonomy, paleoecology and zoogeography; molluscan paleontology and paleoecology; sedimentation, paleolimnology and post-Pleistocene history of temperate lakes; paleosynecological relationships of invertebrates. *Mailing Add:* Dept of Geol St Lawrence Univ Canton NY 13617

ERICKSON, JOHN ROBERT, b Flaxton, NDak, Sept 4, 39. PLANT BREEDING. *Educ:* Wash State Univ, BS, 63; NDak State Univ, PhD(agron), 67. *Prof Exp:* Res geneticist, Crops Res Div, USDA, 67-69; from asst prof to assoc prof agron, NDak State Univ, 69-78; HYBRID WHEAT BREEDER, DEKALB HYBRID WHEAT, INC, 78- *Mem:* Am Soc Agron. *Res:* Winter wheat breeding; genetics. *Mailing Add:* R R 1 PO Box 225 Glenvil NE 68901

ERICKSON, JOHN WILLIAM, b Chicago, Ill, June 13, 25; m 47; c 8. EXPLORATION GEOLOGY. *Educ:* Augustana Col, AB, 50. *Prof Exp:* Jr comput geophys, Atlantic Refining Co, 51-52; stratigr, Chem & Geol Labs, 52-54; geologist, Gulf Oil Corp, 54-58, rep, Denver Div, Gulf Res & Develop Co, 58-60, sr geologist, 60-74; dist geologist, Mich Wis Pipeline Co, 74-77; explor mgr mid-continent, Tex Int Petrol Corp, 77-79; STAFF GEOLOGIST, WALTER DUNCAN OIL PROPERTIES, 79- *Mem:* Am Asn Petrol Geol; Geol Soc Am; Am Inst Prof Geologists. *Res:* Stratigraphy; subsurface and petroleum geology; geological data processing techniques. *Mailing Add:* 4715 Larissa Lane Oklahoma City OK 73112

ERICKSON, JON JAY, b Minot, NDak, Sept 16, 41; m 65; c 2. MEDICAL PHYSICS. *Educ:* St John's Univ, Minn, BS, 63; Vanderbilt Univ, MS, 65, PhD(physics), 72. *Prof Exp:* Res asst physics, Vanderbilt Univ, 64-67; res assoc, 67-73, from instr to asst prof radiol, Div Nuclear Med, Vanderbilt Hosp, 75-81, ASSOC PROF RADIOL, VANDERBILT MED CTR, 81-

Concurrent Pos: Tech expert comput appln nuclear med, Int Atomic Energy Agency, Bolivia, Columbia, Peru, Uruguay & Brazil, 79- *Mem:* NY Acad Sci; Soc Nuclear Med; Am Asn Physicists in Med. *Mailing Add:* Div of Nuclear Med Vanderbilt Hosp Nashville TN 37232

ERICKSON, KAREN LOUISE, b Covington, Mich, Aug 4, 39. ORGANIC CHEMISTRY. *Educ:* Siena Heights Col, BS, 60; Purdue Univ, PhD(org chem), 65. *Hon Degrees:* Siena Heights Col, 81. *Prof Exp:* NIH fel org chem, Cornell Univ, 64-65; from asst prof to assoc prof, 65-79, PROF ORG CHEM, CLARK UNIV, 79- *Concurrent Pos:* NIH spec fel, Univ Hawaii, 72-73; vis lectr, Univ Canterbury, NZ, 75. *Mem:* Am Chem Soc; Sigma Xi. *Res:* Natural products; rearrangement reactions; synthetic inorganic and organometallic chemistry. *Mailing Add:* Dept of Chem Clark Univ Worcester MA 01610

ERICKSON, KENNETH LYNN, b Rapid City, SDak, Apr 13, 46; m 69; c 1. TRANSPORT PHENOMENA, SURFACE PHENOMENA. *Educ:* Univ Ariz, BS, 68, MS, 73; Univ Tex, Austin, PhD(chem eng), 77. *Prof Exp:* Res engr, Tex Div, Dow Chem Co, 74; MEM TECH STAFF, SANDIA NAT LABS, 76- *Mem:* Am Inst Chem Engrs; Am Chem Soc; Mat Res Soc. *Res:* Experimental and theoretical investigations of mass transfer; chemical reactions in geologic systems, particularly with regard to contaminant transport by groundwater, in situ oil shale retorting, and methane and trace metal recovery from unconventional sources. *Mailing Add:* Div 5843 Sandia Nat Labs PO Box 5800 Albuquerqe NM 87185

ERICKSON, KENNETH NEIL, b Minneapolis, Minn, Oct 1, 40; m 65; c 2. ELEMENTARY PARTICLE PHYSICS, SPACE PHYSICS. *Educ:* Augsburg Col, BA, 62; Mich State Univ, MS, 64; Colo State Univ, PhD(physics), 70. *Prof Exp:* Instr, 64-65, assoc prof, 70-81, PROF PHYSICS, AUGSBURG COL, 81- *Concurrent Pos:* Assoc prof, Univ Minn, Minneapolis, 70-81; adj prof physics, Univ Minn, 81- *Mem:* Am Phys Soc; Am Geophys Union. *Res:* Cosmic rays; magnetospheric physics, particularly the behavior of 50-1000 kiloelectron volt electrons trapped in outer radiation belts of the earth. *Mailing Add:* Dept of Physics Augsburg Col Eighth St at 21st Ave S Minneapolis MN 55454

ERICKSON, LAMBERT CORNELIUS, b Goodridge, Minn, May 30, 10; m 40; c 1. WEED SCIENCE, AGRONOMY. *Educ:* Univ Minn, BS, 40, PhD(agron), 59; Univ Wyo, MS, 43. *Prof Exp:* Asst state seed analyst, Minn, 40-41; state seed analyst, Wyo, 41-45; assoc agronomist, 45-63, prof agron, 63-77, EMER PROF AGRON, UNIV IDAHO, 77-, WEED SCIENTIST, 63- *Concurrent Pos:* Tech adv, State Dept Agr, Wyo, 42-45; mem, Columbia Basin Interagency Comt, 49-52; Fulbright fel div weed control, Norweg Plant Protection Inst, 69-70; consult agr, 76- *Mem:* Am Soc Agron; Weed Sci Soc Am. *Res:* Herbicide residues in soils and crops; herbicides and our environment; biological control of weeds; weed ecology. *Mailing Add:* 842 E Seventh St Moscow ID 93943

ERICKSON, LARRY EUGENE, b Wahoo, Nebr, Oct 8, 38; m 62. BIOCHEMICAL & CHEMICAL ENGINEERING. *Educ:* Kans State Univ, BS, 60, PhD(chem eng), 64. *Prof Exp:* From instr to assoc prof, 64-72, PROF CHEM ENG, KANS STATE UNIV, 72- *Concurrent Pos:* US Pub Health Serv spec res fel, 67-68, career develop award, 70-75. *Mem:* Assoc Am Inst Chem Engrs; Am Chem Soc; Am Soc Microbiol; Am Soc Eng Educ; Inst Food Technologists. *Res:* Optimum process design; biochemical engineering; food engineering. *Mailing Add:* Dept Chem Eng Kans State Univ Manhattan KS 66506

ERICKSON, LOUIS CARL, b Wilmington, Calif, Feb 13, 14; m 41; c 2. PLANT PHYSIOLOGY. *Educ:* Univ Calif, Los Angeles, AB, 37, MA, 39; Univ Calif, Berkeley, PhD(bot), 46. *Prof Exp:* Asst plant physiologist, Bur Plant Indust, USDA, 43-45; plant physiologist, Thompson Hort Chem Corp, 46-48; asst plant physiologist, Citrus Res Ctr & Agr Exp Sta, 48-54, assoc plant physiologist, 54-60, plant physiologist, 60-67, prof bot, 67-77, dir botanic gardens, 73-81, EMER PROF BOT, UNIV CALIF, RIVERSIDE, 77- *Mem:* Am Asn Bot Gardens & Arboretums; Am Soc Hort Sci; Royal Hort Soc. *Res:* Plant prop. *Mailing Add:* Dept of Bot & Plant Sci Univ of Calif Riverside CA 92521

ERICKSON, LUTHER E, b Pulaski, Wis, June 30, 33; m 57; c 2. PHYSICAL CHEMISTRY. *Educ:* St Olaf Col, BA, 55; Univ Wis, PhD(phys chem), 59. *Prof Exp:* Asst prof chem, Dickinson Col, 59-62; asst prof, 62-63, from assoc prof to prof, 64-75, DODGE PROF CHEM, GRINNELL COL, 75- *Concurrent Pos:* NSF sci fac fel, Univ NC, 68-69. *Mem:* AAAS; Am Chem Soc. *Res:* Nuclear magnetic resonance spectroscopy; complex ions and coordination compounds; conformational analysis of metal chelates. *Mailing Add:* Dept of Chem Grinnell Col Grinnell IA 50112

ERICKSON, LYNDEN EDWIN, b Ft William, Ont, June 6, 38; m 65; c 3. EXPERIMENTAL ATOMIC PHYSICS, LASERS. *Educ:* Queen's Univ, Ont, BSc, 59; Univ Chicago, SM, 61, PhD(physics), 66. *Prof Exp:* RES OFFICER PHYSICS, NAT RES COUN, 65- *Mem:* Am Phys Soc. *Res:* High resolution spectra of rare earth ions in solids at low temperature using fluorescence line narrowing and saturated and enhanced absorption techniques; optically detected nuclear magnetic resonance of rare earth ions in solids. *Mailing Add:* Nat Res Coun M50 Ottawa ON K1A 0R6 Can

ERICKSON, RALPH LEROY, geology, see previous edition

ERICKSON, RALPH O, b Duluth, Minn, Oct 27, 14; m 45; c 2. BOTANY, DEVELOPMENTAL BIOLOGY. *Educ:* Gustavus Adolphus Col, BA, 35; Wash Univ, MS, 41, PhD(bot), 44. *Prof Exp:* Instr biol, Gustavus Adolphus Col, 35-39; asst bot, Wash Univ, 40-41; asst chemist, Western Cartridge Co, Ill, 42-44; instr bot, Univ Rochester, 44-47; res assoc, 47-49, assoc prof, 49-54, actg chmn dept biol, 61-63, 76-78, chmn biol grad group, 68-76, PROF BOT, UNIV PA, 54- *Concurrent Pos:* Guggenheim fel, 54-55. *Mem:* Bot Soc Am; Soc Develop Biol (secy, 57-58, pres, 59); Am Soc Plant Physiologists; AAAS; Am Inst Biol Sci. *Res:* Analysis of plant growth and morphogenesis; phyllotaxis; packing of structural proteins. *Mailing Add:* Dept Biol Univ Pa Philadelphia PA 19174

ERICKSON, RANDALL L, b Harris, Minn, Apr 24, 39; m 61; c 1. PHYSICAL CHEMISTRY, POLYMER CHEMISTRY. *Educ:* Concordia Col, Moorhead, Minn, BA, 61; NDak State Univ, PhD(phys chem), 65. *Prof Exp:* Res chemist, Textile Fibers Dept, E I du Pont de Nemours & Co, Va, 65-67; sr res chemist, Adhesives, Coatings & Sealers Div, 67-68, supvr, Bldg Serv & Cleaning Prod Div, 68-73, MGR SAFETY SYSTS DIV, 3M CO, 73- *Mem:* Am Chem Soc. *Res:* Solvation of extracted metal complexes by organic solvents; physical chemistry of polymers-structure property relationships. *Mailing Add:* 8 Evergreen Lane North Oaks St Paul MN 55110

ERICKSON, RAY CHARLES, b St Peter, Minn, Jan 30, 18; m 53; c 4. WILDLIFE RESEARCH. *Educ:* Gustavus Adolphus Col, AB, 41; Iowa State Col, MS, 42, PhD(econ zool), 48. *Prof Exp:* Collabr, US Fish & Wildlife Serv, 39-41, jr biologist, Patuxent Res Refuge, Md, 41, asst, Malheur Nat Wildlife Refuge, 42 & 46-47, refuge mgr, 48, wildlife mgt biologist, 48-55, head habitat improv sect, Wildlife Refuges Br, 55-58, res staff specialist, Wildlife Res Div, 58-65, asst dir in-chg endangered wildlife res prog, Patuxent Wildlife Res Ctr, 65-80. *Honors & Awards:* Honor Award, Whooping Crane Conserv Asn, 80. *Mem:* Am Ornith Union; assoc Wildlife Soc; Ecol Soc Am. *Res:* Waterfowl and waterfowl habitat ecology and management studies; preservation of rare and endangered wildlife species; endangered wildlife research supervision. *Mailing Add:* 1943 37th Ave NW Salem OR 97304

ERICKSON, RAYMOND C, microbiology, see previous edition

ERICKSON, RICHARD AMES, b Bryant, SDak, Sept 12, 23; m 43; c 4. PHYSICS. *Educ:* SDak Sch Mines & Technol, BS, 44; Agr & Mech Col, Tex, PhD(physics), 52. *Prof Exp:* Asst prof physics, Univ Tenn, 51-53; from asst prof to prof, 54-79, EMER PROF PHYSICS, OHIO STATE UNIV, 79- *Res:* Neutron diffraction; solid state physics; chemical physics; low temperature physics. *Mailing Add:* Dept Physics Ohio State Univ Columbus OH 43210

ERICKSON, ROBERT JOSEPH, b Chicago, Ill, Sept 20, 41; m 64; c 2. INDUSTRIAL MICROBIOLOGY. *Educ:* Wabash Col, BA, 63; Wesleyan Univ, MA, 65; Rutgers Univ, PhD(microbial genetics), 68. *Prof Exp:* Fel biol & med res, Argonne Nat Lab, 68-70; res scientist genetics, Molecular Biol Lab, 70-76, sr scientist & sect head biosynthesis res, Marschall Div, 76-78, dir, Biosynthesis Res Lab, Indust Prod Group, 78-80, VPRES RES & DEVELOP, BIOTECHNOL GROUP, MILES LABS, INC, 80- *Concurrent Pos:* Fac fel, Lobund Lab, 70-; asst prof, Univ Notre Dame, 73- *Mem:* AAAS; Genetics Soc Am; Am Soc Microbiol; NY Acad Sci. *Res:* Genetics and physiology of industrially important microorganisms. *Mailing Add:* Biosynthesis Res Lab Miles Labs Inc Elkhart IN 46515

ERICKSON, ROBERT PORTER, b South Bend, Ind, Feb 13, 30; m 58; c 3. PHYSIOLOGICAL PSYCHOLOGY. *Educ:* Northwestern Univ, BS, 51; Brown Univ, MSc, 56, PhD(psychol), 58. *Prof Exp:* Res assoc psychol, Brown Univ, 58-59, instr, 59; fel physiol & biophys, Univ Wash, 59-61; from asst prof to prof psychol, 61-77, ASSOC PROF PHYSIOL, DUKE UNIV, 77- *Mem:* Soc Neurosci; Am Physiol Soc; Psychonomic Soc. *Res:* Sensory systems and behavior processes. *Mailing Add:* Dept of Physiol Duke Univ Med Ctr Durham NC 27706

ERICKSON, ROBERT W, b McIntosh, Minn, Jan 31, 29; m 56; c 8. FOREST PRODUCTS. *Educ:* Univ Minn, St Paul, BS, 58, MS, 63, PhD(forest prod eng), 66. *Prof Exp:* Lab technician, Forest Prod Lab, Univ Calif, 58-61; asst forest prod, 61-62, instr wood seasoning, 62-66, from asst prof to assoc prof wood-fluid rels, 66-75, PROF FOREST PROD, COL FORESTRY, UNIV MINN, ST PAUL, 75- *Concurrent Pos:* Vis scientist, Soc Wood Sci & Technol, NC, 71; vis seminarist, Can Forest Prod Labs, BC, 70; sabbatical res in wood drying, Tech Ctr, Weyerhaeuser Co, Wash, 73-74. *Mem:* Soc Wood Sci & Technol (pres, 78). *Res:* Effect of surface tension upon the permeability of wood to distilled water; effects of pre-freezing upon the subsequent accelerated drying behavior of redwood and other collapse susceptible species; factors that influence the flexual creep behavior of wood during dehydration from the green condition; drying of South East Asian hardwoods; nonisothermal moisture movement in wood. *Mailing Add:* Col of Forestry Univ of Minn St Paul MN 55108

ERICKSON, RONALD E, b Peoria, Ill, Apr 20, 33; m 58; c 2. ENVIRONMENTAL CHEMISTRY. *Educ:* Bradley Univ, BS, 55; Univ Iowa, PhD(org chem), 59. *Prof Exp:* Welch fel, Univ Tex, 58-59; NATO fel, Karlsruhe Tech Univ, 60-61; Rosalie B Hite fel, Univ Tex, 61; asst prof chem, Canisius Col, 61-65; assoc prof, 65-70, PROF CHEM, UNIV MONT, 70-, DIR ENVIRON STUDIES PROG, 76- *Res:* environmental problems of coal gasification. *Mailing Add:* Environ Studies Prog Univ of Mont Missoula MT 59801

ERICKSON, STANLEY ARVID, US citizen. SIMULATION, SYSTEMS ANALYSIS. *Educ:* Mass Inst Technol, SB(physics) & SB(math), 64, PhD(math), 74. *Prof Exp:* Proj leader res, Naval Underwater Systs Ctr, 65-77; proj leader, 77-80, GROUP LEADER PHYSICS, LAWRENCE LIVERMORE LAB, UNIV CALIF, BERKELEY, 80- *Concurrent Pos:* Consult, RI Dept Educ, 75-77. *Mem:* Opers Res Soc Am; Inst Elec & Electronics Engrs. *Res:* Simulation and modeling of physical and social systems. *Mailing Add:* L-11 Lawrence Livermore Lab PO Box 808 Livermore CA 94705

ERICKSON, WAYNE DOUGLAS, b Lansing, Mich, Feb 19, 32; m 59; c 1. CHEMICAL ENGINEERING. *Educ:* Mich State Univ, BS, 54, MS, 55; Mass Inst Technol, SM, 58, ScD(chem eng), 62. *Prof Exp:* Res engr, 58-59, head, thermal proj sect, 59-64, res engr, 64-65, head aerothermochem br, 65-70, head life support br, 70-72, SR SCIENTIST, OFF DIR, LANGLEY RES CTR, NASA, 72- *Concurrent Pos:* Mem res staff, phys chem dept, Cambridge Univ, 70-71; vis assoc prof, Dept Chem Eng, Mass Inst Technol, 80-82. *Mem:* Combustion Inst; AAAS; Am Inst Aeronaut & Astronaut; Am Inst Chem Engrs. *Res:* Chemical kinetics of high temperature systems; combustion research; thermodynamics; aerothermochemistry; chemical process systems; life support systems; molecular computations; turbulent flow with combustion. *Mailing Add:* 303 Hamrick Dr Hampton VA 23666

ERICKSON, WAYNE FRANCIS, b Kingston, NY, July 1, 46. ORGANIC CHEMISTRY, MEDICAL PRODUCTS. *Educ:* Univ Mass, BS, 68; Mass Inst Technol, MS, 70; Pa State Univ, PhD(org chem), 72. *Prof Exp:* Res chemist photog sci, 74-80, RES CHEMIST MED PROD, EASTMAN KODAK CO RES LABS, 80- *Res:* High speed color negative films; development medical product systems. *Mailing Add:* Eastman Kodak Co 343 State St Rochester NY 14650

ERICKSON, WILLIAM CLARENCE, b Chicago, Ill, Nov 21, 30; m 52; c 4. ASTRONOMY. *Educ:* Univ Minn, BA, 51, MA, 55, PhD(physics), 56. *Prof Exp:* Lectr physics, Univ Minn, 55-56; fel, Carnegie Inst, 56-57; sr staff scientist, Convair Sci Res Lab Div, Gen Dynamic Corp, 57-62 & Benelux Cross Antenna Proj, 62-63; from assoc prof to prof astron, 63-76, PROF PHYSICS & ASTRON, UNIV MD, COLLEGE PARK, 76- *Mem:* Int Sci Radio Union; Int Astron Union; Am Astron Soc; Royal Astron Soc. *Res:* Theory and observations in radio astronomy. *Mailing Add:* Dept of Physics & Astron Univ of Md College Park MD 20742

ERICKSON, WILLIAM HARRY, b McKeesport, Pa, Apr 4, 16; m 41; c 2. ELECTRICAL ENGINEERING. *Educ:* Univ Pittsburgh, BS, 38; Carnegie Inst Technol, MS, 46. *Prof Exp:* Jr engr, Duquesne Light Co, Pa, 38-42; from instr to assoc prof elec eng, Naval Training Prog, 42-53, asst dir elec eng, 59-65, assoc dean col eng, 65-71, PROF ELEC ENG, CORNELL UNIV, 53- *Mem:* Fel Inst Elec & Electronics Engrs. *Mailing Add:* Dept of Elec Eng Cornell Univ Ithaca NY 14853

ERICSON, ALFRED (THEODORE), b Quincy, Kans, Oct 8, 28; m 48; c 2. BIOCHEMISTRY. *Educ:* Kans State Teachers Col, BSEd, 50; Kans State Univ, MS, 53, PhD(chem), 56. *Prof Exp:* Asst instr chem, Kans State Univ, 53-56; from asst prof to assoc prof, 56-63, PROF CHEM, EMPORIA STATE UNIV, 63- *Mem:* AAAS; Am Chem Soc. *Res:* Chemical education; tracer techniques; protein chemistry. *Mailing Add:* Dept of Chem Emporia State Univ Emporia KS 66801

ERICSON, COREY WILLIAM, theoretical chemistry, physical chemistry, see previous edition

ERICSON, GROVER CHARLES, b Oak Park, Ill, Feb 17, 41; m 64; c 2. HUMAN ANATOMY, MUSCLE BIOLOGY. *Educ:* N Cent Col, BA, 64; Loyola Univ, Chicago, MS, 68, PhD(anat), 72. *Prof Exp:* Asst prof anat, Univ Tex Southwestern Med Sch, Dallas, 72-78; ASSOC PROF ANAT, COL MED & ASSOC PROF ZOOL, OHIO UNIV, 78- *Concurrent Pos:* Anat consult, Med Plastics Lab Inc, 76- *Mem:* Am Asn Zoologists. *Res:* Exercise biology; response of skeletal muscle to weight-lifting exercise. *Mailing Add:* Col of Osteop Med Ohio Univ Athens OH 45701

ERICSON, WILLIAM ARNOLD, b Larchmont, NY, Jan 9, 34; c 2. STATISTICS. *Educ:* Univ Pa, BS, 55, MA, 58; Harvard Univ, PhD(statist), 63. *Prof Exp:* Res asst statist, Harvard Univ, 60-62; from asst prof to assoc prof math, Univ 62-69, assoc prof statist, 69-70, prof statist & chmn dept, 70-75, DIR, STATIST RES LAB, UNIV MICH, ANN ARBOR, 71- *Concurrent Pos:* Assoc ed, J Am Statist Asn, 67-75; vis lectr, Inst Math Statist, 71- *Mem:* Biomet Soc; Inst Math Statist; fel Am Statist Asn. *Res:* Sampling theory; Bayesian inference. *Mailing Add:* Dept of Statist 1447 Mason Hall Univ of Mich Ann Arbor MI 48109

ERIKS, KLAAS, b Alkmaar, Neth, June 16, 22; nat US; m 49; c 3. STRUCTURAL CHEMISTRY. *Educ:* Univ Amsterdam, Chem Cand, 43, Chem Drs, 48, PhD(chem), 52. *Prof Exp:* Res assoc physics, Pa State Univ, 52-53; fel chem, Univ Minn, 53-54; from asst prof to assoc prof, 54-65, PROF CHEM, BOSTON UNIV, 65- *Concurrent Pos:* Fulbright res scholar, Copenhagen Univ, 63-64; mem dent training comt, Nat Inst Dent Res, 65-69; vis res scholar, Neth Reactor Ctr, Petten, 71-72; mem, Nat Comt on Crystallog. *Mem:* Am Chem Soc; Am Crystallog Asn; Royal Neth Chem Soc. *Res:* X-ray structure determination in fields of heteropoly salts; calcium salts of amino acids; transition metal ion complexes, especially with amino acids; organic and inorganic sulphates, phosphates and fluorides. *Mailing Add:* Dept of Chem Boston Univ Boston MA 02215

ERIKSEN, CLYDE HEDMAN, b Santa Barbara, Calif, May 1, 33; div; c 2. PHYSIOLOGICAL ECOLOGY, LIMNOLOGY. *Educ:* Univ Calif, Santa Barbara, BA, 55; Univ Ill, MS, 56; Univ Mich, PhD(zool), 61. *Prof Exp:* Instr biol, Exten Serv, Univ Calif, 54-55, teaching fel, 57; field res asst limnol, Great Lakes Res Inst, 57; field specialist, Nat Sanit Found, 58-59; asst prof zool, Los Angeles State Col, 60-63 & NSF Inst Biol Sci, 61; from asst prof to assoc prof, Univ Toronto, 63-67; assoc prof, 67-72, chmn joint sci dept, 69-73, PROF BIOL, CLAREMONT COLS, 72-, DIR BERNARD BIOL STA, 73- *Concurrent Pos:* Consult, Allen Hancock Found, Univ Southern Calif, 61-63; mem, Environ Resources Task Force, The City of Claremont, 70-71; ecol specialist, US Forest Serv, Beaverhead Nat Forest, Mont, 73; consult, US Forest Serv, Beaverhead Nat Forest, Mont, 74-; vis res entomologist, Div Biol Control, Univ Calif, Berkeley, 81. *Honors & Awards:* Outstanding Educators Am Award, 70; Cert Recognition, US Forest Serv, 73. *Mem:* Ecol Soc Am; Am Soc Limnol & Oceanog; Int Asn Theoret & Appl Limnol; Can Soc Zool. *Res:* Respiratory physiological ecology of aquatic invertebrates; ecology of playa lakes; western limnology. *Mailing Add:* Joint Sci Dept Baxter Sci Lab Claremont Cols Claremont CA 91711

ERIKSEN, STUART P, b San Francisco, Calif, Nov 13, 30; m 55; c 3. PHARMACEUTICAL CHEMISTRY. *Educ:* Univ Calif, BSc, 52, MSc, 54, PhD(pharmaceut chem), 56. *Prof Exp:* Sr res pharmacist, Smith, Kline & French Labs, 55-60; assoc prof pharm, Univ Wis-Madison, 60-65; dir med res, 65-70, dir res opers, 70-72, vpres res & develop, 72-77, V PRES CONTACT LENS PROD RES, ALLERGAN PHARMACEUT, 77- *Concurrent Pos:* Instr, Hahnemann Med Col, 58-60; vis lectr, Sch Pharm, Temple Univ, 59-60. *Mem:* AAAS; Am Chem Soc; Am Pharmaceut Asn; Asn Res Vision & Ophthal; Soc Invest Dermat. *Res:* Physical pharmacy; drug molecules in solution; rheology; drug degradation; lipid chemistry; ophthalmic and derm clinical investigations; surface phenomena on contact lenses. *Mailing Add:* Allergan Pharmaceut 2525 DuPont Irvine CA 92713

ERIKSON, GEORGE EMIL, b Palmer, Mass, May 3, 20; m 50; c 4. ANATOMY. *Educ:* Mass State Col, BS, 41; Harvard Univ, MA, 46, PhD(biol), 48. *Prof Exp:* Reader hist of sci & learning, Harvard Univ, 43-45; instr anat, Harvard Med Sch, 47-49, assoc, 52-55, asst prof, 55-65; PROF MED SCI, BROWN UNIV, 65- *Concurrent Pos:* Guggenheim fel, 49; asst prof gen educ biol, Harvard Univ, 49-52; consult med & pub health, Rockefeller Found, 59; assoc cur, Warren Anat Mus, Harvard Med Sch, 61-65; state dept specialist, Brazil, 62; anatomist, Dept Surg, RI Hosp, 65- *Mem:* AAAS; Am Soc Zool; Am Asn Anat; Am Asn Hist Med; Am Soc Mammal. *Res:* Comparative biology of new world primates. *Mailing Add:* Div Biol & Med Sci Morphol Sect Brown Univ Box G Providence RI 02912

ERIKSON, J ALDEN, b Milwaukee, Wis, Mar 3, 26; m 55; c 3. ORGANIC CHEMISTRY. *Educ:* Univ Wis, BS, 50; Mass Inst Technol, PhD(chem), 53. *Prof Exp:* Chemist, Paint & Brush Div, Pittsburgh Plate Glass Co, 53-59, sr res chemist, Coatings & Resins Div, 59-68, PROJ LEADER, PPG INDUSTS, INC, 68- *Mem:* Am Chem Soc; Fedn Soc Coatings Technol. *Res:* Alkyds; melamine and urea formaldehyde resins; thermosetting free radically polymerised copolymers; oil free polyesters; polyurethanes; silicone modified resins and aqueous dispersions. *Mailing Add:* 4212 E Ewalt Rd Gibsonia PA 15044

ERIKSON, JAY ARTHUR, b Seattle, Wash, May 2, 22; m 55; c 3. SURFACE CHEMISTRY. *Educ:* Univ Wash, BS, 48, MS, 49, PhD(phys chem), 54. *Prof Exp:* Instr petrol ref eng, Colo Sch Mines, 54-55; chemist, Agr Div, Shell Develop Co, 55-61, Santa Barbara Res Ctr, 61-63 & US Polymeric Div, HITCO, 64-67; mat & process engr autonetics, NAm Rockwell Corp, 67-73, mat & process engr, Space Div, Rockwell Int Corp, 73-78; RETIRED. *Mem:* Am Chem Soc; Sigma Xi. *Res:* Reaction kinetics of pesticide decompositions and lead sulfide film depositions; surface treatments of carbon fibers and powders; surface preparation for adhesive bonding. *Mailing Add:* 3697 F Rd Palisade CO 81526

ERIKSON, RAYMOND LEO, b Eagle, Wis, Jan 24, 36; m 58. MOLECULAR BIOLOGY. *Educ:* Univ Wis, BS, 58, MS, 61, PhD(molecular biol), 63. *Prof Exp:* USPHS fel, 63-65, from asst prof to assoc prof, 65-72, PROF PATH, SCH MED, UNIV COLO, DENVER, 72- *Mem:* Am Soc Biol Chemists; Am Soc Microbiol. *Res:* Nucleic acids; biochemical virology, tumor viruses. *Mailing Add:* Dept of Path 4200 E Ninth Ave Denver CO 80220

ERIKSSON, KENNETH ANDREW, b SAfrica, June 6, 46; m 75. GEOLOGY, SEDIMENTOLOGY. *Educ:* Univ Witwatersrand, BSc Hons, 68, MSc, 72, PhD(geol), 77. *Prof Exp:* Lectr geol, Univ Witwatersrand, 69-77, sr lectr geol, 78; asst prof geol, Univ Tex, Dallas, 78-79, assoc prof, 80-81; PROF GEOL, VA POLYTECH INST & STATE UNIV, 81- *Mem:* Geol Soc SAfrica; Geol Soc Am; Soc Econ Paleontologists & Mineralogists; Int Asn Sedimentologists. *Res:* Archean paleoenvironments and crustal evolution; proterozoic and paleozoic shelf sedimentation; sedimentology of Appalachian clastic wedges; atmospheric evolution. *Mailing Add:* Dept Geol Sci Va Polytech Inst & State Univ Blacksburg VA 24061

ERINGEN, AHMED CEMAL, b Kayseri, Turkey, Feb 15, 21; m 49; c 4. APPLIED MECHANICS. *Educ:* Advan Eng Sch Istanbul, MS, 43; Polytech Inst Brooklyn, PhD(appl mech), 48. *Prof Exp:* Res engr, Turkish Aircraft Co, 43-44; int trainee, Glenn L Martin Co, 44-45; group head fuselage sect & head struct sect, Turkish Air League Co, 45-47; from res asst prof to res assoc prof mech, Ill Inst Technol, 48-53; assoc prof eng mech, Purdue Univ, 53-55, prof eng sci, 55-66; prof aerospace & mech sci & chmn solid mech prog, 66-74, PROF CONTINUUM PHYSICS & CIVIL ENG, PRINCETON UNIV, 74- *Concurrent Pos:* Consult, Armour Res Found, 48-50, Gen Motors, Picatinny Arsenal & Gen Tech Corp; ed-in-chief, Int J Eng Sci, Soc Eng Sci, 63- *Honors & Awards:* Outstanding Researcher of Yr Award, Sigma Xi, 63; Distinguished Serv Award, Soc Eng Sci, 73 & Certs of Appreciation, 74 & 75, A C Eringen Award, 76. *Mem:* Soc Eng Sci (pres, 63-73); Am Soc Mech Eng; Am Soc Eng Educ; Soc Rheology; Soc Natural Philos. *Res:* Continuum physics; development of theories of micropolar and micromorphic continua; nonlocal continuum physics, solids, fluids, electromagnetism; material theories. *Mailing Add:* Eng Quadrangle E 307 Princeton Univ Princeton NJ 08540

ERIQUEZ, LOUIS ANTHONY, b Danbury, Conn, Sept 12, 49; m 70; c 1. BIOCHEMISTRY, MICROBIOLOGY. *Educ:* Fairfield Univ, BS, 71; St John's Univ, MS, 73, PhD(biochem), 76. *Prof Exp:* Assoc dir res & develop, Analytab Prod Inc, Div Ayerst Labs, 76-80; WITH CARR SCARBOROUGH, 80- *Mem:* Am Soc Microbiol; Soc Indust Microbiol; Am Chem Soc; Am Asn Clin Chem. *Res:* Microbial physiology, especially enzymolgy, regulatory processes, fermentations and antibiotic biosynthesis; deliniation of metabolic pathways and the interplay of primary and secondary metabolism. *Mailing Add:* Carr Scarborough PO Box 1328 Stone Mountain GA 30086

ERISMAN, ALBERT MAURICE, computational mathematics, mathematical modeling, see previous edition

ERK, FRANK CHRIS, b Evansville, Ind, Dec 17, 24; m 48; c 3. GENETICS. *Educ:* Univ Evansville, AB, 48; Johns Hopkins Univ, PhD(genetics), 52. *Prof Exp:* Jr instr biol, Johns Hopkins Univ, 48-51; assoc prof & head dept, Washington Col, 52-57; prof natural sci, 57-61, prof biol sci, 62-74, chmn dept biol, 58-61, chmn div sci & math, 59-60, chmn dept biol sci, 62-67, prof cellular & comp biol, 74-76, chmn dept biol, 76-78, prof biol, 76-81, PROF BIOCHEM, STATE UNIV NY STONY BROOK, 81- *Concurrent Pos:* Vis assoc prof, Univ Chicago, 54-55; consult, Biol Sci Curriculum Study, 60-70; vis investr, Poultry Res Ctr, Agr Res Coun, Scotland, 64-65, Genetics Inst, Milan, 65, Masonic Med Res Lab, 68-71, Univ Sussex, 71-72, Galton Lab, Univ Col London, 78-79 & Univ Edinburgh, 79; exec ed, Quart Rev Biol, 66-69, ed, 69-; examr advan placement biol, Col Entrance Exam Bd, 67-71; asst examr, Int Baccalaureate Programme, Geneva, 77-; vis prof, Univ Essex, Eng, 78-79. *Mem:* Genetics Soc Am; Am Genetic Asn; Soc Study Evolution; Nat Asn Biol Teachers; Genetics Soc Can. *Res:* Developmental genetics of drosophila; mutagenesis; dermatoglyphics; insect nutrition; aging. *Mailing Add:* Dept Biochem State Univ NY Stony Brook NY 11794

ERKE, KEITH HOWARD, b Rogers City, Mich, Dec 16, 38. MEDICAL MYCOLOGY. *Educ:* Mich State Univ, BS, 64, MS, 66; Tulane Univ, PhD(med mycol), 72. *Prof Exp:* RES MICROBIOLOGIST, WILLIAM BEAUMONT ARMY MED CTR, 73- *Mem:* Sigma Xi; Am Soc Microbiol. *Res:* DNA of the pathogenic yeast organism Cryptococcus neoformans and study of hypha-forming strains. *Mailing Add:* Med Res & Develop William Beaumont Army Med Ctr El Paso TX 79920

ERKILETIAN, DICKRAN HAGOP, JR, b Mayfield, Ky, Sept 22, 13; m 40; c 3. MATHEMATICS. *Educ:* Western Ky State Col, AB, 36; Univ Ill, AM, 38. *Prof Exp:* Asst math, Univ Ill, 40-41; instr, Fenn Col, 41-42; from instr to assoc prof, 42-59, actg chmn dept, 62-63, chmn, 63-64, prof-in-chg-freshman-sophomore math, 65-67, prof math, 59-78, EMER PROF MATH, UNIV MO-ROLLA, 78- *Mem:* Am Math Soc; Am Soc Eng Educ; Math Asn Am. *Res:* Differential equations. *Mailing Add:* 8 Summit Dr Rolla MO 65401

ERLANDSEN, STANLEY L, b Chicago, Ill, May 21, 41; m 62; c 3. HISTOLOGY, MICROSCOPIC ANATOMY. *Educ:* Dana Col, BS, 63; Univ Minn, Minneapolis, PhD(anat), 67. *Prof Exp:* USPHS sr fel electron micros, Univ Wash, 67-69; asst prof anat, Univ Iowa, 69-74; assoc prof, 74-78, PROF ANAT, UNIV MINN, MINNEAPOLIS, 78- *Concurrent Pos:* counsult, Diabetes Ctr, Univ Wash, Seattle, 78- *Mem:* Am Soc Microbiol; Histochem Soc; Am Asn Anatomists; Am Soc Cell Biol. *Res:* Ultrastructure of intestinal microorganisms and their interaction with intestinal mucosa; fine structure and function of the Paneth cell; ultrastructural immunocytochemistry; biology of the intestinal protozoan, Giardia, and it's host response. *Mailing Add:* Dept of Anat Univ of Minn Minneapolis MN 55455

ERLANDSON, ARVID LEONARD, b Norway, Mich, Sept 26, 29; m 55; c 5. BACTERIOLOGY. *Educ:* Univ Mich, BS, 51, MS, 52, PhD, 54. *Prof Exp:* City bacteriologist, Ann Arbor Health Dept, 51-53; asst bact, Univ Mich, 53-54; res bacteriologist, Parke, Davis & Co, 58-64; asst prof microbiol & immunol, Sch Med, Marquette Univ, 64-71; DIR MICROBIOL, BRONSON METHODIST HOSP, 71- *Mem:* Am Soc Microbiol. *Res:* Bacterial physiology; bacillary dysentery; experimental pyelonephritis; pathogenesis of experimental infections; host resistance mechanisms. *Mailing Add:* Bronson Methodist Hosp 252 E Lovell St Kalamazoo MI 49006

ERLANDSON, PAUL M(CKILLOP), b Washington, DC, Oct 27, 20; m 41; c 5. ENGINEERING PHYSICS. *Educ:* Mass Inst Technol, BS, 41; Univ Tex, MA, 49, PhD(physics), 50. *Prof Exp:* Test design engr radio mfg, Crosley Corp, 37-39; cost control engr, electronics mfg, Radio Corp Am, 41-42; res physicist, Defense Res Lab, Univ Tex, 46-50; chmn dept physics, Southwest Res Inst, 50-56, asst vpres, 55-56; dir res physics, Continental Can Co, Inc, 56-59; dir res, Schlumberger Well Surv Corp, 59-61; dir eng res, 61-67, dir corp res, 67-77, gen mgr, Continental Can Co Inc, 77-80, GEN MGR NEW CONCEPTS, CONTINENTAL PACKAGING CO INC, 80- *Mem:* Am Phys Soc; Sigma Xi; Am Soc Mech Eng; Inst Elec & Electronics Engrs. *Res:* Information systems; high energy rate metalworking; energy conversion devices; instrumentation and physical measurements; industrial inspection systems; welding methods; research management; packaging systems. *Mailing Add:* 181 Red Fox Rd Stamford CT 06903

ERLANGER, BERNARD FERDINAND, b New York, NY, July 13, 23; m 46; c 3. BIOCHEMISTRY, IMMUNOLOGY. *Educ:* City Col New York, BS, 43; NY Univ, MS, 49; Columbia Univ, PhD(biochem), 51. *Prof Exp:* Assoc biochem, 51-52, assoc microbiol, 52-55, from asst prof to assoc prof, 55-66, PROF MICROBIOL, COLUMBIA UNIV, 66- *Concurrent Pos:* Vis scientist, Instituto Superiore di Sanita, Univ Rome, 61-62; mem comt Fulbright-Hays Acts Awards, Nat Acad Sci, 66-72; Fulbright scholar, Univ Repub, Uruguay, 67; Guggenheim fel, Inst Biophys & Biochem, Univ Paris, 69-70; adv ed, Immunochemistry, 76-80; vis scientist, Inst Cell Biol, Shanghai, People's Repub of China, 78; scholar, Am Cancer Soc, Inst Pasteur, Paris, 79. *Mem:* AAAS; Am Chem Soc; Am Soc Biol Chemists; Am Soc Cell Biol; Am Soc Photobiol. *Res:* Protein chemistry; peptide synthesis and enzymology; immunochemistry of nucleic acids; receptor biochemistry. *Mailing Add:* Dept Microbiol Columbia Univ 701 W 168th St New York NY 10032

ERLBACH, ERICH, b Wuerzburg, Ger, Dec 17, 33; US citizen; m 57; c 3. PHYSICS. *Educ:* Columbia Univ, AB, 55, AM, 57, PhD(physics), 60. *Prof Exp:* Asst physics, Columbia Col, 55-57; asst, Watson Lab, Int Bus Mach, 57-60, physicist, Res Ctr, 60-62; from asst prof to assoc prof physics, 62-73, chmn dept, 74-80, PROF PHYSICS, CITY COL NEW YORK, 73- *Concurrent Pos:* Lectr, City Col New York, 57-59; NSF res partic, Univ Md, 68-69. *Mem:* Am Phys Soc; Am Asn Physics Teachers; Asn Orthodox Jewish Scientists. *Res:* Cryogenics, especially superconductivity; solid state physics, particularly semiconductors and metals. *Mailing Add:* Dept of Physics 139 St & Convent Ave New York NY 10031

ERLENMEYER-KIMLING, L, b Princeton, NJ, Apr 18, 32; m 51. MEDICAL GENETICS. *Educ:* Columbia Univ, BS, 57, PhD(psychol & genetics), 61. *Prof Exp:* Asst behav genetics & lectr psychol, Columbia Univ, 58-60; from res scientist to prin res scientist, 60-78, RES SCIENTIST VII, MED GENETICS, NY STATE PSYCHIAT INST, 78-, DIR DIV DEVELOP BEHAV STUDIES, 78- *Concurrent Pos:* Asst, Col Physicians & Surgeons, Columbia Univ, 62-66, res assoc, 66-69, asst prof, Dept Psychiat, 69-74, assoc prof, Dept Psychiat & Dept Human Genetics, 74-78, prof, 78-; Genetics Soc Am travel grant, Int Cong Genetics, Neth, 63, USSR, 78; Am Psychol Asn travel grant, Int Cong Psychol, USSR, 66; NIMH res grants, 67-70, 71-80, 76-81 & 81-85; res grant, Scottish Rite Comt Schizophrenia, 71-75, W T Grant Found, 77-81, McArthur Found, 81; vis prof, Dept of Psychol, New Sch Soc Res, 72-; mem peer rev grant appln, NIH Study Sect, 76-80, NIMH Study Sect, 81-85; mem task panel, Cong Comt Huntington's Dis & President's Comn Mental Health. *Mem:* Behav Genetics Asn; Genetics Soc Am; Scientists Ctr Animal Welfare; Soc Life Hist Res Psychopath; Soc Study Soc Biol (secy, 72-75, pres, 75-78). *Res:* Experimental behavior genetics; medical and psychiatric genetics; population-genetic and demographic aspects of schizophrenia. *Mailing Add:* Dept of Med Genetics NY State Psychiat Inst New York NY 10032

ERLICH, DAVID C, b Brooklyn, NY. HIGH PRESSURE PHYSICS. *Educ:* Calif Inst Technol, BS, 68. *Prof Exp:* RES PHYSICIST HIGH PRESSURE PHYSICS, SRI INT, 68- *Res:* Shock-wave propagation in and fracture of condensed media; response of condensed media to high pressure transient loading. *Mailing Add:* SRI Int 333 Ravenswood Ave Menlo Park CA 94025

ERLICH, RONALD HARVEY, b Detroit, Mich, May 14, 45; m 74. ANALYTICAL CHEMISTRY. *Educ:* Wayne State Univ, BS, 67; Mich State Univ, PhD(anal chem), 71. *Prof Exp:* Res fel chem pharmacol, Heart & Lung Inst, NIH, 71-72; sr scientist pharmaceut anal, McNeil Labs, Subsid Johnson & Johnson, 73-77; MEM STAFF, BRISTOL LABS, 77- *Mem:* Am Chem Soc. *Res:* Development of analytical methods for the determination of pharmaceuticals; application of instrumental methods of analysis to the specific assay of drugs in dosage forms. *Mailing Add:* Bristol Labs PO Box 657 Syracuse NY 13201

ERLICHSON, HERMAN, b Brooklyn, NY, Mar 22, 31; m; c 4. PHYSICS. *Educ:* City Col New York, BS, 53; Harvard Univ, AM, 54; Columbia Univ, MA, 61, PhD(philos), 68; Rutgers Univ, MPh, 76, PhD(physics), 80. *Prof Exp:* Res & develop engr, Bell Aircraft Corp, 53; res develop & sales engr, Gen Elec Co, 54-56; res & develop engr, Kollsman Instrument Corp, 56-60; from asst prof to assoc prof, 60-70, PROF PHYSICS, COL STATEN ISLAND, 70- *Mem:* Philos Sci Asn; Am Asn Physics Teachers; Am Phys Soc. *Res:* Quantum mechanics; philosophy of physics; low energy nucleon-nucleon scattering. *Mailing Add:* Dept Appl Sci Col of Staten Island Staten Island NY 10301

ERLICK, BARRY J, genetics, virology, see previous edition

ERMAN, DON COUTRE, b Richmond, Ind, Mar 7, 40; m 65. AQUATIC ECOLOGY, FISHERIES. *Educ:* DePauw Univ, AB, 62; Purdue Univ, MS, 65; Utah State Univ, PhD(fisheries, aquatic ecol), 69. *Prof Exp:* from asst prof to assoc prof, 69-81, vchmn, Dept Forestry & Conserv, 75-77 & 78-81, co-chmn, Dept Conserv & Resources Studies, 81, PROF FISHERIES & AQUATIC ECOL, UNIV CALIF, BERKELEY, 81- *Concurrent Pos:* Mem coord bd, Calif Water Resources Ctr, 76-82. *Mem:* Am Fisheries Soc; Ecol Soc Am; Am Inst Biol Sci; Am Soc Limnol & Oceanog. *Res:* Freshwater benthic invertebrate communities; stream ecology; secondary production; wetland ecology. *Mailing Add:* Dept of Forestry & Conserv Univ of Calif Berkeley CA 94720

ERMAN, JAMES EDWIN, b Lodi, Calif, Dec 16, 40; m 71. PHYSICAL BIOCHEMISTRY. *Educ:* Univ Calif, Berkeley, BS, 62; Mass Inst Technol, PhD(phys chem), 66. *Prof Exp:* Res chemist, Chevron Res Co, 66-68; fel, Johnson Res Found, Univ Pa, 68-70; asst prof chem, 70-76, assoc prof chem, 76-81, PROF CHEM, NORTHERN ILL UNIV, 81- *Mem:* AAAS; Am Soc Biol Chemists; Sigma Xi; Am Chem Soc. *Res:* Enzyme catalyzed oxidation-reduction reactions; rapid reaction techniques. *Mailing Add:* Dept of Chem Northern Ill Univ DeKalb IL 60115

ERMAN, LEE DANIEL, b Chicago, Ill, 1944. ARTIFICIAL INTELLIGENCE. *Educ:* Univ Mich, BS, 66; Stanford Univ, MS, 68, PhD(comput sci), 74. *Prof Exp:* Res assoc comput sci, Carnegie-Mellon Univ, 71-74, res comput scientist, 74-76, asst prof, 76-78; res scientist, Info Sci Inst, Univ Southern Calif, 78-82; DIR KNOWLEDGE ENG TOOLS, TEKNOWLEDGE, INC, 82- *Mem:* Asn Comput Mach; Am Asn Artificial Intel. *Res:* Structures of and tools for building knowledge based artificial intelligence expert systems; control architectures for such systems. *Mailing Add:* Teknowledge Inc 525 University Ave Palo Alto CA 94301

ERMAN, WILLIAM F, b Butler, Mo, May 22, 31; m 60; c 4. ORGANIC CHEMISTRY. *Educ:* Univ Notre Dame, BS, 53; Mass Inst Technol, PhD(org chem), 57. *Prof Exp:* Res chemist & group leader natural prod chem, 57-66, sect head natural prod chem, 66-71, sect head med chem, 71-77, ASSOC DIR RES, PROCTER & GAMBLE CO, 77- *Concurrent Pos:* Lectr, Xavier Univ, Ohio, 63. *Honors & Awards:* Cincinnati Chemist Award, Am Chem Soc, 73. *Mem:* AAAS; Am Chem Soc; NY Acad Sci. *Res:* Natural products chemistry, particularly isolation, structure determination, reactions and synthesis of mono- and sesquiter-penes; organic photochemical transformations; medicinal chemistry; pesticide chemistry; perfume chemistry. *Mailing Add:* Res Dept Miami Vinyl Labs Procter & Gamble Co Cincinnati OH 45239

ERMENC, EUGENE D, b Milwaukee, Wis, Mar 29, 19; m 43; c 1. CHEMICAL ENGINEERING. *Educ:* Univ Wis, BS, 40; Ga Inst Technol, MS, 42. *Prof Exp:* Jr engr, Monsanto Chem Co, 42-46, sr engr, 46-50, plant engr, 50; proj engr, plaskon div, Libbey-Owens-Ford, 50-51; dir eng, Wis Alumni Res Found, 51-55; staff engr, Food Mach & Chem Corp, 55-56; coordr pilot opers, 56-58, mgr process eng, 59-61; dir res, Philip Cary Mfg Co, 61-69; dir, Air Pollution Control, City of Cincinnati, 69-80; prof, Raymond Walters Br, Univ Cincinnati, 76-81; asst county adminr, Hamilton County, 80-81; CONSULT, 81- *Mem:* Fel Am Inst Chem Engrs; Air Pollution Control Asn. *Res:* Engineering economics; process evaluation; oxides of nitrogen; simplification of complex engineering calculations. *Mailing Add:* 2239 Poinsettia Lane DeLand FL 32720

ERMENC, JOSEPH JOHN, b Milwaukee, Wis, Nov 11, 12; m 51; c 3. HISTORY OF TECHNOLOGY. *Educ:* Univ Wis, BS, 34; Univ Mich, MS, 40. *Hon Degrees:* MA, Dartmouth Col, 45. *Prof Exp:* Cadet gas engr, Milwaukee Gas Light Co, 34-36; engr-draftsman, Badger Meter Mfg Co, Milwaukee, 36-37; instr practical mech, Purdue Univ, 37-38; instr mech eng, Rensselaer Polytech Inst, 38-42; asst prof, 42-45, prof, 45-78, EMER PROF MECH ENG, THAYER SCH ENG, DARTMOUTH COL, 78- *Concurrent Pos:* Mem adv comt to Selective Serv Dir, NH, 55-62; NSF sci fac fel, 62-63; hon res assoc, Univ Col, Univ London, 62-63; Nat Acad Sci panel renewable energy resources, 75-76; chmn, Natural Hist & Heritage Comn, Am Assoc Mech Engrs, 78- *Mem:* Am Soc Mech Engrs. *Res:* Heat-power engineering. *Mailing Add:* 77 E Wheelock St Hanover NH 03755

ERMLER, WALTER CARL, b Chicago, Ill, July 22, 46; m 67; c 2. THEORETICAL CHEMISTRY. *Educ:* Northern Ill Univ, BS, 69; Ohio State Univ, MSc, 70, PhD(phys chem), 72. *Prof Exp:* Fel theoret chem, Ohio State Univ, 72-73; res assoc theoret chem, Univ Chicago, 73-76 & Univ Calif, Berkeley, 76-78; ASSOC PROF CHEM, STEVENS INST TECHNOL, 78- *Concurrent Pos:* Vis scientist, Argonne Nat Lab, 74-76; joint study partic, IBM Corp, 74-76. *Mem:* Am Phys Soc; AAAS; Am Chem Soc. *Res:* Application of ab initio quantum mechanical methods for studying potential energy surfaces fo ground and excited electronic states of molecules, properties of large molecules and solids; intra-molecular nuclear motion; relativistic effects on the chemical bond. *Mailing Add:* Dept of Chem & Chem Eng Stevens Inst of Technol Hoboken NJ 07030

ERMUTLU, ILHAN M, b Istanbul, Turkey, June 24, 27; US citizen; m 56; c 2. PSYCHIATRY. *Educ:* Univ Ankara, MD, 52. *Prof Exp:* Intern, Knickerbocker Hosp, NY, 54-55; resident psychiat, Bellevue Hosp, 55-56; resident, Hillside Hosp, 56-58; resident neurol, Goldwater Mem Hosp, 58-59; chief of serv psychiat, Eastern State Hosp, Va, 59-61; dir, Tidewater Ment Health Clin, 61-63; pvt pract, Richmond, Va, 63-64; asst to dir div ment health, Ga Dept Pub Health, 64-65, dir community serv br, 65-70, supt, Ga Regional Hosp, Savannah, 70-73; chief outpatient serv, William S Hall Psychiat Inst, 73-78; assoc prof psychiat, Sch Med, Univ SC, 77-78; dir, DeKalb County Ment Health & Ment Retardation Div, 78-80; dir forensic serv, Ga Ment Health Inst, 80-81; DIR, DIV MENTAL HEALTH & RETARDATION, GA DEPT HUMAN RESOURCES, 81- *Concurrent Pos:* Assoc in psychiat, Sch Med, Emory Univ, 64-73; clin assoc prof psychiat, Sch Med, Emory Univ, 78- *Mem:* Fel Am Psychiat Asn; fel Am Pub Health Asn; AMA. *Res:* Mental health. *Mailing Add:* 4288 Glengary Dr NE Atlanta GA 30342

ERN, ERNEST HENRY, b Irvington, NJ, Apr 27, 33; m 56; c 3. PETROLOGY, GEOLOGY. *Educ:* Bates Col, BS, 55; Lehigh Univ, MS, 57, PhD(geol), 59. *Prof Exp:* Asst geol, Lehigh Univ, 55-59; asst prof, Marshall Univ, 59-62; asst prof, 62-68, asst dean col arts & sci, 66-67, dean admis, 67-73, PROF ENVIRON SCI, UNIV VA, 75-, VPRES STUDENT AFFAIRS, 73- *Concurrent Pos:* Consult, Vt Geol Surv, 56-59 & Va Div Mineral Resources, 62-68. *Mem:* AAAS; fel Geol Soc Am; Am Inst Prof Geol Scientists. *Res:* Metamorphic petrology; geotechnics; metamorphism and structural evolution of the Appalachian Piedmont; foundation investigation studies for engineering structures. *Mailing Add:* Rotunda Univ of Va Charlottesville VA 22903

ERNEST, JOHN ARTHUR, b New York, NY, Dec 12, 35. MATHEMATICS. *Educ:* Drew Univ, BA, 57; Univ Ill, MS, 58, PhD(math), 60. *Prof Exp:* Lectr math, Franklin & Marshall Col, 60; mem, Inst Advan Study, 60-62; asst prof, Univ Rochester, 62-66; vis assoc prof, Tulane Univ, 66-67; assoc prof, 67-70, PROF MATH, UNIV CALIF, SANTA BARBARA, 70-, CHMN DEPT, 80- *Concurrent Pos:* NSF fel, 60-62; vis asst prof, Univ Calif, Berkeley, 65-66. *Mem:* Am Math Soc; Math Asn Am. *Res:* Functional analysis; infinite dimensional representations of topological groups; operator theory. *Mailing Add:* Dept of Math Univ of Calif Santa Barbara CA 93106

ERNEST, JOHN TERRY, ophthalmology, see previous edition

ERNEST, MICHAEL JEFFREY, b New York, NY, Mar 10, 48. MOLECULAR BIOLOGY, ENDOCRINOLOGY. *Educ:* Cornell Univ, BS, 68; Purdue Univ, PhD(biochem), 74. *Prof Exp:* Fel, Inst Cancer Res, Columbia Univ, 74-77; ASST PROF BIOL, YALE UNIV, 77- *Mem:* NY Acad Sci; Sigma Xi; AAAS. *Res:* Gene expression in normal and neoplastic cells. *Mailing Add:* Dept of Biol Yale Univ New Haven CT 06520

ERNSBERGER, FRED MARTIN, b Ada, Ohio, Sept 20, 19; m; c 4. PHYSICAL CHEMISTRY. *Educ:* Ohio Northern Univ, AB, 41; Ohio State Univ, PhD(phys chem), 46. *Prof Exp:* Res chemist, US Naval Ord Test Sta, 47-54, Southwest Res Inst, 54-56 & Mellon Inst of Indust Res, 57; RES CHEMIST, GLASS RES CTR, PPG INDUSTS, INC, 58- *Concurrent Pos:* Adj prof, Dept Mat Sci & Eng, Univ Calif, Los Angeles, 82- *Honors & Awards:* Frank Forrest Award, Am Ceramic Soc, 64, Toledo Glass & Ceramic Award, 70, & G W Morey Award, 74; Indust Res-100 Award, 81. *Mem:* Am Chem Soc; fel Am Ceramic Soc. *Res:* Surface chemistry, surface structure, mechanical properties of glass and glass-ceramics. *Mailing Add:* Glass Res Ctr PPG Industs Inc Box 11472 Pittsburgh PA 15238

ERNSDORFF, LOUIS EDWARD, mathematics, deceased

ERNST, CARL HENRY, b Lancaster, Pa, Sept 28, 38; m 69. HERPETOLOGY, MAMMALOGY. *Educ:* Millersville State Col, BS, 60; West chester State Col, MEd, 63; Univ Ky, PhD(biol), 69. *Prof Exp:* Asst prof biol, Elizabethtown Col, 66-67; cur vert, Univ Ky, 67-69; asst prof biol, Southwest Minn State Col, 69-72; assoc prof, 72-78, PROF BIOL, GEORGE MASON UNIV, 78- *Concurrent Pos:* Sigma Xi res grant-in-aid, 69 & 73; Minn State Col grants, 70,71; res assoc, US Nat Mus Natural Hist, 74-; Am Philos Soc grant, 76 & 81. *Honors & Awards:* Wildlife Publication Award, Wildlife Soc, 73. *Mem:* Am Soc Ichthyologists & Herpetologists; Soc Study Amphibians & Reptiles; Am Soc Mammal; Soc Trop Biol; Sigma Xi. *Res:* Ethology, ecology and taxonomy of turtles. *Mailing Add:* Dept of Biol George Mason Univ Fairfax VA 22030

ERNST, DAVID JOHN, b St Paul, Minn, May 29, 43; m 67; c 2. NUCLEAR PHYSICS. *Educ:* Mass Inst Technol, SB, 65, PhD(physics), 70. *Prof Exp:* Asst prof physics, Ctr Invest Advan Studies, Nat Polytech Inst, 70-71, prof, 71-72; res assoc, Case Western Reserve Univ, 72-74, res assoc & instr, 74-75; asst prof, 75-80, ASSOC PROF PHYSICS, TEX A&M UNIV, 80- *Concurrent Pos:* Vis staff scientist, Los Alamos Sci Lab, 72-; prin investr, NSF grant, 76-; vis asst prof phys, Univ Washington, 79-80. *Mem:* Am Phys Soc; Sigma Xi. *Res:* Theoretical nuclear physics; reactions of nucleons with finite nuclei, particularly at intermediate energies; pion-nucleon interaction; pion induced reactions and elastic scattering with finite nuclei. *Mailing Add:* Dept Physics Tex A&M Univ College Station TX 77843

ERNST, EDWARD W, b Great Falls, Mont, Aug 28, 24; m 50, 75; c 5. ELECTRICAL ENGINEERING. *Educ:* Univ Ill, BS, 49, MS, 50, PhD(elec eng), 55. *Prof Exp:* Res assoc elec eng, Univ Ill, 46-55; res engr, Gen Elec Co, NY, 55 & Stewart-Warner Electronics Corp, 55-58; assoc prof elec eng, 58-68, PROF ELEC ENG, UNIV ILL, URBANA, 68-, ASSOC HEAD DEPT, 71- *Concurrent Pos:* Pres, Nat Electronics Conf, 64; alt, Accreditation Bd Eng & Technol, Inst Elec & Electronics Engrs; mem, Eng Accreditation Comn, 79-, vchmn, 81- *Mem:* Fel AAAS; fel Inst Elec & Electronics Engrs; Am Soc Eng Educ. *Res:* Radiolocation; electronic systems; digital systems; experimentation. *Mailing Add:* Dept of Elec Eng Univ of Ill Urbana IL 61801

ERNST, GEORGE W, b St Marys, Pa, May 25, 39; m; c 1. COMPUTER SCIENCE, ELECTRICAL ENGINEERING. *Educ:* Carnegie Inst Technol, BS, 61, MS, 62, PhD(elec eng), 66. *Prof Exp:* Asst prof eng, 66-70, assoc prof comput & info sci, 70-80, ASSOC PROF, ARTIFICIAL INTELLIGENCE, CASE WESTERN RESERVE UNIV, 80- *Mem:* Asn Comput Mach. *Res:* Artificial intelligence. *Mailing Add:* Dept of Systs Eng Case Western Reserve Univ Cleveland OH 44106

ERNST, JOHN VERLON, b Glencoe, Okla, Mar 2, 35; m 58; c 3. PARASITOLOGY, PROTOZOOLOGY. *Educ:* Portland State Col, BS, 62; Utah State Univ, MS, 67, PhD(zool), 68. *Prof Exp:* NIH trainee, Univ Mass, 67-68; microbiologist, Animal Dis & Parasite Res Div, 68-80, ZOOLOGIST, REGIONAL PARASITE RES LAB, USDA, 80- *Mem:* Am Soc Parasitol; Soc Protozool; Wildlife Dis Asn. *Res:* Mammalian coccidiosis. *Mailing Add:* USDA Regional Parasite Res Lab USDA PO Drawer 952 Auburn AL 36830

ERNST, MARTIN L, b New York, NY, Mar 28, 20; m 53; c 2. PHYSICS. *Educ:* Mass Inst Technol, BS, 41. *Prof Exp:* Physicist, Naval Ord Lab, 41 & Bur Ord, 42; opers analyst, US Air Force, 43-46, electronics engr, Cambridge Res Ctr, 46-48; opers analyst, Opers Eval Group, Off Chief Naval Opers, 48-53, assoc dir, 53-59; sr staff mem & vpres opers res sect, 59-80, VPRES MGT SCI DIV, ARTHUR D LITTLE, INC, 59- *Mem:* Opers Res Soc Am (secy, 55-58, vpres, 59-60, pres, 60-61). *Mailing Add:* Mgt Sci Div Arthur D Little Inc 25 Acorn Park Cambridge MA 02140

ERNST, RALPH AMBROSE, b Saline, Mich, July 5, 38; m 67; c 1. POULTRY SCIENCE, PHYSIOLOGY. *Educ:* Mich State Univ, BS, 59, MS, 63, PhD(avian physiol), 66. *Prof Exp:* Teacher, Milan, Mich, 59-60 & Carson City, Mich, 60-61; EXTEN POULTRY SPECIALIST, UNIV CALIF, DAVIS, 66- *Honors & Awards:* Extension Award, Poultry Sci Asn, 78. *Mem:* Poultry Sci Asn; World Poultry Sci Asn; Sigma Xi. *Res:* Poultry physiology with emphasis on production. *Mailing Add:* Dept of Avian Sci Univ of Calif Davis CA 95616

ERNST, RICHARD DALE, b Long Beach, Calif, Oct 23, 51; m 73; c 3. STRUCTURAL CHEMISTRY. *Educ:* Univ Calif, Berkeley, BS, 73; Northwestern Univ, PhD(chem), 77. *Prof Exp:* ASST PROF CHEM, UNIV UTAH, 77- *Concurrent Pos:* Consult, Phillips Petroleum Co, 79- *Mem:* Am Chem Soc. *Res:* Synthesis, characterization, chemical and structural studies of inorganic and organometallic compounds, particularly those containing allyl or petadienyl ligands. *Mailing Add:* Dept Chem Univ Utah Salt Lake City UT 84112

ERNST, RICHARD EDWARD, b Elgin, Ill, July 2, 42; m 67. INDUSTRIAL CHEMISTRY. *Educ:* Grinnell Col, BA, 64; Univ Wis-Madison, PhD(phys chem), 68. *Prof Exp:* res chemist, 68-80, RES ASSOC, E I DU PONT DE NEMOURS & CO, INC, WILMINGTON, 80- *Mem:* Am Chem Soc; Sigma Xi. *Res:* Stereochemistry of transition metal complexes by nuclear magnetic resonance; radiation chemistry of polymers; pollution control; industrial process development. *Mailing Add:* Unionville-Lenape Rd Kennett Sq PA 19348

ERNST, ROBERTA DOROTHEA, b St Louis, Mo, Oct 12, 44. IMMUNOASSAYS. *Educ:* Univ Ill, Urbana, BS, 66. *Prof Exp:* Res chemist, 72-74, prod specialist, 74-77, supvr mfg & develop, 77-81, RES SCIENTIST, SYVA CO, SYNTEX, 81- *Mailing Add:* Syva Co 900 Arastradero Palo Alto CA 94303

ERNST, STEPHEN ARNOLD, b St Louis, Mo, Mar 31, 40; m 71. CELL BIOLOGY. *Educ:* Brown Univ, AB, 62, PhD(cell biol), 68; Syracuse Univ, MS, 64. *Prof Exp:* Fel cell biol, Brown Univ, 68; res assoc cell biol, Rice Univ, 68-71; from asst prof to assoc prof anat, Sch Med, Temple Univ, 71-78; ASSOC PROF ANAT, MED SCH, UNIV MICH, ANN ARBOR, 78- *Concurrent Pos:* Nat Found Cystic Fibrosis res fel, 68-71; Moody Found res grant, 70-71; Am Heart Asn grant-in-aid, 74-75; NSF res grant, 74-76; NIH res career develop award, 75-80, NIH res grant, 77-80. *Mem:* Histochem Soc; Electron Micros Soc Am; Am Asn Anat; Am Soc Cell Biol. *Res:* Electron microscopy; cytochemistry and biochemistry of electrolyte transporting tissues; histochemistry of the cell surface. *Mailing Add:* Dept of Anat Med Sci II Sch of Med Univ of Mich Ann Arbor MI 48109

ERNST, SUE CARLISLE, parasitology, cell biology, see previous edition

ERNST, SUSAN GWENN, b New York, NY, Sept 21, 46. MOLECULAR BIOLOGY. *Educ:* La State Univ, BS, 68; Univ Mass, PhD(zool), 75. *Prof Exp:* Instr, Div Radiation Biol, Case Western Univ, 74-75; res fel, Kerckhoff Marine Lab, Calif Inst Technol, 75-78, res fel biol, 78-79; ASST PROF BIOL, TUFTS UNIV, 79- *Mem:* AAAS; Soc Develop Biol. *Res:* Transcriptional and translational expression and regulation of gene activity in developing systems; cytoplasmic localization of maternal RNAs in developing embryos. *Mailing Add:* Dept Biol Tufts Univ Medford MA 02155

ERNST, VIVIAN, b Brussels, Belg, Apr 9, 50; Brit citizen; m 78. CELL BIOLOGY. *Educ:* Univ London, BSc, 71, PhD(biochem), 74. *Prof Exp:* Res assoc & scientist, Mass Inst Technol; ASST PROF, DEPT BIOCHEM, BRANDEIS UNIV, 80- *Mem:* AAAS; Asn Women Sci; Women Cell Biol. *Res:* Control of protein synthesis in eukaryotes; phosphorylation-dephosphorylation mechanisms; control of transcription-translation in mammalian cells during differentiation and during nutritional and environmental stress. *Mailing Add:* Grad Dept Biochem Friedland 311 Brandeis Univ Waltham MA 02254

ERNST, WALLACE GARY, b St Louis, Mo, Dec 14, 31; m 56; c 4. PETROLOGY, GEOCHEMISTRY. *Educ:* Carleton Col, BA, 53; Univ Minn, MS, 55; Johns Hopkins Univ, PhD(geol), 59. *Prof Exp:* Geologist, Petrol Br, US Geol Surv, 55-56; fel, Geophys Lab, Johns Hopkins Univ, 58-60; from asst prof to assoc prof, 60-68, chmn dept geol, 70-74, PROF GEOL & GEOPHYS, UNIV CALIF, LOS ANGELES, 68-, CHMN DEPT EARTH & SPACE SCI, 78- *Concurrent Pos:* Fulbright fel, Univ Tokyo, 63; NSF sr fel, Univ Basel, 70-71; Guggenheim fel, Swiss Fed Inst Technol, 75-76. *Honors & Awards:* Mineral Soc Am Award, 69. *Mem:* Nat Acad Sci; AAAS; fel Mineral Soc Am; Am Acad Arts Sci; fel Am Geophys Union. *Res:* Igneous and metamorphic petrology; application of theoretical and experimental phase equilibria to geologic problems; plate tectonics. *Mailing Add:* Dept of Earth & Space Sci Univ of Calif Los Angeles CA 90024

ERNST, WALTER, b Berlin, Ger, Jan 12, 01; nat US; m 33; c 4. MECHANICAL ENGINEERING. *Educ:* Tech Hochsch, Ger, Dipl, 23. *Prof Exp:* Apprentice mech, Mesta Mach Co, 23-24; draftsman & designer, Homestead Valve Mfg Co, 24-26; develop engr, Hydraul Press Mfg Co, 26-32, chief engr, 32-38, dir eng, 38-44; vpres & dir, Commonwealth Eng Co, Ohio, 45-64, pres, 64-65; sr partner, Ernst & Assocs, 65-81; RETIRED. *Honors & Awards:* Award, Nat Fluid Power Asn, 63. *Mem:* Am Soc Mech Engrs. *Res:* Industrial hydraulics; fluid mechanics and power circuits; hydraulic, machine tool and press controls; hydraulic component and special machine design; automation through hydraulics. *Mailing Add:* Ernst & Assocs 225 W Hillcrest Ave Dayton OH 45405

ERNST, WILLIAM PAUL, b New York, NY, July 24, 22; m 44; c 4. MICROWAVE ENGINEERING. *Educ:* Newark Col Eng, BSEE, 57, MSEE, 65. *Prof Exp:* Jr engr microwaves & electronic instrumentation, Lavoie Labs, 48-50; engr, Chatham Electronics, 50-53; resident engr, Stavid Eng, Bell Labs, Murray Hill, 53-59; staff engr, 59-63, SR STAFF ENGR MICROWAVES & ELECTRONIC INSTRUMENTATION, PLASMA PHYSICS LAB, PRINCETON UNIV, 63- *Mem:* Inst Elec & Electronics Engrs. *Res:* Microwave diagnostic systems as applied to controlled fusion research. *Mailing Add:* Plasma Physics Lab PO Box 451 Princeton NJ 08544

ERNST, WILLIAM ROBERT, b Hanover, Pa, June 3, 43; m 66; c 3. CHEMICAL ENGINEERING. *Educ:* Pa State Univ, BS, 65, MS, 71; Univ Del, PhD(chem eng), 74. *Prof Exp:* Proj engr, Allied Chem Corp, 65-69; asst prof, 73-80, ASSOC PROF & CHMN ENG, GA INST TECHNOL, 80- *Mem:* Sigma Xi; Am Inst Chem Engrs. *Res:* Heterogeneous catalysis; chemical reactor design. *Mailing Add:* Sch of Chem Eng Ga Inst of Technol Atlanta GA 30332

ERNST-FONBERG, MARYLOU, b Harrisburg, Pa, Jan 18, 37; m 69; c 1. BIOCHEMISTRY. *Educ:* Susquehanna Univ, BA, 58; Temple Univ, MD, 62; Yale Univ, PhD(biochem), 67. *Prof Exp:* Vis scientist, Dept Chem Immunol, Weizmann Inst Sci, 66-67; res fel chem, Harvard Univ, 68-69; from asst prof to assoc prof biol, Yale Univ, 69-78; ASSOC PROF BIOCHEM, COL MED, EAST TENN STATE UNIV, 78- *Res:* Biochemical characterization of the enzymes of lipid biosynthesis and investigation of alterations in this enzymology in conjunction with the development of organelles. *Mailing Add:* Dept Biochem Col Med Box 19930A E Tenn State Univ Johnson City TN 37601

ERNSTROM, CARL ANTHON, b Draper, Utah, Mar 28, 22; m 49; c 4. DAIRY CHEMISTRY. *Educ:* Utah State Univ, BS, 49, MS, 51; Univ Wis, PhD(dairy indust), 56. *Prof Exp:* Exten specialist dairy indust, State of Wis, 53-55; res assoc, Chris Hansen's Lab, 55-58; assoc prof dairy & food indust, Univ Wis, 60-65; prof dairy sci, 65-67, HEAD DEPT NUTRIT & FOOD SCI, UTAH STATE UNIV, 67- *Concurrent Pos:* Assoc ed, J Dairy Sci, 74- *Honors & Awards:* Pfizer Award, Am Dairy Sci Asn, 68. *Mem:* Fel Inst Food Technologists; Am Dairy Sci Asn. *Res:* Milk coagulating enzymes and chemistry of milk clotting. *Mailing Add:* Dept of Nutrit & Food Sci Utah State Univ Logan UT 84321

EROR, NICHOLAS GEORGE, JR, b Bingham Canyon, Utah, Apr 9, 37; m 59; c 7. SOLID STATE CHEMISTRY, MATERIALS SCIENCE. *Educ:* Yale Univ, BS, 59, MS, 62; Northwestern Univ, PhD(mat sci), 65. *Prof Exp:* Sr scientist solid state chem, Sprague Elec Co, 64-70; ASSOC PROF MAT SCI, ORE GRAD CTR, 70- *Concurrent Pos:* Vis prof math, Williams Col, 66, vis prof chem, 68-70. *Mem:* Am Ceramic Soc. *Res:* Point defects in pure and doped nonmetallic compounds; nonstoichiometric compounds; oxidation-reduction kinetics; electrical properties; Raman spectroscopy; oxide catalysts; synthesis of thermodynamically defined multicomponent compounds. *Mailing Add:* Ore Grad Ctr 19600 NW Walker Rd Beaverton OR 97006

EROSCHENKO, VICTOR PAUL, b May 15, 38; US citizen; m 64; c 2. HUMAN ANATOMY. *Educ:* Univ Calif, Davis, BA, 61, MS, 70, PhD(anat), 73. *Prof Exp:* Asst prof, 73-80, ASSOC PROF HUMAN ANAT, DEPT BIOL SCI, UNIV IDAHO, 80- *Mem:* Soc Study Reproduction; Sigma Xi; AAAS; Am Asn Anatomists. *Res:* Morphological studies on reproductive organs in birds and mammals as altered or effected by environmental pollutants especially insecticide Kepone. *Mailing Add:* Dept Biol Univ of Idaho Moscow ID 83843

ERPENBECK, JEROME JOHN, b Ft Thomas, Ky, Aug 22, 33; m 56; c 8. THEORETICAL CHEMISTRY. *Educ:* Villa Madonna Col, BS, 53; Univ Louisville, MS, 55; Univ Ill, PhD(chem), 57. *Prof Exp:* Asst, Sterling Chem Lab, Yale Univ, 57-59; STAFF MEM, LOS ALAMOS SCI LAB, 59- *Res:* Transport and detonation theories; reactive hydrodynamics; statistical mechanics of fluids. *Mailing Add:* 3 Kiowa Lane White Rock Los Alamos NM 87544

ERPINO, MICHAEL JAMES, b Schenectady, NY, May 30, 39; m 61; c 3. ENDOCRINOLOGY, HISTOLOGY. *Educ:* Pa State Univ, BS, 62; Univ Wyo, MS, 64, PhD(physiol), 67. *Prof Exp:* NIH fel endocrinol, Cornell Univ, 67-68; from asst prof to assoc prof zool, 68-77, PROF BIOL SCI, CALIF STATE UNIV, CHICO, 77- *Mem:* AAAS; Am Soc Zool; Am Ornith Union; fel Int Soc Res Aggression. *Res:* Steroid hormones and behavior; histology of vertebrate endocrines. *Mailing Add:* Dept of Biol Sci Calif State Univ Chico CA 95926

ERREDE, BEVERLY JEAN, b New Britain, Conn, Aug 4, 49. YEAST GENETICS, GENE EXPRESSION. *Educ:* Conn Col, BA, 71; Univ Calif, San Diego, PhD(chem), 76. *Prof Exp:* Fel, Dept Chem, Univ Calif, San Diego, 76-77 & Univ Rochester, 77-81; ASST PROF CHEM, UNIV NC, CHAPEL HILL, 81- *Mem:* Am Chem Soc. *Res:* Identify and define molecular mechanisms utilized by eukaryotic organisms for regulation gene expression; involving genetic and biochemical characterization of defined regulatory mutations in Saccharomyces cereviciae. *Mailing Add:* Dept Chem Univ NC Chapel Hill NC 27514

ERREDE, STEVEN MICHAEL, b Newark, NJ, Dec 24, 52; m 79. ELEMENTARY PARTICLE PHYSICS. *Educ:* Univ Minn, BSc, 75; Ohio State Univ, MSc, 78, PhD(physics), 81. *Prof Exp:* Grad teaching asst physics, Ohio State Univ, 75-78, grad res asst, 78-81; SCHOLAR PHYSICS, UNIV MICH, 81- *Mem:* Sigma Xi; Am Physical Soc. *Res:* Lifetimes of charmed particles (produced in neutrino interactions); proton decay experiment, high resolution particle spectrometry; high energy physics detector hardware and data analysis. *Mailing Add:* Rm 3072 Randall Lab Univ Mich Ann Arbor MI 48109

ERRERA, SAMUEL J(OSEPH), b Hammonton, NJ, Jan 7, 26; m 49; c 2. STRUCTURAL ENGINEERING. *Educ:* Rutgers Univ, BS, 49; Univ Ill, MS, 51; Cornell Univ, PhD(struct), 65. *Prof Exp:* Engr of tests, Fritz Eng Lab, Lehigh Univ, 51-62, from instr to assoc prof, 51-62; mgr struct lab, Cornell Univ, 62-65, assoc prof civil eng, 68-70; sr engr, 70-76, CONSULT ENGR, BETHLEHEM STEEL CORP, 76- *Concurrent Pos:* Consult, Allegheny-Ludlum Steel Corp & R C Mahon Co, 66-70; methods engr, adv composites group, Grumman Aircraft Co, 68-69. *Mem:* Am Soc Civil Engrs. *Res:* Research management; light gauge steel structures; diaphragm bracing; structural materials; composite design; advanced structural composites. *Mailing Add:* 1730 Maple St Bethlehem PA 18017

ERRETT, DARYL DALE, b Gridley, Kans, Dec 2, 22; m 53; c 1. OPTICS. *Educ:* Kans State Teachers Col, BA, 44; Purdue Univ, MS, 48, PhD(physics), 51. *Prof Exp:* Teaching asst, Kans State Teachers Col, 41-44; res asst, Purdue Univ, 46-51; res specialist, Electro Mech Dept, NAm Rockwell Corp, 51-54; res physicist, Santa Barbara Res Ctr, Goleta, 54-67; sr staff physicist, 67-80; CONSULT PHYSICIST, 80- *Concurrent Pos:* Asst, Purdue Res Found, 46-51. *Res:* Electrical discharge through gases; linear electron accelerators; inertial guidance systems; infrared detection systems; infrared optical design; computer programs for optical design and analysis; evaporated thermopile detectors; solid state laser communication systems; infrared proximity detectors; radiometric calibration instrumentation. *Mailing Add:* 345 Conejo Rd Santa Barbara CA 93103

ERSHOFF, BENJAMIN H, b Philadelphia, Pa, Jan 31, 14; m 41; c 2. NUTRITION. *Educ:* Univ Calif, Los Angeles, AB, 37, MPH, 73; Univ Calif, Berkeley, PhD(animal nutrit), 42. *Prof Exp:* Dir res, Emory W Thurston Labs, 42-50, sci dir, 50-53; dir, Western Biol Labs, 54-62; dir, Inst Biol Res, 62-65; sci dir, Inst Arteriosclerosis Res, 65-70; dir, inst nutrit studies, 70-77; RES NUTRITIONIST, DEPT MED, UNIV CALIF, LOS ANGELES, 77- *Concurrent Pos:* Vis prof, Dept Biochem & Nutrit, Univ Southern Calif, 56-59, adj prof, Sch Med, 59-65, adj prof, Sch Dent, 66-72; res prof biochem, Sch Med, Loma Linda Univ, 66-77. *Mem:* Am Inst Nutrit; Inst Food Technologists; Soc Exp Biol & Med; Geront Soc. *Res:* Nutrition and stress; vitamin-endocrine interrelationships; unidentified nutrients; dietary fiber. *Mailing Add:* 858 Woodacres Rd Santa Monica CA 90402

ERSKINE, ANTHONY J, b Whinfield, Eng, June 25, 31; Can citizen; m 55; c 3. WILDLIFE BIOLOGY. *Educ:* Acadia Univ, BSc, 52; Queen's Univ, Ont, MA, 55, PhD(org chem), 57; Univ BC, MA, 60. *Prof Exp:* Tech officer animal chem, Sci Serv, Can Dept Agr, 52-53; Nat Res Coun Can fel, Atlantic Regional Lab, 56-57; biologist, 60-76, SCI MGR, CAN WILDLIFE SERV, DEPT ENVIRON, 77- *Concurrent Pos:* Ed, Can Soc Environ Biologists, 69-74; ed assoc, Can Field Naturalist, 75- *Honors & Awards:* E P Edwards Prize, Wilson Ornithol Soc, 72. *Mem:* Am Ornith Union; Brit Ornith Union; Can Soc Environ Biologists. *Res:* Structures of plant polysaccharides; bird populations, densities, trends and habitats. *Mailing Add:* Dept of the Environ Can Wildlife Serv PO Box 1590 Sackville NB E0A 3C0 Can

ERSKINE, CHRISTOPHER FORBES, b Worcester, Mass, Apr 30, 27; m 52; c 3. GEOLOGY. *Educ:* Harvard Univ, AB, 49. *Prof Exp:* Geologist, Eng Geol Br, US Geol Surv, 50-57; consult eng geologist, E B Waggoner, 57-60; proj geologist, Woodward-Clyde-Sherard & Assocs, 60-62; water geologist, Kennecott Copper Corp, Utah, 62-70, GROUNDWATER GEOLOGIST, AMAX EXPLOR, INC, 70- *Mem:* Geol Soc Am; Am Inst Mining, Metall & Petrol Engrs; Asn Eng Geol; Am Inst Prof Geol; Am Water Resources Asn. *Res:* Engineering geology; groundwater geology. *Mailing Add:* 365 Rangeview Dr Littleton CO 80120

ERSKINE, DONALD B, b Utica, NY, Jan 18, 23; m 53; c 2. CHEMICAL ENGINEERING. *Educ:* Cornell Univ, BCE, 48. *Prof Exp:* Prod engr, Calumet & Hecla Copper Co, 48-49, res engr, 49-50; develop engr, Chem Construct Corp, 50-53; proj engr, Titanium Metals Corp, 53-59, Pittsburgh Chem Co, 59-61 & Fluor Corp, 61-63; systs engr, 63-64, DIR ENG, CALGON CORP, 64- *Mem:* Am Chem Soc; Am Inst Chem Engrs. *Res:* Hydrometallurgy of copper; application of activated carbon. *Mailing Add:* 110 Lang Dr Coraopolis PA 15108

ERSKINE, GORDON JOHN, inorganic chemistry, organometallic chemistry, see previous edition

ERSKINE, JAMES LORENZO, b Seattle, Wash, Oct 25, 42; m 66; c 2. SOLID STATE PHYSICS. *Educ:* Univ Wash, BS, 64, MS, 66, PhD(physics), 73. *Prof Exp:* Res engr nuclear weapons effects, Boeing Co, 66-73; res assoc physics, Univ Wash, 73-74; res asst prof physics, Univ Ill, Urbana, 74-77; ASST PROF PHYSICS, UNIV TEX, AUSTIN, 77- *Concurrent Pos:* Sr res engr consult, Boeing Co, 72-74. *Mem:* Am Phys Soc. *Res:* Optical and magneto-optical properties of solids; physics and chemistry of surfaces and adsorbed atoms; electron spectroscopy applied to the study of bulk and surface electronic and structural properties. *Mailing Add:* Dept of Physics Univ of Tex Austin TX 78712

ERSKINE, JOHN ROBERT, b Milwaukee, Wis, Mar 18, 31; m 56; c 6. NUCLEAR PHYSICS. *Educ:* Univ Rochester, BS, 53; Univ Notre Dame, PhD(physics), 60. *Prof Exp:* Res assoc nuclear physics, Mass Inst Technol, 60-61, instr physics, 61-62; res assoc, 62-63, from asst physicist to assoc physicist, 63-73, SR PHYSICIST, ARGONNE NAT LAB, 73- *Concurrent Pos:* Vis assoc prof, Univ Minn, 71-72; prog officer, US Dept Energy, Washington, DC, 77-79. *Mem:* Fel Am Phys Soc. *Res:* Experimental nuclear physics; heavy ion reactions. *Mailing Add:* Argonne Nat Lab Argonne IL 60439

ERSLEV, ALLAN JACOB, b Copenhagen, Denmark, Apr 20, 19; nat US; m 47; c 4. MEDICINE. *Educ:* Copenhagen Univ, MD, 45. *Prof Exp:* Rosenstock Mem fel, Sloan-Kettering Inst, 46-47; asst res med, Sch Med, Yale Univ, 48-50, instr, 51-53; assoc, Harvard Med Sch, 55-58, asst prof, 58-59; assoc prof, 59-63, CARDEZA RES PROF MED & DIR CARDEZA FOUND HEMAT RES, JEFFERSON MED COL, THOMAS JEFFERSON UNIV, 63- *Concurrent Pos:* Runyon res fel, 50-51; res assoc, Thorndike Mem Lab, Mass, 55-59; consult, US Army, 53-55. *Mem:* Am Soc Clin Invest; Am Fedn Clin Res; Asn Am Physicians; Am Soc Hemat; Int Soc Hemat. *Res:* Hematology. *Mailing Add:* Dept of Med Thomas Jefferson Univ Philadelphia PA 19107

ERSPAMER, JACK LAVERNE, b Chehalis, Wash, Apr 9, 18; m 45; c 1. PLANT MORPHOLOGY, PLANT ANATOMY. *Educ:* Univ Wash, BS, 41; Univ Calif, PhD(bot), 53. *Prof Exp:* Teaching asst, Univ Calif, 48-51, res asst plant path, Citrus Exp Sta, 53-56; PROF BIOL, CALIF STATE POLYTECH UNIV, POMONA, 56- *Mem:* Bot Soc Am. *Res:* Morphology and anatomy of gymnosperms. *Mailing Add:* Dept of Biol Sci Calif State Polytech Univ Pomona CA 91768

ERSTFELD, THOMAS EWALD, b Erie, Pa, Mar 5, 51; m 79. INORGANIC CHEMISTRY. *Educ:* Gannon Col, BS, 73; Brown Univ, PhD(chem), 77. *Prof Exp:* Fel chem, Lunar & Planetary Inst, 77-78; sr scientist chem, Lockheed Electronics Co, Inc, 78-80; ELECTRONIC MAT RES CHEMIST, US AIR FORCE, 80- *Mem:* Am Chem Soc. *Res:* Vapor phase epitaxial growth of III-V quaternary compounds. *Mailing Add:* Electronic Systs Div Rome Air Develop Command Hanscom AFB MA 01731

ERTEL, NORMAN H, b Brooklyn, NY, Nov 15, 32; m 67; c 3. INTERNAL MEDICINE, ENDOCRINOLOGY. *Educ:* Harvard Univ, AB, 53; Columbia Univ, MD, 57. *Prof Exp:* Intern med, Bronx Munic Hosp, Albert Einstein Col Med, 57-58, asst resident, 58-59; NY Heart Asn fel steroid biochem, Col Physicians & Surgeons, Columbia Univ, 59-60; chief, Endocrinol Div, Andrews AFB, Washington, DC, 60-62; resident med, Bronx Munic Hosp Ctr, Albert Einstein Col Med, 62-63; NIH fel endocrinol, Med Sch, Cornell Univ, 63-65; dir, Steroid Res Lab, Jewish Hosp & Med Ctr, Brooklyn, 65-71; from instr to asst prof med, State Univ NY Downstate Med Ctr, 67-71; PROF MED & DIR DIV ENDOCRINOL & METAB, NJ MED SCH, 71-; CHIEF MED SERV, VET ADMIN HOSP, 71- *Concurrent Pos:* Nat Inst Arthritis, Metab & Digestive Dis res grant, Jewish Hosp & Med Ctr, Brooklyn, 68-71, Nat Cancer Inst res grant, 70-71; vis prof, Univ Guadalajara, 74. *Honors & Awards:* Award, Surgeon Gen, US Air Force, 62. *Mem:* Am Fedn Clin Res; fel Am Col Physicians; Endocrine Soc; Am Diabetes Asn; fel NY Acad Sci. *Res:* Clinical endocrinology; steroid biochemistry; metabolic disease. *Mailing Add:* Med Serv 111 Vet Admin Hosp East Orange NJ 07019

ERTEL, ROBERT JAMES, b Buffalo, Minn, May 8, 32; m 58; c 4. PHARMACOLOGY, ENDOCRINOLOGY. *Educ:* Col St Thomas, BS, 54; Univ Minn, Minneapolis, PhD(pharmacol), 65. *Prof Exp:* Jr scientist, Med Sch, Univ Minn, 58-65; res fel biochem, Univ Minn, 65-66; res assoc, Nat Heart Inst, 66-68; asst prof, 68-71, ASSOC PROF PHARMACOL, SCH PHARM, UNIV PITTSBURGH, 71- *Mem:* Soc Neurosci; Endocrine Soc; Am Soc Pharmacol & Exp Therapeut. *Res:* Actions of drugs on the spontaneous activity of heart cells grown in tissue culture; endocrine physiology in chronic stress; neuroendocrinology and protein biosynthesis; effect of dietary sodium on cardiovascular and autonomic nervous function. *Mailing Add:* Dept Pharmacol 1100 Salk Hall Univ Pittsburgh Pittsburgh PA 15261

ERTELT, HENRY ROBINSON, b New Haven, Conn, Apr 29, 24; m 48; c 3. ORGANIC CHEMISTRY. *Educ:* Yale Univ, BS, 49, PhD(org chem), 52; NY Univ, JD, 70. *Prof Exp:* Res chemist, Esso Res & Eng Co, 52-66; patent atty, 66-74, GROUP COUNSEL, CHEM PATENT & LICENSING, FMC CORP, 74- *Mem:* AAAS; Am Chem Soc. *Res:* Organic synthesis; additives for petroleum products; rocket propellants; agricultural pesticides; patent law. *Mailing Add:* FMC Corp 2000 Market St Philadelphia PA 19103

ERTEZA, AHMED, b Rajbari, East Pakistan, Aug 1, 24; nat US; m 57; c 2. ELECTRICAL ENGINEERING. *Educ:* Univ Calcutta, BSc, 45, MS, 47; Stanford Univ, MS, 51, EE, 52; Carnegie Inst Technol, PhD(elec eng), 54. *Prof Exp:* Engr, Dacca Broadcasting Sta, Radio Pakistan, 47-48; sr lectr electronics & radio eng, Univ Dacca, 48-50; elec engr, nuclear instrumentation, Nuclear Res Ctr, Pa, 53-54; asst prof elec eng, Ahsanullah Eng Col, East Pakistan, 55-58 & Bradley Univ, 58; assoc prof, 58-63, PROF ELEC ENG, UNIV N MEX, 63- *Mem:* Inst Elec & Electronics Engrs; assoc mem Inst Eng Pakistan. *Res:* Electromagnetics and microwave; magnetohydrodynamics; nuclear instrumentation; analog and digital computation; energy conversion; controls. *Mailing Add:* Dept of Elec Eng & Comput Sci Univ of NMex Albuquerque NM 87106

ERTINGSHAUSEN, GERHARD, clinical chemistry, see previous edition

ERULKAR, SOLOMON DAVID, b Calcutta, India, Aug 18, 24; m 50; c 2. NEUROPHYSIOLOGY. *Educ:* Univ Toronto, BA, 48, MA, 49; Johns Hopkins Univ, PhD(physiol), 52; Oxford Univ, DPhil, 57. *Prof Exp:* USPHS fel, Johns Hopkins Univ, 52-54; Brit Med Res Coun grant, Oxford Univ, 55-58; asst prof otol & physiol, dir dept & dir res otol, Temple Univ, 59-60; dept demonstr physiol, Oxford Univ, 55-58; from asst prof to assoc prof, 60-67, PROF PHARMACOL, UNIV PA, 67-, ASSOC DIR, INST NEUROL SCI, 81- *Concurrent Pos:* Hon res assoc, Univ Col, Univ London, 67-68; Guggenheim fel, Hadassah Med Sch, Hebrew Univ, Israel, 74-75, vis prof physiol, 74-75. *Res:* Mechanisms of central synaptic transmission. *Mailing Add:* Dept of Pharmacol Med Sch Univ of Pa Philadelphia PA 19104

ERVE, PETER RAYMOND, b Buffalo, NY, June 25, 26; m 61; c 1. CLINICAL CHEMISTRY, TOXICOLOGY. *Educ:* Univ Toronto, BA, 51, MA, 52; Ill Inst Technol, PhD(biochem), 68. *Prof Exp:* Res chemist, Vet Admin Med Ctr, Westside, 68-75; CLIN CHEMIST, VET ADMIN MED CTR, NORTH CHICAGO, 75-; ASSOC PROF, DEPT PATH, CHICAGO MED SCH, 77- *Honors & Awards:* Cert Appreciation, Am Col Surgeons, 71; Cert of Merit, AMA, 72. *Mem:* Am Chem Soc; Am Asn Clin Chem; AAAS; Nat Acad Clin Biochem. *Res:* Pathophysiology of septic shock; bacterial toxins; metabolic derrangements in endotoxic shock. *Mailing Add:* Vet Admin Med Ctr Lab Serv North Chicago IL 60064

ERVEN, BERNARD LEE, b Bowling Green, Ohio, Aug 25, 38; m 61; c 5. AGRICULTURAL ECONOMICS. *Educ:* Ohio State Univ, BSAgr, 60, MS, 63; Univ Wis, PhD(agr econ), 67. *Prof Exp:* Asst prof agr econ, Univ Wis, 67-69; from asst prof to prof, 69-79, PROF AGR ECON & ASSOC CHMN, OHIO STATE UNIV, 79- *Mem:* Am Agr Econ Asn; Nat Asn Col Teachers Agr. *Res:* labor management problems of agricultural employers; farm management problems of part-time farmers. *Mailing Add:* 2120 Fyffe Rd Columbus OH 43210

ERVIN, C PATRICK, b Danville, Ill, Aug 5, 43. GRAVITY, MAGNETICS. *Educ:* Wash Univ, St Louis, BS, 65, MA, 68; Univ Wis, Madison, PhD(geophysics), 72. *Prof Exp:* Res assoc, 72-75, asst prof, 75-82, ASSOC PROF GEOPHYSICS, NORTHERN ILL UNIV, 81- *Concurrent Pos:* Geophysicist, Ill State Geol Surv, 72-73; assoc ed geophysics, Geosci Wis, Wis Geol Surv, 76-; assoc scientist, Dry Valley Drilling Proj, 75-76; mem staff, US Geol Surv, 77-78. *Mem:* Soc Explor Geophysicusts; Am Geophys Union; Europ Asn Explor Geophysicists; Geol Soc Am. *Res:* Applied geophysics, potential fields; computer applications in the earth sciences; geophysics of continental interiors. *Mailing Add:* Dept Geol Northern Ill Univ De Kalb IL 60115

ERVIN, FRANK (RAYMOND), b Little Rock, Ark, Nov 3, 26; m 47; c 5. PSYCHIATRY. *Educ:* Tulane Univ, MD, 51; Am Bd Psychiat & Neurol, dipl. *Prof Exp:* Asst psychiat & neurol, Med Sch, Tulane Univ, 52-57; from instr to asst prof psychiat, Harvard Med Sch, 57-68, assoc clin prof, 68-69, assoc prof, 69-72; PROF PSYCHIAT, UNIV CALIF, LOS ANGELES, 72- *Concurrent Pos:* Dir, Monroe Area Guid Ctr, La, 53-57; consult psychiatrist, State Training Inst, La, 53-57; asst, Mass Gen Hosp, 57-63, psychiatrist, 63-; NIMH career res fel, 62-; adj prof, Hampshire Col & Sch Med, Univ PR; pres, Behav Sci Found; dir, Stanley Cobb Labs Psychol Res, Mass Gen Hosp, 62-72. *Res:* Neurophysiologic aspects of behavior. *Mailing Add:* Neuropsychiat Inst Univ of Calif Sch of Med Los Angeles CA 90024

ERVIN, GUY, JR, b Washington, DC, Nov 14, 15; m 39; c 4. PHYSICAL CHEMISTRY, CERAMICS. *Educ:* George Washington Univ, BS, 37; Univ Md, MS, 41; Pa State Col, PhD(ceramics), 49. *Prof Exp:* Jr chemist, Bur Mines & Md, 37-41, assoc phys chemist, 41-44; res chemist, Westvaco Chem Co, 44-46; res engr ceramic & abrasive prods, Norton Co, 49-57, res assoc, Explor Res Sect, 57-59; sr tech specialist, Atomics Int Div, NAm Rockwell Corp, 59-63, supvr solid state chem, 63-67, tech staff, Atomics Int Div, Rockwell Int Corp, 67-77; CONSULT SOLAR HEATING, 77- *Mem:* AAAS; Am Chem Soc; Am Ceramic Soc; Int Solar Energy Soc. *Res:* Inorganic phase equilibria, high pressure mineral synthesis; alumina and its hydrates; extractive metallurgy of titanium and zirconium; high temperature chemistry; metal oxidation kinetics; porous ceramics; solar heat storage. *Mailing Add:* 8451 Amestoy Ave Northridge CA 91324

ERVIN, MICHAEL ANTHONY, chemical engineering, see previous edition

ERWAY, LAWRENCE CLIFTON, JR, b Lawrenceville, Pa, Apr 27, 38; m 60; c 4. DEVELOPMENTAL GENETICS. *Educ:* Barrington Col, BA, 60; Brown Univ, MA, 63; Univ Calif, Davis, PhD(genetics), 68. *Prof Exp:* Instr biol, Barrington Col, 61-64; trainee genetics, Univ Calif, Davis, 64-66, res technician, 66-68; asst prof, 68-74, ASSOC PROF BIOL, UNIV OF CINCINNATI, 74- *Concurrent Pos:* NIH fel, Pompeiano's Lab, Pisa, Italy, 76-77. *Mem:* Asn Res Otolaryngol. *Res:* Effects of trace elements and genes on birth defects, including pigmentary and neurological defects in mice and man, with particular emphasis on prevention of certain hereditary disorders, specifically otolith defects and deafness. *Mailing Add:* 422 Grove Ave Cincinnati OH 45215

ERWIN, ALBERT R, b Charlotte, NC, May 1, 31; m 54; c 1. PHYSICS. *Educ:* Duke Univ, BS, 53; Harvard Univ, MA, 57, PhD(physics), 59. *Prof Exp:* Jr res assoc, Brookhaven Nat Lab, 57-58; from instr to assoc prof, 58-65, PROF PHYSICS, UNIV WIS-MADISON, 65- *Res:* High energy particle physics. *Mailing Add:* Dept of Physics Chamberlin Hall Univ of Wis Madison WI 53706

ERWIN, CHESLEY PARA, b Okla, June 5, 20; m 49; c 2. MEDICINE, PATHOLOGY. *Educ:* Univ Okla, BA, 42, MD, 51; Am Bd Path, dipl, 56, cert forensic path. *Prof Exp:* Resident path, Milwaukee County Hosp, 52-55; resident, Milwaukee Hosp, 55-56; from instr to assoc prof, 56-74, PROF PATH, MED COL WIS, 74- *Concurrent Pos:* Chief med examr, Milwaukee County, 74. *Mem:* Int Acad Path; NY Acad Sci; Am Acad Forensic Sci; AMA; Col Am Path. *Res:* Study of animal tumors; oncogenic and oncolytic factors; Rickettsiae; viruses; medical education; drug deaths. *Mailing Add:* 8700 W Wisconsin Ave Milwaukee WI 53226

ERWIN, DAVID B(ISHOP), SR, b Flushing, NY, May 30, 24; m 45; c 5. ELECTRICAL ENGINEERING. *Educ:* Purdue Univ, BS, 48. *Prof Exp:* Engr test set develop, Hawthorne Works, 48-53 & St Paul Shops, 53-55, dept chief electronic switching systs develop, Hawthorne Works, 55-60 & Columbus Works, 60-62, asst supt develop eng, 62-66, mgr electronic switching syst eng, Northern Ill Works, 66-72, mgr regional eng, Cent Region, 72-78, mgr eng servs, 78-80, MGR DIST SERV, WESTERN ELEC CO, 80- *Mem:* Sr mem Inst Elec & Electronics Engrs. *Res:* Manufacturing techniques for production of electronic switching system. *Mailing Add:* 315 North Ave St Charles IL 60174

ERWIN, DONALD C, b Concord, Nebr, Nov 24, 20; m 48; c 2. PHYTOPATHOLOGY. *Educ:* Univ Nebr, BS, 49, MA, 50; Univ Calif, PhD(plant path), 53. *Prof Exp:* Asst plant path, Univ Nebr, 49-50 & Univ Calif, Davis, 50-53; from jr plant pathologist to asst plant pathologist, 53-60, assoc prof plant path, 61-66, chmn dept, 77-80, ASSOC PLANT PATHOLOGIST, UNIV CALIF, RIVERSIDE, 60-, PROF PLANT PATH, 66- *Concurrent Pos:* Guggenheim res fel, 59; mem comt cotton study team, Study Problems Pest Control & Technol Assessment, Nat Acad Sci, 73-75; chmn, Cotton Dis Coun, 73-75. *Mem:* Am Phytopath Soc; Mycol Soc Am; Am Inst Biol Sci. *Res:* Study of etiology and control of diseases of alfalfa and cotton; biology and reproduction of Phytophthora; the control of diseases by systemic fungicides and by increasing resistance with growth regulators. *Mailing Add:* Dept Plant Path Univ Calif Riverside CA 92521

ERWIN, JAMES V, b Horton, Kans, Sept 28, 25; m 44; c 4. CHEMICAL ENGINEERING. *Educ:* Univ Nebr, Lincoln, BSc, 50. *Prof Exp:* Res & develop engr, 50-54, proj leader reflective prod, 54-56, supvr res & develop thermal & reflective prod, 56-59, mgr thermal, reflective & decorative prod, 59-61, tech mgr, reflective & decorative prod, 61-64, tech mgr decorative prod dept, 64-67, tech dir visual prod div, 67-72, tech dir commercial tape, 72-76, PROJ MGR PERSONAL CARE PROD, MINN MINING & MFG CO, 76- *Mem:* Am Inst Chem Engrs. *Res:* Radiation physics; surface chemistry and physics; imaging chemistry; surface coatings technology; environmental technology; optics; adhesion physics. *Mailing Add:* Personal Care Prod Bldg 223 3M Ctr 3M Co St Paul MN 55101

ERWIN, LEWIS, b Ind, Apr 2, 51; m 73; c 3. MANUFACTURING ENGINEERING, POLYMER ENGINEERING. *Educ:* Mass Inst Technol, SB, 72, SM, 74, PhD(mech eng), 77. *Prof Exp:* Asst prof mech eng, Univ Wis-Madison, 76-79; asst prof, 79-80, ASSOC PROF MECH ENG, MASS INST TECHNOL, 80- *Mem:* Am Soc Mech Engrs; Soc Mfg Engrs; Soc Rheology; Soc Plastics Engrs. *Res:* Manufacturing issues for plastic and rubber components; mixing of highly viscous liquids; the effect of processing flows on reinforcing fibers; innovative processes in plastics molding. *Mailing Add:* Mass Inst Technol Bldg 35-008 Mass Ave Cambridge MA 02139

ERWIN, ROBERT BRUCE, b Burlington, Vt, Mar 19, 28; m 56; c 4. GEOLOGY. *Educ:* Univ Vt, BA, 52; Brown Univ, ScM, 55; Cornell Univ, PhD, 59. *Prof Exp:* Geologist, Vt Geol Surv, 55 & Texaco, Inc, 59-61; asst prof geol, St Lawrence Univ, 61-64; geologist, 64-65, dir res, 65-66, asst state geologist, 66-69, DIR & STATE GEOLOGIST, WVA GEOL & ECON SURV, 69-; PROF GEOL, WVA UNIV, 74-; PROF GEOL, MARSHALL UNIV, 78- *Mem:* AAAS; Am Asn Petrol Geol; Soc Econ Paleont & Mineral; Geol Soc Am; Am Inst Prof Geol. *Res:* Paleontology and stratigraphy of lower Paleozoic rocks; Gulf Coast stratigraphy and structure; lower Paleozoic time-stratigraphic relationships; paleontology of West Virginia. *Mailing Add:* WVa Geol & Econ Surv Box 879 Morgantown WV 26505

ERWIN, VIRGIL GENE, b Cahone, Colo, Nov 1, 37; m 59; c 3. PHARMACOLOGY, BIOCHEMISTRY. *Educ:* Univ Colo, BS, 60, MS, 62, PhD(pharmacol & biochem), 65. *Prof Exp:* Fel, Sch Med, Johns Hopkins Univ, 65-67; from asst prof to assoc prof, 67-77, PROF PHARM, UNIV COLO, BOULDER, 77- DEAN SCH PHARM, 74- *Mem:* Am Soc Neurochem; Am Soc Pharmacol & Exp Therapeut. *Res:* Biochemical pharmacology; mechanism of action of therapeutic agents on various cellular processes. *Mailing Add:* Sch of Pharm Univ of Colo Boulder CO 80509

ERZURUMLU, HACIK, b Istanbul, Turkey, Mar 7, 34; m 63. STRUCTURAL & CIVIL ENGINEERING. *Educ:* Tech Univ Istanbul, Prof degree civil eng, 57; Univ Tex, Austin, MS, 62, PhD(civil eng), 70. *Prof Exp:* Instr eng, 62-65, from asst prof to assoc prof struct eng, 65-72, head, Civil & Struct Eng Dept, 76-79, PROF STRUCT ENG, PORTLAND STATE UNIV, 72-, HEAD, DIV ENG, 79- *Concurrent Pos:* Consult & qualified instr, Foundry Equip Mfrs Asn, 66- *Mem:* Am Soc Civil Engrs; Sigma Xi; Am Soc Eng Educ; Nat Soc Prof Engrs. *Res:* Static and fatigue investigations of orthotropic plate bridge decks and of tubular joints; ultimate strength considerations of welded steel tubular members. *Mailing Add:* Div Eng Portland State Univ Portland OR 97207

ESACK, ASHMEED, organic chemistry, computer science, see previous edition

ESAIAS, WAYNE EVOR, b Baltimore, Md, May 8, 45; m 68. BIOLOGICAL OCEANOGRAPHY, PHOTOBIOLOGY. *Educ:* Johns Hopkins Univ, BA, 67; Ore State Univ, MS, 70, PhD(biol oceanog), 73. *Prof Exp:* Res asst oceanog, Ore State Univ, 68-72; res assoc biol, Johns Hopkins Univ, 72-74; ASST RES OCEANOG, MARINE SCI RES CTR, STATE UNIV NY STONY BROOK, 74- *Concurrent Pos:* Adj asst prof, Marine Sci Res Ctr, State Univ NY, Stony Brook, 74- *Mem:* AAAS; Am Soc Limnol & Oceanog. *Res:* Ecology and Photophysiology of coastal phytoplankton; physiological ecology of dinoflagellate bioluminescence. *Mailing Add:* Marine Sci Res Ctr State Univ NY Stony Brook NY 11794

ESAKI, LEO, b Osaka, Japan, Mar 12, 25; m 59; c 2. SOLID STATE PHYSICS. *Educ:* Univ Tokyo, BS, 47, PhD(physics), 59. *Hon Degrees:* Doshisha Sch, Japan; Polytech Univ Madrid. *Prof Exp:* Res mem solid state physics, Kobe Kogyo Corp, 47-56; chief physicist, Sony Corp, 56-60; IBM FEL, THOMAS J WATSON RES CTR, IBM CORP, 60- *Concurrent Pos:* Dir, IBM-Japan, Ltd; foreign assoc, Nat Acad Sci, 76- & Nat Acad Eng, 77- *Honors & Awards:* Nobel Prize in Physics, 73; Nishina Found Mem Award, Japan, 59; Asahi Award, 60; Toyo Rayon Found Prom Sci & Tech Award, 61; Stuart Ballentine Medal, Franklin Inst, Pa, 61; Mem Prize Award, Inst Radio Eng, 61; Japan Acad Award, 65; Order of Cult, Japanese Govt, 74. *Mem:* Japan Acad; Am Phys Soc; fel Inst Elec & Electronics Engrs; Phys Soc Japan; Inst Elec Commun Eng Japan. *Res:* Solid state physics and electronics of semiconductors and semimetals, particularly tunneling in the p-n junction of semiconductors. *Mailing Add:* Thomas J Watson Res Ctr IBM Corp PO Box 218 Yorktown Heights NJ 10598

ESARY, JAMES DANIEL, b Seattle, Wash, Apr 8, 26; m 47; c 2. MATHEMATICAL STATISTICS. *Educ:* Whitman Col, AB, 48; Univ Calif, MA, 51, PhD(statist), 57. *Prof Exp:* Asst statist, Univ Calif, 50-51 & 53-57; math statistician, Boeing Airplane Co, 57-58 & Boeing Sci Res Labs, 59-70; assoc prof, 70-74, PROF OPER RES, NAVAL POSTGRAD SCH, 74- *Concurrent Pos:* Vis lectr, Univ Calif, Berkeley, 67; vis lectr prog statist, 68-71. *Mem:* Am Math Soc; Soc Indust & Appl Math; fel Am Statist Asn; fel Inst Math Statist; Opers Res Soc Am. *Res:* Reliability theory; probability; military applications. *Mailing Add:* Dept of Opers Res Naval Postgrad Sch Monterey CA 93940

ESAU, KATHERINE, b Ekaterinoslav, Russia, Apr 3, 98; nat. BOTANY. *Educ:* Univ Calif, PhD, 31. *Hon Degrees:* LLD, Univ Calif, 66; DSc, Mills Col, 62. *Prof Exp:* Instr bot & jr botanist, Univ Calif, Davis, 31-37, asst prof & asst botanist, 37-43, assoc prof & assoc botanist, 43-49, prof & botanist, 49-63; prof, 63-65, EMER PROF BOT, UNIV CALIF, SANTA BARBARA, 65- *Concurrent Pos:* Guggenheim fel, 40; Prather lectr, Harvard Univ, 60. *Mem:* Nat Acad Sci; AAAS; Swedish Royal Acad Sci; Am Philos Soc; Bot Soc Am (pres, 51). *Res:* Anatomy of healthy and virus diseased seed plants. *Mailing Add:* Dept of Biol Sci Univ of Calif Santa Barbara CA 93106

ESAYIAN, MANUEL, b Cleveland, Ohio, Dec 12, 28; m 54; c 2. ORGANIC CHEMISTRY. *Educ:* Western Reserve Univ, BS, 53, MS, 57, PhD(org chem), 60. *Prof Exp:* Chemist, Veg Res Lab, Sherwin Williams Paint Co, 53; cryogenics engr, H L Johnston Inc, 53-54; chemist electronics, Victoreen Instrument Co, 54-55; chemist adhesives, B F Goodrich Co, 55-56; res chemist, Exp Sta, 60-67, tech rep, Mkt Sect, 67-68, mkt rep, plastics dept, 68-76, acct mgr, 76-78, ACCT MGR NAFION MEMBRANES, PLASTICS PROD & RES DEPT, FLUOROCARBONS DIV, E I DU PONT DE NEMOURS & CO, INC, 78- *Mem:* Am Chem Soc; Sci Res Soc Am. *Res:* Chain initiation and transfer in free radical polymerization; polymer characterization; stabilization, coloring and weatherability of plastics; adhesives, gas liquifaction; preparation of electronic components. *Mailing Add:* 2011 Ferndale Dr Westwood Manor Wilmington DE 19810

ESBER, HENRY JEMIL, b El-Mina, Lebanon, Aug 28, 38; US citizen; m; c 2. IMMUNOLOGY, MICROBIOLOGY. *Educ:* Col William & Mary, BS, 61; Univ NC, MS, 63; WVa Univ, PhD(microbiol), 67. *Prof Exp:* Bacteriologist-in-chg, Portsmouth Gen Hosp, 63-64; fel diag virol, Los Angeles County Health Dept, 67; SR SCIENTIST & IMMUNOLOGIST, MASON RES INST, 67- *Concurrent Pos:* Instr immunol, Clark Univ, 69-; clin lab consult, Hahnemann Hosp, Worcester, 69-; affil, Grad Sch, Anna Maria Col, 75-; clin microbiol & immunol lectr, Worcester City Hosp, 79- *Mem:* AAAS; Am Soc Microbiol; Am Pub Health Asn; Am Asn Immunologists; Am Asn Cancer Res. *Res:* Lung antibodies and autoimmunity; silicosis and environmental health; immunosuppressive activity of inhalents; immune enhancement by bacterial fractions; tumor immunology; inflammation; radioimmunoassays of protein hormones and steroids; competitive protein binding of steroids. *Mailing Add:* Dept of Immunol EG&G/Mason Res Inst 57 Union St Worcester MA 01608

ESCH, GERALD WISLER, b Wichita, Kans, June 22, 36; m 58; c 2. ANIMAL PARASITOLOGY, ECOLOGY. *Educ:* Colo Col, BS, 58; Univ Okla, MS, 61, PhD(zool), 63. *Prof Exp:* NIH trainee, Univ NC, 63-65; from asst prof to assoc prof, 65-75, PROF BIOL, WAKE FOREST UNIV, 75-, CHMN DEPT, 75- *Concurrent Pos:* Vis prof, W K Kellogg Biol Sta, 65-74; WHO res fel, Univ London, 70-71; res assoc, Savannah River Ecol Lab, 74-75. *Mem:* Am Inst Biol Sci; Am Soc Parasitol; Am Micros Soc (secy, 74-80). *Res:* Ecology of animal parasites. *Mailing Add:* Dept Biol Wake Forest Univ Winston-Salem NC 27109

ESCH, HARALD ERICH, b Düsseldorf, Ger, Dec 22, 31; m 55; c 3. ANIMAL BEHAVIOR. *Educ:* Univ Wurzburg, Dr rer nat(zool), 60. *Prof Exp:* Res scientist, Ger Res Asn, 60-62; sci asst radiation res, Univ Munich, 62-64; res scientist, 64-65, from asst prof to assoc prof, 65-69, PROF BIOL, UNIV NOTRE DAME, 69- *Concurrent Pos:* Vis prof bee commun, Univ Sao Paulo, 64; mem comt African Honey Bee, Nat Res Coun. *Mem:* AAAS. *Res:* Communication in bees; electrophysiology; radiation effects on cellular level. *Mailing Add:* Dept of Biol Univ of Notre Dame Notre Dame IN 46556

ESCH, LOUIS JAMES, b Grand Rapids, Mich, Apr 11, 32; m 52; c 6. DATA ANALYSIS SYSTEMS DEVELOPMENT. *Educ:* Aquinas Col, BS, 59; Rensselaer Polytech Inst, MS, 62, PhD(nuclear eng & sci), 71. *Prof Exp:* Physicist, 59-80, SR PHYSICIST, KNOLLS ATOMIC POWER LAB, GEN ELEC CO, 80- *Mem:* Am Nuclear Soc. *Res:* Integral and differential measurements of cross sections of fissile and nonfissile nuclides to neutrons of low and intermediate energies; proton recoil neutron spectroscopy; reactor neutronic noise and vibration analysis; data analysis methods development, computer applications. *Mailing Add:* Knolls Atomic Power Lab River Road Niskayuna NY 12309

ESCH, ROBIN ERNEST, b Md, Feb 25, 30; m 66; c 3. APPLIED MATHEMATICS. *Educ:* Harvard Univ, BA, 51, AM, 53, PhD(appl math), 57. *Prof Exp:* Asst prof appl math, Harvard Univ, 58-62; head appl mech dept, Sperry Rand Res Ctr, Sudbury, 62-66; PROF MATH, BOSTON UNIV, 66-, CHMN DEPT, 68- *Mem:* Math Asn Am; Am Math Soc; Soc Indust & Appl Math. *Res:* Numerical analysis. *Mailing Add:* 371 Plainfield Rd Concord MA 01742

ESCHENBACH, R(ICHARD) C(OREY), b Williamsport, Pa, Apr 9, 27; m 66; c 3. MECHANICAL ENGINEERING. *Educ:* Carnegie Inst Technol, BS, 48, MS, 49; Purdue Univ, PhD(mech eng), 57. *Prof Exp:* Res engr, supvr res & div head, 48-55, MGR ADMIN, LINDE DIV, UNION CARBIDE CORP, 57- *Mem:* AAAS; Am Soc Safety Engrs; Combustion Inst. *Res:* Combustion; catalysis; arc radiation; arc gas heaters; high flux heat transfer. *Mailing Add:* Linde Div Union Carbide Corp Tarrytown Tech Ctr Tarrytown NY 10591

ESCHENBERG, KATHRYN (MARCELLA), b St Louis, Mo, Dec 12, 23. ZOOLOGY, EMBRYOLOGY. *Educ:* Miami Univ, BA, 46; Univ Colo, MA, 50; Univ Wash, PhD(zool), 57. *Prof Exp:* Asst biol & vert physiol, Univ Colo, 48-49, instr, 49-51; asst zool, embryol & cell physiol, Univ Wash, 51-56; Nat Cancer Inst res fel, Princeton Univ, 57; asst prof zool, cell biol & embryol, 58-64, assoc prof biol sci, 64-70, prof biol sci & chmn dept, 70-80, IDA & MARION VAN NATTA PROF BIOL SCI, MT HOLYOKE COL, 80- *Mem:* AAAS; Am Inst Biol Sci; Am Soc Zool; Soc Develop Biol. *Res:* Developmental biology; cytology; oogenesis. *Mailing Add:* Dept of Biol Sci Mt Holyoke Col South Hadley MA 01075

ESCHENFELDER, ANDREW HERBERT, b Newark, NJ, June 13, 25; m 49; c 2. PHYSICS. *Educ:* Rutgers Univ, BS, 49, PhD(physics), 52. *Prof Exp:* Ultrasonic res, Aberdeen Proving Ground, 50; physicist, IBM Res Ctr & IBM Corp, 52-55, mgr magnetics dept, 57-60, dir solid state sci, 60-63 & components, 63-66, consult to dir res, Res Div, 66-67, Dir Lab, 67-73, RES CONSULT, IBM CORP, SAN JOSE RES LAB, 73-, SR PHYSICIST, 56- *Mem:* Am Phys Soc; sr mem Inst Elec & Electronics Eng. *Res:* Magnetism; cryogenics; paramagnetic resonance; solid state. *Mailing Add:* San Jose Res Lab IBM Corp 5600 Cottle Rd San Jose CA 95193

ESCHER, DORIS JANE WOLF, b New York, NY, July 1, 17; m 38; c 2. CARDIOLOGY. *Educ:* Columbia Univ, BA, 38; NY Univ, MD, 42. *Prof Exp:* Resident med, Jewish Hosp of Brooklyn, 43-44; asst physician, Cardiac Clin, Bellevue Hosp, 45-48; asst, Med Div, 48-49, HEAD CARDIAC CATHETERIZATION UNIT, MONTEFIORE HOSP & MED CTR, 50- *Concurrent Pos:* Fel, Col Med, NY Univ, 45-46; fel, Med Div, Montefiore Hosp, 46; clin asst, Mt Sinai Hosp, 46-48; Rosenstock Mem Found fel, 47-48; lectr, Columbia Univ, 57-64; assoc attend radiol, Montefiore Hosp & Med Ctr, 57-, attend physician med, 67-; from asst prof to assoc prof med, 66-75, prof, 75-; consult cardiol, Lawrence Hosp, 73-; lectr bioeng, Polytech Inst New York, 74. *Mem:* Am Heart Asn; Am Fedn Clin Res; Asn Advan Med Instrumentation; fel Am Col Cardiol; Am Soc Artificial Internal Organs. *Res:* Diagnosis and clinical research in cardiovascular disease; artificial cardiac pacing; methods, materials, physiology; artificial organs. *Mailing Add:* 1197 Post Rd Scarsdale NY 10583

ESCHLE, JAMES LEE, b Groom, Tex, Jan 20, 37; m 58; c 2. ENTOMOLOGY. *Educ:* Tex Tech Col, BS, 60; Univ Wis, MS, 62, PhD(entom), 64. *Prof Exp:* Asst entom, Univ Wis, 60-64; ENTOMOLOGIST, ENTOM RES DIV, USDA, 64- *Mem:* Entom Soc Am. *Res:* Biology and control of flies affecting livestock; aquaculture. *Mailing Add:* 6710 Hawaii Kai Dr Honolulu HI 96825

ESCHMAN, DONALD FRAZIER, b Granville, Ohio, Oct 22, 23; m 46; c 4. GEOMORPHOLOGY. *Educ:* Denison Univ, AB, 47; Harvard Univ, MA, 50, PhD(geol), 53. *Prof Exp:* Fel geol, Harvard Univ, 47-51; instr Tufts Col, 51-53, actg head dept, 52-53; from instr to assoc prof geomorphol, 53-64, chmn dept geol & mineral, 61-66, PROF GEOMORPHOL, UNIV MICH, 64- *Concurrent Pos:* Geologist, US Geol Surv, 48-70; chmn fac counsr, Col Lit, Sci & Arts, Univ Mich, 58-59 & Dir, Environ Studies Prog, 71-78. *Mem:* AAAS; Sigma Xi; Geol Soc Am; Nat Asn Geol Teachers. *Res:* Glacial geology; engineering geology; Pleistocene of Michigan; geomorphology and Cenozoic history of Rocky Mountains; geology and land use planning; slope processes. *Mailing Add:* Dept Geol Sci Univ of Mich Ann Arbor MI 48109

ESCHMEYER, PAUL HENRY, b New Bremen, Ohio, June 7, 16. BIOLOGY. *Educ:* Univ Mich, BSF, 38, MS, 39, PhD(zool), 49. *Prof Exp:* Fish mgt agent, State Div Conserv & Nat Resources, Ohio, 39-40; dist fisheries biologist, Inst Fisheries Res, Mich, 41-42, asst fisheries biologist, 47-49; aquatic biologist, State Conserv Comn, Mo, 49-50; fishery res biologist, US Fish & Wildlife Serv, 50-56; asst dir, Inst Fisheries Res, Mich, 56-61; asst dir, Great Lakes Biol Lab, US Bur Commercial Fisheries, 61-64, biol ed, Div Biol Res, 65-70; fishery biologist, Great Lakes Fishery Lab, 70-74, FISHERY ED, US FISH & WILDLIFE SERV, 74- *Mem:* Fel Am Inst Fishery Res Biol; Am Fisheries Soc; Am Soc Zoologists; Am Soc Limnol & Oceanog; Wildlife Soc. *Res:* Fishery biology; natural history of freshwater fishes. *Mailing Add:* US Fish & Wildlife Serv Ed Off Colo State Univ Ft Collins CO 80523

ESCHMEYER, WILLIAM NEIL, b Knoxville, Tenn, Feb 11, 39; m 67; c 1. ICHTHYOLOGY. *Educ:* Univ Mich, BS, 62; Univ Miami, MS, 64, PhD(marine biol), 67. *Prof Exp:* Res asst ichthyol, Inst Marine Sci, Miami, 66-67; asst cur, 67-69, CHMN ICHTHYOL & ASSOC CUR, CALIF ACAD SCI, 69- *Concurrent Pos:* Supv ichthyologist, Vanderbilt Proj, Calif Acad Sci, 67-69; prin investr, NSF Grants. *Mem:* Am Soc Ichthyologists & Herpetologists. *Res:* Systematics, zoogeography and biology of fishes. *Mailing Add:* Calif Acad Sci Dept Ichthyol Golden Gate Park San Francisco CA 94118

ESCHNER, ARTHUR RICHARD, b Buffalo, NY, Sept 29, 25; m 51; c 3. FORESTRY, HYDROLOGY. *Educ:* State Univ NY Col Forestry, Syracuse, BS, 50, PhD(silvicult), 65; Iowa State Col, MS, 52. *Prof Exp:* Res forester cent states forest exp sta, US Forest Serv, 53-54, northeastern forest exp sta, Pa, 54-58 & WVa, 59-61, res forester & proj leader, NY, 61-64; from asst prof to assoc prof, 64-70, PROF FOREST INFLUENCES, STATE UNIV NY COL ENVIRON SCI & FORESTRY, 70- *Mem:* Soc Am Foresters; Soil Sci Soc Am; Am Geophys Union; Am Water Resources Asn. *Res:* Effect of forest conditions on the disposition of precipitation and energy; watershed management, especially soil moisture, evaporation, transpiration and snow accumulation and dissipation. *Mailing Add:* State Univ of NY Col Environ Sci & Forestry Syracuse NY 13210

ESCHNER, EDWARD GEORGE, b NY, June 3, 13; m 36; c 5. RADIOLOGY. *Educ:* Univ Buffalo, MD, 36. *Prof Exp:* Resident orthop, Buffalo Gen Hosp, 37-38 & radiol, 38-40, assoc, 40-42; pvt pract, 46-47; actg head dept, 47-72, CLIN PROF RADIOL, SCH MED, STATE UNIV NY BUFFALO, 54- *Concurrent Pos:* Dir radiol, E J Meyer Mem Hosp, 47-72. *Mem:* Radiol Soc NAm; Am Col Radiol; AMA; Pan-Am Med Asn. *Mailing Add:* 1275 Delaware Ave Buffalo NY 14209

ESCOBAR, JAVIER I, b Medellin, Colombia, July 26, 43; m 67; c 2. PSYCHIATRY, PSYCHOPHARMACOLOGY. *Educ:* Col San Ignacio, Medellin, Colombia, BS, 60; Univ Antioquia, Colombia, MD, 67; Univ Minn, Minneapolis, MSc, 73. *Prof Exp:* Resident psychiat, Complutense Univ, Madrid, Spain, 68-69; resident, Univ Minn Hosps, 69-72, res fel psychiat & genetics, 72-73, asst prof psychiat, Univ Minn, 73-76; assoc prof psychiat & pharmacol, Univ Tenn, Memphis, 76-79; ASSOC PROF PSYCHIAT, UNIV CALIF, LOS ANGELES, 79- *Concurrent Pos:* Proj psychiatrist, NIMH-PRB collab study, St Paul Ramsey Hosp, 73-76; staff psychiatrist, St Paul Ramsey Hosp & Med Ctr, 73-76, Memphis Ment Health Inst, 76-78 & Brentwood Vet Admin Med Ctr, 79-; consult psychopharmacol, Ment Health Ctr, Univ Tenn, 76-78, chmn res comt, Dept Psychiat & dir clin res unit, 78; mem task force psychoactive drugs, State Tenn, 78; dir, Vet Admin Neighborhood Ctr, Los Angeles, 79- *Mem:* Am Psychiat Asn; Am Soc Med Genetics; fel Am Col Clin Pharmacol; Soc Biol Psychiat. *Res:* Clinical psychopharmacology; clinical psychiatry; cytogenetics; biological psychiatry; cross cultural psychiatry. *Mailing Add:* Brentwood Va Med Ctr 116A-15 11301 Wilshire Blvd Los Angeles CA 90073

ESCOBAR, MARIO R, b Lima, Peru, Jan 31, 31; US citizen; m 59; c 4. VIROLOGY, IMMUNOLOGY. *Educ:* Univ Louisville, BA, 54; Georgetown Univ, MS, 60; Ind Univ, PhD(microbiol, biochem), 63; Am Bd Med Microbiol, cert pub health & med virol, 72. *Prof Exp:* Med technologist, Clin Path Lab, St Mary & Elizabeth Hosp, Louisville, Ky, 52-54; supvr, Miller Clin, Morgantown, 54-55; res asst hemat, Walter Reed Army Inst Res, 55-57; serologist & supvr, Path & Serol Clin Labs, Children's Hosp, Washington, DC, 57-61; teaching asst bact & med microbiol, Ind Univ, 61-63; Nat Acad Sci-Nat Res Coun res assoc enteric bact, Commun Dis Ctr, USPHS, Ga, 63-64, dir clin path, Clin Pub Health Labs, Ohio, 64-65; Nat Cancer Inst fel cancer & virol, Univ Miami, 65-67; asst prof clin path, 67-71, assoc prof, 71-78, PROF PATH & SCI DIR, CLIN IMMUNOPATH & VIROL SECT, MED COL VA, VA COMMONWEALTH UNIV, 78- *Concurrent Pos:* Head diag, Res Virus & Immunol Labs, 67-76;consult, Vet Admin Med Ctr, Richmond, 74-; adj prof biol sci, Old Dominion Univ, 78- *Mem:* Reticuloendothelial Soc; Am Soc Microbiol; Am Soc Clin Path; Tissue Cult Asn; Am Asn Path & Bact. *Res:* Preservation of human erythrocytes; serology of histoplasma capsulatum; serology of Serratia; bacteriophages and immunogenetics of Salmonella; laboratory diagnosis of viral and immune diseases; virus-host interactions; oncogenic viruses; role of mononuclear cells in cancer immunity; immunopathology of viral hepatitis. *Mailing Add:* Dept Path Va Commonwealth Univ Richmond VA 23298

ESCUE, RICHARD BYRD, JR, b Denton, Tex, Apr 24, 19; m 45; c 3. CHEMISTRY. *Educ:* North Tex State Univ, BA, 39, MA, 40; Calif Inst Technol, PhD(chem, physics), 44. *Prof Exp:* Lab asst chem, North Tex State Univ, 40; Physicist, Neches Butane Prod Co, Tex, 43-45; asst prof chem, 45-47, assoc prof chem & physics, 47-53, PROF CHEM, NTEX STATE UNIV, 53- *Concurrent Pos:* Res grants-in-aid, Res Corp, NY, 45-48, Robert A Welch Found, Tex, 55-64, Am Acad Arts & Sci, 56 & NIH, 57-58; fel Oak Ridge Inst Nuclear Studies, 51, counsr, 58- *Mem:* AAAS; Am Chem Soc. *Res:* Molten Salts; radiochemistry; phase systems; microscopy. *Mailing Add:* Dept of Chem North Tex State Univ Denton TX 76203

ESDERS, THEODORE WALTER, b Buffalo, NY, May 6, 45; m 67; c 3. BIOCHEMISTRY. *Educ:* Gannon Col, BA, 67; Fla State Univ, PhD(chem), 71. *Prof Exp:* NIH fel fac chem, Harvard Univ, 71-73; sr res chemist, 73-80, RES ASSOC, RES LABS, EASTMAN KODAK CO, 80- *Mem:* Am Soc Microbiol. *Res:* Lipid metabolism and the enzymes involved, as well as processes by which lipid metabolism is controlled; isolation and characterization of microbiol enzymes. *Mailing Add:* Res Labs Eastman Kodak Co Rochester NY 14650

ESEN, ASIM, b Fethiye, Turkey, Nov 10, 38; m 66; c 2. BIOCHEMISTRY, AGRONOMY. *Educ:* Univ Ankara, Turkey, Dipl, 65; Univ Calif, Riverside, MS, 68, PhD(plant genetics), 71. *Prof Exp:* Fel plant genetics, Univ Calif, Riverside, 72-74, biochem, 74-75; asst prof, 75-81, ASSOC PROF BOT, VA POLYTECH INST & STATE UNIV, 81- *Mem:* Am Genetic Asn; AAAS; Am Asn Cereal Chemists; Am Chem Soc. *Res:* Molecular genetics of crop plants; structure, variation and expression of storage protein genes in cereals; purification and characterization of maize prolamins; improvement of protein quality and quantity in cereals. *Mailing Add:* Dept Biol Va Polytech Inst & State Univ Blacksburg VA 24061

ESENTHER, GLENN R, b Chicago, Ill, June 23, 26; m 55; c 10. FOREST ENTOMOLOGY. *Educ:* St Ambrose Col, BS, 51; Marquette Univ, MS, 53; Univ Wis, PhD(entom), 61. *Prof Exp:* Instr zool, Marquette Univ, 53-54; instr biol, Xavier Univ, Ohio, 54-55; ENTOMOLOGIST, FOREST PROD LAB, US FOREST SERV, 60- *Mem:* Entom Soc Am; Int Res Group Wood Preservation; Forest Prod Res Soc; AAAS; Int Union Study Social Insects. *Res:* Wood products insects, particularly ecology and control of termites with baits. *Mailing Add:* US Forest Prod Lab PO Box 5130 Madison WI 53705

ESFAHANI, MOJTABA, b Broujerd, Iran, May 7, 39; m 66; c 2. BIOCHEMISTRY. *Educ:* Am Univ Beirut, BS, 63, MS, 65; Duke Univ, PhD(biochem), 70. *Prof Exp:* Res assoc biochem, Duke Univ, 70-71; from instr to asst prof biochem, Baylor Col Med, 71-73; asst biochemist, M D Anderson Hosp & Tumor Res Inst, 73-75; assoc prof biol sci, Drexel Univ, 75-78; ASSOC PROF BIOL CHEM, HAHNEMANN MED COL, 78- *Res:* Membrane structure and function; lipid metabolism. *Mailing Add:* Dept of Biol Chem Hahnemann Med Col Philadelphia PA 19102

ESHBACH, JOHN ROBERT, b Bethlehem, Pa, Oct 7, 22; m 44; c 4. SOLID STATE PHYSICS. *Educ:* Northwestern Univ, BS, 44, BS, 46, MS, 47; Mass Inst Technol, PhD(physics), 51. *Prof Exp:* Res assoc photoconductive cells, Northwestern Univ, 46-47; res asst microwave spectros, Mass Inst Technol, 48-50; mgr light prod studies, 62-68, mgr microwave br, 68-74, RES ASSOC, GEN ELEC RES & DEVELOP CTR, 51- *Mem:* Fel Am Phys Soc; Inst Elec & Electronics Eng. *Res:* Microwave spectroscopy; magnetism; ferrite devices; luminescence; microwave electronics. *Mailing Add:* 2755 Rosendale Rd Schenectady NY 12309

ESHBAUGH, WILLIAM HARDY, b Glen Ridge, NJ, May 1, 36; m 58; c 4. PLANT TAXONOMY, ETHNOBOTANY. *Educ:* Cornell Univ, AB, 59; Ind Univ, MA, 61, PhD(bot), 64. *Prof Exp:* Lectr bot, Ind Univ, 62; asst prof bot & cur herbarium, Southern Ill Univ, 65-67; from asst prof to assoc prof, 67-77, PROF BOT, MIAMI UNIV, 77- *Mem:* Am Soc Plant Taxon; Bot Soc Am; Am Inst Biol Sci; Int Asn Plant Taxon; Soc Econ Bot (secy, 78-81, vpres, 82-83). *Res:* Biosystematic and phytogeographic studies in the Solanaceae, especially the genus Capsicum and allied genera; flora of the Bahamas. *Mailing Add:* Dept Bot Miami Univ Oxford OH 45056

ESHENOUR, TERRY RAY, b Harrisburg, Pa, Mar 12, 44; m 65; c 2. FOOD SCIENCE. *Educ:* Pa State Univ, BS, 66. *Prof Exp:* Supvr res, Welch Foods Inc, 66-70; mgr prod develop, Foods Div, 70-78, DIR PROD DEVELOP, FOODS DIV INT, COCA-COLA CO, 78- *Mem:* Inst Food Technologists; Am Chem Soc. *Res:* Aseptic processing and packaging of food products; development of new nutritious foods using by-products. *Mailing Add:* PO Box 2079 Houston TX 77001

ESHLEMAN, RONALD L, b Shellsville, Pa, Aug 24, 33; m 59. MECHANICAL & AEROSPACE ENGINEERING. *Educ:* Lafayette Col, BSME, 59; Lehigh Univ, MS, 61; Ill Inst Technol, PhD(mech & aerospace eng), 67. *Prof Exp:* Teaching asst mech eng, Lehigh Univ, 59-61; instr, Ill Inst Technol, 61-64; from asst res engr to res engr, Vibration Inst, 64-69, sr res engr, 69-73, sci adv, 73-75, DIR, IIT RES INST, 75- *Concurrent Pos:* Consult, Am Nat Standards Inst, 68-, chmn comt S2; tech ed, Shock & Vibration Digest, 69- *Mem:* Am Soc Mech Engrs; Am Sci Affiliation; Inst Environ Sci; Soc Automotive Engrs. *Res:* Engineering analysis; rotor dynamics; shock and vibration isolation; dynamics of machines; digital simulation of machines; tape dynamics; vehicle dynamics; torsional vibrations. *Mailing Add:* 333 Ridge Ave Clarendon Hills IL 60514

ESHLEMAN, VON R(USSEL), b Darke Co, Ohio, Sept 17, 24; m 47; c 4. ELECTRICAL ENGINEERING. *Educ:* George Washington Univ, BEE, 49; Stanford Univ, MS, 50, PhD(elec eng), 52. *Prof Exp:* Res assoc, radio propagation lab, 52-56, from instr to assoc prof elec eng, 56-61, PROF ELEC ENG & CO-DIR CTR RADAR ASTRON, STANFORD UNIV, 61-, DIR, RADIOSCI LAB, 74- *Concurrent Pos:* Consult, Nat Acad Sci, Nat Bur Standards, SRI Int & Jet Propulsion Lab; mem, Int Astronaut Cong, Int Astron Union & Int Sci Radio Union; dir, Watkins-Johnson Co; radio sci team leader, Voyager missions to Jupiter & Saturn, 76-80; radio sci team mem, Galileo Mission to Jupiter 79-80. *Mem:* Fel AAAS; fel Inst Elec & Electronics Engrs; Am Geophys Union; fel Royal Astron Soc; Nat Acad Eng. *Res:* Radar astronomy; planetary exploration; ionospheric and plasma physics; radio wave propagation; astronautics. *Mailing Add:* Ctr for Radar Astron Stanford Univ Stanford CA 94305

ESKAFI, FRED M, entomology, see previous edition

ESKELSON, CLEAMOND D, b American Fork, Utah, Sept 27, 27; m 46; c 1. BIOCHEMISTRY, ORGANIC CHEMISTRY. *Educ:* Univ Utah, BS, 50; Univ Louisville, MS, 57; Univ Nebr, Omaha, PhD(biochem), 67. *Prof Exp:* Res technician, Dept Internal Med, Univ Utah, 50-51; analyst, Geneva Steel Co, 51-52; biochemist, Army Med Res Lab, Ft Knox, Ky, 52-55; clin chemist, Vet Admin Hosp, Omaha, Nebr, 57-59, biochemist, Vet Admin Radioisotope Lab, 59-67; chemist, Vet Admin Hosp, Tucson, 67-76, RES ASSOC & ADJ ASSOC PROF BIOCHEM, SCH PHARM, UNIV ARIZ, 76- *Concurrent Pos:* Consult, Creighton Univ, 58-59; instr, Col Med, Univ Nebr, 67-68; Licensed Beverage Indust res grant, 68-69; res assoc, Sch Pharm, Univ Ariz, 72-76. *Mem:* AAAS; NY Acad Sci; Am Chem Soc; Soc Nuclear Med; Asn Clin Med. *Res:* Thyroid physiology; effects of x-irradiation on biological systems; mechanisms for controlling cholesterolgenesis; vitaminology; development of radiometric procedures for diagnosing cancer; biochemistry of alcoholism. *Mailing Add:* 7402 Calle Toluca Tucson AZ 85710

ESKELUND, KENNETH H, b Waterville, Maine, Feb 13, 24; m 50; c 3. VETERINARY MEDICINE. *Educ:* Mich State Univ, DVM, 51. *Prof Exp:* Diagnostician, SJersey Diag Lab, 51-52; vet-in-chg poultry, State of Ind, 52-53; vet mgr, Ft Halifax Poultry Co, 53-57; pres & dir, Maine Biol Labs, Inc, 57-66, gen mgr, Maine Biol Lab Div, Morton-Norwich Prod Inc, 66-73; PRES, NORTHEAST LAB SERV, 71-; PRES & MGR, MAINE BIOL LABS, INC, 75- *Concurrent Pos:* Pres, Maine Poultry Serv, 58-72 & Maine Poultry Consults, 59- *Mem:* Am Vet Med Asn; Am Asn Avian Path; Poultry Sci Asn; US Animal Health Asn. *Res:* Development of inactivated avian vaccines. *Mailing Add:* 175 Western Ave Waterville ME 04901

ESKEW, CLETIS THEODORE, b Cloud Chief, Okla, July 10, 04; m 36; c 1. BIOLOGY. *Educ:* Southwestern State Col, Okla, BS, 31; Univ Okla, MS, 37; N Tex State Univ, EdD, 60. *Prof Exp:* Prof biol, Mangum Jr Col, 37-39 & Southwest State Col, Okla, 39-42; prof biol, 42-69, dean admis, 48-56, dean instr, 56-59, dean lib arts, 59-61, dir div sci & math, 61-68, assoc dean instr, 61-69, dean div grad studies, 68-69, EMER PROF BIOL, MIDWESTERN STATE UNIV, 75- *Res:* Taxonomy and ecology; plant physiology; vegetation of Oklahoma and Texas. *Mailing Add:* 2718 Chase Dr Wichita Falls TX 76308

ESKEW, DAVID LEWIS, b Lebanon, Tenn, Nov 18, 50. PLANT PHYSIOLOGY, AGRONOMY. *Educ:* Univ Tenn, BS, 71; Univ Wis, MS, 73, PhD(agron, bot), 75. *Prof Exp:* Res biologist, Univ Calif, Riverside, 75-77; assoc, Boyce Thompson Inst, 77-80, ASSOC, US PLANT, SOIL & NUTRIT LAB, CORNELL UNIV, 80- *Mem:* Am Soc Plant Physiologists; Crop Sci Soc Am; Am Soc Agron. *Res:* Biochemistry and physiology of nitrogen fixation; nitrogen fixing organisms living in association with C-4 plants and rice. *Mailing Add:* 213 Willow Ave Ithaca NY 14850

ESKIN, NEASON AKIVA MICHAEL, b Birmingham, Eng, May 4, 41; m 70. FOOD CHEMISTRY, BIOCHEMISTRY. *Educ:* Univ Birmingham, BSc, 63, PhD(physiol chem), 66. *Prof Exp:* Lectr biochem, Borough Polytech, Eng, 66-68; PROF FOOD CHEM, UNIV MAN, 68-, HEAD, DEPT FOODS & NUTRIT, 80- *Mem:* Can Inst Food Sci & Technol; Brit Inst Food Sci & Technol; Inst Food Technologists; NY Acad Sci; Am Oil Chem Soc. *Res:* Food enzymes, rancidity in foods; cereal chemistry; phytate and mineral availability; vegetable oil quality; titanium chloride properties and applications to food analysis. *Mailing Add:* Dept of Foods & Nutrit Univ of Man Fac of Home Econ Winnipeg MB R3B 2E9 Can

ESKINAZI, SALAMON, b Izmir, Turkey, Nov 25, 22; nat US; m 51; c 2. MECHANICS. *Educ:* Robert Col, Turkey, BS, 46; Univ Wyo, MS, 48; Johns Hopkins Univ, DEng, 54. *Prof Exp:* Res assoc, Johns Hopkins Univ, 50-53, instr mech eng, 53-55; assoc prof, 55-61, PROF MECH ENG, SYRACUSE UNIV, 61-, CHMN DEPT MECH & AEROSPACE ENG, 66- *Concurrent Pos:* Consult, Fairchild Aircraft & Carrier Corp, 59-; Howard, Needles, Tammer & Bergendoff, 67, Tenn Technol Univ, 68-69 & Gen Elec Corp, 70; Fulbright scholar, France & assoc prof, Univ Poitiers, 63-64; lectr, Cambridge Univ & Oxford Univ, 63-64. *Mem:* Am Soc Mech Engrs; Am Soc Eng Educ; Am Inst Aeronaut & Astronaut. *Res:* Fluid and statistical mechanics; heat transfer; thermodynamics; general mechanics of continuum; magnetohydrodynamics; fluid mechanics and thermodynamics of the environment. *Mailing Add:* Dept of Mech & Aerospace Eng Syracuse Univ Syracuse NY 13210

ESKINS, KENNETH, b Beckley, WVa. PHOTOSYNTHESIS, GENETICS. *Educ:* Wheaton Col, BS, 62; Southern Ill Univ, PhD(org chem), 66. *Prof Exp:* Fel, Roswell Park Cancer Res Inst, 66-67; RES CHEM, NORTHERN REGIONAL RES CTR, AGR RES SERV, USDA, 67- *Mem:* Am Soc Plant Physiol. *Res:* Analysis of chloroplast pigments; pigment protein complexes and control of chloroplast development by light, aging and genetic factors; light control of greening and photomorphogenesis. *Mailing Add:* Northern Regional Res Ctr 1815 N University St Peoria IL 61604

ESKRIDGE, CHARLES D(EWITT), III, b Walterboro, SC, Aug 21, 37; m 57; c 3. ENGINEERING MECHANICS. *Educ:* Va Polytech Inst, BS, 59, MS, 63, PhD(eng mech), 64. *Prof Exp:* Instr eng mech, Va Polytech Inst, 59-64; RES ENGR DYNAMICS, DOUGLAS AIRCRAFT CO, INC, 64- *Res:* Spinning bodies with variable mass; solid mechanics of plates. *Mailing Add:* 1004 Lepley Rd Charleston SC 29406

ESLICK, ROBERT FREEMAN, b Walla Walla, Wash, Dec 24, 16; m 39; c 1. PLANT BREEDING, AGRONOMY. *Educ:* Wash State Univ, BS, 39; Univ Wyo, MS, 42. *Prof Exp:* Instr agron & asst agronomist, Univ Wyo, 39-42; asst prof & asst agronomist, Colo State Univ, 42-43 & 46; assoc prof & assoc agronomist, 46-58, PROF AGRON, MONT STATE UNIV, 58- *Mem:* Fel AAAS; fel Am Soc Agron. *Res:* Cultural and plant breeding studies with forage grasses and legumes, oil crops, oats and barley; barley genetics. *Mailing Add:* Dept of Plant & Soil Sci Mont State Univ Bozeman MT 59717

ESLYN, WALLACE EUGENE, b Lawrenceville, Ill, Nov 13, 24; m 47; c 5. FOREST PATHOLOGY. *Educ:* Univ Mont, BS, 50, MS, 53; Iowa State Col, PhD(plant path), 56. *Prof Exp:* Plant pathologist, Forest Prod Lab, US Forest Serv, 57 & Forest Insect & Dis Lab, NMex, 57-60, plant pathologist, Forest Prod Lab, 60-69, SUPV RES PLANT PATHOLOGIST, BIODEGRADATION OF WOOD RES WORK UNIT, FOREST PROD LAB, US FOREST SERV, 69- *Mem:* Soc Am Foresters; Am Phytopath Soc; Mycol Soc Am; Int Union Forestry Res Orgn; Int Res Group Wood Preservation. *Res:* Forest products pathology and mycology. *Mailing Add:* Proc & Protection Forest Prod Lab US Forest Serv PO Box 5130 Madison WI 53705

ESMAIL, MOHAMED NABIL, b Port-Said, Egypt, Jan 22, 42; m 64; c 2. UNIT OPERATIONS, MODELLING. *Educ:* Moscow State Univ, BSc & MSc, 64, PhD(appl math), 72. *Prof Exp:* Lectr mech, Ein-Shams Univ, Egypt, 65-72; asst prof, 72-73; res assoc chem eng, Univ Toronto, Can, 73-76; asst prof, 77-79, ASSOC PROF CHEM ENG, UNIV SASK, 79- *Mem:* Can Soc Chem Eng. *Res:* Fluid mechanics and engineering applications, flows of thin liquid films, stability and analysis; liquid coating process; extrudate swell of newtoniann and nonnewtonian liquids; numerical methods in fluid mechanics and modelling. *Mailing Add:* Dept Chem & Chem Eng Univ Sask Saskatoon SK S7N 0W0 Can

ESMAY, DONALD LEVERN, b Murdo, SDak, Nov 1, 17; m 45; c 6. POLYMER CHEMISTRY. *Educ:* Dakota Wesleyan Univ, BA, 46; Iowa State Univ, PhD(chem), 51. *Prof Exp:* Res chemist, Standard Oil Co, Ind, 52-55; tech dir org prod div, Lithium Corp Am, 56-60; SR RES SPECIALIST, MINN MINING & MFG CO, 61- *Mem:* Am Chem Soc. *Res:* Organometallic and fluorine compounds; heterocycles; hydrocarbon conversions; petroleum, lithium, propellant and fluorine chemistry; polymers; organic syntheses; adhesives; polyurethanes; foams. *Mailing Add:* 1237 98th Lane NW Coon Rapids MN 55433

ESMAY, MERLE L(INDEN), b Greene Co, Iowa, Dec 27, 20; m 42; c 2. AGRICULTURAL ENGINEERING. *Educ:* SDak State Univ, BSAE, 42; Iowa State Univ, MSAE, 47, PhD(agr eng & struct eng), 51. *Prof Exp:* Exten agr engr, SDak State Univ, 46; asst prof teaching & res, Iowa State Univ, 47-51; prof, Univ Mo, 51-55; chief party, univ contract adv team Taiwan, 62-

64, PROF AGR ENG, MICH STATE UNIV, 55- *Concurrent Pos:* Partic in various int symposia & meetings, 62-; agr eng consult in various develop countries, 62- *Honors & Awards:* Metal Bldg Mfrs Asn Award, Am Soc Agr Engrs, 66. *Mem:* Fel Am Soc Agr Engrs; Am Soc Eng Educ. *Res:* Environmental requirements of livestock shelters; rice drying, storage and handling; mechanization in developing countries. *Mailing Add:* Dept of Agr Eng Mich State Univ East Lansing MI 48824

ESMEN, NURTAN A, b Ankara, Turkey, Jan 1, 40; m 69; c 1. INDUSTRIAL HEALTH ENGINEERING, AEROSOL PHYSICS. *Educ:* Northeastern Univ, BS, 65; Univ Pittsburgh, MS, 66, PhD(chem eng), 70. *Prof Exp:* Sr researcher aerosol physics, Univ Pittsburgh, 65-70; asst prof environ eng, Univ Del, 70-74; prin technol dir, Owens-Corning Fiberglas Co, 74-75; assoc prof, 75-80, PROF INDUST HYG, GRAD SCH PUB HEALTH, UNIV PITTSBURGH, 80- *Concurrent Pos:* Mem study sect, Nat Inst Occupational Safety & Health, HEW, 80- *Mem:* Am Inst Chem Engrs; Am Indust Hyg Asn; Am Chem Soc; NY Acad Sci; Air Pollution Control Asn. *Res:* Application of aerosol physics and chemical engineering to the investigation and solution of industrial health problems; development of risk assesment techniques and methodology for occupational exposures to potentially hazardous agents. *Mailing Add:* Univ Pittsburgh 130 Desoto St Pittsburgh PA 15261

ESMON, CHARLES THOMAS, b Centralia, Ill, Apr 3, 47; m 75. BIOCHEMISTRY. *Educ:* Univ Ill, BA, 69; Univ Wash, PhD(biochem), 73. *Prof Exp:* ADJ ASST PROF BIOCHEM & MOLECULAR BIOL, HEALTH SCI CTR, UNIV OKLA, 76-, ASSOC PROF PATH, 80- *Concurrent Pos:* Prin investr various grants, 76-82; established investr, Am Heart Asn, 80; mem, Int Adv Comt, Cong Thrombosis, Haemostasis. *Honors & Awards:* John L Dickson Mem Award, Am Heart Asn, 78 & 79. *Mem:* Am Soc Biol Chemists. *Res:* Control of blood coagulation and fibrinolysis; structure and function of enzymes; cell surface receptors. *Mailing Add:* Health Sci Ctr BMSB-455 Univ Okla PO Box 26901 Oklahoma City OK 73190

ESOGBUE, AUGUSTINE O, b Kaduna, Nigeria, Dec 25, 40. SYSTEMS & ELECTRICAL ENGINEERING. *Educ:* Univ Calif, Los Angeles, BS, 64; Columbia Univ, MS, 65; Univ Southern Calif, PhD(eng & opers res), 68. *Prof Exp:* Res assoc eng & med, Univ Southern Calif, 65-68; asst prof opers res, Case Western Reserve Univ, 68-72; assoc prof eng, 72-77, PROF ENG, GA INST TECHNOL, 77- *Concurrent Pos:* Instr sci, Lagos Ctr Higher Studies, Lagos, Nigeria, 60-61; instr lang, Peace Corps Prog, Univ Calif, Los Angeles, 61-65, develop engr water res, Water Resources Ctr, 66-67; reader & instr, Dept Math, Columbia Univ, 65, assoc fac mem, 70-; consult, Environ Dynamics, Calif, 68-70; prin & consult, Univ Assocs, Inc, Ohio, 69-72; prof in residence, Sch Eng, Howard Univ, 72; vpres, Atlantic Systs Inc, Ga, 72-80, pres, 80-; mem numerous panels, Nat Acad Sci-Nat Res Coun, 73-; adv ed, Int J Fuzzy Sets & Systs & US rep, Int Ctr Cybernetics & Systs, Romania, 76-; assoc ed, J Math Anal & Appln & assoc ed at large, Opers Res Soc Am Health News, 77-; adj prof community med, Morehouse Sch Med, Morehouse Col, 79- *Mem:* Opers Res Soc Am; Sigma Xi; fel AAAS. *Res:* Dynamic programming and optimal control theory; fuzzy sets and decision making in fuzzy environments; large scale systems analysis; operations research; theory and applications to health care, water resources and pollution; urban systems and transportation. *Mailing Add:* Sch of Indust & Systs Eng Ga Inst of Technol Atlanta GA 30332

ESPANA, CARLOS, b Mexico City, Mex, Mar 1, 19; m 49. INFECTIOUS DISEASES. *Educ:* Nat Polytech Inst, Mex, MS, 43; Univ Calif, Berkeley, PhD, 49. *Prof Exp:* Head sect virol, E R Squibb & Sons, 49-51, res assoc microbiol, Squibb Inst Med Res, 51-52, head dept chemother, 52-54; res assoc vet med, Univ Pa, 54-57, res asst prof, 57-63; specialist, Nat Ctr Primate Biol, Univ Calif, Davis, 64-68, res assoc virol, 68-78; RETIRED. *Concurrent Pos:* Prin investr grants, E R Squibb & Sons of Mex Div, Mathieson Corp, 54-60 & Nat Inst Allergy & Infectious Dis, 60-63; rep, Nat Anaplasmosis Conf, 57 & 62; mem ad hoc comt of consult on simian viruses, Diag Virol Sect, Viral Carcinogenesis Br, Nat Cancer Inst, 65-67; partic, Workshops on Virus Dis of Non-Human Primates, 68 & 71 & Int Conf Exp Med & Surg in Primates, 69; mem working team, Prog Compar Virol & Simian Viruses, WHO, Food & Agr Orgn UN, 73- *Mem:* Am Soc Microbiol; fel NY Acad Sci; fel Am Acad Microbiol. *Res:* Diagnosis, pathogenesis, prevention and control of viral diseases of non-human primates; studies on the nature of slow virus diseases also known as spongiform encephalopathies or transmissible virus dementias; Kuru, Creutzfeldt-Jakob disease. *Mailing Add:* 809 Cherry Lane Davis CA 95616

ESPELIE, KARL EDWARD, b New London, Conn, Apr 20, 46; m 74; c 2. LIPID CHEMISTRY, SEED PHYSIOLOGY. *Educ:* Augustana Col, AB, 67; Univ Wis-Madison, MSc, 70, PhD(biochem), 72. *Prof Exp:* Fel biol, Calif Inst Technol, 72-74, protein chem, Imp Cancer Res Fund, London, 74-76; RES SCIENTIST PLANT BIOCHEM, INST BIOL CHEM, WASH STATE UNIV, 76- *Mem:* Am Soc Plant Physiologists. *Res:* Chemistry and biosynthesis of the plant polymers cutin and saberin which serve as protective barriers on the aerial and subterranean surfaces of all plants. *Mailing Add:* Inst Biol Chem Wash State Univ Pullman WA 99164

ESPELIE, (MARY) SOLVEIG, b New London, Conn, Dec 24, 40. MATHEMATICAL FUNCTIONAL ANALYSIS, TOPOLOGY. *Educ:* Luther Col, BA, 62; Univ Md, College Park, MA, 64, PhD(Banach algebras), 68. *Prof Exp:* Asst, Univ Md, College Park, 62-68; asst prof math, Univ Cincinnati, 68-69; asst prof, 69-74, ASSOC PROF MATH, HOWARD UNIV, 74- *Concurrent Pos:* Fel, Univ Edinburgh, Scotland, 75-76. *Mem:* Am Math Soc; Math Asn Am; Asn Women Math; Nat Asn Mathematicians; Nat Inst Sci. *Res:* positive multiplicative and extreme operators between Banach-algebras, their integral representations and geometric properties; study of topological properties which generalize continuity, closure, compactness. *Mailing Add:* Dept of Math Howard Univ Washington DC 20059

ESPENSHADE, EDWARD BOWMAN, JR, b Chicago, Ill, Oct 23, 10; m 39; c 2. PHYSICAL GEOGRAPHY, CARTOGRAPHY. *Educ:* Univ Chicago, BS, 30, MS, 32, PhD(geog), 44. *Prof Exp:* Instr geog, Univ Chicago, 37-44; chmn dept, 57-77, EMER PROF, NORTHWESTERN UNIV, 77- *Concurrent Pos:* Cartog consult, Rand McNally & Co, 45-, adv geog ed, 54-; chmn, Earth Sci Div, Nat Acad Sci-Nat Res Coun, 60-62; mem, Comn Higher Educ, NCent Asn, 70-75, mem exec bd, 72-77. *Mem:* Asn Am Geog (pres, 64-65); Am Cong Surv & Mapping; Am Geog Soc. *Res:* Design and development of thematic maps. *Mailing Add:* Dept of Geog Northwestern Univ Evanston IL 60201

ESPENSON, JAMES HENRY, b Los Angeles, Calif, Apr 1, 37; m 60; c 1. INORGANIC CHEMISTRY, ORGANOMETALLIC CHEMISTRY. *Educ:* Calif Inst Technol, BS, 58; Univ Wis, PhD(inorg chem), 62. *Prof Exp:* Res assoc, Stanford Univ, 62-63; from instr to assoc prof, 63-71, PROF CHEM, IOWA STATE UNIV, 71- *Concurrent Pos:* Fel, Alfred P Sloan Found, 68-70. *Mem:* Fel AAAS; Am Chem Soc; The Chem Soc. *Res:* Inorganic and organometallic reaction mechanisms; kinetics of reactions of metal complexes; formation and cleavage of metal-carbon bonds; electron transfer and substitution reactions; homogeneous catalysis; free radical reactions. *Mailing Add:* Dept of Chem Iowa State Univ Ames IA 50011

ESPEY, LAWRENCE LEE, b Mercedes, Tex, Sept 5, 35; m 78; c 4. REPRODUCTIVE PHYSIOLOGY, ENDOCRINOLOGY. *Educ:* Univ Tex, BA, 58, MA, 61; Fla State Univ, PhD(physiol), 64. *Prof Exp:* Res Technologist physiol, Dent Br, Univ Tex, 59-60; NIH fel & res assoc Univ Mich, 64-66; from asst prof to assoc prof, 66-72, prof physiol & chmn, Dept Environ Studies, 73-80, Cowles prof life sci, 79-82, PROF BIOL, TRINITY UNIV, 80- *Concurrent Pos:* Grants, Nat Inst Child Health & Human Develop, 67-83; Morrison Trust grant, 67-68; adj prof, Dept Obstet & Gynec, Univ Tex Health Sci Ctr, San Antonio, 75-; scholar pop affairs, US Dept State, 76; Fulbright-Hays sr res award, Romania, 77-79. *Mem:* AAAS; Am Physiol Soc; Endocrine Soc; Soc Study Reproduction; World Pop Soc. *Res:* Physical and chemical mechanisms of mammalian ovulation. *Mailing Add:* Dept Biol Trinity Univ San Antonio TX 78284

ESPINO, RAMON LUIS, b Santiago, Cuba, Aug 18, 41; US citizen. CHEMICAL ENGINEERING. *Educ:* La State Univ, BS, 64; Mass Inst Technol, MS, 66, DSc(chem eng), 68. *Prof Exp:* Asst dir chem eng, Mass Inst Technol, 66-67; mgr process develop, Chem Systs Inc, Hackensack, NJ, 68-71, dir res & develop, 71-73; group head eng physics, 73-76, dir eng & appl math lab, 76-81, MGR LONG RANGE RES DIV, EXXON RES & ENG CO, 81- *Concurrent Pos:* Adv bd appl math, Univ Del; adv bd chem engr, State Univ NY-Buffalo; bd dir, Univ Space Res Asn. *Mem:* Am Chem Soc; Am Inst Chem Engrs; NY Acad Sci; Am Petrol Inst. *Res:* Chemical kinetics and reaction engineering; heterogeneous catalysis; cryogenic engineering; research managment. *Mailing Add:* 2200 Willowick Rd 5J Houston TX 77027

ESPINOSA, JAMES MANUEL, b Mexico City, Mex, Nov, 7, 42; US citizen; m 66; c 2. THEORETICAL PARTICLE PHYSICS. *Educ:* Calif Inst Technol, BS, 65; Univ Calif, Los Angeles, MS, 70, PhD(physics), 76. *Prof Exp:* Asst prof physics, Loyola Marymount Univ, 72-78; ASST PROF PHYSICS, TEX WOMAN'S UNIV, 78- *Mem:* Am Phys Soc; Am Asn Physics Teachers; His Sci Soc. *Res:* General relativity; astrophysics; mathematics and history of science. *Mailing Add:* Dept of Math & Physics Tex Woman's Univ Denton TX 76204

ESPOSITO, F PAUL, b Newark, NJ, Aug 24, 44. THEORETICAL PHYSICS. *Educ:* Cornell Univ, AB, 66; Univ Chicago, PhD(physics), 71. *Prof Exp:* Asst prof, 71-77, ASSOC PROF PHYSICS & MATH, UNIV CINCINNATI, 77- *Mem:* Am Phys Asn; Am Math Asn; Am Astron Soc; Int Astron Union; Sigma Xi. *Res:* General relativity; differential geometry. *Mailing Add:* Dept of Physics Univ of Cincinnati Cincinnati OH 45221

ESPOSITO, JOHN NICHOLAS, b Youngstown, Ohio, July 23, 38; m 63; c 3. INORGANIC CHEMISTRY. *Educ:* Youngstown Univ, BS, 60; Case Inst Technol, PhD(chem), 66. *Prof Exp:* Sr res scientist, 66-73, mgr corrosion & solution chem, Res Lab, 74-76, mgr chem technol, Nuclear Steam Generation Div, 76-81, MGR STEAM GENERATOR OPERS, NUCLEAR TECHNOL DIV, WESTINGHOUSE ELEC CORP, 81- *Mem:* Nat Asn Corrosion Engrs; Am Chem Soc. *Res:* Combustion of metals; inorganic chemistry of hexacoordinated silicon and germanium; surface chemistry; high temperature chemistry; corrosion; water chemistry; electrodeposition. *Mailing Add:* Westinghouse Nuclear Technol Div PO Box 855 Pittsburgh PA 15230

ESPOSITO, LARRY WAYNE, b Schenectady, NY, Apr 15, 51; m 75; c 1. CLOUDS, SATURN'S RINGS. *Educ:* Mass Inst Technol, SB, 73; Univ Mass, Amherst, PhD(astron), 77. *Prof Exp:* RES ASSOC, ATMOSPHERIC & SPACE PHYSICS LAB, UNIV COLO, BOULDER, 77- *Concurrent Pos:* Lectr, Dept Astron & Geophys, Univ Colo, 79-; appointee, Mgt Oper Working Group Planetary Atmospheres, NASA, 81- *Mem:* Am Astron Soc; Am Geophys Union; Int Astron Union. *Res:* Spectroscopy, photometry and polarimetry of solar system objects; development of associated radiative transfer methods. *Mailing Add:* Lab Atmospheric & Space Physics Univ Colo Boulder CO 80309

ESPOSITO, MICHAEL SALVATORE, b Brooklyn, NY, Nov 30, 40; c 1. GENETICS, BIOCHEMISTRY. *Educ:* Brooklyn Col, BS, 61; Univ Wash, PhD(genetics), 67. *Prof Exp:* NIH fel, Lab Molecular Biol, Univ Wis-Madison, 67-69; asst prof, 69-74, actg chmn dept, 78, ASSOC PROF BIOL, UNIV CHICAGO, 75- *Concurrent Pos:* NSF grants, 69-70, 71-73, 73-74 & 75-; mem genetics study sect, NIH, 76-78. *Mem:* AAAS; Genetics Soc Am; Am Soc Microbiol. *Res:* Yeast genetics and physiology; biochemical and genetic regulation of gene mutation, recombination, meiosis and sporulation. *Mailing Add:* Dept of Biol Univ Chicago 1116 E 59th St Chicago IL 60637

ESPOSITO, PASQUALE BERNARD, b New York, NY, Feb 28, 40; m 64; c 3. CELESTIAL MECHANICS, GEOPHYSICS. *Educ:* Manhattan Col, BS, 64; Univ Pa, MS, 66; Yale Univ, PhD(celestial mech), 69. *Prof Exp:* MEM TECH STAFF EARTH & SPACE SCI, JET PROPULSION, CALIF INST TECHNOL, 70- *Mem:* Am Geophys Union; Am Astron Soc. *Res:* Planetary science, such as gravity fields of planets; fundamental geodetic constants such as goecentric gravitational constant; solar physics such as solar corona electron density distribution. *Mailing Add:* 1719 Claridge St Arcadia CA 91006

ESPOSITO, ROCHELLE E, b Brooklyn, NY, June 28, 41; c 2. GENETICS. *Educ:* Brooklyn Col, BS, 62; Univ Wash, PhD(genetics) 67. *Prof Exp:* Asst prof, 69-75, ASSOC PROF BIOL, UNIV CHICAGO, 75- *Mem:* Genetics Soc Am; Am Soc Microbiol. *Res:* Genetic recombination; genetic and biochemical control of meiosis. *Mailing Add:* Dept of Biol Univ of Chicago Chicago IL 60637

ESPOSITO, VITO MICHAEL, b Logan, WVa, Sept 11, 40; m 60; c 1. IMMUNOLOGY, MICROBIOLOGY. *Educ:* Marshall Univ, BS, 62; WVa Univ, MS, 65, PhD(biochem genetics), 66. *Prof Exp:* Res asst biochem genetics, WVa Univ, 62-66; scientist, Commissioned Corp, NIH, 67-69, sr staff fel & immunologist, Lab Blood Prod, Div Biologics Standards, 69-71; dir biol res & develop, Dade Div Am Hosp Supply Corp, 71-74; dir, 74-75, vpres res & develop, Quality Assurance & Regulatory Affairs, Bio Quest Div, 75-78, vpres BBL Instruments, 78-80, VPRES RES & DEVELOP, BECTON, DICKINSON & CO, 80- *Mem:* AAAS; Int Soc Blood Transfusion; Am Soc Clin Path; Genetics Soc Am; Am Soc Microbiol. *Res:* Genetic basis of antibody synthesis; biochemistry of host-pathogen relationship; immunohematology biochemistry of development and aging, especially enzymes and subcellular organelles; laboratory instruments and automated systems; mechanisms of immunity; diagnostic reagents; genetics. *Mailing Add:* BBL Microbiol Syst Div Becton Dickinson & Co PO Box 243 Cockeysville MD 21030

ESPOY, HENRY MARTI, b San Francisco, Calif, Oct 22, 17; m 45; c 2. ANALYTICAL CHEMISTRY. *Educ:* Loyola Univ, Calif, BS, 39; Univ Calif, Los Angeles, AM, 42. *Prof Exp:* Res chemist, Van Camp Labs, 41-49; from chemist to chief chemist, Barnett Labs, 59-57; lab dir, Terminal Testing Labs, Inc, 57-59; lab dir, Daylin Labs Inc, 69-77; V PRES, ASSOC LABS, 77- *Concurrent Pos:* Referee chemist, Am Oil Chem Soc, 65- *Mem:* Am Chem Soc; Am Oil Chem Soc; Inst Food Technol. *Res:* Pesticide residues; fats and oils; food and agricultural chemistry. *Mailing Add:* Assoc Labs 806 N Bataria Orange CA 92668

ESPY, HERBERT HASTINGS, b Rochester, NY, June 4, 31; m 53; c 2. PHYSICAL ORGANIC CHEMISTRY, PAPER CHEMISTRY. *Educ:* Harvard Univ, AB, 52; Univ Wis, PhD(phys org chem), 56. *Prof Exp:* Res chemist, 56-70, sr res chemist, 71-78, RES SCIENTIST, HERCULES, INC, 78- *Mem:* Am Chem Soc. *Res:* Vinyl and condensation polymers; paper chemicals; polyelectrolyte interactions. *Mailing Add:* Res Ctr Hercules Inc Wilmington DE 19899

ESQUIVEL, AGERICO LIWAG, b Manila, Philippines, June 5, 32. PHYSICS, ELECTRONICS. *Educ:* Berchmans Col, Philippines, AB, 55, MA, 56; St Louis Univ, PhD(physics), 63. *Prof Exp:* Res physicist, Res Inst Advan Studies, Md, 63-64 & Mats Res Lab, Martin Co, 64-66; sr res engr, Boeing Co, 66-71; res assoc, Univ Southern Calif, 71-73; mem tech staff, Hughes Aircraft Co, 73-76; MEM TECH STAFF, TEX INSTRUMENTS, 76- *Mem:* Am Phys Soc; Inst Elec & Electronics Engrs; Sigma Xi. *Res:* Semiconductor physics; radiation effects; cathodoluminescence; diode lasers; MOS and charge-coupled devices; deep-level impurities; minority carrier lifetimes; x-ray lithography. *Mailing Add:* Tex Instruments Inc MS-118 PO Box 225936 Dallas TX 75265

ESRIG, MELVIN I, b Brooklyn, NY, Mar 15, 30; m 54; c 3. CIVIL ENGINEERING, SOIL MECHANICS. *Educ:* City Col New York, BBA, 51; Polytech Inst Brooklyn, BCE, 54; Univ Ill, MS, 59, PhD(civil eng), 61. *Prof Exp:* Trainee, Corps Engrs, US Army, 54; civil engr, Lockwood, Kessler & Bartlett, Inc, 54-56 & H G Holzmacher & Assocs, 56-57; soils engr, Warzyn Eng, 61-62; from asst prof to assoc prof civil eng, Cornell Univ, 62-70; assoc, Woodward-Moorhouse & Assoc, Inc, Clifton, 70-73; PRIN & V PRES, WOODWARD-CLYDE CONSULTS, 73- *Honors & Awards:* Hogentogler Award, Am Soc Testing & Mats, 80. *Mem:* AAAS; Am Soc Testing & Mats; Am Soc Civil Engrs. *Res:* Foundation engineering; capacity of piles; properties of soils. *Mailing Add:* 43 Royden Rd Tenafly NJ 07670

ESSARY, ESKEL OREN, b Clarkrange, Tenn, June 2, 17; m 39; c 1. POULTRY SCIENCE. *Educ:* Okla State Univ, BS, 47, MS, 49; Mich State Univ, PhD, 61. *Prof Exp:* Asst prof poultry husb, Univ Tenn, 49-52; chemist, Swift Res Labs, Swift & Co, 52-55; PROF FOOD SCI & TECHNOL, VA POLYTECH INST & STATE UNIV, 55- *Mem:* AAAS; Poultry Sci Asn; Inst Food Technol; World Poultry Sci Asn. *Res:* Poultry specialty items; shelf-life and quality of poultry products; influence of ration on quality and yields of poultry; cooking methods on nutritive value of poultry; influence of feed additives in layer rations on qualtiy and functional properties of eggs. *Mailing Add:* Dept of Food Sci Va Polytech Inst & State Univ Blacksburg VA 24061

ESSE, ROBERT CARLYLE, b Walnut Grove, Minn, May 17, 32; m 54; c 2. ORGANIC CHEMISTRY. *Educ:* St Olaf Col, BA, 54; Ore State Univ, PhD(org chem), 59. *Prof Exp:* Group leader antibiotics, Pharmaceut Prod Develop Sect, Lederle Labs Div, 59-66, head chem process develop, 66-74, TECH DIR FINE CHEMICALS DEPT, AM CYANAMID CO, 74- *Mem:* Am Chem Soc. *Res:* Synthesis of coumarins and furocoumarins; synthetic modification of tetracycline antibiotics. *Mailing Add:* Fine Chem Dept Am Cyanamid Co Pearl River NY 10965

ESSELEN, WILLIAM B, b Boston, Mass, July 31, 12; m 47; c 1. FOOD SCIENCE. *Educ:* Mass State Col, BS, 34, MS, 35, PhD(food tech), 38. *Prof Exp:* Asst nutrit, Mass State Col, 36-38; food technologist, Owens-Ill Glass Co, 39-41; from asst res prof to res prof, 41-57, head dept, 57-71, prof, 71-75, EMER PROF FOOD TECHNOL, UNIV MASS, AMHERST, 76- *Concurrent Pos:* Consult, War Food Admin, USDA, 42-45; food technician, Qm Corps, US Dept Army, 45; vis prof, Hokkaido Univ, 60-61 & Univ West Indies, Trinidad, 71-72. *Mem:* Am Soc Microbiologists; Am Chem Soc; Inst Food Technologists. *Res:* Nutritive fruits; effect of canning, freezing and dehydration on nutrition of foods; determination of process times for canned foods; use of glass containers for foods; apple products. *Mailing Add:* 55 Hills Rd Amherst MA 01002

ESSELMAN, W(ALTER) H(ENRY), b Hoboken, NJ, Mar 19, 17; m 43; c 4. ELECTRICAL ENGINEERING. *Educ:* Newark Col Eng, BS, 38; Stevens Inst Technol, MS, 44; Polytech Inst Brooklyn, DrE(elec eng), 53. *Prof Exp:* Elec engr regulating & control systs, Westinghouse Elec Corp, 38-40, elec engr servo & comput systs Navy fire control equip, 40-45, develop engr control & servo-systs, 45-50, mgr power plant syst, Bettis Atomic Power Div, 50-52, mgr syst subdiv atomic power div, 52-53, tech asst to mgr, Test & Develop Nuclear Power Plants, Submarine Thermal Reactor Test Facility, 53-58, mgr adv develop & planning, Bettis Atomic Power Div, 58-59, sr dept mgr, Astronuclear Lab, 59-61, mgr eng develop, Nerva Proj, 61-64, dep mgr, Pa, 64-68, proj mgr, 68-69, exec asst to gen mgr, 69-70; dir, Hanford Eng Develop Lab, 70-72; dir strategic planning, 74-80, TECH DIR, ENG ASSESSMENT, ELEC POWER RES INST, 81- *Concurrent Pos:* Instr, Polytech Inst Brooklyn, 48. *Mem:* Fel Am Nuclear Soc; fel Inst Elec & Electronics Engrs; Am Inst Aeronaut & Astronaut. *Res:* Energy research and development; nuclear power systems; electric utility. *Mailing Add:* 3412 Hillview Ave PO Box 10412 Palo Alto CA 94303

ESSENBERG, MARGARET KOTTKE, b Troy, NY, Apr 21, 43; m 67; c 2. BIOCHEMISTRY, BOTANY. *Educ:* Oberlin Col, AB, 65; Brandeis Univ, PhD(biochem), 71. *Prof Exp:* Res assoc biochem, Univ Leicester, Eng, 71-73; res assoc, 73-74, asst prof, 74-81, ASSOC PROF BIOCHEM, OKLA STATE UNIV, 81- *Concurrent Pos:* NSF fel, 71; NIH fel, 72-73. *Mem:* Am Phytopath Soc; Sigma Xi. *Res:* Bacterial plant disease and disease resistance. *Mailing Add:* Dept of Biochem Okla State Univ Stillwater OK 74074

ESSENBERG, RICHARD CHARLES, b Santa Monica, Calif, Dec 10, 43; m 67; c 2. TRANSPORT PHYSIOLOGY, GENETIC ENGINEERING. *Educ:* Calif Inst Technol, BS, 65; Harvard Univ, PhD(chem), 71. *Prof Exp:* Res fel biochem, Univ Leicester, 71-73; asst prof, 73-78, ASSOC PROF BIOCHEM, OKLA STATE UNIV, 78- *Mem:* Am Inst Biol Sci; Am Soc Microbiol; AAAS. *Res:* Mechanism of energy transduction in membrane transport and oxidative phosphorylation; genetic transformations of plant cells; membrane structure-function relationships. *Mailing Add:* Dept of Biochem Okla State Univ Stillwater OK 74074

ESSENBURG, F(RANKLIN), b Holland, Mich, Aug 2, 24; m 46; c 2. MECHANICS. *Educ:* Univ Mich, BSE, 45, LLB, 48, MS, 49, MSE, 50, PhD(mech), 56. *Prof Exp:* Patent atty, Bell Tel Labs, 50-51; private construct bus, 51-53; from instr to asst prof mech, Univ Mich, 53-58; from assoc prof to prof, Ill Inst Technol, 58-62; chmn dept mech eng, 62-70, chmn dept aerospace eng sci, 76-80, PROF MECH, UNIV COLO, BOULDER, 62-, GRAD SCH FAC, 80- *Mem:* Am Soc Mech Engrs. *Res:* Continuum mechanics; plate and shell theory; dynamics and vibration. *Mailing Add:* 2590 Univ Heights Ave Boulder CO 80309

ESSENE, ERIC J, b Berkeley, Calif, Apr 26, 39; m 63; c 2. PETROLOGY, MINERALOGY. *Educ:* Mass Inst Technol, BS, 61; Univ Calif, Berkeley, PhD(geol), 66. *Prof Exp:* NSF fel geol, Cambridge Univ, 66-68; res fel, Australian Nat Univ, 68-70; from asst prof to assoc prof, 70-80, PROF GEOL, UNIV MICH, 80- *Res:* Petrology and high pressure temperature experimentation on lower crust and upper mantle; thermodynamics and analytical mineralogy; experiments on the origin of the moon; hydrothermal experiments applicable to metamorphic rocks. *Mailing Add:* Dept of Geol & Mineral Univ of Mich Ann Arbor MI 48109

ESSENWANGER, OSKAR M, b Munich, WGer, Aug 25, 20; US citizen; m 47. ATMOSPHERIC PHYSICS, APPLIED STATISTICS. *Educ:* Univ Vienna, Dipl, 43; Univ Würzburg, Dr rer nat, 50. *Prof Exp:* Instr meteorol, Ger Air Force, 44-45; res meteorologist, Ger Weather Serv, 46-57; proj assoc, Univ Wis, 56-57; res meteorologist, Ger Weather Serv, 57 & Nat Weather Records Ctr, 57-61; chief aerophys br, 61-71, group leader, aerophys, 71-73, SUPVR RES PHYSICIST, US ARMY MISSILE COMMAND, 73- *Concurrent Pos:* Ger rep comt statist methods, World Meteorol Org, 57; affil prof, Dept Atmospheric Physics, Colo State Univ, 68-73; adj prof, Univ Ala, Huntsville, 71- *Mem:* Am Meteorol Soc; Am Statist Asn; Am Soc Qual Control; Sigma Xi; Ger Meteorol Soc. *Res:* Physical structure of the atmosphere, especially mathematical analysis and statistical representation of atmospheric parameters for missile design and trajectory analysis; development of statistical methods in climatology. *Mailing Add:* 610 Mountain Gap Dr Huntsville AL 35803

ESSER, ALFRED F, b Lauf, Ger, Feb 11, 40. BIOLOGICAL CHEMISTRY, IMMUNOCHEMISTRY. *Educ:* Univ Frankfurt, Diplomchemiker, 66, PhD(phys biochem), 69. *Prof Exp:* Fel biochem, Univ Calif, Santa Barbara, 69-71; res assoc biophys, NASA-Ames Res Ctr, Moffett Field, 71-73; asst prof biochem, Calif State Univ, Fullerton, 73-75; assoc mem molecular immunol, Scripps Clin & Res Found, 75-81; PROF COMP PATH & BIOCHEM, UNIV FLA, GAINESVILLE, 81- *Concurrent Pos:* Estab investr, Am Heart Asn, 76-81. *Mem:* Am Soc Biol Chemists; Am Chem Soc; Biophys Soc; Am Asn Immunologists. *Res:* Structure-function relationships in biological membranes; complement-immunochemistry. *Mailing Add:* Univ Fla Box J JHMHC Gainesville FL 32610

ESSER, ARISTIDE HENRI, b Padalarang, Indonesia, May 11, 30; US citizen; m 56; c 2. PSYCHIATRY, HUMAN ECOLOGY. *Educ:* Univ Amsterdam, MD, 55. *Prof Exp:* Intern, Amsterdam Univ Hosp, 55-56; resident psychiat, Wolfheze Ment Hosp, Neth, 56-57; staff resident, Endegeest Psychiat Clin, 58-61; Lederle Inst res fel, Yale Univ, 61-62; med dir res ward, Rockland State Hosp, 62-68, dir psychiat res, Letchworth Village, 69-71; dir, Cent Bergen Community Ment Health Ctr, 71-77; chief psychiat servs, Mission of the Immaculate Virgin, 77-80; DIR QUAL ASSURANCE, BRONX PSYCHIATRIC CTR, 80-; ASSOC PROF PSYCHIAT, ALBERT EINSTEIN COL MED, 80- *Concurrent Pos:* City of Leyden travel grant to Ger, Austria & Switz, 60; supvry psychiatrist, Endegeest Psychiat Clin, 64; ed, Man-Environ Systs, 69-; dir social biol labs, Rockland State Hosp, 69-; attend psychiatrist, Col Physicians & Surgeons, Columbia Univ, 70- *Mem:* Fel AAAS; Soc Gen Syst Res; fel Am Psychiat Asn; Animal Behav Soc. *Res:* Methodology for clinical and behavioral evaluations in psychiatry, mental retardation and animal studies; mental health and man-environment relations; social pollution. *Mailing Add:* Quality Assurance Bronx Psychiat Ctr 1500 Waters Pl Bronx NY 10461

ESSER, ROBERT EMMET, b Milwaukee, Wis, July 14, 16; m 41; c 5. BOTANY, INVERTEBRATE ZOOLOGY. *Educ:* Marquette Univ, BS, 38, MS, 40, PhD(cytol), 42. *Prof Exp:* Asst, Marquette Univ, 38-42, instr zool, 42-45; owner-technician, Michaelis-Esser, Inc, Wis, 45-46; asst prof, 46-71, ASSOC PROF BOT & ZOOL, UNIV WIS-PARKSIDE, 71- *Res:* Cytology of ferns; invertebrate zoology; microscopic biological technique. *Mailing Add:* Dept of Bot & Zool Univ of Wis-Parkside Wood Rd Kenosha WI 53140

ESSERY, JOHN M, b Plymouth, Eng, June 15, 36; m 62; c 2. ORGANIC CHEMISTRY, MEDICINAL CHEMISTRY. *Educ:* Univ Exeter, BSc, 57, PhD(chem), 60. *Prof Exp:* Fel, Nat Res Coun Can, 60-62; sr res scientist, Syracuse, 62-79, MGR LICENSING, INT DIV, BRISTOL-MYERS CO, 79- *Mem:* Am Chem Soc; Royal Soc Chem. *Res:* Chemistry of betalactam antibiotics; chemistry of heterocyclic compounds; biosynthesis of natural products. *Mailing Add:* Bristol-Myers Co Int Div 345 Park Ave New York NY 10022

ESSEX, MYRON, b Coventry, RI, Aug 17, 39; m 66; c 2. VIROLOGY, IMMUNOLOGY. *Educ:* Univ RI, BS, 62; Mich State Univ, DVM, 67; Univ Calif, Davis, PhD(microbiol), 70; Harvard Univ, MA, 80. *Prof Exp:* Vis scientist cancer biol, Karolinska Inst, Stockholm, 70-72; from asst prof to assoc prof, 72-78, HEAD DEPT MICROBIOL, SCH PUB HEALTH, HARVARD UNIV, 78- *Concurrent Pos:* Leukemia Soc Am scholar, 72-77; vis prof, Univ Tehran, 75; lectr, Harvard Med Sch, 76-; mem immunotherapy comt, NIH, 77-; mem med & sci adv bd, Leukemia Soc Am, 78-; mem res comt, Am Cancer Soc, Mass, 76- *Honors & Awards:* Bronze Medal, Am Cancer Soc, 80. *Mem:* Am Soc Microbiol; Am Asn Immunologists; Am Asn Cancer Res; Am Vet Med Asn; Am Asn Vet Oncologists. *Res:* Viral oncology; tumor immunology; cancer biology; cell membranes; viral genetics. *Mailing Add:* Dept of Microbiol Sch Pub Health Harvard Univ Boston MA 02115

ESSIEN, FRANCINE B, b Augusta, Ga, Mar 7, 43; c 3. DEVELOPMENTAL GENETICS. *Educ:* Temple Univ, BA, 65; Albert Einstein Col Med, PhD(genetics), 70. *Prof Exp:* Fel cell biol & genetics, Univ Conn, Storrs, 70-71; asst prof, 71-76, ASSOC PROF BIOL, DEPT BIOL SCI, DOUGLASS CAMPUS, RUTGERS UNIV, 76- *Concurrent Pos:* Consult, NJ Dept Higher Educ, 73; Robert Wood Johnson Found, 76; Nyerere Educ Inst, 81-; panelist, Am Coun Educ, NSF, 76-81; mem, NJ Task Force Genetics, 78-; fac fel cell biol & genetics, Univ Tenn, Oak Ridge Biomed Sci Grad Sch, 73-75; co-dir Biomed Careers Prog, Rutgers Univ Med Sch, 75-; Fulbright Award, Comparative & Int Educ Soc, 82. *Mem:* AAAS; Am Soc Cell Biol; Am Soc Zoologists; NY Acad Sci; Am Women Sci. *Res:* Analysis of the genetic control of developmental processes, using mutations in the mouse as tools to investigate the cellular and molecular bases of birth defects. *Mailing Add:* Dept Biol Sci Douglass Campus Rutgers Univ New Brunswick NJ 08903

ESSIG, FREDERICK BURT, b Los Angeles, Calif, Aug 25, 47; m 74. SYSTEMATIC BOTANY. *Educ:* Univ Calif, Riverside, AB, 69; Cornell Univ, PhD(plant taxon), 75. *Prof Exp:* Lectr biol, Cornell Univ, 74-75; asst prof bot & dir, Bot Gardens, 75-80, ASST PROF BIOL, UNIV SOUTH FLA, 80- *Mem:* Int Asn Plant Taxon; Soc Econ Bot; Asn Trop Biol. *Res:* Taxonomy and systematic anatomy-morphology of the monocotyledons, particularly the palms. *Mailing Add:* Dept of Biol Univ of SFla Tampa FL 33620

ESSIG, GUSTAVE ALFRED, b Philadelphia, Pa, June 11, 15; m 42; c 2. PHYSICS. *Educ:* Washington & Lee Univ, BA, 42. *Prof Exp:* Asst radio engr Sig C, US Army, 42, officer in chg radar training, 42-46; asst physicist nucleonics, Monsanto Chem Co, 46-48; supvr phys chem processes & radiog, Mound Lab, Monsanto Res Corp, 48-55, gen supvr radiochem & appl nuclear & phys chem, 55-62, asst to vpres & plant mgr, 62-63, mgr planning & reporting, 63-65, asst to vpres & plant mgr, 65-69, TECH SPECIALIST, MOUND LAB, MONSANTO RES CORP, 69- *Mem:* Am Phys Soc. *Res:* Research and development through pilot plant to production; radio-chemistry; radiography; nuclear physics; physical chemistry; vacuum techniques; electronics; instrumentation. *Mailing Add:* 1215 Meadowview Dr Miamisburg OH 45342

ESSIG, HENRY J, b Eppstein, Ger, Apr 26, 26; US citizen; m 49; c 4. ORGANIC POLYMER CHEMISTRY. *Educ:* Western Reserve Univ, BS, 51, MS, 52, PhD(org chem), 60. *Prof Exp:* Chemist, Grant Photo Prod, 51-52; chemist, 52-60, from assoc develop scientist to develop scientist, 60-68, sr develop scientist, 68-77, SUPVR RES & DEVELOP, B F GOODRICH CHEM CO, 77- *Mem:* Am Chem Soc. *Res:* Kinetic studies of heterogeneous catalysis; monomer synthesis and polymerization. *Mailing Add:* 31480 Detroit Rd Westlake OH 44145

ESSIG, HENRY WERNER, b Paragould, Ark, Dec 9, 30; m 53; c 2. ANIMAL NUTRITION. *Educ:* Univ Ark, BSA, 53, MS, 56; Univ Ill, PhD(animal nutrit), 59. *Prof Exp:* Assoc prof, 59-70, PROF NUTRIT, MISS STATE UNIV, 70- *Mem:* Am Soc Animal Sci; Am Dairy Sci Asn; Animal Nutrit Res Coun. *Res:* Ruminant nutrition research with cattle and sheep. *Mailing Add:* Dept of Animal Sci Miss State Univ Box 5228 Mississippi State MS 39762

ESSIGMANN, JOHN MARTIN, b Woburn, Mass, Apr 26, 47; m 70. TOXICOLOGY, BIOCHEMISTRY. *Educ:* Northeastern Univ, BA, 70; Mass Inst Technol, MS, 72, PhD(toxicol), 76. *Prof Exp:* Nat Inst Environ Health Sci fel, 76-77, res assoc toxicol, 77-80, ASST PROF TOXICOL, MASS INST TECHNOL, 80- *Mem:* Am Chem Soc. *Res:* Chemical carcinogenesis research, especially carcinogen-macromolecule interactions. *Mailing Add:* Dept of Nutrit & Food Sci Mass Inst of Technol Cambridge MA 02139

ESSIGMANN, MARTIN W(HITE), b Bethel, Vt, Jan 14, 17; m 43; c 3. ELECTRICAL ENGINEERING. *Educ:* Tufts Col, BS, 38; Mass Inst Technol, SM, 47. *Prof Exp:* Instr elec eng, Northeastern Univ, 38-44; vis instr, Mass Inst Technol, 44-47; asst prof, 47-50, prof & coordr electronics res, 50-61, head dept elec eng, 54-61, DEAN RES, NORTHEASTERN UNIV, 61-, PROF ELEC ENG, 80- *Concurrent Pos:* Vis asst prof, Mass Inst Technol, 47-48. *Mem:* AAAS; Am Soc Eng Educ; Inst Elec & Electronics Engrs. *Res:* Digital computers; nonlinear devices; speech analysis; principles of radar; information theory. *Mailing Add:* Northeastern Univ 360 Huntington Ave Boston MA 02115

ESSINGTON, EDWARD HERBERT, b Santa Barbara, Calif, Feb 19, 37; m 57; c 2. SOIL SCIENCE. *Educ:* Calif State Polytech Col, BS, 58; Univ Calif, Los Angeles, MS, 64. *Prof Exp:* Lab technician, Dept Nuclear Med & Radiation Biol, Univ Calif, Los Angeles, 57-65; sr assoc soil scientist, Hazleton-Nuclear Sci Corp Div, Isotopes Inc, 65-66; from sr assoc soil scientist to soil scientist, Palo Alto Labs, Teledyne Isotopes, Calif, 66-71, soil scientist, Nev, 71-73; soil scientist, H-7 Indust Waste, 73-75 & H-8 Environ Studies, 75-77, SOIL SCIENTIST LS-6 ENVIRON SCI, LIFE SCI DIV, LOS ALAMOS NAT LAB, 78- *Mem:* AAAS; Health Physics Soc; Soil Sci Soc Am. *Res:* Soil-plant relations; radionuclide uptake by plants; radionuclide and pollutant migration and chemistry in soils and groundwater systems; industrial radioactive and toxic waste management with emphasis on transuranic nuclides. *Mailing Add:* Los Alamos Nat Lab PO Box 1663 MS495 Los Alamos NM 87545

ESSLER, WARREN O(RVEL), b Davenport, Iowa, Apr 22, 24; m 44; c 3. ELECTRICAL ENGINEERING. *Educ:* Univ Iowa, BS, 53, MS, 55, PhD(elec eng, physiol), 60. *Prof Exp:* Res assoc audiol, Univ Iowa, 53-54; res assoc elec eng, Collins Radio Corp, 54-55; from instr to asst prof, SDak State Col, 55-61; prof & dean, Col Technol, Univ Vt, 61-72; chmn dept, 72-80, PROF ELEC ENG, TENN TECHNOL UNIV, 72- *Mem:* Am Soc Eng Educ; Nat Soc Prof Engrs; Inst Elec & Electronics Engrs. *Res:* Medical electronics. *Mailing Add:* Dept of Elec Eng Tenn Technol Univ Cookeville TN 38501

ESSLINGER, JACK HOUSTON, b Ponca City, Okla, July 19, 31; m 55; c 3. PARASITOLOGY. *Educ:* Univ Okla, BS, 53; Rice Inst, MA, 55, PhD(biol), 58. *Prof Exp:* From instr to asst prof, Sch Med, 62-67, ASSOC PROF PARASITOL, SCH PUB HEALTH & TROP MED, TULANE UNIV, 67- *Mem:* Am Soc Parasitologists; Am Soc Trop Med & Hyg; Soc Syst Zool. *Res:* Filarial systematics; filariasis of mammals. *Mailing Add:* Dept of Trop Med Tulane Univ New Orleans LA 70118

ESSLINGER, THEODORE LEE, b Spokane, Wash, Dec 13, 44; m 67; c 1. LICHENOLOGY. *Educ:* Eastern Wash State Col, BA, 68; Duke Univ, PhD(bot), 74. *Prof Exp:* Res fel bot, Smithsonian Inst, 74-75; asst prof, 75-80, PROF BOT, NDAK STATE UNIV, 80- *Mem:* Am Bryol & Lichenological Asn; Mycol Soc Am; Sigma Xi. *Mailing Add:* Dept Bot NDak State Univ Fargo ND 58105

ESSLINGER, WILLIAM GLENN, b Huntsville, Ala, Oct 21, 37; m 58; c 3. ORGANIC CHEMISTRY. *Educ:* Univ Ala, BS, 62, MS, 64, PhD(org chem), 66. *Prof Exp:* Asst prof chem, Union Univ, Tenn, 66-68; from asst prof to assoc prof, 73-77, chmn dept, 73-78, PROF CHEM, WEST GA COL, 77- *Concurrent Pos:* NSF grant dir, Ga Sci Teacher Proj, 70- ; brief org exam comt, Am Chem Soc, 75- *Mem:* Am Chem Soc; Sigma Xi. *Res:* Conformational effects on reactions at exocyclic positions of cycloalkylcarbinyl derivatives; thermal decomposition of esters; conversion of biomass to alcohol and other organics. *Mailing Add:* Dept Chem W Ga Col Carrollton GA 30117

ESSMAN, JOSEPH EDWARD, b Portsmouth, Ore, Nov 15, 35; m 57; c 5. COMMUNICATIONS ENGINEERING. *Educ:* Ohio Univ, BSEE, 57, MS, 61; Purdue Univ, PhD(elec eng), 72. *Prof Exp:* Actg instr elec eng, 57-60, instr, 60-72, asst prof, 72-73, asst chmn, 72-79, assoc prof, 73-77, prof elec eng, 77-79, asst dean, 79-81, ASSOC DEAN, COL ENG, OHIO UNIV, 81- *Concurrent Pos:* Res engr & proj dir, Wright-Patterson AFB, 78- *Mem:* Inst Elec & Electronics Engrs; Sigma Xi. *Res:* Communications and digital signal processing; data compression with applications to images. *Mailing Add:* Col Eng & Technol Ohio Univ Athens OH 45701

ESSMAN, WALTER BERNARD, b New York, NY, Dec 25, 33; m 62; c 1. PSYCHOPHYSIOLOGY. *Educ:* NY Univ, BA, 54; Univ NDak, MA, 55, PhD(psychol), 57; Univ Milan, MD, 72. *Prof Exp:* Asst psychol, Univ NDak, 54-55; asst, Univ Nebr, 55-56; asst, Univ NDak, 56-57; fel neurophysiol, Albert Einstein Col Med, 59-61, res assoc physiol, 61-62; from asst prof to assoc prof, 62-67, PROF PSYCHOL, QUEENS COL, NY, 67- *Concurrent Pos:* Fel neurochem, Mt Sinai Hosp, 64-68. *Mem:* AAAS; Fedn Am Socs Exp Biol; Am Psychol Asn; Am Acad Neurol; fel Am Col Nutrit. *Res:* Neural and chemical basis of learning and memory; physiological stress. *Mailing Add:* Dept of Psychol Queens Col Flushing NY 11367

ESSNER, EDWARD STANLEY, b New York, NY, Mar 31, 27; m 58; c 2. CELL BIOLOGY, ELECTRON MICROSCOPY. *Educ:* Long Island Univ, BS, 47; Univ Pa, PhD(zool), 51. *Prof Exp:* Sr asst scientist, Lab Chem Pharm, Nat Cancer Inst, 52-56; Nat Cancer Inst spec fel path, Albert Einstein Col Med, 56-58; res asst prof, Albert Einstein Col Med, 58-64; assoc mem, Div Cytol, Sloan-Kettering Inst Cancer Res, 64-75; PROF OPHTHAL, SCH MED, WAYNE STATE UNIV, 75- *Mem:* Am Soc Cell Biol; Electron Micros Soc Am; Int Soc Cell Biol; Am Asn Cancer Res; Histochem Soc. *Res:* Cell ultrastructure; enzyme localization; cell organelles. *Mailing Add:* Kresge Eye Inst 3994 John R St Detroit MI 48201

ESTABROOK, FRANK BEHLE, b Nampa, Idaho, June 22, 22; m 50; c 1. PHYSICS. *Educ:* Miami Univ, Ohio, BA, 43; Calif Inst Technol, MA, 47, PhD(physics), 50. *Prof Exp:* From asst prof to assoc prof physics, Miami Univ, Ohio, 50-52; sr engr reactor physics, NAm Aviation, 52-55; physicist, US Army Off Ord Res, 55-60; sr mem tech staff, 60-80, SR RES SCIENTIST, JET PROPULSION LAB, CALIF INST TECHNOL, 80- *Mem:* AAAS; Am Phys Soc. *Res:* Relativity and gravitation; applied mathematics; cosmology. *Mailing Add:* 853 Lyndon St South Pasadena CA 91030

ESTABROOK, GEORGE FREDERICK, b Carlisle Bks, Pa, Nov 1, 42; m 76; c 3. SYSTEMATIC BOTANY, EVOLUTIONARY PLANT ECOLOGY. *Educ:* Darmouth Col, Hanover, NH, AB, 64; Univ Colo, Boulder, MA, 67. *Prof Exp:* Res assoc, NY Bot Garden, 64-65; botanist, Dept Bot & Plant Path, Colo State Univ, 65-67; res mathemetician, Dept Biol, Univ Col, 67-70; asst prof bot & zool, 70-76, RES SCIENTIST HERBARIUM, UNIV MICH, ANN ARBOR, 73-, ASSOC PROF DIV BIOL SCI, 76- *Concurrent Pos:* Assoc ed, Mathematical Biosciences, 76- *Mem:* Am Soc Plant Taxonomists; Am Soc Naturalists; Ecol Soc Am; Soc Study Evolution; Int Asn Plant Taxon. *Res:* Reconstruct evolutionary relationships among kinds of organisms; explain in evolutionary terms when seeds germinate, fruits disperse, etc. *Mailing Add:* Univ Mich Herbarium Ann Arbor MI 48109

ESTABROOK, KENT GORDON, b Astoria, Ore, Oct 12, 43; m 68; c 2. PLASMA PHYSICS, COMPUTER SCIENCES. *Educ:* Vanderbilt Univ, AB, 65; Univ Tenn, PhD(physics), 71. *Prof Exp:* Fel physics, Oak Ridge Assoc Univs, 69-71, Ecole Polytechnique, Paris, 71 & Univ Tenn, 72; PHYSICIST, LAWRENCE LIVERMORE LAB, 72- *Mem:* Fel Am Phys Soc. *Res:* Computer simulation of laser-plasma interaction for laser fusion. *Mailing Add:* 707 Geraldine Livermore CA 94550

ESTABROOK, RONALD (WINFIELD), b Albany, NY, Jan 3, 26; m 47; c 4. BIOCHEMISTRY. *Educ:* Rensselaer Polytech Inst, BS, 50; Univ Rochester, PhD(biochem), 54. *Hon Degrees:* DSc, Univ Rochester, 80; Dr, Karsinska Inst, Stockholm, 80. *Prof Exp:* Fel, Johnson Found Med Physics, Univ Pa, 54-57; res assoc, Univ Pa, 57-58, from asst prof to prof phys biochem, 59-68; dean grad sch biomed sci, 73-76, VIRGINIA LAZENBY O'HARA PROF BIOCHEM & CHMN DEPT, UNIV TEX HEALTH SCI CTR DALLAS, 68- *Concurrent Pos:* Am Heart Asn fel, 57-58; USPHS fel, 58- *Mem:* Inst Med-Nat Acad Sci; Am Soc Pharmacol & Exp Therapeut; Fedn Am Socs Exp Biol; Am Soc Biol Chem; Am Chem Soc. *Res:* Application of physical methods to study of intracellular biochemical processes. *Mailing Add:* Dept Biochem Univ Tex Health Sci Ctr Dallas TX 75235

ESTEE, CHARLES REMINGTON, b Hecla, SDak, Oct 7, 21; m 43; c 3. PHYSICAL CHEMISTRY. *Educ:* Jamestown Col, BS, 42; Univ Iowa, MS, 44, PhD(phys chem), 47. *Prof Exp:* Asst chem, Univ Iowa, 42, asst, 43, instr, 43-44; jr chemist, Tenn Eastman Corp, Oak Ridge, 44-45; instr, Univ Iowa, 46-47; actg prof, 47-48, PROF CHEM, UNIV SDAK, 48-, HEAD DEPT, 52- *Mem:* AAAS; Am Chem Soc; Nat Sci Teachers Asn. *Res:* Electrical properties of colloids; science education. *Mailing Add:* Dept of Chem Univ of SDak Vermillion SD 57069

ESTEP, CHARLES BLACKBURN, b Middlesboro, Ky, Aug 9, 23; m 49; c 3. ENTOMOLOGY, PHARMACOLOGY. *Educ:* Univ Tenn, BA, 48, MS, 53, PhD(entom), 75. *Prof Exp:* Res asst radio-chem, Oak Ridge Inst Nuclear Studies, 48-50 & Univ Tenn, AEC, 50-52; prod supvr radio-pharmaceut, Abbott Labs, Oak Ridge, Tenn, 52-65, CHEM PHARMACOLOGIST, ABBOTT LABS, NORTH CHICAGO, 66- *Mem:* Am Chem Soc; NY Acad Sci; AAAS; Entom Soc Am; Biol Res Inst Am. *Res:* Radiotracer-labeled drugs in absorption, distribution and excretion studies of candidate drugs in vivo in various animal species; wholebody autoradiography for drug distribution studies in different animal species; environmental entomology. *Mailing Add:* 433 McKinley Ave Libertyville IL 60048

ESTEP, HERSCHEL LEONARD, b Dunbar, Va, Nov 29, 29; m 52; c 6. MEDICINE, ENDOCRINOLOGY. *Educ:* King Col, AB, 52; Johns Hopkins Univ, MD, 56. *Prof Exp:* Fel endocrinol, Vanderbilt Univ, 61-62; dir endocrinol res lab, 62-76, ASSOC PROF MED, HEALTH SCI DIV, VA COMMONWEALTH UNIV, 62- *Concurrent Pos:* USPHS res grant, 62-65; Am Cancer Soc grant, 68-70; consult, McGuire Vet Admin Hosp, 68-71. *Mem:* AAAS; fel Am Col Physicians; Endocrine Soc; Am Fedn Clin Res. *Res:* Neuroendocrine regulation of adrenocorticotropic and gonadotropic hormones; mechanisms of control of parathyroid hormone secretion. *Mailing Add:* Dept of Med Health Sci Div Va Commonwealth Univ Richmond VA 23219

ESTERGREEN, VICTOR LINE, b Lynden, Wash, Dec 15, 25; m 50; c 1. ANIMAL PHYSIOLOGY, ENDOCRINOLOGY. *Educ:* Wash State Univ, BS, 50, MS, 56; Univ Ill, PhD(dairy sci), 60. *Prof Exp:* Asst herdsman, Wash State Univ, 50-51; instr, Wash High Schs, 52-54; trainee biol chem, Steroid Training Inst, Univ Utah, 60-61; res assoc animal physiol, 61-62, from asst prof to assoc prof dairy sci, 62-72, PROF DAIRY SCI, WASH STATE UNIV, 72- *Mem:* Am Dairy Sci Asn; Endocrine Soc; Am Soc Animal Sci. *Res:* Bovine reproduction and corticosteroid hormones; endocrinology of reproduction in farm animals. *Mailing Add:* Dept of Animal Sci Wash State Univ Pullman WA 99163

ESTERLING, DONALD M, b Chicago, Ill, Nov 18, 42; m; c 2. THEORETICAL SOLID STATE PHYSICS, MATERIALS SCIENCE. *Educ:* Univ Notre Dame, BS, 64; Brandeis Univ, MA, 66, PhD(physics), 68. *Prof Exp:* From asst prof to assoc prof physics, Ind Univ, Bloomington, 68-75; assoc res prof eng, 75-78, assoc prof eng & appl sci, 78-80, PROF, JOINT INST ADVAN OF FLIGHT SCI, GEORGE WASHINGTON UNIV, NASA-LANGLEY RES CTR, 80- *Mem:* Am Phys Soc; Inst Mech Engrs. *Res:* Application of constructs and methodology of solid state physics to problems in materials engineering, emphasis on strength of solids, fracture and plasticity. *Mailing Add:* NASA-Langley Res Ctr MS-396 Hampton VA 23665

ESTERLY, JOHN ROOSEVELT, b Friedensburg, Pa, Mar 13, 33; m 57; c 4. PATHOLOGY. *Educ:* Yale Univ, BS, 55; Johns Hopkins Univ, MD, 59. *Prof Exp:* USPHS fels, Hammersmith Hosp, Royal Postgrad Med Sch, Univ London, 63-64 & Johns Hopkins Hosp & Med Sch, 64-66; from asst prof to assoc prof, 68-75, PROF PATH, OBSTET & GYNEC, UNIV CHICAGO, 75- *Mem:* Am Thoracic Soc; Am Asn Path; Reticuloendothelial Soc; Histochem Soc. *Res:* Histochemistry of hydrolytic enzymes; pulmonary reactions to injury; pathology of neonatal inflammation and adaptation; cystic fibrosis; pediatric and pulmonary pathology. *Mailing Add:* Dept of Path Univ of Chicago Chicago IL 60637

ESTERLY, NANCY BURTON, b New York, NY, Apr 14, 35; m 57; c 4. PEDIATRICS, DERMATOLOGY. *Educ:* Smith Col, BS, 56; Johns Hopkins Univ, MD, 60; Am Bd Pediat, dipl, 66; Am Bd Dermat, dipl, 70. *Prof Exp:* USPHS fel dermat, Sch Med, Johns Hopkins Univ, 64-67; instr pediat, Johns Hopkins Univ, 67-68; from instr to asst prof, Univ Chicago, 68-70; asst prof dermat, Col Med, Univ Ill Med Ctr, 70-72, assoc prof dermat & pediat, 72-73; assoc prof pediat, Pritzker Med Sch, Univ Chicago, 73-78; PROF PEDIAT & DERMAT, SCH MED, NORTHWESTERN UNIV, 78- *Concurrent Pos:* Attend physician & dir pediat dermat, Michael Reese Hosp & Med Ctr, 73-78; head, Dermat Div, Children's Mem Hosp, 78- *Mem:* Soc Invest Dermat; Soc Pediat Res; Soc Pediat Dermat; Am Acad Dermat. *Res:* Ichthyosis; neonatal skin reactivity; leukocyte chemotaxis in acne vulgaris. *Mailing Add:* Children's Mem Hosp 2300 Children's Plaza Chicago IL 60614

ESTERMANN, EVA FRANCES, b San Francisco, Calif, Feb 26, 32. PLANT PHYSIOLOGY. *Educ:* Univ Calif, BS, 53, PhD(plant nutrit soils), 58. *Prof Exp:* Jr res biochemist, Univ Calif, Berkeley, 58-60; from asst prof to assoc prof, 60-69, PROF BIOL, SAN FRANCISCO STATE UNIV, 69- *Res:* Bacterial nutrition at surfaces; physiological ecology; spore metabolism. *Mailing Add:* Dept of Biol San Francisco State Univ San Francisco CA 94132

ESTERSON, GERALD L(EE), b Baltimore, Md, June 29, 27; m 52; c 2. PROCESS COMPUTER SIMULATION, CHEMICAL PROCESS SCALE-UP. *Educ:* Johns Hopkins Univ, BEng, 51, DEng(elec eng), 56. *Prof Exp:* Res assoc oceanog instrumentation, Inst Co-op Res, Johns Hopkins Univ, 54-56; sr engr air arm div, Westinghouse Elec Co, 56-58; asst prof chem eng, Washington Univ, 58-61, assoc prof appl math, 61-65, dir inst continuing educ, 65-71, from assoc prof to prof eng, 65-76; PROF APPL CHEM, HEBREW UNIV JERUSALEM, 76- *Concurrent Pos:* Consult, Compumatix, Inc, 59, Monsanto Co, 59-61 & 64-68 & McGraw-Hill Bk Co, Inc, 62-63. *Mem:* Inst Elec & Electronics Engrs; Am Inst Chem Engrs; Soc Indust & Appl Math; Instrument Soc Am. *Res:* Simulation and modeling of industrial and environmental systems; automatic control; computer control; pilot plant operations and process development; crystallizer systems; energy and cement from oil shale. *Mailing Add:* Casali Inst of Appl Chem Hebrew Univ Jerusalem Israel

ESTES, DENNIS RAY, b Stradford, Okla, June 18, 41; m 67; c 2. QUADRATIC FORMS, COMMUTATIVE RING THEORY. *Educ:* ECent State Col, Okla, BS, 61; La State Univ, MS, 63, PhD(math), 65. *Prof Exp:* Asst prof math, La State Univ, 65-66; fel, Calif Inst Technol, 66-68; asst prof, 68-72, ASSOC PROF MATH, UNIV SOUTHERN CALIF, 72- *Concurrent Pos:* Vis assoc prof, La State Univ, 74-75; vis prof, Ohio State Univ, 82. *Mem:* Math Asn Am; Am Math Soc. *Res:* Arithmetic theory of quadratic lattices and matrix theory over commutative rings. *Mailing Add:* Dept Math Univ Southern Calif Los Angeles CA 90007

ESTES, EDNA E, b Jasper, Ala, Nov 23, 21. BOTANY, MICROBIOLOGY. *Educ:* Univ Ala, BS, 48, MS, 49, PhD(bot), 57. *Prof Exp:* Asst prof biol, Flora Macdonald Col, 49-53; instr, Mobile Ctr, Univ Ala, 53-54; instr sci & biol, St Mary's Sem-Jr Col, 57-59; asst prof biol, Del Mar Col, 59-60; from assoc prof to prof biol, Salisbury State Col, 60-78; RETIRED. *Mem:* AAAS; Bot Soc Am; Am Inst Biol Sci; Sigma Xi. *Res:* Plant physiology, particularly relation of phosphorus nutrition to photosynthesis; correlating the uptake and distribution of phosphorus-32 in higher plants with certain photosynthetic factors, particularly chlorophyll pattern, light, and carbon dioxide supply. *Mailing Add:* 1177 S Division St Salisbury MD 21801

ESTES, EDWARD HARVEY, JR, b Gay, Ga, May 1, 25; m 48; c 5. MEDICINE. *Educ:* Emory Univ, BS, 44, MD, 47. *Prof Exp:* Intern med, Grady Mem Hosp, Atlanta, Ga, 47-48, asst resident, 49-50; sr asst resident med, Duke Univ Hops, 52-53; fel med, Med Sch, Duke Univ, 53-54; chief cardiovasc sect, Vet Admin Hosp, 54-55; chief cardiol dept, Duke Univ Hosp, 55-58; chief med serv, Vet Admin Hosp, Durham, 58-63; PROF MED, MED CTR, DUKE UNIV, 63-, CHMN DEPT COMMUNITY HEALTH SCI, 66- *Concurrent Pos:* Fel physiol, Emory Univ, 48-49 & cardiovasc physiol, 50. *Res:* Cardiovascular physiology; electrocardiography. *Mailing Add:* Dept of Community Health Sci PO Box 2914 Duke Univ Med Ctr Durham NC 27710

ESTES, FRANCES LORRAINE, b Mendon, Mich, Dec 25, 15. ENVIRONMENTAL CHEMISTRY. *Educ:* Kalamazoo Col, AB, 40; Univ Chicago, MS, 48; Rutgers Univ, PhD, 53. *Prof Exp:* Control chemist, Johnson & Johnson Surg Supplies, 41-42; asst catalysis, Inst Gas Tech, Ill Inst Technol, 43-47; from instr to asst prof, Douglass Col, Rutgers Univ, 48-56; res assoc biochem, Col Med, Baylor Univ, 56-61; res asst prof, Med Br, Univ Tex,

61-67; biochemist, Vet Admin Hosp, Houston, Tex, 67-69; dir environ chem, Gulf South Res Inst, 69-71; CONSULTANT, 71- *Concurrent Pos:* Mem air pollution chem & physics adv comt, US Environ Protection Agency, 72-75. *Mem:* AAAS; Am Chem Soc; NY Acad Sci; fel Am Inst Chem; Soc Appl Spectros. *Res:* Gas phase reactions and biological interactions of environmental concern. *Mailing Add:* 5500 N Braeswood Apt 122 Houston TX 77096

ESTES, JAMES ALLEN, b Sacramento, Calif, Oct 2, 45; m 81. ECOLOGY, VERTEBRATE BIOLOGY. *Educ:* Univ Minn, BA, 67; Wash State Univ, MS, 70; Univ Ariz, PhD(biol), 74. *Prof Exp:* RES BIOLOGIST, DENVER WILDLIFE CTR, US FISH & WILDLIFE SERV, 74- *Concurrent Pos:* Affil asst prof, Ctr Quant Sci, Univ Wash, 76-; res assoc, Ctr Coastal Marine Studies, Univ Calif, Santa Cruz, 78-; adj prof biol, Univ Calif, Santa Cruz, 80- *Mem:* Am Soc Mammalogists; Ecol Soc Am; Am Soc Naturalists; Wildlife Soc; Biomet Soc. *Res:* Sea otter, community interactions in rocky and soft-sediment systems; algae-herbivore interactions; ecology and evolution of marine macroalgae; pinniped population biology. *Mailing Add:* Ctr for Coastal Marine Studies Univ Calif Santa Cruz CA 95064

ESTES, JAMES RUSSELL, b Burkburnett, Tex, Aug 28, 37; m 62; c 2. SYSTEMATIC BOTANY. *Educ:* Midwestern State Univ, BS, 59; Ore State Univ, PhD(bot), 67. *Prof Exp:* Asst prof bot & microbiol, 67-71, asst cur, 71-79, ASSOC PROF BOT, ROBERT BEBB HERBARIUM, UNIV OKLA, 71-, CUR, 79- *Concurrent Pos:* assoc ed botany, Southwesterrn Asn Naturalists. *Mem:* Am Soc Plant Taxon (secy, 81-); Bot Soc Am; Sigma Xi; Int Asn Plant Taxonomists; Southwestern Asn Natualists. *Res:* Pollination ecology; taxonomy of the Poaceae; flora of Oklahoma; evolution of genus Pyrrhopappus; autopolyploidy as an evolutionary process. *Mailing Add:* Rm 135 Dept Bot & Microbiol Univ Okla 770 Van Vleet Oval Norman OK 73019

ESTES, JOHN H, b Youngstown, Ohio, Jan 10, 16; m 46; c 4. ORGANIC CHEMISTRY, METALLURGY. *Educ:* Youngstown Univ, BS, 40; Wash State Univ, MS, 48, PhD(org chem), 52. *Prof Exp:* Metallurgist, Carnegie Ill Steel Co, 40 & Mullins Mfg Corp, 40-42; res chemist, 52-72, SR RES ASSOC, TEXACO RES CTR, 72- *Mem:* Am Chem Soc. *Res:* Zeolite synthesis; commercial process; catalysis in reforming field; gasoline additive studies. *Mailing Add:* Cedar Hill Rd Rte 6 Wappingers Falls NY 12590

ESTES, LELAND LLOYD, b Danville, Va, Nov 6, 20; m 46; c 2. ORGANIC POLYMER CHEMISTRY. *Educ:* Va Mil Inst, BS, 43; Mass Inst Technol, PhD(org chem), 49. *Prof Exp:* Res chemist, 49-55, supvr, 55-65, RES SUPVR, E I DU PONT DE NEMOURS & CO, 65- *Mem:* Am Chem Soc. *Res:* Synthetic chemistry; textile finishes; synthetic polymers and polymerization; cellulose acetate rayon; nylon; dacron; nonwoven fabrics. *Mailing Add:* Res & Develop Lab E I du Pont de Nemours & Co Chattanooga TN 37401

ESTES, RICHARD, b San Rafael, Calif, May 9, 32; m 55; c 1. VERTEBRATE PALEONTOLOGY, HERPETOLOGY. *Educ:* Univ Calif, Berkeley, BA, 55, MA, 57, PhD(paleont), 60. *Prof Exp:* Mus preparator vert paleont, Univ Calif, Berkeley, 57-58, asst, 58-59, mus preparator, 59-60, asst vert zool, 60; from asst prof to prof biol, Boston Univ, 60-73; PROF ZOOL, SAN DIEGO STATE UNIV, 73- *Concurrent Pos:* Res assoc vert paleont, Mus Comp Zool, Harvard Univ, 60-73; NSF res grants, 61-67, 68-70, 73-76, 77-79 & 80-83; Am Philos Soc res grant, 64-65; Sigma Xi res grant, 65; Nat Acad Sci, Marsh Fund res grant, 70; Nat Geog Soc res grant, 73-74. *Mem:* AAAS; Am Soc Ichthyol & Herpet; Soc Vert Paleont; fel Herpetologists League; Soc Study Reptiles & Amphibians. *Res:* Paleoecological and evolutionary phenomena in fossil lower vertebrate faunas; anatomy and relationships of fossil and recent Amphibia and Reptilia. *Mailing Add:* Dept of Zool San Diego State Univ San Diego CA 92182

ESTES, TIMOTHY KING, b Kalamazoo, Mich, Oct 1, 40; m 61; c 2. PAPER CHEMISTRY. *Educ:* Western Mich Univ, BS, 62; Lawrence Univ, MS, 64, PhD(paper chem), 67. *Prof Exp:* SR RES SPECIALIST PAPERBOARD, PACKAGING CORP AM, 66- *Mem:* Am Chem Soc; Tech Asn Pulp & Paper Indust. *Res:* Secondary fibers; semi-chemical pulping; computer modeling; paperboard physics. *Mailing Add:* 30 Manchester Rd SW Grand Rapids MI 49508

ESTEVEZ, ENRIQUE GONZALO, b Havana, Cuba, Nov 25, 48; US citizen; m 76. CLINICAL MICROBIOLOGY. *Educ:* Fla State Univ, BA, 71; Univ Miami, PhD(microbiol), 76. *Prof Exp:* Med technologist clin chem, Lahuis Clin Labs, 72-74; teaching asst microbiol, Univ Miami, 73-76; trainee, 76-78, develop specialist, 78-79, ASST DIR, CLIN MICROBIOL LAB, DUKE UNIV MED CTR, 79- *Mem:* Am Soc Microbiol; Am Soc Clin Pathologist. *Res:* Rapid methods of laboratory diagnosis of infectious diseases; clinical significance of microbiological culture results; formulation and quality control of bacteriologic culture media; lab diagnosis of parasitic infections. *Mailing Add:* Clin Microbiol Labs Duke Univ Med Ctr PO Box 3879 Durham NC 27710

ESTEY, RALPH HOWARD, b Millville, NB, Dec 9, 16; m 44; c 2. PLANT PATHOLOGY. *Educ:* McGill Univ, BSc, 51, PhD(plant path), 56; Univ Maine, MS, 54; Univ NB, BEd, 60; Univ London, DIC, 65. *Prof Exp:* Instr pub sch, NB, Can, 45-53; instr plant path, Univ Conn, 56-57; from asst prof to assoc prof, 57-72, chmn dept, 70-76, PROF PLANT SCI MACDONALD COL, McGILL UNIV, 72- *Mem:* Soc Nematol; Mycol Soc Am; Agr Inst Can; Brit Mycol Soc; Can Phytopath Soc (pres, 78-79). *Res:* Plant root diseases; history of agriculture and plant pathology. *Mailing Add:* Dept of Plant Sci Macdonald Col of McGill Univ Ste Anne de Bellevue PQ H9X 1C0 Can

ESTILAI, ALI, b Iran, Sept 29, 40; m 70; c 2. PLANT BREEDING, CYTOGENETICS. *Educ:* Univ Tehran, BS, 64; Univ Calif, Davis, MS, 68, PhD(genetics), 71. *Prof Exp:* Asst prof teaching & res fac sci, Univ Tehran, 71-77, assoc prof, 77-80; ASST RES AGRONOMIST, UNIV CALIF, DAVIS, 81- *Concurrent Pos:* Mem ed coun, Ministry Educ, Iran, 72-78; Dep dir, Inst Biochem & Biophys, Univ Tehran, 77-78, mem res coun, 78-79; vis prof, Univ Calif, Davis, 78-79. *Mem:* Am Soc Agron; Genetics Soc Am; Guayule Rubber Soc; Genetic Soc Iran (vpres, 76-80). *Res:* Evolution, cytogenetics, and breeding of various crops including safflower and saffron; breeding for increased rubber production in Guayule. *Mailing Add:* Cotton Res Sta USDA 17053 Shafter Ave Shafter CA 93263

ESTILL, WESLEY BOYD, b Enid, Okla, Mar 24, 24; m 48; c 7. ANALYTICAL CHEMISTRY, MATERIAL SCIENCE. *Educ:* Coe Col, BS, 49; Okla State Univ, MS, 51. *Prof Exp:* Mem staff res lab, Armour & Co, 51-52 & res lab, Ozark-Mahoning Co, 52-54; emission spectroscopist, Oak Ridge Nat Lab, 54-57; ELECTRON MICROSCOPIST, SANDIA CORP, 57- *Mem:* Electron Micros Soc Am; Electron Probe Anal Soc Am. *Res:* Complex ions; distillation of fluoride and ruthenium; adhesion of thin films; shock loaded metals; microanalysis; electron microprobe; electron diffraction; electron scanning; transmission microscopy; x-ray computer imaging; hydrogen effects on materials; laser interaction with materials. *Mailing Add:* Div 8316 Sandia Lab Sandia Corp Livermore CA 94550

ESTIN, ARTHUR JOHN, b Feb 15, 27; US citizen; m 48; c 4. MICROWAVE PHYSICS, ELECTRONICS ENGINEERING. *Educ:* Cooper Union, BEE, 49; Univ Colo, MS, 58, PhD(elec eng), 66. *Prof Exp:* Elec engr radio propagation, Nat Bureau Standards, 48-54, elec scientist microwave spectros, 54-58, physicist microwave & plasma physics, 58-66, asst div chief electromagnetics, 66-72, sect chief microwave eng, 72-76, supv physicist satellite commn eng, 76-80; CONSULT ENGR, 80- *Concurrent Pos:* Sci & technol fel, Dept Com, 70-71. *Mem:* AAAS; Inst Elec & Electronics Engrs; Soc Instrumentation & Measurements; Sigma Xi. *Res:* Microvave antenna design and measurement; critical measurements in satellite communications systems. *Mailing Add:* Star Route Paonia CO 81428

ESTIN, ROBERT WILLIAM, b Paterson, NJ, Nov 17, 31; m 64; c 2. PHYSICS, SCIENCE EDUCATION. *Educ:* Ill Inst Technol, BS, 53, MS, 55, PhD(physics), 63. *Prof Exp:* Teacher high sch, Ill, 55-56; from instr to asst prof physics, Ill Inst Technol, 56-65; from assoc prof to prof, Roosevelt Univ, 65-71; staff scientist, Phys Sci Group, Newton Col Sacred Heart, 71-73; assoc prof dept sci & math educ, Boston Univ, 74-75; sr systs instr, 3M/Linolex, Inc, 75-80; SR SYSTS INSTR, HONEYWELL INFO SYSTS, 81- *Concurrent Pos:* Lectr, Univ Ill, 63; mem phys sci study comt, Ed Servs, Inc, 65-66; chmn dept physics, Roosevelt Univ, 67-71. *Mem:* Am Phys Soc; Am Asn Physics Teachers; Fedn Am Sci. *Res:* Physics education at secondary, elementary and intermediate college levels; new curricular developments, including teacher training; mathematics and computer science education. *Mailing Add:* 11 Whitecomb St Belmont MA 02178

ESTLE, THOMAS LEO, b Columbus Junction, Iowa, Jan 8, 31; m 53; c 4. SOLID STATE PHYSICS. *Educ:* Rice Inst, BA, 53; Univ Ill, MS, 54, PhD(physics), 57. *Prof Exp:* Fulbright scholar, 57-58; mem tech staff, Tex Instruments, Inc, 58-62, head defect physics sect, 62-66, sr res physicist, 66-67; PROF PHYSICS, RICE UNIV, 67- *Mem:* Am Phys Soc. *Res:* Magnetic resonance; point imperfections in nonmetals; muon spin rotation. *Mailing Add:* Dept of Physics Rice Univ Houston TX 77001

ESTLER, RON CARTER, b Boonton, NJ, Dec 11, 49. CHEMICAL PHYSICS, CHEMISTRY. *Educ:* Drew Univ, BA, 72; Johns Hopkins Univ, MA, 74, PhD(chem), 76. *Prof Exp:* Res assoc chem, Columbia Univ, 76-77 & Stanford Univ, 77-78; ASST PROF CHEM, UNIV SOUTHERN CALIF, 78- *Mem:* Am Chem Soc; Am Phys Soc. *Res:* Laser-induced chemical reactions; molecular reaction dynamics; laser spectroscopy. *Mailing Add:* Dept of Chem Univ of Southern Calif Los Angeles CA 90007

ESTRIN, GERALD, b New York, NY, Sept 9, 21; m 41; c 3. COMPUTER SCIENCE. *Educ:* Univ Wis, BS, 48, MS, 49, PhD(elec eng), 51. *Prof Exp:* Res engr, Inst Adv Study, Princeton Univ, 50-53 & 55-56; dir electronic comput proj, Weizmann Inst Sci, Israel, 53-55; assoc prof eng, 56-58, PROF ENG, UNIV CALIF, LOS ANGELES, 58-, CHMN, COMPUT SCI DEPT, 79- *Concurrent Pos:* Lipsky fel, 54; consult, Nat Cash Register Co, 57, Telemeter Magnetics, Inc, 58-60 & Ampex Corp, 61-63; Guggenheim fel, 63 & 67; mem adv bd, appl math div, Argonne Nat Lab, 66-68, mem, assoc univs rev comt for chmn, 76-77, mem appl math div, 74-80; dir, Comput Communs, Inc, 66-67; mem int prog comt, Int Fedn Info Processing Cong, 68; int prog chmn, Jerusalem Conf Info Technol, 71; mem bd gov, Weizmann Inst Sci, Israel, 71; Asn Comput Mach lectr; Inst Elec & Electronics Eng distinguished speaker; mem math & comput sci res adv comt, Atomic Energy Comn; dir, Systs Eng Labs, 77-; mem, Scientific Adv Comt, Gould, Inc, Rolling Meadows, Ill, Nitron, Inc, Cupertino, Calif, 81- *Mem:* Fel Inst Elec & Electronics Engrs; Asn Comput Mach; Am Soc Eng Educ; NY Acad Sci. *Res:* Digital computer systems. *Mailing Add:* Dept of Comput Sci Univ of Calif Los Angeles CA 90024

ESTRIN, NORMAN FREDERICK, b Brooklyn, NY, Apr 1, 39; m 61; c 3. SCIENCE ADMINISTRATION, TECHNICAL MANAGEMENT. *Educ:* Brooklyn Col, BS, 59; NY Univ, MS, 62; Fla State Univ, PhD(phys org chem), 68. *Prof Exp:* Teaching asst chem, NY Univ, 60-61; teacher, Morris High Sch, NY, 61-62 & Jane Addams Voc High Sch, 62; chemist, Clairol Res Labs, Conn, 62-64; res asst, Fla State Univ, 64-68; dir sci, 68-72, vpres sci, 72-81, SR VPRES SCI, COSMETIC, TOILETRY & FRAGRANCE ASN INC, DC, 81- *Concurrent Pos:* Consult, Nat Cancer Inst, 75 & 81; ed, Cosmetic Ingredient Dict, Cosmetics, Toiletry & Fragrance Asn, 73, 76 & 82, Tech Guidelines, 74, 82 & Specifications & Descriptions, 71 & 82; ed, Sci & Regulatory Founds of the Cosmetic Indust, 82. *Mem:* Soc Cosmetic Chem; fel Royal Soc Health. *Res:* Synthesis of sequence peptide polymers and study of their structure and possible utility as models for active sites of certain enzymes. *Mailing Add:* 9109 Copenhaver Dr Potomac MD 20854

ESTRIN, THELMA A, b New York, NY, Feb 21, 24; m 41; c 3. ELECTRICAL ENGINEERING, BIOMEDICAL ENGINEERING. *Educ:* Univ Wis, BS, 48, MS, 49, PhD(elec eng), 51. *Prof Exp:* Res engr anat, 60-70, dir, Data Processing Lab, Brain Res Inst, 70-80, PROF ENG, UNIV CALIF, 80- *Concurrent Pos:* Fulbright fel, Weizmann Inst Sci, Rehovot, Israel, 63; prin investr, USPHS grant, Data Processing Lab, Brain Res Inst, Univ Calif, Los Angeles, 70-, adj prof anat & comput sci, 78-80. *Honors & Awards:* Outstanding Engrs Merit Award, Soc Women Engrs, 81. *Mem:* Alliance for Eng in Eng in Med & Biol (vpres, 78); fel Inst Elec & Electronics Engrs; Biomed Eng Soc; fel Inst Advan Eng; Asn Advan Med Instrumentation. *Res:* Application of technology and computers to health care delivery; computer methods in neuroscience; electrical activity of the nervous system; engineering education. *Mailing Add:* Brain Res Inst Univ of Calif Los Angeles CA 90024

ESTRUP, FAIZA FAWAZ, b Joun, Lebanon, Apr 15, 33; US citizen; m 60. BIOPHYSICS, MOLECULAR BIOLOGY. *Educ:* Boston Univ, AB, 53; Yale Univ, MS, 60, PhD(biophys), 61; Brown Univ, MD, 75; Am Bd Internal Med, dipl, 80. *Prof Exp:* Res asst spectros, Huntington Res Labs, Harvard Univ, 53-55; mem tech staff biophys, Bell Tel Labs, Inc, 62-63; fac mem chem, Haverford Col, 64-65, res assoc biol, 65-68; res assoc biol & med sci, Brown Univ, 68-75, resident internal med, RI Hosp, 75-76, resident clin pathol, 76-77, resident internal med, Mem Hosp, 77-78, chief resident internal med, 78, fel rheumatology, Brown Univ Prog, Roger Williams Gen Hosp, 78-80, STAFF RHEUMATOLOGIST, PROG MED, ASSOC HOSPS, BROWN UNIV, 80- *Concurrent Pos:* Res fel, Inst Biophys, Geneva, Switz, 61-62; asst prof biol, RI Jr Col, 69-71; rheumatologist, pvt pract, 80. *Mem:* AAAS; Am Col Physicians; Biophys Soc; Sigma Xi; Am Rheumatism Asn. *Res:* Research on ribosomal proteins using immunochemical techniques; research on host-induced modification of phage deoxyribonucleic acid. *Mailing Add:* 15 Adelphi Ave Providence RI 02906

ESTRUP, PEDER JAN Z, b Copenhagen, Denmark, July 15, 31; m 60. PHYSICAL CHEMISTRY, SOLID STATE PHYSICS. *Educ:* Royal Polytech Inst, Denmark, MSc, 54; Yale Univ, PhD(phys chem), 59. *Prof Exp:* Res assoc nuclear chem, European Ctr Nuclear Res, Switz, 59-61; res scientist phys chem, Bell Tel Labs, NJ, 61-64 & Bartol Res Found, Franklin Inst, 64-67; assoc prof, 67-70, PROF PHYSICS & CHEM, BROWN UNIV, 70- *Mem:* Am Phys Soc; Am Chem Soc; Am Vacuum Soc; Catalysis Soc. *Res:* Physics and chemistry of solid surfaces; low energy electron diffraction; electron spectroscopy; adsorption phenomena. *Mailing Add:* Dept of Physics Brown Univ Providence RI 02912

ETCHELLS, JOHN LINCOLN, bacteriology, deceased

ETESON, DONALD CALVERT, b Worcester, Mass, May 22, 27; m 48; c 2. ELECTRICAL ENGINEERING. *Educ:* Worcester Polytech Inst, BS, 48, MS, 56, PhD(elec eng), 66. *Prof Exp:* Instr elec eng, Worcester Jr Col, 48-56, assoc prof, 56-62; from instr to assoc prof, 62-77, PROF ELEC ENG, WORCESTER POLYTECH INST, 77- *Mem:* Inst Elec & Electronics Engrs. *Res:* Digital transmission networks; hybrid computation; digital computer interfaces; computer interconnections. *Mailing Add:* Dept of Elec Eng Worcester Polytech Inst Worcester MA 01609

ETGEN, GARRET JAY, b Hackensack, NJ, Aug 20, 37; m 60; c 3. MATHEMATICS. *Educ:* Col William & Mary, BS, 59; Univ Wis, MS, 61; Univ NC, PhD(math), 64. *Prof Exp:* Asst chief appl math br, HQ, NASA, 64-67; from asst prof to assoc prof, 67-75, PROF MATH, UNIV HOUSTON, 75-, CHMN DEPT, 78- *Concurrent Pos:* Asst prof lectr, George Washington Univ, 65-67. *Mem:* AAAS; Am Math Soc; Math Asn Am. *Res:* Differential equations; matrix theory. *Mailing Add:* Dept Math Univ Houston Houston TX 77004

ETGEN, WILLIAM M, b Toledo, Ohio, May 7, 29; m 50; c 6. DAIRY SCIENCE, ANIMAL SCIENCE. *Educ:* Ohio State Univ, BS, 51, MSc, 55, PhD(dairy sci), 58. *Prof Exp:* Res assoc dairy sci, Ohio State Univ, 54-55; dairy husbandman, USDA, 55-58; from asst prof to assoc prof dairy sci, Univ RI, 59-64, assoc prof animal sci, 64-68; PROF DAIRY SCI, VA POLYTECH INST & STATE UNIV, 68- *Concurrent Pos:* Chmn, Dept Animal Sci, Univ RI, 67-68. *Mem:* Am Dairy Sci Asn. *Res:* Dairy management and production. *Mailing Add:* Dept Dairy Sci Va Polytech Inst & State Univ Blacksburg VA 24061

ETGES, FRANK JOSEPH, b Chicago, Ill, June 18, 24; m 47; c 5. PARASITOLOGY, MALACOLOGY. *Educ:* Univ Ill, AB, 48, MS, 49; NY Univ, PhD(invert zool), 53. *Prof Exp:* Asst biol, NY Univ, 49-53; asst prof zool, Univ Ark, 53-54; from asst prof to assoc prof, 54-65, dir grad studies, 67-80, PROF ZOOL, UNIV CINCINNATI, 65- *Concurrent Pos:* Interam res fel, 62-63; fel grad sch, Univ Cincinnati, 71; NIH fel, London Sch Hyg & Trop Med, 71-72; WHO fel, Africa, 75. *Honors & Awards:* Distinguished Res Award, Sigma Xi, 66. *Mem:* Am Soc Trop Med & Hyg; Am Soc Parasitol; Soc Protozool; Am Micros Soc. *Res:* Orientation, behavior, growth and reproduction of schistosome vector snails; morphology, life history, taxonomy and physiology of animal parasites. *Mailing Add:* Dept Biol Sci 006 Univ of Cincinnati Cincinnati OH 45221

ETHEREDGE, EDWARD EZEKIEL, b Jacksonville, Fla, May 22, 39; m 61; c 2. SURGERY, TRANSPLANTATION IMMUNOLOGY. *Educ:* Yale Univ, BA, 61, MD, 65; Univ Minn, PhD(surg), 74. *Prof Exp:* Asst resident surg, Univ Minn Hosps, 66-68, fel genetics & cell biol, Univ, 68-69, res fel transplant surg, Hosps, 69-71, chief resident surg, 71-73; staff surgeon, Walter Reed Army Med Ctr, 73-75; asst prof, 75-79, ASSOC PROF SURG, SCH MED, WASHINGTON UNIV, 79- *Mem:* Transplantation Soc; Asn Acad Surg; Am Soc Transplant Surgeons; Soc Univ Surgeons; Asn Immunologists. *Res:* Classes of antibodies against transplantation antigens; leukocyte immunobiology. *Mailing Add:* Dept of Surg Wash Univ Barnes & Wohl Hosps 4960 Audubon Ave St Louis MO 63110

ETHERIDGE, ALBERT LOUIS, b Wilmar, Ark, Aug 9, 40; m 62. ZOOLOGY, DEVELOPMENTAL BIOLOGY. *Educ:* Ark Agr & Mech Col, BS, 64; Univ Miss, MS, 65; Univ Tex, Austin, PhD(zool), 68. *Prof Exp:* Asst prof zool, La State Univ, Baton Rouge, 68-71; assoc prof, 71-77, head, Dept Natural Sci, 78-81, PROF BIOL, UNIV ARK, MONTICELLO, 77-, VCHANCELLOR ACAD AFFAIRS, 81- *Mem:* AAAS; Am Soc Zool; Soc Develop Biol; Sigma Xi. *Res:* Experimental embryology; embryonic induction of the mesonephric kidney in amphibians. *Mailing Add:* Acad Affairs Univ Ark Monticello AR 71655

ETHERIDGE, DAVID ELLIOTT, b Montreal, Que, July 1, 18; m 47; c 4. FOREST PATHOLOGY. *Educ:* Univ NB, BSc, 50; McGill Univ, MSc, 53; Univ London, PhD(plant path) & DIC, 56. *Prof Exp:* Asst forest pathologist, Forest Entom & Path Br, Can Dept of Forestry, NB, 50-52, forest pathologist, Alta, 52-58 & Que, 58-67, res scientist, Pac Forest Res Ctr, Can Dept of Environ, Can Forestry Serv, 67-75; vis scientist, Cent Plantation Crops Res Inst, Kayangulam, Kerala, India & Inst Pertanian, Bogor, Indonesia, 75-76; CONSULTANT, 76- *Concurrent Pos:* Forest pathologist, Food & Agr Orgn, UN, Govt Tanganyika, 63-64; sr res fel, Forest Res Inst, Rotorua, NZ, 66-67; consult trop forest path, UN Develop Prog Forestry Proj, Dominican Republic, 69-70 & Forest Protection, Forestry Dept, Dominica, 78. *Mem:* Can Inst Forestry; Commonwealth Forestry Asn. *Res:* Temperate and tropical forest pest and disease control problems; tropical plantation crop protection; coconut palm; timber identification. *Mailing Add:* 3941 Oakdale Pl Victoria Can

ETHERIDGE, RICHARD EMMETT, b Houston, Tex, Sept 16, 29. HERPETOLOGY, PALEONTOLOGY. *Educ:* Tulane Univ, BS, 51; Univ Mich, MS, 52, PhD(zool), 59. *Prof Exp:* Lectr zool, Univ Southern Calif, 59-61; from asst prof to assoc prof, 61-70, chmn dept, 69-72, PROF ZOOL, SAN DIEGO STATE UNIV, 70- *Concurrent Pos:* NSF fel, 60-61; cur herpet San Diego Natural Hist Mus & res assoc, Los Angeles County Mus, 61-73. *Mem:* AAAS; Am Soc Ichthyologists & Herpetologists; Soc Vert Paleont; Soc Study Evolution. *Res:* Comparative osteology; systematics and evolution of lizards; especially the family Iguanidae; late Cenozoic lizard fossils of North America and the West Indies. *Mailing Add:* Dept of Zool San Diego State Univ San Diego CA 92115

ETHERINGTON, HAROLD, b London, Eng, Jan 7, 00; nat US; m 28; c 1. NUCLEAR ENGINEERING. *Educ:* Univ London, BSc, 21. *Prof Exp:* Supt steel plant, Lena Goldfields, Ltd, 26-30; res engr, A O Smith Corp, 30-32; instr, Milwaukee Voc Sch, 32-36; asst engr, Allis-Chalmers Mfg Co, 37-42, mech engr, eng develop div, 42-46; sect leader, Oak Ridge Nat Lab, 46-47, dir power pile div, 47-48; from dir naval reactor div to dir reactor eng div, Argonne Nat Lab, 48-53; asst to vpres mfg, ACF Industs, Inc, 53-56, vpres, Nuclear Prod, Erco Div, 56-59; mgr atomic energy dept, Allis-Chalmers Mfg Co, 59-61, gen mgr atomic energy div, 61-63; ATOMIC ENERGY CONSULT, 63- *Concurrent Pos:* Ed, Nuclear Eng Handbk; mem adv comt reactor safeguards, US Nuclear Regulatory Comn, 64-74 & 76-80, emer mem, 80- *Honors & Awards:* Atomic Energy Comn Citation, 74. *Mem:* Am Soc Mech Engrs; Nat Acad Eng. *Mailing Add:* 84 Lighthouse Dr Jupiter FL 33458

ETHERINGTON, THEODORE L(AYTON), chemical engineering, see previous edition

ETHERTON, BUD, b Wardner, Idaho, Nov 16, 30; m 57; c 2. BOTANY. *Educ:* Wash State Univ, BS, 56, PhD(bot), 62. *Prof Exp:* Res assoc bot, Wash State Univ, 61-62; NSF fel biophys, Edinburgh, 62-63; lectr plant sci, Vassar Col, 63-64, asst prof biol, 64-67; vis scientist biol & med res, Argonne Nat Lab, 67-68; assoc prof bot, 68-80, PROF BOT, UNIV VT, 80- *Mem:* AAAS; Am Soc Plant Physiol. *Res:* Electrical potentials and ion uptake in plant cells. *Mailing Add:* 42 Elsom Pkwy South Burlington VT 05401

ETHINGTON, ROBERT LOREN, b State Center, Iowa, Feb 13, 32; m 54; c 2. WOOD SCIENCE & TECHNOLOGY, ENGINEERING MECHANICS. *Educ:* Iowa State Univ, BS, 57, MS, 59, PhD(wood technol), 63. *Prof Exp:* Instr, Iowa State Univ, 59-63; technologist, US Forest Prod Lab, 63-64, proj leader fundamental properties, 64-74, asst dir, US Forest Prod Lab, Madison, Wis, 74-76, dir, Forest Prod & Eng Res, 76-79, DIR, PAC NORTHWEST FOREST & RANGE EXP STA, FOREST SERV, USDA, 79- *Honors & Awards:* L J Markwardt Award, Am Soc Testing & Mat, 76. *Mem:* Forest Prod Res Soc; Soc Wood Sci & Technol; Am Soc Testing & Mat. Honors &. *Res:* Fundamental physical and mechanical properties of wood; stress grading; development of allowable stresses for wood; sampling methods for wood property evaluation. *Mailing Add:* Pac Northwest Forest & Range Exp Sta 809 NE Sixth Ave Portland OR 97232

ETHINTON, RAYMOND LINDSAY, b State Center, Iowa, Aug 28, 29; m 55; c 2. GEOLOGY, PALEONTOLOGY. *Educ:* Iowa State Col, BS, 51, MS, 55; Univ Iowa, PhD(geol), 58. *Prof Exp:* Asst prof geol, Ariz State Univ, 58-62; from asst prof to assoc prof, 62-68, PROF GEOL, UNIV MO-COLUMBIA, 68- *Concurrent Pos:* Co-ed, J Paleontol, 69-74. *Mem:* Paleont Soc; Geol Soc Am; Soc Econ Paleontologists & Mineralogists; Am Asn Petrol Geol; Int Palaeont Union. *Res:* Conodonts of North America. *Mailing Add:* Dept of Geol Univ of Mo Columbia MO 65201

ETHRIDGE, FRANK GULDE, b Meridian, Miss, Dec 21, 38; m 64; c 3. SEDIMENTOLOGY. *Educ:* Miss State Univ, BS, 56; La State Univ, MS, 66; Tex A&M Univ, PhD(geol), 70. *Prof Exp:* Prod geologist, Chevron Oil Co, 65-67; asst prof & assoc prof geol, Southern Ill Univ, 70-75; assoc prof, 75-81, PROF EARTH RESOURCES, COLO STATE UNIV, 81- *Concurrent Pos:* Consult petrol & uranium geol; prin investr res, State & Fed agencies & pvt indust. *Mem:* Soc Econ Paleontologists & Mineralogists; Int Asn Sedimentologists; Int Asn Math Geol; Sigma Xi. *Res:* Sedimentology; sandstone petrology; depositional models of Holocene coastal plain, shoreline and shallow marine environments; interpretation of environments of deposition and diagenesis of ancient sedimentary rocks with application to exploration of petroleum, coal, and uranium. *Mailing Add:* Dept of Earth Resources Colo State Univ Ft Collins CO 80523

ETKIN, ASHER, b New York, NY, Mar 12, 43; m 67; c 2. HIGH ENERGY PHYSICS. *Educ:* City Col New York, BS, 64; Yale Univ, MS, 66, MPh, 69, PhD(physics), 71. *Prof Exp:* Res staff physicist physics, Yale Univ, 71-73, res assoc, 73-74, sr res assoc, 74-75; assoc physicist, 76-78, PHYSICIST, BROOKHAVEN NAT LAB, 78- *Concurrent Pos:* asst physicist, City Col New York, 75-76. *Mem:* Am Phys Soc; Inst Elec & Electronics Engrs; AAAS. *Res:* Study of strong interaction physics, particularly multi-particle final states; development of new state of art particle detector systems; study of spin dependence utilizing polarized targets. *Mailing Add:* Bldg 510A Brookhaven Nat Lab Upton NY 11973

ETKIN, BERNARD, b Toronto, Ont, May 17, 18; m 42; c 2. AEROSPACE ENGINEERING. *Educ:* Univ Toronto, BASc, 41, MASc, 47. *Hon Degrees:* DEng, Carleton Univ, Ont, 71. *Prof Exp:* Lectr aerospace eng, 42-48, from asst prof to assoc prof, 48-57, chmn div eng sci, Inst Aerospace Studies, 67-72, dean, Fac Eng, 73-79, PROF AEROSPACE ENG, UNIV TORONTO, 57- *Concurrent Pos:* Indust consult, 40-; mem aerodyn subcomt, Adv Comt Aeronaut Res, Nat Res Coun Can, 44-49, assoc comt aerodyn, 61-, chmn, 62; aerodynamicist, Nat Res Coun Can, 45; mem aerodyn dept, Royal Aircraft Estab, Eng, 58-59. *Honors & Awards:* Centennial Medal, Can Aeronaut & Space Inst, 67, McCurdy Award, 69; Mech & Control Flight Award, Am Inst Aeronaut & Astronaut, 75; Thomas W Eadie Medal, Royal Soc Can, 80; Wright Brothers Lectureship, Am Inst Aeronaut & Astronaut, 80. *Mem:* Fel Am Inst Aeronaut & Astronaut; fel Can Aeronaut & Space Inst; fel Royal Soc Can. *Res:* Subsonic aerodynamics; wing theory; turbulence; dynamics of atmospheric flight; air classification of particles; architectural aerodynamics; university government. *Mailing Add:* Inst for Aerospace Studies Univ of Toronto Toronto ON M5S 1A1 Can

ETLINGER, JOSEPH DAVID, b Albany, NY, Feb 23, 46; m 70; c 3. CELL BIOLOGY, BIOCHEMISTRY. *Educ:* Rensselaer Polytech Inst, BS, 68; Univ Chicago, PhD(biophys), 74. *Prof Exp:* Res assoc physiol, Harvard Med Sch, 74-76; asst prof, 77-80, ASSOC PROF CELL BIOL, STATE UNIV NY, DOWNSTATE MED CTR, 80- *Concurrent Pos:* Muscular Dystrophy Asn fel, 74-76; prin investr, Nat Heart Lung & Blood Inst grant & Muscular Dystrophy Asn grant, 78- *Mem:* Am Physiol Soc; Am Soc Cell Biol; AAAS; Am Heart Asn. *Res:* Mechanisms and physiological control of protein synthesis and degradation in skeletal muscle, cardiac muscle and erythroid cells; muscle hypertrophy and atrophy; myofibrillar assembly; turnover of abnormal proteins. *Mailing Add:* Dept of Anat & Cell Biol Downstate Med Ctr Brooklyn NY 11203

ETNIER, DAVID ALLEN, b St Cloud, Minn, Dec 2, 38; m 64; c 3. ICHTHYOLOGY. *Educ:* Univ Minn, BS, 61, PhD(zool), 66. *Prof Exp:* Asst prof, 66-72, assoc prof, 72-78, PROF ZOOL, UNIV TENN, KNOXVILLE, 78- *Mem:* Am Soc Ichthyologists & Herpetologists; Am Fisheries Soc. *Res:* Taxonomy and ecology of freshwater fishes of eastern United States; biology of aquatic insects, especially Trichoptera taxonomy. *Mailing Add:* Dept of Zool Univ of Tenn Knoxville TN 37916

ETTEL, VICTOR ALEXANDER, b Prague, Czech, Feb 26, 37; Can citizen; m 60; c 2. HYDROMETALLURGY, ELECTROMETALLURGY. *Educ:* Univ Chem Technol, dipl, 60; Prague Univ, PhD(inorg chem), 66. *Prof Exp:* Res engr & scientist inorg chem, Inst Inorg Chem, Czech Acad Sci, 60-68; res chemist electro & sect head hydrometall, J Roy Gordon Res Lab, 68-82, MGR PROCESS TECHNOL, MANITOBA DIV, INCO METALS, 82- *Concurrent Pos:* Fel inorg chem, Univ Toronto, 66-67. *Mem:* Can Inst Metall; Can Inst Chem; Can Soc Chem Eng. *Res:* Hydrometallurgy and electrometallurgy of base metals, mainly copper, nickel and cobalt, and precious metals. *Mailing Add:* Inco Metals Process Res Lab Sheridan Park Mississauga ON L5K 1Z9 Can

ETTELDORF, JAMES N, b Lennox, SDak, Aug 25, 09; m 36; c 2. PEDIATRICS. *Educ:* SDak State Univ, BS, 32; Univ Tenn, MS, 36, MD, 42. *Prof Exp:* Instr med pharmacol, Univ Tenn, 34-40, intern, 42-43; asst resident pediat, Univ Tenn & Washington Univ, 43-45; from assoc prof to prof, 48-70, Goodman prof pediat, 70-76, EMER GOODMAN PROF PEDIAT, CTR HEALTH SCI, COL MED, UNIV TENN, MEMPHIS, 76- *Concurrent Pos:* Mem off exam, Am Bd Pediat, 59-, secy & mem exec comt, 64-69, AMA rep, 64-70, mem written exam comt, 64-70, chmn, 68-70. *Mem:* AAAS; AMA; Soc Pediat Res; Am Pediat Soc; Am Acad Pediat. *Res:* Fluids and electrolytes; renal disease; endocrine and metabolic disorders. *Mailing Add:* Dept of Pediat Univ of Tenn Ctr for Health Sci Memphis TN 38163

ETTENBERG, M(ORRIS), b Canton, Ohio, May 22, 16; m 40; c 1. ELECTRICAL ENGINEERING. *Educ:* City Col New York, BA, 35, MS, 36; NY Univ, PhD(physics), 49; Jewish Theol Sem, BJP, 38. *Prof Exp:* Radar engr, US Navy Yard, NY, 42-45; proj engr, Sperry Gyroscope Co, 45-47 & 49-51, proj engr, 51-54, eng dept head, 54-58; res prof electrophys, Polytech Inst Brooklyn, 58-63; PROF ELEC ENG, CITY COL NEW YORK, 63- *Concurrent Pos:* Fulbright lectr, Israel Inst Technol, 61-62. *Mem:* AAAS; Am Phys Soc; Inst Elec & Electronics Engrs. *Res:* Microwaves; microwave electronic tubes; klystrons; traveling wave tubes. *Mailing Add:* Dept of Elec Eng City Col of New York New York NY 10031

ETTENSOHN, FRANCIS ROBERT, b Cincinnati, Ohio, Feb 6, 47; m 78. PALEONTOLOGY, PALEOECOLOGY. *Educ:* Univ Cincinnnati, BS, 69, MS, 70; Univ Ill, Urbana-Chanpaign, PhD(geol), 75. *Prof Exp:* Combat engr, US Army Corps Engrs, 71; asst prof, 75-81, ASSOC PROF GEOL, UNIV KY, 81- *Concurrent Pos:* Prin investr, US Dept Energy, 76-80. *Mem:* Geol Soc Am; AAAS; Paleont Soc; Int Paleont Asn; Sigma Xi. *Res:* Paleoenvironments and paleoecology of Mississippian carbonates in eastern Kentucky; paleoecology of carboniferous echinoderms; stratigraphy and paleoenvironments of devonian black gas shales of eastern Kentucky. *Mailing Add:* Dept Geol Univ Ky Lexington KY 40506

ETTER, DELORES MARIA, b Denver, Colo, Sept, 25, 47; m 67; c 1. DIGITAL SIGNAL PROCESSING. *Educ:* Wright State Univ, BS, 70, MS, 72; Univ NMex, PhD(elec eng), 79. *Prof Exp:* Fac assoc comput sci, Math Dept, Wright State Univ, 72-73; lectr, 73-78, asst prof, 79-82, ASSOC PROF ELEC ENG, ELEC ENG & COMPUT SCI DEPT, UNIV NMEX, 82- *Concurrent Pos:* Prin investr grants from, Sandia Nat Labs, 79-81, Southwest Resource Ctr, 80-81 & NSF, 81-83. *Mem:* Sigma Xi; Inst Elec & Electronics Engrs. *Res:* Adaptive digital signal processing; algorithms for adaptive time-delay estimation and adaptive recursive filter coefficients. *Mailing Add:* Elec Eng & Comput Eng Dept Univ NMex Albuquerque NM 87131

ETTER, MARGARET C, b Wilmington, Del, Sept 12, 43. SOLID STATE ORGANIC CHEMISTRY. *Educ:* Univ Pa, BA, 65; Univ Del, MS, 71; Univ Minn, PhD(org chem), 74. *Prof Exp:* Chemist, Du Pont Co, 65-67; fel solid state chem, Univ Minn, 74-75; asst prof org chem, Augsburg Col, 75-76; RES CHEMIST, 3M CO, 76- *Concurrent Pos:* Mem, Comt Hazardous Substances in Lab, Nat Res Coun, 81- *Mem:* Am Chem Soc; Am Crystallog Soc. *Res:* Mechanisms of solid state reaction in organic crystals; solid state chemistry and packing patterns of hydrogen bonded organics and dyes; structure property relations in organic materials. *Mailing Add:* Cent Res Dept 201 W 3M Ctr St Paul MN 55101

ETTER, RAYMOND LEWIS, JR, b Sherman, Tex, Aug 10, 31; m 57; c 2. ORGANIC POLYMER CHEMISTRY. *Educ:* Univ Tex, BS, 52, PhD(org chem), 57. *Prof Exp:* Asst org chem, Univ Tex, 52-56; res chemist, 56-62, SR CHEMIST, TEX EASTMAN CO, 62- *Mem:* Am Chem Soc. *Res:* Low molecular weight polymers; heterocyclic nitrogen compounds; polyolefins; synthetic resins; chlorinated polyolefins; paints; high pressure polymerization. *Mailing Add:* Rt 9 Box 178-A Maxey Rd Maxey Rd Longview TX 75601

ETTER, ROBERT MILLER, b Chambersburg, Pa, July 13, 32; m 57; c 3. ORGANIC CHEMISTRY. *Educ:* Gettysburg Col, AB, 54; Pa State Univ, PhD(org chem), 59. *Prof Exp:* Res chemist dyes, Am Cyanamid Co, NJ, 58-62, res chemist explosives, Pa, 62-63; sr res chemist org synthesis, 63-65, res supvr, 65-71, prod res mgr, dir res & develop Europe, 72-78, dir res & develop, Worldwide Indust Prod, 78-80, VPRES RES & DEVELOP, WORLDWIDE INDUST PRODUCTS, S C JOHNSON & SON, INC, 81-, VPRES CORP RES, 81- *Mem:* AAAS; Am Chem Soc; NY Acad Sci. *Res:* Carbenes; reaction mechanisms; dyes; fiber finishes; explosives; insecticides; insect repellents; plant biochemistry; consumer chemical specialties. *Mailing Add:* Corp Res Div S C Johnson & Son Inc 1525 Howe St Racine WI 53403

ETTINGER, ANNA MARIE CONWAY, b Janesville, Wis, Nov 4, 25; m 69. ANATOMY. *Educ:* Univ Wis, BS, 46, MS, 50; Univ Ill, PhD(anat), 67. *Prof Exp:* Teacher, Barrington Sch Syst, Ill, 46-49; teacher, Joliet Sch Syst, 50-55; instr anat, St Louis Univ, 57-63; instr, Univ Ill, 66-67; asst prof, 67-69, assoc prof, 69-76, PROF ANAT, SCH DENT, UNIV DETROIT, 76- CHMN DEPT ANAT, 71- *Concurrent Pos:* Gen res support grants, 67 & 68; univ res grant, 68-69 & 72-; NIH res grant, 69-72. *Mem:* Asn Anat Chmn; Am Asn Immunologists; Am Asn Anat. *Res:* Studies on the ontogeny of immune response in the chick. *Mailing Add:* Dept Anat Sch of Dent Univ Detroit Detroit MI 48207

ETTINGER, HARRY JOSEPH, b New York, NY, July 20, 34; m 58; c 3. INDUSTRIAL HYGIENE. *Educ:* City Col New York, BCE, 56; NY Univ, MCE, 58. *Prof Exp:* Lectr civil eng, City Col New York, 56-58; sanitary engr environ health, NIH, USPHS, 58-61; staff mem indust hyg, 61-67, sect leader aerosol res, 67-71, alt group leader, 71-74, group leader indust hyg, 74-80, PROJ LEADER INDUST HYG STUDIES, LOS ALAMOS NAT LAB, UNIV CALIF, 81- *Concurrent Pos:* Adj prof radiation sci, Sch Pharm, Univ Ark, 69-; consult, Div Reactor Licensing, US AEC, 70-71, Environ Protection Agency, 72-74 & Am Bd Indust Hyg, 79-85; vis mem, Graduate Fac, Texas A&M, 81-; adj fac mem, Div Occup & Environ Health, San Diego State Univ, 81- *Mem:* Am Indust Hyg Asn; Air Pollution Control Asn; Am Acad Indust Hyg; Am Conf Govt Indust Hygienists. *Res:* Properties of fine particles as related to the performance of air cleaning systems and inhalation health hazards; engineering control of toxic material and physical agents in the work environment; evaluation and application of respiratory protection in occupational health. *Mailing Add:* 55 Navajo Los Alamos NM 87544

ETTINGER, MILTON G, b La Crosse, Wis, Aug 3, 30; m 57; c 2. NEUROLOGY. *Educ:* Univ Minn, BA, 51, BS, 52, MD, 54. *Prof Exp:* Intern Internal med, Long Beach Vet Admin Hosp, Calif, 54-55; CHIEF NEUROL, HENNEPIN COUNTY MED CTR, 63-; PROF NEUROL, UNIV MINN, MINNEAPOLIS, 71- *Concurrent Pos:* Fel neurol, Univ Minn & Affil Hosps, 55-58; staff neurologist, Univ Minn, 60- & Hennepin County Gen Hosp, 60-; consult, Kenney Rehab Inst, Minneapolis, 62-68. *Mem:* Am Acad Neurol (asst secy-treas, 73-77; Minn Soc Neurol Sci (past pres); Acad Aphasia; Int Neuropsychol Asn; Pan-Am Neurol Soc. *Res:* Coagulation, lysis and platelet abnormalities in cerebrovascular disease; cerebrovascular disease, including catecholamines and drug therapy; sleep disorders; headache; Huntington's disease. *Mailing Add:* Hennepin Co Med Ctr Dept Neurol 701 Park Ave S Minneapolis MN 55415

ETTRE, LESLIE STEPHEN, b Szombathely, Hungary, Sept 16, 22; US citizen; m 53; c 1. ANALYTICAL CHEMISTRY. *Educ:* Budapest Tech Univ, MS, 45, DSc(anal chem), 69; Am Inst Chem, cert. *Prof Exp:* Process chemist, G Richter Pharmaceut Co, Hungary, 46-49; res assoc, Hungarian Res Inst-Heavy Chem Industs, 49-51, head tech off, 51-53; mgr indust dept, Hungarian Plastics Indust Res Inst, 53-56; chemist, Lurgi Labs, Ger, 57-58; appln chemist, Perkin-Elmer Corp, 58-60, chief appln chemist, 62-68; exec ed, Encycl Indust Chem Anal, John Wiley & Sons, Publ, 68-74; SR STAFF SCIENTIST, PERKIN-ELMER CORP, 72- *Concurrent Pos:* Regional ed, J Chromatographia, 71-77, ed, 78-; res assoc, Dept Eng & Appl Sci, Yale Univ, 77-78; adj prof, Col Natural Sci & Math, Univ Houston, 78-; assoc mem, Comn Nomenclature Anal Chem, Int Union Pure & Appl Chem, 81- *Honors & Awards:* M S Tswett Chromatography Award; Chromatography Mem Medal of the USSR; L S Palmer Award. *Mem:* Am Chem Soc; fel Am Inst

Chem; NY Acad Sci; Am Soc Test & Mat; Brit Chromatography Discussion Group. *Res:* Theory, practice and application of chromatography; analytical instrumentation; scientific editing. *Mailing Add:* 157 Grumman Ave Norwalk CT 06851

ETZEL, HOWARD WESLEY, b Brooklyn, NY, Aug 5, 22; m 44; c 2. SCIENCE ADMINISTRATION, SOLID STATE PHYSICS. *Educ:* Carnegie Inst Technol, BS, 44, MS & DSc(physics), 49. *Prof Exp:* Res physicist, Naval Res Lab, 50-56, head radiation effects sect, 56-62; assoc prog dir physics, Nat Sci Found, Washington, DC, 62-63; prog dir solid state & low temperature physics, 63-71, dep dir, Div Mat Res, 71-79; ASSOC DEAN RES & VIS PROF ELEC ENG, NC STATE UNIV, 79- *Concurrent Pos:* Fulbright res scholar, France, 49-50; mem solid state sci panel, Nat Acad Sci-Nat Res Coun. *Mem:* Fel Am Phys Soc; Sigma Xi; AAAS. *Res:* Electronic and optical properties of solids, lasers. *Mailing Add:* 406 Annandale Dr Cary NC 27511

ETZEL, JAMES EDWARD, b Reading, Pa, Nov 9, 29; m 50; c 5. LIQUID IDUSTRIAL WASTE TREATMENT. *Educ:* Pa State Univ, BSSE, 51; Purdue Univ, MSCE, 55, PhD(sanit eng), 57. *Prof Exp:* Jr engr, Capitol Eng, Inc, 51; construct engr, US Army Corps Engrs, 51-53; serv engr indust wastes, E I du Pont de Nemours & Co, Inc, 57-58; dir res & develop, Environ Eng, R F Weston, Inc, 58-59; asst prof, 59-61, assoc prof, 61-65, PROF ENVIRON ENG, PURDUE UNIV, 65-, CHAIRED PROF, 79- *Concurrent Pos:* Consult, Gen Motors Corp, Monsanto Inc, US Environ Protection Agency, Colgate-Palmolive Corp, Gen Foods Corp & Sime Darby, Malaysia, 61- *Mem:* Water Pollution Control Fedn. *Res:* Treatment of water to remove impurities to make it suitable for industrial use and development of wastewater treatment processes for specific process industries. *Mailing Add:* 710 Cardinal Dr Lafayette IN 47905

ETZLER, DORR HOMER, b Westboro, Wis, Apr 30, 15; m 38; c 2. CHEMISTRY. *Educ:* Univ Wis, BS, 35; Univ Calif, PhD(chem), 38. *Prof Exp:* Res chemist, Standard Oil Co Calif, 38-42 & Calif Res Corp, 45-46, admin asst, 46-50, asst to gen mgr, 50-55, mgr gen serv, 55-63, admin & lab serv, Chevron Res Co, 63-67 & orgn planning, 67-70, mgr res serv dept, 70-78, gen mgr res serv dept, 78-80; RETIRED. *Mem:* Indust Res Inst; Am Chem Soc. *Res:* Photochemistry of acetyl halides; compounded lubricating oils; research administration and management. *Mailing Add:* 130 Miramonte Dr Moraga CA 94556

ETZLER, FRANK M, b Detroit, Mich, March 20, 52; m 74. PHYSICAL CHEMISTRY. *Educ:* Central Mich Univ, BS, 73; Univ Miami, PhD(phys chem), 78. *Prof Exp:* Res specialist, Univ Minn, 78-80; ASST PROF PHYS CHEM, EAST CAROLINA UNIV, 80- *Mem:* Am Chem Soc; NY Acad Sci; Sigma Xi. *Res:* Measurement and structural interpretation of the properties of water near interfaces; relations between structure of interfacial water and biological function. *Mailing Add:* Dept Chem East Carolina Univ Greenville NC 27834

ETZLER, MARILYNN EDITH, b Detroit, Mich, Oct 30, 40. IMMUNOCHEMISTRY, BIOCHEMISTRY. *Educ:* Otterbein Col, BS(biol) & BA(chem), 62; Wash Univ, PhD(biol), 67. *Prof Exp:* Res assoc develop biol, Wash Univ, 66-67; NIH fel immunochem, Dept Microbiol, Col Physicians & Surgeons, Columbia Univ, 67-69; asst prof, 69-75, assoc prof, 75-80, PROF BIOCHEM, UNIV CALIF, DAVIS, 80- *Concurrent Pos:* NIH grants, 71-74 & 75-78. *Mem:* Am Soc Cell Biol; Am Soc Biol Chemists; Soc Complex Carbohydrates. *Res:* Development of cell surface components; structure, specificity and function of plant lectins. *Mailing Add:* Dept of Biochem & Biophys Univ of Calif Davis CA 95616

ETZWEILER, GEORGE ARTHUR, b Lewistown, Pa, Mar 14, 20; m 42; c 3. ELECTRICAL ENGINEERING. *Educ:* Pa State Univ, BS, 49, MS, 50, PhD(elec eng), 64. *Prof Exp:* Develop engr, Ahrendt Instrument Co, Litton Industs, Inc, 50-55, chief develop engr, 55-57; from instr to asst prof elec eng, 57-67, ASSOC PROF ELEC ENG, PA STATE UNIV, 67- *Concurrent Pos:* Lectr, Univ Md, 56-57; consult, Bausch & Lomb, Inc, NY, P R Hoffman Co, Pa & Carborundum Co, Pa; chmn tech comt components & awards comt, Am Automatic Control Coun; mem tech comt components, Int Fedn Automatic Control, US paper selection comt, Fifth Cong. *Mem:* Sr mem Inst Elec & Electronics Engrs; Am Soc Eng Educ. *Res:* Stability and performance of feedback control systems and control system components. *Mailing Add:* Dept of Elec Eng Pa State Univ University Park PA 16802

EU, BYUNG CHAN, b Seoul, Korea, July 7, 35; m 64; c 2. THEORETICAL CHEMISTRY. *Educ:* Seoul Nat Univ, BS, 59; Brown Univ, PhD(chem), 65. *Prof Exp:* Res assoc chem, Brown Univ, 65-66; res fel, Harvard Univ, 66-67; from asst prof to assoc prof, 67-72, PROF CHEM, McGILL UNIV, 75- *Concurrent Pos:* A P Sloan Found fel, 72-74. *Mem:* Am Phys Soc; NY Acad Sci; Korean Chem Soc. *Res:* Theoretical study of molecular collisions of chemically reactive systems and chemical kinetics in gas phase; theory of atomic and molecular scattering; nonequilibrium statistical mechanics; theory of transport processes; nonlinear irreversible thermodynamics. *Mailing Add:* Dept Chem McGill Univ Montreal PQ H3A 2T5 Can

EUBANK, HAROLD PORTER, b Baltimore, Md, Oct 23, 24; m 48; c 3. PHYSICS. *Educ:* Col of William & Mary, BS, 48; Syracuse Univ, MS, 50; Brown Univ, PhD(physics), 53. *Prof Exp:* Asst physics, Syracuse Univ, 48-50; asst physics, Brown Univ, 50-52, res assoc, 52-54, asst prof, 54-59; MEM RES STAFF, PLASMA PHYSICS LAB, PRINCETON UNIV, 59- *Mem:* Am Phys Soc. *Res:* Experimental nuclear and plasma physics. *Mailing Add:* Princeton Univ Plasma Physics Lab PO Box 451 Princeton NJ 08544

EUBANK, PHILIP TOBY, b Greenup, Ill, May 12, 36; m 60. CHEMICAL ENGINEERING. *Educ:* Rose Polytech Inst, BS, 58; Northwestern Univ, PhD(chem eng), 61. *Prof Exp:* From asst prof to assoc prof, 61-68, PROF CHEM ENG, TEX A&M UNIV, 68- *Concurrent Pos:* NSF grant, 73-78. *Mem:* Am Inst Chem Engrs; Am Chem Soc; Am Soc Eng Educ. *Res:* Volumetric and thermodynamic properties of polar fluids and of hydrocarbon fluids. *Mailing Add:* Dept of Chem Eng Tex A&M Univ College Station TX 77843

EUBANK, RANDALL LESTER, b Dallas, Tex, Jan 1, 52. STOCHASTIC PROESSES, APPROXIMATION THEORY. *Educ:* NM State Univ, BS, 74, MS, 75, Tex A&M Univ, MS, 76, PhD(statists), 79. *Prof Exp:* Asst prof, Ariz State Univ, 79-80; ASST PROF STATIST, SOUTHERN METHODIST UNIV, 80- *Mem:* Inst Math Statist; Am Statist Asn; Soc Indust & Appl Math; Sigma Xi. *Res:* Regression analysis and design in the presence of correlated error, splines and stochastic processes; use of quantiles in data analysis; survival data analysis. *Mailing Add:* Dept Statist Southern Methodist Univ Dallas TX 75275

EUBANK, WILLIAM RODERICK, b Cynthiana, Ky, Jan 21, 19; m 45; c 2. PHYSICAL CHEMISTRY. *Educ:* Univ Ky, BS, 40, MS, 41; Johns Hopkins Univ, PhD(phys chem), 47. *Prof Exp:* Asst phys chem, Univ Ky, 40-41; asst ceramic lab, Pa State Univ, 41-42; res phys chemist, Keasbey & Mattison, Pa, 42-43; res assoc, Nat Bur Stand, 44-48; consult, US Naval Ord Test Sta, Calif, 48-51; res chemist, Edgar Bros Co, Ga, 51-52; gen mgr, Ind Hone Mfg Co, Mich, 52-53; sr res chemist, Cent Res Lab, 53-61, proj supvr, Magnetic Prod Lab, 61-64, mgr mat res, Revere-Mincom Div, 64-68, MGR ANAL RES SERV, MAGNETIC PROD DIV, 3M CO, 68- *Mem:* AAAS; Am Chem Soc; Am Ceramic Soc; Electrochem Soc; Electron Micros Soc Am. *Res:* Phase equilibrium; temperature control; microscopy; refractories; enamels; cements; calcination; flame photometry; explosives; electrical ceramics; paint extenders; abrasive honing stones; low-melting glasses; metalloids and intermetallic compounds; ferrites; magnetic metals; electron microscopy; semiconductors; analytical chemistry. *Mailing Add:* Magnetic Prod Div 3M Co 3M Ctr Bldg 236-L127 St Paul MN 55101

EUBANKS, ELIZABETH RUBERTA, b Jacksonville, Fla. MICROBIOLOGY. *Educ:* NTex State Univ, 68, MA, 69; La State Univ, PhD(microbiol), 73. *Prof Exp:* Res assoc microbiol, Univ Tex, Austin, 73-75; asst prof microbiol, Ariz State Univ, 75-79; SR BACTERIOLOGIST, MASS PUB HEALTH BIOLOGIC LABS, 79-; ASST PROF MED, TUFTS UNIV, BOSTON, 79- *Mem:* Am Soc Microbiol; AAAS. *Res:* Pathogenic microbiology; developments of and immune response to subcellular vaccines; pathogenic mechanisms; bacterial flagella; chemistry, location and function of surface components of gram negative bacteria. *Mailing Add:* State Lab Inst 305 South St Jamaica Plain MA 02130

EUBANKS, ISAAC DWAINE, b San Angelo, Tex, Sept 22, 38; m 59; c 3. INORGANIC CHEMISTRY. *Educ:* Univ Tex, BS, 60, PhD(inorg chem), 63. *Prof Exp:* Chemist, Savannah River Lab, E I du Pont de Nemours & Co, Inc, 63-67; asst prof, 67-71, assoc prof, 71-78, PROF CHEM & ASSOC CHMN DEPT, OKLA STATE UNIV, 78- *Mem:* Am Chem Soc; The Chem Soc. *Res:* Coordination chemistry of the lanthanides in nonaqueous solvents; chemical education. *Mailing Add:* Dept of Chem Okla State Univ Stillwater OK 74074

EUBANKS, JULIA FLYNT, b Dublin, Ga, May 17, 24; div; c 3. MEDICAL MICROBIOLOGY. *Educ:* Valdosta State Col, BS, 47; Univ Ga, MS, 66. *Prof Exp:* Asst chief virol lab, Ga Dept Pub Health, 60-67, chief virol lab, 67-69; supvr, 69-77, ASST DIR, DIAG LAB SERV, GA DEPT HUMAN RESOURCES, 77- *Mem:* Am Acad Microbiol; Am Soc Microbiol; Sigma Xi. *Mailing Add:* Lab Sect 47 Trinity Ave SW Atlanta GA 30334

EUBANKS, L(LOYD) STANLEY, b San Antonio, Tex, Sept 24, 31; m 51; c 3. CHEMICAL ENGINEERING. *Educ:* Rice Univ, BA, 52, BS, 53, PhD(chem eng), 57. *Prof Exp:* Res engr, 57-59, sr res engr, 59-61, sr chem engr, 61-64, process specialist, 64-73, fel, 73-80, SR FEL, MONSANTO CO, 80- *Mem:* Am Inst Chem Engrs. *Res:* Phase equilibria. *Mailing Add:* 1143 Sunset Lane Texas City TX 77590

EUBANKS, ROBERT ALONZO, b Chicago, Ill, June 3, 26. THERORETICAL & APPLIED MECHANICS. *Educ:* Ill Inst Technol, BS, 50, MS, 51, PhD, 53. *Prof Exp:* From instr to asst prof mech, Ill Inst Technol, 50-54; sr engr, Bulova Res Lab, NY, 54-55; res engr, Am Mach & Foundry Co, Ill, 55-56; scientist, Borg Warner Res Ctr, 56-60; sr scientist, Armour Res Found, 60-62; mgr vibrations, 62-64; sci adv mech & struct eng, IIT Res Inst, 64-65; George A Miller vis prof, 64-65; PROF CIVIL ENG & THEORET & APPL MECH, UNIV ILL, URBANA, 65- *Concurrent Pos:* Adj prof, Ill Inst Technol, 62-65; consult, Continental Can Co, 68-75 & various govt agencies, 73-; vis distinguished prof civil eng, mech & aerospace eng & math, Univ Del, Newark, 73-74; mem exec comt Nat Consortium for grad degress for minorities in eng, 76- *Mem:* Am Soc Mech; Am Math Soc; Soc Indust & Appl Math; Am Soc Civil Engrs; Acoust Soc Am. *Res:* Mathematical theory of elasticity; rotor stability; elastic wave propagation; protective construction; vibrations and shock; terminal ballistics. *Mailing Add:* 3106 Civil Eng Bldg Univ of Ill Urbana IL 61801

EUBANKS, WILLIAM HUNTER, b Columbus, Miss, Dec 13, 21; m 44; c 3. ENGINEERING GRAPHICS. *Educ:* Miss State Univ, BS, 47, MS, 53. *Prof Exp:* Draftsman, Mobile Dist Corp Eng Design & Construct, Columbus AFB, 41 & 42; from instr to assoc prof, 60-73, PROF ENG GRAPHICS, MISS STATE UNIV, 73- *Mem:* Am Soc Eng Educ; Nat Soc Prof Engrs. *Res:* Interpretation and graphical analysis of research data; use of photography in presenting graphical research data; methods of graphic presentation; graphic analysis; creative projects for freshman engineering students. *Mailing Add:* Dept Eng Graphics Miss State Univ PO Box EG Mississippi State MS 39762

EUBIG, CASIMIR, b Poland, Feb 21, 40; US citizen; m 65; c 2. MEDICAL PHYSICS. *Educ:* Fordham Univ, BS, 62; Univ Ariz, MS, 65, PhD(physics), 70. *Prof Exp:* Instr & res assoc, Dept Physics, Univ Ariz, 70-72, health physicist, Dept Hazards Control, 72-75; asst prof, 75-80, ASSOC PROF RADIOL, MED COL GA, 80- *Mem:* Am Asn Physicists Med; Soc Nuclear Med; Health Physics Soc; Am Inst Ultrasound Med. *Res:* Nuclear medicine; pediatric nuclear cardiology; radiation safety in medical institutions; quality control in radiology imaging equipment. *Mailing Add:* Dept of Radiol Med Med Col of Ga Augusta GA 30902

EUDY, WILLIAM WAYNE, b Oakboro, NC, Sept 1, 39; m 61; c 1. MICROBIOLOGY, BIOCHEMISTRY. *Educ:* Wake Forest Univ, BS, 61, MA, 69; NC State Univ, PhD(microbiol), 69. *Prof Exp:* Sr res microbiologist, Norwich Pharmacal Co, 68-71; sr res microbiologist, 71-76, mgr forest sci, 76-81, ASSOC DIR RES, INT PAPER CO, 81- *Mem:* AAAS; Am Chem Soc; Am Soc Microbiol. *Res:* Developmental biology; enzymology; lignin catabolism. *Mailing Add:* Int Paper Co Box 797 Tuxedo Park NY 10987

EUGERE, EDWARD JOSEPH, b New Orleans, La, May 26, 30; m 54; c 4. PHARMACY, PHARMACOLOGY. *Educ:* Xavier Univ, BS, 51; Wayne State Univ, MS, 53; Univ Conn, PhD(pharmacol), 56. *Prof Exp:* Asst prof pharmacol, Detroit Inst Technol, 56-58; dean sch pharm, 58-70, PROF PHARMACOL, TEX SOUTHERN UNIV, 58- *Concurrent Pos:* Mem pharm rev comt, Pub Adv Group, NIH, 69-72, reviewer consult, Minority Biomed Support Prog & Bur Health Resources Develop; consult, Regional Off Bur Health Resources Develop, USPHS. *Mem:* Am Pharmaceut Asn; Am Asn Cols Pharm; Am Asn Univ Prof; Am Heart Asn. *Res:* Chemotherapy of trichomoniasis; medicinal applications of ion exchange substances; cardiovascular research. *Mailing Add:* Sch of Pharm Tex Southern Univ Houston TX 77004

EUGSTER, A KONRAD, b Langenegg, Austria, Dec 10, 38; US citizen; m 65; c 2. VETERINARY VIROLOGY. *Educ:* Vienna Vet Col, Dr med vet, 63; Colo State Univ, PhD(microbiol), 70; Am Col Vet Microbiol, dipl, 71. *Prof Exp:* Res assoc virol, Southwest Res Ctr, Tex, 64-68; head diag microbiol, 70-80, EXEC DIR, TEX VET MED DIAG LAB, TEX A&M UNIV, 80- *Mem:* Am Vet Med Asn; Am Asn Vet Lab Diagnosticians; Conf Res Workers Animal Dis. *Res:* Improvements of diagnostic techniques in veterinary microbiology and virology; pathogenesis of hitherto unrecognized viruses. *Mailing Add:* Tex Vet Med Diag Lab Drawer 3040 College Station TX 77840

EUGSTER, HANS PETER, b Landquart, Switz, Nov 19, 25; nat; m 53; c 3. GEOCHEMISTRY, SEDIMENTOLOGY. *Educ:* Swiss Fed Inst Technol, Dipl Ing Geol, 48, Dr Sc Nat, 51. *Prof Exp:* Crystallographer, Swiss Inst Study Snow & Avalanches, 48; vis investr, Geophys Lab, Carnegie Inst, 52-53, geochemist, 53-58; assoc prof, 58-60, PROF GEOL, JOHNS HOPKINS UNIV, 60- *Concurrent Pos:* Adj prof, Univ Wyo, 70-; Fairchild scholar, Calif Inst Technol, 73; ed, Contrib Mineral Petrol, 73-; adj prof, Scripps Inst Oceanog, 80- *Honors & Awards:* V M Goldschmidt Medal, Geochem Soc, 76; A L Day Medal, Geol Soc Am, 71. *Mem:* Nat Acad Sci; Geochem Soc; fel Am Geophys Union; fel Mineral Soc Am; Am Acad Arts & Sci. Honors &. *Res:* Petrology, geochemistry and physical chemistry of rockforming minerals; thermodynamics of supercritical fluids and solutions; depositional environments of chemical sediments. *Mailing Add:* Dept of Earth Sci Johns Hopkins Univ Baltimore MD 21218

EUKEL, WARREN W(ENZL), b Plummer, Minn, Mar 4, 21; m 46; c 3. ENGINEERING PHYSICS. *Educ:* Univ Calif, BS, 50. *Prof Exp:* Physicist, Radiation Lab, Univ Calif, 50-53, Chromatic TV, Calif, 53-54 & Appl Radiation Corp, 54-64; mem staff, 64-66, opers mgr, 66-67, V PRES, W M BROBECK & ASSOCS, BERKELEY, 67- *Concurrent Pos:* Mem comt high level dosimetry, Nat Acad Sci; mem adv bd, qm res & develop, Nat Res Coun. *Mem:* AAAS; Inst Elec & Electronics Engrs; Am Nuclear Soc. *Res:* Ion sources and gaseous discharge; electron linear accelerators; peaceful uses of radiation. *Mailing Add:* 1235 Tenth St Berkeley CA 94710

EULER, KENNETH L, b Natrona Heights, Pa, July 25, 37. PHARMACOGNOSY. *Educ:* Univ Pittsburgh, BS, 49, MS, 62; Univ Wash, PhD(pharmacog), 65. *Prof Exp:* Asst prof pharmacog, Univ Md, 65-67; asst prof, 67-68, ASSOC PROF PHARMACOG, UNIV HOUSTON, 68- *Mem:* Am Pharmaceut Asn; Am Acad Pharmaceut Sci; Am Soc Pharmacog; Soc Econ Biol. *Res:* Plant chemistry and biochemistry; isolation and identification of plant constituents having physiological activity and study of their biosynthetic pathways. *Mailing Add:* 3531 Elmridge Houston TX 77025

EURE, HERMAN EDWARD, b Corapeake, NC, Jan 7, 47; m 69; c 1. PARASITOLOGY. *Educ:* Md State Col, BS, 69; Wake Forest Univ, PhD(biol, parasitol), 74. *Prof Exp:* Asst prof, 74-80, ASSOC PROF BIOL, WAKE FOREST UNIV, 80- *Mem:* Am Soc Parasitol; Sigma Xi; Brit Soc Parasitol. *Res:* Parasites of bass and the effects of thermal pollution on their population dynamics. *Mailing Add:* Box 7325 Reynolda Sta Wake Forest Univ Winston-Salem NC 27109

EUSTIS, ROBERT H(ENRY), b Minneapolis, Minn, Apr 18, 20; m 43; c 2. MECHANICAL ENGINEERING. *Educ:* Univ Minn, BMechEng, 42, MS, 44; Mass Inst Technol, ScD(mech eng), 53. *Prof Exp:* Instr mech eng, Univ Minn, 43-44; aeronaut res scientist, Nat Adv Comt Aeronaut, 44-47; from instr to asst prof mech eng, Mass Inst Technol, 48-51; chief engr & asst to pres, Thermal Res & Eng Corp, 51-53; sr mech engr, Stanford Res Inst, 53-56; assoc prof mech eng, 55-62, dir, High Temp Gasodynamics Lab, 61-80, prof mech eng, 61-81, WOODARD PROF, STANFORD UNIV, 81- *Concurrent Pos:* Chmn tech adv coun, Emerson Elec Corp. *Honors & Awards:* High Temp Inst Medal, USSR Sci Acad. *Mem:* Am Soc Mech Engrs; Am Soc Eng Educ; Combustion Inst; fel Am Inst Aeronaut & Astronaut. *Res:* Magnetohydrodynamics; heat transfer; fluid mechanics. *Mailing Add:* Dept Mech Eng Stanford Univ Stanford CA 94305

EUSTIS, WILLIAM HENRY, b Coeur D'Alene, Idaho, Dec 26, 21; m 49; c 1. POLYMER CHEMISTRY. *Educ:* Univ Calif, PhD(chem), 51. *Prof Exp:* Technologist, Shell Oil Co, 51-60; sr engr, Shell Chem Co Div, 60-65; INSTR, YAKIMA VALLEY COL, 65- *Mem:* Am Chem Soc. *Res:* Analytical petroleum; organic reaction mechanisms. *Mailing Add:* Yakima Valley Col Yakima WA 98902

EUWEMA, ROBERT NOEL, theoretical solid state physics, see previous edition

EVALDSON, RUNE L, b Okelbo, Sweden, Nov 21, 18; nat US; m 42; c 5. ENGINEERING MECHANICS. *Educ:* Univ Ill, BS, 41; Stanford Univ, PhD(eng mech), 50. *Prof Exp:* Sr anal engr, Hamilton Standard Propellers, United Aircraft Corp, 41-47; asst dynamics, elasticity, Stanford Univ, 47-50; consult, Booz-Allen & Hamilton, 50-53; assoc prof mech eng, 53-56, assoc dir, Inst Sci & Technol, 58-70, managing dir, Willow Run Labs, 65-67, dir, 67-70, PROF MECH ENG, UNIV MICH, 56- *Res:* Dynamics; elasticity; fatigue of metals; operations research; research administration. *Mailing Add:* Dept of Mech Eng Col of Eng Univ of Mich Ann Arbor MI 48109

EVANEGA, GEORGE R, b Cementon, Pa, Feb 6, 36; m 63; c 2. ORGANIC CHEMISTRY. *Educ:* Lehigh Univ, BS, 57; Yale Univ, MS, 58, PhD(org chem), 60. *Prof Exp:* NIH fel, Univ Freiburg, 60-61; res chemist, Union Carbide Res Inst, NY, 62-69, mgr biomed instrumentation, 69; res chemist, Med Res Labs, Pfizer Inc, 69-70, proj leader diabetes, 70, mgr diag res, 71-73, mgr immunol, Cent Res, 73-75; dir chem res & develop, Boehringer Mannheim Corp, Am, 75-78, head div, Boehringer Mannheim Res Tutzing, WGer, 78-79, vpres, Biodynamics, Indianapolis, 79-81, VPRES NEW PROD DEVELOP, BOEHRINGER MANNHEIM DIAGNOSTICS INC, INDIANAPOLIS & HOUSTON, 81- *Mem:* Am Chem Soc; Royal Soc Chem; Am Asn Clin Chemists; NY Acad Sci; Clin Radioassay Soc. *Res:* Photochemistry; medicinal chemistry; clinical chemistry; immunochemistry; microbiology; instrumentation. *Mailing Add:* Boehringer Mannheim Diagnostics Inc 1901 Hague Rd Indianapolis IN 46250

EVANICH, MYRON JOSEPH, b Edwardsville, Pa, Oct 16, 40; m 66; c 1. PHYSIOLOGY, BIOPHYSICS. *Educ:* Wilkes Col, BA, 63; Univ Tenn, Memphis, PhD(physiol, biophys), 69. *Prof Exp:* Inst physiol & biophys, Med Units, Univ Tenn, Memphis, 69-70; dir, Neuro-respiratory Physiol Lab & asst prof med, Univ Ill, Chicago, 71-77, asst prof physiol, Sch Basic Med Sci & asst prof bio-eng, Grad Col, 74-77; ASSOC PROF PHYSIOL, SCH MED, TULANE UNIV, 77- *Mem:* Am Physiol Soc; Inst Elec & Electronics Engrs; Soc Eng in Med & Biol; Sigma Xi; Am Fedn Clin Res. *Res:* Systems analysis approach for the study of regulation of ventilation; bio-telemetry (radio) in the study of regulation of respiration; statistical analysis of neuronal signals; respiratory muscles, mechanics and neural control. *Mailing Add:* Dept Physiol Tulane Univ Sch Med New Orleans LA 70112

EVANS, ALBERT EDWIN, JR, b Tarrytown, NY, Apr 21, 30; m 56; c 4. NUCLEAR PHYSICS. *Educ:* Yale Univ, BS, 52; Ohio State Univ, MS, 53; Univ Md, PhD(nuclear physics), 65. *Prof Exp:* Engr, Nuclear Div, Martin-Marietta Co, 57-58; sr engr, 58; physicist, Radiation Physics Div, US Naval Ord Lab, 58-67; staff physicist, Nuclear Assay Res Group, 67-75, STAFF PHYSICIST, CRITICAL EXP & DIAG GROUP, LOS ALAMOS NAT LAB, UNIV CALIF, 75- *Mem:* Am Phys Soc; Am Nuclear Soc. *Res:* Neutron and gamma ray spectroscopy of nuclear reactions; low-energy particle accelerators, construction and renovation; measurement of flux and power distributions in nuclear reactors; nondestructive assay of fissionable materials, physics of delayed neutrons; LMFBR fuel-motion diagnostics instrumentation; nuclear reactor critical experiments. *Mailing Add:* Mail Stop 560 Los Alamos Nat Lab Los Alamos NM 87545

EVANS, ALFRED SPRING, b Buffalo, NY, Aug 21, 17; m 50; c 3. EPIDEMIOLOGY, INTERNAL MEDICINE. *Educ:* Univ Mich, AB, 39; MPH, 60; Univ Buffalo, MD, 43; Am Bd Internal Med, dipl, 51. *Hon Degrees:* MA, Yale Univ, 66. *Prof Exp:* Asst prof prev med, Yale Univ, 46-52; assoc prof prev med & med microbiol, Univ Wis, 52-59, prof prev med & chmn dept, 59-66; dir div int epidemiol, 66-77, PROF EPIDEMIOL & DIR WHO SERUM REF BANK, DEPT EPIDEMIOL & PUB HEALTH, SCH MED, YALE UNIV, 66- *Concurrent Pos:* Ed-in-chief, Yale J Biol & Med; vpres, Soc Med Consult to Armed Forces, 79-80, pres, 80-81. *Mem:* AMA; Am Epidemiol Soc (secy-treas, 68-73, pres, 73-74); Soc Epidemiol Res; Int Soc Epidemiol; Infectious Dis Soc Am. *Res:* Infectious mononucleosis; E viruses; respiratory viruses; serological surveys. *Mailing Add:* Yale Univ Sch of Med 333 Cedar St New Haven CT 06520

EVANS, ALLAN ROBERT, energy engineering, policy analysis, see previous edition

EVANS, ALLISON BICKLE, b Erie, Pa, Aug 29, 10. INDUSTRIAL CHEMISTRY. *Educ:* Univ Mich, BSE, 32, MS, 33, AM, 50. *Prof Exp:* Chemist, Firestone Tire & Rubber Co, Akron, 34-36, Erie Lab, Pa, 36-39, US Rubber Reclaiming Co, Buffalo, 39 & Erie Forge Co, Pa, 40-42; chem engr, Bliley Elec Co, 42-45; chemist, Griffin Mfg Co, 45-46; res chemist, Eng Res Inst, Univ Mich, 47-48; anal chemist, QM Food & Container Inst, 50-51; field mfg engr, Assembly & Overhaul Dept, Aircraft Gas Turbine Div, Gen Elec Co, 51-56; tech ed, Redstone Div, Thiokol Chem Corp, 57-62; specif chemist, Lockheed Propulsion Co, 62-66; pub analyst, Gordon M Genge Indust, 66-68; chemist, Prod Dept, Indust Div, Stauffer Chem Co, 68-74 & Kerr McGee Chem Corp, 74-75; RETIRED. *Mem:* Am Chem Soc; Am Soc Metals; Am Inst Chem Eng; Soc Tech Commun. *Res:* Analytical chemistry; elastomers; electrodeposition; manufacturing; jet propulsion; technical editing. *Mailing Add:* 228 N Alvord St Ridgecrest CA 93555

EVANS, ANTHONY GLYN, b Porthcawl, Britain, Dec 4, 42; m 64; c 3. MATERIALS SCIENCE, CERAMICS. *Educ:* Univ London, BSc, 64, PhD(metall), 67. *Prof Exp:* Proj leader ceramics, Atomic Energy Res Estab, NY, 67-71 & Nat Bur Standards, 71-74; group leader, Rockwell Sci Ctr, 74-78; PROF CERAMICS, UNIV CALIF, BERKELEY, 78- *Concurrent Pos:* Consult & mem, Mat Res Coun, 74-; mem, Nat Mat Adv Bd, 76- *Honors & Awards:* Ross Coffin Purdy Award, Am Ceramic Soc, 74. *Mem:* Am Ceramic Soc. *Res:* Mechanical properties of brittle materials, particularly fracture of ceramics under conditions of impact, thermal and mechanical stress; failure production based on non-destructive evaluation. *Mailing Add:* Dept Mat Univ of Calif Berkeley CA 94720

EVANS, ARTHUR T, b Huron, SDak, Nov 26, 19; m 42; c 4. UROLOGY, SURGERY. *Educ:* Miami Univ, AB, 41; Univ Chicago, MD, 44. *Prof Exp:* PROF UROL, MED CTR, UNIV CINCINNATI, 69-, DIR, 61-; DIR, CHRISTIAN R HOLMES HOSP, 69- *Concurrent Pos:* Mem staff, Div Urol, Cincinnati Gen Hosp, 61-; mem staff, Cincinnati Children's Hosp; mem, Residency Rev Comn Urol, 77-; mem coun med educ, Am Urol Asn. *Mem:* AMA; Am Col Surgeons; Am Urol Asn; Soc Genito Urinary Surg; Soc Univ Urologists. *Res:* Translumbar arteriography as presently used in renal angiography and in studying renal circulation. *Mailing Add:* 250 William H Taft Rd Cincinnati OH 45219

EVANS, ARWEL, mathematics, see previous edition

EVANS, AUDREY ELIZABETH, b York, Eng, Mar 6, 25; US citizen. PEDIATRICS, BIOCHEMISTRY. *Educ:* LRCPS(E), 50; Am Bd Pediat, dipl, 57. *Prof Exp:* Resident med & surg, Royal Infirmary, Edinburgh, 51-52; clin fel pediat, Children's Med Ctr, Boston, 53-54, resident tumor ther, 57-58, asst physician, 58-62, assoc med, 62-65; asst prof, Univ Chicago, 65-69; assoc prof, 69-74, PROF PEDIAT, UNIV PA, 74- *Concurrent Pos:* Resident pediat, Johns Hopkins Hosp, 54-56; instr, Harvard Med Sch, 61-65; Fulbright scholar & USPHS spec fel, 63-65. *Mem:* AAAS; Am Acad Pediat; Am Asn Cancer Res; Am Pediat Soc; Royal Soc Med. *Res:* Pediatric hematology and oncology; biochemistry and enzymology of leukemia. *Mailing Add:* Children's Hosp of Philadelphia 34th Civic Center Blvd Philadelphia PA 19104

EVANS, BEN EDWARD, b Wilkes-Barre, Pa, Apr 9, 44. SYNTHETIC ORGANIC CHEMISTRY, ENZYMOLOGY. *Educ:* Kings Col, Pa, BS, 66; Princeton Univ, MA, 69, PhD(org chem), 71. *Prof Exp:* Instr biochem, Univ NC, Chapel Hill, 71-73; sr res chemist, 73-79, RES FEL, MERCK SHARP & DOHME RES LABS, MERCK INC, 78- *Mem:* Am Chem Soc; Sigma Xi; AAAS. *Res:* Organic synthetic methodology; synthesis of pharmacologically active compounds; design and synthesis of enzyme inhibitors; mechanism of enzyme action; peptide synthesis. *Mailing Add:* Med Chem Dept Merck Sharp & Dohme Res Labs West Point PA 19486

EVANS, BERNARD WILLIAM, b London, Eng, July 16, 34; m 62. PETROLOGY. *Educ:* Univ London, BSc, 55; Oxford Univ, DPhil(geol), 59. *Prof Exp:* Asst geol, Glasgow Univ, 58-59; demonstr mineral, Oxford Univ, 59-61; asst res geologist, Univ Calif, Berkeley, 61-66, assoc prof geol, 66-69; chmn dept, 74-79, PROF GEOL, UNIV WASH, 69- *Honors & Awards:* Award, Mineral Soc Am, 70. *Mem:* AAAS; Mineral Soc Am; Am Geophys Union; Geol Soc Am; Brit Geol Soc. *Res:* Petrology and mineralogy of metamorphic and igneous rocks; electron probe microanalysis. *Mailing Add:* Dept of Geol Sci Univ of Wash Seattle WA 98195

EVANS, BILLY JOE, b Macon, Ga, Aug 18, 42; m 63; c 3. SOLID STATE CHEMISTRY, PHYSICS. *Educ:* Morehouse Col, BS, 63; Univ Chicago, PhD(geophys, chem), 68. *Prof Exp:* Nat Res Coun Can fel physics, Univ Man, 68-69; asst prof mineral, 69-73, assoc prof solid state chem, 73-78, PROF INORG/SOLID STATE CHEM, UNIV MICH, ANN ARBOR, 78- *Concurrent Pos:* Asst prof chem, Howard Univ, 69-70; consult, Nat Bur Standards, 70-78; Alfred P Sloan res fel, 72-74; Alexander Von Humboldt fel, 77-78. *Mem:* Am Chem Soc; Am Phys Soc; Am Mineral Soc; Mineral Asn Can; Sigma Xi. *Res:* Mossbauer spectroscopy; x-ray diffraction; crystal growth; magnetism; phase transitions; mixed valence compounds. *Mailing Add:* Dept of Mineral & Geol Univ of Mich Ann Arbor MI 48104

EVANS, BOB OVERTON, b Grand Island, Nebr, Aug 19, 27; m 49; c 4. ELECTRICAL ENGINEERING. *Educ:* Iowa State Univ, BEE, 49. *Prof Exp:* Elec operating engr, Northern Ind Pub Serv Co, Hammond, 49-51; mem staff, 51-62, vpres develop, Data Systs Div, 62-64, pres, Fed Systs Div, 65-69, Systs Develop Div, 70-74 & Systs Commun Div, 75-77, V PRES ENG, PROG & TECHNOL, IBM CORP, 77- *Concurrent Pos:* Mem, Stark Draper Labs, Inc; consult govt agencies; mem, Defense Sci Bd; trustee, Rensselaer Polytech Inst; mem elec eng vis comt, Mass Inst Technol. *Honors & Awards:* Distinguished Pub Serv Award, NASA. *Mem:* Nat Acad Eng; fel Inst Elec & Electronics Engrs; Nat Security Indust Asn; Armed Forces Commun & Electronics Asn; Aerospace Industs Asn. *Mailing Add:* 1000 Westchester Ave White Plains NY 10604

EVANS, BRUCE DOUGLAS, solid state physics, see previous edition

EVANS, BURTON ROBERT, b Harvey, Ill, Sept 26, 29; m 59; c 3. MEDICAL ENTOMOLOGY, VEGETABLE GARDEN INSECTS. *Educ:* Millikin Univ, BA, 51; Univ Md, MEd, 55, PhD(med entom), 58; Tulane Univ, MPH, 65. *Prof Exp:* Sta entomologist, Foreign Quarantine Div, USPHS, 58-67; entomologist, Aedes Aegyptic Eradication Proj, Commun Dis Ctr, 67-69; proj officer, Pesticides Prog, Div Pesticide Community Studies, Environ Protection Agency, 69-73; mem staff pesticide training, 73-78, ASSOC PROF ENTOM, GA COOP EXTEN SERV, UNIV GA, 78- *Mem:* Am Entom Soc; Sigma Xi. *Res:* Transmission of filariae by mosquitoes; evaluation of insecticides for mosquito control; surveys for the presence of various insects of medical importance. *Mailing Add:* Ga Coop Exten Serv Univ Ga Athens GA 30602

EVANS, CHARLES ALBERT, b Minneapolis, Minn, Feb 18, 12; m 39; c 4. MEDICAL MICROBIOLOGY. *Educ:* Univ Minn, BS, 35, MB, 36, MD, 37, PhD(bact), 43. *Prof Exp:* Teaching asst bact, Univ Minn, 37-38; agent dis fur animals & wildlife, Bur Biol Surv, USDA, 38-41; Nat Res Coun fel, Univ Rochester, 41-42; biol res supvr, State Dept Conserv, Minn, 42-43; from asst prof to assoc prof bact, Univ Minn, 42-46; chmn dept microbiol, 46-70, spec asst to pres Univ & dir, Off Spec Student Progs, 68-70, PROF MICROBIOL, UNIV WASH, 46- *Concurrent Pos:* Asst scientist & later assoc scientist, Univ Minn, 38-41; mem microbiol panel, Off Naval Res, 48-51, Microbiol Study Sect, NIH, 51-56 & 57-58 & Nat Adv Cancer Coun, 58-60 & 64-67; mem res adv coun, Am Cancer Soc, 67-70; assoc dir, Fred Hutchinson Cancer Res Ctr, 71-75; mem panel on antiperspirants, Food & Drug Admin, 74-78. *Mem:* Am Soc Microbiol (vpres, Soc Bact, 59, pres, 59-60); Soc Exp Biol & Med; Am Acad Microbiol. *Res:* Microbial flora of normal human skin. *Mailing Add:* Dept of Microbiol Univ of Wash SC-42 Seattle WA 98195

EVANS, CHARLES ANDREW, JR, b Harriman, Tenn, Feb 19, 42; m 78; c 1. ANALYTICAL CHEMISTRY. *Educ:* Cornell Univ, BA, 64, PhD(chem), 68. *Prof Exp:* Anal chemist mass spectros, Ledgemont Lab, Kennecott Copper, 68-70; sr res chemist, Mat Res Lab, Univ Ill, 70-76, prin res chemist, 76-78, assoc prof chem, Dept Chem, 75-78; PRES, CHARLES EVANS & ASSOCS, 78- *Mem:* Am Chem Soc; Am Soc Mass Spectrometry; Microbeam Anal Soc. *Res:* Materials analysis using microanalytical techniques such as secondary ion mass spectrometry; Rutherford backscattering spectrometry and Auger electron spectrometry. *Mailing Add:* Charles Evans & Assocs 1670 S Amphlett Blvd Suite 120 San Mateo CA 94402

EVANS, CHARLES HAWES, b Orange, NJ, Apr 16, 40; m 65; c 1. IMMUNOLOGY, CANCER. *Educ:* Union Col NY, BS, 62; Univ Va, MD & PhD(microbiol, immunol), 69. *Prof Exp:* Intern pediat, Med Ctr, Univ Va, 69-70, resident, 70-71; res assoc, 71-73, sr scientist, 73-76, CHIEF TUMOR BIOL SECT, NAT CANCER INST, NIH, 76- *Concurrent Pos:* Assoc ed, J Nat Cancer Inst, 81- *Mem:* Am Asn Immunologists; Am Asn Cancer Res. *Res:* Immunobiology of carcinogenesis and mammalian cell model systems for the evaluation of carcinogens and study of the phenomenon of carcinogenesis. *Mailing Add:* Rm 2A13 Bldg 37 Nat Cancer Inst NIH Bethesda MD 20205

EVANS, CHARLES P, b New York, NY, May 8, 30; m 57; c 3. ORGANIC CHEMISTRY. *Educ:* Univ Bridgeport, BA, 59. *Prof Exp:* From anal chemist to res chemist, Olin Mathieson Chem Corp, 57-62; res chemist, Escambia Chem Corp, 62-68; vpres res & opers, 68-72, PRES, VITEK RES CORP, STAMFORD, 72- *Mem:* Am Chem Soc; Sigma Xi. *Res:* Suspension and emulsion polymerization reaction. *Mailing Add:* 12 Glenbrook Rd Trumbull CT 06611

EVANS, CLYDE EDSEL, b Arley, Ala, Dec 29, 27; m 51; c 3. SOIL FERTILITY. *Educ:* Abilene Christian Col, BS, 55; Auburn Univ, MS, 57; NC State Univ, PhD(soil sci), 68. *Prof Exp:* ASSOC PROF SOIL SCI, AUBURN UNIV, 57- *Mem:* Am Soc Agron. *Res:* Soil fertility research with phosphorus and potassium, particularly soil testing for fertilizer requirements; fertility requirements for certain vegetable crops. *Mailing Add:* Dept Agron Auburn Univ Auburn AL 36849

EVANS, DANIEL DONALD, b Oak Hill, Ohio, Aug 13, 20; m 46; c 4. HYDROLOGY. *Educ:* Ohio State Univ, BS, 47; Iowa State Univ, MS, 50, PhD(soil physics), 52. *Prof Exp:* Assoc soil physics, Iowa State Univ, 50-52, asst prof, 52-53; from assoc prof to prof soils, Ore State Univ, 53-63; prof agr chem & soils, 63-73, head dept hydrol & water resources, 67-74, PROF HYDROL & WATER RESOURCES, UNIV ARIZ, 63- *Concurrent Pos:* Adv to Kenya Ministry Agr, 60-62. *Mem:* AAAS; fel Soil Sci Soc Am; fel Am Soc Agron; Am Geophys Union; Fel Am Water Resources Asn. *Res:* Soil physics and hydrology. *Mailing Add:* Dept Hydrol & Water Resources Univ Ariz Tucson AZ 85721

EVANS, DAVID ALBERT, b Washington, DC, Jan 11, 41; m 62. ORGANIC CHEMISTRY. *Educ:* Oberlin Col, AB, 63; Calif Inst Technol, PhD(synthetic org chem), 67. *Prof Exp:* Asst prof org chem, Univ Calif, Los Angeles, 67-72, Sloan Found res grant, 72-74; PROF CHEM, CALIF INST TECHNOL, 74- *Concurrent Pos:* Consult, Eli Lilly Co. *Mem:* Am Chem Soc; Royal Soc Chem. *Res:* Synthesis design; chemistry and synthesis of naturally-occurring substances; thermal rearrangements. *Mailing Add:* Calif Inst Technol 1201 E California Blvd Pasadena CA 91125

EVANS, DAVID ARNOLD, b San Mateo, Calif, Sept 24, 38; m 63; c 2. ENTOMOLOGY. *Educ:* Carleton Col, BA, 60; Univ Wis, MS, 62, PhD(entom), 65. *Prof Exp:* Res asst entom, Univ Wis, 60-64, instr, 64-65; asst prof, 65-74, ASSOC PROF BIOL, KALAMAZOO COL, 74- *Concurrent Pos:* Res assoc entom, Univ Ga, 73-74. *Mem:* AAAS; Entom Soc Am. *Res:* Migratory behavior of the corn leaf aphid; taxonomy and bionomics of the velvet ants; chalcidoid reproductive behavior. *Mailing Add:* Dept of Biol Kalamazoo Col Kalamazoo MI 49001

EVANS, DAVID ARTHUR, b Gloucester, Eng, Aug 5, 39; m 62; c 2. STATISTICAL ANALYSIS, MARINE SCIENCES. *Educ:* Cambridge Univ, BA, 60, MA, 64; Oxford Univ, PhD(particle physics), 64. *Prof Exp:* Dept Sci & Indust Res fel particle physics, Nuclear Physics Lab, Oxford Univ, 63-64, dept res asst, 64-65; res assoc, Univ Calif, Riverside, 65-67; asst prof particle physics, State Univ NY Buffalo, 67-74; MARINE SCIENTIST, DEEPSEA VENTURES, INC, 75- *Concurrent Pos:* Res assoc, Rutherford High Energy Lab, Eng, 71. *Res:* Statistical techniques in particle physics data analysis; design of online measuring systems; development of analysis systems for bathymetric and other charting of the deep ocean. *Mailing Add:* Deepsea Ventures Inc Gloucester Point VA 23062

EVANS, DAVID C(ANNON), b Salt Lake City, Utah, Feb 24, 24; m 47; c 7. ELECTRICAL ENGINEERING. *Educ:* Univ Utah, BS, 49, PhD(physics), 53. *Prof Exp:* Dir eng, Comput Div, Bendix Corp, 53-62; prof elec eng & assoc dir comput ctr, Univ Calif, Berkeley, 62-65; prof elec eng & dir comput sci, Univ Utah, 66-76; MEM STAFF, EVANS & SUTHERLAND COMPUT CORP, 76- *Concurrent Pos:* Mem comn on educ, Nat Acad Eng. *Mem:* Nat Acad Eng; Am Phys Soc; Asn Comput Mach; Inst Elec & Electronics Engrs. *Res:* Computing and information processing systems. *Mailing Add:* Evans & Sutherland Comput Corp 580 Arapeen Dr Salt Lake City UT 84108

EVANS, DAVID HUDSON, b Chicago, Ill, June 9, 40; m 62; c 2. COMPARATIVE PHYSIOLOGY, ICHTHYOLOGY. *Educ:* DePauw Univ, BA, 62; Stanford Univ, PhD(biol), 67. *Prof Exp:* NIH fel, Lancaster Univ, 67-69; from asst prof to assoc prof biol & marine sci, 69-78, prof marine sci, 78-80, PROF BIOL & CHMN DEPT, UNIV MIAMI, 78- *Mem:* Am Soc Zoologists; Soc Exp Biol & Med; Am Phys Soc. *Res:* Ion and water balance of fish, crustacea and reptiles. *Mailing Add:* Dept of Biol Univ of Miami Coral Gables FL 33124

EVANS, DAVID HUNDEN, b Philadelphia, Pa, Apr 16, 24; c 2. APPLIED MATHEMATICS. *Educ:* Lehigh Univ, BS, 48; Brown Univ, PhD(appl math), 53. *Prof Exp:* Mem tech staff, Bell Tel Labs, 53-61; sr res mathematician, Res Labs, Gen Motors Corp, 61-68; lectr & res engr, Univ Mich, 68-69; vis prof eng, 69-71, PROF ENG, OAKLAND UNIV, 71- *Mem:* Opers Res Soc Am; Am Soc Qual Control; Am Statist Asn; Sigma Xi; Inst Mgt Sci. *Res:* Statistics applied to tolerancing; operations research; vehicular traffic theory; quality control. *Mailing Add:* Sch of Eng Oakland Univ Rochester MI 48063

EVANS, DAVID L, b Chester, Pa, Apr 28, 46; m 80. PHYSICAL OCEANOGRAPHY, SMALL SCALE DYNAMICS. *Educ:* Univ Pa, BA, 68; Univ RI, PhD(oceanog), 75. *Prof Exp:* Teacher math, Rose Tree Media Sch Dist, 68-71; res assoc, 75-78, ASST PROF PHYS OCEANOG, UNIV RI, 78- *Concurrent Pos:* Consult, SAI, Inc, 80- *Mem:* Am Geophys Union; AAAS. *Res:* Small scale vertical mixing processes and instrumentation development. *Mailing Add:* Grad Sch Oceanog Univ RI Kingston RI 02881

EVANS, DAVID LANE, b Denver, Colo, Sept 16, 54; m 80. ORGANIC CHEMISTRY. *Educ:* Univ Denver, BS, 75; Mass Inst Technol, PhD(org chem), 79. *Prof Exp:* SR RES CHEMIST, MONSANTO CO, 79- *Mem:* Am Chem Soc; Sigma Xi. *Res:* Process improvement in antioxidants for rubber; structure-activity relationships of vulcanization inhibitors; natural products synthesis; plant growth regulators; novel methods of organic synthesis. *Mailing Add:* Monsanto Co 260 Springside Dr Akron OH 44313

EVANS, DAVID STANLEY, b Cardiff, Wales, Jan 28, 16; m 49; c 2. ASTRONOMY. *Educ:* Cambridge Univ, BA, 37, MA & PhD(astron), 41, ScD, 71. *Prof Exp:* Res asst astron, Univ Observ, Oxford Univ, 38-46; second asst, Radcliffe Observ, Pretoria, SAfrica, 46-51; chief asst, Royal Observ, Cape, SAfrica, 51-68; PROF ASTRON, UNIV TEX, AUSTIN, 68- *Concurrent Pos:* NSF sr vis scientist, Univ Tex, 65-66. *Mem:* Fel Royal Astron Soc; fel Royal Soc SAfrica; Astron Soc Southern Africa (past pres & vpres); fel Brit Inst Physics & Phys Soc; Am Astron Soc. *Res:* Observational astronomy; history of astronomy. *Mailing Add:* Dept of Astron Univ of Tex Austin TX 78712

EVANS, DAVID W, b Erie, Pa, Oct 6, 33; m 63; c 2. AGRONOMY, PLANT PHYSIOLOGY. *Educ:* Yale Univ, BS, 55; Cornell Univ, MS, 58, PhD(agron), 62. *Prof Exp:* Res assoc, Univ Mich, Ann Arbor, 61-63; assoc agronomist, 63-80, AGRONOMIST, IRRIGATED AGR RES & EXTEN CTR, WASH STATE UNIV, 80- *Mem:* Am Inst Biol Sci; Am Soc Agron; Crop Sci Soc Am; Am Soc Plant Physiologists. *Res:* Plant root-oxygen relationships; plant-water relationships; forage crop production and management; grass seed production and physiology; alfalfa physiology and forage quality; alfalfa-stem nematode relationships. *Mailing Add:* Irrigated Agr Res & Exten Ctr Wash State Univ Prosser WA 99350

EVANS, DENNIS CHARLES, b Upland, Calif, Feb 16, 38; m 61; c 4. INSTRUMENTATION, CLASSICAL OPTICS. *Educ:* Calif Inst Technol, BS, 60. *Prof Exp:* Mem sci staff geophys, Douglas Aircraft Co, 61-63; mem sci staff astron, 63-71, sect head rockets, 71-74, instrument mgr astron, 74-78, SYSTS ENGR COSMOL, GODDARD SPACE FLIGHT CTR, 79- *Res:* Satellite instrumentation, especially optics; stellar and planetary observations sounding rocket instrumentation-optics; photometry-spectrophotometry; UV-VIS-IR; photography; cosmology; systems management and engineering. *Mailing Add:* Goddard Space Flight Ctr Greenbelt MD 20771

EVANS, DENNIS HYDE, b Grinnell, Iowa, Mar 28, 39; m 58; c 3. ANALYTICAL CHEMISTRY, ELECTROCHEMISTRY. *Educ:* Ottawa Univ, BS, 60; Harvard Univ, AM, 61, PhD(chem), 64. *Prof Exp:* Instr chem, Harvard Univ, 64-66; from asst prof to assoc prof, 66-75, PROF CHEM, UNIV WIS-MADISON, 75- *Mem:* Am Chem Soc. *Res:* Characterization and analytical application of electrode reactions; organic electrochemistry. *Mailing Add:* Dept of Chem Univ of Wis 1101 University Ave Madison WI 53706

EVANS, DONALD B, b Cleveland, Ohio, Oct 11, 33. METALLURGICAL ENGINEERING. *Educ:* Mass Inst Technol, BS, 55; Univ Mich, MS, 59, PhD(metall eng), 63. *Prof Exp:* Develop engr, Mallinckrodt Chem Works, 58; sr engr, Martin Marietta Corp, 63-69; STAFF ENGR, TRW SYSTS GROUP, 69- *Mem:* Am Inst Petrol Engrs; Am Soc Metals. *Res:* New thermoelectric power generation materials and devices; thermodynamics of chemical reactions involved in steel making. *Mailing Add:* 1906 Firmona Ave Redondo Beach CA 90278

EVANS, DONALD LEE, b Clinton, Mo, May 22, 43; m 63; c 3. TUMOR IMMUNOLOGY, VIRAL ONCOLOGY. *Educ:* Univ Mo, Kansas City, BS, 65, MS, 67; Univ Ark, Fayetteville, PhD(microbiol & immunol), 71. *Prof Exp:* fel viral immunol, M D Anderson Hosp & Tumor Inst Univ Tex Syst Cancer Ctr, 71-72, asst prof, 72-73; asst prof immunol, Sch Med, Tex Tech Univ, 73-75; assoc prof immunol Bowman Gray Sch Med, Wake Forest Univ, 75-82; ASSOC PROF, COL VET MED, UNIV GA, 82- *Concurrent Pos:* Prin investr, NIH grant, 76-80 & Am Cancer Soc grant, 79-82; comt mem, Rosalie B Hite Fel, M D Anderson Hosp & Tumor Inst Univ Tex Syst Cancer Ctr, 81- *Mem:* Sigma Xi; Am Soc Microbiol; Reticuloendothelial Soc. *Res:* Characterization of the mechanisms of lymphoid cell and natural killer cell regulation by tumor associated fetal antigens. *Mailing Add:* Col Vet Med Univ Ga Athens GA 30602

EVANS, DONOVAN LEE, b Verona, Ohio, Mar 14, 39; m 60; c 3. MECHANICAL ENGINEERING. *Educ:* Univ Cincinnati, BSME, 62; Northwestern Univ, PhD(mech eng), 67. *Prof Exp:* Res asst mech eng, Northwestern Univ, 65-66; from asst prof to assoc prof, 66-75, PROF MECH ENG, ARIZ STATE UNIV, 75- *Mem:* Am Soc Mech Engrs; Int Solar Energy Soc. *Res:* Thermosciences; high temperature gas dynamics; radiation from gasses; solar energy systems; building heating and cooling. *Mailing Add:* Dept of Mech Eng Ariz State Univ Tempe AZ 85281

EVANS, DORIS L, crystallography, physics, see previous edition

EVANS, DOUGLAS FENNELL, physical chemistry, biophysical chemistry, see previous edition

EVANS, E GRAHAM, JR, US citizen. MATHEMATICS. *Educ:* Dartmouth Col, AB, 64; Univ Chicago, MS, 65, PhD(math), 69. *Prof Exp:* Asst prof math, Univ Calif, Los Angeles, 69-70; instr, Mass Inst Technol, 70-72; From asst prof to assoc prof math, 72-81, PROF MATH, UNIV ILL, URBANA, 81- *Res:* Commutative ring theory; homological algebra; algebraic geometry. *Mailing Add:* Dept Math Univ Ill 1409 W Green St Urbana IL 61801

EVANS, EDWARD WILLIAM, b Frackville, Pa, Sept 1, 32; m 54; c 4. MATHEMATICS. *Educ:* Kutztown State Col, BS, 54; Temple Univ, MEd, 58; Univ Mich, MA, 61, PhD(math, math educ), 64. *Prof Exp:* Teacher high sch, Pa, 55-61; NSF fel, Univ Mich, 61-63, univ & teaching fels, 64; PROF MATH, KUTZTOWN STATE COL, 64-, CHMN DEPT, 65- *Concurrent Pos:* Nat Defense Educ Act vis lectr high schs, 65-; consult high schs math progs, 64- *Mem:* Math Asn Am; Am Math Soc. *Res:* Teaching and learning of mathematics; abstract algebra; foundations of geometry. *Mailing Add:* 3225 Stoudt-Ferry Rd Riverview Park Reading PA 19605

EVANS, EDWIN VICTOR, b Toronto, Ont, Mar 30, 14; m 40; c 2. NUTRITION. *Educ:* Univ Western Ont, BA, 36, MA, 37. *Prof Exp:* From asst prof to assoc prof animal nutrit, Ont Agr Col, 41-48; biochem dir, W R Drynan Nutrit Lab, Hamilton, Ont, 48-50; assoc prof nutrit, Ont Agr Col, 51-68; prof & head dept biochem, nutrit & food sci, Univ Ghana, 68-71; ASSOC PROF NUTRIT, COL BIOL SCI, UNIV GUELPH, 71- *Concurrent Pos:* Assoc prof & actg head dept biochem, nutrit & food sci, Univ Ghana, 65-66. *Mem:* AAAS; Animal Nutrit Res Coun; Am Soc Animal Sci; Can Physiol Soc; Nutrit Soc Can (secy, 60-65). *Res:* Chemical and biological vitamin assays and investigations animal and human nutrition. *Mailing Add:* Dept of Nutrit Univ of Guelph Guelph Can

EVANS, ERNEST C(OLSTON), b New York, NY, July 19, 20; m 42; c 3. ENGINEERING PHYSICS. *Educ:* Univ Tenn, BS, 53, MS, 57. *Prof Exp:* Develop engr, 46-54, sect head barrier testing, 54-56, dept head phys measurements, 56-60, separations systs & biomed eng, 60-67, supt separations syst div, 67-76, DIR, SEPARATION SYSTS DIV, UNION CARBIDE CORP, 76- *Mem:* Fel Instrument Soc Am; Sigma Xi; NY Acad Sci; Nat Soc Prof Engrs. *Res:* Biomedical engineering; sterile containment; centrifuges; isotope separation systems; mass spectrometry; gas flow measurement; analytical instruments; pilot plant design; plant design criteria; manufacturing; plant operation; quality assurance. *Mailing Add:* Union Carbide Corp PO Box P MS 257 Oak Ridge TN 37830

EVANS, ERNEST EDWARD, JR, b Parkersburg, WVa, Dec 14, 22; m 47. MICROBIOLOGY, IMMUNOLOGY. *Educ:* Ohio Univ, AB, 45; Ohio State Univ, MS, 47; Univ Southern Calif, PhD(microbiol), 50. *Prof Exp:* Asst prof bact, Univ Mich, 50-55; assoc prof, Sch Med & Dent, 55-61, chmn dept, 61-70, prof, 61-74, EMER PROF MICROBIOL, SCH MED & DENT, UNIV ALA, BIRMINGHAM, 74- *Concurrent Pos:* Rackham Fund fel, Univ Mich, 51-52; vis investr, Lerner Marine Lab, 66-72; vis res biologist, Univ Calif, Santa Barbara, 70; sr res microbiologist, Mote Marine Lab, Sarasota, Fla, 70-74. *Mem:* Am Soc Microbiol; Am Asn Immunologists; Soc Exp Biol & Med; fel AAAS; Am Asn Univ Prof. *Res:* Antigenic structure of pathogenic fungi; evolution of immunity. *Mailing Add:* PO Box 28355 San Diego CA 92128

EVANS, ERSEL ARTHUR, b Trenton, Nebr, July 17, 22; m 45; c 2. NUCLEAR ENGINEERING, METALLURGY. *Educ:* Reed Col, BA, 45; Ore State Univ, PhD(chem), 47. *Prof Exp:* Sr engr nuclear fuel develop, Gen Elec Co, Richland, Wash, 51-55, mgr ceramic fuels, 56-64, mgr Pu fuels develop, Gen Elec Co, Vallecitos, Calif, 64-67; mgr fuels & mat dept, Battelle Mem Inst, 67-70; mgr mat technol dept, 70-71, assoc dir, Hanford Eng Develop Lab, 72-76, mgr technol dept, 73-76, VPRES, WESTINGHOUSE HANFORD CO, 72-, TECH DIR HANFORD ENG DEVELOP LAB, WESTINGHOUSE ELEC CORP, 76- *Concurrent Pos:* Res fel, Res Corp, 49; DuPont Corp fel, 50-51. *Honors & Awards:* Spec Merit Award, Am Nuclear Soc, 64; Order of Merit, Westinghouse Elec Corp, 75. *Mem:* Nat Acad Eng; fel Am Inst Chem Engrs; fel Am Ceramic Soc; fel Am Soc Metals; fel Am Nuclear Soc. *Res:* High temperature ceramic and metallurgical research, development and engineering involving a variety of nuclear reactors, isotopic heat sources, volcanology. *Mailing Add:* 1850 Stevens Dr Apt 232 Richland WA 99352

EVANS, ESSI H, b Bad-Schwalbach, WGer, Jan 12, 50; US citizen; m 74. ANIMAL NUTRITION. *Educ:* Univ Md, BS, 72; Univ Guelph, MSc, 74, PhD(animal sci), 76. *Prof Exp:* Res & teaching aasst animal sci, Univ Guelph, 72-76; PROJ LEADER NUTRIT, CAN PACKERS INC, 76- *Concurrent Pos:* Nat Res Coun Can indust fel, 76-77. *Mem:* Am Soc Animal Sci; Am Dairy Sci Asn. *Res:* Ruminant nutrition; rumen function modelling; non ruminant herbivor nutrition. *Mailing Add:* Res Ctr 2211 St Clair Ave W Toronto ON M6N 1K4 Can

EVANS, EVAN CYFEILIOG, III, b San Francisco, Calif, Nov 19, 22; m 45; c 3. BIOPHYSICS. *Educ:* Univ Calif, Berkeley, AB, 48, PhD(biophys), 63. *Prof Exp:* Head, Weapon Capabilities Br, US Naval Radiol Defense Lab, 64-66 & Weapon Effects Br, 66-69; DIR MARINE ENVIRON MGT OFF, NAVAL OCEAN SYSTS CTR, HAWAII LAB, 69- *Concurrent Pos:* Naval Radiol Defense Lab fel, 61; lectr, Univ Calif, Berkeley, 64-65; affil grad fac, Univ Hawaii, 71- *Mem:* Nature Conservancy. *Res:* Absorption and translocation of radionuclides in higher plants; effects of ionizing radiation on plants; atomic physics; micromeritics; radioecology of Pacific Ocean basin; underwater acoustics; bioacoustics of marine mammals; environmental survey of harbors and estuaries. *Mailing Add:* 44-702 Nanamoana Pl Kaneohe HI 96744

EVANS, EVAN FRANKLIN, b Kenesaw, Nebr, Mar 17, 18; m 44; c 5. POLYMER CHEMISTRY, COMPUTER SCIENCE. *Educ:* Univ Nebr, BA, 39, MA, 40; Ohio State Univ, PhD(chem), 43. *Prof Exp:* Res chemist, Hercules Powder Co, 44-50; res chemist, 51-52, res supvr, 52-59, res mgr, 59-71, RES ASSOC, E I DU PONT DE NEMOURS & CO, INC, 71- *Mem:*

AAAS; Am Chem Soc. *Res:* Synthesis acyclic sugar derivatives; fundamental and applied research on cellulose and cellulose derivatives; polymers; synthetic fibers; computer system analysis and programming; textiles. *Mailing Add:* 1702 Cambridge Dr Kinston NC 28501

EVANS, FOSTER, b Salt Lake City, Utah, Jan 16, 15; m 78; c 1. THEORETICAL PHYSICS. *Educ:* Brigham Young Univ, BS, 36; Univ Chicago, PhD(physics), 41. *Prof Exp:* Asst physics, Brigham Young Univ, 35-36; instr optics, Northern Ill Univ Col Optom, 40; actg instr physics, Univ Wis, 41; from instr to asst prof, Univ Colo, 41-46; STAFF MEM, LOS ALAMOS NAT LAB, 46- *Concurrent Pos:* Res fel, Radiation Lab, Univ Calif, 42. *Mem:* AAAS; Am Phys Soc; Am Asn Physics Teachers. *Res:* Cosmic rays; hydrodynamics; nuclear physics; transport theory in plasmas. *Mailing Add:* Los Alamos Nat Lab Box 1663 MS 625 Los Alamos NM 87545

EVANS, FRANCIS COPE, b Germantown, Pa, Dec 2, 14; m 42; c 4. ECOLOGY. *Educ:* Haverford Col, BS, 36; Oxford Univ, PhD(animal ecol), 40. *Prof Exp:* Asst, Hooper Found, Univ Calif, 39-41, jr zoologist, Exp Sta & Col Agr, 42-43; from instr to asst prof biol, Haverford Col, 43-58, actg dean, 45; from asst prof to assoc prof, 48-59, PROF ZOOL, UNIV MICH, ANN ARBOR, 59- *Concurrent Pos:* Mem Oxford Univ expeds, Faeroe Islands, 37 & Iceland, 39; lectr, Bryn Mawr Col, 48; asst biologist, Lab Vert Biol, Univ Mich, Ann Arbor, 48-52; ed, Ecol Monogr, 56-62; dir, E S George Reserve, 59-81; Guggenheim fel, 62. *Mem:* Fel AAAS; Am Soc Mammalogists; Ecol Soc Am; Brit Ecol Soc. *Res:* Ecology of natural communities; dynamics of vertebrate populations; patterns of spatial distribution; animal epidemiology. *Mailing Add:* Dept of Zool Univ of Mich Ann Arbor MI 48104

EVANS, FRANCIS EUGENE, b Olney, Ill, June 18, 28; m 50; c 4. ORGANIC CHEMISTRY. *Educ:* DePauw Univ, AB, 50; Mich State Univ, PhD(org chem), 55. *Prof Exp:* Res chemist, Nat Aniline Div, 55-65, sr scientist, Indust Chem Div, 65-70, TECH SUPVR, SPECIALTY CHEM DIV, ALLIED CHEM CORP, 70- *Mem:* Am Chem Soc. *Res:* Organometallics; surfactants; anhydrides; Friedel-Crafts reactions; catalytic chemistry. *Mailing Add:* 4768 Woodside Ave Hamburg NY 14075

EVANS, FRANCIS GAYNOR, b LeMars, Iowa, Dec 7, 07; m 38. ANATOMY, BIOMECHANICS. *Educ:* Coe Col, BA, 31; Columbia Univ, MA, 32, PhD(zool), 39. *Prof Exp:* Instr biol, City Col New York, 35-36; lectr zool, Columbia Univ, 36; instr, Univ NH, 38-41; instr, Duke Univ, 41-43; asst prof human gross anat, Sch Med, Univ Md, 43-45; from asst prof to prof, Col Med, Wayne State Univ, 45-59; prof, 59-77, EMER PROF ANAT, UNIV MICH, ANN ARBOR, 77- *Concurrent Pos:* Fulbright res scholar, Italy, 56-57; vis prof, Gothenburg Univ, 62-63 & Kyoto Prefectural Univ Med, 68. *Honors & Awards:* Morrison Prize, NY Acad Sci, 38. *Mem:* Fel AAAS; Am Asn Anat; Am Physiol Soc; Am Asn Phys Anthrop; Am Soc Biomech. *Res:* Comparative osteology; biomechanics of the human skeleton; stress and strain in bones; mechanical properties and structure of bone. *Mailing Add:* Dept Anat 5805 Med Sci Bldg II Univ of Mich Ann Arbor MI 48109

EVANS, FRANKLIN JAMES, JR, b Hazelton, Pa, June 1, 21; m 47; c 2. ORGANIC CHEMISTRY. *Educ:* Lafayette Col, BS, 42; Pa State Col, MS, 49; Ohio State Univ, PhD(chem), 52. *Prof Exp:* Engr prod explosives, E I du Pont de Nemours & Co, 42-45, engr rayon res, 45-47, from res chemist to sr res chemist, 53-66, res assoc, Textile Fibers, 66-77; CONSULT, 78- *Mem:* Am Chem Soc; Am Inst Chem Eng. *Res:* Textile fibers; organo silicones; steric hindrance. *Mailing Add:* 406 Garland Rd Northwood Wilmington DE 19803

EVANS, FREDERICK EARL, b Springfield, Mass, Nov 11, 48; m 78. BIOCHEMISTRY, PHYSICAL CHEMISTRY. *Educ:* Univ Mass, Amherst, BS, 70; State Univ NY, Albany, PhD(chem), 74. *Prof Exp:* Fel biochem, Univ Calif, San Diego, 75-78; SR RES CHEMIST, NAT CTR TOXICOL RES, 78- *Mem:* Am Asn Cancer Res; Am Chem Soc. *Res:* Nuclear magnetic resonance spectroscopy; chemical carcinogenesis; nucleotide and oligonucleotide conformation; phosphorus-31 nuclear magnetic resonance studies of cells and tissues; structure elucidation. *Mailing Add:* Chem Div/HFT-154 Nat Ctr for Toxicol Res Jefferson AR 72079

EVANS, FREDERICK READ, b Salt Lake City, Utah, Sept 9, 13; m 36; c 4. PROTOZOOLOGY. *Educ:* Univ Utah, BA, 34, MA, 36; Stanford Univ, PhD(protozool), 41. *Prof Exp:* Instr biol, Stanford Univ, 40-45; from asst prof to assoc prof, 45-60, PROF BIOL, UNIV UTAH, 60- *Mem:* Am Inst Biol Sci; fel Am Micros Soc; fel Soc Protozoologists. *Res:* Nutrition of free-living protozoa; cystment in protozoa; protozoan populations; nuclear reorganization in the ciliates; uptake by protozoa of radioactive substances; parasitic protozoa; morphogenesis of ciliates. *Mailing Add:* Dept of Biol Univ of Utah Salt Lake City UT 84112

EVANS, G(EORGE) HARLOWE, b Dallas, Tex, Dec 12, 03; m 27; c 2. PHYSICAL CHEMISTRY. *Educ:* Univ Mich, BS, 25, MS, 26, PhD(chem), 35. *Prof Exp:* Res chemist, Newport Co, Carrollville, Wis, 26-28; prof math & physics, John Fletcher Col, 28-32; prof chem, Taylor Univ, 33-41, Huntingdon Col, 41-45 & Ill Wesleyan Univ, 45-46; prof, 46-72, EMER PROF CHEM, ILL STATE UNIV, 72- *Concurrent Pos:* Vis prof, Southern Ill Univ, 52. *Mem:* AAAS; Am Chem Soc; Nat Sci Teachers Asn. *Res:* Anthraquinone dyes; dielectric constants; viscosity of viscous oils; electrochromatography of metal ions. *Mailing Add:* 1609 N Fell Ave Bloomington IL 61701

EVANS, GARY WILLIAM, b Greybull, Wyo, Jan 5, 40; m 60; c 2. BIOCHEMISTRY, NUTRITION. *Educ:* Eastern Mont State Col, BS, 62; Univ NDak, PhD(biochem), 70. *Prof Exp:* Res chemist, Agr Res Serv, Beltsville, Md, 71, RES CHEMIST, HUMAN NUTRIT LAB, SCI & EDUC ADMIN-AGR RES, USDA, GRAND FORKS, 71-; RES INSTR BIOCHEM, UNIV NDAK, 71- *Mem:* Am Inst Nutrit; Soc Exp Biol & Med; Am Physiol Soc. *Res:* Absorption and metabolism of trace elements. *Mailing Add:* Sci & Educ Admin-Agr Res USDA PO Box D Univ Sta Grand Forks ND 58201

EVANS, GEOFFREY, b Mountain Ash, Wales, Jan 25, 35; m 59; c 3. CARDIOVASCULAR SURGERY. *Educ:* Univ London, MB & BS, 58; FRCS, 62, 78. *Prof Exp:* House surgeon, St Mary's Hosp, London, 58; house physician, Paddington Gen Hosp, 58-59; casualty surgeon, St Mary's Hosp, London, 59, tutor anat & physiol, 59-60; sr house officer, Royal Nat Orthop Hosp, 60; surg registr, Southlands Hosp, Sussex, 61-62; lectr surg, St Mary's Hosp, London, 62-66, sr registr, 64-67; ASSOC PROF SURG, MCMASTER UNIV, 68- *Concurrent Pos:* Can Heart Found fel path, McMaster Univ, 67-69; consult, Hamilton Civic, St Joseph's, Chedoke & Joseph Brant Hosps, 69; mem, Am Heart Found. *Mem:* Asn Acad Surg; Am Heart Asn; Soc Univ Surg. *Res:* Importance of platelet interaction with surfaces in determining the duration of arterial prosthetic replacements and with formed complexes such as antigen antibody complexes in the etiology of disseminated intravascular thrombosis. *Mailing Add:* McMaster Univ Hamilton ON L8S 4L8 Can

EVANS, GEORGE EDWARD, b Great Falls, Mont, Aug 31, 32; m 55; c 2. ORNAMENTAL HORTICULTURE. *Educ:* Mont State Univ, BS, 57; Mich State Univ, MS, 58, PhD(ornamental hort), 69. *Prof Exp:* From instr to assoc prof, 62-75, PROF HORT, MONT STATE UNIV, 75- *Mem:* Am Hort Soc; Int Plant Propagators Soc. *Res:* Graft compatibility studies in intergeneric grafts of members of the rose family and in the genus Juniperus with major emphasis on anatomical aspects; ornamental plant hardiness and adaptability; turfgrass investigations. *Mailing Add:* Dept of Plant & Soil Sci Mont State Univ Bozeman MT 59717

EVANS, GEORGE LEONARD, b Wilkes-Barre, Pa, Aug 3, 31; m 58; c 3. MICROBIOLOGY. *Educ:* King's Col, Pa, BS, 54; Fordham Univ, MS, 57; Temple Univ, PhD(microbiol), 62. *Prof Exp:* Sr scientist, Warner Lambert Res Inst, 62-64 & Univ Labs, 64-65; sr scientist, Hoffman-La Roche, 65-69; dir diag res, Schering Corp, 69-75; DIR MICROBIOL, BBL MICROBIOL SYSTS, 75- *Mem:* Am Soc Microbiol; Am Asn Clin Chem. *Res:* Diagnostic aids; medical microbiology; immunology; clinical chemistry. *Mailing Add:* BBL Microbiol Systs PO Box 243 Cockeysville MD 21030

EVANS, GEORGE WILLIAM, b Chicago, Ill, May 21, 26; m 53; c 5. ANIMAL SCIENCE. *Educ:* Univ Wis-Madison, BA, 55. *Prof Exp:* Lab technician, Res Dept, Oscar Mayer & Co, 47-51, proj engr, 51-58, proj leader, 58-61, res technologist, 61-67, res analyst, 67-73; operator biotron, Grad Sch, 73-74, RES SPECIALIST, DEPT AGR ENG, COL AGR & LIFE SCI, UNIV WIS-MADISON, 74- *Mem:* AAAS; Am Sci Affil. *Res:* Edible rendering; evaluation of cattle, swine; sensory evaluation of meats; stability and sanitation of meat products; food protein sources; irradiation; fermentation of animal and plant tissues and wastes. *Mailing Add:* 5507 Monona Pass Monona WI 53716

EVANS, GLENN THOMAS, b Elizabeth, NJ, July 31, 46; m 69; c 1. CHEMICAL PHYSICS. *Educ:* Seton Hall Univ, BS, 68; Brown Univ, PhD(chem), 73. *Prof Exp:* Fel, Phys Chem Labs, Oxford Univ, 73-74; fel, Sterling Chem Labs, Yale Univ, 74-77; ASST PROF CHEM, ORE STATE UNIV, 77- *Res:* Theory of chemically induced dynamic electron and nuclear spin polarization, CIDEP and CIDNP; magnetic resonance in liquids and theories of the liquid state. *Mailing Add:* Dept of Chem Ore State Univ Corvallis OR 97331

EVANS, GORDON GOODWIN, organic chemistry, deceased

EVANS, HAROLD J, b Woodburn, Ky, Feb 19, 21; m 46; c 2. PLANT NUTRITION, PLANT BIOCHEMISTRY. *Educ:* Univ Ky, BS, 46, MS, 48; Rutgers Univ, PhD(soil chem, plant physiol), 50. *Prof Exp:* Asst prof bot, NC State Univ, 50-51; fel, Johns Hopkins Univ, 51-52; from assoc prof to prof bot, NC State Univ, 51-61; PROF PLANT PHYSIOL, ORE STATE UNIV, 61-, DIR LAB NITROGEN FIXATION, 78- *Concurrent Pos:* Consult, NSF, 64; Rockefeller Found vis prof, Univ Sussex, 69. *Honors & Awards:* Hoblitzelle Nat Award, 65. *Mem:* Nat Acad Sci; Am Soc Plant Physiologists (pres-elect, 70, pres, 71); Am Soc Biol Chemists; Brit Biochem Soc. *Res:* Biochemical role of cations; mechanism of nitrogen fixation. *Mailing Add:* Lab for Nitrogen Fixation Ore State Univ Corvallis OR 97331

EVANS, HARRISON SILAS, b Monroe, Iowa, Aug 4, 11; m 34; c 2. MEDICINE, PSYCHIATRY. *Educ:* Col Med Evangelists, MD, 36; Am Bd Psychiat & Neurol, dipl, 46. *Prof Exp:* Resident psychiat, Harding Hosp, Worthington, Ohio, 36-39, staff psychiatrist, 39-42, co-dir, 46-62; dean sch med, 75-77, vpres med affairs, 77-80, PROF PSYCHIAT & CHMN DEPT, SCH MED, LOMA LINDA UNIV, 62- *Concurrent Pos:* Clin assoc prof, Ohio State Univ, 46-62, asst prof, Sch Social Admin, 58-62. *Mem:* Life fel Am Psychiat Asn; Am Acad Neurol. *Res:* Medical student education in psychiatry and psychotherapy; community mental health. *Mailing Add:* Sch of Med Loma Linda Univ Loma Linda CA 92350

EVANS, HARRY D(EAN), b Arcola, Mo, July 10, 15; m 41; c 1. CHEMICAL ENGINEERING. *Educ:* Univ Ill, BS, 37; Calif Inst Technol, MS, 38. *Prof Exp:* Jr res engr, Shell Develop Co, 38-42, engr, 46-53, develop supvr, 53, engr, Shell Lab, Amsterdam, 53-54, sr technologist, NY, 55-56, develop supvr oil processing, 56-65, dept head, Licensing & Design Eng Dept, 65-68, dept head process eng, Chem Dept, 68-77, dir process eng, 72-75, mgr process eng, Chem Dept, 75-76; RETIRED. *Mem:* Am Inst Chem Engrs. *Res:* Thermodynamic properties of hydrocarbons; high pressure phase equilibria; mass transfer; fluid flow; petroleum process and equipment design and development; chemical process design. *Mailing Add:* 12706 Rock Meadow Houston TX 77024

EVANS, HELEN HARRINGTON, b Cleveland, Ohio, May 11, 24; m 66; c 1. RADIATION BIOLOGY. *Educ:* Purdue Univ, BS, 46; Western Reserve Univ, PhD(biochem), 53. *Prof Exp:* Sr instr biochem, 56-58, from asst prof to assoc prof, 58-75, PROF BIOCHEM & RADIOL, CASE WESTERN RESERVE UNIV, 76- *Concurrent Pos:* Vis scientist, Scripps Clin & Res Found, Calif, 65-66, McCardle Lab, Univ Wis, 73-74 & Radiation Study Sect, NIH, 73-77. *Mem:* Tissue Cult Asn; Radiation Res Soc; Am Soc Biol

Chemists; Am Soc Microbiol. *Res:* Effect of ionizing radiation on DNA; relationship of mutogenesis, carcinogenesis and DNA repair; control of macromolecular synthesis and the mitotic cycle; DNA Replication and repair. *Mailing Add:* Div of Radiation Biol Case Western Reserve Univ Cleveland OH 44106

EVANS, HERBERT JOHN, Franklin, Pa, Jan 22, 37; m 65; c 2. BIOCHEMISTRY OF HEMOSTASIS. *Educ:* Pa State Univ, BS, 63; Case Western Reserve Univ, PhD(biochem), 69. *Prof Exp:* NIH fel biochem, Duke Univ Med Ctr, 69-72; NIH staff fel biochem, Nat Inst Dent Res, 72-74; ASST PROF BIOCHEM, MED COL VA, VA COMMONWEALTH UNIV, 74- *Mem:* AAAS; Sigma Xi; NY Acad Sci. *Res:* Effects of snake venoms on hemostasis, including anticoagulant effects, fibrinolytic effects, antiplatelet effects and hemorrhagic effects of cobra venoms. *Mailing Add:* Dept Biochem Med Col Va Box 614 MCV Sta Richmond VA 23298

EVANS, HIRAM JOHN, b Granville, NY, May 13, 16; m 44; c 4. EMBRYOLOGY. *Educ:* Hamilton Col, BA, 37; Williams Col, MA, 39; Harvard Univ, AM, 41, PhD(biol), 42. *Prof Exp:* Asst, Williams Col, 37-39; res assoc zool, Swarthmore Col, 46; from asst prof to assoc prof, Syracuse Univ, 47-64; prof biol, New Col, 64-65; prof biol & dean, Curry Col, 65-79, vpres res & planning, 73-79; RETIRED. *Concurrent Pos:* Vchmn dept zool, Syracuse Univ, 47-54 & 59-64; secy bd trustees, Biol Abstracts, 50-65. *Mem:* Am Soc Zool; Soc Develop Biol. *Res:* Development and innervation of the chick ear; analysis of microquantities of respiratory gases; adrenal steroids and embryonic development. *Mailing Add:* Pawlet VT 05761

EVANS, HOWARD EDWARD, b New York, NY, Sept 22, 22; m 49; c 2. COMPARATIVE ANATOMY. *Educ:* Cornell Univ, BS, 44, PhD(zool), 50. *Prof Exp:* Asst herpetol, Mus Natural Hist, 38-40; technician zool, Cornell Univ, 40-42, asst, 46-50, from asst prof to assoc prof anat, NY State Vet Col, 50-60, secy vet col, 60-72, PROF ANAT, NY STATE VET COL, CORNELL UNIV, 60- *Concurrent Pos:* NSF fel & vis prof, Univ Calif, 57; vis prof, Phipps Inst, Med Sch, Univ Pa, 64; vis prof, Marine Inst, Univ Ga, 73-74; lectr, Shoals Marine Lab, Maine, 73-75; co-ed & chief reviewer, Avian Anat Nomenclature, 74-76; consult, NIH, 75; vis prof, Univ Hawaii, 79 & Vet Col, Univ Pretoria, 81. *Mem:* Hon mem Am Vet Med Asn; Am Asn Anat; Am Soc Zool; Am Asn Vet Anat; Am Soc Mammal. *Res:* Tooth succession in vertebrates; cyclopia in sheep; fetal skeletal development in dogs. *Mailing Add:* Dept of Anat NY State Vet Col Cornell Univ Ithaca NY 14853

EVANS, HOWARD ENSIGN, b East Hartford, Conn, Feb 23, 19; m 54; c 3. ENTOMOLOGY. *Educ:* Univ Conn, BA, 40; Cornell Univ, MS, 41, PhD(entom), 49. *Hon Degrees:* MA, Harvard Univ, 69. *Prof Exp:* Asst entom, Cornell Univ, 47-49; asst prof, Kans State Col, 49-52; from asst prof to assoc prof insect taxon, Cornell Univ, 52-60; assoc cur, Mus Comp Zool, Harvard Univ, 60-64, cur insects, 64-69, Alexander Agassiz prof zool, 69-73; PROF ENTOM, COLO STATE UNIV, 73- *Concurrent Pos:* Guggenheim fel, Nat Univ Mex, 59 & Commonwealth Sci & Indust Res Orgn, Canberra, Australia, 69. *Honors & Awards:* Daniel Giraud Elliot Medal, Nat Acad Sci, 76. *Mem:* Nat Acad Sci; Soc Study Evolution; Animal Behav Soc. *Res:* Taxonomy of Pompilidae and Bethylidae; comparative ethology of solitary wasps. *Mailing Add:* 304 Off Shore Rd Ft Collins CO 80524

EVANS, HOWARD TASKER, JR, b Ancon, CZ, Sept 9, 19; m 42, 66; c 2. MINERALOGY, INORGANIC CHEMISTRY. *Educ:* Mass Inst Technol, SB, 42, PhD(inorg chem), 48. *Prof Exp:* Mem res staff, Div Indust Coop, Mass Inst Technol, 43-44 & 47-49, instr sect graphics, 45-48; res physicist, Philips Labs, Inc, 49-52; PHYSICIST, US GEOL SURV, 52- *Concurrent Pos:* Guggenheim Found vis res scientist, Royal Inst Technol, Sweden, 60-61. *Mem:* Mineral Soc Am; Am Crystallog Asn (secy, 50-51, vpres, 63, pres, 64); Am Chem Soc. *Res:* Crystal chemistry; x-ray crystallography of inorganic compounds and minerals; x-ray diffraction and crystal structure determination. *Mailing Add:* US Geol Surv Nat Ctr 959 Reston VA 22092

EVANS, HUGH E, b New York, NY, July 6, 34; m 60; c 2. PEDIATRICS, INFECTIOUS DISEASE. *Educ:* Columbia Univ, BA, 54; State Univ NY Downstate Med Ctr, MD, 58; Am Bd Pediat, dipl, 63. *Prof Exp:* Intern pediat, Johns Hopkins Hosp, 58-59, asst resident, 59-60; clin assoc infectious dis, NIH, 60-62; from sr asst resident to chief resident pediat, 62-63; pvt pract, Ohio, 63-65; res assoc, Mt Sinai Hosp, 65-66; from asst prof to assoc prof clin pediat, Columbia Univ, 66-73; PROF PEDIAT, STATE UNIV NY DOWNSTATE MED CTR, BROOKLYN, 73-; DIR, DEPT PEDIAT, JEWISH HOSP & MED CTR BROOKLYN, 73- *Concurrent Pos:* Asst attend pediatrician, Harlem Hosp, NY, 66-69, attend pediatrician, 69-70, vis pediatrician, 70-73, assoc dir pediat, 66-73, consult pediatrician, 73-; assoc prof pediat, Columbia Univ, 73; vis physician, Dept Pediat, Kings County Hosp Ctr, Brooklyn, 73-; consult, St Johns Episcopal Hosp, Brooklyn, Cath Med Ctr, Brooklyn & Health Ins Prog, New York, 73-; mem, Hosp Respiratory Care Consult Team Serv Prog, Am Thoracic Soc; mem, Comt Fac, Downstate Med Ctr, State Univ New York, 81-83; mem comt, Foreign Med Grads, Health & Hosp Corp; grant reviewer, Birth Defect Found, March of Dimes, 81. *Mem:* Am Pediat Soc; NY Acad Sci; Soc Pediat Res; Soc Exp Biol & Med; Am Lung Asn. *Res:* Alpha 1-antitrypsin levels in Respiratory Distress Syndrome; ethnic influence on alpha-1-antitrypsin phenotypes; effect of various drugs on chemotaxis; infection in the neonatal period; bacterial flora of newborns; enzyme inhibitor levels in the Respiratory Distress Syndrome; clinical and laboratory aspects of new respiratory viruses. *Mailing Add:* Dept Pediat Jewish Hosp & Med Ctr 555 Prospect Pl Brooklyn NY 11238

EVANS, HUGH LLOYD, b Brownsville, Pa, Mar 7, 41; m 68; c 1. PSYCHOPHARMACOLOGY, TOXICOLOGY. *Educ:* Rutgers Univ, BA, 63; Temple Univ, MA, 65; Univ Pittsburgh, PhD(psychobiol), 69. *Prof Exp:* NIMH fel toxicol, Univ Rochester, 70, instr radiation biol, 71-73, asst prof radiation biol & environ health sci, 73-77; ASSOC PROF ENVIRON MED, NY UNIV, 77- *Concurrent Pos:* mem, Health Effects Res Rev Panel, US Environ Protection Agency. *Mem:* Am Soc Pharmacol & Exp Therapeut; Soc Neurosci; Am Psychol Asn; Soc Toxicol. *Res:* Behavioral effects of drugs and toxins; brain-behavior relationships. *Mailing Add:* Dept of Environ Med 550 First Ave New York NY 10016

EVANS, J B, b Deniliquin, Australia, July 14, 26; m 55; c 2. MINERAL ENGINEERING. *Educ:* Univ Melbourne, BMinE, 51, BS, 58. *Prof Exp:* Laborer, N Broken Hill Ltd, Australia, 52-53, jr engr, 53-54; jr engr, Howe Sound Mining Co, Can, 54-55; jr engr, Can Explor Ltd, Placer Develop Ltd, 55-56, field engr, 56-57, eval engr, 57-61, chief engr, Craigmont Mines Ltd, 61-62; gen mgr, Molybdenum Corp Am, 62-63, vpres, 63-64; managing dir, Mineral Engrs Proprietary Ltd, 64-69; PROF MINERAL ENG & HEAD DEPT, UNIV BC, 69- *Concurrent Pos:* Managing dir, Austiminex Proprietary Ltd, 64-69; vis prof, Univ Ibadan, 70; mem, Nat Adv Comt Mining & Metall Res, Can, 71-; councillor, BC & Yukon Chamber Mines, 71- *Mem:* Australian Inst Mining & Metall; Can Inst Mining & Metall. *Res:* Mine property evaluation; mine effluent discharges. *Mailing Add:* Dept of Mineral Eng Univ of BC Vancouver Can

EVANS, JAMES BOWEN, b Algonquin, Ill, June 24, 30. RADIOCHEMISTRY. *Educ:* Northwestern Univ, BS, 52; Univ Wis, MS, 54, PhD(chem), 58. *Prof Exp:* Asst prof chem, Univ Colo, 57-64; consult scientist, 64-67; assoc prof chem, Colo Women's Col, 67-81; SR STANDARDS ENGR, ROCKWELL INT, 81- *Mem:* Am Chem Soc. *Res:* Radioisotope applications; radiological physics; instrumentation. *Mailing Add:* Rockwell Int PO Box 464 Golden CO 80401

EVANS, JAMES BRAINERD, b Gainesville, NY, Jan 25, 21; m 45; c 3. BACTERIOLOGY. *Educ:* Houghton Col, BS, 41; Cornell Univ, PhD(bact), 48. *Prof Exp:* Asst prof bact, Cornell Univ, 48; bacteriologist, Am Meat Inst Found, 48-57, chief div bact, 57-59; PROF MICROBIOL, NC STATE UNIV, 60-, HEAD DEPT, 65- *Concurrent Pos:* Res assoc, Univ Chicago, 54-59. *Mem:* Am Acad Microbiol; Am Soc Microbiol; Brit Soc Gen Microbiol. *Res:* Physiology and taxonomy of staphylococci, micrococci and lactic bacteria. *Mailing Add:* Dept of Microbiol NC State Univ Raleigh NC 27650

EVANS, JAMES ERIC LLOYD, b Miniota, Man, May 25, 14; m 40; c 2. EXPLORATION GEOLOGY. *Educ:* Univ Man, BSc, 36; Queens Univ, Ont, MA, 42; Columbia Univ, PhD, 44. *Prof Exp:* Res geologist, Falconbridge Nickel Mines, Ltd, 42-45; field geologist, Frobisher, Ltd, 45-50; mgr, Amco Explor, Inc, 50-54; field mgr, Tech Mines Consult, Ltd, 54-56; chief geologist, Rio Tinto Can Explor, Ltd, 56-70; dir explor, Denison Mines, LTD, 70-79; CONSULT GEOL, 80- *Concurrent Pos:* Adj prof, Univ Toronto, 80- *Honors & Awards:* Can Centennial Medal. *Mem:* Geol Soc Am; Soc Econ Geol; Geol Asn Can (secy, 63-65, pres, 67-68); Can Inst Mining & Metall. *Res:* Petrography and petrology of the mine; identification and metallurgy of various mine, mill and smelter products; mineral exploration in Canada, United States, Chile, Brazil, Costa Rica, Algeria, Italy, Greece, Jordan, Australia, New Zealand and the Philippines. *Mailing Add:* 1375 Stavebank Rd Mississauga ON L5G 2V4 Can

EVANS, JAMES ORNETTE, b Roanoke, Tex, July 27, 20; m 59; c 1. AGRICULTURAL ENGINEERING, SOIL SCIENCE. *Educ:* Univ Wis, BS, 47, MS, 52. *Prof Exp:* Land classification specialist, Bur Reclamation, US Dept Interior, 48-53; conservationist, Div Lands & Soil, Ohio Dept Natural Resources, 53-56 & 57-64; soil scientist, Kuljian Corp Philadelphia, opers in Iraq, 56-57; proj soil scientist, HEW, 64-67; res soil scientist, Cincinnati Water Res Lab, Fed Water Pollution Control Admin, US Dept Interior, 67-68; RES HYDROLOGIST, DIV FOREST ENVIRON RES, FOREST SERV, USDA, 68- *Mem:* Am Soc Agron; Soil Conserv Soc Am; Int Soc Soil Sci; Am Geophys Union. *Res:* Soil and water relationships-infiltration, hydraulic conductivity, drainage; irrigation, salinity; oxidation and assimilation of organic and inorganic sludges and effluents; soil fertility and conditioning; erosion, sedimentation and pollution abatement; water yields; recycling wastes; energy from biomass; reclamation of disturbed lands; assessment of atmospheric deposition on forest watersheds. *Mailing Add:* Forest Serv US Dept of Agr Washington DC 20013

EVANS, JAMES SPURGEON, b Big Sandy, Tenn, Aug 19, 31; m 56; c 2. ANATOMY. *Educ:* Univ Tenn, BS, 58; La State Univ, MS, 60; Univ Ky, PhD(reproductive physiol), 64. *Prof Exp:* NIH fel anat, Med Sch, Univ Ky, 64-65; instr, 65-69, ASST PROF ANAT, UNIV TENN CTR HEALTH SCI, 69- *Mem:* AAAS. *Res:* Neuroendocrinology; general endocrinology and reproductive physiology. *Mailing Add:* Dept of Anat Univ of Tenn Ctr for Health Sci Memphis TN 38163

EVANS, JAMES STUART, b Bridgton, Maine, Jan 16, 41. EDUCATIONAL COMPUTING, INORGANIC CHEMISTRY. *Educ:* Bates Col, BS, 62; Princeton Univ, MA, 64, PhD(chem), 66. *Prof Exp:* Res assoc chem, Princeton Univ, 66; asst prof, 66-74, chmn dept, 68-71, ASSOC PROF CHEM, LAWRENCE UNIV, 75-, DIR COMPUT SERV, 79- *Concurrent Pos:* Vis asst prof, Univ Ore, 72-73; sr vis, Univ Oxford, Eng, 78-79. *Mem:* AAAS; Am Chem Soc; Am Phys Soc; NY Acad Sci. *Res:* Computer applications in chemistry, including simulation programs and computer-controlled instrumentation; coordination compounds, especially sulfato complexes; inorganic biochemistry. *Mailing Add:* Dept of Chem Lawrence Univ Appleton WI 54912

EVANS, JAMES WARREN, b Edna, Tex, Oct 31, 38; m 59; c 1. ANIMAL PHYSIOLOGY. *Educ:* Colo State Univ, BS, 64; Univ Calif, Davis, PhD(physiol), 68. *Prof Exp:* Asst prof & asst physiologist, 68-74, assoc prof & assoc physiologist, 74-78, PROF ANIMAL SCI & ANIMAL PHYSIOLOGIST, EXTEN SERV, UNIV CALIF, DAVIS, 78- *Mem:* Equine Nutrit & Physiol Soc (vpres, 75-77, pres, 77-); Am Soc Animal Sci; Am Physiol Soc; Endocrine Soc. *Res:* Effects of gravity on metabolism; physiology of reproduction in the mare; equine nutrition. *Mailing Add:* Dept of Animal Sci Univ of Calif Davis CA 95616

EVANS, JAMES WILLIAM, b Chilhowee, Mo, Sept 21, 08; m 30; c 1. AGRICULTURAL BIOCHEMISTRY. *Educ:* Cent Mo State Teachers Col, BS, 28; Univ Minn, PhD(agr biochem), 40. *Prof Exp:* Spec analyst, Union Starch & Refining Co, 30-32, res chemist, 32-37; asst biochem, Univ Minn,

38-39, instr, 39-40; res chemist, Union Starch & Refining Co, 40-43; from res chemist to sect leader, Gen Mills, Inc, Minn, 43-50; dir res, Am Maize Prod Co, 50-59, vpres res & develop, 59-64, pres & chief exec officer, 64-75; RES & DEVELOP CONSULT, 75- Concurrent Pos: Mem bd & treas, Central Mo State Univ Found, Inc, 79- Mem: Am Chem Soc; Am Asn Cereal Chem; Am Asn Textile Chem & Colorists; Inst Food Tech. Res: Corn and wheat starches; corn syrups and sugars; caramel coloring; moisture methods for syrups and sugars; composition of starch hydrolysates; development of packaged foods as soups, cake, pie crust and biscuit mixes, breakfast cerals and instant puddings. Mailing Add: Rte 2 Windsor MO 65360

EVANS, JAMES WILLIAM, b Dobcross, Eng, Aug 22, 43; US citizen; div; c 1. EXTRACTIVE METALLURGY, CHEMICAL ENGINEERING. Educ: Univ London, BS, 64; State Univ NY, Buffalo, PhD(chem eng), 70. Prof Exp: Tech adv prog, Int Comput Ltd, 64-65; chemist, Cyanamid Can Ltd, 65-67; chem engr, Ethyl Corp, 70-72; asst prof, 72-76, ASSOC PROF EXTRACTIVE METALL, UNIV CALIF, BERKELEY, 80. Concurrent Pos: Consult, San Louis Mining Co, 74-; Summer Chem Co, 75, Razor Assocs, 76 & 77, Repub Steel Corp, 78 & Dept Energy. Honors & Awards: Extractive Metall Sci Award, Am Inst Mining Metall & Petrol Engrs, 73. Mem: Am Inst Mining, Metall & Petrol Engrs; Iron & Steel Inst Japan; Electrochem Soc. Res: Fluid flow; heat transport; mass transport and chemical reaction kinetics in metallurgical process; fluidized bed electrodes; electrochemistry of metals production and refining, diffusion of gases in porous solids. Mailing Add: Dept Mat Sci & Mineral Eng Univ of Calif Berkeley CA 94720

EVANS, JERRY LYNN, b Portsmouth, Va, Dec 11, 42; m 69; c 4. NUCLEAR PHYSICS, NUCLEAR ENGINEERING. Educ: Southern Missionary Col, BS, 65; Auburn Univ, MS, 68, PhD(physics), 72. Prof Exp: Physicist, Los Alamos Sci Lab, 72-74; NUCLEAR PHYSICIST, US NAVAL WEAPONS EVAL FACIL, 77- Mem: Sigma Xi. Res: Calculation of transport of nuclear radiation; feasibility studies on projects of interest to US Navy. Mailing Add: Naval Weapons Eval Facil code 70 Kirtland AFB Albuquerque NM 87117

EVANS, JOHN C, b Oklahoma City, Okla, Jan 21, 38; m 59; c 3. ASTROPHYSICS, STELLAR ATMOSPHERES. Educ: Univ Okla, BS, 60; Rensselaer Polytech Inst, MS, 62; Univ Mich, MS, 64, PhD(astron), 66. Prof Exp: From asst prof to assoc prof physics, Kans State Univ, 66-76; ASSOC PROF PHYSICS & ASSOC DEAN GRAD SCH, GEORGE MASON UNIV, 76-, ASST DIR, GEORGE MASON INST, 80- Concurrent Pos: Vis prof, Univ Western Ont, 72. Mem: Nat Coun Univ Res Admin; Am Astron Soc; Astron Soc of the Pac; Sigma Xi. Res: Stellar structure, specifically stellar atmospheres, thermal and dynamic structures of stellar atmospheres, line formation, chemical abundances, stellar and solar magnetic fields. Mailing Add: Dept Physics George Mason Univ Fairfax VA 22030

EVANS, JOHN CHARLES, JR, b Jamaica, NY, Dec 19, 44; m 65. RADIOCHEMISTRY. Educ: Fla State Univ, BS, 66; Univ Calif, San Diego, PhD(chem), 71. Prof Exp: Res assoc chem, Brookhaven Nat Lab, 71-73, assoc chemist, 73-76, chemist, Dept Chem, 76-77; SR RES SCIENTIST, DEPT PHYS SCI, PAC NORTHWEST DIV, BATTELLE MEM INST, 77- Res: Cosmic ray interactions in matter; environmental analytical chemistry; high sensitivity nuclear counting techniques; solar neutrino detection. Mailing Add: 106 W Hillview Dr Richland WA 99352

EVANS, JOHN EDWARD, b Sisseton, SDak, July 15, 25; m 50; c 3. BACTERIOLOGY. Educ: Luther Col, Iowa, BA, 49; Univ SDak, MA, 51; Univ London, PhD(bact), 58. Prof Exp: Asst, Univ Wis, 51-52 & Rheumatic Fever Res Inst, Northwestern Univ, 52-54; vis asst prof, 58-59, from asst prof to assoc prof, 59-68, PROF MICROBIOL, UNIV HOUSTON, 68- Mem: AAAS; Genetics Soc Am; Biophys Soc; Am Soc Microbiol; Soc Indust Microbiol. Res: Regulation of growth and cell division in microorganisms; DNA technology. Mailing Add: Dept of Biol Univ of Houston Houston TX 77004

EVANS, JOHN ELLIS, b Oak Hill, Ohio, Oct 2, 14; m 48. PHYSICS. Educ: Ohio State Univ, BSc & BA, 36, MA, 37; Rice Inst, PhD(physics), 47. Prof Exp: Tutor math, Ohio State Univ, 36-37; teacher high sch, Ohio, 37-38; prof physics & math, Civilian Pilot Training Prog, Rio Grande Col, 38-41; asst physics, Ohio State Univ, 41-42; fel physics, Rice Inst, Mass Inst Technol, 42-45; fel physics, Rice Inst, 45-48; staff mem, Los Alamos Sci Lab, 48-52; group leader, Atomic Energy Div, Phillips Petrol Co, 52-54, sect head, 54-56, dir nuclear physics res, 56-61; SR CONSULT SCIENTIST, PHYS SCI LAB, LOCKHEED MISSILES & SPACE CO, 61- Mem: AAAS; fel Am Phys Soc; Am Geophys Union; Am Nuclear Soc; Am Inst Aeronaut & Astronaut. Res: Auroral, atmospheric and nuclear physics; homogeneous reactor development; neutron crystal spectrometry. Mailing Add: Lockheed Palo Alto Res Labs 3251 Hanover St Palo Alto CA 94304

EVANS, JOHN FENTON, b Sewickley, Pa, Mar 20, 49; m 71. ANALYTICAL & SURFACE CHEMISTRY. Educ: Washington & Jefferson Col, BA, 71; Univ Del, PhD(chem), 77. Prof Exp: Teaching & res asst, Dept Chem, Univ Del, 71-75; res assoc, Dept Chem, Ohio State Univ, 75-77; ASST PROF CHEM, UNIV MINN, 77- Mem: Am Chem Soc; Sigma Xi; Am Vacuum Soc. Res: Surface modification using plasma chemistry; photochemistry and conventional chemistry; surface analysis using particle and light spectroscopies. Mailing Add: Dept of Chem 207 Pleasant St SE Minneapolis MN 55455

EVANS, JOHN MCCALLUM, b Hamburg, NY, July 19, 13; m 41; c 1. MEDICINE. Educ: Denison Univ, BA, 35; Univ Buffalo, MD, 39. Prof Exp: Instr med, Sch Med, Univ Buffalo, 41; asst, Harvard Med Sch, 46-48; from asst clin prof to assoc clin prof, 48-54, assoc prof, 54-60, PROF MED, SCH MED, GEORGE WASHINGTON UNIV, 60-, ASSOC, HOSP & DIR CARDIOVASC RES LAB, 48-; DIR CARDIAC CLINS, 51- Concurrent Pos: Fel med, Harvard Med Sch, 46-48; vis physicians, Walter Reed Gen Hosp, 48-58; consult, US Soldiers Home Hosp, 48-70, Newton D Baker Vet Admin Hosp, 50-60, Alto Vet Hosp, 58-62 & Wash Hosp Ctr, 64-; lectr, Cath Univ Am, 58-65. Mem: Asn Univ Cardiologists; fel Am Col Cardiol; fel Am Col Physicians; Am Heart Asn; Am Fedn Clin Res. Res: Cardiovascular diseases. Mailing Add: 5480 Wisconsin Ave Washington DC 20015

EVANS, JOHN STANTON, b Camilla, Ga, Oct 12, 21; m 48; c 3. FLUID DYNAMICS, PHYSICAL CHEMISTRY. Educ: Berry Col, BS, 42; Emory Univ, MS, 48; Univ Tenn, Knoxville, PhD(physics), 59. Prof Exp: Instr physics, Univ Tenn, Martin, 52; AEROSPACE TECHNOLOGIST, LANGLEY RES CTR, NASA, 52- Mem: Am Phys Soc. Res: Computational fluid dynamics. Mailing Add: Langley Res Ctr NASA MS 168 Hampton VA 23665

EVANS, JOHN V, b Manchester, Eng, July 5, 33; m 58; c 3. RADIO PHYSICS. Educ: Univ Manchester, BSc, 54, PhD(physics), 57. Prof Exp: Leverhulme res fel radio astron, Jodrell Bank Exp Sta, Univ Manchester, 57-60; staff mem, Lincoln Lab, Mass Inst Technol, 60-66; George A Miller vis prof elec eng, Univ Ill, 66-67; staff mem, 67-70, from assoc group leader to group leader, 70-75, assoc dir head, 75-77, ASST DIR, LINCOLN LAB, MASS INST TECHNOL, 77-, PROF, DEPT METEOROL & PHYS OCEANOG, 80-; DIR, NORTHEAST RADIO OBSERV CORP, 80- Concurrent Pos: Mem, Int Union Radio Sci, 63-, mem, US Nat Comt, 68-70, secy, 70-72, vchmn, 73-75, chmn, 75-78. Honors & Awards: Appleton Prize, Royal Soc, 75. Mem: AAAS; fel Inst Elec & Electronics Engrs; Am Geophys Union; Sigma Xi. Res: Radar studies of the moon, Venus, meteors and the ionosphere. Mailing Add: Lincoln Lab Mass Inst Technol Lexington MA 02173

EVANS, JOHN W, b Mt Vernon, NY, Jan 20, 35; div; c 2. MATHEMATICAL BIOLOGY. Educ: Cornell Univ, MD, 58; Univ Calif, Los Angeles, PhD(math), 66. Prof Exp: Sr surgeon, Math Res Br, Nat Inst Arthritis & Metab Dis, 66-68; assoc prof, 68-73, PROF MATH, UNIV CALIF, SAN DIEGO, 73- Mem: Am Math Soc. Res: Mathematical models of nerve impulse conduction; mathematical models in pulmonary physiology. Mailing Add: Dept Math Univ Calif San Diego PO Box 109 La Jolla CA 92037

EVANS, JOHN WAINWRIGHT, JR, b New York, NY, May 14, 09; m 32; c 3. ASTROPHYSICS. Educ: Swarthmore Col, AB, 32; Harvard Univ, AM, 36, PhD(astron), 38. Hon Degrees: ScD, Univ NMex, 67 & Swarthmore Col, 70. Prof Exp: Instr astron, Univ Minn, 37-38; from instr to asst prof astron & math, Mills Col, 38-42; optical res worker, Nat Defense Res Comt, Univ Rochester, 42-46, asst prof optics, 45-46; astronomer, High Altitude Observ Harvard-Colo, 46-52; dir, 52-75, SR SCIENTIST, SACRAMENTO PEAK OBSERV, 75- Honors & Awards: Cleveland Prize, AAAS, 57; Distinguished Civilian Serv Award, Dept Defense, 65; Rockefeller Pub Serv Award Sci, Technol & Eng, 69; George Ellery Hale Prize, Am Astron Soc, 82. Mem: AAAS; Am Astron Soc; fel Am Acad Arts & Sci; fel Optical Soc Am. Res: Solar physics; solar terrestrial effects; optical design. Mailing Add: Box 124 High Rolls NM 88325

EVANS, JOHN WILLIAM, b Montreal, Que, Apr 10, 34. ZOOLOGY. Educ: McGill Univ, BSc, 57, MSc, 59; Univ Ore, PhD(ecol), 66. Prof Exp: Asst prof, 66-71, ASSOC PROF BIOL, MEM UNIV NEWF, 71- Mem: Can Soc Zool. Res: Applied terrestial ecology; ecological agriculture and alternative technology. Mailing Add: Dept of Biol Mem Univ of Newf St John's NF A1C 5S7 Can

EVANS, JOSEPH LISTON, b Lebanon, Ky, June 27, 30; m 55; c 2. NUTRITION, ANIMAL NUTRITION. Educ: Univ Ky, BS, 52, MS, 55; Univ Fla, PhD(nutrit, biochem), 59. Prof Exp: Asst animal sci, Univ Ky, 54-55; asst nutrit, Univ Fla, 55-59; from asst prof to assoc prof, 59-69, PROF NUTRIT, RUTGERS UNIV, 69- Mem: Am Soc Animal Sci; Am Inst Nutrit; Am Dairy Sci Asn. Res: Nutritional biochemical mechanisms involving utilization of minerals in rats, man and cattle and nitrogen utilization cattle. Mailing Add: Dept of Animal Sci & Nutrit Rutgers Univ New Brunswick NJ 08903

EVANS, KENNETH, JR, b Decatur, Ill, Jan 25, 41; c 3. PLASMA PHYSICS, CONTROLLED FUSION. Educ: Univ Ill, BS, 63, MS, 64, PhD(physics), 70. Prof Exp: Res teaching asst physics, Univ Ill, 63-70; res asst, Coord Sci Lab, 68-70; res assoc & instr, Univ Wis, 70-74; PHYSICIST, ARGONNE NAT LAB, 74- Mem: Am Phys Soc. Res: Theoretical research in plasma physics and controlled thermonuclear fusion. Mailing Add: Argonne Nat Lab 9700 S Cass Ave Argonne IL 60439

EVANS, KENNETH JACK, b Chickasha, Okla, July 8, 29; m 55; c 4. VERTEBRATE ZOOLOGY, ECOLOGY. Educ: Univ Okla, BS, 57, MS, 58; Univ Calif, Riverside, PhD(zool), 64. Prof Exp: Instr zool, Univ Redlands, 60-61; assoc biol, Univ Calif, Riverside, 63-64; from asst prof to assoc prof, 64-73, PROF BIOL, CALIF STATE UNIV, CHICO, 73- Mem: Ecol Soc Am. Res: Ecology of amphibians and reptiles. Mailing Add: Dept of Biol Sci Calif State Univ Chico CA 95929

EVANS, LANCE SAYLOR, b Philadelphia, Pa, Sept 29, 44; m 65; c 3. PLANT PHYSIOLOGY, CELL CYCLE KINETICS. Educ: Calif State Polytech Col, Kellogg-Voorhis, BS, 67; Univ Calif, Riverside, PhD(plant sci & plant physiol), 70. Prof Exp: Nat Inst Environ Health Sci res fel plant sci, Univ Calif, Riverside, 70-71; res biologist, 71-72; Nat Cancer Inst fel, 72-73; res biologist, Brookhaven Nat Lab, 72-75; ASST PROF BIOL, LAB PLANT MORPHOGENESIS, MANHATTAN COL, 75- Concurrent Pos: Consult, Acid Rain Res Prog, Brookhaven Nat Lab, Upton, NY, 75- Mem: Am Soc Plant Physiologists; Bot Soc Am; Sigma Xi. Res: Cell cycle regulation; air pollution; plant morphogenesis and anatomy; cell cycle kinetics and analysis of cell proliferation and cell arrest; effects of air pollutants on crop growth and yield. Mailing Add: Dept Biol Lab Plant Morphol Manhattan Col Bronx NY 10471

EVANS, LATIMER RICHARD, b Washington, DC, Nov 4, 18; m 42; c 4. CHEMISTRY. Educ: Am Univ, BS, 41; Purdue Univ, PhD(org chem), 45. Prof Exp: Asst chem, Purdue Univ, 41-42, Manhattan Proj fel, 45; res chemist, E I du Pont de Nemours & Co, Inc, 46-50; from asst prof to assoc prof, 50-61, PROF CHEM, NMEX STATE UNIV, 61- Honors & Awards:

Am Inst Chem Medal, 41. *Mem:* Am Chem Soc; Sigma Xi. *Res:* Chlorination; fluorination of chloro compounds; azeotrope distillation as separation method; fluorination with antimony pentafluoride. *Mailing Add:* Dept Chem NMex State Univ University Park NM 88001

EVANS, LAURIE EDWARD, b Unity, Sask, Oct 14, 33; m 60; c 3. CYTOGENETICS, PLANT BREEDING. *Educ:* Univ Sask, BSA, 54; Univ Man, MSc, 56, PhD(plant sci, cytogenetics), 59. *Prof Exp:* From res asst to res assoc, 59-63, from asst prof to assoc prof, 63-73, PROF PLANT SCI, UNIV MAN, 73-, DEPT HEAD, 80- *Concurrent Pos:* Plant breeder, Kenya, 68-69; vis prof, Sydney Australia, 76. *Mem:* Genetics Soc Can. *Res:* Wheat breeding. *Mailing Add:* Dept of Plant Sci Univ of Man Col of Agr Winnipeg Can

EVANS, LAWRENCE B(OYD), b Ft Sumner, NMex, Oct 27, 34; m 63; c 2. CHEMICAL ENGINEERING. *Educ:* Univ Okla, BS, 56; Univ Mich, MSE, 57, PhD(chem eng), 62. *Prof Exp:* From asst prof to assoc prof, 62-76, PROF CHEM ENG, MASS INST TECHNOL, 76- *Concurrent Pos:* pres, Aspen Technol, Inc, 81-; trustee, Cache Corp, 78- *Honors & Awards:* Donald L Katz Lectr, Univ Mich, 80. *Mem:* Am Inst Chem Engrs; Am Chem Soc; Am Soc Mech Engrs; Asn Comput Mach. *Res:* Computer aided chemical process analysis; process dynamics and control; applied mathematics; natural convection; radiative, heat and mass transfer. *Mailing Add:* Dept of Chem Eng Mass Inst of Technol Cambridge MA 02139

EVANS, LAWRENCE EUGENE, b San Antonio, Tex, Sept 18, 32; m 56; c 2. PHYSICS. *Educ:* Birmingham-Southern Col, BS, 53; Johns Hopkins Univ, PhD(physics), 60. *Prof Exp:* Res assoc physics, Univ Wis, 60-62, instr, 62-63; from asst prof to assoc prof, 63-80, PROF PHYSICS, DUKE UNIV, 80- *Mem:* Am Phys Soc. *Res:* Quantum field theory; quantum electrodynamics; theory of elementary particles. *Mailing Add:* Dept of Physics Duke Univ Durham NC 27706

EVANS, LEE E, b Newton, Miss, May 27, 22; m 48; c 3. ANIMAL HUSBANDRY. *Educ:* Alcorn Agr & Mech Col, BS, 43; Iowa State Univ, MS, 47; Univ Ill, PhD(animal sci), 56. *Prof Exp:* Teacher voc agr, Newton Voc Sch, 47-51; dir dept agr, Alcorn Agr & Mech Col, 51-53; asst, Univ Ill, 53-55; head dept animal husb, 55-68, prof, 68-74, PROF RURAL DEVELOP, FLA A&M UNIV, 74- *Mem:* Am Soc Animal Sci; Genetics Soc Am. *Res:* Improvement of farm livestock through better methods and techniques of breeding; experimenting with cattle fed crops fertilized with sewage as part of recycling of human waste. *Mailing Add:* Col of Sci & Technol Fla A&M Univ Tallahassee FL 32307

EVANS, LEONARD, b London, Eng, Feb 21, 39; m 66; c 3. OPERATIONS RESEARCH, HUMAN FACTORS. *Educ:* Queen's Univ, Belfast, BSc, 60; Oxford Univ, DPhil(physics), 65. *Prof Exp:* Fel physics, Div Pure Physics, Nat Res Coun Can, 65-67; assoc sr res physicist, Theoret Physics Dept, 67-74, STAFF RES SCIENTIST, TRANSP RES DEPT, GEN MOTORS RES LABS, 74- *Mem:* Opers Res Soc Am; Human Factors Soc; Soc Automotive Engrs; AAAS; Sigma Xi. *Res:* Traffic safety; driver-vehicle studies; fuel economy and emissions in urban traffic. *Mailing Add:* Transp Res Dept Gen Motors Res Labs Warren MI 48090

EVANS, MARLENE SANDRA, b London, Ont, Jan 26, 46. LIMNOLOGY, OCEANOGRAPHY. *Educ:* Carleton Univ, BSc, 69; Univ BC, PhD(zool, oceanog), 74. *Prof Exp:* Res investr, 74-76, asst scientist, 76-81, ASSOC SCIENTIST LIMNOL, GREAT LAKES RES DIV, UNIV MICH, 81- *Mem:* Can Soc Zool; Am Soc Limnol & Oceanog; Int Asn Great Lakes Res (pres, 81-82); AAAS; Sigma Xi. *Res:* Zooplankton ecology; limnology and biological oceanography; water quality. *Mailing Add:* Great Lakes Res Div Univ of Mich Ann Arbor MI 48109

EVANS, MARY JO, b Maysville, Mo, Nov 28, 35; m 68; c 2. MOLECULAR BIOLOGY, CANCER. *Educ:* William Jewell Col, BA, 57; Univ Mo, MS, 65; Univ Tenn, PhD(microbiol), 68. *Prof Exp:* Res asst virol, Univ Mo, 57-58, res fel, 64-65; teaching fel microbiol, Univ Tenn, 65-66; trainee virol, St Jude Children's Res Hosp, 66-68; cancer res scientist, 68-69, dir grad studies microbiol, 73-75, sr cancer res scientist & asst res prof, 69-78, CANCER RES SCIENTIST IV, ROSWELL PARK MEM INST & ASSOC RES PROF, ROSWELL PARK DIV, STATE UNIV NY BUFFALO, 78- *Mem:* Am Soc Microbiol. *Res:* Mammalian DNA replication. *Mailing Add:* Dept of Viral Oncol Roswell Park Mem Inst 666 Elm St Buffalo NY 14203

EVANS, MICHAEL ALLEN, b New Albany, Ind, Oct 19, 43; m 73; c 3. TOXICOLOGY. *Educ:* St Joseph Col, BS, 67; Ind Univ, PhD(toxicol), 74. *Prof Exp:* Fel, Vanderbilt Med Ctr, 74-76; ASST PROF PHARMACOL, UNIV ILL MED CTR, 76- *Mem:* NY Acad Sci; AAAS; Am Acad Forensic Sci; Soc Toxicol. *Res:* Mechanism of chemical hepatotoxicity; drug disposition during development; relationship between drug metabolism and drug toxicity. *Mailing Add:* Dept Pharmacol Univ Ill Med Ctr PO Box 6998 Chicago IL 60680

EVANS, MICHAEL JOHN, b Glendale, Calif, Jan 29, 38. CELL BIOLOGY. *Educ:* Whittier Col, AB, 62; Univ Southern Calif, PhD(biol), 68. *Prof Exp:* Anal chemist cardiovasc lab, Rancho Los Amigos Hosp, 62-63, res assoc biophys lab, 68-69; res instr electron micros, Univ Southern Calif, 63-68; PROG MGR CELL KINETICS, SRI INT, 69- *Concurrent Pos:* Prin investr grants, Nat Heart, Lung & Blood Inst & Nat Cancer Inst, 70- & Nat Inst Allergy & Infectious Dis, 71-74; consult environ med, Rancho Los Amigos Hosp, 70- & Nat Heart, Lung & Blood Inst, 73- *Mem:* Am Soc Cell Biol; AAAS; Am Fedn Clin Res; Am Thoracic Soc. *Res:* Basic mechanism of cell renewal in the lung and the effects of oxidants on this process; injury and repair in lungs of aging animals; injury and tumor formation in the lung. *Mailing Add:* SRI Int 333 Ravenswood Ave Menlo Park CA 94025

EVANS, MICHAEL LEIGH, b Detroit, Mich, July 26, 41; m 62; c 3. BOTANY. *Educ:* Univ Mich, BA, 63, MS, 65; Univ Calif, Santa Cruz, PhD(biol), 67. *Prof Exp:* Teaching asst biol, Univ Calif, Santa Cruz, 65-67; asst prof, Kalamazoo Col, 67-70; from asst prof to assoc prof, 71-78, PROF BOT, OHIO STATE UNIV, 78- *Concurrent Pos:* NATO fel, Univ Freiburg, WGer, 70-71. *Mem:* Am Soc Plant Physiol; Japanese Soc Plant Physiol. *Res:* Plant growth hormones, especially short-term effects. *Mailing Add:* Dept Bot Ohio State Univ Columbus OH 43210

EVANS, NANCY REMAGE, b Taunton, Mass, May 19, 44; m 68; c 2. ASTRONOMY. *Educ:* Wellesley Col, BA, 66; Univ Toronto, MSc, 69, PhD(astron), 74. *Prof Exp:* Fel astron, 74-76, RES ASSOC, UNIV TORONTO, 76- *Mem:* Am Astron Soc; Int Astron Union; Can Astron Soc. *Res:* Observational studies of variable stars, particularly Cepheids. *Mailing Add:* Dept of Astron Univ of Toronto Toronto ON M5S 1A1 Can

EVANS, NEAL JOHN, II, b San Antonio, Tex, Sept 22, 46; m 73; c 1. INTERSTELLAR MATTER, STAR FORMATION. *Educ:* Univ Calif, Berkeley, AB, 68, PhD(physics), 73. *Prof Exp:* Res fel astron, Owens Valley Radio Observ, Calif Inst Technol, 73-75; res scientist assoc IV astron, 75-76, asst prof astron, 76-81, ASSOC PROF ASTRON, UNIV TEX, AUSTIN, 81- *Concurrent Pos:* Consult, NASA, 77-78; mem, Intermediate Range Task Force Proposal Rev Comt. *Mem:* Am Astron Soc; Int Astron Union; Int Union Radio Sci. *Res:* Molecular line studies of dense interstellar clouds and infrared studies of objects embedded in the clouds to elucidate star formation. *Mailing Add:* Dept of Astron Univ of Tex Austin TX 78712

EVANS, NOEL DEE, mathematics, see previous edition

EVANS, NORMAN A(LLEN), b SDak, Dec 3, 22; m 44; c 4. WATER RESOURCES, IRRIGATION ENGINEERING. *Educ:* SDak State Col, BS, 44; Utah State Univ, MS, 47; Colo State Univ, PhD. *Prof Exp:* Asst, Col Eng, Utah State Univ, 46-47; asst prof agr eng, NDak Agr Col, 47-51; asst civil eng, 51-52, from asst prof to assoc prof, 52-57, assoc prof agr eng, 57-59, head dept, 57-69, dir environ resources ctr, 67-78, assoc dir agr exp sta, 69-70, dir, Off Gen Univ Res, 70-72, PROF AGR ENG, COLO STATE UNIV, 59-; DIR, COLO WATER RES INST, 67- *Concurrent Pos:* Mem, Colo Water Pollution Control Comn, 66-80; mem bd dirs, Engr Coun Prof Develop, 70-76. *Mem:* Fel AAAS; Am Soc Agr Engrs (vpres, 68-70); Am Soc Eng Educ; Soil Sci Soc Am; Am Soc Civil Engrs. *Res:* Fluid mechanics of porous media; drainage; irrigation practices. *Mailing Add:* Environ Resources Ctr Colo State Univ Ft Collins CO 80523

EVANS, RAEFORD G, b Coleman, Tex, Aug 20, 19; m 42; c 3. AGRONOMY, GENETICS. *Educ:* Tex A&M Univ, BS, 41; Univ Wyo, MS, 63, PhD(agron), 69. *Prof Exp:* Agronomist, Tex A&M Univ, 41-44; farm mgr, 55-58, from instr to assoc prof, 59-73, PROF AGRON, TARLETON STATE UNIV, 73- *Concurrent Pos:* Asst, Univ Wyo, 66-67. *Mem:* Am Soc Agron; Crop Sci Soc Am; Am Genetic Asn; Soil Conser- Soc Am. *Res:* Plant breeding; crop production; weed and range science. *Mailing Add:* Dept of Sci Tarleton State Univ Stephenville TX 76402

EVANS, RALPH AIKEN, b Oak Park, Ill, Feb 2, 24. PHYSICS. *Educ:* Lehigh Univ, BS, 44; Univ Calif, PhD(physics), 54. *Prof Exp:* Radio engr, Centimeter Wave Sect, Naval Res Lab, 44-46; physicist, Inst Eng Res, Univ Calif, 47-54; res physicist, Power Transmission & Mat Handling, Linkbelt Res Lab, 54-59, dir res lab, 59-61; sr physicist, Res Triangle Inst, 61-74; PROD ASSURANCE CONSULT, EVANS ASSOCS, 74- *Concurrent Pos:* Ed, Inst Elec & Electronics Engrs Trans on Reliability & Am Soc Qual Control Review. *Mem:* Am Soc Testing & Mat; fel Am Soc Qual Control; fel Inst Elec & Electronics Engrs. *Res:* Electronic instrumentation; mechanical testing; fatigue; engineering statistics; reliability; quality control. *Mailing Add:* 804 Vickers Ave Durham NC 27701

EVANS, RALPH H, JR, b Teaneck, NJ, July 5, 29; m 50; c 1. ANALYTICAL CHEMISTRY. *Educ:* Fairleigh Dickinson Univ, AA, 49, BS, 58; State Univ NY, AS, 52. *Prof Exp:* Res scientist, 58-68, SR RES SCIENTIST, LEDERLE LABS, HOFFMANN-LA ROCHE, INC, 69- *Mem:* Am Chem Soc; Sigma Xi. *Res:* Isolation, assay and structural elucidation of antibiotics and natural products from microbial sources. *Mailing Add:* Chem Res Dept Hoffmann-La Roche Inc Nutley NJ 07110

EVANS, RAYMOND ARTHUR, b Albuquerque, NMex, Mar 31, 25; m 50; c 1. RANGE SCIENCE, WEED SCIENCE. *Educ:* Univ Redlands, AB, 50; Univ Calif, PhD, 56. *Prof Exp:* Asst specialist rangeland soils & plants, Univ Calif, 54-58; RANGE SCIENTIST, PASTURE & RANGE MGT, AGR RES SERV, USDA, 58-, RES LEADER, 72- *Mem:* AAAS; Ecol Soc Am; Soc Range Mgt; Weed Sci Soc Am. *Res:* Range weed control and revegetation; competition studies involving range weeds and forage species emphasizing factors of soil moisture, temperature and nutrients; utilization of field, greenhouse and laboratory techniques; employment of microenvironmental monitoring. *Mailing Add:* Renewable Resources Ctr Univ of Nev 920 Valley Rd Reno NV 89512

EVANS, RICHARD TODD, b Evanston, Ill, Oct 2, 32; m 69; c 3. MICROBIOLOGY, IMMUNOLOGY. *Educ:* Cent Methodist Col, AB, 54; Univ Mo, MS, 59, PhD(microbiol), 63. *Prof Exp:* Asst microbiol, Univ Mo, 57-59, asst instr, 59-62; Am Dent Asn res assoc, NIH, 63-66; asst prof oral biol, Sch Dent, 66-73, asst prof microbiol, Sch Med, 72-75, dir grad studies oral biol, 70-76, ASSOC PROF ORAL BIOL & MICROBIOL & ASSOC CHMN, DEPT ORAL BIOL, SCH DENT, STATE UNIV NY BUFFALO, 75- *Mem:* Am Asn Immunologists; AAAS; Int Asn Dent Res; Am Soc Microbiol; NY Acad Sci. *Res:* Immunochemistry of bacterial antigens; host-parasite relationships of periodontal disease; preventive (chemotherapeutic) measures in oral disease; microbiology of dental caries. *Mailing Add:* Dept Oral Biol 4510 Main St Buffalo NY 14226

EVANS, ROBERT JOHN, b Osage City, Kans, Mar 18, 28; m 51; c 2. ORGANIC CHEMISTRY. *Educ:* Univ Nebr, BSc, 51; Univ Wash, PhD(chem), 59. *Prof Exp:* Org chemist, Merck & Co, NJ, 51-54; org chemist, Hydrocarbons Div, Monsanto Co, 59-66; from asst prof to assoc prof, 66-73, PROF CHEM, ILL COL, 73- *Mem:* Am Chem Soc. *Res:* Oxidation of organic compounds. *Mailing Add:* Dept of Chem Ill Col Jacksonville IL 62650

EVANS, ROBERT JOHN, b Logan, Utah, Mar 18, 09; m 41; c 2. BIOCHEMISTRY, NUTRITION. *Educ:* Utah State Univ, BS, 34, MS, 36; Univ Wis, PhD(biochem), 39. *Prof Exp:* Grad asst biochem, Utah State Univ, 34-36; instr chem, Carbon Col, 39-40; assoc chemist, Wash Agr Exp Sta, 40-47; prof biochem, 47-77, EMER PROF BIOCHEM, MICH STATE UNIV, 77- *Concurrent Pos:* USPHS grant seed proteins in nutrit, Mich State Univ, 63-65, USPHS grant lipoproteins, 66-74. *Honors & Awards:* Poultry & Egg Nat Bd of USA Res Achievement Award, 58. *Mem:* AAAS; Am Chem Soc; Am Inst Nutrit; Poultry Sci Asn. *Res:* Lipid-protein binding in egg yolk lipoproteins which includes the study of lipoprotein structure and the structure of proteins and lipids; nutritive availability of the methionine in dry beans. *Mailing Add:* 760 Polk Ave Ogden UT 84404

EVANS, ROBERT MORTON, b Cleveland, Ohio, Oct 28, 17; m 42, 65; c 4. POLYMER CHEMISTRY. *Educ:* Antioch Col, BS, 41; Case Western Reserve Univ, PhD(chem), 59. *Prof Exp:* VPRES RES & ENG, MAMECO INT, 45- *Concurrent Pos:* Res assoc, Case Inst Technol, 60-61; pres, Prog Design, Inc, 67-70; pres & founder, Isonetics, Inc, 70-75; mem res adv comt, Fedn Socs Paint Technol. *Honors & Awards:* Roon Award, 64 & 77. *Mem:* Am Soc Testing & Mat; Fedn Socs Paint Technol; NY Acad Sci; fel Am Inst Chem; Sigma Xi. *Res:* Specialty coatings and adhesives; sealants and flooring materials; all polymeric and some organic-inorganic alloys; insulated glass; solar heating; abrasion resistance; coauthor or author of over 15 publications. *Mailing Add:* 1365 Forest Hills Blvd Cleveland Heights OH 44118

EVANS, ROBLEY DUNGLISON, b University Place, Nebr, May 18, 07; m 28; c 3. PHYSICS. *Educ:* Calif Inst Technol, BS, 28, MS, 29, PhD(physics), 32; Am Bd Health Physics, dipl, 61. *Prof Exp:* Asst eng, Calif Inst Technol, 28, asst hist, 27-30 & 31-32, teaching fel physics, 29-32; Nat Res Coun fel, Univ Calif, 32-34; from asst prof to prof, 34-72, dir radioactivity ctr, 35-72, EMER PROF PHYSICS & EMER DIR RADIOACTIVITY CTR, MASS INST TECHNOL, 72- *Concurrent Pos:* Consult, Peter Bent Brigham Hosp, 45-72, mem isotopes comt, 64-75, Roger Williams Hosp, 65-; consult, Brookhaven Nat Lab, 47-55, mem vis comn med dept, 65-68; consult, Mass Gen Hosp, 48-73, mem comt isotopes, 50-75; mem joint comn standards, units & constants radioactivity, Int Coun Sci Unions, 48-51, mem joint comn radioactivity, 51-55; consult, Biol & Med Div & Biomed & Environ Res Div, AEC, ERDA, DOE, 50-, mem, Adv Comt Isotope Distribution, 48-53, chmn, 52-53; mem, Aircraft Nuclear Propulsion Med Adv Group, 53-55; mem comt radiation protection, Mass Inst Technol, 55-72, mem comt radioisotope utilization & adv med dept, 59-72, mem clin res ctr policy comt, 64-72; mem adv comt rules & regulations radiation protection, Mass Dept Labor & Industs, 57; mem subcomt rel hazard factors, Nat Comt Radiation Protection & Measurements, 57-; mem subcomt symbols, units & nomenclature, Comt Nuclear Sci, Nat Acad Sci-Nat Res Coun, 62-67, panel adv to Nat Bur Stand, 63, chmn, 64; mem ad hoc adv comt radiation path, Armed Forces Inst Path, 62-64; mem sci adv bd, Cancer Res Inst, New Eng Deaconess Hosp, 63-69; chmn task group high energy & space radiation dosimetry, Int Comn Radiol Units & Measurements, 64-67; adv, Univ Chicago & mem res comt, Radiol Physics Div, Argonne Nat Lab, 64-68, chmn, 67-68, chmn adv comt, Ctr Human Radiobiol, 72-; sr US deleg, Int Asn Radiation Res, 66; vis prof, Ariz State Univ, 66-67; consult, Fed Aviation Agency, 67, chmn standing comt radiation biol aspects of supersonic transport, 67, mem, comt radioactive waste mgt, Nat Acad Sci, 68-70, vchmn adv comt, US Transuranium Registry, 68-, mem tech adv comt, Ariz AEC, 71-72, spec proj assoc, Mayo Clin, 73- *Honors & Awards:* Theobald Smith Medal, AAAS, 37; Hull Gold Medal, AMA, 63; Silvanus Thompson Award & Medal, Brit Inst Radiol, 66. *Mem:* Fel AAAS; fel Am Phys Soc; fel Am Acad Arts & Sci; Health Physics Soc (pres-elect, 71, pres, 72-73); Radiation Res Soc (vpres, 65-66, pres, 66-67). *Res:* Radioactivity; radioactive tracers in engineering and biology; geological age measurement by radioactivity; instrumentation; biological effects of radiation; nuclear medicine; health physics; pure and applied nuclear physics. *Mailing Add:* 4621 E Crystal Lane Scottsdale AZ 85253

EVANS, ROGER JAMES, b Oxford, Eng. STRUCTURAL ENGINEERING, SOLID MECHANICS. *Educ:* Univ Birmingham, BSc, 55; Brown Univ, ScM, 59; Univ Calif, Berkeley, PhD(struct eng), 65. *Prof Exp:* Lectr civil eng, Univ Birmingham, 59-61; preceptor, Civil Eng Dept, Columbia Univ, 65-66; asst prof, 66-77, PROF CIVIL ENG, UNIV WASH, 77- *Res:* Theory of elasticity; elastic wave propagation; geophysical problems including rheological behavior of ice and seismic phenomena. *Mailing Add:* Dept of Civil Eng Univ of Wash Seattle WA 98195

EVANS, ROGER LYNWOOD, b Ipswich, Eng, June 25, 28; m 54; c 3. INORGANIC CHEMISTRY. *Educ:* Oxford Univ, BA, 52, MA, 55, DPhil(natural sci), 58; Univ Minn, MS, 55. *Prof Exp:* Sr chemist, Cent Res Labs, 58-67, sr chemist, Nuclear Prod Lab, 67-78, PATENT LIAISON, MED PROD LAB, 3M CO, 78- *Res:* Elements of periodic groups III and IV; polymer chemistry; radiopharmaceuticals; intellectual property management. *Mailing Add:* Med Prods Lab 3M Ctr Minn Mining & Mfg Co St Paul MN 55144

EVANS, ROGER MALCOLM, b Coronation, Alta, May 27, 35. ANIMAL BEHAVIOR. *Educ:* Univ Alta, BSc, 60, MSc, 61; Univ Wis, PhD(behav of gulls), 66. *Prof Exp:* From asst prof to assoc prof, 66-78, PROF ZOOL, UNIV MAN, 78- *Mem:* Am Ornith Union; Animal Behav Soc; Can Soc Zool. *Res:* Behavioral ecology of colonial water birds. *Mailing Add:* Dept of Zool Univ of Man Winnipeg MB R3T 2N2 Can

EVANS, RONALD DALE, mechanical engineering, applied physics, see previous edition

EVANS, RUSSELL STUART, b Saskatoon, Sask, Nov 18, 23; m 45; c 3. WOOD CHEMISTRY. *Educ:* Univ BC, BA, 49, MA, 51; Univ Sask, PhD(org chem), 56. *Prof Exp:* Res chemist plant residue chem, Prairie Regional Lab, Nat Res Coun Can, 51-56; res chemist wood chem & tech, Rayonier Can Ltd, 56-59, group leader, 59-61; sect leader, East Res Div, Rayonier Inc, 61-65; mgr cellulose res dept, Columbia Cellulose Co, Ltd, 65-73; environ qual officer, 73-74, ASST DIR, WESTERN FOREST PROD LAB, CAN FOREST SERV, 75- *Mem:* Am Chem Soc. *Res:* Wood and fiber chemistry and technology; plant and microbiological chemistry; industrial chemistry of cellulose, lignin and wood extractives. *Mailing Add:* Western Forest Prods Lab 6620 N W Marine Dr Vancouver Can

EVANS, SILAS MCAFEE, b Madison, Wis, Aug 4, 10; m 36; c 4. EXPERIMENTAL MEDICINE. *Educ:* Ripon Col, BA, 30; Univ Wis, MD, 36. *Prof Exp:* Asst dir extramural educ med, Univ Wis, 45-47; jr consult, Vet Admin Hosp, Milwaukee, 46-48; CHIEF MED SERV, MILWAUKEE HOSP, 53-; ASSOC CLIN PROF MED, MED COL WIS, 69- *Concurrent Pos:* Mem med staff, Columbia & Milwaukee Children's Hosps; mem coun arteriosclerosis, Am Heart Asn. *Mem:* Am Thoracic Soc; Am Fedn Clin Res; AMA. *Res:* Arteriosclerosis and fibrotic reactions. *Mailing Add:* 811 E Wisconsin Ave Milwaukee WI 53202

EVANS, T(HOMAS) H(AYHURST), b Los Angeles, Calif, Apr 8, 06; m 45; c 3. CIVIL ENGINEERING. *Educ:* Calif Inst Technol, BS, 29, MS, 30. *Prof Exp:* Instr eng mech, Eng Sch, Yale Univ, 30-35; from asst prof to assoc prof civil eng & mech, Univ Va, 35-42, dir eng sci, mgt & war training, 40-42; prof civil eng & dir, Sch Eng, Ga Tech Univ, 45-49; dean, Colo State Univ, 49-63; dean, 63-73, EMER PROF, SCH ENG, FRESNO STATE UNIV, 73- *Concurrent Pos:* First dean, Asian Inst Technol, Bangkok, Thailand, 59-61. *Mem:* Am Soc Civil Engrs; Am Soc Eng Educ; Nat Soc Prof Engrs; Am Soc Mech Engrs; Inst Elec & Electronics Engrs. *Res:* Mechanics of plates; structural stresses; city planning; administration of engineering education and research. *Mailing Add:* 922 La Tierra Dr Lake San Marcos CA 92069

EVANS, TAYLOR HERBERT, b Edmonton, Alta, Mar 22, 18; m 43; c 4. ORGANIC CHEMISTRY. *Educ:* Univ Alta, BSc, 37, MSc, 38; McGill Univ, PhD(chem), 41. *Prof Exp:* Sessional lectr chem, McGill Univ, 41-43; res chemist, Res Labs, Dominion Rubber Co, Ltd, 43-59, mgr mkt res, Naugatuck Chem Div, 59-62, econ develop dept, 62-64 & develop dept, 64-68, TECH SPECIALIST, GUELPH RES LABS, UNIROYAL LTD, 68- *Mem:* Fel Chem Inst Can. *Res:* Dextran; lignin; vapor phase dehydration reactions; liquid phase oxidation reactions; patents; organic phosphorus compounds; pharmaceuticals; industrial organic chemicals. *Mailing Add:* 38 Suffolk St W Guelph Can

EVANS, THOMAS EDWARD, b Springfield, Vt, July 22, 39; m 66; c 1. MOLECULAR BIOLOGY. *Educ:* DePauw Univ, BA, 61; Case Western Reserve Univ, PhD(biol), 67. *Prof Exp:* asst prof radiol & microbiol, 67-81, DIR EDUC SERV, SCH MED, CASE WESTERN RESERVE UNIV, 81- *Mem:* Radiation Res Soc; AAAS; Am Soc Microbiol; Genetics Soc. *Res:* Nucleic acid metabolism in eukaryotes, especially as related to nuclear division cycles; molecular genetics of DNA replication in Physarum polycephalum; nonnuclear DNA metabolism. *Mailing Add:* Educ Serv Sch Med Case Western Reserve Univ Cleveland OH 44106

EVANS, THOMAS F(REDERICK), b New York, NY, Oct 18, 24; m 59. CHEMICAL ENGINEERING. *Educ:* Univ Wash, BS, 45; Princeton Univ, PhD(chem eng), 50. *Prof Exp:* Res engr, Textile Res Inst, 50-53; develop engr, Gen Elec Co, 53-63; assoc prof, Univ Columbia, 63-64; asst prof chem eng, Pa State Univ, 65-71; chem design engr, 71-76, assoc sr res engr, 76-80, SR RES SPECIALIST, NIAGARA MOHAWK POWER CORP, 80- *Honors & Awards:* Fulbright lectr, Univ Seville, 64-65. *Mem:* Am Chem Soc; Am Inst Chem Engrs. *Res:* Nuclear energy; power generation; environmental control. *Mailing Add:* 219 Strathmore Dr Syracuse NY 13207

EVANS, THOMAS GEORGE, b Taylor, Pa, Feb 16, 34. MATHEMATICS, COMPUTER SCIENCE. *Educ:* Princeton Univ, BA, 55; Mass Inst Technol, PhD(math), 63. *Prof Exp:* Res mathematician, US Air Force Cambridge Res Labs, 62-72; PRES, EVANS GRIFFITHS & HART, 72- *Mem:* Asn Comput Mach; Am Math Soc; Math Asn Am. *Res:* Heuristic programming approach to artificial intelligence, emphasizing description and processing of complex patterns; development of facilities for convenient conversational use of computers, especially for program debugging. *Mailing Add:* Evans Griffiths & Hart Inc 55 Waltham St Lexington MA 02173

EVANS, THOMAS P(ASSMORE), b West Grove, Pa, Aug 19, 21; m 47; c 4. TECHNOLOGY TRANSFER, PATENTS & LICENSING. *Educ:* Swarthmore Col, BS, 42; Yale Univ, MEng, 48. *Prof Exp:* Engr, Atomic Power Div, Westinghouse Elec Corp, Pa, 48-51; dir res & develop, AMF, Inc, NY, 51-60; dir res, O M Scott & Sons Co, Ohio, 60-62; vpres res & develop, W A Sheaffer Pen Co, 62-67; dir res, Mich Technol Univ, 67-80; DIR RES & PROF BUS ADMIN, BERRY COL, 80- *Concurrent Pos:* Mem, Mich Energy & Resource Res Asn, mem bd trustees, 75-80, mem exec comn, 77-80. *Mem:* Inst Elec & Electronics Engrs; Licensing Execs Soc; Am Phys Soc; Am Forestry Asn; Sigma Xi. *Res:* Management of research and development; teaching organization theory and management, new product/process and management counseling, nuclear power plants and reactor shielding; solar energy; water conversion; power generation. *Mailing Add:* Berry Col PO Box 206 Mount Berry GA 30149

EVANS, THOMAS WALTER, b Tioga, NDak, May 27, 23; m 45; c 2. TECHNOLOGICAL ANALYSIS & FORECASTING. *Educ:* NDak State Univ, BS, 47; Univ Wis, PhD(phys chem), 52. *Prof Exp:* Metallurgist, Hanford Works, Gen Elec Co, 52-56, sr engr, Hanford Atomic Prods Oper, 56-67; res assoc, Pac Northwest Labs, Battelle Mem Inst, 67-68, prog consult, 68, assoc dept mgr, Fast Flux Test Facility Div, 68-70; staff consult, Wadco Corp, Westinghouse Elec Corp, 70-72, adv scientist, 72-76, MGR PROG PLANNING, WESTINGHOUSE HANFORD CO, 76- *Mem:* Am Soc

Metals; Am Nuclear Soc. *Res:* X-ray crystallography; physical metallurgy of uranium; irradiation damage; volcanology; design, development and testing of thermal and fast reactor fuel elements. *Mailing Add:* Westinghouse Hanford Co PO Box 1970 Richland WA 99352

EVANS, TOMMY NICHOLAS, b Batesville, Ark, Apr 12, 22; m 45; c 1. MEDICINE. *Educ:* Baylor Univ, AB, 42; Vanderbilt Univ, MD, 45; Am Bd Obstet & Gynec, dipl. *Prof Exp:* From instr to prof obstet & gynec, Univ Mich, 49-65; dean, 70-72, PROF OBSTET & GYNEC & CHMN DEPT, SCH MED, WAYNE STATE UNIV, 65-, DIR, C S MOTT CTR HUMAN GROWTH & DEVELOP, 72- *Concurrent Pos:* Consult, Vet Admin Hosp, 56- *Mem:* AMA; Am Col Surg; Am Col Obstet & Gynec; Am Asn Obstet & Gynec; Am Gynec Soc. *Res:* Human reproduction; gynecologic endocrinology; obstetrics and gynecology. *Mailing Add:* 41 Lochmoore Grosse Pointe Shores MI 48236

EVANS, TREVOR, b Wolverhampton, Eng, Dec 22, 25; m 53; c 4. MATHEMATICS. *Educ:* Oxford Univ, BA, 46, MA, 50, DSc, 60; Manchester Univ, MSc, 48. *Prof Exp:* Asst lectr pure math, Manchester Univ, 46-50; instr math, Univ Wis, 50-51; mem, Inst Advan Study, 52-53; res assoc, Univ Chicago, 53-54; from asst prof to prof, 54-80, head dept, 63-78, FULLER E CALLAWAY PROF MATH, EMORY UNIV, 80- *Concurrent Pos:* Vis prof, Univ Nebr, 59-60; mem comt exam, Math Achievement Test, Col Entrance Exam Bd, 64-69, chmn, 69-; vis prof, Calif Inst Technol, 68 & Technische Hochschule, Darmstadt, WGer, 75. *Mem:* Am Math Soc; Math Asn Am; Sigma Xi; London Math Soc. *Res:* Algebraic aspects of combinatorics; decision problems in algebra; varieties of algebras. *Mailing Add:* Dept Math & Comput Sci Emory Univ Atlanta GA 30322

EVANS, VIRGINIA JOHN, b Baltimore, Md, Mar 19, 13. CELL BIOLOGY, CANCER. *Educ:* Goucher Col, AB, 35; Johns Hopkins Univ, MSc, 40, ScD(biochem), 43. *Prof Exp:* Chem technician, Blood Chem Lab, Johns Hopkins Univ, 38-39; asst tissue culturist, Tissue Cult Lab, Dept Surg, Johns Hopkins Hosp, 40-41; asst to dermatologist, Med Sch, Johns Hopkins Univ, 41-42, instr biochem, Sch Hyg & Nurses Sch, 43-44; fel, Lab Biol, Nat Cancer Inst, 44-46, biologist, 46-64, head, Tissue Cult Sect, 64-73; RETIRED. *Concurrent Pos:* Mem bd gov & chmn exec comt, W Alton Jones Cell Sci Ctr, 70; guest scientist, Am Found Biol Res, 73-; rep, Tissue Cult Asn, Am Type Cult Collection, 80- *Mem:* Soc Develop Biol; Tissue Cult Asn (vpres, 68-72, pres, 72-74); Am Asn Cancer Res; Am Soc Exp Pathologists; Am Soc Cell Biol. *Res:* Nutritional dermatoses of rats; cell physiology with special reference to tissue culture in cancer; nutrition and endocrinology of tissue cultures; carcinogenesis studies in mammalian tissue culture. *Mailing Add:* c/o AFBR 12111 Parklawn Dr Rockville MD 20852

EVANS, WARREN WILLIAM, b Wis, Nov 23, 21. PHYSICAL CHEMISTRY. *Educ:* Univ Wis, BS, 43, PhD(chem), 52. *Prof Exp:* Chemist res & develop, Carbide & Carbon Co, 47-49; sr res chemist photog, 52-70, res assoc, 70-75, RES FEL, PHOTO PRODS DEPT, E I DU PONT DE NEMOURS & CO, INC, 75- *Mem:* Sr mem Am Chem Soc. *Res:* Photographic chemistry; mechanical properties of polymers. *Mailing Add:* 25 S Second Ave Highland Park New Brunswick NJ 08904

EVANS, WAYNE RUSSELL, b Utica, NY, July 2, 21; m 46; c 2. PHYSICS, ENGINEERING. *Educ:* Cornell Univ, BA, 43, MS, 47. *Prof Exp:* Design engr mil infrared projs, Navy Ord Div, 47-50; develop engr syst anal, Apparatus & Optical Div, 50-63, asst prog mgr res & eng, 63-64, asst to gen mgr staff, 64-65, asst mgr com & prof prod develop, 65-68, mgr eng com prod, 68-73, PROD GROUP MGR APPARATUS DIV, EASTMAN KODAK CO, 73- *Concurrent Pos:* Res assoc electronic physics, Cornell Univ, 46-47; teaching assoc electromagnetic theory, Univ Rochester, 47-48. *Mem:* Sigma Xi; Optical Soc Am; Soc Photographic Scientists & Engrs; Nat Microfilm Asn. *Res:* Photographic science and imaging systems for infrared and visible spectrum, applied to data storage and retrieval techniques. *Mailing Add:* 265 Inwood Dr Rochester NY 14625

EVANS, WILLIAM BUELL, b Monticello, Miss, June 5, 18; m 45; c 3. MATHEMATICS, METEOROLOGY. *Educ:* Southern Miss Univ, BS, 39; La State Univ, MS, 41; Mass Inst Technol, MS, 44; Univ Ill, PhD(math), 50. *Prof Exp:* Assoc prof math, Ga Inst Technol, 50-60; assoc prof eng, Univ Calif, Los Angeles & with Eng Gadjah Mada Proj, Indonesia, 60-64; assoc prof, 65-68, PROF MATH & BIOMET, EMORY UNIV, 68-, DIR COMPUT CTR, 65- *Concurrent Pos:* Vis prof, Fed Univ Pernambuco, Recife, Brazil, 73-74. *Mem:* Am Math Soc; Math Asn Am; Soc Indust & Appl Math; Biomet Soc; Sigma Xi. *Res:* Numerical analysis; general methods of approximation; differential equation of potential distribution in a biological cell; pathological analysis. *Mailing Add:* Comput Ctr Uppergate House Emory Univ Atlanta GA 30322

EVANS, WILLIAM DANIEL, physics, computer science, see previous edition

EVANS, WILLIAM GEORGE, b Swansea, Wales, Aug 11, 23; nat US; m 56; c 2. INSECT ECOLOGY. *Educ:* Cornell Univ, BS, 52, MS, 54, PhD(entom), 56. *Prof Exp:* Asst prof entom, Va Polytech Inst, 56-58; from asst prof to assoc prof, 59-69, PROF ENTOM, UNIV ALTA, 69- *Mem:* Entom Soc Am; Ecol Soc Am; Sigma Xi; Entom Soc Can; Am Ornith Union. *Res:* Insect ecology; insect behavior; rhythmic activities; marine insects; insects attracted to forest fires; habitat selection, chemosensory orientation. *Mailing Add:* Dept Entom Univ Alta Edmonton AB T6G 2E8 Can

EVANS, WILLIAM HARRINGTON, b Salem, Ore, Feb 26, 21; m 65. PHYSICAL CHEMISTRY. *Educ:* Willamette Univ, BA, 42; Ore State Col, PhD(phys chem), 47. *Prof Exp:* Tech coordr & mat expeditor, Naval Ord Lab, Wash, DC, 44-45; asst, Ore State Col, 45-47; chemist, Thermochem Sect, Nat Bur Standards, 47-75, chemist, Chem Thermodynamics Div, 75-78; CONSULT, 78- *Concurrent Pos:* Lectr, Cath Univ, 50-54; consult, Key Values Thermodynamics, Codata Task Group, 70- *Mem:* Am Chem Soc. *Res:* Critical evaluation of thermochemical and thermodynamic data for chemical substances. *Mailing Add:* Chem Thermodynamics Div Nat Bur Standards Washington DC 20234

EVANS, WILLIAM JOHN, b Madison, Wis, Oct 14, 47. INORGANIC CHEMISTRY. *Educ:* Univ Wis, Madison, BS, 69; Univ Calif, Los Angeles, PhD(chem), 73. *Prof Exp:* Res assoc chem, Cornell Univ, 73-75; ASST PROF CHEM, UNIV CHICAGO, 75- *Mem:* Am Chem Soc. *Res:* Exploratory synthesis and systematic reaction chemistry of lanthanide and actinide metal complexes and transition metal clusters. *Mailing Add:* Dept of Chem Univ of Chicago 5735 S Ellis Ave Chicago IL 60637

EVANS, WILLIAM L, b Calvert, Tex, Aug 28, 24; m 48; c 3. CYTOLOGY. *Educ:* Univ Tex, BA, 49, MA, 50, PhD(zool), 55. *Prof Exp:* From instr to assoc prof, 55-68, PROF ZOOL, UNIV ARK, FAYETTEVILLE, 68- *Mem:* Am Genetic Asn. *Res:* Environmental effects on the cell and evolutionary cytology; electron microscopy. *Mailing Add:* Dept of Zool Univ of Ark Fayetteville AR 72701

EVANS, WILLIAM PAUL, b Peoria, Ill, July 19, 22; m 49, 81; c 3. PHYSICS. *Educ:* Univ Ill, BS & MS, 47. *Prof Exp:* Instr math, Bradley Univ, 47-48; MEM STAFF ENG, RES DEPT, CATERPILLAR TRACTOR CO, 48- *Mem:* Am Phys Soc; Soc Automotive Eng; Am Soc Metals. *Res:* Fatigue, crack propagation; fracture mechanics; residual stress; radioisotope techniques. *Mailing Add:* Tech Ctr Caterpillar Tractor Co 100 NE Adams Peoria IL 61629

EVANS, WINIFRED DOYLE, b Logansport, La, Sept 10, 34; m 56; c 2. PHYSICS. *Educ:* La Polytech Inst, BS, 56; Univ Calif, Los Angeles, MS, 58; Univ NMex, PhD(physics), 67. *Prof Exp:* Asst prof physics, La Polytech Inst, 58-60; staff mem, Solid State Physics Dept, Langley Res Ctr, NASA, 60-61; staff mem, Physics Div, 61-79, group leader space sci group, 79-81, DEP DIV LEADER, EARTH & SPACE SCI DIV, LOS ALAMOS NAT LAB, 81- *Mem:* Am Geophys Union; Am Astron Soc. *Res:* X-ray emission from the solar corona; stellar x-ray sources; ultra-soft x-ray spectroscopy; gamma-ray astronomy. *Mailing Add:* 390 El Conejo Los Alamos NM 87544

EVANSON, ROBERT VERNE, b Hammond, Ind, Nov 3, 20; m 47; c 2. PHARMACY. *Educ:* Purdue Univ, BS, 47, MS, 49, PhD(pharm admin), 53. *Prof Exp:* Retail sales clerk, E C Minas Co, 40-41; apprentice pharmacist, Physician's Supply Co, 46; asst instr pharm, 47-48, from instr pharm admin to assoc prof, 48-63, head dept, 66-72, PROF PHARM ADMIN, PURDUE UNIV, 63- *Concurrent Pos:* Am Found Pharmaceut Educ fel; mem bd dirs, Am Asn Col Pharm, 73-75. *Mem:* Fel Acad Pharmaceut Sci; Am Pharmaceut Asn; Am Asn Col Pharm. *Res:* Disintegration of compressed tablets; economic study of drug store operation. *Mailing Add:* 400 Lindberg Ave West Lafayette IN 47906

EVARD, RENE, b Geneva, Switz, Oct 25, 27; nat US; m 52; c 1. BIOCHEMISTRY. *Educ:* Emmanuel Col, BA, 52; Mich State Univ, MS, 55, PhD(chem), 59. *Prof Exp:* Asst prof chem, Union Col, Nebr, 58-71; ASSOC PROF BIOCHEM, LOMA LINDA UNIV, 71- *Mem:* Am Chem Soc. *Res:* Mechanism of enzyme action; isolation; purification and characterization of bacteroid pyrophosphatase. *Mailing Add:* Dept of Biochem Loma Linda Univ Loma Linda CA 92350

EVARTS, EDWARD VAUGHAN, b New York, NY, Mar 28, 26; m 50, 71; c 3. PSYCHIATRY, NEUROPHYSIOLOGY. *Educ:* Harvard Univ, MD, 48. *Prof Exp:* Med house officer, Peter Bent Brigham Hosp, 48-49; res assoc, Yerkes Labs Primate Biol, 49-50; Moseley traveling fel neurol, Nat Hosp, London, 50-51; asst res psychiatrist, Payne Whitney Clin, 51-53; chief physiol sect, Lab Clin Sci, NIMH, 53-71, chief, Lab Neurophysiol, 71-77. *Mem:* Nat Acad Sci; Am Physiol Soc; Int Brain Res Soc; Psychiat Res Soc; Soc Neurosci. *Res:* Neurophysiological correlates of behavior. *Mailing Add:* Lab Neurophysiol Bldg 36 Rm 2D-12 Nat Inst Ment Health Bethesda MD 20205

EVARTS, RITVA POUKKA, b Vesilahti, Finland, Jan 27, 32; US citizen; m 71. EXPERIMENTAL PATHOLOGY. *Educ:* Vet Col, Finland, DVM, 60, PhD(muscular dystrophy), 65. *Prof Exp:* Instr biochem, Col Vet Med, 60-71; vis assoc nutrit biochem, Nat Inst Arthritis & Metab Dis, NIH, 71-75; vis scientist path, Carcinogen Metab & Toxicol Br, 75-81, VET MED OFFICER, NAT CANCER INST, NIH, 81- *Mem:* Am Asn Can Res. *Res:* Microsomal enzyme system; experimental pathology. *Mailing Add:* Bldg 37 Rm 3B-27 Nat Inst Health Bethesda MD 20014

EVCES, CHARLES RICHARD, b East Liverpool, Ohio, Dec 31, 38; m 62; c 2. ENGINEERING MECHANICS, MECHANICAL ENGINEERING. *Educ:* Univ Notre Dame, BSME, 60, MSME, 62; Univ WVa, PhD(eng), 67. *Prof Exp:* Asst prof, 67-74, ASSOC PROF MECH ENG, UNIV ALA, TUSCALOOSA, 74- *Mem:* Am Soc Mech Engrs. *Res:* Dynamics and vibrations; acoustical noise control. *Mailing Add:* Dept of Aerospace & Mech Eng Univ of Ala Tuscaloosa University AL 35486

EVELAND, HARMON EDWIN, b Urbana, Ill, Feb 9, 24; m 44; c 4. GEOLOGY. *Educ:* Univ Ill, BS, 47, MS, 48, PhD(geol), 50. *Prof Exp:* Asst prof geol, Univ Tenn, 50-51; PROF GEOL & HEAD DEPT, LAMAR UNIV, 51- *Mem:* Geol Soc Am; Soc Econ Paleontologists & Mineralogists. *Res:* Pleistocene stratigraphy; geomorphology; physiography. *Mailing Add:* Dept of Geol Lamar Univ Box 10031 Lamar Sta Beaumont TX 77710

EVELAND, WARREN C, b Watsonville, Calif, Aug 24, 04; m 40; c 2. MEDICAL BACTERIOLOGY. *Educ:* Univ Calif, AB, 30; Univ Mich, MSPH, 39; Univ Md, PhD, 52; Am Bd Med Microbiol, dipl. *Prof Exp:* Lab technician, Nev State Hyg Lab, 30-35; dir pub health labs, Alaska Territorial Dept Health, 37-41; chief lab serv, US Army Hosp, 41-45, Bact & Serol Sect, US Army Labs, 45-53, Bact Div, Med Gen Lab, Japan, 53-56 & Bact & Immunol Br, Armed Forces Inst Path, 56-59; from assoc prof to prof, 59-75, EMER PROF EPIDEMIOL, SCH PUB HEALTH, UNIV MICH, 75- *Mem:* Am Soc Microbiol; NY Acad Sci; fel Am Acad Microbiol. *Res:* Medical and public health bacteriology; fluorescent antibody techniques in diagnosis. *Mailing Add:* Dept of Epidemiol Univ of Mich Sch of Pub Health Ann Arbor MI 48104

EVELEIGH, DOUGLAS EDWARD, b Croydon, Eng, Dec 6, 33; m 62; c 2. MICROBIOLOGY. *Educ:* Univ London, BSc, 56; Univ Exeter, PhD(mycol), 59. *Prof Exp:* Fel, Nat Res Coun, Halifax, 59-61; Nat Acad Sci-Nat Res Coun vis scientist, US Dept Army, Natick, Mass, 61-63; res assoc bact, Univ Wis, 63-65; assoc res officer, Nat Res Coun, Sask, 65-70; PROF, DEPT BIOCHEM & MICROBIOL, RUTGERS UNIV, 70- *Concurrent Pos:* Assoc ed, Can Soc Microbiol, 70-73 & Europ J Appl Microbiol, 78- *Mem:* Am Soc Microbiol; Brit Soc Gen Microbiol; Can Soc Microbiol; Mycol Soc Am. *Res:* Microbial polysaccharases; non-microbial polysaccharides; leguminous symbiotic nitrogen fixation; fungal ecology. *Mailing Add:* Dept of Biochem & Microbiol Cook Col Rutgers Univ New Brunswick NJ 08903

EVELEIGH, VIRGIL W(ILLIAM), b Dexter, NY, Aug 20, 31; m 56; c 3. ELECTRICAL ENGINEERING. *Educ:* Purdue Univ, BS, 57, MS, 58, PhD(elec eng), 61. *Prof Exp:* Technician commun systs, Gen Elec Co, NY, 53-54, field serv engr, radar systs, 54, engr control systs, 61-64; PROF ELEC & COMPUT ENG, SYRACUSE UNIV, 64-, CHMN DEPT, 79- *Concurrent Pos:* Consult, Syracuse Res Corp, 64- *Mem:* Inst Elec & Electronics Engrs; Am Inst Aeronaut & Astronaut. *Res:* Control systems; computational methods for optimization; adaptive control; radar; signal processing. *Mailing Add:* 271 Link Hall Syracuse Univ Syracuse NY 13210

EVENS, FLOYD MONTE, b Herculaneum, Mo, Jan 21, 32; m 52; c 5. ANALYTICAL CHEMISTRY, SPECTROSCOPY. *Educ:* Southeast Mo State Col, BS, 55; Iowa State Univ, MS, 59, PhD(anal chem), 62. *Prof Exp:* Chem technician, Mallinckrodt Chem Co, 53; jr res assoc, Ames Lab, AEC, Iowa State Univ, 54-62; res chemist, Procter & Gamble Co, 62-63; res scientist, 63-68, ASSOC DIR, CONOCO INC, 68- *Mem:* Am Chem Soc; Soc Appl Spectros. *Res:* Instrumental methods of chemical analysis; atomic and molecular spectroscopy; gas chromatography; chemical separations. *Mailing Add:* 2716 Larchmont Ponca City OK 74601

EVENS, LEONARD, b Brooklyn, NY, June 28, 33; m 58; c 3. MATHEMATICS. *Educ:* Cornell Univ, AB, 55; Harvard Univ, AM, 56, PhD(math), 60. *Prof Exp:* Instr math, Univ Chicago, 60-61; asst prof, Univ Calif, Berkeley, 61-64; assoc prof, 64-69, PROF MATH, NORTHWESTERN UNIV, 69- *Mem:* Am Math Soc. *Res:* Homological algebra; group theory. *Mailing Add:* Dept of Math Northwestern Univ Evanston IL 60201

EVENS, MARTHA WALTON, b Boston, Mass, Jan 1, 35; m 58; c 3. COMPUTER SCIENCE, COMPUTATIONAL LINGUISTICS. *Educ:* Bryn Mawr Col, AB, 55; Radcliffe Col, AM, 57; Northwestern Univ, PhD(comput sci), 75. *Prof Exp:* Instr math, Calif State Univ, Hayward, 61-64 & Nat Col Educ, Evanston, 66-68; lectr, Northwestern Univ, 65-66, lectr eve div, 68-69, asst & consult, Vogelback Comput Ctr, 69-72, instr deptr comput sci, 72-74; asst prof comput sci, 75-81, ASSOC PROF COMPUT SCI, ILL INST TECHNOL, 81- *Concurrent Pos:* Assoc ed, Am Math Monthly & Am J Computational Linguistics; co-ed, Proceedings Nat Comput Conf, 81; prin investr, NSF Awards, Info Sci Div & Math & Comp Sci Directorate. *Mem:* Asn Comput Mach; Asn Comput Ling; Math Asn Am. *Res:* Artificial intelligence; natural language processing; programming languages; compilers; network compilers. *Mailing Add:* Dept of Comput Sci Ill Inst of Technol Chicago IL 60616

EVENSEN, JAMES MILLARD, b McVille, NDak, Nov 8, 31; m 58; c 3. GEOLOGY. *Educ:* Univ Minn, BA, 55; Univ Ariz, MS, 61, PhD(geol), 69. *Prof Exp:* Geologist, Pan Am Petrol Corp, 62-63; PROF GEOL & CHMN DEPT, CALIF LUTHERAN COL, 65- *Concurrent Pos:* Res grant, Union Oil Co, Calif, 74-78. *Mem:* Geol Soc Am; Nat Asn Geol Teachers; Am Geol Inst. *Res:* Petrogenesis and structure of metamorphic rocks as they relate to base metal mineralization. *Mailing Add:* Calif Lutheran Col Thousand Oaks CA 91360

EVENSEN, KATHLEEN BROWN, b Tupper Lake, NY. POSTHARVEST PHYSIOLOGY, PLANT SENESCENCE. *Educ:* State Univ NY Col Potsdam, BA, 74; Univ NH, MS, 76; Univ Fla, PhD(hort), 78. *Prof Exp:* Res assoc fel, Univ Mo, 79-80; ASST PROF POSTHARVEST PHYSIOL, PA STATE UNIV, 80- *Mem:* Am Soc Hort Sci; Am Soc Plant Physiologists; Japanese Soc Plant Physiologists. *Res:* Effects of calcium and plant growth regulators on ripening and senescence; handling and storage of horticultural crops. *Mailing Add:* Dept Hort Pa State Univ University Park PA 16802

EVENSEN, THOMAS JAMES, b Menominee, Mich, Jan 21, 33; m 55; c 2. ORGANIC CHEMISTRY. *Educ:* Augustana Col, Ill, AB, 55; Univ Minn, Minneapolis, PhD(org chem), 59. *Prof Exp:* Teaching asst org chem, Univ Minn, Minneapolis, 55-57; sr chemist, 59-67, res specialist, 68-70, res supvr, 70-73, MGR MAT DEVELOP, COPYING PRODS DIV, 3M CO, 73- *Mem:* Am Chem Soc. *Res:* New product designs; imaging systems. *Mailing Add:* Minn Mining & Mfg Co 3M Ctr St Paul MN 55101

EVENSON, DONALD PAUL, b Story City, Iowa, Oct 30, 40; c 2. CELL BIOLOGY, VIROLOGY. *Educ:* Augustana Col, BA, 64; Univ Colo, PhD(cell biol), 68. *Prof Exp:* Fel, Inst Molecular Biophys, Fla State Univ, 68-70; staff scientist electron micros & virol, Union Carbide Res Inst, NY, 70-72; ASSOC VIRUS ULTRASTRUCT, SLOAN KETTERING INST CANCER RES, 72-; ASST PROF BIOL, GRAD SCH MED SCI, CORNELL UNIV, 72- *Mem:* AAAS; Am Soc Cell Biol; Am Soc Microbiol; NY Acad Sci. *Res:* Controls of DNA synthesis and cell division; ultrastructure of cells, viruses and nucleic acids; replication of DNA and RNA oncogenic viruses. *Mailing Add:* Virus Ultrastruct Lab Sloan Kettering Inst Cancer Res New York NY 10021

EVENSON, EDWARD B, b Milwaukee, Wis, Dec 30, 42; m 63; c 1. GLACIAL GEOLOGY, GEOMORPHOLOGY. *Educ:* Univ Wis, Milwaukee, BS, 65, MS, 69; Univ Mich, PhD(geol), 72. *Prof Exp:* Sr res geologist, Exxon Prod Res Lab, Exxon Corp, 72-73; asst prof, 73-81, ASSOC PROF GEOL, LEHIGH UNIV, 81- *Concurrent Pos:* Dir, Environ Sci & Resource Mgt, Lehigh Univ, 73-; res fel, Univ Western Ont, 75-76. *Mem:* Geol Soc Am; Sigma Xi; Am Asn Quaternary Geologists. *Res:* Glacial geology of the Great Lakes Region and northeast Pennsylvania; deglaciation of Idaho Rockies; sedimentology and fabric of glacial deposits; glacial geomorphology. *Mailing Add:* Dept Geol Sci Lehigh Univ Bethlehem PA 18015

EVENSON, KENNETH MELVIN, atomic physics, molecular physics, see previous edition

EVENSON, MERLE ARMIN, b La Crosse, Wis, July 27, 34; m 57; c 2. ANALYTICAL CHEMISTRY, TOXICOLOGY. *Educ:* Univ Wis-La Crosse, BS, 56; Univ Wis-Madison, MS(guid) & MS(sci educ), 60, PhD(anal chem), 66; Am Bd Clin Chemists, dipl. *Prof Exp:* From instr to asst prof med, Univ Wis-Madison, 65-69, asst dir clin labs, Univ Hosps, 65-67, dir clin chem, 67-69; vis lectr biol chem & NIH spec res fel, Harvard Med Sch, 69-71; assoc prof med, 71-75, PROF MED, UNIV WIS-MADISON, 75-, DIR TOXICOL LABS, UNIV HOSPS, 71- *Concurrent Pos:* Consult, Instrument Prod Div, E I du Pont de Nemours & Co, Inc, 67-71; Nat Inst Gen Med Sci, NIH, 68-72, Anal Div, Oak Ridge Nat Lab, AEC, 69-73; Med Devices Sect, Fed Drug Admin, 75-81 & Millipore Corp, 79-; nat res coun eval panel anal chem, Nat Bur Standards, 81- *Mem:* AAAS; Am Chem Soc; Am Asn Clin Chem; Acad Clin Lab Physicians & Sci; Sigma Xi. *Res:* Development of analytical procedures for drugs and trace elements and the relationship of these results to human health and disease; physical-chemistry studies of structure-function relationships in enzymes and changes of metalloproteins and metalloenzymes in human disease. *Mailing Add:* Dept Med & Path Univ Wis 600 Highland Ave Madison WI 53792

EVENSON, PAUL ARTHUR, b Chicago, Ill, Jan 27, 46; m 68; c 3. COSMIC RAY PHYSICS. *Educ:* Univ Chicago, BS, 67, MS, 68, PhD(physics), 72. *Prof Exp:* Res assoc, 72-76, SR RES ASSOC COSMIC RAY PHYSICS, ENRICO FERMI INST, UNIV CHICAGO, 76- *Concurrent Pos:* NATO fel, Danish Space Res Inst, 73-74; vis scientist, Max Planck Inst, Garching, 81. *Mem:* Am Phys Soc. *Res:* Experimental study cosmic radiation using high altitude balloon and satellite instrumentation. *Mailing Add:* Enrico Fermi Inst 933 E 56th St Chicago IL 60637

EVENSON, WILLIAM EDWIN, b Martinez, Calif, Oct 12, 41; m 64; c 5. THEORETICAL SOLID STATE PHYSICS. *Educ:* Brigham Young Univ, BS, 65; Iowa State Univ, PhD(physics), 68. *Prof Exp:* Res assoc physics, Univ Pa, 68-70; from asst prof to assoc prof, 70-79, assoc dir, 80-81, PROF PHYSICS, BRIGHAM YOUNG UNIV, 79-, DIR GEN EDUC, 81- *Concurrent Pos:* NSF fel, 68-69; vis colleague, Univ Hawaii, 77-78. *Mem:* Am Phys Soc; Am Asn Physics Teachers; Botanical Soc Am. *Res:* Theory of magnetism in metals; theory of dilute magnetic alloys; theory of melting; applications of physics in ecology; theory of defects in solids. *Mailing Add:* Dept of Physics Brigham Young Univ Provo UT 84602

EVERAGE, ARCHIE EDWARD, JR, rheology, see previous edition

EVERARD, NOEL JAMES, b New Orleans, La, Dec 24, 23; m 50; c 2. CIVIL ENGINEERING, MECHANICS. *Educ:* La State Univ, BS, 48, MS, 57; Tex A&M Univ, PhD(civil eng), 62. *Prof Exp:* From instr to asst prof civil eng, La State Univ, 48-60; design engr, David W Godat & Assocs, Consult Engrs, La, 49-53, chief engr, 53-56; from assoc prof to prof eng mech, 60-72, PROF CIVIL ENG & CHMN DEPT, UNIV TEX, ARLINGTON, 72- *Concurrent Pos:* Consult, William Dawson, Civil Engr, La, 56-60, J Weldon Hunnicut, Consult Engr, Tex, 60-, Freese, Nichols & Endress, 63-, Young-Hadawi Assocs, 70-, Welton-Becket Assocs, 75- & Young-Hadawi, 74- *Mem:* Am Soc Civil Engrs; Am Concrete Inst; fel Sigma Xi. *Res:* Theoretical and applied mechanics; column design and torsion in beams of reinforced concrete; computer methods in structural engineering. *Mailing Add:* Dept of Civil Eng Univ of Tex Arlington TX 76019

EVEREST, F(REDERICK) ALTON, b Gaston, Ore, Nov 22, 09; m 34; c 3. ELECTRICAL ENGINEERING. *Educ:* Ore State Col, BS, 32; Stanford Univ, EE, 36. *Hon Degrees:* DSc, Wheaton Col, 59. *Prof Exp:* TV engr, Don Lee Broadcasting Co, 36; asst prof elec eng, Ore State Col, 36-41; engr & sect chief, Calif Div War Res, US Navy Radio & Sound Lab, San Diego, 41-45; assoc dir, Moody Inst Sci, Los Angeles, 45-53, dir, 53-70; sr lectr & head div cinematog, Dept Commun Hong Kong Baptist Col, 70-73; ACOUST CONSULT, 73- *Mem:* Acoust Soc Am; sr mem Inst Elec & Electronics Engrs; fel Am Sci Affiliation; fel Soc Motion Picture & TV Engrs. *Res:* Television video amplifiers; high efficiency radio-telephone transmitters; electric fence controllers; directional broadcast antennae; propagation of underwater sound; underwater sounds of biological origin; cardiac pulse duplicator; scientific films; studio acoustics. *Mailing Add:* 6275 S Roundhill Dr Whittier CA 90601

EVERETT, ALLEN EDWARD, b Kansas City, Mo, July 8, 33; m 66. ELEMENTARY PARTICLE PHYSICS. *Educ:* Princeton Univ, AB, 55; Harvard Univ, AM, 56, PhD(physics), 61. *Prof Exp:* From asst prof to assoc prof, 60-76, chmn dept, 77-80, PROF PHYSICS, TUFTS UNIV, 76- *Mem:* Am Phys Soc. *Res:* Theory of elementary particles. *Mailing Add:* Dept of Physics Tufts Univ Medford MA 02155

EVERETT, ARDELL GORDON, b Cambridge, Mass, July 27, 37; m 60; c 3. GEOLOGY, INORGANIC CHEMISTRY. *Educ:* Cornell Univ, AB, 59; Univ Okla, MS, 62; Univ Tex, Austin, PhD(geol & geochem), 68. *Prof Exp:* Jr geologist, Shell Oil Co, Colo, 60; teaching asst geol & geophys, Univ Okla, 61-62; from instr to asst prof geol, Ohio State Univ, 67-69; staff asst water qual & res, Dept Interior, Washington, DC, 69-70, actg dep asst secy appl sci & eng, 70, dep asst secy, 70, dir, Off Tech Anal, Environ Protection Agency, 70-74; tech adv & dir, Regulatory Litigation Dept, Am Petroleum Inst, 74-77; PRES, EVERETT & ASSOC, 78- *Concurrent Pos:* Consult, Am Petrol Inst, Dept Mineral & Energy, Papua New Guinea & Rocky Nat Oil & Gas Asn. *Honors & Awards:* Franklin Gilliam Prize, Univ Tex Libr, 67. *Mem:* Fel Geol

Soc Am; Am Inst Prof Geol; Geochem Soc; Soc Environ Geochem & Health; Soc Min Eng. *Res:* economic geology; applied geochemistry; environmental geology and resources management; sedimentology; geochemistry of petroleum and economic mineral formations; environmental geochemistry. *Mailing Add:* 203 Dale Dr Rockville MD 20850

EVERETT, GEORGE ALBERT, b Lewiston, Maine, Sept 22, 24. BIOCHEMISTRY. *Educ:* Oberlin Col, AB, 47; Cornell Univ, MS, 59. *Prof Exp:* Chemist pharmaceut res, Norwich Pharmacal Co, 47-49, biochemist, 50-53; jr anal chemist, Purdue Univ, 49-50; asst med res, Yale Univ, 53-54; biochemist, Dept Army, Ft Detrick, 54-55 & Walter Reed Army Med Ctr, 55-56; BIOCHEMIST, AGR RES SERV, USDA, 56- *Res:* Nutritional studies in trace mineral deficiencies particularly zinc. *Mailing Add:* US Plant Soil & Nutrit Lab Tower Rd Ithaca NY 14850

EVERETT, GLEN EXNER, b St George, Utah, Oct 3, 34; m 58; c 3. SOLID STATE PHYSICS. *Educ:* Univ Utah, BA, 56, Univ Chicago, MS, 57, PhD(physics), 61. *Prof Exp:* Actg asst prof, 60-62, from asst prof to assoc prof, 62-74, PROF PHYSICS, UNIV CALIF, RIVERSIDE, 74- *Concurrent Pos:* Consult, US Naval Weapons Ctr, Calif, 63- *Mem:* Am Phys Soc. *Res:* Cyclotron resonance in metals; ferro and antiferromagnetic resonance in binary rare earth compounds. *Mailing Add:* Dept of Physics Univ of Calif Riverside CA 92502

EVERETT, GUY M, b Missouri Valley, Iowa, Feb 6, 15. NEUROPHARMACOLOGY, PSYCHOPHARMACOLOGY. *Educ:* Univ Iowa, BA, 37; Univ Md, PhD(physiol), 43. *Prof Exp:* Sect head neuropharmacol, Abbott Labs, 43-68, res scientist, 68-71; LECTR PHARMACOL, SCH MED, UNIV CALIF, SAN FRANCISCO, 72- *Concurrent Pos:* Consult res div, Abbott Labs, 71-76. *Mem:* Am Soc Pharmacol & Exp Therapeut; Am Col Neuropsychopharmacol; Int Col Neuropsychopharmacol. *Res:* Neuropharmacology, biogenic amines, dopamine in parkinsonism and behavior; interrelation of brain biogenic amines; antiepileptic drugs. *Mailing Add:* Dept Pharmacol S-1210 Sch Med Univ Calif San Francisco CA 94143

EVERETT, HERBERT LYMAN, b New Haven, Conn, Aug 9, 22; m 44; c 2. PLANT BREEDING, GENETICS. *Educ:* Yale Univ, BA, 44, MS, 47, PhD(genetics), 49. *Prof Exp:* Res asst, Dept Plant Breeding, Conn Agr Exp Sta, New Haven, 49-52; from asst prof to assoc prof, 52-64, dir resident instr, Col Agr, 66-77, PROF PLANT BREEDING, CORNELL UNIV, 64- *Concurrent Pos:* Proj leader & vis prof, Cornell Univ Grad Educ Prog, Col Agr, Univ Philippines, 64-65. *Mem:* AAAS; Genetics Soc Am; Am Soc Agron; Am Soc Hort Sci. *Res:* Plant breeding research and genetics research in corn. *Mailing Add:* 409 Bradfield Hall Col of Agr Cornell Univ Ithaca NY 14850

EVERETT, JAMES PEEK, JR, animal nutrition, see previous edition

EVERETT, JOHN WENDELL, b Ovid, Mich, Mar 5, 06; m 32; c 2. ANATOMY, NEUROENDOCRINOLOGY. *Educ:* Olivet Col, AB, 28; Yale Univ, PhD(zool), 32. *Prof Exp:* Instr biol, Goucher Col, 30-31; instr anat, 32-35, assoc, 35-39, from asst prof to prof, 39-76, EMER PROF ANAT, DUKE UNIV, 76- *Concurrent Pos:* Vis prof, Univ Calif, Los Angeles, 52 & Univ Tenn, 54. *Honors & Awards:* Carl G Hartman Lect Award, Soc Study Reprod, 71; Fred Conrad Koch Medal, Endocrine Soc, 78; Sir Henry Dale Medal, Soc Endocrinol, 77. *Mem:* Am Asn Anatomists (pres, 77-78); Endocrine Soc; Am Physiol Soc; Int Soc Neuroendocrinol; fel NY Acad Sci. *Res:* Physiology of reproduction; endocrinology of the ovary and hypophysis; hypothalamic control of hypophysis. *Mailing Add:* Dept of Anat Duke Univ Med Ctr Durham NC 27710

EVERETT, K R, b Corning, NY, Jan 8, 34; m 56; c 2. GEOLOGY. *Educ:* Univ Buffalo, BA, 55; Univ Utah, MS, 58; Ohio State Univ, PhD(geol), 63. *Prof Exp:* Polar & mt geologist, US Army Natick Labs, 64-67; from asst prof to assoc prof agron, Col Agr & Home Econ, 67-78, RES ASSOC GEOMORPHOL, INST POLAR STUDIES, OHIO STATE UNIV, 61-, PROF AGRON, COL AGR & HOME ECON, UNIV, 78- *Mem:* AAAS; fel Arctic Inst NAm; Geol Soc Am; Am Soc Agron. *Res:* Geomorphology and pedology; genesis, classification and distribution of polar and mountain soils, primarily Alaska, Canadian Arctic, Greenland and Antarctica; slope morphology, mass wasting, permafrost and patterned ground development. *Mailing Add:* Dept of Agron Ohio State Univ Col of Agr & Home Econ Columbus OH 43210

EVERETT, KENNETH GARY, b Vicksburg, Miss, Nov 25, 42. INORGANIC CHEMISTRY. *Educ:* Washington & Lee Univ, BS, 64; Stanford Univ, PhD(chem), 68. *Prof Exp:* Asst prof chem, Northeast La State Col, 68-69; asst prof, 69-77, PROF CHEM, STETSON UNIV, 77- *Concurrent Pos:* Consult, Columbian Carbon Co, La, 69- *Mem:* Am Chem Soc. *Res:* Chemical kinetics and mechanisms of inorganic reactions. *Mailing Add:* Dept of Chem Stetson Univ De Land FL 32720

EVERETT, LORNE GORDON, b Thunder Bay, Ont, Jan 1, 43; m 69; c 2. HYDROLOGY, WATER QUALITY. *Educ:* Lakehead Univ, BSc, 66, Hons, 68; Univ Ariz, MS, 69, PhD(hydrol), 72; Tucson Gen Hosp, ASMT, 70. *Prof Exp:* Chemist water qual, Great Lakes Paper Co, Can, 66-67; asst prof hydrol, Univ Ariz, 72-74, Off Water res grant, 72-73; prof staff hydrol, Ctr Advan Studies, 74-76, mgr, Water Resources Prog, Gen Elec-Tempo, 76-78, mgr, Advan Energy Prog & Int Prog, 78-81, MGR, NAT RESOURCES PROG, KAMAN TEMPO, 81- *Concurrent Pos:* Collabr, Nat Park Serv, 71-74; consult, Bell Eng Co, 71-74, Col Eng, Utah State Univ, 72-73, Develop & Assistance Co, 73-74 & CODECU Int Inc, 73-74; proj mgr groundwater monitoring strategies, Environ Protection Agency, 73-76, prog mgr, 76-81; Invited dir, UNESCO Int Symp on water pollution control, Paris, 83. *Mem:* Am Water Resources Asn; Am Med Lab Asn; Am Asn Univ Prof; Am Soc Civil Eng; Int Water Resources Asn. *Res:* Water quality investigations utilizing monitoring, aquatic ecosystem modeling, eutrophication process

studies, physical, biological and chemical reservoir models, remote sensing, saturated and unsaturated flow equations; published over 65 papers in professional journals. *Mailing Add:* Kaman Tempo PO Drawer QQ 816 State St Santa Barbara CA 93102

EVERETT, MARK ALLEN, b Oklahoma City, Okla, May 30, 28. MEDICINE, DERMATOLOGY. *Educ:* Univ Okla, BA, 47, MD, 51; Tulane Univ, 52; Am Bd Dermat, dipl, 58. *Prof Exp:* Intern pediat, Univ Mich, 51-52, resident dermat, 54-56, instr, 56-57; from instr to assoc prof, 57-68, dir res labs, 59, dir resident training & res, 63-64, PROF DERMAT, MED SCH, UNIV OKLA, 68-, HEAD DEPT, 64-, DERMATOLOGIST-IN-CHIEF, UNIV HOSP, 70-, PROF & INTERIM HEAD PATH, 78- *Concurrent Pos:* Consult, Vet Admin Hosp, Oklahoma City & St Anthony Hosp, Oklahoma City; chmn fac bd, Univ Okla, 74- *Mem:* AMA; Am Acad Dermat; Am Dermat Asn; Soc Invest Dermat; Asn Prof Dermat (pres, 76-78). *Res:* Cutaneous photobiology; ultraviolet erythema; clinical dermatology; dermatopathology; medical education and organization. *Mailing Add:* Dept of Dermat Med Sch Univ of Okla Oklahoma City OK 73104

EVERETT, MARK REUBEN, biochemistry, deceased

EVERETT, PAUL HARRISON, b Lake City, Fla, Nov 5, 27; m 51; c 6. SOIL FERTILITY, VEGETABLE CROPS. *Educ:* Univ Fla, BSA, 50, MSA, 55; Purdue Univ, PhD(soil microbiol), 58. *Prof Exp:* From asst prof to assoc prof, 58-68, PROF SOIL SCI, UNIV FLA, 68- *Mem:* Am Soc Agron; Am Soc Hort Sci. *Res:* Soil fertility and plant nutrition, involving macronutrients and micronutrients as related to yield and quality of vegetables. *Mailing Add:* Agr Res Ctr Univ of Fla Rt 1 Box 2G Immokalee FL 33934

EVERETT, PAUL MARVIN, b Toledo, Ohio, Mar 15, 40; m 68; c 1. SOLID STATE PHYSICS. *Educ:* Case Inst Technol, BS, 62; Case Western Reserve Univ, PhD(solid state physics), 68. *Prof Exp:* Res assoc physics, La State Univ, Baton Rouge, 68-71, admin asst, 71-72; asst prof physics, Univ Ky, 72-79, MEM TECH STAFF, TEX INSTRUMENTS, INC, 79- *Mem:* Am Phys Soc; sr mem Inst Elec & Electronics Engrs. *Res:* Properties of electrons in metals; study of fermi surfaces via the de Haas-van Alphen and galvanomagnetic effects; electron bombarded countercurrent distribution imagers, infrared component identification imagers. *Mailing Add:* Dept of Physics & Astron Univ of Ky Lexington KY 40506

EVERETT, ROBERT LINE, b Duquesne, Pa, June 19, 28; m 52; c 2. MECHANICAL ENGINEERING. *Educ:* Univ Pittsburgh, BS, 51 & 57. *Prof Exp:* Res engr, Gen Motors Corp, 57-63, assoc sr res engr, 63-67, sr res engr, 67-73; asst mgr, fed regulations, environ activities staff, 73-75, mgr fed regulations, 75-77, ASST DIR, AUTOMOTIVE EMISSION CONTROL, 77- *Mem:* Soc Automotive Engrs. *Res:* Engine, fuel relationships, emissions; durability; driveability; abnormal combustion. *Mailing Add:* Environ Activities Staff GM Tech Ctr 12 Mile & Mound Rds Warren MI 48090

EVERETT, ROBERT R(IVERS), b Yonkers, NY, June 26, 21; m 44; c 5. ELECTRICAL ENGINEERING. *Educ:* Duke Univ, BS, 42; Mass Inst Technol, MS, 43. *Prof Exp:* Res & develop engr servomechanism lab, Mass Inst Tech, 42-51, assoc dir digital comput lab & assoc head digital comput div, Lincoln Lab, 51-56, head digital comput div, 56-58; tech dir command & control systs, 58-59, vpres tech opers, 59-69, exec vpres, 69, PRES, MITRE CORP, 69- *Concurrent Pos:* Consult, Air Defense Panel, President's Sci Adv Comt, 59-60 & Air Force Systs Command Range Tech Adv Group, 62-68; mem, Air Traffic Control Adv Comt, US Dept Transp, Off Dir Defense Res & Eng, Systs Eng Mgt Panel & Defense Sci Bd Task Force Res & Develop Mgt, 68-69; mem sci adv bd, US Air Force, 69-; mem, Adv Coun Panel Major Systs Acquisition of the Comn Govt Procurement, 70-72 & NASA Tracking & Data Acquisition Adv Panel, 71-72; mem bd trustees, Northern Energy Corp; chief scientist, US Air Force Sci Adv Bd; mem, Defense Commun Agency's Sci Adv Group & Air Force Studies Bd C3 Technol Panel; consult, Defense Sci Bd & Div Adv Group, Electronic Systs Div, US Air Force; mem bd dirs, Inst Educ Serv; mem, McLean Hosp Vis Comt for Arlington Sch. *Mem:* Nat Acad Eng; fel Inst Elec & Electronics Engrs; Asn Comput Mach; Sigma Xi; AAAS. *Res:* Computer technology; military command control, surveillance and communications systems. *Mailing Add:* The Mitre Corp PO Box 208 Bedford MA 01730

EVERETT, ROBERT W, JR, b New Orleans, La, June 13, 21; m 52; c 1. MICROPALEONTOLOGY. *Educ:* Tulane Univ, BS, 42. *Prof Exp:* Seismic computor, Ark Fuel Oil, 42-43; micropaleontologist, 46-53, res geologist, 53-58, micropaleontologist in charge of lab, 59-67, micropaleontologist, 67-70, SR PALEONTOLOGIST, TEXICO, INC, 70- *Mem:* Am Asn Petrol Geol. *Res:* Foraminifera as used in economic work in oil industry; salt dome research; Gulf Coast geology and paleontology; nannofossil research in the Tertiary of Gulf Coast and especially South Louisiana; subsurface deltaic research. *Mailing Add:* 6511 General Diaz New Orleans LA 70124

EVERETT, WILBUR WAYNE, b Benton, Ark, Mar 4, 32; m 54; c 2. BIOPHYSICAL CHEMISTRY. *Educ:* Ouachita Baptist Col, BS, 54; Purdue Univ, PhD(chem), 59. *Prof Exp:* Instr chem, Purdue Univ, 55-56; asst scientist, Geront Br, Nat Heart Inst, 59-61; PROF CHEM, OUACHITA BAPTIST UNIV, 61-, CHMN DEPT, 66- *Mem:* Fel Am Inst Chemists; Am Chem Soc. *Res:* Physical chemistry; structure of proteins and carbohydrate high polymers; application of thermodynamics and hydrodynamics to solutions of macromolecules. *Mailing Add:* Dept of Chem Ouachita Baptist Univ Arkadelphia AR 71923

EVERETT, WILLIS L(YNN), b Birmingham, Mich, June 8, 23; m 49; c 2. NUCLEAR ENGINEERING. *Educ:* Univ Mich, BS, 55, MS, 57, PhD(nuclear eng), 62. *Prof Exp:* Asst, Radiation Lab, Univ Mich, 59-60; proj engr, Bendix Systs Div, 61-62; asst prof physics, Univ Wyo, 62-64, assoc prof eng, 64-65; MEM FAC NUCLEAR ENG, UNIV N MEX, 65- *Mem:* Am Nuclear Soc. *Res:* Plasma systems; thermonuclear devices. *Mailing Add:* Col of Eng Univ of NMex Albuquerque NM 87106

EVERHARD, MARTIN EDWARD, b Pittsburgh, Pa, Jan 28, 33; m 68; c 5. PHYSICAL CHEMISTRY, SURGERY. *Educ:* Col William & Mary, BS, 53; Univ Va, PhD(phys chem), 59; NY Univ, MD, 67; Am Bd Surg, dipl. *Prof Exp:* Sr res scientist phys chem, Squibb Inst Med Res, Olin Mathieson Chem Corp, 59-63; Squibb Inst grant, NY Univ, 63-65; mem surg house staff, St Vincent's Hosp, Bridgeport, Conn, 67-68; surg resident, 68-71, CHIEF RESIDENT SURG, MONTEFIORE HOSP & MED CTR, 71-; DIR, INTENSIVE CARE UNIT, PHELPS MEM HOSP, TARRYTOWN, 74- *Concurrent Pos:* Rubin scholar med, NY Univ, 63-64, univ merit scholar, 64-67; attend surgeon, NY Med Col, Valhalla, 72- & Phelps Mem Hosp, Tarrytown, 72- *Mem:* Am Chem NY Acad Sci; AMA; fel Am Col Surgeons; fel Int Col Surgeons. *Res:* Aqueous solution theory; kinetics of color reactions; differential thermal analysis; medical applications of transport through lipid-like membranes; vitamin B-12 like compounds; clinical and vascular surgery; intestinal blood flow. *Mailing Add:* 308 Chappaqua Rd Briarcliff NY 10510

EVERHART, DONALD LEE, b Erie, Pa, Jan 27, 32; m 55. IMMUNOLOGY, BIOCHEMISTRY. *Educ:* Grove City Col, BS, 54; Boston Univ, AM, 58, PhD(immunochem, biochem), 61. *Prof Exp:* Res assoc, Univ Tenn Mem Res Ctr & Hosp, 61-63; res immunochemist, Res Inst, Ill Inst Technol, 63-66; asst prof microbiol, Med Col Va, 66-72; assoc prof, 72-78, PROF MICROBIOL, COL DENT, NY UNIV, 78-, CHMN DEPT, 72- *Mem:* AAAS; Int Asn Dent Res; Am Chem Soc; NY Acad Sci. *Res:* Immunoglobulin A and its productive effects in oral disease. *Mailing Add:* Dept of Microbiol NY Univ Col of Dent New York NY 10010

EVERHART, DONALD LOUGH, b Troy, Ohio, July 18, 17; m 42; c 4. ECONOMIC GEOLOGY. *Educ:* Denison Univ, AB, 39; Harvard Univ, AM, 42, PhD(geol), 53. *Prof Exp:* Asst geol, Denison Univ, 37-39; fel mineral, Harvard Univ, 40-42; geologist, US Geol Surv, 42-48; geologist & chief, Geol Br, AEC, 49-54, geologist & chief, Geol Adv Div Raw Mat, 54-59; chief geologist, Int Minerals & Chem Corp, 59-70, div vpres, Mining & Explor Div, 70-73 & Geol & Explor Div, 73-77; proj mgr, Nat Uranium Resource Eval Prog, US Dept Energy, 77-79, mgr, Grand Junction Off, 79-81; CONSULT GEOLOGIST, 81- *Mem:* Fel Geol Soc Am; Soc Econ Geologists; Am Inst Mining Engrs. *Res:* Petrology and geology of batholithic igneous rocks; geology of the Franciscan group of California; geology of quicksilver and uranium ore deposits; genesis and economic geology of uranium deposits; economic geology of phosphate and potash deposits. *Mailing Add:* Unit 10 B 2700 G Rd Grand Junction CO 81501

EVERHART, EDGAR, b Akron, Ohio, June 20, 20; m 43; c 2. CELESTIAL MECHANICS, ASTRONOMY. *Educ:* Oberlin Col, AB, 42; Mass Inst Technol, PhD(physics), 48. *Prof Exp:* Staff mem, Radiation Lab, Mass Inst Technol, 42-45, res assoc, 45-48; instr physics, Darthmouth Col, 48-50; from asst prof to prof, Univ Conn, 50-69; PROF PHYSICS, UNIV DENVER, 69-, DIR, CHAMBERLIN OBSERV, 69- *Mem:* Am Phys Soc; Am Astron Soc; Int Astron Union. *Res:* Atomic and ionic collision studies; celestial mechanics; comets; astronomical photography. *Mailing Add:* Dept of Physics Univ of Denver Denver CO 80208

EVERHART, LEIGHTON PHREANER, JR, b Charleston, WVa, Sept 22, 42. BIOLOGY. *Educ:* Univ Del, BA, 63, MS, 66; Univ Calif, Berkeley, PhD(zool), 70. *Prof Exp:* Res assoc cell biol, Univ Colo, 70-73; chemist cent res, 73-76, develop rep agr chem, 76-78, supvr prod regist, 78, asst mgr prod regist, 78-80, REGIONAL MKT MGR, E I DU PONT DE NEMOURS & CO, INC, 80- *Concurrent Pos:* NIH fel, 67-70 & 71-73. *Mem:* Sigma Xi; Am Soc Cell Biol; Am Chem Soc. *Res:* Control of cell division, cell cycle-cell surface interactions; human health and environmental safety aspects of pesticides. *Mailing Add:* Dept Biochem E I du Pont de Nemours & Co Inc Wilmington DE 19898

EVERHART, THOMAS E(UGENE), b Kansas City, Mo, Feb 15, 32; m 53; c 4. ELECTRICAL ENGINEERING, APPLIED PHYSICS. *Educ:* Harvard Univ, AB, 53; Univ Calif, Los Angeles, MSc, 55; Cambridge Univ, PhD(eng), 58. *Prof Exp:* Mem tech staff, Hughes Res Labs, 53-55; from asst prof to assoc prof elec eng, Univ Calif, Berkeley, 58-67, Miller res prof, 69-70, chmn dept elec eng & comput sci, 72-77, prof elec eng, 67-78; DEAN, COL ENGRS, CORNELL UNIV, ITHACA, 79- *Concurrent Pos:* Fel scientist, Westinghouse Res Labs, 62-63; NSF sr fel & guest prof, Univ Tübingen, 66-67; consult, Hughes Res Labs; Guggenheim Mem Found fel, 74-75. *Mem:* AAAS; fel Inst Elec & Electronics Engrs; Electron Micros Soc Am (pres-elect, 76, pres, 77, past pres, 78); Nat Acad Eng. *Res:* Scanning electron microscopy; electron physics; electron beam recording; semiconductor electronics; microfabrication. *Mailing Add:* Dean Col Engrs Cornell Univ Ithaca NY 14853

EVERHART, WATSON HARRY, b Connellsville, Pa, June 5, 18; m 39; c 3. BIOLOGY. *Educ:* Westminster Col, Pa, BS, 40; Univ Pittsburgh, MS, 42; Cornell Univ, PhD(fishery biol), 48. *Prof Exp:* Asst embryol & anat, Univ Pittsburgh, 40-42; asst fishery biol, Cornell Univ, 45, asst biol, 47-48; state fishery biologist, Conn, 47; asst prof fishery biol & ichthyol, Univ Maine 48-53, from assoc prof to prof zool, 53-67; fishery biologist, Maine Inland Fisheries & Game, 48-50, chief fishery res & mgr, 50-67; prof biol & chmn fishery major, Colo State Univ, 67-72; CHMN, DEPT NATURAL RESOURCES, CORNELL UNIV, 72-, PROF NATURAL RESOURCES, 80- *Concurrent Pos:* Mem Atlantic Sea Run Salmon Comn, 53-67; consult, Colo Game, Fish & Parks Dept, 67- *Mem:* Am Fisheries Soc; Am Soc Ichthyologists & Herpetologists; Am Soc Limnol & Oceanog. *Res:* Fishery biology. *Mailing Add:* Dept Natural Resources Cornell Univ Ithaca NY 14853

EVERING, FREDERICK CHRISTIAN, JR, b Baltimore, Md, Mar 20, 36; m 65. ELECTRICAL ENGINEERING. *Educ:* Johns Hopkins Univ, BES, 58, MSE, 60, PhD(elec eng), 65. *Prof Exp:* Electronic engr, US Dept Defense, 60-62; instr elec eng, Johns Hopkins Univ, 62-65; from asst prof to assoc prof, 65-77, PROF ELEC ENG, UNIV VT, 77- *Mem:* Inst Elec & Electronics Engrs; Am Soc Eng Educ. *Res:* Microwave diffraction; low noise systems; special purpose computers; bioengineering; psychological and neurological instrumentation. *Mailing Add:* Dept of Elec Eng Univ of Vt Burlington VT 05405

EVERINGHAM, JOHN RUPE, b Ft Madison, Iowa, Aug 14, 33; m 54; c 4. CHEMICAL ENGINEERING. *Educ:* State Univ Iowa, BS, 56, MS, 57. *Prof Exp:* Engr plant design, Corp Eng, Standard Oil Calif, 57-60, tech serv engr refinery, Chevron Res Corp, 59, res engr pesticides & fertilizers, 60-61, mfg design engr fertilizer plant, 61-64, res engr fertilizer, Ortho Div, 64-66, SUPVR FERTILIZER PROCESS RES & DEVELOP, CHEVRON CHEM CO, 66- *Mem:* Am Inst Chem Engrs. *Res:* Agricultural fertilizer products and processes, including development of new products and processes, process design, plant startup and technical services. *Mailing Add:* Fertilizer Div 940 Hensley St Richmond CA 94804

EVERITT, C W FRANCIS, b Sevenoaks, Eng, Mar 8, 34. SPACE PHYSICS, LOW TEMPERATURE PHYSICS. *Educ:* Univ London, BSc, 55, PhD(physics), 59, ARCS, Royal Col Sci, 55, DIC, 58. *Prof Exp:* Vis res assoc, Phys-Tech Inst, Bundesanstalt, WGer, 55; res assoc, Imp Col, Univ London, 58-60; res assoc & instr, Univ Pa, 60-62; res assoc, 62-66, res physicist, 66-67, sr res physicist, 67-74, ADJ PROF, STANFORD UNIV, 74- *Concurrent Pos:* Instr physics, Univ Pa, 61-63; mem space relativity comt, Int Acad Astronaut, 65- *Mem:* Am Phys Soc; Sigma Xi; Am Asn Physics Teachers. *Res:* Electron optics; paleomagnetism; liquid helium; low temperature and space physics; history of physics. *Mailing Add:* Dept of Physics Stanford Univ Stanford CA 94305

EVERLY, CHARLES RAY, b Oklahoma City, Okla, Oct 13, 44; m 65; c 2. ORGANIC CHEMISTRY. *Educ:* Phillips Univ, BA, 66; Univ Ark, PhD(org chem), 70. *Prof Exp:* Asst prof, 69-73, assoc prof chem, Phillips Univ, 73-78; res chemist, 78-80, SR RES CHEMIST & SUPVR, ETHYL CORP, 80-; D. *Concurrent Pos:* Vis Scholar, Louisiana State Univ, 76-77. *Mem:* Am Chem Soc; Sigma Xi. *Res:* Organic Synthesis, organic reaction mechanics. *Mailing Add:* 1431 Munal Dr Baton Rouge LA 70816

EVERMANN, JAMES FREDERICK, b Van Nuys, Calif, Nov 18, 44; m 65; c 4. CLINICAL VIROLOGY, COMPARATIVE VIROLOGY. *Educ:* Univ Nev, Reno, BS, 69; Univ Wyo, Laramie, MS, 71; Purdue Univ, West Lafayette, PhD(virol), 74. *Prof Exp:* Fel virol, Health Sci Ctr, Univ Ore, 74-76; asst prof, 76-81, ASSOC PROF CLIN VIROL, WASH STATE UNIV, 81- *Mem:* Am Asn Vet Lab Diagnosis; US Animal Health Asn. *Res:* Viruses of domestic animals and wildlife species (bovine leukemia virus, bovine viral diarrhea, border disease viruses, canine encephalitogenic parainfluenza and canine parvovirus type-enteritis-myocarditis) including identification, development of diagnostic capabilities and public health concerns. *Mailing Add:* Dept Vet Microbiol & Path Col Vet Med Wash State Univ Pullman WA 99164

EVERNDEN, JACK FOORD, b Okeechobee, Fla, Mar 12, 22; m 65. SEISMOLOGY, GEOPHYSICS. *Educ:* Univ Calif, PhD(geophys), 51. *Prof Exp:* From asst prof to prof geol & geophys, Univ Calif, Berkeley, 53-65; res assoc, Vela Seismol Ctr, Va, 65-67; res assoc to tech dir, Air Force Technol Appl Ctr, US Dept Defense, 67-69, res assoc & prog monitor, Advan Res Projs Agency, 69-71; res assoc, Arms Control & Disarmament Agency, US Dept State, 71-73; prog mgr, 73-80, SR GEOPHYSICIST, NAT CTR EARTHQUAKE RES, 80- *Concurrent Pos:* Consult, Arms Control & Disarmament Agency, 73- *Honors & Awards:* Newcombe-Cleveland Prize, AAAS, 62; Outstanding Civilian Serv Medal, US Air Force, 68. *Mem:* Geol Soc Am; Seismol Soc Am; Am Asn Petrol Geologists. *Res:* Earthquake seismology; field geology; geochronometry. *Mailing Add:* 7610 Hihn Rd Ben Lomond CA 95005

EVERS, CARL GUSTAV, b Lake Benton, Minn, July 30, 34; m 60; c 3. MEDICINE, PATHOLOGY. *Educ:* Mankato State Col, BA, 55; Univ Minn, MD, 59; Am Bd Path, dipl, 65. *Prof Exp:* Intern, 59-60, resident, 60-64, from instr to assoc prof, 64-74, PROF PATH, MED CTR, UNIV MISS, 74-, ASSOC DEAN, SCH MED, 73- *Concurrent Pos:* USPHS trainee anat & exp path, 63-64, proj dir, Training Proj Cytotech grant, 66- *Mem:* AAAS; Int Acad Path. *Res:* Pathogenesis of human immune disorders and tumor immunology. *Mailing Add:* Dept of Path Univ of Miss Med Ctr Jackson MS 39216

EVERS, PATRICIA WEBER, b Hamilton, Ohio, Dec 29, 27; m 59. PHARMACOLOGY, DRUG DEVELOPMENT. *Educ:* Col Mt St Joseph, AB, 49; St Louis Univ, MS, 51. *Prof Exp:* Res asst, Col Med, Univ Cincinnati, 51-52; instr biol, Rosemont Col, 52-53; lit scientist, 55-57, sr info scientist, 57-73, sr scientist, 73-77, sr investr, 77-81, ASST DIR, SMITH KLINE & FRENCH LABS, 81- *Mem:* AAAS; NY Acad Sci; Sigma Xi. *Res:* Evaluation of clinical and preclinical data in drug development; preparation of communications to Food and Drug Administration; creative analysis of information and identification of new technologies, especially in gastroenterology. *Mailing Add:* Smith Kline & French Labs 1500 Spring Garden St Philadelphia PA 19101

EVERS, ROBERT C, b St Henry, Ohio, Nov 10, 39; m 62; c 5. POLYMER CHEMISTRY. *Educ:* Univ Dayton, BS, 61; Univ Notre Dame, PhD(org chem), 65. *Prof Exp:* Res chemist, 65-72, GROUP LEADER, AIR FORCE MAT LAB, WRIGHT-PATTERSON AFB, 72- *Mem:* AAAS; Am Chem Soc. *Res:* Synthesis of heterocyclic and fluorocarbon monomers and polymers for high temperature applications. *Mailing Add:* Air Force Mat Lab Wright-Patterson AFB Wright Patterson AFB OH 45433

EVERS, WILLIAM JOHN, b Long Branch, NJ, Sept 3, 32. ORGANIC CHEMISTRY. *Educ:* Monmouth Col, NJ, BS, 60; Univ Maine, MS, 62, PhD(org chem), 65. *Prof Exp:* Chemist, Chem Res Ctr, Edgewood Arsenal, Dept of Army, 65-66; PROJ LEADER NATURAL PROD & ORG SYNTHESIS, INT FLAVORS & FRAGRANCES, INC, 66- *Mem:* AAAS; Am Chem Soc. *Res:* Heterocyclic and organosulfur chemistry; natural product chemistry of flavors and fragrances. *Mailing Add:* 1515 State Highway No 36 Union Beach NJ 07735

EVERS, WILLIAM L, b Pittsburgh, Pa, Aug 13, 06; m 64; c 1. RESEARCH ADMINISTRATION. POLYMER. *Educ:* Univ Akron, BS, 28; Northwestern Univ, MS, 29; Pa State Univ, PhD(org chem), 32. *Prof Exp:* Res chemist, Socony Mobil Co, Inc, 31-35; res mgr, Rohm and Haas Co, 35-52; res mgr, Celanese Corp, 52-64; dir univ sci rels, 64-68; EXEC DIR CAMILLE & HENRY DREYFUS FOUND, 68- *Concurrent Pos:* Mem vis comt phys sci, Chicago Univ; mem vis comt chem, Harvard Univ, 82. *Mem:* Am Chem Soc; Asn Res Dirs. *Mailing Add:* Camille & Henry Dreyfus Found 445 Park Ave New York NY 10022

EVERSE, JOHANNES, b Yerseke, Netherlands, Dec 3, 31; m 64; c 3. ENZYMOLOGY. *Educ:* Brandeis Univ, Mass, MA, 71; Univ Calif, San Diego, PhD(chem), 73. *Prof Exp:* Res technician biochem, Philips-Duphar Pharm Co, Holland, 52-60; res assoc, Brandeis Univ, Mass, 60-69; assoc specialist chem, Univ, Calif, San Diego, 69-73; asst res chemist biochem, 76-80; assoc prof, 76-80, PROF BIOCHEM, HEALTH SCI CTR, TEX TECH UNIV, 80- *Concurrent Pos:* NATO sr vis prof, Univ Milan, Italy, 80- *Mem:* Am Soc Biol Chemists; Am Chem Soc; AAAS; Soc Exp Biol Med; Dutch Soc Biochem. *Res:* Relationship between structure and function of enzymes and enzyme mechanisms; application of immobilized enzymes for chemotherapeutic and diagnostic purposes; role of the immune system in cancer development and regression. *Mailing Add:* Dept Biochem Health Sci Ctr Tex Tech Univ Lubbock TX 79430

EVERSMEYER, HAROLD EDWIN, b Randolph, Kans, July 7, 27; m 53; c 4. PLANT PATHOLOGY, BOTANY. *Educ:* Kans State Univ, BS, 51, PhD(plant path), 65. *Prof Exp:* County 4-H Club agent, Exten Serv, Kans State Univ, Olathe, 51-54, Emporia, 56-60; assoc prof, 64-70, PROF BIOL SCI, MURRAY STATE UNIV, 70- *Mem:* Am Phytopath Soc; Soc Nematol; Am Inst Biol Sci. *Res:* Phytonematology-occurrence and damage by plant parasitic nematodes; aeromycology. *Mailing Add:* Dept of Biol Sci Murray State Univ Murray KY 42071

EVERSOLE, WILBURN JOHN, b Jackson, Ky, Oct 29, 15; m 41; c 2. ENDOCRINOLOGY. *Educ:* Berea Col, AB, 36; NY Univ, MSc, 38, PhD(vert zool, endocrinol), 40. *Prof Exp:* Asst, NY Univ, 40-42; res assoc, Princeton Univ, 42-43; instr, Rice Univ, 43-46; from asst prof to assoc prof, Syracuse Univ, 46-51; prof, Univ NMex, 51-59; PROF LIFE SCI, IND STATE UNIV, 60- *Concurrent Pos:* Damon Runyon grant, 51-53; consult, AEC, 51-59; NIH grants, 53-58; Am Cancer Soc grants, 55-57; consult, Vet Admin Hosp, 57-59; Guggenheim fel, 58; Eagle's Max Baer Heart Fund res grant, 74. *Mem:* Fel AAAS; Am Physiol Soc; Am Soc Zool. *Res:* Endocrine physiology of the adrenals and gonads with emphasis on the regulation of reproduction, kidney function, and water and electrolyte metabolism; experimental hypertension and prostaglandins. *Mailing Add:* Dept of Life Sci Ind State Univ Terre Haute IN 47809

EVERSON, ALAN RAY, b Ft Dodge, Iowa, Aug 11, 43; div; c 1. FOREST RECREATION. *Educ:* Iowa State Univ, BS, 65; Univ Mich, MFor, 67; Tex A&M Univ, PhD(recreation resources), 78. *Prof Exp:* Recreation resource specialist, Bur Outdoor Recreation, 66-68; dir field serv, Rocky Mountain Ctr Environ, 68; naturalist, Nat Park Serv, 69; state outdoor recreation planner, Colo Parks & Outdoor Recreation, 69-77; ASSOC PROF OUTDOOR RECREATION & LAND USE, UNIV MO, 77- *Mem:* Soc Am Foresters; Nat Recreation & Park Asn. *Res:* Human carrying capacities of forested lands. *Mailing Add:* 1-30 Agr Bldg Sch of Forestry Univ of Mo Columbia MO 65211

EVERSON, DALE O, b Geneva Lake, Wis, Feb 1, 30; m 54; c 2. STATISTICS, APPLIED STATISTICS. *Educ:* Univ Idaho, BS, 52, MS, 56; Iowa State Univ, PhD(animal breeding), 60. *Prof Exp:* Biometrician, Agr Res Serv, USDA, 60-62; assoc exp sta statistician, 62-66, PROF STATIST & EXP STA STATISTICIAN, UNIV IDAHO, 66- *Concurrent Pos:* Vis prof, Dept of Statist, Ore State Univ, 73-74. *Mem:* Am Dairy Sci Asn; Am Soc Animal Sci; Am Statist Asn. *Res:* Animal breeding and statistic methodology. *Mailing Add:* Exp Sta Col Agr Univ Idaho Moscow ID 83843

EVERSON, EVERETT HENRY, b Whitehall, Wis, Oct 8, 23; m 47; c 2. GENETICS, PLANT BREEDING. *Educ:* Univ Wis, BS, 49; Univ Calif, PhD(genetics), 52. *Prof Exp:* Res agronomist agron, Pillsbury Mills, Inc, 49; asst, Univ Calif, 49-52; asst prof weed control & plant breeding, Univ Ariz, 52-54; res agronomist genetics & plant breeding, USDA, Wash State Univ, 54-56; assoc prof, 56-63, PROF CROP SCI, GENETICS & PLANT BREEDING, MICH STATE UNIV, 64- *Concurrent Pos:* Consult Int Agr, arid regions. *Mem:* Am Soc Agron; Am Genetic Asn; Crop Sci Soc Am. *Res:* Genetics and plant breeding; major organism; wheat; genus Triticum. *Mailing Add:* Dept of Crop & Soil Sci Mich State Univ East Lansing MI 48823

EVERSON, HOWARD E, b Milan, Ohio, Feb 26, 18; m 47; c 3. INORGANIC CHEMISTRY, PHYSICAL CHEMISTRY. *Educ:* Western Reserve Univ, BA, 40, MS, 47, PhD(chem), 48. *Prof Exp:* Res chemist, Wyandotte Chems Corp, 40-42; asst prof chem, Univ Cincinnati, 48-51; res chemist & group leader, Diamond Alkali Co, 51-55; asst to res dir, Res Ctr, Diamond Shamrock Corp, 55-56, chief staff engr, 56-58, from asst dir to dir res, 58-67, tech dir, 67-73, dir safety & environ eng, Diamond Shamrock Chem Corp, Cleveland, 73-78; CONSULT, 80- *Res:* Hydrotropic solvents; effect of salts on the aqueous solubility of non-electrolytes. *Mailing Add:* 6123 Campbell Dr Madison OH 44057

EVERSON, RONALD WARD, b Dodgeville, Wis, Sept 14, 31. OPTOMETRY, PHYSIOLOGICAL OPTICS. *Educ:* Chicago Col Optom, BS, 53, OD, 54; Ind Univ, MS, 59. *Prof Exp:* Lectr optom, Ind Univ, 61-64; assoc prof optom & dir grad prog physiol optics, Pac Univ, 64-67; asst prof, 68-73, ASSOC PROF OPTOM & DIR INTERNAL AFFAIRS, IND UNIV, BLOOMINGTON, 73- *Mem:* Am Optom Asn; fel Am Acad Optom. *Res:* Human color vision; illumination principles; visual acuity; visual system contrast sensitivity; aniseikonia. *Mailing Add:* Sch of Optom Ind Univ Bloomington IN 47405

EVERSTINE, GORDON CARL, b Baltimore, Md, Mar 30, 43; m 68; c 2. COMPUTATIONAL MECHANICS. *Educ:* Lehigh Univ, Pa, BS, 64; Purdue Univ, MS, 66; Brown Univ, PhD(appl math), 71. *Prof Exp:* Mem tech staff, Bell Tel Labs, Inc, 64-66; MATHEMATICIAN NUMERICAL MECHS, DAVID TAYLOR NAVAL SHIP RES & DEVELOP CTR, 68- *Res:* Computational mechanics; finite element method; fluid-structure interaction; structural dynamics; matrix profile reduction algorithms. *Mailing Add:* Numerical Mech Div 184 David Taylor Naval Ship R&D Ctr Bethesda MD 20084

EVERT, CARL F, JR, electrical engineering, computer science, see previous edition

EVERT, HENRY EARL, b Sherwood, Mich, Mar 2, 15; m 46. ORGANIC CHEMISTRY. *Educ:* Mich State Col, BS, 37, MS, 38; Univ Iowa, PhD(sanit chem), 41. *Prof Exp:* Asst org chem, Mich State Col, 37-38; asst inorg chem, Univ Iowa, 38-39; asst sanit chem, 39-40, storeroom asst, 40-41; res chemist, Masonite Corp, 41-43; USPHS consult chemist, Eng Dept, Johns Hopkins Univ, 46-47; asst prof chem, George Washington Univ, 47-48; prof physiol chem, Univ Scranton, 48-49; asst pharmacol, Univ Va, 49-52; asst prof biochem, Sch Med, State Univ NY, 52-62; PROF CHEM & CHMN DEPT, NASSAU COMMUNITY COL, 62- *Mem:* Fel AAAS; fel Am Inst Chemists; Am Chem Soc. *Res:* Carbohydrates; catalysis; wood chemistry; enzymology; chemical oceanography. *Mailing Add:* 11 Harvard St PO Box 326 Garden City NY 11530

EVERT, RAY FRANKLIN, b Mt Carmel, Pa, Feb 20, 31; m 60; c 2. PLANT ANATOMY. *Educ:* Pa State Univ, BS, 52, MS, 54; Univ Calif, Davis, PhD(bot), 58. *Prof Exp:* From instr to asst prof bot, Mont State Col, 58-60; from asst prof to assoc prof, 60-66, chmn dept, 73-74 & 77-79, PROF BOT, UNIV WIS-MADISON, 66-, PROF PLANT PATHOL, 77- *Concurrent Pos:* NSF res grants, 59-83, mem cell biol fel rev panel, NIH, 64-68; Guggenheim Found fel, 65-66; vis prof, Univ Natal, 71 & Univ Gottingen, 71 & 74-75; Alexander von Humboldt Award, 74-75. *Mem:* AAAS; Bot Soc Am; Am Sci Plant Physiologists; Am Inst Biol Sci. *Res:* Light and electron microscopic investigations of the ontogeny, structure and seasonal development of the phloem; leaf structure in relation to solute transport and phloem loading; phloem and leaf structure and function. *Mailing Add:* Dept of Bot Univ of Wis Madison WI 53706

EVERTS, CRAIG HAMILTON, b Appleton, Wis, Apr 18, 39; m 70; c 2. COASTAL ENGINEERING, MARINE GEOLOGY. *Educ:* Univ Southern Calif, BS, 66; Univ Wis, MS, 68, PhD(geol, geophys), 71. *Prof Exp:* Res oceanogr, 71-76, SUPVRY GEOLOGIST, COASTAL ENG RES CTR, 76- *Mem:* Am Soc Civil Engrs; Am Geophys Union. *Res:* Coastal engineering research in harbor and navigation-channel sedimentation, beach erosion and the design of beach restoration projects and coastal structures. *Mailing Add:* Kingman Bldg Coastal Eng Res Ctr Ft Belvoir VA 22060

EVES, CHESTER REDMOND, b Walkerville, Ont, Dec 26, 19; m 46; c 2. ANALYTICAL CHEMISTRY, FORENSIC SCIENCE. *Educ:* McGill Univ, BSc, 45; Univ Ottawa, BSc Hons, 56, PhD(chem), 60. *Prof Exp:* Forensic lab expert, Royal Can Mounted Police, 45-60, officer labs, 60-69, asst comnr identification & labs, 70-73, dep comnr, Nat Police Serv, 73-75; head pub safety proj, Nat Res Coun Can, 75-81; MGR, CUMBERLAND MED CLIN, 82- *Concurrent Pos:* Can rep, Int Criminal Police Orgn, 63 & 72 & Int Asn Forensic Sci, 66 & 75; head Can deleg, Int Sci & Technol Conf Narcotics & Dangerous Drugs, Paris & Washington, DC, 73 & 74; mem bd consults, Dept Criminol, Univ Ottawa, 74-75; mem planning comt, Int Conf Crime Countermeasures, 77- *Mem:* Fel Chem Inst Can; Can Soc Forensic Sci (treas, 65); Can Asn Chiefs Police; Int Asn Chiefs Police; Int Asn Forensic Toxicologists. *Res:* Forensic science and application of science and technology research and development in support of law enforcement; medical clinic administration. *Mailing Add:* Cumberland Med Clin Cumberland BC V0R 1S0 Can

EVESLAGE, SYLVESTER LEE, b Ripley, Ohio, Apr 25, 23; m 55; c 4. ORGANIC CHEMISTRY. *Educ:* Univ Notre Dame, BS, 44, MS, 45, PhD(org chem), 53. *Prof Exp:* From instr to assoc prof, 48-66, PROF CHEM, UNIV DAYTON, 66- *Mem:* AAAS; Am Chem Soc. *Res:* Ion exchange chromatography; synthesis of chemotherapeutic compounds. *Mailing Add:* Dept of Chem Univ of Dayton Dayton OH 45469

EVETT, ARTHUR A, b Pasco, Wash, Apr 12, 25; m 46; c 2. PHYSICS. *Educ:* Wash State Univ, BS, 48, PhD(physics), 51. *Prof Exp:* Adv sci warfare, Weapons Syst Eval Group, US Dept Defense, DC, 51-52; instr physics, Yale Univ, 52-55; asst prof, Wash State Univ, 56-58; from assoc prof to prof, Univ Ariz, 58-68; PROF PHYSICS, CALIF STATE UNIV, DOMINGUEZ HILLS, 68- *Mem:* Am Phys Soc. *Res:* Relativity theory; intermolecular forces; surface physics. *Mailing Add:* Dept of Physics Calif State Univ Dominguez Hills CA 90747

EVETT, JACK B(URNIE), b York, Pa, May 26, 42; m 69; c 1. CIVIL ENGINEERING. *Educ:* Univ SC, BS, 64, MS, 65; Tex A&M Univ, PhD(civil eng), 68. *Prof Exp:* Asst prof civil eng, 67-77, assoc prof environ eng, 77-80, ASSOC PROF CIVIL ENG, UNIV NC, CHARLOTTE, 80- *Mem:* Am Soc Civil Engrs; Am Soc Eng Educ. *Res:* Waste dispersion patterns in an estuarine system; water resources planning and development. *Mailing Add:* Col of Eng Univ of NC UNCC Sta Charlotte NC 28223

EVETT, JAY FREDRICK, b Lewiston, Idaho, Nov 5, 31; m 57; c 1. PHYSICS, BIOPHYSICS. *Educ:* Wash State Univ, BS, 53 & 57; Northwestern Univ, MS, 58; Ore State Univ, PhD(biophys), 68. *Prof Exp:* Nuclear engr, US AEC, 60-61; from asst prof to assoc prof, Moorhead State Col, 61-66; assoc prof, 68-74, PROF PHYSICS, WESTERN ORE STATE COL, 74- *Mem:* AAAS; Am Asn Physics Teachers. *Res:* Viscosity studies of macromolecules. *Mailing Add:* Dept of Natural Sci Western Ore State Col Monmouth OR 97361

EVILIA, RONALD FRANK, b Meriden, Conn, Dec 28, 43; m 67; c 3. ANALYTICAL CHEMISTRY. *Educ:* Lehigh Univ, BA, 65, PhD(chem), 69. *Prof Exp:* Res asst chem, Lehigh Univ, 65-69; res assoc chem, Univ NC, 69-72; asst prof, 72-77, ASSOC PROF CHEM, UNIV NEW ORLEANS, 77- *Mem:* Am Chem Soc; Sigma Xi. *Res:* Utilization of nuclear magnetic resonance techniques for structural and dynamic investigations of coordination compounds; liquid chromatographic separations of enantiomeric substances and new methods of liquid chromatographic detection. *Mailing Add:* Dept of Chem Univ of New Orleans Lake Front New Orleans LA 70122

EVINS, CHARLES VICTOR, b Frankfort, Ky, Feb 16, 41; m 63; c 3. CHEMISTRY. *Educ:* Mass Inst Technol, BS, 63; Purdue Univ, PhD(anal chem), 67. *Prof Exp:* Group leader anal chem, Fiber Industs, Inc, 69-72, group leader polymer develop, 72-74, group leader synthetic fiber process develop, 74-76; res chemist, Celanese Res Co, Summit, 66-69, res supvr, 76, res mgr mat sci, 77-81; RES DIR, AM CYANAMID CO, 81- *Mem:* Am Chem Soc. *Res:* Electroanalytical chemistry; polymer chemistry; polymer morphology; chemical process development; synthetic fiber technology. *Mailing Add:* Celanese Res Co Box 1000 Summit NJ 07901

EVITT, WILLIAM ROBERT, b Baltimore, Md, Dec 9, 23; m 50; c 3. PALYNOLOGY, FOSSIL DINOFLAGELLATES. *Educ:* Johns Hopkins Univ, AB, 42, PhD(geol), 50. *Prof Exp:* Asst, Johns Hopkins Univ, 46-48; from instr to assoc prof geol, Univ Rochester, 48-56; sr res geologist, Jersey Prod Res Co, 56-59, res assoc, 59-62; PROF GEOL, STANFORD UNIV, 62- *Concurrent Pos:* Ed, Jour, Paleont Soc, 53-56. *Mem:* Paleont Soc (vpres, 58); Geol Soc Am; Am Asn Stratig Palynologists; Int Asn Plant Taxon. *Res:* Palynology; dinoflagellate morphology; invertebrate paleontology. *Mailing Add:* Dept Geol Stanford Univ Stanford CA 94305

EVLETH, EARL MANSFIELD, b Evanston, Ill, Dec 7, 31; m 55; c 1. THEORETICAL CHEMISTRY, ORGANIC CHEMISTRY. *Educ:* Calif Inst Technol, BS, 54; Univ Southern Calif, PhD(chem), 63. *Prof Exp:* Chemist, Shell Oil Co, 54-55; res chemist, Am Potash & Chem Co, 55-57 & 60-61 & Int Bus Mach Corp, 62-65; asst prof natural sci, Univ Calif, Santa Cruz, 67-72, assoc prof chem, 72-77; MAITRE DE RECHERCHE, CENTRE NATIONAL DE LA RECHERCHE SCIENTIFIQUE, 74- *Mem:* Am Chem Soc; Royal Soc Chem. *Res:* Proton transfers mechanism; small molecule photochemistry and energy transfer mechanisms; spectra-structure correlations; ab initio and semiempirical molecular orbital calculations of Valence and Rydberg states. *Mailing Add:* Centre Mecanique Ondulatoire Appliquee 23 rue du Maroc Paris France

EVONUK, EUGENE, b Springfield, Ore, Oct 11, 21; m 46. PHYSIOLOGY. *Educ:* Univ Ore, BS, 52, MS, 53; Univ Iowa, PhD(physiol), 60. *Prof Exp:* From instr to asst prof health educ, Univ Ore, 53-58; res physiologist, Arctic Aeromed Lab, US Dept Air Force, 60-63, chief physiol br, 63-67; dir ctr res human develop, 67-74, PROF PHYS EDUC, UNIV ORE, 67- *Mem:* Fel AAAS; Am Physiol Soc; Aerospace Med Asn; Am Polar Soc; Am Soc Zoologists. *Res:* Cardiovascular effects of mild and profound cooling; thermal and metabolic responses to cooling; physiology of work and altitude. *Mailing Add:* Dir Appl Physiol Univ Ore Eugene OR 97403

EVOY, WILLIAM (HARRINGTON), b Philadelphia, Pa, July 1, 38; m 64; c 2. NEUROPHYSIOLOGY. *Educ:* Reed Col, BA, 60; Univ Ore, MA, 62, PhD(biol), 64. *Prof Exp:* Res assoc comp neurophysiol, Stanford Univ, 64-66; asst prof, 66-69, assoc prof, 69-76, PROF BIOL, UNIV MIAMI, 76- DIR LAB QUANT BIOL, 72- *Mem:* Fel AAAS; Am Soc Zool; Soc Gen Physiologists; Soc Exp Biol; Soc Neurosci. *Res:* Comparative physiology of crustacean nervous and neuromuscular systems, particularly the organization and detailed function of central nervous systems in behavior; coordinating mechanisms in locomotion. *Mailing Add:* Lab for Quant Biol Dept of Biol Univ of Miami PO Box 249118 Coral Gables FL 33124

EVTUHOV, VIKTOR, b Poland, May 24, 35; US citizen; m 57; c 2. QUANTUM ELECTRONICS, NONLINEAL OPTICS. *Educ:* Univ Calif, Los Angeles, BS, 56; Calif Inst Technol, MS, 57, PhD(elec eng/physics), 61. *Prof Exp:* Mem tech staff, 56 & 60-65, sr staff physicist, 65-70, head, Quantum Electronics Sect, Laser Dept, Hughes Res Lab, 70-72, asst mgr/mgr, Opto-Electronics Dept, 72-77, sr scientist, Hughes Res Lab, 77-78, mgr tech planning, 78-80, ASST DIR RES & DEVELOP, HUGHES AIRCRAFT CO, 80- *Concurrent Pos:* Res fel & instr elec eng, Calif Inst Technol, 60-61, sr res fel, 70- *Mem:* AAAS; Am Phys Soc; Inst Elec & Electronics Engrs; Optical Soc Am. *Res:* Physical electronics; secondary emission; theory of semiconductors; band structure; quantum electronics; lasers; nonlinear optics; integrated optics; fiber optics. *Mailing Add:* 549 Arbramar Ave Pacific Palisades CA 90272

EWALD, ARNO WILFRED, b Fond du Lac, Wis, May 14, 18; m 43; c 4. SOLID STATE PHYSICS. *Educ:* Wis State Col, BS, 41; Univ Mich, MS, 42, PhD(physics), 48. *Prof Exp:* Fel physics, Univ Mich, 41-44, res assoc, 44-48; from instr to assoc prof, 48-61, PROF PHYSICS, NORTHWESTERN UNIV, ILL, 61- *Concurrent Pos:* Res assoc, Nat Defense Res Comt, 44-45. *Mem:* Fel Am Phys Soc. *Res:* Semiconductors; photoconductivity; energy band structure determinations; infrared phenomena; crystal physics. *Mailing Add:* Dept of Physics Northwestern Univ Evanston IL 60201

EWALD, FRED PETERSON, JR, b Saginaw, Mich, Mar 25, 32. ANALYTICAL CHEMISTRY. *Educ:* Aquinas Col, BS, 54; Univ Kans, PhD(anal chem), 62. *Prof Exp:* Technician anal chem, Haviland Prod, 52-54; asst chem, Univ Kans, 54-59; SUPVR ANAL CHEM, CHEM DIV, PPG INDUSTS, INC, 60- *Mem:* Am Chem Soc. *Res:* Nonaqueous electrochemistry; gas chromatography; mass spectrometry; air and water pollution analysis; infrared spectroscopy, emission and absorption spectroscopy; herbicide residue analysis. *Mailing Add:* PPG Industs Inc PO Box 31 Barberton OH 44203

EWALD, WILLIAM PHILIP, b Whitestone, NY, Mar 27, 22; m 44; c 4. OPTICAL ENGINEERING. *Educ:* Univ Rochester, BS, 53. *Prof Exp:* sr supv engr, Eastman Kodak Co, 44-80; RETIRED. *Concurrent Pos:* Lectr, Univ Rochester, 53-66. *Honors & Awards:* David Richard Medal, Optical Soc Am, 79. *Mem:* Optical Soc Am; Soc Motion Picture & TV Eng; Photog Soc Am. *Mailing Add:* 58 Twin Shores Blvd Longboat Key FL 33548

EWALL, RALPH XAVIER, b Philadelphia, Pa, Aug 14, 42; m 69; c 3. POLYMER & TEXTILE CHEMISTRY. *Educ:* Villanova Univ, BS, 64; Seton Hall Univ, MS, PhD(phys chem), 72. *Prof Exp:* Fel bio-org chem, San Diego State Univ, 72-73; fel biophys chem, Wesleyan Univ, 73-74; res scientist res & develop, Surgikos Johnson & Johnson, 74-77, sr res scientist hosp pack res & develop, 77-80; STAFF, MED DEVICE DEVELOP, ETHICON, 80- *Concurrent Pos:* Chmn, med plastics session, Soc Plastics Indust Conf, Nat Plastics Exposition, 78-79. *Mem:* Am Chem Soc; Asn Advan Med Instrumentation; Soc Plastics Indust; Soc Plastics Engrs; Tech Asn Pulp & Paper Indust. *Res:* Redox reactions of respiratory and photosynthetic metalloenzymes; metal requirements for glycolytic enzyme activity; polymer development and stabilization to gamma radiation; commercial nonwoven fabric finishing; medical device development. *Mailing Add:* Ethicon Rte 22 Somerville NJ 08876

EWALT, JACK R, b Medicine Lodge, Kans, Jan 27, 10; m 31; c 2. PSYCHIATRY. *Educ:* Univ Colo, MD, 33. *Prof Exp:* Commonwealth Fund fel psychiat, Psychopath Hosp, Univ Colo, 34-37; asst prof, Univ Colo, 37-41; prof, Univ Tex, 41-51; clin prof, 52-58, prof, 58-62, Bullard prof psychiat, Harvard Med Sch, 62-76, sr assoc dean clin affairs, 73-76; DIR MENTAL HEALTH SERV, US VET ADMIN, 76- *Concurrent Pos:* Dir psychopath hosp, Univ Tex, 45-50, adminr med br, Hosps, 48-50, dean, Postgrad Sch Med, 50-51; consult, Surgeon Gen, US Dept Air Force, 51-54; comnr, State Dept Ment Health, Mass, 51-58; supt, Mass Ment Health Ctr, 58-73. *Mem:* Am Acad Arts & Sci; fel Am Psychiat Asn (treas, pres, 63-64); fel AMA. *Res:* Neuropyphilis; schizophrenia; amputations; tissue culture. *Mailing Add:* 810 Vermont Ave Washington DC 20420

EWAN, GEORGE T, b Edinburgh, Scotland, May 6, 27; m 52; c 2. NUCLEAR SCIENCE. *Educ:* Univ Edinburgh, BSc, 48, PhD(physics), 52. *Prof Exp:* Asst lectr physics, Univ Edinburgh, 50-52; res assoc, McGill Univ, 52-55; from asst res officer to sr res officer, Atomic Energy Can, Ltd, 55-70; head dept, 74-77, PROF PHYSICS, QUEEN'S UNIV, 70- *Concurrent Pos:* Nat Res Coun fel, 54-55; Ford Found fel, Niels Bohr Inst, Copenhagen, 61-62; vis scientist, Lawrence Radiation Lab, 66; res assoc, Europ Orgn Nuclear Res, 77-78. *Honors & Awards:* Radiation Indust Award, Am Nuclear Soc, 67. *Mem:* Fel Royal Soc Can; Am Inst Physics. *Res:* Nuclear physics; high resolution beta and gamma ray spectroscopy; semiconductor detectors; applications of nuclear techniques. *Mailing Add:* Dept of Physics Queen's Univ Kingston ON K6L 3N6 Can

EWAN, JOSEPH (ANDORFER), b Philadelphia, Pa, Oct 24, 09; m 35; c 3. BOTANY, HISTORY OF BIOLOGY. *Educ:* Univ Calif, AB, 34. *Hon Degrees:* ScD, Col William and Mary, 72, Tulane Univ, 80. *Prof Exp:* Asst phanerogamic bot, Univ Calif, 33-37; instr biol, Univ Colo, 37-44; botanist, For Econ Admin, Colombia, 44-45; asst cur div plants, Smithsonian Inst, 45-46; assoc botanist, Bur Plant Indust, USDA, Md, 46-47; from asst prof to prof, 47-72, Ida A Richardson prof, 72-77, EMER PROF BOT, TULANE UNIV LA, 77- *Concurrent Pos:* Am Philos Soc grant, 49-52, 54, 58, 64 & 72; Guggenheim fel, 54; off del, Int Conf, Nat Sci Res Ctr, France, 56; panelist, Lilly Conf Res Opportunities Am Cultural Hist, Mo, 59; NSF fel, 59-61; ed, Classica Bot Am, 66-; vis prof, Univ Hawaii, 67 & 74 & Univ Ore, 78 & 81. *Honors & Awards:* Eloise Payne Luquer Medal, 78. *Mem:* Fel Linnean Soc London; Am Fern Soc (vpres, 41-47, pres, 58-59); Am Antiquarian Soc; Cooper Ornith Soc; Torrey Bot Club. *Res:* Taxonomy of delphinium, vismia and American gentianaceae; biography and bibliography of naturalists; phytogeography and flora of Louisiana. *Mailing Add:* Dept of Biol Tulane Univ of La New Orleans LA 70118

EWAN, RICHARD COLIN, b Cuba, Ill, Sept 10, 34; m 56; c 4. ANIMAL NUTRITION, BIOCHEMISTRY. *Educ:* Univ Ill, BS, 56, MS, 57; Univ Wis, PhD(animal sci & biochem), 66. *Prof Exp:* PROF ANIMAL SCI, IOWA STATE UNIV, 66- *Mem:* Am Soc Animal Sci; Am Inst Nutrit. *Res:* Vitamin and mineral interactions in nutrition; energy metabolism and utilization. *Mailing Add:* Dept of Animal Sci Iowa State Univ Ames IA 50011

EWART, HUGH WALLACE, JR, b Decatur, Ill, Oct 18, 39; m 63; c 2. ORGANIC CHEMISTRY. *Educ:* Trinity Col, Conn, BS, 61; Yale Univ, MS, 63, PhD(org chem), 67. *Prof Exp:* Res chemist, Olympic Res Div, ITT Rayonier Inc, 68-81; DIR TECH SERV, TREE TOP INC, 81- *Mem:* Am Chem Soc; Sigma Xi; Royal Soc Chem; Inst Food Technol; Am Soc Enologists. *Res:* Fermentation of wood sugars; pulping and bleaching of wood and wood pulp; synthetic chemistry of small ring systems via cycloaddition reactions; separation and identification of natural products and derivatives; photochemistry of organic compounds. *Mailing Add:* Tree Top Inc Box 248 Selah WA 98942

EWART, MERVYN H, b Can, Dec 23, 20; m 57; c 2. BIOCHEMISTRY. *Educ:* Ont Agr Col, BSA, 44; McGill Univ, MSc, 46; Univ Minn, PhD(agr biochem), 51. *Prof Exp:* Res chemist, Can Dept Health & Welfare, 51-54; from asst prof to assoc prof, 54-65, PROF CHEM & CHMN DEPT, ALBANY COL PHARM, UNION UNIV, NY, 65- *Concurrent Pos:* Vis prof, State Univ Col Educ, Albany, 59; consult, Christian Hansen Labs, 56. *Mem:* Am Chem Soc. *Res:* Enzymes; metabolism; chemical analysis. *Mailing Add:* Albany Col of Pharm Union Univ 106 New Scotland Ave Albany NY 12208

EWART, RALPH BRADLEY, b Mt Pleasant, Iowa, Mar 4, 32; m 64. SCIENCE WRITING, BOTANY. *Educ:* Univ Iowa, BA, 56; Wash Univ, MA, 62, PhD(bot), 69. *Prof Exp:* Instr high sch, Ill, 56-59, 60-63 & 64-66 & Guatemala, Cent Am, 63-64; teaching asst biol, Wash Univ, 66-68; asst prof biol & bot, Northwest Mo State Univ, 69-74; instr biol, Mo Western State Col,

75-77, FREELANCE SCI WRITER, 74- *Res:* Anatomical studies of the fossil genus Scolecopteris; developmental studies of cell wall synthesis in the zoospore of Vaucheria sessilis; photography of algae, fungi and lower vascular plants; history of machines that play chess. *Mailing Add:* 1905 N 22nd St St Joseph MO 64505

EWART, TERRY E, b Seattle, Wash, July 6, 34; m 54; c 4. PHYSICS. *Educ:* Univ Wash, BS, 59, PhD(physics), 65. *Prof Exp:* Sr physicist, 59-68, HEAD OCEAN PHYSICS DEPT, APPL PHYSICS LAB, UNIV WASH, 68-, SR RES ASSOC, DEPT OCEANOG, 70- *Concurrent Pos:* Consult, State Bur Fisheries, 62-65. *Mem:* AAAS; Marine Technol Soc; Am Phys Soc. *Res:* High energy particle physics; underwater acoustics. *Mailing Add:* Appl Physics Lab Univ of Wash Seattle WA 98105

EWBANK, WESLEY BRUCE, b Olivet, Kans, Sept 21, 32; m 57; c 2. NUCLEAR PHYSICS, ATOMIC PHYSICS. *Educ:* Univ Kans, BS, 54; Univ Calif, Berkeley, PhD(physics), 60. *Prof Exp:* Asst, Univ Calif, Berkeley, 54-59, res assoc nuclear physics, Lawrence Radiation Lab, 59-62; res assoc, Nuclear Data Proj, Nat Acad Sci-Nat Res Coun, 62-63; res staff mem nuclear physics, 64-68, asst dir, 68-75, dir, Nuclear Data Proj, 75-80, TECH ASST, INFO DIV, OAK RIDGE NAT LAB, 80- *Concurrent Pos:* Lectr, Univ Calif, Berkeley, 61-62. *Mem:* Am Phys Soc; AAAS; Am Soc Info Sci. *Res:* Measurement of nuclear moments by atomic beam spectroscopy; collection and synthesis of experimental results in nuclear-structure physics for publication of nuclear data sheets; use of computers to manage and communicate scientific technical information. *Mailing Add:* Info Div Oak Ridge Nat Lab PO Box X Oak Ridge TN 37830

EWEN, ALWYN BRADLEY, b Saskatoon, Sask, Oct 24, 32; div; c 2. INSECT PATHOLOGY, INSECT PHYSIOLOGY. *Educ:* Univ Sask, BA, 55, MA, 57; Univ Alta, PhD(insect physiol), 61. *Prof Exp:* Res officer, 57-65, RES SCIENTIST, CAN DEPT AGR, 65- *Mem:* Pan-Am Acridological Soc; Entom Soc Can; Soc Invert Path; fel Royal Entom Soc London. *Res:* Grasshopper diseases, especially the Microsporidia, pathology and physiology; insect cancers; physiology of insect reproduction; insect hormones; integrated pest management. *Mailing Add:* Res Sta Agr Can 107 Science Crescent Saskatoon SK S7N 0X2 Can

EWEN, HAROLD IRVING, b Chicopee, Mass, Mar 5, 22; m 56; c 8. MICROWAVE RADIOMETRY, RADIO ASTRONOMY. *Educ:* Amherst Col, BA, 43; Harvard Univ, MA, 48, PhD(physics), 51. *Prof Exp:* Instr math, Amherst Col, 42-43; instr astron, Harvard Univ, 52-57; PRES, EWEN KNIGHT CORP, 52- & EWEN DAE CORP, 58-; Assoc astron, Harvard Univ, 57-80. *Concurrent Pos:* US mem, Int Astron Union, 53- *Honors & Awards:* Morris E Leeds Award, Inst Elec & Electronics Engrs, 70. *Mem:* Fel Am Acad Arts & Sci; fel AAAS; fel Inst Elec & Electronics Engrs. *Res:* Millimeter spectrom of solar proton flares; microwave characteristics of terrain materials; millimeter wave characteristics of the atmosphere. *Mailing Add:* Ewen Knight Corp 60 Beaver Rd Weston MA 02193

EWERT, ADAM, b Mt Lake, Minn, Dec 1, 27; m 60; c 2. PARASITOLOGY. *Educ:* Tabor Col, BA, 51; Univ Tex, MA, 60; Tulane Univ, PhD(parasitol), 63. *Prof Exp:* Asst prof parasitol & lectr, Fac Med, Univ Singapore, 64-67; asst prof, 67-72, ASSOC PROF MICROBIOL, UNIV TEX MED BR, GALVESTON, 72- *Mem:* Am Soc Trop Med & Hyg; Am Soc Parasitol; Inst Filariasis Asn. *Res:* Lymphatic filariae; host-parasite interactions involving microfilaria and mosquitoes. *Mailing Add:* Dept Microbiol Univ Tex Med Br Galveston TX 77550

EWIG, CARL STEPHEN, b Elmira, NY, May 28, 45. COMPUTATIONAL CHEMISTRY. *Educ:* Univ Rochester, BS, 67; Univ Calif, Santa Barbara, PhD(chem), 73. *Prof Exp:* Res asst chem, Univ Calif, Santa Barbara, 67-71; res assoc, 73-76, RES ASST PROF CHEM, VANDERBILT UNIV, 76- *Mem:* Am Chem Soc; Am Phys Soc; Sigma Xi. *Res:* Use of theoretical techniques in quantum mechanics to predict molecular electronic structure and properties; related computer applications in chemistry and physics. *Mailing Add:* Dept of Chem Box 1822 Vanderbilt Univ Nashville TN 37235

EWING, BEN B, b Donna, Tex, Apr 4, 24; m 47; c 3. CIVIL ENGINEERING, ENVIRONMENTAL ENGINEERING. *Educ:* Univ Tex, BSCE, 44, MS, 49; Univ Calif, PhD(sanit eng), 59; Am Acad Environ Engrs, dipl. *Prof Exp:* From instr to asst prof civil eng, Univ Tex, 47-52; civil engr, Hqs Fourth Army, Ft Sam Houston, 52-53; asst prof civil eng, Univ Tex, 53-55; assoc, Univ Calif, 55-56, asst res engr, 56-58; asst prof civil eng, Univ Tex, 58; assoc prof sanit eng, 58-61, dir water resources ctr, 66-72, PROF CIVIL ENG, UNIV ILL, URBANA, 61-, PROF SANIT ENG & NUCLEAR ENG, 67-, DIR, INST ENVIRON STUDIES, 72- *Concurrent Pos:* Pub mem, Water Resources Comn, State of Ill, 74-; chmn comt on lead in human environ, Nat Acad Sci-Nat Res Coun-Environ Studies Bd, 78-80. *Honors & Awards:* Harrison Prescott Eddy Award for Noteworthy Res, Water Pollution Control Fedn, 68. *Mem:* Water Pollution Control Fedn; fel Soc Civil Engrs; Am Soc Eng Educ; Am Water Works Asn; Asn Prof Environ Engrs. *Res:* Water quality and pollution; reactions between organic compounds and clay minerals; radioactive waste disposal; ground water pollution recharge of ground water supplies; water quality management; lead in environment. *Mailing Add:* Inst for Environ Studies Univ of Ill 408 S Goodwin Urbana IL 61801

EWING, CHANNING LESTER, b Jefferson City, Mo, May 28, 27; m 56; c 2. BIOENGINEERING, AEROSPACE MEDICINE. *Educ:* Med Col Va, MD, 52; Johns Hopkins Univ, MPH, 63; Am Bd Prev Med, dipl, 64. *Prof Exp:* US Navy, 52-, intern, US Naval Hosp, Portsmouth, Va, 52-53, flight surgeon, USS Wright & USS Ticonderoga, 53-58, resident prev med, Aerospace Crew Equip Lab, Naval Air Eng Ctr, Philadelphia, 58-60, sr med officer, USS Essex, 60-62, resident, Aerospace Crew Equip Lab, Naval Air Eng Ctr, 63-64, asst dir training, Naval Aerospace Med Inst, 64-67, chief bioeng sci div, Res Dept, 67-69, dist med officer, 17th Naval Dist, Kodiak, Alaska, 69-70, chief bioeng sci div, Naval Aerospace Med Inst, 70-71, officer in chg, 71-76, SCI DIR, NAVAL AEROSPACE MED RES LAB DETACHMENT, NAVAL AEROSPACE MED RES LAB, 76- *Concurrent Pos:* Partic, NASA Gemini 5 Proj, 65, Gemini 9 Proj, 66. *Honors & Awards:* Liljenkrantz Award, Aerospace Med Asn, 77; Legion of Merit, 77. *Mem:* Fel Am Col Prev Med; fel Aerospace Med Asn; Am Inst Aeronaut & Astronaut; Am Asn Automotive Med; Am Nat Standards Inst. *Res:* Biomechanics; physiological basis of protective equipment design, especially dynamic response of living human head neck and torso to impact acceleration, mechanism of ejection vertebral fracture and head protection against crash injury. *Mailing Add:* Naval Aerospace Med Res Lab Box 29407 Michoud Sta New Orleans LA 70189

EWING, CLAIR EUGENE, b Blue Rapids, Kans, Sept 20, 15; m 42; c 5. GEODESY. *Educ:* Kans State Univ, BS, 41; Univ Colo, MS, 50; Ohio State Univ, PhD(geod), 55. *Prof Exp:* Dir range develop, US Air Force, Atlantic Missile Range, Patrick AFB, Fla, 55-58, comdr, Air Technol Intel Ctr, Tex, 59-60, dep comdr, Navy Pac Missile Range, 60-67, vcomdr, Air Force Western Test Range, 67-69; chief scientist, Fed Elec Corp, 69-72; CONSULT & LECTR, 72- *Mem:* Sigma Xi; Am Geophys Union. *Res:* Missile and space range instrumentation; electronic surveying; geodetic computations. *Mailing Add:* PO Box 1965 Vandenberg AFB CA 93437

EWING, DAVID LEON, b Shreveport, La, Aug 20, 41; m 65; c 2. RADIATION BIOLOGY. *Educ:* Centenary Col, BS, 63; Univ Calif, Berkeley, MS, 65; Univ Tex, Austin, PhD(zool), 69. *Prof Exp:* Fel radiation biol, Inst Cancer Res, Surrey, Eng, 70-72; asst prof zool, Univ Tex, Austin, 72-76; ASSOC PROF RADIATION THER, HAHNEMANN MED COL, PHILADELPHIA, 76- *Concurrent Pos:* Radiation Res Soc travel award, 77 & 79. *Mem:* Radiation Res Soc; AAAS; Environ Mutagen Soc; Int Soc Radiation Res; Biophys Soc. *Res:* Chemical mechanisms of radiation damage in cells; modification of radiation sensitivity by chemical processes. *Mailing Add:* Dept of Radiation Ther 230 N Broad Philadelphia PA 19102

EWING, DEAN EDGAR, b Ft Wayne, Ind, Aug 15, 32; m 69. MEDICAL RESEARCH. *Educ:* Mich State Univ, BS, 54, DVM, 56; Univ Rochester, MS, 62. *Prof Exp:* Vet, Bur Poultry Inspection, Dept Agr, State of Calif, 56-58; Chief vet serv, 3605th Air Force Hosp, Ellington AFB, Tex, 58-59 & 821st Med Group, Ellsworth AFB, SDak, 59-61, res vet, 6570th Aerospace Med Res Lab, Wright-Patterson AFB, Ohio, 62-63, chief bioastronaut group, Air Force Weapons Lab, Kirtland AFB, NMex, 63-68, chief vet civic action, 606th Spec Opers Squadron, Nakhon Phanom Royal Thai AFB, Thailand, 68-69 & bioenviron br, Air Force Weapons Lab, 69, chief biomed br, 69-73, med res officer, Defense Civil Preparedness Agency, US Air Force, 73-77, chief, Vet Support Group, Naval Ocean Syst Ctr, San Diego, 77-79. *Concurrent Pos:* Proprietor vet house call service avian med, 79- *Mem:* Am Vet Med Asn. *Res:* Research management in areas ranging from basic biology to radiation effects in both natural and man-made environments; veterinary medicine; emergency and disaster medicine; conservation-ecology; avian medicine. *Mailing Add:* 11262 Via Corroza San Diego CA 92124

EWING, DONALD J(AMES), JR, b Toledo, Ohio, Jan 7, 31; m 57; c 2. ELECTRICAL ENGINEERING. *Educ:* Univ Toledo, BS, 52; Mass Inst Technol, MS, 54; Univ Wis, PhD(elec eng), 71. *Prof Exp:* Asst elec eng, Mass Inst Technol, 52-54; from instr to assoc prof, 54-72, PROF ELEC ENG, UNIV TOLEDO, 72- *Concurrent Pos:* NSF fac fel, 62-63. *Mem:* Inst Elec & Electronics Engrs; Asn Comput Mach; Int Asn Math & Comput Simulation; Soc Comput Simulation. *Res:* Feed back control systems and computers. *Mailing Add:* Dept of Elec Eng Univ of Toledo Toledo OH 43606

EWING, ELMER ELLIS, b Normal, Ill, Sept 16, 31; m 55; c 5. VEGETABLE CROPS, PLANT PHYSIOLOGY. *Educ:* Univ Ill, BS, 53, MS, 54; Cornell Univ, PhD(veg crops), 59. *Prof Exp:* Sci aide, Agr Prog for Latin Am, Rockefeller Found, 56-57; from instr to assoc prof, 58-72, PROF VEG CROPS, CORNELL UNIV, 72- *Concurrent Pos:* NSF fel hort, Purdue Univ, 65-66; vis prof, Dept Bot & Microbiol, Univ Col Wales, Aberystwyth, Wales, 74-75 & Dept Veg Crops, Univ Calif, Davis, 80. *Mem:* Am Soc Hort Sci; Potato Asn Am; Am Soc Plant Physiol; Europ Asn Potato Res. *Res:* Physiological problems of potato. *Mailing Add:* Dept of Veg Crops Cornell Univ Ithaca NY 14850

EWING, GALEN WOOD, b Boston, Mass, Mar 14, 14; m 42; c 3. ANALYTICAL CHEMISTRY, PHYSICAL CHEMISTRY. *Educ:* Col William & Mary, BS, 36; Univ Chicago, PhD(phys chem), 39. *Prof Exp:* Prof chem & physics, Blackburn Col, 39-42; res phys chemist, Sterling Winthrop Res Inst, 42-46; from asst prof to assoc prof chem, Union Col, NY, 46-57; prof, NMex Highlands Univ, 57-64, chmn dept, 59-61; prof chem, Seton Hall Univ, 64-69, chmn dept, 69-72; CONSULT, 69- *Concurrent Pos:* Adj prof, NMex Highlands Univ, 69- *Mem:* AAAS; Soc Appl Spectros; Am Chem Soc; Sigma Xi. *Res:* Instrumental absorption spectrophotometry; electroanalytical chemistry. *Mailing Add:* 707 Myrtle Ave Las Vegas NM 87701

EWING, GEORGE EDWARD, b Charlotte, NC, Nov 28, 33; m; c 6. PHYSICAL CHEMISTRY. *Educ:* Yale Univ, BS, 56; Univ Calif, Berkeley, PhD(chem), 60. *Prof Exp:* Sr scientist, Jet Propulsion Lab, 60-63; from instr to assoc prof, 63-71, PROF CHEM, IND UNIV, BLOOMINGTON, 71- *Concurrent Pos:* Mem tech staff, Bell Tel Labs, NJ, 69-70; dir res, Polytech Sch, Palaiseau, France, 76-77. *Mem:* Am Chem Soc; Am Phys Soc. *Res:* Molecular spectroscopy; low temperature chemistry; energy transfer mechanisms. *Mailing Add:* 1412 E 2nd Bloomington IN 47401

EWING, GEORGE MCNAUGHT, b Lexington, Mo, Sept 30, 07; m 37; c 3. MATHEMATICS. *Educ:* Univ Mo, AB, 29, AM, 30, PhD(math), 35. *Prof Exp:* From instr to prof math, Univ Mo, 30-58; res assoc, Okla Res Inst, Combat Develop Dept, US Army Artillery & Missile Sch, 57-60; prof, 60-63, George L Cross res prof, 63-77, EMER GEORGE L CROSS RES PROF MATH, UNIV OKLA, 77- *Concurrent Pos:* Instr, Princeton Univ, 40-41; mem, Inst Advan Study, 40-41; mathematician, Naval Ord Lab, 44-45, Sandia Corp, 51-52 & Ramo-Wooldridge Corp, 54. *Mem:* Am Math Soc; Soc Indust & Appl Math; Math Asn Am. *Res:* Calculus of variations; optimal control theory; ordinary differential equations. *Mailing Add:* 816 Col Ave Norman OK 73069

EWING, GERALD DEAN, b Alliance, Nebr, Jan 6, 32; m 52; c 3. ELECTRONICS, INSTRUMENTATION. *Educ:* Univ Calif, Berkeley, BSEE, 57, MSEE, 59; Ore State Univ, EE, 62, PhD(elec eng), 64. *Prof Exp:* Elec engr, Lawrence Radiation Lab, Univ Calif, 56-58; electronics engr, Electronics Defense Lab, Sylvania Elec Prod, Inc, Gen Tel & Electronics Corp, 58-60; semiconductor appln engr, Rheem Semiconductor Corp, 60-61; supvr appln eng, Shockley Transistor, Clevelite Corp, 61; instr elec eng, Ore State Univ, 61-63; ASSOC PROF ELEC ENG, NAVAL POSTGRAD SCH, 63- *Concurrent Pos:* Lectr, Foothill Col, 58-61; consult, Lind Instrument Corp, Calif, 60-61 & Sylvania Elec Prod, Inc, Gen Tel & Electronics Corp, 63; lectr, Hartnel Col, 64-; mem staff, Behav Sci Inst, Calif, 66- *Mem:* Inst Elec & Electronics Engrs. *Res:* Solid state devices; oceanography. *Mailing Add:* Dept of Elec Eng Naval Postgrad Sch Monterey CA 93940

EWING, GORDON J, b Smithfield, Utah, Nov 1, 31; m 68; c 12. PHYSICAL CHEMISTRY. *Educ:* Utah State Univ, BS, 54, MS, 57; Pa State Univ, PhD(thermodynamics), 60. *Prof Exp:* Asst prof, 62-68, ASSOC PROF CHEM, N MEX STATE UNIV, 68- *Mem:* AAAS; Am Chem Soc. *Res:* Interactions of gases with respiratory pigments; thermometric titrations; solution thermodynamics; alternate methods for determining chemical oxygen demand. *Mailing Add:* 4040 Cholla Rd Las Cruces NM 88001

EWING, JAMES JOYCE, b Morristown, NJ, Dec 15, 42; m 67; c 1. CHEMICAL PHYSICS. *Educ:* Univ Calif, BA, 64; Univ Chicago, PhD(phys chem), 69. *Prof Exp:* Vis asst prof chem, Univ Ill, 69-71; asst prof, Univ Del, 71-72; prin res scientist atomic & molecular physics, Avco Everett Res Lab, 72-76; MEM STAFF LASER FUSION PROG, LAWRENCE LIVERMORE LAB, 76- *Mem:* Am Phys Soc; AAAS; Sigma Xi. *Res:* Ultra-violet laser research, emphasizing advanced visible lasers for fusion, electronic energy transfer and kinetics. *Mailing Add:* Lawrence Livermore Lab Univ of Calif Livermore CA 94550

EWING, JOAN ROSE, b Rochester, NY, Aug 7, 33. ELECTROPHYSICS. *Educ:* Nazareth Col Rochester, BS, 55; Fordham Univ, MS, 57; Univ Rochester, MS, 67, PhD(elec eng), 73. *Prof Exp:* Chemist, 57-66, SCIENTIST, XEROX CORP, 71- *Res:* Electrical properties of organic photoconductors; corona physics. *Mailing Add:* 103 Washington Rd Pittsford NY 14534

EWING, JOHN ALEXANDER, b Fife Scotland, Mar 17, 23; US citizen; m 46; c 2. PSYCHIATRY. *Educ:* Univ Edinburgh, MB & ChB, 46, MD, 54; Univ London, dipl psychol med, 50. *Prof Exp:* Res psychiat, Cherry Knowle Hosp, Eng, 47-51; sr physician, John Umstead Hosp, Butner, NC, 51-54; from instr to assoc prof, 54-63, chmn dept, 65-70, PROF PSYCHIAT, SCH MED, UNIV NC, CHAPEL HILL, 63-, DIR CTR ALCOHOL STUDIES, 71- *Concurrent Pos:* Asst physician, Psychiat Clin, Sunderland Royal Infirmary, Eng, 49-51 & S Shields Gen Hosp, 49-51; psychiatrist, NC Alcoholic Rehab Ctr, 51-54; clin instr, Univ NC, 53-54; dir, Psychiat In-Patient Serv, NC Mem Hosp, 57-64; consult psychiatrist, Watts Hosp, Durham, NC, 57- *Mem:* Fel Am Psychiat Asn; fel Royal Col Psychiatrists; Am Med Soc Alcoholism; Am Asn Social Psychiat; fel Am Col Psychiat. *Res:* Alcoholism and drug dependency; application of psychiatric principles in medical practice; psychoanalysis. *Mailing Add:* 9 Bluff Trail Chapel Hill NC 27514

EWING, JOHN ARTHUR, b Euchee, Tenn, June 24, 12; m 39; c 3. AGRONOMY, RESEARCH ADMINISTRATION. *Educ:* Univ Tenn, BSA, 33, MS, 46; Harvard Univ, DPA, 56. *Prof Exp:* Teacher high sch, Tenn, 34-35; asst county agent, Demonstration Prog, Tenn Valley Authority, Agr Exten Serv, 35-44, from asst supt to supt, Middle Tenn Exp Sta, 44-49, asst dir, Agr Exp Sta, 49-55, sr vdean col agr, 55-57, dir, Agr Exp Sta, 57-68, dean, 68-75, EMER DEAN, AGR EXP STA, UNIV TENN, KNOXVILLE, 75- *Concurrent Pos:* Admin adv, Water Resource Res South, 53-, exp sta rep, Soybean Res, South, 54- prog leader, Comp Animal Res Lab, Energy Res & Develop Admin, Univ Tenn, 55-, exp sta rep, Seed & Plant Irradiation South, 56- & admin adv Grain Mkt South, 60-; chmn, South Agr Exp Sta Dirs, 61-62 & Exp Sta Sect, Land Grant Col Asn, 62-63; mem, Nat Tobacco Adv Comt, 62-64, Nat Cotton Seed Policy Comt, 65- & agr adv comt, South Regional Educ Bd; adminr adv, Southern Land Econ Res Comt; mem, Bd Univ Tenn Res Corp & State of Tenn Air Pollution Bd. *Mem:* Am Soc Agron. *Res:* Irrigation of pastures; effects of fluorine effluents on Cattle and crops; atomic energy in agricultural research. *Mailing Add:* Rte 1 Ten Mile TN 37880

EWING, JOHN FREDERICK, b East Lansing, Mich, July 12, 22; m 42; c 6. METALLURGICAL ENGINEERING. *Educ:* Univ Mich, BSE, 46, MSE, 48, PhD(metall eng), 53. *Prof Exp:* Asst to metallurgist, US Naval Res Lab, 41-43; chemist, Fed Mogul Res Lab, 47-48; res asst, Eng Res Inst, Univ Mich, 49-50, res assoc, 50-52, res engr, 52-53; res metallurgist, 53-56, metallurgist supvr res, 56-58, mgr qual control, Naval Nuclear Fuel Div, 58-68, mgr opers, 68-73, vpres, 73-80, VPRES QUAL & TECHNOL, BABCOCK & WILCOX CO, 80- *Mem:* Am Soc Metals; Am Mgt Asn. *Res:* Study of metals at elevated temperatures; development of alloys for high temperature service. *Mailing Add:* Babcock & Wilcox Co 1010 Common St New Orleans LA 70161

EWING, JOHN I, b Lockney, Tex, July 5, 24; m 48; c 3. GEOPHYSICS. *Educ:* Harvard Univ, BS, 50. *Prof Exp:* Res assoc geophysics, Lamont-Doherty Geol Observ, Columbia Univ, 50-58, sr res scientist, 58-64, sr res assoc, 64-73, adj prof geol, 74-80, assoc dir res, 73-76; CHMN DEPT GEOL & GEOPHYS, WOODS HOLE OCEANOG INST, 76- *Honors & Awards:* Francis P Shepard Medal, Soc Econ Paleontologist & Mineralogists. *Mem:* Soc Explor Geophys; Am Geophys Union. *Res:* Structure and constitution of the earth; underwater sound propagation. *Mailing Add:* Woods Hole Oceanog Inst Woods Hole MA 02543

EWING, LARRY LARUE, b Valley, Nebr, July 10, 36; m 54; c 4. PHYSIOLOGY, ENDOCRINOLOGY. *Educ:* Univ Nebr, BS, 58; Univ Ill, MS, 60, PhD(agr), 62. *Prof Exp:* From asst prof to prof physiol, Okla State Univ, 62-72; PROF POP DYNAMICS, SCH HYG, JOHNS HOPKINS UNIV, 72- *Concurrent Pos:* NIH trainee, Dept Biochem, Univ Utah, 64-65; NIH spec res fel, Dept Pharmacol, Johns Hopkins Univ, 68-69; NIH career develop award, 71; consult, Reprod Biol Study Sect, NIH, 73-77 & NSF, 73- *Mem:* Am Physiol Soc; Endocrine Soc; Soc Study Fertil; Soc Study Reprod. *Res:* Reproductive physiology and endocrinology; male contraception. *Mailing Add:* Dept Pop Dynamics Sch Hyg Johns Hopkins Univ Baltimore MD 21205

EWING, MARTIN SIPPLE, b Albany, NY, May 4, 45; m 66; c 3. RADIO ASTRONOMY. *Educ:* Swarthmore Col, BA, 66; Mass Inst Technol, PhD(physics), 71. *Prof Exp:* Res asst radio astron, Mass Inst Technol, 66-71; res fel radio astron, 71-73, sr res engr radio astron, 73-75, MEM PROF STAFF, CALIF INST TECHNOL, 75- *Concurrent Pos:* Mem prof staff, Calif Inst Technol, 75-, staff mem, Owens Valley Radio Observ, 75- *Mem:* Int Union Radio Sci; Int Astron Union; Inst Elec & Electronics Engrs; Am Astron Soc; AAAS. *Res:* Instrumentation for radio astronomy; very long baseline interferometry of extragalactic objects and pulsars; interstellar scintillation of pulsars; computer control systems. *Mailing Add:* Radio Astron 102-24 Calif Inst Technol Pasadena CA 91125

EWING, R(OBERT) A(RNO), b Washington, DC, June 20, 15; m 47; c 3. CHEMICAL ENGINEERING. *Educ:* Ohio State Univ, BSc, 36, MSc, 37. *Prof Exp:* Res engr, Monsanto Chem Co, 37-41; res engr, Eagle-Picher Co, 41-44, plant mgr, 44-47; res engr, 47-49, asst div chief, 49-60, res assoc, 61-65, fel, 65-71, SR RES ENGR, BATTELLE MEM INST, 71- *Mem:* Am Inst Chem Engrs. *Res:* Manufacture of elemental phosphorus and phosphates; manufacture of mineral wool insulation; recovery of uranium and thorium from ores; pollution control; environmental effects of toxic substances; environmental impact assessment. *Mailing Add:* Battelle Mem Inst 505 King Ave Columbus OH 43201

EWING, RICHARD DWIGHT, b Lansing, Mich, Jan 17, 30; m 54; c 3. PHYSICS. *Educ:* Univ Chicago, BA, 50; Mich State Univ, MS, 54, PhD(physics), 58. *Prof Exp:* Asst prof, 58-67, res found grant, 59-60, ASSOC PROF PHYSICS, UNIV DEL, 67- *Mem:* Am Phys Soc. *Res:* Electron spin and nuclear magnetic resonance. *Mailing Add:* Dept of Physics Univ of Del Newark DE 19711

EWING, RODNEY CHARLES, b Abilene, Tex, Sept 20, 46; m 73. MINERALOGY, GEOCHEMISTRY. *Educ:* Tex Christian Univ, BS, 68; Stanford Univ, MS, 72, PhD(geol), 74. *Prof Exp:* Cur mineral, Stanford Univ, 73-74; asst prof, 74-78, ASSOC PROF MINERAL, UNIV NMEX, 78-, CHMN DEPT, 79- *Concurrent Pos:* Prin investr, Sandia Corp, 74-81 & Battelle Mem Labs, 77-80. *Mem:* Geol Soc Am; Mineral Soc Am; Mineral Asn Can; Sigma Xi; AAAS. *Res:* Rare-earth, metamict minerals; process of radiation damage in natural materials; relation of texture and fabric of fine grained sedimentary rocks to clay mineralogy and diagenetic history. *Mailing Add:* Dept of Geol Univ of NMex Albuquerque NM 87131

EWING, RONALD IRA, b Dallas, Tex, July 13, 35; m 57; c 4. PHYSICS. *Educ:* Rice Inst, BA, 56, MA, 57, PhD(physics), 59. *Prof Exp:* STAFF MEM PHYS SCI RES, SANDIA CORP, 59- *Mem:* Am Phys Soc. *Res:* Lighting; nuclear physics. *Mailing Add:* 1320 Dakota SE Albuquerque NM 87108

EWING, SIDNEY ALTON, b Emory University, Ga, Dec 1, 34; m 63. VETERINARY PARASITOLOGY. *Educ:* Univ Ga, BSA & DVM, 58; Univ Wis, MS, 60; Okla State Univ, PhD(vet parasitol), 64. *Prof Exp:* Asst vet sci, Univ Wis, 58-60; instr vet parasitol, Okla State Univ, 60-61, asst prof, 61-64, assoc prof vet parasitol & pub health, 64-65; assoc prof vet path, parasitol & pub health, Kans State Univ, 65-67; prof vet sci & head dept, Miss State Univ, 67-68; prof vet parasitol & pub health & head dept, Okla State Univ, 68-72; prof & dean Col Vet Med, Univ Minn, St Paul, 72-78; PROF VET PARASITOL, MICROBIOL & PUB HEALTH, & DEPT HEAD, OKLA STATE UNIV, 79- *Concurrent Pos:* mem adv bd, Morris Animal Found, 67-69, consult, 69-; mem comt animal health, Nat Res Coun-Nat Acad Sci, 71- *Mem:* Am Vet Med Asn; Am Soc Vet Parasitol; Am Soc Parasitol. *Res:* Swine lungworms; canine babesiosis; canine rickettsiosis; anaplasmosis. *Mailing Add:* Col of Vet Med Okla State Univ Dept PARA/MIC/PUB Stillwater OK 74078

EWING, SOLON ALEXANDER, b Headrick, Okla, July 21, 30; m 52; c 2. ANIMAL NUTRITION. *Educ:* Okla State Univ, BS, 52, MS, 56, PhD(animal nutrit), 58. *Prof Exp:* Instr animal sci, Okla State Univ, 56-58; from asst prof to assoc prof, Iowa State Univ, 58-64; prof, Okla State Univ, 64-68; asst dir, Iowa Agr & Home Econ Exp Sta, 68-73, HEAD DEPT ANIMAL SCI, IOWA STATE UNIV, 73- *Mem:* Am Soc Animal Sci. *Res:* Ruminant nutrition studies. *Mailing Add:* 101 Kildee Hall Iowa State Univ Ames IA 50010

EWING, THOMAS EDWARD, b Elgin, Ill, Aug 6, 54. TECTONICS, REGIONAL ANALYSIS. *Educ:* Colo Col, BA, 75; NMex Inst Mining & Technol, MS, 77; Univ BC, PhD(geol sci), 81. *Prof Exp:* Res assoc scientist, 80-81, RES ASSOC, TEX BUR ECON GEOL, 81- *Mem:* Geol Soc Am; Am Asn Petrol Geologists; Geol Asn Can; Asn Geoscientists Int Develop. *Res:* Regional analysis of geological structure, tectonics and structural development, presently focused on the Texas Gulf Coast and in the Pacific Northwest; volcanology and volcanic petrology; petroleum geology. *Mailing Add:* Bur Econ Geol Univ Sta PO Box X Austin TX 78712

EWING, WILLIAM HOWELL, b Carnegie, Pa, Oct 4, 14; m 42; c 2. MEDICAL MICROBIOLOGY. *Educ:* Washington & Jefferson Col, AB, 37, MA, 39; Cornell Univ, PhD(bact), 48. *Prof Exp:* Instr biol, Washington & Jefferson Col, 37-39; asst bact, Univ Mich, 39-41; assoc prof, NY State Vet Col, Cornell Univ, 46-47, from instr to asst prof, 47-48; bacteriologist & asst in charge enteric bact unit, Ctr Dis Control, USPHS, 48-62, in charge Int Shigelia Ctr, 50-74, chief enteric bact unit, 62-69, consult & res microbiologist, 69-74; CONSULT MICROBIOLOGIST, 74- *Concurrent Pos:* Mem, Int Subcomt Enterobacteriaceae, 50-, past secy; consult, WHO, 55, adv, 58, expert adv panel enteric dis, 64-; assoc prof, Sch Pub Health, Univ

NC, 62-; Linton fel from Washington & Jefferson Col, Marine Biol Lab, Woods Hole. *Honors & Awards:* Kimble Methodology Res Award, 56; USPHS Meritorious Serv Award, 63; Wyeth Award Clin Microbiol, Am Soc Microbiol, 75. *Mem:* Am Soc Microbiol; Am Acad Microbiol; Can Soc Microbiol; Brit Soc Gen Microbiol; Infectious Dis Soc Am. *Res:* Antigenic analyses; antigens of enterobacteriaceae, especially Shigella, Escherichia, Salmonella; relationship of these bacteria to disease in man; biochemical characteristics and differentiation; classification and nomenclature. *Mailing Add:* 2364 Wineleas Rd Decatur GA 30033

EXARHOS, GREGORY JAMES, b Milwaukee, Wis, Oct 27, 48; m 79. PHYSICAL CHEMISTRY, SOLID STATE CHEMISTRY. *Educ:* Lawrence Univ, AB, 70; Brown Univ, PhD(chem), 74. *Prof Exp:* Res asst chem, Argonne Nat Lab, 69-70; asst prof chem, Harvard Univ, 74-80; SR RES SCIENTIST, NORTHWEST LAB, BATTELLE MEM INST, 80- *Mem:* Am Chem Soc; Am Ceramic Soc; AAAS. *Res:* Investigations of condensed phases and surfaces by molecular spectroscopy; resonance Raman effects, infrared emission, phase transitions, materials preparation and solid state chemistry of glasses and polymers. *Mailing Add:* Battle Blvd Richland WA 99352

EXTON, JOHN HOWARD, b Auckland, NZ, Aug 29, 33; m 57; c 4. BIOCHEMISTRY. *Educ:* Univ NZ, BMedSc, 55; Univ Otago, NZ, MB, ChB, 58, PhD(biochem), 63. *Prof Exp:* Asst lectr biochem, Univ Otago, NZ, 61-63; from instr to assoc prof physiol, 63-70, PROF PHYSIOL, SCH MED, VANDERBILT UNIV, 70- *Concurrent Pos:* Investr, Howard Hughes Med Inst, 68-74 & 76- *Honors & Awards:* Lilly Award, Am Diabetes Asn, 72. *Mem:* Am Physiol Soc; Am Diabetes Asn; Am Soc Biol Chemists; Biochem Soc. *Res:* Control of metabolism; mechanisms of hormone action; gluconeogenesis, glycogen metabolism, and ketogenesis; effects of glucagon, catecholamines, glucocorticoids, and insulin on liver. *Mailing Add:* Dept of Physiol Vanderbilt Univ Sch of Med Nashville TN 37232

EXTON, REGINALD JOHN, b Folsom, NJ, July 17, 35; m 57; c 3. SPECTROSCOPY, OPTICS. *Educ:* Univ Richmond, BS, 58; WVa Univ, MS, 61, PhD(physics), 72. *Prof Exp:* PHYSICIST, LANGLEY RES CTR, NASA, 61- *Concurrent Pos:* Pres, Res Ventures Inc, 77- *Mem:* Am Phys Soc; AAAS. *Res:* Atomic and molecular spectroscopy; laser spectroscopy; environmental research. *Mailing Add:* NASA Langley Res Ctr MS 235A Hampton VA 23665

EYDE, RICHARD HUSTED, b Lancaster, Pa, Dec 23, 28; m 57; c 2. PLANT ANATOMY, PALEOBOTANY. *Educ:* Franklin & Marshall Col, BS, 56; Ohio State Univ, MSc, 57; Harvard Univ, PhD(biol), 62. *Prof Exp:* Asst, 61-62, assoc cur, 62-69, CUR BOT, SMITHSONIAN INST, 69- *Mem:* Bot Soc Am; Torrey Bot Club; Am Soc Plant Taxon; Int Soc Plant Morphol; Int Orgn Paleobot. *Res:* Tertiary paleobotany; comparative anatomy and phylogeny of angiosperms, especially anatomy of flowers, fruits of Cornaceae and allied groups, including fossils. *Mailing Add:* Dept of Bot Smithsonian Inst Washington DC 20560

EYE, JOHN DAVID, b Franklin, WVa, June 22, 23; m 46; c 4. SANITARY ENGINEERING, ENVIRONMENTAL HEALTH. *Educ:* Va Polytech Inst, BS, 48, MS, 49; Univ Cincinnati, ScD(indust health), 66. *Prof Exp:* Instr civil eng, Univ Southern Calif, 49-51; from asst prof to assoc prof sanit eng, Va Polytech Inst, 51-56; assoc prof, 56-66, PROF ENVIRON HEALTH, UNIV CINCINNATI, 66- *Concurrent Pos:* Consult, Nat Lead Co Ohio, 60-65, Tanners Coun Am, & Naval Ord Syst, 65- & six major leather tanning co, 75- *Mem:* Am Soc Civil Engrs; Am Soc Eng Educ; Am Water Works Asn; Water Pollution Control Fedn. *Res:* Water quality management; industrial waste treatment. *Mailing Add:* 2899 Mt Airy Ave Cincinnati OH 45239

EYER, JAMES ARTHUR, b Rochester, NY, Dec 18, 29; m 60; c 1. OPTICS, PHOTOGRAPHY. *Educ:* Mass Inst Technol, BS, 51; Univ Rochester, PhD(optics, physics), 57. *Prof Exp:* Res assoc optics, Inst Optics, Univ Rochester, 57-61, asst prof, 61-63, asst dir, 63-65; private consult, NY, 65-67; assoc prof optical sci, Univ Ariz, 67-69, assoc dir, Optical Sci Ctr, 67-74, prof 69-75, spec asst to vpres res, 73-74; consult indust & govt, 74-79; RETIRED. *Mem:* Sigma Xi. *Res:* Optical image evaluation; photographic image structure; photographic theory; applications of information theory to optical systems; photointerpretation techniques. *Mailing Add:* PO Box 129 Dundee NY 14837

EYER, JEROME ARLAN, b Orchard, Nebr, Aug 10, 34; m 57; c 2. EXPLORATION GEOLOGY, EXPLORATION GEOPHYSICS. *Educ:* Univ Mo, Columbia, BA, 60, MA, 61; Univ Colo, Boulder, PhD(geol, astrogeophys), 64. *Prof Exp:* Explor geologist, Humble Oil Co, 64-66; from res scientist to group supvr, Continental Oil Co, 66-69, dir geol res, 69-75; chmn, Dept Geol & Geophys, Univ Mo, Rolla, 75-77; explor mgr, Terra Resources, Inc, 77-78; chief geologist, 78-79, VPRES EXPLOR, GRACE PETROL CORP, 79- *Concurrent Pos:* Mem speakers coun, Okla Petrol Coun, 71-; consult geothermal resources, State NMex, 73-74 & NASA, 73-; mem bd dirs, Geosat Comt, Inc, 77-; chmn, Sci Geophys Data Panel, Nat Acad Sci, 80- *Mem:* Am Geophys Union; Am Asn Petrol Geologists; Am Inst Prof Geologists; Soc Explor Geophysicists. *Res:* Petroleum source rock and paleotemperature documentation and determinations; remote detection of chemical variable; petroleum and mineral resource evaluations. *Mailing Add:* Grace Petrol Corp 6501 N Broadway Oklahoma City OK 13116

EYER, LESTER EMERY, b Ithaca, Mich, Apr 9, 12; m 40; c 3. ORNITHOLOGY. *Educ:* Alma Col, Mich, BS, 36; Univ Mich, MS, 42; Mich State Univ, PhD(zool), 54. *Prof Exp:* Teacher pub sch, Mich, 36-43; from instr to prof, 46-77, head dept, 51-71, EMER PROF BIOL, ALMA COL, MICH, 77- *Mem:* Am Ornith Union; Wilson Ornith Soc; Sigma Xi. *Res:* Ecology of birds. *Mailing Add:* 5355 Blue Heron Dr Alma MI 48801

EYERLY, GEORGE B(ROWN), b Canton, Ill, Mar 20, 17; m 47. CERAMICS ENGINEERING. *Educ:* Univ Ill, BS, 40; Univ Wash, MS, 41. *Prof Exp:* US Bur Mines fel, Northwestern Exp Sta, 40-41; chief ceramist, Refractories Corp, Calif, 41-42; chief metall sect, Manhattan Proj & US Atomic Energy Comn, Oak Ridge, 46-47; asst prof ceramic eng, Univ Wash, 47-48; assoc ceramist, Argonne Nat Lab, 48-52; ceramic engr, Allen Bradley Co, 52-55; secy & chief engr, Malvern Brick & Tile Co, 55-67; sr engr, D M Steward Mfg Co, 67-73; MGR ENERGY CONSERV DEPT, TEMTEK-ALLIED DIV, FERRO CORP, 73- *Concurrent Pos:* Consult, US Atomic Energy Comn, 59-62; mem, Ark State Geol Comn, 67 & Gov Tech Adv Comt, 67. *Mem:* AAAS; Am Ceramic Soc; Am Soc Metals; Am Chem Soc. *Res:* High temperature materials; materials for reactor applications; ferromagnetic and nonmetallic ferroelectric materials; structural clay products. *Mailing Add:* Ferro Corp 4150 E 56th St Cleveland OH 44141

EYESTONE, WILLARD HALSEY, b Mulberry, Kans, Jan 7, 18; m 52; c 4. PATHOLOGY. *Educ:* Kans State Col, BS, 39, DVM, 41; Harvard Univ, MPH, 47; Univ Wis, PhD(path), 49. *Prof Exp:* Instr vet sci, Univ Wis, 41; res assoc vet path, Univ Ill, 42; res assoc, Univ Wis, 47-49; head comp path lab, Nat Cancer Inst, 49-55 & vet & chief lab aids br, 55-59, chief regional primate res ctrs br, Nat Heart Inst, 59-62, chief animal resources br, Div Res Facil & Resources, 62-71, CHIEF OPTOM, PHARM, PODIATRY & VET MED EDUC BR, DIV PHYSICIAN & HEALTH PROF EDUC, BUR HEALTH MANPOWER EDUC, NIH, 71-; interim dean, 81, PROF VET PATH & CHMN DEPT, COL VET MED, UNIV MO, 72- *Concurrent Pos:* Pathologist, Nat Zool Park, DC, 50-59; lab consult, Pan-Am Sanit Bur, Ecuador, 52; mem comt vet med res & educ, Nat Res Coun, 68-; mem, Nat Adv Coun Health Prof Educ, Dept Health, Educ & Welfare, 75- *Honors & Awards:* Distinguished Serv Award, Kans State Univ, 69; Meritorious Serv Medal, USPHS, 70; Charles A Griffin Award, Am Asn Lab Animal Sci, 70. *Mem:* Am Vet Med Asn; Am Col Vet Path (pres, 61-62); Am Asn Path & Bact; Am Asn Lab Animal Sci; Int Acad Path. *Res:* Cancer; pathogenesis of tumors; comparative pathology; research administration. *Mailing Add:* 203 Vet Med Complex Univ Mo Columbia MO 65201

EYGES, LEONARD JAMES, b Chelsea, Mass, Oct 30, 20; m 43, 68; c 1. THEORETICAL PHYSICS. *Educ:* Univ Mich, BS, 42; Brown Univ, MS, 43; Cornell Univ, PhD, 48. *Prof Exp:* Staff mem, Radiation Lab, Mass Inst Technol, 43-46; AEC fel, 48-49; res physicist, Radiation Lab, Univ Calif, 49-52; sci attache, State Dept Paris, 52-53; instr physics, Mass Inst Technol, 53-55, staff mem, Lincoln Lab, 55-56 & 57-63; NSF sr fel, 56-57; SR PHYSICIST, AIR FORCE CAMBRIDGE RES LABS, 63- *Mem:* Fel Am Phys Soc. *Res:* Scattering theory; fluid flow. *Mailing Add:* Rome Air Develop Ctr L G Hanscom Field Bedford MA 01730

EYLER, JOHN ROBERT, b Wilmington, Del, May 29, 45; m 67; c 2. PHYSICAL CHEMISTRY. *Educ:* Calif Inst Technol, BS, 67; Stanford Univ, PhD(chem physics), 72. *Prof Exp:* Nat Res Coun-Nat Bur Stand assoc chem, Nat Bur Stand, 72-74; asst prof, 74-79, ASSOC PROF CHEM, UNIV FLA, 79- *Mem:* Am Chem Soc; Inter-Am Photochem Soc; Am Soc Mass Spectrometry. *Res:* Study of gaseous ions utilizing the techniques of ion cyclotron resonance mass spectrometry, with particular emphasis on the interaction of tunable laser radiation with gaseous ions; applications of Fourier transform ion cyclotron resonance mass spectrometry. *Mailing Add:* Dept of Chem Univ of Fla Gainesville FL 32611

EYMAN, DARRELL PAUL, b Mason Co, Ill, Dec 18, 37; m 59; c 3. SYNTHETIC INORGANIC CHEMISTRY, ORGANOMETALLIC CHEMISTRY. *Educ:* Eureka Col, BS, 59; Univ Ill, PhD(inorg chem), 64. *Prof Exp:* Asst prof, 64-69, ASSOC PROF CHEM, UNIV IOWA, 69- *Mem:* Am Chem Soc. *Res:* Structure and reactivity of organo-metallic compounds having two or more transition metal atoms. *Mailing Add:* Dept of Chem Univ of Iowa Iowa City IA 52242

EYMAN, EARL DUANE, b Canton, Ill, Sept 24, 25; m 51; c 2. ENGINEERING, MATHEMATICS. *Educ:* Univ Ill, BS, 49, MS, 50; Univ Colo, PhD(elec eng). 66. *Prof Exp:* Scientist, Atomic Power Div, Westinghouse Elec Corp, 50-51; res engr, Caterpillar Tractor Co, 51-61, proj engr control, 61-66; assoc prof elec & mech eng, 66-69, prof elec eng & head dept, 69-75, PROF ELEC & COMPUT ENG, UNIV IOWA, 75- *Mem:* Sr mem Inst Elec & Electronics Engrs. *Res:* Fluid mechanics; computers; electronics; classical and modern control systems; remote control. *Mailing Add:* Dept Elec Eng Univ Iowa Iowa City IA 52240

EYMAN, LYLE DEAN, b Petersburg, Ill, May 9, 41; m 61; c 2. LIMNOLOGY, AQUATIC ECOLOGY. *Educ:* Bradley Univ, BS, 64; Mich State Univ, MS, 69, PhD(limnol), 72. *Prof Exp:* Biologist aquatic ecol, Water Qual Sect, Ill State Water Surv, 64-67; res scientist limnol, 72-78, PROG MGR NUCLEAR WASTE, ENVIRON SCI DIV, OAK RIDGE NAT LAB, 78- *Mem:* Ecol Soc Am; Am Soc Limnol & Oceanog; Int Soc Theoret & Appl Limnol; Sigma Xi. *Res:* Environmental transport and fate of contaminants generated from advanced energy fuel cycles; disposal of solid wastes from these technologies in an environmentally and socially acceptable manner. *Mailing Add:* Environ Sci Div PO Box X Oak Ridge TN 37830

EYRE, PETER, b Glossop, Eng, Oct 23, 36; m 63; c 2. PHARMACOLOGY, IMMUNOLOGY. *Educ:* Univ Edinburgh, BVM, 60, BSc, 62, PhD(pharmacol), 65; Royal Col Vet Surg, MRCVS, 60. *Prof Exp:* From asst lectr to lectr, Univ Edinburgh, 62-68; assoc prof, 68-73, PROF BIOMED SCI UNIV GUELPH, 74- *Mem:* Brit Pharmacol Soc; Can Physiol Soc; Am Soc Vet Physiol & Pharmacol. *Res:* Chemotherapy of parasitic diseases; pharmacologic actions of anti-parasitic drugs; pharmacologic mechanisms in allergy and anaphylaxis in domesticated herbivores. *Mailing Add:* Dept of Biomed Sci Univ of Guelph Guelph ON N1G 2W1 Can

EYRING, EDWARD J, b Oakland, Calif, Dec 25, 34; m 59; c 5. ORTHOPEDICS, PHYSIOLOGICAL CHEMISTRY. *Educ:* Princeton Univ, BA, 55; Harvard Univ, MD, 59; Univ Calif, San Francisco, PhD(biochem), 67. *Prof Exp:* Asst prof orthop & physiol chem, Ohio State Univ, 67-73; ASST PROF ORTHOP & CONSULT BIOENG, UNIV TENN, 74- *Mem:* Am Rheumatism Asn; Orthop Res Soc; Am Acad Orthop Surg; Am Asn Col Podiatric Med; Am Acad Pediat. *Res:* Anti-inflammatory drug metabolism; surgical implants; pediatric orthopedics; arthritis. *Mailing Add:* Suite N 101 Newland Prof Bldg Knoxville IN 37916

EYRING, EDWARD M, b Oakland, Calif, Jan 7, 31; m 54; c 4. CHEMICAL KINETICS, SURFACE SPECTROSCOPY. *Educ:* Univ Utah, BA, 55, MS, 56, PhD(chem), 60. *Prof Exp:* NSF fel phys chem, Univ Goettingen, 60-61; from asst prof to assoc prof, 61-68, PROF PHYS CHEM, UNIV UTAH, 68- *Concurrent Pos:* Dept chmn chem, Univ Utah, 73-76; Guggenheim fel, 82. *Mem:* Am Chem Soc; Am Phys Soc; AAAS. *Res:* Photoacoustic spectroscopy, particularly of solid surfaces and infrared wavelengths; applications in heterogeneous catalysis, organic semiconductors, metal corrosion, and biocompatible polymers; rapid reactions of macrocyclic ligands in nonaqueous media studied by relaxation techniques and calorimetry. *Mailing Add:* Dept Chem Univ Utah Salt Lake City UT 84112

EYRING, HENRY, b Colonia Juarez, Chihuahua, Mex, Feb 20, 01; US citizen; m 28; c 3. PHYSICAL CHEMISTRY. *Educ:* Univ Az, BS, 23, MS, 24; Univ Calif, PhD(chem), 27. *Hon Degrees:* Numerous from US & foreign univs, 52-64. *Prof Exp:* Instr chem, Univ Ariz, 24-25; teaching fel, Univ Calif, 25-27; instr, Univ Wis, 27-28, res assoc, 28-29; nat res fel, Univ Berlin, 29-30; lectr, Univ Calif, 30-31; res assoc, Princeton Univ, 31-36, from assoc prof to prof, 36-46; prof & dean grad sch, 46-67, DISTINGUISHED PROF CHEM, UNIV UTAH, 67- *Concurrent Pos:* Assoc ed, Textile Res J, Textile Res Inst; dir, Textile Found, 44-46; mem sci adv comt, Welsh Found, 54-; ed, Annual Rev Phys Chem, Phi Kappa Phi, 56; mem, NSF, 63-68. *Honors & Awards:* Nichols Medal, Am Chem Soc, 51; Talmage Award, Brigham Young Univ, 59; Lewis Award, Am Chem Soc, 63, Debye Award, 64; Wolf Prize, Wolf Found, Israel, 80. *Mem:* Nat Acad Sci; AAAS (vpres, 46, pres, 63, pres elect, 64); Am Chem Soc (pres, 65-); Am Philos Soc. *Res:* Radioactivity; application of quantum mechanics to chemistry; theory of reaction rates; theory of liquids. *Mailing Add:* Dept of Chem Univ of Utah Salt Lake City UT 84112

EYRING, LEROY, b Pima, Ariz, Dec 26, 19; m 41; c 4. PHYSICAL CHEMISTRY. *Educ:* Univ Ariz, BS, 43; Univ Calif, PhD(chem), 49. *Prof Exp:* Asst, Univ Calif, Berkeley, 43-44, chemist, Radiation Lab, 46-49; from asst prof to assoc prof chem, Univ Iowa, 49-61; PROF CHEM, ARIZ STATE UNIV, 61- *Concurrent Pos:* Sr fel, NSF, 58-59; Guggenheim fel, 59-60; Fulbright award, 59-60. *Mem:* Am Chem Soc. *Res:* Solid state chemistry, especially electron microscopic, thermodynamic, kinetic and high temperature studies of reactions involving oxide systems of the actinide, lanthanide and transition elements. *Mailing Add:* 6995 E Jackrabbit Rd Scottsdale AZ 85253

EYSTER, EUGENE HENDERSON, b Wheaton, Minn, Mar 21, 14; m 42; c 5. PHYSICAL CHEMISTRY. *Educ:* Univ Minn, BChem, 35; Calif Inst Technol, PhD(phys chem), 38. *Prof Exp:* Nat Res fel molecular spectra, Dept Physics, Univ Mich, 39-40; Hale fel, Calif Inst Technol, 41, group leader explosives res lab, Nat Defense Res Comt & Off Sci Res & Develop, 42-45; subdiv chief explosives div, US Naval Ord Lab, 46-48; alt div leader, Los Alamos Nat Lab, 49-70, div leader, 70-80; RETIRED. *Mem:* AAAS; Am Chem Soc. *Res:* Molecular spectra and structure; physical chemistry of explosives and detonation. *Mailing Add:* 1437 41st St Los Alamos NM 87544

EYSTER, HENRY CLYDE, b Dornsife, Pa, July 10, 10; m 38; c 1. PLANT PHYSIOLOGY, PHYCOLOGY. *Educ:* Bucknell Univ, AB, 32; Univ Ill, AM, 34, PhD(bot), 36. *Prof Exp:* Asst and teaching fel, Univ Ill, 32-36; instr bot, NC State Col, 36-37; from asst prof to assoc prof bot & head dept, Univ SDak, 37-46; res plant physiologist, Charles F Kettering Found, 46-62; sr res biologist, Monsanto Res Corp, 62-66; chmn div natural sci, Mobile Col, 70-76, prof biol, 66-80, distinquished lectr, 76-80; RETIRED. *Concurrent Pos:* From assoc prof to prof biol, Antioch Col, 46-62. *Mem:* Am Phycol Soc; Bot Soc Am; Am Soc Plant Physiol. *Res:* Photosynthesis; auxins; plant enzymes; hybrid vigor; plant genetics; Hill reaction; photophosphorylation; mineral and trace element nutrition of algae and duckweeds; nitrogen fixation; water pollution and eutrophication; aquaculture and mariculture. *Mailing Add:* 417 S Sage Ave Mobile AL 36606

EYSTER, MARSHALL BLACKWELL, b Toledo, Ohio, Sept 25, 23; m 47; c 3. ORNITHOLOGY. *Educ:* Univ Chicago, BS, 45; Univ Ill, MS, 50, PhD(zool), 52. *Prof Exp:* Asst zool, Univ Ill, 46-50; from asst prof to assoc prof, 50-66, PROF BIOL, UNIV SOUTHWESTERN LA, 66- *Mem:* Am Ornith Union; Wildlife Soc; Wilson Ornith Soc; Cooper Ornith Soc; Sigma Xi. *Res:* Daily rhythm and nocturnal unrest in birds; ecological distribution of mammals. *Mailing Add:* Dept of Biol Univ of Southwestern La Lafayette LA 70504

EYZAGUIRRE, CARLOS, b Santiago, Chile, Apr 28, 23; m 47; c 3. NEUROPHYSIOLOGY. *Educ:* Univ Chile, MD, 47. *Hon Degrees:* DSc, Cath Univ Chile, 72; DHon Causa(med), Univ Madrid, 75. *Prof Exp:* Fel med, Johns Hopkins Hosp, 47-50; from asst prof to assoc prof neurophysiol & pharmacol, Cath Univ Chile, 50-57; asst res prof, 57-62, PROF PHYSIOL, COL MED, UNIV UTAH, 62-, HEAD DEPT, 65- *Concurrent Pos:* Guggenheim fel, 53-55; vis praelector, Univ St Andrews, 65; consult, Training Comt B, Nat Inst Neurol & Communicative Dis, NIH, 66-69 & Neurol A Study Sect, 70-74, chmn sect, 73-74; Japan Soc Promotion Sci vis prof, 78; vis prof, A Rosenblueth-Grass Found, 79; mem, Dir Adv Comt, NIH, 80-82. *Honors & Awards:* Distinguished Res Award, Univ Utah, 74; Givaudan lectr, 80. *Mem:* Am Physiol Soc; Soc Neurosci; Sigma Xi. *Res:* Physiology of sensory receptors; physiology of chemoreceptors. *Mailing Add:* 2217 Laird Way Salt Lake City UT 84108

EZEKOWITZ, MICHAEL DAVID, b Durban, Repub SAfrica, Jan 27, 46; m 71; c 1. CARDIOLOGY. *Educ:* Univ Cape Town, MB CHB, 70; Univ London, PhD, 76; MRCP. *Prof Exp:* Intern & resident med, Univ Cape Town, 71-72; resident, Univ Natal, 72-73; res fel sci, Univ London, 73-76; fel med, Johns Hopkins Hosp, 76-78; dir, Coronary Care Unit, 78-80, DIR, HEART STA, VET ADMIN CTR, OKLAHOMA CITY, 78-, DIR ECHOCARDIOGRAPHY, 80-; ASST PROF MED, HEALTH SCI CTR, UNIV OKLA, 78- *Res:* Arterial wall physiology; platelet and vascular disease. *Mailing Add:* 111B1 Cardiol Sect 921 NE 13th St Oklahoma City OK 73104

EZELL, JAMES BEN, JR, b Gorgas, Ala, June 9, 28; m 48; c 2. ANALYTICAL CHEMISTRY. *Educ:* Florence State Teachers Col, BS, 51. *Prof Exp:* Lab asst anal chem, Extractive Metall Div, Ala, Reynolds Metals Co, 51-52, lab supvr, 52-54, asst lab supvr, Alumina Res Div, Ark, 56-62, lab supvr, 62-66, anal dir, Ark, 66-77, anal dir, Alumina Res Div, Va, 77-82. *Concurrent Pos:* Mem task comt, 47 & working group 8, Int Stand Orgn, 65-67 & task group 129, 70-; chmn, Am Stand Testing Mat E16.06, US Tech Adv Group to Int Orgn Tech Comt 129 & Int Stand Orgn Tech Comt 47/SC7, 73- *Mem:* Am Chem Soc; Am Soc Testing & Mat. *Res:* Supervision of analytical section, including atomic absorption, emission spectroscopy, x-ray diffraction, x-ray fluorescence, flame photometry, electron microscopy and conventional wet and colorimetric analytical methods. *Mailing Add:* 1915 South Shore Benton AR 72015

EZELL, RONNIE LEE, b Clarksville, Tenn, Nov 6, 44; m 73; c 1. NUCLEAR PHYSICS. *Educ:* Austin Peay State Univ, BA, 66; Univ Ga, PhD(physics), 73. *Prof Exp:* Asst prof, 73-77, ASSOC PROF PHYSICS, AUGUSTA COL, 77- *Mem:* Sigma Xi; Am Phys Soc. *Res:* Gamma-ray decay of nuclei; neutron spin-flip measurements. *Mailing Add:* Dept of Chem & Physics Augusta Col Augusta GA 30910

EZELL, WAYLAND LEE, b Stockton, Calif, Dec 31, 37; m 61; c 3. SYSTEMATIC BOTANY, EVOLUTIONARY BIOLOGY. *Educ:* Univ of the Pac, BA, 59, MA, 63; Ore State Univ, PhD(syst bot), 70. *Prof Exp:* Instr biol & bot, Ventura Col, 62-66; res asst bot, Ore State Univ, 67-68; from asst prof to assoc prof, 70-79, actg assoc grad dean, 80-81, PROF & CHMN BIOL, ST CLOUD STATE UNIV, 79- *Concurrent Pos:* Deleg, Int Bot Cong, Seattle, 69; lectr, Sigma Xi Regional Lect Exchange Prog, 71. *Mem:* Bot Soc Am; Am Soc Plant Taxonomists; Int Asn Plant Taxonomists; AAAS; Sigma Xi. *Res:* Genetics, evolution and taxonomy of angiosperms, especially genus Mimulus of sections Eunanus and Eumimulus, using field herbarium, hybridization, cytological, biochemical and numerical methods. *Mailing Add:* Dept Biol St Cloud State Univ St Cloud MN 56301

EZELL, WILLIAM BRUCE, JR, medical entomology, environmental health, see previous edition

EZEMENARI, FIDEL REX CHUKWUEMEKA, atmospheric physics, radiation physics, see previous edition

EZRA, ARTHUR ABRAHAM, b Calcutta, India, July 9, 25; US citizen; m 56; c 5. CIVIL & MECHANICAL ENGINEERING. *Educ:* Univ Calcutta, BE, 46; Univ Mich, MSE, 48; Stanford Univ, PhD(eng mech), 58. *Prof Exp:* Engr, Int Eng Co, 48-49; struct & hydraul engr, US Corps Engrs, 49-51; sr struct engr, San Francisco Harbor, 51-56; staff engr, Martin Co, 57-60, chief technol develop, 60-62, mgr aeromech & mat res, 62-66; head mech div, Denver Res Inst & prof mech eng, Univ Denver, 66-72, chmn dept mech sci & environ eng, 68-72; head, Off Res & Develop Incentives, 72-74, PROG DIR WATER RESOURCES, URBAN & ENVRION ENG, NSF, 74- *Mem:* Am Soc Eng Educ; Am Soc Civil Engrs; Am Soc Mech Engrs; AAAS. *Res:* Technology transfer; explosive forming and welding of metals; energy absorbing devices and systems; ultra low cost housing; crashworthiness of motor vehicles; solar energy; water resources and environmental engineering. *Mailing Add:* Eng Div Nat Sci Found Washington DC 20550

EZRIN, ALAN MARK, b Philadelphia, Pa, Mar 21, 52; m 73; c 2. CARDIAC ELECTROPHYSIOGY, BIOPHYSICS. *Educ:* Univ Miami, BS, 73, MS, 77, PhD(pharmacol), 80. *Prof Exp:* RES ASSOC, DEPT PEDIAT & CARDIOL, UNIV MIAMI, 80- *Concurrent Pos:* Adj prof, Fla Int Univ, 75-77. *Mem:* Teratol Soc; Am Physiol Soc. *Res:* Cardiac electropharmacology in the developing heart; cardiovascular pharmaeology; cellular electrophysiology. *Mailing Add:* Dept Pharmacol R-189 Sch Med Univ Miami PO Box 016189 Miami FL 33101

EZRIN, CALVIN, b Toronto, Ont, Oct 1, 26; m 46; c 6. ENDOCRINOLOGY, INTERNAL MEDICINE. *Educ:* Univ Toronto, MD, 49; FRCP(C), 54. *Prof Exp:* Res assoc path, Div Neuropath, Univ Toronto, 53-65, assoc med, Dept Med, 59-76, asst prof path, 65-68, asst prof path & med, 68-70, assoc prof, 70-76, prof med, 76-77; CLIN PROF, UNIV CALIF, LOS ANGELES, 77- *Concurrent Pos:* Stengel res fel, Am Col Physicians, 53-54; physician, Toronto Gen Hosp, 54-; consult, Dept Vet Affairs, Sunnybrook Hosp, Toronto, 54-; mem Int Comt Nomenclature of Adenohypophysis, 63-; vis lectr path, Harvard Med Sch, 74. *Mem:* Endocrine Soc; Am Diabetes Asn; Am Thyroid Asn. *Res:* Anterior pituitary cytology; insulin resistance; metabolic effects of glucagon; obesity; serum binding and kinetics of thyroid hormones; biology of trans-sexualism. *Mailing Add:* 18372 Clark St Suite 226 Tarzana CA 91356

EZRIN, MYER, b Boston, Mass, June 23, 26; m 46; c 3. ANALYTICAL CHEMISTRY, PLASTICS CHEMISTRY. *Educ:* Tufts Col, BS, 48; Yale Univ, PhD(chem), 54. *Prof Exp:* Asst, Org Chem Lab, Yale Univ, 50-52; chemist, coated fabric appln of chlorosulfonated polyethylene, E I du Pont de Nemours & Co, Inc, 48-50 & Plastics Div, Monsanto Co, 53-65; anal group leader, DeBell & Richardson, Inc, 65-69, mgr, Anal Testing Div, 69-72 & Anal Dept, DeBell & Richardson Testing Inst, 72-77; mgr polymer characterization, SL Testing Inst & qual assurance dir, Springorn Inst Bioresearch, 78-80; DIR, ASSOCS PROG & PROG MGR, ELEC INSULATION RES CTR, INST MAT SCI, UNIV CONN, 80- *Mem:* Am

Chem Soc; Soc Plastics Engrs; Sigma Xi. *Res:* Polymer analysis and characterization; molecular weight and molecular weight distribution; thermal analysis; polymers in patent infringement and product liability litigation; electrical insulation. *Mailing Add:* 173 Academy Dr Longmeadow MA 01106

EZZAT, HAZEM AHMED, b Cairo, Egypt, July 12, 42; US citizen; m 72; c 2. MECHANICAL ENGINEERING, ENGINEERING MECHANICS. *Educ:* Cairo Univ, BSc, 63; Univ Wis, MS, 67, PhD(mech eng), 71. *Prof Exp:* Proj engr, Suez Canel Authority, Egypt, 63-65; instr theory mach, Cairo Univ, 65-66; assoc sr res engr, 70-73, sr res engr, 73-77, staff res engr, 77-81, ASST HEAD ENGR, MECH DEPT, GEN MOTORS RES LABS, 81- *Honors & Awards:* Henry Hess Award, Am Soc Mech Engrs, 73. *Mem:* Am Soc Mech Engrs; Soc Automotive Engrs. *Res:* Tribology, particularly lubrication theory; dynamics of physical systems; optimization theory and its application to engineering design. *Mailing Add:* Eng Mech Dept Gen Motors Res Labs Warren MI 48090

F

FAABORG, JOHN RAYNOR, b Hampton, Iowa, Jan 23, 49; m 69, 80; c 2. COMMUNITY ECOLOGY, BIOGEOGRAPHY. *Educ:* Iowa State Univ, BS, 71; Princeton Univ, PhD(ecol), 75. *Prof Exp:* Asst prof, 75-81, ASSOC PROF BIOL, UNIV MO, COLUMBIA, 81- *Mem:* Am Ornithologists Union; Wilson Ornith Soc; Cooper Ornith Soc. *Res:* Ecology of island bird communities, focusing on the role of competition in structuring communities; applied biogeography and non-game bird management; behavioral ecology, particularly the evolution of cooperative polyandry. *Mailing Add:* 110 Tucker Hall Univ Mo Columbia MO 65211

FA'ARMAN, ALFRED, b New York, NY, Nov 29, 17; m 42; c 2. APPLIED PHYSICS, ELECTRONICS ENGINEERING. *Educ:* Brooklyn Col, BA, 39; NY Univ, PhD(physics), 55. *Prof Exp:* Phys sci aide, Eng Bd, US War Dept, 41-43; res adminr, Off Naval Res, 46-49; res assoc, Physics Dept, NY Univ, 49-55; mem tech staff, Hughes Res Labs, 55-65, consult, Hughes Res & Develop Labs, 66-71; physicist, Lawrence Radiation Lab, Univ Calif, 72-74; DIR, APPL PHYSICS CONSULTS, SAN FRANCISCO BAY AREA, 75- *Concurrent Pos:* Lectr, Univ Calif, Los Angeles, 56-67 & NATO Advan Study Inst, 66, 67 & 70; res grant, Sci Affairs Div, NATO, 71; adv, French Govt, Nat Off Aerospace Studies & Res, 78- *Mem:* Am Phys Soc; NY Acad Sci; Sigma Xi; Am Asn Physics Teachers. *Res:* Applied physics/engineering particularly, radiation effects, plasma physics, high voltage technology, liquid dielectrics, solid state physics, reliability, test and measurement procedures, electron and microwave tubes, cosmic ray and nuclear physcis. *Mailing Add:* 2510 Delmer St Oakland CA 94602

FAAS, RICHARD WILLIAM, b Appleton, Wis, Nov 8, 31; m 55; c 3. GEOLOGY, PALEONTOLOGY. *Educ:* Lawrence Col, BA, 53; Iowa State Univ, MS, 62, PhD(geol, ecol), 64. *Prof Exp:* From asst prof to assoc prof, 64-74, PROF GEOL, LAFAYETTE COL, 74-, HEAD DEPT, 70- *Mem:* Geol Soc Am; Soc Econ Paleontologists & Mineralogists; Int Asn Sedimentologist. *Res:* Triassic stratigraphy; estuarine and near-shore marine sedimentation; organic-inorganic interrelationships; paleoecology. *Mailing Add:* Dept of Geol Lafayette Col Easton PA 18042

FABACHER, DAVID LAWRENCE, toxicology, see previous edition

FABBI, BRENT PETER, b Reno, Nev, Mar 1, 38; m 62; c 3. MINING ENGINEERING. *Educ:* Univ Nev, Reno, BS, 63, MS, 65. *Prof Exp:* Sr res assoc, Nev Bur Mines, 63-67; proj chief, US Geol Surv, 64-74, asst br chief, 74-76, br chief, 76-82; PROG COORDR, X-RAY, BAUSCH & LOMB, 82- *Mem:* Soc Appl Spectros; Am Chem Soc; Spectros Soc Can. *Res:* Fundamental and applied x-ray fluorescence and geochemical studies of matrix effects; mathematical algorithms; instrumental design and automation; sample communinution and fusion; quantitative analysis of major through trace elements. *Mailing Add:* Bausch & Lomb Inc 9545 Wentworth Los Angeles CA 91040

FABENS, AUGUSTUS JEROME, b Boston, Mass, Jan 4, 32. PROBABILITY. *Educ:* Harvard Univ, AB, 53; Stanford Univ, PhD(math), 59. *Prof Exp:* John Wesley Young res instr math, Dartmouth Col, 59-61; lectr, Australian Nat Univ, 61-63; asst prof, Univ RI, 63-64; asst prof, 64-67, ASSOC PROF MATH, BOSTON COL, 67- *Mem:* Am Math Soc; Sigma Xi. *Res:* Queuing and inventory theory. *Mailing Add:* 58 Brimmer Boston MA 02108

FABER, BETTY LANE, b Chicago, Ill, Feb 7, 44; m 69. ANIMAL BEHAVIOR, ENTOMOLOGY. *Educ:* Col William & Mary, BS, 66; Rutgers Univ, MS, 70, PhD(entom), 75. *Prof Exp:* Assoc lectr, 73-74, LECTR BIOL SCI, COLUMBIA UNIV, 77-, RES ASSOC ANIMAL BEHAV, AM MUS NATURAL HIST, 75- *Mem:* Animal Behav Soc; Entom Soc Am; NY Acad Sci. *Res:* Ecology and behavior of individual animals in a population of wild American cockroaches. *Mailing Add:* Dept of Animal Behav Cent Park West at 79th St New York NY 10024

FABER, DONALD S, b Buffalo, NY, Mar 3, 43; m 64; c 2. NEUROBIOLOGY. *Educ:* Mass Inst Technol, BS, 64; State Univ NY Buffalo, PhD(physiol), 68. *Prof Exp:* Nat Inst Neurol Dis & Stroke fel, Lab Neurobiol, State Univ NY Buffalo, 68-70; vis res scientist neurophysiol, Max Planck Inst Brain Res, Frankfurt, Ger, 70-72; vis scientist Univ Paris, 72; asst prof physiol, Med Ctr, Univ Cincinnati, 72-74; assoc res scientist neurophysiol, Res Inst Alcoholism, 74-78; res assoc prof, 75-78, assoc prof, 78-81, PROF PHYSIOL & HEAD, DIV NEUROBIOL, STATE UNIV NY BUFFALO, 78- *Concurrent Pos:* Grass Found fel, 69. *Mem:* AAAS; Soc Neurosci; Am Physiol Soc. *Res:* Neuronal excitability; synaptic transmission. *Mailing Add:* Div of Neurobiol Dept of Physiol State Univ NY Buffalo NY 14204

FABER, JAN JOB, b The Hague, Netherlands, June 16, 34; m 57; c 2. PHYSIOLOGY, BIOPHYSICS. *Educ:* Univ Amsterdam, Drs, 57, MD, 60; Univ Western Ont, PhD(biophys), 63. *Prof Exp:* Res asst biophys, Univ Western Ont, 60-62, res assoc, 62-63; from instr to asst prof phys med, Univ Wash, 63-66; From asst prof to assoc prof, 66-73, PROF PHYSIOL, MED SCH, UNIV ORE, HEALTH SCI CTR, PORTLAND, 73- *Concurrent Pos:* Estab investr, Am Heart Asn, 68-73. *Mem:* Am Physiol Soc; Biophys Soc; Perinatal Res Soc; Soc Exp Biol & Med; Am Heart Asn. *Res:* Cardiovascular physiology; prenatal physiology; membrane physiology; physiology of joints; muscle. *Mailing Add:* Dept of Physiol Sch of Med Univ of Ore Health Sci Ctr Portland OR 97201

FABER, LEE EDWARD, b Detroit, Mich, Sept 21, 42. ENDOCRINOLOGY, BIOCHEMISTRY. *Educ:* Duke Univ, AB, 64; Bowling Green State Univ, MA, 67; Ind Univ, PhD(zool), 70. *Prof Exp:* Fel steroid metab, Syntex Res Div, 69-71; sr res fel steroid receptors, Inst Med Res, Toledo Hosp, 71-74, actg dir, 73-74; asst prof, 74-78, ASSOC PROF OBSTET & GYNEC & DIR, ENDOCRINE RES UNIT, MED COL OHIO, 78- *Mem:* Endocrine Soc; AAAS; Am Soc Zoologists. *Res:* Characterization of steroid receptors and their role in mechanism of steroid action. *Mailing Add:* Dept of Obstet & Gynec Med Col of Ohio PO Box 6190 Toledo OH 43614

FABER, MARCEL D, b Leeuwarden, Neth, July 19, 44; US citizen; m 69. MICROBIAL BIOCHEMISTRY. *Educ:* Catawba Col, AB, 66; Rutgers Univ, PhD(microbial biochem), 72. *Prof Exp:* Fel biochem, Princeton Univ, 72-73; vis investr bioeng, Sch Eng, Rutgers Univ, 73-74; SR SCIENTIST MICROBIAL BIOCHEM, AM CAN CO, 74- *Concurrent Pos:* Vis instr chem, Rider Col, 74; consult microbial biochem, Inst Microbiol, Rutgers Univ, 73-74; mem adv comt, Sect Pub Policy & Sci, NY Acad Sci, 76- *Mem:* AAAS; Am Chem Soc; Am Soc Microbiol; NY Acad Sci. *Res:* Microbial attack, degradation and transformation of insoluble polymers; biochemical production of petrochemical substitutes from renewable sources; continuous culture. *Mailing Add:* RFD 1 Box 404 Princeton NJ 08540

FABER, RICHARD LEON, b Winthrop, Mass, May 7, 40; m 64; c 1. MATHEMATICS. *Educ:* Mass Inst Technol, BS, 60; Brandeis Univ, MA, 62, PhD(category theory), 65. *Prof Exp:* Instr math, Regis Col, Mass, 64-65 & Univ Pa, 65-67; asst prof, Univ Calif, San Diego, 67-68; asst prof, 68-71, ASSOC PROF MATH, BOSTON COL, 71- *Mem:* Am Math Soc; Math Asn Am. *Res:* Relativity theory; non-Euclidean and differential geometry. *Mailing Add:* Dept of Math Boston Col Chestnut Hill MA 02167

FABER, ROGER JACK, b Grand Rapids, Mich, Oct 4, 31; m 56; c 3. CHEMICAL PHYSICS. *Educ:* Calvin Col, AB, 53; Mich State Univ, PhD(chem), 58. *Prof Exp:* Res instr chem, Mich State Univ, 57-58; res instr physics, Calvin Col, 58-60, from asst prof to assoc prof, 60-64; NSF fac fel chem, Columbia Univ, 64-65; from asst prof to assoc prof, 65-72, PROF PHYSICS, LAKE FOREST COL, 72- *Concurrent Pos:* Res assoc, Philos Dept, Boston Univ, 73-74. *Mem:* AAAS; Am Phys Soc; Am Asn Physics Teachers; Philos Sci Asn. *Res:* Electron spin resonance; atomic collision processes. *Mailing Add:* Dept of Physics Lake Forest Col Lake Forest IL 60045

FABER, SANDRA MOORE, b Boston, Mass, Dec 28, 44; m 67; c 2. ASTRONOMY. *Educ:* Swarthmore Col, BA, 66; Harvard Univ, PhD(astron), 72. *Prof Exp:* Asst prof, 72-77, assoc prof & astronomer, 77-79, FULL PROF & ASTRONOMER, LICK OBSERV, UNIV CALIF, SANTA CRUZ, 79- *Concurrent Pos:* Alfred P Sloan Found fel, 77- *Honors & Awards:* Bart J Bok Prize, Harvard Univ, 78. *Mem:* Am Astron Soc; Int Astron Union. *Res:* Formation and evolution of normal galaxies; stellar populations in galaxies; galactic structure; stellar spectroscopy; clusters of galaxies; cosmology. *Mailing Add:* Lick Observ Univ of Calif Santa Cruz CA 95064

FABER, SHEPARD MAZOR, b Brooklyn, NY, Aug 8, 28; m 53; c 4. SCIENCE EDUCATION. *Educ:* Emory Univ, BA, 49; Columbia Univ, MA, 50; Univ Fla, EdD(sci ed), 60. *Prof Exp:* Instr sci ed, Univ Fla, 55; assoc prof sci, ECarolina Univ, 59-62; assoc prof, 62-70, PROF PHYS SCI, UNIV MIAMI, 70- *Mem:* Fel AAAS; Nat Asn Res Sci Teaching. *Res:* Science curriculum and instruction. *Mailing Add:* Dept of Physics Univ of Miami Coral Gables FL 33124

FABERGE, ALEXANDER CYRIL, b Moscow, Russia, Feb 26, 12; nat US. GENETICS. *Educ:* Univ Reading, BSc, 33; Univ London, PhD(genetics), 36, DSc(genetics), 45. *Prof Exp:* Res worker, John Innes Inst, London, 33-37; asst lectr, Univ Col, Univ London, 37-45; res assoc genetics, Dept of Bot, Univ Wis, 45-47; assoc prof, Univ Mo, 47-55; scientist, Biol Div, Oak Ridge Nat Lab, 56-57; RES SCIENTIST GENETICS FOUND & LECTR ZOOL, UNIV TEX, AUSTIN, 57- *Concurrent Pos:* Res worker, Rothamsted Exp Sta, Eng, 41-42; exp officer, Army Oper Res Group, Brit Ministry of Supply, 42-45. *Mem:* Electron Micros Soc Am; Brit Genetical Soc. *Res:* Spontaneous and induced mutations and chromosome aberrations; nuclear structure; electron microscopy. *Mailing Add:* Dept of Zool Univ of Tex Austin TX 78712

FABES, EUGENE BARRY, b Detroit, Mich, Feb 6, 37; m 59; c 3. MATHEMATICAL ANALYSIS. *Educ:* Harvard Univ, AB, 59; Univ Chicago, MS, 62, PhD(math), 65. *Prof Exp:* Asst prof math, Rice Univ, 65-66; from asst prof to assoc prof, 66-74, PROF MATH, INST TECHNOL, UNIV MINN, MINNEAPOLIS, 74- *Res:* Singular integrals and partial differential equations. *Mailing Add:* Sch of Math Inst of Technol Univ of Minn Minneapolis MN 55455

FABIAN, LEONARD WILLIAM, b North Little Rock, Ark, Nov 12, 23; m 47; c 3. ANESTHESIOLOGY. *Educ:* Univ Ark, BS, 47, MD, 51; Am Bd Anesthesiol, dipl. *Prof Exp:* Intern, Univ Ark, 51-52, resident anesthesiol, 52-54; fel, Philadelphia Childrens Hosp, 54; instr, Sch Med, Univ Ark, 54-55; asst prof, Duke Univ, 55-58; prof, Univ Miss, 58-71; PROF ANESTHESIOL, SCH MED, WASHINGTON UNIV, 71- *Mem:* Am Soc Anesthesiol; fel Am Col Anesthesiol; AMA. *Res:* Chemistry and pharmacology of anesthetic drugs. *Mailing Add:* Sch of Med Washington Univ St Louis MO 63110

FABIAN, MICHAEL WILLIAM, b Mercer, Pa, Sept 27, 31; m 52; c 1. VERTEBRATE ZOOLOGY, ECOLOGY. *Educ:* Grove City Col, BS, 52; Mich State Univ, MS, 54; Ohio State Univ, PhD(zool), 64. *Prof Exp:* Asst, Mich State Univ, 52-54; teacher pub schs, Ohio, 54-56; instr gen biol, Ariz State Univ, 56-57; asst prof biol, Geneva Col, 57-61; assoc prof physiol, Westminster Col, 61-64; assoc prof physiol & zool, 64-67, PROF ECOL, GROVE CITY COL, 67-, CHMN DEPT BIOL, 64- *Mem:* AAAS; Ecol Soc Am. *Res:* Predatory or carnivorous activity of Crustacea on vertebrates; physiology. *Mailing Add:* Dept of Biol Grove City Col Grove City PA 16127

FABIAN, ROBERT JOHN, b Cleveland, Ohio, Mar 21, 39; m 62. INFORMATION SYSTEMS. *Educ:* Case Western Reserve Univ, BS, 61, MS, 63, PhD(math), 65. *Prof Exp:* Asst prof math, Smith Col, 64-70; ASSOC PROF COMPUT SCI, YORK UNIV, ONT, 70- *Concurrent Pos:* Vis asst prof, Dept Appl Anal & Comput Sci, Univ Waterloo, 68-69; planning consult, Bank of NS, 76; sr consult, Art Benjamin Assoc, 77; pvt consult, 77- *Mem:* Soc Mgt Info Systs; Inst Mgt Sci; Can Info Processing Soc; Asn Comput Mach; Can Comput Sci Asn. *Res:* Organizational use of information systems. *Mailing Add:* Dept of Comput Sci York Univ Downsview ON M3J 2R3 Can

FABIANEK, JOHN, biochemistry, physiology, see previous edition

FABIC, STANISLAV, b Tuzla, Yugoslavia, Nov 14, 25; US citizen; m 61; c 3. NUCLEAR ENGINEERING, MECHANICAL ENGINEERING. *Educ:* Univ Melbourne, Australia, BS, 54, MS, 58; Univ Calif, Berkeley, MS, 59, PhD(nuclear eng), 64. *Prof Exp:* Exp engr automotive res, Standard Motor Co, Port Melbourne, Australia, 54-58; assoc engr nuclear eng, Kaiser Eng, Oakland, Calif, 63-67; adv engr reactor safety, Westinghouse Elec Corp, Pittsburgh, 67-73; chief, Anal Models Br, Off Res, Nuclear Regulatory Comn, Washington, DC, 73-81; PRES, DYNATREK, INC, GAITHERSBURG, MD, 81- *Mem:* Am Nuclear Soc; Sigma Xi. *Mailing Add:* 19152 Roman Way Gaithersburg MD 20879

FABISH, THOMAS JOHN, b Youngstown, Ohio, Feb 27, 38; m 61; c 3. PHYSICAL CHEMISTRY, SURFACE PHYSICS. *Educ:* Ohio State Univ, BAeroEng, 60, MS, 66; Univ Rochester, PhD(mat sci), 75. *Prof Exp:* Res engr aerodynamics, NAm Aviation, Ohio, 61-63; res engr thermal properties of mat, Battelle Mem Inst, 66-69; scientist solid state physics, Xerox Corp, 69-80; SR RES CHEMIST, ASHLAND CHEM CO, 80- *Mem:* Am Chem Soc; Adhesion Soc; Am Phys Soc. *Res:* Insulator physics, with emphasis on the electronic and surface properties of polymers; chemistry and physics of carbon black and particulate-polymer interactions. *Mailing Add:* Ashland Chem Co PO Box 2219 Columbus OH 43216

FABRE, LOUIS FERNAND, JR, b Akron, Ohio, Sept 13, 41; m 62; c 2. PSYCHIATRY, PSYCHOPHARMACOLOGY. *Educ:* Univ Akron, BS, 63; Western Reserve Univ, PhD(physiol), 66; Baylor Univ, MD, 69. *Prof Exp:* Res specialist, Tex Res Inst Ment Sci, 65-67, from actg chief to chief neuroendocrinol, 67-70, from assoc head to head div ment retardation, 70-73; ASST PROF MENT SCI, UNIV TEX GRAD SCH BIOMED SCI, 69- *Concurrent Pos:* NSF res grants, 67-71; intern, Methodist Hosp, Houston, Tex, 69-70; Kelsey Leary Found grant, 69-71; NIMH grant, 70-71; resident, Baylor Univ, 70-73; clin asst prof psychiat, 73-; clin assoc prof, Univ Tex Med Sch Houston; med dir, Tex Alcoholism Found, Inc, Fabre Clin & Res Testing, Inc. *Mem:* Am Physiol Soc; Am Psychiat Asn; Am Group Psychother Soc; Endocrine Soc; Aerospace Med Soc. *Res:* Endocrine function in alcoholism; clinical double-blind studies of new psychopharacologic agents for anxiety, depression, insomnia, schizophrenia and alcoholism; phase one inpatient studies of new drugs. *Mailing Add:* Fabre Clin 5503 Crawford St Houston TX 77004

FABREGA, HORACIO, JR, psychiatry, anthropology, see previous edition

FABREY, JAMES DOUGLAS, b New York, NY, Oct 29, 43; m 67; c 2. COMPUTER SCIENCE, APPLIED MATHEMATICS. *Educ:* Cornell Univ, AB, 65; Mass Inst Technol, PhD(math), 69. *Prof Exp:* Asst prof math, Univ NC, Chapel Hill, 69-75; asst prof, 75-78, ASSOC PROF MATH & COMPUT SCI, WEST CHESTER STATE COL, 78- *Concurrent Pos:* Lectr comput sci, Villanova Univ, 79-; comput analyst, Asn Benefits Corp. *Mem:* Am Math Soc. *Res:* Numerical analysis; software engineering; mathematical physics; applied mathematics. *Mailing Add:* Dept of Math West Chester State Col West Chester PA 19380

FABRICAND, BURTON PAUL, b New York, NY, Nov 22, 23; m 52; c 2. PHYSICS. *Educ:* Columbia Univ, AB, 47, AM, 49, PhD(physics), 53. *Prof Exp:* Proj engr, Philco Corp, 52-54; lectr & res assoc physics, Univ Pa, 54-56; sr res scientist, Hudson Lab, Columbia Univ, 57-69; chmn dept, 69-71, PROF PHYSICS, PRATT INST, 71- *Concurrent Pos:* Consult, Moore Sch Elec Eng, Univ Pa, 54-60 & Indust Electronic Hardware Corp, 60-64. *Mem:* Am Phys Soc. *Res:* Nuclear magnetic resonance; atomic absorption spectroscopy; internal reflection spectroscopy; dosimetry; semiconductors; molecular beams; photonuclear reactions. *Mailing Add:* Dept of Physics Pratt Inst Brooklyn NY 11205

FABRICANT, BARBARA LOUISE, b Ithaca, NY, Mar 2, 50. PHYSICAL CHEMISTRY. *Educ:* Wells Col, BA, 72; Univ Rochester, MS, 74, PhD(phys chem), 77. *Prof Exp:* ADVAN SCIENTIST PHYS CHEM, OWENS-CORNING FIBERGLAS TECH CTR, 77- *Mem:* Am Chem Soc; NAm Thermal Anal Soc; Am Ceramic Soc. *Res:* Understanding gaseous release during glass batch melting via high temperature mass spectroscopy, thermal analysis and laboratory glass melting. *Mailing Add:* Owens-Corning Fiberglas Tech Ctr PO Box 415 Granville OH 43023

FABRICANT, JULIUS, b Philadelphia, Pa, Mar 30, 19; m 45; c 2. POULTRY PATHOLOGY. *Educ:* Univ Pa, VMD, 42; Pa State Col, BS, 45; Cornell Univ, MS, 47, PhD(poultry path), 49. *Prof Exp:* Asst animal path, Pa State Univ, 44-45; asst, 46-49, from asst prof to assoc prof, 49-60, PROF POULTRY DIS, NY STATE COL VET MED, CORNELL UNIV, 60- *Concurrent Pos:* NIH

fel, Inst Gen Path, Aarhus Univ, 64-65. *Mem:* AAAS; Am Vet Med Asn; Poultry Sci Asn. *Res:* Poultry diseases, especially Newcastle, infectious bronchitis, chronic respiratory disease and infectious hepatitis of ducks; mycoplasma; arteriosclerosis; avian tumor viruses. *Mailing Add:* NY State Col of Vet Med Cornell Univ Ithaca NY 14853

FABRICIUS, DIETRICH M, b Bucholz-Aller, Ger, Nov 17, 50; US citizen; m 72; c 1. ORGANIC & POLYMER CHEMISTRY. *Educ:* Luther Col, BA, 73; Northwestern Univ, PhD(org chem), 78. *Prof Exp:* RES CHEMIST ORG/POLYMER CHEM, PHOTOPROD, 78- *Mem:* Am Chem Soc. *Res:* Organic reaction mechanisms especially the Claisen and Cope rearrangements; aromatic and hydrocarbon rearrangements; polycondensation; pyrolysis of organic molecules. *Mailing Add:* 305 Silver Pine Dr Hendersonville NC 28739

FABRIKANT, IRENE BERGER, b Krakow, Poland, Jan 19, 33; US citizen; m 56. TUMOR IMMUNOLOGY, MEDICAL MICROBIOLOGY. *Educ:* McGill Univ, BSc, 54, MSc, 56; Univ Md, PhD(microbiol), 66. *Prof Exp:* USPHS fel microbiol, Sch Med, Univ Md, 66-67, instr, 67-71; asst prof med, Sch Med, Univ Conn, 71-75; asst prof microbiol & immunol, Fac Med, McGill Univ, 75-78, sci exec secy, Biohazards Comt, Fac Grad Studies, 77-78; USPHS vis fel, Ctr Dis Control, San Juan Labs, Puerto Rico, 78-81; RES ASSOC, CANCER RES INST, SCH MED, UNIV CALIF, SAN FRANCISCO, 81- *Concurrent Pos:* Consult typhus, WHO, 69, Pan-Am Health Orgn, 71; ad hoc comt mem typhus vacines, Armed Forces Epidemiol Bd, 66- & assoc mem, Comn Rickettsial Dis, 70-73; hon res fel tumor immunol, Dept Zool, Univ Col London, 73-75. *Mem:* Fel Royal Soc Trop Med & Hyg; Am Soc Microbiol; Am Soc Trop Med & Hyg; Brit Soc Immunol. *Res:* Tumor immunology, cloning human tumors; rickettsiology and arbovirology; epidemiology, pathogenesis and immunology of infectious diseases. *Mailing Add:* 135 Alvarado Rd Berkeley CA 94705

FABRIKANT, VALERY ISAAK, b Minsk, USSR, Jan 28, 40; stateless; m 81. PROGRAMMING. *Educ:* Ivanovo Power Inst, Bachelor, 62; Power Inst, Moscow, USSR, PhD(appl math & eng mech), 66. *Prof Exp:* Asst prof eng mech, Aviation Technol Inst, USSR, 67-69; prof eng mech, Polytech Inst, USSR, 70-73; sr res software systs, Res Inst, USSR, 73-78; RES ASSOC ENG MECH, CONCORDIA UNIV, CAN, 80- *Concurrent Pos:* Prin investr, Power Inst, Ivanavo, USSR, 71-73, adj prof, 76-77. *Mem:* Int Union Theoret & Appl Mech; Soc Eng Sci. *Res:* Elasticity theory; exact solutions of two-dimensional integral equations; contact problems for non-homogeneous bodies; numerical methods of solution of singular integral equations. *Mailing Add:* 1650 Lincoln Ave Apt 1112 Montreal PQ H3H 1H1 Can

FABRIZIO, ANGELINA MARIA, b Italy; US citizen. MEDICAL MICROBIOLOGY, EXPERIMENTAL PATHOLOGY. *Educ:* Villa Maria Col, BS, 44; Univ Ky, MS, 47; Univ Pa, PhD(med microbiol), 52; Hahnemann Med Col & Hosp, cert, 55. *Prof Exp:* Asst bact, Univ Ky, 45-46, instr Italian, 46-47; res bacteriologist antibiotics, Col Med, Univ Cincinnati & Cincinnati Gen Hosp, 47-48; res assoc exp cancer & tissue cult, Presbyterian Hosp, Philadelphia, 51-65; res assoc exp cancer & tissue cult, 65-67, ASST PROF PATH, JEFFERSON MED COL, 67- *Concurrent Pos:* Instr, Sch Med, Univ Pa, 60; res consult, Vet Admin Hosp, Coatesville, Pa, 68- *Mem:* Fel AAAS; Am Soc Microbiol; Tissue Cult Asn; Am Soc Pathologists; Grad Women Sci (past pres). *Res:* Acetylmethylcarbinol production by coliforms; sensitivities of bacteria to antibiotics; tuberculin sensitivity; tissue culture; experimental tumors; experimental heart research. *Mailing Add:* 2045 Spruce St Philadelphia PA 19103

FABRO, SERGIO, b Trieste, Italy, Sept 3, 31; m 58. PHARMACOLOGY, OBSTETRICS & GYNECOLOGY. *Educ:* Univ Milan, MD, 56; Univ Rome, PhD(biol chem), 66 & PhD(pharmacol), 68; Univ London, PhD(biochem), 67. *Prof Exp:* Intern med, Univ Milan, 56-57; asst prof path, Univ Modena, 58-59, asst prof biochem, 60-61; res asst, St Mary's Hosp Med Sch, Univ London, 63-67; RES PROF PHARMACOL, SCH MED, GEORGETOWN UNIV, 67-, PROF OBSTET & GYNEC & PROG DIR, COLUMBIA HOSP WOMEN, 74- *Honors & Awards:* Biochem Award, Nat Acad Lincei, 65. *Res:* Biochemistry of development; teratology; perinatal pharmacology. *Mailing Add:* Columbia Hosp Women Dept Obstet & Gynec Georgetown Univ 2425 L St NW Washington DC 20037

FABRY, ANDRAS, b Budapest, Hungary, Jan 10, 37; m 62; c 2. TOXICOLOGY, VETERINARY PATHOLOGY. *Educ:* Univ Liverpool, BVSc, 62; Colo State Univ, MS, 79. *Prof Exp:* Assoc vet, Gen Pract, 63-65; vet, Meat Inspection Div, Can Dept Agr, 65-67; asst toxicologist, Mason Res Inst, 67-68; supv toxicologist, Schering Corp, 68-76; resident, Dept Path, Col Vet Med & Biomed Sci, Colo State Univ, 76-79; SR RES FEL, DEPT SAFETY ASSESSMENT, MERCK SHARP & DOHME RES LABS, WEST POINT, PA, 79- *Mem:* Am Vet Med Asn; Brit Vet Asn; Am Col Vet Pathologists. *Res:* Clinical aspects of anesthetics; toxicological studies of cancer chemotherapeutic agents and new pharmaceuticals; pathological studies of new pharmaceuticals. *Mailing Add:* 161 Sandy Ridge Rd Doylestown PA 18901

FABRY, MARY E RIEPE, b Iowa, May 17, 42. BIOPHYSICAL CHEMISTRY. *Educ:* Stanford Univ, BA, 64; Yale Univ, PhD(molecular physics), 67. *Prof Exp:* Lectr chem, Yale Univ, 67-68; res assoc biophysics, IBM Watson Lab, Columbia Univ, 68-69; assoc biol sci, 69-71, assoc med, 71-80, ASST PROF, ALBERT EINSTEIN COL MED, 80- *Concurrent Pos:* NY Heart Asn Sr Investr, 71-73; NIH spec fel, 74-75; mem, Biomed Sci Study Sect, NIH, 81- *Mem:* Am Chem Soc; AAAS; Sigma Xi. *Res:* Enzyme mechanisms and metallo-proteins, heme proteins, membrane permeability to small molecules of biological membranes particularly red blood cells; NMR relaxation; high resolution nuclear magnetic resonance of biological systems. *Mailing Add:* Dept Med Albert Einstein Col Med 1300 Morris Park Ave Bronx NY 10461

FABRY, THOMAS LESTER, b Budapest, Hungary, May 30, 37; m 67; c 3. GASTROENTEROLOGY, NUTRITION. *Educ:* St Andrews Univ, BSc, 61; Yale Univ, PhD(phys chem), 63; Albert Einstein Col Med, MD, 73; Am Bd Internal Med, cert. *Prof Exp:* Fel Yale Univ, 63-64, lectr, 64-65; mem res staff biophys chem, Int Bus Mach Corp, 65-70; resident, Mt Sinai Hosp, 73-76, assoc, 76-79, ASST CLIN PROF MED, MT SINAI SCH MED, 79- *Concurrent Pos:* Adj asst prof, Rockefeller Univ, 70-72; res assoc & physician, Bronx Vet Admin Hosp, 76-79. *Honors & Awards:* Irvine Medal, 61. *Mem:* Fel Am Col Gastroenterol. *Res:* Polymer and protein chemistry; chemistry of electrolytic solutions; trace metals and nutrition; hemoproteins. *Mailing Add:* 853 Fifth Ave New York NY 10021

FABRYCKY, WOLTER J, b Springfield, NY, Dec 6, 32; m 54; c 2. INDUSTRIAL ENGINEERING, OPERATIONS RESEARCH. *Educ:* Wichita State Univ, BSIE, 57; Univ Ark, MSIE, 58; Okla State Univ, PhD(eng), 62. *Prof Exp:* Jr design engr, Cessna Aircraft Co, 54-57; instr indust eng, Univ Ark, 57-60; from asst prof to assoc prof indust eng, Okla State Univ, 62-65; assoc dean eng, 70-76, dean, Res Div, 76-81, PROF INDUST ENG & OPERS RES, VA POLYTECH INST & STATE UNIV, 65- *Concurrent Pos:* Prin engr, Brown Eng Co, Ala, 62-65; ser ed, Prentice-Hall, Inc, 70- *Mem:* Am Inst Indust Engrs; Am Soc Eng Educ; Opers Res Soc Am; fel AAAS. *Res:* Systems engineering; engineering economy; operations research; systems engineering management. *Mailing Add:* Dept Indust Eng & Opers Res Va Polytech Inst & State Univ Blacksburg VA 24061

FABUNMI, JAMES AYINDE, b Ile-Ife, Nigeria, Sept 1, 50. AIRCRAFT PROPULSION, ROTORCRAFT DYNAMICS. *Educ:* Kiev Inst Civil Aviation Engrs, USSR, MechE & MSc, 74; Mass Inst Technol, PhD(aeronaut & astronaut), 78. *Prof Exp:* Res assoc fel, Mass Inst Technol, 78; res engr specialist, Kaman Aerospace Corp, 78-80; PRIN CONSULT ASSOC, FABUNMI & ASSOC, 80-; ASST PROF FLIGHT DYNAMICS & FLIGHT PROPULSION, AEROSPACE ENG DEPT, UNIV MD, 81- *Mem:* Am Helicopter Soc. *Res:* Aeroelastic stability of aircraft engines, such as high aspect ratio turbofans; theoretical and experimental methods for rotorcraft dynamics and vibration studies; unsteady aerodynamics of ducted fans; new propulsion concepts. *Mailing Add:* PO Box 1068 College Park MD 20740

FACKELMAN, GUSTAVE EDWARD, b Freeport, NY, May 19, 41; m 64; c 1. VETERINARY SURGERY. *Educ:* Cornell Univ, DVM, 64; Univ Zurich, Dr Med Vet, 71; Univ Pa, MA, 73; Am Col Vet Surgeons, dipl, 75. *Prof Exp:* Practr vet med, Crawford Animal Hosp, 64-65; asst prof surg clinician, Kans State Univ, 65-67; assoc prof surg, Univ Zurich, 67-73; ASSOC PROF ORTHOP SURG VET MED, UNIV PA, 73- *Concurrent Pos:* Res consult, Solco Basel AG, Basel, Switz & Straumann Inst, Waldenburg, Switz, 71- *Mem:* Am Vet Med Asn; Am Col Vet Surgeons; Asn Study Internal Fixation Vet; Vet Orthop Soc. *Res:* Fate of transplanted cancellous bone in the horse; joint mechanics and the biomechanics of equine articular fractures; spinal fusion in the horse; equine osteoarthritis. *Mailing Add:* Univ of Pa New Bolton Ctr Kennett Square PA 19348

FACKLER, WALTER VALENTINE, JR, b Oak Park, Ill, Mar 19, 20; m 47; c 3. SURFACE CHEMISTRY. *Educ:* Iowa State Col, PhD(phys chem), 53. *Prof Exp:* Res chemist, Bauer & Black, 53-56; res supvr, Toni Co, 56-61; adv scientist, Continental Can Co, 61-66; chemist, Van Straaten Chem Co, 66-70; SR RES PROF, ARMOUR-DIAL, INC, 70- *Mem:* AAAS; Am Chem Soc. *Res:* Detergents; polymers; plastic films; adhesives. *Mailing Add:* 8348 E Via de Sereno Scottsdale AZ 85258

FACTOR, ARNOLD, b Boston, Mass, Apr 1, 36; m 61; c 2. PHYSICAL ORGANIC CHEMISTRY. *Educ:* Brandeis Univ, BA, 58; Harvard Univ, MA, 60, PhD(chem), 63. *Prof Exp:* NIH fel, Univ Calif, San Diego, 63-64; res chemist, 64-73, mgr polymer flammability & stabilization proj, 73-80, MGR, POLYMER & SURFACE STABILIZATION UNIT, GEN ELEC RES & DEVELOP CTR, 80- *Honors & Awards:* Award of Excellence, Gen Elec Co Plastic Dept, 70. *Mem:* Am Chem Soc. *Res:* Autoxidation; free radical chemistry; phenol oxidations; polymer stabilization; Redox polymers; polymer flammability. *Mailing Add:* Gen Elec Res & Develop Ctr PO Box 8 Schenectady NY 12301

FADDICK, ROBERT RAYMOND, b Sudbury, Ont, May 18, 38; m 65; c 6. FLUID MECHANICS, HYDRAULIC ENGINEERING. *Educ:* Queen's Univ, Ont, BApS, 61, MApS, 63; Mont State Univ, PhD(civil eng), 70. *Prof Exp:* Res asst hydraul eng, Queen's Univ, Ont, 61-63; hydraul engr, Alden Hydraul Lab, Worcester Polytech Inst, 63-66; res asst civil eng, Mont State Univ, 66-69; asst prof, 69-81, PROF CIVIL ENG, COLO SCH MINES, 81- *Mem:* Hon mem Soc Am Mil Engrs; Am Soc Civil Engrs; Soc Rheology; Slurry Transp Asn; Sigma Xi. *Res:* Transportation of solids in pipelines; rheology of mineral solids; compilation of a slurry pipeline computer data bank; pipeline and rheological aspects of coal-water slurries; hydraulic aspects of thermal pollution; pneumotransport and capsule pipelining. *Mailing Add:* Dept Basic Eng Colo Sch Mines Golden CO 80401

FADDOUL, GEORGE PETER, b Boothbay Center, Maine, July 11, 22; m 53; c 6. VETERINARY MEDICINE, PUBLIC HEALTH. *Educ:* Middlesex Univ, DVM, 44; Univ NH, MS, 48. *Prof Exp:* From instr to asst prof avian path, Univ NH, 47-50; PROF AVIAN MED, UNIV MASS, 50- *Concurrent Pos:* Partic, Nat Salmonella Surveillance Unit, 62- *Mem:* Am Vet Med Asn; Am Asn Avian Path. *Res:* Nature, behavior and effects of pesticides on ecological relationships in urban environments. *Mailing Add:* Farrer Rd Lincoln MA 01773

FADELL, ALBERT GEORGE, b Niagara Falls, NY, Jan 5, 28; m 71. MATHEMATICS. *Educ:* Univ Buffalo, AB, 49, MA, 51; Ohio State Univ, PhD, 54. *Prof Exp:* From asst prof to assoc prof, 54-76, vchmn dept, 69-70, assoc provost fac natural sci math, PROF MATH, STATE UNIV NY BUFFALO, 76- *Mem:* Am Math Soc; Math Asn Am. *Res:* Real variables; measure theory. *Mailing Add:* 407 Countryside Ln Williamsville NY 14221

FADELL, EDWARD RICHARD, b Niagara Falls, NY, March 8, 26; m 53; c 2. MATHEMATICS. *Educ:* Univ Buffalo, BA, 48; Ohio State Univ, MA, 50, PhD(math), 52. *Prof Exp:* Peirce instr math, Harvard Univ, 52-55; from instr to assoc prof, 55-62, PROF MATH, UNIV WIS-MADISON, 62- *Mem:* Am Math Soc; Math Asn Am. *Res:* Algebraic topology; fixed point theory; fiber spaces. *Mailing Add:* Dept Math Univ Wis Madison WI 53706

FADER, WALTER JOHN, b Boston, Mass, Jan 12, 23; m 52; c 1. THEORETICAL PHYSICS. *Educ:* Harvard Univ, AB, 49; Mass Inst Technol, PhD(physics), 55. *Prof Exp:* Physicist, Pratt & Whitney Div, 55-65, PHYSICIST, RES LABS, UNITED TECHNOL 65- *Mem:* Am Phys Soc; AAAS; Sigma Xi; Optical Soc Am. *Res:* Fast reactor criticality studies; theory of laser-produced plasmas and of their interaction with applied magnetic fields; theory of plasma confinement by magnetic fields; theoretical optics. *Mailing Add:* United Technol Res Ctr East Hartford CT 06108

FADLEY, CHARLES SHERWOOD, b Norwalk, Ohio, Sept 4, 41; div. CHEMICAL PHYSICS. *Educ:* Mass Inst Technol, SB, 63; Univ Calif, MS, 65, PhD(chem), 70. *Prof Exp:* Res fel solid state physics, Dept Physics, Chalmers Inst Technol, Gothenburg, Sweden, 70-71; sr lectr physics, Univ Dar es Salaam, Tanzania, 71-72; asst prof, 72-74, assoc prof, 74-78, PROF CHEM, UNIV HAWAII, HONOLULU, 78- *Concurrent Pos:* Vchmn, Gordon Conf Electron Spectros, 74-76, chmn, 76-78; res fel, Alfred P Sloan Found, 75-77; vis prof, Univ Paris, 78-79 & Univ Utah, 79-80. *Mem:* Am Chem Soc; Am Phys Soc; Am Vacuum Soc; AAAS; Sigma Xi. *Res:* Experimental and theoretical studies involving the application of angular-dependent electron spectroscopy to problems in surface chemistry, surface physics, and solid state physics; experimental techniques include x-ray and ultraviolet photoelectron spectroscopy, low energy electron diffraction, and energy loss spectroscopy. *Mailing Add:* Dept of Chem 2545 The Mall Univ of Hawaii Honolulu HI 96822

FADLY, ALY MAHMOUD, b Cairo, Egypt, Nov 3, 41; US citizen; m 71; c 3. POULTRY DISEASES, AVIAN VIROLOGY. *Educ:* Cairo Univ, DVM, 64; Purdue Univ, MS, 73, PhD(vet microbiol), 75. *Prof Exp:* Res vet virol, Vet Res Inst, Cairo, 64-69; asst poultry dis, Sch Vet Med, Purdue Univ, 69-75, asst prof, 75-76; VET RES SCIENTIST POULTRY DIS, REGIONAL POULTRY RES LAB, USDA, 76- *Mem:* Am Asn Avian Pathologists; Am Vet Med Asn; Sci Soc NAm; Asn Egyptian Am Scholars. *Res:* Viral induced diseases of poultry; avian tumor virology; avian diases in general. *Mailing Add:* USDA Regional Poultry Res Lab 3606 E Mount Hope Rd East Lansing MI 48823

FADNER, THOMAS ALAN, b Milwaukee, Wis, Aug 19, 29; div; c 2. POLYMER CHEMISTRY, PRINTING SCIENCES. *Educ:* Wis State Col, Oshkosh, BS, 51; Polytech Inst Brooklyn, PhD(polymer chem), 61. *Prof Exp:* From asst chemist to chemist, S C Johnson & Son, Inc, 51-57, sr chemist, 60-62; lab head paper specialties, Oxford Paper Co, 62-63, from asst dir to dir tech specialties dept, 63-70; mgr, Prod Develop Dept, Fiber Prod Res & Develop, Kendall Co, 70-72; pres, FDX Corp, Bethel, Maine, 72-75; mgr, Chem Div, Graphic Arts Technol Found, 75-79; res scientist, Tech Ctr, Am Can Co, 79-81; MGR MAT RES, ROCKWELL GRAPHIC SYSTS, 81- *Mem:* Tech Asn Pulp & Paper Indust; Am Chem Soc; Am Soc Testing Mat; Soc Mfg Engrs. *Res:* Application of physical properties of polymeric materials to commercial specialty products; paper/plastic, solid-state polymerization; colloidal phenomena; coating development; non-woven fabrics design; lithography and other printing processes. *Mailing Add:* PO Box 3012 Oshkosh WI 54903

FADUM, RALPH EIGIL, b Pittsburgh, Pa, July 19, 12; m 39; c 1. CIVIL ENGINEERING. *Educ:* Univ Ill, BSCE, 35; Harvard Univ, MS, 37, SD, 41. *Hon Degrees:* DEng, Purdue Univ, 63. *Prof Exp:* Asst civil eng, Harvard Univ, 35-37, instr, 37-41, fac instr, 41-43; from asst prof to prof soil mech, Purdue Univ, 43-49; head, Dept Eng, NC State Univ, 49-62, prof civil eng, 49-62, dean, Sch Eng, 62-78. *Concurrent Pos:* Consult, Dept Defense, US Corps Engrs; mem sci adv panel, Dept Army, 59-74; mem res adv comt, Fed Hwy Admin, 63-70; mem adv bd, Ford Found, 63-69; vchmn, Army Sci Adv Panel, Dept Army, 66-70, chmn adv grp to comdr gen, Tank Automotive Command, 67-70; chmn, NC Water Control Adv Coun; mem bd dirs, Nat Driving Ctr, 73-; pres, Atlantic Coast Conf, 66-67, 71-72; chmn bd dirs, NC Water Resources Res Inst, Univ NC. *Mem:* Nat Acad Eng; fel Am Soc Civil Engrs; US Nat Coun Soil Mech & Found Eng; Nat Soc Prof Engrs; Am Soc Eng Educ. *Mailing Add:* Dept Civil Eng NC State Univ Raleigh NC 27650

FAETH, GERARD MICHAEL, b New York, NY, July 5, 36; m 59; c 3. MECHANICAL ENGINEERING, COMBUSTION. *Educ:* Union Col, BME, 58; Pa State Univ, MS, 61, PhD(mech eng), 64. *Prof Exp:* Res asst, 58-64, from asst prof to assoc prof, 64-75, consult ord res lab, 64-78, PROF MECH ENG, PA STATE UNIV, UNIVERSITY PARK, 75- *Mem:* AAAS; Am Soc Mech Engrs; Am Inst Aeronaut & Astronaut; Combustion Inst; Sigma Xi. *Res:* Explosion hazards; physical aspects of fires; evaporation and combustion of sprays; combustion of metals; turbulent natural convection processes; two-phase flow and heat transfer. *Mailing Add:* 214 Mech Eng Bldg Pa State Univ University Park PA 16801

FAFLICK, CARL E(DWARD), b Cleveland, Ohio, Mar 10, 22; m 53; c 3. COMMUNICATIONS, SYSTEMS ENGINEERING. *Educ:* Oberlin Col, BA, 43; Harvard Univ, MA, 48, PhD(appl sci), 53. *Prof Exp:* Instr & res assoc, NeNMex State Univ, 47; Sylvania E Electronic Systs, Gen Tel & Electronics Inc, 55-69; VPRES ENG, GEN TEL & ELECTRONICS INT SYSTS CORP, 69- *Mem:* Inst Elec & Electronics Engrs. *Res:* Antenna; propagation; microwave; space communications; data communications. *Mailing Add:* Gen Tel & Electronics Int Systs Corp 140 First Ave Waltham MA 02154

FAGAN, J(OHN) R(OBERT), b Omaha, Nebr, Sept 17, 35; m 58; c 5. CHEMICAL & NUCLEAR ENGINEERING. *Educ:* Univ Nebr, BS, 57; Kans State Univ, MS, 62; Purdue Univ, PhD(nuclear eng), 68. *Prof Exp:* Jr chem engr, Argonne Nat Lab, Ill, 57-59; from instr to asst prof, Kans State

Univ, 59-63; sr res engr, 63-66, res scientist, 66-67, sect chief, 67-68, mgr theoret res, 68-72, mgr turbine res & develop, 72-73, chief aerothermodyn res, 73-77, CHIEF PROJ ENGR ADVAN TURBINE ENGINE GAS GENERATOR PROG, DETROIT DIESEL ALLISON DIV, GEN MOTORS CORP, 77- *Mem:* Am Inst Aeronaut & Astronaut; Am Nuclear Soc. *Res:* Gas turbine engine design; internal aerodynamics of turbomachinery; nuclear reactor design. *Mailing Add:* 5833 N La Salle Indianapolis IN 46220

FAGAN, JOHN EDWARD, b Manchester, Conn, Oct 17, 43; m 69; c 2. SYSTEMS ENGINEERING. *Educ:* Univ Tex, Arlington, BS, 67, MS, 72, PhD(elec eng), 76. *Prof Exp:* Design engr antisubmarine warfare radar, Tex Instruments Inc, 67-69; design engr comput control test equip, US Air Force, 69-71; asst prof, Col Eng, Univ Okla, 75-78, assoc dean, 78-80; DIR OKLA POWER SYSTS RES CTR, 80- *Honors & Awards:* Dow Award, Dow Chem Co, 78; C Holmes McDonald Award, 78; Jasper P Baldwin Award, 81. *Mem:* Inst Elec & Electronics Engrs; Sigma Xi; Conf Int des Grandes Reseaux Electriques; Am Soc Eng Educ. *Res:* Power system dynamics simulation and use of adaptive real-time control techniques to the control of power systems; transmission line wind loading; development of data aquisition systems. *Mailing Add:* 2329 Blue Creek Parkway Norman OK 73071

FAGAN, JOHN J, b New York, NY, Jan 19, 32. GEOLOGY. *Educ:* City Col New York, BS, 57; Columbia Univ, PhD(geol), 60. *Prof Exp:* From instr to asst prof, 60-69, ASSOC PROF GEOL, CITY COL NEW YORK, 69- *Mem:* Geol Soc Am; Nat Asn Geol Teachers; Soc Econ Paleontologists & Mineralogists. *Res:* Stratigraphy and sedimentary petrology of eugeosynclinal rocks, especially bedded cherts and turbidites; studies in northern Nevada and New York. *Mailing Add:* Dept of Earth & Planetary Sci City Col of New York New York NY 10031

FAGAN, PAUL V, b Newark, NJ, May 22, 27; m 53; c 4. BIOCHEMISTRY, ORGANIC CHEMISTRY. *Educ:* Seton Hall Univ, BS, 49; Fordham Univ, MS, 54. *Prof Exp:* Chemist, Sterone Corp, 51-53; jr scientist, Ethicon Inc, 53-55, asst scientist, 55-59, assoc scientist, Devro Div, 59-66, SR SCIENTIST, DEVRO DIV, JOHNSON & JOHNSON, 66- *Honors & Awards:* Johnson Medal for Res & Develop, Johnson & Johnson, 73. *Mem:* Am Chem Soc; Inst Food Technologists. *Res:* Process development, synthesis of pharmaceuticals and fine chemicals; fiber forming polymer synthesis; chemical modification of natural fibers, edible film and casing; collagen sausage casing technology; tanning processes of proteins. *Mailing Add:* Devro PO Box 858 Somerville NJ 08876

FAGAN, RAYMOND, b Brooklyn, NY, Dec 27, 14; m 36; c 3. EPIDEMIOLOGY, ENVIRONMENTAL SCIENCES. *Educ:* NY Univ, BA, 35; Cornell Univ, DVM, 39; Harvard Univ, MPH, 49. *Prof Exp:* Jr vet, Meat Inspection, USDA, 39-41; jr vet, Milk Sanitation, USPHS, 42, vet officer & epidemiologist, 46-54; assoc prof prev med & hyg & chmn dept, Sch Vet Med, Univ Pa, 54-56; sr investr virol, Wyeth Inst Med Res, 56-67; PRIN SCIENTIST BIOL, PHILIP MORRIS RES CTR, 67- *Concurrent Pos:* Chmn pub health comn, Health & Welfare Coun, Chester County, Pa, 57-60; chmn adv coun, Philadelphia Dept Health, 63-67; consult, WHO, 63-70 & Nat Inst Environ Health Sci, 70-71; adj prof, Drexel Univ, 64-67; adj assoc prof, Med Col Va, 75-; mem, Air Pollution Control Bd, Richmond, 75-81. *Mem:* Am Soc Microbiol; Am Pub Health Asn; Am Vet Med Asn; NY Acad Sci; Sigma Xi. *Res:* Environmental sciences; host-parasite relationships; epidemiology; virology; education. *Mailing Add:* Philip Morris Res Ctr PO Box 26583 Richmond VA 23261

FAGEN, EDWARD ALLEN, solid state physics, see previous edition

FAGEN, ROBERT M, US citizen. ECOLOGY, ANIMAL BEHAVIOR. *Educ:* Mass Inst Technol, BS, 67; Univ Mich, MS, 68; Harvard Univ, PhD(math biol), 74. *Prof Exp:* Asst prof biol, Univ Ill, 74-78; asst prof anat, Sch Vet Med, Univ Pa, 78-82. *Mem:* Animal Behav Soc; Am Soc Naturalists. *Res:* Evolutionary developmental ecology; behavioral ecology; biology of culture. *Mailing Add:* 18 Linden Pl Summit NJ 07901

FAGER, LEI YEN, b China; US citizen. BIOCHEMISTRY. *Educ:* Nat Taiwan Univ, BS, 68; Ohio State Univ, PhD(physiol chem), 71. *Prof Exp:* Res assoc chem, Case Western Reserve Univ, 72-74, res assoc biochem, Univ Va, 74-76, RES ASST PROF PHYSIOL, UNIV VA, 77- *Mem:* Asn for Res Vision & Opthalmology, Inc. *Res:* Biochemical aspects of color vision. *Mailing Add:* 1516 Trailridge Rd Charlottesville VA 22903

FAGERBERG, WAYNE ROBERT, b Denver, Colo, May 16, 44; m 71. MORPHOMETRICS, STEREOLOGY. *Educ:* Univ Wyo, BS, 67; Univ SFla, 72, PhD(algal develop cytol), 75. *Prof Exp:* Fel microecol, Univ Tex, Arlington, 75-77, vis prof biol, 78-79; DIR ELECTRON MICROSCOPE LAB, SOUTHERN METHODIST UNIV, 79- *Mem:* Am Bot Soc; Phycol Soc Am; Int Soc Stereology; Sigma Xi. *Res:* Quantitative morphometric analysis of plant cell structure with the purpose of determining the degree to which internal and external factors affect or change cell structure; correlation of cell structure and function. *Mailing Add:* Dept Biol Southern Methodist Univ Dallas TX 75275

FAGERSON, IRVING SEYMOUR, b Lawrence, Mass, June 7, 20; m 53. FOOD SCIENCE. *Educ:* Mass Inst Technol, SB, 42; Univ Mass, MS, 48, PhD(food tech), 50. *Prof Exp:* Asst food tech, Mass Inst Technol, 42; mkt specialist, USDA, 42-43; from asst prof to assoc prof, 49-58, PROF FOOD CHEM, UNIV MASS, AMHERST, 58- *Mem:* AAAS; Am Chem Soc; Inst Food Technol; fel Am Inst Chem; NY Acad Sci. *Res:* Nutritive value of foods; chemistry of flavor; analysis instrumentation. *Mailing Add:* Chenoweth Lab Univ Mass Amherst MA 01003

FAGERSTROM, JOHN ALFRED, b Ypsilanti, Mich, Jan 4, 30; m 53; c 3. INVERTEBRATE PALEONTOLOGY. *Educ:* Oberlin Col, AB, 52; Univ Tenn, MS, 53; Univ Mich, PhD(geol), 59. *Prof Exp:* From instr to assoc prof, 58-68, chmn dept, 70-74, PROF GEOL, UNIV NEBR-LINCOLN, 68- *Mem:* Int Paleont Asn; Geol Soc Am; Paleont Soc; Brit Palaeont Asn. *Res:* Biostratigraphy and paleoecology of the Devonian rocks of the Great Lakes region; Pennsylvanian paleoecology of the mid-continent region; biometrical aspects of variation and ontogeny. *Mailing Add:* 420 Morrill Hall Dept of Geol Univ of Nebr Lincoln NE 68508

FAGET, MAXIME A(LLAN), b Stann Creek, British Honduras, Aug 26, 21; US citizen; m 47; c 4. AERONAUTICAL ENGINEERING. *Educ:* La State Univ, BS, 43. *Hon Degrees:* DEng, Univ Pittsburgh, 66 & La State Univ, 72. *Prof Exp:* Aeronaut res scientist, Nat Adv Comt Aeronaut, 46-58; chief, Flight Systs Div, 58-62, asst dir eng & develop, Manned Spacecraft Ctr, 62-66, DIR ENG & DEVELOP, MANNED SPACECRAFT CTR, NASA, 66- *Honors & Awards:* Arthur S Flemming Award, 59; Golden Plate Award, Acad Achievement, 62; Medal Outstanding Leadership, NASA, 63, Distinguished Serv Medal, 69 & Medal Except Serv, 69; Spacecraft Design Award, Am Inst Aeronaut & Astronaut, 70; Award Outstanding Accomplishment, Inst Elec & Electronics Engrs, 71, Harry Diamond Award, 76; William Randolph Lovelace II Award, Am Astronaut Soc, 71, Space Flight Award, 76; Daniel & Florence Guggenheim Int Astronaut Award, 73; Gold Medal, Am Soc Mech Engrs, 75; Albert F Sperry Medal, Instrument Soc Am, 76. *Mem:* Nat Acad Eng; fel Am Inst Aeronaut & Astronaut; fel Am Astronaut Soc; Int Acad Astronaut. *Res:* Manned space flight; reentry aerodynamics; propulsion; space power systems; guidance and control; life support systems. *Mailing Add:* Eng & Develop NASA Manned Spacecraft Ctr Houston TX 77058

FAGG, LAWRENCE WELLBURN, b NJ, Oct 10, 23; m 50, 58. NUCLEAR PHYSICS. *Educ:* US Mil Acad, BS, 45; Univ Md, MS, 47; Univ Ill, MA, 48; Johns Hopkins Univ, PhD(physics), 53; George Washington Univ, MA, 81. *Prof Exp:* Physicist coulomb excitation, Naval Res Lab, 53-58; physicist plasma physics, Atlantic Res Corp, 58-63; physicist electron nuclear scattering, US Naval Res Lab, Washington, DC, 63-76; RES PROF ELECTRON NUCLEAR SCATTERING, CATH UNIV AM, 77- *Honors & Awards:* Meritorious Civilian Serv Award, Naval Res Lab, 75. *Mem:* Fel Am Phys Soc. *Res:* Assignment of nuclear energy levels and transition rates; plasma ion density studies; electron-nuclear scattering. *Mailing Add:* Dept of Physics Cath Univ of Am Washington DC 20064

FAGGAN, JOSEPH EDWARD, organic chemistry, see previous edition

FAGIN, CLAIRE M, b New York, NY, Nov 25, 26; m 52; c 2. PSYCHIATRIC NURSING, PEDIATRIC NURSING. *Educ:* Wagner Col, BS, 48; Columbia Univ, MA, 51; NY Univ, PhD, 64. *Prof Exp:* Staff nurse, Seaview Hosp, 47; clin instr nursing, Bellevue Hosp, 48-50; consult, Nat League Nursing, 51-52; asst chief psychiat, Clin Ctr, NIH, 53-54; res proj coordr, Children's Hosp, Washington, DC, 56-58; instr psychiat & mental health, NY Univ, 56-58, from asst prof to assoc prof nursing, 64-69, dir psychol & mental health, 65-69; chmn & prof nursing, Lehman Col, City Univ New York, 69-77, dir health prof, 75-77; DEAN & PROF NURSING, SCH NURSING, UNIV PA, 77- *Concurrent Pos:* Mem expert adv panel on nursing, WHO, 74-; mem bd dirs & audit comt, Provident Mutual Insurance Co, 77-; mem at large, Nat Bd Med Examiners, 80-; mem bd ment health & behav med, Inst Med-Nat Acad Sci, 81-82, gov coun, 81- *Mem:* Inst Med-Nat Acad Sci; Am Acad Nursing. *Res:* Affects of maternal attendance during children's hospitalization. *Mailing Add:* Nursing Educ Bldg S2 Sch Nursing Univ Pa Philadelphia PA 19104

FAGLEY, THOMAS FISHER, b Mt Carmel, Pa, Sept 7, 13. PHYSICAL CHEMISTRY. *Educ:* Bucknell Univ, BS, 35, MS, 37; Univ Chicago, PhD(chem), 49. *Prof Exp:* Instr chem, Bucknell Univ, 38-40 & 42-46; instr, Univ Col, Univ Chicago, 47, teaching fel, 48-49; from asst prof to assoc prof chem, Tulane Univ, 49-61, prof, 61-79; RETIRED. *Mem:* AAAS; Am Chem Soc. *Res:* Microcalorimetry; heats of combustion; kinetics; thermodynamics of solutions. *Mailing Add:* Dept of Chem Tulane Univ New Orleans LA 70118

FAGOT, WILFRED CLARK, b New Orleans, La, Dec 5, 24. APPLIED MATHEMATICS, MATHEMATICAL PHYSICS. *Educ:* Univ Tex, BS, 45; Tulane Univ, MS, 47; Univ Chicago, MS, 52. *Prof Exp:* Physicist, Enrico Fermi Inst Nuclear Studies, 52-53, physicist, Chicago Midway Labs, 53-54; sr systs physicist, Norden Div, United Aircraft Corp, 56-61; sr staff scientist, Kearfott Div, Gen Precision Aerospace, 61-63; prin scientist, Bedford Labs, Missile Systs Div, Raytheon Co, 63-65; asst prof, 65-66, chmn dept, 71-74, ASSOC PROF MATH, JUNIATA COL, 66- *Concurrent Pos:* NSF sci fac fel, Pa State Univ, 70-71. *Mem:* Am Math Soc; Math Asn Am; Soc Indust & Appl Math; Am Phys Soc; sr mem Inst Elec & Electronics Engrs. *Res:* Stochastic processes, electromagnetic theory, antennas, propagation, scattering, noise and radar clutter; perturbation theory; cosmic rays; radar and inertial systems analysis. *Mailing Add:* Dept of Math Juniata Col Huntingdon PA 16652

FAHERTY, KEITH F, b Platteville, Wis, Dec 7, 31; m 51; c 5. CIVIL ENGINEERING, STRUCTURAL ENGINEERING. *Educ:* Wis State Univ, Platteville, BS, 54; Univ Ill, Urbana, MS, 62. *Prof Exp:* Trainee, US Gypsum Co, 54-55, authorities engr, 55, construct foreman, 55-57; from instr to assoc prof civil eng, 57-73, chmn dept, 66-80, PROF CIVIL ENG, UNIV WIS-PLATTEVILLE, 73- *Mem:* Am Soc Civil Engrs; Nat Soc Prof Engrs; Am Soc Eng Educ; Am Concrete Inst. *Res:* Making mathematical models of structures; wood and wood structures. *Mailing Add:* Dept of Civil Eng Univ of Wis Platteville WI 53818

FAHEY, DARRYL RICHARD, b Grand Forks, NDak, July 13, 42; m 66; c 1. ORGANOMETALLIC CHEMISTRY. *Educ:* Univ NDak, BS, 64, PhD(org chem), 69. *Prof Exp:* RES CHEMIST, PHILLIPS PETROL CO, 68- *Mem:* Am Chem Soc; The Chem Soc. *Res:* Organometallic chemistry of transition metals; homogeneous catalysis; transition metals in organic synthesis. *Mailing Add:* Res & Develop Dept Phillips Petrol Co Bartlesville OK 74004

FAHEY, GEORGE CHRISTOPHER, JR, b Weston, WVa, Nov 12, 49. ANIMAL NUTRITION, NUTRITIONAL BIOCHEMISTRY. *Educ:* WVa Univ, BA, 71, MS, 74, PhD(animal nutrit), 76. *Prof Exp:* Res asst agr biochem, WVa Univ, 71-74, res asst animal nutrit, 74-76; asst prof, 76-80, ASSOC PROF ANIMAL SCI, UNIV ILL, URBANA, 80. *Mem:* Am Soc Animal Sci; Am Chem Soc; AAAS; Animal Nutrit Res Coun; Sigma Xi. *Res:* Fiber utilization by ruminant and non-ruminant animals. *Mailing Add:* 124 Animal Sci Lab Univ of Ill Urbana IL 61801

FAHEY, JOHN LEONARD, b Co Durham, UK, Mar 4, 44. MEDICINAL & SYNTHETIC ORGANIC CHEMISTRY. *Educ:* Univ St Andrews, Scotland, BSc, 67; Stevens Inst Technol, PhD(chem), 72. *Prof Exp:* Lab asst inorg & anal chem, Imperial Chem Industs, UK, 60-67; res asst, Warner-Lambert Res Inst, 68-70; sr res chem, Merck, Sharp & Dohme Res Labs, 72-75; res scientist, Stevens Inst Technol, NJ, 75-78; ASST PROF MED CHEM, FAIRLEIGH DICKINSON UNIV, 78- *Concurrent Pos:* Teaching asst, Stevens Inst Technol, 70-71, Delft fel, 71-72; mem adj fac, Kean Col, NJ, 74-75. *Mem:* Sigma Xi (vpres, 76-77, pres, 78); NY Acad Sci; AAAS; fel Chem Soc; Am Chem Soc. *Res:* Medicinal chemistry of beta-lactam antibiotics, antihypertensives and anti-inflammatories; synthetic organic chemistry of natural products, interpretive spectroscopy. *Mailing Add:* Dept of Chem Fairleigh Dickinson Univ Rutherford NJ 07070

FAHEY, JOHN LESLIE, b Cleveland, Ohio, Sept 8, 24; m 54; c 3. IMMUNOLOGY. *Educ:* Wayne State Univ, MS, 49; Harvard Univ, MD, 51. *Prof Exp:* Intern med, Presby Hosp, NY, 51-52, asst res, 52-53; clin assoc, Nat Cancer Inst, NIH, 53-54, sr investr metab, 54-63, chief immunol br, 64-71; prof microbiol & immunol & chmn dept, Sch Med, 71-81, DIR, CTR INTERDISCIPLINARY RES IMMUNOL DIS, UNIV CALIF, LOS ANGELES, 78- *Mem:* Am Physiol Soc; Soc Exp Biol & Med; Am Asn Cancer Res; Am Fedn Clin Res; Am Soc Clin Invest. *Res:* Immunology; oncology. *Mailing Add:* Dept Microbiol & Immunol Sch Med Univ Calif Los Angeles CA 90024

FAHEY, JOHN VINCENT, b New York NY, May 29, 48; m 76. PHYSIOLOGY, IMMUNOLOGY. *Educ:* Mt St Mary's Col, BS, 70; Univ Vt, MS, 74, PhD(cell biol), 77. *Prof Exp:* Teacher biol, Paramus Cath High Sch, 70-71; technologist viral oncol, Pub Health Res Inst, NY, 71-72; teaching fel med microbiol, Univ Vt, 72-74, res fel rheumatology, 74-77; mem fac biol, Clark Univ, 77-78; res assoc physiol, Dartmouth Med Sch, 78-81; MEM FAC SCI, BENNINGTON COL, 81- *Concurrent Pos:* Andrew W Mellon teaching fel, Clark Univ, 77-78. *Mem:* AAAS; Tissue Cult Asn; Am Soc Microbiol; Sigma Xi. *Res:* Mediation and modulation of physiological and immune responses by prostaglandins and cyclic nucleotides. *Mailing Add:* Sci Div Bennington Col Bennington VT 05201

FAHEY, PAUL FARRELL, JR, b Lock Haven, Pa, July 2, 42; m 65; c 2. PHYSICS. *Educ:* Univ Scranton, BS, 64; Univ Va, MS, 66, PhD(physics), 68. *Prof Exp:* Asst prof, 68-73, assoc prof, 73-77, PROF PHYSICS, UNIV SCRANTON, 77- *Concurrent Pos:* Fac sci fel, NSF & vis assoc prof, Cornell Univ, 75-76, vis prof, 77, 78, 80 & 81; vis scientist, Bell Labs, Murray Hill, 82; fac sci develop fel, NSF, 82. *Mem:* Am Phys Soc; The Chem Soc; AAAS; Am Asn Physics Teachers. *Res:* Physical properties of biopolymers; pressure-volume-temperature relations of liquids; fluorescence correlation spectroscopy; lipid bilayer characterizations; cochlear mechanics and electrophysiology of the cochlear nerve. *Mailing Add:* Dept of Physics Univ of Scranton Scranton PA 18510

FAHEY, ROBERT C, b Sacramento, Calif, Feb 8, 36; m 60; c 2. ORGANIC CHEMISTRY, BIOCHEMISTRY. *Educ:* Univ Calif, Berkeley, BS, 57; Univ Chicago, PhD(org chem), 63. *Prof Exp:* Asst prof, 63-70, ASSOC PROF CHEM, UNIV CALIF, SAN DIEGO, 70- *Concurrent Pos:* Alfred P Sloan Found fel, 66-68; John Simon Guggenheim Found fel, 70-71. *Mem:* AAAS; Am Chem Soc; The Chem Soc; Am Soc Biol Chemists. *Res:* Biological chemistry of thiols and disulfides. *Mailing Add:* Dept of Chem Univ of Calif at San Diego La Jolla CA 92093

FAHEY, WALTER JOHN, b Winnipeg, Man, Apr 10, 27; US citizen; m 49; c 4. ELECTRICAL ENGINEERING. *Educ:* Case Inst Technol, BS, 57, MS, 59, PhD(elec eng), 63. *Prof Exp:* Instr elec eng, Case Inst Technol, 59-62; from asst prof to prof, Ohio Univ, 63-69, chmn dept, 66-67, dean col eng & technol, 67-68; dean col eng, 69-77, PROF ELEC ENG, UNIV ARIZ, 69- *Concurrent Pos:* Instr adult div, Cleveland Pub Schs, 59-62; Am Coun Educ fel, 67-68; mem, Ohio Coun Comn, 67-68 & Ariz State Bd Tech Regist, 69-70; dir, Aviation Res & Educ Found, Ariz, 70- *Mem:* Inst Elec & Electronics Engrs; Am Soc Eng Educ. *Res:* Electrical properties of materials; theoretical electromagnets; plasma dynamics and gaseous electronics; methods of engineering education; biomedical instrumentation and measurements engineering; fiber optics; power electronics. *Mailing Add:* Dept of Elec Eng Univ of Ariz Tucson AZ 85721

FAHIDY, THOMAS Z(OLTAN), b Budapest, Hungary, June 17, 34; Can citizen; m 62; c 1. CHEMICAL ENGINEERING, APPLIED MATHEMATICS. *Educ:* Queen's Univ, Ont, BSc, 59, MSc, 61; Univ Ill, Urbana, PhD(chem eng), 65. *Prof Exp:* From asst prof to assoc prof, 64-71, PROF CHEM ENG, UNIV WATERLOO, 71- *Concurrent Pos:* Hon res assoc & Shell vis fel, Univ Col, London, 68-69; partic, Can-France Sci Exchange Prog, 75-76; assoc ed, Can J Chem Eng, 72-80. *Mem:* Am Inst Chem Engrs; Can Soc Chem Engrs; Simulation Coun; NY Acad Sci; fel Chem Inst Can. *Res:* Electrochemical engineering; applied mathematics; process dynamics and control. *Mailing Add:* Dept of Chem Eng Univ of Waterloo Waterloo ON N2L 3G1 Can

FAHIEN, LEONARD A, b St Louis, Mo, July 26, 34; m 58; c 3. PHARMACOLOGY, BIOCHEMISTRY. *Educ:* Washington Univ, AB, 56, MD, 60. *Prof Exp:* Intern med, Univ Wis, 60-61; NIH fel biochem, Washington Univ, 61-62 & physiol chem, Univ Wis, 62-64; from asst prof to assoc prof, 66-74, PROF PHARMACOL, UNIV WIS-MADISON, 74-, ASSOC DEAN, SCH MED, 79- *Concurrent Pos:* NIH res grant, 66-, career develop award, 68-73. *Mem:* AAAS. *Res:* Regulation of enzyme activity; studies of enzyme-enzyme complexes; effects of drugs on enzyme catalyzed reaction. *Mailing Add:* Dept of Pharmacol Univ of Wis Madison WI 53706

FAHIEN, RAY W, b St Louis, Mo, Dec 26, 23. CHEMICAL ENGINEERING. *Educ:* Washington Univ, St Louis, BSChE, 47; Mo Sch Mines, MSChE, 50; Purdue Univ, PhD, 54. *Prof Exp:* Instr chem eng, Mo Sch Mines, 47-50; chem engr, Ethyl Corp, 53-54; from asst prof to prof chem eng, Iowa State Univ, 54-64; chmn dept, 64-69, PROF CHEM ENG, UNIV FLA, 64- *Concurrent Pos:* Sr engr, Ames Lab, US Atomic Energy Comn, 54-64; vis prof, Univ Wis, 59-60; Fulbright lectr, Brazil, 64; ed, Chem Eng Educ J, 67- *Mem:* AAAS; Am Inst Chem Engrs; Am Chem Soc; Am Soc Eng Educ. *Res:* Transport of heat; mass and momentum; turbulent diffusion; applied mathematics. *Mailing Add:* Dept of Chem Eng Univ of Fla Gainesville FL 32601

FAHIM, MOSTAFA SAFWAT, b Cairo, Egypt, Oct 7, 31; c 1. REPRODUCTIVE BIOLOGY. *Educ:* Cairo Univ, BS, 53; Univ Mo-Columbia, MS, 58, PhD(reproductive biol), 61. *Prof Exp:* Asst dir animal sci dept, Ministry of Land Reform, Egypt, 61-63; dir animal reproduction dept, Off of the Pres, Algeria, 63-66; res assoc, 66-68, from asst prof to assoc prof, 68-74, PROF OBSTET & GYNEC, SCH MED, UNIV MO-COLUMBIA, 74- *Concurrent Pos:* Prof, Univ Ain Shams, Cairo, 61-63; consult, Inst de Serotherapie de Toulouse, France & NAfrica Div, Russel Pharmaceut Co, 63-66. *Mem:* Am Col Clin Pharmacol; Am Soc Pharmacol & Exp Therapeut; Soc Environ Geochem & Health; NY Acad Sci; Am Soc Androl. *Res:* Human reproduction biology; effects of drugs and environmental chemicals on the fetus and newborn. *Mailing Add:* Dept Obstet & Gynec Univ Mo Health Sci Ctr Columbia MO 65212

FAHIMI, HOSSEIN DARIUSH, b Teheran, Iran, May 7, 33; m 64; c 2. PATHOLOGY, ELECTRON MICROSCOPY. *Educ:* Univ Heidelberg, MD, 58. *Prof Exp:* Assoc, Harvard Med Sch, 66-69, asst prof, 69-71, assoc prof path, 71-75; PROF ANAT & CHMN DEPT II DIV, UNIV HEIDELBERG, 75- *Concurrent Pos:* Assoc vis physician, Mallory Inst Path, 66-75; NIH career res develop award, 71-75; vis prof anat, Univ Heidelberg, 74-75. *Mem:* AAAS; Am Soc Cell Biol; Histochem Soc; Am Asn Path; Am Fedn Clin Res. *Res:* Experimental cell research; histochemistry; cytochemistry. *Mailing Add:* Dept Anat II Div Univ Heidelberg Neuenheimer Field 307 6900 Heidelberg West Germany

FAHL, ROY JACKSON, JR, b Richmond, Va, Oct 8, 25; m 53; c 2. INDUSTRIAL CHEMISTRY. *Educ:* Washington & Lee Univ, BS, 48; Univ NC, PhD(chem), 53. *Prof Exp:* Asst, Univ NC, 48-51; res chemist metallo-org compounds, 52-56, supvr pigments lab, 56-62, mgr, 63, tech mgr white pigments, 63-69, asst dir tech serv lab, 69-71, lab dir, Pigments Dept, 71-73, mgr titanium dioxide prods, Pigments Dept, 73-77, mkt mgr white pigments, 77-79, MKT MGR SPECIALTY CHEM PROD, CHEM & PIGMENTS DEPT, E I DU PONT DE NEMOURS & CO, INC, 79- *Mem:* Am Chem Soc; NY Acad Sci. *Res:* Pigments. *Mailing Add:* Chem & Pigments Dept E I du Pont de Nemours & Co Inc Wilmington DE 19898

FAHL, WILLIAM EDWIN, b Milwaukee, Wis, Apr 13, 50; m 74. CHEMICAL CARCINOGENESIS, MOLECULAR PHARMACOLOGY. *Educ:* Univ Wis-Madison, BS, 72, PhD(physiol & oncol), 75. *Prof Exp:* Fel, Dept Pharmacol, Med Sch, Univ Wis-Madison, 75-79; ASST PROF PHARMACOL, DEPT PHARMACOL, CANCER CTR, MED SCH, NORTHWESTERN UNIV, 79- *Mem:* Am Asn Cancer Res; AAAS. *Res:* Regulation of carcinogen metabolism and carcinogen modification of DNA in cell systems; molecular studies of gene modification and altered gene expression; cell transformation. *Mailing Add:* Dept Pharmacol Cancer Ctr Med Sch Northwestern Univ 303 E Chicago Ave Chicago IL 60611

FAHLBERG, WILLSON JOEL, b Madison, Wis, July 20, 18; m; c 4. IMMUNOLOGY. *Educ:* Univ Wis, PhB, 48, MS, 49, PhD, 51; Am Bd Microbiol, dipl. *Prof Exp:* Asst microbiol, Univ Wis, 48-50; from instr to asst prof, 51-60, ASSOC PROF MICROBIOL, BAYLOR COL MED, 60-; DIR MED AFFAIRS, MEM BAPTIST HOSP SYST, 69- *Concurrent Pos:* Consult microbiologist, Methodist Hosp, 53-, Vet Admin Lab, 54-, Mem Hosp, Univ Tex M D Anderson Hosp & Tumor Inst, Houston State Psychiatric Inst, Jefferson Davis Hosp Houston, St Tex Inst Rehab & Res. *Mem:* Fel Royal Soc Health; fel NY Acad Sci; fel Am Acad Microbiol. *Res:* Allergy; infectious diseases; hospital infection control. *Mailing Add:* Mem Hosp Syst 7777 Southwest Fwy Suite 252 Houston TX 77074

FAHLEN, THEODORE STAUFFER, b San Francisco, Calif, Sept 5, 41; m 63; c 3. LASERS. *Educ:* Stanford Univ, BS, 63; Univ NMex, MS, 64, PhD(physics), 67. *Prof Exp:* Res asst physics, Univ NMex, 64-67; sr engr, Aerojet-Gen Corp, 67-70; SR ENG SPECIALIST, GTE SYLVANIA INC, 70- *Mem:* Optical Soc Am. *Res:* Single particle scattering; laser applications; high power gas laser research and development, particularly carbon dioxide, copper vapor, xenon, nitrogen and excimons. *Mailing Add:* PO Box 188 Mountain View CA 94040

FAHLMAN, GREGORY GAYLORD, b Lethbridge, Alta, Oct 4, 44; m 69; c 2. ASTRONOMY. *Educ:* Univ BC, BSc, 66; Univ Toronto, MSc, 67, PhD(astron), 70. *Prof Exp:* Fel, Inst Theoret Astron, Cambridge Univ, 70-71; asst prof, 71-76, ASSOC PROF ASTRON, UNIV BC, 76- *Mem:* Am Astron Soc; Can Astron Soc. *Res:* Applications of signal processing theory to astronomical data; time resolved astronomical spectroscopy; observational and theoretical studies of high energy phenomena in astronomy. *Mailing Add:* Dept Geophys & Astron Univ BC 2075 Wesbrook Mall Vancouver BC V6T 1W5 Can

FAHLQUIST, DAVIS A, b Providence, RI, July 16, 26; wid; c 5. GEOPHYSICS, OCEANOGRAPHY. *Educ:* Brown Univ, BS, 50; Mass Inst Technol, PhD(geophys), 63. *Prof Exp:* Engr, Owens Corning Fiberglas Corp, 51-53; from res asst to res assoc geophys, Woods Hole Oceanog Inst, 58-63; from asst prof to assoc prof geophys, 63-74, asst prof oceanog, 69-74, PROF GEOPHYS & OCEANOG, TEX A&M UNIV, 74-, ASST DEAN, COL GEOSCI, 79- *Concurrent Pos:* Mem joint oceanog deep earth sampling prog site selection panel, NSF, 75-78. *Mem:* AAAS; Am Geophys Union; Seismol Soc Am; Soc Explor Geophys. *Res:* Marine geophysics; seismic refraction studies in deep water areas; continuous seismic reflection profiling in ocean areas. *Mailing Add:* Dept of Geophys Tex A&M Univ College Station TX 77843

FAHMY, ABDEL AZIZ, b Giza, Egypt, Apr 24, 25; m 53; c 2. METALLURGY, NUCLEAR ENGINEERING. *Educ:* Cairo Univ, BEng, 47; Sheffield Univ, PhD(metall), 53. *Prof Exp:* Demonstr metall, Cairo Univ, 47-53, lectr, 53-60, assoc prof, 60-65, chair prof, 65-68; vis prof metall eng, 68-69, PROF METALL ENG, NC STATE UNIV, 69- *Concurrent Pos:* Partic int sch nuclear sci & eng, Atoms for Peace Prog, NC State Univ & Argonne Nat Lab, 56-57; spec lectr, NC State Univ, 57-59; resident res assoc, Argonne Nat Lab, 63-64; prof, Am Univ Cairo, 66-68; mem state awards comt eng sci, Egypt, 67-68; consult, Argonne Nat Lab, 68-70, IBM Corp, 68- & US Army & Batelle Mem Inst, 75- *Res:* Formation of austenite; structure of cement; effect of irradiation on properties of materials; interphase stresses in multiphase materials; thermal expansion of multiphase and composite materials; x-ray stress measurement; fiber reinforced composites. *Mailing Add:* Dept of Mat Eng NC State Univ Raleigh NC 27607

FAHMY, ALY, b Cairo, Egypt; US citizen. SURGICAL PATHOLOGY, CLINICAL PATHOLOGY. *Educ:* Fouad Univ, Egypt, MD, 49; Univ London, PhD(med), 56. *Prof Exp:* From instr to asst prof path, Fac Med, Fouad Univ, Egypt, 56-61; Alexander von Humboldt Found res fel, Sch Med, Univ Düsseldorf, 61-62; asst prof, Sch Med, Emory Univ, 62-63; sr pathologist, Sch Med, Univ Dusseldorf, 63-64; from asst prof to assoc prof, Sch Med, Vanderbilt Univ, 65-70; prof, Sch Med Univ Sherbrooke, 70-72; PATHOLOGIST, PATH SERV, VET ADMIN HOSP, OKLAHOMA CITY, 72-; PROF PATH, COL MED, UNIV OKLA, 72- *Concurrent Pos:* Vis prof, Int Tech Coop Prog, Paris, 61; from asst prof to assoc prof, Meharry Med Col, 64-70; asst chief lab serv, Vet Admin Hosp, Nashville, Tenn, 65-70; consult, Bone & Joint Panel, Can Tumor Ref Ctr. *Mem:* Fel Col Am Path; fel Am Soc Clin Path; Int Acad Path; Electron Micros Soc Am; AMA. *Res:* Pathology of tumors; bone and joint pathology; application of electron microscopy to surgical pathology; bone growth problems; hormonal and genetic skeletal disturbances; cancer family syndromes; genodermatoses. *Mailing Add:* Okla Col Sch Med Dept of Path Oklahoma City OK 73104

FAHMY, MOHAMED HAMED, b Ismailia, Egypt, Dec 14, 40; m 67; c 3. GENETICS, ANIMAL HUSBANDRY. *Educ:* Ain Shams Univ, Cairo, BSc, 60, MSc, 64, PhD(animal breeding), 67. *Prof Exp:* Researcher animal breeding, Desert Inst, Egypt, 61-67; RES SCIENTIST, CAN DEPT AGR, 68- *Mem:* Am Soc Animal Sci; Can Soc Animal Sci. *Res:* Swine, beef cattle, dairy cattle and sheep breeding. *Mailing Add:* Res Sta Can Dept of Agr Lennoxville Can

FAHMY, MOUSTAFA MAHMOUD, b Alexandria, Egypt, March 13, 29; Can citizen. DIGITAL SIGNAL PROCESSING, COMPUTER-AIDED FILTER DESIGN. *Educ:* Univ Alexandria, Egypt, BSc, 50; Univ Mich, MSc, 63; PhD(elec eng), 66. *Prof Exp:* Instr elec eng, Univ Alexandria, 50-60; res assoc control systs, Inst Sci & Tech, Univ Mich, 62-65; asst prof elec eng, 66-68, assoc prof, 68-76, PROF ELEC ENG, QUEENS UNIV, CAN, 76- *Concurrent Pos:* Vis prof, Swiss Fed Inst Technol, 71-72, fac eng, Univ Alexandria, Egypt, 74-75, fac eng & petrol, Kuwait Univ, 80-81. *Mem:* Inst Elec & Electronics Engrs; Sigma Xi; Can Asn Univ Teachers. *Res:* Digital signal processing; computer-aided techniques for the analysis and design of two-dimensional digital filters. *Mailing Add:* Dept Elec Eng Queens Univ Kingston ON K7L 3N6 Can

FAHN, STANLEY, b Sacramento, Calif, Nov 6, 33; m 58; c 2. NEUROLOGY, NEUROPHARMACOLOGY. *Educ:* Univ Calif, Berkeley, BA, 55; Univ Calif, San Francisco, MD, 58. *Prof Exp:* Intern, Philadelphia Gen Hosp, 58-59; resident neurol, Neurol Inst, Presby Hosp, 59-62; res assoc neurochem, NIH, 62-65; res assoc neurol, Columbia Univ, 65-67, asst prof, 67-68; from asst prof to assoc prof, Univ Pa, 68-73; prof, 73-78, H HOUSTON MERRITT PROF NEUROL, COLUMBIA UNIV, 78- *Concurrent Pos:* USPHS res grants, 70, 74 & 80; mem sci coun, Comt Combat Huntington's Dis, 72-, chmn, 74-81; attend neurologist, Neurol Inst, Presby Hosp, 73-; mem med adv coun, Dystonia Found, 74-; Fogarty Sr Int fel, 75-76; mem adv coun, Nat Fedn Jewish Genetic Dis, 75-; scientific dir & mem bd dirs, Parkinson's Dis Found, 75-; mem sci adv bd, Hereditary Dis Fedn, 75- & Dystonia Med Res Fedn, 76-; dir, Dystonia Res Ctr, 81-; assoc ed, Neurology, 76- *Honors & Awards:* Levy lectr, Washington Univ, 81; Greenburg lectr, Univ Okla, 81. *Mem:* AAAS; Am Neurol Asn; Am Acad Neurol; Soc Neurosci; Am Soc Neurochem. *Res:* Parkinsonism, Huntington's chorea, dystonia and other movement disorders; neurochemistry; neuropharmacology. *Mailing Add:* Neurol Inst 710 W168th St New York NY 10032

FAHNESTOCK, GEORGE REEDER, b Cincinnati, Ohio, June 25, 14; m 46; c 5. FORESTRY. *Educ:* Univ Cincinnati, AB, 36; Yale Univ, MF, 38; Univ Wash, PhD, 77. *Prof Exp:* Field asst forest mgt, Northern Rocky Mt Forest & Range Exp Sta, 38-39; with Coeur D'Alene Nat Forest, 39, foreman & jr forester, 39-41, asst ranger, Nat Forest Admin, 46; dist ranger, Gallatin Nat Forest, 46-50 & Flathead Nat Forest, 50-51; res forester forest fire, Northern Rocky Mt & Inter-Mt Forest & Range Exp Sta, 51-57; res forester & asst div chief, Southern Forest Exp Sta, 57-60, div chief, 60-64, proj leader, 64-65; proj leader, Pac Northwest Forest & Range Exp Sta, 65-71; CONSULT FOREST FIRE & ENVIRON PROBS, 71- *Concurrent Pos:* Res forester forest mgt, Allegheny Forest Exp Sta, 41-42; fire res coordr, Northern Forest Res Ctr, Can Forestry Serv, 73-75; spec lectr, Fac Forestry, Univ BC, 75-76; affil prof, Univ Wash, 77- *Mem:* AAAS; Soc Am Foresters; Sigma Xi; Can Inst Forestry. *Res:* Physical properties of forest fuels; forest fire behavior; fire danger measurement; fire control planning; fire prevention; forest fire ecology; use of fire in forest management. *Mailing Add:* 16310 Ashworth Ave N Seattle WA 98133

FAHNESTOCK, ROBERT KENDALL, geology, see previous edition

FAHNING, MELVYN LUVERNE, b St Peter, Minn, Apr 28, 36; m 56; c 4. REPRODUCTIVE PHYSIOLOGY, VETERINARY MEDICINE. *Educ:* Univ Minn, BS, 58, MS, 60, DVM & PhD, 64. *Prof Exp:* Asst prof dairy husb, Univ Minn, St Paul, 64-65, asst prof dairy husb & vet anat, 65-66, asst prof vet obstet & gynec, 66-70, assoc prof, 70-72; vpres & dir res, Int Cryobiol Serv, Inc, 72-76; vpres & dir, Tech Serv, Agro-K Corp, 76-77; clin assoc prof large animal clin sci, 78-80, PRES, OVATECH INC, 77-, PROF, DIV THERIOGENEOLOGY, 80- *Mem:* Am Dairy Sci Asn; Am Soc Animal Sci; Am Vet Med Asn; Soc Study Reproduction; Brit Soc Study Fertil. *Res:* Ovum transplantation; superovulation; synchronization of estrus of cattle and swine; insemination of swine; collection and chemical analysis of female reproductive tract fluids. *Mailing Add:* OvaTech Inc Hwy 35N Rte 5 Box 48 River Falls WI 54022

FAHRENBACH, MARVIN JAY, b Buena Vista, Va, Apr 11, 18; m 49; c 3. CLINICAL PHARMACOLOGY. *Educ:* Yale Univ, BS, 39, PhD(org chem), 42. *Prof Exp:* Clin res fel, Sandoz Inc, 74-; mem, Arteriosclerosis Coun, Am Heart Asn. *Concurrent Pos:* Mem, Concurrent. *Mem:* AAAS; Am Chem Soc; Am Inst Chemists; NY Acad Sci; Am Heart Asn. *Res:* Pharmaceuticals; sulfonamides; vitamins; hormones; antiseptics of the quaternary ammonium salt type; anticoagulants; lipid metabolism; atherosclerosis. *Mailing Add:* Buckberg Rd Tomkins Cove NY 10986

FAHRENBACH, WOLF HENRICH, b Berlin, Ger, Apr 21, 32; US citizen; m 77. HISTOLOGY, NEUROCYTOLOGY. *Educ:* Univ Calif, Berkeley, BA, 54; Univ Wash, PhD(invert zool), 61. *Prof Exp:* Asst zool, Univ Wash, 57-60; NSF fel anat, Harvard Med Sch, 61-63; assoc prof, 63-73, PROF EXP BIOL, MED SCH, UNIV ORE, 73-; SCIENTIST ELECTRON MICROS & CHMN LAB, ORE REGIONAL PRIMATE RES CTR, 67- *Mem:* AAAS; Am Asn Anat; Astron League. *Res:* Vertebrate and invertebrate histology and cytology; electron microscopy of invertebrate visual systems. *Mailing Add:* Lab Electron Micros Ore Regional Primate Res Ctr Beaverton OR 97001

FAHRENHOLTZ, KENNETH EARL, b Peoria, Ill, Aug 9, 34; m 58. PHARMACEUTICAL CHEMISTRY, ORGANIC CHEMISTRY. *Educ:* Bradley Univ, BS, 56; Univ Rochester, PhD(org chem), 60. *Prof Exp:* Sr chemist, Strasenburgh Labs, 60-62; sr chemist, 62-71, RES FEL, RES DIV, HOFFMANN-LA ROCHE INC, 71- *Mem:* NY Acad Sci; Am Chem Soc; Sigma Xi. *Res:* Organic synthesis; heterocyclic compounds; medicinal chemistry. *Mailing Add:* 28 Winding Lane Bloomfield NJ 07003

FAHRENHOLTZ, SUSAN ROSENO, b Cologne, Ger, US citizen; m 58. POLYMER CHEMISTRY, ORGANIC CHEMISTRY. *Educ:* Cornell Univ, BA, 57; Univ Rochester, MS, 60. *Prof Exp:* Res chemist, Eastman Kodak Co, 60-62; RES ASSOC CHEM, BELL LABS, 62- *Concurrent Pos:* Adj instr, Fordham Univ, 72-80, adj asst prof, 80- *Mem:* Am Chem Soc. *Res:* Singlet oxygen reactions; chemically induced dynamic nuclear polarization; positive photoresists and electron beam resists; novolak polymers; materials science engineering. *Mailing Add:* 28 Winding Lane Bloomfield NJ 07003

FAHRNEY, DAVID EMORY, b Stapleton, Nebr, Feb 1, 34; m 69. BIOCHEMISTRY. *Educ:* Reed Col, BA, 59; Columbia Univ, PhD(biochem), 63. *Prof Exp:* NIH fel biophys chem, Univ Calif, San Diego, 63-64; asst prof chem, Univ Calif, Los Angeles, 64-69; assoc prof, 69-80, PROF BIOCHEM, COLO STATE UNIV, 80- *Mem:* Am Chem Soc; Am Soc Biol Chemists. *Res:* Structure and function of enzymes; identification of functional groups in active sites of enzymes and proteins. *Mailing Add:* Dept of Biochem Colo State Univ Ft Collins CO 80523

FAHSEL, MICHAEL JOHN, analytical chemistry, see previous edition

FAHSELT, DIANNE, b Cabri, Sask, May 12, 41; m 68. BOTANY. *Educ:* Univ Sask, BA, 63, Hons, 64; Wash State Univ, PhD(bot), 67. *Prof Exp:* Asst prof, 67-71, ASSOC PROF BOT, UNIV WESTERN ONT, 71- *Concurrent Pos:* Nat Res Coun Can grants, 67-74 & 76-83; dept univ affairs grant, 69. *Honors & Awards:* Cooley Award, Am Soc Plant Taxonomists, 68; Dimond Award, Bot Soc Am, 75. *Mem:* AAAS; Bot Soc Am; Am Soc Plant Taxonomists; Can Bot Asn; Int Asn Plant Taxon. *Res:* Biochemical taxonomy, protein characters in lichens; genetics and evolution. *Mailing Add:* Dept of Plant Sci Univ of Western Ont London ON N6A 5B8 Can

FAHY, WILLIAM EARL, b Rochester, NY, Aug 6, 19; m 42; c 3. ICHTHYOLOGY. *Educ:* Cornell Univ, BSc, 46; Univ Rochester, PhD(biol), 51. *Prof Exp:* Asst, Univ Rochester, 47-50, actg instr, 48; res biologist, 51-52, from asst prof to assoc prof, 52-63, PROF MARINE BIOL, INST MARINE SCI, UNIV NC, 63- *Res:* Influence of environmental factors on meristic structures in fishes; taxonomy; ecology; life histories of eastern North American fresh and salt water fishes. *Mailing Add:* Inst of Marine Sci Univ of NC Morehead City NC 28557

FAICH, GERALD ALAN, b Milwaukee, Wis, Oct 7, 42. INFECTIOUS DISEASE. *Educ:* Univ Wis, BS, 64, MD, 68; Harvard Sch Pub Health, MPH, 76. *Prof Exp:* Intern med, Boston City Hosp, 68-70; with prev med, Ctr Dis Control, 72-74; with internal med, Bath Israel Hosp, Boston, 74-75; med epidemiologist, Ctr Dis Control, 70-76; chief, Div Epidemiol, 76-78, ASSOC DIR, RI DEPT HEALTH, 78-; ASST PROF COMMUNITY MED, BROWN UNIV, 76- *Concurrent Pos:* Career develop award, US Pub Health Serv, 74; mem, Nat Inst Health Study Sect, 81- *Mem:* Am Pub Health Asn; fel Am Col Physicians; fel Am Col Prev Med; fel Am Col Epidemiol; Am Coun Sci & Health. *Res:* Epidemiology of infectious and chronic diseases; disease control in Latin America and the United States. *Mailing Add:* 75 Davis St Providence RI 02908

FAILEY, CRAWFORD FAIRBANKS, chemistry, deceased

FAILL, RODGER TANNER, b Niagara Falls, NY, May 1, 36; m 63; c 4. STRUCTURAL GEOLOGY. *Educ:* Columbia Univ, BS, 61, MA, 64, PhD(geol), 66. *Prof Exp:* GEOLOGIST, PA GEOL SURV, 65- *Mem:* Geol Soc Am; Sigma Xi. *Res:* Tectonic analysis of Appalachian mountains, including fold style, faulting and fossil deformation; experimental rock deformation. *Mailing Add:* Pa Geol Surv Harrisburg PA 17120

FAILLA, PATRICIA MCCLEMENT, b New York, NY, Dec 22, 25; wid. BIOPHYSICS. *Educ:* Barnard Col, Columbia Univ, AB, 46, Columbia Univ, PhD(biophys), 58; Univ Chicago, MBA, 76. *Prof Exp:* Asst physicist, Physics Lab, Dept Hosps, NY, 46-48; res scientist, Radiol Res Lab, Col Physicians & Surgeons, Columbia Univ, 50-60; assoc biophysicist, Radiol Physics Div, 60-71, asst dir, Radiol & Environ Res Div, 71-73, prog coordr res, Off Dir, 73-74, asst to lab dir, 74-78, asst lab dir, 78-80, PROG COORDR, BIOMED & ENVIRON RES, OFF DIR, ARGONNE NAT LAB, 80- *Concurrent Pos:* Mem corp, Marine Biol Lab, Woods Hole; mem, Tech Electronic Prod Radiation Safety Standards Comt, Bur Radiol Health, 73-75; mem, Gen Res Support Review Comt, NIH, 78-82. *Mem:* AAAS; Radiation Res Soc; Biophys Soc; Sigma Xi; Health Physics Soc. *Res:* Dosimetry of ionizing radiations and the effects of radiation on biological systems. *Mailing Add:* Off of Dir Argonne Nat Lab 9700 S Cass Ave Argonne IL 60439

FAILLACE, LOUIS A, b Brooklyn, NY, June 7, 32; m 63; c 3. PSYCHIATRY. *Educ:* Marquette Univ, MD, 57; Am Bd Psychiat & Neurol, dipl, 70. *Prof Exp:* Intern med, Boston City Hosp, 57-58; asst resident psychiat, Bellevue Hosp, New York, 58-59; res fel neurochem, Mass Ment Health Ctr, 59-61; asst resident psychiat, Johns Hopkins Hosp, 61-63, resident psychiatrist, 63-64; clin assoc psychopharmacol, Clin Neuropharmacol Res Ctr, NIMH, St Elizabeth's Hosp, 64-66; assoc physician, Psychosom Clin, Johns Hopkins Univ, 66-67; chief psychiat, Baltimore City Hosps, 67-71; PROF PSYCHIAT & CHMN DEPT, UNIV TEX MED SCH HOUSTON, 71- *Concurrent Pos:* Res fels, Harvard Univ & NIH, 60-61; assoc prof, Johns Hopkins Univ, 68-71; consult psychiatrist, Good Samaritan Hosp, 68-71. *Mem:* Am Psychiat Asn; assoc Am Geriat Soc; Am Psychosom Soc; NY Acad Sci. *Res:* Clinical effects of psychoactive drugs; psychological, behavioral and metabolic factors in alcoholism. *Mailing Add:* Dept in Psychiat Univ of Tex Med Sch Houston TX 77025

FAIMAN, CHARLES, b Winnipeg, Man, Dec 6, 39; m 63; c 3. ENDOCRINOLOGY, PHYSIOLOGY. *Educ:* Univ Man, BSc & MD, 62, MSc, 66. *Prof Exp:* Res fel physiol, Univ Man, 64-65; res asst med, Univ Ill, 65-67; res assoc endocrinol, Mayo Found, 67-68; asst prof, 68-71, assoc prof physiol & med, 71-75, assoc prof med, 75-78, PROF PHYSIOL, UNIV MAN, 75-, PROF MED & HEAD, SECT ENDOCRINOL, HEALTH SCI CTR, 78- *Concurrent Pos:* Med Res Coun Can fel, Univ Man, 64-68, scholar, 68-73; dir clin invest unit, Winnipeg Gen Hosp, 71-74; head, Sect Endocrinol & Metab, Univ Man & Health Sci Ctr, 78- *Honors & Awards:* Prowse Prize, Univ Man, 66. *Mem:* Endocrine Soc; Can Soc Endocrinol Metab; Am Fedn Clin Res; Soc Exp Biol & Med; Can Soc Clin Invest. *Res:* Reproductive endocrinology, especially gonadotropin regulation in humans in health and in disease; human fetal pituitary gonadal interrelationships; the use of non-human primates as models for the study of reproductive physiology. *Mailing Add:* G4-Health Sci Ctr 700 William Ave Winnipeg MB R3E 0Z3 Can

FAIMAN, MICHAEL, b London, Eng, Mar 27, 35; m 65; c 2. COMPUTER SCIENCE. *Educ:* Cambridge Univ, BA, 56; Univ Ill, Urbana-Champaign, MS, 64, PhD, 66. *Prof Exp:* Engr, Elliott Automation, Eng, 56-60; asst prof comput sci, 66-70, ASSOC PROF COMPUT SCI, UNIV ILL, URBANA-CHAMPAIGN, 70- *Res:* Computer logic and hardware; digital-analog systems; optical information processing. *Mailing Add:* 708 Harman Urbana IL 61801

FAIMAN, MORRIS DAVID, b Winnipeg, Man, June 24, 32; m 62; c 2. PHARMACOLOGY, TOXICOLOGY. *Educ:* Univ Man, BS, 55; Univ Minn, MS, 61, PhD, 65. *Prof Exp:* From asst prof to assoc prof pharm, 65-73, PROF PHARMACOL & TOXICOL, UNIV KANS, 73- *Mem:* AAAS; Am Soc Pharmacol & Exp Therapeut; Undersea Med Soc; Soc Toxicol; Aerospace Med Asn. *Res:* Drug metabolism; pharmacokinetics; oxygen toxicity; biogenic amines; alcoholism mechanisms. *Mailing Add:* Dept of Pharmacol & Toxicol Univ of Kans Sch of Pharm Lawrence KS 66045

FAIMAN, ROBERT N(EIL), b Excelsior, Minn, June 25, 23; m 44; c 2. ELECTRICAL ENGINEERING. *Educ:* NDak State Col, BSEE, 47; Univ Wash, MSEE, 48; Purdue Univ, PhD, 56. *Prof Exp:* Assoc elec eng, Univ Wash, 47-48; from asst prof to prof & chmn dept, NDak State Col, 48-58; dean col technol, Univ NH, 59-67, vpres res, 67-74; DIR ACAD AFFAIRS, AIR FORCE INST TECHNOL, 74- *Concurrent Pos:* Engr, eng sci prog, NSF, 57-59; mem, NH Bd Registr Prof Engrs, 64-74. *Mem:* Am Soc Eng Educ; sr mem Inst Elec & Electronics Engrs; Soc Am Mil Engrs; Sigma Xi. *Res:* Circuit analysis and synthesis; control systems. *Mailing Add:* Air Force Inst of Technol CAE Wright-Patterson AFB OH 45433

FAIN, JANICE BLOOM, b Hot Springs, Ark, Jan 8, 27; m 48; c 1. PHYSICS. *Educ:* Univ Tex, BA, 48, MA, 51, PhD(physics), 56; Yale Univ, MA, 76. *Prof Exp:* Eng specialist, Chance Vought Aircraft, Tex, 56 & 57-59; mem tech staff, Pac Missile Range, Land-Air, Inc, Point Mugu, 59-61; scientist, Supreme Hq Allied Powers Europe Tech Ctr, Holland, 61-63; exec adv, Douglas Aircraft Co, Calif, 63-66; mem prof staff, Ctr Naval Anal, Va, 66-69; SR ASSOC, CACI, 69- *Concurrent Pos:* Soroptomist Int fel, Univ Paris, 56-57. *Mem:* Am Phys Soc; Inst Mgt Sci. *Res:* Simulation; military operations analysis; quantitative techniques in international relations. *Mailing Add:* CACI 1815 Ft Myer Dr Arlington VA 22209

FAIN, JOHN NICHOLAS, b Jefferson City, Tenn, Aug 18, 34; m 58; c 3. BIOCHEMISTRY. *Educ:* Carson-Newman Col, BS, 56; Emory Univ, PhD(biochem), 60. *Prof Exp:* Res assoc biochem, Emory Univ, 60-61; NSF fel, 61-62; USPHS fel, 62-63; chemist, Nat Inst Arthritis & Metab Dis, 63-65; from asst prof to assoc prof, 65-71, PROF MED SCI, BROWN UNIV, 71-, CHMN SECT PHYSIOL CHEM, 74- *Concurrent Pos:* Macy fac scholar & vis fel, Clare Hall, Cambridge Univ, 77-78. *Mem:* Am Soc Biol Chemists. *Res:* Mechanism of hormone action. *Mailing Add:* Div of Biol & Med Sci Brown Univ Providence RI 02912

FAIN, MARGERY JONES, b New York, NY, Nov 20, 47. INSECT PHYSIOLOGY, DEVELOPMENTAL BIOLOGY. *Educ:* Goucher Col, BA, 70; Harvard Univ, PhD(biol), 75. *Prof Exp:* NIH FEL DEVELOP BIOL, DEVELOP BIOL CTR, UNIV CALIF, IRVINE, 75- *Concurrent Pos:* Res Biologist, Univ Calif, Los Angeles, 80- *Res:* Endocrine physiology of insect development; pattern formation, determination and growth regulation of imaginal discs in Drosophila embryonic and post-embryonic development. *Mailing Add:* Biology Dept Univ Calif Los Angeles CA 90024

FAIN, ROBERT C, b Santa Rosa, Tex, Oct 19, 36; m 58; c 2. ORGANOMETALLIC CHEMISTRY. *Educ:* Southwest Tex State Univ, BS, 58, MA, 59; Univ Tex, PhD(chem), 65. *Prof Exp:* Instr chem, Southwest Tex State Univ, 59-61; res chemist, Celanese Corp, 65-66; assoc prof chem, 66-68, prof phys sci & head dept, 68-74, dean, Sch Arts & Sci, 70-81, VPRES ACAD AFFAIRS, TARLETON STATE UNIV, 79- *Mem:* Am Chem Soc. *Res:* Pi complexes of transition metals. *Mailing Add:* Dept Chem Tarleton State Univ Stephenville TX 76402

FAIN, SAMUEL CLARK, JR, b Jefferson City, Tenn, Aug 13, 42; wid; c 2. SOLID STATE PHYSICS. *Educ:* Reed Col, BA, 65; Univ Ill, Urbana-Champaign, MS, 66, PhD(physics), 69. *Prof Exp:* NATO fel physics, Natuurkundig Lab, Univ Amsterdam, 69-70; from asst prof to assoc prof, 70-80, PROF PHYSICS, UNIV WASH, 80- *Concurrent Pos:* Alfred P Sloan res fel, 71-75. *Mem:* Am Phys Soc; Am Vacuum Soc; AAAS. *Res:* Surface physics. *Mailing Add:* Dept of Physics Univ of Wash Seattle WA 98195

FAIN, WILLIAM WHARTON, b Augusta, Ga, Apr 23, 27; div; c 3. OPERATIONS RESEARCH. *Educ:* Univ Tex, BA, 50, MA, 51, PhD(physics), 55. *Prof Exp:* Res scientist, Electro-Mechanics Co, Tex, 53-56; eng specialist, Chance-Vought Aircraft, 56 & 57-59; mem tech staff, Pac Missile Range, Land-Air Inc, Point Mugu, 60-61; scientist, Supreme Hq, Allied Powers Europe Tech Ctr, Holland, 61-63; exec adv, Douglas Aircraft Co, Calif, 63-66; mem prof staff, Ctr Naval Anal, Va, 66-69; mgr opers res dept, Caci, Inc, Arlington, 69-71, exec vpres, 71-72, pres & chief exec officer, 72-81. *Concurrent Pos:* Inst Defense Anal fel opers anal, 61-63; consult, Steering Comt, Spring Joint Comput Conf, 71, Can Dept Nat Defence, United Aircraft Co, US Army War Col, Indust Col Armed Forces & Univ Southern Calif. *Mem:* AAAS; Opers Res Soc Am; Int Studies Asn. *Res:* Simulation and gaming; military operations research; quantitative techniques in international studies; applications of game theory; computer applications. *Mailing Add:* 1818 N Ode St Arlington VA 22044

FAINBERG, ANTHONY, b London, Eng, Jan 14, 44; US citizen; m 64. NUCLEAR SAFEGUARDS. *Educ:* NY Univ, AB, 64; Univ Calif, Berkeley, PhD(high energy physics), 69. *Prof Exp:* Res assoc high energy physics, Lawrence Radiation Lab, 69 & Univ Turin, Italy, 70-72; res asst prof, Syracuse Univ, 73-77; ASSOC PHYSICIST SAFEGUARDS, DEPT NUCLEAR ENERGY, BROOKHAVEN NAT LAB, 77- *Concurrent Pos:* Adj assoc prof, Syracuse Univ, 77-78. *Mem:* Am Phys Soc; Inst Nuclear Mat Mgt; Am Nuclear Soc. *Res:* Domestic and international nuclear safeguards, particle physics. *Mailing Add:* Bldg 197C TSO Brookhaven Nat Lab Upton NY 11973

FAINBERG, ARNOLD HAROLD, b Brooklyn, NY, Apr 9, 22. PHYSICAL ORGANIC CHEMISTRY. *Educ:* Cornell Univ, BA, 42, PhD(chem), 50. *Prof Exp:* Asst, Cornell Univ, 42-44; res chemist, Manhattan Proj, Monsanto Chem Co, 44-46; asst, Cornell Univ, 46-49; mem staff dept chem, Univ Calif, Los Angeles, 51-56; sr res chemist, Whitemarsh Res Lab, Pennsalt Chem Corp, 56-62, proj leader tech ctr, 62-67, SR RES SCIENTIST, PENNWALT CORP, PA, 67- *Mem:* Am Chem Soc; Mineral Soc Am. *Res:* Polymer chemistry; liquid chromatography; organic fluorine chemistry; mechanism of solvolytic reactions; radiochemistry; gas chromatography; phase equilibria; infrared spectroscopy; mineral identification. *Mailing Add:* Rennwalt Corp 900 First Ave King of Prussia PA 19406

FAINBERG, JOSEPH, b Passaic, NJ, Oct 18, 30; m 56; c 3. RADIO ASTRONOMY. *Educ:* Univ Chicago, AB, 50, BS, 51, MS, 53; Johns Hopkins Univ, PhD(elec eng), 65. *Prof Exp:* Res asst cosmic rays, Univ Chicago, 50-53, res asst meson physics, 53-57; res scientist, Johns Hopkins Univ, 57-66; PHYSICIST, GODDARD SPACE FLIGHT CTR, NASA, 66- *Concurrent Pos:* Instr, Roosevelt Univ, 53-54. *Mem:* AAAS; Int Astron Union; Am Phys Soc; Inst Elec & Electronics Engrs. *Res:* Cosmic rays; meson physics; scattering and diffraction of electromagnetic waves; space physics. *Mailing Add:* 4000 Virgilia Chevy Chase MD 20815

FAINGOLD, CARL L, b Chicago, Ill, Feb 1, 43; m 64; c 3. NEUROPHARMACOLOGY, NEUROPHYSIOLOGY. *Educ:* Univ Ill, BS, 65; Northwestern Univ, PhD(pharmacol), 70. *Prof Exp:* Fel neuropharmacol, Inst Psychiat, Univ Mo, 70-72; asst prof, 72-76, ASSOC PROF PHARMACOL, MED SCH, SOUTHERN ILL UNIV, 76- *Concurrent Pos:* NIH prin investr, Nat Inst Neurol & Comun Disorders & Stroke, 79-82. *Mem:* Am Soc Pharmacol & Exp Therapeut; Soc Neurosci; AAAS; Am Epilepsy Soc; NY Acad Sci. *Res:* Examination of the specific mechanisms of convulsant drug action of brainstem neurons in search of a common action; elucidation of the changes in neuronal response in the brainstem reticular formation which subserve the development of seizures triggered by sensory stimuli. *Mailing Add:* Dept Pharmacol Sch Med Southern Ill Univ PO Box 3926 Springfield IL 62708

FAINSTAT, THEODORE, b Montreal, Que, July 14, 29. OBSTETICS & GYNECOLOGY. *Educ:* McGill Univ, BSc, 50, MSc, 51, MD, 55; Univ Cambridge, PhD, 70. *Prof Exp:* Instr genetics, McGill Univ, 50-51; intern, Univ Montreal, 55-56; asst obstet & gynec, Sch Med, Harvard Univ, 64-66;

from assoc prof to prof, Med Sch, Northwestern Univ, Chicago, 67-74; prof obstet & gynec, Univ Kans Med Ctr, Kans City, 74-77; PROF OBSTET & GYNEC, STANFORD UNIV, 77-; CHMN OBSTET & GYNEC, SANTA CLARA VALLEY MED CTR, 77- Concurrent Pos: Asst resident med, Boston City Hosp, 56-57, surgeon, 60; resident, Boston Lying-In Hosp, 64-66; sr attend, Chicago Wesley Mem Hosp, 69-; fel obstet & gynec, Sch Med, Harvard Univ, 56-63, Josiah Macy Jr Found fel, 57-63, res fel endocrinol, Biol Labs, 57-60; sr investr, NIH grant, 58-63; Am Cancer Soc scholar, Strangeways Res Labs, Eng, 64-66; Kellogg fac fel, Ctr Teaching Prof, Northwestern Univ, 70-73. Honors & Awards: Pres Award, Am Col Obstet & Gynec. Mem: Soc Study Reprod; Am Col Obstet & Gynec; Soc Gynec Invest; Endocrine Soc; Teratology Soc. Res: Biology of reproduction. Mailing Add: Dept Obstet & Gynec Santa Clara Valley Med Ctr San Jose CA 95128

FAIR, FRANK VERNON, b Ford City, Pa, Oct 24, 25; m 49; c 3. ANALYTICAL CHEMISTRY. Educ: Pa State Col, BS, 49; Univ Ill, MS, 51, PhD(chem), 53. Prof Exp: Chemist, Res & Develop Div, Pittsburgh Consolidation Coal Co, 53-57; res mgr, Res Lab, Speer Carbon Co, Pa, 57-66; tech dir, O Hommel Co, Pa, 66-67; RES DIR, RES & DEVELOP LAB, AIRCO SPEER DIV, AIRCO, INC, 67- Mem: Am Chem Soc. Res: Polarography and infrared; carbon and graphite products; high temperature physical measurements. Mailing Add: 802 Pasadena Ave Niagara Falls NY 14302

FAIR, HARRY DAVID, JR, b Indiana, Pa, Dec 2, 36; m 64; c 1. SOLID STATE PHYSICS. Educ: Indiana Univ Pa, BS, 58; Univ Del, MS, 60, PhD(solid state physics), 67. Prof Exp: Teaching asst physics, Univ Del, 58-59; res physicist, Picatinny Arsenal, 60-62; vis scientist, Univ Del, 62-65; solid state physicist, Explosives Lab, 65-69, chief point defect & electron energy level sect, 69-71, chief solid state br, Picatinny Arsenal, 71-74; CHIEF, PROPULSION TECHNOL LAB, ARRADCOM, 77- Concurrent Pos: Vis prof, Univ Paris, 74 & Royal Inst Gr Brit, 75. Mem: Am Phys Soc; Chem Soc; Sigma Xi. Res: Impurity levels in solids; electron spin resonance; optical and electronic of II-VI compound semiconductors and explosive solids; fast reactions in solids; combustion and ignition processes; high pressure physics; photophysics of energetic materials. Mailing Add: Propulsion Technol Lab Arradcom Dover NJ 07801

FAIR, JAMES R(UTHERFORD), b Charleston, Mo, Oct 14, 20; m 50; c 3. CHEMICAL ENGINEERING. Educ: Ga Inst Tech, BS, 42; Univ Mich, MS, 49; Univ Tex, PhD(chem eng), 54. Prof Exp: Chemist & res engr, Monsanto Co, Marshall, Tex, 42-43, res & design engr, 43-45, develop assoc, Mo, 45-47, proj leader, engr, Texas City, 47-52; process design engr, Shell Develop Co, Calif, 54-56; res group leader & sect leader, Monsanto Co, 56-61, eng mgr, 61-69, eng dir, 69-80; ERNEST & VIRGINIA COCKRELL PROF CHEM ENG, UINV TEX, AUSTIN, 80- Concurrent Pos: Affil prof, Wash Univ, 64- Honors & Awards: Walker Award, 73 & Chem Eng Pract Award, 75, Am Inst Chem Engrs. Mem: Am Chem Soc; Am Inst Chem Engrs; Nat Acad Eng. Res: Physical separation methods; heat transfer equipment; chemical reactor design; hydrocarbon pyrolysis operations. Mailing Add: Dept Chem Eng Univ Tex Austin TX 78712

FAIR, RICHARD BARTON, b Los Angeles, Calif, Sept 12, 42; m 64; c 4. SEMICONDUCTORS, ELECTRICAL ENGINEERING. Educ: Duke Univ, BS, 64, PhD(elec eng), 69; Pa State Univ, MS, 66. Prof Exp: mem staff, Bell Labs, 69-73, supvr semiconductors, 73-81; PROF ELEC ENG, DUKE UNIV, 81-; VPRES, MICROELECTRONICS CTR NC, 81- Concurrent Pos: Chmn, Solid State Device Subcomt, Int Electron Develop Mgt, Inst Elec & Electronics Engrs, 77; consult, 81- Mem: Sigma Xi; Inst Elec & Electronics Engrs; Electrochem Soc; AAAS. Res: Fundamental studies of the diffusion of Group III and V impurities in silicon; solubility effects and electrical activity of these impurities; theory and design of semiconductor devices such as transistors and diodes. Mailing Add: 3414 Cambridge Rd Durham NC 27707

FAIRAND, BARRY PHILIP, b Watertown, NY, May 20, 34; m 59; c 5. LASERS. Educ: LeMoyne Col, BS, 55; Univ Detroit, MS, 57; Ohio State Univ, PhD(physics), 69. Prof Exp: SR SCIENTIST PHYSICS, BATTELLE MEM INST, 57- Mem: Am Phys Soc; Soc Photo-Optical Inst Engrs; Mat Res Soc; NY Acad Sci. Res: High-power laser applications, particularly in the areas of laser shock processing, thermal treatment of materials, and nondestructive evaluation. Mailing Add: Columbus Labs Battelle Mem Inst 505 King Ave Columbus OH 43201

FAIRBAIRN, HAROLD WILLIAMS, b Ottawa, Ont, July 10, 06; nat US; m 39; c 4. PETROLOGY. Educ: Queen's Univ, Ont, BSc, 29; Harvard Univ, AM, 31, PhD(mineral, geol), 32. Prof Exp: Field asst, Geol Surv Can, 26-32; Royal Soc Can traveling fel, Innsbruck Univ, Univ Gottingen & Univ Berlin, 32-34; instr mineral, Queen's Univ, Ont, 34-37; from asst prof to prof, 37-72, EMER PROF PETROL, MASS INST TECHNOL, 72- Concurrent Pos: Surv chief, Ont Dept Mines, 35-39, Que Dept Mines, 40 & Geol Surv Can, 42; petrographer, Manhattan Dist Proj, 44. Mem: Fel Geol Soc Am; fel Mineral Soc Am; Am Acad Arts & Sci. Res: Structural petrology; optical crystallography; metamorphism; geochronology. Mailing Add: Dept of Earth & Planetary Sci Mass Inst of Technol Cambridge MA 02139

FAIRBAIRN, JOHN F, II, b Buffalo, NY, Nov 2, 22; m 60; c 2. MEDICINE. Educ: Univ Buffalo, MD, 45. Prof Exp: Pvt pract, Buffalo, NY, 52-53, 54; Nat Heart Inst trainee, Mayo Clin, 54-55; pvt pract, Buffalo, 55-56; from instr to asst prof med, 59-66, ASSOC PROF CLIN MED, MAYO GRAD SCH MED, UNIV MINN, 66-; CONSULT INTERNAL MED, MAYO CLIN, 56- Concurrent Pos: Attend physician & consult, St Mary's & Methodist Hosps, Rochester, 56-; head sect peripheral vascular dis, Mayo Clin, 60-74; mem coun arteriosclerosis, Am Heart Asn, 63, adv bd coun circulation, 64. Mem: Am Fedn Clin Res; Am Heart Asn; fel Am Col Physicians. Res: Atherosclerosis, hypertension and vascular diseases in general. Mailing Add: Mayo Clin 200 First St SW Rochester MN 55901

FAIRBANK, HENRY ALAN, b Lewistown, Mont, Nov 9, 18; m 43; c 3. LOW TEMPERATURE PHYSICS. Educ: Whitman Col, AB, 40; Yale Univ, PhD(physics), 44; Oxford Univ, MA, 53. Hon Degrees: DSc, Whitman Col, 71. Prof Exp: Staff mem, Los Alamos Lab, NMex, 44-45; instr physics, Yale Univ, 45-48, from asst prof to assoc prof, 48-62; chmn dept, 62-73, PROF PHYSICS, DUKE UNIV, 62- Concurrent Pos: Instr physics, Yale Univ, 42-44; Guggenheim fel, Oxford Univ, 53-54; consult, Los Alamos Sci Lab, 57-65. Mem: Fel Am Phys Soc; Am Asn Physics Teachers; fel AAAS. Res: Low temperature physics; properties of liquid and solid helium-3 and helium-4; heat transfer in solids and quantum fluids. Mailing Add: Dept of Physics Duke Univ Durham NC 27706

FAIRBANK, WILLIAM MARTIN, b Minneapolis, Minn, Feb 24, 17; m 41; c 3. PHYSICS. Educ: Whitman Col, AB, 39; Yale Univ, PhD(physics), 48. Hon Degrees: DSc, Whitman Col, 65. Prof Exp: Staff mem, Radiation Lab, Mass Inst Technol, 42-45; asst prof physics, Amherst Col, 47-52; from assoc prof to prof, Duke Univ, 52-59; PROF PHYSICS, STANFORD UNIV, 59- Honors & Awards: Scientist of Year Award, Calif Mus Sci & Indust, 61; Oliver E Buckley Prize, Am Phys Soc, 63; Res Corp Award, 65. Mem: Nat Acad Sci; fel Am Phys Soc. Res: Microwave radar systems and microwave propagation; cryogenics; superconductivity; properties of helium II and III; separation of helium isotopes. Mailing Add: Dept of Physics Stanford Univ Stanford CA 94305

FAIRBANK, WILLIAM MARTIN, JR, b New Haven, Conn, Jan 7, 46; m 75; c 1. QUANTUM OPTICS. Educ: Pomona Col, BA, 68; Stanford Univ, MS, 69, PhD(physics), 74. Prof Exp: Res assoc physics, Optical Sci Ctr, Univ Ariz, 74-75; asst prof, 75-78, ASSOC PROF PHYSICS, COLO STATE UNIV, 78- Mem: Optical Soc Am; Am Phys Soc. Res: High resolution laser spectroscopy; new applications of tunable dye lasers; single atom detection. Mailing Add: Dept of Physics Colo State Univ Ft Collins CO 80523

FAIRBANKS, DANIEL F(URTH), chemical engineering, see previous edition

FAIRBANKS, GILBERT WAYNE, b Hartford, Conn, July 26, 37; m 69. PHYSIOLOGY. Educ: Trinity Col, Conn, BS, 59; Wesleyan Univ, MA, 61; Univ SC, PhD, 64. Prof Exp: ASSOC PROF BIOL, FURMAN UNIV, 64-, PREMED ADV, 75- Mem: AAAS. Res: Effect of hyperthermic conditions on lipids in animal tissues; membrane lipids of protozoans. Mailing Add: Dept of Biol Furman Univ Greenville SC 29613

FAIRBANKS, HAROLD V, b Des Plaines, Ill, Dec 7, 15; m 51. METALLURGY. Educ: Mich State Col, BS, 37, MS, 39. Prof Exp: Instr gen chem, Mich State Col, 37-39; instr chem eng, Univ Louisville, 40-42; asst prof, Rose Polytech Inst, 42-47; from asst prof to assoc prof metall, 47-55, prof metall, 55-78, EMER PROF, WVA UNIV, 78- Concurrent Pos: Adv, Purdue Team Int Coop Admin, Chen Kung Univ, Tainan, Taiwan, 57-59; co-dir grad studies mat sci eng, WVa Univ, 63. Mem: Nat Asn Corrosion Engrs; Am Soc Metals; Int Solar Energy Soc; Am Inst Chem Engrs. Res: Application of high intensity sonics to various processes. Mailing Add: 909 Riverview Dr Morgantown WV 26506

FAIRBANKS, LAURENCE DEE, b Wilson Co, Kans, May 23, 26; m 53; c 3. INVERTEBRATE ZOOLOGY. Educ: Univ Kans, AB, 49, MA, 56; Tulane Univ, PhD(zool), 59. Prof Exp: Instr zool, 58-66, asst prof med, 66-70, ASSOC PROF MED, SCH MED, TULANE UNIV, 70- Mem: AAAS; Am Soc Zoologists; Entom Soc Am; Am Inst Biol Sci. Res: Physiology and ecology of invertebrates, Mollusca and Insecta; general biology of aging; human and environmental biology. Mailing Add: Tulane Univ Sch of Med 1430 Tulane Ave New Orleans LA 70112

FAIRBANKS, MICHAEL BRUCE, b Rogers City, Mich, Aug 31, 44; m 62; c 2. COMPARATIVE PHYSIOLOGY. Educ: Mich State Univ, BS, 66, MS, 68, PhD(physiol), 70. Prof Exp: Asst prof anat & physiol, Ohio State Univ, 70-72; ASSOC PROF BIOL, CENT MICH UNIV, 72- Mem: Am Soc Zoologists; Sigma Xi. Res: Ocular oxygen concentration in teleosts; retinal oxygen toxicity; lactic dehydrogenase isoenzymes in fish. Mailing Add: Dept of Biol Cent Mich Univ Mt Pleasant MI 45558

FAIRBANKS, VIRGIL, b Ann Arbor, Mich, June 7, 30; m 55; c 3. INTERNAL MEDICINE, HEMATOLOGY. Educ: Univ Utah, BA, 51; Univ Mich, MD, 54. Prof Exp: Intern internal med, Bellevue Hosp, New York, 54-55; resident, Col Med, Univ Utah, 57-59; fel hemat, Scripps Clin, La Jolla, Calif, 59-60; asst physician, City of Hope Med Ctr, Duarte, 60-61, assoc physician, 61-63; asst prof internal med, Calif Col Med, 63-64; assoc prof, 72-78, PROF INTERNAL MED & LAB MED, MAYO MED SCH, 78-, MEM RES & TEACHING STAFF, MAYO CLIN, 65- Concurrent Pos: Sr attend physician, Los Angeles County Hosp & consult, Vet Admin Hosp, Long Beach, 63-64. Mem: AAAS; Am Soc Hemat; Am Fedn Clin Res; Am Col Physicians; Int Soc Hemat. Res: Pharmacology of veratrum alkaloids; glycolytic functions of human erythrocyte; hemoglobin structure and function; iron metabolism; human genetics. Mailing Add: Dept of Lab Med Mayo Clin Rochester MN 55901

FAIRBRIDGE, RHODES WHITMORE, b Pinjarra, Australia, May 21, 14; m 43; c 1. GEOLOGY. Educ: Queen's Univ, BA, 36; Univ Oxford, BS, 40; Univ Western Australia, DSc, 44. Prof Exp: Field geologist, Iraq Petrol Co, 38-41; lectr geol, Univ Western Australia, 46-53; assoc prof, Univ Ill, 53-54; PROF GEOL, COLUMBIA UNIV, 55- Concurrent Pos: Consult, Hydro-Elec Comn Tasmania, 47, Richfield Oil Co, 48, Australian Bur Mineral Resources, 50, Snowy Mountains Hydro-Elec Auth, 51, Pure Oil Co, 55-56, Life Mag, 56-, Nat Acad Sci, 58-59, Off Naval Res, 56-, Readers Digest Books, 72-, Fabbri Publ Co, Milano, 78-; leader, Nile Exped, Columbia Univ, 61; vis prof, Univ Sorbonne, 62; ed, Geol Series, Hutchinson & Ross Publ Co, 58-, Encycl Earth Sci, 63- & Benchmark Series, 70- Honors & Awards: Alexander von Humboldt Prize, 77. Mem: Fel Geol Soc Am; Soc Econ Paleontologists & Mineralogists; fel Am Geog Soc; Nat Asn Geol Teachers;

Am Asn Petrol Geologists. *Res:* Gravitational processes in sedimentation and tectonics; littoral sedimentation; coral reefs; eustatic changes of sea-level; paleoclimatology; geomorphology; geosynclines; world geotectonics. *Mailing Add:* Dept of Geol Columbia Univ New York NY 10027

FAIRBROTHERS, DAVID EARL, b Absecon, NJ, Sept 24, 25; m 49; c 2. BOTANY. *Educ:* Syracuse Univ, BS, 50; Cornell Univ, MS, 52, PhD(bot), 54. *Prof Exp:* Asst bot, Cornell Univ, 50-54, instr, 54; from instr to assoc prof, 54-65, chmn dept, 72-78, PROF BOT, RUTGERS UNIV, 65- *Concurrent Pos:* Rockefeller Res Found grant, 52; NSF grant, 57, 60, 63, 65, 67, 69, 71, 73 & 75. *Mem:* Int Soc Plant Taxonomists; Bot Soc Am; Am Soc Plant Taxonomists; Soc Study Evolution; Torrey Bot Club. *Res:* Chemosystematics; experimental taxonomy; rare and endangered plant species of New Jersey; scanning electron microscope. *Mailing Add:* Dept of Bot Rutgers Univ Busch Campus New Brunswick NJ 08903

FAIRCHILD, CLIFFORD EUGENE, b Philip, SDak, Sept 19, 34; m 60; c 2. ATOMIC PHYSICS. *Educ:* Fresno State Col, BA, 56; Univ Wash, PhD(physics), 62. *Prof Exp:* From asst prof to assoc prof, 62-77, PROF PHYSICS, ORE STATE UNIV, 77- *Concurrent Pos:* Sr postdoctoral assoc, US Air Force Cambridge Res Labs, 68-69; vis fel, Joint Inst Lab Astrophys & Lab Atmospheric & Space Physics, 75-76. *Mem:* Am Phys Soc. *Res:* Laser excitation of molecules; photofragment spectroscopy; spectra, polarizations, and lifetimes of laser excited fluorescence; upper atmospheric physics; auroral physics. *Mailing Add:* Dept of Physics Ore State Univ Corvallis OR 97331

FAIRCHILD, DAVID GEORGE, b Albany, Calif, Jan 7, 39; m 61; c 4. VETERINARY PATHOLOGY, TOXICOLOGY. *Educ:* Univ Calif, BS, 60, DVM, 62; Tex A&M Univ, MS, 66. *Prof Exp:* Chief path br, Res & Nutrit Br, US Army, Denver, 62-65; chief path div, Biomed Lab, Edgewood Arsenal, MD, 68-71; chief vet med dept, US Naval Res Lab, Cairo, Egypt, 71-72; chief vet path, Biomed Lab, Edgewood Arsenal, 72-74 & Letterman Inst Res, Presidio of San Francisco, 74-76; PATHOLOGIST, SYNTEX LABS, 76- *Mem:* Am Vet Med Asn; Wildlife Dis Asn; Soc Pharmacol & Environ Pathologists; Am Col Vet Pathologists; Int Acad Path. *Res:* Industrial pharmaceutical toxicology; laboratory animal pathology; wildlife diseases; oncology. *Mailing Add:* Syntex Res Labs 3401 Hillview Ave Palo Alto CA 94304

FAIRCHILD, EDWARD ELWOOD, JR, b Morgantown, WVa, Sept 21, 49; m 70; c 4. MATHEMATICAL PHYSICS. *Educ:* WVa Univ, BS, 71, MS, 72; Univ Tex, Austin, PhD(physics), 75. *Prof Exp:* ASST PROF PHYSICS, WASH UNIV, 75- *Concurrent Pos:* NATO fel, Dept Astrophys, Oxford Univ, 76-77. *Mem:* Am Phys Soc; Int Soc Gen Relativity & Gravitation. *Res:* Quantization of the gravitational field. *Mailing Add:* Dept of Physics Box 1105 St Louis MO 63130

FAIRCHILD, EDWARD JOSEPH, II, occupational health, toxicology, see previous edition

FAIRCHILD, GRAHAM BELL, b Washington, DC, Aug 17, 06; m 38; c 2. ENTOMOLOGY. *Educ:* Harvard Univ, BS, 32, MS, 34, PhD, 42. *Prof Exp:* Asst entomologist, Exp Sta, Univ Fla, 34-35; entomologist, Yellow Fever Serv, Int Health Div, Rockefeller Found, 35-37; jr med entomologist & later entomologist, Gorgas Mem Lab, 38-71; COURTESY PROF ENTOM, UNIV FLA, 71- *Concurrent Pos:* Asst prof, Univ Minn, 49-50 & Douglas Lake Biol Sta, Univ Mich, 56-57; asst dir, Gorgas Mem Lab, 58-71; mem trop med & parasitol sect, Nat Inst Allergy & Infectious Dis, 61-65; res assoc, Mus Comp Zool, Harvard Univ, 65- & Fla State Collection Arthropods, 70- *Honors & Awards:* Founders Mem Award, Entom Soc Am, 68. *Mem:* AAAS; Entom Soc Am; Soc Syst Zool. *Res:* Taxonomy of arthropods of medical importance; insects affecting man and animals, especially Tabanidae, Simuliidae, Psychodidae and Ixodidae. *Mailing Add:* Dept Entom McCarty Hall Univ Fla Gainesville FL 32611

FAIRCHILD, HOMER EATON, medical entomology, deceased

FAIRCHILD, JACK, b Houston, Tex, Oct 25, 28; m 51; c 7. AEROSPACE ENGINEERING. *Educ:* Univ Tex, BS, 53; Univ Southern Calif, MS, 59; Univ Okla, PhD(eng sci), 64. *Prof Exp:* Aerodynamicist, Bell Helicopter Corp, 53-54; sr aerodynamics engr, Chance Vought Aircraft Corp, 54-56; lectr aerospace eng, Aviation Safety Div, Univ Southern Calif, 56-60; instr & res engr, Univ Okla, 60-62; assoc prof, 64-70, PROF AEROSPACE ENG, UNIV TEX, ARLINGTON, 70- *Concurrent Pos:* Adv, US Army Bd Aircraft Accident Invest, 57-59; consult, Aircraft Div, Hughes Tool Co, 58-59, Bell Helicopter-Textron, 77-79 & Am Airlines Flight Acad, 66-80. *Mem:* Am Inst Aeronaut & Astronaut; Am Soc Eng Educ; Nat Soc Prof Engrs. *Res:* Flying qualities of airplanes; operational aerodynamics; automobile simulation and experimental testing; helicopter anti-torque systems; unsteady aerodynamics. *Mailing Add:* Dept of Aerospace Eng Univ of Tex Arlington TX 76010

FAIRCHILD, JOSEPH VIRGIL, JR, b New Orleans, La, Nov 26, 33; m 61; c 3. GEOLOGY, MANAGEMENT SCIENCE. *Educ:* La State Univ, BS, 56, MBA, 63, PhD(accounting), 75. *Prof Exp:* Geologist, United Core Inc, 56-57; assoc accountant, Humble Oil & Refining Co, 63-64; sr accountant, L A Champagne & Co CPA's, 64-68, partner, 68-69; from asst prof to assoc prof, 69-76, PROF ACCOUNTING, NICHOLLS STATE UNIV, 76- *Res:* Business research, particularly asset revaluation and depreciation. *Mailing Add:* 412 Plater Dr Thibodaux LA 70301

FAIRCHILD, MAHLON DAVID, pharmacology, neurophysiology, see previous edition

FAIRCHILD, MAHLON LOWELL, b Spencer, Iowa, Oct 13, 30; m 54; c 3. ENTOMOLOGY. *Educ:* Iowa State Univ, BS, 52, MS, 53, PhD(entom), 59. *Prof Exp:* Asst entom, Iowa State Univ, 52-53 & 55-56; entomologist Europ corn borer res lab, Agr Res Serv, USDA, 57-59; from asst prof to assoc prof, 59-67, chmn dept, 69-80, coordr, Integrated Pest Mgt, 80-81, PROF ENTOM, UNIV MO-COLUMBIA, 67- *Mem:* Am Entom Soc. *Res:* Insecticidal control of the European corn borer; biology and control of corn insects. *Mailing Add:* Dept Entom Univ Mo Columbia MO 65201

FAIRCHILD, RALPH GRANDISON, b Trenton, NJ, Sept 24, 35; m 58; c 4. RADIOLOGICAL PHYSICS, NEUTRON CAPTURE THERAPY. *Educ:* St Lawrence Univ, BS, 58; Cornell Univ, MS, 61; Adelphi Univ, PhD, 75. *Prof Exp:* PHYSICIST, BROOKHAVEN NAT LAB, 61-; ASSOC PROF, SCH MED, STATE UNIV NY STONY BROOK, 79- *Concurrent Pos:* Consult, Radiol Dept, Vet Admin Hosp, Northport, NY, 75- *Mem:* Am Asn Physicists in Med; Health Physics Soc; Soc Nuclear Med. *Res:* Mixed field dosimetry; use of neutrons in diagnosis and therapy; diagnostic x-ray physics; nuclear medicine; neutron capture therapy. *Mailing Add:* Nuclear Med Div Brookhaven Nat Lab Upton NY 11973

FAIRCHILD, ROBERT WAYNE, b Williamsport, Pa. EXPERIMENTAL PHYSICS, COMPUTER INTERFACING. *Educ:* Rensselaer Polytech Inst, BS, 71; Cornell Univ, PhD(nuclear sci), 75. *Prof Exp:* ASST PROF PHYSICS, NEBR WESLEYAN UNIV, 75-, DIR COMPUT SERV, 80- *Concurrent Pos:* Res assoc, Univ Nebr, Lincoln, 76-78. *Mem:* Am Phys Soc; Am Asn Physics Teachers. *Res:* Computer interfacing and experiment control. *Mailing Add:* Dept Physics Nebr Wesleyan Univ Lincoln NE 68504

FAIRCHILD, WILLIAM WARREN, b Rutland, Vt, July 30, 38. MATHEMATICS. *Educ:* Swarthmore Col, BA, 60; Univ Pa, MA, 63; Univ Ill, PhD(math), 67. *Prof Exp:* Physicist, Bartol Res Found, Franklin Inst, 60-62; asst prof math, Northwestern Univ, 67-70; ASSOC PROF MATH, UNION COL, NY, 70-, CHMN DEPT, 80- *Mem:* Am Math Soc. *Res:* Functional analysis, particularly convolution algebras. *Mailing Add:* Dept of Math Union Col Schenectady NY 12308

FAIRCLOTH, WAYNE REYNOLDS, b Whigham, Ga, Jan 15, 32; m 66; c 3. SYSTEMATIC BOTANY. *Educ:* Valdosta State Col, BS, 55; Univ NC, MEd, 59; Univ Ga, PhD(bot), 71. *Prof Exp:* Teacher high sch, Ga, 51-61; from asst prof to assoc prof, 61-71, PROF BIOL & CUR HERBARIUM, VALDOSTA STATE COL, 71- *Mem:* AAAS; Bot Soc Am; Am Fern Soc. *Res:* Ecology and systematics of vascular flora of the Atlantic and Gulf Coastal plains, particularly phytogeography; taxonomy of the genus Ophioglossum. *Mailing Add:* Dept Biol Valdosta State Col Valdosta GA 31698

FAIRES, BARBARA TRADER, b Washington, DC, Apr 25, 43. PURE MATHEMATICS, GENERAL MATHEMATICS. *Educ:* ECarolina Univ, BS, 65; Univ SC, MS, 68; Kent State Univ, PhD(math), 74. *Prof Exp:* Instr math, Governor's Sch NC, 68; instr math, Westminster Col, 70-71; asst prof math, Carnegie-Mellon Univ, 74-76; asst prof, 76-80, ASSOC PROF MATH, WESTMINSTER COL, 80- *Mem:* Am Math Soc; Math Asn Am; Asn Women Math. *Res:* Theory of vector measures and applications of vector measures to Banach space theory and control theory. *Mailing Add:* Dept of Math Westminster Col New Wilmington PA 16142

FAIRES, JOHN DOUGLAS, b Sharon, Pa, Apr 27, 41; m 64, 69. MATHEMATICAL ANALYSIS. *Educ:* Youngstown State Univ, BS, 63; Univ SC, MS, 65, PhD(math), 70. *Prof Exp:* From asst prof to assoc prof, 69-79, PROF MATH, YOUNGSTOWN STATE UNIV, 79- *Mem:* Am Math Soc; Math Asn Am; Sigma Xi; Soc Indust & Appl Math. *Res:* Functional analysis, emphasis on operator theory in Banach Spaces; numerical analysis. *Mailing Add:* Dept of Math Youngstown State Univ Youngstown OH 44555

FAIRES, WESLEY LEE, b El Dorado, Kans, Aug 28, 32; m 55; c 5. SPEECH PATHOLOGY. *Educ:* Wichita State Univ, BS, 58, MS, 62, PhD(speech path), 65. *Prof Exp:* Speech pathologist, Inst Logopedics, 58-62, preceptor, 62-65; dir clin serv, 65-70; asst prof, 65-75, ASSOC PROF LOGOPEDICS, WICHITA STATE UNIV, 75- *Mem:* Am Speech & Hearing Asn. *Res:* Auditory processing ability of cerebral palsied children. *Mailing Add:* Dept of Logopedics Wichita State Univ Wichita KS 67208

FAIRFAX, SALLY KIRK, b Bainbridge, Md, Feb 21, 44. FORESTRY. *Educ:* Hood Col, BA, 65; NY Univ, MA, 69; Duke Univ, MA(forestry), & PhD(polit sci), 74. *Prof Exp:* Asst prof natural resources, Univ Mich, Ann Arbor, 74-78; asst prof & asst economist, Agr Exp Sta, 78-80, ASSOC PROF NATURAL RESOURCE POLICY, COL NATURAL RESOURCES, UNIV CALIF, BERKELEY, 80- *Mem:* Soc Am Foresters; Am Polit Sci Asn. *Res:* Public involvement; natural resource law and environmental regulation; public land management; water law and policy range management policy. *Mailing Add:* Col of Natural Resources Univ of Calif Berkeley CA 94720

FAIRHALL, ARTHUR WILLIAM, b Hamilton, Ont, Mar 2, 25; nat US; m 53; c 3. CHEMISTRY. *Educ:* Queen's Univ, Ont, BSc, 46; Mass Inst Technol, PhD(chem), 52. *Prof Exp:* Res chemist, Eldorado Mining & Refining Co, Ltd, 46-48; res assoc chem, Mass Inst Technol, 52-54; from asst prof to assoc prof, 54-63, PROF CHEM, UNIV WASH, 63-, ACTG CHMN DEPT, 75- *Concurrent Pos:* Guggenheim fel, 63-64. *Mem:* Am Chem Soc; AAAS. *Res:* Nuclear reactions; nuclear fission; radiocarbon dating. *Mailing Add:* Dept of Chem Univ of Wash Seattle WA 98195

FAIRHURST, C(HARLES), m 57; c 7. MINING ENGINEERING. *Educ:* Sheffield Univ, BEng, 52, PhD(mining), 55. *Prof Exp:* Mining engr, Northwest Div, Nat Coal Bd, 55-56; res fel mineral & metall eng, 56-57, from asst prof to prof, 57-70, from assoc head dept to head dept, 65-70, PROF CIVIL & MINERAL ENG, UNIV MINN, MINNEAPOLIS, 70-, HEAD DEPT, 72- *Mem:* Int Soc Rock Mech; Am Inst Mining, Metall & Petrol Engrs; Am Soc Civil Engrs; Am Underground-Space Asn (pres, 76-77, past pres); foreign mem Royal Swedish Acad Eng Sci. *Res:* Rock mechanics. *Mailing Add:* Dept of Civil & Mineral Eng Univ of Minn 221 Church St SE Minneapolis MN 55455

FAIRLESS, CHARLES MICHAEL HASKEL, b Kennett, Mo, Nov 9, 44. ANALYTICAL CHEMISTRY. *Educ:* Southeast Mo State Univ, BS, 66; Univ Tex, Austin, PhD(anal chem), 74. *Prof Exp:* SR ANAL CHEMIST, DOW CHEM CO, 74- *Mem:* Am Chem Soc; Electrochem Soc. *Res:* Industrial applications of plasma optical atomic emission spectroscopy. *Mailing Add:* Dow Chem Co Mich Div 1602 Bldg Midland MI 48640

FAIRLEY, HENRY BARRIE FLEMING, b London, Eng, Apr 24, 27; Can citizen; m 50; c 3. ANESTHESIOLOGY. *Educ:* Univ London, MB & BS, 49; FFARCS, 54; RCPS(C), dipl anaesthesia, 56, FRCP(C), 73. *Prof Exp:* Clin asst anaesthesia, Univ Toronto, 55-56, clin teacher, 56-61, assoc, 61-64, prof, 64-69; PROF ANESTHESIOL, UNIV CALIF, SAN FRANCISCO, 69-, ASSOC DEAN, 79- *Mem:* Asn Univ Anesthetists; Can Anaesthetists Soc; Am Soc Anesthesiologists; hon mem Australian & NZ Socs Anaesthetists. *Res:* Respiratory physiology as applied to anesthesia and the management of respiratory failure. *Mailing Add:* Dept of Anesthesiol Univ of Calif San Francisco CA 94143

FAIRLEY, JAMES LAFAYETTE, JR, b Orland, Calif, Oct 15, 20; m 48. BIOCHEMISTRY. *Educ:* San Jose State Col, AB, 42; Stanford Univ, PhD(chem), 50. *Prof Exp:* Instr meteorol, Univ Calif, Los Angeles, 43-44; instr physics & chem, San Jose State Col, 46-47; asst biochem, Stanford Univ, 47-49, res assoc, 49-51; res biochemist, Radiation Lab, Univ Calif, 51-52; from asst prof to assoc prof chem, 52-62, PROF BIOCHEM, MICH STATE UNIV, 62- *Mem:* AAAS; Am Chem Soc; Am Soc Biol Chemists. *Res:* Deoxyribonucleases; pyrimidine biosynthesis; glycoprotein structure and function. *Mailing Add:* Dept Biochem Mich State Univ East Lansing MI 48824

FAIRLEY, WILLIAM MERLE, b Millinocket, Maine, Oct 13, 28; m 60; c 2. GEOLOGY. *Educ:* Colby Col, AB, 49; Univ Maine, MS, 51; Johns Hopkins Univ, PhD, 62. *Prof Exp:* Geologist, Ga Marble Co, 57-58; asst prof, 58-65, ASSOC PROF GEOL, UNIV NOTRE DAME, 65-, ASST DEAN COL SCI, 75- *Mem:* Geol Soc Am; Soc Econ Paleontologists & Mineralogists; Sigma Xi. *Res:* Petrology and structure of metamorphic rocks, especially marble and soapstone. *Mailing Add:* Dept of Earth Sci Univ of Notre Dame Notre Dame IN 46556

FAIRMAN, FREDERICK WALKER, b Montreal, Que, May 29, 35; m 57; c 2. ELECTRICAL ENGINEERING, APPLIED MATHEMATICS. *Educ:* McGill Univ, BE, 59; Univ Pa, MSEE, 62, PhD(elec eng), 68. *Prof Exp:* Engr, Honeywell, Inc, 60-62; instr elec eng, Drexel Univ, 62-67; lectr, Univ Del, 67-69; assoc prof, 69-80, PROF, QUEEN'S UNIV, ONT, 80- *Mem:* Inst Elec & Electronics Engrs; Can Asn Univ Teachers. *Res:* On-line identification of dynamic system models; design of observers for estimating system states from input-output data. *Mailing Add:* Dept of Elec Eng Queen's Univ Kingston ON K7L 3N6 Can

FAIRMAN, WILLIAM DUANE, b Paducah, Ky, June 7, 29; m 57; c 5. ANALYTICAL CHEMISTRY, RADIOLOGICAL HEALTH. *Educ:* Marquette Univ, BS, 50, MS, 58. *Prof Exp:* From asst chemist to assoc chemist, 58-72, CHEMIST, ARGONNE NAT LAB, 73-, BIOASSAY GROUP LEADER, 74- *Concurrent Pos:* Abstractor, Chem Abstracts, 65-70. *Mem:* Sigma Xi; Health Physics Soc. *Res:* Radiochemical and instrumental determination of radionuclides in humans; environmental impact assessments; analytical tracer chemistry; radiation spectroscopy; computer applications in radiation measurement; liquid scintillation counting techniques; whole body counting; internal dosimetry. *Mailing Add:* Argonne Nat Lab 9700 S Cass Ave Argonne IL 60439

FAIRWEATHER, GRAEME, b Dundee, Scotland, Apr 18, 42; m 65; c 3. NUMERICAL ANALYSIS. *Educ:* Univ St Andrews, BSc, 63, PhD(appl math), 66. *Prof Exp:* Lectr appl math, Univ St Andrews, 63-66; vis lectr math, Rice Univ, 66-67; lectr appl math, Univ St Andrews, 67-69; asst prof math, Rice Univ, 69-71; ASSOC PROF MATH, UNIV KY, 71- *Concurrent Pos:* Vacation assoc, UK Atomic Energy Auth, 68; vis sr res officer, Numerical Anal Div, Nat Res Inst Math Sci, SAfrica, 71, vis scientist, 76; vis prof, Univ Tulsa, 77-78; vis assoc prof, Univ Toronto, 80-81. *Mem:* Soc Indust & Appl Math; Can Appl Math Soc; SAfrican Math Soc. *Res:* Numerical solution of partial differential equations. *Mailing Add:* Dept of Math Univ of Ky Lexington KY 40506

FAIRWEATHER, WILLIAM ROSS, US citizen. STATISTICS. *Educ:* Univ Calif, Berkeley, AB, 64; Cornell Univ, MS, 66; Univ Wash, PhD(statist), 73. *Prof Exp:* Syst analyst, MITRE Corp, 66-68; statistician, Nat Heart & Lung Inst, NIH, 68-70; statistician, 73-79, CHIEF, STATIST APPL BR, US FOOD & DRUG ADMIN, 79- *Mem:* Sigma Xi; Am Statist Asn; Biomet Soc; Inst Math Statist. *Res:* Statistical methodology for longitudinal data; multivariate analysis; mathematical modeling. *Mailing Add:* Food & Drug Admin HFD-234 5600 Fishers Lane Rockville MD 20857

FAISSLER, WILLIAM L, b Hammond, Ind, Nov 23, 38; m 66. COMPUTER INTERFACING, ELECTRONICS. *Educ:* Oberlin Col, BA, 61; Harvard Univ, MA, 62, PhD(physics), 67. *Prof Exp:* Res assoc, 67-70, asst prof, 70-74, assoc prof, 74-78, PROF PHYSICS, NORTHEASTERN UNIV, 78- *Concurrent Pos:* Vis prof, Max Planck Inst High Energy Physics, 77-78. *Mem:* Am Phys Soc; AAAS. *Mailing Add:* Dept of Physics Northeastern Univ Boston MA 02115

FAITH, CARL CLIFTON, b Covington, Ky, Apr 28, 27; div; c 2. MATHEMATICS. *Educ:* Univ Ky, BS, 51; Purdue Univ, MS, 53, PhD(math), 56. *Prof Exp:* Asst math, Purdue Univ, 51-55; from instr to asst prof, Mich State Univ, 55-57; from asst prof to assoc prof, Pa State Univ, 57-62; PROF MATH, RUTGERS UNIV, 62- *Concurrent Pos:* NATO fel, Univ Heidelberg, 59-60; NSF fel, Inst Advan Study, 60-61, mem, 61-62; consult, Inst Defense Anal, 64; Rutgers fac fel, Univ Calif, Berkeley 65-66 & 69-70; mem screening comt int exchange of persons, Sr Fulbright Awards, 70-73; vis, Inst Advan Study, 73-74, 77-78 & Israel Inst Technol, 76; mem nominating panel, Harvey Prize, Israel, 81- *Mem:* Am Math Soc; Asn Mem Inst Adv Study. *Res:* Galois theory; ring theory; commutativity theorems; structure of injective and projective modules; quotient rings; semiprime Noetherian and quasi-Frobenius rings; Dedekind prime rings; module theory; category theory. *Mailing Add:* 199 Longview Dr Princeton NJ 08540

FAITH, RAY EDWIN, statistics, see previous edition

FAIX, JAMES JACOB, agronomy, see previous edition

FAJANS, EDGAR W, b Manchester, Eng, Feb 24, 11; nat US; m 36; c 2. INDUSTRIAL CHEMISTRY. *Educ:* Univ Frankfurt, PhD(chem), 34. *Prof Exp:* Fel photochem res, Univ Col, London, 35; mem staff, Colloid Chem, Agr Res Sta, Univ Bristol, 36-37; res chemist, Imp Chem Industs, 37-44; controller res dept, Boron Chem, Borax Consol, Ltd, London, 44-51; assoc dir chem res, US Borax Res Corp, 51-59, spec asst to vpres, 59-63, mgr chem econ, 63-74, mgr eng econ, 74-76; CONSULT INDUST & MINERAL ECON, 77- *Mem:* Am Chem Soc. *Res:* Physical, inorganic and boron chemistry; chemical economics. *Mailing Add:* 12432 Ranchwood Rd Santa Ana CA 92705

FAJANS, JACK, b USA, Nov 17, 22; m 44; c 2. PHYSICS. *Educ:* City Col, BChE, 44; Mass Inst Technol, PhD(physics), 50. *Prof Exp:* Sr engr, Sylvania Elec Co, 50-53; assoc prof, 53-75, assoc dean grad studies, 74-77, PROF PHYSICS, STEVENS INST TECHNOL, 75-, DEAN GRAD STUDIES, 77- *Concurrent Pos:* Consult, Huyck Indust Controls, 56-; prof physics, Kabul Univ, Afghanistan, 63-69. *Mem:* Optical Soc Am; Am Asn Physics Teachers. *Res:* Low-temperature physics; superfluid helium; optical systems; instrumentation. *Mailing Add:* Grad Studies Stevens Inst of Technol Hoboken NJ 07030

FAJANS, STEFAN STANISLAUS, b Munich, Ger, Mar 15, 18; nat US; m 47; c 2. INTERNAL MEDICINE. *Educ:* Univ Mich, BS, 38, MD, 42. *Prof Exp:* Am Col Physicians res fel, 49-50; from asst prof to assoc prof, 51-61, PROF INTERNAL MED, SCH MED, UNIV MICH, ANN ARBOR, 61-, HEAD DIV ENDOCRINOL & METAB, 73- *Concurrent Pos:* Life Ins Med Res fel, 50-52; consult to Surgeon Gen, USPHS, 58-62 & 66-70; dir, Mich Diabetes Res & Training Cent, 77- *Mem:* Am Soc Clin Invest; Endocrine Soc; Am Diabetes Asn (pres, 71-72); Asn Am Physicians; Am Fedn Clin Res. *Res:* Endocrinology and metabolism; carbohydrate metabolism; diabetes; hypoglycemia; pituitary adrenal function. *Mailing Add:* Univ Mich Univ Hosp Ann Arbor MI 48104

FAJER, ABRAM BENCJAN, b Piaski, Poland, Sept 12, 26; m 56; c 3. PHYSIOLOGY, ENDOCRINOLOGY. *Educ:* Univ Sao Paulo, MD, 51. *Prof Exp:* Asst prof physiol, Sch Med, Univ Sao Paulo, 51-59, head lab exp endocrinol, 59-63; scientist, Worcester Found Exp Biol, 63-64; from asst prof to assoc prof, 64-74, PROF PHYSIOL & OBSTET-GYNEC, SCH MED, UNIV MD, BALTIMORE, 74- *Concurrent Pos:* Res fel, Inst Biol & Exp Med, Arg, 54, pharmacol lab, Univ Edinburgh, 56-58. *Res:* Ovarian and steroid physiology. *Mailing Add:* Dept of Physiol Univ of Md Sch of Med Baltimore MD 21201

FAJER, JACK, b Brussels, Belg, June 22, 36; US citizen; m 59; c 3. PHYSICAL CHEMISTRY. *Educ:* City Col New York, BS, 57; Brandeis Univ, PhD(phys chem), 63. *Prof Exp:* Res assoc, 62-64, from asst chemist to assoc chemist, 64-69, chemist, 69-76, GROUP LEADER, BROOKHAVEN NAT LAB, 76-, SR SCIENTIST, 80- *Concurrent Pos:* Adj prof, State Univ NY Stony Brook, 78; vis scholar, Stanford Univ, 79. *Mem:* Am Chem Soc; Biophys Soc; The Chem Soc. *Res:* Electron spin resonance; electronic spectroscopy of metalloporphyrins and chlorophylls; photochemistry; mechanisms of photosynthetic and enzymatic reactions. *Mailing Add:* Brookhaven Nat Lab Upton NY 11973

FAKUNDINY, ROBERT HARRY, b Manitowoc, Wis, Feb 11, 40. ENVIRONMENTAL GEOLOGY, REGIONAL GEOLOGY. *Educ:* Univ Calif, Riverside, BA, 62; Univ Tex, Austin, MA, 67, PhD(geol), 70. *Prof Exp:* Vol regional geol, US Peace Corps, Ghana, 63-65; sr scientist, 71-73, assoc scientist environ geol, 74-78, PRIN SCIENTIST & HEAD, ENERGY & ENVIRON GEOL SECT, NY STATE MUS-GEOL SURV & STATE GEOLOGIST & CHIEF, NY STATE GEOL SURV, 78- *Concurrent Pos:* Hogg fel, Univ Tex, 70; adj asst prof environ geol, State Univ NY Albany, 75-; ed, Northeastern Geol, 78-& Geol, 82- *Mem:* Geol Soc Am; Asn Am State Geologists; Am Asn Petrol Geologists; Am Geophys Union; Am Inst Prof Geologists. *Res:* Geology, geohydrology, geomorphology, and radionuclide migration at radioactive waste burial ground, West Valley, NY; study of brittle structural features in western NY; development of seismic hazard potential in the northeastern United States; sand and gravel economics. *Mailing Add:* NY State Geol Surv CEC 3136 ESP Albany NY 12230

FALB, LINFORD NEVIN, b Dalton, Ohio, Dec 22, 46. PLANT PHYSIOLOGY. *Educ:* Ohio State Univ, BS, 73, MS, 76; Univ Ga, PhD(agron), 80. *Prof Exp:* ASST PROF BIOL, OLIVET NAZARENE COL, 80- *Mem:* Am Soc Plant Physiologists; AAAS. *Res:* Herbicide metabolism in plants. *Mailing Add:* Biol Dept Olivet Nazarene Col Kankakee IL 60901

FALB, PETER L, b New York, NY, July 26, 36; m 71. APPLIED MATHEMATICS. *Educ:* Harvard Univ, AB, 56, MA, 57, PhD(math), 61. *Prof Exp:* Mem staff, Lincoln Lab, Mass Inst Technol, 56-65; assoc info & control, Univ Mich, 65-67; assoc prof, 67-69, PROF APPL MATH, BROWN UNIV, 69- *Concurrent Pos:* Consult, Electronics Res Ctr, NASA, 65-70 & Bolt Beranek & Newman, Inc, 66 & 71; chmn & treas, Barberry Corp, 68-; dir, Data Ledger, Inc, 70-72; vis prof, Lund Inst Technol, Sweden, 71, 72, 74, 76 & 78; prin, Dane, Falb, Stone & Co, 77- *Mem:* Am Math Soc; Inst Elec & Electronics Engrs; Soc Indust & Appl Math. *Res:* Control theory; control system design; algebraic geometry; human factors; convertible securities. *Mailing Add:* Dept of Appl Math Brown Univ Providence RI 02912

FALB, RICHARD D, b Ft Wayne, Ind, July 29, 36; m 58; c 5. BIOCHEMISTRY, BIOMEDICAL ENGINEERING. *Educ:* Wheaton Col, BS, 58; Ohio State Univ, PhD(phys org chem), 63. *Prof Exp:* Sr res chemist, Battelle Mem Inst, 63-66, proj leader, 66-68, assoc chief, 68-69, chief, Div Biochem & Biomed Eng, 69-76; vpres res & develop, 76-81, PRES, AMES CO, 81- *Concurrent Pos:* Sem assoc, Columbia Univ, 67- *Mem:* Am Chem Soc; Am Soc Artificial Internal Organs; Soc Biomat. *Res:* Biomaterials; blood coagulation chemistry; insolubilized enzymes. *Mailing Add:* Ames Div Miles Labs Inc 505 King Ave Elkhart IN 43201

FALCK, FRANK JAMES, b New York, NY, Oct 27, 25; m 50; c 1. AUDIOLOGY, SPEECH PATHOLOGY. *Educ:* Univ Ky, AB, 50, MA, 51; Pa State Univ, PhD(speech path), 55. *Prof Exp:* Asst prof & dir speech path, Sch Med, Vanderbilt Univ, 55-57; assoc prof & dir speech & hearing, Col Med, Univ Vt, 57-69; PROF SPEECH PATH & AUDIOL, UNIV HOUSTON, 69- *Concurrent Pos:* State consult, Vt Dept Health, 57- *Mem:* Am Speech & Hearing Asn; Am Psychol Asn. *Res:* Localization of auditory lesions; stuttering; audile-visile modability. *Mailing Add:* 2805 Bissonnet Houston TX 77005

FALCO, CHARLES MAURICE, b Ft Dodge, Iowa, Aug 17, 48; m 73; c 2. PHYSICS. *Educ:* Univ Calif, Irvine, BA, 70, MA, 71, PhD(physics), 74. *Prof Exp:* asst physicist, 74-77, PHYSICIST, SOLID STATE SCI DIV, ARGONNE NAT LAB, 77- *Concurrent Pos:* Group leader, Tunneling & Transport Properties Group, 78- *Mem:* Am Phys Soc; Inst Elec & Electronic Engrs. *Res:* Superconductivity, especially transport properties, Josephson effects, quantum interference, superconductive devices and high temperature superconductors; transport, electronic and phonon properties of normal metals; artificially layered metallic superlattices. *Mailing Add:* Solid State Sci Div Argonne Nat Lab Argonne IL 60439

FALCO, ELVIRA ALLEGRA (MRS BASS), medicinal chemistry, see previous edition

FALCO, JAMES WILLIAM, b Chicago, Ill, May 14, 42; m 75. CHEMICAL ENGINEERING, APPLIED MATHEMATICS. *Educ:* Univ Tenn, BS, 64; Univ Fla, MS, 69, PhD(chem eng), 71. *Prof Exp:* Exp test engr, Jet & Rocket Res, Pratt & Whitney Aircraft, 64-67; res engr, Environ Res, 69- Environ Protection Agency, 71-73 & US Army Corps Engrs, 73-74; res engr, 74-80, DIR EXPOSURE ASSESSMENT GROUP, US ENVIRON PROTECTION AGENCY, 80- *Mem:* Am Chem Soc; Am Inst Chem Engrs; Sigma Xi; Am Soc Testing & Mat. *Res:* Mathematical modeling of environmental systems; development protocols and models to assess toxic chemicals' impact on human health and the environment. *Mailing Add:* Off Health & Environ Assessment Environ Protection Agency 401 M St SW Washington DC 20460

FALCON, CARROLL JAMES, b Rayne, La, Mar 15, 41; m 68. REPRODUCTIVE PHYSIOLOGY, ANIMAL SCIENCE. *Educ:* Univ Southwestern La, BS, 63; Univ Ky, MS, 65, PhD(genetics), 67. *Prof Exp:* Res asst animal sci, Univ Ky, 63-67; asst prof, 67-70, head dept agr, 71-77, ASSOC PROF ANIMAL SCI, NICHOLLS STATE UNIV, 70-, DEAN COL LIFE SCI & TECHNOL, DEPT AGR, 77- *Mem:* AAAS; Am Inst Biol Sci; Am Soc Animal Sci; Am Soc Study Reprod; Am Dairy Sci Asn. *Res:* Role of the uterus in hormone metabolism; sexual behavior of animals; growth stimulants; environmental influences on fertility; nutrition of ruminants. *Mailing Add:* Dept of Life Sci & Technol Nicholls State Univ Thibodaux LA 70301

FALCON, LOUIS A, b Tarrytown, NY, Sept 6, 32; m 59; c 4. ENTOMOLOGY. *Educ:* Univ Calif, Berkeley, BS, 59, PhD(entom), 64. *Prof Exp:* Res asst, 59-63, asst insect pathologist, 63-70, lectr, 68-77, assoc insect pathologist, 70-77, PROF ENTOM, UNIV CALIF, BERKELEY, 77- INSECT PATHOLOGIST, 70- *Concurrent Pos:* Consult, FAO, Nicaragua, 70-, Univ Calif/US AID, 72- & Cent Am Res Inst Indust, 73- *Mem:* Entom Soc Am; Soc Invert Path. *Res:* Development and implementation of microbial control and integrated control, especially cotton and pome fruit; application of insect pathogens; applied ecology; systems analyses; developing countries; Latin America. *Mailing Add:* Dept of Entom Sci Univ of Calif Berkeley CA 94720

FALCONE, A B, b Bryn Mawr, Pa; m; c 2. ENDOCRINOLOGY, BIOCHEMISTRY. *Educ:* Temple Univ, AB, 44, MD, 47; Univ Minn, PhD(biochem), 54. *Prof Exp:* Intern, Philadelphia Gen Hosp, 47-48, resident physician, 48-49; teaching fel internal med, Univ Hosps, Univ Minn, 49-51, fel biochem, 51-54; asst prof, 54-65, Inst Enzyme Res, Univ Wis-Madison, 63-64, vis prof, 66-67; CONSULT PRACTR ENDOCRINOL & METAB DIS, FRESNO, CALIF, 68- *Concurrent Pos:* Asst clin prof internal med, Univ Wis-Madison, 56-57; assoc clin prof, 59-63; mem honorary staff, Valley Med Ctr, Fresno, 68-; mem staff, St Agnes Hosp, Fresno, 68-; mem staff, Fresno Community Hosp, 68-, chmn dept med, 73; sr corresp, Ettore Majorana Ctr Sci Cult, Erice, Italy, 77- *Mem:* Fel Am Col Physicians; Am Soc Biol Chem; Cent Soc Clin Res; Am Asn Study Liver Dis; Am Fedn Clin Res. *Res:* Mechanisms of adenosine triphosphate synthesis; oxidative phosphorylation; biological energy transformation mechanisms; mechanisms of drug action; membrane biochemistry; mechanism of enzyme action and use of radioactive and stable isotopes in biological systems. *Mailing Add:* 2240 E Illinois Ave Fresno CA 93701

FALCONE, JAMES SALVATORE, JR, b Bryn Mawr, Pa, Sept 17, 46; m 70; c 2. PHYSICAL CHEMISTRY, INORGANIC CHEMISTRY. *Educ:* Univ Pa, BS, 68; Univ Del, PhD(chem), 72. *Prof Exp:* Res assoc chem, Univ Fla, 72-73; res scientist, Union Camp Corp, 73-74; sr chemist, 74-76, res supvr, 76-77, TECH MGR, PQ CORP, 77- *Mem:* Am Chem Soc; Sigma Xi; Tech Soc Pulp & Paper Indust; Soc Glass Technol. *Res:* Properties of aqueous electrolyte solutions in general and soluble silicates in particular and the applications of these properties to industrial processes. *Mailing Add:* PQ Corp Res & Develop Ctr PO Box 258 Lafayette Hill PA 19444

FALCONER, DAVID G, optical physics, computer science, see previous edition

FALCONER, ETTA ZUBER, b Tupelo, Miss, Nov 21. 33; m 55; c 3. ALGEBRA. *Educ:* Fisk Univ, BA, 53; Univ Wis, MS, 54; Emory Univ, PhD(math), 69. *Prof Exp:* Instr math, Okolona Jr Col, 54-63; teacher, Chattanooga Pub Schs, 63-64; assoc prof, Spelman Col, 65-71 & Norfolk State Col, 71-72; CHMN DEPT MATH, SPELMAN COL, 72- *Mem:* Math Asn Am; Nat Asn Mathematicians (secy, 70-72); Am Math Soc. *Res:* Quasigroups and loops. *Mailing Add:* Dept of Math Spelman Col Atlanta GA 30314

FALCONER, JOHN LUCIEN, b Baltimore, Md, Aug 2, 46. CHEMICAL ENGINEERING. *Educ:* Johns Hopkins Univ, BES, 67; Stanford Univ, MS, 69, PhD(chem eng), 74. *Prof Exp:* Res chem engr catalysis, Exxon Res & Eng, 67; res assoc chem kinetics, Stanford Univ, 68-69; process res engr semiconductors, Fairchild Semiconductor Res & Develop, 69; fel catalysis, Stanford Res Inst, 74-75; asst prof, 75-80, ASSOC PROF CHEM ENG, UNIV COLO, 80- *Mem:* Am Chem Soc; Am Inst Chem Engrs; Am Vacuum Soc; Am Catalysis Soc. *Res:* Mechanisms of catalytic reactions on supported metal catalysts; reactions of gases with well-defined surfaces using surface analysis techniques. *Mailing Add:* Dept Chem Eng Box 424 Univ of Colo Boulder CO 80309

FALCONER, WARREN EDGAR, b Brandon, Man, Apr 13, 36; m 57; c 2. PHYSICAL CHEMISTRY. *Educ:* Univ Man, BSc, 57, MSc, 58; Univ Edinburgh, PhD, 61. *Prof Exp:* Res officer kinetics & catalysis, Nat Res Coun Can, 61-63; mem tech staff, Bell Tel Labs, Inc, 63-69, head phys chem res & develop dept, 69-73, asst chem dir, Bell Labs, 73, dir, Phys Chem Res, 73-78, dir, Network Configuration Planning Ctr, 78-81, DIR, TRANSMISSION FACILITIES PLANNING, BELL LABS, 81- *Concurrent Pos:* NATO sci fel, Cath Univ Louvain, 61. *Mem:* Am Chem Soc; Chem Inst Can; Am Phys Soc; Inst Elec & Electronics Engrs. *Res:* Photochemistry; chemical kinetics; free and trapped radicals; combustion chemistry; noble gas chemistry; flouride chemistry; ion molecule reactions; telecommunications network planning. *Mailing Add:* Bell Labs Bldg WB Rm 1L-249 Holmdel NJ 07733

FALEK, ARTHUR, b New York, NY, Mar 23, 24; m 49; c 2. HUMAN GENETICS. *Educ:* Queen's Col, NY, BS, 48; NY Univ, MA, 49; Columbia Univ, PhD(human genetics), 57. *Prof Exp:* Res worker med genetics, NY State Psychiat Inst, 49-50, psychol asst, 50-51, res scientist, NY State Dept Ment Hyg, 51-57; sr res scientist, 58-65; asst prof, 65-71, assoc prof, 67-75, PROF PSYCHIAT, EMORY UNIV, 76- CHIEF DIV HUMAN GENETICS, GA MENT HEALTH INST, 65- *Concurrent Pos:* Asst, Columbia Univ, 50-53, assoc, 53-65; consult, Ct Dept Health, 61-; mem, Inst Study Human Variation; mem comt Huntington's chorea, WHO; genetic consult, Nat Inst Drug Abuse, 74, mem study sect, 47-; ed, Soc Biol, 77- *Mem:* AAAS; Am Soc Human Genetics; Am Eugenics Soc; fel Gerontol Soc; Soc Biol Psychiat. *Res:* Medical genetics; cytogenetics, psychogenetics and related fields. *Mailing Add:* Div Human Genet & Dept Psychiat Ga Ment Health Inst Emory Univ Atlanta GA 30306

FALER, KENNETH TURNER, b Rock Springs, Wyo, Mar 13, 31. NUCLEAR CHEMISTRY. *Educ:* Idaho State Univ, BS, 53; Univ Calif, Berkeley, PhD(chem), 59. *Prof Exp:* Jr chemist, Am Cyanamid Co & Phillips Petrol Co Chem Processing Plant, Idaho, 53-54, res chemist mat testing reactor, Atomic Energy Div, Phillips Petrol Co, 59-61, group leader nuclear chem group, 61-67; affil asst prof, 67-69, ASSOC PROF CHEM, IDAHO STATE UNIV, 69-, ASSOC DEAN, COL LIB ARTS, 78- *Concurrent Pos:* Mem staff, Idaho Nuclear Corp, 67-69. *Mem:* Am Chem Soc. *Res:* Nuclear fission and decay schemes; fuel waste disposal; neutron cross sections; biological use of radioisotopes; biological fluid and electrolyte balance; geothermal site location using slow chemical kinetic systems. *Mailing Add:* Dept Chem Idaho State Univ PO Box 8023 Pocatello ID 83209

FALES, FRANK WECK, b Missoula, Mont, Sept 24, 14. BIOCHEMISTRY, CLINICAL CHEMISTRY. *Educ:* Ore State Univ, BS, 39; Stanford Univ, MA, 41, PhD(physiol), 51. *Prof Exp:* Res assoc physiol, Stanford Univ, 50-51; instr, 51-54, asst prof, 54-65, ASSOC PROF BIOCHEM, EMORY UNIV, 65- *Concurrent Pos:* Clin chemist, Hosp & Clin Res Ctr, Emory Univ, 51-70, NSF grant, 53-56. *Mem:* Fel AAAS; Am Soc Biol Chemists; Am Asn Clin Chem; fel Am Inst Chemists; Nat Acad Clin Biochem. *Res:* Physical and chemical characteristics of S-hemoglobin and sickle cell erythrocytes; clinical chemistry methods; cellular metabolism; relationship between structure and iodine staining of the amyloglucans. *Mailing Add:* Dept Biochem Emory Univ Div Basic Health Sci Atlanta GA 30322

FALES, STEVEN LEWIS, b Providence, RI, Mar 14, 47; m 74. FORAGE CROP PHYSIOLOGY. *Educ:* Univ RI, BA, 70, MS, 77; Purdue Univ, PhD(agron), 80. *Prof Exp:* Res assoc, Univ RI, 77; asst prof, 80-82, ASSOC PROF, DEPT AGRON, EXP STA, UNIV GA, 82- *Honors & Awards:* Scarseth Award, Purdue Res Found, 79. *Mem:* Am Soc Agron; Crop Sci Soc Am; Int Grassland Cong; Sigma Xi. *Res:* Identifying environmental and physiological constraints to the production of high quality forage feedstuff for ruminant livestock; systems analysis of livestock forage systems. *Mailing Add:* Dept Agron Univ Ga Experiment GA 31212

FALES, WILLIAM HAROLD, b Redding, Calif, Dec 29, 40; m 63; c 2. VETERINARY MICROBIOLOGY. *Educ:* San Jose State Univ, BA, 64; Univ Idaho, MS, 71, PhD(bacteriol), 74. *Prof Exp:* Microbiologist, Orange County Health Dept, Calif, 64-66; res assoc, 74-75, asst prof, 75-81, ASSOC PROF VET MICROBIOL & CLIN MICROBIOLOGIST VET MED, DIAG LAB, COL VET MED, UNIV MO, 81- *Mem:* Am Soc Microbiol; Sigma Xi. Diagnostic response anaerobic bacteriology and immunology; AAAS; NY Acad Sci; US Animal Health Asn. *Res:* Clinical veterinary microbiology; anaerobic bacteriology. *Mailing Add:* Diag Lab Col Vet Med Univ of Mo Columbia MO 65211

FALETTI, DUANE W, b Spring Valley, Ill, Apr 3, 34; m 59; c 2. CHEMICAL ENGINEERING. *Educ:* Univ Ill, BS, 56; Univ Wash, PhD(chem eng), 59. *Prof Exp:* Res engr, Boeing Airplane Co, Wash, 59-60; chem engr, Appl Physics Lab, Univ Wash, 60-62, sr chem engr, 62-77; SR RES ENGR, BATTELLE MEM INST, WASH, 77- *Mem:* Am Inst Chem Engrs. *Res:* Power plant systems and economics; nuclear power plant operations and licensing; underwater ordnance and thermal propulsion; electrochemistry; two-phase critical flow. *Mailing Add:* Battelle Mem Inst 2231 Enterprise Dr Richland WA 99352

FALICOV, LEOPOLDO MAXIMO, b Buenos Aires, Arg, June 24, 33; US citizen; m 59; c 2. THEORETICAL PHYSICS, SOLID STATE PHYSICS. *Educ:* Univ Buenos Aires, Lic en cie, 57; Balseiro Inst Physics, Arg, PhD(physics), 58; Cambridge Univ, PhD(physics), 60, ScD, 77. *Prof Exp:* Res assoc physics, Inst Study Metals, Univ Chicago, 60-61, from instr to prof, 61-69; Miller res prof, 79-80, PROF PHYSICS, UNIV CALIF, BERKELEY, 69-, CHMN DEPT, 81- *Concurrent Pos:* Vis staff mem, Bell Labs, 61; Sloan res fel, 64-68; vis mem, Cavendish Lab, Cambridge Univ & vis fel, Fitzwilliam Col, 66; Fulbright fel, Univ Colombia, 69; Nordita vis prof, Univ Copenhagen, 71-72; Fulbright lectr, Spain, 72; coordr workshop, Valence Fluctuations in Solids, Inst Theoret Physics, Univ Calif, Santa Barbara, 80-; lectr, NATO Sch, Mich State Univ, 81; mem adv comt, Div Mat Res, NSF, 78; mem rev comt, Solid State Sci Div, Argonne Nat Lab, 78-, chmn, 80; mem rev panel, Solid State Physics & Chem, Exxon Labs, 79 & 81. *Mem:* Am Phys Soc. *Res:* Electronic band structure of solids; superconductivity; many-body physics; theroretical chemistry. *Mailing Add:* Dept Physics Univ Calif Berkeley CA 94720

FALK, CATHERINE T, b Louisville, Ky, Aug 9, 39; m 63. POPULATION GENETICS. *Educ:* Pomona Col, BA, 61; Univ Pittsburgh, PhD(human genetics), 68. *Prof Exp:* Res fel, 68-70, res assoc, 70-81, ASSOC INVESTR GENETICS, NY BLOOD CTR, 81- *Concurrent Pos:* Vis investr, Rockefeller Univ, 69-71. *Mem:* Genetics Soc Am; Biomet Soc; Soc Study Evolution; Am Soc Naturalists. *Res:* Study of mathematical models of genetic populations; analysis and computer simulation; analysis of human genetics data to estimate linkage between known genetic markers; genetics of complex traits. *Mailing Add:* NY Blood Ctr 310 E 67th St New York NY 10021

FALK, CHARLES DAVID, b Chicago, Ill, July 18, 39; m 65, 81. PHYSICAL INORGANIC CHEMISTRY. *Educ:* Univ Chicago, BS, 61, PhD(chem), 66. *Prof Exp:* USPHS fel coord chem, Univ Sussex, 66-67; chemist, Explosives Dept, Exp Sta, E I du Pont de Nemours & Co, Inc, 67-70; mgr & adminr, Clifford Chem Corp, 70-74; CHEMIST-MGR, ENGELHARD INDUSTS, EDISON, 74- *Mem:* Am Chem Soc; The Chem Soc. *Res:* Kinetics and mechanisms of coordination complexes; ligand exchange reactions; hydride transfer; oxidation reactions with metal complexes; homogeneous and heterogeneous catalysis; auto exhaust catalysts. *Mailing Add:* 3 Jacata Rd Marlboro NJ 07746

FALK, CHARLES EUGENE, b Hamm, Ger, Oct 20, 23; nat US; m 48; c 3. PHYSICS, SCIENCE POLICY. *Educ:* NY Univ, BA, 44, MS, 46; Carnegie Inst Technol, DSc(physics), 50. *Prof Exp:* Instr physics, Carnegie Inst Technol, 49-50; assoc physicist, Brookhaven Nat Lab, 50-53, admin scientist, 53-56, admin scientist, Div Res, US Atomic Energy Comn, 56-58, asst to dir of lab, 58-61, from asst dir to assoc dir, 61-66; planning dir, 66-70, DIR DIV SCI RESOURCES STUDIES, NAT SCI FOUND, 70- *Concurrent Pos:* Vis fel, Sci Policy Res Unit, Univ Sussex, 72-73; consult, Orgn Econ Develop & Coop, France, 72- *Mem:* AAAS; Am Phys Soc; Sigma Xi; NY Acad Sci. *Res:* High energy physics; particle accelerators; neutron scattering; deuteron stripping; research administration; science manpower and policy. *Mailing Add:* 8116 Lilly Stone Dr Bethesda MD 20034

FALK, DARREL ROSS, b New Westminster, BC, Aug 25, 46; m 67; c 2. DEVELOPMENTAL GENETICS. *Educ:* Simon Fraser Univ, BSc, 69; Univ Alta, PhD(genetics), 73. *Prof Exp:* Fel genetics, Univ BC, 73-74; res scientist genetics, Univ Calif, Irvine, 74-76, asst prof, 76-81, ASSOC PROF BIOL, BIOL RES LAB, SYRACUSE UNIV, 81- *Mem:* Genetics Soc Am. *Res:* Mutagenesis and gene organization in Drosophilo melanogaster. *Mailing Add:* Dept Biol Res Lab 130 College Pl Syracuse Univ Syracuse NY 13210

FALK, EDWARD D, b Tonopah, Nev, Mar 13, 25; m 52; c 1. INSTRUMENTATION. *Educ:* Univ Calif, Berkeley, AB, 52; Ore State Col, MS, 56. *Prof Exp:* Physicist, Gen Elec Co, Wash, 52-54; sr scientist, Lockheed Aircraft Corp, Calif, 55-56; res engr, Atomics Int Div, NAm Aviation, Inc, Calif, 56-57; sr res engr, 57, eng supvr, 57-64, exec adv tech planning, 64-65, eng supvr irradiation testing, 65-68; asst dir, 68-79, EXEC DIR, INSTRUMENTATION SYSTS CTR, UNIV WIS-MADISON, 79- *Concurrent Pos:* Consult, various Middle East nations, 77- *Mem:* Sigma Xi; sr mem Inst Elec & Electronics Engrs; sr mem Instrument Soc Am. *Res:* Reactor instrumentation; in-pile fully instrumented capsule irradiations of fuels and fuel materials; design and development of instruments and instrumentation systems used in interdisciplinary research. *Mailing Add:* Instrumentation Systs Ctr Univ of Wis Madison WI 53706

FALK, GERTRUDE, b New York, NY, Aug 24, 25. BIOPHYSICS. *Educ:* Antioch Col, BS, 47; Univ Rochester, PhD(physiol), 52. *Prof Exp:* Fel physiol, Univ Chicago, 52, instr natural sci, 53-54; Porter fel psychiat, Med Sch, Univ Ill, 52-53; from instr to asst prof pharmacol, Univ Wash, 54-61; hon res asst, 61-72, LECTR BIOPHYS, UNIV COL, LONDON, 72- *Concurrent Pos:* Nat Inst Neurol Dis & Blindness spec fel, 61-63; Guggenheim fel, 63-64. *Mem:* Am Physiol Soc; Brit Biophys Soc; Brit Photobiol Soc; Brit Physiol Soc. *Res:* Excitation and contraction of muscle; visual excitation. *Mailing Add:* Dept of Biophys Univ Col Univ of London London England

FALK, HANS LUDWIG, b Breslau, Ger, Sept 15, 19; nat US; m 50; c 3. ENVIRONMENTAL HEALTH. *Educ:* McGill Univ, BSc, 44, PhD, 47. *Prof Exp:* Instr biochem, Dept Path & res assoc cancer, Univ Chicago, 47-52; vis asst prof biochem & nutrit, Univ Southern Calif, 52-56, adj assoc prof path, 56-62; head chem sect, Carcinogenesis Studies Br, Nat Cancer Inst, 62-63, chief, 63-66, assoc sci dir carcinogenesis & etiology, 66-68; assoc dir lab res, 68-71, assoc dir prog, 71-76, ASSOC DIR HEALTH HAZARD ASSESSMENT, NAT INST ENVIRON HEALTH SCI, NIH, 76- *Concurrent Pos:* Consult, WHO, Switz & Int Agency Res Cancer, France, 73-74. *Honors & Awards:* USPHS Award, 68. *Mem:* AAAS; Am Asn Cancer Res; NY Acad Sci; Am Soc Cell Biol; Am Soc Exp Path. *Res:* Carcinogenesis; metabolism of carcinogenic agents; spectroscopic analyses; tobacco and health research; toxicology of pesticides; teratogenicity of environmental chemicals. *Mailing Add:* Nat Inst Environ Health Sci NIH PO Box 12233 Research Triangle Park NC 27709

FALK, HAROLD, b Sioux City, Iowa, Nov 5, 33; m 63. STATISTICAL MECHANICS. *Educ:* Iowa State Univ, BS, 56; Univ Ariz, MS, 57; Univ Wash, PhD(physics), 62. *Prof Exp:* Mem tech staff, Bell Tel Labs, Inc, 60; res asst theoret physics, Univ Wash, 60-62; res assoc, Univ Pittsburgh, 64-66; PROF THEORET PHYSICS, CITY COL NEW YORK, 66- *Mem:* Am Phys Soc; Math Asn Am. *Res:* Statistical mechanics of model systems. *Mailing Add:* Dept of Physics City Col of New York New York NY 10031

FALK, HAROLD CHARLES, b Mitchell, SDak, May 9, 34; m 56; c 2. ELECTRICAL ENGINEERING. *Educ:* SDak State Univ, BS, 56, MS, 58; Okla State Univ, PhD(elec eng), 66. *Prof Exp:* Instr elec eng, SDak State Univ, 58-59; electronics engr, Aeronaut Systs Div, Wright-Patterson AFB, 59-63; from instr to assoc prof, US Air Force Acad, 66-71; assoc prof, Pakistan AF Col Aeronaut Eng, 71-73; chief software br, 73-76, dep dir, Directorate Avionics Eng, Aero Systs Div, 76-80, dep elect tech, Rome Air Develop Ctr, 80-81, DIR ADVAN CONCEPTS & TECHNOL, ELEC SYSTS DIV, 81- *Mem:* Inst Elec & Electronics Engrs. *Res:* Integrated circuits systems design, systems analysis; engineering management. *Mailing Add:* USAF/ESD/XRV Hanson AFB Bedford MA 01731

FALK, HENRY, b New York, NY, Feb 7, 43; m 71; c 3. PEDIATRICS, PUBLIC HEALTH. *Educ:* Yeshiva Col, BA, 64; Albert Einstein Col Med, MD, 68; Harvard Sch Pub Health, MPH, 76. *Prof Exp:* Intern, Children's Hosp, Philadelphia, 68-69; resident, Bronx Munic Hosp Ctr, 69-72; MED EPIDEMIOLOGIST, CTR DIS CONTROL, 72-75 & 76- *Concurrent Pos:* Liaison mem, Comt Environ Health, Am Acad Pediat, 78- *Mem:* Am Acad Pediat; Soc Pediat Res; Am Col Epidemiol; Soc Epidemiol Res. *Res:* Epidemiologic research on the etiology of cancer; environmental and occupational exposures; evaluation of vinyl chloride exposed individuals and development of hepatic tumors. *Mailing Add:* Ctr for Dis Control 1600 Clifton Rd NE Atlanta GA 30333

FALK, JAMES EDWARD, operations research, see previous edition

FALK, JOHN CARL, b Algonac, Mich, May 28, 38. ORGANIC CHEMISTRY. *Educ:* Kalamazoo Col, BA, 60; Univ Mich, MS, 62, PhD(org chem), 64. *Prof Exp:* Fel phys biochem, Northwestern Univ, 64-65; res chemist, Dow Chem Co, 65-67; sr res chemist, 67-70, group leader polymer synthesis, 70-74, SECT MGR, BORG WARNER RES CTR, 74- *Mem:* AAAS; Am Chem Soc; Sigma Xi. *Res:* Organic reaction mechanisms; physical biochemistry; polymer synthesis. *Mailing Add:* Borg Warner Res Ctr Des Plaines IL 60018

FALK, LAWRENCE A, JR, b Houston, Tex, May 5, 38. VIROLOGY, IMMUNOLOGY. *Educ:* Centenary Col La, BA, 62; Univ Houston, MS, 66; Univ Ark, PhD(microbiol), 70. *Prof Exp:* Asst prof, 71-75, Rush-Presby-St Luke's Med Ctr, 71-75, assoc prof microbiol, 75-78; ASSOC PROF MICROBIOL & MOLECULAR GENETICS & CHMN, DIV MICROBIOL, NEW ENGLAND REGIONAL PRIMATE RES CTR, HARVARD MED SCH, 78-, ASSOC PROF MICROBIOL, HARVARD SCH PUB HEALTH, 80- *Mem:* AAAS; Am Soc Microbiol; Am Asn Immunol; Am Asn Cancer Res; Soc Exp Biol & Med. *Res:* Herpesviruses; lymphotropic viruses; oncogenic viruses of man and animals. *Mailing Add:* New England Regional Primate Res Ctr Southborough MA 01772

FALK, LESLIE ALAN, b St Louis, Mo, Apr 19, 15; c 4. OCCUPATIONAL HEALTH, ENVIRONMENTAL HEALTH. *Educ:* Univ Ill, AB, 35; Johns Hopkins Univ, MD, 42. *Prof Exp:* Intern med, Johns Hopkins Hosp, 42-43; med dir, UN Relief & Rehab Admin Mission to Byelorussia, 46-47; med dir, Migratory Labor Health Asn, USPHS Southeast Region, Atlanta, 47-48; area med adminr, Welfare Fund, United Mine Workers Am, Pittsburgh, 48-67; proj dir, Matthew Walker Ctr, Nashville, Tenn, 67-68, co-dir, 68-70; PROF OCCUP & COMMMUNITY HEALTH & CHMN DEPT, MEHARRY MED COL, 67- *Concurrent Pos:* Fel med econ & admin, Med Admin Serv & Comt Res in Med Educ, 43-44; coordr primary medicare, educ health consult, Food Employees Health & Welfare Fund, Pittsburgh, 54-70 & Off Econ Opportunity, 70-72; from adj assoc prof to adj prof prev med, Vanderbilt Univ, 70- *Mem:* Am Col Prev Med; Am Asn Hist Med; Soc Health & Human Values; Am Pub Health Asn; Nat Med Asn. *Res:* Antibiotics; medical care organization; international health; social history of medicine, especially black medical history. *Mailing Add:* Dept Family & Community Health Meharry Med Col Nashville TN 37208

FALK, LLOYD L(EOPOLD), b Ocean Grove, NJ, Nov 6, 19; m 45; c 3. ENVIRONMENTAL ENGINEERING. *Educ:* Rutgers Univ, BSc, 41, PhD(sanit), 49. *Prof Exp:* Res assoc, Rutgers Univ, 45-49; consult, Eng Dept, E I Du Pont de Nemours & Co, 49-67, sr consult, 67-75, prin consult, 75-81; CONSULT, 81- *Mem:* Am Chem Soc; Water Pollution Control Fedn. *Res:* Air pollution; waste and sewage treatment; industrial climatology and meteorology; water pollution control. *Mailing Add:* 123 Bette Rd Wilmington DE 19803

FALK, MARSHALL ALLEN, b Chicago, Ill, May 23, 29; m; c 2. PSYCHIATRY. *Educ:* Bradley Univ, BS, 50; Univ Ill, Urbana, MS, 52; Chicago Med Sch, MD, 56; Am Bd Psychiat, dipl, 69. *Prof Exp:* Med dir, London Mem Hosp, 64-74; PROF PSYCHIAT & DEAN, CHICAGO MED SCH, 74-, VPRES MED AFFAIRS, 81- *Concurrent Pos:* Chmn coun mental health & addiction, Ill State Med Soc, 69-74; actg chmn dept psychiat, Chicago Med Sch, 73-75. *Honors & Awards:* Physician's Recognition Award Continuing Med Educ, AMA, 69 & 72. *Mem:* Fel Am Psychiat Asn; AMA; Am Asn Univ Prof; fel Am Col Psychiatrists. *Mailing Add:* Off Dean & VPres Chicago Med Sch Chicago IL 60064

FALK, MICHAEL, b Warsaw, Poland, Sept 22, 31; Can citizen; m 59; c 2. PHYSICAL CHEMISTRY. *Educ:* McGill Univ, BSc, 52; Laval Univ, DSc(chem), 58. *Prof Exp:* Res chemist, Can Copper Refiners, Montreal E, 52-54; fel spectros, Nat Res Coun Can, Ottawa, 58-60; res assoc, Mass Inst Technol, 60-62; assoc res officer, 62-68, SR RES OFFICER, ATLANTIC

REGIONAL LAB, NAT RES COUN CAN, HALIFAX, 68- *Concurrent Pos:* Vis scholar phys chem, Univ Cambridge, 76-77. *Mem:* Chem Inst Can; Spectros Soc Can. *Res:* Molecular structure; infrared spectroscopy; hydration of biopolymers; hydrogen bonding; crystalline hydrates; water. *Mailing Add:* Atlantic Regional Lab Nat Res Coun of Can Halifax Can

FALK, RICHARD H, b Peru, Ill, Oct 12, 38; m 58; c 5. BOTANY, CYTOLOGY. *Educ:* Univ Ill, Urbana, BS, 64, MS, 65, PhD(bot), 68. *Prof Exp:* NIH fel, Harvard Univ, 68-69; asst prof, 69-75, ASSOC PROF BOT, UNIV CALIF, DAVIS, 75- *Mem:* AAAS; Bot Soc Am; Am Soc Plant Physiologists. *Res:* Biological ultrastructure; scanning electron microscopy; x-ray microanalysis. *Mailing Add:* Dept of Bot Univ of Calif Davis CA 95616

FALK, THEODORE J(OHN), b Meriden, Conn, Oct 9, 31; m 55; c 3. AERODYNAMICS, PHYSICS. *Educ:* Rensselaer Polytech Inst, BAero, 53; Cornell Univ, MAeroEng, 56, PhD(aero eng), 63. *Prof Exp:* Res engr, Res Dept, United Aircraft Corp, 53-54; sr aerodyn engr, Gen Dynamics/Convair, 56-59; prin aerodynamicist, Calspan Corp, Buffalo, 63-81; SR MEM TECH STAFF, WILSON GREATBATCH LTD, CLARENCE, NY, 81- *Mem:* Am Inst Aeronaut & Astronaut. *Res:* Shock tubes, chemical lasers and chemical transfer lasers; metallic evaporation and condensation; electromechanical devices; bioengineering. *Mailing Add:* 10880 Boyd Dr Clarence NY 14031

FALK, THOMAS, b Budapest, Hungary, Feb 9, 26; US citizen; m 60; c 2. INFORMATION THEORY, IMAGE PROCESSING. *Educ:* Graz Tech Univ, Austria, Dipl Ing, 51; Univ Buffalo, MSc, 61; Columbia Univ, DSc, 67. *Prof Exp:* Develop supvr analog electronics, Am Optical Co, Buffalo, NY, 58-60; staff consult infrared instrumentation, Barnes Eng Co, Stanford, Conn, 60-67; sr engr radar, Norden, Div United Technol, 67-78; SR SCIENTIST RADAR, SCI APPL INC, 78- *Mem:* Inst Elec & Electronics Engrs; Sigma Xi; Optical Soc Am. *Res:* High resolution radar imagery; data compression; transmission; change detection; electronic counter-counter measures aspects of synthetic aperture systems; radar applications in oceanography. *Mailing Add:* 4925 N Calle Bendita Tucson AZ 85718

FALK, WILLIE ROBERT, b Dundurn, Sask, Mar 12, 37; m 60; c 3. NUCLEAR PHYSICS. *Educ:* Univ Sask, BSc, 59, MSc, 62; Univ BC, PhD(physics), 65. *Prof Exp:* Nat Res Coun Can overseas fel nuclear physics, Swiss Fed Inst Technol, 65-67; from asst prof to assoc prof, 67-78, PROF NUCLEAR PHYSICS, UNIV MANITOBA, 78- *Concurrent Pos:* Vis scientist, Inst Nuclear Physics, Jülich, WGer, 73-74, Tri Univ Meson Facil, Univ BC, 80-81. *Mem:* Am Phys Soc; Can Asn Physicists. *Res:* Annihilation of positrons in gases; nuclear reaction studies. *Mailing Add:* Dept of Physics Univ of Manitoba Winnipeg MB R3T 2N2 Can

FALKE, ERNEST VICTOR, b Brooklyn, NY, Mar 31, 42; m 72; c 2. GENETICS. *Educ:* Cornell Univ, BS, 64, MS, 65; Univ Va, PhD(genetics), 75. *Prof Exp:* Fel genetics, Albert Einstein Col Med, 75-78; res scientist, 78-80, TOXIC EFFECTS BR CHIEF, US ENVIRON PROTECTION AGENCY, 80- *Mem:* Environ Mutagen Soc; Soc Risk Anal. *Res:* Mutagenicity data; determination of genetic risk to humans due to exposure to chemicals; regulation of RNA and ribosome synthesis; governmental regulation of toxic chemicals. *Mailing Add:* US Environ Protection Agency (TS-796) 401 M St SW Washington DC 20460

FALKEHAG, S INGEMAR, b Falkenberg, Sweden, May 28, 30; m 55; c 2. ORGANIC CHEMISTRY, SURFACE CHEMISTRY. *Educ:* Chalmers Univ Technol, Sweden, MS, 59, PhD(org chem), 62. *Prof Exp:* Res chemist, Res Dept, WVa Pulp & Paper Co, 62-64, group leader lignin & pulping, res ctr, Westvaco, Inc, 64-78; INDEPENDENT CONSULT, 78- *Mem:* AAAS; Tech Asn Pulp & Paper Indust; Soc Gen Systems Res; Swed Soc Futures Res; World Future Soc. *Res:* Structure, reactions and technical utilization of wood chemicals; natural polymers; renewable resources; dietary fiber; nutrition; solution properties of macromolecules; research management and technology transfer; self-organizing and evolutionary processes; future studies; systems science. *Mailing Add:* 706 Creekside Dr Mt Pleasant SC 29464

FALKENBACH, GEORGE J(OSEPH), b Columbus, Ohio, July 24, 27; m 53; c 4. ELECTRICAL ENGINEERING. *Educ:* Univ Dayton, BEE, 48; Univ Ill, MSEE, 50. *Prof Exp:* Asst instr elec eng, Univ Ill, 48-50; electronics engr, Bell Aircraft Corp, NY, 50-55; res assoc, Lee Labs, Pa, 55; prin elec engr, 55-59, sr elec engr, 59-66, assoc chief, Electromagnetic Div, 66-74, prin elec engr, Phys Sci Sect, 74-76, RES ENGR, QUAL ASSURANCE SECT, COLUMBUS DIV, BATTELLE MEM INST, 76- *Mem:* Inst Elec & Electronics Engrs; Am Soc Nondestructive Testing. *Res:* Electronic circuit design; electronics instrumentation; ferromagnetism; magnetics testing; ultrasonics and eddy current testing; microwave engineering; ultrahigh-frequency techniques; electromagnetic theory; dielectric and magnetic materials. *Mailing Add:* Columbus Div Battelle Mem Inst 505 King Ave Columbus OH 43201

FALKENSTEIN, GARY LEE, b Bottineau, NDak, Oct 8, 37; m 69, 81; c 2. CHEMICAL ENGINEERING, POLYMER PROCESSING. *Educ:* Mass Inst Technol, SB, 59, SM, 61, PhD(chem eng), 64. *Prof Exp:* Asst dir sch chem eng practice, Mass Inst Technol, 60-61; sr res engr, Res Dept, Rocketdyne Div, NAm Rockwell Corp, 63-66, prin scientist, 66-67, mgr advan progs, Canoga Park, 67-71; mgr, Sesame Div, Polaroid Corp, 71-77; managing dir, 77-80, VPRES RES & DEVELOP, FLEXIBLE & GRAPHICS PACKAGING, AM CAN CO, 80- *Mem:* Am Inst Chem Engrs. *Res:* Polymer processing; coatings; surface chemistry; adhesion; diffusion in plastics. *Mailing Add:* Am Can Co American Lane Greenwich CT 06830

FALKENSTEIN, KATHY FAY, b Frederick, Md, Feb 17, 50; m 79. PLANT PHYSIOLOGY. *Educ:* Gettysburg Col, BA, 72; WVa Univ, MS, 74; Pa State Univ, PhD(bot), 79. *Prof Exp:* Res fel & assoc lectr biol, Princeton Univ, 79-81; ASST PROF BIOL, HOOD COL, 81- *Mem:* Am Soc Plant Physiologists. *Res:* Phyto-hormone interaction and plant tissue culture; extraction of auxins from caulerpa, a coenocytic alga; crown gall induction; plasmid isolation and recombinant DNA research. *Mailing Add:* Biol Dept Hood Col Frederick MD 21701

FALKIE, THOMAS VICTOR, b Mt Carmel, Pa, Sept 5, 34; m 57; c 5. MINING ENGINEERING, MANAGEMENT SCIENCE. *Educ:* Pa State Univ, BS, 56, MS, 58, PhD(mining eng), 61. *Prof Exp:* Res asst mining, Pa State Univ, 56-58; opers res consult, Int Minerals & Chem Corp, 61-62, oper res engr, 63-64, chief minerals planning, 64-65, asst mgr spec projs, 65-66, minerals planning & prod control mgr, 66-68, prod supt, 68-69; prof mineral eng & head dept & chmn mineral eng mgt prog, Col Earth & Mineral Sci, Pa State Univ, 69-74; dir, Bur Mines, Dept Interior, 74-77; PRES BERWIND NAT RESOURCES CO, 77- *Concurrent Pos:* Mem indust adv comt, Col Eng, Univ SFla, 65-69, adj prof, 66; consult, Fla State Bd Regents, 66-67; US del, Conf on Tunnelling, Orgn Econ Coop & Develop, 70; invited partic, Panel on Mineral Sci & Technol Educ Policy, Nat Acad Eng & US Bur Mines, 71; consult, UN, 71-73; neutral chmn, BCOA/UMWA Jt Comt Health & Safety, 73; mem, NAS/NAE Comt Mine Waste Disposal, 73-74; chmn, US Govt Interagency Task Force Coal, 74-75. *Honors & Awards:* Henry Krumb lectr, Am Inst Mining, Metall & Petrol Engrs, 78. *Mem:* Mining & Metall Soc Am; distinquished mem Soc Mining Engrs; Metall & Petrol Engrs (vpres, 77-79). *Res:* Operations research; mine systems engineering; land reclamation and other phases of mine environmental control; industrial engineering; economic analysis; mineral resource management; surface and underground mining; national mineral and coal policy. *Mailing Add:* Berwind Corp Ctr Sq West Philadelphia PA 19102

FALKIEWICZ, MICHAEL JOSEPH, b Brooklyn, NY, Oct 8, 42; m 66; c 2. COLLOID SCIENCE, TECHNICAL MANAGEMENT. *Educ:* City Col New York, BS, 65; Syracuse Univ, PhD(phys chem), 70. *Prof Exp:* Res chemist, Colgate-Palmolive Co, 70-75; proj mgr, Church & Dwight Co, Inc, 75-78, MGR PHYS PROPERTY TESTING, FMC CORP, 78- *Concurrent Pos:* Consult surface chem, 78. *Mem:* Am Chem Soc; Royal Soc Chem; Soc Cosmetic Chemists. *Res:* Absolute viscosities of molten metals and alloys by an oscillating closed cup method; surface chemistry of glass surface in contact with liquid phase; consumer product development; food, personal care products, rheology and colloid science. *Mailing Add:* PO Box 40 Rosemont NJ 08556

FALKINHAM, JOSEPH OLIVER, III, b Oakland, Calif, May 3, 42; m 67; c 1. MICROBIAL GENETICS. *Educ:* Univ Calif, Berkeley, AB, 64, PhD(microbiol), 69. *Prof Exp:* Teaching asst bacteriol, Univ Calif, Berkeley, 66-67; dir clin lab, David Grant Med Ctr, US Air Force, 69-71; dir lab serv, US Air Force Hosp, Castle AFB, Calif, 71-72; fel, Univ Ala Med Ctr, Birmingham, 72-74; asst prof, 74-80, ASSOC PROF MICROBIOL, VA POLYTECH INST & STATE UNIV, 80- *Mem:* Am Soc Microbiol; Genetics Soc Am. *Res:* Physiology, genetics and regulation of microbes, especially Esherichia coli; genetic linkage relationships in male strains of Escherichia coli; DNA replication in bacteria and its regulation; plasmid replication and inheritance; mechanism of gene transmission; structure and function of membranes; biosynthesis of alanine. *Mailing Add:* Dept of Biol Va Polytech Inst & State Univ Blacksburg VA 24061

FALKLER, WILLIAM ALEXANDER, JR, b York, Pa, Sept 9, 44; m 69; c 2. IMMUNOLOGY. *Educ:* Western Md Col, BA, 66; Univ Md, MS, 69, PhD(immunol), 71. *Prof Exp:* Fel & Clin instr immunol, Dept Trop Med & Med Microbiol, Sch Med, Univ Hawaii, 71-73; asst prof, 73-77, assoc prof immunol, 77-80, ASSOC PROF MICROBIOL, DENT SCH, UNIV MD, 80- *Honors & Awards:* J Howard Brown Award, Am Soc Microbiol, 71. *Mem:* Am Soc Microbiol; Sigma Xi; Int Asn Dent Res. *Res:* Radioimmunoassay for detecting antibody in gonococcal infected asymptomatic females; immunogenic relationships of oral peptostreptococci; immunology and periodontal disease; immunopathology and human arbovirus infections; activation of alternate complement pathway by oral microorganisms. *Mailing Add:* Dept of Microbiol Dent Sch Univ of Md Baltimore MD 21201

FALKNER, FRANK TARDREW, b Hale, Eng, Oct 27, 18; nat US; m 47; c 2. PEDIATRICS. *Educ:* Cambridge Univ, BA, 45; Univ London, LRCP & MRCS, 45, MRCP, 62; FRCP, 72. *Prof Exp:* Chief res, London Hosp, 45-48; res physician, Childrens Hosp & Res Found, Cincinnati, Ohio, 48-49; res med officer, Inst Child Health, Univ London, 51-53, lectr child health, 53-56; from asst prof to prof pediat & chmn dept, Univ Louisville, 56-68; assoc dir, Nat Inst Child Health, 68-71; dir, Fels Res Inst, Yellow Springs & fels prof, Col Med, Univ Cincinnati, 71-79; prof mat & child health, Univ Mich, Ann Arbor, 79-81; PROF MAT & CHILD HEALTH, UNIV CALIF, BERKELEY, 81- *Concurrent Pos:* Res scholar pediat, Univ Liverpool, 49-51; Markle scholar, 57-61; asst consult, Hosp Sick Children, France, 53; dir growth study sect, Int Ctr Children, Paris, 53, coord officer, 54; asst, Hosp Sick Children, London, 54-56; consult, Nat Inst Child Health, Nat Inst Neurol Dis & Stroke & Maternal & Child Health Servs & HEW; chmn comt, Comn Human Develop, Int Union Nutrit Sci; ser ed, Monogr Pediat; co-ed, Mod Probs Pediat; vis prof pediat, Col Med, Univ Cincinnati, 79-81. *Mem:* Soc Pediat Res; Soc Res Child Develop; fel Royal Soc Med; Am Pediat Soc; fel Am Acad Pediat. *Res:* Prenatal biology; normal-abnormal growth. *Mailing Add:* Dept of Mat & Child Health Univ Calif Warren Hall Berkeley CA 94720

FALKOW, STANLEY, b Albany, NY, Jan 24, 34; m 58; c 2. MICROBIOLOGY. *Educ:* Univ Maine, BS, 55; Brown Univ, MS, 59, PhD(biol), 60. *Hon Degrees:* ScD, Univ Maine, 79. *Prof Exp:* Chief, Dept Bact, Newport Hosp, RI, 56-58; res microbiologist, Walter Reed Army Inst Res, 60-66; from assoc prof to prof microbiol, Sch Med & Sch Dent, Georgetown Univ, 66-72; prof microbiol, Sch Med, Univ Wash, 72-81; PROF & CHMN MED MICROBIOL, STANFORD UNIV, 81- *Concurrent Pos:* Soc Am Bacteriologists president's fel, 60-61; mem comn enteric infections, Armed Forces Epidemiol Bd; mem, Recombinant DNA Molecule Adv Comt, NIH, 75-76, Microbiol Immunol Adv Comt, 81- *Honors & Awards:* Paul Ehrlich-Ludwig Darmstaeder Prize, WGer, 81. *Mem:* AAAS; Am Soc Microbiol; Genetics Soc Am; Am Inst Biol Sci; Infectious Dis Soc. *Res:* Molecular biology of bacterial plasmids; pathogenesis of enteric infections; antibiotic resistance of microorganisms; microbial genetics; molecular biology. *Mailing Add:* Dept Med Microbiol Stanford Univ Stanford CA 94305

FALKOWSKI, PAUL GORDON, b New York, NY, Jan 4, 51; div. BIOLOGY, OCEANOGRAPHY. *Educ:* City Col NY, BS, 72, MA, 73; Univ BC, PhD(biol), 75. *Prof Exp:* Res assoc oceanog, Univ RI, 75-76; SCIENTIST OCEANOG, BROOKHAVEN NAT LAB, 76- *Concurrent Pos:* Adj prof, State Univ NY, Stony Brook, 76- *Mem:* Am Soc Limnol & Oceanog; Am Soc Plant Physiol. *Res:* Marine phytoplankton physiology, biochemistry and ecology. *Mailing Add:* Brookhaven Nat Lab Oceanog Sci Div Upton NY 11973

FALL, HARRY H, b Lucenec, Czech, Dec 8, 20; nat US; m 47; c 3. PHYSICAL ORGANIC CHEMISTRY. *Educ:* Pa State Col, BS, 42, PhD(chem), 50. *Prof Exp:* Res chemist, Sylvania Indust Corp, 42-44; sr res chemist, Upjohn Co, 51-56; sr res chemist, Mobay Chem Co, 56-57; sr res chemist, Gen Tire & Rubber Co, 57-64; sr res chemist, Goodyear Tire & Rubber Co, 64-80; CONSULT, OMNITRONICS RES CORP, 81- *Mem:* Am Chem Soc; fel Am Inst Chemists. *Res:* Cellulose ethers; cellophane coatings; origin of petroleum; pterine chemistry; chemotherapy of experimental neoplastic diseases; kinetics of polyether glycol formation and polymerization; block and graft polymers; thermoplastic elastomers; pharmaceuticals. *Mailing Add:* 3959 Cardinal Rd Akron OH 44313

FALL, MICHAEL WILLIAM, b Port Clinton, Ohio, Dec 17, 42; m 66; c 1. PEST MANAGEMENT, ECOLOGY. *Educ:* Bowling Green State Univ, BS, 63, MA, 66; Pa State Univ, PhD(pest mgt), 78. *Prof Exp:* Wildlife biologist animal damage control, Denver Wildlife Res Ctr, 70-71, wildlife biologist rodent control, Philipine Rodent Res Ctr, AID, 71-75, wildlife biologist int progs vert pest control, 75-81, CHIEF, SECT PREDATOR MGT RES, DENVER WILDLIFE RES CTR, US FISH & WILDLIFE SERV, 81- *Concurrent Pos:* Grad res adv entom & appl zool, Univ Philippines, 72-75, vis asst prof zool, 75. *Mem:* Am Soc Mammalogists; AAAS; Wildlife Soc. *Res:* Ecology and behavior of pest vertebrates; development of vertebrate pest management methods and programs. *Mailing Add:* Denver Wildlife Res Ctr Bldg 16 Fed Ctr Lakewood CO 80225

FALLER, ALAN JUDSON, b Boston, Mass, Mar 4, 29; m 51; c 4. METEOROLOGY. *Educ:* Mass Inst Technol, SB, 51, MS, 53, ScD(meteorol), 57. *Prof Exp:* Asst, Univ Chicago, 57-58 & Woods Hole Oceanog Inst, 58-63; res assoc prof, 63-66, RES PROF, INST PHYS SCI & TECHNOL, UNIV MD, COLLEGE PARK, 66- *Concurrent Pos:* Guggenheim fel, 60-61. *Mem:* AAAS; Am Meteorol Soc; Am Geophys Union; fel Am Phys Soc. *Res:* Hydrodynamic model experiments applied to the circulations of the oceans and the atmosphere. *Mailing Add:* Inst Phys Sci & Technol Univ of Md College Park MD 20782

FALLER, JAMES E, b Mishawaka, Ind, Jan 17, 34; m 59; c 2. PHYSICS, ASTROPHYSICS. *Educ:* Ind Univ, AB, 55; Princeton Univ, MA, 57, PhD(physics), 63. *Prof Exp:* Instr physics, Princeton Univ, 59-62; Nat Res Coun fel, Joint Inst Lab Astrophys, Nat Bur Standards, 63-64, physicist, 64-66; from asst prof to prof physics, Wesleyan Univ, 66-73; FEL JOINT INST LAB ASTROPHYS & ADJOINT PROF PHYSICS & ASTROPHYS, UNIV COLO, BOULDER, 72- *Concurrent Pos:* Alfred P Sloan fel, 72-73. *Honors & Awards:* Arnold O Beckman Award, Instrument Soc Am, 70; Medal Excep Sci Achievement, NASA, 73. *Mem:* AAAS; Am Phys Soc; Optical Soc Am; Sigma Xi; Am Geophys Union. *Res:* Precision experiments; atomic physics; physical optics; gravitation; fundamental constants and invariants; geophysics; experimental relativity; geophysics. *Mailing Add:* Joint Inst for Lab Astrophys Univ of Colo Boulder CO 80309

FALLER, JAMES GEORGE, b Wheeling, WVa, Sept 29, 34; m 59. MATERIALS ENGINEERING. *Educ:* WVa Univ, BChE, 59; Univ Del, MChE, 62, PhD, 66. *Prof Exp:* Phys metallurgist, Ballistics Lab, US Army Terminal, 64-66; sr mat engr, Vertol Div, Boeing Co, 66-70; pvt pract eng consult, 70-72; asst prof mat, US Naval Acad, 72-74; mat engr, David Taylor Naval Ship Res & Develop Ctr, 74-78; SR MECH ENGR, US ARMY MATERIEL TESTING DIRECTORATE, 78- *Concurrent Pos:* Resident indust scientist, State Pa, 69; adv, Armed Serv Comt, US House Rep, 75-78. *Mem:* Sigma Xi; Am Soc Metals; Am Soc Nondestructive Testing. *Res:* Nondestructive testing, welding. *Mailing Add:* STEAP-MT-G(B400) Aberdeen Proving Ground MD 21005

FALLER, JOHN WILLIAM, b Louisville, Ky, Jan 7, 42. INORGANIC CHEMISTRY, ORGANOMETALLIC CHEMISTRY. *Educ:* Univ Louisville, BS, 63, MS, 64; Mass Inst Technol, PhD(inorg & phys chem), 67. *Prof Exp:* Asst prof, 66-71, assoc assoc prof, 71-76, PROF CHEM, YALE UNIV, 76- *Concurrent Pos:* Petrol Res Fund grant, 67-; A P Sloan fel, 70-72; NSF grant, 72-; Guggenheim fel, 72-73. *Mem:* Am Chem Soc; The Chem Soc. *Res:* Synthesis and elucidation of structure and bonding of inorganic and organometallic compounds; stereospecific synthesis using transition metal complexes; mechanisms of catalysis; intramolecular rearrangement mechanisms of organometallics. *Mailing Add:* Dept of Chem Yale Univ New Haven CT 06520

FALLETTA, CHARLES EDWARD, b Phoenix, Ariz, Feb 8, 44; m 66; c 3. PHYSICA & INORGANIC CHEMISTRY. *Educ:* Johns Hopkins Univ, AB, 66; Univ Pittsburgh, PhD(chem), 72. *Prof Exp:* Jr res chemist catalysis, W R Grace & Co, 66-68; asst prof inorg chem, Denison Univ, 72-74; asst prof anal chem, Bates Col, 74-75; sr res chemist inorg chem, Foote Mineral Co, 75-77; SR RES CHEMIST CATALYSIS, JOHNSON-MATTHEY, INC, 77- *Res:* Precious metal catalysis. *Mailing Add:* Johnson-Matthey Inc 1401 King Rd West Chester PA 19380

FALLETTA, JOHN MATTHEW, b Arma, Kans, Sept 3, 40; m 63; c 2. ONCOLOGY, IMMUNOLOGY. *Educ:* Univ Kans, Lawrence, AB, 62;xUni 62, MD, 66. *Prof Exp:* Intern mixed med, Kans Univ Med Ctr, 66-67; from asst instr to resident pediat, Baylor Col Med, 67-71, fel hematol oncol, 71-73, asst prof pediat, 73-76; ASSOC PROF PEDIAT & CHIEF, DIV PEDIAT HEMAT-ONCOL, DUKE UNIV MED CTR, 76- *Mem:* Int Soc Exp Hematol; Soc Pediat Res. *Res:* Immunologic features of childhood cancer and its therapy; epidemiology of childhood cancer. *Mailing Add:* Duke Univ Med Ctr PO Box 2916 Durham NC 27710

FALLGATTER, MICHAEL, physical chemistry, see previous edition

FALLIERS, CONSTANTINE J, b Athens, Greece, Dec 10, 24; nat US; m 53; c 4. ALLERGY, PEDIATRICS. *Educ:* Nat Univ Athens, MD, 51; Am Bd Pediat, dipl, 58, cert pediat allergy, 65. *Prof Exp:* Intern, Evangelismos Hosp, Athens, Greece, 51; Fulbright fel basic med sci & clin pediat & resident, Med Ctr, Univ Colo, 51-53; resident pediat, Calif Babies & Children's Hosp, Los Angeles, 53-54; resident, Kaiser Found Hosp, Oakland, 54-55; mem Permanente Med Group, Walnut Creek, Calif, 55-57; dir clin serv, 59-63, med dir, children's Asthma Res Inst, 63-69; assoc clin prof pediat, Univ Colo Med Ctr, Denver, 73-77; DIR CLIN RES, CHILDREN'S ASTHMA RES INST & HOSP, 69-; 77- *Concurrent Pos:* Fel pediat allergy, Jewish Nat Home Asthmatic Children & Children's Asthma Res Inst & Hosp, Denver, 57-59; co-investr, USPHS grants, 62-68, res support grant, 64; co-investr, Fleischman Found grant, 64-65; instr, Univ Colo Med Ctr, Denver, 61-64, asst clin prof pediat, 64-73; ed, J Asthma. *Mem:* Am Acad Allergy; Am Col Allergists; Am Psychosom Soc; Soc Biol Rhythm. *Res:* Longitudinal study of asthma; growth and development, especially in relation to allergy and immunology; metabolic and endocrine aspects of allergic disease and therapy; clinical pharmacology; cybernetics and information theory as applied to biology and medicine. *Mailing Add:* 155 Cook St Denver CO 80206

FALLIS, ALBERT MURRAY, b Wellington Co, Ont, Jan 2, 07; m 38; c 3. PARASITOLOGY. *Educ:* Univ Toronto, BA, 32, PhD(parasitol), 37, FRSC, 58. *Prof Exp:* Asst biol, Univ Toronto, 31-32, demonstr parasitol, Sch Hyg, 37-43, lectr, 42-45, from assoc prof to prof, 45-75, head dept, 66-72, assoc dean, Sch Grad Studies, 67-70; res fel, Ont Res Found, 32-47, dir parasitol, 47-66, consult, 66-70; EMER PROF PARASITOL, UNIV TORONTO, 75- *Concurrent Pos:* Chmn adv comn entom res, Defense Res Bd, 69-70; Erskine fel, Univ Canterbury, 75. *Mem:* Am Soc Parasitologists (vpres, 69-70, pres, 79); Entom Soc Am; Entom Soc Can; Royal Can Inst (hon ed, 49-54, pres, 55-56); Can Soc Zoologists. *Res:* Animal parasites; protozoa; helminths; insects. *Mailing Add:* Dept Microbiol & Parasitol Univ Toronto Toronto ON M5S 1A1 Can

FALLIS, ALEXANDER GRAHAM, b Toronto, Ont, Aug 20, 40; m 67; c 2. ORGANIC CHEMISTRY. *Educ:* Univ Toronto, BSc, 63, MA, 64, PhD(org chem), 67. *Prof Exp:* Nat Res Coun Can fel, Oxford Univ, 67-69; asst prof, 69-74, assoc prof, 74-78, PROF ORG CHEM, MEM UNIV NFLD, 78-; PROF ORG CHEM, NFLD INST COLD OCEAN SCI, 78- *Concurrent Pos:* Nat Res Coun Can res grants, 69- & IBM Can, 75-78. *Mem:* Am Chem Soc; Chem Inst Can; Royal Soc Chem; fel Chem Inst Can. *Res:* Structural and synthetic organic chemistry especially the total synthesis of terpenes; marine natural products, synthetic methods and reactions of bridged-ring systems; reactions of bridged-ring systems and marine natural products. *Mailing Add:* Dept of Chem Mem Univ of Nfld St John's NF A1B 3X7 Can

FALLON, FREDERICK WALTER, b Washington, DC. ASTRONOMY. *Educ:* Harvard Univ, AB, 61; Univ SFla, MA, 72; Univ Fla, PhD(astron), 75. *Prof Exp:* Astronr, GS 5-12, US Army Map Serv, Defense Mapping Agency, 61-69; asst astron, Univ Fla, 71-74; instr, Univ SFla, 74-77, asst prof astron, 78-80; MEM STAFF, LAB ASTRON, GODDARD SPACE FLIGHT CTR, NASA, 80- *Mem:* Am Astron Soc; Royal Astron Soc. *Res:* Astrometry and stellar kinematics; photographic and optical techniques. *Mailing Add:* Lab Astron Goddard Space Flight Ctr NASA Greenbelt MD 20771

FALLON, HAROLD JOSEPH, b New York, NY, Aug 13, 31; m 55; c 4. PHARMACOLOGY. *Educ:* Yale Univ, BA, 53, MD, 57; Am Bd Internal Med, dipl, 65. *Prof Exp:* Instr internal med, Univ NC, Chapel Hill, 61-62, asst prof internal med, 64-69, prof med & pharmacol, 69-74; PROF MED & CHMN DEPT, MED COL VA, 74- *Concurrent Pos:* Fel liver dis, Yale Univ, 62-63; NIH spec fel biochem, Duke Univ, 63-64; Sinsheimer Fund award, 65-70; Burroughs-Wellcome scholar, 70; consult, metabolism study sect, USPHS. *Mem:* Asn Am Physicians; Asn Profs Med; AMA; Exp Am Gastroenterol Asn; Am Asn Study Liver Dis. *Res:* Liver disease; Pyrimidine metabolism in man; regulation of metabolic pathways; lipid biosynthesis; serine metabolism; gastroenterology. *Mailing Add:* Med Col VA Richmond VA 23298

FALLON, JOSEPH GREENLEAF, b Los Angeles, Calif, Oct 2, 11; m 34; c 3. PUBLIC HEALTH. *Educ:* Pac Union Col, BA, 38; Mass Inst Technol, MPH, 44. *Prof Exp:* Asst prof biol, 38-42, assoc prof biol & health, 44-45, assoc prof biol, nursing & health, 47-55, assoc prof biol, 55-57, assoc prof biol & health, 57-65, prof biol, 65-76, EMER PROF BIOL, PAC UNION COL, 76- *Concurrent Pos:* Fel Int Union for Health Educ of Public; instr, Sch Med, Loma Linda Univ; mem, UN Relief & Rehab Admin, China, 46; vis prof, Pac Union Col Exten, Honolulu, 50. *Mem:* AAAS; Am Soc Microbiologists; Am Soc Parasitologists; fel Am Pub Health Asn; fel Royal Soc Health. *Res:* Pollution studies on rivers; health surveys. *Mailing Add:* PO Box 203 Angwin CA 94508

FALLON, LESLIE DODDS, b Plattekill, NY, Feb 1, 16; m 42; c 4. PHYSICS. *Educ:* Geneva Col, BS, 36; Yale Univ, PhD(phys chem), 39. *Prof Exp:* From asst prof to prof chem, Geneva Col, 39-44; indust fel, Mellon Inst, 44-46; prof physics, Geneva Col, 46-61; assoc prof, 61-79, prof, 79-81, EMER PROF PHYSICS, NMEX INST MINING & TECHNOL, 81- *Mem:* AAAS; Am Asn Physics Teachers. *Res:* Electrolytes of solution; adhesives; ionization of water; water-dioxane mixtures; atomic physics. *Mailing Add:* 726 Bagley St Socorro NM 87801

FALLS, JAMES BRUCE, b Toronto, Ont, Dec 18, 23; m 52; c 3. ANIMAL BEHAVIOR, ECOLOGY. *Educ:* Univ Toronto, BA, 48, PhD(zool), 53. *Prof Exp:* Lectr zool, Univ Toronto, 52-53; Nat Res Coun Can Overseas fel, 53-54; lectr, 54-58, from asst prof to assoc prof, 58-66, assoc chmn dept, 75-80, PROF ZOOL, UNIV TORONTO, 66- *Concurrent Pos:* Royal Soc & Nuffield Found Commonwealth bursary, 64; vis fel, Wolfson Col, Oxford, 81. *Mem:* Am Ornith Union; Am Soc Mammal; Ecol Soc Am; Animal Behav Soc; Can Soc Zoologists. *Res:* Behavior contributing to population regulation, dispersion and resource use by animals; bioacoustics (structure and function of signals, individual recognition, repertoires) and territoriality in birds; populations, behavior and activity of mammals. *Mailing Add:* Dept of Zool Univ of Toronto Toronto ON M5S 1A1 Can

FALLS, WILLIAM MCKENZIE, b Muncie, Ind, May 13, 48. NEUROANATOMY, NEUROCYTOLOGY. *Educ:* Hanover Col, BA, 70; Ohio State Univ, MS, 73, PhD(anat), 75. *Prof Exp:* Grad teaching assoc anat, Ohio State Univ, 71-75; staff fel neuroanat, Nat Inst Dent Res, 75-78, sr staff fel, 78-79; ASST PROF ANAT, MICH STATE UNIV, 79- *Mem:* Soc Neurosci; Am Asn Anatomists; AAAS. *Res:* Golgi technique, Horseradish Peroxidase technique and electron microscopic analysis of sensory trigeminal nuclei; elucidation of basic pain and tactile mechanisms and understanding of chronic pain states which affect the face and oral cavity. *Mailing Add:* Dept Anat Mich State Univ East Lansing MI 48824

FALLS, WILLIAM RANDOLPH, SR, b Ironton, Ohio, Sept 15, 29; m 56; c 3. SCIENCE EDUCATION. *Educ:* Rio Grande Col, BS, 53; Marshall Univ, MA, 59; Ind Univ, Bloomington, EdD(sci educ), 70. *Prof Exp:* Assoc prof, 61-75, PROF SCI, MOREHEAD STATE UNIV, 75-, HEAD DEPT SCI EDUC, 61- *Concurrent Pos:* AEC res grant & resident physicist, 65- *Mem:* AAAS; Nat Sci Teachers Asn; Am Asn Physics Teachers. *Res:* Trace elements present in post oak trees as revealed through activation analysis; intense gamma field's effects on metals. *Mailing Add:* Dept of Sci Educ Lappin Hall Morehead State Univ Morehead KY 40351

FALOON, WILLIAM WASSELL, b Pittsburgh, Pa, July 6, 20; m 48; c 3. GASTROENTEROLOGY. *Educ:* Allegheny Col, AB, 41; Harvard Univ, MD, 44; Am Bd Internal Med, dipl. *Prof Exp:* Intern, Pa Hosp, Philadelphia, 44-45; asst resident med, Albany Hosp, NY, 45-46, resident, 46-47; res fel, Thorndike Mem Lab, Harvard Med Sch & Boston City Hosp, 47-48; asst prof oncol & instr med, Albany Med Col, 48-50; from instr to prof med, State Univ NY Upstate Med Ctr, 50-68; physician-in-chief, Cottage & Gen Hosp, Santa Barbara, Calif, 68-69; PROF SCH MED & DENT, UNIV ROCHESTER, 69-; chief med, 70-80, DIR GASTROENTEROL & NUTRIT, HIGHLAND HOSP, NY, 70- *Concurrent Pos:* Consult, Adv Comt, Surgeon Gen; vis prof, Cleveland Clin Found, 79, Univ Kans, 80 & Pensacola, Fla, 81. *Mem:* Fel Am Col Physicians; Am Gastroenterol Asn; Am Inst Nutrit; Am Fedn Clin Res; Am Asn Study Liver Dis. *Res:* Nutrition; gastrointestinal and metabolic disease. *Mailing Add:* Highland Hosp South Ave at Bellevue Rochester NY 14620

FALSETTI, HERMAN LEO, b Niagara Falls, NY, Oct 8, 34. CARDIOLOGY. *Educ:* Univ Rochester, BA, 57, MD, 60. *Prof Exp:* Chief med serv, Edwards AFB Hosp, US Air Force, 64-66; res instr med, State Univ NY Buffalo & Buffalo Gen Hosp, 66-68, asst res prof, 68-69; asst prof med, State Univ NY Buffalo & E J Meyer Mem Hosp, 69-73; assoc prof, 73-75, PROF MED, UNIV IOWA HOSPS & CLINS, 75- *Concurrent Pos:* Adj prof eng, 77- *Mem:* Am Heart Asn; Fedn Clin Res; Am Col Physicians; Am Col Cardiol; Am Physiol Soc. *Res:* Cardiac mechanics; blood velocity-flow relationship; coronary artery disease; computer applications in cardiology. *Mailing Add:* Dept of Internal Med Univ of Iowa Hosps & Clins Iowa City IA 52242

FALTER, JOHN MAX, b West Bend, Wis, Dec 13, 30; m 59; c 3. ENTOMOLOGY. *Educ:* Univ Wis, BS, 52, MS, 59, PhD(entom), 64. *Prof Exp:* Instr entom, Univ Wis, 61-64; asst prof, 64-67, ASSOC PROF ENTOM, NC STATE UNIV, 67- *Mem:* Entom Soc Am. *Res:* Economic entomology; biology and control of economic pests. *Mailing Add:* Dept of Entom NC State Univ Gardner Hall Raleigh NC 27650

FALTYNEK, ROBERT ALLEN, b Chicago, Ill, Sept 1, 48; m 70. INORGANIC & ORGANOMETALLIC CHEMISTRY. *Educ:* Augustana Col, AB, 70; Univ Minn, Minneapolis, PhD(inorg chem), 76. *Prof Exp:* Instr chem, Coe Col, Iowa, 75-76; fel inorg chem, Mass Inst Technol, 76-78; STAFF CHEMIST, CORP RES & DEVELOP, GEN ELEC, 78- *Mem:* Am Chem Soc; AAAS; NY Acad Sci. *Res:* Synthetic and structural inorganic and organometallic chemistry; transition metal photochemistry; silicon, silicone chemistry. *Mailing Add:* Gen Elec Corp Res & Develop PO Box 8 Schenectady NY 12301

FAMBROUGH, DOUGLAS MCINTOSH, b Durham, NC, July 22, 41; c 2. NEUROBIOLOGY. *Educ:* Univ NC, AB, 63; Calif Inst Technol, PhD(biochem), 68. *Prof Exp:* STAFF MEM EMBRYOL, CARNEGIE INST OF WASHINGTON, 68- *Concurrent Pos:* Asst prof biol & biophys, Johns Hopkins Univ, 70-74, assoc prof, 74-78, prof, 78- *Mem:* Soc Develop Biol; Soc Neurosci; Soc Gen Physiologists. *Res:* Nerve-muscle interactions; physical and metabolic aspects of cell membranes. *Mailing Add:* Carnegie Inst of Washington 115 W University Pkwy Baltimore MD 21210

FAMIGLIETTI, EDWARD VIRGIL, JR, b Providence, RI, June 2, 43. NEUROBIOLOGY. *Educ:* Yale Univ, BA, 65; Boston Univ, MD, 72, PhD(neuroanat), 72. *Prof Exp:* Commissioned officer, US Pub Health Serv, NIH, 72-74, fel, Nat Eye Inst, 74-76; fel, Keio Univ Sch Med, Tokyo, 77 & Washington Univ Sch Med, 77-79; ASST PROF, DEPT ANAT, WAYNE STATE UNIV SCH MED, 79- *Mem:* Asn Res Vision & Ophthal; Am Asn Anatomists; NY Acad Sci; Soc Neurosci. *Mailing Add:* Dept Anat Wayne State Univ Sch Med 540 E Canfield Detroit MI 48201

FAMULARO, KENDALL FERRIS, b Pasadena, Calif, June 8, 28. NUCLEAR PHYSICS. *Educ:* Calif Inst Technol, BS, 49; Rice Inst, PhD(physics), 53. *Prof Exp:* Res assoc physics, Univ Minn, 52-57; STAFF MEM, PHYSICS, LOS ALAMOS SCI LAB, 57- *Mem:* Am Phys Soc. *Res:* Nuclear reactions. *Mailing Add:* 555 Myrtle St Los Alamos NM 87544

FAN, CHANG-YUN, b Nantong, Jiangsu, China, Jan 7, 18; m 50; c 3. HIGH ENERGY ASTROPHYSICS, ATOMIC MOLECULAR PHYSICS. *Educ:* Nanking Univ, BA, 42; Univ Chicago, MS, 50, PhD(physics), 52. *Prof Exp:* Res assos astrophysics, Univ Chicago, 52-57; asst prof physics, Univ Ark, 57-58; sr physicist space physics, Lab Appl Sci, Univ Chicago, 58-67; PROF PHYSICS, UNIV ARIZ, 67- *Mem:* Am Phys Soc; Am Geophys Union. *Res:* Measurements of the compositions and energies of charged particles in space

for the understanding of plasma processes which energize these particles. *Mailing Add:* Dept Physics Univ Ariz Tucson AZ 85721

FAN, CHIEN, b Kiang-Su, China, Apr 1 30; m 58; c 3. ENGINEERING SCIENCE, MECHANICAL ENGINEERING. *Educ:* Univ Taiwan, BS, 54; Univ Ill, MS, 58, PhD(mech eng), 64. *Prof Exp:* Asst prof eng sci, Fla State Univ, 61-65; res specialist, 65-78, STAFF ENGR, LOCKHEED MISSILES & SPACE CO, 78- *Concurrent Pos:* Assoc prof, Univ Ala, Huntsville, 67-69; vis scientist, Repub China, 70. *Mem:* NY Acad Sci; Am Inst Aeronaut & Astronaut; Am Soc Mech Engrs. *Res:* Fluid mechanics; heat transfer; reliability engineering; spacecraft thermodynamics. *Mailing Add:* Lockheed Missiles & Space Co PO Box 504 Sunnyvale CA 94086

FAN, DAH-NIEN, b Hupei, China, Sept 3, 37; c 1. FLUID MECHANICS, AEROSPACE ENGINEERING. *Educ:* Nat Taiwan Univ, BS, ME, 58; Cornell Univ, MAeroE, 63, PhD(aerospace eng), 66. *Prof Exp:* Res assoc, Cornell Univ, 66-68 & 68-69; from asst prof to assoc prof, 69-77, PROF MECH ENG, HOWARD UNIV, 77- *Concurrent Pos:* Pres & consult, WHF & Assocs, Md, 76-; consult, Resource Recovery Servs Inc, 75- *Mem:* AAAS; Am Inst Aeronaut & Astronaut; AAUP; Am Phys Soc. *Res:* Aerodynamics of sounding rockets; tether dynamics in aerospace systems; acoustics; resource recovery from municipal solid waste; magneto-fluid dynamics. *Mailing Add:* Dept of Mech Eng Howard Univ Washington DC 20059

FAN, DAVID P, b Hong Kong, Jan 18, 42; US citizen; m 69. BIOLOGY. *Educ:* Purdue Univ, BS, 61; Mass Inst Technol, PhD(biol), 65. *Prof Exp:* Fel, Med Res Coun Lab Molecular Biol, Eng, 65-67, fel, Univ Geneva, 67-69; asst prof, 69-73, assoc prof, 73-77, PROF GENETICS & CELL BIOL, UNIV MINN, ST PAUL, 77- *Mem:* Am Soc Microbiologists. *Res:* Biochemisty of the bacterial cell envelope growth as related to growth and division; antigen recognition by mammalian cytolytic thymus- dependent lymphocytes. *Mailing Add:* Dept Genetics & Cell Biol Univ Minn St Paul MN 55108

FAN, HSIN YA, b Kiangsi, China. APPLIED MATHEMATICS. *Educ:* Ordnance Eng Col, China, BS, 56; Chenkung Univ, China, MS, 61; Univ Calif, Los Angeles, PhD(math), 70. *Prof Exp:* Instr mech eng, Ordnance Eng Col, 56-59; physicist, US Army Cold Regions Res & Eng Lab, 63; assoc prof, 69-77, PROF MATH, CALIF STATE POLYTECH UNIV, 77- *Honors & Awards:* Jeme Tien Yow Gold Medal, Chinese Inst Engrs, 61. *Mem:* Soc Indust & Appl Math. *Res:* Design and production of instructional models for mathematics. *Mailing Add:* Dept of Math 3801 W Temple Ave Pomona CA 91768

FAN, HSING YUN, b Changsha, China, Apr 27, 14; m 47; c 1. AGRICULTURAL BIOCHEMISTRY. *Educ:* Nat Tsing Hua Univ, BS, 35; Univ Minn, PhD(agr biochem), 45. *Prof Exp:* Asst, Nat Tsing Hua Univ, 35-40; China Found res fel insect physiol, Univ Minn, 45-46, res assoc, 48; res chemist, Julius Hyman & Co, 48-52; SR RES CHEMIST, SHELL DEVELOP CO, 53- *Mem:* Am Chem Soc. *Res:* Organic analysis; vitamins; pesticides; permeability of insect cuticle. *Mailing Add:* 1933 La Villa Rose Ct Modesto CA 95350

FAN, HSU YUN, b Shanghai, China, July 15, 12; nat US; m 41; c 4. SOLID STATE PHYSICS. *Educ:* Mass Inst Technol, MS, 34, ScD, 37. *Prof Exp:* From assoc prof to prof, Nat Tsing Hua Univ, China, 37-47; mem staff, Electron Res Lab, Mass Inst Technol, 48; vis prof, 48-49, from assoc prof to prof, 49-63, Duncan distinguished prof, 63-78, EMER PROF PHYSICS, PURDUE UNIV, 78- *Concurrent Pos:* Past mem var comts & panels, Nat Acad Sci-NSF; cor mem semiconductor comn, Int Union Pure & Appl Physics; mem solid state sci panel, Nat Res Coun. *Mem:* Am Phys Soc. *Res:* Semiconductors. *Mailing Add:* Dept of Physics Purdue Univ Lafayette IN 47907

FAN, JOHN C C, b Shanghai, China, Dec 5, 43; US citizen. ENERGY TECHNOLOGY. *Educ:* Univ Calif, Berkeley, BS, 66; Harvard Univ, MS, 67, PhD(applied physics), 72. *Prof Exp:* Tech staff, 72-80, ASST GROUP LEADER ELECTRON MAT, LINCOLN LAB, MASS INST TECHNOL, 80- *Mem:* AAAS; Sigma Xi; Electrochem Soc. *Res:* Thin films; electronic materials; solar selective coatings; solar cells; materials for integrated circuits. *Mailing Add:* Lincoln Lab Mass Inst Technol 244 Wood St Lexington MA 02173

FAN, JOYCE WANG, b China, Oct 2, 19; nat US; m 43; c 2. ORGANIC CHEMISTRY. *Educ:* Wheaton Col, BS, 42; Univ Iowa, MS, 44, PhD(chem), 46. *Prof Exp:* Fel, Northwestern Univ, 46-47; lectr chem, Univ Southern Calif, 47-48; from asst prof to assoc prof, Univ Houston, 49-63; PROF CHEM & CHMN PREMED ADV COMT, HOUSTON BAPTIST UNIV, 63-, HEAD DEPT, 67- *Mem:* Am Chem Soc; fel Am Inst Chemists. *Res:* Polarography as applied to organic compounds. *Mailing Add:* Dept of Chem 7502 Fondren Houston TX 77074

FAN, KY, b Hangchow, China, Sept 19, 14; nat US; m 36. MATHEMATICS. *Educ:* Univ Peking, BS, 36; Univ Paris, DSc(math), 41. *Prof Exp:* Fr Nat Sci fel, Univ Paris & Inst Henri Poincare, 42-45; mem, Inst Advan Study, 45-47; from asst prof to prof math, Univ Notre Dame, 47-60; prof, Wayne State Univ, 60-61; prof, Northwestern Univ, 61-65; chmn dept, 68-69, PROF MATH, UNIV CALIF, SANTA BARBARA, 65- *Concurrent Pos:* Assoc ed, J Math Anal & Appln, 60- *Mem:* Am Math Soc; Math Asn Am; Acad Sinica. *Res:* Functional analysis; topology. *Mailing Add:* Dept of Math Univ of Calif Santa Barbara CA 93106

FAN, LIANG-SHIH, b Fu-Wei, Taiwan, Dec 15, 47; m 78. REACTION ENGINEERING, FLUIDIZATION. *Educ:* Nat Taiwan Univ, BS, 70; WVa Univ, MS, 73, PhD(chem eng), 75; Kans State Univ, MS, 78. *Prof Exp:* Res asst chem eng, WVa Univ, 71-75, res assoc, 75; vis asst prof, Kans State Univ, 76-78, adv & judge, 76-77, coord grad res, 76-78; asst prof, 78-81, ASSOC PROF CHEM ENG, OHIO STATE UNIV, 81- *Concurrent Pos:* Res eng, Amoco Res Center, 79; Sigma Xi grant, 79; prin investr, Off Water Res & Technol, Dept Interior, 79-82, NSF, 79-82, Battelle Columbus Lab, 80-82; res assoc Argonne Nat Lab, 80; co-investr, Nat Sci Found, 81-83; consult, Argonne Nat Lab Chem Eng Div, 80-81; Battelle Mem Inst, 81- *Mem:* Sigma Xi; Am Inst Chem Engrs. *Res:* Energy conversion, fluidization, fluid solid reaction and mathematical modeling; author and co author of over sixty technical papers. *Mailing Add:* 1286 Castleton Rd N Columbus OH 43220

FAN, LIANG-TSENG, b Taiwan, Aug 7, 29; nat US; m 58; c 2. CHEMICAL ENGINEERING, MATHEMATICS. *Educ:* Nat Taiwan Univ, BS, 51; Kans State Univ, MS, 54; WVa Univ, PhD(chem eng), 57, MS(math), 58. *Prof Exp:* Jr chem engr, Taiwan Agr Chem Works, 51-52; asst chem eng, Kans State Univ, 52-54 & WVa Univ, 54-58; from instr to prof, 58-67, Kans Power & Light distinguished prof, 67-73, DIR, INST SYSTS DESIGN & OPTIMIZATION, KANS STATE UNIV, 67-, HEAD DEPT CHEM ENG, 68- *Concurrent Pos:* Phys chemist, US Bur Mines, 56-58, chem engr, 58-59; consult, Nat Air Pollution Control Admin, 69-75. *Mem:* AAAS; Am Chem Soc; Am Inst Chem Engrs; Soc Eng Sci; Japanese Soc Chem Engrs. *Res:* Mass and heat transfer; fluidization; chemical process design; applied mathematics; optimization; chemical process dynamics; mathematical optimization technique; air and water pollution control; desalination; energy resources conversion. *Mailing Add:* Dept of Chem Eng Kans State Univ Manhattan KS 66506

FAN, POW-FOONG, b Palenbang, Indonesia, Sept 4, 33; m 65. GEOLOGY. *Educ:* Wheaton Col, Ill, BS, 55; Univ Calif, Los Angeles, MA, 63, PhD(geol), 65. *Prof Exp:* Asst geophysicist, 65-70, asst prof, 66-70, ASSOC PROF GEOSCI & ASSOC GEOPHYSICIST, INST GEOPHYS, UNIV HAWAII, 70- *Mem:* Geol Soc Am; Soc Econ Paleontologists & Mineralogists. *Res:* Mineralogy of sediments; marine geology; hydrothermal alteration of geothermal fields; geology of China; geology of Asia. *Mailing Add:* Inst of Geophys Univ of Hawaii Honolulu HI 96822

FAN, STEPHEN S(HU-TU), b Shanghai, China, Jan 2, 34; m 59; c 4. CHEMICAL ENGINEERING. *Educ:* Stanford Univ, BS, 57, MS, 60, PhD(chem eng), 62. *Prof Exp:* From asst prof to assoc prof, 62-77, actg chmn dept, 70-71, PROF CHEM ENG, UNIV NH, 77-, CHMN DEPT, 71- *Mem:* Am Inst Chem Engrs; Am Soc Eng Educ. *Res:* Properties and heat transfer in chemically reacting systems; adsorption of gases; flow through porous media; applied kinetics. *Mailing Add:* Dept of Chem Eng Univ of NH Durham NH 03824

FANALE, FRASER P, planetology, see previous edition

FANALE, LOUISA P, b Fall River, Mass; m; c 2. ZOOLOGY, IMMUNOLOGY. *Educ:* Brown Univ, PhB, 50; Rutgers Univ, MS, 59, PhD, 67. *Prof Exp:* Instr biol, Fairleigh Dickinson Univ, 50-52; from instr to assoc prof, 52-75, prof, 75-80, EMER PROF BIOL, UPSALA COL, 80-, DIR ALLIED HEALTH, 81- *Mem:* Am Soc Microbiologists; Sigma Xi; NY Acad Sci. *Res:* Relation of tyrosinase to melanotic masses in Drosophilia; erythrocyte receptor sites for influenza A virus; immunological comparison of the endotoxins of various gram negative bacteria. *Mailing Add:* Dept of Biol Upsala Col East Orange NJ 07019

FANCHER, DAVID LOUIS, b Chicago, Ill, May 7, 47. EXPERIMENTAL HIGH ENERGY PHYSICS. *Educ:* Univ Ill, Urbana, BS, 69; Univ Calif, Santa Barbara, MA, 72, PhD(physics), 77. *Prof Exp:* PHYSICIST HIGH ENERGY PHYSICS, LAWRENCE BERKELEY LAB, 76- *Mem:* Am Phys Soc. *Res:* High energy physics research including experimental, lepton interactions and electron-positron colliding beam research. *Mailing Add:* One Cyclotron Rd Berkeley CA 94720

FANCHER, LLEWELLYN W, b Merced, Calif, Mar 30, 17; m 42; c 1. ORGANIC CHEMISTRY, AGRICULTURAL CMEMISTRY. *Educ:* Univ Calif, Berkeley, AB, 41. *Prof Exp:* Observer, US Steel Corp, 41-42, raw mat inspector, 42-44; res chemist, Ragooland-Broy Labs, 44-45; res chemist, Multiphase, Inc, 45-52; group leader, Stauffer Chem Co, 52-59, sect leader, 59-64, res assoc, 64-70, sr res assoc, 70-79; RETIRED. *Mem:* Am Chem Soc. *Res:* Industrial products and processes; new agricultural compounds such as pesticides, herbicides, fungicides and bactericides. *Mailing Add:* 233 Old Oak Rd New Castle CA 94658

FANCHER, OTIS EARL, b McCool, Miss, Jan 17, 16; m 46. CHEMISTRY. *Educ:* Miss State Col, BS, 38; Northwestern Univ, PhD(org chem), 42. *Prof Exp:* Res assoc, Nat Defense Res Comt Contract, Northwestern Univ, 42-45; res chemist, G D Searle & Co, 45-46; asst prof chem, Miss State Col, 46-47; head org sect, Miles-Ames Res Lab, 47-59, dir chem therapeut res lab, Miles Labs, Inc, 59-63, dir therapeut res labs, 63-66; vpres & sci dir, 66-72, CONSULT, INDUST BIOTEST LABS, INC, 72- *Mem:* Am Chem Soc; Soc Toxicol. *Res:* Synthesis of pharmacologically active organic compounds; toxicological studies. *Mailing Add:* PO Box 576 Pinetop AZ 85935

FANCHER, PAUL S(TRIMPLE), b San Antonio, Tex, Jan 5, 32; m 54; c 4. INSTRUMENTATION, ENGINEERING. *Educ:* Univ Mich, BSE, 53, MSE, 59, InstmE, 64. *Prof Exp:* Asst, 57-59, res assoc, 59-61, assoc res engr, 61-70, RES SCIENTIST, HWY SAFETY RES INST, UNIV MICH, ANN ARBOR, 70- *Mem:* Soc Comput Simulation; Am Soc Testing & Mat. *Res:* Highway vehicle dynamics; analysis, control, and simulation of dynamical systems. *Mailing Add:* Hwy Safety Res Inst Huron Parkway & Baxter Rd Ann Arbor MI 48105

FANCONI, BRUNO MARIO, b Merced, Calif, May 20, 39; m 65; c 3. POLYMER PHYSICS. *Educ:* Univ Calif, BS, 62; Univ Wash, PhD(chem), 68. *Prof Exp:* Teaching asst chem, Univ Wash, 63-64; from res asst to res assoc, Univ Ore, 64-71; SUPVRY CHEMIST POLYMERS, NAT BUR STANDARDS, 71- *Mem:* AAAS; Am Phys Soc. *Res:* Vibrational spectroscopy of polymers. *Mailing Add:* Rm A209 Bldg 224 Nat Bur Standards Washington DC 20234

FAND, RICHARD MEYER, b Janow, Poland, Aug 13, 23; US citizen; m 66; c 3. HEAT TRANSFER, FLUID MECHANICS. *Educ:* Rensselaer Polytech Inst, BS, 45; Columbia Univ, MS, 49; Cornell Univ, PhD(mech eng), 59. *Prof Exp:* Mech engr, US Civil Serv, 46-48; res engr, Bendix Aviation, 51; engr dynamics, Canadair Ltd, 52; instr mech eng, Cornell Univ, 52-55; res engr, Mass Inst Technol, 55-61; sr eng scientist, Bolt Beranet & Newman Inc, 61-66; PROF MECH ENG, UNIV HAWAII, 66- *Mem:* Am Soc Mech Engrs; Am Soc Eng Educ. *Res:* Influence of vibrations and intense sound, combined boiling and forced convection; combined forced and natural convection; influence of property variation on heat transfer; removal of scale by acoustically induced cavitation. *Mailing Add:* Dept Mech Eng Univ Hawaii Hawaii HI 96822

FAND, THEODORE IRA, b Brooklyn, NY, Dec 1, 15; m 41; c 2. ORGANIC CHEMISTRY, PHARMACEUTICAL CHEMISTRY. *Educ:* Brooklyn Col, BS, 35; Univ Mich, MS, 36; Polytech Inst Brooklyn, PhD(chem), 54. *Prof Exp:* Jr chemist anal, Vet Admin, 36-38; asst chemist, Bd Transp, NY, 38-42; asst dir develop & eng, Nepera Chem Co, Inc, 42-57; dir prod develop, 57-62, dir pharmaceut res & develop, 62-74, VPRES NEW PROD DEVELOP, WARNER-LAMBERT RES INST, 74- *Mem:* AAAS; Am Chem Soc; Am Pharmaceut Asn; Soc Cosmetic Chem; NY Acad Sci. *Res:* Pharmaceutical research and development; new dosage forms; drug absorption; pharmaceutical technology; pyridine chemistry; heterocycles and vitamines. *Mailing Add:* Warner-Lambert Res Inst 170 Tabor Rd Morris Plains NJ 07950

FANELLI, GEORGE MARION, JR, b Pelham, NY, Oct 5, 26; c 4. PHARMACOLOGY. *Educ:* George Washington Univ, BS, 50; NY Univ, MS, 57, PhD(biol), 62. *Prof Exp:* Biologist, Hazleton Labs, Inc, 51-52; pharmacologist, Chas Pfizer & Co, Inc, 52-58; res scientist, Lederle Labs Div, Am Cyanamid Co, 58-63; SR INVESTR PHARMACOL, MERCK SHARP & DOHME RES LABS, 65- *Concurrent Pos:* USPHS res fel physiol, Harvard Med Sch, 63-65. *Mem:* Am Physiol Soc; Am Soc Pharmacol & Exp Therapeut; Am Soc Nephrol; Brit Pharmacol Soc; Brit Primate Soc. *Res:* Comparative renal physiology; effects of drugs on renal transport processes; organic acid transport especially uric acid in nonhuman primates; chimpanzee renal function; pharmacology of diuretics; renin-angiotensin-aldosterone system. *Mailing Add:* Merck Sharp & Dohme Res Labs West Point PA 19486

FANESTIL, DARRELL DEAN, b Great Bend, Kans, Oct 31, 33; m 55; c 4. INTERNAL MEDICINE, NEPHROLOGY. *Educ:* Univ Kans, BA, 55, MD, 58. *Prof Exp:* Intern internal med, Los Angeles County Gen Hosp, 58-59; resident, Lahey Clin, 59-60; trainee cardiol, Scripps Clin & Res Found, 60-61; from asst prof to assoc prof internal med, Sch Med, Univ Kans, 66-70; assoc prof, 70-72, PROF INTERNAL MED, SCH MED, UNIV CALIF, SAN DIEGO, 72- *Concurrent Pos:* USPHS res fel biochem, Scripps Clin & Res Found, 61-62; Am Heart Asn adv res fel nephrology, Univ Calif Med Ctr, San Francisco, 64-66; Markle scholar acad med, 66-71; Am Heart Asn estab investr, 66-71. *Mem:* AAAS; Am Soc Clin Invest; Am Fedn Clin Res; Am Physiol Soc; Am Soc Nephrology. *Res:* Mechanism of action of hormones on transport of sodium, hydrogen and ions and of water; relationships between metabolism and ion transport. *Mailing Add:* Dept of Internal Med Sch of Med Univ of Calif at San Diego La Jolla CA 92093

FANG, CHENG-SHEN, b Taipei, Taiwan, Mar 29, 36; US citizen; m 72. CHEMICAL ENGINEERING. *Educ:* Nat Taiwan Univ, BS, 58; Univ Houston, MS, 65, PhD(chem eng), 68. *Prof Exp:* Supvr chem eng, Taiwan Fertilizer Co, 60-62; ASSOC PROF CHEM ENG, UNIV SOUTHWESTERN LA, 69- *Concurrent Pos:* Fel chem eng dept, Univ Houston, 68-69; prin investr, Dept Conserv, State La, 75-76; consult, Col Com, Univ Southwestern La, 77-78; tech consult, Chem Eng Dept, Lamar Univ, Tex, 77-78. *Mem:* Am Inst Chem Engrs; Sigma Xi. *Res:* Energy conservation and alternative energy sources; alternative chemical feedstocks; process design. *Mailing Add:* Dept of Chem Eng USL Box 44130 Lafayette LA 70504

FANG, CHING SENG, b China, Nov 23, 38; US citizen; m 66; c 2. HYDROMECHANICS, ENVIRONMENTAL ENGINEERING. *Educ:* Nat Taiwan Univ, BS, 61; NC State Univ, MS, 64, PhD(hydromech), 68. *Prof Exp:* Water resources engr, Camp, Dresser & McKee, 68-69; assoc scientist marine sci, 69-70, SR SCIENTIST PHYS OCEANOG & HYDRAUL & HEAD DEPT, VA INST MARINE SCI, 70-; assoc prof 72-78, PROF MARINE SCI, WILLIAM & MARY COL, 79- *Concurrent Pos:* Gen mgr & treas, Coastal Environ Asn, Inc, 71-; assoc prof marine sci, Univ Va, 72-78. *Mem:* Am Soc Civil Engrs; Am Geophys Union. *Res:* Water resource systems analysis; mathematical models for thermal and water pollution management; flood routing; wave mechanics; ground water and estuarine circulation. *Mailing Add:* 325 Yorkville Rd Grafton VA 23692

FANG, FABIAN TIEN-HWA, b Nanking, China, Oct 14, 29; nat US; m 55; c 1. ORGANIC CHEMISTRY. *Educ:* Nat Cent Univ, China, BS, 49; Univ Ill, MS, 52, PhD(chem), 54. *Prof Exp:* Res assoc chem, Univ Notre Dame, 54-55; res assoc, Iowa State Univ, 55-57; sr res chemist, Rohm & Haas Co, 57-64; asst prof chem, Univ Wis, Milwaukee, 64-69; vis assoc, Calif Inst Technol, 70; assoc prof, 70-72, PROF CHEM, CALIF STATE COL, BAKERSFIELD, 72-, CHMN DEPT, 70- *Mem:* Am Chem Soc; Am Inst Chemists; Catalysis Soc. *Res:* Macromolecular chemistry; heterogeneous catalysis. *Mailing Add:* Dept of Chem Calif State Col Bakersfield CA 93309

FANG, FRANK F, b Peiping, China, Sept 11, 30; m 57; c 4. SEMICONDUCTOR PHYSICS. *Educ:* Nat Univ Taiwan, BS, 52; Univ Notre Dame, MS, 54; Univ Ill, PhD(elec eng), 59. *Prof Exp:* Assoc phys electronics, Univ Ill, 57-59; res engr, Boeing Airplane Co, 59-60; RES STAFF MEM, IBM CORP, 60- *Honors & Awards:* John Price Wetherill Medal, Franklin Inst, 81. *Mem:* Inst Elec & Electronics Engrs; Sigma Xi; Am Phys Soc. *Res:* Solid state science; semiconductor physics and devices; solid state electronics. *Mailing Add:* Thomas J Watson Res Ctr IBM Corp PO Box 218 Yorktown Heights NY 10598

FANG, JEN-HO, b Tainan, Formosa, Oct 21, 29; m 61; c 3. MINERALOGY. *Educ:* Nat Taiwan Univ, BS, 53; Univ Minn, MS, 57; Pa State Univ, PhD(geochem), 61. *Prof Exp:* Res assoc chem, Boston Univ, 61-62; mem staff, Mass Inst Technol, 62-64; from asst prof to assoc prof, 64-71, PROF GEOL, SOUTHERN ILL UNIV, 71- *Mem:* Am Crystallog Asn; fel Mineral Soc Am; Am Geochem Soc. *Res:* X-ray crystallography; x-ray and neutron diffraction; physics of minerals; geostatistics. *Mailing Add:* Dept Geol Southern Ill Univ Carbondale IL 62901

FANG, JOONG, b Piongyang, Korea, Mar 30, 23; US citizen; m 56; c 1. MATHEMATICS, PHILOSOPHY. *Educ:* Yale Univ, MA, 50; Univ Mainz, Dr Phil, 57. *Prof Exp:* Asst prof math, Jinhae Col & Pusan Nat Univ, Korea, 45-48, Defiance Col, 57-58; Valparaiso Univ, 58-59 & St John's Univ, Minn, 59-62; assoc prof, Northern Ill Univ, 62-67; from assoc prof to prof philos & math, Memphis State Univ, 67-71; VIS PROF MATH, UNIV MUNSTER, 71- *Concurrent Pos:* Ed, Philosophia Mathematica, Asn Philos Math, 64- *Mem:* Math Asn Am; Am Math Soc; Am Philos Asn. *Res:* Foundation and philosophy of mathematics; sociology, history, and philosophy of science. *Mailing Add:* 251 Portview Norfolk VA 23503

FANG, KAUNG-KING, b China, Feb 8, 48. NUCLEAR PHYSICS. *Educ:* Fu-Jen Univ, BS, 68; State Univ NY, Binghamton, MA, 73; Rensselaer Polytech Inst, PhD(physics), 76. *Prof Exp:* Fel physics, Univ Sask, 76-78; RES ASSOC PHYSICS, TEMPLE UNIV, 78- *Res:* Quantum mechanical three-body scattering problems and electro and photo pion production from nuclei; quantum cluster coefficients in statistical mechanics. *Mailing Add:* Dept of Physics Temple Univ Philadelphia PA 19122

FANG, SHENG CHUNG, b Foochow, Fukien, China, June 27, 16; nat US; m 48. AGRICULTURAL CHEMISTRY. *Educ:* Fukien Christian Univ, BS, 37; Ore State Col, MS, 44, PhD(biochem), 48. *Prof Exp:* Instr, 48-53, from asst prof & asst chemist to assoc prof & assoc chemist, 53-71, PROF AGR CHEM, ORE STATE UNIV, 71- *Mem:* Weed Sci Soc Am; Am Soc Plant Physiologists; Am Chem Soc; Am Soc Biol Chemists. *Res:* Radioactive tracer studies in agricultural and biological chemistry; herbicides; plant growth regulators. *Mailing Add:* Dept of Agr Chem Ore State Univ Corvallis OR 97331

FANG, TA-YUN, Chinese citizen. PROTEIN CHEMISTRY, ENZYMOLOGY. *Educ:* Chung-Hsing Univ, Taiwan, BS, 67; Ore State Univ, MS, 71, PhD(biochem), 76. *Prof Exp:* Res fel, Dept Psychiat, McGill Univ, 76-78; RES ASSOC, ORE REGIONAL PRIMATE RES CTR, 79- *Mem:* AAAS. *Res:* Protein isolation, purification and characterization via column chromatography, electrophoresis and centrifugation; radioimmunoassay and enzymatic study. *Mailing Add:* 4800 NW Kahneeta Ct Portland OR 97229

FANG, TSUN CHUN, b Wuyuan, China, Mar 11, 14; US citizen; m 39; c 2. APPLIED MECHANICS, APPLIED MATHEMATICS. *Educ:* Tsinghua Univ, China, BS, 36; Polytech Inst, Brooklyn, MS, 47, PhD(appl mech), 69. *Prof Exp:* Prin sr engr, Repub Aviation Corp, 59-64, specialist mathematician, 64-65; res engr, 65-69, res scientist, 69-76, STAFF RES SCIENTIST, GRUMMAN AEROSPACE CORP, 76- *Res:* Guidance and control; optimization technique. *Mailing Add:* Res Dept Plant 35 Grumman Aerospace Corp Bethpage NY 11714

FANGBONER, RAYMOND FRANKLIN, b Waukegan, Ill, July 10, 43. DEVELOPMENTAL BIOLOGY, DEVELOPMENTAL NEUROBIOLOGY. *Educ:* Transylvania Col, BA, 65; Purdue Univ, MS, 68, PhD(biol), 72. *Prof Exp:* ASST PROF BIOL, TRENTON STATE COL, 72- *Mem:* Am Soc Zoologists; Am Inst Biol Sci; AAAS; NY Acad Sci. *Res:* Studies in in vivo nerve growth patterns; resolution of competition between appropriate and inappropriate innervation for a given end-organ; cell death as mechanism of central nervous system morphogenesis. *Mailing Add:* Dept of Biol Trenton State Col Trenton NJ 08625

FANGER, CARLETON G(EORGE), b Wolsey, SDak, Mar 22, 24; m 45; c 3. MECHANICAL ENGINEERING, ENGINEERING MECHANICS. *Educ:* Ore State Univ, BS, 47, MS, 48. *Prof Exp:* Asst prof eng, Vanport Exten Ctr, 48-52 & Portland State Exten Ctr, 52-55; assoc prof, 55-69, PROF MECH ENG, PORTLAND STATE UNIV, 69- *Concurrent Pos:* Qual instr nuclear defense, Defense Civil Preparedness Agency, 66- *Mem:* Am Soc Mech Engrs; Nat Soc Prof Engrs; Am Soc Eng Educ. *Mailing Add:* 10234 SE Market Dr Portland OR 97216

FANGER, HERBERT, b Millis, Mass, Sept 15, 14; m 42; c 2. PATHOLOGY. *Educ:* Harvard Univ, AB, 36; NY Med Col, MD, 40. *Prof Exp:* Instr path, Sch Med, Boston Univ, 43-44, 46-47 & 49-52, from asst prof to assoc prof, 52-65; PROF PATH & MED SCI, BROWN UNIV, 65-; PATHOLOGIST-DIR DEPT PATH, RI HOSP, 49- *Concurrent Pos:* Assoc pathologist, Peter Bent Brigham Hosp, Boston, Mass, 47-49; instr, Harvard Med Sch, 47-49; assoc pathologist & actg dir, Dept Path, RI Hosp, 49; consult, Vet Admin Hosp, RI & Morton Hosp, Taunton, Mass. *Mem:* Soc Clin Path; AMA; Am Asn Path & Bact; Col Am Path. *Res:* Histochemistry in neoplastic diseases; biology of neoplasms; malignant melanomas; thrombocythemia; uterine and breast cancer. *Mailing Add:* Dept of Path RI Hosp Providence RI 02902

FANGER, MICHAEL WALTER, b Ft Wayne, Ind, July 3, 40; m 62; c 2. BIOCHEMISTRY, IMMUNOLOGY. *Educ:* Wabash Col, BA, 62; Yale Univ, PhD(biochem), 67. *Prof Exp:* Asst prof microbiol, Case Western Reserve Univ, 70-76, assoc prof, 76-81; PROF MICROBIOL & MED, DARTMOUTH MED SCH, 81- *Concurrent Pos:* NIH fel, Nat Inst Med Res, London, 67-68; fel, Med Sch, Univ Ill, 68-69, NIH fel, 69-70. *Mem:* Am Asn Immunol. *Res:* Characterization of lymphocyte subpopulations; initiation of the immune response by the mechanism of transformation of the small lymphocyte. *Mailing Add:* Dept Microbiol Dartmouth Med Sch Hanover NH 03755

FANGMEIER, DELMAR DEAN, b Hubbell, Nebr, Oct 27, 32; m 69; c 2. AGRICULTURAL ENGINEERING, IRRIGATION. *Educ:* Univ Nebr, BSc, 54 & 60, MSc, 61; Univ Calif, Davis, PhD(eng), 67. *Prof Exp:* Agr engr, Agr Res Serv, USDA, 61; asst prof civil eng, Univ Wyo, 66-68; assoc prof agr eng, 68-72, PROF AGR ENG, UNIV ARIZ, 72- *Concurrent Pos:* Agr Water Conserv Panel, Calif Dept Water Res, 79; chmn, Soil & Water Div, Am Soc Agr Engrs, 78-80. *Mem:* Am Soc Agr Engrs; Am Soc Civil Engrs; Am Soc Eng Educ; US Comn Irrig & Drainage. *Res:* Hydraulics of surface irrigation; water requirements for urban plants; water and energy requirements for irrigation; water management for guayule. *Mailing Add:* Dept of Soils Water & Eng Univ of Ariz Tucson AZ 85721

FANGUY, ROY CHARLES, b New Orleans, La, Nov 23, 29; m 51; c 2. IMMUNOGENETICS. *Educ:* Miss State Univ, BS, 51; Auburn Univ, MS, 53; Tex A&M Univ, PhD(poultry breeding), 58. *Prof Exp:* From asst prof to assoc prof immunogenetics, 58-74, ASSOC PROF POULTRY SCI, TEX A&M UNIV, 74-, ASSOC PROF GENETICS, 80- *Concurrent Pos:* USPHS grant, 58- *Mem:* Poultry Sci Asn. *Res:* Poultry breeding; physiology. *Mailing Add:* Dept of Poultry Sci Tex A&M Univ College Station TX 77843

FANKBONER, PETER VAUGHN, b Mare Island, Calif, Feb 9, 38; m 67; c 1. INVERTEBRATE PHYSIOLOGY. *Educ:* Calif Polytech State Univ, BS, 64; Univ Pac, MS, 70; Univ Victoria, PhD(invert biol), 72. *Prof Exp:* Marine tech, Scripps Inst Oceanog, 64-65; ASSOC PROF BIOL, SIMON FRASER UNIV, BC, 72- *Concurrent Pos:* Lectr, Univ Victoria, BC, 71; researcher, Cambridge Univ, 71-72; vis prof, Stazione Zoologica, Napoli, 72. *Mem:* Marine Biol Asn UK; Western Soc Naturalists. *Res:* Physiology and functional ultrastructure of invertebrate nutrition with particular emphasis upon giant clams (Tridacnidae) and sea cucumbers; growth, recruitment and development in the commercial sea cucumber parastichopus californicus. *Mailing Add:* Dept Biol Sci Simon Fraser Univ Burnaby BC V5A 1S6 Can

FANN, HUOO-LONG, b Formosa, China, Mar 29, 31; m 62. NUCLEAR PHYSICS. *Educ:* Taiwan Norm Univ, BS, 56; Univ Md, PhD(physics), 64. *Prof Exp:* Asst prof, 64-68, ASSOC PROF PHYSICS, MERRIMACK COL, 68- *Mem:* Am Phys Soc. *Res:* Experimental nuclear physics concerning reaction theories for light nuclei. *Mailing Add:* Dept of Physics Merrimack Col North Andover MA 01845

FANNELOP, TORSTEIN KJELL, fluid mechanics, heat transfer, see previous edition

FANNIN, BOB M(EREDITH), b Midland, Tex, June 9, 22; m 47; c 3. ELECTRICAL ENGINEERING. *Educ:* Univ Tex, BA, 44, MS, 47, PhD(elec eng), 56. *Prof Exp:* Instr math, Arlington State Col, 47-48; res assoc sch elec eng, Cornell Univ, 48-51; res engr, Elec Eng Res Lab, Univ Tex, 51-56; assoc prof elec eng, Univ NMex, 56-58; assoc prof, 58-72, PROF ELEC ENG, UNIV TEX, AUSTIN, 72-, ENG COUNR, 77- *Concurrent Pos:* Mem comn II, US Nat Comt of Int Sci Radio Union. *Res:* Tropospheric radio wave program. *Mailing Add:* 4709 Crestway Austin TX 78731

FANNING, DELVIN SEYMOUR, b Copenhagen, NY, July 13, 31; m 58; c 3. SOIL SCIENCE. *Educ:* Cornell Univ, BS, 54, MS, 59; Univ Wis, PhD(soil sci), 64. *Prof Exp:* Soil scientist, Soil Conserv Serv, USDA, 53-63; asst prof, 64-69, assoc prof, 69-77, PROF SOIL MINERAL & CLASSIFICATION, UNIV MD, COLLEGE PARK, 77- *Concurrent Pos:* Guest prof, Soil Sci Inst, Munich Tech Univ, 71-72; res assoc, Tex A&M Univ, 79. *Mem:* AAAS; Am Soc Agron; Soil Sci Soc Am; Mineral Soc Am; Clay Minerals Soc. *Res:* Mineralogy of soils in relation to their genesis; clay mineral and x-ray spectroscopic analytical techniques; highly man-influenced soils; soil moisture regimes; acid sulfate weathering. *Mailing Add:* Dept of Agron Univ of Md College Park MD 20742

FANNING, JAMES COLLIER, b Atlanta, Ga, Nov 8, 31; m 57; c 3. INORGANIC CHEMISTRY. *Educ:* The Citadel, BS, 53; Ga Inst Technol, MS, 56, PhD(chem), 60. *Prof Exp:* Instr chem, Ga Inst Technol, 57-59; fel, Tulane Univ, 60-61; from asst prof to assoc prof, 61-71, PROF CHEM, CLEMSON UNIV, 71- *Concurrent Pos:* Vis lectr, Univ Ill, 66-67. *Mem:* Am Chem Soc. *Res:* Chemistry of transition metals. *Mailing Add:* Dept of Chem Clemson Univ Clemson SC 29631

FANNING, KENT ABRAM, b Lawton, Okla, May 22, 41; m 62; c 2. OCEANOGRAPHY, GEOCHEMISTRY. *Educ:* Colo Sch Mines, BS, 64; Univ RI, PhD(oceanog), 73. *Prof Exp:* Oceanog specialist marine chem, Univ RI, 64-66; asst prof, 73-77, ASSOC PROF MARINE SCI, UNIV S FLA, 77- *Concurrent Pos:* Prin investr, NSF, 74-78, Off Naval Res, 76-78, US Dept Energy, 78-81. *Mem:* Am Soc Limnol & Oceanog; Geochem Soc; Am Geophys Union. *Res:* Chemical oceanography; interstitial chemistry of sediments; transport processes in sediments; geochemistry of anoxic basins; marine geochemistry of radionuclides. *Mailing Add:* Dept Marine Sci 830 First St S St Petersburg FL 33701

FANO, ROBERT M(ARIO), b Torino, Italy, Nov 11, 17; nat US; m 49; c 3. EDUCATION, INFORMATION THEORY. *Educ:* Mass Inst Technol, SB, 41, ScD(elec eng), 47. *Prof Exp:* Asst elec eng, 41-43, instr, 43-44, mem staff, Radiation Lab, 44-46, res assoc, Res Lab Electronics, 46-47, from asst prof to prof elec commun, 47-62, dir, Proj MAC, 63-68, group leader, Lincoln Lab,

51-53, assoc head, Elec Eng Dept, head comput sci & eng, 71-74, FORD PROF ENG, MASS INST TECHNOL, 62- *Mem:* Nat Acad Sci; Nat Acad Eng; Am Acad Arts & Sci; Asn Comput Mach; fel Inst Elec & Electronics Engrs. *Res:* Microwave circuit components; network synthesis; transmission of information; computer sciences; theoretical limitations on the broad band matching of arbitrary impedances. *Mailing Add:* Dept of Elec Eng Mass Inst of Technol Cambridge MA 02139

FANO, UGO, b Torino, Italy, July 28, 12; nat US; m 39; c 2. THEORETICAL PHYSICS. *Educ:* Univ Turin, DSc(math), 34. *Hon Degrees:* Queen's Univ, Belfast, DSc, 78; Dr, Univ Pierre, Marie Curie, Paris, 79. *Prof Exp:* Ital Dept Educ Int fel, Univ Leipzig, 36-37; instr physics, Univ Rome, 38-39; res assoc, Washington Biophys Inst, 39-40; res fel genetics, Carnegie Inst, 40-41, res assoc, 42-43, physicist & mathematician, 43-45; consult & ballistician, Ballistics Res Lab, Aberdeen Proving Ground, 44-45; res assoc, Carnegie Inst, 46; physicist, Nat Bur Standards, 46-66; chmn dept, 72-74, PROF PHYSICS, UNIV CHICAGO, 66- *Concurrent Pos:* Prof lectr, George Washington Univ, 46-47 & 57-58 & Univ Calif, 58 & 68; vis prof, Cath Univ Am, 63-64. *Honors & Awards:* Rockefeller Pub Serv Award, 56-57. *Mem:* Nat Acad Sci; Am Acad Arts & Sci; Am Phys Soc; Radiation Res Soc. *Res:* Atomic physics; molecular physics; quantum physics; radiological physics; statistical mechanics; genetics; radiobiology. *Mailing Add:* Dept Physics Univ Chicago Chicago IL 60637

FANSHAWE, JOHN RICHARDSON, II, b Philadelphia, Pa, Oct 20, 06; m 37; c 3. PETROLEUM GEOLOGY. *Educ:* Princeton Univ, AB, 29, MA, 31, PhD(geol), 39; Univ Lille, Dr es Sc, 30. *Prof Exp:* Asst geol, Princeton Univ, 30-32; master physics & geol, Deerfield Acad, Mass, 33-35; instr geol, Williams Col, 35-39; geologist, Ohio Oil Co, 40-42; dist geologist & dist dir reserves, Dist IV, Petrol Admin War, 43-45; sr geologist, Gen Petrol Corp, 45-47; dist mgr & mgr explor, Seaboard Oil Co of Del, 47-51; consult geologist, 51-62; vpres & res mgr, Forest Cyprus Corp, 63-64; staff geologist, Mont Power Co, 64-71; CONSULT GEOLOGIST, 71- *Concurrent Pos:* Vis prof, Rocky Mt Col, 71-80. *Mem:* Geol Soc Am; Am Asn Petrol Geologists; Am Inst Prof Geologists. *Res:* Structural theory and interpretation; regional stratigraphy; application of geophysics to petrol exploration; geology of fossil fuels, and geothermal resources. *Mailing Add:* 3116 E MacDonald Dr Billings MT 59102

FANSHAWE, WILLIAM JOSEPH, b Brooklyn, NY, May 7, 26; m 52; c 8. ORGANIC CHEMISTRY. *Educ:* St John's Univ, BS, 50. *Prof Exp:* SR RES CHEMIST, LEDERLE LABS, AM CYANAMID CO, 51- *Mem:* Am Chem Soc. *Res:* Chemical synthesis of central nervous system and hypoglycemic agents. *Mailing Add:* Cyanamid Med Res Div Lederle Labs Pearl River NY 10965

FANSLER, BRADFORD S, b Clarksburg, WVa, Sept 12, 39. GENETICS. *Educ:* Drexel Inst Tech, BSc, 62; Ohio State Univ, MSc, 64; Univ Pa, PhD(biol), 72. *Prof Exp:* Res asst assoc, Inst Cancer Res, Fox Chase, Pa, 67-74; Damon Runyon-Walter Winchel fel, 74-76, RES ASST PROF PATH, THOMAS JEFFERSON UNIV, 76- *Concurrent Pos:* Adj res asst prof biochem, Thomas Jefferson Univ, 79- *Mem:* Am Soc Cell Biol; AAAS; Am Soc Photobiol; Sigma Xi. *Res:* Human DNA repair enzymology, especially DNAses; DNA repair defective human syndromes; aging; carcinogenesis and oncology; DNA polymerases and their functions. *Mailing Add:* Thomas Jefferson Univ Dept Path 1020 Locust St Philadelphia PA 19107

FANSLER, KEVIN SPAIN, b Thomas, Okla, Jan 13, 38; m 69; c 2. AEROSPACE ENGINEERING, PHYSICS. *Educ:* Okla State Univ, BS, 60; Univ Hawaii, MS, 64; Univ Del, PhD(aerospace eng), 74. *Prof Exp:* Physicist, naval ordnance lab, Silver Spring, MD, 60-62; res & teaching asst, Dept Physics, Univ Hawaii, 62-64; physicist, US Army Electronics Lab, Ft Monmouth, NJ, 65 & US Army Chem Lab, Edgewood Arsenal, Md, 65-67; RES PHYSICIST, BALLISTICS RES, US ARMY BALLISTIC RES LAB, ABERDEEN PROVING GROUND, 67- *Mem:* Am Inst Astronaut & Aeronaut; Am Defense Preparedness Asn. *Res:* Pressure fields about weapons; effect of muzzle blast on trajectory of projectiles; motions of projectiles within guntubes; electronic populations in nuclear blast and aerosol dispersion. *Mailing Add:* 501 Jamestown Ct Edgewood MD 21040

FANSLOW, DON J, b Yankton, SDak, Apr 16, 36. ZOOLOGY, ENDOCRINOLOGY. *Educ:* Yankton Col, BA, 58; Univ SDak, MA, 60; Ind Univ, PhD(zool), 65. *Prof Exp:* Assoc prof, 65-77, PROF BIOL, NORTHEASTERN ILL UNIV, 77- *Mem:* AAAS; Am Soc Zoologists; Sigma Xi; AAUP; Nat Asn Adv Health Prof. *Mailing Add:* Dept of Biol Northeastern Ill Univ Chicago IL 60625

FANSLOW, GLENN E, b Minot, NDak, Sept 5, 27; m 60; c 2. ELECTRICAL ENGINEERING, PHYSICS. *Educ:* NDak Agr Col, BS, 53; Iowa State Univ, MS, 57, PhD(elec eng), 62. *Prof Exp:* Elec engr, Gen Elec Co, 53-55; from instr to asst prof elec eng, 55-69, ASSOC PROF ELEC ENG, IOWA STATE UNIV, 70- *Concurrent Pos:* NSF grant, 64-65. *Mem:* Inst Elec & Electronics Engrs; Sigma Xi; Int Microwave Power Inst. *Res:* Applications of microwave power in the processing of materials; microwave generation, instrumentation and design. *Mailing Add:* Dept of Elec Eng Iowa State Univ Coover Hall Ames IA 50011

FANTA, GEORGE FREDERICK, b Chicago, Ill, Aug 30, 34; m 57; c 3. ORGANIC POLYMER CHEMISTRY. *Educ:* Purdue Univ, BS, 56; Univ Ill, PhD(org chem), 60. *Prof Exp:* Res chemist, Ethyl Corp, 60-63; RES CHEMIST, NORTHERN REGIONAL RES LAB, US DEPT AGR, 63- *Mem:* Am Chem Soc. *Res:* Chemistry of starch and starch derivatives; synthesis and properties of starch graft copolymers. *Mailing Add:* 1815 N University St Peoria IL 61604

FANTA, PAUL EDWARD, b Chicago, Ill, July 24, 21; m 49; c 2. ORGANIC CHEMISTRY. *Educ:* Univ Ill, BS, 42, Univ Rochester, PhD(chem), 46. *Prof Exp:* Asst chem, Univ Rochester, 42-44, asst, Manhattan Proj, 44-46, fel, 46-47; instr, Harvard Univ, 47-48; from asst prof to assoc prof, 48-61, PROF CHEM, ILL INST TECHNOL, 61- *Concurrent Pos:* NSF fel, Imp Col, Univ London, 56-57; exchange scholar, Czech Acad Sci, 63-64 & Acad Sci USSR, 70-71. *Mem:* AAAS; Am Chem Soc. *Res:* Nitrogen heterocycles; stereochemistry; chemical information. *Mailing Add:* Dept of Chem Ill Inst of Technol Chicago IL 60616

FANTE, RONALD LOUIS, b Philadelphia, Pa, Oct 27, 36; m 61; c 3. MICROWAVE PHYSICS. *Educ:* Univ Pa, BS, 58; Mass Inst Technol, MS, 60; Princeton Univ, PhD(elec eng), 63. *Prof Exp:* Sr physicist, Space Sci Inc, 63-64; staff scientist, Res & Adv Develop Div, Avco Corp, 64-70, sr consult scientist, Avco Systs Div, 70-71; sr scientist, US Air Force Cambridge Res Lab, 71-80; ASST VPRES, AVCO SYSTS DIV, 80- *Concurrent Pos:* Adj prof, Univ Mass, 73- *Honors & Awards:* Marcus O'Day Prize, US Air Force, 75. *Mem:* Inst Elec & Electronics Engrs; Optical Soc Am. *Res:* Propagation of microwaves and laser beams on turbulent media. *Mailing Add:* 26 Sherwood Rd Reading MA 01867

FANTINI, AMEDEO ALEXANDER, b New York, NY, Feb 11, 22; m 54; c 3. MICROBIAL GENETICS. *Educ:* NY Univ, BA, 52; Columbia Univ, MA, 59, PhD(genetics), 61. *Prof Exp:* Virol, Chas Pfizer & Co, 46-50; biologist cancer res, Lederle Labs Div, Am Cyanamid Co, 52-54, biologist mycol, 54-56, asst, Columbia Univ, 56-58; from res microbiologist to sr res microbiologist, 60-73, PRIN RES MICROBIOLOGIST, LEDERLE LABS DIV, AM CYANAMID CO, 73- *Mem:* Genetics Soc Am; Am Soc Microbiol; Soc Indust Microbiol; Sigma Xi. *Res:* Genetics and physiology of fungi and streptomyces in relation to increased yields of antibiotics; microbial fermentations; bioconversions. *Mailing Add:* Med Res Div Am Cyanamid Co Pearl River NY 10965

FANTZ, PAUL RICHARD, b St Louis, Mo, Mar 12, 41; m 65; c 2. PLANT SYSTEMATICS. *Educ:* Southern Ill Univ, BSEd, 64, MSEd, 69; Wash Univ, MA, 72; Univ Fla, PhD(bot), 77. *Prof Exp:* Sci teacher, Mehlville Sch Dist, St Louis, 64-72; sci coordr, 67-72; grad instr biol sci, Univ Fla, 74-76, adj asst prof bot, 77-78; res assoc taxonomy & hort, Fairchild Trop Garden, 78-79; ASST PROF HORT SCI, NC STATE UNIV, 79- *Mem:* Am Asn Plant Taxonomists; Bot Soc Am; AAAS; Am Inst Biol Sci; Sigma Xi. *Res:* Systematic biology of the Glycineae; monographic studies on Clitoria; systematics of horticultural plants. *Mailing Add:* Dept Hort Sci NC State Univ Box 5216 Raleigh NC 27650

FANUCCI, JEROME B(EN), b Glen Lyon, Pa, Oct 7, 24; m 52; c 2. AERODYNAMICS. *Educ:* Pa State Univ, BS, 44, MS, 52, PhD(aeronaut eng), 56. *Prof Exp:* Aeronaut engr, Eastern Aircraft Corp, NJ, 44-45 & Repub Aviation Corp, NY, 47-50; instr aeronaut eng, Pa State Univ, 52-56, asst prof, 56-57; res eng gas dynamics, Missile & Space Vehicle Div, Gen Elec Co, Pa, 57-59; sr res scientist, plasma & space appl physics, Radio Corp Am, NJ, 59-64; chmn dept, 64-81, PROF AEROSPACE ENG, WVA UNIV, 64- *Concurrent Pos:* Consult, RCA Corp, NJ, 64- *Res:* Heat transfer; Laminar incompressible and compressible boundary layer theory; mass addition in boundary layer; ablation of reentry vehicles; blast wave theory of conducting fluids in magnetic fields; magnetohydrodynamic alternating current power generation; low speed aerodynamics. *Mailing Add:* 1313 Anderson Ave Morgantown WV 26505

FARADAY, BRUCE (JOHN), b New York, NY, Dec 9, 19; m 50; c 5. SOLID STATE PHYSICS. *Educ:* Fordham Univ, AB, 40, MS, 47; Cath Univ, PhD, 63. *Prof Exp:* Solid state supvry physicist, 48-72, head semiconductor sect, 65-72, consult radiation effects, 72-74, head, Radiation Effects Br, 74-80, PROG MGR, US NAVAL RES LAB, 80- *Concurrent Pos:* Lectr, Prince George's Community Col, 60-79, Northern Va Community Col, 70-; lectr, Univ Md, 67-70; sci prog adminr, Off Naval Res, 70-71; prog adminr electronics support, Naval Mat Command, 73. *Mem:* Fel Am Phys Soc; Sigma Xi; NY Acad Sci. *Res:* Radiation effects in materials and devices; modification of materials by radiation; energy conversion; radar absorbing materials. *Mailing Add:* Solid State Div US Naval Res Lab Code 6604 Washington DC 20375

FARAGO, JOHN, b Budapest, Hungary, Sept 12, 17; nat US; m 45; c 2. POLYMER CHEMISTRY, APPLIED PSYCHOLOGY. *Educ:* Budapest Tech Univ, Dipl Chem Eng, 39, Dr Tech Sc, 47; Va Commonwealth Univ, MS, 68. *Prof Exp:* Asst to org chair, Univ of Sci, Budapest, 39-40; res supvr, Egger Pharmaceut, 40-43; res engr, Grab Textile Factory, Hungary, 44; asst to org chair, Univ of Sci, Budapest, 44-45; asst dir, Chem Inst City Budapest, 46-47; res assoc, George Washington Univ, 47-51, res prof, 52; from res chemist to sr res chemist, 52-60, res assoc, 60, res supvr, 61-70, RES FEL, TEXTILE FIBERS DEPT, E I DU PONT DE NEMOURS & CO, INC, 70- *Concurrent Pos:* Lectr, George Washington Univ, 48-52. *Mem:* Am Psychol Asn. *Res:* Structure, application and analysis of polymers; learning; motivation. *Mailing Add:* 10424 Iron Mill Rd Richmond VA 23235

FARAH, ALFRED EMIL, b Nazareth, Palestine, July 10, 14; m 71. MEDICAL RESEARCH, PHARMACOLOGY. *Educ:* Am Univ Beirut, BA, 37, MD, 40. *Prof Exp:* From instr to asst prof pharmacol, Am Univ Beirut, 40-45; vis lectr, Harvard Med Sch, 45-47; asst prof, Med Sch, Univ Wash, 47-50; assoc prof, State Univ of NY Upstate Med Ctr, 50-53, prof & chmn dept, 53-68; dir biol div, 68-71, chmn, Sterling-Winthrop Res Inst, 72-78; VPRES RES, STERLING DRUG INC, 72- *Concurrent Pos:* Res fel, Harvard Med Sch, 45-47; secy, State Univ NY, Albany Found, 75- *Mem:* Am Soc Pharmacol; Soc Exp Biol & Med; Cardiac Muscle Soc; hon mem Ger Pharmacol Soc. *Res:* Cardiac and kidney pharmacology; cardiac glycosides; mercurial diuretics; secretory activity of kidney; pharmacology of enzyme inhibitors; drug development. *Mailing Add:* Sterling Drug Inc Rensselaer NY 12144

FARAS, ANTHONY JAMES, b Chisholm, Minn, Dec 23, 42; m 66; c 2. VIROLOGY, MOLECULAR BIOLOGY. *Educ:* Univ Minn, BA, 65; Univ Colo, PhD(path), 70. *Prof Exp:* Fel microbiol & virol, Med Sch, Univ Calif, 70-73; asst prof, Med Sch, Univ Mich, 73-75; assoc prof, 75-78, PROF MICROBIOL & VIROL, MED SCH, UNIV MINN, 78- *Concurrent Pos:* Consult med oncol, Med Sch, Univ Minn, 75-; mem, Exp Virol Study Sect, NIH, 79-83; mem ad bd, Battell Int Conf Genetic Eng; assoc ed, Virol; founder, Molecular Genetics Inc, 79. *Mem:* Am Soc Microbiol; AAAS; Sigma Xi; NY Acad Sci. *Res:* Molecular mechanisms by which viruses, particularly RNA tumor viruses and papilloma viruses, replicate and induce disease. *Mailing Add:* Dept Microbiol Med Sch Univ Minn Minneapolis MN 55455

FARB, EDITH, b Philadelphia, Pa, Aug 7, 28; div; c 3. ORGANIC CHEMISTRY. *Educ:* Univ Pa, BA, 49, MS, 51; Bryn Mawr Col, PhD(phys & org chem), 58. *Prof Exp:* Asst chem, Rohm & Haas Co, 49-50; demonstr, Bryn Mawr col, 51-52; asst prof, Long Island Univ, 58-67; lectr, Hunter Col, 67-70; lit chemist, Texaco Develop Corp, 70-73; analyst, New York Dept Health Environ Health Serv, 73-76, analyst, Bur Lead Poisoning Control, 76-78, sr res assoc & chief, Environ Unit, 78-81. *Mem:* NY Acad Sci; Am Inst Chemists; AAAS; Am Chem Soc. *Res:* Aromatic substitution; physical properties of aromatic compounds; toxic materials; air contaminants. *Mailing Add:* 63-58 78th St Middle Village NY 11379

FARBER, ELLIOT, b New York, NY, May 7, 32. PHYSICS. *Educ:* Brooklyn Col, BS, 54; Columbia Univ, AM, 56; Stevens Inst Technol, PhD(physics), 66. *Prof Exp:* From jr physicist to physicist, Naval Res Lab, 53-54; microwave engr, Sylvania Elec Prods, Inc, 56; from instr to asst prof physics, Pratt Inst, 57-67; ASSOC PROF PHYSICS, NJ INST TECHNOL, 67- *Concurrent Pos:* Res assoc, Stevens Inst Technol, 65-67. *Mem:* Am Asn Physics Teachers. *Res:* Plasma physics. *Mailing Add:* Dept of Physics NJ Inst of Technol Newark NJ 07102

FARBER, EMMANUEL, b Toronto, Ont, Oct 19, 18; US citizen; m 42; c 1. BIOCHEMISTRY, PATHOLOGY. *Educ:* Univ Toronto, MD, 42; Univ Calif, Berkeley, PhD(biochem), 49; FRCP(C), 75. *Prof Exp:* Instr path, Sch Med, Tulane Univ, 50-51, asst prof path & lectr biochem, 51-55, assoc prof path & biochem, 55-59, Am Cancer Soc res prof, 59-61; prof path & chmn dept, Sch Med, Univ Pittsburgh, 61-70; Am Cancer Soc res prof path & biochem & sr investr, Fels Res Inst, Sch Med, Temple Univ, 70-74, prof path & biochem & dir, 74-75; PROF & CHMN DEPT OF PATH, UNIV TORONTO, 75- *Concurrent Pos:* Am Cancer Soc fel cancer res, Cook County Hosp, Ill, 49-50; mem adv comt smoking & health, Surgeon Gen, 62; chmn path B study sect, NIH, 62-66; consult, Div Chronic Dis, Dept Health, Educ & Welfare; vis prof, Middlesex Hosp, Med Sch, Univ London, 68-69; vpres, Asn Cancer Res, 71-72, bd dirs, 70-73. *Honors & Awards:* Second Annual Parke-Davis Award, 58; Fourth Annual Teplitz Mem Award, 61; Samuel R Noble Found Award, 76. *Mem:* Am Gastroenterol Asn; Am Soc Biol Chem; Am Chem Soc; Am Soc Exp Path; Am Asn Path & Bact. *Res:* Biochemical pathology; carcinogenesis, cytochemistry and histochemistry. *Mailing Add:* Dept of Path Univ of Toronto Toronto ON M5S 1A1 Can

FARBER, ERICH A(LEXANDER), b Vienna, Austria, Sept 7, 21; nat US; m 49; c 2. MECHANICAL ENGINEERING. *Educ:* Univ Mo, BS, 43, MS, 46; Univ Iowa, PhD(mech eng), 49. *Prof Exp:* Mach operator, Erving Paper Mills, Mass, 40-41; drafting & blueprinting, City of Columbia, Mo & Univ Mo, 41-43; instr physics & math, Univ Mo, 43-46; instr mech eng, Univ Iowa, 46-49; asst prof, Univ Wis, 49-54, assoc prof, 54; prof mech eng & res prof, 54-80, DISTINGUISHED SERV PROF, UNIV FLA, 80-, DIR SOLAR ENERGY LAB, 65- *Concurrent Pos:* Consult to various indust & govt agencies, 46- *Honors & Awards:* Worcester Reed Warner Gold Medal, Am Soc Mech Engrs. *Mem:* Fel Am Soc Mech Engrs; Am Soc Eng Educ; Solar Energy Soc. *Res:* Heat transfer; solar energy; fluid flow; thermodynamics; energy conversion. *Mailing Add:* Dept of Mech Eng Univ of Fla Gainesville FL 32601

FARBER, EUGENE M, b Buffalo, NY, July 24, 17; m 44; c 4. DERMATOLOGY. *Educ:* Oberlin Col, AB, 39; Univ Buffalo, MD, 43; Univ Minn, MS, 46. *Prof Exp:* Intern, Buffalo Gen Hosp, NY, 43-44; fel dermat & syphilol, Mayo Clin, 44-48, asst, 47-48; instr dermat, 48, asst prof path, 49-50, assoc prof dermat, 50-54, clin prof, 54-59, PROF DERMAT, SCH MED, STANFORD UNIV, 59-, CHMN DEPT, 50-, DIR PSORIASIS DAY CARE CTR, 73- *Concurrent Pos:* Consult, Surg Gen, US Air Force, 57-64; consult, Calif State Dept Pub Health, 63-; mem gen clin res ctr comt, NIH, 65; pres, Found Int Dermat Educ; pres, Orinoco Found; Howard Fox Mem lectr, NY Acad Med, 71; founder & ed, Int Psoriasis Bull, 73- *Honors & Awards:* Jose Maria Vargas Award, Cent Univ, Caracas, 72; Taub Int Mem Award Psoriasis Res, 74. *Mem:* Soc Exp Biol & Med; Am Soc Clin Invest; Soc Invest Dermat (vpres, 65); Am Acad Dermat; Am Asn Prof Dermat (secy, 67, pres, 68). *Res:* Peripheral vascular diseases; psoriasis; mycosis fungoides; tropical dermatology; epidemiology; cutaneous blood flow in various dermatoses and psoriasis. *Mailing Add:* Dept of Dermat Stanford Univ Sch of Med Stanford CA 94305

FARBER, FLORENCE EILEEN, b New York, NY, Aug 11, 39. MOLECULAR BIOLOGY, VIROLOGY. *Educ:* Mt Holyoke Col, AB, 61; Columbia Univ, PhD(biochem), 66. *Prof Exp:* Lectr cell physiol, Univ Calif, Berkeley, 68-69; asst prof physiol & biophys, Col Med, Univ Vt, 69-71; asst prof genetics & microbiol, Mt Holyoke Col, 71-72; res assoc, Baylor Col Med, 72-73, asst prof virol, 74-78; asst prof genetics & microbiol, Carleton Col, 78-81; ASST PROF MICROBIOL, UNIV NH, 81- *Concurrent Pos:* NSF fel, Free Univ Brussels, 66-68; Am Heart Asn sr fel, Univ Calif, Berkeley, 68-69; Am Cancer Soc grant, Col Med, Univ Vt, 70-71; Edmond de Rothschild Found int observer, Weizmann Inst Sci, 68. *Mem:* Am Soc Microbiol. *Res:* Mechanism of herpes simplex virus-induced malignancy; exogenous gene transfer mechanisms. *Mailing Add:* 514 E Second St Northfield MN 55057

FARBER, HERMAN, b New York, NY, Dec 3, 19; m 43; c 2. ELECTROPHYSICS. *Educ:* Brooklyn Col, BA, 41; Polytech Inst Brooklyn, MEE, 52. *Prof Exp:* Res engr, Bristol Co, 46-49; from asst to assoc prof elec eng, 54-60, ASSOC PROF ELECTROPHYSICS, POLYTECH INST NY, BROOKLYN, 60-, DIR EVE ELEC ENG STUDIES, 73-, DIR ELEC ENG LABS, 74- *Concurrent Pos:* Res chemist, Manhattan Proj, 43-46. *Mem:* NY Acad Sci; Am Asn Physics Teachers; sr mem Inst Elec & Electronics Engrs; AAAS; Sigma Xi. *Res:* Electromagnetic properties of materials, including the electric strength of solids and liquids at microwave frequencies; cryogenic engineering; plasma diagnostics; chemical synthesis using discharge and plasmas; relaxation phenomena at microwave frequencies. *Mailing Add:* Polytech Inst of NY Brooklyn NY 11201

FARBER, HUGH ARTHUR, b Muskegon, Mich, Oct 6, 33; m 54; c 3. ORGANIC CHEMISTRY. *Educ:* Mich State Univ, BSCh, 56; Northwestern Univ, PhD(org chem), 60. *Prof Exp:* Res org chemist, 59-66, proj leader, 66-68, group leader res & develop, 68-76, mgr environ affairs, 76-80, SR MGR ENVIRON AFFAIRS, DOW CHEM CO, 80- *Mem:* Am Chem Soc; Sigma Xi. *Res:* Preparation of monomer, polymer modification and agricultural chemicals; study of reaction mechanisms; chlorinated solvents; ecology of chlorinated solvents; toxicology and environmental effects research; product stewardship; government regulation and legislative liaison/management. *Mailing Add:* 2030 Dow Ctr Midland MI 48640

FARBER, JAY PAUL, b New York, NY, Jan 25, 42; m 68; c 1. PHYSIOLOGY. *Educ:* City Col New York, BS, 63; State Univ NY, Buffalo, PhD(physiol), 69. *Prof Exp:* Fel respiratory physiol, Dartmouth Med Sch, 69-71; asst prof, Univ Iowa, 71-78; ASSOC PROF PHYSIOL, UNIV OKLA HEALTH SCI CTR, 78- *Concurrent Pos:* Res grant, NIH, 72-, res career develop award, 80-84. *Mem:* Am Physiol Soc; Am Col Sports Med; AAAS; Soc Neurosci. *Res:* Respiratory physiology particularly the control of breathing and its development. *Mailing Add:* Dept Physiol & Biophysics PO Box 26901 Oklahoma City OK 73190

FARBER, JORGE, b Buenos Aires, Arg, Feb 29, 48; US citizen; m 77; c 1. NEUROPHYSIOLOGY, SLEEP. *Educ:* City Col NY, BA, 70, PhD(psychol), 75. *Prof Exp:* Adj lectr psychol, City Col NY, 72-74; NIMH fel, Albert Einstein Col Med, 74-76 & Montefiore Hosp & Med Ctr, 76-77; ASST PROF PSYCHIAT, HEALTH SCI CTR, UNIV TEX, 77- *Concurrent Pos:* Res fel, Alfred P Sloan Found, 77-80. *Honors & Awards:* Gardner Murphy Award; Henry L Moses Award; Olto Peterson Award. *Mem:* NY Acad Sci; Soc Neurosci; AAAS; Asn Psychophysiol Study of Sleep. *Res:* Neurophysiological and neurochemical mechanisms involved in the mediation of the sleep and wake state; the role of rapid eye movement sleep in the maturation of the central nervous system in the newborn. *Mailing Add:* Dept Psychiat Univ Tex Med Sch Dallas TX 75235

FARBER, JOSEPH, b Newark, NJ, June 1, 24; m 51; c 2. ENERGY CONVERSION, FLUID PHYSICS. *Educ:* City Col New York, BS, 45; Univ Wis, PhD(phys chem), 51. *Prof Exp:* From res engr to sr thermodyn engr, Convair Div, Gen Dynamics Corp, Calif, 51-55; mgr real gas eng, Gen Elec Co, 55-56, mgr aerophys sect, Space Sci Lab, 56-64, mgr adv systs eng, 64-67; chief engr, Space & Reentry Systs Div, Philco-Ford Corp, 67-69, prog mgr, Mid-Course Surv Systs, 69-70; pres & gen mgr, KMS Technol Ctr, Div KMS Industs, Inc, 70-73; consult & lectr, J F Assocs, 73-75; PRES, SOLAR RES SYSTS, 75- *Concurrent Pos:* Consult & lectr solar energy, J F Assocs & Univ Calif, Irvine, 73- *Mem:* Am Chem Soc; Am Phys Soc; Am Inst Aeronaut & Astronaut; Int Solar Energy Soc; Sigma Xi. *Res:* Systems engineering; fluid dynamics; space science; aerophysics; magnetohydrodynamics; solar thermal power generation; solar plastic heaters. *Mailing Add:* 1605 Sherrington Pl Suite Y212 Newport Beach CA 92660

FARBER, MARILYN DIANE, b Los Angeles, Calif, Apr 21, 45. EPIDEMIOLOGY, PUBLIC HEALTH. *Educ:* Univ Calif, Los Angeles, BA, 67, MPH, 71, DrPH(epidemiol), 77. *Prof Exp:* Surv supvr hypertension res, Univ Calif, Los Angeles, Sch Pub Health, 73-77; instr, 77-78, ASST PROF EPIDEMIOL, UNIV ILL MED CTR SCH PUB HEALTH, 78- *Mem:* Am Pub Health Asn; Soc Epidemiol Res; Am Heart Asn; Int Soc & Fedn Cardiol. *Res:* Epidemiology of cardiovascular diseases, especially hypertension; cancer, especially cancer of the breast; sickle cell anemia; sickle cell retinopathy; compliance studies in hypertension; social epidemiology. *Mailing Add:* Univ Ill Med Ctr PO Box 6998 Chicago IL 60680

FARBER, MILTON, b Los Angeles, Calif, Oct 6, 16; m 42; c 3. PHYSICAL CHEMISTRY. *Educ:* Univ Calif, BS, 38; Univ Minn, MS, 39; Calif Western Univ, PhD, 76. *Prof Exp:* Chief chem engr, Colloidal Prod, 41-42; area supvr, Ky Ord Works, 42-43; sr res engr, Manhattan Proj, 43-46; sr res engr, Jet Propulsion Lab, Calif Inst Technol, 46-55; assoc dir res, Aerojet-Gen Corp Div, Gen Tire & Rubber Co, 55-57, head propulsion lab, Hughes Tool Co, 57-59; vpres, Maremont Corp, Rocket Power, Inc, 59-67; PRES, SPACE SCI, INC, 67- *Mem:* Am Chem Soc; Am Inst Physics; Am Chem Soc; The Chem Soc; Am Inst Aeronaut & Astronaut. *Res:* Thermodynamics; separation of isotopes; thermal diffusion; mass spectroscopy; kinetics; air pollution. *Mailing Add:* Space Sci Inc 135 W Maple Ave Monrovia CA 91016

FARBER, MORTON SHELDON, microwave physics, see previous edition

FARBER, PAUL ALAN, b Brooklyn, NY, Sept 13, 38; m 60; c 2. MICROBIOLOGY, DENTISTRY. *Educ:* Univ Mich, AB, 60, DDS, 62; Univ Rochester, PhD(microbiol), 67. *Prof Exp:* Asst prof microbiol, 67-72, assoc prof, 72-78, PROF PATH, SCH DENT, TEMPLE UNIV, 78-; CLIN PROF ORAL MED, DENT COL, NY UNIV, 80- *Concurrent Pos:* NIH spec fel, Nat Inst Dent Res, 70-71; guest worker, Albert Einstein Med Ctr, 75-76. *Mem:* AAAS; Am Soc Microbiol; Am Asn Pathologists; Int Asn Dent Res. *Res:* Periodontal disease; immunology of bacterial and virus infection. *Mailing Add:* Dept of Path Temple Univ Sch of Dent Philadelphia PA 19140

FARBER, PHILLIP ANDREW, b Wilkes-Barre, Pa, Sept 19, 34; m 65, 74; c 3. HUMAN GENETICS, CYTOGENETICS. *Educ:* King's Col, BS, 56; Boston Col, MS, 58; Cath Univ Am, PhD(biol), 63. *Prof Exp:* Asst biol, Boston Col, 56-57; asst, St Louis Univ, 58-59; asst, Cath Univ Am, 60-62; asst instr, Georgetown Univ, 62-63; res biologist, Lab Perinatal Physiol, NIH, 63-64; res instr phys med & rehab, Med Ctr, NY Univ, 64-66; PROF BIOL, BLOOMSBURG STATE COL, 66- *Concurrent Pos:* USPHS res grant, 65; consult cytogenetics, Geisinger Med Ctr, 67- *Mem:* Nat Soc Histotechnol; Am Soc Human Genetics; Teratology Soc; Sigma Xi; NY Acad Sci. *Res:* Human and mammalian cytogenetics; histology. *Mailing Add:* Dept Biol & Allied Health Sci Bloomsburg State Col Bloomsburg PA 17815

FARBER, ROBERT JAMES, b Oak Ridge, Tenn, May 2, 46. ATMOSPHERIC CHEMISTRY. *Educ:* Yale Univ, BS, 68; Univ Wash, MS, 71, PhD(aerosol chem), 75. *Prof Exp:* Res asst, Univ Wash, 68-72; mgr environ sci, STD Res Corp, 75-76; SR RES SCIENTIST, SOUTHERN CALIF EDISON CO, 76- *Mem:* Air Pollution Control Asn; Am Meterol Soc. *Res:* Air pollution, meteorology, cloud physics and weather modification as these affect the environment; quantifying the measurement and monitoring of visibility impairment and sky coloration phenomena; chemical formations of major constituents in particulate smog in the Los Angeles area. *Mailing Add:* Southern Calif Edison Co 2244 Walnut Grove Ave Rosemead CA 91770

FARBER, ROSANN ALEXANDER, b Charlotte, NC, Nov 21, 44; m 73; c 1. GENETICS, CELL BIOLOGY. *Educ:* Oberlin Col, AB, 66; Univ Wash, PhD(genetics), 73. *Prof Exp:* Fel genetics, Nat Inst Med Res, Mill Hill, London, 73-75 & Children's Hosp Med Ctr, Boston, 75-77; ASST PROF MICROBIOL & GENETICS, UNIV CHICAGO, 77- *Concurrent Pos:* Fel Jane Coffin Childs Mem Fund Med Res, 73-75; researcher, Career Develop Award, NIH, 81-86. *Mem:* AAAS; Am Soc Human Genetics; Am Soc Cell Biol. *Res:* Somatic cell genetics; control of chromosome replication in cell hybrids; expression of recessive mutations in cultured mammalian cells; repeated DNA sequences in the mouse genoma. *Mailing Add:* Dept of Microbiol 920 E 58th St Chicago IL 60637

FARBER, SAUL JOSEPH, b New York, NY, Feb 11, 18; m 49; c 2. MEDICINE. *Educ:* NY Univ, AB, 38, MD, 42; Am Bd Internal Med, dipl, 55. *Prof Exp:* From instr to prof med, 49-66, actg dean, Sch Med, 63-66 & 79-81, Nathan Friedman Prof Med, 65-75, PROF MED & CHMN DEPT, SCH MED, NY UNIV & DIR MED, UNIV HOSP & BELLEVUE HOSP, 66-, FREDERICK KING PROF INTERNAL MED & DEAN FAC AFFAIRS, 78- *Concurrent Pos:* mem bd dirs, NY Heart Asn, 63-, pres, 73-75; mem, Nat Adv Res Resources Coun, 67-71; mem adv coun, New York Kidney Dis Inst, 68-; mem adv comt, Inter-Soc Comn Heart Dis Resources, 68-; bd mem, Am Bd Internal Med, 68-, mem exec comt, 72-, chmn, 73-; mem med adv comt, Hosp Corp Task Force, New York, 69-71; mem bd dirs, Russell Sage Inst Path, 70-; mem med adv bd, Found Study Wilson's Dis, 71-; mem & trustee, Riverside Res Inst, 71-; mem, Irma T Hirschl Charitable Trust Sci Adv Comt, 72-; chmn comt resource requirements Vet Admin health care syst, Nat Res Coun, 74-; ed, Am J Med Sci; mem adv comt, Spaciality & Geog Distribution Physicians, Inst Med, 74-; mem, Health Adv Coun, NY State, 75; mem adv comt, Program for Long Term Care, Robert Johnson Found, 79-; trustee, Riverside Res Inst, 79-; mem, Comn on Nursing, 80-; mem bd trustees, Sackler Sch Med, 77-; mem bd gov, Tel Aviv Univ, 79- *Mem:* Inst of Med of Nat Acad Sci; Am Soc Clin Invest (secy-treas, 57-60); Harvey Soc (treas, 63-67, vpres, 67-68, pres, 68-69); master Am Col Physicians; Asn Prof Med (pres, 73-74). *Res:* Physiological and biochemical clinical investigation related to human disease. *Mailing Add:* NY Univ Sch Med 550 First Ave New York NY 10016

FARBER, SERGIO JULIO, b Argentina, Jan 30, 38; m 60; c 2. ORGANIC CHEMISTRY, CLINICAL PATHOLOGY. *Educ:* Univ Buenos Aires, MS, 62, PhD(org chem), 65. *Prof Exp:* Teaching asst org chem, Univ Buenos Aires, 62-64, instr, 64-66; res chemist, Univ Calif, Santa Barbara, 67-68; sr res chemist, Calbiochem, Inc, 68-70; lab dir, Nuclear Dynamics, Inc, El Monte, 70-72; res assoc biochem procedures, 72-74, biochemist, 74-80, CHIEF BIOCHEMIST, CEDARS-SINAI MED CTR, LOS ANGELES, 80- *Mem:* Can Soc Clin Chemists; NY Acad Sci; Am Asn Clin Chem; Nat Acad Clin Biochem. *Res:* Current methodology in clinical chemistry with emphasis in immunoassays and enzymology. *Mailing Add:* 475 Ladera St Monterey Park CA 91754

FARBER, SEYMOUR MORGAN, b Buffalo, NY, June 3, 12; m 40; c 3. THORACIC DISEASES & PULMONARY DISEASES. *Educ:* Univ Buffalo, BA, 31; Harvard Univ, MD, 39. *Prof Exp:* From instr to prof, 42-62, vchancellor pub prog & continuing educ, 73-78, CLIN PROF MED, SCH MED, UNIV CALIF, SAN FRANCISCO, 62- *Concurrent Pos:* In-chg tuberc & chest serv, San Francisco Gen Hosp, 45-62; lectr, Sch Pub Health, Univ Calif, Berkeley, 48-60, spec asst to pres, 64-; spec consult, Nat Cancer Inst, 58-60; nat consult to Surgeon Gen, US Air Force, 62-68; mem President's Comt Status of Women, 62-63. *Mem:* Am Col Chest Physicians (pres elect, 59, pres, 59-60); Am Col Cardiol; AMA; Am Fedn Clin Res; NY Acad Sci. *Res:* Cancer of lung; pulmonary cytology; chemotherapy of lung cancer; chemotherapy of tuberculosis pulmonary pathophysiology; continuing education in medicine and the health sciences. *Mailing Add:* Med Ctr Univ Calif San Francisco CA 94122

FARBER, THEODORE MYLES, b New York, NY, July 20, 35; m 60; c 3. PHARMACOLOGY, TOXICOLOGY. *Educ:* Long Island Univ, BS, 57; Med Col Va, PhD(parmacol), 62. *Prof Exp:* Instr pharmacol, Med Col Va, 60-61; asst prof, George Washington Univ Med Sch, 61-65; pharmacologist, 65-73, sr res pharmacologist, 73-78, SUPVRY PHARMACOLOGIST, FOOD & DRUG ADMIN, 78- *Concurrent Pos:* Lectr, Howard Univ Med Sch, 75-, US Dept Agr Grad Sch, 73- & NIH Eve Sch, 76- *Mem:* Sigma Xi; Soc Toxicol; Am Soc Pharmacol & Exp Therapeut; Soc Exp Biol & Med. *Res:* Drug metabolism; drug interactions; biochemical pharmacology and toxicology of drugs; food additives and veterinary drugs. *Mailing Add:* Food Animal Additives Eval Br 200 C St SW Washington DC 20850

FARBMAN, ALBERT IRVING, b Boston, Mass, Aug 25, 34; div; c 3. HISTOLOGY, CYTOLOGY. *Educ:* Harvard Univ, AB, 55, DMD, 59; NY Univ, MS, 61, PhD(basic med sci), 64. *Prof Exp:* Instr anat, Sch Med, NY Univ, 62-64; from asst prof to assoc prof, 64-72, PROF ANAT, NORTHWESTERN UNIV, 72-, ASSOC DEAN GRAD SCH, 75- *Concurrent Pos:* Res career develop award, Nat Inst Dent Res, 66-71; vis scientist, Strangeways Res Lab, Cambridge, 68-69; mem bd dir, McGaw Med Ctr, 75- *Mem:* AAAS; Am Asn Anat; Am Soc Cell Biol. *Res:* Cytodifferentiation of taste buds; keratinization of oral epithelium and epidermis; differentiation of olfactory mucosa. *Mailing Add:* Dept of Anat Northwestern Univ Chicago IL 60611

FARCASIU, DAN, b Carei, Romania, Aug 22, 37; US citizen; m 60; c 1. ORGANIC CHEMISTRY. *Educ:* Polytech Inst, Bucharest, BS & MS, 59; Polytech Inst Timisoara, Romania, PhD(org chem), 68. *Prof Exp:* Sr researcher, Inst Atomic Physics, Romania, 64-69; res assoc, City Univ New York, 69-71; res assoc, Princeton Univ, 71-72, instr, 72-73; mem staff org chem, Squibb Inst Med Res, 73-74; STAFF CHEMIST, CORP RES LABS, EXXON RES & ENG CO, 74- *Mem:* Am Chem Soc; Sigma Xi. *Res:* Physical organic chemistry, especially organic reaction mechanisms; synthetic organic chemistry. *Mailing Add:* Corp Res Labs PO Box 45 Linden NJ 07036

FARDO, ROBERT D, b Ambridge, Pa, Dec 8, 36. APPLIED STATISTICS. *Educ:* Geneva Col, BS, 60; Ariz State Univ, MA, 62. *Prof Exp:* Mathematician, 62-68, SR MATHEMATICIAN APPL STATIST, WESTINGHOUSE ELEC CORP, 69- *Mem:* Am Statist Asn. *Res:* Response surface studies; regression; data analysis and interpretation; Monte Carlo methods. *Mailing Add:* Westinghouse Res & Develop Ctr Churchill Boro Pittsburgh PA 15235

FAREL, PAUL BERTRAND, b Camden, NJ, Sept 29, 44; m 67. NEUROPHYSIOLOGY. *Educ:* Univ Calif, Berkeley, AB, 66; Univ Calif, Los Angeles, MA, 67, PhD(psychol), 70. *Prof Exp:* Instr, 72-73, asst prof, 73-79, ASSOC PROF PHYSIOL, SCH MED, UNIV NC, CHAPEL HILL, 79- *Concurrent Pos:* Nat Inst Ment Health fel, Univ Calif, Irvine, 70-72; NSF res grant, Univ NC, Chapel Hill, 74-77 & 77-80; NIH res grant, 80- *Mem:* AAAS; Soc Neurosci. *Res:* Development and regeneration of specific neuronal connections in spinal cord. *Mailing Add:* Dept of Physiol Univ of NC Sch of Med Chapel Hill NC 27514

FAREWELL, JOHN P, b Worcester, Mass, May 29, 42; m 68; c 2. PAPER CHEMISTRY, PHYSICAL CHEMISTRY. *Educ:* State Univ NY Col Plattsburgh, BSEd, 64; State Univ NY Buffalo, PhD(chem), 69. *Prof Exp:* Res scientist, 68-72, res engr, Bleached Papers, 72-76; SR RES SCIENTIST, AM CYANAMID CORP, 76- *Honors & Awards:* Hugh Camp Award Singular Achievement in Res, Union Camp Corp, 73. *Mem:* Am Chem Soc; Tech Asn Pulp & Paper Indust. *Res:* Physical chemistry of polymers; properties of paper; process modeling and optimization; process stability; emulsion stability. *Mailing Add:* Am Cyanamid Corp 1937 N Main St Stamford CT 06906

FARHADIEH, ROUYENTAN, b Tehran, Iran, Nov 3, 44; m 76; c 3. FLUID MECHANICS, HEAT TRANSFER. *Educ:* Univ Ariz, BS, 68; Stanford Univ, MS, 70; Northwestern Univ, PhD(mech eng), 74. *Prof Exp:* asst mech engr, 75-81, MECH ENG, REACTOR ANAL & SAFETY, ARGONNE NAT LAB, 81- *Concurrent Pos:* Fel, Argonne Nat Lab, 74-75. *Mem:* Am Soc Mech Eng; Am Soc Nuclear Eng; Sigma Xi. *Res:* Natural laminar or turbulent convection in direct or internally heated liquid layers; melting and freezing coupled with convection in solid-liquid system of different density; double diffusive convection; high temperature studies. *Mailing Add:* RAS 208 Argonne Nat Lab 9700 S Cass Ave Argonne IL 60439

FARHATAZIZ, b Amritsar, India, Dec 19, 32; Pakistan citizen; m 70; c 3. PHYSICAL CHEMISTRY, RADIATION CHEMISTRY. *Educ:* Panjab Univ, Pakistan, BSc, 53, MSc, 54; Cambridge Univ, PhD(chem), 59. *Prof Exp:* Lectr pharmaceut chem, Panjab Univ, 54-56, lectr chem, 59-60; sr sci officer, Pakistan AEC, 60-68, prin sci officer, 68-76; asst prof specialist, Univ Notre Dame, 74-76; asst prof, 77-81, ASSOC PROF CHEM, TEX WOMAN'S UNIV, 81- *Concurrent Pos:* Columbo Plan fel, UK Atomic Energy Authority, 61-62; fel Radiation Lab, Univ Notre Dame, 64-67, 70-74; prin investr, Robert A Welch Found, Tex Woman's Univ, 78- *Mem:* Am Chem Soc; AAAS; Radiation Res Soc. *Res:* Primary processes in radiation chemistry; fast chemical kinetics; chemical and physical effects at high pressures up to 7000 atmospheres and low temperatures down to 4 degress K. *Mailing Add:* Dept of Chem Tex Woman's Univ Denton TX 76204

FARHI, LEON ELIE, b Cairo, Egypt, Oct 9, 23; US citizen; m 49; c 2. CARDIOPULMONARY PHYSIOLOGY, ENVIRONMENTAL PHYSIOLOGY. *Educ:* Am Univ Beirut, BSc, 40; Univ St Joseph, Lebanon, MD, 47. *Prof Exp:* Resident, Hadassah Univ Hosp, Israel, 50-52; res fel, Trudeau Sanatorium, 53; res fel physiol, Univ Rochester, 53-54; res fel & asst physician, Sch Med, Johns Hopkins Univ, 54-55; instr physiol & pulmonary dis, Hebrew Univ, Israel, 56-58; from asst prof to assoc prof, 58-66, PROF PHYSIOL, STATE UNIV NY BUFFALO, 66- *Concurrent Pos:* Vis prof, Univ Fribourg & NSF sr fel, 65-66; consult, Erie County Health Dept & USPHS. *Mem:* Am Physiol Soc; Aerospace Med Asn; Undersea Med Soc. *Res:* Pulmonary physiology and physiopathology; environmental and cardio-respiratory physiology. *Mailing Add:* Dept of Physiol State Univ of NY Buffalo NY 14214

FARIELLO, RUGGERO G, b Turin, Italy, Sept 27, 42; m 67; c 3. NEUROLOGY, CLINICAL NEUROPHYSIOLOGY. *Educ:* Univ Turin, MD, 66, dipl neurol, 69; Univ Aix-Marselle, dipl EEG, 73. *Prof Exp:* Assoc prof EEG, Med Sch, Univ Turin, 73-74; asst prof neurol, Med Sci Ctr, Univ Wis-Madison, 76-77, assoc prof, 77-80; ASSOC PROF NEUROL, HEALTH SCI CTR, UNIV TEX, SAN ANTONIO, 80- *Concurrent Pos:* Fel, Nat Ctr Sci Res, Marseille, France, 72-73, Can Med Res Coun, Clarke Inst Psychiat, Toronto, 74-75 & Can Muscular Dystrophy Assoc Hosp for Sick Children,

75-76. *Honors & Awards:* H H Jasper Prize, Can Soc Electroencephalographers & Electromyographers, 76. *Mem:* AAAS; NY Acad Sci; Soc Neurosci; Am Acad Neurol; Am Epilepsy Asn. *Res:* Neurophysiology and neuropharmacology of epilepsy, extrapyramidal and limbic system; development and testing of new drugs for treatment of convulsions, movement disorders and dimentia. *Mailing Add:* Health Sci Ctr 7400 Merton Minter Blvd San Antonio TX 78284

FARIES, DILLARD WAYNE, b Mooreland, Okla, Sept 28, 41; m 65; c 3. QUANTUM OPTICS. *Educ:* Rice Univ, BA, 63; Univ Calif, Berkeley, PhD(physics), 69. *Prof Exp:* Geophys trainee, Shell Oil Co, 63; res asst physics, Univ Calif, Berkeley, 65-69; from asst prof to assoc prof, 69-81, PROF PHYSICS & CHMN DEPT, WHEATON COL, 81- *Mem:* Am Asn Physics Teachers; Am Sci Affiliation. *Res:* Nonlinear interaction of electromagnetic fields with matter. *Mailing Add:* Dept Physics Wheaton Col Wheaton IL 60187

FARINA, JOSEPH PETER, b Queens, NY, May 11, 31; m 55; c 4. MICROBIAL PHYSIOLOGY, HEALTH SCIENCES. *Educ:* St John's Col, BS, 53; St John's Col, NY, MS, 58, MSE, 60, PhD(microbiol), 67. *Prof Exp:* Teacher, NY High Sch, 58-67; assoc prof, 67-71, spec asst to dean, Sch Allied Health & Natural Sci, 74-75, PROF BIOL, UNIV LOWELL, 71-, DIR MED TECHNOL MAJ, 70-, CHMN DEPT CLIN LAB SCI, COL HEALTH PROFESSIONS, 74- *Concurrent Pos:* Sr lab technician, Mercy Hosp, NY, 58-63, instr, 62-67, instr radiol physics, 67-; instr radiol physics, Peninsular Gen Hosp, NY, 65-66; chmn prof educ comt, Am Cancer Soc, 73-75; admin internship allied health professions, State Univ NY Albany, 74-75. *Mem:* AAAS; Am Soc Zoologists; NY Acad Sci; Soc Protozoologists; Am Inst Biol Sci. *Res:* Axenic cultivation and nutritional requirements of Blepharisma, a pink ciliate. *Mailing Add:* 7 Singlefoot Rd Chelmsford MA 01824

FARINA, PETER R, b New York, NY, Apr 30, 46; m 68; c 2. BIO-ORGANIC CHEMISTRY. *Educ:* Hofstra Univ, BS, 67; State Univ NY Buffalo, PhD(org chem), 72. *Prof Exp:* Fel, Pa State Univ, 71-73; res scientist, Corp Res Lab, Union Carbide Corp, 74-78, group leader med prod div, 78-79; SR PRIN BIOCHEMIST, BOEHRINGER INGELHEIM, 80- *Mem:* Am Chem Soc. *Res:* Synthesis of biologically active molecules; isotopic and non-isotopic immunoassay; elucidation of mechanism of drug action; development of bioanalytical methods for pharmacokinetic studies. *Mailing Add:* RFD 1 Sunset Dr S Salem NY 10560

FARINA, ROBERT DONALD, b Schenectady, NY, Sept 29, 34; m 66; c 2. BIOINORGANIC CHEMISTRY. *Educ:* Rensselaer Polytech Inst, BChE, 57; Union Col, MS, 63; State Univ NY Buffalo, PhD(chem), 68. *Prof Exp:* Engr, Stauffer Chem Co, 57-60; test engr, Knolls Atomic Power Lab, Gen Elec Co, 60-63; fels chem, Univ Calif, 67-69 & Univ Utah, 69; PROF CHEM, W KY UNIV, 69- *Mem:* Am Chem Soc; Am Inst Chem Eng. *Res:* Kinetic studies of fast reactions in solution; coordination chemistry of transition metal complexes; kinetic studies of metalloenzymes in biological systems. *Mailing Add:* Dept of Chem Western Ky Univ Bowling Green KY 42101

FARINA, THOMAS EDWARD, b Brooklyn, NY, Dec 9, 41; m 66; c 2. ORGANIC CHEMISTRY. *Educ:* St Bernadine of Siena Col, BS, 64; State Univ NY Buffalo, PhD(org chem), 70. *Prof Exp:* Res scientist, Union Camp Corp, 69-78; ORG CHEMIST, GLYCO CHEM, INC, 78- *Mem:* Am Chem Soc; Am Oil Chemist's Soc. *Res:* Fatty acid; rosin acid; hydantoin chemistry. *Mailing Add:* Glyco Chem Inc PO Box 3187 Williamsport PA 17701

FARIS, DONALD GEORGE, genetics, plant physiology, see previous edition

FARIS, JOHN JAY, b Grandview, Wash, Nov 7, 21; m 42; c 4. PHYSICS. *Educ:* Reed Col, BA, 43; Univ Wash, PhD(physics), 51. *Prof Exp:* Assoc prof physics, Pac Univ, 50-54; from asst prof to prof, Colo State Univ, 54-68; chmn dept, 68-80, PROF PHYSICS, UNIV OF WIS-STOUT, 68- *Mem:* Am Phys Soc; Am Asn Physics Teachers. *Res:* Secondary emission of electrons; electroretinagram; microwaves; magnetism. *Mailing Add:* Dept of Physics Univ of Wis-Stout Menomonie WI 54751

FARIS, SAM RUSSELL, b Moore, Okla, Nov 5, 17; m 42; c 5. PHYSICAL CHEMISTRY, ANALYTICAL CHEMISTRY. *Educ:* Univ Okla, BS, 42, MS, 46, PhD(chem), 49. *Prof Exp:* Sr res technologist, 49-54, RES ASSOC, FIELD RES LAB, MOBIL RES & DEVELOP CORP, 54- *Mem:* Fel AAAS; Am Chem Soc; NY Acad Sci. *Res:* Electrochemistry; electrokinetics. *Mailing Add:* Mobil Res & Develop Corp Field Res Lab PO Box 900 Dallas TX 75221

FARIS, WILLIAM GUIGNARD, b Montreal, Que, Can, Nov 22, 39; US citizen. MATHEMATICAL PHYSICS. *Educ:* Univ Wash, BA, 60; Princeton Univ, PhD(math), 65. *Prof Exp:* Asst prof math, Cornell Univ, 64-70; mathematician, Battelle Inst, Geneva, Switz, 70-74; assoc prof, 74-80, PROF MATH, UNIV ARIZ, 80- *Mem:* Am Math Soc; Int Asn Math Physics. *Res:* Operator theory and quantum mechanics; probability and statistical mechanics. *Mailing Add:* Dept Math Univ Ariz Tucson AZ 85721

FARISH, DONALD JAMES, ethology, population genetics, see previous edition

FARISON, JAMES BLAIR, b McClure, Ohio, May 26, 38; m 61; c 2. SYSTEMS ENGINEERING, BIOMEDICAL ENGINEERING. *Educ:* Univ Toledo, BS, 60; Stanford Univ, MS, 61, PhD(elec eng), 64. *Prof Exp:* From asst prof to assoc prof elec eng, 64-74, asst dean grad studies, 69-70, actg dean, 70-71, dean, 71-80, PROF ELEC ENG, UNIV TOLEDO, 74- *Concurrent Pos:* Consult, Med Col Ohio, 81- *Honors & Awards:* Outstanding Young Elec Engr Award, Eta Kappa Nu Nat Elec Eng Hon, 71; Young Engr of the Year Award, Ohio Soc Prof Engrs, 73. *Mem:* Sr mem Inst Elec & Electronics Engrs; Am Soc Eng Educ; sr mem Instrument Soc Am; Nat Soc Prof Engrs. *Res:* Systems analysis and design; biomedical imaging; communication and control; random processes; discrete-time systems; system identification. *Mailing Add:* Col of Eng Univ of Toledo Toledo OH 43606

FARISS, BRUCE LINDSAY, b Allisonia, Va, July 22, 34; c 5. ENDOCRINOLOGY, INTERNAL MEDICINE. *Educ:* Roanoke Col, BS, 57; Univ Va, MD, 61; Am Bd Internal Med, dipl endocrinol metabolism. *Prof Exp:* Gen med officer, US Army Hosp, Ft Monroe, Va, 62-63; chief endocrine serv, Madigan Army Med Ctr, Tacoma, Wash, 68-76; consult endocrinol & internal med, Hq US Army Med Command, Europe, 76-79; CHIEF, DEPT CLIN INVEST & DIR, ENDOCRINE FEL PROG, MADIGAN ARMY MED CTR, TACOMA, 79- *Concurrent Pos:* Intern, Univ Va Hosp, 61-62; resident internal med, Brooke Gen Hosp, Ft Sam Houston, Tex, 63-66; fel endocrinol metab res unit, Univ Calif, San Francisco, 66-68. *Honors & Awards:* Meritorious Serv Medal, Off Surgeon Gen, 77. *Mem:* Am Fedn Clin Res; Endocrine Soc; Am Diabetes Asn; Am Col Physicians. *Res:* Endocrinology and metabolism; carbohydrate metabolism; adrenal gland; testicular function; pineal gland. *Mailing Add:* Hq US Army Med Command Europe APO New York 09102 Fed Repub of Ger

FARISS, ROBERT HARDY, b St Louis, Mo, May 31, 28; m 50; c 5. CHEMICAL ENGINEERING. *Educ:* Wash Univ, BS, 50; Mass Inst Technol, MS, 51, DSc(chem eng), 54. *Prof Exp:* Chem engr, Mallinckrodt Chem Works, 54-59; chem engr, 59-67, TECHNOL DIR, MONSANTO CO, 67- *Mem:* Am Inst Chem Engrs; Am Chem Soc; Soc Plastics Engrs. *Res:* Thermodynamics of phase equilibria; kinetics of heterogeneous catalysis; applied mathematics; optimization; statistics. *Mailing Add:* Monsanto Co 190 Grochmal Ave Indian Orchard MA 01151

FARKAS, DANIEL FREDERICK, b Boston, Mass, June 20, 33; m 59; c 2. FOOD DEHYDRATION, FOOD PRESERVATION. *Educ:* Mass Inst Technol, BS, 54, MS, 55, PhD(food sci), 60. *Prof Exp:* Staff scientist food & flavor, Arthur D Little, Inc, 60-62; asst prof food processing, Cornell Univ, 62-66; head food eng develop, Western Regional Res Ctr, USDA, 67-79; CHAIR & PROF FOOD SCI, DEPT FOOD SCI & HUMAN NUTRIT, UNIV DEL, 80- *Concurrent Pos:* Assoc prof, Dept Nutrit Sci, Univ Calif, Berkeley, 71-79. *Mem:* Inst Food Technologists; Am Chem Soc; Am Inst Chem Eng; NY Acad Sci; AAAS. *Res:* Food process engineering design; dehydration; heat transfer; biofermentations technology. *Mailing Add:* Dept Food Sci & Human Nutrit Alison Hall Univ Del Newark DE 19711

FARKAS, EUGENE, b Melvindale, Mich, Dec 11, 26; m 56; c 3. ORGANIC CHEMISTRY, MEDICINAL CHEMISTRY. *Educ:* Wayne State Univ, BS, 49, PhD(org chem), 52. *Prof Exp:* Res assoc, Mass Inst Technol, 52-53; res assoc, Wayne State Univ, 53-54; sr scientist, 54-70, sr scientist, Anal Develop Metab, 70-80, SR SCIENTIST PROCESS RES, LILLY RES LABS, 80- *Mem:* Am Chem Soc; Royal Soc Chem; Am Pharm Asn. *Res:* Steroids; alkaloids and natural products; organic synthesis. *Mailing Add:* Anal Develop Lilly Res Lab Indianapolis IN 46205

FARKAS, HERSHEL M, b New York, NY, Dec 2, 39; m 60; c 3. MATHEMATICS. *Educ:* Yeshiva Univ, BS, 61, MS, 63, PhD(math), 65. *Prof Exp:* Res assoc math, Belfer Grad Sch Sci, Yeshiva Univ, 65-66; asst prof, Johns Hopkins Univ, 66-68; assoc prof, State Univ NY, Stoney Brook, prof math, 71-79; PROF MATH, UNIV MD, COLLEGE PARK, 79- *Concurrent Pos:* Sloan Found fel, 70-72. *Mem:* Am Math Soc. *Res:* Moduli of compact Riemann surfaces; theory of theta functions. *Mailing Add:* Dept of Math Univ Md College Park MD 20740

FARKAS, LESLIE GABRIEL, b Ruzomberok, Czech, Apr 18, 15; Can citizen; m 71; c 1. PLASTIC SURGERY. *Educ:* Univ Bratislava, MD, 41; Charles Univ, Prague, CSc, 59, DSc(plastic surg), 68; FRCS(C), 73. *Prof Exp:* Resident surg, Mil Hosp & Field Serv, Slovakia, 41-45; resident plastic surg, Charles Univ, Prague, 45-48, from asst prof to assoc prof, 48-68; asst prof, 70-78, assoc prof, Plastic Surg, 78-80, EMER PROF PLASTIC SURG & SPEC LECTR, DEPT SURG, UNIV TORONTO, 80- *Concurrent Pos:* Dep dir, Plastic Surg Res Lab & dir, Div Congenital Anomalies, Acad Sci, Prague, 63-68; clin fel, Div Plastic Surg, Hosp Sick Children, Toronto, 68-69, res fel, Div Exp Surg, 69-70, asst scientist, Res Inst, 70-77, sr scientist, 77-, dir, Plastic Surg Res Lab, Res Inst, 70-; consult, Cleft Palate Prog, Univ Iowa, 75-78; consult, Res Inst, Univ Toronto, 80- *Mem:* Am Soc Plastic & Reconstruct Surgeons; Can Soc Plastic Surgeons; Plastic Surg Res Coun; Can Asn Anatomists; Biomat Soc Can. *Res:* Experimental plastic surgery; tendon repair; quantitative anatomical and functional assessment; anatomy and growth of experimentally reconstructed urethra; quantitative surface anatomy of growing, healthy, congenitally and traumatically damaged face; use of anthropometry in evaluation of morphological changes in patients with congenital anomalies of the cranio-orbito-facial complex; application of newly established rules about facial proportions in study of facial syndromes. *Mailing Add:* Dept of Surg 555 University Ave Toronto ON M5G 1X8 Can

FARKAS, WALTER ROBERT, b New York, NY, June 30, 33; m 56; c 2. BIOCHEMISTRY. *Educ:* City Col New York, BS, 55; Duke Univ, PhD(biochem), 60. *Prof Exp:* Res asst biochem, Duke Univ, 55-60; res assoc, Sch Med, NY Univ, 60-63; fel hemat, Col Physicians & Surgeons, Columbia Univ, 63-66; from asst prof to assoc prof, 66-75, PROF MED BIOL, MEM RES CTR, UNIV TENN, 75-, ACTG HEAD DEPT, 81- *Concurrent Pos:* Life Ins Med Res Fund grant, 67-70; NIH grant, 68-75; Am Cancer Soc res grant, 77-80; NIH res grants, 75-78, 79-82 & 81-, USDA grant, 80-82. *Mem:* Am Chem Soc; Am Soc Biol Chemists; Am Col Toxicologists. *Res:* Saturrine gout; biosynthesis of lysine; control mechanisms in hemoglobin biosynthesis; biological effects of metals; transfer RNA of erythroid cells; discovery of guanylation of tRNA; discovery that lead depolymerizes RNA. *Mailing Add:* Mem Res Ctr Univ of Tenn Knoxville TN 37920

FARKAS-HIMSLEY, HANNAH, b Moscow, Russia, May 3, 18; Can citizen; m 40; c 2. MEDICAL MICROBIOLOGY, ONCOLOGY. *Educ:* Hebrew Univ, Israel, MSc, 40, PhD(bact), 46. *Prof Exp:* Asst bact, Hadassah Med Sch, Hebrew Univ, 49-53; attache sci, Israel Embassy, Eng, 53-55; asst bact, Hadassah Med Sch, Hebrew Univ, 55-57; fel, Univ Toronto, 58-59, grant, 59, asst prof, 59-62, assoc prof microbiol, Fac Med, 62-80; ASSOC SCIENTIST, MT SINAI HOSP, 81- *Concurrent Pos:* Res grants, Nat Res Coun Can, 60-

61, Med Res Coun Can, 61-70, Can Nat Health, 67-69, 73-75, WHO, 72-73 & Nat Cancer Inst, 75-78; vis prof, Lautenberg Ctr Gen & Tumor Immunol, Hebrew Univ Med Sch, Jerusalem, 78-79. *Mem:* Am Soc Microbiol; NY Acad Sci; Can Soc Microbiol; Can Pub Health Asn; Royal Inst Gt Brit. *Res:* Streptomycin and penicillin resistance; Vibriocin production by Vibrio comma, mode of action; halogen resistant bacteria; microassay in-vitro for recognition of enterotoxins; bacterial proteinaceous products as cytotoxic agents of neoplasia; diagnosis of pseudomallei; survey of staphylococci on Easter Island; bacteriocins in diagnsosis of neoplasia. *Mailing Add:* Dept of Microbiol & Parasitol Univ of Toronto Fac of Med Toronto ON M5S 1A1 Can

FARKASS, IMRE, b Budapest, Hungary, Sept 26, 19; nat US; m 51. APPLIED PHYSICS, TELECOMMUNICATIONS. *Educ:* Budapest Tech Univ, Dipl, 42. *Prof Exp:* Asst prof physics, Budapest Tech Univ, 42-46, lectr, Inst Physics, 47-49, assoc head, Vacuum Res Lab, 50-56; head dept math & physics, Agr Univ Budapest, 54-56; sr physicist, Nat Res Corp, 57-60; dir appl physics dept, Ilikon Corp, 61-65; MEM TECH STAFF, BELL LABS, 65- *Concurrent Pos:* Invited lectr, Mass Inst Technol, 64, Northeastern Univ, 65 & Johns Hopkins Univ, 69. *Mem:* Am Phys Soc. *Res:* Applied physics; vacuum physics and technology. *Mailing Add:* Bell Labs Whippany NJ 07981

FARLEE, RODNEY DALE, b Albany, Ore, Oct 9, 52. SPECTROSCOPY, NUCLEAR MAGNETIC RESONANCE. *Educ:* Univ Idaho, BS, 74; Univ Ill, Urbana, 79. *Prof Exp:* CHEMIST, CENT RES & DEVELOP DEPT, E I DU PONT DE NEMOURS & CO, INC, 79- *Mem:* Am Chem Soc; Sigma Xi. *Res:* Spectroscopic, particularly nuclear magnetic resonance; studies of solid materials, including polymers, fossil fuels and catalysts. *Mailing Add:* Cent Res Dept Exp Sta Bldg 328 E I du Pont de Nemours & Co Inc Wilmington DE 19898

FARLEY, BELMONT GREENLEE, b Cape Girardeau, Mo, Dec 29, 20; m 53; c 3. BIOPHYSICS, INFORMATION SCIENCE. *Educ:* Univ Md, BS, 41; Yale Univ, MS, 46, PhD(physics), 48. *Prof Exp:* Asst math, Mass Inst Technol, 41-42, mem staff, Radiation Lab, 42-45; instr physics, Yale Univ, 47-48; mem tech staff, Bell Labs, 48-53; mem staff, Lincoln Labs, Mass Inst Technol, 53-64; assoc prof biophys, Johnson Found, Sch Med, Univ Pa, 64-70; assoc prof, 70-73, PROF INFO SCI, TEMPLE UNIV, 73- *Mem:* Am Math Soc; Am Physiol Soc; Am Phys Soc; Inst Elec & Electronics Engrs; Biophys Soc. *Res:* Theoretical and experimental neurophysiology. *Mailing Add:* Dept of Info Sci Temple Univ Philadelphia PA 19122

FARLEY, DONALD T, JR, b New York, NY, Oct 26, 33; m 56; c 3. IONOSPHERIC PHYSICS, PLASMA PHYSICS. *Educ:* Cornell Univ, BEngPhys, 56, PhD(ionospheric physics), 60. *Prof Exp:* NATO fel ionospheric physics, Cambridge Univ, 59-60; docent, Chalmers Univ Technol, Sweden, 60-61; physicist, Jicamarca Radar Observ, Lima, Peru, US Nat Bur Standards, 61-64, dir, 64-67; PROF ELEC ENG, CORNELL UNIV, 67- *Concurrent Pos:* Assoc ed, Rev Geophys & Space Physics, 63-69 & J Geophys Res, 74-77 & Radio Sci, 76-78; mem comn III & IV, Int Sci Radio Union, Exec Comt Comn IV, 66-69. *Honors & Awards:* Nat Bur Standards Award, 63; Environ Sci Serv Admin Award, 64; US Dept Commerce Gold Medal, 67. *Mem:* Am Geophys Union; Inst Elec & Electronics Engrs; AAAS. *Res:* Scattering of radio waves from thermal fluctuations in a plasma; plasma instabilities in the ionosphere. *Mailing Add:* Dept of Elec Eng Cornell Univ Ithaca NY 14850

FARLEY, EUGENE SHEDDEN, JR, b Upland Borough, Pa, Feb 6, 27; m 55; c 4. MEDICINE, PUBLIC HEALTH. *Educ:* Swarthmore Col, BA, 50; Univ Rochester, MD, 54; Johns Hopkins Univ, MPH, 67. *Prof Exp:* Intern, Philadelphia Gen Hosp, 54-55; resident gen pract, Med Ctr, Univ Colo, 55-56; asst instr prev med, Med Col, Cornell Univ, 56-58; resident internal med, Univ Vt & De Goesbriand Hosp, 58-59; pvt pract, 59-66; resident fel pub health, Sch Hyg & Pub Health, Johns Hopkins Univ, 66-67; from assoc prof to prof family med, Sch Med, Univ Rochester, 67-78, dir family med prog, 67-78; PROF & CHMN DEPT FAMILY MED, UNIV COLO MED CTR, 78- *Mem:* Am Acad Gen Practice; Am Pub Health Asn; Asn Teachers Prev Med; Soc Teachers Family Med. *Res:* Development and implementation of systems of primary care; use of ancillaries who allow provision of more efficient and effective medical care to those needing it; built-in research potential to all primary care practices. *Mailing Add:* Dept Family Med Univ Colo Med Ctr Denver CO 80220

FARLEY, JAMES D, b Olney, Ill, Sept 28, 38; m 65; c 2. PHYTOPATHOLOGY. *Educ:* Ill Wesleyan Univ, BS, 61; Mich State Univ, MS, 63, PhD(plant path), 68. *Prof Exp:* Asst res plant path, Univ Calif, Berkeley, 68-69; ASSOC PROF PLANT PATH, OHIO STATE UNIV, 69- *Mem:* Am Phytopath Soc. *Res:* Soil borne diseases; tomato breeding. *Mailing Add:* Dept of Plant Path Ohio State Univ Columbus OH 43210

FARLEY, JOHN, b Eng, Apr 23, 36; Can citizen; m 60; c 4. HISTORY OF BIOLOGY. *Educ:* Univ Sheffield, BSc, 59; Univ Western Ont, MSc, 61; Univ Man, PhD(zool), 64. *Prof Exp:* From asst prof to assoc prof, 64-78, PROF BIOL, DALHOUSIE UNIV, 78- *Concurrent Pos:* Res fel hist of sci, Harvard Univ, 70-71 & 77-78; Can Coun fel, 71- *Mem:* Hist of Sci Soc; Am Soc Hist of Med; Can Soc Hist & Philos Sci. *Res:* History of parasitology and tropical medicine; spontaneous generation controversy; nineteenth century views on reproduction. *Mailing Add:* Dept of Biol Dalhousie Univ Halifax NS B3H 3J5 Can

FARLEY, REUBEN WILLIAM, b Richmond, Va, Sept 21, 40; m 81. MATHEMATICS. *Educ:* Randolph-Macon Col, BS, 61; Univ Tenn, MA, 65, PhD(math), 68. *Prof Exp:* Instr math, Randolph-Macon Col, 61-63; asst prof math, Mary Washington Col, 66-67; assoc prof, 68-81, PROF MATH SCI, VA COMMONWEALTH UNIV, 81- *Mem:* Am Math Soc. *Res:* Topological semigroups. *Mailing Add:* 901 W Franklin St Richmond VA 23284

FARLEY, ROGER DEAN, b Jefferson, Iowa, Feb 2, 35; m 61; c 1. NEUROPHYSIOLOGY. *Educ:* Univ Northern Iowa, BA, 57; Univ Iowa, MS, 62; Univ Calif, Santa Barbara, PhD(insect neurophysiol), 66. *Prof Exp:* NIH fel, Tufts Univ, 66-67; asst prof, 67-74, ASSOC PROF ZOOL, UNIV CALIF, RIVERSIDE, 74- *Mem:* Am Soc Zoologists; Am Inst Biol Sci; AAAS. *Res:* Behavior and sensory physiology of desert scorpions and solpugids. *Mailing Add:* Dept of Biol Univ of Calif Riverside CA 92521

FARLEY, THOMAS ALBERT, b Washington, DC, Feb 10, 33; m 58; c 2. ENGINEERING DESIGN. *Educ:* George Washington Univ, BS, 54; Mass Inst Technol, PhD(physics), 59. *Prof Exp:* Mem tech staff, Space Technol Labs, Thompson-Ramo-Wooldridge, Inc, 59-61; res geophysicist, Inst Geophys & Planetary Physics, Univ Calif, Los Angeles, 61-73; mgr, Technol Ctr, 73-77, mgr advan develop, 76-81, PRIN SCIENTIST, XEROX CORP, 81- *Mem:* Am Phys Soc. *Mailing Add:* 287 Brooksboro Dr Webster NY 14580

FARLIN, STANLEY DEAN, animal nutrition, see previous edition

FARLOW, STANLEY JEROME, b Emmetsburg, Iowa, Mar 7, 37; m 67. APPLIED MATHEMATICS. *Educ:* Iowa State Univ, BS, 59; Univ Iowa, MS, 62; Ore State Univ, PhD(math), 67. *Prof Exp:* Mathematician, NIH, 62-68; ASST PROF MATH, UNIV MAINE, ORONO, 68- *Mem:* Am Math Soc; Math Asn Am. *Res:* Mathematical modeling of biological systems; partial differential equations; control theory; numerical analysis; computer systems. *Mailing Add:* 104 Forest Ave Orono ME 04473

FARMANFARMAIAN, ALLAHVERDI, b Teheran, Iran, June 10, 29; m 58; c 2. PHYSIOLOGY. *Educ:* Reed Col, BA, 52; Stanford Univ, MA, 55, PhD(physiol), 59. *Prof Exp:* Assoc prof physiol, Pahlavi Univ, Iran, 61-66 & Univ Tehran, 66-67; assoc prof, 72, chmn sect physiol, 74-75, chmn & grad dir, 79-81, PROF PHYSIOL, RUTGERS UNIV, 72- *Concurrent Pos:* Mem, Marine Biol Lab Corp, 63; US Agency Internat Develop fel, 63; prin investr, NSF grant, 66-69, coordr, 68-69; sr investr, Marine Biol Lab, Woods Hole, Mass, 66-71; coordr, NIH grant, 69-71; assoc ed, J Exp Zool, 74-; NSF grant, 74-78; Sci Educ Admin grant, USDA, 79-81. *Mem:* Fel AAAS; Am Physiol Soc; Am Gen Physiol; Am Soc Zool. *Res:* Comparative approach to the mechanisms of membrane transport; nutrition and ecological physiology of marine animals. *Mailing Add:* Dept of Physiol Nelson Lab Rutgers Univ New Brunswick NJ 08903

FARMER, CHARLES HENRY, b Littlefield, Tex, July 17, 39; wid; c 1. MATHEMATICS. *Educ:* Southwest Tex State Univ, BS, 63; Univ Tex, Austin, MS, 66, PhD(math), 68. *Prof Exp:* Teaching assoc math, Univ Tex, Austin, 63-67; res scientist, Tracor, Inc, Austin, 66-68; PROF MATH, UNIV TULSA, 68- *Concurrent Pos:* Consult commun theory, Midwestern Instruments, 68-69; consult statist, Ark Crime Comn, 69-73; consult biomath, Warren Res Found, Tulsa, Okla, 69-71. *Mem:* Am Inst Decision Sci. *Res:* Digital filtering; nonlinear programming; numerical analysis. *Mailing Add:* Dept Math Univ Tulsa 600 S College Ave Tulsa OK 74104

FARMER, CROFTON BERNARD, b Rumney, Wales. INFRARED SPECTROSCOPY, RADIATION TRANSPORT. *Educ:* Univ London, BSc, 52, PhD(physics), 68. *Prof Exp:* Head dept infrared res, EMI Electronics Eng, 60-67; mem tech staff, Space Sci Div, 67-70, mgr planetary atmospheres sect, 70-73, SR MEM TECH STAFF, SPACE SCI DIV, JET PROPULSION LAB, CALIF INST TECHNOL, 73- *Concurrent Pos:* Mem, Adv Comt, NASA, 68-81; prin investr, Viking, 76, Mars Atmospheric Water Exp, Spacelab, 69-78 & 78-; vis prof, Div Geol & Planetary Sci, Calif Inst Technol, 78-81; mem Int Comn Planetary Atmospheres, 80- *Mem:* Am Astron Soc; AAAS. *Res:* Remote sensing of planetary atmospheres; radiative transfer; infrared spectroscopy; spectroscopy of earth's upper atmosphere; history and present distribution of water on Mars. *Mailing Add:* Jet Propulsion Lab 4800 Grove Dr Pasadena CA 91103

FARMER, DONALD JACKSON, b Morenci, Ariz, Apr 7, 25; m 49; c 3. PHYSICS. *Educ:* Univ Wash, BS, 50, PhD(physics), 54. *Prof Exp:* Res assoc, Univ Wash, 54-55; mem tech staff, Ramo-Wooldridge Corp, 55-58; sr staff, Space Tech Labs, Inc, 58-60, assoc dept mgr, 59-60; mgr quantum electronics, Gen Tech Corp, 60-63, from vpres to pres, 63-69; from vpres to sr vpres, Tracor, Inc, 64-71; consult, 71-74; PRES, EXTEK MICROSYSTS, INC, 74- *Mem:* Am Phys Soc. *Res:* Atomic and nuclear physics; upper atmosphere physics; radio propagation; physical electronics. *Mailing Add:* 6955 Hayvenhurst Ave Van Nuys CA 91406

FARMER, FLORENCE AMELIA, b Ste Anne de Bellevue, Que, May 10, 18. NUTRITION, PHYSIOLOGY. *Educ:* McGill Univ, BHS, 39, MSc, 44, PhD(nutrit), 47. *Prof Exp:* Asst prof nutrit, MacDonald Col, McGill Univ, 48-59; lectr home sci, Women's Christian Col, Univ Madras, 59-64; PROF NUTRIT, MACDONALD COL, MCGILL UNIV, 64- *Mem:* Can Dietetic Asn; Can Home Econ Asn; Can Inst Food Sci & Technol; Nutrit Soc Can. *Res:* Nutrient analysis of meat and fish from the Arctic, incorporation of fish protein concentrate in Canadian foods; bioavailability of folic acid; flavor testing of irradiated chicken; flavor testing of paper mill effluent-treated fish. *Mailing Add:* Sch of Food Sci Macdonald Col Box 276 Ste Anne de Bellevue PQ H9X 1C0 Can

FARMER, FRANKLIN HARRIS, b Boothbay Harbor, Maine, Dec 18, 38; m 62; c 3. REMOTE SENSING, PHYCOLOGY. *Educ:* Tufts Univ, BS, 60; Va Polytech Inst & State Univ, MS, 65, PhD(food sci), 76. *Prof Exp:* MICROBIOLOGIST, LANGLEY RES CTR, NASA, 65- *Mem:* Am Soc Microbiol. *Res:* Remote sensing of phytoplankton concentration and composition from aircraft and satellites using active and passive sensors; in situ sensor development for same parameters; high temperature resistance of bacterial spores. *Mailing Add:* Mail Stop 272 Langley Res Ctr NASA Hampton VA 23665

FARMER, GEORGE THOMAS, JR, geology, paleontology, see previous edition

FARMER, JAMES BERNARD, b Liverpool, Eng, Dec 13, 28. PHYSICAL CHEMISTRY. *Educ:* Univ Liverpool, BSc, 50, PhD(chem), 53. *Prof Exp:* Fel chem, Nat Res Coun Can, 53-55 & Laval Univ, 55-56; fel, 56-57, from asst prof to assoc prof, 57-69, PROF CHEM, UNIV BC, 69- *Mem:* Am Phys Soc; The Chem Soc. *Res:* Electron spin resonance spectrometry. *Mailing Add:* Dept of Chem Univ of BC Vancouver Can

FARMER, JAMES LEE, b South Gate, Calif, Aug 8, 38; m 67; c 5. BIOCHEMISTRY. *Educ:* Calif Inst Technol, BS, 60; Brown Univ, PhD(biol), 66. *Prof Exp:* Instr biophys, Med Ctr, Univ Colo, 66-68; asst prof, 69-78, ASSOC PROF ZOOL, BRIGHAM YOUNG UNIV, 78- *Mem:* AAAS; Fedn Am Scientists; Genetics Soc Am. *Res:* Biochemical genetics of Drosophila. *Mailing Add:* Dept of Zool Brigham Young Univ Provo UT 84602

FARMER, JOHN HENRY, b Killeen, Tex, May 16, 33; m 63; c 3. STATISTICS. *Educ:* Southwest Tex State Univ, BA, 59; St Mary's Univ, MS, 66; Tex A&M Univ, PhD(statist), 71. *Prof Exp:* Teacher math, Dickinson Independent Sch Dist, 59-60 & Army Educ Ctr, Ft Hood, Tex, 60-61; statistician, Sch Aerospace Med, Brooks AFB, 61-67; res statistician, Environ Protection Agency, 71-73; MATH STATISTICIAN, NAT CTR TOXICOL RES, 73-; asst prof, 73-80, PROF BIOMET, MED SCH, UNIV ARK, 80- *Mem:* Am Statist Asn; Sigma Xi. *Res:* Applications of multivariate statistical methods and bioassay techniques to toxicological data. *Mailing Add:* Biomet Dept Nat Ctr Toxicol Res Jefferson AR 72079

FARMER, JOHN JAMES, III, b Newnan, Ga, Aug 12, 43; m 68; c 2. MICROBIOLOGY. *Educ:* Ga Inst Technol, BS, 65; Univ Ga, PhD(microbiol), 68. *Prof Exp:* Sr asst scientist, NIH, 68-70; asst prof microbiol, Univ Ala, Tuscaloosa, 70-72; DIR, NAT LAB ENTERIC BACTERIOPHAGE TYPING, CTR DIS CONTROL, USPHS, 72- *Concurrent Pos:* Attend microbiologist, Druid City Hosp, 70-72; mem, Int Pseudomonas Typing Comt, 71-; adj assoc prof, Col Arts & Sci, Univ Ala, 72- & Sch Pub Health, Univ NC, 73-; mem, Int Comt, Vibrio, & Enteric Bacteriophage Typing. *Honors & Awards:* Bausch & Lomb Sci Medal, 61; Chem Rubber Co Award, 66. *Mem:* AAAS; Am Soc Microbiol. *Res:* Epidemiology of hospital-acquired infections; medical and clinical microbiology; microbial ecology of the hospital and other environments; marine bacteria which cause human disease, enterobacteriaceae and vibrionaceae. *Mailing Add:* Bldg 1 Rm B-341 Ctr Dis Control USPHS 1600 Clifton Rd Atlanta GA 30333

FARMER, JOHN NEVILLE, parasitology, see previous edition

FARMER, JOHN WILLIAM, b Springfield, Mo, May 2, 47; m 72; c 2. PHYSICS. *Educ:* Kans State Univ, PhD(physics), 74. *Prof Exp:* Fel, Argonne Nat Lab, 74-76; res physicist, Univ Dayton, 76-80; SR RES SCIENTIST GEN PHYSICS, RES REACTOR, UNIV MO, 80- *Concurrent Pos:* Prin investr, Res Corp Grant, 81- *Mem:* Am Phys Soc. *Res:* Defects in solids, in particular semiconductors; electron irradiation induced; neutron irradiation induced; intrinsic. *Mailing Add:* Res Reactor Univ Mo Columbia MO 65211

FARMER, LARRY BERT, b Greenville, SC, Jan 5, 36; m 60; c 3. ORGANIC CHEMISTRY. *Educ:* Wofford Col, BS, 58; Univ Tenn, PhD(org chem), 63. *Prof Exp:* Res chemist, 64-65, sr res chemist, Chem Div, 65-70, sr res chemist, Res Div, 70-77, dept mgr, Res Serv Div, 77-80, PROJ MGR, RES SERV DIV, MILLIKEN RES CORP, 80- *Mem:* Am Chem Soc; Am Asn Textile Chemists & Colorists; Am Soc Testing & Mat. *Res:* Organic syntheses; natural products; textile fibers. *Mailing Add:* Milliken Res Corp, M-700 PO Box 1927 Spartanburg SC 29304

FARMER, PATRICK STEWART, b Saskatoon, Sask, Jan 27, 42; m 67. MEDICINAL CHEMISTRY. *Educ:* Univ Sask, BSP, 62, MSc, 64; Portsmouth Col Tech, Eng, PhD(pharm & chem), 68. *Prof Exp:* Asst prof, 68-75, ASSOC PROF PHARMACEUT CHEM, COL PHARM, DALHOUSIE UNIV, 75- *Mem:* Chem Inst Can; Acad Pharmaceut Sci; Am Asn Cols Pharm; NY Acad Sci. *Res:* Synthesis of potential antiradiation compounds; indomethacin analogs for study of mode of action. *Mailing Add:* Col of Pharm Dalhousie Univ Halifax NS B3H 3J5 Can

FARMER, ROBERT E, JR, b Rehoboth Beach, Del, Dec 3, 30; m 60; c 2. FORESTRY, PLANT PHYSIOLOGY. *Educ:* Univ Mich, BSF, 53, MF, 57, PhD(forestry), 61. *Prof Exp:* Res forester, Southern Hardwoods Lab, US Forest Serv, 61-67; plant physiologist, Tenn Valley Authority, 67-81; ASSOC PROF, SCH FORESTRY, LAKEHEAD UNIV, ONT, 81- *Mem:* AAAS; Ecol Soc Am; Soc Am Foresters; Am Soc Plant Physiol. *Res:* Genecology of plants in the North American forest. *Mailing Add:* Lakehead Univ Thunder Bay ON 37828 P7B 5E1 Can

FARMER, SUSAN WALKER, endocrinology, see previous edition

FARMER, T ALBERT, JR, b Smithfield, NC, Jan 28, 32; m 56; c 4. ENDOCRINOLOGY. *Educ:* Univ NC, BS, 53, MD, 57. *Prof Exp:* From asst prof to prof, Med Col, Univ Ala, Birmingham, 65-72, from asst dean to exec assoc dean, 65-68; dean col med, Univ Tenn, Memphis, 72-75, chancellor, Ctr Health Sci & vpres health affairs, Univ Tenn Syst, 75-80; CHANCELLOR, UNIV MD, BALTIMORE, 81- *Concurrent Pos:* NIH fel endocrinol, 59-60; ward physician, Walson Army Hosp, Ft Dix, NJ, 61-63. *Mem:* fel Am Col Physicians. *Res:* Endocrinology of the adrenal gland; medical education; internal medicine. *Mailing Add:* Sch Med Univ Baltimore 655 W Baltimore St Baltimore MD 21201

FARMER, THOMAS WOHLSEN, b Lancaster, Pa, Sept 18, 14; m 41; c 2. NEUROLOGY. *Educ:* Harvard Univ, AB, 35, MD, 41; Duke Univ, MA, 37. *Prof Exp:* From asst prof to prof neurol, Southwestern Med Sch, Tex, 48-52, prof med & actg chmn dept, 51-52; PROF NEUROL MED, SCH MED, UNIV NC, CHAPEL HILL, 52- *Concurrent Pos:* NIH spec fel, Inst Neurophysiol, Denmark, 57-58. *Mem:* AMA; Am Col Physicians; Am Neurol Asn; Am Acad Neurol (secy, 55-57). *Res:* Virus infections of the nervous system, including lymphocytic choriomeningitis and Coxsackie viruses; neurosyphilis; radioactive iodine in brain tumor localizations; electrophysiology of muscle. *Mailing Add:* Dept of Neurol Univ of NC Sch of Med Chapel Hill NC 27514

FARMER, WALTER ASHFORD, b Schenectady, NY, Nov 11, 27; m 54; c 4. SCIENCE EDUCATION. *Educ:* State Univ NY Albany, BA, 51, MA, 53; Ohio State Univ, PhD(sci educ), 64. *Prof Exp:* Sec educ teacher sci, Chatham Cent Sch, Chatham, NY, 51-58; instr educ, Ohio State Univ, 58-60; dept chmn sci, Chatham Cent Sch, 60-62; assoc prof, 62-65, PROF SCI EDUC, STATE UNIV NY ALBANY, 65- *Concurrent Pos:* Consult, NY State Educ Dept, 67-72, 77-82. *Mem:* Am Educ Res Asn; Asn Educ Teachers Sci; Nat Asn Res Sci Teaching; Sigma Xi. *Res:* Instructional methodology in science instruction; science teacher education; Piagetian model of cognitive development. *Mailing Add:* State Univ NY EdB13 1400 Washington Ave Albany NY 12222

FARMER, WALTER JOSEPH, b Anderson, Ind, Nov 1, 38; m 62; c 2. SOIL CHEMISTRY. *Educ:* Ind Univ, BS, 61; Purdue Univ, PhD(soil chem), 66. *Prof Exp:* Asst chemist, 66-70, asst prof soil sci, 70-73, ASSOC PROF SOIL SCI, UNIV CALIF, RIVERSIDE, 73- *Mem:* Am Soc Agron; Soil Sci Soc Am; Am Chem Soc; Sigma Xi. *Res:* Adsorption, movement and volatilization of organic pesticides and other synthetic organic compounds in soils and their reactions with soils, clays and other soil materials; fate of pesticides in soils. *Mailing Add:* Dept of Soil & Environ Sci Univ of Calif Riverside CA 92521

FARMER, WILLIAM MICHAEL, b Nashville, Tenn, May 10, 44; m 66; c 2. AEROSOLS, ELECTRO-OPTICAL INSTRUMENTATION. *Educ:* Univ Tenn, BS, 67, MS, 68, PhD(physics), 73. *Prof Exp:* Coop engr, Arnold Res Orgn, 62-66; res asst, Space Inst, Univ Tenn, 67-68; res engr, Arnold Res Orgn, 68-73; staff scientist, Sci Applications, Inc, 73-75; lab mgr & res scientist, Spectron Develop Labs, 75-77; staff scientist, 77-78, ASSOC PROF PHYSICS, OPTICS & CLASSICAL ELECTRODYNAMICS, SPACE INST, UNIV TENN, 78- *Concurrent Pos:* Consult, San-Div Int Harvestor, 77-79; mem, Plasma Dynamics Tech Comt, Am Inst Aeronaut & Astronaut, 79-81. *Mem:* Am Optical Soc; Soc Photographic Inst Engrs. *Res:* Development of laser instrumentation for aerosol measurement; aerosol research using wide spectrum of instrumentation for the measurement of smoke and obscurants. *Mailing Add:* 1414 Country Club Dr Tullahoma TN 37388

FARMER, WILLIAM S(ILAS), JR, b Waterville, Maine, Apr 16, 22; m 47; c 4. ENGINEERING DESIGN, ENGINEERING MANAGEMENT. *Educ:* Tufts Univ, BS, 44; Univ Tenn, MS, 50. *Prof Exp:* Chem engr, Texas Co, 44; tech supvr, Fercleve Corp, 45; develop engr, Oak Ridge Nat Lab, 46-49, sr develop engr, 50-53; proj engr, Advan Design Sect, Pratt & Whitney Aircraft Co, 54-55, proj engr, Aircraft Nuclear Propulsion, 56-57; sr nuclear engr & sect head, ACF Industs, Inc, 58; proj mgr, Elk River Nuclear Power Reactor, Allis-Chalmers Mfg Co, 59, mgr planning dept, 60-62, tech dir, 62-70; mem staff, AEC, 70-74, PROG MGR, US NUCLEAR REGULATORY COMN, 74- *Mem:* Am Chem Soc; Am Nuclear Soc; Am Inst Chem Engrs. *Res:* Nuclear engineering; heat transfer and fluid mechanics; chemical engineering. *Mailing Add:* 10115 Green Forest Dr Silver Spring MD 20903

FARN, CHARLES LUH-SUN, b Checkiang, China, Sept 19, 34; m 62; c 2. FLUID MECHANICS. *Educ:* Nat Taiwan Univ, BS, 58; NC State Col, MS, 62; Univ Mich, PhD(mech eng), 65. *Prof Exp:* Asst prof fluid mech, Carnegie-Mellon Univ, 65-68; sr engr, 68-76, MGR FLUID DYNAMICS RES, WESTINGHOUSE RES & DEVELOP CTR, 76- *Mem:* Am Soc Mech Engrs. *Res:* Boundary layers; magnetohydrodynamic generators; wave propagations; electrokinetics; turbulence; aerodynamics of turbomachines; steam turbine; gas turbine; pump; axial flow fan; gas dynamics; numerical analysis. *Mailing Add:* Westinghouse Res & Develop Ctr Pittsburgh PA 15235

FARNELL, ALBERT BENNETT, b Shreveport, La, July 18, 17; m 41; c 3. MATHEMATICS. *Educ:* Centenary Col, AB, 38; La State Univ, MS, 40; Univ Calif, PhD(math), 44. *Prof Exp:* Asst prof math, Univ Colo, 46-48; lectr, Princeton Univ, 48-49; asst prof, Univ Colo, 49-51; sr res engr, NAm Aviation, 53-56; sr staff scientist, Convair Sci Res Lab Div, Gen Dynamics Corp, 56-63; prof math, Colo State Univ, 63-65; sr staff scientist, Convair Sci Res Lab Div, Gen Dynamics Corp, 65-66; prof, 66-77, EMER PROF MATH, COLO STATE UNIV, 77- *Mem:* Math Asn Am. *Res:* Matrix algebra; nonlinear differential equations; characteristic roots of matrix polynomials and infinite matrices; digital computation. *Mailing Add:* 850 Mt Champion Livermore CO 80536

FARNELL, DANIEL REESE, b Mobile, Ala, Feb 7, 32; m 54; c 4. TUMOR PATHOLOGY, LABORATORY ANIMAL PATHOLOGY. *Educ:* Auburn Univ, DVM, 57, MS, 62; Mich State Univ, PhD(path), 69; Am Col Lab Animal Med, dipl, 66. *Prof Exp:* Res scientist, Southern Res Inst, 57-61; assoc prof animal dis res, Auburn Univ, 62-67; prof vet sci & head dept, Miss State Univ, 69-73; prof comp med, Col Med, Univ Southern Ala, 73-75; dir animal resources, 73-78, SR PATHOLOGIST, SOUTHERN RES INST, 78- *Mem:* Am Vet Med Asn; Am Asn Lab Animal Sci. *Res:* Pathology & oncology; nutrition; toxicology; endocrinology. *Mailing Add:* Southern Res Inst PO Box 3307-A Birmingham AL 35255

FARNELL, G(ERALD) W(ILLIAM), b Toronto, Ont, Aug 31, 25; m 48; c 2. ELECTRICAL ENGINEERING, PHYSICS. *Educ:* Univ Toronto, BASc, 48; Mass Inst Technol, SM, 50; McGill Univ, PhD, 57. *Prof Exp:* Asst, Res Lab Electronics, Mass Inst Technol, 48-50; lectr elec eng, 50-54, from asst prof to assoc prof elec eng & physics, 54-61, chmn dept elec eng, 67-73, PROF ENG PHYSICS, McGILL UNIV, 61-, DEAN, FAC ENG, 73- *Concurrent Pos:* Nuffield fel, Clarendon Lab, Oxford, 60-61. *Mem:* Fel Inst Elec & Electronics Engrs. *Res:* Solid state electronics; ultrasonics and elastic surface waves. *Mailing Add:* McGill Univ Fac of Eng 817 Sherbrooke St W Montreal PQ H3A 2T5 Can

FARNER, DONALD SANKEY, b Waumandee, Wis, May 2, 15; m 40; c 2. PHYSIOLOGY, ZOOLOGY. *Educ:* Hamline Univ, BS, 37; Univ Wis, MA, 39, PhD(zool), 41. *Hon Degrees:* DSc, Hamline Univ, 62. *Prof Exp:* Asst biol, Hamline Univ, 35-37; asst zool, Univ Wis, 37-41, instr, 41-43; asst prof & asst cur birds, Univ Kans, 46-47; from assoc prof to prof zoophysiol, Wash State Univ, 47-65, dean grad sch, 60-64; chmn dept zool, 66-81, PROF ZOOPHYSIOL, UNIV WASH, 65- *Concurrent Pos:* Fulbright res scholar & hon lectr, Otago, NZ, 53-54; Guggenheim fel, Western Australia, 58-59; Alexander von Humboldt Sr US Sci, Aschoff Div, Max Planck Inst Physiol Behav, Andechs, 78. *Mem:* AAAS; Am Chem Soc; Endocrinol Soc; Am Soc Zoologists; Am Physiol Soc. *Res:* Avian and comparative physiology; control of annual physiologic cycles. *Mailing Add:* Dept of Zool Univ of Wash Seattle WA 98195

FARNES, PATRICIA, b Portland, Ore, May 16, 31. HEMATOLOGY. *Educ:* Willamette Univ, BA, 53; Univ Ore, MS & MD, 56. *Prof Exp:* Intern med, Presby Hosp, Chicago, 56-57, resident internal med, 57-58, resident med, 60-61, res assoc path, 61-68, asst prof med res, 68-74, ASSOC PROF MED SCI, BROWN UNIV, 74-; CHIEF EXP CELL BIOL SECT, RI HOSP, PROVIDENCE, 68- *Concurrent Pos:* Fel hemat, Presby Hosp, Chicago, 58-60; Nat Heart Inst fel, Presby-St Luke's Hosp, Chicago, 59-60; NIH res grants, 60-; USPHS grants, 61-65; Am Cancer Soc grant, 66-68; internist, Civil Hosp of Beni Messous, Algiers, 62 & Avicenna Hosp, Kabul, 72, 74 & 75; mem med adv bd, Hemophilia Guild, 65. *Mem:* AAAS; Am Soc Cell Biol; Am Fedn Clin Res; Reticuloendothelial Soc; Int Soc Exp Hemat. *Res:* Tissue culture; Haemic cell culture, especially in vitro differentiation of granulocytes and in vitro modulations of lymphocytes; phytomitogens and modes of action; histochemistry of in vitro cells. *Mailing Add:* 66 Bowden Ave Barrington RI 02806

FARNG, RICHARD KWANG, b Apr 1, 43; US citizen; m 72; c 3. PHARMACEUTICS. *Educ:* Nat Taiwan Univ, BS, 67; Univ Minn, PhD(pharm), 73. *Prof Exp:* Scientist pharm res & develop, 3M Co, 73-76; SR SCIENTIST PHARM RES & DEVELOP, JOHNSON & JOHNSON, 76- *Mem:* Am Pharmaceut Asn; Acad Pharmaceut Sci. *Res:* Diffusion; skin penetration; preformulation; formulation. *Mailing Add:* 14 Revock Rd East Brunswick NJ 08816

FARNHAM, PAUL REX, b St Louis, Mo, Nov 2, 31; m 55. STRUCTURAL GEOLOGY, GEOPHYSICS. *Educ:* Western Md Col, BS, 53; Va Polytech Inst, MS, 60; Univ Minn, PhD(structural geol), 67. *Prof Exp:* Assoc engr, Martin Co, Md, 56-57; teaching asst phys geol & mineral, Va Polytech Inst, 58-59, instr, 59-61; teaching assoc phys geol, Univ Minn, Minneapolis, 61-66; res geophysicist, Seismic Data Lab, Earth Sci Co, Teledyne, Inc, 67-69; dir tech educ, Bison Instruments, 69-70; asst prof, 70-77, mem fac geol, 77-80, ASST PROF GEOL, COL ST THOMAS, 80- *Res:* Instrumentation and data processing in earthquake seismology and synthesis of geophysical and geological data to establish structural geologic relationships. *Mailing Add:* Dept of Geol Col of St Thomas St Paul MN 55105

FARNHAM, ROUSE SMITH, b Evergreen, Ala, Jan 29, 18; m 51; c 2. SOIL SCIENCE. *Educ:* Ala Polytech Inst, BS, 41; Ohio State Univ, PhD(agron), 51. *Prof Exp:* Soil surveyor, Agr Exp Sta, Ala Polytech Inst, 41-42 & 46; soil scientist, Soil Conserv Surv, 50-58, asst prof, 58-69, PROF SOIL SCI, UNIV MINN, MINNEAPOLIS, 69- *Res:* Soil genesis and classification; peat and organic soils, use for energy and biomass production for energy. *Mailing Add:* Dept of Soil Sci Univ of Minn St Paul MN 55108

FARNSWORTH, ARCHIE VERDELL, JR, b Mesa, Ariz, July 12, 41; m 66; c 5. FLUID MECHANICS, HEAT TRANSFER. *Educ:* Ariz State Univ, BSE, 66, MSE, 68; Brown Univ, PhD(eng), 71. *Prof Exp:* MEM TECH STAFF ENG, SANDIA LABS, 70- *Mem:* Am Phys Soc. *Res:* Target design for particle-beam driven inertial confinement fusion; investigation of high intensity ion beam sources for inertial confinement fusion application. *Mailing Add:* Sandia Labs Albuquerque NM 87115

FARNSWORTH, CARL LEON, b Lincoln, Nebr, Aug 5, 30. ORGANIC CHEMISTRY. *Educ:* Univ Tex, BS, 55, MA, 58, PhD(chem), 61. *Prof Exp:* Res chemist, Spruance Film Res & Develop Lab, Film Dept, E I du Pont de Nemours & Co, Inc, 60-66; chemist, W H Brady Co, 66-67; ASSOC PROF CHEM, UNIV WIS-STEVENS POINT, 67- *Mem:* Am Chem Soc. *Mailing Add:* Dept of Chem Univ of Wis Stevens Point WI 54481

FARNSWORTH, MARIE, b Holden, Mo, July 19, 96. CHEMISTRY. *Educ:* Univ Chicago, BS, 18, PhD(chem), 22. *Prof Exp:* Instr chem, Iowa State Col, 22-23; res chemist, US Bur Mines, 23-26; instr chem, NY Univ, 26-35; res, Munich & London, 35-36; res chemist, Fogg Art Mus, Harvard Univ, 36-37; chemist, Agora Excavations, Greece, 38-40; res supvr, Res & Develop Lab, M & T Corp, 40-61; Ford Found fel, 61-64; res assoc dept hist & archaeol, Columbia Univ, 64-79. *Concurrent Pos:* Vis prof, Univ Mo-Columbia, 70- *Honors & Awards:* First Pomerance Award, Archaeol Inst Am, 80. *Mem:* Am Chem Soc; Archaeol Inst Am. *Res:* Analytical chemistry; technical problems of archaeology. *Mailing Add:* 803 W 48th St #301 Kansas City MO 64112

FARNSWORTH, MARJORIE WHYTE, b Detroit, Mich, Nov 18, 21; m 45; c 2. GENETICS. *Educ:* Mt Holyoke Col, BA, 44; Cornell Univ, MS, 46; Univ Mo, PhD(zool), 51. *Prof Exp:* Asst entom, Cornell Univ, 44-46; instr zool, Univ Mo, 46-49, res fel, 49-50, from instr to asst prof, 50-52; cytologist, Roswell Park Mem Inst, 52-53; lectr & res assoc biol, 53-64, assoc prof, 65-79, ADJ ASSOC PROF BIOL, STATE UNIV NY BUFFALO, 79- *Mem:* Fel AAAS; Genetics Soc Am; Am Soc Zoologists. *Res:* Biochemical genetics of Drosophila. *Mailing Add:* 505 N Lake Shore Dr Chicago IL 60611

FARNSWORTH, NORMAN R, b Lynn, Mass, Mar 23, 30; m 53. PHARMACOGNOSY, PHYTOCHEMISTRY. *Educ:* Mass Col Pharm, BS, 53, MS, 55; Univ Pittsburgh, PhD(pharm), 59. *Hon Degrees:* Dr, Univ Paris, 78. *Prof Exp:* Instr biol sci, Univ Pittsburgh, 55-59, from asst prof to prof pharmacog, 59-70, chmn dept, 64-70; PROF PHARMACOG & HEAD DEPT PHARMACOG & PHARMACOL, COL PHARM, UNIV ILL MED CTR, 70- *Concurrent Pos:* Consult, Schering AG, Berlin, Amazon Natural Drug Co, Gillette, WHO, Nat Cancer Inst & A D Little. *Mem:* Am Soc Pharmacog (vpres, 59-61, pres, 61-62); Soc Econ Bot; Am Pharmaceut Asn; fel Acad Pharm Sci. *Res:* Evaluation of medicinal folklore; computer analysis of chemical and biological data on natural products; isolation, identification and structure elucidation of biologically active plant constituents; investigation of plants for biologically active substances. *Mailing Add:* Col of Pharm Univ of Ill at the Med Ctr Chicago IL 60680

FARNSWORTH, PATRICIA NORDSTROM, b Sioux City, Iowa, Aug 17, 30; m 52; c 4. PHYSIOLOGY, BIOCHEMISTRY. *Educ:* Morningside Col, BA, 51; Columbia Univ, MS, 52, PhD(physiol), 60. *Prof Exp:* Instr zool, Hofstra Col, 52-54; instr genetics & zool, Marymount Col, 56-57; asst physiol, Columbia Univ, 58-59, instr occup & phys ther, 59-60, fel med, Col Physicians & Surgeons, 62-63; asst prof genetics & physiol, Fairleigh Dickinson Univ, 63-67; asst prof physiol, Barnard Col, Columbia Univ, 67-69, asst prof biol, 69-73; assoc prof, 73-76, PROF PHYSIOL & OPHTHAL, COL MED & DENT NJ, NEWARK, 76- *Concurrent Pos:* Consult, Dept Health, Englewood, NJ, 66- & Arthur D Little, Inc, 71; vis lectr, Harvard Univ, 70-; NIH sr res fel, 71; bd sci coun, Nat Eye Inst, 80-; consult, Nat Adv Eye Coun, 80. *Mem:* AAAS; NY Acad Sci; Am Physiol Soc; Sigma Xi; Int Soc Eye Res. *Res:* cell membrane chemistry; lipid metabolism. *Mailing Add:* Dept of Physiol Col Med & Dent NJ Newark NJ 07103

FARNSWORTH, PHILLIP L, b Panguitch, Utah, July 5, 36; m 55; c 5. MATERIALS SCIENCE, ENGINEERING. *Educ:* Univ Utah, BS, 58; Mass Inst Technol, ScD(ceramics), 64. *Prof Exp:* Engr, Gen Elec Co, Wash, 58-61; sr scientist, Pac Northwest Labs, Battelle Mem Inst, 65-66, mgr ceramics res, 66-69, spec asst to pres, 69-70, mgr ceramics & graphite sect, 70-73; mgr control performance, 73-76, mgr process eng, 76-78, mgr mat develop, 78-79, MGR PROD COST ENG, EXXON NUCLEAR CO, 80- *Mem:* Fel Am Ceramic Soc; Sigma Xi; Am Nuclear Soc. *Res:* Research and development on processes and materials for production of nuclear fuel. *Mailing Add:* Rte 1 Box 5338 Richland WA 99352

FARNSWORTH, RICHARD KENT, b Salt Lake City, Utah, July 21, 34; m 59; c 4. HYDROLOGY, REMOTE SENSING. *Educ:* Univ Utah, BA, 61; Brigham Young Univ, MS, 66; Univ Mich, PhD(natural resources), 76. *Prof Exp:* Supvr physics, Tritium Lab, Water Resources Div, US Geol Surv, 65-67; RES HYDROLOGIST, HYDROL RES LAB, OFF HYDROL, NAT WEATHER SERV, NAT OCEANIC & ATMOSPHERIC ADMIN, 67- *Mem:* Am Geophys Union. *Res:* Mathematical modeling of soil surface layers to compute the likelihood of signigicant changes in permeability due to impervious frost; satellite estimates of current rainfall; implications of tritium in natural waters. *Mailing Add:* Nat Weather Serv W23 Silver Spring MD 20910

FARNSWORTH, ROY LOTHROP, b Shirley, Mass, Mar 4, 28; m 57; c 3. GEOLOGY. *Educ:* Boston Univ, AB, 49, AM, 56, PhD(geol), 61. *Prof Exp:* Pub sch teacher, Mass, 53-55; instr geol, Trinity Col, Conn, 57-59, pub sch teacher, Mass, 60-61; asst prof geol, 61-68, ASSOC PROF GEOL, BATES COL, 68- *Mem:* Soc Econ Paleontologists & Mineralogists; Am Asn Univ Prof; Geol Soc Am; Nat Asn Geol Teachers; Am Quaternary Asn. *Res:* Glaciol geology; sedimentology; environmental geology; coastal geology; genesis analysis of land forms. *Mailing Add:* Dept of Geol Bates Col Lewiston ME 04240

FARNSWORTH, WELLS EUGENE, b Hartford, Conn, July 10, 21; m 45; c 2. BIOCHEMISTRY. *Educ:* Trinity Col, Conn, BS, 46; Univ Mo, MA, 49, PhD(endocrine physiol, chem), 51. *Prof Exp:* Endocrinologist, Wm S Merrell Co, Ohio, 51-52; res biochemist, US Vet Admin Hosp, 52-61, dir biochem res, 61-80; assoc prof biochem, State Univ NY Buffalo, 67-80, assoc res prof urol, 75-80; PROF & CHMN BIOCHEM, CHICAGO COL OSTEOP MED, 80- *Concurrent Pos:* Consult, Edward J Meyer Hosp, 57-58; asst prof, State Univ NY Buffalo, 64-67. *Mem:* Endocrine Soc; Brit Biochem Soc; Am Physiol Soc; fel Am Inst Chemists; Am Chem Soc. *Res:* Steroid metabolism; influence of steroid on prostate metabolism and protein synthesis in vitro. *Mailing Add:* Chicago Col Osteop Med 1122 E 53rd St Chicago IL 60615

FARNUM, BRUCE WAYNE, b Fargo, NDak, Apr 5, 35; m 59; c 1. ORGANIC CHEMISTRY. *Educ:* NDak State Univ, BS, 57, MS, 59; Univ Del, PhD(org chem), 69. *Prof Exp:* Instr chem, Moorhead State Col, 59; from assoc prof to prof chem, Minot State Col, 64-76; res chemist, 76-80, CHIEF ORG ANAL BR, GRAND FORKS ENERGY TECHNOL CTR, US DEPT ENERGY, 80- *Mem:* Am Chem Soc. *Res:* Mechanism of coal liquefaction; characterization of gasifier tar, waste water and coal liquids. *Mailing Add:* Grand Forks Energy Technol Ctr Box 8213 Univ Sta Grand Forks ND 58202

FARNUM, DONALD G, b Oakland, Calif, Apr 3, 34; m 53; c 4. ORGANIC CHEMISTRY. *Educ:* Harvard Univ, AB, 56, PhD(org chem), 59. *Prof Exp:* Chemist, Arthur D Little, Inc, 53-59; from instr to asst prof chem, Cornell Univ, 59-66; assoc prof, 66-72, PROF CHEM, MICH STATE UNIV, 72- *Concurrent Pos:* Sloan Found fel, 62. *Mem:* Am Chem Soc. *Res:* Organic synthesis; stable carbonium ions; structures which test current concepts; bridged polycyclic olefins; pheromone synthesis and structure; reactive intermediates; photochemical synthesis. *Mailing Add:* Dept of Chem Mich State Univ East Lansing MI 48824

FARNUM, EUGENE HOWARD, b Athol, Mass, July 7, 42; m 65; c 2. MATERIAL SCIENCE ENGINEERING. *Educ:* Clark Univ, AB, 64; Princeton Univ, MS, 66, PhD(solid state & mat sci), 68. *Prof Exp:* Mem staff mat sci, Sandia Labs, 68-73; mem staff laser fusion, 73-77, assoc group leader laser fusion, 77-79, DEP GROUP LEADER TARGET FABRICATION, LOS ALAMOS NAT LAB, 79- *Mem:* Am Phys Soc; AAAS; Am Vacuum Soc. *Res:* Radiation damage in materials; defects in crystalline solids; physical properties of ceramics; hydrogen and hydrogen isotope diffusion; permeation and embrittlement in metals; microscopic machining and assembly techniques; cleanliness control; technical management; inertially confined fusion target fabrication. *Mailing Add:* Chem & Mat Sci Div Los Alamos Nat Lab Los Alamos NM 87545

FARNUM, PETER, b Orange, NJ, Sept 24, 46; m 71; c 2. FORESTRY. *Educ:* Princeton Univ, AB, 68; Univ Washington, PhD(forestry), 77. *Prof Exp:* RES SCIENTIST, WEYERHAEUSER FORESTRY RES CENTRALIA, 77- *Mem:* Soc Am Foresters; Am Statist Asn. *Res:* Increasing and quantifying basic biological productivity of managed forest stands, silviculture, long term growth and yield biometries. *Mailing Add:* 505 N Pearl St Centrelia WA 98531

FARNUM, SYLVIA ARLYCE, b St Paul, Minn, Dec 29, 36; m 59; c 1. PHYSICAL CHEMISTRY. *Educ:* NDak State Univ, BS, 58, MS, 59; Univ NDak, PhD(chem), 79. *Prof Exp:* Instr chem, Washington Col, Md, 60-61; chemist org synthesis, US Army Ballistics Res Lab, 61-62; chemist metal anal, Univ Del, 62-64; instr chem & math, Minot State Col, 64-76; res fel enzyme kinetics, Univ NDak, 76-78; RES CHEMIST COAL LIQUEFACTION, GRAND FORKS ENERGY TECHNOL CTR, US DEPT ENERGY, 78- *Mem:* Am Chem Soc. *Res:* Nuclear magnetic resonance; enzyme structure and mechanism; chemical kinetics; heterocyclic synthesis and structure; date and origin of antique metals from chemical analysis. *Mailing Add:* Univ Sta US Dept Energy Box 8214 Grand Forks ND 58202

FARNWORTH, EDWARD ROBERT, b Thorold, Ont, Aug 13, 47; m 70; c 2. NUTRITION, AGRICULTURE. *Educ:* Brock Univ, BSc, 70; McMaster Univ, MSc, 72; Guelph Univ, PhD(nutrit), 78. *Prof Exp:* RES SCIENTIST NUTRIT, AGR CAN, 78- *Concurrent Pos:* Tutor chem, Univ Papua, New Guinea, 72-74. *Mem:* Can Soc Nutrit Sci; Agr Inst Can. *Res:* Nutrition and biochemistry of lipids; nutritional and toxicological implications of mycotoxins in diets of domestic animals. *Mailing Add:* Animal Res Ctr K W Neatby Bldg Ottawa Can

FARONA, MICHAEL F, b Cleveland, Ohio, Jan 30, 35; m 60; c 1. INORGANIC CHEMISTRY. *Educ:* Western Reserve Univ, BS, 56; Ohio State Univ, MS, 62, PhD(chem), 64. *Prof Exp:* From asst prof to assoc prof, 64-72, PROF CHEM, UNIV AKRON, 72-, HEAD DEPT, 76- *Concurrent Pos:* Consult, Goodyear Tire & Rubber Co, 71-78. *Mem:* Catalysis Soc; Am Chem Soc; The Chem Soc. *Res:* Transition metal chemistry, including homogeneous catalysis, metal carbonyls and organometallics. *Mailing Add:* Dept of Chem Univ of Akron Akron OH 44325

FARONE, WILLIAM ANTHONY, b Cortland, NY, Feb 1, 40; c 1. PHYSICAL CHEMISTRY. *Educ:* Clarkson Tech, BS, 61, MS, 63, PhD(chem), 65. *Prof Exp:* Res physicist, US Army Electronics Res & Develop Activity, White Sands Missile Range, NMex, 64-65; assoc prof phys chem, Va State Col, 65-67; sr res assoc, Lever Bros Co, 67-69, sect chief, New Prod Group, Res & Develop Div, 69-70 & Detergents Eval Sect, 70-72, dir sci res, 72-75; vpres res & develop, Chem Specialties Div, PVO Int, Inc, 75-76; DIR, APPL RES, PHILIP MORRIS, INC, 77- *Concurrent Pos:* Prin investr, Res Corp res grant, 65-67; co-prin investr, NSF res grant, 66-67. *Mem:* Optical Soc Am; Sigma Xi; Am Chem Soc; AAAS. *Res:* Colloid science, particularly use of electromagnetic scattering to determine particle properties and interactions. *Mailing Add:* Philip Morris Res Ctr PO Box 26583 Richmond VA 23261

FARQUHAR, GALE BURTON, b Oakland, Calif, Jan 5, 27; m 51; c 3. ORGANIC CHEMISTRY. *Educ:* Occidental AB, 50, MA, 51. *Prof Exp:* Res & develop engr, Superior Oil Co, 51-60, from staff corrosion engr to sr corrosion engr, 60-72, gen corrosion engr, 72-78; RES SCIENTIST, EXPLOR & PROD RES LAB, GETTY OIL CO, 78- *Mem:* Am Chem Soc; Am Inst Chemists; Nat Asn Corrosion Engineers. *Res:* Waterflood and bacterial corrosion; cathodic protection; inhibitor evaluation. *Mailing Add:* 5814 Portal Dr Houston TX 77096

FARQUHAR, JOHN WILLIAM, b Winnipeg, Man, June 13, 27; nat US. MEDICINE, PREVENTIVE MEDICINE. *Educ:* Univ Calif, AB, 49, MD, 52. *Prof Exp:* Fel med, Univ Minn, 54-56; fel, Univ Calif, 56-57, instr & chief resident, 57-58; res assoc, Rockefeller Univ, 58-62; from asst prof to assoc prof, 62-73, PROF MED, SCH MED, STANFORD UNIV, 73-, PROF FAMILY, COMMUNITY & PREV MED, 78- *Mem:* Nat Acad Sci; Am Soc Clin Invest; Inst Med; Am Heart Asn; Sigma Xi. *Res:* Epidemiology of cardiovascular disease, human nutrition and atherosclerosis; behavior and communication in respect to human health. *Mailing Add:* Dept of Med Stanford Univ Sch of Med Stanford CA 94305

FARQUHAR, MARILYN GIST, b Tulare, Calif, July 11, 28; m 51, 70; c 2. CELL BIOLOGY, EXPERIMENTAL PATHOLOGY. *Educ:* Univ Calif, MA, 53, PhD(exp path), 55. *Prof Exp:* Jr res pathologist, Univ Calif, 53-54, asst res pathologist, 55-58; guest investr, Rockefeller Inst, 58-59, res assoc, 59-62; assoc res pathologist, Univ Calif, San Francisco, 62-64, assoc prof path, 64-68, prof in residence, 68-70; prof, Rockefeller Univ, 70-73; PROF CELL BIOL & PATH, SCH MED, YALE UNIV, 73- *Concurrent Pos:* Adj prof, Rockefeller Univ, 70- NIH cell biol study sect, 75- *Mem:* Am Soc Cell Biol (pres, 81-82); Am Soc Exp Path; Am Anat Anat; Electron Micros Soc Am; Endocrine Soc. *Res:* Electron microscopy, cytochemistry and cell fractionation of anterior pituitary gland, kidney and leukocytes; glomerular permeability and pathology; cell secretion; structure and function of Golgi complex and lysosomes; composition of glonuclear basement membrane; intracellular membrane traffic. *Mailing Add:* Sect of Cell Biol Yale Univ Sch of Med New Haven CT 06510

FARQUHAR, OSWALD CORNELL, b Gt Brit, Sept 26, 21; m 53; c 3. ECONOMIC GEOLOGY. *Educ:* Univ Oxford, BA, 40, MA, 47; Aberdeen Univ, PhD(geol), 51. *Prof Exp:* Lectr geol & mineral, Aberdeen Univ, 48-53; asst prof geol, Univ Kans, 54-57; assoc prof, 57-61, PROF GEOL, UNIV MASS, AMHERST, 61- *Concurrent Pos:* Sr res fel, Dept Sci &-Indust Res, Wellington, NZ, 63-64. *Mem:* Soc Econ Geologists; Geol Soc Am; Am Asn Petrol Geologists; Brit Geol Soc. *Res:* Engineering geology; mineral deposits. *Mailing Add:* Dept Geol Univ Mass Amherst MA 01003

FARQUHAR, PETER HENRY, b Boston, Mass, May 7, 47; m 69; c 3. MANAGEMENT SCIENCE, OPERATIONS RESEARCH. *Educ:* Tufts Univ, BS, 69; Cornell Univ, MS, 72, PhD(oper res), 74. *Prof Exp:* Assoc mathematician res & consult, Info Sci Dept, Rand Corp, 74-75; asst prof, Dept Indust Eng & Mgt Sci, Northwestern Univ, 75-78; asst prof, Grad Sch Bus Admin, Harvard Univ, 78-80; ASSOC PROF, GRAD SCH ADMIN & DEPT AGR ECON, UNIV CALIF, DAVIS, 80- *Concurrent Pos:* Consult, Rand Corp, 75-76. *Mem:* Oper Res Soc Am; Inst Mgt Sci; Am Stat Asn; Psychometric Soc; Am Mkt Asn. *Res:* Decision analysis; management policy; measurement theory; multivariate statistical methods; risk assessment. *Mailing Add:* Grad Sch Admin Univ Calif Davis CA 95616

FARQUHAR, RONALD MCCUNN, b Montreal, Que, Nov 25, 29; m 55; c 3. GEOCHRONOLOGY. *Educ:* Univ Toronto, BA, 51, MA, 52, PhD(physics), 54. *Prof Exp:* Fel physics, McMaster Univ, 54-55; lectr, 55-56, from asst prof to assoc prof, 56-71, assoc chmn dept, 74-78, PROF PHYSICS, UNIV TORONTO, 71- *Concurrent Pos:* Royal Soc Can traveling fel, 64; ed, Can Geophys Bull, 75-78. *Mem:* Fel Royal Soc Can; Can Asn Physicists; Can Geophys Union. *Res:* Geological age determinations; mass spectrometry; natural isotopic variations. *Mailing Add:* Dept of Physics Univ of Toronto Toronto ON M5S 1AF Can

FARR, DAVID FREDERICK, b Salinas, Calif, Nov 15, 41; m 63. MYCOLOGY. *Educ:* Humboldt State Col, BA, 63; Univ Kans, MA, 65; Va Polytech Inst & State Univ, PhD(bot), 75. *Prof Exp:* RES BOTANIST MYCOL, SCI & EDUC ADMIN-AGR RES SERV, USDA, 74- *Mem:* Mycol Soc Am; Am Inst Biol Sci; Int Asn Plant Taxon; Sigma Xi. *Res:* Taxonomy, morphology and speciation in basidiomycetous fungi through study of cultural characters, genetics and fruit body production in conjunction with field and herbarium work. *Mailing Add:* Mycol Lab Bldg 011A Rm 313 Agr Res Ctr-West Beltsville MD 20705

FARR, KENNETH E(DWARD), b Philadelphia, Pa, May 6, 17; m 68. ELECTRONIC ENGINEERING. *Educ:* Bucknell Univ, BSEE, 59; Drexel Inst, MSEE, 63. *Prof Exp:* Field serv engr, Philco Corp, 40-41; inspector radio mat, US Army Signal Corps, 42; sr engr licensee lab, adv develop, field serv engr & engr in-chg field serv sch, Hazeltine Corp, 42-48; eng sect mgr advan develop, Westinghouse Elec Co, 48-57; sr eng specialist underwater systs eng, Philco Corp, 60-61; mgr indust prod eng, Jerrold Electronics Corp, 61-63; ADV ENGR CONTROL & INSTRUMENTATION RES, WESTINGHOUSE ELEC CO, 63- *Mem:* Sr mem Inst Elec & Electronics Engrs. *Res:* Color, slow-scan and educational television; band-width compression; magnetic video recording; internal connection design; computer-aided design, computer-aided manufacturing application. *Mailing Add:* 732 Garden City Dr Monroeville PA 15146

FARR, RICHARD STUDLEY, b Detroit, Mich, Oct 30, 22; m 44; c 2. MEDICINE, ALLERGY. *Educ:* Univ Chicago, BS, 45, MD, 46. *Prof Exp:* Intern, US Navy Hosp, Annapolis, 46-47, hematologist, Naval Med Res Inst, 47-48; res assoc anat, Univ Chicago, 48-50; hematologist, Naval Med Res Inst, 50-53; from instr to asst prof med, Univ Chicago, 54-56; assoc res prof anat, Univ Pittsburgh, 56-57, asst prof med & head sect clin immunol, 57-62, head div allergy, immunol & rheumatology, Scripps Clin & Res Found, 62-69, chmn dept clin biol, 66-69; chmn dept med, 69-77, staff physician, 77-80, PROF MED, NAT JEWISH HOSP & RES CTR, DENVER, 80-; PROF MED, UNIV COLO SCH MED, DENVER, 69- *Concurrent Pos:* Sr res fel chem & immunochem, Calif Inst Technol, 53-54. *Honors & Awards:* Borden Award, Chicago, 46. *Mem:* AAAS; Am Soc Clin Invest; Am Acad Allergy (pres, 70); Am Asn Immunol; hon fel Can Soc Allergy & Clin Immunol. *Res:* Morphogenesis of blood cells; irradiation illness; body temperature regulating mechanisms; immunochemistry; clinical immunology. *Mailing Add:* Dept of Med Nat Jewish Hosp & Res Ctr Denver CO 80206

FARR, WILLIAM MORRIS, b Kansas City, Mo, Oct 20, 38; m 60; c 2. PLASMA PHYSICS, REACTOR PHYSICS. *Educ:* Rice Univ, BA, 60; Univ Mich, MS, 62, PhD(nuclear sci), 66. *Prof Exp:* Res engr, Atomics Int, 62-63; physicist, Oak Ridge Nat Lab, 66-69; asst prof nuclear eng, 69-74, ASSOC PROF NUCLEAR ENG, UNIV ARIZ, 74- *Mem:* Am Phys Soc; Am Nuclear Soc. *Res:* Theoretical study of microinstabilities in plasma with emphasis on those instabilities of importance to controlled fusion. *Mailing Add:* Dept of Nuclear Engineering Univ of Ariz Tucson AZ 85721

FARRAN, CHARLES FREDERICK, physical chemistry, photography, see previous edition

FARRAND, STEPHEN KENDALL, b Bremerton, Wash, Nov 28, 45; m 70. MICROBIOLOGY, MOLECULAR BIOLOGY. *Educ:* Whitman Col, AB, 67; Univ Rochester, PhD(microbiol), 73. *Prof Exp:* Nat Cancer Inst fel microbiol, Univ Wash, 72-73, sr res fel, 73-74, Nat Cancer Inst fel, 74-75; asst prof, 75-80, ASSOC PROF MICROBIOL, STRITCH SCH MED, LOYOLA UNIV CHICAGO, 80- *Concurrent Pos:* Res consult microbiol, Univ Ill, 76- *Mem:* Am Soc Microbiol. *Res:* Plasmids of Agrobacterium tumefaciens as they related to virulence; drug resistance plasmids of Pseudomonas Aeruginosa; molecular biology of DNA tumor viruses and DNA tumor virus transformed mammalian cells. *Mailing Add:* Dept Microbiol Stritch Sch of Med Loyola Univ of Chicago Maywood IL 60153

FARRAND, WILLIAM RICHARD, b Columbus, Ohio, Apr 27, 31; m 62; c 2. QUATERNARY GEOLOGY. *Educ:* Ohio State Univ, BSc, 55, MSc, 56; Univ Mich, PhD(Pleistocene geol), 60. *Prof Exp:* Res assoc Pleistocene geol, Lamont Geol Observ, Columbia Univ, 60-61, asst prof, Dept Geol, 61-64; vis prof, Inst Geol, Univ Strasbourg, 64-65; from asst prof to assoc prof pleistocene geol, 65-74, PROF GEOL SCI & CUR MUS ANTHROP, UNIV MICH, 74- *Concurrent Pos:* Nat Acad Sci res fel, Univ Strasbourg, 63-64; vis prof, Hebrew Univ, 71-72. *Mem:* AAAS; Geol Soc Am; Am Quaternary Asn. *Res:* Pleistocene geology; history of the Great Lakes and glacio-isostatic rebound; Quaternary paleoclimate; chronology and paleoecology of prehistoric men and their environment. *Mailing Add:* Dept Geol Sci Univ of Mich Ann Arbor MI 48109

FARRAR, DAVID TURNER, b Nashville, Tenn, Feb 4, 41; m 64. PHYSICAL CHEMISTRY. *Educ:* Vanderbilt Univ, BA, 63; Univ SC, PhD(phys inorg chem), 68. *Prof Exp:* From asst prof to assoc prof, 68-78, PROF CHEM, TENN TECHNOL UNIV, 78- *Mem:* Am Chem Soc; Sigma Xi. *Res:* Analysis of environmental plutonium. *Mailing Add:* Dept of Chem Box 5055 Tenn Technol Univ Cookeville TN 38501

FARRAR, GEORGE ELBERT, JR, b Winter Park, Fla, Mar 12, 06; m 33; c 2. INTERNAL MEDICINE. *Educ:* Wesleyan Univ, BS, 27; Johns Hopkins Univ, MD, 31. *Prof Exp:* Asst pharmacol, Johns Hopkins Univ, 28-31; intern, Univ Mich Hosp, 31-32, asst resident med, 32-33, instr, Univ & T H Simpson Mem Inst, 33-35; assoc pharmacologist, Food & Drug Admin, USDA, 35-36; from asst prof to clin prof med, Sch Med, Temple Univ, 36-71; field rep, Joint Comn Accreditation Hosps, 71 & Dept Grad Educ, AMA, 72-74; dir med affairs, 74-78, MED CONSULT, EXCERPTA MEDICA, 78- *Concurrent Pos:* Consult pharmaceut advert, Wyeth Labs, Inc, 40-49, dir med serv, 49-71; assoc physician, Episcopal Hosp, Philadelphia, 44-46, chief med serv, 46-49; mem rev comt, US Pharmacopoeia, 50-60, vpres, 70-75. *Mem:* AAAS; Am Soc Pharmacol & Exp Therapeut; fel AMA; Am Rheumatism Asn; fel Am Col Physicians. *Res:* Metabolism of iron; nutritional anemia; osteoporosis in adults; hyaluronidase in rheumatic diseases. *Mailing Add:* Tahoe 18 Village 2 New Hope PA 18938

FARRAR, GROVER LOUIS, b Lynchburg, Va, May 22, 36; m 63; c 2. ORGANIC CHEMISTRY. *Educ:* Randolph-Macon Col, BS, 56; Calif Inst Technol, PhD(org chem), 61. *Prof Exp:* Res chemist, Nitrogen Div, Allied Chem Corp, Va, 60-64 & Denver Res Ctr, Marathon Oil Co, 64-67; sr res chemist, Celanese Plastics Co, 67-70, group leader, 70-78, res & develop supt, 78-80; SR RES ASSOC, AM HOECHST CORP, 80- *Mem:* Am Chem Soc. *Res:* Chemistry of organic nitrogen compounds; reagent additions to olefins; chlorination of aralkyl compounds; naphthalene dicarboxylates; polyester film. *Mailing Add:* Am Hoechst Corp Box 1400 Greer SC 29652

FARRAR, JAMES MARTIN, b Pittsburgh, Pa, June 15, 48; m 71; c 2. PHYSICAL CHEMISTRY. *Educ:* Wash Univ, AB, 70; Univ Chicago, MS, 72, PhD(chem), 74. *Prof Exp:* Res asst chem, Univ Chicago, 70-74; res assoc, Univ Calif, Berkeley, 74-76; ASST PROF CHEM, UNIV ROCHESTER, 76- *Concurrent Pos:* Alfred P Sloan res fel, 81-83. *Mem:* Am Phys Soc. *Res:* Molecular beam kinetics; ion molecule reaction dynamics; photodissociation of gas phase cations; state-to-state chemistry. *Mailing Add:* Dept Chem Univ Rochester Rochester NY 14627

FARRAR, JOHN, b Manchester, Eng, Mar 30, 27; US citizen; m 55; c 3. PHYSICAL CHEMISTRY. *Educ:* Univ Manchester, BSc, 48, PhD(chem), 51. *Prof Exp:* Chemist, E I du Pont de Nemours & Co, 52-53, Shell Develop Co, 53-56 & Technicolor Corp, 56-59; prin scientist, Rocketdyne Div, NAm Rockwell Corp, 59-67, MGR AUTONETICS DIV, ROCKWELL INT CORP, 67- *Mem:* Am Chem Soc; Electrochem Soc. *Res:* Electrochemistry and microelectronics; process development; desalination; batteries; photographic materials; crystal growth; microelectronics; solar energy conversion. *Mailing Add:* Rockwell Int Corp 3370 Miraloma Ave Anaheim CA 92803

FARRAR, JOHN KEITH, b Columbus, Ohio, Oct 9, 48; m 71; c 2. CEREBRAL BLOOD FLOW, CEREBRAL METABOLISM. *Educ:* Univ Western Ont, BSc, 71, PhD(biophysics), 74. *Prof Exp:* Res asst, Dept Physiol, Univ Glasgow & Dept Neurosurg, Southern Gen Hosp, 74-75; lectr, clin neurol sci/biophysics, 75-77, ASST PROF, UNIV WESTERN ONT, 77- *Honors & Awards:* Fel Can Heart Found, 74-75, sr fel, 75-; fel Am Heart Asn, 77. *Mem:* Can Stroke Soc; Am Heart Asn; Am Stroke Soc; Int Soc Cerebral Blood Flow & Metabolism. *Res:* The study of cerebral blood flow and metabolism and physiological control and alterations during ischemia-stroke. *Mailing Add:* Dept Clin Neurol Sci Univ Hosp 339 Windermere Rd London ON N6A 5A5 Can

FARRAR, JOHN LAIRD, b Hamilton, Ont, Dec 31, 13; m 46. FORESTRY. *Educ:* Univ Toronto, BScF, 36; Yale Univ, MF, 39, PhD, 55. *Prof Exp:* Forester, Can Int Paper Co, 36-37; forest ecol, Can Forestry Br, 37-41 & 45-56; prof forestry, Univ Toronto, 56-78; RETIRED. *Concurrent Pos:* Ed, Can J Forest Res, 70-80. *Mem:* Can Inst Forestry; Can Bot Asn. *Res:* Forest ecology and tree physiology. *Mailing Add:* Fac Forestry Univ Toronto Toronto ON M5S 1A1 Can

FARRAR, JOHN THRUSTON, b St Louis, Mo, June 26, 20; m 47; c 2. INTERNAL MEDICINE, GASTROENTEROLOGY. *Educ:* Princeton Univ, AB, 42; Univ Wash, MD, 45; Am Bd Internal Med, dipl, 54; Am Bd Gastroenterol, dipl, 62. *Prof Exp:* Asst res path, Boston City Hosp, 48-49; intern med, Mass Mem Hosp, Boston, 49-50, asst resident, 50-51, res assoc, 51-54; chief gastroenterol sect, Med Serv, Vet Admin Hosp, New York, 55-63, asst dir prof serv res, 56-63; assoc prof med, Med Col Va, 63-65, prof, 65-80, chief Gastroenterol Sect, 63-80; MEM FAC, HEALTH SCI DIV, VA COMMONWEALTH UNIV, 80- *Concurrent Pos:* Asst, Sch Med, Boston Univ, 50-54, instr, 54-55; ed, Am J Digestive Dis, 68- *Mem:* AMA; Am Gastroenterol Asn; Am Fedn Clin Res; Inst Elec & Electronics Engrs. *Res:* Gastrointestinal physiology, particularly absorption and motility; pancreatic exocrine physiology; medical electronics. *Mailing Add:* Health Sci Div Va Commonwealth Univ Richmond VA 23219

FARRAR, MARTIN WILBUR, b Hazlehurst, Miss, Dec 25, 22; m 44; c 2. ORGANIC CHEMISTRY, POLYMER CHEMISTRY. *Educ:* Miss Col, BS, 43; Univ Pittsburgh, PhD(org chem), 50. *Prof Exp:* Res chemist, Monsanto Chem Co, 50-54; proj leader, Ethyl Corp, 54-55; res group leader, Monsanto Chem Co, 55-60, asst res dir, 60-62, mgr res, 63-74, DIR RES & DEVELOP, PLASTICIZERS DIV, MONSANTO CO, 74- *Concurrent Pos:* Mem exec comt, Mo Acad Sci, 75-77. *Mem:* Soc Plastics Engrs; Am Chem Soc. *Res:* Organic synthesis. *Mailing Add:* Monsanto Co 800 N Lindbergh Blvd St Louis MO 63166

FARRAR, R(ICHARD) E(DWARD), b Lynchburg, Va, Mar 13, 17; m 46; c 1. CHEMICAL ENGINEERING. *Educ:* Va Polytech Inst, BS, 38; Johns Hopkins Univ, ME, 50, DrEng, 51. *Prof Exp:* Asst chemist, Control Div, Mead Corp, 38-40; chief chemist, Columbia Paper Co, 40-41; prod supvr, Prod Div, US Army Chem Ctr, 41-43, area engr, Develop Div, 45-48; mgr res & develop, Colgate-Palmolive Co, 51-60, res coordr, Household Prod Div, 60-62, dir res & develop, Europ Div, London, Colgate-Palmolive Int, Inc, 62-67; dir prod develop, R J Reynolds Tobacco, ND, 67-70; mem staff, Dairy Res, Inc, 70, exec vpres, 70-77; CONSULT PROD & PROCESS DEVELOP, RICHARD E FARRAR, CONSULT, 77- *Concurrent Pos:* VPres prod develop, Lisher & Co Inc, New York, 77- *Mem:* Am Chem Soc; Am Inst Chem Engrs. *Res:* Administration of research and development. *Mailing Add:* Bermuda Run Box 717 Advance NC 27006

FARRAR, RALPH COLEMAN, b Cabool, Mo, Sept 22, 30; m 53; c 2. ORGANIC CHEMISTRY. *Educ:* Univ Wichita, BS, 53; Univ Ill, PhD(org chem), 56. *Prof Exp:* Chemist, Rubber Res Prog, Univ Ill, 54-56; res chemist, 56-79, res assoc synthetic rubber, Res & Develop Br, 79-82, SECT SUPVR, RUBBER CHEM RES & DEVELOP BR, PHILLIPS PETROL CO, 82- *Mem:* Am Chem Soc; Am Inst Chemists; Sigma Xi. *Res:* New types of synthetic rubber. *Mailing Add:* Phillips Petrol Co Bartlesville OK 74004

FARRAR, ROBERT LYNN, JR, b Nashville, Tenn, Sept 3, 21; m 45; c 3. PHYSICAL CHEMISTRY. *Educ:* Vanderbilt Univ, AB, 43; Univ Wash, MS, 48; Univ Tenn, PhD(chem), 53. *Prof Exp:* Chemist, Carbide & Carbon Chem Corp, 47-54, res chemist, 54-58, head phys chem sect, Oak Ridge Gaseous Diffusion Plant, Union Carbide Nuclear Co, 58-61, spec assignment, Y12 Plant, 61-62, DEVELOP CONSULT CHEM, OAK RIDGE GASEOUS DIFFUSION PLANT, UNION CARBIDE NUCLEAR CO, 62- *Concurrent Pos:* Instr, Eve Sch, Univ Tenn, 57, vis assoc prof, Oak Ridge Grad Prog, 58. *Mem:* AAAS; Am Chem Soc; Sigma Xi; fel Am Inst Chemists. *Res:* Fluorine and uranium chemistry; kinetics of solid-gas reactions; adsorption; corrosion; physical properties of inorganic fluorine compounds. *Mailing Add:* Oak Ridge Gaseous Diffusion Plant PO Box P MS 271 Oak Ridge TN 37830

FARRAR, THOMAS C, b Independence, Kans, Jan 14, 33; m 63; c 3. PHYSICAL CHEMISTRY. *Educ:* Univ Wichita, BS, 54; Univ Ill, PhD(phys chem), 59. *Prof Exp:* NSF fel, Cambridge Univ, 59-61; asst prof chem, Univ Ore, 61-63; chemist, Nat Bur Stand, 63-67, chemist, Inorg Chem Sect, 67-69, head magnetism group, 69-71; dir res & develop, Geol, Inc, 71-76; dir, Chem Instrumentation Prog, NSF, 76-79; PROF CHEM, UNIV WIS-MADISON, 79- *Concurrent Pos:* Chmn, Enc Inc, 73-74; secy, Joint Comt Atomic & Molecular Phys Data, 76- *Honors & Awards:* US Dept Commerce Silver Medal; Indust Res Mag Award, 75. *Mem:* Fel Am Inst Chemists; Am Phys Soc; Am Chem Soc; NY Acad Sci. *Res:* Experimental and theoretical nuclear magnetic resonance spectroscopy; theoretical chemistry; research and development in analytical spectroscopy (ms, ir, nmr); development of new instrumentation. *Mailing Add:* Dept of Chem Univ of Wis Madison WI 53706

FARRAR, WILLIAM EDMUND, JR, b Macon, Ga, May 28, 33; m 57; c 2. INFECTIOUS DISEASE, MICROBIOLOGY. *Educ:* Mercer Univ, BS, 55; Med Col Ga, MD, 58. *Prof Exp:* Intern med, Talmadge Mem Hosp, Augusta, 58-59, asst resident, 59-60; sr asst resident, Grady Mem Hosp, Atlanta, 60-61; assoc med, Emory Univ, 65-67, from asst prof to assoc prof prev med, 65-71, from asst prof to assoc prof med, 67-71, dir div infectious dis, Dept Med, 69-71; PROF MED & MICROBIOL & DIR, DIV INFECTIOUS DIS, DEPT MED, MED UNIV SC, 72- *Concurrent Pos:* USPHS fel, Sch Med, Emory Univ, 61-62; vis mem staff, Grady Mem Hosp, 65-; partic, Int Conf Molecular Biol of Gram-Negative Bacteria, NY Acad Sci, 65, Int Conf Biol Effects of Gram-Negative Bacteria, Nat Ctr Sci Res, France, 68 & Int Conf Recombinant DNA Molecules, Nat Res Coun, Nat Acad Sci, Calif, 75; consult, Emory Univ Clin, 65-71; consult malaria res prog, NIH, Atlanta Fed Prison, 67- *Mem:* AAAS; Am Fedn Clin Res; Royal Soc Med; Am Soc Microbiol; fel Am Col Physicians. *Res:* Resistance of bacteria to antibiotics; bacterial flora of gastrointestinal tract; bacterial endotoxins; infections due to Gram-negative bacteria. *Mailing Add:* Dept of Med Med Univ of SC Charleston SC 29403

FARRAR, WILLIAM WESLEY, b Birmingham, Ala, July 29, 40; 67; c 2. BIOCHEMISTRY, ANATOMY. *Educ:* Samford Univ, BS, 64; Med Col Va, MS, 68; Va Polytech Inst & State Univ, PhD(biochem), 70. *Prof Exp:* NIH trainee biochem, Univ Utah, 70-71; NIH fel, Mich State Univ, 71-74; res assoc oncol, Med Col Va, 74-76; asst prof 76-79, ASSOC PROF BIOL, EASTERN KY UNIV, 79- *Mem:* Sigma Xi; Biochem Soc; Int Soc Neurochemistry. *Res:* Physical, chemical and kinetic properties of glycolytic enzymes from flight muscle of birds; developmental enzymology of birds. *Mailing Add:* 218 Magnolia Dr Richmond KY 40475

FARRELL, DAVID E, b May 9, 39; US citizen. PHYSICS. *Educ:* Univ London, BSc, 60, PhD(physics), 64. *Prof Exp:* Res asst physics, Univ London, 64; fel, Western Reserve Univ, 64-66, instr, 66-67; asst prof, 67-72, assoc prof, 72-80, PROF PHYSICS, CASE WESTERN RESERVE UNIV, 80- *Mem:* Am Phys Soc. *Res:* Low temperature physics; superconductivity; biomagnetism. *Mailing Add:* Dept of Physics Case Western Reserve Univ Cleveland OH 44106

FARRELL, EDWARD JOSEPH, b San Francisco, Calif, Mar 28, 17; m 54; c 2. MATHEMATICS. *Educ:* Univ San Francisco, BSc, 39; Stanford Univ, MA, 42. *Prof Exp:* Assoc prof, 41-68, PROF MATH, UNIV SAN FRANCISCO, 68-, DIR MATH INST, 60- *Concurrent Pos:* NSF dir inst progs, 60- & dir NSF Summer Conf Geom, 67-75. *Mem:* AAAS; Am Inst Phys; Math Asn Am. *Res:* Differential equations. *Mailing Add:* Dept of Math Univ of San Francisco San Francisco CA 94117

FARRELL, EUGENE PATRICK, b Wamego, Kans, July 3, 11; m 35; c 5. FOOD ENGINEERING. *Educ:* Kans State Univ, BS, 35, MS, 53. *Prof Exp:* Trainee, Gen Mills, Inc, Minn, 35-38, miller, NY, 38-42, plant supt, Ky, 42-43 & Iowa, 43-45, div supt, Minn, 45-47; prod mgr, Maney Milling Co, Nebr,

47-49; milling technologist, 49-53, assoc prof flour & feed milling indust, 53-67, PROF GRAIN SCI & INDUST, KANS STATE UNIV, 67- *Concurrent Pos:* Consult, 51- *Res:* Flour milling; flow diagrams; equipment layout and operation; wheat quality evaluation and conditioning; feed grain grinding; corn and sorghum milling. *Mailing Add:* Dept of Grain Sci & Indust Kans State Univ Manhattan KS 66506

FARRELL, HAROLD MARON, JR, b Pottsville, Pa, Sept 5, 40; m 63; c 2. PROTEIN CHEMISTRY, ENZYMOLOGY. *Educ:* Mt St Mary's Col, Md, BS, 62; Pa State Univ, MS, 65, PhD(biochem), 68. *Prof Exp:* Asst biochem, Pa State Univ, 63-66, res asst, 66-67; res assoc protein chem, 67-69, res chemist, 69-75, SUPVRY RES CHEMIST, EASTERN REGIONAL LAB, USDA, 75- *Mem:* AAAS; Am Chem Soc; NY Acad Sci; Am Dairy Sci Asn; Am Soc Biol Chem. *Res:* Protein chemistry, especially the relation of protein structure to biological function; milk proteins and enzymes of lactation. *Mailing Add:* Eastern Regional Lab USDA 600 E Mermaid Lane Philadelphia PA 19118

FARRELL, J(OSEPH) B(RENDAN), b New York, NY, May 3, 23; m 51; c 7. CHEMICAL ENGINEERING. *Educ:* Univ Notre Dame, BS, 43; Mass Inst Technol, MS, 47; Cornell Univ, PhD(chem eng), 54. *Prof Exp:* Chem engr, Kellex Corp, 44-45; instr chem eng, Univ Notre Dame, 47-49; res chem engr, M W Kellogg Co, 51-55; res assoc, Am Mach & Foundry Co, 56-61; assoc prof chem eng, Manhattan Col, 61-67; chem engr, RA, Taft Water Res Ctr, US Dept Interior, Fed Water Pollution Control Admin, 67-75; SECT CHIEF, US ENVIRON PROTECTION AGENCY, 75- *Concurrent Pos:* Indust consult; adj prof chem eng, Univ Cincinnati, 79- *Mem:* Am Chem Soc; Am Inst Chem Engrs; Water Pollution Control Asn. *Res:* Flow of non-Newtonian liquids; film casting; drying; electrodialysis; wet oxidation of graphite; ultimate disposal of solid and liquid wastes from conventional and advanced methods for treatment of wastewater to eliminate pollution. *Mailing Add:* US Environ Protection Agency St Clair & Vine Cincinnati OH 45268

FARRELL, JOHN A, b Ft Worth, Tex, Dec 25, 35; m 58; c 1. NUCLEAR PHYSICS. *Educ:* Tex Christian Univ, BA, 59; Duke Univ, PhD(physics), 64. *Prof Exp:* Res assoc physics, Duke Univ, 64-66; STAFF MEM GROUP W-8, LOS ALAMOS SCI LAB, UNIV CALIF, 66- *Mem:* Am Phys Soc. *Res:* Neutron total cross sections in the kilovolt energy region. *Mailing Add:* Physics Div MS 808 Los Alamos Sci Lab Los Alamos NM 87545

FARRELL, LARRY DON, b Woodward, Okla, Nov 5, 42; m 65; c 2. MICROBIOLOGY, MICROBIAL GENETICS. *Educ:* Univ Okla, BS, 64, MS, 66; Univ Calif, Los Angeles, PhD(bact), 70. *Prof Exp:* Fel & instr microbiol, Univ Ill Col Med, 70-72; asst prof, 72-78, ASSOC PROF MICROBIOL, IDAHO STATE UNIV, 78-, CHMN DEPT, 77- *Mem:* Am Soc Microbiol; AAAS; Sigma Xi. *Res:* Bacterial DNA-membrane associations; replication and repair of bacterial DNA; bacterial virology; extremely thermophilic bacteria. *Mailing Add:* Dept of Microbiol & Biochem Idaho State Univ Pocatello ID 83209

FARRELL, MARGARET ALICE, b Troy, NY, Mar 9, 32. MATHEMATICS EDUCATION. *Educ:* Col St Rose, Albany, AB, 53; Boston Col, MEd, 54; Ind Univ, PhD(math educ), 67. *Prof Exp:* Teacher math, Brasher Falls Cent Sch, NY, 54-55, Chatham Cent Sch, NY, 55-58 & Shaker High Sch, NY, 58-60; from assist prof to assoc prof, 60-73, PROF MATH EDUC, STATE UNIV NY ALBANY, 73- *Concurrent Pos:* Mem, Nat Comn Educ Teachers, 75- *Mem:* Sigma Xi. *Res:* Piagetian research in mathematics education; mathematics teacher education. *Mailing Add:* 32 Oak Rd Delmar NY 12054

FARRELL, RICHARD ALFRED, b Providence, RI, Apr 22, 39; m 61; c 2. PHYSICS, BIOPHYSICS. *Educ:* Providence Col, BS, 60; Univ Mass, MS, 62; Cath Univ Am, PhD(physics), 65. *Prof Exp:* NASA grant, Cath Univ Am, 64-65; sr staff physicist, 65-70, prin prof staff physicist, 70-77, SUPVR THEORET PROBS GROUP, APPL PHYSICS LAB, JOHNS HOPKINS UNIV, 77- *Concurrent Pos:* Prin investr, USPHS grant, Nat Eye Inst, NIH, 73-; prin investr, US Army Med Res & Develop Command Contract, 77- & Geosci Div, US Army Res Off Contract, 80- *Mem:* Am Phys Soc; NY Acad Sci; Asn Res Vision & Ophthal. *Res:* Application of theoretical physics to the fields of eye research; statistical mechanics and light scattering. *Mailing Add:* Appl Physics Lab Johns Hopkins Rd Laurel MD 20810

FARRELL, ROBERT LAWRENCE, b Zanesville, Ohio, Oct 6, 25; m 45; c 4. VETERINARY PATHOLOGY. *Educ:* Ohio State Univ, DVM, 50, MSc, 51, PhD(vet path), 54. *Prof Exp:* From instr to prof vet path, Ohio State Univ, 51-73; PROF, DEPT PATH, UNIV GA, 73- *Concurrent Pos:* Consult, Procter & Gamble Co, 73- *Mem:* AAAS; Am Col Vet Path; Am Vet Med Asn; Conf Res Workers Animal Dis; Int Acad Path. *Res:* Effects of toxic aerosols on respiratory tract of animals; study of bovine pneumonia. *Mailing Add:* Dept of Path Col of Vet Med Univ of Ga Athens GA 30602

FARRELL, ROBERT MICHAEL, b Honesdale, Pa, Nov 5, 47; m 72; c 2. COMPUTER SCIENCE. *Educ:* Villanova Univ, BEE, 69; Univ Pa, MSE, 71, PhD(sci eng), 79. *Prof Exp:* Engr, 69-74, sr engr, 74-79, MGR ADVAN TECHNOL, SPACE DIV, GEN ELEC, 79- *Concurrent Pos:* Lectr comput archit & orgn, Villanova Univ, 82- *Mem:* Inst Elec & Electronics Engrs; Asn Comput Mach. *Res:* Computer network mathematical models, performance estimation, and optimization; distributed database modeling, performance estimation and optimization; computer network architectures and designs to meet specific requirements. *Mailing Add:* 544 Deerfield Dr Norristown PA 19401

FARRELL, ROGER HAMLIN, b Greensboro, NC, July 23, 29; m 67. MATHEMATICAL STATISTICS. *Educ:* Univ Chicago, PhB, 47, MS, 51; Univ Ill, PhD(math), 59. *Prof Exp:* From instr to assoc prof, 59-67, PROF MATH, CORNELL UNIV, 67- *Mem:* Am Math Soc; Inst Math Statist; Am Statist Asn. *Res:* Measure theory; probability theory; mathematical statistics. *Mailing Add:* Dept of Math Cornell Univ Ithaca NY 14853

FARRELL, ROY KEITH, b Bend, Ore, Apr 10, 26; m 50; c 1. VETERINARY MEDICINE. *Educ:* Ore State Col, BS, 51; Wash State Univ, DVM, 55. *Prof Exp:* Coop agt, USDA, 55-58, vet med officer, Sci & Educ Admin, Col Vet Med, Wash State Univ, 58-66, vet med officer, USDA Agr Res Serv, Endoparasite Vector Pioneering Res Lab, Col Vet Med, 66-80, PROF, DIV PHARMACOL & TOXICOL, WASH STATE UNIV, 80- *Mem:* Wildlife Dis Asn; Am Vet Med Asn; Am Col Vet Toxicol; US Animal Health Asn; AAAS. *Res:* Veterinary cryobiology. *Mailing Add:* Col Vet Med Wash State Univ Pullman WA 99163

FARREN, ANN LOUISE, b Portage, Pa, Dec 5, 26. BIOCHEMISTRY, INFORMATION SCIENCE. *Educ:* Univ Pa, AB, 48. *Prof Exp:* Biochemist, Valley Forge US Army Hosp, Pa, 49-50 & Jefferson Med Col, 50-52; org chemist, Smith Kline & French Labs, 52-53; anal chemist, Rohm & Haas Co, 53-56; with info off pub rels, News Serv, Am Chem Soc, NY, 56-59; asst to dir, Biol Abstracts, Inc, 59-61; actg head, Lit Acquisition Dept, 61-62, prof rels off, 62-74, mgr educ bur, 74-78, mgr, User Commun, 78-80, SR EDUC ASSOC, BIOSCI INFO SERV, 80- *Concurrent Pos:* Mem, Nat Fedn Sci Abstracting & Indexing Serv. *Mem:* Fel AAAS; Am Chem Soc; Nat Asn Sci Writers; Am Inst Biol Sci; Drug Info Asn. *Res:* Hepatic and metabolic diseases; organic syntheses; colchicine derivatives; ion exchange resins; abstracting, indexing, information retrieval; education. *Mailing Add:* Biosis 2100 Arch St Philadelphia PA 19103

FARRIER, MAURICE HUGH, b Washington Co, Iowa, Sept 18, 26; m 56; c 1. ACAROLOGY, FOREST ENTOMOLOGY. *Educ:* Iowa State Univ, BS, 48, MS, 50; NC State Col, PhD(entom), 55. *Prof Exp:* Asst to state entomologist, State of Iowa, 50-52; asst entom, 54-55, asst res prof, 55-60, assoc prof, 60-71, PROF ENTOM, NC STATE UNIV, 71- *Honors & Awards:* Southern Insect Work Conf Outstanding Contrib Award, 70. *Mem:* Entom Soc Am; Int Soc Soil Sci. *Res:* Taxonomy of Veigaiidae and other gamasid mites in forest soils; forest entomology and bibliographic documentation in biology. *Mailing Add:* NC State Univ Dept Entom PO Box 5215 Raleigh NC 27607

FARRIER, NOEL JOHN, b Pittsburgh, Pa, Dec 9, 37; m 73. ENVIRONMENTAL HEALTH, BIOINORGANIC CHEMISTRY. *Educ:* Carnegie Inst Technol, BS, 60, Univ Pittsburgh, MS, 64, MPH, 80; Ohio State Univ, PhD(inorg coord chem), 69. *Prof Exp:* Lab technician chem, Mellon Inst, 61; trainee metalloenzyme chem, Clin Study Ctr, Children's Hosp, Columbus, Ohio, 64; asst prof chem, Wittenberg Univ, 68-69; vis res assoc physiol chem, Col Med, Ohio State Univ, 69-70; asst prof chem, Raymond Walters Gen & Tech Col, Univ Cincinnati, 70-76, instr nutrit, 75-76; instr chem & phys sci, Edison State Community Col, Piqua, Ohio, 76-78; FEL, DEPT EPIDEMIOL, GRAD SCH PUB HEALTH, UNIV PITTSBURGH, 78- *Mem:* Am Chem Soc; Soc Epidemiol Res. *Res:* Coordination compounds of cobalt III, copper II and copper I containing unusual monodentate ligands; kinetics; infrared studies; blood lead studies in children; trace metals and cardiovascular diseases; trace metals in foods; carbon monoxide in blood of smokers, former smokers and never smokers. *Mailing Add:* Dept of Epidemiol Univ of Pittsburgh Pittsburgh PA 15261

FARRINGER, LELAND DWIGHT, b Lena, Ill, May 28, 27; m 50; c 3. PHYSICS. *Educ:* Manchester Col, BA, 49; Bethany Biblical Sem, BD, 52; Ohio State Univ, MA, 55, PhD(physics), 58. *Prof Exp:* Asst physics, Ohio State Univ, 52-58; from asst prof to assoc prof, 58-69, PROF PHYSICS, MANCHESTER COL, 69-, HEAD DEPT, 59-, CHMN, DIV SCI, 80- *Mem:* Am Phys Soc; Am Asn Physics Teachers. *Res:* Nuclear magnetic resonance; physical electronics; electronic circuitry; scintillation spectrometry of gamma rays. *Mailing Add:* Dept of Physics Manchester Col North Manchester IN 46962

FARRINGTON, GREGORY CHARLES, b Bronxville, NY, Aug 4, 46; m 70. PHYSICAL CHEMISTRY, ELECTROCHEMISTRY. *Educ:* Clarkson Col, BS, 68; Harvard Univ, AM, 70, PhD(chem), 72. *Prof Exp:* Res chemist, Gen Elec Res & Develop Corp, 72-79; ASSOC PROF, DEPT MAT SCI, UNIV PA, PHILADELPHIA, 79- *Mem:* AAAS; Electrochem Soc; Am Chem Soc. *Res:* Conduction in solid electrolytes; interfacial electrochemistry of Na beta alumina and derivatives; solid state batteries; dielectric properties of solids. *Mailing Add:* Gen Elec Res & Develop Corp PO Box 8 Schenectady NY 12301

FARRINGTON, JOHN WILLIAM, b New Bedford, Mass, Sept 25, 44; m 66; c 2. MARINE GEOCHEMISTRY. *Educ:* Southeastern Mass Univ, BS, 66, MS, 68; Univ RI, PhD(oceanog), 72. *Prof Exp:* Chem investr, 71-72, asst scientist, 72-76, ASSOC SCIENTIST CHEM, WOODS HOLE OCEANOG INST, 76-, DIR, COASTAL RES CTR, 81- *Mem:* Sigma Xi; AAAS; Am Chem Soc. *Res:* Sediment-water interface; organic geochemical processes in the marine environment; marine biochemistry. *Mailing Add:* Dept of Chem Woods Hole Oceanog Inst Woods Hole MA 02543

FARRINGTON, PAUL STEPHEN, b Indianapolis, Ind, May 9, 19; m 46; c 5. ANALYTICAL CHEMISTRY. *Educ:* Calif Inst Technol, BS, 41, MS, 47, ChE, 48, PhD(chem), 50. *Prof Exp:* Control & res chemist, Kelco Co, 41-42; asst chem, Calif Inst Technol, 42-45 & 48-49; from instr to assoc prof, 52-62, PROF CHEM & ASSOC DEAN COL LETTERS & SCI, UNIV CALIF, LOS ANGELES, 62- *Concurrent Pos:* Guggenheim Found fel, Ger, 58-59. *Mem:* Am Chem Soc. *Res:* Coulometric and other instrumental methods of analysis, inorganic complexes. *Mailing Add:* Dept of Chem Univ of Calif Los Angeles CA 90024

FARRINGTON, WILLIAM BENFORD, b New York, NY, Mar 10, 21; div; c 3. STRUCTURAL GEOLOGY. *Educ:* Cornell Univ, BCE, 47, MS, 49; Mass Inst Technol, PhD(geol), 53. *Prof Exp:* Radio engr radar design, Naval Res Labs, 42-43; plant engr, Hope's Windows, Inc, 50-51; instr geol, Univ Mass, 53-54; res geophysicist, Humble Oil & Ref Co, 54-56; investment analyst, Continental Res Corp, 56-61; vpres, Empire Resources Corp, Empire Trust Co, 61-64; sci dir, US Cong House Select Comt Govt Res, 64-65;

PARTNER, FARRINGTON & LIGHT ASSOCS, 67- *Concurrent Pos:* Eve lectr, Univ Houston, 55-56; pres, Farrington Eng Corp, 58-67; eve lectr, Univ Calif, Los Angeles, 68- *Mem:* Geol Soc Am; Am Inst Aeronaut & Astronaut; Am Petrol Inst; fel AAAS; fel Financial Analyst Fedn. *Res:* Theory and measurement of stress distribution in rocks. *Mailing Add:* Farrington & Light Assocs 1565 Skyline Dr Laguna Beach CA 92651

FARRIS, DAVID ALLEN, b Bloomington, Ind, Mar 26, 28; m 56; c 2. FISHERIES. *Educ:* Ind Univ, AB, 50; Stanford Univ, PhD(biol), 58. *Prof Exp:* Field asst fisheries, Ind Lake & Stream Surv, 43-50; asst biol, Stanford Univ, 53-54; res fisheries biologist, Bur Commercial Fisheries, 55-60; from asst prof to assoc prof biol, 60-66, PROF BIOL, SAN DIEGO STATE UNIV, 66- *Mem:* AAAS; Am Soc Limnol & Oceanog; Am Inst Fishery Res Biol. *Res:* Population dynamics of egg and larval fish populations; the intrinsic and extrinsic factors which govern growth and death of fish larvae; factors which govern changes in the biochemistry of fishes. *Mailing Add:* Dept of Biol San Diego State Univ San Diego CA 92182

FARRIS, HANSFORD WHITE, b Blackford, Ky, Oct 7, 19; m 42; c 2. ELECTRONICS, COMMUNICATIONS. *Educ:* Eastern Ky State Teachers Col, BS, 41, MA, 42; Univ Ill, MS, 48; Univ Mich, PhD(elec eng), 58. *Prof Exp:* Asst electronics, Univ Ill, 47-48, 51-53; asst prof elec eng, Univ Ky, 48-51; res assoc eng res inst, 53-58, from asst prof to assoc prof elec eng, 58-61, dir electronics res lab, 58-62, assoc dir inst sci & tech & dir indust develop div, 63-65, chmn dept elec eng, 65-68, assoc dean col eng, 68-73, PROF ELEC ENG, UNIV MICH, ANN ARBOR, 61-, PROF COMPUT ENG, 80- *Concurrent Pos:* Secy, Nat Electronics Conf, 64, vpres, 65, pres, 66, bd chmn, 69-70; eng educ consult & evaluator. *Honors & Awards:* Amoco Found Undergrad Teaching Award, 76. *Mem:* Inst Elec & Electronics Engrs. *Res:* Communication systems; engineering concepts for the layman. *Mailing Add:* Dept of Elec Eng Univ of Mich Ann Arbor MI 48109

FARRIS, RICHARD AUSTIN, b Baltimore, Md, July 24, 43; m 66; c 1. MARINE ECOLOGY. *Educ:* Calif Luthern Col, BA, 66; Calif State Univ, Humboldt, MA, 68; Univ NC, Chapel Hill, PhD(zool), 76. *Prof Exp:* Teacher biol, Newbury Park High Sch, 68-70; ASSOC PROF BIOL, LINFIELD COL, 74- *Concurrent Pos:* Montgomery-Moore fel, Bermuda Biol Sta, 74; chmn, Sci State Adv Bd, 79-81. *Mem:* Asn Meiobenthologists; Sigma Xi; AAAS; Am Soc Zoologists. *Res:* Ecology and systematics of marine interstitial organisms in the Northwest and Bermuda, with emphasis on the phylum Gnathostomulida. *Mailing Add:* Dept of Biol Linfield Col McMinnville OR 97128

FARRISSEY, WILLIAM JOSEPH, JR, b Fall River, Mass, Nov 19, 31; m 57; c 4. ORGANIC POLYMER CHEMISTRY. *Educ:* Yale Univ, BS, 53, MS, 55, PhD, 57. *Prof Exp:* Fel, Rice Univ, 56-57; instr chem, Rutgers Univ, 57-58; res chemist, Humble Oil & Refining Co, 58-61, sr res chemist, 61-63; group leader, 63-64, head new prod, 64-66, mgr process res, 66-69, mgr polymer res, Carwin Res Labs, 69-78, GROUP MGR POLYMER RES & RES ADMIN, D S GILMORE LABS, UPJOHN CO, 78- *Mem:* Am Chem Soc. *Res:* High temperature polymers; polyimides; isocyanate polymers. *Mailing Add:* Maltby Lane Northford CT 06472

FARROW, LEONILDA ALTMAN, b Brooklyn, NY, May 11, 29; m 56. CHEMICAL PHYSICS. *Educ:* Cornell Univ, BEngPhysics), 51; Mass Inst Technol, PhD(physics), 56. *Prof Exp:* Res asst physics, Mass Inst Technol, 51-56; MEM TECH STAFF RES CHEM, BELL LABS, 56- *Mem:* Am Phys Soc. *Res:* Chemical kinetics; reaction rate measurements; absorption spectroscopy; infared lasers; molecular spectroscopy; optoacoustics; atmospheric chemical reactions; chemistry of the contaminated troposphere; computer simulation; environmental physics and chemistry; plasma etching. *Mailing Add:* 66 Seaview Terr Monmouth Hills NJ 07732

FARROW, WENDALL MOORE, b Winchester, Mass, June 20, 22; m 49; c 2. MICROBIOLOGY. *Educ:* Univ Iowa, BA, 49, MS, 51, PhD(bot, mycol), 53. *Prof Exp:* Asst, Univ Iowa, 49-53; microbiologist, Commercial Solvents Corp, 53-56, Hoffman-La Roche, Inc, 56-63, Marine Lab, Fla Bd Conserv, 63-65 & Germ-free Prod, Inc, 65-68; res assoc, 68-80, DIR LAB & SAFETY OFF, LIFE SCI, INC, 80- *Mem:* Mycol Soc Am; Am Soc Microbiol. *Res:* Microbial fermentations; fungicides; carotenoids of microorganisms; soil fungi; marine bacteria and phytoplankton; animal breeding and development; gnotobiology. *Mailing Add:* Life Sci Inc 2900 72nd St N St Petersburg FL 33710

FARTHING, BARTON ROBY, b Watauga Co, NC, Feb 20, 16; m 38; c 3. APPLIED STATISTICS. *Educ:* Wake Forest Col, BS, 38; NC State Col, MS, 54, PhD(animal breeding), 58. *Prof Exp:* Res instr, NC State Col, 54-58, asst prof, 58-59; exp sta statistician, La State Univ, Baton Rouge, 59-64, head dept, 64-77, prof exp statist, 77-81; RETIRED. *Mem:* Biomet Soc; Am Soc Animal Sci; Am Dairy Sci Asn. *Res:* Design of experiments; analysis and interpretation of data. *Mailing Add:* Rte 2 Box 279 Vilas NC 28692

FARVOLDEN, ROBERT NORMAN, b Forestburg, Alta, May 22, 28; m 54; c 2. HYDROGEOLOGY. *Educ:* Univ Alta, BSc, 51, MSc, 58; Univ Ill, PhD, 63. *Prof Exp:* Head groundwater div, Res Coun Alta, 56-60; res assoc, Desert Res Inst, Univ Nev, 62-64; from asst prof to assoc prof geol, Univ Ill, Urbana, 64-67; assoc prof, Univ Western Ont, 67-70; chmn dept earth sci, 70-76, ASSOC PROF GEOL, UNIV WATERLOO, 70-, DEAN FAC SCI, 77- *Mem:* Fel Geol Soc Am; Am Geophys Union; fel Geol Asn Can. *Res:* Water resources development; solid-waste disposal; scientific hydrology. *Mailing Add:* Dept of Earth Sci Univ of Waterloo Waterloo Can

FARWELL, DONALD CHARLES, biochemistry, molecular biology, see previous edition

FARWELL, GEORGE WELLS, b Oakland, Calif, Feb 15, 20; m 45; c 4. PHYSICS. *Educ:* Harvard Univ, BS, 41; Univ Chicago, PhD(physics), 48. *Prof Exp:* Asst physics, Radiation Lab, Univ Calif, 42-43, physicist, Los Alamos Sci Lab, NMex, 43-46; from asst prof to assoc prof, 48-59, assoc dean, Grad Sch, 59-65, asst vpres, 65-67, vpres res, 67-76, PROF PHYSICS, UNIV WASH, 59- *Concurrent Pos:* Sr fel, NSF, 60-61. *Mem:* Fel Am Phys Soc. *Res:* Nuclear physics; radiochronology, ultrasensitive mass spectrometry with accelerators. *Mailing Add:* Dept of Physics Univ of Wash FM-15 Seattle WA 98195

FARWELL, ROBERT WILLIAM, b Providence, RI, May 11, 27; div; c 2. PHYSICS. *Educ:* Yale Univ, BS, 50; Pa State Univ, MS, 55, PhD(physics), 60. *Prof Exp:* Res asst physics, Ord Res Lab, 51, res assoc, 51-58, asst, Dept Physics, 58-59, asst prof eng res, 60-65, ASSOC PROF ENG RES, APPL RES LAB, PA STATE UNIV, 65- *Concurrent Pos:* Mem, Int Oceanog Found. *Mem:* Acoust Soc Am. *Res:* Underwater sound transmission; reverberation; sound scat scattering; transducer calibrations; acoustic torpedoes; sonar; effect of sound on tissues; enzyme kinetics; ultraviolet and visible spectrophotometers. *Mailing Add:* Pa State Univ Appl Res Lab PO Box 30 State College PA 16801

FARY, ISTVAN, b Gyula, Hungary, June 30, 22; m 57; c 1. MATHEMATICS. *Educ:* Eotvos Lorand Univ, Budapest, MA, 44; Szeged Univ, PhD, 48; Sorbonne, DSc, 55. *Prof Exp:* Asst math, Nat Sci Res Ctr, France, 48-52, in charge res, 52-55; res fel, Nat Res Coun Can, 55-56; assoc prof math, Montreal Univ, 56-57; assoc prof, 57-71, PROF MATH, UNIV CALIF, BERKELEY, 71- *Mem:* Am Math Soc; Math Asn Am; Math Soc France. *Res:* Algebraic topology; geometry. *Mailing Add:* Dept Math 970 Evans Hall Univ Calif Berkeley CA 94720

FARY, RAYMOND W, JR, b Long Branch, NJ, Apr 14, 18; m 41; c 6. GEOLOGY. *Educ:* Wash Univ, AB, 47, MA, 48. *Prof Exp:* Explor geologist, Pure Oil Co, Inc, 48-60; geologist, Subsurface Sect, Ohio Geol Surv, 60-61; geologist, Strategic Studies Sect, Mil Geol Br, 61-62, res supvr, 62-64, chief eastern area unit, Geol Group, 64-66, chief remote sensing eval & coord staff, 66-71, asst mgr training & info progs, Earth Resources Observ Systs Prog, 71-74, coordr remote sensing, 74-76, OFF INT GEOL, US GEOL SURV, 76- *Concurrent Pos:* Consult, Adv Group Minerals Develop, Cent Treaty Orgn, 71-; res geologist energy resources, 76-79; dep chief, Br Am & African Geol, 79-81, actg chief, 81- *Res:* Development and coordination of programs for international cooperation in scientific exchange and technology transfer. *Mailing Add:* Off of Int Geol MS 917 US Geol Surv Reston VA 22092

FASANO, ANTHONY VINCENT, b Montclair, NJ, Dec 28, 36; m 65; c 2. ANATOMY, NEUROENDOCRINOLOGY. *Educ:* Colo State Univ, AB, 64; Stritch Sch Med, Loyola Univ, PhD(anat), 72. *Prof Exp:* Instr anat & neuroanat, Philadelphia Col Osteopath Med, 71-72; instr, 72-73, ASST PROF ANAT, COL MED & DENT NJ, 73- *Concurrent Pos:* Consult, East Orange Vet Admin Hosp, NJ, 73; mem supvry comt, Fed Credit Union, Col Med & Dent NJ, 74- *Mem:* Am Soc Zool; Am Asn Univ Prof. *Res:* Interrelationship of the pineal gland and the estrous and reproductive mechanisms in the albino rat as studied by histochemical and biochemical methods. *Mailing Add:* Dept of Anat Col of Med & Dent NJ 100 Bergen St Newark NJ 07103

FASBENDER, M VERONICA, invertebrate zoology, palynology, see previous edition

FASCHING, JAMES LE ROY, b Dickinson, NDak, Mar 15, 42; m 69. ANALYTICAL CHEMISTRY, CHEMOMETRICS. *Educ:* NDak State Univ, BS, 64; Mass Inst Technol, SM, 67, PhD(chem), 70. *Prof Exp:* Res asst chem, NDak State Univ, 62-63, instr, 63; asst, Mass Inst Technol, 64-70; from instr to assoc prof, 69-81, PROF CHEM, UNIV RI, 81- *Mem:* Sigma Xi; AAAS; Am Phys Soc; Am Chem Soc; Soc Appl Spectros. *Res:* Neutron activation analysis of biological samples; effects of trace element on cancer pattern recognition techniques; minicomputers; microprocessors for data acquisition and control and development of piezoelectric sorption devices; aerosols, global pollution transport. *Mailing Add:* Dept Chem Univ RI Kingston RI 02881

FASHENA, GLADYS JEANNETTE, b New York, NY, June 3, 10; m 38; c 2. PEDIATRICS, PEDIATRIC CARDIOLOGY. *Educ:* Hunter Col, BA, 29; Columbia Univ, MA, 30; Cornell Univ, MD, 34. *Prof Exp:* Instr pediat, Med Col, Cornell Univ, 37-38; instr, Baylor Col Med, 39-43; from instr to assoc prof, 43-49, PROF PEDIAT, UNIV TEX SOUTHWESTERN MED SCH, DALLAS, 49-, DIR REGIONAL CONGENITAL HEART DIS PROG, 52- *Honors & Awards:* Piper Prof, Minnie Stevans Piper Found, 74. *Mem:* Am Acad Pediat; Am Pediat Soc; Soc Pediat Res; Am Soc Clin Invest; Am Col Cardiol. *Res:* Development of methods for assay of various substances in blood; bilirubin metabolism in infancy; physiological aspects of congenital heart disease. *Mailing Add:* Univ of Tex Health Sci Ctr 5323 Harry Hines Blvd Dallas TX 75235

FASHING, NORMAN JAMES, b Walker, Minn, Aug 14, 43; m 69; c 2. ACAROLOGY. *Educ:* Calif State Univ, Chico, BA, 65, MA, 67; Univ Kans, PhD(entom), 73. *Prof Exp:* ASST PROF BIOL, COL WILLIAM & MARY, 73- *Mem:* Acarological Soc Am; Entom Soc Am. *Res:* Orientation behavior of insects and arachnids; taxonomy and biology of acarid mites. *Mailing Add:* Dept of Biol Col of William & Mary Williamsburg VA 23185

FASK, ALAN S, b New York, NY, Oct 26, 45. STATISTICS, OPERATIONS RESEARCH. *Educ:* City Col New York, BS, 68; NY Univ, MS, 72, PhD(statist), 73. *Prof Exp:* ASSOC PROF COMPUT & DECISION SYSTS, FAIRLEIGH DICKINSON UNIV, 73- *Mem:* Am Statist Asn; Opers Res Soc Am; Inst Mgt Sci; Economet Soc. *Res:* Applications of multivariate and time series statistical techniques to economics and marketing; optimal control of industrial processes. *Mailing Add:* 5445 Netherland Ave Riverdale NY 10471

FASMAN, GERALD DAVID, b Drumheller, Alta, May 28, 25; nat US; m 53; c 3. BIOCHEMISTRY, BIOPHYSICS. *Educ:* Univ Alta, BSc, 48; Calif Inst Technol, PhD(chem), 52. *Prof Exp:* Royal Soc Can scholar, Cambridge Univ, 51-53; Merck fel natural sci, Eng Tech Inst, Zurich, 53-54; Weizmann fel, Weizmann Inst, 54-55; asst, Children's Res Found, Boston, 55-56, res assoc, 57-61, asst head biophys chem, 59-61; from asst prof to prof biochem, 61-71, ROSENFIELD PROF BIOCHEM, BRANDEIS UNIV, 71- *Concurrent Pos:* Asst, Med Sch, Harvard Univ, 57-58, res assoc, 58-61, tutor, univ, 60-61; estab investr, Am Heart Asn, 61-66; ed, Biol Macromolecules & Critical Rev in Biochem, 72-; ed, Handbk Biochem & Molecular Biol, 73-; John Guggenheim fel, 74-75; res scholar, Japan Soc Prom Sci, 79; mem, NSF Adv Panel, 79. *Mem:* Fel AAAS; fel Am Inst Chemists; Am Chem Soc; Am Soc Biol Chem; NY Acad Sci. *Res:* Enzymes, proteins, nucleic and polyamino acids; chromatin; conformational studies of biopolymers. *Mailing Add:* Grad Dept of Biochem Brandeis Univ Waltham MA 02154

FASOLA, ALFRED FRANCIS, b Pa, Mar 29, 19; m; c 2. CARDIOPULMONARY PHYSIOLOGY. *Educ:* Oberlin Col, AB, 48; Ohio State Univ, MS, 50, PhD(physiol), 53, MD, 57. *Prof Exp:* Res assoc, Ohio State Univ, 53-55, instr physiol, 55-57; intern, Mt Carmel Hosp, Columbus, Ohio, 57-58; resident internal med, Wishard Mem Hosp, Indianapolis, 59-60 & 60-61; ASST PROF MED, MED CTR, IND UNIV, INDIANAPOLIS, 68- *Concurrent Pos:* Res fel cardiol, Robert Moore Heart Clin, Indianapolis, 58-59; staff physician, Lilly Lab Clin Res, Wishard Mem Hosp, Indianapolis, 61-66, sr physician, 66-75, sr clin pharmacologist, 75-; mem coun arteriosclerosis, Am Heart Asn; mem, Med Adv Bd Coun High Blood Pressure. *Mem:* Am Heart Asn; Aerospace Med Asn; fel Am Col Cardiol; Am Col Physicians. *Res:* Space research, effects of deceleration and negative gravity; general cardiovascular research; renin-angiotensin system in hypertension. *Mailing Add:* Lilly Lab Clin Res Wishard Mem Hosp Indianapolis IN 46202

FASS, ARNOLD LIONEL, b New York, NY, Apr 2, 22. MATHEMATICS. *Educ:* City Col New York, BS, 42; Columbia Univ, MA, 47, PhD(math), 51. *Prof Exp:* Lectr math, Columbia Univ, 48-51; tutor, 51, from instr to assoc prof, 51-76, PROF MATH, QUEENS COL, NY, 77- *Concurrent Pos:* Lectr, NSF Inst Teacher Training, 61-62. *Mem:* AAAS; Am Math Soc; Math Asn Am. *Res:* Homology and cohomology of linear algebras; topological methods in algebra; general linear algebra. *Mailing Add:* 41-25 Kissena Blvd Flushing NY 11355

FASS, RICHARD A, b Brooklyn, NY, June 13, 43; m 64; c 1. PHYSICAL CHEMISTRY. *Educ:* Cooper Union, BE; Univ Wis, PhD(phys chem), 69. *Prof Exp:* Res assoc photochem kinetics & radiation chem, Univ Wis, 69; asst prof chem, 69-73 & 77-79, assoc dean, 73-76, DEAN STUDENTS, POMONA COL, 76-, VPRES, 79- *Res:* Reactions of hot and thermal hydrogen atoms produced by photolysis of hydrogen halides; reactions of hot free radicals in the gas phase; gas kinetics. *Mailing Add:* Sumner Hall Pomona Col Claremont CA 91711

FASS, STEPHEN M, b New York, NY, Aug 22, 38; m 66; c 2. CHEMICAL ENGINEERING. *Educ:* Cooper Union, BChE, 60; Univ Colo, MS, 64, PhD(chem eng), 67. *Prof Exp:* Engr, FMC Corp, 60-62; sr res engr, US Steel Corp, 66-68; sr res engr, Gulf Res & Develop Co, 68-73; sr processing engr, Ralph M Parsons Co, 73-77, Crawford & Russell, 77-78; prin processing engr, 78-81, SECT MGR, FMC CORP, NJ, 81- *Mem:* Am Inst Chem Engrs. *Res:* Reaction kinetics; reactor design and process research in steel, petroleum and organic chemicals industries. *Mailing Add:* FMC Corp PO Box 8 Princeton NJ 08540

FASSBENDER, CAROL ANNE, b Jamaica, NY, Jan 24, 43. ANALYTICAL CHEMISTRY, ANALYTICAL MICROBIOLOGY. *Educ:* Upsala Col, AB, 65, Rutgers Univ, BS, 73, PhD(microbiol), 82. *Prof Exp:* From res asst to assoc, Dept Agr Chem, Rutgers Univ, 65-71, res assoc, Dept Biochem & Microbiol, 71-78; res assoc, 78-80, RES INVESTR, SQUIBB INST MED RES, 80- *Concurrent Pos:* Lectr, York Col, 80-81, Rutgers Univ, 81-; asst prof, Baruch Col, 81- *Mem:* Am Soc Microbiologists; Sigma Xi; Asn Off Anal Chemists. *Res:* Methods development in analytical microbiology and chemistry of pharmaceuticals; metabolisom of agriculture chemicals. *Mailing Add:* E R Squibb Inc PO Box 191 New Brunswick NJ 08902

FASSEL, VELMER ARTHUR, b Frohna, Mo, Apr 26, 19; m 43. PHYSICAL CHEMISTRY, ANALYTICAL CHEMISTRY. *Educ:* Southeast Mo State Col, BA, 41; Iowa State Univ, PhD(phys chem), 47. *Prof Exp:* Asst spectros, Nat Defense Res Comt contract, 42-43, jr chemist, Manhattan Proj, 43-46, assoc chemist, Inst Atomic Res, 46-47, from asst prof to assoc prof chem, 47-54, PROF CHEM, IOWA STATE UNIV, 54-, DEP DIR ENERGY & MINERAL RESOURCES RES INST & AMES LAB, DEPT ENERGY, IOWA STATE UNIV, 69- *Concurrent Pos:* Lectr tour, Sci Coun Japan, 62; US ed, Spectrochimica Acta. *Honors & Awards:* Soc Appl Spectros Medal Award, 64; Pittsburgh Spectros Award, 69; Maurice F Hasler Award, 71; Anachem Award, 71; Fisher Award Anal Chem, Am Chem Soc, 78; Japan Soc Anal Chem Medal. *Mem:* Fel AAAS; Am Chem Soc; fel Optical Soc Am; Soc Appl Spectros. *Res:* Analytical emission spectroscopy; spectrographic analysis; infrared spectra and molecular structure correlations; fluorescence spectroscopy; analytical chemistry. *Mailing Add:* Ames Lab-DOE Iowa State Univ Ames IA 50010

FASSETT, DAVID WALTER, b Broadalbin, NY, Nov 13, 08; m 34; c 3. TOXICOLOGY. *Educ:* Columbia Univ, AB, 33; NY Univ, MD, 40. *Prof Exp:* Biochemist, Dept Exp Surg, NY Univ, 35-36; pharmacologist, Wellcome Res Lab, 36-38; intern, Bellevue Hosp, 40-41; asst therapeut, Col Med, NY Univ, 42-45; cardiologist, James M Jackson Mem Hosp, Fla, 45-48; dir health & safety lab, Eastman Kodak Co, 48-73; CONSULT, INDUST TOXICOL, 73- *Concurrent Pos:* Wellcome fel therapeut, NY Univ, 41; actg chief div pharmacol, Food & Drug Admin, Fed Security Agency, DC, 42-44; clin assoc prof prev med, Univ Rochester, 65-73; vis lectr, Harvard Sch Pub Health, 65-; consult toxicol, Nat Acad Sci, 73-76. *Honors & Awards:* Cummings Award, Am Indust Hyg Asn, 78. *Mem:* Fel AAAS; Am Soc Pharmacol & Exp Therapeut; Soc Exp Biol & Med; Am Indust Hyg Asn (pres, 69-70); Soc Toxicol. *Res:* Pharmacology; industrial toxicology; industrial hygiene. *Mailing Add:* 13 Summer St Box 739 Kennebunk ME 04043

FASSNACHT, JOHN HARTWELL, b Wenonah, NJ, Oct 22, 33; m 60; c 2. ORGANIC CHEMISTRY. *Educ:* Middlebury Col, AB, 55; Mass Inst Technol, PhD(org chem), 59. *Prof Exp:* Res chemist, Org Chem Dept, Jackson Lab, 59-62, res chemist, Freon Prod Div, 62-67, proj leader, 67-68, tech asst, 68-69, tech assoc, 70-74, territory mgr, 75-78, sr territory mgr, Freon Prod Div, 78-80, AREA MGR, INTERMEDIATES PROD DIV, E I DU PONT DE NEMOURS & CO INC, 80- *Mem:* Am Chem Soc; Sigma Xi. *Mailing Add:* 451 Beverly Pl Lake Forest IL 60045

FAST, ARLO WADE, b Mt Clemens, Mich, Nov 22, 40; m 63. AQUACULTURE, LIMNOLOGY. *Educ:* Mich State Univ, BS, 62, PhD(limnol), 71; San Diego State Univ, MS, 68. *Prof Exp:* Fishery biologist, Calif Dept Fish & Game, 63-68; aquatic ecologist, Union Carbide Corp, 71-75; owner, Limnol Assocs, 75-78; AQUACULTURIST, UNIV HAWAII, 78- *Mem:* Am Soc Limnol & Oceanog; Am Fisheries Soc; Soc Int Limnol; World Maricult Soc; Am Inst Fishery Res Biologists. *Res:* Environmental impact assessments; assessments of freshwater habitats; lake restoration; lake aeration technology. *Mailing Add:* Univ Hawaii PO Box 1346 Kaneohe HI 96744

FAST, C(LARENCE) R(OBERT), b Tulsa, Okla, Feb 12, 21; m 44; c 4. PETROLEUM ENGINEERING. *Educ:* Univ Tulsa, BS, 43. *Prof Exp:* Liaison engr, Douglas Aircraft Co, 43; Apprentice engr, Standard Oil Co, Ind, 43-56, res group supvr, Amoco Prod Co, 56-77; OWNER, FAST ENG, CONSULT PETROL ENGRS, 77- *Concurrent Pos:* Chmn nat subcomt perforating, Am Petrol Inst, exec comt prod pract; Soc Petrol Engrs distinguished lectr, 70-71; consult petrol eng probs. *Honors & Awards:* Uren Award, Soc Petrol Engrs. *Mem:* Soc Petrol Engrs; Am Petrol Inst. *Res:* Direct research on drilling, well completion, stimulation, well operation and production practice. *Mailing Add:* 4037 E 49th Tulsa OK 74135

FAST, DALE EUGENE, b Kansas City, Kans, Oct 2, 45; m 70. GENETICS, DEVELOPMENTAL BIOLOGY. *Educ:* Tabor Col, BS, 67; Univ Chicago, PhD(biol), 78. *Prof Exp:* Teacher & asst dir sci, Kikwit Sec Sch, Dem Rep Congo, 67-69; ASST PROF BIOL, ST XAVIER COL, 76- *Mem:* Genetics Soc Am; Sci for the People; AAAS. *Res:* Genetics and biochemistry of yeast sporulation; political and ethical issues in the life sciences. *Mailing Add:* Dept of Biol 103rd & Central Park Chicago IL 60655

FAST, HENRYK, b Bochnia, Poland, Oct 4, 25; nat US; div; c 1. MATHEMATICAL ANALYSIS. *Educ:* Univ Wroclaw, PhM, 50; Polish Acad Sci, PhD(math), 58. *Prof Exp:* Asst math, Univ Wroclaw, 50-51, adj, 56-60; sr asst, Polish Acad Sci, 51-55; asst prof, Univ Notre Dame, 62-66; ASSOC PROF MATH, WAYNE STATE UNIV, 66- *Concurrent Pos:* Vis scholar, Stichting Math Centrum, Amsterdam, Holland, 73-74. *Mem:* Am Math Soc; Math Asn Am. *Res:* General measure and integration, especially geometrical measure theory; functions of real variables; convex sets and set theoretical geometry; integral geometry. *Mailing Add:* Dept Math Wayne State Univ Detroit MI 48202

FAST, PATRICIA E, b Santa Monica, Calif, July 21, 43; c 1. IMMUNOLOGY. *Educ:* Univ Calif, Los Angeles, AB, 65, PhD(microbiol), 69. *Prof Exp:* Teaching asst bact, Univ Calif, Los Angeles, 66-67; asst prof microbiol, Calif State Univ, Los Angeles, 69-70; asst res biologist, Univ Calif, Los Angeles, 70; staff scientist, Wellcome Res Labs, 70-72; asst prof pediat, microbiol & immunol, Univ Calif, Los Angeles & Harbor Gen Hosp, Torrance, 72-75; RES SCIENTIST, UPJOHN CO, 75- *Concurrent Pos:* Nat Res Coun Italy grant, 74. *Mem:* AAAS; Tissue Cult Asn; Am Asn Immunol; Am Soc Microbiol; Brit Soc Immunol. *Mailing Add:* Hypersensitivity Dis Res Upjohn Co 2109 Glenwood Dr Kalamazoo MI 49008

FAST, PAUL GERHARDT, entomology, see previous edition

FAST, RONALD WALTER, b Toledo, Ohio, Apr 2, 34; m 59; c 2. PHYSICS. *Educ:* Washington & Lee Univ, BS, 56; Univ Va, MS, 58, PhD(physics), 60. *Prof Exp:* Physicist, US Army Nuclear Defense Lab, 60-62 & Midwestern Univs Res Asn, 62-67; assoc scientist, Phys Sci Lab, Univ Wis, 67-69; MEM STAFF, FERMI NAT ACCELERATOR LAB, 69- *Mem:* Am Phys Soc. *Res:* Low temperature physics, especially on superconductivity and its technical applications. *Mailing Add:* Fermilab Box 500 Batavia IL 60510

FAST, THOMAS NORMAND, b Selma, Calif, Sept 10, 22; m 52; c 2. MARINE BIOLOGY. *Educ:* Univ Santa Clara, BS, 49; Stanford Univ, PhD, 60. *Prof Exp:* Oceanog technician, Stanford Univ, 52-56; instr biol, 57-67, chmn dept, 73-77, ASSOC PROF BIOL, UNIV SANTA CLARA, 67-, CHMN DEPT, 80- *Mem:* AAAS; Am Soc Ichthyologists & Herpetologists. *Res:* Ecology of bathypelagic fishes; cardiovascular dynamics in stress. *Mailing Add:* Dept of Biol Univ of Santa Clara Santa Clara CA 95053

FASTIE, WILLIAM GEORGE, b Baltimore, Md, Dec 6, 16; m 46; c 3. ASTRONOMY. *Prof Exp:* Lab instr physics, Johns Hopkins Univ, 38-41, res asst, 41-45; res physicist, Leeds & Northrup Co, 45-51; res contract dir & res scientist, 51-68, ADJ RES PROF, JOHNS HOPKINS UNIV, 68-; CONSULT, NASA, 69- *Honors & Awards:* David Richardson Medal, Optical Soc Am, 72; Exceptional Sci Achievement Medal for Outstanding Contrib to Space Prog, NASA, 73. *Res:* Optics; radiation pyrometry; general physical instrumentation; spectrometric instrumentation; space science. *Mailing Add:* Dept of Physics Johns Hopkins Univ Baltimore MD 21218

FATELEY, WILLIAM GENE, b Franklin, Ind, May 17, 29; m 53; c 5. STRUCTURAL CHEMISTRY. *Educ:* Franklin Col, AB, 51; Kans State Univ, PhD(chem), 56. *Hon Degrees:* DSc, Franklin Col, 65. *Prof Exp:* Asst chem, Northwestern Univ, 51-53 & Kans State Univ, 53-55; res assoc, Univ

Md, 56; res fel, Univ Minn, 56-57; res chemist & head spectros lab, James River Div, Dow Chem Co, 57-60; fel chem, Carnegie-Mellon Univ, 60-62, head sci rels, 62-63, asst to pres, 63-67, sr fel, 65-67, from assoc prof to prof chem, 67-72, asst to vpres res, 67-72; head dept, 72-79, PROF CHEM, KANS STATE UNIV, 72- *Concurrent Pos:* Treas, Fourier Transform Users Group, 70- & 1st, 4th & 6th Int Conf Raman Spectros; vis prof, Univ Tokyo, 72-73 & 81; ed-in-chief, J Appl Spectros, 74-; ed, Raman Newsletter, 75-79; pres, DOM Assocs, Int, 79-; lectr, Boudoin Col, 81. *Honors & Awards:* Coblentz Award, 65; H H King Award, 79. *Mem:* Am Chem Soc; fel Optical Soc; Soc Appl Spectros. *Res:* Infrared and Raman spectroscopy; structure of matter. *Mailing Add:* Dept of Chem Kans State Univ Manhattan KS 66506

FATEMAN, RICHARD J, b New York, NY, Nov 4, 46; m 68; c 2. COMPUTER SCIENCE, MATHEMATICS. *Educ:* Union Col, NY, BS, 66; Harvard Univ, PhD(appl math), 71. *Prof Exp:* Lectr math, Mass Inst Technol, 71-74; asst prof, 74-78, ASSOC PROF COMPUT SCI, UNIV CALIF, BERKELEY, 78- *Concurrent Pos:* Mem staff comput sci, Proj MAC, Mass Inst Technol, 69-73. *Mem:* Asn Comput Mach; Soc Indust & Appl Math. *Res:* Algebraic manipulation by computer; programming languages; analysis of algorithms; scientific software. *Mailing Add:* Elec Eng & Comput Sci Univ of Calif Berkeley CA 94720

FATH, JOSEPH, b Frankfurt, Ger, Aug 31, 25; m 45; c 4. ORGANIC CHEMISTRY. *Educ:* Cornell Univ, BChem, 44. *Prof Exp:* Res chemist, Montrose Chem Co, 46-50; group leader, org sect, Nuodex Prods Co, 50-55; dir res, Thompson Chem Co, 55-65, vpres, 65-69; vpres bus develop & planning, Nuodex Div, Tenneco Chem, Inc, 69-71; gen mgr, Org & Polymers Div & vpres, Piscataway, 71-75, vpres, Planning & Develop, 76-80, SR VPRES PLANNING & DEVELOP, TENNECO CHEM CO, SADDLEBROOK, 80- *Mem:* Am Chem Soc. *Res:* Vinyl plasticizers and resins; organic intermediates; metalloorganics. *Mailing Add:* 501-B Kingston Terrace Princeton NJ 08540

FATIADI, ALEXANDER JOHANN, b Kharkov, Ukraine, Oct 22, 23; US citizen; m 52; c 4. ORGANIC CHEMISTRY. *Educ:* Tech Husbandry Inst, Ger, DrNatSc, 50; George Washington Univ, BS, 57, MS, 59. *Prof Exp:* Res asst chemist, George Washington Univ, 56-59; org chemist, 59-67, RES CHEMIST & PROJ LEADER, NAT BUR STAND, 68- *Honors & Awards:* Hillebrand Prize, Wash Chem Soc, 81. *Mem:* Am Chem Soc; NY Acad Sci; Royal Soc Chem; Ger Chem Soc. *Res:* New periodic acid oxidations; clinical standards and chemistry; cyclic ketones; aromatization of cyclitols; polyhydroxy phenols; phenylhydrazine osazones and osotriazoles; oxidation of polycyclic aromatic hydrocarbons; stable free radicals; oxidation mechanisms; malononitrile and tetracyanoethylene chemistry; new oxocarbons; active manganese dioxide. *Mailing Add:* 7516 Carroll Ave Takoma Park MD 20012

FATT, IRVING, b Chicago, Ill, Sept 16, 20; m 42; c 1. PHYSIOLOGICAL OPTICS. *Educ:* Univ Calif, Los Angeles, BS, 47, MS, 48; Univ Southern Calif, PhD, 55. *Prof Exp:* Instr commun, Yale Univ, 44-45; sr res chemist, Calif Res Corp, 48-57; prof eng sci, Col Eng, 57-80, PROF PHYSIOL OPTICS, SCH OPTOM, UNIV CALIF, BERKELEY, 67- *Mem:* Bioeng Soc; Am Acad Optom. *Res:* Fluid flow through porous media; structure of porous media; bioengineering; corneal physiology. *Mailing Add:* 360 Minor Hall Univ of Calif Berkeley CA 94720

FATTIG, W DONALD, b DeKalb Co, Ga, Feb 22, 36; m 58; c 1. GENETICS. *Educ:* Emory Univ, AB, 59, MS, 60, PhD(genetics), 63. *Prof Exp:* Fel microbiol, Sch Med, Emory Univ, 63-64; asst prof biol, Southwestern Univ, Memphis, 64-68; assoc prof, 68-74, assoc dean, Sch Natural Sci & Math, 74-76, PROF BIOL, UNIV ALA, BIRMINGHAM, 74- *Mem:* AAAS; Am Genetic Asn; Am Inst Biol Sci; Am Soc Human Genetics; Genetics Soc Am. *Res:* Bacteriophage, human and drosophilia genetics; biological controls. *Mailing Add:* Dept of Biol Univ of Ala Birmingham AL 35294

FATTORINI, HECTOR OSVALDO, b Buenos Aires, Arg, Oct 28, 38; m 61; c 3. APPLIED MATHEMATICS. *Educ:* Univ Buenos Aires, Lic en Mat, 60; NY Univ, PhD(math), 65. *Prof Exp:* Res assoc math, Nat Sci & Tech Res Coun, Arg & assoc prof, Sch Exact & Natural Sci, Univ Buenos Aires, 65-66; res assoc, Brown Univ, 67; asst prof, 67-70, assoc prof, 70-77, PROF MATH, ENG & APPL SCI, UNIV CALIF, LOS ANGELES, 77- *Concurrent Pos:* US Air Force Off Sci Res & Off Aerospace Res grant, 67; NASA grant, 67; Off Naval Res contract, 67-68; NSF grant, 69-; prof, Sch Exact & Natural Sci, Univ Buenos Aires, 70-75. *Mem:* Am Math Soc; Soc Indust & Appl Math; Arg Math Union. *Res:* Control theory; differential equations in linear topological spaces; partial differential equations; control systems in infinite dimensional spaces; system theory. *Mailing Add:* Dept Math Univ Calif Los Angeles CA 90024

FATZINGER, CARL WARREN, b Albany, NY, June 9, 38; m 76. FOREST ENTOMOLOGY. *Educ:* Univ Mich, BS, 60, MS, 61; NC State Univ, PhD(entom), 68. *Prof Exp:* Entomologist, NC, 62, Fla, 62-64, res entomologist, 64, Res Triangle Park, 64-68, Fla, 68-70, PRIN INSECT ECOLOGIST, SOUTHEASTERN FOREST EXP STA, FLA, 70- *Mem:* Entom Soc Am; Soc Am Foresters. *Res:* Behavior of insects affecting pine cones; effects of light and temperature on insect behavior; trapping systems for bark beetles; radiography for detection of forest insects. *Mailing Add:* Southeastern Forest Exp Sta PO Box 70 Olustee FL 32072

FAUBION, BILLY DON, b Breckenridge, Tex, May 24, 42; m 63; c 3. PHYSICAL CHEMISTRY. *Educ:* Tex A&M Univ, BS, 64, MS, 65, PhD(phys chem), 68. *Prof Exp:* Asst prof phys chem, Adams State Col, 68-70; SCIENTIST, MASON & HANGER-SILAS MASON CO, INC, 70- *Mem:* Am Chem Soc. *Res:* Molecular and electronic structure of molecules; thermal analysis and compatibility of high explosives. *Mailing Add:* Mason & Hanger-Silas Mason Co Box 30020 Amarillo TX 79177

FAUBL, HERMANN, b Hungary, Feb 8, 42; US citizen; m 66; c 3. ORGANIC CHEMISTRY, BIOCHEMISTRY. *Educ:* Loyola Univ, Ill, BS, 65; Northwestern Univ, PhD(chem), 69. *Prof Exp:* Sr res scientist, Pfizer, Inc, 69-77; sr res scientist, Clinton Corn Processing Co, 77-80; GROUP LEADER, ABBOTT LABS, 80- *Mem:* AAAS; Am Mgt Asn. Am Chem Soc; Sigma Xi. *Res:* Synthetic organic chemistry; natural product synthesis; synthesis and properties of strained olefins; pharmaceutical chemistry; chemotherapy; antibiotics; antivirals; carbohydrate chemistry; protein isolation. *Mailing Add:* Abbott Labs North Chicago IL 60064

FAUCETT, ROBERT E, b Dearborn, Mich, Nov 21, 26; m 46, 65; c 3. ELECTRICAL ENGINEERING. *Educ:* Case Inst Technol, BS, 47, MS, 51. *Prof Exp:* Eng asst, Cleveland Elec Illum Co, Ohio, 47-49, 50-51; mgr photom lab, Tech Develop & Eval Ctr, Civil Aeronaut Admin, Ind, 51-53; asst mgr photom dept, Elec Testing Labs, NY, 53-55; chief eng res & develop lab, US Corps Engrs, Va, 55-56; sr appln engr, Lighting Systs Dept, Gen Elec Co, 56-75; PRES, INDEPENDENT TESTING LABS INC, 75-, CHIEF EXEC OFFICER & PUB RELATIONS OFFICER, 80- *Honors & Awards:* Gen Elec Co Managerial Awards, 59 & 63. *Mem:* Fel Illum Eng Soc. *Res:* Basic glare research; photometry; testing of lighting systems; design of outdoor floodlighting and roadway lighting systems; interior commerical and industrial lighting systems; computer application for solving complex lighting problems; photometric testing of lighting equipment; general lighting consulting and computer services. *Mailing Add:* Independent Testing Labs Inc 3386 Longhorn Rd Boulder CO 80302

FAUCETT, T(HOMAS) R(ICHARD), b Hatton, Mo, Aug 22, 20; m 42; c 4. MECHANICAL ENGINEERING. *Educ:* Univ Mo, BS, 42; Purdue Univ, MS, 49, PhD(mech eng), 52. *Prof Exp:* Design analyst, Cleveland Diesel Engine Div, Gen Motors Corp, 42-46; instr mech eng, Purdue Univ, 46-52; assoc prof, Univ Rochester, 52-60; prof sch mines, Univ Mo-Rolla, 60-62; prof & head dept, Univ Iowa, 62-65; chmn, Dept Mech & Aerospace Eng, 65-78, PROF MECH ENG, UNIV MO-ROLLA, 65- *Mem:* Am Soc Mech Engrs; Am Soc Eng Educ. *Res:* Vibrations; dynamics; stress analysis. *Mailing Add:* Dept of Mech & Aerospace Eng Univ of Mo Rolla MO 65401

FAUCETT, WILLIAM MUNROE, b Union, SC, Sept 16, 16; m 46; c 1. MATHEMATICS. *Educ:* Univ SC, BS, 42, MS, 50; Tulane Univ, PhD(math), 54. *Prof Exp:* Asst, Off Naval Res Contract, Tulane Univ, 52-54; asst prof math, Univ Ky, 54-55; sr aerophysics engr, 55-58, sr opers analyst, 58-61, proj opers analyst, 61-63, design specialist, 63-77, sr eng specialist, 77-78, STAFF CONSULT, GEN DYNAMICS/FT WORTH, 78- *Mem:* Am Math Soc; Sigma Xi; Opers Res Soc Am. *Res:* Operations research; management science. *Mailing Add:* 3500 Creston Ave Ft Worth TX 76133

FAUCHALD, KRISTIAN, b Oslo, Norway, July 1, 35; nat US. SYSTEMATIC ZOOLOGY, MARINE BIOLOGY. *Educ:* Univ Bergen, Cand Mag, 59, Cand Real, 61; Univ Southern Calif, PhD(biol), 69. *Prof Exp:* Vitenskapelig asst biol, Univ Bergen, 59-64, amanuensis, 64-65; from res assoc to assoc prof biol, Univ Southern Calif, 75-79; ASSOC CUR INVEST ZOOL, SMITHSONIAN INST, 79- *Mem:* Am Soc Zool. *Res:* Systematics and biology of polychaetous annelids from world wide areas; benthic ecology. *Mailing Add:* Dept Invest Zool Smithsonian Inst Washington DC 20560

FAUCHER, JOSEPH A, b San Francisco, Calif, Oct 2, 27; m 59; c 2. CORROSION CHEMISTRY. *Educ:* Princeton Univ, AB, 49; Yale Univ, PhD(chem), 53. *Prof Exp:* Chemist plastics, 56-57; licensing mgr, 68-71, RES SCIENTIST CORROSION CHEM, UNION CARBIDE CORP TECH CTR, 71- *Mem:* Am Chem Soc; Nat Asn Corrosion Eng. *Mailing Add:* 45 Maple Hill Pleasantville NY 10570

FAUDREE, RALPH JASPER, JR, b Durant, Okla, Aug 23, 39; m 62; c 2. GRAPH THEORY. *Educ:* Okla Baptist Univ, BS, 61; Purdue Univ, MS, 63, PhD(math), 64. *Prof Exp:* Instr math, Univ Calif, Berkeley, 64-66; asst prof, Univ Ill, Urbana, 66-70; assoc prof, 70-75, PROF MATH, MEMPHIS STATE UNIV, 75- *Concurrent Pos:* Vis prof math, Univ Aberdeen, Scotland, 80; res mathematician, Hungarian Acad Sci, Budapest, 81. *Mem:* Am Math Soc. *Res:* Theory of groups; graph theory. *Mailing Add:* Dept of Math Memphis State Univ Memphis TN 38111

FAUGHNAN, BRIAN WILFRED, solid state physics, see previous edition

FAUGHT, JOHN BRIAN, b Toronto, Ont, Mar 18, 42; m 68. INORGANIC CHEMISTRY, X-RAY CRYSTALLOGRAPHY. *Educ:* Univ Windsor, BSc, 65; Univ Ill, Urbana, MS, 67, PhD(inorg chem), 69; St Mary's Univ, BEd, 77. *Prof Exp:* Res assoc, Univ Fla, 69-70; asst prof chem, Dalhousie Univ, 70-76; proj leader & chemist, Environ Can, Environ Protection Serv, 77-78; teacher chem & math, Dartmouth Acad, 78-79; HEAD SCI DEPT, HALIFAX GRAMMAR SCHOOL, 79- *Concurrent Pos:* Lectr chem, St Mary's Univ, 80- *Mem:* Am Chem Soc; Am Crystallog Asn. *Res:* Synthesis and structural studies of phosphorus-nitrogen and arsenic-nitrogen compounds; structural analysis utilizing the techniques of x-ray crystallography, infra-red and Raman spectroscopy. *Mailing Add:* 5750 Atlantic St Halifax NS Can

FAUL, HENRY, GEOPHYSICS. *Educ:* Mass Inst Technol, PhD(geol, physics), 49. *Prof Exp:* Prof geophys, Southwestern Ctr Advan Studies, 63-66; chmn dept, 66-73, PROF GEOL, UNIV PA, 66- *Res:* Nuclear geophysics. *Mailing Add:* Dept Geol Univ Pa Philadelphia PA 19174

FAUL, WILLIAM HENRY, organic chemistry, photographic chemistry, see previous edition

FAULCONER, ROBERT JAMIESON, b Sussex, Eng, July 11, 23; nat US; m 45; c 4. PATHOLOGY. *Educ:* Col of William & Mary, BS, 43; Johns Hopkins Univ, MD, 47. *Prof Exp:* Instr path, Univ Pa, 49-52; pathologist, DePaul Hosp, 54-78, dir labs, 66-78; PROF PATH, EASTERN VA MED SCH, 74-, CHMN DEPT, 78- *Concurrent Pos:* Fel gynecol path, Johns Hopkins Univ, 48-49; clin assoc, Med Col Va, 66-70, clin prof, 72-79; consult pathologist, US

Naval Hosp, Portsmouth, USPHS Hosp, Norfolk & Vet Admin Ctr, Hampton. *Mem:* AAAS; fel Am Soc Clin Path; Am Asn Anat; Am Asn Hist Med; Col Am Path. *Res:* Pathologic anatomy; human embryology; immunology of cancer; pathology of endocrine organs. *Mailing Add:* Dept of Path 700 Olney Rd Norfolk VA 23507

FAULDERS, CHARLES R(AYMOND), b Spokane, Wash, May 21, 27; m 54; c 5. MECHANICAL ENGINEERING. *Educ:* Univ Calif, BS, 48; Mass Inst Technol, SM, 50, ME, 51, ScD(mech eng), 54. *Prof Exp:* Asst mech eng, Mass Inst Technol, 49-54; aerodynamicist aerophysics dept, NAm Aviation, Inc, 54-55, supvr propulsion aerodyn, Missile Div, 55-57, res specialist eng dept, 57-58, res specialist aerospace labs, 58-60; assoc prof, Univ Aix-Marseille, 60-62; mgr flight technol, Paraglider Prog, NAm Aviation, Inc, 63-65, mgr systs eng, 65-66, mgr flight sci, Space Div, NAm Rockwell Corp, 66-73, proj engr, Energy Systs Studies, Space Div, Rockwell Int, 73-76, proj mgr, Energy Conserv Systs, 76-77, mkt rep advan progs, 77-80, PROJ MONITOR, OIL SHALE PROG, ENERGY SYSTS GROUP, ROCKWELL INT, 80- *Res:* Fluid mechanics; aerodynamics of compressors and turbines; space flight mechanics; optimization of powered space flight trajectories; magnetohydrodynamics; atmospheric flight dynamics of lifting vehicles; thermodynamics; cost analysis; coal gasification and liquefaction; oil shale. *Mailing Add:* Energy Systs Group 8900 DeSoto Ave Canoga Park CA 91304

FAULK, DENNIS DERWIN, b Searcy, Ark, Nov 29, 36; m 58; c 2. ORGANIC CHEMISTRY. *Educ:* Ark State Teachers Col, BS, 58; Univ Ark, PhD(org chem), 66. *Prof Exp:* Chemist, Gulf Oil Corp, 58-61; asst chem, Univ Ark, 61-66; res chemist, Shell Oil Co, Deer Park, 66-67; asst chem, 67, asst prof, 67-71, assoc prof, 71-81, PROF CHEM, CENT MO STATE UNIV, 81- *Mem:* Am Chem Soc; Sigma Xi. *Res:* Heterogeneous catalysis; organic reaction mechanisms; acid-catalysed ketone rearrangements; spectroscopic identifications and correlations; structural correlations using nuclear magnetic resonance shift reagents. *Mailing Add:* Dept Chem Cent Mo State Univ Warrensburg MO 64093

FAULKENBERRY, GERALD DAVID, b Wapanucka, Okla, May 28, 37; m 61; c 2. STATISTICS. *Educ:* Southeastern State Col, BS, 59; Okla State Univ, MS, 61, PhD(statist), 65. *Prof Exp:* Asst prof statist, Okla State Univ, 65; asst prof statist, Ore State Univ, 65-69; supvr statist group, Litton Sci Support Lab, Litton Industs, Calif, 69-71; vis assoc prof, 71-72, assoc prof, 72-81, PROF STATIST & CHMN DEPT, ORE STATE UNIV, 81- *Mem:* Am Statist Asn. *Res:* Statistical theory and methodology, particularly estimation; predictive inferences: analysis of survey data; survey research. *Mailing Add:* Dept Statist Ore State Univ Corvallis OR 97330

FAULKIN, LESLIE J, JR, b Peoria, Ill, July 4, 30; m 50; c 2. ANATOMY. *Educ:* Univ Calif, Berkeley, BA, 55, MA, 57, PhD(zool), 64. *Prof Exp:* Asst prof, 64-69, chmn dept, 72-78, ASSOC PROF ANAT, SCH VET MED, UNIV CALIF, DAVIS, 69- *Mem:* AAAS; Am Asn Cancer Res; Am Asn Anat. *Res:* Experimental oncology; growth and development; growth regulation; endocrinology. *Mailing Add:* Dept of Anat Univ of Calif Sch of Vet Med Davis CA 95616

FAULKNER, D JOHN, b Bournemouth, Eng, June 10, 42; m 66. ORGANIC CHEMISTRY. *Educ:* Imp Col, London, BSc, 62; Univ London, PhD(org chem), 65. *Prof Exp:* Fel, Harvard Univ, 65-67; fel, Stanford Univ, 67-68; assoc prof, 68-80, PROF MARINE CHEM, SCRIPPS INST OCEANOG, UNIV CALIF, 80- *Mem:* Am Chem Soc; The Chem Soc. *Res:* Synthesis of complex molecules; studies of synthetic methods; isolation and identification of natural products. *Mailing Add:* Scripps Inst of Oceanog La Jolla CA 92093

FAULKNER, DAVID, b St Helens, Eng, June 13, 42; Can citizen; m 76. PHYSICAL METALLURGY. *Educ:* Univ Manchester, BSc, 64, MSc, 66, PhD(metall), 67. *Prof Exp:* ASSOC RES OFFICER METALL, ATOMIC ENERGY CAN LTD, 67- *Mem:* Fel Royal Micros Soc. *Res:* Radiation damage; use of high energy ion beams to simulate neutron irradiation damage; electron microscopy. *Mailing Add:* Mat Sci Br Atomic Energy of Can Ltd Pinawa MB R0E 1L0 Can

FAULKNER, FRANK DAVID, b Humansville, Mo, Apr 6, 15; m 41; c 6. APPLIED MATHEMATICS. *Educ:* Kans State Teachers Col, BS, 40; Kans State Col, MS, 42; Univ Mich, Ann Arbor, PhD(appl math), 69. *Prof Exp:* Jr physicist, Appl Physics Lab, Johns Hopkins Univ, 44-46; res mathematician, Eng Res Inst, Univ Mich, 46-50; from assoc prof to prof, 50-71, DISTINGUISHED PROF MATH, NAVAL POSTGRAD SCH, 71- *Mem:* Am Math Soc; Am Astronaut Soc; Math Asn Am; Soc Indust & Appl Math. *Res:* Numerical methods in optimization; mechanics; calculus of variations; applications in missile problems; numerical methods applied to partial differential equations. *Mailing Add:* Dept of Math Naval Postgrad Sch Monterey CA 93940

FAULKNER, GARY DOYLE, b Aberdeen, Miss, Sept 20, 44; m 72; c 2. MATHEMATICS. *Educ:* Ga State Univ, BS, 71; Univ SC, MS, 73; Ga Inst Technol, PhD(math), 76. *Prof Exp:* ASSOC PROF MATH, NC STATE UNIV, 76- *Mem:* Am Math Soc. *Res:* Analysis; functional analysis; topology and applied mathematics. *Mailing Add:* Math Dept NC State Univ Raleigh NC 27650

FAULKNER, GAVIN JOHN, b Edinburgh, Scotland; Brit citizen. ROCK MECHANICS. *Educ:* Univ Strathclyde, Glasgow, BS, 77, PhD(mining eng), 80. *Prof Exp:* ASST PROF MINING ENG, VA POLYTECH INST & STATE UNIV, 80- *Mem:* Am Inst Mining Engrs; Inst Mining & Metall, UK. *Res:* Pump packing systems in longwall gate roads and strata movement on steeply inclined longwall facelines; underground measuring techniques. *Mailing Add:* Dept Mining & Minerals Eng Va Polytech Inst & State Univ Blacksburg VA 24061

FAULKNER, JAMES DOUGLAS, b Griffin, Ga, Apr 1, 45; m 72. ORGANIC CHEMISTRY. *Educ:* Columbus Col, BS, 70; Emory Univ, MS, 73, PhD(org chem), 75. *Prof Exp:* Chief chemist, 75-76, TECH DIR INDUST RES, LESTER LABS, INC, 76- *Mem:* Am Chem Soc. *Res:* Electrochemical and corrosion phenomena; corrosion inhibition; computer simulation; static electricity control. *Mailing Add:* Lester Labs Inc 2370 Lawrence St Atlanta GA 30344

FAULKNER, JAMES EARL, b Brigham City, Utah, Nov 22, 28; m 62; c 7. STATISTICS. *Educ:* Utah State Univ, BS, 50; Kans State Univ, MS, 52; Univ Minn, PhD(biostatist), 64. *Prof Exp:* Instr math, Utah State Univ, 52-54 & Univ Minn, 56-62; from asst prof to assoc prof statist, 63-72, PROF STATIST, BRIGHAM YOUNG UNIV, 72- *Concurrent Pos:* Assoc res engr, Aero Div, Minneapolis-Honeywell Regulator Co, 57; consult, Toole Army Depot, 64-65, Hercules Inc, 66-68, Technol Div, GCA Corp, 68-72 & H E Cramer Co, Inc, 72- *Mem:* Am Statist Asn; Biomet Soc. *Res:* Probability; mathematical statistics. *Mailing Add:* Dept of Statist 214 TMCB Brigham Young Univ Provo UT 84602

FAULKNER, JAMES EARL, mathematical physics, see previous edition

FAULKNER, JOHN, b Hayes, Middlesex, Eng, Apr 29, 37; m 66; c 2. ASTROPHYSICS, THEORETICAL PHYSICS. *Educ:* Cambridge Univ, BA, 59, MA, 63, PhD(appl math & theoret physics), 64. *Prof Exp:* Asst res astrophys, Cambridge Univ, 63-64; res fel physics, Calif Inst Technol, 64-66; staff mem astrophys, Inst Theoret Astron, Cambridge, 67-69; assoc prof, 69-73, prof astron & astrophys, 73-80, PROF STELLAR STRUCT & RELATIVITY, UNIV CALIF, SANTA CRUZ, 80- *Concurrent Pos:* Vis res assoc, Mass Inst Technol, 65-67; vis res scientist, Nat Radio Astron Observ, 77. *Honors & Awards:* William Stone Prize, Peterhouse, Cambridge, 65; Gravity Prize, Gravity Found, 72; Judy A Seydoux Mem Prize, Griffith Observ, 72-73. *Mem:* Fel Royal Astron Soc; fel Am Astron Soc; Int Astron Union. *Res:* Newtonian and general relativistic stellar structure and evolution; horizontal branch, helium content, dwarf novae and gravitational radiation; tides in general relativity, occasional general relativity and/or cosmology. *Mailing Add:* Lick Observ Crown Col Univ of Calif Santa Cruz CA 95064

FAULKNER, JOHN A, b Kingston, Ont, Dec 12, 23; m 55; c 2. PHYSIOLOGY. *Educ:* Queen's Univ, Ont, BA, 49, BPHE, 50; Ont Col Ed, Toronto, cert, 51; Univ Mich, MS, 56, PhD(educ), 62. *Prof Exp:* Teacher high sch, Ont, 51-52; teacher sci & phys educ, Glebe Collegiate Inst, Ont, 52-56; asst prof phys educ, Univ Western Ont, 56-60; asst prof educ, 60-66, assoc prof physiol, 66-71, PROF PHYSIOL, UNIV MICH, 71- *Concurrent Pos:* Mich Heart Asn grants, 63-67 & 69-; NIH grants, 63-67, 71-; Muscular Dystrophy Asn of Am grant; pres, Am Col Sports Med, 71-72. *Mem:* AAAS; Am Physiol Soc. *Res:* Physiological adaptation to exercise and hypoxia; skeletal muscle transportation and regeneration; contractile and biochemical properties of masticatory muscles. *Mailing Add:* Dept Physiol Univ Mich Med Sch Ann Arbor MI 48104

FAULKNER, JOHN EDWARD, b Plattsburg, Ohio, Oct 5, 20; m 46; c 2. APPLIED PHYSICS. *Educ:* Oberlin Col, BA, 42; Univ Wis, PhD(physics), 50. *Prof Exp:* Mem staff radiation lab, Mass Inst Technol, 42-46; physicist, Hanford Labs, Gen Elec Co, Wash, 50-52; supvr exp nuclear physics, 52-57, mgr nuclear physics res, 57-63; consult exp physics, 63-64, mgr safeguards eng, 64-66, consult appl physics, Astronuclear Lab, 66-77, CONSULT APPL PHYSICS, ADV ENERGY SYSTS DIV, WESTINGHOUSE ELEC CO, 77- *Concurrent Pos:* Consult, Secy War, 45. *Honors & Awards:* Cert of Appreciation, US War Dept & US Navy Dept, 47. *Mem:* Am Phys Soc; Am Nuclear Soc. *Res:* Low energy neutron physics; reactor physics; x-rays. *Mailing Add:* Westinghouse Elec Co PO Box 10864 Pittsburgh PA 15236

FAULKNER, JOHN SAMUEL, b Memphis, Tenn, Sept 30, 32; m 57; c 2. PHYSICS. *Educ:* Auburn Univ, BS, 54, MS, 55; Ohio State Univ, PhD(physics), 59. *Prof Exp:* Asst prof physics, Univ Fla, 59-62; MEM STAFF, METALS & CERAMICS DIV, OAK RIDGE NAT LAB, 62- *Concurrent Pos:* Sr Fulbright res scholar, Univ Sheffield, UK, 68-69; vis prof, Univ Bristol, UK, 76-77. *Mem:* Fel AAAS; fel Am Phys Soc. *Res:* Theoretical solid state physics; electronic states in ordered and disordered systems. *Mailing Add:* Metals & Ceramics Div Oak Ridge Nat Lab PO Box X Oak Ridge TN 37830

FAULKNER, KENNETH KEITH, b Barbourville, Ky, Apr 28, 26; m 55; c 3. ANATOMY. *Educ:* Lincoln Mem Univ, BS, 49; Univ Okla, MS, 51, PhD(med sci), 55. *Prof Exp:* From instr to assoc prof, 54-70, actg head, 75-76, PROF ANAT, HEALTH SCI CTR, UNIV OKLA, 70-, INTERIM HEAD, 81- *Concurrent Pos:* Instr, Lincoln Mem Univ, 49. *Mem:* AAAS; Soc Exp Biol & Med. *Res:* Neurophysiology; neuroanatomy; effects of low temperatures on intermediary metabolism of nervous tissue; hibernation; audiovisual aids and methodology in medical education; anatomy of marine mammals; morphologic parameters of ossicles of middle ear; morphometry of cardiac muscle. *Mailing Add:* Dept Anat Sci PO Box 26901 Oklahoma City OK 73190

FAULKNER, LARRY RAY, b Shreveport, La, Nov 26, 44; m 65; c 2. ELECTROCHEMISTRY, LUMINESCENCE SPECTROSCOPY. *Educ:* Southern Methodist Univ, BS, 66; Univ Tex, Austin, PhD(chem), 69. *Prof Exp:* Asst prof chem, Harvard Univ, 69-73; from asst prof to assoc prof, 73-79, PROF CHEM, UNIV ILL, URBANA-CHAMPAIGN, 79- *Concurrent Pos:* Div ed, J Electrochem Soc, 74-80; US regional ed, J Electroanal Chem, 80- *Mem:* Am Chem Soc; Electrochem Soc. *Res:* Chemical reactions of excited states; chemiluminescent electron transfer processes; fluorescence and phosphorescence phenomena and techniques; electrochemistry and electroanalytical chemistry. *Mailing Add:* Dept Chem Univ Ill 1209 W Calif St Urbana IL 61801

FAULKNER, LINDSEY RALPH, plant nematology, see previous edition

FAULKNER, LLOYD (CLARENCE), b Longmont, Colo, Oct 24, 26; m 54; c 5. REPRODUCTIVE PHYSIOLOGY. *Educ:* Colo State Univ, DVM, 52; Cornell Univ, PhD(animal physiol), 63; Am Col Theriogenologists, dipl, 71. *Prof Exp:* From asst prof to assoc prof vet clins & surg, Colo State Univ, 55-63, assoc prof vet clins, surg, physiol & endocrinol, 63, 66, prof vet clins & surg, 66-70, prof physiol & biophys & chmn dept, 70-78; assoc dean vet res, Univ Mo, 79-81; DIR VET RES, OKLA STATE UNIV, 81- *Concurrent Pos:* Consult, Ft Dodge Labs, 73-; Cong Sci & Eng fel, Fedn Am Socs Exp Biol. *Mem:* Fel AAAS; Am Vet Med Asn; Am Soc Animal Sci; Soc Study Reproduction; Am Col Theriogenologists (secy, 71-74, pres, 74-75). *Res:* Testis-accessory sex gland relationships; hypothalamo-hypophyseal relationships in the rat; alterations in semen quality in bulls with lesions of the reproductive system; population control in companion animals. *Mailing Add:* Dir Vet Res Okla State Univ Stillwater OK 74078

FAULKNER, LYNN L, b Ft Wayne, Ind, June 24, 41; m 61; c 2. MECHANICAL ENGINEERING, ACOUSTICS. *Educ:* Purdue Univ, BS, 65, MS, 66, PhD(mech eng), 69. *Prof Exp:* Apprentice draftsman eng, Gen Elec Co, Ind, 59-63; res asst mech eng, Herrick Labs, Purdue Univ, 65-70; asst prof, 70-74, ASSOC PROF MECH ENG, OHIO STATE UNIV, 74- *Concurrent Pos:* Fel, Purdue Univ, 69-70. *Mem:* Am Soc Mech Engrs; Acoust Soc Am; Soc Exp Stress Anal; Am Soc Eng Educ. *Res:* Engineering acoustics; noise control; noise analysis of household appliances; vehicle noise; building acoustics; outdoor power equipment. *Mailing Add:* Dept of Mech Eng Ohio State UniV Columbus OH 43210

FAULKNER, PETER, b Cardiff, Wales, July 8, 29; m 50; c 4. VIROLOGY. *Educ:* Univ London, BSc, 50; McGill Univ, PhD(biochem), 54. *Prof Exp:* Res student, Montreal Gen Hosp, 50-54; agr res officer, Lab Insect Path, Can Dept Agr, 54-63; mem sci staff med res coun, Virus Res Unit, Carshalton Surv, Eng, 63-65; assoc, 65-80, CAREER INVESTR, MED RES COUN CAN, 80-; PROF MICROBIOL, QUEEN'S UNIV, ONT, 73- *Mem:* Brit Biochem Soc; Soc Gen Microbiol; Can Soc Microbiol. *Res:* Insect virus genetics. *Mailing Add:* Dept Microbiol Queen's Univ Kingston ON K7L 3N6 Can

FAULKNER, RUSSELL CONKLIN, JR, b Barbourville, Ky, Jan 31, 20; m 54; c 2. ZOOLOGY, EXPERIMENTAL MORPHOLOGY. *Educ:* Lincoln Mem Univ, BS, 48; Univ Okla, MS, 52, PhD(zool), 58. *Prof Exp:* Asst zool, Univ Okla, 48-55; asst prof biol, Okla Baptist Univ, 55-57; from asst prof to assoc prof, Tex Christian Col, 57-67; PROF BIOL, STEPHEN F AUSTIN STATE UNIV, 67- *Mem:* Am Inst Biol Sci; Am Micros Soc; Sigma Xi. Prof Exp: Effects of radioisotopes on growth and development and use of histochemical methods in detecting effects; microtechnique; radioecological techniques. *Mailing Add:* S F Austin State Univ Dept Biol Box 13003 Nacogdoches TX 75962

FAULKNER, THOMAS RICHARD, b Detroit, Mich, Dec 3, 47; m 74. SOFTWARE DEVELOPMENT, COMPUTER SYSTEMS. *Educ:* Oakland Univ, BA & MS, 70; Univ Minn, PhD(chem), 76. *Prof Exp:* Fel chem, Univ Minn, 76; instr chem, Univ Va, 76-79; software analyst, 79-80, ANAL MGR, CRAY RES INC, 81- *Mem:* Am Chem Soc; Am Phys Soc; AAAS; Asn Comput Mach. *Res:* Theoretical and experimental spectroscopy; molecular vibrations; quantum chemistry; design, development and installation of computer software. *Mailing Add:* Cray Res Inc Laurel MD 20707

FAULKNER, WILLARD RILEY, b Jerry, Wash, Jan 2, 15; m 50. BIOCHEMISTRY. *Educ:* Univ Idaho, BS, 40; Univ Denver, MS, 50; Vanderbilt Univ, PhD, 56; Am Bd Clin Chem, dipl. *Prof Exp:* Asst biochem, Vanderbilt Univ, 52-56; clin chemist, Cleveland Clin Found, 56-58; ASSOC PROF BIOCHEM, SCH MED & DIR CLIN CHEM LABS, MED CTR, VANDERBILT UNIV, 68-, ACTG DIR CLIN LABS, 71- *Concurrent Pos:* Mem med bd dirs, Nat Registry Clin Chem, 68-; chmn licensure adv comt, Tenn Med Lab Act, 69-; co-ed, CRC, Critical Rev Clin Lab Sci, 70- *Honors & Awards:* Bronze Award, Am Soc Clin Pathologists & Col Am Pathologists, 58. *Mem:* AAAS; Am Microchem Soc; Am Chem Soc; Am Asn Clin Chemists. *Res:* Myoglobin; blood pH, urinary amino acids; blood ammonium; clinical microchemistry; normal clinical laboratory values; ionic calcium. *Mailing Add:* Clin Chem Labs Sta 17 Vanderbilt Univ Med Ctr Nashville TN 37232

FAUNTLEROY, AMASSA COURTNEY, algebra, see previous edition

FAUPEL, JOSEPH H(ERMAN), b Waukegan, Ill, Oct 25, 16; m 40; c 9. ENGINEERING MECHANICS. *Educ:* Pa State Univ, BS, 39, PhD(eng mech), 48; Univ Pittsburgh, MS, 42. *Prof Exp:* Res metallurgist, Aluminum Co Am, 39-42; asst, Pa State Univ, 45-47; res engr, 48-52, proj engr, 52-55, res assoc, 55-62, CONSULT, E I DU PONT DE NEMOURS & CO, INC, 62- *Concurrent Pos:* Spec lectr mech eng, Univ Del, 49-51; mem, Pressure Vessel Res Comt, Boiler & Pressure Vessel Comt & indust & prof adv comt, Pa State Univ. *Mem:* Am Soc Metals; fel Am Soc Mech Engrs; Am Soc Testing & Mat; Sigma Xi. *Res:* Mechanics of materials; stress analysis; pressure vessels; plasticity; elasticity; viscoelasticity; limit design; high temperature and high pressure mechanics. *Mailing Add:* 400 Crest Rd W Crocraft Wilmington DE 19803

FAURE, GUNTER, b Tallinn, Estonia, May 11, 34; US citizen; m 59; c 4. GEOCHEMISTRY, GEOCHRONOLOGY. *Educ:* Western Ont Univ, BSc, 57; Mass Inst Technol, PhD(geol), 61. *Prof Exp:* Res assoc geochronology, Mass Inst Technol, 61-62; from asst prof to assoc prof, 62-68, PROF GEOL, OHIO STATE UNIV, 68- *Concurrent Pos:* NSF res grants, 64-81; ed-in-chief, Isotope Geosci, Elsevier, Amsterdam. *Mem:* AAAS; Geol Soc Am; Geochem Soc. *Res:* isotopic composition of strontium in volcanic rocks, in oceans and fresh water on continents, and its isotope geochemistry in the base metal deposits of the Red Sea; petrogenesis of basalt in Antarctica; sediment mixing in the Ross Sea and Black Sea; provenance of feldspar in glacial deposits of Ohio. *Mailing Add:* Dept Geol Ohio State Univ 125 S Oval Mall Columbus OH 43210

FAUSCH, HOMER DAVID, b Buffalo Center, Iowa, Apr 5, 19; m 43; c 3. ANIMAL GENETICS. *Educ:* Univ Minn, BS, 47, MS, 50, PhD(animal breeding), 53. *Prof Exp:* Assoc prof & animal husbandman, Northwest Exp Sta, Univ Minn, 47-56; dir res, 68-74, PROF ANIMAL SCI, CALIF STATE POLYTECH UNIV, POMONA, 56- *Concurrent Pos:* Lectr, Univ Alta, 64-65. *Mem:* AAAS; Am Soc Animal Sci. *Res:* Effect of inbreeding on variability of economic traits in the Minnesota number one and number two breeds of swine; lipid metabolism in swine. *Mailing Add:* Dept of Animal Sci 3801 W Temple Ave Pomona CA 91768

FAUSEY, NORMAN RAY, b Fremont, Ohio, Oct 28, 38; m 59; c 4. SOIL PHYSICS. *Educ:* Ohio State Univ, BS, 62, MS, 66, PhD(agron), 75. *Prof Exp:* SOIL DRAINAGE SCIENTIST, USDA, 67- *Mem:* Am Soc Agron; Soil Sci Soc Am; Soil Conserv Soc Am; Am Soc Agr Engrs. *Res:* Farm drainage for more efficient farming operations and increased production. *Mailing Add:* 491 E Dunedin Rd Columbus OH 43214

FAUST, CHARLES HARRY, JR, b Allentown, Pa, Jan 10, 43. MOLECULAR BIOLOGY, IMMUNOLOGY. *Educ:* Franklin & Marshall Col, AB, 64; Colo State Univ, PhD(biochem), 70. *Prof Exp:* Asst prof, 74-80, ASSOC PROF SURG, BIOCHEM & MICROBIOL, MED SCH, UNIV ORE, 80- *Concurrent Pos:* Max Planck Soc fel, Max Planck Inst Exp Med, Ger, 70-71; Am Cancer Soc fel, Dept Path, Univ Geneva, 71-73, Am-Swiss Coun Sci Exchange fel, 73-74. *Mem:* NY Acad Sci; Am Chem Soc. *Res:* Molecular biology of normal and malignant animal cells with emphasis on control of gene expression. *Mailing Add:* Dept Surg Univ Ore Med Sch Portland OR 97201

FAUST, CHARLES L(AWSON), b St Louis, Mo, Nov 8, 06; m 34; c 3. CHEMICAL ENGINEERING. *Educ:* Univ Washington, St Louis, BS, 30, MS, 31; Univ Minn, PhD(chem eng), 34. *Prof Exp:* Grad asst, Univ Minn, 31-34; res engr, Battelle Mem Inst, 34-41, asst supvr electrochem res, 41-44, supvr electrochem eng res, 44-53, chief electrochem eng div, 53-69, assoc mgr chem & chem eng dept, 69-71; CONSULT, 71- *Concurrent Pos:* Mem Int Coun Electrodeposition, 64-67; consult, Mining & Mat Adv Bd. *Honors & Awards:* Atcheson Medal, Electrochem Soc, 62; Proctor award, Am Electroplaters Soc, 42, gold medal, 51, Heusner Award, 55, sci award, 61; res gold medal, Soc Mfg Engrs, 66; Hothersall Medal, Brit Inst Metal Finishing, 67. *Mem:* Am Chem Soc; hon mem Electrochem Soc (vpres, 48-50, pres, 50-51); Am Electroplaters Soc; Soc Mfg Engrs; Am Soc Metals. *Res:* Electrodeposition of metals and alloys; electroforming; electropolishing; pickling; metal finishing; protection; alumina from clays; fuel cells; batteries; electrolysis; electrowinning; electrorefining; electrochemical machining. *Mailing Add:* 2763 Wellesley Dr Columbus OH 43221

FAUST, (SISTER) CLAUDE MARIE, b San Antonio, Tex, Nov 18, 17. MATHEMATICS. *Educ:* Incarnate Word Col, BA, 39; Cath Univ Am, MA, 54; Marquette Univ, MS, 55; Univ Notre Dame, PhD(math), 61. *Prof Exp:* From instr to assoc prof, 46-61, Minnie Stevens Piper prof, 67, dir NSF In-Serv Insts High Sch Teachers Math, 63-71, PROF MATH, INCARNATE WORD COL, 61- *Concurrent Pos:* Vis scientist, NSF Vis Scientist Prog, Tex Acad Sci, 64-65; dir, Tex Ctr for Minn Math & Sci Teaching Proj, NSF, 63-68. *Mem:* Math Asn Am; Am Math Soc. *Res:* Complex analysis; boundary behavior of holomorphic functions in the unit disc. *Mailing Add:* Dept of Math Incarnate Word Col San Antonio TX 78209

FAUST, GEORGE TOBIAS, b Philadelphia, Pa, Aug 27, 08; m 36; c 5. MINERALOGY, GEOLOGY. *Educ:* Pa State Univ, BS, 30; Univ Mich, MS, 31, PhD(mineral), 34. *Prof Exp:* Asst mineralogist, Univ Mich, 30-35; asst prof ceramic mineral, Rutgers Univ, 35-38; asst chemist-petrogr, US Bur Mines, Ala, 38-40; asst mineralogist-petrogr, Bur Plant Indust, USDA, Md, 40-42; from asst mineralogist to head mineral group, US Geol Surv, 42-53, staff assoc solid state group, 53-60, geologist, 60-63, res geologist, 63-77; RETIRED. *Concurrent Pos:* Instr, Gemological Inst, Am, 35-38; lectr grad sch, Am Univ, 57. *Mem:* Fel Mineral Soc (vpres, 64, pres, 65); fel Ceramic Soc; fel Geol Soc; Geochem Soc (treas, 55-61); Crystallog Asn. *Res:* Mineralogy, geochemistry and petrology; Watchung basalt flows of New Jersey. *Mailing Add:* PO Box 411 Basking Ridge NJ 07920

FAUST, JOHN PHILIP, b New Orleans, La, Sept 26, 24; m 52; c 3. WATER CHEMISTRY. *Educ:* Loyola Univ, La, BS, 44; Univ Ill, MS, 48; Univ Notre Dame, PhD(chem), 52. *Prof Exp:* Chemist, Olin Mathieson Chem Corp, 52-53, res group leader, 53-54, chief inorg res sect, Olin Corp, 54-57, proj supvr, 58-62, mem staff, 63-71, sr res assoc, 71-78, CONSULT SCIENTIST POOL CHEM, OLIN CORP, 78- *Mem:* Am Chem Soc; Sigma Xi; fel Am Inst Chemists. *Res:* Infrared and ultraviolet studies of inorganic coordination compounds in the solid state; metal hydrides, boranes; catalysis high vacuum techniques; high energy fuels; high energy oxidizers; fluorine and pesticides; borazine polymers; hypochlorites; sanitizers; pollution control; water purification; swimming pool treatment. *Mailing Add:* Olin Corp Box 30 275 Winchester Ave New Haven CT 06511

FAUST, JOHN WILLIAM, JR, b Pittsburgh, Pa, July 25, 22; m 47; c 8. SURFACE PHYSICS & CHEMISTRY. *Educ:* Purdue Univ, BS, 44; Univ Mo, MA, 49, PhD(phys chem), 51. *Prof Exp:* Res chemist, Westinghouse Elec Corp, 51-59, supvry engr, 59-63, sect mgr, Mat Characterization Lab, 63-65, mgr semiconductor crystals growth, 65-67; prof solid state sci, Mat Res Labs, Pa State Univ, 67-69; PROF ENG, UNIV SC, 69- *Concurrent Pos:* Consult, Silage Corp, 79-80 & res & develop, Arionics Lab, 78; res physicist, Naval Res Labs, Washington, DC, 80-81. *Honors & Awards:* Gordon Conf Cert Recognition. *Mem:* Am Inst Mining, Metall & Petrol Engrs; Electrochem Soc; Sigma Xi; fel Am Inst Chemists; Am Chem Soc. *Res:* Etching and surface problems of semiconductors and metals; growth of metal and semiconductor crystals; submicron electronics processing; characterization of materials; solar cell materials and processing. *Mailing Add:* Col of Eng Univ of SC Columbia SC 29208

FAUST, MARIA ANNA, b Budapest, Hungary; US citizen. MARINE MICROBIOLOGY, MARINE PHYCOLOGY. *Educ:* Agr Univ Budapest, BS, 51; Rutgers Univ, MS, 62; Univ Md, PhD(microbiol), 70. *Prof Exp:* Biologist, Ethicon, Inc, NJ, 59-61; res asst soil microbiol, Rutgers Univ, 61-62; res assoc microbiol, Cornell Univ, 62-66; teaching asst, Univ Md, 67-70; res assoc phycologist, Radiation Biol Lab, 71-72, MICROBIOLOGIST, CHESAPEAKE BAY CTR ENVIRON STUDIES, SMITHSONIAN INST, 73- *Mem:* Sigma Xi; Am Soc Microbiol; Phycol Soc Am; Am Soc Limnol & Oceanog; Estuarine Res Fed. *Res:* Structure and function of phytoplankton and bacterial communities in a watershed-estuarine ecosystem; effects of environmental stress on microorganisms; ultrastructure of flagellates and nannoplankton; photoadaptation of phytoplankton. *Mailing Add:* Chesapeake Bay Ctr Smithsonian Inst PO Box 28 Edgewater MD 21037

FAUST, MIKLOS, b Nagybereny, Hungary, Dec 12, 27; m 54; c 1. POMOLOGY. *Educ:* Agr Univ Budapest, BS, 52; Rutgers Univ, MS, 60; Cornell Univ, PhD(pomol), 65. *Prof Exp:* Mgr, Csaszartoltes State Farm, Hungary, 52-54; regional supvr, Ministry of State Farms, 55-57; res assoc, Rutgers Univ, 58-60; res horticulturist, United Fruit Co, NY, 60-62; res assoc, Cornell Univ, 63-65 & NY State Agr Exp Sta, 65-66; res assoc, 66-69, leader pome fruit invests, 69-72, CHIEF FRUIT LAB, BELTSVILLE AGR RES CTR, AGR RES SERV, USDA, 73- *Mem:* Am Soc Hort Sci; Int Soc Hort Sci. *Res:* Postharvest physiology; biochemistry of fruits; metabolic changes in fruits exposed to different environmental conditions. *Mailing Add:* Agr Res Serv USDA Beltsville MD 20705

FAUST, RICHARD AHLVERS, b Terre Haute, Ind, Sept 6, 21; m 43; c 2. MICROBIOLOGY. *Educ:* Purdue Univ, BS, 48, MS, 52, PhD(bact), 58. *Prof Exp:* Instr bact, Purdue Univ, 51-55; asst prof, 58-66, ASSOC PROF MICROBIOL, UNIV MONT, 66- *Mem:* AAAS; Am Soc Microbiol. *Res:* Physiology of Bordetella pertussis; microbial ecology of alpine soils. *Mailing Add:* Dept of Microbiol Univ of Mont Missoula MT 59812

FAUST, RICHARD EDWARD, b Greenfield, Mass, Oct 26, 27; m 53; c 3. PHARMACEUTICAL CHEMISTRY. *Educ:* Mass Col Pharm, BS, 51; Purdue Univ, MS, 53, PhD(pharmaceut chem), 55; Columbia Univ, MBA, 68. *Prof Exp:* Res assoc, Sterling-Winthrop Res Inst, 54-55; asst prof pharm, Ferris State Col, 55-57; dir res, Potter Drug & Chem Corp, 57-61; mgr new prod creation, Merck & Co, 61-63; asst dir res, Johnson & Johnson Res Ctr, 63-66, consult, 66-67; corp planning mgr, 68-69, DIR RES PLANNING & DEVELOP, HOFFMANN-LA ROCHE, INC, 69- *Concurrent Pos:* Prof lectr, Mass Col Pharm, 58-61; adj prof, Fairleigh Dickinson Univ, 76- *Mem:* AAAS; Am Pharmaceut Asn; Am Chem Soc; Soc Res Adminr; Acad Pharmaceut Sci. *Res:* Cosmetic and dermatologic preparations; topical therapeutics; toiletries; soaps; research administration and planning. *Mailing Add:* Hoffmann-La Roche Inc Nutley NJ 07110

FAUST, ROBERT GILBERT, b Brooklyn, NY, Nov 9, 32; m 56; c 1. CELL PHYSIOLOGY, BIOPHYSICS. *Educ:* NY Univ, AB, 53; Univ Southern Calif, MS, 57; Princeton Univ, PhD(biol), 60. *Prof Exp:* Asst zool, Univ Southern Calif, 55-57; asst biol, Princeton Univ, 57-59; res assoc biophys, Harvard Med Sch, 62-63; asst prof physiol, 63-68, dir space sci prog, 68-72, assoc prof, 68-75, PROF PHYSIOL, SCH MED, UNIV NC, CHAPEL HILL, 75- *Concurrent Pos:* NIH fel, Oxford Univ, 60-62 & Harvard Med Sch, 62-63; NIH grants, 64-83; NASA grant, 68-72; mem physiol study sect, NIH, 70-74; NIH sr int fel, Max-Planck Inst Biophys, Frankfurt, Ger, 76-77; Erna & Jakob Michael vis prof, Weizman Inst Sci, Rehovot, Israel, 82. *Mem:* AAAS; Am Physiol Soc; Sigma Xi; Biophys Soc; Brit Biochem Soc. *Res:* Permeability of cells and tissues; mechanisms of active transport of electrolytes and non-electrolytes; use of model and reconstituted systems to interpret solute penetration into cells and tissues. *Mailing Add:* Dept of Physiol Univ of NC Sch of Med Chapel Hill NC 27514

FAUST, SAMUEL DENTON, b Shiloh, NJ, Aug 11, 29; m 60. ENVIRONMENTAL SCIENCES. *Educ:* Gettysburg Col, BS, 50, PhD(environ sci), 58. *Prof Exp:* Chemist, W A Taylor & Co, Md, 50-54; res fel, 54-58, from asst prof to assoc prof, 58-65, prof environ sci, 65-80, RES PROF ENVIRON SCI, RUTGERS UNIV, 80- *Mem:* Am Chem Soc; Am Soc Limnol & Oceanog; Am Water Works Asn; Am Geophys Union; Am Soc Testing & Mat. *Res:* Water chemistry; water quality management; water resources. *Mailing Add:* Wikwames Yapewi PO Box 94 Change Water NJ 07831

FAUST, WALTER LUCK, b Benton, Ark, Feb 13, 34; m 57; c 3. LASERS, EXPERIMENTAL PHYSICS. *Educ:* Columbia Univ, AB, 56; Columbia Univ, PhD(physics), 61. *Prof Exp:* Mem tech staff, Bell Labs, 61-67; from assoc prof to prof physics & elec eng, Univ Southern Calif, 67-72; head, Optical Physics Br, 72-75, SR SCIENTIST, OPTICAL SCI DIV, NAVAL RES LAB, 75- *Mem:* Fel Am Phys Soc. *Res:* Short pulse optical spectroscopy. *Mailing Add:* Naval Res Lab Code 5504.4 Washington DC 20375

FAUSTO, NELSON, b Sao Paulo, Brazil, Dec 12, 36; m 66. BIOCHEMICAL PATHOLOGY. *Educ:* Univ Sao Paulo, Brazil, BS, 54, MD, 60. *Prof Exp:* Asst prof, Dept Histol & Embryol, Med Sch, Univ Sao Paulo, 61; res assoc, Dept Path & Regional Primate Ctr, Med Sch, Univ Wis, 62-63; res assoc & fel, Damon Runyon Mem Fund Cancer Res, 64-65; instr med sci, 66; asst prof, 66-71, assoc prof, 71-75, PROF MED SCI, DEPT PATH, BROWN UNIV, 75-, CHMN, SECT PATH, 78- *Concurrent Pos:* Mem, Path B Study Sect, NIH, 75-79, chmn, Clin Sci Fel Review Comt, Div Cancer Biol & Diag, 80-81, consult, Bd Sci Counselors, Nat Cancer Inst, 81; vis prof, Dept Path, MD Anderson Hosp & Tumor Inst, Univ Tex, 79. *Mem:* Am Soc Cell Biol; Am Asn Pathologists; NY Acad Sci. *Res:* Gene expression in regenerating, neoplastic and fetal liver. *Mailing Add:* Div Biol & Med Brown Univ Box G Providence RI 02912

FAUSTO-STERLING, ANNE, b New York City, NY, July 30, 44; m 66. EMBRYOLOGY. *Educ:* Univ Wis, BA, 65; Brown Univ, PhD(develop genetics), 70. *Prof Exp:* Asst prof, 71-77, ASSOC PROF BIOL & MED, BROWN UNIV, 77- *Mem:* Soc Develop Biol; Genetics Soc Am; Nat Women's Studies Asn; Int Soc Develop Biol; AAAS. *Res:* Developmental genetics of drosophila melanogaster; biological theories about women. *Mailing Add:* Box G Brown Univ Providence RI 02912

FAUT, OWEN DONALD, b Allentown, Pa, July 8, 36; m 59; c 4. INORGANIC CHEMISTRY. *Educ:* Muhlenburg Col, BS, 58; Mass Inst Technol, PhD(chem), 62. *Prof Exp:* From asst prof to assoc prof chem, Hanover Col, 62-67; assoc prof, 67-77, PROF CHEM, WILKES COL, 77- *Mem:* Am Chem Soc. *Res:* Electronic and molecular structures of first row transition metal compounds. *Mailing Add:* Dept of Chem Wilkes Col Wilkes-Barre PA 18073

FAUTH, DAVID JONATHAN, b Erie, Pa, Aug 9, 51; m 76. INORGANIC CHEMISTRY, ORGANOMETALLIC CHEMISTRY. *Educ:* Thiel Col, BA, 73; Univ SC, PhD(chem), 78. *Prof Exp:* RES CHEMIST NUCLEAR CHEM, SAVANNAH RIVER LAB, E I DU PONT DE NEMOURS & CO, INC, 78- *Mem:* Am Chem Soc. *Res:* Metal cluster chemistry, catalysis, metal carbonyl, thiocarbonyl and nitrosyl chemistry, phase transfer catalysis; solvent extraction. *Mailing Add:* Savannah River Lab E I du Pont de Nemours & Co Inc Aiken SC 29801

FAUTH, MAE IRENE, b Wrightsville, Pa, June 12, 13. ANALYTICAL CHEMISTRY, RESOURCE MANAGEMENT. *Educ:* Lebanon Valley Col, BS, 33; Columbia Univ, AM, 46; Pa State Univ, PhD(chem), 55. *Prof Exp:* Attend nursing, Wernersville State Hosp, Pa, 35-43; asst engr elec eng, Western Elec Co, NJ, 43-45; head dept sci, NY Pub Sch, 46-47; instr chem, Hazleton Ctr, Pa State Univ, 47-49, instr, Univ, 49-55; mgr anal br, Naval Ord Sta, Indian Head, Md, 55-72; asst to pres environ res, Charles County Community Col, Md, 72-73; HEAD POLLUTING CONTROL GROUP, NAVAL SURFACE WEAPONS CTR, WHITE OAK LAB, INDIAN HEAD, 73- *Concurrent Pos:* Prof lectr, Charles County Community Col, 59- *Mem:* Am Chem Soc; Am Defense Preparedness Asn; Inst Environ Sci. *Res:* Chemistry of rocket fuels; analysis and evaluation of solid propellants; propellant reclamation; pollution abatement; environmental effects of chemicals. *Mailing Add:* Box 217 Indian Head MD 20640

FAUVER, VERNON A(RTHUR), b Hammond, Ind, Mar 25, 28; m 47; c 2. CHEMICAL ENGINEERING. *Educ:* Purdue Univ, BS, 52, MS, 53. *Prof Exp:* Chem engr, Eastman Kodak Co, NY, 53; chem engr, Styrene Polymerization Lab, 54-58, Process Eng Dept, 58-59 & C J Strosacker Res & Develop Lab, 59-61, res engr, Edgar C Britton Res Lab, 61-66, process specialist, Process Eng Dept, 66-72, SR PROCESS SPECIALIST, PROCESS ENG DEPT, DOW CHEM CO, 72- *Mem:* Am Inst Chem Engrs; Am Chem Soc. *Res:* Process development; reaction engineering; separations processes; plant start-up; fluid flow/pumps. *Mailing Add:* Process Eng Dept 633 Bldg Dow Chem Co Midland MI 48640

FAVALE, ANTHONY JOHN, b New York, NY, Feb 28, 35; m 72; c 3. NUCLEAR PHYSICS. *Educ:* Polytech Inst Brooklyn, BS, 56; NY Univ, MS, 63. *Prof Exp:* Res physicist, 56-62, head high energy physics & astrophysics, 62-74, HEAD, ENERGY RES OFF, GRUMMAN AEROSPACE CORP, GRUMMAN CORP, 74-, DEP DIR FUSION, 81- *Concurrent Pos:* Guest scientist, Reactor Div, Brookhaven Nat Lab, 61-64; lectr, C W Post Col, 64- *Mem:* Am Phys Soc; Inst Elec & Electronics Engrs; Am Nuclear Soc. *Res:* High energy physics experiments in space; gamma ray astronomy; solar energy research; fusion energy development. *Mailing Add:* 22 Major Trescott Lane Northport NY 11768

FAVAZZA, ARMANDO RICCARDO, b New York, NY, Apr 14, 41; m 71; c 2. PSYCHIATRY. *Educ:* Columbia Univ, BA, 62; Univ Va, MD, 66; Univ Mich, MPH, 71. *Prof Exp:* Resident psychiat, Univ Mich, 66-71; staff psychiatrist, US Naval Hosp, Oakland, Calif, 71-73; assoc prof, 73-80, PROF PSYCHIAT, UNIV MO-COLUMBIA, 80- *Concurrent Pos:* Psychiat consult, Vet Admin Hosp, Columbia, 73-; assoc ed, MD Mag, 73-; ed-in-chief, J Oper Psychiat, 73- *Mem:* Fel Am Psychiat Asn; Am Col Psychiatrists; fel Am Asn Social Psychiat; Am Anthrop Asn; Sigma Xi. *Res:* Cultural psychiatry; psychiatric epidemiology. *Mailing Add:* Dept Psychiat Univ Mo Sch Med Columbia MO 65201

FAVERO, MARTIN, b Butte, Mont, May 3, 37; m 61; c 4. MICROBIOLOGY. *Educ:* Gonzaga Univ, BS, 59; Wash State Univ, MS, 61, PhD(bact), 64. *Prof Exp:* RES MICROBIOLOGIST HEPATITIS LAB DIV, CTR DIS CONTROL, USPHS, 64- *Honors & Awards:* Superior Serv Award, Health Serv & Ment Health Admin, 71; J D Culligan Award, World Water Soc. *Mem:* Am Soc Microbiol. *Res:* Resistance of microorganisms to chlorine and iodine; microbial flora of chlorinated and iodinated swimming pools; environmental health; aerospace microbiology; microbial contamination of spacecraft; spacecraft sterilization; hospital acquired infections; viral hepatitis; dialysis associated diseases. *Mailing Add:* Ctr for Dis Control USPHS 4402 N Seventh St Phoenix AZ 85014

FAVORITE, FELIX, b Quincy, Mass, Mar 18, 25; m 51; c 4. OCEANOGRAPHY, ECOLOGY. *Educ:* Mass Maritime Acad, BS, 46; Univ Wash, BS, 55, MS, 65; Ore State Univ, PhD(oceanog, meteorol), 68. *Prof Exp:* Res asst oceanog, Univ Wash, 55-57; oceanogr phys oceanog, Seattle Biol Lab, Bur Com Fisheries, Northwest & Alaska Fisheries Ctr, Nat Marine Fisheries Serv, 57-59, chief oceanog invest, 59-70, prog dir oceanog, Seattle Biol Lab, Nat Marine Fisheries Serv, 70-75, coordr resource ecol, 75-80; CONSULT OCEANOGR, 80- *Concurrent Pos:* Expert oceanog, Int NPac Fish Comn, 57-76; partic, US-Japan Coop Sci Prog & US-USSR Oceanog Exchange Prog, 64 & US-Japan Bering Sea Prog & Nat Oceanic & Atmospheric Admin-Bur Land Mgt Outer Continental Shelf Environ Assessment Prog, 73-80. *Honors & Awards:* Silver Medal, US Dept Com, 73. *Mem:* New York Acad Sci; Oceanog Soc Japan; Am Inst Fishery Res Biologists. *Res:* Physical oceanography and resource ecology studies in the North Pacific Ocean and Bering Sea. *Mailing Add:* 16103 41st N E Seattle WA 98155

FAVORITE, JOHN R, b Muskegon, Mich, June 26, 16; m 42; c 2. CHEMICAL ENGINEERING. *Educ:* Purdue Univ, BS, 38. *Prof Exp:* Engr, Goodyear Tire & Rubber Co, 38-49 & Clopay Co, 49-50; supvr, Thermo-Fax prod develop, 50-55, tech dir, Duplicating Prod Div, 55-64, group mkt mgr duplicating & microfilm prod, Int Div, 64-67, PROJ MGR PHOTOG PROD DIV, MINN MINING & MFG CO, 67- *Mem:* Am Chem Soc; Am Inst Chem Engrs. *Res:* Product research and development. *Mailing Add:* 1292 Hillcrest Ave St Paul MN 55116

FAVOUR, CUTTING BROAD, b Toreva, Ariz, July 19, 13; m 41, 74; c 3. MEDICINE. *Educ:* Hendrix Col, AB, 36; Johns Hopkins Univ, MD, 40; Am Bd Internal Med, dipl, 54. *Prof Exp:* Intern, Osler Wards, Hopkins Hosp, 40-41; asst resident, Peter Bent Brigham Hosp, Boston, 41-42, resident, 42-43; instr & asst, Harvard Med Sch, 43-47, assoc, 47-54; asst clin prof, Med Sch, Stanford Univ, 55-60; prof prev med & chmn dept, Sch Med, Georgetown Univ, 60-62; chief dept physiol, Nat Jewish Hosp, Denver, 62-64, chief dept exp epidemiol, 64-66; dir med educ, St Mary's Hosp, 66-70; med dir, Kaiser Industs Corp, 70-73; dir ambulatory serv, San Joaquin County Gen Hosp, 73; dir, Ambulatory Serv, Scenic Gen Hosp, 73-74; ASSOC CLIN PROF MED, SCH MED, UNIV CALIF, SAN FRANCISCO, 75- *Concurrent Pos:* Head dept immunol, Palo Alto Med Res Found, 54-60; asst vis physician, Stanford Serv, City & County Hosp, San Francisco, 55-60; mem staff, Palo Alto Hosp, 55-56; lectr & consult, US Navy Hosp, Oak Knoll, Calif, 56-60; chief, Georgetown Med Serv, Washington, DC, Gen Hosp, 60-62; mem attend staff, St Mary's Hosp, San Francisco, 66-74, consult staff, 75-, San Francisco Gen Hosp, 69-73, Highland Gen Hosp, Oakland, 70-73 & St Joseph's Hosp, 71-73; mem, Emergency Med Systs, Inc. 73-; active staff, Scenic Gen Hosp, Modesto, 73-; courtesy staff, San Francisco Gen Hosp & Mem Hosps, Modesto, 76-; consult staff, Oak Valley District Hosp, Oakdale, 74-75, active staff, 76-; med dir, Driftwood Convalescent Hosp, Modesto, 76- & Oakdale Convalescent Hosp, Oakdale, 79-; pvt pract, Oakdale 76-; consult tuberculosis, Pub Health Dept Stanislaus County, Modesto, 77- *Mem:* Soc Exp Biol & Med; fel Am Col Physicians; Am Thoracic Soc; affil Royal Soc Med; Am Rheumatism Asn. *Res:* Immunology and microbiology applied to clinical medicine. *Mailing Add:* PO Box 399 Oakdale CA 95361

FAVRE, HENRI ALBERT, b Payerne, Switz, Dec 4, 26; m 58; c 3. ORGANIC CHEMISTRY. *Educ:* Swiss Fed Inst Technol, Ing Chem Dipl, 48, DrSc, 51. *Prof Exp:* Brit Coun student, Sheffield Univ, 51-52; from asst prof to assoc prof org chem, 52-60, dir dept chem, 59-63, PROF ORG CHEM, UNIV MONTREAL, 60- *Mem:* Chem Inst Can. *Res:* Stereochemistry. *Mailing Add:* Univ of Montreal Dept of Chem PO Box 6128 Montreal PQ H3C 3S7 Can

FAVREAU, ROGER F, physics, see previous edition

FAVRET, A(NDREW) G(ILLIGAN), b Cincinnati, Ohio, May 9, 25; m 49; c 11. ELECTRONICS. *Educ:* US Mil Acad, BS, 45; Univ Pa, MS, 50; Cath Univ Am, DEng(elec eng), 64. *Prof Exp:* Staff mem, Lincoln Lab, Mass Inst Technol, 54-55; actg dir planning, Defense Prod Group, Am Mach & Foundry Co, 55-56, mgr syst anal dept, Alexandria Div, 56-59; sr sci adv to asst chief staff intel, US Dept Army, 59-63; assoc prof elec eng, 63-67, dir comput ctr, 68-73, PROF ELEC ENG, CATH UNIV AM, 67-, DEAN, SCH ENG & ARCHIT, 81- *Concurrent Pos:* Sr analyst, Cent Intel Agency, 73-78. *Mem:* Sr mem Inst Elec & Electronics Engrs; Asn Comput Mach. *Res:* Digital computer applications; statistical decision theory; signal processing; digital computer systems; biomedical instrumentation; computer simulation. *Mailing Add:* 2105 Gatewood Pl Silver Spring MD 20903

FAVRO, LAWRENCE DALE, b Pittsburgh, Pa, Apr 17, 32; m 57; c 2. THEORETICAL PHYSICS. *Educ:* Harvard Univ, AB, 54, AM, 55, PhD(physics), 59. *Prof Exp:* Instr physics, Columbia Univ, 59-62; from asst prof to assoc prof, 62-72, PROF PHYSICS, WAYNE STATE UNIV, 72- *Mem:* Am Phys Soc. *Res:* Stochastic processes; statistical theory of energy levels; coherent processes in particle beams; acoustics; optics; photoacoustics. *Mailing Add:* Dept of Physics Wayne State Univ Detroit MI 48202

FAW, RICHARD E, b Adams Co, Ohio, June 22, 36; m 61; c 2. CHEMICAL & NUCLEAR ENGINEERING. *Educ:* Univ Cincinnati, BS, 59; Univ Minn, PhD(chem eng), 62. *Prof Exp:* From asst prof to assoc prof, 62-68, PROF NUCLEAR ENG, KANS STATE UNIV, 68- *Mem:* Am Nuclear Soc; Am Soc Eng Educ. *Res:* Radiation protection; nuclear reactor safety. *Mailing Add:* 1100 Thurston St Manhattan KS 66502

FAW, WADE FARRIS, b Eubank, Ky, Feb 23, 42; m 65; c 1. AGRONOMY, PLANT PHYSIOLOGY. *Educ:* Berea Col, BS, 65; WVa Univ, PhD(agron), 69. *Prof Exp:* Trainee farm planning, US Soil Conserv Serv, 63-65; asst prof agron, Rice Br Exp Sta, Univ Ark, 69-74; exten agronomist, Auburn Univ, 74-75; assoc prof & chmn, Plant Sci Dept, Tenn Technol Univ, 75-77; exten agronomist, Auburn Univ, 77-80; ASSOC SPECIALIST AGRON, LA STATE UNIV, 80- *Mem:* Am Soc Agron; Crop Sci Soc Am; Am Forage & Grassland Coun; Weed Sci Soc Am. *Res:* Response of plants to their environment; physiology of grain and forage crops. *Mailing Add:* Coop Exten Serv Auburn Univ Baton Rouge LA 70803

FAWAZ, GEORGE, b Deirminas, Lebanon, Nov 22, 13; nat US; m 46; c 2. PHARMACOLOGY, BIOCHEMISTRY. *Educ:* Am Univ, Beirut, AB, 33, MS, 35; Graz Univ, PhD(org chem), 36; Univ Heidelberg, MD, 55. *Prof Exp:* From instr to asst prof biochem, 39-49, assoc prof pharmacol, 49-53, PROF PHARMACOL, AM UNIV, BEIRUT, 53- *Concurrent Pos:* Rockefeller fel, Harvard Univ, 46-47. *Mem:* Ger Pharmacol Soc. *Res:* Organic phosphorus compounds of biological interest; cardiac and renal pharmacology and metabolism; synthetic antimalarials. *Mailing Add:* Dept Pharmacol Am Univ of Beirut Beirut Lebanon

FAWCETT, COLVIN PETER, b Blyth, Eng, Feb 16, 35; m 61; c 2. ENDOCRINOLOGY, NEUROENDOCRINOLOGY. *Educ:* Univ Durham, BSc, 56; Univ Newcastle, PhD(org chem), 59. *Prof Exp:* Fel biochem, Brandeis Univ, 59-61; mem sci staff, Nat Inst Med Res, Eng, 61-66; vis asst prof neurochem, Western Reserve Univ, 66-67; asst prof physiol, 67-75, ASSOC PROF PHYSIOL, UNIV TEX HEALTH SCI CTR, DALLAS, 75-, DIR, GRAD PROG PHYSIOL & BIOPHYSICS, 75- *Mem:* Brit Biochem Soc; Endocrine Soc; Am Physiol Soc; Int Soc Neuroendocrinol. *Res:* Control of hormonal secretion from anterior pituitary; isolation and characterization of hypophysiotrophic hormones from the hypothalamus particularly the gonadotropin releasing factors; biochemistry of the hypothalamus. *Mailing Add:* Dept of Physiol Univ of Tex Health Sci Ctr Dallas TX 75235

FAWCETT, DON WAYNE, b Springdale, Iowa, Mar 14, 17; m 42; c 4. ANATOMY, HISTOLOGY. *Educ:* Harvard Univ, AB, 38, MD, 42. *Hon Degrees:* DSc, Univ Siena, 74; DSc, New York Med Col, 75; DVetMed, Justus Liebig Univ, 77; MD, Univ Heidelberg, 77; DSc, Univ Chicago, 78 & Univ Cordoba, 78. *Prof Exp:* Surg intern, Mass Gen Hosp, 42-43; from instr to asst prof anat, Harvard Med Sch, 46-55; prof & head dept, Med Col, Cornell Univ, 55-59; cur, Warren Anat Mus, 61-70, sr assoc dean preclin affairs, Harvard Med Sch, 75-77, Hersey prof anat & head dept, 59-81, James Stillman prof comp anat, 62-81; SR SCIENTIST, INTERNATIONAL LAB RES ANIMAL DISEASES, NAIROBI, KENYA, 80- *Concurrent Pos:* Res fel anat, Harvard Med Sch, 46; Markle scholar med sci, 49-54; Lederle Med Fac Award, 54-56; consult, NIH, 55-59, 64-; Ferris lectr, Yale Univ, 57; Phillips lectr, Haverford Col, 58; Christiana Smith lectr, Mt Holyoke Col, 66; Charnock Bradley lectr, Royal (Dick) Sch Vet Studies, Edinburgh, Sigmund Pollitzer lectr, NY Univ & Adam Miller lectr, State Univ NY Downstate Med Ctr, 69; Robert Terry lectr, Sch Med, Wash Univ, Daniel Kempner lectr, Univ Tex Med Br, Galveston, Harold Chaffer lectr, Univ Otago, NZ & Sigma Xi nat lectr, 70. *Mem:* Nat Acad Sci; Fedn Socs Electron Micros (pres, 75-78); Am Asn Anat (1st vpres, 59-60, pres, 65-66); Tissue Cult Asn (vpres, 54-55); Am Soc Cell Biol (pres, 61-62). *Res:* Electron microscopy; cytology; growth and differentiation; spermatogenesis; histophysiology of male reproductive tract; ultrastructure of cardiac muscle; ultrastructure of liver; host-parasite relations in Theileriosis. *Mailing Add:* Int Lab Res Animal Dis PO Box 30709 Nairobi Kenya

FAWCETT, ERIC, b Blackburn, Eng, Aug 23, 27; m 54; c 3. EXPERIMENTAL SOLID STATE PHYSICS, METAL PHYSICS. *Educ:* Cambridge Univ, MA, 52, PhD(physics), 54. *Prof Exp:* Div Low Temperature & Solid State Physics, Nat Res Coun Can, 54-56; sci officer physics, Royal Radar Estab, Eng, 56-61; mem tech staff, Bell Tel Labs, Inc, 61-70; PROF PHYSICS, UNIV TORONTO, 70- *Concurrent Pos:* chmn, Canadian Comt Scientists & Scholars, 80-; pres, Sci for Peace, 81- *Mem:* Am Phys Soc; Can Asn Physicists; fel Brit Inst Physics & Phys Soc. *Res:* Experimental study of electronic structure of metals, including neutron scattering, thermal expansion, magnetostriction and sound velocity, especially in transition and magnetically ordered metals. *Mailing Add:* Dept of Physics Univ of Toronto Toronto ON M5S 1A1 Can

FAWCETT, JAMES JEFFREY, b Blyth, Eng, July 6, 36; m 60; c 2. GEOLOGY. *Educ:* Univ Manchester, BSc, 57, PhD(geol), 61. *Prof Exp:* Asst geol, Univ Manchester, 60-61; fel, Carnegie Inst Geophys Lab, 61-64; assoc chmn dept, 70-75, assoc dean, Sch Grad Studies, 77-80, PROF GEOL, UNIV TORONTO, 64-, ASSOC DEAN SCI, ERINDALE COL, 80- *Mem:* Am Geophys Union; Mineral Soc Am; Geol Asn Can; Mineral Soc Gt Brit & Ireland; Mineral Asn Can. *Res:* Application of high temperature and pressure studies of rocks and minerals to problems of igneous and metamorphic petrogenesis. *Mailing Add:* Dept of Geol Univ of Toronto Toronto ON M5S 1A1 Can

FAWCETT, MARK STANLEY, b Jamestown, NDak, Oct 17, 32. ORGANIC CHEMISTRY. *Educ:* Northwestern Univ, BS, 54; Univ Minn, PhD(org chem), 58. *Prof Exp:* Res chemist, Elastomers Dept, 58-64; mkt develop asst, 64-70, mem staff mkt res, 70-80, MKT RES PROG MGR, E I DU PONT DE NEMOURS & CO, INC, WILMINGTON, 80- *Res:* Structure of polyphenyl cyclopentadienes; elastomeric polymers. *Mailing Add:* Rd 1 21 Arthur Dr Hockessin DE 19707

FAWCETT, NEWTON CREIG, b Fargo, NDak. ELECTROANALYTICAL CHEMISTRY, POLYMER CHEMISTRY. *Educ:* Univ Denver, BS, 64; Univ NMex, MS, 72, PhD(chem), 73. *Prof Exp:* Staff asst, Sandia Corp, 65-68; staff mem, Los Alamos Sci Lab, 72-75; asst prof chem, Southwest Tex State Univ, 75-76; asst prof, 76-80, ASSOC PROF CHEM, UNIV SOUTHERN MISS, 80- *Concurrent Pos:* Consult, Tex Res Inst, 76-; Robert A Welch fel, Southwest Tex State Univ, 76. *Mem:* Am Chem Soc. *Res:* Anti-corrosion coatings; corrosion mechanisms. *Mailing Add:* Southern Sta Box 8273 Hattiesburg MS 39401

FAWCETT, RICHARD STEVEN, b Iowa City, Iowa, Apr 26, 48; m 72. WEED SCIENCE. *Educ:* Iowa State Univ, BS, 70; Univ Ill, PhD(agron), 74. *Prof Exp:* Asst prof res & exten weed control specialsist, Dept Agron, Univ Wis-Madison, 74-76; ASSOC PROF & EXTEN WEED CONTROL SPECIALIST, DEPT PLANT PATH, SEED & WEED SCI, IOWA STATE UNIV, AMES, 76- *Concurrent Pos:* Fac exchange, Univ Costa Rica, San Jose, 80. *Honors & Awards:* Am Soybean Asn Award, 81. *Mem:* Weed Sci Soc Am; Am Soc Agron; Crop Sci Soc Am. *Res:* Weed control systems for corn and soybeans in conservation tillage; herbicide interactions with soil microorganisms; selective applicators for herbicides; perennial weed control. *Mailing Add:* Dept Plant Path Seed & Weed Sci Iowa State Univ Ames IA 50011

FAWCETT, SHERWOOD LUTHER, b Youngstown, Ohio, Dec 25, 19; m 53; c 3. PHYSICS, RESEARCH ADMINISTRATION. *Educ:* Ohio State Univ, BS, 41; Case Inst Technol, MS, 48, PhD(physics), 50. *Hon Degrees:* DSc, Ohio State Univ, 71; DPS, Detroit Inst Technol, 74; DL, Otterbein Col,

77. *Prof Exp:* Instr physics, Case Inst Technol, 46-48; physicist, Battelle Mem Inst, 50-52, from asst chief to chief eng mech div, 52-57, from asst mgr to mgr physics dept, 57-62, mgr metall & physics dept, 62-64, dir, Pac Northwest Lab, 65-67, exec vpres, Inst, 67-68, PRES, BATTELLE MEM INST, 68- *Honors & Awards:* Medal for Advan Res, Am Soc Metals, 77. *Mem:* Am Phys Soc; Am Nuclear Soc; Am Soc Metals; AAAS (vpres, 70); Metall Soc Am Inst Metall Engrs. *Res:* Reactor engineering; heat transfer; fluid flow; methods of electronic beam ejection from Betatrons; reactor irradiation experiments on reactor fuel elements; research and development management. *Mailing Add:* Battelle Memorial Inst 505 King Ave Columbus OH 43201

FAWCETT, TIMOTHY GOSS, b Boston, Mass, Nov 18, 53; m 77. STRUCTURAL CHEMISTRY. *Educ:* Univ Mass, Amherst, BS, 75; Rutgers Univ, PhD(chem), 79. *Prof Exp:* Teaching asst chem, Douglass Col, 75-78, res asst bioinorg chem, Rutgers Univ, 78-79; SR RES CHEMIST, DOW CHEM CO, 79- *Concurrent Pos:* Mem, Joint Comt Powder Diffraction Standards, Int Ctr Diffraction Data, 82- *Mem:* Am Crystallog Asn; Am Chem Soc. *Res:* Development and application of high resolution x-ray powder diffraction techniques used to analyze structural relationships in organic, inorganic polymer and pharmaceutical fields. *Mailing Add:* Anal Lab 1602 Bldg Dow Chem Co Midland MI 48640

FAWLEY, JOHN PHILIP, b Auburn, NY, July 23, 45; m 68; c 1. PHYSIOLOGY. *Educ:* Kent State Univ, BS, 67, MS, 70, PhD(physiol), 72. *Prof Exp:* Instr biol, Kent State Univ, 68-72; asst prof biol, 72-80, ASSOC PROF BIOL, WESTMINSTER COL, 80- *Mem:* AAAS; Nat Speleol Soc. *Res:* Responses of rodents to exercise and environmental stress. *Mailing Add:* Dept of Biol Westminster Col New Wilmington PA 16142

FAXVOG, FREDERICK ROGGEMAN, b Minneapolis, Minn, Jan 7, 43; m 65; c 2. APPLIED PHYSICS, ELECTRICAL ENGINEERING. *Educ:* Univ Minn, BS, 65, MSEE, 68, PhD(elec eng), 71. *Prof Exp:* Sr res scientist physics, Gen Motors Res Labs, 71-80; SECT CHIEF ACTIVE DEVICES SYSTS, HONEYWELL RES CTR, 80- *Mem:* Am Phys Soc; Optical Soc Am; AAAS. *Res:* Laser physics; photo-acoustic spectroscopy; particle light scattering; coherent optics; optical data processing. *Mailing Add:* 23938 Research Dr Farmington Hills MI 48024

FAY, FRANCIS HOLLIS, b Melrose, Mass, Nov 18, 27; m 52; c 2. MARINE MAMMALOGY. *Educ:* Univ NH, BS, 50; Univ Mass, MS, 52; Univ BC, PhD(vert zool), 55. *Prof Exp:* Med biologist, Arctic Health Res Ctr, USPHS, 55-67, res biologist, 67-74; ASSOC PROF, INST MARINE SCI, UNIV ALASKA, FAIRBANKS, 74- *Concurrent Pos:* Mem comt sci adv, Marine Mammal Comn, 75-77. *Mem:* Fel AAAS; Am Soc Mammal; Ecol Soc Am; Wildlife Dis Asn; fel Arctic Inst NAm. *Res:* Biology of pinnipeds; vertebrate populations; animal ecology. *Mailing Add:* Inst Marine Sci Univ of Alaska Fairbanks AK 99701

FAY, HOMER, b Brooklyn, NY, Aug 3, 28; m 55; c 2. GAS SEPARATION & PURIFICATION. *Educ:* Bowdoin Col, AB, 49; Mass Inst Technol, PhD(anal chem), 53. *Prof Exp:* Asst anal chem, Mass Inst Technol, 50-53; chemist, 53-70, sr scientist, Res Inst, Tarrytown, 70-79, SR RES ASSOC, LINDE DIV, UNION CARBIDE CORP, TONAWANDA, NY, 79- *Concurrent Pos:* Chemist, Ionics, Inc, 51. *Mem:* AAAS; Am Chem Soc; Am Phys Soc; Am Ceramic Soc. *Res:* Materials and processes for gas separation and purification; adsorption and absorption; instrumentation for gas analysis; optical instrumentation for the detection of fluorescent minerals; solid-state materials synthesis and properties; dielectrics and ferroelectrics; electrical and optical properties of crystals; electrochemical behavior of semiconductors. *Mailing Add:* Linde Div Union Carbide Corp 61 E Park Dr Tonawanda NY 14150

FAY, JAMES A(LAN), b Southold, NY, Nov 1, 23; m 46; c 6. FLUID MECHANICS, HEAT TRANSFER. *Educ:* Webb Inst Naval Archit, BS, 44; Mass Inst Technol, MS, 47; Cornell Univ, PhD(mech eng), 51. *Prof Exp:* Res engr, Lima-Hamilton Corp, 47-49; asst prof eng mech, Cornell Univ, 51-55; PROF MECH ENG, MASS INST TECHNOL, 55- *Concurrent Pos:* Consult, Avco-Everett Res Lab, 55-69, Exec Dept, State of Maine, 71-72, Natural Resources Coun Maine, 77- & Mass Energy Facil Siting Coun, 77-78; chmn, Boston Air Pollution Control Comn, 69-72 & Mass Port Authority, 72-77; mem, Environ Studies Bd, Nat Res Coun, 73-78 & 80-, Comt on Radioactive Waste Mgt, 78-81; dir, Union Concerned Scientists, 78-; consult, SCA Servs, Inc, 77- *Mem:* Am Soc Mech Engrs; fel Am Phys Soc; fel Am Inst Aeronaut & Astronaut; fel Am Acad Arts & Sci; fel AAAS. *Res:* Gaseous detonations; hypersonic heat transfer; magnetohydrodynamics; plasma physics; high temperature gas dynamics; ionization phenomena; air and oil pollution; liquified energy gas safety. *Mailing Add:* Rm 3-246 Mass Inst of Technol Cambridge MA 02139

FAY, JOHN EDWARD, II, b Rochester, NY, July 28, 34. CHEMICAL ENGINEERING. *Educ:* Univ Mich, Ann Arbor, BSE, 56, MSE, 57; Mass Inst Technol, ScD, 71. *Prof Exp:* Process engr chem eng, capital budgets coordr, economist, process supvr & sr engr, Humble Oil & Refining Co, Bayonne Refinery, NJ, 57-68; res engr chem & metall, 72-73, sect head, proj eval, 73-79, sect head, 80-81, SUPT, CHEM ENG, CENT RES LABS, ASARCO, INC, 82- *Concurrent Pos:* Chmn subcomt Energy Conserv Non-Ferrous Metals, Am Mining Cong. *Mem:* Am Inst Mining, Metall & Petrol Engrs; Asn Energy Engrs; Am Asn Cost Engrs. *Res:* Economic and technical evaluation of research projects; energy conservation; process metallurgy; computer modeling. *Mailing Add:* ASARCO Inc Cent Res Labs 901 Oak Tree Rd South Plainfield NJ 07080

FAY, MARCUS J, b Adair, Iowa, July 5, 21; m 44; c 2. PLANT TAXONOMY. *Educ:* Univ Iowa, PhD(bot), 53. *Prof Exp:* Asst, Univ Iowa, 49-53, instr, 53; from asst prof to assoc prof, 53-57, head dept, 53-55, PROF BIOL, UNIV WIS-EAU CLAIRE, 57-, HEAD DEPT, 57- *Res:* Floristics and plant distribution studies. *Mailing Add:* Dept of Biol Univ of Wis Eau Claire WI 54701

FAY, PHILIP S, b Ballard, Wash, Jan 24, 21; m 42; c 3. PETROLEUM. *Educ:* Cornell Col, AB, 41; Western Reserve Univ, PhD(chem), 49. *Prof Exp:* PROJ LEADER, CHEM & PHYS RES DIV, STAND OIL CO OHIO, 42-44 & 49- *Mem:* Am Chem Soc. *Res:* Reaction of phosphorous pentasulfide with olefins; gasoline additives; combustion chamber deposits; reaction of hydrocarbons; organoboron chemistry; petrochemicals; geochemical instrumentation and exploration. *Mailing Add:* Stand Oil Co of Ohio 4440 Warrensville Rd Cleveland OH 44128

FAY, RICHARD ROZZELL, b Holden, Mass, May 5, 44; m 68; c 2. PSYCHOPHYSIOLOGY, NEUROSCIENCES. *Educ:* Bowdoin Col, BA, 66; Conn Col, MA, 68; Princeton Univ, PhD(psychol), 70. *Prof Exp:* Res asst prof sensory sci, Sensory Sci Lab, Univ Hawaii, 72-74; asst prof otolaryngol, Bowman Gray Sch Med, 74-75; ASSOC PROF PSYCHOL, LOYOLA UNIV, CHICAGO, 75- *Concurrent Pos:* USPHS fel, Auditory Res Labs, Princeton Univ, 70-72; res career develop award, Nat Inst Neurol & Commun Disorders & Stroke, 80- *Mem:* Acoust Soc Am; Am Psychol Asn; Sigma Xi; Soc Neurosci; Asn Res Otolaryngol. *Res:* Processing by the brain of sensory information and the coding of information by the nervous system; neurophysiological correlates of sensory behavior. *Mailing Add:* Dept of Psychol Loyola Univ 6525 N Sheridan Rd Chicago IL 60626

FAY, ROBERT CLINTON, b Kenosha, Wis, Mar 14, 36; m 60. INORGANIC CHEMISTRY. *Educ:* Oberlin Col, AB, 57; Univ Ill, MS, 60, PhD(inorg chem), 62. *Prof Exp:* From asst prof to assoc prof, 62-75, PROF CHEM, CORNELL UNIV, 75- *Concurrent Pos:* NSF fac fel, Univ EAnglia & Univ Sussex, 69-70. *Mem:* Am Chem Soc; Royal Soc Chem; Am Crystallog Asn. *Res:* Stereochemistry of metal complexes; applications of nuclear magnetic resonance spectroscopy to inorganic chemistry. *Mailing Add:* 318 Eastwood Ave Ithaca NY 14850

FAY, ROGER RICHARD, biological oceanography, marine ecology, see previous edition

FAY, WARREN HENRY, b Scottsbluff, Nebr, Jan 3, 29; m 52; c 1. SPEECH PATHOLOGY, INFANTILE AUTISM. *Educ:* Colo State Col, BA, 51; Univ Ore, MEd, 59; Purdue Univ, PhD(speech path, audiol), 63. *Prof Exp:* High sch instr, Ore, 56-58; speech therapist, Pub Schs, 58-60; instr, 62-67, assoc prof, 67-78, PROF SPEECH PATH, ORE HEALTH SCI UNIV, 78- *Mem:* Am Speech & Hearing Asn. *Res:* Physiological aspects of language development and disorders, especially in the areas of echolalia and temporal coding of linguistic units; speech of childhood autism. *Mailing Add:* Univ of Ore Health Sci Ctr Portland OR 97201

FAYER, MICHAEL DAVID, b Los Angeles, Calif, Sept 12, 47; m 68. CHEMICAL PHYSICS. *Educ:* Univ Calif, Berkeley, BS, 69, PhD(chem), 74. *Prof Exp:* asst prof, 74-80, ASSOC PROF CHEM, STANFORD UNIV, 80- *Mem:* Am Phys Soc. *Res:* Energy transport in organic solids and liquids at liquid helium to room temperatures utilizing optical spectroscopic and picosecond laser techniques. *Mailing Add:* Dept of Chem Stanford Univ Stanford CA 94305

FAYER, RONALD, b Philadelphia, Pa, Oct 12, 39. PARASITOLOGY, PROTOZOOLOGY. *Educ:* Univ Alaska, BS, 62; Utah State Univ, MS, 64, PhD(zool), 68. *Prof Exp:* Parasitologist, Beltsville Parasite Lab, USDA, 68-72, PROJ LEADER, ANIMAL PARASITOL INST, USDA, 72- *Concurrent Pos:* Adj prof, Sch Vet Med, Univ Pa, 78- *Honors & Awards:* USDA Cert of Merit, 74 & 78 & Super Serv Award, 78; H B Ward Medal, Am Soc Parasitologists, 78. *Mem:* Am Soc Parasitologists; Soc Protozoologists; Wildlife Dis Asn; Am Asn Vet Parasitologists. *Res:* Veterinary and wildlife parasitology; pathology; serology; in vitro cultivation. *Mailing Add:* Animal Parasitol Inst USDA Beltsville MD 20705

FAYLE, HARLAN DOWNING, b Hibbing, Minn, July 24, 07; m 36; c 1. BIOCHEMISTRY, PHARMACOLOGY. *Educ:* Hamline Univ, BA, 31; Univ Minn, MS, 36, PhD(biochem, pharmacol), 63. *Prof Exp:* Instr chem, Eveleth Jr Col, 33-36, Hibbing Jr Col, 36-46; & Duluth Jr Col, 46-48; from instr to asst prof, Univ Minn, Duluth, 48-56; asst, Univ Minn, Minneapolis, 54-55; from assoc prof to prof, 56-73, chmn sect, 56-73, EMER PROF CHEM, PURDUE UNIV, CALUMET CAMPUS, 73- *Concurrent Pos:* Consult, Butler Mining Co, 40-42, Elliott Packing Co, 48-50 & Mitchell Oil Co, 50-51; rep pres adv coun on retirement, Purdue Univ, Calumet Campus, 76-; adj prof chem, Ind Univ Northwest, 78. *Mem:* AAAS; Am Chem Soc; fel Am Inst Chemists; NY Acad Sci; Am Asn Univ Professors. *Res:* Distribution and determination of cadmium in biological material; toxicology of cadmium. *Mailing Add:* 7512 Knickerbocker Pkwy Hammond IN 46323

FAYMON, KARL A(LOIS), b St Louis, Mo, Sept 9, 27; m 60; c 2. SYSTEMS ANALYSIS. *Educ:* Univ Mich, BS, 51, MS, 52; Case Inst Technol, PhD(aerodyn), 57. *Prof Exp:* Instr, St Louis Univ, 52-53; instr & asst, Case Inst Technol, 53-57; theoret aerodynamicist, Convair Div, Gen Dynamics Corp, 57-60; systs analyst, Thompson-Ramo-Wooldridge, Inc, 60-63; chief systs anal off, Launch Vehicles Div, 63-74, asst chief, Systs Anal & Assessment Off, 74-80, DEP CHIEF, PLANNING, ANAL, & SYSTS OFF, ENERGY PROGS DIRECTORATE, LEWIS RES CTR, NASA, CLEVELAND, 81- *Res:* Trajectory analysis; thermodynamics; applied mathematics; space launch vehicles systems analysis; structural and control dynamics; energy systems analysis; propulsion systems analysis; power and energy conversion systems analysis. *Mailing Add:* 2066 Marshfield Rd Mayfield Heights OH 44124

FAYON, A(BRAM) M(IKO), b Sofia, Bulgaria, Apr 1, 20; US citizen; m 58; c 3. CHEMICAL ENGINEERING. *Educ:* Istanbul Univ, BS, 47; Johns Hopkins Univ, MSE, 52; NY Univ, EngScD(chem eng), 59. *Prof Exp:* Chemist, Baltimore Paint & Color Works, 48-51; chem engr res & develop, US Indust Chem, 51-52 & Chem Construct Corp, 52-54; asst chem eng, NY Univ, 56-57; from instr to asst prof, 57-60; res chem engr, Am Cyanamid Co, Conn, 60-62; sr res chem engr, 62-65; sr process engr, Sci Design Co, Inc,

65-66; assoc engr, Mobil Oil Corp, 66-67 & Mobil Res & Develop Corp, 67-70, opers res coordr, 70-75, sr planning assoc, New York, 75-80, SR ENG ASSOC, MOBIL CHEM CO, HOUSTON, TEX, 80- *Concurrent Pos:* Consult, Nuclear Energy Prod Div, Am Car & Foundry, 56-57. *Mem:* Am Inst Chem Engrs. *Res:* Thermodynamics; heat transfer; fluid flow; process simulation of petroleum and petrochemical plants; development of computer methods related to process and process design problems; financial and technical appraisal of petrochemical processes. *Mailing Add:* 510 Siwanoy Pl Pelham Manor NY 10803

FAYOS, JUAN VALLVEY, b Camaguey, Cuba, Nov 24, 29; US citizen; m 61; c 4. RADIOLOGY. *Educ:* Inst de Camaguey, BS, 48; Univ Havana, MD, 55. *Prof Exp:* From instr to assoc prof, 61-72, PROF RADIOL, UNIV MICH, ANN ARBOR, 72-, DIR RADIATION THER DIV, 72- *Concurrent Pos:* Mem staff, Wayne County Gen Hosp, 66; consult, Vet Admin Hosp, Ann Arbor. *Mem:* AMA; Radiol Soc NAm; Am Radium Soc; Am Soc Therapeut Radiol. *Res:* Clinical radiation therapy. *Mailing Add:* 1805 Ivywood Dr Ann Arbor MI 48103

FAYTER, RICHARD GEORGE, JR, b Woodbury, NJ, Nov 26, 37; m 61; c 1. ORGANIC CHEMISTRY. *Educ:* Temple Univ, AB, 69; Brown Univ, PhD(org chem), 73. *Prof Exp:* Sr res chemist resins group, 73-74, group leader cent res, 74-79, mgr ctr res, 79-80, DIR CTR RES, EMERY INDUST, OHIO, 80- *Mem:* Am Chem Soc; Am Inst Chemists; Sigma Xi. *Res:* Mechanistic organic chemistry; bridged polycyclic compounds; molecular rearrangements and ionic additions; synthetic organic chemistry; organic ultrasonic chemistry; agriculture chemistry; pesticide chemistry; polymer chemistry. *Mailing Add:* Emery Industs Inc Cent Res Cincinnati OH 45232

FAZEKAS, ARPAD GYULA, b Szeged, Hungary, Aug 30, 36; Can citizen; m 66; c 1. EXPERIMENTAL SURGERY, BIOCHEMISTRY. *Educ:* Med Univ Szeged, MD, 60; Hungarian Acad Sci, CMedSci, 65. *Prof Exp:* Asst lectr biochem, Med Univ Szeged, 60-62, lectr, 62-63; lectr path, Royal Infirmary, Univ Glasgow, 64-65; lectr biochem, Med Univ Szeged, 65-68; ASST PROF MED, UNIV MONTREAL, 69-; asst prof, 74-80, ASSOC PROF EXP SURG, MCGILL UNIV, 80- *Concurrent Pos:* Res assoc med, Columbia Univ, NY, 71-74. *Mem:* Endocrine Soc; Can Soc Endocrinol & Metab; Brit Biochem Soc. *Res:* Biosynthesis, metabolism and mechanism of action of steroid hormones; biosynthesis of flavin coenzymes, riboflavin metabolism. *Mailing Add:* 5025 Sherbrooke W Montreal PQ H4A 1S9 Can

FAZIO, GIOVANNI GENE, b San Antonio, Tex, May 26, 33; wid; c 2. INFRARED ASTRONOMY, HIGH ENERGY ASTROPHYSICS. *Educ:* St Mary's Univ, BS & BA, 54; Mass Inst Technol, PhD(physics), 59. *Prof Exp:* Res assoc, Univ Rochester, 59, from instr to asst prof physics, 59-62; PHYSICIST, HARVARD SMITHSONIAN ASTROPHYS CTR, 62-; LECTR ASTRON, HARVARD UNIV, 62- *Concurrent Pos:* Mem, NASA Airborne Astron Mgt Opr Working Group, 76-; Int Astron Union rep to Comt Space Res Comn E-1, 80-; prin investr, Spacelab 2 infrared telescope exp & balloon-borne for infrared telescope exp. *Mem:* Am Astron Soc; Int Astron Union; fel Am Phys Soc; fel Royal Astron Soc; fel AAAS. *Res:* Infrared astronomy; gamma-ray astronomy. *Mailing Add:* Harvard Smithsonian Ctr Astrophys 60 Garden St Cambridge MA 02138

FAZIO, PAUL P(ALMERINO), b Italy, Apr 1, 39; Can citizen; m 66; c 3. SOLID MECHANICS. *Educ:* Univ Windsor, BASc, 63, MASc, 64, PhD(struct), 68. *Prof Exp:* Sessional instr, Univ Windsor, 64-67; from asst prof to assoc prof, 67-74, chmn dept civil eng, 73-77, PROF CIVIL ENG, CONCORDIA UNIV, 74-, DIR CTR FOR BLDG STUDIES, 77- *Concurrent Pos:* Jr struct engr, Can Bridge Co, 63; struct engr, Montreal Eng Co, 68; mem cent comt, Can Cong Appl Mech, 71-77, chmn papers comt, 71. *Honors & Awards:* Galbraith Prize, Eng Inst Can, 67. *Mem:* Am Soc Civil Engrs; Eng Inst Can; Am Concrete Inst; Am Soc Eng Educ; Int Asn Shell Struct. *Res:* Building engineering; building science; energy conservation; management; structures, especially structural analysis and design of folded plates, sandwich elements, panel connections and panelized building systems; development of wall panels; panel connections. *Mailing Add:* 118 Ashington Rd Pointe Claire PQ H9R 2Z2 Can

FAZIO, STEVE, b Phoenix, Ariz, Sept 2, 16; m 40; c 2. HORTICULTURE. *Educ:* Univ Ariz, BS, 40, MS, 51. *Prof Exp:* Head dept, 65-71, PROF HORT, UNIV ARIZ, 64- HORTICULTURIST & HORT SPECIALIST, AGR EXTEN SERV, 72- *Mem:* Am Soc Hort Sci; Int Plant Propagators Soc (vpres, 78-79, pres, 79). *Res:* Propagation of woody and herbaceous plants in arid desert regions. *Mailing Add:* Dept Plant Sci Univ Ariz Tucson AZ 85721

FEAD, JOHN WILLIAM NORMAN, b Wetaskiwin, Alta, Oct 23, 23; m 47; c 3. CIVIL ENGINEERING. *Educ:* Univ Alta, BS, 45, MS, 49; Northwestern Univ, PhD, 57. *Prof Exp:* Instr civil eng, Univ Alta, 46-48 & Univ Sask, 48-49; from instr to assoc prof, SDak State Col, 49-57; lectr, Northwestern Univ, 51-53; assoc civil eng & asst res engr, Inst Transp & Traffic Eng, Univ Calif, 54-55; assoc prof, 57-61, PROF CIVIL ENG, COLO STATE UNIV, 61-, HEAD DEPT, 63- *Concurrent Pos:* Mem city coun, Ft Collins, Colo, 71-75, mayor, 74-75. *Mem:* Am Soc Civil Engrs; Am Soc Eng Educ; Am Concrete Inst. *Res:* Structures and structural mechanics; soil mechanics and foundations. *Mailing Add:* Dept of Civil Eng Colo State Univ Ft Collins CO 80521

FEAGANS, WILLIAM MARION, b Fortescue, Mo, Feb 2, 27; m 50; c 3. ANATOMY. *Educ:* Univ Mo-Kansas City, DDS, 54; Med Col Va, PhD(anat), 60. *Prof Exp:* From instr to asst prof clin dent, Sch Dent, Univ Mo-Kansas City, 54-56; from instr to assoc prof anat, Med Col Va, 58-66, curric coordr med educ, 64-66; assoc prof anat, Schs Med & Dent Med, Tufts Univ, 66-70, from asst dean to assoc dean, Sch Dent Med, 66-70; PROF ANAT SCI, SCH MED & DEAN SCH DENT, STATE UNIV NY, BUFFALO, 70- *Concurrent Pos:* Consult, Surg Serv, US Naval Hosp, Va, 58-66, Dent Serv, 60-66. *Mem:* Histochem Soc; Am Asn Anat; NY Acad Sci. *Res:* Physiology of male reproduction; histochemistry and electron microscopy of oral tissues. *Mailing Add:* Sch of Dent State Univ of NY Buffalo NY 14214

FEAGIN, FRANK J, b Kaufman, Tex, Mar 14, 14; m 36; c 3. GEOPHYSICS. *Educ:* Agr & Mech Col Tex, BSEE, 34. *Prof Exp:* Asst elec eng, Agr & Mech Col Tex, 34-35; attached helper, Seismog Party, Humble Oil & Refining Co, 35-37, seismog operator, 37-41; asst prof elec eng, Agr & Mech Col Tex, 41-42; electronic develop work, War Contracts, Humble Oil & Refining Co, 42-46, res specialist, 46-54, sr res specialist, Geophys Res Sect, 54-57, asst chief geophysics res, 57-60, chief geophys res & eng sect, 60-64; mgr appl geophys div, Esso Prod Res Co, 64-66, sr res assoc, 66-73, sr res adv, 73-79; RETIRED. *Mem:* Soc Explor Geophys; Inst Elec & Electronics Engrs; Soc Info Display. *Res:* Geophysical instruments; geophysical displays; research management. *Mailing Add:* 7 Beavertail Houston TX 77086

FEAGIN, FREDERICK F, b Pike Co, Ala, Nov 22, 31; m; c 3. DENTISTRY. *Educ:* Auburn Univ, BS, 58; Univ Ala, Birmingham, DMD, 64, PhD(physiol, pharmacol), 69. *Prof Exp:* Res asst, 60-64, res assoc & instr, 65-69, asst prof clin dent, Sch Dent, 69-77, investr, Inst Dent Res, 69-77, asst prof physiol & biophys, Grad Fac, 69-77, PROF PHYSIOL & BIOPHYS, SCH MED & SCH DENT & ASSOC PROF DENT, UNIV ALA, BIRMINGHAM, 77- *Concurrent Pos:* Staff dentist & prin investr, Vet Admin Hosp, Birmingham, Ala, 68-69, clin investr, 69-72. *Mem:* Int Asn Dent Res. *Res:* Mechanisms of biological calcifications. *Mailing Add:* 2675 Southgate Dr Birmingham AL 35243

FEAGIN, ROY C(HESTER), b Andersonville, Ga, July 23, 14; m 38; c 2. CHEMICAL ENGINEERING. *Educ:* Ala Polytech Inst, BS, 36, MS, 37. *Prof Exp:* Res chemist, Gen Elec Co, NY, 37-39; res chemist, Austenal Microcast Div, Howmet Corp, 39-45, chief chemist, 45-56, mgr chem res, 56-67, assoc res dir, 67-68, mgr int opers, Superalloy Group, 68-73; consult, 73-75; tech dir, 75-77, vpres, 77-80, CONSULT, REMET CORP, 80- *Mem:* Am Chem Soc; Am Ceramic Soc; Int Asn Dent Res; Am Soc Testing & Mat; Am Inst Ceramic Engrs. *Res:* Development of compositions and applications of plastics, cements, refractories to dental and high temperature alloy casting field. *Mailing Add:* 1971 W McNab Rd Pompano Beach FL 33060

FEAGIN, TERRY, b Houston, Tex, Mar 27, 45; m 68; c 2. COMPUTER SCIENCE, AEROSPACE ENGINEERING. *Educ:* Rice Univ, BA, 67; Univ Tex, Austin, MA, 69, PhD(aeorspace eng), 72. *Prof Exp:* Nat Acad Sci-Nat Res Coun res assoc astrodynamics, 72-73; asst prof comput sci & aerospace eng, 73-78, assoc prof comput sci & aerospace eng & assoc dir res & devel, Comput Ctr, 78-79, HEAD COMPUT SCI DEPT, UNIV TENN, KNOXVILLE, 80- *Mem:* Am Inst Aeronaut & Astronaut; Asn Comput Mach; Am Astron Soc; Am Phys Soc. *Res:* Astrodynamics; optimal control theory; numerical analysis; small computer systems; parallel processing. *Mailing Add:* Comput Sci Dept Univ Tenn 8 Ayres Hall Knoxville TN 37996

FEAIRHELLER, STEPHEN HENRY, b Philadelphia, Pa, Nov 4, 33; m 59; c 3. NATURAL POLYMER CHEMISTRY. *Educ:* Pa State Univ, BS, 60; Mass Inst Technol, PhD(org chem), 64. *Prof Exp:* Res chemist, Eastern Utilization Res & Develop Div, USDA, 64-69; asst prof chem, Ogontz Campus, Pa State Univ, 69-70; res scientist, 70-73, res leader, 73-76, CTR CHIEF, EASTERN REGIONAL RES CTR, USDA, 76- *Honors & Awards:* Alsop Award, Am Leather Chemists Asn, 73. *Mem:* Am Chem Soc. *Res:* Chemical modification of proteins. *Mailing Add:* USDA Eastern Regional Res Ctr 600 E Mermaid Lane Philadelphia PA 19118

FEAIRHELLER, WILLIAM RUSSELL, JR, b Camden, NJ, Nov 25, 31; m 56; c 4. ENVIRONMENTAL CHEMISTRY. *Educ:* Rutgers Univ, BA, 54; Univ Md, MS, 58. *Prof Exp:* Anal chemist, Am Viscose Corp, 59-60; chemist, Avisun Corp, 60-63; sr res chemist, 63-68, res group leader, 68-74, sr res group leader, 74-77, RES SPECIALIST, MONSANTO RES CORP, 77- *Mem:* Air Pollution Control Asn. *Res:* Environmental monitoring and testing; air, stationary source and water emissions measurement; environmental source assessment; project and government contract management. *Mailing Add:* Monsanto Res Corp Sta B Box 8 Dayton OH 45407

FEAR, J(AMES) VAN DYCK, b Morgantown, WVa, Nov 7, 25; m 52; c 3. CHEMICAL ENGINEERING. *Educ:* Univ Louisville, BChE, 45, MChE, 47. *Prof Exp:* Res engr, Sun Co, 48-60, sect chief process develop, 60-66, mgr process develop, 66-71, mgr res & develop spec projs, 71-75, mgr raw mat storage & distrib, 75-77, vpres res & eng, Suntech, Inc, 75-77, vpres mkt, 77-80, vpres fuels, Sun Petrol Prod Co, 80-81, VPRES, FUELS DIV, SUN REFINING & MKT CO, SUN CO, 81- *Mem:* Am Inst Chem Engrs; Am Petrol Inst. *Res:* Development of petroleum processes, especially in lubricating and waxes; hydrogenation and reforming; recovery of tar from Athabasca tar sands. *Mailing Add:* Sun Refining & Mkt Co 18th & Market Sts Philadelphia PA 19103

FEARING, OLIN S, b Lawrence, Kans, Mar 30, 28; m 54; c 2. BOTANY. *Educ:* Univ Kans, AB, 50, MA, 51; Univ Tex, PhD, 59. *Prof Exp:* From asst prof to assoc prof, 59-75, PROF BIOL, TRINITY UNIV, TEX, 75- *Mem:* AAAS; Am Soc Plant Taxonomists; Bot Soc Am. *Res:* Cytotaxonomy of flowering plants; specifically the genus Cologania, Amphicarpaea and related genera; physiology and development of lichen symbionts. *Mailing Add:* Dept Biol Trinity Univ 715 Stadium Dr San Antonio TX 78284

FEARING, RALPH BURTON, b Oak Park, Ill, Aug 20, 18; m 46; c 2. ORGANIC CHEMISTRY, TEXTILE CHEMISTRY. *Educ:* Univ Chicago, BS, 40, MS, 43; Iowa State Col, PhD(org chem), 51. *Prof Exp:* Res assoc war gases, Univ Chicago, 43; res assoc anal chem, Los Alamos Sci Lab, 44-45; res assoc org synthesis, Monsanto Chem Co, 46-47; instr chem, Iowa State Col, 47-51; asst prof org chem, Utica Col, 51-56; res chemist, Victor Div, Eastern Res Labs, Stauffer Chem Co, Dobbs Ferry, 57-65, sr chemist, 65-82; RETIRED. *Res:* Organic synthesis; organic phosphorus chemistry; pesticide chemistry; textile finishing chemistry; synthesis of organophosphorus compounds and oligomers. *Mailing Add:* Eastern Res Ctr Stauffer Chem Co Dobbs Ferry NY 10522

FEARN, JAMES ERNEST, b Chattanooga, Tenn, Nov 21, 20; m 40; c 3. PHYSICAL ORGANIC CHEMISTRY, POLYMER CHEMISTRY. *Educ:* Howard Univ, BS, 49, MS, 50; Cath Univ Am, PhD(chem, physics), 54. *Prof Exp:* Org chemist, Nat Cancer Inst, 50-52; res chemist, Patuxent Res Refuge, US Dept Interior, 55-57; res chemist, Polymer Chem Sect, 57-73, RES CHEMIST, MAT & COMPOSITES SECT, NAT BUR STAND, 73- *Mem:* AAAS; Am Chem Soc; Royal Soc Chem; fel Am Inst Chemists. *Res:* Synthesis of fluorocarbons and high thermostable polymers; kinetic studies; mechanism studies, free radical polymerization; high pressure reactions; abrasion of rubber; microstructure studies of building materials; microscopy; porosimetry. *Mailing Add:* 4446 Alabama Ave SE Washington DC 20019

FEARN, RICHARD L(EE), b Mobile, Ala, Mar 24, 37; m 69; c 2. AERODYNAMICS. *Educ:* Auburn Univ, BS & MS, 60; Univ Fla, PhD(physics), 65. *Prof Exp:* Asst prof, 65-75, assoc prof, 75-80, PROF ENG SCI, UNIV FLA, 80- *Mem:* Am Inst Aeronaut & Astronaut. *Res:* Jet in a cross flow; lifting surface theory. *Mailing Add:* Dept of Eng Sci Univ of Fla Gainesville FL 32611

FEARNLEY, LAWRENCE, b Bradford, Eng, July 18, 32; m 56. TOPOLOGY. *Educ:* Univ London, BSc, 53; Univ Utah, PhD(math, topology), 59. *Prof Exp:* Asst math, Univ Utah, 54-57; from asst prof to assoc prof, 57-70, PROF MATH, BRIGHAM YOUNG UNIV, 70- *Mem:* Am Math Soc; Math Asn Am. *Res:* Topology of manifolds, limit spaces, continua. *Mailing Add:* Dept of Math Brigham Young Univ Provo UT 84602

FEARNSIDES, JOHN JOSEPH, b Philadelphia, Pa. AUTOMATIC CONTROL SYSTEMS, TRANSPORTATION ENGINEERING. *Educ:* Drexel Univ, BSEE, 62, MSEE, 64; Univ Md, PhD(elec eng), 71. *Prof Exp:* Instr elec eng, Drexel Univ, 62-64; instr, Univ Md, 64-68; mem tech staff controls, Bellcomm, Inc, 68-71; mem tech staff decision theory, Bell Tel Labs, 71-72; mgr advan res prog transp systs anal, US Dept Transp, 72-75, chief res & develop policy div, 74-75, exec asst to dep secy, 75-77, dep under secy & chief scientist, 77-79; dir Economies & Mgt Sci, Analytic Sci Corp, 80, DIR PLANNING & POLICY ANAL, MITRE CORP, 80- *Concurrent Pos:* Assoc ed Trans, Inst Elec & Electronics Engrs, 76 & 77; Nat Sci Found fel. *Mem:* Inst Elec & Electronics Engrs; Sigma Xi. *Res:* Control systems analysis, especially aerospace; investment decision analysis under uncertainty; application of research and development to transportation problems. *Mailing Add:* MITRE Corp 1820 Dolley Madison Blvd McLean VA 22102

FEARON, FREDERICK WILLIAM GORDON, b London, Eng, June 4, 38; m 63; c 2. CHEMISTRY, MATERIALS SCIENCE. *Educ:* Univ Leeds, BSc, 61; Univ Wales, PhD(chem), 65. *Prof Exp:* Chemist res, Laporte Chem, Luton, Eng, 61-63; demonstr chem, Univ Col Wales, 63-65; res assoc, Iowa State Univ, 65-67; chem polymer res, Dow Corning Corp, 68-70, from group leader to sr group leader fluids, 70-74, res & develop mgr new ventures, 74-78; dir res, Cent Chem Div, BEE Chem 78-80; TECHNOL MGR NEW VENTURES, DOW CORNING CORP, 80- *Mem:* Am Chem Soc; Royal Soc Chem; Soc Plastic Engrs; Am Ceramic Soc. *Res:* Structure property relationships in organosilicone polymers; ceramics. *Mailing Add:* Dow Corning Corp Midland MI 48640

FEARS, FULTON KELLER, b Caney, Okla, Aug 1, 20. CIVIL ENGINEERING. *Educ:* Univ Okla, BS, 43; Purdue Univ, MS, 50, PhD(civil eng), 57. *Prof Exp:* Asst prof, 46-57, ASSOC PROF CIVIL ENG, UNIV OKLA, 57- *Res:* Structural analysis; effect of air entrainment on durability of concrete. *Mailing Add:* Dept of Civil Eng Col of Eng Univ of Okla Norman OK 73019

FEASLEY, CHARLES FREDERICK, b Lexington, Ill, Jan 21, 15; m 40; c 4. ENVIRONMENTAL HEALTH. *Educ:* Hanover Col, AB, 37; Purdue Univ, MS, 40, PhD(org chem), 42. *Prof Exp:* Asst chem, Purdue Univ, 37-41; res chemist, Res Dept, Mobil Oil Corp, 41-44, sr chemist, 45-57, supv technologist, 57-62, asst to mgr toxicol & pollution, 63-68, toxicol adv, Res Dept, 68-70, toxicol adv, Med Dept, 70-76, sr toxicologist, Med Dept, 76-78, sr toxicologist, Environ Affairs & Toxicol, 76-80; RETIRED. *Mem:* AAAS; Am Indust Hyg Asn; Soc Toxicol; Am Chem Soc; Am Soc Testing & Mat. *Res:* Antiseptics; utilization of nitroalkanes; chemicals from petroleum; synthetic fuels from natural gas and coal; condensation of aryl diazonium salts and hydroxides with secondary nitroalkanes; development of laboratory tests for petroleum products; air and water pollution; toxicology and labeling of chemicals and petroleum products. *Mailing Add:* 37 N Columbia St Woodbury NJ 08096

FEASTER, CARL VANCE, b Monon, Ind, Aug 11, 21; m 78; c 3. PLANT BREEDING. *Educ:* Purdue Univ, BS, 44; Univ Mo, MA, 47, PhD(field crops), 50. *Prof Exp:* Agronomist, Soybean Res, Bur Plant Indust, Soils & Agr Eng, 44-50, Field Crops Res Br, 50-56, AGRONOMIST, COTTON BREEDING, SCI & EDUC ADMIN-AGR RES, USDA, 56-; PROF, ARIZ STATE UNIV, 73- *Mem:* Sigma Xi. *Res:* Genetics; fiber plants. *Mailing Add:* 9715 E Michigan Ave Sun Lake AZ 85224

FEASTER, GENE R(ICHARD), b Winfield, Kans, Sept 19, 18; m 51. MEDICAL PHYSICS, RADIATION THERAPY. *Educ:* Univ Kans, BS, 40, PhD(physics), 53. *Prof Exp:* Physicist thermionic tubes, RCA Corp, NJ, 42-47; instr physics, Univ Kans, 47-52; adv engr thermionic tubes, Westinghouse Elec Corp, 53-66; adv engr image intensifier & thermionic tubes, 66-67; eng assoc, Corning Glass Works, 67-70; res assoc, Med Ctr, Univ Va, 76-77; ASST PROF, MED CTR, UNIV KANS, 77- *Mem:* Am Asn Physicists Med. *Res:* Thermionic emission; photon beam compensators in radiation therapy; hematoporphyrin and photoradiation therapy. *Mailing Add:* Dept of Radiation Therapy Med Ctr Univ of Kans Kansas City KS 66103

FEASTER, JOHN PIPKIN, b St Petersburg, Fla, Oct 1, 20; m 44; c 3. BIOLOGICAL CHEMISTRY. *Educ:* Col of William & Mary, BA, 43; Emory Univ, MS, 48; Univ NC, PhD(biochem), 51. *Prof Exp:* Assoc biochemist, Agr Exp Sta, 51-68, biochemist & prof, 68-82, EMER PROF, INST FOOD & AGR SCI, UNIV FLA, 82- *Mem:* Am Chem Soc; Am Soc Animal Sci; Am Inst Nutrit. *Res:* Mineral nutrition; placental transfer; lipid metabolism; pesticide toxicity. *Mailing Add:* 3021 S W 70th Lane Gainesville FL 32601

FEATHER, A(LAN) L(EE), b Mich, Aug 31, 23; m 50; c 2. FOOD TECHNOLOGY. *Educ:* Mich State Col, BS, 47, MS, 48. *Prof Exp:* Asst horticult, Mich State Col, 47-48; canning technologist, 48-49, customer res rep, 49-52, dist chief customer res, 52-67, prod coordr beer prod, 67-70, mgr customer packaging opers, Pac Metal Div, 70-74, customer tech serv consult, Food Div, 74-77, MGR FIELD SERV, PAC DIV, CONTINENTAL CAN CO, USA, 77- *Mem:* Inst Food Technol; Master Brewers Asn Am; Am Soc Brewing Chem; Soc Soft Drink Technol. *Res:* Packaging operations engineering; metal containers; new container development; canning methods and equipment; food spoilage and claims investigation. *Mailing Add:* Western Div 357 E Taylor St PO Box 1210 San Jose CA 95108

FEATHER, DAVID HOOVER, b Orange, NJ, Apr 27, 43. MATERIALS SCIENCE. *Educ:* Alfred Univ, BS, 68; Univ Calif, Berkeley, MS, 69, PhD(mat sci), 72. *Prof Exp:* Scientist phys chem, Aluminum Co Am; SCIENTIST HIGH TEMP CHEM, JOSEPH C WILSON CTR TECHNOL, XEROX CORP, 75- *Res:* Heterogeneous kinetics and high temperature chemistry; free surface and equilibrium vaporization processes. *Mailing Add:* 31 C Brook Hill Lane Rochester NY 14625

FEATHER, MILTON S, b Massillon, Ohio, Mar 14, 36; m 57; c 1. BIOCHEMISTRY. *Educ:* Heidelberg Col, BS, 58; Purdue Univ, MS, 61, PhD(biochem), 63. *Prof Exp:* Chemist, US Forest Serv, 63-67; from asst prof to assoc prof agr chem, 67-73, PROF BIOCHEM, UNIV MO-COLUMBIA, 73- *Concurrent Pos:* USDA trainee, Swedish Forest Prod Res Lab, Stockholm, 64-65. *Mem:* Am Chem Soc. *Res:* Chemistry of nonenzymatic browning and dehydration reactions; structural studies on polysaccharides. *Mailing Add:* Dept of Biochem Univ of Mo Columbia MO 65201

FEATHERS, WILLIAM D, b Pittsburgh, Pa, Sept 14, 27; m 50; c 6. CHEMICAL ENGINEERING. *Educ:* Univ Pittsburgh, BS, 50. *Prof Exp:* Technician, Color Unlimited, Pa, 47-50; engr, Mellon Inst, 50; from engr to sr res engr, Photo Prod Dept, Parlin, NJ, 51-69, Wilmington, 69-73 & Towanda, Pa, 73-74, RES ASSOC, E I DU PONT DE NEMOURS & CO, INC, TOWANDA, PA, 74- *Res:* Coating application methods and equipment development for photographic products. *Mailing Add:* RD 1 Box 76A Towanda PA 18848

FEATHERSTON, FRANK HUNTER, b Washington, DC, Mar 9, 29; m 51; c 2. PHYSICS. *Educ:* US Naval Acad, BS, 50; US Naval Postgrad Sch, MS, 57, PhD(physics), 63, JD, 82. *Prof Exp:* US Navy, 50-, asst nuclear physics, Radiation Lab, Univ Calif, Berkeley, 56-57, mem opers res staff, Off Comdr, Aircraft Early Warning Barrier, Pac, 57-58, SNAP reactor proj officer, Div Reactor Develop, US AEC, 58-60, res officer astronaut, US Naval Missile Ctr, Calif, 63-65, Phoenix Proj Mgr, Hq, Naval Mat Command, DC, 66-68, dep for avionics & armament, F-14/Phoenix Proj, Naval Air Systs Command, 68-70, commanding officer, Naval Training Device Ctr, 70-72, chief, Naval Training Support, Off Naval Res, 72-73, dep & asst chief, 74-75; CONSULT, VEDA, INC, 75- *Mem:* Am Phys Soc; Inst Elec & Electronics Engrs. *Res:* K-meson research in nuclear emulsions; low temperature elastic constants of body-centered cubic transition metals; law and practice of military major system acquisitions. *Mailing Add:* 15 Deer Path Charlottesville VA 22901

FEATHERSTON, WILLIAM ROY, poultry nutrition, metabolism, deceased

FEATHERSTONE, JOHN DOUGLAS BERNARD, b Stratford, New Zealand, Apr 26, 44; m 67; c 2. CHEMISTRY DENTAL CARIES. *Educ:* Victoria Univ Wellington, NZ, BSc, 65, PhD(chem), 77; Univ Manchester, Eng, MSc, 75. *Prof Exp:* Qual control chemist, Unileves Ltd, NZ, 64-66; tech mgr, Chem Indust Ltd, NZ, 66-72; prod mgr, Quinodesm Pharmaceut, Eng, 72-74; lectr pharmaceut, Cent Inst Technol, NZ, 77-79; Med Res Coun sr fel, Med Res Coun Dent Res Univ, NZ, 79-80; SR RES ASSOC DENT CHEM, EASTMAN DENT CTR, 80- *Concurrent Pos:* Res fel, Sandoz Pharmaceut Sch, Univ Manchester, 74-75; Med Res Coun Training fel & lectr chem, Victoria Univ Wellington, 75-77; Colgate travel award, Int Asn Dent Res, New Zealand & Colgate res award, Australia Div, 76; dir res proj, Med Res Coun, New Zealand, 77-80, sr fel, 79-80; mem, Flouridation Adv Comt, New Zealand Govt, 79-, Expert Groups Flouridated Dentifres, WHO, 81-; co-prin investr, NIH & Nat Inst Dent Res Grant, 80-; asst prof, Dept Dent Res, Univ Rochester, 80- *Mem:* Fel NZ Inst Chem; Int Asn Dent Res; Europ Orgn Caries Res; Australia & NZ Asn Advan Sci. *Res:* Chemistry of dental decay; structure and acid reactivity of carbonated apatites; diffusion processes in dental enamel; remineralization of dental enamel; trace elements in dental enamel. *Mailing Add:* Eastman Dent Ctr 625 Elmwood Ave Rochester NY 14620

FEAY, DARRELL CHARLES, b Larchwood, Iowa, Mar 13, 27; m 52. POLYMER CHEMISTRY. *Educ:* Univ Iowa, BS, 50; Univ Calif, PhD(chem), 54. *Prof Exp:* Asst chem, Univ Calif, 50-51, chemist, radiation lab, 51-54; res chemist, 54-65, proj leader, 64-70, res specialist, Dow Chem Co, 70-79, RES LEADER, DOW CHEM USA, 79- *Mem:* Soc Plastic Engrs; Am Chem Soc. *Res:* Application and development of polymerization catalysts; stereoselective catalysts; inorganic and polymer solvent extraction; plastics extrusion and molding; spectroscopy; analytical chemistry; water purification. *Mailing Add:* Dow Chem USA 2800 Mitchell Dr Walnut Creek CA 94598

FEAZEL, CHARLES ELMO, JR, b Crockett, Tex, Aug 10, 21; m 42; c 2. ORGANIC CHEMISTRY. *Educ:* Harvard Univ, AB, 41; Univ Md, MS, 50, PhD(chem), 53. *Prof Exp:* Chemist, B F Goodrich Co, 41-46; chemist, Appl Physics Lab, Johns Hopkins Univ, 46-53; res chemist & dir phys sci res, Southern Res Inst, 53-78; CONSULT, 78- *Concurrent Pos:* Prof, Birmingham-Southern Col, 54-55 & 59-60. *Res:* Organic synthesis; cellulose; plastics; polymer synthesis; technical editing and writing. *Mailing Add:* 3753 Forest Run Rd Birmingham AL 35223

FEAZEL, THOMAS A(NDERSON), chemical engineering, see previous edition

FECHHEIMER, NATHAN S, b Cincinnati, Ohio, May 24, 25; m 46; c 2. ANIMAL GENETICS. *Educ:* Ohio State Univ, BS, 49, MSc, 50, PhD(dairy sci), 57. *Prof Exp:* From asst to assoc prof, 50-65, dir animal reprod teaching & res ctr, 74, PROF DAIRY SCI, OHIO STATE UNIV, 65- *Concurrent Pos:* NATO fel, Univ Edinburgh, 59-60; sr res fels genetics, 70-71 & 77-78; mem animal health comt, Nat Res Coun, 68-72. *Mem:* Fel AAAS; Genetics Soc Am; Am Soc Animal Sci; Soc Study Reproduction; Am Dairy Sci Asn. *Res:* Mammalian and avian genetics and cytogenetics; genetic influence on reproductive performance. *Mailing Add:* Dept Dairy Sci Ohio State Univ 2027 Coffey Rd Columbus OH 43210

FECHNER, GILBERT HENRY, b Northbrook, Ill, Dec 20, 22; m 48; c 3. FOREST GENETICS. *Educ:* Colo State Univ, BS, 47, MS, 55; Univ Minn, PhD(forestry), 64. *Prof Exp:* Wood technologist, Hallack & Howard Lumber Co, 47-49; staff forester, Tenn Valley Authority, 49-53; from instr to assoc prof forest mgt, 54-67, PROF FOREST GENETICS, COLO STATE UNIV, 67- *Honors & Awards:* Charles A Lory Award Outstanding Teaching, 69. *Mem:* Soc Am Foresters; Bot Soc Am. *Res:* Ecotypic variation of coniferous and broadleaved species. *Mailing Add:* Dept Forest & Wood Sci Colo State Univ Ft Collins CO 80521

FECHTER, LAURENCE DAVID, b New York NY. NEUROSCIENCE, NEUROTOXICOLOGY. *Educ:* Clark Univ, BA, 67; Kent State Univ, MA, 69; Univ Rochester, PhD(biopsychol), 73. *Prof Exp:* Instr social sci, Mohawk Valley Community Col, 68-69; asst prof, Genesee Community Col, 69-72; fel pharmacol, Biomed Ctr, Uppsala Univ, 73-74; fel physiol, 74-76, res assoc toxicol, 76-77, ASST PROF NEUROTOXICOL, JOHNS HOPKINS UNIV, 77- *Mem:* Soc Neurosci; Soc Toxicol; Behav Teratology Soc; Int Soc Develop Neurosci; Eastern Psychol Asn. *Res:* Susceptibility of the developing central nervous sytem to toxic agents; prediction of pattern of effects and determination of mechanisms of action using behavioral, biochemical and pharmacological methods. *Mailing Add:* 615 N Wolfe St Sch Hyg Johns Hopkins Univ Baltimore MD 21205

FECHTER, ROBERT BERNARD, b Cleveland, Ohio, Oct 8, 40; m 79. POLYMER SYNTHESIS AND CHARACTERIZATION. *Educ:* Western Reserve Univ, BA, 62; Ohio State Univ, PhD(org chem), 66. *Prof Exp:* Res assoc nitrogen fixation, Stanford Univ, 66-69; sr scientist org & polymer chem, Owens-Ill Inc, 69-80; SR CHEMIST POLYMER CHEM, ASHLAND CHEM CO, 80- *Concurrent Pos:* Instr, Univ Toledo, 75-79. *Mem:* Am Chem Soc; AAAS; Sigma Xi. *Res:* Synthesis of polymeric, organic, and organotransition metal compounds; characterization, evaluation, and processing of both thermoplastic and thermoset polymers of potential commercial interest. *Mailing Add:* Ashland Chem Co PO Box 2219 Columbus OH 43216

FEDAK, GEORGE, b Hudson Bay, Sask, Dec 28, 40; m 69; c 2. CYTOGENETICS. *Educ:* Univ Saskatchewan, BSA, 63, MSc, 65; Univ Man, PhD(cytogenetics), 69. *Prof Exp:* Fel cytogenetics, 69-70; res scientist, 70-79, SECT HEAD CYTOGENETICS, OTTAWA RES BR AGR CAN, 79- *Mem:* Genetics Soc Can. *Res:* Conducting cytogenetic research on intergeneric hybrids in cereal crop species. *Mailing Add:* Cytogenetics Sect Ottawa Res Sta Agr Can Ottawa ON K1A 0C6 Can

FEDDE, MARION ROGER, b Ionia, Kans, Oct 1, 35; m 56; c 3. PULMONARY PHYSIOLOGY. *Educ:* Kans State Univ, BS, 57; Univ Minn, MS, 59, PhD(avian physiol), 63. *Prof Exp:* Asst prof vet anat, Univ Minn, 63-64; from asst prof to assoc prof, 64-73, PROF PHYSIOL, KANS STATE UNIV, 73- *Honors & Awards:* Res Award, Poultry Sci Asn, 64; Fac Res Award, Col Vet Med, Kans State Univ, 70; US Sr Scientist Award, Alexander von Humboldt Found, 73. *Mem:* AAAS; Poultry Sci Asn; World Poultry Sci Asn; Am Physiol Soc; Am Soc Vet Physiol & Pharmacol. *Res:* Avian physiology, respiration; neurophysiology; myophysiology. *Mailing Add:* Dept of Anat & Physiol Kans State Univ Manhattan KS 66506

FEDDE, VICKI HYMEL, b Pascagoula, Miss, Nov 12, 45; m 70; c 1. ENTOMOLOGY, ECOLOGY. *Educ:* Univ Montevallo, BS, 67; NC State Univ, MS, 70. *Prof Exp:* Res biologist entom, US Forest Serv, Res Triangle Park, NC, 68-70; res entomologist, 70-76, ASSOC RES ENTOMOLOGIST, US FOREST SERV, ATHENS, GA, 76- *Mem:* Entom Soc Am. *Res:* Biological control of destructive forest insects including hardwood defoliators, pine sawflies and seed orchard pests. *Mailing Add:* Forestry Sci Lab Carlton St Athens GA 30602

FEDDER, STEVEN LEE, b Denver, Colo, July 28, 50. GEOCHEMISTRY, ANALYTICAL CHEMISTRY. *Educ:* Colo Col, BA, 72; Ariz State Univ, PhD(chem), 78. *Prof Exp:* Teaching & res assoc chem, Ariz State Univ, 72-78, vis asst prof, 78-82. *Mem:* Am Chem Soc; Soc Appl Spectros; Sigma Xi. *Res:* Trace metal behavior in natural waters with special interest in adsorption processes; trace metal detection by flameless atomic absorption. *Mailing Add:* 813 W Rice Dr Tempe AZ 85283

FEDDERN, HENRY A, b Poughkeepsie, NY, May 22, 38; m 68. ICHTHYOLOGY. *Educ:* Univ Miami, BS, 60, MS, 63, PhD(ichthyol), 68. *Prof Exp:* Asst, Inst Marine Sci, Univ Miami, 66-68; aquatic biologist, Precision Valve Corp, 68-69; dir marine lab, 69-73; aquaculturist, Neptunian

Maricult, 73; COLLECTOR-AQUACULTURIST, 73- *Mem:* Am Soc Ichthyologists & Herpetologists; Am Littoral Soc. *Res:* Tolerances of marine inshore fishes to insecticides; factors influencing the survival and breeding of marine coral fishes and the mass-culture of the same. *Mailing Add:* 156 Dove Ave Tavernier FL 33070

FEDDERS, PETER ALAN, b Minneapolis, Minn, Feb 8, 39; m 63; c 2. PHYSICS. *Educ:* Yale Univ, BS, 61; Harvard Univ, MA, 62, PhD(physics), 65. *Prof Exp:* Res assoc physics, Princeton Univ, 65-66; instr, 66-68; from asst prof to assoc prof, 68-74, PROF PHYSICS, WASHINGTON UNIV, 74- *Mem:* Am Phys Soc. *Res:* Solid state physics. *Mailing Add:* Dept of Physics Washington Univ St Louis MO 63130

FEDER, BERNARD HERBERT, b New York, NY, Feb 11, 13; m 41; c 2. RADIOTHERAPY, RADIOLOGY. *Educ:* Univ Southern Calif, BA, 36, MD, 40; Am Bd Radiol, dipl, 49. *Prof Exp:* Intern & resident, Los Angeles County Hosp, Calif, 39-41, resident, 46-49; head roentgenologist, Los Angeles County Harbor Gen Hosp, Torrance, 49-52; chief radiother sect, Vet Admin Hosp, Long Beach, 52-58, chief radiol sect, 58-68, chief radiother sect, 68-70; assoc radiotherapist, Los Angeles County-Univ Southern Calif Med Ctr, 70-80, prof, 70-80, EMER PROF RADIOL, SCH MED, UNIV SOUTHERN CALIF, 80- *Concurrent Pos:* Assoc investr, NIH grant, 60-66; prin investr, Am Cancer Soc grant, 63-69; Defense Atomic Support Agency grant, 67-70; Nat Cancer Inst grant, 73-76; from clin instr to clin prof radiol, Sch Med, Univ Calif, Los Angeles, 50-70; mem attend staff, Los Angeles County Harbor Gen Hosp, Torrance, 52- *Mem:* Fel Am Col Radiol; AMA; Am Radium Soc; Am Soc Therapeut Radiol; Health Physics Soc. *Res:* Radiation therapy; evaluation of preoperative irradiation utilizing a solid tumor model; detection of minute doses of ionizing irradiation by mammals; autologous marrow storage and reinfusion in management of human cancer; immunologic response in cancer irradiation; optimization of endoradiotherapy. *Mailing Add:* Radiation Ther Sect Univ Southern Calif Med Ctr Los Angeles CA 90033

FEDER, DONALD PERRY, b Rochester, NY, Feb 2, 18; m 48; c 3. OPTICS. *Educ:* Univ Rochester, AB, 40. *Prof Exp:* Physicist, Geomet Optics, Univ Rochester, 41-45; supt optical design, Argus, Inc, 44-49; physicist in chg optical design, Nat Bur Standards, 49-56; OPTICAL DESIGNER, EASTMAN KODAK CO, 57- *Res:* Application of computing machinery to optical design; numerical analysis and programming digital computers. *Mailing Add:* 800 Thayer Rd Fairport NY 14450

FEDER, HARVEY HERMAN, b New York, NY, Mar 28, 40; m 61; c 3. ANATOMY, REPRODUCTIVE PHYSIOLOGY. *Educ:* City Col New York, BS, 61; Univ Ore, PhD(anat), 66. *Prof Exp:* Asst scientist, Ore Regional Primate Res Ctr, 63-70; assoc prof psychol, 70-74, PROF PSYCHOL, INST ANIMAL BEHAV, RUTGERS UNIV, 74- *Concurrent Pos:* USPHS res fel, 65-67, at Oxford Univ, 66-67; NIH res grant, 69-72; NIMH career develop award, 70- *Mem:* Endocrine Soc; Int Soc Psychoneuroendocrinol; AAAS; Brit Soc Endocrinol. *Res:* Role of gonadal steroids in differentiation of sexual behavior of females; estimations of circulation gonadal steroids. *Mailing Add:* Inst Animal Behav Rutgers Univ 101 Warren St Newark NJ 07102

FEDER, HOWARD MITCHELL, b New York, NY, June 8, 22; m 50; c 4. MARINE BIOLOGY. *Educ:* Univ Calif, Los Angeles, AB, 48, MA, 51; Stanford Univ, PhD(marine biol), 57. *Prof Exp:* Asst gen zool, Univ Calif, Los Angeles, 48, asst protozool & human anat, 50-51; asst marine biol, Kerckhoff Marine Lab, Calif Inst Technol, 49; asst, Arctic Res Lab, Point Barrow, Alaska, 49-50; oceanographic technician, Hopkins Marine Sta, Stanford Univ, 51-52, asst marine invert zool, 52 & 54; instr biol, Hartnell Col, 55-65, prof, 65-70; assoc prof zool & marine sci, 70-76, PROF ZOOL & MARINE SCI, UNIV ALASKA, FAIRBANKS, 76- *Concurrent Pos:* Am Acad Arts & Sci res grants, 60-64; NSF res grants, 62-67 & 79-81; Sea Grant res grant, 70-81. *Mem:* Marine Biol Asn UK; Sigma Xi; Nat Shellfisheries Asn. *Res:* Benthic biology of the Gulf of Alaska, the Bering Sea and the Beaufort Sea; marine ecology; intertidal biology; sea star biology; fisheries biology clams; feeding biology of shrimps, crabs, demersal fishes. *Mailing Add:* Inst Marine Sci Univ of Alaska Fairbanks AK 99701

FEDER, JOSEPH, b St Louis, Mo, Feb 20, 32; m 53; c 4. BIOCHEMISTRY. *Educ:* Roosevelt Univ, BS, 53; Ill Inst Technol, MS, 61, PhD(biochem), 64. *Prof Exp:* asst prof, 66-70, assoc prof, 70-75, PROF, UNIV MO-ST LOUIS, 75-; SR SCI FEL, MONSANTO CO, 77- *Concurrent Pos:* Res biochemist, Monsanto Co, 65-70, res group leader, 70-73, sci fel, 73-77. *Mem:* Am Soc Biol Chemists; AAAS; Am Chem Soc; Sigma Xi. *Res:* Mechanism of action of enzymes; kinetics of enzyme catalyzed reactions, primarily proteolytic enzymes; cell culture; growth regulators; tumor factors, angiogenesis. *Mailing Add:* New Enterprise Div Monsanto Co St Louis MO 63166

FEDER, RALPH, b Philadelphia, Pa, Jan 12, 22; m 50; c 3. SOLID STATE PHYSICS. *Educ:* Ind Univ, BA, 50; Univ Pa, MS, 55. *Prof Exp:* Physicist, Pitman-Dunn Lab, Frankford Arsenal, Philadelphia, 49-61; PHYSICIST, THOMAS J WATSON RES CTR, IBM CORP, 61- *Mem:* NY Acad Sci; Am Phys Soc; Am Vacuum Soc; Sigma Xi. *Res:* X-ray microscopy and x-ray lithography. *Mailing Add:* Thomas J Watson Res Ctr IBM Res Ctr Yorktown Heights NY 10598

FEDER, RAYMOND L, b New York, NY, Apr 1, 20; m 43; c 2. CHEMICAL ENGINEERING. *Educ:* Polytech Inst Brooklyn, BChE, 43, MChE, 47, DChE, 49. *Prof Exp:* Sr engr penicillin develop, Schenley Lab, 43-46; plant engr indust enzymes, Takamine Lab, 48-51; supvr process develop, Plastics Div, Allied Chem Corp, 51-62; mgr develop lab, 62-63 & nylon res & develop, 63-65, mgr polyolefins res & develop, 65-67, tech mgr, Frankford Plant, 67-72, plant mgr, 72-76, tech dir, 77-79. *Concurrent Pos:* Instr, Eve Div, Drexel Inst Technol, 52-58, adj prof, 58-62. *Mem:* Am Chem Soc; Am Inst Chem Engrs. *Res:* Process development of organic chemicals; polyolefins and nylons; economic evaluation and process design; process improvement; quality control; process engineering for phenol from cumene, phthalic anhydride from naphthalene; natural tar acids from carbolic oil; environmental science relative to inorganic and organic chemicals. *Mailing Add:* Allied Chem Corp PO Box 3000R Morristown NJ 07960

FEDER, WILLIAM ADOLPH, b New York, NY, Oct 15, 20; m 45; c 3. POLLUTION BIOLOGY. *Educ:* Johns Hopkins Univ, AB, 41; Univ Calif, PhD(plant path), 50. *Prof Exp:* Asst bot & plant physiol, Univ Calif, 48-49; storage dis pathologist, Indust Res Adv Coun, Exp Sta, Univ Hawaii, 50-51; from asst prof to assoc prof plant path, NY State Col Agr, Cornell Univ, 51-54; plant pathologist, Crops Res Div, Agr Res Serv, USDA, 54-66; PROF PLANT PATH & LEADER AIR POLLUTION RES PROJS, UNIV MASS, AMHERST, 66- *Concurrent Pos:* NSF sr fel, Eng, 58-59; Fulbright res scholar, Israel, 64- *Mem:* AAAS; Am Phytopath Soc; Bot Soc Am; Air Pollution Control Asn. *Res:* Environmental impact of saline aerosols from cooling towers; biological control of plant diseases; effects of air pollution on plant growth. *Mailing Add:* Suburban Exp Sta Univ of Mass 240 Beaver St Waltham MA 02154

FEDERBUSH, PAUL GERARD, b Newark, NJ, Mar 23, 34; m 56; c 1. THEORETICAL PHYSICS. *Educ:* Mass Inst Technol, BS, 55; Princeton Univ, PhD(physics), 58. *Prof Exp:* From instr to asst prof physics, Mass Inst Technol, 58-65; lectr, 65-67, assoc prof, 67-71, PROF MATH, UNIV MICH, ANN ARBOR, 71- *Mem:* Am Phys Soc. *Res:* Axiomatic field theory. *Mailing Add:* Dept of Math Univ of Mich Ann Arbor MI 48109

FEDERER, C ANTHONY, b New York, NY, Jan 19, 39; m 60; c 2. FOREST SOILS, FOREST METEOROLOGY. *Educ:* Univ Mass, BS, 59; Univ Wis, MS, 62, PhD(soils), 64. *Prof Exp:* Assoc meteorologist, 64-70, prin meteorologist, 70-80, PRIN SOIL SCIENTIST, NORTHEASTERN FOREST EXP STA, US FOREST SERV, 80- *Concurrent Pos:* Adj assoc prof, Univ NH, 70- *Mem:* Am Meteorol Soc; Am Geophys Union; Am Soc Agron; Soil Sci Soc Am; Ecol Soc Am. *Res:* Evapotranspiration from forests; nutrient cycling in forests; stomatal behavior; water relations of trees; nitrogen in forest soils. *Mailing Add:* Northeastern Forest Exp Sta PO Box 640 Durham NH 03824

FEDERER, HERBERT, b Vienna, Austria, July 23, 20; nat US; m 49; c 3. MATHEMATICAL ANALYSIS. *Educ:* Univ Calif, AB, 42, PhD(math), 44. *Prof Exp:* From instr to prof, 45-66, FLORENCE PIRCE GRANT UNIV PROF MATH, BROWN UNIV, 66- *Concurrent Pos:* Sloan res fel, 57-60; NSF fel, 64-65; mem, Nat Res Coun, 66-69; Guggenheim fel, 75-76. *Mem:* Nat Acad Sci; Am Math Soc (assoc secy, 67-68); Am Acad Arts & Sci. *Res:* Geometric measure theory. *Mailing Add:* Dept of Math Brown Univ Providence RI 02912

FEDERER, WALTER THEODORE, b Cheyenne, Wyo, Aug 23, 15; c 1. BIOSTATISTICS. *Educ:* Colo State Col, BS, 39; Kans State Col, MS, 41; Iowa State Univ, PhD(math statist), 48. *Prof Exp:* Asst corn invests, USDA & Kans State Col, 39-41, Bur Agr Econ & Iowa State Col, 41-42, assoc geneticist, Special Guayule Res Proj, Bur Plant Indust, USDA, 42-44, assoc agr statistician, Bur Agr Econ & Iowa State Col, 44-48; prof biostatist & in charge biometric unit, 48-77, LIBERTY HYDE BAILEY PROF BIOSTATIST, CORNELL UNIV, 77-, PROF BIOSTATIST & IN CHARGE BIOMETRIC UNIT, 81- *Concurrent Pos:* Mem consult panel, 53-61; head dept exp statist, Hawaiian Sugar Planters' Asn & consult, Pineapple Res Inst, 54-55; reviewer, Math Rev & Math Tables & Other Aids Comput, 57-58; prof, Univ & US Army Math Res Ctr, Univ Wis, 62-63 & 69-70; chmn & exec secy, Comt Pres of Statist Socs, 64-71; bk rev ed, Biomet, 64-72; assoc ed, Biomet, 72-76; assoc ed, J Statist Planning & Inference, 77- & Int J Math & Statist, 79- *Mem:* Fel AAAS; Int Statist Inst; fel Am Statist Asn; fel Inst Math Statist; fel Royal Statist Soc. *Res:* Statistical design, statistical education and statistical analyses. *Mailing Add:* Biomet Unit 337 Warren Hall Cornell Univ Ithaca NY 14853

FEDERICI, BRIAN ANTHONY, b Paterson, NJ, May 28, 43. INVERTEBRATE PATHOLOGY, VIROLOGY. *Educ:* Rutgers Univ, New Brunswick, BS, 66; Univ Fla, MS, 67, PhD(med entom), 70. *Prof Exp:* NIH fel, Boyce Thompson Inst, Yonkers, NY, 72-74; asst prof, 74-80, ASSOC PROF ENTOM, UNIV CALIF, RIVERSIDE, 80- *Mem:* Entom Soc Am; Soc Invert Path; AAAS. *Res:* Pathogens and pathology of invertebrates, particularly aquatic invertebrates; diseases of medically important human and animal disease vectors, especially mosquitoes. *Mailing Add:* Div Biol Control Univ Calif 990 Univ Ave Riverside CA 92521

FEDERICO, OLGA MARIA, b New York, NY, Dec 12, 23. ANIMAL PHYSIOLOGY. *Educ:* Hunter Col, BA, 46; Long Island Univ, MS, 60; NY Univ, PhD(biol), 68. *Prof Exp:* Res asst rheumatologic dis, Hosp Spec Surg, 50-60; instr biol, Long Island Univ, 60-65; USPHS trainee hemat, NY Univ, 65-68; instr biol, Hunter Col, 66-67; instr biol, Queens Col, NY, 67-68; asst prof, 68-72, ASSOC PROF BIOL SCI & GEOL, QUEENSBOROUGH COMMUNITY COL, 72- *Res:* Hematology; medical laboratory science; plant ecology; environmental science. *Mailing Add:* Queensborough Community Col City Univ NY Bayside Queens NY 11364

FEDERIGHI, ENRICO THOMAS, b Norfolk, Va, Nov 1, 27; m 65; c 1. ALGEBRA. *Educ:* Antioch Col, AB, 50; Johns Hopkins Univ, MA, 54; Ind Univ, PhD, 57. *Prof Exp:* Jr instr math, Johns Hopkins Univ, 50-53; jr engr, Bendix Radio, 53-55, asst proj engr, 56-57; SR MATHEMATICIAN, APPL PHYSICS LAB, JOHNS HOPKINS UNIV, 58- *Res:* Algebra and number theory; finite groups; statistics. *Mailing Add:* 5029 Round Tower Pl Columbia MD 21044

FEDERIGHI, FRANCIS D, b Xenia, Ohio, Oct 19, 31; m 55; c 2. COMPUTER SCIENCE. *Educ:* Oberlin Col, BA, 53; Harvard Univ, MA, 55, PhD(physics), 61. *Prof Exp:* Theoret physicist, Knolls Atomic Power Lab, Gen Elec Co, 59-66; ASSOC PROF COMPUT SCI, STATE UNIV NY ALBANY, 66- *Concurrent Pos:* Guest scientist, Swiss Fed Inst Reactor Res, 63-64. *Honors & Awards:* Mgt Award, Gen Elec Co, 60. *Mem:* Asn Comput Mach; Math Asn Am; Soc Indust & Appl Math. *Res:* Nuclear reactor physics; programming languages; numerical methods. *Mailing Add:* Dept of Comput Sci State Univ NY 1400 Wash Ave Albany NY 12222

FEDERLE, THOMAS WALTER, b Cincinnati, Ohio, June 5, 52; m 76; c 1. ENVIRONMENTAL MICROBIOLOGY, MICROBIAL ECOLOGY. *Educ:* Univ Cincinnati, BS, 74, MS, 76, PhD(biol & microbiol), 81. *Prof Exp:* Instr microbial ecol, Univ Cincinnati, 81; RES ASSOC, FLA STATE UNIV, 81- *Mem:* Sigma Xi; Am Soc Microbiol; Am Soc Limnol & Oceanog. *Res:* Ecology of microorganisms including the role of the microorganism in the degradation of natural and xenobiotic compounds; effect of pollutants on microbial processes. *Mailing Add:* 310 Nuclear Res Bldg Fla State Univ Tallahassee FL 32306

FEDERMAN, MICHELINE, b Paris, France, Jan 1, 39; US citizen. CELL BIOLOGY, ELECTRON MICROSCOPY. *Educ:* Long Island Univ, BS, 61; Rutgers Univ, PhD(cell biol), 66. *Prof Exp:* Res assoc cell biol & electron micros, Douglass Col, Rutgers Univ, 66-67 & Rutgers Med Sch, 67-68; RES ASSOC CELL BIOL & ELECTRON MICROS, CANCER RES INST, NEW ENG DEACONESS HOSP, 68-, SCI ASSOC, DEPT PATH, 75-; assoc path, Harvard Med Sch, 75- *Mem:* AAAS; Electron Micros Soc Am; Am Soc Cell Biol. *Res:* Ultrastructural aspects and function of normal and pathological tissues. *Mailing Add:* Cancer Res Inst New Eng Deaconess Hosp Boston MA 02215

FEDEROWICZ, ALEXANDER JOHN, b Hartford, Conn, May 28, 35; m 59; c 2. APPLIED MATHEMATICS. *Educ:* Carnegie Inst Technol, BS, 57, MS, 58, PhD(math), 63. *Prof Exp:* Sr mathematician, 62-73, FEL MATHEMATICIAN, WESTINGHOUSE RES & DEVELOP CTR, 73- *Mem:* Sigma Xi; Math Prog Soc. *Res:* Mathematical programming techniques in electrical and nuclear fission and fusion design problems; geometric, integer and linear programming; electrical utility planning techniques. *Mailing Add:* 113 Country Club Dr Pittsburgh PA 15235

FEDERSPIEL, CHARLES FOSTER, b Flint, Mich, May 3, 29; m 57. BIOSTATISTICS. *Educ:* Univ Mich, AB, 50, AM, 52; NC State Col, PhD(statist), 59. *Prof Exp:* Statistician, Communicable Dis Ctr, USPHS, 52-54; assoc prof biostatist, 59-76, PROF BIOSTATIST, SCH MED, VANDERBILT UNIV, 76-, DIR, BIOSTATIST DIV, 80- *Mem:* Biomet Soc; Am Statist Asn; Am Pub Health Asn. *Res:* Statistical methodology and its applications in biology and medicine; health services research. *Mailing Add:* Div of Biostatist Vanderbilt Med Ctr Nashville TN 37232

FEDINEC, ALEXANDER, b Uzhorod, Czech, Jan 29, 26; nat US; m 52; c 2. ANATOMY. *Educ:* Univ Kans, MA, 57, PhD(anat), 58. *Prof Exp:* Instr anat, State Univ NY Downstate Med Ctr, 58-60; asst prof, Hahnemann Med Col, 60-62; from asst prof to assoc prof, 62-74, asst dean col med, 71-73, PROF ANAT, CTR HEALTH SCI, UNIV TENN, MEMPHIS, 74-, ASSOC DEAN STUDENT AFFAIRS, COL MED, 73- *Mem:* Am Soc Microbiol; Int Soc Toxicol; Soc Neurosci; Am Asn Anat; Am Soc Exp Path. *Res:* Mode of dispersal and action of neurotropic toxins; blood-brain barrier and placental permeability; teratology. *Mailing Add:* Dept of Anat Univ of Tenn Ctr Health Sci Memphis TN 38163

FEDOR, EDWARD JOHN, b Braddock, Pa, Feb 15, 24. PHYSIOLOGY. *Educ:* Waynesburg Col, BS, 47; Univ WVa, MS, 50; Princeton Univ, MA & PhD(physiol), 53. *Prof Exp:* Instr biol & chem, Waynesburg Col, 47-48; instr physiol, Univ WVa, 48-50; res assoc & instr biol, Princeton Univ, 50-53; instr clin physiol, Sch Med, Univ Tenn, 53-54; res assoc exp surg, Sch Med, Univ Pittsburgh, 54-57, asst res prof surg, 57-61; sr physiologist, Wallace Labs, NJ, 61-64; sr physiologist, Abbott Labs, 64-69, head cardiovasc sect, 69-71, head blood physiol sect, 71-72, proj mgr, 72-74, clin monitor, 74-79; DIR SCI AFFAIRS, ALPHA THERAPEUT CORP, 80. *Concurrent Pos:* Proctor fel, Princeton Univ, 53-54. *Mem:* Am Physiol Soc; Soc Exp Biol & Med; Soc Nuclear Med; Am Soc Pharmacol & Exp Therapeut; Am Heart Asn. *Res:* Cardiovascular physiology and fibrinolysis. *Mailing Add:* Dir Sci Affairs R&D Dept Alpha Therapeutic Corp 5555 Valley Blvd Chicago IL 60064

FEDOR, LEO RICHARD, b Boston, Mass, Jan 11, 34; m 62; c 2. ORGANIC CHEMISTRY. *Educ:* Mass Col Pharm, BS, 55, MS, 57; Ind Univ, PhD(org chem), 63. *Prof Exp:* Instr chem, ETex State Col, 58-59; fel, Cornell Univ, 63-64 & Univ Calif, Santa Barbara, 64-65; asst prof, 65-69, ASSOC PROF MED CHEM, STATE UNIV NY BUFFALO, 69- *Mem:* Am Chem Soc. *Res:* Mechanisms of organic reactions related to enzymic reactions. *Mailing Add:* Sch Pharm Cooke 457 State Univ of NY Buffalo NY 14260

FEDOROFF, NINA V, b Cleveland, Ohio, Apr 9, 42; div; c 2. MOLECULAR BIOLOGY. *Educ:* Syracuse Univ, BS, 66; Rockefeller Univ, PhD(molecular biol), 72. *Prof Exp:* Asst prof biol, Univ Calif, Los Angeles, 74-75; Damon Runyan fel molecular biol, Sch Med, 74-75; NIH fel, 75-77, res assoc, 77-78, STAFF SCIENTIST, CARNEGIE INST WASHINGTON, 78- *Concurrent Pos:* Mem, Develop Biol Panel, NSF, 79-80; mem, Sci Adv Panel Appl Genetics, Office Technol Assessment, Cong US, 79-80; mem, NIH Recombinant DNA Adv Comt, 80- *Mem:* Sigma Xi; AAAS. *Res:* Transposable elements in maize. *Mailing Add:* Dept of Embryol 115 W University Pkwy Baltimore MD 21210

FEDOROFF, SERGEY, b Daugavpils, Latvia, Feb 20, 25; nat US; m 54; c 4. EMBRYOLOGY, HISTOLOGY. *Educ:* Univ Sask, BA, 52, MA, 55, PhD(histol), 58. *Prof Exp:* Demonstr histol, 53-55, instr anat, 55-57, spec lectr, 57-58, from asst prof to assoc prof, 58-64, admin asst to dean med, 60-62, asst dean Col Med, 70-77, dir cell biol study Prog, 73-77, PROF ANAT & HEAD DEPT, UNIV SASK, 64- *Concurrent Pos:* Lederle med fac award, 57-60; mem steering comt study basic biol res Can, Sci Secretariat, 66; mem, Med Res Coun Assessment Group Anat Res Can, 67; mem studentship comt, Med Res Coun Can, 69-, mem, Coun, 73-; mem bd gov, W Alton Jones Cell Sci Ctr, NY, 70-72, vchmn, 80- *Mem:* Can Asn Anat (vpres, 65-66, pres, 66-67); Am Asn Anatomists; Pan-Am Asn Anat (pres, 72-75, hon pres, 75-); Can Soc Cell Biologists; Tissue Cult Asn (vpres, 64-68, pres, 68-72). *Res:* Cytogenetics; immunobiology; tissue culture; cell differentiation; author or coauthor of numerous scientific publications. *Mailing Add:* Dept of Anat Univ of Sask Saskatoon Can

FEDORS, ROBERT FRANCIS, b Bayonne, NJ, Jan 16, 34; m 61; c 3. POLYMER CHEMISTRY. *Educ:* Purdue Univ, BS, 55; Akron Univ, PhD(polymer chem), 62. *Prof Exp:* Chemist plastics, Gen Cable Corp, 55-56; chemist rubber & plastics, Edgewood Arsenal, 56-58; MEM TECH STAFF POLYMERS, JET PROPULSION LAB, CALIF INST TECHNOL, 62- *Mem:* Am Chem Soc. *Res:* Studies of the time dependent physical and mechanical properties of polymers, including extensive work on the time and temperature dependence of the ultimate properties of elastomers. *Mailing Add:* Jet Propulsion Lab 4800 Oak Grove Dr Pasadena CA 91103

FEDRICK, JAMES LOVE, b Lordsburg, NMex, Apr 17, 30; m 64; c 4. MEDICINAL CHEMISTRY, PHARMACEUTICS. *Educ:* Univ Ariz, BS, 53, MS, 55; Univ Ill, PhD(chem), 59. *Prof Exp:* Org chemist, Org Chem Res Sect, Lederle Lab, Am Cyanamid Co, 59-61, group leader, 61-63, tech dir fine chem dept, Pearl River, NY, 63-66, dir prod & process develop, Med Res, Lederle Labs, Cyanamid Int, 66-74, dir pharmaceut & mech develop, Lederle Labs, 75-77, FOREIGN PATENT COORDR & AGENT, AM CYANAMID CO, STAMFORD, CONN, 77- *Concurrent Pos:* Teacher, Bergen Col. *Mem:* Am Chem Soc; NY Acad Sci. *Res:* Heterocyclic synthesis; medicinal chemistry; management of international research and development; pharmaceutical product and process; foreign Patent Agent. *Mailing Add:* 51 Sparrow Bush Rd Mahwah NJ 07430

FEDUCCIA, JOHN ALAN, b Mobile, Ala, Apr 25, 43. ZOOLOGY, EVOLUTIONARY BIOLOGY. *Educ:* La State Univ, BS, 65; Univ Mich, MA, PhD(zool), 69. *Prof Exp:* Lectr zool, Univ Mich, 69; asst prof biol, Southern Methodist Univ, 69-71; from asst prof to assoc prof, 71-79, PROF ZOOL, UNIV NC, CHAPEL HILL, 79-, ASSOC CHMN DEPT, 81-; RES ASSOC, DEPT VERT ZOOL, SMITHSONIAN INST, 78- *Mem:* Fel Am Ornith Union; Soc Study Evolution; Soc Syst Zool; Soc Vert Paleont; AAAS; Sigma Xi. *Res:* Avian evolution and systematics; avian paleontology. *Mailing Add:* Dept of Zool Univ of NC Chapel Hill NC 27514

FEE, JAMES ARTHUR, b Nokomis, Sask, Aug 30, 39; US citizen; m 60; c 2. PHYSICAL BIOCHEMISTRY. *Educ:* Pasadena Col, BA, 61; Univ Southern Calif, PhD(biochem), 67. *Prof Exp:* NSF fel biochem, Gothenburg Univ, 67-69; NIH trainee & res assoc biophys, Univ Mich, Ann Arbor, 69-70; asst prof chem, Rensselaer Polytech Inst, 70-74; assoc prof biol chem & assoc res biophysicist, 74-81, PROF BIOL CHEM & RES BIOPHYSICIST, UNIV MICH, ANN ARBOR, 81- *Mem:* Am Chem Soc; Am Soc Biol Chemists. *Res:* Oxygen metabolism; role of metal ions in biological systems; mechanistic aspects of enzymatically catalyzed oxidation-reduction reactions. *Mailing Add:* Biophys Res Div Univ of Mich Ann Arbor MI 48109

FEELEY, JOHN CORNELIUS, b Los Angeles, Calif, Mar 7, 33; m 57; c 3. IMMUNOLOGY. *Educ:* Univ Calif, Los Angeles, AB, 55, PhD, 58; Am Bd Microbiol, dipl, 64. *Prof Exp:* Asst bact, Univ Calif, Los Angeles, 55-58; from sr asst scientist to scientist, Div Biol Standards, 58-65, chief sect bact vaccines, 65-71, mem cholera adv comt, 68-72, chief bact immunol br, 71-81, ASST DIR, BACT DIS DIV, CTR DIS CONTROL, USPHS, NIH, 81- *Concurrent Pos:* Mem cholera panel, US-Japan Coop Med Sci Prog, 65-73 & 78-; sr scientist, USPHS, 66-73; scientist dir, 73-; mem, WHO Expert Panel Bact Dis, 67-; adj assoc prof parasitol & lab pract, Sch Pub Health, Univ NC, 68-; consult, US AID, 70- & Food & Drug Admin, 72-81; clin assoc prof path, Sch Med, Emory Univ, 77- *Honors & Awards:* Meritorious Serv Medal, USPHS, 74. *Mem:* AAAS; fel Am Acad Microbiol; Soc Exp Biol & Med; Am Soc Microbiol; fel Infectious Dis Soc Am. *Res:* Hypersensitivity; hemagglutination; serum bactericidal action; standardization of biological and immunodiagnostic products; bacteriology and immunology of enteric diseases. *Mailing Add:* Bldg 1 Rm 5035 Ctr for Dis Control Atlanta GA 30333

FEELY, FRANK JOSEPH, JR, b Chicago, Ill, Aug 26, 18; m 69; c 7. MECHANICAL ENGINEERING. *Educ:* Univ Mich, BS, 40. *Prof Exp:* Engr, Design Div, Standard Oil Develop Co, 40-48, group head, 48-51, asst supv engr, 51-55, asst dir, 55-59, assoc dir planning eng div, Esso Res & Eng Co, 59-61, dir gen eng div, 61-64, asst gen mgr gen mgr off, 64-66, vpres & dir, 66-71; mgr opers coordr, Logistics Dept, Standard Oil Co, NJ, 71-77; VPRES ENG, EXXON RES & ENG CO, FLORHAM PARK, 77- *Concurrent Pos:* Mem, Am Petrol Inst, 53-; vpres & mem bd dir & exec comt, Am Nat Standards Inst. *Mem:* Fel Am Soc Mech Engrs. *Res:* Mechanical engineering developments in catalytic cracking including stress analysis of piping expansion joints; brittle fracture in steel. *Mailing Add:* Exxon Res & Eng Co PO Box 101 Florham Park NJ 07932

FEELY, HERBERT WILLIAM, b Brooklyn, NY, Apr 29, 28; m 67; c 4. GEOCHEMISTRY. *Educ:* City Col NY, BS, 50; Columbia Univ, MA, 52, PhD(geol), 56. *Prof Exp:* Instr, Upsala Col, 55-57; sr res geochemist, Isotopes, Inc, 57-67; assoc prof earth sci, Queens Col, NY, 67-76; ENVIRON SCIENTIST, US DEPT ENERGY, NEW YORK, 76- *Concurrent Pos:* Res assoc, Columbia Univ, 56-57; sr res assoc, 67- *Mem:* Am Geophys Union; Am Meteorol Soc. *Res:* Atmospheric and marine geochemistry. *Mailing Add:* 31 Seneca Ave Emerson NJ 07630

FEELY, RICHARD ALAN, b Farmington, Minn, Feb 26, 47; m 71; c 2. CHEMICAL OCEANOGRAPHY, GEOCHEMISTRY. *Educ:* Col St Thomas, BA, 69; Tex A&M Univ, MS, 71, PhD(oceanog), 74. *Prof Exp:* Res asst chem oceanog, Tex A&M Univ, 69-73, res assoc, 73-74; RES ASSOC CHEM OCEANOG, UNIV WASH, 74-; OCEANOGR, PAC MARINE ENVIRON LAB, NAT OCEANOG & ATMOSPHERIC ADMIN, 74- *Mem:* AAAS; Am Geophy Union; Am Soc Limnol & Oceanog. *Res:* Factors influencing the major and trace element composition of marine particulate matter and sediments; reactions of trace metals at the freshwater-seawater interface; exchange of elements between sediments and seawater. *Mailing Add:* Pac Marine Environ Lab 7600 Sand Point Way NE Seattle WA 98115

FEEMAN, GEORGE FRANKLIN, b Lebanon, Pa, Apr 16, 30; m 71; c 4. MATHEMATICS. *Educ:* Muhlenberg Col, BS, 51; Lehigh Univ, MS, 53, PhD(math), 58. *Prof Exp:* From instr to asst prof math, Muhlenberg Col, 54-59; instr, Mass Inst Technol, 59-61; from asst prof to assoc prof, Williams Col, 61-69; from actg chmn to chmn dept, 71-75, chmn dept, 78-81, PROF MATH, OAKLAND UNIV, 69-, ASSOC PROVOST, 81- *Concurrent Pos:* NSF sci fac fel, 65-66; math coordr, African Math Proj, 65-66; Detroit Teacher Intern Proj, 69-70 & Urban Corps Proj, 69-70 & 70-71; math specialist, USAID team, Nepal, 75-77; math evaluator, Univ Qatar, 81. *Mem:* Am Math Soc; Math Asn Am; Am Asn Univ Prof. *Res:* Differential geometry, especially geometry of Riemannian manifolds; problems in mathematics education. *Mailing Add:* Dept Math Sci Oakland Univ Rochester MI 48063

FEEMAN, JAMES FREDERIC, b Lebanon, Pa, June 1, 22; m 47; c 4. INDUSTRIAL ORGANIC CHEMISTRY, RESEARCH ADMINISTRATION. *Educ:* Muhlenberg Col, BS, 45; Lehigh Univ, MS, 47, PhD(chem), 49. *Prof Exp:* Res Found fel, Ohio State Univ, 49-50; res chemist, Althouse Div, 50-68, asst dir res, 68-72, assoc dir res, Dyes & Chem Div, 72-74, dir, 74-80, VPRES RES & DEVELOP, DYES & CHEM DIV, CROMPTON & KNOWLES CORP, READING, 80- *Mem:* Fel AAAS; NY Acad Sci; fel Am Inst Chemists; Am Chem Soc; Am Asn Textile Chem & Colorists. *Res:* Textile dyes and auxiliaries; textile chemistry; dye intermediates; chemical information management; synthetic organic chemistry. *Mailing Add:* 1500 Garfield Ave Wyomissing PA 19610

FEENEY, GLORIA COMULADA, b NJ, July 11, 25; m 53; c 2. PHARMACOLOGY, TOXICOLOGY. *Educ:* Univ Va, BS, 45; George Washington Univ, MS, 48, PhD(pharmacol), 53. *Prof Exp:* Instr pharmacol, Sch Med & Dent, Georgetown Univ, 54-57, asst prof, 57-59; toxicologist-pharmacologist, Bur Foods, Div Toxicol, Food & Drug Admin, 73-74; info scientist life sci, Smithsonian Sci Info Exchange, 74-75; consult info scientist, Technassociates, Inc, 78-79 & JRB Assocs, Inc, 79-80. *Mem:* Soc Exp Biol & Med; Soc Petrol Engrs; Soc Cosmetic Chemists; Sigma Xi. *Res:* Endocrinological influence of salicylates; cocaine and the autonomic nervous system; environmental, earth and marine sciences; ecology; technical management. *Mailing Add:* 1650 Harvard St NW Washington DC 20009

FEENEY, ROBERT EARL, b Oak Park, Ill, Aug 30, 13; m 54; c 2. BIOCHEMISTRY, PROTEIN CHEMISTRY. *Educ:* Northwestern Univ, BS, 38; Univ Wis, MS, 40, PhD(biochem), 42. *Prof Exp:* Asst, Univ Wis, 40-42; res assoc, Harvard Med Sch, 42-43; chemist, Western Regional Res Lab, Bur Agr & Indust Chem, USDA, 46-53; prof biochem & nutrit & chmn dept, Univ Nebr, 53-60; PROF FOOD SCI & TECHNOL, UNIV CALIF, DAVIS, 60- *Concurrent Pos:* Chemist, Exp Sta, Univ Nebr, 53-60; prin investr, NIH & NSF, 56-; vis scholar, Univ Cambridge, Eng, 71; vis prof, Swiss Fed Inst Technol, Zurich, 72, Univ Bergen, 76, Univ Bielefeld, 79 & Hokkaido Univ, 81; distinguished vis prof, Mem Univ Nfld, 78-79. *Mem:* Am Soc Biol Chem; Am Chem Soc; Inst Food Technol. *Res:* Investigation of chemical, biochemical and physical techniques and their effects on proteins, including chemical improvement of food proteins for better function and nutritional properties; iron-binding sites of transferrins; water ice proteins interactions of antifreeze proteins; chemical modifications of proteins. *Mailing Add:* Dept of Food Sci & Technol 3450 Chem Annex Univ Calif Davis CA 95616

FEENEY-BURNS, MARY LYNETTE, b Burnsville, WVa, Mar 5, 31; m 78. CELL BIOLOGY, OPHTHALMOLOGY. *Educ:* Col Mt St Joseph-on-the-Ohio, BA, 53; Univ Calif, San Francisco, MA, 64, PhD(endocrinol), 68. *Prof Exp:* From asst prof to assoc prof ophthal, Med Sch, Univ Ore, 70-79; assoc prof, 79-81, PROF OPHTHAL, SCH MED, UNIV MO-COLUMBIA, 81- *Concurrent Pos:* Nat Inst Neurol Dis & Blindness fel, Harvard Univ, 69-70; mem visual sci A study sect, NIH, 74-78. *Mem:* NY Acad Sci; AAAS; Am Soc Cell Biol; Asn Res Vision & Ophthal; Am Asn Anat. *Res:* Correlated morphological and biochemical studies of normal and pathological ocular tissues. *Mailing Add:* Dept Ophthal Univ Mo Sch Med 807 Stadium Rd Columbia MO 65212

FEENSTRA, ERNEST STAR, b Grand Rapids, Mich, Oct 22, 17; m 44; c 3. VETERINARY PATHOLOGY. *Educ:* Mich State Univ, DVM, 42, MS, 44, PhD(animal path), 47; Am Col Vet Pathologists, dipl; Am Col Lab Animal Med, dipl. *Prof Exp:* Asst animal path, Mich State Univ, 42-47, asst prof, 47-48; sect head res div, Upjohn Co, 48-56, mgr path & toxicol res, 56-81; RETIRED. *Concurrent Pos:* Res prof path, Mich State Univ, 70- *Mem:* AAAS; Int Acad Path; Am Sci Affiliation; Am Vet Med Asn; Am Asn Pathologists & Bacteriologists. *Res:* Experimental pathology and toxicology; diseases of laboratory animals. *Mailing Add:* 6046 Torrington Kalamazoo MI 49009

FEENY, PAUL PATRICK, b Birmingham, Eng, Feb 8, 40; m 68; c 2. ECOLOGY, ENTOMOLOGY. *Educ:* Oxford Univ, BA, 60 & 63, BSc, 61, MA, 63, PhD(zool), 66. *Prof Exp:* Asst prof ecol, 67-72, fac trustee, 71-73, assoc prof entom, ecol & systs, 72-78, PROF ENTOM, ECOL & SYSTS, CORNELL UNIV, 78- *Mem:* AAAS; Ecol Soc Am. *Res:* Chemical ecology; evolution and ecological significance of secondary plant and animal chemical compounds, including attractants and repellants. *Mailing Add:* Dept of Entom Comstock Hall Cornell Univ Ithaca NY 14853

FEERST, IRWIN, b New York, NY, Nov 18, 27; m 50; c 2. ELECTRONIC ENGINEERING. *Educ:* City Col New York, BEE, 51; NY Univ, MEE, 55; Polytech Inst New York, MSEE, 74. *Prof Exp:* Pvt consult, 60-62; asst prof physics, Adelphi Univ, 62-69; PVT CONSULT, 69- *Concurrent Pos:* Consult, Am Mach & Foundry Co, 62-64 & Bucode Co, 69-75; NSF grant, 64-66; contrib ed, New Engr, 77-79; vis lectr, Nat Proj Philos & Eng Ethics, 78. *Mem:* Inst Elec & Electronics Engrs. *Res:* Servomechanisms; tape transport design and development; cathode ray tube deflection systems; spectral analysis of signals; pulse and digital circuits and systems. *Mailing Add:* 368 Euclid Ave Massapequa Park NY 11762

FEESE, BENNIE TAYLOR, b Cane Valley, Ky, Dec 21, 37; m 60; c 2. MOLECULAR BIOLOGY. *Educ:* Centre Col Ky, AB, 59; Wash Univ, PhD(molecular biol), 65. *Prof Exp:* Asst prof biol, 64-71, chmn life sci prog, 67-69, chmn molecular biol prog comt, 69-73, assoc prof biol, 71-76, PROF BIOL, CENTRE COL KY, 76- *Mem:* AAAS. *Res:* Erythropoietic aspects of amphibian metamorphosis. *Mailing Add:* Div of Sci & Math Centre Col of Ky Danville KY 40422

FEESER, LARRY JAMES, b Hanover, Pa, Feb 23, 37; m 61; c 2. CIVIL ENGINEERING, COMPUTERS. *Educ:* Lehigh Univ, BS, 58; Univ Colo, MS, 61; Carnegie Inst Technol, PhD(civil eng), 65. *Prof Exp:* From instr to prof civil eng, Univ Colo, Boulder, 58-74, res assoc, Comput Ctr, 70-73; PROF CIVIL ENG & CHMN DEPT, RENSSELAER POLYTECH INST, 74- *Concurrent Pos:* Mem, Nat Coop Hwy Res Prog; mem adv comt interactive comput graphics, NSF fac fel, Swiss Fed Inst Technol, 71-72. *Mem:* Am Soc Civil Engrs (nat dir, 79-82); Am Concrete Inst; Am Soc Eng Educ; Int Asn Bridge & Struct Engrs; Int Asn Shell Struct. *Res:* Dynamics and optimization of structures; computer applications; interactive computer graphics; highway computer graphics. *Mailing Add:* Dept Civil Eng Rensselaer Polytech Inst Troy NY 12181

FEFFERMAN, CHARLES LOUIS, b Washington, DC, Apr 18, 49; m 75. MATHEMATICAL ANALYSIS. *Educ:* Univ Md, BS, 66; Princeton Univ, PhD(math), 69. *Prof Exp:* Lectr math, Princeton Univ, 69-70; from asst prof to prof, Univ Chicago, 70-74; PROF MATH, PRINCETON UNIV, 74- *Concurrent Pos:* Alfred P Sloan fel, 70-71; NATO fel, 71. *Honors & Awards:* Salem Prize, 71; First Recipient, Alan T Waterman Award, 76; Fields Medal, 78. *Mem:* Am Math Soc; Am Acad Arts & Sci. *Res:* Fourier analysis; partial differential equations; several complex variables. *Mailing Add:* Fine Hall Princeton Univ Princeton NJ 08540

FEGEL, ARTHUR C(HRISTIAN), mechanical engineering, deceased

FEGLEY, KENNETH A(LLEN), b Mont Clare, Pa, Feb 14, 23; m 51; c 3. ELECTRICAL ENGINEERING, SYSTEMS ENGINEERING. *Educ:* Univ Pa, BS, 47, MS, 50, PhD(elec eng), 55. *Prof Exp:* Instr, 47-53, assoc, 53-55, asst prof, 55-58, assoc prof elec eng, 58-66, PROF ELEC ENG, MOORE SCH ELEC ENG, UNIV PA, 66- *Mem:* Am Soc Eng Educ; fel Inst Elec & Electronics Engrs; fel AAAS; AAUP. *Res:* Navigation, control, optimization, modeling and simulation; applications of mathematical programming and other optimization techniques to engineering and medical problems; hazard analysis. *Mailing Add:* Sch Eng & Appl Sci Univ Pa Philadelphia PA 19104

FEHER, ELSA, b Buenos Aires, Arg, Dec 1, 32; US citizen; m 61; c 2. SCIENCE EDUCATION, PHYSICS. *Educ:* Univ Buenos Aires, BA, 56; Columbia Univ, PhD(physics), 64. *Prof Exp:* Res asst physics, Columbia Univ, 59-61; res physicist, Univ Calif, San Diego, 61-67; Radcliffe scholar, Radcliffe Inst Independent Study, 67-68; lectr, 69-71, ASSOC PROF PHYS SCI, SAN DIEGO STATE UNIV, 71-, CHMN, NATURAL SCI DEPT, 80- *Mem:* Am Asn Physics Teachers. *Res:* Science education of prospective elementary school teachers. *Mailing Add:* Dept Natural Sci San Diego State Univ San Diego CA 92182

FEHER, GEORGE, b Czech, May 29, 24; m 49; c 3. PHYSICS, BIOPHYSICS. *Educ:* Univ Calif, SB, 50, MS, 51, PhD(physics), 54. *Prof Exp:* Res physicist, Bell Tel Labs, 54-60; PROF SOLID STATE PHYSICS & BIOPHYS, UNIV CALIF, SAN DIEGO, 60- *Concurrent Pos:* Vis assoc prof, Columbia Univ, 59-60; vis prof, Mass Inst Technol, 67-68; mem bd gov, Israel Inst Technol, 68- *Honors & Awards:* Prize, Am Phys Soc, 60, Buckley Prize, 75. *Mem:* Nat Acad Sci; fel Am Acad Arts & Sci; Am Phys Soc. *Res:* Solid state physics; paramagnetic resonance; photosynthesis. *Mailing Add:* Dept of Physics Univ of Calif at San Diego La Jolla CA 92037

FEHER, JOSEPH JOHN, b Derby, Conn, Apr 2, 49. CARDIOVASCULAR PHYSIOLOGY, CELL PHYSIOLOGY. *Educ:* Cornell Univ, BS, 71, MNS, 73, PhD(nutrit), 78. *Prof Exp:* Instr, 78-79, ASST PROF RENAL PHYSIOL, DEPT PHYSIOL, MED COL VA, 79- *Mem:* Biophys Soc; AAAS. *Res:* Characterization of the mechanism of calcium transport across intestinal epithelium and across sarcoplasmic reticulum membranes. *Mailing Add:* Med Col Va MCV Sta PO Box 551 Richmond VA 23298

FEHLER, MICHAEL C, b Riverside, Calif, Nov 15, 51. GEOPHYSICS, SEISMOLOGY. *Educ:* Reed Col, BA, 74; Mass Inst Technol, PhD(geophysics), 79. *Prof Exp:* ASST PROF SEISMOL, ORE STATE UNIV, 79- *Mem:* Am Geophy Union; Seismol Soc Am; Soc Explor Geophysics. *Res:* Geothermal energy; volcanoes. *Mailing Add:* Sch of Oceanog Ore State Univ Corvallis OR 97331

FEHLNER, FRANCIS PAUL, b Dolgeville, NY, Aug 3, 34; m 62; c 3. PHYSICAL CHEMISTRY. *Educ:* Col Holy Cross, BS, 56; Rensselaer Polytech Inst, PhD(phys chem), 59. *Prof Exp:* Mgr, Res & Develop Lab, 62-80, MEM STAFF, RES & DEVELOP DIV, CORNING GLASS WORKS, 80- *Mem:* Am Chem Soc; Am Vacuum Soc; Electrochem Soc. *Res:* Glass chemistry; chemical kinetics; ultra-high vacuum; thin films; oxidation of metals. *Mailing Add:* 83 E Fourth St Corning NY 14830

FEHLNER, THOMAS PATRICK, b Dolgeville, NY, May 28, 37; m 62; c 3. PHYSICAL INORGANIC CHEMISTRY. *Educ:* St Bernardine of Siena Col, BS, 59; Johns Hopkins Univ, MA, 61, PhD(phys chem), 63. *Prof Exp:* Res assoc inst coop res, Johns Hopkins Univ, 63-64; from asst prof to assoc prof, 64-75, PROF CHEM, UNIV NOTRE DAME, 75- *Mem:* Am Chem Soc; AAAS. *Res:* Characterization of unstable inorganic molecules and radicals by mass spectrometry; kinetics of unstable species; ultraviolet photoelectron spectroscopy of inorganic species; synthesis of metalloborane clusters. *Mailing Add:* Dept of Chem Univ of Notre Dame Notre Dame IN 46556

FEHNEL, EDWARD ADAM, b Bethlehem, Pa, Apr 22, 22; m 44; c 2. ORGANIC CHEMISTRY. *Educ:* Lehigh Univ, BS, 43, MS, 44, PhD(org chem), 46. *Prof Exp:* Instr, Moravian Prep Sch, Pa, 43-44; res chemist, Cent Res Lab, Allied Chem & Dye Corp, NJ, 44-45; lectr chem & Am Chem Soc fel, Univ Pa, 46-48; from asst prof to prof, 48-72, EDMUND ALLEN PROF CHEM, SWARTHMORE COL, 72- *Concurrent Pos:* NSF sci fac fel, Cambridge Univ, 62; vis prof, Ind Univ, 68. *Mem:* Am Chem Soc. *Res:* Synthetic organic chemistry; preparation and properties of organic sulfur compounds; ultraviolet absorption spectroscopy; quinoline derivatives; arene oxides; photocycloaddition reactions of norbornadiene and quadricyclane. *Mailing Add:* Dept of Chem Swarthmore Col Swarthmore PA 19081

FEHON, JACK HAROLD, b Irvington, NJ, Dec 14, 26; m 50; c 3. ZOOLOGY. *Educ:* Univ Fla, BS, 50, MS, 52; Fla State Univ, PhD, 55. *Prof Exp:* Instr biol, Fla State Univ, 55-56; from assoc prof to prof, 56-62, DANA PROF BIOL, QUEENS COL, NC, 62-, HEAD DEPT, 59- *Mem:* Am Soc Bariatrics. *Res:* Amino acid flux in marine invertebrates. *Mailing Add:* 2411 Vernon Dr Charlotte NC 28211

FEHR, ROBERT O, b Germany, Sept 12, 11; nat US; m 41; c 2. ACOUSTICS. *Educ:* Inst Technol, Berlin, Vordiplom, 33; Swiss Fed Inst Technol, Dipl Ing, 34; Dr Tech Sc, 39. *Prof Exp:* Test engr, Gen Elec Co, 37-38, develop engr, Gen Eng Lab, 39-46, sect engr, 46-53, consult engr, 53-56, mgr mech eng lab, 56-61; prof eng, Cornell Univ, 61-64; vpres Europ opers, Branson Europa NV, Branson Instruments, Inc, Neth, 64-66; vpres int opers, Conn, 66-68; pres, Fehr & Fiske Inc, 68-76; CONSULT ENGR, 76- *Concurrent Pos:* Ed, J Audio Engrs Soc; secy-treas, Int Microwave Corp. *Honors & Awards:* Audio Engrs Soc Award. *Mem:* Fel Acoust Soc Am; fel Audio Eng Soc; Inst Noise Control Engrs; Inst Elec & Electronics Engrs; Am Soc Mech Engrs. *Res:* Acoustics; vibration; mechanical shock. *Mailing Add:* 294 Round Hill Rd Greenwich CT 06830

FEHR, WALTER R, b East Grand Fork, Minn, Dec 4, 39. PLANT BREEDING. *Educ:* Univ Minn, BS, 61, MS, 62; Iowa State Univ, PhD(plant breeding), 67. *Prof Exp:* Res asst, Univ Minn, 61-62; agronomist, Congo Polytech Inst, Zaire, 62-64; res assoc, 64-67, from asst prof to assoc prof, 67-74, PROF AGRON, IOWA STATE UNIV, 74- *Concurrent Pos:* Mem, Nat Soybean Res Coord Comt; mem corn-soybean study team, Nat Acad Sci; mem, Nat Cert Soybean Variety Rev Bd; assoc ed, Crop Sci; mem, Germplasm Team, People's Republic China, USDA. *Res:* Development of superior soybeans. *Mailing Add:* Dept of Agron Iowa State Univ Ames IA 50011

FEIBELMAN, PETER JULIAN, b New York, NY, Nov 12, 42. THEORETICAL SOLID STATE PHYSICS. *Educ:* Columbia Univ, BA, 63; Univ Calif, San Diego, PhD(physics), 67. *Prof Exp:* NSF fel physics, Saclay Nuclear Res Ctr, France, 68-69; Nat Ctr Sci Res researcher, 69; res asst prof, Univ Ill, Urbana-Champaign, 69-71; asst prof, State Univ NY Stony Brook, 71-74; MEM TECH STAFF SANDIA LABS, 74- *Mem:* Am Phys Soc. *Res:* Theoretical surface physics; dielectric properties of surfaces; photoemission spectroscopy; auger spectroscopy; electron stimulated desorption; electronic structure of surfaces; many-electron problems. *Mailing Add:* Sandia Labs Orgn 5151 Albuquerque NM 87185

FEIBELMAN, WALTER A, b Berlin, Ger, Oct 30, 25; US citizen. ASTRONOMY, ASTROPHYSICS. *Educ:* Carnegie Inst Technol, BS, 56. *Prof Exp:* Res specialist, Westinghouse Res Labs, 48-56, res engr, 56-63; asst res prof physics, Univ Pittsburgh, 64-69, observer, Allegheny Observ, 55-69; PHYSICIST, LAB OPTICAL ASTRON, GODDARD SPACE FLIGHT CTR, NASA, 69- *Concurrent Pos:* Consult, Westinghouse Elec Corp, 66- *Mem:* Am Astron Soc; fel Meteoritical Soc; Royal Astron Soc Can; Int Astron Union. *Res:* Microwave spectroscopy; thin films; planetary nebulae; infrared, visible and ultraviolet image converters; cold cathode electron emission; meteor spectroscopy; astrometry; interforometry; astronomical and upper-atmosphere instrumentation. *Mailing Add:* Lab for Astron & Solar Physics 685 Goddard Space Flight Ctr Greenbelt MD 20771

FEIBES, WALTER, b Aachen, Ger, Jan 26, 28; US citizen; m 50; c 3. STATISTICS, OPERATIONS RESEARCH. *Educ:* Union Col, NY, BS, 52; Western Reserve Univ, MS, 53; State Univ NY Buffalo, PhD(opers res), 68. *Prof Exp:* Doc analyst, Libr Cong, 53-55; head librn, Appliance Park, Gen Elec Co, 55-62; assoc prof math, 67-76, PROF MATH, WESTERN KY UNIV, 76-, PROF COMPUT SCI, 80- *Mem:* Math Asn Am; Am Statist Asn; Inst Mgt Sci; Opers Res Soc Am; Sigma Xi. *Res:* Applied statistics; time series. *Mailing Add:* Dept of Math Western Ky Univ Bowling Green KY 42101

FEICHTNER, JOHN DAVID, b Erie, Pa, July 6, 30; m 57. QUANTUM ELECTRONICS. *Educ:* Stanford Univ, BS, 53; NMex State Univ, MS, 60; Univ Colo, PhD(physics), 64. *Prof Exp:* Physicist, Gen Elec Co, 55-57; res asst physics, Univ Colo, 60-65; sr res scientist, 65-71, fel scientist, 71-74, MGR OPTICAL PHYSICS, WESTINGHOUSE RES LABS, 74- *Mem:* Am Phys Soc; Inst Elec & Electronics Engrs; Optical Soc Am; Soc Photog Instrumentation Engrs; Am Asn Physics Teachers. *Res:* Atomic and molecular physics; nonlinear and acoustooptic materials; laser chemistry; laser isotope separation. *Mailing Add:* Westinghouse Res Labs Churchill Borough Pittsburgh PA 15235

FEIERTAG, THOMAS HAROLD, b Rockford, Ill, Sept 25, 35; m 68; c 2. ELECTRICAL ENGINEERING, NONDESTRUCTIVE TESTING. *Educ:* Monmouth Col, BA & Case Inst Technol, BS, 61; New York Univ, MS, 63. *Prof Exp:* Mem tech staff elec eng, Bell Tel Labs, 61-66; MEM STAFF ELEC ENG, LOS ALAMOS NAT LAB, 66- *Concurrent Pos:* Mem, Acoustic Emission Working Group. *Mem:* Am Soc Nondestructive Testing. *Res:* Acoustic emission testing; stress emission from metals and the practical application of this phenomenon. *Mailing Add:* Los Alamos Nat Lab Box 1663 MS-912 Los Alamos NM 87545

FEIG, GERALD, b Newark, NJ, July 29, 32; m 56; c 2. ORGANIC CHEMISTRY. *Educ:* Rutgers Univ, BA, 54, MS, 57, PhD(org chem), 59. *Prof Exp:* Sr res chemist, Nat Cash Register Co, 59-62; res chemist, Sun Chem Corp, 62-63, res group leader, 63-66, res sect head, 66-69, dir corp res lab, 69-75, resin prog mgr, 75-78; mgr, Specialty Prod Div, Polychrome Corp, 78-80; CONSULT, 80- *Mem:* Textile Res Inst; Tech Asn Graphic Arts; Am Chem Soc; Soc Photog Sci & Eng. *Res:* Mechanisms of organic peroxide decompositions; photopolymerization systems and photoinitiators; photochromic compounds; thermography; electrostatic printing; polymer synthesis; textile chemical finishes; graphic arts. *Mailing Add:* 10 Eton Pl Springfield NJ 07081

FEIGELSON, MURIEL, b New York, NY, July 15, 26; m 47; c 2. BIOCHEMISTRY. *Educ:* Queen's Col, NY, BS, 46; NY Univ, MS, 57, PhD(cell physiol), 61. *Prof Exp:* Trainee oncol biochem, 60-62, res assoc biochem, 63-71, asst prof biochem, 71-80, SR RES ASSOC, DEPT OBSTET & GYNEC, COL PHYSICIANS & SURGEONS, COLUMBIA UNIV, 80-; DIR, BASIC RES LAB, DEPT OBSTET & GYNEC, ST LUKES ROOSEVELT HOSP CTR, 73- *Concurrent Pos:* USPHS fel, Lab Exp Embryol, Col France, 62-63; dir res & clin labs, Dept Obstet & Gynec, Harlem Hosp, New York, 65-73; corresp ed, J Steroid Biochemistry; mem maternal & child health res comt, Nat Inst Child Health Develop, 80-83. *Mem:* Fel AAAS; Am Soc Biol Chem; Soc Study Reproduction; World Pop Soc; Perinatal Res Soc. *Res:* Developmental endocrine and reproductive biochemistry. *Mailing Add:* St Lukes Roosevelt Hosp Ctr 428 W 59th St New York NY 10019

FEIGELSON, PHILIP, b New York, NY, Apr 20, 25; m 47; c 2. BIOCHEMISTRY. *Educ:* Queens Col, NY, BS, 47; Syracuse Univ, MS, 48; Univ Wis, PhD(biochem), 51. *Prof Exp:* Asst prof biochem, Antioch Col, 51-54; res assoc, Fels Res Inst, 51-54; from asst prof to assoc prof, 54-70, PROF BIOCHEM, COL PHYSICIANS & SURGEONS, COLUMBIA UNIV, 70- *Concurrent Pos:* Career investr, Health Res Coun, NY, 59-75. *Mem:* Fel NY Acad Sci (pres, 75); Am Soc Biol Chem; Am Chem Soc; Am Asn Cancer Res; Harvey Soc. *Res:* Mechanism of hormone action; control of gene expression in normal and neoplastic cells. *Mailing Add:* Col of Physicians & Surgeons Columbia Univ New York NY 10032

FEIGEN, GEORGE ALEXANDER, b Rostov-on-Don, Russia, Nov, 19, 16; nat US; m 48. IMMUNOCHEMISTRY, PHYSIOLOGY. *Educ:* Univ Calif, AB, 38; Calif Inst Technol, PhD(immunol), 47. *Prof Exp:* Asst pharmacol, Calif Inst Technol, 39-42; physiologist, Inst Med Physics, Res Labs, Univ Calif & biochemist, Dept Obstet & Gynec, Med Sch, 43; asst chem, Calif Inst Technol, 43-47; res assoc pharmacol & toxicol, Sch Med, Univ Southern Calif, 48-49; from instr to assoc prof, 49-70, PROF PHYSIOL, SCH MED, STANFORD UNIV, 70- *Concurrent Pos:* USPHS sr res fel, Calif Inst Technol, 47-48; Am Heart Asn traveling fel, Oxford Univ, 56-57, NSF sr fel, 63-64; consult, Sch Med, Univ Calif, Los Angeles, 54 & White Mountain High Altitude Res Sta, Calif; vis prof, Monash Univ, Australia, 72 & State Univ NY, Albany, 78. *Mem:* Am Physiol Soc; Am Asn Immunol; Brit Asn Immunologists; Biophys Soc; fel NY Acad Sci. *Res:* Hemorrhagic and burn shock; anaphylactic shock and blood substitutes; hemodynamics; myocardial failure; mechanism of erythrocyte sedimentation; spinal conduction; stimulants and depressants; immunophysiology; effects of hormones on antibody production; immunochemistry of anaphylactic mediator release. *Mailing Add:* Dept Physiol Stanford Univ Sch Med Stanford CA 94305

FEIGEN, LARRY PHILIP, b Everett, Mass, Mar 27, 42; m 65; c 2. MEDICAL PHYSIOLOGY. *Educ:* Northeastern Univ, BA, 64, MS, 66; Chicago Med Sch, Univ Health Sci, PhD(physiol & biophys), 74. *Prof Exp:* Instr physiol, Chicago Med Sch, Univ Health Sci, 73-74; asst prof, 74-81, ASSOC PROF PHYSIOL, MED SCH, TULANE UNIV, 81- *Concurrent Pos:* Prin investr, NIH, 81- *Mem:* Am Heart Asn; AAAS; Am Physiol Soc; NY Acad Sci; Sigma Xi. *Res:* Control of peripheral vascular resistance with emphasis on renal blood flow and function as influenced by the prostaglandin system; control of blood pressure. *Mailing Add:* Tulane Med Ctr 1430 Tulane Ave New Orleans LA 70112

FEIGENBAUM, ABRAHAM SAMUEL, b New York, NY, Mar 11, 29; m 52; c 3. BIOCHEMISTRY, NUTRITION. *Educ:* Rutgers Univ, BS, 51, MS, 59, PhD(nutrit), 62. *Prof Exp:* Inspection chemist, E R Squibb & Sons Div, Olin Mathieson Chem Corp, 54-56, assay methods anal chemist, 56-57; res asst nutrit, Poultry Dept, Rutgers Univ, 57-61; res scientist, NJ Bur Res Neurol & Psychiat, 61-73; assoc dir med servs, Warren-Teed Labs, Inc, 73-81; CLIN PROJ DIR, PHARMACEUT RES INST, 81- *Mem:* NY Acad Sci; Am Inst Nutrit; Am Chem Soc; Soc Exp Biol & Med; Am Oil Chem Soc. *Res:* Lipid metabolism in chickens, including fatty liver etiology and atherosclerosis; genetic variation in susceptibility to experimentally-induced atherosclerosis and spontaneous arteriosclerosis in rabbits; potassium metabolism; clinical use chemically defined diets. *Mailing Add:* 2447 Seneca Park Pl Bexley OH 43209

FEIGENBAUM, EDWARD A(LBERT), b Weehawken, NJ, Jan 20, 36; m 58; c 2. COMPUTER SCIENCE, PSYCHOLOGY. *Educ:* Carnegie Inst Technol, BS, 56, PhD(indust admin), 60. *Prof Exp:* Fulbright res scholar, Gt Brit, 59-60; asst prof bus admin, Univ Calif, Berkeley, 60-64; assoc prof comput sci, 65-69, dir comput ctr, 65-69, PROF COMPUT SCI, STANFORD UNIV, 69-, CHMN DEPT, 76- *Concurrent Pos:* Consult indust & govt, 57-; mem comput & biomath sci study sect, NIH, 68-72. *Mem:* AAAS; Asn Comput Mach; Am Psychol Asn. *Res:* Information processing models of cognitive processes; artificial intelligence; programming languages; verbal learning; models of human memory. *Mailing Add:* Dept of Comput Sci Stanford Univ Stanford CA 94305

FEIGENBAUM, HARVEY, b East Chicago, Ind, Nov 20, 33; m 57; c 3. MEDICINE. *Educ:* Ind Univ, AB, 55, MD, 58. *Prof Exp:* Sr res assoc, Krannert Inst Cardiol, 62; from instr to assoc prof, 62-71, PROF MED, MED CTR, IND UNIV, 71- *Concurrent Pos:* Assoc med, Wishard Mem Hosp, 65. *Mem:* Am Fedn Clin Res; fel Am Col Physicians; fel Am Col Cardiol; Am Soc Echocardiography; Am Soc Clin Invest. *Res:* Clinical cardiology; electrophysiology; hemodynamics; echocardiography. *Mailing Add:* Ind Univ Med Ctr Indianapolis IN 46202

FEIGENBAUM, MITCHELL JAY, b Philadelphia, Pa, Dec 19, 44. DYNAMICAL SYSTEMS, CHAOS. *Educ:* City Col, NY, BEE, 64; Mass Inst Technol, PhD(theoret physics), 70. *Prof Exp:* Res assoc & instr physics, Cornell Univ, 70-72; res assoc physics, Va Polytech State Univ, 72-74; staff mem theoret physics, 74-80, LAB FEL, LOS ALAMOS NAT LAB, 81- *Concurrent Pos:* Vis mem, Inst Adv Studies, Princeton, 78 & Inst des Hautes Etudes Sci, France, 80-81; vis prof, Physics Dept, Cornell Univ, 81; ed, J Statist Physics, 81- *Mem:* Sigma Xi; NY Acad Sci. *Res:* Discoverer of metrically universal behaviors in dynamical systems; subject matter represent the major thrust in the theory of the onset of chaos, leading towards an understanding of turbulence in flows and other contexts. *Mailing Add:* Los Alamos Nat Lab Mail Stop 258 Los Alamos NM 87545

FEIGHAN, MARIA JOSITA, b Philadelphia, Pa, Aug 29, 32. PHYSICAL CHEMISTRY. *Educ:* Immaculata Col, Pa, AB, 64; Harvard Univ, MEd, 67; St Louis Univ, PhD(phys chem), 69. *Prof Exp:* Teacher high schs, Pa, 57-66; assoc prof chem, 69-80, asst acad dean, 74-76, PROF CHEM, IMMACULATA COL, 80-, DIR, EVENING DIV, 76- *Mem:* Am Chem Soc. *Res:* Educational programs on pollution; spectroscopic studies of nitro compounds. *Mailing Add:* Dept of Chem Immaculata Col Immaculata PA 19345

FEIGHNER, SCOTT DENNIS, b Alma, Mich, Apr 1, 51; m 72; c 2. ANAEROBIC BACTERIOLOGY, INFECTIOUS DISEASES. *Educ:* Western Mich Univ, BS, 73, MA, 75; Va Commmonwealth Univ, PhD(microbiol), 79. *Prof Exp:* Res assoc, Mich State Univ, 79-80, Syracuse Res Corp, 80; SR RES MICROBIOL, MERCK SHARP & DOHME RES LABS, MERCK & CO, INC, 81- *Mem:* Am Soc Microbiol; AAAS; NY Acad Sci. *Res:* Elucidation of the mechanisms of action of growth permittants in monogastric animals; interactions between gastrointestinal microflora and their hosts. *Mailing Add:* Merck Sharp & Dohme Res Labs PO Box 2000 Rahway NJ 07065

FEIGIN, IRWIN HARRIS, b New York, NY, May 13, 15; m 49; c 2. NEUROPATHOLOGY. *Educ:* Columbia Univ, BA, 34; NY Univ, MD, 38. *Prof Exp:* Res neuropathologist, Vet Admin Hosp, Bronx, 47-51; asst prof, Col Physicians & Surgeons, Columbia Univ, 52-56; assoc prof, 56-59, PROF NEUROPATH, COL MED, NY UNIV, 59- *Concurrent Pos:* Neuropathologist, Bellevue Hosp, 59-; pathologist, Sydenham Hosp, New York, 50-51; assoc pathologist, Mt Sinai Hosp, 51-56. *Mem:* Histochem Soc; Am Asn Neuropath. *Mailing Add:* Dept Path NY Univ Med Ctr New York NY 10016

FEIGIN, RALPH DAVID, b New York, NY, Apr 3, 38; m 60; c 3. PEDIATRICS, INFECTIOUS DISEASES. *Educ:* Columbia Univ, AB, 58; Boston Univ, MD, 62. *Prof Exp:* From intern to resident, Boston City Hosp, 62-64; resident, Children's Serv, Mass Gen Hosp, 64-65, chief resident, 67-68; from instr to prof pediat, Washington Univ, St Louis, 68-77, dir, Div Infectious Dis, Dept Pediat, 73-77; J S ABERCROMBIE PROF PEDIAT & CHMN DEPT, BAYLOR COL MED, 77- *Concurrent Pos:* Fel pediat, Harvard Med Sch, 64-65 & 67-68; Nat Inst Allergy & Infectious Dis res career develop award, 70; clin asst, Mass Gen Hosp, Boston, 67-68; asst pediatrician, St Louis Children's, St Louis Maternity & McMillan Hosps, 68; assoc pediatrician, Mo Crippled Children's Serv, 68; assoc dir, Clin Res Ctr, Wash Univ, 68, mem adv comt, 68-77, mem safety comt, Joint Med Adv Bd, 71-77; mem med records comt, St Louis Children's Hosp, 70-71; physician-in-chief, Tex Children's Hosp & Pediat Serv, Harris County Hosp Dist, Houston, 77- *Mem:* AAAS; Am Fedn Clin Res; Am Soc Microbiol; Soc Pediat Res; Infectious Dis Soc Am (pres elect, 81-82). *Res:* Metabolic response of the host to infectious diseases, including the effect of time of infectious exposure upon the outcome of disease. *Mailing Add:* Dept of Pediat 1200 Moursund Ave Houston TX 77030

FEIGL, DOROTHY MARIE, b Evanston, Ill, Feb 25, 38. ORGANIC CHEMISTRY. *Educ:* Loyola Univ, Ill, BS, 61; Stanford Univ, PhD(org chem), 66. *Prof Exp:* Res assoc org chem, NC State Univ, 65-66; from asst prof to assoc prof, 66-75, PROF ORG CHEM, ST MARY'S COL, IND, 75-, CHMN DEPT CHEM & PHYSICS, 77- *Concurrent Pos:* Consult, Int Bakers Serv, Inc, 74-76; Extramural Assoc, NIH, 81-82. *Mem:* Am Chem Soc; Royal Soc Chem; Sigma Xi. *Res:* Structure of the Grignard reagent; mechanism of the Grignard reduction reaction; steroid chemistry; polymer chemistry; flavor chemistry. *Mailing Add:* Dept of Chem St Mary's Col Notre Dame IN 46556

FEIGL, ERIC O, b Iowa City, Iowa, June 5, 33; m 57; c 2. PHYSIOLOGY. *Educ:* Univ Minn, BA & BS, 54, MD, 58. *Prof Exp:* Intern, Philadelphia Gen Hosp, 58-59; instr physiol, Sch Med, Univ Pa, 59-61; vis scientist, Gothenburg Univ, 61-62; instr physiol, Sch Med, George Washington Univ, 62-64; asst prof, Sch Med, Univ Pa, 64-69; assoc prof, 69-72, PROF PHYSIOL, SCH MED, UNIV WASH, 72- *Concurrent Pos:* NIH fel, 59-62 & res career develop award, 64-69; res assoc, Nat Heart Inst, 62-64; mem, Basic Sci Coun, Circulation Coun & adv bd, High Blood Pressure Coun, Am Heart Asn. *Mem:* AAAS; Am Physiol Soc; Microcirculation Soc; Cardiac Muscle Soc. *Res:* Coronary circulation; neural control of the circulation; cardiovascular instrumentation. *Mailing Add:* Dept of Physiol SJ-40 Univ of Wash Sch of Med Seattle WA 98105

FEIGL, FRANK JOSEPH, b Chicago, Ill, Mar 5, 36; m 60; c 3. SOLID STATE PHYSICS. *Educ:* Univ Notre Dame, AB, 58; Univ Pittsburgh, PhD(physics), 65. *Prof Exp:* Res assoc metal physics, Mat Res Lab, Univ Ill, Urbana-Champaign, 65-67; from asst prof to assoc prof, 67-76, PROF PHYSICS, LEHIGH UNIV, 76-, SR STAFF MEM, MAT RES CTR, 67-, COORDR, SHERMAN FAIRCHILD LAB SOLID STATE STUDIES, 78- *Mem:* Am Phys Soc. *Res:* Physical properties of thin solid films and solid-solid interfaces; solid state transport; optical processes; magnetic resonance. *Mailing Add:* Fairchild Lab 161 Lehigh Univ Bethlehem PA 18015

FEIGL, POLLY CATHERINE, b Minneapolis, Minn, July 30, 35; m 57; c 2. BIOSTATISTICS. *Educ:* Univ Chicago, BA & BS, 56; Univ Minn, MA, 57, PhD(biostatist), 61. *Prof Exp:* Statistician, Smith Kline & French Labs, 58-61; math statistician, Nat Cancer Inst, 62-64; Res Assoc Med Statist, Sch Med, Univ Pa, 64-67, asst prof, 67-69; from asst prof to assoc prof, 69-77, PROF BIOSTATIST, SCH PUB HEALTH & COMMUNITY MED, UNIV WASH, 77- *Mem:* Am Statist Asn; Biomet Soc; fel Am Statist Asn; mem Int Statist Inst. *Res:* Statistical design and analysis of biomedical experiments. *Mailing Add:* Dept of Biostatist SC32 Univ of Wash Seattle WA 98195

FEIGN, DAVID, b New York, NY, Apr 28, 23; m 54; c 4. COMPUTER SCIENCE. *Educ:* City Col New York, BMechE, 44; Univ Buffalo, MS, 53; Univ Calif, Irvine, PhD(comput sci), 80. *Prof Exp:* Res aerodynamicist, Nat Adv Comt Aeronaut, 44-48; Cornell Aeronaut Labs, 48-59, head digital comput sect, 53-59; head, Software Develop Autonetics Div, NAm Aviation, Inc, 59-75; mem tech staff, Space Div, Rockwell Int, 75-79; CONSULT SOFTWARE & SYSTS, 67. *Concurrent Pos:* Instr, Canisius Col, 58, Univ Calif, Irvine, 66-69 & West Coast Univ, 75-77; teacher, Eldorado Sch Gifted Child, 61-66; assoc prof & dir, Comput Ctr, Champman Col, 78-79; res engr, Univ Calif, Irvine, 69-71. *Mem:* Asn Comput Mach; Inst Elec & Electronic Engrs. *Res:* Digital computers; artificial intelligence; software engineering; programming languages. *Mailing Add:* 1301 Landfair Circle Santa Ana CA 92705

FEIKER, GEORGE E(DWARD), JR, b Northampton, Mass, May 6, 18; m 40; c 3. ELECTRICAL ENGINEERING. *Educ:* Worcester Polytech Inst, BS, 39; Harvard Univ, MS, 40. *Prof Exp:* Asst elec eng, Calif Inst Technol, 40-41; engr, 41-48, mgr microwave eng, 48-57, mgr radio frequency & commun eng, 57-64, mgr electronic eng lab, 64-65, mgr electronic physics lab, 65-69, mgr advan systs studies, 69-78, CONSULT, GEN ELEC CO, 78- *Concurrent Pos:* Instr, Rensselaer Polytech Inst, 46-48. *Honors & Awards:* Coffin Award, Gen Elec Co. *Mem:* Inst Elec & Electronics Engrs. *Res:* Research and development in electrical power conversion and control; communications; microwave generation and radiation. *Mailing Add:* 883 Inman Rd Schenectady NY 12309

FEILER, WILLIAM A, JR, b Paducah, Ky, Oct 9, 40; m 62; c 3. INDUSTRIAL CHEMISTRY. *Educ:* Univ Ky, BS, 62; Univ Fla, PhD(chem), 65. *Prof Exp:* Res chemist, Monsanto Co, 65-70, res group leader, 70-79, mgr technol, 79-81; DIR PROCESS & ANAL RES, EDWIN COOPER DIV, ETHYL CORP, 81- *Mem:* Am Chem Soc; Am Inst Chem Engrs. *Res:* Process development, with emphasis on solvent extraction technology for inorganic materials; phosphate salts, household detergents and elemental phosphorus; oil additives. *Mailing Add:* 1891 Charmwood Ct St Louis MO 63122

FEIN, ALVIN ELI, b Cleveland, Ohio, Jan 29, 31; m 56; c 2. APPLIED MATHEMATICS. *Educ:* Case Inst Technol, BS, 52; Mass Inst Technol, PhD(physics), 58. *Prof Exp:* Res physicist, Westinghouse Res & Develop Ctr, 56-62, assoc dir appl math, Surface Div, Westinghouse Defense & Space Ctr, 62-68; PRES, FEIN-MARQUART ASSOCS, INC, 68- *Mem:* Asn Comp Mach; Am Phys Soc; Am Math Soc; Inst Elec & Electronics Engrs; Soc Indust & Appl Math. *Res:* Custom computer software; chemical information systems; information science; data processing; system analysis; statistics; information retrieval; operations research. *Mailing Add:* Fein-Marquart Assocs Inc 7215 York Rd Baltimore MD 21212

FEIN, BURTON IRA, b New York, NY, May 20, 40; m 68; c 1. ALGEBRA. *Educ:* Polytech Inst Brooklyn, BSc, 61; Univ Wis, MSc, 62; Univ Ore, PhD(math), 65. *Prof Exp:* Asst prof math, Univ Calif, Los Angeles, 65-70; assoc prof, 70-77, PROF MATH ORE STATE UNIV, 77- *Concurrent Pos:* Res fel, Alexander von Humboldt Found, 76-77. *Mem:* Am Math Soc. *Res:* Braner groups of fields, division algebras, algegraic number theory; Schur index questions in the representation theory of finite groups. *Mailing Add:* Dept Math Ore State Univ Cowallis OR 97330

FEIN, HARVEY L(ESTER), b Washington, DC, Mar 4, 36; m 73; c 2. CHEMICAL ENGINEERING. *Educ:* Cornell Univ, BChE, 59; Mass Inst Technol, SM, 61, ScD(chem eng), 63. *Prof Exp:* Res engr, Atlantic Res Corp, 63-66, head thermodyn sect, 66-67, staff scientist, Propulsion & Eng Res Dept, 67-75; sr chem engr & task mgr, Energy Eng Div, TRW, Inc, 75-80, mgr process eng, 80-81; PROJ LEADER, US SYNTHETIC FUELS CORP, 81- *Mem:* Am Chem Soc; Am Inst Aeronaut & Astronaut; Am Inst Chem Engrs. *Res:* Coal gasification; coal liquefaction; systems analysis; thermodynamic cycle analysis; energy conversion processes; theoretical and experimental combustion kinetics; gas dynamics; propulsion system analysis; solid propellants; chemical thermodynamics; polymer physics; diffusion. *Mailing Add:* 6444 Elmdale Rd Alexandria VA 22312

FEIN, JACK M, b New York, NY, Mar 10, 40; c 1. SURGERY. *Educ:* New York Univ, BA, 61, MD, 65. *Prof Exp:* Instr surg neurosurg & attend surg, Georgetown Univ Sch Med, 73-74; asst prof neurosurg, 74-77, ASST PROF VASCULAR SURG, A EINSTEIN COL MED, 77-, ASSOC PROF NEUROSURG, 78- *Concurrent Pos:* Vis prof microsurg, Theo Gildred Ctr, Univ Fla, 77, Downstate Med Ctr, NY & Karolinska Inst, Sweden, 78, Loyola Univ & NY Univ Med Ctr, 79, Neurol Inst, Columbia Univ & Jefferson Med Col, 80; res career develop award, NIH, 76-81; consult, The Pres Comn Ethical Issues in Med, 81-85. *Honors & Awards:* Irving Wright Award Res Cerebrovascular Dis, Am Heart Asn, 74. *Res:* Cerebral ischemia and the biochemical and physiological changes associated with its treatment. *Mailing Add:* Albert Einstein Col Med 1300 Morris Park Ave Bronx NY 10461

FEIN, JAY SHELDON, b Brooklyn, NY, July 6, 37; m 66. ATMOSPHERIC SCIENCE. *Educ:* Rutgers Univ, BS, 62; Fla State Univ, MS, 66, PhD(meteorol), 72. *Prof Exp:* Weather forecaster, US Air Force, 62-65; asst prof meteorol, Univ Okla, 73-79; assoc prog dir, 76-80, PROG DIR ATMOSPHERIC SCI, NSF, 80- *Mem:* Am Meteorol Soc. *Res:* Large-scale atmospheric circulations; geophysical fluid dynamics. *Mailing Add:* Global Atmospheric Res Prog Nat Sci Found Washington DC 20550

FEIN, MARVIN MICHAEL, b Brooklyn, NY, July 31, 23; m 46; c 2. ORGANIC CHEMISTRY. *Educ:* Brooklyn Col, AB, 43; Purdue Univ, MS, 48, PhD(org chem), 49. *Prof Exp:* Res chemist, Schenley Labs, 49-50 & Nat Aniline Div, Allied Chem & Dye Corp, 50-55; sect supvr appl chem res, Reaction Motors Div, Thiokol Chem Corp, 56-64; mgr indust org chem & acetylenic chem res & develop, GAF Corp, 64-67, asst mgr res & develop dept, 67, tech dir dyestuff & chem prod, 67-70; vpres res & develop, Chem Specialties, 70-72, VPRES RES & DEVELOP, CHEM-PLASTICS GROUP, DART INDUSTS INC, 72- *Mem:* AAAS; Am Inst Chemists; Sigma Xi; Am Chem Soc; Asn Res Dirs. *Res:* Nitration; fluorination; organometallics; polymers; detergents; acetylenics; dyestuffs; pollution control; catalysts; agricultural chemistry; polymer additives. *Mailing Add:* Chem-Plastics Group Dart Industs Inc PO Box 37 Paramus NJ 07652

FEIN, R(ICHARD) S(AUL), b Milwaukee, Wis, Apr 25, 23; m 48; c 3. CHEMICAL ENGINEERING. *Educ:* Univ Wis, BS, 47, PhD(chem eng), 49. *Prof Exp:* Asst, Naval Res Lab, Univ Wis, 46-49; chem engr, 49-57, group leader, 57-64, res assoc, 64-68, fundamental res supvr, 68-77, SR RES ASSOC, TEXACO, INC, 77- *Honors & Awards:* Hunt Award, Am Soc Lubrication Engrs, 66. *Mem:* AAAS; Am Chem Soc; Sigma Xi; fel Am Soc Lubrication Engrs; Am Soc Mech Engrs. *Res:* Laminar flame speeds and temperatures; fuel applications, primarily in engines and vehicles; engine lubrication; fundamentals of boundary lubrication; combustion chemistry; atmospheric chemistry and physics. *Mailing Add:* 35 Sheldon Dr Poughkeepsie NY 12603

FEINBERG, BARRY N(ORMAN), b Chicago, Ill, Dec 24, 38; m 63. CLINICAL & ELECTRICAL ENGINEERING. *Educ:* Univ Mich, BSEMath & BSEE, 62; Univ Louisville, MEE, 64; Case Western Reserve Univ, PhD(systs eng), 69. *Prof Exp:* Instr math, Univ Louisville, 62-64; lectr control systs, Univ Edinburgh, 68-69; from asst prof to assoc prof elec eng, Cleveland State Univ, 69-76; assoc prof elec eng, sch elec eng, Purdue Univ, 76-81; SR SCIENTIST, BARRINGTON RES CTR, KENDALL CO, 81- *Concurrent Pos:* Res grant, Cleveland State Univ, 70; consult, Vet Admin Hosp, Cleveland, 71; chmn, bd examr in Clin Eng, 81. *Mem:* AAAS; Inst Elec & Electronics Engrs; Asn Advan Med Instrumentation; Nat Soc Prof Engrs. *Res:* Application of systems theory and control theory to the biomedical area, especially the use of mathematical models and optimization techniques for the detection and diagnosis of obstructive lung disease, asthma, bronchitis and emphysema; applied electrical engineering to instrumentation, x-ray and other medical radiation systems and patient electrical safety. *Mailing Add:* Kendall Res Ctr 411 Lake Zurich Rd Barrington IL 60010

FEINBERG, BENEDICT, plasma physics, see previous edition

FEINBERG, BENJAMIN ALLEN, b St Louis, Mo, Mar 23, 44; m 69. ANALYTICAL CHEMISTRY, BIOCHEMISTRY. *Educ:* Wash Univ, AB, 66; Univ Kans, PhD(chem), 71. *Prof Exp:* Res & teaching fel, Pa State Univ, 71-72; res fel, Northwestern Univ, 72-75; ASST PROF CHEM, UNIV WIS-MILWAUKEE, 75- *Mem:* Am Chem Soc. *Res:* Electroanalytical, biochemical and biophysical study of electron transfer mechanisms of redox proteins and enzymes; study of the influence of selective chemical modification upon the redox potential, structure and function of redox proteins. *Mailing Add:* Dept of Chem Univ of Wis Milwaukee WI 53201

FEINBERG, DONALD LESTER, b Brooklyn, NY, Dec 17, 25; m 62. NEUROLOGY, PEDIATRICS. *Educ:* Hamilton Col, NY, BA, 45; NY Univ, MD, 49. *Prof Exp:* Intern, NY Polyclin Med Sch & Hosp, 49-50; intern, Children's Med Ctr, Harvard Univ, 50-51; asst resident, Children's Hosp of Mich, 51-52; from jr resident to sr resident, Sarah Morris Children's Hosp of Michael Reese Hosp, Chicago, 52-54; from asst clin prof to asst prof pediat, NY Med Col, 56-69, neurologist, Med Retardation Inst, 74-76; neurol consult, Bernard Fineson Develop Ctr, 73-76, dir seizure serv, 76-79, MED SPECIALIST FOR THE BLIND, STATEN ISLAND DEVELOP CTR, 79- *Concurrent Pos:* Fel neurol, neurochem & pediat neurol, NY Mt Sinai Sch Med, 70-73; chief pediat outpatient dept, Metropolitan Hosp, 56-57; pediat consult maternity, Family Planning & Newborn Bur, New York City Health Dept, 61-69; clin prof, NY Polyclin Med Sch & Hosp, 60-64; dir pediat, Knickerbocker Hosp, New York, 62-64; assoc attend pediatrician neurol, Roosevelt-St Lukes Hosp Ctr, New York, 76-; asst clin prof pediat neurol, Col Physicians & Surgeons, Columbia Univ, 79- *Mem:* Fel Am Acad Pediat. *Mailing Add:* NY State Off Ment Retardation 2760 Victory Blvd Staten Island NY 10314

FEINBERG, GERALD, b New York, NY, May 27, 33; m 68; c 2. THEORETICAL HIGH ENERGY PHYSICS. *Educ:* Columbia Univ, BA, 53, MA, 54, PhD(physics), 57. *Prof Exp:* Mem sch math, Inst Advan Study, Princeton Univ, 56-57; res assoc, Brookhaven Nat Lab, 57-59; from asst prof to assoc prof, 59-65, PROF PHYSICS, COLUMBIA UNIV, 65-, CHMN, 80- *Concurrent Pos:* Adj asst prof & consult physics, NY Univ, 59; consult, Brookhaven Nat Lab, 59-74; overseas fel, Churchill Col, Cambridge, 63-64; vis prof, Rockefeller Univ, 73-74; Guggenheim fel, 73-74. *Mem:* Am Phys Soc. *Res:* Elementary particles; field theory. *Mailing Add:* Dept of Physics Columbia Univ New York NY 10027

FEINBERG, HAROLD, b Chicago, Ill, June 20, 22; div; c 2. PHARMACOLOGY. *Educ:* Univ Calif, Los Angeles, BA, 48, MA, 50; Univ Calif, Berkeley, PhD(physiol), 52. *Prof Exp:* Life Ins med res fel, Univ Calif, 52-53; chief biochemist, Children's Mem Hosp & instr biochem, Med Sch, Northwestern Univ, 53-55; res assoc, Cardiovasc Dept, Med Res Inst,

Michael Reese Hosp, 55-61; res assoc biochem, Univ Birmingham, 61-63; assoc prof, 63-70, PROF PHARMACOL, UNIV ILL COL MED, 70- *Concurrent Pos:* Am Heart Asn res fel, 56-58 & adv res fel, 58-60, estab investr, 60-65. *Mem:* Am Chem Soc; Am Physiol Soc; Am Soc Pharmacol & Exp Therapeut; Am Asn Advan Animal Lab Care (pres, 79-80). *Res:* Cardiovascular physiology, platelets and hemostasis; metabolism of cardiac muscle; ionflux of human blood platelets in response to physiologic stimuli; metabolism and function of heart. *Mailing Add:* Dept of Pharm Univ of Ill Sch Med Chicago IL 60612

FEINBERG, IRWIN, b Brooklyn, NY, June 11, 28; m 59. PSYCHIATRY. *Educ:* Brooklyn Col, BA, 49; Swarthmore Col, MA, 51; NY Univ, MD, 55. *Prof Exp:* Asst psychol, Swarthmore Col, 49-50; intern, Boston City Hosp, 55-56; resident psychiat, Boston Psychopathic Hosp, 56-57; res psychiatrist, Nat Inst Ment Health, 57-64; from asst prof to prof psychiat, State Univ NY Downstate Med Ctr, 64-69; PROF PSYCHIAT, UNIV CALIF, SAN FRANCISCO, 69-, VCHMN DEPT, 70- *Concurrent Pos:* Fel, Harvard Med Sch, 56-57; Nat Inst Ment Health trainee, Inst Sci Educ, Geneva, 60-61; prof psychiat, Med Sch NY Univ, 79-80; chief psychiat serv, Ft Miley Vet Admin Hosp, 69-79. *Mem:* AAAS. *Res:* Clinical and experimental psychiatry; sleep patterns in mental illness and in normal and pathological aging. *Mailing Add:* Ft Miley Vet Admin Hosp 42nd Ave & Clement St San Francisco CA 94121

FEINBERG, JERRY MARK, mathematics, physics, see previous edition

FEINBERG, MARTIN ROBERT, b New York, NY, Apr 2, 42; m 65. CHEMICAL ENGINEERING. *Educ:* Cooper Union, BChE, 62; Purdue Univ, MS, 63; Princeton Univ, PhD(chem eng), 68. *Prof Exp:* asst prof, 67-80, ASSOC PROF CHEM ENG, UNIV ROCHESTER, 80- *Concurrent Pos:* Dreyfus teacher-scholar, Camille & Henry Dreyfus Found, 73. *Mem:* Am Inst Chem Engrs; Soc Natural Philos. *Res:* Applied mathematics; thermodynamics; mathematics of complex chemical reaction systems. *Mailing Add:* Dept of Chem Eng Univ of Rochester Rochester NY 14627

FEINBERG, MELVYN JOEL, chemical physics, see previous edition

FEINBERG, ROBERT JACOB, b Chelsea, Mass, Apr 6, 31; m 64; c 2. HEALTH PHYSICS, ENVIRONMENTAL SCIENCES. *Educ:* Boston Col, BS, 53, MS, 54; Univ Rochester, MS, 55; Oak Ridge Sch Reactor Technol, dipl(nuclear eng), 56; Am Bd Health Physics, cert, 61 & 80. *Prof Exp:* Weapons physicist, Picatinny Arsenal, Divor, NJ, 51-52; physicist, Nat Bur Standards, 52-53; astrophysicist, Air Force Cambridge Res Ctr, 53-54; health physicist, Brookhaven Nat Lab, 54-55; nuclear engr, Oak Ridge Nat Lab, 55-56; physicist, 56-58, supv physicist radiol physics & eng, 58-62, proj engr radiol eng, 62-63, supvr nuclear & radiol safety, 63-66, MGR HEALTH PHYSICS & NUCLEAR SAFETY, GEN ELEC CO, KNOLLS ATOMIC POWER LAB, 66- *Concurrent Pos:* Mem, Atomic Indust Forum, 58- *Mem:* Int Health Physics Soc; Am Nuclear Soc. *Res:* Radiological dosimetry; environmental hazards analyses; nuclear criticality safety evaluation; health effects of low-level ionizing radiation; atmospheric diffusion of effluents; internal dosimetry. *Mailing Add:* 1223 Godfrey Lane Schenectady NY 12309

FEINBERG, ROBERT SAMUEL, b Baltimore, Md, June 10, 40; m 71; c 1. BIO-ORGANIC CHEMISTRY. *Educ:* Harvard Univ, BA, 61; Oxford Univ, PhD(org chem), 65. *Prof Exp:* Res assoc, McCollum Pratt Inst, Johns Hopkins Univ, 65-66 & org chem dept, 66-69; res assoc, Rockefeller Univ, 69-74, asst prof org chem, 74-76; secy-treas, 76-80, PRES, DURON, INC, 81- *Mem:* Am Chem Soc. *Res:* Hemoglobin model compounds; solid-phase synthesis of peptides and proteins. *Mailing Add:* Duron Inc 10406 Tucker St Beltsville MD 20705

FEINBERG, STEWART CARL, b Brooklyn, NY, July 7, 47; m 72; c 2. ORGANIC POLYMER CHEMISTRY. *Educ:* Brooklyn Col, BS, 69; Univ Akron, PhD(polymer sci), 76. *Prof Exp:* res chemist org polymers, Washington Res Ctr, W R Grace & Co, 75-79; RES CHEMIST, NEW POLYMER PROD RES & DEVELOP, ARCO CHEM CO, PA, 79- *Mem:* Am Chem Soc. *Res:* Applied research and product development in thermoplastic elastomers. *Mailing Add:* 3801 West Chester Pike Newton Square PA 19073

FEINBLUM, DAVID ALAN, b New York, NY, May 20, 40; m 64; c 2. APPLIED PHYSICS, ENGINEERING. *Educ:* Cooper Union, BME, 60; Rensselaer Polytech Inst, PhD(physics), 66. *Prof Exp:* Asst prof physics, State Univ NY, Albany, 64-71; prin mathematician mil res & develop, Sperry/Univac, 71-75; PRIN SCIENTIST, MIL RES & DEVELOP, XYBION CORP, 75- *Concurrent Pos:* Consult, Nuclear Fuel Serv, Inc, 65-66; vis fel, Princeton Univ, 67-68; fel, Weitzman Inst Sci, 69-70. *Mem:* Sigma Xi. *Res:* Engineering of software systems; signal processing. *Mailing Add:* Xybion Corp 7 Ridgedale Ave Cedar Knolls NJ 07927

FEINDEL, WILLIAM HOWARD, b Bridgewater, NS, July 12, 18; c 6. NEUROSURGERY. *Educ:* Acadia Univ, BA, 39; Dalhousie Univ, MSc, 42; McGill Univ, MD & CM, 45; Oxford Univ, DPhil(neuroanat), 49; Am Bd Neurol Surg, dipl 55; FRCS(C), 55. *Hon Degrees:* DSc, Acadia Univ, 63. *Prof Exp:* Med researcher, Exp Head Injuries, Montreal Neurol Inst, 42-44; lectr neurosurg, McGill Univ, 52-55; prof, Univ Sask, 55-59; chmn dept neurol & neurosurg, 72-77, CONE PROF NEUROSURG, McGILL UNIV, 59-, DIR MONTREAL NEUROL INST, 72- *Concurrent Pos:* Nat Res Coun Can fel med, Montreal Neurol Inst, 49-50, Reford fel, 53-55; Med Res Coun Can res grant, 56-; Can Cancer Found grant, 56-59; neurosurgeon-in-chief, Montreal Neurol Inst, 63-72; hon asst librn, Osler Libr, McGill Univ, 64-72; vis lectr, Yale Univ, 66; dir, Fourth Can Cong Neurol Sci, Montreal, 69; vis prof, Univ BC, 70-71; vis lectr, Univ Calif, San Francisco, 71- *Mem:* Am Acad Neurol; Am Acad Neurol Surg; Soc Neurol Surg; Am Asn Neurol Surg; Can Neurosurg Soc (pres, 68). *Res:* Clinical neurosurgery; cerebral edema; immersion foot; neurohistology of peripheral nervous system; anatomy of pain; temporal lobe function; radioisotopes in cerebral localization and circulation; 17th century medical history. *Mailing Add:* Montreal Neurol Inst 3801 University St Montreal PQ H3A 2B4 Can

FEINER, ROSE RESNICK, b New York, NY, May 23, 14; m 36; c 2. BACTERIOLOGY. *Educ:* Hunter Col, BA, 34; Columbia Univ, MA, 36, PhD(bact), 41. *Prof Exp:* Res asst bact, Columbia Univ, 35-37; instr physiol, Hunter Col, 37-39; res asst bact, Columbia Univ, 40-42; res asst, NY Univ, 43-44; res asst, Columbia Univ, 44-46, 49-52; instr, 52-55, lectr, 55-59, from instr to prof, 59-78, EMER PROF BIOL, CITY COL NEW YORK, 78- *Concurrent Pos:* Res assoc & vis scientist, Dept Microbiol, Col Physicians & Surgeons, Columbia Univ, 69-73. *Mem:* AAAS; Am Soc Microbiol. *Res:* Effects of physical and chemical agents on bacteria and bacteriophages. *Mailing Add:* Dept of Biol City Col of New York New York NY 10031

FEINGOLD, ADOLPH, b Poltava, USSR, Mar 8, 20; m 64; c 2. MECHANICAL ENGINEERING, ENGINEERING ECONOMICS. *Educ:* Univ Genoa, Italy, PhD, 52, DEng(naval archit & mech eng), 53. *Prof Exp:* From assoc prof to prof mech eng, Univ Mo-Rolla, 63-66; prof civil eng, 66-67, chmn, Dept Mech Eng, 67-71, gov, 76-79, PROF MECH ENG, UNIV OTTAWA, 67-; MGR, DESIGN ENG DIV, SYNCRUDE CAN LTD, 80- *Mem:* Brit Inst Marine Eng; Israel Soc Naval Archit & Marine Eng (pres, 61); Am Soc Mech Engrs; fel Eng Inst Can; Can Soc Mech Eng (vpres, 77-79). *Res:* Internal combustion engines; application of computers in design; heat transfer; arctic technology; low temperature environmental problems; marine engineering; ocean bed technology; resource policy alternatives. *Mailing Add:* Syncrude Can Ltd 10030 107th St Edmonton AB K1N 6N5 Can

FEINGOLD, ALEX JAY, b Baltimore, Md, Apr 1, 50; m 77. ALGEBRA. *Educ:* Johns Hopkins Univ, BA & MA, 71; Yale Univ, PhD(math), 77. *Prof Exp:* Jr instr math, Johns Hopkins Univ, 70-71; officer comput, US Pub Health Serv, 71-73; teaching asst math, Yale Univ, 75-77; asst prof, Drexel Univ, 77-79; ASST PROF MATH, STATE UNIV NY, 79- *Concurrent Pos:* Prin investr, NSF grant, Drexel Univ, 78-79 & State Univ NY, 80-82. *Mem:* Math Asn Am; Am Math Soc; Sigma Xi. *Res:* Pure mathematics in an area of algebra known as Kac-Moody Lie algebras. *Mailing Add:* Dept Math State Univ NY Binghamton NY 13901

FEINGOLD, ALFRED, b Sellersville, Pa, Jan 31, 41; m 66; c 2. ANESTHESIOLOGY. *Educ:* Dartmouth Col, BA, 62; Tufts Univ, MD, 66; Northwestern Univ, MS, 71. *Prof Exp:* Intern med, Univ Chicago Hosps & Clins, 66-67, resident anesthesia, 67-69; fel, Northwestern Univ Sch Med, 69-70; physician, Wright-Patterson AFB Hosp, 70-72; from asst prof to assoc prof anesthesia, Sch Med, Univ Miami, 72-77; STAFF MEM & DIR CARDIAC ANESTHESIA, CEDARS OF LEBANON HEALTH CARE CTR, 77- *Concurrent Pos:* Consult, AMA Panel Eval Fentanyl, 70; fel biomed eng, Technol Inst, Northwestern Univ, 70; staff mem, Jackson Mem Hosp & Miami Vet Admin Hosp, 72-77; dir anesthesiol, Bascom Palmer Eye Inst-Ann Bates Leach Eye Hosp, Miami, 76; adj assoc prof biomed eng, Univ Miami, 77- *Mem:* Am Soc Anesthesiol; Int Res Anesthesia Soc. *Res:* Pharmacokinetics of anesthetics; biotransformation of anesthetics; computer applications to anesthesiology and medicine; biomedical engineering; human factors engineering. *Mailing Add:* Dept of Anesthesiol Cedars of Lebanon Health Care Ctr Miami FL 33136

FEINGOLD, ARNOLD MOSES, b Brooklyn, NY, Dec 30, 20; m 54; c 2. NUCLEAR PHYSICS. *Educ:* Brooklyn Col, AB, 41; Princeton Univ, MS, 48, PhD(physics), 52. *Prof Exp:* Physicist, Langley Mem Aeronaut Lab, 41-46; from instr to asst prof, Univ Pa, 50-55; asst prof, Univ Ill, 55-57; assoc prof, Univ Utah, 57-60; PROF PHYSICS, STATE UNIV NY STONY BROOK, 60- *Mem:* AAAS; fel Am Phys Soc; Am Asn Physics Teachers. *Res:* Theoretical nuclear physics; tensor force effects in nuclei. *Mailing Add:* Dept of Physics State Univ of NY Stony Brook NY 11794

FEINGOLD, BEN F, b Pittsburgh, Pa, June 15, 00. ALLERGY, IMMUNOLOGY. *Educ:* Univ Pittsburgh, BS, 21, MD, 24. *Prof Exp:* Instr pediat, Med Sch, Northwestern Univ, 29-32; attend pediatrician, Cedars of Lebanon Hosp, Los Angeles, Calif, 32-40, chief dept pediat, 40-50; chief dept, 51-71, EMER CHIEF ALLERGY DEPT, PERMANENTE MED GROUP, KAISER FOUND HOSPS, 71-, DIR LAB MED ENTOM, RES INST, 59- *Concurrent Pos:* Attend pediatrician, Chicago Lying-In Hosp, 29-32 & Los Angeles County Hosp, 32-39; attend pediatrician & assoc allergy, Los Angeles Children's Hosp, 32-51. *Mem:* Fel Am Acad Allergy; fel Am Col Allergists; fel Am Acad Pediat. *Res:* Problems of clinical allergy; problems of immunology and immunochemistry, especially behavior of low molecular weight fractions and compounds in the antigen-antibody reaction. *Mailing Add:* 2200 O'Farrell St San Francisco CA 94115

FEINGOLD, DAVID SIDNEY, b Chelsea, Mass, Nov 15, 22; m 49; c 3. BIOCHEMISTRY. *Educ:* Mass Inst Technol, BS, 44; Hebrew Univ, PhD(biochem), 56. *Prof Exp:* Chemist, Lucidol Corp, 44; instr, Northeastern Univ, 46-47; chemist, Hadassah Hosp, Jerusalem, 50-51; asst, Med Sch, Hebrew Univ, 51-56; jr res biochemist, Univ Calif, Berkeley, 56-58, asst res biochemist, 58-60; from asst prof to prof biol, Fac Arts & Sci, 60-74, PROF MICROBIOL, SCH MED, UNIV PITTSBURGH, 66- *Concurrent Pos:* NIH res career develop award, 65-75. *Honors & Awards:* State of Israel Prize, 57. *Mem:* Am Chem Soc; Am Soc Biol Chem. *Res:* Intermediary carbohydrate metabolism; enzymic transformations of carbohydrates; biosynthesis of poly- and oligosaccharides; transglycosylation; structure of polysaccharides; enzyme mechanism; dehydrogenases. *Mailing Add:* Dept of Microbiol Univ of Pittsburgh Sch of Med Pittsburgh PA 15261

FEINGOLD, EARL, b Philadelphia, Pa, Dec 4, 24; m 47; c 2. SOLID STATE PHYSICS. *Educ:* Temple Univ, AB, 50, AM, 51, PhD(physics), 59. *Prof Exp:* Asst instr physics, Temple Univ, 49-51; res physicist, Brown Instrument Div, Minneapolis Honeywell Regulator Co, 51-52 & res ctr, Burroughs Corp, 52-54; solid state res physicist, Atlantic Refinery Co, 54-59; SOLID STATE PHYSICIST & MGR MAT ENG, ADVAN ENERGY PROGS DEPT, ENERGY SYSTS & TECHNOL DIV, GEN ELEC CO, 59- *Mem:* AAAS; Am Phys Soc; Sigma Xi; Int Metallog Soc. *Res:* Physical and chemical characterization of matter; electron and optical microscopy; x-ray diffraction and spectroscopy; refractory-high-strength-special purpose materials; materials sciences; surface properties; thin films; physical metallurgy. *Mailing Add:* King of Prussia PA 19406

FEININGER, TOMAS, b Stockholm, Sweden, Sept 21, 35; US citizen; m 63; c 3. GEOLOGY. *Educ:* Middlebury Col, BA, 56; Brown Univ, MSc, 60, PhD(geol), 64. *Prof Exp:* Geologist, Eng Geol Br, US Geol Surv, 56-59, Br Regional Geol, New Eng, 60-64 & Off Int Geol, 64-69; vis res assoc, Smithsonian Inst, 69-70; chmn, Dept Geol, Mining & Petrol, Nat Polytech Sch, Quito, Ecuador, 70-78; RESEARCHER, DEPT GEOL, LAVAL UNIV, QUEBEC, 78- *Mem:* AAAS; Geol Soc Am; Ecuadorian Inst Natural Sci; Geol Asn Can; Mineral Soc Am. *Res:* Metamorphic petrology and regional geology of the northern Andes. *Mailing Add:* Dept Geol Laval Univ Quebec PQ G1K 7P4 Can

FEINLAND, RAYMOND, b New York, NY, Oct 12, 28; m 59. COSMETIC CHEMISTRY. *Educ:* Brooklyn Col, BS, 49; Polytech Inst Brooklyn, MS, 52, PhD(chem), 57. *Prof Exp:* Sr res chemist, Am Cyanamid Co, Conn, 57-65; mgr anal res, 65-71, assoc dir, 71-80, DIR, PROD DEVELOP, CLAIROL INC, 80- *Mem:* Soc Cosmetic Chemists; Am Chem Soc. *Res:* Cosmetic products; ion exchange resins; hair bleaching; chromatography; spectrophotometry; general analytical techniques; hair color products. *Mailing Add:* Clairol Inc 2 Blachley Rd Stamford CT 06922

FEINLEIB, JULIUS, b Brooklyn, NY, Sept 17, 36; m 61. SOLID STATE PHYSICS. *Educ:* Cornell Univ, BEngPhys, 58; Harvard Univ, MA, 59, PhD(appl & solid state physics), 63. *Prof Exp:* Fel, Harvard Univ, 63-64; staff physicist, Lincoln Lab, Mass Inst Technol, 64-69; mem staff, Energy Conversion Devices, Inc, 69-71; MGR, PHYSICS LAB, ITEK CORP, 71- *Mem:* Am Phys Soc. *Res:* High pressure physics of semiconductors; nuclear resonance in magnetic materials; optical properties of magnetic materials; amorphous semiconductors and optical computer memories. *Mailing Add:* 22 Whittier St Cambridge MA 02140

FEINLEIB, MANNING, b Brooklyn, NY, July 19, 35; m 57; c 3. BIOSTATISTICS, EPIDEMIOLOGY. *Educ:* Cornell Univ, AB, 56; State Univ NY Downstate Med Ctr, MD, 61; Harvard Univ, MPH, 63, DrPH, 66. *Prof Exp:* Instr statist, State Univ NY, 58-59; med officer epidemiol, 66-68, CHIEF FIELD EPIDEMIOL RES SECT, NAT HEART LUNG & BLOOD INST, NIH, 68-, CHIEF EPIDEMIOL BR, 79- *Concurrent Pos:* Fel epidemiol, Sch Pub Health, Harvard Univ, 63-66; asst med, Peter Bent Brigham Hosp, 62-66; assoc registr, Mass Tumor Registry, 64-66; asst prof, Sch Pub Health, Harvard Univ, 66-68. *Mem:* AAAS; Am Pub Health Asn; Am Statist Asn; Biomet Soc; Am Epidemiol Soc. *Res:* Epidemiology of heart disease. *Mailing Add:* Epidemiol Br Fed Bldg 2C08 Nat Heart & Lung Inst Bethesda MD 20205

FEINLEIB, MARY ELLA (HARMAN), b Italy, May 21, 38; US citizen. PLANT PHYSIOLOGY. *Educ:* Cornell Univ, AB, 59; Radcliffe Col, AM, 61; Harvard Univ, PhD(biol), 66. *Prof Exp:* From instr to asst prof, 65-72, ASSOC PROF BIOL, TUFTS UNIV, 72-, CHMN DEPT, 76- *Mem:* AAAS; Am Soc Photobiol. *Res:* Phototaxis in algae, specifically in Chlamydomonas. *Mailing Add:* Dept of Biol Tufts Univ Medford MA 02155

FEINLEIB, MORRIS, b Berlin, Ger, July 16, 24; nat US; wid; c 2. CHEMICAL ENGINEERING, ELECTROCHEMISTRY. *Educ:* Columbia Univ, BS, 44, MS, 45, PhD(chem eng), 48. *Prof Exp:* Res electrochemist, metals res dept, Armour Res Found, Ill, 48-52; res electrochemist & group leader, reduction res sect, Kaiser Aluminum & Chem Corp, Wash & Calif, 52-58; res scientist, electrochem sect, missiles & space div, Lockheed Aircraft Corp, 58-59; sr res engr, tube res dept, 59-63, mgr tube process develop, 63-67, chem vapor deposition pilot facility, cent res, 67-69, mgr photoconductor prep, electrophotog unit, 69-75, mgr mat & processes, Graphics Div, 75-79, MGR MAT RES & DEVELOP, PALO ALTO MICROWAVE TUBE DIV, VARIAN ASSOCS, 79- *Mem:* Electrochem Soc; Am Chem Soc. *Res:* High temperature materials and methods, including fused salts, chemical vapor deposition; batteries; electroplating; materials and chemical processes in electronics; special photoconductors and materials for electrophotography and electrostatic printing. *Mailing Add:* Palo Alto Microwave Tube Div 611 Hansen Way Palo Alto CA 94303

FEINMAN, J(EROME), b Brooklyn, NY, Mar 18, 28; m 54; c 3. FLUIDIZED BED TECHNOL. *Educ:* Polytech Inst Brooklyn, BChE, 49; Ill Inst Technol, MSChE, 56; Univ Pittsburgh, PhD(chem eng), 64. *Prof Exp:* From proj engr to sr proj engr, US Steel Corp, 52-60, sect head, ore reduction technol sect, 60-64, sr process engr process eng div, 64-65, assoc res consult, 65-, res consult, Raw Mat & Ore Reduction Div, Res Lab, 76-80; DIR, TECH DEVELOP, OCCIDENTAL OIL SHALE, INC, 80- *Concurrent Pos:* Mem bd dir & tech adv comt, Particulate Solid Res, Inc, 77- *Mem:* Am Chem Soc; Am Inst Chem Engrs; Metall Soc; Iron & Steel Soc; Am Inst Mining, Metall & Petrol Engrs. *Res:* Ferrous and nonferrous metallurgical process development and design; direct reduction of iron ore; fluidization; coal gasification and high temperature cleanup; process technical and economic evaluation and engineering; recovery and treatment of shale oil. *Mailing Add:* Occidental Oil Shale Inc PO Box 2687 Grand Junction CO 81502

FEINMAN, MAX L, b New York, NY, May 13, 05; m 33; c 2. SURGERY, ANATOMY. *Educ:* State Univ NY Downstate Med Ctr, MD, 28. *Prof Exp:* Assoc anat, Long Island Col Hosp, 50-54; attend surgeon, Wyckoff Heights Hosp, Brooklyn, NY, 58-64; DIR MED EDUC, DOCTORS HOSP, 64-; PROF ANAT & SURG, M J LEWI COL PODIATRY, 65- *Concurrent Pos:* Fel anat, Long Island Col Hosp, 47-51; surgeon, Coney Island Hosp, 49-54; dir surg, Lefferts Gen Hosp, Brooklyn, NY, 58-63. *Res:* General surgery; traumatic surgery. *Mailing Add:* 25 Sutton Pl S New York NY 10022

FEINMAN, RICHARD DAVID, b Brooklyn, NY, July 19, 40. BIOCHEMISTRY. *Educ:* Univ Rochester, BA, 63; Univ Ore, PhD(chem), 69. *Prof Exp:* asst prof biochem, 69-80, ASSOC PROF BIOCHEM, STATE UNIV NY DOWNSTATE MED CTR, 80- *Concurrent Pos:* Fac mem, New Sch Social Res, 73- *Res:* Enzyme mechanism; blood coagulation; mechanism of inhibitors of proteolytic enzymes from blood plasma and stimulus response coupling in blood platelets and neurons. *Mailing Add:* Biochem Dept State Univ NY Downstate Med Ctr 450 Clarkson Ave Brooklyn NY 11203

FEINMAN, SUSAN (BIRNBAUM), b Atlanta, Ga, Sept 16, 30; c 3. MICROBIOLOGY. *Educ:* Wellesley Col, BA, 51; George Washington Univ, MS, 52, PhD(microbiol), 69. *Prof Exp:* Res asst pharmacol, Beth Israel Hosp, Harvard Med Sch, 52-53; teaching fel microbiol, Med Sch, George Washington Univ, 66-68; supvry microbiologist immunol, Lab Serol, Div Labs, Govt Washington, DC, 68-69; tech info specialist pharmacol, NIMH, HEW, 71-74; microbiologist drug resistance antibiotics, Bur Vet Med, Food & Drug Admin, 74-79; BIOLOGIST SUPVR IMMUNOL/TOXICOL, HEALTH SCI, US CONSUMER PROD SAFETY COMN, 79- *Concurrent Pos:* Nat Cancer Inst fel, Lab Microbiol, Nat Inst Allergy & Infectious Dis, NIH, Bethesda, 69-71. *Honors & Awards:* Commendation, Food & Drug Admin, 77; Qual Increase Award, Bur Vet Med, 77. *Mem:* Am Soc Microbiol; AAAS; Sigma Xi; Am Col Toxicol. *Res:* Effect of antibiotics in animal feeds on drug resistance; environmental impacts of antibiotics; arsenic-resistant E coli R-plasmids; hypersensitivity effects and toxicology of environmental chemicals; immunology of streptococcal L-forms; immunology of atypical mycobacteria. *Mailing Add:* Div Poison Prev Consumer Prod Safety Comn 5401 Westbard Ave Bethesda MD 20207

FEINSINGER, PETER, b Madison, Wis, July 16, 48. ECOLOGY. *Educ:* Colo Col, BA, 69; Cornell Univ, PhD(ecol, evolutionary biol), 74. *Prof Exp:* Vis asst prof zool, Ind Univ, 74; asst prof biol sci, Univ Denver, 75-76; asst prof, 76-80, ASSOC PROF ZOOL, UNIV FLA, 80- *Concurrent Pos:* NSF grant, 80. *Mem:* Ecol Soc Am; Soc Study Evolution; Asn Tropical Biol; Am Ornithologists Union; Brit Ecol Soc. *Res:* Community organization and coevolution in neotropical nectar-feeding birds and bird-pollinated plants. *Mailing Add:* Dept Zool Univ Fla Gainesville FL 32611

FEINSTEIN, ALEJANDRO, b La Plata, Arg, May 30, 29; m 59; c 3. ASTROPHYSICS. *Educ:* Univ La Plata, astronr, 56, DrAstron, 60. *Prof Exp:* Observer asst astron, 48-56, instr, 52-56, tech asst, 56-62, asst prof astrophys, 62-63, instr math, Fac Phys Sci & Math, 58-61, PROF ASTROPHYSICS, ASTRON OBSERV, UNIV LA PLATA, 63- *Concurrent Pos:* Nat Coun Sci & Tech Res, Arg fel, Lick Observ, Univ Calif, 61-62; Guggenheim Mem Found fel, Steward Observ, Univ Ariz, 69-70. *Mem:* Arg Astron Asn; Royal Astron Soc; Astron Soc Pac; Int Astron Union; NY Acad Sci. *Res:* Stellar photoelectric photometry, including infrared; open clusters; galactic structure. *Mailing Add:* Observ Astron Paseo Del Bosque La Plata 1900 Argentina

FEINSTEIN, ALLEN IRWIN, b Brooklyn, NY, Apr 9, 40; m 62; c 3. ORGANIC CHEMISTRY. *Educ:* Brooklyn Col, BS, 62; Iowa State Univ, PhD(alkaloid biosynthesis), 67. *Prof Exp:* Wax chemist, Austenal Co Div, Howe Sound Corp, 62; res chemist, 67-78, SR RES CHEMIST, AMOCO CHEM CORP, 78- *Concurrent Pos:* Instr, Aurora Col, 70- & chem, Elmhurst Col, 75- *Mem:* Am Chem Soc. *Res:* Vapor phase oxidations; heterogeneous catalysis. *Mailing Add:* Amoco Chem Corp Res & Develop Box 400 Naperville IL 60540

FEINSTEIN, ALVAN RICHARD, b Philadelphia, Pa, Dec 4, 25; m 68; c 2. INTERNAL MEDICINE. *Educ:* Univ Chicago, BS, 47, MS, 48, MD, 52. *Prof Exp:* Asst med, Rockefeller Inst, 54-56; clin dir rheumatic heart dis, Irvington House, 56-60, med dir, 60-62; clin biostatist, Eastern Res Support Ctr, Vet Admin Hosp, West Haven, 62-67, chief, 67-74; assoc prof, 64-69, PROF MED & EPIDEMIOL, SCH MED, YALE UNIV, 69-, DIR JOHNSON CLIN SCHOLAR PROG, 74- *Concurrent Pos:* Asst prof internal med, Col Med, NY Univ Med Ctr, 59-62; consult, Spec Serv Div, USPHS & PR Dept Health, 60. *Mem:* Inst Med-Nat Acad Sci; Am Fedn Clin Res; Asn Am Physicians; Am Epidemiol Soc; Am Soc Clin Invest. *Res:* Rheumatic fever; obesity; prognosis of cancer; clinical pharmacology and biostatistics; clinical epidemiology; clinimetrics. *Mailing Add:* Dept of Med Yale Univ Sch of Med New Haven CT 06510

FEINSTEIN, CHARLES DAVID, b New York, NY, Oct 23, 46; m 80. OPTIMIZATION THEORY, MATHEMATICAL MODELING. *Educ:* Cooper Union, BSME, 67; Stanford Univ, MS, 68, MS, 78, PhD(eng & econ syst), 80. *Prof Exp:* Engr, Stanford Res Inst, 75-76, Xerox Corp, 76-81; SR DECISION ANALYST, APPL DECISION ANAL, INC, 81- *Concurrent Pos:* Consult asst prof, Eng & Econ Syst, Stanford Univ, 80- *Res:* Optimal control theory; mathematical programming; dynamic systems; forecasting; stochastic choice theory. *Mailing Add:* 390 Bethany Dr Scotts Valley CA 95066

FEINSTEIN, HYMAN ISRAEL, b Brooklyn, NY, Apr 9, 11; m 43. ANALYTICAL CHEMISTRY. *Educ:* Univ Mich, AB, 30; Columbia Univ, MA, 32. *Prof Exp:* Asst instr, Long Island Univ, 30-36; chemist, Nat Bur Stand, 36-40, Customs Bur Labs, 40-41 & Nat Bur Stand, 41-54; anal chemist, US Geol Surv, 54-58; lectr & assoc prof chem, George Mason Univ, 58-79. *Concurrent Pos:* Instr, Howard Univ, 43-48 & grad sch, Nat Bur Stand, 50-53; lectr, Cath Univ Am, 54. *Mem:* Am Chem Soc; Nat Sci Teachers Asn; Am Inst Chem. *Res:* Rare elements; trace analysis; mineral and rock analysis; uranium; thorium; vanadium; coordination compounds of chromium; chemical literature and education; chemical microscopy; microchemistry. *Mailing Add:* 10411 Forest Ave Fairfax VA 22030

FEINSTEIN, IRWIN K, b Chicago, Ill, Aug 29, 14; m 54; c 2. MATHEMATICAL ANALYSIS. *Educ:* Ill Inst Technol, BS, 36; Northwestern Univ, MA, 46, PhD(math educ), 52. *Prof Exp:* From instr to asst prof math, 46-60, from assoc prof to prof math educ, 60-66, PROF MATH, UNIV ILL, CHICAGO CIRCLE, 66- *Concurrent Pos:* Schwab Found lectr, Mus Sci & Indust, Ill, 65-67. *Mem:* AAAS; Am Math Asn; Nat Coun Teachers Math; Sch Sci & Math Asn; Am Asn Univ Professors. *Mailing Add:* Dept of Math Univ of Ill at Chicago Circle Chicago IL 60680

FEINSTEIN, JOSEPH, b New York, NY, July 8, 25; m 52; c 3. PHYSICS, ELECTRICAL ENGINEERING. *Educ:* Cooper Union, BEE, 44; Columbia Univ, MA, 47; NY Univ, PhD(physics), 51. *Prof Exp:* Res physicist, Nat Bur Standards, 49-54; mem tech staff, Bell Tel Labs, 54-59; dir res, S-F-D Labs,

59-64; vpres res, Varian Assocs, 64-80; DIR, ELECTRONICS & PHYS SCI, OFF UNDER SECY DEFENSE RES & ENG, RES & ADVAN TECHNOL, DEPT DEFENSE, WASHINGTON, DC, 80- *Mem:* Nat Acad Eng; AAAS; fel Inst Elec & Electronics Engrs. *Res:* Electromagnetic theory; microwave electron tubes; power conversion; computers and peripherals. *Mailing Add:* Off Under Secy Defense Res & Eng Pentagon Rm 3D1079 Washington DC 20301

FEINSTEIN, LOUIS, b Philadelphia, Pa, Apr 20, 12; m 35; c 2. BIOCHEMISTRY. *Educ:* Univ Pa, AB, 33, BS, 34, MS, 39; Georgetown Univ, PhD(chem), 46. *Prof Exp:* Res chemist, Barrett Co, 34-35 & Sch Med, Univ Pa, 35-39; from jr chemist to chemist, Grain Br, Agr Res Serv, USDA, 39-47 & Bur Entom & Plant Quarantine, 47-53, sr res biochemist animal & poultry husb res, 53-56, supvry chemist & prin biochemist, Biol Sci Br, 56-60, asst chief, Field Crops & Animal Prods Res Br, Agr Res Serv, 60-67, chief, 67-73, chief, Seed Qual Lab, 73-74; CONSULT, 74- *Mem:* AAAS; Am Chem Soc; Entom Soc Am; Asn Off Anal Chem; fel Am Inst Chem. *Res:* Coal tar chemicals; liver and kidney metabolism; cereal chemistry; vitamins; plant alkaloids and insecticides; insect attractants and repellants; animal composition; quality evaluation of agricultural products. *Mailing Add:* 14757 Wild Flower Lane Delray Beach FL 33446

FEINSTEIN, MAURICE B, b New York, NY, Nov 28, 29; m 51; c 3. PHARMACOLOGY. *Educ:* Columbia Univ, BS, 52, MS, 54; State Univ NY, PhD(pharmacol), 60. *Prof Exp:* Res assoc physiol, Inst Muscle Dis, 60-62; from instr to assoc prof pharmacol, State Univ NY Downstate Med Ctr, 62-69; assoc prof, 69-80, PROF PHARMACOL, SCHS MED & DENT MED, UNIV CONN, 80- *Concurrent Pos:* USPHS grant, 63-65 & 69-74. *Mem:* Am Pharmacol Soc; Harvey Soc. *Res:* High energy phosphates; calcium fluxes in muscle; mechanisms of rigor in muscle and local anesthetic action; membrane structure; fluorescent probes; anesthetic effects on cell permeability and ion-channel proteins; ionophorous antibiotics; blood platelets; myelin structure. *Mailing Add:* Dept of Pharmacol Univ of Conn Health Ctr Farmington CT 06032

FEINSTEIN, MYRON ELLIOT, b New York, NY, Jan 7, 43; m 64; c 2. SURFACE CHEMISTRY. *Educ:* City Col New York, BS, 63, MA, 65; City Univ New York, PhD(phys chem), 67. *Prof Exp:* Lectr chem, City Col New York, 64-67; from res chemist to sr res chemist, Allied Chem Corp, 67-68; estab scientist, Unilever Res Lab, Eng, 68-70, mgr process develop soaps & detergents, Unilever Scand, 70-74, area prod mgr, Lever-Gibbs, Italy, 74-77, mfg mgr, Hammond, Ind, 77-81, PLANT MGR, LEVER BROS CO, LOS ANGELES, 81- *Concurrent Pos:* E I du Pont de Nemour res asst, 66. *Mem:* Am Chem Soc. *Res:* Production control; chemical process engineering; environmental engineering; wetting and detergency; colloidal surfactants; emulsions and foams; insoluble monolayers; surface potentials; fluorinated surfactants. *Mailing Add:* 965 S Grinnell St Anaheim Hills CA 92807

FEINSTEIN, ROBERT, b New York, NY, Nov 19, 40; m 64; c 2. BIOENGINEERING, ANESTHESIOLOGY. *Educ:* Pratt Inst, BS, 65; Univ Mich, MS, 67 & 68, PhD(bioeng), 70; Tex A&M, MD, 82. *Prof Exp:* Res assoc bioeng, Univ Mich, 70-71, asst res engr, 70-71; chief bioeng, Marine Biomed Inst, 71-75; asst prof physiol, Univ Tex Med Br, Galveston, 71-75, res scientist, Dept Surg, 75-78. *Concurrent Pos:* Consult, Highway Safety Res Inst & Human Performance Ctr, Univ Mich, 70-71; asst prof bioeng prog, Univ Tex Austin, 74-78. *Mem:* AAAS; Biomed Eng Soc; Inst Elec & Electronic Engrs; Asn Comput Mach. *Res:* Concepts of modern systems theory and control theory applied to the analysis and modeling of neurophysiological systems; intelligent use of computers in medicine. *Mailing Add:* 3019 Beluche Galveston TX 77551

FEINSTEIN, ROBERT NORMAN, b Milwaukee, Wis, Aug 10, 15; m 40; c 2. ENZYMOLOGY, BIOCHEMISTRY. *Educ:* Univ Wis, BS, 37, MS, 38, PhD(physiol chem), 40. *Prof Exp:* Asst, McArdle Mem Inst, Univ Wis, 38-39; res assoc metab & endocrinol, Michael Reese Hosp, Chicago, 40-41 & May Inst Med Res, Cincinnati, 46; from instr to assoc prof biochem, Univ Chicago, 47-79, researcher, US Air Force Radiation Lab, 47-54, res assoc, 47-79; sr biochemist, Argonne Nat Lab, 79-80; RETIRED. *Concurrent Pos:* Assoc scientist, Argonne Nat Lab, 54-59; Guggenheim fel, Inst Radium, Paris, 59-60. *Mem:* AAAS; Am Chem Soc; Am Soc Biol Chem; Soc Exp Biol & Med; Radiation Res Soc. *Res:* Radiation; enzymes; cancer; isozymes. *Mailing Add:* 4624 Highland Ave Downers Grove IL 60515

FEINSTEIN, SHELDON ISRAEL, b Brooklyn, NY, Sept 17, 50. MOLECULAR GENETICS, GENETIC ENGINEERING. *Educ:* Yeshiva Univ, BA, 71; Yale Univ, MPhil, 74. PhD(biol), 77. *Prof Exp:* Assoc bact genetics, Radiobiol Labs, Dept Therapeut Radiol, Sch Med, Yale Univ, 77-81. *Concurrent Pos:* vis scientist, Weizmann Inst Sci, Rehorot, Israel, 81- *Mem:* Sigma Xi. *Res:* Suppression of nonsense mutations; mutations that increase genetic recombination; mutator genes; mechanisms of integration of insertion sequences and transposons; genetics of human interferon and related genes; isolation, mapping and expression. *Mailing Add:* 33 Franham Ave Apt 40 New Haven CT 06515

FEINSTONE, WOLFFE HARRY, b Pultusk, Poland, Oct 1, 13; nat US; m 38; c 3. BACTERIOLOGY, SCIENCE ADMINISTRATION. *Educ:* Univ Ark, BS, 36; Johns Hopkins Univ, ScD(bact), 39. *Prof Exp:* Asst chemother, Johns Hopkins Univ, 37-39; res bacteriologist, Am Cyanamid Co, 39-43; dir biol res, Pyridium Corp, 43-47; dir res, Cent Pharmacol Co, 47-49; sci dir, C B Kendall Co, 49-58; vpres sci admin, Plough Inc, 58-76; DISTINGUISHED PROF MICROBIOL, MEMPHIS STATE UNIV, 76- *Concurrent Pos:* Consult, 49-58. *Mem:* NY Acad Sci; Am Inst Biol Sci; AAAS; Am Chem Soc; Soc Exp Biol & Med. *Res:* Chemotherapy; pharmaceutical development; pharmaceutics and cosmetics. *Mailing Add:* 3745 S Galloway Dr Memphis TN 38111

FEIOCK, FRANK DONALD, b Murray, Ky, June 22, 36; m 54; c 2. PHYSICS, OPTICS. *Educ:* Murray State Col, AB, 58; Univ Iowa, PhD(physics), 64. *Prof Exp:* Res assoc physics, Tufts Univ, 64-65; assoc res scientist, Univ Notre Dame, 65-69; staff physicist, KMS Technol Ctr, KMS Industs, Inc, 69-72; sr scientist, McDonnell Douglas Astronaut, 72-77; assoc group leader, Lawrence Livermore Lab, Univ Calif, 77-78; prog mgr, Rocketdyne Lasers, 78-82; DEPT MGR, MAXWELL LABS, 82- *Concurrent Pos:* Instr mgt, Univ Southern Calif. *Mem:* Am Phys Soc; Optical Soc Am; Am Soc Mech Eng. *Res:* Lasers; optics; atomic physics; materials response; statistical mechanics; numerical analysis. *Mailing Add:* Maxwell Labs 8835 Balboa Ave San Diego CA 92123

FEIR, DOROTHY JEAN, b St Louis, Mo, Jan 29, 29. INSECT PHYSIOLOGY. *Educ:* Univ Mich, BS, 50; Univ Wyo, MS, 56; Univ Wis, PhD(entom), 60. *Prof Exp:* Instr biol, Univ Buffalo, 60-61; from asst prof to assoc prof, 61-67, PROF BIOL, ST LOUIS UNIV, 67- *Concurrent Pos:* Ed, Environ Entom, 77- *Mem:* AAAS; NY Acad Sci; Am Physiol Soc; Entom Soc Am; Sigma Xi. *Res:* Feeding behavior of insects; hematology and immunology of insects; action of hormones in insects; air pollutants and insects. *Mailing Add:* Dept of Biol St Louis Univ St Louis MO 63103

FEISEL, LYLE DEAN, b Tama, Iowa, Oct 16, 35; m 57; c 3. ELECTRICAL ENGINEERING. *Educ:* Iowa State Univ, BS, 61, MS, 63, PhD(elec eng), 64. *Prof Exp:* From asst prof to assoc prof, 64-76, PROF ELEC ENG & HEAD DEPT, SDAK SCH MINES & TECHNOL, 76- *Concurrent Pos:* Nat vis prof, Cheng Kung Univ, Taiwan. *Mem:* Inst Elec & Electronics Engrs; Am Vacuum Soc; Int Soc Hybrid Microelectronics; Am Soc Eng Educ; Am Underground Space Asn. *Res:* Thin film circuitry and components, especially phenomena in thin insulating films with emphasis on active components. *Mailing Add:* Dept of Elec Eng SDak Sch of Mines & Technol Rapid City SD 57701

FEISS, PAUL GEOFFREY, b Cleveland, Ohio, Mar 7, 43; m 66; c 4. ECONOMIC GEOLOGY, GEOCHEMISTRY. *Educ:* Princeton Univ, AB, 65; Harvard Univ, MA, 67, PhD(geol), 70. *Prof Exp:* Asst prof geol, Albion Col, 70-75; asst prof, 75-78, ASSOC PROF GEOL & CHMN DEPT, UNIV NC, CHAPEL HILL, 78- *Mem:* Sigma Xi; Geol Soc Am; AAAS; Soc Econ Geologists. *Res:* Metallogeny and plate tectonics; ore deposits of Southern Appalachians; sulfide geothermometry and geobarometry; igneous processes and ore deposition; uranium geochemistry. *Mailing Add:* Dept Geol Univ NC Chapel Hill NC 27514

FEIST, DALE DANIEL, b Cincinnati, Ohio, Feb 24, 38; m 62; c 2. ZOOLOGY, PHYSIOLOGY. *Educ:* Univ Cincinnati, AB, 60; Univ Calif, Berkeley, PhD(zool), 69. *Prof Exp:* NIH fel physiol, Karolinska Inst, Sweden, 70-71; asst prof, 71-74, ASSOC PROF ZOOPHYSIOL, INST ARCTIC BIOL, UNIV ALASKA, 74- *Mem:* AAAS; Am Soc Zool; Am Soc Mammal; Am Physiol Soc. *Res:* Adrenergic mechanisms in cold acclimation and hibernation; neuroendocrine aspects of acclimatization and adaptation to cold; role of catecholamines in thermogenesis. *Mailing Add:* Inst of Arctic Biol Univ of Alaska Fairbanks AK 99701

FEIST, WILLIAM CHARLES, b St Paul, Minn, Nov 13, 34; m 56; c 2. WOOD CHEMISTRY, POLYMER CHEMISTRY. *Educ:* Hamline Univ, BS, 56; Univ Colo, PhD(org chem), 61. *Prof Exp:* Res chemist, Esso Res & Eng Co, Stand Oil Co NJ, 60-64; RES CHEMIST, FOREST PROD LAB, US FOREST SERV, 64- *Mem:* Am Chem Soc; Soc Wood Sci & Technol; Forest Prod Res Soc; Sigma Xi. *Res:* Wood and water interactions; durability and dimensional stabilization of wood; weathering of wood; interaction of polymers with wood substance; wood finishing; surface chemistry of wood. *Mailing Add:* 6809 Forest Glade Ct Middleton WI 53562

FEIST, WOLFGANG MARTIN, b Oppeln, Ger, Mar 12, 27; m 57; c 3. SOLID STATE PHYSICS, SOLID STATE ELECTRONICS. *Educ:* Univ Frankfurt, dipl, 54; Univ Mainz, Dr rer nat, 57. *Prof Exp:* Electronic scientist, Diamond Ord Fuze Labs, DC, 57-60; prin scientist, 60-79, CONSULT SCIENTIST, RES DIV, RAYTHEON CO, 80- *Mem:* Inst Elec & Electronics Engrs; Am Vacuum Soc. *Res:* Solid state devices; integrated circuits; thin films. *Mailing Add:* Raytheon Co Res Div 28 Seyon St Waltham MA 02154

FEIT, CARL, b New York, NY, Oct 3, 45; m 68; c 2. IMMUNOLOGY. *Educ:* Yeshiva Univ, AB, 67; Rutgers Univ, PhD(microbiol), 73. *Prof Exp:* Res fel immunol, Waksman Inst Microbiol, Rutgers Univ, 73-75; RES ASSOC IMMUNODIAG, SLOAN-KETTERING INST, 75- *Concurrent Pos:* Vis asst prof biol, Yeshiva Univ, 75- *Mem:* Am Soc Microbiol. *Res:* Detection and analysis of tumor specific and tumor associated antigens; modulation of the immune response by tumors. *Mailing Add:* 115 E 87th New York NY 10028

FEIT, DAVID, b New York, NY, Sept 17, 37; m 59; c 3. ACOUSTICS, MECHANICS. *Educ:* Columbia Univ, MS, 61, EngScD(eng mech), 64. *Prof Exp:* Res engr, Davidson Lab, Stevens Inst Technol, 59-60; res scientist, TRG, Inc, NY, 60-61; sr scientist, Cambridge Acoust Assocs, 64-73; SUPVRY MECH ENGR, DAVID W TAYLOR NAVAL SHIP RES & DEVELOP CTR, 73- *Mem:* Am Acad Mech; fel Acoust Soc Am; Am Soc Mech Engrs. *Res:* Vibrations; mathematics. *Mailing Add:* David W Taylor Naval Ship Res & Develop Ctr Carderock MD 20084

FEIT, EUGENE DAVID, b Chicago, Ill, Sept 23, 35; m 64; c 3. ORGANIC POLYMER CHEMISTRY. *Educ:* Univ Chicago, MS, 64, PhD(phys org chem), 68. *Prof Exp:* Chemist, Am Meat Inst Found, 62-64; chemist, Bell Labs, 68-79; SR SCIENTIST, HARRIS SEMICONDUCTOR, 79- *Mem:* Am Chem Soc; Electrochem Soc; Am Vacuum Soc. *Res:* Microlithography; plasma etching; radiation chemistry; photopolymerization; organic photochemistry; process developments for integrated circuits. *Mailing Add:* 425 Rio Casa Indialantic FL 32903

FEIT, IRA (NATHAN), b Brooklyn, NY, Feb 28, 40; m 71. DEVELOPMENTAL BIOLOGY, MICROBIOLOGY. *Educ:* Brooklyn Col, BS, 60; Princeton Univ, MA, 64, PhD(biol), 69. *Prof Exp:* From instr to asst prof, 64-75, ASSOC PROF BIOL, FRANKLIN & MARSHALL COL, 75- *Concurrent Pos:* NSF trainee lab quant biol, Univ Miami, 69-70. *Mem:* AAAS. *Res:* Developmental control mechanisms in the cellular slime molds; changes in the polyribosome complement during cellular slime mold development. *Mailing Add:* Dept of Biol Franklin & Marshall Col Lancaster PA 17604

FEIT, IRVING N, b Providence, RI, Oct 15, 42. ORGANIC CHEMISTRY. *Educ:* Univ RI, BS, 64; Univ Rochester, PhD(chem), 69, St John's Univ, JD, 79. *Prof Exp:* Fel, Univ Calif, Santa Cruz, 69-70; asst prof, 70-74, assoc prof chem, C W Post Col, Long Island Univ, 74-79, PATENT ATTY, LEVER BROS, 80- *Mem:* Am Chem Soc. *Res:* Base catalyzed and solvolytic elimination reactions; rearrangement and disproportionation of oligohalobenzenes. *Mailing Add:* 455 W 43rd St New York NY 10036

FEIT, JULIUS, b New York, NY, Nov 24, 19; m 53; c 2. SPACE PHYSICS, SOLAR PHYSICS. *Educ:* City Col New York, BS, 42; Columbia Univ, MA, 59; Adelphi Univ, MS, 63, PhD(physics), 67. *Prof Exp:* Lectr physics, Adelphi Univ, 65-66; assoc prof, 67-70, PROF PHYSICS, QUEENSBOROUGH COMMUNITY COL, CITY UNIV NEW YORK, 70- *Mem:* Am Geophys Union; Am Asn Physics Teachers. *Res:* Diffusion of solar flare cosmic rays through interplanetary space; effects of slow acceleration, external and internal boundaries and convection and energy loss in diffusion; modulation of galactic cosmic rays. *Mailing Add:* 101 Violet St Massapequa Park NY 11762

FEIT, MICHAEL DENNIS, b Easton, Pa, Nov 15, 42; m 67; c 2. FIBER OPTICS, MAGNETOHYDRODYNAMICS. *Educ:* Lehigh Univ, BA, 64; Rensselaer Polytech Inst, PhD(physics), 70. *Prof Exp:* Res asst physics, Rensselaer Polytech Inst, 66-69; res assoc, Univ Ill, Urbana, 69-72; RES PHYSICIST, LAWRENCE LIVERMORE LAB, 72- *Mem:* AAAS; Am Phys Soc. *Res:* Interaction of intense laser pulses with plasmas; fiber optics; numerical methods; nonlinear propagation; self-focusing. *Mailing Add:* Lawrence Livermore Lab PO Box 808 L-71 Livermore CA 94550

FEIT, SIDNIE MARILYN, b Hackensack, NJ, Nov 29, 35; m 57; c 2. MATHEMATICS. *Educ:* Cornell Univ, BA, 57, MA, 63, PhD(math), 68. *Prof Exp:* Mathematician, Labs Appl Sci, Univ Chicago, 60-61; lectr math, Cornell Univ, 61-63; mathematician, Inst Naval Studies, 63-64; asst prof math, Quinnipiac Col, 68-70; asst prof math, Albertus Magnus Col, 70-77; RES ASSOC, DEPT MATH, YALE UNIV, 77- *Concurrent Pos:* Consult, Yale Univ, 75. *Mem:* Math Asn Am; Am Math Soc. *Res:* Topology; geometry; use of computers in teaching mathematics. *Mailing Add:* Dept of Math Yale Univ New Haven CT 06511

FEIT, WALTER, b Vienna, Austria, Oct 26, 30; nat US; m 57; c 2. MATHEMATICS. *Educ:* Univ Chicago, BA & MS, 51; Univ Mich, PhD(math), 54. *Prof Exp:* Instr math, Cornell Univ, 53-55, from asst prof to assoc prof, 56-64; PROF MATH, YALE UNIV, 64- *Concurrent Pos:* NSF fel, Inst Advan Study, 58-59. *Honors & Awards:* Cole Prize, Am Math Soc, 65. *Mem:* Nat Acad Sci; Am Math Soc; Math Asn Am. *Res:* Group theory and algebra. *Mailing Add:* Dept of Math Yale Univ New Haven CT 06520

FEITLER, DAVID, b Chicago, Ill, Oct 5, 52. ORGANIC CHEMISTRY, CATALYSIS. *Educ:* Univ Calif, BS, 73; Mass Inst Technol, PhD(org chem), 77. *Prof Exp:* Res chemist, 77-80, SR RES CHEMIST CATALYSIS, AIR PROD & CHEM, 80- *Mem:* Am Chem Soc; Sigma Xi. *Res:* Homogeneous catalysis; design and synthesis of catalytic materials; reactions of small molecules; synthetic inorganic and organometallic chemistry; zeolites. *Mailing Add:* Air Prod & Chem PO Box 538 Allentown PA 18105

FEJER, JULES A, b Budapest, Hungary, Jan 22, 14; m 43, 69; c 1. ATMOSPHERIC PHYSICS, PLASMA PHYSICS. *Educ:* Swiss Fed Inst Technol, dipl, 36; Witwatersrand Univ, MSEng, 49, DSc(eng), 57. *Prof Exp:* Res engr, Hungarian Tungsten Lampworks, Ltd, 36-38; geophysicist, Oscar Weiss Consult Geophysicists Ltd, SAfrica, 39-42; res officer, Nat Inst Telecommun Res, 46-58; defence sci serv officer, Defence Res Telecommun Estab, Can, 59-61; tech specialist, Gen Motors Defense Res Labs, Calif, 61-62; prof upper atmospheric & space sci, Southwest Ctr Advan Studies, 62-66; prof appl physics, Univ Calif San Diego, 66-76; consult aeronomy, Max-Planck Inst, Katlenburg, Lindan, 76-82; SR RES ASSOC, ARECIBO OBSERV, PR, 82- *Concurrent Pos:* Mem Comn IV, Int Sci Radio Union, 62- *Honors & Awards:* John Dellinger Gold Medal, Union Radio Sci Int, 81. *Mem:* Am Geophys Union; Am Inst Physics. *Res:* Wave propagation through irregular media; incoherent scattering of electromagnetic waves by plasmas; hydromagnetic propagation and stability; dynamo theory of geomagnetic variations; magnetic storm theory; ionospheric modification; radio-frequency plasma probes. *Mailing Add:* Arecibo Observ PO Box 995 Arecibo PR 00612

FEJER, STEPHEN OSCAR, b Budapest, Hungary, Dec 27, 16; Can citizen; m 50; c 1. GENETICS. *Educ:* Pazmany Peter Univ, Budapest, Dr jur, 39; Univ NZ, MAgrSci, 52; Swiss Fed Inst Technol, DrTechSc(genetics), 67. *Prof Exp:* Plant breeder grass genetics, Grasslands Div, Dept Sci & Indust Res, NZ, 50-61; geneticist, Res Sta, Can Dept Agr, 62-71. *Concurrent Pos:* Ger Acad Exchange Serv vis scientist, Tech Univ Munich, 75 & 79. *Mem:* Genetics Soc Am; Genetics Soc Can; Can Soc Hort Sci. *Res:* Plant breeding for yield and its components; quantitative genetics and selection index; relations to environmental factors, adaptation and homeostasis; biochemical background of plant hormones; competition; frost resistance. *Mailing Add:* 9 LeRoy St Ottawa ON K1J 6X1 Can

FEKETY, F ROBERT, JR, b Pittsburgh, Pa, June 29, 29; m 54; c 2. INTERNAL MEDICINE, INFECTIOUS DISEASES. *Educ:* Wesleyan Univ, AB, 51; Yale Univ, MD, 55. *Prof Exp:* Intern & resident internal med, Yale Med Ctr, 55-56, 58-60; from instr to asst prof med, Sch Med, Johns Hopkins Univ, 60-67; assoc prof internal med, Sch Med, 67-70, PROF INTERNAL MED & HEAD SECT INFECTIOUS DIS, MED CTR, UNIV MICH, ANN ARBOR, 70- *Concurrent Pos:* Res fel infectious dis, Sch Med, Johns Hopkins Univ, 57-58. *Mem:* AAAS; Infectious Dis Soc Am; Am Soc Microbiol. *Res:* Bacterial infections; epidemiology; clinical pharmacology of antibiotics; cellular immunology. *Mailing Add:* Dept of Internal Med Univ Mich Med Ctr Ann Arbor MI 48109

FELAND, SARAH ELIZABETH, nutritional biochemistry, see previous edition

FELBECK, DAVID K(NISELEY), b Mt Vernon, NY, Apr 2, 26; c 3. MECHANICAL ENGINEERING, MATERIALS SCIENCE. *Educ:* Cornell Univ, BME, 48; Mass Inst Technol, MS, 49, MechE, 51, ScD(mech eng), 52. *Prof Exp:* Fulbright lectr, Delft Univ Technol, 52-53; asst prof mech eng, Mass Inst Technol, 53-55; exec dir, Nat Acad Sci-Nat Res Coun, 55-61; assoc prof mech eng, 61-65, PROF MECH ENG, UNIV MICH, ANN ARBOR, 65- *Honors & Awards:* Wilson Award, Am Soc Metals, 73. *Mem:* Am Soc Mech Engrs; Am Soc Metals; Am Inst Mining, Metall & Petrol Engrs; Am Soc Testing & Mat; Nat Soc Prof Engrs. *Res:* Fractography and failure analysis; high-performance composites. *Mailing Add:* 2060 Scottwood Ann Arbor MI 48104

FELBECK, GEORGE THEODORE, JR, b Buffalo, NY, Sept 18, 24; m 50; c 3. ORGANIC GEOCHEMISTRY. *Educ:* Mass Inst Technol, BS, 49; Pa State Univ, MS, 55, PhD(agron), 57. *Prof Exp:* Asst prof agron, W Va Univ, 56-57; lectr biol, Yonsei Univ, Korea, 57-58; asst prof agron, Univ Del, 58-64; assoc prof agr chem, 64-70, PROF SOIL SCI, UNIV RI, 70-, CHMN DEPT, 72- *Mem:* AAAS; Am Soc Agron; Soil Sci Soc Am. *Res:* Chemistry of soil organic matter; organic geochemistry. *Mailing Add:* Dept of Plant & Soil Sci Univ of RI Kingston RI 02881

FELBER, FRANKLIN STANTON, b Newark, NJ, June 11, 50. PLASMA PHYSICS, THEORETICAL PHYSICS. *Educ:* Princeton Univ, AB, 72; Univ Southern Calif, MA, 73, PhD(physics), 75; Univ Chicago, MS, 74. *Prof Exp:* Fel, Univ Southern Calif, 75-76; Nat Res Coun assoc, Naval Res Lab, 76-77; sr scientist, Gen Atomic Co, 77-79; sr staff scientist, Maxwell Labs, 79-81; THEORY GROUP MGR, WESTERN RESEARCH CORP, 81- *Concurrent Pos:* Nat Res Coun Assoc, 76; NATO fel, 77. *Honors & Awards:* Res Award, Sigma Xi, 75. *Mem:* Am Phys Soc; Sigma Xi. *Res:* Plasma physics and instabilities; fusion; imploding plasmas; magneto-hydrodynamics; high-current accelerators; interaction of intense radiation with matter; nonlinear optics. *Mailing Add:* 15194 Amalia St San Diego CA 92129

FELCH, RICHARD ELROY, agronomy, see previous edition

FELCHER, GIAN PIERO, b Milano, Italy, June 14, 36; m 70; c 2. SOLID STATE PHYSICS. *Educ:* Univ Milan, Dr physics, 58. *Prof Exp:* Res assoc physics, Centro Italiano Studi Esperienze, 59-62; res assoc, Centro Nazionale Energia Nucleare, 62-63; fel, Brookhaven Nat Lab, 63-66; asst physicist, 66-71, PHYSICIST, ARGONNE NAT LAB, 71- *Concurrent Pos:* Int Atomic Energy Agency fel, 60-62; asst prof, Univ Rome, 62-63; vis prof, NATO, 75-76, res grant, 77-79. *Mem:* Am Phys Soc. *Res:* Neutron scattering from solids; magnetism and magnetic structures; properties of surfaces and their interaction with gases. *Mailing Add:* Solid State Div Argonne Nat Lab Argonne IL 60439

FELD, BERNARD TAUB, b New York, NY, Dec 21, 19; m 47; c 2. ELEMENTARY PARTICLE PHYSICS, HIGH ENERGY PHYSICS. *Educ:* City Col New York, BS, 39; Columbia Univ, PhD(physics), 45. *Prof Exp:* Instr eve session, City Col New York, 40-41; res assoc, Columbia Univ, 41-42; physicist metall lab, Univ Chicago, 42-44 & Los Alamos Lab, Univ Calif, 44-46; from instr to assoc prof physics, 46-57, actg dir lab nuclear sci, 61-62, PROF PHYSICS, MASS INST TECHNOL, 57- *Concurrent Pos:* Consult, Brookhaven Nat Lab, 48-; asst ed, Ann of Physics; Guggenheim fel & vis prof, Univ Rome, 53-54; vis scientist & Ford fel, Europ Orgn Nuclear Res, 60-61; vis prof, Polytech Sch Paris, 66-67; vis prof theoret physics, Imp Col Sci & Technol, London, 73-75; Fulbright-Hays res fel, 74-75; secy-gen, Pugwash Conf on Sci & World Affairs, 72-77; ed-in-chief, Bull Atomic Scientists, 75- *Honors & Awards:* Leo Szilard Award, Am Phys Soc, 75. *Mem:* Fel Am Acad Arts & Sci; fel Am Phys Soc; Fedn Am Scientists. *Res:* Neutron physics; atomic and molecular hyperfine structure and nuclear moments; meson physics and elementary particles, theory and experiment. *Mailing Add:* Dept of Physics Mass Inst of Technol Cambridge MA 02139

FELD, MICHAEL S, b New York, NY, Nov 11, 40; m 63; c 2. PHYSICS. *Educ:* Mass Inst Technol, SB & SM, 63, PhD(physics), 67. *Prof Exp:* Fel physics, 67-68, asst prof, 68-74, assoc prof, 74-79, PROF PHYSICS, MASS INST TECHNOL, 79-, DIR SPECTROS LAB, 76-, DIR, REGIONAL LASER, CTR, 79- *Concurrent Pos:* Sloan fel, 73- *Mem:* AAAS; fel Optical Soc Am; Am Phys Soc; Sigma Xi. *Res:* Laser physics; quantum electronics; superradiance. *Mailing Add:* Spectros Lab Mass Inst of Technol Cambridge MA 02139

FELD, WILLIAM ADAM, b Sandwich, Ill, Nov 20, 44; m 67; c 2. SYNTHESIS, MICROCOMPUTER APPLICATIONS. *Educ:* Loras Col, Dubuque, Iowa, BS, 66; Univ Iowa, Iowa City, PhD(chem), 71. *Prof Exp:* Asst prof org & anal chem, Northern State Col, SDak, 71-72; adj asst prof, 72-77, asst prof, 77-82, ASSOC PROF ORG CHEM, WRIGHT STATE UNIV, 82- *Mem:* Am Chem Soc; Sigma Xi. *Res:* Synthesis of biologically active molecules (benzotriazoles); synthesis of thermally stable polymer precursors; application of microcomputers in organic and polymer chemistry. *Mailing Add:* Dept Chem Wright State Univ Dayton OH 45435

FELDBALLE, JEANETTE, b Chicago, Ill, Jan 6, 18. ZOOLOGY. *Educ:* Edgewood Col, BS, 43; Univ Wis, MS, 55, PhD, 60. *Prof Exp:* Instr zool, 55-58, assoc prof biol, 57-65, PROF BIOL, EDGEWOOD COL, 65-, CHMN DIV NATURAL SCI, 58- *Concurrent Pos:* NSF fac fel, 58-59. *Mem:* AAAS; Nat Asn Biol Teachers. *Res:* Endocrinology; physiology of reproduction. *Mailing Add:* 2302 Edgewood Dr Madison WI 53711

FELDBERG, ROSS SHELDON, b Chicago, Ill, Sept 7, 43; m 67. BIOCHEMISTRY. *Educ:* Univ Ill, BS, 65; Univ Mich, Ann Arbor, PhD(biochem), 70. *Prof Exp:* Fel biochem, Univ Aberdeen, 70-72; fel, Brandeis Univ, 72-75; asst prof biochem, 75-81, ASSOC PROF BIOL, TUFTS UNIV, 81- *Concurrent Pos:* NIH fel, Brandeis Univ, 74-75. *Mem:* AAAS; Tissue Cult Asn. *Res:* Repair of ultraviolet-light induced DNA damage in human cells. *Mailing Add:* Dept of Biol Tufts Univ Medford MA 02155

FELDBERG, STEPHEN WILLIAM, b New York, NY, July 22, 37. ELECTROCHEMISTRY. *Educ:* Princeton Univ, AB, 58, PhD(chem), 61. *Prof Exp:* Res assoc, Brookhaven Nat Lab, 61-63; vis asst prof, Univ Kans, 64; CHEMIST, BROOKHAVEN NAT LAB, 64- *Concurrent Pos:* Vis assoc chemist, Univ Kans, 68; vis prof, Colo State Univ, 72. *Mem:* Sigma Xi. *Res:* Studies of mechanism and kinetics of chemical reactions coupled with heterogeneous electron transfer; computer simulation techniques; studies of semi-conductor photophenomena. *Mailing Add:* Brookhaven Nat Lab 60 Rutherford Dr Upton NY 11973

FELDBUSH, THOMAS LEE, b Canton, Ohio, Apr 18, 39; m 63; c 3. IMMUNOBIOLOGY. *Educ:* Mt Union Col, BS, 61; Ohio State Univ, MSc, 64, PhD(microbiol), 66. *Prof Exp:* Sr res microbiologist, Merck Inst Therapeut Res, 66-70; from asst prof to assoc prof, 71-79, PROF IMMUNOL-MICROBIOL, DEPT MICROBIOL, COL MED, UNIV IOWA, 79- *Concurrent Pos:* Vis lectr, Dept Microbiol, Rutgers Univ, 68-70; vis worker, Sir Williams Dunn Sch Path, Oxford, Eng, 69-70; Res Career Scientist Award, Vet Admin. *Mem:* Brit Soc Immunol; Am Asn Immunologists; Am Soc Microbiol; AAAS; Sigma Xi. *Res:* Influence of antigen on development, maintenance and characteristics of immunologic memory; immune response to prostatic carcinoma following cryosurgery. *Mailing Add:* Dept Microbiol Col of Med Univ Iowa Iowa City IA 52242

FELDER, DARRYL LAMBERT, b Kingsville, Tex, Oct 21, 47; m 70. SYSTEMATIC ZOOLOGY, INVERTEBRATE PHYSIOLOGY. *Educ:* Tex A&I Univ, BS, 69, MS, 71; La State Univ, PhD(zool), 75. *Prof Exp:* asst prof, 75-79, ASSOC PROF BIOL, UNIV SOUTHWESTERN LA, 79- *Concurrent Pos:* Taxon consult, US Bur Land Mgt Proj, Univ Tex Marine Sci Inst, Port Aransas, Tex, 76-77 & Southwest Res Inst, Houston, 78-80; dir planning off, La Maine Consortium, 79-80. *Mem:* Am Soc Zoologists; AAAS; Estuarine Res Fedn. *Res:* Systematics of decapod crustaceans; ecology of decapod crustaceans in the Gulf of Mexico; physioecology of estuarine invertebrates. *Mailing Add:* Dept Biol Univ Southwestern La Lafayette LA 70504

FELDER, RICHARD MARK, b New York, NY, July 21, 39; m 63; c 3. CHEMICAL ENGINEERING. *Educ:* City Col New York, BChE, 62; Princeton Univ, PhD(chem eng), 66. *Prof Exp:* NATO fel, theoret physics div, Atomic Energy Res Estab, Eng, 66-67; res scientist, nuclear eng dept, Brookhaven Nat Lab, 67-69; PROF CHEM ENG, NC STATE UNIV, 69- *Honors & Awards:* Fac achievement, Sigma Xi, 74. *Mem:* Am Inst Chem Engrs; Am Chem Soc. *Res:* Chemical reaction engineering; process simulation and optimization; coal conversion; air pollution control technology. *Mailing Add:* Dept of Chem Eng NC State Univ Raleigh NC 27650

FELDER, WILLIAM, b Greensburg, Pa, Mar 20, 43; m 67; c 2. PHYSICAL CHEMISTRY. *Educ:* Univ Pa, AB, 64; Mass Inst Technol, SM, 66, PhD(phys chem), 69. *Prof Exp:* Fel physics & chem, Ctr Res Exp Space Sci, York Univ, Toronto, Can, 69-72; RES SCIENTIST, AEROCHEM RES LABS, INC, 72- *Mem:* Am Phys Soc; Am Chem Soc. *Res:* Chemical kinetics of high temperature gas phase reactions; excited species reactions; chemiluminescence; ion-molecule reactions; atmospheric chemistry; chemical lasers. *Mailing Add:* AeroChem Res Labs PO Box 12 Princeton NJ 08540

FELDHAMER, GEORGE ALAN, b Minneapolis, Minn, Feb 20, 47; m 74; c 2. WILDLIFE BIOLOGY. *Educ:* Univ Minn, BS, 69; Idaho State Univ, MS, 72; Ore State Univ, PhD(wildlife biol), 77. *Prof Exp:* res assoc, 77-80, ASST PROF WILDLIFE ECOL, CTR ENVIRON & ESTUARINE STUDIES, UNIV MD, 80- *Mem:* Am Soc Mammalogists; Wildlife Soc. *Res:* Ecology of sika deer; white-tailed deer. *Mailing Add:* Appalachian Environ Lab Gunter Hall Frostburg State Col Frostburg MD 21532

FELDHAUS, RICHARD JOSEPH, b Omaha, Nebr, May 6, 29; m 53; c 5. SURGERY. *Educ:* Creighton Univ, BS, 53, MS, 55, MD, 59. *Prof Exp:* Intern, St Joseph Mem Hosp, Omaha, Nebr, 59-60; resident surg, Creighton Univ Affil Hosps, 60-62; resident, Vet Admin Hosp, 62-64; staff surgeon, 64-65; chief surg, Vet Admin Hosp, Phoenix, Ariz, 67-71; dir surg educ, Good Samaritan Hosp, 71-74; ASSOC PROF SURG, SCH MED, CREIGHTON UNIV, 74- *Concurrent Pos:* From instr to asst prof, Sch Med, Creighton Univ, 62-67. *Mem:* Fel Am Col Surgeons. *Res:* Peripheral vascular surgery; esophageal surgery. *Mailing Add:* 18 Swanson Prof Ctr 8601 W Dodge Rd Omaha NE 68114

FELDHERR, CARL M, b New York, NY, Jan 3, 34; m 59; c 1. ANATOMY. *Educ:* Hartwick Col, BA, 55; Univ Pa, PhD(physiol), 60. *Prof Exp:* Damon Runyon fel, Univ Pa, 60-62; asst prof physiol, Univ Alta, 62-65; asst prof anat, Sch Med, Univ Pa, 65-67; asst prof, 67-70, assoc prof, 70-77, PROF ANAT, COL MED, UNIV FLA, 77- *Mem:* AAAS; Am Soc Cell Biol. *Res:* Permeability characteristics of nuclear envelope. *Mailing Add:* Dept of Anat Sci Univ of Fla Col of Med Gainesville FL 32601

FELDMAN, ALAN SIDNEY, b New York, NY, Feb 19, 27; m 50; c 2. AUDIOLOGY, SPEECH PATHOLOGY. *Educ:* Syracuse Univ, AB, 49, MS, 51, PhD(audiol, speech path), 56. *Prof Exp:* Audiologist & speech pathologist, Mass Eye & Ear Infirmary, 52-58; from asst prof to assoc prof, 58-71, dir, Commun Dis Unit, 64-82, PROF OTOLARYNGOL, STATE UNIV NY UPSTATE MED CTR, 71-; PRES, ENVIRON HEARING & VISION CONSULT LTD, 72- *Concurrent Pos:* Res fel, Lab Sensory Commun, Syracuse Univ, 58-; consult, Syracuse Vet Admin Hosp, 58- *Mem:* Acoust Soc Am; Int Soc Audiol; Am Speech & Hearing Asn. *Res:* Audition; problems in measurement and differential diagnosis of auditory disorders and speech communication. *Mailing Add:* 404 Univ Ave Syracuse NY 13210

FELDMAN, ALBERT, b Jersey City, NJ, May 20, 36; m 59; c 3. PHYSICS. *Educ:* City Col New York, BS, 59; Univ Chicago, MS, 60, PhD(physics), 66. *Prof Exp:* PHYSICIST, NAT BUR STANDARDS, 66- *Honors & Awards:* Spec Achievement Award, US Dept Com, Nat Bur Standards, 72; Bronze Medal, US Dept Com, 80. *Mem:* Am Phys Soc; Optical Soc Am; Am Soc Testing & Mat. *Res:* Optical properties of solid materials including piezo-optic and thermo-optic effects; optically bistable systems; optical properties of thin films. *Mailing Add:* Nat Bur of Standards A257 Mat Bldg Washington DC 20234

FELDMAN, ALBERT WILLIAM, b Gardner, Ill, Aug 6, 18; c 2. PLANT PATHOLOGY. *Educ:* Univ Ill, AB, 42; NC State Col, MS, 44; Univ Minn, PhD(plant path), 47. *Prof Exp:* Asst plant path, NC State Col, 42-43; agent, Bur Plant Indust, USDA, NC, 43-44; res assoc plant path, Univ Minn, 47; asst res prof, Exp Sta, RI State Col, 47-51; sr res biologist & prod develop mgr, Naugatuck Chem Div, US Rubber Co, 51-58; plant pathologist, Citrus Exp Sta, 58-74, PROF PLANT PATH, AGR RES & EDUC CTR, UNIV FLA, 58- *Mem:* AAAS; Int Orgn Citrus Virol; Am Phytopath Soc; Am Soc Plant Physiol; Int Soc Citricult. *Res:* Physiology of citrus diseases. *Mailing Add:* Agr Res & Educ Ctr Univ of Fla Lake Alfred FL 33850

FELDMAN, ALFRED PHILIP, b Hamburg, Ger, Aug 7, 23; US citizen; m 54; c 2. ORGANIC CHEMISTRY. *Educ:* Univ Chicago, MS, 56; Johns Hopkins Univ, MS, 78. *Prof Exp:* Asst ed, Chem Abstr Serv, 56-60; chief coding sect, 60-69, asst to dir, Div Biomet & Med Info Processing, 70-74, systs analyst, 74-79, HEAD, CHEM INFO SECT, NAT CANCER INST, NIH, 79- *Honors & Awards:* US Army Res & Develop Award. *Mem:* AAAS; Am Chem Soc; Asn Comput Mach. *Res:* Management of scientific information; man-machine interaction; chemical data processing. *Mailing Add:* Div Biomet Med Info Processing Walter Reed Army Inst of Res Washington DC 20012

FELDMAN, ARNOLD, radiological physics, see previous edition

FELDMAN, ARTHUR, b St Louis, Mo, Apr 6, 31; m 53; c 1. STRUCTURAL ENGINEERING, NUCLEAR WEAPONS EFFECTS. *Educ:* Washington Univ, St Louis, BS, 52; Univ Ill, MS, 54, PhD(civil eng), 60. *Prof Exp:* Asst civil eng, Univ Ill, 52-54, res assoc, 54-59, asst prof, 59-61; assoc prof, Univ Denver, 61-63; asst res scientist, 63-66, sr res scientist, 66-81, DEPT STAFF ENGR, MARTIN MARIETTA CORP, 81- *Concurrent Pos:* Instr, Off Civil Defense, 62- *Honors & Awards:* Martin Author Award, 68 & 69. *Mem:* Soc Exp Stress Anal; Am Soc Civil Engrs. *Res:* Composite pressure vessels; buckling and vibration of composite materials; reinforced concrete, blast and earthquake resistance; prestressed concrete; radiation protection. *Mailing Add:* Mail No D-6039 PO Box 179 Denver CO 80201

FELDMAN, BARRY JOEL, b Providence, RI, Feb 25, 44; m 68; c 1. QUANTUM OPTICS, LASERS. *Educ:* Brown Univ, ScB, 65; Mass Inst Technol, PhD(physics), 71. *Prof Exp:* STAFF PHYSICIST, LOS ALAMOS SCI LAB, 71- *Mem:* Am Phys Soc. *Res:* Theoretical and experimental research in nonlinear interactions of photons and matter; laser isotope separation; laser fusion; new laser development; coherent multiphoton processes. *Mailing Add:* 346 Hillside Ave Santa Fe NM 87501

FELDMAN, BERNARD JOSEPH, b San Francisco, Calif, July 20, 46; m 70; c 2. SEMICONDUCTOR PHYSICS. *Educ:* Univ Calif, Berkeley, AB, 67; Harvard Univ, AM, 69, PhD(physics), 72. *Prof Exp:* Asst res physicist, Univ Calif, Berkeley, 72-74; asst prof, 74-80, ASSOC PROF PHYSICS, UNIV MO-ST LOUIS, 80- *Concurrent Pos:* Equip grant, Res Corp, 74-; NSF travel grant, 75. *Mem:* Am Phys Soc. *Res:* Experimental studies of optical properties of thin film solar cell materials. *Mailing Add:* Dept Physics Univ Mo St Louis MO 63121

FELDMAN, BERNARD ROBERT, b New York, NY, July 5, 34; m 60; c 2. MEDICINE. *Educ:* Col William & Mary, BS, 55; Chicago Med Sch, MD, 59. *Prof Exp:* Intern, Michael Reese Hosp & Med Ctr, 59-60; resident pediat, 60-62, fel allergy, 62-63; fel pediatric allergy, Babies Hosp, Columbia-Presby Med Ctr, 63-64; ASST PROF CLIN PEDIAT, COLUMBIA COL PHYSICIANS & SURGEONS, 68- *Concurrent Pos:* Am Acad Pediat fel, 68 & Am Acad Allergy, 75; consult pediat allergy, Nyack Hosp, 73- & St Mary's Hosp Children, 75-; assoc dir, Div Allergy, Babies Hosp, Columbia-Presby Med Ctr, 74- *Mem:* Fel Am Acad Allergy. *Res:* Pharmacotherapy of bronchial asthma; clinical research on newer therapeutic agents. *Mailing Add:* Babies Hosp 3959 Broadway New York NY 10032

FELDMAN, CHARLES, b Baltimore, Md, Mar 20, 24; m 46; c 2. SOLID STATE PHYSICS. *Educ:* Johns Hopkins Univ, AB, 44, AM, 49; Univ Paris, PhD(physics), 52. *Prof Exp:* Physicist, Aberdeen Proving Ground, 48; asst inst coop res, Johns Hopkins Univ, 49-50; physics master grammar sch, Eng, 50-51; asst, Nat Ctr Sci Res, Paris, France, 51-53; physicist, Crystal Br, Naval Res Lab, 53-60; sect head, Melpar, Inc, 60-63, lab mgr, 64-67; sr staff mem, 67-68, prin prof staff mem, 68-72, SUPVR SOLID STATE RES GROUP, APPL PHYSICS LAB, JOHNS HOPKINS UNIV, 72- *Concurrent Pos:* Adj prof, George Washington Univ, 69-76. *Honors & Awards:* Award, Sci Res Soc Am, 58. *Mem:* Am Phys Soc; Sigma Xi; Optical Soc Am. *Res:* Metal films; dielectric films; solid state physics, luminescence; thin film electronics; amorphous semiconductors. *Mailing Add:* 2855 Davenport St NW Washington DC 20008

FELDMAN, CHARLES LAWRENCE, b Yonkers, NY, Dec 18, 35; m 56; c 4. MECHANICAL ENGINEERING. *Educ:* Mass Inst Technol, SB & SM, 58, MechE, 60, ScD(mech eng), 62. *Prof Exp:* Res asst, Brookhaven Nat Lab, 56; scientist commun theory, Edgerton, Germeshausen & Grier, Inc, 58-59;

asst, Mass Inst Technol, 59-60; sr prof engr, Joseph Kaye & Co, Inc, 61-62, dir res, 62-65; from asst prof to prof mech eng, Worcester Polytech Inst, 65-78; sr vpres, Electronics for Med, Inc, 71-81; PRES, CANDIO DATA CORP, 81- *Concurrent Pos:* Instr, Lowell Inst, 58-59; consult, Autonetics Div, N Am Aviation, Inc, 59-61 & Joseph Kaye & Co, Inc, 60-61; lectr indust mgt, Northeastern Univ, 62-63, lectr eng, 63-; res assoc biomath, med sch, Harvard Univ, 66-69, lectr, 69-72; consult math, dept psychiat, Mass Gen Hosp, 67-72; adj prof, Univ Mass Med Sch, 76- & Worcester Polytech Inst, 78- *Mem:* Asn Advan Med Instrumentation. *Res:* Application of statistical communication theory to computers and medicine. *Mailing Add:* 344 Boston Post Rd Marlboro MA 01752

FELDMAN, CHESTER, b South Bend, Ind, June 26, 20; m 54; c 1. MATHEMATICS. *Educ:* Univ Chicago, SB, 40, SM, 41, PhD(math), 50. *Prof Exp:* Asst prof, Antioch Col, 51-52; consult, Air-Craft-Marine Prod, Inc, 52-53; instr math, Purdue Univ, 53-55; asst prof, Univ NH, 55-57 & Univ Conn, 57-63; assoc prof, Kent State Univ, 63-68; assoc ed math rev, Univ Mich, Ann Arbor, 68-78; ASSOC PROF, IND UNIV, KOKOMO, 81- *Mem:* Fel AAAS; Am Math Soc. *Res:* Topological and Banach algebras. *Mailing Add:* Indiana Univ 2300 S Washington St KoKomo IN 46902

FELDMAN, DANIEL S, b Philadelphia, Pa, Feb 26, 26; m 57; c 3. NEUROLOGY, NEUROPHYSIOLOGY. *Educ:* Univ Pa, AB, 45, MD, 49. *Prof Exp:* From asst prof to assoc prof neurol, State Univ NY Downstate Med Ctr, 61-72; PROF NEUROL & MED, MED COL GA, 72- *Concurrent Pos:* Fel, Nat Inst Neurol Dis & Blindness, 53-54; Abrahamson fel, Mt Sinai Hosp, NY, 56; dir neurol, Maimonides Hosp, Brooklyn, 60-66; mem med adv bd, Myasthenia Gravis Found, 62-, chmn, 80-81; guest investr, Dept Pharmacol, Univ Lund, 64-65; career scientist, Health Res Coun, City of New York, 66-72; consult, Maimonides-Coney Island Med Ctr, Brooklyn, 66-72; vis neurologist, Kings County Hosp, 66-72; attend neurologist, State Univ Hosp, 66-72 & E Talmadge Hosp, Augusta, Ga, 72-; consult neurol, Vet Admin Hosp, Augusta, US Army Hosp, Ft Gordon & Univ Hosp, Augusta, 72- *Mem:* Am Physiol Soc; Am Neurol Asn; Am Acad Neurol; Am Fedn Clin Res; AMA. *Res:* Electrophysiological studies in vitro of parameters affecting chemical transmitter release and post-synaptic response in vertebrate, including human muscle; application of physiological systems and methods to study of human neuromuscular function in health and disease. *Mailing Add:* Dept of Neurol Med Col of Ga Augusta GA 30912

FELDMAN, DAVID, b Brooklyn, NY, June 16, 21; m 46; c 2. THEORETICAL PHYSICS. *Educ:* City Col New York, BS, 40; NY Univ, MS, 46; Harvard Univ, PhD(physics), 49. *Prof Exp:* AEC fel, Inst Advan Study, 49-50; asst prof physics, Univ Rochester, 50-56; assoc prof, 56-59, PROF PHYSICS, BROWN UNIV, 59- *Concurrent Pos:* NSF sr fel, Univ Paris, 62-63; mem adv panel for physics, NSF, 68- *Mem:* Fel Am Phys Soc; Ital Phys Soc. *Res:* Quantum theory of fields; nuclear and high-energy physics. *Mailing Add:* Dept of Physics Brown Univ Providence RI 02912

FELDMAN, DAVID, b New York, NY, Oct 16, 27; m 51; c 3. ELECTRICAL ENGINEERING. *Educ:* Newark Col Eng, BS, 47, MS, 49. *Prof Exp:* Asst prof elec eng, Cooper Union, 49-54; res engr non-linear magnetics, Polytech Res & Develop Co, 54-56; DIR COMPONENTS LAB, BELL TEL LABS, INC, 56- *Concurrent Pos:* Consult, Aerospace Industs Asn, 62-66, Electronic Industs Asn, 66-71 & Fedn Mat Sci. *Honors & Awards:* Contrib Award, Inst Elec & Electronics Engrs. 77. *Mem:* Fel Inst Elec & Electronics Engrs. *Res:* Thick and thin film component development, electronic materials, feedback control. *Mailing Add:* Bell Tel Labs Inc 555 Union Blvd Allentown PA 18103

FELDMAN, DONALD WILLIAM, b Memphis, Tenn, Oct 5, 31; m 55; c 2. PHYSICS. *Educ:* Southwestern at Memphis, BS, 52; Pa State Univ, MS, 54; Univ Calif, Berkeley, PhD(physics), 59. *Prof Exp:* PHYSICIST, SOLID STATE SCI DEPT, WESTINGHOUSE RES LABS, 59- *Mem:* Am Phys Soc. *Res:* Solid state physics; electron spin resonance; nuclear magnetic resonance; Raman spectroscopy. *Mailing Add:* Solid State Sci Dept Westinghouse Res Labs Beulah Rd Pittsburgh PA 15235

FELDMAN, DOREL, b Romania, Mar 16, 24; Can citizen; m 79; c 1. THERMODYNAMICS, MATERIAL PROPERTIES. *Educ:* Polytech Inst, Iasi, Romania, BA, 49, DrEng, 58, DrSci, 71. *Prof Exp:* Prof polymer chem & technol, Polytech Inst, Iasi Romania, 50-78; ASSOC PROF ENG MAT, ENG FAC, CONCORDIA UNIV, MONTREAL, 78- *Concurrent Pos:* Researcher, Inst Macromolecular Chem, Iasi, Romania, 52-58, head Polymerization Dept, 58-78. *Mem:* Am Chem Soc; Plastics & Rubber Inst; Cancer Res Soc. *Res:* Polymer technology; polymerization; copolymerization; sraft-copolymerization; photopolymerization; polymer blends; polymer compatibility; applications as plastics, synthetic fibers, adhesives, sealants; polymer characterization. *Mailing Add:* Concordia Univ 1455 De Maisonneuve Blvd W Montreal PQ H39 1M8 Can

FELDMAN, DOROTHY, biology, see previous edition

FELDMAN, EDGAR A, b New York, NY, May 11, 37; m 62; c 2. GEOMETRY. *Educ:* Mass Inst Technol, BS, 58; Columbia Univ, PhD(math), 63. *Prof Exp:* Instr math, Princeton Univ, 63-65; from asst prof to assoc prof, 65-74, PROF MATH, CITY UNIV NEW YORK, GRAD CTR, 75- *Mem:* Am Math Soc; Math Asn Am. *Res:* Relationship between the low eigen values of the Laplacian of a compact Riemannian manifold and its topology and differential geometry. *Mailing Add:* City Univ New York Grad Ctr 33 W 42nd St New York NY 10036

FELDMAN, EDWIN B(ARRY), b Atlanta, Ga, Apr 30, 25; m 47; c 3. INDUSTRIAL ENGINEERING. *Educ:* Ga Inst Technol, BIE, 50. *Prof Exp:* Plant engr, Puritan Chem Co, 49-52, plant mgr, 52-58, vpres & dir eng, 58-60; PRES, SERV ENG ASSOCS, INC, 61- *Honors & Awards:* Outstanding Serv Award, Nat Soc Prof Engrs, 67; Distinguished achievement award, Educ Press Asn Am, 74. *Mem:* Nat Soc Prof Engrs; Am Inst Indust Engrs; Am Inst Plant Engrs; Environ Mgt Asn; Am Mgt Asn. *Res:* Application of engineering principles to industrial and institutional housekeeping and sanitation; facilities maintenance and energy conservation; author of over 150 publications. *Mailing Add:* 1023 Burton Dr NE Atlanta GA 30329

FELDMAN, ELAINE BOSSAK, b New York, NY, Dec 9, 26; m 57; c 3. MEDICINE. *Educ:* NY Univ, AB, 45, MS, 48, MD, 51. *Prof Exp:* From intern to resident path, Mt Sinai Hosp, NY, 51-52, asst resident med, 53, asst, 55-57; from instr to assoc prof, State Univ NY Downstate Med Ctr, 57-72; PROF MED, MED COL GA, 72-, CHIEF SECT NUTRIT, 77- *Concurrent Pos:* Fel, Mt Sinai Hosp, NY, 54-55, NY Heart Asn res fel, 55-57; USPHS spec fel physiol chem, Univ Lund, 64-65; from asst vis physician to assoc vis physician, Kings County Hosp, 57-72; attend physician, State Univ Hosp, 66-72 & Eugene Talmadge Mem Hosp; mem nutrit study sect, NIH, 76-80; dir, Ga Inst Human Nutrit, 78- & Clin Nutrit Res Unit, 80- *Mem:* Endocrine Soc; Am Heart Asn; Am Soc Clin Nutrit. *Res:* Nutrition and metabolism, especially the effect of diet and drugs on serum lipids; dietary control of cholesterol absorption and intestinal lipoprotein formation. *Mailing Add:* Dept Med Med Col Ga Augusta GA 30912

FELDMAN, FRED, b Baku, USSR, Dec 4, 42; US citizen; m 65. BIOCHEMISTRY, MEDICAL RESEARCH. *Educ:* Univ Chicago, BS, 66; Purdue Univ, PhD(biochem), 71. *Prof Exp:* Teaching asst biochem, Purdue Univ, 67; res assoc biochem, Ind Univ, 71-74; SR RES SCIENTIST PROCESS DEVELOP, ARMOUR PHARMACEUT CO, 74- *Res:* Human plasma protein purification and characterization; protein chemistry; cell biology; membrane-protein interactions; mitochondrial protein synthesis. *Mailing Add:* 407 Gettysburg St Park Forest 60466 IL

FELDMAN, FREDRIC J, b Brooklyn, NY, Feb 9, 40; m 62; c 2. ANALYTICAL CHEMISTRY, INORGANIC CHEMISTRY. *Educ:* Brooklyn Col, BS, 60; Univ Md, MS, 64, PhD(anal chem), 67. *Prof Exp:* Prin investr, Walter Reed Army Inst Res, 64-68; pres, Chrisfeld Precision Instruments Corp, 64-70, dir anal lab, Instrumentation Lab, 68-70; prog mgr, 70-77, OPERS MGR & DIR EUROP OPERS, BECKMAN INSTRUMENTS INC, 81- *Mem:* AAAS; Am Chem Soc; Am Asn Clin Chem; Soc Appl Spectros. *Res:* Research and development of atomic absorption and emission methods for the analysis of substances of clinical, biological and industrial importance; physiological mechanisms of chromium; coulometric and polarographic studies of biologically important substances. *Mailing Add:* 200 S Kraemer Brea CA 92621

FELDMAN, GARY JAY, b Cheyenne, Wyo, Mar 22, 42; m 67; c 2. ELEMENTARY PARTICLE PHYSICS. *Educ:* Univ Chicago, BS, 64; Harvard Univ, AM, 65, PhD(physics), 71. *Prof Exp:* Res assoc physics, 71-74, staff physicist, 74-79, ASSOC PROF, STANFORD LINEAR ACCELERATOR CTR, 79- *Mem:* Am Phys Soc. *Res:* Electroproduction of hadrons and electron-positron annihilation. *Mailing Add:* Stanford Linear Accelerator Ctr Stanford Univ Stanford CA 94305

FELDMAN, GORDON, b Windsor, Ont, Dec 6, 28. THEORETICAL PHYSICS. *Educ:* Univ Toronto, BA, 50, MA, 51; Univ Birmingham, PhD(physics), 53. *Prof Exp:* Asst physics, Univ Birmingham, 53-55; mem, Inst Advan Study, Princeton Univ, 55-56; res assoc physics, Univ Wis, 56-57; asst prof, 57-64, PROF PHYSICS, JOHNS HOPKINS UNIV, 65- *Concurrent Pos:* Guggenheim fel, 62-63; vis prof physics, Imp Col, London, 68-69 & 74-75. *Res:* High energy physics; elementary particles and field theory. *Mailing Add:* Dept of Physics Johns Hopkins Univ Baltimore MD 21218

FELDMAN, HAROLD SAMUEL, b Boston, Mass, May 8, 17; m 45; c 3. PSYCHIATRY, PSYCHOPHARMACOLOGY. *Educ:* Mass Col Pharm, BS, 39, MS, 42; Boston Univ, PhD(pharmacol), 45, MD, 49. *Prof Exp:* Asst pharmacol, Sch Med, Boston Univ, 42-45, prof mat med, New Eng Col Pharm, 45-49; DIR MED RES, MALTBIE LABS, NEWARK, 50-; DIR DEPT NEUROPSYCHOPHARMACOL, ESSEX COUNTY, OVERBROOK HOSP, CEDAR GROVE, 63-; ASSOC PROF PSYCHIAT, COL MED & DENT NJ, 67- *Concurrent Pos:* Staff psychiatrist & res psychiat training, Essex County, Overbrook Hosp, 64-; dir Quinn Rehab Prog Drug Addicts, Essex County, 67-; dir, Essex County Penitentiary Rehab Prog Narcotics Addicts, 68-71; clin instr, NY Med Col & Seton Hall Col Med; adj prof law, Seton Hall Law Sch; forensic psychiatrist, Essex County Jail & Martland Community Ment Health Ctr; comnr, Millburn-Short Hills Comn Against Alcohol, Crime & Drug Abuse; chief forensic psychiat & assoc prof, Col Med & Dent, NJ. *Honors & Awards:* Am Druggist Award, 40. *Mem:* Fel Am Geriat Soc; Am Soc Pharmacol & Exp Therapeut; AMA; assoc Am Pharmaceut Asn; Am Acad Forensic Sci. *Res:* Internal medicine; clinical and experimental pharmacology; pharmacognosy. *Mailing Add:* Dept of Psychiat Col of Med & Dent NJ Newark NJ 07103

FELDMAN, HARRY ALFRED, b Newark, NJ, May 30, 14; m 39; c 4. MEDICINE. *Educ:* George Washington Univ, AB, 35, MD, 39. *Prof Exp:* Res assoc bact, George Washington Univ, 36-39; intern, Gallinger Hosp, Washington, DC, 39-40; asst resident med, George Washington Univ, 40-41; assoc prof med, 49-55, PROF PREV MED & CHMN DEPT, STATE UNIV NY UPSTATE MED CTR, 55- *Concurrent Pos:* Fel bact infections, George Washington Univ, 41-42; fel med, Harvard Univ, 42; sr fel virus dis, Nat Res Coun, 46-48; dir res, Wieting-Johnson Hosp, 49-55; mem, Nat Bd Med Exam, 65-70, chmn prev med test comt, 67-69; mem comn acute respiratory dis & chmn comt meningococcal infections, Armed Forces Epidemiol Bd; mem comn toxoplasmosis, Int Cong Microbiol. *Honors & Awards:* Sir Spencer Lister Mem Lectr Medal, SAfrican Inst Med Res, 79; Maxwell Finland lectr, Infectious Dis Soc Am, 79. *Mem:* Am Pediat Soc; Am Soc Clin Invest; Am Asn Immunologists; Asn Am Physicians; Int Epidemiol Asn. *Res:* Evaluation of bacterial chemotherapeutic and sero-therapeutic agents; toxoplasmosis; epidemiology; respiratory diseases and meningitis. *Mailing Add:* State Univ of NY Upstate Med Ctr 750 E Adams St Syracuse NY 13210

FELDMAN, HENRY ROBERT, b New York, NY, June 28, 32; m 56; c 1. UNDERWATER ACOUSTICS. *Educ:* Harvard Univ, AB, 53; Columbia Univ, AM, 58, PhD(physics), 63. *Prof Exp:* Res asst prof physics, 63-65, SR PHYSICIST, APPL PHYSICS LAB, UNIV WASH, 66- *Mem:* Sigma Xi; Acoust Soc Am; Am Phys Soc. *Res:* Acoustic lenses; underwater acoustic studies in the Arctic; marine bioacoustics. *Mailing Add:* Univ of Wash Appl Physics Lab 1013 NE 40th St Seattle WA 98105

FELDMAN, ISAAC, b Washington, DC, Mar 6, 18; m 56. CHEMISTRY, BIOPHYSICS. *Educ:* George Washington Univ, BS, 41; Univ Ill, Urbana, PhD(phys chem), 47. *Prof Exp:* Instr electronics, US Army Air Force Tech Sch, Scott Field, Ill, 42-43; instr chem, George Washington Univ, 43-44; jr scientist toxicol, 47-48, from instr to asst prof phys chem, 48-56, assoc prof phys chem, 56-58, assoc prof radiation biol, 58-65, PROF RADIATION BIOL & BIOPHYS, SCH MED & DENT, UNIV ROCHESTER, 65- *Concurrent Pos:* USPHS spec res fel, Univ Col London, 62-63. *Mem:* Am Chem Soc; Biophys Soc; Int Soc Supramolecular Biol; Am Soc Photobiology; Sigma Xi. *Res:* Bioinorganic chemistry; application of magnetic resonance and fluorescence to biophysics; role of metal ions in normal and abnormal biochemistry. *Mailing Add:* Dept of Radiation Biol & Biophys Sch of Med & Dent Rochester NY 14642

FELDMAN, J(AMES) A(RTHUR), b Canton, Minn, Aug 31, 17; m 46. CHEMICAL ENGINEERING. *Educ:* Iowa State Univ, BSc, 39. *Prof Exp:* Chemist, Glidden Co, Ill, 40; chemist, Phillips Petrol Co, 41, group leader, 47-50, chief plant engr, 51-55, proj engr, 56, pilot plant supvr, 57-61, proj mgr process optimization, 61-68; proj mgr, 68-74, SR PROCESS ANAL ENGR, APPL AUTOMATION, INC, 74- *Mem:* Am Inst Chem Engrs. *Res:* Operation of pilot plants and semicommercial plants in chemical and petrochemical branches; improvement of profit potential of processes and plants through coordinated study by multidiscipline teams; feasibility studies for plant/process computer control systems; economic evaluation of benefits; conservation of energy through control applications. *Mailing Add:* Appl Automation Inc Pawhuska Rd Bartlesville OK 74004

FELDMAN, JACOB, b Philadelphia, Pa, Jan 10, 28; div; c 2. MATHEMATICS. *Educ:* Univ Pa, BA, 50; Univ Ill, MA, 51; Univ Chicago, PhD(math), 54. *Prof Exp:* NSF fel, Inst Advan Study, 54-56; vis asst prof, Columbia Univ, 56-57; asst prof, 57-64, PROF MATH, UNIV CALIF, BERKELEY, 64- *Concurrent Pos:* NSF fel, Inst Advan Study, 60-61; exchange visitor, USSR, 67. *Mem:* Am Math Soc; Math Asn Am. *Res:* Stochastic processes; operator algebras; ergodic theory. *Mailing Add:* Dept of Math Univ of Calif Berkeley CA 94704

FELDMAN, JAMES MICHAEL, b Pittsburgh, Pa, Sept 29, 33; m 55; c 1. ELECTRICAL ENGINEERING, PHYSICS. *Educ:* Carnegie Inst Technol, BS, 57, MS, 58, PhD(elec eng), 60. *Prof Exp:* Asst prof elec eng, Carnegie Inst Technol, 60-65; assoc prof, 65-71, dir, Power Systs Eng Prog, 74-82, PROF ELEC ENG, NORTHEASTERN UNIV, 71- *Concurrent Pos:* Res engr quantum electronics, Westinghouse Res Labs, 61-64; vis prof, Technion, Haifa, Israel, 71-72; vis prof, Telaviv Univ, 80-81. *Mem:* Am Phys Soc; Inst Elec & Electronics Engrs. *Res:* Semiconductor devices; optical properties of semiconductors; applied superconductivity; transformer theory. *Mailing Add:* Dept of Elec Eng Northeastern Univ Boston MA 02115

FELDMAN, JEROME A, b Pittsburgh, Pa, Dec 5, 38; m 61; c 2. COMPUTER SCIENCE, MATHEMATICS. *Educ:* Univ Rochester, BA, 60; Univ Pittsburgh, MA, 61; Carnegie Inst Technol, PhD(comput sci), 64. *Prof Exp:* Res scientist comput sci, Carnegie Inst Technol, 63-64; staff mem data systs, Lincoln Lab, Mass Inst Technol, 64-66; from asst prof to assoc prof comput sci, Stanford Univ, 66-75; chmn dept, 75-81, PROF COMPUT SCI, UNIV ROCHESTER, 75- *Concurrent Pos:* Fulbright lectr & vis prof math & comput sci, Hebrew Univ, Jerusalem, 70-71. *Mem:* Asn Comput Mach. *Res:* Programming languages; aritifical intelligence. *Mailing Add:* Dept of Comput Sci Univ of Rochester Rochester NY 14627

FELDMAN, JERRY F, b Philadelphia, Pa, May 11, 42. GENETICS. *Educ:* Swarthmore Col, BA, 63; Princeton Univ, MA, 65, PhD(biol), 67. *Prof Exp:* USPHS res fel biol, Calif Inst Technol, 67-69; asst prof, State Univ NY Albany, 69-74; asst prof, 75-77, assoc prof, 77-81, PROF BIOL, UNIV CALIF, SANTA CRUZ, 81- *Mem:* Am Soc Plant Physiologists; Am Soc Cell Biol; Am Soc Microbiol; Genetics Soc Am; Biophys Soc. *Res:* Biological clocks - genetic and biochemical approaches in neurospora; sexual differentiation in Neurospora. *Mailing Add:* Thimann Labs Univ of Calif Santa Cruz CA 95064

FELDMAN, JOSE M, b Entre Rios, Arg, Sept 27, 27; m 54, 68; c 5. PLANT VIROLOGY. *Educ:* Cuyo Univ, IngAgron, 55. *Prof Exp:* From asst to assoc prof, 56-75, ASSOC PATHOLOGIST, FAC AGRON, NAT UNIV CUYO, 63-, PATHOLOGIST, NAT COUN SCI & TECHNOL RES, 75- *Concurrent Pos:* Nat Coun Sci & Technol Res grants, Arg, 59, 62 & 63; fel, 62-63; lectr, 64-65, prin researcher, 68; consult, Plant Path, Food & Agr Orgn, UN, 81. *Mem:* Arg Soc Plant Physiol; Latin Am Phytopath Asn. *Res:* Plant virus diseases, especially vegetable crops and grapes; plant virus serology; inhibition of plant viruses; physiology of virus-diseased plants. *Mailing Add:* Loria 5882 Chacras de Coria Mendoza Argentina

FELDMAN, JOSEPH AARON, b Fall River, Mass, Feb 2, 25; m 48; c 3. PHARMACEUTICAL CHEMISTRY. *Educ:* RI Col Pharm, BS, 50; Univ Wis, MS, 52, PhD(pharm), 56. *Prof Exp:* Assoc prof, 55-64, PROF PHARMACEUT CHEM, DUQUESNE UNIV, 64- *Concurrent Pos:* Vis anal consult, Ciba-Geigy Co, Basel, Switz, 71. *Mem:* Am Chem Soc; Am Pharmaceut Asn; Acad Pharmaceut Sci. *Res:* Nonaqueous titration; analysis using chelometric methods; fluorimetry; pharmaceutical analysis; effects of solvent systems on drug stability. *Mailing Add:* Sch of Pharm Duquesne Univ Pittsburgh PA 15219

FELDMAN, JOSEPH DAVID, b Hartford, Conn, Dec 13, 16; m 49; c 3. PATHOLOGY. *Educ:* Yale Univ, BA, 37; LI Col Med, MD, 41. *Prof Exp:* From assoc prof to prof path, Sch Med, Univ Pittsburgh, 54-61; chmn, Dept Immunopath, 76-79, MEM STAFF, SCRIPPS CLIN & RES FOUND, LA JOLLA, 61- *Concurrent Pos:* Lectr, Hadassah Med Sch, Hebrew Univ Jerusalem, 50-54; consult, USPHS, 67-, chmn, Path B Study Sect, 67-70; adj prof path, Univ Calif, San Diego, 68-; ed-in-chief, J Immunol, 71-; consult, Nat Cancer Inst Virus Cancer Prog, Sci Rev Comt & Sci Adv Bd, Coun Tobacco Res, 74. *Mem:* Int Acad Path; Histochem Soc; Endocrine Soc; Electron Micros Soc Am; Am Asn Path. *Res:* Immunopathology; cytology. *Mailing Add:* Scripps Clin & Res Found 10666 N Torrey Pines Rd La Jolla CA 92037

FELDMAN, JOSEPH GERALD, b New York, NY, Sept 5, 40; m 64; c 2. BIOSTATISTICS, EPIDEMIOLOGY. *Educ:* Lehman Col, BA, 62; City Univ New York, MBA, 67; Univ NC, DrPH(biostatist), 72. *Prof Exp:* Res assoc statist, Health & Hosp Coun South NY, 63-67; instr statist, Dept Social & Prev Med, State Univ NY Buffalo, 67-71; asst prof, 72-75, ASSOC PROF BIOSTATIST & EPIDEMIOL, DEPT ENVIRON MED & COMMUNITY HEALTH, DOWNSTATE MED CTR, STATE UNIV NY, 75- *Concurrent Pos:* Statist consult, Eval Training Prog, Dept Epidemiol, Sch Pub Health, Univ NC, 72- & Manhattan Vet Admin Hosp, 74-; consult, Breast Cancer Prog Eval, Div Cancer Control, Nat Cancer Inst, 75-, Kings County Med Soc, 80- & data mgt, Kings County Health Care Rev Orgn, 80- *Mem:* Am Statist Asn; Biometric Soc; Am Pub Health Asn; Int Epidemiol Asn. *Res:* Application of biostatistics to problems in epidemiology and public health with emphasis on the epidemiology of cancer; coronary heart disease; evaluation of health services. *Mailing Add:* Dept of Environ Med Downstate Med Ctr Box 43 Brooklyn NY 11203

FELDMAN, JOSEPH LOUIS, b New York, NY, June 6, 38; m 63; c 2. SOLID STATE PHYSICS. *Educ:* Queens Col, BS, 60; Rutgers Univ, MS, 62, PhD(physics), 66. *Prof Exp:* Res fel physics, Rensselaer Polytech Inst, 65-68; RES PHYSICIST, US NAVAL RES LAB, 68- *Mem:* Sigma Xi; Am Phys Soc. *Res:* Lattice vibrations and thermal properties of solids; electronic properties of solids. *Mailing Add:* US Naval Res Lab Matter Physics Br Code 6683 Washington DC 20375

FELDMAN, JULIAN, b Brooklyn, NY, May 24, 15; m 44; c 3. ORGANIC CHEMISTRY. *Educ:* City Col New York, BS, 35; Brooklyn Col, AM, 40; Univ Pittsburgh, PhD(chem), 50. *Prof Exp:* Chief chemist, Pro-Medico Labs, 35-40 & Gold-Leaf Pharmacal Co, 40-41; asst chemist, Bur Animal Indust, USDA, 41; asst plant mgr, Trubek Labs, 41-42; res assoc explosives res lab, Nat Defense Res Comn, 42-45; res chemist, Bur Mines, 45-53; group leader, Nat Distillers Prod & Chem Corp, 53-57, res supvr, 57-59, sr res assoc, 59-74, mgr explor chem res, US Indust Chem Co Div, Nat Distillers & Chem Corp, 74-81, RES SCIENTIST, USI CHEM CO, 81- *Mem:* AAAS; Am Chem Soc. *Res:* Separations and purifications; phase equilibria; distillation; kinetics; isomerization; catalysis; composition of fuels and carbonization products; molecular complexes; polynuclear compounds; catalytic organic processes. *Mailing Add:* 7511 Sagamore Dr Cincinnati OH 45236

FELDMAN, KARL THOMAS, JR, mechanical engineering, see previous edition

FELDMAN, LARRY HOWARD, b Brooklyn, NY, Feb 25, 42; m 64; c 3. PHOTOGRAPHIC CHEMISTRY. *Educ:* Brooklyn Col, BS, 62; Mich State Univ, PhD(chem), 66. *Prof Exp:* Sr res chemist, Res Labs, 66-70, sr develop engr, 70-73, tech assoc, 73-76, SUPVR, KODAK PARK DIV, EASTMAN KODAK CO, 76- *Mem:* Am Chem Soc; Soc Photog Sci & Eng. *Res:* Photographic science and technology of silver halide systems; electron attachment reactions in anhydrous ethylenediamine; photographic paper quality control and product development. *Mailing Add:* 99 Hillhurst Lane Rochester NY 14617

FELDMAN, LAWRENCE, b Havana, Cuba, Apr 5, 22; US citizen; m 52. NUCLEAR PHYSICS, ACCELERATORS. *Educ:* Brooklyn Col, BA, 43; Univ NC, MS, 44; Columbia Univ, PhD(physics), 50. *Prof Exp:* Instr physics, Univ NC, 43-44; physicist, Naval Ord Lab, 44-46; asst physics, Columbia Univ, 46-48, res assoc, 50-63, Higgins fel, 51-52, dir 36'' cyclotron, 52-63; sr res assoc, Univ Pa, 63-64; assoc prof, 64-69, PROF PHYSICS, ST JOHN'S UNIV, NY, 69- *Concurrent Pos:* Lectr, City Col New York, 52-64. *Mem:* Am Phys Soc. *Res:* Lambda beta decay; weak interactions; nuclear reactions; giant resonance phenomena; C-W cyclotron; high forbidden nuclear beta decay; calculations of atomic energy levels in helium. *Mailing Add:* Dept Physics St John's Univ Jamaica NY 11439

FELDMAN, LAWRENCE A, b Brooklyn, NY, Oct 11, 38; m 61; c 1. MICROBIOLOGY, VIROLOGY. *Educ:* Univ Wis, BS, 60; Pa State Univ, MA, 62, PhD(microbiol), 64. *Prof Exp:* USPHS training fel virol & epidemiol, Col Med, Baylor Univ, 64-66; from instr to asst prof microbiol, 66-71, asst dean student affairs, 71-73, assoc prof microbiol, 71-78, asst dean admin, 73-76, assoc dean planning & mgt, 76-77, PROF MICROBIOL, COL MED & DENT NJ, NEWARK, 78- *Mem:* AAAS; Am Soc Microbiol; Brit Soc Gen Microbiol. *Res:* Viral diseases of the central nervous system; viral oncogenesis; abortive viral infections. *Mailing Add:* Dept of Microbiol Col of Med & Dent of NJ Newark NJ 07103

FELDMAN, LEONARD, b Jamaica, NY, Oct 3, 23; m 48; c 2. MATHEMATICS EDUCATION, MATHEMATICAL LITERACY. *Educ:* Queen's Col, NY, BS, 48; Columbia Univ, MA, 50; Univ Calif, Berkeley, EdD(counseling psychol), 57. *Prof Exp:* Tech writer electron tube group, NY Univ, 48-49; teacher pub schs, NY & Calif, 49-57; from asst prof to assoc prof, 57-70, PROF MATH & EDUC, SAN JOSE STATE UNIV, 70- *Concurrent Pos:* Dir, NSF Acad Year Inst, 62-63, 66-68, NSF sci fac fel, 64-65; vis assoc prof, Columbia Univ on assignment to Makerere Univ, Uganda, 68-70. *Mem:* Asn Women in Math; Am Math Asn Two Yr Cols; Math Asn Am; Nat Coun Teachers Math; Res Coun Diag & Prescriptive Math. *Res:* Evaluation of mathematics education; in-service education for teachers; learning theory; mathematics for reluctant and anxious learners. *Mailing Add:* Dept of Math San Jose State Univ San Jose CA 95192

FELDMAN, LEONARD CECIL, b New York, NY, June 8, 39; m 64; c 2. SOLID STATE PHYSICS, ATOMIC PHYSICS. *Educ:* Drew Univ, BA, 61; Rutgers Univ, MS, 63, PhD(atomic physics), 67. *Prof Exp:* MEM TECH STAFF SOLID STATE PHYSICS, BELL LABS, 67- *Concurrent Pos:* Res assoc physics, Rutgers Univ, 69-; guest scientist solid state physics, Aarhus Univ, Denmark, 70-71; guest lectr physics, Drew Univ, 75 & 77; mem, Int Comn Ion Beam Anal Conf & Int Comn Atomic Collisions in Solids Conf, 75-; chmn, Gordon Conf Particle-Solid Interactions, 76-78; res assoc, Univ Guelph, 77-; vis prof mat sci, Cornell Univ, 81. *Mem:* Am Phys Soc; Am Vacuum Soc; AAAS. *Res:* Use of energetic ion beams for the modification and analysis of solids and solid surfaces; physics of ion-solid interactions; surface science. *Mailing Add:* Rm 1E-434 Bell Labs Murray Hill NJ 07974

FELDMAN, LOUIS A, b Bay City, Mich, Nov 26, 41. TOPOLOGY, GEOMETRY. *Educ:* Univ Mich, BS, 63; Univ Calif, Berkeley, MA, 65, PhD(math), 69. *Prof Exp:* Asst math, Univ Calif, Berkeley, 64-68; from asst prof to assoc prof 68-76, PROF MATH, CALIF STATE COL, STANISLAUS, 76- *Mem:* Am Math Soc; Oper Res Soc Am. *Res:* Algebraic topology; the relationship between fibre bundles and topological transformation groups. *Mailing Add:* Dept of Math Calif State Col Stanislaus Turlock CA 95380

FELDMAN, MARC ALAN, b Madison, Wis, May 25, 52; m 77. CRIMINALISTICS, FORENSIC CHEMISTRY. *Educ:* Cornell Univ, AB, 73; Kans State Univ, PhD(anal chem), 81. *Prof Exp:* Analyst, Crucible Steel, Colt Indust, 70; chemiker, Ciba-Geigy, Basel, Switz, 71; line off, US Navy, 73-77; grad teaching asst & res asst, Kans State Univ, 77-81; RES CHEMIST, E I DUPONT DE NEMOURS CO, INC, 81- *Mem:* Sigma Xi; Anal Div Affil. *Res:* Analytical methods for chemical manufacture and environment analysis past. *Mailing Add:* Jackson Lab E I DuPont Deepwater NJ 08023

FELDMAN, MARCUS WILLIAM, b Perth, Australia, Nov 14, 42; m 64; c 1. MATHEMATICAL BIOLOGY. *Educ:* Univ Western Australia, BSc, 64; Monash Univ, Australia, MSc, 66; Stanford Univ, PhD(math biol), 69. *Prof Exp:* Tutor math, Monash Univ, Australia, 64-65; res asst, 65-69, asst prof, 69-74, assoc prof, 74-77, PROF BIOL, STANFORD UNIV, 77- *Concurrent Pos:* Ed, Theoret Pop Biol. *Mem:* Am Soc Naturalists; Genetics Soc Am. *Res:* Mathematical models of genetical phenomena, primarily selection and recombination; population genetics and ecology of a theoretical nature. *Mailing Add:* Dept of Biol Stanford Univ Stanford CA 94305

FELDMAN, MARTIN, b New York, NY, July 13, 35; m 61; c 3. PHYSICS. *Educ:* Rensselaer Polytech Inst, BS, 57; Cornell Univ, PhD(physics), 62. *Prof Exp:* Res assoc physics, Cornell Univ, 62-63; asst prof, Univ Pa, 63-68; MEM TECH STAFF, BELL LABS, 68- *Mem:* Am Phys Soc; Optical Soc Am; Inst Elec & Electronics Engrs. *Res:* Experimental high energy physics; electronics; optics. *Mailing Add:* 141 Murray Hill Blvd Murray Hill NJ 07974

FELDMAN, MARTIN LEONARD, b New York, NY, May 22, 37; c 2. NEUROANATOMY. *Educ:* Brown Univ, AB, 58; Boston Univ, MA, 64, PhD(psychol), 69. *Prof Exp:* Res assoc, 70-71, asst prof, 71-77, ASSOC PROF ANAT, BOSTON UNIV, 77- *Concurrent Pos:* NIH fels, New Eng Regional Primate Res Ctr, 68-69 & Boston Univ, 69-70. *Mem:* AAAS; Am Asn Anat; Int Brain Res Orgn; Gerontol Soc. *Res:* Neurocytology of the aging brain; neuroanatomy of the central auditory system and cerebral cortex. *Mailing Add:* Dept of Anat Boston Univ Sch of Med Boston MA 02118

FELDMAN, MARTIN LOUIS, b Brooklyn, NY, June 14, 41; m 62; c 2. ORGANIC CHEMISTRY. *Educ:* City Col New York, BS, 63; Univ Pittsburgh, PhD(org chem), 66. *Prof Exp:* Chemist, Am Cyanamid Corp, 66-72; sr chemist, 72-77, LAB MGR, ORG & POLYMERS DIV, TENNECO CHEM, 77- *Mem:* Soc Coatings Technol; Am Chem Soc. *Res:* Pigments; colorants for coatings; thermoset and thermoplastics; coating additives. *Mailing Add:* 9 Fieldcrest Dr East Brunswick NJ 08816

FELDMAN, MARTIN ROBERT, b New York, NY, Apr 23, 38; m 59; c 2. ORGANIC CHEMISTRY. *Educ:* Columbia Univ, AB, 58; Univ Calif, Los Angeles, PhD(phys & org chem), 63. *Prof Exp:* Res chemist, Univ Calif, Berkeley, 62-63; from asst prof to assoc prof, 63-71, PROF CHEM, HOWARD UNIV, 71- *Concurrent Pos:* NSF sci fac fel, Univ Calif, Irvine, 69-70; vis scientist, King's Col, London, 77-78. *Mem:* Am Chem Soc; The Chem Soc. *Res:* Physical-organic chemistry. *Mailing Add:* Dept Chem Howard Univ Washington DC 20059

FELDMAN, MILTON H, b New York, NY, Mar 17, 18; m 46; c 4. PHYSICAL CHEMISTRY. *Educ:* NY Univ, BS, 39, PhD(phys chem), 44. *Prof Exp:* Scientist, Oak Ridge Nat Lab, 46-49; res engr, NAm Aviation Co, 49-53; adv scientist, Bettis Atomic Power Lab, 53-59; dep tech dir, Defense Atomic Support Agency, 59-60; tech dir, Winchester Environ Lab, 60-61; chief radiation & radiochem sect, Walter Reed Army Inst Res, 61-66; res chemist, Environ Protection Agency, 66-81. *Concurrent Pos:* Consult indust req, Dept Defense, Environ Protection Agency & Occupational Safety & Health Admin. *Mem:* Fel AAAS; fel Am Inst Chem; fel Royal Soc Arts. *Res:* Radiation effects; nuclear technology; environmental and planetary sciences; biophysics; chemical and biological oceanography; ecological response of trace materials. *Mailing Add:* 3625 N Roosevelt Dr Corvallis OR 97330

FELDMAN, NATHANIEL E, b New London, Conn, Oct 7, 25; m 46; c 4. ELECTRONICS. *Educ:* Univ Calif, Berkeley, BS, 48, MS, 50. *Prof Exp:* Asst elec eng, Univ Calif, Berkeley, 49-50, engr, Lawrence Radiation Lb, 51-54; instr fire control radar, Hughes Aircraft Co, 55; leader adv develop defense electronic prod div, Radio Corp Am, 56-60; proj leader, systs anal, Rand Corp, 60-78; chief scientist, Systs Res Oper, Sci Appln Inc, 78-81; SYSTS DIR, ADVAN SPACE COMMUN, AEROSPACE CORP, 81- *Mem:* Sr mem Inst Elec & Electronics Engrs; assoc fel Am Inst Aeronaut & Astronaut; Sigma Xi. *Res:* Satellite communications; components for microwave systems for radar, electronic counter measures and aerospace communications; systems analysis and exploratory design. *Mailing Add:* 2350 El Segundo Blvd PO Box 92957 El Segundo CA 90245

FELDMAN, NICHOLAS, b Mukacevo, Czech, Sept 25, 24; US citizen; m 58; c 2. PETROLEUM CHEMISTRY, ANALYTICAL CHEMISTRY. *Educ:* Prague Tech Univ, MS, 49. *Prof Exp:* Anal chemist, Fiber Chem Corp, NJ, 50-52, chief chemist, 52-57; from res chemist to sr res chemist, 57-68, res assoc, 68-75, SR RES ASSOC, PROD RES DIV, EXXON RES & ENG CO, 75- *Mem:* Am Chem Soc. *Res:* Effect of fuel and lube additives on product quality; interaction of additives; mechanism of wax crystal modification; leather and textile specialties; analytical methods; compositional analysis. *Mailing Add:* Prod Res Div Exxon Res & Eng Co PO Box 51 Linden NJ 07036

FELDMAN, PAUL ARNOLD, b Everett, Mass, Apr 22, 40; c 2. RADIO ASTRONOMY, ASTROPHYSICS. *Educ:* Mass Inst Technol, BS, 61; Stanford Univ, PhD(physics), 69. *Prof Exp:* Res fel astrophys, Inst Theoret Astron, Univ Cambridge, 68-70 & Dept Physics, Queen's Univ, Ont, 70-72; lectr astron & astrophys, York Univ, 72-74; res officer astron, Dominion Radio Astron Observ, Penticton, BC, 74-75; RES OFFICER ASTRON, HERZBERG INST ASTROPHYS, NAT RES COUN CAN, 75- *Concurrent Pos:* NATO fel sci, Univ Cambridge, 68-69. *Honors & Awards:* First Prize, Gravity Res Found, 70. *Mem:* Int Astron Union; Am Astron Soc; Can Astron Soc. *Res:* Stellar radio astronomy and astrophysics; microwave spectroscopy of complex interstellar molecules; general radio astrophysics; infrared astronomy. *Mailing Add:* Herzberg Inst Astrophys Nat Res Coun Can 100 Sussex Dr Ottawa Can

FELDMAN, PAUL DONALD, b Brooklyn, NY, Nov 4, 39; m 65; c 2. ATMOSPHERIC PHYSICS, ULTRAVIOLENT ASTRONOMY. *Educ:* Columbia Univ, AB, 60, MA, 62, PhD(atomic physics), 64. *Prof Exp:* Instr physics, Columbia Univ, 64-65, res assoc, Naval Res Lab, 65-67; asst prof, 67-72, assoc prof, 72-76, PROF PHYSICS, JOHNS HOPKINS UNIV, 76- *Concurrent Pos:* Sloan Found res fel, 69-73. *Mem:* Am Geophys Union; Am Astron Soc; Am Phys Soc; Int Astron Union. *Res:* Aurora; comets; ultraviolet astronomy. *Mailing Add:* Dept Physics Johns Hopkins Univ Baltimore MD 21218

FELDMAN, RICHARD MARTIN, b Wyandotte, Mich, July 19, 44; m 67; c 2. OPERATIONS RESEARCH, PROBABILITY. *Educ:* Hope Col, AB, 66; Mich State Univ, MS, 67; Ohio Univ, MS, 70; Northwestern Univ, PhD(indust eng), 75. *Prof Exp:* Mathematician, Goodyear Atomic Corp, 67-70; instr indust eng, Ohio Univ, 70-72; opers res analyst, Michael Reese Med Ctr, 74-75; asst prof, 75-80, ASSOC PROF INDUST ENG, TEX A&M UNIV, 80- *Mem:* Opers Res Soc Am; Am Inst Indust Engrs; Sigma Xi. *Res:* Mathematical modeling of plant-pest agricultural systems; probabilistic description of biological and ecological phenomena; applications of Markov renewal theory to both biological and industrial processes. *Mailing Add:* Dept of Indust Eng Tex A&M Univ College Station TX 77843

FELDMAN, SAMUEL M, b Philadelphia, Pa, Sept 26, 33; div; c 2. NEUROSCIENCE. *Educ:* Univ Pa, AB, 54; Northwestern Univ, AM, 55; McGill Univ, PhD(physiol psychol), 59. *Prof Exp:* Fel, Univ Wash, 58-60; from instr to assoc prof physiol, Albert Einstein Col Med, 60-71; PROF PSYCHOL, NY UNIV, 71- *Concurrent Pos:* Consult, NIMH, 68-72, 74-78 & 80-84; assoc ed, Brain Res, 70-74. *Mem:* Soc Neurosci; Am Physiol Soc; NY Acad Sci; Sigma Xi. *Res:* The role of catecholamines in the regulation of cerebral circulation and behavior; role of the locus coeruleus in behavior; aging brain; cellular activity of neurons in midbrain. *Mailing Add:* 37 Washington Square W New York NY 10011

FELDMAN, STUART, b Bronx, NY, Feb 14, 41; m 63; c 2. PHARMACEUTICS, BIOPHARMACEUTICS. *Educ:* Columbia Univ, BS, 62, MS, 66; State Univ NY Buffalo, PhD(pharmaceut), 69. *Prof Exp:* From asst prof to assoc prof biopharmaceut, Sch Pharm, Temple Univ, 69-74; ASSOC PROF PHARMACEUT, DEPT PHARMACEUT, COL PHARM, UNIV HOUSTON, 74-, CHMN DEPT, 76- *Mem:* Fel Acad Pharmaceut Sci; AAAS; Am Pharmaceut Asn; Am Col Clin Pharmacol; NY Acad Sci. *Res:* Effect of surface active agents on drug absorption; study of the biopharmaceutical factors influencing drug absorption, distribution and elimination; pharmacokinetics. *Mailing Add:* Dept Pharmaceut Univ Houston 1441 Moursund Houston TX 77030

FELDMAN, SUSAN C, b Brooklyn, NY, Oct 1, 43. NEUROANATOMY, NEUROENDOCRINOLOGY. *Educ:* Hofstra Univ, BA, 63; Rutgers Univ, MS, 67; City Univ NY, PhD(biol), 76. *Prof Exp:* Fel neurol, Albert Einstein Col Med, Col Physicians & Surgeons, Columbia Univ, 75-77, fel anat, 77-79; ASST PROF ANAT, MED SCH, UNIV MED & DENT NJ, 79- *Mem:* Am Asn Anatomists; AAAS; Soc Neurosci; NY Acad Sci. *Res:* Organization of the central nervous system by determining the biochemistry of neurons using immunohistochemistry and related techniques to identify transmitters and other molecules intrinsic to particular neuronal populations, and correlating these with projections; development of neurons in vitro as a means of studying the organization of neurons and the regulation of gene expression. *Mailing Add:* Dept Anat Sch Med Univ Med & Dent NJ NJ Med Sch 100 Bergen St Newark NJ 07103

FELDMAN, URI, b Tel-Aviv, Israel. ATOMIC SPECTROSCOPY, SOLAR PHYSICS. *Educ:* Hebrew Univ Jerusalem, MSc, 63, PhD(physics), 65. *Prof Exp:* Fel spectros, Goddard Space Flight Ctr, Greenbelt, Md, 65-67; lectr spectros, 67-69, sr lectr astrophys, 69-71, dir, Wise Astron Observ, 69-72, assoc prof astrophys, Tel-Aviv Univ, 71-74; ASTROPHYSICIST, NAVAL RES LAB, 74- *Mem:* Royal Astron Soc; fel Optical Soc Am; Int Astron Union. *Res:* Investigation of ultraviolet and x-ray from the sun; physical conditions in laser produced plasmas, and konamat plasmas. *Mailing Add:* EO Hulburt Ctr Space Res Naval Res Lab Washington DC 20375

FELDMAN, WILLIAM, b New London, Conn, Sept 15, 17; m 49; c 3. PHYSICS, RESEARCH ADMINISTRATION. *Educ:* Purdue Univ, BS, 39; Univ Pa, PhD(physics), 42. *Prof Exp:* Sr physicist, Radiation Lab, Univ Calif, 42-43; supt pilot plant, Tenn Eastman Corp, Oak Ridge, 43, asst supt prod dept, 43-45; res physicist, 45-51, asst supt eng & develop, Guided Missiles Sect, Naval Ord Div, 51-56, asst dir res & develop, Apparatus & Optical Div, 56-64, proj group mgr res & eng, 64-65, prog mgr apparatus div, 65-74, mgr lunar orbiter prog, 66-74, MGR RES LAB, KODAK APPARATUS DIV, EASTMAN KODAK CO, 74- *Honors & Awards:* Pub Serv Award, NASA, 67, Apollo Achievement Award, 70. *Mem:* AAAS; Am Phys Soc; Am Inst Physics; NY Acad Sci. *Res:* Electromagnetic isotope separation; nuclear physics; camera and shutter design; guided missiles; data processing; information storage and retrieval; professional motion picture and television equipment; space satellite projects; lunar orbiter. *Mailing Add:* Eastman Kodak Co Apparatus Div 901 Elmgrove Rd Rochester NY 14650

FELDMAN, WILLIAM A, b Brookline, Mass, Mar 28, 45; m 76; c 3. FUNCTION SPACES. *Educ:* Tufts Univ, BS, 67; Northwestern Univ, MS, 68; Queen's Univ, PhD(math), 71. *Prof Exp:* Asst prof, 71-76, assoc prof, 76-81, PROF MATH, UNIV ARK, 81- *Mem:* Math Asn Am; Am Math Soc. *Res:* Functional analysis and topology on function spaces. *Mailing Add:* Dept Math Univ Ark Fayetteville AR 72701

FELDMAN, WILLIAM CHARLES, b New York, NY, Apr 15, 40; m 65; c 2. SPACE PHYSICS. *Educ:* Mass Inst Technol, BS, 61; Stanford Univ, PhD(physics), 68. *Prof Exp:* Fel space physics, Univ Wis, 70-71; MEM STAFF SPACE PHYSICS, LOS ALAMOS SCI LAB, 71- *Mem:* Am Geophys Union. *Res:* Solar and interplanetary physics. *Mailing Add:* Los Alamos Sci Lab MS 436 Los Alamos NM 87545

FELDMANN, EDWARD GEORGE, b Chicago, Ill, Oct 13, 30; m 52; c 4. PHARMACEUTICAL CHEMISTRY. *Educ:* Loyola Univ, Ill, BS, 52; Univ Wis, MS, 54, PhD(pharmaceut chem, biochem), 55. *Prof Exp:* Lab asst, Loyola Univ, Ill, 51-52; Alumni Res Found asst, Univ Wis, 52-53; sr chemist, Chem Div, Am Dent Asn, 55-58, dir, 58-59; chmn elect comt nat formulary & assoc dir rev, 59-60, chmn comt & dir rev, 60-69, ed, J Pharmaceut Sci, 60-74, asst exec dir sci affairs, 69-70, ASSOC EXEC DIR, AM PHARMACEUT ASN, 70- *Concurrent Pos:* Spec lectr, George Washington Univ, 60-65; deleg, US Pharmacopeia, 70-; mem, Nat Res Coun, 71-; mem, Nat Coun on Drugs, 76-; mem food codex panel, Nat Acad Sci-Nat Res Coun & expert panel pharmaceut, WHO. *Mem:* Am Chem Soc; Am Pharmaceut Asn; NY Acad Sci; assoc mem AMA; Int Pharmaceut Fedn. *Res:* Analysis of pharmaceutical products; standards and specifications for drugs and dosage forms; chemistry of local anesthetics; chemical structure-therapeutic activity relationships; synthetic organic medicinal chemistry; federal drug law. *Mailing Add:* Am Pharmaceut Asn 2215 Constitution Ave NW Washington DC 20037

FELDMANN, GEORGE WILFRED, b Wilkes-Barre, Pa, Feb 5, 15; m. CHEMICAL ENGINEERING. *Educ:* Columbia Univ, AB, 39, BS, 40, ChE, 41. *Prof Exp:* Res chemist, Jackson Lab, 41, develop engr, 41-45, indust engr, eng dept, 45-49, res chemist, textile res & rayon mfg, textile fibers dept, 49-54 & pigments dept, 54-61, RES CHEMIST, TRAFFIC RES & DEVELOP, E I DU PONT DE NEMOURS & CO, INC, 61- *Mem:* Am Inst Chem Engrs; Soc Naval Archit & Marine Engrs. *Res:* Rubber chemicals; flourine, titanium, titanium oxide process development; cost reduction; financial analysis; marine engineering; movement of bulk dangerous products by barge and vessel. *Mailing Add:* Traffic & Develop Dept 4 Hoiland Dr Wilmington DE 19898

FELDMANN, RODNEY MANSFIELD, b Steele, NDak, Nov 19, 39; m 64; c 1. INVERTEBRATE PALEONTOLOGY. *Educ:* Univ NDak, BS, 61, MS, 63, PhD(paleont), 67. *Prof Exp:* Teaching asst geol, Univ NDak, 62-65; from instr to assoc prof, 65-75, asst dean col arts & sci, 66-67, PROF GEOL, KENT STATE UNIV, 75-, ASST CHMN DEPT, 76- *Concurrent Pos:* Ed, Compass, Sigma Gamma Epsilon, 72-76; co-ed, J Paleont, Paleont Soc, 77- *Mem:* Geol Soc Am; Paleont Soc; Am Asn Petrol Geol. *Res:* Cretaceous stratigraphy of the midcontinent; taxonomy, biogeography and paleoecology of decapod crustaceans. *Mailing Add:* Dept Geol Kent State Univ Kent OH 44242

FELDMEIER, JOSEPH ROBERT, b Niles, Ohio, Feb 17, 16; m 42; c 5. NUCLEAR PHYSICS. *Educ:* Carnegie Inst Technol, BS, 38; Univ Notre Dame, MS, 40, PhD(nuclear physics), 42. *Prof Exp:* Asst physics, Univ Notre Dame, 38-42; staff mem, Radiation Lab, Mass Inst Technol, 42-46; asst prof physics, Rutgers Univ, 46-48; prof & chmn dept, Col St Thomas, 48-52; physics mgr, Bettis Atomic Power Lab, Westinghouse Elec Corp, 52-60; assoc dir & dir sci lab, Philco Corp, 60-64; dir res labs, Franklin Inst, 64-73, vpres, Inst, 67-73; vpres, STV Engrs, 73-76; DEAN, MONTGOMERY COUNTY COMMUNITY COL, 76- *Concurrent Pos:* Tech consult, Fed Telecommun Labs, NJ, 46-48; mem adv coun sci, Univ Notre Dame, 70- *Mem:* AAAS; Am Nuclear Soc; fel Am Phys Soc; sr mem Inst Elec & Electronics Engrs; Sigma Xi. *Res:* Nuclear physics using Van der Graaf generator; design of radar transmitters; low temperature research using Collins liquefier; excitation of nuclei by x-ray; reactor physics; electronics. *Mailing Add:* 631 Midway Lane Blue Bell PA 19422

FELDMESSER, JULIUS, b New York, NY, Oct 23, 18; m 44; c 2. PLANT NEMATOLOGY, INVERTEBRATE ZOOLOGY. *Educ:* Brooklyn Col, AB, 40; NY Univ, MS, 51, PhD(invert zool, parasitol), 53. *Prof Exp:* Asst biol, NY Univ, 48-49; from jr nematologist to prin nematologist, 48-63, RESEARCH NEMATOLOGIST, AGR RES, USDA, 63-, TECH ADV NAT RES PROGS AGR CHEM TECHNOL & RES LEADER, 75- *Concurrent Pos:* Consult, Spencer Chem Co, 57 & 58 & Int Mineral & Chem Corp, 64. *Mem:* Fel AAAS; Soc Nematol; Am Soc Zool; Sigma Xi; Controlled Release Soc. *Res:* Parasitology; nematicide evaluation and development of evaluation techniques; host-parasite relationships; zoology and chemical control of plant-parasitic nematodes; controlled release nematicide formulations; forage grass nematode biology; new safer nematicides. *Mailing Add:* Nematol Lab Plant Protect Inst USDA BARC-W Beltsville MD 20705

FELDMETH, CARL ROBERT, b Los Angeles, Calif, Mar 16, 42; m 64. ZOOLOGY, ENVIRONMENTAL PHYSIOLOGY. *Educ:* Calif State Col, Los Angeles, BS, 64; Univ Toronto, MSc, 66, PhD(zool), 68. *Prof Exp:* Lectr zool, Univ Calif, Los Angeles, 68-71; asst prof, 71-74, ASSOC PROF BIOL, JOINT SCI DEPT, CLAREMONT COLS, 74- *Mem:* Am Soc Limnol & Oceanog; Can Soc Zoologists. *Res:* Environmental physiology; marine crustacea; aquatic insects; respiratory and osmotic regulation; effect of thermal effluent on marine invertebrates and fish; comparative energy studies on swimming marine and freshwater fish; thermal tolerance of desert pupfish. *Mailing Add:* Joint Sci Dept Claremont Cols Claremont CA 91711

FELDSTEIN, ALAN, b Pittsburgh, Pa, Feb 28, 33; m 55; c 4. COMPUTER SCIENCE, NUMERICAL ANALYSIS. *Educ:* Ariz State Univ, BA, 54; Univ Calif, Los Angeles, PhD(math), 64. *Prof Exp:* Staff mem comput prog, Los Alamos Sci Lab, 56-60; res asst numerical anal, Univ Calif, Los Angeles, 60-64; asst prof math, Univ Calif, Los Angeles, 64-65; asst prof appl math, Brown Univ, 65-68; assoc prof comput sci, Univ VA, 68-70; assoc prof, 70-74, PROF MATH, ARIZ STATE UNIV, 74- *Concurrent Pos:* Consult, US Naval Res Lab, 70-74. *Mem:* Asn Comput Mach; Soc Indust & Appl Math. *Res:* Computer arithmetic; numerical solution of and theory of functional differential equations; iteration theory; parallel algorithms. *Mailing Add:* Dept of Math Ariz State Univ Tempe AZ 85281

FELDSTEIN, NATHAN, b Haifa, Israel, Jan 4, 37; US citizen; m 61; c 3. PHYSICAL CHEMISTRY. *Educ:* City Col New York, BChE, 60; NY Univ, MS, 64, PhD(chem), 66. *Prof Exp:* Engr, Corning Glass Works, 60; lectr chem, Brooklyn Col, 64-66; res scientist, David Sarnoff Res Ctr, RCA Labs, 66-73; PRES, SURFACE TECHNOL, INC, 73- *Concurrent Pos:* Div ed, J Electrochem Soc. *Honors & Awards:* David Sarnoff Achievement Awards, 68, 72 & 73. *Mem:* Am Chem Soc; Electrochem Soc; fel Am Inst Chemists. *Res:* Adsorption effects in electrochemistry; electroless plating catalysis; composite electroless deposition. *Mailing Add:* Surface Technol Inc Box 2027 Princeton NJ 08540

FELDT, LEONARD SAMUEL, b Long Branch, NJ, Nov 2, 25; m 54; c 2. APPLIED STATISTICS. *Educ:* Rutgers Univ, BSc, 50, MEd, 51; Univ Iowa, PhD(educ), 54. *Prof Exp:* From asst prof to prof educ measurement, 55-81, chmn, Div Educ Psychol, 77-81, E F LINDQUIST DISTINGUISHED PROF EDUC MEASUREMENT & DIR, IOWA TESTING PROGS, UNIV IOWA, 81- *Mem:* Psychomet Soc; Am Educ Res Asn; Am Statist Asn; Inst Math Statist. *Res:* Experimental design; educational measurement; psychometrics. *Mailing Add:* Col Educ Univ Iowa Iowa City IA 52242

FELGER, MAURICE MONROE, b Ft Wayne, Ind, Feb 5, 08; m 33; c 3. CHEMISTRY. *Educ:* Ind Univ, AB, 30, AM, 31, PhD(chem), 33. *Prof Exp:* Instr chem, Exten Div, Ind Univ, 33-39, asst prof, Ft Wayne Ctr, 39-41; assoc chemist, US Nitrate Plant, Wilson Dam, 41-45; develop chemist, Gen Elec Co, 45-73; CONSULT POLYMER CHEM & PLASTICS, 73- *Mem:* Am Chem Soc; Soc Plastics Eng. *Res:* Electrolytic deposition of metals; high pressure synthesis; synthetic resins as electrical insulation. *Mailing Add:* 315 Arcadia Ct Ft Wayne IN 46807

FELICETTA, VINCENT FRANK, b Seattle, Wash, July 20, 19; m 42; c 2. ORGANIC POLYMER CHEMISTRY. *Educ:* Univ Wash, BS, 42; MS, 51. *Prof Exp:* Chemist, US Rubber Co, Mich, 42-45; res chemist, Pulp Mills Res Proj, Univ Wash, 45-53, res assoc, 53-57, res asst prof, 57-59; from res chemist to sr chemist, 59-69, admin asst, 69-72, coordr chem res, 72-76, ASSOC DIR PROD DEVELOP, BELLINGHAM DIV, GA-PAC CORP, 76- *Mem:* Am Chem Soc. *Res:* Organic natural polymers, structure and ulitization of lignin, building materials, polymer fractionation and characterization; product development. *Mailing Add:* 2958 Plymouth Dr Bellingham WA 98225

FELICIANO-DODONOFF, MANUEL, b Mayaguez, PR, Nov 5, 28; m 51; c 8. MATHEMATICS. *Educ:* Polytech Inst PR, BA, 47; Columbia Univ, MA, 51; Univ Tenn, PhD(math), 70. *Prof Exp:* From instr to assoc prof math, Cath Univ PR, 51-57; mathematician, Oak Ridge Nat Lab, 57-74; MEM STAFF, AEROSPACE CORP, 74- *Concurrent Pos:* Prog group leader, Oak Ridge Nat Lab, 62-70, prog consult, 70-74. *Mem:* Math Asn Am; Asn Comput Math. *Res:* Programming languages, especially the algorithmic; special functions; ordinary differential equations. *Mailing Add:* Aerospace Corp B-A2 Rm 2043 Box 92957 Los Angeles CA 90009

FELICIOTTI, ENIO, b Southbridge, Mass, Oct 9, 26; m 50; c 3. FOOD CHEMISTRY. *Educ:* Univ Boston, AB, 49, AM, 52; Univ Mass, PhD(food technol), 56. *Prof Exp:* Instr food technol, Univ Mass, 53-55; mgr customer res, Hazel Atlas Glass Div, Continental Can Co, Inc, 55-60; from mgr prod develop to vpres res, 60-77, vpres, 77-81, SR VPRES RES, DEVELOP & QUAL ASSURANCE, THOMAS J LIPTON, INC, 81- *Concurrent Pos:* Tech consult, For Agr Serv, USDA, 53-54. *Mem:* AAAS; Am Chem Soc; Inst Food Technol. *Res:* Food research; administration. *Mailing Add:* Thomas J Lipton Inc 800 Sylvan Ave Englewood Cliffs NJ 07631

FELIG, PHILIP, b New York, NY, Dec 18, 36; m 58; c 3. INTERNAL MEDICINE, ENDOCRINOLOGY. *Educ:* Princeton Univ, AB, 57; Yale Univ, MD, 61. *Hon Degrees:* DMed, Karolinska Inst, Sweden, 78. *Prof Exp:* From intern to asst resident internal med, Yale-New Haven Hosp, Conn, 61-63, asst resident to chief resident, 65-67; from asst prof to assoc prof, 69-75, vchmn dept, 75-80, PROF INTERNAL MED, SCH MED, YALE UNIV, 75- *Concurrent Pos:* USPHS spec res fel metab-endocrinol, Joslin Res Lab, Harvard Med Sch & Peter Bent Brigham Hosp, Boston, Mass, 67-69; Am Col Physicians teaching & res scholar, 69-72; estab investr award, Am Diabetes Asn, 77. *Honors & Awards:* Alvarenga Prize, Swedish Med Asn, 75; Lilly Award, Am Diabetes Asn, 76; John Claude Kellion lectr, Australian Diabetes Asn, 77. *Mem:* Am Fedn Clin Res; Am Diabetes Asn; Am Soc Clin Invest (nat councilor, 78-81); Endocrine Soc; Am Physiol Soc. *Res:* Regulation of gluconeogenesis; amino acid metabolism in the regulation of insulin secretion and gluconeogenesis; clinical diabetes mellitus; development of an insulin infusion pump; metabolism of exercise. *Mailing Add:* Sch Med Yale Univ 333 Cedar St New Haven CT 06510

FELIX, ARTHUR M, b New York, NY, June 15, 38; m 67; c 2. BIO-ORGANIC CHEMISTRY. *Educ:* NY Univ, BA, 59; Polytech Inst Brooklyn, PhD(chem), 64. *Prof Exp:* NIH res fel, Harvard Univ, 64-66; sr res chemist, 66-76, res fel, 76-80, GROUP CHIEF, HOFFMANN-LA ROCHE, INC, 80- *Concurrent Pos:* Guest investr, Rockefeller Univ, 68-69; instr, Fairleigh Dickinson Univ, 68- *Mem:* Am Chem Soc; The Chem Soc; NY Acad Sci; Am Inst Chemists; Sigma Xi. *Res:* Classical and solid phase peptide synthesis; synthesis and physical chemistry of polypeptides; detection and analysis of amino acids. *Mailing Add:* Hoffmann-La Roche Inc Res Div Nutley NJ 07110

FELIX, CHARLES JEFFREY, paleobotany, see previous edition

FELIX, JAMES ANTHONY, microbiology, see previous edition

FELIX, RAYMOND ANTHONY, b Los Angeles, Calif, Aug 25, 46. ORGANIC CHEMISTRY. *Educ:* Calif State Col, Los Angeles, BS, 69; Univ Southern Calif, PhD(chem), 72. *Prof Exp:* Res chemist, 72-80, SR RES CHEMIST, STAUFFER CHEM CO, 80- *Mem:* Am Chem Soc. *Res:* Preparation of novel agrochemicals; phase transfer catalysis; homogeneous catalysis; organic synthesis. *Mailing Add:* Dept Chem 1200 S 47th St Richmond CA 94804

FELIX, ROBERT HANNA, b Downs, Kans, May 29, 04; m 33; c 1. PSYCHIATRY. *Educ:* Univ Colo, AB, 26, MD, 30; Johns Hopkins Univ, MPH, 42. *Hon Degrees:* ScD, Univ Colo, 53, Boston Univ, 53, Univ Rochester, 64; LLD, Univ Chattanooga, 57, Ripon Col, 59, St Louis Univ, 75. *Prof Exp:* Staff psychiatrist, Hosp for Fed Prisoners, Mo, 33-35, clin dir, 35-36; chief psychiat serv, USPHS Hosp, Ky, 36-38, dir res, 38-40, exec officer, 40-41; psychiatrist, US Coast Guard Acad, 42-43, sr med officer, 43-44; asst chief hosp div, USPHS, 44, chief ment hyg div, 44-49, dir, Nat Inst Ment Health, 49-64; prof psychiat & dean sch med, 64-74, dir bi-state regional med prog, 74-76, EMER PROF PSYCHIAT & EMER DEAN SCH MED, ST LOUIS UNIV, 74- *Concurrent Pos:* Commonwealth Fund fel, Colo Psychopath Hosp, 31-33. *Mem:* Fel AMA; fel Am Psychiat Asn (treas, 58-59, pres, 60-61); Am Pub Health Asn; fel Am Col Physicians. *Res:* Medical education; drug addiction; mental public health; mental hygiene and socio-environmental factors; medical school administration. *Mailing Add:* 10501 Indian Wells Dr Sun City AZ 85373

FELKER, JEAN HOWARD, b Centralia, Ill, Mar 14, 19; m 43; c 2. ELECTRICAL ENGINEERING. *Educ:* Wash Univ, BEE, 41. *Prof Exp:* Mem staff, Bell Tel Labs, 45-59; mem staff, Am Tel & Tel, 59-60, asst chief engr, 60-62; vpres opers & dir, NJ Bell Tel Co, 62-69; bus consult, 69-71; VPRES, BELL LABS, 71- *Concurrent Pos:* Dir & mem exec comt, Colonial Life Ins Co Am & Shulman Transport Enterprises. *Mem:* Nat Acad Eng; fel Inst Elec & Electronics Engrs. *Mailing Add:* Bell Labs Rm 2A200 6 Corporate Pl Piscataway NJ 08854

FELKNER, IRA CECIL, b Alice, Tex, Jan 3, 36; m 69; c 2. MICROBIAL GENETICS, MOLECULAR BIOLOGY. *Educ:* Univ Tex, Austin, BA, 58, MA, 60, PhD(microbiol), 66. *Prof Exp:* Med Res Coun Gt Brit fel, Inst Animal Genetics, Univ Edinburgh, 65-66; res scientist molecular biol, Southwest Ctr Advan Studies, 66-68; asst prof microbiol, Tex Tech Univ, 68-74, assoc prof biol sci, 74-79, prof, 79-81; ASSOC DIR, DIV LIFE SCI, CLEMENT ASSOC, INC, 81- *Concurrent Pos:* Asst prof genetics, Austin Col, 66-68; Brown Hazen Fund-Res Corp & Eli Lilly Co grants, 69-71; deleg, Int Cong Microbiol, Mexico City, 70; dir, Inst Mech Carcinogen Action, 76-81; ed-in-chief, J Environ Risk Assessment, 80- *Honors & Awards:* Sci Award Res & Develop, Asn US Army, 62. *Mem:* Am Soc Microbiol. *Res:* Nature of and regulation mechanisms controlling uptake and recombination in Bacillus subtilis; chemical and irradiation mutagenesis in bacteria; biochemical and physico-chemical aspects of microbial genetics. *Mailing Add:* Clement Assocs Inc 1010 Wisconsin Ave NW Lubbock TX 79409

FELL, COLIN, b Flint, Mich, June 21, 30; m 50; c 4. PHYSIOLOGY. *Educ:* Antioch Col, AB, 51; Wayne State Univ, MS, 53, PhD(physiol), 57. *Prof Exp:* Asst, Wayne State Univ, 51-57; cardiovasc res trainee, Med Col, Univ Ga, 57-58 & Univ Washington, 58-60; instr physiol, Col Physicians & Surgeons, Columbia Univ, 60-62; asst prof, 62-71, ASSOC PROF PHYSIOL, MED COL, CORNELL UNIV, 71- *Mem:* Am Physiol Soc; Harvey Soc. *Res:* Cardiovascular physiology. *Mailing Add:* Dept of Physiol Cornell Univ Med Col New York NY 10021

FELL, GEORGE BRADY, b Elgin, Ill, Sept 27, 16; m 48. ECOLOGY. *Educ:* Univ Ill, BS, 38; Univ Mich, MS, 40. *Prof Exp:* Teacher pub sch, Ill, 40-41; bacteriologist & serologist, City Health Dept Lab, Rockford, Ill, 46-48; soil conservationist, US Soil Conserv Serv, 48-49; exec dir, Nature Conserv, 50-58; DIR, NATURAL LAND INST, 58- *Concurrent Pos:* Mem, Ill Nature Preserves Comn, 64-70, exec secy, 70- *Mem:* Wildlife Soc; Ecol Soc Am; Nat Areas Asn (secy-treas, 78-). *Res:* Methods of preserving and maintaining natural areas; analysis and management of natural vegetation. *Mailing Add:* 320 S Third St Rockford IL 61108

FELL, HOWARD BARRACLOUGH, b Lewes, Eng, June 6, 17; m 42; c 3. INVERTEBRATE ZOOLOGY. *Educ:* Univ NZ, BSc, 38, MSc, 39; Univ Edinburgh, PhD(zool), 41, DSc(zool), 55. *Hon Degrees:* AM, Harvard Univ, 65. *Prof Exp:* Demonstr zool, Univ Edinburgh, 39-41; sr lectr, Univ Victoria, NZ, 45-57, assoc prof, 57-64; cur invert zool, Mus Comp Zool, 64-65, prof, 65-77, cur, Mus Comp Zool, 74-77, EMER PROF INVERT ZOOL, MUS COMP ZOOL, HARVARD UNIV, 77- *Honors & Awards:* Hector Medal & Prize, Royal Soc NZ, 59, Hutton Medal, 62. *Mem:* Emer fel Am Acad Arts & Sci; fel Royal Soc NZ; NZ Asn Scientists (secy, 46, pres, 48); fel Explorer's Club; fel Sci Explor Soc. *Res:* Evolution; general problems of marine biogeography; biology of deep-sea bottom faunas; systematics, morphology and paleontology of the Echinodermata. *Mailing Add:* 6625 Bamburgh Dr San Diego CA 92117

FELL, JAMES MICHAEL GARDNER, b Vancouver, BC, Dec 4, 23; m 57; c 2. PURE MATHEMATICS. *Educ:* Univ BC, BA, 43; Univ Calif, Berkeley, MA, 45, PhD(math), 50. *Prof Exp:* Jr res physicist, Nat Res Coun, Can, 45-46; instr, Calif Inst Technol, 53-55; res assoc, Univ Chicago, 55-56; from asst prof to prof math, Univ Wash, 56-65; PROF MATH, UNIV PA, 65- *Mem:* Am Math Soc. *Res:* Functional analysis; group representations. *Mailing Add:* Dept of Math Univ of Pa Philadelphia PA 19104

FELL, PAUL ERVEN, b Richmond, Va, Oct 4, 37; m 71. INVERTEBRATE EMBRYOLOGY, MARINE BIOLOGY. *Educ:* Hope Col, BA, 60; Stanford Univ, PhD(biol), 68. *Prof Exp:* Instr biol, Stanford Univ, 64-65; res assoc, Univ Calif, San Diego, 66-68; from asst prof to assoc prof, 68-78, PROF ZOOL, CONN COL, 78- *Mem:* AAAS; Am Soc Zool; Soc Develop Biol; Int Soc Invertebrate Reproduction. *Res:* Reproduction and dormancy in marine sponges and tidal marsh ecology. *Mailing Add:* Dept Zool Box 1484 Conn Col New London CT 06320

FELL, RONALD DEAN, b Clinton, Iowa, May 4, 49; m 72; c 2. EXERCISE PHYSIOLOGY, MUSCLE METABOLISM. *Educ:* Iowa State Univ, BS, 72, MS, 74, PhD(zool), 77. *Prof Exp:* Muscular Dystrophy Asn fel, Sch Med, Wash Univ, 77-79; ASST PROF, UNIV LOUISVILLE, 80- *Mem:* Sigma Xi; Am Physiol Soc; Am Col Sports Med. *Res:* Physiological and biochemical adaptations which occur in response to exercise training; muscle utilization of energy providing substrates during and after chronic exercise training is being investigated using small animal models. *Mailing Add:* Exercise Physiol Lab Crawford Gym Univ Louisville Belknap Campus Louisville KY 40292

FELLER, DANNIS R, b Monroe, Wis, Oct 27, 41; m 63; c 2. BIOCHEMICAL PHARMACOLOGY, LIPID PHARMACOLOGY. *Educ:* Univ Wis, BS, 63, MS, 66, PhD(pharmacol), 68. *Prof Exp:* Guest worker, Nat Heart Inst, NIH, 67-69; asst prof, 69-74, assoc prof, 74-80, PROF PHARMACOL, OHIO STATE UNIV, 80- *Mem:* Am Soc Pharmacol & Exp Therapeut; Am Pharmaceut Asn; Sigma Xi. *Res:* Evaluation of the mechanism of adrenoceptor, antilipemic and antiplatelet actions of pharmacologically active drugs; biochemical aspects of drug action and relationship to toxicity. *Mailing Add:* 2846 Wellesley Dr Columbus OH 43210

FELLER, DAVID DOUGLAS, physiology, see previous edition

FELLER, RALPH PAUL, b Quincy, Mass, Aug 31, 34; m 59; c 3. DENTISTRY, PROSTHODONTICS. *Educ:* Tufts Univ, BS, 56, DMD, 64; Univ Tex, MS & cert prosthodontics, 75; Loma Linda Univ, MPH, 81. *Prof Exp:* Res asst biochem, Protein Found, 56-57; res asst dent, Sch Dent Med, Tufts Univ, 60-64, res assoc biochem, 64-66, clin instr oral diag, 66-69; coordr, Vet Admin Dent Res Trainee Prog & chief, Oral Biol Res Lab, Vet Admin Outpatient Clin, Boston, 69-71; asst prof community dent, Univ Tex, Houston, 71-74; chief, Dent Serv, Vet Admin Hosp, Lyons, NJ, 75-77; assoc prof prosthodontics, Sch Dent, Fairleigh Dickinson Univ, 75-77; CHIEF, DENT SERV, VET ADMIN HOSP, LOMA LINDA, CA, 77-; ASSOC PROF PROSTHODONTICS, SCH DENT, LOMA LINDA UNIV, 77- *Concurrent Pos:* Sigma Xi res grant-in-aid, 63-64; gen pract, Hingham, Mass, 64-69; res dentist, Boston Vet Admin Hosp, 66-69; asst prof prosthetic dent, Sch Dent, Harvard Univ, 69-71; clin investr, Houston Vet Admin Hosp, 71-74. *Mem:* Am Dent Asn; Int Asn Dent Res; Am Col Prosthodontists. *Res:* Salivary gland physiology; olfaction and taste; preventive dentistry. *Mailing Add:* Dent Serv Vet Admin Hosp Loma Linda CA 92357

FELLER, ROBERT JARMAN, b Fayetteville, NC, Jan 31, 45. BIOLOGICAL OCEANOGRAPHY, BENTHOS ECOLOGY. *Educ:* Univ Va, Charlottesville, BA, 66; Univ Wash, Seattle, MS, 72, PhD(oceanog), 77. *Prof Exp:* Fel res assoc, Dept Oceanog, Univ Wash, 77-79; res asst prof, 79-81, ASST PROF BIOL, OCEANOG & MARINE SCI PROG, UNIV SC, 81- *Mem:* AAAS; Am Soc Limnol & Oceanog; Sigma Xi; Ecol Soc Am; Am Soc Naturalists. *Res:* Applications of immunological methods for investigating marine benthic food webs; secondary production processes; benthos ecology; biological oceanography. *Mailing Add:* Dept Biol Univ SC Columbia SC 29208

FELLER, ROBERT LIVINGSTON, b Newark, NJ, Dec 27, 19. PHYSICAL ORGANIC CHEMISTRY. *Educ:* Dartmouth Col, AB, 41; Rutgers Univ, MS, 43, PhD(chem), 50. *Prof Exp:* Instr & lectr, Rutgers Univ, 46-49; Nat Gallery Art fel, 50-63, SR FEL, CARNEGIE-MELLON INST RES, 63- *Concurrent Pos:* Vis scientist, Inst Fine Arts, NY Univ, 61; pres comt conserv, Int Coun Mus, 69-75; mem exec comt, Nat Conserv Adv Coun, 74-, pres, 75-79. *Mem:* Fel Illum Eng Soc; fel Int Inst Conservation; fel Am Inst Conservation; AAAS; Am Chem Soc. *Res:* Properties of methacrylate polymers; scientific examination of materials in the fine arts, particularly spirit varnishes; artists' pigments. *Mailing Add:* Carnegie-Mellon Inst Res 4400 Fifth Ave Pittsburgh PA 15213

FELLER, WILLIAM, b St Paul, Minn, Nov 2, 25; m 64; c 2. SURGERY, CANCER RESEARCH. *Educ:* Univ Minn, BA, 48, BS, 52, MD, 54, PhD(surg), 62. *Prof Exp:* Instr surg, Med Sch, Univ Minn, 61-62; asst prof, 64-69, ASSOC PROF SURG, SCH MED, GEORGETOWN UNIV, 69- *Concurrent Pos:* Vis scientist, Nat Cancer Inst, 62-64. *Mem:* AAAS; NY Acad Sci; Am Asn Cancer Res; Am Col Surg. *Res:* Cancer virology; human breast cancer. *Mailing Add:* Sch of Med Georgetown Univ Washington DC 20007

FELLERS, DAVID ANTHONY, b Northampton, Mass, Jan 3, 35; m 61; c 2. FOOD SCIENCE. *Educ:* Univ Mass, BS, 57; Rutgers Univ, MS, 62, PhD(food sci), 64. *Prof Exp:* Res food technologist, 63-69, chief cereal lab, 69-73, RES FOOD TECHNOLOGIST, WESTERN REGIONAL RES CTR, USDA, 73- *Mem:* Inst Food Technol; Am Asn Cereal Chem; Am Chem Soc. *Res:* Discoloration of beef by myoglobin auto-oxidation; development of protein concentrates and high protein foods from wheat and rice; nutrient composition, enrichment, and stability of cereals; development of pregelatinized flours; introduction of soy fortified flour in Bolivia. *Mailing Add:* USDA 800 Buchanan St Albany CA 94710

FELLERS, FRANCIS XAVIER, b Seattle, Wash, Feb 6, 22. NEPHROLOGY, GERIATRICS. *Educ:* Amherst Col, BA, 44; Cornell Univ, MD, 46. *Prof Exp:* Intern pediat, New York Hosp, 46-47; asst resident, Boston Floating Hosp, 53-56; from asst to assoc, Harvard Med Sch, 58-63, asst prof pediat, 63-69, assoc prof clin pediat, 69-75; MED DIR, MONTELLO MANOR NURSING HOME, 74- & RUSSELL PARK MANOR, 81- *Concurrent Pos:* Res fel, Harvard Med Sch, 56-58; asst, Med Col, Tufts Univ, 54-55; from asst to sr assoc physician, Children's Med Ctr, 56- *Mem:* AAAS; NY Acad Sci. *Res:* Metabolic disease in children. *Mailing Add:* PO Box 107 New Gloucester ME 04260

FELLERS, RUFUS GUSTAVUS, b Columbia, SC, Sept 26, 20; m 67; c 3. ELECTRICAL ENGINEERING. *Educ:* Univ SC, BS, 41; Yale Univ, PhD(elec eng), 43. *Prof Exp:* Asst instr elec eng, Yale Univ, 42-43, instr, 43-44; electronic scientist & sect head, res & develop ultra-high frequencies, naval res lab, 44-55; chmn dept elec eng, 55-60, dean col, 60-69, PROF ELEC ENG, UNIV SC, 55-, CHMN ELEC & COMPUT ENG, COL ENG, 76- *Concurrent Pos:* Lectr, Univ Md, 48-54; mem nat comt, Int Sci Radio Union, 68-71; mem tech staff, Bell Tel Labs, 70-71. *Mem:* Fel Inst Elec & Electronics Engrs; Int Sci Radio Union; Am Soc Eng Educ. *Res:* Millimeter waves; electromagnetic theory; microwave techniques. *Mailing Add:* Col of Eng Univ of SC Columbia SC 29208

FELLEY, DONALD LOUIS, b Memphis, Tenn, Feb 7, 21; m 49; c 5. ORGANIC CHEMISTRY. *Educ:* Ark State Col, BS, 41; Univ Ill, PhD(org chem), 49. *Prof Exp:* Mem staff tech sales, 49-57, mgr Societe Minoc Div, France, 57-64, asst gen mgr foreign opers div, 64-68, vpres & prod mgr chem div, 68-71, bd dirs, 71, vpres & gen mgr int div, 71-76, vpres & dir NAm region, 76-78, group vpres, 77, PRES & CHIEF OPERATING OFFICER, ROHM AND HAAS CO, 78- *Mem:* Am Chem Soc. *Res:* Synthesis of heterocyclic nitrogen compounds. *Mailing Add:* Rohm and Haas Co Independence Mall W Philadelphia PA 19105

FELLIN, DAVID GENE, forest entomology, see previous edition

FELLIN, PHILIP, b Trento, Italy, Jan 9, 49; Can citizen; m 74; c 1. SAMPLING ATMOSPHERIC TRACE CONSTITUENTS. *Educ:* Univ Toronto, BSc Hons, 72; York Univ, MSc, 77. *Prof Exp:* Teacher math & physics, Can Univ Serv, 72-74; scientist, Ont Ministry Environ, 74-78; CHEMIST, ENVIRON CAN, 78- *Mem:* Can Inst Chem. *Res:* Environmental research and monitoring, particularly atmospheric sampling for inorganic and organic chemical constituents; analytical methods development; process chemistry in the atmosphere. *Mailing Add:* 4905 Dufferin St Toronto ON M3H 5T4 Can

FELLING, WILLIAM E(DWARD), b St Louis, Mo, Nov 26, 24; m 48; c 10. RESEARCH & DEVELOPMENT MANAGEMENT. *Educ:* Iowa State Univ, BS, 45; St Louis Univ, MS, 49, PhD(math), 59. *Prof Exp:* Dept dir, Parks Col, St Louis Univ, 48-58; res sci dynamical astron, McDonnell Aircraft Corp, 58-61; corp dir res indust R&D, Raytheon Co, 61-65; prog officer sci & eng, Ford Found, 65-67, res & environ, 67-75; ASSOC DIR TO EXEC DIR R&D MANAGEMENT, OAK RIDGE ASSOC UNIVS, 75- *Concurrent Pos:* Consult, Holcomb Res Inst & Int Inst Applied Syst Anal, 75-78; pres, Felling Assocs, Inc & Found Adv Serv, 75-; advisor, Sci Comt Problems Environ 76-78. *Mem:* Fel AAAS; Sigma Xi; Am Soc Eng Educ; fel Am Inst Aeronaut & Astronaut. *Res:* Regional environmental resource management; energy policy analysis; social consequences of energy policies. *Mailing Add:* Oak Ridge Assoc Univs PO Box 117 Oak Ridge TN 37830

FELLINGER, L(OWELL) L(EE), b Norris City, Ill, Sept 7, 15; m 41; c 2. CHEMICAL ENGINEERING. *Educ:* Univ Ill, BS, 37; Mass Inst Technol, ScD(chem eng), 41. *Prof Exp:* Res chem engr, Monsanto Chem Co, 42-43, group leader interim prod, 43-47, asst dir res, 47-51, asst eng mgr, 51-57, proj sect mgr, 57-60, asst dir eng, 60-62, eng proj mgr, 62-65, dir process eng dept, Monsanto Co, 65-67, mgr proj sect, Cent Eng Dept, 67-70, mgr chem eng sect, 70-81; RETIRED. *Mem:* Am Inst Chem Engrs. *Res:* Unit operations; process development; engineering project management. *Mailing Add:* 1289 Weatherby Dr St Louis MO 63141

FELLINGER, ROBERT C(ECIL), b Burlington, Iowa, Aug 10, 22; m 43; c 2. MECHANICAL ENGINEERING. *Educ:* Univ Iowa, BS, 47; Iowa State Univ, MS, 48. *Prof Exp:* Mech engr, Manhattan Proj, Chicago, 44, res mech eng, Mass Inst Technol, 44-46; from instr to assoc prof, 47-60, actg chmn, Dept Mech Eng, 79-80, PROF MECH ENG, IOWA STATE UNIV, 60-, DIV LEADER THERODYNAMICS & ENERGY UTILIZATION, 72- *Concurrent Pos:* Consult, prod liability, fires & explosions. *Mem:* Fel Am Soc Mech Engrs. *Res:* Thermodynamics; fuels and combustion; compressible flow. *Mailing Add:* Dept Mech Eng Iowa State Univ Ames IA 50011

FELLMAN, JACOB HAROLD, b New York, NY, Apr 25, 27; m 50; c 4. BIOCHEMISTRY. *Educ:* Univ Kans, BA, 48, MA, 52, PhD, 54. *Prof Exp:* Assoc neurol, 56-58, asst prof biochem, 58-60, assoc prof biochem & asst prof neurol, 60-66, assoc prof neurochem, 66-67, PROF BIOCHEM, MED SCH, UNIV ORE, 67- *Res:* Chemistry of neurohumoral substances. *Mailing Add:* Univ of Ore Med Sch Portland OR 97201

FELLMANN, ROBERT PAUL, b Chicago, Ill, July 22, 24; m 47. CHEMISTRY. *Educ:* Univ Pa, AB, 47. *Prof Exp:* GROUP LEADER, RES DEPT, ROHM AND HAAS CO, 56- *Mem:* Am Chem Soc. *Res:* Polymerization of acrylic monomers; monomer synthesis; polymer chemistry. *Mailing Add:* Res Dept Rohm and Haas Co PO Box 219 Bristol PA 19007

FELLNER, CARL HEINZ, b Vienna, Austria, Aug 24, 17; m 48; c 2. PSYCHIATRY. *Educ:* Univ Lausanne, MD, 52. *Prof Exp:* Intern & resident psychiat, Mapperley Hosp, Eng, 52-54; resident, Hadassah Univ Hosp, Israel, 54-55 & Albert Einstein Col Med, 55-56; lectr, Med Sch, Univ Wis-Madison, 57, from asst prof to prof, 58-72; PROF PSYCHIAT & BEHAV SCI, UNIV WASH, 72- *Concurrent Pos:* Fel, Albert Einstein Col Med, 56. *Mem:* Am Psychosom Soc; Soc Appl Anthrop; AMA; Am Psychiat Asn; Asn Advan Psychother. *Res:* Psychosomatic problems of adaptation; psychotherapeutic processes; family therapy; hospital psychiatry. *Mailing Add:* Dept Psychiat & Behav Sci Sch Med Univ Wash Seattle WA 98195

FELLNER, SUSAN K, b Hartford, Conn, Nov 14, 36; div; c 2. NEPHROLOGY. *Educ:* Smith Col, AB, 58; Univ Fla, MD, 66. *Prof Exp:* Res asst pharmacol, Med Sch, Univ Fla, 58-61; med intern, Duval Med Ctr, 66-67; fel cardiol, 67-68, res med, 68-69, fel nephrol, 69-71, asst prof med, 71-75, ASSOC PROF MED, MED SCH, EMORY UNIV, 75- *Mem:* Am Soc Nephrol; Int Soc Nephrol. *Res:* Problems of clinical nephrology and kidney transplantation. *Mailing Add:* 1365 Clifton Rd Atlanta GA 30322

FELLNER, WILLIAM HENRY, b New York, NY, Sept 27, 42. STATISTICS. *Educ:* Brooklyn Col, BS, 63; Univ Calif, Berkeley, MA, 65, PhD(biostatist), 71. *Prof Exp:* Asst prof math, Univ Calif, Irvine, 69-73; asst prof biostatist, Med Col Va, Richmond, 73-76; statistician, Nat Inst Occup Safety & Health, Morgantown, WVa, 76-77; tech serv statistician, 77-80, SR STATISTICIAN, ENG SERV DIV, E I DU PONT DE NEMOURS & CO, 80- *Mem:* Am Statist Asn; Inst Math Statist; Sigma Xi. *Res:* Robust estimation of variance components. *Mailing Add:* Eng Dept E I Du Pont de Nemours & Co Louviers Bldg Wilmington DE 19898

FELLOWES, OLIVER NELSON, b Steubenville, Ohio, July 23, 08; m 38; c 1. MEDICAL MICROBIOLOGY, IMMUNOLOGY. *Educ:* Mt Union Col, BS, 30; Ohio State Univ, MS, 34, PhD(virol), 38; Am Bd Microbiol, dipl. *Prof Exp:* Instr bact, Ohio State Univ, 36-38 & Univ Iowa, 38-41; instr, Univ Tenn, 41-42, dir diag lab, 41-42; res assoc virol, Sharp & Dohme, Inc, Pa, 42-44, head prod virus vaccines, 44-48; chief virus br, Chem Corps, Ft Detrick, US Dept Army, 48-52, chief tech opers, Ft Terry, 52-54; prin res microbiologist, Plum Island Animal Dis Lab, USDA, 54-69; vpres, Gray Industs, Fla, 69-71; SCI DIR, SANDERS MED RES FOUND, 71- *Mem:* AAAS; Am Soc Microbiol; Am Acad Microbiol; Int Soc Toxinology; Am Asn Immunol. *Res:* Cultivation, adaptation, inactivation and immunology of human and animal viruses; use of snake venoms in the treatment of neuromuscular diseases. *Mailing Add:* Sanders Med Res Found 33 SE Third St Boca Raton FL 33432

FELLOWS, JOHN A(LBERT), b Greenfield, Mass, July 27, 06; wid; c 3. METALLURGICAL ENGINEERING, FAILURE ANALYSIS. *Educ:* Williams Col, AB, 28; Mass Inst Technol, MS, 32, ScD(phys metall), 42. *Prof Exp:* Asst metallurgist, Am Brake Shoe & Foundry Co, 37-39, foundry metallurgist, Am Manganese Steel Div, 39-41, asst chief metallurgist, Co, 41-45; proj engr, Manhattan Proj, Kellex Corp, 43-45; proj engr, Carbide & Carbon Chems Corp, 45-46, metallurgist, 46-47; asst chief metallurgist, Am Brake Shoe Co, 48-50, res metallurgist, 51-53; chief staff metallurgist, Mallinckrodt Chem Works, 53-55, mgr metall develop dept, 56-58, asst tech dir, 59-66; dir tech prog, Am Soc Metals, 66-70; CONSULT, 70- *Concurrent Pos:* Consult ed, Metals Handbk, Am Soc Metals, 70-75; metall consult, Harney & Moore, Atty At Law, 76- *Honors & Awards:* Howe Medal, Am Soc Metals, 44. *Mem:* Am Inst Mining, Metall & PEtrolxEngrs; fel Am Soc Metals (pres, 64-65); Metals Soc UK; Am Soc Testing & Mat; Inst Metallurgists UK. *Res:* Physical and process metallurgy of cast irons, highly alloyed steels, nonferrous metals; high temperature creep testing; metallurgy of uranium. *Mailing Add:* 650 S Grand Ave Ste 1200 Los Angeles CA 90017

FELLOWS, LARRY DEAN, b Magnolia, Iowa, May 29, 34; m 60; c 3. STRATIGRAPHY, ENVIRONMENTAL GEOLOGY. *Educ:* Iowa State Univ, BS, 55; Univ Mich, MA, 57; Univ Wis, PhD(geol), 63. *Prof Exp:* Geologist, Carter Oil Co, 57-59; asst prof geol, Southwest Mo State Col, 62-65; chief stratig, Mo Geol Surv & Water Resources, 66-71, geologist, 65-80, asst state geologist, 71-80; ASST DIR & STATE GEOLOGIST, ARIZ BUR GIOL & MINERAL TECHNOL, 79- *Mem:* Geol Soc Am; Soc Econ Paleontologists & Mineralogists. *Mailing Add:* Bur Geol & Mineral Technol 845 N Park Ave Tucson AZ 85719

FELLOWS, ROBERT ELLIS, JR, b Syracuse, NY, Aug 4, 33; c 2. PHYSIOLOGY, ENDOCRINOLOGY. *Educ:* Hamilton Col, AB, 55; McGill Univ, MD, 59; Duke Univ, PhD(biochem), 66. *Prof Exp:* Asst prof physiol & med, 66-69, assoc prof physiol & asst prof med, Sch Med, Duke Univ, 70-76; PROF PHYSIOL & BIOPHYS & CHMN DEPT, COL MED, UNIV IOWA, 76- *Concurrent Pos:* USPHS fel, 64-66. *Mem:* Soc Neurosci; Endocrine Soc; Am Soc Cell Biol; Am Physiol Soc; Am Soc Biol Chem. *Res:* Chemistry and structure-function relationship of protein and peptide hormones; neuroendocrinology of reproduction; neurobiology of central nervous system development. *Mailing Add:* Dept Physiol & Biophys Univ Iowa Col Med Iowa City IA 52242

FELLOWS, ROBERT FRANCIS, b Cleveland, Ohio, July 27, 20; m 43; c 4. PLANETARY ATMOSPHERES. *Educ:* Baldwin-Wallace Col, BS, 43; Brown Univ, PhD(chem), 51. *Prof Exp:* Test observer, Lubrizol Corp, 41-43; instr chem, Williams Col, Mass, 43-44; res chemist, Dow Chem Co, 51-53; head anal sect, Sprague Elec Co, 53-58; chief planetary atmospheres prog, NASA, 59-77; RETIRED. *Concurrent Pos:* Instr chem, Slippery Rock State Col, Pa, 81-82. *Mem:* Am Chem Soc; Soc Appl Spectros. *Res:* Spectroscopy; instrumentation; space sciences. *Mailing Add:* PO Box 226 West Sunbury PA 16061

FELMLEE, WILLIAM JOHN, b Bay City, Mich, Feb 14, 30; m 57; c 2. PHYSICS, CHEMISTRY. *Educ:* Alma Col, BS, 53; Univ Mich, Ann Arbor, MS, 57. *Prof Exp:* Res physicist, Dow Chem USA, 57-72; sales eng mgr, Audn Corp, 72-74; sr engr, 74-80, SR RES SCIENTIST, KMS FUSION, INC, KMS INDUST, 80- *Mem:* Am Vacuum Soc; Microbeam Anal Soc. *Res:* Preparation of DT solid layer cryogenic laser fusion targets complete manufacture of targets for laser fusion energy research; DT gas permeation into hollow glass shells. *Mailing Add:* 2144 Georgetown Blvd Ann Arbor MI 48105

FELS, IRVING GORDON, b New York, NY, Dec 24, 16; c 3. BIOCHEMISTRY. *Educ:* Brooklyn Col, BA, 40; Univ Minn, MA, 41; Ore State Univ, PhD(biochem), 49. *Prof Exp:* Am Scand fel chem & Am Cancer Soc fel, 50-51; res assoc inst exp biol, Univ Calif, 51-54; chief biochem sect, Radioisotope Serv, Hines Vet Admin Hosp, 57-61; Old Dom Found res fel, 61-64; sr res biochemist, Va Inst Sci Res, 61-67, head div biochem, 67-73; dir, Monitor Med Lab, 73-75; RES ASSOC, DIV MED ONCOL, MED COL VA, 75- *Mem:* Biochem Soc; Am Chem Soc; NY Acad Sci; Geront Soc. *Res:* Collagen aging; collagen in cancer research. *Mailing Add:* 1928 N Junaluska Dr Richmond VA 23225

FELS, MORTON, chemical & biomedical engineering, see previous edition

FELS, STEPHEN BROOK, b New York, NY, July 2, 40; m 66; c 2. DYNAMIC METEOROLOGY, PLANETARY ATMOSPHERES. *Educ:* Harvard Univ, AB, 62, PhD(physics), 68. *Prof Exp:* Fel & asst prof physics, Univ Calif, Los Angeles, 67-71; Nat Ctr Atmospheric Res fel, Univ Chicago, 71-72; RES PHYSICIST, GEOPHYS FLUID DYNAMICS LAB, PRINCETON UNIV, 72- *Res:* Radiative transfer in terrestrial and planetary atmospheres. *Mailing Add:* Geophys Fluid Dynamics Lab Forrestal Campus Princeton Univ Princeton NJ 08540

FELSEN, LEOPOLD BENNO, b 1924; US citizen. ELECTRICAL ENGINEERING, ELECTROPHYSICS. *Educ:* Polytech Inst Brooklyn, DEE, 52. *Hon Degrees:* Dr tecnices, Tech Univ Denmark, 79. *Prof Exp:* Prof, 61-78, dean eng, 74-78, INST PROF ELECTROPHYS, POLYTECH INST NEW YORK, 78- *Concurrent Pos:* Guggenheim Mem fel, 73-74. *Honors & Awards:* Distinguished Res Citation, Sigma Xi, 73; Van der Pol Gold Medal, Int Union Radio Sci, 75; Humboldt Sr Scientist Award, 80. *Mem:* Nat Acad Eng; fel Inst Elec & Electronics Engrs; Int Union Radio Sci; fel Optical Soc Am; Am Soc Eng Educ. *Res:* Electromagnetics; optics. *Mailing Add:* Sch of Eng 333 Jay St Brooklyn NY 11201

FELSENFELD, AMBHAN DASANEYAVAJA, b Dhonburi, Thailand, Oct 8, 22; US citizen; m 61. VIROLOGY. *Educ:* Univ Med Sci, Bangkok, MD, 50; Johns Hopkins Univ, MPH, 55. *Prof Exp:* From instr to asst prof path, Chulalongkorn Hosp Med Sch, 50-62; res virologist, Armed Forces Inst Path, 63-65; RES SCIENTIST VIROLOGY, DELTA PRIMATE RES CTR, TULANE UNIV, 65- *Concurrent Pos:* Fels, Commun Dis Ctr, Ga, 53-54 & Univ Ill, Urbana, 54; res fel, Rockefeller Found Virus Lab, India, 57-58 & Virus Lab, New York, 60; fel, Sch Pub Health, Univ Pittsburgh, 59; lectr, Sch Pub Health, Tulane Univ, 65- *Mem:* AAAS; Med Asn Thailand; hon mem Asn Mil Surg US; Am Soc Trop Med & Hyg. *Res:* Arbo viruses; infectious hepatitis; tissue cultures. *Mailing Add:* 123 Magnolia Dr Covington LA 70433

FELSENFELD, GARY, b New York, NY, Nov 18, 29; m 56; c 3. BIOPHYSICS. *Educ:* Harvard Univ, AB, 51; Calif Inst Technol, PhD(chem), 55. *Prof Exp:* Officer, NIH, USPHS, 55-58; asst prof biophys, Univ Pittsburgh, 58-61; CHIEF PHYS CHEM, LAB MOLECULAR BIOL, NAT INST ARTHRITIS, DIABETES, DIGESTIVE & KIDNEY DIS, 61- *Concurrent Pos:* Vis prof, Harvard Univ, 63. *Mem:* Nat Acad Sci; Am Soc Biol Chem; Am Chem Soc; Biophys Soc; fel AAAS. *Res:* Physical chemistry of nucleic acids and proteins; chromatin structure; nucleoprotein complexes. *Mailing Add:* Lab of Molecular Biol Nat Inst of Arthritis Bethesda MD 20205

FELSENSTEIN, JOSEPH, b Philadelphia, Pa, May 9, 42. POPULATION GENETICS. *Educ:* Univ Wis-Madison, BS, 64; Univ Chicago, PhD(zool), 68. *Prof Exp:* NIH fel, Inst Animal Genetics, Scotland, 67-68; from asst prof to assoc prof, 67-78, PROF GENETICS, UNIV WASH, 78- *Concurrent Pos:* Assoc ed, Theoret Pop Biol, 75- & Evolution, 78- *Mem:* Am Soc Naturalists; Genetics Soc Am; Biomet Soc; Soc Syst Zool. *Res:* Theoretical population genetics, applied to evolution; statistical estimation of evolutionary trees. *Mailing Add:* Dept of Genetics Univ of Wash Seattle WA 98195

FELSHER, MURRAY, b New York, NY, Oct 8, 36; m 61; c 3. GEOLOGY, OCEANOGRAPHY. *Educ:* City Col New York, BS, 59; Univ Mass, Amherst, MS, 63; Univ Tex, Austin, PhD(geol & oceanog), 71. *Prof Exp:* Asst prof geol, Syracuse Univ, 67-69; assoc dir coun educ in geol sci, Am Geol Inst, 69-71; sr staff scientist, US Environ Protection Agency, 71-75; fed affairs officer, Off Appln, NASA, 75-77, chief, Geol & Energy Appln, 77-80; PRES, ASSOC TECH CONSULT, 80- *Concurrent Pos:* Consult oceanog, Syracuse Univ Res Corp, 67-69; publ, Washington Fed Sci Newsletter, 80- & Washington Remote Sensing Letter, 80- *Mem:* AAAS; Fine Particle Soc; fel Geol Soc Am; Int Asn Math Geol; Int Asn Planetology. *Res:* Coastal morphology; marine geology; remote sensing; educational administration; sedimentology and sedimentary petrology; cosmology and planetary geology; mathematical geology. *Mailing Add:* 1067 Nat Press Bldg Washington DC 20045

FELSHER, ZACHARY, b Russia, Nov 21, 10; nat US; m 45; c 1. DERMATOLOGY. *Educ:* Univ Chicago, BS, 31; Rush Med Col, MD, 36. *Prof Exp:* Asst dermat, Univ Chicago Clin, 43-44, instr, 44-47; instr, Univ Ill, 48-55; asst prof, 56-64, ASSOC PROF DERMAT, NORTHWESTERN UNIV, CHICAGO, 64- *Concurrent Pos:* Consult, US Army Hqs, Chicago, 54-59 & USPHS Hosp, 59- *Mem:* AAAS; Soc Invest Dermat; AMA; Am Acad Dermat; NY Acad Sci. *Res:* Diseases of the skin; physiology and biochemistry of the skin, particularly fibrous proteins. *Mailing Add:* Dept of Dermat Northwestern Univ Med Sch Chicago IL 60611

FELSON, BENJAMIN, b Newport, Ky, Oct 21, 13; m 36; c 5. RADIOLOGY. *Educ:* Univ Cincinnati, BS, 31, MD, 35. *Prof Exp:* Intern, Cincinnati Gen Hosp, 35-36; resident path, Cincinnati Gen Hosp & Univ Cincinnati, 36-37, resident radiol, 37-40; pvt pract, Tulsa, Okla, 41-42; from asst prof to assoc prof, 45-51, dir radiol, 51-73, PROF RADIOL, UNIV CINCINNATI, 51- *Concurrent Pos:* Fel cancer therapy, Indianapolis City Hosp, 40-41; radiologist, Cincinnati Gen Hosp, 45-48, assoc dir, 48-51, dir dept radiol, 51-73; hon fel fac radiologists, Royal Col Surgeons, Ireland & Australia; consult, Dayton Vet Admin Hosp, Cincinnati Vet Admin Hosp, USPHS, Walter Reed Army Hosp, Armed Forces Inst Path & Cent Off US Vet Admin; chancellor, Am Col Radiol, 66-69; ed, Seminars in Roentgenology. *Honors & Awards:* Gold Medalist, Am Col Radiol, 77. *Mem:* Radiol Soc NAm(vpres, 59); fel Am Col Radiol; fel Am Col Chest Physicians; Am Roentgen Ray Soc (1st vpres, 72); Fleischner Chest Soc (pres, 75). *Res:* Radiology of diseases of the chest; fundamentals of chest roentgenology. *Mailing Add:* 3994 Rose Hill Ave Cincinnati OH 45229

FELT, ROWLAND EARL, b Idaho Falls, Idaho, Aug 3, 36; m 66; c 4. CHEMICAL ENGINEERING. *Educ:* Univ Idaho, BS, 58, MS, 59; Iowa State Univ, PhD(chem eng), 64. *Prof Exp:* Instr chem eng, Univ Idaho, 59-60; res asst, Ames Lab, 60-64; staff engr, Gen Elec Co, Wash, 64-66 & Isochem Inc, 66-67; staff engr, Atlantic Richfield Hanford Co, 67-73, mgr plutonium process eng, 73-77; mgr eng develop, Rockwell Hanford Opers, 77-78; mgr chem engr, 78-81, MGR PROCESS ENG, EXXON NUCLEAR, 81- *Mem:* Am Inst Chem Engrs; Am Nuclear Soc; Sigma Xi. *Res:* Plutonium processing; plutonium scrap management; nuclear fuel cycle technology; nuclear fuel fabrication. *Mailing Add:* 619 Lynnwood Loop Richland WA 99352

FELTEN, DAVID L, b Sheboygan, Wis, Feb 27, 48; m 68. NEUROANATOMY. *Educ:* Mass Inst Technol, BS, 69; Univ Pa, MD & PhD(anat), 74. *Prof Exp:* Asst prof, 74-77, ASSOC PROF ANAT, SCH MED, IND UNIV, 77- *Concurrent Pos:* Alfred P Sloan Found fel, 79-80. *Mem:* AAAS; Am Asn Anat; Soc Neurosci; Elec Micros Soc Am. *Res:* Catecholamine and indoleamine neuroanatomy in primates; role of aminergic and amino acid transmitters in spinal cord injury and brain disorders; diabetic neuropathy; neural control of immune system; central control of autonomics. *Mailing Add:* Dept Anat Ind Univ Indianapolis IN 46202

FELTEN, JAMES EDGAR, b Duluth, Minn, Sept 8, 34. ASTROPHYSICS. *Educ:* Univ Minn, Duluth, BA, 56; Cornell Univ, PhD(astrophys), 65. *Prof Exp:* Asst res physicist, Univ Calif, San Diego, 65-68; vis fel, Inst Theoret Astron, Cambridge Univ, 68-70; vis assoc prof, Univ Ariz, 70-72, assoc prof astron, 72-75, assoc astronr, 70-75; Nat Acad Sci/Nat Res Coun sr resident res assoc, Goddard Space Flight Ctr, 76-78; vis prof astron, 78-80, RES ASSOC SPACE PHYSICS, UNIV MD, 80- *Concurrent Pos:* Int Astron Union vis fel, Tata Inst Fundamental Res, Bombay, 70; vis prof, Univs Padua & Bologna, 70; vis prof astron, Univ Md, 78-79; vis res physicist, Univ Calif, San Diego, 80. *Mem:* Int Astron Union. *Res:* Theoretical high-energy astrophysics; theories of celestial x-ray and gamma-ray astronomy; cosmic rays; interstellar and intergalactic medium; galaxies. *Mailing Add:* Code 660 Goddard Space Flight Ctr Greenbelt MD 20771

FELTEN, JOHN JAMES, b Louisville, Ky, July 19, 37; m 67; c 4. ORGANOMETALLIC CHEMISTRY. *Educ:* St Meinrad Col, AB, 59; Ind Univ, Bloomington, MS, 68; Univ Del, PhD(chem), 73. *Prof Exp:* Teaching asst chem, Ind Univ, Bloomington, 65-68; inorg chemist, Pigments Dept, E I du Pont de Nemours & Co, Del, 68-69; teaching asst chem, Univ Del, 69-73; res chemist, Photo Prod Dept, E I du Pont de Nemours & Co, Inc, Del, 73-74, res chemist, Niagara Falls, 74-76, sr res chemist, 76-80, RES ASSOC, PHOTO PROD DEPT, ELECTRONIC MAT DIV, E I DU PONT DE NEMOURS & CO, INC, NIAGARA FALLS, 80- *Mem:* Am Chem Soc; Int Soc Hybrid Microelectronics; AAAS. *Res:* Properties and composition of materials used in production of thick film microcircuits, both during processing and in functioning circuits. *Mailing Add:* 4682 Hickory Lane Lewiston NY 14092

FELTHAM, LEWELLYN ALLISTER WOODROW, b Nfld, Oct 23, 26; m 53; c 3. BIOCHEMISTRY. *Educ:* Dalhousie Univ, BSc, 47; Univ Toronto, MA, 52, PhD(path chem), 60. *Prof Exp:* Chemist, Pub Health Labs, St John's, Nfld, 49-50, biochemist, 52-55, chief biochemist, 58-67; head dept biochem, 67-73, PROF BIOCHEM, MEM UNIV NFLD, 67- *Concurrent Pos:* Consult biochemist, Grace Hosp, St John's, 58-66 & St Clare's Mercy Hosp, St John's, 58-67; vis lectr biol, Mem Univ Nfld, 59-62, part-time assoc prof, 62-67. *Mem:* Can Biochem Soc; The Biochem Soc. *Res:* Properties of regulatory enzymes in marine animals; seasonal amino acid variation in marine fish; pheromones in marine fish; the effect of temperature on proteolytic enzymes in marine fish. *Mailing Add:* Dept of Biochem Mem Univ of Nfld St John's NF A1B 3X9 Can

FELTHAM, ROBERT DEAN, b Roswell, NMex, Nov 18, 32; m 54; c 2. INORGANIC CHEMISTRY, PHYSICAL CHEMISTRY. *Educ:* Univ NMex, BSc, 54; Univ Calif, PhD(chem), 57. *Prof Exp:* Asst, Univ NMex, 54 & Univ Calif, 54-57; Fulbright study grant, Denmark, 57-58; res fel, Mellon Inst, 58-64; from asst prof to assoc prof, 64-70, PROF CHEM, UNIV ARIZ, 71- *Concurrent Pos:* NATO fel, Univ Col, London, 63-64; vis prof, Univ Paul Sabatier, 81. *Mem:* Am Chem Soc; Royal Soc Chem; NY Acad Sci. *Res:* Synthesis and spectroscopic studies of transition metal derivatives of the group V elements; infrared, electron spin resonance and photoelectron spectroscopy; bioinorganic chemistry. *Mailing Add:* Dept of Chem Univ of Ariz Tucson AZ 85721

FELTMAN, REUBEN, b Newark, NJ, Nov 3, 07; m 30; c 2. ORAL MEDICINE. *Educ:* Univ Pa, DDS, 30; Am Bd Oral Med, dipl, 67. *Prof Exp:* Vis attend surgeon, Dept Periodontia, Midtown Hosp, New York, 30-42; prin investr, Div Res Grants, USPHS, 50-55; PRES, BD HEALTH, CLIFTON, 55- *Concurrent Pos:* Assoc dent surgeon, Passaic Gen Hosp, 30-67, dir dept dent & sr oral surgeon, 67-, prin investr dent res lab, pres med-dent staff; dir, Power Conversion Inc, Calif, 67-; alcohol, narcotic & drug abuse grant rev comn, NJ State Dept Health; secy, Bergson-Passaic Health Systs Agency, 80-81. *Mem:* Int Col Appl Nutrit; fel AAAS; fel Am Acad Oral Med (pres elect, pres, 66-67); fel Am Inst Chem; Am Inst Oral Biol. *Res:* Determining effects of fluorides ingested during pregnancy and after birth; storage in placenta and transfer to fetus. *Mailing Add:* 211 Main Ave Passaic NJ 07055

FELTNER, KURT C, b Rock Springs, Wyo, May 23, 31; m 51; c 3. AGRONOMY. *Educ:* Univ Wyo, BS, 56, MS, 59; Univ Ariz, PhD(crop physiol), 63. *Prof Exp:* Mgr seed cert serv, Univ Wyo, 57-60, asst prof crop physiol, 62-64; assoc prof plant sci, Kans State Univ, 65-70, prof, 70-71; prof agron & head dept plant & soil sci, Mont State Univ, 71-79; DEAN, COL LIFE SCI & AGR & DIR, NH AGR EXP STA, UNIV NH, 79- *Mem:* Weed Sci Soc Am; Am Soc Agron; Int Crop Improv Asn. *Res:* Physiology and ecology of higher economic plants, especially hardiness and competition. *Mailing Add:* Dean Col Life Sci & Agr Univ NH Durham NH 03824

FELTON, JAMES STEVEN, b San Francisco, Calif, Jan 31, 45; m 68; c 2. BIOCHEMISTRY, TOXICOLOGY. *Educ:* Univ Calif, Berkeley, AB, 67; State Univ NY Buffalo, PhD(molecular biol), 73. *Prof Exp:* Staff fel develop pharmacol, Nat Inst Child Health & Human Develop, 73-76; SR BIOMED RES SCIENTIST BIOCHEM & TOXICOL, LAWRENCE LIVERMORE

NAT LAB, UNIV CALIF, 76- *Mem:* AAAS; Environ Mutagen Soc; Am Asn Cancer Res. *Res:* Biochemical and genetic aspects of drug and carcinogen metabolism; effect of environmental pollutants on the reproductive systems of mammals. *Mailing Add:* L-452 Biomed Div PO Box 808 Livermore CA 94550

FELTON, JEAN SPENCER, b Oakland, Calif, Apr 27, 11; m 37; c 3. OCCUPATIONAL MEDICINE. *Educ:* Stanford Univ, AB, 31, MD, 35. *Prof Exp:* Intern & resident surg, Mt Zion & Dante Hosps, San Francisco, 35-38; pract physician & surgeon, Calif, 36-40; med dir, Oak Ridge Nat Lab, 46-53; prof, Dept Med & Dept Prev Med & Pub Health & dir employees health serv, Sch Med, Univ Okla, 53-58; prof occup health, Dept Prev Med & Pub Health, Sch Med, Univ Calif, Los Angeles, 58-68; dir occup health serv, Dept Personnel, County of Los Angeles, 68-74; chief occup health serv, Naval Regional Med Ctr, Long Beach & med dir, Br Clin, Terminal Island, 74-78; CLIN PROF COMMUN MED PUB HEALTH, SCH MED, UNIV SOUTHERN CALIF, 68-, CLIN PROF COMMUNITY MED, COL MED, UNIV CALIF, IRVINE, 75- *Concurrent Pos:* Lectr sociol, Univ Tenn, 46-53; mem Nat Safety Coun Comt Indust Eye Protection, 47-51; mem Nat Publicity Coun Health & Welfare Servs, 47-49, dir, 49-54; chmn adv bd, Family Serv Bur, Oak Ridge, 47-48, mem, 48-49; consult, Atlanta area, US Vet Admin, 49-53, St Louis area, 53-58, Vet Admin Ctr, Los Angeles, 65-, Oak Ridge Hosp & Okla State Dept Health, 53-58; ed, Indust Med & Surg, 50-51; occup health adminr, Calif State Dept Health, 58- & NASA, 64-; mem, President's Comt on Employ of Handicapped. *Mem:* Fel Am Pub Health Asn; Am Indust Hyg Asn; fel Am Occup Med Asn; fel Am Acad Occup Med; Nat Rehab Asn. *Res:* Occupational health methods and practices; health status of employee groups; mental health in industry; job performances of the physically impaired; communication in occupational health; history of occupational medicine; public speaking and medical writing. *Mailing Add:* Col Med Univ Calif Irvine CA 92717

FELTON, KENNETH E(UGENE), b Kenton, Ohio, Aug 18, 20; m 43; c 1. AGRICULTURAL ENGINEERING. *Educ:* Univ Md, BS(agr), 50, BS(civil eng), 51; Pa State Univ, MS, 62. *Prof Exp:* Engr, eng div, Assoc Factory Mutual Fire Ins Co, 51-52; sanit engr, Interstate Comn, Potomac River Basin, 52-54; agr engr irrig, Southern States Co-op, 54; asst prof, 54-63, assoc prof, 63-80, PROF AGR ENG, UNIV MD, 80- *Concurrent Pos:* Adv, Repub Korea on rice storage, 75-76, Repub Somalia, 78. *Mem:* Am Soc Agr Engrs. *Res:* Structural components of farm and light industrial buildings; environmental requirements of poultry for maximum performance; proper design and arrangement of farm structures for optimum operation; application of solar energy to poultry production. *Mailing Add:* Dept of Agr Eng Col of Agr Univ of Md College Park MD 20742

FELTON, LEWIS P(ETER), b Brooklyn, NY, Dec 14, 38; m 60; c 2. STRUCTURAL & CIVIL ENGINEERING. *Educ:* Cooper Union, BCE, 59; Carnegie Inst Technol, MS, 61, PhD(civil eng), 64. *Prof Exp:* Mem tech staff, appl mech div, Aerospace Corp, 63-64; asst prof eng, 64-71, ASSOC PROF MECH & STRUCT ENG, UNIV CALIF, LOS ANGELES, 71- *Mem:* Am Soc Civil Engrs; Am Inst Aeronaut & Astronaut. *Res:* Structural mechanics and design; optimum structural design. *Mailing Add:* Dept of Mech & Struct Univ of Calif 6731 Boelter Hall Los Angeles CA 90024

FELTON, RONALD H, b Washington, DC, Jan 12, 38. CHEMICAL PHYSICS. *Educ:* Mass Inst Technol, BS, 58; Harvard Univ, PhD(chem physics), 64. *Prof Exp:* Fel chem, Brandeis Univ, 65-67; NSF fel, Mass Inst Technol, 67-68; from asst to assoc prof, 68-77, PROF CHEM, GA INST TECHNOL, 77- *Concurrent Pos:* Res collabr, Brookhaven Nat Lab, 68- *Mem:* Am Inst Physics; NY Acad Sci. *Res:* Redox behavior of metalloporphyrins; electronic spectra of organic radicals; Raman spectroscopy; magnetic circular dichroism spectroscopy. *Mailing Add:* Sch of Chem Ga Inst of Technol Atlanta GA 30332

FELTON, SAMUEL PAGE, b Petersburg, Va, Sept 7, 19; m 55; c 1. AQUATIC CHEMISTRY, BIOLUMINESCENCE. *Educ:* Univ Wash, BS, 51. *Prof Exp:* Res assoc, Scripps Clin & Res Found, 62-64, asst mem, 64-66; asst biochemist, Childrens Orthopedic Hosp, Seattle, 66-68; res technician, 52-55, from res asst to res assoc, 55-62, res assoc, Dept Anethesiol, 69-73, res assoc, Fisheries Res Inst, 73-78, DIR WATER QUAL LAB, UNIV WASH, 76-, SR RES ASSOC, FISHERIES RES INST, 78- *Mem:* Am Chem Soc; NY Acad Sci; Am Inst Fishery Res Biologists. *Res:* Biochemistry (enzymology); fish, including environmental chemistry, the effects of nutrition in diseases, drugs and aquatic pollutant interactions, elucidation of vitamin C's role in detoxification and tumorgenesis, and fish as a model in biomedical research. *Mailing Add:* 8415 Talbot Rd Edmonds WA 98020

FELTON, STALEY LEE, b Whaleyville, Va, Oct 23, 20; m 51; c 4. AGRICULTURAL CHEMISTRY. *Educ:* Va Polytech Inst, BS, 50. *Prof Exp:* Chemist, Va Dept Agr, 50-51 & Tobacco Byprod & Chem Corp, 51-55; asst mgr res & develop dept, Diamond Black Leaf Co, 55-57; sr chemist, Va-Carolina Chem Corp, 57-64; prod mgr pesticides, Indust Chem Div, 64-81, COORDR INT SALES, MOBIL CHEM CO, 81- *Mem:* Am Chem Soc. *Res:* Formulation of agricultural chemicals; field development of new agricultural chemicals such as insecticides, nematocides, herbicides, repellents and plant growth regulators. *Mailing Add:* 1704 Brentwood Rd Richmond VA 23222

FELTS, JOHN HARVEY, b Lumberton, NC, Apr 2, 24; m 55; c 2. INTERNAL MEDICINE. *Educ:* Wofford Col, BS, 49; Med Col SC, MD, 49; Am Bd Internal Med, dipl, 57. *Prof Exp:* Intern, Walter Reed Army Hosp, Washington, DC, 49-50; intern, NC Baptist Hosp, Winston-Salem, 50-51, from asst resident to resident med, 51-53; resident physician, Western NC Sanatorium Treat Tuberc, Black Mountain, 53; from instr to assoc prof, 55-70, PROF INTERNAL MED, BOWMAN GRAY SCH MED, 70-, ASSOC DEAN ADMIS, 78- *Concurrent Pos:* Attend physician cardiac & diabetic clin, Regional Off, Vet Admin Hosp, Winston-Salem, 52-53; consult physician, Vet Admin Hosp, Salisbury, 66-74; ed, NC Med J, 74- *Mem:* Am Fedn Clin Res; fel Am Col Physicians; Am Soc Artificial Internal Organs. *Res:* Renal disease and toxicology. *Mailing Add:* Bowman Gray Sch of Med Wake Forest Univ Winston-Salem NC 27103

FELTS, WILLIAM JOSEPH LAWRENCE, b Saginaw, Mich, Dec 29, 24; m 46; c 3. ANATOMY. *Educ:* Univ Mich, AB, 48, AM, 51, PhD(anat), 52. *Prof Exp:* Instr anat, Ind Univ, 51-52; instr, Tulane Univ, 52-55; from asst prof to prof, Univ Minn, Minneapolis, 55-68; chmn dept, 68-75, PROF ANAT SCI, HEALTH SCI CTR, UNIV OKLA, 68- *Concurrent Pos:* Res assoc, Eng Res Inst, Univ Mich, 52; vis prof, Univ Otago, NZ, 75. *Mem:* Am Asn Anat; Orthop Res Soc; Am Asn Phys Anthrop; Am Soc Zool. *Res:* Human growth and development; growth processes in bone and cartilage; connective tissue transplantation; mechanical organization of bone; skeletal aging; functional anatomy and adaptation in marine mammals; antarctic and arctic seals. *Mailing Add:* Dept of Anat Sci PO Box 26901 Oklahoma City OK 73190

FELTS, WILLIAM ROBERT, b Judsonia, Ark, Apr 24, 23; div; c 4. INTERNAL MEDICINE. *Educ:* Univ Ark, BS, 45, MD, 46. *Prof Exp:* Intern, Garfield Mem Hosp, Washington, DC, 46-47; from jr resident to resident med, Gallinger Munic Hosp, Washington, DC, 49-51; from resident to chief resident, George Washington Univ Hosp, 51-53; asst chief arthritis res unit, Vet Admin Hosp, Washington, DC, 53-54; trainee rehab med, Univ Hosp, 55-57, from instr to assoc prof, 58-79, dir div rheumatol, 70-79, PROF MED, SCH MED, GEORGE WASHINGTON UNIV, 80- *Concurrent Pos:* Consult-lectr, US Naval Hosp, Md, 57-70; chief arthritis res unit, Vet Admin Hosp, 58-62; mem, Nat Comn Arthritis & Related Musculoskeletal Dis, 75-77; prof adv bd, Cartel Data Corp, 76-; mem adv bd, Nat Arthritis, 77-; pres, Nat Capital Med Found, 80-81; chmn ed adv panel, AMA, 80- *Mem:* Inst Med-Nat Acad Sci; AMA; Am Rheumatism Asn; Am Soc Internal Med (pres, 76-77); Am Fedn Clin Res. *Res:* Arthritis and rheumatic diseases; computers in medicine. *Mailing Add:* Dept of Med George Washington Univ Sch of Med Washington DC 20037

FELTY, EVAN J, b Columbus, Ohio, Dec 22, 32; m 58; c 3. PHYSICAL CHEMISTRY, ELECTROPHOTOGRAPHY. *Educ:* Bowling Green State Univ, BA, 54; Ohio State Univ, PhD(phys chem), 63. *Prof Exp:* Sr chemist mat res, 63-64, scientist, 64-66, mgr photoconductor systs develop, 66-68, mgr mat sci lab, 68-71, mgr photoreceptor technol, 71-73, mgr explor photoreceptors, 73-80, MGR MAT SCI LAB, XEROX CORP, 80- *Concurrent Pos:* Mem panel tellurium, Comt Tech Aspects Critical & Strategic Mat, Nat Mat Adv Bd, Nat Res Coun-Nat Acad Sci, 69 & Comt Fundamentals Amorphous Mat, 70-71. *Mem:* AAAS; Sigma Xi; fel Am Inst Chem; Am Chem Soc. *Res:* Electrical, optical and structural properties of photoconductor materials and devices; structure of inorganic materials by x-ray diffraction techniques. *Mailing Add:* Xerox Corp 800 Phillips Rd Webster NY 14580

FELTZ, DONALD EVERETT, b Sherman, Tex, Aug 23, 33; m 55; c 2. NUCLEAR & MECHANICAL ENGINEERING. *Educ:* Tex A&M Univ, BS, 59, MS, 63. *Prof Exp:* Reactor supvr, 61-63, chief facil opers, 63-65, asst dir, 65-78, ASSOC DIR, NUCLEAR SCI CTR, TEX A&M UNIV, 78- *Mem:* Am Soc Mech Engrs; Am Nuclear Soc. *Res:* Investigations of neutron flux perturbations and the development on non-perturbing foils; reactor design, installation and operations; mechanical heat transfer systems; isotope production and applications; systems engineering. *Mailing Add:* Nuclear Sci Ctr Tex A&M Univ College Station TX 77843

FELTZIN, JOSEPH, b New York, NY, Mar 2, 21; m 47; c 1. ORGANIC CHEMISTRY. *Educ:* Brooklyn Col, BA, 43, MA, 50; Polytech Inst Brooklyn, PhD(chem), 54. *Prof Exp:* Asst pharmaceut chem, E R Squibb & Sons, 47-51; res chemist, Norda Chem Co, 53-58; res chemist, Aero-Jet Gen Corp, Gen Tire & Rubber Co, 58-64; group leader mat res & develop, Struct Mat Div, 64-65; supvr new prod develop, Atlas Chem Indust, 65-75; MGR NEW PROD DEVELOP, ICI US, 75- *Mem:* Am Chem Soc; NY Acad Sci. *Res:* Epoxies; phenolics and related polymers; reinforced plastics applications; polyesters; urethane foams; elastomers; chemical additives to resins and plastics; thermoset and thermoplastic materials; polymer chemistry. *Mailing Add:* ICI US Concord Pike & Murphy Rd Wilmington DE 19897

FEMAN, STEPHEN SOSIN, b Perth Amboy, NJ, Aug 3, 40. OPHTHALMOLOGY, RETINAL SURGERY. *Educ:* Franklin & Marshall Col, BA, 62; Univ of Pa, MD, 66. *Prof Exp:* Asst prof ophthal, Albany Med Col Union Univ, 74-78; ASSOC PROF OPHTHAL & DIR OF RETINAL SERV, SCH OF MED VANDERBILT UNIV, 78- *Concurrent Pos:* Consult retinal dis, Vet Admin Hosp, Nashville, Metro Nashville Gen Hosp, 78-; NIH fel, 68-69, Heed Found fel, Jules Stein Eye Inst, 72-73, Seeing Eye Found fel, Wilmer Ophthal Inst, Johns Hopkins Univ Hosp, 73-74. *Mem:* AMA; Asn Res Vision & Ophthal; Am Acad Ophthal & Otolaryngol; fel Am Col Surg. *Res:* Diabetic retinal disease; rhegmatogenous retinal disease; vitreo-retinal disease. *Mailing Add:* Sch of Med Vanderbilt Univ Nashville TN 37232

FENBURR, HERBERT L(ESTER), b New York, NY, Dec 11, 13; m 36; c 1. CHEMICAL ENGINEERING. *Educ:* Ohio State Univ, BChE, 34, MS, 35, PhD(chem eng), 37. *Prof Exp:* Asst chem eng, Ohio State Univ, 34-35, instr, 35-37; chem engr, Indust Div, Hanna Chem Coatings Corp, 37-76; PRES, REED-O-MATIC INC, 56-, CHEM COATINGS CONSULT, 76- *Concurrent Pos:* Pres, Fedn Socs Paint Technol, 67-68 & Paint Res Inst, 69-73. *Mem:* AAAS; Am Chem Soc; Am Inst Chem Engrs; Am Inst Chemists; NY Acad Sci. *Mailing Add:* 2742 Bryden Columbus OH 43209

FENDALL, ROGER K, b Newberg, Ore, Aug 20, 35; m 57; c 4. AGRONOMY. *Educ:* Ore State Univ, BS, 60; NDak State Univ, PhD(agron), 64. *Prof Exp:* Asst prof agron, Wash State Univ, 64-68; from asst prof to assoc prof, 68-77, PROF AGRON, ORE STATE UNIV, 77-, ASST DEAN SCH AGR & HEAD ADV, 70- *Mem:* Am Soc Agron. *Res:* Physiology of seed germination; mechanisms of seed dormancy, inhibition and stimulation; physiology of flowering. *Mailing Add:* Sch of Agr Ore State Univ Corvallis OR 97331

FENDER, DEREK HENRY, b Hethe, Eng, Dec 4, 18; m 44; c 2. BIOLOGY, APPLIED SCIENCE. *Educ:* Univ Reading, BSc, 39 & 47, PhD(physics), 56. *Prof Exp:* Sr lectr physics, Royal Mil Col Sci, Eng, 46-53; lectr, Univ Reading, 53-61; assoc prof biol & elec eng, 61-66, PROF BIOL & APPL SCI, CALIF INST TECHNOL, 66- *Concurrent Pos:* NIH grant, Univ Reading, 56-61 & Calif Inst Technol, 61-; mem comt, Photobiol Group, 58-61; mem res bd, Dept Sci & Indust Res, Gt Brit, 59-61; consult, Electronic Color Assocs, 63- *Mem:* Human Factors Soc; Optical Soc Am; Brit Biol Eng Soc. *Res:* Interaction between the scanning motions of the human eye and the pattern recognition processes of which it is capable. *Mailing Add:* Jorgensen Lab of Info Sci Calif Inst of Technol Pasadena CA 91125

FENDLER, ELEANOR JOHNSON, b Danville, Pa, June 27, 39; div; c 2. PHYSICAL ORGANIC CHEMISTRY, BIO-ORGANIC CHEMISTRY. *Educ:* Bucknell Univ, BA, 61; Univ Calif, Santa Barbara, PhD(phys org chem), 66. *Prof Exp:* Res assoc statist, Upper Susquehanna Valley Prog Coop Res, Bucknell Univ, 61-62; teacher pub schs, Pa, 62-63; part-time instr chem, Univ Calif, Santa Barbara, 63-64, res assoc, 65-66; NASA fel, Univ Pittsburgh, 66-68, res asst prof, 68-70; vis assoc prof chem, Tex A&M Univ, 70-74, assoc prof, 74-80; MEM STAFF, KIMBERLY CLARK PIONEERING RES, 80- *Concurrent Pos:* Health Res Serv Found grant, 68-70; Soc Sigma Xi grant-in-aid, 70-71; NIH career develop award, 71-76. *Mem:* Am Chem Soc; The Chem Soc; Am Asn Univ Prof; NY Acad Sci; Sigma Xi. *Res:* Bio-organic and physical organic reaction mechanisms; biomedical chemistry; interactions and catalyses in bile salt systems; drug interactions and transport; colon cancer; micellar interactions and catalysis; nucleophilic aromatic substitution; H-1 and C-13 nuclear magnetic resonance of reactive bioorganic substrates and micellar systems. *Mailing Add:* Kimberly Clark Pioneering Res 2100 Winchester Rd Neenah WI 54956

FENDLER, JANOS HUGO, b Budapest, Hungary, Aug 12, 37; m 75. ORGANIC BIOCHEMISTRY. *Educ:* Leicester Univ, BSc, 60; Leicester Col Technol, Eng, dipl radiochem, 62; Univ London, PhD(phys-org chem), 64; Univ London, DSc(membrane mimetic chemistry), 78. *Prof Exp:* NSF fel phys-org chem, Univ Calif, Santa Barbara, 64-66; fel radiation chem, Radiation Res Labs, Mellon Inst Sci, Carnegie-Mellon Univ, 66-70; assoc prof, Tex A&M Univ, 70-75, prof chem, 75-81; PROF CHEM, CLARKSON COL TECHNOL, 81- *Concurrent Pos:* Abstractor, Chem Abstr, 65-70. *Mem:* AAAS; Royal Soc Chem; Am Chem Soc; Faraday Soc. *Res:* Membrane mimetic chemistry; characterization and utilization for synthesis, energy conversion and drug delivery; stereochemistry in the excited state; circularly polarized laser induced excited state processes; photophysical investigations of chiral discrimination and enantiomeric recognition; picosecond spectroscopy; fluorescence detected circular dichroism and circularly polarized luminescence. *Mailing Add:* Dept of Chem Clarkson Col Potsdam NY 13676

FENDLEY, TED WYATT, b Eatonton, Ga, Oct 28, 39; m 64; c 1. CLINICAL CHEMISTRY, BIOCHEMISTRY. *Educ:* Mercer Univ, BA, 61; Auburn Univ, MS, 68, PhD(biochem), 71; Am Bd Clin Chem, cert. *Prof Exp:* Fel clin chem, Med Lab Assoc, 71-73, asst dir, 73-75, assoc dir, 75-76; regional tech dir clin lab, Med Diagnostic Serv, 76-78; TECH DIR CLIN LABS, PATH & CYTOL LABS, 78- *Concurrent Pos:* Clin instr, Univ Ala, Birmingham, 73-76; mem adv coun, Auburn Univ Arts & Sci Health Prof, 73-76, vchmn, 76; instr, Jefferson State Jr Col, 72-76. *Mem:* Am Asn Clin Chem; Am Chem Soc; Am Asn Bioanal. *Res:* Analytical methods in endocrinology; clinical toxicology. *Mailing Add:* Path & Cytol Labs 2370 Nicholasville Rd Lexington KY 40503

FENECH, HENRI J, b Alexandria, Egypt, Mar 14, 25; US citizen; m 52; c 2. NUCLEAR ENGINEERING, ENGINEERING SCIENCES. *Educ:* Nat d'Ingenieurs des Arts et Metiers, France, Dipl Ecole, 46; Mass Inst Technol, SM, 57, ScD(nuclear eng), 59. *Prof Exp:* Engr, Foster Wheeler, France, 52-55; staff mem, Gen Atomic Div, Gen Dynamics Corp, 59-60; from asst prof to assoc prof nuclear eng, Mass Inst Technol, 60-69; PROF NUCLEAR ENG, UNIV CALIF, SANTA BARBARA, 69-, V CHMN DEPT, 70- *Concurrent Pos:* Atomic Energy Comn res grant, 57-62; NATO sr sci fel, 69; lectr, USSR, Acad Sci, Moscow-Leningrad, 71. *Mem:* Fel Am Nuclear Soc; Am Soc Mech Engrs. *Res:* Thermal contact resistance between surfaces; analysis of nuclear reactors; methods of optimization of power systems; nuclear power safety; thermal and hydraulics in energy systems; nuclear fuel management. *Mailing Add:* Dept of Chem & Nuclear Eng Univ of Calif Santa Barbara CA 93106

FENG, ALBERT SHIH-HUNG, b Indonesia; US citizen. NEUROBIOLOGY, BIOENGINEERING. *Educ:* Univ Miami, BS, 68, MS, 70; Cornell Univ, PhD(neurobiol), 75. *Prof Exp:* Asst res neuroscientist, Univ Calif, San Diego, 74-76; trainee neurobiol, Wash Univ, 76-77; ASST PROF PHYSIOL, UNIV ILL, URBANA-CHAMPAIGN, 77- *Concurrent Pos:* NIH fel, 75. *Mem:* AAAS; Soc Neurosci; Sigma Xi; Acoust Soc Am. *Res:* Neurol basis of acoustic communication; development of the nervous system. *Mailing Add:* Dept Physiol & Biophys Burrill Hall Univ Ill 407 S Goodwin Urbana IL 61801

FENG, CHIA-CHING, US citizen. COMBUSTION, FLUID MECHANICS. *Educ:* Nat Taiwan Univ, BS, 63; Univ BC, MASc, 69; Princeton Univ, PhD(aerospace & mech sci), 73. *Prof Exp:* Res assoc, Princeton Univ, 73-74; ASST PROF ENG TECHNOL, TRENTON STATE COL, 74- *Concurrent Pos:* Prin investr, Trenton State Col grant, 76-79 & NASA grant, 78. *Mem:* Sigma Xi; Am Soc Mech Engrs; Combustion Inst. *Res:* Flame propagation and extinction. *Mailing Add:* Dept Eng Technol Trenton State Col Trenton NJ 08625

FENG, CHUAN C(HUNG) D(AVID), b Shanghai, China, Sept 15, 22; m; c 3. STRUCTURAL & CIVIL ENGINEERING. *Educ:* Chiao Tung Univ, BS, 45; Univ Mo, MS, 55, PhD(civil eng), 59. *Prof Exp:* Assoc prof, 63-67, PROF CIVIL ENG, UNIV COLO, BOULDER, 67- *Concurrent Pos:* Mem staff, Calif Inst Technol & Stanford Univ. *Mem:* Am Soc Civil Engrs; Am Concrete Inst; Am Soc Eng Educ. *Res:* Relaxation method for structural problems; optimization; flow graph analysis; systems engineering analysis. *Mailing Add:* Col of Eng Univ of Colo Boulder CO 80302

FENG, DA-FEI, b Shanghai, China; US citizen. RADIATION CHEMISTRY. *Educ:* DePauw Univ, BA, 67; Wayne State Univ, PhD(radiation chem), 73. *Prof Exp:* Fel radiation chem, Wayne State Univ, 73-74; fel radiochem, Univ Calif, Davis, 74-76; FEL RADIOCHEM, SAN DIEGO MESA COL, 76- *Res:* Theoretical studies of high energy reactions. *Mailing Add:* Dept Chem San Diego Mesa Col San Diego CA 92111

FENG, DAHSUAN, b New Delhi, India; Singapore citizen; m 72; c 1. THEORETICAL NUCLEAR PHYSICS, THEORETICAL QUANTUM OPTICS. *Educ:* Drew Univ, BA, 68; Univ Minn, Minneapolis, PhD(physics), 72. *Prof Exp:* UK Sci Res Coun res fel theoret physics, Univ Manchester, 72-74; res assoc, Ctr Nuclear Studies, Univ Tex, Austin, 74-76; ASST PROF PHYSICS & ATMOSPHERIC SCI, DREXEL UNIV, 76- *Mem:* Southeast Asia Theoret Physics Asn; Sigma Xi. *Res:* Theoretical studies of nucleon transfer reactions; nuclear structure; statistical and thermodynamics; optical bistability. *Mailing Add:* Dept Physics & Atmospheric Sci Drexel Univ Philadelphia PA 19104

FENG, PAUL YEN-HSIUNG, b Peking, China, Aug 29, 26; nat US; m 47; c 3. NUCLEAR CHEMISTRY, RADIATION CHEMISTRY. *Educ:* Cath Univ, China, BS, 47; Washington Univ, PhD(chem), 54. *Prof Exp:* Asst chem, Washington Univ, 50-51, res chemist geochem, 51-54; chemist, Manu Mine Res & Develop Co, 54, chief chemist, 54-55, tech dir, 55; assoc physicist, IIT Res Inst, 55-56, res physicist, 56-57, group leader, 57-58, asst supvr nuclear physics, 58-59, supvr chem physics, 59-62, sci adv, 62-67; assoc prof, 67-71, PROF CHEM, MARQUETTE UNIV, 71- *Concurrent Pos:* Asst, AEC Res Prog, Washington Univ, 53-54; lectr, Ill Inst Technol, 56-58, adj assoc prof, 66-67; vis prof, Tsinghus Univ Inst Nuclear Sci, Formosa, 58; tech adv US deleg, Int Conf Peaceful Uses Atomic Energy, Geneva, Switz, 58; Fulbright lectr, Taiwan Nat Univ, 65. *Mem:* AAAS; The Chem Soc; Am Asn Physics Teachers; Am Chem Soc; Radiation Res Soc. *Res:* Radiation effects; electric discharge and electron impact phenomena; high polymer physics; mass spectrometry; geochemistry and silicate chemistry; reactions at extreme temperatures. *Mailing Add:* Dept of Chem 535 N 14th St Marquette Univ Milwaukee WI 53233

FENG, SUNG YEN, b Shanghai, China, Oct 1, 29; US citizen; m 63; c 1. PHYSIOLOGICAL ECOLOGY. *Educ:* Univ Taiwan, BS, 54; Col William & Mary, MA, 58; Rutgers Univ, PhD(parasitol), 62. *Prof Exp:* Res asst, Dept Zool & NJ Oyster Res Lab, Rutgers Univ, 60-62, res assoc, NJ Oyster Res Lab, 62-66; asst prof systs & environ biol, 66-68, assoc prof biol, 68-74, asst dir marine sci inst, 72-77, PROF BIOL SCI, MARINE SCI INST & BIOL SCI GROUP, UNIV CONN, 74-, DIR MARINE SCI INST, UNIV CONN, 77- *Mem:* Am Soc Parasitol; Am Soc Protozool; Nat Shellfisheries Asn; Soc Invert Path; Am Soc Zool. *Res:* Invertebrate pathobiology; diseases, pathology and defense mechanisms of marine molluscs; physiological ecology of marine molluscs; pathobiology of invertebrates. *Mailing Add:* Marine Sci Inst Univ of Conn Groton CT 06340

FENG, TSE-YUN, b Hangchow, China, Feb 6, 28; US citizen; m 65; c 4. COMPUTER ENGINEERING, ELECTRICAL ENGINEERING. *Educ:* Nat Taiwan Univ, BS, 50; Okla State Univ, MS, 57; Univ Mich, PhD(comput eng), 67. *Prof Exp:* Sr designer elec eng, Ebasco Serv, Inc, 57-61; teaching fel, Univ Mich, 62-65, from res asst to res assoc, 65-67; from asst prof to assoc prof elec & comput eng, Syracuse Univ, 67-75; prof elec & comput eng, Wayne State Univ, 75-79; PROF COMPUT & INFO SCI, OHIO STATE UNIV, COLUMBUS, 80- *Concurrent Pos:* Proj leader, Rome Air Develop Ctr, 66-75, proj dir, 76-; consult, Transidyne Gen Inc & Syracuse Univ, 67-68, Pattern Anal & Recognition Corp, 76- & World Bank & Asia Found, 81-; proposal reviewer, US Army Res Off, 73-; panelist & proposal reviewer, NSF, 76-; dir, Northeast Consortium Eng Educ, 76- *Mem:* fel Inst Elec & Electronics Engrs; Asn Comput Mach. *Res:* Computer architecture; associative, parallel, concurrent and distributed processors-processing; processor-memory interconnection networks; communication processors; fault- tolerant computing; switching theory and logic design. *Mailing Add:* Ohio State Univ Dept Comput & Info Sci 2036 Neil Ave Mall Columbus OH 43210

FENG, TSUAN H, b Hangchow, China, Feb 17, 18; nat US; m 51; c 4. SANITARY ENGINEERING. *Educ:* Nat Pei-Yang Univ, China, BS, 40; Univ Wis, MS, 46, PhD, 50. *Prof Exp:* Engr, Eng Serv, Mass, 50-51; from instr to assoc prof civil eng, 51-61, PROF CIVIL ENG, UNIV MASS, AMHERST, 61-, COORDR ENVIRON ENG PROG, 67- *Mem:* Am Soc Civil Engrs; Water Pollution Control Fedn. *Res:* Disinfection of water and sewage; biological treatment of sewage; filtration of water; sludge deposits in waters. *Mailing Add:* Dept of Civil Eng Univ of Mass Sch of Eng Amherst MA 01003

FENICHEL, GERALD M, b New York, NY, May 11, 35; m 58; c 3. NEUROLOGY. *Educ:* Johns Hopkins Univ, AB, 55; Yale Univ, MD, 59. *Prof Exp:* Fel neurol, Sch Med, Yale Univ, 63-64. Prof Exp: From instr to asst prof neurol, Sch Med, George Washington Univ, 64-69; PROF NEUROL, SCH MED, VANDERBILT UNIV, 69- *Mem:* Am Acad Neurol; Am Neurol Asn; AMA; Am Acad Cerebral Palsy. *Res:* Muscle development; neuromuscular diseases of infancy and childhood. *Mailing Add:* Dept of Neurol Vanderbilt Univ Sch of Med Nashville TN 37203

FENICHEL, HENRY, b The Hague, Neth, Apr 13, 38; US citizen; m 61; c 2. LOW TEMPERATURE PHYSICS, HOLOGRAPHY. *Educ:* Brooklyn Col, BS, 60; Rutgers Univ, MS, 62, PhD(physics), 65. *Prof Exp:* From asst prof to assoc prof physics, 65-76, PROF PHYSICS, UNIV CINCINNATI, 76- *Mem:* Optical Soc Am; Am Phys Soc; Am Asn Physics Teachers. *Res:* Lattice dynamics; measurements of specific heats of inert gas solids; thermal properties of solids at low temperatures; holographic interferometry with application to diffusion in liquids. *Mailing Add:* Dept of Physics Univ of Cincinnati Cincinnati OH 45221

FENICHEL, RICHARD LEE, b New York, NY, July 23, 25; m 51; c 2. BIOCHEMISTRY, PHYSIOLOGY. *Educ:* NY Univ, AB, 47; Polytech Inst Brooklyn, MS, 51; Wayne State Univ, PhD(physiol, biochem), 56. *Prof Exp:* Biochemist, Med Dept, Chrysler Corp, 51-54; asst, Wayne State Univ, 54-56, res assoc, 56-57; investr, Aviation Med Accelerator Lab, 57-59; sr res scientist, Ortho Res Found, 59-63; SR SCIENTIST, WYETH LABS, 63- *Mem:* AAAS; Am Chem Soc; Am Soc Biol Chemists; NY Acad Sci. *Res:* Protein isolation and characterization; blood coagulation; enzymatic studies; mechanisms of protein interactions; cellular immunology; immunomodulating agents. *Mailing Add:* Wyeth Labs Radnor PA 19088

FENIMORE, DAVID CLARKE, b Evansville, Ind, Jan 27, 30; m 65. ANALYTICAL CHEMISTRY, BIOCHEMISTRY. *Educ:* DePauw Univ, BA, 52; Univ Houston, PhD(chem), 66. *Prof Exp:* Chemist, Thomas & Skinner, Inc, 54-57; sect leader instrumental anal, Baroid Div, Nat Lead Co, 57-64; fel chem, Univ Houston, 66-67; sect head anal chem, Tex Res Instrumental Sci, 67-69, div head instrumental anal, 69-81; PRES, CLARK ANAL SYSTS, 81- *Concurrent Pos:* Instr, Grad Sch Biomed Sci, Univ Tex, 67-69, asst prof, 69-; clin asst prof, Dept Biophys, Univ Houston, 70-; mem biomed res review comt, Nat Inst Drug Abuse. *Mem:* AAAS; Am Chem Soc; fel Am Inst Chemists; NY Acad Sci; Am Soc Mass Spectrometry. *Res:* Gas chromatographic instrumentation with emphasis on electron capture detector design and studies of electron capture processes; application of electron capture detection to ultramicro biochemical analysis; development of high performance thin-layer chromatographic instrumentation. *Mailing Add:* 180 S Michillinda Ave Sierra Madre CA 91024

FENLON, FRANCIS HUGH, b Dublin, Ireland, Oct 7, 39; US citizen; m 64; c 4. ENGINEERING SCIENCE, ACOUSTICS. *Educ:* Univ Col Dublin, BE, 60; Univ Liverpool, Eng, PhD(elec eng), 64. *Prof Exp:* Numerical analyst elec eng, Hydro-Elec Power Comn Ont, 64-66; sr res staff mem acoust, Gen Dynamics, 66-69; sr engr, Res & Develop Ctr, Westinghouse Elec Co, 69-75; SR RES ASSOC ACOUST, APPL RES LAB, PA STATE UNIV, 75-, ASSOC PROF ENG SCI, DEPT ENG SCI & MECH, 79- *Honors & Awards:* Sci Award, Brit Inst Elec Engrs, 63. *Mem:* Sr mem Inst Elec & Electronics Engrs; Acoust Soc Am; Sigma Xi. *Res:* Nonlinear acoustics; parametric acoustical array technology; physical acoustics; acoustic signal processing; engineering acoustics. *Mailing Add:* Dept of Eng Sci & Mech Pa State Univ State College PA 16801

FENN, H(OWARD) N(ATHAN), b Milford, Conn, Nov 11, 07; m 48; c 1. CHEMICAL ENGINEERING. *Educ:* Yale Univ, BS, 29. *Prof Exp:* Chem engr org chem, Dow Chem Co, 29-37, develop group engr cellulose prods, 37-43, supt silicone prod mgr silicone mfr, Dow Corning Corp, 44-62, dir mfg, 62-63, vpres mfg, 63-65, vpres eng & mfg, 65-71, vpres & asst to pres, 71-72; DIR, TRI-CITY PLASTICS, INC, 73-; MGT CONSULT, 73- *Mem:* AAAS; Am Inst Chem Engrs; Am Chem Soc; NY Acad Sci. *Res:* Manufacture of silicones; development of silicone products; industrial management; industrial safety. *Mailing Add:* 2200 Wingate Village Apt 37 Midland MI 48640

FENN, JOHN BENNETT, b New York, NY, June 15, 17; m 39; c 3. CHEMISTRY. *Educ:* Berea Col, AB, 37; Yale Univ, PhD(phys chem), 40. *Prof Exp:* Res chemist, Monsanto Chem Co, Ala, 40-42 & Sharples Chem, Inc, Mich, 43-45; vpres & res supvr, Exp, Inc, Va, 45-52; dir proj Squid, Forrestal Res Ctr, Princeton Univ, 52-62, lectr aerospace & mech sci, 59-60, prof, 60-67; PROF APPL SCI & CHEM, YALE UNIV, 67- *Mem:* AAAS; Am Chem Soc; Combustion Inst; Am Inst Chem Engrs. *Res:* Combustion thermodynamics; propulsion; kinetics; molecular beams; rarefied gas dynamics. *Mailing Add:* Sch Eng & Appl Sci Yale Univ New Haven CT 06520

FENN, ROBERT WILLIAM, III, b Philadelphia, Pa, Feb 1, 41; m 64; c 3. CHEMICAL ENGINEERING. *Educ:* Villanova Univ, BE, 62; Carnegie-Mellon Univ, MS, 65; Univ Rochester, PhD(chem eng), 68. *Prof Exp:* Sr res engr, 67-76, res supvr electrochem res & develop, 76-77, group leader, 77-78, mgr electrochem res & develop, 78-81, SPEC PROJS LEADER, DIAMOND SHAMROCK CORP, 81- *Mem:* Am Inst Chem Engrs; Electrochem Soc. *Res:* Application of electrochemistry and electrochemical engineering principles to water and air pollution control and energy storage and conservation as well as research and development on industrial electrochemical processes. *Mailing Add:* Diamond Shamrock Corp Indust Pkwy Chardon OH 44024

FENN, W(ILLARD) H(ENRY), b Portland, Ore, Jan 18, 16; m 44; c 1. ELECTRONIC ENGINEERING. *Educ:* Univ Calif, BS, 38, MS, 39. *Prof Exp:* Assoc head test equip group, radiation lab, Mass Inst Technol, 41-45; from head commercial develop to sales mgr, Polytech Res & Develop Co, 46-51; head primary standards & instr prod group planning, Hughes Aircraft Co, 52-60, asst to dir physics lab, 58-60; vpres west coast div, FXR, Inc, 60-62; electronic consult, 62; southwest dist mgr, Energy Systs, Inc, 63-64; dir eng, Guide Industs, 64-65; ASST PROG MGR, TRW SPACE & TECHNOL GROUP, REDONDO BEACH, 65- *Concurrent Pos:* Bd dir, Western Electronic Show & Conv, 74-78. *Mem:* Electronic Industs Asn; Inst Elec & Electronics Engrs; fel Inst Advan Eng. *Res:* Microwave tubes and instrumentation; satellite communications systems. *Mailing Add:* TRW Inc Space & Technol Group 1 Space Park Redondo Beach CA 90278

FENNA, ROGER EDWARD, b Stafford, Eng, Jan 6, 47; m 72. MOLECULAR BIOLOGY, X-RAY CRYSTALLOGRAPHY. *Educ:* Univ Leeds, BSc, 69; Univ Oxford, DPhil(molecular biophys), 73. *Prof Exp:* Res assoc molecular biol, Univ Ore, 73-76; res assoc molecular biol, Univ Calif, Los Angeles, 76-80; MEM FAC, MED SCH, UNIV MIAMI, 80- *Mailing Add:* Biochem Dept Univ Miami Med Sch Box 016129 Miami FL 33101

FENNEL, WILLIAM EDWARD, b Moberly, Mo, Mar 4, 23. INVERTEBRATE ZOOLOGY. *Educ:* Univ Mo, AB, 46, MA, 49; Univ Mich, PhD(zool), 59. *Prof Exp:* Asst zool, Univ Mo, 46-49; instr, Eastern Ill State Col, 48, Univ Mo, 49-50 & biol, Flint Jr Col, Mich, 50-53; from instr to asst prof, Brooklyn Col, 58-67; from assoc prof to prof, Pace Col, 67-70; PROF BIOL, EASTERN MICH UNIV, 70- *Mem:* Am Micros Soc; Soc Syst Zool; Ecol Soc Am; Am Soc Zool; Sigma Xi. *Res:* Aquatic invertebrate ecology. *Mailing Add:* Dept Biol Eastern Mich Univ Ypsilanti MI 48197

FENNELL, ROBERT E, b Peoria, Ill, Apr 21, 42; m 69; c 3. MATHEMATICS. *Educ:* Bradley Univ, BA, 64; Univ Iowa, MS, 66, PhD(math), 69. *Prof Exp:* Instr math, Grinnell Col, 68-69; asst prof, 69-73, ASSOC PROF MATH, CLEMSON UNIV, 73- *Concurrent Pos:* Sabbatical leave, Langley Res Ctr, NASA, 79-80. *Mem:* Am Math Soc; Soc Indust & Appl Math; Math Asn Am. *Res:* Differential equations; control theory. *Mailing Add:* Dept of Math Sci Clemson Univ Clemson SC 29631

FENNELLY, PAUL FRANCIS, b Frackville, Pa, Aug 1, 45; m 70; c 3. POLLUTION CONTROL, COAL COMBUSTION. *Educ:* Villanova Univ, BS, 67; Brandeis Univ, MA, 68, PhD(chem), 72. *Prof Exp:* Teaching fel phys chem, Brandeis Univ, 67-72, Ctr Res Exp Space Sci, York Univ, Toronto, 72-73; phys chemist environ sci, Aero Chem Res Lab, Princeton, NJ, 73-74; PROG MGR & PRIN SCIENTIST ENERGY & ENVIRON SCI, GCA CORP, 74- *Concurrent Pos:* Nat Res Coun Can fel, 72-73; vis lectr air pollution sci, Univ Lowell, 77-78. *Mem:* Air Pollution Control Asn; Am Chem Soc. *Res:* Fluidized bed combustion; coal combustion; air pollution control; incineration of chemical waste atmospheric chemistry. *Mailing Add:* Technol Div GCA Corp 213 Burlington Rd Bedford MA 01730

FENNEMA, OWEN RICHARD, b Hinsdale, Ill, Jan 23, 29; m 48; c 3. FOOD SCIENCE. *Educ:* Kans State Univ, BS, 50; Univ Wis, MS, 51, PhD(food sci), 60. *Prof Exp:* Proj leader food process res, Pillsbury Co, Minn, 54-57; from asst prof to assoc prof, 60-69, PROF FOOD SCI, UNIV WIS, MADISON, 69-, CHMN DEPT, 77- *Mem:* Inst Food Technol; Am Chem Soc; Am Dairy Sci Asn; Soc Cryobiol. *Res:* Low temperature preservation; physical chemistry of food. *Mailing Add:* Dept of Food Sci Babcock Hall Univ of Wis Madison WI 53706

FENNER, DON FRANK, b Seattle, Wash, June 16, 38. PHYSICAL OCEANOGRAPHY, CHEMICAL OCEANOGRAPHY. *Educ:* Univ Wash, BS(chem), 60, BS(oceanog), 62. *Prof Exp:* Oceanographer phys oceanog, Naval Oceanog Off, 64-68, oceanographer sound speed, 68-76; RES OCEANOGRAPHER SOUND SPEED, NAVAL OCEAN RES & DEVELOP ACTIV, 76- *Mem:* Am Geophys Union. *Res:* Underwater sound speed; environmental effects on acoustic propagation; underwater acoustics; water masses and oceanic circulation in North Atlantic, North Indian, and South Atlantic Oceans, and in the Caribbean and Mediterranean Seas. *Mailing Add:* Naval Ocean Res & Develop Activ Code 341 NSTL Station MS 39529

FENNER, GUNTHER ERWIN, solid state physics, see previous edition

FENNER, HEINRICH, b Arolsen, Ger, Sept 23, 24; US citizen; m 56; c 2. ANIMAL NUTRITION. *Educ:* Hohenheim Agr Univ, dipl, 51, DSc(animal nutrit), 56. *Prof Exp:* Consult animal nutrit, H Fundel K G, Ger, 55-56; res instr, 56-61, asst res prof, 61-72, ASSOC PROF ANIMAL NUTRIT, UNIV MASS, AMHERST, 72- *Concurrent Pos:* Consult, Peace Corps, Ivory Coast, 72-73. *Mem:* AAAS; Am Dairy Sci Asn; Am Soc Animal Sci; Am Geog Soc; Am Inst Biol Sci. *Res:* Nutrient and energy metabolism in horses and ruminants; macro and minor elements in feed stuff and milk; improvement and development of analytical methods in nutritional research; forage utilization and preservation; the interaction of base forming feed constituents in the cow's rumen. *Mailing Add:* 188 West St RFD 5 Amherst MA 01002

FENNER, PETER, b Zurich, Switz, Oct 2, 37; US citizen; c 3. GEOLOGY, SCIENCE EDUCATION. *Educ:* City Col New York, BS, 59; Univ Ill, MS, 61, PhD(sedimentology, clay mineral), 63. *Prof Exp:* From instr to asst prof geol, Univ Pa, 63-67; from assoc dir to exec dir, Coun Educ Geol Sci, Am Geol Inst, 67-70; from asst dean to dean, Col Environ & Appl Sci, Governors State Univ, 70-79, prof geol, 70-81, spec asst to provost, 79-81; VCHANCELLOR ACAD AFFAIRS & PROF GEOL SCI, PURDUE UNIV CALUMET, 81- *Concurrent Pos:* Chmn instructional mat panel, Coun Educ Geol Sci; adv geol ed, Appleton-Century-Crofts; scientist, Smithsonain Inst-Coast Guard Oceanog Res Cruises; mem bd adv, Nat Study Math Req of Scientists & Engrs. *Mem:* AAAS; Geol Soc Am; Soc Econ Paleont & Mineral; World Future Soc. *Res:* Application of quantitative methods to geology, particularly in clay mineral and trace element studies; environmental and earth-science education; oceanography; higher education planning, especially implementing basic skills; developmental studies programs. *Mailing Add:* Purdue Univ Calumet Hammond IN 46323

FENNER, WAYNE ROBERT, b Butte, Mont, Aug 6, 39; m 61; c 3. INTEGRATED OPTICS, OPTICAL COMMUNICATIONS. *Educ:* Univ Calif, Berkeley, BS, 62; Univ Ill, MS, 64, PhD(physics), 69. *Prof Exp:* Res assoc physics, Univ Southern Calif, 69-71; mem tech staff elec eng, 72-80, mgr signal processing, 80-81, HEAD, DEPT LASERS & OPTICS, ELECTRONICS RES LAB, AEROSPACE CORP, 81- *Concurrent Pos:* Lectr, Univ Calif, Los Angeles, 77; instr, El Camino Col, 78-79. *Mem:* Am Phys Soc; Inst Elec & Electronics Engrs. *Res:* Laser raman spectroscopy; ultrasonic imaging; digital signal processing; adaptive antenna arrays; integrated optics; optical communications. *Mailing Add:* Aerospace Corp A6/1467 PO Box 92957 Los Angeles CA 90009

FENNER-CRISP, PENELOPE ANN, b Milwaukee, Wis, Apr 18, 39; m 65; c 2. NEUROTOXICOLOGY, REPRODUCTIVE TOXICOLOGY. *Educ:* Univ Wis, Milwaukee, BS, 62; Univ Tex Med Br Galveston, MS, 64, PhD(pharmacol), 68. *Prof Exp:* Fel pharmacol-morphol, Sch Med & Dent, Georgetown Univ, 71-73, adj instr, 73-74, res assoc pharmacol, 76-78; pharmacologist, 78-80, SR TOXICOLOGIST REGULATORY AFFAIRS, US ENVIRON PROTECTION AGENCY, 80- *Concurrent Pos:* Consult, USV Pharmaceut Co, Tuckahoe, NY, 70; vis scientist, Dept Physiol, Univ Birmingham, 74-75. *Mem:* Sigma Xi; AAAS. *Res:* Regulations and non-regulatory health effects guidance concerning chemical contamination of drinking water. *Mailing Add:* 5920 N 35th St Arlington VA 22207

FENNESSEY, PAUL V, b Oklahoma City, Okla, Oct 3, 42; m 62; c 3. MASS SPECTROMETRY. *Educ:* Univ Okla, BS, 64; Mass Inst Technol, PhD(chem), 68. *Prof Exp:* Fel, Mass Inst Technol, 64-69; sr res scientist, Monsanto Corp, 68-69; asst prog scientist, Martin Marietta Corp, 69-72, prog scientist, 72-74; asst prof, 75-81, ASSOC PROF PEDIAT PHARMACOL, SCH MED, UNIV COLO, 81- *Mem:* Am Soc Mass Spectros; AAAS; Soc Inherited Metab Dis; Am Chem Soc; Am Soc Pharmacol & Exp Therapeuts. *Res:* Application of mass spectrometry to clinical medicine; inborn errors of metabolism; steroid imbalances; marine animals in collaboration with the Naval Ocean Systems center for organic and physiological analysis. *Mailing Add:* Mass Spectros Res Resource Med Sch Univ Colo 4200 9th Ave Denver CO 80262

FENNESSY, JOHN JAMES, b Clonmel, Ireland, Mar 8, 33; m 60; c 7. RADIOLOGY. *Educ:* Nat Univ Ireland, MB, BCH & BAO, 57. *Prof Exp:* From instr to assoc prof radiol, 63-74, chief chest & gastrointestinal radiol, 73-74, actg chief diag radiol, 74, PROF RADIOL & CHMN DEPT, UNIV CHICAGO HOSPS & CLINS, 74- *Mem:* Am Asn Univ Radiologists; Am Gastroenterol Soc; Am Med Asn; Soc Gastrointestinal Radiol; Am Asn Univ Prof. *Mailing Add:* Dept Radiol Univ Chicago Hosp & Clin Chicago IL 60637

FENNEWALD, MICHAEL ANDREW, b Jefferson City, Mo, Sept 8, 51; m 74. MICROBIOLOGY. *Educ:* Carleton Col, BA, 73; Univ Chicago, PhD(microbiol), 79. *Prof Exp:* Fel biochem, Univ Chicago, 79-81; ASST PROF MICROBIOL, UNIV NOTRE DAME, 81- *Mem:* Am Soc Microbiol; Genetics Soc Am; AAAS. *Res:* Transpositions and insertion elements; nucleic acid enzymes; microbial hydrocarbon metabolism. *Mailing Add:* Dept Microbiol Univ Notre Dame Notre Dame IN 46556

FENNEY, NICHOLAS WILLIAM, b New Haven, Conn, July 18, 06; m 30; c 2. PHARMACY. *Educ:* Columbia Univ, PhG, 25; Univ Conn, PhC, 30; Yale Univ, MPH, 46. *Prof Exp:* From instr to prof, 25-68, EMER PROF PHARM, UNIV CONN, 68- *Concurrent Pos:* Vis lectr, Dept Pharmacol, Sch Med, Yale Univ, 35-42; Dept Pub Health, 48, Cancer Control Sect, 48-49; mem, Conn Adv Comt Foods & Drugs, 50-; estab Nicholas W Fenney scholar, Conn Pharm Asn, 65; mem, Conn Regional Med Prog, 66-70 & Conn Comprehensive Health Planning Coun, 68-72; pharmaceut consult, Conn Blue Cross/Blue Shield, 68-, mem, 71- *Honors & Awards:* Sydney Rome Achievement Award, 64; Bowl of Hygeia Award, 69; Nard-Lederle Nat Interprof Serv Award, 69. *Mem:* Am Pharmaceut Asn; Am Pub Health Asn; fel Am Col Apothecaries. *Res:* Detoxication of toxic chemicals with vitamin C; bacteriology; sanitation; public health. *Mailing Add:* 62 Broadfield Rd Hamden CT 06517

FENNINGER, LEONARD DAVIS, b Hampton, Va, Oct 3, 17; m 43; c 2. MEDICINE. *Educ:* Princeton Univ, AB, 38; Univ Rochester, MD, 43. *Prof Exp:* From instr to prof med, Sch Med & Dent, Univ Rochester, 47-67, assoc dean, 58-61; dir bur health manpower, USPHS, Div HEW, 67-69; assoc dir health manpower, NIH, 69-73; dir, Dept Grad Med Educ, 73-76, VPRES MED EDUC & SCI ACTIV, AMA, 76- *Concurrent Pos:* Head clin med sect, Nat Cancer Inst, NIH, 52-54; med dir, Strong Mem Hosp, NY, 61-67. *Mem:* AAAS; NY Acad Sci. *Res:* Protein and energy metabolism in cancer. *Mailing Add:* AMA 535 N Dearborn St Chicago IL 60610

FENOGLIO, CECILIA M, b New York, NY, Nov 28, 43; c 1. PATHOLOGY. *Educ:* Col Saint Elizabeth, BS, 65; Sch Med, Georgetown Univ, MD, 69. *Prof Exp:* Instr path, Col Physicians & Surgeons, Columbia Univ, 73-74, asst prof, 74-77; asst attend pathologist, 74-77, ASSOC ATTEND PATHOLOGIST, PRESBYTERIAN HOSP, 77-; DIR, ELECTRON MICRO LAB, INT INST HUMAN REPRODUCTION, 78-; CO-DIR PATH, COL PHYSICIANS & SURGEONS, COLUMBIA UNIV, 78-, PROF, 82- *Concurrent Pos:* Fel immunol, Mem Sloan Kettering Cancer Ctr, 73; mem, path comt, Nat Cancer Inst, Div Cancer Control & Rehab, 75-; mem, NIH study sect, cancer control intervention, 80-; mem, Nat Ileitis & Colitis Found, 78- *Mem:* AAAS; Am Asn Pathologists; Int Acad Path; NY Acad Med; NY Acad Sci. *Res:* Problems in cancer research and tumor markers; gastrointestinal and gynecologic cancer. *Mailing Add:* Col Physicians & Surgeons Columbia Univ 630 W 168th St New York NY 10032

FENOGLIO, DAVID JOHN, b Joliet, Ill, Oct 2, 43; m 69; c 3. PHYSICAL ORGANIC CHEMISTRY. *Educ:* Univ Ill, BS, 65; Mich State Univ, PhD(chem), 69. *Prof Exp:* RES CHEMIST, AMOCO CHEM CORP RES & DEVELOP CTR, 70- *Mem:* Am Chem Soc. *Res:* Chemicals in tertiary oil recovery; oil additives. *Mailing Add:* Amoco Chem PO Box 400 Naperville IL 60540

FENOGLIO, RICHARD ANDREW, b Joliet, Ill, Jan 4, 41; m 65; c 2 ORGANIC CHEMISTRY. *Educ:* Univ Ill, BS, 62; Yale Univ, PhD(org chem), 67. *Prof Exp:* RES CHEMIST, E I DU PONT DE NEMOURS & CO, INC, 67- *Mem:* Am Chem Soc. *Res:* Study of solvolyses and thermochemistry of small ring compounds; study of dye chemistry; study of titanium dioxide pigments. *Mailing Add:* Dept Chem & Pigments Edge Moor Plant Hay Rd Edge Moor DE 19809

FENRICK, HAROLD WILLIAM, b Janesville, Wis, Mar 31, 35; m 63; c 3. PHYSICAL CHEMISTRY. *Educ:* Beloit Col, BS, 57; Univ Wis-Madison, PhD(chem), 65. *Prof Exp:* Instr chem, Carleton Col, 65-66; asst prof, Monmouth Col, Ill, 66-68; assoc prof, 68-80, PROF CHEM, UNIV WIS-PLATTEVILLE, 80- *Mem:* Am Chem Soc. *Res:* Radiation chemistry of solids; electron spin resonance studies of free radicals. *Mailing Add:* Dept of Chem Univ of Wis Platteville WI 53818

FENRICK, MAUREEN HELEN, b Toronto, Ont, Feb 8, 46; US citizen. ALGEBRA. *Educ:* Edgewood Col, BS, 67; Northern Ill Univ, MS, 69; Univ Fla, PhD(math), 73. *Prof Exp:* Instr, 73-74, ASST PROF MATH, WICHITA STATE UNIV, 74- *Mem:* Math Asn Am. *Res:* Noncommutative ring theory, in particular preradical classes and their associated torsion filters. *Mailing Add:* Dept of Math Wichita State Univ Wichita KS 67208

FENSELAU, ALLAN HERMAN, b Philadelphia, Pa, May 17, 37; div; c 2. ORGANIC CHEMISTRY. *Educ:* Yale Univ, BS, 58; Stanford Univ, PhD(org chem), 64. *Prof Exp:* Teacher, Univ Sch, 58-60; fel org chem, Inst Molecular Biol, Syntex Res Ctr, Calif, 64-65; fel biochem, Univ Calif, Berkeley, 65-67; from asst prof to assoc prof physiol chem, Johns Hopkins Univ, 73-81; SR SCIENTIST, PAPANICOLAOU CANCER RES INST, 81-; ASSOC PROF ANAT & CELL BIOL, SCH MED, UNIV MIAMI, 81- *Concurrent Pos:* USPHS res career develop award, 72-77. *Honors & Awards:* Myers Honor Award Ophthal. *Mem:* AAAS; Am Chem Soc; Royal Soc Chem; Am Soc Biol Chemists. *Res:* Protein chemistry; cancer; biochemistry of angiogenesis. *Mailing Add:* Dept Physiol Chem Sch Med Johns Hopkins Univ 725 N Wolfe St Baltimore MD 21205

FENSELAU, CATHERINE CLARKE, b York, Nebr, Apr 15, 39; m 62; c 2. PHARMACOLOGY, MASS SPECTROMETRY. *Educ:* Bryn Mawr Col, AB, 61; Stanford Univ, PhD(org chem), 65. *Prof Exp:* Res chemist, NASA, Univ Calif, Berkeley, 66-67; from instr to asst prof pharmacol, 67-73, ASSOC PROF PHARMACOL, SCH MED, JOHNS HOPKINS UNIV, 73- *Concurrent Pos:* Am Asn Univ Women fel, Univ Calif, Berkeley, 65-66; USPHS res career develop award, 72-77; ed-in-chief, Biomed Mass Spectrometry, 73-; consult, Med Chem Study Sect, NIH, 75-79. *Mem:* AAAS; Am Chem Soc; Am Soc Mass Spectrometry. *Res:* Biomedical applications of mass spectrometry; drug metabolism; chemistry of gaseous ions; chemistry of glucuronides. *Mailing Add:* Dept of Pharmacol Johns Hopkins Univ Sch of Med Baltimore MD 21205

FENSKE, PAUL RODERICK, b Ellensberg, Wash, May 15, 25; m 52; c 4. HYDROGEOLOGY. *Educ:* SDak Sch Mines & Technol, BS, 50; Univ Mich, MS, 51; Univ Colo, PhD(geol), 63. *Prof Exp:* Geologist, Magnolia Petrol Co, 51-56 & Delfern Oil Co, 56-59; asst prof geol, Idaho State Univ, 63-65; mgr earth sci & eng, Teledyne Isotopes Palo Alto Labs, 65-71; res assoc, 71-73, asst exec dir, 79-80, RES PROF, WATER RES CTR, DESERT RES INT, UNIV NEV, RENO, 73-, DEP EXEC DIR, 80-, ACTG EXEC DIR, 81- *Concurrent Pos:* Consult hydrogeol, mining hydrol & waste mgt. *Mem:* Am Inst Mining Engineers; Am Geophys Union; Am Water Resources Asn; Sigma Xi. *Res:* Origin of porosity in oil producing reefs; origin and significance of concretions; geochemistry of sedimentary rocks; hydrogeochemistry; hydrologic systems analysis; groundwater transport of contaminants; well hydraulics; porous media flow. *Mailing Add:* Desert Res Inst Univ Nev Syst PO Box 60220 Reno NV 89506

FENSOM, DAVID STRATHERN, b Toronto, Ont, Apr 10, 16; m 44; c 2. PLANT BIOPHYSICS, PLANT PHYSIOLOGY. *Educ:* Univ Toronto, BASc, 38. *Prof Exp:* Master sci & head dept, Ridley Col, Ont, 46-63; assoc prof, 63-65, head dept, 69-76, PROF BIOL, MT ALLISON UNIV, 65- *Mem:* Fel Royal Inst Chem; fel Royal Soc Arts; Can Soc Plant Physiologists (secy-treas, 69-71); Soc Cryobiol; Brit Soc Exp Biol. *Res:* Electroosmosis, electrophysiology; long distance transport in plants; membrane phenomena. *Mailing Add:* Dept of Biol Mt Allison Univ Sackville NB E0A 3C0 Can

FENSTER, SAUL, b New York, NY, Mar 22, 33; m 59; c 3. MECHANICAL ENGINEERING. *Educ:* City Col New York, BME, 53; Columbia Univ, MS, 55; Univ Mich, PhD(heat transfer), 59. *Prof Exp:* Tool designer, Tech Facilities, Inc, 52; lectr mech eng, City Col New York, 53-56; mech engr, res inst, Univ Mich, 58; res engr aerospace, Sperry Gyroscope Div, Sperry Rand Corp, 59-62; prof physics, Fairleigh Dickinson Univ, 62-63; chmn dept physics, 62-63, chmn dept mech eng, 63-70, prof, 63-72, grad admin asst to dean col sci & eng, 65-70, assoc dean col sci & eng, 70-71, exec asst to pres, 71-72, provost, Rutherford Campus, 72-78; PRES, NJ INST TECHNOL, 78- *Concurrent Pos:* Indust consult, 62-; mem bd dirs, NJ Asn Cols & Univs; mem bd trustees, Newark Boys Chorus Sch; chmn, Gov Citizens Task Force on Water Mgt Emergency. *Mem:* Am Soc Mech Engrs; Am Soc Eng Educ; AAAS; Sigma Xi. *Res:* Heat transfer; machine dynamics and design; structural analysis; cryogenic and societal engineering. *Mailing Add:* 524 Bernita Dr River Vale NJ 07675

FENSTER, STANLEY, accelerator physics, see previous edition

FENSTERMACHER, CHARLES ALVIN, b Scranton, Pa, Mar 31, 28. EXPERIMENTAL PHYSICS. *Educ:* Philadelphia Col Pharm, BS, 50; Swarthmore Col, BA, 53; Yale Univ, MS, 55, PhD(physics), 57. *Prof Exp:* Staff mem weapons test div, 57-59, group leader test div, Rover Prog, 59-69, group leader res & develop electrically excited gas lasers, 69-75, assoc div leader, Laser Div, 75-79, PROG MGR ADVAN LASERS, LOS ALAMOS NAT LAB, 79- *Mem:* Am Phys Soc. *Res:* Gamma ray spectroscopy of neutron capture gamma rays from rare earths; weapons test measurements; Rover nuclear rocket reactor systems design and test. *Mailing Add:* 3215 Arizona Los Alamos NM 87544

FENSTERMACHER, ROBERT LANE, b Scranton, Pa, May 30, 41; c 1. SOLID STATE PHYSICS, RADIO ASTRONOMY. *Educ:* Drew Univ, BA, 63; Pa State Univ, PhD(physics), 68. *Prof Exp:* From asst prof to assoc prof, 68-80, PROF PHYSICS, DREW UNIV, 80-, CHMN DEPT, 75- *Concurrent Pos:* NASA fel, Jet Propulsion Lab, 79, NSF fac fel, Bell Telephone Labs, 80-81. *Mem:* AAAS; Am Asn Univ Prof; Am Asn Physics Teachers; Am Phys Soc. *Res:* Particle-solid interactions; solar radio astronomy. *Mailing Add:* Dept of Physics Drew Univ Madison NJ 07940

FENSTERMAKER, ROGER WILLIAM, b Akron, Ohio, Aug 17, 42; m 64; c 1. CHEMISTRY. *Educ:* Case Inst Technol, BS, 64; Univ Wis, PhD(chem), 70. *Prof Exp:* Res assoc, Wayne State Univ, 70-71; fel, Rice Univ, 71-72; asst prof chem, Northern Mich Univ, 72-73; RES CHEMIST, PHILLIPS PETROL CO, 73- *Mem:* Soc Automotive Engrs; Am Chem Soc. *Res:* Fundamental and applied studies of combustion. *Mailing Add:* 2929 Ridge Court Bartlesville OK 74003

FENTER, FELIX WEST, b Paris, Tex, Sept 16, 26; m 51; c 1. AERONAUTICAL ENGINEERING. *Educ:* Univ Tex, BS, 53, MS, 54, PhD(aeAonaut & space eng), 60. *Prof Exp:* Asst aeromech div, Defense Res Lab, Tex, 52-53, res engr, 53-55, syst develop specialist, 55-58; eng specialist, aerodyn sect, Chance Vought Aircraft, Inc, 58-60, sr scientist, Vought Res Ctr, 60-61, supvr, aerophysics group, Ling-Temco-Vought Res Ctr, 61-62, asst dir, 62-66, assoc dir, LTV Res Ctr, Ling-Temco-Vought, Inc, 66-71, vpres Advan Technol Ctr, Inc, 71-76; CHMN BD & PRES, ADVAN TECHNOL CTR, INC, 73-; V PRES RES & ADVAN TECHNOL, VOUGHT CORP, 76- *Mem:* AAAS; Am Ord Asn; Am Inst Aeronaut & Astronaut. *Res:* Supersonic and hypersonic aerodynamics; mechanics of viscous fluids. *Mailing Add:* Vought Corp PO Box 225907 Dallas TX 75265

FENTERS, JAMES DEAN, b Attica, Ind, Sept 23, 36. VIROLOGY, MICROBIOLOGY. *Educ:* Purdue Univ, BS, 58; Univ Iowa, MS, 61, PhD(bact), 62. *Prof Exp:* Res virologist, Abbott Labs, 62-67; res virologist, 67-74, HEAD MICROBIOL & IMMUNOL RES, IIT RES INST, 74- *Mem:* AAAS; Am Soc Microbiol; NY Acad Sci; Tissue Cult Asn; Sigma Xi. *Res:* Environmental pollutant effects on infectious processes; water microbiology, viral vaccines, immune responses and serology, antiviral chemotherapy, organ and tissue culture, in vitro bioassay systems. *Mailing Add:* IIT Res Inst 10 W 35th St Chicago IL 60616

FENTIMAN, ALLISON FOULDS, JR, b Pittsburgh, Pa, Apr 21, 37; m 57; c 2. ORGANIC CHEMISTRY. *Educ:* Muskingum Col, BS, 61; Ohio State Univ, MS, 66, PhD(org chem), 69. *Prof Exp:* PRIN RES CHEMIST ORG CHEM, COLUMBUS DIV, BATTELLE MEM INST, 63- *Mem:* AAAS; Am Chem Soc; Sigma Xi. *Res:* Organic synthesis, mechanism, and spectrometric analysis, including synthesis of deuterium-labeled drugs; mechanistic study of the competition between aryl substituents and neighboring groups; identification of insect pheromones and marihuana constituents and metabolites; nuclear magnetic resonance of solids. *Mailing Add:* Columbus Div Battelle Mem Inst 505 King Ave Columbus OH 43201

FENTON, DAVID GEORGE, b London, Eng, June 8, 32; m; c 2. PHYSICS. *Educ:* Univ London, Eng, BSc, 55; Univ Conn, PhD, 64. *Prof Exp:* Asst, Purdue Univ, 55-57; prod engr, Taylor Instrument Co, 57-58; from instr to assoc prof, 58-73, PROF PHYSICS, CONN COL, 73- *Mem:* Hist Sci Soc; Am Asn Physics Teachers. *Res:* Quantum mechanics of the electronic structure of molecules and of atomic collision processes. *Mailing Add:* Dept of Physics Conn Col New London CT 06320

FENTON, DONALD MASON, b Los Angeles, Calif, May 23, 29; m 53; c 2. PETROLEUM CHEMISTRY. *Educ:* Univ Calif, Los Angeles, BS, 52, PhD, 58. *Prof Exp:* Res chemist, Rohm and Haas Co, 58-61; RES CHEMIST, UNION OIL CO, 62- *Mem:* Am Chem Soc. *Res:* Organometallic chemistry. *Mailing Add:* Union Oil Co PO Box 76 Brea CA 92621

FENTON, EDWARD WARREN, b Lucky Lake, Sask, Mar 5, 37; m 66; c 1. SOLID STATE PHYSICS. *Educ:* Univ Alta, BSc, 59, MSc, 62, PhD(physics), 65. *Prof Exp:* Nat Res Coun fel physics, Simon Fraser Univ, Vancouver, 65-67; res officer physics, Noranda Res Ctr, Montreal, 67; from asst res officer to sr res officer, 67-77, SR RES OFFICER PHYSICS, NAT RES COUN CAN, 77- *Mem:* Can Asn Physicists; Am Phys Soc. *Res:* Experimental and theoretical solid state physics, including properties of semiconductors, metals, and itinerant-electron condensates. *Mailing Add:* Physics Div Nat Res Coun Can Ottawa ON K1A 0R6 Can

FENTON, JOHN WILLIAM, II, b Salamanaca, NY, Feb 4, 39; m 65; c 2. BIOCHEMISTRY, IMMUNOLOGY. *Educ:* Cornell Univ, BS, 61; Univ Wis-Madison, MS, 64; Univ Calif, San Diego, PhD(biochem), 68. *Prof Exp:* SR RES SCIENTIST, DIV LABS & RES, NY STATE DEPT HEALTH, 68- *Concurrent Pos:* USPHS grants, 69-73 & 75-83; Brown-Hazen Fund grant, 74; adj asst prof, Dept Microbiol, Albany Med Col, 70-74; mem coun thrombosis, Am Heart Asn, grant, 77-78. *Mem:* Am Heart Asn; AAAS; Am Soc Biol Chemists; NY Acad Sci; Am Chem Soc. *Res:* Purification, properties, structures, enzymic specificity and functionality of human thrombins and other blood components; coagulation; purification of antibodies and diagnostic application; antibody and enzyme active sites. *Mailing Add:* Div of Labs & Res NY State Dept Health Albany NY 12201

FENTON, M BROCK, b Guyana, Oct 20, 43; Can citizen; m 69. MAMMALOGY. *Educ:* Queen's Univ, Ont, BSc, 65; Univ Toronto, MSc, 66, PhD(zool), 69. *Prof Exp:* Assoc prof, 69-81, PROF BIOL, CARLETON UNIV, 81- *Concurrent Pos:* Res assoc mammal, Royal Ont Mus. *Honors & Awards:* A B Howell Award, Am Soc Mammal, 69. *Mem:* AAAS; Am Soc Mammal; Can Soc Zool; Soc Vert Paleont; Nat Speleol Soc. *Res:* Chiroptology; speleology; ecology of bats with special references to their behavior; biology and paleontology of caves. *Mailing Add:* Dept of Biol Carleton Univ Ottawa ON K1S 5B6 Can

FENTON, PAUL FREDRIC, b Stuttgart, Ger, Nov 28, 15; nat US; m 41; c 2. BIOCHEMISTRY. *Educ:* Univ Rochester, BS, 38; Univ Vt, MS, 40, PhD(biochem), 44. *Prof Exp:* Asst, Univ Vt, 38-40, from instr to asst prof biochem, 40-45; Nutrit Found fel, Yale Univ, 45-46, asst prof nutrit, 46-49; assoc prof biol, 49-54, chmn exec coun, Div Biol & Med Sci, 64-68, prof, 54-81, EMER PROF BIOL, BROWN UNIV, 81- *Concurrent Pos:* Mem nutrit panel, Comt Growth, Nat Res Coun, 49-52; Guggenheim Mem fel & vis prof, Emory Univ, 57-58; mem physiol training comt, Nat Inst Gen Med Sci, 61-65. *Mem:* Am Inst Nutrit; Am Physiol Soc; Soc Exp Biol & Med. *Res:* Nutritional biochemistry; physiology of digestive system; endocrinology and metabolism. *Mailing Add:* Div of Biol & Med Sci Brown Univ Providence RI 02912

FENTON, ROBERT E, b Brooklyn, NY, Sept 30, 33; m 55; c 2. ELECTRICAL ENGINEERING. *Educ:* Ohio State Univ, BEE, 57, MSc, 60, PhD(elec eng), 65. *Prof Exp:* Res engr, N Am Aviation, Inc, 57; from instr to assoc prof elec eng, 60-73, asst supvr, Commun & Controls Syst Labs, 65-67, actg dir, 67-70, PROF ELEC ENG, OHIO STATE UNIV, 73-, DIR, TRANSP CONTROL LAB, 70- *Concurrent Pos:* Mem, Hwy Res Bd Comt Hwy Commun, 66-; consult, Transp Systs Div, 73-74 & Gen Motors Corp, 76- *Mem:* Inst Elec & Electronics Engrs. *Res:* Automatic control and computer systems; automated transportation systems. *Mailing Add:* Dept of Elec Eng 2015 Neil Ave Columbus OH 43210

FENTON, ROBERT GEORGE, b Budapest, Hungary, Apr 3, 31; m 57; c 2. MECHANICAL ENGINEERING. *Educ:* Univ Budapest, Dipl Ing, 53; Univ NSW, PhD(mech eng), 68. *Prof Exp:* Sr lectr mech eng, Univ NSW, 62-68; assoc prof, 68-81, PROF MECH ENG, UNIV TORONTO, 81- *Honors & Awards:* Water Arbit Prize, Inst Mech Engrs, 69; Handerson Mem Prize, Inst Mech Engrs, 70. *Res:* Experimental and analytical investigation of metal flow during machining and forming; yield criteria, thermal effects; machine tool vibration; wear analysis; tool life and machining economy; computerized design; reliability; simulation models; computer graphics. *Mailing Add:* Dept of Mech Eng Univ of Toronto Toronto ON M5S 1A1 Can

FENTON, STUART WILLIAM, b London, Ont, Apr 29, 22; m 62. ORGANIC CHEMISTRY. *Educ:* Queen's Univ, Ont, BSc, 45, MSc, 46; Mass Inst Technol, PhD(chem), 50. *Prof Exp:* Asst prof org chem, 50-55, assoc prof chem & assoc chmn dept, 55-61, chmn dept, 61-68, PROF CHEM, UNIV MINN, MINNEAPOLIS, 61- *Mem:* AAAS; Am Chem Soc; The Chem Soc. *Res:* Organic synthesis and peroxides. *Mailing Add:* Dept of Chem Univ of Minn Minneapolis MN 55455

FENTON, THOMAS E, b Cabery, Ill, July 19, 33; m 59; c 4. SOIL GENESIS, SOIL CLASSIFICATION. *Educ:* Univ Ill, Urbana, BS, 59, MS, 60; Iowa State Univ, PhD(soil genesis & classification), 66. *Prof Exp:* Instr, US Army Europe Qm Sch, 54-55; res soil scientist, USDA, summers 61-64; res assoc agron, 64-66, from asst prof to assoc prof soil genesis & classification, 66-74, asst prof, Res Found, 68, PROF SOIL GENESIS & CLASSIFICATION, IOWA STATE UNIV, 74- *Concurrent Pos:* Consult, Attorney Gen Off, State of Iowa, 67-69. *Mem:* AAAS; Clay Mineral Soc; Am Soc Agron; Soil Sci Soc Am; Soil Conserv Soc Am. *Res:* Soil genesis and classification combined with geomorphology. *Mailing Add:* Dept of Agron Iowa State Univ Ames IA 50011

FENTRESS, JOHN CARROLL, b East Chicago, Ind, Feb 4, 39. ETHOLOGY, NEUROBIOLOGY. *Educ:* Amherst Col, BA, 61; Cambridge Univ, PhD(zool), 65. *Prof Exp:* From asst prof to assoc prof biol-psychol, Univ Ore, 67-75; PROF PSYCHOL & CHMN DEPT, DALHOUSIE UNIV, 75- *Concurrent Pos:* USPHS fel, Ctr Brain Res, Univ Rochester, 65-67; mem bd dirs, Wild Canid Survival & Res Ctr, 71- & Ore Zool Res Ctr, 72-; assoc ed, Behav Biol, 74-; res award, Nat Res Coun, 75- *Mem:* AAAS; Animal Behav Soc; Am Soc Zool; Soc Neurosci. *Res:* Integration and development of species-characteristic behaviors; brain mechanisms and behavior. *Mailing Add:* Psychol Dept Dalhousie Univ Halifax NS B3H 3J5 Can

FENVES, STEVEN J(OSEPH), b Subotica, Yugoslavia, June 6, 31; US citizen; m 55; c 4. CIVIL & SOFTWARE ENGINEERING. *Educ:* Univ Ill, BS, 57, MS, 58, PhD(eng), 61. *Prof Exp:* Draftsman, Erik Floor & Assoc, Ill, 50-52; from asst prof to prof civil eng, Univ Ill, 57-71; prof & head dept, 72-75, UNIV PROF CIVIL ENG, CARNEGIE-MELLON UNIV, 75- *Concurrent Pos:* Indust & govt consult, 57-; vis prof, Mass Inst Technol, 62-63, Nat Univ Mex, 65 & Cornell Univ, 70-71. *Mem:* Nat Acad Eng; Am Soc Civil Engrs; Asn Comput Mach. *Res:* Computer applications in civil engineering; structural dynamics, analysis and design; problem-oriented computer languages. *Mailing Add:* Dept Civil Eng Carnegie-Mellon Univ Pittsburgh PA 15213

FENWICK, HARRY, b Filer, Idaho, Sept 24, 22; m 46; c 3. PLANT PATHOLOGY. *Educ:* Mont State Univ, BS, 49, MS, 52; Ore State Col, PhD(plant path), 56. *Prof Exp:* Assoc prof plant path, 68-72, PROF PLANT SCI, UNIV IDAHO, 72-, EXTEN PLANT PATHOLOGIST, 56- *Mem:* Am Phytopath Soc. *Res:* Seedling diseases of sugarbeets; control of cereal rusts by chemotherapy; studies of dwarf bunt in cereals and grasses. *Mailing Add:* Dept of Plant Path Univ of Idaho Moscow ID 83843

FENWICK, JAMES CLARKE, b New West Minster, BC, Jan 5, 40; m 67; c 2. COMPARATIVE ENDOCRINOLOGY. *Educ:* Univ Man, BS, 62, MS, 65; Univ BC, PhD(zool), 69. *Prof Exp:* Lectr biol, St Johns Col, Man, 64-65; fel, Nat Res Coun Can, 69-70; asst prof, 70-75, assoc prof, 75-81, PROF BIOL, UNIV OTTAWA, 81- *Concurrent Pos:* Vis prof, Univ Nijmegen, The Netherlands, 81. *Mem:* Can Soc Zoologists; Am Zool Soc; Can Physiol Soc; European Soc Comp Biochem Physiol. *Res:* Calcium metabolism in lower vertebrates with special emphasis on transport processes in fish. *Mailing Add:* Dept of Biol Univ of Ottawa Ottawa ON K1N 6N5 Can

FENWICK, ROBERT B, b Indianapolis, Ind, Apr 13, 36; m 60; c 3. ELECTRICAL ENGINEERING. *Educ:* Purdue Univ, BS, 58; Stanford Univ, MS, 59, PhD(elec eng), 63. *Prof Exp:* Res assoc, Radiosci Lab, Stanford Univ, 60-68; vpres, 66-76, sr scientist, 68-76, PRES, BARRY RES CORP, 76- *Mem:* Am Geophys Union; Inst Elec & Electronics Engrs. *Res:* High frequency radio wave propagation via the ionosphere; techniques of ionospheric measurement, especially ionospheric sounders; frequency management systems including methods of measuring spectrum occupancy; data modern research. *Mailing Add:* 1249 Innsbruck Dr Sunnyvale CA 94088

FENYES, JOSEPH GABRIEL EGON, b Paszto, Hungary, Mar 19, 25; US citizen; m 57; c 3. SYNTHETIC ORGANIC CHEMISTRY. *Educ:* Univ Szeged, BSc, 48; McGill Univ, PhD(org chem), 55. *Prof Exp:* Lectr org chem, Royal Mil Col, Ont, 55-56; res chemist, Shawinigan Chem Ltd, Que, 56-58; res group leader, Hyman Labs, Inc, Calif, Berkeley, 58-62; res chemist, Ortho Div, Calif Chem Co, Richmond, 62 & Chevron Chem Co, Calif, 62-69; CHIEF ORGANIC RES CHEMIST, BUCKMAN LABS, INC, MEMPHIS, TENN, 69- *Mem:* Am Chem Soc. *Res:* Synthesis of biologically active and agriculturally useful organic compounds; sulfenyl halides; halogen and sulfur containing fungicides; plant growth regulators; organophosphorous insecticides; B-substituted naphthalenes; heterocyclic chemicals; plastics additives; ultraviolet light absorbers; fire retardants; agricultural and industrial microbicides and herbicides. *Mailing Add:* 1827 Oakhill Cove Germantown TN 38138

FENYVES, ERVIN J, b Budapest, Hungary, Aug 29, 24; m 51; c 2. HIGH ENERGY PHYSICS, COSMIC RAY PHYSICS. *Educ:* Eotvos Lorand Univ, Budapest, MS, 46, PhD(physics), 50; Hungarian Acad Sci, Cand Phys Sci, 55, Dr Phys Sci, 60. *Prof Exp:* Asst prof physics, Eotvos Lorand Univ, 46-51; res fel, Cent Res Inst Physics, Hungarian Acad Sci, 51-59, head lab cosmic rays, 59-65, dep sci dir, 65-69; res fel physics, Univ Pa, 69-70; PROF PHYSICS & ENVIRON SCI, UNIV TEX, DALLAS, 70-, ACTG DIR, CTR ENVIRON STUDIES, 80- *Concurrent Pos:* Asst prof, Eotvos Lorand Univ, 60-64, prof, 64-69; cor mem high energy nuclear physics comn, Int Union Pure & Appl Physics, 63-69, mem cosmic ray comn, 66-70; vdir, Joint Inst Nuclear Res, Dubna, 64-66; head physics sect, Int Atomic Energy Agency, Vienna, 68-69. *Honors & Awards:* Brodi-Schmidt Prize, Hungarian Phys Soc, 52; Nat Kossuth Prize, Hungarian Govt, 65; Prize for Books, Hungarian Acad Sci, 67. *Mem:* Fel Am Phys Soc; NY Acad Sci. *Res:* Nuclear radiation measurements; neutrino astrophysics. *Mailing Add:* Univ Tex at Dallas PO Box 668 Richardson TX 75080

FEOLA, JOSE MARIA, b Buenos Aires, Arg, May 30, 26; US citizen; m 50; c 3. RADIATION BIOLOGY, PHYSICS. *Educ:* Univ Rochester, MS, 61; Univ La Plata, Arg, licenciate physics & math, 63; Univ Minn, Minneapolis, PhD(environ health), 74. *Prof Exp:* Mem res staff radiobiol, Arg Atomic Energy Comn, 56-65; Donner Lab, Univ Calif, Berkeley, 65-69; instr radiobiol, Univ Minn, Minneapolis, 70-73, instr sci methods, Exten Div, 74-75; ASSOC PROF CLIN MED, DEPT RADIATION MED, UNIV KY, 75- *Concurrent Pos:* Asst prof, Fac Eng, Univ Buenos Aires, 56-64; Nat Cancer Inst grant, 77-80; Univ Ky Res Found grant, 78, NIH grant, 78-79. *Mem:* Radiation Res Soc; Southeastern Cancer Res Asn. *Res:* Cancer radiation and chemotherapy in experimental systems; biological effects of low doses of ionizing radiation of high and low linear energy transfer; biological effects of magnetic fields. *Mailing Add:* Dept of Radiation Med 800 Rose St Lexington KY 40506

FERADAY, MELVILLE ALBERT, b Toronto, Ont, Jan 13, 29; m 58; c 3. MECHANICAL ENGINEERING, MATERIALS SCIENCE. *Educ:* Queen's Univ, Ont, BSc, 54; Univ Waterloo, MSc, 70. *Prof Exp:* Engr, Chalk River Nuclear Labs, 56-58, commissioning engr, Colombo Plan, India, 59-60, fuel develop engr, 60-80, MGR NUCLEAR WASTE, CHALK RIVER NUCLEAR LABS, ATOMIC ENERGY CAN, LTD, 80- *Res:* Design, development, metallurgy and irradiation of uranium based fuel elements, particularly metallic fuels and powder packed uranium dioxide fuels; design of a remotely operated plant to fabricate gamma active nuclear fuels; long term environmental planning of low level radioactive waste management sites. *Mailing Add:* Chalk River Nuclear Labs Chalk River ON K0J 1J0 Can

FERBEL, THOMAS, b Radom, Poland, Dec 12, 37; US citizen; m 63; c 2. PARTICLE PHYSICS. *Educ:* Queens Col, NY, BS, 59; Yale Univ, MS, 60, PhD(physics), 63. *Prof Exp:* Res staff physicist, Yale Univ, 63-65; from asst prof to assoc prof, 65-73, PROF PHYSICS, UNIV ROCHESTER, 73- *Concurrent Pos:* Sloan Found res fel, 70; Guggenheim Found fel, 71; chmn, Meson Dept, Comt Fermilab, 78-79; Mgt Dept contract, Dept Energy, 77-80; sci dir, Advand Study Inst, NATO, St Croix, 80 & Adirondacks, 82; mem, High Energy Adv Comt, Brookhaven Lab, 81-83. *Mem:* Am Phys Soc. *Res:* Experimental elementary particle physics; strong interactions. *Mailing Add:* Dept of Physics & Astron Univ of Rochester Rochester NY 14627

FERBER, KELVIN HALKET, b Brooklyn, NY, Oct 18, 10; m 37; c 2. INDUSTRIAL HYGIENE, OCCUPATIONAL HEALTH. *Educ:* Cornell Univ, BChem, 32; State Univ NY Buffalo, MBA, 71. *Prof Exp:* Supvr anal lab, Allied Chem Corp, 38-42, supt qual control, 42-44, asst to plant mgr, 45-49, supt tests & inspections, 49-64, tech mgr, 64-71, tech asst to mgr, 71-72, mgr occup health, 72-75; CONSULT OCCUP HEALTH, 76- *Mem:* Am Chem Soc; fel Am Soc Testing & Mat; fel Am Inst Chemists; Am Indust Hyg Asn. *Res:* Industrial toxicology; environmental control; occupational hazards and industrial hygiene control of carcinogens. *Mailing Add:* Buffalo Color Corp Box 7027 Buffalo NY 14240

FERBER, RICHARD HENRY, New York, NY, Nov 8, 43; m 70; c 1. CARDIO-VASCULAR PHARMACOLOGY, VASCULAR DISEASES. *Educ:* Brooklyn Col Pharm, Long Island Univ, BS, 66; Univ Minn, MS, 77. *Prof Exp:* Advan Pharmacologist, Riker Labs, 72-78, SR PHARMACOLOGIST, BIO-SCI LABS, 3M CO, 78- *Mem:* Int Soc Radio-Pharmacol. *Res:* Blood and vessel wall interactions; non-invasive thrombosis detections. *Mailing Add:* 6160 Rice Creek Dr Fridley MN 55432

FERBER, ROBERT R, b Monongahela, Pa, June 11, 35; m 64. ELECTRICAL ENGINEERING. *Educ:* Univ Pittsburgh, BS, 58; Carnegie-Mellon Univ, MS, 66, PhD(elec eng), 67. *Prof Exp:* Audio engr, Radio Sta WWSW, 52-56; head dept eng, WRS Motion Picture Labs, 54-58; res engr radiation detection, Westinghouse Res Labs, 58-66, adv engr, Westinghouse Astronuclear Labs, 67-71, power systs planning, Westinghouse Elec Corp, 71-77; mem tech staff, 77-80, MGR COLLECTOR TECHNOL DEVELOP, PHOTOVOLTAIC LEAD CTR, JET PROPULSION LAB, 80- *Concurrent Pos:* Lectr, Inst Safety & Systs Mgt, Univ Southern Calif, 81- *Mem:* Inst Elec & Electronics Engrs; Int Solar Energy Soc. *Res:* Advanced concepts in electric power generation; nuclear radiation effects; nuclear power; solar power; semiconductor physics. *Mailing Add:* Jet Propulsion Lab 4800 Oak Grove Dr Pasadena CA 91109

FERCHAU, HUGO ALFRED, b Mineola, NY, July 22, 29; m 52; c 4. BOTANY. *Educ:* Col William & Mary, BS, 51; Duke Univ, PhD(bot), 59. *Prof Exp:* Actg jr botanist, Div Indust Res, 53-54; assoc prof biol, Wofford Col, 58-62; from asst prof to assoc prof, 62-69, PROF BIOL, WESTERN STATE COL COLO, 69- *Concurrent Pos:* Dir, Bact Testing Serv, Western State Col, 62-; mem fac, Inst Mountain Ecol, Rocky Mountain State Univ, Ft Collins, 72-73, fac affil agron, 75-; vis prof environ sci, Colo Sch Mines, Golden, 81-82. *Mem:* AAAS; Ecol Soc Am; Bot Soc Am; Soc Range Mgt; Sigma Xi. *Res:* Ecology of mycorrhizae; vegetation analysis; environmental analysis; reclamation mines. *Mailing Add:* Dept Biol Western State Col Colo Gunnison CO 81230

FERCHAUD, JOHN B(ARTHOLOMEW), b New Orleans, La, June 14, 12; m 47; c 3. CHEMICAL ENGINEERING. *Educ:* La State Univ, BS, 35. *Prof Exp:* Process engr, Standard Oil Co, La, 35-36; plant chemist, Ark Fuel Oil Co, 36-37; state chem eng, Conserv Dept, La, 37-42; supt construct & oper, Chem Construct Corp, NY, 42-51; tech asst to mfg mgr, Lion Oil Co Div, Monsanto Co, 51-56; eng mgr, 56-61, eng mgr agr div, 61-65 & cent eng dept, 65-77; RETIRED. *Mem:* Am Inst Chem Engrs. *Res:* Engineering and construction of manufacturing units. *Mailing Add:* 182 Meadow Lark Dr St Louis MO 63141

FEREBEE, ROBERT NEWTON, microbiology, see previous edition

FERENCE, MICHAEL, JR, b Whiting, Ind, Nov 6, 11; m 37; c 5. PHYSICS. *Educ:* Univ Chicago, BS, 33, MA, 34, PhD(physics), 37. *Hon Degrees:* DSc, Kenyon Col, 69. *Prof Exp:* From instr to assoc prof physics, Univ Chicago, 37-46; chief meteorol br, Signal Corps Eng Labs, Evans Signal Lab, 46-48, chief scientist, 48-51, tech dir, 51-53; chief scientist, 53-54, from assoc dir to exec dir, 54-62, V PRES RES, SCI LAB, FORD MOTOR CO, 62- *Concurrent Pos:* Trustee, Rand Corp; mem panel, Res & Develop Bd, tech panel earth satellite prog & comt atmospheric sci, Nat Acad Sci & res panel, Signal Corps Res & Develop Adv Coun; mem adv group on weather modification, Nat Sci Found, spec adv comt to Dept of Com, Rocket & Satellite Res Panel, adv comt, US Weather Bur & President's Sci Adv Comt; mem bd of trustees, Carnegie Inst, Dirs Indust Res & adv comt, PR Nuclear Ctr, Univ PR. *Mem:* Nat Acad Eng; Am Phys Soc; Am Geophys Soc; Am Meteorol Soc; Soc Automative Eng; fel Inst Elec & Electronics Engrs. *Res:* Physics of the upper atmosphere; experimental hydrodynamics; designs of radiosondes; radar; electronics; microwave propagation; x-ray spectroscopy. *Mailing Add:* Anglers Cove 12-203 1456 NE Ocean Blvd Stuart FL 33494

FERENCZ, CHARLOTTE, b Budapest, Hungary, Oct 28, 21; US citizen. PEDIATRIC CARDIOLOGY, EPIDEMIOLOGY. *Educ:* McGill Univ, BSc, 44, MD, CM, 45; Johns Hopkins Univ, MPH, 70. *Prof Exp:* Demonstr pediat, McGill Univ, 52-54; asst prof pediat, Johns Hopkins Univ, 54-59; asst prof, Med Col, Univ Cincinnati, 59-60; from asst prof to assoc prof, Sch Med, State Univ NY Buffalo, 60-73, clin asst prof social & prev med, 71-73; assoc prof prev med, 73-74, ASSOC PROF PEDIAT, SCH MED, UNIV MD, 73-, PROF PREV MED, 74- *Mem:* Am Acad Pediat; Am Col Cardiol; Am Pub Health Asn. *Res:* Changes in the pulmonary vascular bed associated with congenital heart disease; normal growth of pulmonary vessels; epidemiology of heart disease in pediatric age group, children with long term illnesses and infant mortality; environmental teratology. *Mailing Add:* Dept Epidemiol & Prev Med 655 W Baltimore St Baltimore MD 21201

FERENCZ, NICHOLAS, b Cleveland, Ohio, Apr 22, 37; m; c 2. DENTISTRY. *Educ:* Hiram Col, AB, 59; Cath Univ Am, MS, 62, PhD(cell biol), 67; Case Western Reserve Univ, DDS, 74. *Prof Exp:* Instr radiol, 67-69, asst prof radiation biol, 69-71, clin instr, 74-77, ASST CLIN PROF PROSTHODONT, SCH DENT, CASE WESTERN RESERVE UNIV, 77- *Res:* Tissue culture; radiology; prosthodontics; dental materials. *Mailing Add:* Sch of Dent Case Western Reserve Univ Cleveland OH 44106

FERENTZ, MELVIN, b New York, NY, Oct 14, 28; m 48, 64; c 3. COMPUTER SCIENCE. *Educ:* Brooklyn Col, BS, 49; Univ Pa, PhD(physics), 53. *Prof Exp:* Asst instr physics, Univ Pa, 48-50; assoc physicist, Argonne Nat Lab, 52-57; sr mathematician analyst, Int Bus Mach Corp, 57-59; assoc prof physics, St John's Univ, NY, 59-65, prof & chmn dept, 65-66; dept chmn grad studies, Dept Physics, Brooklyn Col, 67-74, prof physics, 66-79; DIR COMPUT SERV, ROCKEFELLER UNIV, 78- *Concurrent Pos:* Res assoc, Columbia Univ, 64-66; vis prof, NY Univ, 66; assoc dir, City & State Univs NY Joint Inst Learning & Instr, 67-70; pres, Ferentz Assoc, Inc; consult, IBM Corp, Univac Div, Sperry Rand Corp & Grumman Aerospace. *Mem:* Asn Comput Mach. *Res:* digital computers. *Mailing Add:* 535 East 86 New York NY 10028

FERGIN, RICHARD KENNETH, b Tacoma, Wash, Dec 9, 33; m 67; c 1. ENGINEERING, PHYSICAL CHEMISTRY. *Educ:* Wash State Col, BS, 55; NMex State Univ, MS, 61, ScD(mech eng), 64. *Prof Exp:* Tool engr, Boeing Airplane Co, 55-57; mech engr, Ft Belvoir, Va, 58-59; res assoc, Rocket Sect, Phys Sci Lab, NMex State Univ, 59-60, asst mech eng, 60-61, instr, 61-63; assoc prof eng, San Diego State Col, 64-68; assoc prof math, US Int Univ, 68; staff scientist, Geosci Ltd, 69-72; dir res & develop, NRG Technol, 73-74; sr thermodyn engr, Teledyne Ryan, 75-76; chief mech engr, HVAC, Carter Engrs, 76-79; LEAD ENGR & MGR ENERGY CONSERV, NAVY PUB WORKS CTR, 80- *Mem:* Am Soc Heat, Refrig & Air-Conditioning Engrs; Am Soc Eng Educ; Am Soc Mech Engrs; Sigma Xi. *Res:* Binary liquid jet refrigeration using immiscible fluids; heat, mass and momentum transfer and enhancement with applications in energy recovery; micrometeorology; air and thermal pollution; solar energy; environmental control; energy optimization. *Mailing Add:* 1779 Ocean Front St San Diego CA 92107

FERGUS, CHARLES LEONARD, b Ottawa, Kans, Nov 11, 17; m 42; c 3. MYCOLOGY. *Educ:* Ottawa Univ, AB, 40; Univ Kans, MA, 42; Pa State Univ, PhD(bot), 48. *Prof Exp:* Lab instr biol, Ottawa Univ, 38-40; lab instr bot & med mycol, Univ Kans, 40-41; from instr to assoc prof, 48-60, PROF BOT, PA STATE UNIV, 60- *Mem:* Mycol Soc Am. *Res:* Physiology and taxonomy of thermophilic molds and actinomycetes. *Mailing Add:* Dept of Biol 202 Buckhout Lab Pa State Univ University Park PA 16802

FERGUSON, ALBERT BARNETT, b New York, NY, June 10, 19; m 43; c 3. ORTHOPEDIC SURGERY. *Educ:* Dartmouth Col, BA, 41; Harvard Univ, MD, 43. *Prof Exp:* Asst orthop surg, Harvard Univ, 51-52; from assoc prof to prof, 53-58, SILVER PROF ORTHOP SURG & CHMN DEPT, SCH MED, UNIV PITTSBURGH, 58- *Mem:* Am Acad Orthop Surg; Am Acad Pediat; Am Acad Neurol; Am Bd Orthopaedic Surgery (past pres); Am Orthopaedic Asn (past pres). *Res:* Physiology of muscles; growth. *Mailing Add:* Dept of Orthop Surg Univ of Pittsburgh Sch of Med Pittsburgh PA 15213

FERGUSON, ALBERT HAYDEN, b Big Timber, Mont, Sept 12, 28; m 51; c 2. SOIL PHYSICS. *Educ:* Mont State Col, BS, 50; Wash State Univ, MS, 56, PhD(soils), 59. *Prof Exp:* Soil scientist, US Bur Reclamation, 50-51; asst soils, Wash State Univ, 53-58; PROF SOILS, MONT STATE UNIV, 58- *Mem:* fel Am Soc Agron; Soil Sci Soc Am. *Res:* Water movement in soils; soil-plant relationships. *Mailing Add:* Dept of Plant & Soil Sci Mont State Univ Bozeman MT 59717

FERGUSON, ALEXANDER CUNNINGHAM, b Scotland. ALLERGY, IMMUNOLOGY. *Educ:* Univ Glasgow, MB, ChB, 67; Royal Col Physicians Glasgow, DCH, 69; FRCP(C), 72; Am Bd Allergy & Immunol, dipl, 75. *Prof Exp:* Intern/resident med, surg, pediat & infectious dis, Univ Glasgow, 67-69; resident pediat, Univ Western Ont, 69-70 & Hosp for Sick Children, Toronto, 70-72; res fel pediat immunol/allergy, Univ Calif, Los Angeles, 72-74; lectr pediat, Queen's Univ, 74-76; ASST PROF PEDIAT, UNIV BC, 76- *Concurrent Pos:* Can Pediat Soc fel, 72-74; grants, Med Res Coun Can, 75-, BC Health Res Found, BC Med Serv Found & BC Lung Asn, 77- *Honors & Awards:* Ross Award, Can Pediat Soc, 74. *Mem:* Am Acad Allergy; Can Pediat Soc; DELETE THIS FIELD; Royal Col Physicians Can; Can Med Asn. *Res:* Developmental immunology; immunologic function and nutrition; immunologic therapy of asthma; growth and development in allergic children. *Mailing Add:* Dept of Pediat 250 W 59th Ave Vancouver Can

FERGUSON, CHARLES WESLEY, b Los Angeles, Calif, July 27, 22; m 60. DENDROCHRONOLOGY. *Educ:* Mont State Univ, BS, 48; Univ Ariz, MS, 50, PhD(range mgt), 60. *Prof Exp:* Res asst, 50-54, res assoc, 61-63, from asst prof to assoc prof, 63-74, PROF DENDROCHRONOLOGY, LAB TREE-RING RES, UNIV ARIZ, 74- *Mem:* AAAS; Tree-Ring Soc (secy-treas, 58-); Am Soc Range Mgt; Ecol Soc Am. *Res:* Growth ring studies in big sagebrush and other nonconifers; development of a 8680 year tree-ring chronology of bristlecone pine. *Mailing Add:* Lab Tree-Ring Res Univ Ariz Tucson AZ 85721

FERGUSON, COLIN C, b Winnipeg, Man, Oct 3, 21; m 49; c 4. SURGERY. *Educ:* Univ Man, MD, 45; McGill Univ, dipl, 52; FRCS(C), 53. *Prof Exp:* Demonstr path, 44-45, head dept, 53-69, PROF SURG, UNIV MAN, 53- *Concurrent Pos:* Harrison fel surg, Univ Pa, 48-49; res fel pediat surg, Boston Children's Hosp, 51-52; teaching fel surg, Harvard Univ, 52-53; surgeon-in-chief, Children's Hosp, 54-73; guest lectr, Univ Edinburgh, 56; mem coun, Royal Col Physicians & Surgeons Can, 62-70, chmn comt gen surg, 68-72; mem, Can Coun Hosp Accreditation, 70-74; head pediat surg, Children's Ctr, 73-81. *Mem:* Am Col Surg; Am Surg Asn. *Res:* Cardiac and pediatric surgery. *Mailing Add:* Dept Surg Univ Man Winnipeg MB R3T 2N2 Can

FERGUSON, DALE CURTIS, b Dayton, Ohio, Aug 21, 48; m 71. RADIO ASTRONOMY, ASTROPHYSICS. *Educ:* Case Western Reserve Univ, BS, 70; Univ Ariz, PhD(astrophys), 74. *Prof Exp:* Vis asst prof astron, La State Univ, 74-75; res fel, Max Planck Inst Radio Astron, 75-77; asst prof physics, NY Univ, 77-78; resident pulsar-observer, Nat Astron & Ionosphere Ct, Cornell Univ, Arecibo, 78-81; ASST PROF PHYSICS, SOUTHEAST MO STATE UNIV, 81- *Mem:* AAAS; Am Astron Soc; Royal Astron Soc. *Res:* Pulsars; special relativity; polarization of light. *Mailing Add:* 3008 Themis Apt A Cape Girardeau MO 63701

FERGUSON, DALE VERNON, b Tulsa, Okla, Nov 24, 43; m 63; c 2. MICROBIOLOGY. *Educ:* Okla State Univ, BS, 66, MS, 67, PhD(microbiol), 70. *Prof Exp:* Res scientist virol, Armour-Baldwin Labs, 67-68; assoc prof biol, 70-80, PROF BIOL, UNIV ARK, LITTLE ROCK, 81- *Mem:* Am Soc Microbiol. *Res:* antimicrobial action of antibiotics and chemotherapeutic agents; immunotoxicology. *Mailing Add:* Dept of Biol Univ of Ark Little Rock AR 72204

FERGUSON, DAVID B, b Conrad, Mont, May 19, 26; m 50; c 2. PLANT BREEDING. *Educ:* Mont State Univ, BS, 50; Univ Minn, PhD(plant genetics), 62. *Prof Exp:* Asst agron, Mont State Univ, 54-57; asst plant genetics, Univ Minn, 57-62; supt plant breeding, Plains Br Sta, NMex State Univ, 62-66; res mgr plant breeding, Northrup, King & Co, Lubbock, Tex Br, 66-70 & Woodland, Calif Br, 70-74; plant breeder, David & Sons, Inc, Fresno, Calif, 74-80; PLANT BREEDER, SEEDS GROUP, STAUFFER CHEM CO, 80- *Mem:* AAAS; Am Soc Agron; Crop Sci Soc Am; Am Genetic Asn. *Res:* Corn breeding; wheat, sorghum and sudan breeding; breeding cucurbita for seed; breeding confectionary sunflowers; breeding oil sunflowers. *Mailing Add:* 6225 N Callisch Ave Fresno CA 93710

FERGUSON, DAVID JOHN, b Sandwich, Ill, May 24, 39; m 60; c 2. MATHEMATICS. *Educ:* Univ Idaho, BS, 64, PhD(math), 71. *Prof Exp:* Asst prof, 70-74, ASSOC PROF MATH, BOISE STATE UNIV, 74- *Mem:* Am Math Soc; Math Asn Am. *Res:* Structure of nonassociative nilalgebras. *Mailing Add:* Dept of Math Boise State Univ Boise ID 83725

FERGUSON, DAVID LAWRENCE, b St Louis, Mo, Aug 19, 49. INTELLIGENT SYSTEMS. *Educ:* Southeast Mo State Univ, BS, 71; Univ Calif, Los Angeles, MA, 75; Univ Calif, Berkeley, PhD(math educ), 80. *Prof Exp:* Consult math & sci, Harper & Row, Scott Foresman & Co, 74-76; res assoc group math sci educ, Univ Calif, Berkeley, 77-79, teaching assoc math, 79-81; ASST PROF TECHNOL SOC, STATE UNIV NY, STONY BROOK, 81- *Concurrent Pos:* Dir acad math & sci, Partnership Prog, Univ Calif, Berkeley, 79-81. *Mem:* Math Asn Am; Fedn Am Scientists; Am Statist Asn; AAAS. *Res:* Quantitative methods; applications of cognitive science and artificial intelligence to problem solving in mathematics, science, and engineering; mathematics, science, and engineering education. *Mailing Add:* Dept Technol Soc Col Eng & Appl Sci State Univ NY Stony Brook NY 11794

FERGUSON, DENZEL EDWARD, vertebrate zoology, see previous edition

FERGUSON, DON ERNEST, b Roswell, NMex, Oct 12, 23; m 44; c 4. CHEMICAL ENGINEERING, PHYSICAL CHEMISTRY. *Educ:* Tenn Tech, BS, 44; Univ Tenn, MA, 51. *Prof Exp:* Chief chem develop sect, Chem Tech Div, 55-63, asst dir, Chem Tech Div, 63-64, DIR, CHEM TECH DIV, OAK RIDGE NAT LAB, 64- *Concurrent Pos:* Mem transplutonium prog comt, Atomic Energy Comn, 64- *Mem:* Am Nuclear Soc; Am Inst Chem Engrs. *Res:* Research and development in the fuel cycle for nuclear reactors and the production of transuranium elements; coal conversion. *Mailing Add:* Chem Technol Div Oak Ridge Nat Lab Oak Ridge TN 37830

FERGUSON, DONALD ALLEN, JR, microbial biochemistry, see previous edition

FERGUSON, DONALD JOHN, b Minneapolis, Minn, Nov 19, 16; m 43; c 3. SURGERY. *Educ:* Yale Univ, BS, 39; Univ Minn, MD, 43, MS & PhD(surg), 51. *Prof Exp:* From asst prof to prof surg, Univ Minn, 52-60; PROF SURG, UNIV CHICAGO, 60- *Mem:* Am Col Surg; Am Surg Asn; Soc Univ Surg. *Res:* Surgical research. *Mailing Add:* 5629 S Blackstone Chicago IL 60637

FERGUSON, DONALD LEON, b Logan, Utah, Nov 23, 30; m 61; c 2. VETERINARY PARASITOLOGY. *Educ:* Utah State Univ, BS, 56, MS, 60; Univ Nebr-Lincoln, PhD(parasitol), 66. *Prof Exp:* Parasitologist, Jensen-Salsbury Res Labs, Mo, 60-62; assoc prof, 62-74, PROF VET SCI & PARASITOLOGIST, UNIV NEBR-LINCOLN, 62- *Mem:* Am Soc Parasitologists; Am Soc Animal Sci; Japanese Soc Parasitologists. *Res:* Immunologic properties of parasites, in vitro cultivation of nematodes, x-irradiation of parasites and development and field evaluation of anthelmintic drugs and coccidiostats. *Mailing Add:* Dept of Vet Sci Univ of Nebr Lincoln NE 68503

FERGUSON, DOUGLAS CAMPBELL, insect taxonomy, see previous edition

FERGUSON, EARL J, b Dallas, Tex, June 30, 25; m 46; c 3. INDUSTRIAL ENGINEERING. *Educ:* Tex A&M Univ, BS, 49; Okla State Univ, MS, 59, PhD(indust eng), 64. *Prof Exp:* Time study engr, Montgomery Ward & Co, 49-51; mfg engr, Gen Dynamics Corp, 51-56; assoc prof indust eng, 56-69, PROF INDUST ENG & MGT, OKLA STATE UNIV, 69- *Mem:* Am Inst Indust Engrs; Nat Soc Prof Engrs. *Res:* Management and management science; safety engineering; statistical quality control. *Mailing Add:* Sch of Indust Eng & Mgt Okla State Univ Stillwater OK 74074

FERGUSON, EARL WILSON, b Lebanon, Pa, Aug 29, 43; m 65; c 3. INTERNAL MEDICINE, CARDIOVASCULAR DISEASES. *Educ:* Baylor Univ, BA, 65; Univ Tex Med Br, Galveston, MD, 70, PhD(physiol), 70. *Prof Exp:* Intern, Univ Tex Med Br, Galveston, 70-71; resident, Duke Univ Med Ctr, NC, 71-73, fel cardiol, 73-75; cardiologist, Wilford Hall US Air Force Med Ctr, Lackland AFB, 75-76; asst prof biochem & med, 76-80, ASSOC PROF, PHYSIOL & MED, UNIFORMED SERV HEALTH SCI UNIV, BETHESDA, MD, 80- *Concurrent Pos:* Consult, Surgeon Gen US Air Force Internal Med, Physiol & Cardiol, 80-; rep, Interagency Tech Comt Heart, Blood Vessel, Lung, Blood Dis & Blood Resources, 81-; nat fac, Advan Cardiac Life Support, Am Heart Asn, 81- *Mem:* Am Physiol Soc; Am Fedn Clin Res; fel Am Col Cardiol; fel Am Col Physicians; Aerospace Med Asn. *Res:* Fibrinogen structure and fibrin crosslinking; evaluating effects of exercise and physical conditioning on blood clotting, fibrinolysis, platelets, red blood cells, selected endocrine studies and thermal adaptations. *Mailing Add:* Uniformed Serv Univ Health Sci 4301 Jones Bridge Rd Bethesda MD 20814

FERGUSON, EDWARD C, III, b Beaumont, Tex, Mar 11, 26. OPHTHALMOLOGY. *Educ:* Northwestern Univ, BS, 46, BM, 49, MD, 50; Am Bd Ophthal, dipl, 57. *Prof Exp:* Asst prof ophthal, Col Med, Univ Iowa, 56-57; assoc prof, 64-69, PROF OPHTHAL, UNIV TEX MED BR GALVESTON, 69-, CHMN DEPT, 64- *Concurrent Pos:* Fel, Howe Lab Ophthal, Mass Eye & Ear Infirmary, 56-57; Heed fel ophthal, 57. *Mem:* AMA; Asn Res Vision & Ophthal; Am Acad Ophthal & Otolaryngol; Am Col Surgeons. *Mailing Add:* Dept of Ophthal Univ of Tex Med Br Galveston TX 77550

FERGUSON, ELDON EARL, b Rawlins, Wyo, Apr 23, 26. AERONOMY. *Educ:* Univ Okla, BS, 49, MS, 50, PhD(physics), 53. *Prof Exp:* Physicist, Phillips Petrol Co, 54-55 & Naval Res Lab, 55-57; from asst prof to assoc prof physics, Univ Tex, 57-62; chief atmospheric collision processes sect, 63-69, DIR AERONOMY LAB, NAT OCEANIC & ATMOSPHERIC ADMIN ENVIRON RES LABS, 69- *Concurrent Pos:* Guggenheim fel, Max Planck Inst Physics & Astrophys, 60-61; adj prof chem, Univ Colo, Boulder, 66-; Humboldt fel, 79-80. *Mem:* Am Phys Soc; Am Geophys Union; Am Chem Soc. *Res:* Atomic physics; gaseous electronics; atmospheric chemistry. *Mailing Add:* Aeronomy Lab Environ Res Labs Nat Oceanic & Atmospheric Admin Boulder CO 80302

FERGUSON, FREDERICK PALMER, b Middletown, Conn, March 19, 16; m 41; c 5. PHYSIOLOGY. *Educ:* Wesleyan Univ, BA, 38, MA, 39; Univ Minn, PhD(zool), 43. *Prof Exp:* Asst biol, Wesleyan Univ, 38-39; asst zool, Univ Minn, 39-43; instr physiol, Sch Med, La State Univ, 43-45; res assoc, Biochem Lab, Rutgers Univ, 45-46; asst prof, 46-47; asst prof biol, Wesleyan Univ, 47-49; from asst prof to prof physiol, Sch Med, Univ Md, 49-60; chief res fel sect, Div Gen Med Sci, NIH, 60-63, chief res fels br, Nat Inst Gen Med Sci, 63-73, dep dir biomed eng prog, 73-76, dir biomed eng prog, 76-78,

PROG COORDR PHYSIOL & BIOMED ENG PROG, NAT INST GEN MED SCI, 78- *Concurrent Pos:* Mem corp, Marine Biol Lab, Woods Hole, 49- & Mt Desert Island Biol Lab, 53- *Honors & Awards:* Sustained High Qual Performance Award, US Dept Health, Educ & Welfare, 70; NIH Dirs Award, 78. *Mem:* Fel AAAS; Am Physiol Soc; Soc Exp Biol & Med; Biomed Eng Soc; fel NY Acad Sci. *Res:* Physiology of melanophores; electrocardiography; renal physiology; protein metabolism; hypoxia. *Mailing Add:* Physiol & Biomed Eng Prog Nat Inst Gen Med Sci NIH Bethesda MD 20205

FERGUSON, GARY GENE, b East St Louis, Ill, Jan 2, 40; m 63; c 1. PHARMACOLOGY. *Educ:* Univ Houston, BS, 63; Baylor Univ, MS, 65; Univ Colo, Boulder, PhD(pharmacol), 69. *Prof Exp:* Instr pharmacol, Univ NMex, 65-69; asst prof, 69-73, ASSOC PROF PHARMACOL, NORTHEAST LA UNIV, 73- *Concurrent Pos:* Consult pharmacol, Enviro-Med Labs, Ruston, La, 80- *Res:* Cardiovascular pharmacology; psychopharmacology; drug screening; writing articles for continuing education for pharmacists in a variety of areas; participating in continuing education survivors for pharmacists in Louisiana. *Mailing Add:* Sch Pharmacy Northeast La Univ Monroe LA 71209

FERGUSON, GARY GILBERT, b London, Ont, Aug 30, 41; m 64; c 3. NEUROSURGERY, BIOPHYSICS. *Educ:* Univ Western Ont, BA, 61, MD, 65, PhD(biophysics), 70; FRCS(C), 73, FACS, 77. *Prof Exp:* asst prof, 73-81, ASSOC PROF NEUROSURG & BIOPHYS, UNIV WESTERN ONT, 81-, ASST PROF SURG, 74- *Honors & Awards:* Annual Award, Am Acad Neurol Surg, 70. *Mem:* Can Med Asn; Can Neurosurg Soc; Cong Neurol Surgeons; Royal Col Physicians & Surgeons Can; Am Asn Neurol Surgeons. *Res:* Cerebral blood flow; application to cerebrovascular disease. *Mailing Add:* Univ Hosp 339 Windermere Rd London ON N6A 5A5 Can

FERGUSON, GARY WRIGHT, herpetology, evolutionary biology, see previous edition

FERGUSON, GEORGE ALONZO, b Washington, DC, May 25, 23; m 66; c 5. NUCLEAR ENGINEERING, SOLID STATE PHYSICS. *Educ:* Howard Univ, BS, 47, MS, 48; Cath Univ Am, PhD(physics), 65. *Prof Exp:* Res asst physics, Univ Pa, 48-50; chmn dept physics, Clark Col, Ga, 50-53; res scientist, Naval Res Lab, Washington, DC, 54-67; prof physics, 67-80, PROF ENG, HOWARD UNIV, 80- *Concurrent Pos:* AEC/NASA/Pepco res grants, 67-; consult, Nuclear Regulatory Comn, 73- *Mem:* Am Phys Soc; AAAS; Am Nuclear Soc; Am Asn Physics Teachers. *Res:* Properties of materials and instrumentation in nuclear engineering; solid state physics, especially structure determination. *Mailing Add:* Sch of Eng Howard Univ Washington DC 20059

FERGUSON, GEORGE E(RNEST), b Stillwater, Minn, Apr 2, 06; m 29; c 1. HYDRAULIC ENGINEERING. *Educ:* Univ Minn, BCE, 28. *Prof Exp:* Hydraul engr, Tex, 28-31, Hawaii, 31-37 & Washington, DC, 37-40, dist engr, Fla, 40-46, staff officer, Water Resources Div, 46-48, chief prog control br, 48-55, regional hydrologist, Atlantic Coast, 55-72, hydrologist, 74-81, MEM STAFF, US GEOLOGICAL SURV, 81- *Mem:* Am Soc Civil Engrs; hon mem Am Water Works Asn; Am Geophys Union. *Res:* Hydrologic investigations. *Mailing Add:* US Geol Surv Nat Ctr Mail Stop 439 Reston VA 22092

FERGUSON, GEORGE RAY, b Bolivar, La, Jan 8, 15; m 56; c 5. ENTOMOLOGY. *Educ:* Ore State Col, BS, 36, MS, 39; Ohio State Univ, PhD(entom), 41. *Prof Exp:* Asst, Ore State Col, 37-39, asst entomologist, 41-43; res assoc, Crop Protection Inst, 43-45; chief entomologist, Geigy Chem Corp, 45-47, tech dir, 48-53, pres agr chem div, 53-69, exec vpres corp, 69-70, vpres, Ciba-Geigy Corp, 70-72; PROF ENTOM, ORE STATE UNIV, 73- *Mem:* Fel AAAS; Entom Soc Am; Weed Sci Soc Am; Am Chem Soc. *Res:* Insecticides; agriculture pest control. *Mailing Add:* Dept of Entom Ore State Univ Corvallis OR 97331

FERGUSON, HARRY, b Dayton, Ohio, May 1, 14; m 41. MATHEMATICS, MECHANICS. *Educ:* Boston Univ, BS, 39; Harvard Univ, AM, 49; Univ Pittsburgh, PhD(math), 58. *Prof Exp:* Instr math, Northeastern Univ, 39-43, Bowdoin Col, 43-44, Tufts Univ, 44-47, Northeastern Univ, 47-48 & Ohio Univ, 48-50; mathematician, Wright-Patterson AFB, Ohio, 50-56, aeronaut res engr fluid mech, 56-59; assoc prof math, 59-66, PROF ENG SCI, UNIV CINCINNATI, 66- *Concurrent Pos:* Mem, Appl Math Br, Wright Air Develop Ctr, 50-59. *Mem:* Am Math Soc; Math Asn Am; Am Soc Eng Educ. *Res:* Boundary value problems; turbulence; complex variables; Laplace transform; rigid body mechanics. *Mailing Add:* 5105 Weston Circle Dayton OH 45429

FERGUSON, HARRY IAN SYMONS, b High Wycombe, Eng, June 25, 20; Can citizen; m 46; c 3. PHYSICS. *Educ:* Univ Western Ont, BSc, 51, MSc, 53, PhD(physics), 58. *Prof Exp:* Res assoc physics, Univ Western Ont, 55-57; physicist, Ont Cancer Treatment & Res Found, London Clin, Victoria Hosp, 57-59; lectr, 59-60, from asst prof to assoc prof, 60-68, PROF PHYSICS, UNIV WESTERN ONT, 68- *Res:* Molecular spectroscopy; optics and spectroscopy, particularly applied to laboratory astrophysics and molecular excitation. *Mailing Add:* Dept of Physics Univ of Western Ont London ON N6A 5B8 Can

FERGUSON, HELAMAN ROLFE PRATT, b Salt Lake City, Utah, Aug 11, 40; m 63; c 7. MATHEMATICS. *Educ:* Hamilton Col, AB, 62; Brigham Young Univ, MS, 66; Univ Wash, MS & PhD(math), 71. *Prof Exp:* Technician, Control Lab, Garlock Packing Corp, 58; mem staff math, Hamilton Col, 60-61; writer, Teaching Mach, Hamilton Res Assocs, 62; programmer & systs analyst, Data Processing Ctr, Church of Jesus Christ of Latter-day Saints, 63-64; asst math, Brigham Young Univ, 65-66; asst & instr, Univ Wash, 66-71; from asst prof to assoc prof, 71-78, PROF MATH, BRIGHAM YOUNG UNIV, 79- *Concurrent Pos:* Consult, Urban Data Ctr, Univ Wash, 70-71. *Mem:* Am Math Soc; Math Asn Am. *Res:* Harmonic analysis; group representations; Lie groups and algebras; number theory; mathematical geography; mathematics of biological systems—the eye; mathematical exploration geophysics. *Mailing Add:* Dept of Math 314 MSCB Brigham Young Univ Provo UT 84602

FERGUSON, HERMAN WHITE, b Chapel Hill, Tenn, Dec 28, 16; m 43; c 2. ECONOMIC GEOLOGY. *Educ:* Vanderbilt Univ, BA, 39, MS, 40. *Prof Exp:* Geol aide to asst geologist, Div Geol, Tenn Dept Conserv, 40-46, asst state geologist, 46-51, state geologist, 51-52; geologist, Tenn Coal & Iron Div, 52-57, sr geologist, Mich Limestone Div, 57-64, mgr geol invests stone & coal, 64-65, SR GEOLOGIST, INT & RESOURCE DEVELOP DEPT, US STEEL CORP, 65- *Mem:* Inst Mining Engrs; fel Geol Soc Am; Soc Econ Geologists. *Res:* Structural and economic geology. *Mailing Add:* Rm 2757 US Steel Bldg 600 Grant St Pittsburgh PA 15219

FERGUSON, HUGH CARSON, b Detroit, Mich, July 13, 21; m 55; c 2. PHARMACOLOGY. *Educ:* Wayne State Univ, BS, 48; Purdue Univ, MS, 50, PhD, 52. *Prof Exp:* Asst prof pharmacol, Univ NMex, 52-58; assoc prof, Col Pharm, Ohio Northern Univ, 58-61; head, Pharmacol Lab, Distillation Prod Indust Div, Eastman Kodak Co, 61-66; group leader, 66-69, sect leader, 69-70, prin investr, 70-74, SR PRIN INVESTR PHARMACOL, RES CTR, MEAD JOHNSON & CO, 74- *Mem:* Am Pharmaceut Asn; Am Chem Soc; Am Soc Pharmacol & Exp Therapeut. *Res:* Pharmacological investigation of plant products; cause of hypertension with relation to kidney function; relationship of stress to disease; new methods to evaluate drug action. *Mailing Add:* 310 Hunter Dr Evansville IN 47711

FERGUSON, JAMES HOMER, b San Antonio, Tex, July 26, 36; m 59; c 1. ENVIRONMENTAL PHYSIOLOGY. *Educ:* Sul Ross State Univ, BS, 58; Univ Ariz, PhD(zool), 64. *Prof Exp:* Asst zool, Univ Ariz, 61-64; from asst prof to assoc prof zool, Univ Idaho, 64-73; prof, Univ Tex, San Antonio, 73-74; PROF ZOOL, UNIV IDAHO, 75- *Concurrent Pos:* Vis asst prof, Univ Iowa, 69; NIH spec fel, 69. *Mem:* AAAS; Am Soc Ichthyol & Herpet; Am Soc Zool; Am Physiol Soc. *Res:* Evolution; physiology of temperature adaptations in vertebrates; mammalian and environmental physiology. *Mailing Add:* Dept of Biol Sci Univ of Idaho Moscow ID 83843

FERGUSON, JAMES JOSEPH, JR, b Glen Cove, NY, Feb 1, 26; m 52; c 4. BIOCHEMISTRY, MEDICINE. *Educ:* Univ Rochester, BA, 46, MD, 50. *Prof Exp:* From intern to asst resident, Mass Gen Hosp, 50-52, resident, 55; assoc, 59-63, from asst prof to assoc prof, 63-71, PROF BIOCHEM & MED, 71-, ASSOC DEAN INSTNL RES & GRAD EDUC, 75- *Concurrent Pos:* Res fel biochem, Western Reserve Univ, 56-58; Markel fel, 60-64. *Mem:* Am Soc Biol Chem; Endocrine Soc. *Res:* Metabolic regulation; hormone action. *Mailing Add:* Dept of Biochem & Biophys Univ of Pa Sch of Med Philadelphia PA 19104

FERGUSON, JAMES KENNETH WALLACE, b Tamsui, Formosa, Japan, Mar 19, 07; m 33; c 4. PHARMACOLOGY. *Educ:* Univ Toronto, BA, 28, MA, 29, MD, 32. *Prof Exp:* From instr to asst prof physiol, Sch Med, Univ Western Ont, 34-36; asst prof, Ohio State Univ, 36-38; asst prof pharmacol, Univ Toronto, 38-41; prof & head dept, 45-55; dir, Connaught Med Res Labs, 55-72; RETIRED. *Concurrent Pos:* Nat Res Coun fel, 33-34. *Mem:* Am Soc Pharmacol & Exp Therapeut; Am Physiol Soc; Can Physiol Soc; fel Royal Soc Can. *Res:* Anoxia and oxygen equipment; antithyroid drugs; carbon dioxide in tissues; uterine motility; anti-alcoholic drugs. *Mailing Add:* 56 Clarkehaven St Thornhill ON L4J 2B4 Can

FERGUSON, JAMES L, b Thomas, Okla, July 9, 47; m 78; c 2. CARDIOVASCULAR PHYSIOLOGY, CIRCULATORY SHOCK. *Educ:* Southwestern State Col, Okla, BS, 69; NTex State Univ, MS, 72; Purdue Univ, PhD(physiol), 75. *Prof Exp:* Fel, La State Univ Med Ctr, 75-78; ASST PROF PHYSIOL, UNIV ILL MED CTR, 78- *Concurrent Pos:* Lectr, Am Physiol Soc; prin investr, Chicago Heart Asn, 81-83. *Mem:* Am Physiol Soc; Shock Soc; Sigma Xi. *Res:* Study of alterations of regional distribution of blood flow during states of shock and trauma; mechanisms of control of skeletal muscle, splanchnic and cerebral blood flow; pharmacological approaches to altering blood flow to the above vascular beds. *Mailing Add:* Dept Physiol & Biophysics Col Med Univ Ill Med Ctr PO Box 6998 Chicago IL 60680

FERGUSON, JAMES MALCOLM, b Chicago, Ill, June 6, 31. NUCLEAR PHYSICS. *Educ:* Antioch Col, BS, 53; Mass Inst Technol, PhD, 57. *Prof Exp:* Physicist, US Naval Radiol Defense Lab, 57-69; PHYSICIST, LAWRENCE LIVERMORE LAB, 69- *Mem:* Fel Am Phys Soc; Am Nuclear Soc. *Res:* Neutron transport; nuclear reactions; theory; nuclear fission. *Mailing Add:* Lawrence Livermore Lab L-35 PO Box 808 Livermore CA 94550

FERGUSON, JAMES MECHAM, b Washington, DC, Apr 16, 41; m 68; c 2. PSYCHIATRY, BEHAVIORAL BIOLOGY. *Educ:* Stanford Univ, BA, 64, MD, 71. *Prof Exp:* Res asst & assoc psychiat, Med Sch, Stanford Univ, 64-69; intern med & surg, Med Sch, Univ Utah, 71-72; resident, Med Sch, Stanford Univ, 72-75; ASST PROF PSYCHIAT, MED SCH, UNIV CALIF SAN DIEGO, 75-; CHIEF AMBULATORY PSYCHIAT & MENT HYG CLIN, VET ADMIN HOSP, SAN DIEGO, 75- *Concurrent Pos:* Attend physician, Univ Hosp, San Diego, 75- *Mem:* Am Psychiat Asn; Asn Advan Behav Ther; Asn Psychophysiol Study Sleep; Biofeedback Res Soc. *Res:* Behavior therapy; behavioral medicine; development of behavior and behavior change programs for use by non-physicians. *Mailing Add:* Dept of Psychiat Univ of Calif at San Diego PO Box 109 La Jolla CA 92037

FERGUSON, JOHN ALLEN, b Cincinnati, Ohio, Dec 20, 45; m 68; c 4. INDUSTRIAL CHEMISTRY. *Educ:* Univ Cincinnati, BS, 67; Univ NC, PhD(chem), 71. *Prof Exp:* Fel chem, Univ NC, Chapel Hill, 71; sr res chemist, Drackett Co, 73-75; group leader prod develop, Clairol Res Labs, 75-76, sect head prod develop, 76-78; SECT MGR PROD DEVELOP, DRACKETT CO, 78- *Mem:* Soc Cosmetic Chemists; Am Chem Soc. *Res:* Analytical techniques; electrochemistry; emulsion theory; fragrance evaluation. *Mailing Add:* Drackett Res Labs 5020 Spring Grove Ave Cincinnati OH 45232

FERGUSON, JOHN BARCLAY, b Baltimore, Md, July 5, 47; m 70; c 1. BIOCHEMISTRY. *Educ:* Brown Univ, ScB, 69; Yale Univ, M Phil, 71, PhD(biol), 73. *Prof Exp:* Res fel chem, Harvard Univ, 73-77, ASST PROF BIOL, BARD COL, 77- *Concurrent Pos:* NIH fel, 74-76. *Mem:* AAAS; Am Chem Soc; Am Inst Biol Sci; NY Acad Sci. *Res:* Enzymology; purification and characterization of enzymes; substrate specificity; active-site-directed inhibition. *Mailing Add:* Dept Biol Bard Col Annandale-on-Hudson NY 12504

FERGUSON, JOHN CARRUTHERS, b Tuscaloosa, Ala, Mar 2, 37; m 61; c 3. INVERTEBRATE ZOOLOGY, PHYSIOLOGY. *Educ:* Duke Univ, BA, 58; Cornell Univ, MA, 61, PhD(invert zool), 63. *Prof Exp:* From asst prof to assoc prof, 63-72, PROF BIOL, ECKERD COL, 72- *Concurrent Pos:* NSF grants, 64-; vis investr, Marine Biol Lab, Woods Hole, 66; proj leader, Marine Biol Prog, Jamaica, 68 & 69; vis investr, Friday Harbor Labs, Wash, 70. *Mem:* AAAS; Am Soc Zoologists; Am Micros Soc; Int Oceanog Found. *Res:* Physiology and ecology of starfish nutrition; nutrient translocation; utilization of dissolved nutrients by marine invertebrates. *Mailing Add:* Dept of Biol Box 12560 Eckerd Col St Petersburg FL 33733

FERGUSON, JOHN HOWARD, b Edinburgh, Scotland, Mar 1, 02; nat US; m 27, 55; c 6. PHYSIOLOGY. *Educ:* Univ Cape Town, BA, 21, DrSc, 57; Oxford Univ, BA, 25, MA, 31; Harvard Univ, MD, 28. *Prof Exp:* Lectr pharmacol, Univ Cape Town, 23, asst prof bact, 28-31; asst path, Harvard Univ, 26-28; instr physiol, Sch Med, Yale Univ, 31-34; asst prof physiol & pharmacol, Sch Med, Univ Ala, 34-35, assoc prof, 35-37; asst prof pharmacol, Univ Mich, 37-43; from actg head dept to head dept, 43-67, prof physiol, 43-70, EMER PROF PHYSIOL, MED SCH, UNIV NC, CHAPEL HILL, 70- *Mem:* AAAS; fel Am Col Physicians; Am Physiol Soc; Int Soc Hemat. *Res:* Blood coagulation and related fields. *Mailing Add:* 226 Glandon Dr Chapel Hill NC 27514

FERGUSON, JOSEPH GANTT, b Charleston, WVa, May 26, 21; m 48, 79; c 1. RESEARCH ADMINISTRATION. *Educ:* Clemson Univ, BS, 42. *Prof Exp:* Lab analyst mfg tech, Southern Kraft Div, 47-51, develop engr, 51-54, second asst chief chemist, 54-55, res proj leader pulp & paper res & develop, 55-57, first asst chief chemist mfg tech, 57, group leader, res assoc, sr res assoc, chief paper res & first asst dir res, 57-66, dir res res admin, 66-75, mgr mfg res, Mfg & Eng Serv, 75-77, MGR TECH & ADMIN SERV, ERLING RIIS RES LAB, INT PAPER CO, 77- *Mem:* Tech Asn Pulp & Paper Indust. *Res:* Management of applied research for the pulp, paper and wood products business; chemical and mechanical engineering; wood and paper chemistry; polymer and environmental sciences; management of creativity. *Mailing Add:* Erling Riis Res Lab Sci & Technol Int Paper Co PO Box 2787 Mobile AL 36652

FERGUSON, JOSEPH LUTHER, JR, b Utica, Miss, May 22, 41. PLASMA PHYSICS, OPTICS. *Educ:* Miss State Univ, BS, 63; Vanderbilt Univ, PhD(plasma physics), 69. *Prof Exp:* From asst prof to assoc prof, 68-80, PROF PHYSICS, MISS STATE UNIV, 80- *Mem:* Am Asn Physics Teachers. *Res:* Electromagnetic shock tube studies and laser-produced plasma studies. *Mailing Add:* Dept of Physics Box 5167 Miss State Univ State College MS 39762

FERGUSON, KAREN ANNE, b Nebo, Ill, Oct 25, 42. BIOCHEMISTRY, LIPID CHEMISTRY. *Educ:* Western Ill Univ, BS, 63; Bryn Mawr Col, PhD(biochem), 71. *Prof Exp:* Fel biochem, Washington Univ, 72-74; asst prof chem, Eastern Ill Univ, 74-78; ASST PROF BIOCHEM, STATE UNIV NY BUFFALO, 78- *Mem:* AAAS; NY Acad Sci; Am Chem Soc. *Res:* Membrane-bound enzymes; fatty acid desaturation and elongation in Tetrahymena; metabolic control by sterols. *Mailing Add:* Dept of Biochem State Univ of NY Buffalo NY 14214

FERGUSON, LAING, b Dunfermline, Scotland, Apr 25, 35; m 60; c 3. GEOLOGY, PALEONTOLOGY. *Educ:* Univ Edinburgh, BSc, 57, PhD(paleont), 60. *Prof Exp:* Nat Res Coun Can fel, Univ Alta, 60-62; from asst prof to assoc prof, 62-78, PROF GEOL, MT ALLISON UNIV, 78-HEAD DEPT, 73- *Concurrent Pos:* Fel, Univ Edinburgh, 69-70. *Mem:* Paleont Soc; Soc Econ Paleont & Mineral; Asn Petrol Geol; fel Geol Soc London; fel Geol Soc Am. *Res:* Upper Paleozoic paleoecology, especially brachiopods; effects of environmental factors on criteria used in brachiopod taxonomy; Permian faunas from the high Arctic; distortion of fossils by compaction; trace fossils; Carboniferous ostracods. *Mailing Add:* Dept of Geol Mt Allison Univ Sackville Can

FERGUSON, LE BARON O, b Oak Bluffs, Mass, Apr 20, 39; div; c 3. MATHEMATICS. *Educ:* Mass Inst Technol, SB, 61; Univ Wash, MA, 63, PhD(math), 65. *Prof Exp:* Assoc res engr, Boeing Airplane Co, 61-62; asst prof, 65-70, ASSOC PROF MATH, UNIV CALIF, RIVERSIDE, 70- *Concurrent Pos:* Vis assoc prof, Rensselaer Polytech Inst, 70-71 & Univ Nancy, 71-72; US Air Force Off Sci Res grant, 71- *Mem:* Am Math Soc; Math Asn Am. *Res:* Approximation theory. *Mailing Add:* Dept of Math Univ of Calif Riverside CA 92521

FERGUSON, LLOYD C, b Lebanon, Ind, Sept 10, 12; m 35; c 1. MICROBIOLOGY. *Educ:* Ohio State Univ, DVM, 34; Univ Wis, MS, 36, PhD(immunogenetics), 40. *Prof Exp:* Asst vet sci, Univ Wis, 34-36, instr vet sci & genetics, 36-41; from asst prof to assoc prof bact, Ohio State Univ, 46-53; prof vet sci, Agr Exp Sta, Ohio Univ, 53-56; prof microbiol & pub health, head dept & dir div biol sci, Mich State Univ, 56-59, dean col sci & arts, 59-63, prof microbiol, 63-68; chmn dept vet sci, 68-76, EMER PROF, OHIO AGR RES & DEVELOP CTR, 76- *Concurrent Pos:* Consult, Off State Exp Sta, USDA, 58-62; mem agr bd, Nat Acad Sci-Nat Res Coun, 59-63; Am Cancer Soc scholar, 62-63; sci adv, Univ Nigeria, 65-67. *Mem:* AAAS; Am Soc Microbiol; Am Asn Immunol; Am Vet Med Asn. *Res:* Immunology; pathogenesis of infectious diseases. *Mailing Add:* 8608 Pickerill Rd Russellville OH 45168

FERGUSON, LLOYD NOEL, b Oakland, Calif, Feb 9, 18; m 44; c 3. CHEMISTRY. *Educ:* Univ Calif, BS, 40, PhD(chem), 43. *Hon Degrees:* DSc, Howard Univ, 70, Coe Col, 79. *Prof Exp:* Asst chem, Nat Defense Res Comt Proj, Univ Calif, 41-44; asst prof, Agr & Tech Col, NC, 44-45; from assoc prof to prof, Howard Univ, 45-65, head dept, 58-65; chmn dept, 68-71, PROF CHEM, CALIF STATE UNIV, LOS ANGELES, 65- *Concurrent Pos:* Guggenheim fel, Carlsberg Lab, Copenhagen, 53-54; NSF fac fel, Swiss Fed Inst Technol, 61-62; vis prof, Univ Nairobi, 71-72; consult, Col Chem Consult Serv; vis scientist, Div Chem Educ, Am Chem Soc; mem chemother adv comt, Nat Cancer Inst, 72-75; mem US nat comt, Int Union Pure & Appl Chem, 73-76; mem, US Nat Sea Grant Rev Panel, 78-81; mem bd sci counselors, Nat Inst Environ Health Sci, 79-83. *Mem:* Fel AAAS; Am Chem Soc (chmn, Div Chem Educ, 80); fel Royal Soc Chem. *Res:* Taste and molecular properties; homoconjugation; chemistry of alicycles; cancer chemotherapy. *Mailing Add:* Dept Chem Calif State Univ 5151 State University Dr Los Angeles CA 90032

FERGUSON, MALCOLM STUART, b St Thomas, Ont, Apr 1, 08; nat US; m 38. MEDICAL PARASITOLOGY, COMMUNICATION SCIENCE. *Educ:* Univ Western Ont, BA, 32, MA, 34; Univ Ill, PhD(invert zool, parasitol), 37. *Prof Exp:* Demonstr zool, Univ Western Ont, 32-34; asst, Univ Ill, 34-36; res investr, Inst Parasitol, Macdonald Col, McGill Univ, 38; Royal Soc Can fel, Rockefeller Inst, 38-39, fel, 39-40, asst, 40-47; scientist dir, Commun Dis Ctr, USPHS, 47-61, chief med arts & photog br, NIH, 61-67; multi-media specialist, Nat Libr Med, 67-72; admin dir, Am Sci Film Asn, 72-74; EXPERT PREV MED, NAT NAVAL MED CTR, 74- *Mem:* Fel AAAS; Am Soc Parasitol; Am Soc Trop Med & Hyg. *Res:* Life cycles of trematodes; sterile culture of helminths; migration and localization of parasites within the host; application of the motion picture camera as a tool in study of living organisms; production of technical motion pictures on medical and public health subjects; development of learning resource centers in libraries. *Mailing Add:* 3522 Twin Br Dr Silver Spring MD 20906

FERGUSON, MARION LEE, b Washington, Iowa, Nov 27, 23; m 46; c 2. PHSIOLOGY. *Educ:* Univ Iowa, BA, 49; Iowa State Univ, MS, 55, PhD(physiol), 59. *Prof Exp:* Instr zool, Iowa State Univ, 53-55 & 57-60; head physiol lab, Life Sci Res Dept, Goodyear Aerospace Corp, 60-65; assoc prof, 65-69, PROF BIOL, KENT STATE UNIV, 69-, DIR CONSERV LAB, 67- *Concurrent Pos:* Vis lectr, Univ Colo, 61; dir joint flight res prog, US Air Force-Goodyear Aerospace Corp, 62-63; res investr, NASA Biosatellite Prog, Ames Res Ctr, 63-65; partic, BS/MD Prog, Col Med, Northeastern Ohio Univ, 75- *Mem:* AAAS; Am Inst Biol Sci; Am Soc Zool. *Res:* General and protozoan physiology; environmental biology; developmental phenomena. *Mailing Add:* Dept of Biol Sci Kent State Univ Kent OH 44242

FERGUSON, MARY HOBSON, b Canton, Miss, Apr 3, 27; m 46, 69; c 1. PHARMACY, COMMUNICATION SCIENCE. *Educ:* Univ Miss, BS, 61, PhD(pharm), 64. *Prof Exp:* Sr scientist, Alcon Labs, 64-67; from asst ed to assoc ed, 67-74, ED, J PHARMACEUT SCI, AM PHARMACEUT ASN, 74-, LIT SCIENTIST, SCI DIV, 67- *Mem:* Coun Biol Ed. *Res:* Pharmaceutical product development; scientific technical writing and editing; scientific information computerized systems. *Mailing Add:* 2215 Constitution Ave NW Washington DC 20037

FERGUSON, MICHAEL WILLIAM, b Chelsea, Mass, Sept 29, 47; m 77; c 1. PHYTOPATHOLOGY, BACTERIOLOGY. *Educ:* Calif State Univ, Long Beach, BA, 74; Calif State Polytech Univ, MS, 76; Kans State Univ, PhD(plant path), 81. *Prof Exp:* ASST PROF PLANT PATH, SDAK STATE UNIV, 81- *Mem:* Am Plytopathological Soc; Am Soc Microbiol. *Res:* Host-parasite interaction; plant disease physiology. *Mailing Add:* Dept Plant Sci Box 2109 SDak State Univ Brookings SD 57007

FERGUSON, NOEL MOORE, b East St Louis, Ill, Dec 20, 07; m 33; c 2. PHARMACOGNOSY, BOTANY. *Educ:* St Louis Col Pharm, PhG, 30, PhC, 32, BS, 33; Washington Univ, AB, 34, MS, 35, PhD(chem), 42. *Prof Exp:* Asst chem, St Louis Col Pharm, 30-32, from instr to prof bot & pharmacog, 32-43; sr res chemist, Drs Hess & Clark, Inc, 43-49; asst prof chem, Ashland Col, 43-49; dean, Col Pharm, Univ Houston, 49-73, prof pharmacog & dean emer, 73-78; SR RES SCIENTIST, UNIV SOUTHERN CALIF, 78- *Concurrent Pos:* Consult pharmaceut chemist; spec consult in connection with AID Develop Prog, Fed Univs, Brazil, 69-; res, anticancer plants, Mex & Los Angeles; dir, Drug Plant Res Lab, Univ Autonoma DeGuadaiara, Mex, 73-78. *Mem:* Am Chem Soc; Am Pharmaceut Asn. *Res:* Plant physiology; laxative drugs; anthelmintics; coccidiostatistics; vitamine assay methods; study of natural drugs, quinine, and volatile oils of Indonesia; anticancer plants of Mexico. *Mailing Add:* 999-3 E Valley Blvd Alhambra CA 91801

FERGUSON, PHIL MOSS, b Bartlett, Tex, Nov 10, 99; div; c 1. CIVIL ENGINEERING. *Educ:* Univ Tex, BSCE, 22, CE, 23; Univ Wis, MS, 24. *Prof Exp:* Tutor physics, 22-23, from assoc prof to prof civil eng, 28-76, T U Taylor prof, 68-72, chmn dept, 43-57, EMER PROF CIVIL ENG, UNIV TEX, AUSTIN, 76- *Honors & Awards:* Wason Res Medal, Am Concrete Inst, 54, 58 & 68, Lindau Award, 72, Raymond C Reese Res Medal, 73, Turner Medal, 76, Kelly Award, 77; Res Award, Am Soc Civil Engrs, 61. *Mem:* Nat Acad Eng; hon mem Am Concrete Inst; hon mem Am Soc Civil Engrs; Int Asn Bridge & Struct Eng; Sigma Xi. *Res:* Plate girder theory; reinforced concrete; frame analysis. *Mailing Add:* 3102 Beverly Rd Austin TX 78703

FERGUSON, RAYMOND CRAIG, b Ft Morgan, Colo, May 28, 22; m 55; c 2. PHYSICAL CHEMISTRY. *Educ:* Iowa State Univ, BS, 48, MS, 50; Harvard Univ, PhD(phys chem), 53. *Prof Exp:* Jr chemist, Ames Lab, AEC, 48-50; teaching fel, Harvard Univ, 50-53; chemist, 53-68, supvr, 68-74, RES CHEMIST, E I DU PONT DE NEMOURS & CO, INC, 74- *Mem:* AAAS; Am Chem Soc; Am Phys Soc; Soc Appl Spectros; Am Inst Chemists. *Res:* Nuclear magnetic resonance; infrared and microwave spectroscopy; polymer structure analysis; computer analysis of spectra. *Mailing Add:* Cent Res & Develop Dept E I du Pont de Nemours & Co Inc Wilmington DE 19898

FERGUSON, ROBERT BURY, b Cambridge, Ont, Feb 5, 20; m 48; c 3. MINERALOGY. *Educ:* Univ Toronto, BA, 42, MA, 43, PhD(mineral), 48. *Prof Exp:* Asst, Royal Ont Mus Mineral, 42-43; meteorologist, Can Dept Transp, 43-45; demonstr geol sci, Univ Toronto, 45-47; from asst prof to assoc prof, 47-59, PROF MINERAL, UNIV MAN, 59- *Concurrent Pos:* Nat Res Coun Can fel, Crystallog Lab, Cambridge Univ, 50-51; vis scientist, Dept Geol & Mineral, Oxford Univ, 72-73 & Dept Geol & Mineral, Adelaide Univ, Australia, 79-80. *Honors & Awards:* Hawley Award, Mineral Asn Can, 80. *Mem:* Am Crystallog Asn; fel Mineral Soc Am; Mineral Asn Can (pres, 77); fel Royal Soc Can. *Res:* Crystal structures and crystal chemistry of rock-forming silicate minerals. *Mailing Add:* Dept Earth Sci Univ Man Winnipeg MB R3T 2N2 Can

FERGUSON, ROBERT LYNN, b Mayfield, Ky, Apr 1, 32; m 54; c 2. NUCLEAR SCIENCE. *Educ:* Murray State Col, BA, 54; Wash Univ, PhD(chem), 59. *Prof Exp:* Chemist, 59-66, RES STAFF MEM, OAK RIDGE NAT LAB, 66- *Concurrent Pos:* Vis scientist, Tech Univ Munich, 70-71. *Mem:* Am Chem Soc; Sigma Xi; Am Phys Soc. *Res:* Fission; heavy-ion induced nuclear reactions. *Mailing Add:* PO Box X Oak Ridge Nat Lab Oak Ridge TN 37830

FERGUSON, ROBERT NICHOLAS, b Washington, DC, Apr 17, 44; m 71; c 1. BIO-ORGANIC CHEMISTRY, ANALYTICAL CHEMISTRY. *Educ:* Cath Univ Am, BA, 66; Johns Hopkins Univ, PhD(org chem), 71. *Prof Exp:* Staff fel biochem, Nat Inst Arthritis, Metab & Digestive Dis, 71-74; res scientist chem, 74-79, ASSOC SR SCIENTIST RES & DEVELOP, PHILIP MORRIS, USA, 79- *Mem:* AAAS; Am Chem Soc; Sigma Xi. *Res:* Intramolecular isotope effects; protein structure and function; structure biological activity relationships; isolation and identification of natural products; pyrolysis reactions. *Mailing Add:* Philip Morris USA Res & Develop PO Box 26583 Richmond VA 23261

FERGUSON, RONALD JAMES, b Toronto, Ont, Sept 18, 39. PREVENTIVE MEDICINE. *Educ:* Univ Western Ont, BA, 63; Univ Mich, MSc, 65, PhD(phys educ), 67. *Prof Exp:* Asst prof, 67-70, ASSOC PROF PHYS EDUC, UNIV MONTREAL, 70-, ASSOC PROF PREV MED, 74- *Concurrent Pos:* Res assoc, Montreal Heart Inst, 70-; chmn res comt, Can Asn Sport Sci, 71-73. *Mem:* Fel Am Col Sports Med; Can Asn Sport Sci. *Res:* Exercise physiology; cardiac rehabilitation. *Mailing Add:* Montreal Heart Inst Montreal Can

FERGUSON, SAMUEL A, b Philadelphia, Pa, Feb 4, 32; m 80; c 3. PHARMACOLOGY, PHYSIOLOGY. *Educ:* Oakwood Col, BA, 52; Univ Pa, PhD(gen physiol), 61. *Prof Exp:* Pharmacologist, Smith Kline & French Labs, 58-61; chief pharmacol br, Resources Res, Inc, 61-62; pharmacologist, Panoramic Res, Inc, 62 & Stanford Res Inst, 62-69; chmn div life sci, 69-71, assoc dean arts & sci, Col San Mateo, 74-76; dean instr, Canada Col, Redwood City, Calif, 76-79, pres, 79-81; SUPT/PRES, CHAFFEY COL, ALTA LOMA, CALIF, 81- *Concurrent Pos:* Lectr, Univ San Francisco, 62; asst prof pharmacol, Col Dent, Univ Pac, 69-71. *Res:* Analgetics; psychopharmacology, depressants, anti-depressants, tranquilizers; cerebrospinal fluid electrolytes and behavior; narcotic addiction. *Mailing Add:* Chaffey Col Alta Loma CA 91701

FERGUSON, SHIRLEY MARTHA, b Syracuse, NY, Mar 9, 23; m 51; c 3. PSYCHIATRY. *Educ:* Syracuse Univ, BA, 45, MD, 47; McGill Univ, dipl psychiat, 55. *Prof Exp:* Res fel psychiat, McGill Univ, 54-55; res fel neurol, Montreal Neurol Inst, 57-58; res assoc, Columbia Univ, 58-60; res assoc psychiat, Albert Einstein Col Med, 60-65, asst clin prof, 65-68; ASSOC PROF PSYCHIAT & NEUROSCI, MED COL OHIO, 69- *Concurrent Pos:* Spec fel, Interdept Inst Training & Res Behav & Neurol Sci, 63-65; adj prof, Mt Zion Hosp & Med Ctr, 69; dir med col units, Toledo Ment Health Ctr, 69- *Mem:* Soc Biol Psychiat; Am Psychiat Asn; Int Asn Study Pain; Am Epilepsy Soc. *Res:* Epilepsy. *Mailing Add:* Med Col of Ohio CS 10008 Toledo OH 43699

FERGUSON, STEPHEN MASON, b Bozeman, Mont, Oct 29, 39; m 63; c 2. EXPERIMENTAL NUCLEAR PHYSICS. *Educ:* Mont State Univ, BS, 62; Univ Wash, MS, 64, PhD(nuclear physics), 69. *Prof Exp:* Assoc atomic physics, Kans State Univ, 69-71; res fel nuclear physics, Australian Nat Univ, 71-74; ACCELERATOR PHYSICIST, WESTERN MICH UNIV, 74- *Mem:* Am Phys Soc; Am Asn Physics Teachers. *Res:* Practical applications of particle accelerators; trace element analysis with particle induced x-ray emission. *Mailing Add:* Dept of Physics Western Mich Univ Kalamazoo MI 49008

FERGUSON, THOMAS, b Union, SC, June 30, 21. ZOOLOGY. *Educ:* Fisk Univ, BA, 43; Univ Iowa, MS, 48, PhD(zool), 55. *Prof Exp:* From instr to prof, J C Smith Univ, 48-62; PROF BIOL, DEL STATE COL, 62-, CHMN DEPT, 74- *Mem:* Am Soc Zoologists; Nat Inst Sci. *Res:* Neuroembryology. *Mailing Add:* Dept of Biol Del State Col Dover DE 19901

FERGUSON, THOMAS LEE, b Dallas, Tex, Nov 8, 42; m 68; c 3. CHEMICAL ENGINEERING. *Educ:* Tex A&M Univ, BS, 64. *Prof Exp:* Chem engr petrochem prod, Monsanto Co, 64-65; chem engr viral & rickettsial agent prod, US Army Chem Corps, 65-67; chem engr petrochem prod, Monsanto Co, 67-68; chem engr, 68-76, PRIN CHEM ENGR, MIDWEST RES INST, 76- *Concurrent Pos:* Consult expert, US Environ Protection Agency, 75. *Mem:* Am Inst Chem Engrs. *Res:* Systems studies of the operation and environmental control of chemical and biological production facilities, especially pesticides and toxic chemicals. *Mailing Add:* Midwest Res Inst 425 Volker Blvd Kansas City MO 64110

FERGUSON, THOMAS MORGAN, b Burnet, Tex, Nov 8, 15; m 38; c 4. AVIAN PHYSIOLOGY. *Educ:* Southwestern Univ, Tex, BA, 36; Tex A&M Univ, MS, 46, PhD(zool, biochem), 54. *Prof Exp:* Teacher high schs, Tex, 36-42; civilian instr aircraft instruments, Army Air Force Tech Training Command, 42-43; asst prof biol, 46-55, USPHS res fel, 53-55, from assoc prof to prof, 55-79, EMER PROF POULTRY SCI, TEX A&M UNIV, 79- *Mem:* AAAS; Fedn Am Socs Exp Biol; Am Inst Nutrit; Soc Exp Biol & Med; Poultry Sci Asn. *Res:* Nutritional deficiencies in avian embryos; physiological measurements on breeder turkeys as affected by nutrition and management; bone strength of laying hens in relation to diet. *Mailing Add:* Dept of Poultry Sci Tex A&M Univ College Station TX 77843

FERGUSON, THOMAS S, b Oakland, Calif, Dec 14, 29; m 58; c 2. MATHEMATICAL STATISTICS. *Educ:* Univ Calif, PhD(statist), 56. *Prof Exp:* PROF MATH, UNIV CALIF, LOS ANGELES, 56- *Res:* Determination of distributions; decision theory. *Mailing Add:* Dept of Math Univ of Calif Los Angeles CA 90024

FERGUSON, WILLIAM ALLEN, b Roanoke, Mo, Mar 6, 17; m 42; c 4. MATHEMATICS. *Educ:* Mo Valley Col, BA, 37; Univ Ill, MA, 38, PhD(math), 46. *Prof Exp:* Asst instr, 38-41, 45-46, from instr to asst prof, 46-55, ASSOC PROF MATH, UNIV ILL, URBANA, 55-, EXEC SECY DEPT, 68- *Mem:* Math Asn Am. *Mailing Add:* Dept of Math 274 Altgeld Hall Univ of Ill Urbana IL 61801

FERGUSON, WILLIAM E, b Oakland, Calif, July 11, 21; m 47; c 2. ENTOMOLOGY, ZOOLOGY. *Educ:* Univ Calif, Berkeley, BS, 46, MS, 56, PhD(entom), 61. *Prof Exp:* Teacher high sch, Calif, 47-56, counsr, 48-56; sr lab technician entom, Univ Calif, Berkeley, 56-60, NIH fel, 60-62; from asst prof to assoc prof, 62-70, NSF res grant, 64-66, dir ctr res & advan studies, 66-68, prof entom, 70-81, EMER PROF, SAN JOSE STATE UNIV, 81- *Mem:* Entom Soc Am; Soc Syst Zool; Asn Trop Biol. *Res:* Systematic entomology; biology and systematics of the hymenopterous family Mutillidae; insect parasite-predator-pathogen complexes; insect postembryonic development, especially differentiation of environmental from genetic influences; insect photography; protective coloration, form and behavior. *Mailing Add:* 245 Vista Sierra Los Gatos CA 95030

FERGUSON, WILLIAM SIDNEY, b Chatfield, Minn, Nov 15, 27; m 48; c 2. ANALYTICAL CHEMISTRY, GEOCHEMISTRY. *Educ:* Ore State Univ, BS, 49, MS, 53; Univ Ill, PhD(chem), 56. *Prof Exp:* Chemist, Gen Elec Co, 49-53; res geochemist, Marathon Oil Co, 56-70; dir, Anal Chem Facil, Colo State Univ, 70-79; RES SUPVR, AMOCO PROD CO, RES, 80- *Mem:* AAAS; Am Chem Soc. *Res:* Laboratory services management; environmental chemistry; trace metal analysis; microanalytical techniques; oceanography; organic geochemistry; fused salt electrochemistry. *Mailing Add:* AMOCO Prod Res PO Box 591 Tulsa OK 74102

FERGUSON-MILLER, SHELAGH MARY, b Toronto, Ont, Mar 12, 42; m 73; c 1. BIOENERGETICS, MEMBRANE PROTEINS. *Educ:* Univ Toronto, BSc, 64, MA, 66; Univ Wis, PhD(biochem), 71. *Prof Exp:* Fel, Dept Biochem, Univ Oxford, Eng, 71-72; res assoc, Dept Chem, Northwestern Univ, Evanston, Ill, 72-77; ASST PROF, DEPT BIOCHEM, MICH STATE UNIV, EAST LANSING, 78- *Mem:* Am Soc Biol Chemists; NY Acad Sci; Sigma Xi; Am Chem Soc; Biophys Soc. *Res:* Structure and kinetic properties of electron transfer proteins involved in energy conservation in mitochondria; purified proteins and their interaction in the intact membrane. *Mailing Add:* Biochem Dept Biochem Bldg Mich State Univ East Lansing MI 48824

FERGUSSON, GORDON JOHN, physics, geophysics, see previous edition

FERGUSSON, WILLIAM BLAKE, b Boston, Mass, Apr 24, 24; m 48; c 6. GEOLOGY. *Educ:* Boston Univ, BA, 52, MA, 53; Univ Ariz, PhD(geol), 65. *Prof Exp:* Instr geol, Boston Univ, 52-53; explor geologist, USAEC, 53-54; explor geologist & consult, Grand Junction, Colo, 54-55; instr geol, Univ Ariz, 55-59; geologist, Pa RR Co, 59-67; ASSOC PROF GEOL, VILLANOVA UNIV, 67- *Concurrent Pos:* Consult geologist, Valley Forge Labs, Berwyn, Pa, 68-, Pa Dept Natural Resources, 72- & McCormick, Taylor & Co, Philadelphia, 73-; adj prof, Drexel Univ, 77-78. *Mem:* Fel Geol Soc Am; AAAS; Asn Eng Geologists; Int Asn Eng Geol. *Res:* Geological processes relative to engineering and environmental geology, particularly slope stability, Karst topography, groundwater, weathering and erosion. *Mailing Add:* Dept of Civil Eng Villanova Univ Villanova PA 19085

FERIN, JURAJ, b Topolcany, Czech; m 53; c 2. ENVIRONMENTAL MEDICINE, INHALATION TOXICOLOGY. *Educ:* Slovak Univ, Bratislava, MD, 50; Charles Univ, Prague, PhD(indust med), 55. *Prof Exp:* Physician, Med Sch, Slovak Univ, Bratislava, 50-51; res scientist, Inst Indust Med & Occup Dis, Bratislava, 54-59; sr scientist environ health, Inst Exp Hyg, Slovak Acad Sci, 59-68; prof environ med, dept biophysics & environ sci, Sch Med & Dent, 68-80, PROF TOXICOL, DEPT RADIATION BIOL & BIOPHYSICS, DIV TOXICOL, SCH MED & DENT, UNIV ROCHESTER, 80- *Concurrent Pos:* Environ Res & Develop Agency & Nat Inst Environ Health Sci res grant, Sch Med & Dent, Univ Rochester, 69-74, US Dept Energy & Environ Protection Agency grants, 74-81; dep dir, Inst Exp Med, Slovak Acad Sci, 61-65; assoc prof, Sch Med, Slovak Univ, 65-68. *Mem:* AAAS; Am Indust Hyg Asn; Am Thoracic Soc; Reticuloendothelial Soc. *Res:* Air pollutants and the response of the respiratory system; particle clearance from the lung; occupational and environmental health; experimental pathology of the lung. *Mailing Add:* Dept of Biophysics & Environ Sci Univ Rochester Sch Med & Dent Rochester NY 14642

FERINGA, EARL ROBERT, b Grand Rapids, Mich, May 30, 32. NEUROLOGY. *Educ:* Calvin Col, BS, 53; Northwestern Univ, MD, 57. *Prof Exp:* Intern, Philadelphia Gen Hosp, Pa, 57-58; clin pharmacologist cancer chemotherapy, Nat Serv Ctr, NIH, 58, neuroanatomist, Lab Neuroanat Sci, 59-62; neuroanatomist, Col Physicians & Surgeons, Columbia Univ, 59; resident & assoc neurol, Colo Med Ctr, 62-64; from instr to prof neurol, Med Ctr, Univ Mich, Ann Arbor, 64-79, prof neurol, Dept Path, 75-79, chief neurol serv, Ann Arbor Vet Admin Hosp, 64-79; CHIEF NEUROL SERV, SAN DIEGO VET ADMIN HOSP, 79- *Concurrent Pos:* Consult, Wayne County Gen Hosp, 66-; adj prof neurosci, Univ Calif, San Diego, 79- *Mem:* Fel Am Acad Neurol; fel Am Col Physicians; Soc Clin Neurol; Asn Res Nerv & Ment Dis; Soc Neurosci. *Res:* Neurology and neuroanatomy; regeneration of central nervous system, particularly the spinal cord. *Mailing Add:* 3350 La Jolla Village San Diego CA 92161

FERINGTON, THOMAS EDWIN, b Lockport, NY, Oct 19, 26; m 49; c 2. POLYMER CHEMISTRY. *Educ:* Univ Buffalo, BA, 49; Calif Inst Technol, MS, 52; Princeton Univ, PhD(chem), 57. *Prof Exp:* Res chemist, Chemstrand Corp, 51-54; from instr to asst prof chem, Col Wooster, 57-61; res chemist, 61-65, res supvr, 65-69, res mgr, 69-73, SR DEVELOP ASSOC, W R GRACE & CO, 73- *Mem:* Am Chem Soc. *Res:* Physical chemistry of high polymers; dilute solution properties; kinetics; chemistry of organic sulfur compounds; rheology; chemistry of metallorganic compounds; materials science; processing and properties of polymers; photopolymerization; cross-linked systems. *Mailing Add:* Res Div W R Grace & Co Columbia MD 21044

FERKO, ANDREW PAUL, b Trenton, NJ, Aug 19, 42; m 71; c 3. PHARMACOLOGY, TOXICOLOGY. *Educ:* Philadelphia Col Pharm & Sci, BS, 65; Hahnemann Med Col, PhD(pharmacol), 69. *Prof Exp:* From jr instr to asst prof, 67-81, ASSOC PROF, PHARMACOL, HAHNEMANN MED COL & HOSP, 81- *Concurrent Pos:* Co-investr, HEW grant, 72-74. *Mem:* AAAS; Am Soc Pharmacol & Exp Therapeut; Soc Toxicol; Int Soc Study Xenobiotics. *Res:* Narcotic analgesics; dopamine; leuodopa; lead; abused drugs; ethanol and physical dependence on ethanol. *Mailing Add:* Hahnemann Med Col & Hosp 230 N Broad St Philadelphia PA 19102

FERL, ROBERT JOSEPH, b Conneaut, Ohio, Jan 19, 54; m 80. RECOMBINANT DNA. *Educ:* Hiram Col, BA, 76; Ind Univ, MA, 78, PhD(genetics), 80. *Prof Exp:* ASST PROF GENETICS, DEPT BOT, UNIV FLA, 80- *Concurrent Pos:* Vis scientist, Div Plant Indust, Commonwealth Sci & Indust Res Orgn, Canberra, Australia, 81. *Mem:* Genetics Soc Am; Bot Soc Am. *Res:* Gene expression, structure and function in plants. *Mailing Add:* Dept Bot Univ Fla Gainesville FL 32611

FERLING, JOHN ALBRECHT, b Koenigsberg, Ger, Sept 16, 28; nat US; m 55; c 2. MATHEMATICS. *Educ:* Upsala Col, BS, 52; Univ Southern Calif, PhD(math), 59. *Prof Exp:* Asst math, Univ Southern Calif, 52-55, lectr, 55-57; from asst prof to assoc prof, 57-66, PROF MATH, CLAREMONT MEN'S COL, 66- *Concurrent Pos:* Asst, Off Naval Res, 55-57. *Mem:* Am Math Soc; Math Asn Am. *Res:* Non-linear integral equations. *Mailing Add:* Dept of Math Claremont Men's Col Claremont CA 91711

FERM, JOHN CHARLES, b East Liverpool, Ohio, Mar 21, 25; m 49; c 3. GEOLOGY OF COAL. *Educ:* Pa State Univ, BS, 46, MS, 48, PhD(mineral), 57. *Prof Exp:* Instr mineral, Pa State Univ, 51-52; geologist, US Geol Surv, 52-57; from asst prof to prof geol, La State Univ, 57-69; dir grad studies geol, Univ SC, 69-74, prof geol, 69-80, dir, Caro Coal Group, 77-80; PROF GEOL, UNIV KY, 80-, DIR GRAD STUDIES, 81- *Concurrent Pos:* Consult various industs. *Honors & Awards:* Esso distinguished lectr, 81. *Mem:* AAAS; Geol Soc Am; Soc Econ Paleont & Mineral; Sigma Xi. *Res:* Coal geology; fluvial deltaic sedimentation; carboniferous stratigraphy; underground mine planning; resource estimates; computer applications. *Mailing Add:* 812 Surrey Lane Lexington KY 40503

FERM, RICHARD L, b Kansas City, Mo, June 18, 24; m 53; c 3. CHEMICAL ENGINEERING. *Educ:* Univ Kans, BS, 44, MS, 45, PhD(chem), 48. *Prof Exp:* From instr to asst prof chem eng, Univ NMex, 48-55; res engr, Calif Res Corp, 55-61, sr res chemist, 61-69, SR RES ASSOC, CHEVRON RES CO, 69- *Mem:* Am Chem Soc. *Res:* Petroleum products; emulsions and surface chemistry; ecological uses of asphalt; sulfur products; building materials; fuel chemistry and additives. *Mailing Add:* 3282 Theresa Lane Lafayette CA 94549

FERM, ROBERT JAMES, b Kansas City, Mo, Dec 22, 25. PETROLEUM CHEMISTRY. *Educ:* Univ Kans, BS, 46, MS, 47; Univ NMex, PhD(chem), 50. *Prof Exp:* SR STAFF CHEMIST, AM OIL CO, 50- *Mem:* Am Chem Soc; Sigma Xi; Inst Chem Eng. *Res:* Petroleum chemistry; heterocyclic nitrogen compounds. *Mailing Add:* Amaco Oil Co 11400 E Kentucky Rd Sugan Creek MO 64054

FERM, VERGIL HARKNESS, b West Haven, Conn, Sept 13, 24; m 48; c 4. BIOLOGY, EMBRYOLOGY. *Educ:* Col Wooster, BA, 46; Western Reserve Univ, MD, 48; Univ Wis, MS, 50, PhD, 55. *Prof Exp:* Intern, St Luke's Hosp, Cleveland, Ohio, 48-49; asst zool, Univ Wis, 49-51 & 54-55; asst prof anat, Ind Univ, 55-57; assoc prof, Univ Fla, 57-61; assoc prof path, 61-66, PROF ANAT-CYTOL & CHMN DEPT, DARTMOUTH MED SCH, 66- *Concurrent Pos:* USPHS sr res fel, Univ Fla, 58-63. *Mem:* Am Asn Anat; Am Soc Zool; Am Soc Human Genetics; Am Soc Exp Path. *Res:* Placental physiology; teratology; experimental embryology. *Mailing Add:* Dept of Anat-Cytol Dartmouth Med Sch Hanover NH 03755

FERMI, GIULIO, b Rome, Italy, Feb 16, 36; US citizen; m 60; c 2. MOLECULAR BIOLOGY, SYSTEMS ANALYSIS. *Educ:* Princeton Univ, MA, 57; Univ Calif, Berkeley, PhD(biophys), 62. *Prof Exp:* NSF fel, Max Planck Inst Biol, 61-62; Nat Inst Neurol Dis & Blindness fel, 62-63; staff mem, Inst Defense Anal, 64-69; dir systs eval group, Ctr Naval Anal, 69; consult systs anal, Inst Defense Anal, 70-71; TECH OFFICER, LAB MOLECULAR BIOL, MED RES COUN, 71- *Res:* Mutation and replication mechanisms in bacteriophages; optomotor reaction of musca domestica; system evaluation techniques for military communications and antisubmarine warfare; crystal structure of haemoglobin and derivatives. *Mailing Add:* Med Res Coun Lab Molecular Biol Hills Rd Cambridge England

FERNALD, ARTHUR THOMAS, b Nottingham, NH, Dec 13, 17; m 55; c 1. GEOLOGY. *Educ:* Univ NH, BS, 41; Harvard Univ, AM, 51, PhD(geomorphol), 56. *Prof Exp:* Instr geol, Colby Col, 46-47; GEOLOGIST, US GEOL SURV, 51- *Mem:* AAAS; Geol Soc Am; Arctic Inst NAm; Glaciol Soc; Am Quaternary Asn. *Res:* Geologic, geomorphic and engineering studies of polar and desert regions, particularly Alaska, Greenland, Nevada, New Mexico. *Mailing Add:* US Geol Surv Fed Ctr Box 25046 MS 954 Denver CO 80225

FERNALD, ROBERT LESLIE, b Larchland, Ill, Aug 27, 14. EMBRYOLOGY. *Educ:* Monmouth Col, AB, 37; Univ Calif, PhD(zool), 41. *Prof Exp:* Instr zool, Coe Col, 41-42; from instr to assoc prof, 46-68, actg dir, Friday Harbor Labs, 58-60, dir, 60-76, PROF ZOOL, UNIV WASH, 68- *Concurrent Pos:* bd trustees, Western Wash Univ, 76- *Mem:* AAAS; Am Soc Zool. *Res:* Experimental and comparative embryology of marine invertebrates. *Mailing Add:* Friday Harbor Labs Univ Wash Friday Harbor WA 98250

FERNALD, RUSSELL DAWSON, b Chuquicamata, Chile, Nov 20, 41; US citizen; m 69; c 2. NEUROBIOLOGY. *Educ:* Swarthmore Col, BSEE, 63; Univ Pa, PhD(biophys), 68. *Prof Exp:* Fel neurophysiol of visual cortex, Max Planck Inst Psychiat, 68-70; staff scientist neurobiol, Mac Planck Inst Behav Physiol, 70-76; ASSOC PROF BIOL, UNIV ORE, 76- *Concurrent Pos:* Proj leader, Cybernetic Study Group 50, 72-76. *Mem:* Animal Behav Soc; NY Acad Sci; Neurosci Soc; AAAS; Europ Brain & Behav Soc. *Res:* Quantitative analysis of visual communication signals in fish and the central nervous system processing of those signals. *Mailing Add:* Dept of Biol Univ of Ore Eugene OR 97403

FERNANDES, JOHN HENRY, b Tiverton, RI, Aug 21, 24; m 47; c 6. MECHANICAL ENGINEERING. *Educ:* RI State Col, BS, 49; Lehigh Univ, MS, 53; Calvin Coolidge Col, ScD, 60. *Prof Exp:* Serv engr, Combustion Eng, Inc, 49-50; from instr to assoc prof mech eng, Lafayette Col, 50-60; prof & head dept, Manhattan Col, 60-63; chief prof engr, New Prod Div, 63-68, admin asst to vpres, 68-70, coordr, Pollution Control Systs, Indust Group, 70, dir tech activities, 70-72, coordr, Environ Control Systs, 72-76, dir, Corp Tech Liaison, 76-81, DIR CORP TECH RESOURCES, COMBUSTION ENG, 81- *Concurrent Pos:* Consult, McGinley Mills, NJ, 54-56; dir eve col, Lafayette Col, 57-60. *Mem:* Fel Am Soc Mech Engrs; Nat Soc Prof Engrs; Am Soc Eng Educ; Instrument Soc; Am Acad Environ Engrs. *Res:* Broad areas of thermodynamics and compressible flow; particularly steam power plants and gas turbines; broad fields of fuel combustion; power generation and related equipment. *Mailing Add:* 65 Ludlow Rd Windsor CT 06095

FERNANDEZ, ALBERTO ANTONIO, b Buenos Aires, Arg, July 12, 25; m 49; c 1. BIOCHEMISTRY, CLINICAL CHEMISTRY. *Educ:* Univ Buenos Aires, MS, 54, PhD(chem), 60. *Prof Exp:* Chemist prod control, Behring Inst, Arg, 52-55, chief control, 55-58; chief chem res, Quimica Estrella, 58-61; res chemist, Bio-Sci Labs, 61-63, chief chem res, 63-66; head res & develop, Pfizer Int Subsidiaries, Arg, 66-67; dir res, Biochem Procedures, Inc, North Hollywood, 67-77; CONSULT, RIA, 77-; CANCER RESEARCHER, UNIV SOUTHERN CALIF, 79- *Mem:* Am Asn Clin Chem. *Res:* Chemical methods of clinical analysis; industrial organic synthesis; basic biochemical research; radioimmunoassays; cancer research. *Mailing Add:* 6322 Ellenview Ave Canoga Park CA 91303

FERNANDEZ, BERNAL, microbial physiology, see previous edition

FERNANDEZ, HECTOR R C, b Jaruco, Cuba, Feb 18, 37; US citizen. VISUAL PHYSIOLOGY, MARINE BIOLOGY. *Educ:* Univ Miami, BC, 60, PhD(zool), 65. *Prof Exp:* Fel, Biol Dept, Yale Univ, 65-67, res assoc, 67-69; asst prof, Biol Dept, Univ Southern Calif, 69-76; ASSOC PROF BIOL, WAYNE STATE UNIV, 76- *Concurrent Pos:* NIH fel, USPHS, 65; investr, Woods Hole Marine Biol Lab, 65-67 & Naval Arctic Res Lab, 70-77; vis prof, Physiol Dept, Keio Univ, 67-68 & Physics Dept, Konstanz Univ, 75; investr, Alpha Helix Southeast Asia Expedition, 76; vis prof, Dept Biol, Keio Univ, 82. *Mem:* Am Soc Photobiol; Asn Res Vision & Ophthalmol; fel AAAS; Am Soc Zoologists; Sigma Xi. *Res:* Investigate the role of enzymes in visual receptor excitation; histochemical localization of the enzymes; physiological studies of the enzyme and/or their products and by biochemical characterization of the enzymes. *Mailing Add:* Dept Biol Sci Wayne State Univ Detroit MI 48202

FERNANDEZ, HUGO LATHROP, b Rengo, Chile, Jan 16, 40; m 61; c 2. NEUROSCIENCE, NEUROBIOLOGY. *Educ:* Cath Univ Valparaiso, BS, 65; Mass Inst Technol, MS, 69; Univ Kans, PhD(physiol & cell biol), 71. *Prof Exp:* Res assoc neurosci, Dept Physiol, Univ Kans, 71; asst prof, Dept Neurobiol, Cath Univ, 72-73, assoc prof neurophysiol, 74-76; asst prof neurol, 77-79, ASSOC PROF PHYSIOL, UNIV KANS MED CTR, 79-; co-dir, Neuroscis Res Lab, 79-80, ASST PROF PHYSIOL, NEUROSCIS RES LAB, VET ADMIN MED CTR, 80- *Concurrent Pos:* Prin investr, UNESCO-PNUD, Cath Univ grant, 74-76; assoc investr, Muscular Dystrophy Asn Am grant, 77-79; prin investr, Vet Admin Merit Review grant, 79-; prin investr, NIH grant, 79-81. *Honors & Awards:* P Newmark Award, Univ of Kans, 71. *Mem:* AAAS; Soc Neurosci; Int Brain Res Org; Sigma Xi; NY Acad Sci. *Mailing Add:* Univ Kans Med Ctr 39th & Rainbow Blvd Kansas City KS 66103

FERNANDEZ, JACK EUGENE, b Tampa, Fla, May 18, 30; m 51; c 3. ORGANIC CHEMISTRY. *Educ:* Univ Fla, BSCh, 51, MS, 52, PhD(chem), 54. *Prof Exp:* Chemist, Naval Stores Sta, USDA, 54; instr & res assoc, Duke Univ, 56-57; chemist, Tenn Eastman Co, 57-60; from asst prof to assoc prof, 60-77, PROF CHEM, UNIV S FLA, 77- *Mem:* Am Chem Soc. *Res:* Kinetics and mechanisms; infrared spectroscopy; polymers; history of chemistry; chemistry for the non-scientist. *Mailing Add:* Dept of Chem Univ of S Fla Tampa FL 33620

FERNANDEZ, JOSE MARTIN, b La Coruna, Spain; US citizen. ENVIRONMENTAL HEALTH, ORGANIC CHEMISTRY. *Educ:* City Col New York, BS, 63; Yale Univ, PhD(org chem), 68. *Prof Exp:* Sr res chemist, 68-73, assoc org chem, 73-78, MEM STAFF, HEALTH & SAFETY LAB, EASTMAN KODAK CO RES LABS, 78- *Mem:* Am Chem Soc. *Res:* Couplers and developers for the photographic system; dyes; environmental regulations; toxicology; environmental sciences. *Mailing Add:* 525 Fox Meadow Rd Rochester NY 14626

FERNANDEZ, LOUIS AGNELO, b Karachi, Pakistan, May 30, 44; Can citizen; m 73; c 1. HEMATOLOGY. *Educ:* Univ Karachi, MS & BS, 66; FRCP(C), cert med, 73, hemat, 74. *Prof Exp:* Lectr, 74-76, asst prof, 76-81, ASSOC PROF MED, DALHOUSIE UNIV, 81- *Concurrent Pos:* Consult hemat, Camp Hill Hosp, Dalhousie Univ, 74-, Victoria Gen Hosp, 77- *Mem:* Can Soc Hemat; fel Am Col Physicians; Am Soc Hemat; Can Soc Clin Invest. *Res:* Characterization of lymphocyte subpopulations and functions in chronic lymphocytic leukemia; normal young and aging individuals. *Mailing Add:* Bldg 7 Camp Hill Hosp 1763 Robie St Halifax NS B3H 3G2 Can

FERNANDEZ, LOUIS ANTHONY, b New York, NY, Oct 5, 39; m 65; c 1. GEOLOGY, PETROLOGY. *Educ:* City Col New York, BS, 62; Univ Tulsa, MS, 64; Syracuse Univ, PhD(geol), 69. *Prof Exp:* Res geologist, Yale Univ, 68-71; asst prof, 71-74, actg asst dean, Col Sci, 76, assoc prof, 74-77, PROF GEOL, UNIV NEW ORLEANS, 77-, CHMN DEPT, 81- *Mem:* Geol Soc Am; Mineral Soc Am; Nat Asn Geol Teachers; Sigma Xi. *Res:* Igneous petrology; volcanology. *Mailing Add:* Dept of Earth Sci Univ of New Orleans New Orleans LA 70122

FERNANDEZ, REMIGIO, b Cuba, Aug 23, 41; US citizen; m 63; c 2. CHEMICAL ENGINEERING. *Educ:* Calif Inst Technol, BSc, 63; Syracuse Univ, PhD(chem eng, math), 68. *Prof Exp:* CHEM ENGR, RES LABS, HALCON INT, INC, 67- *Res:* Chemical reaction kinetics; homogeneous and heterogeneous gas phase reactions; heterogeneous liquid phase; heat and mass transfer in moving boundary systems; applied mathematics. *Mailing Add:* 781 River Rd New Milford NJ 07646

FERNANDEZ, SALVADOR M, b Guantanamo, Cuba, Mar 14, 43. BIOPHYSICS. *Educ:* Wayne State Univ, BA, 65, MS, 68, PhD(physics), 75. *Prof Exp:* ASST PROF PHYSIOL, UNIV CONN HEALTH CTR, 75- *Concurrent Pos:* Consult, NIH, 79-; ed, Elsevier/NHolland, 79- *Res:* Time resolved fluorescence spectroscopy in living cells; membrane biophysics. *Mailing Add:* Physiol Dept Univ Conn Health Ctr Farmington CT 06032

FERNANDEZ-POL, JOSE ALBERTO, b Buenos Aires, Arg, Mar 17, 43; m 71; c 1. GROWTH FACTORS, MEMBRANE RECEPTORS. *Educ:* Col Nat de Vincente Lopez, Buenos Aires, BA, 63; Univ de Buenos Aires, MD, 69. *Prof Exp:* Physician, Hosp Escuela Jose de San Martin, Univ Buenos Aires, 69-70, res assoc, Endocrine Res Lab, Cent de Med Nuclear Comn, 70-71; resident physician, State Univ NY at Buffalo, 72-72, res fel, Nuclear Med Lab, 72-75; fel, Lab Molecular Biol, Nat Cancer Inst, NIH, 75-77; asst prof med, St Louis Univ, 77-80; ASSOC PROF MED, ST LOUIS UNIV, 80-, ASSOC PROF RADIOL, 81- *Concurrent Pos:* Fel, Dept Internal Med, Inst Med Sci, Can, 72; dir, Radioimmunoassay Lab & prin investr, Vet Admin Med Ctr, St Louis, Mo, 77- *Mem:* Am Soc Microbiol; Am Asn Cancer Res; Arg Soc Biochem Invest. *Res:* Growth control mechanisms in normal and cancerous cells. *Mailing Add:* Nuclear Med Lab Dept Internal Med St Louis Univ 915 N Grand Blvd St Louis MO 63125

FERNANDEZ Y COSSIO, HECTOR RAFAEL, b Jaruco, Cuba, Feb 18, 37. PHYSIOLOGY. *Educ:* Univ Miami, Fla, BSc, 60, PhD(zool), 65. *Prof Exp:* Teaching asst zool, Univ Miami, Fla, 60-65; NIH fel, 65-67; staff res biologist, Yale Univ, 67-69; asst prof biol, Univ Southern Calif, 69-76, dir, Arctic Res Proj, 71-77; ASSOC PROF BIOL & CHMN DIV REGULATORY BIOL & BIOPHYS, WAYNE STATE UNIV, 77- *Mem:* Fel AAAS; Am Soc Zool; Am Soc Photobiol; Soc Res Vision & Ophthal; Soc Neurosci. *Res:* Biochemical and electrophysiological properties of photoreceptors; physiological adaptations of arctic and deep sea organisms; visual physiology, extraction and identification of crustacean visual pigments; electrophysiological studies of arthropod photoreceptors; plant physiology, study of electrical properties of plant cell membranes. *Mailing Add:* Div Regulatory Biol & Biophys Wayne State Univ Detroit MI 48202

FERNANDO, CONSTANTINE HERBERT, b Colombo, Ceylon, Apr 4, 29; m 57; c 3. LIMNOLOGY, RESERVOIR FISHERIES. *Educ:* Univ Ceylon, BSc, 52; Oxford Univ, DPhil(entom), 56. *Prof Exp:* Asst lectr zool, Univ Ceylon, 56-59; lectr, Univ Singapore, 60-64; sr res officer, Dept Fisheries, Ceylon, 64-65; assoc prof, 65-67, PROF BIOL, UNIV WATERLOO, 67- *Concurrent Pos:* Consult, Filariasis Res Unit, WHO, Rangoon, Burma, 63, Freshwater Fisheries, 79. *Mem:* Int Soc Limnol; Brit Freshwater Biol Asn; Brit Ecol Soc; Brit Inst Biol. *Res:* Taxonomy and ecology of Potamonidae and aquatic Coleoptera and Hemiptera; fish parasites; reservoir ecology; tropical lake and reservoir fisheries; introduced fishes; lacustrine fishes; taxonomy and ecology of freshwater microcrustaceans; predator/prey relations in freshwater zooplankton. *Mailing Add:* Dept of Biol Univ of Waterloo Waterloo ON K2L 3G1 Can

FERNANDO, QUINTUS, b Colombo, Ceylon, Nov 23, 26; m 50; c 2. ANALYTICAL CHEMISTRY. *Educ:* Univ Ceylon, BS, 49; Univ Louisville, MS, 51, PhD(chem), 53; FRIC. *Prof Exp:* Lectr chem, Univ Ceylon, 49; asst analyst, Govt Ceylon, 53; lectr chem, Univ Ceylon, 54-57; res assoc, Univ Pittsburgh, 57-58, asst prof, 58-61; assoc prof, 61-64, PROF CHEM, UNIV ARIZ, 64-, PROF TOXICOL & FORENSIC SCI, 80- *Res:* Development of techniques for trace element analysis; determination of mixtures of acids in rainwater; multielement analysis of environmental and forensic samples by proton induced x-ray emmission/x-ray crystallographic structure determination and photoelectron spectroscopy of metal complexes of importance in analytical chemistry; extraction of metals from deep-sea ferromanganese nodules; toxicology of metals and their compounds. *Mailing Add:* Dept of Chem Univ of Ariz Tucson AZ 85721

FERNBACH, DONALD JOSEPH, b Brooklyn, NY, Apr 10, 25; m 54; c 4. PEDIATRICS, HEMATOLOGY. *Educ:* Tusculum Col, AB, 48; George Washington Univ, MD, 52. *Prof Exp:* Instr zool, Tusculum Col, 47-48; Jesse Jones fel pediat hemat, Children's Med Ctr, Boston, Mass, 56-57; from instr to assoc prof, 57-71, PROF PEDIAT, BAYLOR COL MED, 71- *Concurrent Pos:* Consult, Wilford Hall Army Hosp, Lackland AFB, 60- *Mem:* Am Acad Pediat; Am Pediat Soc; AMA; Am Asn Cancer Res; Am Soc Hemat. *Res:* Cancer chemotherapy in children; possible viral etiology; clinical and epidemiological investigations of pediatric neoplasia, especially childhood leukemia. *Mailing Add:* Tex Children's Hosp 6621 Fannin St Houston TX 77025

FERNBACH, SIDNEY, b Philadelphia, Pa, Aug 4, 17; m 55; c 3. THEORETICAL PHYSICS, COMPUTER SCIENCE. *Educ:* Temple Univ, AM, 40; Univ Calif, PhD(physics), 52. *Prof Exp:* Physicist, Frankford Arsenal, 40-43; asst instr, Univ Pa, 43-44; asst, Univ Calif, 46-48, physicist, Lawrence Radiation Lab, 48-51; mem staff, Stanford Univ, 51-52; head, Theoret Div, Lawrence Livermore Nat Lab, 58-68, head, Comput Dept, 62-77, dep assoc dir sci support, 77-79; CONSULT, INFO SYSTS, 79- *Concurrent Pos:* Mem bd dirs, Advan Memory Systs, Sunnyvale, Calif, 69-76; consult, US Dept of Defense, 71-; consult, Comput Systs Tech Adv Comt, Domestic & Int Bus Admin Bur East West Trade, US Dept Com, 72-80; mem steering comt, Comput Sci & Eng Res Study, NSF, 74-80; mem bd dir, Solar Energy Sales, 78- *Mem:* Fel Am Phys Soc; Asn Comput Mach; fel AAAS; Math Asn Am; Inst Elec & Electronics Engrs. *Res:* Neutron physics; cosmic ray shower theory; computation. *Mailing Add:* 4 Holiday Dr Alamo CA 94507

FERNEKESS, HANS G, b Frankenthul, WGer, July 26, 31. ORGANIC CHEMISTRY. *Educ:* Univ Muinz, WGer, BS, 55, MS, 58, Dr rer nat, 60. *Prof Exp:* Fel, Agr & Med Col, Tex, 60-61; fel, Yale Univ, 61-62; scientist, Kulle, Niederlossing der Hoechst, 62-63, RES & DEVELOP MGR, TECH INFO SYSTS, DIV AM HOECHST CORP, 63- *Mem:* Ges Deut Chemike. *Res:* Photopolymerization systems; pre-sensitized printing plates and their aluminum substrates and color proofing systems; the light sensitive systems include positive and negative working coatings. *Mailing Add:* 179 Grove St Somerville NJ 08876

FERNELIUS, NILS CONARD, b Columbus, Ohio, Nov 10, 34. SURFACE PHYSICS, EXPERIMENTAL SOLID STATE PHYSICS. *Educ:* Harvard Univ, AB, 56; Univ Ill, Urbana, MS, 59, PhD(physics), 66. *Prof Exp:* Res assoc, Dept Physics, Univ Ill, Urbana, 66-67; asst physicist, Mat Sci Div, Argonne Nat Lab, 68-71; vpres, Res Consults, Inc, 71-72; Nat Res Coun resident res assoc, Aerospace Res Lab, 73-75, vis scientist, Air Force Mat Lab, Wright-Patterson AFB, 75-77; RES PHYSICIST, UNIV DAYTON RES INST, 77- *Mem:* Am Phys Soc; Optical Soc Am; Am Asn Physics Teachers; Sigma Xi; Am Vacuum Soc. *Res:* Studies of point defects using nuclear magnetic resonance and nuclear quadrupole resonance; laser applications, particularly scattering of laser light and holography; x-ray photoelectron, Auger electron, appearance potential, and photoacoustic spectroscopies. *Mailing Add:* 829 Edinboro Ct Dayton OH 45431

FERNELIUS, W(ILLIS) CONARD, b Riverdale, Utah, Aug 7, 05; m 31; c 2. CHEMISTRY. *Educ:* Stanford Univ, AB, 26, AM, 27, PhD(chem), 28. *Hon Degrees:* ScD, Franklin & Marshall Col, 59. *Prof Exp:* Asst, Stanford Univ, 26-27; from instr to prof chem, Ohio State Univ, 28-42; prof chem, Purdue Univ, 42-47; chmn dept chem, Syracuse Univ, 47-49; prof chem & head dept, Pa State Univ, 49-60; assoc dir res, Koppers Co, Inc, 60-70; distinguished prof chem, Univ SFla, 70-75, distinguished emer prof chem, 75; ADJ PROF CHEM, KENT STATE UNIV, 75- *Concurrent Pos:* Asst lab dir, Manhattan Dist, 43-45, lab dir, 45-46; Guggenheim fel, Oxford Univ, 56-57; Fulbright fel, Univ Cairo, 60; asst ed, Chem Abstracts, 39-49; mem comt documentation & nomenclature, Nat Res Coun; mem comn nomenclature inorg compounds, Int Union Pure & Appl Chem, 63-71, chmn, 71-75, mem inorg div comn, 73-77. *Honors & Awards:* Pittsburgh Award, Am Chem Soc, 69; Patterson-Crane Award, Am Chem Soc, 81. *Mem:* AAAS; Am Chem Soc; Mfg Chem Asn; fel Am Inst Chem; fel The Chem Soc. *Res:* Chemical nomenclature; nitrogen systems of compounds; chemistry of liquid ammonia solutions; chemical and physical study of coordination compounds; radioactivity; less familiar elements; electron spectroscopy. *Mailing Add:* Dept of Chem Kent State Univ Kent OH 44242

FERNIE, JOHN DONALD, b Pretoria, SAfrica, Nov 13, 33; Can citizen; m 55; c 2. ASTRONOMY. *Educ:* Univ Cape Town, BSc, 53, Hons, 54, MSc, 55; Ind Univ, PhD(astron), 58. *Prof Exp:* Lectr astron, Univ Cape Town, 58-61; asst prof, 61-64, assoc prof, 64-67, PROF ASTRON, DAVID DUNLAP OBSERV, UNIV TORONTO, 67-, DIR OBSERV & CHMN ASTRON DEPT, 78- *Mem:* Am Astron Soc; fel Royal Astron Soc; Int Astron Union; Royal Astron Soc Can (pres, 74-76); Can Astron Soc. *Res:* History of modern astronomy; variable stars; galactic structure; photoelectric photometry. *Mailing Add:* David Dunlap Observ Univ of Toronto Richmond Hill ON M5S 2R8 Can

FERNOW, RICHARD CLINTON, b Newark, Ohio, Feb 5, 47; m 70; c 2. HIGH ENERGY PHYSICS. *Educ:* Ohio Univ, BS, 69; Syracuse Univ, MS, 71, PhD(physics), 73. *Prof Exp:* Res assoc physics, Univ Mich, 73-78; assoc physicist, 78-81, PHYSICIST, BROOKHAVEN NAT LAB, 81- *Mem:* Am Phys Soc; Am Asn Physics Teachers. *Res:* Experimental particle physics; hadron spectroscopy; super conducting; polarized target development. *Mailing Add:* Physics Dept Bldg 510 Brookhaven Nat Lab Upton NY 11973

FERNSTROM, JOHN DICKSON, b New York, NY, July 9, 47; m 78. NEUROPHARMACOLOGY, NEUROENDOCRINOLOGY. *Educ:* Mass Inst Technol, SB, 69, PhD(nutrit biochem & metab), 72. *Prof Exp:* Fel neuroendocrinol, Roche Inst Molecular Biol, Hoffmann-LaRoche Inc, NJ, 72-73; asst prof, 73-77, ASSOC PROF NEUROENDOCRINOL, MASS INST TECHNOL, 77- *Concurrent Pos:* Consult life sci, Gen Tel & Electronics Res Labs, 73-75; fel neurochem, Alfred P Sloan Found, 74-76; consult, A D Little, 77; mem, Neurol Disorders Spec Projs A Study Sect, Nat Inst Neurol & Commun Disorders & Stroke, 78-82, chmn, 81-82; NIMH res develop award, 79-; mem, Life Sci Adv Comt, NASA, 80- *Honors & Awards:* Mead-Johnson Award, Am Inst Nutrit, 80. *Mem:* Am Physiol Soc; Endocrine Soc; Am Soc Pharmacol & Exp Therapeut; Soc Neurosci; Am Inst Nutrit. *Res:* Effects of diet and drugs on brain neurotransmitter synthesis and utilization; control of pituitary hormone secretion by the brain; malnutrition and brain function; amino acid utilization in the body; nutrition; neuropeptide synthesis and function in the brain. *Mailing Add:* Bldg 56 Rm 137 Mass Inst Technol Cambridge MA 02139

FEROE, JOHN ALBERT, b Grand Forks, NDak, Dec 6, 46. MATHEMATICS. *Educ:* St Olaf Col, BS, 68; Univ Calif, San Diego, MA, 70, PhD(math), 74. *Prof Exp:* ASST PROF MATH, VASSAR COL, 74- *Mem:* Am Math Soc; Math Asn Am; Soc Indust & Appl Math. *Res:* Differential equations; reaction-diffusion equations; mathematical modeling. *Mailing Add:* Dept Math Vassar Col Box 335 Poughkeepsie NY 12601

FERONE, ROBERT, b Mt Vernon, NY, Nov 8, 36; m 60; c 4. MICROBIOLOGY, BIOCHEMISTRY. *Educ:* NY Univ, BA, 58, MS, 63. *Prof Exp:* Res microbiologist, 58-68, sr res microbiologist, 68-79, GROUP LEADER, WELLCOME RES LABS, BURROUGHS WELLCOME & CO, 79- *Mem:* Am Soc Microbiol; Am Soc Biol Chem. *Res:* Chemotherapy; antifolate inhibitors; folate metabolism in malaria; antibacterial and antimalarial drugs. *Mailing Add:* Burroughs Wellcome & Co Research Triangle Park NC 27709

FERRANTE, FRANK L, physiology, see previous edition

FERRANTE, JEANNE, mathematical logic, computer science, see previous edition

FERRANTE, MICHAEL JOHN, b New York, NY, Feb 1, 30; m 53; c 3. PHYSICAL INORGANIC CHEMISTRY, THERMODYNAMICS. *Educ:* Eastern Wash Col, BA(chem) & BA(educ), 52. *Prof Exp:* Res chemist metall, 56-69, RES CHEMIST THERMODYNAMICS, US BUR MINES, ALBANY METALL RES CTR, 69- *Mem:* Sigma Xi; Am Inst Chem Engrs. *Res:* Experimental and theoretical studies of thermodynamic properties of substances by conducting research in high-temperature calorimetry. *Mailing Add:* Albany Metall Res Ctr PO Box 70 Albany OR 97321

FERRANTE, W(ILLIAM) R(OBERT), b Providence, RI, Mar 9, 28; m 68; c 2. ENGINEERING MECHANICS. *Educ:* Univ RI, ScB, 49; Brown Univ, ScM, 55; Va Polytech Inst, PhD(eng mech), 62. *Prof Exp:* Instr math, Univ RI, 49-50; asst prof mech, Lafayette Col, 52-56; assoc prof mech eng, 56-68, assoc dean, 67-69, dean grad sch, 69-71, actg vpres for acad affairs, 71-72, vpres for acad affairs, 72-73, actg pres, 73-74, PROF MECH ENG & APPL MECH, UNIV RI, 68-, VPRES FOR ACAD AFFAIRS, 74- *Concurrent Pos:* Fulbright fel, Al-Hikma Univ, Baghdad, 63-64. *Mem:* Asn Higher Educ; Am Soc Mech Engrs; Am Soc Eng Educ; Math Asn Am; Sigma Xi. *Res:* Applied mechanics; elasticity; shell theory; applied mathematics. *Mailing Add:* 50 Ferry Rd Saunderstown RI 02874

FERRAR, JOSEPH C, b Lansing, Mich, Dec 10, 39; m 61; c 4. MATHEMATICS. *Educ:* Mich State Univ, BS, 60; Yale Univ, PhD(math), 66. *Prof Exp:* assoc prof, 65-80, PROF MATH, OHIO STATE UNIV, 80- *Concurrent Pos:* Vis lectr, State Univ Utrecht, 67-68. *Mem:* Am Math Soc. *Res:* Classification of Lie algebras and the related algebraic structures. *Mailing Add:* Dept of Math Ohio State Univ Columbus OH 43210

FERRARA, ANGELO, b Brooklyn, NY, July 25, 31; m 61; c 5. PEDIATRICS. *Educ:* City Univ NY, BS, 53; Univ Rome, MD, 58; NY Univ, PhD(pub admin), 77. *Prof Exp:* Dir, Pediat Allergy Clin, Long Island Col Hosp & Lutheran Hosp, 63-65; clin asst, Roosevelt Hosp, 63-66; attend physician pediat, St Vincents Hosp & Med Ctr, med coordr teaching & res, 63-69; coordr teaching & pediat, ambulatory comprehensive care, New York Foundling Hosp, 63-69; dir, Allergy Clin & Regional Med Progs, St Mary's Hosp, NY & Pediat Serv & Community Progs, 69-71; asst attend, 68-70, ASSOC ATTEND, UNIV BELLEVUE HOSP, 69-, DIR, PEDIAT ALLERGY & INFANT TRANSP SERV, 71-; ASSOC PROF PEDIAT, SCH MED, NY UNIV, 71- *Concurrent Pos:* Prin investr, Nat Ctr Health Sci res grant, 80-82. *Mem:* Am Pediat Soc; Am Pub Health Asn; Asn Am Med Col; fel Am Acad Pediat; fel NY Acad Med. *Res:* Epidemiology in health care systems; research design; neonatac problems. *Mailing Add:* NY Univ Med Ctr Univ Hosp 560 First Ave New York NY 10016

FERRARA, LOUIS W, b Chicago, Ill, Aug 27, 23; m 53; c 6. ANALYTICAL CHEMISTRY, BIOCHEMISTRY. *Educ:* Univ Ill, BS, 52. *Prof Exp:* Sr res chemist, 52-65, supvr anal chem, 65-67, anal serv specialist, 67-68, mgr anal serv, 68-78, MGR ANAL CHEM TECH DEVELOP, INT MINERALS & CHEM CORP, 78- *Mem:* Am Chem Soc; Am Soc Testing & Mat; Asn Off Agr Chem; Inst Food Technol; Soc Appl Spectros. *Res:* Organic and inorganic chemistry; microbiology; plants and soils. *Mailing Add:* IMC Corp Res & Develop Ctr PO Box 207 Terre Haute IN 47808

FERRARA, THOMAS CIRO, b Sacramento, Calif, Mar 27, 47; m 70; c 2. TRANSPORTATION ENGINEERING. *Educ:* Univ Calif, Davis, BS, 69, MS, 70, PhD(civil eng), 75. *Prof Exp:* Instr eng, Ft Lewis Col, 70-71; asst prof, 71-77, ASSOC PROF CIVIL ENG, CALIF STATE UNIV, CHICO, 77-, HEAD DEPT, 78- *Concurrent Pos:* Traffic engr, D J Faustman Consult Traffic Engr, 71- *Mem:* Am Soc Civil Engrs; Inst Transp Engrs; Am Soc Eng Educ; Transp Res Bd. *Res:* Bicycle traffic. *Mailing Add:* Div of Eng Calif State Univ Chico CA 95929

FERRARI, HARRY M, b Detroit, Mich, May 20, 32; m 60; c 2. METALLURGICAL ENGINEERING. *Educ:* Wayne State Univ, BS, 54; Univ Mich, MS, 55, PhD(metall eng), 58. *Prof Exp:* Metallurgist, Pontiac Div, Gen Motors Corp, 53-54; assoc metallurgist, eng res inst, Univ Mich, 54-58; sr engr thermoelec mat, 58-60, tech adv nuclear mat, European Atomic Energy Comn, Brussels, Belg, 60-63, supvry engr, 63-64, mgr nuclear fuel tech, 64-69 & fuel assembly develop, 69-72, CONSULT ENGR, ATOMIC POWER DIV, WESTINGHOUSE ELEC CO, 72- *Concurrent Pos:* Fel, Univ Mich, 58; lectr, Milan Polytech Inst, 61-62; consult, US Dept Energy, 79- *Mem:* Fel Am Nuclear Soc; Am Soc Metals; Am Inst Mining, Metall & Petrol Engrs. *Res:* Studies on nuclear fuel materials; advanced fuel assembly designs and effects of irradiation on material properties. *Mailing Add:* Westinghouse Nuclear Fuel Div Box 3912 Pittsburgh PA 15230

FERRARI, LAWRENCE A, b Hackensack, NJ, Nov 30, 37; m 64; c 1. PHYSICS. *Educ:* Stevens Inst Technol, ME, 58, MS, 60, PhD(physics), 65. *Prof Exp:* Vis res assoc physics, Plasma Physics Lab, Princeton Univ, 64-65; asst prof, 65-69, chmn dept, 70-77, PROF PHYSICS, QUEENS COL, NY, 69- *Mem:* Am Phys Soc. *Res:* Experimental plasma physics. *Mailing Add:* Dept of Physics Queens Col Flushing NY 11367

FERRARI, RICHARD ALAN, b Minneapolis, Minn, June 13, 32; m 58; c 3. BIOCHEMICAL PHARMACOLOGY. *Educ:* Cornell Univ, BA, 54, MFS, 55; Pa State Univ, PhD(biochem), 59. *Prof Exp:* From assoc res biologist to sr res biologist biochem, 59-76, GROUP LEADER PHARMACOL, STERLING-WINTHROP RES INST, 76- *Mem:* AAAS; Am Chem Soc; Sigma Xi. *Res:* Photosynthesis of plant lipids; purification and kinetics of enzymes; central nervous system biochemistry; radiobiology; biochemical pharmacology; dermatology. *Mailing Add:* Sterling-Winthrop Res Inst Rensselaer NY 12144

FERRARIS, JOHN PATRICK, b Stamford, Conn, Apr 6, 47. ORGANIC CHEMISTRY, SOLID STATE CHEMISTRY. *Educ:* St Michael's Col, Vt, BA, 69; Johns Hopkins Univ, MA, 71, PhD(chem), 73. *Prof Exp:* Nat Res Coun res assoc, Nat Bur Standards, 73-75; asst prof chem, 75-80, ASSOC PROF CHEM & PHYSICS, UNIV TEX, DALLAS, 80- *Mem:* Am Chem Soc; Royal Soc Chem; AAAS; Sigma Xi; Am Phys Soc. *Res:* Design, synthesis and characterization of organic charge transfer materials; investigation of transport, optical and magnetic properties of organic metals and semiconductors; study of piezo- and pyroelectricity in polar polymers. *Mailing Add:* Dept Chem Box 688 Univ Tex Dallas Richardson TX 75080

FERRARO, CHARLES FRANK, b New York, NY, Sept 14, 24; m 59; c 3. ANALYTICAL CHEMISTRY. *Educ:* Polytech Inst Brooklyn, BS, 44; Columbia Univ, MA, 46, PhD(chem), 50. *Prof Exp:* From instr to asst prof chem, Fordham Univ, 49-56; MGR ANAL SERV, CTR TECH DEPT, FMC CORP, 56- *Mailing Add:* 12 Millbrook Lane Lawrenceville NJ 08648

FERRARO, JOHN ANTHONY, b Pueblo, Colo, Dec 21, 46; m 73; c 2. NEUROPHYSIOLOGY. *Educ:* Southern Colo State Col, BS, 68; Univ Denver, MS, 70, PhD(speech & hearing sci), 72. *Prof Exp:* NIH fel, Northwestern Univ, 72-74; asst prof, 74-78, ASSOC PROF SPEECH & HEARING SCI, OHIO STATE UNIV, 78-; CLIN NEUROPHYSIOLOGIST, SWED MED CTR, 81- *Concurrent Pos:* NIH res asst, Nat Inst Neurol Dis & Stroke, 72-73; prin investr, 73-74; consult, Speech & Hearing Sci Sect, Dept Otolaryngol, Ohio State Univ, 74-81; asst dir, 80-81. *Mem:* Acoust Soc Am; Am Speech & Hearing Asn; Asn Res Otolaryngol; Sigma Xi. *Res:* Application of evoked potentials as diagnostic, and prognostic tools in a clinical setting; evoked potentials including: auditory, visual, vestibulor, somatosensory, as well as surgical monitoring using evoked potentials. *Mailing Add:* Neurosensory Diag Ctr Swed Med Ctr Englewood CO 80110

FERRARO, JOHN J, b New York, NY, Apr 20, 31; m 54; c 5. ORGANIC CHEMISTRY, BIOCHEMISTRY. *Educ:* Fordham Univ, BS, 52; Polytech Inst Brooklyn, PhD(org chem), 61. *Prof Exp:* Res assoc peptide chem, Med Col, Cornell Univ, 62-63; instr biochem, 63-64; asst prof biochem & org chem, St John's Univ, NY, 64-69; assoc prof, 69-74, PROF CHEM, LONG ISLAND UNIV, 69- *Mem:* AAAS; Am Chem Soc; Royal Soc Chem. *Mailing Add:* Dept of Chem Long Island Univ Brooklyn NY 11201

FERRARO, JOHN RALPH, b Chicago, Ill, Jan 27, 18; m 47; c 3. MOLECULAR SPECTROSCOPY. *Educ:* Ill Inst Technol, BS, 41, PhD(chem), 54; Northwestern Univ, MS, 48. *Prof Exp:* Supv chemist, Tetryl Labs, Kankakee Arsenal, Ill, 41-43; lab asst, Northwestern Univ, 46-48; assoc chemist, Argonnne Nat Lab, 48-68, sr scientist, 68-81; SEARLE PROF CHEM, LOYOLA UNIV, CHICAGO, 81- *Concurrent Pos:* Vis prof, Univ Rome, Italy, 66-67; ed jour, Soc Appl Spectros, 68-74; mem spec adv bd, Chem Rubber Co, 71-; vis prof, Univ Ariz, 73-74; adj prof planetary sci, 74- *Honors & Awards:* Spectros Award, Soc Appl Spectros, 70, Meggers Award & Prof Achievement Award Spectros, 75; Distinguished Scientist Award, Argonne Univs Asn, 73; NATO recipient, Sr Scientist Award, 78. *Mem:* Am Chem Soc; AAAS; NY Acad Sci; Soc Appl Spectros (pres, 65); Coblentz Soc. *Res:* Infrared spectroscopy of inorganic complexes, coordination compounds and electrical conductors; Raman spectra; vibrational spectroscopy at high pressures. *Mailing Add:* Chem Dept Loyola Univ 6525 N Sheridan Rd Chicago IL 60439

FERRAUDI, GUILLERMO JORGE, b Buenos Aires, Argentina, Dec 9, 42; m 74; c 2. INORGANIC CHEMISTRY, PHYSICAL CHEMISTRY. *Educ:* Univ Buenos Aires, MS, 70; Univ Chile, PhD(inorg chem), 74. *Prof Exp:* Res assoc, Wayne State Univ, 74-76; asst prof, Fac Sci, Univ Chile, 76-78; SCIENTIST, RADIATION LAB, UNIV NOTRE DAME, 78- *Mem:* Am Chem Soc; Interam Photochem Soc; Sigma Xi. *Res:* Physical inorganic chemistry; photochemistry of coordination complexes; reactions of radicals with coordination complexes; chemistry of the complexes in unusual oxidation states. *Mailing Add:* Radiation Lab Univ of Notre Dame Notre Dame IN 46556

FERREE, CAROLYN RUTH, b Liberty, NC, Jan 29, 44; m 68. RADIATION ONCOLOGY. *Educ:* Univ NC, Greensboro, BA, 66; Bowman Gray Sch Med, MD, 70. *Prof Exp:* Intern med, NC Baptist Hosp, Winston-Salem, 70-71; resident radiation ther, 71-74; asst prof, 75-81, ASSOC PROF RADIATION THER, BOWMAN GRAY SCH MED, 81- *Concurrent Pos:* Am Cancer Soc jr fac clin fel, 76-79. *Mem:* Am Col Radiol; Am Soc Therapeut Radiologists. *Res:* Psychology of terminal patients; Hodgkin's disease. *Mailing Add:* Bowman Gray Sch of Med 300 Hawthorne Rd Winston-Salem NC 27103

FERREE, DAVID C, b Lock Haven, Pa, Feb 9, 43; m 68. HORTICULTURE, POMOLOGY. *Educ:* Pa State Univ, BS, 65; Univ Md, College Park, MS, 68, PhD, 69. *Prof Exp:* Assoc prof, 71-80, PROF HORT, OHIO AGR RES & DEVELOP CTR, 80- *Mem:* Am Soc Hort Sci. *Res:* Integrating present knowledge and techniques of apple production management into efficient systems for high density orchards, with emphasis on light relations as affected by pruning, training systems and root stocks. *Mailing Add:* Dept of Hort Ohio Agr Res & Develop Ctr Wooster OH 44691

FERREIRA, LAURENCE E, b Livermore, Calif, Mar 23, 28; m 54; c 3. CERAMICS ENGINEERING. *Educ:* Univ Calif, Berkeley, BS, 52, MS, 55. *Prof Exp:* Ceramic engr, Western Gold & Platinum Co, Calif, 53-56; dir res, Coors Procelain Co, 56-71, consult ceramist, 71-77; MEM STAFF, CYPRUS MINES CORP, 77- *Honors & Awards:* PACE Award, Nat Inst Ceramics Engrs. *Mem:* Fel Am Ceramic Soc; Am Soc Testing & Mat. *Res:* Research management development of oxide ceramics for industrial use; ceramic processing method development. *Mailing Add:* Cyprus Mines Corp 2435 Military Ave Los Angeles CA 90064

FERRELL, BLAINE RICHARD, b Upper Darby, Pa, Feb 2, 52; m 73. PHYSIOLOGICAL ECOLOGY, CIRCADIAN RHYTHMS. *Educ:* Univ Pa, BA, 73; Western Ky Univ, MS, 75; La State Univ, PhD(vert zool), 79. *Prof Exp:* ASST PROF ZOOL BEHAV, WESTERN KY UNIV, 78- *Mem:* Am Soc Zoologists; Am Ornith Union; Coopers Ornith Soc; Wilson Ornith Soc. *Res:* Mechanisms by which photoperiod length and temperature time the occurrence of seasonal physiological and behavioral condition in vertebrates, the approach used is based on the premise that such mechanisms have a circadian basis. *Mailing Add:* Dept Biol Western Ky Univ Bowling Green KY 42101

FERRELL, D THOMAS, JR, b Durham, NC, Sept 28, 22; m 65; c 1. ELECTROCHEMISTRY. *Educ:* Eastern Ky State Col, BS, 43; Duke Univ, AM, 48, PhD(chem), 50. *Prof Exp:* Chemist, Naval Ord Lab, Md, 50-56; mgr res & develop, Battery Lab, Am Mach & Foundry Co, 57-58, asst lab mgr, 58-59; asst gen mgr, Missile Battery Div, Elec Storage Battery Co, 59-60, from assoc dir to asst dir eng, Exide Indust Div, 60-65, tech coordr, ESB Inc, 65-69, mgr lead acid eng, Exide Power Systs Div, 69-74, assoc dir technol, 74-78, V PRES, ESB TECHNOL CO, 78- *Mem:* Am Chem Soc; Electrochem Soc. *Res:* Electrode reactions; batteries. *Mailing Add:* ESB Technol Co 19 W College Ave Yardley PA 19067

FERRELL, EDWARD F(RANCIS), b Louisa, Ky, Apr 19, 14; m 45; c 3. PHYSICAL METALLURGY. *Educ:* Western Ky State Col, BS, 39; Vanderbilt Univ, MS, 40, PhD, 50. *Prof Exp:* Analyst, Electro Metall Co, WVa, 41-42; mem staff, Battelle Mem Inst, 47-55; instr chem, Bowling Green State Univ, 55-57; asst prof, Colo Sch Mines, 57-64; PHYS METALLURGIST, US BUR MINES, 64- *Mem:* Am Chem Soc; Am Soc Eng Educ; Metall Soc; Am Ceramic Soc. *Res:* Properties of metallic carbides and silicides; cermets; refractory metals; powder metallurgy; vapor phase deposition; oxidation rare earth metals; metal-ceramic bonding; refractory metals; ceramics. *Mailing Add:* Reno Ctr US Bur of Mines 1605 Evans Ave Reno NV 89503

FERRELL, HOWARD H, b Shreveport, La, Apr 11, 29; m 54; c 3. PETROLEUM ENGINEERING. *Educ:* Okla State Univ, BS, 51, MS, 57; Tex A&M Univ, PhD(petrol eng), 61. *Prof Exp:* Eng trainee, Stanolind Oil & Gas Co, 51-52; res engr, 59-61, res group supvr, 61-65, res group leader, 65-77, SR STAFF ENGR, CONTINENTAL OIL CO, 77- *Mem:* Soc Petrol Engrs. *Res:* Water-oil displacement in porous underground rock; application of the displacement mechanism for development of oil recovery processes; techniques to evaluate the characteristics of underground oil bearing strata. *Mailing Add:* Continental Oil Co Box 1267 Ponca City OK 74261

FERRELL, JAMES K(IO), b Maryville, Mo, Jan 18, 23; m 43; c 2. CHEMICAL ENGINEERING. *Educ:* Univ Mo, BS, 48, MS, 49; NC State Univ, PhD(chem eng), 54. *Prof Exp:* Asst prof chem eng, NC State Univ, 53-56; design specialist, Martin Marietta Corp, 56-58; sect chief design, Babcock & Wilcox, Co, 58-61; PROF CHEM ENG, NC STATE UNIV, 61-, DEPT HEAD, 66- *Concurrent Pos:* Pres, Triangle Univ Comput Ctr, 65-66. *Mem:* Am Inst Chem Engrs; Am Chem Soc; Sigma Xi. *Res:* Heat transfer applied to the chemical industry; coal gasification and environmental control for the coal processing industry. *Mailing Add:* NC State Univ Raleigh NC 27650

FERRELL, RAY EDWARD, JR, b New Orleans, La, Jan 29, 41; m 62; c 4. MINERALOGY, GEOCHEMISTRY. *Educ:* Univ Southwestern La, BS, 62; Univ Ill, MS, 65, PhD(geol), 66. *Prof Exp:* From asst prof to assoc prof, 66-77, PROF GEOL & CHMN DEPT, LA STATE UNIV, BATON ROUGE, 78- *Mem:* Mineral Soc Am; Clay Minerals Soc. *Res:* Origin and geologic importance of clay minerals. *Mailing Add:* Dept of Geol La State Univ Baton Rouge LA 70803

FERRELL, ROBERT EDWARD, b Meridian, Miss, July 15, 43; m 70. BIOCHEMICAL GENETICS. *Educ:* Miss Col, Clinton, BS, 66; Univ Tex, Austin, PhD(biochem), 71. *Prof Exp:* Fel human genetics, Dept Human Genetics, Univ Mich, Ann Arbor, 70-72, res assoc, 72-75; asst prof pop genetics & head genetic markers lab, 75-79, ASSOC PROF POP GENETICS, CTR POP & DEMOG GENETICS, HEALTH SCI CTR, UNIV TEX, HOUSTON, 79- *Mem:* AAAS; Am Chem Soc; Sigma Xi; Am Asn Phys Anthrop. *Res:* Genetic and meaning of genetically determined biochemical variability in natural populations with particular interest in human populations; biochemical evolution of human and other populations. *Mailing Add:* Ctr for Demog & Pop Genetics Health Sci Ctr Univ of Tex Houston TX 77030

FERRELL, WILLIAM JAMES, b Wheeling, WVa, Apr 7, 40; m 60; c 3. BIOCHEMISTRY, ORGANIC CHEMISTRY. *Educ:* West Libery State Col, BS, 61; WVa Univ, MS, 63; Univ Pittsburgh, PhD(biochem), 67. *Prof Exp:* Asst prof biochem, Univ Detroit, 67-74; asst prof biol chem, Univ Mich, Ann Arbor, 74-81; DIR CLIN CHEM, CHILDREN'S HOSP, DETROIT, 81-; ASSOC PROF PATH, WAYNE STATE UNIV, 81- *Concurrent Pos:* Grant-in-aid, Mich Heart Asn, 68-69 & 71-72 & Licensed Beverage Industs, 68-69 & 70-71; NIH grant, 70-73. *Mem:* Am Asn Clin Chemists. *Res:* Isolation, characterization and biosynthesis of aldehydogenic lipids and glycerol thioethers; biosynthesis and metabolism of free fatty aldehydes; changes in plasma and heart adenosine triphosphate, adenosine diphosphate and creatine phosphate during shock; enzymatic interconversion of fatty acids, alcohols and aldehydes; applications of high performance liquid chromatography to therapeutic drug monitoring. *Mailing Add:* Dept Lab Med Children's Hosp 3901 Beaubien Blvd Detroit MI 48201

FERRELL, WILLIAM KREITER, b Barberton, Ohio, Oct 18, 19; m 49; c 3. FORESTRY. *Educ:* Univ Mich, BS, 41; Duke Univ, MF, 46, PhD(forest soils), 49. *Prof Exp:* Asst forest soils specialist, Univ Idaho, 48-53, asst prof forestry, 53-56; from asst prof to assoc prof, 56-65, PROF FOREST MGT, ORE STATE UNIV, 65- *Concurrent Pos:* NSF sci fac fel, Denmark, 64-65; vis prof ecol syst, Cornell Univ, 71-72; ed forest sci, Soc Am Foresters, 75-79. *Mem:* AAAS; Soc Am Foresters; Am Soc Plant Physiol; Ecol Soc Am. *Res:* Photosynthesis, respiration and drought resistance studies of tree seedlings; ecotypic variation. *Mailing Add:* Sch of Forestry Ore State Univ Corvallis OR 97331

FERRELL, WILLIAM RUSSELL, b Cleveland, Ohio, June 19, 32; m 54; c 2. SYSTEMS & HUMAN FACTORS ENGINEERING. *Educ:* Swarthmore Col, BA, 54; Mass Inst Technol, SB & SM, 61, ME, 63, PhD(mech eng), 64. *Prof Exp:* Res asst mech eng, Mass Inst Technol, 61-62, from instr to assoc prof, 62-69; PROF SYSTS & INDUST ENG, UNIV ARIZ, 69- *Concurrent Pos:* Ford fel, Mass Inst Technol, 64-66; ed, Trans Man-Mach Systs, 69-70, co-ed, Trans Systs, Man & Cybernetics, 70-71. *Mem:* Human Factor Soc; Inst Elec & Electronics Engrs. *Res:* Human performance in engineering systems; remote manipulation; decision making; subjective probability and utility; mathematical models of performance; work methods and measurement. *Mailing Add:* Dept of Systs & Indust Eng Univ of Ariz Tucson AZ 85721

FERREN, LARRY GENE, b Emporia, Kans, Oct 13, 48; m 69; c 2. BIOCHEMISTRY. *Educ:* Univ Mo, BS, 70, PhD(biochem), 74. *Prof Exp:* Fel biochem, Univ Iowa, 74-75; ASST PROF CHEM, OLIVET NAZARENE COL, 75- *Mem:* Am Chem Soc; Biophys Soc. *Res:* Metal ion catalyzed hydrolysis of dipeptides; metalloenzymes; proteolytic enzymes requiring metal ions for activity. *Mailing Add:* Dept of Chem Olivet Nazarene Col Kankakee IL 60901

FERREN, RICHARD ANTHONY, b New Brunswick, NJ, Jan 19, 31; m 56; c 5. PHYSICAL ORGANIC CHEMISTRY. *Educ:* Villanova Univ, 52; Univ Pa, MS, PhD(chem), 56. *Prof Exp:* RES CHEMIST, PENNWALT CHEM CO, 56- *Mem:* Am Chem Soc; Soc Rheol. *Res:* Polymer chemistry. *Mailing Add:* Cent Res & Develop Lab Pennwalt Corp 900 First Ave King of Prussia PA 19406

FERRENDELLI, JAMES ANTHONY, b Trinidad, Colo, Dec 5, 36; m 57; c 3. NEUROLOGY, NEUROPHARMACOLOGY. *Educ:* Univ Colo, BA, 58, MD, 62. *Prof Exp:* Intern, Med Ctr, Univ Ky, 62-63; med officer, US Army, 63-65; resident neurol & neuropath, Cleveland Metrop Gen Hosp, 65-68; USPHS fel pharmacol, 68-71, from asst prof to assoc prof neurol & pharmacol, 70-77, PROF NEUROL & PHARMACOL, SCH MED, WASHINGTON UNIV, 77- SEALY PROF CLIN NEUROPHARMACOL, NEUROL, 77- *Concurrent Pos:* Asst neurologist, Barnes Hosp, 72-75, assoc neurologist, 75-78, neurologist, 78-; fel adv comn, Pharmacol-Morphol, Pharmaceut Mgrs Asn Found Inc, 79-; mem comt, Epilepsy Adv Comn, NINCDS, chmn subcomt, Anticonvulsant Drugs, 81- *Honors & Awards:* Epilepsy Award, Am Soc Pharmacol & Exp Therapeut, 81. *Mem:* Am Neurol Asn; Am Acad Neurol; Am Soc Pharmacol & Exp Therapeut; Soc Neurosci; Am Soc Neurochem. *Res:* Neurochemistry and neuropharmacology of epilepsy; role of cyclic nucleotides in nervous tissue; mechanisms of action of neuropharmacological agents; molecular mechanisms of retinal function; pathophysiological mechanisms of seizure disorders. *Mailing Add:* Dept Neurol & Neurol Surg Sch Med Wash Univ 660 Euclid Ave St Louis MO 63110

FERRER, JOSE M, b New York, NY, Nov 25, 12; m 39; c 5. SURGERY. *Educ:* Princeton Univ, AB, 34; Columbia Univ, MD, 38; Am Bd Surg, dipl, 44. *Prof Exp:* Dir surg, First Surg Div, Bellevue Hosp, 62-67; dir surg, Harlem Hosp Ctr, Col Physicians & Surgeons, 67-73, PROF SURG, COLUMBIA UNIV, 67-, ASSOC DEAN POSTGRAD EDUC, FAC MED, 73- *Concurrent Pos:* Attend surgeon, Presby & Babies Hosps, Columbia Univ-Presby Med Ctr, 64- *Mem:* Fel Am Col Surg; fel AMA; Int Soc Surg; Soc Surg Alimentary Tract; Int Col Digestive Surg. *Mailing Add:* 962 Park Ave New York NY 10028

FERRETTI, ALDO, b Rome, Italy, Jan 22, 29; US citizen; m 56; c 2. ORGANIC CHEMISTRY. *Educ:* Univ Rome, PhD(chem), 53. *Prof Exp:* Org chemist, Nat Hydrocarbon Corp, Italy, 53-57; Fulbright fel, Univ Ill, 57-59; res chemist, Farmitalia Div, Montecatini SA, 59-62; res assoc, Vanderbilt Univ, 62-63; res chemist, US Naval Propellant Plant, 63-64; sr scientist, Tenco Div, Coca-Cola Co, NJ, 64-68; RES CHEMIST, USDA, 68- *Mem:* Am Chem Soc; NY Acad Sci; Am Oil Chemists' Soc; The Chem Soc; Am Inst Chemists. *Res:* Synthetic organic chemistry; chemistry and biochemistry of natural products; lipid chemistry. *Mailing Add:* 8516 Howell Rd Bethesda MD 20817

FERRETTI, JAMES ALFRED, b Sacramento, Calif, Aug 1, 39; m 70; c 2. PHYSICAL & ANALYTICAL CHEMISTRY. *Educ:* San Jose State Col, BS, 61; Univ Calif, Berkeley, PhD(chem), 65. *Prof Exp:* Bio-org chemist, Stanford Res Inst, 61-62; res asst chem, Lawrence Radiation Lab, 62-65; instr, Univ Naples, Italy, 65-66; chemist, Food & Drug Admin, 66-67; RES CHEMIST, NIH, 67- *Mem:* Am Chem Soc; Am Phys Soc; Biophys Soc; Sigma Xi. *Res:* Nuclear magnetic resonance spectroscopy applied to biological polymers and to the conformation of intermediate molecular weight peptides. *Mailing Add:* NIH Bldg 12A Rm 2007 Bethesda MD 20205

FERRETTI, JOSEPH JEROME, b Chicago, Ill, Dec 23, 37; m 65; c 2. BIOCHEMISTRY, MICROBIOLOGY. *Educ:* Loyola Univ Chicago, BS, 60; Univ Minn, Minneapolis, MS, 65, PhD(biochem), 67. *Prof Exp:* Res asst biochem, Med Sch, Northwestern Univ, 60-62; assoc prof microbiol, 69-76, PROF MICROBIOL, HEALTH SCI CTR, UNIV OKLA, 76- *Concurrent Pos:* USPHS fel, Johns Hopkins Univ, 67-69; NSF grant, 73; NIH grants, 73-; Nat Acad Sci vis scientist, Ger Dem Repub, 80; mem, NSF US-France Coop Sci Prog, Pasteur Inst, 82. *Mem:* AAAS; Am Soc Microbiol. *Res:* Plasmids in Streptococci; immunologic cross-reactions with Streptococcal antigens; genetic studies on group A Streptococci and their bacteriophage; molecular cloning in streptococci. *Mailing Add:* Dept Microbiol PO Box 26901 Oklahoma City OK 73190

FERRIANS, OSCAR JOHN, JR, b Touchet, Wash, Mar 9, 28; m 53. GEOLOGY. *Educ:* State Col Wash, BS, 52, MS, 58. *Prof Exp:* GEOLOGIST, US GEOL SURV, 53- *Mem:* AAAS; Geol Soc Am; Arctic Inst NAm; Am Quaternary Asn. *Res:* Areal, surficial, glacial, economic, engineering and environmental geology; geomorphology; permafrost; earthquake effects; gold placer deposits; remote sensing. *Mailing Add:* US Geol Surv 345 Middlefield Rd Menlo Park CA 94025

FERRIER, BARBARA MAY, b Edinburgh, Scotland, Aug 7, 32; m 63; c 2. BIOCHEMISTRY. *Educ:* Univ Edinburgh, BSc, 54, PhD(chem), 58. *Prof Exp:* Asst chem, Univ Edinburgh, 54-58; res fel, Hickrill Chem Res Found, NY, 58-59; asst lectr, Bedford Col, Univ London, 59-61; res fel, Yale Univ, 61-62; res assoc biochem, Med Col, Cornell Univ, 62-63, instr, 63-66; res assoc obstet physiol, Clin Hosp, Montevideo, Uruguay, 66-68; assoc prof biochem, 69-76, PROF BIOCHEM, McMASTER UNIV, 76- *Mem:* Am Chem Soc; The Chem Soc; Can Biochem Soc; Int Soc Res Reproduction. *Res:* Metabolism of peptide and protein hormones in pregnancy. *Mailing Add:* 165 Chedoke Ave Hamilton ON L8S S4L8 Can

FERRIER, JACK MORELAND, b Cleveland, Ohio, Aug 8, 43; Can citizen; m 66; c 1. ELECTROPHYSIOLOGY, THEORETICAL BIOLOGY. *Educ:* Ohio State Univ, BSc, 66, MSc, 68, PhD(physics), 73. *Prof Exp:* Lectr physics, Dept Physics, Ohio State Univ, 73-75; res assoc, Bot Dept, 75-79, ASST PROF PERIODONT PHYSIOL, UNIV TORONTO, 79- *Mem:* Am Phys Soc. *Res:* Ion and water transport in biological cells and tissues: electrophysiology of mammalian cells and algal cells; elasticity and water transport in plant and animal tissue. *Mailing Add:* 4384 Med Sci Bldg Kings Col Circle Univ Toronto Toronto ON M5S 1A8

FERRIER, LESLIE KENNETH, b Welland, Ont, Apr 13, 41; m 74. FOOD SCIENCE, PROTEIN CHEMISTRY. *Educ:* Univ Guelph, BSA, 63, MSc, 65; Univ Wis, PhD(food sci), 72. *Prof Exp:* Res chemist brewing res, Can Breweries Ltd, 65-67; fel enzym, Dept Food Sci, Univ Wis, 71-72; asst prof food sci, Dept Food Sci & Int Soybean Prog, Univ Ill, 72-77; PROJ LEADER, GEN FOODS TECH CTR, TARRYTOWN, NY, 77- *Mem:* Am Asn Cereal Chemists; Inst Food Sci; Am Chem Soc. *Res:* Processing soybeans for human food; use of enzymes for food processing; effects of processing on protein functionality and nutrition. *Mailing Add:* Gen Foods Tech Ctr 555 S Broadway Tarrytown NY 10591

FERRIGNO, PETER D, b Washington, DC, Aug 26, 27; m 52; c 4. DENTISTRY. *Educ:* Georgetown Univ, BS, 50, DDS, 55; Cath Univ Am, MS, 52; Ohio State Univ, MS, 57; Am Bd Endodont, dipl, 65. *Prof Exp:* From instr to assoc prof, 59-68, PROF PERIODONT, SCH DENT, GEORGETOWN UNIV, 68-, CHMN DEPT, 60- *Concurrent Pos:* Consult, Vet Admin, 63-, Montgomery Jr Col, 61 & US Navy. *Mem:* Am Dent Asn; Am Asn Endodont; Am Acad Periodont; Int Asn Dent Res. *Res:* Fibrogenesis on periodontal ligament in rats by radioautolosis. *Mailing Add:* 4400 Jennifer St NW Washington DC 20015

FERRIGNO, THOMAS HOWARD, b Newark, NJ, Dec 3, 25; m 47; c 2. ORGANIC CHEMISTRY. *Educ:* Seton Hall Univ, BS, 51. *Prof Exp:* Plant chemist, Pabco Prod, Inc, 50-55; res supvr minerals & chem, Philipp Corp, 55-63; asst tech dir, United Clay Mines Corp, 63-65; mgr appl res, United Sierra Div, Cypress Mines Corp, 65-67; group leader, Tenneco Plastics Div, 67-70; MINERAL INDUST CONSULT, 71- *Mem:* Soc Plastics Engrs; Asn Consult Chemists & Chem Engrs; Am Inst Chemists; Am Chem Soc; Soc Plastics Indust. *Res:* Application of minerals in paints, plastics, rubber and allied fields; surface treatment of minerals; product development and promotion. *Mailing Add:* 29 Clover Hill Circle Trenton NJ 08638

FERRILL, MITCHELL, b Cobden, Ill, Feb 16, 34; m 57; c 3. RESOURCES POLICY & MANAGEMENT. *Educ:* Univ Mo, BSF, 57; La State Univ, MF, 58; Duke Univ, DF(forest ecol), 63. *Prof Exp:* Lectr mensuration & wood technol, Southern Ill Univ, 60-61; from asst prof to assoc prof forest ecol & chmn dept natural resources, Univ Conn, 63-75; chmn, 75-81, PROF, DEPT FORESTRY, FISHERIES & WILDLIFE, UNIV NEBR-LINCOLN, 81- *Mem:* Am Soc Photogram; Ecol Soc Am; Soc Am Foresters. *Res:* Forest ecology and aerial photo interpretation; ecology of bottomland hardwoods; radioecological techniques for study of longleaf pine root extension. *Mailing Add:* Dept of Forestry Fisheries & Wildlife Univ of Nebr Lincoln NE 68583

FERRIS, BENJAMIN GREELEY, JR, b Watertown, Mass, Jan 24, 19; m 42; c 5. ENVIRONMENTAL HEALTH, PULMONARY DISEASES. *Educ:* Harvard Col, AB, 40, Harvard Med Sch, MD, 43. *Prof Exp:* From intern to asst resident pediat, Children's Hosp, Boston, 43-48; from asst prof to assoc prof, 50-71, PROF ENVIRON HEALTH, SCH PUB HEALTH, HARVARD UNIV, 71- *Concurrent Pos:* Res fel physiol, Sch Pub Health, Harvard Univ, 48-50; asst physician med, Phillips Acad, Andover, Ma, 49-50; dir res & med care, Mary MacArthur Respirator Unit, 50-58; indust res physician, Ludlow Jute Co, India, 51; consult, Mass Gen Hosp, Lemuel Shattuck Hosp & Children's Med Ctr, 56-; dir environ health & safety, Harvard Univ Health Servs, 58-; lectr med, Med Sch, Tufts Univ, 65-; vis prof, Univ BC, 72-78. *Mem:* AAAS; Am Physiol Soc; Am Pub Health Asn; Am Epidemiol Soc; Int Epidemiol Asn. *Res:* Effects of air-borne pollutants on human health; low levels of air pollution and exposures at work. *Mailing Add:* Dept of Physiol Harvard Univ Sch Pub Health Boston MA 02115

FERRIS, BERNARD JOE, b Denver, Colo, Nov 16, 22; m; c 2. PETROLEUM GEOLOGY, ORGANIC GEOCHEMISTRY. *Educ:* Colo Sch Mines, GeolE, 47, MGeolE, 48. *Prof Exp:* Geologist, Shell Oil Co, 48-53, dist geologist, 53-54, div explor mgr, 54-56, sr geologist, 56-60, mgr geol dept, Shell Develop Co, 60-63, chief geologist, Midland Area, Shell Oil Co, 63-66, div explor mgr, 66-69, sr res assoc, Shell Develop Co, 69-70, mgr geol dept, 70-71, mgr explor training dept, Shell Oil Co, 71-73, chief geologist, Western Region, 73-76, chief geologist, Int Region, 76-79; INDEPENDENT GEOL CONSULT, 79- *Mem:* Am Asn Petrol Geologists; Geol Soc Am. *Res:* Use of fossil calcareous algae in biostratigraphy; geological and chemical investigations of the origin and migration of petroleum hydrocarbons in the subsurface. *Mailing Add:* 4038 S Wisteria Way Denver CO 80237

FERRIS, CLIFFORD D, b Philadelphia, Pa, Nov 19, 35. BIOENGINEERING, ELECTRICAL ENGINEERING. *Educ:* Univ Pa, BS, 57, MS, 58; George Washington Univ, DSc(math, physics), 62. *Prof Exp:* Engr, electronic instrument div, Burroughs Corp, Pa, 53, basic physics div, res ctr, 55-56; res asst, Univ Pa, 56-57, res assoc electromed res lab & consult, dept pharmacol & dept therapeut res, univ hosp, 57-59, asst instr elec eng, 58-59; from instr to assoc prof, George Washington Univ, 59-63; assoc prof, Drexel Inst Technol, 63-64 & Univ Md, 64-68; assoc prof, 68-73, actg dean, Col Eng, 73-74, PROF ELEC ENG, UNIV WYO, 73-, DIR BIOENG PROG, 74- *Concurrent Pos:* Systs analyst, res lab, Melpar, Inc, Va, 59; consult, instrument eng & develop br, NIH, 60-62; vis scientist, Armed Forces Inst Path, Walter Reed Army Med Ctr, DC, 61-68. *Mem:* AAAS; Inst Elec & Electronics Engrs; NY Acad Sci. *Res:* Interaction of electromagnetic fields with biological systems; bioinstrumentation; bioelectrodes. *Mailing Add:* Dept Elec Eng Univ Wyo Laramie WY 82070

FERRIS, CLINTON S, JR, b Chicago, Ill, Aug 13, 33; m 59; c 3. EXPLORATION GEOLOGY. *Educ:* Colo Col, BS, 55; Univ Sask, MSc, 61; Univ Wyo, PhD(geol), 65. *Prof Exp:* From geologist to sr geologist, Kerr-McGee Corp, 64-69, explor adv, 70-71; proj mgr, Tex Gulf Inc, 72-73; chief geologist, Urania Explor Inc, 73-77; CHIEF GEOLOGIST, RESERVE OIL & MINERALS CORP, 77- *Mem:* Soc Econ Geol; Am Inst Prof Geologists. *Res:* Sandstone uranium genesis and ore controls; porphyry copper genesis and relation to rock alteration; structural geology; occurrences and formation of the uranium mineral brannerite; Athabasca region uranium geology. *Mailing Add:* 11421 W 59 Ave Arvada CO 80004

FERRIS, CRAIG, b Los Angeles, Calif, Mar 22, 13; m 34; c 2. GEOPHYSICS. *Educ:* Friends Univ, AB, 34. *Hon Degrees:* LLD, Friends Univ, 74. *Prof Exp:* Geophysicist, Am Seismograph Co, 36-38 & Mott-Smith Corp, 38-43; partner, E V McCollum & Co, 43-79; PRES, GRAVIMETRICS, INC, 80- *Concurrent Pos:* Pres, Tulsa Sci Found, 69. *Mem:* Soc Explor Geophys (secy-treas, 64); Am Asn Petrol Geologists; Am Geophys Union; Soc Independent Petrol Earth Scientists; Am Inst Prof Geologists. *Res:* Exploration for petroleum and minerals. *Mailing Add:* 1243 E 28th St Tulsa OK 74114

FERRIS, DEAM HUNTER, b Mankato, Minn, July 8, 12; m 35; c 4. VETERINARY MICROBIOLOGY. *Educ:* Drake Univ, AB, 34, MA, 38; Univ Wis, PhD(vet sci, zool), 53. *Prof Exp:* Teacher high schs, Iowa & Kans, 35-42; instr AV educ, Univ Wis, 46-48; prof biol & natural hist, Graceland Col, 48-57; from assoc prof to prof, 57-74, EMER PROF VET PATH & HYG, COL VET MED, UNIV ILL, URBANA, 74-; RES MICROBIOLOGIST, PLUM ISLAND ANIMAL DIS CTR, USDA, 74- *Concurrent Pos:* Virologist, Near East Animal Health Inst, Food & Agr Orgn, UN, 64-66. *Mem:* Fel AAAS; Am Soc Microbiol; Am Soc Parasitol; Wildlife Dis Asn; fel Royal Soc Health. *Res:* Host range and pathobiology of African malignant catarrhal fever and African swine fever; foot-and-mouth disease and rinderpest in deer; cytauxzoon-like protozoon of domestic cat; development of microfiche; handbooks and manuals on emergency diseases as well as research on computer-based and self-instructional autotutorial systems; development of a new immunofluorescence and peroxidase for trypanosomarypanosoma vivax and the adaptation of Colombian bovine T vivax to mice; development of simplified immunoelectroosmophoresis methods for diagnosis of African Swine Fever; lyophilization of reference antisera and African mink cell focus-inducing virus. *Mailing Add:* Plum Island Animal Dis Ctr USDA Greenport NY 11944

FERRIS, HORACE GARFIELD, b Los Angeles, Calif, Aug 3, 13; m 45; c 2. PHYSICS. *Educ:* Pomona Col, BA, 36; Univ Calif, Los Angeles, MA, 39, PhD(physics), 49. *Prof Exp:* Asst physics, Univ Calif, Los Angeles, 39-40; instr, Long Beach Jr Col, 41-42; civilian physicist, US Navy, 42-43, instr mil training prog, Pomona Col, 43-44; res assoc, Calif Inst Technol, 44-45; physicist, US Naval Ord Test Sta, 45-46; lectr physics, Univ Southern Calif, 46-49; instr, San Diego State Col, 49-51; asst res physicist, Scripps Inst, Univ Calif, 51-55; assoc prof physics, Chapman Col, 55-58; from asst prof to prof, 58-78, EMER PROF PHYSICS, CALIF STATE POLYTECH UNIV, POMONA, 78- *Concurrent Pos:* Consult, Robert Shaw Fulton Controls Co, 56-57, US Naval Radiol Defense Lab, 56-59, Civil Eng Lab, 59-60 & Hughes Aircraft Co, 57-69; assoc instr, Univ Calif, Los Angeles, 64-66. *Mem:* AAAS;

Acoust Soc Am; Am Asn Physics Teachers. *Res:* Geothermal gradient in ocean floor by probe methods; hydrodynamics of stratified fluids including the ocean; partial differential equations of physics; methods of mathematical physics; measurement of thermal conductivities at high temperatures by transient methods; underwater acoustics, including theory of sound transmission in the ocean. *Mailing Add:* 4934 Gentry Ave North Hollywood CA 91607

FERRIS, JAMES PETER, b Nyack, NY, July 25, 32; m 55; c 2. BIOCHEMISTRY, ORGANIC CHEMISTRY. *Educ:* Univ Pa, BS, 54; Ind Univ, PhD, 58. *Prof Exp:* Lectr chem, Ind Univ, 58; res assoc, Mass Inst Technol, 58-59; instr org chem, Fla State Univ, 59-60, asst prof, 61-64; res assoc, Salk Inst Biol Studies, 64-67; assoc prof, 67-74, PROF CHEM, RENSSELAER POLYTECH INST, 74-, CHMN DEPT, 80- *Concurrent Pos:* USPHS career award, 69-74; sr res assoc, NASA Ames Res Ctr, Moffett Field, Calif, 76. *Mem:* Inter-Am Photochem Soc; Am Chem Soc; The Chem Soc; Int Soc Study Origins of Life; AAAS. *Res:* Chemistry of the origins of life; atmospheric photochemistry; chemistry of hydrocyanic acid and nitriles; oxidase enzymes and cytochrome P-450; nucleoside synthesis. *Mailing Add:* Dept of Chem Rensselaer Polytech Inst Troy NY 12181

FERRIS, JOHN MASON, b Mt Vernon, NY, July 9, 27; m 53; c 2 NEMATOLOGY. ECOLOGY, PHYTOPATHOLOGY. *Educ:* Cornell Univ, BS, 51, PhD(plant path), 56. *Prof Exp:* Asst plant path, Cornell Univ, 51-56; asst plant pathologist, State Natural Hist Surv, Ill, 57-58; from asst prof to assoc prof, 58-75, PROF NEMATOL, PURDUE UNIV, 75- *Concurrent Pos:* Ed, Nematol News Letter, Soc Nematol, 63-65. *Mem:* AAAS; Am Phytopath Soc; Soc Nematol (treas, 74-77, secy, 80, vpres, 79-80, pres, 80-81); Soc Europ Nematol. *Res:* Ecology of soil and freshwater nematodes; integrated pest management. *Mailing Add:* Dept of Entom Purdue Univ West Lafayette IN 47906

FERRIS, PHILIP, b New York, NY, Mar 17, 30; m 53; c 2. ONCOLOGY. *Educ:* City Col New York, BS, 52, MS, 57; NY Univ, PhD(biol), 70. *Prof Exp:* Pub sch teacher, NY, 53-59; res asst, 60-69, RES ASSOC ONCOL, WALDEMAR MED RES FOUND, 69- *Concurrent Pos:* NSF res grant, 65-71; adj assoc prof cell biol, State Univ NY Col Old Westbury, 78. *Mem:* NY Acad Sci. *Res:* Cancer virology; immunology and cytokinetics of chloroleukemia; biomedical research. *Mailing Add:* 8 Cedar Dr S Old Bethpage NY 11804

FERRIS, ROBERT MONSOUR, biochemistry, neurochemistry, see previous edition

FERRIS, STEVEN HOWARD, b New York, NY, June 27, 43; c 2. GERONTOLOGY, NEUROBIOLOGY. *Educ:* Rensselaer Polytech Inst, BA, 65; Queens Col, MA, 67; City Univ NY, PhD(exp psychol), 70. *Prof Exp:* NRC res associateship, Submarine Med Res Lab, Naval Submarine Med Ctr, 70-72; asst prof, 79-81, EXEC DIR GERIAT PROG, DEPT PSYCHIAT, MED CTR NY UNIV, 73-, ASSOC PROF, 81- *Concurrent Pos:* Vis scientist, Brookhaven Nat Lab, 79-; consult, Psychiat Serv, Manhattan Vet Admin Med Ctr, 80- *Mem:* Am Psychol Asn; Am Geront Soc; Neurosci Soc; Int Neuropsychol Soc; Am Col Neuropsychopharmacology. *Res:* Gerontology; neuropsychology, neurobiology and psychopharmacology of memory; cognitive deficits in aging and senile dementia. *Mailing Add:* Dept Psychiat NY Univ Med Ctr 550 First Ave New York NY 10016

FERRIS, THOMAS FRANCIS, b Boston, Mass, Dec 27, 30; m 57; c 4. INTERNAL MEDICINE. *Educ:* Georgetown Univ, AB, 52; Yale Univ, MD, 56. *Prof Exp:* Intern, Osler Serv, Johns Hopkins Hosp, Baltimore, Md, 56-57; resident, New Haven Hosp, Conn, 60-62; from instr to asst prof med, Sch Med, Yale Univ, 63-67; from assoc prof to prof med, Col Med, Ohio State Univ, 67-78, dir renal dis, Univ Hosp, 67-78; PROF MED & CHMN DEPT, UNIV MINN, MINNEAPOLIS, 78- *Concurrent Pos:* USPHS clin fel renal dis, New Haven Hosp, Conn, 59-60, USPHS res fel, 62-63; John & Mary Markle scholar acad med, 64-69; vis investr, Regius Dept Med, Oxford Univ, 66-67. *Mem:* Am Fedn Clin Res; Am Soc Clin Invest; Am Soc Nephrology. *Res:* Renal physiology; hypertension; diseases of the kidney. *Mailing Add:* Univ of Minn 420 Delaware St SE Minneapolis MN 55455

FERRIS, VIRGINIA ROGERS, b Abilene, Kans, Mar 26, 27; m 53; c 2. NEMATOLOGY. *Educ:* Wellesley Col, BA, 49; Cornell Univ, MS, 52, PhD(plant path), 54. *Prof Exp:* Asst plant path, Cornell Univ, 49-52, asst prof, 54-56; consult plant path, 56-65; asst dean, Grad Sch, 71-75, asst provost, 76-79, from asst prof to assoc prof, 65-74, PROF ENTOM, PURDUE UNIV, WEST LAFAYETTE, 74- *Concurrent Pos:* Consult, NSF, 79- *Mem:* Soc Nematol (secy, 65-68, vpres, 68-69, pres, 69-70); Am Phytopath Soc; Ecol Soc Am; Soc Syst Zool; Asn Systematics Collections. *Res:* Nematode systematics, bionomics and ecology; plant diseases caused by nematodes. *Mailing Add:* Dept of Entom Purdue Univ West Lafayette IN 47906

FERRIS, WAYNE ROBERT, b Lockman, Iowa. CYTOLOGY. *Educ:* Univ Chicago, PhD(zool), 59. *Prof Exp:* Asst zool, Univ Chicago, 50-58; from instr to assoc prof, 58-66, PROF ZOOL, UNIV ARIZ, 66- *Res:* Myogenesis of vertebrates striated muscle; cytochemistry and ultrastructural aspects of induction mechanisms; electron microscopy. *Mailing Add:* Dept of Cell Biol Univ of Ariz Tucson AZ 85721

FERRIS-PRABHU, ALBERT VICTOR MICHAEL, b Meerut, Uttar Pradesh, India, Sept 5, 32; m 67; c 1. SOLID STATE PHYSICS, MEMORY TECHNOLOGY. *Educ:* Univ Dayton, BME, 57; Princeton Univ, MSE & MA, 60; Cath Univ Am, PhD(solid state physics), 63. *Prof Exp:* Res assoc mat theory group, Mass Inst Technol, 63-64; physicist, Goddard Space Flight Ctr, NASA, 64-66; assoc prof appl sci, George Washington Univ, 66-68; ADV PHYSICIST, COMPONENTS DIV, IBM CORP, 68- *Concurrent Pos:* Consult, Wolf Res & Develop Corp, 67-68 & Adaptronics Inc, 68; adj prof, Univ Vt, 78- *Mem:* Am Phys Soc; sr mem Inst Elec & Electronics Engrs; fel AAAS. *Res:* Diffusion kinetics; semiconductors; nonvolatile memories; magnetism; error correction; systems performance evaluation; bipolar products yield management. *Mailing Add:* Gen Tech Div B18-970 COL E214 IBM Corp Essex Junction VT 05452

FERRISS, DONALD P, b Rutherford, NJ, Apr 17, 24; m 52; c 3. PHYSICAL METALLURGY, CERAMICS. *Educ:* Stevens Inst Technol, ME, 50, MS, 54; Mass Inst Technol, ScD(metall), 61. *Prof Exp:* Res engr powder metall, Stevens Inst Technol, 50-57; instr metall, Mass Inst Technol, 57-61; res metallurgist, 61-66, res assoc, 66-77, SR RES ASSOC, ENG TECHNOL LAB, E I DU PONT DE NEMOURS & CO, INC, 77- *Mem:* Am Soc Metals; Am Inst Mining, Metall & Petrol Engrs; Sigma Xi; Am Powder Metall Inst. *Res:* Special processing of metal powders; deformation and fracture of metals; mechanical properties of ceramics; wear of materials. *Mailing Add:* Eng Technol Lab Exp Sta E I du Pont de Nemours & Co Wilmington DE 19898

FERRISS, GREGORY STARK, b Summit, NJ, Aug 2, 24; m 57; c 2. NEUROLOGY. *Educ:* Harvard Univ, AB, 46; Tulane Univ, MD, 51. *Prof Exp:* From instr to assoc prof, 55-67, PROF NEUROL, SCH MED, LA STATE UNIV, 67- *Concurrent Pos:* Vis physician, Charity Hosp La, New Orleans, 55- & South Baptist Hosp, 63-; consult, DePaul Hosp, Coliseum House, Childrens' Hosp; head neurol sect, Collab Child Develop Proj, Charity Hosp La, 60- *Mem:* Am Acad Neurol; Am Electroencephalog Soc; Am Epilepsy Soc; Asn Res Nerv & Ment Dis. *Res:* Clinical electroencephalography, ambulatory monitoring, evoked potentials, epilepsy and sleep. *Mailing Add:* Dept of Neurol State Univ Sch of Med New Orleans LA 70112

FERRO, DAVID NEWTON, b San Bernardino, Calif, Sept 26, 46; m 67; c 2. ENTOMOLOGY. *Educ:* San Jose State Univ, BA, 69; Wash State Univ, MS, 73, PhD(entom), 75. *Prof Exp:* Technician entom, Univ Calif, Riverside, 68-70; res asst, Wash State Univ, 70-74; lectr, Lincoln Col, Univ Canterbury, 74-77; asst prof, 78-81, ASSOC PROF ENTOM, UNIV MASS, 81- *Mem:* Entom Soc Am; Sigma Xi; NY Acad Sci. *Res:* Insect pest management; effects of the insects microclimate on insect pest management. *Mailing Add:* Dept of Entom Univ Mass Amherst MA 01003

FERRON, JEAN H, b Montreal, Que, Mar 5, 48; m 77; c 1. ETHOLOGY. *Educ:* Univ Montreal, BSc, 69, MSc, 71, PhD(biol & ethol), 74. *Prof Exp:* Res fel, Dept Zool, Univ Alta, 75; PROF ETHOL & ECOL, DEPT PURE SCI, UNIV QUE, RIMOUSKI, 75- *Mem:* Animal Behav Soc; Am Soc Mammal; Wildlife Soc Can; Wildlife Soc. *Res:* An evolutionary and ecological approach of the ethology of Sciurid rodents; interspecific comparison of ontogeny, individual and social behavior; activity cycles and foraging behavior; snowshoe hare social behavior. *Mailing Add:* Dept of Pure Sci Univ of Que 300 av des Ursulines Rimouski PQ G5L 3A1 Can

FERRON, JOHN R(OYAL), b Anoka, Minn, Oct 29, 26; m 51; c 4. CHEMICAL ENGINEERING, PHYSICAL CHEMISTRY. *Educ:* Univ Minn, BChE, 48, MS, 50; Univ Wis, PhD(chem eng), 58. *Prof Exp:* Instr chem, Macalester Col, 48-49; asst chem eng, Univ Minn, 49-50; engr, E I du Pont de Nemours & Co, 50-54; instr chem eng, Univ Wis, 54-57; from asst prof to prof, Univ Del, 58-69; PROF CHEM ENG, UNIV ROCHESTER, 69- *Concurrent Pos:* NSF sci fac fel, Univ Naples, 66-67; vis prof, Calif Inst Technol & Univ Calif, Berkeley, 78-79. *Mem:* Am Chem Soc; Am Inst Chem Engrs; NY Acad Sci; Soc Natural Philos. *Res:* High temperature reactions and transport phenomena; fluidization; optimization; applied mathematics. *Mailing Add:* Dept of Chem Eng Univ of Rochester Rochester NY 14627

FERRONE, FRANK ANTHONY, b New York, NY, Aug 13, 47. BIOLOGICAL SELF ASSEMBLY, MACROMOLECULAR DYNAMICS. *Educ:* Manhattan Col, BS, 69; Princeton Univ, MA, 71, PhD(physics), 74. *Prof Exp:* Instr physics, Princeton Univ, 74-75, vis fel, 75-76; staff fel, Lab Chem Physics, NIH, 76-80; ASST PROF PHYSICS, DREXEL UNIV, 80- *Mem:* Am Phys Soc; Biophys Soc; Sigma Xi. *Res:* Conformational kinetics of normal hemoglobin & kinetic mechanism of the self assembly of sickle-cell hemoglobin using optical techniques. *Mailing Add:* Dept Physics Drexel Univ Philadelphia PA 19104

FERRONE, RONALD ANTHONY, b Altoona, Penn, June 16, 48; m 76. CARDIOVASCULAR PHYSIOLOGY. *Educ:* Pa State Univ, BS, 70, MS, 72, PhD(physiol), 76. *Prof Exp:* Fel, Alton Ochsner Med Found, 76-78; RES INVESTR, SQUIBB INST MED RES, 78- *Concurrent Pos:* Instr physiol, Dept Continuing Educ, Pa State Univ, 73-75; adj instr, Dept Pharmacol, Sch Med, Tulane Univ, 76-78; Am Heart Asn fel grant, 77-78. *Mem:* AAAS; Am Heart Asn. *Res:* Hypertensive diseases; atherosclerosis. *Mailing Add:* Dept of Pharmacol PO Box 4000 Princeton NJ 08540

FERRRARIO, CARLOS MARIA, US citizen. CARDIOVASCULAR PHYSIOLOGY, CARDIOVASCULAR DISEASES. *Educ:* Mariano Moreno Col, Agr, BS, 56; Univ Buenos Aires, MD, 63. *Prof Exp:* Asst physiol, Med Sch, Univ Buenos Aires, 63-64; assoc mem res staff, 70-71, MEM RES STAFF, CLEVELAND CLIN RES DIV, 71-, ACTG CHMN, DEPT CARDIOVASCULAR RES, 81- *Concurrent Pos:* Nat Sci Coun Agr fel, Univ Buenos Aires, 63-64; Swedish Int Agency fel, Gothenberg Univ, 64-66; Nat Lung & Heart Insts grant, Cleveland Clin Found, 67-; estab investr cardiovasc res, Am Heart Asn, 72-77, mem med adv bd, Coun High Blood Pressure Res. *Mem:* Am Heart Asn; Am Col Cardiol; Physiol Soc. *Res:* Investigation into the cause of arterial hypertension, especially in reference to its hemodynamic, humoral and nervous system participation. *Mailing Add:* Cleveland Clin Res Div 9500 Euclid Ave Cleveland OH 44106

FERRY, ANDREW P, b New York, NY, June 15, 29; m 64. OPHTHALMOLOGY, PATHOLOGY. *Educ:* Manhattan Col, BS, 50; Georgetown Univ, MD, 54. *Prof Exp:* Intern med, Duke Univ Hosp, 54-55; asst resident, Hosp, Univ Mich, Ann Arbor, 57-58; resident ophthal, NY Hosp-Cornell Med Ctr, 58-61; dir Jordan Eye Bank, St John Ophthalmic Hosp, Jerusalem, Jordan, 64-65; assoc prof opthal, Mt Sinai Sch Med, 65-76, prof, 76-78, asst prof path, 65-78; PROF & CHMN, DEPT OPHTHAL, MED COL, VA COMMONWEALTH UNIV, 79- *Concurrent Pos:* Inst Neurol Dis & Blindness spec fel, Armed Forces Inst Path, 61-64; instr, Col Med, Cornell Univ, 60-61; consult, Manhattan Eye, Ear & Throat Hosp, NY, 66-78, Beth Israel Med Ctr, 67-78, Am Acad Ophthal & Otolaryngol, 69-,

City Hosp Ctr, Elmhurst, 74-78 & Richmond Vet Admin Hosp, 78- *Honors & Awards:* Kober Medal & Gold Medal Prev Med, Sch Med, Georgetown Univ, 54; Billings Bronze Medal, AMA, 65; appointed by Queen Elizabeth II to position of Officer in Grand Priory in Brit Realm of Most Venerable Order of Hosp of St John of Jerusalem, 68 and promoted to Comdr, 74. *Mem:* Fel Am Col Surg; Asn Res Vision & Ophthal; AMA; Am Ophthal Soc. *Res:* Ophthalmic pathology, especially pathology of ocular tumors. *Mailing Add:* Dept Opthal Med Col Va Richmond VA 23298

FERRY, DAVID K, b San Antonio, Tex, Oct 25, 40; m 62. ELECTRICAL ENGINEERING, SOLID STATE PHYSICS. *Educ:* Tex Tech Col, BS, 62, MS, 63; Univ Tex, Austin, PhD(elec eng), 66. *Prof Exp:* NSF fel physics, Univ Vienna, 66-67; from asst prof to assoc prof elec eng, Tex Tech Univ, 66-73; with res off, Off Naval Res, 73-77; PROF ELEC ENG & HEAD DEPT, COLO STATE UNIV, 77- *Mem:* Fel Am Phys Soc; Inst Elec & Electronics Engrs. *Res:* High field transport in semiconductors, physics and modeling of sub-micron semiconductor devices; optical interactions in semiconductors. *Mailing Add:* Dept of Elec Eng Colo State Univ Ft Collins CO 80523

FERRY, JAMES A, b Mazomanie, Wis, Sept 9, 37; m 64; c 2. NUCLEAR PHYSICS. *Educ:* Univ Wis, BS, 59, MS, 62, PhD(physics), 65. *Prof Exp:* Res assoc physics, Univ Wis, 65-66; mgr accelerator div & vpres, 66-70, vpres prod, 70-78, EXEC VPRES & CHIEF RES EXEC PROD, NAT ELECTROSTATICS CORP, 70- *Mem:* Am Phys Soc. *Res:* Low energy nuclear physics particle accelerator design and construction; ultra high vacuum technology. *Mailing Add:* Nat Electrostatics Corp Box 117 Middleton WI 53562

FERRY, JOHN DOUGLASS, b Dawson, YT, May 4, 12; US citizen; m 44; c 2. POLYMER CHEMISTRY. *Educ:* Stanford Univ, AB, 32, PhD(chem), 35. *Prof Exp:* Attached worker, Nat Inst Med Res, London, 32-34; pvt asst, Hopkins Marine Sta, Stanford, 35-36; instr biochem sci, Harvard Univ, 36-38, jr fel, Soc Fels, 38-41; assoc chemist, Oceanog Inst, Woods Hole, 41-45; from asst prof to prof, 46-73, chmn dept, 59-67, FARRINGTON DANIELS RES PROF CHEM, UNIV WIS-MADISON, 73- *Concurrent Pos:* NSF fel, Brussels, 59, Strasbourg & Kyoto, 68; vis lectr, Kyoto, 68; chmn, Int Comt Rheology, 63-68; vis lectr, Univ Grenoble, 73. *Honors & Awards:* Lilly Award, Am Chem Soc, 46, Kendall Award, 60 & Witco Award, 74; Bingham Medal, Soc Rheol, 53; High Polymer Physics Prize, Am Phys Soc, 66; Colwyn Medal, Brit Inst of the Rubber Indust, 72; Tech Award, Int Inst Synthetic Rubber Producers, 77; Charles Goodyear Medal, Rubber Div, Am Chem Soc, 81. *Mem:* Nat Acad Sci; fel Am Acad Arts & Sci; Am Chem Soc; Am Soc Biol Chemists; hon mem Fr Group Rheol. *Res:* Ultrafiltration; polymers of high molecular weight; proteins; mechanical properties of viscoelastic materials. *Mailing Add:* Dept of Chem Univ of Wis Madison WI 53706

FERRY, JOHN MOTT, b Madison, Wis, Mar 21, 49; m 77; c 2. PETROLOGY, GEOCHEMISTRY. *Educ:* Stanford Univ, BS & MS, 71; Harvard Univ, PhD(geol sci), 75. *Prof Exp:* Fel petrol, Geophys Lab, Carnegie Inst Washington, 75-77; asst prof, 77-80, ASSOC PROF GEOL, ARIZ STATE UNIV, 80- *Mem:* Mineral Soc Am; Am Geophys Union; AAAS; Sigma Xi. *Res:* Determination of temperature, pressure, fluid compositions, mass transfer, heat transfer and mineral reactions in the earth's crust during metamorphism. *Mailing Add:* Dept of Geol Ariz State Univ Tempe AZ 85281

FERSTANDIG, LOUIS LLOYD, b Brooklyn, NY, Apr 26, 24; m 46; c 3. ORGANIC CHEMISTRY. *Educ:* Univ Ill, BS, 44; Cornell Univ, PhD(chem), 49. *Prof Exp:* Res assoc, Univ Minn, 49-50; res chemist, Calif Res Corp, 50-56, group supvr, 56-60, res assoc, 60-64; res dir, 64-70, TECH DIR, HALOCARBON PROD CORP, 70-, V PRES, 77- *Mem:* Am Chem Soc; Am Soc Anesthesiologists. *Res:* Chemicals for use in plastics, fiber and surface coating; stereospecific polymers; isocyanates; molecular complexes; allophanates; hydrogen bonding; organic halogen compounds; toxicity of trace concentrations of anesthetics; metabolism of anesthetics. *Mailing Add:* Halocarbon Prod Corp 82 Burlews Ct Hackensack NJ 07601

FERTIG, JOHN WILLIAM, b Lebanon, Pa, Oct 13, 11; m 39; c 2. BIOSTATISTICS, PUBLIC HEALTH. *Educ:* Ursinus Col, AB, 31; Univ Minn, Minneapolis, PhD(statist), 35. *Hon Degrees:* Dr, Fac Med, Univ Montevideo. *Prof Exp:* Assoc biometrician, Mem Found Neuroendocrine Res, Worcester, Mass, 35-37; res assoc biostatist, Sch Hyg & Pub Health, Johns Hopkins Univ, 37-40; prof, 40-76, EMER PROF BIOSTATIST, SCH PUB HEALTH, COLUMBIA UNIV, 76- *Concurrent Pos:* Vis lectr, Univ Ky, 38-40, Univ PR, 48-53 & Yale Univ & Univ Minn, 49; vis prof, NY Univ, 43-45; consult, Pan-Am Health Orgn, 53- *Honors & Awards:* Hon prof, Univ Chile & Univ Cayetano Heredia, Peru. *Mem:* AAAS; Am Pub Health Asn; Am Statist Asn; Inst Math Statist; Biomet Soc. *Res:* Tests of statistical hypotheses; bioassay; analysis of followup data; calibration curves; analysis of dental research, public health and medical data. *Mailing Add:* Columbia Univ Sch Pub Health 600 W 168th St New York NY 10032

FERTIG, STANFORD NEWTON, b Marlinton, WVa, July 10, 19; m 49; c 1. WEED SCIENCE. *Educ:* Univ WVa, BS, 46, MS, 47; Cornell Univ, PhD(weed sci), 50. *Prof Exp:* From asst prof to prof agron, Cornell Univ, 50-66; adminr, Am Res Ctr, 76-78, CHIEF, PESTICIDE IMPART ASSESSMENT STAFF, USDA, 78-; MEM STAFF, AM RES CTR, USDA, 77- *Concurrent Pos:* Vis assoc prof bot, Univ Philippines, Los Banos, 54-56; mem weeds sub-comt, Nat Acad Sci, 64-66, mem pesticide study panel, Agr Res Inst, 72-, secy, 73-75, chmn, 76 & 80, mem gov bd, 81; mem sub-comt fertilizers & pesticides, Nat Indust Pollution Control Coun, Dept of Com, 71-72; mem 73-, comtes dirs comt, Nat Agr Chem Asn, 73-, vchmn, 76, mem pest mgt comt, 73-, comt crop yields, 73-75, long range planning comt, 74, chmn sub-comt dirs relationships with USDA, 74-75; mem, Environ Protection Agency comt study pesticides, 72-73; US rep, Codex Comt Pesticides, 79-82. *Mem:* Weed Sci Soc Am; Am Soc Agron; Sigma Xi; Philippines Asn Adv Res; fel Weed Sci Soc Am. *Res:* Weed control; research in herbicides and growth regulators for agriculture; benefits of pesticides in agriculture. *Mailing Add:* Agr Res Ctr-USDA 351 Admin Bldg Washington DC 20250

FERTIS, DEMETER G(EORGE), b Athens, Greece, July 25, 26; nat US; m 53; c 2. STRUCTURAL DYNAMICS. *Educ:* Mich State Univ, BS, 52, MS, 55; Nat Tech Univ Athens, DE, 64. *Prof Exp:* Bridge design engr, Mich State Hwy Dept, 52-55, phys res engr, 56-57; asst prof eng mech, Wayne State Univ, 57-63; assoc prof civil eng, Univ Iowa, 64-66; PROF CIVIL ENG, UNIV AKRON, 66- *Concurrent Pos:* Consult, Atomic Power Develop Assocs, 57-, Power Reactor Develop Co, 57-, Ford Motor Res Ctr, 61- & Gen Motors Proving Grounds, 62- *Mem:* Am Soc Civil Engrs; Am Concrete Inst; Indust Math Soc; NY Acad Sci; Am Soc Eng Educ. *Res:* Structures; vibrations; urban planning; theoretical mechanics; acoustic stochastic method and approach to determine concrete material properties; developer of the method of the equivalent systems and the concept of the dynamic hinge. *Mailing Add:* Dept of Civil Eng Univ of Akron Akron OH 44325

FERTL, WALTER HANS, b Vienna, Austria, Mar 16, 40; m 65; c 2. GEOPHYSICS. *Educ:* Mining & Metall Col, Austria, Dipl Ing, 63, Dr mont, 71; Univ Tex, Austin, MS, 66, PhD(petrol eng), 68. *Prof Exp:* Asst mgr, Well Serv & Workover Dept, Austrian State Oil Co, Vienna, 63-65; res scientist, Prod Res Div, Continental Oil Co, 68-72, sr res scientist, 72-76; dir, Interpretation & Field Develop, 76-81, VPRES, DRESSER PETROL ENG SERV, DRESSER ATLAS, 81- *Concurrent Pos:* Lectr, Univ Zulia, Venezuela, 67 & 73; guest lectr, Mining & Metall Col, Austria, 71 & Tech Univ Istanbul, 71; ed, Log Analyst, Soc Prof Well Log Analysts. *Mem:* Soc Prof Well Log Analysts (pres, 78-81); Soc Petrol Eng; Can Well Logging Soc; Soc Explor Geophys; Am Asn Petrol Geologists. *Res:* Geophysical well logging research and tool responses; development and improvement of interpretation methods; laboratory and field investigations of physical and chemical rock properties with special emphasis on abnormally pressured formations. *Mailing Add:* Dresser Atlas Dresser Industs Inc Box 1407 Houston TX 77001

FERTZIGER, ALLEN PHILIP, b New York, NY, June 27, 41; m 70. NEUROPHYSIOLOGY, NEUROBIOLOGY. *Educ:* City Col New York, BS, 63; Univ Mich, PhD(physiol), 68. *Prof Exp:* Fel anat, Albert Einstein Col Med, 68-70; asst prof physiol, Med Sch, Univ Md, Baltimore, 70-78; FEL, JOHNS HOPKINS SCH PUB HEALTH & HYG, 78- *Mem:* Am Physiol Soc; Electroencephalog Soc; Soc Neurosci; Am Inst Biol Sci. *Res:* Electrophysiology of epilepsy; mechanism of action of anticonvulsant drugs; developmental neurobiology; health and behavior; health education; behavior and cardiovascular health. *Mailing Add:* 1801 Fairbank Rd Baltimore MD 21209

FERY, RICHARD LEE, b Salem, Ore, Dec 4, 43; m 70; c 1. GENETICS, PLANT BREEDING. *Educ:* Ore State Univ, BS, 66; Purdue Univ, PhD(plant genetics & breeding), 70. *Prof Exp:* Res horticulturist, 70-72, RES GENETICIST, US VEG LAB, AGR RES SERV, USDA, 72- *Concurrent Pos:* Assoc ed, J Am Soc Hort Sci, 81- *Honors & Awards:* Marian W Meadows Award, Am Soc Hort Sci, 71, Asgrow Award, 76. *Mem:* AAAS; Am Genetic Asn; Am Soc Hort Sci; Crops Sci Soc Am; Am Soc Agron. *Res:* Genetics of plant resistance to diseases and insects; breeding vegetable crop plants for disease and insect resistance. *Mailing Add:* US Veg Lab 2875 Savannah Hwy Charleston SC 29407

FERZIGER, JOEL H(ENRY), b Brooklyn, NY, Mar 24, 37; m 61; c 3. MECHANICAL ENGINEERING. *Educ:* Cooper Union, BChE, 57; Univ Mich, MSE, 59, PhD(nuclear eng), 62. *Prof Exp:* From asst prof to assoc prof nuclear eng, 61-72, PROF MECH ENG, STANFORD UNIV, 72- *Concurrent Pos:* Consult, Gen Elec Co & Encycl Britannica Films, 61-67 & Nielsen Eng & Res, 75-; Fulbright res fel, Netherlands, 67-68; vis prof, Queen Mary Col, London, 79. *Mem:* Am Phys Soc; Int Solar Energy Soc; Am Inst Aeronaut & Astronaut. *Res:* Kinetic theory of fluids; radiative transfer; numerical fluid mechanics; solar energy. *Mailing Add:* Dept Mech Eng Stanford Univ Stanford CA 94305

FESCIYAN, SEZAR, b Dec 7, 43. STATISTICAL MECHANICS. *Educ:* Ohio Univ, BS, 66; Yeshiva Univ, PhD(physics), 73. *Prof Exp:* Res assoc statist mech, Res Found State of NY, State Univ NY Albany, 72-78; res assoc, Dept Chem, Univ Minn, Minneapolis, 78-81; ASST PROF, DEPT PHYSICS, MANHATTAN COL, BRONX, NY, 81- *Res:* Equilibrium and nonequilibrium fluids; polymer physics. *Mailing Add:* Dept Physics Manhattan Col Bronx NY 10471

FESHBACH, HERMAN, b New York, NY, Feb 2, 17; m 40; c 3. PHYSICS. *Educ:* City Col New York, BS, 37; Mass Inst Technol, PhD(physics), 42; Lowell Technol Univ, ScD. *Prof Exp:* Tutor physics, City Col New York, 37-38; from asst prof to prof physics, 45-76, dir ctr theoret physics, 67-73, HEAD DEPT PHYSICS, MASS INST TECHNOL, 73-, CECIL & IDA GREEN PROF, 76- *Concurrent Pos:* Guggenheim fel, 54-55; Ford Found fel, 62-63; mem nuclear sci adv comt, Dept Energy/NSF, chmn, 79-80. *Honors & Awards:* Bonner Prize, Am Phys Soc, 73; Townsend-Harris Medal, City Col New York, 77. *Mem:* Nat Acad Sci; Am Acad Arts & Sci (vpres, 73-76); fel Am Phys Soc (vpres, 79, pres, 80). *Res:* Theoretical nuclear physics. *Mailing Add:* Dept Physics 6-113 Mass Inst Technol Cambridge MA 02139

FESSENDEN, PETER, b Newton, Mass, Sept 5, 37; m 59; c 2. RADIOLOGIC PHYSICS. *Educ:* Williams Col, AB, 59; Brown Univ, ScM, 63, PhD(physics), 65. *Prof Exp:* Fel nuclear physics, Los Alamos Sci Lab, 65-66; assoc prof physics, Ore State Univ, 67-72; postdoctoral appointment, Dept Radiol, 72-74, asst prof radiol, 74-81, ADJ PROF & DIR RADIOL PHYSICS, SCH MED, STANFORD UNIV, 81- *Mem:* Am Asn Physicists Med; Am Phys Soc; Radiation Res Soc. *Res:* Pion radiotherapy research; hyperthermia. *Mailing Add:* Dept of Radiol Stanford Univ Sch of Med Stanford CA 94305

FESSENDEN, RALPH JAMES, b Chicago, Ill, Oct 25, 32; m 55; c 1. CHEMISTRY. *Educ:* Univ Ill, BS, 55; Univ Calif, PhD(chem), 58. *Prof Exp:* From asst prof to assoc prof chem, San Jose State Col, 58-67; chmn dept, 67-73, PROF CHEM, UNIV MONT, 67- *Concurrent Pos:* Alfred P Sloan fel, 65-67. *Mem:* Am Chem Soc. *Res:* Organo-metallic chemistry; organo-silicon chemistry; author of numerous books. *Mailing Add:* Dept of Chem Univ of Mont Missoula MT 59801

FESSENDEN, RICHARD WARREN, b Northampton, Mass, Jan 22, 34; m 57; c 2. PHYSICAL CHEMISTRY. *Educ:* Univ Mass, BS, 55; Mass Inst Technol, PhD(phys chem), 58. *Prof Exp:* NSF fel, Calif Inst Technol, 58-59; fel, Mellon Inst, 59-62, sr fel, Radiation Res Labs, 62-78, prof chem, Carnegie-Mellon Univ, 67-78; MEM STAFF, RADIATION LAB, UNIV NOTRE DAME, 78- *Mem:* AAAS; Am Chem Soc; Am Phys Soc. *Res:* Electron spin resonance; radiation cehmistry. *Mailing Add:* Radiation Lab Univ of Notre Dame Notre Dame IN 46556

FESSENDEN-RADEN, JUNE MARION, b Whitinsville, Mass, Sept 2, 37; wid; c 1. BIOCHEMISTRY, TOXICOLOGY. *Educ:* Brown Univ, AB, 59; Tufts Univ, PhD(biochem), 63. *Prof Exp:* NSF fel biochem, Pub Health Res Inst of City of New York, Inc, 63-65 & Am Cancer Soc fel, 65-66; consult, Am Pub Health Serv, 66; asst prof, 66-74, NIH career develop award, 70-74, assoc dir acad affairs, Div Biol Sci, 74-75, vprovost undergrad educ, 75-78, ASSOC PROF BIOCHEM, BIOL & SOC, CORNELL UNIV, 74- *Concurrent Pos:* Mem, NIH Biochem Study Sect, 75-77, Middle States, 78-; vis res scholar humanities, Dartmouth Col, 81-83; NSF interdisciplinary incentive award, 82-83; chmn, Cornell Recombinant DNA res comt. *Mem:* AAAS; Am Soc Biol Chemists; Asn Women Sci. *Res:* Environmental chemicals, reproductive and fetal effects; chemical risk perception and management; environmental chemicals and the ethics with emphasis on laboratory health and safety; biology and society; undergraduate education. *Mailing Add:* 107 Cobb Ithaca NY 14850

FESSLER, JOHN HANS, b Vienna, Austria, June 15, 28; m 58; c 2. MOLECULAR BIOLOGY. *Educ:* Oxford Univ, BA, 49, BSc, 51, BA & MA, 52, PhD(biochem), 56. *Prof Exp:* Res fel biochem & med, Mass Gen Hosp & Harvard Med Sch, 56-58; sci officer biochem, Unit Body Temperature Res, Med Res Coun Eng, 58-61; sr res fel biophys & molecular biol, Calif Inst Technol, 61-66; assoc prof, 66-70, PROF MOLECULAR BIOL & BIOL, UNIV CALIF, LOS ANGELES, 70- *Concurrent Pos:* Arthritis & Rheumatism Found fel & Fulbright grant, Wellcome fel, Royal Soc Med, 59-60. *Mem:* Soc Biol Chem; Brit Biochem Soc; Soc Develop Biol. *Res:* Macromolecules of connective tissue; physical chemistry of proteins; developmental biology; ultracentrifugal analysis. *Mailing Add:* Molecular Biol Inst Dept Biol Univ of Calif Los Angeles CA 90024

FESTER, DALE A(RTHUR), b Sterling, Colo, Nov 7, 32; m 53; c 4. AEROSPACE ENGINEERING. *Educ:* Univ Denver, BS, 53, MS, 61. *Prof Exp:* Engr, Phillips Petrol Co, 53; proj assoc, GOG Lof, Consult Chem Eng, 56-61; sr engr, 61-62, design specialist, 62-67, staff engr, 67-70, sr res scientist, 70-72, sr group engr, 72-77, prog mgr, 77-79, MGR, DENVER DIV, MARTIN MARIETTA CORP, 79- *Concurrent Pos:* Proj asst solar energy, Univ Wis, 56-61. *Mem:* AAAS; Am Inst Chem Engrs; Am Inst Aeronaut & Astronaut. *Res:* Low gravity fluid behavior, high energy liquid propellants; cryogenic systems; pressurization systems; fluid mechanics; heat transfer; mass transfer; pressurized gas absorption; material compatibility; solar energy utilization. *Mailing Add:* 2916 S Fenton Denver CO 80227

FESTER, KEITH EDWARD, b Glendale, Calif, Nov 16, 42; m 67; c 2. ELECTROCHEMISTRY. *Educ:* Loyola Univ, Calif, BS, 64; Creighton Univ, MS, 66; Univ of the Pac, PhD(phys chem), 68. *Prof Exp:* ELECTROCHEMIST, MEDTRONIC, INC, 69- *Mem:* Am Chem Soc; Electrochem Soc; NY Acad Sci. *Res:* Complex ion polarography; applied research in the design and use of chemical cells as implantable power sources. *Mailing Add:* 5141 Brighton Lane New Brighton MN 55112

FETCHER, E(DWIN) S(TANTON), b Winnetka, Ill, Aug 9, 09; m 53; c 4. HEALTH SCIENCES. *Educ:* Harvard Univ, BS, 31; Univ Chicago, PhD(phys chem), 34. *Prof Exp:* Res chemist, Universal Oil Prod Co, 35-36 & Rockefeller Inst Med Res, 37; instr physiol, Univ Chicago, 37-40 & Univ Minn, 40-43; res physiologist, environ physiol & equip develop, Air Mat Command, US Air Force, 43-49; rancher & stockman, Fetcher Ranch, 49-62; res assoc, lab physiol hyg sch pub health, Univ Minn, Minneapolis, 62-70; cur, environ sci, Sci Mus Minn, St Paul, 70-72; prog exec, Mt Sinai Hosp, Minneapolis & Univ Minn, 72-75; CONSULT, 75- *Mem:* AAAS. *Res:* Membrane chemistry and physiology; water balance of marine mammals; emergency ocean survival personal equipment; special protective flight clothing; livestock production; agribusiness; epidemiology of cardiovascular diseases. *Mailing Add:* 12 Crocus Hill St Paul MN 55102

FETH, GEORGE C(LARENCE), b Pittsburgh, Pa, Aug 17, 31; m 57; c 3. DIGITAL INTEGRATED CIRCUITS & DEVICES. *Educ:* Carnegie Inst Technol, BS, 53, MS, 54, PhD(elec eng), 56. *Prof Exp:* Engr, Gen Elec Co, 56-61; mgr magnetic film devices res, 61-62, exploratory memory res, 62-64, integrated circuits & systs res, 64-65, res tech planning staff, 65-67, res staff mem memory & storage res, 67-69, mgr eng & syst anal, 69-71, RES STAFF MEM, THOMAS J WATSON RES CTR, IBM CORP, 71- *Mem:* Sr mem Inst Elec & Electronics Engrs. *Res:* Self-aligned bipolar transistors, devices and circuits fo integrated digital circuits (VLSI); control memory and storage devices and systems; computer power supplies; magnetic memories; tunnel-diode memories; integrated circuits and systems; computer power supplies, memory and storage devices and systems. *Mailing Add:* Thomas J Watson Res Ctr IBM Corp PO Box 218 Yorktown Heights NY 10598

FETKOVICH, JOHN GABRIEL, b Aliquippa, Pa, June 9, 31; m 58; c 2. HIGH ENERGY PHYSICS, ENERGY CONVERSION. PHYSICS. *Educ:* Carnegie Inst Technol, BS, 53, MS, 55, PhD(physics), 59. *Prof Exp:* Res physicist, 59-61, from asst prof to assoc prof, 61-68, PROF PHYSICS, CARNEGIE-MELLON UNIV, 68- *Concurrent Pos:* Consult, Argonne Nat Lab, 60-70, Argonne Univs Asn appointee, 70-71; consult, Rutherford High Energy Lab, Eng, 71-72. *Mem:* AAAS; Am Phys Soc; Am Asn Physics Teachers; Sigma Xi. *Res:* Physics of elementary particles; ocean thermal energy conversion. *Mailing Add:* Dept of Physics Carnegie-Mellon Univ Pittsburgh PA 15213

FETNER, ROBERT HENRY, b Savannah, Ga, Feb 22, 22; m 44; c 2. BIOLOGY. *Educ:* Univ Miami, BS, 50, MS, 52; Emory Univ, PhD(biol), 55. *Prof Exp:* Res asst prof appl biol, Eng Exp Sta, 55-58, res assoc prof, 59-64, res prof, 64-77, dir, Sch Biol, 65-77, PROF BIOL, NUCLEAR RES CTR, GA INST TECHNOL, 77- *Res:* Radiation biology; cellular physiology; cytogenetics. *Mailing Add:* 2219 Walker Dr Lawrenceville GA 30245

FETSCHER, CHARLES ARTHUR, b New York, NY, Dec 7, 12; m 42; c 3. ORGANIC POLYMER CHEMISTRY. *Educ:* Col of the Holy Cross, BS, 34, MS, 35; Columbia Univ, PhD(org chem), 38. *Prof Exp:* Res chemist, Cuban Mining Co, Cuba, 38-40 & Shawinigan Resins Corp, Mass, 41-45; asst dir res, Cluett Peabody & Co, NY, 45-55; dir cent res labs, Nopco Chem Co, 55-65; group mgr res, Hysol Div, Dexter Corp, 65-76; RETIRED. *Mem:* Fel AAAS; Fiber Soc; Am Chem Soc. *Res:* Resins, plastics and additives. *Mailing Add:* PO Box 523 Troy NY 12181

FETSKO, JACQUELINE MARIE, b Allentown, Pa, Jan 14, 26. PHYSICAL CHEMISTRY. *Educ:* Univ Pa, BA, 46; Lehigh Univ, MS, 53. *Prof Exp:* Tech asst, 49-55, res supvr, 55-61, asst res dir, 61-66, asst to dir, Ctr for Surface & Coating Res, 66-69, ed, 69-74, ASST RES DIR, NAT PRINTING INK RES INST, LEHIGH UNIV, 74-, ADMIN ASST, CTR FOR SURFACE & COATINGS RES, 76- *Concurrent Pos:* Asst ed, Encycl Org Coatings, 56-58; consult, Scott Paper Co, 56-58 & Handy & Harman, 59-60. *Mem:* Tech Asn Pulp & Paper Indust. *Res:* Printing ink-paper relationships; transfer; surface strength; optical properties. *Mailing Add:* Nat Printing Ink Res Inst Lehigh Univ Bethlehem PA 18015

FETT, E REINOLD, b Grand Haven, Mich, Sept 18, 27; m 51; c 2. ANALYTICAL CHEMISTRY. *Educ:* Hope Col, AB, 51; Univ Ill, MS, 53, PhD(chem), 55. *Prof Exp:* From asst res chemist to res chemist, 55-61, sr res scientist, 62-70, RES ASSOC, UNION OIL CO CALIF, 71- *Mem:* Am Chem Soc. *Res:* Development and application of instrumentation as applied to analytical chemistry. *Mailing Add:* Union Res Ctr Box 76 Brea CA 92621

FETT, GILBERT H(OWARD), electrical engineering, deceased

FETT, JOHN D, b New York, NY, Mar 2, 33; m 56; c 3. GEOLOGY, GEOPHYSICS. *Educ:* Redlands Univ, BS, 54; Univ Calif, Riverside, MA, 67. *Prof Exp:* Chemist, Naval Ord Test Sta, Calif, 54-55; gravity observer, Lamont Geol Observ, Columbia Univ, 56-57; res asst, Inst Geophys, Univ Calif, Los Angeles, 57-59; geologist, Beylik Drilling Co, 59-60; consult, John D Fett & Assocs, 60-69; prin consult, Earth Sci Assocs, 69-73; PRES, EARTH SCI & ENG, 73- *Concurrent Pos:* Dir & vpres, Eastern Munic Water Dist. *Mem:* Fel Geol Soc Am; Soc Explor Geophys; Seismol Soc Am; Am Geophys Union; Am Water Resources Asn. *Res:* New techniques for the application of geophysics to problems in engineering geology and ground water studies. *Mailing Add:* 27770 Pachea Trail Hemet CA 92343

FETTE, CLARENCE WILLIAM, mathematical physics, see previous edition

FETTER, ALEXANDER LEES, b Philadelphia, Pa, May 16, 37; m 62; c 2. THEORETICAL CONDENSED MATTER PHYSICS. *Educ:* Williams Col, AB, 58; Rhodes Scholar, Oxford Univ, BA, 60, MA, 64; Harvard Univ, PhD(physics), 63. *Prof Exp:* Miller res fel physics, Univ Calif, Berkeley, 63-65; from asst prof to assoc prof, 65-74, assoc dean undergrad studies, 76-79, PROF PHYSICS, STANFORD UNIV, 74- *Concurrent Pos:* Sloan res fel, 68-70. *Mem:* Fel Am Phys Soc; AAAS. *Res:* Low-temperature behavior of quantum fluids, especially superfluid helium and type-II superconductors; general theory of many-particle systems; quantum hydrodynamics. *Mailing Add:* Dept of Physics Stanford Univ Stanford CA 94305

FETTER, ARTHUR WILLIAMS, b Lakeville, Ohio, Apr 4, 37; m 60; c 2. VETERINARY PATHOLOGY. *Educ:* Ohio State Univ, DVM, 61, MSc, 68, PhD(vet path), 70. *Prof Exp:* Gen vet pract, 63-66; NIH fel vet path, Ohio State Univ, 66-70, assoc prof vet path, 70-78; ASSOC PROF & HEAD, LAB LARGE ANIMAL PATH, SCH VET MED, UNIV PA, 78- *Concurrent Pos:* Consult vet path, Procter & Gamble Co, 73- *Mem:* AAAS; Int Acad Path; Electron Micros Soc Am; Am Vet Med Asn; Res Workers Animal Dis. *Res:* Comparative orthopedic pathology with emphasis on nutritional, metabolic and neoplastic bone disease; evaluation of the effects of orthopedic techniques on the structure and function of bone. *Mailing Add:* Lab of Large Animal Path Univ of Pa Kennett Sq PA 19348

FETTER, BERNARD FRANK, b Baltimore, Md, Jan 21, 21; m 45; c 4. PATHOLOGY. *Educ:* Johns Hopkins Univ, AB, 41; Duke Univ, MD, 44. *Prof Exp:* From instr to assoc prof, 51-67, PROF PATH, MED CTR, DUKE UNIV, 67- *Mem:* AMA; Am Asn Path & Bact; Col Am Path. *Res:* Surgical pathology. *Mailing Add:* Med Ctr Duke Univ Box 3220 Durham NC 27710

FETTER, CHARLES WILLARD, JR, b Dayton, Ohio, Apr 15, 42; m 65; c 3. HYDROGEOLOGY, HYDROLOGY. *Educ:* DePauw Univ, AB, 64; Ind Univ, MA, 66, PhD(hydrol), 71. *Prof Exp:* Staff hydrogeologist, Holzmacher, McLendon & Murrell, 66-70; asst prof, 71-75, assoc prof, 75-78, dept chmn, 78-81, PROF GEOL, UNIV WIS-OSHKOSH, 78- *Concurrent Pos:* Prog mgr, Law Eng Testing Co, 81-82. *Mem:* Am Inst Prof Geologists; Am Geophys Union; Am Water Resources Asn; Am Water Works Asn; Nat Water Well Asn. *Res:* Contaminant transport in groundwater flow systems; monitoring of groundwater quality; regional groundwater flow systems; groundwater flow models. *Mailing Add:* Dept of Geol Univ of Wis Oshkosh WI 54901

FETTER, NEIL ROSS, analytical chemistry, see previous edition

FETTERMAN, HAROLD RALPH, b Jamaica, NY, Jan 17, 41; m 65; c 2. LASERS, EXPERIMENTAL SOLID STATE PHYSICS. *Educ:* Brandeis Univ, BA, 62; Cornell Univ, PhD(physics), 67. *Prof Exp:* Asst prof physics, Univ Calif, Los Angeles, 67-69; STAFF PHYSICIST, LINCOLN LAB,

MASS INST TECHNOL, 69- *Mem:* Am Phys Soc; fel Optical Soc Am; sr mem Inst Elec & Electronics Engrs; Sigma Xi. *Res:* Development and application of submillimeter sources and detectors, including the use of optically pumped molecular lasers and Schottky diode receivers in solid state physics. *Mailing Add:* Lincoln Lab Box 73 Lexington MA 02173

FETTEROLF, CARLOS DE LA MESA, JR, b Glenridge, NJ, Dec 28, 26; m 52; c 4. FISHERIES, POLLUTION BIOLOGY. *Educ:* Univ Conn, BS, 50; Mich State Univ, MS, 52. *Prof Exp:* From fishery biologist reservoir res to dist fishery biologist, Tenn Game & Fish Comn, 52-57; from chief biologist to supvr water qual appraisal, Bur Water Mgt, Mich Dept Natural Resources, 57-71; sci coordr water qual criteria develop, Nat Acad Sci & Eng, 71-72; chief environ scientist, Bur Water Mgt, Mich Dept Natural Resources, 72-75; EXEC SECY, GREAT LAKES FISHERY COMN, 75- *Concurrent Pos:* Mem, US Govt Interstate Water Pollution Tech Comts, 66-71; mem sci adv bd, Int Joint Comn, 72-; mem comt stand methods, Am Pub Health Asn, 72-73; chmn water qual objectives comt, Int Joint Comn, 72-75. *Mem:* NAm Benthol Soc (vpres, 64, pres, 66); Int Asn Great Lakes Res (vpres, 75, pres, 76); Am Fisheries Soc (Southern Div pres, 56); Fel Am Inst Fishery Res Biologists. *Mailing Add:* 1451 Green Rd Ann Arbor MI 48105

FETTERS, KARL L(EROY), b Alliance, Ohio, Nov 28, 09; m 32, 68; c 5. METALLURGICAL ENGINEERING. *Educ:* Carnegie Inst Technol, BS, 31; Mass Inst Technol, DSc(metall eng), 40. *Prof Exp:* Asst metallurgist, Nat Tube Co, 33-36; open hearth metallurgist, Youngstown Sheet & Tube Co, Ohio, 36-38, asst, 38-39, metallurgist, 40-41; asst prof metall & staff mem, Metals Res Lab, Carnegie Inst Technol, 41-43; spec metal engr, Youngstown Sheet & Tube Co, 43-50, asst to vpres in chg opers, 50-59, vpres res & develop, 59-70 & tech serv, 70-77; CONSULT ENGR, 77- *Mem:* Nat Acad Eng; Am Soc Metals; Am Inst Mining, Metall & Petrol Engrs (pres, 64-65); Am Iron & Steel Inst; Brit Iron & Steel Inst. *Res:* Slag metal reactions as applied to steelmaking; basic open hearth research; ingot structures; corrosion studies; electrolytic tin plate. *Mailing Add:* 7099 Oak Dr Poland OH 44514

FETTERS, LEWIS, b Toledo, Ohio, Mar 29, 36. PHYSICAL CHEMISTRY, POLYMER CHEMISTRY. *Educ:* Col Wooster, AB, 58; Univ Akron, PhD(chem), 62. *Prof Exp:* NSF fel polymer chem, Univ Akron, 62-63; Nat Acad Sci-Nat Res Coun fel, Nat Bur Standards, 63-65; prof polymer chem, 67-77, PROF CHEM & PROF POLYMER SCI, INST POLYMER SCI, UNIV AKRON, 77- *Res:* Ionic polymerization kinetics; polymer rheology and synthesis; solution properties of polymers; radiation polymerization. *Mailing Add:* Inst of Polymer Sci Univ of Akron Akron OH 44325

FETTES, EDWARD MACKAY, b Brooklyn, NY, Jan 10, 18; m 41, 53, 80; c 9. POLYMER CHEMISTRY. *Educ:* Mass Inst Technol, SB, 40; Polytech Inst Brooklyn, PhD(chem), 57. *Prof Exp:* Develop chemist, US Rubber Co, RI, 40-41; res chemist, Kendall Co, Mass, 41-42; res chemist, Thiokol Chem Corp, NJ, 42-44, group leader, 44-45, asst develop mgr, 45-46, mgr develop dept, 46-50 & res & develop dept, 51-58, dir res & develop, 58-60; mgr plastics res, Koppers Co, Inc, 60-70; tech dir, Northern Petrochem Co, 70-81; RETIRED. *Concurrent Pos:* Consult, 81- *Mem:* AAAS; Soc Plastics Engrs; Plastics & Rubber Inst; The Chem Soc; Sigma Xi. *Res:* Elastomers; plastics; resins. *Mailing Add:* 61 Azalea Dr Harwich MA 02645

FETTES, JAMES JOSEPH, b Ottawa, Ont, Oct 30, 14; m 45; c 3. FOREST ENTOMOLOGY. *Educ:* Univ NB, BSc, 45; Univ Toronto, PhD(forest entom), 51. *Prof Exp:* Res officer, Forest Biol Div, Can Dept Agr, 45-50, head chem control sect, Can Dept Forestry, 51-64, DIR CHEM CONTROL RES INST, ENVIRON CAN, 64- *Concurrent Pos:* Mem, Interdept Comt Forest Spraying Opers, 58-66, entom panel subcomt, Defence Res Bd, 62-66 & Fed Interdept Comt Pesticides, 63-66; dir, Int Agr Aviation Centre, The Hague, Netherlands, 64-; mem assoc comt agr & forestry aviation, Nat Res Coun Can, 65-66. *Mem:* Entom Soc Can; Can Inst Forestry. *Res:* Direct control of forest pests; airplane spraying and forestry aviation; forest insect toxicology; research and development of aircraft spraying equipment. *Mailing Add:* RR 2 Ottawa ON K2C 3H1 Can

FETTIS, HENRY EASON, b East Orange, NJ, May 17, 15; m 59. APPLIED MATHEMATICS. *Educ:* Wittenberg Univ, AB, 39; Ohio State Univ, MS, 52. *Prof Exp:* Res math, Aircraft Lab, US Air Force Wright-Patterson AFB, 42-50, res math, Aerospace Res Labs, 50-72; consult appl math, Technol Inc, 72-73; PVT CONSULT, 73- *Concurrent Pos:* NSF fel, Standford Univ, 60-61; consult, Aerospace Res Labs, 72-73. *Mem:* Soc Indust & Appl Math; Am Inst Aeronaut & Astronaut; Math Asn Am; Am Acad Mech. *Res:* Numerical and classical analysis and aeroelasticity; scientific writing. *Mailing Add:* Apt 62 1885 California Mountain View CA 94041

FETZER, HOMER D, b San Antonio, Tex, Oct 19, 32; m 54; c 5. ATOMIC PHYSICS, NUCLEAR PHYSICS. *Educ:* St Mary's Univ, Tex, BS, 54; Univ Tex, MA, 59, PhD(electron scattering), 65. *Prof Exp:* From instr to assoc prof, 59-69, chmn dept, 65-69 & 73-75, PROF PHYSICS, ST MARY'S UNIV, 70-, CHMN DEPT, 77- *Concurrent Pos:* NSF sci fac fel, 63-65. *Mem:* Am Asn Physics Teachers; Sigma Xi. *Res:* Use of low energy accelerator for education and research; x-ray analysis of trace elements. *Mailing Add:* Dept of Physics St Mary's Univ San Antonio TX 78284

FEUCHT, DONALD LEE, b Akron, Ohio, Aug 25, 33; m 58; c 2. ELECTRICAL ENGINEERING. *Educ:* Valparaiso Univ, BS, 55; Carnegie Inst Technol, MS, 56, PhD(elec eng), 61. *Prof Exp:* From instr to prof elec eng, Carnegie-Mellon Univ, 58-77, assoc head dept, 69-73, assoc dean eng, 73-77; br chief photovoltaic res & develop, Solar Technol Div, US Dept Energy, 77-78; mgr, Photovoltaic Prog Off, 78-80, mgr, Photovoltaics Div, 80, assoc dir, Res & Develop, 81, DEP DIR, SOLAR ENERGY RES INST, 81- *Concurrent Pos:* Consult, Technograph Printed Circuits, Inc, 61, Union Carbide Corp, 63, Power Components, 65-67, PPG Industs, 67-69, Aluminum Asn Am, 67-69 & Essex Int, 67-74. *Mem:* Am Phys Soc; Am Vacuum Soc; fel Inst Elec & Electronics Engrs; Electrochem Soc. *Res:* Theoretical and experimental properties of semiconductor heterojunctions; fabrication and electrical and optical properties of semiconductor devices; integrated circuits; solar energy; photovoltaic devices. *Mailing Add:* Solar Energy Res Inst 1617 Cole Blvd Golden CO 80401

FEUCHT, JAMES ROGER, b Denver, Colo, June 6, 33; m 56; c 3. HORTICULTURE, BOTANY. *Educ:* Colo State Univ, BS, 56; Mich State Univ, MS, 57, PhD(hort), 60. *Prof Exp:* Teaching asst hort, Mich State Univ, 56-60; asst prof, Western Ill Univ, 60 & Rutgers Univ, 61-66; EXTEN PROF HORT & EXTEN HORTICULTURIST, COLO STATE UNIV, 66- *Concurrent Pos:* Consult landscape mgt. *Res:* Landscape horticulture; air-layering of pine and spruce using several potential rooting hormones; effects of gibberellin A-3 on cell growth in Phaseolus vulgaris L, an anatomical study; various applied research in insect control on landscape plants. *Mailing Add:* 909 York St Denver CO 80206

FEUCHTWANG, THOMAS EMANUEL, b Budapest, Hungary, May 21, 30; m 53; c 4. SOLID STATE PHYSICS, SURFACE PHYSICS. *Educ:* Ga Inst Technol, BEE, 53; Calif Inst Technol, MS, 54; Stanford Univ, PhD(microwave theory), 60. *Prof Exp:* Res asst, Microwave Lab, Stanford Univ, 54-59; res assoc physics, Univ Ill, 60-62; asst prof physics, Univ Minn, Minneapolis, 62-65; assoc prof, 65-70, PROF PHYSICS, PA STATE UNIV, UNIVERSITY PARK, 70- *Concurrent Pos:* Vis prof, Dept Physics, Tel-Aviv Univ, Israel, 71-72; Lady Davis vis prof, Israel Inst Technol, 78-79; vis prof, Dept Physics, Univ Hawaii, 80-81. *Mem:* Am Phys Soc; Sigma Xi. *Res:* Lattice dynamics; electronic structure of point defects in ionic crystals; theory of low energy electron scattering from single crystals; many and single particle tunneling phenomena across interfaces; field and photoemission. *Mailing Add:* Dept of Physics Pa State Univ University Park PA 16802

FEUER, GEORGE, b Szeged, Hungary, Mar 12, 21; m 49; c 3. BIOCHEMICAL PHARMACOLOGY, PATHOLOGICAL CHEMISTRY. *Educ:* Univ Szeged, BS, 43, PhD(phys chem) & high sch teaching dipl, 44; Hungarian Acad Sci, Cand Med Sci, 52. *Prof Exp:* Asst lectr org chem, Univ Szeged, 45-46, sr lectr biochem, 46-48; sr lectr, Univ Budapest, 48-50; sr res assoc, Hungarian Acad Sci, 50-53, head muscular & neurochem, 53-56; head biochem, Cancer Res Inst, Budapest, 56; guest worker, Pasteur Inst, Paris, 57; sr res assoc neurochem, Inst Psychiat, Univ London, 57-62; sr res assoc neuropsychiat, Med Res Coun, Carshalton, Eng, 62-63; head biochem, Brit Indust Biol Res Asn, Carshalton, 63-68; from asst prof to assoc prof path chem, 68-74, PROF CLIN BIOCHEM, UNIV TORONTO, 74-, PROF PHARMACOL & TOXICOL, 79- *Concurrent Pos:* Prof biochem, Eotvos Lorand Univ, 50-53; secy biochem comt, Hungarian Acad Sci, 52-56; chmn session, Fourth Int Goitre Conf, London, Eng, 60; vis prof, Warner-Lambert Res Inst, Can, 69-73 & Food & Drug Admin, 75-77. *Honors & Awards:* Res Award, Budapest County Coun, 45; Order of Merit, 2nd Class, Hungarian People's Repub, 53. *Mem:* Fel Royal Inst Chem; NY Acad Sci; Am Chem Soc; Soc Toxicol; Can Biochem Soc. *Res:* Mechanism of muscular contraction; neurochemistry; metabolism of thyroid and other hormones in connection with emotional behavior; biochemical organization of the liver function in relation to its response to drugs and toxic compounds; iatrogenic diseases. *Mailing Add:* Dept Clin Biochem Univ Toronto Rm 521 Banting Inst Toronto ON M5G 1L5 Can

FEUER, HENRY, b Stanislau, Austria, Apr 4, 12; nat US; m 46. ORGANIC CHEMISTRY. *Educ:* Univ Vienna, MS, 34, PhD(org chem), 37. *Prof Exp:* Fel, Sorbonne, 39 & Purdue Univ, 43-46; pharmacist, Toledo Hosp, Ohio, 41-43; instr chem, Univ Exten, Ind Univ, 46; from asst prof to prof, 46-68, EMER PROF CHEM, PURDUE UNIV, WEST LAFAYETTE, 68- *Concurrent Pos:* Vis prof, Hebrew Univ, Israel, 64-71 & Beijing Inst Technol, China, 79. *Mem:* AAAS; Am Chem Soc; Sigma Xi. *Res:* Organic nitrogen compounds; synthesis and reactions of nitro compounds and heterocyclic systems. *Mailing Add:* Dept Chem Purdue Univ West Lafayette IN 47906

FEUER, PAULA BERGER, b New York, NY, Feb 11, 22; m 46. PHYSICS. *Educ:* Hunter Col, BA, 41; Purdue Univ, MS, 46, PhD(physics), 51. *Prof Exp:* Instr physics, 46-55, from asst prof to assoc prof eng sci, 55-65, PROF ENG SCI, PURDUE UNIV, WEST LAFAYETTE, 65- *Concurrent Pos:* Vis prof, Hebrew Univ Israel, 64. *Mem:* Am Phys Soc; Soc Eng Sci (treas, 64-69). *Res:* Solid state physics; electronic properties solids; gas-surface interactions. *Mailing Add:* Purdue Univ Sch Aeronaut & Astronaut Eng West Lafayette IN 47906

FEUER, RICHARD DENNIS, b New York, NY, Sept 2, 40. ALGEBRA. *Educ:* Cornell Univ, BA, 62; Courant Inst, NY Univ, MS, 65, PhD(math), 70. *Prof Exp:* Adj Lectr math, New York City Community Col, 70-74; instr, Queens Col, City Univ New York, 71-77; adj asst prof, Medgar Eiers Col & York Col, City Univ New York, 72-74; ASST PROF MATH, NY INST TECHNOL, 74- *Mem:* Math Asn Am; Am Math Soc. *Res:* Combinational group theory. *Mailing Add:* 230 Westend Ave New York NY 10023

FEUER, ROBERT CHARLES, b New York, NY, Feb 23, 36; m 69. ENVIRONMENTAL BIOLOGY, HERPETOLOGY. *Educ:* Cornell Univ, BS, 56; Tulane Univ, MS, 58. Univ Utah, PhD, 66. *Prof Exp:* Asst, Tulane Univ, 56-58; asst prof biol, Hartwick Col, 60-61; asst, Univ Utah, 61-63; instr biol sci, Purdue Univ, Calumet Campus, 63-64; from instr to asst prof, Philadelphia Col Pharm, 64-74; consult, McCormick, Taylor Assocs, Inc, 74-76; CONSULT, 76- *Mem:* Sigma Xi; Soc Study Amphibians & Reptiles; Am Soc Ichthyol & Herpet. *Res:* Taxonomic herpetology, especially Chelydridae; ecology. *Mailing Add:* 102 S New Ardmore Ave Broomall PA 19008

FEUERSTEIN, ERWIN, electrical engineering, deceased

FEUERSTEIN, IRWIN, b New York, NY, Sept 18, 39. CHEMICAL ENGINEERING, FLUID MECHANICS. *Educ:* City Col New York, BChE, 62; Newark Col Eng, MSChE, 65; Univ Mass, Amherst, PhD(chem eng), 69. *Prof Exp:* Process engr, Esso Res & Eng Co, 62-64; fel exp med, McGill Univ, 69-70; asst prof, 70-77, ASSOC PROF CHEM ENG, McMASTER UNIV, 77- *Concurrent Pos:* Can Heart Found sr res fel, 78. *Mem:* Am Soc Artificial Internal Organs; Am Inst Chem Engrs; Can Soc Chem Eng. *Res:* Biological fluid mechanics, especially model studies of flow in arterial shapes prone to artery disease; blood platelet transport and adhesion to artificial surfaces; red blood cell damage. *Mailing Add:* Dept Chem Eng McMaster Univ Hamilton ON L8S 4L8 Can

FEUERSTEIN, SEYMOUR, b New York, NY, Dec 12, 31; m 57; c 3. SPACECRAFT MATERIALS, SPACECRAFT TECHNOLOGY. *Educ:* Univ Ariz, BS, 53; Univ Calif, Berkeley, MS, 58, PhD(metall), 62. *Prof Exp:* Metallurgist, Gen Elec Co, NY, 53 & Goodyear Aircraft Co, Ariz, 56; res engr, Univ Calif, 56-61, res engr, Lawrence Radiation Lab, Univ Calif, Berkeley, 60-61; mem tech staff, mat sci lab, 61-66, head, surface & lubrication phenomena sect, chem & physics lab, 67-75, head interfacial sci dept, 76-80, DIR, CHEM & PHYSICS LAB, AEROSPACE CORP, CALIF, 81- *Concurrent Pos:* Lectr eng exten, Univ Calif, Los Angeles, 64-68. *Mem:* Am Vacuum Soc. *Res:* Mechanical properties of materials; crystal and surface physics; crystal growth; vacuum and radiation effects on materials; lubrication phenomena; adhesion; electronic and infrared sensor materials, battery electrochemistry. *Mailing Add:* 2350 E El Segundo Blvd Los Angeles CA 90245

FEULNER, RICHARD LEE, b Trenton, NJ, Feb 28, 44; m 67; c 2. HORTICULTURE, WEED SCIENCE. *Educ:* Univ Del, BS, 66, MS, 68. *Prof Exp:* Regist specialist, Geigy Agr Chem, 68-72; MGR PROD REGIST AGR DIV, CIBA-GEIGY CORP, 73- *Mem:* Weed Sci Soc Am; Sigma Xi. *Res:* Research and development of agricultural pesticides including biological screening, residue and metabolism chemistry, environmental chemistry, toxicology and fish and wildlife. *Mailing Add:* 4611 Charlottesville Rd Greensboro NY 27410

FEUSTEL, EDWARD ALVIN, b Fort Wayne, Ind, June 18, 40. COMPUTER SCIENCE, ELECTRICAL ENGINEERING. *Educ:* Mass Inst Technol, BSEE & MSEE, 64; Princeton Univ, MA, 66, PhD(elec eng), 67. *Prof Exp:* Res fel, Calif Inst Technol, 67; syst programmer, Commun Res Div, Inst Defense Anal, NJ, 68; asst prof comput sci, Rice Univ, 68-73, assoc prof elec eng & comput sci, 73-78; mem tech staff, Commun Res Div, Inst Defense Anal, 79-80; SR RES CONSULT, PRIME COMPUT, 80- *Concurrent Pos:* Lectr elec eng, Princeton Univ, 68; consult, Inst Defense Anal, 68-80, Los Alamos Nat Labs, 73-76, NSF, 75-76 & Dept Pub Welfare, State Tex, 76; syst programmer, Lawrence Livermore Labs, 72. *Mem:* Asn Comput Mach; Inst Elec & Electronics Engrs; Soc Indust & Appl Math; Brit Comput Soc; Australian Comput Soc. *Res:* Computer architecture; protection in operating systems; high-level-language computer architecture; programming language design; artificial intelligence. *Mailing Add:* Prime Comput Res Dept 500 Old Conn Path Framingham MA 01701

FEVOLD, HARRY RICHARD, b Madison, Wis, Jan 28, 35; m 58; c 3. BIOCHEMISTRY, ENDOCRINOLOGY. *Educ:* Univ Mont, BS, 56; Univ Utah, PhD(biochem), 61. *Prof Exp:* Asst biochem, Univ Utah, 61; NIH fel, Biochem Inst, Uppsala Univ, 61-63; from asst prof to assoc prof, Univ Mont, 63-70; proj assoc, Univ Wis-Madison, 70-71; PROF CHEM, UNIV MONT, 71- *Concurrent Pos:* NIH res grant, 64-78, career develop award, 65-70; NSF res grant, 64-70. *Mem:* AAAS; Am Soc Biol Chem; Endocrine Soc; Am Chem Soc; NY Acad Sci. *Res:* Biosynthesis of steroid hormones and their regulation; avian endocrinology; metabolic regulation during food and water deprivation. *Mailing Add:* Dept of Chem Univ of Mont Missoula MT 59812

FEW, ARTHUR ALLEN, b Jasper, Tex, Nov 30, 39; m 62; c 3. THUNDERSTORMS, LIGHTNING. *Educ:* Southwestern Univ, Tex, BS, 62; Univ Colo, MBS, 65; Rice Univ, PhD(space sci), 69. *Prof Exp:* Syst analyst gas pipeline simulation, Tenneco, Inc, 62-63; res assoc thunderstorm res, 68-70, adj assoc prof, 70-75, ASSOC PROF SPACE PHYSICS, RICE UNIV, 78- *Concurrent Pos:* Prin investr, thunderstorm elec res, NSF & Off Naval Res, 70-, NASA, 78-81. *Honors & Awards:* Mitchell Prize, Third Biennial Woodlands Conf Growth Policy, 79. *Mem:* Am Geophys Union; Am Meteorol Soc; Sigma Xi; AAAS; Am Forestry Asn. *Res:* Experimental and theoretical research in the areas of atmospheric electricity and atmospheric acoustics, especially lightning and thunderstorm research. *Mailing Add:* Dept Space Physics Rice Univ PO Box 1892 Houston TX 77251

FEWER, DARRELL R(AYMOND), b Perth, NB, Mar 12, 23; m 49; c 1. PHYSICS, ELECTRONICS. *Educ:* Univ NB, BSc, 50; Univ Western Ont, MSc, 52. *Prof Exp:* Mem tech staff, Bell Tel Labs, NJ, 52-57; sr proj engr, semiconductor components div, Tex Instruments Inc, 57-58, br mgr semiconductor surface studies, res & eng dept, 58-60; vpres res & eng & mem bd dirs, Tex Res & Electronic Corp, 60-63; br mgr reliability sci, semiconductor res & develop labs, Tex Instruments Inc, 63-69, br mgr optoelectronics dept, 69-74; PRES, ENSA CORP, 74- *Honors & Awards:* W R G Baker Award, Inst Elec & Electronics Engrs, 57. *Mem:* Am Phys Soc; sr mem Inst Elec & Electronics Engrs; Soc Petrol Engrs. *Res:* Semiconductor device characterization and applications; semiconductor surface physics; electrochemical devices. *Mailing Add:* PO Box 12112 Dallas TX 75225

FEWKES, ROBERT CHARLES JOSEPH, b Colonial Manor, NJ, Mar 25, 35; m 70; c 3. PROCESS ENGINEERING. *Educ:* Univ Del, BChE, 62; Mass Inst Technol, MS, 72, PhD(biochem eng), 77. *Prof Exp:* Proj engr chem eng, Gulf Res & Develop Co, 62-70; sr res engr biochem eng, Lederle Labs, 76-80; RES ASSOC BIOCHEM ENG, EASTMAN KODAK RES LABS, 80- *Mem:* Am Chem Soc; Am Inst Chem Engrs. *Res:* Enzyme and bioconversion processes; process development; process scaleup. *Mailing Add:* Eastman Kodak Res Labs Bldg 82 Kodak Park Rochester NY 14650

FEX, JÖRGEN, b Stockholm, Sweden, Mar 24, 24; US citizen; m 57; c 3. HEARING. *Educ:* Univ Stockholm, BA, 45; Univ Lund, MD, 52; Karolinska Inst, PhD(neurophysiol), 62. *Prof Exp:* Docent neurophysiol, Nobel Inst Neurophysiol, Karolinska Inst, Stockholm, 64-66; sr res fel, Dept Physiol, John Curtin Sch Med Res, Australian Nat Univ, 64-66; vis scientist, Lab Neurobiol, Dept Health, Educ & Welfare, NIMH, 66-69; prof neural sci, Ind Univ, 69-73; CHIEF, LAB NEURO-OTOLARYNGOL, PUB HEALTH SERV, DEPT HEALTH & HUMAN SERV, NAT INST NEUROL & COMMUN DIS & STROKE, NIH, 73- *Mem:* NY Acad Sci; fel Acoust Soc Am; Am Soc Neurochem; Soc Neurosci. *Res:* Function and mechanisms of the mammalian organ of hearing from a multidisciplinary point of view, using experimental techniques in the fields of anatomy, biochemistry, immunology, pharmacology and physiology. *Mailing Add:* Bldg 36 Rm 5-D-32 NIH Bethesda MD 20205

FEY, CURT F, b Berlin, Ger, May 19, 32; US nat. OPERATIONS RESEARCH, FINANCE. *Educ:* Haverford Col, BS Hons, 54; Univ Pa, PhD(opers res), 60; Univ Rochester, MBA, 76. *Prof Exp:* Prin scientist mach intel, Gen Dynamics Corp, 60-61; adv scientist opers res, IBM Corp, 61-65; mem corp staff, Tex Instruments, Inc, 65-70; MGR PLANNING, XEROX CORP, 70- *Concurrent Pos:* Prof & lectr math, Am Univ, 63-65; lectr, Indust Col Armed Forces, 64; lectr opers res, NTex State Univ, 68-69. *Mem:* Inst Elec & Electronic Engrs; Instr Mgt Sci. *Res:* Corporate planning; securities analysis; operations res. *Mailing Add:* 181 Chartwell Ct Rochester NY 14618

FEY, GEORGE TING-KUO, b Shanghai, China, July 4, 40; Can & Chinese citizen; c 1. CHEMISTRY, CHEMICAL ENGINEERING. *Educ:* Nat Taiwan Univ, BS, 65; Univ Mass, MS, 70, PhD(chem), 73. *Prof Exp:* Fel coordr chem, Univ Guelph, 73-74; lectr & fel electrochem, Univ Western Ont, 74-77; res assoc organometallic chem, Univ Guelph, 77-78; res assoc catalysis chem eng, Univ Waterloo, 78-80; anal chemist gas chromatography, Labstat Inc, Kitchener, Ont, 80-81; RES CHEMIST, LITHIUM SEC BATTERY, BALLARD RES INC, NORTH VANCOUVER, 81- *Mem:* Am Chem Soc. *Res:* Vibrational spectroscopy; pentacoordinated phosphorus compounds; phosphine transition metal complexes; platinum metals chemistry; organometallic electrochemistry; homogeneous catalysis of transition metal complexes. *Mailing Add:* Ballard Res Inc 1164 - 15th St W North Vancouver BC Can

FEY, RICHARD S(MOUSE), b Cumberland, Md, Apr 11, 24; m 53; c 1. CHEMICAL ENGINEERING. *Educ:* Univ SC, BS, 45; Univ Md, PhD(chem eng), 53. *Prof Exp:* Engr coal res, US Bur Mines, 49-51; assoc proj engr, plastics res, US Naval Ord Lab, 51-52; instr chem eng, Univ Md, 52-53; res assoc rocket res, 53-57, group supvr rocket develop, 57-58, asst supt dept, 58-59, supt dept, 59-62, div mgr, 62-64, mgr adv tech studies, 64-65, mgr adv design dept, 65, mgr adv innovation proj, 66, mgr adv ord studies, 67, mgr progs, Bacchus Works, Utah, 68-70, mgr propulsion mkt, 70-78, dir propulsion mkt, 78-80, DIR PROPULSION PROD, HERCULES AEROSPACE DIV, HERCULES INC, 80- *Mem:* Am Chem Soc; Sigma Xi; Am Inst Aeronaut & Astronaut. *Res:* Development of numerous successful military and civilian space agency high performance rockets. *Mailing Add:* Hercules Inc PO Box 26625 Salt Lake City UT 84125

FEYERHERM, ARLIN MARTIN, b West Point, Nebr, May 21, 25; m 51; c 3. EXPERIMENTAL STATISTICS. *Educ:* Univ Minn, BS, 46; State Univ Iowa, MS, 48; Iowa State Univ, PhD(math), 52. *Prof Exp:* Instr math, Northwest Mo State Col, 48-49; asst prof, Iowa State Univ, 52-53; from asst prof to assoc prof, 53-64, PROF STATIST, KANS STATE UNIV, 53- *Concurrent Pos:* Consult, US Air Force, 51-70. *Mem:* Am Statist Asn; Inst Math Statist; Am Soc Agron. *Res:* Operations research and statistical climatology. *Mailing Add:* Dept of Statistics Calvin Hall Kans State Univ Manhattan KS 66506

FEYERHERM, MARVIN PAUL, b West Point, Nebr, Feb 10, 17; m 59; c 3. PHYSICS. *Educ:* Nebr Wesleyan Univ, BA, 39; Univ Iowa, MS, 42. *Prof Exp:* Design engr, 42-50; appln engr, 50-55, engr, 55-60, adminr, 60-69, PROD ASSURANCE ADMINR, RCA CORP, 69- *Mem:* Inst Elec & Electronic Engrs. *Res:* Electronic circuits, systems and component parts; reliability analysis of electronic systems. *Mailing Add:* Astroelectronics Div RCA Corp Box 800 Princeton NJ 08540

FEYNMAN, JOAN, b New York, NY, Mar 30, 27; div; c 3. SOLAR PHYSICS, SPACE SCIENCE. *Educ:* Oberlin Univ, BA, 48; Syracuse Univ, PhD(theoret physics), 58. *Prof Exp:* Instr physics, Syracuse Univ, 58-59; geophysicist, Lamont Observ, Columbia Univ, 61-64; geophysicist, Ames Res Ctr, NASA, 64-72; res scientist, High Altitude Observ, Nat Ctr Atmospheric Res, 72-76; phys sci adminr, NSF, 76-78; SR RES PHYSICIST, BOSTON COL, 79- *Concurrent Pos:* Res assoc appl mech, Stanford Univ, 69-71; sr resident res assoc, Nat Res Coun-Nat Acad Sci, 71-, lectr, Colo Univ, 76-78. *Mem:* Am Phys Soc; Am Geophys Union; Am Astron Soc. *Res:* Geomagnetics and space research; solar and interplanetary and magnetospheric physics. *Mailing Add:* Dept of Physics Boston Col Chestnut Hill MA 02167

FEYNMAN, RICHARD PHILLIPS, b New York, NY, May 11, 18; m 60; c 2. THEORETICAL PHYSICS. *Educ:* Mass Inst Technol, BS, 39; Princeton Univ, PhD(theoret physics), 42. *Prof Exp:* Physicist, Atomic Energy Proj, Princeton Univ, 41-42 & Los Alamos Proj, NMex, 42-45; assoc prof physics, Cornell Univ, 45-51; TOLMAN PROF PHYSICS, CALIF INST TECHNOL, 51- *Honors & Awards:* Nobel Prize in Physics, 65; Einstein Award, 54. *Mem:* AAAS; Am Phys Soc; foreign mem Royal Soc. *Res:* Quantum electrodynamics; principles of least action in quantum mechanics; liquid helium; beta-decay and weak interactions. *Mailing Add:* Dept of Physics Calif Inst of Technol Pasadena CA 91125

FEYNS, LIVIU VALENTIN, b Bucharest, Romania, May 5, 38; m 64; c 2. MEDICINAL CHEMISTRY, PHARMACEUTICAL CHEMISTRY. *Educ:* Polytech Inst, Bucharest, MS, 69; Timisoara, Polytech Inst, PhD(org chem), 73. *Prof Exp:* Chemist drugs mfg, Biofarm, Bucharest, 59-64; chemist design & synthesis anticancer agents, Oncological Inst, Bucharest, 64-71, head, Anal Lab Cancer Res, 71-76; vis fel, Drug Design & Chem Sect, Nat Cancer Inst, NIH, 76-78; assoc scientist drugs anal, 78-80, SUPVR METHOD DEVELOP, US PHARMACOPEIA, 80- *Mem:* Am Chem Soc; Am Inst Chemists. *Res:* Drug design; synthesis and analysis; analytical methods development; drug purity profiles. *Mailing Add:* 12601 Twinbrook Pkwy Rockville MD 20852

FEYOCK, STEFAN, b Austria, June 24, 42; m 68; c 3. COMPUTER SCIENCES. *Educ:* Colo Col, BA, 64; Univ Kans, MA, 66; Univ Wis, PhD(comput sci), 71. *Prof Exp:* Asst prof comput sci, Univ Okla, 71-76, ASSOC PROF MATH & COMPUT SCI, COL WILLIAM & MARY, 76- *Mem:* Asn Comput Mach; Inst Elec & Electronics Engrs. *Res:* Artificial intelligence; programming languages; compiler construction; portable and extensible software design. *Mailing Add:* Dept of Math & Comput Sci Col of William and Mary Williamsburg VA 23185

FEZER, KARL DIETRICH, b Englewood, NJ, Mar 2, 30; m 52; c 4. SCIENCE EDUCATION, PHILOSOPHY OF SCIENCE. *Educ:* Cornell Univ, BS, 51, PhD(plant path), 57; Haverford Col, MA, 53. *Prof Exp:* Asst plant path, Cornell Univ, 52-55; from instr to asst prof, Univ Minn, St Paul, 57-62; div sci & math, Univ Minn, Morris, 62-63; tutor, St John's Col, 63-66; assoc prof, 66-67, PROF & CHMN DEPT BIOL, CONCORD COL, 67- *Concurrent Pos:* Dir workshop high sch biol, NSF, 71. *Mem:* AAAS; Nat Asn Biol Teachers. *Res:* Philosophy and history of science in relation to science education; interaction between science and religion. *Mailing Add:* Dept of Biol Concord Col Athens WV 24712

FIALA, ALAN DALE, b Beatrice, Nebr, Nov 9, 42. ASTRONOMY. *Educ:* Carleton Col, BA, 63; Yale Univ, MS, 64, PhD(astron), 68. *Prof Exp:* ASTRONR, US NAVAL OBSERV, 63-67 & 68- *Concurrent Pos:* Instr, US Dept Agr Grad Sch, 69- *Mem:* AAAS; Am Astron Soc; Am Inst Navig; Am Inst Aeronaut & Astronaut; NY Acad Sci. *Res:* Celestial mechanics; general and special perturbations; numerical analysis; ephemerides; astronomical constants; eclipses and transits; computerized data handling; natural satellite dynamics. *Mailing Add:* US Naval Observ Washington DC 20390

FIALA, EMERICH SILVIO, b Prague, Czechoslovakia, Aug 24, 38; US citizen; m 63; c 3. CANCER RESEARCH, PHARMACOLOGY. *Educ:* Columbia Col, BS, 59; Rutgers Univ New Brunswick, PhD(biochem), 64. *Prof Exp:* Res assoc, Fels Res Inst, 64-67; res chemist, Veterans Admin Hosp, 67-73; res assoc, 73-76, head sec biochem & pharmacol, 76-80, ASSOC CHIEF, DIV MOLEC BIOL & PHARMACOL, NAYLOR DANA INST, 80- *Concurrent Pos:* adj assoc prof Dept Pharmacol, NY Med Col, 80-; Bd Dirs, NY Chromatography Club, 81- *Mem:* Am Assoc Cancer Res; Am Chem Soc; Soc Exp Biol & Med. *Res:* Mechanics of action of chemical carcinogens; pharmacology; analytical chemistry; toxicology; biochemistry; metabolism. *Mailing Add:* 2 Southview Rd Chappaqua NY 10514

FIALA, SILVIO EMERICH IVAN, b Prague, Czech, Jan 1, 12; nat US; m 37; c 2. PHYSIOLOGY, CANCER. *Educ:* Charles Univ, Prague, MD, 37. *Prof Exp:* Head dept virus res, NIH, Czech, 42-46; res assoc path, Columbia Univ, 53-62; chief, Cell Physiol Lab, Vet Admin Hosp, San Fernando, Calif, 62-71; CHIEF CELL PHYSIOL LAB, VET ADMIN CTR, WVA, 71- *Concurrent Pos:* Rockefeller fel, Rockefeller Inst, 46-47; Nat Cancer Inst res fel, Univ Pa, 48-50; adj assoc prof, Univ Southern Calif, 62-71. *Mem:* Am Asn Cancer Res; Am Soc Biol Chemists; Am Soc Cell Biol; Soc Exp Biol & Med; Int Soc Preventive Oncol. *Res:* Cell physiology; cancer research. *Mailing Add:* Cell Physiol Lab Vet Admin Ctr Martinsburg WV 25401

FIALER, PHILIP A, b San Francisco, Calif, Nov 6, 38; m 67; c 2. ELECTRICAL ENGINEERING. *Educ:* Stanford Univ, BS, 60, MS, 64, PhD(elec eng), 70. *Prof Exp:* Sr res engr electronics, Lockheed Missiles & Space Co, Calif, 61-67; res assoc, radiosci lab, Stanford Univ, 67-70; asst dir, 70-80, DEP DIR, REMOTE MEASUREMENTS LAB, SRI INT, 80- *Concurrent Pos:* Consult, Barry Res Corp, 68-69 & western develop labs, Philco-Ford, 69-70. *Mem:* AAAS; Inst Elec & Electronics Engrs. *Res:* Ionospheric structure and physics; radar cross-section analysis; radio propagation in irregular media; computer methods in signal and image processing. *Mailing Add:* Remote Measurements Lab SRI Int 333 Ravenswood Ave Menlo Park CA 94025

FIALKOW, AARON DAVID, b New York, NY, Aug 9, 11; m 40; c 3. MATHEMATICS. *Educ:* City Col New York, BS & MS, 31; Columbia Univ, PhD(math), 36. *Prof Exp:* Teacher high sch, NY, 32-33 & 35; Nat Res fel, Inst Advan Study & Princeton Univ, 36-37; instr, Brooklyn Col, 37-42; lectr, Columbia Univ, 42-45; math res engr, Fed Telecommun Labs, 45-46; head math sect, Control Instrument Co, 46-54; adj prof, 46-47, from assoc prof to prof, 47-76, EMER PROF MATH, POLYTECH INST NEW YORK, 76- *Mem:* Am Math Soc. *Res:* Differential geometry; electric network theory. *Mailing Add:* 3125 Tibbett Ave Bronx NY 10463

FIALKOW, PHILIP JACK, b New York, NY, Aug 20, 34; m 60; c 2. INTERNAL MEDICINE, MEDICAL GENETICS. *Educ:* Univ Pa, AB, 56; Tufts Univ, MD, 60. *Prof Exp:* From intern to resident med, Sch Med, Univ Calif, San Francisco, 60-62; resident, Univ Wash Hosps, Seattle, 62-63, fel med & genetics, Sch Med, 63-65, from instr to assoc prof med, 65-72, vchmn, dept med, 74-80, PROF MED & GENETICS, SCH MED, UNIV WASH, 72-, CHMN, DEPT MED & PHYSICIAN-IN-CHIEF, UNIV HOSP, 80-; CHIEF MED SERV, SEATTLE VET ADMIN HOSP, 74- *Mem:* Genetics Soc Am; Am Soc Human Genetics; Am Soc Clin Invest; Asn Am Physicians; fel Am Col Physicians. *Res:* Human genetics; etiology of chromosomal abnormalities; origin and development of tumors. *Mailing Add:* Dept Med RG-20 Univ Wash Seattle WA 98195

FICALORA, PETER, physical chemistry, solid state chemistry, see previous edition

FICENEC, JOHN ROBERT, b Rochester, Minn, Oct 29, 38; m 59; c 4. EXPERIMENTAL HIGH ENERGY PHYSICS. *Educ:* St John's Univ, Minn, BS, 60; Univ Ill, Urbana, MS, 61, PhD(physics), 66. *Prof Exp:* Asst prof, 68-73, ASSOC PROF PHYSICS, VA POLYTECH INST & STATE UNIV, 73- *Concurrent Pos:* Guest asst physicist, Brookhaven Nat Lab, 68-71, res collabr, 74-75; Res Corp grants, 69-70; Petrol Res Fund grants, 69-72; NSF grants, 79-82. *Mem:* AAAS; Am Phys Soc; Sigma Xi; Am Asn Univ Prof. *Res:* Bubble chamber physics; electron scattering from nickel, tin and zirconium isotopes at 300 MeV/c; counter-spark chamber experiments to study high momentum transfer, high multiplicity p-p interactions; magnetic monopole search; search for high mass resonance states. *Mailing Add:* Dept of Physics Va Polytech Inst & State Univ Blacksburg VA 24061

FICH, SYLVAN, b New York, NY, Aug 8, 10; m 44. ELECTRICAL ENGINEERING, BIOMEDICAL ENGINEERING. *Educ:* Cooper Union, BSc, 31; Rutgers Univ, MSc, 32. *Prof Exp:* Instr math & eng, Union Jr Col, 33-39, dean eve session, 40-42; instr elec eng, Rutgers Univ, 42-44; mem staff, wave propagation res, Columbia Univ, 44-45; from asst prof to assoc prof elec eng, 45-55, PROF ELEC ENG, RUTGERS UNIV, 55-, DIR, GRAD PROGS ELEC ENG, 68- *Concurrent Pos:* Consult, Essex Electronics Co, 49-52 & Plastron Co, 69-70. *Honors & Awards:* Cert of appreciation, Sci Res Soc N Am, 76. *Mem:* Inst Elec & Electronics Engrs; Soc Math Biol; Int Soc Ventricular Dynamics. *Res:* Electromagnetic waves and radiation; biomedical engineering; hemodynamics and models of the circulatory system; wave phenomena in biomedical systems. *Mailing Add:* Dept Elec Eng PO Box 909 Rutgers Univ Busch Campus Piscataway NJ 08854

FICHER, MIGUEL, b Buenos Aires, Arg, July 24, 22; US citizen; m 50; c 3. ENDOCRINOLOGY, CHEMISTRY. *Educ:* Univ Buenos Aires, Lic in Chem, 48, PhD, 50. *Prof Exp:* Instr biol anal, Sch Chem, Univ Buenos Aires, 50; sub-dir clin lab, Moron County Hosp, Arg, 56-57; dir clin lab, Pvt Policlin, Arg, 57-61; dir endocrine diag lab, Jewish Hosp, St Louis, Mo, 61-65; res mem endocrinol, Univ Buenos Aires, 65-66; res mem steroid chem, Dept Endocrinol, Albert Einstein Med Ctr, 66-71; assoc prof pediat, Temple Univ, 71-74; med res scientist, Div Psychoendocrinol, Eastern Pa Psychiat Inst, 74-80; res assoc prof, 75-80, RES PROF PSYCHIAT & HUMAN BEHAV, JEFFERSON MED COL, THOMAS JEFFERSON UNIV, 80- *Concurrent Pos:* Consult chem invest, St Louis State Sch & Hosp, 64-65; consult psychoendocrinol, Vet Admin Hosp, Coatesville, Pa, 76- *Mem:* Am Asn Clin Chem; Endocrine Soc; Soc Study Reproduction; Am Soc Andrology; AAAS. *Res:* Biosynthesis of steroid hormones by gonads in humans and animals; study of pituitary-gonad axis; reproduction and spermatogenesis; psychoendocrinology of sexual functioning, of sleep, and of aging. *Mailing Add:* Dept Psychiat & Human Behavior Thomas Jefferson Univ Philadelphia PA 19107

FICHTEL, CARL EDWIN, b St Louis, Mo, July 13, 33. ASTROPHYSICS. *Educ:* Wash Univ, BS, 55, PhD(physics), 60. *Prof Exp:* Asst physics, Wash Univ, 56-59; scientist, 59-60, head nuclear emulsion sect, 60-66, head gamma ray & nuclear emulsion sect, 66-70, HEAD GAMMA RAY & NUCLEAR EMULSION BR, GODDARD SPACE FLIGHT CTR, NASA, 70- *Concurrent Pos:* Vis lectr, Univ Md, 63-; chmn, High Energy Astrophys Div, Am Astron Soc, 80-81. *Honors & Awards:* John C Lindsay Mem Award, Goddard Space Flight Ctr, 68; Exceptional Sci Achievement Medal, NASA, 71. *Mem:* Int Astron Union; Am Phys Soc; Am Astron Soc. *Res:* High energy astrophysics; galactic cosmic rays; solar cosmic rays, especially solar particle composition and its relation to solar abundances; gamma ray astronomy; cosmic ray propagation and confinement; spark chambers. *Mailing Add:* Goddard Space Flight Ctr NASA Code 662 Greenbelt MD 20771

FICK, BESSIE DAVEY, b Detroit, Mich, Nov 8, 20; m 64. NUTRITION. *Educ:* Wayne Univ, BS, 43; Ore State Col, MS, 45, PhD(foods, nutrit), 49. *Prof Exp:* Grad res asst, Ore State Col, 43-49; assoc prof food & nutrit & res assoc, Lab Human Nutrit, Univ Ala, 49-53, prof & head, Dept Food & Nutrit, 53-61; prof home econ & head dept, NMex State Univ, 61-66; instr home econ, Eastern Ariz Col, 66-70, head dept, 67-70; PROF NUTRIT & FOODS, AUBURN UNIV, 70-, HEAD DEPT, 77- *Mem:* Am Dietetic Asn; Am Inst Nutrit; Am Home Econ Asn. *Res:* Human nutrition; ascorbic acid metabolism during adolescence; utilization of ascorbic acid. *Mailing Add:* Dept Nutrit & Foods Sch Home Econ Auburn Univ Auburn AL 36830

FICK, GARY WARREN, b O'Neill, Nebr, July 10, 43; m 69. AGRONOMY, CROP PHYSIOLOGY. *Educ:* Univ Nebr, Lincoln, BS, 65; Massey Univ, NZ, Dipl Agr Sci, 68; Univ Calif, Davis, PhD(plant physiol), 71. *Prof Exp:* Asst prof, 71-76, ASSOC PROF AGRON, CORNELL UNIV, 76- *Mem:* Am Soc Plant Physiol; Am Soc Agron; Crop Sci Soc Am. *Res:* Forage crop physiology; computer modelling of crop growth. *Mailing Add:* Dept of Agron Cornell Univ Ithaca NY 14853

FICK, GERHARDT NELSON, plant breeding, genetics, see previous edition

FICK, HERBERT JOHN, b Minn, Jan 4, 37; m 60; c 3. PLASTICS CHEMISTRY, POLYMER CHEMISTRY. *Educ:* St Olaf Col, BA, 59; Univ Chicago, MS, 60. *Prof Exp:* Supvr corp chem lab, 63-65, mgr mat eng, Elec Prod Div, 65-66, eng mgr, UK Div, 66-69, chemist, 69, mgr display devices mfg, 69-71, prog mgr new process develop, 71-72, mgr tape & laminations prod line, 72-74, SR STAFF TECH SPECIALIST, G T SCHJELDAHL CO, 75- *Mem:* Am Chem Soc. *Res:* Flexible printed wiring; adhesives; electroluminescent display; electrical insulating materials; materials for flexible, inflatable structures; adhesives; adhesives. *Mailing Add:* 519 E Eighth St Northfield MN 55057

FICKEISEN, DUANE H, b Bremerton, Wash, June 9, 47. AQUATIC ECOLOGY. *Educ:* Univ Wash, BS(biol oceanog) & BS(zool), 70, MS, 72. *Prof Exp:* RES SCIENTIST AQUATIC ECOL, PAC NORTHWEST DIV, BATTELLE MEM INST, 71- *Mem:* Am Fisheries Soc; AAAS; Pac Fishery Biologists. *Res:* Ecological modelling; environmental effects of hydroelectric generation; effects of water level fluctuations on fishes; gas bubble disease of aquatic biota. *Mailing Add:* Pac Northwest Div Battelle Mem Inst PO Box 999 Richland WA 99352

FICKEN, MILLICENT SIGLER, b Washington, DC, July 27, 33; m 55; c 2. ETHOLOGY. *Educ:* Cornell Univ, BS, 55, PhD(zool), 60. *Prof Exp:* Res assoc zool, Univ Md, 63-68; from asst prof to assoc prof, 67-75, PROF ZOOL, UNIV WIS-MILWAUKEE, 75-, DIR FIELD STA, 67- *Mem:* Am Ornith Union; Soc Study Evolution; Animal Behav Soc. *Res:* Ornithology; animal communication; sociobiology. *Mailing Add:* Dept Zool Univ Wis Milwaukee WI 53201

FICKEN, ROBERT W, b Brooklyn, NY, Feb 26, 32; m 55; c 2. ETHOLOGY. *Educ:* Cornell Univ, BS, 53, PhD(vert zool), 60. *Prof Exp:* Res assoc animal behav, Cornell Univ, 60-62; asst prof zool, Univ Md, 62-68; RES ASSOC ZOOL, UNIV WIS-MILWAUKEE, 68- *Mem:* AAAS; Am Ornith Union. *Res:* Comparative avian ethology; ecology; interspecific communication; evolution of signalling systems; analysis of vocalizations. *Mailing Add:* 1623 16th Ave Grafton WI 53024

FICKESS, DOUGLAS RICARDO, b Piedmont, Okla, Aug 25, 31; m 53; c 2. ZOOLOGY, PHYSIOLOGY. *Educ:* Univ Okla, BS, 54, MS, 56; Univ Mo, PhD(zool), 63. *Prof Exp:* From asst prof to assoc prof, 62-69, chmn dept, 66-74, PROF BIOL, WESTMINSTER COL, MO, 69- *Mem:* Am Soc Mammalogists; Am Soc Zoologists. *Res:* Effects of population density dependent factors on the histology and physiology of adrenal glands in mammals and reptiles. *Mailing Add:* Dept of Biol Westminster Col Fulton MO 65251

FICKETT, FREDERICK ROLAND, b Portland, Maine, Sept 30, 37; m 61; c 2. PHYSICS. *Educ:* Univ NH, BS, 60; Univ Ariz, MS, 62; Ore State Univ, PhD(physics), 67. *Prof Exp:* Nat Bur Standards-Nat Res Coun res assoc, 67-69; MEM STAFF, CRYOGENICS DIV, NAT BUR STANDARDS, 69- *Mem:* Am Nuclear Soc; Am Phys Soc; Inst Elec & Electronics Engrs. *Res:* Properties of metals and alloys at cryogenic temperatures; materials science; solid state physics. *Mailing Add:* 3660 Cloverleaf Dr Boulder CO 80302

FICKETT, WILDON, b Tucson, Ariz, Mar 25, 27; m 45; c 5. FLUID PHYSICS. *Educ:* Univ Ariz, BS, 48; Calif Inst Technol, PhD(chem), 51. *Prof Exp:* MEM STAFF, LOS ALAMOS NAT LAB, UNIV CALIF, 51- *Mailing Add:* Los Alamos Nat Lab Univ Calif PO Box 1663 Los Alamos NM 87545

FICKINGER, WILLIAM JOSEPH, b New York, NY, July 18, 34. HIGH ENERGY PHYSICS. *Educ:* Manhattan Col, BS, 55; Yale Univ, PhD(physics), 61. *Prof Exp:* Asst prof physics, Univ Ky, 61-62; asst physicist, Brookhaven Nat Lab, 62-63 & 64-65; assoc physicist, Saclay Nuclear Res Ctr, France, 63-64 & 65-66; asst prof physics, Vanderbilt Univ, 66-67; assoc prof, 67-76, PROF PHYSICS, CASE WESTERN RESERVE UNIV, 76- *Mem:* Am Phys Soc; Am Asn Univ Professors. *Res:* Experimental particle physics; Intermediate energy scattering processes and particle production. *Mailing Add:* Dept of Physics Case Western Reserve Univ Cleveland OH 44106

FICSOR, GYULA, b Kiskunhalas, Hungary, Apr 11, 36; US citizen; m 65; c 2. GENETICS, GENETIC TOXICOLOGY. *Educ:* Colo State Univ, 60; Univ Mo-Columbia, PhD(genetics), 65. *Prof Exp:* NIH fel, 65-66; res assoc, Molecular Biol Lab, Univ Wis, 67; asst prof, 67-71, assoc prof biol, 72-80, PROF BIOMED SCI, WESTERN MICH UNIV, 80- *Concurrent Pos:* Nat Acad Sci exchange scientist, Hungary, 73; consult, Nat Inst Environ Health Sci, 76-78. *Mem:* Environ Mutagen Soc; Am Genetics Asn; Am Soc Primatologists. *Res:* Methods development for detecting mutagens, carcinogens and teratogens in mammals. *Mailing Add:* Dept of Biomed Sci Western Mich Univ Kalamazoo MI 49008

FIDDLER, WALTER, b Vienna, Austria, Feb 5, 36; US citizen. ANALYTICAL CHEMISTRY. *Educ:* Temple Univ, AB, 59, PhD(org chem), 65. *Prof Exp:* RES CHEMIST, MEAT LAB, QUAL & COMPOS, USDA, 65- *Mem:* AAAS; Am Chem Soc; Inst Food Technol; Am Meat Sci Asn. *Res:* Pyrimidine containing sulfonamides; retrieval of chemical information; smoke flavor investigations; determination of carcinogens in cured meat products. *Mailing Add:* Eastern Regional Res Ctr USDA 600 E Mermaid Lane Philadelphia PA 19118

FIDLER, ISAIAH J, b Jerusalem, Israel, Dec 4, 36; m 75; c 3. CANCER BIOLOGY, IMMUNOLOGY. *Educ:* Okla State Univ, BS, 61, DVM, 63; Univ Pa, PhD(path), 70. *Prof Exp:* Instr vet surg, 66-68, from asst prof to assoc prof path, 70-75, PROF PATH, SCH MED, UNIV PA, 81-; head lab, 75-80, DIR LAB, CANCER METASTASIS & TREATMENT PROG, FREDERICK CANCER RES FACIL, NAT CANCER INT, 80-; PROF PATH, SCH MED, UNIV MD, BALTIMORE, 81- *Concurrent Pos:* Mem, Study Sect Path B, NIH, 77-81; chief ed, Cancer Metastasis Review, 81- *Mem:* Am Vet Med Asn; Am Asn Cancer Res; Am Asn Path; AAAS. *Res:* Mechanisms of cancer metastasis; investigations into the nature of the metastatic cancer cell and its relationship with host factors; the manipulation of host defense toward eradication of metastases. *Mailing Add:* Cancer Metastasis & Treatment Lab Frederick Cancer Res Ctr PO Box B Frederick MD 21701

FIDONE, SALVATORE JOSEPH, b New York, NY, June 10, 39; m 62; c 2. PHYSIOLOGY, NEUROCHEMISTRY. *Educ:* Georgetown Univ, BS, 62; State Univ NY, PhD(physiol), 67. *Prof Exp:* From instr to assoc prof, 69-81, PROF PHYSIOL, SCH MED, UNIV UTAH, 81- *Concurrent Pos:* NIH fel neurophysiol, Col Med, Univ Utah, 67-69, prin investr, NIH res grants, 75-78, 78-81 & 81-86; co-investr, NIH prog proj grants, 68-73, 73-78, 78-81 & 81-84; mem, Neurol A Study Sect, NIH. *Mem:* Soc Neurosci; Am Physiol Soc. *Res:* Neurochemistry and neurophysiology of carotid body chemoreception. *Mailing Add:* Dept Physiol Univ Utah Sch Med Salt Lake City UT 84112

FIEDELMAN, HOWARD W(ILLIAM), b Sheboygan, Wis, Apr 23, 16; m 47; c 2. CHEMICAL ENGINEERING. *Educ:* Univ Wis, BS, 38. *Prof Exp:* From chem engr to res supvr, cent res lab, Morton Salt Co, 39-67, dir salt res, Morton Salt Div, Morton-Norwich Prod, Inc, 67-77; EXEC DIR, SOLUTION MINING RES INST, 78- *Res:* Salt technology; purification of salt from brines; theoretical aspects of caking. *Mailing Add:* 812 Muriel St Woodstock IL 60098

FIEDLER, H(OWARD) C(HARLES), b Chicago, Ill, June 24, 24; m 49; c 5. PHYSICAL METALLURGY. *Educ:* Purdue Univ, BS, 49; Mass Inst Technol, MS, 50, ScD(metall), 53. *Prof Exp:* Res assoc, metal dept res lab, 53-59, metallurgist, 59-66, METALLURGIST, RES & DEVELOP CTR, GEN ELEC CO, 66- *Mem:* Am Soc Metals; Am Inst Mining, Metall & Petrol Engrs. *Res:* Soft magnetic materials; recrystallization; surface alloying; amorphous metals. *Mailing Add:* Res & Develop Ctr Gen Elec Co Schenectady NY 12301

FIEDLER-NAGY, CHRISTA, b Marienbad, Czech, July 8, 43; Ger citizen; m 69. CONNECTIVE TISSUE, ENZYMES. *Educ:* Fairleigh Dickinson Univ, BS, 67, MS, 74; Rutgers Univ, PhD(biochem), 81. *Prof Exp:* Res asst & assoc toxicol, biochem nutrit & pharmacol, 68-80, SR SCIENTIST PHARMACOLOGY, HOFFMANN-LA ROCHE, INC, 81- *Mem:* AAAS. *Res:* Factors affecting collagen metabolism; collagenase, inhibition of collagen biosynthesis by proline analogs; mediators of inflammation and immediate hypersensitivity reactions arachidonic acid cascade. *Mailing Add:* Hoffmann-La Roche Inc Nutley NJ 07110

FIEHLER, HARLAN EDWARD, analytical chemistry, see previous edition

FIELD, ARTHUR KIRK, b North Adams, Mass, Jan 6, 38; m 60; c 2. IMMUNOBIOLOGY, VIROLOGY. *Educ:* Cornell Univ, BS, 60, MS, 61; Univ Calif, Berkeley, PhD(virol, biochem), 65. *Prof Exp:* Res fel, 65-72, sr res fel, 72-80, SR INVESTR, MERCK INST THERAPEUT RES, 80- *Concurrent Pos:* Instr, Gwnedd Mercy Col, 71- *Mem:* Soc Exp Biol & Med; Am Asn Immunol; Am Soc Microbiol; NY Acad Sci; Sigma Xi. *Res:* Mode of action of interferon and means of interferon induction; cellular immune response to viral antigens; antiviral chemotherapy. *Mailing Add:* Dept of Virol & Cell Biol Merck Inst Therapeut Res West Point PA 19486

FIELD, BYRON DUSTIN, b Charlotte, Mich, June 2, 18; m 41; c 2. SPECTROSCOPY. *Educ:* Mich State Univ, BS, 39, MS, 42. *Prof Exp:* Asst spectroscopist, Wyandotte Chem Corp, Mich, 41-43; spectroscopist, 43-56, HEAD, PHYS METHODS LAB, MALLINCKRODT INC, 56- *Mem:* Am Chem Soc; Soc Appl Spectros; Spectros Soc Can. *Res:* Spectrochemical analysis of chemical products; absorption spectra; infrared spectroscopy; x-ray diffraction and fluorescence spectroscopy; general instrumental and analytical chemistry; atomic absorption spectroscopy; computer applications in analytical chemistry. *Mailing Add:* Corp Anal Serv Mallinckrodt Inc PO Box 5439 St Louis MO 63147

FIELD, CHRISTOPHER BOWER, b Dinuba, Calif, Mar 12, 53. PHYSIOLOGICAL PLANT ECOLOGY. *Educ:* Harvard Univ, AB, 75; Stanford Univ, PhD(biol), 81. *Prof Exp:* ASST PROF PLANT ECOL, DEPT BIOL, UNIV UTAH, 81- *Mem:* AAAS; Am Soc Plant Physiologists. *Res:* Ways that physiological processes determine the distribution and abundance of plant species, specifically photosynthesis, water relations and nutrient uptake. *Mailing Add:* Dept Biol Univ Utah Salt Lake City UT 84112

FIELD, CYRUS WEST, b Duluth, Minn, May 5, 33; m 58; c 4. ECONOMIC GEOLOGY, GEOCHEMISTRY. *Educ:* Dartmouth Col, BA, 56; Yale Univ, MS, 57, PhD(geol), 61. *Prof Exp:* Res asst geol, Yale Univ, 58-60; geologist, Bear Creek Mining Co, Kennecott Copper Corp, 60-63; asst prof, 63-68, assoc prof, 68-76, PROF GEOL, ORE STATE UNIV, 76- *Mem:* Soc Econ Geol; Geochem Soc; Geol Soc Am; Am Inst Mining, Metall & Petrol Engrs. *Res:* Sulfur isotope abundances in minerals; geochemistry and mineralogy of ore deposits. *Mailing Add:* Dept of Geol Ore State Univ Corvallis OR 97331

FIELD, FRANK HENRY, b Keansburg, NJ, Feb 27, 22; m 44, 59, 77; c 2. PHYSICAL CHEMISTRY. *Educ:* Duke Univ, BS, 43, MA, 44, PhD(chem), 48. *Prof Exp:* Instr & asst prof chem, Univ Tex, 47-52; res chemist, Humble Oil & Refining Co, 52-53, sr res chemist, 53-60, res specialist, 60-62, res assoc, 62-65 & Esso Res & Eng Co, 65-68, sr res assoc, 68-70; PROF CHEM, ROCKEFELLER UNIV, 70- *Concurrent Pos:* Guggenheim fel, 63-64. *Mem:* Am Chem Soc; Am Soc Mass Spectrometry (pres, 72-74, past pres, 74-76, vpres, 70-72). *Res:* Mass spectrometry, electron impact studies, energies and reactions of gaseous ions; radiation chemistry. *Mailing Add:* Rockefeller Univ New York NY 10021

FIELD, GEORGE BROOKS, b Providence, RI, Oct 25, 29; m 56; c 2. THEORETICAL ASTROPHYSICS. *Educ:* Mass Inst Technol, BS, 51; Princeton Univ, PhD(astron), 55. *Prof Exp:* Physicist, Naval Ord Lab, 51-52; res asst, Princeton Univ, 52-54; jr fel astron, Harvard Soc Fels, 55-57; from asst prof to assoc prof astron, Princeton Univ, 57-65; prof, Univ Calif, Berkeley, 65-72, chmn dept, 70-71; PROF ASTRON, HARVARD UNIV, 72-, DIR CTR ASTROPHYS, HARVARD COL OBSERV & SMITHSONIAN ASTROPHY OBSERV, 73-, PAINE PROF PRACTICAL ASTRON, 80- *Concurrent Pos:* Guggenheim fel, 60-61; mem planetology subcomt, Space Sci Steering Comt, NASA, 64-66, mem astron missions bd, 68-70, mem space telescope working group, 73-77, mem shuttle astron working group, 74-76 & space prog adv coun, 75-77, chmn phys sci comt, 75-77; Phillips visitor, Haverford Col, 65 & 71; mem panel on astron adv to Off Naval Res, 65-66, mem physics surv comt, 69-72, mem astron surv comt, 69-72, mem panel on radio astron, Astron Surv Comt, 69-72, chmn panel astrophys & relativity, Physics & Astron Survs, 69-72; NSF grants astrophys, 65-73, mem astron panel, NSF, 66-67, chmn, 67-69; mem space sci panel, President's Sci Adv Comt, 66-67; mem vis comt, Nat Radio Astron Observ, 67-69; co-ed, Gordon & Breach Ser Astrophys & Space Sci, 68-75; corresp, Comments on Astrophys & Space Sci, 68-71; vis prof, Cambridge Univ, 69; trustee-at-large, Assoc Univs, Inc, 69-72; trustee, mem corp & exec comt, Aspen Ctr Physics, 72-74; mem adv bd, Nat Astron & Ionosphere Ctr, 71-74; mem vis comt div physics, math & astron, Calif Inst Technol, 71-; vpres comn 34, Int Astron Union, 73-76, pres, 76-79; lectr, Sch Theoret Physics, Les Houches, France, 74; chmn, Boyden Observ Coun, 74-76; mem vis comt, Lowell Observ, 75; mem comt on study of uses for balloons for sci purposes, Nat Acad Sci, 75-76; mem adv panel on orientation & roles, Univ Space Res Asn, 75; mem corp vis comt, Dept of Physics, Mass Inst Technol, 76-79; liaison rep NASA phys sci comt, Space Sci Bd, Nat Res Coun, 76-77; mem vis comt, Dept Physics & Astrophys, Univ Colo, Boulder, 77; mem exec comt, Space Adv Coun, NASA, 78-; chmn Nat Res Coun astron surv, Nat Acad Sci, 78- *Mem:* AAAS; fel Am Phys Soc; Am Astron Soc; Int Astron Union. *Res:* Dynamics of interstellar matter, including galaxy and star formation; instabilities in dilute gases; cosmology, including background radiation and intergalactic matter. *Mailing Add:* Ctr for Astrophys 60 Garden St Cambridge MA 02138

FIELD, GEORGE FRANCIS, b Stockton, Calif, Dec 26, 34; m 62; c 2. ORGANIC CHEMISTRY. *Educ:* Pomona Col, AB, 56; Harvard Univ, PhD(org chem), 62. *Prof Exp:* Sr chemist, 62-70, RES FEL, HOFFMAN-LA ROCHE, INC, 70- *Mem:* Am Chem Soc. *Res:* Medicinal chemistry; heterocyclic synthesis. *Mailing Add:* Chem Res Dept Hoffman-La Roche Inc Nutley NJ 07110

FIELD, GEORGE ROBERT, b Vienna, Austria, Oct 16, 19; US citizen; m 46; c 3. ELECTRICAL ENGINEERING. *Educ:* Washington Univ, St Louis, BSEE, 48; Drexel Univ, MSEE, 60, MSEngMgt, 71, MBA, 78. *Prof Exp:* Design & develop engr, 48-55, design & develop leader, 55-55-56, mgr radar data conversion eng, 56-61, design support & integration, 61-62, eng opers, 62-63 & design & develop eng, 63-64; mgr tech assurance, 64-69, MGR TECH OPERS, MISSILE & SURFACE RADAR DIV, RCA CORP, 69- *Mem:* Sr mem Inst Elec & Electronics Engrs. *Res:* Design and development of electronic equipment for missile range instrumentation; strategic and defensive systems and space exploration. *Mailing Add:* Missile & Surface Radar Marne Hwy & Borton's Landing Rd Moorestown NJ 08057

FIELD, HENRY, b Chicago, Ill, Dec 15, 02; m 53; c 2. PHYSICAL ANTHROPOLOGY, ARCHAEOLOGY. *Educ:* Oxford Univ, BA, 25, MA, 28, DSc(anthrop), 37. *Prof Exp:* From asst cur to cur phys anthrop, Field Mus Natural Hist, Chicago, 26-41; govt researcher Near East, Libr Cong, 41-45; pvt researcher, Mex, 46-47; phys anthropologist, Univ Calif exped, Africa, 47-48; HON ASSOC PHYS ANTHROP, PEABODY MUS, HARVARD UNIV, 50- *Concurrent Pos:* Leader, Marshall Field expeds, NArabian Desert; asst, Field Mus, Oxford Univ exped, Kish, Iraq, 25-26 & 27-28; leader, archaeological expeds, Western Europe, Near East exped, 34 & Peabody Mus exped, southwest Asia, 50 & WPakistan, 55. *Honors & Awards:* Annandale Medal, Calcutta Asiatic Soc, 66. *Mem:* AAAS; Am Anthrop Asn; fel Royal Anthrop Inst Gt Brit & Ireland; fel Royal Geog Soc; fel Royal Asiatic Soc. *Res:* Anthropometric survey and prehistory of southwestern Asia; anthropology of Iraq, Iran, India, Caucasus, West Pakistan and Mongolia, 73. *Mailing Add:* 3551 Main Hwy Coconut Grove Miami FL 33133

FIELD, HERBERT CYRE, b Cleveland, Ohio, Nov 2, 30; m 53; c 4. REACTOR PHYSICS. *Educ:* Case Univ, BS, 53; Purdue Univ, MS, 57. *Prof Exp:* Physicist exp physics div, Lawrence Radiation Lab, Calif, 53-54 & exp shock hydrodyn div, 54-55; physicist exp physics group, Atomic Int Div, NAm Aviation, Inc, 57-59, sr physicist reactor physics group, 59-63; reactor safety specialist, Div Oper Safety, US Atomic Energy Comn & US Energy Res & Develop Admin, 63-77, SR EXEC, OFF EVIRON, US DEPT ENERGY, 77- *Concurrent Pos:* Consult, US Navy, 70-71. *Mem:* AAAS; Am Phys Soc; Am Nuclear Soc; Antarctican Soc. *Res:* Nuclear reactors, especially their safety evaluation; experimental neutron physics; administration of safety programs. *Mailing Add:* 8185 Inverness Ridge Rd Potomac MD 20854

FIELD, HOWARD LAWRENCE, b Buffalo, NY, May 1, 28; m 60; c 3. PSYCHIATRY. *Educ:* Univ NC, AB, 49; Jefferson Med Col, MD, 54. *Prof Exp:* PROF PSYCHIAT, JEFFERSON MED COL, 60- *Mem:* AAAS; Am Psychiat Asn; Am Med Asn. *Res:* Psychiatric treatment of patients in a general hospital. *Mailing Add:* Dept of Psychiat Jefferson Med Col Philadelphia PA 19107

FIELD, JACK EVERETT, b Gary, Ind, June 3, 27; m 58; c 3. INORGANIC CHEMISTRY, TRACE METAL ANALYSIS. *Educ:* Harvard Univ, AB, 52; Tulane Univ, MS, 55, PhD(inorg chem), 57. *Prof Exp:* Chemist, E I du Pont de Nemours & Co, 57-63; res chemist, Corning Glass Works, 64-66; prof phys sci, 66-71, head dept, 71-77, PROF CHEM, NICHOLLS STATE UNIV, 71- *Mem:* AAAS; Am Chem Soc; Am Soc Testing & Mat. *Res:* Inorganic chemistry of the solid states and surfaces, including crystal growth; water pollution. *Mailing Add:* Dept Chem Nicholls State Univ Thibodaux LA 70301

FIELD, JAMES BERNARD, b Ft Wayne, Ind, May 28, 26; m 54; c 4. MEDICINE. *Educ:* Harvard Univ, MD, 51. *Prof Exp:* From intern to resident, Mass Gen Hosp, 51-54; sr investr clin endocrinol br, NIH, 54-62; from assoc prof to prof med, Sch Med, Univ Pittsburgh, 61-78, dir clin res unit, 62-78; RUTHERFORD PROF MED, BAYLOR COL MED, 78- *Concurrent Pos:* USPHS training grant, 70-74; consult diabetes & arthritis prog, Div Chronic Dis, USPHS, 62-68, mem endocrinol study sect, 65-69 & chmn, 68-69, mem diabetes & endocrinol training grant comt, 70-74; ed, Metab, 70-; res collabr, Brookhaven Nat Lab, 72-; mem clin sci panel, Utilization Human Resources Comn, Nat Res Coun, 76-79; mem gen clin res ctr review comt, USPHS, 76-80; mem nat diabetes adv bd, USPHS, 77- *Honors & Awards:* Eli Lilly Award, Am Diabetes Asn, 58; Van Meter Prize, Am Goiter Asn, 61. *Mem:* Am Soc Clin Invest; Endocrine Soc; Am Physiol Soc; Am Diabetes Asn; Asn Am Physicians. *Res:* Diabetes mellitus and endocrinology. *Mailing Add:* Dept of Med Baylor Col of Med Houston TX 77030

FIELD, JAY ERNEST, b Roanoke, Va, Nov 4, 47; m 70; c 1. PHYSICAL CHEMISTRY. *Educ:* Va Polytech Inst, BS, 70; Univ Fla, PhD(phys chem), 75. *Prof Exp:* RES CHEMIST HERMETIC SYSTS, MAJOR APPLIANCES LAB, GEN ELEC CO, 76- *Mem:* Am Soc Testing & Mat. *Res:* Chemical aspects of hermetic refrigeration systems and electrical properties evaluations of electrical insulating materials. *Mailing Add:* 7014 Fontendleau Way Fern Creek KY 40291

FIELD, JOSEPH H(ERMAN), b Pittsburgh, Pa, May 29, 20; m 47; c 2. CHEMICAL ENGINEERING. *Educ:* Carnegie Inst Technol, BS, 40; Univ Pittsburgh, MS, 44. *Prof Exp:* From jr engr to supv chem engr, US Bur Mines, 41-58, actg chief, Gas Synthesis Sect, 58-60, proj coordr eng, 60-69; VPRES ENG, BENFIELD CORP, 69- *Mem:* Am Chem Soc; Air Pollution Control Asn; Am Inst Chem Engrs; Brit Inst Fuel. *Res:* Synthetic liquid and high-British thermal unit gas from coal; air pollution, sulfur oxide removal from flue gas; gas purification. *Mailing Add:* Benfield Corp 666 Washington Rd Pittsburgh PA 15228

FIELD, KURT WILLIAM, b Akron, Ohio, Mar 29, 44; m 67; c 2. CHEMISTRY. *Educ:* Hiram Col, BS, 66; Case Western Reserve Univ, PhD(org chem), 70. *Prof Exp:* Fel org chem, Johns Hopkins Univ, 70-72; asst prof, Univ Wis-Whitewater, 72-76; asst prof, 76-82, ASSOC PROF ORG CHEM, BRADLEY UNIV, 82- *Mem:* Am Chem Soc. *Res:* The formation and cleavage of carbon-nitrogen bonds; the chlorination of alkenes with nitrogen trichloride; rotational isomerism in substituted acylamides; synthesis of small ring heterocycles; organic reaction mechanisms; organic synthesis via organometallics. *Mailing Add:* Dept Chem Bradley Univ Peoria IL 61625

FIELD, LAMAR, b Montgomery, Ala, July 19, 22; m 48; c 2. CHEMISTRY, ORGANOSULFUR CHEMISTRY. *Educ:* Mass Inst Technol, SB, 44, PhD(chem), 49. *Prof Exp:* Asst chemist res lab, Merck & Co, Inc, 44-46; from instr to assoc prof chem, 49-59, chmn, Dept Chem, 61-67, PROF CHEM, VANDERBILT UNIV, 59- *Concurrent Pos:* Consult chem indust, 55-; vis assoc, Am Chem Soc, 63-, vis scientist, 66-73; consult, NIH, 65-69 & NY State Educ Dept, 74; Coulter lectr, Univ Miss, 68; vis fel, John Curtin Sch Med Res, Australian Nat Univ & hon fel, Res Sch Chem, 74. *Honors & Awards:* William Barton Rogers Award, 44; L C Glenn Award, 52. *Mem:* Am Chem Soc; The Chem Soc. *Res:* Synthetic, structural, medicinal and biological aspects of organic chemistry, especially with reference to organic sulfur compounds; medicinal chemistry. *Mailing Add:* Box 1507 Sta B Vanderbilt Univ Nashville TN 37235

FIELD, LESLIE A, b Oct 1, 56. CATALYSIS, OXYGENATED FUELS. *Educ:* Mass Inst Tech, BS, 78, MS, 78. *Prof Exp:* RES ENGR, CHEVRON RES CO, STANDARD OIL CALIF, 78- *Mem:* Am Inst Chem Engrs; Am Chem Soc; AAAS. *Res:* Zeolite catalysis; hydrocarbon catalysis; oxygenated compound; crystallization technology. *Mailing Add:* Chevron Res Co 576 Standard Ave Richmond CA 94802

FIELD, MARVIN FREDERICK, b Manistee, Mich, Oct 3, 26; m 51; c 3. MICROBIOLOGY. *Educ:* Cent Mich Univ, AB, 48; Mich State Univ, MS, 50; Univ Minn, PhD(microbiol), 57. *Prof Exp:* Instr microbiol, Univ Rochester, 50-51; res microbiologist, Chas Pfizer & Co, NY, 51-53, microbiologist, Ind, 57-62; sr virologist, Jensen Salsbery Labs Div, Richardson-Merrell, Inc, 62-63; asst prof dent, Univ Mo-Kansas City, 63-70, assoc prof, 70-73; res mgr, Haver Lockhart Labs, 73-76; res dir, Douglas Industs, 76-80; RES DIR, CEVA LABS, 80- *Concurrent Pos:* Asst prof microbiol, Med Ctr, Univ Kans, 63-69. *Mem:* AAAS; Am Chem Soc; Am Soc Microbiol. *Res:* Electron microscopy; virology. *Mailing Add:* 10316 Mohawk Lane Kansas City MO 64116

FIELD, MICHAEL, b New York, NY, Feb 21, 14; m 42; c 2. PHYSICS. *Educ:* City Col New York, BME, 37; Columbia Univ, MS, 38; Univ Cincinnati, PhD(physics), 48. *Prof Exp:* Res engr, Cincinnati Milling Mach Co, 38-45, res physicist, 46-48; partner, 48-58, pres, 59-78, CHMN BD & CHIEF EXEC OFFICER, METCUT RES ASSOCS, INC, 78- *Mem:* Nat Acad Eng; AAAS; Am Soc Metals; Soc Automotive Engrs; Soc Exp Stress Anal. *Res:* Physics and mechanics of metal cutting; machinability; high temperature mechanical testing; machine tools; metallurgy. *Mailing Add:* Metcut Res Assoc Inc 3980 Rosslyn Dr Cincinnati OH 45209

FIELD, MICHAEL EHRENHART, b Baltimore, Md, June 27, 45; m 67; c 2. MARINE GEOLOGY. *Educ:* Univ Del, BS, 67; Duke Univ, MA, 69; George Washington Univ, PhD(geol), 76. *Prof Exp:* Res geologist, US Army Coastal Eng Res Ctr, 69-75; MARINE GEOLOGIST, US GEOL SURV, 75- *Mem:* Geol Soc Am; Soc Econ Paleontologists & Mineralogists; Sigma Xi. *Res:* Sedimentary processes and patterns on continental margins; quaternary evolution of coastal areas and continental shelves; modern tectonic and sedimentary processes on the continental margin as they relate to basin evolution, hydrocarbon accumulation, placer deposits of minerals, and geologic hazards. *Mailing Add:* US Geol Surv 345 Middlefield Rd Menlo Park CA 94025

FIELD, NATHAN DAVID, b New York, NY, Aug 21, 25; m 49; c 3. POLYMER SCIENCE, ORGANIC CHEMISTRY. *Educ:* City Col New York, BS, 45; Columbia Univ, AM, 49; Polytech Inst Brooklyn, PhD(polymer chem), 56. *Prof Exp:* Res chemist polymer chem & textile fibers, E I du Pont de Nemours, Inc, 56-62; supvr polymer chem, Atlantic Refining Co, 62-64; mgr, GAF Corp, 64-68, mgr, Cent Res Lab, 68-70; res dir chem & consumer prod, Int Playtex Co, Inc, 70-80; DIR RES & DEVELOP, DART INDUSTRIES, 81-; PROF, DEPT CHEM ENG, CITY UNIV NEW YORK, 81- *Concurrent Pos:* Mem adv bd, Jour Polymer Sci, 64-, Sch Theoret & Appl Sci, Ramapo Col, 77- *Mem:* Am Chem Soc; Asn Res Dirs; AAAS; Sigma Xi. *Res:* Polymer science; water soluble and swellable polymers; materials; surface active agents; absorbency; organic chemistry; consumer products; catamenial devices. *Mailing Add:* 170 Fox Hollow Rd Wyckoff NJ 07481

FIELD, NORMAN J, b New York, NY, Dec 5, 22; m 46; c 4. PHYSICS, RESEARCH ADMINISTRATION. *Educ:* City Col New York, BS, 42; Polytech Inst Brooklyn, MS, 59. *Hon Degrees:* LHD, Monmouth Col, 79. *Prof Exp:* Electronic engr, Signal Corps Radar Lab, 42-44, chief optical micros, Eng Labs, 46-53, external researcher, 53-54, asst to dir res, 54-58; asst dir inst explor res, US Army Signal Res & Develop Lab, 58-62, dep dir res, US Army Electronics Labs, 62-65, chief sci & technol, US Army Electronics Command, 65-70, dir prog mgt, 70-74, spec asst logistics, 74-76, DIR INT LOGISTICS, US ARMY ELECTRONICS COMMAND, 76- *Concurrent Pos:* Adj prof, Monmouth Col, 56- *Mem:* Am Phys Soc; Optical Soc Am; Am Chem Soc; Am Asn Physics Teachers; NY Acad Sci. *Res:* Crystal physics and chemistry; optical properties of solids; administration of research. *Mailing Add:* 726 Sycamore Ave Shrewsbury NJ 07701

FIELD, PAUL EUGENE, b Easton, Pa, June 16, 34; m 60; c 3. PHYSICAL CHEMISTRY, INORGANIC CHEMISTRY. *Educ:* Moravian Col, BS, 57; Pa State Univ, MS, 61, PhD(chem), 63. *Prof Exp:* Asst prof, 63-68, ASSOC PROF CHEM, VA POLYTECH INST & STATE UNIV, 68- *Mem:* AAAS; Am Chem Soc; Sigma Xi. *Res:* Thermodynamic properties of solutions; high temperature calorimetry; microcomputer interfacing for measurement and control. *Mailing Add:* Dept of Chem Va Polytech Inst & State Univ Blacksburg VA 24061

FIELD, RAY A, b Ogden, Utah, Dec 15, 33; m 58; c 5. MEAT SCIENCE. *Educ:* Brigham Young Univ, BS, 58; Univ Ky, MS, 60, PhD(animal sci), 63. *Prof Exp:* Meat specialist, Nat Livestock & Meat Bd, 58; res asst, Univ Ky, 59-62; from asst prof to assoc prof, 62-70, PROF MEAT SCI, UNIV WYO, 70- *Concurrent Pos:* Consult meat deboning, Beehive Equip Co, 74- *Honors & Awards:* Award in Meat Sci, Am Soc Animal Sci, 75. *Mem:* Am Meat Sci Asn; Inst Food Technol; Am Soc Animal Sci. *Res:* Live animal and carcass evaluation; inheritance of quality in meat; consumer acceptance, and palatability characteristics of meat; postmortem biochemistry of collagen as related to tenderness; mechanically deboned meat. *Mailing Add:* Dept Animal Sci Univ Wyo Univ Sta Box 3354 Laramie WY 82071

FIELD, RICHARD D, b Pasadena, Calif, Apr 13, 44; m 66; c 3. ELEMENTARY PARTICLE PHYSICS. *Educ:* Univ Calif, Berkeley, BS, 66, PhD(theoret physics), 71. *Prof Exp:* Fel physics res, Brookhaven Nat Lab, 71-73; res fel physics, Calif Inst Technol, 73-78, res assoc prof, 78-80; PROF PHYSICS, UNIV FLA, 80- *Mem:* Am Phys Soc. *Res:* Theory and phenomenology of the strong wear, and electromagnetic forces in elementary particle physics. *Mailing Add:* Dept Physics 215 WN Univ Fla Gainesville FL 32611

FIELD, RICHARD JEFFREY, b Attleboro, Mass, Oct 26, 41; m 66. CHEMICAL KINETICS. *Educ:* Univ Mass, BS, 63; Col Holy Cross, MS, 64; Univ RI, PhD(phys chem), 68. *Prof Exp:* Res assoc phys chem, Univ Ore, 68-74 & vis asst prof, 70-73; sr res chemist, Radiation Res Lab, Carnegie-Mellon Univ, 74-75; asst prof, 75-78, ASSOC PROF CHEM, UNIV MONT, 78- *Mem:* Am Chem Soc. *Res:* Experimental gas and solution phase kinetics of complex chemical reactions, especially those exhibiting oscillatory behavior related to an unstable or excitable steady state; thermo-chemical kinetics, diffusive properties of free radicals and numerical methods in physical chemistry. *Mailing Add:* Dept of Chem Univ of Mont Missoula MT 59812

FIELD, ROBERT WARREN, b Wilmington, Del, June 13, 44. CHEMICAL PHYSICS. *Educ:* Amherst Col, BA, 65; Harvard Univ, MA & PhD(phys chem), 72. *Prof Exp:* Fel spectros, Quantum Inst, Univ Calif, Santa Barbara, 71-74; asst prof, 74-78, ASSOC PROF CHEM, MASS INST TECHNOL, 78- *Concurrent Pos:* Sloan Found res fel, 75. *Mem:* Am Chem Soc. *Res:* Tunable laser spectroscopy, particularly optical-optical double resonance on diatomic and triatomic molecules; optically pumped lasers; collision induced transitions; long-lived electronic states; analysis and consequences of intramolecular perturbations. *Mailing Add:* Dept of Chem 2-121 Mass Inst of Technol Cambridge MA 02139

FIELD, RONALD JAMES, b Grand Rapids, Mich, Jan 3, 46; m 69; c 1. WILDLIFE MANAGEMENT, ENVIRONMENTAL SCIENCES. *Educ:* Mich State Univ, BS, 68, MS, 70, PhD(zool), 71. *Prof Exp:* Asst prof zool, Howard Univ, 71-73; chmn, Dept Earth & Life Sci, Univ DC, 73-78; head, Dept Agr Sci, Tuskegee Inst, 78-80; PROG MGR, WILDLIFE RES DEVELOP, TENN VALLEY AUTHORITY, 80- *Concurrent Pos:* Consult rodent control, Synecology, Inc, 70-72; res grants, US Dept Interior, 72, NIH, 72-73; be dirs, Friends Nat Zoo, 72-78; wildlife res, US Fish & Wildlife Serv, 72; assoc dean, Agr & Nat Res, Washington Tech Inst, 75-76; vis prof wildlife mgt, Tenn Technol Univ, 76; asst pres & asst vpres, Univ DC, 76-77; consult furbearers, Tenn Valley Authority, 76. *Mem:* Wildlife Soc; Am Soc Mammalogists; Soc Am Foresters; Bear Biol Asn. *Res:* Population structures of several species of wildlife, expecially semiaquatic furbearers; population demography and control through chemical sterilization in wild rats. *Mailing Add:* 108 S Purdue Ave Oak Ridge TN 37830

FIELDER, D(ANIEL) C(URTIS), b North Kingstown, RI, Oct 9, 17; m 44. ELECTRICAL ENGINEERING. *Educ:* Univ RI, BS, 40, EE, 50; Ga Inst Technol, MS, 48, PhD(elec eng), 57. *Prof Exp:* Jr design engr transformers & switchgear, Westinghouse Elec Corp, 40-41; design engr degaussing & compass compensation, Bur Ships, Washington, DC, 41-46; asst elec eng, Ga Inst Technol, 46-47; instr, Syracuse Univ, 47-48; from asst prof to assoc prof, 48-63, PROF ELEC ENG, GA INST TECHNOL, 63- *Mem:* Sr mem Inst Elec & Electronics Engrs; Math Asn Am. *Res:* Graph theory; combinatorics; electric circuit theory; digital computer theory. *Mailing Add:* Sch of Elec Eng Ga Inst of Technol Atlanta GA 30332

FIELDER, DOUGLAS STRATTON, b Washington, DC, July 22, 40; m 68; c 1. PHYSICS. *Educ:* Va Mil Inst, BS, 62; Univ Va, MS, 64, PhD(physics), 67. *Prof Exp:* Asst prof, 69-70, ASSOC PROF PHYSICS & CHMN DEPT, STATE UNIV NY COL ONEONTA, 70- *Mem:* AAAS; Am Phys Soc; Am Asn Physics Teachers. *Res:* Determination of absolute cross sections for several photoneutron reactions; photonuclear physics; low energy nuclear reactions. *Mailing Add:* Dept of Physics State Univ of NY Oneonta NY 13820

FIELDHOUSE, DONALD JOHN, b Dodgeville, Wis, Nov 18, 25; m 49; c 4. SEED-BORNE BACTERIAL DISEASES, VEGETABLE PHYSIOLOGY. *Educ:* Univ Wis, PhD(hort), 54. *Prof Exp:* From asst prof to assoc prof, 54-70, PROF HORT, UNIV DEL, 70- *Mem:* Am Soc Hort Sci; Am Phytopath Soc. *Res:* Irrigation of vegetable crops; vegetable physiology; seed technology; soil, plant, and water relationships; plant growth regulators; crop physiology; plant pathology. *Mailing Add:* Dept Plant Sci Univ Del Col Agr Sci Newark DE 19711

FIELDHOUSE, JOHN W, b Rensselaer, Ind, Oct 17, 41; m 63; c 1. SYNTHETIC ORGANIC CHEMISTRY. *Educ:* Hope Col, BA, 63; Purdue

Univ, PhD(sulfenes), 68. *Prof Exp:* Res scientist, 68-73, sr res scientist, 73-78, ASSOC SCIENTIST, FIRESTONE TIRE & RUBBER CO, 78- *Mem:* Am Chem Soc. *Res:* Olefin and rubber intermediates synthesis; synthesis of polyfluoroalkoxyphosphazenes; emulsion polymerization of olefins. *Mailing Add:* Firestone Tire & Rubber Co 1200 Firestone Pkwy Akron OH 44317

FIELDING, CHRISTOPHER J, b Cheadle, Eng, Jan 26, 42; m 68. METABOLISM, BIOCHEMISTRY. *Educ:* Univ London, BSc, 62, PhD(genetics), 65. *Hon Degrees:* MA, Oxford Univ, 65. *Prof Exp:* Am Heart Asn estab investr, Dept Med, Univ Chicago, 70-71; Am Heart Asn estab investr biochem, Sch Med, 71-75, asst prof physiol & assoc staff, 75-77, ASSOC PROF PHYSIOL & SR MEM STAFF, CARDIOVASC RES INST, UNIV CALIF, SAN FRANCISCO, 78- *Concurrent Pos:* Res fel biochem, Oxford Univ, 65-67, fel, New Col, 65-69; Med Res Coun grant, 67-69; Am Heart Asn grant, 71-75; USPHS grant, Nat Heart & Lung Inst, 71- *Mem:* Am Soc Biol Chemists; fel Am Heart Asn. *Res:* Lipid metabolism; metabolism and structure of plasma lipoproteins; enzymology of lipases and acyl transferases; cellular cholesterol metabolism. *Mailing Add:* Sch of Med Cardiovasc Res Inst Univ of Calif San Francisco CA 94143

FIELDING, MAX JAE, b Orem, Utah, Jan 17, 26; m 48; c 4. NEMATOLOGY. *Educ:* Brigham Young Univ, BS, 48; La State Univ, MS, 56. *Prof Exp:* Nematologist, USDA, 48-56; res biologist, 56-66, SR RES BIOLOGIST, E I DU PONT DE NEMOURS & CO, 66- *Res:* Nematode taxonomy, physiology, ecology; control of parasitic nematodes by chemicals; control of soil fungi. *Mailing Add:* Plant Res Lab 900 Wilson Rd Wilmington DE 19898

FIELDING, STUART, b Bronx, NY, Oct 31, 39; m 62; c 2. PSYCHOPHARMACOLOGY, NEUROPHARMACOLOGY. *Educ:* Monmouth Col, BA, 62; Howard Univ, MS, 64; Univ Del, PhD(psychol), 68. *Prof Exp:* Teaching asst psychol, Howard Univ, 62-64; res psychologist, Commun Sci Res Ctr, 64; mgr psychopharmacol, Ciba-Geigy, 67-75; asst dir pharmacol, 75-76, ASSOC DIR BIOL SCI, HOECHST-ROUSSEL PHARMACEUT, INC, 77- *Concurrent Pos:* Adj asst prof, Fairleigh Dickinson Univ, 72-74; adj assoc prof, 74-; adj prof drug develop res, Univ RI, 80- *Mem:* AAAS; Am Psychol Asn; Soc Neurosci; Behav Pharmacologist Soc; Am Soc Pharmacol & Exp Therapeut. *Res:* Psychopharmacology, physiological basis of behavior, aggression, analgesia and operant behavior. *Mailing Add:* Dept of Pharmacol Rte 202-206 N Somerville NJ 08876

FIELDING-RUSSELL, GEORGE SAMUEL, b Calcutta, India, Dec 10, 39; Brit citizen; m 66; c 2. POLYMER SCIENCE. *Educ:* Loughborough Univ Technol, BSc Hons & dipl, 63, PhD(polymer sci), 67; Univ Leicester, MSc, 65. *Prof Exp:* Indust chemist, Brit Celanese Ltd, 61-62; SR RES CHEMIST POLYMER SCI, RES DIV, GOODYEAR TIRE & RUBBER CO, 68- *Mem:* Am Chem Soc. *Res:* Physical chemistry of high polymers; mechanical, dielectric, rheological and viscoelastic properties of solid polymers; polymer crystallization and morphology; polymer characterization via thermal methods. *Mailing Add:* 3901 Greentree Rd Stow OH 44224

FIELDS, ALFRED E, b Rochester, NY, July 2, 37. POLYMER PHYSICS. *Educ:* St John Fisher Col, NY, BS, 59; Univ Akron, PhD(polymer sci), 67. *Prof Exp:* Mgr, Voplex Corp, NY, 67-69 & Polymer Prod Corp, 69-72; sr res chemist, Photomat Lab, 72-73, sect coordr, Environ Chem Sect, 74, group leader, 75, SUPVR ENVIRON SERV LAB, EASTMAN KODAK CO, 76- *Res:* Environmental studies and physical chemistry of polymers in the photographic industry. *Mailing Add:* 260 Dunning Ave Webster NY 14580

FIELDS, BERNARD N, b Brooklyn, NY, Mar 24, 38; c 5. VIROLOGY, GENETICS. *Educ:* Brandeis Univ, AB, 58; NY Univ, MD, 62. *Hon Degrees:* AM, Harvard Univ, 76. *Prof Exp:* Asst-assoc prof med & cell biol, Albert Einstein Col Med, 67-75; PROF MICROBIOL, HARVARD MED SCH, 75- *Concurrent Pos:* Mem, NSF Genetic Biol Adv Panel, 73-76, Multiple Sclerosis Soc Adv Panel Fundamental Res, 76- & NIH Task Force Virology, 76-77; assoc ed, J Infectious Dis, 76-; vis prof, Wash Univ, 77; NIH grants; ed, Infection & Immunity, 79-; mem, Bd Scientific Counr, Nat Inst Allergy & Infectious Dis, NIH, 81. *Honors & Awards:* Fac Res Assoc Award, Am Cancer Soc, 69-74. *Mem:* Am Soc Clin Invest; Infectious Dis Soc Am; Harvey Soc; Am Asn Immunologists; AAAS. *Res:* Viral genetics; virus-host interaction; infectious disease. *Mailing Add:* Harvard Med Sch Boston MA 02115

FIELDS, CLARK LEROY, b Pipestone, Minn, Oct 25, 37; m 63; c 1. INORGANIC CHEMISTRY. *Educ:* Pasadena Col, BA, 59; Univ Iowa, MS, 62, PhD(inorg chem), 64. *Prof Exp:* Assoc prof, 64-74, PROF CHEM, UNIV NORTHERN COLO, 74- *Mem:* AAAS; Am Chem Soc. *Res:* Chemistry of boron and transition metal hydrides. *Mailing Add:* Dept of Chem Univ of Northern Colo Greeley CO 80639

FIELDS, D(AVIS) S(TUART), JR, b Lexington, Ky, Apr 17, 29; m 55; c 3. PHYSICAL METALLURGY. *Educ:* Univ Ky, BS, 50; Mass Inst Technol, MS, 54, ScD(metall), 57. *Prof Exp:* Phys metallurgist, Watertown Arsenal Labs, 51-52; res metallurgist, Res Labs, Aluminum Co Am, 57-60; from asst prof to assoc prof metall, Univ Ky, 60-62; staff metallurgist, 62-64, adv metallurgist, 64-67, SR ENGR, IBM CORP, 67- *Concurrent Pos:* Lectr, Univ Ky, 62-67; adj prof, Univ Ariz, 80. *Mem:* Am Soc Metals; Am Inst Mining, Metall & Petrol Engrs; Sigma Xi. *Res:* Mechanical metallurgy; strain hardening behavior of metals and alloys; relationship to working and forming operations; relationship to microstructural characteristics; practical applications of superplastic alloys; reliability modeling and maintenance philosophy of computer systems; technology advancement in digital magnetic recording systems. *Mailing Add:* 2630 Santa Lucia Tucson AZ 85715

FIELDS, DAVID EDWARD, b Hickman, Ky, Oct 25, 44; m 71. APPLIED PHYSICS. *Educ:* Murray State Univ, BS, 66; Univ Wis, Madison, MS, 68, PhD(solid state physics), 72. *Prof Exp:* Teaching asst physics, Univ Wis, 66-67, res asst, 67-72; APPL PHYSICIST, HEALTH & SAFETY RES DIV, UNION CARBIDE CORP, NUCLEAR DIV, OAK RIDGE NAT LAB, 72- *Concurrent Pos:* Vis lectr electronics & comput sci, Murray State Univ, Murray, Ky, 76-77. *Mem:* Am Inst Physics; Am Geophys Union; Am Phys Soc. *Res:* Environmental modeling; numerical analysis; hydrologic sediment transport; windblown seed dispersal; solid state physics; pattern recognition; solar energy usage. *Mailing Add:* Box X Oak Ridge Nat Lab Oak Ridge TN 37831

FIELDS, DONALD LEE, b Louisville, Ky, May 16, 32; m 53; c 4. ORGANIC CHEMISTRY. *Educ:* East Ky State Col, BS, 54; Ohio State Univ, PhD(chem), 58. *Prof Exp:* Res chemist, 58-60, sr res chemist, 60-64, res assoc chem, 64-74, lab head, 74-75, SR LAB HEAD, ORG RES LAB, EASTMAN KODAK CO, 75- *Mem:* Am Chem Soc. *Res:* Exploratory research in synthetic organic chemistry. *Mailing Add:* Eastman Kodak Co 343 State Rochester NY 14608

FIELDS, ELLIS KIRBY, b Chicago, Ill, May 10, 17; m 39; c 3. ORGANIC CHEMISTRY. *Educ:* Univ Chicago, BS, 36, PhD(org chem), 38. *Prof Exp:* Eli Lilly res fel, Univ Chicago, 38-41; dir res, Develop Lab, Univ Chicago, 41-50; res assoc, Standard Oil Co (Ind), 50-62, sr res assoc, 62-75, RES CONSULT, AMOCO CHEM CORP DIV, STANDARD OIL CO (IND), 75- *Concurrent Pos:* Mem staff, Kings Col, London, 62-; mem petrol res fund adv bd, Am Petrol Inst; assoc ed, Chem Revs, Petrol Preprints, Am Chem Soc; Almquist lectr, Univ Idaho, 79. *Honors & Awards:* Petrol Chem Award, Am Chem Soc, 78. *Mem:* AAAS; Am Chem Soc; Faraday Soc; The Chem Soc. *Res:* Petrochemicals; oxidation process; lube oils and additives; pesticides; catalysis; photochemistry. *Mailing Add:* Davenport House 559 Ashland Ave River Forest IL 60305

FIELDS, HOWARD LINCOLN, b Chicago, Ill, Dec 12, 39; m 66; c 2. NEUROPHYSIOLOGY. *Educ:* Univ Chicago, BS, 60; Stanford Univ, MD, 65, PhD(neurosci), 66. *Prof Exp:* Fel neurol, Harvard Med Sch, 70-72; instr, 72-73, asst prof, 73-78, ASSOC PROF NEUROL & PHYSIOL, UNIV CALIF, SAN FRANCISCO, 78- *Concurrent Pos:* Macy Found fel, 79. *Honors & Awards:* Res Career Develop Award, NIH, 74. *Mem:* Soc Neurosci; Am Physiol Soc; Am Acad Neurol; Am Neurol Asn; Int Asn Study Pain. *Res:* Neurophysiological mechanisms of pain transmission; modulation of sensory transmission by central nervous system. *Mailing Add:* Dept of Neurol M794 Univ of Calif San Francisco CA 94143

FIELDS, JAMES PERRY, b Sherman, Tex, July 30, 32; m 58; c 2. DERMATOLOGY, DERMATOPATHOLOGY. *Educ:* Univ Tex, Austin, BS, 53, MS, 57; Univ Tex Med Br, Galveston, MD, 58. *Prof Exp:* Asst dermat to assoc clin prof dermat & path, Columbia Univ Col Physicians & Surgeons, New York, 63-80; dir dermat, US Pub Health Serv Hosp, 64-79; ASSOC PROF MED & PATH, VANDERBILT UNIV MED SCH, 79- *Concurrent Pos:* J D Lane Clin Res Award, USPHS, 78. *Mem:* Fel Am Col Physicians; fel Am Acad Dermat; fel Am Soc Dermatopath; fel Am Acad Allergy; fel Am Col Allergists. *Res:* Pharmacology of cobalt; immunopathology of leprosy; cancer of the skin (leiomyosarcoma). *Mailing Add:* 620 Med Arts Bldg Vanderbilt Med Ctr Nashville TN 37212

FIELDS, JERRY L, b Green City, Mo, Aug 5, 36. MATHEMATICS. *Educ:* Harvard Univ, AB, 58, AM, 61, PhD(math), 64. *Prof Exp:* Sr mathematician, Midwest Res Inst, 64-68; vis assoc prof math, Tsing Hua Univ, Taiwan, 68-69; ASSOC PROF MATH, UNIV ALTA, 69- *Mem:* Math Asn Am; Am Math Soc; Soc Indust & Appl Math. *Res:* Approximation theory, asymptotic analysis. *Mailing Add:* Dept of Math Univ of Alta Edmonton AB T6G 2E1 Can

FIELDS, KAY LOUISE, b Palo Alto, Calif, July 22, 41. MOLECULAR BIOLOGY, NEUROSCIENCES. *Educ:* Radcliffe Col, AB, 63; Mass Inst Technol, PhD(biol), 68. *Prof Exp:* Am Cancer Soc fel molecular biol, Univ Geneva, Switz, 68-70; res assoc, Inst Molecular Biol, Univ Geneva, 70-71; hon res fel neuroimmunol, Univ Col, London, 71-77; ASST PROF NEUROL & NEUROSCI, ALBERT EINSTEIN COL MED, 78- *Res:* Definition and characterization of cell surface antigens and receptors on normal and tumor cells of the nervous system using biochemical and immunological approaches. *Mailing Add:* Dept of Neurol F-131 Morris Park Ave Bronx NY 10461

FIELDS, MARION LEE, b Plainfield, Ind, Dec 15, 26; m 46; c 4. FOOD SCIENCE, MICROBIOLOGY. *Educ:* Univ Ind, AB, 50; Purdue Univ, MS, 56, PhD(food tech), 59. *Prof Exp:* Sanitarian, Ind State Bd Health, 51-54; asst hort, Purdue Univ, 54-56, instr, 56-59, asst prof, 59-60; from asst prof to assoc prof hort, 60-67, assoc prof food sci & nutrit, 67-69, PROF FOOD SCI & NUTRIT, UNIV MO-COLUMBIA, 69- *Mem:* Inst Food Technol; Am Soc Microbiol. *Res:* Microbial ecology; heat resistance of bacterial spores; protein quality evaluation; microbial protein for food for man. *Mailing Add:* Dept of Food Sci & Nutrit Univ of Mo Columbia MO 65201

FIELDS, MELVIN, organic chemistry, see previous edition

FIELDS, PAUL ROBERT, b Chicago, Ill, Feb 4, 19; m 43; c 3. HEAVY ELEMENT CHEMISTRY, NUCLEAR CHEMISTRY. *Educ:* Univ Chicago, BS, 41. *Prof Exp:* Chemist, Tenn Valley Authority, 41-43, Metall Lab, 43-45, Monsanto Chem Co, 45; Standard Oil Ind, 45-46; chemist, 46-48, assoc chemist, 48-58, sr chemist, 58-71, dir, Chem Div, 71-80, ASSOC LAB DIR, PHYSICAL RES, ARGONNE NAT LAB, 80- *Concurrent Pos:* Mem, Adv Comt Transplutonium Elements, 58-76; mem, Nat Acad Sci Ad Hoc Comt Heavy Ion Facil & Res, 70-71. *Mem:* Am Chem Soc; Am Phys Soc; fel Am Nuclear Soc; AAAS. *Res:* Heavy element chemistry; nuclear chemistry; chemistry of rare gas compounds; lunar soil analysis. *Mailing Add:* Chem Div Argonne Nat Lab 9700 S Cass Ave Argonne IL 60439

FIELDS, REUBEN ELBERT, b Society Hill, SC, Sept 30, 16; m 45; c 3. NUCLEAR SCIENCE, NUCLEAR STRUCTURE. *Educ:* Ga Inst Technol, BS, 40; Univ Wis, MS, 51, PhD(physics), 54. *Prof Exp:* Assoc engr, Rural Electrification Admin, 40-42; physicist nuclear physics, Argonne Nat Lab, 44-46 & 47-49; STAFF SCIENTIST NUCLEAR PHYSICS, FT WORTH DIV, GEN DYNAMICS CORP, 53- *Concurrent Pos:* Lectr, Southern Methodist Univ; adj prof, Tex Christian Univ. *Mem:* Am Phys Soc; Am Nuclear Soc; Am Asn Physics Teachers; Sigma Xi. *Res:* Photoneutron sources; neutron cross sections; nuclear forces; nuclear reactor hazards; analysis of survivability/vulnerability of military aircraft subjected to nuclear weapon threat fields, including blast, thermal, neutron, gamma and x-radiation, and electromagnetic pulse. *Mailing Add:* 4132 Clayton Rd W Fort Worth TX 76116

FIELDS, RICHARD JOEL, b Philadelphia, Pa, Nov 21, 47; c 4. METALLURGY, CHEMISTRY. *Educ:* Univ Pa, BA & Bsc, 71; Harvard Univ, MSc, 73; Cambridge Univ, PhD(eng), 77. *Prof Exp:* res assoc metall, 77-79, METALLURGIST, NAT BUR STANDARDS, 79- *Concurrent Pos:* Consult, Automotive Training Ctr, 76- *Mem:* Am Soc Metals; Am Soc Test & Mat; Am Ceramic Soc. *Res:* High temperature fracture and effects of inclusions on strength of metals; strength differential in managing steel; precipitation kinetics in high-strength low-alloy steel. *Mailing Add:* Nat Bur Standards Rm A113 Bldg 223 Washington DC 20234

FIELDS, ROBERT WILLIAM, b San Leandro, Calif, Sept 17, 20; m 45; c 2. PALEONTOLOGY, SEDIMENTOLOGY. *Educ:* Univ Calif, BA, 49, PhD(vert paleont), 52. *Prof Exp:* Asst teacher vert paleont, Univ Calif, 49-51; geologist, Shell Oil Co, 52-55; from asst prof to assoc prof, 55-64, chmn dept, 64-70 & 77-79, PROF GEOL, UNIV MONT, 64- *Concurrent Pos:* Field leader exped, Colombia, SAm, Univ Calif; geol consult, var petrol & mineral co, 70- *Mem:* Soc Vert Paleont; Geol Soc Am. *Res:* Evolution, sedimentology and paleoecology of Tertiary intermontane basins of the Northern Rocky Mountain province; mammalian vertebrate paleontology; evolution of South American hystricomorph rodents; comparative anatomy and evolution of Tertiary mammals. *Mailing Add:* Dept of Geol Univ of Mont Missoula MT 59812

FIELDS, THEODORE, b Chicago, Ill, Jan 23, 22; m 45; c 3. MEDICAL PHYSICS. *Educ:* Univ Chicago, BS, 42; DePaul Univ, MS, 53; Am Bd Radiol, dipl, 50; Am Bd Health Physics, dipl, 60. *Prof Exp:* Physicist, Manhattan Proj, Univ Chicago, 43-45; chief engr, Precision Radiation Instrument Co, 48-49; instr radiation physics, Med Sch, Northwestern Univ, 49-61; asst prof, 61-74, clin assoc prof radiol, 74-78, LECTR RADIOL, STRITCH SCH MED, LOYOLA UNIV, CHICAGO, 80- *Concurrent Pos:* Chief physics sect, Vet Admin Hines Hosp, 49-65; physicist, Radiation Ctr, Cook County Hosp, Chicago, 58-, radiation physicist, 66-; pres, Health Physics Assocs, 60-; pres, Isotope Measurement Labs, Highland Park, 69-; pres, Mobile Imaging Labs, Highland Park, 77- *Mem:* Am Phys Soc; Soc Nuclear Med; Am Pub Health Asn; Inst Elec & Electronics Engrs; fel Am Col Radiol. *Res:* Radiation safety in medicine, industry, and teaching; quality control evaluations of x-ray diagnostic procedures and nuclear medicine; neutron activation analysis; whole body counting. *Mailing Add:* 1141 Hohlfelder Rd Glencoe IL 60022

FIELDS, THOMAS HENRY, b Kearny, NJ, Oct 23, 30; m 58; c 4. EXPERIMENTAL PHYSICS, COMPUTERS. *Educ:* Carnegie-Mellon Univ, BS, 51, PhD(physics), 55. *Prof Exp:* Assoc prof physics, Carnegie-Mellon Univ, 58-60; prof physics, Northwestern Univ, 60-69; dir, High Energy Physics Div, 65-74, assoc lab dir, 74-77, SR PHYSICIST, ARGONNE NAT LAB, 77- *Concurrent Pos:* Vis scientist, Univ Birmingham, 70-71 & Europ Orgn Nuclear Res, Switzerland, 77-78. *Mem:* Am Phys Soc. *Res:* Experimental study of antiproton annihilation, large transverse momentum hadron reactions and proton decay. *Mailing Add:* High Energy Physics Div Argonne Nat Lab Argonne IL 60439

FIELDS, THOMAS LYNN, b Baltimore, Md, Oct 12, 25; m 47; c 2. ORGANIC CHEMISTRY. *Educ:* Ala Polytech Inst, BS, 52, MS, 54. *Prof Exp:* RES CHEMIST, LEDERLE LABS, AM CYANAMID CO, 54- *Mem:* Am Chem Soc. *Res:* Chemistry of natural products; total synthesis and chemical modifications of tetracyclines; medicinal chemistry. *Mailing Add:* Lederle Labs Am Cyanamid Co Pearl River NY 10965

FIELDS, WILLIAM GORDON, b Victoria, BC, Mar 29, 12; m 50; c 3. INVERTEBRATE ZOOLOGY. *Educ:* Univ BC, BA, 37; Stanford Univ, AM, 49, PhD(biol), 63. *Prof Exp:* Pub sch teacher, BC, 38-40; from instr to assoc prof biol & zool, 40-61, head dept, 51-71, prof, 61-77, EMER PROF BIOL, UNIV VICTORIA, BC, 77- *Mem:* AAAS; Soc Syst Zool; Can Soc Zoologists. *Res:* Marine biology; structure, development, food relations, reproduction, life histories and taxonomy of marine invertebrate animals, particularly cephalopods; biological oceanography. *Mailing Add:* 2221 Arbutus Rd Victoria Can

FIELDS, WILLIAM STRAUS, b Baltimore, Md, Aug 18, 13; m 41; c 2. NEUROLOGY. *Educ:* Harvard Univ, AB, 34, MD, 38; Am Bd Psychiat & Neurol, dipl, 50. *Prof Exp:* From assoc prof to prof, Baylor Col Med, 49-67, chmn dept, 59-65; prof, Univ Tex Med Sch Dallas, 67-69; prof, Univ Tex Grad Sch Biomed Sci Houston, 69-70; PROF NEUROL, UNIV TEX MED SCH HOUSTON, 70-, CHMN DEPT, 72- *Concurrent Pos:* Rockefeller fel, Sch Med, Washington Univ, St Louis, 46-49; consult neurologist, St Luke's Episcopal Hosp, Tex Children's Hosp & M D Anderson Hosp, Houston; chief neurol serv, Hermann Hosp, St Anthony Ctr, Houston, 70-79; mem exec comt & study group chmn, Joint Comt Stroke Res, Washington, DC, 68-76; mem adv comt, Psychiat, Neurol & Psychol Serv, Vet Admin, 66-74; consult, Hearings & Appeals Bds, Social Security Admin, US Dept Health, Educ & Welfare, 65-78. *Honors & Awards:* Mem Order of Brit Empire, 46. *Mem:* Am Acad Neurol; Am Asn Neurol Surg; Am Cong Rehab Med; Am Epilepsy Soc; AMA. *Res:* Epilepsy; cerebrovascular disease; anti-thrombotic drugs. *Mailing Add:* 6431 Fannin Houston TX 77030

FIELDSTEEL, ARNOLD HOWARD, b New York, NY, May 14, 18; m. VIROLOGY. *Educ:* Johns Hopkins Univ, BA, 39; Univ Mich, PhD(bact), 50. *Prof Exp:* Virologist, Pitman-Moore Co, 53-55; virologist, Cutter Labs, 55-57; dir virus lab, Mont State Bd Health, 57-61; assoc res virologist, Dept Path, Med Ctr, Univ Calif, San Francisco, 61-62, sr virologist, 62-69; mgr virol prog, 69-74, MGR INFECTIOUS DIS PROG, SRI INT, 74- *Concurrent Pos:* Nat Found Infantile Paralysis fel virol, Children's Hosp Res Found, Cincinnati, 50-53. *Mem:* AAAS; Soc Exp Biol & Med; Am Asn Cancer Res; Am Soc Microbiol; Int Leprosy Asn. *Res:* Murine leukemias; viral carcinogenesis; in vivo and in vitro studies of virus transformed malignant cells; defective leukemia virus; tissue culture studies on Mycobacterium leprae; tissue culture studies on Treponema pallidum; immunosuppression and susceptibility to disease. *Mailing Add:* Life Sci Div SRI Int Menlo Park CA 94025

FIENBERG, STEPHEN ELLIOTT, b Toronto, Ont, Nov 27, 42; m 65; c 2. STATISTICS. *Educ:* Univ Toronto, BSc, 64; Harvard Univ, AM, 65, PhD(statist), 68. *Prof Exp:* Instr psychol, Wellesley Col, 68; asst prof statist & theoret biol, Univ Chicago, 68-72; assoc prof, Univ Minn, 72-76, chmn dept, 72-78, prof appl statist, 78-80; PROF STATIST & SOC SCI, CARNEGIE-MELLON UNIV, 80-, HEAD DEPT STATIST, 81- *Concurrent Pos:* Mem adv & planning comt social indicators, Social Sci Res Coun, 72-77; vis assoc dir, Ctr Health Practs, Sch Pub Health, Harvard Univ & vis lectr, Dept Statist, 75-76; coord & appl ed, J Am Statist Asn, 77-79; mem bd dirs, Social Sci Res Coun, 80-83; chmn, Comt Nat Statist, Nat Res Coun, Nat Acad Sci, 81-84. *Mem:* fel AAAS; fel Am Statist Asn; Biomet Soc; fel Inst Math Statist; Psychomet Soc. *Res:* Analysis of cross classified data; Bayesian inference; data analysis; stochastic modelling. *Mailing Add:* Dept Appl Statist Carnegie-Mellon Univ Pittsburgh PA 15213

FIENUP, JAMES R, b St Louis, Mo, Apr 17, 48; m 70; c 4. INFORMATION PROCESSING, HOLOGRAPHY. *Educ:* Holy Cross Col, BA, 70; Stanford Univ, MS, 72, PhD(appl physics), 75. *Prof Exp:* Res asst, Electronics Lab, Stanford Univ, 72-75; RES PHYSICIST, RADAR & OPTICS DIV, ENVIRON RES INST MICH, 75- *Honors & Awards:* Rudolf Kingslake Medal & Prize, Soc Photo-Optical Instrumentation Engrs, 80. *Mem:* Optical Soc Am; Soc Photo-Optical Instrumentation Engrs; Sigma Xi. *Res:* Coherent optical and digital image processing; image reconstruction; holographic optical elements; computer-generated holograms. *Mailing Add:* 3426 Gettysburg Rd Ann Arbor MI 48105

FIERER, JOSHUA A, b New York, NY, Nov 25, 37; m 59; c 4. PATHOLOGY, IMMUNOPATHOLOGY. *Educ:* Alfred Univ, BA, 59; State Univ NY Downstate Med Ctr, MD, 63. *Prof Exp:* Asst surg, Sch Med, Univ Rochester, 64-65; resident path, Columbia-Presby Med Ctr, 67-68, vis fel, 68-70; asst prof path, Columbia Univ Col Physicians & Surgeons, 70-76; prof path, Sch Med, Creighton Univ, 76-78; PROF & CHMN DEPT PATH, COL MED, UNIV ILL, PEORIA, 78- *Concurrent Pos:* Vis lectr path, Sch Dent, Farleigh Dickinson Univ, 68-72; guest investr immunol, Rockefeller Univ, 69-70; asst med examr, Off Chief Med Examr, City of New York, 69-; dir immunopath, Columbia-Presby Med Ctr, 72-76; consult renal path, Holy Name Hosp, 72-; consult immunopath, Kidney Hypertension Unit, Lenox Hill Hosp, 73-75; assoc dir labs, Francis Delafield Div, Columbia-Presby Med Ctr, 74-75; dir, Div Anat Path, Creighton-Omaha Med Ctr, 76-78; dir lab, Col med, Univ Ill, 78- *Mem:* Am Soc Exp Path; Am Asn Pathologists & Bacteriologists; Am Asn Immunologists; fel Col Am Pathologists; Int Acad Path. *Res:* Ultrastructure of lung connective tissue; tumor associated antigens; proteolytic enzymes and enzyme inhibitors; cellular aspects of aging. *Mailing Add:* Dept Path Univ Ill PO Box 1649 Peoria IL 61656

FIERING, MYRON B, b New York, NY, Apr 5, 34; m 57; c 2. CIVIL ENGINEERING, APPLIED MATHEMATICS. *Educ:* Harvard Univ, AB, 55, SM, 58, PhD(eng), 60. *Prof Exp:* Soils engr, Tippetts, Abbott, McCarthy, Stratton, 55-57; asst prof eng, Univ Calif, Los Angeles, 60-61; res fel environ eng, 61-62, lectr appl math, 62-63, asst prof eng & appl math, 63-70, GORDON McKAY PROF ENG & APPL MATH, HARVARD UNIV, 70- *Concurrent Pos:* Consult, USPHS, 63-; Fulbright lectr & vis assoc prof, Univ New South Wales, Australia, 64. *Honors & Awards:* Gold Medal, Am Asn Sanitary Engrs, 62. *Mem:* Am Soc Civil Engrs; Am Geophys Union; Sigma Xi; Int Asn Sci Hydrol. *Res:* Water resources; statistics. *Mailing Add:* Pierce Hall 118 Harvard Univ Cambridge MA 02138

FIERO, GEORGE WILLIAM, JR, b Buffalo, NY, Jan 16, 36; m 59; c 3. GEOLOGY, ENVIRONMENTAL SCIENCES. *Educ:* Dartmouth Col, BA, 57; Univ Wyo, MS, 59; Univ Wis, PhD(geol), 68. *Prof Exp:* Explor geologist, Texaco, Inc, 59-61, exploitation geologist, 61-63; teacher geol, Mt Hermon Sch, 63-66; PROF GEOL, UNIV NEV, LAS VEGAS, 68- *Honors & Awards:* Stanley A Tyler Award, Univ Wis, 68. *Mem:* AAAS; Am Asn Petrol Geol; Am Geophys Union; Am Water Resources Asn; Geol Soc Am. *Res:* Ground water effects on geothermal gradients; remote sensing in water resource studies; hydrogeological aspects of water pollution; regional geology of the Great Basin; geology of the national parks. *Mailing Add:* Dept of Geosci Univ of Nev Las Vegas NV 89154

FIERSTINE, HARRY LEE, b Long Beach, Calif, Aug 14, 32; m 58; c 3. COMPARATIVE ANATOMY, ICHTHYOLOGY. *Educ:* Long Beach State Col, BS, 57; Univ Calif, Los Angeles, MA, 61, PhD(zool), 65. *Prof Exp:* From instr to asst prof zool, Calif State Col Long Beach, 64-66; from asst prof to assoc prof, 66-74, PROF ZOOL, CALIF POLYTECH STATE UNIV, SAN LUIS OBISPO, 74- *Mem:* Am Soc Zool; Am Soc Ichthyol & Herpet; Soc Vert Paleont. *Res:* Functional fish anatomy; tertiary fish paleontology. *Mailing Add:* Dept of Biol Sci Calif Polytech State Univ San Luis Obispo CA 93407

FIESINGER, DONALD WILLIAM, b Corning, NY, Aug 4, 43; m 67; c 2. IGNEOUS PETROLOGY. *Educ:* State Univ NY Col, Potsdam, BA, 66; Wayne State Univ, MS, 69; Univ Calgary, PhD(geol), 75. *Prof Exp:* Asst prof geol, State Univ NY Col, New Paltz, 74-76; ASST PROF GEOL, UTAH STATE UNIV, 76- *Concurrent Pos:* Investr fac res fel & grant-in-aid, Res Found State Univ NY, 76-77; co-investr fac res grant, Utah State Univ, 77-79; co-investr, US Geol Surv res grant, 78-79. *Mem:* Geol Soc Am; Am Geophys Union; Geol Asn Can; Mineral Asn Can. *Res:* Chemical evolution of magma systems; study of tertiary volcanism in the basin and range province; computer modeling of igneous processes. *Mailing Add:* Dept of Geol UMC07 Utah State Univ Logan UT 84322

FIESS, HAROLD ALVIN, b Ringoes, NJ, Apr 28, 17; m 43; c 4. CHEMISTRY. *Educ:* Wheaton Col, Ill, BS, 39; Univ Ill, MS, 42, PhD(chem), 44. *Prof Exp:* Chemist, Am Cyanamid Co, NJ, 39-40; asst chem, Univ Ill, 40-43; from instr to assoc prof, 44-58, chmn dept, 75-80, PROF CHEM, WHEATON COL, 58- *Concurrent Pos:* Res assoc, Northwestern Univ, 49-50. *Mem:* Am Chem Soc. *Res:* Analytical chemistry. *Mailing Add:* Dept of Chem Wheaton Col Wheaton IL 60187

FIETZ, WILLIAM ADOLF, b Corinna, Maine, Sept 20, 31; m 60; c 2. LOW TEMPERATURE PHYSICS. *Educ:* Cornell Univ, BEE, 57, MS, 63, PhD(appl physics), 67. *Prof Exp:* Field engr, Fla Power & Light Co, Miami, 57-60; res physicist, Linde Div Lab, Union Carbide Corp, NY, 66-71; staff scientist, Intermagnetics Gen Corp, 71-74; GROUP LEADER, OAK RIDGE NAT LAB, 74- *Mem:* AAAS; Am Phys Soc; Inst Elec & Electronics Eng. *Res:* Superconductivity of high field-high current materials; properties of plasma-plated metal powders. *Mailing Add:* Union Carbide Corp Nuclear Div Y-12 Site PO Box Y Oak Ridge TN 37830

FIEVE, RONALD ROBERT, b Stevens Point, Wis, Mar 5, 30; m 63; c 2. PSYCHIATRY. *Educ:* Univ Wis, BMS, 51; Harvard Med Sch, MD, 55; Am Bd Psychiat & Neurol, dipl, 62. *Prof Exp:* Intern, Columbia Med Div, Bellevue Hosp, 55-56; asst resident internal med, NY Hosp, Cornell Univ, 56-57; resident psychiat, NY State Psychiat Inst, 57-60; instr, 60-62 & assoc, 64-67, from asst prof to assoc prof, 67-73, PROF CLIN PSYCHIAT, COL PHYSICIANS & SURGEONS, COLUMBIA UNIV, 73-; CHIEF PSYCHIAT RES, NY STATE PSYCHIAT INST, 76- *Concurrent Pos:* NIMH res grant psychopharmacol; dir personnel med clin & acute psychiat serv, NY State Psychiat Inst, 60-; prin res scientist & chief psychiat res, Lithium Clin, 62-, dir metab res serv, 63-; mem, WHO, 60-; asst exam, Am Bd Psychiat & Neurol, 66- *Honors & Awards:* Richard H Hutchings Award. *Mem:* AMA; Am Psychiat Asn; Acad Psychoanal; Am Col Neuropsychopharmacol; Am Psychopath Asn. *Res:* Behavioral and biological psychiatry; lithium; manic depressive illness and psychopharmacology. *Mailing Add:* 161 Fort Washington Ave New York NY 10032

FIFE, PAUL CHASE, b Cedar City, Utah, Feb 14, 30; m 59; c 3. MATHEMATICS, CONTINUUM MECHANICS. *Educ:* Univ Chicago, BA, 51; Univ Calif, Berkeley, BA, 53; NY Univ, PhD(math), 59. *Prof Exp:* From instr to asst prof math, Stanford Univ, 59-63; from asst prof to assoc prof, Univ Minn, 63-68; PROF MATH, UNIV ARIZ, 69- *Concurrent Pos:* Res grants, Off Naval Res, Air Force Off Sci Res & NSF, 59-; US Dept State Fulbright res grant, Ger, 66-67; teaching grant, Peru, 71; sr res fel, US Sci Res Coun, 74-75. *Mem:* Am Math Soc; Soc Natural Philos. *Res:* Various aspects of partial differential equations of elliptic and parabolic types; singular perturbations of partial differential equations; elastic plate theory; fluid dynamics. *Mailing Add:* Dept of Math Univ of Ariz Tucson AZ 85721

FIFE, THOMAS HARLEY, b Oak Park, Ill, Feb 6, 31; m 58; c 2. PHYSICAL ORGANIC. *Educ:* Univ Ill, BS, 55; Univ Minn, PhD(chem), 59. *Prof Exp:* Fel, Johns Hopkins Univ, 59-60, Cornell Univ, 60-62; asst prof, 62-65, assoc prof, 65-70, PROF BIOCHEM, UNIV SOUTHERN CALIF, 70- *Mem:* Am Chem Soc; Am Soc Biol Chemists. *Res:* kinetics and mechanisms of chemical and enzymatic reactions. *Mailing Add:* Dept Biochem Univ Southern Calif Mudd-612 2025 Zonal Ave Los Angeles CA 90033

FIFE, WILLIAM PAUL, b Plymouth, Ind, Nov 23, 17; m 47; c 2. PHYSIOLOGY, ANATOMY. *Educ:* Univ Ore, BS, 56; George Washington Univ, 56-58; Ohio State Univ, PhD(physiol), 62. *Prof Exp:* Asst chief aerospace med res div, US Air Force Sch Aerospace Med, 62-67; asst dir, Inst Life Sci, 67-77, PROF BIOL, TEX A&M UNIV, 70-, ASSOC DEAN, COL SCI & DIR, HYPERBARIC LAB, 77-, INTERIM HEAD DEPT, 80- *Concurrent Pos:* Actg head dept biol, Tex A&M Univ, 67-70 & 73-74. *Mem:* Am Physiol Soc; Aerospace Med Asn; Undersea Med Soc. *Res:* Cardiovascular and diving physiology, including environmental physiology; study of deep diving and use of hydrogen|oxygen mixtures for diving. *Mailing Add:* Dept of Biol Texas A&M Univ College Station TX 77843

FIFE, WILMER KRAFFT, b Wellsville, Ohio, Oct 19, 33; m 59; c 3. BIO-ORGANIC CHEMISTRY. *Educ:* Case Inst Technol, BSc, 55; Ohio State Univ, PhD(org chem), 60. *Prof Exp:* From asst prof to prof chem, Muskingum Col, 60-71 & chmn dept, 66-71; chmn dept, 71-80, PROF CHEM, IND UNIV-PURDUE UNIV, INDIANAPOLIS, 71- *Concurrent Pos:* Res grants, Res Corp, 60-61 & NSF, 62-66, 71 & 75; NIH spec fel, Harvard Univ, 65-66 & Chandler Lab, Columbia Univ, 68-69. *Mem:* AAAS; Am Chem Soc. *Res:* Function of metal ions in enzymes; enzyme models; catalysis and pathway control of organic reactions with transition metal ions. *Mailing Add:* Dept Chem Ind Univ-Purdue Univ PO Box 647 Indianapolis IN 46223

FIFER, ROBERT ALAN, b Abington, Pa, Nov 25, 43; m 65, 80; c 2. PHYSICAL CHEMISTRY. *Educ:* Gordon Col, BS, 65; Temple Univ, PhD(phys chem), 69. *Prof Exp:* Res fel chem, Cornell Univ, 69-71; sr res assoc, Boston Col, 71-72; res chemist, US Army Frankford Arsenal, 72-76, RES CHEMIST, US ARMY BALLISTIC RES LAB, 77- *Concurrent Pos:* NSF presidential internship, 72. *Mem:* Am Chem Soc; Am Phys Soc. *Res:* High temperature chemical kinetics behind shock waves; reactions of high energy materials and air-polluting systems; kinetics of reactions of nitrogen oxides, sulfur- and fluorine-containing species; low temperature vibrational spectroscopy; thermodynamics. *Mailing Add:* US Army Ballistic Res Lab Aberdeen Proving Ground MD 21005

FIGDOR, SANFORD KERMIT, b New York, NY, Mar 3, 26; m 48; c 2. ORGANIC CHEMISTRY, DRUG METABOLISM. *Educ:* NY Univ, BA, 49; Univ New Brunswick, MS, 51, PhD(chem), 53. *Prof Exp:* Am Heart Asn fel, Wayne State Univ, 53-54; res chemist, 54-68, HEAD RADIOCHEM, CENT RES, PFIZER INC, 68- *Mem:* Am Chem Soc. *Res:* Natural products; alkaloids; steroids; organic synthesis medicinals; radiochemistry. *Mailing Add:* Cent Res Pfizer Inc Groton CT 06340

FIGGE, DAVID C, b Twin Falls, Idaho, May 20, 25; m 51; c 2. OBSTETRICS & GYNECOLOGY. *Educ:* Northwestern Univ, BS & MD, 50. *Prof Exp:* Am Cancer Soc fel gynec, 54-56; res fel obstet & gynec, 55-56, from instr to assoc prof, 56-69, PROF OBSTET & GYNEC, SCH MED, UNIV WASH, 70-, DIR GYNEC, UNIV HOSP, 69-, DIR GYNEC ONCOL, 74- *Concurrent Pos:* Obstetrician-gynecologist-in-chief, King's County Hosp, 63-69. *Res:* Investigation and management of gynecologic cancer; tissue culture investigations in uterine tissues. *Mailing Add:* 5624 55th NE Seattle WA 98155

FIGLEY, MELVIN MORGAN, b Toledo, Ohio, Dec 5, 20; m 46; c 3. RADIOLOGY. *Educ:* Harvard Univ, MD, 55; FRCRadiol. *Prof Exp:* From asst prof to assoc prof radiol, Univ Mich, 48-58; prof radiol & chmn dept, 58-78, PROF RADIOL & MED, UNIV WASH, 79- *Concurrent Pos:* Markle Found scholar, 53-58; mem bd trustees, Am Bd Radiol, 67-73; mem bd dirs, James Picker Found, 70-; ed, Am J Roentgenology, 79-; mem, Radiation Study Sect, NIH; chmn comt radiol, Nat Acad Sci-Nat Res Coun. *Mem:* Radiol Soc NAm; NAm Soc Cardiac Radiol; Am Roentgen Ray Soc; hon mem Royal Soc Med; Asn Univ Radiol. *Res:* Thoracic and cardiovascular radiology. *Mailing Add:* 7010 51st Ave NE Seattle WA 98115

FIGUEIRA, JOSEPH FRANKLIN, b Paris, Ill, Mar 7, 43; m 65; c 2. LASERS. *Educ:* Univ Ill, BS, 65; Cornell Univ, MS & PhD(physics), 71. *Prof Exp:* Staff mem, 71-75, alt group leader, 75-76, GROUP LEADER, LOS ALAMOS NAT LAB, 76- *Mem:* Am Phys Soc. *Res:* Ultraviolet, visible and infrared lasers; laser systems and laser effects in direct support of Los Alamos programs in inertial confinement fusion; advanced isotope separation; directed energy weapons. *Mailing Add:* Los Alamos Nat Lab AP-5 MS 535 Los Alamos NM 87545

FIGUERAS, JOHN, b Rochester, NY, Oct 28, 24; m 70. ANALYTICAL CHEMISTRY, STRUCTURE ELUCIDATION. *Educ:* Univ Rochester, BS, 49; Univ Ill, MS, 50, PhD(chem), 52. *Prof Exp:* Instr chem, Ill Inst Technol, 52-53; SR RES ASSOC, EASTMAN KODAK CO, 53- *Mem:* AAAS; Am Chem Soc. *Res:* Organic synthesis; analytical chemistry; chemical kinetics; physical chemistry; applied mathematics, applied statistics, numerical analysis and computer modeling. *Mailing Add:* 65 Steele Rd Victor NY 14564

FIGUERAS, PATRICIA ANN MCVEIGH, b Detroit, Mich, Jan 23, 33; m 70. ORGANIC CHEMISTRY. *Educ:* Univ Mich, BS, 53, MA, 57, PhD(chem), 58; Univ Minn, MS, 54. *Prof Exp:* RES ASSOC, EASTMAN KODAK CO, 58- *Mem:* Am Chem Soc; AAAS. *Res:* Photographic applications of chemistry; computer systems and software; applied mathematics; applied statistics. *Mailing Add:* 65 Steele Rd Victor NY 14564

FIGUEROA, WILLIAM GUTIERREZ, b El Paso, Tex, May 25, 21; m 46; c 4. INTERNAL MEDICINE. *Educ:* Tex Western Col, AB, 42; St Louis Univ, MD, 46; Am Bd Internal Med, dipl. *Prof Exp:* Intern, Robert B Green Hosp, San Antonio, Tex, 46 & Los Angeles County Gen Hosp, 46-47; resident internal med, Vet Admin Hosp, Los Angeles, 50-53; jr res metabolist, 52-53, from instr to asst prof, 53-61, assoc prof, 61-75, PROF MED, UNIV CALIF, LOS ANGELES, 75- *Concurrent Pos:* Attend physician, Vet Admin Hosp, Los Angeles, 53- *Mem:* AMA. *Res:* Diseases of metabolism; iron metabolism in various diseases states using radioactive iron; the nature and mechanism of anemia in various blood dyscrasias. *Mailing Add:* Sch of Med Univ of Calif Los Angeles CA 90024

FIGURSKI, DAVID HENRY, b Erie, Pa, Apr 12, 47; m 69; c 2. MOLECULAR BIOLOGY. *Educ:* Univ Pittsburgh, BS, 69; Univ Rochester, PhD(microbiol), 74. *Prof Exp:* USPHS fel molecular biol, Univ Calif, San Diego, 74-78; ASST PROF MICROBIOL, COL PHYSICIANS & SURGEONS , COLUMBIA UNIV, 78- *Mem:* Am Soc Microbiol. *Res:* Replication of extrachromosomal elements in bacteria; broad host range R-plasmids. *Mailing Add:* Dept Microbiol Columbia Univ New York NY 10032

FIGWER, J(OZEF) JACEK, b Mielec, Poland, Mar 16, 28; US citizen; m 55; c 2. ACOUSTICS, ELECTROACOUSTICS. *Educ:* Silesian Polytech Inst, Gliwice, Poland, MS, 51; NIKFI, Moscow, Ussr, DS, 58. *Prof Exp:* Supervry consult acoustics, Bolt Beranek Newman, Inc, 62-78; PRIN CONSULT ACOUSTICS, JACEK FIGWER ASSOC, INC, 78- *Concurrent Pos:* Consult, Inst Elec & Electron Eng, Inc, 72-75. *Mem:* fel Acoust Soc Am; Audio Eng Soc. *Res:* Architectural acoustics. *Mailing Add:* Jacek Figwer Assoc Inc 85 The Valley Rd Concord MA 01742

FIKE, HAROLD LESTER, b Toledo, Ohio, Jan 30, 26; m 56; c 4. ORGANIC CHEMISTRY. *Educ:* Univ Toledo, BS, 50; Northwestern Univ, MBA, 63. *Prof Exp:* Res chemist, Int Mineral & Chem corp, 52-56, sr res chemist, 56-59, asst dir res, 60-63, economist, 63-68; DIR RES, SULPHUR INST, 68- *Mem:* Am Chem Soc; Chem Mkt Res Asn. *Res:* Development of processes for the recovery of amino acids from natural sources and resolution of racemic mixtures of amino acids; mechanisms of sulfur reactions and development of new uses for sulfur. *Mailing Add:* Sulphur Inst 1725 K St NW Rm 508 Washington DC 20006

FIKE, WILLIAM THOMAS, JR, b McKeesport, Pa, Nov 22, 28; m 52; c 1. AGRONOMY. *Educ:* Pa State Univ, BS, 52, MS, 56; Univ Minn, PhD(agron), 62. *Prof Exp:* From asst prof to assoc prof, 59-76, PROF CROP SCI, NC STATE UNIV, 76- *Mem:* Am Soc Agron. *Res:* Introduction, evaluation and improvement of new and established crops; oil, fiber, forage and feed for industrial and agricultural uses; maximizing net return per acre for corn, sorghum and small grains. *Mailing Add:* Dept of Crop Sci NC State Univ Raleigh NC 27650

FIKE, WINSTON, b Pittsfield, Mass, Feb 15, 21; m; c 4. ANALYTICAL CHEMISTRY. *Educ:* NY State Col, Albany, AB, 41; Rensselaer Polytech Inst, PhD(chem), 50. *Prof Exp:* Analyst pharmaceut control, Sterling-Winthrop Corp, 41-45; anal chemist, Tenn Eastman Corp, 45-46; asst prof org chem, Thiel Col, 50-52; res chemist, Ansco Div, Gen Aniline & Film Corp, 52-55; asst prof anal chem, Utica Col, 55-63; res assoc chromatog, County Coroner's Off, 63-65; CHEMIST, ANAL METHODS DEVELOP, MERRELL DOW PHARM, 65- *Concurrent Pos:* NIH grant, 63-65; consult, Sch Med, Case Western Reserve Univ, 63-65. *Mem:* Am Chem Soc. *Res:* Thin layer, gas, and liquid chromatography. *Mailing Add:* Dept of Anal Chem Merrell Dow Pharm Cincinnati OH 45215

FILACHIONE, EDWARD MARIO, b Concord, NH, Oct 10, 09; m 45; c 4. CHEMISTRY. *Educ:* Univ Ill, BS, 31; Northwestern Univ, PhD(org chem), 35. *Prof Exp:* Asst chem, Northwestern Univ, 31-35; instr, De Paul Univ, 35-37 & Univ Maine, 37-38; du Pont fel, Cornell Univ, 38-39; res chemist, Columbia Chem Div, Pittsburgh Plate Glass Co, Ohio, 39-41; res chemist, Eastern Regional Res Ctr, USDA, 41-77; RETIRED. *Honors & Awards:* Alsop Award, Am Leather Chem Asn. *Mem:* Am Chem Soc; Am Leather Chem Asn. *Res:* Pyrolysis of triphenylmethyl ethers; organoboron chemistry; synthetic organic chemistry; lactic acid esters, amide and other derivatives; vinyl monomers and polymers; tanning and leather chemistry. *Mailing Add:* 706 Avondale Rd Philadelphia PA 19118

FILANDRO, ANTHONY SALVATORE, b New York, NY, Oct 10, 30; m 58; c 2. ORGANIC CHEMISTRY. *Educ:* Fordham Univ, BS, 50. *Prof Exp:* Chemist, Florasynth labs, 50-51; chemist, 51-56, chief chemist, 56-64, tech dir, 64-77, V PRES, VIRGINIA DARE EXTRACT CO, 77- *Mem:* Inst Food Technologists; Flavor & Extract Mfrs Asn US (vpres); NY Acad Sci; Soc Soft Drink Technologists; Nat Asn Fruits Flavors & Syrups. *Res:* Flavoring extracts; natural and synthetic flavoring compounds; analytical methods for flavors. *Mailing Add:* Virginia Dare Extract Co 882 Third Ave Brooklyn NY 11232

FILANO, ALBERT E, b Penfield, Pa, Aug 17, 25; m 50; c 4. MATHEMATICS. *Educ:* Univ Pa, BS, 48, MS, 49; Pa State Univ, PhD(math ed), 54. *Prof Exp:* Instr math, Hobart Col, 49-50, State Univ NY Oswego, 50-52 & Pa State Univ, 52-56; chmn dept math, 58-69, dir div sci & math, 67-69, interim dean fac & acad affairs, 69-70, vpres acad affairs, 70-74, PROF MATH, WEST CHESTER STATE COL, 56- *Concurrent Pos:* Dir & prof, Math Insts, NSF, 62-71. *Mem:* Math Asn Am; Nat Coun Teachers Math. *Res:* Mathematics education. *Mailing Add:* Dept Math West Chester State Col West Chester PA 19380

FILBERT, AUGUSTUS MYERS, b Hazleton, Pa, Sept 28, 33; m 63; c 2. PHYSICAL CHEMISTRY. *Educ:* Lehigh Univ, BS, 55; Univ Pa, PhD(phys chem), 62. *Prof Exp:* Lab asst, Univ Pa, 55-61; from sr chemist to sr res chemist, 61-73, res supvr, 73-74, mgr biomat res & develop, 74-77, mgr, Tech Staffs Div, 78, DIR RES & DEVELOP ANAL SERV, CORNING GLASS WORKS, 78- *Mem:* AAAS; Am Chem Soc; Am Ceramic Soc; Am Ord Asn. *Res:* Metal-ammonia solutions; solution chemistry; glass composition; chemistry and physics of glass; conductivity studies; surface chemistry of glass; immobilized enzymes; electrophoresis; biochemistry; immunochemistry; analytical chemistry. *Mailing Add:* 210 W Fourth St Corning NY 14830

FILBEY, ALLEN HOWARD, b Wis, Jan 14, 27; m 49; c 4. ORGANIC CHEMISTRY. *Educ:* Univ Wis, BS, 48; Univ Mich, MS, 49, PhD(chem), 53. *Prof Exp:* Res chemist, 52-58, asst res supvr chem res, 58-60, res supvr, 60-63, asst dir, 63-81, ASSOC DIR CHEM RES & DEVELOP, ETHYL CORP, 81- *Mem:* Am Chem Soc; AAAS. *Res:* Homogeneous catalysis; bromine chemicals; alkylated aromatics; antioxidants. *Mailing Add:* Ethyl Corp 1600 W Eight Mile Rd Ferndale MI 48220

FILBY, ROYSTON HERBERT, b London, Eng, Feb 16, 34; m 65; c 2. NUCLEAR CHEMISTRY, GEOCHEMISTRY. *Educ:* Univ London, BSc, 55; McMaster Univ, MSc, 57; Wash State Univ, PhD(chem), 71. *Prof Exp:* Res fel geochem, Univ Oslo, 61-64; head dept chem, Univ El Salvador, 64-67; chemist, 67-70, asst prof chem, 70-71, assoc prof chem & asst dir Nuclear Radiation Ctr, 70-74, prof chem & assoc dir nuclear radiation ctr, 74-76, PROF CHEM & DIR NUCLEAR RADIATION CTR, WASH STATE UNIV, 76- *Concurrent Pos:* Org Europ Econ Coop sr vis fel, Europ Atomic Energy Comn, Mol, Belg, 62; guest worker, Nat Bur Stand, Washington, DC, 75-76. *Mem:* AAAS; Geochem Soc; Am Chem Soc; Geol Soc Finland; fel Am Inst Chem. *Res:* Neutron activation analysis; coal and petroleum geochemistry; environmental geochemistry of metals. *Mailing Add:* Nuclear Radiation Ctr Wash State Univ Pullman WA 99163

FILE, JOSEPH, b Lecce, Italy, May 6, 23; US citizen; m 44; c 3. MECHANICAL ENGINEERING, APPLIED SUPERCONDUCTIVITY. *Educ:* Cornell Univ, BME, 44; Columbia Univ, MS, 55, PhD(mech eng), 68. *Hon Degrees:* Dr Physics, Univ Lecce, 78. *Prof Exp:* Design engr mech eng, Petro-Chem Develop Co, 48-56; RES ASSOC & SR TECH STAFF MEM FUSION ENERGY RES, PLASMA PHYSICS LAB, PRINCETON UNIV, 56- *Concurrent Pos:* Sr consult, Radio Corp Am, 67-70 & Univ Calif, Los Angeles, 78-; Fulbright-Hays teaching grant, 78. *Mem:* Sigma Xi. *Res:* Application of superconducting magnets to fusion reactors; research in fusion technology; design of fusion energy research devices. *Mailing Add:* Plasma Physics Lab Princeton Univ Princeton NJ 08544

FILER, CRIST NICHOLAS, b Hartford, Conn, May 12, 49; m 75; c 1. SYNTHETIC ORGANIC CHEMISTRY, MEDICINAL CHEMISTRY. *Educ:* Trinity Col, Conn, BS, 71; Mass Inst Technol, Phd(org chem), 75. *Prof Exp:* Sr chemist org synthesis, 77-78, SUPVR LIGANDS, NEW ENG NUCLEAR CORP, BOSTON, 78- *Concurrent Pos:* Res assoc med chem, Dept Med Chem, Northeastern Univ, 75-77. *Mem:* Am Chem Soc. *Res:* Central nervous system radiolabeled (carbon 14, tritium) neurotransmitter synthesis. *Mailing Add:* New Eng Nuclear Corp 575 Albany St Boston MA 02118

FILER, LLOYD JACKSON, JR, b Grove City, Pa, Sept 30, 19; m 42; c 3. PEDIATRICS, NUTRITION. *Educ:* Univ Pittsburgh, BS, 41, PhD(biochem), 44; Univ Rochester, MD, 52. *Prof Exp:* Intern, Strong Mem Hosp, 52-53; med dir, Ross Labs, 53-65; PROF PEDIAT, COL MED, UNIV IOWA, 65- *Concurrent Pos:* Sr res fel, Univ Pittsburgh, 44-45; res fel, Univ Rochester, 45-52, instr physiol, 45-47; asst clin prof pediat, Sch Med, Ohio State Univ, 53-65. *Honors & Awards:* Am Med Asn Goldberger Award, 78; Am Col Nutrit Award, 79. *Mem:* Am Pediat Soc; Soc Pediat Res; Am Soc Clin Nutrit; AMA; Am Inst Nutrit. *Res:* Autoxidation of fats and oils; x-ray diffraction studies in glycerides; vitamin E in animal and human nutrition; nutritional studies on infants; studies on body composition; food additives; biochemistry. *Mailing Add:* Univ Hosp Univ of Iowa Iowa City IA 52242

FILER, THEODORE H, JR, b Galveston, Tex, Aug 15, 28; m 50; c 2. PLANT PATHOLOGY, SOILS. *Educ:* Tex A&M Univ, BS, 50, MS, 58; Wash State Univ, PhD(plant path), 64. *Prof Exp:* Instr forest & gen path, Wash State Univ, 62-63; plant pathologist, 63-74, PRIN PLANT PATHOLOGIST & PROJ LEADER, US FOREST SERV, 74- *Mem:* Am Phytopath Soc; Mycol Soc Am; Am Forestry Asn; Int Soc Plant Path. *Res:* Factors concerned with development and control of root rot, decay and cankers of hardwood trees; fungi and significance of hardwood mycorrhizae; regeneration diseases in hardwood nurseries and plantations. *Mailing Add:* Southern Hardwood Lab PO Box 227 Stoneville MS 38776

FILGO, HOLLAND CLEVELAND, JR, b Van Alstyne, Tex, Mar 28, 26. MATHEMATICAL ANALYSIS. *Educ:* Baylor Univ, BS, 48; Rice Univ, MA, 51, PhD(math), 53. *Prof Exp:* Asst math, Rice Univ, 51-53; from asst prof to assoc prof, Univ Ala, 53-60; asst prof, Univ Ga, 60-61; assoc prof, 61-70, PROF MATH, NORTHEASTERN UNIV, 70- *Mem:* Am Math Soc; Math Asn Am. *Res:* Complex analysis. *Mailing Add:* Dept of Math Northeastern Univ Boston MA 02115

FILICE, FRANCIS P, b Hollister, Calif, Aug 19, 22; m 47; c 6. ZOOLOGY. *Educ:* Univ San Francisco, BS, 43; Univ Calif, MA, 45, PhD(zool), 49. *Prof Exp:* From instr to prof, 47-78, EMER PROF BIOL, UNIV SAN FRANCISCO, 78- *Res:* Protozoan cytology; invertebrate ecology. *Mailing Add:* 578 24th Ave San Francisco CA 94121

FILIPESCU, NICOLAE, b Predeal, Rumania, July 30, 35; US citizen; m 63; c 3. ORGANIC CHEMISTRY, MEDICINE. *Educ:* Bucharest Polytech Inst, PhD(chem engr), 57; George Washington Univ, PhD(phys & org chem), 64, MD, 75. *Prof Exp:* Chem engr, Res Labs, Anticorrosion Plant, Rumania, 57-59; sr chemist, Res Inst Construct Mat, 59; sr scientist, Melpar, Inc, 60-63; from asst prof to assoc prof, 63-71, PROF CHEM, GEORGE WASHINGTON UNIV, 71- *Concurrent Pos:* Res grant & consult, Goddard Space Flight Ctr, NASA, 64-; consult, Lockheed Elec Co, 66-70 & TAAG, Inc, 70-71; res grant, AEC, 69-75 & Energy Res & Develop Admin, 75-79. *Honors & Awards:* Hillebrand Prize, Chem Soc Wash, 71. *Mem:* Am Chem Soc; NY Acad Sci; Am Med Asn. *Res:* Photochemistry; intra- and intermolecular energy transfer; molecular spectroscopy; reaction mechanisms; free radicals; endocrinology; obstetrics and gynecology. *Mailing Add:* Dept of Chem George Washington Univ Washington DC 20052

FILIPOWSKY, R(ICHARD) F(REDERICK) J, physics, electronic engineering, deceased

FILIPPENKO, VLADIMIR I, b Belgrade, Yugoslavia, Aug 23, 30; US citizen; m 52; c 2. APPLIED MATHEMATICS. *Educ:* Univ Calif, Berkeley, BA, 53, PhD(appl math), 64. *Prof Exp:* Res mathematician, Inst Eng Res, Univ Calif, Berkeley, 57-59, assoc math, 59-62, res asst, 62-64; sr res mathematician high velocity physics, Gen Motors Corp, 64-68; asst prof, 68-71, ASSOC PROF MATH, CALIF STATE UNIV, NORTHRIDGE, 71- *Concurrent Pos:* Off Naval Res fel, 64. *Mem:* Am Math Soc. *Res:* Partial and ordinary differential equations; fluid mechanics. *Mailing Add:* Dept of Math Calif State Univ Northridge CA 91330

FILKINS, JAMES P, b Milwaukee, Wis, Apr 10, 36; m 59; c 6. PHYSIOLOGY. *Educ:* Marquette Univ, BS, 57, MS, 59, PhD(physiol), 64. *Prof Exp:* Instr physiol, Sch Med, Marquette Univ, 64-65; from asst prof to assoc prof physiol & biophys, Univ Tenn, 65-71; assoc prof, 71-75, PROF PHYSIOL & CHMN DEPT, STRITCH SCH MED, LOYOLA UNIV CHICAGO, 75- *Concurrent Pos:* USPHS fel, 64-65. *Mem:* AAAS; Reticuloendothelial Soc; Am Physiol Soc. *Res:* Physiopathology of the reticuloendothelial system; mechanism of hepatic phagocytosis; physiology of shock; insulin and glucose regulation. *Mailing Add:* Dept of Physiol 2160 S First Ave Maywood IL 60153

FILKKE, ARNOLD M(AURICE), b Viroqua, Wis, July 8, 19; m 42; c 3. AGRICULTURAL ENGINEERING. *Educ:* Univ Wis, BS, 41; Univ Minn, MS, 43; Auburn Univ, PhD(agr eng), 72. *Prof Exp:* From instr to assoc prof, 46-64, PROF AGR ENG & RURAL ELECTRIFICATION, UNIV MINN, MINNEAPOLIS, 64-, HEAD DEPT, 72- *Mem:* Fel Am Soc Agr Engrs; Am Soc Eng Educ; Inst Elec & Electronics Engrs. *Res:* Application of electricity to agriculture; alternate energy from agricultural biomass; fermentation and combustion; power and machinery design; soil, machine dynamics. *Mailing Add:* Dept of Agr Eng Univ of Minn St Paul MN 55108

FILLER, LEWIS, b New York, NY, Feb 15, 28; m 54; c 3. APPLIED MECHANICS. *Educ:* NY Univ, BAE, 51, MAE, 53, DEngSci, 58. *Prof Exp:* Instr aeronaut eng, NY Univ, 52-57; res specialist, Boeing Airplane Co, 57-59; vis asst prof aeronaut eng, Univ Wash, 59; assoc res scientist, Denver Div, Martin Co, 59-62; assoc prof, 26-68, PROF MECH ENG, SEATTLE UNIV, 68- *Concurrent Pos:* Lectr, Univ Colo, 60-62. *Mem:* AAAS; Am Phys Soc. *Res:* Fluid mechanics; applied mathematics. *Mailing Add:* Dept of Mech Eng Seattle Univ Seattle WA 98122

FILLER, ROBERT, b Brooklyn, NY, Feb 2, 23; m 45, 59; c 5. ORGANIC CHEMISTRY. *Educ:* City Col New York, BS, 43; Univ Iowa, MS, 47, PhD(chem), 49. *Prof Exp:* Asst chemist, Off Sci Res & Develop, Columbia Univ, 43-44; asst dept pharmacol, Univ Iowa Col Med, 47-49; asst prof chem, Albany Col Pharm, 49-50; res fel, Purdue Univ, 50-51; res chemist, Wright Air Develop Ctr, US Air Force, 51-53; asst prof chem, Ohio Wesleyan Univ, 53-55; from asst prof to assoc prof, 55-66, chmn dept, 68-76, PROF CHEM, ILL INST TECHNOL, 66-, DEAN, LEWIS COL SCI & LETTERS, 76- *Concurrent Pos:* Actg chmn dept chem, Ill Inst Technol, 66-68; NIH spec fel, Cambridge Univ, 62-63; vis scientist, Weizmann Inst Sci, Israel, 74; chmn div fluorine chem, Am Chem Soc, 76. *Mem:* AAAS; Am Chem Soc; The Chem Soc; NY Acad Sci. *Res:* Organic fluorine chemistry; heterocyclic chemistry; synthetic and medicinal chemistry. *Mailing Add:* Dept of Chem Ill Inst of Technol Chicago IL 60616

FILLER, RONALD STUART, b Brooklyn, NY, Sept 11, 42; m 68; c 2. MOLECULAR TERATOLOGY, DEVELOPMENTAL BIOLOGY. *Educ:* Brooklyn Col, BS, 65; Temple Univ, PhD(biochem), 73. *Prof Exp:* Fel molecular biol, Inst Chem Biol, Strasbourg Fac Med, 73-75; res assoc develop biol, Inst Cancer Res, Fox Chase Cancer Ctr, 75-77; UNIT LEADER MAMMALIAN EMBRYOL & TERATOGENESIS, BIOL DIV, OAK RIDGE NAT LAB, 77- *Concurrent Pos:* Fac mem, Oak Ridge Grad Sch Biomed Sci, Univ Tenn, 77-; extramural reviewer cell biol, NSF, 78-; external reviewer toxicol, Toxicol J, 78-; mem orgn comt, Reproductive & Develop Biol Group, Univ Tenn, 78- *Mem:* Teratol Soc; Int Soc Differentiation; Southeastern Cancer Res Asn. *Res:* Effects of environmental chemicals on altering the normal developmental processes in differentiating mammalian embryos and elucidating initiating mechanisms in teratogenesis; developmental toxicology. *Mailing Add:* Biol Div PO Box Y Oak Ridge Nat Lab Oak Ridge TN 37830

FILLEY, GILES FRANKLIN, b New York, NY, Apr 30, 15; m 42; c 4. PHYSIOLOGY. *Educ:* Williams Col, BA, 37; Johns Hopkins Univ, MD, 42. *Prof Exp:* Assoc physiologist, Edward L Trudeau Found, 47-53; dir dept physiol, Trudeau-Saranac Inst, 53-55; from asst prof to assoc prof, Sch Med, Univ Colo, Denver, 55-69, prof med, 69-80. *Concurrent Pos:* Clinical physiologist, Webb-Waring Inst Med Res, 55- *Mem:* Am Thoracic Soc; Am Physiol Soc; Am Clin & Climat Asn; fel Am Col Physicians. *Res:* Respiratory physiology. *Mailing Add:* Webb-Waring Lung Inst 4200 East Ninth Ave Denver CO 80220

FILLIBEN, JAMES JOHN, b Philadelphia, Pa, Dec 14, 43; m 67; c 4. COMPUTER LANGUAGE. *Educ:* LaSalle Col, BA, 65; Princeton Univ, PhD(statist), 69. *Prof Exp:* Programmer, Radio Corp Am, 65; mathematician, Bell Telephone Res Lab, 66, Rand Corp, 67; STATIST CONSULT, NAT BUR STANDARDS, 69- *Mem:* Am Statist Soc; Am Comput Mach. *Res:* Design and development of dataplot-A widely used comprehensive, high-level (English-syntax), portable computer language with extensive capabilities in graphics, non-linear fitting, data analysis and mathematics. *Mailing Add:* Admin Bldg Room A337 Statist Eng Lab Nat Bur Standards Washington DC 20034

FILLIOS, LOUIS CHARLES, b Boston, Mass, July 1, 23; m 47; c 3. BIOCHEMISTRY, NUTRITION. *Educ:* Harvard Univ, AB, 48, MS, 53, ScD, 56. *Prof Exp:* From asst to assoc nutrit, Harvard Univ, 53-60; res assoc biochem, Mass Inst Technol, 60-61, asst prof physiol chem, 61-64, assoc prof, 64-66; assoc res prof biochem & path, Sch Med, 66-68, assoc prof biochem, Sch Med & assoc prof nutrit, Sch Grad Dent, 68-69, dir Div Basic Sci, 69-74, co-chmn div med & dent sci, Grad Sch, 70-71, PROF BIOCHEM, SCH MED & SCH GRAD DENT, BOSTON UNIV, 69-, CHMN DEPT NUTRIT SCI, 74- *Concurrent Pos:* Res fel, Harvard Univ, 56-57; Am Heart Asn estab investr, 61-66. *Mem:* Fel AAAS; Am Inst Nutrit; Brit Biochem Soc; fel Am Heart Asn; Am Asn Univ Prof. *Res:* Endocrinology; experimental atherosclerosis; lipid, cholesterol, thyroid and nucleic acid metabolism; protein and lipoprotein synthesis; growth and development; periodontal res; glyprotein met. *Mailing Add:* Boston Univ Med Ctr Boston MA 02118

FILLIPI, GORDON MICHAEL, b Warren, Minn, Oct 17, 40; m 60; c 5. MICROBIOLOGY, MEDICAL TECHNOLOGY. *Educ:* Univ NDak, BS, 62, MS, 70, PhD(microbiol), 73. *Prof Exp:* Chief med technologist, Clin Tuberc Lab, Nopeming Sanatorium, 62-68; teaching asst microbiol, Univ NDak, 68-69; instr, 73-74, ASST PROF PATH & MICROBIOL, MED SCH, UNIV NDAK, 74-; DIR CLIN MICROBIOL, UNITED HOSP, 73- *Concurrent Pos:* NIH trainee, 73. *Mem:* Am Soc Microbiol; affil Am Soc Clin Path. *Mailing Add:* United Hosp Microbiol Lab 1200 S Columbia Rd Grand Forks ND 58201

FILLIPPONE, WALTER R, b Newark, NJ, Mar 17, 21; m 43; c 2. GEOLOGY, GEOPHYSICS. *Educ:* Marietta Col, BA, 42; Calif Inst Technol, MSc, 44. *Prof Exp:* Seismologist, United Geophys Co, 43-45; party chief, 46-51, area mgr, Alaska, 52 & Rocky Mts, 53-55; sr geophysicist, 55-60, div geologist, 61-65, SR RES ASSOC, UNION OIL CO CALIF, 65- *Mem:* Soc Explor Geophys. *Res:* Applied geophysics; exploration seismic interpretation and techniques; data processing and interpretation of remote sensing from space. *Mailing Add:* 421 Larry Lane Placentia CA 92670

FILLIUS, WALKER, b Washington, DC, Mar 22, 37; c 1. MAGNETOSPHERIC PHYSICS, SCIENTIFIC INSTRUMENTATION. *Educ:* Cornell Univ, BEP, 60; State Univ Iowa, MS, 63, PhD(physics), 65. *Prof Exp:* From asst res physicist to assoc res physicist, 65-80, RES PHYSICIST, UNIV CALIF, SAN DIEGO, 80- *Mem:* Am Geophys Union; Sigma Xi. *Res:* Measuring the properties of energetic charged particles trapped in the magnetospheres of earth, Jupiter, Saturn, and the sun; building instrumentation to make these measurements aboard satellites and space probes. *Mailing Add:* CASS C-011 Univ Calif San Diego La Jolla CA 92093

FILLMORE, PETER ARTHUR, b Moncton, NB, Oct 28, 36; m 60; c 3. PURE MATHEMATICS. *Educ:* Dalhousie Univ, BSc, 57; Univ Minn, Minneapolis, MA, 60, PhD(math), 62. *Prof Exp:* Instr math, Univ Chicago, 62-64; from asst prof to prof math, Ind Univ, 64-72; sr fel, 72-73, Killam Res prof, 73-76, PROF MATH, DALHOUSIE UNIV, 76- *Concurrent Pos:* Vis assoc prof, Univ Toronto, 70-71. *Mem:* Am Math Soc; Math Asn Am; Can Math Cong (vpres, 73-75); fel Royal Soc Can. *Res:* Functional analysis; operator theory. *Mailing Add:* Dept Math Dalhousie Univ Halifax NS B3H 4H8 Can

FILMER, DAVID LEE, b Youngstown, Ohio, June 4, 32; m 57; c 3. BIOCHEMISTRY, BIOPHYSICS. *Educ:* Youngstown Univ, AB, 54; Univ Wis, MS, 58, PhD(biochem), 61. *Prof Exp:* Res assoc enzyme mechanisms, Brookhaven Nat Lab, 61-63, asst biochemist, 63-65; asst prof, 65-68, ASSOC PROF BIOPHYS, PURDUE UNIV, 68- *Concurrent Pos:* Mem analog comput educ users group. *Mem:* AAAS; Asn Comput Mach; Soc Comput Simulation; Inst Elec & Electronic Engrs. *Res:* Physical biochemistry; biomedical applicattions of computers; fast reaction kinetics; enzyme mechanisms; bio-instrumentation; computer applications to life science and medicine. *Mailing Add:* Dept of Biol Sci Purdue Univ Lafayette IN 47907

FILNER, BARBARA, b Philadelphia, Pa, Nov 15, 41. SCIENCE POLICY. *Educ:* Queen's Col, BS, 62; Brandeis Univ, PhD(biol), 67. *Prof Exp:* Res assoc, Atomic Energy Comn Plant Res Lab, Mich State Univ, 67-69; Pub Health Serv fel, Inst Cancer Res, 69-71; asst prof cell biol, Columbia Univ, 71-76; asst prof cell & molecular biol, Kalamazoo Col, 77-78; staff officer, Div Health Promotion & Dis Prevention, Inst Med, Nat Acad Sci, 78-79, sr staff officer, 80-81, ASSOC DIR, DIV HEALTH SCI POLICY, INST MED, NAT ACAD SCI, 81- *Concurrent Pos:* Prin investr, Columbia Univ, 72-75. *Mem:* AAAS; NY Acad Sci; Am Pub Health Asn; Asn Women Sci. *Res:* Health sciences research policy; science based health policy; aging; child health; medical education; alcohol abuse and other behavioral components to health. *Mailing Add:* Inst Med-Nat Acad Sci 2101 Constitution Ave Washington DC 20418

FILNER, PHILIP, b Philadelphia, Pa, July 12, 39; m 67; c 3. BIOCHEMISTRY. *Educ:* Johns Hopkins Univ, BA, 60; Calif Inst Technol, PhD(biochem), 65. *Prof Exp:* From asst prof to prof biochem, Mich State Univ, AEC Plant Res Lab, Mich State Univ, 73-82, actg dir, Dept Energy Plant Res Lab, 79-80; ASSOC DIR, ARCO PLANT CELL RES INST, 81- *Mem:* Am Soc Biol Chemists; Am Soc Plant Physiologists. *Res:* Plant biochemistry; mechanisms of enzyme regulation and role of enzymes in development; biochemistry of cultured plant cells; enzymes of nitrate and sulfate assimilation; microtubule proteins. *Mailing Add:* Arco Plant Cell Res Inst 6560 Trinity Ct Dublin CA 48824

FILSETH, STEPHEN V, b Portland, Ore, Nov 7, 36; m 58; c 3. PHYSICAL CHEMISTRY. *Educ:* Stanford Univ, BS, 58; Univ Wis, PhD(phys chem), 62. *Prof Exp:* From asst prof to assoc prof chem, Harvey Mudd Col, 62-71; assoc prof, 71-81, PROF CHEM, YORK UNIV, ONT, 81- *Mem:* Am Phys Soc. *Res:* kinetics of elementary, homogeneous gas phase reactions; laser chemistry; gas phase photochemistry and energy transfer. *Mailing Add:* Dept of Chem York Univ Toronto ON M3J 1P3 Can

FILSON, DON P, b Chicago, Ill, Feb 6, 31; m 57; c 5. PHYSICAL CHEMISTRY. *Educ:* Park Col, AB, 52; Univ Ill, MS, 62, PhD, 67. *Prof Exp:* Assoc prof, 60-67, chem prof, 67-77, STRAWN PROF CHEM, ILL COL, 77- *Mem:* AAAS; Am Chem Soc; Asn Educ Data Syst; Asn Develop Comput Based Instrnl Systs. *Res:* Precipitation problems; hydrodynamic properties of macromolecules; computer-based instruction in chemistry. *Mailing Add:* Dept of Chem Ill Col Jacksonville IL 62650

FILSON, MALCOLM HAROLD, b Chattanooga, Tenn, Oct 19, 07; m 32, 60; c 3. CHEMISTRY. *Educ:* Univ Ky, BS, 29, MS, 31; Univ Mich, PhD(anal chem), 36. *Prof Exp:* Asst anal chem, Univ Ky, 29-31, asst res chemist, Exp Sta, 29; prof inorg chem, Ohio Northern Univ, 34-35; prof chem & head dept chem & physics, Miss Woman's Col, 35-36; asst prof, 35-42, prof chem, 42-72, chmn dept chem & physics, 55-65, chmn dept chem, 65-71, EMER PROF CHEM, CENT MICH UNIV, 72- *Concurrent Pos:* Consult, chem eng; assoc mem, Winter Haven Libr Bd & Winter Haven Human Rels Comt & Community Develop Comn. *Honors & Awards:* US Treas Citation, 45; President Truman Citation, 48. *Mem:* Fel AAAS; Am Chem Soc; Sigma Xi; Nat Sci Teachers Asn. *Res:* Analytical chemistry; chromyl chloride; chromium plating baths; chromyl fluoride; periodates; perchloric acid in analytical chemistry; solubilities and fiscosity as applied to silver, lead and mercury compounds. *Mailing Add:* 442 Ave A NE Winter Haven FL 33880

FILTEAU, GABRIEL, b Quebec, Que, Oct 16, 18; m 46; c 2. MARINE ECOLOGY. *Educ:* Laval Univ, BA, 39, BScA, 44, PhD(biol), 51. *Prof Exp:* Asst biologist, Biol Sta, St Laurent, Que, 44-46; lectr zool, 46-50, asst prof, 50-55, PROF ZOOL, LAVAL UNIV, 55-, HEAD DEPT BIOL, 61-, ASST DEAN FAC SCI, 70- *Concurrent Pos:* Asst biologist, Biol Sta, St Laurent, Que, 46-50; fel, Nuffield Found, Eng, 56; dir res, Fisheries & Oceans, Can, 77-; pres, Interuniv Res Group, 81. *Mem:* French-Can Asn Advan Sci; Can Soc Zool; Royal Soc Can. *Res:* Freshwater and marine biology, especially plankton; invertebrate zoology. *Mailing Add:* Fac of Sci Laval Univ Quebec PQ G1K 7P4 Can

FIMIAN, WALTER JOSEPH, JR, b New York, NY, May 22, 26; m 50; c 5. MORPHOLOGY, RADIOBIOLOGY. *Educ:* Univ Vt, AB, 50; Notre Dame Univ, MS, 52, PhD, 55. *Prof Exp:* Instr & res investr, Marquette Univ, 54-55; asst prof, 55-60, ASSOC PROF ZOOL, BOSTON COL, 60- *Concurrent Pos:* Premed & predent adv, Boston Col, 74- *Mem:* AAAS; Radiation Res Soc; Am Soc Zool. *Res:* Tissue culture studies; amphibian regeneration; melanin synthesis; experimental morphogenesis; radiation biology. *Mailing Add:* Dept of Biol Boston Col Chestnut Hill MA 02167

FINA, LOUIS R, b Cleveland, Ohio, Dec 13, 18; m 46; c 3. MICROBIAL PHYSIOLOGY. *Educ:* Univ Ill, AB, 42, MS, 48, PhD(bact, chem), 50. *Prof Exp:* Asst prof bact, Univ Wyo, 50-52 & Univ Ark, 52-54; PROF BACT & MICROBIOLOGIST, KANS STATE UNIV, 54- *Concurrent Pos:* Vis prof, Rowett Res Inst, Scotland, 62. *Mem:* Am Soc Microbiol; Int Water Resources Asn. *Res:* Methane fermentation; industrial problems; Rumen microbiology; disinfectants. *Mailing Add:* Div of Biol Kans State Univ Manhattan KS 66506

FINAMORE, FRANK JOSEPH, biochemistry, physiological chemistry, deceased

FINBERG, LAURENCE, b Chicago, Ill, May 20, 23; m 45; c 3. PEDIATRICS, PHYSIOLOGY. *Educ:* Univ Chicago, BS, 44, MD, 46. *Prof Exp:* From instr to asst prof pediat, Sch Med, Johns Hopkins Univ, 51-63, pediatrician, Hosp, 51-63; PROF PEDIAT, ALBERT EINSTEIN COL MED, 63-; CHMN PEDIAT DEPT, MONTEFIORE HOSP & MED CTR, 63- *Concurrent Pos:* From asst chief pediatrician to assoc chief pediatrician, Baltimore City Hosp, 51-63. *Mem:* Am Pediat Soc; Soc Pediat Res; Am Fedn Clin Res; Am Acad Pediat; Am Inst Nutrit. *Res:* Electrolyte physiology, especially relating to disturbances of sodium and water osmotic equilibrium; metabolic and infectious diseases. *Mailing Add:* Dept Pediat Montefiore Hosp & Med Ctr Bronx NY 10467

FINBY, NATHANIEL, b New York, NY, May 31, 17; m 47. RADIOLOGY. *Educ:* Johns Hopkins Univ, AB, 38, MD, 42. *Prof Exp:* Intern, Grasslands Hosp, NY, 42-43; pvt pract, 46-52; resident radiol, NY Hosp, 52-55, attend radiologist, 55-61; DIR DEPT RADIOL, ST LUKE'S HOSP, 61-; PROF CLIN RADIOL, COL PHYSICIANS & SURGEONS, COLUMBIA UNIV, 61- *Concurrent Pos:* From asst prof to assoc prof, Med Col, Cornell Univ, 56-61; consult, Rockefeller Univ, 56-70, Vet Admin Hosp, Northport, Long Island, 57-72 & St Barnabas Hosp Chronic Dis, NY; pres, Seminars & Symposia. *Mem:* Radiol Soc NAm; fel Am Col Radiol; fel AMA. *Res:* Diagnostic radiology. *Mailing Add:* Dept of Radiol St Luke's Hosp 421 W 113th St New York NY 10025

FINCH, C(HARLES) R(ICHARD), b Memphis, Tenn, Nov 30, 28; m 56; c 4. CHEMICAL ENGINEERING. *Educ:* Univ Md, BS, 50, PhD(chem eng), 55. *Prof Exp:* Asst chem eng, Univ Md, 51-53, instr, 53-54; proj leader, 56-60, GROUP LEADER, DOW CHEM CO, 60- *Mem:* Soc Plastics Engrs; Am Inst Chem Engrs. *Res:* Plastics development. *Mailing Add:* Dow Chem Co 433 Bldg Midland MI 48640

FINCH, CALEB ELLICOTT, b July 4, 39; US citizen. ENDOCRINOLOGY, GERONTOLOGY. *Educ:* Yale Univ, BS, 61; Rockefeller Univ, PhD(cell biol), 69. *Prof Exp:* Asst prof anat, Med Col, Cornell Univ, 70-72; from asst prof to assoc prof, 72-78, PROF BIOL, UNIV SOUTHERN CALIF, LOS ANGELES, 78- *Concurrent Pos:* NIH fel, Rockefeller Univ, 69-70. *Mem:* Geront Soc; Endocrine Soc; Sigma Xi; Neurosci Soc. *Res:* Neuroendocrine control of aging. *Mailing Add:* Geront Ctr Univ of Southern Calif Los Angeles CA 90007

FINCH, CLEMENT ALFRED, b Broadalbin, NY, July 4, 15. MEDICINE. *Educ:* Union Col, BA, 36; Univ Rochester, MD, 41. *Prof Exp:* From intern to asst resident med, Peter Bent Brigham Hosp, Boston, 41-43, resident, 44-46; instr, Harvard Med Sch, 46-48, assoc, 48-49; assoc prof med, 49-55, prof med & head div, 55-81, PROF MED, SCH MED, UNIV WASH, 81-; DIR HEMAT RES, PROVIDENCE HOSP, 81- *Concurrent Pos:* Res fel hemat, Evans Mem Hosp, 43-44. *Mem:* Nat Acad Sci; Am Soc Clin Invest; Asn Am Physicians; Am Soc Hemat; Int Soc Hemat. *Mailing Add:* Hemat Res 4-East Providence Hosp 500 17th Ave Seattle WA 98124

FINCH, CONSTANCE ANNE, b Hays Kans, July 2, 48. PUBLIC HEALTH ADMINISTRATION. *Educ:* Univ Kans, BA, 70; Univ NC, Chapel Hill, MPH, 76, DrPH, 78. *Prof Exp:* Bacteriologist, St Jospeh Med Ctr, Wichita, Kans, 70-71; microbiologist, Off Labs & Res, Kans Dept Health & Environ, 71-75, Dept Dir, 78-81; DIR, JACKSON BR LAB, TENN DEPT PUB HEALTH, 81- *Mem:* Am Soc Microbiol; Conf Pub Health Lab Dir. *Res:* Evaluation of the use of counter immunoelectrophoresis in the identification of organisms causing bacterial meningitis. *Mailing Add:* 1336 Campbell St # 5 Jackson TN 38301

FINCH, GAYLORD KIRKWOOD, b Owosso, Mich, Nov 16, 23; m 45; c 4. ORGANIC CHEMISTRY. *Educ:* Univ Mich, BSChE, 45, MS, 48, PhD(chem), 54. *Prof Exp:* Ord engr, US Govt, 46; sr chemist, 50-60, chief chemist, 60-64, supvr acid develop & control dept, 64-66, asst div supt, Acid Div, 66-70, asst div supt, Polymers Div, 70-71, asst div supt, Org Chem Div, 71-72, asst gen mgr chem, Europ Region, Kodak Int Photog Div, 72-75, staff asst, 75-76, ASST DIR RES LABS, EASTMAN CHEMS DIV, KINGSPORT, TENN, 76- *Mem:* Am Chem Soc; Am Inst Chem Engrs; Sigma Xi. *Res:* Synthesis, development and process improvement of aliphatic and aromatic oxygenated compounds; statistical design and interpretation of experiments; polymer chemistry; manufacture of polyesters; synthesis of dyes and fine organic chemicals; manufacture of photographic chemicals. *Mailing Add:* Eastman Chem Div Kingsport TN 37662

FINCH, HARRY C, b Ringsted, Iowa, Jan 15, 17; m 45; c 2. PLANT PATHOLOGY. *Educ:* Iowa State Univ, BA, 46, MS, 47, PhD(plant path), 50. *Prof Exp:* Asst prof plant path, NC State Univ, 50-54; assoc prof, Pa State Univ, 54-59; proj leader fungicides-nematicides, Monsanto Chem Co, 59-62; from asst prof to assoc prof, 62-74, PROF BIOL SCI, CALIF POLYTECH STATE UNIV, SAN LUIS OBISPO, 74- *Concurrent Pos:* Res fel AID technologist, Guatemala, 70-71. *Mem:* AAAS; Am Phytopath Soc; Mycol Soc Am. *Res:* Diseases of fruit trees; virus diseases of plants; fungicide-nematicides. *Mailing Add:* Dept of Biol Sci Calif Polytech State Univ San Luis Obispo CA 93407

FINCH, JACK NORMAN, b Esbon, Kans, Sept 26, 23; m 47; c 2. PHYSICAL CHEMISTRY. *Educ:* Ft Hays Kans State Col, BS, 48, MS, 49; Kans State Univ, PhD, 57. *Prof Exp:* Instr chem, Northern Okla Jr Col, 49-53; asst prof, Northeastern State Col, 53; instr, Kans State Univ, 55-56; RES CHEMIST, PHILLIPS PETROL CO, 56- *Mem:* Am Chem Soc. *Res:* Molecular structure, spectroscopy, catalysis and synthetic fuels. *Mailing Add:* 4762 Dartmouth Dr Bartlesville OK 74003

FINCH, JOHN VERNOR, b Madison, Wis, Mar 4, 17; m 43; c 2. MATHEMATICS. *Educ:* Oberlin Col, AB, 38; Univ Wis, MA, 40; Univ Chicago, PhD(math), 51. *Prof Exp:* Asst math, Univ Wis, 38-39; instr meteorol, Univ Chicago, 46, asst math, 47-49; actg instr, Univ Wis, 49-50; from asst prof to assoc prof, 50-59, PROF MATH, BELOIT COL, 59-, CHMN DEPT, 72- *Mem:* AAAS; Am Math Soc; Math Asn Am. *Res:* Banach spaces. *Mailing Add:* Dept of Math Beloit Col Beloit WI 53511

FINCH, LEIKO HATTA, b Peking, China, Apr 19, 45; Japanese citizen; m 71; c 1. APPLIED MATHEMATICS. *Educ:* Utah State Univ, BS, 70, MS, 71; Univ Houston, PhD(math), 72. *Prof Exp:* Comput specialist, Brown & Root Inc, 73-77; ASST PROF, DOWNTOWN COL, UNIV HOUSTON, 77- *Mem:* Am Math Soc; Soc Indust & Appl Math. *Mailing Add:* PO Box 8952 Houston TX 77009

FINCH, ROBERT ALLEN, b Cleveland, Ohio, Mar 15, 41; m 68; c 2. TOXICOLOGY, CELL BIOLOGY. *Educ:* Oberlin Col, AB, 63; Case Western Reserve Univ, PhD(anat), 68. *Prof Exp:* NIH trainee biol, Brandeis Univ, 68-70; asst prof anat, Bowman Gray Sch Med, 70-78; Nat Inst Environ Health Sci fel toxicol, Univ Rochester, 78-79; HEAD GENETIC TOXICOL, RALTECH SCI SERV, MADISON, WIS, 79- *Mem:* Tissue Culture Asn; Am Col Toxicol; Environ Mutagen Soc; Genetic Toxicol Asn; Sigma Xi. *Res:* Cell and tissue culture; in vitro and in vivo mutagenesis and carcinogenesis. *Mailing Add:* 785 Pilgrim Trail Sun Prairie WI 53590

FINCH, ROGERS B(URTON), b Broadalbin, NY, Apr 16, 20; m 42; c 5. TEXTILE TECHNOLOGY. *Educ:* Mass Inst Technol, SB, 41, SM, 47, ScD, 50. *Prof Exp:* Textile technologist, Broadalbin Knitting Co, Inc, NY, 41; res assoc mech eng, textile div, Mass Inst Technol, 46-47, asst prof textile tech, 47-53, dir, US Opers Mission, Burma, 53-54; asst dir res div, Rensselaer Polytech Inst, 54-58, assoc dean, sch sci, 58-60, dir res div, 60-61; dir univ rels, Peace Corps, DC, 61-63; assoc dean, Hartford Grad Ctr, Rensselaer Polytech Inst, 63-66, dir acad planning, 66-70, vpres planning, 70-72; exec dir, Am Soc Mech Engrs, 72-81; FINCH CONSULTS, 81- *Mem:* Fel AAAS; fel Am Soc Mech Engrs; Am Soc Eng Educ; Soc Automotive Engrs; Am Inst Aeronaut & Astronaut. *Res:* Association management; long-range planning. *Mailing Add:* Am Soc Mech Engrs 345 E 47th St New York NY 10017

FINCH, STEPHEN JOSEPH, b St Louis, Mo, Mar 20, 45. STATISTICS. *Educ:* St Louis Univ, BS, 67; Princeton Univ, MA, 69, PhD(statist), 74. *Prof Exp:* asst prof, 74-80, ASSOC PROF STATISTIC, STATE UNIV NY, STONY BROOK, 80- *Concurrent Pos:* Consult, Brookhaven Nat Labs, 75- *Mem:* Am Statist Asn; Am Pub Health Asn; AAAS. *Res:* Robust tests of structural properties of random variables, such as symmetry; applications of statistics in policy studies. *Mailing Add:* Dept of Appl Math & Statist State Univ of NY Stony Brook NY 11794

FINCH, STUART CECIL, b Broadalbin, NY, Aug 6, 21; m 46; c 4. INTERNAL MEDICINE. *Educ:* Univ Rochester, MD, 44. *Prof Exp:* Intern surg, Baltimore City Hosp, Md, 44-45, asst resident path, 45-46; res fel med, Harvard Med Sch, 48-49; asst, Dept Hemat, Peter Bent Brigham Hosp, 48-49, asst resident, 49-50; asst, Sch Med, Boston Univ, 50-52, instr, 52-53; from asst prof to assoc prof, 53-67, PROF MED, SCH MED, YALE UNIV, 67- *Concurrent Pos:* Res assoc, Evans Mem-Mass Mem Hosps, 50-52; asst mem, 52-53; assoc physician, Grace-New Haven Community Hosp, 53-; consult, West Haven Vet Admin Hosp, Conn, 53-, Laurel Heights Hosp, Derby, 58- & Meriden Hosps, 58-; clin prof, Yale Univ, 78-79. *Mem:* Am Soc Hemat; Am Soc Clin Invest; Asn Am Physicians; Am Fedn Clin Res; Int Soc Hemat. *Res:* Iron metabolism; leukemia; leucocyte kinetics and immunology. *Mailing Add:* Yale Univ Sch of Med New Haven CT 06510

FINCH, STUART MCINTYRE, b Salt Lake City, Utah, Aug 16, 19; m 41; c 2. PSYCHIATRY. *Educ:* Univ Colo, MD, 43. *Prof Exp:* Intern, Alameda County Hosp, Oakland, Calif, 43-44; resident psychiat, Sch Med, Temple Univ, 46-49, instr, 49-53, assoc prof to prof, Med Sch, Univ Mich, Ann Arbor, 56-73; LECTR MED, COL MED, UNIV ARIZ, 73- *Concurrent Pos:* Dir child psychiat, Sch Med, Temple Univ, 49-56; attend psychiatrist, St Christopher's Hosp for Children, 53-56; consult, Vet Admin Hosp, Battle Creek, 56-58, Battle Creek Child Guid Clin, 56-58, Kalamazoo State Hosp, 56-58 & fresh air camp, Univ Mich, 57-; mem comt cert child psychiat, Am Bd Psychiat & Neurol; mem, Gov Ment Health Adv Coun. *Mem:* Am Psychosom Soc; AMA; Am Psychiat Asn; Am Psychoanal Asn; Am Orthopsychiat Asn. *Res:* Psychophysiologic illness. *Mailing Add:* 109 Camino Espanol Tucson AZ 85716

FINCH, THOMAS LASSFOLK, b Madison, Wis, Nov 26, 26. PHYSICS. *Educ:* Univ Wis, BA, 47, MA, 49, PhD(physics), 57. *Prof Exp:* Asst prof physics, Union Univ, NY, 55-57; asst prof, 57-60, ASSOC PROF PHYSICS, ST LAWRENCE UNIV, 60- *Concurrent Pos:* Vis lectr, Univ Col NWales, 64-65. *Mem:* AAAS; Am Phys Soc; Am Asn Physics Teachers; Acoust Soc Am. *Res:* Low-temperature physics; intermediate state of super conductors; musical acoustics. *Mailing Add:* Dept of Physics St Lawrence Univ Canton NY 13617

FINCH, WARREN IRVIN, b Union Co, SDak, Oct 27, 24; m 51; c 3. GEOLOGY. *Educ:* SDak Sch Mines & Technol, BS, 48; Univ Calif, MS, 54. *Prof Exp:* Geologist, US Geol Surv, 48-72, chief supvry geologist, 72-77, URANIUM COMMODITY GEOLOGIST, BR URANIUM & THORIUM RESOURCES, US GEOL SURV, 77- *Concurrent Pos:* Chmn, Int Atomic Energy Agency Working Group Sandstone Uranium Deposits, 79- *Mem:* Fel Geol Soc Am; Soc Econ Geol; Int Asn Genesis Ore Deposits. *Res:* Exploration for uranium deposits of the Colorado Plateau and beryllium; geology of uranium deposits in sandstone formations of the United States; regional geology of Jackson Purchase region, Kentucky; resource assessment methodology. *Mailing Add:* US Geol Surv Box 25046 MS 916 Denver Fed Ctr Denver CO 80225

FINCHER, BOBBY LEE, b Clarksville, Ark, Aug 28, 34; m 54; c 2. ALGEBRA. *Educ:* Univ Ark, BS, 56; Okla State Univ, MS, 62; Ind Univ, PhD(algebra), 72. *Prof Exp:* Radiation engr, McCullough Tool Co, 56-58; teacher geol & math, Ft Smith High Sch, Ark, 58-60; from instr to asst prof, 63-72, ASSOC PROF MATH, TEX WOMAN'S UNIV, 72- *Mem:* Math Asn Am; Sigma Xi. *Res:* Relationship between mathematics and music. *Mailing Add:* Box 22865 Tex Woman's Univ Denton TX 76204

FINCHER, EDWARD LESTER, b Atlanta, Ga, Jan 16, 21; m 48; c 2. MICROBIOLOGY. *Educ:* Mercer Univ, BA, 48; Emory Univ, MSc, 49; Univ Ga, PhD(bact), 62. *Prof Exp:* Res biologist, Eng Exp Sta, Ga Inst Technol, 50-58, asst res scientist, 58-60, asst prof res biol, 60-63; res microbiologist, Biophys Sect, Tech Br, Commun Dis Ctr, USPHS, 64-65; assoc prof environ sci & eng, Univ NC, 65-68; actg dir dept, 70-72, assoc prof, 68-80, PROF BIOL, GA INST TECHNOL, 80- *Concurrent Pos:* USPHS trainee, 58-59, res fel, 59-60. *Mem:* AAAS; Am Soc Microbiol. *Res:* Aerobiology; bacterial growth and cytology; infection, host-parasite relationships; microbiology of the hospital environment; bacterial degradation of synthetic molecules; effect of chemical and physical factors on bacterial cells; electron microscopy. *Mailing Add:* Sch of Biol Ga Inst of Technol Atlanta GA 30332

FINCHER, GEORGE TRUMAN, b Arlington, Ga, Sept 28, 39; m 63; c 3. VETERINARY ENTOMOLOGY, PARASITOLOGY. *Educ:* Univ Ga, BSA, 61, MS, 66, PhD(entom), 68. *Prof Exp:* Zoologist parasitol, 68-78, RES ENTOMOLOGIST BIO-CONTROL, USDA, 78- *Mem:* Entom Soc Am; Am Soc Parasitologists. *Res:* Use of dung-burying beetles as biological control agents for control of livestock inst pests that breed in cattle dung. *Mailing Add:* Vet Toxicol & Entom Res Lab USDA SEA VTERL PO Box GE College Station TX 77840

FINCHER, JOHN ALBERT, b Union, SC, Sept 8, 11; m 39; c 3. ZOOLOGY. *Educ:* Univ SC, BS, 33, MS, 35; Univ NC, PhD(zool), 39. *Prof Exp:* Prin pub sch, SC, 33-34; instr biol, Univ SC, 34-35; lab asst zool, Univ NC, 35-39; instr biol, Cumberland Col, 39-40; from asst prof to assoc prof, Millsaps Col, 40-46; prof & head dept, Samford Univ, 47-57, asst to the pres, 55-57; dean, 57-68, pres, 68-77, EMER PRES, CARSON-NEWMAN COL, 77- *Concurrent Pos:* Fel, Highlands Biol Lab, 39; trustee, Gorgas Scholar Found, State Sci Talent Search, 52-68 & East End Mem Hosp, Birmingham, Ala, Educ Consult, Baptist Med Ctr, Sch Anesthesia Samford Univ & prof biol, 78- *Mem:* Fel AAAS; Am Soc Zool. *Res:* Invertebrate zoology; cell behavior and gametogenesis in sponges; growth of sponges from gemmules. *Mailing Add:* 315 Gran Ave Birmingham AL 35209

FINCHER, JULIAN H, b Cross Keys, SC, July 22, 35; m 66; c 3. PHYSICAL PHARMACY. *Educ:* Univ SC, BS, 58; Univ Ga, MS, 62; Univ Conn, PhD(pharm), 64. *Prof Exp:* Instr pharm, Univ SC, 58-59 & Univ Ga, 59-61; from asst prof to assoc prof pharmaceut, Univ Miss, 64-72 & chmn dept, 70-72; PROF PHARMACEUT, UNIV SC, 72-, DEAN & PROF, COL PHARM, 72- *Concurrent Pos:* Chmn, Coun Deans, Am Asn Col Pharm, 81-82. *Mem:* Am Pharmaceut Asn; Am Chem Soc; Sigma Xi; Acad Pharmaceut Sci; Am Asn Cols Pharm. *Res:* Biopharmaceutics; physical and chemical properties affecting drug release and absorption from dosage forms. *Mailing Add:* Col of Pharm Univ of SC Columbia SC 29208

FINCK, HENRY, anatomy, cell biology, see previous edition

FINCO, ARTHUR A, b Ely, Minn, Mar 1, 32; m 60; c 2. MATHEMATICS. *Educ:* St Cloud State Univ, BS, 53; Northern Iowa Univ, MA, 59; Purdue Univ, PhD(math educ), 66. *Prof Exp:* Instr high sch, Minn, 56-58; instr math, Mankato State Col, 59-61; from asst prof to assoc prof 61-74, PROF MATH & MATH EDUC, PURDUE UNIV, FT WAYNE, 74- *Mem:* Math Asn Am; Nat Coun Teachers Math. *Res:* Mathematics education. *Mailing Add:* 4744 Innsbruck Dr Ft Wayne IN 46815

FINCO, DELMAR R, b Roundup, Mont, Nov 5, 36; m 59; c 4. VETERINARY MEDICINE. *Educ:* Univ Minn, St Paul, BS, 57, DVM, 59, PhD(canine leptospirosis), 66. *Prof Exp:* Fel, Univ Minn, St Paul, 61-66, asst prof clin vet med, 66-70; prof clin vet med, 70-75, PROF PHYSIOL, COL VET MED, UNIV GA, 75- *Mem:* Am Vet Med Asn; Am Asn Vet Clinicians. *Res:* Canine leptospirosis and studies of leptospira canicola; urogenital diseases of dog and cat. *Mailing Add:* Dept of Physiol Univ of Ga Col of Vet Med Athens GA 30602

FINDLAY, JOHN A, b Manchester, Eng, May 29, 36; Can citizen; m 63; c 3. ORGANIC CHEMISTRY. *Educ:* Univ NB, BSc, 59, PhD(org chem), 62. *Prof Exp:* NATO-Dept Indust & Sci Res UK fel org chem, Cambridge Univ, Eng, 62-63; lectr, 63-65, from asst prof to assoc prof, 65-74, PROF CHEM, UNIV NB, 74- *Concurrent Pos:* Asst dean sci, Univ NB, 73-75, actg chmn chem dept, 75. *Mem:* Fel Chem Inst Can. *Res:* Structural elucidation and synthesis of natural products, especially compounds of biological interest, including those of marine origin. *Mailing Add:* Dept of Chem Univ of NB Fredericton NB E3B 4Z7 Can

FINDLAY, JOHN WILSON, b Kineton, Eng, Oct 22, 15; nat US; m 53; c 2. PHYSICS. *Educ:* Cambridge Univ, BA, 37, PhD(physics), 50. *Prof Exp:* Researcher, Cambridge Univ, 37-39; univ demonstr & fel & lectr physics, Queens' Col, 45-53; mem staff, Brit Ministry Supply, 54-56; mem staff, Nat Radio Astron Observ, 57-65; dir, Arecibo Ionospheric Observ, 65-66; MEM STAFF, NAT RADIO ASTRON OBSERV, 66- *Concurrent Pos:* Mem, Order of the Brit Empire. *Mem:* Fel Inst Elec & Electronics Engrs. *Res:* Physics of the ionosphere; radio astronomy. *Mailing Add:* Nat Radio Astron Observ Charlottesville VA 22901

FINDLAY, RAYMOND D(AVID), b Toronto, Ont, Aug 10, 38; m 61; c 4. ELECTRICAL ENGINEERING. *Educ:* Univ Toronto, BASc, 63, MASc, 65, PhD(elec eng), 68. *Prof Exp:* Lectr elec eng, 67-68, asst prof elec eng & comput sci, 68-70, from asst prof to assoc prof elec eng, 70-78, dir grad studies, Elec Eng Dept, 75-78, PROF ELEC ENG, UNIV NB, 78- *Concurrent Pos:* Nat Res Coun Can operating grant, 68-79; Nat Res Coun sr indust fel & proj dir, Can Gen Elec Co, 72-73. *Honors & Awards:* Am Soc Eng Educ/DOW Award, 72. *Mem:* Am Soc Eng Educ; Inst Elec & Electronics Engrs. *Res:* Electrical power and apparatus; pole face losses in synchronous machines; current and loss distributions in aluminum conductor steel-reinforced cable. *Mailing Add:* Dept of Elec Eng PO Box 4400 Fredericton NB E3B 5A3 Can

FINDLER, NICHOLAS VICTOR, b Budapest, Hungary, Nov 24, 30; US citizen; m 55; c 2. COMPUTER SCIENCE, APPLIED MATHEMATICS. *Educ:* Budapest Tech Univ, BEng, 53, PhD(math, physics), 56. *Prof Exp:* Sr lectr, Theoret Physics, Budapest Tech Univ, 56; vis lectr, Univ Vienna, 56-57; res fel theoret physics & comput sci, Univ Sydney, 57-59; staff appl mathematician, CSR Co, Ltd, Australia, 59-63; res assoc comput sci, Univ Pittsburgh, 64; assoc prof comput sci & math, Univ Ky, 64-66; PROF COMPUT SCI & MATH, STATE UNIV NY BUFFALO, 66- *Concurrent Pos:* Adj asst prof math, Univ New South Wales, 62-63; res scientist & Adv Res Proj Agency fel, Carnegie Inst Technol, 63-64; invited lectr, NATO Adv Study Insts, 65-80, dir, 70; consult, var indust firms, 64-; sr Fulbright scholar vis prof, Tech Univ Vienna, 72-73, Univ Amsterdam & Free Univ Amsterdam, 79-80. *Mem:* AAAS; Asn Comput Mach; Brit Comput Soc; Asn Comput Linguistics; Am Asn Artificial Intel. *Res:* Heuristic programming; special purpose computer languages; simulation of human cognitive behavior; theory of competition and strategies; man-machine relations; computer graphics; self-adaptive systems; computational linguistics; information retrieval; mathematical physics; mathematical psychology; mathematical biophysics. *Mailing Add:* Dept of Comput Sci State Univ NY Buffalo Amherst NY 14226

FINDLEY, JAMES SMITH, b Cleveland, Ohio, Dec 28, 26; m 49; c 4. VERTEBRATE ZOOLOGY. *Educ:* Western Reserve Univ, AB, 50; Univ Kans, PhD, 55. *Prof Exp:* Asst instr, Univ Kans, 50-53, asst, Mus Natural Hist, 53-54; instr zool, Univ SDak, 54-55; from asst prof to assoc prof biol, 55-70, PROF BIOL, UNIV NMEX, 70-, CHMN DEPT, 78- *Mem:* AAAS; Am Soc Mammal; Ecol Soc Am; Soc Syst Zool; Am Soc Naturalists; Soc Study Evolution. *Res:* Taxonomic mammalogy; ecology and zoogeography. *Mailing Add:* Dept of Biol Univ of NMex Albuquerque NM 87131

FINDLEY, MARSHALL E(WING), b Arkansas City, Kans, Oct 13, 27; m 55; c 2. CHEMICAL ENGINEERING. *Educ:* Agr & Mech Col Tex, BS, 49; Inst Paper Chem, MS, 51; Univ Fla, PhD(chem eng), 55. *Prof Exp:* Chem engr, Celotex Corp, La, 51-52; asst, Univ Fla, 52-55; res engr, E I du Pont de Nemours & Co, Tenn, 55-58; assoc res prof chem eng, Auburn Univ, 58-65; from asst prof to assoc prof, 65-69, PROF CHEM ENG, UNIV MO-ROLLA, 69- *Concurrent Pos:* Fulbright lectr, Univ Alexandria, 62-63; eng educ adv, USAID, SVietnam, 69-71; prof, Inst Algerien du Petrole, 78-79. *Mem:* Am Chem Soc; Am Inst Chem Engrs; Tech Asn Pulp & Paper Indust; Am Soc Eng Educ. *Res:* Pulp and paper; process control; water desalination; wood gasification. *Mailing Add:* Dept of Chem Eng Univ of Mo Rolla MO 65401

FINDLEY, WILLIAM N(ICHOLS), b Mankato, Minn, Feb 12, 14; m 39; c 1. APPLIED MECHANICS, MECHANICS OF MATERIALS. *Educ:* Ill Col, AB, 36; Univ Mich, BSE(mech eng) & BSE(math), 37; Cornell Univ, MS, 39. *Hon Degrees:* DSc, Ill Col, 70. *Prof Exp:* Asst eng mech, Univ Mich, 36-37; instr civil eng, George Washington Univ, 38-39; from instr to asst prof theoret & appl mech, Univ Ill, 39-47, res assoc prof, 47-54; dir cent facility mech testing, 66-69, PROF ENG, BROWN UNIV, 54- *Concurrent Pos:* Consult, Lawrence Radiation Lab, 62-78; mem sci adv coun, Picatinny Arsenal, 51-62; mem orgn comt, Joint Int Conf Creep, NY & London, 63. *Honors & Awards:* Prize paper, Soc Plastics Engrs, 49, 50; Dudley Medal, Soc Testing & Mat, 45, Templin Award, 53 & 64. *Mem:* Soc Testing & Mat; Soc Exp Stress Anal; Am Soc Eng Educ; Soc Rheol. *Res:* Creep, fatigue and other strength properties of plastics at various temperatures; fatigue and creep of metals in combined stress; photoelasticity; mechanics of creep; theories of fatigue; viscoelasticity. *Mailing Add:* Div of Eng Box D Brown Univ Providence RI 02912

FINDLEY, WILLIAM RAY, JR, b Manhattan, Kans, June 26, 20; m 43; c 2. PLANT BREEDING. *Educ:* Kans State Univ, BS, 49, MS, 50; Univ Md, PhD(plant breeding), 60. *Prof Exp:* From asst agronomist to assoc agronomist, Div Cereal Crops & Dis, 50-56, RES AGRONOMIST, CEREAL CROPS RES BR, USDA, 56- *Mem:* Am Soc Agron. *Res:* Corn breeding and genetics, with emphasis on virus disease of corn. *Mailing Add:* Dept Agron Ohio Agr Res & Develop Ctr Wooster OH 44691

FINDLEY, WILLIAM ROBERT, b Detroit, Mich, Apr 26, 35. APPLIED CHEMISTRY. *Educ:* Denison Univ, BS, 57; Ohio Univ, MSc, 61, PhD(chem), 63. *Prof Exp:* Chemist, dyestuffs & Chem Div, 63-64, prod mgr chelates, 64-66, tech develop mgr whiteners, 66-74, tech develop mgr, 74-80, DIR, TECH DEVELOP & SERV, SPEC CHEMS, CIBA-GEIGY CORP, 80. *Mem:* Tech Asn Pulp & Paper Indust. *Res:* Chelates. *Mailing Add:* Ciba-Geigy Corp 410 Swing Rd Greensboro NC 27409

FINE, ADRIAN, b Dublin, Ireland, June 28, 45; m 68; c 2. MEDICINE. *Educ:* Trinity Col, Dublin, MB, BCh & BAO Hons, 68, MD, 72. *Prof Exp:* Med Res Coun Ireland fel, 69-70; sr registrar nephrology med, Royal Infirmary, Glasgow, 74-77; consult, Greater Glasgow Health Bd, 77-78; ASST PROF MED, MEM UNIV NFLD, 78- *Concurrent Pos:* Med Res Coun fel, Univ West Indies, 75-76. *Mem:* Int Soc Nephrology; Renal Asn Brit. *Res:* Intermediary metabolism of the kidney; hormone metabolism by the kidney; drug metabolism in uraemia. *Mailing Add:* Fac of Med Mem Mem Univ Nfld St John's NF A1C 5S7 Can

FINE, ALBERT SAMUEL, b Philadelphia, Pa, Oct 24, 23; m 59; c 1. BIOCHEMISTRY. *Educ:* Brooklyn Col, BA, 50, MA, 53; NY Univ, PhD, 70. *Prof Exp:* Asst biochem & enzymol, Col Med, NY Univ, 50-52; biochemist, Col Physicians & Surgeons, Columbia Univ, 52-56; biochemist, Spec Dent Res Prog, 56-66 & Spec Res Lab Oral Tissue Metab, 66-70, CHIEF DENT RES LAB, VET ADMIN HOSP, 70- *Concurrent Pos:* Assoc prof periodont, Dent Ctr, NY Univ. *Mem:* AAAS; Am Chem Soc; NY Acad Sci; Am Inst Biol Sci; Int Asn Dent Res. *Res:* Intermediary metabolism of the oral tissues; biochemistry of oxidative and electron transport enzymes of oral mucosa; collagen synthesis during wound healing of epithelium; cyclic nucleotide regulation of cellular proliferation during regeneration of oral tissues. *Mailing Add:* Dent Res Lab Vet Admin Hosp New York NY 10010

FINE, BEN SION, b Peterborough, Ont, Sept 29, 28. OPHTHALMOLOGY. *Educ:* Univ Toronto, MD, 53; Am Bd Ophthal, dipl, 59. *Prof Exp:* Assoc prof, 64-70, ASSOC RES PROF OPHTHAL, GEORGE WASHINGTON UNIV, 70-, RES ASSOC, ARMED FORCES INST PATH, 58- *Concurrent Pos:* Clin prof pathol, Uniformed Serv Univ Health Sci, Bethesda, Md, 77- *Mem:* Electron Micros Soc Am. *Res:* Ophthalmic pathology; investigations into the structure of the eye, both normal and abnormal. *Mailing Add:* Ophthalmic Path Dept Armed Forces Inst of Path Washington DC 20305

FINE, BENJAMIN, b New York, NY, Oct 12, 48; m 70; c 2. GROUP THEORY. *Educ:* Brooklyn Col, BS, 69; NY Univ, MS, 71, PhD(math), 73. *Prof Exp:* Instr math, Fashion Inst Technol, 73-74; asst prof, 74-78, ASSOC PROF MATH & CHMN DEPT, FAIRFIELD UNIV, 78- *Concurrent Pos:* Lilly Found res grant, Yale Univ, 77, assoc fel, 77-78; consult statist, Ctr Creative Living, 77- *Mem:* Am Math Soc; Math Asn Am. *Res:* Combinatorial group theory; structure of discrete groups of matrices; applications of discrete group theory to ring theory and number theory. *Mailing Add:* 24 West Bank Lane Stamford CT 06902

FINE, DAVID H, b Johannesburg, SAfrica, Sept 17, 42; US citizen; m 64; c 2. CHEMISTRY, CHEMICAL ENGINEERING. *Educ:* Univ Witwatersrand, BSc, 64; Univ Leeds, PhD(chem), 67. *Prof Exp:* Fel chem, Univ Leeds, 67-68; fel, Univ Man, 68-69; res assoc chem eng, Mass Inst Technol, 69-72; sr scientist chem & head, Cancer Res Div, Thermo Electron Corp, 72-79; DIR RES, NEW ENGLAND INST LIFE SCI, 79- *Mem:* Am Chem Soc; Soc Occup & Environ Health; Am Inst Chem Engrs; The Chem Soc. *Res:* Nitrosamines; nitroso compounds; worker and environmental exposure; analytical chemistry; combustion; explosions; air pollution chemistry; instrumentation; author of over 50 research papers. *Mailing Add:* Cancer Res Div 101 First Ave Waltham MA 02154

FINE, DONALD LEE, b Nanticoke, Pa, Jan 14, 43; m 65; c 2. MICROBIOLOGY. *Educ:* Wilkes Col, AB, 64; Pa State Univ, MS, 66, PhD(microbiol), 68. *Prof Exp:* Res asst limnol, Wilkes Col, 62-64; trainee microbiol, Pa State Univ, 64-68, res assoc, 68-69; proj leader, Virus & Rickettsia Div, US Army Biol Ctr, 69-71; chief oncol, virol & cell biol, Bionetics Res Labs, Inc, 71-72; sect head, RNA Virus Lab, 72-79, MGR, NIH INTRAMURAL RES PROG, FREDERICK CANCER RES CTR, NAT CANCER INST, 79- *Mem:* AAAS; Sigma Xi; NY Acad Sci; Am Soc Microbiol; Am Asn Cancer Res. *Res:* Limnology; ecology; cell physiology; virus biochemistry; virology and immunology with particular reference to arboviruses; viral oncology, with special interest in primates; immunology, biochemistry and virology of mammary tumor viruses. *Mailing Add:* Frederick Cancer Res Ctr PO Box B Frederick MD 21701

FINE, DWIGHT ALBERT, b Los Angeles, Calif, Sept 17, 33. INORGANIC CHEMISTRY. *Educ:* Univ Calif, Los Angeles, BS, 56; Univ Calif, Berkeley, PhD(inorg chem), 60. *Prof Exp:* Asst chem, Univ Calif, Berkeley, 56-57 & Lawrence Radiation Lab, 57-60; CHEMIST, NAVAL WEAPONS CTR, 60- *Concurrent Pos:* Vis res & Teaching assoc, Univ Calif, Irvine, 73-74. *Mem:* Am Chem Soc; AAAS. *Res:* Coordination chemistry; solution chemistry of metals of Group VIII; electroanalytical chemistry. *Mailing Add:* Code 3851 Michelson Lab Naval Weapons Res Ctr China Lake CA 93555

FINE, LAWRENCE OLIVER, b Sheyenne, NDak, May 14, 17; m 41; c 3. SOIL CHEMISTRY, WATER CHEMISTRY. *Educ:* NDak Agr Col, BS, 38; Univ Wis, PhD(soil chem), 41. *Prof Exp:* Soil surveyor, USDA, 41-42; resident instr agron, Univ Ark, 42 & asst agronomist, 45-46; from asst prof to assoc prof, 46-53, PROF AGRON, S DAK STATE UNIV, 53- *Concurrent Pos:* Assoc agronomist, SDak State Univ, 48-50, agronomist, Exp Sta, 53-69, head dept agron, 58-69; collabr soil & water div, Agr Res Serv, USDA, 53- *Mem:* Fel Am Soc Agron; AAAS; Soil Sci Soc Am; Am Inst Chemists. *Res:* Salinity, phosphate supply and nutrition; general soil fertility; irrigation. *Mailing Add:* Dept of Plant Sci SDak State Univ Brookings SD 57007

FINE, LEONARD W, b Bridgeport, Conn, Apr 19, 35; m 58; c 3. ORGANIC CHEMISTRY. *Educ:* Marietta Col, BS, 58; Univ Md, PhD(org chem), 62. *Prof Exp:* Res chemist, Harris Res Lab, Gillette Co, 62-64, Ethyl Corp, Mich, 64-66 & Am Cyanamid Co, Bridgeport, 66-70; assoc prof, 70-76, PROF, HOUSATONIC COMMUNITY COL, 76- *Concurrent Pos:* Lectr, Columbia Univ, 75- *Mem:* AAAS; Am Chem Soc; NY Acad Sci; Hist Sci Soc; Soc Hist Technol. *Res:* Synthesis and reactions of pyrimidine heterocycles; peroxide oxidations of organic compounds; synthesis of alpha-amino acids; natural auxins and synthetic plant growth regulators; organometallic synthesis; catalysis; chemical education; history of chemistry. *Mailing Add:* 15 Grey Hollow Rd Norwalk CT 06850

FINE, MICHAEL LAWRENCE, b Brooklyn, NY, Feb 10, 46; m 77; c 1. NEUROETHOLOGY, BIOCOMMUNICATIONS. *Educ:* Univ Md, BS, 67; Col William & Mary, MA, 70; Univ RI, PhD(oceanog), 76. *Prof Exp:* Fel, Cornell Univ, 76-79; ASST PROF, VA COMMONWEALTH UNIV, 79- *Concurrent Pos:* Oceanographer, US Naval Oceanog Off, 76-77; res physiologist, Tunison Lab Fish Nutrit, Fish & Wildlife Serv, 79. *Mem:* Soc Neurosci; AAAS; Animal Behav Soc; Am Soc Ichthyologists & Herpetologists. *Res:* In the oyster toadfish--described seasonal and geographical variation of mating call, evoked sound production by electrical brain stimulation, recorded extracellularly from single units of VIIIth nerve, localized hydrogen 3 testosterone receptors in brainstem. *Mailing Add:* Dept Biol Va Commonwealth Univ Richmond VA 23284

FINE, MORRIS EUGENE, b Jamestown, NDak, Apr 12, 18; m 50; c 2. METALLURGY. *Educ:* Univ Minn, BMetE, 40, MS, 42, PhD(phys metall), 43. *Prof Exp:* Instr phys metall, Univ Minn, 42-44; assoc metallurgist, Manhattan Proj, Chicago, 44-45; assoc metallurgist, Univ Calif, Los Alamos, NMex, 45; mem tech staff, Bell Tel Labs, 46-54; prof metall, Tech Inst, 54-64, chmn, Dept Mat Sci, 54-60, chmn res ctr, 60-64, WALTER P MURPHY PROF MAT SCI & ENG, NORTHWESTERN UNIV, EVANSTON, 64-, ASSOC DEAN, TECHNOL INST RES & GRAD STUDIES, 74- *Concurrent Pos:* Mem mat adv bd, Nat Acad Sci, 65-69; vis prof, Stanford Univ, 67-68; current chmn mem comt, Nat Acad Eng; vis prof, Japan Soc for Prom Sci, 79. *Honors & Awards:* Campbell lectr, Am Soc Metals, 79; Mathewson Gold Medal, Am Inst Mining, Metall & Petrol Engrs Metall Soc, 81. *Mem:* Nat Acad Eng; fel Am Soc Metals; fel Am Phys Soc; fel Metall Soc; fel Am Ceramic Soc. *Res:* Phase transformations in solids; precipitation hardening; theory of the strength of metals and alloys; elasticity and internal friction of solids; magnetic properties of metals and ceramics; materials science; fatigue of metals. *Mailing Add:* Dept of Mat Sci & Eng Northwestern Univ Evanston IL 60201

FINE, MORRIS M(ILTON), b St Louis, Mo, Nov 15, 14; m 37; c 1. EXTRACTIVE METALLURGY. *Educ:* Wash Univ, BS, 35. *Prof Exp:* Chemist, Mo, US Bur Mines, 35-40, metallurgist, 41-55, sect chief mineral dressing, 56-59, proj coordr metall, Minn, 59-70, res dir, Rolla Metall Res Ctr, 71-79; RETIRED. *Honors & Awards:* Superior performance award, US Bur Mines, 64, Meritorious Serv Award, 69. *Mem:* Am Inst Mining, Metall & Petrol Eng; Sigma Xi (pres, 59). *Res:* Agglomeration and reduction of iron ore raw materials; extractive metallurgy of lead and zinc; iron and steel process metallurgy. *Mailing Add:* 1405 Liberty Dr Rolla MO 65401

FINE, PAUL CHARLES, b Dallas, Tex, June 28, 15. THEORETICAL PHYSICS. *Educ:* Univ Okla, BA, 35; Calif Inst Technol, MS, 36, PhD(physics), 39. *Prof Exp:* Asst, Calif Inst Technol, 36-38; instr physics, Univ Ore, 39 & Univ Tex, 39-42; tech aide, Nat Defense Res Comt, 42-45; fel, Calif Inst Technol, 45-46; sci adv, US delegation, UN Atomic Energy Agency, NY, 46-47; special asst, Div Mil Appln, US AEC, 48-55, asst to comnr, 55-56, dir div opers anal & forecasting, 56-71, sr cost-benefit specialist, 72-74, sr cost benefit specialist, US Nuclear Regulatory Comn, 75-76, tech asst, Environ Projs, 76-78, TECH ASST, OFF NUCLEAR REACTOR REGULATION, US NUCLEAR REGULATORY COMN, 79- *Res:* Normal modes of vibration of the atoms in crystal lattices; nuclear power; load-duration curves of electric utilities; load forecasting. *Mailing Add:* Off Nuclear Reaction Regulation US Nuc Reg Comn Washington DC 20555

FINE, RANA ARNOLD, b New York, NY, Apr 17, 44. PHYSICAL OCEANOGRAPHY, CHEMICAL OCEANOGRAPHY. *Educ:* New York Univ, BA, 65; Univ Miami, MA, 73, PhD(marine sci), 75. *Prof Exp:* Fel chem oceanog, Rosenstiel Sch Marine & Atmospheric Sci, Univ Miami, 76-77, res asst prof, 77-80, res assoc prof, 80-81; ASSOC PROG DIR PHYS OCEANOG, NSF, 81- *Mem:* Am Geophys Union; AAAS. *Res:* Use of radioactive tracers found in the oceans as a result of the nuclear testing, such as tritium and radiocarbon, to study circulation and mixing. *Mailing Add:* Nat Sci Found 1800 G St NW Washington DC 20550

FINE, RICHARD ELIOT, b Pueblo, Colo, May 27, 42; m 69; c 2. CELL BIOLOGY, BIOCHEMISTRY. *Educ:* Univ Calif, Berkeley, AB, 64; Brandeis Univ, PhD(biochem), 69. *Prof Exp:* Am Cancer Soc fel, Med Res Coun Lab Molecular Biol, Cambridge, Eng, 69-71; asst prof physiol, 71-78, ASSOC PROF PHYSIOL & BIOCHEM, SCH MED, BOSTON 78- *Mem:* AAAS. *Mailing Add:* Dept of Physiol Boston Univ Sch of Med Boston MA 02118

FINE, SAMUEL, b Baranowiczach, Poland, Jan 21, 25; Can citizen. MEDICINE, BIOPHYSICS. *Educ:* Univ Toronto, BASc, 46, MD, 57; Mass Inst Technol, SM, 53. *Prof Exp:* Jr engr, Can Gen Elec Co, 47-48; staff mem, Res Lab Electronics, Mass Inst Technol, 51-53; civil serv app, NIH, 58-59; res assoc med, Brookhaven Nat Lab, 59-61; assoc prof elec eng, 61-64, PROF BIOMED ENG, NORTHEASTERN UNIV, 64-, CHMN DEPT, 70- *Concurrent Pos:* Mem adv comt optical masers, Surgeon Gen, US Army, 64- *Mem:* Inst Elec & Electronics Engrs; Soc Nuclear Med. *Res:* Electrical engineering; biomedical engineering; nuclear medicine; biological effects of laser radiation. *Mailing Add:* Dept of Biophys & Biomed Eng Northeastern Univ Boston MA 02115

FINE, TERRENCE LEON, b New York, NY, Mar 9, 39; m 64. ELECTRICAL ENGINEERING. *Educ:* City Col New York, BEE, 58; Harvard Univ, SM, 59, PhD(appl physics), 63. *Prof Exp:* Res fel, Harvard Univ, 63-64; Miller Inst fel, Univ Calif, Berkeley, 64-66; asst prof, 66-70, assoc prof, 70-79, PROF ELEC ENG, CORNELL UNIV, 79- *Concurrent Pos:* Consult, TASC, Inc, 73- & Lawrence Livermore Lab, 77- *Mem:* Inst Elec & Electronics Eng; Inst Math Statist. *Res:* Foundations of probability and statistics; decision theory. *Mailing Add:* Sch of Elec Eng Cornell Univ Col of Eng Ithaca NY 14853

FINEBERG, CHARLES, b Philadelphia, Pa, Jan 1, 21; m 46; c 3. THORACIC SURGERY. *Educ:* Wake Forest Col, BS, 40; Hahnemann Med Col, MD, 50; Am Bd Surg, dipl, 56; Am Bd Thoracic Surg, dipl, 57. *Prof Exp:* Intern med, Mt Sinai Hosp, 50-51; resident surg, 51-55, asst, 55-56, from instr to assoc prof, 55-72, PROF SURG, THOMAS JEFFERSON UNIV, 72-; CHMN DEPT SURG, DAROFF DIV, ALBERT EINSTEIN MED CTR, 68- *Concurrent Pos:* Res fel, Thomas Jefferson Univ, 51-52; USPHS fel, Nat Cancer Inst, 52-54; dir, Clin Cancer Training, Tumor Adv Group, 66-68. *Mem:* Fel Am Col Surgeons; fel Am Asn Thoracic Surgeons; AMA. *Res:* Surgical correction of coronary artery disease and malabsorption syndromes; surgical uses of hyperbaric oxygenation; carcinoma of the breast. *Mailing Add:* Dept of Surg Thomas Jefferson Univ Philadelphia PA 19107

FINEBERG, HERBERT, b Portland, Maine, Jan 16, 15; m 41; c 2. ORGANIC CHEMISTRY, PHYSICS. *Educ:* Trinity Col, BS, 35; Univ Ill, PhD(org chem), 41. *Prof Exp:* Res chemist org, Eastman Kodak Co, 35-38; res mgr, Conn Hard Rubber Co, 41-45; pres, Geral Chem Co, 45-48; vpres res, Glyco Chem Co, 48-62; res mgr fat derivatives, Archer-Daniels-Midland Co, 62-67; res mgr fat derivatives, 67-75, RES MGR, TECH INFO CTR & PLANNING, ASHLAND CHEM CO, 75- *Mem:* Am Oil Chemists Asn; Am Chem Soc; Lic Exec Soc. *Res:* Technical information storage and retrieval and technical and economic evaluations of projects in fatty derivatives and petrochemicals. *Mailing Add:* 2848 Maryland Ave Columbus OH 43209

FINEBERG, RICHARD ARNOLD, b St Paul, Minn, Mar 8, 22; m 43; c 1. BIOCHEMISTRY. *Educ:* Univ Chicago, SB, 42, MD, 45; Univ Calif, PhD(biochem), 54. *Prof Exp:* Intern, Naval Hosps, Shoemaker & Oakland, Calif, 45-46; asst prof biochem, 54-60, ASSOC PROF BIOCHEM & BIOPHYS, UNIV CALIF, SAN FRANCISCO, 60- *Concurrent Pos:* Asst resident, Kaiser Hosp, San Francisco, 60-61. *Mem:* AAAS. *Res:* Protein chemistry and biosynthesis. *Mailing Add:* Rm S-960 Univ of Calif San Francisco CA 94143

FINEG, JERRY, b Buffalo, NY, Jan 7, 28; m 55; c 4. LABORATORY ANIMAL SCIENCE. *Educ:* Tex A&M Univ, BS, 49, DVM, 53; Univ Southern Calif, MS, 64. *Prof Exp:* Chief vet sci, 6571st Aeromed Res Lab, US Air Force, 58-62, chief biodynamics, 64-67, chief, Vet Sci Div, Sch Aerospace Med, Brooks AFB, Tex, 69-73; DIR, ANIMAL RESOURCES CTR & PROF PHARM & PHYSIOL, COL PHARM, UNIV TEX, AUSTIN, 73- *Concurrent Pos:* Consult lab animal facil, Architects-Barnes, Landes, Goodman, Youngblood, White, Budd VanNess Partnership, 76- *Mem:* Am Vet Med Asn; Am Asn Lab Animal Sci; Int Primatol Soc; Am Soc Lab Animal Practitioners. *Res:* Drug effects and distribution in disease states of laboratory animals. *Mailing Add:* Animal Resources Ctr Univ of Tex Austin TX 78712

FINEGOLD, HAROLD, b Lawrence, Mass, Jan 13, 29. MOLECULAR SPECTROMETRY. *Educ:* Boston Univ, AB, 51; Harvard Univ, AM, 53. *Prof Exp:* Instr chem, Boston Univ, 52-53; phys chemist, Nat Bur Standards, 57-65; phys & anal chemist, Agr Res Serv, USDA, 65-80; CONSULT, 80- *Mem:* Am Chem Soc; NY Acad Sci; Am Soc Mass Spectrometry. *Res:* Structural and/or spectroscopic studies, utilizing nuclear magnetic resonance, mechanically accelerated Sabot System, iridium spectrometry of pesticides, herbicides, insecticides, plant growth regulators, lipids, steroids, proteins and polypeptides, vitamins and organo-phosphorous materials. *Mailing Add:* Agr Res Ctr US Dept of Agr Beltsville MD 20705

FINEGOLD, LEONARD X, b London, Eng, Feb 15, 35; m 65; c 2. MOLECULAR BIOPHYSICS, POLYMER PHYSICS. *Educ:* Univ London, BSc, 56, PhD(physics), 59. *Prof Exp:* Res fel, Div Eng & Appl Physics, Harvard Univ, 59-62; res assoc, Lawrence Radiation Lab, Univ Calif, Berkeley, 62-65; from asst prof to assoc prof physics, Univ Colo, Boulder, 65-74; PROF PHYSICS, DREXEL UNIV, 74- *Concurrent Pos:* Am Cancer Soc res scholar biol, Univ Calif, San Diego, 71-72 & NIH spec fel biol, 72-73; Watkins prof, 78. *Mem:* Am Phys Soc; Am Inst Physics; Soc Basic Irreproducible Res; Electron Micros Soc Am; Biophys Soc. *Res:* Cell membranes; physics of biopolymers; electron microscopy; computer simulations. *Mailing Add:* Dept of Physics Drexel Univ Philadelphia PA 19104

FINEGOLD, SYDNEY MARTIN, b New York, NY, Aug 12, 21; m 47; c 3. INFECTIOUS DISEASES, MICROBIOLOGY. *Educ:* Univ Calif, Los Angeles, AB, 43; Univ Tex, MD, 49; Am Bd Internal Med, dipl, 57. *Prof Exp:* Intern, US Marine Hosp, 49-50; resident, Wadsworth Vet Hosp, Los Angeles, 53-54; from instr to assoc prof, 55-68, PROF MED, SCH MED, UNIV CALIF, LOS ANGELES, 68-; SECT CHIEF INFECTIOUS DIS, WADSWORTH VET HOSP, 57- *Concurrent Pos:* Fel med, Med Sch, Univ Minn, 50-52; attend physician, Minn Gen Hosp, 51-52; mem comt infectious dis res prog, Vet Admin, 61-65, mem, Merit Rev Bd, 72-74 & Infectious Dis Adv Comt, 74-; mem adv panel, US Pharmacopeia, 70-75; mem, Nat Res Coun-Nat Acad Sci Drug Efficacy Study Group, 66-69; mem subcomt, Int Comn Nomenclature Bacteria, 66-, chmn, 72-78. *Mem:* Fel AAAS; fel Am Acad Microbiol; fel Am Col Physicians; Infectious Dis Soc Am. *Res:* Infectious diseases; intestinal flora; anaerobic bacteria and anaerobic infections. *Mailing Add:* Wadsworth Vet Hosp Los Angeles CA 90073

FINELLI, ANTHONY FRANCIS, b Newton, Mass, June 18, 22; m 56; c 3. ORGANIC CHEMISTRY. *Educ:* Boston Col, BS, 43; Univ Pa, MS, 47, PhD(chem), 50. *Prof Exp:* Org res chemist, 50-64, head urethane elastomers res, 64-74, mgr, rubber applns res, 74-77 & urethanes, 77-78, MGR URETHANE PROD & POLYMER CHARACTERIZATION, GOODYEAR TIRE & RUBBER CO, 78- *Mem:* Am Chem Soc; Am Inst Chemists; Am Soc Artificial Internal Organs. *Res:* Artificial heart valves, ventricles and arterial grafts; morphine chemistry; vinyl chloride polymers; natural and synthetic latices, natural and synthetic rubbers, urethane elastomers; foams and coatings; polyester characterization; polyesters for solution adhesives, hot melt adhesives, powder coatings. *Mailing Add:* Goodyear Res Lab 142 Goodyear Blvd Akron OH 44316

FINELLI, VINCENT NICOLA, b Castelvetere Val Fortore, Italy, Apr 5, 35; US citizen; m 69; c 2. BIOCHEMISTRY, ENVIRONMENTAL HEALTH. *Educ:* Univ Rome, PhD(biochem), 68. *Prof Exp:* Res asst biochem, McLean Hosp Res Lab & Harvard Med Sch, 68-72; asst prof, 72-76, ASSOC PROF ENVIRON HEALTH, COL MED, UNIV CINCINNATI, 76- *Concurrent Pos:* Fel environ health, Univ Cincinnati, 69-72; coordr, co-author & reviewer Multimedia Criteria Documents, US Environ Protection Agency, 79- *Mem:* Am Chem Soc; Soc Environ Geochem & Health; NY Acad Sci. *Res:* Studies of the effects of environmental pollutants on metal-dependent biological systems; interactions of chelating agents and heavy metals with the functions of essential metals. *Mailing Add:* Dept of Environ Health Univ of Cincinnati Col of Med Cincinnati OH 45267

FINEMAN, MORTON A, b Kearny, NJ, Aug 9, 19; m 49; c 2. PHYSICAL CHEMISTRY. *Educ:* Ind Univ, BA, 41; Univ Pittsburgh, PhD(chem), 48. *Prof Exp:* Asst, Univ Pittsburgh, 41-44; mem res staff, Sprague Elec Co, 48-50; res fel, Univ Minn, 50-52; from asst prof to prof chem, Providence Col, 52-61; sr res staff mem, Gen Atomic Div, Gen Dynamics Corp, 61-66; chmn dept physics, 66-75, PROF PHYSICS, LYCOMING COL, 66- *Concurrent Pos:* Vis prof physics, Univ Calif, San Diego, 74-75. *Mem:* Am Phys Soc; Am Chem Soc; Am Asn Physics Teachers. *Res:* Thermodynamics of solid solutions; chemical kinetics; electron impact studies of gases; negative ions; chemical reactive cross sections via crossed beam techniques; angular scattering of electrons from atoms. *Mailing Add:* 2608 Blair St R D 3 Montoursville PA 17754

FINERMAN, A(ARON), b New York, NY, Apr 1, 25; m 68; c 4. COMPUTER SCIENCE. *Educ:* City Col New York, BCE, 48; Mass Inst Technol, SM, 51, ScD(civil eng), 56. *Prof Exp:* Instr, City Col New York, 48-49, lectr, 51-54; engr, Thomas Worcester & Co, 49; proj engr struct design, Voorhees, Walker, Foley & Smith, 51-54; res engr, Mass Inst Technol, 54-55, instr struct eng, 55-56; mgr digital comput & data process, Repub Aviation Corp, 56-61; prof eng & dir comput ctr, State Univ NY, Stony Brook, 61-69, prof comput sci, 69-71; mgr off comput & info systs, Jet Propulsion Lab, 71-73; prof comput sci, State Univ NY, 73-78, chmn dept, 75-77; DIR COMPUT CTR & PROF COMPUT & COMMUN SCI, UNIV MICH, 78- *Concurrent Pos:* Pres, SHARE, 61-62; sr res assoc, Jet Propulsion Lab, 68-69. *Mem:* AAAS; Asn Comput Mach (treas, 73-); Am Fed Info Processing Soc; Asn Am Univ Profs. *Res:* Management of computing ctr; education in computing science and data processing; computing applications. *Mailing Add:* Dir Comput Ctr Univ of Mich Ann Arbor MI 48109

FINERTY, JOHN CHARLES, b Chicago, Ill, Oct 20, 14; m 40; c 2. ANATOMY. *Educ:* Kalamazoo Col, AB, 37; Kans State Col, MS, 39; Univ Wis, PhD(zool), 42. *Prof Exp:* Asst zool, Kans State Univ, 37-39; asst, Univ Wis, 39-42, asst physiol, 42; instr, Univ Mich, 43, instr anat, 43-46; from asst prof to assoc prof, Sch Med, Wash Univ, 46-49; from assoc prof to prof, Univ Tex Med Sch, 49-56, asst dean, 54-56; prof, Sch Med, Univ Miami, 56-66, chmn dept, 56-66, from asst dean to assoc dean, 56-66; dean sch med, 66-71, PROF ANAT, SCH MED, LA STATE UNIV MED CTR, NEW ORLEANS, 66-, VCHANCELLOR ACAD AFFAIRS, 71-, DEAN, SCH GRAD STUDIES, 74- *Concurrent Pos:* Rackham Found fel, Univ Mich, 42-43. *Mem:* AAAS; Am Asn Anat (pres, 75-76); Am Physiol Soc; Soc Exp Biol & Med; Endocrine Soc. *Res:* Experimental endocrinology; pituitary cytophysiology; correlation of microscopic structure and function; neurohumoral control of respiration; gross human anatomy; parabiosis; protection from x-irradiation; effects of fat deficiency. *Mailing Add:* La State Univ Med Ctr 1440 Canal St New Orleans LA 70112

FINESTONE, ALBERT JUSTIN, b Philadelphia, Pa, May 12, 21; m 51; c 3. MEDICINE. *Educ:* Temple Univ, AB, 42, MD, 45, MSc, 51. *Prof Exp:* Asst prof, 58-64, CLIN PROF MED, SCH MED, TEMPLE UNIV, 64-, DEAN CONTINUING MED EDUC, 73- *Concurrent Pos:* Dir continuing educ, Col Physicians Philadelphia, 74-79. *Mem:* AMA; Am Diabetes Asn; Am Col Physicians; Am Psychosom Soc; Am Fedn Clin Res. *Res:* Metabolic diseases. *Mailing Add:* Dept of Med Temple Univ Sch of Med Philadelphia PA 19140

FINGAR, WALTER WIGGS, b Nashville, Tenn, Jan 14, 34; m 55; c 6. DENTISTRY. *Educ:* Univ Tenn, DDS, 56; Univ Iowa, MS, 65. *Prof Exp:* From instr to asst prof dent technol, Col Dent, Univ Iowa, 64-67; asst prof oper dent, Col Dent, Univ Tenn, 67-68; assoc prof, 68-73, chmn dept, 71-77, PROF OPER DENT, MED UNIV SC, 73-, ASST DEAN, 76- *Concurrent Pos:* Dir maternity & infant care proj, Dent Clin, Med Univ SC, 68-70; mem nat rev comt, Proj ACORDE. *Res:* Dental materials especially composite resins and pit and fissure sealants; pulpal response to dental materials and operations. *Mailing Add:* Dept Oper Dent Med Univ SC Charleston SC 29403

FINGER, IRVING, b Peekskill, NY, Sept 23, 24. GENETICS. *Educ:* Swarthmore Col, BA, 50; Univ Pa, PhD(zool), 55. *Prof Exp:* Am Cancer Soc fel, Columbia Univ, 56-58; from asst prof to assoc prof, 57-69, PROF BIOL, HAVERFORD COL, 69- *Concurrent Pos:* USPHS spec fel, Univ Calif, San Diego, 63-64. *Mem:* Genetics Soc Am; Soc Protozool; Am Soc Zool. *Res:* Immunology; microbial genetics; protozoology; cellular differentiation. *Mailing Add:* Dept of Biol Haverford Col Haverford PA 19041

FINGER, KENNETH F, b Antigo, Wis, Jan 2, 29; m 51; c 1. BIOCHEMICAL PHARMACOLOGY. *Educ:* Univ Wis, BS, 51, MS, 53, PhD(pharm, pharmacol), 55. *Prof Exp:* Sr investr pharmaceut chem, Chas Pfizer & Co, 55-57, res supvr, 59-61, res mgr, 61-63; guest worker, Nat Heart Inst, 57-59; from assoc prof to prof pharmacol, Sch Pharm, Univ Wis, Madison, 63-68; dean Col Pharm, 68-74, ASSOC VPRES HEALTH AFFAIRS, UNIV FLA, 74- *Mem:* Am Soc Pharmacol & Exp Therapeut; Am Pharmaceut Asn. *Res:* Biochemistry of function; drug metabolism; drug-receptor interactions; catecholamines; anti-diabetic drugs and drugs affecting behavior. *Mailing Add:* J Hillis Miller Health Ctr Univ of Fla Gainesville FL 32610

FINGER, LARRY W, b Terril, Iowa, May 22, 40; m 62; c 2. MINERALOGY, CRYSTALLOGRAPHY. *Educ:* Univ Minn, BPhys, 62, PhD(crystal struct), 67. *Prof Exp:* Fel, 67-69, MEM STAFF, GEOPHYS LAB, CARNEGIE INST, 69- *Mem:* AAAS; Mineral Soc Am; Am Crystallog Asn; Am Geophys Union. *Res:* Crystallography and crystal structure of minerals in solid-solution series and the computations required in these studies. *Mailing Add:* 5015 Druid Dr Kensington MD 20895

FINGER, TERRY RICHARD, b Saugerties, NY, July 21, 48; m 79. FISH ECOLOGY, STREAM ECOLOGY. *Educ:* NEastern Univ, BS, 71; State Univ NY, Syracuse, MS, 75; Ore State Univ, PhD(fisheries), 79. *Prof Exp:* Res assoc, Dept Fisheries & Wildlife, Ore State Univ, 79-80; ASST PROF POP DYNAMICS & FISHERY BIOL, SCH FORESTRY, FISHERIES & WILDLIFE, UNIV MO, 80- *Mem:* Am Soc Ichthyologists & Herpetologists; Ecol Soc Am; Am Fisheries Soc; Sigma Xi. *Res:* Investigation of ecology of stream fishes, especially species interactions among benthic species; relations between ecology and systematics of benthic stream fishes; ecology of larval fishes especially in seasonally flooded lowland hardwood habitats. *Mailing Add:* Sch Forestry, Fisheries & Wildlife 112 Stephens Hall Univ Mo Columbia MO 65211

FINGER, THOMAS EMANUEL, b Orange, NJ, Aug 30, 49; m 74; c 2. NEUROANATOMY, IMMUNOCYTOCHEMISTRY. *Educ:* Mass Inst Technol, SB, 72, SM, 73, PhD(psychol & brain sci), 75. *Prof Exp:* Res assoc psychiat, Res Found State Univ NY, Stony Brook, 75; NIH fel vision res, Dept Anat, Sch Med, Wash Univ, 75-78; ASST PROF, DEPT ANAT, MED SCH, UNIV COLO, 78- *Concurrent Pos:* Investr, Marine Biol Lab, Wood Hole, Mass, 81- *Mem:* Soc Neurosci; Am Asn Anatomists. *Res:* Comparative neuroanatomy especially of teleost fish; neuroembryology; localization of neuropeptides and neurotransmitters; chemosensory systems; lateral line system; cerebellum; evolution of the nervous system. *Mailing Add:* Dept of Anat Med Sch Univ Colo Denver CO 80220

FINGERHUT, MARILYN ANN, b Brooklyn, NY, Oct 3, 40. CELL BIOLOGY, MICROBIOLOGY. *Educ:* Col of St Elizabeth, BS, 64; Cath Univ Am, PhD(cell biol), 70. *Prof Exp:* Instr biol, Col St Elizabeth, 70-71; res assoc biochem, Col Med & Dent NJ, 71-73; asst prof, 73-77, ASSOC PROF BIOL, ST PETER'S COL, NJ, 77- *Mem:* Am Inst Biol Sci; Sigma Xi. *Res:* Induction and enzymology of the flavoprotein, sarcosine dehydrogenase in Pseudomonas strains and levels of covalently bound flavoproteins and folic acid in selected bacteria. *Mailing Add:* Dept of Biol St Peter's Col Kennedy Blvd Jersey City NJ 07306

FINGERMAN, MILTON, b Boston, Mass, May 21, 28; m 58; c 2. COMPARATIVE PHYSIOLOGY. *Educ:* Boston Col, BS, 48; Northwestern Univ, MS, 49, PhD(biol), 52. *Prof Exp:* Asst, Northwestern Univ, 49-51; from instr to assoc prof, 54-63, PROF BIOL, TULANE UNIV, 63-, CHMN, DEPT BIOL, 90- *Concurrent Pos:* mem adv panel regulatory biol, NSF, 66-69; mem supply dept comt, Marine Biol Lab, Woods Hole, 70-73 & comt chmn, 71-73; chmn nominating comt, Div Comp Endocrinol, Am Soc Zoologists, 72, prog officer, 77-78 & mem, Comt Hist, 78-; Comt Animal Models Biomed Res Invertebrate, Inst Lab Animal Resources, Nat Res Coun, 72-73, comt marine invertebrate, 76-81; Environ Sci Prog Planning Coun, Gulf Univ Res Consortium, 77- *Mem:* AAAS; Am Inst Biol Sci; Int Soc Chronobiol; Am Soc Zool. *Res:* Comparative endocrinology; biological chronometry; animal color changes; crustacean physiology and endocrinology; chromatophores. *Mailing Add:* Dept of Biol Tulane Univ New Orleans LA 70118

FINGERMAN, SUE WHITSELL, b Earlington, Ky, May 4, 32; m 58; c 2. ENVIRONMENTAL TOXICOLOGY. *Educ:* Transylvania Col, BA, 55; Tulane Univ, MS, 59, PhD(biol), 75. *Prof Exp:* Instr biol, Ursuline Acad, 67-68, Dominican Col, 68-69 & Xavier Univ, 69-71; res assoc biol, Tulane Univ, 72-80; res fac, 80-81, BIOL CONSULT, OKLA STATE UNIV, 80- *Mem:* Sigma Xi; Soc Environ Toxicol & Chem; Am Soc Zoologists. *Res:* Study of effects of insecticides and other environmental pollutants on the physiology and behavior of fishes and crabs. *Mailing Add:* 1730 Broadway New Orleans LA 70118

FINGL, EDWARD (GEORGE), b Oak Park, Ill, Oct 24, 23; m 56. PHARMACOLOGY. *Educ:* Purdue Univ, BS, 43, MS, 49; Univ Utah, PhD(pharmacol), 52. *Prof Exp:* Asst pharmaceut chem, Purdue Univ, 46-49; asst pharmacol, 49-51, USPHS fel, Col Med, 52-53, asst res prof, 53-54, from asst prof to assoc prof, 54-72, PROF PHARMACOL, COL MED, UNIV UTAH, 72- *Mem:* AAAS; Am Soc Pharmacol & Exp Therapeut. *Res:* Pharmacodynamics; pharmacokinetics; biostatistics; drug tolerance. *Mailing Add:* Dept of Pharmacol Univ of Utah Col of Med Salt Lake City UT 84112

FINHOLT, ALBERT EDWARD, b Chicago, Ill, Jan 28, 18; m 41; c 4. CHEMISTRY. *Educ:* Knox Col, AB, 38; Univ Chicago, PhD(chem), 46. *Prof Exp:* Res chemist, Gen Printing Ink Co, Ill, 39-42; res assoc chem dept staff & assoc dir hydride proj, US Navy, 45-47; chief chemist, Metal Hydrides, Inc, 47-49; assoc prof, 49-54, PROF CHEM, ST OLAF COL, 54-64, 71- *Concurrent Pos:* Chmn dept chem, St Olaf Col, 57-64, dean, 64-71, vpres, 66-71. *Mem:* AAAS; Am Chem Soc. *Res:* Inorganic and metal hydrides; preparation of aluminum hydrides and their use in inorganic and organic chemistry; organometallics. *Mailing Add:* Dept of Chem St Olaf Col Northfield MN 55057

FINHOLT, JAMES E, b Oak Park, Ill, Oct 28, 33; m 56; c 1. PHYSICAL CHEMISTRY, INORGANIC CHEMISTRY. *Educ:* St Olaf Col, BA, 55; Univ Calif, Berkeley, PhD(chem), 60. *Prof Exp:* Asst prof chem, Albion Col, 59-60; from asst prof to assoc prof, 60-72, Chmn Dept, 75-78, PROF CHEM, CARLETON COL, 73- *Concurrent Pos:* Petrol Res Found grant theoret inorg chem, Columbia Univ, 65-66; AEC res assoc, Argonne Nat Lab, 72-73; vis scientist, Oak Ridge Nat Lab, 80; vis prof, The Univ, England, 81. *Mem:* Am Chem Soc; Sigma Xi; AAAS. *Res:* Physical properties of coordination compounds in aqueous solution; chromium species; x-ray diffraction. *Mailing Add:* Dept of Chem Carleton Col Northfield MN 55057

FINITZO-HIEBER, TERESE, b Chicago, Ill, Apr 8, 47; m 69. AUDIOLOGY. *Educ:* Northwestern Univ, BS, 69, MA, 71, PhD(auditory res), 75. *Prof Exp:* Clin audiologist, Otol Prof Asn, 71-73; consult audiol, Univ Affil Ctr, 76-77; RES CONSULT, AUDIOL, SOUTHWESTERN MED UNIV, PEDIAT, 74- & ASST PROF AUDIOL, UNIV TEX, DALLAS, 75- *Concurrent Pos:* Consult, Suburban Low Incidence Develop Exemplary Serv, 70-71, Children's Med Ctr, 76-; grant, Univ Tex, Dallas, 76-77, 77-78, Schering Drug Co, 78-79. *Mem:* Am Speech & Hearing Asn. *Res:* Audiological assessment and habilitation of infants using auditory evoked potentials; evaluation of acoustical environments for the sensorially handicapped. *Mailing Add:* Callier Ctr for Commun Disorders 1966 Inwood Rd Dallas TX 75235

FINIZIO, MICHAEL, b Naples Italy, Nov 27, 38; m 66; c 2. ORGANIC CHEMISTRY, MEDICINAL CHEMISTRY. *Educ:* Univ Naples, PhD(org chem), 62. *Prof Exp:* Res chemist, Endo Labs, Inc, 63-76, RES CHEMIST MED CHEM, E I DU PONT DE NEMOURS & CO, INC, 76- *Mem:* Am Chem Soc. *Res:* Synthesis of biological active compounds. *Mailing Add:* 3034 Mapleshade Lane Wilmington DE 19810

FINK, ANTHONY LAWRENCE, b Hertford, Eng, Jan 25, 43; m 66. BIO-ORGANIC CHEMISTRY. *Educ:* Queen's Univ (Ont), BSc, 64, PhD(org chem), 68. *Prof Exp:* Nat Res Coun Can fel, Northwestern Univ, 67-69; asst prof, 69-76, ASSOC PROF CHEM, UNIV CALIF, SANTA CRUZ, 76- *Concurrent Pos:* Staff, Lab Molecular Biophysics, Univ Oxford, England, 78-; vis fel, All Souls Col, Oxford, 80-81. *Mem:* AAAS; Am Chem Soc; Biochem Soc; Am Soc Biol Chemists. *Res:* Mechanisms of enzyme reactions; cryobiochemistry; protein folding; polyfunctional and intramolecular catalysis; chemical communication in marine organisms; investigations of enzyme mechanisms; protein folding; cryobiochemistry and cryoenzymology; development of anti-penicillinase compounds. *Mailing Add:* Dept of Chem Univ of Calif Santa Cruz CA 95060

FINK, ARLINGTON M, b Armour, SDak, Dec 15, 32. MATHEMATICS. *Educ:* Wartburg Col, BA, 56; Iowa State Univ, MS, 58, PhD(math), 60. *Prof Exp:* Res assoc math, Mathematica, Princeton, NJ, 60; instr, Univ Va, 60-62; asst prof, Univ Nebr, Lincoln, 62-67; assoc prof, 67-71, PROF MATH, IOWA STATE UNIV, 71- *Mem:* Am Math Soc; Math Asn Am. *Res:* Almost periodic functions; ordinary differential equations. *Mailing Add:* Dept of Math Iowa State Univ Ames IA 50011

FINK, AUSTIN IRA, b New York, NY, Nov 18, 20; m 56; c 3. OPHTHALMOLOGY. *Educ:* Univ Mich, AB, 42; Long Island Col Med, MD, 44. *Prof Exp:* Instr, Med Col, Cornell Univ, 50-57; from asst prof to assoc prof, 55-72, PROF OPHTHAL, COL MED, STATE UNIV NY DOWNSTATE MED CTR, 72- *Res:* Blood vessels of conjunctiva and retina in relation to disease; surgery of congenital cataracts; electron microscopy of Schlemms canal and surrounding structures. *Mailing Add:* Dept of Ophthal State Univ NY Downstate Med Ctr Brooklyn NY 11203

FINK, BERNARD RAYMOND, b London, Eng, May 25, 14; nat US; m 44; c 2. ANESTHESIOLOGY. *Educ:* Univ London, BSc, 35, MB & BS, 38. *Prof Exp:* Med supt, Methodist Mission Hosp, SAfrica, 47-49; from instr to assoc prof anesthesiol, Columbia Univ, 52-64; PROF ANESTHESIOL, SCH MED, UNIV WASH, 64- *Concurrent Pos:* Commonwealth Fund fel, Monaco, 63; assoc prof anesthesiologist, Presby Hosp, NY, 55-64; fel fac anaesthetists, Royal Col Surgeons, Eng, 80. *Honors & Awards:* Fulbright lectr, Turku, 59. *Mem:* AAAS; Am Soc Pharmacol; Am Physiol Soc; Soc Neurosci; Am Soc Neurochem; Int Asn Study Pain (secy). *Res:* Cellular biology of anesthesia; rapid axoplasmic transport; neuropharmacology of local anesthetics; mechanics of the human larynx. *Mailing Add:* Dept of Anesthesiol RN-10 Univ of Wash Sch of Med Seattle WA 98195

FINK, CHARLES L, b Pittsburgh, Pa, May 29, 44; m 67. INSTRUMENTATION DESIGN, ANALYSIS. *Educ:* Univ Pittsburgh, BS, 66, PhD(nuclear physics), 71. *Prof Exp:* Nuclear physicist, Argonne Nat Lab, 71-73, Los Alamos Nat Lab, 73-74; NUCLEAR ENGR, ARGONNE NAT LAB, 74- *Mem:* Am Phys Soc; Am Nuclear Soc; Inst Elec & Electronics Engrs. *Res:* Diagnostic instrumentation and new data analysis techniques for the imaging of destructive fuel motion tests; synthesis of these experimental results with computer codes for use in safety studies of the fast breeder reactor. *Mailing Add:* Argonne Nat Lab Reactor Anal & Safety Argonne IL 60439

FINK, CHESTER WALTER, b New York, NY, May 6, 28; m 55; c 3. PEDIATRICS. *Educ:* Duke Univ, BA, 47, MD, 51. *Prof Exp:* From instr to assoc prof, 57-71, PROF PEDIAT, UNIV TEX HEALTH SCI CTR DALLAS, 71- *Concurrent Pos:* Fel pediat, Sch Med, Western Reserve Univ, 56-57. *Mem:* Am Pediat Soc; Soc Pediat Res; Am Rheumatism Asn. *Res:* Rheumatoid arthritis and allied diseases. *Mailing Add:* Dept Pediat Southwestern Med Sch Univ Tex Health Sci Ctr Dallas TX 75235

FINK, COLIN ETHELBERT, b Columbia, Pa, Aug 21, 10; m 48; c 1. INORGANIC CHEMISTRY. *Educ:* Pa State Col, BS, 32; Mass Inst Technol, MS, 33; Columbia Univ, PhD(chem eng), 44. *Prof Exp:* Prod engr, Cracking Dept, Atlantic Refining Co, 33-36; prod engr res lubricating oils, Pa State Univ, 36-40; asst chem eng, Columbia Univ, 40-44; asst pilot plant & develop, Am Cyanamid Co, 44-45; asst res & develop floor coverings, Armstrong Cork Co, 45-46; asst develop & prod cathode ray tubes, Radio Corp Am, 46-47; assoc prof chem eng, Drexel Inst, 47-51, prof, 51-57; from assoc prof to prof chem, 57-76, EMER PROF CHEM, FRANKLIN & MARSHALL COL, 76- *Mem:* AAAS; Am Chem Soc; Am Soc Eng Educ; Am Inst Chem Eng. *Res:* Viscosity-density-pressure characteristics of lubrication oils; binders in activated carbons; pulsating flow of fluids; heart-lung machine for cardiac surgery. *Mailing Add:* Maple Farm Akron PA 17501

FINK, DAVID JORDAN, b Columbus Ohio, Aug 5, 43; m 67. BIOCHEMICAL ENGINEERING. *Educ:* Univ Cincinnati, BSChE, 66; Univ Mich, MSE, 68, PhD(chem eng), 73. *Prof Exp:* Staff scientist, 74-77, prin scientist, 77-81, PROJS MGR BIOCHEM ENG, COLUMBUS LABS, BATTELLE MEM INST, 81- *Concurrent Pos:* Res assoc, Dept Biochem, Purdue Univ, 73-74. *Mem:* Am Inst Chem Engrs. *Res:* Enzyme technology in industrial processing, medical and analytical applications; immunoassay systems; controlled-release technology; microencapsulation; biocompatible materials. *Mailing Add:* 1275 Arlington Columbus OH 43212

FINK, DAVID WARREN, b Brooklyn, NY, Mar 30, 44; m 67; c 2. ANALYTICAL CHEMISTRY. *Educ:* Brooklyn Col, BS, 64; Lehigh Univ, PhD(anal chem), 69. *Prof Exp:* Sr res chemist, Res Ctr, Lever Bros Co, Edgewater, 69-71; sr res chemist, 71-72, sect leader, 72-75, ASST DIR, MERCK, SHARP & DOHME RES LABS, 75- *Mem:* Am Chem Soc; Am Pharmaceut Asn. *Res:* Luminescence of metal chelates; properties of excited states; analytical applications of fluorescence spectroscopy. *Mailing Add:* Merck Sharp & Dohme Res Labs Rahway NJ 07065

FINK, DIANE JOANNE, b Chicago, Ill, July 27, 36; wid; c 2. ONCOLOGY, HEMATOLOGY. *Educ:* Stanford Univ, BS, 57, MD, 60. *Prof Exp:* Intern, Kaiser Found Hosp, San Francisco, 60-61, resident internal med, 61-63; resident internal med, cancer chemother & immunohemat, Vet Admin Hosp, San Francisco, 63-65, res assoc immunohemat, 65-66, staff physician in chg of cancer chemother sect, 66-69, chmn tumor bd, 67-71, chief sect oncol, 69-71; prog dir chemother, Div Cancer Res Resources & Ctrs, Nat Cancer Inst, 71-73, chief treat br, Cancer Control Prog, 73-74, assoc dir cancer control, Nat Cancer Inst, 74, dir, Cancer Control & Rehabilitation, 74-79, assoc dir, Nat Cancer Inst, 79-81, VPRES DETECTION SERV, REHABILITATION, AM CANCER SOC, 81- *Concurrent Pos:* Chmn, US Deleg on US-USSR Exchange on Cancer Control & Cancer Ctrs, 74-; mem expert adv panel, WHO, 77-82. *Honors & Awards:* Superior Serv Honor Award, US Dept Health, Educ & Welfare, 75; Gerard B Lambert Award, Gerard B Lambert Found, 75. *Mem:* Am Asn Cancer Res; Am Soc Clin Oncol; Am Soc Hemat; Am Asn Cancer Educ. *Res:* Clinical trials in cancer treatment, screening, rehabilitation and prevention; cancer related health services research. *Mailing Add:* Nat Cancer Inst Blair Bldg Rm 732 Bethesda MD 20205

FINK, DON ROGER, b Reading, Pa, Apr 27, 31; m 52; c 6. GEOPHYSICS, ELECTRONICS. *Educ:* Harvard Univ, AB, 52; Wash Univ, AM, 54. *Prof Exp:* Asst, Geophys Anal Group, Mass Inst Technol, 54-56; asst geophysicist, Woods Hole Oceanog Inst, 56-59; res geophysicist, Humble Oil & Refining Co, 59-63; res scientist, Melpar, Inc, 63-64, sr scientist, 64; sr eng specialist, Philco Corp, 64-65, proj mgr, 65-67; sr eng specialist, Gen Atronics Corp, 67-70, chief geophysicist, Magnavox, 70-72; mgr Oceanog & Environ Serv, Raytheon Co, 72-78; EXEC DIR, NEW ENG CONF PUB UTILITIES COMMISSIONERS INC, 78- *Mem:* Soc Explor Geophys; Inst Elec & Electronics Engrs. *Res:* Elastic wave propagation; geomagnetism; oceanography and underwater systems; information theory; computer applications; communication systems; geophysical exploration. *Mailing Add:* PO Box 557 North Falmouth MA 02556

FINK, DONALD G(LEN), b Englewood, NJ, Nov 8, 11; m 48; c 3. ELECTRICAL ENGINEERING, ELECTRONICS. *Educ:* Mass Inst Technol, BSc, 33; Columbia Univ, MSc, 42. *Prof Exp:* Asst, Mass Inst Technol, 33-34, staff mem, Radiation Lab, 41-43; asst ed, McGraw-Hill Publ Co, 34-37, managing ed electronics, 37-41, exec ed, 45-46, ed-in-chief, 46-52; expert consult, Off Secy War, 43-45; consult, Bur Ships US Navy, 46; dir res, Philco Corp, 52-61, vpres, 61; gen mgr, 62-63, gen mgr & exec dir, 63-75, exec consult, 75-76, EMER DIR, INST ELEC & ELECTRONICS ENGRS, 74- *Concurrent Pos:* Consult, TV standards, Belg Govt, 52; ed, Standard Handbk for Elec Engrs, 68-; mem & consult, Army Sci Adv Panel, 57-78; ed, Proc Inst Radio Engrs, 56-57; mem, Bd Int Orgns & Progs, Nat Acad Sci, 74-81; mem, US Nat Comn, UNESCO, 76-81. *Honors & Awards:* Medal of Freedom, 46; Presidential Cert Merit, 48; Outstanding Civilian Serv Medal, Dept of the Army, 69; Founders Medal, Inst Elec & Electronics Engrs, 78, Consumer Electronics Award, 78; Progress Medal, Soc Motion Picture & Television Engrs, 79. *Mem:* Nat Acad Eng; fel Inst Elec & Electronics Engrs (pres, 58); fel Brit Inst Elec Eng; Soc Motion Picture & TV Engrs. *Res:* Computer systems; radio and radar navigation systems; pulsed transmitters; television, color systems and standards; semiconductor devices; stereophonic sound systems. *Mailing Add:* 103-B Heritage Hills Somers NY 10589

FINK, DWAYNE HAROLD, b Albert Lea, Minn, June 15, 32; m 60; c 3. AGRONOMY. *Educ:* Univ Minn, BS, 60; Va Polytech Inst, MS, 63, PhD(agron), 65. *Prof Exp:* Fel, Univ Minn, 65-66; SOIL SCIENTIST, US WATER CONSERV LAB, AGR RES SERV, USDA, 69- *Mem:* Clay Minerals Soc; Int Asn Study Clays; Am Soc Agron. *Res:* Surface chemistry of clay minerals, especially new methods for determination of surface area and adsorption of pollutants; reduction of surface energy of natural soils to induce precipitation runoff. *Mailing Add:* US Water Conserv Lab Agr Res Serv USDA Phoenix AZ 85040

FINK, FREDERICK CHARLES, microbiology, see previous edition

FINK, GERALD RALPH, b Brooklyn, NY, July 1, 40; m 61; c 2. GENETICS. *Educ:* Amherst Col, BA, 62; Yale Univ, MS, 64, PhD(biol), 65. *Prof Exp:* Fel biochem genetics, NIH, 65-67; asst prof 67-71, assoc prof, 71-76, prof genetics, 76-80, PROF BIOCHEM, NY STATE COL AGR & LIFE SCI, CORNELL UNIV, 81- *Concurrent Pos:* Mem, NSF Adv Panel Genetic Biol, 70-; assoc ed jour, Genetics Soc Am, 70-; Guggenheim fel, 74-75; prof, Am Cancer Soc, 81. *Honors & Awards:* US Steel Prize Molecular Biol, 81. *Mem:* Nat Acad Sci; Genetics Soc Am (secy, 77-80). *Res:* Regulation of gene activity in eucaryotes; control of histidine biosynthesis in yeast. *Mailing Add:* 1 Hunter Lane Slaterville Springs NY 14850

FINK, GREGORY BURNELL, b Outlook, Mont, Aug 3, 28; m 57; c 3. PHARMACOLOGY. *Educ:* Mont State Univ, BS, 50; Univ Utah, PhD(pharmacol), 60. *Prof Exp:* Asst prof, Wash State Univ, 60-63; asst prof, Univ Kans, 64; head dept, 64-70, PROF PHARMACOL, ORE STATE UNIV, 64- *Concurrent Pos:* Consult, Ore State Drug Adv Coun. *Mem:* Am Pharmaceut Asn; Am Soc Pharmacol & Exp Therapeut. *Res:* Neuropharmacology; psychopharmacology. *Mailing Add:* Dept of Pharmacol Ore State Univ Sch of Pharm Corvallis OR 97331

FINK, HERMAN JOSEPH, b Neutitschein, Czech, Aug 16, 30; c 3. SOLID STATE PHYSICS. *Educ:* Univ BC, BASc, 55, MASc, 56, PhD(physics), 59. *Prof Exp:* Nat Res Coun Can fel, Oxford Univ, 59-61; mem tech staff parametric amplifiers & magnetic properties solids, Bell Tel Labs, NJ, 61-63; res specialist electronic structure solids, Atomics Int Div, NAm Aviation, Inc, 63-69; actg prof, 69-70, PROF ELEC ENG, UNIV CALIF, DAVIS, 70- *Mem:* Fel Am Phys Soc. *Res:* Properties of superconductors, semiconductors at low temperatures and microwave frequencies; resonance properties of magnetic materials. *Mailing Add:* Dept of Elec Eng Univ of Calif Davis CA 95616

FINK, JAMES PAUL, b Calumet, Mich, Nov 10, 40; m 66; c 1. APPLIED MATHEMATICS. *Educ:* Drexel Inst Technol, BS, 63; Stanford Univ, MS, 65, PhD(math), 67. *Prof Exp:* Eng technician, Clifton Precision Prod Co, Inc, 59-62; instr physics, Drexel Inst Technol, 62-63; instr math, Stanford Univ, 66-67; asst prof, 67-73, ASSOC PROF MATH, UNIV PITTSBURGH, 73- *Mem:* Am Math Soc; Soc Indust & Appl Math; Math Asn Am; hon mem Sigma Xi. *Res:* Differential equations; functional analysis; nonlinear differential equations; nonlinear wave motion; mathematical modeling; analysis, bifurcation theory, continuation methods and numerical analysis. *Mailing Add:* Dept Math & Stat Univ of Pittsburgh Pittsburgh PA 15260

FINK, JOANNE KRUPEY, b Greensburg, Pa, Feb 19, 45; m 67. CHEMICAL ENGINEERING, PHYSICS. *Educ:* Univ Pittsburgh, BS, 66, PhD(physics), 72. *Prof Exp:* Appointee physics, Argonne Nat Lab, 72-73; prof classical mech, Univ NMex, Los Alamos Exten, 74; appointee physics, Los Alamos Sci Lab, 74; res assoc, 74-75, asst physicist chem eng, 75-79, CHEM ENGR, ARGONNE NAT LAB, 79- *Mem:* Am Phys Soc; Am Nuclear Soc. *Res:* Experimental and theoretical determination of physical properties use in reactor safety analysis; material interaction experiments and computer code development related to post-accident heat removal and waste handling. *Mailing Add:* Chem Eng Div 9700 S Cass Ave Argonne IL 60439

FINK, JORDAN NORMAN, b Milwaukee, Wis, Oct 13, 34; m 56; c 3. ALLERGY, IMMUNOLOGY. *Educ:* Univ Wis, BS, 56, MD, 59. *Prof Exp:* Asst instr, Sch Med, Marquette Univ, 60-63; NIH fel allergy & immunol & assoc, Med Sch, Northwestern Univ, 63-65; from instr to assoc prof med, 65-73, PROF MED, MED COL WIS, 73- *Concurrent Pos:* Clin investr, Vet Admin, 65-68. *Mem:* AAAS; Am Asn Immunologists; Am Asn Clin Invest; fel Am Acad Allergy. *Res:* Basic mechanisms in human hypersensitivity, and their diagnosis and treatment; internal medicine. *Mailing Add:* 8700 W Wisconsin Milwaukee WI 53226

FINK, KATHRYN FERGUSON, b State Center, Iowa, Feb 13, 17; m 41; c 2. BIOCHEMISTRY. *Educ:* Univ Iowa, BA, 38; Univ Rochester, PhD(biochem), 43. *Prof Exp:* Res technician, Mayo Inst Exp Med, Minn, 38-39; res assoc, Manhattan Proj, Rochester, 43-46 & Atomic Energy Proj, 46-47; assoc clin prof biophys, Sch Med, 48-63, assoc prof res, biophys & nuclear med, 64-66, prof, 66-67, resident prof med, 67-74, PROF MED, SCH MED, UNIV CALIF, LOS ANGELES, 74-, ASST DEAN, 76- *Concurrent Pos:* Res biochemist, Vet Admin Hosp, 47-61. *Mem:* Soc Exp Biol & Med; Am Soc Biol Chem; Sigma Xi. *Res:* Intestinal secretion; traumatic shock; biological effects of radiation; thyroid chemistry; amino acids; pyrimidine and purine metabolism; erythrocyte pyrimidine 5-nucleotidase deficiency in a hereditary hemolytic anemia and in hemolytic anemia associated with lead poisoning. *Mailing Add:* Dept of Med Univ of Calif Med Ctr Los Angeles CA 90024

FINK, KENNETH HOWARD, b Omaha, Nebr, Dec 11, 14; m 40; c 2. FOOD CHEMISTRY. *Educ:* Univ Denver, BS, 36. *Prof Exp:* Analyst, Great Western Sugar Co, 38-39 & Wilson & Co, 39-41; analyst, Joliet Ord Works, Army Ord, 41-44, resident inspector, 44-45; res engr, Podbielniak, Inc, 45-49; res chemist, Food Res Div, Armour & Co, 49-54, chief chemist, Refinery, 54-56, asst sect head fats & oils, Food Res Div, 56-67, res analyst, 67-79; RETIRED. *Mem:* Am Chem Soc; Am Oil Chemists Soc. *Res:* Technology of edible fats and oils; food analysis. *Mailing Add:* 1461 Selleck St Crete IL 60417

FINK, LOUIS MAIER, b Brooklyn, NY, Mar 28, 42; m 62; c 3. PATHOLOGY. *Educ:* Boston Univ, BA, 61; Albany Med Col, MD, 65. *Prof Exp:* Asst prof path, Col Physicians & Surgeons, Columbia Univ, 70-72; asst prof path, Med Sch, Univ Colo, 72-77, assoc prof, 77-81; PROF PATH, MED SCH, VANDERBILT UNIV, 81- *Mem:* Am Asn Cancer Res; Am Asn Pathologists; Harvey Soc; Int Acad Pathologists; Col Am Pathologists. *Res:* Plasma membrane protein interactions and neoplasic processes. *Mailing Add:* Vet Admin Ctr 1310 24th St Nashville TN 37203

FINK, LOYD KENNETH, JR, b Canton, Ill, Dec 26, 36; m 63; c 1. MARINE GEOLOGY. *Educ:* Univ Ill, BS, 61; Univ Miami, PhD(marine geol, geophys), 68. *Prof Exp:* Fel geophys, Inst Marine Sci, Univ Miami, 68-69; asst prof, 69-77, ASSOC PROF OCEANOG, UNIV MAINE, ORONO, 77-, COOP ASST PROF GEOL SCI, IRA C DARLING RES CTR, WALPOLE, 74- *Mem:* Geol Soc Am; Am Geophys Union. *Res:* Tectonics of the seafloor; origin of island arcs. *Mailing Add:* Dept of Oceanog Univ of Maine Orono ME 04473

FINK, LYMAN R, b Elk Point, SDak, Nov 14, 12; m 37; c 3. ELECTRICAL ENGINEERING. *Educ:* Univ Calif, Berkeley, BS, 33, MS, 34, EE, 35, PhD(elec eng), 37. *Prof Exp:* Mgr, Electronics Lab, Gen Elec Co, 47-49, chief engr, Radio & TV Dept, 49-55, mgr, Res Appln Dept, Res Lab, 55-57, gen mgr, X-ray Dept, 57-59 & Atomic Prod Div, 59-63, vpres, 62-63, pres, Gen Elec X-ray of Can, 57-59; vpres, Otis Elevator Co, 63-66, vpres & chief tech officer, Singer Co, 66-68, group vpres, Off Equip Group, 68-70; exec vpres, Church's, Inc, 70-73; PRES, DIVERSITEK CO, 73- *Concurrent Pos:* Chmn ad hoc comt digital comput, Res & Develop Bd, 49-50; mem comt atomic energy, US Chamber Commerce, 59-63; dir, Atomic Indust Forum, 60-63, vpres, 63; trustee, Southwest Res Inst, 76-; adv coun, Univ Tex, San Antonio, 78- *Mem:* Fel Inst Elec & Electronics Engrs. *Res:* Administration of engineering and research; television receivers; x-ray and medical electronics; commercial applications of atomic energy; atomic power plants; atomic fuel cycle; computer music. *Mailing Add:* Diversitek Co 4438 Center View San Antonio TX 78228

FINK, MANFRED, b Berlin, Ger, Aug 16, 37; m 64; c 2. ATOMIC PHYSICS. *Educ:* Univ Karlsruhe, vordiplom, 58, diplom, 61, PhD, 64. *Prof Exp:* Fel physics, Ind Univ, 65-66, res assoc, 66-67; fac assoc, 67-69, asst prof, 69-73, assoc prof, 73-80, PROF PHYSICS, UNIV TEX, AUSTIN, 80- *Mem:* Am Phys Soc; Ger Phys Soc. *Res:* Electron scattering from gases and numerical evaluation of the scattering theories; biophysics of viruses. *Mailing Add:* Dept of Physics Univ of Tex Austin TX 78712

FINK, MARY ALEXANDER, b Camden, Tenn, Oct 18, 19; m 50. CANCER. *Educ:* Okla Agr & Mech Col, BS, 39; Univ Mich, MS, 45; George Washington Univ, PhD(bact), 49. *Prof Exp:* Immunologist, Camp Detrick, 46-49; res assoc, R B Jackson Mem Lab, 49-51 & Dept Microbiol, Univ Colo Sch Med, 51-58; immunologist, Nat Cancer Inst, 59-66, head immunol sect, Viral Leukemia & Lymphoma Br, 66-70, chmn test & monitoring segment, Spec Virus Leukemia Prog, 68 & immunol-epidemiol segment, 68-70, prog dir immunol, Extramural Area, 70-74, assoc dir res progs, 74-77, SPEC ASST FOR SPEC PROJS, DIV EXTRAMURAL ACTIV, NAT CANCER INST, 77- *Mem:* Am Asn Immunologists; Soc Exp Biol & Med; Am Asn Cancer Res; Am Acad Microbiol; Brit Soc Immunol. *Res:* Tularemia in humans; immunology and hypersensitivity, particularly in mice; immune response to tumors; oncogenic viruses, especially leukemia. *Mailing Add:* Cancer Res Resources & Ctrs Nat Cancer Inst NIH Bethesda MD 20014

FINK, MAX, b Vienna, Austria, Jan 16, 23; nat US; m 49; c 3. NEUROPSYCHIATRY. *Educ:* NY Univ, BA, 42, MD, 45. *Prof Exp:* Supvry psychiatrist, Dept Exp Psychiat, Hillside Hosp, 53-54, dir, 54-62; res prof psychiat, Sch Med, Wash Univ, 62-66; prof psychiat, New York Med Col, 66-72, dir div biol psychiat, 67-72; PROF PSYCHIAT, HEALTH SCI CTR, STATE UNIV NY STONY BROOK, 72- *Concurrent Pos:* Dir, Mo Inst Psychiat, 62-65; mem comt clin drug eval, NIMH, 62-65; prof, Univ Mo, 65-66; exec dir, Int Asn Psychiat Res, 67- & Div Clin Sci, Long Island Res Inst, 76- *Honors & Awards:* Award, Electroshock Res Asn, 56; Bennett Award, Soc Biol Psychiat, 58; S Hamilton Award, Am Psychopath Asn, 74; Anna Monika Prize, 79. *Mem:* Am Electroencephalog Soc; Soc Biol Psychiat; fel Am Psychiat Asn; Am Psychopath Asn; Am Col Neuropsychopharmacol. *Res:* Experimental alteration of human behavior by neurophysiologic agents; evaluation of psychiatric therapies; opiate dependence; cannabis research; convulsive therapy; electroencephalography. *Mailing Add:* Health Sci Ctr Dept Psychiat State Univ NY Stony Brook NY 11794

FINK, RICHARD DAVID, b New York, NY, July 14, 36; m 61; c 2. PHYSICAL CHEMISTRY. *Educ:* Harvard Univ, AB, 58; Mass Inst Technol, PhD(nuclear chem), 62. *Hon Degrees:* MA, Amherst Col, 71. *Prof Exp:* NSF fel chem, Yale Univ, 62-63, NIH fel, 63-64; from asst prof to prof, 64-77, MELLON PROF CHEM, AMHERST COL, 77-, CHMN DEPT, 70- *Concurrent Pos:* Lectr, Yale Univ, 62-64; NSF sci fac fel, King's Col, Univ London, 68-69 & Amherst Col, 76-77; Sloan res fel, 70-74; Dreyfus Teacher-Scholar Prize, 71-75; vis prof, King's Col, Univ London, 72-73 & 80-81; vis prof sci & humanities, Univ Kans, 81. *Mem:* Am Phys Soc; Am Chem Soc. *Res:* Chemistry of molecular beams; photochemistry of atomic and molecular interactions. *Mailing Add:* Dept of Chem Amherst Col Amherst MA 01002

FINK, RICHARD WALTER, b Detroit, Mich, Jan 13, 28. NUCLEAR CHEMISTRY, PHYSICS. *Educ:* Univ Mich, BS, 48; Univ Calif, MS, 49; Univ Rochester, PhD(chem), 53. *Prof Exp:* Res chemist, Univ Calif Radiation Lab, 48-49 & Knolls Atomic Power Lab, 48-50; assoc prof chem, Univ Ark, 53-61; prof physics, Marquette Univ, 61-65; PROF CHEM, GA INST TECHNOL, 65- *Concurrent Pos:* Consult, Phillips Petrol Co, 57-65; vis prof, Werner Inst Nuclear Chem, Univ Uppsala, 59-60; mem staff, Argonne Nat Lab, 63; vis prof, Univ Hamburg, 63-64; consult, Lawrence Radiation Lab, Univ Calif, 63- & Int Atomic Energy Agency, Nuclear Res Ctr, Athens, 74-76; mem exec bd, Univ Isotope Separator, Oak Ridge, 70-; vis exchange lectr, Yugoslavia, 71. & Poland, 77. *Honors & Awards:* Outstanding Res Awards, Sigma Xi, 71, 77 & 79. *Mem:* Fel Am Phys Soc. *Res:* Investigations of nuclei far from stability with an on-line isotope separator and heavy ion beams; x-ray fluorescence and Coster-Kronig yields; radioactivity studies and separations. *Mailing Add:* Sch of Chem Ga Inst of Technol Atlanta GA 30332

FINK, ROBERT DAVID, b Brooklyn, NY, Oct 1, 42; c 4. BIOCHEMISTRY. *Educ:* St Lawrence Univ, BS, 64; Univ Tenn, MD, 67. *Prof Exp:* Intern, Baptist Mem Hosp, 67-68; resident psychiat, Univ Tenn, 68-71; dir psychiat serv, alcohol & drug unit, 71-74, clin dir, 74-76, asst supt adult serv, 76-77, dep supt, 77-78, SUPT PSYCHIAT, MEMPHIS MENT HEALTH INST, 78- *Concurrent Pos:* Am Psychiat Asn Falk fel, 70-71. *Mem:* Am Med Soc Alcoholism. *Res:* Alcohol and drug abuse; psychopharmacology. *Mailing Add:* PO Box 4966 865 Poplar Ave Memphis TN 38104

FINK, RODNEY JAMES, b Oregon, Mo, Apr 10, 34; m 58; c 4. AGRONOMY, WEED SCIENCE. *Educ:* Univ Mo, BS, 56, MS, 61, PhD(field crops), 66. *Prof Exp:* Exten agronomist, Coop Exten Serv, Iowa State Univ, 61-64; instr field crops, Univ Mo, 64-66; assoc prof agr, Murray State Univ, 66-68, Univ Found grant, 66-67; from assoc prof to prof agr & chmn dept, 68-74, DEAN APPL SCI, WESTERN ILL UNIV, 74- *Concurrent Pos:* Partic conf comt educ in agr & natural resources, Nat Res Coun, 67; chmn resident educ sect, North Cent Weed Control Conf, vpres, 74-76, pres, 76-; Western Ill Univ contract, Agency Int Develop Progs, USDA, 74-; contact, Univ Title XII & Inst Soc Econ Change. *Mem:* Weed Sci Soc Am; Soil Conserv Soc Am; Sigma Xi. *Res:* Effectuating new, better and safer methods of controlling weeds in crop and non-crop areas; effects of herbicides on crop species; effects of fertilizer sources on nitrate pollution in soil; factors affecting soil persistence of herbicides; administration of academic and international programs in agriculture and applied sciences. *Mailing Add:* Col Appl Sci Western Ill Univ Macomb IL 61455

FINK, THOMAS ROBERT, b Indianapolis, Ind, June 5, 43; m 67; c 2. BIOPHYSICAL CHEMISTRY, SURFACE CHEMISTRY. *Educ:* Ind Univ, AB, 65; Yale Univ, PhD(biophys chem), 70. *Prof Exp:* Fel biophys chem, Wash State Univ, 70-72; asst prof biochem, Univ Tulsa, 72-74; sr res chemist, Res & Develop Dept, Atlantic Richfield Corp, 74-78, MGR, ENVIRON CONSERV, ARCO ALASKA INC, 78- *Concurrent Pos:* NIH & NSF fel, 65-70; NIH fel, 71-72. *Mem:* Am Chem Soc. *Res:* Physical polymer chemistry of polynucleotides, helix-coil transitions; surface chemistry of enhanced recovery of petroleum, chemical flooding; chemical dispersion of oil spills; Arctic environmental research. *Mailing Add:* 6359 Colgate Anchorage AK 99504

FINK, WILLIAM HENRY, b Marshfield, Wis, Nov 4, 41; m 68. CHEMICAL PHYSICS, THEORETICAL CHEMISTRY. *Educ:* Univ Wis, BS, 63; Princeton Univ, PhD(phys chem), 66. *Prof Exp:* Res assoc chem, Princeton Univ, 66-67; NATO res fel appl math, Queen's Univ Belfast, 67-68; asst prof, 68-73, assoc prof, 73-80, PROF CHEM, UNIV CALIF, DAVIS, 80- *Mem:* Am Chem Soc; Am Phys Soc; Sigma Xi. *Res:* Application of quantum mechanical methods to problems of chemical interest; especially ab initio molecular structure calculations. *Mailing Add:* Dept of Chem Univ of Calif Davis CA 95616

FINK, WILLIAM LEE, b Coleman, Tex, July 22, 46; m 72. ICHTHYOLOGY, SYSTEMATIC BIOLOGY. *Educ:* Univ Miami, BS, 67; Univ Southern Miss, MS, 69; George Wash Univ, PhD(biol), 76. *Prof Exp:* asst cur fishes & asst prof, Mus Comp Zool, 76-80, ASSOC PROF BIOL, HARVARD UNIV, 80- *Concurrent Pos:* Prin & co-prin investr, NSF grants, 78-81. *Mem:* Am Soc Ichthyol & Herpetol; Soc Syst Zool; Soc Study Evolution; Am Soc Zool. *Res:* Systematics of neotropical freshwater fishes; systematics of mesopelagic fishes; systematic theory. *Mailing Add:* Mus of Comp Zool Harvard Univ Cambridge MA 02138

FINKBEINER, DANIEL TALBOT, II, b Aspinwall, Pa, Oct 7, 19; m 45; c 4. MATHEMATICS. *Educ:* Washington & Jefferson Col, AB, 41, MA, 43; Calif Inst Technol, PhD(math), 49. *Prof Exp:* Instr math, Washington & Jefferson Col, 41-43; asst, Calif Inst Technol, 46-49; instr, Yale Univ, 49-51; assoc prof, 51-56, PROF MATH, KENYON COL, 56- *Concurrent Pos:* Actg dean, Kenyon Col, 56-58; NSF fel, Princeton Univ, 58-59; vis prof, Univ Western Australia, 64; Fulbright lectr, Australia, 69 & 72; mem adv screening comt sci educ, Coun Int Exchange Scholars, 75-78. *Mem:* Am Math Soc; Math Asn Am. *Res:* Lattice theory; convex sets in abstract linear spaces; linear algebra. *Mailing Add:* Dept Math Kenyon Col Gambier OH 43022

FINKBEINER, HERMAN LAWRENCE, b Syracuse, NY, July 20, 31; m 54. PHYSICAL CHEMISTRY, ORGANIC CHEMISTRY. *Educ:* Park Col, AB, 52; Univ Mich, PhD(chem), 60. *Prof Exp:* Staff asst org chem, Spencer Chem Co, 53-56; res scientist, Corp Res & Develop, 59-70, mgr chem synthesis & processing opers, 70-72, mgr synthesis & characterization br, 72-76, mgr employee rels oper, CRD, 76-78, MGR PLANNING & RESOURCES, MAT SCI & ENG, GEN ELEC CO, 78- *Mem:* Am Chem Soc. *Res:* Action of metal ions on organic reactions, especially biological reactions. *Mailing Add:* Gen Elec Co PO Box 8 Schenectady NY 12301

FINKBEINER, JOHN ARIS, b Freeport, Pa, Sept 3, 17; m; c 2. MEDICINE. *Educ:* Univ Pittsburgh, BS, 39; Western Reserve Univ, MD, 42. *Prof Exp:* Asst med, Harrisburg Polyclin Hosp, 46-51; ASST PROF CLIN MED, COL MED, CORNELL UNIV, 56- *Concurrent Pos:* Dir tumor clin, Harrisburg Polyclin Hosp, 49-51, consult, 53-; clin asst, Mem & James Ewing Hosps, 53-55, asst attend physician, 55-74, assoc attend physician, 74-; assoc, Sloan-Kettering Inst Cancer Res, 53-62, asst clinician, 62-65; adj physician, Lenox Hill Hosp, 64-66, assoc physician, 66-78, physician, 78-, chief med neuplasia serv, 65- *Mem:* Am Radium Soc; AMA; Am Fedn Clin Res; fel Am Col Physicians; Am Soc Cytol. *Res:* Medical oncology; Hodgkin's disease and other lymphomas; therapy of advanced cancer. *Mailing Add:* 34 E 67th St New York NY 10021

FINKE, GUENTHER BRUNO, b Minden, Ger, May 31, 30; m 57; c 3. SOLID STATE PHYSICS, METALLURGY. *Educ:* Brunswick Tech Univ, dipl, 55, Dr rer Nat(semiconductors), 57. *Prof Exp:* Asst tech physics, Brunswick Tech Univ, 55-57; asst magnetic mat, Widia-Factory-Krupp-Essen, Ger, 57-58, asst proj head, 58-60; DIR RES & DEVELOP, MAGNETIC METALS CO, 60- *Mem:* Inst Elec & Electronics Engrs; Ger Phys Soc. *Res:* Fuel cells; semiconductors; magnetic alloys and devices. *Mailing Add:* Magnetic Metals Co Hayes Ave at 21st St Camden NJ 08101

FINKE, JAMES HAROLD, immunology, see previous edition

FINKE, REINALD GUY, b San Francisco, Calif, June 10, 28; Div; c 3. SYSTEMS MODELING, TRAJECTORY ANALYSIS. *Educ:* Univ Calif, Berkeley, AB, 49, MA, 51, PhD(nuclear physics), 54. *Prof Exp:* Teaching asst physics, Univ Calif, Berkeley, physicist, Radiation Lab, 50-54, sr physicist, Radiation Lab, Livermore, 54-62; MEM SR TECH STAFF, INST DEFENSE ANAL, 62- *Mem:* Am Inst Aeronaut & Astronaut; Sigma Xi. *Res:* Study of operations and configurations of military aerospace systems, particularly space launch vehicles, spacecraft, and supporting ground facilities, with emphasis on performance, and technological and economic feasibility. *Mailing Add:* Inst Defense Anal 1801 N Beauregard St Alexandria VA 22311

FINKE, RICHARD GERALD, b Scottsbluff, Nebr, July 1, 50; m 73; c 1. ORGANOTRANSITION METAL CHEMISTRY, BIOINORGANIC CHEMISTRY. *Educ:* Univ Colo, BA, 72; Stanford Univ, PhD(chem), 76. *Prof Exp:* NSF fel chem, Stanford Univ, 76-77; ASST PROF CHEM, UNIV ORE, 77- *Mem:* Am Chem Soc. *Mailing Add:* Dept of Chem Univ of Ore Eugene OR 97403

FINKEL, ASHER JOSEPH, b Chicago, Ill, June 5, 15; m 43; c 4. MEDICINE, ZOOLOGY. *Educ:* Univ Chicago, SB, 36, PhD(zool), 47, MD, 48. *Prof Exp:* Asst zool, Univ Chicago, 36-42, intern, Univ Clins, 48-49, asst med, 50-60, res assoc, 60-70; dir dept environ, pub & occup health, AMA, 70-76, dir div sci activities, 72-76, group vpres sci activities & continuing med studies, 75-82. *Concurrent Pos:* Mem, Nat Coun Radiation Protection, 74-80; assoc biologist, Argonne Nat Lab, Ill, 48, assoc physician, 49-55, dir health div, 55-70. *Mem:* Ecol Soc Am; Am Soc Zool; Radiation Res Soc; Soc Exp Biol & Med; fel Am Col Physicians. *Res:* Radium metabolism; biological aspects of xenon compounds; lipids in mealworm larvae; experimental beryllium poisoning; experimental burns with NaK alloy; biological effects of deuterium; radium toxicity in man; occupational toxicology. *Mailing Add:* 10314 S Oakley Ave Chicago IL 60643

FINKEL, HERMAN J(ACOB), b Chicago, Ill, Mar 9, 18; m 41; c 2. AGRICULTURAL ENGINEERING, CIVIL ENGINEERING. *Educ:* Univ Ill, BS, 40; Hebrew Univ, PhD, 57. *Prof Exp:* Dairy farm inspector, Health Dept, St Louis, Mo, 40-41; civil engr, Great Lakes Div, Corps Eng, Ill, 41-43; agr engr & farm planner, Soil Conserv Serv, NY, 43-46; consult structural engr, Ill, 46-49; chief engr, Soil Conserv Serv, Israel Ministry Agr, 49-52; lectr agr eng, Israel Inst Technol, 52-57; expert irrig adv to Govt Peru, Food & Agr Orgn, UN, 57-59; assoc prof agr eng, 59-67, prof & consult engr, 67-70, vpres acad affairs, 70-73, dean fac agr eng, 73-77, EMER PROF AGR ENG, ISRAEL INST TECHNOL, 77- *Concurrent Pos:* Consult water dept, Israel Ministry Agr, 56-57 & UN Spec Fund Peru, 60; mem agr mission Haute Volta, WAfrica, 61; mem UNESCO teams ed planning, Chile, Peru, Trinidad, Jamaica & Brit Honduras, 64; mem agr mission & consult, Brit WIndies, Thailand & Panama, 62-64; consult engr, Cyprus, Nigeria, Iran, Uganda, Ivory Coast, Thailand & Brazil, 70-; head, Finkel & Finkel, Consult Engrs, Haifa. *Res:* Irrigation methods and efficiency; soil conservation, especially sand-dune control and economic water utilization; development of underground dams; modernization of the traditional Arab village. *Mailing Add:* Finkel & Finkel Consult Engrs 42 Einstein St 34602 Haifa Israel

FINKEL, LEONARD, b Brooklyn, NY, Jan 7, 31; m 49; c 2. ELECTRONICS. *Educ:* Rutgers Univ, BS, 52; Harvard Univ, MS, 53. *Prof Exp:* Test engr, Chelsea Fan & Blower Co, NJ, 51-52; develop engr, Raymond Rosen Eng Prod, Pa, 53-56, group supvr, 56-58; sect mgr, Teledynamics, Inc, 58-60, asst to chief engr, Tele Dynamics Div, Am Bosch Arma Corp, Pa, 60-62, chief engr, 62-66, dir tech planning, 66-71; prog mgr advan systs develop, 71-75, mgr advan progs, Missile & Surface Radar Div, 75-81, MGR SYSTS CONCEPTS, GOV SYSTS DIV, RCA CORP, 81- *Mem:* Inst Elec & Electronics Engrs. *Res:* Radar; weapon systems; instrumentation; air traffic control; communications; space systems; telemetry. *Mailing Add:* 14 Glen Lane Cherry Hill NJ 08002

FINKEL, MADELON LUBIN, b Mt Vernon, NY, Oct 11, 49; m 73; c 1. DEMOGRAPHY. *Educ:* NY Univ, BA, 71; Grad Sch Pub Admin, MPA, 73, Grad Sch Arts & Sci, PhD(health serv res), 80. *Prof Exp:* Res asst pub health & demog), Grad Sch Pub Health, NY Univ, 72-74; staff assoc pub health, Sch Pub Health, Columbia Univ, 74-75; res consult demog, Dept Health, New York City, 75-77; res assoc, 77-80, ASST PROF PUB HEALTH & EPIDEMOL, MED COL, CORNELL UNIV, 80- *Concurrent Pos:* Organizer & co-sponsor, Conf Second Surg Opinion Progs, 81; consult, Amalgamated Meat Cutters, 80-81, Mobil Oil Corp, 80-81, Am Pub Health Asn, 80- *Mem:* Am Health Asn; Am Fedn Clin Res; Pop Asn Am; Int Epidemol Asn. *Res:* Medical care (health services); demographic research; occupational epidemiological studies. *Mailing Add:* Dept Pub Health Med Col Cornell Univ 1300 York Ave New York NY 10021

FINKEL, MIRIAM POSNER, b Chicago, Ill, Jan 22, 16; m 43; c 4. ONCOGENESIS, RADIOBIOLOGY. *Educ:* Univ Chicago, SB, 38, PhD(zool), 44. *Prof Exp:* Assoc biologist, Metall Lab, Univ Chicago, 44-46; assoc biologist, 46-62, SR BIOLOGIST, ARGONNE NAT LAB, 62- *Concurrent Pos:* Mem subcomt, Nat Coun Radiation Protection & Measurements; mem subcomt internal emitters, Nat Acad Sci-Nuclear Res Coun. *Mem:* Health Physics Soc; Am Soc Zool; Soc Exp Biol & Med; Radiation Res Soc; Am Soc Exp Path. *Res:* Toxicity of radionuclides; radio-oncogenesis; viral oncogenesis; experimental pathology. *Mailing Add:* Div of Biol & Med Res Argonne Nat Lab Argonne IL 60439

FINKEL, RAPHAEL ARI, b Chicago, Ill, June 13, 51. COMPUTER SCIENCE. *Educ:* Univ Chicago, BA & MAT, 72; Stanford Univ, PhD(comput sci), 76. *Prof Exp:* ASST PROF COMPUT SCI, UNIV WIS-MADISON, 76- *Mem:* Sigma Xi; Asn Comput Mach; AAAS. *Res:* Operating systems; distributed computing. *Mailing Add:* Dept of Comput Sci Univ Wis 1210 W Dayton St Madison WI 53706

FINKELMAN, ROBERT BARRY, b New York, NY, Feb 17, 43; m 65; c 2. MICROMINERALOGY, COAL SCIENCE. *Educ:* City Col New York, BS, 65; George Washington Univ, MS, 70; Univ Md, PhD(chem), 80. *Prof Exp:* Cartographer, US Coast & Geodetic Surv, 65; geologist, US Geol Surv, 65-80; SR RES SPECIALIST, EXXON PROD RES CO, 80- *Concurrent Pos:* Prin investr, Nat Aeronaut & Space Admin, 74-75; lectr geol, Northern Va Community Col, Loudoun Campus, 74-80. *Mem:* Mineral Soc Am; Geochem Soc; Mineral Asn Can. *Res:* Geochemistry of coal, peat and burning coal-waste banks; mineralogy and petrography of lunar soil and cosmic dust; mineralogy of geodes; micromineralogical techniques. *Mailing Add:* Exxon Prod Res Co PO Box 2189 Houston TX 77001

FINKELSTEIN, ABRAHAM BERNARD, b New York, NY, Feb 11, 23; m 47; c 3. APPLIED MATHEMATICS. *Educ:* City Col New York, BS, 43; NY Univ, MS, 47, PhD(math), 53. *Prof Exp:* Asst prof math, Long Island Univ, 48-53; sr res assoc aero eng & appl mech, Polytech Inst Brooklyn, 53-57; prof eng sci, 57-64, PROF MATH, PRATT INST, 64-, CHMN DEPT, 66- *Concurrent Pos:* Consult, Eastern Res Group, 55- *Mem:* Am Math Soc; Math Asn Am. *Res:* Water waves; underwater propulsion systems; transpiration cooling; differential equations. *Mailing Add:* Dept of Math Pratt Inst Brooklyn NY 11205

FINKELSTEIN, DAVID, b New York, NY, July 19, 29; m 81; c 3. THEORETICAL PHYSICS. *Educ:* City Col New York, BS, 49; Mass Inst Technol, PhD(physics), 53. *Prof Exp:* Asst physics, Mass Inst Technol, 50-53; from instr to asst prof, Stevens Inst Technol, 53-56, assoc prof, 57-60; from assoc prof to prof physics, Yeshiva Univ, 60-78, dean, 78-79; dir, Sch Physics, 79-80, PROF PHYSICS, GA INST TECHNOL, 79- *Concurrent Pos:* Res assoc, NY Univ, 54-56; consult, Brookhaven Nat Lab, 57-; Ford fel, Europ Orgn Nuclear Res, Geneva, 58-59; ed, Int J Theoret Physics, 77- *Mem:* Am Phys Soc. *Res:* Quantum mechanics; general relativity; geophysics. *Mailing Add:* Sch of Physics Ga Inst of Technol Atlanta GA 30332

FINKELSTEIN, DAVID, b Philadelphia, Pa, Apr 27, 11; m 39; c 1. CARDIOLOGY. *Educ:* Temple Univ, BS, 32, MD, 35; Am Bd Internal Med, dipl. *Prof Exp:* From instr to asst prof, 50-67, ASSOC PROF CARDIOL, SCH MED, UNIV PA, 67- *Concurrent Pos:* Asst cardiologist, Philadelphia Gen Hosp, 37-75; chief cardiac clin, St Luke's & Children's Hosps, Philadelphia, 47-50; chief cardiac clin, Grad Hosp Univ Pa, 64- *Mem:* AMA; Am Heart Asn; Am Col Physicians; Am Col Cardiol. *Res:* Clinical research in relationship to cardiovascular parameters. *Mailing Add:* Med Grad Bldg Suite 104 419 S 19th St Philadelphia PA 19146

FINKELSTEIN, JACOB, b New York, NY, Oct 27, 10; m 45; c 2. ORGANIC CHEMISTRY, MEDICINAL CHEMISTRY. *Educ:* City Col, New York, BS, 33; Columbia Univ, AM, 34, PhD(chem), 39. *Prof Exp:* Res chemist, Res Corp, New York, 35 & Merck & Co, NJ, 35-43; res scientist, Hoffmann-La Roche, Inc, 43-75; prof org chem, St Peter's Col, Jersey City, 77-79. *Concurrent Pos:* Mem fac, Fairleigh Dickinson Univ; chem consult, 77- *Mem:* AAAS; fel Am Inst Chemists; Am Chem Soc. *Res:* Vitamins; sulfanilamides, antimalarials; contrast media; renal clearance; synthetic organic chemicals; antihistamines; antispasmodics; analgesics; alkaloidal salts of organic acids and quaternary hydroxides in the resolution of optically active substances; glucose lowering and antiviral agents; tetracyclines; stimulants; anticholesterol and antihypertensive drugs. *Mailing Add:* 648 Sunderland Rd Teaneck NJ 07666

FINKELSTEIN, JAMES DAVID, b New York, NY, Oct 16, 33; m 59; c 2. GASTROENTEROLOGY, BIOCHEMISTRY. *Educ:* Harvard Univ, AB, 54; Columbia Univ, MD, 58; Am Bd Internal Med, dipl, 67. *Prof Exp:* From intern to asst resident med, Presby Hosp, NY, 58-61; clin assoc, Nat Inst Arthritis & Metab Dis, 63-65; from asst prof to assoc prof, 66-74, PROF MED, GEORGE WASHINGTON UNIV, 74-; chief gastroenterol & hepatology, 70-79, assoc chief of staff for res, 75-80, CHIEF BIOCHEM RES LAB, VET ADMIN HOSP, 68-, CHIEF MED SERV, 79- *Concurrent Pos:* USPHS trainee gastroenterol, Col Physicians & Surgeons, Columbia Univ, 61-63; clin investr, Vet Admin, 65-68, med investr, 70-75; consult, Children Hosp, Washington, DC, 67- & Nat Inst Arthritis, Metab & Digestive Dis, 73- *Honors & Awards:* Arthur S Flemming Award, 71. *Mem:* AAAS; Am Fedn Clin Res; Am Gastroenterol Asn; Am Soc Clin Invest; Am Soc Clin Nutrit. *Res:* Sulfur amino acid metabolism; active transport across cell membranes; intestinal malabsorption. *Mailing Add:* Vet Admin Hosp 50 Irving St NW Washington DC 20422

FINKELSTEIN, MANUEL, b Scranton, Pa, Oct 18, 28; m 58; c 2. ORGANIC CHEMISTRY. *Educ:* Univ Scranton, BS, 50; Williams Col, MA, 52; Yale Univ, PhD(chem), 56. *Prof Exp:* Asst chem, Williams Col, 50-52; sr engr org chem res, 56-62, SR RES SCIENTIST, SPRAGUE ELEC CO, 62- *Concurrent Pos:* Vis instr, Williams Col, 57-61 & 68-75, lectr, 75- *Mem:* Am Chem Soc. *Res:* Organic electrochemistry; organic synthesis; reaction mechanisms. *Mailing Add:* 4 Birchwood Terrace North Adams MA 01247

FINKELSTEIN, PAUL, b New York, NY, Nov 20, 22; m 55; c 2. BIOCHEMISTRY. *Educ:* Brooklyn Col, BA, 43; Polytech Inst Brooklyn, PhD(chem), 49. *Prof Exp:* Res assoc, Ohio State Univ, 50-51; res biochemist, US Naval Med Res, 51-52; assoc dir res, Toni Co Div, Gillette Co, 52-64, lab dir, Gillette Med Res Inst, 64-68; dir clin dermat, Carter Prod Res Div, Carter-Wallace, Inc, 68-74; asst dir med res, Health Care Div, 74-77, ASSOC DIR MED RES, PROF PROD RES & DEVELOPMENT, JOHNSON & JOHNSON, INC, 77- *Concurrent Pos:* Fel, Univ Chicago, 49-50. *Mem:* Am Chem Soc; Soc Cosmetic Chem; Soc Invest Dermat; Am Soc Clin Pharmacol & Therapeut. *Res:* Photochemistry of proteins; biochemical effects of radiation; protein isolation and characterization; structure and functions of skin; clinical dermatological evaluations; pharmacology; toxicology. *Mailing Add:* Prof Res & Develop Johnson & Johnson Inc New Brunswick NJ 08903

FINKELSTEIN, RICHARD ALAN, b New York, NY, Mar 5, 30; m 52, 76; c 3. MICROBIOLOGY. *Educ:* Univ Okla, BS, 50; Univ Tex, MA, 52, PhD(bact), 55; Am Bd Med Microbiol, dipl. *Prof Exp:* Res scientist, Univ Tex, 52-55, fel microbiol, Med Sch, Dallas, 55-58, instr, 58; chief bio-assay sect, Div Commun Dis & Immunol, Walter Reed Army Inst Res, 58-67; assoc prof microbiol, Univ Tex Health Sci Ctr Dallas, 67-74, prof microbiol, 74-79; PROF & CHMN, DEPT MICROBIOL, SCH MED, UNIV MO-COLUMBIA, 79- *Concurrent Pos:* Dep chief & chief dept bact & immunol, Med Res Lab, SEATO, Thailand, 64-67; vis assoc prof, Fac Grad Studies, Univ Med Sci, Bangkok, 64-67; mem, Nat Comt Cholera Res, Thailand, 64-67; consult, WHO; mem, NIH Cholera Adv Comt, 71-; consult to comndg gen, US Army Med Res & Develop Command, 75-; vis scientist, Japanese Sci Coun, 76; vis prof, Med Sch, Univ Chicago, 77; chmn, Prog Comt, 79-82. *Honors & Awards:* Cert Outstanding Achievement, US Army Sci Conf, 64; Robert Koch Prize Sci & Med, Ger, 76. *Mem:* Am Soc Microbiol; Soc Gen Microbiol; Am Asn Immunol; Path Sci Gt Brit & Ireland; fel Am Acad Microbiol. *Res:* Pathogenesis and immunology of cholera, enteric diseases and gonorrhea; role of iron in microbial-host interactions. *Mailing Add:* Dept Micro Sch Med Univ Mo-Columbia Columbia MO 65212

FINKELSTEIN, ROBERT, b New York, NY, Oct 13, 42; m 64; c 3. OPERATIONS RESEARCH. *Educ:* Temple Univ, BA, 64; Lowell Technol Inst, MS, 66; George Washington Univ, MS, 74. *Prof Exp:* Systs analyst mil syst, Missile Intel Agency, 66-68; physicist, Mass Inst Technol Draper Lab, 68-70; task leader space physics, Comput Sci Corp, 70-72; proj mgr oper res, Atlantic Res Corp, 72-75 & Ketron, Inc, 75-76; proj mgr opers res, Mantech NJ Corp, 76-77; proj mgr, Opers Res, 77-80, SYSTS SCIENTIST, MITRE CORP, MCLEAN, VA, 80- *Concurrent Pos:* Instr physics, Lowell Technol Inst & Univ Ala, 64-68; prof lectr mgt sci, Southeastern Univ, 75-76; lectr oper res, Cent Mich Univ, 75-78; lectr mgt, Prince Georges Community Col, 75- *Mem:* Oper Res Soc Am; Inst Mgt Sci; Am Phys Soc; AAAS; Soc Gen Systs Res. *Res:* Unmanned weapons systems; artificial intelligence and cybernetics; countermeasures for sensor-dependent weapons; combat modeling; command, control, communications and intelligence. *Mailing Add:* 10001 Crestleigh Lane Potomac MD 20854

FINKELSTEIN, ROBERT JAY, b Pittsfield, Mass, Mar 26, 16. PHYSICS. *Educ:* Dartmouth Col, BA, 37; Harvard Univ, PhD(physics), 41. *Prof Exp:* Theoret physicist, Bur Ord, US Navy Dept, 41-46 & Argonne Nat Lab, 46-47; fel, Inst Advan Study, 47-48 & Calif Inst Technol, 48-49; from asst prof to assoc prof physics, 49-57, PROF PHYSICS, UNIV CALIF, LOS ANGELES, 57- *Res:* Quantum theory; elementary particle theory. *Mailing Add:* Dept of Physics Univ of Calif Los Angeles CA 90024

FINKELSTEIN, STANLEY MICHAEL, b Brooklyn, NY, June 16, 41; m 67; c 2. BIOENGINEERING, BIOMEDICAL COMPUTING. *Educ:* Polytech Inst Brooklyn, BS, 62, MS, 64, PhD(elec eng, syst sci), 69. *Prof Exp:* Instr mech eng, Polytech Inst NY, 65-67, instr elec eng, 67-68, from asst prof to assoc prof bioeng & syst eng, 68-77; ASSOC PROF LAB MED, UNIV MINN, 77- *Concurrent Pos:* Mem fac NIH Bioeng Training Prog, Mt Sinai Sch Med, 66-72, lectr, 74-77; prin investr NSF res grant, 69-70, fel, 75-77; co-investr, NIH res grant, 71-73, NIH training prog, 77-, NIH prog proj, 80-, prin investr, NIH grant, 81- *Mem:* Inst Elec & Electronics Engrs; Eng Med & Biol Soc; Biomed Eng Soc; AAAS; NY Acad Sci. *Res:* Biomedical engineering; signal processing; computer applications in health science; simulation of physiological systems; patient monitoring systems; computer assisted instruction; electrocardiographic analysis. *Mailing Add:* Div of Health Comput Sci 420 Delaware St SE Minneapolis MN 55455

FINKL, CHARLES WILLIAM, II, b Chicago, Ill, Sept 19, 41; m 65; c 2. COASTAL GEOMORPHOLOGY, COASTAL ZONE MANAGEMENT. *Educ:* Ore State Univ, BSc, 64, MSc, 66; Univ Western Australia, PhD(soil sci), 71. *Prof Exp:* Instr natural resources, Ore State Univ, 66-67; demonstr phys geog, Univ Western Australia, 67-68; staff geochemist, explor geochem, Int Nickel Australia, 70-74; DIR & PROF, MARINE SCI INST COASTAL STUDIES, NOVA UNIV, 77- *Concurrent Pos:* Ed, Encyclopedia Earth Sci Series, 74-; consult, Multinat Agribus Systs, 75-; courtesy prof, Fla Int Univ, 76- *Honors & Awards:* Order of the Orange Oar, Ore State Univ, 64. *Mem:* Am Geophys Union; Geol Soc Am; Soil Sci Soc Am; Soc Econ Paleontologists & Mineralogists; Soc Mining Engrs. *Res:* Soil-geomorphic relationships in tropical cratonic regions, modes of landscape sculpture in deeply weathered terranes, soil micromorphology and soil stratigraphy ; coastal and submarine soils are of current interest. *Mailing Add:* Inst Coastal Studies Nova Univ Port Everglades Dania FL 33004

FINKLE, BERNARD JOSEPH, b Chicago, Ill, Mar 17, 21; m 44; c 2. PLANT BIOCHEMISTRY. *Educ:* Univ Chicago, BS, 42; Univ Calif, Los Angeles, PhD(plant biochem), 50. *Prof Exp:* Chemist, Manhattan Proj, Univ Chicago & Oak Ridge Nat Lab, 43-46; AEC fel, Molteno Inst, Eng, 50; biochemist, Univ Calif, 51-53; lab dir, Atomic Res Lab, 53-54; biochemist, Univ Utah, 54-57; CHEMIST, FRUIT LAB, USDA, 57- *Concurrent Pos:* Fel, US-Japan Coop Sci Prog, Dept Med Chem, Kyoto Nat Univ, 66-67. *Honors & Awards:* Japan Soc Prom Sci Award, 74. *Mem:* Am Soc Biol Chem; Phytochem Soc NAm (vpres, 64-65, pres, 65-66); Am Soc Plant Physiologists; Soc Cryobiol. *Res:* Factors in tissue freezing viability; biosynthesis and metabolism of phenolic acids, ascorbate and oxalate; thiol groups of papain; chlorophyll biogenesis; culture of green algae. *Mailing Add:* US Dept of Agr 800 Buchanan St Berkeley CA 94710

FINKLEA, HARRY OSBORN, b Columbia, SC, Feb 26, 49; m 76; c 2. ELECTROCHEMISTRY, SURFACE ANALYSIS. *Educ:* Duke Univ, BS, 70; Calif Inst Technol, PhD(chem), 76. *Prof Exp:* NSF res fel, Royal Inst of Gt Brit, London, 75-76; res assoc, Univ NC, Chapel Hill, 76-78; res assoc, Fla Atlantic Univ, 78-79; ASST PROF ANAL CHEM, VA POLYTECH INST & STATE UNIV, 79- *Mem:* Am Chem Soc; Electrochem Soc. *Res:* Semiconductor, electrochemistry and photoelectrochemistry; photo-electrochemical solar cells; chemically modified electrodes. *Mailing Add:* Dept Chem Va Polytech Inst & State Univ Blacksburg VA 24061

FINKLEA, JOHN F, b Florence, SC, Aug 27, 33; m 58; c 2. PREVENTIVE MEDICINE, RESEARCH ADMINISTRATION. *Educ:* Davidson Col, BS, 54; Med Univ SC, MD, 58; Univ Mich, DPH, 66. *Prof Exp:* Assoc med, Sch Med, Northwestern Univ, 66-67; from asst prof to assoc prof prev med, Med Col SC, 66-69; chief ecol res br environ health, Nat Air Pollution Control Admin, 69-71; from dir div health effects res to dir environ health, Nat Environ Res Ctr, Environ Protection Agency, 71-75; dir health res, Nat Inst Occup Safety & Health, 75-78; PROF PUB HEALTH, UNIV ALA, BIRMINGHAM, 78- *Concurrent Pos:* Teaching asst epidemiol, Univ Mich Sch Pub Health, 66; consult epidemiologist, Northwestern Univ, 67-71; mem, Nat Ctr Health Statist Adv Bd, 71-; chmn, Nat Air Qual Adv Comt, 72-73; mem, Adv Comt Atomic Bomb Casualty Comn, Nat Acad Sci, 72-74 & Comt on Hearing, Bioacoust & Biomech, 72-; consult & sci adv, Environ Health Prog, 73-74; mem adv comt conserv of energy, Nat Power Surv, Fed Power Comn, 74; examr, Am Bd Prev Med, 75. *Mem:* Soc Occup & Environ Health; Am Occup Med Asn; Am Pub Health Asn; Am Col Prev Med; Am Acad Pediat. *Res:* Occupational health research with emphasis on epidemiology of chronic diseases; health effects of air pollutants and pesticides. *Mailing Add:* Med Ctr University Station Birmingham AL 35294

FINKLER, PAUL, b Brooklyn, NY, Nov 29, 36; m 65; c 1. PARTICLE PHYSICS, NUCLEAR PHYSICS. *Educ:* Brooklyn Col, BS, 58; Purdue Univ, PhD(physics), 63. *Prof Exp:* Res appointee theoret physics, Lawrence Radiation Lab, Univ Calif, 63-65; asst prof, 65-74, ASSOC PROF PHYSICS, UNIV NEBR, LINCOLN, 74- *Mem:* Am Phys Soc. *Res:* High energy physics; dispersion relations; Regge pole theory; high energy phenomenology; electromagnetic interactions of particles. *Mailing Add:* Dept of Physics Univ of Nebr Lincoln NE 68508

FINKNER, ALVA LEROY, b Akron, Colo, May 8, 17; m 46; c 3. STATISTICS. *Educ:* Colo State Univ, BS, 38; Kans State Univ, MS, 40; NC State Univ, PhD(exp statist), 50. *Prof Exp:* Jr agr statistician, Statist Reporting Serv, USDA, NC State Univ, 40-41, asst agr statistician, 41-42, head, Raleigh Res Off, 46-60; sr statistician, Statist Res Div, Res Triangle Inst, 59-71, group leader, 59-62, assoc dir, Statist Res Div, 62-64, dir, 64-71, vpres, Res Triangle Inst, 71-74; assoc dir statist standards & methodol, US Bur Census, 74-77; SR V PRES, RES TRIANGLE INST, 77- *Concurrent Pos:* From assoc prof to prof exp statist, NC State Univ, 50-60, adj prof, 60-; analyst, Standby Unit, US Air Force, Univ NC, 50-70. *Mem:* Am Statist Asn; Biomet Soc; Int Statist Inst; Int Asn Surv Statisticians; Int-Am Statist Inst. *Res:* Development of theory and methodology of sample surveys and their application to the fields of education, economics, demography and the social sciences. *Mailing Add:* Res Triangle Inst PO Box 12194 Research Triangle Park NC 27709

FINKNER, MORRIS DALE, b Akron, Colo, Feb 11, 21; m 49; c 2. EXPERIMENTAL STATISTICS. *Educ:* Colo State Univ, BS, 43; Kans State Univ, MS, 47; NC State Univ, PhD(agron), 52. *Prof Exp:* Asst prof forage crops, Miss State Col, 47-49; asst cotton breeding, NC State Col, 49-52; asst prof exp statist, NMex Agr & Mech Col, 52-55; biometrician, Agr Res Serv, USDA, Md, 56-58; assoc prof, 58-64, PROF EXP STATIST, NMEX STATE UNIV, 64-, HEAD, DEPT EXP STATIST, & DIR, STATIST CTR, 70- *Mem:* Am Soc Agron; Biomet Soc; Crop Sci Soc Am; Am Statist Asn. *Res:* Design and analysis of experiments; data processing; climatology; plant breeding. *Mailing Add:* Dept of Exp Statist Box 3130 NMex State Univ Las Cruces NM 88003

FINKNER, RALPH EUGENE, b Akron, Colo, Mar 24, 25; m 50; c 3. PLANT BREEDING, AGRONOMY. *Educ:* Colo State Univ, BS, 50; Iowa State Col, MS, 52, PhD(plant breeding, path), 53. *Prof Exp:* Asst agron, Iowa State Col, 50-53; plant breeder, Am Crystal Sugar Co, 53-55, chief plant breeder, 55-56, res sta mgr, 56-66; SUPT & PROF AGRON, PLAINS BR STA, NMEX STATE UNIV, 66- *Concurrent Pos:* US AID consult, Paraguay, 70, Turkey, 71 & Egypt, 78-79. *Mem:* Am Soc Sugar Beet Technol; Crop Sci Soc Am; Am Soc Agron; Sigma Xi; Am Peanut Res & Educ Soc. *Res:* Development of improved beet varieties; development of high yielding, high protein grain sorghum hybrids. *Mailing Add:* Plains Br Exp Sta NMex State Univ Clovis NM 88101

FINKS, ROBERT MELVIN, b Portland, Maine, May 12, 27. INVERTEBRATE PALEONTOLOGY, PALEOECOLOGY. *Educ:* Queens Col, NY, BS, 47; Columbia Univ, MA, 54, PhD(geol), 59. *Prof Exp:* Asst zool, Columbia Univ, 47-48, cur asst paleontol, 48-49; lectr geol, Hofstra Col, 49-50; asst instr, Rutgers Univ, 50-54; lectr, Brooklyn Col, 55-58, instr, 59-61; lectr, 61-62, asst prof, 62-65, assoc prof, 66-70, PROF GEOL, QUEENS COL, NY, 71- *Concurrent Pos:* Lectr, Hunter Col, 52-54; geologist, US Geol Surv, 52-54, 63-; mus aide, Smithsonian Inst, 56-57, res assoc, 68-; res assoc, Am Mus Natural Hist, 61-77; vis prof, Syracuse Univ, 62 & Univ Wyo, 65. *Mem:* Fel AAAS; fel Geol Soc Am; Int Paleont Asn; Paleont Soc. *Res:* Fossil sponges; paleoecology; longevity and growth-rates in fossil populations; natural selection in fossil populations; biostratigraphy; evolution of ecosystems; Paleozoic corals. *Mailing Add:* Dept Earth & Environ Sci Queens Col Flushing NY 11367

FINLAND, MAXWELL, b Russia, Mar 15, 02; nat US. INFECTIOUS DISEASES. *Educ:* Harvard Univ, BS, 22, MD, 26. *Hon Degrees:* DSc, Western Reserve Univ, 64; DHL, Thomas Jefferson Univ, 78. *Prof Exp:* Asst resident physician, Boston Sanitarium, 26-27; med house officer, 2nd Med Serv, Boston City Hosp, 27-28; from asst to George Richards Minot prof med, 29-68, EMER MINOT PROF MED, HARVARD MED SCH, 68- *Concurrent Pos:* Folsom fel, Harvard Med Sch, 28-29 & Peabody fel, 32-37; resident physician, 2nd Med Serv & Pneumonia Patients, Boston City Hosp, 28-29, asst physics, 28-38, jr vis physician, 38-54, chief 4th Med Serv, 39-63, dir, 2nd & 4th Med Servs, 63-68; from asst resident physician to assoc physician, Thorndike Mem Lab, 29-46, assoc dir, 46-63, dir, 63-68, hon physician & epidemiologist, 68-74; vis physician, Pondville Hosp, Wrentham, 33-57; mem subcomt infectious dis, Nat Res Coun, 46-58; mem drug res bd, Nat Acad Sci, 64-71. *Honors & Awards:* Chapin Award, 65; Bristol Award, 66, Modern Med Award, 69; John Phillips Mem Award, Oscar B Hunter Award & Sheen Award, 71; Distinguished Physician, US Vet Admin; Kober Medal, Asn Am Physicists, 78; Bristol-Myers Award, 12th Int Cong Chemother. *Mem:* Nat Acad Sci; AAAS; Am Soc Clin Invest (vpres, 47); fel AMA; Infectious Dis Soc Am (pres, 64). *Res:* Clinical and laboratory investigations of infectious diseases, including chemotherapy and antibiotics. *Mailing Add:* Boston City Hosp 818 Harrison Ave Boston MA 02118

FINLAY, GORDON ROY, b Innisfail, Alta, Oct 24, 13; m 53. INORGANIC CHEMISTRY. *Educ:* Univ Alta, BSc, 38, MSc, 39; Cornell Univ, PhD(inorg chem), 42. *Prof Exp:* Asst chem, Cornell Univ, 39-42; res chemist, Norton Co, 42-55, sect head, 55-57, asst dir res, 57-66, res assoc, 66-68; sr demonstr, Dept Chem, Brock Univ, 68-78; RETIRED. *Concurrent Pos:* Consult, 78- *Mem:* AAAS; Am Chem Soc; Am Ceramic Soc; Nat Inst Ceramic Engrs; fel Chem Inst Can. *Res:* Boron compounds; high temperature materials; boron trifluoride complexes. *Mailing Add:* Dept of Chem Brock Univ St Catharines ON L2S 3A1 Can

FINLAY, JOSEPH BRYAN, b Meriden, Eng, Feb 28, 43; m 68; c 3. ORTHOPAEDIC BIOMECHANICS, CLINICAL ENGINEERING. *Educ:* Lanchester Polytech, BSc, 66; Univ Strathclyde, PhD(bioeng), 70. *Prof Exp:* Control systs engr, Gyroscope Div, Sperry Rand, 66-67; lectr, Univ Strathclyde, 67-72; MGR BIOMED ENG, UNIV HOSP, LONDON, ONT, 72-; PROF BIOPHYSICS, UNIV WESTERN ONT, 82- *Concurrent Pos:* Mem, Health Devices J, Emergency Res Care Inst, 74-; co-prin investr, Med Res Coun Can grants, 74- & Ont Heart Found grant, 77-78; assoc prof, Dept Biophysics, Univ Western Ont, 76-82; chmn, Technol Adv Comt, Fanshawe Community Col, London, Ont, 80-81; mem, Biomed Eng Grant Comt, Med Res Coun Can, 81- *Mem:* Can Med & Biol Eng Soc; Inst Mech Engrs; Inst Elec Engrs; Am Soc Mech Engrs; Inst Elec & Electronic Engrs. *Res:* Distribution of the principal strains in the human leg as they are affected by surgical procedures and the implantation of prosthetic components; optimum design of prostheses for the hip and knee. *Mailing Add:* 61 Hampton Crescent London ON N6H 2P1 Can

FINLAY, JOSEPH BURTON, b Collins, Ohio, Sept 15, 21; m 42; c 2. ORGANIC CHEMISTRY. *Educ:* Bowling Green State Univ, BA, 43; Univ NC, PhD(org chem), 52. *Prof Exp:* Instr chem, Bowling Green State Univ, 46-48; chemist, 51-79, RES FEL, E I DU PONT DE NEMOURS & CO, INC, 79- *Mem:* AAAS; Am Chem Soc; Sigma Xi. *Res:* Elastomeric materials. *Mailing Add:* 1229 Lakewood Dr Wilmington DE 19803

FINLAY, MARY FLEMING, b Columbia, SC, Oct 3, 44; m 66; c 2. DEVELOPMENTAL GENETICS. *Educ:* Sweet Briar Col, BA, 66; Univ SC, PhD(zool), 70. *Prof Exp:* Res trainee genetics, Population Coun, Rockefeller Univ, 66; instr biol, Allen Univ, 69; from asst prof to assoc prof, 70-76, PROF BIOL, BENEDICT COL, 76- *Concurrent Pos:* Prin investr, Nat Inst Child Health & Human Develop, NIH, 70-72, Div Res Resources, 74-, Nat Inst Gen Med Sci, 77-; prog dir, Minority Biomed Support Prog, 74-; prog dir, Minority Access Res Careers, 77-, fac fel, 79-80. *Mem:* Sigma Xi; Am Soc Zoologists; Am Genetics Asn. *Res:* Developmental changes in isozymes in rodents, particularly as markers of stress or dysfunction; circadian patterns of activity, and hybridization in Peromyscus. *Mailing Add:* Dept Biol Benedict Col Harden & Blanding St Columbia SC 29204

FINLAY, PETER STEVENSON, b Montclair, NJ, Oct 12, 24; m 56; c 3. ZOOLOGY. *Educ:* Williams Col, Mass, BA, 49; Univ Vt, MS, 53; Syracuse Univ, PhD(zool), 57. *Prof Exp:* Assoc prof, 56-70, PROF BIOL, ALFRED UNIV, 70- *Mem:* Soc Protozool; Am Soc Parasitol; Am Soc Zool. *Res:* Red cell parasites of amphibia. *Mailing Add:* Dept of Biol Alfred Univ Alfred NY 14802

FINLAY, ROGER W, b Pittsburgh, Pa, Oct 22, 35; m 56; c 2. NUCLEAR PHYSICS. *Educ:* Johns Hopkins Univ, AB, 57, PhD(physics), 62. *Prof Exp:* Asst, Johns Hopkins Univ, 60-62; from asst prof to assoc prof, 62-69, PROF PHYSICS, OHIO UNIV, 69- *Concurrent Pos:* Vis scientist, Max Planck Inst Nuclear Physics, Heidelberg, 68-69. *Mem:* Am Phys Soc. *Res:* Nuclear structure and nuclear reaction mechanisms; nuclear radiation detectors. *Mailing Add:* Dept of Physics Ohio Univ Athens OH 45701

FINLAY, THOMAS HIRAM, b Brooklyn, NY, Nov 28, 38; m 61; c 2. MOLECULAR ENDOCRINOLOGY. *Educ:* Univ Md, BS, 64; PhD(biochem), 69. *Prof Exp:* Fel biochem, Brandeis Univ, 69-71; asst prof, Rockefeller Univ, 71-74; asst prof, 75-79, ASSOC PROF OBSTET & GYNECOL, MED CTR, NY UNIV, 79- *Concurrent Pos:* Res career develop award, Med Ctr, Nat Heart, Lung & Blood Inst, 77-81. *Mem:* Am Soc Biol Chemists; Am Chem Soc; NY Acad Sci. *Res:* Role of proteolytic enzymes and inhibitors of proteolytic enzymes in the regulation of cellular activity. *Mailing Add:* Dept Obstet & Gynecol NY Univ Med Ctr 550 First Ave New York NY 10016

FINLAY, WALTER L(EONARD), b Brooklyn, NY, Mar 10, 13; m 37; c 2. PHYSICAL METALLURGY. *Educ:* Lehigh Univ, BS, 36; Yale Univ, MSc, 47, DEng, 48. *Prof Exp:* Supvr chem & metall res, Remington Arms Co, 39-51; res mgr, Rem-Cru Titanium, Inc, 51-55, vpres res, 54-58; dir res, Crucible Steel Co Am, 58-62, asst vpres adv technol, 62-65; asst vpres res, 65-67, dir res, 67-70, vpres res & develop, 70-77, DIR RES, COPPER RANGE CO, 77- *Concurrent Pos:* Chmn mat adv bd, Nat Acad Sci. *Mem:* Am Soc Metals; Electrochem Soc; Am Inst Mining, Metall & Petrol Engrs; Brit Inst Metals; Brit Iron & Steel Inst. *Res:* Small arms ballistics; titanium; steels; refractory metals. *Mailing Add:* Copper Range Co Rte 43 PO Box 100 Port Townsend WA 98368

FINLAYSON, BIRDWELL, b Pocatello, Idaho, Oct 28, 32; m 55; c 2. UROLOGY, BIOPHYSICS. *Educ:* Univ Chicago, MD, 57, PhD(biophys), 67. *Prof Exp:* From intern to resident, Univ Chicago, 57-63; from asst prof to assoc prof urol, 67-73, prof surg, 73-76, PROF UROL, UNIV FLA, 76- *Concurrent Pos:* Mem, Nat Kidney Found. *Res:* Urolithiasis. *Mailing Add:* Div Urol Box J-247 Univ of Fla Sch of Med Gainesville FL 32601

FINLAYSON, BRUCE ALAN, b Waterloo, Iowa, July 18, 39; m 61; c 3. CHEMICAL ENGINEERING, APPLIED MATH. *Educ:* Rice Univ, BA, 61, MS, 63; Univ Minn, PhD(chem eng), 65. *Prof Exp:* Proj officer appl physics, Off Naval Res, 65-67; from asst prof to assoc prof chem eng, 67-77, PROF CHEM ENG & APPL MATH, UNIV WASH, 77- *Mem:* Soc Rheol; Am Inst Chem Engrs; Soc Petrol Engrs; Am Chem Soc; Soc Indust & Appl Mech. *Res:* Fluid mechanics; rheology; approximate and variational methods of analysis; finite element methods; flow through porous media. *Mailing Add:* Dept of Chem Eng Univ of Wash Seattle WA 98105

FINLAYSON, HENRY C, b Vulcan, Alta, July 5, 30; m 57; c 3. MATHEMATICAL ANALYSIS. *Educ:* Univ Alta, BSc, 52, MSc, 54; Univ Minn, PhD(math), 64. *Prof Exp:* Lectr math, Univ Alta, 54-55; lectr, 56-62, asst prof, 62-69, ASSOC PROF MATH, UNIV MAN, 69- *Mem:* Math Asn Am; Am Math Soc. *Res:* Integration in function space. *Mailing Add:* Fac of Math Univ of Man Winnipeg MB R3T 2N2 Can

FINLAYSON, JAMES BRUCE, b Montrose, Colo, July 3, 37; m 70. ANALYTICAL CHEMISTRY, GEOCHEMISTRY. *Educ:* Univ Ore, BA, 59; La State Univ, Baton Rouge, MS, 62; Univ Hawaii, PhD(anal chem), 67. *Prof Exp:* Scientist, Chem Div, Dept Sci & Indust Res, NZ Govt, 67-70; from asst prof to assoc prof, chem, 70-75, Hilo Col, Univ Hawaii, 70-75; SCIENTIST, CHEM DIV, DEPT SCI & INDUST RES, NZ, 75- *Mem:* Am Chem Soc; NZ Geochem Group. *Res:* Volcano chemistry; volcanic gases and volatiles; gas analysis by gas chromatography; geothermal chemistry; trace methods of analysis; water analysis, especially trace metals in natural waters; inorganic environmental water analysis. *Mailing Add:* Chem Div Wairakei Private Bag Taupo New Zealand

FINLAYSON, JOHN SYLVESTER, b Philadelphia, Pa, Sept 19, 33; m 57; c 2. BIOCHEMISTRY. *Educ:* Marietta Col, BA, 53; Univ Wis, MS, 55, PhD(biochem), 57. *Prof Exp:* Asst, Wis Alumni Res Found, 53-55; Nat Cancer Inst fel, Univ Wis, 55-57 & Inst Radiophysics, Stockholm, Sweden,

57-58; biochemist, Lab Blood & Blood Prod, Div Biol Standards, NIH, 58-72; res chemist, 72-75, DIR PLASMA DERIVATIVES BR, DIV BLOOD & BLOOD PROD, BUR BIOLOGICS, FOOD & DRUG ADMIN, 75- *Concurrent Pos:* Instr, Found Advan Educ Sci, 61-75; vis scientist & prof, Inst Protein Res, Osaka Univ, Japan, 76; mem, Coun Thrombosis, Am Heart Asn. *Mem:* Soc Exp Biol & Med; Int Soc Thrombosis & Hemostasis; Am Heart Asn. *Res:* Plasma proteins; blood coagulation. *Mailing Add:* Bur Biologics Food & Drug Admin Bethesda MD 20014

FINLEY, ARLINGTON LEVART, b Newburn, NC, Mar 17, 48; m 70; c 2. SOLID STATE CHEMISTRY, INORGANIC CHEMISTRY. *Educ:* Tougaloo Col, BS, 70; Brown Univ, PhD(inorg chem), 75. *Prof Exp:* Res asst chem, Brown Univ, 70-74; PROJ LEADER, DOW CHEM CO, 74- *Mem:* AAAS; Am Chem Soc. *Res:* Development of solid state technology in Dow processes. *Mailing Add:* Cent Res Lab Inorg Chem Bldg 1776 Dow Chem Co Midland MI 48640

FINLEY, ARTHUR MARION, b La Monte, Mo, Apr 15, 18; m 43; c 6. PLANT PATHOLOGY. *Educ:* Univ Mo, BS, 41, MA, 48, PhD(plant path), 50. *Prof Exp:* Asst plant pathologist, 50-54, assoc prof plant path & assoc plant pathologist, 54-55, head dept plant path, 55-63, head dept plant sci, 63-71, PROF PLANT PATH & PLANT PATHOLOGIST, UNIV IDAHO, 55- *Mem:* Am Phytopath Soc. *Res:* Diseases of vegetable crops; soil borne pathogenic organisms. *Mailing Add:* Dept of Plant Sci Univ of Idaho Moscow ID 83843

FINLEY, DAVID ANTHONY, b LaCrosse, Wis, May 15, 47; m 70; c 3. A-DEPENDENCE, BEAM SPLITTING. *Educ:* Purdue Univ, BS, 70, MS, 72, PhD(physics), 78. *Prof Exp:* Fel, State Univ NY, Stony Brook, 78-81; ASSOC SCIENTIST, FERMILAB, 81- *Mailing Add:* Fermilab PO Box 500 Batavia IL 60510

FINLEY, DAVID EMANUEL, b Springfield, Ill, July 23, 35; m 60; c 2. BIOLOGY, BOTANY. *Educ:* Western Ill Univ, BS, 62, MS, 64; Univ Ill, PhD(bot), 67. *Prof Exp:* Teaching asst bot, Univ Ill, Urbana, 63-67; assoc prof biol, 67-73, PROF BIOL, LINCOLN UNIV, MO, 73- *Mem:* Mycol Soc Am; Bot Soc Am. *Res:* Taxonomy of the Stilbellaceae; fungal cytology. *Mailing Add:* Dept of Natural Sci & Math Lincoln Univ Jefferson City MO 65101

FINLEY, J(OHN) BROWNING, b Crowley, La, July 18, 19; m 43; c 4. CHEMICAL ENGINEERING. *Educ:* Southwestern La Univ, BS, 41, BSChE, 42, MS, 60; Okla State Univ, PhD(chem eng), 64. *Prof Exp:* Petrol chemist, Humble Oil & Refining Co, 42-47; pvt consult, 47-50; mgr, Crowley Motor Co, Inc, 50-56 & Am Rice Milling Co, Inc, 56-58; PROF CHEM ENG, TEX A&I UNIV, 63- *Mem:* Am Inst Chem Engrs; Am Chem Soc; Am Soc Eng Educ. *Res:* Diffusion in electrolytes and mass transfer studies; nuclear engineering and radioisotope applications in research. *Mailing Add:* Box 2139 Sta 1 Kingsville TX 78363

FINLEY, JAMES DANIEL, III, b Louisville, Ky, Aug 2, 41; m 62. THEORETICAL PHYSICS, RELATIVITY. *Educ:* Univ Tex, Austin, BS & BA, 63; Univ Calif, Berkeley, PhD(physics), 68. *Prof Exp:* From asst prof to assoc prof, 68-78, PROF PHYSICS, UNIV NMEX, 78- *Concurrent Pos:* Vis prof, Centro de IEA del Inst Politecnico Nacional, 75. *Res:* General relativity. *Mailing Add:* Dept Physics & Astron Univ NMex Albuquerque NM 87106

FINLEY, JOANNE ELIZABETH, b Brockport, NY, Dec 28, 22; m 50; c 4. PUBLIC HEALTH, PREVENTIVE MEDICINE. *Educ:* Antioch Col, BA, 44; Yale Univ, MPH, 51; Case-Western Reserve Univ, MD, 62; Am Bd Prev Med, Dipl, 72. *Prof Exp:* Econ Res Anal, US Off Alien Property Custodian, 44-45; admin asst, US House of Repr, 45-48; field dir, Nat Inst Soc Rels, 48-49; Pub Affairs Anal, Nat Comt Effective Cong, 49-50; dir health educ, Montgomery County TB & Heart Asn, 52-55; exec dir, Montgomery County Planned Parenthood League, 55-56; founder & dir, Parent & Child, Inc, 56-57; res dir, Cleveland Health Goals Proj, 63-66; dep comnr & actg comnr, Cleveland Div Pub Health, 66-68; dir health planning, Dept Pub Health, Philadelphia, 68-72; vpres med affairs, Blue Cross, Philadelphia, 72-73; dir, Pub Health New Haven Dept Health, 73-74; COMNR NJ STATE DEPT OF HEALTH, 74- *Concurrent Pos:* Asst clin prof, Med Col Pa, 69- vis lectr, NJ Col Med & Dent, 74- comnr, Kellogg Found Comn Educ Health Admin, 72-74; mem, HEW Task Force Future Nat Immunization Pol, 77; mem adv comn immunization practices, Ctr Dis Control, USPHS, 81. *Mem:* Asn State & Territorial Health Off; Am Pub Health Asn; Am Soc Pub Admin. *Mailing Add:* NJ State Dept of Health C N 360 Trenton NJ 08625

FINLEY, JOHN WESTCOTT, b Auburn, NY, Sept 21, 42; m 67; c 2. FOOD SCIENCE. *Educ:* Le Moyne Col, BS, 64; Cornell Univ, PhD(food sci), 68. *Prof Exp:* Fel food sci, Mich State Univ, 68-69; res chemist, Sci & Educ Admin-Agr Res, USDA, 69-81; SCIENTIST, RALSTON PURINA CO, ST LOUIS, 81- *Mem:* Am Chem Soc; Inst Food Technologists; Am Asn Cereal Chemists; NY Acad Sci; AAAS. *Res:* Effects of food processing on the lipids and proteins in foods, especially amino acids and their degradation products with regard to nutrition and food safety. *Mailing Add:* 2030 Med Bow Dr Ballwin MO 63011

FINLEY, JOSEPH HOWARD, b Newark, NJ, Jan 15, 31; m 54; c 6. ORGANIC CHEMISTRY. *Educ:* Seton Hall Univ, BS, 53, MS, 61; Rutgers Univ, PhD(org chem), 68. *Prof Exp:* Chemist control, Am Cyanamid Co, 55; chemist anal, Air Reduction Co, Inc, 55-60; RES ASSOC PROCESS & PROD DEVELOP, FMC CORP, 80- *Mem:* Am Chem Soc. *Res:* Active chlorine and peroxygen bleaches; development of new detergent products; development of new industrial processes. *Mailing Add:* FMC Corp PO Box 8 Princeton NJ 08540

FINLEY, KAY THOMAS, b Elmira, NY, Aug 29, 34; m 78; c 2. PHYSICAL ORGANIC CHEMISTRY. *Educ:* Rochester Inst Technol, BS, 59; Univ Rochester, PhD(chem), 63. *Prof Exp:* From asst prof to assoc prof chem, Rochester Inst Technol, 62-66; sr res chemist, Eastman Kodak Co, 66-70;

PROF CHEM, STATE UNIV NY COL BROCKPORT, 70- *Res:* Nucleophilic addition to quinonoid systems; chromatography; history of chemistry. *Mailing Add:* Dept of Chem State Univ NY Col Brockport Brockport NY 14420

FINLEY, ROBERT BYRON, JR, b Pittsfield, Mass, Aug 22, 17; m 46, 74; c 3. VERTEBRATE ZOOLOGY. *Educ:* Univ Calif, AB, 41; Univ Kans, PhD(zool), 56. *Prof Exp:* Instr zool & asst cur mus natural hist, Univ Kans, 50-51; sci intel analyst, Off Naval Intel, 55-59; mem staff, Denver Wildlife Res Ctr, 59-65, chief sect wildlife ecol pub lands, 65-73, zoologist, Nat Fish & Wildlife Lab, 73-80, ZOOLOGIST, DENVER WILDLIFE RES CTR, US FISH & WILDLIFE SERV, 80- *Mem:* Soc Syst Zool; Soc Study Evolution; Wildlife Soc; Am Soc Mammal; Am Soc Ichthyol & Herpet. *Res:* Biogeography; evolution of mammals and reptiles; paleobiology of Pleistocene; ecology; wildlife management; effects of chemicals on wildlife. *Mailing Add:* Denver Wildlife Res Ctr 1300 Blue Spruce Dr Ft Collins CO 80524

FINLEY, ROBERT JAMES, b New York, NY, Apr 14, 47; m 68; c 2. GEOLOGICAL REMOTE SENSING, PETROLEUM GEOLOGY. *Educ:* City Univ NY, BS, 67; Syracuse Univ, MS, 69; Univ SC, PhD(geol), 75. *Prof Exp:* Geologist, Chevron Oil Co, 69-71; assoc res scientist, 75-78, RES SCIENTIST, BUR ECON GEOL, UNIV TEX, 78- *Concurrent Pos:* Mem, Austin City Environ Bd, 77-81, co-chmn, 78-79; mem, Remote Sensing & Cartog Comt, Tex Natural Resources Info Syst, 77-; instr, 79-81; consult, Computech Energy & Explor, 80-82. *Mem:* Am Asn Petrol Geologists; Soc Econ Paleontologists & Mineralogists; Int Asn Sedimentologists; Am Soc Photogram; Am Geophys Union. *Res:* Interpretation of clastic depositional systems and their relationship to hydrocarbon and geothermal resources; applications of remote sensing to resource exploration through geomorphic, structural and surface analysis. *Mailing Add:* Bur Econ Geol Univ Tex Austin TX 78712

FINLEY, SARA CREWS, b Lineville, Ala, Feb 26, 30; m 52; c 2. MEDICAL GENETICS, PEDIATRICS. *Educ:* Univ Ala, BS, 51; Med Col Ala, MD, 55. *Prof Exp:* From instr to assoc prof, 60-75, PROF PEDIAT, SCH MED, UNIV ALA, BIRMINGHAM, 75-, CO-DIR, LAB MED GENETICS, 66-, ASST PROF PHYSIOL & BIOPHYS, 67- *Concurrent Pos:* NIH fel pediat, Sch Med, Univ Ala, Birmingham, 56-60 & NIH trainee, Inst Med Genetics, Univ Uppsala, 61-62; mem, White House Conf Health, 65; mem res manpower rev comt, Nat Cancer Inst, 77-81. *Mem:* Am Soc Human Genetics; Am Fedn Clin Res; NY Acad Sci. *Res:* Cytogenetics; congenital malformations; human growth and development; genetic counseling. *Mailing Add:* 3412 Brookwood Rd Birmingham AL 35223

FINLEY, WAYNE HOUSE, b Goodwater, Ala, Apr 7, 27; m 52; c 2. MEDICAL GENETICS, BIOCHEMISTRY. *Educ:* Jacksonville State Col, BS, 47; Univ Ala, MA, 50, MS, 55, PhD(biochem), 58, MD, 60. *Prof Exp:* Sr high sch teacher, Ala, 49-51; from asst prof to assoc prof pediat, 62-66, asst prof biochem, 65-75, asst prof physiol & biophys, 67-75, assoc prof biochem, 75-77, PROF PEDIAT, SCH MED, UNIV ALA, BIRMINGHAM, 70-, ASSOC PROF PHYSIOL & BIOPHYS, 75-, PROF PUB HEALTH & EPIDEMIOL, 75-, DIR LAB MED GENETICS, 66- *Concurrent Pos:* Fel, Inst Med Genetics, Univ Uppsala, 61-62; prin investr, USPHS res grant, 62-68; co-prin investr, US Dept Health, Educ & Welfare training grant, 64-; sr scientist, Comprehensive Cancer Ctr; mem nat adv res resources coun, NIH, 76-80. *Mem:* AAAS; Am Soc Human Genetics; Am Fedn Clin Res; Am Chem Soc; Am Inst Chem. *Res:* Medical genetics; organic syntheses of new alkylating agents and their screening against transplantable animal tumors; cell culture techniques and human cytogenetics including mitotic and meiotic studies. *Mailing Add:* Lab Med Genetics Univ Ala Birmingham AL 35294

FINLON, FRANCIS P(AUL), b Carbondale, Pa, Sept 2, 24; m 47; c 2. ELECTRICAL ENGINEERING. *Educ:* Pa State Univ, BS, 47, MS, 48. *Prof Exp:* Assoc prof, 47-64, PROF ENG RES, PA STATE UNIV, 64-, HEAD DEPT ACOUST, 76- *Mem:* Inst Elec & Electronics Engrs. *Res:* Underwater ordnance. *Mailing Add:* Appl Res Lab Pa State Univ University Park PA 16801

FINN, ARTHUR LEONARD, b Boston, Mass, Mar 24, 34; m 56; c 3. PHYSIOLOGY, BIOPHYSICS. *Educ:* Harvard Univ, AB, 54; Boston Univ, MD, 58. *Prof Exp:* Intern med, Mass Mem Hosp, Boston, 58-59; resident, Duke Hosp, Durham, 59-60 & 62-63; asst prof physiol & med, Sch Med, Yale Univ, 65-70; assoc prof, 70-74, PROF MED & PHYSIOL, SCH MED, UNIV NC, CHAPEL HILL, 74- *Concurrent Pos:* Fel metab, Univ NC, Chapel Hill, 60-62; adv res fel membrane transport, Nat Heart Inst, 63-65. *Mem:* AAAS; Biophys Soc; Am Physiol Soc; Soc Gen Physiol; Am Soc Clin Invest. *Res:* Membrane biophysics; transport of ions and water in the isolated amphibian urinary and gall bladder. *Mailing Add:* Dept of Med Univ of NC Sch of Med Chapel Hill NC 27514

FINN, D(AVID) L(ESTER), b Memphis, Tenn, Mar 24, 24; m 48; c 3. ELECTRICAL ENGINEERING. *Educ:* Purdue Univ, BSEE, 48, MS, 50, PhD(elec eng), 52. *Prof Exp:* PROF ELEC ENG, GA INST TECHNOL, 52- *Mem:* Inst Elec & Electronics Eng. *Res:* Applied mathematics; random processes; sampling theory. *Mailing Add:* Dept of Elec Eng Ga Inst of Technol Atlanta GA 30332

FINN, EDWARD J, b Ridgefield Park, NJ, July 24, 30; m 54; c 4. THEORETICAL MOLECULAR SPECTROSCOPY. *Educ:* Col Holy Cross, BS, 51; Catholic Univ, MS, 55; Georgetown Univ, PhD(physics), 62. *Prof Exp:* Instr physics, Georgetown Univ, 52-54 & St Vincent Col, 54-55; physicist, Naval Res Lab, 55-56; asst prof, 56-64, assoc prof, 64-77, PROF PHYSICS, GEORGETOWN UNIV, 77- *Concurrent Pos:* Physicist, Naval Res Lab, 56-; lectr, Nat Univ Mex, 71. *Mem:* Am Asn Physics Teachers; Am Phys Soc; Sigma Xi. *Res:* Computer managed instruction; direction of scientific symposia; vibrational energies of diatomic molecules; systems analysis of unmanned vehicles; science curriculum development; management of bilateral United States-Latin American scientific projects. *Mailing Add:* Dept of Physics Georgetown Univ Washington DC 20057

FINN, FRANCES M, biochemistry, see previous edition

FINN, JAMES CRAMPTON, JR, b Detroit, Mich, Oct 18, 24; m 55; c 2. PLANT PHYSIOLOGY. *Educ:* Mich State Univ, BS, 52, MS, 53; Univ Calif, Los Angeles, PhD(bot), 58. *Prof Exp:* Plant physiologist cotton physiol, Delta Exp Sta, USDA, Miss, 58; asst prof hort, Agr & Mech Col, Tex, 58-59; prin scientist bio, Aero-space Labs, Missile Div, NAm Aviation, Inc, 59-62, asst dir life sci dept, Space & Info Systs Div, 62-63, tech dir res planning aerospace sci, 63-65, staff scientist, Life Sci Opers, 65-68, sci adv, Autonetics Div, NAm Rockwell Corp, 68; asst mgr microbics mkt & admin, Microbics Opers, 68-75, asst mgr mkt planning, Biol & Fine Chems Div, 75-81, PROG MGR MICROBICS, BECKMAN INSTRUMENTS, INC, 81- *Mem:* AAAS. *Res:* Photoperiodism; plant growth regulators; biological rhythms; closed ecological systems; research administration. *Mailing Add:* Microbics Beckman Instruments Inc 6200 El Camino Real Carlsbad CA 92008

FINN, JAMES WALTER, b St Paul, Minn, Oct 3, 46; m 80; c 2. CHEMISTRY. *Educ:* Univ Minn, BChem, 70; Kans State Univ, PhD(chem), 81. *Prof Exp:* Res prof chemist, Pillsbury Co, 71-77; RES CHEMIST, ICI AMERICAS, 81- *Mem:* Am Chem Soc; Am Asn Cereal Chemists; Asn Off Anal Chemists; Sigma Xi. *Res:* High pressure liquid chromatography of polymeric materials; fluorine combustion; elemental analysis by gas chromatography. *Mailing Add:* Corp Res & Develop ICI Americas Wilmington DE 19897

FINN, JOHN MCMASTER, b Washington, DC, Jan 8, 47; m 77; c 2. NONLINEAR PLASMA PHYSICS. *Educ:* Ga Inst Technol, BS, 69; Univ Houston, MS, 71; Univ Md, PhD(physics), 74. *Prof Exp:* Res assoc plasma physics, Princeton Univ, 74-76 & Cornell Univ, 76-79; physicist, Sci Applications Inc, 79-81; PHYSICIST, NAVAL RES LAB, 81- *Res:* Ideal and resistive magneto hydrodynamic stability of various types of magnetic fusion devices; the effects of ergodic particle orbits on such instabilities; the destruction of magnetic surfaces due to such instabilities. *Mailing Add:* Code 4790 Naval Res Lab Washington DC 20375

FINN, JOHN MARTIN, b Philadelphia, Pa, Nov 16, 19; m 54; c 3. APPLIED CHEMISTRY, RESEARCH ADMINISTRATION. *Educ:* Harvard Univ, AB, 48; Univ Pa, MS, 49, PhD(chem), 53. *Prof Exp:* Chemist, E I du Pont de Nemours & Co, 40-42, shift supvr, 42-43, area engr, 43-44; asst instr, Univ Pa, 48-51, asst, 51-52; proj engr chem, Horizons, Inc, 52-55; res chemist, Union Carbide Corp, 55-70, sr res scientist, 70-72; asst prof eng, Kent State Univ, 72-73; dir inorg res & develop, 73-80, DIR CORP RES, HARSHAW CHEM CO, 80- *Mem:* Am Chem Soc. *Res:* Liquid ammonia chemistry; phosphide chemistry; complex ions; boron chemistry; anode processes; fused salts and glasses; high temperature chemistry; pigments; fire retardant chemistry; polymer and composite technology. *Mailing Add:* 7663 Alan Pkwy Cleveland OH 44130

FINN, JOHN THOMAS, b Washington, DC, Oct 23, 48; m 71; c 1. ECOLOGY, SYSTEMS SCIENCE. *Educ:* Georgetown Univ, BS, 70; Univ Ga, PhD(ecol), 77. *Prof Exp:* Res asst membrane transp, Renal Lab, Beth Israel Hosp & Harvard Med Sch, 71-73; assoc systs ecol Ecosystems Ctr, Marine Biol Lab, 77-78; ASST PROF SYSTS ECOL, DEPT FORESTRY & WILDLIFE MGT, UNIV MASS, 78- *Concurrent Pos:* Res consult, Ecol Simulations, Inc, 76- *Mem:* AAAS; Am Inst Biol Sci; Ecol Soc Am; Int Soc Trop Ecol; Soc Comput Simulation. *Res:* Application of general systems theory, modeling, simulation and systems analysis to ecological problems; particular interest in nutrient cycling, watershed management, remote sensing and methods of qualitative analysis including flow analysis, loop analysis and path analysis. *Mailing Add:* Dept of Forestry & Wildlife Mgt Univ of Mass Amherst MA 01003

FINN, PATRICIA ANN, b Oak Park, Ill. THERMODYNAMICS & MATERIAL PROPERTIES, COMPUTER SCIENCES. *Educ:* Mundelein Col, BS, 67; Univ Calif, Berkeley, PhD(physinorg chem), 71. *Prof Exp:* Fel organo metal chem, Chem Dept, Iowa State Univ, 72-73; fel, Chem Div, 73-75, CHEMIST, CHEM ENG DIV, ARGONNE NAT LAB, 75- *Mem:* Am Nuclear Soc; Sigma Xi; Am Ceramic Soc; Am Chem Soc. *Res:* System design for nuclear fusion reactors; lithium systems, physical properties, corrosion, for use in fusion reactors as breeding medium; tritium systems in fusion reactors. *Mailing Add:* 339 S Park Westmont IL 60559

FINN, R(OBERT) K(AUL), b Waukesha, Wis, May 3, 20; m 49; c 5. CHEMICAL ENGINEERING. *Educ:* Cornell Univ, BCh, 41, ChE, 42; Univ Minn, PhD(chem eng), 49. *Prof Exp:* Res chem engr, Merck & Co, Inc, 42-46; asst prof chem eng, Univ Ill, 49-55; assoc prof, 55-65, PROF CHEM ENG, CORNELL UNIV, 65- *Concurrent Pos:* Consult; Fulbright fel, 62-63; vis prof, Univ Calif, Berkeley, 69; Guggenheim fel, 75-76. *Mem:* AAAS; Am Chem Soc; Am Soc Microbiol; Am Inst Chem Engrs. *Res:* Applied microbiology; fermentation engineering. *Mailing Add:* 342 Olin Hall Cornell Univ Ithaca NY 14853

FINN, RONALD DENNET, b Weymouth, Mass, Aug 15, 44; m 69. RADIOCHEMISTRY. *Educ:* Worcester Polytech Inst, BS, 66; Va Polytech Inst, PhD(nuclear & radiochem), 71. *Prof Exp:* Res assoc chem, Brookhaven Nat Lab, 71-72, res assoc med, 72-73, assoc chemist solid state physics, 73-74; radiochemist, 74-75, tech dir radiochem & radiopharmacol, 75-79, DIR CYCLOTRON FACIL, MT SINAI MED CTR, 79- *Concurrent Pos:* Collabr dept chem, Brookhaven Nat Lab, 74-; asst res prof, Med Sch, Univ Miami, 74-77, asst prof, 78- *Mem:* Am Chem Soc; Sigma Xi; NY Acad Sci. *Res:* Reactions of hot atoms produced by nuclear processes; synthesis of labelled compounds incorporating short half-life nuclides for potential clinical utility. *Mailing Add:* Cyclotron Facil Mt Sinai Med Ctr 4300 Alton Rd Miami Beach FL 33140

FINN, SIDNEY BERNARD, dentistry, deceased

FINN, WILLIAM DANIEL LIAM, b Cork, Ireland, Aug 25, 33. SOIL MECHANICS. *Educ:* Nat Univ Ireland, BE, 54; Univ Wash, MSc, 57, PhD, 60. *Prof Exp:* Instr, Univ Wash, 56-60; asst prof civil eng, 61, head dept, 64-70, PROF CIVIL ENG, UNIV BC, 64- *Concurrent Pos:* Partner, Pan-Am Eng & Comput Serv, Ltd. *Mem:* Am Soc Civil Engrs; Am Soc Eng Educ. *Res:* Creep of soils; plasticity theory in soil mechanics; soil structure interaction during earthquakes; seismic response of earth dams; ocean engineering. *Mailing Add:* Fac of Appl Sci Univ of BC Vancouver BC B6T 1W5 Can

FINNEGAN, CYRIL VINCENT, b Dover, NH, July 17, 22; m 47; c 9. EXPERIMENTAL EMBRYOLOGY, DEVELOPMENTAL BIOLOGY. *Educ:* Bates Col, BS, 46; Notre Dame Univ, MS, 48, PhD(zool), 51. *Prof Exp:* Instr gen biol, Wabash Col, 49-50; res fel, Stanford Univ, 51-52; from instr to asst prof embryol & anat, St Louis Univ, 52-56; asst prof, Notre Dame Univ, 56-58; from asst prof to assoc prof zool, 58-64, chmn biol prog, 69-78, assoc dean fac sci, 72-79, PROF DEVELOP BIOL & MORPHOGENESIS, UNIV BC, 64-, DEAN FAC SCI, 79- *Mem:* Am Soc Zoologists; Soc Develop Biol; Int Soc Develop Biol; Tissue Culture Asn; Can Soc Cell Biol. *Res:* Tissue interactions in induction in Amphibia; history and philosophy of biology. *Mailing Add:* Off Dean Fac Sci Univ BC 6270 Univ Blvd #2354 Vancouver BC V6T 2A9 Can

FINNEGAN, MICHAEL, b Appleton, Wis, Jan 17, 41; m 71; c 2. PHYSICAL ANTHROPOLOGY. *Educ:* Univ Colo, BA, 67, MA, 70, PhD(anthrop), 72; Am Bd Forensic Anthropol, dipl. *Prof Exp:* Fel, Smithsonian Res Found, 72-73; asst prof, 73-77, ASSOC PROF ANTHROP, KANS STATE UNIV, 77- *Concurrent Pos:* Osteologist, archaeologist, Kans Hist Soc, 73-; consult osteologist, Kans Bur Invest, 74-; field consult, Van Doren-Hazard-Stallings, 75. *Mem:* Am Asn Phys Anthropologists; Am Acad Forensic Sci; Int Asn Identification; Soc Am Archaeol; Paleopath Asn. *Res:* Non-metric skeletal variation; forensic osteology; paleopathology. *Mailing Add:* Osteology Lab Kans State Univ Manhattan KS 66506

FINNEGAN, RAYMOND JOSEPH, b Cochran, Ont, Mar 2, 22; m 71; c 2. FOREST ENTOMOLOGY. *Educ:* Univ NB, BSc, 48, MSc, 50; Univ BC, PhD(zool), 59. *Prof Exp:* Res scientist, Can Dept Agr, 48-60 & Can Dept Forestry, 60-67; res scientist, Laurentian Forest Res Ctr, Can Dept Fisheries & Forestry, 67-71, RES SCIENTIST, LAURENTIAN FOREST RES CTR, ENVIRON CAN, 71- *Concurrent Pos:* Vis prof, Univ Fla, Gainesville, 81. *Mem:* Entom Soc Am; Entom Soc Can; French Asn Advan Sci. *Res:* Ecological study of nursery, plantation, and woodlot insects; vectors of Dutch elm disease; scolytid damaging maple regeneration; needle miner on pines; ants as limiting factor of insect pests; weevils attacking pines. *Mailing Add:* Laurentian For Res Ctr Environ Can 1080 Rte du Vallon Quebec PQ G1V 4C7 Can

FINNEGAN, RICHARD ALLEN, b Minneapolis, Minn, Feb 5, 32; m 56; c 3. ORGANIC CHEMISTRY. *Educ:* Univ Minn, BA, 53; Mass Inst Technol, PhD(org chem), 57. *Prof Exp:* Res fel, Univ Chicago, 57-58 & Wayne State Univ, 58-59; asst prof chem, Ohio State Univ, 59-63; assoc prof med chem, 63-66, PROF MED CHEM, STATE UNIV NY BUFFALO, 66- *Mem:* Am Chem Soc; NY Acad Sci; Am Pharmaceut Asn; The Chem Soc. *Res:* Natural products chemistry; photochemistry; organoalkali metal chemistry. *Mailing Add:* Dept of Med Chem State Univ of NY Sch of Pharm Buffalo NY 14214

FINNEGAN, WALTER DANIEL, b Anaconda, Mont, Mar 31, 23; m 48; c 2. METALLURGY. *Educ:* Mont Col Mineral Sci & Tech, BS, 48, MS, 49. *Prof Exp:* Engr metall, US Bur Mines, 49-52; res metallurgist, 52-55, from asst supvr to supvr joining br, Dept Metall Res, Wash, 55-70, SR RES ASSOC, CTR TECHNOL, KAISER ALUMINUM & CHEM CORP, CALIF, 70- *Mem:* Am Welding Soc; Am Soc Metals. *Res:* Metallurgy and joining of aluminum alloys. *Mailing Add:* Ctr for Technol PO Box 877 Pleasanton CA 94566

FINNEGAN, WILLIAM GEORGE, atmospheric chemistry, see previous edition

FINNEMORE, DOUGLAS K, b Cuba, NY, Sept 9, 34; m 56; c 2. SOLID STATE PHYSICS. *Educ:* Pa State Univ, BS, 56; Univ Ill, MS, 58, PhD(superconductivity), 62. *Prof Exp:* Res assoc physics, Univ Ill, 62 & Ames Lab, 62-63; from asst prof to assoc prof, 63-68, PROF PHYSICS, IOWA STATE UNIV, 68- *Mem:* Fel Am Phys Soc. *Res:* Superconductivity. *Mailing Add:* Dept of Physics Iowa State Univ Ames IA 50010

FINNERTY, FRANK AMBROSE, JR, b Montclair, NJ, Nov 3, 23; m 46, 75; c 6. CARDIOLOGY. *Educ:* Georgetown Univ, AB, 43, MD, 47; Am Bd Internal Med, cert, 55. *Prof Exp:* Vis physician, Georgetown Med Div, Gen Hosp, Washington, DC, 52, chief cardiovascular res, 52-76; asst prof med & pharmacol, Med Sch, Georgetown Univ, 55-65, prof med & obstet & gynec, 65-72, prof obstet & gynec, 72-76; chief med, Columbia Hosp Women, 63-73; CLIN PROF MED, GEORGE WASHINGTON UNIV MED CTR, 77-; DIR, HYPERTENSION CTR, WASHINGTON, DC, 77- *Concurrent Pos:* Vis physician, Med Ctr, Georgetown Univ, 52-76; Am Heart Asn res fel, 55, estab investr, 57; adj prof med, Grad Sch Nursing, Cath Univ, 75-; mem, Coun High Blood Pressure Res & Task Force Hypertension, Am Heart Asn; charter mem, Task Force Nat Hypertension Info & Educ Prog & mem Task Force Drug Protocol, Nat High Blood Pressure Info Prog, NIH; assoc ed, Dialogues in Hypertension. *Mem:* AMA; fel Am Col Cardiol; fel Am Col Physicians; fel Am Col Angiol. *Res:* Cardiovascular research hypertension toxemias of pregnancy; postural hypotension; patient comliance. *Mailing Add:* 1341 Pennsylvania Ave SE Washington DC 20003

FINNERTY, JAMES LAWRENCE, b Sioux Falls, SDak, Mar 9, 27. BIOCHEMISTRY, INFORMATION SCIENCE. *Educ:* Marquette Univ, BS, 48; Univ Ill, MS, 50; Loyola Univ, Ill, PhD(chem), 60. *Prof Exp:* Prof, Sogang Univ, Korea, 66-75; prof, Basic Sci & librn, Health Sci, Peoria Sch Med, Univ Ill, 75-80; CHIEF MED LIBRN, MED LIBR, COLUMBUS HOSP, CHICAGO, ILL, 80- *Concurrent Pos:* Fulbright sci educ prof, Korea, 66-68. *Mem:* Am Chem Soc; Med Libr Asn; Spec Libr Asn; Sigma Xi. *Res:* Information retrieval in the health sciences. *Mailing Add:* Columbus Hosp Med Libr 2520 N Lakeview Chicago IL 61614

FINNERTY, WILLIAM ROBERT, b Keokuk, Iowa, May 2, 29; m 53; c 6. MICROBIAL PHYSIOLOGY, BIOCHEMISTRY. *Educ:* Univ Iowa, BA, 55, PhD(microbiol), 61. *Prof Exp:* Teaching fel microbiol, Univ Iowa, 57-58, res asst, 58-60, instr, 60, res assoc, 60-61; USPHS fel biochem & enzym, Oak Ridge Nat Labs, 61-62; from asst prof to assoc prof microbiol, Ind Univ Sch Med, 62-68; assoc prof, 68-75, PROF MICROBIOL, UNIV GA, 75-, HEAD DEPT, 77- DIR ENERGY RES OFF, 75- *Concurrent Pos:* Vis prof, Univ Gottingen, 73; mem ed bd, J of Bact, 73. *Honors & Awards:* P R Edwards Award, Am Soc Microbiol, 80. *Mem:* AAAS; Am Soc Microbiol; Am Soc Biol Chemists; Am Chem Soc. *Res:* Mechanism of oxidation of aliphatic hydrocarbons by microorganisms; control mechanisms; lipids; petroleum microbiology; membranes. *Mailing Add:* Dept of Microbiol Univ of Ga Athens GA 30602

FINNEY, ESSEX EUGENE, JR, b Powhatan, Va, May 16, 37; m 59; c 2. AGRICULTURAL ENGINEERING. *Educ:* Va Polytech Inst, BS, 59; Pa State Univ, MS, 61; Mich State Univ, PhD(eng), 63. *Prof Exp:* Res agr engr, Sci & Educ Admin-Agr Res, 65-77, ASST DIR, BELTSVILLE AGR RES CTR, USDA, 77- *Concurrent Pos:* Sr policy anal, Presidential Sci Adv Off, Washington, DC, 80-81. *Mem:* Am Soc Agr Engrs; Inst Food Technol. *Res:* Instrumentation and techniques for measuring physical properties and characteristics associated with quality within agricultural and food products. *Mailing Add:* 11206 Chantly Lane Mitchellville MD 20716

FINNEY, JOSEPH J, b New York, NY, Mar 11, 27; m 61; c 3. GEOLOGY, MINERALOGY. *Educ:* US Merchant Marine Acad, BS, 50; Univ NMex, MS, 59; Univ Wis, PhD(struct mineral), 62. *Prof Exp:* PROF GEOL & HEAD DEPT, COLO SCH MINES, 62- *Concurrent Pos:* Res grants, Colo Sch Mines Found, Inc, 62- & Res Corp, 63. *Mem:* Mineral Soc Am; Mineral Asn Can; Mineral Soc Gt Brit & Ireland; Am Crystallog Asn. *Res:* Structural mineralogy; investigations in structure of minerals; crystal chemistry. *Mailing Add:* Dept of Geol Colo Sch of Mines Golden CO 80401

FINNEY, KARL FREDERICK, b Salina, Kans, July 25, 11; m 35; c 3. CHEMISTRY. *Educ:* Kans Wesleyan Univ, AB, 35; Kans State Univ, BS, 36, MS, 37. *Prof Exp:* Assoc chemist, Hard Winter Wheat Qual Lab, USDA, Kans State Univ, 38-43; from assoc chemist to chemist, Soft Wheat Lab, Ohio Exp Sta, 43-46; prof grain sci & res chemist in chg hard winter wheat qual lab, 46-72, RES CHEMIST & RES LEADER, GRAIN QUAL & END USE PROPERTIES UNIT, US GRAIN MKT RES CTR, USDA & PROF GRAIN SCI, KANS STATE UNIV, 72- *Mem:* Fel AAAS; Am Chem Soc; Am Soc Agron; Am Asn Cereal Chemists; Sigma Xi. *Res:* Role of wheat flour components in breadmaking by fractionating and reconstituting techniques; optimized physical and breadmaking methods for evaluating functional properties of wheat; effects of environmental factors and varying stages of wheat maturity on quality. *Mailing Add:* US Grain Mkt Res Ctr USDA-ARS-NCR 1515 College Ave Manhattan KS 66502

FINNEY, ROSS LEE, b Springfield, Mass, May 31, 33; m 63. TOPOLOGY. *Educ:* Univ Mich, BA, 54, MA, 55, PhD(math), 62. *Prof Exp:* Instr math, Mass Inst Technol, 61-63 & Princeton Univ, 63-66; asst prof, 66-68, ASSOC PROF MATH, UNIV ILL, URBANA-CHAMPAIGN, 68- *Concurrent Pos:* Fulbright scholar, Poincare Inst, 56-57, lectr, Bo, Sierra Leone, 68 & 69 & Addis Ababa, Ethiopia, 71; chmn curriculum comt, African Math Prog, USAID, 62, secondary C writing group, 65-67; codir, Ghana Teaching Intern Prog, 71-74; sr mathematician, Proj CALC, 76; dir NSF undergrad math appln proj, 77- *Mem:* Am Math Soc; Math Asn Am; Nat Coun Teachers Math. *Res:* Combinatorial and general topology. *Mailing Add:* Dept of Math Univ of Ill Urbana-Champaign Urbana IL 61801

FINNEY, STANLEY CHARLES, b Chula Vista, Calif, Oct 14, 47; m 77. GEOLOGY, PALEONTOLOGY. *Educ:* Univ Calif, Riverside, BS, 69, MS, 71; Ohio State Univ, PhD(geol), 77. *Prof Exp:* Res assoc geol, Field Mus Nat Hist, 78-79; instr, Ohio State Univ, 79-80; asst prof, Northern Ariz Univ, 80-81; ASSOC PROF GEOL, OKLA STATE UNIV, 81- *Concurrent Pos:* Fels, Mem Univ Nfld, 77-78 & Field Mus Natural Hist, 78- *Mem:* Geol Soc Am; Am Asn Petrol Geologists; Paleont Soc; Paleaont Asn; Int Paleont Asn. *Res:* Invertebrate paleontology-stratigraphy; graptolites- morphology, taxonomy, biostratigraph; receptaculitids- morphology, paleoecology; ordovician biostratigraphy and biogeography. *Mailing Add:* Dept Geol Okla State Univ Stillwater OK 74078

FINNIE, I(AIN), b Hong Kong, July 18, 28; nat US. MECHANICAL ENGINEERING. *Educ:* Glasgow Univ, BSc, 49, DSc, 75; Mass Inst Technol, SM, 50, ME, 51, ScD(mech eng), 53. *Prof Exp:* Instr mech eng, Mass Inst Technol, 52-53; engr, Shell Develop Co, 53-61; assoc prof mech eng, 61-63, PROF MECH ENG, UNIV CALIF, BERKELEY, 63- *Mem:* Soc Exp Stress Anal; Am Soc Mech Engrs; Am Soc Testing & Mat; Brit Inst Mech Engrs. *Res:* Mechanical behavior of engineering materials, especially creep, wear and fracture. *Mailing Add:* Dept of Mech Eng Univ of Calif Berkeley CA 94720

FINNIGAN, FREDERICK T(HOMAS), b New Haven, Conn, Mar 4, 17; m 41; c 2. MECHANICAL ENGINEERING. *Educ:* Tri-State Col, BS, 40. *Prof Exp:* Res engr petrol prod, Res Ctr, Pure Oil Co, 40-49, fleet supvr prod performance, 49-56, div dir engines & fuels, 56-67; supvr prod eval, Prod Res Div, 67-78, MGR PROD RES, PROD RES DIV, UNION OIL CO CALIF, 78- *Mem:* Soc Automotive Engrs; Coord Res Coun. *Res:* Research and development in the areas of gasoline composition, alternative fuels research, internal combustion engine lubricants, distillate fuels, industrial oils, greases and wax; development and application of associated hardware. *Mailing Add:* Prod Res Div PO Box 76 Brea CA 92621

FINNIGAN, J(EROME) W(OODRUFF), b Oak Park, Ill, Feb 9, 24; m 49; c 4. CHEMICAL ENGINEERING. *Educ:* Northwestern Univ, BS, 50; Univ Idaho, MS, 53; Ore State Univ, PhD(chem eng), 58. *Prof Exp:* Reactor engr, Hanford Atomic Prod Oper, Gen Elec Co, 50-56, supvr reactor tech develop oper, 58-62; proj mgr & res & develop mgr, TRW Systs, 62-70; mgr Fuels & Mat Dept, Battelle-Northwest Labs, 70-81; DEAN & RESIDENT DIR, JOINT CTR GRAD STUDY, 81- *Mem:* Am Nuclear Soc; Am Inst Chem Engrs; Am Ord Asn. *Res:* Nuclear reactor and systems engineering; materials development and technology applied to nuclear and non-nuclear projects for government and industry. *Mailing Add:* Joint Ctr Grad Study 100 Sprout Rd Richland WA 99352

FINSETH, DENNIS HENRY, b Bremerton, Wash, July 24, 45; m 69. SPECTROCHEMISTRY. *Educ:* Western Wash State Col, BA, 67; Univ Pittsburgh, MS, 69, PhD(chem), 73. *Prof Exp:* instr chem, Univ Pittsburgh, 73-76; RES CHEMIST DEPT OF ENERGY, PITTSBURGH ENERGY TECHNOL CTR, 76- *Mem:* Am Chem Soc. *Res:* Vibrational spectroscopy of theoretically interesting small molecules; analytical applications of spectroscopy; chemistry of coal conversion. *Mailing Add:* Pittsburgh Energy Technol Ctr PO Box 10940 Pittsburgh PA 15236

FINSTEIN, MELVIN S, b Cambridge, Mass, June 25, 31; m 51; c 3. MICROBIOLOGY. *Educ:* Cornell Univ, BS, 59, MS, 61; Univ Calif, Berkeley, PhD(soil microbiol), 64. *Prof Exp:* Asst prof, 64-70, assoc prof, 70-73, PROF ENVIRON SCI, RUTGERS UNIV, NEW BRUNSWICK, 73- *Mem:* Am Soc Microbiol; Am Soc Limnol & Oceanog. *Res:* Physiology of autotrophic bacteria; microbiology of polluted waters; waste water treatment processes; ecology of nitrifying waste treatment and bacteria in polluted water; composting for the treatment of sludge and solid waste; environmental regulation and management. *Mailing Add:* Dept of Environ Sci Rutgers Univ New Brunswick NJ 08903

FINSTER, MIECZYSLAW, b Lwow, Poland, Aug 1, 24; US citizen; m 51; c 2. PHYSIOLOGY, PHARMACOLOGY. *Educ:* Univ Geneva, MD, 57. *Prof Exp:* Resident anesthesiol, Columbia Univ-Presby Med Ctr, 58-60; from instr to assoc prof, 61-75, prof anesthesia, 75-78, PROF ANESTHESIA, OBSTET & GYNEC, COL PHYSICIANS & SURGEONS, COLUMBIA UNIV, 78- *Concurrent Pos:* NIH res fel anat, Col Physicians & Surgeons, Columbia Univ, 60-61. *Mem:* Am Soc Anesthesiologists; Asn Univ Anesthetists; Am Soc Pharmacol & Exp Therapeut; Soc Obstet Anesthesiologists & Perinatologists; assoc fel Am Col Obstetricians & Gynecologists. *Res:* Transmission of drugs across the placenta; neonatal pharmacology. *Mailing Add:* 622 W 168th St New York NY 10032

FINSTON, HARMON LEO, b Chicago, Ill, Feb 16, 22; m 50; c 4. NUCLEAR CHEMISTRY. *Educ:* Ill Inst Technol, BSAS, 43; Ohio State Univ, PhD(chem), 50. *Prof Exp:* Cur chem, Lewis Inst Br, Ill Inst Technol, 42-43; jr chemist, Manhattan Dist, Metall Lab, Univ Chicago, 43-45; asst cyclotron chem, Ohio State Univ, 45-50; assoc chemist, Dept Chem, Brookhaven Nat Lab, 50-51, assoc chemist & supvr, Radiochem Anal Sect, Dept Nuclear Eng, 51-58, chemist, 58-60, leader, Radiochem Anal Group, 60-63; PROF CHEM, BROOKLYN COL, CITY UNIV NEW YORK, 63- *Concurrent Pos:* Mem subcmt radiochem, Nat Res Coun, 57-60 & subcmt use radioactivity standards, 62; fel Israel AEC, 65; consult, US Army Nuclear Defense Lab; I M Kolthoff fel & vis prof inorg & anal chem, Hebrew Univ, 73. *Mem:* Am Chem Soc; Am Nuclear Soc; fel Japan Soc Prom Sci. *Res:* Nuclear, radio and analytical chemistry; mechanisms of synergic solvent extraction; homogeneous liquid-liquid extraction and extraction at near neutral pH. *Mailing Add:* Dept of Chem Brooklyn Col City Univ of New York Brooklyn NY 11210

FINSTON, MORTON, b Chicago, Ill, Oct 18, 19; m 55; c 2. AERONAUTICS. *Educ:* Northwestern Univ, BS, 41; Brown Univ, PhD(appl math), 49. *Prof Exp:* Asst aeronaut eng, Calif Inst Technol, 42-45; res assoc appl math, Brown Univ, 45-48; mem staff, Naval Supersonic Lab, 48-51, asst prof aeronaut eng, 51-56, assoc prof aeronaut & astronaut, 56-63, PROF AERONAUT & ASTRONAUT, MASS INST TECHNOL, 63- *Mem:* Am Inst Aeronaut & Astronaut; Am Math Soc. *Res:* Applied mechanics; aerodynamics; heat transfer; fluid mechanics. *Mailing Add:* Dept of Aeronaut & Astronaut Mass Inst of Technol Cambridge MA 02139

FINSTON, ROLAND A, b Chicago, Ill, Jan 27, 37; m 60; c 2. HEALTH PHYSICS, RADIOLOGICAL PHYSICS. *Educ:* Univ Chicago, AB & SB, 57; Vanderbilt Univ, MS, 59; Cornell Univ, PhD(biophys), 65. *Prof Exp:* Assoc prof radiol physics, Ore State Univ, 65-66; sr health physicist, 66-77, DIR HEALTH PHYSICS, STANFORD UNIV, 77- LECTR RADIOL, 70- *Mem:* Health Physics Soc; Soc Nuclear Med; Am Asn Physicists in Med. *Res:* Radiation dosimetry; radiation biology; radiological health; radiological physics; dosimetry in nuclear medicine. *Mailing Add:* Health Physics Off 67 Encina Hall Stanford Univ Stanford CA 94305

FINZEL, RODNEY BRIAN, b Monroe, Mich, Dec 23, 51; m 80. PHYSICAL ORGANIC CHEMISTRY. *Educ:* Eastern Mich Univ, BS, 73, MS, 77; Northwestern Univ, PhD(chem), 81. *Prof Exp:* Instr org chem, Northwestern Univ, 80; ASST PROF ORG CHEM, HOFSTRA UNIV, 81- *Mem:* Am Chem Soc. *Res:* Organic reaction mechanisms; conformational analysis; nuclear magnetic resonance; molecular orbital theory. *Mailing Add:* Dept Chem Hofstra Univ Hempstead NY 11550

FIORE, ANTHONY WILLIAM, b Youngstown, Ohio, Oct 26, 20; m 44. AERONAUTICAL & ASTRONAUTICAL ENGINEERING. *Educ:* Univ Cincinnati, BS, 48, MS, 49; Ohio State Univ, PhD(aeronaut & astronaut eng), 66. *Prof Exp:* Instr aeronaut, Col Eng, Univ Cincinnati, 48-49; aeronaut develop engr, Aircraft Lab, Air Mat Command, 49-52, aeronaut res engr, Aircraft Lab, Wright Air Develop Ctr, 52-54, aeronaut res engr, Aeronaut Res Lab, 54-65, asst for exp aerodyn res, Hypersonic Res Lab, Aerospace Res Lab, Air Force Syst Command, 65-75, tech mgr, 75-82, SR AERODYNAMIC RES SCIENTIST, AIR FORCE FLIGHT DYNAMICS LAB, US AIR FORCE, WRIGHT PATTERSON AFB, 82- *Mem:* Assoc fel Am Inst Aeronaut & Astronaut. *Res:* Theoretical and experimental basic research in aerodynamics; subsonic, transonic, supersonic and hypersonic aerodynamic research. *Mailing Add:* Flight Dynamics Lab Wright Patterson AFB OH 45433

FIORE, CARL, b New Haven, Conn, Sept 9, 28; m 56. INSECT PHYSIOLOGY, INSECT DEVELOPMENT. *Educ:* Yale Univ, BA, 50; Fordham Univ, MS, 56, PhD(physiol), 59. *Prof Exp:* Instr physiol, Fordham Univ Col Pharm, 56-58, res assoc biol, 58-61; asst prof, City Univ New York, 61-63; fel, Develop Biol Ctr, Western Reserve Univ, 63-65; researcher, Am Mus Natural Hist, 65-66; assoc prof, 66-69, PROF BIOL, CENT CONN STATE COL, 69- *Mem:* AAAS; Am Soc Zool; Entom Soc Am. *Res:* Physiology and biochemistry of aging; environmental effects on development; cell biology. *Mailing Add:* Dept of Biol Sci Cent Conn State Col New Britain CT 06050

FIORE, JOSEPH VINCENT, b NY, Oct 9, 20; m 50; c 3. BIOCHEMISTRY, SEPARATION PROCESSES. *Educ:* Fordham Univ, BS, 43, MS, 47, PhD(chem), 50. *Prof Exp:* Chief biochem & clin biochem, Rochester Gen Hosp, 50-53; group leader cereal chem, Fleischmann Labs Div, Standard Brands, Inc, 53-60; mgr tobacco res group, 60-64, area mgr chem develop lab, 64-66, mgr food & tobacco lab, Res Div, 66-70, mgr tobacco & anal lab, 70-78, DIR APPLIED CHEM, AMF INC, 78- *Mem:* Am Chem Soc; Inst Food Technol; NY Acad Sci; Water Pollution Control Fedn; Tech Asn Pulp & Paper Indust. *Res:* Enzymology; fermentation; clinical biochemistry; ecological sciences; analytical chemistry. *Mailing Add:* AMF Tech Ctr 689 Hope St Stamford CT 06907

FIORE, NICHOLAS F, b Pittsburgh, Pa, Sept 24, 39; m 60; c 4. MATERIALS ENGINEERING, PHYSICAL METALLURGY. *Educ:* Carnegie Inst Technol, BS, 60, MS, 63, PhD(metall), 64. *Prof Exp:* From asst prof to prof metall, Univ Notre Dame, 66-82, chmn, Dept Metall Eng & Mat Sci, 69-82; DIR CORP TECHNOL, CABOT CORP, 82- *Concurrent Pos:* Consult, Ford Motor Co, Miles Lab, Argonne Nat Lab, Corning Glass Works, US Army & NSF, 68-; mem basic res subcomt, Welding Res Coun; Allegheny Ludlum Corp fel, 63. *Mem:* Am Soc Metals; Am Welding Soc; Am Inst Mining, Metall & Petrol Engrs. *Res:* Internal friction, non-destructive testing, wear, corrosion, environment-sensitive degradation of materials. *Mailing Add:* Cabot Corp 125 High St Boston MA 02110

FIORI, BART J, b Passaic, NJ, Dec 7, 30; m 56; c 4. ENTOMOLOGY. *Educ:* Univ Ga, BSA, 54; Cornell Univ, PhD(entom), 63. *Prof Exp:* Field res specialist, Ortho Div, Calif Chem Co, 63-64; RES ENTOMOLOGIST & RES LEADER, SCI & EDUC ADMIN AGR RES, USDA, 64- *Concurrent Pos:* Assoc prof, Cornell Univ, 68- *Mem:* Entom Soc Am; Sigma Xi. *Res:* Petroleum oils as ovicides; evaluation of insecticides; physical, chemical and biological control of the European chafer Amphimallon majalis; plant resistance against insects. *Mailing Add:* Melvin Hill Rd Sci & Educ Admin Agr Res USDA Geneva NY 14456

FIORICA, VINCENT, endocrinology, see previous edition

FIORITO, RALPH BRUNO, b New York, NY, Oct 24, 41. PHYSICS. *Educ:* Col Holy Cross, BS, 63; Cath Univ Am, MSE, 66, PhD(physics), 71. *Prof Exp:* Res asst space sci physics, Cath Univ Am, 65-71; comput consult, 73; physicist acoust, 73-78, RES PHYSICIST ELECTRON BEAM PROPAGATION, WHITE OAK LAB, NAVAL SURFACE WEAPONS CTR, 76- *Concurrent Pos:* Lectr, Cath Univ, 73-74; vis res physicist electron beam propagation, Naval Res Lab, 78-80 & Lawrence Livermore Nat Lab, 81- *Mem:* Am Phys Soc; Acoust Soc Am; Sigma Xi. *Res:* Relativistic electron beam propagation in gases; acoustic wave propagation in materials. *Mailing Add:* White Oak Lab Naval Surface Weapons Ctr Silver Spring MD 20910

FIOTO, GEORGE ANTHONY, b Brooklyn, NY, Nov 22, 33; m 56; c 3. COSMETIC CHEMISTRY. *Educ:* Manhattan Col, BS, 55. *Prof Exp:* Res chemist, Revlon Inc, 55-59, sr res chemist, 59-61, tech staff asst, 61-63, dept head emulsion & colloid chem, 63-65, asst dir res, Skin Treatment, Toiletries & Make-up Prod, 65-68; vpres, 68-77, SR VPRES RES & DEVELOP, NOXELL CORP, 77- *Mem:* Soc Cosmetic Chemists. *Res:* Emulsion technology; colloid chemistry; rheological properties of dispersions; chemistry of surface active agents. *Mailing Add:* Noxell Corp PO Box 1799 Baltimore MD 21023

FIRBY, JAMES R, b Detroit, Mich, Nov 28, 33; m 56; c 1. INVERTEBRATE PALEONTOLOGY, STRATIGRAPHY. *Educ:* San Francisco State Col, BA, 60; Univ Calif, Berkeley, PhD(paleont), 69. *Prof Exp:* Asst prof, 66-74, asst dean, 74-80, ASSOC PROF GEOL, MACKAY SCH MINES, UNIV NEV, RENO, 74- *Mem:* Am Asn Petrol Geologists. *Res:* Cenozoic non-marine Mollusca, especially of Western North America. *Mailing Add:* Dept Geol Sci Mackay Sch Mines Univ of Nev Reno NV 89557

FIRE, PHILIP, b Paterson, NJ, Dec 18, 25; m 51; c 2. ELECTRICAL ENGINEERING. *Educ:* Masst Inst Technol, BS & MS, 52; Stanford Univ, PhD(elec eng), 64. *Prof Exp:* Staff engr, Lincoln Lab, Mass Inst Technol, 52-54; sr scientist, 55-80, SR SCIENTIST, GTE-SYLVANIA SYSTS, GTE CORP, 82- *Concurrent Pos:* Liason scientist, Off Naval Res, London, 80-82; ed, Trans on Commun, Inst Elec & Electronics Engrs, 78-79. *Mem:* Fel Inst Elec & Electronics Engrs. *Res:* Error-correcting codes for communication systems; analysis and synthesis of electronic systems. *Mailing Add:* GTE-Sylvania Systs-WD PO Box 188 Mountain View VA 94042

FIREBAUGH, MORRIS W, b Freeport, Ill, July 5, 37; m 60; c 2. MICROCOMPUTERS, ENERGY CONVERSION. *Educ:* Manchester Col, AB, 59; Univ Ill, MS, 60, PhD(physics), 66. *Prof Exp:* Res assoc high-energy physics, Univ Ill, 66-67; instr physics, Univ Wis, 67-69, PROF PHYSICS, UNIV WIS-PARKSIDE, 69- *Concurrent Pos:* Vis scientist, Inst Energy Anal, Oak Ridge, Tenn, 79-80. *Mem:* Am Phys Soc; Am Asn Physics Teachers; Sigma Xi. *Res:* Instructional applications of interactive computer graphics; energy policy; energy management; nuclear power. *Mailing Add:* Dept Physics Box 2000 Univ of Wis-Parkside Kenosha WI 53140

FIREHAMMER, BURTON DEFOREST, b Franklin, Mont, Apr 29, 23; m 64. VETERINARY MICROBIOLOGY, VETERINARY IMMUNOLOGY. *Educ:* Mont State Col, BS, 48, MS, 51. *Prof Exp:* Asst vet res, Vet Res Lab, Agr Exp Sta, 48-53, from asst prof to assoc prof, 53-66, PROF VET BACT, MONT STATE UNIV, 66- *Mem:* AAAS; Sigma Xi; Am Soc Microbiol; Conf Res Workers Animal Dis. *Res:* Mastitis of sheep; vibrionic abortion of sheep; bovine abortion due to Haemophilus; intestinal vibrios of sheep; bovine vibriosis vaccines; mycoplasma; calf scours; reproductive diseases of cattle and sheep; applied immunology. *Mailing Add:* Vet Res Lab Mont State Univ Bozeman MT 59715

FIREMAN, EDWARD LEONARD, b Pittsburgh, Pa, Mar 23, 22; m 47; c 3. PHYSICS. *Educ:* Carnegie Inst Technol, BS, 42, MS, 45; Princeton Univ, PhD(physics), 48. *Prof Exp:* Asst solid state physics, Carnegie Inst Technol, 42-46; AEC fel, Princeton Univ, 48-50; assoc scientist physics, Brookhaven Nat Lab, 50-56; PHYSICIST, SMITHSONIAN ASTROPHYS OBSERV, 56- *Concurrent Pos:* Guest scientist, Brookhaven Nat Lab, 56-; pres comn meteorites, Int Astron Union; res assoc, Harvard Observ, 56-, lectr, 64- *Mem:* Fel AAAS; Am Phys Soc; Am Astron Soc; Am Meteorol Soc; Am Geophys Union. *Res:* Meteorites; radioactive and stable isotopes in meteorites; age determinations; beta decay; cloud chambers; natural tritium; lunar materials; radioactive and stable isotopes in lunar material. *Mailing Add:* Smithsonian Astrophys Observ Harvard Col Observ Cambridge MA 02138

FIREMAN, PHILIP, b Pittsburgh, Pa, Feb 28, 32; m 57; c 5. PEDIATRICS, IMMUNOLOGY. *Educ:* Univ Pittsburgh, BS, 53; Univ Chicago, MD, 57. *Prof Exp:* Clin assoc, NIH, 60-62; from instr to assoc prof, 63-74, PROF PEDIAT, SCH MED, UNIV PITTSBURGH, 74- DIR ALLERGY-IMMUNOL, CHILDREN'S HOSP, 68- *Concurrent Pos:* Mead-Johnson fel pediat, 58-60; USPHS res fel, Harvard Med Sch, 62-63; Interstate Postgrad Med Asn res award, 64; USPHS res career develop award, 65; res collabr, Brookhaven Nat Lab, 64-69 & Univ Lausanne & Swiss Inst Cancer Res, 72-73. *Res:* Immediate and delayed hypersensitivity; clinical immunology; allergy. *Mailing Add:* Children's Hosp 125 DeSoto St Pittsburgh PA 15213

FIRESTONE, ALEXANDER, b New York, NY, July 22, 40. HIGH ENERGY PHYSICS. *Educ:* Columbia Univ, BS, 62; Yale Univ, MA, 64, PhD(physics), 66. *Prof Exp:* Res physicist, Lawrence Berkeley Lab, 66-71; asst prof high energy physics, Calif Inst Technol, 71-75; assoc prof, 75-78, PROG DIR, AMES LAB, IOWA STATE UNIV, 78-, PROF HIGH ENERGY PHYSICS, 79- *Mem:* Am Phys Soc. *Res:* Problems in strong interactions; particle dynamics; resonance production, diffractive effects, correlations, high transverse momentum effects, inclusive cross sections, charge and rapidity structure and jet structure. *Mailing Add:* Dept of Physics Iowa State Univ Ames IA 50010

FIRESTONE, RAYMOND A, b New York, NY, Jan 20, 31; m 52; c 4. ORGANIC CHEMISTRY. *Educ:* Cornell Univ, AB, 51; Columbia Univ, PhD(org chem), 54. *Prof Exp:* Sr chemist, 56-73, res fel, 73-77, sr res fel, 77-80, SR INVESTR, MERCK & CO, RAHWAY, 80- *Concurrent Pos:* Chmn, Gordon Heterocyclic Conf, 78. *Honors & Awards:* Directors Award, Merck Sharp & Dohme, 68. *Mem:* The Chem Soc. *Res:* Synthesis and mechanism in organic chemistry; enzyme inhibitors; cancer chemotherapy. *Mailing Add:* 60 Hunter Ave Fanwood NJ 07023

FIRESTONE, RICHARD FRANCIS, b Canton, Ohio, June 18, 26; m 54; c 3. PHYSICAL CHEMISTRY. *Educ:* Oberlin Col, AB, 50; Univ Wis, PhD, 54. *Prof Exp:* Asst chem, Univ Wis, 50-51, asst radiochem, 51-54; resident res assoc chem div, Argonne Nat Lab, 54-55, instr, Int Sch Nuclear Sci & Eng, 55-56; asst prof chem, Western Reserve Univ, 56-60; assoc prof, 61-67, PROF CHEM, OHIO STATE UNIV, 67- *Mem:* Fel AAAS; Am Phys Soc; Am Chem Soc; Sigma Xi. *Res:* Radiation chemistry; kinetics of ionizing-radiation induced reactions; fast reactions of excited atoms in the gaseous phase. *Mailing Add:* Dept of Chem Ohio State Univ 140 W 18th Ave Columbus OH 43210

FIRESTONE, WILLIAM L(OUIS), b Chicago, Ill, June 20, 21; m 53; c 3. ELECTRICAL ENGINEERING. *Educ:* Univ Colo, BS, 46; Ill Inst Technol, MS, 49; Northwestern Univ, PhD(elec eng), 52. *Prof Exp:* Elec engr, Manhattan Proj, Univ Calif, 46; microwave engr, Motorola Radio, 46-49; grad asst, Northwestern Univ, 49-50; chief engr, Res Dept, Motorola Inc, Ill, 51-60, dir eng, Commun Div, 60-62, asst gen mgr, Chicago Mil Electronics Ctr, 62-64; vpres, Hallecrafte Corp, 65-66; vpres, Whittaker Corp, Calif, 66-70, gen mgr, Tech Prod Div, 66-69, group exec, Corp, 69-70; vpres & gen mgr, F W Sickles Div, Gen Instruments Corp, 70-71, vpres & group exec entertainment prod, Chicopee, 71-75; DIV V PRES & GEN MGR, AVIONICS SYSTS, RCA INC, 75- *Concurrent Pos:* Instr, US Radio Mat Sch, 42 & Ill Inst Technol 48-49 & 55-56; lectr, Northwestern Univ, 57. *Mem:* Fel Inst Elec & Electronics Engrs. *Res:* Communication engineering; communication theory and single sideband; engineering managements. *Mailing Add:* RCA Inc 8500 Balboa Blvd Van Nuys CA 91409

FIREY, JOSEPH CARL, b Roundup, Mont, Oct 22, 18; m 51; c 3. MECHANICAL ENGINEERING. *Educ:* Univ Wash, BS, 40; Univ Wis, MS, 41. *Prof Exp:* Instr mech eng, Univ Wis, 41-42; res engr, Calif Res Corp, 42-43, 46-54; from asst prof to prof mech eng, 54-80, EMER PROF MECH ENG, UNIV WASH, 80- *Mem:* Am Soc Mech Engrs; Soc Automotive Engrs; Am Soc Lubrication Engrs. *Res:* Combustion and lubrication problems in power generating equipment. *Mailing Add:* Dept of Mech Eng Univ of Wash Seattle WA 98105

FIREY, WILLIAM JAMES, b Roundup, Mont, Jan 23, 23; m 46; c 2. MATHEMATICS. *Educ:* Univ Wash, BS, 49; Univ Toronto, MA, 50; Stanford Univ, PhD(math), 54. *Prof Exp:* From instr to asst prof math, Wash State Univ, 53-61; assoc prof, 61-64, PROF MATH, ORE STATE UNIV, 64- *Concurrent Pos:* Mem staff, Fulbright Res Sch, Univ Otago, NZ, 67; vis prof, Mich State Univ, 69-70, Univ Freiburg, West Germany, 75-76. *Mem:* Am Math Soc; Math Asn Am; Can Math Cong. *Res:* Theory of convex sets and integral geometry. *Mailing Add:* Dept of Math Ore State Univ Corvallis OR 97331

FIRK, FRANK WILLIAM KENNETH, b London, Eng, Nov 2, 30; m 52; c 3. NUCLEAR PHYSICS. *Educ:* Univ London, BSc, 56, MSc, 65, PhD(physics), 67. *Prof Exp:* Asst exp officer physics, Atomic Energy Res Estab, Eng, 52-56, exp officer, 56-59, sr sci officer, 59-62, prin sci officer, 62-65; sr res assoc, 65-68, assoc prof, 68-77, PROF PHYSICS, YALE UNIV, 77-, DIR, ELECTRON ACCELERATOR LAB, 76-, CHMN DEPT, 80- *Concurrent Pos:* Vis scientist, Oak Ridge Nat Lab, 60-61. *Mem:* Am Inst Physics; Brit Inst Physics & Phys Soc. *Res:* Low energy neutron spectroscopy; nuclear photo-disintegration. *Mailing Add:* Dept of Physics Yale Univ New Haven CT 06520

FIRKINS, JOHN LIONEL, b Victoria, BC, Feb 13, 42; m 66; c 2. PHYSICAL ORGANIC CHEMISTRY. *Educ:* Univ Victoria, BC, BSc, 65; Calif Inst Technol, PhD(chem, bus econ), 70. *Prof Exp:* Sr res & develop chemist, Celanese Fibers Co, 69-75; mem staff fiber chem, 75-78, group leader paper, 79-80, CORP METRIC COORDR, WEYERHAEUSER CO, 80- *Mem:* AAAS; Am Chem Soc; Chem Inst Can; Tech Asn Pulp & Paper Indust. *Res:* Free radical reaction mechanisms; wood and cellulose chemistry; wood pulps for disposable products; chemical derivatives of renewable resources; cellulose acetate and other textile fibers. *Mailing Add:* Weyerhaeuser Co Weyerhaeuser Technol Ctr Tacoma WA 98401

FIRLE, TOMAS E(RASMUS), b Berlin, Ger, July 4, 26; nat US; div; c 3. ENVIRONMENTAL SCIENCE, COMMUNICATIONS. *Educ:* Univ Calif, Los Angeles, BS, 52, MS, 55. *Prof Exp:* Res physicist & head develop group, Semiconductor Lab, Hughes Aircraft Co, 52-58; res physicist, Gulf Energy & Environ Systs Inc, San Diego, 58-72; spec asst to supt, San Dieguito High Sch, 72-73; head environ anal, City San Diego, Environ Qual Div, 73-74; DEPT HEAD ENVIRON MGT, PORT OF SAN DIEGO, 74- *Concurrent Pos:* Lectr, Univ Calif, Los Angeles, 57-58 & Univ Calif, San Diego, 59-61; discussion leader, Univ Calif, San Diego & univ exten, 62-; trustee, Bd Educ, Del Mar Union Sch Dist, 67; mem ombudsman comt, Dept Educ, 69; bd dirs, Indust-Educ Coun, 69; pres, Inter-Focus, Calif, 70-; mem bd dirs & regional dir, Calif Asn Environ Profs, 74-77; lectr environ mgt, Sch Bus Admin, San Diego State Univ, 75-; environ comt chmn, Airport Opers Coun Int, 75-77; vchmn environ comt, Pac Coast Airport Authorities, 78-; mem environ comt, Calif Asn Port Authorities. *Mem:* AAAS; Am Phys Soc; Sigma Xi; Marine Technol Soc. *Res:* Environmental effects; interpersonal human relationships; group and individual behaviorism; social and political psychology; human communications; effectiveness training; management consulting; establishment of integrated eco-systems; environmental management; salt marsh and shoreline rehabilitation. *Mailing Add:* PO Box 9782 San Diego CA 92109

FIRLIT, CASIMIR FRANCIS, b Chicago, Ill, Dec 7, 39; m 65; c 2. PEDIATRICS, UROLOGY. *Educ:* Loyola Univ, Chicago, MS & MD, 65, PhD(pharmacol), 71. *Prof Exp:* Intern med, Mercy Hosp Med Ctr, Chicago, 65-66; resident gen surg, Vet Admin Hosp, Hines, 68-70; from instr to asst prof pharmacol, Stritch Sch Med, Loyola Univ, Chicago, 70-73; asst prof urol & physiol, 73-80, PROF UROL, NORTHWESTERRN UNIV, CHICAGO, 80-; HEAD PEDIAT RENAL TRANSPLANTATION, CHILDREN'S MEM HOSP, 73-, UROL FEL, 77-, CHMN PEDIAT UROL, 76- *Concurrent Pos:* Resident urol & res & educ assoc, Vet Admin Hosp, Hines, 70-73; attend pediat urologist, Children's Mem Hosp, Chicago, 73-; attend urologist, Northwestern Mem Hosp, 73- & Vet Admin Lakeside Hosp, 73-; head pediat urol, Childrens Mem Hosp; lectr urol & pharmacol, Stritch Sch Med, Loyola Univ, 73-; consult urol, Vet Admin Hosp, Hines, 73-; attend urologist, Loyola McGaw Med Ctr, Maywood, 73- *Honors & Awards:* Resident Prize, Chicago Urol Soc, 72. *Mem:* fel Am Acad Pediat; fel Am Bd Urol; Am Soc Transplant Surgeons; Am Fedn Clin Res. *Res:* Testicular metabolism and male fertility; neurogenic bladder research; pediatric renal transplantation; pediatric embryolory. *Mailing Add:* Children's Mem Hosp 2300 Childrens Plaza Chicago IL 60614

FIRMAGE, D(AVID) ALLAN, b Nephi, Utah, Feb 15, 18; m 40; c 6. CIVIL ENGINEERING. *Educ:* Univ Utah, BS, 40; Mass Inst Technol, MS, 41. *Prof Exp:* Stress analyst, E G Budd Mfg Co, Pa, 41-42; res engr struct eng, Res & Develop Labs, Ft Belvoir, Va, 42-47; assoc prof civil eng, Univ Fla, 47-52; asst, Mass Inst Technol, 52-53; asst chief struct engr, Patchen & Zimmerman, Engrs, Ga, 53-55; assoc prof civil eng, Brigham Young Univ, 55-57; chief bridge design engr, Capitol Engrs, Saigon, Vietnam, 57-59; assoc prof civil eng, 59-60, chmn dept, 69-72, PROF CIVIL ENG, BRIGHAM YOUNG UNIV, 60- *Concurrent Pos:* Adv, Guindy Col Eng, India, 63-64. *Mem:* Am Soc Eng Educ; Am Soc Civil Engrs; Int Asn Bridge & Struct Eng. *Res:* Structural design including mechanics and materials; design of highway bridges; textbooks. *Mailing Add:* Dept of Civil Eng Brigham Young Univ Provo UT 84602

FIRMAN, MELVIN CURTIS, b Glenside, Pa, Jan 11, 19; m 45. BACTERIOLOGY. *Educ:* Philadelphia Col Pharm, BSc, 40. *Prof Exp:* Res chemist milk prods, Abbott's Dairies, 45-46; res bacteriologist, Solvents & Vitamins, Publicker Alcohol Co, 46-48 & antibiotics, Heyden Chem Corp, 48-53; res bacteriologist, Am Cyanamid Co, 53-55, tech rep food indust, 55-56 & field develop, 56-60, asst tech dir, Fine Chem Dept, 60-61, asst to mgr res & develop, Agrodiv, 60-69, mgr sales coord, 69-70, asst to mgr, 70-77, asst mgr animal indust, 77-80; RETIRED. *Concurrent Pos:* Vis lectr, Serv Training Sch, USPHS. *Mem:* Fel AAAS; Am Chem Soc; Inst Food Technologists. *Res:* Antibiotics; fermentation improvement; use in foods and new antibiotic research, including isolation of tetracycline; microbiological tests of antibiotics; antifungal agent; chemotherapeutic agents and antifungals; research administration; plant and animal products for health and nutrition. *Mailing Add:* 10 B Drake St Whiting NJ 08759

FIRMENT, LAWRENCE EDWARD, b Elyria, Ohio, Mar 24, 50. PHYSICAL CHEMISTRY. *Educ:* Mass Inst Technol, SB, 72; Univ Calif, Berkeley, PhD(phys chem), 77. *Prof Exp:* CHEMIST, E I DU PONT DE NEMOURS & CO, INC, 77- *Mem:* Am Chem Soc; Am Phys Soc; Am Vacuum Soc. *Res:* Surface chemistry and heterogeneous catalysis. *Mailing Add:* Cent Res & Develop Dept E I du Pont de Nemours & Co Inc Wilmington DE 19898

FIRMINGER, HARLAN IRWIN, b Minneapolis, Minn, Dec 31, 18; m 42; c 3. PATHOLOGY. *Educ:* Wash Univ, AB, 39, MD, 43; Am Bd Path, dipl, 49. *Prof Exp:* Asst path, Sch Med, Wash Univ, 43-44; sr resident, Mass Gen Hosp, 46-47; pathologist, Nat Cancer Inst, 48-51; from asst prof to prof path & oncol, Med Sch, Univ Kans, 51-57; head dept path, Sch Med, Univ Md, Baltimore, 57-67, prof path, 57-75; dir anat path, Gen Rose Mem Hosp, 75-76, PROF PATH, UNIV COLO, SCH MED, 75- *Concurrent Pos:* Consult, Ft Howard Vet Hosp; mem sci adv bd consults, Armed Forces Inst Path, 65-70, ed, Atlas Tumor Path, 66-75; mem comt path, Nat Acad Sci-Nat Res Coun, 65-71. *Mem:* Am Soc Exp Path; Am Asn Cancer Res; Am Asn Path & Bact; Soc Exp Biol & Med; Int Acad Path. *Res:* Testicular tumors; chemical carcinogenesis; induced tumors of the liver; endocrine pathology. *Mailing Add:* 4200 E Ninth Ave Denver CO 80262

FIRNKAS, SEPP, b Rinnberg, Ger, Nov 16, 25; US citizen. CIVIL ENGINEERING. *Educ:* Munich Tech Univ, Dipl Ing, 53; Columbia Univ, CE, 78. *Prof Exp:* Assoc struct eng, CETBA, Algeria, 54-56; proj engr, Raymond Int Inc, NY, & Venezuela, 56-59, chief engr, Northeast Concrete Prod, 59-61; PRES, SEPP FIRNKAS ENG INC, 61; ASSOC PROF CIVIL ENG, NORTHEASTERN UNIV, 62- *Honors & Awards:* Progressive Archit Struct Design Award, 64; Prestressed Concrete Inst Struct Design Award, 66. *Mem:* Am Concrete Inst; Int Asn Shell Struct; Prestressed Concrete Asn. *Res:* Design and applications of reinforced and prestressed concrete; precast structural systems; analysis and design for seismic forces. *Mailing Add:* Sepp Firnkas Eng Inc 251 Newbury St Boston MA 02116

FIROR, JOHN WILLIAM, b Athens, Ga, Oct 18, 27; wid; c 4. SOLAR PHYSICS, RADIO ASTRONOMY. *Educ:* Ga Inst Technol, BS, 49; Univ Chicago, PhD(physics), 54. *Prof Exp:* Staff mem, Dept Terrestrial magnetism, Carnegie Inst, 53-61; from assoc dir to dir, Nat Ctr Astmospheric Res, 61-74, dir high altitude observ, 61-68, exec dir, 80, DIR ADVAN STUDY PROG, CTR ATMOSPHERIC RES, 80- *Concurrent Pos:* Mem US nat comt, on Global Atmospheric Res Prog, 68-72; Am Astron Soc vis prof, adj prof astrophys, Univ Colo, 62-68; mem, Dept of Com Weather Modification Adv Bd, 77-78; chmn, NASA Space & Terrestrial Appln Adv Comt, 78-81; mem, NASA Adv Coun, 78-81; trustee, Environ Defense Fund, & mem, Exec Comt, 74-, chmn, 75-80. *Mem:* Am Astron Soc; Am Geophys Union; Am Meteorol Soc; Int Astron Union. *Res:* Physical conditions in solar atmosphere; solar-terrestrial relations; physics of earth's atmosphere; impact of climate change. *Mailing Add:* Nat Ctr for Atmospheric Res PO Box 3000 Boulder CO 80307

FIRRIOLO, DOMENIC, b Brooklyn, NY, Sept 4, 33; m 59; c 2. PHYSIOLOGY, ANATOMY. *Educ:* St Francis Col, NY, BS, 54; St John's Univ, NY, MS, 56, PhD(physiol), 64. *Prof Exp:* From instr to asst prof biol, 56-63, assoc prof, 64-66, asst dean, Col Lib Arts & Sci, 66-70, PROF BIOL, LONG ISLAND UNIV, 70-, CHMN DEPT, 76- *Mem:* AAAS. *Res:* Comparative hematology; vertebrate erythropoiesis. *Mailing Add:* Dept of Biol Long Island Univ Brooklyn Ctr Brooklyn NY 11201

FIRSCHEIN, HILLIARD E, b Brooklyn, NY, Apr 7, 27. BIOCHEMISTRY. *Educ:* Ohio State Univ, BS, 48; Univ Wis, MS, 50; Univ Rochester, PhD(biochem), 58. *Prof Exp:* Asst, Univ Wis, 48-50; biochemist, Army Med Res Lab, Ft Knox, Ky, 51-55; res assoc, Atomic Energy Proj, Univ Rochester, 55-58, asst scientist, 58-60, instr biochem, Sch Med & Dent, 58-60, instr radiation biol, 59-60; from instr to asst prof biochem, Sch Med, NY Univ, 60-64; asst prof biochem orthop surg, Med Col, Cornell Univ, 64-69; assoc res biochemist, Univ Calif, Los Angeles, 69-71; asst dir, 72-80, ASSOC DIR, CIBA-GEIGY CORP, 72- *Concurrent Pos:* Sr scientist, Hosp for Spec Surg, 64-69. *Mem:* Am Chem Soc; Am Physiol Soc. *Res:* Endocrinology; vitamins; metabolism; clinical research. *Mailing Add:* 141 Laauwe Ave Wayne NJ 07470

FIRSCHING, FERDINAND HENRY, b Utica, NY, June 22, 23; m 55; c 6. ANALYTICAL CHEMISTRY. *Educ:* Syracuse Univ, MS, 51, PhD(chem), 55. *Prof Exp:* Res chemist, Skenandoa Rayon Corp, NY, 51-52; anal chemist, Cowles Chem Co, 52-53; sr chemist, Diamond Alkali Co, Ohio, 55-58; asst prof anal chem, Univ Ga, 58-63; assoc prof, 63-69, PROF ANAL CHEM, SCI & TECHNOL DIV, SOUTHERN ILL UNIV, EDWARDSVILLE, 69- *Mem:* Am Chem Soc. *Res:* Precipitation from homogeneous solution; development of analytical methods; use of radioactive tracers. *Mailing Add:* Sch Sci Eng Southern Ill Univ Edwardsville IL 62026

FIRSHEIN, WILLIAM, b New York, NY, Aug 28, 30; m 54, 71. MICROBIOLOGY. *Educ:* Brooklyn Col, BS, 52; Rutgers Univ, MS, 53, PhD, 58. *Prof Exp:* Microbiol physiologist, Camp Detrick, Md, 54-55; asst prof, 58-65, assoc prof, 65-70, chmn dept, 70-74, PROF BIOL, WESLEYAN UNIV, 70- *Concurrent Pos:* USPHS career develop award, 65-70. *Mem:* AAAS; Am Soc Microbiol; Am Soc Biochemists. *Res:* Microbial genetics; biochemistry; DNA synthesis. *Mailing Add:* Shanklin Lab Wesleyan Univ Middletown CT 06457

FIRST, MELVIN WILLIAM, b Boston, Mass, Dec 23, 14; m 38; c 2. PUBLIC HEALTH. *Educ:* Mass Inst Technol, BS, 36; Harvard Univ, MS, 47, ScD(indust hyg eng), 50; Environ Eng Intersoc Bd, dipl; Am Bd Indust Hyg, dipl. *Prof Exp:* Indust hyg engr, Dept of Health, Detroit, Mich, 36-39 & Mich State Health Dept, 39-41; res assoc, Sch Pub Health, Harvard Univ, 50-53; CONSULT ENGR, 53-; PROF ENVIRON HEALTH ENG, SCH PUB HEALTH, HARVARD UNIV, 71- *Concurrent Pos:* Assoc prof appl indust hyg, Harvard Univ, 62-71. *Mem:* Am Chem Soc; Nat Soc Prof Engrs; Am Indust Hyg Asn; Air Pollution Control Asn. *Res:* Air and gas purification equipment and techniques for control of industrial atmospheres and prevention of air pollution. *Mailing Add:* 295 Upland Ave Newton Highlands MA 02161

FIRST, NEAL L, b Ionia, Mich, Oct 8, 30; m 51; c 4. REPRODUCTIVE PHYSIOLOGY. *Educ:* Mich State Univ, BS, 52, MS, 57, PhD(animal physiol), 59. *Prof Exp:* Instr animal husb, Mich State Univ, 59-60; from asst prof to assoc prof meat & animal sci, 60-69, PROF MEAT & ANIMAL SCI, UNIV WIS-MADISON, 69- *Mem:* Am Soc Animal Sci; Am Genetic Asn; Am Soc Study Reproduction; Soc Study Fertil. *Res:* Reproductive physiology, especially of male livestock; artificial insemination. *Mailing Add:* 1717 Heim Ave Madison WI 53705

FIRSTBROOK, JOHN BRADSHAW, b Toronto, Ont, Oct 29, 19; m 45; c 3. PHYSIOLOGY, INTERNAL MEDICINE. *Educ:* Univ Toronto, MD, 45, PhD(physiol), 51; Royal Col Physicians & Surgeons, Can, cert internal med, 57. *Prof Exp:* Asst physiol, Banting & Best Dept Med Res, Toronto, 48-51, res assoc, 51-52; asst prof, Queen's Univ, Ont, 52-53; resident internal med, var hosps, 53-56; assoc dir field studies, Sch Hyg, Univ Toronto, 56-60, assoc prof physiol hyg, 60-63, prof appl physiol, 63-64; assoc dean fac med, Queen's Univ, Ont, 64-68; exec secy, Asn Can Med Cols, 68-70, exec dir, 70-75; DIR TRAINING & EVAL, ROYAL COL PHYSICIANS & SURGEONS CAN, 75- *Res:* Atherosclerosis; medical education. *Mailing Add:* 74 Stanley Ave Ottawa Can

FIRSTENBERGER, B(URNETT) G(EORGE), b Seneca, Kans, July 18, 17; m 43; c 3. ENGINEERING, CHEMISTRY. *Educ:* Univ Kans, BS, 39; Iowa State Col, PhD(chem eng), 42. *Prof Exp:* Chemist res & develop, Nat Aniline Div, 42-44, engr & group leader eng res, 45-48, asst operating supvr, Detergents Div, 48-53, chief chemist, Moundsville Plant, WVa, 53-57, supt quality control, 57-60, tech asst to plant mgr, 60-69, environ engr, Corp Eng Dept, 69-80, PRIN ENGR, ENVIRON ALLIED CHEM ENG DEPT, ALLIED CHEM CORP, MORRISTOWN, 80- *Mem:* Am Inst Chem Engrs. *Res:* Utilization of agricultural wastes; synthetic organics; synthetic detergents; design, construction and operation of pilot plants; process design for pollution abatement. *Mailing Add:* Pheasant Hill Dr Far Hills NJ 07931

FIRSTMAN, SIDNEY I(RVING), engineering, materials science, see previous edition

FIRTH, WILLIAM CHARLES, JR, b Buffalo, NY, Apr 9, 34; m 61; c 3. CHEMISTRY. *Educ:* Rensselaer Polytech Inst, BS, 56; Univ Colo, PhD(org chem), 60. *Prof Exp:* Asst gen chem, Univ Colo, 56-57; res chemist, Am Cyanamid Co, 60-64, sr res chemist, 64-76; RES SCIENTIST, UNION CAMP CORP, 76- *Mem:* Am Chem Soc; Tech Asn Pulp & Paper Indust. *Res:* Stereochemistry of reactions in a bridged polycyclic system; brominative decarboxylation reactions; fluorine chemistry; polymer synthesis; product and process development; bleaching technology; monomer synthesis. *Mailing Add:* 40 Galston Dr RD 4 Robbinsville NJ 08691

FISANICK, GEORGIA JEANNE, b New York, NY, Dec 29, 50. LASER-INDUCED CHEMISTRY. *Educ:* Polytech Inst Brooklyn, BS, 70, MS, 70; Princeton Univ, MA, 72, PhD(chem), 75. *Prof Exp:* MEM TECH STAFF, BELL LABS, 74- *Mem:* Am Chem Soc; Am Phys Soc; Sigma Xi. *Res:* Multiphoton ionization mass spectroscopy; chemical dynamics; non-linear laser absorption effects in molecules. *Mailing Add:* Bell Labs 600 Mountain Ave Murray Hill NJ

FISCH, CHARLES, b Poland, May 11, 21; nat US; m 43; c 3. MEDICINE. *Educ:* Ind Univ, AB, 42, MD, 44; Am Bd Internal Med, dipl, 53, cert cardiovasc med, 60. *Prof Exp:* Resident internal med, Vet Admin Hosp, Indianapolis, 48-50; fel gastroenterol, Marion County Gen Hosp, 50-51, fel cardiol, 51-53; prof med & dir, Cardiovasc Div, 63-80, DISTINGUISHED PROF MED, SCH MED, IND UNIV, 80-; DIR, KRANNERT HEART RES INST, 53- *Concurrent Pos:* Consult, La Rue Carter & St Vincent's Hosps; fel coun cardiol, Am Heart Asn. *Mem:* Am Fedn Clin Res; fel Am Col Physicians; Am Col Cardiol (pres 75-77); Am Physiol Soc. *Res:* Electrolytes and drugs in cardiovascular disease. *Mailing Add:* Ind Univ Sch of Med 1100 W Michigan Indianapolis IN 46202

FISCH, FOREST NORLAND, b Cope, Colo, July 6, 18; m 43; c 2. MATHEMATICS. *Educ:* Univ Northern Colo, AB, 40, MA, 47. *Prof Exp:* From asst prof to assoc prof math, Univ Northern Colo, 47-69, Chmn Dept, 66-69, prof math, 69-80; RETIRED. *Mem:* Math Asn Am. *Res:* General mathematics. *Mailing Add:* Dept of Math Univ of Northern Colo Greeley CO 80639

FISCH, HERBERT A(LBERT), b Cleveland, Ohio, Oct 6, 23; m 51; c 3. CHEMICAL ENGINEERING. *Educ:* Case Inst Technol, BSc, 44; Ohio State Univ, MSc, 48, PhD(chem eng), 51. *Prof Exp:* Asst chem eng, Ohio State Univ, 47-48; chem engr, Lubrizol Corp, Ohio, 48-49; chem engr, Gaseous Diffusion Plant, Union Carbide Nuclear Co, Tenn, 51-53; phys chemist, Oak Ridge Nat Lab, 53-56; chem engr, US Atomic Energy Comn, NY, 56-58; phys chemist, Knolls Atomic Power Lab, Gen Elec Co, 58-62, res metallurgist, Lamp Metals & Components Div, 62-67; PRIN ENGR, TRW, INC, 67- *Res:* Reactions between metals and gaseous or liquid environments; effects of nuclear radiation on corrosion; vacuum technology; high temperature oxidation/sulfidation resistant coatings; electrocoating. *Mailing Add:* 3590 Beacon Dr Cleveland OH 44122

FISCH, ROBERT O, b Budapest, Hungary, June 12, 25; m 53; c 1. PEDIATRICS. *Educ:* Med Sch Budapest, MD, 51. *Prof Exp:* Resident, 59-60, res fel, 61, from instr to assoc prof, 61-78, PROF PEDIAT, UNIV MINN, MINNEAPOLIS, 78- *Concurrent Pos:* Pediat coord, Child Develop Study, 61-63, dir, 63-65; dir, Phenylketonuric Clin, 61-, Child Care Clin, 72- & Speech, Language & Hearing Proj, 75-77. *Mem:* Am Acad Pediat; Asn Ambulatory Pediat Serv; Int Col Pediat; Am Pediat Soc. *Mailing Add:* Mayo Mem Hosp Univ Minn Box 384 Minneapolis MN 55455

FISCH, RONALD, Forest Hills, NY, Jan 24, 51. THEORETICAL CONDENSED MATTER PHYSICS. *Educ:* Cornell Univ, AB, 72; Univ Pa, PhD(physics), 77. *Prof Exp:* Res assoc, Princeton Univ, 77-80; ASST PROF PHYSICS, WASHINGTON UNIV, 80- *Concurrent Pos:* Consult, Bell Telephone Labs, 78-80. *Mem:* Am Phys Soc. *Res:* Theoretical condensed matter physics; phase transitions and cooperative phenomena; non-crystalline solids, glass and spin-glass. *Mailing Add:* Dept Physics Washington Univ St Louis MO 63130

FISCHANG, WILLIAM JOHN, entomology, see previous edition

FISCHBACH, DAVID BIBB, b Beckley, WVa, Oct 28, 26; m 52; c 2. MATERIALS SCIENCE ENGINEERING. *Educ:* Denison Univ, BA, 50; Yale Univ, MS, 51, PhD(physics), 55. *Prof Exp:* From res engr to sr res engr, Mat Sect, Jet Propulsion Lab, Calif Inst Technol, 55-61, res specialist, 61-69; res assoc prof, 69-77, RES PROF CERAMIC ENG, UNIV WASH, 77- *Concurrent Pos:* Assoc ed, Carbon J, 79- *Mem:* Am Phys Soc; Metall Soc; Am Inst Mining, Metall & Petrol Engrs; Am Ceramic Soc; Am Carbon Soc. *Res:* Properties and structure of carbons and graphite and other ceramic materials; internal friction; ferromagnetic materials; defects in solids. *Mailing Add:* Dept Mining Metall & Ceramic Eng Univ Wash FB-10 Seattle WA 98145

FISCHBACH, EPHRAIM, b Brooklyn, NY, Mar 29, 42; m 71; c 3. PHYSICS. *Educ:* Columbia Univ, AB, 63; Univ Pa, MS, 64, PhD(physics) 67. *Prof Exp:* Res assoc physics, Inst Theoret Physics, State Univ NY, Stony Brook, 67-69 & Niels Bohr Inst, Copenhagen, 69-70; asst prof, 70-74, assoc prof, 74-78, PROF PHYSICS, PURDUE UNIV, WEST LAFAYETTE, 79- *Concurrent Pos:* Vis assoc prof physics, Inst Theoret Physics, State Univ NY, Stony Brook, 78-79. *Mem:* Am Phys Soc. *Res:* Elementary particle theory. *Mailing Add:* Dept of Physics Purdue Univ West Lafayette IN 47907

FISCHBACH, FRITZ ALBERT, b Kenosha, Wis, June 16, 37; m 63; c 2. BIOPHYSICS, BIOCHEMISTRY. *Educ:* Univ Wis, BS, 59, MS, 61, PhD(biophys), 65. *Prof Exp:* NIH fels biophys, Univ Sheffield, 65-66, 67-68 & Purdue Univ, 66-67; asst prof physics, 68-70, assoc prof, 71-73, assoc prof ecosysts anal, 73-77, ASSOC PROF SCI & ENVIRON CHANGE, UNIV WIS-GREEN BAY, 77- *Mem:* AAAS; Biophys Soc. *Res:* Structure of large biological molecules, viruses and iron storage molecules; mineral structure of biological iron crystals; natural atmospheric minerals and aerosols. *Mailing Add:* 3044 Colleen Dr Green Bay WI 54301

FISCHBACH, GERALD DAVID, b New Rochelle, NY, Nov 15, 38. NEUROBIOLOGY. *Educ:* Colgate Univ, AB, 60; Cornell Univ, MD, 65. *Prof Exp:* Intern, Univ Wash Hosp, 65-66; sr surgeon, Lab Neurophysiol, Pub Health Serv, Nat Inst Neurol Dis & Stroke, NIH, 66-69; staff fel, Behav Biol Br, Nat Inst Child Health, 69-73; assoc prof pharmacol, Med Sch, Harvard Univ, 73-78, prof, 78-81; EDISON PROF NEUROBIOL & CHMN, DEPT ANAT & NEUROBIOL, SCH MED, WASHINGTON UNIV, 81- *Concurrent Pos:* Assoc ed, Develop Biol, 74-78, J Neurophysiol, 75-81; mem, Neurobiol B Study Sect, NIH, 78-80; sci adv bd, Am Paraplegia Found, 78- *Honors & Awards:* Mathilde Solowey Award in Neurosci, 75. *Mem:* Am Physiol Soc; Soc Neurosci; Soc Gen Physiologists; Am Soc Pharmacol & Exp Therapeut; Am Asn Anatomists. *Mailing Add:* Dept Anat & Neurobiol Sch Med Washington Univ St Louis MO 63130

FISCHBACH, HENRY, b New York, NY, May 2, 14; m 45; c 3. CHEMISTRY. *Educ:* Ind Univ, AB, 35, AM, 36, PhD(inorg chem), 38. *Prof Exp:* Asst chem, Ind Univ, 35-38; dir educ prog, Joseph E Seagram & Sons, Inc, 39; food & drug inspector, Food & Drug Admin, Dept Health, Educ & Welfare, 39-41, res chemist, Washington, DC, 41-45, in chg chem res antibiotics, Med Div, 45-53, Antibiotics & Alkaloids Div Pharmaceut Chem, 53-56, asst to dir, Bur Biol & Phys Sci, 56-59, dir, Div Food, 59-69, Div Pesticides, Bur Sci, 69-71, Dir Off Sci, Bur Foods, 71-72, asst dir phys sci, 72-73, assoc dir, 74; RETIRED. *Concurrent Pos:* Secy, Tech Comt Lab Equipment & Supplies, Fed Specifications Bd, 48-54; mem panel, Bd US Civil Serv Exam, 57-; mem, Adv Panel & vchmn, Chem Comt, Food Chems Codex, Food Protection Comt, Nat Acad Sci-Nat Res Coun, 61-65, chmn, 65-; chmn, Trace Substances Comn, Int Union Pure & Appl Chem, 64-73; mem, Subcomt Ref Mat, Div Anal Chem, Nat Acad Sci-Nat Res Coun, 65-; chmn, Joint Asn Off Anal Chem-Am Oil Chemists Soc-Am Asn Cereal Chemists, Mycotoxin Comt, 65-74. *Honors & Awards:* Superior Serv Award, Dept Health, Educ & Welfare, 61, Distinguished Serv Award, 67. *Mem:* AAAS; Am Chem Soc; fel Asn Off Anal Chem; Inst Food Technologists. *Res:* Antibiotics; food chemistry; chlorophyllins; continuous ascending chromatography; aflatoxins; pesticides; analytical research. *Mailing Add:* 5627 Bradley Blvd Alexandria VA 22311

FISCHBACH, JOSEPH W(INSTON), b New York, NY, Nov 12, 17; m 45; c 4. ENGINEERING. *Educ:* City Col New York, BME, 38; NY Univ, MME, 44, MAE, 46, DrEngSc, 52. *Prof Exp:* Marine engr submarines, Navy Yard, NH, 39-41, mech engr, Brooklyn Navy Yard, 41-44; ord engr rocket res, Ord Ballistics Res Labs, 45-46, chief rocket br, 56-59, mathematician, Comput Lab, 49-52, chief anal & comput br, 52-54; asst chief engr, US Time Corp, 54-55; partner, Fischbach, Hamilton & Co, 55-56; mgr consult, Booz, Allen & Hamilton, 56-59; PRES, FISCHBACH, McCOACH & ASSOCS, INC, 59- *Mem:* Am Soc Mech Engrs; Opers Res Soc Am; Asn Comput Mach; Inst Mgt Sci. *Res:* Management and administration; mergers; organization studies; cost reductions; marketing; general surveys of operations systems and procedures; inventory, production, cost and management control; feasibility and application for electronic data processing; operations research; gradient methods for solution of differential equations; aerodynamics; rocket research; automatic processes and servo control; rockets and missiles. *Mailing Add:* Fischbach & McCoach & Assocs Inc 30 E 42nd St New York NY 10017

FISCHBACK, BRYANT C, b Alhambra, Calif, Nov 29, 26; m 50; c 3. ORGANIC CHEMISTRY. *Educ:* Univ Calif, Los Angeles, BS, 49. *Prof Exp:* Chemist, Res Dept, 49-56, proj leader, 56-68, tech res & develop mgr, Prod Depts-West, 68-72, res mgr, 72-79, MGR ENVIRON SERV, WESTERN

DIV, DOW CHEM USA, 79- *Mem:* Am Chem Soc; Royal Soc Chem. *Res:* Organic synthesis of new insecticides; herbicides; general agricultural chemicals; coccidiostats; animal health products; pharmaceuticals; mechanism of nitration reactions; synthesis of ore flotation agents; research and development of secondary oil recovery, mining and environmental control systems. *Mailing Add:* Dow Chem USA PO Box 1398 Pittsburg CA 94565

FISCHBARG, JORGE, b Buenos Aires, Arg, Aug 14, 35; nat US; m 64; c 2. PHYSIOLOGY, OPHTHALMOLOGY. *Educ:* Univ Buenos Aires, BS, 53, MD, 62; Univ Chicago, PhD(physiol), 71. *Prof Exp:* Asst biophys, Sch Med, Univ Buenos Aires, 62-64; trainee ophthal, Eye Res Lab, Univ Louisville, 64-65; trainee math biol & physiol, Univ Chicago, 65-70; asst prof ophthal, 70-73, asst prof physiol, 73-78, ASSOC PROF PHYSIOL & OPHTHAL, COLUMBIA UNIV, 78- *Concurrent Pos:* Vis Scientist, Dept Biol, Centre D'Energie Nucleaire, Saclay, France, 73 & 78; res career develop award, Nat Eye Inst & NIH, 75-80, mem visual sci A study sect, Div Res Grants, 80- *Mem:* Am Physiol Soc; NY Acad Sci; Biophys Soc; Asn Res Vision & Ophthal. *Res:* Transport of fluid and electrolytes across and electrophysiology of epithelial cells and membranes; theoretical modeling of fluid transport and transepithelial osmosis; physiology of cornea and ciliary body; fluorometry of redox states in corneal cells. *Mailing Add:* Dept of Ophthal Columbia Univ New York NY 10032

FISCHBECK, HELMUT J, b Tübingen, Ger, Oct 19, 28; m 55; c 2. PHYSICS. *Educ:* Univ Heidelberg, MA, 55; Ind Univ, PhD(physics), 60. *Prof Exp:* Instr physics, Univ Mich, 60-61, asst prof, 62-66; assoc prof, 66-71, PROF PHYSICS, UNIV OKLA, 71-, CHMN ENG PHYSICS, 80- *Concurrent Pos:* Vis scientist, Argonne Nat Lab, 75. *Mem:* Am Phys Soc; Am Soc Eng Educ. *Res:* Nuclear spectroscopy; atomic physics; solid state physics. *Mailing Add:* Dept of Physics Univ of Okla Norman OK 73069

FISCHBECK, K(ENNETH) H(ENRY), b Wallington, NJ, Mar 30, 24; m 47; c 3. ENGINEERING. *Educ:* Mass Inst Technol, BS, 47; Wayne State Univ, MS, 54; Univ Pa, MS, 58, PhD(elec eng), 61. *Prof Exp:* Sr engr, Res Labs, Bendix Aviation Corp, 47-54; mem tech staff defense elec prod, Radio Corp Am, 54-66, mgr printing res, RCA Labs, 66-68, staff tech adv, RCA Corp, 68-76; MGR, INK JET TECHNOL, WEBSTER RES CTR, XEROX CORP, 76- *Mem:* AAAS; Am Phys Soc; Inst Elec & Electronics Engrs. *Res:* Automata and control; nuclear technology; energy conversion; electronic data processing; graphic arts. *Mailing Add:* Webster Res Ctr 1341 W Mockingbird Lane Dallas TX 75220

FISCHEL, DAVID, b Du Bois, Pa, Sept 12, 36; m 60; c 3. ASTROPHYSICS. *Educ:* Brown Univ, ScB, 58; Ind Univ, MA, 61, PhD(astrophys), 63. *Prof Exp:* Res scientist astrophys, Space Sci Div, Ames Res Ctr, 63-65, head anal sect, 70-78, RES SCIENTIST ASTROPHYS LAB ASTRON & SOLAR PHYSICS, DATA ANAL & OBSERV BR, GODDARD SPACE FLIGHT CTR, NASA, 65-, SR PHYS SCIENTIST & LAND SAT-D ASSESSMENT SYST SCI MGR, 78- *Mem:* Asn Comput Mach; Soc Photo-Optical Instrument Engrs; Int Astron Union; Sigma Xi. *Res:* Theoretical model stellar atmospheres and interiors; image processing; numerical methods for electronic computers; plasma thermodynamics. *Mailing Add:* Code 932 Goddard Space Flight Ctr NASA Greenbelt MD 20771

FISCHEL, EDWARD ELLIOT, b New York, NY, July 29, 20; m 43; c 2. INTERNAL MEDICINE. *Educ:* Columbia Univ, BA, 41, MD, 44, ScD(med), 48. *Prof Exp:* Asst physician, Presby Hosp, 47-54; assoc clin prof, Albert Einstein Col Med, 57-69; assoc clin prof med, Columbia Univ, 69-72; prof med, Albert Einstein Col Med, 72-81; dir, Dept Med, Bronx-Lebanon Hosp Ctr, 54-80; PROF MED, UNIV CONN SCH MED, 80-; CHIEF, DEPT MED, MT SINAI HOSP, HARTFORD, 80- *Concurrent Pos:* Assoc, Dept Med, Columbia Univ, 50-55; chmn med admin coun, Arthritis Found, 68-69; mem med & sci adv comt, Arthritis & Rheumatism Found; mem coun rheumatic fever & congenital heart dis, Am Heart Asn. *Mem:* AAAS; Am Soc Clin Invest; Am Soc Exp Biol & Med; AMA; Am Rheumatism Asn (pres, 68-69). *Res:* Immunochemistry; hypersensitivity reaction; rheumatic diseases; nephritis; inflammation; serum complement activity; immunosuppression by cortisone. *Mailing Add:* Mt Sinai Hosp 500 Blue Hills Ave Hartford CT 06112

FISCHELL, ROBERT E, b New York, NY, Feb 10, 29; m 51; c 3. SPACE PHYSICS, BIOMEDICAL ENGINEERING. *Educ:* Duke Univ, BSME, 51; Univ Md, MS, 53. *Prof Exp:* Physicist, US Naval Ord Lab, Md, 51-56; prin staff physicist, Emerson Res Labs, 56-59; sr staff physicist, 59-60, proj supvr, 60-64, chief engr, Space Dept, 73-81, GROUP SUPVR, APPL PHYSICS LAB, JOHNS HOPKINS UNIV, 64-, PRIN STAFF PHYSICIST, 63-, ASST HEAD, SPACE DEPT, 78-, CHIEF TECHNOL TRANSFER, 81- *Concurrent Pos:* Consult, US Air Force, 59-61; mem ad hoc comt, NASA Dept Defense, 63; consult, French Space Agency, 65; prin proj scientist, Navy Navig Satellites, 69-; consult, NASA Hq, 71; mem space comt, Int Fedn Automatic Control, 71-78; dir, Pacesetter Syst, Inc, 70- & Patlex Corp, 81- *Honors & Awards:* Award, Am Soc Mech Engrs, 63; three IR-100 Awards, Indust Res Mag, 67-70. *Mem:* Am Inst Aeronaut & Astronaut; Am Soc Mech Engrs; Inst Elec & Electronics Engrs; Am Heart Asn. *Res:* Altitude control systems for earth satellites; space electric power systems; cardiac pacemakers; implantable biomedical instrumentation; electronic pancreas. *Mailing Add:* Johns Hopkins Univ Appl Physics Lab Laurel MO 20707

FISCHER, (ALBERT) ALAN, b Indianapolis, Ind, June 30, 28; m; c 4. FAMILY MEDICINE. *Educ:* Ind Univ, MD, 52; Am Bd Family Pract, dipl. *Prof Exp:* Intern, St Vincent Hosp, Indianapolis, 52-53; pvt pract, 53-70; dir family pract residency prog, St Vincent Hosp, 69-75; PROF FAMILY MED & CHMN DEPT, IND UNIV, INDIANAPOLIS, 74- *Concurrent Pos:* Med dir, Lakeview Convalescent Ctr; mem, Nat Joint Pract Comn, Nat Acad Sci. *Mem:* Inst of Med of Nat Acad Sci; Am Acad Family Physicians (vpres, 71-72); Sigma Xi; Int Acad Family Physicians (pres, 64-66); AMA. *Mailing Add:* Ind Univ Sch of Med 1100 W Michigan St Indianapolis IN 46202

FISCHER, ALBERT G, b Ilmenau, Ger, July 5, 28; US citizen; m 56; c 3. SOLID STATE ELECTRONICS. *Educ:* Univ Giessen, Diplom-Physiker, 55, Dr phil nat, 57. *Prof Exp:* Scientist, Lamp Div, Gen Elec Co, 58-59; mem tech staff, RCA Labs, 59-71; adv scientist, Res & Develop Ctr, Westinghouse Elec Corp, 71-72; PROF ELEC ENG, UNIV DORTMUND, WGER, 73- *Mem:* Electrochem Soc; Inst Elec & Electronics Engrs. *Res:* Electro luminescence; materials science; single crystal growth; films; liquid crystals; thin-film transistors. *Mailing Add:* Dept Elec Eng PO Box 500500 46 Dortmund 50 West Germany

FISCHER, ALBERT KARL, b Newark, NJ, Oct 15, 31; m 59; c 3. PHYSICAL INORGANIC CHEMISTRY, MORPHOLOGICAL ELECTROCHEMISTRY. *Educ:* NY Univ, BA, 53; Harvard Univ, MA, 55, PhD(chem), 58. *Prof Exp:* Res chemist, Union Carbide Metals Co Div, Union Carbide Corp, 57-60 & Union Carbide Chem Co Div, 60-62; assoc chemist, 62-73, CHEMIST, ARGONNE NAT LAB, 73- *Mem:* Am Chem Soc. *Res:* Metal carbonyls; organometallics; fused salt and liquid metal chemistry; surface chemistry of liquid metals; morphology of electrodeposition. *Mailing Add:* Chem Eng Div Argonne Nat Lab Argonne IL 60439

FISCHER, ALFRED GEORGE, b Rothenburg, Ger, Dec 10, 20; US citizen; m 39; c 3. GEOLOGY. *Educ:* Univ Wis, BA, 39, MA, 40; Columbia Univ, PhD, 50. *Prof Exp:* Instr geol, Va Polytech Inst, 41-43; geologist, Stanolind Oil & Gas Co, Kans, 43-44, Fla, 44-46; instr geol, Univ Rochester, 47-48; from instr to asst prof, Univ Kans, 48-51; sr geologist, Int Petrol Co, Peru, 51-56; from asst prof to assoc prof, 56-63, PROF GEOL, PRINCETON UNIV, 63- *Concurrent Pos:* Guggenheim fel, 69-70. *Mem:* Geol Soc Am; Soc Econ Paleont & Mineral; Paleont Soc; Am Asn Petrol Geol. *Res:* Invertebrate paleontology; paleoecology; historical geology; carbonate sediments; sedimentation. *Mailing Add:* Dept of Geol & Geophys Sci Princeton Univ Princeton NJ 08540

FISCHER, C RUTHERFORD, b New York, NY, June 21, 34; m 62; c 1. MOLECULAR PHYSICS, SOLID STATE PHYSICS. *Educ:* City Col New York, BS, 54; Yale Univ, MS, 55, PhD(physics), 60. *Prof Exp:* Asst prof physics, NMex State Univ, 59-61 & Adelphi Univ, 61-64; assoc prof, 64-70, PROF PHYSICS, QUEENS COL, NY, 70- *Concurrent Pos:* NSF grant, Adelphi Univ, 62-64; consult, US Army Res Off, Durham, 70-71 & Sandia Labs, 75- *Mem:* Am Phys Soc. *Res:* Molecular structure and spectra; point defects in ionic crystal; ionic interactions; optical properties of solids; fast reactions in solids. *Mailing Add:* Dept Physics Queens Col Flushing NY 11367

FISCHER, CHARLOTTE FROESE, b Ukraine, Russia, Sept 21, 29; nat US; m 67; c 1. APPLIED MATHEMATICS. *Educ:* Univ BC, BA, 52, MA, 54; Cambridge Univ, PhD(appl math), 57. *Prof Exp:* From asst prof to prof math, Univ BC, 57-67; prof appl anal & comput sci, Univ Waterloo, 67-68; vis prof, Pa State Univ, 68-69, prof comput sci, 69-72, prof appl math, 72-75, prof comput sci, 74-79; PROF COMPUT SCI, VANDERBILT UNIV, 80- *Concurrent Pos:* Programmer, numerical analyst & consult, Pac Oceanog Group, BC, 57-59; res fel, Harvard, 63; Sloan fel, 64; grant, Nat Res Coun Can, 64-76, US Dept of Energy, 77. *Mem:* Asn Comput Mach; Soc Indust & Appl Math. *Res:* Atomic structure calculations; numerical analysis. *Mailing Add:* Vanderbilt Univ PO Box 6035 B Nashville TN 37235

FISCHER, DAVID JOHN, b Jefferson City, Mo, Apr 30, 28; m 54; c 2. MATERIALS & PROCESS RESEARCH, QUALITY ASSURANCE. *Educ:* Univ Mo, BS, 50, MS, 52, PhD(phys chem), 54. *Prof Exp:* Proj group leader, Polymer Res Lab, Dow Corning Corp, 56-59, dept supvr, Hyper-Pure Silicon Div, 59-62; sr chemist, Midwest Res Inst, 62-65; mgr microcircuits res dept, Corning Glass Works, 65-68, mgr spec projs, Advan Mkt Develop, 68-69, res assoc, 69-70, mgr, Bio-Organic Develop, 70-73, phys scientist, Corning Mus Glass, 73-75; dir res & develop, Ophthalmic Group, Milton Roy Co, 75-79; pres, Universal Res & Develop Corp, 79-81; sr res advr, Gulf South Res Inst, 81-82; CHIEF QUAL ENG, MICHOUD DIV, MARTIN MARIETTA AEROSPACE, 82- *Mem:* Am Chem Soc; Electrochem Soc; Am Inst Conserv Hist & Artistic Works; Asn Advan Med Instrumentation. *Res:* Quality engineering, aerospace materials and processes; renewable energy sources, anaerobic digestion for producing methone; lasers for spectrophotometric measurements and machining plastics. *Mailing Add:* Martin Marietta Aerospace Michoud Div Mail 3770 PO Box 29304 New Orleans LA 70189

FISCHER, DAVID LLOYD, b Calif, June 7, 28; m 56. NUCLEAR PHYSICS. *Educ:* Univ Calif, BS, 50, PhD(physics), 56. *Prof Exp:* PHYSICIST, ATOMIC POWER EQUIP DEPT, NUCLEAR ENERGY PRODS DIV, GEN ELEC CO, 56- *Mem:* Am Nuclear Soc. *Res:* Reactor physics. *Mailing Add:* 6834 Hampton Dr San Jose CA 95120

FISCHER, DIANA BRADBURY, b Mt Vernon, NY, May 5, 34. STATISTICS, EPIDEMIOLOGY. *Educ:* Mt Holyoke Col, BA, 56; Yale Univ, MPH, 66, PhD(biomet), 74. *Prof Exp:* Res asst endocrinol, Med Sch, Harvard Univ, 56-63, comput programmer biostatist, Sch Pub Health, 63-64; from sr programmer statistician to mgr appln prog, Comput Ctr, Yale Univ, 66-71; res assoc fac statistician, Dept Epidemiol Pub Health & Yale Comprehensive Cancer Ctr, 74-75, DIR EPIDEMIOL STATIST UNIT, YALE COMPREHENSIVE CANCER CTR & ASST PROF PUB HEALTH, SCH MED, YALE UNIV, 76- *Mem:* Am Statist Asn; Biomet Soc; Sigma Xi. *Res:* Statistical methods for time-dose relationships in radiotherapy; life table and survivorship analysis with covariates; clinical trials methodology; computer methodology. *Mailing Add:* 82 Pickwick Rd New Haven CT 06517

FISCHER, EDMOND H, b Shanghai, China, Apr 6, 20; m 48; c 2. BIOCHEMISTRY. *Educ:* State Col Geneva, Mat Fed, 39; Univ Geneva, Lic es Sc, 43, dipl, 44, PhD(chem), 47. *Prof Exp:* Asst org chem labs, Univ Geneva, 46-48, Swiss Found res fel chem, 48, privat-docent, 50, Rockefeller Found res fel, 50-53; from asst prof to assoc prof biochem, 53-61, PROF BIOCHEM, UNIV WASH, 61- *Concurrent Pos:* Lederle med fac award,

56-59. *Honors & Awards:* Warner Medal, Swiss Chem Soc, 52; Jaubert Prize, 68. *Mem:* Nat Acad Sci; Am Acad Arts & Sci; Am Chem Soc; Am Soc Biol Chemists; Swiss Chem Soc. *Res:* Enzymology; carbohydrate metabolism; protein structure. *Mailing Add:* 5540 NE Windermere Rd Seattle WA 98105

FISCHER, EDWARD G(EORGE), b New York, NY, Mar 31, 16; m 44; c 4. MECHANICAL ENGINEERING. *Educ:* Cooper Union, BS, 36, MS, 39, PhD(math eng), 46. *Prof Exp:* CONSULT ENGR, RES LAB, WESTINGHOUSE ELEC CORP, 36- *Concurrent Pos:* Instr, Grad Sch, Univ Pittsburgh, 46-59. *Honors & Awards:* Cert Appreciation, US Army Corps Engrs. *Mem:* Am Soc Mech Engrs; Soc Exp Stress Anal; Inst Environ Sci; Seismol Soc Am; Inst Elec & Electronics Engrs. *Res:* Vibration; shock; noise; seismic design. *Mailing Add:* 5525 Third St Verona PA 15147

FISCHER, EUGENE CHARLES, b New York, NY, Apr 7, 40; m 64; c 4. RESEARCH ADMINISTRATION, MARINE BIOLOGY. *Educ:* Iona Col, BS, 61; St John's Col, NY, MS, 63, PhD(marine microbiol), 66. *Prof Exp:* Staff scientist microbiol, US Naval Appl Sci Lab, 64-65; res oceanogr, 65-70, HEAD OCEAN ENVIRON BR, US NAVAL SHIP RES & DEVELOP LAB, ANNAPOLIS, 70- *Honors & Awards:* Cmndg Officer & Dir Award, US Naval Appl Sci Lab, 66. *Mem:* Am Soc Microbiol; Sigma Xi. *Res:* Deep ocean-high pressure microbial physiology; marine fouling; pollution abatement; polymer chemistry; antifouling materials. *Mailing Add:* 107 Chautaugua Rd Indian Hills Arnold MD 21012

FISCHER, FERDINAND JOSEPH, b Kansas City, Mo, June 13, 40; m 62; c 1. ENGINEERING MECHANICS, APPLIED MATHEMATICS. *Educ:* Univ Kans, BS, 62; Rice Univ, MS, 64; Harvard Univ, MA, 65, PhD(appl math), 68. *Prof Exp:* Res asst eng mech, Harvard Univ, 66-68; mathematician, 67-70, sr res engr, 70-73, staff res engr, 73-75, staff engr,75-78, staff supvr, 79-81, SR STAFF SUPVR, SHELL DEVELOP CO, 81- *Concurrent Pos:* Lectr, Univ Houston, 68-71. *Mem:* Am Soc Mech Engrs. *Res:* Elastic shell theory; continuum mechanics; numerical analysis; ocean engineering. *Mailing Add:* 13130 Rummel Creek Houston TX 77079

FISCHER, FREDERICK THOMAS, b Carmel, NY, Mar 15, 28; m 55; c 2. ECONOMIC GEOLOGY, HYDROGEOLOGY. *Educ:* Yale Univ, BS, 49. *Prof Exp:* Geologist oil & gas res, US Geol Surv, 49-50; geologist, B H Putnam & Assocs, 50-60; mgr Tenn explor, 60-77, CHIEF GEOLOGIST, NJ ZINC CO, DIV GULF & WESTERN INDUST, 77- *Mem:* Soc Econ Geologists; Am Asn Mining, Metall & Petrol Engrs. *Res:* Investigation of base-metal deposits with emphasis on size, configuration, modes of emplacement as guides to exploration. *Mailing Add:* Gulf & Western Natural Resources Group 65 E Elizabeth Ave Nashville TN 37239

FISCHER, GEORGE A, b Cleveland, Ohio, Mar 27, 39; m 62; c 3. BIOCHEMISTRY, CLINICAL CHEMISTRY. *Educ:* Univ Detroit, BS, 61, MS, 64, PhD(biochem), 67; Am Bd Clin Chem, dipl, 72. *Prof Exp:* CLIN CHEMIST, HARPER HOSP, 66-, DIR CHEM, GRACE HOSP, 75- *Mem:* AAAS; Am Chem Soc; Nat Acad Clin Biochem; Am Asn Clin Chemists; Clin Radioassay Soc. *Res:* Immunochemistry; mechanisms and chemistry of hypertension; radioligand binding analyses; laboratory computerization. *Mailing Add:* Harper-Grace Hosp 3990 John R St Detroit MI 48201

FISCHER, GEORGE J, b Bronx, NY, Mar 30, 25; m 48; c 2. METALLURGICAL ENGINEERING. *Educ:* Polytech Inst Brooklyn, BMetE, 49, MMetE, 53. *Prof Exp:* Instr metall, Polytech Inst Brooklyn, 48-50; plant metallurgist, Western Elec Co, 50-53; dept head, Sam Tour & Co, 53-55; from asst prof to assoc prof, 55-65, admin officer, Div Metall Eng, 61-71, head dept, 71-76, dean student serv, 76-80, PROF ENG METALL, POLYTECH INST BROOKLYN, 65- *Concurrent Pos:* Res grants, Int Nickel Co, 60-61 & Curtiss-Wright Corp, 62-65; NSF res grant, 63-65. *Mem:* Am Soc Metals; Am Inst Mining, Metall & Petrol Engrs; Am Soc Testing & Mat. *Res:* Physical metallurgy; weldability criteria of metallic materials. *Mailing Add:* Metall Eng Dept 333 Jay St Brooklyn NY 11201

FISCHER, GEORGE J, b Chicago, Ill, Aug 6, 18; m 48; c 1. PHYSICS. *Educ:* Univ Chicago, BS, 46, MS, 50; Univ Iowa, PhD(physics), 57. *Prof Exp:* Instr physics, Coe Col, 51-54; asst, Univ Iowa, 55-56; asst physicist, Reactor Eng Div, Argonne Nat Lab, 56-58, assoc physicist, 58-69, sr physicist, 69-73, head accident anal & safety eval group, Reactor Anal & Safety Div, 66-73; head, Fast Reactor Safety Div, 73-76, head, Fast-Mixed Spectrum Reactor Concept Group, 77-79, HEAD, ADV BREEDER CONCEPTS GROUP, BROOKHAVEN NAT LAB, 79- *Concurrent Pos:* US Nuclear Regulatory Comn rep, French AEC, 75-76. *Mem:* Am Phys Soc; Am Nuclear Soc. *Res:* Theoretical and experimental reactor physics and safety studies. *Mailing Add:* Dept Nuclear Energy Brookhaven Nat Lab Upton NY 11973

FISCHER, GERHARD EMIL, b Berlin, Ger, Mar 1, 28; nat US; m 51; c 2. HIGH ENERGY PHYSICS. *Educ:* Univ Toronto, BASc, 49; Univ Calif, PhD(physics), 54. *Prof Exp:* From instr to asst prof physics, Columbia Univ, 54-59; res fel, Harvard Univ, 59-63, sr res assoc, 63-65; STAFF MEM STANFORD LINEAR ACCELERATOR CTR, 65- *Concurrent Pos:* Vis scientist, DESY, Hamburg, Ger, 74 & CERN, Geneva, Switz, 75. *Mem:* Am Phys Soc. *Res:* Storage ring physics. *Mailing Add:* Stanford Linear Accelerator Ctr Box 4349 Stanford CA 94305

FISCHER, GLENN ALBERT, b Pritchett, Colo, Nov 18, 22; m 46; c 2. GENETICS, PHARMACOLOGY. *Educ:* Univ Colo, BS, 49; Calif Inst Technol, MS, 51, PhD(genetics), 54. *Prof Exp:* Res assoc, Univ Mich, 54; asst res prof, Sch Med, George Washington Univ, 55; asst prof pharmacol, Univ PR, 55; from asst prof to assoc prof, Sch Med, Yale Univ, 58-69; PROF BIOCHEM PHARMACOL, BORWN UNIV, 69- *Mailing Add:* Dept of Biol & Med Sci Brown Univ Providence RI 02912

FISCHER, GRACE MAE, b Weatherly, Pa, Nov 25, 27. PHYSIOLOGY, CARDIOVASCULAR DISEASE. *Educ:* Bucknell Univ, BS, 49; Temple Univ, MD, 53; Drexel Univ, MS, 64. *Prof Exp:* Res assoc, 66-67; asst prof, 69-72, ASSOC PROF PHYSIOL, DEPT PHYSIOL, SCH MED, UNIV PA, 72- *Concurrent Pos:* Nat Heart Inst fel, 63-64, spec fel, 65-66; res fel cardiovasc res, Bockus Res Inst & Dept Physiol, Sch Med, Univ Pa, 64-66. *Mem:* Am Heart Asn; Am Physiol Soc. *Res:* Arterial connective tissue, especially chemical and endocrine effects on arterial wall properties and collagen and elastin metabolism in arterial wall; regulation of cardiovascular processes. *Mailing Add:* Dept Physiol Univ Pa Philadelphia PA 19104

FISCHER, HARRY WILLIAM, b St Louis, Mo, June 4, 21; m 43; c 5. RADIOLOGY. *Educ:* Univ Chicago, BS, 43, MD, 45. *Prof Exp:* Intern surg, Barnes Hosp, St Louis, 45-46; resident, Wash Univ, 48-51; resident radiol, St Louis City Hosp, 52-54, mem teaching staff, 56; pvt pract, 54-56; from asst prof to prof radiol, Col Med, Univ Iowa, 56-66; prof, Med Sch, Univ Mich, 66-71; PROF RADIOL & CHMN DEPT, SCH MED, UNIV ROCHESTER, 71-; RADIOLOGIST IN CHIEF, STRONG MEM HOSP, 71- *Concurrent Pos:* Fel, Wash Univ, 48-51; fel pediat surg, Children's Mem Hosp, Chicago, 51-52; dir dept radiol, Wayne County Gen Hosp, 66-71. *Mem:* AMA; Am Col Radiol; Radiol Soc NAm; Asn Univ Radiol; Soc Exp Biol & Med. *Res:* Contrast visualization of liver, spleen and lymph nodes; toxicity of contrast media; excretion of contrast media by liver and kidney; adherence of contrast media to mucosal surfaces. *Mailing Add:* Univ of Rochester Sch of Med Dept of Radiol Rochester NY 14642

FISCHER, HUGO B, b Lakehurst, NJ, Mar 16, 37; m 62; c 2. CIVIL ENGINEERING. *Educ:* Calif Inst Technol, BS, 58, MS, 63, PhD(civil eng), 66. *Prof Exp:* From asst prof to assoc prof, 66-74, PROF CIVIL ENG, UNIV CALIF, BERKELEY, 74-, CHMN SANIT, ENVIRON, COASTAL & HYDRAUL ENG, 81- *Concurrent Pos:* Res hydraul engr, US Geol Surv, 66-76; NATO fel, Univ Cambridge, 70-71; guest investr, Woods Hole Ocean Inst, 77. *Honors & Awards:* Lorenz G Straub Award, 66; J James R Croes Medal, Am Soc Civil Engrs, 69, Hilgard Hydraul Prize, 71 & Huber Res Prize, 74. *Mem:* Am Soc Civil Engrs; Am Geophys Union; Int Asn Hydraul Res. *Res:* Hydraulic aspects of pollutant dispersion in rivers, reservoirs, estuaries and coastal areas. *Mailing Add:* Dept of Civil Eng Univ of Calif Berkeley CA 94720

FISCHER, IMRE A, b Budapest, Hungary, Apr 12, 35; US citizen; m 61. CLINICAL BIOCHEMISTRY, QUALITY CONTROL. *Educ:* Univ Louvain, MS, 62, PhD(microbial biochem), 65. *Prof Exp:* Res asst microbial biochem, Univ Louvain, 62-65; res microbiologist, Univ Calif, Davis, 65-67; res biochemist, Sch Med, Univ Calif, Los Angeles, 67-69; biochemist, Xerox/ Med Diag Opers, 69-70; res assoc, Harbor Gen Hosp, Torrance, Calif & Sch Med, Univ Calif, Los Angeles, 70; tech dir, Bio-Technics Labs, Inc, Los Angeles, 70-72; CLIN BIOCHEMIST, LONG BEACH GEN HOSP, CALIF, 72-; ASST PROF PATH IN RESIDENCE, UNIV CALIF MED SCH, LOS ANGELES, 78-, HEAD, EMERGENCY LAB SERV COUN HARBOR, MED CTR, 78- *Concurrent Pos:* Asst prof, Calif State Univ, Dominguez Hills, 74-79. *Honors & Awards:* Clinical Chemists Recognition Award, Am Asn Clin Chemists, 81. *Mem:* Fel Am Soc Qual Control; Am Asn Clin Chem; fel Asn Clin Scientists; fel Nat Acad Clin Biochem; fel Inst Advan Eng. *Res:* Enzyme isolation and kinetics; red blood cell aging; medical diagnostics; clinical chemistry; laboratory medicine; biomedical quality control and assurance; laboratory management. *Mailing Add:* Dept Path Harbor-UCLA Med Ctr 1000 W Carson St Torrance CA 90509

FISCHER, IRENE KAMINKA, b Vienna, Austria, July 27, 07; US citizen; m 30; c 2. GEODESY. *Educ:* Univ Vienna, MA, 31. *Hon Degrees:* Hon Doctorate, Univ Karlsruhe, 75. *Prof Exp:* Mathematician, Geoid Br, Defense Mapping Agency Topog Ctr, 52-58, geodesist, 58-62; supvry geodesist, 62-65, supvry res geodesist, Geod Br, 65-77, br chief, 62-77; RETIRED. *Concurrent Pos:* Mem, Int Union Geod & Geophys, 54- & comt SAm datum, Pan-Am Inst Geog & Hist; mem spec study group hist geod, Int Asn Geod. *Honors & Awards:* Meritorious Civilian Serv Award, Dept of Army, 57, Bronze Leaf Cluster, 66, Res & Develop Achievement Award, 66 & Decoration for Except Civilian Serv, 67; Distinguished Civilian Serv Award, Dept of Defense, 67; Outstanding Career Woman, Defense Mapping Agency, 75, Meritorious Serv Medal, 77; Nat Civil Serv League Career Award, 76; Voto de Aplauso, Pan Am Inst Geog & Hist, 65, 77. *Mem:* Nat Acad Eng; fel Am Geophys Union; Int Asn Geod. *Res:* Figure of the earth; shape of the geoid; parallax and distance of the moon; geodetic world datum; Fischer ellipsoid; mercury datum for space flights; Mercury, Gemini and Apollo projects; South American datum of 1969; deflections at sea; mean sea level slopes; history of geodesy. *Mailing Add:* 301 Philadelphia Ave Takoma Park MD 20912

FISCHER, IRWIN, b New York, NY, Nov 23, 27; m 54; c 2. MATHEMATICS. *Educ:* City Col New York, BS, 48; Harvard Univ, AM, 49, PhD(math), 53. *Prof Exp:* Mathematician, Air Force Cambridge Res Ctr, 52-54; instr math, Univ Minn, 54-55 & Dartmouth Col, 55-57; from asst prof to assoc prof, 57-69, PROF MATH, UNIV COLO, BOULDER, 69- *Mem:* Am Math Soc. *Res:* Algebraic geometry. *Mailing Add:* Dept of Math Univ of Colo Boulder CO 80309

FISCHER, JAMES JOSEPH, b Hazleton, Pa, Aug 17, 36. RADIOBIOLOGY, RADIOTHERAPY. *Educ:* Yale Univ, BS, 57; Harvard Med Sch, MD, 61; Harvard Univ, PhD(pharmacol), 64. *Hon Degrees:* MA, Yale Univ, 73. *Prof Exp:* PROF THERAPEUT RADIOL, SCH MED, YALE UNIV, 72- *Concurrent Pos:* Nat Cancer Inst clin & res fel radiother, Yale Univ, 65-68; consult, West Haven Vet Admin Hosp, 68-, Hosp St Raphael & Waterbury Hosp. *Mem:* AAAS; Am Asn Cancer Res; Am Soc Therapeut Radiol; Radiation Res Soc; Asn Univ Radiol. *Res:* Experimental therapeutic radiology; mammalian cell radiobiology; radioprotective and sensitizing agents; cell kinetics. *Mailing Add:* Dept of Therapeut Radiol Yale Univ Sch of Med New Haven CT 06520

FISCHER, JANET JORDAN, b Pittsburgh, Pa, Apr 28, 23; m 51; c 5. INTERNAL MEDICINE, INFECTIOUS DISEASES. *Educ:* Vassar Col, AB, 44; Johns Hopkins Univ, MD, 48; Am Bd Internal Med, dipl, 56. *Prof Exp:* Asst physician, Outpatient Dept, Johns Hopkins Hosp, 50-52; from instr to assoc prof, 54-70, prof, 70-80, SARAH GRAHAM KENAN PROF MED & ASSOC PROF BACTERIOL & IMMUNOL, UNIV NC, CHAPEL HILL, 80- *Concurrent Pos:* Fel infectious dis, Sch Med, Johns Hopkins Univ, 50-51; Nat Found Poliomyelitis Found fel, 51-52; fel infectious dis, Sch Med, Univ NC, 52-53; consult physician, Watts Hosp, Durham, NC, 54-; attend physician, NC Mem Hosp, Chapel Hill, 54- & Gravely Sanatorium, 54-74. *Mem:* AAAS; AMA; Am Fedn Clin Res; Am Thoracic Soc. *Res:* Pyelonephritis; urinary tract infections; bacterial endocarditis; laboratory medicine in microbiology; antibiotic sensitivity testing. *Mailing Add:* Dept of Med Mem Hosp Univ of NC Sch of Med Chapel Hill NC 27514

FISCHER, JOHN EDWARD, b Albany, NY, June 8, 39; m 63; c 3. SOLID STATE PHYSICS. *Educ:* Rensselaer Polytech Inst, BME, 61, PhD(nuclear sci & eng), 66; Calif Inst Technol, MS, 62. *Prof Exp:* Res assoc, Univ Paris, 66-67; res physicist, Michelson Lab, Naval Weapons Ctr, 67-70, br head, 70-73; assoc prof, 73-77, PROF ELEC ENG & SCI, UNIV PA, 77- *Concurrent Pos:* Vis assoc prof, Univ Pa, 71-72; consult, Naval Air Develop Ctr, 75- *Mem:* Am Phys Soc. *Res:* Optical properties of solids; characterization and electronic properties of synthetic metals, such as graphite intercalation compounds; point defects, compositional and topological disorder in semiconductors; radiation effects; thin films; energy band structure. *Mailing Add:* Moore Sch Elec Eng Univ Pa Philadelphia PA 19174

FISCHER, LAWRENCE J, b Chicago, Ill, Sept 2, 37; c 3. BIOCHEMICAL PHARMACOLOGY, TOXICOLOGY. *Educ:* Univ Ill, BS, 59, MS, 61; Univ Calif, PhD(pharmaceut chem), 65. *Prof Exp:* Sr res pharmacologist, Merck Inst Therapeut Res, 66-68; from asst prof to assoc prof, 68-76, PROF PHARMACOL, COL MED, UNIV IOWA, 76- *Concurrent Pos:* NIH fel biochem, St Mary's Hosp Med Sch, London, Eng, 65-66; vis prof, Univ Geneva, 76-77. *Mem:* AAAS; Am Soc Pharmacol & Exp Therapeut; Am Pharmaceut Asn; Soc Toxicol. *Res:* Absorption; distribution; metabolism and excretion of drugs and chemicals; toxicity of chemicals to the endocrine pancreas. *Mailing Add:* Dept of Pharmacol Univ of Iowa Sch of Med Iowa City IA 52242

FISCHER, LEEWELLYN C, b Litchfield, Minn, May 23, 37; div; c 2. PHOTOGRAPHIC CHEMISTRY. *Educ:* Univ Minn, BS, 59; Carnegie Inst Tech, MS, 61, PhD(phys chem), 64. *Prof Exp:* RES CHEMIST, PHOTO PRODS DEPT, E I DU PONT DE NEMOURS & CO, INC, 63- *Mem:* Soc Photog Scientists & Engrs. *Res:* Kinetics of fast reactions, specifically photolysis; photochemistry of liquids and thin films; free radical reactions in gas phase; photographic imaging and emulsion research. *Mailing Add:* E I du Pont de Nemours & Co Inc 666 Driving Park Rochester NY 14613

FISCHER, LOUIS, b Seattle, Wash, Aug 18, 05; m 29; c 2. PHARMACEUTICAL CHEMISTRY. *Educ:* Univ Wash, PhC & BS, 26, MS, 28, PhD(pharmaceut chem), 33. *Prof Exp:* Pharm stockman, Univ Wash, 26-28; asst state chemist, Wash, 29-35; instr pharm, Univ Wash, 35-37, from asst prof to prof pharmaceut chem, 37-74, asst to dean, 49- 60, assoc dean, 60-72, chmn dept pharmaceut chem, 45-74, dir student affairs, 72-74, EMER PROF PHARMACEUT CHEM, UNIV WASH, 74- *Concurrent Pos:* Chemist & bacteriologist, La Villa & Kristoferson Dairy, 25-29; med rep, Consol Dairy Prod, 40; off grader, USDA, 42-74; mkt specialist, Food Distribution Agency, USDA, 42, grand vice regent, 49-55, grand regent, 55-57, chmn nominating comt, 65-83; mem, US Pharmacopoeia Rev Comt, 50-70 & adv panel Nat Formulary, 61-70; fel, Rev Panel, NIH, 64-67 & Nat Prescription Surv Bd. *Mem:* AAAS; Am Pharmaceut Asn; Sigma Xi; Inst Food Technologists. *Res:* Phytochemistry; food chemistry. *Mailing Add:* 13875 108th Dr Sun City AZ 85351

FISCHER, MARK BENJAMIN, b San Francisco, Calif, Mar 23, 49. CATALYSIS, SYNTHETIC FUELS. *Educ:* Univ Calif, Berkeley, BS, 71, Univ Wis-Madison, PhD(inorg chem), 78. *Prof Exp:* Fel dept chem, Univ Toronto, 78-79, Tulane Univ, 79-80; RES CHEMIST, MW KELLOG RES & DEVELOP CTR, 80- *Mem:* Am Chem Soc; Sigma Xi; Am Inst Chemists. *Res:* Performance of experimental programs leading to process innovation in synfuels production and upgrading; development and evaluation of novel catalysts for process applications in synfuels production. *Mailing Add:* 4635 Turf Valley Dr Houston TX 77084

FISCHER, MARK SAMUEL, biochemistry, see previous edition

FISCHER, NIKOLAUS HARTMUT, b Kunzendorf, Ger, Aug 8, 36. NATURAL PRODUCTS CHEMISTRY, SYNTHETIC ORGANIC CHEMISTRY. *Educ:* Univ Tuebingen, Ger, BS, 60, MS, 63, Dr Natural Sci(org chem), 65. *Prof Exp:* R A Welch fel natural prod chem, Univ Tex, Austin, 65-67; asst prof chem, La State Univ, 67-73; asst biosynthesis betalains, Univ Zurich, 68-70; assoc prof, 73-78, PROF NATURAL PROD CHEM, LA STATE UNIV, BATON ROUGE, 78- *Mem:* Am Chem Soc; Phytochem Soc NAm; The Chem Soc; Sigma Xi. *Res:* Isolation and structure elucidation of natural products; biochemical systematics in the compositae; generation and chemistry of sulfenes; synthetic applications of sulfenes; plant-insect and insect-insect interaction. *Mailing Add:* Dept Chem La State Univ Baton Rouge LA 70803

FISCHER, PATRICK CARL, b St Louis, Mo, Dec 3, 35; m 67; c 2. COMPUTER SCIENCE. *Educ:* Univ Mich, BS, 57, MBA, 58; Mass Inst Technol, PhD(math), 62. *Prof Exp:* Asst prof appl math, Harvard Univ, 62-65; assoc prof comput sci, Cornell Univ, 65-68; vis prof, Univ Waterloo, 68-69, prof, 69-74, chmn dept appl anal & comput sci, 72-74; head, Dept Comput Sci, Pa State Univ, 74-78, prof, 74-79; PROF & CHMN, DEPT COMPUT SCI, VANDERBILT UNIV, 80- *Concurrent Pos:* Grants, NSF, 64-66, 66-68 & 79-81, Nat Res Coun Can, 68-76; vis assoc prof, Univ BC, 67-68; mem,

Grant Selection Comt, Nat Res Coun Can, 73-76; ed-in-chief, Asn Comput Mach Spec Publ; ed, J Comput Syst Sci; ed, SIAM J on Comput. *Mem:* Asn Comput Mach; Am Math Soc; Inst Elec & Electronics Engrs. *Res:* User-oriented data-base systems; computational complexity. *Mailing Add:* Dept Comput Sci Vanderbilt Univ Nashville TN 37235

FISCHER, PAUL EDGAR, b Kansas City, Kans, Nov 26, 19; m 50, 76; c 6. PETROLEUM CHEMISTRY, INFORMATION SCIENCE. *Educ:* Cent Col Mo, AB, 41; Univ Chicago, PhD(chem), 47. *Prof Exp:* Res chemist, Nat Defense Res Comt Prog, Univ Chicago, 42-44 & rubber reserve, 44-46; res chemist, 47-69, MGR TECH INFO SERV, CHEVRON RES CO, STANDARD OIL CO CALIF, 60- *Concurrent Pos:* Mem, Comt Res Data & Info Serv & Subcomt Tech Info, Am Petrol Inst. *Mem:* Am Chem Soc; Am Petrol Inst. *Res:* Petroleum processes; hydrocarbon separations; polymerization; free radical reactions; hydrogenation; rubber chemistry. *Mailing Add:* Tech Info Ctr Chevron Res Co PO Box 1627 Richmond CA 94802

FISCHER, R(OLAND) B(ARTON), b Denver, Colo, Feb 28, 20; m 42; c 2. PHYSICAL METALLURGY. *Educ:* Colo Sch Mines, MetE, 42. *Prof Exp:* Asst metallurgist, Am Smelting & Refining Co, El Paso, Tex, 46; res engr, Battelle Mem Inst, 46-49, asst supvr, 49-53, div chief, 53-63; sr develop specialist, 63-66, sr res metallurgist, Dow Chem Co, 66-75, SR RES SPECIALIST, ROCKY FLATS PLANT, ROCKWELL INT, 75- *Mem:* Am Soc Metals; Am Inst Mining, Metall & Petrol Engrs. *Res:* Non-ferrous metals, hard metals technology; tungsten carbide, powder metallurgy and others; high pressure research; nuclear materials; diamond technology. *Mailing Add:* 12035 Applewood Knolls Dr Lakewood CO 80215

FISCHER, RICHARD BERNARD, b Boston, Mass, Jan 19, 19; m 53; c 3. BIOLOGY. *Educ:* Queens Col, NY, BS, 42; Columbia Univ, MA, 43; Cornell Univ, PhD(zool), 53. *Prof Exp:* Asst press serv, 51-52, asst biol, 52-53, PROF ENVIRON EDUC, CORNELL UNIV, 53- *Mem:* Asn Interpretive Naturalists; Conserv Educ Asn; Am Nature Study Soc; Am Ornith Union; Wilson Ornith Soc. *Res:* Chimney swift; environmental quality; ecology; natural history writing and photography; natural history. *Mailing Add:* 135 Pine Tree Rd Ithaca NY 14850

FISCHER, RICHARD MARTIN, JR, b Vancouver, Wash, Apr 23, 47; m 69; c 2. POLYMER & PHOTOCHEMISTRY. *Educ:* NDak State Univ, BS, 69, PhD(polymer chem), 74. *Prof Exp:* Process develop chemist, heterogeneous catalysis, Shell Chem Co, 69-70; sr res chemist, 74-80, RES SPECIALIST, POLYMER PHOTOCHEM, 3M CO, 80- *Concurrent Pos:* NSF grant, 70-74. *Honors & Awards:* Roon Award, Fedn Soc Paint Technol, 74. *Res:* Ultraviolet curing chemistry; photodegradation of polymer systems; accelerated weathering and durability test development. *Mailing Add:* 803 Eighth St Hudson WI 54016

FISCHER, ROBERT BLANCHARD, b Hartford, Conn, Oct 24, 20; m 46; c 5. ANALYTICAL CHEMISTRY, ACADEMIC ADMINISTRATION. *Educ:* Wheaton Col, Ill, BS, 42; Univ Ill, PhD(anal chem), 46. *Prof Exp:* Radio broadcast engr, Chicago 41; asst anal chem, Univ Ill, 42-44; instr, 46-48; res chemist, Metall Lab, Univ Chicago, 44-46; from asst prof to prof chem, Ind Univ, 48-63; prof chem, 63-79, dean, Sch Natural Sci & Math, 63-79, EMER PROF CHEM, CALIF STATE UNIV, DOMINGUEZ HILLS, CARSON, 79-; VPRES ACAD AFFAIRS, BIOLA UNIV, 79- *Concurrent Pos:* Vis assoc, Calif Inst Technol, 59-60. *Mem:* AAAS; Am Chem Soc; Am Sci Affil. *Res:* Science and society quantitative chemical analysis; electron microscopy; instrumentation. *Mailing Add:* Biola Univ 13800 Biola Ave La Mirada CA 90639

FISCHER, ROBERT GEORGE, b St Paul, Minn, Oct 17, 20; m 47; c 3. MICROBIOLOGY. *Educ:* Univ Minn, BA, 42, MS, 47, PhD, 48; Am Bd Microbiol, dipl. *Prof Exp:* Asst bact, Univ Minn, 45-48; from asst prof to assoc prof, 48-62, PROF MICROBIOL & CHMN DEPT, UNIV NDAK, 62- *Mem:* Am Soc Microbiol; Am Acad Microbiol. *Res:* Viruses; experimental leukemia transmission; poliomyelitis; virus tumors. *Mailing Add:* 447 Campbell Dr Grand Forks ND 58201

FISCHER, ROBERT GEORGE, JR, inorganic chemistry, industrial organic chemistry, see previous edition

FISCHER, ROBERT LEIGH, b Chicago, Ill, July 29, 26; m 54; c 3. CLINICAL CHEMISTRY. *Educ:* Northern Ill State Teachers Col, BS, 50; Univ Ill, MS, 51, PhD(biochem), 54. *Prof Exp:* Asst, Univ Ill, 51-54; res chemist, E I du Pont de Nemours & Co, 54-55; asst prof chem, Med Sch, Univ Tenn, 55-61, res assoc pediat, 55-61; sr res chemist, Campbell Soup Co, 61-64, div head proteins, 64-67; chief clin chemist, Philadelphia Gen Hosp, 67-78; dir, Philadelphia Police Lab, 78-80; RES SCIENTIST, NJ DEP, 80- *Mem:* AAAS; Am Chem Soc; Am Asn Clin Chemists. *Res:* Clinical chemistry methods. *Mailing Add:* 714 Hilltop Rd Cinnaminson NJ 08077

FISCHER, ROLAND LEE, b Detroit, Mich, Sept 9, 24; m 46; c 3. ENTOMOLOGY. *Educ:* Univ Mich, BS, 46; Mich State Col, MS, 48; Kans State Col, PhD(entom), 52. *Prof Exp:* Teacher pub schs, Mich, 46-47; asst entom, Mich State Col, 47-48; asst, Kans State Col, 48-50, instr, 51; res assoc, Univ Kans, 52; res fel, Univ Minn, 52-53; from asst prof to assoc prof entom, 53-64, cur entom, Mus, 59-64, PROF ENTOM, MICH STATE UNIV, 64- *Mem:* Entom Soc Am; Soc Syst Zool; Entom Soc Can; Int Union Study Social Insects; fel Royal Entom Soc London. *Res:* T Taxonomy of the Aculeate Hymenoptera, particularly the Apoidea; biological and phenological investigations in the Aculeate Hymenoptera; insect morphology; pollination of legume seed crops. *Mailing Add:* Dept of Entom Mich State Univ East Lansing MI 48824

FISCHER, RONALD HOWARD, b New York, NY, May 1, 42. FUELS ENGINEERING, CHEMICAL ENGINEERING. *Educ:* City Col New York, BS, 63; Princeton Univ, MA, 66, PhD(chem), 67. *Prof Exp:* Sr res chemist, Mobil Res & Develop Corp, 67-75; proj mgr coal technol, 75-78, dir coal liquefaction, US Dept Energy, Washington, DC, 78-80; MGR PRODUCING & TECHNOL, MOBIL OIL CORP, 80- *Mem:* Am Inst Chem Engrs; AAAS; Am Chem Soc; Sigma Xi. *Res:* Upgrading of petroleum residue; synthetic fuels processing, refining of synthetic fuels, synthesis gas conversion reactions; conversion of coal to fuel oil and gasoline. *Mailing Add:* 5557 S Hillsdale St Englewood CO 80111

FISCHER, THEODORE E, b St Louis, Mo, Mar 10, 10; c 2. DENTISTRY. *Educ:* Nat Inst Eng, BS, 32; St Louis Univ, DDS, 36. *Prof Exp:* Prof dent & chmn, Dept Dent Mat, Sch Dent, Univ Ala, Birmingham, 63-76, mem staff, Med Ctr & prof eng, 76-80; RETIRED. *Concurrent Pos:* Consult, US Army, Ft Benning & Vet Admin, Tuskegee & Birmingham; mem dent health res & educ comt, USPHS; chmn subcomt zinc oxide, Int Standards Orgn; consult, Sch Dent, Univ Ala, Southern Res Inst. *Mem:* Fel AAAS; fel Am Col Dent; Am Dent Asn; Int Asn Dent Res; Am Asn Dent Res. *Res:* Dental materials; silicate cements; acrylic resins; amalgam; maxillofacial prostheses. *Mailing Add:* Dept of Dent Mat Univ of Ala Sch of Dent Birmingham AL 35294

FISCHER, THEODORE VERNON, b Brillion, Wis, July 25, 39; m 69; c 2. HUMAN ANATOMY. *Educ:* NCent Col, Ill, BA, 61; Univ Wis, PhD(anat), 66. *Prof Exp:* Fel reproductive physiol, Univ Wis, 66-67; asst prof anat, 67-76, ASSOC PROF ANAT, UNIV MICH, 76- *Mem:* Am Asn Anat; Soc Study Reproduction. *Res:* Mammalian placentation; physiology of reproduction; histochemistry and organ culture of prostate. *Mailing Add:* Dept of Anat Univ of Mich Ann Arbor MI 48109

FISCHER, TRAUGOTT ERWIN, b Aarau, Switz, Jan 21, 32; m 58; c 3. SURFACE PHYSICS. *Educ:* Swiss Fed Inst Technol, dipl, 56, PhD(solid state physics), 63. *Prof Exp:* Asst solid state physics, Swiss Fed Inst Technol, 57-63; mem tech staff surface physics, Bell Labs, NJ, 63-66; assoc prof eng & appl sci, Yale Univ, 66-72; SR RES ASSOC, EXXON RES & ENG CO, 72- *Concurrent Pos:* co-ed, Advan Med & Physics Surfaces; mem organizing comt, NATO Conf Adv Comt, Dept Metall, Ohio State Univ, 80- *Honors & Awards:* Kern Prize, Swiss Fed Inst Technol, 62. *Mem:* AAAS; Am Vacuum Soc; fel Am Phys Soc; Swiss Phys Soc. *Res:* Physical properties of surfaces; optical properties and energy-band structure of solids; surface-physical aspects of catalysis and metallurgy; tribology. *Mailing Add:* Exxon Corp Res Lab PO Box 45 Linden NJ 07036

FISCHER, WILLIAM ALFRED, b Chicago, Ill, Apr 15, 17; m 45; c 4. INVERTEBRATE PALEONTOLOGY. *Educ:* Beloit Col, BS, 39, MS, 41; Univ Colo, PhD, 53. *Prof Exp:* Asst geol, Beloit Col, 39-41; petrol geologist, Carter Oil Co, 41-43; from asst prof to assoc prof geol, 49-58, chmn dept, 58-74, PROF GEOL, COLO COL, 58- *Concurrent Pos:* Ford Found Advan of Educ fac fel, 54-55. *Res:* Micropaleontology. *Mailing Add:* Dept of Geol Colo Col Colorado Springs CO 80903

FISCHER, WILLIAM CARL, JR, agricultural biochemistry, see previous edition

FISCHINGER, PETER JOHN, cancer, animal virology, see previous edition

FISCHLER, MARTIN A(LVIN), b New York, NY, Feb 15, 32; m 60; c 2. COMPUTER SCIENCE, ARTIFICIAL INTELLIGENCE. *Educ:* City Col New York, BEE, 54; Stanford Univ, MS, 58, PhD(elec eng), 62. *Prof Exp:* Electronic engr, Nat Bur Standards, 56; scientist, Lockheed Missiles & Space Co, 58-61, sr scientist, 61-62, res scientist, 62-71, staff scientist, 71-77; SR COMPUTER SCIENTIST, SRI INT, 77- *Mem:* Pattern Recognition Soc; Asn Comput Mach; Math Asn Am; Inst Elec & Electronics Eng. *Res:* Artificial intelligence; switching theory; information theory; computer organization; information retrieval; operations research. *Mailing Add:* 966 Bonneville Way Sunnyvale CA 94087

FISCHLSCHWEIGER, WERNER, b Bremen, Ger, May 4, 32; m 60; c 2. ELECTRON MICROSCOPY. *Educ:* Graz Univ, PhD(zool), 57. *Prof Exp:* Dir tissue cult, Austrian Cancer Res Inst, 58-62; asst prof histol, Med Sch, Graz Univ, 62-63; asst prof, Med Sch, St Louis Univ, 63-65; assoc prof, Dent Sch, Univ Md, Baltimore, 65-69; assoc prof, 69-73, PROF BASIC DENT SCI, COL DENT, UNIV FLA, 73-, DIR, E M LAB, 74- *Mem:* Int Asn Dent Res; Ger Zool Soc. *Res:* Dental research. *Mailing Add:* Dept of Basic Dent Sci Univ of Fla Col of Dent Gainesville FL 32610

FISCHMAN, DONALD A, b New York, NY, Apr 27, 36; m 60; c 3. MEDICINE. *Educ:* Kenyon Col, AB, 57; Cornell Univ, MD, 61. *Prof Exp:* Res fel anat, Med Col, Cornell Univ, 61-63; fel embryol, Strangeways Lab, Cambridge, Eng, 63-64; instr anat, Med Col, Cornell Univ, 64-65; asst prof zool, Univ Chicago, 65-66, asst prof biol & anat, 68-71, assoc prof biol & anat, 71-77, assoc dean curric, div biol sci, 70-77; mem fac, 77-80, PROF & CHMN, DEPT ANAT & CELL BIOL, DOWNSTATE MED CTR, STATE UNIV NY, 80- *Concurrent Pos:* NY Heart Asn res fel, 61-63; USPHS fel, 63-64 & res grant, 64-66 & 71-; res grants, NSF, 68- & Chicago Heart Asn, 69-71. *Mem:* Am Asn Anatomists; Am Soc Cell Biologists; Soc Develop Biol; Biophys Soc; Soc Gen Physiol. *Res:* Anatomy; developmental biology; electron microscopy; development, growth and physiology of muscle; ultrastructure of bacterial cell walls and membranes. *Mailing Add:* Dept of Anat & Cell Biol State Univ NY Downstate Med Ctr Brooklyn NY 11203

FISCHMAN, HARLOW KENNETH, b New York, NY, Dec 19, 32; div; c 2. MEDICAL GENETICS, CYTOGENETICS. *Educ:* Brooklyn Col, BA, 55; Univ Ark, MS, 60; NY Univ, PhD(genetics), 68. *Prof Exp:* Sr res assoc cancer, Sloan-Kettering Inst, 60; instr biol, Long Island Univ, 60-61 & Nassau Community Col, 61-63; asst prof biol, Queensboro Community Col, 65-69; res assoc genetics, Col Physicians & Surgeons, Columbia Univ, 69-72; asst prof genetics, Fairleigh Dickinson Univ, 72-73; ASSOC RES SCIENTIST MED GENETICS, NY STATE PSYCHIAT INST, 73- *Concurrent Pos:* Fac res fel, State Univ NY, 68; res assoc, Col Physicians & Surgeons, Columbia Univ, 73-; NIH grant, 75-; travel grant, Environ Mutagenesis Symp, 81. *Mem:* Environ Mutagenesis Soc; Am Soc Human Genetics; Am Soc Cell Biologists; Somatic Cell Genetics Soc; Genetic Toxicol Asn. *Res:* Human chromosome structure and function; behavioral genetics; genetic toxicology; karyotype analyses; chromosome localization; meiosis; cellular aging; gene mapping. *Mailing Add:* NY State Psychiat Inst 722 W 168 St New York NY 10032

FISCHMAN, MARIAN WEINBAUM, b New York, NY, Oct 13, 39; c 3. BEHAVIORAL PHARMACOLOGY, PSYCHOLOGY. *Educ:* Barnard Col, BA, 60; Columbia Univ, MA, 62; Univ Chicago, PhD(psychol), 72. *Prof Exp:* Res assoc anat, Cornell Med Sch, 61-63; res asst psychol, Univ Chicago, 65-66; res assoc, Inst Behav Res, 66-68; res asst psychol, 68-69, RES ASSOC & ASST PROF PSYCHIAT, UNIV CHICAGO, 72- *Mem:* Fel, Am Psychol Asn; Behav Pharmacol Soc; Am Soc Pharmacol & Exp Therapeut; AAAS; Nat Inst Drug Abuse. *Res:* Behavioral pharmacology; drug abuse; psychology; behavioral medicine. *Mailing Add:* Dept of Psychiat Univ Chicago 950 E 59th St Chicago IL 60637

FISCHMAN, STUART L, b Buffalo, NY, Nov 29, 35; m 60; c 2. ORAL PATHOLOGY. *Educ:* Harvard Univ, DMD, 60; Am Bd Oral Path, dipl, 69. *Prof Exp:* Intern dent, Boston Vet Admin Hosp, Mass, 60-61; instr clin dent, 61-64, from asst prof to assoc prof oral path, 64-72, asst dean acad develop & facil planning, 70-73, PROF ORAL MED, SCH DENT, STATE UNIV NY BUFFALO, 72- *Concurrent Pos:* Res assoc, Vet Admin Hosp, Buffalo, NY, 63-64; consult, USPHS, 65-70; vis prof, Nat Univ Asuncion, Paraguay, 69-; univ assoc dent, Buffalo Gen Hosp, 69-; consult, WHO, 70-; consult oral med, Univ PR, 74; dir dent, Meyer Mem Hosp, Buffalo, 74-78 & Erie County Med Ctr, Buffalo, 78-; consult, Coun Hosp Dent & Coun Dent Educ, Am Dent Asn, 76-; Lady Davis fel, Hebrew Univ, Jerusalem, 81; consult, Lever Bros Co, 76- *Mem:* AAAS; fel Am Col Dent; fel Am Acad Oral Path; Am Dent Asn; Int Asn Dent Res. *Res:* Experimental oral pathology and periodontal diseases; clinical testing of therapeutic dentifrice; oral diseases; tropical oral pathology. *Mailing Add:* Dept of Oral Med State Univ NY Sch of Dent Buffalo NY 14214

FISCHTHAL, JACOB HENRY, b Brooklyn, NY, Apr 18, 17; m 42; c 4. PARASITOLOGY. *Educ:* Long Island Univ, BS, 37; Univ Iowa, MS, 38; Univ Mich, PhD(zool), 50. *Prof Exp:* Aquatic biologist, NAtlantic Fisheries Invests, US Fish & Wildlife Serv, 43 & fish mgt div, State Conserv Dept, Wis, 43-48; instr biol, Triple Cities Col, Syracuse, 48-50; from asst prof to assoc prof, 50-61, head dept, 56-59, PROF BIOL, STATE UNIV NY BINGHAMTON, 61- *Concurrent Pos:* NIH res grant, 53-55; Sigma Xi-Sci Res Soc Am res grant, 55; Off Naval Res, US Navy res grant, 56; Fulbright grants, Univ Col Cape Coast, Ghana, 65-66 & Haile Sellassie I Univ, 68-69; State Univ NY fac res fel, 67, 68, 71 & 74; consult, Parasitol Dept, US Naval Med Res Inst, 55-75 & law dept, Div Water Supply, City New York, 56-65, 72 & 74. *Mem:* Am Soc Parasitologists. *Res:* Ecology, allometry, taxonomy and zoogeography of trematodes of vertebrates. *Mailing Add:* Dept of Biol Sci State Univ of NY Binghamton NY 13901

FISCUS, ALVIN G, b Newell, SDak, July 6, 30; m 56; c 3. VIROLOGY, MICROBIOLOGY. *Educ:* SDak State Univ, BS, 56, MS, 57; Univ Ariz, PhD(microbiol), 66. *Prof Exp:* Dir lab clin microbiol, Tucson Med Ctr, Ariz, 66-67; assoc prof, 67-77, PROF MICROBIOL, MONT STATE UNIV, 77- *Concurrent Pos:* Consult, Mont Regional Med Prog, 67- *Mem:* Am Soc Microbiol. *Res:* Clinical microbiology; viral and chemical oncology. *Mailing Add:* Dept of Bot & Microbiol Mont State Univ Bozeman MT 59715

FISCUS, EDWIN LAWSON, b Ellwood City, Pa, Jan 20, 42; m 69. PLANT PHYSIOLOGY. *Educ:* Slippery Rock State Col, BSEd, 64; Univ Ariz, MS, 66; Duke Univ, PhD(bot), 69. *Prof Exp:* Res assoc plant physiol, Auburn Univ, 69-70; res assoc plant physiol, Duke Univ, 70-76; PLANT PHYSIOLOGIST, AGR RES, SCI & EDUC ADMIN, USDA, 76- *Mem:* Sigma Xi; Am Soc Plant Physiologists; Am Inst Biol Sci; Am Soc Agron. *Res:* Plant and soil water relations; root-oxygen relations; factors influencing salt and water uptake by roots and water movement through the plant; stress physiology. *Mailing Add:* Crops Res Lab Colo State Univ Ft Collins CO 80523

FISER, PAUL STANLEY, b Roznava, Czech, Apr 30, 38; Can citizen; m 62; c 1. REPRODUCTIVE PHYSIOLOGY, GENETICS. *Educ:* Univ Agr, Brno, Ing Zoot, 63; Univ Guelph, PhD(genetics & reproductive physiol), 72. *Prof Exp:* Res scientist biol, Vet Col, Brno, 63-69; res assoc reproductive physiol, Univ Guelph, 72-78; RES SCIENTIST REPRODUCTIVE PHYSIOL, ANIMAL RES INST, OTTAWA, 78- *Concurrent Pos:* Consult, Hybrid Turkeys LTD, Kitchener, Ont, 76-78; assoc fac mem, Dept of Animal & Poultry Sci, Univ Guelph, 76- *Mem:* Soc Study Reproduction; Can Soc Animal Sci; World's Poultry Sci Asn. *Res:* Low temperature preservation of mammalian gametes; experimental embryology (mammalia and aves); lethal factors in avian species. *Mailing Add:* Agr Can Animal Res Inst Ottawa Can

FISET, PAUL, b Quebec, Que, Nov 7, 22; m 53; c 3. MICROBIOLOGY. *Educ:* Laval Univ, BA, 44, MD, 49; Cambridge Univ, PhD(microbiol), 56. *Prof Exp:* Asst bact, Laval Univ, 55-57; asst prof, Sch Med & Dent, Univ Rochester, 58-64, asst med, 58-64; assoc prof, 64-75, PROF MICROBIOL, SCH MED, UNIV MD, BALTIMORE CITY, 75- *Mem:* AAAS; Am Soc Microbiol; Ny Acad Sci; Am Asn Immunol. *Mailing Add:* Dept of Microbiol Sch Med Univ of Md Baltimore MD 21201

FISH, ARTHUR GEOFFREY, b Pictou, NS, Apr 24, 33; m 58; c 2. INVERTEBRATE ZOOLOGY. *Educ:* Carleton Univ, Ont, BSc, 56; McGill Univ, MSc, 58; Univ BC, PhD(biol oceanog), 68. *Prof Exp:* Res asst biol oceanog, Bellairs Res Inst, McGill Univ, 58-60; asst prof biol, 64-69, ASSOC PROF BIOL, UNIV SOUTHERN MISS, 69- *Concurrent Pos:* Benthonic study sea grant, Univs Marine Ctr Miss, NASA Contract, Earth Resources

Data & Technol Studies, Miss, 70-; interstitial faunal study of Timbalier Bay, La, Offshore Ecol Invest, Gulf Univs Res Consortium, 72-74; Miss/Ala Sea grant consortium, 74-75. *Mem:* Am Inst Biol Sci. *Res:* Nonparasitic marine zooplankton; zooplankton of the Mississippi Sound; interstitial faunal studies of marine and estuarine environments of the Mississippi Sound. *Mailing Add:* Dept of Biol Univ of Southern Miss Box 445 Hattiesburg MS 39401

FISH, BARBARA, b New York, NY, July 31, 20; m 53; c 2. PSYCHIATRY. *Educ:* Columbia Univ, BA, 42; NY Univ, MD, 45; Am Bd Psychiat & Neurol, dipl, 55, cert child psychiat, 60; W A White Inst Psychiat, cert, 56. *Prof Exp:* Intern & asst resident med, Bellevue Hosp, 45-47; resident pediat, New York Hosp, 47-48 & NY Univ-Bellevue Med Ctr, 48-49, resident psychiat, Bellevue Hosp, 49-52, clin asst psychiat, 51-55; from instr to asst prof pediat & psychiat, Med Col, Cornell Univ, 55-60; assoc prof psychiat, 60-70, prof child psychiat, 70-72, ADJ PROF CHILD PSYCHIAT, SCH MED, NY UNIV, 72-; PROF PSYCHIAT, UNIV CALIF, LOS ANGELES, 72- *Concurrent Pos:* Dir child psychiat, NY Univ Med Ctr, 60-72; mem comt cert child psychiat, Am Bd Psychiat & Neurol, 69-77; prin investr, Schizophrenic Offspring From Birth To Adulthood, 78- & mem clin prog projs res rev comt, Nat Inst Mental Health, 76-79. *Mem:* Soc Res Child Develop; fel Am Psychiat Asn; Am Acad Child Psychiat; Asn Res Nerv & Ment Dis; fel Am Col Neuropsychopharmacol. *Res:* Child psychiatry, especially childhood schizophrenia and pharmacotherapy; infant development and the aantecedents of schizophrenia and other neuropsychiatric disorders in infancy. *Mailing Add:* Dept of Psychiat Univ of Calif Sch of Med Los Angeles CA 90024

FISH, DONALD C, b New York, NY, Apr 19, 37; m 58; c 3. MICROBIOLOGY, IMMUNOLOGY. *Educ:* Cornell Univ, BS, 58; Univ Mich, MS, 61, PhD(microbiol), 64. *Prof Exp:* Asst bact, Cornell Univ, 57-58; lab instr, Univ Mich, 58-61, asst, 61-64; microbiologist anthrax res, US Army Biol Labs, 64-71; dir microbiol div, Woodard Res Corp, 71-72; MGR DIS CONTROL LAB, FREDERICK CANCER RES CTR, 72- *Concurrent Pos:* Instr microbiol, Sci Prog, Interlochen Arts Acad, Univ Mich, 63. *Mem:* Tissue Cult Asn; Am Soc Microbiol; Am Chem Soc; NY Acad Sci; Sigma Xi. *Res:* Immunological, biochemical and genetic studies on the control over expression of endogenous virus and its relationship to spontaneous cancer; development of potential vaccines; monitor immune reactivity during cancer progression. *Mailing Add:* 116 W 14th St Frederick MD 21701

FISH, F(LOYD) H(AMILTON), JR, b Bryan, Tex, May 8, 23; m 53; c 5. MECHANICS. *Educ:* Va Polytech Inst, BS, 43, MS, 50. *Prof Exp:* Asst prof fluid mech, Va Polytech Inst, 48-50; sr res engr, Textile Fibers Dept, 50-60, RES SUPVR, TECH DIV FIBERS DEPT, E I DU PONT DE NEMOURS & CO, INC, 60- *Mem:* Am Soc Mech Engrs; Soc Automotive Engrs. *Res:* Mechanics of paper, fabrics and non-woven fabrics and cushioning structures, including manufacturing processes as well as products. *Mailing Add:* Christina Lab E I du Pont de Nemours & Co Inc Wilmington DE 19898

FISH, FEROL F, JR, b East Chicago, Ind, Jan 15, 30; m 56; c 5. THERMODYNAMICS & MATERIAL PROPERTIES. *Educ:* Ind Univ, BS, 55, AM, 57; Pa State Univ, PhD(geophys), 61. *Prof Exp:* Geophys investr, NJ Zinc Co, 60-63; sr res scientist, Gen Dynamics/Ft Worth, 63-64; sr scientist, Douglas Aircraft Co, 64-68; mgr appl physics, Roy C Ingersoll Res Ctr, Borg-Warner Corp, Des Plaines, 68-79; MGR PHYSICAL SCI, GAS RES INST, CHICAGO, 79- *Mem:* Am Geophys Union; Sigma Xi. *Res:* Research administration of geosciences, materials, and thermophysical properties of fluids. *Mailing Add:* 1502 S Fernandez Arlington Heights IL 60005

FISH, GORDON E, b Dayton, Tenn, Jan 4, 51. SOLID STATE PHYSICS. *Educ:* Wheaton Col, Ill, BS, 72; Univ Ill, Urbana, MS, 73, PhD(physics), 77. *Prof Exp:* Teaching asst & fel, Univ Ill, Urbana, 72-73, res asst physics, 73-77; physicist, US Nat Bur Standards, 77-79; PHYSICIST, ALLIED CORP, 79- *Concurrent Pos:* Nat Merit scholar, Wheaton Col, 68-72; Nat Bur Standards-Nat Res Coun fel, Nat Bur Standards, 77- *Mem:* Am Phys Soc; Am Sci Affil; Inst Elec & Electronics Engrs; Sigma Xi. *Res:* Magnetic materials; neutron scattering; magnetic resonance and relaxation; phase transitions; structure of amorphous materials. *Mailing Add:* Mat Lab Corp Res & Develop Allied Corp Morristown NJ 07960

FISH, IRVING, b Montreal, Can, May 1, 38; m 67; c 3. PEDIATRIC NEUROLOGY. *Educ:* McGill Univ, BSc, 59; Dalhousie Univ, MD, 64. *Prof Exp:* Instr Neurol, Cornell Univ, 67-69; asst prof, 69-76, ASSOC PROF NEUROL, MED CTR, NEW YORK UNIV, 76-, DIR PEDIAT NEUROL, 77- *Concurrent Pos:* Consult neurol, Vet Admin Hosp, 69- *Mem:* Am Acad Neurol. *Res:* Amino acid transport; effects of nutrition on development; spina bifida, hydrocephalus, and epilepsy. *Mailing Add:* New York Univ Med Ctr 560 First Ave New York NY 10016

FISH, JAMES FRANKLIN, JR, biological oceanography, animal behavior, see previous edition

FISH, JOHN G, b Chicago, Ill, Mar 30, 38; m 61; c 4. POLYMER CHEMISTRY. *Educ:* Western Mich Univ, BS, 62; Univ Cincinnati, PhD, 68. *Prof Exp:* Mem tech staff, Mat Group, 66-68, mem tech staff, Cent Anal & Characterization Lab, 68-79, MGR, UNIV PHD RECRUITING & UNIV RELS, TEX INSTRUMENTS, INC, 79- *Mem:* Am Chem Soc; Creation Res Soc. *Res:* Analysis and characterization of polymers and plastics used in electronic processing, equipment and devices. *Mailing Add:* Tex Instruments Inc PO Box 225936 Mail Sta 145 Dallas TX 75265

FISH, JOSEPH LEROY, b Portland, Ore, Feb 10, 43; m 64; c 3. VERTEBRATE ECOLOGY, POPULATION ECOLOGY. *Educ:* Walla Walla Col, BS, 65, MA, 67; Wash State Univ, PhD(zool biomet), 72. *Prof Exp:* Instr Biol, Walla Walla Col, 67-68; asst prof biol, Oakwood Col, 72-77; ASSOC PROF BIOL, SOUTHWESTERN ADVENTIST COL, 77- *Concurrent Pos:* Consult, Teledyne Brown Eng, 74-75; fel, Lawrence Livermore Lab, 77. *Mem:* Wildlife Soc; Nat Wildlife Fedn. *Res:* Population biology of coyotes (canis latrans) and heavy metal toxicity to freshwater and marine vertebrates. *Mailing Add:* Dept of Biol Southwestern Adventist Col Keene TX 76059

FISH, RICHARD WAYNE, b Gowrie, Iowa, Aug 27, 34; m 64; c 1. ORGANIC CHEMISTRY. *Educ:* Iowa State Univ, BS, 56; Mich State Univ, PhD(org chem), 60. *Prof Exp:* Res chemist, Calif Res Corp, Standard Oil Co, Calif, 60-61; res assoc phys org chem, Brandeis Univ, 61-63; NSF fel, Univ Calif, Berkeley, 63-64; from asst prof to assoc prof, 64-70, dir, NSF Undergrad Res Partic Prog, 65-71, PROF CHEM, CALIF STATE UNIV, SACRAMENTO, 70- *Concurrent Pos:* Petrol Res Fund grant, 64-66; sr res fel, Brandeis Univ, 71-72. *Mem:* AAAS; Am Chem Soc. *Res:* Physical organic chemistry; synthesis and reactions of aromatic, nonclassical aromatic and organometallic compounds; electrophilic reactions of metallocenes; stabilized carbonium on intermediates; benzyne intermediates and charge transfer studies. *Mailing Add:* Dept of Chem Calif State Univ Sacramento CA 95819

FISH, STEWART ALLISON, b Benton, Ill, Nov 4, 25; m 57; c 4. OBSTETRICS & GYNECOLOGY. *Educ:* Univ Pa, MD, 49. *Prof Exp:* Asst prof obstet & gynec, Univ Tex Southwestern Med Sch, 54-58, clin asst prof, 58-62; pvt pract, 56-62; asst prof, Univ Ark, 62-66; prof obstet & gynec & chmn dept, Univ Tenn, Memphis, 66-75; CHIEF DEPT GYNEC, NACOGDOCHES MED CTR HOSP, 75- *Mem:* Am Col Surg; AMA; Am Col Obstet & Gynec; Am Asn Obstet & Gynec. *Res:* Mammalian teratology; infectious diseases in pregnancy. *Mailing Add:* 4800 NE Stallings Dr Suite 115 Nacogdoches TX 75961

FISH, WAYNE WILLIAM, b Helena, Okla, Apr 21, 41; m 62; c 3. BIOCHEMISTRY. *Educ:* Okla State Univ, BS, 63, PhD(biochem), 67. *Prof Exp:* Res assoc, Med Ctr, Duke Univ, 67-68; from asst prof to assoc prof, 70-78, PROF BIOCHEM, MED UNIV SC, 78- *Concurrent Pos:* NIH fel, Duke Univ, 68-70; Swedish Med Res Coun vis scientist fel, Univ Uppsala, 78. *Mem:* Am Soc Biol Chem; Am Chem Soc. *Res:* Intrinsic physical and chemical properties of biological macromolecules, principally proteins; the subunit nature of proteins; characterization of the iron storage and transport proteins and the structure/function relationships of membrane glycoproteins. *Mailing Add:* Dept of Biochem Med Univ of SC Charleston SC 29403

FISH, WILLIAM ARTHUR, b Boston, Mass, Aug 2, 21; m 41; c 7. EMBRYOLOGY. *Educ:* Notre Dame Univ, BSc, 42; Ohio State Univ, MSc, 46, PhD, 48. *Prof Exp:* Asst zool, Ohio State Univ, 46, instr, 46-48; instr comp anat, 48-49, from asst prof to assoc prof, 49-55, PROF COMP ANAT & EMBRYOL, PROVIDENCE COL, 55- *Mem:* AAAS; NY Acad Sci. *Res:* Insect embryology; metabolism of thyroid in rats and of cholesterol in normal, neoplastic and embryonic tissue. *Mailing Add:* 168 Garden City Dr Cranston RI 02920

FISHBACK, WILLIAM THOMPSON, b Milwaukee, Wis, Jan 28, 22; m 60; c 1. MATHEMATICS. *Educ:* Oberlin Col, AB, 43; Harvard Univ, AM, 47, PhD(math), 52. *Prof Exp:* Mem staff, Radiation Lab, Mass Inst Technol, 43-46; from instr to asst prof math, Univ Vt, 50-53; from asst prof to prof, Ohio Univ, 53-66; PROF MATH, EARLHAM COL, 66- *Concurrent Pos:* Vis prof, New Paltz State Teachers Col, 54; vis lectr, Clark Univ, 59, Harvard Univ, 60 & Denison Univ, 64. *Mem:* Am Math Soc; Math Asn Am. *Res:* Mathematical education; geometry. *Mailing Add:* Dept of Math Earlham Col Richmond IN 47374

FISHBEIN, EILEEN GREIF, b Baltimore, Md, April 17, 36; m 56; c 3. NURSING, EDUCATION. *Educ:* Univ Md, BS, 58, MS, 59; Catholic Univ Am, DNSc, 82. *Prof Exp:* Mem staff, Obstet Nursing, Univ Md Hosp, 58-59 & in-serv educ instr, 61-62; instr nursing, Sch Nursing, Catholic Univ Am, 71-73, asst prof, 73-78; ASST PROF NURSING, SCH NURSING, UNIV MD, 81- *Concurrent Pos:* Nat res serv award, Dept Educ & Welfare, 78-81; consult, Asn Am Med Cols, 77; guest worker, NIH, 78. *Mem:* Nat League Nursing; Nurses Asn Am Col Obstet & Gynec. *Res:* Paternal parenting behavior by expectant couples and its relationship to attitudes toward womens roles and anxiety in the prospective father; maternal and neonatal nursing. *Mailing Add:* 14201 Woodcrest Dr Rockville MD 20853

FISHBEIN, LAWRENCE, b Brooklyn, NY, Oct 27, 23; m 48; c 2. ORGANIC CHEMISTRY, BIOCHEMISTRY. *Educ:* Brooklyn Col, BS, 48; Georgetown Univ, MS, 55, PhD(org chem), 58. *Prof Exp:* Anal chemist, US Naval Propellant Plant, Md, 48-51, org chemist, 51-56; lectr chem, Georgetown Univ, 56-58; sr org chemist, Tracer Lab, Inc, Mass, 58, E R Squibb & Sons, NJ, 58-60 & Albright & Wilson, Ltd, Eng, 60-61; dir prod & develop, Chemed, Inc, Md, 61-63; staff scientist, Bionetics Res Labs, Inc, Md, 63-67; chief org synthesis & anal chem br, Nat Inst Environ Health Sci, 67-77; MEM STAFF, OFF OPERS, NAT CTR TOXICOL RES, 77- *Concurrent Pos:* Adj prof entom & toxicol, NC State Univ, 70- *Mem:* Am Chem Soc; Coblentz Soc; Soc Chem Indust; fel Am Inst Chemists; NY Acad Sci. *Res:* Paper, thin-layer and gas chromatography of carbamates, isomeric ureas and thioureas, synergistic agents; relationship of environmental agents in mutagenesis, carcinogenesis and teratogenesis; metabolism and photolysis of pesticides. *Mailing Add:* Off of Opers Nat Ctr for Toxicol Res Jefferson AR 72079

FISHBEIN, MORRIS, food bacteriology, deceased

FISHBEIN, WILLIAM, b New York, NY. RADAR. *Educ:* City Col NY, BEE, 48; Rutgers Univ, MS, 55. *Prof Exp:* Supvr electronics engr, 64-74, DIR, RADAR DIV, COMBAT SURVEILLANCE & TARGET ACQUISITION LAB, US ARMY ELECTRONICS RES & DEVELOP COMMAND, 74- *Mem:* Sr mem Inst Elec & Electronic Engrs. *Res:* Antenna and signal processing technology; for radars which can detect targets in the presence of competing reflections from terrain, foliage and precipitation. *Mailing Add:* 283 Norgrove Pl Elberon NJ 07740

FISHBEIN, WILLIAM NICHOLS, b Baltimore, Md, July 21, 33; m 56; c 3. BIOCHEMISTRY, MEDICINE. *Educ:* Johns Hopkins Univ, BA, 53, MD, 57; Univ Md, Baltimore, PhD(biochem), 66. *Prof Exp:* From intern to resident med, Univ Hosp, Baltimore, Md, 57-60; clin assoc, Nat Cancer Inst, 62-64; instr biochem, Med Sch, Univ Md, Baltimore, 64-65; CHIEF

BIOCHEM DIV, ARMED FORCES INST PATH, 65- *Concurrent Pos:* NIH trainee neurochem, Pediat Res Lab, Univ Hosp, Baltimore, Md, 60-62, NIH spec fel neurochem, 64-65; res grants cryobiol & hepatic coma, US Army Med Res & Develop Command, Washington, DC, 66-72; res grant urease, Nat Inst Arthritis, Metab & Digestive Dis, 67-81; Am Cancer Soc res grant cryobiol, 74-80; scientist assoc, Univs Assoc Res & Educ in Path, Md, 67-81; res grant adenylate deaminase, Muscular Dystrophy Asn, 79- *Honors & Awards:* A Cressy Morrison Award, NY Acad Sci, 68. *Mem:* Soc Cryobiol; Am Soc Biol Chem; Am Asn Path; Am Soc Cell Biol; Am Fedn Clin Res. *Res:* Enzyme structure and function; urease; cryobiology; hepatic coma; adenylate deaminase deficiency; hydroxamic acids; pathology. *Mailing Add:* Biochem Div Armed Forces Inst of Path Washington DC 20306

FISHBONE, LESLIE GARY, b Elizabeth, NJ, Feb 20, 46; m 77; c 1. NUCLEAR SAFEGUARDS, ENERGY ANALYSIS. *Educ:* Calif Inst Technol, BS, 68; Univ Md, PhD(physics), 72. *Prof Exp:* Fel physics, Univ Md, 72-73; exch fel physics, Landau Inst Theoret Physics, Acad Sci USSR, 73; res assoc & assoc instr physics, Univ Utah, 74-76; res assoc, Energy & Environ, Utah State Adv Coun Sci & Technol, 76-77; asst scientist energy & environ, 77-79, ASSOC SCIENTIST, NUCLEAR ENERGY, BROOKHAVEN NATR LAB, 79- *Mem:* Am Phys Soc; AAAS; Sigma Xi. *Res:* Research and development in support of domestic and international nuclear materials safeguards, computer modeling studies of national energy supply and demand systems; also black hole astrophysics. *Mailing Add:* Dept Nuclear Energy Bldg 197C Brookhaven Nat Lab Upton NY 11973

FISHBURNE, EDWARD STOKES, III, b Charleston, SC, Feb 8, 36; m 56; c 2. MOLECULAR PHYSICS, AERONAUTICAL ENGINEERING. *Educ:* The Citadel, BS, 57; Ohio State Univ, PhD(aeronaut & astronaut eng), 63; Hofstra Univ, MBA, 72. *Prof Exp:* Scientist, Crosley Div, Avco Corp, Ohio, 57 & Booz-Allen Appl Res Inc, 57-59; res assoc gas dynamics, Rocket Res Lab, Ohio State Univ, 59-63, asst supvr rocket propulsion, 63-67; asst prof aeronaut & astronaut eng, Univ, 63-67; res scientist, Grumman Aerospace Corp, 67-68, head aerophys sect, Res Dept, 68-73; vpres, Aeronaut Res Assocs Princeton, Inc, 73-79; PRES, SCI TECHNOL ASSOCS, INC, 79- *Mem:* AAAS; Am Phys Soc; Combustion Inst. *Res:* High temperature chemistry; energy exchange between molecules; spectroscopy; chemical physics; fluid dynamics; combustion. *Mailing Add:* Sci Technol Assocs Inc CN 5203 Princeton NJ 08540

FISHEL, DERRY LEE, b Findlay, Ohio, July 15, 29; m 67; c 2. ORGANIC CHEMISTRY. *Educ:* Bowling Green State Univ, BA, 52; Ohio State Univ, PhD(org chem), 59. *Prof Exp:* Asst prof chem, SDak Univ, 58-60; asst prof, 60-65, assoc prof, 65-73, PROF CHEM, KENT STATE UNIV, 73-; CONSULT, D&S CONSULT, 75- *Mem:* Sigma Xi; Am Soc Mass Spectrometry; Am Chem Soc. *Res:* Carbon-nitrogen rearrangement mechanisms; syntheses and properties of liquid crystals; organic mass spectrometry; digital data acquisition and control. *Mailing Add:* Dept of Chem Kent State Univ Kent OH 44242

FISHEL, JOHN B, b Hagerstown, Md, Sept 24, 14; m 45; c 2. ORGANIC CHEMISTRY. *Educ:* Lehigh Univ, BS, 36; Ohio State Univ, MS, 48. *Prof Exp:* Chemist, Neville Co, 38-39 & Gulf Res & Develop Co, 39-42; prin chemist, Battelle Mem Inst, 48-56; org res chemist, Res Lab, 56-64, res mgr, 64-69, mgr res & develop projs, 69-79, CONSULT, GEN CIGAR & TOBACCO CO, 79- *Mem:* Am Chem Soc; Am Soc Qual Control. *Res:* Chemistry of tobacco and tobacco smoke. *Mailing Add:* Gen Cigar & Tobacco Co R&D Ctr 602 N Charlotte St Box 4217 Lancaster PA 17604

FISHER, ALBERT MADDEN, b Toronto, Ont, May 27, 07; m 45; c 2. CHEMISTRY. *Educ:* Univ Toronto, BA, 31, MA, 32, PhD, 34. *Prof Exp:* Asst chem, Univ Toronto, 31-32, asst, Connaught Med Res Labs, 32-39, res assoc, 39-48, res & admin assoc, 48-50, from asst dir to assoc dir, 50-72, from assoc prof to prof physiol hyg, Sch Hyg, 50-72, actg chmn environ health, 69-72, EMER PROF PHYSIOL HYG, UNIV TORONTO, 72- *Concurrent Pos:* From secy to exec secy, Insulin Comt, Univ Toronto, 44-71, assoc, Sch Hyg, 45-48. *Mem:* Am Soc Biol Chem; Can Diabetes Asn (pres, 74-76); fel Chem Inst Can; Can Physiol Soc; Royal Can Inst (pres, 67 & 79). *Res:* Chemistry of insulin; blood substitutes. *Mailing Add:* 53 Dalewood Rd Toronto ON M4P 2N4 Can

FISHER, BEN, b Chicago, Ill, Jan 8, 24. HEMATOLOGY. *Educ:* Univ Ill, BS, 46, Col Med, MD, 48. *Prof Exp:* Instr med, Sch Med, Tulane Univ, 49-50; instr path, Col Med, Univ Ill, 50-53; assoc med to assoc prof med, Sch Med, State Univ NY, Buffalo, 59-77; CHIEF STAFF, VET ADMIN MED CTR, NORTH CHICAGO, ILL, 77-; ASSOC DEAN & PROF MED & PATH, CHICAGO MED SCH, UNIV HEALTH SCI, 77- *Concurrent Pos:* Resident clin path, Marine Hosp, US Pub Health Serv, New Orleans, 49-50; res fel path, Michael Reese Hosp, Chicago, 50-51 & asst dir hemat, 61-53; clin pathologist, Wayne Co Gen Hosp, 53-54; res hematologist, Roswell Park Mem Inst, 54-56; dir clin labs, Deaconess Hosp, Buffalo, NY, 59-68; chief hematol, Vet Admin Hosp, Buffalo, NY, 68-77. *Mem:* Sigma Xi; Am Col Physicians; Col Am Pathologists; Int Soc Hemat; Am Soc Hemat. *Res:* Hereditary hemoglobinopathies. *Mailing Add:* 1112 Garfield Ave Libertyville IL 60048

FISHER, BERNARD, b Pittsburgh, Pa, Aug 23, 18; m 48; c 3. SURGERY. *Educ:* Univ Pittsburgh, BS, 40, MD, 43; Am Bd Surg, dipl, 52. *Prof Exp:* Rotating intern, Mercy Hosp, 43-44, Surg resident, 44-48; from asst instr to instr surg, 47-53, asst prof surg & assoc dir Gibson Lab, 53-55, assoc prof, 56-59, dir lab surg res, 56-74, PROF SURG, UNIV PITTSBURGH, 59-, DIR ONCOL, 74- *Concurrent Pos:* Fel surg, Mercy Hosp; teaching fel path, Univ Pittsburgh, 44-45, fel surg, 45-47, res fel exp endocrinol, 47-50; fel, Univ Pa, 50-52; Markle scholar, 53-58; mem staff, Pittsburgh Med Ctr Hosps; consult, Oakland Vet Admin Hosp; exec comt coop group chairmen; consult, Nat Cancer Inst & chmn nat surg adjuvant proj for breast & bowel cancers. *Honors & Awards:* David Earle lectr, Sch Med, Northwestern Univ, 78; 11th Ann Karnofsky Mem lectr, 80; Wadsworth Mem Fund lectr, Rush Univ, 80; Karnofsky Award, Am Soc Clin Oncol, 80; Lucy Wortham James Clin Res Award, Soc Surg Oncol, 81; Henrietta Banting Mem lectr, Womens Col Hosp, Toronto, 81; Mary Ann Ervin Mem lectr, Jacksonville, 81. *Mem:* AAAS; Soc Univ Surg; Am Physiol Soc; AMA; fel Am Col Surg. *Res:* Experimental surgery; 332 publications. *Mailing Add:* Dept Surg Sch Med Univ Pittsburgh Pittsburgh PA 15261

FISHER, C(HARLES) P, water resources, see previous edition

FISHER, C(HARLES) PAGE, JR, b Richmond, Va, Sept 24, 21; m 72; c 2. CIVIL ENGINEERING. *Educ:* Univ Va, BSCE, 49; Harvard Univ, SM, 50; NC State Univ, PhD(civil eng, physics), 62. *Prof Exp:* Rodman, Va Hwy Dept, 39-41; with land surv, W W La Prade & Bros, 45-46; engr, Metcalf & Eddy, 51; found engr, Robertson & Assocs, 52-53 & H S Porter, 53-55; from instr to assoc prof civil eng, NC State Univ, 55-69; pres, Depcon Group, 69-78; CONSULT ENGR, 78- *Concurrent Pos:* Dir & secy corp, Troxler Electronics Labs, Inc, 62-; chmn bd & pres, Geotech Eng Co, 63-78; prin, Gardner-Kline Assoc, 67-71 & Fisher Assoc, 73- *Mem:* Fel Am Soc Civil Engrs; Am Soc Testing & Mat; fel Am Consult Eng Coun; Sigma Xi. *Res:* Measurement of the properties of earth materials in situ and in the laboratory; application of modern physics to civil engineering problems; quality control of engineering materials. *Mailing Add:* One Stoneridge Circle Durham NC 27705

FISHER, CHARLES HAROLD, b Hiawatha, WVa, Nov 20, 06; m 33, 68. ORGANIC CHEMISTRY. *Educ:* Roanoke Col, BS, 28; Univ Ill, MS, 29, PhD(org chem), 32. *Hon Degrees:* DSc, Tulane Univ, 53 & Roanoke Col, 63. *Prof Exp:* Instr org chem, Harvard Univ, 32-35; org chemist, US Bur Mines, Pa, 35-40; head org acids sect, Eastern Regional Res Lab, USDA, 40-46, head carbohydrate div, 46-50, dir southern mkt & nutrit res div, Agr Res Serv, 50-72; CONSULT, 72- *Concurrent Pos:* Mem comt chem utilization of coal, Nat Res Coun, 39-41; adj res prof, Roanoke Col, 72- *Honors & Awards:* Southern Chemists Award, 56; Herty Award, 59; Chem Pioneer Award, Am Inst Chemists, 66. *Mem:* AAAS; Am Chem Soc; Am Asn Textile Chemists & Colorists; hon mem Am Inst Chemists (pres, 62-63); Royal Soc Chem. *Res:* Cotton textiles; cellulose; chemistry and utilization of farm crops; polymers; organic synthesis. *Mailing Add:* Dept of Chem Roanoke Col Salem VA 24153

FISHER, CHARLES RAY, b Carrollton, Mo, July 30, 40; m 61; c 2. MICROBIOLOGY. *Educ:* Cent Col, Mo, BA, 61; Purdue Univ, MS, 63; Ill State Univ, PhD(microbiol), 68. *Prof Exp:* Res biologist, Oak Ridge Nat Lab, 66-73; radiation biologist, Int Atomic Energy Agency, UN, 71-72; biophysicist, US AEC, 73-76; assoc prof microbiol, Radford Col, 76-79; Fulbright prof, Ege Univ, Turkey, 79-80; vis prof biol & chem, Cent Methodist Col, 80-81; PROF MICROBIOL, SCH MED, UNIV DOMINICA, 81- *Concurrent Pos:* Fel, Oak Ridge Nat Lab, 66-68; res microbiologist, Sch Vet Med, Univ Mo, 79-80. *Mem:* Am Soc Microbiol; AAAS; Soc Indust Micrbiol; Sigma Xi; Am Inst Biol Sci. *Mailing Add:* 505 N Linn St Fayette 65248

FISHER, CLARK ALAN, b Torrance, Calif, Sept 5, 33; m 61; c 1. MICROBIOLOGY, IMMUNOLOGY. *Educ:* Ore State Col, BS(pharm) & BS(bact), 60; Univ Calif, Berkeley, MA, 64, PhD(immunol), 69. *Prof Exp:* Asst res scientist microbiol, NY Univ Sch Med, 70-72; instr, 72-75, ASST PROF MICROBIOL, NEW YORK MED COL, 75- *Mem:* Am Chem Soc; Am Soc Microbiol; Int Leprosy Asn; NY Acad Sci; Sigma Xi. *Res:* Immunochemistry and biological properties of envelope antigens of anaerobic corynebacteria; pathogenesis of persistent bacterial infections. *Mailing Add:* Dept of Microbiol New York Med Col Valhalla NY 10595

FISHER, CLETUS G, b Canton, Ohio, Sept 22, 22; m 46; c 2. SPEECH PATHOLOGY, AUDIOLOGY. *Educ:* Kent State Univ, BS, 49; Univ Iowa, MA, 50; Ohio State Univ, PhD(audiol), 63. *Prof Exp:* Instr speech, Kans State Col, 50-53; exec dir, Hearing & Speech Ctr, Dayton, Ohio, 53-60; instr speech, Ohio State Univ, 62-63; asst prof speech path & audiol, Univ Iowa, 63-68; dir speech & hearing div, Dept Speech, 68-69, assoc prof speech, 69-71, PROF SPEECH, NORTHERN ILL UNIV, 71-, CHMN DEPT COMMUN DIS, 74- *Mem:* Acad Rehab Audiol; Am Speech & Hearing Asn. *Res:* Visual and aural perception of oral signals, including those with normal or with pathological hearing. *Mailing Add:* Dept of Commun Dis Northern Ill Univ De Kalb IL 60115

FISHER, D(ANIEL) JEROME, b Canton, NY, June 14, 96; m 19; c 3. MINERALOGY, CRYSTALLOGRAPHY. *Educ:* Univ Chicago, BS, 17, MS, 20, PhD(geol), 22. *Prof Exp:* From instr to prof mineral, 21-61, EMER PROF MINERAL, UNIV CHICAGO, 61- *Concurrent Pos:* Geologist, Ill Geol Surv, 21-34; from jr geologist to sr geologist, US Geol Surv, 24-43; geologist, SDak Geol Surv, 41-42; vis prof, Northwestern Univ, 65 & Ariz State Univ, 68-70; prof, Dept Geol, Ariz State Univ, 70-74. *Mem:* Fel AAAS; fel Geol Soc Am; fel Mineral Soc Am (vpres, 56, pres, 57); hon mem Mineral Soc India; Int Mineral Asn (treas, 58-60, pres, 60-64). *Res:* Pegmatites; fuel geology; areal and stratigraphic geology; projection protractor to prepare gnomonic and stereographic projections; x-ray precession methods; optical crystallography; projections in structural studies; mineral phosphates; refractometry; goniometry. *Mailing Add:* 2101 E Maryland Ave Phoenix AZ 85016

FISHER, DALE JOHN, b Omro, Wis, June 4, 25; m 57; c 1. INSTRUMENTATION. *Educ:* Univ Wis-Oshkosh, BS, 47; Ind Univ, PhD(chem), 51. *Prof Exp:* Chemist, Ionic Anal Group, Oak Ridge Nat Lab, 51-52, group leader anal instrumentation, Anal Chem Div, 52-72, dirs staff, 72-73; physicist, Vet Admin Hosp, 73-74, tech dir nuclear med, 74-76; PHYSICIST, BUR MED DEVICES, FOOD & DRUG ADMIN, SILVER SPRING, 76- *Honors & Awards:* Am Chem Soc Award, 69. *Mem:* Am Chem Soc; Sigma Xi; Am Soc Testing & Mat. *Res:* Design and new applications of instruments and methods for chemical analysis and research; nuclear medicine and research with computer-based instrumentation to obtain better diagnostic information for patient care; concerns with clinical laboratory instrument systems including hazards, problems, standards and specifications. *Mailing Add:* 6319 Golden Hook Columbia MD 21044

FISHER, DAVID A(LEXANDER), b Kitchener, Ont, June 16, 07; US citizen; m 36; c 2. MECHANICAL ENGINEERING. *Educ:* Cornell Univ, ME, 31; Columbia Univ, MS, 39. *Prof Exp:* Instr mech eng, Cornell Univ, 31-33; engr, Bronx Gas & Elec Co, 35; instr mech eng, City Col New York, 36-40; asst prof, Tufts Col, 40-48; from assoc prof to prof, 48-73, EMER PROF MECH ENG, UNIV CONN, 77- *Concurrent Pos:* Mech engr, Jackson & Moreland, Mass, 45-48. *Mem:* Am Soc Mech Engrs; Am Soc Eng Educ. *Res:* Applied thermodynamics. *Mailing Add:* 17 Storrs Heights Rd Storrs CT 06268

FISHER, DAVID E, b Philadelphia, Pa, June 22, 32; m 54; c 3. GEOCHRONOLOGY, METEORITICS. *Educ:* Trinity Col, BS, 54; Univ Fla, PhD(chem physics), 58. *Prof Exp:* Oak Ridge Inst Nuclear Studies fel, Oak Ridge Nat Lab, 57-58; res assoc, Brookhaven Nat Lab, 58-60; asst prof eng physics, Cornell Univ, 60-66; assoc prof, 66-70, PROF MARINE & GEOPHYS, INST MARINE SCI, UNIV MIAMI, 70- *Mem:* AAAS; Meteoretical Soc; Am Phys Soc; Am Chem Soc; Am Geophys Union. *Res:* Nuclear cosmochronology; cosmic-ray nuclear reactions in meteorites; activation analysis; isotopic abundances in meteorites and tektites; cosmic chemistry; marine geology and geochemistry; geochronology. *Mailing Add:* Inst of Marine Sci Univ of Miami Miami FL 33149

FISHER, DELBERT A, b Placerville, Calif, Aug 12, 28; m 51; c 3. MEDICINE, PEDIATRICS. *Educ:* Univ Calif, AB, 50, MD, 53; Am Bd Pediat, dipl, 59. *Prof Exp:* Instr & res assoc pediat, endocrinol & metab, Sch Med, Univ Ore, 57-60; from asst prof to prof pediat, Sch Med, Univ Ark, 60-68, asst dir clin study ctr, 62-68; prof pediat, 68-73, PROF PEDIAT & MED, SCH MED, UNIV CALIF, LOS ANGELES, 73-; RES PROF DEVELOP BIOL, HARBOR GEN HOSP, TORRANCE, 75- *Concurrent Pos:* USPHS career develop award, 64-68; examr, Am Bd Pediat, 70-; ed, J Clin Endocrinol Metab, 78-83. *Honors & Awards:* Nutrit Res Award, Am Acad Pediat, 81. *Mem:* Soc Pediat Res; Am Soc Clin Invest; Lawson Wilkins Pediat Endocrine Soc; Am Acad Pediat; Am Pediat Soc. *Res:* Pediatric endocrinology and metabolism; thyroid disease; maternal-fetal metabolism and endocrinology. *Mailing Add:* Los Angeles County Harbor 1000 W Carson St Torrance CA 90509

FISHER, DON LOWELL, b Salt Lake City, Utah, June 14, 41; m 67; c 4. EMBRYOLOGY, TERATOLOGY. *Educ:* Brigham Young Univ, BS, 66, MS, 68; Univ Minn, PhD(anat), 71. *Prof Exp:* Instr histol, Univ Mich, 71-72; ASST PROF GROSS ANAT, UNIV MINN, ANN ARBOR, 72-, PROF EMBRYOL, 78- *Concurrent Pos:* Consult embryol, Eastern Mich Univ, 81 & Oakland Univ, 81 & 82. *Mem:* Teratology Soc; Am Asn Anatomists; Soc Study Reproduction; Sigma Xi. *Res:* Early experimental embryology and teratology. *Mailing Add:* 2100 Churchill Ann Arbor MI 48103

FISHER, DONALD B, b Philadelphia, Pa, Oct 14, 35; m 63. BOTANY. *Educ:* Univ Wash, BS, 57; Univ Wis, MS, 61; Iowa State Univ, PhD(biochem), 65. *Prof Exp:* Asst bot, Univ Wis, 59-61 & biochem, Iowa State Univ, 61-63; NIH fel bot, Univ Calif, Berkeley, 65-67, res botanist, 67-68; from asst prof to assoc prof, Univ Ga, 68-78; assoc prof, 78-80, PROF BOT, WASH STATE UNIV, 80- *Mem:* AAAS; Am Soc Plant Physiol; Am Inst Biol Sci. *Res:* Transport of materials in plants. *Mailing Add:* Dept of Bot Wash State Univ Pullman WA 99164

FISHER, DONALD D, b Spokane, Wash, Dec 20, 29; m 51; c 3. INFORMATION PROCESSING, COMPUTER SCIENCE EDUCATION. *Educ:* Wash State Univ, BA, 51, MA, 53; Stanford Univ, PhD(math), 62. *Prof Exp:* Asst math, State Col Wash, 51-53; mathematician, Douglas Aircraft Co, Inc, 53-54; asst math, Stanford Univ, 54-57, actg instr, 57-58; appl sci rep, Int Bus Mach Corp, 58-60, mathematician, 60-62; res assoc comput sci, Stanford Univ, 62-65; dir res, Comput Ctr & assoc prof prev med & math, Ind Univ, 65-69; prof & head comput & info sci dept, 69-73, dir, Sch Math Sci, 73-81, PROF COMPUT & INFO SCI DEPT, OKLA STATE UNIV, 73- *Mem:* Asn Comput Mach; Soc Indust & Appl Math; Sigma Xi. *Res:* Computer architecture; data flow architecture; data structures; numerical solution of partial differential equations - particulary free boundary problems; computer-based scheduling and simulation. *Mailing Add:* Dept Comput & Info Sci Okla State Univ Stillwater OK 74074

FISHER, DONALD WILLIAM, b Schenectady, NY, Sept 8, 22; m 55; c 2. PALEONTOLOGY. *Educ:* Univ Buffalo, AB, 44, AM, 48; Univ Rochester, PhD(geol), 52. *Prof Exp:* Instr geol, Union Col, 49-51, asst prof, 52-53; sr paleontologist & stratigrapher, 53-55, STATE PALEONTOLOGIST, NY STATE MUS, STATE SCI SERV NY, 55- *Concurrent Pos:* Field geologist, State Geol Surv, NY, 47-53. *Mem:* AAAS; fel Geol Soc Am; Int Paleont Union; Paleont Soc; Geol Asn Can. *Res:* Cambrian, Ordovician and Silurian stratigraphy and paleontology of New York; Taconic geology; tentaculitids; New York Pleistocene mammals; history of New York geology and paleontology. *Mailing Add:* 1 Lindenwald Ct Kinderhook NY 12106

FISHER, E(ARL) EUGENE, b Monongahela, Pa, Dec 18, 22; m 44; c 4. ORGANIC CHEMISTRY, RESEARCH ADMINISTRATION. *Educ:* Washington & Jefferson Col, BS, 43; Ohio State Univ, MS, 44; Carnegie Inst Technol, PhD(chem), 48. *Prof Exp:* Asst, Ohio State Univ, 43-44; asst, Carnegie Inst Technol, 46-47, res assoc, 47-48; res chemist org chem, E I du Pont de Nemours & Co, Inc, 48-52; res chemist fabrics & finishes dept, 52-58; head explor sect, Chem Dept, A E Staley Mfg Co, 58-61; dir chem res, 61-69, dir food prod res & develop, 69-70; dir, 70-73, VPRES, RES & DEVELOP, WILLIAM WRIGLEY JR CO, 73- *Mem:* AAAS; Am Chem Soc; Sigma Xi; Inst Food Technologists; Am Soc Qual Control. *Res:* Organic syntheses; carbohydrates; polymers; analytical methods. *Mailing Add:* Wm Wrigley Jr Co Res & Develop 410 N Michigan Ave Chicago IL 60611

FISHER, EDWARD, b Boston, Mass, Sept 3, 13; m 57. MATHEMATICAL PHYSICS. *Educ:* Mass Inst Technol, BS, 33; Cornell Univ, PhD(theoret physics), 45. *Prof Exp:* Instr physics, Univ Md, 42-43; instr, Cornell Univ, 43-45; asst prof, Univ Wyo, 46-48; assoc prof, Mo Sch Mines, 48-52; physicist, Gen Precision Lab, 52-53, consult, 53-54; physicist, Atomic Power

Develop Assocs, 54-56; staff scientist, Lockheed Aircraft Corp, 57-59; prin scientist, United Tech Ctr, 59-63; PROF PHYSICS, STATE UNIV NY COL OSWEGO, 63- *Mem:* Am Phys Soc. *Res:* Concepts in wave mechanics; electrical rocket propulsion; nuclear reactor shielding; noise theory; calculation of the fine-structure constant. *Mailing Add:* Dept of Physics State Univ of NY Col Oswego NY 13126

FISHER, EDWARD RICHARD, b Detroit, Mich, Mar 24, 38; m 73; c 5. CHEMICAL PHYSICS, ENGINEERING. *Educ:* Univ Calif, Berkeley, BSc, 61; Johns Hopkins Univ, PhD(chem eng sci), 65. *Prof Exp:* Res chemist, Lawrence Radiation Lab, 61; asst prof chem, Univ Copenhagen, 65-66; phys chemist, Space Sci Lab, Gen Elec Co, Pa, 66-68; assoc prof chem eng, 68-74, PROF CHEM ENG, WAYNE STATE UNIV, 74-; DIR, RES INST ENG SCI, 77- *Concurrent Pos:* Lectr, Univ Copenhagen, 66 & Gen Elec Grad Prog, Rensselaer Polytech Inst, 67. *Mem:* Am Inst Physics; Am Inst Chem Engrs. *Res:* Experimental and theoretical study of the details of energy transfer mechanisms in molecular collisions; plasma chemistry and molecular laser studies. *Mailing Add:* Res Inst 220 Eng Bldg Wayne State Univ Detroit MI 48202

FISHER, EDWARD S, b Minneapolis, Minn, Apr 23, 21; m 53; c 3. PHYSICAL METALLURGY. *Educ:* Univ Minn, BS, 48; Ill Inst Technol, MS, 54. *Prof Exp:* Asst metallurgist, 48-55, assoc metallurgist, 55-80, RES METALLURGIST, ARGONNE NAT LAB, 80- *Mem:* Am Inst Mining, Metall & Petrol Engrs; Metall Soc. *Res:* Elastic constants in metal single crystals, particularly relation between elastic constant changes and phase changes. *Mailing Add:* Metall Div Argonne Nat Lab Argonne IL 60439

FISHER, EDWIN RALPH, b Pittsburgh, Pa, Sept 2, 23; m 53. PATHOLOGY. *Educ:* Univ Pittsburgh, BS, 45, MD, 47. *Prof Exp:* Assoc pathologist, Cleveland Clin, 52, 54 & USPHS, 52-54; assoc prof, 54-58, PROF PATH, UNIV PITTSBURGH, 58-; DIR LABS, SHADYSIDE HOSP, 70- *Concurrent Pos:* Chief lab serv, Vet Admin Hosp, 54-70. *Honors & Awards:* Parke-Davis Award, 63. *Mem:* Am Soc Clin Pathologists; Am Soc Exp Pathologists; Am Asn Pathologists & Bacteriologists; Col Am Pathologists; Int Acad Path. *Res:* Histochemistry; pathology of gastrointestinal tract and thyroid. *Mailing Add:* Shadyside Hosp 5230 Centre Ave Pittsburgh PA 15232

FISHER, ELLSWORTH HENRY, b Ottawa, Kans, Dec 30, 11; m 37; c 2. ENTOMOLOGY. *Educ:* ECent State Teachers Col, BS, 34; Okla Agr & Mech Col, MS, 39; Univ Wis, PhD(entom), 48. *Prof Exp:* From asst prof to assoc prof, 45-61, PROF ENTOM, UNIV WIS-MADISON, 61-, COORDR PESTICIDE USE EDUC, 65- *Mem:* Am Entom Soc; Entom Soc Am. *Res:* Insects of field crops, man, livestock and household; rats and mice; coordination of educational programs in the safe and economical uses of pesticides. *Mailing Add:* Col of Agr Dept of Entomol Univ of Wis Madison WI 53706

FISHER, ELWOOD, b New Martinsville, WVa, Apr 12, 26; m 56; c 1. PARASITOLOGY, ECOLOGY. *Educ:* Fairmont State Col, BSc, 53; Miami Univ, MSc, 60; Va Polytech Inst, PhD(biol), 67. *Prof Exp:* Instr high sch, Ohio, 53-59; asst prof, Miami Univ, 59-60; asst prof biol, 60-67, assoc prof, 67-77, PROF BIOL, JAMES MADISON UNIV, 77- *Mem:* Am Soc Parasitol; Am Pomol Soc. *Res:* Parasites of wildlife; genetics of fruit trees. *Mailing Add:* Dept of Biol James Madison Univ Harrisonburg VA 22807

FISHER, FARLEY, b Cleveland, Ohio, Apr 30, 38. CHEMISTRY, CHEMICAL ENGINEERING. *Educ:* Mass Inst Technol, SB, 60; Univ Ill, PhD(chem), 65. *Prof Exp:* Asst prof chem, Tex A&M Univ, 65-69; vis lectr, Bucknell Univ, 69-70; res assoc, Ctr Sci Pub Interest, 71-72; chemist, Environ Protection Agency, 72-73, dir hazard assessment, 73-77; prog mgr chem threats, 77-79, PROG DIR KINETICS CATALYSIS & REACTION ENG, NSF, 79- *Mem:* Am Chem Soc; Am Inst Chem Eng; Soc Environ Geochem & Health; AAAS. *Res:* Environmental transport and fate; hazard assessment of chemicals; catalysis; photochemistry; research management. *Mailing Add:* Div Chem & Process Eng NSF Washington DC 20550

FISHER, FRANCIS JOHN FULTON, b Roxburgh, NZ, Oct 31, 26; Can citizen; m 49; c 5. EVOLUTIONARY BIOLOGY, PLANT PHYSIOLOGY. *Educ:* Univ Canterbury, BSc, 47, MSc, 49; Univ NZ, PhD(exp taxon), 54. *Prof Exp:* Lectr bot, Univ Melbourne, 54-57; sr lectr, Univ Tasmania, 57-58; prin sci off, Bot Div, NZ Dept Sci & Indust Res, 58-65; assoc prof, 65-67, PROF BIOL SCI, SIMON FRASER UNIV, 67- *Concurrent Pos:* Nuffield Found biol res grant, Australian Nat Univ, 54-55; Brit Coun travel grant, 55-56; Carnegie Corp travel grant, 56; Carnegie Inst Wash res fel, 56-57; dir, Tasmanian Bot Gardens, 57-58; USPHS int fel, 63-64, int follow-up grant, 66-67; biol consult, Sch Social Welfare, Univ Calgary, 67- & Can Environ Sci Ltd, 68-; consult, Environ Res Consults, Ltd, 71- *Mem:* AAAS; Am Inst Biol Sci; Can Bot Asn; Royal Soc NZ; fel Linnaean Soc London. *Res:* Ecophysiology of New Zealand alpine screes; genecology of mountain ranunculus of New Zealand and North and South America; evolution of reproductive isolation in plants; morphogenesis of leaves; adaptive change processes in living systems including human; biological criteria for value systems. *Mailing Add:* Dept of Biosci Simon Fraser Univ Burnaby BC V5A 1S6 Can

FISHER, FRANK M, JR, b Louisville, Ky, Oct 16, 31; m 56; c 2. PARASITOLOGY, INVERTEBRATE PHYSIOLOGY. *Educ:* Hanover Col, BA, 53; Purdue Univ, MS, 56, PhD(invert physiol), 61. *Prof Exp:* NIH fel, 61-63, asst prof, 63-69, assoc prof, 69-73, PROF BIOL, RICE UNIV, 73- *Concurrent Pos:* Instr invert zool, Marine Biol Lab, Woods Hole, Mass, 64-70; mem ARB study sect, NIH, 75-, chairperson, 76- *Res:* Chemical basis parasitism; distribution and flux of organic materials in wetland ecosystems; toxic materials in wetland environments. *Mailing Add:* Dept of Biol Rice Univ Houston TX 77001

FISHER, FRANK ROYAL, b Denver, Colo, Sept 1, 18; m 44, 80; c 6. ENVIRONMENTAL ENGINEERING, PIPELINE TECHNOLOGY. *Educ:* Colo Sch Mines, BPE, 40. *Prof Exp:* Process engr, Sinclair Refining Co, 40-42 & 45-47, admin asst to mgr, 47-51, mem jr bd dirs, Sinclair Oil Corp, 52-53, corp sect, Sinclair Res, Inc, 51-58, chmn exec prod comt, Sinclair Refining Co, 55-65, vpres opers, Sinclair Res, Inc, 58-65, vpres & dir res, Sinclair Oil & Gas Co, 65-68, dir prod res, Sinclair Oil Corp, 68-69; asst dept mgr prod res, Atlantic Richfield Co, 69-73; mgr environ protection, 73-80, ALASKA MGR ANETS RELS, ALYESKA PIPELINE SERV CO, 81- *Mem:* Am Inst Chem Engrs; Soc Petrol Engrs. *Res:* Environmental management; petroleum research; pipeline operations. *Mailing Add:* Alyeska Pipeline Serv Co 1835 S Bragaw Anchorage AK 99504

FISHER, FRANKLIN E(UGENE), b Robinson, Ill, Mar 8, 33; m 59; c 1. MECHANICAL ENGINEERING, ENGINEERING MECHANICS. *Educ:* Rose Polytech Inst, BS, 60; Univ Md, College Park, MS, 65, PhD(mech eng), 69. *Prof Exp:* Aerospace engr, Aeronaut Systs Div, Wright-Patterson AFB, Ohio, 60-63; instr mech eng, Univ Md, College Park, 64-69; assoc prof, 69-80, PROF MECH ENG & CHMN, LOYOLA MARYMOUNT UNIV, 80- *Concurrent Pos:* Res mech eng, Naval Res Lab, Washington, DC, 65-66; consult, Ralph M Parson Co, 73-75; mem tech staff, Hughes Aircraft Co, 77- *Mem:* Am Soc Mech Engrs; Am Soc Eng Educ; Soc Automotive Engrs. *Res:* Shock loading and vibration of structures as applied to mechanical engineering design. *Mailing Add:* Dept of Mech Eng 7101 W 80th St Los Angeles CA 90045

FISHER, FREDERICK HENDRICK, b Aberdeen, Wash, Dec 30, 26; m 55; c 4. PHYSICS. *Educ:* Univ Wash, BS, 49, PhD(physics), 57. *Prof Exp:* Asst physics, Univ Calif, Los Angeles, 54-55; from res physicist to assoc res physicist, 55-68, RES OCEANOGR & LECTR, MARINE PHYS LAB, SCRIPPS INST OCEANOG, UNIV CALIF, SAN DIEGO, 68-, ASSOC DIR, 74- *Concurrent Pos:* Res fel acoust, Harvard Univ, 57-58; co-designer & proj scientist res platform FLIP, 60-62; dir res, Havens Indust, 63-64; prof & chmn dept physics, Univ RI, 70-71; assoc ed, J Acoust Soc Am, 69-76. *Mem:* Fel Acoust Soc Am (vpres elect, 79-80, vpres, 80-81); AAAS; Am Chem Soc; Sigma Xi; sr mem Inst Elec & Electronics Engrs. *Res:* Acoustics; physical chemistry; underwater sound; oceanography; how acoustic propagation in the ocean is affected by oceanographic environmental fluctuations and chemical ion-speciation, especially at elevated pressures. *Mailing Add:* Marine Phys Lab Scripps Inst Oceanog Univ Calif LaJolla CA 92093

FISHER, FREDERICK STEPHEN, b Highland Park, Mich, Aug 5, 37; m 61; c 2. GEOLOGY, GEOCHEMISTRY. *Educ:* Wayne State Univ, BS, 61, MS, 62; Univ Wyo, PhD(geol), 66. *Prof Exp:* asst prof geol, Rocky Mountain Col, 75-78; GEOLOGIST, US GEOL SURV, 66- *Mem:* Geol Soc Am; Soc Econ Geologists; Am Inst Prof Geologists. *Res:* Geology and geochemistry of hydrothermal deposits. *Mailing Add:* US Geol Surv Denver Fed Ctr Denver CO 80225

FISHER, GAIL FEIMSTER, b Washington, DC, Sept 18, 28; c 2. APPLIED STATISTICS, DEMOGRAPHY. *Educ:* Univ Md, BA, 49, MA, 51; Univ NC, PhD, 77. *Prof Exp:* Analyst health, Air Pollution Med Prog, Dept Health, Educ & Welfare, 56-58, analyst, Accident Prev Prog, 58-60, chief statistician, Diabetes & Arthritis Prog, 60-66, eval officer, Bur Health Servs, 66-68, dir off prog planning & eval, 68-73, ASSOC DIR COOP HEALTH STATIST PROG, NAT CTR HEALTH STATIST, HEW, 73- *Concurrent Pos:* Mem staff, President's Comn Health Care Facil, 67-68. *Res:* Health research; health statistics. *Mailing Add:* Nat Ctr for Health Statist Ctr Bldg Hyattsville MD 20782

FISHER, GALEN BRUCE, b Bethesda, Md, Jan 14, 45; m 76; c 1. SURFACE SCIENCE, CATALYSIS. *Educ:* Pomona Col, BA, 66; Stanford Univ, MS, 67, PhD(solid state physics), 74. *Prof Exp:* Res assoc, Div Eng, Brown Univ, 72-75; physicist, Surface Sci Div, Nat Bur Standards, 75-78; sr res scientist, 78-82, STAFF RES SCIENTIST, PHYS CHEM DEPT, GEN MOTORS RES LABS, 82- *Concurrent Pos:* Lectr, NATO Advan Study Inst, 74; vis asst prof, Physics Dept, Brown Univ, 75. *Mem:* Am Vacuum Soc; Am Phys Soc; Am Chem Soc; Catalysis Soc; Mat Res Soc. *Res:* Surface science, heterogeneous catalysis, and chemisorption; the bonding, electronic structure, and vibrations of adsorbates on metal surfaces. *Mailing Add:* Physical Chem Dept Gen Motors Res Labs Warren MI 48090

FISHER, GENE JORDAN, b Quitman, Miss, March 26, 31; m 54; c 2. ORGANIC CHEMISTRY. *Educ:* Univ Tex, BS, 52. *Prof Exp:* From res chemist to sr res chemist, 52-59, group leader, 59-67, res mgr, 67-77, DIR RES, CELANESE CHEM CO, 77- *Mem:* Am Chem Soc; fel Am Inst Chemists. *Res:* Reactions of ketene; reactions of formaldehyde; synthesis of monomers; heterogeneous catalysis. *Mailing Add:* Celanese Chem Co Tech Ctr PO Box 9077 Corpus Christi TX 78408

FISHER, GEORGE HAROLD, JR, b San Antonio, Tex, July 19, 43. ORGANIC BIOCHEMISTRY. *Educ:* Rollins Col, Fla, BS, 65; Univ Fla, MS, 68; Univ Miami, PhD(org chem), 73. *Prof Exp:* Res asst org chem, Univ Fla, 68; res fel biomed chem, Inst Biomed Res, Univ Tex, Austin, 73-75; res scientist peptide chem, Papanicolaou Cancer Res Inst, 75-77; RES ASST PROF MED & RES ASST PROF CHEM, UNIV MIAMI, 76- *Mem:* Am Heart Asn; Am Chem Soc; Sigma Xi. *Res:* Synthesis, purification and biological activity studies of peptide hormones such as bradykinin, angiotensins, substance P, and luteinizing hormone-releasing hormone. *Mailing Add:* Dept Med PO Box 0106960 Miami FL 33101

FISHER, GEORGE PHILLIP, b Quincy, Mass, May 10, 38; m 79. APPLIED PHYSICS. *Educ:* Mass Inst Technol, BS, 59; Univ Ill, MS, 61, PhD(physics), 65. *Prof Exp:* Res assoc physics, Univ Colo, Boulder, 64-65; asst prof, 65-71; assoc physicist, Physics Dept, Brookhaven Nat Lab, 71-73; PHYSICIST, R&D ASSOCS, 73- *Concurrent Pos:* NSF fel, Europ Ctr Nuclear Res, 67-68; US AEC nuclear educ & training appointment, Lawrence Radiation Lab, Berkeley, 69, Brookhaven Nat Lab, 70; consult, Dow Chem Co, 71. *Mem:* AAAS; Am Phys Soc; Am Asn Physics Teachers. *Res:* Pulsed power systems; x-ray sources; nuclear effects; broad range of problems in energy, fusion and national security. *Mailing Add:* R&D Assocs Box 9695 Marina Del Rey CA 90291

FISHER, GEORGE ROBERT, b Long Prairie, Minn, Aug 29, 28; m 58; c 4. DAIRY HUSBANDRY. *Educ:* Univ Minn, St Paul, BS, 51, PhD(agr invests bovine semen), 66. *Prof Exp:* Teacher pub sch, 52-53 & 56-57, instr, 58-59; res asst dairy husb, Univ Minn, St Paul, 55-61; PROF DAIRY HUSB, N DAK STATE UNIV EXTEN, 61- *Mem:* Am Soc Animal Sci; Am Dairy Sci Asn. *Res:* Investigations on bovine semen extenders and their application. *Mailing Add:* Dept of Animal Sci NDak State Univ Fargo ND 58102

FISHER, GEORGE WESCOTT, b New Haven, Conn, May 16, 37; m 59; c 3. GEOLOGY. *Educ:* Dartmouth Col, BA, 59; Johns Hopkins Univ, MA, 62, PhD(geol), 63. *Prof Exp:* Fel, Carnegie Inst Geophys Lab, 64-66; lectr, 65-66, from asst prof to assoc prof, 66-74, PROF GEOL, JOHNS HOPKINS UNIV, 74-, CHMN DEPT EARTH & PLANETARY SCI, 78- *Mem:* Geochem Soc; Mineral Soc Am; Geol Soc Am. *Res:* Field and laboratory studies of the chemistry, structure and origin of metamorphic and igneous rocks; kinetics of petrologic processes. *Mailing Add:* Dept of Earth & Planetary Sci Johns Hopkins Univ Baltimore MD 21218

FISHER, GERALD LIONEL, b Malden, Mass, Aug 28, 46. ENVIRONMENTAL CHEMISTRY, METABOLISM. *Educ:* Northeastern Univ, BA, 68; Univ Calif, Santa Barbara, MA, 71; Univ Calif, Davis, Phd(chem ecol), 74. *Prof Exp:* ASSOC RES ENVIRON CHEMIST POLLUTION TOXICOL, RADIOBIOL LAB, UNIV CALIF, DAVIS, 75-; MGR, TOXICOL & HEALTH SCI SECT, BATTELLE MEM INST, COLUMBUS, 80- & ADJ PROF, PHARMACOL, OHIO STATE UNIV, 80- *Concurrent Pos:* Adj assoc prof, Div Environ Studies, Univ Calif, Davis, 75-80, fac mem, Biomed Eng Grad Group, 75-80 & Ecol Grad Group & Nutrit Grad Group, 76-80. *Mem:* NY Acad Sci; Am Chem Soc; Int Asn Bioinorg Scientists; Soc Environ Geochem & Health; AAAS. *Res:* Trace mineral metabolism and homeostasis; evaluation of health hazard and mechanisms of damage from pollutant exposure. *Mailing Add:* Battelle Columbus Lab 515 King Ave Columbus OH 43201

FISHER, GORDON MCCREA, b St Paul, Minn, Oct 5, 25; m 56; c 2. MATHEMATICS, HISTORY OF SCIENCE. *Educ:* Miami Univ, BA, 51; La State Univ, PhD(math), 59. *Prof Exp:* Instr math, Miami Univ, 53 & 56-57; instr, La State Univ, 57-59; instr, Princeton Univ, 59-62; lectr math & hon lectr hist & philos sci, Univ Otago, NZ, 62-64; sr lectr hist & philos sci & hon sr lectr math, 64-66; sr lectr math & sr lectr hist philos sci, Univ Waikato, 66-67; PROF MATH, JAMES MADISON UNIV, 67- *Mem:* AAAS; Hist Sci Soc; Phil Sci Asn; Am Math Soc; Math Asn Am. *Res:* Analysis; history of mathematics. *Mailing Add:* Dept of Math Madison Col Harrisonburg VA 22801

FISHER, GORDON P(AGE), b Baltimore, Md, July 26, 22; m 44; c 4. CIVIL ENGINEERING. *Educ:* Johns Hopkins Univ, BE, 42, DEng, 48. *Prof Exp:* Engr, Struct Res Div, NASA, 42-44; from asst prof to assoc prof civil eng, 48-59, assoc dean col eng, 60-66, dir water resources ctr, 62-64, head dept environ systs eng, 66-71, PROF CIVIL ENG, CORNELL UNIV, 59- *Concurrent Pos:* Sr engr, Pittsburgh Des Moines Steel Co, Pa, 54-55, consult, 57; consult, Power Reactor Develop Co, Mich, 57-64; vis prof, Chalmers Univ, 62-63; mem, Transp Res Forum & Hwy Res Bd, Nat Acad Sci-Nat Res Coun; expert mem, European Comt Concrete. *Honors & Awards:* Norman Medal, Am Soc Civil Engrs, 62. *Mem:* Am Soc Civil Engrs; Am Concrete Inst; Column Res Coun; Opers Res Soc Am. *Res:* Buckling; foundation design; matrix formulation of structural theory; industrialization of building construction; water resources planning and management; analysis and design of transportation systems; traffic flow theory. *Mailing Add:* Sch of Civil & Environ Eng Cornell Univ Ithaca NY 14853

FISHER, HANS, b Ger, Mar 4, 28; nat US; m 51; c 3. NUTRITION. *Educ:* Rutgers Univ, BS, 50; Univ Conn, MS, 52; Univ Ill, PhD(nutrit), 54. *Prof Exp:* From asst prof to prof nutrit, 54-62, chmn nutrit coun, 61-63, CHMN DEPT NUTRIT, RUTGERS UNIV, 66- *Concurrent Pos:* Mem bd trustees, Rutgers Univ; assoc ed, Nutrit Reports Int, 70- & J Nutrit, 71-75. *Honors & Awards:* Am Feed Mfrs Award, 59; Poultry Sci Award, 57. *Mem:* Fel AAAS; Poultry Sci Asn; Am Inst Nutrit; fel NY Acad Sci; Am Bd Nutrit. *Res:* Amino acid requirements; cholesterol metabolism; histamine stress; carnosine metabolism. *Mailing Add:* Dept of Nutrit Rutgers Univ New Brunswick NJ 08903

FISHER, HAROLD DEAN, b Kamloops, BC, Apr 8, 22; m 47; c 3. ZOOLOGY. *Educ:* Univ BC, BA, 44, MA, 47; McGill Univ, PhD, 54. *Prof Exp:* Admin asst wildlife mgt, Can Wildlife Serv, 47-48; assoc biologist, Atlantic Biol Sta, Fisheries Res Bd Can, NB, 49-50, biologist, 50-55, sr scientist, Arctic Unit, 56-58, prin scientist & dir, 58-63; assoc prof, 63-66, comnr, Can-Norway Sealing Comn, Can, 73-77; PROF ZOOL, UNIV BC, 66- *Concurrent Pos:* Seasonal field asst, Dom Entom Lab, BC, 40-43; sci asst, Pac Biol Sta, Fisheries Res Bd Can, 44-46; mem comt seals & sealing, Fed Minister Fisheries, 71- *Mem:* Wildlife Soc; Am Soc Mammal; Can Soc Zool. *Res:* Functional anatomy and ecology of aquatic mammals. *Mailing Add:* Dept of Zool Univ of BC Vancouver BC V6T 1W5 Can

FISHER, HAROLD M, b Fayetteville, NC, Feb 19, 40; m 63; c 2. POLYMER TECHNOLOGY, INORGANIC CHEMISTRY. *Educ:* Davidson Col, BS, 62; Univ Fla, MS, 64, PhD(inorg chem), 66. *Prof Exp:* Asst gen chem, Univ Fla, 62-66; res chemist, Atlantic-Richfield Co, 66; fiber engr, 69-77, POLYMER GROUP LEADER, FIBER INDUSTS, INC, 77- *Res:* Inorganic chemistry, transition metal complexes, magnetically anomalous cobalt II spectra; propellant chemistry, burning rate modifiers, polybutadine, ferrocene derivatives; homogeneous catalysis, vaska-type complexes; fiber engineering, polyester, nylon; polyester polymer engineering. *Mailing Add:* 6500 Windyrush Rd Charlotte NC 28211

FISHER, HAROLD WALLACE, b Rutland, Vt, Oct 27, 04; m 30; c 1. CHEMICAL ENGINEERING. *Educ:* Mass Inst Technol, BS, 27. *Hon Degrees:* DSc, Clarkson Col Technol, 60. *Prof Exp:* Mem staff res lab, Standard Oil Co La, 27-29; mem staff, Standard Oil Develop Co, NJ, 29-30, mem staff hydro-eng & chem, 30-32, mem staff, Esso Labs, 32-33, asst dir, 35-36, mgr com dept, NY, 36-41, asst mgr sales eng, Standard Oil Co, NJ, 33-35, mgr chem prod dept, 41, dir, 45-47, mgr chem prod dept & vpres, Stanco Distributors, Inc, 41-44, pres, Standard Alcohol Co, 44-47, pres, Enjay Co, Inc, 47-48, dir mfg opers ECoast & mgr chem prod dept, Esso Standard Oil Co, 48-49, dept refining coordr, Standard Oil Co, NJ, 49-50, refining coordr, 50-54, rep in UK, 54-57, managing dir, Iraq Petrol Co, London, 57-59, dir contact for MidE refining & transp activities, Standard Oil Co, NJ, 59-62, vpres & dir chem res & refining, 62-69; RETIRED. *Concurrent Pos:* Trustee, Sloan-Kettering Inst Cancer Res, 64-, chmn bd, 70-74; vchmn & chmn exec comt, Community Blood Coun Greater New York, 69-71. *Honors & Awards:* Chem Indust Medal, 68. *Mem:* Nat Acad Eng; fel AAAS; Am Chem Soc; Am Inst Chem Engrs; Brit Soc Chem Indust. *Mailing Add:* PO Box 1792 Duxbury MA 02332

FISHER, HAROLD WILBUR, b Galt, Ont, Nov 29, 28; US citizen; m 49; c 2. BIOPHYSICS, MOLECULAR BIOLOGY. *Educ:* Univ Mich, BS, 51, MS, 53; Univ Colo, PhD(biophys), 59. *Prof Exp:* Res assoc biophys, Univ Mich, 50-53; chemist, Eli Lilly Res Labs, 53-55; instr biophys, Univ Colo, 56-59, asst prof, 60-63; assoc prof, 63-68, PROF BIOPHYS, BIOCHEM & MICROBIOL, UNIV RI, 68- *Concurrent Pos:* Am Cancer Soc fel, 60-62. *Mem:* Biophys Soc; Am Soc Cell Biol. *Res:* Electron microscopy; bacteriophage; mammalian cell culture and genetics; cell fractionation and membranes; tumor viruses. *Mailing Add:* Dept of Chem Univ of RI Kingston RI 02881

FISHER, HARVEY FRANKLIN, b Cleveland, Ohio, June 12, 23; m 64; c 1. BIOCHEMISTRY. *Educ:* Western Reserve Univ, BS, 47; Univ Chicago, PhD(biochem), 52. *Prof Exp:* Biochemist, Col Physicians & Surgeons, Columbia Univ, 52-54; res assoc chem, Univ Wis, 54-56; instr, Univ Mass, 56-57; sr assoc biochem, Edsel B Ford Inst, 57-63; assoc prof, 63-65, PROF BIOCHEM, SCH MED, UNIV KANS MED CTR, KANSAS CITY, 65-; DIR MOLECULAR BIOCHEM LAB, VET ADMIN HOSP, 63- *Concurrent Pos:* Mem, Nat Sci Found Molecular Biol adv panel, 77; mem ed bd, J Biol Chem, 73-78. *Mem:* Am Chem Soc; Am Soc Biol Chem. *Res:* Mechanisms and energetics of enzymatic catalyses. *Mailing Add:* Vet Admin Hosp Res Dept 4801 Linwood Blvd Kansas City MO 64128

FISHER, HARVEY IRVIN, b Edgar, Nebr, June 15, 16; m 37; c 3. VERTEBRATE MORPHOLOGY. *Educ:* Kans State Col, BS, 37; Univ Calif, PhD(comp anat), 42. *Prof Exp:* Asst zool, Univ Calif, 37-41, asst vert zool, Mus Vert Zool, 41-42, tech cur, 42-45; asst prof, Univ Hawaii, 45-48; from asst prof to assoc prof, Univ Ill, 48-55; prof zool, 55-80, chmn dept, 55-71, asst dean, Sch Med, 71-80, EMER PROF ZOOL, SOUTHERN ILL UNIV, 80- *Concurrent Pos:* Exchange prof, Univ Nev, 47-48; ed, The Auk, Wilson Ornith Soc. *Mem:* AAAS; Soc Study Evolution; Am Soc Zoologists; Am Soc Mammalogists; Am Ornith Union. *Res:* Avian and functional anatomy; vertebrate natural history; natural history and behavior of birds. *Mailing Add:* Fenwood Toft Triplett MO 65286

FISHER, IRVING SANBORN, b Augusta, Maine, May 21, 20; m 45; c 3. GEOLOGY. *Educ:* Bates Col, AB, 41; Harvard Univ, MA, 48, PhD(geol), 52. *Prof Exp:* Asst instr geol, Dartmouth Col, 41-42; field asst, US Geol Surv, 42; asst prof, 49-56, ASSOC PROF GEOL, UNIV KY, 56- *Mem:* Fel AAAS; fel Meteoritical Soc; Mineral Soc Am; fel Geol Soc Am; Soc Econ Paleont & Mineral. *Res:* Petrology; mineralogy. *Mailing Add:* Dept of Geol Univ of Ky Lexington KY 40506

FISHER, JACK BERNARD, b New York, NY, July 13, 43. TROPICAL BOTANY, PLANT ANATOMY. *Educ:* Cornell Univ, BS, 65, MS, 66; Univ Calif, Davis, PhD(bot), 69. *Prof Exp:* Cabot Found res fel, Harvard & Fairchild Trop Garden, Miami, 69-71; PLANT MORPHOLOGIST, FAIRCHILD TROP GARDEN, MIAMI, 72- *Concurrent Pos:* Asst prof, Ohio Univ, 71-72; vis prof, Univ Calif, Berkeley, 76. *Mem:* Bot Soc Am; Asn Trop Biol; Int Soc Plant Morphologists; Linnean Soc London; Int Asn Wood Anatomists. *Res:* Developmental anatomy and morphology, especially of monocotyledons and tropical trees; tropical botany and agriculture. *Mailing Add:* Fairchild Trop Garden Miami FL 33156

FISHER, JAMES DELBERT, b Lebanon, Ohio, June 23, 42; m 64; c 2. PESTICIDE CHEMISTRY. *Educ:* Ohio State Univ, BS, 64; Univ Ill, MS, 67, PhD(plant physiol), 70. *Prof Exp:* Group leader XT-11, 69-74, GROUP LEADER XT-10 PESTICIDE CHEM, ROHM AND HAAS CO, 74- *Mem:* Am Chem Soc. *Res:* To develop procedures for laboratory and field studies which delineate the environmental fate of pesticides; to supervise scientists in actually carrying out the above environmental studies. *Mailing Add:* Rohm and Haas Co Norristown & McKean Rds Spring House PA 19477

FISHER, JAMES HAROLD, b Mayfield, Ky, Nov 8, 19; m 43; c 3. PETROLEUM GEOLOGY. *Educ:* Univ Ill, AB, 43, BS, 47, MS, 49, PhD(geol), 53. *Prof Exp:* Asst, Univ Ill, 47-48; geologist, McCurtain Limestone Co & Pure Oil Co, 48-51; asst prof geol, Univ Ill, 52-55; asst prof, Univ Nebr, 55-57; from asst prof to assoc prof, 57-69, PROF GEOL, MICH STATE UNIV, 70- *Mem:* Geol Soc Am; An Asn Petrol Geologists. *Res:* Stratigraphy and structure of the Rocky Mountains and the Great Plains province; petroleum geology of the Michigan Basin; fuel energy resources of the US. *Mailing Add:* Dept Geol Mich State Univ East Lansing MI 48824

FISHER, JAMES RUSSELL, b New Castle, Pa, Sept 24, 40. GEOCHEMISTRY, PHYSICAL INORGANIC CHEMISTRY. *Educ:* Harvard Univ, AB, 62; Pa State Univ, PhD(geochem), 69. *Prof Exp:* Nat Acad Sci res assoc geochem, 69-71, GEOLOGIST, US GEOL SURV, 71- *Mem:* AAAS; Mineral Soc Am. *Res:* Chemistry of aqueous solutions at elevated temperature and pressure; hydrothermal synthesis of crystalline materials; pressure-volume-temperature properties of gases and aqueous solutions. *Mailing Add:* US Geol Surv 803 National Ctr Reston VA 22092

FISHER, JAMES THOMAS, b Bryan, Tex, June 28, 46; m 65; c 3. FOREST TREE PHYSIOLOGY. *Educ:* WTEx State Univ, BS, 69; Colo State Univ, MS, 72, PhD(forest tree physiol), 75. *Prof Exp:* Res fel forest tree physiol, Colo State Univ, 69-70; chmn biol, Le Tourneau Col, 71-72; res fel forest tree physiol, Colo State Univ, 72-75; ASSOC PROF SILVICULT TREE PHYSIOL, NMEX STATE UNIV, 75-; MGR SILVICULT TREE PHYSIOL, MORA RES CTR, 75- *Concurrent Pos:* Adj asst prof forestry, NMex Highlands Univ, 76-78; mem, NMex Forest Planning Comt, 76-, Int Parasitic Seed Plant Res Group, 78-, NMex State Reforestation Comt, 82-, Res Adv Comt, NMex Agr Exp Sta, 82-; delegate, Eisenhower Consortium, 80-; chmn, GP-13 Regional Tree Improvement Comt, 82- *Mem:* AAAS; Soc Am Foresters; Sigma Xi. *Res:* Forest tree physiology; physiological genetics and tree improvement as related to forestation and intensive silvicultural management of conifer plantations. *Mailing Add:* Box 3530 Dept Hort Col Agr & Home Econ NMex State Univ Las Cruces NM 88003

FISHER, JAMES W, b Startex, SC, May 22, 25; m 47; c 6. PHARMACOLOGY. *Educ:* Univ SC, BS, 47; Univ Louisville, PhD, 58. *Prof Exp:* Chemist org synthesis, Abbott Pharmaceut Labs, Ill, 48; pharmacologist, Armour Pharmaceut Labs, 50-54; sr pharmacologist, Res Div, Lloyd Bros, Inc, Ohio, 54-56; from instr to prof pharmacol, Med Units, Univ Tenn, Memphis, 58-68; PROF PHARMACOL & CHMN DEPT, SCH MED, TULANE UNIV, 68- *Concurrent Pos:* USPHS career develop award, Univ Tenn, 60-65; guest lectr & investr, Christie Hosp, Holt Radium Inst & Sch Med, Victoria Univ Manchester, 63-64; mem comt erythropoietin, Nat Heart & Lung Inst, 71-74; mem res comt, Cooley's Anemia Found, 74-; mem career develop award comt, Vet Admin; mem, Nat Heart & Lung Inst training grants adv comt, 75-; dir Pan Am Health Orgn training prog physiol sci, Tulane Univ-Nat Univ North-East, Arg, 72-; consult, Schering Corp, NJ, 76- & Upjohn Co, Mich, 77- *Mem:* AAAS; Am Soc Hemat; Am Soc Pharmacol & Exp Therapeut; Int Soc Nephrology; Soc Exp Biol & Med. *Res:* Hematopharmacology; erythropoietin, hormones and erythropoiesis; erythropoietic function of the kidney; adrenocortical steroids; anemia and kidney disease. *Mailing Add:* Dept Pharmacol Tulane Univ 1430 Tulane Ave New Orleans LA 70112

FISHER, JOHN BERTON, b McKees Rocks, Pa, Sept 28, 51; m 73. GEOCHEMISTRY, BIOLOGY. *Educ:* Yale Univ, BS, 73; Case Western Reserve Univ, MS, 76, PhD(geol), 79. *Prof Exp:* Res asst geol, Yale Univ, 71-73; res assoc environ sci, Normandeau Asn, Inc, 73-74; res asst, Case Western Reserve Univ, 75-78, res assoc geol, 78-80; res asst, Univ Calif, 80-81; RES ASST, AMOCO PROD CO, 81- *Concurrent Pos:* Asst, Case Western Reserve Univ, 75-78, fel, 78- *Honors & Awards:* Belknap Prize, Dept Geol & Geophys, Yale Univ, 73. *Mem:* Soc Econ Paleont & Mineralogists. *Res:* Sedimentary geochemistry; early sediment diagenesis, animal-sediment interaction; formation water-rock interaction. *Mailing Add:* Amoco Prod Co Res Ctr Tulsa OK 74102

FISHER, JOHN CROCKER, b Ithaca, NY, Dec 19, 19; m 43; c 3. PHYSICS, NATURAL SCIENCE. *Educ:* Ohio State Univ, AB, 41; Mass Inst Technol, ScD, 47. *Prof Exp:* Res engr, Battelle Mem Inst, 41-42; asst & later instr mech, Mass Inst Technol, 42-47; res assoc, Gen Elec Co, 47-51, mgr phys metall sect, 51-57, physicist, 57-63, mgr liaison & transition, Res Lab, 63-64, mgr phys sci & info disciplines, Tech Mil Planning Oper, Calif, 64-68, consult scientist, Re-Entry & Environ Systs Prod Div, Pa, 69-72, mgr energy technol anal, Power Generation Bus Group, 72-78, consult res & develop, Corp Res & Develop, 78-81; CONSULT & ENTREPRENEUR, 81- *Concurrent Pos:* Chief scientist, US Air Force, Washington, DC, 68-69; Campbell mem lectr; Gillette mem lectr; mem, Bus & Indust Comt Energy & Raw Mat, 75-77 & Comn Sociotech Systs of Nat Res Coun, 76-78. *Honors & Awards:* Alfred Noble Prize. *Mem:* AAAS; Am Inst Physics; Am Phys Soc; Am Soc Metals. *Res:* Physical sciences. *Mailing Add:* 189 Forts Ferry Rd Latham NY 12110

FISHER, JOHN F, b East Liverpool, Ohio, July 23, 37; m 59. ANALYTICAL CHEMISTRY, PHYSICAL CHEMISTRY. *Educ:* Univ WVa, BS, 59, MS, 61, PhD(chem), 63. *Prof Exp:* Anal chemist, Res & Develop Dept, 62-70, PRIN ENGR, ENG DEPT, UNION CARBIDE CORP, 70- *Res:* Gas chromatography; non-aqueous titrations; spectrophotometry; infrared spectroscopy; analytical instrumentation; microprocessors; process instrumentation. *Mailing Add:* 313 Parkview Dr St Albans WV 25177

FISHER, JOHN GATEWOOD, b McLaughlin, SDak, June 9, 24; m 45; c 5. ORGANIC CHEMISTRY. *Educ:* Western Ky State Col, BS, 47; Ohio State Univ, PhD(chem), 51. *Prof Exp:* From asst res chemist to sr res chemist, Tenn Eastman Co, 51-67, res assoc, 67-81; RETIRED. *Res:* Azo dyes and their intermediates; heterocyclic compounds; quarternary ammonium compounds; metal chelate compounds; general synthetic organic chemistry. *Mailing Add:* 1157 Wataugua St Kingsport TN 37660

FISHER, JOHN HERBERT, b Tipton, Mich, Dec 19, 21; m 47; c 4. SURGERY. *Educ:* Harvard Med Sch, MD, 46; Tufts Univ, MS, 52. *Prof Exp:* Surgeon, 56-59, pediat surgeon in chief, Boston Floating Hosp, 60-73; asst prof surg, Sch Med, Tufts Univ, 59-72; ASSOC CLIN PROF SURG, HARVARD UNIV, 77-, SR ASSOC SURG, CHILDREN'S HOSP MED CTR, 76- *Res:* Pediatric surgery. *Mailing Add:* Children's Hosp Med Ctr 300 Longwood Ave Boston MA 02115

FISHER, JOHN WILLIAM, b Ancell, Mo, Feb 15, 31; m 52; c 4. CIVIL ENGINEERING. *Educ:* Washington Univ, BSCE, 56; Lehigh Univ, MS, 58, PhD(struct joints), 64. *Prof Exp:* Struct res asst, Lehigh Univ, 56-58; asst bridge res engr, Hwy Res Bd, Nat Acad Sci-Nat Res Coun, 58-61; struct res instr, 61-64, from asst prof to assoc prof, 64-69, PROF CIVIL ENG, LEHIGH UNIV, 69- *Concurrent Pos:* Mem, Res Coun Riveted & Bolted Struct Joints; mem transp res bd, Nat Acad Sci-Nat Res Coun; consult, Nelson Div, TRW, Ont Ministry Transp, Can Nat RR, Bethlehem Steel, Allied Struct Steel & Ammann & Whitney, Sea Land, US Steel, La Dept Transp, Bechtel Power Corp, Dravo, NJ Transit, Modjeski & Masters &

DeLeuw-Cather, 77-81. *Honors & Awards:* Walter L Huber Res Prize, Am Soc Civil Engrs, 69; A W S Adams Memorial Mem Award, Am Welding Soc, 74; Ernest E Howard Award, Am Soc Civil Engrs, 79; Raymond C Reese Res Prize, Am Soc Civil Engrs, 81. *Mem:* Fel Am Soc Civil Engrs; Am Soc Eng Educ; Nat Soc Prof Engrs; Am Welding Soc; Int Asn Bridge & Struct Engrs. *Res:* Behavior of welded connections; fatigue studies of bridge components; behavior of bridge structures; high strength bolts; bolted joints and composite beams. *Mailing Add:* Fritz Eng Lab Bldg 13 Lehigh Univ Bethlehem PA 18015

FISHER, KATHLEEN MARY, b Long Branch, NJ, Aug 4, 38; m 59; c 3. BIOLOGY, SCIENCE EDUCATION. *Educ:* Rutgers Univ, BS, 60; Univ Calif, PhD(genetics), 69. *Prof Exp:* Lab technician malaria res, Christ Hosp Inst Med Res, Cincinnati, 60-63; res specialist, Nat Ctr Primate Biol, 63, lab technician, Dept Genetics, 64-68, res cytogeneticist, 69, AEC fel, 69-71, dir, Teaching Res Ctr, 74-79, ASSOC PROF BIOL SCI & EDUC, UNIV CA LIFE, DAVIS, 71- *Concurrent Pos:* prog assoc, Res Sci Educ, NSF, 80-81. *Mem:* AAAS; Am Educ Res Asn; Nat Asn Res Sci Teaching; Genetics Soc Am. *Res:* Development of new methods of genetics instruction; teaching and learning processes, use of computers and visual media in education; life cycle and drug response of Plasmodium cynomolgi; recombination and dominance in bacteriophage T4; chromosome ultrastructure. *Mailing Add:* Bact Dept Div Biol Sci Univ Calif Davis CA 95616

FISHER, KENNETH D, b Lowell, Mass, Mar 3, 32; m 56; c 3. RESEARCH ANALYSIS, SCIENCE COMMUNICATION. *Educ:* Oberlin Col, Univ Vt, BS, 53, MS, 55; NC State Univ, PhD(plant path), 60. *Prof Exp:* Asst bot, Univ Vt, 53-55; asst plant path, NC State Univ, 57-60; asst prof, SDak State Univ, 60-63; asst prof bot, Univ Vt, 63-66, plant pathologist, Vt Agr Exp Sta & Exten Serv, 63-68; res assoc, 68-75, assoc dir, 75-77, DIR, LIFE SCI RES OFF, FEDN AM SOCS EXP BIOL, 77- *Concurrent Pos:* Adj prof biol, Montgomery Col, 69- *Mem:* AAAS; Am Inst Nutrit; Soc Nematol. *Res:* Research analysis and evaluation in the life sciences; research analysis and evaluation in the life sciences; phytonematology. *Mailing Add:* Life Sci Res Off FASEB 9650 Rockville Pike Bethesda MD 20814

FISHER, KENNETH ROBERT STANLEY, b Toronto, Ont, Dec 8, 42. DEVELOPMENTAL BIOLOGY. *Educ:* Univ Toronto, BS, 63, MS, 67, PhD(zool), 73. *Prof Exp:* Researcher embryol, Animal Biol Lab, Nat Ctr Sci Res, Univ Paris, 64-65; demonstr zool, Univ Toronto, 65-71; instr anat, Univ Sask, 72-73, Med Res Coun Can fel, 73-76; ASST PROF MICROS ANAT, DEPT BIOMED SCI, ONT VET COL, UNIV GUELPH, 76- *Mem:* Can Asn Anatomists; Can Soc Cell Biol; Soc Develop Biol; Tissue Cult Asn; AAAS. *Res:* Embryological development of biological control mechanisms, sexual organogenesis and developmental neurobiology. *Mailing Add:* Dept Biomed Sci Ont Vet Col Univ of Guelph Guelph Can

FISHER, KENNETH WALTER, b Heston, Eng, Dec 30, 31; m 65; c 5. MOLECULAR GENETICS. *Educ:* Univ London, BSc, 53, MSc, 54, PhD(bact genetics), 57. *Prof Exp:* Res worker med res coun, Microbial Genetics Res Unit, Hammersmith Hosp, London, 57-66; assoc prof biol, Kans State Univ, 66-70; actg chmn dept biol, 72-73, chmn dept, 73-78, dir, Univ Grad Prog Microbiol, 75-78, PROF BIOL, FAC ARTS & SCI, RUTGERS UNIV, NEW BRUNSWICK, 70- *Concurrent Pos:* Vis worker, Physiol Microbial Serv, Pasteur Inst Paris, 57-58; Rockefeller traveling fel med, Group Biochem Studies, Princeton Univ, 62-63; temp assoc prof physics, Kans State Univ, 64; NSF res grant, 66-68; Eli Lilly grant-in-aid, 67-70; mem cause grant review panel, NSF, 76-78; mem fel review sect, Microbiol Chem Study Sect, NIH. *Mem:* Genetics Soc Am; Brit Soc Gen Microbiol; Brit Biochem Soc; Brit Genetical Soc; Am Soc Microbiol. *Res:* Bacterial genetics and chemistry; mechanism of conjugation in the bacterium Escherichia coli; isolation of auxotrophic mutants in Solanum tuberosum tissue cultures. *Mailing Add:* Dept of Biol Douglass Col Rutgers Univ New Brunswick NJ 08903

FISHER, LEON HAROLD, b Montreal, Que, July 11, 18; nat US; m 41; c 4. ELECTRON PHYSICS, ACADEMIC ADMINISTRATION. *Educ:* Univ Calif, BS, 38, MS, 40, PhD(physics), 43. *Prof Exp:* Instr pre-meteorol physics, Univ Calif, 43-44; instr physics, Univ NMex, 44; assoc scientist, Los Alamos Sci Lab, Univ Calif, 44-46; from asst prof to prof physics, NY Univ, 46-61; mgr plasma physics, Lockheed Missiles & Space Co, 61-62; head plasma physics, Gen Tel & Electronics Labs, 62-63; sr mem & sr consult scientist, Lockheed Palo Alto Res Lab, 63-70, asst mgr, Electronic Sci Lab, 67-68; prof elec eng & head dept info eng, Univ Ill, Chicago Circle, 71; PROF PHYSICS & DEAN SCH SCI, CALIF STATE UNIV, HAYWARD, 71- *Concurrent Pos:* Chmn, Gaseous Electronics Conf, 48, 67 & 68; assoc ed Phys Review, 55-58; consult, Edgerton, Germeshausen & Grier, 54-55, Harry Diamond Labs, 58-61, Xerox Corp, 58-61, Army Res Off Durham, 58-63, Rome Air Develop Ctr, 59-63, Re-entry Physics Panel, Nat Acad Sci, 65-66 & Monsanto Envirochem, 71. *Mem:* AAAS; fel Am Phys Soc; Am Asn Physics Teachers. *Res:* Low temperature heat capacities; ionization coefficients in gases; mechanism of electrical breakdown in gases; formation of negative ions; corona discharges; plasma physics; contact potentials. *Mailing Add:* Calif State Univ Sch of Sci 25800 Hillary St Hayward CA 94542

FISHER, LEONARD V, b Elizabeth, NJ, May 22, 29; m 63; c 2. MEDICINE. *Educ:* Rutgers Univ, BSc, 48; Yale Univ, MS, 50; Univ Chicago, MD, 54; Am Bd Internal Med, cert internal med, 64, cert endocrinol & metab, 72. *Prof Exp:* From intern to resident med, Montefiore Hosp, NY, 54-57; asst prof, Seton Hall Col Med & Dent, 60-61, clin asst prof, 61-64; asst prof, 64-70, ASSOC PROF MED, NY MED COL, 70-, ASST PROF RADIOL & NUCLEAR MED, 70-, CHIEF SECT ENDOCRINOL & METAB, B S COLER HOSP, 64-, ASSOC DIR MED, 70- *Concurrent Pos:* Vis res fel med, Col Physicians & Surgeons, Columbia Univ, 57-60; Nat Found fel, 57-59; spec fel, Nat Inst Arthritis & Metab Dis, 59-60; dir endocrinol & biochem, St Michael Hosp, Newark, NJ, 60-64; assoc vis physician, Metrop Hosp, 64- *Mem:* Soc Nuclear Med; Am Diabetes Asn; Endocrine Soc; Am Geriatrics Soc; Asn Aging Res. *Res:* Geriatric endocrinology. *Mailing Add:* NY Med Col Ctr Chronic Dis B S Coler Hosp Roosevelt Island New York NY 10044

FISHER, LESLIE JOHN, b New York, NY, Feb 26, 40; m 62. NEUROBIOLOGY. *Educ:* Rensselaer Polytech Inst, BEE, 61; Tufts Univ, MS, 66, PhD(biol), 69. *Prof Exp:* Vis asst prof physiol, Sch Med, Univ Md, Baltimore, 71-72; asst prof anat, Med Sch, Univ Mich, Ann Arbor, 72-80; DIR RES, DEPT OPHTHAL, HENRY FORD HOSP, DETROIT, 80- *Concurrent Pos:* NIH fel, Sch Med, Johns Hopkins Univ, 69-71; NIH & NSF res grant; partic NATO Neurobiol Advan Study Inst, 71. *Mem:* Soc Neurosci; Asn Res Vision & Ophthal. *Res:* Electron microscopic studies of the development of neurons and synaptic arrays in the retina. *Mailing Add:* Dept Ophthal 2799 W Grand Blvd Detroit MI 48202

FISHER, LINDA E, b Kansas City, Kans, Dec 3, 47; m 70. VIROLOGY. *Educ:* Univ Kans, BA, 69, PhD(microbiol), 74. *Prof Exp:* fel, Roche Inst Molecular Biol, 74-76 & Pa State Univ Col Med, 76-78; ASST PROF MICROBIOL, UNIV MICH, DEARBORN, 78- *Concurrent Pos:* Adj asst prof microbiol, Lebanon Valley Col, 77; prin investr res grant, NatMultiple Sclerosis Soc, 80-82. *Mem:* Am Soc Microbiol; Sigma Xi; NY Acad Sci; AAAS. *Res:* Virus persistence, particularly what contribution selection of virus variants and totally or partially resistant cells in a population makes in determining whether a persistent infection occurs. *Mailing Add:* Dept Natural Sci Univ Mich Dearborn MI 48128

FISHER, LLOYD D, JR, b Baltimore, Md, June 8, 39; m 61; c 2. BIOSTATISTICS. *Educ:* Mass Inst Technol, SB, 61; Dartmouth Col, MA, 65, PhD(math), 66. *Prof Exp:* Sci programmer, Lockheed Missiles & Space Co, 61-63; asst prof math, 66-70, assoc prof, 70-74, PROF BIOSTATIST, 75-DIR, COORD CTR COLLAB STUDIES CORONARY ARTERY SURG, UNIV WASH, 73- *Concurrent Pos:* Consult, Aerospace Corp, 66-67, Minneapolis-Honeywell Regulator Co, 68, Vet Admin, 74-75, Fed Drug Admin, 75- & Am Arthritis Asn, 78. *Mem:* Am Col Cardiol; Biomet Soc; fel Am Statist Asn; Royal Statist Soc; Inst Math Statist. *Mailing Add:* Dept of Biostatist SC-32 Univ of Wash Seattle WA 98195

FISHER, LYMAN MCA, b Appin, Ont, Mar 21, 23; m 53; c 4. CLINICAL PATHOLOGY, HEMATOLOGY. *Educ:* Univ Western Ont, BA, 51; Univ Sask, MA, 54, PhD(physiol), 57, MD, 60; Am Bd Clin Path, dipl, 65. *Prof Exp:* Lectr physiol, Univ Sask, 57-58; from asst prof to assoc prof clin path, 60-70, PROF CLIN PATH, MED COL VA, 70- *Mem:* Can Physiol Soc; Am Soc Exp Path; Am Soc Clin Path. *Res:* Blood coagulation and atherosclerosis. *Mailing Add:* Div Clin Path Med Col Va Richmond VA 23298

FISHER, MARTIN JOSEPH, b Pittsburgh, Pa, Mar 18, 44; m 68; c 2. MEDICAL PHYSIOLOGY. *Educ:* Wheeling Col, BS, 66; WVa Univ, PhD(physiol & biophys), 71. *Prof Exp:* Res asst biochem, WVa Univ, 66-67, res asst physiol & biophys, 67-71; instr anesthesiol physiol, Univ Ala, 71-72; NIH fel respiratory physiol, Univ Fla, 72-74, asst prof physiol, 74-81; ASSOC PROF & CHMN, DEPT OF PHYSIOL, SCH MED, WORLD UNIV, SANTO DOMINGO, DOMINICAN REPUBLIC, 81- *Concurrent Pos:* NIH fel, 71 & 74; fel respiratory physiol, Univ Fla, 74. *Mem:* Am Physiol Soc. *Res:* Respiratory physiology; pulmonary mechanics; enzyme inhibitors and pulmonary emphysema; models of lung disease and stereology. *Mailing Add:* Dept Physiol Univ of Fla Santo Domingo Dominican Republic

FISHER, MICHAEL ELLIS, b Fyzabad, Trinidad, Sept 3, 31; m 54; c 4. MATHEMATICAL PHYSICS, CHEMISTRY. *Educ:* Univ London, BSc, 51, PhD(physics), 57. *Prof Exp:* Lectr math, Royal Air Force Tech Col, 52-53; tutor physics, King's Col, Univ London, 53-57, lectr theoret physics, 57-62, reader physics, 62-64, prof, 65-66; prof chem & math, 66-73, chmn chem dept, 75-78, HORACE WHITE PROF CHEM, PHYSICS & MATH, CORNELL UNIV, 73- *Concurrent Pos:* Dept Sci & Indust Res sr res fel, 56-58; guest investr, Rockefeller Inst, 63-64; John Simon Guggenheim mem fel & vis prof, Stanford Univ, 70-71; Buhl lectr theoret physics, Carnegie-Mellon Univ, 71; Guggenheim fel, 78-79. *Honors & Awards:* Irving Langmuir Prize, Am Phys Soc, 71; 32nd Richtmyer Mem Lectr Award, Am Asn Physics Teachers, 73; Bakerian lectr, Royal Soc, 79; Guthrie Medal & Prize, Inst Physics, 80; Wolf Prize, 80. *Mem:* Fel Am Phys Soc; fel Royal Soc; Inst Physics; Soc Indust & Appl Math; Math Asn Am. *Res:* Theory and practice of electronic analog computing; statistical mechanics of phase transitions and critical phenomena; magnetism; polymer configurations; combinatorial mathematics; mathematical foundations of statistical mechanics. *Mailing Add:* Baker Lab Cornell Univ Ithaca NY 14853

FISHER, MORRIS ALAN, neurology, see previous edition

FISHER, NEWMAN, b San Francisco, Calif, Mar 21, 28. MATHEMATICS. *Educ:* Univ Calif, AB, 50, MA, 51; Univ Idaho, PhD(math), 62. *Prof Exp:* Res aeronaut scientist, Ames Aeronaut Lab, NASA, 52-55; instr math, San Francisco State Col, 57-59; instr, Univ Idaho, 59-61; from asst prof to assoc prof, 61-71, chmn dept, 68-75, PROF MATH, SAN FRANCISCO STATE UNIV, 71-, ASSOC DEAN SCI, 75- *Mem:* Am Math Soc; Soc Indust & Appl Math; Math Asn Am. *Res:* Transonic flow theory; stability theory of ordinary differential equations. *Mailing Add:* Dept of Math San Francisco State Univ San Francisco CA 94132

FISHER, NICHOLAS SETH, b New York, NY, Apr 29, 49; m 74; c 1. PHYTOPLANKTON ECOLOGY, MARINE POLLUTION. *Educ:* Brandeis Univ, BA, 70; State Univ NY Stony Brook, PhD(marine biol), 74. *Prof Exp:* Fel investr, Woods Hole Oceanog Inst, 74-77; res scientist, Marine Sci Labs, Ministry Conserv, Australia, 77-80; RES SCIENTIST, INT LAB MARINE RADIOACTIVITY, INT ATOMIC ENERGY AGENCY, MONACO, 80- *Mem:* Phycological Soc Am; Am Soc Limnol & Oceanog; NY Acad Sci. *Res:* Physiology and ecology of marine phytoplankton; marine pollution research; metal effects on marine biota; transuranics in the sea; community ecology. *Mailing Add:* Int Lab Marine Radioactivity Int Atomic Energy Agency Musee Oceanog Monaco

FISHER, PEARL DAVIDOWITZ, b New York, NY, May 22, 20; m 41; c 2. BIOSTATISTICS, EDUCATIONAL ADMINISTRATION. *Educ:* Brooklyn Col, BA, 41; Columbia Univ, MS, 51; Univ Okla, PhD(prev med, pub health), 58. *Prof Exp:* Asst parasitol & epidemiol, Sch Med, Univ Okla, 53-58, res assoc prev med & publ health, 58-60, asst prof, 60-64; life scientist advan studies, Marshall Space Flight Ctr, NASA, 64-66; math statistician & sr analyst, Off Biomet, Nat Inst Neurol Dis & Blindness, 67-71; chief, br serv delivery res, Nat Ctr Family Planning Serv, Health Serv & Ment Health Admin, Rockville, 71-75; CHIEF APPL STATIST TRAINING INST, NAT CTR HEALTH STATIST, 75- *Concurrent Pos:* Instr statist, Grad Sch, NIH, 68- *Res:* Survival of man in space; radiation hazards; sterilization of spacecraft; duration of life studies on parasitic nematodes; survival evaluation of cancer patients; etiological factors of leukemia in children. *Mailing Add:* 13324 Sherwood Forest Dr Silver Spring MD 20904

FISHER, PERRY WRIGHT, b New York, NY; m 68. AIR POLLUTION, METEOROLOGY. *Educ:* Cornell Univ, BEngrPhysics, 62; Univ Mich, Ann Arbor, MS, 67, Am 68, PhD(meteorol), 70. *Prof Exp:* Res asst meteorologist, Univ Mich, Ann Arbor, 66-70; asst prof geophys & eng, Case Western Reserve Univ, 71-73; proj meteorologist, 73-80, ASSOC, DAMES & MOORE, 80- *Mem:* Am Meteorol Soc; Air Pollution Control Asn. *Mailing Add:* Dames & Moore 1550 Northwest Hwy Park Ridge IL 60068

FISHER, PHILIP CHAPIN, b Rochester, NY, Aug 3, 26; m 48; c 1. PHYSICS, ASTRONOMY. *Educ:* Univ Rochester, BS, 47; Univ Ill, MS, 48, PhD(physics), 53. *Prof Exp:* Staff mem, Los Alamos Sci Lab, Univ Calif, 53-59; consult scientist, Phys Sci Lab, Lockheed Missiles & Space Co, 59-74; owner & consult scientist, Ruffner Assocs, 75-77; SENSOR ENG MGR, GAS TECH INC, 77- *Concurrent Pos:* Sr physicist, Rasor Assocs, Inc, 76-77. *Mem:* Am Phys Soc; Am Astron Soc; Int Astron Union; Inst Elec & Electronics Engrs; Soc Photo-Optical Inst Eng. *Res:* Bremsstrahlung; delayed gammas from fission; x-ray astronomy and instrumentation; space particle measurements; optics; astrophysics. *Mailing Add:* 2401 Sharon Oaks Dr Menlo Park CA 94025

FISHER, RAY W, b Anamosa, Iowa, Nov 27, 21; m 45; c 4. COAL RESEARCH, ETHANOL PRODUCTION. *Educ:* Iowa State Univ, BS, 48. *Prof Exp:* Asst atomic res & phys chem, 43-48, admin aide, 49-61, asst prof mech eng, 61-63, plant mgr, Ames Lab, 69-77, ASSOC PROF MECH ENG, IOWA STATE UNIV, 63-, DIR, FOSSIL ENERGY PROG, 75-, DIR, MINING & MINERAL RESOURCES RES INST, 81- *Concurrent Pos:* Res assoc, Ames Lab, Iowa State Univ, 49-57, assoc engr, 57-62, engr, 62-64, assoc prof nuclear eng, 63-71, head bldg & eng serv, 64-69; prin lectr coal preparation res, The Royal Swedish Acad Eng Sci, Stockholm, 79. *Mem:* Soc Mining Engrs. *Res:* High temperature corrosion studies of components used in molten metal reactor concepts; design of research facilities; production of pure chemicals; coal mining, preparation, and conversion; land restoration; ethanol separation by absorption. *Mailing Add:* Spedding Hall Rm 320 Iowa State Univ Ames IA 50011

FISHER, RICHARD GARY, b Philadelphia, Pa, Nov 24, 52. PROTEIN STRUCTURE, INTERACTIVE GRAPHICS. *Educ:* Northwestern Univ, BA & MS, 74; Univ Calif, Los Angeles, PhD(molecular biol), 80. *Prof Exp:* Fel, Biol Lab, Harvard Univ, 80; RES ASSOC, INST MOLECULAR BIOL, UNIV ORE, 80- *Concurrent Pos:* Fel, Damon Runyon-Walter Winchell Cancer Fund, 80. *Mem:* AAAS; Sigma Xi; Am Crystallog Asn. *Res:* Development of computer methods in protein crytallography, in particular real-time interactive graphics. *Mailing Add:* Inst Molecular Biol Univ Ore Eugene OR 97403

FISHER, RICHARD PAUL, b Alameda, Calif, Feb 10, 48; m 73. BORATE CHEMISTRY, BORANE CHEMISTRY. *Educ:* Univ Calif, Berkeley, BS, 70; Univ Calif, Davis, PhD(chem), 74. *Prof Exp:* Res chemist, 74-79, SR RES CHEMIST, US BORAX RES CORP, 74- *Mem:* Am Chem Soc. *Res:* Development of borate products and processes; application of analytical instrumentation to such processes; res analytical instrumentation. *Mailing Add:* Borate Process Res Pilot Plant Ctr Boron CA 93516

FISHER, RICHARD R, b Wichita, Kans, June 2, 41; m 62; c 1. ASTROPHYSICS, SOLAR ASTRONOMY. *Educ:* Grinnell Col, BA, 61; Univ Colo, PhD(astrophys), 65. *Prof Exp:* Res asst solar astrophys res, High Altitude Observ, Univ Colo, 62-65; from asst astrophysicist to assoc astrophysicist, Univ Hawaii, 69-71, resident astronr, Mees Solar Observ & asst fiscal off, Univ, 70-71; astrophysicist, Sacramento Peak Observ, 71-76; PROJ SCIENTIST, CORONAL DYNAMICS PROJ, HIGH ALTITUDE OBSERV, BOULDER, 76- *Concurrent Pos:* Lectr, Dept Gen Sci, Maui Community Col, 70; telescope scientist, Solar Optical Telescope Proj, NASA, 81-; sci leader, Joint US-USSR Siberiary Eclipse Expeditory, 81. *Mem:* Am Astron Soc; Optical Soc Am; Int Astron Union. *Res:* Solar research, including solar activity, coronal structure and chromospheric structure; instrument design and geometrical optics. *Mailing Add:* High Altitude Observ Box 3000 Boulder CO 80307

FISHER, RICHARD VIRGIL, b Whittier, Calif, Aug 8, 28; m 47; c 4. GEOLOGY. *Educ:* Occidental Col, BA, 52; Univ Wash, PhD, 57. *Prof Exp:* Actg instr geol, Univ Calif, Santa Barbara, 55-57, from instr to prof & chmn dept, 57-73 chmn dept, 79-80, PROF GEOL SCI, UNIV CALIF, SANTA BARBARA, 73- *Concurrent Pos:* NSF grants, 61-67 & 76-81; vis assoc prof, Univ Hawaii, 65-66; res affil, Hawaii Inst Geophys, 65-; NASA grant, 67-73; vis lectr, Am Geol Inst, 70; prin investr, NASA Apollo 12 lunar samples, consult, synthesis proposals rev panel, NASA, 73-77; mem subcomn syst igneous rocks, Int Union Geol Sci, mem working group effusive & pyroclastic rocks, 74- & rep subcomn, Int Asn Volcanology & Chem Earth's Interior, 76-; chmn, Volcanic Adv Group, Lithostratigraphic Subcomt, NAm Comn Stratigraphic Nomendature, 79-80; mem subcomn syst igneous rocks, Int Union Geol Sci, 80-; Alexander von Humboldt Found, US Sr Scientist award, WGer, 80-81. *Mem:* Fel Geol Soc Am; Soc Econ Paleont & Mineral. *Res:* Process oriented interdisciplinary field, volcanological sedimentology and stratigraphy (volcaniclastic rocks); pyroclastic flow and pyroclastic surge deposits, fallout tephra, turbidites and lahars. *Mailing Add:* Dept of Geol Sci Univ of Calif Santa Barbara CA 93106

FISHER, ROBERT (WILLIAM), entomology, see previous edition

FISHER, ROBERT ALAN, b Berkeley, Calif, Apr 19, 43; m 67; c 2. LASERS, OPTICS. *Educ:* Univ Calif, Berkeley, AB, 65, MA, 67, PhD(physics), 71. *Prof Exp:* Scientist laser physics, Lawrence Livermore Lab, 71-74; STAFF MEM GROUP AP-5, LOS ALAMOS NAT LAB, 74- *Concurrent Pos:* Lectr solid state physics & nonlinear optics, Dept of Appl Sci, Univ Calif, Davis, 72-73. *Mem:* Am Phys Soc; Optical Soc Am; Inst Elec & Electronics Engrs; Soc Photo-Optical Instrumentation Engrs. *Res:* Nonlinear optical effects; linear optics; spectroscopy; x-ray optics; optical phase conjugation. *Mailing Add:* Los Alamos Nat Lab Mail Stop 535 Los Alamos NM 87544

FISHER, ROBERT AMOS, JR, b Honey Grove, Pa, Mar 25, 34; m 58; c 1. LOW TEMPERATURE PHYSICS, THERMODYNAMICS. *Educ:* Juniata Col, BS, 56; Pa State Univ, PhD(phys chem), 61. *Prof Exp:* RES CHEMIST, UNIV CALIF, BERKELEY, 60- *Mem:* AAAS; Am Phys Soc; Sigma Xi. *Res:* Physical and chemical adsorption; low temperature, chemical and magneto thermodynamics; cryogenics; magnetism; calorimetry; single crystal growth. *Mailing Add:* Low Temperature Lab Univ Calif Berkeley CA 94720

FISHER, ROBERT CHARLES, b Shelbyville, Ind, July 30, 26; m 46; c 3. MATHEMATICS. *Educ:* Univ Kans, PhD(math), 52. *Prof Exp:* Prof math, Ohio State Univ, 52-71; prof math sci & chmn dept math & statist, 71-74, assoc vpres acad affairs, 74-77, vpres, 77-80, PROF COMPUT SCI, FLA INT UNIV, 80- *Mem:* Math Asn Am; Soc Indust & Appl Math; Asn Comput Mach; AAAS. *Res:* Software design; numerical methods; approximation theory. *Mailing Add:* Dept of Math Fla Int Univ Miami FL 33199

FISHER, ROBERT EARL, b Salt Lake City, Utah, Apr 22, 39; m 60; c 8. CHEMICAL ENGINEERING. *Educ:* Univ Utah, BS, 61; Mass Inst Technol, ScD(chem eng), 66. *Prof Exp:* Sr process engr, Air Prod & Chem, Inc, 66-67, staff engr, Pa, 67-70; res engr, 70-71, res supvr, 71-76, RES DIV DIR, AMOCO CHEM CORP, 76- *Concurrent Pos:* Lectr, Lehigh Univ, 66-68. *Mem:* Am Inst Chem Engrs. *Res:* Chemical process engineering and development. *Mailing Add:* Amoco Chem Corp 25 W 124st Summit Naperville IL 60540

FISHER, ROBERT GEORGE, b Bound Brook, NJ, Jan 6, 17; m 42; c 3. NEUROSURGERY. *Educ:* Rutgers Univ, BS, 38; Univ Pa, MD, 42; Univ Minn, PhD, 51; Am Bd Neurol Surg, dipl, 68. *Prof Exp:* Instr neurosurg, Johns Hopkins Hosp, 49-51; from instr to prof, Dartmouth Med Sch, 51-67; prof surg & chmn dept neurosurg, Med Sch, Univ Okla, 67-74; CHIEF SURG, MUHLENBERG HOSP, PLAINFIELD, 74- *Concurrent Pos:* Chmn dept neurosurg, Hitchcock Clin, Dartmouth Med Sch; consult, Vet Hosp, White River Junction, Vt; prof clin surg & neurosurg, Rutgers Med Sch, Col Med & Dent, NJ, 74-; mem liaison comt grad med educ, AMA, 75- *Mem:* Am Asn Neurol Surgeons; AMA; Asn Res Nerv & Ment Disease; Am Acad Neurol; Am Acad Neurol Surg. *Res:* Cerebrovascular hemodynamics; brain circulatory system research; brain healing. *Mailing Add:* Muhlenberg Hosp Randolph Rd Plainfield NJ 07060

FISHER, ROBERT JOHN, bacterial physiology, see previous edition

FISHER, ROBERT L, b San Jose, Calif; div; c 3. ANIMAL ECOLOGY, MAMMALOGY. *Educ:* San Jose State Col, AB, 58; Cornell Univ, PhD(vert zool), 68. *Prof Exp:* Assoc prof, 63-77, PROF BIOL, JUNIATA COL, 77- *Mem:* Am Soc Mammal; Sigma Xi; Orgn Inland Biol Field Stas; Japanese Soc Pop Ecol. *Res:* Ecology of microtine rodents. *Mailing Add:* Dept of Biol Juniata Col Huntingdon PA 16652

FISHER, ROBERT LLOYD, b Alhambra, Calif, Aug 19, 25; div; c 1. MARINE GEOLOGY, GEOPHYSICS. *Educ:* Calif Inst Technol, BS, 49; Univ Calif, MS, 52, PhD(oceanog), 57. *Prof Exp:* Jr geologist, US Geol Surv, 49; assoc dir, 74-80, RES GEOLOGIST, SCRIPPS INST OCEANOG, UNIV CALIF, SAN DIEGO, 50- *Concurrent Pos:* Mem, Int Hydrographic Orgn-Intergovt Oceanog Comn, Gen Bathymetric Chart of Oceans, 78- *Mem:* Geol Soc Am; Am Geophys Union; Challenger Soc. *Res:* Shipborne geophysical explorations of Pacific, Indian and South Atlantic Oceans; deep-sea topography; crustal structure and igneous composition in oceanic regions; oceanic trenches and fracture zones; tectonic evolution and plate motions. *Mailing Add:* Scripps Inst Oceanog A-015 Univ Calif San Diego La Jolla CA 92093

FISHER, RONALD RICHARD, b Peoria, Ill, Oct 3, 41; m 69. BIOCHEMISTRY. *Educ:* Ariz State Univ, BA, 64; Cornell Univ, PhD(biochem), 70. *Prof Exp:* Chemist, Solid State Diffusion, Motorola, Inc, 63-64; asst chem, Ariz State Univ, 64-66; fel biochem, Univ Calif, San Diego, 70-71; from asst prof to assoc prof, 71-78, PROF CHEM & BIOCHEM, UNIV SC, 78-, CHMN, DEPT CHEM, 76- *Concurrent Pos:* NIH fel, Cornell Univ, 66-70. *Mem:* AAAS; Am Chem Soc; Am Soc Biol Chemists; NY Acad Sci. *Res:* Mitochondrial oxidative phosphorylation; bacterial photosynthesis; pyridine nucleotide enzymology; active ion transport. *Mailing Add:* Dept of Chem Univ of SC Columbia SC 29208

FISHER, RUSSELL SYLVESTER, b Bernie, Mo, Nov 15, 16; m 37; c 2. PATHOLOGY. *Educ:* Med Col Va, MD, 42; Am Bd Path, dipl path anat, 50, dipl forensic path, 59. *Prof Exp:* Intern & resident med, Henry Ford Hosp, 42-44; res fel legal med, Harvard Med Sch, 46-49; PROF FORENSIC PATH, SCH MED, UNIV MD, BALTIMORE CITY, 49-; CHIEF MED EXAMR, MD, 49- *Concurrent Pos:* Lectr, Sch Med, Johns Hopkins Univ, 50- & Sch Hyg & Pub Health, 52-; consult, US Army Chem Ctr, 53, NIH Clin Ctr, 57-, US Armed Forces Inst Path, 58- & Fed Aviation Agency, 60- *Mem:* Am Asn Path; Am Soc Clin Path; Col Am Path; AMA; Am Bd Path. *Res:* Barbiturate poisoning and methods of determining barbiturates; effects of trauma on the central nervous system; causes of sudden death of infants; coronary artery disease; medicolegal pathology. *Mailing Add:* 111 Penn St Baltimore MD 21201

FISHER, SALLIE ANN, b Green Bay, Wis, Sept 10, 23. WATER CHEMISTRY, POLLUTION CHEMISTRY. *Educ:* Univ Wis, BS, 45, MS, 46, PhD(anal chem, inorg chem), 49. *Prof Exp:* Instr quant anal, Mt Holyoke Col, 49-50; asst prof, Univ Minn, Duluth, 50-51; res chemist, Rohm and Haas Co, 51-60; assoc dir res, Robinette Res Labs, Inc, 60-72; vpres, 72-76, PRES, PURICONS, INC, 76- *Honors & Awards:* Award of Merit, Am Soc Testing & Mat, 74, Max Hecht Award, 75. *Mem:* Am Chem Soc; fel Am Soc Testing & Mat; Nat Asn Corrosion Engrs; Am Water Works Asn. *Res:* Ion exchange applications; industrial water production; metal recovery. *Mailing Add:* Puricons Inc 16 Central Ave Berwyn PA 19312

FISHER, SAMUEL STURM, b Pinconning, Mich, Feb 25, 38; m 59; c 3. FLUID MECHANICS. *Educ:* Univ Cincinnati, ME, 61; Univ Calif, Los Angeles, MS, 63, PhD(eng), 67. *Prof Exp:* From asst to assoc prof, 67-81, PROF AEROSPACE ENG, SCH ENG & APPL SCI, UNIV VA, 81- *Concurrent Pos:* Consult, Nuclear Div, Union Carbide Corp, 71-73; vis scientist, Los Alamos Sci Lab, 75-77. *Mem:* Am Phys Soc; Am Inst Aeronaut & Astronaut; Sigma Xi. *Res:* Low-density fluid mechanics; molecule-surface interactions; homogeneous condensation processes; flow-diagnostic techniques; isotope separation methods; electromagnetic suspension systems. *Mailing Add:* 722 Shamrock Rd Charlottesville VA 22903

FISHER, SAUL HARRISON, b Brooklyn, NY, Feb 20, 13; m 45; c 1. PSYCHIATRY. *Educ:* City Col New York, BS, 32; NY Univ, MD, 36. *Prof Exp:* Asst physiol, 36-37, instr med, 43-45, clin asst psychiat, 48-50, clin instr, 50-54, asst clin prof, 54-57, from asst prof to assoc prof clin psychiat, 57-72, CLIN PROF PSYCHIAT, SCH MED, NY UNIV, 72- *Mem:* AMA; Am Psychiat Asn; Am Orthopsychiat Asn; Acad Psychoanal. *Res:* Relationship of brain damage to personality; effect of severe stress on personality; biological studies in acute psychosis. *Mailing Add:* Dept of Psychiat NY Univ Sch of Med New York NY 10016

FISHER, SEYMOUR, b Baltimore, Md, May 13, 22; m 47; c 2. PSYCHIATRY. *Educ:* Univ Chicago, PhD(psychol), 48. *Prof Exp:* Chief psychologist, Elgin State Hosp, Ill, 49-51; USPHS career res investr & assoc prof, Baylor Col Med, Houston, 57-61; PROF, DEPT PSYCHIAT, MED CTR, STATE UNIV NY, SYRACUSE, 61- *Concurrent Pos:* Adj prof, Syracuse Univ, NY, 72-; consult ed, J Nonverbal Behav, 76- *Mem:* Am Psychol Asn. *Res:* How people organize and integrate their body perceptions; nature of changes in body perception during stress, psychosis, and illness; personality factors involved in sexual responsiveness; determinants of psychosomatic symptom choice. *Mailing Add:* Dept Psychiat State Univ Hosp 750 E Adams St Syracuse NY 13210

FISHER, STANLEY PARKINS, b Suffern, NY, Dec 9, 19; m 43; c 2. PETROLEUM GEOLOGY. *Educ:* Univ Va, BA, 42; Univ Okla, MS, 48; Cornell Univ, PhD(geol), 52. *Prof Exp:* Instr geol, Rutgers Univ, 47-49; asst prof geol, Univ NDak & asst state geologist, NDak Geol Surv, 52-53; geologist oil explor, Nat Petrol Coun, Brazil, 53-54; regional explor geologist, Mene Grande Oil Co Div, Gulf Oil Corp, 54-60; from asst prof to assoc prof, 60-68, chmn dept, 70-75, prof, 68-80, assoc dean arts & sci, 78-80, EMER PROF GEOL, OHIO UNIV, 80- *Mem:* Geol Soc Am; Am Asn Petrol Geologists. *Res:* Sedimentology & petroleum geology of northern Appalachian basin; structure and stratigraphy of Andes Mountains and Caribbean area; landslides of central Ohio River Valley; strip mine land reclamation. *Mailing Add:* Dept of Geol Ohio Univ Athens OH 45701

FISHER, STEPHEN D, b Chicago, Ill, July 23, 41; m 65. MATHEMATICS. *Educ:* Mass Inst Technol, BS, 63; Univ Wis, Madison, PhD(math), 67. *Prof Exp:* Instr math, Mass Inst Technol, 67-69; from asst prof to assoc prof, 69-79, PROF MATH, NORTHWESTERN UNIV, 79- *Mem:* Am Math Soc. *Res:* Complex analysis; variational problems. *Mailing Add:* Dept of Math Northwestern Univ Evanston IL 60201

FISHER, STEVEN KAY, b Rochester, Ind, July 18, 42; m 71; c 1. NEUROBIOLOGY. *Educ:* Purdue Univ, BS, 64, MS, 66, PhD(neurobiol), 69. *Prof Exp:* USPHS fel biophys, Johns Hopkins Univ, 69-71; ASSOC PROF BIOL, UNIV CALIF, SANTA BARBARA, 71- *Concurrent Pos:* Prin investr, USPHS res grant, Nat Eye Inst, 72; res career develop award, NIH, 79. *Mem:* AAAS; Asn Res Vision & Ophthal. *Res:* Studies of the developing and adult vertebrate visual system using light and electron microscopy and autoradiography; cell ultrastructure, protein synthesis, membrane renewal and synaptogenesis. *Mailing Add:* Dept of Biol Sci Univ of Calif Santa Barbara CA 93106

FISHER, STUART GORDON, b Elmhurst, Ill, Mar 1, 43; div; c 1. ECOLOGY, LIMNOLOGY. *Educ:* Wake Forest Col, BS, 65, MA, 67; Dartmouth Col, PhD(biol), 71. *Prof Exp:* Asst prof biol, Amherst Col, 70-76; ASSOC PROF ZOOL, ARIZ STATE UNIV, 78- *Mem:* Ecol Soc Am; Am Soc Limnol & Oceanog; Int Asn Theoret & Appl Limnol. *Res:* Ecosystem biology; Aquatic ecology; energy flow and nutrient cycling in stream ecosystems; ecology of desert streams; metabolism of running water ecosystems; stream ecology. *Mailing Add:* Dept of Zool Ariz State Univ Tempe AZ 85281

FISHER, T RICHARD, b Brownstown, Ill, Dec 23, 21; m 44; c 4. BOTANY. *Educ:* Eastern Ill Univ, BS, 47; Ind Univ, PhD(bot), 54. *Prof Exp:* Asst prof, Appalachian State Teachers Col, 54-56; asst prof bot, Ohio State Univ, 56-68; chmn dept biol, 68-74, PROF BOT, BOWLING GREEN STATE UNIV, 68- *Mem:* Sigma Xi; Am Soc Plant Taxon; Int Asn Plant Taxon. *Res:* Biosystematic investigations of Silphium and other Compositae; taxonomy and cytotaxonomy of compositae. *Mailing Add:* Dept of Biol Bowling Green State Univ Bowling Green OH 43403

FISHER, THEODORE ROOSEVELT, agriculture, soil chemistry, see previous edition

FISHER, THEODORE WILLIAM, b San Francisco, Calif, May 26, 21; m 46; c 1. ENTOMOLOGY. *Educ:* San Jose State Col, AB, 43; Univ Calif, Riverside, PhD(entom), 52. *Prof Exp:* Prin lab technician, Citrus Exp Sta, 48-57, asst entomologist, 57-64, assoc specialist, 64-66, SPECIALIST ENTOM, DIV BIOL CONTROL, UNIV CALIF, RIVERSIDE, 66- *Mem:* Am Entom Soc. *Res:* Biological control of pest mollusks; citrus pest management. *Mailing Add:* Dept of Entom Div of Biol Cont Univ of Calif Riverside CA 92521

FISHER, THOMAS HENRY, b Fulton, Mo, Aug 22, 38; m 56; c 3. ORGANIC CHEMISTRY, PHYSICAL CHEMISTRY. *Educ:* Westminster Col, Mo, BA, 60; Univ Ill, Urbana, MS, 62, PhD(org chem), 64. *Prof Exp:* Asst prof org chem, 66-74, ASSOC PROF CHEM, MISS STATE UNIV, 74- *Mem:* Am Chem Soc. *Res:* Organic reaction mechanisms; free radical decompositions; factors affecting free radical stability. *Mailing Add:* Box CH Dept of Chem Miss State Univ State College MS 39762

FISHER, THORNTON ROBERTS, b Santa Monica, Calif, Feb 16, 37. NUCLEAR PHYSICS. *Educ:* Wesleyan Univ, BA, 58; Calif Inst Technol, PhD(physics), 63. *Prof Exp:* Res assoc nuclear struct physics, Calif Inst Technol, 63; res assoc, Stanford Univ, 63-69; res scientist, 69-75, STAFF SCIENTIST, LOCKHEED PALO ALTO RES LAB, 75- *Mem:* Am Phys Soc. *Res:* Nuclear structure physics; charged particle, gamma ray, and neutron producing reactions; cryogenics; laser-driven fusion. *Mailing Add:* Lockheed Palo Alto Res Lab 3251 Hanover St Palo Alto CA 94304

FISHER, TOM LYONS, b Cincinnati, Ohio, Aug 13, 42; m 72. BIOCHEMISTRY. *Educ:* Old Dom Col, BS, 64; Iowa State Univ, PhD(biochem), 71. *Prof Exp:* Res assoc, Va Polytech Inst, 70-72; asst prof, St Mary's Col Md, 72-76; asst prof, 76-81, ASSOC PROF, JUNIATA COL, 81- *Concurrent Pos:* Adj prof, Va Polytech, Reston, 73; grantee, Res Corp, 78-79; NSF grant, 80. *Mem:* Am Chem Soc. *Res:* Bioorganic chemistry; synthesis and characterization of analogs of vitamins, especially nicotinamide adenine dinucleotide. *Mailing Add:* Dept of Chem Juniata Col Huntingdon PA 16652

FISHER, WALDO REYNOLDS, b Philadelphia, Pa, Sept 10, 30; m 60; c 3. BIOCHEMISTRY, METABOLISM. *Educ:* Wesleyan Univ, BA, 52; Univ Pa, MD, 56, PhD(biochem), 64; Am Bd Internal Med, dipl, 66. *Prof Exp:* From intern to asst resident med, Presby Hosp, Philadelphia, 56-58; instr biochem, Sch Med, Univ Pa, 63-64; sr resident, Peter Bent Brigham Hosp, Boston, 64-65; asst prof med, 65-71, asst prof biochem, 68-71, PROF MED & BIOCHEM, COL MED, UNIV FLA, 78- *Concurrent Pos:* NIH res grants, 66-72, res career develop award, 67-72; Am Heart Asn res grant, 67-73; fac develop award, Univ Fla, 70; vis scientist, Lab Chem Biol, NIH, 71-72; mem coun atherosclerosis, Am Heart Asn; mem, Nat Inst Health Metab Study Sect, 81-84. *Mem:* AAAS; Am Soc Biol Chem. *Res:* Biochemistry and physiology of metabolic disease; structure and metabolism of plasma lipoproteins and pathophysiology of hyperlipemic diseases; apolipoprotein kinetics. *Mailing Add:* Dept of Med Box J-226 Univ of Fla Col of Med Gainesville FL 32610

FISHER, WARNER DOUGLASS, b Sharon, Tenn, Aug 17, 23; m 48; c 4. AGRONOMY. *Educ:* Purdue Univ, BS, 47; Utah State Agr Col, MS, 49; Agr & Mech Col Tex, PhD(plant breeding), 54. *Prof Exp:* Instr agron, Univ Tenn, Martin, 48-51; asst, Agr & Mech Col Tex, 51-53; assoc prof, Ala Polytech Inst, 53-54; PLANT BREEDER, COTTON RES CTR, UNIV ARIZ, 54- *Mem:* Am Soc Agron. *Res:* Cotton production and breeding. *Mailing Add:* Cotton Res Ctr Univ of Ariz 4201 E Broadway Phoenix AZ 85040

FISHER, WILLIAM DAVID, b Volens, Va, Mar 18, 30; m 56; c 2. CELL PHYSIOLOGY. *Educ:* Duke Univ, AB, 50, PhD(zool), 57. *Prof Exp:* From instr to asst prof physiol, Fla State Univ, 57-60; asst prof physiol & radiol, State Univ NY Upstate Med Ctr, 60-63; BIOLOGIST, BIOL DIV, OAK RIDGE NAT LAB, 63- *Concurrent Pos:* Lectr, Oak Ridge Biomed Grad Sch, 69; molecular biologist, Biol Div, US AEC, 69-70. *Mem:* Am Soc Microbiol; Biophys Soc; Radiation Res Soc. *Res:* Control of cell division in bacterial cells; biochemistry of anucleate cells, DNA-membrane association; cellular fractionations; radiation effects. *Mailing Add:* 120 Wendover Circle Oak Ridge TN 37830

FISHER, WILLIAM FRANCIS, b Mobile, Ala, Nov 3, 41; m 62; c 5. IMMUNOLOGY, PARASITOLOGY. *Educ:* Col St Joseph, BS, 63; NMex Highlands Univ, MS, 65. *Prof Exp:* Res lab technician histol, Vet Admin Hosp, 65; lab instr biol, Univ Albuquerque, 65-66; biol lab technician parasitol, Agr Res Serv, Parasite Res Lab, 66-67, res asst, 67-77, RES SCIENTIST IMMUNOL & ACAROLOGY, US LIVESTOCK INSECTS LAB, AGR RES SERV, SCI & EDUC, USDA, 77- *Mem:* Am Soc Parasitologists; Acarological Soc Am; Entom Soc Am. *Res:* Immunological and physiological responses of animals to parasitic mites; host-parasite relationships; biology and control of parasitic mites. *Mailing Add:* US Livestock Insects Lab Agr Res Ser Sci & Educ USDA Kerrville TX 78028

FISHER, WILLIAM GARY, b Cleveland, Ohio, Aug 15, 47. MEDICAL PHYSICS. *Educ:* Ariz State Univ, BS, 69, MS, 71. *Prof Exp:* Res asst, Orange County Med Ctr, Calif, 72-73; dept supvr nuclear med, Mesa Gen Hosp, Mesa, Ariz, 74-78; PRES, FISHER MED PHYSICS, TEMPE, ARIZ, 79- *Concurrent Pos:* lectr, Saint Joseph's Hosp & Med Ctr, Phoenix, Ariz, 76- *Mem:* Am Asn Physicists Med; Am Phys Soc; Health Physics Soc; Radiol Soc NAm; Soc Nuclear Med. *Mailing Add:* Suite 112 2039 E Broadway Rd Tempe AZ 85282

FISHER, WILLIAM LAWRENCE, b Marion, Ill, Sept 16, 32; m 54; c 3. GEOLOGY, PALEONTOLOGY. *Educ:* Southern Ill Univ, BS, 54; Univ Kans, MS, 58, PhD(geol), 61. *Prof Exp:* Geologist, Aluminum Co Am, 57; asst, Kans Geol Surv, 57-58; asst geol, Univ Kans, 58-60; res assoc, Bur Econ Geol, Univ Tex, Austin, 60-64, res scientist, 64-68, assoc dir, 68-70, dir, 70-75, spec lectr geol & assoc mem grad fac, Univ, 64-69, prof geol sci & mem grad fac, 69-75; dep asst secy energy & minerals, Dept Interior, 75-76, asst secy, 76-77; DIR, UNIV TEX, AUSTIN, 77-, PROF PUBLIC AFFAIRS, 81- *Mem:* Geol Soc Am; Am Asn Petrol Geol; Soc Econ Geol; Asn Am State Geol; Soc Mining Eng. *Res:* Depositional systems; seismic stratigraphy; oil, gas and mineral exploration; energy and minerals policy. *Mailing Add:* Univ Sta Box X Austin TX 78712

FISHKIN, ARTHUR FREDERIC, b New York, NY, May 27, 30; m 56; c 4. BIOCHEMISTRY. *Educ:* Ind Univ, AB, 51, AM, 53; Univ Iowa, PhD(biochem), 57. *Prof Exp:* From instr to asst prof biochem, Sch Med, La State Univ, 58-64; asst prof chem, NMex State Univ, 64-68; ASSOC PROF BIOCHEM, SCH MED, CREIGHTON UNIV, 68- *Mem:* AAAS; NY Acad Sci; Am Chem Soc; fel Am Inst Chemists. *Res:* Glycoproteins of cardiovascular connective tissue; connective tissue biochemistry. *Mailing Add:* Creighton Univ Sch of Med Omaha NE 68178

FISHLER, MAURICE CHARLES, b Chicago, Ill, Nov 9, 12; m 34; c 2. PHYSIOLOGY. *Educ:* Univ Calif, Los Angeles, AB, 36; Univ Calif, PhD(physiol), 43, MD, 47. *Prof Exp:* Asst physiol, Univ Calif, 39-42, physiologist, Off Sci Res & Develop, 42-43; asst surgeon, USPHS Marine Hosp, San Francisco, 47-48; chief biol div, Naval Radiol Defense Lab, 48-53 & Dept Med, Kaiser Found Hosp, 50-59, staff physician, 59-65; res scientist, 59-65, INVESTR, KAISER FOUND RES INST, 66- *Concurrent Pos:* Dep mem joint panel, Res & Develop Bd, Dept Defense, 51-53. *Res:* Metabolism of phospholipids with radioactive phosphorus; thoracic duct lymph; liverless animals; effects of radiation on living tissue. *Mailing Add:* 1645 Scenic Ave Berkeley CA 94709

FISHMAN, ALFRED PAUL, b New York, NY, Sept 24, 18; wid; c 2. PHYSIOLOGY. *Educ:* Univ Mich, AB, 38, MS, 39; Univ Louisville, MD, 43. *Prof Exp:* Intern med, Jewish Hosp, Brooklyn, NY, 43-44; from asst resident to resident med, Mt Sinai Hosp, 47-48; Am Heart Asn estab investr, Columbia Univ, 51-55, from asst prof to assoc prof med, Col Physicians & Surgeons, 55-67; prof, Univ Chicago, 67-69; prof med, 69-72, assoc dean sch med, 69-76, WILLIAM MAUL MEASEY PROF MED, SCH MED, UNIV PA, 72-, DIR, ROBINETTE FOUND, CARDIOVASC PULMONARY DIV & CARDIOVASC RES CTR, 69-, DIR CARDIOVASC PULMONARY DIV, 77- *Concurrent Pos:* Dazian Found fel path, Mt Sinai Hosp, New York, 46-47; fel cardiovasc physiol, Michael Reese Hosp, Chicago, Ill, 48-49; Am Heart Asn fels physiol, Bellevue Hosp, New York, 49-50 & Harvard Univ, 50-51; Commonwealth fel physiol, Nuffield Inst Med Res, Eng, 64-65; dir cardiorespiratory lab, Columbia-Presby Med Ctr, 55-66; trustee, Mt Desert Island Biol Lab, 55-60; consult, Vet Admin Hosp, Bronx, NY, 61-67 & Off Sci Technol, 62-; hon consult med, St Mary's Hosp Med Sch, London, 64; Sir Ernest Finch prof, Univ Sheffield, 65; dir cardiovasc inst, Michael Reese Med Ctr, Chicago, 67-69; mem, Nat Adv Heart Coun, 68-72; James Howard Means vis prof, Harvard Med Sch, 70; Litchfield lectr, Oxford Univ, 72; Arthur E Strauss vis prof, Sch Med, Washington Univ, 73; mem adv panel cardiovasc dis, WHO, 73; consult to chancellor, Univ Mo-Kansas City, 73-78; mem adv comt respiratory dis coal miners, Gov Pa, 74; vis scientist, Johns Hopkins Univ & Univ Md, 74; Zyskind hon vis prof, Ben Gurion Univ, Israel, 75; visitor, Nat Heart Lung Blood Inst, People's Repub China, 80. *Mem:* Nat Acad Sci; Am Soc Clin Invest; Am Soc Exp Biol & Med; Am Fedn Clin Res; fel Am Col Physicians. *Res:* Physiology of respiration and circulation; comparative physiology; internal medicine; interactions of the heart and lungs for purposes of gas exchange; regulation of the pulmonary circulation, heart failure, control of breathing in health and disease; comparative biology. *Mailing Add:* Dept Med Univ Pa Hosp 3600 Spruce St Philadelphia PA 19104

FISHMAN, DAVID H, b Brooklyn, NY, Aug 21, 39; m 62; c 3. POLYMER SCIENCE. *Educ:* Columbia Col, AB, 60; Pa State Univ, PhD(org chem), 64. *Prof Exp:* Res chemist org chem dept, E I du Pont de Nemours & Co, Inc, 64-66; Celanese Plastics Co, 66-69, group leader plastic molding resins, 69-74, tech mgr, 74-76; mgr tech acquisitions, 76-80, DIR TECH PLANNING & DEVELOP, INMONT CORP, UNITED TECHNOL CORP, 80- *Mem:* Am Chem Soc; Soc Plastics Engrs; Licensing Exec Soc; Soc Chem Indust France. *Res:* Coatings; printing inks; sealants; adhesives; cellular rubber; colorants; concentrates; plastics; composites. *Mailing Add:* 1255 Broad St Clifton NJ 07015

FISHMAN, FRANK J, JR, b Chicago, Ill, Jan 18, 31; m 54; c 5. THEORETICAL PHYSICS. *Educ:* Univ Ill, BS, 52; Harvard Univ, AM, 53, PhD(physics), 57. *Prof Exp:* Prin res scientist, Avco-Everett Res Lab, Avco Corp, 57-68; assoc prof physics, Adrian Col, 68-76; INSTR PHYS SCI, GRAND RAPIDS JR COL, 76- *Mem:* Am Phys Soc; Am Asn Physics Teachers; Am Sci Affiliation. *Res:* Magnetohydrodynamics; generators, shock wave structure, kinetic models of gases and plasmas; physics of music. *Mailing Add:* Phys Sci Div 143 Bostwick NE Grand Rapids MI 49502

FISHMAN, GEORGE SAMUEL, b Everett, Mass, July 3, 37; m 69; c 2. OPERATIONS RESEARCH, APPLIED STATISTICS. *Educ:* Mass Inst Technol, BS, 60; Stanford Univ, MA, 63; Univ Calif, Los Angeles, PhD(biostatist), 70. *Prof Exp:* Economist, Rand Corp, 63-70; assoc prof opers res and assoc dir health serv res training prog, Yale Univ, 70-74; PROF OPERS RES & SYSTS ANAL, UNIV NC, CHAPEL HILL, 74-, CHMN, OPERS RES & SYSTS ANAL, 80- *Concurrent Pos:* Consult, New York City Rand Inst, 70-71; Bur Manpower Educ, Health Serv & Ment Health Admin, 72-73 & Housing Auth, City of New Haven & Ford Found, 72-74. *Mem:* Am Statist Asn; Opers Res Soc Am; Inst Mgt Sci. *Res:* Statistical analysis of discrete event digital simulation; experimental design and techniques aimed at statistical evaluation of simulation results. *Mailing Add:* Curric in Opers Res & Systs Anal Smith Bldg 128A Univ NC Chapel Hill NC 27514

FISHMAN, GERALD JAY, b St Louis, Mo, Feb 10, 43; m 67; c 2. ASTROPHYSICS, GAMMA-RAY ASTRONOMY. *Educ:* Univ Mo-Columbia, BS, 65; Rice Univ, MS, 68, PhD(space sci), 69. *Prof Exp:* Res assoc space sci, Rice Univ, 69; sr physicist, Teledyne Brown Eng Co, 69-74; res

physicist, Marshall Space Flight Ctr, 74-77, staff scientist, Hq, 77-78, RES PHYSICIST, MARSHALL SPACE FLIGHT CTR, NASA, 78- *Mem:* AAAS; Am Astron Soc; Am Phys Soc. *Res:* Nuclear instrumentation; gamma-ray and x-ray astronomy; high energy and nuclear astrophysics. *Mailing Add:* 8024 Tea Garden Rd Huntsville AL 35802

FISHMAN, HARVEY MORTON, b Lynn, Mass, Oct 27, 37; m 62; c 3. BIOPHYSICS, PHYSIOLOGY. *Educ:* Mass Inst Technol, BS, 54; Univ Calif, Berkeley, MS, 64, PhD(biophys), 68. *Prof Exp:* Design engr, Hewlett-Packard Co, 59-63; staff fel, Lab Biophys, Nat Inst Neurol Dis & Stroke, 68-70; asst prof biol sci, State Univ NY Albany, 70-73; assoc prof physiol & biophys, 73-77, PROF PHYSIOL & BIOPHYS, UNIV TEX MED BR GALVESTON, 77- *Concurrent Pos:* Develop engr, Space Sci Lab, Univ Calif, Berkeley, 64-66, vis prof, Dept Biophysics, 79; investr, Marine Biol Lab, Woods Hole, Mass, 68-, mem corp, 71- *Mem:* Biophys Soc; Inst Elec & Electronics Eng; Soc Gen Physiol; Sigma Xi. *Res:* Ion conduction in excitable membranes. *Mailing Add:* Dept of Physiol & Biophys Univ of Tex Med Br Galveston TX 77550

FISHMAN, IRVING YALE, b Ardmore, Okla, Sept 12, 20; m 42; c 2. SENSORY PHYSIOLOGY. *Educ:* Univ Okla, BS, 42, MS, 48; Fla State Univ, PhD(physiol, biochem), 55. *Prof Exp:* Spec lectr physiol, Fla State Univ, 51-54; from instr to assoc prof, 54-70, PROF BIOL, GRINNELL COL, 71- *Concurrent Pos:* NSF res grants, 54- *Mem:* AAAS; Am Physiol Soc; Am Soc Zoologists. *Res:* Electrophysiological studies of chemoreception in mammals. *Mailing Add:* Dept of Biol Grinnell Col Grinnell IA 50112

FISHMAN, JACK, b Poland, Sept 27, 30; nat US; m 64; c 3. ORGANIC CHEMISTRY, BIOCHEMISTRY. *Educ:* Yeshiva Univ, BA, 50; Columbia Univ, MA, 52; Wayne State Univ, PhD, 55. *Prof Exp:* Fel, Oxford Univ, 55-56; res assoc, Sloan-Kettering Inst Cancer Res, 56-58, asst, 58-62; assoc, Inst Steroid Res, Montefiore Hosp & Med Ctr, 62-74, dir, 74-78; PROF BIOCHEM, ROCKEFELLER UNIV, 78- *Concurrent Pos:* From assoc prof to prof biochem, Albert Einstein Col Med, Yeshiva Univ, 67-78. *Mem:* Endocrine Soc; Am Chem Soc; Am Soc Biol Chemists. *Res:* Natural products, particularly steroids and alkaloids; metabolism of steroids. *Mailing Add:* Rockefeller Univ 1230 York Ave New York NY 10021

FISHMAN, JERRY HASKEL, b June 21, 23. CHEMISTRY. *Educ:* Sir George Williams Univ, BSc, 52; Brooklyn Col, MS, 58; Stevens Inst Technol, PhD(chem), 60. *Prof Exp:* Res mgr, Leesona Moos Lab, Div Leesona Corp, 60-71; prin investr, Med Ctr, Montefiore Hosp, 71-73; res chemist, Inst Steroid Res, 74-77; SR RES ASSOC, ROCKEFELLER UNIV, 77- *Mem:* Electrochem Soc; Sigma Xi; Am Inst Chemists. *Res:* Electrochemical reactions at interfaces; steroid hormones; hormone receptors and cancer. *Mailing Add:* 227 Cent Park W New York NY 10024

FISHMAN, LOUIS, b Brooklyn, NY, June 20, 22; m 48; c 3. BIOCHEMISTRY. *Educ:* NY Univ, AB, 49, MS, 53, PhD(biochem), 57. *Prof Exp:* Res assoc, 57-60, asst res prof, 60-66, assoc prof, 66-74, PROF BIOCHEM & ACTG CHMN DEPT, COL DENT, NY UNIV, 74- *Concurrent Pos:* Consult, Manhattan Vet Admin Hosp. *Mem:* AAAS; Am Chem Soc. *Res:* Protein chemistry; protein structure; proteolytic and blood clotting enzymes; human lysozymes. *Mailing Add:* NY Univ Col of Dent 342 E 26th St New York NY 10010

FISHMAN, MARSHALL LEWIS, b Philadelphia, Pa, July 2, 37; m 66; c 2. POLYMER CHEMISTRY. *Educ:* Temple Univ, BA, 59; Villanova Univ, MS, 61; Polytech Inst Brooklyn, PhD, 69. *Prof Exp:* RES CHEMIST, SCI & EDUC ADMIN, USDA, 69- *Mem:* Am Chem Soc. *Res:* Isolation and characterization of proteins; development of new or improved methods for characterizing proteins in complex mixtures such as those found in plants; development of automated analysis of plant proteins by gel filtration; development of new methods of extracting proteins from plants. *Mailing Add:* Richard B Russell Agr Res Ctr PO Box 5677 Athens GA 30604

FISHMAN, MARVIN, b New York, NY, Mar 17, 28; m 57; c 2. IMMUNOLOGY. *Educ:* City Col New York, BS, 49; Univ Ky, MS, 51; Wash Univ, PhD(microbiol), 54. *Prof Exp:* Assoc mem, 62-66, MEM, PUB HEALTH RES INST, CITY OF NEW YORK, INC, 66-; res prof path, 70-76, ADJ PROF PATH, POSTGRAD MED SCH, NY UNIV, 76- *Concurrent Pos:* Res assoc prof path, Postgrad Med Sch, 68-70. *Honors & Awards:* Selman A Waksman Award, 65. *Mem:* Am Soc Microbiol; Am Asn Immunol. *Res:* Investigation in the mechanism of antibody formation and antibody action. *Mailing Add:* Pub Health Res Inst City of New York Inc New York NY 10016

FISHMAN, MARVIN JOSEPH, b Denver, Colo, Apr 15, 32; m 57; c 3. WATER CHEMISTRY. *Educ:* Univ Colo, BA, 54, MS, 56. *Prof Exp:* CHEMIST, WATER RESOURCES DIV, US GEOL SURV, 56- *Mem:* Am Chem Soc; Soc Appl Spectros; Am Soc Testing & Mat. *Res:* Water analysis; development of new or improved methods for determining inorganic constituents found in water; automation of analytical methods; development of atomic absorption methods for determining metals in water. *Mailing Add:* 3353 S Niagara Way Denver CO 80224

FISHMAN, MAX, electrical engineering, see previous edition

FISHMAN, MORRIS, b Montreal, Que, Mar 2, 39; m 67; c 2. ORGANIC CHEMISTRY. *Educ:* McGill Univ, BSc, 60; Univ NB, PhD(chem), 66. *Prof Exp:* Lab asst chem, Ayerst, McKenna & Harrison, Que, 60-62; SR RES CHEMIST, F M C CORP, 66- *Mem:* Am Chem Soc; Chem Inst Can. *Res:* Synthesizing organic compounds to be evaluated in medicinal or agricultural biological programs; process development work. *Mailing Add:* Agr Chem Div FMC Corp PO Box 8 Princeton NJ 08540

FISHMAN, MYER M, b Boston, Mass, Apr 27, 18; m 48; c 2. BIOCHEMISTRY. *Educ:* City Col New York, BS, 38; Univ Minn, MS, 40, PhD, 42. *Prof Exp:* Assoc chemist, Sig Corps, US Army, 42-43; chemist, Stein, Hall & Co, 43-44; from instr to assoc prof, 46-67, PROF CHEM, CITY COL NEW YORK, 67- *Concurrent Pos:* Assoc dean Col Lib Arts & Sci, 69-76. *Mem:* Am Chem Soc; NY Acad Sci. *Res:* Physical biochemistry. *Mailing Add:* Dept of Chem City Col of New York New York NY 10031

FISHMAN, NORMAN, b Petaluma, Calif, July 18, 24; m 53; c 2. POLYMER TECHNOLOGY, CHEMICAL ENGINEERING. *Educ:* Univ Calif, BS, 48. *Prof Exp:* Chem engr, Western Regional Utilization Lab, USDA, 49-53; proj engr, Food Mach & Chem Corp, 53-54; sr chem engr, 54-61, mgr propellant eval, 61-67, mgr polymer technol, 67-76, sr indust economist, 76-79, DIR, POLYMERS DEPT, SRI INT, 79- *Honors & Awards:* USDA Award, 54. *Mem:* Soc Plastics Engrs; Sigma Xi; Am Technion Soc; Am Chem Soc. *Res:* Applications of polymeric materials; fire retardance in polymers; market research; acquisition and diversification studies; technoeconomics. *Mailing Add:* 2316 Blueridge Ave Menlo Park CA 94025

FISHMAN, PETER HARVEY, b Boston, Mass, Dec 8, 39. BIOCHEMISTRY. *Educ:* Mass Inst Technol, BS, 61; George Washington Univ, MS, 67, PhD(biochem), 70. *Prof Exp:* From res asst to teaching fel biochem, George Washington Univ, 65-69; staff fel, 70-75, res assoc biochem, 75-80, CHIEF MEMBRANE BIOCHEM SECT, NAT INST NEUROL & COMMUN DISORDERS & STROKE, 80- *Concurrent Pos:* Lectr biochem, George Washington Univ, 70- & Georgetown Univ, 71-; Prof lectr, 78- *Mem:* Am Soc Biol Chemists; Sigma Xi. *Res:* Biosynthesis of complex carbohydrates; abnormal biosynthesis of gangliosides in neoplasia and genetic diseases; role of surface glycoconjugates in transmission of information across cell membranes; role of gangliosides in cellular differentiation; regulation of ademylate cyclase. *Mailing Add:* Develop & Metab Br Nat Inst Neurol & Commun Dis NIH Bethesda MD 20014

FISHMAN, ROBERT ALLEN, b New York, NY, May 30, 24; m 56; c 3. NEUROLOGY. *Educ:* Columbia Univ, AB, 44; Univ Pa, MD, 47. *Prof Exp:* Intern & asst resident med, New Haven Hosp, 47-49; resident neurol, Mass Gen Hosp, 49-50; asst resident neurol, Neurol Inst, 50-51; from instr to assoc prof neurol, Col Physicians & Surgeons, Columbia Univ, 54-66; PROF NEUROL & CHMN DEPT, SCH MED, UNIV CALIF, SAN FRANCISCO, 66- *Concurrent Pos:* Asst med, Yale Univ, 47-49; teaching fel, Harvard Med Sch, 49-50; neurophysiologist, Army Med Serv Grad Sch, DC, 51-53; chief res, Neurol Inst, 53-54; asst attend neurologist, 55-62, assoc attend neurologist, 62-66; Markle scholar med sci, 60-65; co-dir, Neurol Clin Res Ctr, 61-66; consult neurologist, San Francisco Gen Hosp, San Francisco Vet Admin Hosp & Letterman Gen Hosp, San Francisco. *Honors & Awards:* Moses Res Prize, Columbia Univ, 70, Royer Award, 73. *Mem:* Am Epilepsy Soc; Int Soc Neurochem; Am Neurol Asn; Asn Res Nerv & Ment Dis; Am Acad Neurol (vpres, 71-73, pres, 75-77). *Res:* Metabolic disorders of the nervous system; the blood brain barrier; cerebrospinal fluid. *Mailing Add:* Dept Neurol Rm 794M Sch Med Univ Calif San Francisco CA 94122

FISHMAN, ROBERT SUMNER, b Boston, Mass, May 17, 32; m 57; c 4. MATHEMATICS. *Educ:* Northeastern Univ, BS, 54; Univ Vt, MA, 56; Boston Univ, PhD(math), 61. *Prof Exp:* From assoc prof to prof math, Emmanuel Col, Mass, 61-65; prof, Mass State Col Salem, 65-68; sr mathematician, Missle Systs Div, Raytheon Co, Bedford, 68-74; consult, QEI Consult Firm, 74-79; SR ENG SCIENTIST, RCA, 79- *Concurrent Pos:* Lectr, Mass Col Pharm, 61-65. *Mem:* Soc Indust & Appl Math; Am Math Soc; Math Asn Am; Asn Symbolic Logic. *Res:* The average of a function over a group of translations in a subinvariant measure space. *Mailing Add:* 20 Ruby Ave Marblehead MA 01945

FISHMAN, SHERMAN SAMPSON, b Miami, Fla, Feb 20, 26. PHARMACOLOGY, ULTRASOUND. *Educ:* Tufts Univ, AB, 48; Univ Chicago, MS, 52; Univ Calif, Berkeley, Cert(med care admin), 70. *Prof Exp:* Sci investr, US Naval Radiol Defense Lab, 56-59; DIR RES & DEVELOP & GEN MGR, SARA SCI CO, 60- *Concurrent Pos:* Mem, Am Nat Stand Comt Med Electronics. *Mem:* Am Chem Soc; Am Soc Advan Instrumentation; Western Pharmacol Soc; Instrument Soc Am. *Res:* Biological effects of ultrasound. *Mailing Add:* Sara Sci Co PO Box 321 San Francisco CA 94101

FISHMAN, SHEROLD, b Winnipeg, Man, Jan 24, 25; m 54; c 2. NUCLEAR MEDICINE, INTERNAL MEDICINE. *Educ:* Univ Sask, BA, 45; McGill Univ, PhD(biochem), 53; Univ BC, MD, 59; FRCP(C), 65; Am Bd Nuclear Med, cert, 73. *Prof Exp:* Biochemist, Montreal Gen Hosp, 51-54; clin chemist, Univ BC, 60-62, partic residency prog internal med, 62-63; CONSULT NUCLEAR MED, SHAUGHNESSY HOSP, 65-; REGIONAL LAB COORDR, ROYAL COLUMBIAN HOSP, 72-; DIR NUCLEAR MED, 73- *Concurrent Pos:* Res fel, Univ Wash, 63-64; consult internal med & endocrinol, Vancouver Gen Hosp, 64-72. *Res:* Endocrinology. *Mailing Add:* 7170 Hudson Vancouver BC Can

FISHMAN, WILLIAM HAROLD, b Winnipeg, Man, Mar 2, 14; nat US; m 39; c 3. BIOCHEMISTRY, ONCOLOGY. *Educ:* Univ Sask, BS, 35; Univ Toronto, PhD(biochem), 39. *Prof Exp:* From instr to asst prof biochem, Bowman Gray Sch Med, 41-45; res assoc biochem & asst prof surg, Univ Chicago, 45-48; res prof biochem & nutrit, Sch Med, Tufts Univ, 48-59, res prof oncol, 59-70, prof path & dir cancer res ctr, 70-77, PRES, LA JOLLA CANCER RES FOUND, 76-, DIR, CANCER RES CTR, 81- *Concurrent Pos:* Fedn fel, Int Physiol Cong, Oxford, Eng, 47; assoc dir cancer res & chief biochemist, New Eng Ctr Hosp, 48-59, dir cancer res, 59-; vis prof, NSF travel award, Japan, 59; mem tissue & cell biol study sect, Vet Admin; mem, Int Study Group Carcinoembryonic Proteins; ed-in-chief, J Oncol Develop Biol & Med, 79- *Honors & Awards:* Gov Gen Medal, 31. *Mem:* Am Soc Exp Path; Am Soc Biol Chemists; Am Asn Cancer Res; Histochem Soc; Soc Exp Biol & Med. *Res:* Enzymes; beta-glucuronidase; prostatic acid phosphatase; alkaline phosphatase isoenzymes; steroids; renal beta-glucuronidase response to androgens; glucuronic acid metabolism; biochemical diagnostic tests; enzyme histochemistry; enzymorphology; experimental pathology; oncodevelopmental gene expression. *Mailing Add:* 10901 N Torrey Pines Rd La Jolla CA 92037

FISK, DONALD, b Sterling, Mich, Dec 12, 37; m 56; c 3. MATHEMATICS. *Educ:* Mich State Univ, BA, 59, MA, 60, PhD(statist), 63. *Prof Exp:* Asst prof math, Knox Col, 63-64; Kent State Univ, 64-65 & Northwestern Univ, 65-67; assoc prof, Kent State Univ, 67-69; PROF MATH, CENT MICH UNIV, 69- *Mem:* Am Math Soc. *Res:* Probability; decomposition of stochastic processes; stochastic integrals. *Mailing Add:* Dept of Math Cent Mich Univ Mt Pleasant MI 48858

FISK, FRANK WILBUR, b Logan, Utah, Apr 15, 14; m 44; c 2. INSECT PHYSIOLOGY, INSECT TAXONOMY. *Educ:* Univ Ill, BS, 36; Univ Minn, MS, 39, PhD(entom), 49. *Prof Exp:* Jr entomologist, USPHS, 38-40, asst entomologist, 41-43, sanitarian, 43-45, assoc entomologist, 45-46; from asst prof to prof zool & entom, 49-76, EMER PROF ENTOM, OHIO STATE UNIV, 76- *Mem:* Entom Soc Am. *Res:* Blattaaria (cockroach) taxonomy. *Mailing Add:* Dept Entom Ohio State Univ Columbus OH 43210

FISK, HENRY EUGENE, high energy physics, see previous edition

FISK, JAMES BROWN, physics, deceased

FISK, LANNY HERBERT, b Edmore, Mich, Feb 24, 44; m 67. PALYNOLOGY, PETROLEUM GEOLOGY. *Educ:* Andrews Univ, BA, 71; Loma Linda Univ, PhD(biol), 76. *Prof Exp:* Asst prof paleobiol, Walla Walla Col, 74-78, assoc prof, 78-79; ASSOC PROF GEOL & BIOL, LOMA LINDA UNIV, 79- *Concurrent Pos:* Consult, Amoco Oil Co, 79-81 & Davis Oil Co, 81-82. *Mem:* Am Asn Stratig Palynologists; Am Asn Petrol Geologists; Sigma Xi; Paleont Soc; Soc Econ Paleontologists & Mineralogists. *Res:* Paleoecological interpretation of the fossil plant record; Tertiary stratigraphic palynology; petroleum source rock analysis; petroleum potential of West Coast Cretaceon-Tortiary basins. *Mailing Add:* Dept Geol Sci Loma Linda Univ Riverside CA 92515

FISK, LEROY (HENRY), b San Francisco, Calif, Nov 11, 19; m 51; c 2. PARASITOLOGY. *Educ:* Col of the Pac, BA, 48, MA, 49; Univ Southern Calif, PhD, 49. *Prof Exp:* Lab asst physiol, Univ Southern Calif, 49-50; chief lab technician, Figueroa Med Labs, Calif, 50; lab dir, Trinity Gen Hosp, 52-54; from asst prof to assoc prof parasitol, 54-67, chmn med assocs div, 57-74, PROF PARASITOL, ORE INST TECHNOL, 67-, Coordr Water Qual Control Environ Technol, 77- *Mem:* Am Soc Parasitol; Am Micros Soc. *Res:* Hematology; biochemistry. *Mailing Add:* Ore Inst of Technol Box 2177 Klamath Falls OR 97601

FISK, ROBERT SPENCER, b Chicago, Ill, Dec 21, 39; c 1. APPLIED MATHEMATICS. *Educ:* Univ Wyo, BS, 60, MS, 62, PhD(math), 72. *Prof Exp:* Dean of Inst, Sheridan Col, 66-67; from instr to assoc prof, Pac Lutheran Univ, 68-78; ASST PROF MATH, COLO SCH MINES, 78- *Concurrent Pos:* Vis asst prof, Colo Sch Mines, 76-77; vis lectr, Univ Calif, Davis, 81-82. *Mem:* Math Asn Am; Soc Indust & Appl Math; Sigma Xi. *Res:* Partial differential equations. *Mailing Add:* Dept of Math Colo Sch of Mines Golden CO 80401

FISKE, MILAN DERBYSHIRE, b Sharon, Wis, Nov 15, 14; m 36; c 3. SOLID STATE PHYSICS. *Educ:* Beloit Col, BS, 37; Univ Wis, PhD(physics), 41. *Prof Exp:* Asst physics, Univ Wis, 37-40; res assoc, Res Lab, Gen Elec Co, 41-57, mgr personnel & sci rels, 57-59, res personnel, 59-62, physicist, 62-66, mgr personnel & admin, Gen Phys Lab, 66-68, progs & admin, Phys Sci & Eng, 68-69, mgr, Phys Sci Br, 69-77; CONSULT, 78- *Concurrent Pos:* Mem, US Nat Comt, Int Union Pure & Appl Physics, 68-74. *Mem:* Fel Am Phys Soc; Biophys Soc; AAAS. *Res:* Thermionics; gas discharges; T-R switches for radar; cryogenics; high-pressure effects at low temperature; radiation damage; superconductivity; management of multidisciplinary group engaged in exploratory research. *Mailing Add:* 215 Lakehill Rd Burnt Hills NY 12027

FISKE, RICHARD SEWELL, b Baltimore, Md, Sept 5, 32; m 59; c 2. GEOLOGY. *Educ:* Princeton Univ, BSE, 54, MSE, 55; Johns Hopkins Univ, PhD(geol), 60. *Prof Exp:* Geologist, Union Oil Co, Calif, 55-56; Am Chem Soc Petrol Res Fund Lectr, Univ Tokyo, 60-61; res assoc, Johns Hopkins Univ, 61-63; geologist, US Geol Surv, 64-76; geologist, 76-80, DIR, NAT MUS NATURAL HIST, SMITHSONIAN INST, 80- *Mem:* Geol Soc Am; Am Geophys Union. *Res:* Petrology; Cenozoic volcanic geology of the Pacific Northwest and Japan; volcanic sedimentation; applied geophysics; monitoring active Hawaiian and Caribbean volcanoes; Mesozoic volcanism of the Sierra Nevada. *Mailing Add:* Smithsonian Inst NHB-119 Washington DC 20560

FISKELL, JOHN GARTH AUSTIN, b Clearwater, Man, May 8, 17; nat US; m 41; c 7. SOIL CHEMISTRY. *Educ:* Univ Toronto, BSA, 47; McGill Univ, MSc, 49, PhD(agr chem), 51. *Prof Exp:* Asst chemist, Welland Chem Works, 41-44; asst biochemist, 51-56, assoc prof soils, 56-61, PROF SOILS & BIOCHEMIST, UNIV FLA, 61- *Mem:* Am Chem Soc. *Res:* Soil mineralogy and chemistry; micronutrient relationships in plant nutrition; soil amendments; analytical methods; root absorption and desorption studies. *Mailing Add:* Dept of Soils Agr Exp Sta Univ of Fla Gainesville FL 32611

FISLER, GEORGE FREDERICK, b Saginaw, Mich, Nov 29, 31. BIOLOGY, ZOOLOGY. *Educ:* Mich State Univ, BS, 54, MS, 56; Univ Calif, Berkeley, PhD(zool), 61. *Prof Exp:* Res zoologist, Hastings Natural Hist Reservation, Univ Calif, Carmel Valley, 60-61, jr res zoologist, 61-62; asst prof biol, Portland State Col, 62-64; from asst prof to assoc prof, 64-70, PROF BIOL, CALIF STATE UNIV, NORTHRIDGE, 70- *Mem:* Am Soc Mammal; Ecol Soc Am; Am Ornith Union; Cooper Ornith Soc; Animal Behav Soc. *Res:* Behavior, ecology and systematics of mammals; behavior of birds. *Mailing Add:* Dept Biol Calif State Univ Northridge CA 91330

FISSER, HERBERT GEORGE, b Ames, Iowa, Mar 9, 26; m 52; c 3. RANGE MANAGEMENT, ECOLOGY. *Educ:* Mont State Col, BS, 58, MS, 61; Univ Wyo, PhD(range mgt), 62. *Prof Exp:* From instr to assoc prof, 59-70, PROF RANGE MGT, UNIV WYO, 70- *Concurrent Pos:* Consult, Rangeland Inventory. *Mem:* Ecol Soc Am; Am Soc Range Mgt; Wildlife Soc; Sigma Xi; Int Asn Ecol. *Res:* Game range improvement; plant pattern and distribution; grazing systems and wildlife interrelationships; plant phenology and seed production; range site productivity potential. *Mailing Add:* Div of Range Mgt Univ of Wyo Laramie WY 82071

FISTEDIS, STANLEY H, b Constantinople, Turkey, June 25, 25; US citizen; m 53; c 2. NUCLEAR ENGINEERING, ENGINEERING MECHANICS. *Educ:* Robert Col, Istanbul, BS, 47; Mont State Univ, MS, 49; Univ Mo, PhD(eng mech), 53; Univ Chicago, MBA, 65. *Prof Exp:* Designer, Babcock & Wilcox Co, 48-49; instr eng mech, Univ Mo, 49-52; struct engr, Western Knapp Eng Co, 52-53, Johnson & Johnson Co, 53 & Allen & Garcia Co, 53-54; spec assignments engr, Girdler Co, 54-57; assoc engr, 57-63, group head eng mech, 63-66, mgr, 66-71, PROG MGR, ARGONNE NAT LAB, 71- *Concurrent Pos:* Prin ed, Int J Nuclear Eng & Design, 80-; sci & gen chmn, 7th Int Conf Struct Mech Reactor Technol, Chicago, 83. *Mem:* Fel Am Soc Civil Engrs; Am Nuclear Soc; Nat Soc Prof Engrs; Am Soc Mech Engrs; Int Asn Struct Mech Reactor Technol (pres, 81-83). *Res:* Structural mechanics; application of advances in mechanics of materials to industrial plant construction; prestressed and reinforced concrete; nuclear plant components; nuclear safety and containment; safety and design of fast breeder nuclear reactors. *Mailing Add:* 500 N Parkwood Park Ridge IL 60068

FITCH, COY DEAN, b Marthaville, La, Oct 5, 34; m 56; c 2. MEDICINE, BIOCHEMISTRY. *Educ:* Univ Ark, BS, 56, MS & MD, 58; Am Bd Internal Med, dipl, 65, dipl endocrinol, 72. *Prof Exp:* Instr biochem, Sch Med, Univ Ark, Little Rock, 59-62, from asst prof to assoc prof med & biochem, 62-67; assoc prof internal med & biochem, 67-73, PROF INTERNAL MED, SCH MED, ST LOUIS UNIV, 73-, PROF BIOCHEM, 76-, DIR DIV ENDOCRINOL, 77- *Concurrent Pos:* Russell M Wilder-Nat Vitamin Found fel, 59-62; mem nutrit study sect, NIH, 67-71; dep dir, Div Biochem, Walter Reed Army Inst Res, 69. *Mem:* Endocrine Soc; Am Soc Clin Invest; Am Inst Nutrit; Am Soc Biol Chemists. *Res:* Metabolism and nutrition; membrane transport processes; role of vitamin E in hematopoiesis and muscle function; diseases of skeletal muscle; drug resistance in malaria. *Mailing Add:* Dept Internal Med Sch Med St Louis Univ 1402 S Grand Blvd St Louis MO 63104

FITCH, ELLIOT BRYANT, b Los Gatos, Calif, Apr 30, 10; m 38; c 2. CHEMICAL ENGINEERING. *Educ:* Calif Inst Technol, BS, 32; Univ Conn, MS, 64. *Prof Exp:* Operator, Am Potash & Chem Corp, 33-34, shift boss, 34-35, chem engr, 35-41, sr res chem engr, 41-44; sales engr, Dorr Co, 44-46, res engr, 46-48, from asst to dir res to dir res, 48-57, dir res, Westport Labs, Dorr-Oliver, Inc, 57-64, res dir, 64-66, tech adv, Murphy Div, 66-69, chief scientist, 69-74; vis indust prof, Carnegie-Mellon Univ, 74-78; adj prof, Univ Auburn, 78-81; MEM STAFF, PHYS SEPARATIONS RES, 81- *Mem:* Fel Am Inst Chem Engrs. *Res:* Physical separation processes. *Mailing Add:* Phys Separations Res 705 Sch St Napa CA 94559

FITCH, ERNEST CHESTER, JR, b Wichita, Kans, Nov 30, 24; m 48; c 3. MECHANICAL ENGINEERING, FLUID POWER ENGINEERING. *Educ:* Okla State Univ, BS, 50, MS, 51; Univ Okla, PhD(eng sci), 64. *Prof Exp:* Res engr, Jersey Prod Res Corp, Okla, 51-53; PROF MECH ENG, OKLA STATE UNIV, 53-, DIR RES, FLUID POWER RES CTR, 65-, FLUID POWER INDUST PROF, 76- *Concurrent Pos:* Deleg, US Fluid Power Indust, Int Orgn Standard, 71-80; chmn, US Dept Com, Int Trade Mission, Korea & Taiwan, 77; chmn, 7th Int Conf Fluid Mech & Fluid Power, Baroda, India, 77; mem bd adv, NSF, 77-78; consult. *Honors & Awards:* Arch T Colwell Award, Soc Automotive Engrs, 70; Ann Achievement Award, Nat Fluid Power Asn, 70. *Mem:* Nat Soc Prof Engrs; Am Soc Testing & Mat. *Res:* Fluid power component and system design; diagnostics and conditionn monitoring; system reliability and component service life; filtration and fluid contamination control. *Mailing Add:* Fluid Power Res Ctr Okla State Univ Stillwater OK 74074

FITCH, FRANK WESLEY, b Bushnell, Ill, May 30, 29; m 51; c 2. PATHOLOGY. *Educ:* Univ Chicago, MD, 53, MS, 57, PhD(path), 60. *Prof Exp:* Intern, Hosp, Univ Mich, 53-54; from instr to prof, 57-76, ALBERT D LASKER PROF PATH & ASSOC DEAN EDUC AFFAIRS, UNIV CHICAGO, 76- *Concurrent Pos:* USPHS fel path, Univ Chicago, 54-57; Lederle med fac award, 58-61; Markle scholar acad med, 61-66; vis scientist, Inst Biochem, Univ Lausanne, 65-66; Guggenheim fel, 74-75. *Mem:* AAAS; Am Asn Pathologists; Radiation Res Soc; Asn Am Med Cols; Am Asn Immunologists. *Res:* Experimental pathology; immunology. *Mailing Add:* Dept of Path Univ of Chicago Chicago IL 60637

FITCH, HENRY SHELDON, b Utica, NY, Dec 25, 09; m 46; c 3. ECOLOGY. *Educ:* Univ Ore, BA, 30; Univ Calif, MA, 33, PhD(zool), 37. *Prof Exp:* Wildlife technician, Hastings Wildlife Reserve, Univ Calif, 37-38; biologist, US Fish & Wildlife Serv, Wash, 38-47; from instr to assoc prof, 48-59, prof zool, 59-70, prof systs & ecol, 70-80, EMER PROF SYSTS & ECOL, UNIV KANS, 80-, SUPT NATURAL HIST RESERVATION, 48- *Mem:* Am Soc Ichthyol & Herpet; Ornith Soc Am; Cooper Ornith Soc; Soc for Study Amphibians & Reptiles. *Res:* Systematics and natural history of North American and neotropical reptiles; economics and ecology of rodent populations; predator ecology; reproductive cycles in reptiles. *Mailing Add:* Natural Hist Reservation Univ of Kans RR 3 Box 142 Lawrence KS 66044

FITCH, HOWARD MONTGOMERY, b Cobden, Ill, Sept 25, 11; m 37. CHEMISTRY. *Educ:* Tex Christian Univ, BS, 33; Univ Va, PhD(org chem), 37. *Prof Exp:* Res chemist, E I du Pont de Nemours & Co, Inc, 37-44; res assoc org med chem, Col Med, NY Univ, 44-49; res chemist, Campbell Pharmaceut Co, 49-57; RES CHEMIST, HANOVIA LIQUID GOLD DIV, ENGELHARD INDUST, INC, 57- *Mem:* Am Chem Soc; NY Acad Sci. *Res:* Synthesis of organic chemicals and their use as petroleum additives and medicinals, particularly alkaloids and related compounds; nuclear alkylated derivatives of morphine; phosphorus esters; metallo-organic compounds of precious metals. *Mailing Add:* 19 Colony Dr Summit NJ 07901

FITCH, JOHN EDGAR, b San Diego, Calif, June 27, 18; m 42; c 3. SYSTEMATIC ICHTHYOLOGY. *Educ:* San Diego State Col, AB, 41; Univ Calif, Los Angeles, MA, 63. *Prof Exp:* Biologist, Calif State Dept Fish & Game, 46-54; asst dir, Calif State Fisheries Lab, Long Beach, 54-56, dir, 56-60, res dir, 60-79; CONSULT, 79- *Concurrent Pos:* Asst, Univ Calif, Los Angeles, 51; marine ed, Calif Fish & Game 52-62, ed-in-chief, 62-66; res assoc, Los Angeles County Mus, 63-; mem, Working Group Tuna Taxon, UN Food & Agr Orgn, 65-; res assoc, Scripps Inst Oceanog, Univ Calif, San Diego, 66- & Santa Barbara Mus Natural Hist, 67-; adj prof biol, Grad Sch, Univ Southern Calif, 72- *Honors & Awards:* Prof Excellence Fishery Res Award, Am Fisheries Soc, 71. *Mem:* Am Soc Ichthyol & Herpet; Am Soc Vert Paleontologists. *Res:* Comparative morphology of fish otoliths; fish biology, age composition, habit, habitats, and systematics; fossil fishes of North America; use of teleost fish otoliths in fishery biology, food-habit studies, taxonomy, archaeology and paleontology. *Mailing Add:* 2657 Averill Ave San Pedro CA 90731

FITCH, JOHN HENRY, b Medford, Ore, Mar 1, 44; m 79. BEHAVIORAL ECOLOGY, ENVIRONMENTAL SCIENCE POLICY. *Educ:* Univ Kans, BA, 66; Mich State Univ, MA, 72, PhD(zool), 75. *Prof Exp:* Asst prof biol, Mich State Univ, 75-78; staff scientist ecol, Exec Off President, Coun Enivron Qual, 78-79; asst prof biol, Univ NDak, 79-80; DIR, ENIVRON SCI DEPT, MASS AUDUBON SOC, 80- *Concurrent Pos:* Bd mem, Detroit Zoo Med Adv Coun, 75-78; adj prof, Tufts Univ, 81- *Mem:* AAAS; Am Soc Mammalogists; Animal Behav Soc; Sigma Xi; Ecol Soc Am. *Res:* Studies of pelagic birds, bat homing behavior and population dynamics; behavioral ecology of rodents; sociobiology of ungulates. *Mailing Add:* Environ Sci Dept Mass Audubon Soc S Great Rd Lincoln MA 01773

FITCH, JOHN WILLIAM, III, b San Antonio, Tex, July 28, 38. ORGANOMETALLIC CHEMISTRY. *Educ:* Univ Tex, Austin, BS, 60, PhD(chem), 65. *Prof Exp:* Res chemist, E I du Pont de Nemours & Co, Inc, 65-67; from asst prof to assoc prof chem, 67-77, PROF CHEM, SOUTHWEST TEX STATE UNIV, 77- *Concurrent Pos:* Robert A Welch Found grant, 69-81. *Mem:* Am Chem Soc. *Res:* Organometallic synthesis; unusual olefin-metal complexes; organosilicon chemistry. *Mailing Add:* Dept of Chem Southwest Tex State Univ San Marcos TX 78666

FITCH, KENNETH LEONARD, b Genoa, Nebr, Mar 8, 29; m 50; c 3. ANATOMY. *Educ:* Univ Nebr, BS, 51; Univ Kans, MA, 52; Univ Mich, PhD(zool), 56. *Prof Exp:* Asst zool, Univ Kans, 51-52; instr, Ohio Univ, 55-56; from instr to asst prof anat, Univ Mo, 56-59; asst prof, Col Med, Univ Nebr, 59-63; ASSOC PROF ANAT, ILL STATE UNIV, 63- *Mem:* AAAS; Am Asn Anat; Am Soc Zool. *Res:* Amphibian embryology and reproduction; chemical embryology. *Mailing Add:* Dept of Biol Ill State Univ Normal IL 61761

FITCH, RICHARD ARNOLD, b Bartlesville, Okla, July 17, 33; m 59; c 3. PETROLEUM ENGINEERING. *Educ:* Univ Okla, BS, 56; Univ Ill, MS, 57. *Prof Exp:* Asst develop high pressure apparatus, Univ Ill, 56-57; mem staff reservoir eng res, Pan Am Petroleum Corp, 57-66; mem staff reservoir & prod eng, 66-74, eng supvr, 75-78, dist prod supt, 78-82, DIV OPERS SUPT, AMOCO PROD CO, NEW ORLEANS, 82- *Mem:* Am Inst Mining, Metall & Petrol Engrs; Am Petrol Inst. *Res:* Enhanced oil recovery methods; reservoir engineering. *Mailing Add:* 114 South Dr Covington LA 70433

FITCH, ROBERT MCLELLAN, b Shanghai, China, Apr 30, 28; US citizen; m 55; c 3. POLYMER CHEMISTRY, COLLOID CHEMISTRY. *Educ:* Dartmouth Col, AB, 49; Univ Mich, PhD(chem), 54. *Prof Exp:* Res chemist, Marshall Lab, E I du Pont de Nemours & Co, Inc, 54-62; from asst prof to assoc prof chem, NDak State Univ, 62-67; assoc prof & asst head dept, 67-73, PROF CHEM, UNIV CONN, 73- *Concurrent Pos:* chmn polymer colloids, Gorden Res Conf, 81. *Mem:* Fel AAAS; Am Chem Soc. *Res:* Macromolecular chemistry; mechanism of particle formation in polymer colloids; polymerization kinetics; chemical reactions at the polymer colloidal interface. *Mailing Add:* Dept Chem & Inst Mat Sci Univ Conn Storrs CT 06268

FITCH, STEVEN JOSEPH, b Chicago, Ill, Feb 25, 30; m 52, 67; c 4. INDUSTRIAL CHEMISTRY. *Educ:* Univ Ill, BS, 52; Cornell Univ, PhD(inorg chem), 58. *Prof Exp:* Sr res chemist phosphorus chem, Monsanto Chem Co, 57-64; dir corp res dept, Glidden Co, 64-65, dir chem res dept, 65-66, mgr pigments res dept, Inorg Res Ctr, 66-68, MGR RES DEPT, GLIDDEN PIGMENTS GROUP, SCM CORP, 68- *Mem:* Am Chem Soc; Am Inst Chemists; Fine Particle Soc. *Res:* Titanium dioxide chemistry, technology and processes; pigments; inorganic and organic phosphorus chemistry; pollution control processes, research, development and engineering; waste acid neutralization; gypsum; iron precipitation; fine particle silica. *Mailing Add:* Glidden Pigments Group SCM Corp 3901 Glidden Rd Baltimore MD 21226

FITCH, VAL LOGSDON, b Merriman, Nebr, Mar 10, 23; m 49; c 2. PHYSICS. *Educ:* McGill Univ, BE, 48; Columbia Univ, PhD(physics), 54. *Prof Exp:* Mem staff, Los Alamos Sci Lab, 46-47; instr physics, Columbia Univ, 53-54; from instr to prof, 54-60, CYRUS FOGG BRACKETT PROF PHYSICS, PRINCETON UNIV, 76- *Concurrent Pos:* Sloan fel, 60-64; trustee, Assoc Univs, Inc, 61-; mem, President's Sci Adv Comt, 70-73. *Honors & Awards:* Nobel Prize Physics, 80; E O Lawrence Award, AEC, 68; Res Corp Award, 68; E D Lawrence Award, AEC, 68. *Mem:* Nat Acad Sci; Am Acad Arts & Sci; fel Am Phys Soc. *Res:* Particle physics. *Mailing Add:* Jadwin Hall PO Box 708 Princeton Univ Princeton NJ 08540

FITCH, W(ILLIAM) CHESTER, b Billings, Mont, Nov 12, 16; m 46; c 1. INDUSTRIAL ENGINEERING. *Educ:* Mont State Col, BS, 38; Iowa State Col, MS, 39, PhD(eng valuation), 40. *Prof Exp:* Instr eng drawing, Iowa State Col, 39-41, instr mech eng, 41-45; asst prof indust eng, Mont State Col, 45-46; lectr mech eng, Univ Calif, 46-47; assoc prof, Iowa State Col, 47-52; asst dir valuation div, Gannett, Fleming, Corddry & Carpenter, Inc, 52-58; prof mech eng & head dept, Utah State Univ, 58-59; asst dir valuation div, Gannett,

Fleming, Corddry & Carpenter, Inc, 59-64; prof mech eng & head dept, Mich Technol Univ, 64-68; PROF ENG & TECHNOL & CHMN DEPT, WESTERN MICH UNIV, 68-, DEAN, COL APPL SCI, 73-; PRES, DEPRECIATION PROGS INC, 78- *Concurrent Pos:* Consult engr, 64- *Mem:* Am Soc Eng Educ; Am Soc Mech Engrs; Am Inst Indust Engrs; Nat Soc Prof Engrs. *Res:* Statistical analyses of industrial property; depreciation and engineering economy. *Mailing Add:* Col of Appl Sci Western Mich Univ Kalamazoo MI 49008

FITCH, WALTER M, b San Diego, Calif, May 21, 29; m 51; c 3. BIOCHEMISTRY. *Educ:* Univ Calif, Berkeley, AB, 53, PhD(biochem), 58. *Prof Exp:* Lab technician, Calif Res Corp, 51-52 & Pac Guano Co, Calif, 53; res physiologist, Univ Calif, Berkeley, 57-58; NIH fels physiol, Univ Calif, Berkeley, 58-59 & pharmacol, Sch Med, Stanford Univ, 59-61; Fulbright fel & lectr biochem, Univ Col, London, 61-62; from asst prof to assoc prof physiol chem, 62-72, PROF PHYSIOL CHEM, SCH MED, UNIV WIS-MADISON, 72- *Concurrent Pos:* Nat Inst Neurol Dis & Blindness res grant, 63-69; NSF res grant, 65-; examr physiol chem, Wis State Bd Examrs, 66-75; mem adv bd, Biochem Genetics, 66-; mem subcomt cytochrome nomenclature, Int Univs Bur, 72-76; NIH spec fel & vis prof, Univ Hawaii & mem bd reviewers, Fedn Proc, 73-74; NIH grant, 74-78; ed, Classification Lit Automated Res Serv, 75-; assoc ed, J Molecular Evolution & Syst Zool, 76- *Mem:* Am Soc Naturalists; Am Chem Soc; Classification Soc; Am Soc Biol Chemists; Soc Syst Zool. *Res:* Enzymology; kinetics; molecular genetics; evolution. *Mailing Add:* Dept of Physiol Chem Univ of Wis Sch of Med Madison WI 53706

FITCH, WALTER STEWART, b Oak Park, Ill, Mar 6, 26; m 47; c 3. ASTRONOMY. *Educ:* Univ Chicago, AB, 48, PhD(astron), 55. *Prof Exp:* From instr to assoc prof, 51-63, PROF ASTRON, UNIV ARIZ, 63- *Mem:* Am Astron Soc; Int Astron Union. *Res:* Astronomical photoelectric photometry; intrinsic variable stars. *Mailing Add:* Steward Observ Univ of Ariz Tucson AZ 85721

FITCH, WILLIAM LAWRENCE, bio-organic chemistry, see previous edition

FITCHEN, FRANKLIN CHARLES, b New Rochelle, NY, June 15, 28; m 50; c 3. ELECTRICAL ENGINEERING. *Educ:* Univ RI, BS, 50; Northeastern Univ, MS, 57; Yale Univ, DEng, 64. *Prof Exp:* Design engr, Meter & Instrument Dept, Gen Elec Co, 50-56; assoc prof elec eng, Univ RI, 56-65; prof & head dept, SDak State Univ, 65-72; dean eng, 72-80, PROF ELEC ENG, UNIV BRIDGEPORT, 81- *Concurrent Pos:* Consult tech educ, 72- *Mem:* Sr mem Inst Elec & Electronics Engrs. *Res:* Transistor and integrated circuits. *Mailing Add:* Col of Eng Univ of Bridgeport Bridgeport CT 06601

FITCHETT, GILMER TROWER, b Cape Charles, Va, June 16, 20; m 53; c 2. ORGANIC CHEMISTRY. *Educ:* Col William & Mary, BS, 42; Univ Va, PhD(chem), 51. *Prof Exp:* Anal chemist, Norfolk Naval Shipyard, 42-43; develop chemist, Pharmaceut Dept, Am Cyanamid Co, NJ, 51-66; develop chemist, Gane's Chem Works, Inc, NJ, 66-68; sr chemist, 68-73, SR STAFF SCIENTIST, CIBA-GEIGY LTD, 73- *Res:* Phenylcyclopropyl amine derivatives and 5-, 8-dimethoxyquinoline derivatives. *Mailing Add:* 13 Briar Circle Green Brook NJ 08812

FITE, LLOYD EMERY, b Litchfield, Ill, Dec 12, 30; m 55. ELECTRICAL ENGINEERING. *Educ:* Agr & Mech Col Tex, BS, 60, MS, 61; Tex A&M Univ, PhD(elec eng), 68. *Prof Exp:* Staff, 58-60, chief engr & proj engr, 60-62, ASSOC HEAD, ACTIVATION ANAL RES LAB, TEX A&M UNIV, 62-, ASSOC PROF ELEC ENG, 69-, TRAINING SPECIALIST, INST ELECTRONIC SCI, 71- *Mem:* Inst Elec & Electronic Engrs. *Res:* Instrumentation and electronic data reduction equipment required to support and improve the technique of neutron activation analysis. *Mailing Add:* Activation Anal Res Lab Tex A&M Univ College Station TX 77843

FITE, WADE LANFORD, b Apperson, Okla, Oct 4, 25; m 47; c 4. PHYSICS. *Educ:* Univ Kans, AB, 47; Harvard Univ, MA, 49, PhD(physics), 51. *Prof Exp:* Physicist, Res Labs, Philco Corp, 51-52; instr physics, Univ Pa, 52-54; NSF hon res asst, Univ Col, Univ London, 54-55; mem staff, Gen Atomic Div, Gen Dynamics Corp, 56-63; PROF PHYSICS, UNIV PITTSBURGH, 63-; PRES, EXTRANUCLEAR LABS, INC, 72- *Concurrent Pos:* Chmn, Int Conf Physics Electronic & Atomic Collisions, 63-67, Extranuclear Labs, Inc, 67- & Nat Acad Sci, Nuclear Res Coun Comt, Atomic & Molecular Sci, 77-80. *Mem:* AAAS; fel Am Phys Soc; Am Soc Mass Spectrometry. *Res:* Plasma, atomic and atomic collision physics; collision properties of atomic hydrogen; laboratory experimentation on upper atmosphere and astrophysics; chemical reactions; gas-surface phenomena; atomic beams; aerosols; mass spectrometry. *Mailing Add:* Dept of Physics Univ of Pittsburgh Pittsburgh PA 15260

FITT, PETER STANLEY, b La Punta, Peru, Oct 12, 31; Brit & Can citizen; m 61; c 2. BIOCHEMISTRY. *Educ:* Univ London, BSc & ARCS, 53, Imp Col, PhD(org chem) & dipl, 56. *Prof Exp:* Sci officer, Royal Aircraft Estab, Eng, 56-57; res assoc biochem, Med Col, Cornell Univ, 57-58; tech officer, Imp Chem Industs, Ltd, 58-59; vis res fel, Sloan-Kettering Inst Cancer Res, 59-62; vis scientist, Inst Physico-Chem Biol, Paris, France, 62-64; from asst prof to assoc prof, 64-73, PROF BIOCHEM, UNIV OTTAWA, 73- *Concurrent Pos:* Vis assoc prof biochem virol, Baylor Col Med & Med Res Coun Can vis scientist, 70-71. *Mem:* AAAS; Can Biochem Soc; Brit Biochem Soc; The Chem Soc; Am Soc Biol Chemists. *Res:* Nucleic acid enzymology; molecular biology. *Mailing Add:* Dept of Biochem Univ of Ottawa Ottawa Can

FITTERER, G(EORGE) R(AYMOND), b Newark, Ohio, Apr 10, 01; m 25; c 1. METALLURGY. *Educ:* Rose Polytech Inst, BS, 24; Carnegie Inst Technol, MS, 27; Univ Pittsburgh, PhD(metall), 30. *Hon Degrees:* DSc, Rose Polytech Inst, 61; DEng, Universidad Tecnica Federico Santa Maria, Chile, 65; Dr, Cath Univ Cordoba, 67. *Prof Exp:* Metallurgist, Am Chain Co, Ind, 24-25; metallographer, Stanley Works, Conn, 25-26; from asst metallurgist to asst dir res, US Bur Mines, 27-31, head dept metall, 31-33; pres, Fitterer Pyrometer Co, 34-38; chmn dept metall eng, 38-51, dean schs eng & mines & dir eng res div, 51-63, first distinguished prof metall eng & dir ctr study thermodyn properties mat, 63-77, EMER PROF METALL ENG, SCH ENG, UNIV PITTSBURGH, 77- *Concurrent Pos:* Supvr navy res contracts, Nat Defense Res Comt, 42-; dir res, Acid Open Hearth Res Asn, 42-; eng ed contract, Int Co-op Admin, Chile; US deleg, UN, 1st Pan-Am Metall Conf, Bogota, Colombia & 2nd conf, Sao Paulo, Brazil; chmn, Fitterer Eng Inc, 69-79; pres, Sci Applns, Inc, 79-; pres, Thermosensors, Inc, 80- *Mem:* Am Soc Metals; Am Inst Mining, Metall & Petrol Engrs; Brit Iron & Steel Inst. *Res:* Metallurgical thermodynamics; physical chemistry of steel making; high temperature measurement in liquid metals; liquid steel process metallurgy. *Mailing Add:* 825 12th St Oakmont PA 15139

FITTING, MARJORIE ANN PREMO, b Detroit, Mich, Nov 29, 33; m 72; c 3. MATHEMATICS EDUCATION. *Educ:* Mich State Univ, BS, 54, PhD(math educ), 68; Wayne State Univ, MEd, 58; Univ Mich, Ann Arbor, AM, 66. *Prof Exp:* Teacher var high schs, 54-60; instr math, Lawrence Inst Technol, 61-65; asst, Mich State Univ, 66-68; from asst prof to assoc prof, 68-77, dir, Comput Sci Inst, 79-80, PROF MATH, SAN JOSE STATE UNIV, 77- *Concurrent Pos:* Consult, NSF comprehensive grant, 69-73; dir, Metra Instruments, Inc, 71-81. *Mem:* Math Asn Am; Asn Data & Comput Info Systs; NY Acad Sci; Nat Coun Teachers Math. *Res:* Curriculum study; encouraging undergraduate research on number theory and group theory; manipulatives in teaching mathematics; using microcomputers in teaching mathematics. *Mailing Add:* Dept Math San Jose State Univ San Jose CA 95193

FITTS, CHARLES THOMAS, b Jackson, Tenn, July 4, 32; m 54; c 4. SURGERY. *Educ:* Princeton Univ, BA, 53; Univ Pa, MD, 57. *Prof Exp:* Chief trauma study br, US Army Surg Res Unit, Brooke Army Med Ctr, Ft Sam Houston, Tex, 63-65; from asst prof to assoc prof surg, 65-74, PROF SURG, MED UNIV SC, 74-, CHIEF TRANSPLANTATION SERV, 70- *Concurrent Pos:* Attend surgeon, Med Univ SC Hosp & Vet Admin Hosp, Charleston, 65-; consult surg, US Naval Hosp, Charleston, 65- *Honors & Awards:* Gold Medal, Southeastern Surg Cong, 61. *Mem:* Am Asn Surg Trauma; Am Col Surg; Soc Univ Surgeons; Am Surg Asn; Southern Surg Asn. *Res:* General surgery; transplantation immunology; burn therapy, fluid replacement therapy in hemorrhagic shock. *Mailing Add:* Dept of Surg Med Univ of SC Charleston SC 29425

FITTS, DONALD DENNIS, b Concord, NH, Sept 3, 32; m 64; c 2. PHYSICAL CHEMISTRY, CHEMICAL PHYSICS. *Educ:* Harvard Univ, AB, 54; Yale Univ, PhD(chem), 57. *Prof Exp:* NSF fel, Univ Amsterdam, 57-58; res fel chem, Yale Univ, 58-59; from asst prof to assoc prof, 59-69, actg vdean, Col Lib Arts & Sci, 63-64, asst chmn dept, 65-72, PROF CHEM, UNIV PA, 69-, ASSOC DEAN, 78- *Concurrent Pos:* NATO sr sci fel, Imp Col, Univ London, 71. *Mem:* Am Phys Soc; Royal Soc Chem. *Res:* Quantum-statistical mechanics; thermodynamics and statistical theory of irreversible processes; theory of liquids; theoretical chemistry. *Mailing Add:* Dept of Chem Univ of Pa Philadelphia PA 19104

FITTS, JAMES WALTER, b Ft Riley, Kans, July 17, 13; m 35; c 3. SOIL FERTILITY. *Educ:* Nebr State Teachers Col, BSc, 35; Univ Nebr, MS, 37; Iowa State Col, PhD, 52. *Prof Exp:* Instr agron, Univ Nebr, 37-42, asst prof agron & asst exten agronomist, 42-48; res asst prof agron, exten asst prof & in chg soil testing lab, Iowa State Col, 48-52; in chg soil testing div, Dept Agr, 52-56, prof soils & head dept, 56-64, dir int soil testing proj, 64-69, dir int soil fertility eval proj, 70-75, EMER PROF SOILS, NC STATE UNIV, 75-; PRES, AGRO SERV INT, 78- *Concurrent Pos:* Chmn, Nat Soil Test Work Group, 52-55; pres, Agr Serv Int Inc, 73- *Honors & Awards:* Soil Sci Soc NC Res Award, 65; Distinguished Serv Award, Nebr State Col, Chadron, 77. *Mem:* Fel Soil Sci Soc Am (vpres, 59, pres, 60); fel Am Soc Agron; Int Soil Sci Soc. *Res:* Alkali soil; movement of water in soil during irrigation; commercial fertilizers; procedures and factors affecting soil testing; nitrogen availability. *Mailing Add:* 550 N Leavitt Ave Orange City FL 32763

FITTS, RICHARD EARL, b Montpelier, Vt, Nov 12, 31; m 53; c 7. ELECTRICAL ENGINEERING. *Educ:* Yale Univ, BE, 53; Mass Inst Technol, SM, 55, PhD(elec eng), 66. *Prof Exp:* Proj officer, Rome Air Develop Ctr, Griffiss AFB, NY, 55-57 & 61-63, co-pilot, Pease AFB, NH, 58-61, forward air controller, Da Nang Air Base, Vietnam, 66-67; from instr to assoc prof, US Air Force Acad, 67-73; staff analyst, Prog Anal & Eval, Off of Asst Secy Defense, 73-77; SR ANALYST, GEN RES CORP, 77- *Mem:* Inst Elec & Electronics Engrs. *Res:* Nonlinear feedback control theory; electronic warfare; military force balance analysis. *Mailing Add:* 7655 Old Springhouse Rd McLean VA 22102

FITTS, WILLIAM THOMAS, JR, surgery, deceased

FITZ, HAROLD CARLTON, JR, b Charleston, SC, Aug 30, 26; m 49; c 3. SPACE PHYSICS, ATMOSPHERIC PHYSICS. *Educ:* US Mil Acad, BS, 49; Univ Ala, MS, 55; Univ Va, PhD(solid state physics), 62. *Prof Exp:* Instr physics, Spec Weapons Proj, US Army, 55-57, syst analyst, 57-59, syst analyst, Satellite Commun Agency, 61-64; from asst prof to assoc prof physics, US Mil Acad, 64-67; test plans officer, Atmospheric Effects Div, Defense Atomic Support Agency, Washington, DC, 67-70; staff scientist, Gen Res Corp, Va, 70; chief atmospheric effects div, Defense Atomic Support Agency, Washington, DC, 70-71, chief atmospheric effects div, 71-77, chief electronics vulnerability div, 77-79, CHIEF ATMOSPHERIC EFFECTS DIV, DEFENSE NUCLEAR AGENCY, 79- *Mem:* Am Phys Soc; Am Inst Aeronaut & Astronaut; Am Geophys Union. *Res:* Design and effects of nuclear weapons; atmospheric and space environment; cosmic ray physics; satellite communications systems. *Mailing Add:* 1152 Steam Boat Rd PO Box 82 Shady Side MD 20764

FITZER, JACK, b Joplin, Mo, Oct 5, 26; m 50; c 3. ELECTRICAL ENGINEERING. *Educ:* Univ Mo, BS, 51; Wash Univ, MS, 60, DSc(elec eng), 62. *Prof Exp:* Design engr, Chance Vought Aircraft Co, 51-54; design engr, Emerson Elec Mfg Co, 54-59, consult, 59-62, sr res engr, 62-63; mem res & develop staff, LTV Electrosysts, 63-67; from asst prof to assoc prof elec eng, 67-77, PROF ELEC ENG, UNIV TEX, ARLINGTON, 77- *Mem:* Inst Elec & Electronics Engrs; Am Inst Aeronaut & Astronaut. *Res:* Automatic control, guidance; network theory. *Mailing Add:* Dept of Elec Eng Univ of Tex Arlington TX 76019

FITZGERALD, CHARLES H, forest physiology, pesticide chemistry, see previous edition

FITZGERALD, DONALD RAY, b Pomeroy, Wash, June 18, 23; m 55; c 2. ATMOSPHERIC PHYSICS. *Educ:* Univ Chicago, BS, 47, MS, 49, PhD(meteorol), 56. *Prof Exp:* Asst, Univ Chicago, 51-54, res assoc, 54-61; PHYSICIST, US AIR FORCE GEOPHYS LAB, 61- *Mem:* Am Meteorol Soc; Am Geophys Union; Sigma Xi. *Res:* Electrical structure of thunderstorms; general atmospheric electrostatic phenomena; radar meteorology; instrumentation for cloud physics; research aircraft. *Mailing Add:* US AF Geophys Lab L G Hanscom AFB Bedford MA 01730

FITZGERALD, DOROTHEA BABBITT, b Boston, Mass, Mar 3, 12; m 45. BIOCHEMISTRY. *Educ:* Boston Univ, BS, 33. *Prof Exp:* Asst pharmacol, Sch Med, Johns Hopkins Univ, 36-41; res biochemist, Am Cyanamid Co, 41-45; res pharmacologist, Sch Med, Duke Univ, 46-48; pharmacologist, Nat Cancer Inst, 49-53, biochemist, 53-63; consult, Nat Inst Dent Res Gnotobiotics, 64-65; biomed consult, 65-67; biochemist, Nat Inst Dent Res, 67-68; res scientist, 69-72, RES ASST PROF, DEPT MICROBIOL, SCH MED, UNIV MIAMI, 72- *Concurrent Pos:* Guest investr, Germ-Free Lab, Karolinska Inst, Sweden, 63. *Res:* Gnotobiotics; animal models in cardiology. *Mailing Add:* Lab of Microbiol Univ of Miami Med Sch Miami FL 33101

FITZGERALD, DUANE GLENN, b Jackson, Mich, Oct 6, 31; m 55; c 4. NUCLEAR & ELECTRICAL ENGINEERING. *Educ:* Univ Mich, BS, 57, MS, 59; Univ Mo, PhD(elec eng), 66. *Prof Exp:* Proj engr, Bendix Corp, 59-62; reactor supvr, Univ Mo, 62-67; mgr systs anal, Eng Div, 67-74, mgr int bus develop, 74-77, regional gen mgr, 77-79, VPRES, INT OPERS, NUS CORP, 79- *Mem:* Am Nuclear Soc. *Res:* Reliability analysis; protection system design and analysis; system kinetics analysis; direct digital control. *Mailing Add:* NUS Corp 4 Res Pl Rockville MD 20850

FITZGERALD, EDWARD ALOYSIUS, b Washington, DC, Feb 11, 42; m 67; c 5. VIROLOGY, MICROBIOLOGY. *Educ:* Georgetown Univ, BS, 63; Cath Univ Am, PhD(microbiol), 70. *Prof Exp:* Contract officer res contracts, Div Biol Standards, NIH, 67-69, res microbiologist vaccine control, Lab Control Activites, 69-74; DEP DIV DIR VACCINE CONTROL, BUR BIOL, FOOD & DRUG ADMIN, 74- *Concurrent Pos:* Mem rev comt, Urban Studies Proj, 80-85. *Mem:* AAAS; Am Soc Microbiol; Sigma Xi; Int Asn Biol Standardization. *Res:* Control testing of biological products, specifically vaccines; development and testing of human rabies vaccine and rabies immune globulin; development and testing of reference preparations for use in biological testing. *Mailing Add:* Div Prod Qual Control Bur of Biol 8800 Rockville Pike Bethesda MD 20014

FITZGERALD, EDWIN ROGER, b Oshkosh, Wis, July 14, 23; m 46; c 8. PHYSICS. *Educ:* Univ Wis, BS, 44, MS, 50, PhD(physics), 52. *Prof Exp:* Mem tech staff, B F Goodrich Co, 44-46; asst physics & math, Univ Wis, 46-48, asst chem, 48-51, proj assoc, 51-53; from asst prof to prof physics, Pa State Univ, 53-61; PROF MECHANICS, JOHNS HOPKINS UNIV, 61- *Mem:* Am Phys Soc; Acoust Soc Am; Mats Res Soc. *Res:* Solid state physics; dynamic mechanical properties of solids; polymers, metals and long chain hydrocarbon compounds; dielectric properties of liquids and solids; wave mechanical explanations of deformation and other mechanical behavior. *Mailing Add:* Dept Mechanics Johns Hopkins Univ Baltimore MD 21218

FITZGERALD, GEORGE PATRICK, b Milwaukee, Wis, Sept 22, 22; m 43; c 2. FRESH WATER ECOLOGY. *Educ:* Univ Wis, BS, 48, MS, 49, PhD(bot), 50. *Prof Exp:* Asst bot, Univ Wis-Madison, 48-50, res assoc, 50-68, sr scientist, 68-75; INDUST & GOVT CONSULT, 75- *Mem:* Phycol Soc Am. *Res:* Mineral nutrition of algae; control of algae. *Mailing Add:* 3644 Rivercrest Rd McFarland WI 53558

FITZGERALD, GERARD JOHN, b Nfld, Sept 9, 49. ANIMAL BEHAVIOR, BEHAVIORAL ECOLOGY. *Educ:* Mem Univ, BSc, 70; McGill Univ, BSc, 72; Univ Western Ont, PhD(zool), 76. *Prof Exp:* PROF AGREGE BIOL, UNIV LAVAL, 76- *Mem:* Animal Behav Soc; Can Soc Zoologists; Nat Geog Soc. *Res:* Reproduction and parental behavior in fish; interspecific competition and predator-prey relationships; fish ecology in unstable environments. *Mailing Add:* Dept of Biol Laval Univ Quebec Can

FITZGERALD, GLENNA GIBBS (CADY), b Westfield, Mass; m. PHARMACOLOGY, NEUROCHEMISTRY. *Educ:* Univ Mass, Amherst, BS & MS; Yale Univ, PhD(pharmacol), 68. *Prof Exp:* Res assoc pharmacol, Yale Univ, 61-62; instr, George Washington Univ, 68-71; staff fel, Lab Cerebral Metab, Sect Develop Neurochem, NIMH, 71-77; PHARMACOLOGIST, DIV NEUROPHARMACOL, BUR DRUGS, FOOD & DRUG ADMIN, 77- *Res:* Neurochemistry; development and differentiation of the central nervous system; mechanism of action of centrally acting drugs. *Mailing Add:* 620 Bennington Dr Silver Spring MD 20910

FITZGERALD, J(OHN) EDMUND, b Chelsea, Mass, Oct 29, 23; m 45; c 4. CIVIL ENGINEERING, MATERIALS SCIENCE. *Educ:* Harvard Univ, MS, 47; Univ Col, Cork, MSc, 70; Nat Univ Ireland, DSc(math & physics), 72. *Prof Exp:* Mgr appl mech, Am Mach & Foundry Res Labs, 53-57 & Borg-Warner Res Labs, 57-60; dir res eng, Lockheed Propulsion Co, 60-66; assoc dean, Col Eng, Univ Utah, 66-75; PROF & DIR SCH CIVIL ENG, GA INST TECHNOL, 75- *Concurrent Pos:* Consult, Lockheed Propulsion Co, 66-70,

Math Sci Corp, 66-75, US Army Missile Command, 67-77, Battelle Mem Inst, 68- 78, United Technol Corp, 70-75 & Aerojet Gen Corp, 76-78, chief, Naval Res, 66-72. *Honors & Awards:* US Sr Scientist, Alexander von Humboldt Inst, 73. *Mem:* Fel Inst Physics; fel Am Soc Civil Engrs; assoc fel Am Inst Aeronaut & Astronaut; Am Phys Soc; Soc Rheology. *Res:* Characterization of irreversible effects in polymers especially damage; applications to solid propellants, asphalt concrete and fabrics. *Mailing Add:* Sch of Civil Eng Ga Inst Technol Atlanta GA 30332

FITZGERALD, JAMES ALLEN, b Albany, NY, Apr 7, 41; m 64; c 2. FIBER SCIENCE. *Educ:* Univ Rochester, BS, 62; Carnegie Inst Technol, MS, 64, PhD(org chem), 66. *Prof Exp:* Res chemist, 66-73, res supvr, 74-78, sr res supvr textile fibers, 78-79, RES MGR HIGH PERFORMANCE FIBERS, TEXTILE FIBERS DEPT, E I DU PONT DE NEMOURS & CO, INC, 79- *Mem:* Am Chem Soc; AAAS. *Res:* Research and supervision in organic and polymer chemistry, polymer processing, fiber science and process development; specialty areas include high performance polymers and fibers including Kevlar and Nomex. *Mailing Add:* Textile Res Lab E I du Pont de Nemours & Co Inc Wilmington DE 19898

FITZGERALD, JAMES EDWARD, b Paris, Ill, Feb 14, 31; m 59; c 3. VETERINARY PATHOLOGY, TOXICOLOGY. *Educ:* Univ Ill, Urbana, BS, 53; DVM, 55, MS, 62, PhD(vet med), 64. *Prof Exp:* Instr vet clin med, Univ Ill, Urbana, 55-56; instr vet, Agr Res Ctr, Pfizer, Inc, 58-60; NIH trainee vet path & hyg, Col Vet Med, Univ Ill, Urbana, 61-64; pathologist, Dept Toxicol, 64-72, asst dir, 72-76, dir, Dept Toxicol, 77-81, DIR, TOXICOL LAB, PARKE DAVIS & CO, 81- *Mem:* Am Vet Med Asn; Am Col Vet Path; Soc Toxicol. *Res:* Experimental pathology and toxicology; animal neoplasia. *Mailing Add:* Parke Davis & Co Dept Toxicol PO Box 1047 Ann Arbor MI 48106

FITZGERALD, JAMES W, b New York, NY, May 1, 42; m 69; c 1. ATMOSPHERIC PHYSICS. *Educ:* City Col New York, BS, 63; Univ Chicago, MS, 64, PhD(atmospheric sci), 72. *Prof Exp:* RES PHYSICIST, US NAVAL RES LAB, 72- *Mem:* Am Meteorol Soc; Sigma Xi. *Res:* Cloud, fog and aerosol physics; physical meteorology; boundary layer meteorology; electro-optical meteorology. *Mailing Add:* US Naval Res Lab Washington DC 20375

FITZGERALD, JERRY MACK, b Alliance, Nebr, Jan 20, 37. ANALYTICAL CHEMISTRY. *Educ:* Univ Colo, BA, 59; Princeton Univ, MA, 61, PhD(anal chem), 63. *Prof Exp:* Res assoc chem, Purdue Univ, 63-64; asst prof, Seton Hall Univ, 64-68; assoc prof chem, Univ Houston, 68-76; qual control dir, Eastern US Nat Health Labs, Inc, Vienna, 76-79; HEAD, ANAL CHEM, LITTON BIONETICS, INC, KENSINGTON, MD, 79- *Mem:* Am Asn Clin Chem; Sigma Xi; Soc Appl Spectros; Am Chem Soc. *Res:* Photochemical reactions for analytical determinations; electron spin resonance and fluorescence spectroscopy; continuous and automated analysis. *Mailing Add:* 10907 Ambleside Ct Reston VA 22090

FITZGERALD, JOSEPH ARTHUR, b Cleveland, Ohio, Apr 22, 25; m 55; c 8. MEDICINE, PSYCHIATRY. *Educ:* Case Western Reserve Univ, BS, 46; Loyola Univ, Chicago, MD, 51; Am Bd Psychiat & Neurol, dipl, 59. *Prof Exp:* Intern gen med, Milwaukee County Gen Hosp, 51-52; resident psychiat, Cleveland Psychiat Inst & Hosp, 52-54; sr resident, 57-58, from instr to assoc prof, 58-71, PROF PSYCHIAT, MED CTR, SCH MED, IND UNIV, INDIANAPOLIS, 71-; PSYCHIATRIST, LARUE D CARTER HOSP, 58-, DIR OUTPATIENT CLIN, 62- *Concurrent Pos:* Actg dir, Riley Child Guid Clin, 58; lectr, postgrad progs gen practitioners & nonpsychiat specialists, 60-; residency training comt psychiat, Med Sch, Ind Univ, 60-, lectr personality theory, psychopath & psychopharmacol, Sch Nursing, 67-; dir diag ctr, Marydale Sch for Girls, 61-68; mem attend staff, Tenth St Vet Admin Hosp, 62-70; consult, St Mary's Child Ctr, 66-; dir psychiat serv, Cath Social Serv, 73-; consult psychiatrist, Adult & Child Ctr, 81- *Mem:* Fel Am Psychiat Asn. *Res:* Anxiety; group process; primary prevention of mental disability through identifying high risk groups from perinatal and other preschool studies. *Mailing Add:* Larue D Carter Hosp 1315 W Tenth Indianapolis IN 46202

FITZGERALD, LAURENCE ROCKWELL, b Boston, Mass, Sept 15, 16; m 42; c 3. PHYSIOLOGY. *Educ:* Tufts Col, BS, 39; Univ Iowa, MS, 41, PhD(zool), 49. *Prof Exp:* Res assoc zool, Univ Iowa, 44-49; from instr to asst prof anat, 49-58, ASSOC PROF ANAT, CTR HEALTH SCI, UNIV TENN, MEMPHIS, 58- *Concurrent Pos:* Chmn sect anat sci, Am Asn Dent Schs, 71-74. *Mem:* AAAS; Soc Develop Biol; Am Soc Zoologists; Am Asn Anatomists; Int Asn Dent Res. *Res:* Physiology of neonatal period. *Mailing Add:* Dept of Anat Univ of Tenn Ctr for Health Sci Memphis TN 38163

FITZGERALD, LAWRENCE TERRELL, b Tampa, Fla, Sept 19, 38. MEDICAL RADIATION PHYSICS. *Educ:* Univ Tampa, BS, 60; Univ Fla, MS, 62, PhD(med radiation physics), 74. *Prof Exp:* Instr med radiation physics, 64-69, res assoc, 70-74, asst prof, 74-75, ASSOC PROF MED RADIATION PHYSICS, DEPT RADIO, UNIV FLA, 75- *Mem:* Am Asn Physicists Med; Asn Comput Mach; Inst Elec & Electronics Engrs; Health Physics Soc. *Res:* Computer applications in medicine; medical radiation physics; radiation dosimetry. *Mailing Add:* Univ of Fla-Shands Teaching Hosp Box J-385 Gainesville FL 32610

FITZGERALD, MARIE ANTON, b Boston, Mass, Apr 10, 22; m 45; c 3. PHYSIOLOGY. *Educ:* Columbia Univ, BS, 50; Mass Inst Technol, PhD(physiol), 54. *Prof Exp:* Asst biol, Mass Inst Technol, 52-54, res assoc, 54-55; fel biophys, New Eng Inst Med Res, 58-59; assoc, Inst Biophys Res, 60-68; ASSOC PROF BIOL, HOLYOKE COMMUNITY COL, 68- *Res:* Protein, physical chemistry; scientific illustration. *Mailing Add:* Dept Biol Holyoke Community Col 303 Homestead Ave Holyoke MA 01040

FITZGERALD, MAURICE E, b Holyoke, Mass, Dec 16, 32; m 60; c 2. ANALYTICAL CHEMISTRY. *Educ:* St Anselm's Col, BA, 54; St John's Univ NY, MS, 56. *Prof Exp:* Lab asst quant anal, St John's Univ NY, 54-56; develop chemist, Borden Chem Co, Pa, 56-57; jr chemist, 57-64, res chemist & group leader, Mass Spectros & Comput Lab, 64-67, sr chemist & supvr, Mass Spectros & Comput Lab, 67-78, SR CHEMIST & SUPVR ELEMENTAL ANAL, RES & ENG, ARCO CHEM CO DIV, ATLANTIC RICHFIELD CO, PHILADELPHIA, 78- *Concurrent Pos:* Ed, Annual Rev, Am Soc Testing & Mat, 65-67. *Mem:* Am Chem Soc; Am Soc Mass Spectros; Soc Appl Spectros; Am Soc Testing & Mat. *Res:* Application of mass spectrometry to quantitative analysis and structure determinations; application of time-shared computer for the automation of analytical instrumentation; application of x-ray fluorescence, x-ray differation and atomic absorption spectroscopy to the analysis of organic, inorganic, polymeric and catalyst materials. *Mailing Add:* 517 Upland Rd Havertown PA 19083

FITZGERALD, MAURICE PIM, b Manchester, Eng, Aug 14, 39; Can citizen; m 64; c 2. ASTROPHYSICS. *Educ:* Univ Toronto, BSc, 62, MA, 63; Case Western Reserve Univ, PhD(astron), 67. *Prof Exp:* assoc prof, 67-80, PROF PHYSICS, UNIV WATERLOO, 80- *Mem:* AAAS; Am Astron Soc; Royal Astron Soc; Royal Astron Soc Can; Int Astron Union. *Res:* Galactic structure; interstellar dust; spectroscopic binary stars; photometry; space density studies; spectroscopy; radial velocities; open clusters. *Mailing Add:* Dept of Physics Univ of Waterloo Waterloo Can

FITZGERALD, PATRICK HENRY, b Utica, NY, Sept 5, 43; m 67; c 3. PHYSICAL ORGANIC CHEMISTRY. *Educ:* Univ Toronto, BS, 66, MS, 68, PhD(phys org chem), 73. *Prof Exp:* Res assoc, Dept Chem, Ill Inst Technol, 73; res chemist, Res & Develop, Pigments Dept, 73-77, sr res chemist, 77-81, RES ASSOC, RES & DEVELOP, PIGMENTS DEPT, E I DU PONT DE NEMOURS & CO, INC, 81- *Mem:* Am Chem Soc. *Res:* Organic reaction mechanisms; organic pigments, synthesis and processing; organic analysis and instrumentation. *Mailing Add:* Jackson Lab Chambers Works E I du Pont de Nemours & Co Inc Deepwater NJ 08023

FITZGERALD, PATRICK JAMES, b Haverhill, Mass, Aug 9, 13; m 49; c 1. PATHOLOGY. *Educ:* Univ Mass, BS, 36; Tufts Univ, MD, 40. *Prof Exp:* Resident med, Boston City Hosp, 40-41; res & asst pathologist, Mallory Inst Path, 42-43 & 46-47; fel, Nat Cancer Inst, Mem Ctr Cancer & Allied Dis, 47-48; spec res fel biophys techs, Sloan-Kettering Inst, 48-49, asst biophys 49-53; prof path & chmn dept, Col Med, State Univ NY Downstate Med Ctr, 53-72; PROF PATH, MED COL, CORNELL UNIV, 72- *Concurrent Pos:* Sloan-Kettering Inst fel, Nobel Med Inst, Karolinska Inst, Stockholm, Sweden, 49-50; Sloan scholar, Sloan-Kettering Inst, 50-53; asst attend pathologist, Mem Ctr Cancer & Allied Dis, 50-53; asst prof, Sloan-Kettering Div, Med Col, Cornell Univ, 52-53; dir, Inst Path, Kings County Hosp, 53-67; consult, Path Study Sect, USPHS, 58-62; vis scientist biochem, Oxford Univ, 59-60; pathologist-in-chief, Downstate Med Ctr, State Univ NY, 67-72, State Univ NY distinguished res fel, Fac Sci, Inst Biol Chem, Marseille, France & vis fel, St Catherine's Col, Oxford Univ, 68; mem, Sloan-Kettering Inst, 72-79; chmn dept path, Mem Hosp, NY, 72-79, attending pathologist, 79-81; prof pathol, Med Ctr, Univ Kans, Kansas City, Kans, 80- *Mem:* Am Soc Clin Path; Am Soc Exp Path; Histochem Soc; Electron Micros Soc Am; Am Asn Path & Bact (pres, 66-67). *Res:* Nucleoprotein metabolism in growth and cancer; pancreatic differentiation and pancreatic cancer. *Mailing Add:* Med Ctr Univ Kans 39th & Rainbow Blvd Kansas City KS 66103

FITZGERALD, PAUL JACKSON, b Nashville, Tenn, July 20, 24; m 50; c 3. PLANT BREEDING, PLANT PATHOLOGY. *Educ:* Univ Tenn, BS, 50; Purdue Univ, MS, 52, PhD(plant path, breeding & genetics), 54. *Prof Exp:* Breeder hard red winter wheat, Intermountain Area & res agronomist, Plant Sci Res Div, USDA, 54-60; forage improve leader, Rockefeller Found, Santiago, Chile, 60-62; mem staff, Northern Grain Insects Res Lab, SDak, 62-68; from asst chief to chief cereal crops res br, Plant Indust Sta, 68-72, area dir, Lake States Area, 72-74, assoc dep adminr, 74-80, REGIONAL ADMINR, NORTH CENT REGION, AGR RES SERV, USDA, 80- *Mem:* Am Soc Agron. *Res:* Inheritance of resistance to insects and insect-transmitted disease in plants. *Mailing Add:* USDA Agr Res Serv North Cent Region Peoria IL 61614

FITZGERALD, PAUL RAY, b Elsinore, Utah, May 2, 20; m 41; c 4. ZOOLOGY, PARASITOLOGY. *Educ:* Utah State Univ, BS, 49, MS, 50; Univ Ill, PhD, 61. *Prof Exp:* Instr zool & biol, Utah State Univ, 49-53; res parasitologist, Animal Dis & Parasite Res Div, USDA, 53-66, coop agt, 50-53; PROF VET PARASITOL, COL VET MED, UNIV ILL, URBANA-CHAMPAIGN, 66- *Concurrent Pos:* Proj dir grants, NIH, State of Ill & commercial; Fulbright fel, Arg; La State Univ fel, 71. *Mem:* Am Soc Parasitol; Soc Protozool; Am Soc Zool; Am Inst Biol Sci. *Res:* Parasitic protozoa, helminths; arthropods; domestic livestock; wild ruminants; parasites of fish; physiology of parasites and effects upon hosts; studies in environmental biology; public health aspects of sewage sludge utilization; parasites, heavy metals in animal tissues. *Mailing Add:* Col of Vet Med Univ of Ill Urbana IL 61801

FITZGERALD, ROBERT JAMES, b New York, NY, Nov 3, 18; m 45. MICROBIOLOGY, ORAL BIOLOGY. *Educ:* Fordham Univ, BS, 39; Va Polytech Inst, MS, 41; Duke Univ, PhD(pharmacol), 48. *Prof Exp:* Microbiologist, Chemother Div, Am Cyanamid Co, 41-45; jr asst sanitarian, Tuberc Control, USPHS, 45-46, scientist to scientist dir dent res, NIH, 48-69; res prof oral biol, Sch Med, Univ Miami, 69-77; RES MICROBIOLOGIST ORAL BIOL, VET ADMIN HOSP, MIAMI, 69-; PROF MICROBIOL, SCH MED, UNIV MIAMI, 77- *Concurrent Pos:* Clin prof endodont, Col Dent, Univ Fla; consult, Nat Inst Dent Res, 69-80, Merck & Co, 70-75 & Naval Dent Res Inst, 72-; Vet Admin career res scientist, 79- *Honors & Awards:* Res Award, Chicago Dent Soc, 60; Albert Joachim Res Prize, Int Fedn Dent, 62; Caries Res Award, Int Asn Dent Res, 77. *Mem:* Fel AAAS; Int Asn Dent Res; Am Soc Microbiol; Asn Gnotobiotics; Acad Microbiol. *Res:* Etiology and control of oral diseases; chemotherapy; oral microbiology. *Mailing Add:* Vet Admin Hosp Dent Res Unit 1201 NW 16th St Miami FL 33125

FITZGERALD, ROBERT SCHAEFER, b Detroit, Mich, July 12, 31; m 73. PHYSIOLOGY. *Educ:* Xavier Univ, Ohio, LittB, 54; Spring Hill Col, MA, 57; Univ Chicago, PhD(physiol), 63; Woodstock Col, STB, 65, STM, 67. *Prof Exp:* Fel physiol, 63-67, assoc prof environ med, 68-76, PROF ENVIRON HEALTH SCI, JOHNS HOPKINS UNIV, 77-, ASSOC CHMN, 80- *Concurrent Pos:* Vis scientist, Univ Wash, 66, Univ Nancy, 67 & Univ Paris, 68; USPHS res career develop award, 68-73; vis assoc prof physiol, Univ Calif, San Francisco, 73-74. *Mem:* AAAS; Am Physiol Soc; Am Thoracic Soc; Sigma Xi. *Res:* Examination of the elements and reflexes involved in the control of respiration and circulation, especially in response to different gaseous environments. *Mailing Add:* Dept Environ Health Sci Johns Hopkins Univ Baltimore MD 21205

FITZGERALD, ROBERT WILLIAM, b Canton, Ohio, May 30, 31; m 54; c 2. SAFETY ENGINEERING, STRUCTURAL ENGINEERING. *Educ:* Worcester Polytech Inst, BS, 53, MS, 60; Univ Conn, PhD(civil eng), 69. *Prof Exp:* Struct engr, Harvey & Tracy Consult Engrs, Mass, 55-58; instr mech, Worcester Jr Col, 58-62; instr struct eng & mech, Univ Conn, 62-63; from asst prof to assoc prof, 63-78, PROF STRUCT ENG & MECH, WORCESTER POLYTECH INST, 78- *Mem:* Am Soc Civil Engrs; Am Concrete Inst; Soc Fire Protection Engrs; Nat Fire Protection Asn. *Res:* Building design for fire safety; building codes; building design and construction. *Mailing Add:* Dept of Civil Eng Worcester Polytech Inst Worcester MA 01609

FITZGERALD, THOMAS JAMES, b Troy, NY, May 7, 38; m 74; c 4. PHARMACOLOGY, MEDICINAL CHEMISTRY. *Educ:* Union Univ, BS, 60; Ohio State Univ, MS, 62, PhD(med chem), 65. *Prof Exp:* NIH fel, Inst Cancer Res, Univ Heidelberg, Ger, 65-66, Alexander von Humboldt fel, 66-67; NIH trainee fel, Sch Pharm, Univ Minn, 68-69; from instr to asst prof pharmacol, Univ Kans Med Ctr, 69-73; asst prof, 73-76, ASSOC PROF PHARMACOL, SCH PHARM, FLA A&M UNIV, 76- *Mem:* Am Chem Soc; Sigma Xi; Am Soc Pharmacol & Exp Therapeut; AAAS. *Res:* Molecular pharmacology; mitotic inhibitors; cancer chemotherapy. *Mailing Add:* Sch of Pharm Fla A&M Univ Tallahassee FL 32307

FITZGERALD, THOMAS JAMES, b Chicago, Ill, Dec 12, 43; m 71. MICROBIOLOGY. *Educ:* St Mary's Col, Minn, BA, 66; Loyola Univ Ill, MS, 68, PhD(microbiol), 71. *Prof Exp:* Fel microbiol, Harvard Univ, 71-72; fel, Univ Calif, Los Angeles, Med Sch, 72-73, lectr, 73-74; res assoc, 74-80, ASST PROF MICROBIOL, MED SCH, UNIV MINN, 80- *Mem:* Sigma Xi; Am Soc Microbiol; AAAS; NY Acad Sci. *Res:* In vitro cultivation of treponema pallidum in tissue culture; pathogenic mechanisms of treponema pallidum with emphasis on cell mediated immunity. *Mailing Add:* Dept of Microbiol Sch of Med Univ of Minn 1060 Mayo Box 196 Minneapolis MN 55455

FITZGERALD, THOMAS MICHAEL, b Boston, Mass, Oct 20, 36; m 58; c 3. ACOUSTICS. *Educ:* Boston Col, ScB, 58; Brown Univ, ScM, 61, PhD(physics), 63. *Prof Exp:* Res assoc solid state physics, Brown Univ, 63-65; physicist, NASA Electronics Res Ctr, 65-70; physicist, Naval Underwater Syst Ctr, 70-76 & Rand Corp, Calif, 76-77; physicist, 77-80, SCI ADV, COMDR-IN-CHIEF, ATLANTIC FLEET, NAVAL UNDERWATER SYST CTR, 80- *Mem:* Sigma Xi; Am Phys Soc. *Res:* Phonon-phonon, electron-phonon interactions; elastic constants; effects of irradiation on ultrasonic properties of materials; radiation damage; underwater acoustics; acousto-optics; systems analysis; microwave acoustics; infra-red spectroscopy. *Mailing Add:* Naval Underwater Systems Ctr 101 Newport RI 02840

FITZGERALD, WILLIAM FRANCIS, b Boston, Mass. CHEMICAL OCEANOGRAPHY, MARINE GEOCHEMISTRY. *Educ:* Boston Col, BS, 60; Col of the Holy Cross, MS, 61; Mass Inst Technol, PhD(chem oceanog), 70; Woods Hole Oceanog Inst, PhD(chem oceanog), 70. *Prof Exp:* Res asst chem oceanog, Woods Hole Oceanog Inst, 61-66, investr, 69-70; ASSOC PROF CHEM OCEANOG, MARINE SCI INST, UNIV CONN, 70- *Mem:* Sigma Xi; Am Chem Soc; AAAS. *Res:* Chemical routes and transport of mercury to the marine environment; trace metal speciation in sea water; sedimentary geochemistry and the biological interactions of heavy metals in the coastal zones; marine pollution and air-sea exchange. *Mailing Add:* Marine Sci Inst Univ of Conn Groton CT 06340

FITZGIBBON, WILLIAM EDWARD, III, b Cambridge, Mass, July 21, 45. MATHEMATICS. *Educ:* Vanderbilt Univ, BA, 68, PhD(math), 72. *Prof Exp:* From asst prof to assoc prof, 72-80, PROF MATH, UNIV HOUSTON, 81- *Concurrent Pos:* Vis assoc prof math, Univ Calif, San Diego, 80-81. *Mem:* Am Math Soc; Soc Indust & Appl Math; Sigma Xi. *Res:* Pure and applied mathematics; ordinary and partial differential equations; operator theory; nonlinear analysis approximation theory; integral equations. *Mailing Add:* Dept of Math Univ Houston Houston TX 77004

FITZGIBBONS, J(OHN) D(AVID), b Ithaca, NY, Apr 18, 22; m 46; c 1. NUCLEAR ENGINEERING. *Educ:* NC State Univ, BS, 53; Oak Ridge Sch Reactor Technol, cert, 55. *Prof Exp:* Indust radiographer, Los Alamos Sci Lab, 46-47; nuclear engr, Atomic Energy Div, 53-58, proj engr res reactors, 58-59, proj mgr & engr res reactors, 59-64, planner, Div Long Range Planning, 64-68, supvr systs data mgt, Naval Nuclear Fuel Div, 68-69, sr systs analyst, 69-72, proj admin, 72-79, ENG SUPVR, BABCOCK & WILCOX, CO, 79-; supvr systs data mgt, Naval Nuclear Fuel Div, 68-69, sr systs analyst, 69-72, PROJ ADMIN, NAVAL NUCLEAR FUEL DIV, BABCOCK & WILCOX CO, 72- *Res:* Research reactor design and development; systems analysis. *Mailing Add:* Naval Nuclear Fuel Div Babcock & Wilcox PO Box 785 Lynchburg VA 24505

FITZHARRIS, TIMOTHY PATRICK, b New York, NY, Oct 31, 44; m 67; c 2. CELL BIOLOGY, DEVELOPMENTAL BIOLOGY. *Educ:* State Univ NY Col Potsdam, AB, 66; State Univ NY Albany, MS, 69, PhD(biol sci), 71. *Prof Exp:* NSF fel, Dept Molecular, Cellular & Develop Biol, Univ Colo, 71-73; assoc anat, 73-74, Nat Inst Neurol Dis & Stroke grant, 74-76, asst prof,

74-77, ASSOC PROF ANAT, MED UNIV SC, 77- *Concurrent Pos:* Affil marine scientist, SC Marine Resources Ctr, 73-; SC Heart Grant-in Aid, 77-78; estab investr, Am Heart Asn, 80-; Am Heart-grant-in-aid, 79-82; exchange scientist, Nat Acad Sci, Charles Univ, Prague, 80. *Mem:* AAAS; Am Soc Cell Biologists; Soc Develop Biol; NY Acad Sci; Am Asm Anatomists. *Res:* Extracellular matrix and morphogenesis; early heart development; cell motility and intracellular transport; congenital heart defects. *Mailing Add:* Dept Anat Med Univ SC 171 Ashley Ave Charleston SC 29425

FITZHUGH, HENRY ALLEN, b San Antonio, Tex, July, 2, 39; c 1. AGRICULTURAL SYSTEMS, ANIMAL BREEDING. *Educ:* Tex A&M Univ, BS, 61, MS, 63, PhD(animal breeding), 65. *Prof Exp:* Res & teaching asst genetics, Tex A&M Univ, 63-65, assoc prof animal sci statist, 65-73; exec vpres, Agri-Link Corp, 73-75; ANIMAL SCIENTIST & PROG OFFICER, WINROCK INT LIVESTOCK CTR, 75- *Concurrent Pos:* NATO fel, Agr Res Serv, Animal Breeding Res Orgn, 65-66; partner, Genetics Appl Prod Inc, 66-73; consult, Southwest Res Found, 71-72; US Feed Grains Coun, 76, Enterprise Brasil Invest Agr, Brasil, 79 & Inst Nat Invest Pecuarias, Mex, 80; res geneticist, US Meat Animal Res Ctr, Agr Res Serv, USDA, 75. *Mem:* Am Soc Animal Sci; AAAS; Asn Latin Am Prod Animal. *Res:* Development and testing of biological and socioeconomic interventions to improve efficiency of animal component of agricultural production systems. *Mailing Add:* Winrock Int Livestock Res Ctr Petit Jean Mountain Rte 3 Morrilton AR 72110

FITZHUGH, OSCAR GARTH, b Hood, Va, Aug 26, 01; m 29; c 4. PHARMACOLOGY. *Educ:* Univ Va, BS, 27, MS, 33, PhD(physiol), 36. *Prof Exp:* Instr physiol & pharmacol, Univ Vt, 34-36, asst prof, 36-37; res assoc pharmacol, Sch Med, Vanderbilt Univ, 37-39; pharmacologist, Food & Drug Admin, 39-47, chief chronic toxicity sect, Div Pharmacol, 47-53, chief toxicity br, 53-64, dep dir div toxicol eval, 64-68, toxicol dir, Bur Sci, 68-70, assoc dir toxicol res, Off Pesticides, Bur Foods & Pesticides, 70-71; toxicol adv, Off Pesticide Progs, Environ Protection Agency, 71-72; consult toxicol, 72-81; RETIRED. *Mem:* AAAS; Soc Toxicol; Inst Food Technol; Am Soc Pharmacol & Exp Therapeut; Soc Exp Biol & Med. *Res:* Adrenal cortex; anesthetics; chronic toxicology; coal tar colors; pesticides; food additives. *Mailing Add:* 4208 Dresden St Kensington MD 20795

FITZHUGH, RICHARD, b Concord, Mass, Mar 30, 22; m 63; c 2. BIOPHYSICS, BIOMATHEMATICS. *Educ:* Univ Colo, BA, 48; Johns Hopkins Univ, PhD(biophys), 53. *Prof Exp:* Instr physiol optics, Med Sch, Johns Hopkins Univ, 53-55; BIOPHYSICIST, NIH, USPHS, 56- *Mem:* AAAS; Biophys Soc. *Res:* Physiology of the nerve membrane; mathematical models of nerve cells, statistical detection of single channel signals, and of muscular control. *Mailing Add:* Nat Inst Health Bldg 36 2A29 Bethesda MD 20205

FITZHUGH-BELL, KATHLEEN, b Kansas City, Mo. NEUROPSYCHOLOGY. *Educ:* Univ Mo, Kansas City, BA, 51, MA, 54; Purdue Univ, PhD(clin psychol), 58. *Prof Exp:* Psychologist, New Castle State Hosp, Ind, 58-66; vis assoc prof phys med, Sch Med, Tufts Univ, 69-70; asst prof, Dept Neurol, 66-69, assoc prof neurol & clin psychol, 70-78, PROF NEUROL & CLIN PSYCHOL, SCH MED, IND UNIV, 78-, DIR, NEUROPSYCHOL LAB, 70- *Concurrent Pos:* Consult, Marion County Asn Retarded Persons, Ind, 71- & Larue Carter Mem Hosp, 74- *Mem:* Am Psychol Asn; Am Acad Retardation; Am Asn Mental Deficiency; AAAS; Int Neuropsychol Soc. *Mailing Add:* Neuropsychol Lab Ind Univ Med Ctr Indianapolis IN 46202

FITZ-JAMES, PHILIP CHESTER, b Vancouver, BC, Nov 25, 20; m 48; c 4. MICROBIAL BIOCHEMISTRY. *Educ:* Univ BC, BSA, 43; Univ Toronto, MSA, 45; Univ Western Ont, MD, 49, PhD(bact, biochem), 53. *Prof Exp:* Asst penicillin prod, Banting Inst, Toronto, 43-44; assoc prof bact & immunol, 53-67, PROF BACT, IMMUNOL & BIOCHEM, SCH MED, UNIV WESTERN ONT, 67- *Concurrent Pos:* Res assoc, Nat Res Coun Can, 56- *Honors & Awards:* Harrison Award, Royal Soc Can, 63. *Mem:* Brit Biochem Soc. *Res:* Structure, composition and activities of bacteria, particularly the process of spore formation; role of the membrane in cell wall assembly. *Mailing Add:* Dept of Microbiol & Immunol Health Sci Ctr London ON N6A 5B8 Can

FITZLOFF, JOHN FREDERICK, b Jan 7, 40; US citizen; m 69; c 3. MEDICINAL CHEMISTRY, TOXICOLOGY. *Educ:* San Jose State Col, BS, 61; Univ Calif, San Francisco, PhD(pharmaceut chem), 72. *Prof Exp:* Chemist, Stanford Res Inst, 61-65; teaching asst chem, Univ Calif, San Francisco, 66-68; asst prof, 72-77, ASSOC PROF MED CHEM, UNIV ILL MED CTR, 77- *Concurrent Pos:* Vis scientist, Inst Toxicol & Pharmacol, Phillips Univ, Fed Repub of Ger, 79-80. *Mem:* Sigma Xi; Acad Pharmaceut Sci; Am Chem Soc. *Res:* Metabolism of drugs and other foreign compounds; methods of analyses of foreign compounds in biological media; relationship of chemical structure and metabolizing enzymes. *Mailing Add:* Univ of Ill Dept of Med Chem PO Box 6998 Rm 545 Pharmacy Chicago IL 60680

FITZNER, RICHARD EARL, b Belding, Mich, June 25, 46; m 70. VERTEBRATE ECOLOGY, ZOOLOGY. *Educ:* Mich State Univ, BS, 69, MS, 70; Wash State Univ, PhD(zool), 78. *Prof Exp:* RES SCIENTIST TERRESTRIAL ECOL, PAC NORTHWEST LABS, BATTELLE MEM INST, 71- *Concurrent Pos:* Mem, Wash State, Natural Preserves Adv Comt, 77-80. *Mem:* Cooper Ornith Soc; Am Ornithologists Union; Wildlife Soc; Sigma Xi. *Res:* Vertebrates and their role in ecosystem functioning; environmental perturbations (land disturbances, and chemical contaminants) and their impact on the environment; natural history and behavior of vertebrates, particularly birds. *Mailing Add:* 6652 I Bldg 600 Area Northwest Lab Battelle Mem Inst Richland WA 99352

FITZPATRICK, BEN, JR, b Miami, Fla, Sept 28, 32; m 53; c 3. MATHEMATICS. *Educ:* Ala Polytech Inst, BS, 52; Univ Tex, MA & PhD, 58. *Prof Exp:* Asst math, Univ Tex, 55-56, spec instr, 56-58, asst prof, 58-59; from asst prof to assoc prof, 59-66, PROF MATH, AUBURN UNIV, 66- & HEAD DEPT MATH, 78- *Mem:* Am Math Soc; Math Asn Am. *Res:* Continua and point set theory; abstract spaces; theory of integration. *Mailing Add:* Dept of Math Auburn Univ Auburn AL 36830

FITZPATRICK, FRANCIS ANTHONY, b Wilmington, Del, July 5, 47. ANALYTICAL BIOCHEMISTRY. *Educ:* Villanova Univ, BS, 69; Univ Mass, PhD(anal chem), 72. *Prof Exp:* Sr anal chemist, Vick Chem Co, Div Richardson-Merrill, 72-74; SCIENTIST & ANAL BIOCHEMIST, UPJOHN CO, 74- *Mem:* AAAS; Am Chem Soc. *Res:* Cell biology, pharmacology, biochemistry and analytical chemistry of lipids including steroids, prostaglandins, leukotrienes, thromboxanes, and glyceryl ether phospholipids; elucidation of mechanism of action of drugs, identification of modulators of lipid biosynthesis and pharmacology. *Mailing Add:* 2730 Kensington Dr Kalamazoo MI 49008

FITZPATRICK, GARY OWEN, b Petaluma, Calif, Dec 20, 43; c 2. PHYSICS, ENGINEERING. *Educ:* Calif Inst Technol, BSc, 66. *Prof Exp:* Sr engr thermionics, Gulf Gen Atomic, 66-73; sr engr, EMC, Intelcom Rad Technol, 73-74; prog mgr, Direct Energy Conversion, 74-79, VPRES, RASOR ASSOC, INC, 79- *Mem:* AAAS; Inst Elec & Electronic Engrs. *Res:* Thermionics; high temperature materials; energy converters; systems behavior; electromagnetic pulse effects; astronomical instrumentation. *Mailing Add:* 2612 Tahoe Dr Livermore CA 94550

FITZPATRICK, GEORGE, b Trenton, NJ, Oct 7, 46; m 69; c 2. ENVIRONMENTAL BIOLOGY, HORTICULTURE. *Educ:* Trenton State Col, BA, 68, MA, 72; Rutgers Univ, PhD(entom & econ zool), 75. *Prof Exp:* res assoc entom, Miss State Univ, 75-76; asst res scientist, 76-79, ASST PROF, INST FOOD & AGR SCI, AGR RES CTR, UNIV FLA, 79- *Mem:* AAAS; Ecol Soc Am; Sigma Xi. *Res:* Effects of toxicants on biological systems; effects of agricultural technologies on water quality; quantitative and qualitative water relations in plants. *Mailing Add:* Univ of Fla Agr Res Ctr 3205 SW 70th Ave Ft Lauderdale FL 33314

FITZPATRICK, HUGH MICHAEL, b Pittsburgh, Pa, Apr 22, 20; m 44; c 5. PHYSICS. *Educ:* George Washington Univ, BS, 44. *Prof Exp:* Naval architect, David Taylor Model Basin, 42-48, physicist, 48-59; physicist, Syst Eng Div, Cleveland Pneumatic Indust Inc, 59-63; PHYSICIST, OFF NAVAL RES, 63- *Mem:* Acoust Soc Am. *Res:* Fluid mechanics; acoustics; hydromechanics; cavitation; hydrodynamic noise; propulsion; radio; astronomy. *Mailing Add:* 4709 Merivale Rd Chevy Chase VA 20815

FITZPATRICK, J(OSEPH) F(ERRIS), JR, b New Orleans, La, Mar 8, 32; m 61; c 4. INVERTEBRATE ZOOLOGY, FRESHWATER CRUSTACEA. *Educ:* Tulane Univ, BS, 59, MS, 61; Univ Va, PhD(biol), 64. *Prof Exp:* Asst zool, Tulane Univ, 60, asst bot & zool, 61; asst biol, Univ Va, 62-64; instr, dept zool, Univ Ky, 64; asst prof zool, Miss State Univ, 64-69; assoc prof biol, Randolph-Macon Woman's Col, 69-73; assoc prof, 73-78, PROF, UNIV SOUTH ALA, 78- *Concurrent Pos:* Assoc ed, Northeast Gulf Sci, 80- *Mem:* Fel AAAS; Sigma Xi; Soc Syst Zool; found mem Crustacean Soc. *Res:* Systematics of North American crawfishes and other freshwater crustacea. *Mailing Add:* Dept of Biol Sci Univ SAla Mobile AL 36688

FITZPATRICK, JIMMIE DOILE, b Jonesboro, La, Aug 6, 38; m 59; c 2. ORGANIC CHEMISTRY, ANALYTICAL CHEMISTRY. *Educ:* La Polytech Inst, BS, 60; Iowa State Univ, MS, 63; Univ Tex, Austin, PhD(org chem), 66. *Prof Exp:* Res chemist, Phillips Petrol Co, 65-66; res assoc, Purdue Univ, 66-67; res chemist, GAF Corp, 67-68; asst prof org chem, 68-76, ASSOC PROF ORG CHEM, UNIV SOUTHWESTERN LA, 77- *Mem:* Am Chem Soc. *Res:* Organic synthesis; organometallic and polymer chemistry; homogenous and heterogenous catalysis; flavor chemistry. *Mailing Add:* Dept Chem Box 4370 Univ of Southwestern La Lafayette LA 70501

FITZPATRICK, JOHN MICHAEL, b Topeka, Kans, May 25, 45; m 73. CHEMICAL PHYSICS. *Educ:* Univ NC, Chapel Hill, BS, 67; Fla State Univ, PhD(physics), 72. *Prof Exp:* Fel physics, Fla State Univ, 72-73; fel chem, Univ BC, 73-74; vis instr, Clemson Univ, 74-75; ASST PROF PHYSICS, NEWBERRY COL, 75- *Mem:* Am Phys Soc. *Res:* Kinetic theory of gases relaxing from a non-equilibrium state; two-temperature gas mixtures; Fokker-Planck equation for particles of disparate mass; gas phase reactions in non-equilibrium states. *Mailing Add:* Dept of Physics Newberry Col Newberry SC 29108

FITZPATRICK, JOHN WEAVER, b St Paul, Minn, Sept 17, 51. ORNITHOLOGY, ECOLOGY. *Educ:* Harvard Univ, BA, 74; Princeton Univ, PhD(biol), 78. *Prof Exp:* ASST CUR & HEAD BIRD DIV, FIELD MUS NATURAL HIST, 78- *Mem:* Soc Syst Zool; Am Ornith Union; Wilson Ornith Soc; Cooper Ornith Soc; Sigma Xi. *Res:* Systematics, ecology, and zoogeography of neotropical birds, especially Tyrannidae; adaptive radiation in morphology and behavior among birds; evolution of cooperative breeding social systems in birds; tropical bird community structure. *Mailing Add:* Div Birds Field Mus Natural Hist Roosevelt Rd at Lake Shore Dr Chicago IL 60605

FITZPATRICK, JOSEPH A, b Albany, NY, Oct 20, 44; m 67; c 5. ENVIRONMENTAL CHEMISTRY, CIVIL ENGINEERING. *Educ:* Univ Notre Dame, BS, 66; Harvard Univ, MS, 67, PhD(eng), 72. *Prof Exp:* Res sanitary engr, Metcalf & Eddy Engrs, Boston, 66; asst prof civil engr, Clarkson Col, 71-72; asst prof, 72-76, ASSOC PROF CIVIL ENG, NORTHWESTERN UNIV, 77- *Concurrent Pos:* Sci adv, ECO, Inc, Cambridge, 70-; consult, Common-wealth Edison Co, 73-75, Environ Equip Div, FMC Corp, 74-, Tech Prod Div, Brunswick Corp, 75-77 & Argonne Nat Lab, 77-78; prin investr, Environ Protection Agency, 74-77, co-prin investr, Am Iron & Steel Inst, 77-78. *Mem:* Am Chem Soc; Am Inst Chem Engrs; Am

Soc Civil Engrs; Am Water Works Asn; Filtration Soc. *Res:* Chemistry, mechanics and removal of particulates in water and wastewater; solid-liquid separation process design; filtration theory and practice; ground water quality modeling. *Mailing Add:* Technol Inst Northwestern Univ Evanston IL 60201

FITZPATRICK, JOSEPH MICHAEL, synthetic organic chemistry, see previous edition

FITZPATRICK, LLOYD CHARLES, b Erie, Pa, May 12, 37; div; c 3. ECOLOGY. *Educ:* Mt Union Col, BS, 60; Kent State Univ, MA, 66; PhD(ecol), 70. *Prof Exp:* High sch instr, Fla, 60-61; jr high instr, 61-66; instr biol sci, Kent State Univ, 68-70; asst prof, 70-75, assoc dir res, Inst Environ Studies, 73-76, chmn ecol div, Dept Biol Sci, 76-80, assoc dir, Anal Water Qual Lab, 75-78, coordr grad studies, 78-79, assoc prof, 75-81, PROF BIOL, NTEX STATE UNIV, 81- *Mem:* Am Soc Naturalists; Ecol Soc Am; Am Soc Zool; Sigma Xi; NAm Benthological Soc. *Res:* Ecological, geographical and evolutionary effects on intra- and interspecific energetics, physiologies and reproductive strategies in animals; population dynamics and trophic dynamics of aquatic and terrestrial ecosystems; assessment of environmental impacts. *Mailing Add:* Dept of Biol Sci NTex State Univ Denton TX 76203

FITZPATRICK, MICHAEL MORSON, geophysics, see previous edition

FITZPATRICK, PATRICK MICHAEL, b Youghal, Ireland, Mar 14, 46; US citizen; m 70; c 2. PURE MATHEMATICS. *Educ:* Rutgers Univ, BS, 66, PhD(math), 71. *Prof Exp:* Vis mem, Courant Inst, NY Univ, 71-72; lectr, Rutgers Univ, 72-73; L E Dickson instr, Univ Chicago, 73-75; ASST PROF MATH, UNIV MD, COLLEGE PARK, 75- *Concurrent Pos:* NSF res awards, 70-76. *Mem:* Am Math Soc; Am Math Asn. *Res:* Application of functional analysis and topological methods to the solution of abstract nonlinear equations and to integral and partial differential equations. *Mailing Add:* Dept of Math Univ of Md College Park MD 20742

FITZPATRICK, PHILIP MATTHEW, b New York, NY, Sept 17, 15; m 42; c 2. APPLIED MATHEMATICS. *Educ:* Univ Okla, BS, 50, MS, 51, PhD(physics), 55. *Prof Exp:* Asst physics, Univ Okla, 53-55; physicist, US Navy Mine Defense Lab, Fla, 55-59; physicist, Air Proving Ground Ctr, Eglin AFB, 59-62; assoc prof, 62-68, PROF MATH, AUBURN UNIV, 68- *Mem:* AAAS; Am Phys Soc; Am Geophys Union; Math Asn Am. *Res:* Astrodynamics. *Mailing Add:* 107 Ryan St Auburn AL 36830

FITZPATRICK, ROBERT CHARLES, b Port Huron, Mich, Jan 18, 26; m; c 2. GEOPHYSICS. *Educ:* Univ Mich, BS, 48, MS, 50. *Prof Exp:* Packaging-mat handling engr, Kaiser-Frazer Corp, 50-51; geophysicist, Air Force Cambridge Res Ctr, 53-54, chief geodesy sect, 54-56; res assoc, Seismol & Acoustics, Willow Run Labs, Univ Mich, 56-60, mem staff, Res Admin, 60-65, from asst dir to assoc dir, 65-69; mgr mkt res, Datamax Corp, 69-70; asst vpres res, 70-80, ASSOC VPRES RES, STATE UNIV NY BUFFALO, 80- *Concurrent Pos:* Geophysicist, Off Naval Res, 51-53; mem, Nat Coun Univ Res Adminrs. *Mem:* Geol Soc Am; Soc Explor Geophys; Int Asn Gt Lakes Res; Am Geophys Union. *Res:* Physical oceanography; gravimetry; seismology. *Mailing Add:* 99 Parkledge Dr Snyder NY 14226

FITZPATRICK, THOMAS BERNARD, b Madison, Wis, Dec 19, 19; m 44; c 6. MEDICINE. *Educ:* Univ Wis, AB, 41; Harvard Univ, MD, 45; Univ Minn, PhD, 52; Am Bd Dermat, dipl, 52. *Prof Exp:* Asst prof, Univ Mich, 51-52; prof & head div, Med Sch, Univ Ore, 52-58; EDWARD WIGGLESWORTH PROF DERMAT, HARVARD MED SCH, 59-; CHIEF DERMAT SERV, MASS GEN HOSP, 59- *Concurrent Pos:* Chief dept dermat, Multnomah & Children's Hosps, Portland, Ore, 52-58; guest lectr, Univs Tokyo, Tohoku & Kyoto, Japan, 56; consult, Nat Inst Arthritis, Metab & Digestive Dis, 60-; mem dermat training grants comt, USPHS, 60-65; Pollitzer lect, NY Univ, 62; consult, Peter Bent Brigham Hosp, 62-; Prosser White Oration, Royal Soc Med, 64; mem, Climatic Impact Comt, Nat Acad Sci, 71-74 & Comt on Impacts of Stratospheric Change, 74-; pres, Dermat Found, 71-73; pres, Int Pigment Cell Soc, 78-; pres-elect, Asn Prof Dermat, 80. *Honors & Awards:* Mayo Found Award, 51; Achievement Award, Univ Mich, 64; Myron Gordon Award, Int Union Against Cancer, 65; Stephen Rothman Gold Medal Award Distinguished Achievement, Soc Invest Dermat, 70; Dome lectr, Am Acad Dermat, 79; Taub Psoriasis Award, 80. *Mem:* Soc Invest Dermat (pres, 59-60); Am Acad Arts & Sci; Am Dermat Asn; Am Soc Photobiology; Asn Am Physicians. *Res:* Melanin biosynthesis; normal and abnormal reactions of man to light; molecular biology of melanin; origin of racial color; dermatology. *Mailing Add:* Mass Gen Hosp Boston MA 02114

FITZPATRICK, THOMAS JOSEPH, agricultural chemistry, see previous edition

FITZROY, NANCY DELOYE, b Pittsfield, Mass, Oct 5, 27; m 51. ENGINEERING. *Educ:* Rensselaer Polytech Inst, BChE, 49. *Prof Exp:* Asst engr, Knolls Atomic Power Lab, 50-52; develop engr, Hermes Missile Proj, 52-53, develop engr, Gen Eng Lab, 53-63, heat transfer engr, Advan Technol Labs, 63-65, consult heat transfer, Res & Develop Ctr, 65-71, mgr heat transfer consult, 71-74, strategy planner, 74-76, advan concepts planner & proposal mgr, 76-79, PROG DEVELOP MGR, GAS TURBINE DIV, GEN ELEC CO, 79- *Concurrent Pos:* Lectr, Advan Eng Course, Gen Elec Co, 62-67; res comt adv, NSF, 72-75; bd mem, Bd Eng Manpower & Educ Policy, Nat Acad Eng, 74-76. *Honors & Awards:* Achievement Award, Soc Women Engrs, 72; Centennial Medallion, Am Soc Mech Engrs, 80. *Mem:* Fel Am Soc Mech Engrs; Am Inst Chem Engrs; Nat Soc Prof Engrs; Soc Women Engrs. *Res:* Heat transfer; thermal engineering; thermal properties of materials; high temperature radiation from nuclear source; cooling of integrated circuits; heat transfer in regenerator matrices; patentee in field of cooling of integrated circuits. *Mailing Add:* Gas Turbine Div Gen Elec Co Schenectady NY 12345

FITZSIMMONS, DELBERT WAYNE, b Bazine, Kans, Jan 20, 32; m 52; c 4. AGRICULTURAL & IRRIGATION ENGINEERING. *Educ:* Univ Idaho, BS, 59, MS, 62; Wash State Univ, PhD(eng sci), 70. *Prof Exp:* From instr to assoc prof, 59-71, actg chmn, 70-72, PROF AGR ENG, UNIV IDAHO, 71-, CHMN DEPT, 72- *Mem:* Am Soc Agr Engrs; Am Soc Eng Educ; Nat Soc Prof Engrs. *Res:* Unsteady flow into and through porous media; hydraulic characteristics of porous media; mathematical modeling of flow through soils; effects of irrigated agriculture on water quality. *Mailing Add:* Dept Agr Eng Univ Idaho Moscow ID 83848

FITZSIMMONS, VINCENT G(EORGE), lubrication engineering, deceased

FITZWATER, DONALD (ROBERT), b Kansas City, Mo, Oct 5, 30; m 51; c 2. COMPUTER SCIENCE. *Educ:* William Jewell Col, BA, 50; Iowa State Col, MS, 52, PhD(chem), 58. *Prof Exp:* Asst chem, Ames Lab, Atomic Energy Comn, 50-52, jr chemist, 51-52, 55-58, assoc chemist, 58-64, chemist, 64-67, from asst prof to assoc prof chem, Iowa State Univ, 59-67; ASSOC PROF COMPUT SCI, UNIV WIS-MADISON, 67- *Mem:* Asn Comput Mach. *Res:* Real time control; programming systems; information processing; system & language structures. *Mailing Add:* Dept of Comput Sci Univ of Wis Madison WI 53706

FITZWATER, ROBERT N, b Elkins, WVa, Apr 8, 24; m 50; c 1. CHEMISTRY. *Educ:* Rollins Col, BS, 49; Univ Fla, PhD, 58. *Prof Exp:* Asst, Bur Entom & Plant Quarantine, USDA, 51-53; asst, Univ Fla, 53-55; sr chemist, Res Labs, Gen Motors Corp, 58-61 & Martin Col, 62; asst prof chem, Rollins Col, 62-65; asst prof pharmacol, Sch Med, Univ Miami, 65-69; assoc prof chem, 69-74, ASSOC PROF CHEM, GA SOUTHERN COL, 74- *Mailing Add:* Dept of Chem Ga Southern Col Statesboro GA 30458

FITZWATER, SUSAN JANE, physical chemistry, see previous edition

FIUMARA, NICHOLAS J, b Boston, Mass, Oct 31, 12; m 44; c 1. PUBLIC HEALTH, VENEREAL DISEASES. *Educ:* Boston Col, AB, 34; Boston Univ, MD, 39; Harvard Univ, MPH, 47. *Prof Exp:* Assoc clin prof, 51-69, CLIN PROF DERMAT, SCH MED, BOSTON UNIV, 69-; INSTR EPIDEMIOL, SCH PUB HEALTH, HARVARD UNIV, 57- *Concurrent Pos:* Lectr, Sch Med, Tufts Univ, 52-; instr dermat, Harvard Med Sch, 63-; vis physician, Mass Mem Hosps, 57-; asst clin dermatologist, Mass Gen Hosp, 53-; assoc vis physician, Boston City Hosp, 58-; physician, Dept Dermat & Syphil, Boston Dispensary, 59-; dir div commun & venereal dis, Boston. *Mem:* Fel AMA; fel Am Venereal Dis Asn (pres, 73-74); Conf State & Territorial Epidemiol (pres, 71-73); fel Am Col Prev Med; assoc Am Acad Dermat. *Res:* Common health; clinical and public health aspects of communicable and venereal diseases and dermatology. *Mailing Add:* Mass Dept Pub Health 600 Washington St Boston MA 02178

FIVEL, DANIEL I, b Baltimore, Md, Oct 12, 32; m 57; c 1. THEORETICAL PHYSICS. *Educ:* Johns Hopkins Univ, PhD(physics), 59. *Prof Exp:* Res assoc physics, Univ Pa, 59-61; NSF fels, Synchrotron Lab, Frascati, Rome, Italy, 61-62 & Mass Inst Technol, 62-63; asst prof, 63-68, ASSOC PROF PHYSICS, UNIV MD, COLLEGE PARK, 68- *Concurrent Pos:* Mem exec comt, Aspen Ctr Physics, Colo. *Mem:* Am Phys Soc. *Res:* Weak interactions; quantum field theory; dispersion relations; elementary particles; symmetry properties; potential theory. *Mailing Add:* Dept of Physics Univ of Md College Park MD 20742

FIVES-TAYLOR, PAULA MARIE, b Brooklyn, NY, Oct 9, 33; m 71. MEDICAL MICROBIOLOGY. *Educ:* St Thomas Aquinas Col, BS, 58; Villanova Univ, MS, 65; Univ Vt, PhD(med microbiol), 73. *Prof Exp:* Sci teacher, Our Lady Perpetual Help Sch, 55-60, St Helena's High Sch, 60-68; instr biol, St Thomas Aquinas Col, 67; teaching asst, Univ Vt, 68-71; instr biol, Trinity Col, 72-74; asst prof med microbiol, 74-78, ASSOC PROF MED MICROBIOL, COL MED UNIV VT, 78- *Concurrent Pos:* Prin investr, NIH grant; vpres, Genetics Resources, Inc. *Mem:* Am Soc Microbiol; Sigma Xi; Infectious Dis Soc Am; Int Asn Dent Res; Am Asn Sci. *Res:* Mechanisms involved in the assembly of surface structures on the bacterial cell and the role these structures play in adherence to mucous membranes. *Mailing Add:* Univ Vt Col Med Dept Med Microbiol Burlington VT 05405

FIVIZZANI, ALBERT JOHN, JR, b Chicago, Ill, Sept 11, 46; m 71. COMPARATIVE PHYSIOLOGY, ENDOCRINOLOGY. *Educ:* DePaul Univ, BS, 68, MS, 71; La State Univ, PhD(physiol), 77. *Prof Exp:* Instr, La State Univ, 76-78; ASST PROF PHYSIOL, UNIV N DAK, 78- *Mem:* AAAS; Am Inst Biol Sci; Am Soc Zoologists; Int Soc Chronobiol; Sigma Xi. *Res:* Biological rhythms; animal migration and orientation; regulation of seasonal conditions of vertebrates. *Mailing Add:* Dept of Biol Univ NDak Grand Forks ND 58202

FIVOZINSKY, SHERMAN PAUL, b Hartford, Conn, Aug 2, 38; m 61; c 2. NUCLEAR PHYSICS. *Educ:* Univ Conn, BA, 61, MS, 63, PhD(nuclear physics), 71. *Prof Exp:* nuclear physicist electron scattering, Ctr Radiation Res, 66-76, ASST TO CHIEF, OFF STANDARD REF DATA, NAT BUR STANDARDS, 76- *Concurrent Pos:* Adj prof, Montgomery Col, Rockville, Md, 78- *Mem:* AAAS; Am Phys Soc; Am Asn Physicists Med. *Res:* Electron scattering, nuclear structure; medical physics; critical data evaluation. *Mailing Add:* Off of Standard Ref Data Nat Bur Standards Washington DC 20234

FIX, DELBERT DALE, b Pierce, Nebr, Dec 10, 26; m 46; c 4. PHOTOGRAPHIC CHEMISTRY. *Educ:* Univ Nebr, BS, 48, MS, 50; Univ Colo, PhD(chem), 52. *Prof Exp:* Asst, Univ Nebr, 48-49; asst, Univ Colo, 49-52; res chemist, 52-65, RES ASSOC, EMULSION RES DIV, RES LAB, EASTMAN KODAK CO, 65- *Mem:* AAAS; Am Chem Soc; Soc Photographic Scientists & Engrs. *Res:* Organic synthesis; nitrogen heterocyclic chemistry; reaction mechanisms; photographic emulsions; black and white and color photographic systems. *Mailing Add:* Eastman Kodak Co Res Labs 343 State St Rochester NY 14650

FIX, GEORGE JOSEPH, b Dallas, Tex, May 10, 39; m; c 2. FINITE ELEMENT METHODS, PARTIAL DIFFERENTIAL EQUATIONS. *Educ:* Tex A&M Univ, BS, 63; Rice Univ, MS, 65; Harvard Univ, PhD(math), 68. *Prof Exp:* Engr, Tex Instruments, 63-64; asst prof math, Harvard Univ, 68-72; assoc prof, Dept Comput Sci, Univ Md, College Park, 72-73; assoc prof, Dept Math, Univ Mich, Ann Arbor, 73-75; PROF & HEAD MATH, CARNEGIE-MELLON UNIV, 75- *Concurrent Pos:* Consult, Westinghouse Res & Develop Ctr, 75-; prin investr, NASA Langley Res Ctr, 72-; vis prof, Inst Angewandte Math, Univ Bonn, Ger, 76-77, 77-78 & 79-80. *Mem:* Am Math Soc; Soc Ind & Appl Math; AAAS. *Res:* Scientific computing with a special emphasis on acoustics, fluid dynamics, and free boundary problems; numerical analysis; author or coauthor of over 49 technical publications. *Mailing Add:* Dept Math Carnegie-Mellon Univ Pittsburgh PA 15213

FIX, JAMES D, b Atlantic City, NJ, Jan 24, 31; m 54; c 4. ANATOMY, PHYSICAL ANTHROPOLOGY. *Educ:* Univ Del, BA, 58; Univ Tuebingen, Dr rer nat(anat & phys anthrop), 67. *Prof Exp:* From instr to asst prof anat, Sch Med, Univ Louisville, 67-70, asst prof ophthal, 70-71; assoc prof path & anat, Sch Med, Ind Univ, 71-79; PROF & CHMN ANAT, SCH MED, MARSHALL UNIV, 80- *Concurrent Pos:* Assoc prof anat, Sch Med, ECarolina Univ, 69-80; NIH spec res fel opthal, 70-71. *Mem:* Am Asn Anatamists; Am Asn Neuropathologists; fel Royal Micros Soc. *Res:* Cytoarchitecture of the central nervous system; neuropathology; quantitative neuropathology of the autonomic nervous system in diabetes. *Mailing Add:* Dept Anat Med Sch Marshall Univ Huntington WV 25701

FIX, JOHN DEKLE, b Melrose Park, Ill, Dec 23, 41; m 67; c 3. ASTROPHYSICS. *Educ:* Purdue Univ, BS, 63; Ind Univ, Bloomington, MA, 67, PhD(astrophys), 69. *Prof Exp:* from asst prof to assoc prof, 69-80, PROF ASTRON, UNIV IOWA, 80- *Mem:* Am Astron Soc; Royal Astron Soc; Int Astron Union. *Res:* Particulate matter in stellar atmospheres and interstellar space; stellar masers; physical properties and observations of planetary surfaces. *Mailing Add:* Dept Physics & Astron Univ Iowa Iowa City IA 52240

FIX, RICHARD CONRAD, b Milwaukee, Wis, Dec 26, 30; m 58; c 3. ENVIRONMENTAL CHEMISTRY. *Educ:* Univ Wis, BS, 52; Mass Inst Technol, PhD(chem), 56. *Prof Exp:* Sr scientist, Tracerlab, Inc, 56-57; asst tech dir, Controls for Radiation, Inc, 57-63; vpres & dir res & develop, 63-65; sr staff scientist, Tracerlab Div, Lab for Electronics, Inc, 65-69; mgr tech serv dept, ICN/Tracerlab, 69-72; MGR ENVIRON SCI, INTEREX CORP, NATICK, 72- *Mem:* Sigma Xi; Am Nuclear Soc; Health Physics Soc. *Res:* Radiation physics; nuclear and medical instrumentation; dosimetry; environmental radioactivity; site surveys. *Mailing Add:* 484 Hosmer St Marlboro MA 01752

FIXMAN, MARSHALL, b St Louis, Mo, Sept 21, 30; m 59; c 3. THEORETICAL CHEMISTRY. *Educ:* Washington Univ, AB, 50; Mass Inst Technol, PhD(chem), 54. *Prof Exp:* Instr chem, Harvard Univ, 56-59; sr fel, Mellon Inst, 59-61; prof, Univ Ore, 61-65; PROF CHEM, YALE UNIV, 65- *Concurrent Pos:* Sloan vis prof chem, Harvard Univ, 65. *Mem:* Nat Acad Sci; Am Chem Soc; Am Phys Soc. *Res:* Statistical mechanics; polymer theory. *Mailing Add:* 225 Prospect St New Haven CT 06520

FIXOTT, HENRY CLINE, b Portland, Ore, Aug 28, 14; m 40; c 4. ROENTGENOLOGY. *Educ:* Univ Ore, DMD, 38. *Prof Exp:* Clin instr dent, Sch Med, 39-46, clin assoc, Sch Dent, 46-52, assoc prof oral roentgenol, 52-57, clin assoc, Sch Med, 46-77, head dept, 52-76, prof roentgenol, 57-77, EMER PROF ROENTGENOL, SCH DENT, HEALTH SCI CTR, UNIV ORE, 78- *Concurrent Pos:* Consult, Vet Admin, Ore & Barnes Hosps, 46-; consult & chief dent serv, Shriner's Hosp for Crippled Children, 58-; consult, US Army Madigan Gen Hosp, 52-; Fulbright lectr, Dept Oral Radiol, Sch Dent, Univ Tehran, 70-71. *Mem:* Am Dent Asn; fel Am Col Dent; fel Am Acad Dent Radiol (pres, 54); Am Acad Oral Path; Int Acad Dento-Maxillofacial Radiol (pres 77-80, chmn, 80). *Res:* Radiation dosage; effects of radiation on color film; section roentgenology; coinventor grid used in dental roentgenology; oral roentgenology. *Mailing Add:* Dept Oral Roentgenol Dent Sch Univ Ore Health Sci Ctr Portland OR 97201

FJARLIE, EARL J, b Nanaimo, BC, Apr 10, 32; m 59; c 3. APPLIED PHYSICS. *Educ:* Univ BC, BASc, 55, MASc, 58; Univ Sask, PhD(physics), 65. *Prof Exp:* Defence serv tech officer, Defence Res Bd-Defence Res Estab Valcartier, 55, defence serv sci officer, 57-59; mem II res & develop, RCA Ltd, 65-76; ASSOC PROF MECH ENG, ROYAL MIL COL CAN, 76- *Concurrent Pos:* Part-time lectr physics, Sir George Williams Univ, 66-73; mem comt reflection spectros, Can Ctr Remote Sensing, 75-77; mem comt optical surveillance, Defence Res Bd, 75-76; mem comt phys sci Valcariter, Defence Res Estab Valcartier, 76-77; dir, Tekerg, Inc, PQ, 76-79. *Mem:* Optical Soc Am; Am Asn Physics Teachers; Can Asn Physicists; Soc Photo-Optical & Instrumentation Engrs. *Res:* Optoelectronic systems; infrared spectroscopy; radiometry; display devices; laser doppler anemometry; atmospheric and space physics; air pollution; interferometry; remote sensing; photodiode circuitry; fluid flow; thermal convection; liquid crystals; laser systems. *Mailing Add:* 4 Copperfield Dr Kingston ON K7M 1M4 Can

FJELD, ROBERT ALAN, b Greensboro, NC, Dec 28, 47; m 68; c 2. NUCLEAR ENVIRONMENTAL SCIENCE ENGINEERING. *Educ:* NC State Univ, BS, 70; Pa State Univ, MS, 73, PhD(nuclear eng), 76. *Prof Exp:* Asst prof, Nuclear Eng, Tex A&M Univ, 76-80; ASSOC PROF ENVIRON SYSTS ENG, CLEMSON UNIV, SC, 81- *Concurrent Pos:* NSF grant prin investr, 77- *Mem:* Sigma Xi; Am Nuclear Soc; Health Phys Soc. *Res:* Nuclear environmental engineering; occupational and environmental health physics with emphasis on the generation, transport, fate and effects of radioactive material; theoretical and experimental aerosol physics. *Mailing Add:* Environ Systs Eng Clemson Univ Clemson SC 29631

FLACCUS, EDWARD, b Lansdowne, Pa, Feb 4, 21; m 47; c 3. PLANT ECOLOGY. *Educ:* Haverford Col, BS, 42; Univ NH, MS, 52; Duke Univ, PhD(bot), 59. *Prof Exp:* Teacher pvt sch, 48-50 & 51-55; asst zool, Univ NH, 50-51; asst bot, Duke Univ, 55-57; asst prof, Univ Minn, Duluth, 58-62, assoc prof, 63-68; vis prof, State Univ NY, Stony Brook, 68-69; PROF BIOL SCI, BENNINGTON COL, 69- *Concurrent Pos:* Vis scientist, Brookhaven Nat Lab, 68-69. *Mem:* AAAS; Ecol Soc Am; Bot Soc Am; Am Inst Biol Sci; Sigma Xi. *Res:* Plant successions; forest ecology. *Mailing Add:* Sci Div Bennington Col Bennington VT 05201

FLACH, FREDERIC FRANCIS, b New York, NY, Jan 25, 27; m 51; c 4. PSYCHIATRY. *Educ:* St Peters Col, BA, 47; Cornell Univ, MD, 51. *Prof Exp:* Intern, Bellevue Hosp, 51-52; from asst resident psychiatrist to resident psychiatrist, Payne Whitney Clin, 53-58; asst prof, 58-62, ASSOC PROF CLIN PSYCHIAT, MED COL, CORNELL UNIV, 62- *Concurrent Pos:* From asst attend psychiatrist to attend psychiatrist, Payne Whitney Clin, 58-; assoc attend psychiatrist, St Vincent's Hosp, 58. *Mem:* Am Pub Health Asn; fel Am Psychiat Asn; Endocrine Soc; AMA. *Res:* Electrolyte and endocrine metabolism in psychiatric disorders; integration of chemotherapy and analytic psychotherapy in clinical practice; development of programs in preventive psychiatry. *Mailing Add:* 420 E 51st St New York NY 10022

FLACH, KLAUS WERNER, b Kolbermoor, Ger, Mar 24, 27; nat US; m 59; c 2. SOIL SCIENCE. *Educ:* Munich Tech Inst, Dipl, 50; Cornell Univ, MS, 54, PhD(soils), 60. *Prof Exp:* Asst soils, Cornell Univ, 53-58; soil scientist, Soil Surv Lab, 58-72, dir soil survey invest, 72-76, asst adminr in chg of soil survey, 76-80, ASSOC DEP CHIEF NATURAL RESOURCE ASSESSMENTS, SOIL CONSERV SERV, USDA, 80- *Mem:* Soil Sci Soc Am. *Res:* Soil and soil mineralogy; thinsection techniques; clay mineralogy; soil classification and mapping. *Mailing Add:* USDA Soil Conserv Serv Rm 5207 S Agr Bldg Washington DC 20250

FLACHSBART, PETER GEORGE, b St Louis, Mo, Apr 15, 44; m 76. ENVIRONMENTAL PLANNING, LAND USE PLANNING. *Educ:* Wash Univ, BS, 66; Northwestern Univ, MS, 68, PhD(civil eng), 71. *Prof Exp:* Sr res assoc, Univ Southern Calif, 71-72; lectr urban & environ mgt, Calif State Univ, Dominguez Hills, 72-73, asst prof, 73, asst prof public admin, 73-76; asst prof civil eng, Stanford Univ, 76-80; ASST PROF URBAN & REGIONAL PLANNING, UNIV HAWAII, MANOA, 80- *Concurrent Pos:* Prin investr, Stanford Univ, 77-80 & Univ Hawaii, Manoa, 80-; consult, US Environ Protection Agency, 79- *Mem:* Sigma Xi; Sci Soc. *Res:* Development of methodologies to estimate human exposure to air pollution using personal monitoring instruments; public policy analysis for energy conservation in urban passenger travel. *Mailing Add:* Urban & Regional Planning Prog Univ Hawaii at Manoa 2424 Maile Way Honolulu HI 96822

FLACHSKAM, ROBERT LOUIS, JR, b Joliet, Ill, Oct 11, 46; m 70. ORGANIC CHEMISTRY. *Educ:* Lewis Univ, BA, 68; Ohio State Univ, PhD(chem), 73. *Prof Exp:* asst prof, 75-80, ASSOC PROF CHEM, KY WESLEYAN COL, 75- *Mem:* Am Chem Soc; Asn Astron Educators. *Mailing Add:* Dept of Chem Ky Wesleyan Col Owensboro KY 42301

FLACK, J(OHN) E(RNEST), b Ft Collins, Colo, Jan 28, 29; m 51; c 3. WATER RESOURCES ENGINEERING. *Educ:* Colo State Univ, BSc, 50; Univ Iowa, MSc, 54; Stanford Univ, PhD(civil eng), 65. *Prof Exp:* From asst prof to assoc prof civil eng, Univ Colo, Boulder, 57-68; vis prof eng & econ planning, Water Resources Ctr, Ga Inst Technol, 68-69; PROF CIVIL ENG, UNIV COLO, BOULDER, 69- *Concurrent Pos:* NSF fac fel, 62-63; trustee, Rocky Mt Hydraul Lab; deleg, Univs Coun Water Resources, exec bd, 72-75 & 77-80; Eng Found fel, 78-79; vis prof, New South Wales Inst Technol, Australia, 80. *Mem:* AAAS; fel Am Soc Civil Engrs; Am Geophys Union; Am Water Resources Asn; Sigma Xi. *Res:* Hydrology; fluid mechanics; water resources. *Mailing Add:* Dept Civil Environ & Archit Eng Campus Box 428 Univ Colo Boulder CO 80309

FLACK, RONALD DUMONT, JR, b South Bend, Ind, Dec 24, 47; m 69; c 2. EXPERIMENTAL FLUID MECHANICS, LUBRICATION. *Educ:* Purdue Univ, BS, 70, MS, 73, PhD(mech eng), 75. *Prof Exp:* Anal design engr, Pratt & Whitney Aircraft, 70-71; teaching & res asst fluid mech, Purdue Univ, 71-75; asst prof, 76-81, ASSOC PROF FLUID MECH, UNIV VA, 81- *Concurrent Pos:* Prin investr res grants, NASA, NIH, Dept Energy & NSF, 76-; consult several industs, 76- *Mem:* Am Soc Mech Engrs; Am Soc Eng Educ; Am Soc Lubrication Eng; Optical Soc Am. *Res:* Experimental fluid mechanics, gas dynamics, lubrication, rotor dynamics, convective heat transfer and optical instrumentation; application in rotating machinery. *Mailing Add:* Dept Mech & Aerospace Eng Thornton Hall McCormick Rd Univ Va Charlottesville VA 22901

FLACKE, WERNER ERNST, b Recke, Ger, July 14, 24; nat US; m 57; c 3. PHARMACOLOGY. *Educ:* Univ Düsseldorf, MD, 50. *Prof Exp:* Asst pharmacol, Univ Düsseldorf, 51-52; asst path, Koblenz, Rhein, 52-53; resident internal med, St Elisabeth Hosp, Essen, Ruhr, 53-54; from instr to assoc prof pharmacol, Harvard Med Sch, 55-70; prof pharmacol & chmn dept, Univ Ark, Little Rock, 70-77; PROF ANESTHESIOL & PHARMACOL, UNIV CALIF, LOS ANGELES, 77- *Concurrent Pos:* Fel pharmacol, Harvard Med Sch, 54. *Mem:* Pavlovian Soc; Am Soc Pharmacol & Exp Therapeut; sr fel Max Planck Soc; Biophys Soc; Ger Pharmacol Soc. *Res:* Pharmacology of excitable membranes; circulation; sensory input to central nervous system; respiration; skeletal muscle. *Mailing Add:* Dept Anesthesiol Univ Calif Los Angeles CA 90024

FLAGAN, RICHARD CHARLES, b Spokane, Wash, June 12, 47; m 79; c 2. COMBUSTION, AEROSOL PHYSICS. *Educ:* Univ Mich, BSME, 65; Mass Inst Technol, SM, 71, PhD(mech eng), 73. *Prof Exp:* Res assoc mech eng, Mass Inst Technol, 73-75, lectr, 75; asst prof, 75-81, ASSOC PROF ENVIRON ENG SCI, CALIF INST TECHNOL, 81- *Mem:* Combustion Inst; Am Inst Chem Engrs; Am Asn Aerosol Res. *Res:* Formation, control and atmospheric transformations of gaseous and particulate pollutants, combustion processes and fundamental aerosol physics. *Mailing Add:* Calif Inst Technol 138-78 Pasadena CA 91125

FLAGG, JOHN FERARD, b Wellsville, NY, Dec 30, 14; m 40; c 2. ANALYTICAL CHEMISTRY, RESEARCH ADMINISTRATION. *Educ:* Univ Rochester, BS, 36; Princeton Univ, AM, 37, PhD(chem), 39. *Prof Exp:* Instr chem, Univ Rochester, 39-43, asst prof, 43-46; res assoc, Gen Elec Co, 46-52, mgr chem & chem eng, Knolls Atomic Power Lab, 52-56, proj analyst, GE Res Lab, 56-59, mgr mat eng lab, 59-61; dir res, Cent Res Div, Am Cyanamid Co, 61-64; dir & gen mgr, 64-72; VPRES & DIR RES, UOP, INC, 72- *Mem:* Am Chem Soc; The Chem Soc. *Res:* Radioactivity in inorganic and analytical chemistry; organic analytical reagents; processing of nuclear fuels; planning and evaluation of research; materials development; fuels; petrochemicals; environmental control. *Mailing Add:* 10 UOP Plaza Des Plaines IL 60016

FLAGG, RAYMOND OSBOURN, b Martinsburg, WVa, Jan 31, 33; m 56; c 3. BOTANY, SCIENCE ADMINISTRATION. *Educ:* Shepherd Col, BA, 57; Univ Va, PhD(biol), 61. *Prof Exp:* Teacher, High Sch, Md, 57; res assoc biol, Univ Va, 61-62; head bot, 62-79, VPRES, CAROLINA BIOL SUPPLY CO, 80- *Mem:* AAAS; Bot Soc Am; Am Inst Biol Scis. *Res:* Plant cytogenetics and bisystematics; nutrition of Drosophila. *Mailing Add:* Carolina Biol Supply Co Burlington NC 27215

FLAGLE, CHARLES D(ENHARD), b Scottdale, Pa, Apr 26, 19; m 46, 65; c 4. OPERATIONS RESEARCH. *Educ:* Johns Hopkins Univ, BE, 40, MSc, 54, DrEng, 55. *Prof Exp:* Design engr mech eng, Westinghouse Elec Corp, 40-46; res assoc fluid mech, Inst Co-op Res, 50-53, mem staff, Opers Res Off, 53-55, consult, 55-62, PROF OPERS RES & INDUST ENG, SCH ENG SCI, JOHNS HOPKINS UNIV, 61-, PROF PUB HEALTH ADMIN, 63-, DIR OPERS RES, HOSP, 56- *Concurrent Pos:* Consult, USPHS, 58-, New York Health Dept, 62-, Res Anal Corp, 62-, Calif Dept Pub Health, 63-, Vet Admin & Community Systs Found; mem, Nat Adv Comt Epidemiol & Biometry, 63-66. *Mem:* Nat Inst Med; Opers Res Soc Am; Inst Mgt Sci; Am Pub Health Asn. *Res:* Operations research applied to health services, particularly applications of decision theory and stochastic processes. *Mailing Add:* Dept of Pub Health Admin Johns Hopkins Univ Baltimore MD 21205

FLAHERTY, EDWARD JOHN, JR, theoretical physics, see previous edition

FLAHERTY, FRANCIS JOSEPH, b Chicago, Ill, July 26, 35; m 62; c 2. GEOMETRY. *Educ:* Univ Wis-Madison, BA, 56; Univ Notre Dame, MS, 59; Univ Calif, Berkeley, PhD(math), 65. *Prof Exp:* Mathematician, Rand Corp, 56-57; asst prof math, San Francisco State Col, 59-65; asst prof, Univ Southern Calif, 65-67; from asst prof to assoc prof, 67-77, PROF MATH, ORE STATE UNIV, 77- *Concurrent Pos:* Vis prof, Math Inst, Univ Bonn, 71-72 & 75; vis scholar, Inst Astron, Cambridge, Eng, 75. *Mem:* Am Math Soc. *Res:* Differential and integral geometry; differential topology; general relativity. *Mailing Add:* Dept of Math Ore State Univ Corvallis OR 97331

FLAHERTY, FRANKLIN TRIMBY, JR, b Philadelphia, Pa, Aug 7, 34; m 56; c 2. MECHANICAL ENGINEERING, APPLIED MATHEMATICS. *Educ:* Mass Inst Technol, BS, 56, MS, 58; NY Univ, EngScD, 63. *Prof Exp:* Res asst, Dynamic Anal & Control Labs, Mass Inst Technol, 56-58; mem tech staff, 58-65, supvr eng mech group, 65-69, HEAD POWER SYSTS PHYS DESIGN DEPT, BELL TEL LABS, 69- *Res:* Dynamic behavior of discrete and continuous mechanical systems; communications equipment design. *Mailing Add:* Power Systs Phys Design Whippany Rd Whippany NJ 07981

FLAIM, FRANCIS RICHARD, b Sublet, Wyo, Nov 2, 13; m 44; c 2. ZOOLOGY. *Educ:* Univ Utah, BA, 36, MA, 38; Stanford Univ, PhD, 56. *Prof Exp:* Asst zool, Univ Utah, 34-35; instr, 38-44; from asst prof to assoc prof zool & biol, 46-56, chmn dept biol, 60-66, PROF ZOOL & BIOL, UNIV SANTA CLARA, 56- *Concurrent Pos:* Food technologist, Food Mach Corp, Calif, 44-46. *Mem:* AAAS; Am Soc Mammal; Sigma Xi; Am Asn Univ Prof. *Res:* Anatomy of muskrat; problems in comparative anatomy. *Mailing Add:* Dept of Biol Univ of Santa Clara Santa Clara CA 95053

FLAIM, KATHRYN ERSKINE, b Oakland, Calif, Nov 5, 49; m 75; c 2. PHYSIOLOGY. *Educ:* Univ Calif, Davis, BS, 71, PhD(physiol), 75. *Prof Exp:* res fel physiol, 75-78, res assoc, 78-81, ASST PROF PHYSIOL, MILTON S HERSHEY MED CTR, PA STATE UNIV, 81- *Res:* Roles of hormones in controlling protein metabolism in liver and skeletal muscle. *Mailing Add:* Dept of Physiol Hershey Med Ctr Pa State Univ Hershey PA 17033

FLAIM, STEPHEN FREDERICK, b San Jose, Calif, May 28, 48; m 75. PHYSIOLOGY. *Educ:* Univ Santa Clara, BS, 70, sec credential, 71; Univ Calif, Davis, PhD(physiol), 75. *Prof Exp:* Res assoc, Univ Calif, Davis, 71-72 & 73-75, teaching asst, 72-73; Fel physiol, 75-78, ASST PROF MED & PHYSIOL, SCH MED, PA STATE UNIV, 78- *Concurrent Pos:* Adj instr, Sch Med, Pa State Univ, 75-78. *Mem:* Am Physiol Soc; fel Am Col Clin Pharmacol; AAAS; Am Asn Univ Profs; Am Heart Asn. *Res:* Regulation of the peripheral circulation in health and disease. *Mailing Add:* Div of Cardiol Hershey Med Ctr Sch of Med Pa State Univ Hershey PA 17033

FLAIM, THOMAS ALFRED, b Paris, Tex, July 11, 46; m 70; c 2. MATERIALS SCIENCE, SURFACE ANALYSIS. *Educ:* Univ Mo-Rolla, BS, 68, MS, 70, PhD(mat sci), 71; Univ Detroit, MBA, 74. *Prof Exp:* STAFF RES ENGR, RES LABS, GEN MOTORS CORP, 71- *Concurrent Pos:* Adj prof mgt sci, Interpersonal & Pub Commun Dept, Cent Mich Univ, 73-; chmn, Troy Bldg Code Adv Comt, 75-76. *Mem:* Am Ceramic Soc; Am Vacuum Soc; Sigma Xi; Am Inst Physics. *Res:* Aluminum alloy processing and joining; surface studies of high temperature oxidation of metals and alloys and studies of brake friction and rotor materials; physics of the solid-solid interface. *Mailing Add:* 5072 Blair Dr Troy MI 48098

FLAJSER, STEVEN HENRY, b Rome, Italy, Dec 5, 43; US citizen; m; c 2. INTERDISCIPLINARY SCIENCES, SCIENCE POLICY. *Educ:* Univ Calif, Berkeley, BS, 65; Univ Wash, PhD(chem), 70. *Prof Exp:* Res asst, Dept Chem, Univ Wash, 65-70, res assoc, Social Mgt Technol Prog, 70-73, res asst prof, 73-74, asst prof, 74-75; PROF STAFF MEM SCI POLICY, US SENATE, COMMERCE COMT, 75- *Concurrent Pos:* Mem, Seattle 2000 Comn, 72-73, Gov Alternatives Wash Comt, 74-75; consult several pvt corps & govt agencies, 72-75. *Mem:* Am Chem Soc; World Future Soc; AAAS. *Res:* Technology assessment; futures; energy policy and oceans policy; technological innovation; space policy; materials policy. *Mailing Add:* Comt on Commerce 5202 Dirksen Senate Off Bldg Washington DC 20510

FLAKE, JOHN C, b Goliad, Tex, Mar 13, 14; m 42. DAIRY SCIENCE. *Educ:* Univ Tenn, BSA, 36; Purdue Univ, MS, 37; Univ Wis, PhD(dairy indust), 40. *Prof Exp:* Asst dir, 40-55, DIR SANIT STANDARDS, EVAPORATED MILK ASN, 55-, EXEC V PRES, 73- *Mem:* Am Dairy Sci Asn; Inst Food Technologists; Int Asn Milk, Food & Environ Sanitarians. *Res:* Dairy bacteriology and chemistry; activated flavor in irradiated milk. *Mailing Add:* Evap Milk Asn PO Box 188 Rockville MD 20850

FLAKS, JOEL GEORGE, b New York, NY, Oct 20, 27; m 61; c 2. BIOCHEMISTRY. *Educ:* Brooklyn Col, BA, 50; Univ Pa, PhD(biochem), 57. *Prof Exp:* Asst instr biochem, Univ Pa, 51-53; instr, Mass Inst Technol, 55-57; Damon Runyon Mem Fund fel, 57-58; from instr to assoc prof, 58-73, PROF BIOCHEM, SCH MED, UNIV PA, 73- *Concurrent Pos:* USPHS career develop award, 61-70; consult microbial chem study sect, NIH, 69-73; ed, Antimicrobial Agents & Chemother, 71-; Fogarty Sr Int fel, Imp Cancer Res Fund, 77-78. *Mem:* AAAS; Am Chem Soc; Am Soc Biol Chemists; Am Soc Microbiol; Genetics Soc Am. *Res:* Purine and pyrimidine biosynthesis and metabolism; microbial metabolism and alterations induced by bacteriophage infection; antimetabolite action; ribosome structure, function and genetics. *Mailing Add:* Dept of Biochem Univ of Pa Sch of Med Philadelphia PA 19174

FLAM, ERIC, b Vienna, Austria, Feb 14, 35; US citizen; m 63; c 2. BIOMEDICAL ENGINEERING, CHEMICAL ENGINEERING. *Educ:* City Col New York, BChE, 56; Southern Methodist Univ, MS, 61; NY Univ, PhD(biomed eng), 68. *Prof Exp:* Test engr aerospace, LTV Industs, 58-60; mat scientist electronics, Tex Instruments, Inc, 60-62; proj engr, Gen Precision Div, Singer Corp, 62-63; res scientist, Biomed Eng, Res Div, Johnson & Johnson, 68-74, group leader, 74-76, sr group leader, 76-80; MGR, RES & DEVELOP, BARD HOME HEALTH DIV, C R BARD, INC, 80- *Concurrent Pos:* Adj lectr, Rutgers Univ, 70-71 & Polytech Inst NY, 71; res dir, Breast Exam Bras, Inc, 74-; adj asst prof, Rutgers Med Sch, Col Med & Dent NJ, 77- *Mem:* NY Acad Sci; Am Thermographic Soc; Biomed Eng Soc; Am Soc Testing & Mat. *Res:* Biomaterials and connective tissues; biomechanics and support systems; absorbents; menstrual protection and fluid management; diagnostics and temperature measurement, hemostasis, ostomy management, incontinence control, wound management. *Mailing Add:* 29 Ainsworth Ave East Brunswick NJ 08816

FLAMMAN, M MURIEL, b Crafton, Pa, Aug 23, 07. BOTANY. *Educ:* Seton Hill Col, BA, 30; Univ Pittsburgh, MS, 35, PhD(bot), 44. *Prof Exp:* Instr biol, 30-44, from asst prof to assoc prof bot, 44-52, dean col, 52-68, DEAN ADMIN, SETON HILL COL, 68- *Res:* Bacteriology; biology. *Mailing Add:* Seton Hill Col Greensburg PA 15601

FLAMMANG, RICHARD ALAN, b Los Angeles, Calif, June 1, 46. THEORETICAL ASTROPHYSICS, RELATIVISTIC ASTROPHYSICS. *Educ:* Calif Inst Technol, BS, 68, PhD(physics), 82; Harvard Univ, AM, 71. *Prof Exp:* Teaching asst & res asst, Calif Inst Technol, 74-81; FEL, ASTRON, UNIV TEX, 81- *Res:* Accretion into black holes. *Mailing Add:* Dept Astron Univ Tex Austin TX 78712

FLAMMER, GORDON H(ANS), b St Johns, Ariz, June 9, 26; m 49; c 6. CIVIL ENGINEERING. *Educ:* Utah State Univ, BS, 52, MS, 53; Univ Minn, PhD(civil eng), 58. *Prof Exp:* Asst, Utah State Univ, 52-53; asst, Univ Minn, 53-55, instr civil eng, 55-58; from asst prof to assoc prof, 58-64, PROF CIVIL ENG, UTAH STATE UNIV, 64- *Concurrent Pos:* Prof, Asian Inst Technol, 66-67, acad dean, 67-68; vis prof, Stanford Univ, 70-71. *Mem:* Am Soc Civil Engrs; Am Soc Eng Educ. *Res:* Fluid mechanics; hydrodynamics; hydrology; hydraulic models; education research and methodology. *Mailing Add:* Dept Civil Eng Utah State Univ Logan UT 84321

FLANAGAN, CARROLL EDWARD, b Price Co, Wis, Dec 18, 11; m 39; c 2. MATHEMATICS. *Educ:* Univ Wis-Oshkosh, EdB, 33; Univ Wis, PhM, 43, PhD(math educ, statist), 60. *Prof Exp:* Prin, Waukau State Graded Sch, Wis, 33-36, teacher high sch, 36-42; instr math, Univ Wis-Superior, 42-44; from instr to assoc prof, 46-60, dir lib arts & sec educ, 50-63, PROF MATH, UNIV WIS-WHITEWATER, 60-, COORDR SEC EDUC, 63- *Concurrent Pos:* Math curric consult, 38- & modern math elem schs, 62-; tech consult math, Northern Nigeria Teacher Educ Proj, 65-68. *Mem:* Am Math Soc; Math Asn Am; Nat Coun Teachers Math. *Res:* Mathematics curriculum; algebra. *Mailing Add:* Dept of Math Univ Wis-Whitewater Whitewater WI 53190

FLANAGAN, CHARLES LARKIN, b Chicago, Ill, July 3, 26; m 57; c 1. INTERNAL MEDICINE. *Educ:* Univ Chicago, PhB, 47, MD, 51. *Prof Exp:* Resident med, Univ Chicago, 52-55; from instr to asst prof, 56-62, ASSOC PROF MED, NORTHWESTERN UNIV, CHICAGO, 62- *Concurrent Pos:* Attend physician, Northwestern Mem Hosp; dir Army med res proj, Ill, 54-56; med consult to pres, Chicago Bd Health, 62-; pvt pract, 62-73; asst dir med serv, Int Harvester Co, 73- *Mem:* AAAS; Am Fedn Clin Res. *Res:* Renal tubular function. *Mailing Add:* 720 N Michigan Ave Chicago IL 60611

FLANAGAN, JAMES L(OTON), b Greenwood, Miss, Aug 26, 25. ELECTRICAL ENGINEERING. *Educ:* Miss State Univ, BS, 48; Mass Inst Technol, SM, 50, ScD(elec eng), 55. *Prof Exp:* Res engr, Acoust Lab, Mass Inst Technol, 48-50, 53-54; asst prof elec eng, Miss State Univ, 50-52; electronic scientist, US Air Force Cambridge Res Ctr, 54-57; mem tech staff, 57-61, head speech & auditory res dept, 61-67, HEAD ACOUST RES DEPT, BELL TEL LABS, 67- *Mem:* Nat Acad Eng; fel Acoust Soc Am (pres, 78-79); fel Inst Elec & Electronics Engrs. *Res:* Digital communications; optimal coding of speech signals; acoustic theory of speech production; psychoacoustics of speech perception; digital filtering; computer simulation. *Mailing Add:* Acoust Res Dept Bell Tel Labs Murray Hill NJ 07974

FLANAGAN, PATRICK WILLIAM, b Dublin, Ireland, Nov 21, 42; div; c 3. MYCOLOGY, ADMINISTRATION RESEARCH. *Educ:* Dublin Univ, BSc, 64; McGill Univ, Montreal, PhD(bot), 68. *Prof Exp:* Asst prof bot, Dept Biol, Univ Alaska, 68-71, assoc prof bot/microbiol, 71-74 & Inst Arctic Biol, 72-74; sr lectr microbiol, Univ Col Galway, Ireland, 74-76; assoc prof microbiol, 76-78, PROF MICBROBIAL ECOL, INST ARCTIC BIOL, UNIV ALASKA, 78- *Concurrent Pos:* Mem, Decomposition/Microbiol Steering Comt, Int Biol Prog, 71-74, Tundra Decomposition/Microbiol Working Comt, 71-75; prin investr, var grants, 71-75, 75-79, 79-82. *Mem:* Am Bot Soc; Can Bot Soc; Am Mycol Soc; Brit Mycol Soc; Am Ecol Soc. *Res:* Microbial ecology of soils, forest floors and northern aquatic environments; microbial physiology; nutrient cycling; cytogenetics of fungi and genetic manipulation of fungi; aeromicrobiology (spores as ice nuclei and sublimation nuclei). *Mailing Add:* Inst Arctic Biol Univ Alaska Fairbanks AK 99701

FLANAGAN, R(ALPH) C(LARENCE), mechanical engineering, see previous edition

FLANAGAN, ROBERT JOSEPH, b Alexandria, Minn, Aug 10, 24; m 47, 77; c 7. SYSTEM ANALYSIS. *Educ:* Univ NMex, BS, 49. *Prof Exp:* Math analyst, Sandia Corp, 48-49, supvr data reduction, 49-52, staff mem systs anal, 52-57; res engr, Dikewood Industs, Inc, 57-59, sr res engr, 59-64, dir, 64-69, vpres, 69-72 & sr vpres, 72-80; SR VPRES, HANCOCK/DIKEWOOD SERV, INC, 80- *Mem:* Opers Res Soc Am; Soc Advan Med Systs; AAAS. *Res:* Administration of systems analyses of military and civil systems; current emphasis on health systems. *Mailing Add:* 1009 Bradbury Dr SE Albuquerque NM 87106

FLANAGAN, STEVEN DOUGLAS, b Columbus, Ga, Sept 9, 48; m 74. NEUROSCIENCES, MEMBRANE STRUCTURE & FUNCTION. *Educ:* Calif Inst Technol, BSc, 70; Univ Calif, San Diego, PhD(biol), 75. *Prof Exp:* HEAD, MEMBRANE NEUROCHEM SECT, CITY OF HOPE RES INST, 77- *Mem:* Soc Neurosci. *Res:* The biochemical structure of synopses, with the long term aim of determining the supramolecular basis for synaptic activity and modulation. *Mailing Add:* Div Neurosci City Hope Res Inst 1450 E Duarte Rd Duarte CA 91010

FLANAGAN, TED BENJAMIN, b Oakland, Calif, July 11, 29; m 55; c 3. PHYSICAL CHEMISTRY. *Educ:* Univ Calif, Berkeley, BS, 51; Univ Wash, PhD(phys chem), 55. *Prof Exp:* Res chemist, Picatinny Arsenal, NJ, 55-57; fel phys chem, Queen's Univ, Belfast, 57-59; assoc physicist, Brookhaven Nat Lab, 59-61; from asst prof to assoc prof phys chem, 61-68, PROF PHYS CHEM, UNIV VT, 68- *Concurrent Pos:* Fulbright res scholar, Univ Münster, 67-68; Petrol Res Fund int fac award, 67-68; Fulbright res scholar, Univ Utrecht, 77-78. *Mem:* Am Chem Soc; Am Phys Soc; Faraday Soc. *Res:* Heterogeneous catalysis; hydrogen storage in solids; hydrogen in Palladium and its alloys; kinetics of the thermal decomposition of solids; diffusion in solids. *Mailing Add:* Dept of Chem Univ of Vt Burlington VT 05405

FLANAGAN, THEODORE ROSS, b New York, NY, May 9, 20; m 43; c 1. AGRONOMY. *Educ:* Rutgers Univ, BS, 48; Pa State Col, MS, 50, PhD, 51. *Prof Exp:* Plant mgr & field agronomist, Grange League Fedn, 51-52; asst prof plant & soil sci & asst agronomist, Univ Vt, 53-72, assoc prof plant & soil sci, 72-76, specialist, garden, crop & weeds, 76-82; RETIRED. *Mem:* AAAS; Weed Sci Soc Am; Am Soc Agron. *Res:* Cold resistance of Ladino clover; development and adaptation of birdsfoot trefoil; herbicides; weed control-extension; environmental pollution; ecology; natural resources. *Mailing Add:* Dept of Plant & Soil Sci Univ of Vt Burlington VT 05401

FLANAGAN, THOMAS DONALD, b Providence, RI, Jan 6, 35; m 55; c 5. VIROLOGY, IMMUNOLOGY. *Educ:* Univ RI, AB, 57, MS, 62; State Univ NY Buffalo, PhD(virol), 65; Am Bd Med Microbiol, dipl, 78. *Prof Exp:* Chemist, US Rubber Co, 56-60; res asst, Dept Animal Path, Univ RI, 60-62; from instr to assoc prof, 66-76, PROF MICROBIOL, STATE UNIV NY BUFFALO, 76- *Concurrent Pos:* Fel, Dept Bacteriol & Immunol, State Univ NY Buffalo, 65-66; vis res worker, Dept Tumor Biol, Karolinska Inst, Sweden, 73-74; vis prof microbiol, Univ Linkoping, Sweden, 74; dir, Erie County Virol Lab, 74. *Mem:* Am Soc Microbiol; fel Am Acad Microbiol; Am Asn Immunol; Tissue Cult Asn. *Res:* Biology of paramyxoviruses; cellular response to virus infection. *Mailing Add:* Dept of Microbiol State Univ of NY Med Sch Buffalo NY 14214

FLANAGAN, THOMAS LEO, b Philadelphia, Pa, Sept 25, 16; m 47; c 9. BIOCHEMISTRY. *Educ:* Drexel Univ, dipl, 43. *Prof Exp:* Technician anal chem, Rohm and Haas Co, 35-38, jr chemist, 38-41, chemist anal & textile chem, 41-47; jr scientist anal chem, 48, biochemist, 48-50, sr scientist, 50-56, group leader biochem res, 56-62, asst sect head biochem serv, 62-67, from asst sect head to sect head, Drug Metab Sect, 63-67, assoc dir biochem, 67-75, ASSOC DIR BIOL SCI, SMITH KLINE & FRENCH LABS, 75- *Mem:* Am Chem Soc; NY Acad Sci. *Res:* Drug metabolism, biochemical methods development; isotope tracer studies; instrumental methodology. *Mailing Add:* Drug Metab Sect 1500 Spring Garden St Philadelphia PA 19101

FLANAGAN, WILLIAM F(RANCIS), b Cambridge, Mass, Apr 27, 27; m 58; c 5. PHYSICAL METALLURGY. *Educ:* Mass Inst Technol, SB, 51, SM, 53, ScD(metall), 59. *Prof Exp:* Asst, Mass Inst Technol, 51-53, 55-59, instr phys metall, 53-55; asst prof metall eng, Univ Wash, 59-66; sr res physicist, Gen Motors Res Lab, 66-68; assoc prof mat sci & eng, 68-72, PROF MAT SCI & ENG, VANDERBILT UNIV, 72- *Mem:* Am Soc Metals; Am Inst Mining, Metall & Petrol Eng. *Res:* Materials engineering embracing solid state physics; deformation mechanisms; physics of solids; materials resources policy. *Mailing Add:* Box 17 Sta B Vanderbilt Univ Nashville TN 37235

FLANDERS, CLIFFORD AUTEN, b Rutherford, NJ, May 3, 11; m 38; c 4. ANALYTICAL CHEMISTRY. *Educ:* Wagner Col, BS, 33; Columbia Univ, MA, 34; WVa Univ, PhD(agr biochem), 51. *Prof Exp:* Asst instr chem, Wagner Col, 35-36; instr, NC State Col, 36-37 & 38-40; instr, Univ Louisville, 40-45; asst biochemist, Exp Sta, WVa Univ, 45-51; dir chem prod, Fisher Sci Co, 51-66; assoc prof chem, Pace Univ, 66-69; assoc prof chem, William Paterson Col NJ, 69-81; INSTR, MORRIS COUNTY COL, DOVER, 81- *Mem:* Sigma Xi; Am Chem Soc; Am Inst Chemists. *Res:* Analytical chemistry. *Mailing Add:* 81 Beechwood Dr Wayne NJ 07470

FLANDERS, HARLEY, b Chicago, Ill, Sept 13, 25; div; c 2. PURE MATHEMATICS, APPLIED MATHEMATICS. *Educ:* Univ Chicago, BS, 46, MS, 47, PhD(math), 49. *Prof Exp:* Bateman fel math, Calif Inst Technol, 49-51; from instr to assoc prof math, Univ Calif, 51-60; prof math, Purdue Univ, 60-70; prof math, Tel-Aviv Univ, 70-77; PROF MATH, FLA ATLANTIC UNIV, 78- *Concurrent Pos:* NSF fel, Cambridge Univ, 57-58; ed-in-chief, Am Math Monthly, 68- *Honors & Awards:* Lester Ford Award, 69. *Mem:* Am Math Soc; Math Asn Am (vpres, 59-61); London Math Soc; AAAS; Inst Elec & Electronics Engrs. *Res:* Algebra; differential geometry; electric circuit theory. *Mailing Add:* Dept of Math Fla Atlantic Univ Boca Raton FL 33431

FLANDERS, ROBERT B(ERNARD), b Boston, Mass, Nov 12, 15; m 76; c 5. NUCLEAR ENGINEERING. *Educ:* Tufts Univ, BS, 38; Mass Inst Technol, SM, 58. *Prof Exp:* Asst qual anal, Tufts Univ, 36-38; asst fire assayer, Eastern Smelting & Refining Co, 38-39; asst chem engr, Whitlock Coil Pipe Co, 39-40; plant engr, Kelbar Powder Co, 40; asst chem engr, Nat Fireworks Co, Am Fireworks Co, 40-45; chem engr, Process Eng Co, 45-46; actg chief engr, M & C Nuclear, Inc Div, Tex Instruments, Inc, 57-60, res staff proj mgr, 60-67; nuclear engr, Stone & Webster Eng Corp, 67-78; MGR APPL ENG, NRC INC, 78- *Mem:* Am Nuclear Soc; Am Inst Chem Engrs; Am Soc Mech Engrs. *Res:* Nuclear materials research and development; chemical engineering; metallurgy; ceramics; electrochemistry; radiochemistry; nuclear safety; nuclear power plant engineering; licensing; economic evaluation; engineered safeguards; chemistry process equipment design. *Mailing Add:* NRC Inc 45 Industrial Pl Newton MA 02164

FLANDERS, ROBERT VERN, b Orange, Calif, Oct 28, 47; m 69; c 2. BIOLOGICAL CONTROL. *Educ:* Calif State Polytech Univ, Pomona, BS, 74; Univ Calif, Riverside, MS, 76, PhD(biol control), 79. *Prof Exp:* Res assoc, Entom Dept, Univ Calif, Riverside, 74, res asst, Div Biol Control, 74-79; ASST PROF, DEPT ENTOM, PURDUE UNIV, 79- *Mem:* Entom Soc Am; Int Orgn Biol Control; Entom Soc Can. *Res:* Biological and ecological interactions between arthropod pests, insects and/or mites, and their indigenous or exotic natural enemies, parasitious, predators and/or pathogens, in agricultural ecosystems. *Mailing Add:* Dept Entom Purdue Univ West Lafayette IN 47907

FLANDRO, GARY A, b Salt Lake City, Utah, Mar 30, 34; m 61; c 1. MECHANICAL & AERONAUTICAL ENGINEERING. *Educ:* Univ Utah, BS, 57; Calif Inst Technol, MS, 60, PhD(aeronaut), 67. *Prof Exp:* Sci teacher, Liahona Col, Tonga, SPac, 59; res engr, Jet Propulsion Lab, Calif Inst Technol, 60; sr proj engr, Sperry Utah Co, 60-61; instr mech eng, Univ Utah, 61-63; teaching asst aeronaut, Calif Inst Technol, 63-64, sr res engr, Jet Propulsion Lab, 64-66, mem tech staff, 66-67; assoc prof mech eng, 67-76, PROF MECH & INDUST ENG, UNIV UTAH, 76- *Mem:* Am Inst Aeronaut & Astronaut. *Res:* Acoustic combustion instability and internal ballistics of rocket motors; astrodynamics; low thrust trajectory and mission analysis for interplanetary space missions. *Mailing Add:* Dept of Mech Eng Univ of Utah Salt Lake City UT 84112

FLANIGAN, EVERETT, b Atlanta, Ga, Apr 10, 44; m 68; c 4. ORGANIC CHEMISTRY, BIOCHEMISTRY. *Educ:* Clark Col, BSc, 65; Howard Univ, MSc, 70; Wash Univ, PhD(molecular biol-biochem), 71. *Prof Exp:* Res scientist organ chem, Armour Pharmaceut Co, 74-77, head anal res, 77-78; SECT HEAD PEPTIDE CHEM, REVLON HEALTH CARE RES & DEVELOP, 78- *Concurrent Pos:* Fel, Brookhaven Nat Lab, 71-74, vis scientist, 74-75; grant reviewer, Comprehensive Assistance Undergrad Sci Educ, NSF, 78, 79 & 81. *Mem:* Sigma Xi; AAAS; NY Acad Sci. *Res:* Analytical peptide-protein; isolation and purification of peptide hormones. *Mailing Add:* Revlon Health Care Res & Develop 1 Scarsdale Rd Tuckahoe NY 10707

FLANIGAN, NORBERT JAMES, b Green Bay, Wis, Aug 12, 18; m 46; c 6. ANATOMY. *Educ:* St Norbert Col, AB, 40; Univ Iowa, MS, 53, PhD, 58. *Prof Exp:* Instr biol, St Francis Col Col, Pa, 46-47 & Creighton Univ, 48-52; instr zool, Univ Iowa, 52-55; instr anat, Sch Med, Univ Southern Calif, 55-58, asst prof biol, 58-63; from asst prof to assoc prof, 63-68, chmn dept, 65-70, PROF BIOL, ST NORBERT COL, 68- *Mem:* AAAS; Am Asn Anat; Am Soc Zool; Int Asn Aquatic Animal Med. *Res:* Comparative and functional neuroanatomy, especially Cetacea; Cetacean behavior. *Mailing Add:* Div of Natural Sci St Norbert Col De Pere WI 54115

FLANIGAN, STEVENSON, b Lebanon, Tenn, July 2, 26; m 48; c 3. MEDICINE. *Educ:* Wash Univ, AB, 49, MD, 53. *Prof Exp:* From asst prof to assoc prof, Sch Med, Yale Univ, 61-67; PROF NEUROSURG, MED CTR, UNIV ARK, LITTLE ROCK, 67-, HEAD DEPT, 72- *Concurrent Pos:* Consult, Vet Admin Hosp, West Haven, Conn, 61-; mem, Forum Univ Neurosurgeons, 64- *Mem:* Am Asn Neurol Surg; Cong Neurol Surg; Am Col Surg; Asn Res Nerv & Ment Dis. *Res:* Biology of glial tumor cells; electrophysiology of basal nuclear groups and the urinary bladder; clinical neurosurgery. *Mailing Add:* Dept of Neurosurg Univ of Ark Med Ctr Little Rock AR 72201

FLANIGAN, VIRGIL JAMES, JR, b Higginsville, Mo, Dec 31, 38; m 64; c 2. MECHANICAL ENGINEERING, SYSTEMS ENGINEERING. *Educ:* Mo Sch Mines, BSME, 60, MSME, 62; Univ Mo-Rolla, PhD(mech eng), 68. *Prof Exp:* Prod engr, Western Elec Co, 60-61; instr, Mech Eng Dept, Mo Sch Mines, 62-64; res engr, Boeing Co, 64-65; from instr to assoc prof, 65-77, PROF MECH ENG, UNIV MO-ROLLA, 77- *Concurrent Pos:* Consult, var law firms, 72-, Naval Weapons Ctr, 73, Noranda Aluminum & Sverdrup & Parcel & Assocs, 72- *Mem:* Am Soc Mech Engrs; Forest Prod Res Soc; Sigma Xi. *Res:* Energy research with primary emphasis on coal and biomass utilization including direct combustion, gasification and pyrolysis. *Mailing Add:* Dept of Mech Eng Univ of Mo-Rolla Rolla MO 65401

FLANIGAN, WILLIAM FRANCIS, JR, b Montreal, Que, Nov 25, 39; US citizen; m 68; c 1. COMMAND CONTROL AND COMMUNICATIONS, ANTENNA DESIGN. *Educ:* Clarkson Col Technol, BS, 61; Cornell Univ, MBA, 63; George Washington Univ, MA, 68; Univ Chicago, PhD(biol psychol), 73. *Prof Exp:* Financial analyst, Securities & Exchange Comn, 63-66; res psychologist, Nat Naval Med Ctr, 68; eng res psychologist, 73-78, SR ELECTRONIC ENGR, NAVAL OCEAN SYSTS, 79- *Mem:* AAAS; Armed Forces Com & Electronics Asn; Inst Elec & Electronics Engrs; NY Acad Sci. *Res:* Vulnerability reduction of communication, navigation, and electronic warfare antennas and electronic systems; nonconventional design, modification and reconfiguration. *Mailing Add:* Naval Ocean Systs Ctr Code 8122 San Diego CA 92132

FLANIGAN, WILLIAM J, b Hot Springs, Ark, June 2, 30; c 5. MEDICINE, PHYSIOLOGY. *Educ:* Univ Ark, BS, 53, MD, 55. *Prof Exp:* Med house officer, Peter Bent Brigham Hosp, 55-56; asst resident med, Sch Med, Univ Ark, 56; asst, Peter Bent Brigham Hosp, 59-63; from asst prof to assoc prof, 63-72, PROF MED, SCH MED, UNIV ARK, LITTLE ROCK, 72-, DIR DIV DIALYSIS & TRANSPLANTATION, 74- *Concurrent Pos:* Res fels, Harvard Med Sch, 59 & 60-61; res fel, Peter Bent Brigham Hosp, 61-63 & NSF, 60-62; Am Heart Asn adv res fel, 62-63; chmn coun dialysis & transplantation, Nat Kidney Found, 73-74. *Res:* Renal physiology and tissue transplantation. *Mailing Add:* 4301 W Markham Little Rock AR 72205

FLANIGEN, EDITH MARIE, b Buffalo, NY, Jan 28, 29. INORGANIC CHEMISTRY. *Educ:* D'Youville Col, BA, 50; Syracuse Univ, MS, 52. *Prof Exp:* Asst, Syracuse Univ, 50-51; res chemist, Tonawanda Res Lab, Linde Co, 52-60, sr res chemist, Linde Div Labs, Union Carbide Corp, 60-62, from res assoc to sr res assoc, 67-69, sr res scientist, 69-73, CORP RES FEL, LINDE DIV LABS, UNION CARBIDE CORP, 73- *Mem:* AAAS; Mineral Soc Am; Am Chem Soc. *Res:* Inorganic and physical chemistry research in crystalline molecular sieves, zeolites adsorbents, and catalysts; hydrothermal synthesis of mineral phases, particularly silicates; crystal growth. *Mailing Add:* Linde Div Labs Union Carbide Corp Tarrytown Tech Ctr Tarrytown NY 10591

FLANK, WILLIAM H, b Akron, Ohio, Jan 7, 32; m 56; c 2. MOLECULAR SIEVES, CATALYSIS. *Educ:* Temple Univ, AB, 58; Univ Del, PhD(chem), 65. *Prof Exp:* Res chemist, Houdry Labs, Air Prod & Chem Inc, 58-71; res chemist, 71-72, sr staff chemist, 72-77, TECHNOL CONSULT, MOLECULAR SIEVE DEPT, UNION CARBIDE CORP, 77- *Concurrent Pos:* Lectr, Temple Univ, 67-70. *Mem:* Clay Minerals Soc; Am Chem Soc; Catalysis Soc; Int Zeolite Asn; Int Confedn Thermal Anal. *Res:* Zeolite chemistry; heterogeneous catalysis; surface science, clays; preparation, characterization and application of zeolites and catalytic materials; adsorption and catalytic mechanisms; thermoanalytical and other physicochemical characterization techniques. *Mailing Add:* Molecular Sieve Dept Union Carbide Corp Tarrytown Tech Ctr Tarrytown NY 10591

FLANNAGAN, JOHN FULLAN, b Glasgow, Scotland, Jan 10, 40; Can citizen; m 61; c 3. FRESHWATER BIOLOGY, TOXICOLOGY. *Educ:* Paisley Col Sci & Technol, Scotland, HNC, 66; Inst Biol, London, MIBiol, 74. *Prof Exp:* Sr technician, Dept Zool, Glasgow Univ, 61-66, Can Land Inventory Proj, Govt Man, 66-67 & Freshwater Inst, Fisheries Res Bd Can, 67-72; PROJ LEADER, FRESHWATER INST, ENVIRON CAN, 72- *Concurrent Pos:* Mem, Alta Blackfly Control Res Comt, 74-; chmn, 3rd Int Mayfly Symp Orgn Comt, 75-79. *Mem:* Sigma Xi; Entom Soc Can; Can Coun Freshwater Fisheries Res; NAm Benthological Soc; Int Limnol Asn. *Res:* Investigation and improvement of sampling methodology for macrobenthic research; investigation of effect of insecticides on freshwater ecosystems; development of environmental protocols to assess environmental impact of toxic substances; ecology of aquatic invertebrates. *Mailing Add:* Freshwater Inst 501 University Crescent Winnipeg MB R3T 2N3 Can

FLANNELLY, WILLIAM G, b Scranton, Pa, May 15, 31; m 55; c 2. STRUCTURAL DYNAMICS. *Educ:* Rensselaer Polytech Inst, BS, 54. *Prof Exp:* Mech engr, Consol Molded Prod Corp, Pa, 54-55 & Sylvania Elec Prod Co, Pa, 55-56; design engr, Hamilton Standard Div, United Aircraft Corp, 56-57; stress engr, 57-58, dynamicist, 58-59, 60-63, test engr, 59-60, asst chief vibrations res, 63-69, staff res engr, 69-73, prin res engr, 73-80, PRES CHIEF RES ENGR, KAMAN, 80- *Mem:* Sigma Xi. *Res:* Structural dynamics system identification; structural vibrations analyses; antiresonant theory; vibration control instruments; applied matrix algebra. *Mailing Add:* 108 Hilton Dr South Windsor CT 06074

FLANNERY, BRIAN PAUL, b Utica, NY, July 30, 48; m 70; c 2. APPLIED MATHEMATICS. *Educ:* Princeton Univ, BA, 70; Univ Calif, Santa Cruz, PhD(astrophysics), 74. *Prof Exp:* Res assoc, Inst Advan Study, Princeton, 74-76; asst prof astron, Harvard Univ, 76-80, assoc prof, 80; SR STAFF PHYSICIST, EXXON RES & ENG CO, 80- *Mem:* Am Astron Soc; Int Astron Union. *Res:* Stellar structure and evolution; radiative transfer fluids; climate. *Mailing Add:* Exxon Res & Eng PO Box 45 Linden NJ 07036

FLANNERY, JOHN B, JR, b Providence, RI, Mar 15, 41; m 68; c 2. PHYSICAL CHEMISTRY. *Educ:* St Vincent Col, BS, 62; Rensselaer Polytech Inst, PhD(phys chem), 65. *Prof Exp:* Chemist, Phys Res Lab, Dow Chem Co, Mich, 64; from assoc scientist to sr scientist, Res Labs, 65-74, mgr optical mat & devices res, 71-74, mgr, Mat Sci Lab, 74-80, MGR TECH STRATEGY, XEROX CORP, ROCHESTER, 80- *Mem:* AAAS; Am Chem Soc; Soc Info Display. *Res:* Information display; optical systems; photochemistry; thermochemistry; liquid crystals; spectroscopy; organic synthesis; dyes and pigments; electrooptics; optical data storage; photochromism; thermochromism. *Mailing Add:* 1258 Wildflower Dr Webster NY 14580

FLANNERY, MARTIN RAYMOND, b Co Derry, Northern Ireland, Jan 8, 41; m 67; c 4. ATOMIC PHYSICS, THEORETICAL PHYSICS. *Educ:* Queens Univ, Belfast, BSc, 61, PhD(atomic & molecular physics), 64. *Prof Exp:* Lectr theoret physics, Queens Univ, 64-66; res assoc astrophys, Joint Inst Lab Astrophys, 66-67; physicist & lectr, Harvard Col Observ & Smithsonian Astrophys Observ, 68-71; from asst prof to assoc prof, 67-74, PROF PHYSICS, GA INST TECHNOL, 74- *Honors & Awards:* Cert Higher Achievement, Smithsonian Inst, 72; Monie A Ferst Award, Sigma Xi, 74 & 75. *Mem:* Fel Inst Physics London; fel Am Phys Soc; Sigma Xi; fel Inst Physics. *Res:* Theoretical studies of atomic and molecular collision processes with application to plasmas, laser fusion, astrophysics and to the laboratory. *Mailing Add:* Sch Physics Ga Inst Technol Atlanta GA 30332

FLANNERY, WILLIAM LOUIS, b Jamestown, NDak, Dec 22, 22; m 48; c 1. BACTERIOLOGY. *Educ:* Univ NDak, BA, 48; Univ Md, PhD(bact), 53. *Prof Exp:* Asst bact, Univ Md, 50-52, bacteriologist, USDA, 53; from instr to asst prof microbiol, Baylor Col Med, 53-56; prof, Med Sch, Univ El Salvador, 56-59; head dept, 59-76, PROF MICROBIOL UNIV SOUTHWESTERN LA, 59- *Concurrent Pos:* Med ed adv, Int Coop Admin, San Salvador, 56-59. *Mem:* AAAS; Am Soc Microbiol; Brit Soc Gen Microbiol. *Res:* Nutrition, metabolism and physiology of bacteria; halophilic bacteria; thermophiles. *Mailing Add:* Dept of Microbiol Univ of Southwestern La Lafayette LA 70504

FLASAR, F MICHAEL, b East St Louis, Ill, Feb 20, 46; m 69; c 1. PLANETARY PHYSICS, ASTROPHYSICS. *Educ:* Mass Inst Technol, BS, 67, PhD(physics), 72. *Prof Exp:* Res fel planetary physics, Harvard Univ, 71-75; RES SCIENTIST PLANETARY PHYSICS & ASTROPHYS, GODDARD SPACE FLIGHT CTR, NASA, 75- *Concurrent Pos:* Res assoc, Nat Res Coun, 75-77. *Mem:* Am Astron Soc. *Res:* Planetary interiors and atmospheres; extragalactic astrophysics; geophysical and astrophysical fluid dynamics. *Mailing Add:* Goddard Space Flight Ctr NASA Code 693 Greenbelt MD 20771

FLASCHEN, STEWART SAMUEL, b Berwyn, Ill, May 28, 26; m 49; c 4. SCIENCE POLICY, RESOURCE MANAGEMENT. *Educ:* Univ Ill, BS, 47; Miami Univ, MA, 48; Pa State Univ, PhD(geochem), 53. *Prof Exp:* Instr geol, Miami Univ, 47-48; mem chem res staff, Bell Tel Labs, 52-55, group supvr, Chem Res Dept, 55-59; dir res & develop, Semiconductor Prods Div, Motorola, Inc, 59-64; dir component res & develop, 64-66, dep tech dir, 66-69, V PRES & DEP GEN TECH DIR, INT TEL & TEL CORP, 69- *Mem:* AAAS; Am Chem Soc; Am Ceramic Soc; Inst Elec & Electronics Engrs; Electrochem Soc. *Res:* Solid state materials; glasses; electronic ceramics; piezoelectrics; ferroelectrics; dielectrics; semiconductors. *Mailing Add:* IT&T Corp 320 Park Ave New York NY 10022

FLASCHKA, HERMENEGILD ARVED, b Cilli, Austria, June 10, 15; US citizen; m 45; c 2. ANALYTICAL CHEMISTRY. *Educ:* Graz Univ, DrPhil, 38. *Prof Exp:* Demonstr, Graz Univ, 37-38; sci co-worker, Kaiser Wilhelm Inst, Ger, 45-46; chemist, Fa Schultz, 46-47; asst, Graz Univ, 48-49; res dir, Fa A Zankl-SOhne, Austria, 49-53; privatdozent, Graz Univ, 53; lectr, Graz Tech Univ, 53-55; head anal dept, Nat Res Ctr, Egypt, 55-57; guest prof, Univ NC, 57-58; from assoc prof to prof chem, Ga Inst Technol, 58-65, Regent's prof chem, 65-81; RETIRED. *Concurrent Pos:* Consult, Grazer Glass Works, Austria, 50-55 & J T Baker Chem Co, NJ, 58-76; co-ed, Microchem J, 63- *Honors & Awards:* Fritz Feigl Award, Austrian Chem Soc, 53; L Gordon Mem Award, 68; Benedetti-Pichler Award, Am Microchem Soc, 81. *Mem:* Am Chem Soc; Am Microchem Soc; Austrian Chem Soc. *Res:* Ethylenediamine-tetraacetic acid and related titrations; organic reagents; indicator theories; complexes in analytical chemistry; complementary tristimulus colorimetry; long-path photometry; photometric titrations. *Mailing Add:* Dept of Chem Ga Inst of Technol Atlanta GA 30332

FLASHMAN, STUART MILTON, b Boston, Mass, Feb 14, 48. SOMATIC CELL GENETICS, PLANT TISSUE CULTURE. *Educ:* Brown Univ, AB & ScM, 69; Harvard Univ, PhD(biochem), 76. *Prof Exp:* Teaching fel biol, Harvard Univ, 70-73, res asst biochem, 73-75; res assoc, ERDA Plant Res Lab, Mich State Univ, 75-76; asst prof genetics, Sch Agr, NC State Univ, 77-80; RES BIOLOGIST, STAUFFER CHEM CO, 81- *Mem:* Am Soc Plant Pysiologists; Int Asn Plant Cell & Tissue Cult. *Res:* Application of plant somatic cell genetics to problems of crop improvements; genetic regulation in higher plants; mechanisms of genetic change in cultured plant cells. *Mailing Add:* DeGuigne Tech Ctr Stauffer Chem Co 1200 S 47th St Richmond CA 94804

FLASHNER, MARCIA S, see Steinberg, Marcia Irene

FLASHNER, MICHAEL, b Brooklyn, NY, Aug 16, 42. BIOCHEMISTRY. *Educ:* Brooklyn Col, BS, 65; Univ Mich, MA, 70, PhD(biochem), 71. *Prof Exp:* Fel microbiol, Univ Mich, 72-73; asst prof chem, 73-80, ASSOC PROF CHEM, COL ENVIRON SCI & FORESTRY, STATE UNIV NY, 80- *Mem:* Am Soc Biol Chem; Am Chem Soc; Am Soc Microbiol; Sigma Xi. *Res:* Basic enzymology; mechanisms of enzyme reactions; bacterial physiology; cell and molecular biology. *Mailing Add:* Dept of Chem Col Environ Sci & Forestry Syracuse NY 13210

FLATH, ROBERT ARTHUR, b St Louis, Mo, Mar 14, 33; m 55; c 2. NATURAL PRODUCTS CHEMISTRY. *Educ:* Concordia Teachers Col, Ill, BS, 55; Long Beach State Col, BS, 60; Univ Calif, Berkeley, PhD(org chem), 64. *Prof Exp:* RES CHEMIST FRUIT COMPOSITION INVEST, WESTERN UTILIZATION RES & DEVELOP DIV, USDA, 64- *Mem:* AAAS; Am Chem Soc; Royal Soc Chem; Am Soc Enologists; Am Phytochem Soc. *Res:* Terpenoid and food flavor chemistry; instrumental analysis. *Mailing Add:* 207 Colgate Kensington CA 94708

FLATO, JUD B, b Brooklyn, NY, Feb 21, 40; m 63; c 2. PHYSICAL CHEMISTRY. *Educ:* Polytech Inst Brooklyn, BS, 61; NY Univ, MS, 63, PhD(phys chem), 68. *Prof Exp:* Sr res chemist, Technicon, Inc, 66-67; sr res chemist, 67-71, mgr chem instrument group, 71-72, mkt mgr, 72-73, vpres, 74-81, SR VPRES, EG&G & PRINCETON APPL RES CORP, 81- *Mem:* Am Chem Soc; Instrument Soc Am; Soc Appl Spectros. *Res:* Paramagnetic resonance and absorption spectroscopy in molten salts; design and development of scientific instrumentation in electrochemistry and spectroscopy; applications of electronics to chemistry. *Mailing Add:* 244 Glenn Ave Trenton NJ 08638

FLATT, ADRIAN EDE, b Frinton, Eng, Aug 26, 21; nat US; m 55; c 1. SURGERY. *Educ:* Cambridge Univ, BA, 42, MB, BCh & MA, 45, MD, 51; FRCS, 53. *Prof Exp:* Instr anat, Cambridge Univ, 50-51 & Royal Col Surgeons Eng, 51; from asst to prof surg, London Hosp, London Univ, 51-53, asst orthop, 53-56; from asst prof to assoc prof, 57-66, PROF ORTHOP SURG, UNIV IOWA, 66- *Concurrent Pos:* Fulbright grant, 54-55; civilian consult hand surg, US Air Force Aerospace Med Hosp, Wilford Hall, Tex. *Mem:* Am Soc Surg of the Hand; Am Soc Plastic & Reconstruct Surg; AMA; fel Am Col Surg. *Res:* Reconstructive surgery of the congenitally deformed, diseased or injured hand, especially the biomechanical influence of disease or injury on hand function. *Mailing Add:* Dept of Orthop Surg Univ of Iowa Iowa City IA 52242

FLATT, HORACE PERRY, b Wichita Falls, Tex, Aug 28, 30; m 57; c 2. MATHEMATICS, COMPUTER SCIENCE. *Educ:* Rice Inst, BA, 51, MA, 53, PhD(math), 58. *Prof Exp:* Physicist, Shell Oil Co, 53; asst math, Rice Inst, 53-54 & 56-58; mathematician, Thompson-Ramo-Woolbridge, Inc, 56; sr res engr math & supvr, Programming Unit, Atomics Int Div, NAm Aviation, Inc, 58, group leader appl math, 58-61; from spec rep, Western Regional Off, to mgr, Problem Anal Dept, Systs Res & Develop Ctr, 61-66, mgr, Wash Sci Ctr, 66-69, MGR, PALO ALTO SCI CTR, IBM CORP, 69- *Mem:* Am Math Soc; Soc Indust & Appl Math. *Res:* Numerical analysis in the fields of ordinary and partial differential equations. *Mailing Add:* 12445 Greenmeadow Ln Saratoga CA 95070

FLATT, RONALD EUGENE, b Des Moines, Iowa, Dec 10, 35; m 58; c 6. PATHOLOGY, LABORATORY ANIMAL MEDICINE. *Educ:* Univ Calif, Davis, BS, 60, DVM, 62, PhD(comp path), 67; Am Col Vet Path, dipl; Am Col Lab Animal Med, dipl. *Prof Exp:* Asst prof vet path, Univ Mo-Columbia, 67-68, assoc prof, 68-70; assoc prof, 70-74, coordr lab animal med, 70-77, PROF VET PATH, VET COL, IOWA STATE UNIV, 74-, DIR LAB ANIMAL RESOURCES, 77- *Concurrent Pos:* Chief morphol path, Sinclair Comp Med Res Farm, 67-70. *Mem:* Am Asn Lab Animal Sci; Am Vet Med Asn. *Res:* Spontaneous diseases of laboratory animals. *Mailing Add:* Lab Animal Resources Iowa State Univ Ames IA 50011

FLATT, WILLIAM PERRY, b Newbern, Tenn, June 17, 31; m 49; c 2. ANIMAL NUTRITION. *Educ:* Univ Tenn, BS, 52; Cornell Univ, PhD(animal nutrit), 55. *Prof Exp:* Res resident, Dept Animal Husb, Cornell Univ, 55; dairy cattle nutritionist & head, Energy Metab Lab, Nutrit & Physiol Sect, Dairy Cattle Res Br, Agr Res Serv, USDA, 56-68, asst dir animal husbandry res div, 68-69; prof animal sci & head dept, 69-70, dir, Agr Exp Sta, 70-81, DEAN & COORDR, COL AGR, UNIV GA, 81- *Concurrent Pos:* Chmn, Southern Asn Agr Exp Sta Dirs, 74-75 & Legis Subcomt Exp Stas Comt Orgn & Policy, 76-78; mem, Bd Agr & Renewable Resources, Nat Res Coun-Nat Acad Sci, 75-78. *Honors & Awards:* Presidential Citation, USDA, 65, Superior Serv Award, 68; Hoblitzelle Nat Award Agr Res, 68. *Mem:* AAAS; Am Soc Animal Sci; Am Dairy Sci Asn; Am Inst Nutrit. *Res:* Biochemistry; physiology; energy metabolism of dairy cattle, especially the nutritive evaluation of forages and the energy requirements of cattle performing various functions; factors affecting rumen development. *Mailing Add:* 101 Conner Hall Univ of Ga Athens GA 30602

FLATTE, STANLEY MARTIN, b Los Angeles, Calif, Dec 2, 40; m 66; c 2. FLUIDS. *Educ:* Calif Inst Technol, BSc, 62; Univ Calif, Berkeley, PhD(physics), 66. *Prof Exp:* Res physicist, Lawrence Berkeley Lab, 66-71; asst prof, 71-73, assoc prof, 73-78, PROF PHYSICS, UNIV CALIF, SANTA CRUZ, 78- *Concurrent Pos:* Zero Gradient Synchrotron, Argonne Nat Lab, 73-79; Guggenheim fel, 75; vis scientist, Orgn Europ Res Nuclear, 75-76 & La Jolla Inst, 80-81; sr vis, Univ Cambridge, 81; dir, Ctr Studies Nonlinear Dynamics, La Jolla, 82- *Mem:* Am Physical Soc; Sigma Xi; fel Acoust Soc Am. *Res:* Study of wave propagation through random media, including sound in the ocean, radio waves in plasmas, light and sound in the atmosphere, for the purpose of understanding the physical processes in the media. *Mailing Add:* Natural Sci II Univ Calif Santa Cruz CA 95064

FLATTO, LEOPOLD, b Antwerp, Belg, Aug 20, 29; US citizen; m 66; c 2. MATHEMATICS. *Educ:* City Col New York, BS, 50; Johns Hopkins Univ, MA, 51; Mass Inst Technol, PhD, 55. *Prof Exp:* Mathematician, Reeves Instrument Corp, 55-57; prof math, Brooklyn Polytech Inst, 57-60; mathematician, IBM Res Ctr Yorktown Heights, 60-61; prof math, Belfer Grad Sch Sci, Yeshiva Univ, 61-79; MATHEMATICIAN, BELL LABS, 79- *Concurrent Pos:* NSF grant, 63-68; vis prof, Hebrew Univ, 68-69. *Mem:* Am Math Soc. *Res:* Mean value problems related to harmonic functions; finite reflection groups and their invariant theory; probability theory with emphasis on random walk problems; queuing theory; ergodic theory. *Mailing Add:* Bell Labs 600 Mountain Ave Murray Hill NJ 07974

FLAUGH, MICHAEL EDWARD, b Findlay, Ohio, Nov 14, 41; m 66. SYNTHETIC ORGANIC CHEMISTRY. *Educ:* Univ Dayton, BS, 63; Univ Calif, Berkeley, PhD(chem), 68. *Prof Exp:* SR CHEMIST, ELI LILLY RES LABS, 67- *Mem:* Am Chem Soc. *Res:* Synthesis of organic structures, particularly heterocyclic compounds. *Mailing Add:* 9224 Kinlock Dr Indianapolis IN 46256

FLAUTT, THOMAS JOSEPH, JR, b Glendora, Miss, Feb 8, 32. CITRUS TECHNOLOGY. *Educ:* Univ St Louis, BS, 53; Univ Calif, PhD(chem), 57. *Prof Exp:* Res chemist, 57-67, sect head, 67-72, HEAD PROD RES SECT, PROCTER & GAMBLE CO, 72- *Mem:* Int Microwave Power Inst; Am Chem Soc. *Res:* Nuclear magnetic resonance, mesmorphic phases; citrus and paper product development; microwave applications. *Mailing Add:* Winton Hill Tech Ctr 6210 Center Hill Rd Cincinnati OH 45224

FLAVIN, JOHN WILLIAM, b Boston, Mass, July 16, 14. CYTOLOGY. *Educ:* Boston Col, AB, 36, AM, 41; Fordham Univ, MS, 43; Brown Univ, PhD(biol), 54. *Prof Exp:* Instr, Cranwell Prep Sch, 43-44; instr biol, Col of Holy Cross, 53-54 & Boston Col, 54-58; from asst prof to assoc prof, 58-68, chmn dept, 62-80, PROF BIOL, COL OF HOLY CROSS, 68- *Mem:* AAAS; Am Soc Zool; NY Acad Sci. *Res:* Cytophysiology of tumor cells in spontaneous hepatomas of C3H mice. *Mailing Add:* Dept of Biol Col of the Holy Cross Worcester MA 01610

FLAVIN, MARTIN, b Chicago, Ill, Mar 18, 20. BIOCHEMISTRY. *Educ:* Stanford Univ, BA, 44; Univ Calif, MD, 47; Columbia Univ, PhD(biochem), 51. *Prof Exp:* Sr asst surgeon, Nat Heart Inst, 52-54; mem dept biochem, NY Univ, 54-56; Am Heart Asn estab investr, Dept Agr Biochem, Univ Calif, 56-57; mem enzyme sect, 57-61, med dir, 61-77, HEAD SCIENTIST, ORGANELLE BIOCHEM, NAT HEART & LUNG INST, NIH, 78- *Mem:* Am Soc Biol Chem. *Res:* Enzymatic reaction mechanisms; chemical pathways of metabolism. *Mailing Add:* Nat Heart Inst Bethesda MD 20014

FLAVIN, MICHAEL AUSTIN, b New York, NY, Nov 27, 32; m 55; c 4. ELECTRICAL ENGINEERING. *Educ:* Univ Conn, BSE, 54; Columbia Univ, MSEE, 61. *Prof Exp:* Mem tech staff commun, 54-65, dept head tel, 65-71, dir ocean technol, 71-74, dir semiconductors, 74-79, EXEC DIR BUS COMMUN, BELL LABS, INC, 79- *Mem:* Inst Elec & Electronics Engrs. *Res:* Semiconductor memory; metal oxide semiconductor integrated circuits; telephone systems. *Mailing Add:* 11900 N Pecos St Denver CO 80234

FLAWN, PETER TYRRELL, b Miami, Fla, Feb 17, 26; m 46; c 2. GEOLOGY, ACADEMIC ADMINISTRATION. *Educ:* Oberlin Col, BA, 47; Yale Univ, MS, 48, PhD(geol), 51. *Prof Exp:* Jr geologist, US Geol Surv, 48-49; res scientist & geologist, Bur Econ Geol, Univ Tex, Austin, 49-60, dir bur & prof geol, 60-70, dir div natural resources & environ & vpres acad affairs, 70-72, exec vpres, 72-73, pres, Univ Tex, San Antonio, 73-77, PROF GEOL SCI & PUB AFFAIRS, UNIV TEX, AUSTIN, 78-, PRES, 79- *Concurrent Pos:* Mem mineral resources bd & space appln bd, Nat Acad Sci-Nat Res Coun, 75- *Mem:* Nat Acad Eng; hon mem Asn Am State Geologists; fel Geol Soc Am; Am Geol Inst (dir, 67-70); Soc Econ Geologists. *Res:* Economic and environmental geology; geology of Texas and Mexico. *Mailing Add:* Univ Tex Austin TX 78712

FLAX, ALEXANDER H(ENRY), b New York, NY, Jan 18, 21; m 51; c 1. AERONAUTICAL ENGINEERING. *Educ:* NY Univ, BAeE, 40; Univ Buffalo, PhD(physics), 58. *Prof Exp:* Stress analyst, Curtiss-Wright Corp, NY, 40-44; chief aerodyn & struct, Piasecki Helicopter Corp, Philadelphia, 44-46, asst head aeromech dept, Cornell Aeronaut Lab, 46-49, head aerodyn res dept, 49-55, asst dir, 55-59; chief scientist, US Dept Air Force, 59-61; vpres-tech dir, Cornell Aeronaut Labs, 61-63; asst secy res & develop, US Dept Air Force, 64-69; vpres res, 69, PRES, INST DEFENSE ANAL, 69- *Concurrent Pos:* Instr eng sci & mgt war training, Cornell Univ, 43, 48; instr exten course, Pa State Col, 45-46; mem comt aerodyn, Nat Adv Comt Aeronaut, 52-53, mem subcomt high speed aerodyn, 54-58; mem res adv comt aircraft aerodyn, NASA, 59-63; mem adv comt, Defense Sci Bd, Dept Defense, 70-; mem, Air Force Sci Adv Bd, 70-; adv, Dept of Transp, 70-74 & Off Sci Technol, 70-73. *Honors & Awards:* Sperry Award, Inst Aeronaut Sci, 49; Air Force Except Civilian Serv Award, 61 & 69; NASA Distinguished Serv Medal, 69; von Karman Medal, NATO Adv Group for Aerospace Res & Develop, 78. *Mem:* Nat Acad Engrs; fel Am Inst Aeronaut & Astronaut. *Res:* Aircraft flutter and vibration; aero-elastic effects on stability and control; helicopter dynamics and aerodynamics; supersonic aerodynamics; missile dynamics; lifting surface theory; high temperature gas dynamics. *Mailing Add:* Inst for Defense Analysis 400 Army-Navy Dr Arlington VA 22202

FLAX, LAWRENCE, b Brooklyn, NY, May 17, 34; m 56; c 3. ACOUSTICS. *Educ:* Brooklyn Col, BS, 59; John Carroll Univ, MS, 66; Colo State Univ, PhD(physics), 69. *Prof Exp:* Theoret physicist, NASA, 60-72; physicist, Naval Res Lab, Washington, DC, 72-81; DIV HEAD, HIGH DEFINITION SONAR NAVAL COASTAL SYSTS, PANAMA CITY, FLA, 81- *Concurrent Pos:* Prof, Cuyahoga Community Col, 68-72; instr, Am Univ, 75- *Mem:* Am Phys Soc; Sigma Xi; fel Acoust Soc Am; Cong Int du Froid. *Res:* Acoustic reflection and scattering from finite bodies; acoustic field interaction with nonabsorptive and absorptive materials; fourier optical analysis of acoustic schlieren systems; theory of parametric sound transmission. *Mailing Add:* 745 Brandeis Ave Panama City FL 32405

FLAX, MARTIN HOWARD, b New York, NY, Jan 19, 28; m 55; c 3. PATHOLOGY. *Educ:* Cornell Univ, AB, 46; Columbia Univ, AM, 48, PhD, 53; Univ Chicago, MD, 55. *Prof Exp:* Asst zool, Columbia Univ, 46-49; intern, Mt Sinai Hosp, New York, 55-56; asst path, Med Sch, Univ Chicago, 56-57; chief biophys br, Armed Forces Inst Path, 57-59; res & clin fel path, Mass Gen Hosp, 59-61; from instr to assoc prof path, Harvard Med Sch, 61-70; PROF PATH & CHMN DEPT, SCH MED, TUFTS UNIV, 70- *Concurrent Pos:* Asst path, Mass Gen Hosp, 61-70, consult path B study sect, 70-74; NIH career develop award, 66- *Mem:* Am Soc Exp Path; Am Asn Path & Bact; Int Acad Path; Am Asn Immunologists. *Res:* Immunopathology; electron microscopy. *Mailing Add:* Dept of Path Tufts Univ Sch of Med Boston MA 02111

FLAX, STEPHEN WAYNE, b Denver, Colo, Apr 10, 46; m 71. ULTRASONICS, MEDICAL IMAGING. *Educ:* Univ Colo, BS, 68; Univ Wis, MS & PhD(elec eng), 75. *Prof Exp:* Asst prof eng, Portland State Univ, 75-78; SR PHYSICIST MED IMAGING, MED SYSTS GROUP, GEN ELEC, 78- *Mem:* Sigma Xi; Inst Elec & Electronics Engrs. *Res:* Medical imaging systems; basic ultrasound research and the computer modeling of ultrasound instrumentation as applied to medical applications. *Mailing Add:* Med Systs Group Gen Elec PO Box 414 NB-924 Milwaukee WI 53201

FLEAGLE, JOHN G, b US. PHYSICAL ANTHROPOLOGY, BIOLOGY. *Educ:* Yale Univ, BS, 71; Harvard Univ, MS, 73, PhD(anthrop), 76. *Prof Exp:* Res consult, Dept Nutrit, Sch Health, Harvard Univ, 73-74; lectr, 75-76, asst prof, 76-78, ASSOC PROF, DEPT ANAT SCI, STATE UNIV NY, STONY BROOK, 78- *Mem:* Am Asn Phys Anthropologists; Soc Study Evolution; Soc Vert Paleont; Am Inst Biol Sci; Am Soc Mammalogists. *Res:* Evolution and radiation of higher primates; growth and development, and evolutionary biology of primates. *Mailing Add:* Dept of Anat Sci Health Sci Ctr State Univ NY Stony Brook Stony Brook NY 11794

FLEAGLE, ROBERT GUTHRIE, b Baltimore, Md, Aug 16, 18; m 42; c 2. METEOROLOGY. *Educ:* Johns Hopkins Univ, AB, 40; NY Univ, MS, 44, PhD(physics), 49. *Prof Exp:* High sch teacher, Md, 40-41; asst, NY Univ, 46-48; from asst prof to assoc prof atmospheric sci, 48-56, chmn dept, 67-77, PROF ATMOSPHERIC SCI, UNIV WASH, 56- *Concurrent Pos:* NSF sr fel, Imp Col, Univ London, 58-59; tech asst, Off Sci & Technol, 63-64; chmn comt atmospheric sci, Nat Acad Sci, 69-73; chmn bd trustees, Univ Corp Atmospheric Res, 75-77. *Honors & Awards:* Cleveland Abbe Award, Am Meteorol Soc, 72. *Mem:* Am Meteorol Soc (pres, 81-82); Am Geophys Union; Royal Meteorol Soc. *Res:* Description and theory of large scale atmospheric motions; physics of air near the earth's surface; air sea interaction; atmospheric science policy problems. *Mailing Add:* Dept of Atmospheric Sci Univ of Wash Seattle WA 98195

FLECHSIG, ALFRED J, JR, b Tacoma, Wash. ELECTRICAL ENGINEERING. *Educ:* Wash State Univ, BS, 57, MS, 59; La State Univ, PhD(elec eng), 70. *Prof Exp:* assoc prof, 60-80, PROF ELEC ENG, WASH STATE UNIV, 80- *Mem:* Inst Elec & Electronics Engrs. *Res:* Power system protection; digital relaying. *Mailing Add:* Dept of Elec Eng Wash State Univ Pullman WA 99163

FLECHTNER, THOMAS WELCH, b Fostoria, Ohio, July 7, 43; m 67; c 2. ORGANIC CHEMISTRY, PHOTOCHEMISTRY. *Educ:* Dartmouth Col, AB, 65; Univ Wis, PhD(chem), 70. *Prof Exp:* Technician, Upjohn Co, 65; res assoc chem, Columbia Univ, 70-72; asst prof, 72-78, ASSOC PROF CHEM, CLEVELAND STATE UNIV, 78- *Concurrent Pos:* NIH res fel, 70-72. *Mem:* Am Chem Soc; AAAS. *Res:* Exploratory organic photochemistry; development of new synthetic reactions; physical organic chemistry. *Mailing Add:* Dept of Chem Cleveland State Univ Cleveland OH 44115

FLECK, ARTHUR C, b Chicago, Ill, Oct 29, 36; m 57; c 3. COMPUTER SCIENCE. *Educ:* Univ Western Mich, BS, 59; Mich State Univ, MA, 60, PhD(math), 64. *Prof Exp:* Dir prog comput, Mich State Univ, 64-65; asst prof math & comput, 65-67, assoc prof comput sci, 67-71, PROF COMPUT SCI, UNIV IOWA, 71- *Concurrent Pos:* Vis prof, Dept Appl Math & Comput Sci, Univ Va, 73-74. *Mem:* Asn Comput Mach. *Res:* Automata theory; programming languages; theory of data structures. *Mailing Add:* Comput Ctr Dept of Math Univ of Iowa Iowa City IA 52242

FLECK, GEORGE MORRISON, b Warren, Ind, May 13, 34; m 59; c 2. PHYSICAL CHEMISTRY, HISTORY OF SCIENCE. *Educ:* Yale Univ, BS, 56; Univ Wis, PhD(phys chem), 61. *Prof Exp:* Asst prof, 61-67, assoc prof, 67-77, PROF CHEM, SMITH COL, 78- *Res:* Systems chemistry; kinetics and mechanisms of chemical reactions in solution; mutiple equilibria involving metal complexes in solution; history of physical chemistry. *Mailing Add:* Dept Chem Smith Col Northampton MA 01063

FLECK, JOSEPH AMADEUS, JR, b Kansas City, Mo, Mar 10, 28; m 61; c 2. LASERS. *Educ:* Harvard Univ, AB, 48; Rice Inst, MA, 50, PhD(physics), 52. *Prof Exp:* Assoc physicist, Brookhaven Nat Lab, 52-57; physicist, 57-69, group leader theoret div, 69-74, ASSOC DIV LEADER THEORET PHYSICS DIV, LAWRENCE LIVERMORE LAB, UNIV CALIF, 74- *Concurrent Pos:* Fulbright adv res fel, Norway, 57-58; consult, AEC Halden Proj, Norway, 58-59 & Atomic Energy Res Inst, Japan, 61; lectr, Univ Calif, Davis, 67- *Mem:* Fel Am Phys Soc. *Res:* Reactor and nuclear weapons physics; Monte Carlo methods; radiative transfer; laser physics and quantum optics; numerical methods; laser effects; atmospheric propagation of laser beams; optical wave guide theory; hydrodynamics. *Mailing Add:* Theoret Physics Div Lawrence Livermore Lab Livermore CA 94550

FLECK, STEPHEN, b Frankfurt-am-Main, Ger, Sept 18, 12; nat US; m 45; c 3. PSYCHIATRY. *Educ:* Harvard Univ, MD, 40. *Prof Exp:* Intern med, Beth Israel Hosp, Boston, 40-42; intern, Johns Hopkins Hosp, 46, resident psychiat, 46-48, asst, 48, instr psychiat & asst med, 48-49; from instr to asst prof psychiat, Med Sch, Univ Wash, 49-53; assoc prof psychiat, 53-54, assoc prof psychiat & pub health, 54-63, PROF PSYCHIAT & PUB HEALTH, SCH MED, YALE UNIV, 63-, PSYCHIATRIST-IN-CHIEF, YALE PSYCHIAT INST, 63- & CONN MENT HEALTH CTR, 69- *Concurrent Pos:* Attend staff, King County Hosp & Vet Admin Hosp, Seattle, 51-53; consult, Vet Admin Hosp, West Haven, Conn, 53-; med dir, Yale Psychiat Inst, 54-63; consult, State Hosp, Middletown, Conn, 54- *Mem:* Am Psychosom Soc; Geront Soc; Am Psychiat Asn; Am Pub Health Asn; Am Fedn Clin Res. *Res:* Schizophrenia, emotional aspects of motherhood outside marriage; conditioning and integration of the central nervous system; social structure of mental hospitals; family psychiatry and medicine; population control. *Mailing Add:* Dept of Psychiat Yale Univ Sch of Med 25 Park St New Haven CT 06519

FLECK, WILLIAM G(EORGE), b Havertown, Pa, Nov 17, 40; m 67; c 3. CIVIL & STRUCTURAL ENGINEERING. *Educ:* Villanova Univ, BCE, 62; Carnegie-Mellon Univ, MS, 64, PhD(civil eng), 68. *Prof Exp:* ASSOC PROF CIVIL ENG, CLEVELAND STATE UNIV, 70- *Concurrent Pos:* Interim dean, Fenn Col Eng, 76-77. *Mem:* Am Soc Eng Educ. *Res:* Mechanics of materials; reinforced concrete. *Mailing Add:* Dept of Civil Eng Cleveland State Univ Cleveland OH 44115

FLECKENSTEIN, WILLIAM OWEN, b Scranton, Pa, Apr 6, 25; m 47; c 2. ELECTRICAL ENGINEERING. *Educ:* Lehigh Univ, BS, 49. *Prof Exp:* Mem tech staff, Bell Tel Labs, 49-54, supvr switching syst design, 54-56, head dept data commun systs, 56-60, dir data commun develop, 60-66, dir phys design commun equip, 66, exec dir data & PBX systs, 66-68; gen mgr res & develop, Western Elec Co, Inc, 68-70; exec dir switching eng & local crossbar develop div, 70-73, V PRES SWITCHING SYST, BELL TEL LABS, 73- *Concurrent Pos:* Mem, bd trustees, Lehigh Univ, 81-, vis comt chmn, Comput Ctr, 80- *Mem:* Inst Elec & Electronics Engrs. *Res:* Switching system exploratory development and design; switching theory; digital systems, including data communication systems; manufacturing process technology; systems engineering. *Mailing Add:* Bell Tel Labs Inc Holmdel NJ 07733

FLEDDERMANN, RICHARD G(RAYSON), b Havana, Cuba, June 4, 22; US citizen; m 51; c 3. AERONAUTICAL ENGINEERING, PHYSICS. *Educ:* Loyola Univ, La, BS, 41; Univ Mich, BSE, 43, MSE, 47, PhD(aeronaut eng), 50. *Prof Exp:* Aerodynamicist, El Segundo Div, Douglas Aircraft Co, 43 & Higgins Industs Inc, La, 43-44; res assoc, Eng Res Inst, Univ Mich, 45-60; assoc prof aeronaut eng, Ga Inst Technol, 50-54; engr aeronaut res & develop, Arnold Eng Develop Ctr, USAF, 54-56; sr staff scientist & chmn theoret aerodyn group, Avco Mfg Co, 56-59; sr eng scientist, Radio Corp Am, 59-61; prin staff engr, staff of vpres eng, Martin Co, 61-65, staff of dir res & eng, Denver Div, 65-66, mgr space physics, 66-68; PROF AERONAUT SYSTS & CHMN DEPT, OMEGA COL, UNIV W FLA, 68-, PROF PHYSICS, 76- *Concurrent Pos:* Consult, Arnold Eng Develop Ctr, USAF, 51, 53-54. *Mem:* Am Inst Aeronaut & Astronaut. *Res:* Hypersonic aerodynamics and heat transfer; ablation materials; properties of turbulent flow; fuel sprays. *Mailing Add:* Dept Physics Univ West Fla Pensacola FL 32504

FLEEGER, JOHN WAYNE, b Ann Arbor, Mich, May 21, 49; m 69; c 1. ESTUARINE BIOLOGY, MARINE ECOLOGY. *Educ:* Slippery Rock State Col, BA, 71; Ohio Univ, MS, 74; Univ SC, PhD(biol), 77. *Prof Exp:* Res asst marine sci, Univ SC, 75-76; ASST PROF ZOOL & PHYSIOL, LA STATE UNIV, 77- *Concurrent Pos:* Instrnl Equip grant, Off Educ, La State Univ, 78- *Mem:* Ecol Soc Am; Am Soc Zoologists; Sigma Xi; Estuarine Res Fedn; Int Asn Meiobenthologists. *Res:* Population dynamics, energetics and community structure of estuarine microfauna and macrofauna. *Mailing Add:* Dept of Zool & Physiol La State Univ Baton Rouge LA 70803

FLEEK, JAMES BURTON, b Jamestown, NY, Sept 19, 20; m 42; c 2. PHYSICAL CHEMISTRY. *Educ:* Allegheny Col, BS, 42; Univ Mo, AM, 47; Fla State Univ, EdD, 56. *Prof Exp:* Instr chem, Miami Univ, 47-48 & Fla State Univ, 48-50; asst prof, Jacksonville Jr Col, 54-56; chmn div sci & math, 56-58, ASSOC PROF CHEM, JACKSONVILLE UNIV, 56- *Res:* Science teachers training. *Mailing Add:* Dept of Chem Jacksonville Univ Jacksonville FL 32211

FLEEKER, JAMES R, b Emporia, Kans, Aug 11, 37; m 49; c 4. PESTICIDE BIOCHEMISTRY. *Educ:* Kans State Teachers Col, BS, 60; Mich State Univ, PhD(biochem), 65. *Prof Exp:* Res assoc, Mich State Univ, 65-66; asst prof, NDak State Univ, 66-67, assoc prof biochem, 77-81. *Mem:* AAAS. *Res:* Metabolism of pesticides; immunoassay of drugs and pesticides. *Mailing Add:* Dept of Biochem NDak State Univ Fargo ND 58105

FLEESON, WILLIAM, b Sterling, Kans, May 21, 15; m 43; c 5. MEDICINE, PSYCHIATRY. *Educ:* Univ Kans, AB, 37; Yale Univ, MD, 42; Am Bd Psychiat & Neurol, dipl, 58. *Prof Exp:* Intern, Univ Minn Hosps, 42-43; assoc psychiatrist & dir child guid div, Minn Psychiat Inst, 46-55; from asst to assoc prof psychiat, Col Med Sci, Univ Minn, 56-63, asst dean col, 60-63; assoc dean sch med, 63-74, PROF PSYCHIAT, SCH MED, UNIV CONN, FARMINGTON, 63- *Concurrent Pos:* USPHS fel, Judge Baker Guid Ctr, Boston, Mass, 50-51; NIH spec fel psychiat & rehab, Univ Minn, 55; mem adv mgt prog, Harvard Univ, 64; lectr psychiat, Sch Med, Yale Univ, 65-72; actg head dept psychiat & chief psychiat serv, Univ Conn-McCook Hosp, 67-68; bd dirs, Comt Int Med Exchange, 74-; vis prof social & behav sci, Univ Lille, France, 74- *Mem:* Fel Am Psychiat Asn. *Res:* Medical education and administration. *Mailing Add:* Dept of Psychiat Univ of Conn Sch of Med Farmington CT 06032

FLEETWOOD, CHARLES WESLEY, b Ghent Ind, Nov 10, 04; m 39; c 1. CHEMISTRY. *Educ:* Hanover Col, AB, 30; St Louis Univ, MS, 32, PhD(inorg chem), 37. *Prof Exp:* Asst chem, St Louis Univ, 32-37; indust res chemist, US Rubber Co, Indianapolis, 37-41; asst supt explosives dept, Des Moines Ord, 41-42; explosives supt, Eau Claire Ord Plant, Wis, 42-44; indust chemist, Gillette Plant, US Rubber Co, 44-46; prof chem, 46-47, prof anal chem, 47-71, EMER PROF ANAL CHEM, NDAK STATE UNIV, 71- *Res:* Photoelectric colorimeter and its use in determining some elements of physiological importance found in deep well water; rubber; explosives; glass fabrication. *Mailing Add:* 1309 Ball Blvd PO Box 1180 Waldport OR 97394

FLEETWOOD, MILDRED KAISER, b Keyser, WVa, Jan 10, 45; m 67. IMMUNOPATHOLOGY. *Educ:* Univ Richmond, BS, 66; Med Col Va, MS, 68, PhD(clin path), 72. *Prof Exp:* ASSOC PATH, GEISINGER MED CTR, 72- *Mem:* Am Soc Microbiol; Sigma Xi; NY Acad Sci; Am Soc Clin Chemists. *Res:* Cellular immunity; development of immunology tests for the clinical laboratory. *Mailing Add:* Div of Lab Med Geisinger Med Ctr Danville PA 17821

FLEGAL, ARTHUR RUSSELL, JR, b Oakland, Calif, Aug 30, 46; m 71; c 2. MARINE GEOCHEMISTRY, BIOLOGICAL OCEANOGRAPHY. *Educ:* Univ Calif, Santa Barbara, BA, 68; Calif State Univ, Hayward, MA, 76; Ore State Univ, PhD(oceanog), 79. *Prof Exp:* RES ASSOC OCEANOG, MOSS LANDING MARINE LABS, CALIF STATE UNIVS, 78- *Concurrent Pos:* Vis lectr chem & biol, Univ Calif, Santa Cruz, 78 & 81; res fel geochem, Calif Inst Tech, 80, vis assoc geochem, 80- *Mem:* Am Soc Limnol & Oceanog; Am Chem Soc. *Res:* Biogeochemical cycles of trace elements; radioecology; analytical and nuclear chemistry. *Mailing Add:* Moss Landing Marine Labs Moss Landing CA 95039

FLEGAL, CAL J, b Kalamazoo, Mich, Feb 25, 36; m 58; c 3. POULTRY NUTRITION. *Educ:* Mich State Univ, BS, 58, MS, 62, PhD(poultry nutrit), 65. *Prof Exp:* Asst, 60-63, nutrit technician, 63-65, EXTEN SPECIALIST, DEPT POULTRY SCI, COOP EXTEN SERV, MICH STATE UNIV, 65- *Mem:* Poultry Sci Asn; World Poultry Sci Asn. *Res:* Vitamin A-Beta-Carotene relationships and activity; utilization of raw soybeans in poultry rations, the nutritional aspects of the fatty-liver syndrome in chickens and recycling animal wastes. *Mailing Add:* Dept Poultry Sci Mich State Univ Coop Exten Serv East Lansing MI 48824

FLEGAL, ROBERT MELVIN, b Salt Lake City, Utah, Dec 22, 41; m 66; c 1. COMPUTER SCIENCE. *Educ:* Univ Utah, BA, 66, MA, 68. *Prof Exp:* Teacher math, US Peace Corps, 68-69; mem staff comput sci, Univ Utah, 69-70; RES SCIENTIST COMPUT SCI, XEROX PALO ALTO RES CTR, 70- *Res:* Computer graphics and mathematical representations of images. *Mailing Add:* Xerox Palo Alto Res Ctr 3333 Coyote Hill Rd Palo Alto CA 94304

FLEGENHEIMER, HAROLD H(ANSLEO), b Heilbronn, Ger, Feb 18, 24; nat US; m 47; c 1. CHEMICAL ENGINEERING. *Educ:* Cooper Union, BChE, 44; Polytech Inst Brooklyn, MChE, 47. *Prof Exp:* Formulator org coatings, Devoe & Raynolds Co, Inc, 47-54, tech dir, Newark Plant, 54-66; Eastern tech mgr, Celanese Coatings Co, 66-70, mgr prod develop planning, 70-74, MGR ENVIRON, HEALTH & PROD SAFETY AFFAIRS, CELANSES PLASTICS & SPECIALTIES CO, 74- *Mem:* Am Chem Soc. *Res:* Development of protective and decorative coatings; and related materials, especially polymers, resins, solvents and pigments. *Mailing Add:* 2556 Cherhosen Rd Louisville KY 40231

FLEHARTY, EUGENE, b Beaver Falls, Pa, Oct 16, 34; m 55; c 2. MAMMALIAN ECOLOGY. *Educ:* Hastings Col, BA, 56; Univ NMex, MS, 58, PhD(biol), 63. *Prof Exp:* Asst prof biol, Nebr Wesleyan Univ, 60-62; asst prof, 62-65, assoc prof, 65-70, PROF ZOOL, FT HAYS STATE UNIV, 70-, CHMN DEPT, 79- *Mem:* Am Soc Mammal; Ecol Soc Am. *Res:* Mammalogy and herpetology distribution, taxonomy and ecology. *Mailing Add:* Dept of Biol Ft Hays State Univ Hays KS 67601

FLEIG, ALBERT J, JR, b Rochester, NY, May 17, 37; m 65; c 2. SCIENCE MANAGEMENT, ATMOSPHERIC SCIENCE. *Educ:* Purdue Univ, BS, 58; Catholic Univ, PhD, 68. *Prof Exp:* Design engr, Convair Astronaut, 58-60; systs engr, Vitro Corp Am, 60-62; systs analyst, 62-68, spec asst to dir admin & mgt, 68-70, head technol applns, 70-72, dep proj mgr, 72-76, MGR OZONE PROCESSING TEAM, GLOBAL ATMOS RES PROJ, GODDARD SPACE FLIGHT CTR, NASA, 76-, NIMBUS PROJ SCIENTIST, 79- *Concurrent Pos:* Lectr aerospace eng, Univ Md, 69- *Res:* Management of large scale scientific and/or technical research interests; development of algorithms and concepts for interpreting experimental data; atmospheric research in stratosphere and climate. *Mailing Add:* Code 910 Goddard Space Flight Ctr NASA Greenbelt MD 20771

FLEISCH, JEROME HERBERT, b Bronx, NY, June 6, 41. PHARMACOLOGY. *Educ:* Columbia Univ, BS, 63; Georgetown Univ, PhD(pharmacol), 67. *Prof Exp:* Res fel pharmacol, Harvard Med Sch, 67-68; res assoc, Nat Heart & Lung Inst, 68-70, sr staff fel, 70-74; sr pharmacologist, 74-77, RES SCIENTIST, LILLY RES LABS, ELI LILLY & CO, 77- *Concurrent Pos:* Lectr pharmacol & physiol sci, Univ Chicago, 75-78. *Mem:* AAAS; Am Soc Pharm & Exp Therapeut; Soc Exp Biol Med; Col Int Allergologicum; NY Acad Sci. *Res:* Smooth muscle, cardiovascular and mediator release lung. *Mailing Add:* Lilly Res Labs MC 905 Indianapolis IN 46285

FLEISCHAUER, PAUL DELL, b Buffalo, NY, Sept 23, 42; m 78; c 1. PHYSICAL CHEMISTRY, SURFACE SPECTROSCOPY. *Educ:* Wesleyan Univ, BA, 64; Univ Southern Calif, PhD(phys chem), 68. *Prof Exp:* NSF exchange fel, Rome, 68-69; mem tech staff, 69-75, HEAD SURFACE PHENOMENA SECT, AEROSPACE CORP, 75- *Concurrent Pos:* Vis asst prof, Univ Southern Calif, 75-76. *Mem:* Am Inst Chemists; Sigma Xi; Am Chem Soc; Am Vacuum Soc. *Res:* Characterization of chemical and physical processes, including photochemical ones, on solid surfaces; identification of the chemical composition of interface states; infrared and electron spectroscopy of solids. *Mailing Add:* Aerospace Corp PO Box 92957 Los Angeles CA 90009

FLEISCHER, ALLAN A, b Hartford, Conn, Feb 6, 31; m 56; c 2. NUCLEAR MEDICINE, NUCLEAR SCIENCE. *Educ:* Yale Univ, BS, 52, MS, 56, PhD(physics), 59. *Prof Exp:* Mem tech staff, Ramo-Wooldridge Corp, 59-60; dept mgr, Edgerton, Germeshavsen & Grier, 60-63, tech adv to mgr, 63; dir res, W M Brobeck & Assocs, 63-65; vpres res & develop, Cyclotron Corp, Calif, 65-70; pres & chief exec officer, Medi-Physics, Inc, 70-79; CONSULT, 79- *Mem:* AAAS; Am Phys Soc; sr mem Inst Elec & Electronics Engrs; Am Nuclear Soc; Soc Nuclear Med. *Res:* Radiopharmaceuticals; radioisotopes; nucleonics; accelerator development. *Mailing Add:* 543 Tahos Rd Orinda CA 94563

FLEISCHER, BECCA CATHERINE, b Brooklyn, NY, Feb 12, 30; m 62. BIOCHEMISTRY. *Educ:* Brooklyn Col, BS, 52; Ind Univ, MA, 55, PhD(biochem), 58. *Prof Exp:* Proj assoc, Dept Genetics, Univ Wis, 58-62, trainee, Enzyme Inst, 62-64; res assoc molecular biol, 64-72, res asst prof, 72-74; RES ASSOC PROF MOLECULAR BIOL, VANDERBILT UNIV, 74- *Mem:* NY Acad Sci; Am Soc Cell Biol; AAAS; Am Chem Soc; Am Soc Biol Chemists. *Res:* Comparative biochemistry of membranes; isolation and characterization of subcellular organelles of liver and kidney, particularly Golgi apparatus. *Mailing Add:* Dept of Molecular Biol Vanderbilt Univ Nashville TN 37235

FLEISCHER, EVERLY B, b Salt Lake City, Utah, June 5, 36; m 59; c 2. BIOINORGANIC CHEMISTRY. *Educ:* Yale Univ, BS, 58, MS, 59, PhD(chem), 61. *Prof Exp:* From asst prof to assoc prof chem, Univ Chicago, 61-71; chmn dept chem, Univ Calif, Irvine, 72-74, prof chem, 71-80, dean, sch phys sci, 74-80; DEAN ARTS & SCI, UNIV COLO, BOULDER, 80- *Concurrent Pos:* Sloan fel, Sloan Found, 67-68. *Mem:* Am Chem Soc; The Chem Soc. *Res:* Role of metal ions in biology; porphyrin and metalloporphyrin chemistry; coordination chemistry. *Mailing Add:* Col Arts & Sci Univ Colo Boulder CO 80309

FLEISCHER, GERALD A, b St Louis, Mo, Jan 7, 33; m 60; c 2. INDUSTRIAL ENGINEERING, SYSTEMS ANALYSIS. *Educ:* St Louis Univ, BS, 54; Univ Calif, Berkeley, MS, 59; Stanford Univ, PhD(indust eng, eng-econ planning), 62. *Prof Exp:* Instr eng ed, Heald Eng Col, 58-59; opers analyst, Consol Freightways, Inc, 59-61; asst prof indust eng, Univ Mich, 63-64; assoc prof, 64-71, dir, Traffic & Safety Ctr, 76-79, PROF INDUST & SYSTEMS ENG, UNIV SOUTHERN CALIF, 71- *Concurrent Pos:* Statist analyst, Maritime Cargo Transp Conf Div, Nat Acad Sci-Nat Res Coun, 58; res mgr, Hawaiian Marine Freightways, 60; actg asst prof, Stanford Univ, 60-62; consult, USAID, 65-66; US Navy, 66; Rand Corp, 66- & Nat Coop Hwy Res Prog, Nat Acad Sci, 70-; Fulbright sr lectr, Ecuador, 74; Dir, NATO Advan Study Inst, 79. *Mem:* Fel Am Inst Indust Engrs; Am Soc Eng Educ; fel Inst Advan Eng; Inst Mgt Sci. *Res:* Engineering-economic planning and systems analysis, especially in public sector. *Mailing Add:* Dept of Indust & Systs Eng Univ of Southern Calif Los Angeles CA 90007

FLEISCHER, HERBERT OSWALD, b Lake Geneva, Wis, June 22, 13; m 40, 67; c 2. FORESTRY, GENERAL BIOLOGY. *Educ:* Northwestern Col, BA, 35; Univ Mich, BS & MF, 38; Univ Mich, PhD, 52. *Prof Exp:* Field asst, Lake States Forest & Range Exp Sta, US Forest Serv, 38, jr forester, Nicolet Nat Forest, Wis, 39; forester, Consol Water Power & Paper Co, 39-40; forest prod technologist, Forest Prod Lab, US Forest Serv, USDA, 42-57, chief div timber processing, 57-64; dir forest prod utilization & eng res, 64-67, dir forest prod lab, 67-75; RETIRED. *Concurrent Pos:* Consult, Foreign Econ Admin, 45; tech consult forestry & forest prod, UN Develop Prog, India, 76 & 78 & Brazil, 78. *Mem:* Fel Soc Am Foresters; Forest Prod Res Soc (pres, 64-65); Soc Wood Sci & Technol; fel Int Acad Wood Sci; Int Union Forestry Res Orgns. *Res:* Forest products utilization and engineering research, and research administration; history and philosophy of science. *Mailing Add:* 2508 Santa Maria Ct Middleton WI 53562

FLEISCHER, ISIDORE, b Leipzig, Ger, June 4, 27; US citizen; c 1. MATHEMATICS. *Educ:* Brooklyn Col, BSc, 48; Univ Chicago, MSc, 49, PhD(math), 52. *Prof Exp:* Res asst, Univ Chicago, 50-52; Nat Res Coun fel, Paris, France, 52-53; lectr math, Northwestern Univ, 55-56; mem tech staff, Bell Tel Labs, 56-57; mathematician, Eastern Res Group, 57-58 & Appl Res Lab, Sylvania Elec Prod, Inc, 59-60; assoc prof math, Purdue Univ, 61 & Univ Clermont-Ferrand, France, 61-62; prof agr & fel, Univ Montreal, 63-65; fel, Queen's Univ, Ont, 67-68; vis scientist, Dept Math, 68-73, VIS SCIENTIST, RES CTR, UNIV MONTREAL, 74- *Res:* Ordered, universal, topological and logical algebra. *Mailing Add:* Ctr of Math Res Univ of Montreal C P 6128 Montreal PQ H3C 3S7 Can

FLEISCHER, JOSEPH, b Bridgeport, Conn, Dec 27, 05; m 39; c 2. PHYSICAL CHEMISTRY. *Educ:* Yale Univ, BS, 27, PhD(chem), 30. *Prof Exp:* Res chemist, Frigidaire Corp, 30-32, chem consult, 32-34; chem & patent consult, Olin Industs, Inc, 34-56; tech adv & patent mgr, Olin Mathieson Chem Corp, 56-60, sr patent assoc, 60-70; CHEM & PATENT CONSULT, 71- Am Chem Soc; Sigma Xi. *Res:* Phase rule; phenol-formaldehyde type polymers; drying oils; thermodynamic properties of chlorofluorides; liquid absorbents for refrigerant gases; congealing brines; cellulose; explosives; synthetic organic polymers; galvanic cells; nonferrous metals; chemical patent literature; polyesters polyamides. *Mailing Add:* 210 Yale Ave New Haven CT 06515

FLEISCHER, MICHAEL, b Bridgeport, Conn, Feb 27, 08; m 34; c 2. MINERALOGY, GEOCHEMISTRY. *Educ:* Yale Univ, BS, 30, PhD(chem), 33. *Prof Exp:* Fel, Yale Univ, 33-34; asst to ed, Dana's Syst Mineral, 35-36; asst phys chemist, Geophys Lab, Carnegie Inst Technol, 36-39; GEOCHEMIST, US GEOL SURV, 39- *Concurrent Pos:* Asst ed, Chem Abstr, 40-; vpres comn geochem, Int Union Chem, 51-53, pres, 53-57; prof lectr, George Washington Univ, 57-65; chmn comn new minerals, Int Mineral Asn, 59-74; mem, US Nat Comt Geochem, 69-74. *Honors & Awards:* Roebling Medal, Mineral Soc Am, 75; Becke Medal, Mineral Soc Austria, 77. *Mem:* Am Chem Soc; fel Mineral Soc Am(vpres, 51, pres, 52); fel Geol Soc Am (vpres, 53); fel Soc Econ Geol; Geochem Soc (vpres, 63, pres, 64). *Res:* Geochemical abundance and distribution of elements; chemical mineralogy. *Mailing Add:* US Geol Surv Reston VA 22092

FLEISCHER, PETER, b Coburg, Ger, Sept 10, 41; US citicitizen; m 72. GEOLOGICAL OCEANOGRAPHY, SEDIMENTOLOGY. *Educ:* Univ Minn, BA, 63; Univ Southern Calif, PhD(geol), 70. *Prof Exp:* Lectr geol, Loyola Univ Los Angeles, 69 & Univ Calif, Los Angeles, 70; NSF fel biol oceanog, Marine Lab, Duke Univ, 70-71; asst prof geol oceanog, Old Dominion Univ, 71-78; GEOLOGIST, NAVAL OCEAN RES & DEVELOP ACTIV, 78- *Mem:* Geol Soc Am; Soc Econ Paleontologists & Mineralogists; Sigma Xi; Am Asn Petrol Geologists; AAAS. *Res:* Beach processes and beach erosion; continental margin sedimentation and structure; fine-grained sediment transport. *Mailing Add:* Sea Floor Div Naval Ocean Res & Develop Activ NSTL Station MS 39529

FLEISCHER, ROBERT, astronomy, science administration, see previous edition

FLEISCHER, ROBERT LOUIS, b Columbus, Ohio, July 8, 30; m 54; c 2. PHYSICS, GEOPHYSICS. *Educ:* Harvard Univ, AB, 52, AM, 53, PhD(appl physics), 56. *Prof Exp:* Asst prof metall, Mass Inst Technol, 56-60; WITH RES LAB, GEN ELEC CO, 60- *Concurrent Pos:* Sr res fel physics, Calif Inst Technol, 65-66; adj prof, Rensselaer Polytech Inst, 67-68; consult, US Geol Surv, 67-70; assoc ed, Geochem & Cosmochem Acta, Lunar Sci Conf Proc, 70-73; vis scientist, Nat Ctr Atmospheric Res, Nat Oceanic & Atmospheric Admin & Atmospheric Physics & Chem Lab, 73-74; consult, Calif Inst Technol, 80. *Honors & Awards:* Am Nuclear Soc Award, 64; Ernest O Lawrence Award, 71; Gen Elec Co Inventor's Awards, 67 & 71; Except Sci Achievement Medal, NASA, 73. *Mem:* Fel Am Geophys Union; fel Am Phys Soc; fel Meteoritical Soc; Health Physics Soc; Am Meteorol Soc. *Res:* Solid state physics; charged particle tracks in solids; superconductivity; crystal plasticity; geochronology and application of geochronology to anthropology;

applications of charged particle tracks in space sciences; nuclear physics and engineering; cosmic ray physics; radiobiology of alpha emitters; uranium exploration; infoor radon and health, earthquake prediction. *Mailing Add:* Res Lab Gen Elec Co Schenectady NY 12301

FLEISCHER, SIDNEY, b New York, NY, May 10, 30; m 62. BIOCHEMISTRY. *Educ:* City Col New York, BS, 52; Ind Univ, PhD(biochem), 57. *Prof Exp:* Res chemist, Heyden Chem Corp, NJ, 52-56; asst, Ind Univ, 54-56, res asst with Prof F Haurowitz, 57-58; res fel, Inst Enzyme Res with Prof D Green, Univ Wis, 58-60, from asst prof to assoc prof, 60-68, PROF MOLECULAR BIOL, VANDERBILT UNIV, 68- *Concurrent Pos:* Mem, Physiol Chem Study Sect, Am Heart Asn, 68-72; mem, Sci Adv Comt, Am Cancer Soc, 73-77, Biochem Study Sect, NIH, 74-; rep, Int Comt Bioenergetics, 74-75. *Mem:* Am Soc Biol Chemists; Am Chem Soc; Am Soc Cell Biol; NY Acad Sci. Biophys Soc. *Res:* Structure and function of biological membranes and subcellular organelles; physiological role of lipids; electron transport and oxidative phosphorylation. *Mailing Add:* Dept of Molec Biol Vanderbilt Univ Nashville TN 37240

FLEISCHER, THOMAS B, b Oslo, Norway, Mar 27, 29; m 58; c 3. PAPER CHEMISTRY. *Educ:* Univ Oslo, BS, 50, 52 & 53, PhD(phys chem), 56. *Prof Exp:* Res chemist, WVa Pulp & Paper Co, Md, 57-59; res assoc papermaking, Scott Paper Co, Pa, 59-61; res group leader pulp-paper prod, A/B Borregaard, Sarpsborg, Norway, 61-66; mgr res & develop phys & chem res, 66-68, mgr felt & fabrics, 68-71, dir res, Huyck Res Ctr, 71-79, VPRES TECHNOL, HUYCK FORMEX, 80- *Mem:* Am Tech Asn Pulp & Paper Industs. *Res:* Structure of polymers; fillers and additives in paper; paper coating forming fabric development; dryer fabric development. *Mailing Add:* FORMEX PO Box 471 Wake Forest NC 27587

FLEISCHMAJER, RAUL, b Buenos Aires, Arg, Dec 17, 24; US citizen; m 57; c 1. DERMATOLOGY, BIOCHEMISTRY. *Educ:* NY Univ, dipl, 62. *Prof Exp:* Instr dermat, NY Univ, 60-62, asst prof dermat & res assoc biochem, 62-63; assoc prof dermat, Hahnemann Med Col, 63-69, prof med & dir dermat, 69-79; PROF DERMAT & CHMN DEPT, MT SINAI MED CTR, NY, 79- *Concurrent Pos:* Asst vis dermatologist, Bellevue Hosp, New York, 61-63; fel, Arthritis & Rheumatism Found, 62-64; asst attend physician, Philadelphia Gen Hosp, 64-67; consult, Vet Admin Hosps, Philadelphia, 64-67 & Wilkes-Barre, 65-67. *Honors & Awards:* Henry Silver Award, 63. *Mem:* AAAS; AMA; Soc Invest Dermat; Am Acad Dermat. *Res:* Disturbances of lipid metabolism; chemical structure of human connective tissue; role of connective tissue in experimental carcinogenesis; chemical structure of collagen in scleroderma; immunology; connective tissue disease. *Mailing Add:* 1200 Fifth Ave New York NY 10029

FLEISCHMAN, ALAN ISADORE, biochemistry, microbiology, see previous edition

FLEISCHMAN, ALAN R, b NY, Mar 8, 46; m 68; c 1. PEDIATRICS, NEONATOLOGY. *Educ:* City Col New York, BS, 66; Albert Einstein Col Med, MD, 70. *Prof Exp:* Clin assoc pregnancy res br, Nat Inst Child Health & Human Develop, 72-74; assoc dir new born serv, Morrisania City Hosp, 75-76; assoc dir newborn serv, 76-78, dir, 78-81, DIR NEONATOL, MONTEFIORE HOSP & MED CTR, 81-; asst prof, 75-80, ASSOC PROF PEDIAT, ALBERT EINSTEIN COL MED, 80- *Concurrent Pos:* Royal Soc Med Found grant, 74. *Mem:* Am Acad Pediat; AAAS; Harvey Soc; NY Acad Sci; Am Fedn Clin Res. *Res:* Perinatal physiology; clinical neonatology; metabolic bone diseases; calcium and vitamin D metabolism. *Mailing Add:* Dept of Pediat 111 E 210th St New York NY 10467

FLEISCHMAN, DARRELL EUGENE, b Gooding, Idaho, Apr 7, 34. BIOPHYSICS. *Educ:* Calif Inst Technol, BS, 58; Univ Ariz, PhD(chem), 65. *Prof Exp:* Fel, 64-65, staff scientist, 65-70, INVESTR, CHARLES F KETTERING RES LAB, 70- *Mem:* Biophys Soc. *Res:* Photosynthesis; vision; nitrogen fixation. *Mailing Add:* Charles F Kettering Res Lab 150 E South College St Yellow Springs OH 45387

FLEISCHMAN, JULIAN B, b Philadelphia, Pa, Dec 6, 33. MICROBIOLOGY. *Educ:* Yale Univ, BS, 55; Harvard Univ, PhD(biochem), 60. *Prof Exp:* NSF fel, Stanford Univ, 59-61; Am Cancer Soc fel, St Mary's Hosp, London & Pasteur Inst, Paris, 61-63; Weizmann Inst, Israel, 63-64; asst prof, 64-77, ASSOC PROF MICROBIOL & IMMUNOL, SCH MED, WASHINGTON UNIV, ST LOUIS, 78- *Mem:* AAAS; Am Asn Immunol. *Res:* Structure and biosynthesis of immunoglobulins and antibodies. *Mailing Add:* Dept of Microbiol Washington Univ Sch of Med St Louis MO 63110

FLEISCHMAN, ROBERT WERDER, b New York, NY, Feb 13, 37; m 63; c 2. VETERINARY PATHOLOGY. *Educ:* State Univ NY Vet Col, Cornell Univ, DVM, 61. *Prof Exp:* Sr asst vet, Lab Perinatal Physiol, Nat Inst Neurol Dis & Blindness, 62-63; assoc bacteriologist, Nat Ctr Primate Biol, 64-65; fel comp path, Sch Med, Johns Hopkins Univ, 66-69; PATHOLOGIST, EG&G MASON RES INST, 69- *Concurrent Pos:* Consult, Worcester Found Exp Biol, Mass, 70-; dir, Northboro Vet Clinic, 70- *Mem:* Am Vet Med Asn; Am Asn Lab Animal Sci; NY Acad Sci; Am Col Vet Path. *Res:* Primate care and pathology; laboratory animal medicine and pathology; zoo animal pathology; drug induced toxicology and pathology. *Mailing Add:* EG&G Mason Res Inst 57 Union St Worcester MA 01608

FLEISCHMANN, CHARLES WERNER, b New York, NY, Jan 22, 36; m 59; c 3. PHYSICAL CHEMISTRY, ELECTROCHEMISTRY. *Educ:* Queens Col, NY, BS, 57; Polytech Inst NY, MS, 65, PhD(chem), 70. *Prof Exp:* Jr chemist bio org, Jacques Loewe Res Lab, 57-58; chemist fuel-cell batteries, Leesona Moos Labs, 58-59; lieutenant ammunition, USAF, 59-62; chemist fuel cells & batteries, Leesona Moos Lab, 62-66; NASA trainee chem, Polytech Inst NY, 66-69; res engr, Mallory Battery Co, 69-70; res scientist, NL Industs, 70-74; MGR RES, C & D BATTERIES DIV, ELTRA CORP, 74- *Mem:* Am Chem Soc; Electrochem Soc; Sigma Xi; Am Soc Metals. *Res:* Electrochemical power sources, presently lead acid batteries; alkaline zinc cells; fuel cells; magnesium cells; solid state cells; electrochemistry in molten salts; electrolytic production of magnesium and tungsten bronzes; magnetochemical measurement. *Mailing Add:* C & D Batteries Div 3043 Walton Rd Plymouth Meeting PA 19462

FLEISCHMANN, HANS HERMANN, b Munich, Ger, June 2, 33. NUCLEAR PHYSICS. *Educ:* Tech Univ, Munich, dipl, 59, Dr rer nat(physics), 62. *Prof Exp:* Res assoc physics, Tech Univ, 62-63; staff mem fusion, Gen Atomic Div, Gen Dyn Corp, 63-67; assoc prof, 67-81, PROF APPL PHYSICS, CORNELL UNIV, 81- *Concurrent Pos:* Consult, Rohde & Schwarz, Munich, 60-63 & Naval Res Lab, 69-75. *Mem:* Am Nuclear Soc; fel Am Phys Soc; Inst Elec & Electronics Engrs; sr mem Am Asn Univ Professors. *Res:* Thermonuclear fusion, in particular application of intense relativistic electron and ion beams, field-reversed configurations, atomic collision physics. *Mailing Add:* Sch of Appl & Eng Physics Cornell Univ Ithaca NY 14850

FLEISCHMANN, WILLIAM ROBERT , JR, b Baltimore, Md, Oct 16, 44; m 66; c 1. VIROLOGY, CELL BIOLOGY. *Educ:* Capital Univ, BS, 66; Purdue Univ, PhD(viral genetics), 72. *Prof Exp:* NIH fel genetics, Ind Univ, 71-72, vis asst prof genetics & virol, 72-73; asst prof microbiol, Idaho State Univ, 73-76; McLaughlin fel, 76-77, asst prof, 77-80, ASSOC PROF MICROBIOL, UNIV TEX MED BR, GALVESTON, TEX, 80- *Mem:* Am Soc Microbiol; NY Acad Sci; AAAS; Sigma Xi. *Res:* Interferon production and action, including studies of interferon inhibitors and of cooperative effects of interferons, potentiation. *Mailing Add:* Dept Microbiol Univ Tex Med Br Galveston TX 77550

FLEISHER, DANIEL S, b Philadelphia, Pa, Mar 4, 27; m 50; c 3. PEDIATRICS. *Educ:* Villanova Univ, BS, 48; Hahnemann Med Col, MD, 53; Univ Ill, MEd, 67. *Prof Exp:* Assoc prof pediat, Sch Med, Temple Univ, 63-72, dir continuing educ, Ctr Health Educ Studies, Health Sci Ctr, 67-72; prof health professions educ, Univ of the Pac, 72-74; qual assurance consult, Children's Hosp Med Ctr, 74-77; PROF PEDIAT, MED COL WIS, 77-, ASSOC DEAN CURRICULAR AFFAIRS, 77- *Concurrent Pos:* Dir nephrology, St Christopher's Hosp for Children, Philadelphia, 58- *Mem:* AAAS; Soc Pediat Res; Am Fedn Clin Res. *Res:* Renal disease in children; education in the health sciences. *Mailing Add:* Med Educ Bldg PO Box 26509 Milwaukee WI 53226

FLEISHER, GERARD ADALBERT, b Dresden, Ger, Nov 10, 11; nat US; m 37; c 2. CHEMISTRY. *Educ:* Danzig Tech Inst, PhD(chem), 36. *Prof Exp:* Res chemist, Schering Corp, NJ, 37-42; res assoc chem, Med Col, Cornell Univ, 42-44; res chemist, Gelatin Prod Corp, Mich, 44-45; consult, Mayo Clin, 47-76, prof biochem, Mayo Grad Sch Med, Univ Minn, 64-76, prof, 73-76, EMER PROF BIOCHEM, MAYO MED SCH, 76- *Mem:* AAAS; Soc Exp Biol & Med; Am Chem Soc; Am Soc Biol Chemists. *Res:* Steroidal hormones; testosterone adrenal hormones; prolactin and gonadotrophic hormones; contributions to the chemistry of the progesterone group; steroids related to cortisone; kinetics of enzyme reactions; peptidases, transaminases and aldolase in human blood and tissues. *Mailing Add:* 2059 Lenwood Dr SW Rochester MN 55901

FLEISHER, HAROLD, b Kharkov, Russia, Oct 12, 21; nat US; m 45; c 3. PHYSICS, MATHEMATICS. *Educ:* Univ Rochester, BA, 42, MS, 43; Case Inst Technol, PhD, 51. *Prof Exp:* Res assoc physics, Univ Rochester, 42-43; mem staff radar circuitry, Radiation Lab, Mass Inst Technol, 43-45; sr engr, Video Circuitry, Rauland Corp, 45-46; instr physics, Case Inst Technol, 46-50; mem staff physics & comput, Res Lab, Int Bus Mach Corp, 50-61, sr physicist, Systs Develop Div, 61-65, mgr adv tech develop, Poughkeepsie Systs Develop Div, 65-68, prog mgr, Systs Develop Div Lab, 68-74, FEL, DATA SYSTS DIV, IBM CORP, 74- *Concurrent Pos:* Vis prof, Vassar Col. *Mem:* Am Phys Soc; fel Inst Elec & Electronics Eng; Sigma Xi; AAAS. *Res:* Semiconductors and cryogenic physics and devices; optics and quantum electronics; computer organization theory and design. *Mailing Add:* IBM Corp Data Systs Div C14/704 PO Box 390 Poughkeepsie NY 12602

FLEISHER, LYNN DALE, b Brooklyn, NY, Jan 2, 47. HUMAN BIOCHEMICAL GENETICS. *Educ:* City Univ New York, BA, 67, PhD(biomed sci), 74. *Prof Exp:* res scientist human biochem genetics, NY State Inst Basic Res Ment Retardation, 74-80; asst prof pediat, Children's Mem Hosp, Northwestern Univ, Ill, 80-81; ASST PROF PEDIAT, SCH MED, WAYNE STATE UNIV, DETROIT, 81- *Concurrent Pos:* Lalor Found fel, 74-75; adj asst prof genetics & pediat, Mt Sinai Sch Med, City Univ New York, 78-80. *Mem:* Am Soc Human Genetics; AAAS; Soc Pediat Res. *Res:* Human genetics, amino acid metabolism, inborn errors of metabolism, vitamin-responsive genetic diseases, prenatal diagnosis, tissue culture. *Mailing Add:* Sch Med Wayne State Univ Detroit MI 48202

FLEISHER, MARTIN, b Liberty, NY, May 15, 35; m 58; c 3. CLINICAL CHEMISTRY, IMMUNOCHEMISTRY. *Educ:* Harpur Col, State Univ NY, BA, 58; NY Univ, MS, 61, PhD(biochem), 66. *Prof Exp:* Instr radiol, Col Med, NY Univ, 66-67; ASST PROF, SLOAN-KETTERING DIV, GRAD SCH MED SCI, CORNELL UNIV, 69-; ASSOC, SLOAN-KETTERING INST, 69- *Concurrent Pos:* Assoc attend biochemist, Dept Biochem, Mem Hosp Cancer & Allied Dis, 72-81, attend biochemist, 81-; adj prof clin chem, Richmond Col, 73-75; adj prof pharmaceut sci, Columbia Univ, 74-75. *Mem:* Am Asn Clin Chemists; Am Chem Soc; NY Acad Sci; AAAS; Am Inst Chemists. *Res:* Development of immunologic and enzymatic diagnostic laboratory procedure; characterization of tumor associated antigens; clinical chemical methodology. *Mailing Add:* Mem Hosp Dept of Biochem 1275 York Ave New York NY 10021

FLEISHER, PENROD JAY, b Liberty, NY, Aug 2, 37; m 62; c 2. GEOMORPHOLOGY, GLACIOLOGY. *Educ:* St Lawrence Univ, BS, 61; Univ NC, Chapel Hill, MS, 63; Wash State Univ, PhD(glacial geol), 67. *Prof Exp:* Geophysicist, Pan Am Petrol Corp, 63-64; ASSOC PROF GEOL, STATE UNIV NY COL ONEONTA, 67- *Mem:* Geol Soc Am; Nat Asn Geol Teachers. *Res:* Glacial geology and periglacial geomorphology; model studies in glacier dynamics. *Mailing Add:* Dept of Earth Sci State Univ of NY Col Oneonta NY 13820

FLEISHMAN, BERNARD ABRAHAM, b New York, NY, June 16, 25; m 50; c 3. APPLIED MATHEMATICS, SCIENCE EDUCATION. *Educ:* City Col New York, BA, 44; NY Univ, MS, 48, PhD(math), 52. *Prof Exp:* Spec instr ling, US Army Specialized Training Prog, Univ Pa, 43-44; asst physics, NY Univ, 46-48, res asst & instr math, 48-52; sr staff mathematician, Appl Physics Lab, Johns Hopkins Univ, 52-55; from asst prof to assoc prof, 55-61, PROF MATH, RENSSELAER POLYTECH INST, 61- *Concurrent Pos:* Vis prof, US Army Math Res Ctr, Univ Wis, 61-62; sr Fulbright-Hays res scholar, Delft Tech Univ, 73; fac res partic & consult, Davidson Lab, Stevens Inst Technol, 74. *Mem:* Am Math Soc; Soc Indust & Appl Math; AAAS. *Res:* Nonlinear vibrations; diffusion and heat conduction. *Mailing Add:* Colehamer Ave Troy NY 12180

FLEISIG, ROSS, b Montreal, Can, Oct 12, 21; nat US; m 43; c 2. AERONAUTICAL ENGINEERING. *Educ:* Polytech Inst Brooklyn, BAeroEng, 42, MS, 55. *Prof Exp:* From aerodynamicist to aerodyn design engr, Chance Vought Aircraft, 42-50; flight control systs engr, Sperry Gyroscope Co, 50-54, eng sect head, Missile Systs, 54-58 & Astronaut Syst, 58-60; group head, Guidance Dynamics, 60-62, head lunar excursion module dynamics & performance anal, 62-65, head lunar excursion module guid, Navig & Control Anal & Integration, 65-67, LM-5 space craft team mgr, 67-69, space systs proj mgr, Grumman Aircraft Corp, 69-80, SYSTS PROJ MGR, GRUMMAN AEROSPACE CORP, 80- *Concurrent Pos:* Mem space rescue studies comt, Int Acad Astronaut. *Mem:* Fel AAAS; fel Am Astronaut Soc (pres, 57-58, nat dir, 59-67); assoc fel Am Inst Aeronaut & Astronaut; fel Brit Interplanetary Soc. *Res:* Aerodynamics; flight dynamics; flight control and guidance systems analyses and development; astronautics; aerospace systems integration. *Mailing Add:* 58 Kilburn Rd Garden City NY 11530

FLEISS, JOSEPH L, b Brooklyn, NY, Nov 13, 37; m; c 3. BIOSTATISTICS. *Educ:* Columbia Col, AB, 59; Columbia Univ, MS, 61, PhD(math statist), 67. *Prof Exp:* Asst, Div Biostatist, Sch Pub Health, Columbia Univ, 60-65; sr biostatistician, NY State Psychiat Inst, 61-65, assoc biostatistician, 65-66; instr, Columbia Univ, 65-68; prin biostatistician, NY State Psychiat Inst, 67, assoc res scientist, 67-76; from adj asst prof to adj assoc prof, 72-75, PROF BIOSTATIST & HEAD DIV, SCH PUB HEALTH, COLUMBIA UNIV, 75- *Concurrent Pos:* Assoc ed, Biometrics, 75-; mem data monitoring comt, Ctr Prev Premature Arteriosclerosis, 75-; biostatistician, Presby Hosp, New York, 76-; mem bd dirs, Nat Comn Confidentiality of Health Records, 79- *Honors & Awards:* Spiegelman Gold Medal, Am Pub Health Asn, 73. *Mem:* Am Col Neuropsychopharmacol; Am Psychopath Asn; Am Pub Health Asn; fel Am Statist Asn; Biometric Soc. *Mailing Add:* Div of Biostatist Columbia Univ Sch of Pub Health New York NY 10032

FLEMAL, RONALD CHARLES, b Two Rivers, Wis, Feb 17, 42; m 64; c 4. GEOLOGY. *Educ:* Northwestern Univ, BA, 63; Princeton Univ, AM, 65, PhD(geol), 67. *Prof Exp:* Asst prof, 67-74, ASSOC PROF GEOL, NORTHERN ILL UNIV, 74- *Mem:* AAAS; Geol Soc Am; Am Quaternary Asn. *Res:* Water quality; pollution control; application of quantitative techniques in geology and geomorphology; quaternary geology. *Mailing Add:* Dept of Geol Northern Ill Univ DeKalb IL 60115

FLEMING, ALAN WAYNE, b Kansas City, Mo, Dec 2, 39; m 61; c 2. CONTROL SYSTEMS, DYNAMICS. *Educ:* Univ Kans, BS, 61; Stanford Univ, MS, 62, PhD(aeronaut & astronaut sci), 66. *Prof Exp:* Asst engr, Boeing Co, 61; assoc eng, Lockheed Missiles & Space Co, 62-63; res engr, Stanford Univ, 66-72; sr staff eng, 72-77, MGR CONTROL SYSTS ENG DEPT, TRW SPACE & TECHNOL GROUP, 77- *Mem:* Am Inst Aeronaut & Astronaut; Inst Elec & Electronics Engrs. *Res:* Spacecraft and missile control system engineering; design; analysis; modelling; simulation instrumentation; testing; flexible structure control; attitude determination; navigation; microprocessor control implementation. *Mailing Add:* TRW/Space & Technol Group 82/2024 One Space Park Redondo Beach CA 90278

FLEMING, ATTIE ANDERSON, b Russellville, Ala, Dec 3, 21. PLANT GENETICS. *Educ:* Auburn Univ, BS, 43, MS, 49; Univ Minn, PhD(plant genetics), 51. *Prof Exp:* Asst county agr agent, Calhoun County, Ala, 43-45; asst agron, Ala Polytech Inst, 47-49; asst agron & plant genetics, Univ Minn, 49-51; from asst prof to assoc prof plant genetics, 51-61, PROF PLANT GENETICS, UNIV GA, 62- *Mem:* Am Soc Agron; Am Genetic Asn; Genetics Soc Can; Crop Sci Soc Am. *Res:* Corn improvement; genetics of corn; disease and insect resistance of corn; field-plot technique. *Mailing Add:* Dept of Agron Univ of Ga Athens GA 30602

FLEMING, BRUCE INGRAM, b Bradford, Eng, Jan 30, 41; Can citizen; m 66; c 2. REDOX REACTIONS, REACTION KINETICS. *Educ:* Oxford Univ, BA, Hons, 63, MA, 68; McGill Univ, PhD(org chem), 74. *Prof Exp:* Chemist, Shell Can, Ltd, 64-66; SCIENTIST, PULP & PAPER RES INST CAN, 74- *Mem:* Chem Inst Can; Can Pulp & Paper Asn; Tech Asn Pulp & Paper Indust. *Res:* Chemistry and technology of alkaline pulping and bleaching, including the chemistry of lignin, and the development of new technical processes to produce superior types of pulp. *Mailing Add:* Pulp & Paper Res Inst Can 570 St John's Blvd Pointe Claire PQ H9R 3J9 Can

FLEMING, DONOVAN ERNEST, b Ogden, Utah, Aug 16, 32; m 55; c 3. PSYCHOPHYSIOLOGY. *Educ:* Brigham Young Univ, BS, 56, MS, 57; Wash State Univ, PhD(physiol psychol), 62. *Prof Exp:* Trainee, Vet Admin Hosp, Salt Lake City, Utah, 60-61; res psychologist brain res, 61-64, dir res unit, Phoenix, Ariz, 64-71; PROF PSYCHOL, BRIGHAM YOUNG UNIV, 71-, CHMN DEPT PSYCHOL, 77- *Concurrent Pos:* Spec instr, Brigham Young Univ, 60-64; res instr, Div Neurol, Col Med & lectr psychol, Univ Utah, 62-64; res asst prof psychol, Ariz State Univ, 65-67, vis assoc prof, 67-71. *Mem:* Am Psychol Asn; Am Physiol Soc; Soc Neurosci. *Res:* Behavioral neurophysiology; physiological and psychological study of central nervous system functions. *Mailing Add:* Dept of Psychol Brigham Young Univ Provo UT 84602

FLEMING, EDWARD HOMER, JR, b University City, Mo, Feb 27, 25. NUCLEAR CHEMISTRY, SCIENCE ADMINISTRATION. *Educ:* Wabash Col, AB, 49; Univ Calif, PhD(chem), 52. *Prof Exp:* Chemist, Lawrence Radiation Lab, Univ Calif, Berkeley, 49-52; res chemist, Calif Res Corp, 52-55; asst head dept chem, Lawrence Livermore Lab, Univ Calif, 55-7S; dir, Div Appl Technol, US AEC, 73-75; SPEC ASST TO DIR, LAWRENCE LIVERMORE LAB, UNIV CALIF, 75- *Concurrent Pos:* Tech dir, Proj Sulky & chmn, Radioactivity Working Group, Atlantic-Pac Interoceanic Canal Studies Comn, 67-70. *Mem:* AAAS; Am Nuclear Soc; Sigma Xi. *Res:* Half-lives of uranium isotopes; gamma-ray scattering; oil soluble tracers; fallout from nuclear explosions; fission product decay chains; radiation doses from radionuclides; international treaties on nuclear explosives. *Mailing Add:* Lawrence Livermore Lab PO Box 808 Livermore CA 94550

FLEMING, GLENN ALLEN, medical entomology, see previous edition

FLEMING, GORDON N, b Pittsburgh, Pa, Apr 14, 36; m 58; c 2. THEORETICAL PHYSICS. *Educ:* Univ Pittsburgh, BS, 58; Univ Pa, PhD(physics), 64. *Prof Exp:* Res asst prof theoret physics, Univ Wash, 63-65; from asst prof to assoc prof, 65-74, PROF PHYSICS, PA STATE UNIV, UNIVERSITY PARK, 74- *Mem:* Am Phys Soc. *Res:* Relatavistic quantum theory; theory of elementary particles; foundations of quantum mechanics. *Mailing Add:* Dept of Physics Davey Lab Pa State Univ University Park PA 16802

FLEMING, HENRY PRIDGEN, b New Haven, Conn, Aug 9, 32; m 54; c 3. FOOD SCIENCE, MICROBIOLOGY. *Educ:* NC State Univ, BS, 54, MS, 58; Univ Ill, PhD(food sci), 63. *Prof Exp:* Instr animal sci, NC State Univ, 58-60; microbiologist, Merck & Co, Inc, 63-64; assoc prof food sci, NC State Univ, 71-77, FOOD TECHNOLOGIST FERMENTATION, DEPT FOOD SCI, USDA & NC STATE UNIV, 64-, PROF FOOD SCI, NC STATE UNIV, 77- *Mem:* Inst Food Technologists; Am Soc Microbiol; AAAS. *Res:* Microbiology and chemistry of vegetable fermentations; lactic acid bacteria; spore forming bacteria; yeasts; fungi; pickles. *Mailing Add:* Dept of Food Sci NC State Univ Raleigh NC 27650

FLEMING, JAMES CHARLES, b Lancaster, Ohio, Aug 25, 38; m 68; c 1. PHOTOGRAPHIC CHEMISTRY. *Educ:* Ohio Univ, BS, 60; Ohio State Univ, PhD(diazooxides), 64. *Prof Exp:* Org res chemist, 65-70, RES ASSOC, EASTMAN KODAK CO, 70- *Mem:* Am Chem Soc; Soc Photographic Scientists & Engrs. *Res:* Photographic and synthetic organic chemistry. *Mailing Add:* 1241 Holley Rd Webster NY 14580

FLEMING, JAMES JOSEPH, b Chicago, Ill, Feb 26, 17; m 50; c 4. COMPUTER SCIENCE. *Educ:* Northwestern Univ, BS, 38. *Prof Exp:* Physicist, Naval Res Lab, 41-62, head, Opers Res Br, 45-62; assoc supt applns res div, 56-62; chief data systs div, Goddard Space Flight Ctr, NASA, 62-67, depasst dir, 67-70, asst dir, Ctr Automatic Data Processing, 70-81; RETIRED. *Honors & Awards:* Meritorious Civilian Serv Award, US Navy, 47, Distinguished Civilian Serv Award, 60. *Mem:* Am Phys Soc; Asn Comput Mach; Inst Elec & Electronics Engrs; Am Inst Aeronaut & Astronaut. *Res:* Systems engineering; electronics; radar; digital computers. *Mailing Add:* 7216 Windsor Lane Hyattsville MD 20782

FLEMING, JOHN F, b Indiana, Pa, Dec 15, 34; m 57; c 2. CIVIL ENGINEERING. *Educ:* Carnegie Inst Technol, BS, 57, MS, 58, PhD(civil eng), 60. *Prof Exp:* Assoc prof civil eng, Northwestern Univ, 60-65; proj engr, Gen Analytics, Inc, Pa, 65-69; ASSOC PROF CIVIL ENG, UNIV PITTSBURGH, 69- *Concurrent Pos:* Consult, Westinghouse Nuclear Systs. *Mem:* Am Soc Civil Engrs; Soc Exp Stress Anal. *Res:* Structural dynamics; computer applications in structural design; structural model analysis. *Mailing Add:* Dept of Civil Eng Univ of Pittsburgh Pittsburgh PA 15261

FLEMING, LAWRENCE THOMAS, b Tacoma, Wash, Sept 26, 13; m 37; c 1. APPLIED PHYSICS, RESEARCH ADMINISTRATION. *Educ:* Calif Inst Technol, BS, 37. *Prof Exp:* Examr, US Patent Off, DC, 37-41; engr, US Naval Ord Lab, 41-46, sect head, 46-50; head mech group, Electron Tube Lab, Nat Bur Stand, 50-53, group leader, 55-56; chief instrumentation sect, Diamond Ord Fuze Labs, US Army, 53-55; prin res engr, Res Ctr, Bell & Howell Co, 59-67; PRES, INNES INSTRUMENTS, 67- *Mem:* Fel Acoust Soc Am. *Res:* Instrumentation; mechanical measurements; vibration and shock; history, sociology and legal aspects of invention. *Mailing Add:* 1830 Reiter Dr Pasadena CA 91106

FLEMING, MICHAEL PAUL, b Hingham, Mass, Feb 18, 48. CHEMISTRY. *Educ:* Mankato State Col, BS, 70; Ore State Univ, MS, 73; Univ Calif, Santa Cruz, PhD(chem), 76. *Prof Exp:* NIH fel, Colo State Univ, 77-79; RES CHEMIST, ARAPAHOE CHEM, INC, 79- *Mem:* Am Chem Soc. *Res:* Synthetic organic research and development of pharmaceuticals and fine chemicals. *Mailing Add:* 2075 N 55th St Boulder CO 80301

FLEMING, PATRICK JOHN, b Springfield, Mass, June 6, 47. BIOCHEMISTRY. *Educ:* Kalamazoo Col, BA, 69; Univ Mich, Ann Arbor, PhD(biochem,), 75. *Prof Exp:* fel, Health Ctr, Univ Conn, 75-77, instr biochem, 78-79; ASST PROF BIOCHEM, MED SCH, GEORGETOWN UNIV, 79- *Concurrent Pos:* Estab investr, Am Heart Asn, 80- *Mem:* AAAS; NY Acad Sci. *Res:* Structure, function, and biosynthesis of membrane-bound proteins. *Mailing Add:* Dept Biochem Med Sch Georgetown Univ 3900 Reservoir Rd Washington DC 20007

FLEMING, PAUL DANIEL, III, b Tampa, Fla, June 1, 43; m 67; c 2. CHEMICAL PHYSICS, CHEMICAL ENGINEERING. *Educ:* Ohio State Univ, BSc, 64; Harvard Univ, AM, 66, PhD(chem physics), 70. *Prof Exp:* Res assoc chem, Columbia Univ, 70-71 & Brown Univ, 71-74; res physicist enhanced oil recovery, 74-79, RES ASSOC, PROD RES BR, PHILLIPS PETROL CO, 79- *Mem:* Soc Petrol Engrs; Am Phys Soc. *Res:* Statistical mechanics; many body theory; theory of condensed matter; interfacial phenomena; phase transitions and critical phenomena; rate processes and fluid mechanics with applications to enhanced oil recovery. *Mailing Add:* 127 GB Phillips Res Ctr Phillips Petrol Co Bartlesville OK 74004

FLEMING, PAUL LAWRENCE, b New York, NY, Aug 3, 32; m 54; c 4. MICROWAVE TECHNOLOGY. *Educ:* City Col NY, BSEE, 57; Columbia Univ, MS, 60. *Prof Exp:* Mem tech staff, Res Div, IBM, 57-60, adv syst, 60-63, fed syst, 63-68; mem tech staff, 68-73, mgr device physics, 73-81, DIR MICROELECTRONICS, COMSAT LAB, 81- *Mem:* Inst Elec & Electronics Engrs. *Res:* Microwave solid state devices mainly in III-V compounds; originated the concept of an active transmission line in gallium arsenide as well as transmission line switches. *Mailing Add:* Comsat Lab 22300 Comsat Dr Clarksburg MD 20871

FLEMING, PETER B, b Trenton, NJ, Apr 9, 41; m 63; c 4. INORGANIC CHEMISTRY. *Educ:* Union BS, 63; Iowa State Univ, PhD(inorg chem), 68. *Prof Exp:* Sr chemist, Cent Res Lab, 68-73, res specialist, 73-74, res & develop supvr, 74-75, res & develop mgr, 75-80, MGR TECH CERAMICS LAB, 3M CO, 80- *Mem:* Am Chem Soc. *Res:* Metal-metal bonded complexes; niobium and tantalum clusters and complexes; copper chemistry; optical spectra and photochemistry of transition metal complexes; fire protection systems; intumescent compounds; ceramic materials. *Mailing Add:* 3M Co Bldg 207|1W St Paul MN 55101

FLEMING, PHYLLIS JANE, b Shelbyville, Ind, Oct 9, 24. EXPERIMENTAL SOLID STATE PHYSICS. *Educ:* Hanover Col, BA, 46; Univ Wis, MS, 48, PhD, 54. *Prof Exp:* Instr physics, Mt Holyoke Col, 48-50; from instr to assoc prof, 53-67, dean col, 68-72, prof, 67-80, SARAH FRANCES WHITING PROF PHYSICS, WELLESLEY COL, 80-, DEPT CHMN, 80- *Mem:* Am Phys Soc. *Res:* Film flow of liquid helium II; photoconductivity of lead sulfide films. *Mailing Add:* Wellesley Col Wellesley MA 02181

FLEMING, RICHARD ALLAN, b Chicago, Ill, Sept 16, 29; m 53; c 3. PLASTICS CHEMISTRY. *Educ:* Knox Col, AB, 51; Iowa State Univ, MS, 55, PhD(chem), 57. *Prof Exp:* Res chemist, 57-62, res assoc, 62-64, staff scientist, 64, res supvr, 64-71, SR RES SUPVR, E I DU PONT DE NEMOURS & CO, INC, 71- *Mem:* Sigma Xi; Am Chem Soc. *Res:* Plastic products and resins for home and industrial use, especially extrusion, molding and glazing applications. *Mailing Add:* 3202 Kammerer Dr Wilmington DE 19803

FLEMING, RICHARD CORNWELL, b Blue Island, Ill, Mar 10, 32; m 58; c 5. ZOOLOGY, ENTOMOLOGY. *Educ:* Kalamazoo Col, AB, 54; Univ Kans, MA, 56; Mich State Univ, PhD, 68. *Prof Exp:* Asst instr zool, Univ Kans, 54-56; teacher, High Sch, Mich, 58-61; from asst prof to assoc prof biol, 61-71, PROF BIOL, OLIVET COL, 71- *Concurrent Pos:* Instr, Western Mich Univ, 59-60. *Mem:* Lepidop Soc; Nat Audubon Soc. *Res:* Entomology, especially distribution, behavior and morphology of Lepidoptera. *Mailing Add:* Dept Biol Olivet Col Olivet MI 49076

FLEMING, RICHARD HOWELL, b Victoria, BC, Sept 21, 09; nat US; m 33; c 3. OCEANOGRAPHY. *Educ:* Univ BC, BA, 29, MA, 31; Univ Calif, PhD(oceanog), 35. *Prof Exp:* Asst chem, Univ BC, 29-31; asst oceanog, Scripps Inst, Univ Calif, 31-35, res assoc, 35-36, from instr to asst prof, 36-46; chief div oceanog, Hydrographic Off, Dept Navy, 46-50; exec officer dept oceanog, 50-51, chmn dept, 51-77, PROF OCEANOG, UNIV WASH, 50- *Concurrent Pos:* Sr oceanogr div war res, Scripps Inst, Univ Calif, 41-42, chief oceanog sect, 42-44, admin asst & sr oceanogr, 44-45, asst dir, 45-46; mem comt geophys & geog, Res & Develop Bd; mem comt marine ecol, Pac Sci Bd, Nat Res Coun; chmn, Comt Atlantic Weather Ships. *Mem:* Am Geophys Union. *Res:* Chemical oceanography; biochemistry; naval applications of oceanography; oceanography of Central American Pacific. *Mailing Add:* Dept of Oceanog Univ of Wash Seattle WA 98195

FLEMING, RICHARD JOSEPH, b Stuart, Iowa, July 26, 38; m 60; c 3. MATHEMATICS. *Educ:* Northwest Mo State Col, BS, 60; Fla State Univ, MS, 62, PhD(math), 65. *Prof Exp:* Instr math, Fla State Univ, 62-63 & 64-65, asst prof, 65; asst prof, Univ Mo-Columbia, 65-71; assoc prof, 71-80, PROF MATH, MEMPHIS STATE UNIV, 80- *Mem:* Math Asn Am; Am Math Soc. *Res:* Banach spaces; operators on Banach spaces and locally convex spaces; isometries and hermitian operators on Banach spaces. *Mailing Add:* Dept of Math Memphis State Univ Memphis TN 38152

FLEMING, RICHARD SEAMAN, b La Jolla, Calif, Apr 30, 39; m 75. ECOLOGY, ENVIRONMENTAL SCIENCES. *Educ:* Univ Wash, BA, 61, PhD(zool), 73; Univ Alaska, MS, 68. *Prof Exp:* Actg asst prof, 73-75, lectr environ studies, 75-76, res asst prof, Univ Wash, 76-77; sr res scientist, 78-79, PRIN SCIENTIST, R W BECK & ASSOC CONSULTS, 79- *Mem:* Ecol Soc Am; Wildlife Soc. *Res:* Alpine-Arctic ecosystems; use of environmental sciences in land use planning; environmental analysis of hydroelectric development; wildlife mitigation planning. *Mailing Add:* 5622 12th NE Seattle WA 98105

FLEMING, ROBERT WILLERTON, b Bon Aire, Pa, May 28, 19; m 43; c 4. MEDICINAL CHEMISTRY. *Educ:* Univ Pittsburgh, BS, 40; Univ Cincinnati, MS, 41, PhD(org chem), 43. *Prof Exp:* Chemists asst, Calgon Inc, Pa, 37-42; chemist, Gen Dyestuff Corp, NY, 43-44; asst, Manhattan Dist, Rochester, 44-46; res chemist, Parke, Davis & Co, 46-63; head dept org res, William S Merrell Co Div, Richardson-Merrell, Inc, 63-72; res scientist, 72-77, SR RES ASSOC, PHARMACEUT RES DIV, WARNER-LAMBERT/PARKE DAVIS, 77- *Mem:* AAAS; Am Chem Soc. *Res:* Synthetic organic medicinals. *Mailing Add:* Warner-Lambert/Parke Davis 2800 Plymouth Rd Ann Arbor MI 48106

FLEMING, ROBERT WILLIAM, b Macomb, Ill, Oct 12, 36; m 58; c 3. GEOLOGY, ENGINEERING GEOLOGY. *Educ:* Okla Univ, BS, 62; Brown Univ, MS, 64; Stanford Univ, PhD(geol), 72. *Prof Exp:* Geologist, US Army Corps Engrs, Sacramento, 63-68, US Army Eng Nuclear Cratering Group, 68-69; asst prof geol, Univ Cincinnati, 72-74, actg head dept, 74-75; GEOLOGIST, US GEOL SURV, 75- *Concurrent Pos:* Mgr, Nat Prog Landslide Hazard Reduction, US Geol Surv, 75- *Mem:* Geol Soc Am; Int Asn Eng Geol. *Res:* Mass wasting processes on hillsides. *Mailing Add:* Eng Geol Br US Geol Surv MS 903 KAE Denver Fed Ctr Denver CO 80225

FLEMING, SHARON ELAYNE, b Tisdale, Sask, Aug 20, 49. NUTRITION. *Educ:* Univ Saskatchewan, BSc, 71, PhD(food sci & nutrit), 75. *Prof Exp:* Food serv supvr, Univ Saskatchewan, 69-70; org chem lab asst, Saskatchewan Res Coun, 70-71; food scientist, Dept Crop Sci, Govt Can Res Grant, 73-74; res assoc, Prairie Regional Lab, Nat Res Coun Can, 75-79; ASST FOOD SCIENTIST, AGR EXP STA, UNIV CALIF, BERKELEY, 79- *Mem:* Can Inst Food Sci & Technol; Am Asn Cereal Chemists; Am Inst Nutrit; Inst Food Technol; Asn Anal Chemists. *Res:* Influence of food and their indigestible residues on gastrointestinal function; fermentation and the influence of the resulting compounds on health and nutrition. *Mailing Add:* Dept Nutrit Sci Univ Calif Berkeley CA 94720

FLEMING, SUZANNE M, b Detroit, Mich, Feb 4, 27. INORGANIC CHEMISTRY. *Educ:* Marygrove Col, BS, 57; Univ Mich, MS, 59, PhD(inorg chem), 63. *Prof Exp:* Teacher, St Mary Convent, Mich, 48-58; asst chem, Univ Mich, 61; from instr to assoc prof, 62-70, chmn natural sci div, 70-75, vpres & dean, 75-78, acad vpres, 78-80, PROF CHEM, MARYGROVE COL, 70-; ASST ACAD VPRES, EASTERN MICH UNIV, 80-, ADJ PROF CHEM, 80- *Concurrent Pos:* Res grants, Gulf Equip, 64, Sigma Xi, 64-65, NIH, 64-67 & Am Chem Soc Petrol Res Fund, 67-75; vis lectr, Univ Mich, 68-69, vis scholar, Ctr Study Higher Educ, 78-79. *Mem:* Am Chem Soc; Sigma Xi; fel Am Inst Chemists. *Res:* Synthesis and study of bonding characteristics of transition metal complexes and Lewis acid-Lewis base complexes; boron hydride chemistry; spectroscopic studies of bonding. *Mailing Add:* Eastern Mich Univ 146 Pierce Hall Ypsilanti MI 48197

FLEMING, SYDNEY WINN, b Thomasville, Ga, July 12, 24; m 49; c 4. PHYSICAL CHEMISTRY. *Educ:* Emory Univ, BA, 47, MS, 48; Univ Pa, PhD(chem), 54. *Prof Exp:* Instr chem, Emory Univ, 48-49; from res phys chemist to sr res phys chemist, 53-61, res supvr, 61-68, RES ASSOC ENG PHYSICS LAB, EXP STA, E I DU PONT DE NEMOURS & CO, INC, 68- *Mem:* Am Chem Soc; Optical Soc Am; Sigma Xi. *Res:* Polymer physical chemistry; optics; color. *Mailing Add:* Eng Phys Lab Exp Sta E I du Pont de Nemours & Co Wilmington DE 19898

FLEMING, THEODORE HARRIS, b Detroit, Mich, Mar 27, 42; m 65; c 2. ZOOLOGY, MAMMALIAN ECOLOGY. *Educ:* Albion Col, BA, 64; Univ Mich, MS, 68, PhD(zool), 69. *Prof Exp:* Syst zoologist, US Nat Mus, 66-67; asst prof biol, Univ Mo-St Louis, 69-74, assoc prof, 74-78; assoc prof, 78-80, PROF BIOL, UNIV MIAMI, 80- *Mem:* AAAS; Am Soc Mammal; Ecol Soc Am; Soc Study Evolution; Asn Trop Biol. *Res:* Evolution of mammalian reproductive rates; comparative demography of temperate and tropical rodent populations; foraging behavior of tropical bats; plant-animal coevolution. *Mailing Add:* Dept Biol Univ Miami Coral Gables FL 33124

FLEMING, WALTER, b Langham, Sask, May 20, 19; nat US; m 45; c 1. MATHEMATICS. *Educ:* Univ Sask, BA, 42; Univ Minn, MA, 44, PhD(math), 49. *Prof Exp:* Asst prof math, Univ NB, 45-46; lectr, Univ Man, 46-48; asst prof, Ft Hays Kans State Col, 48-49; assoc prof & chmn dept, Mankato State Col, 49-57; chmn dept, 57-73, PROF MATH, HAMLINE UNIV, 57- *Concurrent Pos:* Consult, St Paul High Schs, 59- *Mem:* Math Asn Am; Am Math Soc. *Res:* Integration in Wiener space. *Mailing Add:* Dept of Math Hamline Univ St Paul MN 55104

FLEMING, WARREN R, b Enterprise, Ore, Nov 30, 22; wid; c 2. PHYSIOLOGY. *Educ:* Univ Portland, BS, 49, MS, 52; Univ Ore, PhD(biol), 55. *Prof Exp:* Instr biol, Univ Ore, 53-55; from asst prof to assoc prof zool, 55-63, PROF ZOOL, UNIV MO-COLUMBIA, 63-, DIR, DIV BIOL SCI, 80- *Mem:* Am Soc Zool; Am Physiol Soc. *Res:* General physiology; hormonal control of salt and water metabolism in freshwater teleosts. *Mailing Add:* Div Biol Sci Univ of Mo Columbia MO 65201

FLEMING, WENDELL HELMS, b Guthrie, Okla, Mar 7, 28; m 48; c 3. MATHEMATICS. *Educ:* Univ Wis, PhD(math), 51. *Prof Exp:* Mathematician, Rand Corp, 51-53; res proj assoc, Univ Wis, 53-54; mathematician, Rand Corp, 54-55; asst prof math, Purdue Univ, 55-58; from asst prof to assoc prof, 58-63, chmn dept, 65-68, PROF MATH, BROWN UNIV, 63- *Concurrent Pos:* Mem staff, Math Res Ctr, Univ Wis, 62-63; NSF fel, 68-69; Guggenheim fel, 76-77. *Mem:* Soc Indust & Appl Math; Am Math Soc; Math Asn Am. *Res:* Stochastic control; calculus of variations; stochastic differential equations; population genetics theory. *Mailing Add:* Dept of Math Brown Univ Providence RI 02912

FLEMING, WILLIAM HERBERT, b Galt, Ont, Sept 3, 25; m 45; c 1. PHYSICS. *Educ:* McMaster Univ, BSc, 50, MSc, 51, PhD(physics), 54. *Prof Exp:* Fel, 54-58, reactor supt, 58-69, ASSOC PROF APPL MATH, McMASTER UNIV, 66-, MGR COMPUT SYSTS & PROG, 69- *Mem:* Am Nuclear Soc; Can Asn Physicists. *Res:* Nuclear reactor operation; digital computer programming systems. *Mailing Add:* Dept of Appl Math McMaster Univ Hamilton ON L8S 4L8 Can

FLEMING, WILLIAM LEROY, b Morgantown, WVa, Aug 29, 05; m 34; c 4. PREVENTIVE MEDICINE. *Educ:* Vanderbilt Univ, BA, 25, MS, 27, MD, 32. *Prof Exp:* Asst bact, Sch Med, Vanderbilt Univ, 25-28; intern & house physician, Bellevue Hosp, New York, 33-34; asst resident & resident physician med serv, Vanderbilt Univ Hosp, 34-37; Milbank fel syphilis clin, Johns Hopkins Hosp, 37-39, instr med, Sch Med, Johns Hopkins Univ, 37-39; mem staff internal health div, Rockefeller Found, 39; res prof syphil, Sch Pub Health, Univ NC, 39-45; assoc prof med, Sch Med, Boston Univ, 46-48, prof prev med & chmn dept, 48-52; chmn dept, 52-70, asst dean, 57-70, prof prev med, 52-78, EMER PROF PREV MED, SCH MED, UNIV NC, CHAPEL HILL, 78- *Concurrent Pos:* Mem staff, Evans Mem Hosp, Boston, 46-52; vis physician, Mass Mem Hosp, 46-52, chief genito infectious dis clin, 46-52; dir gen clin, NC Mem Hosp, 52-64; vis prof & consult prev med, Paulista Sch Med, Sao Paulo, 62; serv with Proj Hope, Ceylon, 68-69, Jamaica, 71, Natal, Brazil, 72, Maceio, Brazil, 73, Egypt & Tunisia, 77. *Mem:* Am Soc Clin Invest; Am Pub Health Asn; Am Venereal Dis Asn (pres, 54-55); Asn Teachers Prev Med (pres, 59-60); Am Col Prev Med. *Res:* Research bacteriology; venereal disease control; internal medicine; clinical experimental syphilology. *Mailing Add:* Univ of NC Sch of Med Chapel Hill NC 27514

FLEMING, WILLIAM WRIGHT, b Washington, DC, Jan 30, 32; m 52; c 3. PHARMACOLOGY. *Educ:* Harvard Univ, AB, 54; Princeton Univ, MA, 56, PhD(biol), 57. *Prof Exp:* NIH res fel pharmacol, Harvard Med Sch, 57-60; from asst prof to assoc prof, 60-66, PROF PHARMACOL & TOXICOL & HEAD DEPT, MED SCH, WVA UNIV, 66- *Concurrent Pos:* Vis prof, Univ Melbourne, 69 & St George's Hosp Med Sch, Univ London, 78; mem pharmacol-toxicol prog comt, Nat Inst Gen Med Sci, 73-77, chmn, 75-77. *Mem:* AAAS; Soc Exp Biol & Med; Am Soc Pharmacol & Exp Therapeut (pres-elect, 80-81, pres, 81-82); Fedn Am Soc Exp Biol. *Res:* Autonomic and cardiovascular pharmacology; electrophysiology; cellular control of sensitivity. *Mailing Add:* Dept Pharmacol & Toxicol WVa Univ Med Ctr Morgantown WV 26506

FLEMINGER, ABRAHAM, b New York, NY, Feb 4, 25; m 49; c 1. INVERTEBRATE ZOOLOGY. *Educ:* Brooklyn Col, BS, 50; Harvard Univ, MS, 52, PhD(biol), 56. *Prof Exp:* Biologist fishery res, US Fish & Wildlife Serv, 56-60; res biologist, 60-68, assoc res biologist, 68-77, assoc cur & lectr sci support div, 69-77, RES BIOLOGIST & CUR & LECTR SCI SUPPORT DIR, SCRIPPS INST OCEANOG, UNIV CALIF, SAN DIEGO, 77- *Mem:* AAAS; Am Soc Limnol & Oceanog; Ecol Soc Am; Soc Syst Zool; Marine Biol Asn UK. *Res:* Ecology, distribution and systematics of marine zooplankton, especially the Copepoda; principles underlying spatial distribution and speciation of the oceans pelagic fauna. *Mailing Add:* 1156 Ritter Hall Scripps Inst of Oceanog La Jolla CA 92093

FLEMINGS, MERTON CORSON, b Syracuse, NY, Sept 20, 29; c 3. METALLURGY, MATERIALS ENGINEERING. *Educ:* Mass Inst Technol, SB, 51, SM, 52, ScD(metall), 54. *Prof Exp:* Metallurgist, Am Brake Shoe Res Lab, 54-56; from asst prof to assoc prof metall, 56-69, Abex prof, 70-75, assoc dir, Ctr Mat Sci & Eng, 73-77, Ford Prof, 75-81, PROF METALL, MASS INST TECHNOL, 69-, TOYOTA PROF MAT PROCESSING, 81-, DIR, MAT PROCESSING CTR, 79- *Concurrent Pos:* Consult var govt labs & industs, 70-; overseas fel, Churchill Col, Eng, 70-71; vis prof, Univ Cambridge, Eng, 70-71. *Honors & Awards:* Simpson Gold Medal, Am Foundrymen's Soc, 61; Mathewson Gold Medal, Am Inst Mining, Metall & Petrol Engrs, 69; Henry Marion Howe Medal, Am Soc Metals, 73, Albert Sauveur Achievement Award, 78. *Mem:* Nat Acad Eng; Am Foundrymen's Soc; fel Am Soc Metals; Inst Metals London; Am Inst Metall Engrs. *Res:* Materials processing; solidification processing; foundry and ingot-making; technical education; innovation in industrial research; primary materials production. *Mailing Add:* Rm 8-407 Mass Inst of Technol Cambridge MA 02139

FLEMINGS, MILTON BAKER, b Fulshear, Tex, Apr 24, 17; m 41; c 3. INSECT PHYSIOLOGY. *Educ:* Prairie View Agr & Mech Col, BS, 39; Kans State Univ, MS, 54; Fordham Univ, PhD(biol), 64. *Prof Exp:* Teacher high sch, Tex, 39-42; dir entom div, First US Army Med Lab, 57-64; assoc prof, 64-69, PROF BIOL, C W POST COL, LONG ISLAND UNIV, 69-, CHMN DEPT, 74- *Mem:* Entom Soc Am; Am Mosquito Control Asn; Am Inst Biol Sci. *Res:* Ecology and control of insects; parasitology of medically important insects. *Mailing Add:* Dept of Biol C W Post Col Greenvale NY 11548

FLEMISTER, LAUNCELOT JOHNSON, b Atlanta, Ga, Dec 11, 13; m 41. PHYSIOLOGY. *Educ:* Duke Univ, AB, 35, MA, 39, PhD(physiol), 41. *Prof Exp:* Asst physiol, Duke Univ, 38-41; instr pharmacol, Sch Med, George Washington Univ, 41-43; res assoc, Sharp & Dohme, Philadelphia, 46-47; from asst prof to assoc prof, 47-66, PROF ZOOL, SWARTHMORE COL, 66- *Concurrent Pos:* Fulbright fel, Peru, 59-60; consult, NSF Facil Prog, 63-64. *Mem:* Fel AAAS; Am Physiol Soc; Am Soc Zool; Ecol Soc Am; Sigma Xi. *Res:* Comparative aspects of water balance and metabolism; environmental adaptation. *Mailing Add:* PO Box F Swarthmore PA 19081

FLESHER, JAMES WENDELL, b Chicago, Ill, June 24, 25; m 52; c 3. PHARMACOLOGY. *Educ:* Northwestern Univ, BS, 49; Loyola Univ Chicago, PhD(pharmacol), 58. *Prof Exp:* Control chemist edible fats & oils, Lever Bros Co, 51-55; res assoc, Ben May Lab Cancer Res, Chicago, 58-62; asst prof, 62-67, assoc prof, 67-80, PROF PHARMACOL, UNIV KY, 80- *Concurrent Pos:* Vis prof, Inst Cancer Res, Columbia Univ, 70-71. *Mem:* Soc Toxicol; Am Asn Cancer Res; Am Chem Soc; Am Soc Pharmacol & Exp Therapeut. *Res:* Chemical carcinogenesis; steroid hormones; mechanism of drug action; bio-transformation of aromatic hydrocarbon procarcinogens especially meso-hydroxyalkyl metabolite formation and subsequent possible activation via reactive esters; development of drugs to inactivate and eliminate procarcinogens and the active metabolites. *Mailing Add:* Dept of Pharmacol Univ of KY Col of Med Lexington KY 40506

FLESHLER, BERTRAM, b New York, NY, May 1, 28; m 56; c 2. GASTROENTEROLOGY. *Educ:* Univ Wis, AB, 48; Boston Univ, MD, 51. *Prof Exp:* Intern med, Mass Mem Hosp, 51-52; asst resident, Georgetown Univ Hosp, 52-53; asst resident, Mt Alto Vet Admin Hosp, 55-56; fel gastroenterol, Mass Mem Hosp, 56-58; from sr instr to assoc prof, 58-72, ASSOC CLIN PROF MED, SCH MED, CASE WESTERN RESERVE UNIV, 72-; SR STAFF GASTROENTEROL & DIR TRAINING PROG GASTROENTEROL, CLEVELAND CLIN FOUND, 76- *Concurrent Pos:* Assoc vis physician, Cleveland Metrop Gen Hosp, 58-59, dir gastroenterol, 58-72, vis physicial, 59-; consult, Vet Admin Hosp, 58- & Lutheran Hosp, 63-; NIH res career develop award, 66-71; hon sr lectr & consult, Kings Col Hosp Med Sch, London, Eng, 66-69; dir dept med, St Vincent Charity Hosp, Cleveland, 72-75. *Mem:* AAAS; Soc Exp Biol in Med; Am Fedn Clin Res; Am Gastroenterol Asn; fel Am Col Physicians. *Res:* Esophageal motility studies; amino acid absorption. *Mailing Add:* Sch Med Case Western Reserve Univ 2119 Abington Rd Cleveland OH 44106

FLESSA, KARL WALTER, b Nuremberg, Ger, Aug 3, 46. PALEONTOLOGY. *Educ:* Lafayette Col, AB, 68; Brown Univ, PhD(geol sci), 73. *Prof Exp:* Asst prof earth & space sci, State Univ NY Stony Brook, 72-77; asst prof, 77-81, ASSOC PROF GEOSCI, UNIV ARIZ, 81- *Mem:* AAAS; Geol Soc Am; Soc Syst Zool; Soc Econ Paleontologists & Mineralogists; Paleont Soc. *Res:* Quantitative analysis of taxonomic diversity, evolutionary rates and morphology; biogeography. *Mailing Add:* Dept of Geosci Univ of Ariz Tucson AZ 85721

FLETCHALL, OSCAR HALE, b Grant City, Mo, May 4, 20; m 50. WEED SCIENCE. *Educ:* Univ Mo, BS, 42, PhD(field crops), 54. *Prof Exp:* Asst field crops, USDA & Univ Mo, 38-42, asst instr & sci aide field crops, 47-51, instr field crops & agronomist, 52-54; from asst prof to assoc prof, 54-61, PROF AGRON, UNIV MO-COLUMBIA, 61- *Mem:* Am Soc Agron; fel Weed Sci Soc Am. *Res:* Development of more effective, more efficient, safer methods of controlling weeds in agronomic crops and on non-crop land. *Mailing Add:* 204 Waters Hall Dept Agron Univ of Mo-Columbia Columbia MO 65211

FLETCHER, AARON NATHANIEL, b Los Angeles, Calif, Dec 24, 25; m 51; c 5. PHYSICAL CHEMISTRY, ANALYTICAL CHEMISTRY. *Educ:* Calif Inst Technol, BS, 49; Univ Calif, Los Angeles, PhD(anal chem), 61. *Prof Exp:* Lab technician, Southern Pac Co, 49-50, chemist, 50-54; res chemist, 54-75, head gen res br, 75-78, HEAD ENERGY CHEM BR, NAVAL WEAPONS CTR, CHINA LAKE, 78- *Mem:* Fel AAAS; Electrochem Soc; Am Chem Soc. *Res:* Dye laser systems; photoluminescence; self-association of alcohols; chemiluminescence; photogalvanic and thermal batteries; quantitative spectrophotometry; electroanalytical chemistry. *Mailing Add:* Mail Code 3852 Naval Weapons Ctr China Lake CA 93555

FLETCHER, ALAN G(ORDON), b Gibson's Landing, BC, Jan 2, 25; m 49; c 4. FLUID MECHANICS, WATER RESOURCES. *Educ:* Univ BC, BASc, 48; Calif Inst Technol, MSc, 52; Northwestern Univ, PhD(civil eng), 65. *Prof Exp:* Engr-in-training, BC Elec Co, Ltd, 48-51, hydraul design engr, 52-56, supvr hydro-planning, 56-59; asst prof civil eng, Univ Idaho, 59-60, assoc prof, 60-62; assoc prof, Univ Utah, 64-69; DEAN SCH ENG & MINES, UNIV N DAK, 69- *Concurrent Pos:* Danforth Assoc, 65. *Mem:* Am Soc Civil Engrs; Am Soc Eng Educ; Nat Soc Prof Engrs; Sigma Xi. *Res:* Hydraulic engineering; flood waves in natural channels. *Mailing Add:* Sch of Eng & Mines Univ of N Dak Grand Forks ND 58202

FLETCHER, ANTHONY PHILLIPS, b Maidenhead, Eng, Feb 25, 19; nat US; m 61. INTERNAL MEDICINE. *Educ:* Univ London, MB, BS, 43, MD, 49. *Prof Exp:* Lectr human physiol, St Mary's Hosp Med Sch, London, 47-48; sr med registr, St Mary's Hosp & Wright-Fleming Inst Microbiol, 50-53; res assoc med, NY Univ, 54-56; asst prof, 56-62, ASSOC PROF MED, SCH MED, WASH UNIV, 62- *Concurrent Pos:* Merck Inst fel microbiol, Col Med, NY Univ, 53-54; asst attend physician, Barnes Hosp Group, 56- *Mem:* Am Physiol Soc; Am Soc Clin Invest; Am Fedn Clin Res. *Res:* Physiological fibrinolysis and the development of enzymatic methods for the treatment of thrombo-embolic vascular disease; blood coagulation and plasma proteins. *Mailing Add:* Med Ctr 113JB Vet Admin Hosp St Louis MO 63125

FLETCHER, BARRY DAVIS, b London, Can, June 25, 35; m 78; c 3. DIAGNOSTIC RADIOLOGY, PEDIATRIC RADIOLOGY. *Educ:* Univ Western Ont, BA, 57; McGill Univ, Can, MD & CM, 61. *Prof Exp:* Radiologist & instr radiol, Johns Hopkins Hosp, 66-67, asst prof, 67; asst prof, McMaster Univ, 67-69; asst prof diag radiol, McGill Univ, Can, 69-74, assoc prof, 74-76; PROF RADIOL, CASE WESTERN RESERVE UNIV, 76-; DIR, DIV PEDIAT RADIOL, UNIV HOSPS CLEVELAND, 76- *Concurrent Pos:* Radiologist, Montreal Childrens Hosp, 69-76. *Mem:* Am Col Radiol; Radiol Soc NAm; Soc Pediat Radiol; Can Asn Radiologists; Asn Univ Radiologists. *Res:* Pulmonary maturation and development in neonates and infants using radiologic techniques with clinical research in pediatric radiology; applications of new technologic methods (digital radiography and nuclear magnetic resonance) to pediatric diagnosis. *Mailing Add:* Dept Radiol Univ Hosps 2074 Abington Rd Cleveland OH 44106

FLETCHER, C(HARLES) L(EONARD), b Columbus, Ohio, Sept 30, 07; m 30; c 2. CHEMICAL ENGINEERING. *Educ:* Ohio State Univ, BChE, 30. *Hon Degrees:* ChE, Ohio State Univ, 39. *Prof Exp:* Chem engr cellulose esters develop, Eastman Kodak, NY, 30-33; engr cellulose esters develop & qual control, Tenn Eastman Co, 33-36, asst div supt, 36-41, div supt, 41-58, gen supt, 58-63, asst worksmgr, 63-72; RETIRED. *Mem:* Am Chem Soc; Am Inst Chem Engrs; fel Am Inst Chem; Nat Soc Prof Engrs. *Res:* Plasticizers, photographic chemicals, dyes, inhibitors, antioxidants, antiozanants, aliphatic and aromatic chemicals and polyester resins production and development; production of cellulose esters, cellulose esters plastics and polyolefins plastics. *Mailing Add:* 1536 Fairidge Dr Kingsport TN 37664

FLETCHER, DEAN CHARLES, b Logan, Utah, June 14, 21; m 44; c 3. BIOCHEMISTRY, NUTRITION. *Educ:* Utah State Univ, BS, 43, MS, 48; Univ Del, PhD(biochem), 51. *Prof Exp:* Instr physiol, Utah State Univ, 43, 48-49; res assoc biochem, Res Found, Franklin Inst, 49-51; chemist, Stine Lab, E I du Pont de Nemours & Co, Inc, 51-57; dir, Dept Invest Med, Washoe Med Ctr, 57-72; dir, Ctr Learning Res, Med Ctr, Univ Ky, 72-73; dir planning, Health Sci Ctr, Univ Utah, 73; dir sect food sci, AMA, Chicago, 73-77; CHMN DEPT HUMAN NUTRIT & FOODS, WASH STATE UNIV, 77- *Concurrent Pos:* Lectr, Univ Del, 52-57; lectr pharmacol, Univ Nev, Reno, 57-60, Allie M Lee prof biochem, 61-72, chmn dept biochem, 62-71, dir allied health, Sch Med Sci, 69-71, assoc dean, 71-72; asst clin prof postgrad med, Col Med, Univ Utah, 68-; dir, Reno Cancer Ctr; mem, Nev Cancer Coord Comt; consult, St Mary's Hosp, Reno, Reno Vet Admin Hosp, Washoe Med Ctr, Dade Chem Co & Lamar Chem Co, Calif. *Mem:* Am Chem Soc; Am Asn Clin Chem; NY Acad Sci; Am Dietetics Asn; Am Col Clin Biochem. *Res:* Stress physiology; cancer chemotherapy; clinical investigations; toxicology. *Mailing Add:* Dept of Foods-Nutrit-Inst Mgt Wash State Univ Pullman WA 99163

FLETCHER, DONALD JAMES, b Atlanta, Ga, Mar 21, 51; m 74; c 1. ENDOCRINOLOGY, CELL BIOLOGY. *Educ:* Ga Inst Technol, BS, 73; Emory Univ, PhD(biol), 77. *Prof Exp:* Res fel cell biol, Dept Anat, Sch Med, Emory Univ, 77-79; RES FEL PHYSIOL, DEPT MED, MED COL VA, 80- *Concurrent Pos:* Nat Arthritis, Metab & Digestive Dis trainee grant, 77-79. *Mem:* Am Soc Zoologists; Am Soc Cell Biol; Am Diabetes Asn. *Res:* Separation of dispersed islet cells and characterization of secretion and attachment of those cells; parcrine aspects of hormone secretion in situ and in vitro. *Mailing Add:* Box 693 Dept Med Med Col Va Richmond VA 23298

FLETCHER, DONALD WARREN, b Phoenix, Ariz, June 8, 29; m 63; c 2. MICROBIAL ECOLOGY. *Educ:* Ore State Univ, BS, 51, MS, 53; Wash State Univ, PhD(bact), 56. *Prof Exp:* Instr bact, Wash State Univ, 56-59; assoc prof biol, San Francisco State Univ, 59-67, exec dir, Ctr Advan Med Technol & assoc dean, Sch Natural Sci, 70-74, prof biol, 67-75; ASSOC DEAN EXTENDED EDUC, OFF CHANCELLOR, CALIF STATE UNIV & COLS, LONG BEACH, 75- *Concurrent Pos:* Lectr & consult, Sch Med, Univ Calif, San Francisco, 62-64; Fulbright lectr, Univ Belgrade, 67-68; dean col arts & sci, Univ Bridgeport, 69-70; asst dir health manpower educ proj, Calif State Univ & Cols, 75- *Mem:* Fel AAAS; Am Soc Microbiol; Brit Soc Gen Microbiol; Sigma Xi. *Res:* Microbial physiology; bacterial ecology; rumen and soil microbiology; bacterial nutrition; microbiology of the gut of herbivorous fish; allied health manpower. *Mailing Add:* Calif State Univ & Cols 400 Golden Shore Long Beach CA 90802

FLETCHER, EDWARD A(BRAHAM), b Detroit, Mich, July 30, 24; m 48; c 3. CHEMISTRY, THERMODYNAMICS. *Educ:* Wayne State Univ, BS, 48; Purdue Univ, PhD(inorg chem), 52. *Prof Exp:* Aeronaut res scientist, NASA, 52-56, head flame mech sect, 56-57, head propellant chem sect, 57-59; assoc prof, 59-60, PROF MECH ENG, UNIV MINN, MINNEAPOLIS, 60-, DIR GRAD STUDIES, 71- *Concurrent Pos:* Vis exchange scientist, Byellorussian Acad Sci, 64; vis prof, Univ Poitiers, 68; mem comt waste heat mgt, Dept Com, 74-75; co-chmn safety hydraul comn fluids, Nat Res Coun, Nat Acad Sci, 77- *Mem:* Am Chem Soc; Combustion Inst (secy, 68-69, vchmn, 78-); Solar Thermal Test Facil Users Asn. *Res:* Combustion; ignition; fluorine chemistry; chemical kinetics; thermochemical solar energy storage; fluidized bed combustion. *Mailing Add:* Univ Minn 111 Church St SE Minneapolis MN 55455

FLETCHER, EDWARD ROYCE, b Hays, Kans, May 20, 37. BIODYNAMICS. *Educ:* Univ NMex, BS, 58, MS, 60, PhD(physics), 64. *Prof Exp:* Electronic technician, 56, math analyst, 57-60, physicist, 61-63, head theoret anal sect, Dept Physics, 64-70, HEAD, DEPT PHYSICS, LOVELACE BIOMED & ENVIRON RES INST, 71- *Mem:* Inst Elec & Electronics Engrs. *Res:* Analysis of biological and physical systems in terms of the physical process and the development of mathematical models to simulate these systems. *Mailing Add:* Lovelace Biomed & Environ Res Inst 5200 Gibson Blvd SE PO Box 5890 Albuquerque NM 87185

FLETCHER, FRANK WILLIAM, b Camden, NJ, Oct 7, 37; m 60; c 3. GEOLOGY. *Educ:* Lafayette Col, BA, 59, Univ Rochester, PhD(geol), 64. *Prof Exp:* Eng aide soils div, NJ State Hwy Dept, 58-59; asst geol, Univ Rochester, 59-62; geologist, NY State Mus & Sci Serv, 59-64; instr, 62-64, from asst prof to assoc prof, 64-73, PROF GEOL, SUSQUEHANNA UNIV, 73-, DIR INST ENVIRON STUDIES, 70- *Concurrent Pos:* Cooperating geologist, Pa Geol Surv, 66- *Mem:* AAAS; Geol Soc Am; Soc Econ Paleont & Mineral; Int Asn Sedimentol. *Res:* Paleozoic stratigraphy; sedimentology; tectonics; environmental geology. *Mailing Add:* Inst for Environ Studies Susquehanna Univ Selingsgrove PA 17870

FLETCHER, FREDERICK BENNETT, b Latrobe, Pa, Jan 17, 46; m 69; c 2. METALLURGY. *Educ:* Lehigh Univ, BS, 67; Mass Inst Technol, ScD, 72; Univ Mich, MBA, 79. *Prof Exp:* Res metallurgist, Medium Steam Turbine Dept, Gen Elec Co, 72-74; sr res assoc oil indust steels, 74-79, res supvr, 79-80, RES MGR LOW ALLOY STEELS, CLIMAX MOLYBDENUM CO MICH, AMAX, INC, 80- *Mem:* Am Soc Metals; Am Railway Eng Asn; AAAS; Am Inst Mining Metall & Petrol Engrs. *Res:* Low alloy steels for the oil industry; elevated temperature steels; rail steels; steels for the automotive industry. *Mailing Add:* 1245 Bardstown Trail Ann Arbor MI 48105

FLETCHER, GARTH L, b Glasgow, Scotland, Apr 15, 36; Can citizen; m 64; c 2. ANIMAL PHYSIOLOGY. *Educ:* Univ BC, BSc, 63; Univ Calif, Santa Barbara, PhD(biol), 67. *Prof Exp:* Res scientist, Halifax Lab, Fisheries Res Bd, Can, 67-70, Marine Ecol Lab, Bedford Inst, 70-71; RES SCIENTIST, MARINE SCI RES LAB, MEM UNIV NFLD, 71- *Mem:* AAAS; Am Soc Zoologists; Can Soc Zoologists. *Res:* Water and electrolyte regulation in birds; steroid hormones in fish; toxicology of elemental phosphorus; mechanisms controlling heavy metal levels in fish; red blood cell production and senescence in fish; regulation of protein anti-freeze levels in fish blood. *Mailing Add:* Marine Sci Res Lab Mem Univ of Nfld St John's NF A1C 5S7 Can

FLETCHER, GILBERT HUNGERFORD, b Paris, France, Mar 11, 11; nat US; m 44; c 2. MEDICINE. *Educ:* Univ Paris, BA, 29; Cath Univ Louvain, 32; Free Univ Brussels, MS, 35, MD, 41. *Hon Degrees:* Dr Sci, Hahnemann Med Col & Hosp, Philadelphia, Pa, 79; Dr, Univ Granada, Spain, 81. *Prof Exp:* head dept, 48-81, PROF RADIOTHER, UNIV TEX M D ANDERSON HOSP & TUMOR INST, 48- *Concurrent Pos:* Jr asst radiologist, New York Hosp, 44-45; consult, Hermann Hosp, 50-; chmn comt radiation ther studies, Nat Cancer Inst, 63-71; consult, St Joseph Hosp, Houston, Tex, 67-; nat consult to Surgeon Gen, US Air Force, Washington, DC, 68-; prof, Sch Med, Univ Tex, Houston. *Honors & Awards:* Ann lectr, Del Ragato Found Award, Med Col Milwaukee, 79; Pierluigi Nervi Int Award Cancer Res, Rome Italy, 80. *Mem:* Fel Am Col Radiol; Am Radium Soc (treas, 59-61, pres, 62-63); Radiol Soc NAm; Inter-Am Col Radiol. *Res:* Radiotherapy. *Mailing Add:* Dept of Radiother Univ of Tex M D Anderson Hosp & Tumor Inst Houston TX 77030

FLETCHER, HARRY HUNTINGTON, b Pittsburgh, Pa, Nov 4, 07; m 37; c 3. ORGANIC POLYMER CHEMISTRY. *Educ:* Yale Univ, BS, 29; Columbia Univ, PhD(chem), 39. *Prof Exp:* Res chemist, US Rubber Co, 29-31; asst, Columbia Univ, 31-35; res chemist, Res Ctr, US Rubber Co, 36-63; teacher chem, Fairleigh Dickinson, 64-67; patent examr, US Patent Off, Arlington, 67-77; RETIRED. *Mem:* Am Chem Soc. *Res:* Action of aqueous chlorine and hypochlorite on starches; adhesion of rubber to metal; antioxidants and accelerators for rubber; agricultural organic chemicals; transfer chemicals; chemical modification of cotton; patent liaison work; analytical-organic research; teaching. *Mailing Add:* 3308 Holloman Rd Falls Church VA 22042

FLETCHER, HARVEY, physics, deceased

FLETCHER, HARVEY JUNIOR, b New York, NY, Apr 9, 23; m 53; c 6. APPLIED MATHEMATICS. *Educ:* Mass Inst Technol, BS, 44; Calif Inst Technol, MS, 48; Univ Utah, PhD(math), 54. *Prof Exp:* Instr physics, Univ Utah, 53; from instr to prof math, Brigham Young Univ, 54-63, chmn dept, 58-61 & 62-63; mem tech staff, Bellcom, 63-64; prof math, Brigham Young Univ, 64-74; prof, Staten Island Community Col, 74-75; mem staff, Eyring Res Inst, 75-80; MEM STAFF, BRIGHAM YOUNG UNIV, 80- *Concurrent Pos:* Mem tech staff, Bell Labs, 61-62 & 73-74; sr tech specialist, Hercules, Inc, 67-68. *Mem:* Math Asn Am. *Res:* Bending of plates; Fourier series; attitude of satellite; Apollo trajectories; diffusion theory; minuteman simulation; intercept trajectories; delta modulation coding; beta battery; EM diffraction. *Mailing Add:* 1175 Locust Circle Provo UT 84601

FLETCHER, JAMES CHIPMAN, b Millburn, NJ, June 5, 19; m 46; c 4. PHYSICS. *Educ:* Columbia Univ, AB, 40; Calif Inst Technol, PhD(physics), 48. *Hon Degrees:* various from Univ Utah, Brigham Young Univ & Lehigh Univ. *Prof Exp:* Res physicist, Bur Ord US Navy, 40-41; spec res assoc, Cruft Lab, Harvard Univ, 41-42; instr, Princeton Univ, 42-45; teaching fel, Calif Inst Technol, 45-48; instr, Univ Calif, Los Angeles, 48-50; dir theory & anal lab, Hughes Aircraft Co, 48-54; from assoc dir guided missile lab to dir electronics, guided missile res div, Space Tech Labs, Ramo-Wooldridge Corp, 54-58; pres, Space Electronics Corp, 58-60; pres, Space-Gen Corp, 60-62, chmn bd, 60-64, vpres systs, Aerojet-Gen Corp, 62-64; pres, Univ Utah, 64-71; adminr, NASA, NASA, 71-77; DIR, BURROUGHS CORP & STANDARD OIL, IND, 77-; WHITEFORD PROF TECHNOL & ENERGY RESOURCES, UNIV PITTSBURGH, 77- *Concurrent Pos:* Mem subcomt stability & control, Nat Adv Comt Aeronaut, 50-54; consult & mem, President's Sci Adv Comt, 58-70, mem strategic weapons panel, 59-61, command, control & intel panel, 62-63 & mil aircraft panel, 64-67; chmn ad hoc comt rev, Minuteman Command & Control Syst, 61; mem command, control & intel comt, US Dept Defense, 61-62; mem, Woods Hole Summer Study Group Arms Control, 62; consult, Arms Control & Disarmament Agency, 62-64; mem, Air Force Sci Adv Bd, 63; mem, Pan Am Adv Bd, 77-; trustee, Rockefeller Found, 78-; mem technol adv assessment comn, US Cong Off Tech Assessment, 78-; mem, Energy Res Adv Bd, Dept Energy, 78-, Defense Sci Bd, 81-, TMI 2 safety adv bd, 81-, gov bd, Nat Res Coun, 78-, exec comt, 81- & gov coun, Nat Acad Eng, 78- *Mem:* Nat Acad Eng; fel Inst Elec & Electronics Engrs; Am Astron Soc; hon fel Am Inst Aeronaut & Astronaut. *Res:* Underwater acoustics; aerodynamics; shock waves; cosmic rays; magnetic survey of naval vessels; servomechanisms; radar; guided missiles and space electronics; guidance; instrumentation; adminstration of large scale research and development programs; communications, systems engineering, space technology and energy resources. *Mailing Add:* 7726 Old Springhouse Rd McLean VA 22207

FLETCHER, JAMES W, b Belleville, Ill, Oct 6, 43; m 67; c 3. INTERNAL MEDICINE, NUCLEAR MEDICINE. *Educ:* St Louis Univ, MD, 68. *Prof Exp:* Intern med, Sch Med, St Louis Univ, 68-69, asst resident, 69-70, resident fel nuclear med, 70-71; resident fel nuclear med, Harvard Med Sch, 71-72; asst prof, 72-75, ASSOC PROF MED, SCH MED, ST LOUIS UNIV, 75-; asst chief nuclear med, St Louis Vet Admin Hosp, 76-79; ASSOC PROF RADIOL, SCH MED, ST LOUIS UNIV, 78- *Concurrent Pos:* Staff physician, St Louis Univ Hosp, 72- *Mem:* Am Fedn Clin Res; Soc Exp Biol & Med; Soc Nuclear Med; AAAS; NY Acad Sci. *Res:* Cardiovascular nuclear medicine; computer applications and computer-assisted data analysis in nuclear medicine. *Mailing Add:* St Louis Vet Admin Hosp St Louis MO 63125

FLETCHER, JESSE LANE, b New Verda, La, May 31, 16; m 41; c 1. ANIMAL BREEDING. *Educ:* Southwestern La Inst, BS, 37; Tex A&M Col, MS, 39, PhD(animal breeding), 55. *Prof Exp:* Instr biol, McNeese Col, 41-44; res assoc animal indust, La State Univ, 44-46; instr animal sci, Miss State Col, 46-47, asst prof, 47-49, assoc prof, 49-53; environ physiologist, USDA Agr Res Serv Nat Ctr, 56, geneticist, Iberia Sta, 56-61; assoc prof, 61-64, PROF BIOL, MID TENN STATE UNIV, 64- *Mem:* Sigma Xi; AAAS; Am Genetics Asn. *Res:* Polymorphism of Drosophila melanogoster in relationship to season and habitat adaptations. *Mailing Add:* 420 Second Ave Murfreesboro TN 37130

FLETCHER, JOEL EUGENE, b Logan, Utah, Jan 7, 11; m 34; c 2. SOILS. *Educ:* Utah State Agr Col, BS, 34, MS, 37. *Prof Exp:* Asst soil surveyor, Utah State Agr Col, 35; jr soil expert, Soil Conserv Serv, USDA, Univ Ariz, 36, jr soil technologist, 36-38, asst soil technologist, 38-41, col agr, Univ Calif, 41-43 & Univ Ariz, 43-44, soil scientist & proj supvr soil conserv exp sta, 44-45, soil conservationist, 45-54, watershed tech res br, Agr Res Serv, 54-59, soil scientist, Univ Idaho, 59-63; PROF HYDROL, UTAH STATE UNIV, 63-, PROF CIVIL & ENVIRON ENG, 73- *Mem:* Soil Sci Soc Am; Am Soc Agron; Sigma Xi; Am Geophys Union. *Res:* Erodibility of western soils; soil properties affecting infiltration; electrical methods for determining soil moisture; effect of tillage on soil structure and compaction; base exchange equilibria; freezing and moisture phenomena in frozen soils; rainfall-runoff relations; hydrologic instrumentation; weather modification; flood forecasting; erosion estimation and control. *Mailing Add:* Utah Water Res Lab Utah State Univ Box 1304 Logan UT 84321

FLETCHER, JOHN EDWARD, b Banner Elk, NC, June 12, 37; m 64; c 2. APPLIED MATHEMATICS. *Educ:* NC State Univ, BS, 59, MS, 61; Univ Md, PhD(math), 72. *Prof Exp:* Res asst differential equations, NC State Univ, 59-61; opers res sr analyst, Adv Concepts Sect, Adv Studies Div, Lockheed-Ga Co, 64-66; res mathematician, 66-69, CHIEF, APPL MATH SECT, LAB APPL STUDIES, DIV COMPUT RES & TECHNOL, NIH, 69- *Concurrent Pos:* Chmn math & comp sci fac, Found Advan Educ in Sci, 75- *Mem:* Soc Indust & Appl Math; NY Acad Sci; Int Soc Oxygen Transport to Tissue. *Res:* Application of deterministic mathematical models to problems of biological sciences; mathematical simulation models in biology and medicine; numerical methods; data fitting and analysis methods. *Mailing Add:* 12 A 2041 Div Comput Res & Technol 9000 Rockville Pike Bethesda MD 20205

FLETCHER, JOHN GEORGE, b Aberdeen, SDak, Oct 28, 34; m 56; c 3. COMPUTING NETWORKS. *Educ:* George Washington Univ, BS, 55; Princeton Univ, AM, 57, PhD(physics), 59. *Prof Exp:* Mem tech staff, Bell Tel Labs, 59; instr, Princeton Univ, 59-60; PHYSICIST, LAWRENCE LIVERMORE LAB, UNIV CALIF, 61- *Concurrent Pos:* Consult, Grumman Aircraft Eng Corp, 59-63; fel, Miller Inst, 60-62; consult, Ed Serv, Inc, 61-63; lectr, Univ Calif, Davis & Univ Calif, Berkeley, 62-; mem, Comt, Am Nat Standards Inst, 70-73. *Mem:* Fel Am Phys Soc; Asn Comput Mach. *Res:* Computer networks and operating systems; symbol manipulation; relativity; automata. *Mailing Add:* L-60 Lawrence Livermore Lab Univ of Calif Box 808 Livermore CA 94550

FLETCHER, JOHN SAMUEL, b Columbus, Nebr, Jan 7, 38; m 60; c 2. PLANT PHYSIOLOGY, CELL BIOLOGY. *Educ:* Ohio State Univ, BSE, 60; Ariz State Univ, MNS, 65; Purdue Univ, PhD(plant physiol), 69. *Prof Exp:* Asst prof, 69-77, ASSOC PROF BOT & MICROBIOL, UNIV OKLA, 77- *Mem:* Am Soc Plant Physiologists; Am Inst Biol Sci. *Res:* Synthesis and utilization of amino acids in higher plant cells; growth and development of plant tissue cultures. *Mailing Add:* Dept of Bot & Microbiol Univ of Okla Norman OK 73019

FLETCHER, KENNETH STEELE, III, b Springfield, Mass, May 4, 41; m 63; c 2. ANALYTICAL CHEMISTRY. *Educ:* Trinity Col, Conn, BS, 63; Univ Mass, Amherst, PhD(chem), 68. *Prof Exp:* RES CHEMIST, FOXBORO CO, 68- *Mem:* Am Chem Soc. *Res:* Solid state ionic conductivity; ion selective electrode materials; refractory borides, nitrides and carbides for voltammetry and coulometry; voltammetric hydrodynamics. *Mailing Add:* Res Ctr Foxboro Co Foxboro MA 02035

FLETCHER, LEROY S(TEVENSON), b San Antonio, Tex, Oct 10, 36; m 66; c 2. MECHANICAL & AEROSPACE ENGINEERING. *Educ:* Tex A&M Univ, BS, 58; Stanford Univ, MS, 63, Engr, 64; Ariz State Univ, PhD(mech eng), 68. *Prof Exp:* Aeronaut engr, Ames Aeronaut Lab, Nat Adv Comt Aeronaut, 58-60, aerospace engr, Ames Res Ctr, NASA, 61-63; asst heat transfer, Dept Mech Eng, Stanford Univ, 62-63; asst thermodynamics, 63-64; asst mech eng, Ariz State Univ, 64-65, instr, 65-68; from asst prof to prof aerospace eng, Rutgers Univ, 68-75, actg assoc dean, 74-75; prof & chmn mech eng dept, Univ Va, 75-77, prof mech & aero eng & chmn dept, 77-80; ASSOC DEAN, COL ENG, TEX A&M UNIV, 80- *Concurrent Pos:* Mem President's adv comt energy conservation, Univ Va, 75-80; mem governor's comt conservation energy resources, Commonwealth Va, 76-80. *Honors & Awards:* Ralph R Teeter Award, Soc Automotive Engrs, 70; Centennial Medallion, Am Soc Mech Engrs, 80; George Westinghouse Award, Am Soc Eng Educ, 81. *Mem:* Fel Am Soc Mech Engrs; assoc fel Am Inst Aeronaut & Astronaut; Am Soc Eng Educ; AAAS. *Res:* Heat transfer; conduction, convection, radiation; aerothermodynamics; energy conservation, energy systems, aerodynamics, fluid mechanics. *Mailing Add:* Col Eng Tex A&M Univ College Station TX 77843

FLETCHER, LOWELL W, b Princeton, WVa, Aug 18, 20; m 49; c 4. ENTOMOLOGY. *Educ:* Concord Col, BS, 47; WVa Univ, MS, 58; Rutgers Univ, PhD(entom), 61. *Prof Exp:* Res med entomologist, USDA, 61-69, res entomologist, Tobacco Insect Invest, 69-70, INSECT ECOLOGIST, TOBACCO INSECT INVEST, USDA, 70- *Mem:* Entom Soc Am; AAAS. *Res:* Basic insect biology; physical and biological methods of insect control. *Mailing Add:* USDA Tobacco Insect Invest PO Box 10125 Richmond VA 23240

FLETCHER, MARTIN J, b New York, NY, Aug 24, 32; m 60; c 1. BIOCHEMISTRY. *Educ:* Columbia Col, AB, 53; Purdue Univ, MS, 58, PhD(biochem), 59. *Prof Exp:* Biochemist, NIH, 59-62; chemist natural prods, Wallace Labs, Carter Prods, Inc, 62-68; DIR BIOCHEM, AFFIL MED ENTERPRISES INC, 68-, VPRES, 74- *Mem:* AAAS; Am Chem Soc; NY Acad Sci. *Res:* Biochemistry of energy metabolism; isolation, purification and identification of natural products. *Mailing Add:* Sleepy Hollow Ln Belle Mead NJ 08502

FLETCHER, MARY ANN, b Little Rock, Ark, July 23, 37; c 1. IMMUNOLOGY. *Educ:* Tex Technol Col, BS, 59; Univ Tex, MA, 61; Baylor Univ, PhD(microbiol, biochem), 66. *Prof Exp:* Res assoc immunochem, Evanston Hosp, 66-69; asst dir, Div Hemat, Michael Reese Hosp, Chicago, 69-72; from asst prof to assoc prof, 72-80, PROF IMMUNOL, SCH MED, UNIV MIAMI, 80- *Concurrent Pos:* Asst prof, Dept Microbiol, Northwestern Univ, 67-69; asst prof, Dept Biol, Ill Inst Technol, 70-72. *Mem:* Am Asn Immunol; Am Soc Microbiol; Soc Complex Carbohydrates; AAAS; Asn Women in Sci. *Res:* Immunochemistry of membrane antigens. *Mailing Add:* Dept Med Univ Miami Sch Med PO Box 520875 Miami FL 33152

FLETCHER, NEIL RUSSEL, b Morenci, Mich, Oct 17, 33; m 58; c 3. NUCLEAR PHYSICS. *Educ:* Mich State Univ, BS, 55; Duke Univ, PhD(physics), 61. *Prof Exp:* Res assoc physics, Duke Univ, 60-61; res assoc, 61-63, from asst prof to assoc prof, 63-74, PROF PHYSICS, FLA STATE UNIV, 74-, MEM GRAD FAC, 80- *Mem:* Am Phys Soc. *Res:* Low energy nuclear physics; direct reactions and reaction mechanisms; angular correlations; structure of light nuclei. *Mailing Add:* Dept of Physics Fla State Univ Tallahassee FL 32306

FLETCHER, OSCAR JASPER, JR, b Bennettsville, SC, Oct 18, 38; m 63; c 2. PATHOLOGY. *Educ:* Wofford Col, BS, 60; Univ Ga, DVM, 63, MS, 65; Univ Wis, PhD(vet sci), 68; Am Col Vet Path, dipl. *Prof Exp:* Res asst path, Univ Ga, 64-65; trainee, Univ Wis, 65-68; asst prof path, 68-72, assoc prof path, 75-78, PROF AVIAN MED & PATH, UNIV GA, 78-, ASSOC DEAN, COL VET MED, 76- *Mem:* Am Vet Med Asn; Am Asn Avian Pathologists; Conf Res Works Animal Dis. *Res:* Rheumatoid; neoplastic diseases of domestic animals especially serum protein alterations; immunopathology; avian histopathy. *Mailing Add:* Col Vet Med Univ of Ga Athens GA 30602

FLETCHER, PAUL CHIPMAN, b New York, NY, Jan 10, 26; m 55; c 4. SOLID STATE PHYSICS. *Educ:* Mass Inst Technol, BS, 47; Columbia Univ, PhD, 57. *Prof Exp:* Res physicist, Res Labs, Hughes Aircraft Co, 57-61; mgr quantum physics lab, Electro-Optical Systs, Inc, 61-66; chief space optics lab, NASA Electronic Res Ctr, 66, chief optics lab, 66-70; head Electromagnetic Systs Dept, Naval Electronics Lab Ctr, 70-80; HEAD DEPT ENG SCI, US NAVAL OCEAN SYSTS CTR, 80- *Mem:* AAAS; Am Phys Soc; sr mem Inst Elec & Electronics Engrs. *Res:* Gaseous microwave spectroscopy; magnetism; lasers; electro-optics. *Mailing Add:* Eng Sci Dept Naval Ocean Systs Ctr 271 Catalina Blvd San Diego CA 92152

FLETCHER, PAUL LITTON, JR, b Raleigh, NC, Aug 19, 41; m 73. PROTEIN CHEMISTRY. *Educ:* Va Polytech Inst, BS, 64; Univ NC, Greensboro, MA, 68; Vanderbilt Univ, PhD(microbiol), 71. *Prof Exp:* Res assoc biochem, Rockefeller Univ, 71-74; res assoc, Med Sch, Yale Univ, 74-75, asst prof cell biol, 75-79; ASSOC PROF MICROBIOL, SCH MED, EAST CAROLINA UNIV, GREENVILLE, NC, 79- *Mem:* Sigma Xi; NY Acad Sci; Am Chem Soc. *Res:* Isolation and characterization and sequence analysis of proteins from cell membranes; mechanisms of exocytosis from pancreatic acinar cells. *Mailing Add:* Sect Cell Biol IE-26 IHR Bldg Med Sch Yale Univ 333 Cedar St New Haven CT 06510

FLETCHER, PAUL WAYNE, b Woodbury, NJ, Feb 20, 51; m 73. BIOCHEMICAL ENDOCRINOLOGY, GONADOTROPIC RECEPTORS. *Educ:* Univ Del, BS, 74; Clemson Univ, MS, 75; Univ Wyo, PhD(reproduction phys), 78. *Prof Exp:* Fel, Colo State Univ, 78-80; ASST PROF MED BIOCHEM, ALBANY MED COL, UNION UNIV, 80- *Mem:* Soc Study Reproduction. *Res:* Mechanism of gonadotropin action in the testis; regulation of hormone-receptor interaction; activation of adenylate cyclase. *Mailing Add:* Dept Biochem Albany Med Col 47 New Scotland Ave Albany NY 12208

FLETCHER, PETER, b New York, NY, July 6, 39; m 62. TOPOLOGY. *Educ:* Washington & Lee Univ, BS, 62; Univ NC, Chapel Hill, MA, 64, PhD(math), 66. *Prof Exp:* assoc prof, 67-80, PROF MATH, VA POLYTECH INST & STATE UNIV, 80- *Mem:* Am Math Soc; Math Asn Am. *Res:* Quasi-uniform spaces. *Mailing Add:* Dept Math McBryde Hall Va Polytech Inst & State Univ Blacksburg VA 24060

FLETCHER, PETER C, b Shrewsbury, Eng, Nov 16, 35; m 67. PHYSICAL CHEMISTRY, CERAMICS. *Educ:* Univ Liverpool, BSc, 56, PhD(surface chem), 59. *Prof Exp:* Gulf Oil fel, State Univ NY, 59-60; sr scientist physics & surface chem, Owens-Ill Co, Ohio, 60-70; MAT ENGR ELECTRONIC MAT DIV, BELL & HOWELL CO, PASADENA, 70- *Mem:* Am Chem Soc; Am Ceramic Soc; sr mem Am Vacuum Soc. *Res:* Surface physics and chemistry; heterogeneous catalysis; glass. *Mailing Add:* 890 Ridgeside Dr Monrovia CA 91016

FLETCHER, ROBERT CHIPMAN, b New York, NY, May 27, 21; m 45; c 8. PHYSICS. *Educ:* Mass Inst Technol, BS, 43, PhD(physics), 49. *Prof Exp:* Mem staff, Radiation Lab, Mass Inst Technol, 43-45, asst, Insulation Lab, 47-49; mem tech staff, Bell Tel Labs, 49-58, dir solid state device develop, 58-64; vpres res, Sandia Corp, 64-67; exec dir mil systs res div & ocean systs div, 67-71, EXEC DIR, INTEGRATED CIRCUIT DESIGN DIV, BELL LABS, 71- *Mem:* Fel Am Phys Soc; fel Inst Elec & Electronics Engrs. *Res:* Electron dynamics; magnetrons; traveling wave tubes; gas discharge; impulse breakdown of air; semiconductors; magnetic and ultrasonic devices; masers; solid state devices; optical devices; integrated circuits. *Mailing Add:* Integrated Circuit Design Bell Labs Murray Hill NJ 07974

FLETCHER, ROBERT HILLMAN, b Abington, Pa, Mar 26, 40; m 63; c 2. INTERNAL MEDICINE, EPIDEMIOLOGY. *Educ:* Wesleyan Univ, BA, 62; Harvard Univ, MD, 66; Johns Hopkins Univ, MSc, 73. *Prof Exp:* Asst prof med & epidemiol, McGill Univ, 73-78; ASSOC PROF MED & EPIDEMIOL & DIR ROBERT WOOD JOHNSON CLIN SCHOLARS PROG, UNIV NC, CHAPEL HILL, 78-; CO-CHIEF DIV GEN MED & RES ASSOC, HEALTH SERV RES CTR, 78- *Concurrent Pos:* Dir med poly clin, Royal Victoria Hosp, 73-78. *Mem:* Fel Am Col Physicians; Am Fedn Clin Res; Sigma Xi; Asn Health Rec; Soc Res & Educ Primary Care Med. *Res:* Clinical epidemiology and health care research. *Mailing Add:* Clin Scholars Prog Wing B Box 5 207H Chapel Hill NC 27514

FLETCHER, ROBERT HOLTON, b Lansing, Mich, June 19, 06; m 33; c 2. MECHANICAL ENGINEERING. *Educ:* Pa State Univ, BS, 28. *Prof Exp:* Exp tester aeronaut eng, Lycoming Mfg Co, 28-31; owner, Adkins Ice Cream Co, 33-41; instr ord vehicles, US Army, 41-43; res engr combat vehicles, Aberdeen Proving Grounds Md, 43-45; coordr diversified occupations, Pub Sch Syst, Waco, Tex, 45-46; from instr to prof, 47-74, EMER PROF MECH ENG, TEX A&M UNIV, 74- *Concurrent Pos:* Consult var comt & state industs; results engr, Houston Lighting & Power Co, 65, 68 & 70; proj engr, Tex Elec Power Inst, 66-67. *Mem:* Soc Automotive Engrs; Am Soc Eng Educ. *Res:* Automotive and aircraft engineering; reciprocating, gas turbine and high energy engines; plant efficiencies; oil string casing design. *Mailing Add:* 749 N Rosemary Dr Bryan TX 77801

FLETCHER, RONALD AUSTIN, b Cape Comorin, India, July 1, 31; Can citizen; m 62; c 2. PLANT PHYSIOLOGY. *Educ:* Univ Delhi, BSc, 54; Univ BC, MSc, 61; Univ Alta, PhD(physiol), 64. *Prof Exp:* Sect officer landscape hort, Govt India, 54-59; Nat Res Coun Can-NATO overseas res fel sci, Eng, 64-65; from asst prof to assoc prof bot, 65-72, PROF ENVIRON BIOL, UNIV GUELPH, 72- *Concurrent Pos:* Nat Res Coun Can exchange fel, France, 73. *Mem:* Can Soc Plant Physiologists (secy, 67-68); Am Soc Plant Physiologists; Scand Soc Plant Physiologists. *Res:* Hormonal regulation of plant growth and development; mode of action of herbicides. *Mailing Add:* Dept of Environ Biol Univ of Guelph Guelph Can

FLETCHER, RONALD D, b Foxboro, Mass, Jan 18, 33; m; c 3. VIROLOGY, MYCOPLASMA BIOLOGY. *Educ:* Univ Conn, BS, 54, MS, 59, PhD(bact), 63. *Prof Exp:* Nat Inst Allergy & Infectious Dis fel microbiol, Vet Bact Inst, Univ Zürich, 63-64; res virologist, Antimicrobial Ther Dept, Lederle Labs, Am Cyanamid Co, 64-67; ASSOC PROF MICROBIOL & ASSOC HEAD DEPT, SCH DENT MED, UNIV PITTSBURGH, 67- *Concurrent Pos:* Gen res support grant, Univ Pittsburgh, 67-68; Am Cancer Soc instnl res grant, 68-69; Dept Army life sci div grant, 69-72; Nat Inst Dent Res grant, 75-79, res develop fund, 80-81. *Mem:* Fel AAAS; fel Am Acad Microbiol; Am Soc Microbiol; Tissue Cult Asn; Int Asn Dent Res. *Res:* Relationship between mycoplasma species and selected respiratory viruses, in vitro and in vivo; adhesion of animate human cells with inanimate materials; adhesion in biological systems. *Mailing Add:* Dept Microbiol 645 Salk Hall Univ Pittsburgh Sch Dent Med Pittsburgh PA 15261

FLETCHER, ROY JACKSON, b Red Deer, Alta, Feb 1, 35; c 3. CLIMATOLOGY. *Educ:* Univ Alta, BA, 57, Univ Minn, MA, 59; Clark Univ, PhD(geog), 68. *Prof Exp:* Lectr geog, State Univ NY Buffalo, 61-68; assoc prof, 68-76, PROF GEOG, UNIV LETHBRIDGE, 76- *Mem:* Asn Am Geog; Am Soc Photogram; Arctic Inst NAm; Can Asn Geog. *Res:* Synoptic and dynamic climatology; biometeorology; arctic, especially physical geography; transportation and human ecology. *Mailing Add:* Dept of Geog Univ of Lethbridge Lethbridge AB T1K 3M4 Can

FLETCHER, STEWART G(AILEY), b Wilkinsburg, Pa, Jan 20, 18; m 42; c 4. METALLURGY. *Educ:* Carnegie Inst Technol, BS, 38; Mass Inst Technol, ScD(phys metall), 43. *Prof Exp:* Lab instr metall, Carnegie Inst Technol, 37-39; asst, Mass Inst Technol, 39-42; res assoc, 42-45; chief res metallurgist, Latrobe Steel Co, 45-47, chief metallurgist, 47-57, vpres & tech dir, 57-73; sr vpres, Am Iron & Steel Inst, 73-80; CONSULT & PRES, FERROTECHNOL, INC, 80- *Concurrent Pos:* Lab instr, Lowell Inst Sch, 39-41, instr, 42-44. *Honors & Awards:* Howe Medal, Am Soc Metals, 46 & 49. *Mem:* Fel AAAS; fel Am Soc Metals (secy, 62-64, vpres, 64-65, pres, 65-66); Am Iron & Steel Inst; Am Inst Mining, Metall & Petrol Engrs; Metals Soc London. *Res:* Heat treatment of tool and die steels; alloying tool steels; electric steel making; vacuum melting of steels; superalloys; electroslag melting; technical and engineering administration. *Mailing Add:* 4407 Tournay Rd Bethesda MD 20816

FLETCHER, THOMAS FRANCIS, b New York, NY, Mar 26, 37; m 60; c 5. VETERINARY ANATOMY. *Educ:* Cornell Univ, DVM, 61; Univ Minn, PhD(vet anat), 65. *Prof Exp:* From asst prof to assoc prof, 65-72, PROF VET ANAT, COL VET MED, UNIV MINN, ST PAUL, 72- *Concurrent Pos:* USPHS grants, 65-66 & 67-81. *Mem:* Am Asn Anatomists; Am Asn Vet Anat; World Asn Vet Anatomists. *Res:* Neuroanatomy and neurophysiology of the spinal cord; anatomicophysiological basis of nervous disorders in domestic animals; morphometry; pathogenesis of canine globoid leukodystrophy. *Mailing Add:* Dept of Vet Biol Univ of Minn St Paul MN 55101

FLETCHER, THOMAS LLOYD, b Boydton, Va, Jan 4, 17; m 41; c 4. ORGANIC CHEMISTRY. *Educ:* Clark Univ, AB, 37, MA, 38; Univ Wis, PhD(biochem, org chem), 49. *Prof Exp:* Chemist, Lever Bros Co, Mass, 39-42; chemist, Colonial-Beacon Oil Co, 42; teacher chem, Adm Billard Acad, 42-43; chemist, Forest Prod Lab, US Forest Serv, 43-48; chemist, Pulp Mills Res, 48-51, res chemist, Dept Surg, Sch Med, 51-55, from res assoc prof to res prof surg, 55-67, PROF SURG, CHEM RES LAB, SCH MED, UNIV WASH, 67-; MEM, FRED HUTCHINSON CANCER RES CTR, 72- *Concurrent Pos:* Nat Cancer Inst res career develop award, 61-71. *Mem:* Fel AAAS; Am Chem Soc; The Chem Soc; Soc Exp Biol & Med; Am Cancer Soc. *Res:* Chemistry of fluorene and other aryl polycyclics; carcinogenicity; cancer chemotherapy

FLETCHER, WILLIAM ELLIS, b Colfax, La, Nov 11, 36; m; c 3. HORTICULTURE. *Educ:* Univ Southwestern La, BS, 58; Iowa State Univ, MS, 61, PhD, 64. *Prof Exp:* Asst, Iowa State Univ, 58-63, instr, 63-64; asst prof ornamental hort, Univ Fla, 64-67; asst prof, 67-69, assoc prof, 69-76, PROF HORT, UNIV SOUTHWEST LA, 76- *Res:* Woody ornamentals; general nursery stock and foliage plants. *Mailing Add:* Dept of Hort Col of Agr Univ of Southwest La Lafayette LA 70504

FLETCHER, WILLIAM HENRY, b Eureka, Kans, Apr 25, 16; m 49; c 4. PHYSICAL CHEMISTRY. *Educ:* Col Idaho, BS, 39; Univ Minn, PhD(chem), 49. *Prof Exp:* Res chemist, Norwich Pharmacal Co, 40-42; res chemist, Lubrizol Corp, 42-46; from asst prof to assoc prof, 49-59, PROF CHEM, UNIV TENN, KNOXVILLE, 59- *Concurrent Pos:* Consult, Union Carbide Nuclear Co, 57. *Mem:* Optical Soc Am; Coblentz Soc; Soc Appl Spectros; Am Chem Soc; Am Phys Soc. *Res:* Molecular spectroscopy; molecular force fields; high resolution Raman spectroscopy. *Mailing Add:* 7132 Cheshire Dr Knoxville TN 37919

FLETCHER, WILLIAM L, US citizen. ENGINEERING. *Educ:* New England Col, BS, 57; Northeastern Univ, MS, 62. *Prof Exp:* Proj engr, Camp, Dresser & McKee, Inc, 57-67; prin sanit engr, NH Water Supply & Pollution Control Comn, 67-69; mem staff, Environ Engrs, Inc, 69-76; VPRES, WESTON, 76- *Concurrent Pos:* Advr to Gov Coun on Energy, 74-78. *Mem:* Am Soc Civil Engrs; dipl Am Acad Environ Engrs. *Res:* Engineering management; project management; environmental engineering; civil engineering. *Mailing Add:* Weston Weston Way West Chester PA 19380

FLETCHER, WILLIAM SIGOURNEY, b Arlington, Mass, May 7, 27; m 49; c 3. SURGERY. *Educ:* Dartmouth Col, AB, 52; Harvard Med Sch, MD, 55. *Prof Exp:* Am Cancer Soc clin fel, Middlesex Hosp, London, Eng, 58-59; from instr to assoc prof, 60-70, PROF SURG, HEALTH SCI CTR, UNIV ORE, 70-, HEAD DIV SURG ONCOL, 75- *Concurrent Pos:* Advan clin fel, 60-63; Markle scholar med sci, 62-67. *Mem:* Am Col Surg; Soc Surg Oncol; Am Soc Clin Oncol; Am Fedn Clin Res; AMA. *Res:* Medical education; basic experimental and clinical cancer research; breeding a large standard laboratory dog. *Mailing Add:* Dept of Surg Univ of Ore Health Sci Ctr Portland OR 97201

FLETCHER, WILLIAM THOMAS, b Durham, NC, Aug 19, 34. MATHEMATICS. *Educ:* NC Col Durham, BS, 56, MS, 58; Univ Idaho, PhD(math), 66. *Prof Exp:* From assoc prof to prof math, LeMoyne-Owen Col, 57-72; PROF & CHMN DEPT MATH, NC CENT UNIV, 72- *Mem:* Math Asn Am; Am Math Soc. *Res:* Lie algebras; abstract algebra; associative and non associative. *Mailing Add:* Dept of Math NC Cent Univ Durham NC 27707

FLETTERICK, ROBERT JOHN, b Cleveland, Ohio, July 22, 43. MOLECULAR BIOPHYSICS. *Educ:* Marietta Col, BS, 65; Cornell Univ, PhD(chem), 70. *Prof Exp:* Fel biochem, Yale Univ, 70-74; asst prof biochem, Univ Alta, 74-79; ASSOC PROF BIOCHEM, UNIV CALIF, SAN FRANCISCO, 79- *Mem:* Am Crystallog Asn; Brit Biophys Soc; Can Biochem Soc. *Res:* Structure and function of proteins; investigations using x-ray diffraction; regulation of glycogen metabolism. *Mailing Add:* Dept Biochem Univ Calif San Francisco CA 94122

FLEURY, PAUL A, b Baltimore, Md, July 20, 39; m 64; c 3. SOLID STATE PHYSICS, SPECTROSCOPY. *Educ:* John Carroll Univ, BS, 60, MS, 62; Mass Inst Technol, PhD(physics), 65. *Prof Exp:* Mem tech staff, 65-70, dept head physics, 70-79, DIR MAT RES, BELL TEL LABS, 79- *Mem:* Fel Am Phys Soc; AAAS. *Res:* Nonlinear optical and inelastic laser light scattering studies of solids and simple fluids including semiconductors, ferroelectrics, magnets and their phase transitions; fiber optics, semiconductors, ceramics, metals and alloys. *Mailing Add:* Room 1A161 Bell Tel Labs Murray Hill NJ 07974

FLEXMAN, EDMUND A, JR, b Harrisburg, Liberia, Aug 13, 40; US citizen; m 64; c 2. POLYMER CHEMISTRY. *Educ:* Bradley Univ, BA, 62; Ind Univ, Bloomington, PhD(org chem), 67. *Prof Exp:* Phys sci aide paper chem, Northern Regional Lab, USDA, 61-64; RES CHEMIST, EXP STA, E I DU PONT DE NEMOURS & CO, INC, 65- *Mem:* Am Chem Soc; Sigma Xi. *Res:* Polymer chemistry and physics. *Mailing Add:* Exp Sta Lab E I Du Pont de Nemours & Co Inc Wilmington DE 19898

FLEXNER, JOHN M, b Louisville, Ky, Mar 29, 26; m 54; c 4. INTERNAL MEDICINE, HEMATOLOGY. *Educ:* Yale Univ, BA, 50; Johns Hopkins Univ, MD, 54. *Prof Exp:* Intern, Vanderbilt Univ Hosp, 54-55, asst resident internal med, 55-56; Grace New Haven Hosp, Conn, 56-57; from instr to asst prof, 59-71, ASSOC PROF MED, SCH MED, VANDERBILT UNIV, 71- *Concurrent Pos:* USPHS fel hemat, Sch Med, Vanderbilt Univ, 57-59; asst & vis hematologist, Vanderbilt Univ Hosp, 57-59, vis hematologist & dir, Hemat Labs & Blood Bank, 59-; consult, Thayer Vet Admin Hosp, Nashville, Tenn, 59- & Regional Blood Ctr Labs, 65- *Mem:* AAAS; Am Soc Hemat. *Res:* Effect of oral fat intake on blood coagulation; megaloblastic anemia due to anti-convulsants; paroxysmal nocturnal hemoglobinuria; myleran induced pulmonary pneumonitis and fibrosis. *Mailing Add:* 4213 Wallace Lane Nashville TN 37215

FLEXNER, LOUIS BARKHOUSE, b Louisville, Ky, Jan 7, 02; m 37. ANATOMY. *Educ:* Univ Chicago, BS, 22; Johns Hopkins Univ, MD, 27. *Hon Degrees:* LLD, Univ Pa. *Prof Exp:* Loeb fel, Johns Hopkins Univ, 27-28; resident house officer, Clins, Chicago, 28-29; instr & assoc anat, Sch Med, Johns Hopkins Univ, 30-40; mem staff, Dept Embryol, Carnegie Inst, 40-51; chmn dept anat, 51-67, dir inst neurol sci, 53-65, PROF ANAT, SCH MED, UNIV PA, 51- *Concurrent Pos:* Mem tech aide comt aviation med, Nat Res Coun, 42-45; mem study sects, USPHS, 51-70; res assoc, Carnegie Inst, 51-; mem adv bd, United Cerebral Palsy Asn, 56 & Nat Found, 59-64. *Honors & Awards:* Weinstein Award, 57. *Mem:* Nat Acad Sci; Am Physiol Soc; Am Soc Biol Chemists; Am Acad Arts & Sci; Am Asn Anatomists (secy-treas, 56-64). *Res:* Meninges and cerebrospinal fluid; learning and memory; fetal physiology. *Mailing Add:* Dept Anat Univ Pa Sch Med Philadelphia PA 19104

FLEXSER, LEO AARON, b New York, NY, June 20, 1910; m 39; c 1. CHEMISTRY. *Educ:* Columbia Univ, AB, 31, AM, 32, PhD(chem), 35. *Prof Exp:* Asst chem, Columbia Univ, 31-34; res chemist, Montrose Chem Co, NJ, 35-36, plant supt, 36-38; instr chem, Brooklyn Col, 38; res chemist, NY Quinine & Chem Co, 38-41; sr chemist, Hoffmann-La Roche, Inc, 41-45, group chief mfg & develop dept, 45-59, dir chem prod, 59-63, vpres, 63-75, consult, 75-77; RETIRED. *Concurrent Pos:* Mem bd trustees, Jersey City State Col, NJ, 68-; pres, R P, Inc, Puerto Rico, 74-75, consult, 75-77. *Mem:* AAAS; Am Chem Soc; fel Am Inst Chemists; Am Inst Chem Eng. *Res:* Process research and development in synthesis and manufacture of vitamins and pharmaceutical chemicals; administration of fine chemical manufacturing and development. *Mailing Add:* 3 The Fairway Upper Montclair NJ 07043

FLICK, CATHY, b Bryn Mawr, Pa, June 19, 49. PHYSICS, CHEMICAL PHYSICS. *Educ:* Marywood Col, BS, 71; Kent State Univ, MA, 74, PhD(chem physics), 76. *Prof Exp:* asst prof physics, Earlham Col, 76-79; SCI TRANSLR & CONSULT, 78- *Mem:* Am Phys Soc; Am Chem Soc. *Res:* Liquid crystals; biomembrane model systems; magnetic resonance spectroscopy. *Mailing Add:* 302 S W 5th St Richmond IN 47374

FLICK, GEORGE JOSEPH, JR, b New Orleans, La, May 30, 40; m 67; c 3. FOOD SCIENCE. *Educ:* La State Univ, Baton Rouge, BA, 63, MS, 66, PhD(food sci), 69. *Prof Exp:* Asst prof, 69-73, assoc prof, 73-78, PROF FOOD SCI & TECHNOL, VA POLYTECH INST & STATE UNIV, 78- *Concurrent Pos:* Vis prof, Southern Regional Res Ctr, US Dept Agr, 73-; mem bd dirs, Nat Fisheries Educ & Res Found, 81- *Mem:* AAAS; Am Chem Soc; Inst Food Technol; Marine Technol Soc; Am Sch Food Serv Asn. *Res:* Separation and isolation of compounds in marine organisms; chemical and microbiological contaminants in processed seafood products; utilization and biochemical properties of marine products and sub-tropical fruits and vegetables. *Mailing Add:* Food Sci & Technol Va Polytech Inst & State Univ Blacksburg VA 24061

FLICK, JOHN A, b Camden, NJ, May 10, 17; m 43, 67; c 5. IMMUNOLOGY. *Educ:* Haverford Col, BS, 39; Harvard Univ, MD, 43. *Prof Exp:* Instr, 44-53, chmn dept, Div Grad Med, 55-72, ASSOC PROF MED MICROBIOL, SCH MED, UNIV PA, 53- *Mem:* AAAS; Am Asn Immunol; Reticuloendothelial Soc. *Res:* Allergy; immunology. *Mailing Add:* Dept of Microbiol Univ of Pa Sch of Med Philadelphia PA 19104

FLICK, PARKE KINSEY, b French Lick, Ind, Oct 3, 46; m 77. BIOCHEMISTRY. *Educ:* Purdue Univ, BSChE, 68, MS, 70; Harvard Univ, PhD(chem), 75. *Prof Exp:* Fel biochem, Sch Med, Wash Univ, 75 & Merck Sharp & Dohme Res Labs, 75-77; ASST PROF BIOCHEM, SCH MED, WRIGHT STATE UNIV, 77- *Concurrent Pos:* NIH grant, 78- *Mem:* Am Chem Soc; AAAS. *Res:* Regulation of lipid metabolism in mammals and bacteria; structure and function of biological membranes; regulation of gene expression. *Mailing Add:* Dept of Biol Chem Sch Med Wright State Univ Dayton OH 45435

FLICKER, HERBERT, b Brooklyn, NY, Jan 28, 30; m 53; c 2. LASERS, MOLECULAR SPECTROSCOPY. *Educ:* Cornell Univ, AB, 51; Univ Pa, MS, 53, PhD(physics), 59. *Prof Exp:* Mem tech staff, RCA Labs, 59-64; vis assoc prof eng, Brown Univ, 64-65; mem staff, TRW Systs Group, 65-66; mgr semiconductor dept, Electrooptical Systs, Xerox Corp, 66-68, chief scientist advan systs & requirements, 68-72; MEM STAFF, LOS ALAMOS SCI LAB, 72- *Mem:* Am Phys Soc; Inst Elec & Electronics Engrs. *Res:* Semiconductor physics; radiation damage in semiconductors; cryogenics; optical and electrical properties of semiconductors; infrared photodetectors, systems analysis; molecular spectroscopy using tunable diode lasers, and fourier transform spectrometer. *Mailing Add:* 535 Totavi Los Alamos NM 87544

FLICKER, YUVAL ZVI, b Tel Aviv, Israel, Jan 3, 55. AUTOMORPHIC FORMS. *Educ:* Tel Aviv Univ, BA, 73; Hebrew Univ, MA, 74; Cambridge Univ, PhD(math), 78. *Prof Exp:* Vis, Inst Advan Study, Princeton, 78-79; asst prof, Columbia Univ, 79-81; vis, Univ Paris, 80-81; ASST PROF, PRINCETON UNIV, 81- *Res:* Automorphic representations, trace formula. *Mailing Add:* Fine Hall Box 37 Princeton Univ Princeton NJ 08544

FLICKINGER, GEORGE LATIMORE, JR, b Hanover, Pa, May 21, 33; m 58; c 3. COMPARATIVE PATHOLOGY, REPRODUCTIVE PHYSIOLOGY. *Educ:* Pa State Univ, BS, 54; Univ Pa, VMD, 58, PhD(path), 63. *Prof Exp:* Assoc dir path, Penrose Res Lab, 62-63; from instr to assoc path, 63-66, from assoc to asst prof obstet & gynec, 64-73, ASSOC PROF OBSTET & GYNEC, UNIV PA, 73- *Mem:* AAAS; Endocrine Soc. *Res:* Hormone secretion by gonadal tissues; relationship of social behavior to reproductive performance. *Mailing Add:* Univ Hosp Rm 581 Dulles Bldg 34th & Spruce Sts Philadelphia PA 19104

FLICKINGER, REED ADAMS, b Council Bluffs, Iowa, Apr 5, 24; m 49; c 2. DEVELOPMENTAL BIOLOGY. *Educ:* Stanford Univ, BA, 46, PhD, 49. *Prof Exp:* Instr embryol, Univ Pa, 49-52; asst prof, Univ Calif, Los Angeles, 52-58; assoc prof, Univ Iowa, 58-61 & Univ Calif, Davis, 61-64; PROF EMBRYOL, STATE UNIV NY BUFFALO, 64- *Concurrent Pos:* Rockefeller res fel, Brussels, Belg, 50-51; Stockholm, Sweden, 51-52; USPHS spec fels, Paris, 61 & Honolulu, 72. *Mem:* Soc Develop Biol; Am Soc Cell Biologists. *Mailing Add:* Dept of Biol State Univ of NY Buffalo NY 14214

FLICKINGER, STEPHEN ALBERT, b Savanna, Ill, Feb 12, 42; m 66; c 1. FISH BIOLOGY. *Educ:* Southern Ill Univ, Carbondale, BA, 64, MA, 66; Colo State Univ, PhD(fishery biol), 69. *Prof Exp:* Asst prof, Univ Ill, 69-77, ASSOC PROF FISHERY BIOL, COLO STATE UNIV, 77- *Mem:* Am Fisheries Soc. *Res:* Culture of food, bait, and sport fishes. *Mailing Add:* Dept of Fish & Wildlife Biol Colo State Univ Ft Collins CO 80521

FLIEDNER, LEONARD JOHN, JR, b Flushing, NY, Mar 16, 37. MEDICINAL CHEMISTRY, CLINICAL RESEARCH. *Educ:* Princeton Univ, AB, 58; Fordham Univ, MS, 60; Univ Mass, PhD(org chem), 65. *Prof Exp:* SR RES CHEMIST, ENDO LABS, INC, GARDEN CITY, 65- *Concurrent Pos:* Clin res monitor, Ayerst Labs, New York, NY, 81- *Mem:* Am Chem Soc; Am Inst Chemists; AAAS. *Res:* Synthetic organic chemistry; synthesis of fibrinolytics, analgetics and antidepressants; heterocyclic chemistry. *Mailing Add:* 109 Mineola Ave PO Box 498 Point Lookout NY 11569

FLIEGEL, HENRY FREDERICK, b Ridley Park, Pa, Apr 25, 36. ASTRONOMY, GEODESY. *Educ:* Univ Pa, BA, 58, PhD(astron), 63; Ohio State Univ, MA, 59. *Prof Exp:* Staff astronr, US Naval Observ, 63-65; asst prof astron, Georgetown Univ, 65-68; prof astron & physics, Del State Col, 68-69; MEM TECH STAFF EARTH PHYSICS APPLN, JET PROPULSION LAB, CALIF INST TECHNOL, 69- *Concurrent Pos:* Mem, Com l'Heure, Int Astron Union, 75- *Mem:* Am Astron Soc; Am Geophys Union. *Res:* Applications of astronomical data, especially optical observations of time and polar motion; radio interferometry to spacecraft navigation and studies of earth crustal motion. *Mailing Add:* PO Box 8682 La Crescenta CA 91214

FLINDERS, JERRAN T, b Salt Lake City, Utah, July 2, 37; m 56; c 5. WILDLIFE ECOLOGY, RANGE ECOLOGY. *Educ:* Univ Utah, BS, 67, MS, 68; Colo State Univ, PhD(animal ecol), 71. *Prof Exp:* Asst prof, Dept Range & Wildlife Mgt, Tex Tech Univ, 71-74; assoc prof wildlife resources & affil fac range resources, Col Forestry Wildlife & Range Resources, Univ Idaho, 74-76; assoc prof, 76-80, PROF & DIR WILDLIFE & RANGE RESOURCES GRAD PROG, BRIGHAM YOUNG UNIV, 76-, CHMN DEPT BOT & RANGE SCI, 80- *Mem:* Wildlife Soc; Soc Range Mgt; Am Soc Mammalogists; Nat Wildlife Fedn. *Res:* Mule deer habitat selection and deer fawn mortality; baseline wildlife habitat studies prior to strip mining; ecological studies of bobcats leading to management purposes; dietary studies of pygmy rabbits; habitat selection of sage grass in relation to fire and grazing practices. *Mailing Add:* 407 WIDB Brigham Young Univ Provo UT 84602

FLINK, EDMUND BERNEY, b Isanti, Minn, Jan 27, 14; m 40; c 4. MEDICINE. *Educ:* Univ Minn, BS & MB, 37, MD, 38, PhD(internal med), 45. *Prof Exp:* From instr to asst prof internal med, Sch Med, Univ Minn, 42-45, from asst prof to prof med, 45-60; chmn dept, 60-76, PROF MED, MED CTR, W VA UNIV, 60- *Concurrent Pos:* Commonwealth Fund fel, Harvard Univ, 48-49; chief med serv, Vet Admin Hosp, Minn, 52-60. *Mem:* Endocrine Soc; Am Soc Clin Invest; fel Am Col Physicians; Asn Am Physicians. *Res:* Hemoglobin metabolism; clinical endocrinology; mineral metabolism. *Mailing Add:* Dept Med WVa Univ Med Ctr Morgantown WV 26506

FLINN, EDWARD AMBROSE, b Oklahoma City, Okla, Aug 27, 31; m 62; c 1. GEOPHYSICS. *Educ:* Mass Inst Technol, SB, 53; Calif Inst Technol, PhD(geophys), 60. *Prof Exp:* Seismologist, United Electrodynamics, Inc, 60-68, assoc dir, Alexandria Labs, Teledyne Geotech, Va, 68-74; dir lunar progs, 75, dep dir & chief scientist, Planetary Progs, 75-77, CHIEF SCIENTIST, GEODYNAMICS PROG, NASA HQ, 77- *Concurrent Pos:* Vis assoc prof geophys, Brown Univ, 69; vis res assoc, Calif Inst Technol, 78; secy comt math geophys, chmn comn planetary sci & ed, J Geophys Res, Int Union Geod & Geophys; secy-gen, Inter-Union Comn Lithosphere, Int Coun Sci Unions, 80- *Mem:* AAAS; Am Geophys Union; Seismol Soc Am; Royal Astron Soc. *Res:* Seismology; general geophysics; coastal movements. *Mailing Add:* NASA Hq Code ERG Washington DC 20546

FLINN, JAMES EDWIN, b Cincinnati, Ohio, Sept 3, 34; m 56; c 3. CHEMICAL ENGINEERING. *Educ:* Purdue Univ, BS, 56; Univ Cincinnati, PhD(chem eng), 65. *Prof Exp:* Design engr, Dow Corning Corp, Mich, 56-57; develop engr, Nat Lead Co, Ohio, 60-62; sr res engr, Battelle Mem Inst, 65-66, assoc div chief, Battelle-Columbus Labs, 66-72, mgr waste control & process technol sect, 73-75, mgr energy & environ systs sect, 75-76, mgr, Chem Process Develop Sect, 76-80, ASSOC DIR CORP TECH DEVELOP, BATTELLE-COLUMBUS LABS, 80- *Mem:* AAAS; Am Inst Chem Engrs; Sigma Xi. *Res:* Biotechnology; separations technology; microencapsulation; environmental control technology; toxic and hazardous waste; oil shale and coal processing; fluidized bed technology; laboratory, bench and pilot scale process development. *Mailing Add:* Battelle-Columbus Labs 505 King Ave Columbus OH 43201

FLINN, JANE MARGARET, b Warrington Lanes, UK, Feb 12, 38; m 62; c 1. PHYSIOLOGICAL PSYCHOLOGY, BRAIN SCIENCES. *Educ:* Oxford Univ, BA, 60; Univ Calif, Los Angeles, MSc, 62; Cath Univ Am, PhD(physics), 69; George Washington Univ, PhD(psychol), 74. *Prof Exp:* Lectr physics, 69-74, asst prof, 74-80, ASSOC PROF PHYSICS & PSYCHOL, GEORGE MASON UNIV, 80- *Mem:* Am Psychol Asn. *Res:* Sensory psychology; brain function; evoked potentials. *Mailing Add:* Dept of Psychol George Mason Univ Fairfax VA 22030

FLINN, PAUL ANTHONY, b New York, NY, Mar 25, 26; m 49; c 5. PHYSICS, METALLURGY. *Educ:* Columbia Col, Ill, AB, 48, AM, 49; Mass Inst Technol, ScD, 52. *Prof Exp:* Asst prof physics, Wayne State Univ, Detroit, Mich, 52-54; res staff, Westinghouse Res Lab, Pittsburgh, Pa, 54-63; from assoc prof to prof physics & metall, Carnegie Inst Technol, 63-78; SR STAFF SCIENTIST, INTEL CORP, 78- *Concurrent Pos:* Vis prof, Univ Nancy, 67-68; distinquished appointment, Argonne Univs Asn, 71; mem adv bd, Mossbauer Effect, Int Comn Applications, 75-; vis scientist, Argonne Nat Lab, 77-78. *Mem:* AAAS; fel Am Phys Soc; Am Inst Metall, Mining & Petrol Eng. *Res:* Structure of solids; Mossbauer effect; dynamics of highly viscous liquids; Raman spectroscopy; diffusion. *Mailing Add:* Intel Corp SC2-258 3065 Bowers Ave Santa Clara CA 95051

FLINN, RICHARD A(LOYSIUS), b New York, NY, May 31, 16; m 44; c 5. METALLURGY. *Educ:* City Col New York, BS, 36; Mass Inst Technol, MS, 37, ScD(phys metall), 41. *Prof Exp:* Res metallurgist, Int Nickel Co, NJ, 37-39; from metall asst to asst chief metallurgist, Am Brake Shoe Co, 41-52; PROF METALL ENG, UNIV MICH, 52-, IN CHARGE, CAST METALS LAB, 52- *Concurrent Pos:* With Atomic Energy Comn & Off Sci Res & Develop, 44. *Honors & Awards:* Howe Medal, Am Soc Metals, 44 & 63; Simpson Medal, Am Foundrymen's Soc, 47, Hoyt Mem lectr, 81. *Mem:* Am Foundrymen's Soc; fel Am Soc Metals. *Res:* Failure analysis; physical and production metallurgy of cast metals; casting design and stress analysis; basic cupola melting; shell molding; basic oxygen steel making; metal casting. *Mailing Add:* 140 Underdown Rd Ann Arbor MI 48105

FLINNER, JACK L, b Canton, Ohio, June 6, 31; m 55; c 3. NUCLEAR PHYSICS. *Educ:* Wittenberg Univ, AB, 53; Univ Ill, MS, 55; Ohio State Univ, PhD(physics), 65. *Prof Exp:* Prof physics, Wittenberg Univ, 57-69; PROF PHYSICS, MANKATO STATE UNIV, 69-, CHMN DEPT PHYSICS & ELECTRONIC ENG TECHNOL, 75- *Mem:* Sigma Xi; Am Asn Physics Teachers. *Res:* Low energy nuclear physics; gas scatteri scattering experiments; angular correlation. *Mailing Add:* Dept of Physics Mankato State Univ Mankato MN 56001

FLINT, ARTHUR EMERSON, b Owanka, SDak, Feb 20, 13; m 39; c 2. ECONOMIC GEOLOGY. *Educ:* Univ Chicago, BS, 48, MS, 49, PhD(geol), 54. *Prof Exp:* Geologist, US Geol Surv, 49-50, chief, Iowa party, 50-53, Bull Canyon Proj, 53-55; chief geologist, Radium King Mines, Inc, 55-59; consult econ geologist, 59-62; sr geologist, Fed Resources Corp, 63-64; prof, 64-77, EMER PROF GEOL & CHMN DIV NATURAL SCI, CHAPMAN COL, 77- *Mem:* Geol Soc Am; Am Inst Mining, Metall & Petrol Engrs; Nat Asn Geol Teachers. *Res:* Research in the origin, occurrence and controls, particularly stratigraphic, of economic metalliferous deposits and in improved techniques for finding them. *Mailing Add:* 26031 Ave Mariposa San Juan Capistrano CA 92675

FLINT, DELOS EDWARD, b Pasadena, Calif, Dec 5, 18; m 50; c 5. ECONOMIC GEOLOGY. *Educ:* Calif Inst Technol, BS, 39; Northwestern Univ, MS, 41. *Prof Exp:* Asst, Northwestern Univ, 40-41; jr geologist, US Geol Surv, 41-42, geologist, 42-57; geologist, Freeport Sulphur Co, 57-64, chief geologist, 64-70; CHIEF GEOLOGIST, FREEPORT MINERALS CO, 70- *Mem:* Am Inst Mining, Metall & Petrol Engrs; Geochem Soc; fel Geol Soc Am; Soc Econ Geologists. *Res:* Areal, economic and military geology. *Mailing Add:* 1120 Mt Rose St Reno NV 89509

FLINT, DUANE L(ESLIE), b Cedaredge, Colo, Feb 23, 30. CHEMICAL ENGINEERING. *Educ:* Wash State Col, BS, 52; Univ Ill, MS, 56, PhD(chem eng), 58. *Prof Exp:* Res engr, 58-71, sr res engr, 71-75, ASSOC ENGR, UNION OIL CO, 75- *Res:* Engineering services. *Mailing Add:* PO Box 76 Brea CA 92621

FLINT, EINAR PHILIP, b Wardner, Idaho, Aug 10, 08; m 37; c 2. CHEMISTRY. *Educ:* Univ Wash, BS, 30; George Washington Univ, AM, 32; Univ Md, PhD(phys chem), 36. *Prof Exp:* Jr chemist, Bur Stand, 30-36, assoc chemist, 36-41, chemist, 41-44; supvr inorg chem sect, Armour Res Found, 44-46, mgr ceramics & minerals dept, 46-54; dir inorg res, Mallinckrodt Chem Works, 54-55; sr staff assoc, Arthur D Little, Inc, 55-62; asst to pres, Ipsen Industs, Inc, 62-65; mgr mat dept, Alexandria Div, Am Mach & Foundry Co, 65-66; staff metallurgist, Div Metall, US Bur Mines, 66-73; tech writer hist of sci, 74. *Mem:* Fel AAAS; Am Chem Soc; fel Am Ceramic Soc; Nat Inst Ceramic Engrs; Am Inst Min, Metall & Petrol Engrs. *Res:* Phase equilibria; hydrothermal synthesis; fine chemicals and pharmaceuticals; diamond, graphite and related materials; portland cement; ceramics; metallurgy; history of science. *Mailing Add:* 6229 Radcliffe Rd Alexandria VA 22307

FLINT, ELIZABETH PARKER, b Washington, DC, July 1, 51; m 79. PLANT ECOLOGY, WEED SCIENCE. *Educ:* Mt Holyoke Col, AB, 72; Duke Univ, PhD(bot & plant ecol), 80. *Prof Exp:* RES ASSOC, DEPT BOT, DUKE UNIV, 80- *Concurrent Pos:* Res tech, Southern Weed Sci Lab, USDA, 80-81. *Mem:* Ecol Soc Am; Weed Sci Soc Am; Sigma Xi. *Res:* Investigation of plant growth responses to temperature, light, carbon dioxide in controlled environments; competition of weeds and crops in controlled environments. *Mailing Add:* Dept Bot Duke Univ Durham NC 27706

FLINT, FRANKLIN FORD, b Va, Aug 4, 25; m 48; c 3. BIOLOGICAL STRUCTURE. *Educ:* Lynchburg Col, BS, 49; Univ Va, MS, 50, PhD(biol), 55. *Prof Exp:* From instr to prof biol, Randolph-Macon Woman's Col, 51-68, chmn dept, 62-68; staff biologist, Comn Undergrad Educ Biol Sci, NSF, Washington, DC, 68-69; PROF BIOL & CHMN DEPT, RANDOLPH-MACON WOMAN'S COL, 69- *Concurrent Pos:* Res grants, Am Philos Soc, 57 & Am Acad Arts & Sci, 58; Fulbright res scholar, Portugal, 64-65; dir, Lee Soil & Water Conserv Dist, Va, 73-; bd dirs, Va Chap Nature Conservancy, 75- *Mem:* Bot Soc Am. *Res:* Cell research; gametogenesis in the angiosperms. *Mailing Add:* Dept of Biol Randolph-Macon Woman's Col Lynchburg VA 24503

FLINT, HARRISON LEIGH, b Barre, Vt, Nov 5, 29; m 57; c 4. LANDSCAPE HORTICULTURE. *Educ:* Cornell Univ, BS, 51, PhD(floricult), 58; Mich State Univ, MS, 52. *Prof Exp:* Asst, Mich State Univ, 51-52 & Cornell Univ, 53 & 56-58; asst prof hort, Univ RI, 58-62; assoc, Univ Vt, 62-66; assoc horticulturist, Arnold Arboretum, Harvard Univ, 66-68; PROF HORT, PURDUE UNIV, WEST LAFAYETTE, 68- *Mem:* Am Soc Hort Sci; Am Asn Bot Gardens & Arboretums; Ecol Soc Am; Int Plant Propagators Soc. *Res:* Woody landscape plants; adaptation and comparative physiology; cold resistance in plants. *Mailing Add:* Dept Hort Purdue Univ West Lafayette IN 47906

FLINT, HOLLIS MITCHELL, b Miami, Fla, May 28, 38; m 60; c 4. ENTOMOLOGY, RADIATION BIOLOGY. *Educ:* Stetson Univ, BS, 60; Univ Fla, PhD(entom), 64. *Prof Exp:* Res entomologist, metab & radiation res lab, Entom Res Div, Agr Res Serv, USDA, NDak, 64-71, RES ENTOMOLOGIST, ENTOM RES DIV, AGR RES SERV, USDA, WESTERN COTTON INSECTS LAB, 71- *Mem:* Entom Soc Am. *Res:* Effects of radiation on insect sterility, longevity, oviposition and mating behavior; use of sex pheromones for control of pest Lepidoptera. *Mailing Add:* Western Cotton Insects Lab 4135 E Broadway Phoenix AZ 85040

FLINT, JEAN-JACQUES, b Le Vesinet, France, Aug 14, 43. GEOMORPHOLOGY, HYDROLOGY. *Educ:* Colby Col, BA, 66; State Univ NY Binghamton, MSc, 68, PhD(geol), 72. *Prof Exp:* Res asst geol, State Univ NY Binghamton, 68-70; asst prof, 70-77, ASSOC PROF GEOL, BROCK UNIV, 77- *Mem:* Geol Soc Am; Am Geophys Union; Int Asn Great Lakes Res; Ont Asn Remote Sensing. *Mailing Add:* Dept of Geol Sci Brock Univ St Catharines ON L2S 3A1 Can

FLINT, NORMAN KEITH, b North Newport, NH, Oct 16, 21; m 46; c 4. GEOLOGY. *Educ:* Univ NH, BS, 44; Ohio State Univ, MA, 46, PhD(geol), 48. *Prof Exp:* Instr geol, Ohio State Univ, 48-49; from asst prof to assoc prof, 49-66, actg head dept, 57-60, PROF GEOL, UNIV PITTSBURGH, 66- *Concurrent Pos:* Geologist, State Geol Surv, Ohio, 48; geologist, US Geol Surv, 49; coop geologist, State Geol Surv, Pa, 50-53, 56 & 59-64; prof geol, Cent Univ Ecuador, 64-66. *Mem:* Geol Soc Am; Nat Asn Geol Teachers; Asn Prof Geol Scientists. *Res:* Upper Paleozoic stratigraphy and areal geology; engineering geology; nonmetallic economic geology; environmental geology. *Mailing Add:* Dept of Earth & Planetary Sci Univ of Pittsburgh Pittsburgh PA 15260

FLINT, OLIVER SIMEON, JR, b Amherst, Mass, Oct 10, 31; m 54; c 3. SYSTEMATIC ENTOMOLOGY. *Educ:* Univ Mass, BS, 53, MS, 55; Cornell Univ, PhD(entom), 60. *Prof Exp:* Assoc cur, 60-65, CUR ENTOM, NAT MUS NATURAL HIST, SMITHSONIAN INST, 65-, IN CHG, DIV NEUROPTERIODS, 63- *Mem:* Am Entom Soc; Benthological Soc; Asn Trop Biol. *Res:* Taxonomy and biology of caddis flies and dobson flies, especially those of the New World. *Mailing Add:* Nat Mus of Natural Hist Smithsonian Inst Washington DC 20560

FLIPO, JEAN, b St Eustache, Que, Oct 7, 24; m 50; c 3. VETERINARY MEDICINE. *Educ:* Univ Montreal, BA, 44, DVM, 49. *Prof Exp:* Asst, 50-58, head small animals clin, 58-78, PROF SURG, SCH VET MED UNIV MONTREAL, 50- . *Honors & Awards:* Gaines Vet Award, Can, 70. *Res:* Small animals surgery. *Mailing Add:* Sch Vet Med Univ Montreal St Hyacinthe PQ H3C 3J7 Can

FLIPPEN, RICHARD BERNARD, b Williamson, WVa, Aug 23, 30; m 61; c 2. SOLID STATE PHYSICS. *Educ:* WVa Univ, AB, 53, MS, 54; Carnegie Inst Technol, PhD(physics), 60. *Prof Exp:* PHYSICIST, CENT RES DEPT, E I DU PONT DE NEMOURS & CO, INC, 60- *Mem:* Sigma Xi; Am Phys Soc; AAAS. *Res:* Magnetic properties of materials; magnetic ordering transitions; superconductivity; low temperature thermal properties of materials; electrical transport properties of materials; laser light scattering. *Mailing Add:* Exp Sta 223-300 E I du Pont de Nemours & Co Wilmington DE 19898

FLIPPEN-ANDERSON, JUDITH LEE, b Winthrop, Mass, Apr 21, 41; m 78; c 1. X-RAY CRYSTALLOGRAPHY. *Educ:* Northeastern Univ, Boston, BA, 63; Ariz State Univ, MS, 66. *Prof Exp:* Lab technician, Cancer Res Inst, 58-63; CHEMIST X-RAY CRYSTALLOG, NAVAL RES LAB, 66- *Mem:* Am Chem Soc; Am Crystallog Asn; Sigma Xi. *Res:* X-ray diffraction analysis of small to medium sized organic and biochemical materials; adaptation and optimization of programs for a large array processor computer. *Mailing Add:* Code 6030 Naval Res Lab Washington DC 20375

FLIPSE, MARTIN EUGENE, b Monteville, NJ, Apr 27, 19; m 49; c 6. PREVENTIVE MEDICINE. *Educ:* Hope Col, AB, 40; Harvard Med Sch, MD, 43; Am Bd Internal Med, dipl. *Prof Exp:* Intern med, Boston City Hosp, Mass, 44, resident med & contagious dis, 44-45; asst res path, Jackson Mem Hosp, Miami, Fla, 48-49; fel med, Mayo Found & Clin, Univ Minn, 49-51; resident pulmonary dis, Nopening Sanatorium, 51; staff asst, Mayo Found & Clin, Univ Minn, 52; from asst prof to assoc prof, 56-59, PROF MED, SCH MED, UNIV MIAMI, 59-, DIR UNIV HEALTH SERV, 57- *Mem:* AMA; Am Col Health Asn; fel Am Col Physicians. *Res:* Pulmonary disease; public health. *Mailing Add:* Univ of Miami Health Ctr 5513 Merrick Dr Coral Gables FL 33146

FLIPSE, ROBERT JOSEPH, b Topeka, Kans, July 18, 23; m 44; c 5. DAIRY SCIENCE. *Educ:* Kans State Col, BS, 47; Mich State Col, MS, 48, PhD(animal nutrit), 50. *Prof Exp:* Asst dairy husb, Mich State Col, 47-49; from asst prof to assoc prof, 50-66, PROF DAIRY SCI, PA STATE UNIV, 66-, ASST DIR, AGR EXP STA, 68- *Concurrent Pos:* Mem, Sci Group Chem & Physiol Gametes, WHO, 65. *Honors & Awards:* Borden Award Res Dairy Sci, 69. *Mem:* Fel AAAS; Am Inst Biol Sci; Soc Study Reproduction; Am Soc Animal Sci; Am Dairy Sci Asn. *Res:* Cellular metabolism; nutrition and reproductive physiology; rumen physiology. *Mailing Add:* Agr Exp Sta Pa State Univ University Park PA 16802

FLISZAR, SANDOR, b Lugano, Switz, May 11, 27; Can citizen; m 61; c 3. PHYSICAL ORGANIC CHEMISTRY, QUANTUM CHEMISTRY. *Educ:* Univ Geneva, PhD(chem), 62. *Prof Exp:* Res chemist, Cyanamid Europ Res Inst, Geneva, Switz, 62-64; from asst prof to assoc prof, 64-71, PROF PHYS CHEM, UNIV MONTREAL, 71- *Res:* Ozone chemistry; theoretical. *Mailing Add:* Dept of Chem Univ of Montreal Montreal PQ H3C 3J7 Can

FLITCRAFT, R(ICHARD) K(IRBY), II, b Woodstown, NJ, Sept 5, 20; m 42; c 4. CHEMICAL ENGINEERING. *Educ:* Rutgers Univ, BS, 42; Washington Univ, St Louis, MS, 48. *Prof Exp:* Mem tech serv, Org Chem Div, Monsanto Co, 42-46, group leader, Tech Serv, 46-48, supvr prod dept, 48-50, supt tech serv, 50-52, asst dir res, Meramec Div, 52-55; asst dir res, Inorg Chem Div, 55-60, prod bd dir, 60, dir res, 60-65, dir mgt info & systs dept, 65-67, asst to pres, 67-68, group mgr, Electronics Enterprise, 68-69, gen mgr, Electronic Prod Div, 69-71; dir, Mound Labs & vpres, 71-76, PRES, MONSANTO RES CORP, 76- *Mem:* AAAS; Am Chem Soc; Am Inst Chem Engrs; Sigma Xi; NY Acad Sci. *Res:* Surface active agents and detergents; phosphates; production and process development; management information systems; electronic data processing; electronic materials; light emitting devices; environmental analyses; government contracts. *Mailing Add:* Monsanto Res Corp PO Box 8 Sta B Dayton OH 45407

FLITTER, DAVID, b Philadelphia, Pa, Aug 1, 13; m 42; c 3. ORGANIC CHEMISTRY. *Educ:* Univ Pa, BS, 34; Pa State Col, MS, 50, PhD(chem), 52. *Prof Exp:* Chemist, R T French Co, 34-38; asst, Sun Oil Co, 38-41; jr chemist, US Govt, 41-42; chemist, Celanese Corp Am, 42-45, supvr, 45-48; chemist, E I du Pont de Nemours & Co, 52-61; sr chemist, Wyeth Labs, Inc, 61-81; RETIRED. *Mem:* Am Chem Soc. *Res:* Organic coatings; development of new drugs. *Mailing Add:* 270 Ellis Rd Havertown PA 19083

FLITTNER, GLENN ARDEN, b Los Angeles, Calif, Sept 10, 28; m 57; c 2. MARINE ECOLOGY, METEOROLOGY. *Educ:* Univ Calif, Berkeley, AB, 51, MA, 53; Univ Mich, PhD(fisheries), 64. *Prof Exp:* Fishery res biologist, Biol Lab, Bur Com Fisheries, US Dept Interior, Mich, 57-61 & Tuna Resources Lab, Calif, 61-70; dir bur marine sci, 70-74, prof biol, San Diego State Univ, 70-74; CHIEF OCEAN SERV DIV, NAT WEATHER SERV, NAT OCEANIC & ATMOSPHERIC ADMIN, 74- *Honors & Awards:* Commendation, Marine Technol Soc, 68. *Mem:* Am Inst Fishery Res Biol; Am Fisheries Soc; Am Meteorol Soc; Ecol Soc Am; Am Soc Zool. *Res:* Life history, ecology of marine fishery stocks; effects of physical characteristics of the environment on abundance, availability and distribution of stocks, special interest in forecasting availability and distribution of tuna stocks in relation to predicted changes in physical oceanographic parameters such as upper mixed layer temperature. *Mailing Add:* Ocean Serv Div Nat Weather Serv NOAA Silver Spring MD 20910

FLOCK, DONALD LOUIS, b Calgary, Alta, Feb 19, 30; m 52; c 4. PETROLEUM ENGINEERING. *Educ:* Univ Okla, BSc, 52, MSc, 53; Agr & Mech Col, Tex, PhD, 56. *Prof Exp:* Res engr, Cities Serv Res & Develop Co, Ltd, 56-57; from assoc prof to prof, 57-67, assoc dean fac eng, 69-73, prof petrol eng, 73-79, CHMN DEPT MINERAL ENG, UNIV ALTA, 79- *Mem:* Am Inst Mining, Metall & Petrol Engrs. *Res:* Petroleum production and reservoir engineering. *Mailing Add:* Fac of Eng Univ of Alta Edmonton AB T6G 2E1 Can

FLOCK, EUNICE VERNA, b Kellogg, Idaho, Aug 20, 04. BIOCHEMISTRY. *Educ:* Univ Wash, BS, 26; Univ Chicago, MS, 30; Univ Minn, PhD(physiol chem), 35. *Prof Exp:* Asst physiol chem, Mayo Clin, 30-33, instr, Mayo Grad Sch Med, 36-39, from asst prof to prof, 39-57, EMER PROF BIOCHEM, MAYO GRAD SCH MED, UNIV MINN, ROCHESTER, 69- *Concurrent Pos:* Vs scientist, Clin Res Sect, Phoenix Indian Med Ctr, Nat Inst Arthritis & Metab Dis, 71-80. *Mem:* Fel AAAS; Thyroid Asn Am; NY Acad Sci; Am Chem Soc; Am Soc Biol Chemists. *Res:* Fat metabolism; amino acids; thyroxine; serotonin; epinephrine. *Mailing Add:* 1287-A E Maryland Ave Phoenix AZ 85014

FLOCK, JOHN WILLIAM, b Denver Colo, Feb 4, 47; m 69; c 2. CHEMICAL ENGINEERING. *Educ:* Univ Colo, Boulder, BS, 69; Univ Calif, Berkeley, MS, 72, PhD(chem eng), 76. *Prof Exp:* Mem tech staff chem eng, TRW Systs Group, 70-71; res asst, Dept Chem Eng, Univ Calif, Berkeley, 71-76; staff chem engr, 76-80, MGR, CHEM ENERGY TECHNOL UNIT, CORP RES & DEVELOP, GEN ELEC CO, 80- *Mem:* Am Inst Chem Engrs; AAAS; Sigma Xi. *Res:* Thermodynamic analysis and development of closed loop chemical systems for transport and storage of energy; thermodynamic analysis of the irreversible processes associated with heat pumps and chemical processes. *Mailing Add:* Gen Elec Corp Res & Develop PO Box 8 Schenectady NY 12301

FLOCK, WARREN L(INCOLN), b Kellogg, Idaho, Oct 26, 20; m 57. ELECTRICAL ENGINEERING, GEOPHYSICS. *Educ:* Univ Wash, BS, 42; Univ Calif, Berkeley, MS, 48; Univ Calif, Los Angeles, PhD(eng), 60. *Prof Exp:* Staff mem radiation lab, Mass Inst Technol, 42-45; partner, Radar Engrs, Wash, 45-46; lectr & asst engr, Col Eng, Univ Calif, Los Angeles, 50-56, lectr assoc engr, 56-60; from assoc prof to prof geophys, Geophys Inst, Univ Alaska, 60-64; PROF ELEC ENG, UNIV COLO, BOULDER, 64- *Concurrent Pos:* Mem tech staff, Jet Propulsion Lab, Pasadena, CA, 80-81. *Mem:* AAAS; Inst Elec & Electronics Engrs; Am Geophys Union; Int Solar Energy Soc; Arctic Inst NAm. *Res:* Propagation effects on electromagnetic waves in satellite and deep-space communications; radio science; remote sensing of the environment; telecommunications; radar ornithology; solar energy. *Mailing Add:* Dept of Elec Eng Univ of Colo Boulder CO 80309

FLOCKEN, JOHN W, b Sioux Falls, SDak, Sept 2, 39; m 64; c 2. THEORETICAL SOLID STATE PHYSICS. *Educ:* Augustana Col, SDak, BA, 61; Univ Nebr, Lincoln, MS, 64, PhD(physics), 69. *Prof Exp:* Scientist, Raven Industs, SDak, 64-65; physicist, Bendix Labs, Mich, 65-66; from asst prof to assoc prof physics, 69-75, asst dean arts & sci, 75, PROF PHYSICS, UNIV NEBR, OMAHA, 75-, CHMN DEPT, 80- *Mem:* Am Phys Soc; Sigma Xi. *Res:* Lattice statics calculations; determination of atomic displacements about point defects in metals; formation and activation energies; interactions between pairs of defects in crystals. *Mailing Add:* Dept of Physics Univ of Nebr Omaha NE 68182

FLODIN, N(ESTOR) W(INSTON), b Chicago, Ill, Jan 30, 15; m 41; c 2. BIOCHEMISTRY, NUTRITION. *Educ:* Univ Chicago, BS, 35, PhD(chem), 38. *Prof Exp:* Instr chem, Cent State Teachers Col, Stevens Point, 38-40; chemist electrochem, E I du Pont de Nemours & Co, Inc, 40-61, chemist indust & biochem, 61-66, sr chemist pharmaceut, 66-73; PROF BIOCHEM, UNIV S ALA COL MED, 74- *Mem:* NY Acad Sci; AAAS; Am Col Nutrit; Am Inst Nutrit; Sigma Xi. *Res:* Organic boron compounds; vinyl monomers and polymers; amino acids in nutrition; food technology; pharmaceuticals marketing and research; kinetics of nutritional responses; vitamins; trace elements. *Mailing Add:* Univ of SAla Col of Med Dept of Biochem Mobile AL 36688

FLOKSTRA, JOHN HILBERT, b Chicago, Ill, Apr 17, 25; m 48; c 3. CLINICAL CHEMISTRY. *Educ:* Calvin Col, AB, 47; Mich State Col, MS, 50, PhD(biochem), 52. *Prof Exp:* Asst biochem, Mich State Col, 47-51; res assoc biochem, 52-59, HEAD CLIN RES LAB, UPJOHN CO, 60- *Mem:* Am Chem Soc; Am Asn Clin Chem; Am Soc Clin Path; Can Soc Clin Chem. *Mailing Add:* Upjohn Co Clin Res Lab 301 Henrietta St Kalamazoo MI 49001

FLOM, DONALD GORDON, b Kenyon, Minn, May 8, 24; m 57; c 3. PHYSICAL CHEMISTRY. *Educ:* St Olaf Col, BA, 44; Purdue Univ, MS, 49; Pa State Col, PhD(chem), 52. *Prof Exp:* Instr chem, St Olaf Col, 46-47; asst, Purdue Univ, 47-49; res assoc, Res Lab, 51-59, phys chemist, 59-61, mgr chem res, Space Sci Lab, Valley Forge Space Tech Ctr, 61-71, mgr chem eng br, Res & Develop Ctr, 71-74, mgr mat removal & lubrication prog, 74-80, MGR ADVAN MACHINING & WEAR CONTROL PROG, RES & DEVELOP CTR, GEN ELEC CO, 80- *Honors & Awards:* Nat Award, Am Soc Lubrication Engrs. *Mem:* Am Chem Soc; Am Soc Lubrication Eng. *Res:* Vapor liquid equilibria; chemical use of high frequency oscillators; surface chemistry; electrical contacts; friction and wear; polymer chemistry; reinforced composites; ablation; machining; superhard materials. *Mailing Add:* Res & Develop Ctr Gen Elec Co PO Box 8 Schenectady NY 12301

FLOM, MERTON CLYDE, b Pittsburgh, Pa, Aug 19, 26; m 68; c 4. OPTOMETRY. *Educ:* Univ Calif, Berkeley, BS, 50, MOpt, 51, PhD(physiol optics), 57. *Prof Exp:* Clin instr optom, 51-57, instr, 57-58, from asst prof to assoc prof physiol optics & optom, 58-66, vchmn sch optom, 62-63, asst dean, 69-72, PROF PHYSIOL OPTICS & OPTOM, SCH OPTOM, UNIV CALIF, BERKELEY, 67- *Concurrent Pos:* Pvt pract optom, 60-70; USPHS res grants, Sch Optom, Univ Calif, Berkeley, 62-67 & 77-80; NASA grant, Smith-Kettlewell Inst Visual Sci, 72, US Army Basic contract grants, 72-; assoc res mem, Inst Med Sci, Pac Med Ctr, San Francisco, 68-; consult, Optical Sci Group, San Rafael, 69-; ed, J Optom & Physiol Optics, 77- *Mem:* AAAS; Am Acad Optom (pres elect, 78); Am Asn Univ Prof; Am Optom Asn; Optical Soc Am. *Res:* Physiological optics; binocular vision and space perception. *Mailing Add:* 420 Minor Hall Univ of Calif Sch of Optom Berkeley CA 94720

FLOOD, BRIAN ROBERT, b Phelps, NY, Feb 21, 48; m 70. ENTOMOLOGY, WEED SCIENCE. *Educ:* Purdue Univ, Lafayette, BS, 70; Univ Wis-Madison, MS, 72, PhD(entom), 75. *Prof Exp:* Consult, Agr Chem Serv Corp, Sodus, NY, 74-75; SR ENTOMOLOGIST APPL RES, DEL MONTE CORP, ROCHELLE, ILL, 75-, AGR RES MGR, 80- *Mem:* Entom Soc Am; Am Registry Prof Entomologists; Coun Agr Sci & Technol; NCent Weed Sci Soc. *Res:* Develop, maintain and oversee effective economical weed and insect control programs and cultural practices for sweet corn, snap beans, lima beans, peas, cabbage and pumpkins; development of alternate fuels from processing waste. *Mailing Add:* Del Monte Corp PO Box 89 Rochelle IL 61068

FLOOD, CHARLES W, JR, b New York, NY, Mar 24, 32; m 54. HEALTH PHYSICS. *Educ:* Adelphi Col, BS, 63; Am Bd Health Physics, cert, 66. *Prof Exp:* Technician, 54-63, HEALTH PHYSICIST, BROOKHAVEN NAT LAB, 63- *Mem:* Health Physics Soc. *Mailing Add:* 247 N Prospect Ave Patchogue NY 11772

FLOOD, CLIFFORD ARRINGTON, JR, b Jacksonville, Fla, Oct 17, 39; m 68; c 2. AGRICULTURAL ENGINEERING. *Educ:* Univ Fla, BAGE, 62; Univ Ky, MSAE, 66; Purdue Univ, PhD(agr eng), 71. *Prof Exp:* asst prof, 71-79, ASSOC PROF AGR ENG, AUBURN UNIV, 79- *Concurrent Pos:* Vis assoc prof agr eng, Univ Ky, 81-82. *Mem:* Am Soc Agr Engrs; Coun Agr Sci & Technol. *Res:* Heat and mass transfer in agricultural products; feed and grain drying and storage; environmental control in livestock housing; agricultural application of solar energy for heating and cooling. *Mailing Add:* Dept of Agr Eng Auburn Univ Auburn AL 36849

FLOOD, JAMES FELIX, b Mar 15, 45. PSYCHOPHARMACOLOGY. *Educ:* Univ Calif, Berkeley, AB, 69, PhD(psychol), 73. *Prof Exp:* RES PSYCHOPHARMACOLOGIST, NEUROPSYCHIAT INST, MED SCH, UNIV CALIF, LOS ANGELES, 73- *Concurrent Pos:* Res Psychopharmacologist, Vet Admin Med Ctr, Sepulveda, Calif, 80- *Res:* Mechanisms of memory formation; preclinical assessment of drug on demensias of aging. *Mailing Add:* Box 227 308 Westwood Plaza Los Angeles CA 90024

FLOOD, THOMAS CHARLES, b Wilmington, Del, June 5, 45; m 67. ORGANIC CHEMISTRY, ORGANOMETALLIC CHEMISTRY. *Educ:* Trinity Col, BS, 67; Mass Inst Technol, PhD(org chem), 72. *Prof Exp:* Asst prof, 72-78, ASSOC PROF CHEM, UNIV SOUTHERN CALIF, 78- *Mem:* Am Chem Soc; The Chem Soc. *Res:* New metallic reagents for organic synthesis, stereochemistry and mechanism of organometallic reactions, homogeneous catalysis, models for metallo-enzymes. *Mailing Add:* Dept of Chem Univ of Southern Calif Los Angeles CA 90007

FLOOD, WALTER A(LOYSIUS), b New York, NY, Apr 27, 27; m 54; c 3. ELECTRICAL ENGINEERING. *Educ:* Cornell Univ, BEE, 50, MEE, 52, PhD, 54. *Prof Exp:* Asst ionosphere lab, Cornell Univ, 50-54, res engr aeronaut lab, 54-59, head radio physics sect, 59-64, staff scientist, 64-67; PROF ELEC ENG, NC STATE UNIV, 67- *Concurrent Pos:* Consult, Res Triangle Inst, Stanford Res Inst & Gen Elec Tempo Ctr Advan Study, Calif. *Mem:* AAAS; Inst Elec & Electronics Engrs; Am Geophys Union; Int Sci Radio Union. *Res:* Upper atmospheric physics; ionospheric and tropospheric propagation; D-region backscatter; ionospheric drifts; rough surface backscatter; radio wave propagation; ionospheric scintillation and multipath phenomena. *Mailing Add:* Dept of Elec Eng NC State Univ Raleigh NC 27650

FLOOK, WILLIAM MOWAT, JR, b Briarcliff, NY, July 7, 21; m 45; c 5. PHYSICS. *Educ:* Harvard Univ, AB, 43; Brown Univ, MS, 49, PhD(physics), 52. *Prof Exp:* Asst physvs, Woods Hole Oceanog Inst, Mass, 46-47; res supvr, E I du Pont de Nemours & Co, 51-61, res assoc, 61-69, RES ASSOC, PELTRON LAB, E I DU PONT DE NEMOURS & CO, 69- *Mem:* AAAS; Optical Soc Am; Sigma Xi; Am Inst Aeronaut & Astronaut. *Res:* Instrumentation; process control; optical and electronic measurements. *Mailing Add:* Peltron Lab Box 3748 Greenville DE 19807

FLORA, EDWARD B(ENJAMIN), b Phillipsburg, Ohio, June 23, 29; m 52; c 3. STRUCTURAL MECHANICS, MECHANICAL ENGINEERING. *Educ:* Carnegie Inst Technol, BS, 51, MS, 53. *Prof Exp:* Nuclear Res Ctr, Carnegie Inst Technol, 51-52; proj engr, Nevis Cyclotron Lab, Columbia Univ, 53-58; sr engr, Dalmo Victor Co, 58-63; VPRES, ANAMET LABS, INC, 63-, MGR AEROSPACE STRUCTURES INFO & ANAL CTR, 72- *Mem:* Am Soc Mech Engrs; Soc Exp Stress Anal; Soc Automotive Engrs; Am Inst Aeronaut & Astronaut; Am Soc Testing & Mat. *Res:* Analytical and experimental stress analysis; vibration; failure analysis; fracture mechanics. *Mailing Add:* Anamet Labs Inc 100 Industrial Way San Carlos CA 94070

FLORA, GEORGE CLAUDE, b Clark, SDak, Apr 8, 23; m 51; c 3. NEUROLOGY. *Educ:* Univ SDak, BS, 48; Temple Univ, MD, 50. *Prof Exp:* Prof neurol, Univ Minn, Minneapolis, 63-74; PROF NEUROL & HEAD, SCH MED, UNIV SOUTH DAK, 74- *Concurrent Pos:* Consult neurol, Fargo Vet Admin Hosp, 63-74; consult neuropath, Ramsey-Ancker County Hosp, St Paul, 63-68 & State of Minn, Anoka, 63-68; acad consult, Sioux Valley Hosp, McKennen Hosp, Vet Admin Hosp, Sioux Falls, Sacred Heart Hosp, Yankton, Human Serv Ctr, Yankton & St Annes Hosp, Watertown, 74- *Mem:* AMA; Acad Neurol; Am Soc Internal Med; Asn Univ Prof Neurol. *Res:* Cerebrovascular disease, epidemiology and ultrastruc- ultrastructure of the arthrosclerotic plaque; chemophilia; role of medical profession in the handling of alcoholism and chemical dependency. *Mailing Add:* Univ of SDak Sch of Med 2501 W 22nd Sioux Falls SD 57105

FLORA, JAIRUS DALE, (JR), b Northfield, Minn, Mar 27, 44; m 67. BIOSTATISTICS, MEDICAL STATISTICS. *Educ:* Midland Lutheran Col, BS, 65; Fla State Univ, MS, 68, PhD(statist), 71. *Prof Exp:* Assoc res scientist, Hwy Safety Res Inst, 76-81, asst prof biostatist, 71-76, asst res scientist, 73-76, assoc prof, 76-81, PROF BIOSTATIST, SCH PUB HEALTH, UNIV MICH, ANN ARBOR, 81- *Concurrent Pos:* Dir statist anal & data collection, Inst Burn Med, 72-77; Bicycle Mfrs Asn grant bicycle accidents & injuries, Hwy Safety Res Inst, Univ Mich, 74-78. *Mem:* Int Biomet Soc; Am Statist Asn; Inst Math Statist; Sigma Xi; Int Soc Burn Injuries. *Res:* Statistical methodology; analysis of accident statistics; cooperative medical trials, particularly of burn treatment, cardiology and cancer treatments; analysis of accident statistics, evaluation of standards effectiveness; design and implementation and evaluation of prevention programs. *Mailing Add:* Univ of Mich Dept of Biostatist M4208 T Francis Jr Bldg Ann Arbor MI 48104

FLORA, LEWIS FRANKLIN, b Frederick, Md, June 9, 47; m 69; c 2. FOOD SCIENCE, FOOD CHEMISTRY. *Educ:* Univ Md, College Park, BS, 69, MS, 71, PhD(food sci), 73; Susquehanna Univ, cert mgt, 81. *Prof Exp:* Food technologist, Div Food Technol, Food & Drug Admin, Dept Health, Educ & Welfare, 74; asst prof, Dept Food Sci, Exp Sta, Univ Ga, 74-80; PROJ LEADER, CENT RES LAB, AM HOME FOODS, 80- *Mem:* Inst Food Technologists. *Res:* Product and process technology, quality evaluation and maintenance, and chemistry of fruits and fruit juices, low-acid and acidified vegetables, dry pasta, canned pasta and meat, and frozen specialties. *Mailing Add:* 75 Fairmount Dr Lewisburg PA 17837

FLORA, ROBERT MONTGOMERY, b Richmond, Va, Oct 1, 38; m 65; c 2. BIOCHEMISTRY, ENZYMOLOGY. *Educ:* Bridgewater Col, BA, 60; Va Polytech Inst & State Univ, PhD(biochem), 65. *Prof Exp:* NIH fel microbiol, Vanderbilt Univ, 64-66; asst prof chem, Am Univ, 66-68; sr res biochemist, 68-72, dir res prod develop, 72-77, HEAD BIOTECHNOL, WORTHINGTON BIOCHEM CORP, DIV MILLIPORE CORP, 77- *Mem:* AAAS; Am Chem Soc; NY Acad Sci; Sigma Xi. *Res:* New products and process development; applications and formulations; technical support of products and production. *Mailing Add:* Worthington Biochem Corp Freehold NJ 07728

FLORA, ROGER E, b Roanoke, Va, Feb 5, 39; m 63; c 2. BIOSTATISTICS. *Educ:* Univ Va, BA, 60; Va Polytech Inst, MS, 64, PhD(statist), 66. *Prof Exp:* Asst prof statist, WVa Univ, 65-68; from asst prof to assoc prof biostatist, Med Col Va, Va Commonwealth Univ, 68-77; SR RES STATISTICIAN, A H ROBINS CO, 77- *Mem:* Am Statist Asn; Biostatist Soc. *Res:* Multivariate analysis; statistical inference; analysis of clinical trials. *Mailing Add:* A H Robins Co 1211 Sherwood Ave Richmond VA 23220

FLORAN, ROBERT JOHN, b Bronx, NY, June 4, 47; m 71; c 2. PETROLOGY, MINERALOGY. *Educ:* City Col New York, BS, 69; Columbia Univ, MA, 71; State Univ NY, Stony Brook, PhD(petrol), 75. *Prof Exp:* Res assoc petrol, Johnson Space Ctr, 75-76 & Am Mus Natural Hist, 76-77; res assoc geol, Oak Ridge Nat Lab, 78-80; RES GEOLOGIST, UNION OIL CO, 81- *Concurrent Pos:* Nat Res Coun fel, 75-76; NASA res grants co-investr, 76-77. *Mem:* Geol Soc Am; Mineral Soc Am; Am Geophys Union. *Res:* Economic geology of base metals; radioactive waste management; meteoritics; impact cratering processes; mineralogy and petrology of iron formations. *Mailing Add:* Union Oil Co 376 S Valencia Ave Brea CA 92621

FLORANCE, EDWIN R, b Lewiston, Idaho, Mar 2, 42; div; c 1. CELL BIOLOGY, BOTANY. *Educ:* Eastern Wash State Col, BA, 65; Ore State Univ, MS, 71, PhD(bot), 74. *Prof Exp:* Asst instr biol, Eastern Wash State Col, 65-68; instr biol, Columbia Basin Community Col, 74-77; asst prof, 77-80, ASSOC PROF BIOL, LEWIS & CLARK COL, 80- *Concurrent Pos:* Res assoc, Wash State Univ Tree Fruit Res Ctr, 77-79; coop aid, USDA Forest Serv, 78-82; grad res asst Ore State Univ, 71-73. *Mem:* Am Inst Biol Sci; Electron Micros Soc Am; Am Phytopath Soc. *Res:* General interests: developmental cytology and three-dimensional cell structure; specifically, developmental ultrastructural cytology of viruses, mycoplasma, bacteria, fungi and algae, cytopathology; the cytology of host parasite interactions. *Mailing Add:* 3800 SW Botticelli Lake Oswego OR 97034

FLORANT, GREGORY LESTER, b New York, NY, Aug 31, 51. ENDOCRINOLOGY, NEUROPHYSIOLOGY. *Educ:* Cornell Univ, BS, 73; Stanford Univ, PhD(biol), 78. *Prof Exp:* Fel neurol res, Montefiore Hosp, NY, NIH, 78-80; ASST PROF BIOL, SWARTHMORE COL, 80- *Mem:* Am Physiol Soc; AAAS; Am Soc Zoologists; Sigma Xi. *Res:* Hibernation physiology, specifically how hormones regulate metabolic processes during euthermia and hibernation. *Mailing Add:* Dept Biol Swarthmore Col Swarthmore PA 19081

FLOREA, HAROLD R(OBERT), b New York, NY, July 24, 14; m 47. ENGINEERING. *Educ:* Stevens Inst Technol, ME, 37. *Prof Exp:* Dist head, US Navy Field Off, Ind, 41-45, Vt, 45-46, & NY, 47-51; prof eng, Off Naval Res, 51-57, head weapon syst, Trainers Flight Br, 57-60, adv tech dept, 60-72; ENG CONSULT, 72- *Res:* Development and applications in training devices. *Mailing Add:* 2912 Ambergate Rd Winter Park FL 32792

FLOREEN, STEPHEN, b Chicago, Ill, July 19, 32; m 61; c 1. PHYSICAL METALLURGY. *Educ:* Mass Inst Technol, BS, 54; Univ Mich, MS, 55, PhD(metall), 60. *Prof Exp:* Res asst, Univ Mich, 57-60; metallurgist steels & nickel alloys, 60-62, sect head, 62-64, res assoc, 64-73, RES FEL, INT NICKEL CO, 73- *Mem:* Am Soc Metals; Am Inst Mining, Metall & Petrol Engrs; Sigma Xi. *Res:* High temperature metallurgy; surface effects; nickel alloys; high strength steels; fracture behavior. *Mailing Add:* Inco Res & Develop Ctr Sterling Forest Suffern NY 10901

FLORENTINE, GERALD JOSEPH, b Brooklyn, NY, Mar 13, 36; m 59; c 3. INSECT PHYSIOLOGY. *Educ:* Cornell Univ, BS, 59; Purdue Univ, PhD(entom), 65. *Prof Exp:* ENTOMOLOGIST, US ARMY NATICK LABS, 65- *Mem:* Entom Soc Am; Sigma Xi. *Res:* Physiology; toxicology; biochemistry. *Mailing Add:* Pa Dept of Agr Bur Plant Ind 2301 N Cameron St Harrisburg PA 17122

FLORES, IVAN, b New York, NY, Jan 3, 23; m 54; c 2. COMPUTER SCIENCE, ELECTRICAL ENGINEERING. *Educ:* Brooklyn Col, BA, 48; Columbia Univ, MA, 49; NY Univ, PhD(ed), 55. *Prof Exp:* Sr engr, Mergenthaler Linotype Co, 50-53; proj engr, Balco Labs, 53-55 & Nuclear Develop Corp, 55-57; proj supvr comput design, Remington Rand, 57-59; comput consult, Dunlap & Assocs, 59-60; assoc prof elec eng, Polytech Inst Brooklyn, 61-62; adj prof, NY Univ, 62-63; assoc prof, Stevens Inst Technol, 65-67; INDEPENDENT CONSULT COMPUT DESIGN, 60-; PROF STATIST, CITY UNIV NEW YORK, 67- *Concurrent Pos:* Ed, J Asn Comput Mach, 63-67; consult, US Army Sci Adv Panel, 69-70 & UN Develop Prog Surv, India & Philippines. *Mem:* AAAS; Inst Elec & Electronics Engrs; Asn Comput Mach; fel Brit Comput Soc. *Res:* Theory and design of general and special digital computers; programming computers; optical, magnetic character recognition; mathematical analysis, modeling; programming and software development; author or coauthor of sixty publications. *Mailing Add:* 108 Eighth Ave Brooklyn NY 11215

FLORES, ROMEO M, b San Fernando, Philippines, Apr 28, 39; m 70; c 1. SEDIMENTOLOGY, GEOLOGY. *Educ:* Univ Philippines, BS, 59; Univ Tulsa, MS, 62; La State Univ, PhD(geol), 66. *Prof Exp:* Jr geologist & micropaleontologist, Island Oil Co, Inc, Philippines, 59-60; from asst prof to prof geol, Sul Ross State Univ, 66-75, chmn dept, 67-75; RES GEOLOGIST, BR COAL RESOURCES, US GEOL SURVEY, 75- *Concurrent Pos:* Adj prof, Colo State Univ & NC State Univ, 78-; lectr, Am Asn Petrol Geologists, 81- *Mem:* Int Asn Math Geol; Am Asn Petrol Geol; Soc Econ Paleontologists & Mineralogists; Geol Soc Am. *Res:* Sedimentology and stratigraphy of the Paleozoic sedimentary rocks, Marathon Basin, Texas; fluvial and lake sedimentation of Lake Erie, New York; coal resources and coal depositional environments of Tertiary and Cretaceous basins in Wyoming, Montana, North Dakota, Colorado, New Mexico, Utah, Kentucky and West Virginia; Fluvio-deltaic-barrier sediments of Rio Grande, Mustang Island and Gulf Coast continental shelf sediments. *Mailing Add:* Br Coal Resources US Geol Survey MS 972 Fed Ctr Denver CO 80225

FLORES, SAMSON SOL, b Luzon, Philippines, Jan 6, 22; US citizen; m 51; c 2. PROSTHODONTICS. *Educ:* Centro Escolar Univ, Manila, DMD, 44; Univ Ill, DDS, 58. *Prof Exp:* From asst to assoc prof prosthodontics, 48-68, consult-chancellor adv coun, 69-71, from clin dir to actg head dept, 68-75, PROF PROSTHODONTICS, COL DENT, UNIV ILL MED CTR, 68-, DIR ADVAN PROSTHODONTICS, 75- *Concurrent Pos:* Consult, Mouth Guard Proj, USPHS, 63, Spec Patient Geriat Proj, Ill State Pub Health, 63 & VA Hosp, Chicago, 75; dir dent div, Pac Garden Mission Clins, Chicago; exec dir, Philippine Dent Soc Midwest, 72-77; consult, Ill State Dent Bd Examrs, 72- *Mem:* Am Col Dent; Am Dent Asn; Am Prosthodont Soc; Acad Gen Dent; Am Asn Univ Prof. *Res:* Oral surgical prosthesis after cancer patients are released; mouth protectors for use in general anesthesia. *Mailing Add:* Dept Prosthodontics Univ Ill Col of Dent Chicago IL 60612

FLORES-GALLARDO, HECTOR, b Naguabo, PR, Nov 28, 18; m 44; c 2. ORGANIC CHEMISTRY. *Educ:* Univ PR, BS, 39; Univ Fla, MS, 42, PhD(chem), 47. *Prof Exp:* Dir distillation dept, Butanol Plant, Arroyo, PR, 39-41, chief chemist, 47-49; res chemist, Monsanto Chem Co, Ala, 49-53; tech dir, Am Steroids, Inc, 53 55; vpres prod, Root Chems, Inc, 55-60; vpres prod & develop, Productos Esteroides, SA, 60-67, vpres & mgr, Chem Div, 67-79, SR VPRES & DIR MFG, SEARLE DE MEX, SA, 79- *Mem:* AAAS; NY Acad Sci. *Res:* Organic isocyanates; detergents; antioxidants; steroids. *Mailing Add:* Searle de Mex SA PO Box 1848 Mexico City DF Mexico

FLOREY, KLAUS, b Dresden, Ger, July 4, 19; nat US; m 56; c 2. ORGANIC CHEMISTRY. *Educ:* Univ Heidelberg, dipl, 47; Univ Pa, PhD(biochem), 54. *Prof Exp:* Asst org chem, I G Farben, Ger, 44-45; res chemist, Merck & Co, 49-50; res asst, 54-59, DIR DEPT ANAL RES & PHYS CHEM, E R SQUIBB & SONS, 59- *Concurrent Pos:* Mem, USP Comt on Revision, 70-; ed, Anal Profiles of Drug Substances, 72-; mem expert advisory panel int pharmacopeia, WHO, 76- *Mem:* fel AAAS; Am Chem Soc; fel Acad Pharmaceut Sci (pres, 80-81). *Res:* Isolation, chemistry and development of natural products, steroids and medicinals; analytical research; chromatography; radiopharmaceuticals. *Mailing Add:* E R Squibb & Sons New Brunswick NJ 08903

FLORIDIS, THEMISTOCHLES PHILOMILOS, b Alexandroupolis, Greece, Nov 5, 24; US citizen; m 53; c 1. METALLURGY. *Educ:* Nat Tech Univ, Athens, Dipl, 47; Mass Inst Technol, MS, 54, ScD(metall), 57. *Prof Exp:* Chem engr, Viamyl Ltd, Greece, 50-53; res engr, Foundry Dept, Gen Elec Co, 57-59; sect head phys chem, Appl Res Lab, US Steel Corp, 59-64; assoc prof, 64-68, PROF METALL ENG, VA POLYTECH INST & STATE UNIV, 68- *Mem:* Am Inst Mining, Metall & Petrol Engrs; Am Soc Metals. *Res:* Physical chemistry of extraction and refining of metals; analysis of metallurgical processes. *Mailing Add:* PO Box 546 Blacksburg VA 24060

FLORIN, ROLAND ERIC, b Chicago, Ill, Jan 18, 15; m 49; c 2. POLYMER CHEMISTRY. *Educ:* Univ Ill, BS, 36, PhD(phys chem), 48. *Prof Exp:* Abstractor, Standard Oil Co, Ill, 37-38, technologist, Ill, 38-41; asst, Univ Ill, 46-47; instr phys chem, Univ Nebr, 48-51; chemist, 51-80, GUEST WORKER, NAT BUR STANDARDS, 80- *Mem:* AAAS; Am Chem Soc. *Res:* Mechanism of polymerization; polymer degradation; deuterium compounds; fluorine compounds; copolymer composition; free radicals. *Mailing Add:* Polymer Stab & React Sect Nat Bur of Standards Washington DC 20234

FLORINI, JAMES RALPH, b Gillespie, Ill, Sept 22, 31; m 55; c 2. BIOCHEMISTRY. *Educ:* Blackburn Col, BA, 53; Univ Ill, PhD(biochem), 56. *Prof Exp:* Asst chem, Univ Ill, 53-56; res chemist, Lederle Labs, Am Cyanamid Co, 56-60, group leader & sr res chemist, 60-66; assoc prof biochem, 66-70, PROF BIOCHEM, SYRACUSE UNIV, 70- *Concurrent Pos:* Chmn, Gordon Res Conf on Biol of Aging, 80. *Mem:* Am Soc Cell Biol; Am Soc Biol Chemists; Geront Soc; Tissue Cult Asn; Endocrine Soc. *Res:* Control of muscle cell growth and differentiation in culture; hormone action; muscular dystrophy; cardiac disease. *Mailing Add:* Dept of Biol Syracuse Univ 108 College Pl Syracuse NY 13210

FLORMAN, ALFRED LEONARD, b Jersey City, NJ, Oct 11, 12; m 44; c 3. PEDIATRICS, INFECTIOUS DISEASES. *Educ:* Princeton Univ, AB, 34; Johns Hopkins Univ, MD, 38. *Prof Exp:* Intern, Johns Hopkins Hosp, 38-40; Dazian fel, Harvard Med Sch, 40-41; resident, Mt Sinai Hosp, 42; Welt fel, Rockefeller Inst Hosp & Mt Sinai Hosp, 46-47; adj pediatrician, Mt Sinai Hosp, 47-52, asst attend pediat, 52-56, assoc attend, 56-68; dir pediat, NShore Hosp, 52-68; prof pediat, Sch Med, NY Univ, 68-81; PROF PEDIAT, UNIV NMEX SCH MED, 82- *Mem:* Am Pediat Soc; Soc Pediat Res; fel Am Acad Pediat; NY Acad Med; fel Infectious Dis Soc Am. *Res:* Nosocomial infections; hospital epidemiology; clinical virology and bacteriology; nonspecific enhancement of resistance to infection; neonatal and intrauterine infections. *Mailing Add:* 2011 Dartmouth NE Albuquerque NM 87106

FLORMAN, EDWIN F(RANK), b Venice, Ill, Feb 16, 04; m 47; c 3. ELECTRONICS. *Educ:* Washington Univ, MS, 34. *Prof Exp:* Res physicist, Western Cartridge Co, Ill, 34-41; radio engr, Nat Bur Standards, 41-44, Philco Radio Co, 44-46 & Nat Bur Standards, DC & Colo, 46-65; radio telecommun consult, Defense Commun Agency, 65-74; RETIRED. *Concurrent Pos:* Mem, Int Radio Consult Comt. *Honors & Awards:* Meritorious Award, Dept of Com, 56. *Mem:* AAAS; Sigma Xi; Inst Elec & Electronics Engrs. *Res:* Ballistic research; meteorological measurements; low frequency radio wave propagation studies; precise measurement of the velocity of propagation of radio waves; characteristics of atmospheric lightning discharges; tropospheric radio wave propagation; research and engineering of broadband telecommunication systems. *Mailing Add:* 10239 Brigade Dr Fairfax VA 22030

FLORMAN, MONTE, b New York, NY, Nov 19, 26; m; c 3. ENGINEERING ADMINISTRATION, ELECTRICAL ENGINEERING. *Educ:* NY Univ, BEE, 46. *Prof Exp:* Test engr bur standards, R H Macy & Co, 46-48; proj engr, Consumers Union US, Inc, 48-52; engr, Am Bosch Arma Corp, 52-53; proj engr, 53-57, head appliance div, 57-64, assoc tech dir, 64-70, TECH DIR, CONSUMERS UNION US, INC, 71- *Concurrent Pos:* Mem, Underwriters Lab Consumer Adv Coun. *Mem:* Inst Elec & Electronics Engrs; Am Soc Mech Engrs; Am Soc Heat, Refrig & Air Conditioning Engrs; AAAS; Asn Food & Drug Officials of US. *Res:* Evaluation of food, chemical, electrical, automotive electronic and electro-mechanical products intended for consumer use. *Mailing Add:* 31 Vernon Pkwy Mt Vernon NY 10552

FLORSCHUETZ, LEON W(ALTER), b Sublette, Ill, Aug 11, 35; m 57; c 3. MECHANICAL ENGINEERING. *Educ:* Univ Ill, BS, 58, MS, 59, PhD(eng), 64. *Prof Exp:* Asst mech eng, Univ Ill, 62-63; from asst prof to assoc prof, 64-77, PROF ENG, ARIZ STATE UNIV, 77- *Concurrent Pos:* NSF res grant, 65-67. *Mem:* Am Soc Eng Educ; Am Soc Mech Engrs. *Res:* Heat transfer; vapor bubble dynamics and boiling in single and binary component systems. *Mailing Add:* Dept of Eng Ariz State Univ Tempe AZ 85287

FLORSHEIM, WARNER HANNS, b Hamburg, Ger, Dec 11, 22; nat US; m 52; c 2. ENDOCRINOLOGY. *Educ:* Univ Calif, Los Angeles, BA, 43, MA, 44, PhD(chem), 48. *Prof Exp:* Asst chem, Univ Calif, Los Angeles, 43-46, res assoc zool, 48-51, anat, Med Sch, 51-53, asst clin prof biol chem, 55-71, assoc clin prof physiol, Irvine, 71-81; BIOCHEMIST, US VET ADMIN HOSP, LONG BEACH, CALIF, 53- *Concurrent Pos:* USPHS fel anat, Oxford Univ, 63-64. *Mem:* Endocrine Soc; Soc Exp Biol & Med; Am Thyroid Asn; Am Fedn Clin Res; Am Physiol Soc. *Res:* Neuroendocrinology; thyroid function. *Mailing Add:* Vet Admin Hosp 5901 E Seventh St Long Beach CA 90822

FLORY, LESLIE E(ARL), b Sawyer, Kans, Mar 17, 07; m 31; c 2. ELECTRICAL ENGINEERING. *Educ:* Univ Kans, BS, 30. *Prof Exp:* Engr, RCA Corp, Camden, 30-42; res engr, RCA Labs, 42-64, fel, 61, leader spec systs res, Astroelectronics Appl Res Lab, 64-67, chief scientist, RCA Med Electronics, 67-68; chief scientist, Roche Med Electronics Div, Hoffmann-La Roche, Inc, 68-71; RETIRED. *Concurrent Pos:* Secy-gen, Int Fedn Med Electronics & Biol Eng. *Mem:* Fel Inst Elec & Electronics Engrs; Sigma Xi. *Res:* Television and television tubes; electronic computers; special electronic tubes and circuits; industrial television; transistor applications; medical electronics; astronomical and space television. *Mailing Add:* 153 Philip Dr Princeton NJ 08540

FLORY, PAUL JOHN, b Sterling, Ill, June 19, 10; m 36; c 3. PHYSICAL CHEMISTRY. *Educ:* Manchester Col, BSc, 31; Ohio State Univ, MS, 31, PhD(phys chem), 34. *Hon Degrees:* ScD, Manchester Col, 50 & Ohio State Univ, 70; Laurea, Milan Polytech Inst, 64; DSc, Univ Manchester, 69. *Prof Exp:* Res chemist, Exp Sta, E I du Pont de Nemours & Co, Del, 34-38; res assoc basic sci lab, Univ Cincinnati, 38-40; res chemist, Esso Labs, Stand Oil Co, NJ, 40-43; sect head res lab, Goodyear Tire & Rubber Co, 43-48; Baker lectr, Cornell Univ, 48, prof chem, 48-56; exec dir res, Mellon Inst, 56-61; prof chem, 61-65, chmn dept, 69-71, J G Jackson-C J Wood Prof Chem, 65-76, EMER PROF CHEM, STANFORD UNIV, 76- *Concurrent Pos:* Chmn comt macromolecular chem, Nat Res Coun, 55-59 & div chem & chem technol, 66-68; mem coun, Nat Acad Sci, 67-70. *Honors & Awards:* Nobel Prize in Chem, 74; Sullivant Medal, Ohio State Univ, 45; Baekeland Award, Am Chem Soc, 47, Nichols Medal, 62, Goodyear Medal, 68, Debye Award, 69, Gibbs Medal, 73 & Priestley Medal, 74; Colwyn Medal, Brit Inst Rubber Indust, 54; High-Polymer Physics Prize, Am Phys Soc, 62; Int Award Plastics & Sci Eng, Soc Plastics Engrs, 67; Chandler Medal, Columbia Univ, 70; First Award for Excellence-Chem, Carborundum Co, 71; Cresson Medal, Franklin Inst, 71; Kirkwood Medal, Yale Univ, 71; Nat Medal of Sci, 75. *Mem:* Nat Acad Sci; Am Chem Soc; fel Am Phys Soc; Am Acad Arts & Sci; fel AAAS. *Res:* Polymerization mechanisms; constitution; configurational statistics; physical and thermodynamic properties of high polymers; theory of solutions; biopolymers. *Mailing Add:* 210 Golden Oak Dr Portola Valley CA 94025

FLOSS, HEINZ G, b Berlin, Germany, Aug 28, 34; m 56; c 4. BIOCHEMISTRY. *Educ:* Tech Univ, Berlin, BS, 56, MS, 59; Munich Tech, PhD(org chem), 61. *Prof Exp:* Sci asst, Munich Tech, 61-64 & 64-65, dozent, 66; assoc prof, 66-69, prof, 69-77, head dept, 68-79, LILLY DISTINGUISHED PROF MEDICINAL CHEM, PURDUE UNIV, WEST LAFAYETTE, 77- *Concurrent Pos:* Fel biochem, Univ Calif, Davis, 64-65; mem med chem study sect, NIH, 74-78. *Mem:* Phytochem Soc NAm (pres, 74-75); Am Chem Soc; Am Soc Biol Chemists; fel Acad Pharmaceut Sci; Am Soc Pharmacog (pres, 77-78). *Res:* Biosynthesis of secondary plant and mold metabolites; regulation of secondary metabolism; stereochemistry and mechanism of biological reactions; chemical carcinogenesis. *Mailing Add:* Sch of Pharm & Pharmacol Sci Purdue Univ Lafayette IN 47907

FLOTOW, HOWARD EDWARD, b Maywood, Ill, May 18, 22; m 44; c 3. PHYSICAL CHEMISTRY. *Educ:* Univ Chicago, BS, 43, MS, 48. *Prof Exp:* Chemist anal, Standard Oil Co, 43-44; chemist inorg, Manhattan Proj, 44-45; CHEMIST PHYS CHEM, ARGONNE NAT LAB, 46- *Mem:* Am Chem Soc. *Res:* Calorimetry, thermodynamics, transport properties of inorganic substance, including metal hydrides and radioactive compounds. *Mailing Add:* Argonne Nat Lab 9700 S Cass Ave Argonne IL 60439

FLOURET, GEORGE R, b Rosario, Arg, Jan 5, 35; US citizen; m 63; c 3. BIOCHEMISTRY, ENDOCRINOLOGY. *Educ:* Columbia Univ, BS, 57, MS, 59; Univ Wis, PhD(org med chem), 63. *Prof Exp:* Instr org chem, Univ Wis, 61, asst prof org med chem, 62-63; res assoc biochem, Med Sch, Cornell Univ, 63-65, instr, 64-65; sr chemist, Abbott Labs, 65-71; assoc prof, 72-81, PROF PHYSIOL, NORTHWESTERN UNIV, CHICAGO, 81- *Res:* Chemistry, biochemistry and physiology of hypothalamic and neurohypophyseal peptide hormones. *Mailing Add:* Dept of Physiol Northwestern Univ Med Sch Chicago IL 60611

FLOURNOY, ROBERT WILSON, b Tulsa, Okla, Dec 12, 36; div; c 4. PHYSIOLOGY. *Educ:* Tex A&M Univ, BS, 59, MS, 61, PhD(physiol), 66. *Prof Exp:* Instr biol, Tex A&M Univ, 61-65; from asst prof to assoc prof zool, La Tech Univ, 66-74, prof, 75-77; PRES & CHIEF EXEC OFFICER, FOUND TESTING LABS, INC, 77- *Concurrent Pos:* Consult toxicologist, Hazardous Waste Mgt Prog, La Dept Natural Resources, Baton Rouge, 79-; consult environ scientist, La Dept Transp & Develop, Baton Rouge, 80- *Mem:* Am Water Works Asn; Am Water Resources Asn; Am Heart Asn; Am Physiol Soc; AAAS. *Res:* Effects of sympathomimetic amines and related compounds on the cardiovascular system of mammals; action of saponins on uterine motility in rodents; effects of environmental products on mammalian systems. *Mailing Add:* 3003 Lakeview Pl Ruston LA 71270

FLOUTZ, WILLIAM VAUGHN, b Defiance, Ohio, Nov 12, 35; m 59; c 2. ANALYTICAL CHEMISTRY. *Educ:* Kent State Univ, BS, 57; Purdue Univ, MS, 59. *Prof Exp:* Chemist, 59-61, res chemist, 61-67, sr res chemist, 67-76, RES ASSOC, BASF WYANDOTTE CORP, 76- *Mem:* Am Chem Soc; Coblentz Soc; Sci Res Soc Am. *Res:* The use of infrared spectroscopy and nuclear magnetic resonance spectroscopy for the elucidation of chemical structure. *Mailing Add:* BASF Wyandotte Corp Biddle Ave Wyandotte MI 48192

FLOWER, PHILLIP JOHN, b Toledo, Ohio, Feb 4, 48; m 70; c 1. ASTROPHYSICS. *Educ:* Univ Toledo, BS, 70; Univ Wash, PhD(astron), 76. *Prof Exp:* Res assoc astrophys, Joint Inst Lab Astrophys, 76-78; ASST PROF PHYSICS & ASTRON, CLEMSON UNIV, 78- *Mem:* Am Astron Soc; Am Phys Soc. *Res:* Stellar evolution; stellar interiors; Magellanic clouds; dwarf galaxies; distance scale; evolution of galaxies. *Mailing Add:* Dept of Physics & Astron Clemson Univ Clemson SC 29631

FLOWER, ROBERT WALTER, b Baltimore, Md, July 6, 41; m 68; c 2. MEDICAL PHYSICS. *Educ:* Johns Hopkins Univ, BA, 66. *Prof Exp:* Assoc staff, Appl Physics Lab, 66-71, sr staff, 71-76, instr ophthal, Sch Med, 72-73, asst prof, 73-81, spec adv to dir biomed prog, 74-81, PRIN STAFF, APPL PHYSICS LAB, JOHNS HOPKINS UNIV, 76-, PROF, SCH MED, 81-, DIR BIOMED PROG, 81- *Concurrent Pos:* Instr ophthal, Johns Hopkins Univ, 72-73, asst prof, 73-, spec adv to dir biomed eng prog, Appl Physics Lab, 74- *Honors & Awards:* Award for Achievement, Soc Tech Commun, 72; Meyers Honor Award for Basic Sci Res, 77. *Mem:* Asn Res Vision & Ophthal; Int Soc Oxygen Transport to Tissue; Wilmer Res Group; Sigma Xi. *Res:* Relationship of ocular blood flow dynamics to distribution and maintenance of metabolites, particularly oxygen, within tissues of the eye during perinatal development; development of techniques for routine clinical monitoring of retinal and choroidal blood flow. *Mailing Add:* Appl Physics Lab Johns Hopkins Univ Laurel MD 20707

FLOWER, ROUSSEAU HAYNER, b Center Brunswick, NY, Mar 21, 13; m 50; c 2. GEOLOGY, PALEONTOLOGY. *Educ:* Cornell Univ, AB, 34, AM, 35; Univ Cincinnati, PhD(paleont), 39. *Prof Exp:* Temp paleontologist, NY State Mus, 38; cur univ mus, Univ Cincinnati, 40-43, 44; lectr, Bryn Mawr Col, 43-44; temp expert, NY State Mus, 44-45, asst state paleontologist, NY, 45-51; stratigraphic geologist, NMex Inst Mining & Technol, 51-66, sr paleontologist, 66-78, EMER SR PALEONTOLOGIST, NMEX BUR OF MINES & MINERAL RESOURCES, N MEX INST MINING & TECHNOL, 78- *Concurrent Pos:* NSF res grant, 67-71 & 78-83; paleontologist, US Geol Survey, 75- *Mem:* Soc Syst Zool; Paleont Soc; fel Geol Soc Am; Soc Study Evolution; Soc Geol France. *Res:* Paleozoic cephalopods, primarily Nautiloidea-evolution, taxonomy, morphology, stratigraphy, faunal realms with implicatios relating to plate tectonics and continental drift; Ordovician colonial corals; cyathaspids, graptolites, general stratigraphy and faunas Cambrian-Devonian. *Mailing Add:* 205 Pena Pl Socorro NM 87801

FLOWERDAY, ALBERT DALE, b Nebr, June 14, 27; m 51; c 3. CROP PHYSIOLOGY. *Educ:* Univ Nebr, BS, 50, MS, 51, PhD(agron), 58. *Prof Exp:* From supt Northeastern Nebr Exp Sta to asst prof agron, 57-66, assoc prof, 66-73, mem staff, Mission to Nat Univ Colombia, 67-69, dir exten, 67-

70, PROF AGRON, UNIV NEBR, LINCOLN, 73- *Honors & Awards:* Outstanding Teacher, Univ Nebr Lincoln Builders, 74. *Mem:* Am Soc Agron. *Res:* Crop production system with special emphasis on conservation of energy, soil and water. *Mailing Add:* Dept of Agron 229 Keim Hall Univ of Nebr Lincoln NE 68583

FLOWERS, ALLAN DALE, b New Castle, Ind, Mar 21, 46; m 68. OPERATIONS RESEARCH. *Educ:* Ind Univ, BS, 67, MBA, 70, DBA(opers mgt), 72. *Prof Exp:* Systs coordr comput, Univ Div, Ind Univ, 70-72; from asst prof to assoc prof opers mgt, Tex Tech Univ, 72-78; ASSOC PROF OPERS MGT, CASE WESTERN RESERVE UNIV, 78- *Concurrent Pos:* Ed, Decision Line, Am Inst Decision Sci, 72-73, opers mgt chmn, 77-78, coun mem, 78-80; consult, Tex Instruments, Inc, 77-78 & Devro, Inc, 77-78. *Mem:* Am Inst Decision Sci; Opers Res Soc Am; Inst Mgt Sci; Soc Mgt Info Systs. *Res:* Production planning and inventory control; forecasting; operations scheduling; quality control; assembly line balancing; materials requirements planning. *Mailing Add:* Dept of Opers Res Case Western Reserve Univ Cleveland OH 44106

FLOWERS, CHARLES E, JR, b Zebulon, NC, July 20, 20; m 72; c 2. OBSTETRICS & GYNECOLOGY. *Educ:* The Citadel, BS, 41; Johns Hopkins Univ, MD, 44. *Prof Exp:* Asst obstet & gynec, Johns Hopkins Hosp, 48-50; from instr to asst prof, Col Med, State Univ NY, 51-53; from assoc prof to prof, Sch Med, Univ NC, 53-66; prof obstet & gynec & chmn dept, Col Med, Baylor Univ, 66-69; obstetrician & gynecologist-in-chief, Ben Taub & Jefferson Davis Hosps, Houston, 66-69; PROF OBSTET & GYNEC & CHMN DEPT, MED CTR, UNIV ALA, BIRMINGHAM, 69- *Mem:* Fel Am Col Surgeons; fel Am Col Obstet & Gynec; fel Am Gynec Soc; fel Am Asn Obstet & Gynec. *Res:* Obstetrical anesthesia and analgesia; metabolism in toxemia of pregnancy; studies of the endometrium and the menstrual cycle. *Mailing Add:* Dept of Obstet & Gynec Univ of Ala Med Ctr Birmingham AL 35294

FLOWERS, DANIEL F(ORT), b New York, NY, Jan 21, 20; m 58. MECHANICAL ENGINEERING. *Educ:* Va Mil Inst, BS, 40; Mass Inst Technol, SM, 42, ScD(mech eng), 49. *Prof Exp:* Engr, 46-47 & 49-56, vpres, 56-75, CHMN BD, DIFFERENTIAL CORP, 75- *Mem:* Am Soc Mech Engrs; Am Inst Mining, Metall & Petrol Engrs. *Res:* Aircraft vibration and flutter; gas turbine control; railway vehicles; oil and gas production. *Mailing Add:* Differential Corp 2001 Kirby Dr No 513 Houston TX 77019

FLOWERS, EARL SHEDERICK, environmental health, chemistry, see previous edition

FLOWERS, HAROLD L(EE), b Hickory, NC, June 25, 17; m 41; c 2. ELECTRONICS. *Educ:* Duke Univ, BS, 38; Univ Cincinnati, MS, 48. *Prof Exp:* Asst, Proctor & Swartz, Inc, Pa, 38-41; asst radio engr radio & radar, Off Chief Sig Off, US War Dept, Washington, DC, 41-42; br head missile command & report links, Naval Res Lab, 42-50; dir weapon syst, Goodyear Aircraft Corp, 50-61; gen eng mgr, Avco Electronics, Ohio, 61-63; eng mgr, McDonnell Aircraft Corp, Mo, 63-66, chief engr tactical missiles, Fla Div, McDonnell Douglas Corp, 66-69, dept prog mgr, 69-74, CHIEF PROG MGR, MCDONNELL DOUGLAS ASTRONAUT CO, MO, 74- *Concurrent Pos:* Mem guided missile com, Res & Develop Bd, Dept Defense, 49-53. *Mem:* Assoc fel Am Inst Aeronaut & Astronaut; fel Inst Elec & Electronics Engrs. *Res:* Electronic guidance and missile systems; radar; weapon systems. *Mailing Add:* McDonnell Douglas Astronaut Co PO Box 516 St Louis MO 63166

FLOWERS, JOHN WILSON, b Memphis, Tenn, Aug 20, 10; m 41; c 1. PHYSICS. *Educ:* Southwestern (Tenn), BS, 31; Univ Va, MS, 33, PhD(physics), 35. *Prof Exp:* Mem staff, Gen Elec Co, 37-47; assoc prof, 47-53, PROF PHYSICS, UNIV FLA, 53- *Concurrent Pos:* Sr physicist, Aerojet Gen Corp, 61; consult, Union Carbide Co, 52- & Gen Dynamics/Ft Worth, 59, 60, Sperry Rand, 61 & Radiation Res Corp, 64- *Mem:* AAAS; Am Phys Soc. *Res:* Plasma, thermonuclear and space physics. *Mailing Add:* Williamson Hall Univ of Fla Gainesville FL 32611

FLOWERS, NANCY CAROLYN, b McComb, Miss, Sept 28, 28; m 66; c 3. CARDIOVASCULAR DISEASES. *Educ:* Miss State Col Women, BS, 50; Univ Tenn, Memphis, MD, 58; Am Bd Internal Med, dipl, 66; Am Bd Cardiovasc Dis, dipl, 70. *Prof Exp:* Preceptorship under Dr Ralph R Braund, 58; intern med, Roanoke Mem Hosp, 58-59; preceptorship internal med, Beckley Mem Hosp, WVa, 60, resident, 60-62; instr med, Col Med, Univ Tenn, Memphis, 63-65; NIH fel & trainee, 62-65, asst prof, 65-67, asst prof physiol, 66-67; from assoc prof to prof med, Med Col Ga, 67-73; PROF MED & CHIEF DIV CARDIOL, SCH MED, UNIV LOUISVILLE, 73- *Concurrent Pos:* Res physician cardiol, Kennedy Vet Admin Hosp, Memphis, Tenn, 63-67; dir heart sta, John Gaston Hosp, 64-65; consult, William F Bowld Hosp, 65-66 & WTenn Tuberc Hosp, 66-67; prin investr, Am Heart Asn grant-in-aid, 69-72; sect chief cardiol, Forest Hills Div, Vet Admin Hosp, Augusta, Ga, 67-73, dir training prog, 70; co-investr, NIH grant-in-aid, 67-74; fel coun clin cardiol, Am Heart Asn, 70. *Mem:* AMA; Am Fedn Clin Res; fel Am Col Physicians; fel Am Col Cardiol; fel Am Col Chest Physicians. *Res:* Distribution of electrocardiographic potential on the body surface with respect to the limits of the contained information, equivalent cardiac generator representation, clinical significance and A-V conduction system of the heart. *Mailing Add:* Health Sci Ctr Univ of Louisville Sch of Med Louisville KY 40202

FLOWERS, RALPH GRANT, b North Platte, Nebr, Apr 11, 15; m 40; c 2. PHYSICAL CHEMISTRY. *Educ:* Univ WVa, AB, 38, MS, 39; NY Univ, PhD(phys chem), 42. *Prof Exp:* Asst, Nat Defense Res Comt, Columbia Univ, 41-42; res chemist, 42-56, SR CHEMIST, GEN ELEC CO, 56- *Concurrent Pos:* Civilian with Off Sci Res & Develop, 41-42. *Res:* Kinetics; polymers and resins; organic synthesis; oils; waxes; photolysis of azomethane in the presence of hydrogen; cellulose chemistry; electrical insulation and wire enamels. *Mailing Add:* 177 E New Lenox Rd Pittsfield MA 01201

FLOWERS, RALPH WILLS, b Pittsfield, Mass, Oct 2, 48. ENTOMOLOGY, MALACOLOGY. *Educ:* Cornell Univ, BS, 70; NC State Univ, MS, 72; Univ Wis, PhD(entom), 75. *Prof Exp:* Res asst entom, NC State Univ, 70-71 & Univ Wis, 72-75; ASST PROF ENTOM, FLA A&M UNIV, 75- *Mem:* Entom Soc Am; Lepidopterists Soc; Asn Trop Biol. *Res:* Taxonomy and biology of Ephemeroptera. *Mailing Add:* Box 111 Univ Sta Fla A&M Univ Tallahassee FL 32307

FLOWERS, RUSSELL SHERWOOD, JR, microbiology, food science, see previous edition

FLOYD, ALTON DAVID, b Henderson, Ky, July 17, 41; m 62; c 2. ANATOMY. *Educ:* Univ Ky, BS, 63; Univ Louisville, PhD(anat), 68. *Prof Exp:* From instr to asst prof anat, Univ Mich, Ann Arbor, 67-72; asst prof, 72-79, ASSOC PROF ANAT, MED SCI PROG, IND UNIV, BLOOMINGTON, 79- *Mem:* Am Asn Anatomists; Tissue Cult Asn; Teratol Soc; Histochem Soc. *Res:* Cell nuclear differentiation and specialization; quantitative cytology. *Mailing Add:* 4811 N Hite Rd Bloomington IN 47401

FLOYD, DENIS RAGAN, algebra, see previous edition

FLOYD, DON EDGAR, b Iowa City, Iowa, Feb 26, 18; m 43; c 1. ORGANIC POLYMER CHEMISTRY. *Educ:* Univ Iowa, BA, 40, PhD(org chem), 43. *Prof Exp:* Asst chem, Univ Iowa, 40-43; res chemist, Gen Mills, Inc, 43-73, PRIN SCIENTIST, GEN MILLS CHEM INC, 73- *Res:* Ester condensations; synthesis of amino acids; derivatives of fatty acids; resins and surface coatings; polyamide resins; basic research on new polymer development. *Mailing Add:* 2672 Parkview Ave Robbinsdale MN 55422

FLOYD, EDWIN EARL, b Eufaula, Ala, May 8, 24; m 45; c 3. TOPOLOGY. *Educ:* Univ Ala, BA, 43; Univ Va, PhD(math), 48. *Prof Exp:* Instr math, Princeton Univ, 48-49; from asst prof to assoc prof, 53-56, chmn dept, 66-69, prof, 56-80, ROBERT C TAYLOR PROF MATH, UNIV VA, 80-, DEAN FAC, ARTS & SCI, 74- *Concurrent Pos:* Mem, Inst Advan Study, 58-59 & 63-64; Sloan res fel, 60-64. *Mem:* Am Math Soc; Math Asn Am. *Res:* Differential topology; cobordism; periodic maps; transformation groups. *Mailing Add:* 419 Cabell Hall Univ of Va Charlottesville VA 22903

FLOYD, ERNEST HAZEL, b Aiken, SC, Apr 5, 14; m 38; c 1. ENTOMOLOGY. *Educ:* Clemson Univ, BS, 37; La State Univ, MS, 39. *Prof Exp:* PROF ENTOM, LA STATE UNIV, BATON ROUGE, 41- *Mem:* Entom Soc Am. *Res:* Insects of corn, stored rice and grain sorghum. *Mailing Add:* 1838 Stuart Ave Baton Rouge LA 70808

FLOYD, J F R(ABARDY), b Pagosa Springs, Colo, May 22, 15; m 44; c 3. AERONAUTICAL ENGINEERING. *Educ:* Carnegie Inst Technol, BS, 37. *Prof Exp:* Aerodynamicist, Glenn L Martin Co, 37-43, chief aerodyn, 43-47; sr engr & mem prin prof staff, Appl Physics Lab, 47-78, MISSILE SYST PROJ ENGR, JOHNS HOPKINS UNIV, 67- *Mem:* Am Inst Aeronaut & Astronaut. *Res:* Design and development of aircraft and guided missiles, particularly missile system design and launching techniques. *Mailing Add:* 9217 Crownwood Rd Ellicott City MD 21043

FLOYD, JOHN CLAIBORNE, JR, b Olla, La, July 3, 27; m 52; c 4. DIABETOLOGY, ENDOCRINOLOGY. *Educ:* La State Univ, BS, 49, MD, 54. *Prof Exp:* Instr internal med, Med Ctr, Univ Mich, 58-59; instr internal med, Sch Med, La State Univ, 59-60; instr, 60-61, asst prof, 61-64, assoc prof, 64-70, PROF INTERNAL MED, MED CTR, UNIV MICH, 70- *Concurrent Pos:* Vis prof, Univ Aarhus, 78-79. *Mem:* Am Diabetes Asn; Am Fedn Clin Res; Endocrine Soc; Cent Soc Clin Res. *Res:* Research activities in physiological and pathophysiological regulation of endocrine pancreatic (islet) function in man (healthy, diabetes, obesity, starvation); evaluation of programs of care of diabetes mellitus. *Mailing Add:* Univ Mich Hosp 1405 E Ann St D4109 SACB Box 02 Ann Arbor MI 48109

FLOYD, JOSEPH CALVIN, b La Grange, Ga, June 6, 41; m 65; c 2. ORGANIC CHEMISTRY. *Educ:* Ga Inst Technol, BChE, 65, PhD(org chem), 69. *Prof Exp:* Res chemist, Exxon Res & Eng Co, 68-74; staff chemist, 74-77, SR STAFF CHEMIST, EXXON CHEM CO, 77- *Mem:* Am Chem Soc; Am Inst Chem Engrs. *Res:* Organic synthesis; oxidative stabilization of polymers; polymer process development. *Mailing Add:* 5106 Arrowhead Baytown TX 77521

FLOYD, ROBERT A, b Yosemite, Ky, Oct 7, 40; m 65. BIOPHYSICS. *Educ:* Univ Ky, BS, 63, MS, 65; Purdue Univ, PhD(agron), 69. *Prof Exp:* Fel agron, Univ Calif, Davis, 68-69; fel, Johnson Res Found, Univ Pa, 69-71; res assoc, Ctr Biol Natural Systs, Washington Univ, 71-74; asst prof, 74-78, ASSOC PROF BIOCHEM MOLEC BIOL, HEALTH SCI CTR, UNIV OKLA, 78-; ASSOC MEM, OKLA MED RES FOUND, 77- *Mem:* AAAS; Am Soc Biol Chemists; Am Chem Soc; Biophys Soc; Am Soc Photochem & Photobiol. *Res:* Carcinogenesis; carcinogen free radicals; spin trapping in biological systems; bioenergetics; plant root-soil interface; photosynthesis; electron spin resonance in biological systems; oxygen free radicals; aging brain membranes. *Mailing Add:* Okla Med Res Found 825 NE 13th St Oklahoma City OK 73104

FLOYD, ROBERT W, b New York, NY, June 8, 36; div; c 3. COMPUTER SCIENCE. *Educ:* Univ Chicago, BA, 55, BS, 58. *Prof Exp:* Elec engr, Westinghouse Elec, 55-56; comput oper programmer & analyst, Armour Res Found, 56-62; sr proj scientist, Comput Assoc, 62-65; assoc prof comput sci, Carnegie-Mellon Univ, 65-68; assoc prof, 68-70, chmn, 73-76, PROF COMPUT SCI, STANFORD UNIV, 70- *Concurrent Pos:* Assoc ed, J Asn Comput Mach, 67-69. *Honors & Awards:* Turing Award, Asn Comput Mach, 78. *Mem:* Fel Am Acad Arts & Sci; Asn Comput Mach; AAAS. *Res:* Optimal methods for computation; computer programming languages. *Mailing Add:* Dept of Comput Sci Stanford Univ Stanford CA 94305

FLOYD, WILLIAM BECKWITH, b Atlanta, Ga, Dec 27, 30; m 53; c 1. COMPUTER SCIENCE. *Educ:* Harvard Univ, AB, 52; Emory Univ, MS, 53. *Prof Exp:* Sr res engr, Appl Sci Div, Melpar, Inc, 56-59, head systs res lab, 59-60; sr staff engr, Info Sci Lab, Litton Systs, Inc, 60-66, tech mgr, Signal Processing Dept, Data Systs Div, 66-67; assoc tech dir, B-D Spear Med Systs Div, Becton, Dickinson & Co, 67-73; pres, Ruskin Data Systs, LTD, 73-81. *Mem:* Inst Elec & Electronics Engrs; Asn Comput Mach. *Res:* Pharmaceutical manufacturing system, design and development. *Mailing Add:* 59 Ash St Weston MA 02193

FLUCK, EUGENE RICHARDS, b Hazleton, Pa, Dec 10, 34; m 57; c 2. BIOCHEMISTRY. *Educ:* Pa State Univ, BS, 56, MS, 60, PhD(biochem), 62. *Prof Exp:* Metabolic chemist, R J Reynolds Tobacco Co, 62-69; METABOLIC CHEMIST, WYETH LABS, INC, 69- *Mem:* Am Chem Soc; NY Acad Sci. *Res:* Drug metabolism and drug safety evaluations. *Mailing Add:* Metab Chem Sect Wyeth Labs PO Box 8299 Philadelphia PA 19101

FLUCK, MICHELE MARGUERITE, b Geneva, Switzerland, Aug 5, 50. VIRAL ONCOLOGY. *Educ:* Univ Geneva, MS(physics), 64, MS(molecular biol), 66, PhD(molecular biol), 72. *Prof Exp:* Instr viral oncol, Harvard Med Sch, 72-78, asst prof, 78-79; ASSOC PROF VIRAL ONCOL, MICH STATE UNIV, 79- *Mem:* Am Women Sci; Am Soc Virologists. *Res:* Neoplastic transformation by polyoma virus: how a virus transforms a normal cell into a cancer cell. *Mailing Add:* Microbiol Dept Mich State Univ East Lansing MI 48824

FLUCK, RICHARD ALLEN, b Litchfield, Minn, June 21, 45; m 70; c 3. CELL PHYSIOLOGY. *Educ:* Iowa State Univ, BS, 66; Univ Calif, Berkeley, PhD(zool), 71. *Prof Exp:* Res assoc bot, Ohio Univ, 71-74; asst prof, 74-81, ASSOC PROF BIOL, FRANKLIN & MARSHALL COL, 81- *Concurrent Pos:* NSF fel, Ohio Univ, 71-72. *Mem:* Am Soc Cell Biologists; Soc Gen Physiologists; Soc Develop Biol; Am Soc Plant Physiologists; AAAS. *Res:* Intercellular communication during early development; the role of acetylcholine in nonnervous tissues and cells. *Mailing Add:* Dept of Biol Franklin & Marshall Col Lancaster PA 17604

FLUCK, RICHARD CONARD, b Clemmons, NC, May 22, 38; m 60; c 3. AGRICULTURAL ENGINEERING. *Educ:* NC State Univ, BS, 60, MS, 63, PhD(agr eng), 66. *Prof Exp:* Asst prof agr eng & asst agr engr, 65-69, assoc prof agr eng & assoc agr engr, 69-77, PROF & AGR ENGR, UNIV FLA, 77- *Mem:* Am Soc Agr Engrs; Nat Soc Prof Engrs; Sigma Xi. *Res:* Agricultural energy analysis and management; agricultural machinery management and engineering economy; agricultural engineering instrumentation. *Mailing Add:* Dept of Agr Eng Univ of Fla Gainesville FL 32611

FLUECK, JOHN A, b Apr 13, 33; US citizen; c 2. BIOMETRICS. *Educ:* Beloit Col, BS, 55; Univ Chicago, MBA, 58, PhD(statist), 67. *Prof Exp:* Lectr statist, Univ Chicago, 64-65, res assoc geophys, 65-69; assoc prof statist, 68-72, DIR, DATA ANAL LAB, TEMPLE UNIV, 72-, PROF STATIST, 77- *Concurrent Pos:* Vis lectr, Univ Ill, Chicago, 67-68; consult, Panel Weather & Climate Modification, Nat Acad Sci-Nat Res Coun, 68-70; consult, Bur of Budget, Washington, DC, 70, vis appointment, Off Mgt & Budget, Exec Off President, 70-71; consult, Campbell Inst of Food Res, 73-; chmn, Coun of Am Statist Asn, 75; mem, NSF Adv Panel on Weather Modification, 75- *Mem:* Am Statist Asn; Royal Statist Soc; Inst Math Statist; Biomet Soc; Am Meteorol Soc. *Res:* Data analysis, survey sampling, design of experiments, distributional theory and weather modification research. *Mailing Add:* Dept of Statist Temple Univ Philadelphia PA 19122

FLUHARTY, ARVAN LAWRENCE, b Haines, Ore, June 10, 34; m 61; c 3. BIOCHEMISTRY. *Educ:* Univ Wash, BS, 56; Univ Calif, Berkeley, PhD(biochem), 59. *Prof Exp:* From asst prof to assoc prof biochem, Univ Southern Calif, 62-68; res specialist, Pac State Hosp-Calif State Dept Ment Hyg, 68-73, assoc res biochemist, 73-75, adj prof psychiat, Neuropsychiat Inst, Pac State Hosp Res Group, 75-79, PROF IN RESIDENCE, MENTAL RETARDATION RES CTR GROUP, LANTERMAN STATE HOSP, UNIV CALIF, LOS ANGELES, 79-, RES GROUP COORDR, 80- *Concurrent Pos:* Adj assoc prof biochem, Sch Med, Univ Southern Calif, 69-72, adj prof, 72-75. *Mem:* AAAS; Am Chem Soc; Am Soc Biol Chemists; Am Soc Neurochem; Biochem Soc. *Res:* Biochemistry of metabolic diseases; biochemistry of mental retardation; neurobiochemistry; metabolism of four carbon sugars; enzymatic dithiols; cellular energy transformations. *Mailing Add:* Ment Retardation Res Ctr Univ Calif Lanterman State Hosp Box 100-R Pomona CA 91769

FLUHARTY, DAVID LINCOLN, b Seattle, Wash, Jan 30, 46. OFFSHORE OIL, FISHERIES. *Educ:* Univ Wash, BA, 68, MA, 72; Univ Mich, Ann Arbor, PhD(natural resource conserv), 77. *Prof Exp:* Fel, Inst Marine Studies, 76-78, RES ASSOC, UNIV WASH, 78- *Concurrent Pos:* Fel, US Int Commun Agency, 77; lectr, Dept Geog, Univ Wash, 78-79. *Mem:* AAAS. *Res:* Marine natural resource management at the international level primarily with respect to the North Pacific and Baltic Sea; integration of management policies for natural resources. *Mailing Add:* Inst Marine Studies HA-35 Univ Wash Seattle WA 98105

FLUHARTY, DEAN MILTON, b Culdesac, Idaho, June 18, 16; m 53; c 5. VETERINARY PUBLIC HEALTH, VETERINARY BACTERIOLOGY. *Educ:* Univ Idaho, BS, 39; Mich State Univ, DVM, 42; Univ Idaho, MS, 62. *Prof Exp:* Asst bact, Mich State Univ, 39-42; supvry veterinarian, Badger Breeders Co-op, Wis, 46-49; poultry dis diagnostician, Wash State Dept Agr, 49-52; ASSOC PROF VET PATH, COL VET MED, WASH STATE UNIV, 52- *Concurrent Pos:* Vet pvt pract, 49. *Mem:* Am Vet Med Asn; AAAS; Am Asn Vet Clin Pathologists. *Res:* Bovine mastitis; veterinary laboratory diagnostic methods; veterinary clinical pathology and meat hygiene; canine blood groups; hemolytic anemia of newborn puppies; staphylococcal diseases in animals and man. *Mailing Add:* Western Washington Res & Exten Ctr Wash State Univ Puyallup WA 98371

FLUHARTY, REX GILBERT, b Corvallis, Ore, Nov 22, 18; m 43; c 2. NUCLEAR PHYSICS. *Educ:* Univ Idaho, BS, 39; Mass Inst Technol, PhD(physics), 49. *Prof Exp:* Mem staff, Radiation Lab, Mass Inst Technol, 42-45, res assoc, 45-59; physicist, Oak Ridge Inst Nuclear Studies, 49-52; physicist & mgr nuclear technol br, Phillips Petrol Co, 52-66; mgr nuclear technol br, Idaho Nuclear Corp, 66-68; mem staff, Los Alamos Sci Lab, 68-80; MEM STAFF, UNIVERSE RACIATIONS, INC, 80- *Mem:* Fel Am Phys Soc; Am Nuclear Soc. *Res:* Radioactive and medical tracer research; low energy neutron cross sections; reactors as neutron sources; pulsed cyclic reactors; spallatim neutron sources; accelerator target and shielding design, weapons neutron research facility design concepts and solar energy. *Mailing Add:* 111 Los Pueblos Los Alamos NM 87544

FLUHR, WALLACE EMORY, b Louisville, Ky, Jan 3, 32; m 53; c 5. STRUCTURAL DYNAMICS, NUCLEAR ENGINEERING. *Educ:* Univ Ky, BS, 54; Univ Ill, MS, 59, PhD(struct dynamics), 60. *Prof Exp:* Base engr, Gunter AFB, Ala, 54-57, chief appl res, Ballistic Syst Div, Calif, 60-63, assoc prof mech, 63-66, PROF CIVIL ENG & HEAD DEPT, US AIR FORCE ACAD, 66- *Concurrent Pos:* Chmn dynamic forces adv panel, US Air Force, 60-; lectr, Univ Calif, Los Angeles, 62- *Mem:* Am Soc Civil Engrs; Am Soc Eng Educ; Am Concrete Inst. *Res:* Nuclear weapons effects and design of underground protective structures; structural dynamics. *Mailing Add:* Dept of Civil Eng US Air Force Acad CO 80840

FLUKE, DONALD JOHN, b Nankin, Ohio, Feb 17, 23; m 54; c 2. RADIATION BIOPHYSICS. *Educ:* Wooster Col, BA, 47; Yale Univ, MS, 48, PhD(physics), 50. *Prof Exp:* Instr physics, Yale Univ, 50-52; biophysicist, Brookhaven Nat Lab, 52-57; assoc prof zool, 58-65, chmn acad coun, 69-71, chmn dept, 69-78, PROF ZOOL, DUKE UNIV, 65- . *Concurrent Pos:* Lectr, Univ Calif, 56-57, vis assoc prof, Donner Lab, 58; vis lectr, Am Inst Biol Scientists, 61-63; vis prof, Inst Molecular Biophysics, Fla State Univ, 64-65; tech rep biophys, Div Biol & Med, US Atomic Energy Comn, 68-69; vis prof, Univ Utrecht, 73-74. *Mem:* AAAS; Radiation Res Soc; Biophys Soc; Am Asn Physics Teachers; Am Soc Photobiol. *Res:* Ultraviolet action spectroscopy; biophysical application of accelerated ions on virus and enzyme; radiation biology; temperature dependence, direct effect; ultraviolet photobiology. *Mailing Add:* Dept Zool Duke Univ Durham NC 27706

FLUKER, SAM SPRUILL, entomology, see previous edition

FLUM, ROBERT S(AMUEL), SR, b Indianapolis, Ind, July 3, 25; m 47; c 7. SYSTEMS ANALYSIS. *Educ:* Univ Ind, BS, 49, MS, 56. *Prof Exp:* Asst physics, Univ Ind, 49-50; asst discharge in gases, Univ Md, 51-52; proj engr underwater acoust, US Naval Ord Lab, 52, physicist aero boundary layer, 52-54, physicist ord eng, 54-55, staff consult aerodyn, 55-58 & aerodevelop eng, 58-61; mem staff, Univ Chicago, 61-63; physicist, 63-65, sr analyst, Systs Anal Off, Anti-submarine Warefare, Spec Proj Off, 65-70, sr analyst, US Naval Ord Lab, 70-75, sr analyst, Navy Dept, 75-79, PHYSICAL SCIENTIST, ANTI-SUBMARINE WARFARE SYSTS PROJ OFF, US NAVAL ORD LAB, 79- *Mem:* Opers Res Soc Am; Am Phys Soc. *Res:* Application of logic and common sense to the basic problems of optimization of the Naval antisubmarine warfare posture. *Mailing Add:* Anti-Sub Warfare Systs Proj Dept of Navy Washington DC 20362

FLUMERFELT, RAYMOND W, b Hobbs, NMex, Nov 18, 39; m 59; c 2. CHEMICAL ENGINEERING. *Educ:* Lamar State Col, BS, 61; Northwestern Univ, MS, 63, PhD, 65. *Prof Exp:* Asst prof eng sci, Univ Notre Dame, 65-67; fel, Univ Wis, 67-68; from asst prof to assoc prof chem eng, 68-75, assoc chmn dept, 77-79, PROF CHEM ENG, UNIV HOUSTON, 75- *Mem:* Am Inst Chem Engrs; Soc Rheol; Am Chem Soc. *Res:* Rheology; fluid mechanics; interfacial phenomena. *Mailing Add:* Dept of Chem Eng Univ of Houston Houston TX 77004

FLURRY, ROBERT LUTHER, JR, b Hattiesburg, Miss, Nov 15, 33; m 57; c 4. THEORETICAL CHEMISTRY. *Educ:* Emory Univ, AB, 58, MS, 59, PhD(org chem), 61. *Prof Exp:* NIH fel, 61-62; from asst prof to assoc prof chem, 62-70, PROF CHEM, UNIV NEW ORLEANS, 70- *Concurrent Pos:* Vis prof, Math Inst, Eng, 68; pres, La Chap, Am Inst Chemists, 73-74. *Mem:* Am Chem Soc; NY Acad Sci; fel Am Inst Chemists. *Res:* Applications of quantum chemistry and group theory to chemical and biological problems. *Mailing Add:* Dept of Chem Univ of New Orleans New Orleans LA 70122

FLURY, ALVIN GODFREY, b Austin, Tex, Nov 1, 20; m 44; c 4. HERPETOLOGY. *Educ:* Univ Tex, BA, 48, MA, 51; Tex Tech Univ, PhD(zool), 72. *Prof Exp:* Aquatic biologist, Freshwater Fisheries, Tex Game & Fish Comn, 51-62; info-ed officer, Tex Parks & Wildlife Dept, 62-65; instr biol, 65-69, asst prof, 69-77, ASSOC PROF BIOL, ANGELO STATE COL, 77- *Mem:* Am Soc Ichthyol & Herpet; Soc Study Evolution; Soc Study Amphibians & Reptiles; Asn Study Animal Behav; Ecol Soc Am. *Res:* Reptiles; amphibians; fish; fish and wildlife conservation. *Mailing Add:* Dept of Biol Angelo State Col San Angelo TX 76901

FLUSSER, PETER R, b Vienna, Austria, July 3, 30; US citizen; m 58; c 4. MATHEMATICS. *Educ:* Ottawa Univ, BA, 58; Univ Kans, MA, 60; Okla State Univ, EdD(higher educ), 71. *Prof Exp:* From asst prof to prof math, Ottawa Univ, 60-78; ASST PROF MATH, FORT HAYS STATE UNIV, 78- *Mem:* Am Math Soc; Math Asn Am. *Res:* Probability theory; characterization theorems in probability, especially characterization theorems for random variables with values in topological groups. *Mailing Add:* Dept of Math Fort Hays State Univ Hays KS 67601

FLY, CLAUDE LEE, b Fulbright, Tex, June 23, 05; m 27; c 2. SOIL CHEMISTRY, PLANT PHYSIOLOGY. *Educ:* Okla Agr & Mech Col, BS, 27, MS, 28; Iowa State Col, PhD(soil chem), 31. *Prof Exp:* Prof chem & head dept sci, Panhandle Agr & Mech Col, 31-35; asst soil survr, Soil Conserv Serv, USDA, 35, assoc soil scientist, 35-39, soil scientist, Tex, 39-42, Nebr, 42-47, state soil scientist, Kans, 47-52; head land develop dept, Int Eng Co & Morrison-Knudsen-Afghanistan Co, 52-58; area dir, Northern Great Plains,

Soil & Water Conserv, Agr Res Serv, USDA, 58-59, res proj leader, Western Br, 59-63; PRES, CLAUDE L FLY & ASSOCS, 63- *Concurrent Pos:* Soil scientist to Greece, Italy & Sicily, UN Relief & Rehab Admin, 46-47, Kaiser Engrs, Ghana, WAfrica, Ivory Coast, 63-64, Int Eng Co-Peru, 64-67; partner & dir, Agriconsult, 65-67; consult, Eng Consult, Inc, Jamaica & Turkey, 66-67, Food & Agr Orgn, UN, Jordan, Yugoslavia, Nigeria, Uruguay, Panama, 67-69; polit hostage, Tupamaro guerillas, Uruguay, 70-71; consult, Develop, Planning & Res Assocs, Brazil, 72, Great Western Sugar Co, 73, Develop Planning, Inc, Kans, 72-, Am Agr Industs, Ill, 75- & Platte River Power Authority, Colo, 75; lectr & writer; mem, Subcomt Southern Great Plains, President's Nat Resources Bd, 28. *Mem:* Hon mem Am Soc Agron; Soil Sci Soc Am; fel Soil Conserv Soc Am; Am Soc Agr Consult (pres, 75); Int Soc Soil Sci. *Res:* Soil-plant-climate interrelationships affecting land and water resource development and resource conservation; research, program planning and administration. *Mailing Add:* Apt 1107 415 S Howes St Ft Collins CO 80521

FLYGARE, WILLIS H, chemical physics, deceased

FLYGER, VAGN FOLKMANN, b Aalborg, Denmark, Jan 4, 22; nat US; m 46; c 2. WILDLIFE ECOLOGY. *Educ:* Cornell Univ, BS, 48; Pa State Univ, MS, 52; Johns Hopkins Univ, ScD, 56. *Prof Exp:* Game biologist, Md Dept Res & Educ, 48-51 & Wildlife Res, Md Game & Inland Fish Dept, 54-55; sr biologist, Inland Res Div, Md Dept Res & Educ, 55-61; res assoc prof, 61-67, actg dir, 64-65, chmn dept forestry, Fish & Wildlife, 71-74, PROF, NATURAL RESOURCES INST, UNIV MD, 67-, PROF ANIMAL SCI, 79- *Mem:* AAAS; Am Soc Mammal; Wildlife Soc; Ecol Soc Am. *Res:* Mammal behavior; factors influencing animal populations and especially biology of tree squirrels. *Mailing Add:* Animal Sci Dept Univ of Md College Park MD 20742

FLYNN, ARTHUR, b Cleveland, Ohio, Aug 25, 44; m 70; c 2. BIOINORGANIC CHEMISTRY. *Educ:* Baldwin-Wallace Col, BS, 68; Univ Pittsburgh, PhD(biol), 72. *Prof Exp:* Res assoc, Cleveland Metrop Gen Hosp, 71-73, biochemist, 73-74, dir labs surg, 75-78; STAFF SCIENTIST, CLEVELAND CLIN FOUND, 78- *Concurrent Pos:* Instr biochem, Case Western Reserve Univ, 73-74, asst prof, 74-77, assoc prof, 77-78; assoc, F-2 Wildlife Res Consult Serv Inc, 75-; dir, Cancer Ctr for Northeast Ohio, 76-78. *Mem:* AAAS; Am Col Nutrit Am Fedn Clin Res; Soc Environ Geochem & Health. *Res:* Bioinorganic correlates in hormonal functions, mineral element nutrition in disease states and geochemical variations in biological mineralization. *Mailing Add:* Res Div Cleveland Clin Found Cleveland OH 44106

FLYNN, ARTHUR DAVIS, entomology, see previous edition

FLYNN, COLIN PETER, b Stockton-on-Tees, Eng, Aug 18, 35; m 61, 71; c 1. SOLID STATE PHYSICS. *Educ:* Univ Leeds, BSc, 57, PhD(physics), 60; Cambridge Univ, MA, 66. *Prof Exp:* Res assoc, 60-62, res asst prof, 62-64, from asst prof to assoc prof, 64-68, PROF PHYSICS, UNIV ILL, URBANA, 68-, DIR, MAT RES LAB, 78- *Concurrent Pos:* Fel, Christ's Col, Cambridge Univ, 66-67; NSF int prog fel, Sao Carlos, Brazil, 77-78. *Mem:* Am Soc Metals; fel Am Phys Soc. *Res:* Impurities and thermal defect structure in crystals; impurity magnetism and nuclear magnetic resonance in metals; diffusive hopping of ions and electrons in crystals; kinetics of defect equilibration. *Mailing Add:* Dept of Physics & Mat Res Lab Univ of Ill Urbana IL 61801

FLYNN, EDWARD JOSEPH, b Waltham, Mass, Apr 4, 42; m 65; c 2. PHARMACOLOGY. *Educ:* Northeastern Univ, BS, 64, MS, 66; NY Univ, PhD(pharmacol), 71. *Prof Exp:* Pharmacologist, US Army Res Inst Environ Med, Natick, Mass, 66; asst prof, 71-80, ASSOC PROF PHARMACOL, NJ MED SCH, UNIV MED & DENT NJ, 80- *Concurrent Pos:* Fel, Roche Inst Molecular Biol, Nutley, NJ, 70-71; Pharmaceut Mfrs Asn Found starter grant, 74; NIH grant, 74; consult curric div & instr, NJ State Dept Educ, 71- *Mem:* AAAS; NY Acad Sci. *Res:* Drug metabolism; barbiturate pharmacology; immunopharmacology. *Mailing Add:* NJ Med Sch Col of Med & Dent of NJ Newark NJ 07103

FLYNN, EDWARD ROBERT, b Joliet, Ill, July 7, 34; m 54; c 6. PHYSICS. *Educ:* Univ Ill, BS, 56; Univ NMex, MS, 64, PhD(physics), 66. *Prof Exp:* Accelerator engr, Univ Ill, 56-58; MEM STAFF, LOS ALAMOS SCI LAB, 58- *Concurrent Pos:* NATO fel, Niels Bohr Inst, Copenhagen, 70-71. *Mem:* Am Phys Soc. *Res:* Nuclear physics. *Mailing Add:* Los Alamos Sci Lab PO Box 1663 Los Alamos NM 87545

FLYNN, GARY ALAN, b Jacksonville, Ill, Nov 2, 50; m 72. ORGANIC CHEMISTRY. *Educ:* Northern Ill Univ, BS, 72, MS, 73; Northwestern Univ, PhD(chem), 77. *Prof Exp:* SR RES CHEMIST ORG CHEM, MERRELL NAT LABS DIV, RICHARDSON-MERRELL, 77- *Mem:* Am Chem Soc; Sigma Xi. *Res:* Synthesis and biological evaluation of organic compounds related to or derived from naturally occurring substances. *Mailing Add:* Merrell Res Ctr 2110 E Galbraith Rd Cincinnati OH 45215

FLYNN, GEORGE P(ATRICK), b Fall River, Mass, Aug 12, 36. PHYSICAL CHEMISTRY. *Educ:* Providence Col, BS, 57; Brown Univ, PhD(phys chem), 62. *Prof Exp:* Res asst chem, Yale Univ, 61-63; res assoc, Brown Univ, 64-67; res assoc chem, Mass Inst Technol, 67-70 & 72-80. *Mem:* Am Chem Soc. *Res:* Textbook writing; viscosity of gases. *Mailing Add:* 27 Sowamsett Ave Warren RI 02885

FLYNN, GEORGE WILLIAM, b Hartford, Conn, July 11, 38; m 70. CHEMICAL PHYSICS. *Educ:* Yale Univ, BS, 60; Harvard Univ, AM & PhD(chem), 64. *Prof Exp:* Fel physics, Mass Inst Technol, 64-66; from asst prof to assoc prof, 67-76, PROF CHEM, COLUMBIA UNIV, 76- *Concurrent Pos:* NSF fel, 64-65; Alfred P Sloan fel, 68-71; res collabr, Brookhaven Nat Lab, 69-; John Simon Guggenheim Found fel, 74-75; vis assoc prof, Mass Inst of Technol, 75; dir, Columbia Radiation Lab, 79-; adv

ed, Chem Physics, 78-, J Phys Chem, 80-, Chem Physics Lett, 81-, Ann Rev Phys Chem, 80-85. *Mem:* Am Phys Soc; Am Chem Soc; NY Acad Sci. *Res:* Relaxation phenomena in molecular systems; development and uses of lasers; photo fragmentation dynamics; matrix isolation studies. *Mailing Add:* Dept Chem Columbia Univ 315 Havemeyer Hall New York NY 10027

FLYNN, JAMES PATRICK, b Wilkes Barre, Pa, Aug 1, 24; m 54; c 3. PHYSICAL CHEMISTRY, INORGANIC CHEMISTRY. *Educ:* Bucknell Univ, BS, 48; Iowa State Univ, PhD(chem), 53. *Prof Exp:* Res engr, Battelle Mem Inst, 48-49; asst, Ames Lab, AEC, 49-53; res & develop engr, Magnesium Dept, 53-58, res chemist, Sci Proj Lab, 58-67, proj leader, Prod Dept Labs, 67-70, RES ASSOC, DOW CHEM CO, 70- *Mem:* Nat Acad Sci; Sigma Xi; Am Soc Testing & Mat; Am Chem Soc. *Res:* Magnesium alloy and recovery of metals; propellant testing and compatibility; evaluation of chemical hazards; hazardous waste disposal; health and environmental regulations. *Mailing Add:* The Dow Chem Co Midland MI 48640

FLYNN, JOHN JOSEPH, JR, b Salida, Colo, Sept 16, 31. ORGANIC CHEMISTRY. *Educ:* Western State Col Colo, BA, 53; Okla State Univ, MS, 55; Purdue Univ, PhD(chem), 61. *Prof Exp:* ASSOC PROF CHEM, PURDUE UNIV FT WAYNE, 58- *Mem:* Am Chem Soc. *Res:* Diels-Alder reactions. *Mailing Add:* Dept of Chem Purdue Univ 2101 Coliseum Blvd E Ft Wayne IN 46805

FLYNN, JOHN M(ATHEW), b Cleveland, Ohio, Dec 9, 29; div; c 7. CHEMICAL ENGINEERING. *Educ:* Case Inst Technol, BSChE, 51, MSChE, 53, PhD, 56. *Prof Exp:* Instr, Case Inst Technol, 51-52, asst, 52, res assoc, 53-56; proj leader, High Pressure Lab, Dow Chem Co, 56-60, lab dir, 60-63, prod supt pelaspan, 63-66, sales mgr chlorine based polymers, 66-67, bus mgr, 67, mgr res & develop, Plastics Dept, 67-72, dir prod res, Res & Develop, 72-73, gen mgr, Styrene Plastics Dept, 73-77, PROD DIR, AGR CHEM, METALS & SPECIALTY PROD, EXEC DEPT, DOW CHEM CO, 77- *Mem:* Am Chem Soc; Sigma Xi; Soc Plastics Indust. *Res:* Plastics technology; polyolefins and polystyrene. *Mailing Add:* Exec Dept Dow Chem Co 2030 Dow Ctr Midland MI 48640

FLYNN, JOHN THOMAS, b Chester, Pa, Mar 14, 48; m 70; c 2. CARDIOVASCULAR PHYSIOLOGY. *Educ:* Widener Univ, BS, 70; Hahnemann Med Col, PhD(physiol), 74. *Prof Exp:* fel, Thomas Jefferson Univ, 74-75, NIH fel, 75-76, ASST PROF PHYSIOL, JEFFERSON MED COL, THOMAS JEFFERSON UNIV, 76- *Mem:* Am Physiol Soc; Shock Soc; Sigma Xi; NY Acad Sci. *Res:* Role of prostglandin-like materials in circulatory shock and cellular injury; mechanisms of pulmonary edema; physiology of the leukotriene-liposygenase cascade; regulation of prostanoid synthesis and metabolism. *Mailing Add:* Dept Physiol Thomas Jefferson Univ 1020 Locust St Philadelphia PA 19107

FLYNN, JOSEPH HENRY, b Washington, DC, Oct 28, 22; m 52; c 9. POLYMER SCIENCE, THERMAL SCIENCES. *Educ:* Georgetown Univ, BS, 43; Cath Univ, PhD(phys chem), 54. *Prof Exp:* Asst, Cath Univ, 46-50; RES CHEMIST, NAT BUR STANDARDS, 52- *Honors & Awards:* Mettler Award, 80. *Mem:* AAAS; Am Chem Soc; Am Soc Testing & Mat; fel NAm Thermal Anal Soc; Int Confedn Thermal Anal. *Res:* Thermal analysis; polymer degradation; chemical kinetics; photochemistry and radiation chemistry of polymers; diffusion in polymers. *Mailing Add:* 5309 Iroquois Rd Bethesda MD 20816

FLYNN, MARGARET A, b Hurley, Wis, Nov 22, 15; m 38; c 2. NUTRITION. *Educ:* Col St Catherine, BS, 37; Univ Iowa, MS, 38; Univ Mo, PhD(nutrit), 66; Am Bd Nutrit, cert, 71, dipl. *Prof Exp:* Teaching dietitian, Levi Hosp, Hot Springs, Ark, 42-46 & Holy Name Hosp, 48-54; res assoc, 61-63, from asst prof to assoc prof nutrit, 66-75, PROF NUTRIT, UNIV MO-COLUMBIA, 75- *Mem:* Am Inst Nutrit. *Res:* Body composition changes with age and disease. *Mailing Add:* 1121 S Glenwood Columbia MO 65201

FLYNN, MICHAEL J, b New York, NY, May 20, 34; m 57; c 4. COMPUTER SCIENCE, ELECTRICAL ENGINEERING. *Educ:* Manhattan Col, BS, 55; Syracuse Univ, MS, 60; Purdue Univ, PhD(elec eng), 61. *Prof Exp:* Engr & mgr, IBM Corp, 55-65; assoc prof systs eng, Univ Ill, Chicago Circle, 65-66; assoc prof indust & elec eng, Northwestern Univ, 66-70; prof computer sci, Johns Hopkins Univ, 70-74; PROF ELEC ENG, STANFORD UNIV, 75- *Res:* Organization of computer systems. *Mailing Add:* Comput Sci Lab Stanford Univ Stanford CA 94305

FLYNN, PATRICK, b Ireland; Can citizen. PSYCHOPHARMACOLOGY. *Educ:* Univ Col Dublin, MPSIPhC, 51, MDBChBAO, 57; FRCP(C), 62; Am Col Psychiat, FACP, 74. *Prof Exp:* Clin dir psychiat, Waterford Hosp, St John's, Nfld, 62-64; dir psychiat res, May & Baker, Ltd, Dogenham, Essex, 64-65; asst prof, 65-72, ASSOC PROF PSYCHIAT, MED SCH, DALHOUSIE UNIV, 72- *Concurrent Pos:* Consult psychiatrist var Halifax orgns, Victoria Gen Hosp, Halifax Infirmary, TriServ Hosp, Stadacona & Camp Hill Vet Hosp. *Mem:* Can Med Asn; Can Psychiat Asn; Am Col Psychiat. *Res:* Long acting neuroleptic agents; lithium toxicity. *Mailing Add:* Victoria Gen Hosp Centennial 9A Halifax Can

FLYNN, PAUL D(AVID), b Baltimore, Md, Oct 23, 26. EXPERIMENTAL MECHANICS, PHOTOELASTICITY. *Educ:* Johns Hopkins Univ, BE, 48, MSE, 50; Ill Inst Technol, PhD(mech), 54. *Prof Exp:* Inst mech eng, Johns Hopkins Univ, 48-51; engr, Gen Elec Co, 54-59; assoc prof mech, Ill Inst Technol, 59-62; consult, Frankford Arsenal, 60-62, res physicist, 62-77; RETIRED. *Honors & Awards:* Karl Fairbanks Mem Award, Soc Photo-Optical Instrumentation Engrs, 64; Army Res & Develop Achievement Award, 65. *Mem:* Am Soc Mech Engrs; Soc Exp Stress Anal. *Res:* Engineering mechanics; theoretical and experimental stress analysis; photoelasticity; strain gages; ballistics; high-speed photography; high-speed radiography; instrumentation. *Mailing Add:* 215 Tuscany Rd Baltimore MD 21210

FLYNN, ROBERT J, computer systems, applied mathematics, see previous edition

FLYNN, ROBERT JAMES, b Chicago, Ill, Jan 8, 23; m 42; c 6. LABORATORY ANIMAL MEDICINE, VETERINARY PUBLIC HEALTH. *Educ:* Mich State Univ, DVM, 44; Am Col Lab Animal Med, dipl, 57. *Prof Exp:* Supvr animal facil, Argonne Nat Lab, 48-55, assoc vet, 48-66, asst dir, Div Biol & Med Res, 62-76, sr vet, 66-81; CONSULT VET, LA RABIDA, CHICAGO, 81- *Concurrent Pos:* Vet inspector, State of Ill, 44-57; consult, Pan-Am Health Orgn, 56-62; secy-treas, Am Col Lab Animal Sci, 56-62, pres, 63; mem adv coun, Inst Lab Animal Resources, Nat Acad Sci-Nat Res Coun, 57-64; county vet, Lake County, Ill, 57-, rabies inspector, 70-73, animal control adminr, 74-; adv bd vet specialties, Am Vet Med Asn, 60-66; consult, NIH, 60-76 & Biomed Res Found, AMA, 64-66; mem coun accreditation, Am Asn Accreditation Lab Animal Care, 64-66, consult, 64-76; consult, Vet Admin, 64-76; mem, Nat Res Coun, 67-70 & Comt Vet Med Res & Educ, 68-71; mem, NIH Adult Develop & Aging Res & Training Comt, 70-74; ed, Lab Animal Sci, 76-78. *Honors & Awards:* Griffin Award, 68 & Robert J Flynn Award, 69, Am Asn Lab Animal Sci. *Mem:* AAAS; Am Asn Lab Animal Sci (secy-treas, 53-62, pres, 64); Am Vet Med Asn; Am Soc Lab Animal Practitioners; Soc Exp Biol & Med. *Res:* environmental impact studies. *Mailing Add:* 421 E Westleigh Rd Lake Forest IL 60045

FLYNN, ROBERT W, b Brooklyn, NY, July 26, 34. PLASMA PHYSICS. *Educ:* US Naval Acad, BS, 58; Mass Inst Technol, SM, 65, ScD(nuclear eng), 68. *Prof Exp:* From asst prof to assoc prof, 68-76, PROF PHYSICS, UNIV SOUTH FLA, 76- *Concurrent Pos:* Scientist-aquanaut, Scientist-in-the-Sea Prog, 73- *Mem:* Am Phys Soc; Am Asn Physics Teachers. *Res:* Large amplitude plasma waves; plasma mode coupling; plasma turbulence. *Mailing Add:* Dept of Physics Univ of SFla Tampa FL 33620

FLYNN, RONALD THOMAS, b Cleveland, Ohio, Dec 6, 47; m 69. GEOCHEMISTRY, GLASS SCIENCE. *Educ:* Temple Univ, BA, 69, MA, 72; Penn State Univ, PhD(geochem), 77. *Prof Exp:* Teaching asst geol, Temple Univ, 70-72; res asst geochem, Penn State Univ, 72-77; adv scientist glass sci, 77-78, supvr glass structure, 78-80, SUPVR FUNDAMENTAL STUDIES, OWENS-CORNING FIBERGLAS CORP, 80- *Mem:* Geochem Soc; Am Geophys Union; Am Ceramic Soc. *Res:* Redox equilibria; experimental geochemistry; glass structure. *Mailing Add:* Owens-Corning Fiberglas Corp PO Box 415 Granville OH 43023

FLYNN, T(HOMAS) F(RANCIS), b New Haven, Conn, Feb 27, 27; m 50; c 6. ELECTRICAL ENGINEERING. *Educ:* Yale Univ, BE, 50, ME, 51. *Prof Exp:* Engr, 51-56, group leader, 56-60, chief engr, 60-69, dir eng, Instrument Div, 70-80, GEN MGR SPECTROS DIV, PERKIN-ELMER CORP, 80- *Concurrent Pos:* Lectr, Univ Conn, 55-57. *Mem:* Optical Soc Am; Inst Elec & Electronics Engrs. *Res:* Scientific instrument development. *Mailing Add:* Perkin-Elmer Corp Main Ave Norwalk CT 06856

FLYNN, THOMAS GEOFFREY, b Ystradgynlais, Wales, Feb 20, 37; m 61; c 3. BIOCHEMISTRY. *Educ:* Univ Wales, BSc, 60, MSc, 62, PhD(biochem), 66. *Prof Exp:* Res asst clin chem, Med Unit, Royal Infirmary, Cardiff, Wales, 60-62; fel biochem, Univ Col, Cardiff, 66-67; fel & lectr, Queen's Univ, Ont, 67-69; from asst prof to assoc prof, 69-77, PROF BIOCHEM, QUEEN'S UNIV, ONT, 77- *Concurrent Pos:* Del, NATO Conf Protein Struct & Function, Venice, Italy, 70. *Mem:* Am Chem Soc; Brit Biochem Soc; Can Biochem Soc; Am Soc Biol Chem. *Res:* Structure of enzymes in relation to their function, especially monomeric oxidoreductases aldehyde reductares; alodose reductare and the complications of diabetes. *Mailing Add:* Dept Biochem Queen's Univ Kingston Can

FLYNN, THOMAS M(URRAY), b Huntsville, Tex, July 19, 33; m 58; c 4. CHEMICAL ENGINEERING, CRYOGENIC ENGINEERING. *Educ:* Rice Inst Technol, BA, 54, BS, 55; Univ Colo, MS, 56, PhD(chem eng), 58. *Prof Exp:* Asst explor res, Magnolia Petrol Co, 51-52; process engr catalytic cracking, Shell Oil Co, 53-54; instr chem eng, Univ Colo, 55-58; proj leader, Cryogenic Eng Labs, Nat Bur Standards, 56-61; mgr cryogenic res & develop, Bendix Corp, 61-63; chief cryogenic metrol sect, 63-66, sr scientist, Inst Mat Res, 66-68, chief prog coord off, Inst Basic Standards, 68-70, dirs staff, 70-72, SR CHEM ENGR, US GOVT, NAT BUR STANDARDS, 72- *Concurrent Pos:* NSF lectr, 64; lectr, Univ Colo, 64- & Am Inst Chem Engrs, 80- *Mem:* Am Inst Chem Engrs; Sigma Xi. *Res:* Cryogenic engineering; unit operations; cryogenic instrumentation; separation phenomena; membranes. *Mailing Add:* Nat Bur of Standards 325 Broadway Boulder CO 80303

FOA, J(OSEPH) V(ICTOR), b Turin, Italy, July 10, 09; nat US; m 42; c 4. AERONAUTICAL ENGINEERING, ENGINEERING PHYSICS. *Educ:* Univ Turin, PhD(mech eng), 31; Univ Rome, PhD(aeronaut eng), 33. *Prof Exp:* From res engr to proj engr, Piaggio Aircraft Co, Italy, 33-35 & 37-39; chief engr, Studi Caproni, 35-37; proj engr, Bellanca Aircraft Corp, Del, 39-40; chief engr, Am Aero-Marine Indust, Inc, Mass, 42-43; head design res, Curtiss-Wright Corp, NY, 42-45; head propulsion br, Cornell Aeronaut Lab, 45-52; prof aeronaut eng, Rensselaer Polytech Inst, 52-58, head dept aeronaut eng & astronaut, 58-67; PROF ENG & APPL SCI, GEORGE WASHINGTON UNIV, 70- *Res:* Fluid mechanics; propulsion; transportation; energy exchange, ground transportation, and air conditioning; cryptosteady flow and interactions; propulsion, transportation, heating, and air conditioning; author and coauthor of professional books and journal articles. *Mailing Add:* Sch of Eng & Appl Sci George Washington Univ Washington DC 20052

FOA, PIERO PIO, b Torino, Italy, Apr 13, 11; nat US; m 41; c 2. PHYSIOLOGY. *Educ:* Univ Milan, MD, 34, ScD(chem), 38. *Prof Exp:* Instr biochem, Univ Milan, 34-36; asst prof physiol, Univ Pavia, 36-38; Mendelson fel surg, Univ Mich, 39-42; from asst prof to prof physiol & pharmacol, Chicago Med Sch, 42-61; prof physiol & pharmacol, 61-81, interim chmn, 80-81, EMER PROF, SCH MED, WAYNE STATE UNIV, 81- *Concurrent Pos:* Fel med, Univ Mich, 42-43; consult in res; chmn dept res, Sinai Hosp Detroit, 61-66, mem attend staff, 61-80. *Mem:* Am Physiol Soc; Soc Exp Biol & Med; Endocrine Soc; Am Diabetes Asn; Am Fedn Clin Res. *Res:* Arterial hypertension; metabolism of thiamine; choline deficiency; functional innervation of the bone marrow; metabolism of lactic and pyruvic acids; glucagon; insulin; growth hormone; oral antidiabetic drugs. *Mailing Add:* Wayne State Univ Sch of Med 540 E Canfield Detroit MI 48201

FOARD, DONALD EDWARD, b Alexandria, Va, Dec 17, 29; m 55; c 3. BOTANY. *Educ:* Univ Va, BA, 52, MA, 54; NC State Col, PhD, 60. *Prof Exp:* Asst bot, Longwood Col, 54-56; asst prof, Univ Tenn, 59-60; asst prof, Univ Calif, Los Angeles, 60-63; BIOLOGIST, OAK RIDGE NAT LAB, 63-; BIOLOGIST COMP ANIMAL RES, UNIV TENN, 77- *Mem:* Am Soc Plant Physiol. *Res:* Morphogenesis; morphology; anatomy. *Mailing Add:* Comp Animal Res Univ of Tenn Oak Ridge TN 37830

FOBES, MELCHER PRINCE, b Portland, Maine, Sept 18, 11; m 42. MATHEMATICAL ANALYSIS. *Educ:* Bowdoin Col, AB, 32; Harvard Univ, AM, 33, PhD(math), 47. *Prof Exp:* Instr math, Harvard Univ, 34-37 & Bryn Mawr Col, 38-39; from instr to prof, 40-81, EMER PROF MATH, COL WOOSTER, 81- *Mem:* Math Asn Am. *Res:* Topology; a conjectured inequality related to the product of Lipschitz Skeleton Cochains. *Mailing Add:* Col Wooster Wooster OH 44691

FOCELLA, ANTONINO, b Baucina-Palermo, Italy, Dec 11, 24; US citizen; m 55; c 4. SUGAR ANALYST. *Educ:* Univ Palermo, Italy, Dr(org chem & biochem), 55. *Prof Exp:* Chemist food chem, Pepsi-Cola, Co, 56-59; ASST RES GROUP CHIEF, HOFFMAN-LA ROCHE, INC, 59- *Mem:* Am Chem Soc; Sigma Xi; Sci Res Soc. *Res:* Synthetic organic chemistry; food chemistry; oil emulsion for beverages. *Mailing Add:* Hoffman-La Roche Inc 340 Kingsland St Nutley NJ 07110

FOCHT, DENNIS DOUGLASS, b West Reading, Pa, Aug 30, 41; m 66. SOIL MICROBIOLOGY. *Educ:* Rutgers Univ, BS, 63; Iowa State Univ, MS, 65, PhD(bact), 68. *Prof Exp:* Fel microbiol, Cornell Univ, 68-70; asst prof soil microbiol, 70-74, asst microbiologist, Citrus Res Exp Sta, 70-74, assoc prof, 74-80, PROF SOIL MICROBIOL, UNIV CALIF, RIVERSIDE, 80- *Concurrent Pos:* Proj leader, Western Regional Res Comt on Nitrogen in Environ, 70-75; consult, Stanford Res Inst, 73-74. *Mem:* Am Soc Microbiol; Am Soc Agron; Can Soc Microbiologists. *Res:* Biodegradation; nitrogen transformations; microbial ecology; methylation of metals. *Mailing Add:* Dept of Soil Sci & Agr Eng Univ of Calif Riverside CA 92502

FOCKE, ALFRED BOSWORTH, b Cleveland, Ohio, Sept 30, 06; m 28, 44; c 6. PHYSICS. *Educ:* Case Western Reserve Univ, BS, 28; Calif Inst Technol, PhD(physics), 32. *Prof Exp:* Fel, Calif Inst Technol, 32-33; Nat Res fel, Yale Univ, 33-34; instr physics, Brown Univ, 34-38, asst prof, 38-45; head res div, Navy Radio & Sound Lab, 45-46; sr consult, Navy Electronics Lab, 46-52, head syst div, 52-53, assoc tech dir res, 53; res physicist & dir marine phys lab, Scripps Inst, Calif, 54-59; from prof to sr prof, 59-74, EMER SR PROF PHYSICS, HARVEY MUDD COL, 74- *Concurrent Pos:* Tech dir, Pac missile range, Naval Missile Ctr, 58-59; sci dir, Off Naval Res, London, 68-70; WIGWAM, US Dept Defense; mem mine adv comt, Nat Acad Sci-Nat Res Coun; contract physicist, Bur Ord, Navy Dept, 40-43, prin physicist, 43-45. *Honors & Awards:* Meritorious civilian serv awards, 45, 53. *Mem:* AAAS; fel Am Phys Soc; fel Acoust Soc Am; Am Geophys Union; Inst Elec & Electronics Eng. *Res:* Geophysics; properties of crystals; underwater ordnance; sound propagation; general electronics. *Mailing Add:* 741 W 11th Claremont CA 91711

FOCKE, ARTHUR E(LDRIDGE), b Cleveland, Ohio, June 17, 04; m 29, 68. METALLURGY. *Educ:* Ohio State Univ, BMetE, 25, MS, 26, PhD(metall), 28. *Prof Exp:* Metallurgist, Cleveland Wire Div, Gen Elec Co, 27-29; chief engr, P R Mallory & Co, 29-30; res metallurgist, Diamond Chain & Mfg Co, 30-45, chief metallurgist, 45-51; mgr mat develop, Aircraft Nuclear Power Dept, Gen Elec Co, 51-61; from assoc prof to prof metall eng, 62-74, EMER PROF METALL ENG, UNIV CINCINNATI, 74-; PRES, A E FOCKE CORP, 63- *Concurrent Pos:* Bur Standards fel. *Mem:* fel Am Soc Metals (pres, 50); Am Soc Testing & Mat; Am Inst Mining, Metall & Petrol Engrs; Am Nuclear Soc; Am Soc Eng Educ. *Res:* Mechanical metallurgy; wear and fatigue; factor influencing the quality of tungsten incandescent lamp filaments; selection and development of materials for aircraft nuclear power plants. *Mailing Add:* A E Focke Corp 8041 Hosbrook Cincinnati OH 45236

FODDEN, JOHN HENRY, b Halifax, Eng, June 16, 18; m 42; c 6. PATHOLOGY. *Educ:* Univ Leeds, MB, ChB, 41, MD, 46; FRCP(C), 56. *Prof Exp:* Asst path, Univ Leeds, 41-44; asst clin pathologist, Royal Hosp, Sheffield, 45-46; asst prof path, Univ Liverpool, 46-48; assoc prof, Dalhousie Univ, 48-52; assoc prof, Med Sch, Univ SDak, 52-57; assoc dir labs, Mt Sinai Hosp, 57-60; dir labs, Manitowoc County Hosp, 60-65; DIR LABS, MANITOWOC MEM, TWO RIVERS COMMUNITY & ALGOMA MEM HOSPS, 65- *Concurrent Pos:* Registr, Cancer Control Orgn, Radium Inst, 46-48; Markle Found scholar, Univ SDak, 51-56, Lederle Med Fac award scholar, 56-57; forensic pathologist, Manitowoc County, 70- *Mem:* Fel Col Am Path; Am Soc Exp Path; Am Soc Clin Path; Am Asn Path & Bact; Am Acad Forensic Sci. *Res:* Etiologic and pathogenetic factors in peptic ulceration; hormonal factors in abnormal carbohydrate metabolism; clinical and experimental pathology. *Mailing Add:* Dept of Path Mem Hosp 333 Reed Ave Manitowoc WI 54220

FODERARO, ANTHONY HAROLDE, b Scranton, Pa, Apr 3, 26; m 53; c 3. PHYSICS, REACTOR ENGINEERING. *Educ:* Univ Scranton, BS, 50; Univ Pittsburgh, PhD(physics), 55. *Prof Exp:* Consult nuclear physics, Westinghouse Atomic Power Div, 52-53, supvry scientist radiation shielding, 54-65; sr nuclear physicist reactor physics, Gen Motors Res Labs, 56-60; PROF NUCLEAR ENG, PA STATE UNIV, 60- *Concurrent Pos:* Consult, Gilbert Assoc, Inc, 73-77, Westinghouse Elec Corp, 60-77 & Stone & Webster Eng Corp, 76-; tech expert, Int Atomic Energy Agency, 76-77. *Mem:* Fel Am Nuclear Soc; Am Phys Soc; Am Asn Physics Teachers. *Res:* Reactor physics, reactor safety, radiation transport and shielding. *Mailing Add:* Pa State Univ 231 Sackett Bldg University Park PA 16802

FODOR, GABOR, b Budapest, Hungary, Dec 5, 15; US citizen; m 39, 64, 78; c 5. ORGANIC CHEMISTRY. *Educ:* Graz Tech Univ, state exam, 34; Univ Szeged, PhD(org chem), 37, Veniam Legendi, 45; Hungarian Acad Sci, DSc(org chem), 52. *Prof Exp:* Univ demonstr org chem, Univ Szeged, 35-38, from assoc prof to prof, 45-57, res assoc, Chinoin Pharmaceut Ltd, Hungary, 38-45; head lab stereochem, Hungarian Acad Sci, 58-65; prof org chem, Laval Univ, 65-69; CENTENNIAL PROF CHEM, W VA UNIV, 69- *Concurrent Pos:* Overseas fel, Churchill Col, 61; vis scientist, Nat Res Coun Can, 64-65; vis prof, Polytech Inst, Darmstadt, Ger, 75-76. *Honors & Awards:* Kossuth Award, Hungary, 50 & 54; Silver Medalist, Univ Helsinki, 58. *Mem:* Am Chem Soc; Can Inst Chem; Hungarian Acad Sci; Swiss Chem Soc; The Chem Soc. *Res:* Constitutional and synthetic work in isoquinolines, ephedrines, adrenaline and its derivatives; elucidation of configuration, chloromycetine, the tropines, scopolamine, cocaines, sedridine and sphingosine; total synthesis of valeroidine and hyoscine; selective quaternization; new reactions of ascorbic acid with highly electrophilic aldehydes. *Mailing Add:* Dept of Chem W Va Univ Morgantown WV 26506

FODOR, GEORGE EMERIC, b Mako, Hungary, Feb 13, 32; US citizen; m; c 2. ORGANIC CHEMISTRY. *Educ:* Univ Szeged, dipl, 55; Rice Univ, PhD(chem), 65. *Prof Exp:* Chemist, Hungarian Oil Refining Co, 55; mem sci staff, Hungarian Oil & Gas Res Inst, 56; chemist, Pontiac Refining Co, Tex, 57-60; asst org chem, Rice Univ, 60-62; res chemist, Photo Prod Dept, E I du Pont de Nemours & Co, Inc, NJ, 65-66; sr res scientist, 66-81, STAFF SCIENTIST, SOUTHWEST RES INST, 81- *Mem:* Am Chem Soc; Sigma Xi. *Res:* Synthetic organic and petroleum chemistry. *Mailing Add:* Southwest Res Inst PO Box 28510 San Antonio TX 78284

FODOR, LAWRENCE MARTIN, b Cleveland, Ohio, Dec 1, 37; m 62; c 3. ORGANIC CHEMISTRY, POLYMER CHEMISTRY. *Educ:* Western Reserve Univ, AB, 59; Cornell Univ, PhD(inorg chem), 63. *Prof Exp:* res chemist, 63-76, SUPVR CHEM RES, PHILLIPS PETROL CO, 76- *Mem:* Am Chem Soc. *Res:* Olefin polymerization; organic chemicals processes; fertilizer research; impact polystyrene; organometallic compounds. *Mailing Add:* Phillips Petrol Co 255 CPL Bartlesville OK 74003

FOECKE, HAROLD ANTHONY, b Crofton, Nebr, Mar 7, 26; m 51; c 7. SCIENCE EDUCATION. *Educ:* Iowa State Univ, BS, 45, MS, 48; Univ Notre Dame, PhD(educ), 62. *Prof Exp:* Jr res fel, Iowa State Univ, 46, instr elec eng, 46-48; sr res fel, Polytech Inst Brooklyn, 48-49; from instr to asst prof elec eng, 49-52; asst prof, Univ Notre Dame, 54-58, assoc prof, 58-61; specialist eng educ, US Off Educ, 62-65; dean eng, Gonzaga Univ, 65-68; dir div sci teaching, 68-76, DEP ASST DIR-GEN, EDUC, UNESCO, PARIS, FRANCE, 76- *Honors & Awards:* Arthur L Williston Award, Am Soc Eng Educ, 68. *Mem:* AAAS; Am Soc Eng Educ. *Res:* Engineering education; higher education. *Mailing Add:* US Deleg UNESCO US Embassy APO New York NY 09777 France

FOECKLER, FRANCIS H, JR, pharmacology, see previous edition

FOEGE, WILLIAM HERBERT, b Decorah, Iowa, Mar 12, 36; m 58; c 3. MEDICINE, EPIDEMIOLOGY. *Educ:* Pac Lutheran Univ, BA, 57; Univ Wash, MD, 61; Harvard Univ, MPH, 65. *Prof Exp:* Intern, USPHS Hosp, Staten Island, NY, 61-62; epidemiologist, Epidemic Intel Serv, Nat Commun Dis Ctr, 62-64; med officer, Emmanuel Med Ctr, Lutheran Church-Mo Synod, Nigeria Mission, 65-66; epidemiologist, Ctr Dis Control, 66-70, dir smallpox eradication prog, 70-73; med epidemiologist, Southeast Asia Smallpox Eradication Prog, WHO, New Delhi, India, 73-75, asst dir, 75-77, DIR, CTRS FOR DIS CONTROL, ATLANTA, 77- *Concurrent Pos:* Consult, Smallpox Eradication Prog, Nigeria, 66-67. *Honors & Awards:* Dept Health, Educ & Welfare Superior Serv Award; Joseph C Wilson Award, 78. *Mem:* Inst Med-Nat Acad Sci; Royal Soc Trop Med & Hyg; AAAS; Am Epidemiol Soc; Am Col Prev Med. *Res:* Epidemiology and control of communicable diseases in the tropics. *Mailing Add:* Ctrs for Dis Control 1600 Clifton Rd NE Atlanta GA 30333

FOEHR, EDWARD GOTTHARD, b Philadelphia, Pa, Sept 22, 17; m 41; c 1. CHEMISTRY. *Educ:* Pa State Col, BS, 38, MS, 41, PhD(org chem), 44. *Prof Exp:* Asst petrol refinery lab, Pa State Col, 38-44; RES CHEMIST & SUPVR RES, CHEVRON RES CO, 44- *Concurrent Pos:* With Off Sci Res & Develop, 44. *Mem:* Am Chem Soc; Am Soc Lubrication Engrs. *Res:* Type analysis of lubricating oils; industrial lubricants; hydraulic transmission fluids; analysis of lubricating oil additives. *Mailing Add:* Chevron Res Co 576 Standard Ave Richmond CA 94802

FOELSCHE, HORST WILHELM JULIUS, b Darmstadt, Ger, Oct 28, 37; m 61; c 2. HIGH ENERGY PHYSICS. *Educ:* Univ NMex, BS, 59; Yale Univ, MS, 60, PhD(physics), 63. *Prof Exp:* Res assoc physics, Yale Univ, 63-65; from asst physicist to assoc physicist, Accelerator Dept, 65-69, PHYSICIST, ACCELERATOR DEPT, BROOKHAVEN NAT LAB, 69- *Res:* Experimental apparatus. *Mailing Add:* Accelerator Dept Brookhaven Nat Lab Upton NY 11973

FOERNZLER, ERNEST CARL, b Indianapolis, Ind, Apr 12, 35; m 64; c 2. PHARMACEUTICAL CHEMISTRY. *Educ:* Purdue Univ, BS, 57, MS, 59, PhD(phys chem), 62. *Prof Exp:* Instr radiochem, Purdue Univ, 57-59; mem opers res staff, Arthur D Little, Inc, 62-65; MGR COMPUT SYSTS, HOFFMANN-LA ROCHE, INC, NUTLEY, 65- *Mem:* Am Pharmaceut Asn; Asn Comput Mach; Opers Res Soc Am; Am Chem Soc. *Res:* Biomedical computer techniques; operations research; quantum biochemistry; computer systems and programming. *Mailing Add:* 340 Kingsland St Nutley NJ

FOERSTER, EDWARD L(EROY), SR, b Chicago, Ill, Sept 17, 19; m 48; c 3. CHEMICAL ENGINEERING. *Educ:* Univ Ill, BS, 41; Univ Va, ChemE, 42. *Prof Exp:* Asst chem engr, Merck & Co, Inc, 42-48, chem engr, 48-52, sect leader, 52-58, mgr develop & control, Electronic Chem Div, 58-59; consult, 59-60; INDUST & COMMERCIAL CONSULT, 60- *Mem:* Am Inst Chem Engrs; Am Chem Soc; Water Pollution Fedn; Nat Soc Prof Engrs. *Res:* Waste disposal; by-product recovery; food processing; fermentation; ion exchange; organic chemical manufacturing; rendering. *Mailing Add:* Box 779 Harrisonburg VA 22801

FOERSTER, GEORGE STEPHEN, b New Orleans, La, Sept 29, 29; div; c 6. METALLURGY. *Educ:* Tulane Univ, BS, 50. *Prof Exp:* Res & develop engr, Metall Lab, 50-56, group leader, 56-61, assoc scientist, 61-72; prin res scientist, Metall Lab, 72-79, SR PROCESS ENGR NL PERMANENT MOLD CASTINGS, NL INDUSTS, INC, 79- *Mem:* Fel Am Soc Metals. *Res:* Metal alloy design, magnesium, aluminum, lead other non-ferrous metals; metal processing, battery grids; lead shot and body solder; die casting; alumuminum permanent mold casting. *Mailing Add:* NL Industs Inc PO Box 3013 Greeneville TN 37743

FOFONOFF, NICHOLAS PAUL, b Queenstown, Alta, Aug 18, 29; m 51; c 4. MECHANICS. *Educ:* Univ BC, BA & MA, 51; Brown Univ, PhD(appl math), 55. *Prof Exp:* From asst scientist to sr scientist, Pac Oceanog Group, Fisheries Res Bd Can, 54-62; sr scientist, Woods Hole Oceanog Inst, 62-69; GORDON McKAY PROF PRACT OF PHYS OCEANOG, HARVARD UNIV, 69- *Concurrent Pos:* Nat Res Coun Can overseas fel, 55. *Res:* Fluid mechanics; dynamics of ocean circulation; thermodynamics of sea water; measurement of ocean currents. *Mailing Add:* Dept of Eng & Appl Physics Harvard Univ Cambridge MA 02138

FOFT, JOHN WILLIAM, b Los Angeles, Calif, May 13, 28; m 57; c 2. PATHOLOGY. *Educ:* Univ Nebr, BS, 51, MD, 54. *Prof Exp:* Pathologist, Sch Aerospace Med, US Air Force, 61-63, chief dept path, 63-64; asst prof path, Univ Chicago, 64-68; assoc prof, Univ Hosps, 68-70, prof clin path & chmn dept, Sch Med, Univ Ala, Birmingham, 70-75; CHMN DEPT PATH, CARRAWAY METHODIST MED CTR & NORWOOD CLIN, 75- *Concurrent Pos:* Vis prof path, Univ Ala, Birmingham, 75- *Mem:* Am Asn Pathologists; Col Am Path; Am Soc Clin Path; AMA. *Res:* Computer applications inn diagnosis and monitoring of disease; clinical laboratory equipment design for developing countries. *Mailing Add:* Carraway Methodist Med Ctr 1615 N 25th St Birmingham AL 35234

FOGARTY, CHARLES F(RANKLIN), mining engineering, geology, deceased

FOGARTY, JOHN CHARDE, b Leamington, UK, Dec 16, 34; US citizen. ALGEBRA. *Educ:* Harvard Univ, AB, 61, PhD(math), 66. *Prof Exp:* Asst prof math, Univ Pa, 66-71; assoc prof, 71-80, PROF MATH, UNIV MASS, 80- *Res:* Invariant theory. *Mailing Add:* Dept of Math & Statist Univ of Mass Amherst MA 01003

FOGARTY, WILLIAM JOSEPH, b Toronto, Ont, Nov 18, 32; US citizen; m 58; c 3. CIVIL ENGINEERING. *Educ:* Univ Miami, BSCE, 58; Purdue Univ, MSCE, 61; Ga Inst Technol, PhD(transp), 68. *Prof Exp:* Engr trainee, Fla State Rd Dept, 58-59; instr civil eng, Purdue Univ, 59-61; from asst prof to assoc prof, 61-73, PROF CIVIL ENG, UNIV MIAMI, 73- *Concurrent Pos:* Pvt consult, 61- *Res:* Multidisciplinary accident analysis, vehicular crash incidents, human, vehicle and environmental factors; environmental wastewater operations; water pollution and purification. *Mailing Add:* Sch of Eng & Environ Design Univ of Miami Coral Gables FL 33124

FOGEL, BERNARD J, b New York, NY, Nov 30, 36; m 58; c 3. IMMUNOLOGY, PEDIATRICS. *Educ:* Univ Miami, MD, 61. *Prof Exp:* Intern pediat, Jackson Mem Hosp, Miami, Fla, 61-62, resident, 62-63; fel, Sch Med, Johns Hopkins Univ, 63-64; asst chief pediat, Walter Reed Army Med Ctr & researcher immunol, Walter Reed Army Inst Res, 64-66; ASSOC PROF PEDIAT, SCH MED, UNIV MIAMI, 66-, ASSOC DEAN EDUC, 67-, ASST VPRES MED AFFAIRS, 74-, PROF PEDIAT, 74-, VPRES & DEAN, SCH MED, 81- *Concurrent Pos:* Chief resident, Sinai Hosp, Baltimore, Md, 63-64; Am Cancer Soc fel, Jackson Mem Hosp, Miami, Fla, 66-68. *Mem:* Am Fedn Clin Res. *Res:* Complement system in human and animal diseases; osmotic fragility of erythrocytes; malaria; the human neonate. *Mailing Add:* Dept of Pediat Univ of Miami Sch of Med Miami FL 13136

FOGEL, CHARLES M(ORTON), b Syracuse, NY, June 21, 13; m 47; c 3. CIVIL ENGINEERING. *Educ:* Univ Buffalo, BA, 35, MA, 38. *Prof Exp:* Teacher sci pub schs, Buffalo, 37-41; instr physics, Univ Buffalo, 41-44; res engr, Nat Union Radio Corp, 44-46; from asst prof to assoc prof, 46-63, asst dean, 47-52, dir div gen & tech studies, 52-57, indust liaison officer, 52-58, asst exec vpres, 67-77, actg grad dean, 77-78, PROF ENG, STATE UNIV NY BUFFALO, 63-, ACTG EXEC V PRES, 78- *Mem:* Am Soc Eng Educ. *Res:* Tapered columns; general engineering. *Mailing Add:* Capen Hall State Univ of NY Buffalo NY 14214

FOGEL, NORMAN, b Chicago, Ill, May 20, 24; m 60; c 2. PHYSICAL INORGANIC CHEMISTRY. *Educ:* Univ Ill, BS, 50; Univ Wis, MS, 51, PhD(chem), 56. *Prof Exp:* Instr chem, Exten Div, Univ Wis, 52-53, asst, 53-54, Univ Wis Alumni Res Found asst, 54-56; from asst prof to assoc prof chem, 56-68, PROF CHEM, UNIV OKLA, 68- *Mem:* The Chem Soc; Sigma Xi; Am Chem Soc. *Res:* Inorganic complex ions in solution and in solid state; dissociation pressure, spectra and magnetism of transition metal halide hydrates. *Mailing Add:* Dept Chem Rm 116 620 Parrington Oval Univ of Okla Norman OK 73069

FOGEL, ROBERT DALE, b Spokane, Wash, Jan 16, 47; m 68; c 2. HYPOGEOUS FUNGI. *Educ:* Ore State Univ, BS, 69, PhD(mycol), 75; Univ Colo, MS, 70. *Prof Exp:* Res asst, Sch Forestry, Ore State Univ, 72-75, res assoc, 75-78; ASST PROF BOT & FUNGI ECOL, DIV BIOL SCI & ASST CUR, HERBARIUM, UNIV MICH, 78- *Mem:* Mycol Soc Am; British Mycol Soc; Ecol Soc Am; Japanese Mycol Soc. *Res:* Ecology and systematics of hypogeous fungi-truffles; role of mycorrhizae in nutrient cycling in forest ecosystems. *Mailing Add:* Herbarium N Univ Bldg Univ Mich Ann Arbor MI 48109

FOGEL, SEYMOUR, b New York, NY, Sept 27, 19; m 62; c 2. GENETICS. *Educ:* Queen's Col, BS, 41; Univ Mo, PhD(genetics), 46. *Prof Exp:* Asst biol, Univ Mo, 42-43, instr zool, 46; instr biol, Queen's Col, 46-50; from assoc prof to prof, Brooklyn Col, 50-69, exec officer PhD prog, 65-69; PROF GENETICS & CHMN DEPT, UNIV CALIF, BERKELEY, 69- *Concurrent Pos:* Sigma Xi grant in aid, Queen's Col, NY, 47; USPH training fel, 59, res grant, 60; vis assoc prof, Stanford Univ; Guggenheim fel, Univ Calif, 67-68; vis prof, Univ Paris-Seed, Orsay, 80; vis res fel, Stanford Univ, 80. *Mem:* Genetics Soc Am; Am Soc Microbiol; AAAS. *Res:* Molecular mechanisms of recombination; gene conversion and recombinant DNA in yeast; fungal genetics; genetics of wine yeasts; fermentations. *Mailing Add:* Dept of Genetics 345 Mulford Hall Univ of Calif Berkeley CA 94720

FOGELSON, DAVID EUGENE, b St Paul, Minn, Sept 13, 26; m 56; c 1. GEOPHYSICS. *Educ:* Univ Minn, BA, 52, MS, 56. *Prof Exp:* Asst seismol oil explor, Shell Oil Co, 50-52; geologist, Minn Dept Hwys, 52-56; geophysicist, Appl Physics Lab, US Bur Mines, 57-61, res geophysicist, 61-68, head explosive fragmentation lab, 61-70, sci res mgr, 70-71, res supvr, Advan Fragmentation Tech, 71-74, res supvr, environ effects mining, 74-77; RES ASSOC, NUCLEAR REPOSITORY DESIGN STUDIES, UNIV MINN, 79- *Concurrent Pos:* Prog mgr, NASA Contract on Lunar Mining Studies, 70-73; consulting geophysicist, 77- *Mem:* Seismol Soc Am; Int Soc Rock Mech. *Res:* Engineering seismology; generation and propagation of explosive waves; damage to structure from blasting; rock mechanics; lunar mining studies. *Mailing Add:* 1800 Valley Curve St Paul MN 55118

FOGG, DONALD ERNEST, b Camden, NJ, Jan 26, 22; m 43; c 3. VETERINARY PATHOLOGY. *Educ:* Univ Pa, VMD, 45. *Prof Exp:* Pvt pract, 45-49; with Bur Animal Indust, USDA, 49; with State of Del, 50; mgr clin res, Merck & Co, Inc, 51-60; tech serv dir, Del Poultry Labs, Inc, 60-66; dir vet serv, Eshams Farms Corp, 66-71; vet med officer, Consumer & Mkt Serv, 71-73, SUPVRY VET MED OFFICER, ANIMAL & PLANT HEALTH INSPECTION SERV, USDA, 73- *Mem:* Am Asn Avian Path. *Res:* Diseases of poultry. *Mailing Add:* PO Box 215 Dagsboro DE 19939

FOGG, EDWARD T(HOMPSON), b Salem, NJ, Mar 24, 27; m 50. CHEMICAL ENGINEERING. *Educ:* Univ Va, BChE, 49; Univ Pa, MS, 51, PhD(chem eng), 53. *Prof Exp:* Asst instr chem eng, Univ Pa, 49-50, instr, 50-51; res engr, Jackson Lab, E I Du Pont de Nemours & Co, Inc, Chambers Works, 53-56, res supvr, 56-60, div head, 60-66, mgr lab, 66-68, design supt, 68-70, works engr, 70-73, gen supt, Environ Serv Dept, 73-78; RETIRED. *Mem:* Am Chem Soc; Am Inst Chem Engrs. *Mailing Add:* Greenwich St Alloway NJ 08001

FOGG, GEORGE GARRETT, b Greensburg, Ind, Jan 27, 38; m 61. PLANT ECOLOGY, SYSTEMATIC BOTANY. *Educ:* Wabash Col, AB, 60; Butler Univ, MS, 62; Univ Okla, PhD(bot), 66. *Prof Exp:* Instr bot, Univ Hawaii, 62-63; asst prof biol, State Univ NY Stony Brook, 66-70, lectr biol sci & exec vpres, 70-76; proj engr, Turner Int Industs, 76-80; ASST TO PRES, VULCAN CINCINNATI, INC, 80- *Res:* Ecology, systematics and evolution in conifers with emphasis in the genus Pinus. *Mailing Add:* 7137 Royal Green Dr Cincinnati OH 45244

FOGG, JOHN MILTON, JR, b Philadelphia, Pa, Nov 8, 98; m; c 2. BOTANY. *Educ:* Univ Pa, BS, 25; Harvard Univ, PhD(bot), 29; La Salle Col, ScD, 49. *Prof Exp:* Jessup fel, Acad Nat Sci, Philadelphia, 21-22; cur herbarium, 22-63, from instr to asst prof bot, 25-41, assoc prof bot & dean col arts & sci, 41-44, prof bot, 44-74, vprovost, 44-53, dir, Morris Arboretum, 54-67, dir, Barnes Arboretum, 67-79, EMER PROF BOT, UNIV PA, 74- *Mem:* AAAS; Bot Soc Am; Torrey Bot Club. *Res:* Systematic study of flowering plants; floristics; plant geography; flora of Pennsylvania. *Mailing Add:* Barnes Arboretum Merion PA 19066

FOGG, PETER JOHN, b Bristol, Eng, June 14, 31; m 58; c 3. WOOD SCIENCE, WOOD TECHNOLOGY. *Educ:* Univ Wales, BSc, 52; La State Univ, MF, 61, PhD(forestry), 68. *Prof Exp:* Asst conservator, Forest Dept, Govt of Brit Honduras, 55-58; from instr to asst prof, 60-72, ASSOC PROF FORESTRY, LA STATE UNIV, BATON ROUGE, 72- *Mem:* Forest Prod Res Soc; Soc Wood Sci & Technol. *Res:* Wood quality in relation to genetic and environmental factors; permeability of wood to liquids and gases; relation of wood properties to anatomical structure. *Mailing Add:* Sch of Forestry & Wildlife Mgt La State Univ Baton Rouge LA 70803

FOGH, JORGEN (ENGELL), b Copenhagen, Denmark, Feb 6, 23; m 47; c 2. MEDICINE. *Educ:* Univ Copenhagen, MD, 49. *Prof Exp:* Asst chief physician res, Danish Nat Found Infantile Paralysis, 51-53; asst res virologist, Virus Lab, Univ Calif, 53-58; assoc med virologist, Div Labs & Res, NY State Dept Health, 58-60; ASSOC MEM VIRUS CELL RES SECT, SLOAN-KETTERING INST CANCER RES, 60-; ASSOC PROF MICROBIOL, SLOAN-KETTERING DIV, MED COL, CORNELL UNIV, 66- *Concurrent Pos:* Assoc, dept microbiol, Albany Med Col, 59-61; assoc prof path, Sloan-Kettering Div, Med Col, Cornell Univ, 61-66. *Honors & Awards:* Lifetime Career Award, Nat Cancer Inst, 64. *Mem:* Am Soc Cell Biologists; Tissue Cult Asn; Am Asn Cancer Res; Am Asn Immunologists; Am Soc Exp Path. *Res:* Human viruses; tumor viruses; human tumor cells; mycoplasmas; tissue culture; micromorphology of cells and viruses. *Mailing Add:* Sloan-Kettering Inst Cancer Res 145 Boston Post Rd Rye NY 10580

FOGIEL, ADOLF W, POLYMER CHEMISTRY, RUBBER CHEMISTRY. *Educ:* Karlsruhe Tech Univ, dipl, 49; Wayne State Univ, PhD(phys chem), 62. *Prof Exp:* Chemist, By-Prod & Chem, Australia, 50-52; res chemist, Am Agr Chem Co, Mich, 54-60, res supvr, 60-62; res chemist, 62-79, RES ASSOC, E I DU PONT DE NEMOURS & CO, INC, 79- *Mem:* Am Chem Soc. *Res:* Physical chemistry of polymers, especially elastomers. *Mailing Add:* Polymer Prods Dept Exp Sta E I du Pont de Nemours & Co Inc Wilmington DE 19898

FOGLE, BENSON TARRANT, b Springfield, SC, Sept 8, 35; m 62; c 2. AERONOMY, METEOROLOGY. *Educ:* Univ SC, BS, 56, MS, 58; Univ Alaska, PhD(geophys), 66. *Prof Exp:* Physicist, Boeing Sci Res Labs, 58-59; res physicist, Stanford Res Inst, 59-62; asst geophysicist, Geophys Inst, Univ Alaska, 62-66, asst prof geophys, 66-67; fel, Nat Ctr Atmospheric Res, 67-68, staff scientist, 68-75; assoc prog dir, 75-76, PROG MGR, NSF, 76- *Mem:* AAAS; Am Geophys Union; Am Meteorol Soc. *Res:* Noctilucent clouds; atmospheric aerosols, magnetosphere-ionosphere interactions. *Mailing Add:* NSF 180 G St NW Washington DC 20550

FOGLE, HAROLD WARMAN, b Morgantown, WVa, Apr 23, 18; m 47; c 2. HORTICULTURE. *Educ:* WVa Univ, BS, 40, MS, 41; Univ Minn, PhD(hort, plant genetics), 49. *Prof Exp:* Asst WVa Univ, 38-41; asst county supvr, Charlestown & Martinsburg, WVa, 41-42; county supvr, Farm Security Admin, USDA, West Union, Morgantown & Buckhannon, 42-46; asst, Univ Minn, 46-49; horticulturist, Irrigation Exp Sta, USDA & Wash State Univ, 49-63; stone fruit invest leader, Plant Sci Res Div, Plant Indust Sta, USDA, Beltsville, 63-72, res horticulturist, Fruit Lab, Agr Res Ctr, 72-80; RETIRED. *Honors & Awards:* Wilder Medal, Am Pomol Soc, 78. *Mem:* Am Soc Hort Sci; Am Pomol Soc (vpres, pres, 73-75); Int Soc Hort Sci; Genetics Soc Am. *Res:* Stone fruit breeding and varietal investigations; winter hardiness of tree fruits; ultrastructure of fruit and pollen surfaces; inheritance studies with tomatoes and stone fruits; vegetative propagation of stone fruits. *Mailing Add:* 2014 Forest Date Dr Silver Springs MD 20903

FOGLEMAN, RALPH WILLIAM, b McDonald, Kans, Mar 18, 26; m; c 3. TOXICOLOGY, VETERINARY MEDICINE. *Educ:* Kans State Univ, DVM, 47. *Prof Exp:* Asst vet, R A Self Animal Hosp, Tex, 47-48; vet, R W Fogleman Small Animal Hosp, Nebr, 48-50; head agr chem dept, Hazleton Labs, Inc, Va, 53-57, mgr western div, 57-60; vpres, Hazleton-Nuclear Sci Corp, Calif, 60-61, sr res pharmacologist, Am Cyanamid Co, 61-62; vpres, AME Assocs, 62-65; pres, Biographics, Inc, 65; toxicologist & registrations supvr, CIBA Agrochem Co, 65-69; dir toxicol, 69-71, vpres, Affil Med Enterprises, Inc, 71-75; DIR & OWNER, R W FOGLEMAN & ASSOCS, 75- *Mem:* Am Vet Med Asn; Am Col Vet Toxicol; Soc Toxicol; Coun Agr Sci & Technol; Am Soc Agr Consult. *Res:* Research administration; applied biological sciences; toxicology of pesticides, drugs and xenobiotics in man and animals; metabolism of pesticides in plants and animals; industrial hygiene. *Mailing Add:* River Rd Rd 1 Box 590-D Upper Black Eddy PA 08551

FOGLEMAN, WAVELL WAINWRIGHT, b Winston-Salem, NC, July 17, 42. ENVIRONMENTAL CHEMISTRY, INORGANIC CHEMISTRY. *Educ:* Univ NC, Chapel Hill, BS, 64, MSPH, 76; Tulane Univ, PhD(chem), 68. *Prof Exp:* Asst prof chem, Old Dom Univ, 68-74; ASST PROF NATURAL SCI, 77- *Mem:* Am Chem Soc; Water Pollution Control Fedn. *Res:* Analysis and impact assessment of metals, gases and nutrients in water. *Mailing Add:* Dept of Natural Sci Plymouth State Col Plymouth NH 03264

FOGLER, HUGH SCOTT, b Normal, Ill, Oct 28, 39; m 62; c 3. CHEMICAL ENGINEERING. *Educ:* Univ Ill, BS, 62; Univ Colo, MS, 63, PhD(chem eng), 65. *Prof Exp:* Asst prof, Univ Mich, 65; mem res staff, Jet Propulsion Labs, US Army, Pasadena, 66-68; from asst prof to assoc prof, 68-75, PROF CHEM ENG, UNIV MICH, ANN ARBOR, 75- *Concurrent Pos:* Consult, Packaging Corp Am, 65-66, Chevron Oil Field Res, 67- & Mich Consol Gas, 76-; Fulbright scholar, 74. *Honors & Awards:* Dow Outstanding Young Fac Award, Am Soc Eng Educ, 71. *Mem:* Am Inst Chem Engrs; Acoust Soc Am; Am Soc Eng Educ. *Res:* Applications of sonic and ultrasonic waves to transport phenomena and reaction kinetics; flow and reaction in porous media, dissolution kinetics; acoustically former emulsions. *Mailing Add:* 2028 E Eng Bldg Univ of Mich Ann Arbor MI 48104

FOGLESONG, MARK ALLEN, b Keokuk, Iowa, June 20, 49; m 71; c 2. MICROBIOLOGY, FERMENTATION TECHNOLOGY. *Educ:* Univ Iowa, BS, 71, MS, 72, PhD(microbiol), 74. *Prof Exp:* sr microbiologist res & develop, 74-80, SR MICROBIOLOGIST FERMENTATION TECHNOL, ELI LILLY & CO, 80- *Mem:* Am Soc Microbiol. *Res:* Microbiological assay development and therapeutic drug monitoring; control and regulation of macrolide antibiotic synthesis. *Mailing Add:* Eli Lilly & Co Indianapolis IN 46206

FOGLIA, THOMAS ANTHONY, b Philadelphia, Pa, Apr 11, 40; m 63; c 3. ORGANIC CHEMISTRY, AGRICULTURAL & FOOD CHEMISTRY. *Educ:* Drexel Univ, BS, 64; Temple Univ, PhD(org chem), 68. *Prof Exp:* RES LEADER, EASTERN REGIONAL RES CTR, NORTHEASTERN REGION, AGR RES SERV, USDA, 68- *Concurrent Pos:* Asst prof, Dept Chem, Eve Col, Drexel Univ, 68-; lectr, St Joseph's Univ. *Mem:* Am Chem Soc; Am Oil Chemist Soc; Sigma Xi; AAAS. *Res:* Chemistry of fats and oils; lipid chemistry; food safety and quality; interaction of food components; lipid-protein interactions; membrane structure and function. *Mailing Add:* Agr Res Div USDA Eastern Res Lab 600 E Mermaid Lane Wyndmoor PA 19118

FOGLIA, VIRGILIO GERARDO, b Buenos Aires, Arg, Feb 13, 05; m 50; c 3. PHYSIOLOGY, ENDOCRINOLOGY. *Educ:* Univ Buenos Aires, MD, 28. *Prof Exp:* From assoc prof to prof physiol & dir dept, Fac Med, Univ Buenos Aires, 54-71; DIR, INST BIOL & EXP MED, 71- *Concurrent Pos:* Fel biochem, McGill Univ, 37-38; NIH spec res fel, 49-50; hon prof, Fac Med, Univ Cochabamba, 62 & Fac Med, Univ Madrid; mem, UNESCO Int Sci Comn, Venezuela, 64; pres VII cong, Int Fedn Diabetes, 70. *Honors & Awards:* Miguel Couto Award, Acad Med, Brazil, 44; B A Houssay Award, WHO, 81. *Mem:* Soc Exp Biol & Med; Arg Biol Soc (pres, 78); Arg Soc Endocrinol (pres, 44-48); Arg Soc Diabetes (pres, 55-57); Arg Acad Med. *Res:* Physiology of endocrine glands and diabetes. *Mailing Add:* Callao No 1695 Piso 12 Dto B Buenos Aires Argentina

FOGLIO, MARIO EUSEBIO, b Buenos Aires, Arg, Apr 25, 31; m 57; c 3. INTERMEDIATE VALENCE, LINEAR RESPONSE. *Educ:* Univ Buenos Aires, Lic en Quimica, 54, Dr en Quimica, 58; Bristol Univ, PhD(physics), 62. *Prof Exp:* Researcher phys chem, Arg Atomic Energy Comn, 54-56, researcher physics, 56-61; res assoc, Bristol Univ, 61-62; researcher, Arg Atomic Energy Comn, 62-68; res assoc, Harvard Univ, 68-69; assoc prof, Southern Ill Univ, 69-74; MEM STAFF, INST FISICA, 74- *Concurrent Pos:* S J Guggenheim Mem Found fel, 68-69. *Mem:* Am Phys Soc; NY Acad Sci; Phys Soc Brasil. *Res:* Spin lattice relaxation; electron spin resonance; magnetic impurities in dielectrics; ferrimagnetic relaxation in europium iron garnet; statistical mechanics of impurities; neutron scattering in intermediate valence compounds. *Mailing Add:* Inst Fisica Unicamp-CP 1170 13100 Campinsa Sao Paulo Brazil

FOGLIO, SUSANA, b Bahia Blanca, Arg, June 6, 24; m 57; c 3. MATHEMATICS, STATISTICS. *Educ:* Univ Buenos Aires, MS, 49, PhD(math), 59. *Prof Exp:* Asst prof math, Nat Univ of the South, Arg, 49-52 & Univ Buenos Aires, 52-54; assoc prof, Nat Univ of the South, Arg, 54-56 & Bariloche Atomic Ctr, Arg, 56-70; PROF MATH, FED UNIV SAO CARLOS, 77- *Mem:* Arg Math Union; Am Math Soc. *Res:* Theory of integration; stochastic integrals. *Mailing Add:* Fed Univ Sao Carlos Sao Carlos Est Sao Paulo Brazil

FOGWELL, JOSEPH WRAY, b Topeka, Kans, Dec 11, 15; m 42; c 2. MECHANICAL ENGINEERING. *Educ:* Univ Kans, BS, 40, MS, 45. *Prof Exp:* Res mech engr, Aluminum Co Am, 40-42; instr mech eng, Univ Kans, 42-44; mgr indust eng, Corning Glass Works, 44-45; prod design engr, Cuno Eng Corp, 45-47; chief engr, Stock Equip Co, 47-51; sr res engr, Southwest Res Inst, 51-56; pvt consult engr, 56-57; from gen mgr to pres, Prestressing, Inc, 57-61; staff engr, Southwest Res Inst, 61-81. *Mem:* Am Soc Mech Engrs. *Res:* Electromechanical research and development. *Mailing Add:* 4934 View Dr San Antonio TX 78228

FOHL, TIMOTHY, b Pittsburgh, Pa, Apr 21, 34; m 61; c 3. FLUID DYNAMICS. *Educ:* Dartmouth Col, AB, 56; Mass Inst Technol, MS, 59, PhD(geophys), 63. *Prof Exp:* Res scientist physics, Itek Corp, 62-63; res scientist & dir, Mt Auburn Res Assoc, Inc, 63-72; MGR, NEW PROD RES, GTE SYLVANIA, INC, 72- *Concurrent Pos:* Res affil, Mass Inst Technol, 63-65. *Res:* Vortex motion and turbulent flows with application to atmospheric motions and flows in arcs. *Mailing Add:* 681 South St Carlisle MA 01741

FOHLEN, GEORGE MARCEL, b San Francisco, Calif, Jan 3, 19; m 46. ORGANIC CHEMISTRY, POLYMER CHEMISTRY. *Educ:* Univ Calif, BS, 40, PhD(pharmaceut chem), 44. *Prof Exp:* Asst pharm, Univ Calif, 40-43; res chemist, Oronite Chem Co, Calif, 44-45; sr res chemist, Sterling-Winthrop Inst, NY, 45-47, Res & Develop Dept, Barrett Div, Allied Chem & Dye Corp, 47-55 & Reichhold Chem, Inc, Calif, 55-60; mgr anal servs, Cutter Labs, Berkeley, 60-62; sr res chemist process develop, Kaiser Chem Corp, Calif, 62-67 & Appl Space Prod, Inc, 67-70; RES SCIENTIST CHEM RES PROJS, AMES RES CTR, NASA, 70- *Concurrent Pos:* Civilian with Off Sci Res & Develop, 44. *Honors & Awards:* NASA Award for develop achievement, 69. *Mem:* AAAS; Am Chem Soc. *Res:* Analytical methods; spectroscopy; organic synthesis; dipole moments and structures of urea, thiourea and some sex hormones; industrial organic chemistry; plastics; high temperature polymers; intumescent coatings; transparent polymers. *Mailing Add:* Chem Res Projs Off Ames Res Ctr NASA Moffett Field CA 94035

FOHLMEISTER, JURGEN FRITZ, b Znaim, Ger, Nov 18, 41; US citizen. NEUROPHYSIOLOGY, BIOPHYSICS. *Educ:* Univ Minn, BS, 64, MS, 65, PhD(physics), 71. *Prof Exp:* Fel, 71-73, lectr, 73-78, ASST PROF NEUROPHYSIOL, UNIV MINN, 78- *Mem:* Soc Neurosci; Biophys Soc. *Res:* Basic mechanisms of neural excitation; membrane biophysics. *Mailing Add:* Dept of Physiol Univ of Minn Minneapolis MN 55455

FOIL, ROBERT RODNEY, b Bogalusa, La, Aug 12, 34; m 59; c 2. FORESTRY, RESEARCH ADMINISTRATION. *Educ:* La State Univ, Baton Rouge, BS, 56, MFor, 60; Duke Univ, DFor(forest soils), 65. *Prof Exp:* Forester, Union Bag Corp, 56; instr forestry, La State Univ, 59-62, asst prof, 62-67; assoc specialist, La Exten Serv, 67-68, specialist, 68-69; prof & head dept, Miss State Univ, 69-73, dean, Sch Forest Resources, 74-78; DIR MISS AGR & FORESTRY EXP STA, 78- *Mem:* Soc Am Foresters; Am Forestry Asn. *Res:* Forest resource management and use, particularly efficient harvesting of timber crops without damaging soils or desirable vegetation; science policy; agricultural and forest policy. *Mailing Add:* PO Drawer ES Mississippi State MS 39762

FOILES, CARL LUTHER, b Hardin, Ill, Oct 1, 35; m 63; c 2. PHYSICS. *Educ:* Univ Ariz, BS, 57, MS, 60, PhD(physics), 64. *Prof Exp:* Res assoc physics, Mich State Univ, 64-66; NSF fel Imp Col London, 66-67; asst prof, 67-70, assoc prof, 70-76, PROF PHYSICS, MICH STATE UNIV, 76- *Concurrent Pos:* Vis assoc prof, Univ Wash, 73-74. *Mem:* Am Phys Soc. *Res:* Low temperature properties of metals and alloys; transport properties and magnetic properties. *Mailing Add:* Dept of Physics Mich State Univ East Lansing MI 48823

FOISY, HECTOR B, b Ft Covington, NY, Feb 8, 36; m 58; c 5. MATHEMATICS. *Educ:* St Michael's Col, Vt, BA, 58; Univ Ill, Urbana, MA, 62; George Peabody Col, PhD(math), 71. *Prof Exp:* Teacher & chmn dept, High Sch, NY, 58-61; assoc prof, 62-80, PROF MATH, STATE UNIV NY COL POTSDAM, 80- *Mem:* Math Asn Am; Nat Coun Teachers Math. *Res:* Qualifications, duties and training of elementary school mathematics specialists. *Mailing Add:* Dept of Math State Univ of NY Col Potsdam NY 13676

FOIT, FRANKLIN FREDERICK, JR, b Buffalo, NY, Jan 15, 42; m 65; c 2. GEOLOGY, MINERALOGY. *Educ:* Univ Mich, BS, 64, MS, 65, PhD(mineral), 68. *Prof Exp:* Asst prof, 71-77, ASSOC PROF GEOL, WASH STATE UNIV, 77- *Concurrent Pos:* Res assoc, Va Polytech Inst & State Univ, 70-71. *Mem:* Mineral Asn Can; Mineral Soc Am; Int Zeolite Asn. *Res:* Crystal chemistry of silicates and borosilicates, geology and geochemistry of thermal springs, mineralogy and chemistry of alkaline lake sediments. *Mailing Add:* Dept of Geol Wash State Univ Pullman WA 99164

FOK, AGNES KWAN, Hong Kong, Brit Crown Colony, Dec 11, 40; m 65; c 2. CELL BIOLOGIST, ELECTRON MICROBIOLOGIST. *Educ:* Col Great Falls, BA, 65; Utah State Univ, MS, 66; Univ Tex, Austin, PhD(biochem), 71. *Prof Exp:* ASST RES, UNIV HAWAII, 71- *Concurrent Pos:* Fel, Ford Found, 75. *Mem:* Am Soc Cell Biologists; Soc Protozoologists; Sigma Xi. *Res:* Intracellular digestion using paramecium as a model cell system to understand this process using a multidisciplinary approach. *Mailing Add:* Snyder 306, 2538 The Mall Dept Microbiol Univ Hawaii Honolulu HI 96822

FOK, SAMUEL S(HIU) M(ING), b Macao, China, Feb 15, 26; US citizen; m 52; c 3. CHEMICAL ENGINEERING. *Educ:* Ohio State Univ, BChe, 49; Case Inst Technol, MS, 51, PhD(chem eng), 55. *Prof Exp:* Res asst, Case Inst Technol, 50-54; res engr, Indust Rayon Corp, Ohio, 54-56; sr staff engr, Shockley Transistor Corp, Calif, 56-60; mem tech staff, Res & Develop Lab, Fairchild Semiconductor Corp, 60-70; microphotog consult, 70-71; group leader, Siliconix, Inc, 71-73; engr mgr, 73-74; consult, 74-77; mgr processing & mach acceptance, ETEC Corp, 77-79; MGR PROCESS TECHNOL, PERKIN-ELMER ETEC, INC, 79- *Concurrent Pos:* Tech adv, Ledel Semiconductor, Hong Kong, 73; dep managing dir, F C T Bros Co; exec dir, Int Frozen Foods Co; dir, Inter-Asian Tobacco Exporters Co, Bangkok, Thailand, 57-81. *Mem:* Am Chem Soc; Electrochem Soc; Soc Photog Sci & Eng; Am Soc Test Mat; Semiconductor Equip Mat Inst. *Res:* Large scale integration, metal-oxide-silicon or LSI/MOS mask making; masking; photoresists; photofabrication; microphotography; semiconductor process development; plastic packaging; high polymers; chrome mask making; transparent mask; one to one projection system; electron beam mask making and processing. *Mailing Add:* 820 Talisman Dr Palo Alto CA 94303

FOK, SIU YUEN, b Macau, China, Nov 23, 37. POLYMER PHYSICS, CHEMICAL ENGINEERING. *Educ:* Nat Taiwan Univ, BS, 60; Univ Cincinnati, MS, 62; Va Polytech Inst, PhD(chem eng), 65. *Prof Exp:* Fel chem, Clarkson Col Technol, 65-66; sr res chemist, Fibers & Laminates Div, Enjay Chem Co, 66-69; prin chemist, Dart Indust, 69-73; PLANT MGR, BEAU PLASTIC CO, 73- *Mem:* Am Chem Soc; Am Inst Chem Engrs; Soc of Plastics Engrs. *Res:* Polymer physics and characterization; fiber spinning; coated fabrics. *Mailing Add:* Beau Plastic Co 158 Tin Hau Temple Rd D1 19F Kowloon Hong Kong

FOK, THOMAS DSO YUN, b Canton, China, July 1, 21; nat US; m 49. CIVIL ENGINEERING. *Educ:* Nat Tung-Chi Univ, China, BEng, 45; Univ Ill, MS, 48; NY Univ, MBA, 50; Carnegie Inst, PhD(civil eng), 56. *Prof Exp:* Design engr, Richardson, Gordon & Assocs, Pa, 56-58; assoc prof civil eng, Youngstown Univ, 58-67, dir comput ctr, 63-67; partner, Mosure & Fok, consult engrs, 67-76; CHMN, THOMAS FOK & ASSOCS, LTD, 77- *Concurrent Pos:* Consult to indust & pub agencies Ohio & Pa, 58- *Mem:* Am Soc Eng Educ; Am Soc Civil Engrs; Am Concrete Inst; Int Asn Bridge & Struct Engrs. *Res:* Structural engineering; applied mechanics and programming for digital computers. *Mailing Add:* 325 S Canfield-Niles Rd Youngstown OH 44515

FOK, YU SI, b China, Jan 15, 32. WATER RESOURCES, IRRIGATION. *Educ:* Nat Taiwan Univ, BS, 55; Utah State Univ, MS, 59, PhD(civil eng), 64. *Prof Exp:* Res asst civil & irrig eng, Utah State Univ, 57-63, asst prof agr & irrig eng & asst res engr, Utah Water Res Lab, 63-66; res assoc, Univ Ill, Urbana, 66-68; head basin hydrol sect, Tex Water Rights Comn, Tex, 68-70; assoc prof, 70-77, PROF CIVIL ENG, WATER RESOURCES RES CTR, UNIV HAWAII, 77- *Concurrent Pos:* Hydrologist, Ill State Water Surv, Ill, 66-68. *Mem:* Am Geophys Union; Int Water Resources Asn; Am Soc Civil Engrs; Am Soc Agr Eng; Sigma Xi. *Res:* Soil physics; stream system morphology-mechanics of stream morphological systems; hydrology-urban hydrology, flood hydrology, water conservation and availability and streamflow forecasting; water resources systems analysis-optimization of water resources; irrigation and drainage science. *Mailing Add:* Univ Hawaii Dept Civil Eng 2540 Dole St Honolulu HI 96822

FOLAND, NEAL EUGENE, b Parnell, Mo, Dec 9, 29; m 56; c 5. MATHEMATICS. *Educ:* Northeast Mo State Teachers Col, BS, 54; Univ Mo, MA, 58, PhD(math), 61. *Prof Exp:* From asst prof to assoc prof math, Kans State Univ, 61-65; assoc prof, 65-70, PROF MATH, SOUTHERN ILL UNIV, 70-, CHMN DEPT, 71- *Mem:* Am Math Soc; Math Asn Am. *Res:* Topological dynamics. *Mailing Add:* Dept of Math Southern Ill Univ Carbondale IL 62901

FOLAND, WILLIAM DOUGLAS, b Knoxville, Tenn, Jan 15, 26; m 55. PHYSICS. *Educ:* Univ Tenn, AB, 51, MS, 55, PhD(physics), 58. *Prof Exp:* Asst physics, Univ Tenn, 51-55, instr, 55-58; from asst prof to assoc prof, Univ Mass, Amherst, 58-68; assoc prof, 68-76, PROF PHYSICS, WASHINGTON & JEFFERSON COL, 76-, DEPT CHMN, 75- *Res:* Atomic collisions; theory. *Mailing Add:* Dept Physics Washington & Jefferson Col Washington PA 15301

FOLCH-PI, JORDI, biochemistry, deceased

FOLDEN, DEWEY BRAY, JR, b Charleston, WVa, Dec 2, 23; m 49. ANIMAL PHYSIOLOGY. *Educ:* Morris Harvey Col, BS, 47, BA, 48; WVa Univ, MS, 49. *Prof Exp:* Instr biol, Memphis State Col, 49-55 & Dickinson Col, 55-57; from instr to asst prof, 57-61, ASSOC PROF BIOL, MEMPHIS STATE UNIV, 61- *Concurrent Pos:* NIH res grant, 59-60. *Mem:* AAAS. *Res:* Spectrophotometry of selected crab meat samples; renal blood flow in the decapsulated kidney. *Mailing Add:* Dept of Biol Memphis State Univ Memphis TN 38152

FOLDES, FRANCIS FERENC, b Budapest, Hungary, June 13, 10; nat US; m 38; c 3. ANESTHESIOLOGY. *Educ:* Univ Budapest, MD, 34; fel Royal Australasian Col Surgeons, 70 & FRCS, 71. *Prof Exp:* Res physician, Svabhegyi Sanatorium, Budapest, 35-39; pvt pract, 39-41; res fel anesthesia, Mass Gen Hosp, Boston, 41-42, resident, 42-43, asst anesthetist, 44-47; dir dept anesthesiol, Mercy Hosp, Pittsburgh, Pa, 47-62; chmn dept anesthesiol,

62-75, CONSULT ANESTHESIOL, MONTEFIORE HOSP & MED CTR, 75-, EMER PROF ANESTHESIOL, ALBERT EINSTEIN COL MED, 75- *Concurrent Pos:* Asst, Harvard Med Sch, 43-47; assoc prof, Med Sch, Univ Pittsburgh, 48-57, clin prof, 57-62; mem med adv bd, Myasthenia Gravis Found, 59-, from vchmn to chmn, 62-68; vpres, World Fedn Socs Anesthesiologists, 60-64, mem sci adv & membership comts, 65-68, pres fedn, 68-72; mem subcomt anesthesiol, Comt Revision US Pharmacopeia, 60-75; clin prof, Col Physicians & Surgeons, Columbia Univ, 62-64; res assoc, Mt Sinai Hosp, NY, 62-75; prof anesthesiol, Albert Einstein Col Med, 64-75; vis prof, Cath Univ Nijmegen, Holland, 75; prof anesthesiol, Sch Med, Miami Univ, 76- *Honors & Awards:* Semmelweis Award, Am Hungarian Med Asn, 66, George Washington Award, 70; Am Soc Anesthesiol Distinguished Serv Award, 72; Span Soc Anesthesiologists Gold Medal, 74; Heidbrink Award, Am Dent Soc Anesthesiol, 75; Ralph M Waters Award, Int Anesthesia Award Comn, 76. *Mem:* Am Soc Anesthesiol; Am Soc Pharmacol & Exp Therapeut; NY Acad Med; NY Acad Sci; Int Anesthesia Res Soc. *Res:* Neuropharmacology; enzymes; co-enzymes. *Mailing Add:* Dept of Anesthesiol Montefiore Hosp & Med Ctr New York NY 10467

FOLDI, ANDREW PETER, b Budapest, Hungary, Feb 24, 31; US citizen; m 66. ORGANIC CHEMISTRY, POLYMER CHEMISTRY. *Educ:* Budapest Tech Univ, dipl Chem Eng, 53; Univ Del, PhD(org chem), 63. *Prof Exp:* Design & prod chem engr, Chem Complex, Hungary, 53-56; chem engr, 57-60, RES CHEMIST, E I DU PONT DE NEMOURS & CO, 62- *Mem:* Am Chem Soc. *Res:* Industrial fibers; rubber technology; thermoplastics; polyurethanes; pharmaceutical and synthetic organic chemistry; theoretical organic and industrial chemistry; textile technology. *Mailing Add:* E I du Pont de Nemours & Co Wilmington DE 19898

FOLDS, JAMES DONALD, b Augusta, Ga, Sept 26, 40; m 62; c 2. MICROBIOLOGY, IMMUNOLOGY. *Educ:* Univ Ga, BS, 62; Med Col Ga, PhD(microbiol), 67. *Prof Exp:* USPHS fel immunol, Sch Med, Case Western Reserve Univ, 67-69; instr, 69-70, asst prof, 70-75, ASSOC PROF BACT & IMMUNOL, SCH MED, UNIV NC, CHAPEL HILL, 75- & DIR CLIN MICROBIOL LABS, NC MEM HOSP, 76- *Mem:* AAAS; Am Asn Immunol; Am Soc Microbiol. *Res:* Antibody synthesis and secretion; control and regulation of antibody synthesis; immunity to treponema pallium; degradative mechanisms of human polymorphonuclear neutrophils. *Mailing Add:* Dept of Bacteriol & Immunol Univ of NC Sch of Med Chapel Hill NC 27514

FOLDVARY, ELMER, b Youngstown, Ohio, Mar 9, 35; m 65; c 2. ORGANIC CHEMISTRY. *Educ:* Youngstown State Univ, BS, 58; Tex A&M Univ, MS, 61, PhD(chem), 64. *Prof Exp:* Asst prof, 63-68, assoc prof, 68-77, PROF CHEM, YOUNGSTOWN STATE UNIV, 77- *Mem:* Am Chem Soc; Sigma Xi. *Res:* Linear free energy relationships; synthetics; polyester plastics; kinetics. *Mailing Add:* Dept of Chem Youngstown State Univ Youngstown OH 44555

FOLDY, LESLIE LAWRANCE, b Sabinov, Czech, Oct 26, 19; US citizen; m 44; c 2. THEORETICAL PHYSICS. *Educ:* Case Inst Technol, BS, 41; Univ Wis, PhM, 42; Univ Calif, PhD(physics), 48. *Prof Exp:* Res physicist, Div War Res, Columbia Univ, 42-45; res physicist, Radiation Lab, Univ Calif, 45-46; from asst prof to prof, 48-66, INST PROF PHYSICS, CASE WESTERN RESERVE UNIV, 66- *Concurrent Pos:* Fulbright & Guggenheim fel, Inst Theoret Physics, Copenhagen, 53-54; NSF sr fel, Europ Orgn Nuclear Res, Geneva, 63-64. *Mem:* Fel Am Phys Soc; fel Acoust Soc Am; Fedn Am Sci. *Res:* Acoustical theory; theoretical nuclear physics; quantum theory; quantum field theories; theory of high energy accelerators; elementary particle physics. *Mailing Add:* Dept of Physics Case Western Reserve Univ Cleveland OH 44106

FOLEN, VINCENT JAMES, b Scranton, Pa, Jan 17, 24; m 54. MAGNETISM. *Educ:* La Salle Col, BA, 49; Univ Pa, MA, 54; Am Univ, PhD(physics), 72. *Prof Exp:* Res asst, Univ Pa, 50-54; physicist, 54-59, HEAD FERRO MAGNETISM SECT, US NAVAL RES LAB, 59- *Honors & Awards:* Res Publ Awards, Naval Res Lab, 68, 70 & 79; Pure Sci Award, Sci Res Soc Am, 71. *Mem:* Fel Am Phys Soc; Sigma Xi. *Res:* Electron spin and ferromagnetic resonance, magnetoelectric effect, magnetocrystalline anisotropy, quantum electronics. *Mailing Add:* Code 6892 Naval Res Lab Washington DC 20375

FOLEY, DAVID ALLEN, b Baltimore, Md, May 6, 47. PATHOBIOLOGY, PARASITOLOGY. *Educ:* Lafayette Col, BA, 69; Lehigh Univ, MS, 72, PhD(biol), 74; New York Univ, MD, 81. *Prof Exp:* Fel parasitol, Sch Med, NY Univ, 74-75; instr prev med, 75-76, asst prof parasitol, 76-79, fel pathol, Bellevue Hosp, 80-81; fel internal med, Johns Hopkins Univ, 81-82. *Honors & Awards:* Res Serv Award, NIH, 75. *Mem:* Soc Invert Path; AMA; Am Soc Parasitologists; Am Micros Soc; Am Soc Tropical Med. *Res:* Comparative disease processes in the vertebrate and invertebrate metazoa, particularly in the cellular component of internal defense mechanisms in arthropods, molluscs and mammals; physiology of malarial infections; chemotherapy against malaria infections. *Mailing Add:* 6625 Bonnie Ridge Dr 201 Baltimore MD 21209

FOLEY, DEAN CARROLL, b Pomeroy, Wash, Nov 25, 25; m 55. PHYTOPATHOLOGY. *Educ:* Univ Idaho, BS, 49; WVa Univ, MS, 51; Pa State Univ, PhD(plant path), 55. *Prof Exp:* Asst plant path, WVa Univ, 49-51 & Pa State Univ, 51-55; asst prof, 55-61, ASSOC PROF PLANT PATH, IOWA STATE UNIV, 61- *Mem:* AAAS; Am Phytopath Soc; Bot Soc Am; Am Inst Biol Sci. *Res:* Diseases resistance; diseases of cereals. *Mailing Add:* Dept of Bot & Plant Path Iowa State Univ Ames IA 50011

FOLEY, DENNIS D(ONALD), b Bainville, Mont, Mar 17, 23; m 47; c 1. CHEMICAL ENGINEERING. *Educ:* Ohio State Univ, BChEng, 47, MS, 49, PhD(chem eng), 54. *Prof Exp:* Asst engr, Tenn Eastman Corp, Oak Ridge, 44-46; asst physics, Ohio State Univ, 47-50 & Battelle Mem Inst, 51-58; head mat technol nuclear power eng, Alco Prods, Inc, 58-61; mgr, Nuclear Prod

Dept, Am Standard Adv Tech Lab, 62-64; dir eng, Neptune Meter Co, 65-77; VPRES TECHNOL, ALEAN ALUMINUM CORP, 77- *Mem:* Am Inst Mining, Metall & Petrol Engrs; Am Soc Metals. *Res:* Mass spectroscopy; beta ray spectroscopy; extraction and purfication of thorium and uranium; distillation theory; nuclear power equipment; metering and measurement equipment and systems; aluminum fabrication. *Mailing Add:* Alean Aluminum Corp 100 Ericview Plaza Cleveland OH 44114

FOLEY, DENNIS JOSEPH, b Brooklyn, NY, Dec 28, 45; m 68; c 3. PHARMACOLOGY. *Educ:* Fordham Univ, BS, 68; WVa Univ, PhD(pharm), 72. *Prof Exp:* Res pharmacologist, Walter Reed Army Inst Res, 72-75; group leader Clin Study Anal, 75-81, DEPT HEAD, CLIN RES INFO, MED RES DIV, LEDERLE LABS, AM CYANAMID CO, 81- *Mailing Add:* Med Res Div Lederle Labs Am Cyanamid Co Pearl River NY 10965

FOLEY, EDWARD LEO, b Butte, Mont, Apr 15, 30; m 55; c 8. PHYSICS. *Educ:* Mont State Col, BS, 54; Lehigh Univ, MS, 57, PhD(physics), 62. *Prof Exp:* Instr physics, Lehigh Univ, 60-62; asst prof, Univ Vt, 62-66; from asst prof to assoc prof, 66-71, chmn dept, 67-77, PROF PHYSICS, ST MICHAEL'S COL, 71- *Mem:* Am Asn Physics Teachers; Int Solar Energy Soc. *Res:* Thermal diffusivities of metals; surface physics; solar energy, insolation on tilt. *Mailing Add:* Dept of Physics St Michael's Col Winooski VT 05404

FOLEY, GEORGE EDWARD, b Mechanicville, NY, Dec 1, 12; m 41; c 1. MEDICAL MICROBIOLOGY. *Educ:* Univ Amsterdam, ScD(microbiol), 54; Am Bd Med Microbiol, dipl. *Prof Exp:* Asst, NY State Dept Health, 35-40; serologist, Roosevelt Hosp, New York, 40-41; assoc epidemiol, Harvard Med Sch & Sch Pub Health, 43-45; asst bacteriologist, Mass Gen Hosp, 45-47; chief microbiol and cell biol labs, Children's Cancer Res Found, 47-73, assoc dir labs, 68-74, dir res admin, 74-78, EMER STAFF, SIDNEY FARBER CANCER INST, 78- *Concurrent Pos:* Res assoc path, Children's Hosp Med Ctr, 52, bacteriologist, 52-70; ed bd, Antibiotics & Chemother, 60-62; regional ed, Exp Cell Res, 62-78. Nat Cancer Inst res career award, 64-73; lectr path, Harvard Med Sch, 64- *Mem:* Fel AAAS; Am Soc Microbiol; Am Asn Path; Royal Soc Health; Am Asn Cancer Res. *Res:* Cell biology; microbiology; cancer; chemotherapy; experimental pathology. *Mailing Add:* 16 Clifton Pk Melrose MA 02176

FOLEY, H THOMAS, b Pittsburgh, Pa, Mar 27, 33; m 54; c 2. INTERNAL MEDICINE. *Educ:* Univ Pittsburgh, BS, 54; NY Univ, MD, 60; Georgetown Univ, JD, 77. *Prof Exp:* Intern & resident, III & IV Med Div, Bellevue Hosp, New York, 60-63; liaison officer to eastern solid tumor group, Nat Cancer Inst, 63-65; sr investr radiation & med br, 65-69, Baltimore Cancer Res Ctr, med officer, Georgetown Med Serv, DC Gen Hosp, 70-81; MED OFFICER, ARMED FORCES INST PATH, 81- *Concurrent Pos:* Clin asst prof, Georgetown Univ. *Mem:* Fel Am Col Physicians; fel Col Legal Med. *Mailing Add:* Dept Legal Med Armed Forces Inst Path Walter Reed Army Med Ctr Washington DC 20306

FOLEY, HENRY GRANT, organic chemistry, see previous edition

FOLEY, HENRY MICHAEL, b Palmer, Mass, June 1, 17; m; c 2. PHYSICS. *Educ:* Univ Mich, BS, 38, MA, 39, PhD(physics), 42. *Prof Exp:* Asst physics, Univ Mich, 36-40, res assoc, Off Sci Res & Develop Proj, 42-44; res physicist, Appl Physics Lab, Johns Hopkins Univ, 44-45; assoc physics, 46-47, from asst prof to assoc prof, 48-54, chmn dept physics, 57-60 & 71-73, PROF PHYSICS, COLUMBIA UNIV, 54- *Concurrent Pos:* Guggenheim fel, 54-55; Fulbright lectr, Univ Utrecht, 55; liaison scientist, Off Naval Res, London, 68-69. *Mem:* Am Phys Soc. *Res:* Pressure broadening of spectral lines; atomic and molecular structure; atomic beams and magnetic moments; nuclear quadruple moments; radiation theory; atmospheric physics. *Mailing Add:* Dept of Physics Columbia Univ New York NY 10027

FOLEY, HOWARD KENNETH, b Youngstown, Ohio, Jan 6, 20; m 45; c 2. POLYMER CHEMISTRY. *Educ:* Youngstown Univ, BS, 42; Univ Akron, MS, 56, PhD(polymer chem), 64. *Prof Exp:* Chem operator, Plum Brook Ord Works, Trojan Powder Co, Ohio, 42-44; qual control chemist, 44-46, res chemist, 46-63, sr res chemist, 63-71, RES SCIENTIST, GOODYEAR TIRE & RUBBER CO, 71- *Mem:* Am Chem Soc. *Res:* Emulsion polymerization variables; shortstopping; popcorn polymer inhibition; analytical procedures pertaining to styrene-butadiene rubber and related polymers and the polymerization process; network properties of styrene-butadiene rubber, polymer-solvent interaction and stress versus strain; molecular weight distribution of styrene-butadiene rubbers. *Mailing Add:* Goodyear Tire & Rubber Co Dept 455B 142 Goodyear Blvd Akron OH 44316

FOLEY, JAMES DAVID, b Palmerton, Penn, July 20, 42; m 64; c 2. INTERACTIVE COMPUTER GRAPHICS, USER-COMPUTER INTERFACES. *Educ:* Lehigh Univ, BS, 64; Univ Mich, MS, 65, PhD(comput info & control eng), 69. *Prof Exp:* Asst prof comput sci, Univ NC, 70-76; assoc prof, 77-81, PROF ELEC ENG & COMPUT SCI, GEORGE WASHINGTON UNIV, 81- *Concurrent Pos:* assoc ed, Transactions Graphics, 81-; pres, Comput Graphics Consult, Inc, 79- *Mem:* Asn Comput Mach; Inst Elec & Electronic Engrs; Comput Soc; Nat Comput Graphics Asn. *Res:* Interactive computer graphics software, hardware, systems, and applications; human factors of user-computer interfaces; cognitive psychology. *Mailing Add:* 713 Sixth St SW Washington DC 20024

FOLEY, JOHN F, b Buffalo, NY, Feb 1, 31; m 55; c 5. INTERNAL MEDICINE. *Educ:* Univ Buffalo, MD, 55; Univ Minn, PhD(internal med), 62. *Prof Exp:* Res specialist, Univ Minn, 60-62; res fel internal med, 62-63; asst prof med, 63-68, PROF MED, UNIV NEBR MED CTR, 68- *Mem:* Am Asn Cancer Res; Tissue Cult Asn; Am Soc Clin Oncol; Am Asn Cancer Educ; fel Am Col Physicians. *Res:* Tissue culture; cell interactions; chemical chemotherapy; preventive medicine; hormonal action on tissue culture cells. *Mailing Add:* Dept of Internal Med Univ of Nebr Med Ctr Omaha NE 68105

FOLEY, JOSEPH MICHAEL, b Dorchester, Mass, Mar 9, 16; m 44. NEUROLOGY. *Educ:* Col of the Holy Cross, AB, 37; Harvard Univ, MD, 41. *Hon Degrees:* ScD, Col of the Holy Cross, 62. *Prof Exp:* Intern, Bellevue Hosp, NY, 41-43; asst neurol, Harvard Med Sch, 46-48, from instr to asst prof, 48-59; prof, Seton Hall Col Med & Dent, 59-61; PROF NEUROL, SCH MED, CASE WESTERN RESERVE UNIV, 61-; DIR DIV NEUROL, UNIV HOSPS CLEVELAND, 66- *Concurrent Pos:* Rockefeller asst, Boston City Hosp, 46-48; asst prof, Med Sch, Univ Boston, 48-51; dir dept neurol, Jersey City Med Ctr, 59-61; consult, US Air Force, 59-63; chmn med adv bd & res rev panel, Nat Multiple Sclerosis Soc; coordr continuing med educ, Case Western Reserve Univ, 67-; mem bd trustees, Col Holy Cross; trustee, Cleveland Med Libr Asn, 72- *Honors & Awards:* Bronze Hope Chest Award, Nat Multiple Sclerosis Soc, 75. *Mem:* Am Neurol Asn (pres, 74-75); Am Asn Neuropath; Asn Res Nerv & Ment Dis; Am Acad Neurol (pres, 63-65); Am Fedn Clin Res. *Res:* Neurological medicine and pathology. *Mailing Add:* Div of Neurol Univ Hosps of Cleveland Cleveland OH 44106

FOLEY, KATHLEEN M, b Flushing, NY, Jan 28, 44; m 68; c 2. NEUROLOGY. *Educ:* St John's Univ, BA, 65; Cornell Univ, MD, 69. *Prof Exp:* Fel genetics, New York Hosp, 70-71, resident neurol, New York Hosp-Cornell Med Ctr, 71-74, chief resident neurol, 74; ASST PROF NEUROL, COL MED, CORNELL UNIV, 75-; ASST ATTEND PHYSICIAN, SLOAN KETTERING INST CANCER RES, 75- *Mem:* Am Soc Neurol; Int Asn Study Pain; Am Women's Med Asn; NY Acad Sci; Am Fedn Clin Res. *Res:* Cancer pain; neurological complications of cancer. *Mailing Add:* Sloan Kettering Inst Cancer Res 1275 York Ave New York NY 10021

FOLEY, MICHAEL GLEN, b Independence, Mo, July 23, 45; m 68. GEOMORPHOLOGY, GEOLOGY. *Educ:* Calif Inst Technol, BS, 67, MS, 68, PhD(geol), 76. *Prof Exp:* Res engr aeronaut, Boeing Co, 68-69; analyst, Jet Propulsion Lab, 69-70; asst prof geol, Univ Mo-Columbia, 76-80; SR GEOLOGIST, BATTELLE PAC NORTHWEST LABS, 80- *Mem:* Am Geophys Union; Am Quaternary Asn; Brit Geomorphol Res Group; Geol Soc Am; Soc Econ Paleontologists & Mineralogists. *Res:* Laboratory and deterministic stochastic mathematical modeling of sediment transport mechanics and fluvial system behavior; field study of modern and late Cenozoic channels and drainage basins; computer modeling of geologic/hydrologic systems for nuclear-waste containment studies. *Mailing Add:* 2305 Towhee Lane West Richland WA 99352

FOLEY, ROBERT THOMAS, b Turners Falls, Mass, Dec 21, 18; m 45; c 2. ELECTROCHEMISTRY. *Educ:* Univ Mass, BS, 40; Lafayette Col, MS, 41; Univ Tex, PhD(phys chem), 48. *Prof Exp:* Res chemist, Am Cyanamid Co, NJ, 41-45; instr phys chem, Univ Tex, 45-48; res chemist, Gen Elec Co, 48-52, supvr gen metall, 52-54, specialist surface chem, 54-61; supvr electrochem, Melpar, Inc, Va, 61-64; PROF CHEM, AM UNIV, 64- *Concurrent Pos:* Consult, Union Carbide Corp, US Army, Silver Inst, Washington, DC, 72-; WR Grace Co, 76- *Honors & Awards:* William Blum Award, 78. *Mem:* Am Chem Soc; Electrochem Soc; Int Electrochem Soc; Am Inst Chem; Nat Asn Corrosion Eng. *Res:* Energy conversion; fuel cells; batteries; corrosion mechanisms; fuel cell electrolytes. *Mailing Add:* Dept of Chem Am Univ Washington DC 20016

FOLEY, WILLIAM M, b Hoquiam, Wash, Mar 12, 29; m 53; c 4. FLUID MECHANICS. *Educ:* Univ Minn, BS, 51; Stanford Univ, MS, 56, PhD(aeronaut & astronaut), 62. *Prof Exp:* Supvr gaseous physics group, Res Labs, United Aircraft Corp, 58-65, chief aerophysics sect, 65-66, mgr fluid dynamics lab, 67-76, DEP DIR RES, UNITED TECHNOL CORP, 76- *Concurrent Pos:* Mem res adv comt aircraft aerodyn, NASA, 66-71. *Mem:* Am Phys Soc; Am Inst Aeronaut & Astronaut. *Res:* Rarefied gas dynamics; fluid mechanics of gaseous core nuclear reactors; physics of gas-surface interactions. *Mailing Add:* United Technol Res Ctr Silver Lane East Hartford CT 06108

FOLEY, WILLIAM THOMAS, b New York, NY, Oct 30, 11; m; c 5. MEDICINE. *Educ:* Columbia Univ, AB, 33; Cornell Univ, MD, 37; Am Bd Internal Med, dipl. *Prof Exp:* Asst prof, 51-59, assoc prof, 59-77, EMER ASSOC PROF CLIN MED, MED COL, CORNELL UNIV, 77- *Concurrent Pos:* Assoc attend physician, NY Hosp; consult, Hosps. *Mem:* Sr mem Am Soc Clin Invest; Harvey Soc; Am Heart Asn; fel Am Col Physicians; Am Col Cardiol. *Res:* Clinical research in thromboembolism and vascular diseases; lymphedema; cerebrovascular disease. *Mailing Add:* 441 E 68th St New York NY 10021

FOLGER, DAVID W, b Woburn, Mass, Nov 21, 31; wid; c 3. GEOLOGICAL OCEANOGRAPHY. *Educ:* Dartmouth Col, BA, 53; Columbia Univ, MA, 58, PhD(submarine geol), 68. *Prof Exp:* Petrol geologist, Chevron Oil Co, 58-63; res asst submarine geol & geophys, Lamont Geol Observ, Columbia Univ, 64-68; investr submarine geol, Woods Hole Oceanog Inst, 68-69; asst prof geol, Middlebury Col, 69-75, actg chmn dept geol & geog, 70; coordr environ assessment, 75-78, CHIEF ATLANTIC & GULF BR MARINE GEOL, US GEOL SURVEY, WOODS HOLE, 78- *Mem:* AAAS; Am Geophys Union; Soc Econ Peleont & Mineral; Geol Soc Am. *Res:* Submarine geology; processes of estuarine, continental shelf and deep sea sedimentation; composition of air and waterborne particulate matter; environmental effects of continental shelf exploitation. *Mailing Add:* Off of Marine Geol US Geol Surv Woods Hole MA 02543

FOLINAS, HELEN, b Montpelier, Vt, June 5, 27. CELL PHYSIOLOGY. *Educ:* Trinity Col, Vt, BS, 52; St Michael's Col, Vt, MS, 59; Fordham Univ, PhD(physiol), 69. *Prof Exp:* From instr to asst prof, 57-71, assoc prof, 71-80, PROF BIOL, TRINITY COL, VT, 80-, CHMN DEPT, 65- *Mem:* AAAS; Am Soc Cell Biol; Am Soc Zool; Am Inst Biol Sci. *Res:* Cell physiology with emphasis on the physiological and cellular aspects of development and inheritance. *Mailing Add:* Dept of Biol Trinity Col Colchester Ave Burlington VT 05401

FOLINSBEE, ROBERT EDWARD, b Edmonton, Alta, Apr 16, 17; m 42; c 4. GEOLOGY. *Educ:* Univ Alta, BSc, 38; Univ Minn, MS, 40, PhD(petrol), 42. *Prof Exp:* Asst geologist, Geol Surv Can, 41-43; from asst prof to assoc prof, 46-55, PROF GEOL, UNIV ALBERTA, 55- *Concurrent Pos:* Pres, 24th Int Geol Cong, Montreal, 72. *Honors & Awards:* The Order of Can, Gov Gen of Can, 73. *Mem:* Geol Soc Am (pres, 76); Soc Econ Geol; Royal Soc Can (pres, 77); Can Inst Mining & Metall; Geol Asn Can. *Res:* Petrology; economic geology; geochemistry. *Mailing Add:* Dept of Geol Univ of Alta Edmonton AB T6G 2E3 Can

FOLK, GEORGE EDGAR, JR, b Natick, Mass, Nov 12, 14; m; c 1. PHYSIOLOGY. *Educ:* Harvard Univ, AB, 37, MA, 40, PhD(biol), 47. *Prof Exp:* Instr biol, St Mark's Sch, 40-43; res assoc, Fatigue Lab, Harvard Univ, 43-47; asst prof biol, Bowdoin Col, 47-52, dir, Bowdoin Sci Sta; assoc prof physiol, 52-65, PROF PHYSIOL, UNIV IOWA, 65- *Concurrent Pos:* Physiologist, Climatic Res Lab, 47; Univ Iowa Col Med res fel, Kings Col, Univ London, 57-58; vis res prof, Arctic Aeromed Lab, Ft Wainwright, Alaska, 64-65; mem, Hibernation Info Exchange, Off Naval Res. *Mem:* AAAS; Am Physiol Soc; Soc Exp Biol & Med; Am Soc Zool; NY Acad Sci. *Res:* Environmental physiology; factors influencing dissipation of heat by the human body and lower animals; mammalian physiology; biological rhythms. *Mailing Add:* Lab of Environ Physiol Dept of Physiol Univ of Iowa Iowa City IA 52242

FOLK, JOHN EDWARD, biochemistry, see previous edition

FOLK, ROBERT LOUIS, b Cleveland, Ohio, Sept 30, 25; m 46; c 3. SEDIMENTARY PETROLOGY. *Educ:* Pa State Col, BS, 46, MS, 50, PhD(mineral), 52. *Prof Exp:* Asst & instr mineral, Pa State Col, 46-50; res geologist, Gulf Res & Develop Co, 51-52; from asst prof to assoc prof geol, 52-61, prof geol, 61-77, J NALLE GREGORY PROF OF SEDIMENTARY GEOL, UNIV TEX, AUSTIN, 77- *Honors & Awards:* WH Twenhofel Medal, Soc Econ Paleontologists & Mineralogists, 79. *Res:* Petrography and genesis of limestones, dolomites, cherts and sandstones; particle size distribution of recent sediments; geomorphology; sedimentary petrology; electron microscopy; texture of carbonate sands; natural history; archaeological geology. *Mailing Add:* Dept of Geol Univ of Tex Austin TX 78712

FOLK, ROBERT THOMAS, b Reading, Pa, Oct 17, 27; m 58; c 3. NUCLEAR PHYSICS. *Educ:* Lehigh Univ, BS, 53 & 54, MS, 55, PhD(physics), 58. *Prof Exp:* Instr physics, Princeton Univ, 57-59, 60-61; NSF fel, Ger, 59-60; from asst prof to assoc prof, 61-66, PROF PHYSICS, LEHIGH UNIV, 66- *Mem:* Am Phys Soc. *Res:* Theoretical nuclear physics. *Mailing Add:* Dept of Physics Lehigh Univ Bethlehem PA 18015

FOLK, THEODORE LAMSON, b Aurora, Ill, June 19, 40. ANALYTICAL CHEMISTRY. *Educ:* Knox Col, Ill, BA, 62; Univ Ariz, MS, 65; Univ Hawaii, PhD(org chem), 68. *Prof Exp:* Res chem, Univ Ariz, 62-64 & Univ Hawaii, 65-68; SR RES CHEMIST, GOODYEAR TIRE & RUBBER CO, 68- *Mem:* Am Chem Soc; Am Soc Mass Spectrometry; Sigma Xi. *Res:* Addition reactions of organolithium compounds on acetylenic systems; synthetic studies of polyhydroxynaphthoquinones; mass spectrometry of organic compounds. *Mailing Add:* Res Div Goodyear Tire & Rubber 142 Goodyear Blvd Akron OH 44316

FOLK, WILLIAM ROBERT, b Little Rock, Ark, July 4, 44; m 66; c 2. BIOCHEMICAL GENETICS. *Educ:* Rice Univ, BA, 66; Stanford Univ, PhD(biochem), 71. *Prof Exp:* Helen Hay Whitney fel, Imp Cancer Res Fund, London, 71-73; asst prof, 73-75, ASSOC PROF BIOL CHEM, UNIV MICH, ANN ARBOR, 75- *Mem:* Am Soc Microbiol; Genetics Soc Am; Am Soc Biol Chemists. *Res:* Structure and function of nucleic acids and of macromolecules which regulate gene expression. *Mailing Add:* Dept of Biol Chem Univ of Mich Med Sch Ann Arbor MI 48104

FOLKERS, KARL AUGUST, b Decatur, Ill, Sept 1, 06; m 32; c 2. CHEMISTRY. *Educ:* Univ Ill, BS, 28; Univ Wis, PhD(org chem), 31. *Hon Degrees:* ScD, Philadelphia Col Pharm, 62; Univ Wis, 69; DPharm, Univ Uppsala, 69; DSc, Univ Ill, 73. *Prof Exp:* Squibb & Lilly res fel, Yale Univ, 31-34; lab pure res, Merck & Co, Inc, 34-38, asst dir res, 38-45, dir org & biol chem res div, 53-56, exec dir fundamental res, 56-62, vpres explor res, 62-63; pres, Stanford Res Inst, 63-68; ASHBEL SMITH PROF CHEM & DIR INST BIOMED RES, UNIV TEX, AUSTIN, 68- *Concurrent Pos:* Mem div 9, Nat Defense Res Comt, 43-46; Harrison-Howe lectr, 49; Baker nonresident lectr, Cornell Univ, 53; lectr med fac, Lund, Stockholm, Uppsala Gothenborg Univs, Sweden, 54; Sturmer lectr, 57; chmn adv coun, Dept Chem, Princeton Univ, 58-64; guest lectr, Am-Swiss Found Sci Exchange, 61; Robert A Welch Found lectr, 63; courtesy prof, Stanford Univ, 63-; courtesy lectr, Univ Calif, Berkeley, 63-; Marchon vis lectr, Univ Newcastle, 64; F F Nord lectr, Fordham Univ, 71; mem rev comt, US Pharmacopoeia. *Honors & Awards:* Co-recipient, Mead Johnson & Co Award, 40 & 49; Presidential Cert of Merit, 48; Merck & Co, Inc Award, 51; Spencer Award, 59; Perkin Medal, 60; co-recipient, Van Meter Prize, Am Thyroid Asn, 69; Robert A Welch Int Award, 72; APhA Achievement Award, 74. *Mem:* Nat Acad Sci; AAAS; Am Soc Biol Chem; Am Inst Chemists; Am Inst Nutrit. *Res:* Organic chemistry; catalytic hydrogenation; pyrimidine; alkaloids; vitamins; synthetic medicinals; antibiotics; hormones; coenzymes. *Mailing Add:* 6406 Mesa Dr Austin TX 78731

FOLKERT, JAY ERNEST, b Holland, Mich, Dec 16, 16; m 46; c 3. MATHEMATICS. *Educ:* Hope Col, AB, 39; Univ Mich, MA, 40; Mich State Univ, PhD(math), 55. *Prof Exp:* Teacher pub schs, 40-42, 46; chmn, Dept Math, 57-71, prof math, Hope Col, 46-81; EMER PROF MATH, HOPE COL, 82- *Mem:* Math Asn Am; Am Math Soc; Am Sci Affil; Nat Coun Teachers Math. *Res:* General mathematics; education. *Mailing Add:* Dept Math Hope Col Holland MI 49423

FOLKERTS, GEORGE WILLIAM, b Beardstown, Ill, Nov 26, 38; m 65; c 2. HERPETOLOGY, AQUATIC COLEOPTERA. *Educ:* Southern Ill Univ, BA, 61, MA, 63; Auburn Univ, PhD(zool), 68. *Prof Exp:* Instr zool, Auburn Univ, 66-68; asst prof, Clemson Univ, 68-69; from asst prof to assoc prof, 69-77, ALUMNI PROF ZOOL, AUBURN UNIV, 77- *Mem:* Soc Study Org Evolution; Sigma Xi; Coleopterists Soc. *Res:* Systematics and ecology of reptiles and amphibians; systematics and ecology of aquatic coleoptera; ecology of southeastern bogs. *Mailing Add:* Dept of Zool/Entom Auburn Univ Auburn AL 36830

FOLKERTS, THOMAS MASON, b Peoria, Ill, Sept 5, 26; m 48; c 7. VETERINARY MICROBIOLOGY. *Educ:* Univ Ill, BS, 50 & 52, DVM(vet med), 54. *Prof Exp:* Practr vet med, Wes-Lyn Animal Hosp, Ill, 54-61; teaching asst animal health & feeding, Southern Ill Univ, 61-62; field vet tech serv, 63-65, mgr, 65-66, head field res, 66-68, head vet res, 68-79, HEAD INT ANIMAL SCI FIELD RES, ELI LILLY & CO, 79- *Mem:* Am Soc Microbiol; AAAS; Am Vet Med Asn; Am Asn Bovine Practr; Am Col Vet Toxicologists. *Res:* Compound screening and testing for useful antibacterial and antiviral activity; target species toxicology of drugs being developed for animal agriculture; resistance studies on antibiotic compounds used and developed for animal agriculture; field evaluation of animal health products. *Mailing Add:* 8100 Allisonville Rd Indianapolis IN 46250

FOLKMAN, MOSES JUDAH, b Cleveland, Ohio, Feb 24, 33; m 60; c 1. SURGERY. *Educ:* Ohio State Univ, BA, 53; Harvard Med Sch, MD, 57; Am Bd Surg, dipl, 66; Am Bd Thoracic Surg, dipl, 68. *Prof Exp:* From intern to chief resident surg, Mass Gen Hosp, 57-65; instr, 65-66, assoc, 66-67, prof surg, Harvard Med Sch, 67-77, SURGEON-INCHIEF, CHILDREN'S HOSP MED CTR, 77- JULIA DYCKMAN ANDRUS PROF PEDIAT SURG, 68- *Concurrent Pos:* Nat Cancer Inst res career develop award, 65-70; surgeon & chief, Children's Hosp Med Ctr, 68- *Mem:* NY Acad Sci. *Res:* Tissue culture; diffusion of drugs and administration of anesthetics through silicone rubber; cancer research. *Mailing Add:* Children's Hosp Med Ctr 300 Longwood Ave Boston MA 02115

FOLKS, HOMER CLIFTON, b Hydro, Okla, Aug 6, 23; m 50; c 3. SOILS. *Educ:* Okla State Univ, BS, 50; Iowa State Univ, PhD(soils), 54. *Prof Exp:* Instr soils, Iowa State Univ, 53-54, exten area agronomist, 54-55; asst prof soils, NC State Col, 55-58, assoc prof, 58-59, asst dir instr, 59-63; assoc dean, Col Agr, 63-80, PROF AGRON, UNIV MO-COLUMBIA, 63- *Mem:* Am Soc Agron. *Res:* Soil genesis and morphology; mechanics of soil profile development. *Mailing Add:* Dept Agr Univ Mo 143 Mumford Hall Columbia MO 65201

FOLKS, JOHN LEROY, b Hydro, Okla, Oct 12, 29; m 56; c 4. ANALYTICAL STATISTICS, APPLIED STATISTICS. *Educ:* Okla State Univ, BA, 53, MS, 55; Iowa State Univ, PhD(statist), 58. *Prof Exp:* Scientist opers res, Tex Instruments, Inc, 58-60, mgr opers res, 60-61; assoc prof math & statist, Okla State Univ, 61-67, chmn statist unit, 69-73, PROF MATH & STATIST, OKLA STATE UNIV, 67-, CHMN STATIST DEPT, 73- *Concurrent Pos:* NSF sci fac fel, Univ Calif, Berkeley, 66-67. *Mem:* Fel Am Statist Asn; Inst Math Statist; Biomet Soc. *Res:* Significance testing. *Mailing Add:* Statist Dept Okla State Univ Stillwater OK 74075

FOLLAND, GERALD BUDGE, b Salt Lake City, Utah, June 4, 47. MATHEMATICS. *Educ:* Harvard Univ, BA, 68; Princeton Univ, MA, 70, PhD(math), 71. *Prof Exp:* Instr math, Courant Inst, NY Univ, 71-73; from asst prof to assoc prof, 73-80, PROF MATH, UNIV WASH, 80- *Concurrent Pos:* Vis asst prof math, Princeton Univ, 74; vis mem, Inst Advan Study, 79; vis prof, Tata Inst Fundamental Res, 81. *Mem:* Am Math Soc; Math Asn Am. *Res:* Partial differential equations and Fourier analysis. *Mailing Add:* Dept of Math Univ of Wash Seattle WA 98195

FOLLAND, NATHAN ORLANDO, b Greenbush, Minn, Jan 12, 37; m 60; c 2. PHYSICS. *Educ:* Concordia Col, BA, 59; Iowa State Univ, PhD(physics), 65. *Prof Exp:* NATO fel, Univ Messina, 65-66; asst prof physics, 66-72, ASSOC PROF PHYSICS, KANS STATE UNIV, 73- *Mem:* Am Phys Soc. *Res:* Theoretical solid state physics; band theory; transport; optical properties. *Mailing Add:* Dept of Physics Kans State Univ Manhattan KS 66502

FOLLETT, ROY HUNTER, b Cowdrey, Colo, Feb 27, 35; m 59; c 2. AGRONOMY, SOIL SCIENCE. *Educ:* Colo State Univ, BS, 57, MS, 63, PhD(soil sci), 69. *Prof Exp:* Soil scientist, US Geol Surv, Norton, Kans, 57-58, Soil Conserv Serv, Ft Collins, Colo, 58-60, 63-64; jr agronomist, Colo State Univ, 60-63, exten agronomist soils, 64-70; asst prof, Ohio State Univ, 70-74; from assoc prof to prof soils, Kans State Univ, 74-81; PROF SOILS, COLO STATE UNIV, 81- *Concurrent Pos:* Assoc ed, J of Agron, ed, 78. *Mem:* Am Soc Agron; Soil Sci Soc Am; Soil Conserv Soc Am; Sigma Xi. *Res:* Soil fertility, fertilizer materials, rates and time of application; conservation tillage and reduced tillage system. *Mailing Add:* Dept of Agron Colo State Univ Ft Collins KS 80523

FOLLETT, WILBUR IRVING, b Newark, NJ, Mar 10, 01; m 29. ICHTHYOLOGY. *Educ:* Univ Calif, Berkeley, AB, 24, JD, 26. *Prof Exp:* Asst ichthyol, Calif State Fish & Game Comn, 26; from actg cur to cur, 47-69, EMER CUR ICHTHYOL, CALIF ACAD SCI, 70- *Concurrent Pos:* Atty at law, 27-; deleg, Int Cong Zool & Colloquium Zool Nomenclature Denmark, 53. *Mem:* Soc Syst Zool (pres, 60); Am Soc Ichthyologists & Herpetologists (pres, 69). *Res:* Nomenclature, taxonomy, osteology and distribution of California fishes; identification of fish remains from archaeological sites. *Mailing Add:* Calif Acad Sci Golden Gate Park San Francisco CA 94118

FOLLOWS, ALAN GREAVES, b Normanton, Eng, Dec 20, 21; nat US; m 50; c 3. CHEMISTRY. *Educ:* Queen's Univ, Can, BSc, 44, MSc, 45; Univ Toronto, PhD(elec), 48. *Prof Exp:* Chem res, Nat Res Coun Can, Queen's Univ, 44-45; lectr phys chem, Univ Toronto, 47-48; res chemist, Solvay Process Div, 48-59, asst dir res, 59-69, mgr technol, 69-72; mgr tech serv, Indust Chem Div, Allied Chem Corp, 72-79; PRES, NEOS CHEM CORP, 79- *Mem:* Am Chem Soc. *Res:* Electrochemistry; industrial research and management; titanium; alkalies. *Mailing Add:* NEOS Chem Corp Box 201 Camillus NY 13031

FOLLSTAD, MERLE NORMAN, b Milwaukee, Wis, May 14, 31; m 63; c 2. BOTANY. *Educ:* Univ Wis, BS, 55; Univ Minn, MS, 61, PhD(plant path), 64. *Prof Exp:* Res asst, Inst Paper Chem, Lawrence Univ, 56-58; res asst plant path, Univ Minn, 58-64; res plant pathologist, Mkt Qual Res Div, US Dept Agr, 64-66; res assoc, NC State Univ, 66-67; microbiologist, Northern Regional Res Lab, Ill, 67-68; ASST PROF BIOL, UNIV WIS, WHITEWATER, 68- *Mem:* AAAS; Botanical Soc Am; Am Inst Biol Sci; Am Forestry Asn. *Res:* Developmental anatomy of seed plants; plant histochemistry. *Mailing Add:* Rte 4 Whitewater WI 53190

FOLLSTAEDT, DAVID MARTIN, b Haskell, Tex, Aug 18, 47; m 71. SOLID STATE PHYSICS. *Educ:* Tex Technol Univ, BS, 69; Univ Ill, MS, 70, PhD(physics), 75. *Prof Exp:* Staff mem, nuclear magnetic resonance, 74-76, STAFF MEM, ION IMPLANTATION, SANDIA NAT LABS, 76- *Concurrent Pos:* NSF fel, 69-70. *Mem:* Am Phys Soc. *Res:* Nuclear magnetic resonance in metals (pure and with magnetic impurities), and in superionic conductors; ion implantation in metals; electron microscopy; laser and electron beam pulsed melting of solids. *Mailing Add:* Div 5111 Sandia Nat Labs Albuquerque NM 87185

FOLLWEILER, DOUGLAS MACARTHUR, b Allentown, Pa, June 28, 42; m 64; c 2. ANALYTICAL CHEMISTRY. *Educ:* Muhlenberg Col, BS, 64; Univ Pa, PhD(org chem), 68. *Prof Exp:* Fel org chem, Princeton Univ, 68-69; ENGR ANAL CHEM, BETHLEHEM STEEL CORP, 69- *Mem:* Sigma Xi. *Res:* Gas chromatography; liquid chromatography; minicomputers and analysis of industrial pollutants. *Mailing Add:* Homer Res Labs Bethelem Steel Corp Bethlehem PA 18016

FOLLWEILER, JOANNE SCHAAF, b Philadelphia, Pa, Aug 8, 42; m 64; c 2. ORGANIC CHEMISTRY. *Educ:* Muhlenberg Col, BS, 64; Univ Pa, MS, 68, PhD(chem), 77. *Prof Exp:* Libr chemist, E I du Pont de Nemours & Co, Inc, 64-66; lab asst chem, Radiocarbon Lab, Univ Pa, 66-67; consult, FMC Corp, 68; instr, Mercer County Community Col, 68-69; ASST PROF CHEM, LAFAYETTE COL, 70- *Res:* Organo-sulfur compounds; organometallic compounds. *Mailing Add:* Dept of Chem Lafayette Col Easton PA 18042

FOLSE, DEAN SYDNEY, b Kansas City, Mo, Dec 19, 21; m 47. VETERINARY PATHOLOGY, VETERINARY PARASITOLOGY. *Educ:* Agr & Mech Col, Univ Tex, BS & DVM, 45; Kans State Col, MS, 46; Univ Tex, PhD, 70. *Prof Exp:* Asst prof path, Ala Polytech Inst, 48-50, assoc prof, 50-52; assoc prof, Kans State Univ, 52-66; US AEC histopathologist, Inst Biol & Agr, Seibersdorf Reactor Ctr, Austria, 66-68; res instr path, 69-71, RES ASST PROF PATH, UNIV TEX MED BR GALVESTON, 71- *Mem:* AAAS; Am Soc Parasitol; Am Vet Med Asn. *Mailing Add:* Dept of Path Univ of Tex Med Br Galveston TX 77550

FOLSE, RAYMOND FRANCIS, JR, b New Orleans, La, Sept 4, 40; m 74; c 1. FLUID DYNAMICS. *Educ:* Loyola Univ South, BS, 63; La State Univ, PhD(physics), 68. *Prof Exp:* Vis asst prof physics, La State Univ, 68; asst prof, 68-70, ASSOC PROF PHYSICS, UNIV SOUTHERN MISS, 70- *Concurrent Pos:* NSF teacher proj dir, NSF & Univ Southern Miss, 74-75. *Mem:* Am Phys Soc; AAAS; Sigma Xi. *Res:* The effects of unsteady flows in density stratified fluids studied experimentally in order to determine the importance of buoyant forces to various geophysical phenomena. *Mailing Add:* Dept of Physics & Astron Box 9198 Univ of Southern Miss Hattiesburg MS 39401

FOLSOM, CLARENCE B(URTON), JR, b Denver, Colo, June 14, 17; m 41; c 2. PETROLEUM ENGINEERING. *Educ:* Colo Sch Mines, MSc(petrol MSc, 52. *Prof Exp:* Petrol engr, Phillips Petrol Co, 41-46; head petrol eng dept, NMex Sch Mines, 47-53; CHIEF PETROL ENGR, STATE GEOL SURV, N DAK, 53-; ASSOC PROF GEOL, UNIV N DAK, 70- *Res:* Oil and gas reserves; oil and gas conservation; secondary recovery of oil and gas. *Mailing Add:* Dept of Geol Univ of NDak Grand Forks ND 58202

FOLSOM, RICHARD G(ILMAN), b Los Angeles, Calif, Feb 3, 07; m 29; c 3. MECHANICAL ENGINEERING, AERONAUTICAL ENGINEERING. *Educ:* Calif Inst Technol, BS, 28, MS, 29, PhD(mech eng), 32. *Hon Degrees:* DSc, Northwestern Univ, 62, Union Col, 64, Albany Med Col, 71 & Lehigh Univ, 72; DEng, Rose Polytech Inst, 71; LLD, Rensselaer Polytech Inst, 73. *Prof Exp:* Engr, Pasadena, Calif, 32-33; instr mech eng, Dept Eng, Univ Calif, Berkeley, 33-37, from asst prof to prof, 37-53, chmn div mech eng, 48-53; prof & dir eng res inst, Univ Mich, 53-58; pres, 58-71, EMER PRES, RENSSELAER POLYTECH INST, 71- *Concurrent Pos:* Staff engr, Jet Propulsion Lab, Calif Inst Technol, 43-44; pvt pract, 71-; counr, Nat Acad Eng, 75-78. *Mem:* Nat Acad Eng; hon mem Am Soc Mech Engrs (pres, 72-73); hon mem Am Soc Eng Educ; assoc fel Inst Aeronaut & Astronaut; Am Inst Chem Engrs. *Res:* Pumps; fluid metering; fluid flow and heat transfer at low pressures; fundamental fluid mechanics; mechanical equipment. *Mailing Add:* 585 Oakville Crossroad Napa CA 94558

FOLSOM, THEODORE ROBERT, b San Diego, Calif, Mar 20, 08; m 35; c 2. PHYSICS, OCEANOGRAPHY. *Educ:* Calif Inst Technol, BS, 31, MS, 32; Univ Calif, PhD(phys oceanog), 52. *Prof Exp:* Asst physicist, Soiland Clin, 33 & Lincoln Gen Hosp, 33-36; assoc physicist, Mem Hosp, 37-42; physicist, Mass Inst Technol, 42-44 & Food Mach Corp, 44-45; pvt consult, 46-52; asst res oceanographer, 52-59, sr engr, 59-64, res oceanographer, 64-75, RECALLED STATUS, SCRIPPS INST OCEANOG, UNIV CALIF, 75- *Mem:* AAAS. *Res:* Techniques in oceanography and radiology, particularly measurements traces fallout radioactivity in marine environment, especially by gamma and alpha spectrometry. *Mailing Add:* Scripps Inst Oceanog Univ of Calif at San Diego La Jolla CA 92093

FOLSOME, CLAIR EDWIN, b Ann Arbor, Mich, June 26, 35; m 56; c 4. MICROBIAL GENETICS, EXOBIOLOGY. *Educ:* Harvard Univ, AB, 56, MS, 59, PhD(biol), 60. *Prof Exp:* Res asst prof genetics, Grad Sch Med, Boston Univ, 60-62; sr lectr, Univ Melbourne, 62-64; assoc prof, 64-67, PROF MICROBIOL, UNIV HAWAII, 67- *Concurrent Pos:* Nat Res Coun sr res assoc, Ames Res Ctr, NASA, 70-71. *Mem:* AAAS; Genetics Soc Am; Am

Chem Soc; fel Brit Interplanetary Soc; Int Soc for Study Origin Life. *Res:* Analysis of extraterrestrial organic matter; origin of life and origin of the genetic code, synthetic protocells and organic matter in meteorites. *Mailing Add:* Dept of Microbiol Lab Exobiol Univ of Hawaii Honolulu HI 96822

FOLT, V(ERNON) L(OUIS), b Minneapolis, Minn, Aug 2, 18; m 46; c 5. POLYMER SCIENCE. *Educ:* Univ Minn, BChE, 41. *Prof Exp:* Res chemist, 41-60, SR RES ASSOC, RES CTR, B F GOODRICH CO, 60- *Mem:* AAAS; Soc Rheol; Am Chem Soc; Soc Plastics Engrs; Am Inst Chemists. *Res:* Rheology; structure and properties of polymers. *Mailing Add:* Res Ctr B F Goodrich Co Brecksville OH 44141

FOLTS, DWIGHT DAVID, b Fillmore, NY, Mar 24, 47; m 71; c 2. ENTOMOLOGY. *Educ:* State Univ NY Col Environ Sci & Forestry, BS, 69, MS, 73. *Prof Exp:* sr biologist entomol, 72-77, SYSTS ANALYST/PROGRAMMER, AGR CHEM GROUP, FMC CORP, 77- *Mem:* Entomol Soc Am; Ecol Soc Am; Acarological Soc Am; Data Retrieval Syst Users Soc (pres, 80-82). *Res:* Screening of chemicals for potential use as insecticides and miticides; studies on the effects of organic pesticides on soil microarthropods. *Mailing Add:* Agr Chem Group FMC Corp 100 Niagara St Middleport NY 14105

FOLTZ, CALVIN MARTIN, b Akron, Pa, Nov 29, 24; m 53; c 2. ORGANIC CHEMISTRY, MEDICINAL CHEMISTRY. *Educ:* Philadelphia Col Pharm, BSc, 48, MSc, 49; Purdue Univ, PhD(med chem), 54. *Prof Exp:* Res fel, 55-56, RES CHEMIST, LAB CHEM, NAT INST ARTHRITIS, DIABETES, DIGESTIVE & KIDNEY DIS, NIH, USPHS, 56- *Res:* Synthesis of adrenergic blocking agents; stereochemistry; chemistry of amino acids, peptides and proteins; characterization of Factor 3, a source of selenium in deficiency diseases; heterocyclic chemistry; photochemistry; biology of metastasis. *Mailing Add:* 3938 Rickover Rd Silver Springs MD 20902

FOLTZ, CRAIG BILLIG, b Shamokin, Pa, June 28, 52; m 80; c 1. ASTRONOMICAL INSTRUMENTATION. *Educ:* Dartmouth Col, AB, 74; Ohio State Univ, PhD(astron), 79. *Prof Exp:* Fel, Dept Astron, Ohio State Univ, 79-80, instr, Dept Physics, 80, res assoc, Dept Astron, 81-82; FEL, STEWARD OBSERV, UNIV ARIZ, 81- *Mem:* Am Astron Soc; NY Acad Sci. *Res:* Analysis of emission-line spectra of active galactic nuclei and quasars; development of astronomical spectrophotometers; problems in quasar absorption-line spectra; development of software for instrument control and data handling. *Mailing Add:* Steward Observ Univ Ariz Tucson AZ 85721

FOLTZ, ELDON LEROY, b Ft Collins, Colo, Mar 28, 19; m 43; c 4. NEUROSURGERY. *Educ:* Mich State Col, BS, 41; Univ Mich, MD, 43. *Prof Exp:* Asst resident surg, Univ Mich, 46-47; neurosurg resident, Med Sch, Dartmouth Col, 47-49; clin asst, Univ Louisville, 49-50; NIMH fel & res assoc surg, Univ Wash, 50-51, from instr to prof neurosurg, 51-69; chmn div, 69-77, PROF NEUROL SURG, UNIV CALIF, IRVINE-CALIF COL MED, 69-, CHIEF NEUROL SURG, 77- *Concurrent Pos:* Markle scholar, 54. *Mem:* Am Asn Neurol Surg; Am EEG Soc; Am Col Surgeons; Am Acad Neurologists; Am Acad Neurol Surgeons. *Res:* Cerebral concussion; consciousness; cerebral vascular disease; central factors of psychosomatic diseases; hydrocephalus. *Mailing Add:* Irvine Med Ctr Univ Calif 101 City Dr S Orange CA 92668

FOLTZ, FLOYD MATHEW, b Mitchell, SDak, Feb 27, 27; m 48; c 2. ANATOMY. *Educ:* Dakota Wesleyan Univ, BS, 51; Univ SDak, MA, 54; Univ Kans, PhD, 58. *Prof Exp:* Instr anat, Univ Kans, 57-58; asst prof, Univ SDak, 58-65; assoc prof, 65-72, PROF ANAT, SCH MED, MED CTR, UNIV KANS, 72- *Mem:* Am Asn Anat. *Res:* Comparative neuroanatomy. *Mailing Add:* Dept of Anat Univ of Kans Med Ctr Kansas City KS 66103

FOLTZ, GEORGE EDWARD, b Pittsburgh, Pa, May 20, 24; m 45, 55; c 2. SYNTHETIC ORGANIC CHEMISTRY. *Educ:* Carnegie Inst Technol, BS, 47, MS, 51, PhD(chem), 52. *Prof Exp:* Control chemist resins & solvents, Neville Co, 47-48; sr res chemist, Explor Org, Columbia-Southern Chem Corp, 52-54; asst chemist, 54-80, MGR, PROD DEVELOP & ANAL LABS, NEVILLE CHEM CO, 80- *Res:* Polymer chemistry; antioxidants; ultraviolet stabilizers. *Mailing Add:* 339 Goldsmith Rd Pittsburgh PA 15237

FOLTZ, NEVIN D, b Akron, Pa, Feb 12, 40; m 65; c 2. MOLECULAR PHYSICS. *Educ:* Pa State Univ, BSc, 62, MSc, 64, PhD(physics), 68. *Prof Exp:* Instr physics, Commonwealth Campus, Pa State Univ, 64-66; asst prof, 68-74, ASSOC PROF PHYSICS, MEM UNIV, NFLD, 74- *Mem:* Optical Soc Am; Am Inst Physics; Am Phys Soc. *Res:* Stimulated light scattering from liquids and gases; dye lasers; nonlinear optics techniques for Raman spectroscopy. *Mailing Add:* Dept of Physics Mem Univ of Nfld St John's NF A1C 5S7 Can

FOLTZ, RODGER L, b Milwaukee, Wis, Feb 10, 34; m 56; c 2. ANALYTICAL CHEMISTRY, MASS SPECTROMETRY. *Educ:* Mass Inst Technol, 56; Univ Wis, PhD(org chem), 61. *Prof Exp:* sr res leader chem, Battelle-Columbus Labs, 61-79; ASSOC DIR, CTR HUMAN TOXICOL, UNIV UTAH, 79-, RES ASSOC PROF, COL PHARMACOL, 80- *Concurrent Pos:* Adj prof, Col Pharm, Ohio State Univ, 72-76, adj assoc prof, Col Med, 76- *Mem:* Am Chem Soc; Am Soc Mass Spectrometry; Royal Soc Chem. *Res:* Application of mass spectrometry to analysis of organic and biochemical materials. *Mailing Add:* Ctr Human Toxicology Univ Utah Salt Lake City UT 84112

FOLTZ, THOMAS ROBERTS, JR, b Philadelphia, Pa, July 8, 20; m 45; c 2. ENVIRONMENTAL SCIENCES. *Educ:* Philadelphia Col Pharm, BS, 42; Temple Univ, AM, 52. *Prof Exp:* Mem staff, Gulf Refining Co, 41; res chemist, Philadelphia Quartz Co, 42-46; instr textile chem, Philadelphia Textile Inst, 46-49, asst prof, 49-54; chief chemist & dir chem res, Lockport Felt Co, 54-63; prod mgr, Armour Food Co, Collagen & Protein Specialties, 63-75, opers specialist, fresh meats div, 75-80; CHIEF CHEMIST, WASTE WATER TREAT DIV, CITY PHOENIX, 81- *Mem:* Am Chem Soc; fel Am Inst Chemists; Am Leather Chem Asn; Inst Food Technologists; AAAS. *Res:* Analytical methodology of textile chemistry; wool protein; denaturation; wool fabric finishing; leather chemistry, by-product utilization, meat or poultry; microwave, collagen and protein technology; rendering technology; hazardous wastes techology and testing. *Mailing Add:* 7726 E Oak St Scottsdale AZ 85257

FOLTZ, VIRGINIA C, b Ashtabula, Ohio, Aug 3, 11; m 33; c 2. RADIATION BIOLOGY, GENETICS. *Educ:* Baldwin-Wallace Col, BS, 33; Univ Houston, MS, 67; Tex Woman's Univ, PhD(radiation biol), 69. *Prof Exp:* Instr biol, Univ Houston, 63-64; asst prof zool, La Polytech Univ, 69-70; asst prof, 70-73, ASSOC PROF BIOL, PAN AM UNIV, 73- *Concurrent Pos:* Vis sci consult, Southern Asn, 74 & 77. *Mem:* AAAS; Genetics Soc Am. *Res:* Neonatal birth defects in lower Rio-Grande Valley of Texas; nutritional studies; mutogenic effects of specific fluorinated hydrocarbons found in polluted air; radiation mutation studies. *Mailing Add:* Dept Biol Pan Am Univ Edinburg TX 78539

FOLWEILER, ROBERT COOPER, b Tallahassee, Fla, Aug 2, 33; m 61; c 3. MATERIALS SCIENCE. *Educ:* Rice Univ, BA, 55, BS, 56, MS, 58. *Prof Exp:* Res asst metall, Rice Univ, 56-58; metallurgist ceramics, Gen Elec Res Lab, 59-61; sr scientist, Res & Adv Develop Div, Avco Corp, 61; vpres & lab dir, Lexington Labs, Inc, 61-68; mgr mat technol, Defensive Systs Div, Sanders Assocs, Inc, 68-79; sr mat scientist, Microwave Assocs, Inc, 79-80; PRIN INVESTR, GEN TEL ELEC LABS INC, 80- *Concurrent Pos:* Vis scientist, Mass Inst Technol, 69-74. *Mem:* Am Asn Crystal Growth; Am Ceramic Soc; AAAS; Sigma Xi. *Res:* Investigation of optical communication fiber preparation and properties; crystal growth solution and vapor phase techniques; development of process control for materials preparation; investigation of new laser hosts; high temperature materials technology. *Mailing Add:* Gen Tel Elec Labs Inc 40 Sylvan Rd Waltham NH 02254

FOLZ, SYLVESTER D, b Marshfield, Wis, Feb 26, 41; m 62; c 3. VETERINARY PARASITOLOGY, MEDICAL PARASITOLOGY. *Educ:* Univ Wis, BS, 64, MS, 66, PhD(parasitol), 68. *Prof Exp:* Res asst parasitol, Univ Wis, 64-66, asst, 66-68; res assoc, 68-69, scientist, 69-72, sr res scientist, 72-75, RES HEAD, UPJOHN CO, 75- *Concurrent Pos:* Ed, Int J Vet Parasitol, 75- *Mem:* Am Soc Parasitol; Am Soc Protozool; Am Heartworm Soc; Wildlife Dis Asn; Australian Soc Parasitologists. *Res:* Helminthology; protozoology; coccidiosis; malaria; helminth studies in man and animals; veterinary and medical entomology. *Mailing Add:* The Upjohn Co Kalamazoo MI 49001

FOMON, SAMUEL JOSEPH, b Chicago, Ill, Mar 9, 23; m 48; c 5. PEDIATRICS, NUTRITION. *Educ:* Harvard Univ, AB, 45; Univ Pa, MD, 47. *Hon Degrees:* Dr, Cath Univ Cordoba, Arg, 74. *Prof Exp:* Resident pediat, Philadelphia Children's Hosp, 48-50; Res Found fel biochem, Cincinnati Children's Hosp, 50-52; from asst prof to assoc prof pediat, 54-60, PROF PEDIAT, UNIV IOWA, 60- *Concurrent Pos:* USPHS career develop award, 62-67; consult nutrit, Bur Community Health Serv, Health Serv Admin, 65-81; chmn sect II, panel 2, White House Conf on Food, Nutrit & Health, 69; vpres, 12th Int Cong Nutrit, 81. *Honors & Awards:* Borden Award, Am Acad Pediat, 66; Rosen von Rosenstein Medal, Swed Pediat Asn, 74; McCollum Award, Am Soc Clin Nutrit, 79; Award F Cuenca Villoro Found, Zaragoza, Spain, 81. *Mem:* Am Acad Pediat; Am Pub Health Asn; Soc Pediat Res; Am Pediat Soc; Am Inst Nutrit. *Res:* Infant nutrition, growth, and body composition. *Mailing Add:* Dept of Pediat Univ of Iowa Hosps Iowa City IA 52242

FONAROFF, LEONARD SCHUYLER, b Philadelphia, Pa, Nov 30, 28; m 51. BIOGEOGRAPHY. *Educ:* Univ Ariz, BA, 55; Johns Hopkins Univ, PhD(geog), 61. *Prof Exp:* From instr to asst prof anthrop & int health, Johns Hopkins Univ, 59-63; from asst prof to assoc prof geog, Calif State Univ, Northridge, 63-67; assoc prof, 67-69, PROF GEOG, UNIV MD, COLLEGE PARK, 69- *Concurrent Pos:* Clin assoc prof community med & int health, Med Sch, Georgetown Univ, 68-76; mem subcomt geochem environ & health & dis, Nat Comt Geochem, Nat Acad Sci, 70-72. *Mem:* Asn Am Geogr; Am Anthrop Asn; Brit Ornith Union; Int Soc Tropical Ecol; Am Geog Soc. *Res:* Disease ecology; zoogeography; animal ecology; man-environment relationships, especially adaption and faunal change. *Mailing Add:* Dept of Geog Univ of Md College Park MD 20742

FONASH, STEPHAN J(OSEPH), b Philadelphia, Pa, Oct 28, 41; m 68; c 1. SOLID STATE ELECTRONICS, ENERGY CONVERSION. *Educ:* Pa State Univ, BS, 63; Univ Pa, PhD(eng), 68. *Prof Exp:* Fel surface physics, Univ Pa, 68; asst prof eng sci, 68-77, PROF ENG SCI, ENG SCI PROG, PA STATE UNIV, 77- *Concurrent Pos:* NASA fac fel, Jet Propulsion Lab, 70; vis mem tech staff, Bell Tel Labs, Murray Hill, 72; vis fac mem, Dept Physics, Univ Lyon, France, 73. *Mem:* Am Phys Soc; sr mem Inst Elec & Electronics Engrs; Am Vacuum Soc. *Res:* Solid state and thin film devices; photovoltaics; interface and bulk phenomena exhibited by materials; solid state sensors. *Mailing Add:* Dept of Eng Sci Pa State Univ University Park PA 16802

FONCK, RAYMOND JOHN, b Joliet, Ill, Nov 1, 51; m 77. ATOMIC PHYSICS, PLASMA PHYSICS. *Educ:* Univ Wis-Madison, BA, 73, PhD(physics), 78. *Prof Exp:* Res asst plasma physics, Dept Astrophys Sci, Princeton Univ, 73-74; NSF fel & res asst physics, Univ Wis-Madison, 74-78; res assoc, 78-80, MEM RES STAFF, PLASMA PHYSICS LAB, PRINCETON UNIV, 80- *Mem:* Am Phys Soc; Optical Soc Am. *Res:* Optical and UV atomic spectroscopy; atomic diamagnetism; spectroscopic instrumentation; plasma diagnostics. *Mailing Add:* Plasma Physics Lab PO Box 451 Princeton NJ 08544

FONDA, MARGARET LEE, b Cleveland, Ohio, July 13, 42; m 76. ENZYMES, COENZYMES. *Educ:* Univ Del, BS, 64; Univ Tenn, Knoxville, PhD(biochem), 68. *Prof Exp:* Res assoc biochem, Iowa State Univ, 68-70; asst prof, 70-76, ASSOC PROF BIOCHEM, SCH MED, UNIV LOUISVILLE,

76- *Concurrent Pos:* NIH res assoc, Iowa State Univ, 69-70. *Mem:* AAAS; Am Soc Biol Chemists; Am Chem Soc. *Res:* Mechanism of enzyme action; interaction of coenzymes and substrates with enzymes; control of enzyme action; metabolism of viatmins and coenzymes. *Mailing Add:* Dept of Biochem Univ of Louisville Sch of Med Louisville KY 40292

FONDA, RICHARD WESTON, b Chicago, Ill, June 14, 40; m 63; c 2. PLANT ECOLOGY. *Educ:* Duke Univ, BA, 62; Univ Ill, MS, 65, PhD(bot), 67. *Prof Exp:* Asst prof biol, Western Ill Univ, 67-68; from asst prof to assoc prof biol, 68-79, PROF BIOL, WESTERN WASH UNIV, 79-, BIOL GRAD PROG DIR, 69- *Concurrent Pos:* Grants, Western Ill Univ Res Coun, 68 & US Forest Serv, 78. *Mem:* Ecol Soc Am; Torrey Bot Club. *Res:* Vegetation ecology in western Washington especially forest, timberline and alpine. *Mailing Add:* Dept of Biol Western Wash Univ Bellingham WA 98225

FONDAHL, JOHN W(ALKER), b Washington, DC, Nov 4, 24; m 46; c 4. CIVIL ENGINEERING. *Educ:* Dartmouth Col, BS, 47, MS, 48. *Prof Exp:* Struct detailer, Bridge Div, Am Bridge Co, 48; from instr to asst prof civil eng, Univ Hawaii, 48-51; engr & estimator heavy construct, Winston Bros Co, 51-52, off engr, 52; proj engr, Nimbus Dam & Powerhouse contract, Al Johnson Construct Co, 53-55; from asst prof to assoc prof, 55-68, PROF CIVIL ENG, STANFORD UNIV, 68- *Concurrent Pos:* Dir, Scott Co, Calif, 63-; pres, Proj Mgt Inst, 74 & 75; chmn bd, 76 & 77, dir, 78-; dir, Caterpillar Tractor Co, 76- *Honors & Awards:* Construct Mgt Award, Am Soc Civil Engrs, 77. *Mem:* Am Soc Civil Engrs. *Res:* Construction engineering; administration; planning and scheduling. *Mailing Add:* Dept of Civil Eng Stanford Univ Stanford CA 94305

FONDY, THOMAS PAUL, b Pittsburgh, Pa, Dec 24, 37; m 63; c 3. BIOCHEMISTRY, CHEMOTHERAPY. *Educ:* Duquesne Univ, BS, 59, PhD(biochem), 61. *Prof Exp:* Fel biochem, Duquesne Univ, 61-62 & Brandeis Univ, 62-65; from asst prof to assoc prof, 65-75, PROF BIOCHEM, SYRACUSE UNIV, 75- *Concurrent Pos:* Res trainee, Nat Inst Neurol Dis & Blindness, 62-65; Nat Cancer Inst career develop award, 72-77; vis prof pharmacol, Yale Univ Sch Med, 75-76. *Mem:* Am Soc Biol Chem; Am Asn Cancer Res. *Res:* carbohydrate analogs in cell membrane directed chemotherapy and chemoimmunotherapy of cancer; in vivo host response to tumor cells modified in vitro; host response modifiers in host-tumor interaction. *Mailing Add:* Dept of Biol Syracuse Univ Syracuse NY 13210

FONER, SAMUEL NEWTON, b New York, NY, Mar 21, 20. CHEMICAL PHYSICS, MASS SPECTROMETRY. *Educ:* Carnegie-Mellon Univ, BS, 40, MS, 41, DSc(physics), 45. *Prof Exp:* Asst physics, Carnegie-Mellon Univ, 40-43, instr, 43-44, res assoc, 44-45; physicist, Appl Physics Lab, 45-, Supvr, Mass Spectrometry Group, 47-52, SUPVR ELECTRONIC PHYSICS GROUP, APPL PHYSICS LAB, JOHNS HOPKINS UNIV,53-, VCHMN, MILTON S EISENHOWER RES CTR, 75- *Concurrent Pos:* Mem comt, Nat Acad Sci-Nat Res Coun; adv, Army Res Off, 61-64. *Honors & Awards:* Phys Sci Award, Wash Acad Sci, 54. *Mem:* AAAS; fel Am Phys Soc; Am Vacuum Soc; Combustion Inst. *Res:* Reaction kinetics, surface science; electron spin resonance; free radicals; molecular beams; electronic physics; scanning electron microscopy; acoustics. *Mailing Add:* Appl Physics Lab Johns Hopkins Univ Laurel MD 20707

FONER, SIMON, b Pittsburgh, Pa, Aug 13, 25; m 55; c 2. SOLID STATE PHYSICS. *Educ:* Carnegie Inst Technol, BS, 47, MS, 48, DSc(physics), 52. *Prof Exp:* Asst physics, Carnegie Inst Technol, 47-52, res physicist, 52-53; physicist, Lincoln Lab, 53-61, group leader, Nat Magnet Lab, 61-63, proj leader magnetism & superconductivity, 71, leader transport & resonance group, 63-77, leader magnetism & superconductivity group, 74-77, CHIEF SCIENTIST & HEAD RES DIV, NAT MAGNET LAB, MASS INST TECHNOL, 77- *Concurrent Pos:* Mem adv comt to Army Res Off, Nat Res Coun, 67-73; dir, NATO Advan Study Inst, 70, 73, 76 & 80. *Mem:* Fel Am Phys Soc. *Res:* Magnetism; high field superconductors; magnetic resonance; high magnetic fields; magnetometry. *Mailing Add:* Nat Magnet Lab Mass Inst of Technol Cambridge MA 02139

FONG, CHING-YAO, b Soochow, China, May 23, 35. SOLID STATE PHYSICS. *Educ:* Nat Taiwan Univ, BS, 58; Univ Calif, Berkeley, MS, 62, PhD(physics), 68. *Prof Exp:* Res physicist, Lawrence Radiation Lab, Univ Calif, Berkeley, 68; asst prof, 69-74, assoc prof, 74-78, PROF PHYSICS, UNIV CALIF, DAVIS, 78- *Concurrent Pos:* Vis scientist, Argonne Nat Lab, 80. *Mem:* Am Phys Soc. *Res:* Optical properties of solids; semiconductor alloys; amorphous semiconductor. *Mailing Add:* Dept of Physics Univ of Calif Davis CA 95616

FONG, FRANCIS K, b Shanghai, China, Mar 21, 38; m 63; c 2. CHEMICAL PHYSICS, BIOPHYSICS. *Educ:* Princeton Univ, AB, 59, PhD(chem), 62. *Prof Exp:* Res assoc, Princeton Univ, 62-63; mem tech staff, RCA Labs, 63-64 & NAm Aviation Sci Ctr, Calif, 64-68; assoc prof, 68-71, PROF CHEM, PURDUE UNIV, 71- *Mem:* Am Chem Soc; Am Phys Soc. *Res:* Photochemistry; primary light reaction in photosynthesis; radiationless processes in large molecules; chlorophyll chemistry; theory of molecular relaxation; solid state chemical physics. *Mailing Add:* Dept of Chem Purdue Univ West Lafayette IN 47907

FONG, FRANKLIN, b San Francisco, Calif, Apr 16, 47. PLANT PHYSIOLOGY. *Educ:* Univ Calif, Davis, BS, 69; Univ Calif, Riverside, PhD(biol), 75. *Prof Exp:* NSF fel, Inst Photobiol Cells & Organelles, Brandeis Univ, 75-78; ASST PROF DEPT PLANT SCI, TEX A&M UNIV, 78- *Mem:* Am Soc Plant Physiologists; AAAS; Air Pollution Control Asn. *Res:* Air pollution physiology, photobiology; stress physiology. *Mailing Add:* Dept of Plant Sci Tex A&M Univ College Station TX 77843

FONG, GODWIN WING-KIN, b Kwang-Tung, China, Oct 11, 50. ANALYTICAL CHEMISTRY. *Educ:* State Univ NY, Stony Brook, BS, 74; State Univ NY, Buffalo, PhD(chem), 80. *Prof Exp:* Res asst chem, State Univ NY, Buffalo; GROUP LEADER ANAL RES & DEVELOP, AYERST

LABS, INC, AM HOME PROD CORP, 78- *Mem:* Am Chem Soc; AAAS; Acad Pharmaceut Sci; NY Acad Sci. *Res:* Analytical chemistry, especially chromatography, both theoretical and experimental; bonded phase chemistry as applied in chromatography; pharmaceutical analysis; development and validation of analytical procedures. *Mailing Add:* Anal Res & Develop Ayerst Labs Inc Rouses Pt NY 12979

FONG, HARRY H S, b Kwangtung, China, June 30, 35; US citizen; m 64; c 3. PHARMACOGNOSY. *Educ:* Univ Pittsburgh, BS, 59, MS, 62; Ohio State Univ, PhD(pharm), 65. *Prof Exp:* Res asst prof pharmacog, Sch Pharm, Univ Pittsburgh, 65-68, assoc prof, 68-70; assoc prof, 70-72, PROF PHARMACOG, COL PHARM, UNIV ILL, 72-, DIR PHARMACOG & HORT FIELD STA, 81- *Concurrent Pos:* Consult, WHO, 77; hon vis res fel, Inst Sci & Technol, Chinese Univ, Hong Kong, 77. *Mem:* Am Soc Pharmacog (vpres, 77-78, pres, 78-79, past-pres, 79-80); Am Pharmaceut Asn; Acad Pharmaceut Sci; Soc Econ Bot (treas, 75-77). *Res:* Phytochemistry, isolation, characterization and/or identification of pharmacologically active principles from plants; biological and phytochemical evaluation of fertility regulating agents from plants. *Mailing Add:* Col of Pharm Univ of Ill 833 S Wood St Chicago IL 60612

FONG, JACK SUN-CHIK, b Hong Kong, Jan 6, 41; Can citizen; m 68; c 3. PEDIATRICS, IMMUNOLOGY. *Educ:* McGill Univ, BS, 64, MS, MD & CM, 68. *Prof Exp:* Intern med, St Josephs Hosp, Ont, 68-69; res fel immunol, Univ Minn, Minneapolis, 69-72, med fel pediat, 72-74; asst prof, 74-77, ASSOC PROF PEDIAT, McGILL UNIV, 77- *Mem:* Am Asn Immunologists; Am Fedn Clin Res; Soc Exp Biol & Med; Can Pediat Soc. *Res:* Mechanism of immunologic injury, immune mediated coagulopathy, the complement system and immunodeficiency state. *Mailing Add:* Montreal Childrens Hosp 2300 Tupper St Montreal PQ H3H 1P3 Can

FONG, JAMES T(SE-MING), b Shanghai, China, Aug 23, 27; nat US; m 64; c 3. ENGINEERING, MATERIALS SCIENCE. *Educ:* Mass Inst Technol, SB, 48; Columbia Univ, MS, 51. *Prof Exp:* Develop engr, Griscom-Russell Co, 48-51; mech engr, Burns & Roe, Inc, 51-54; proj engr, Res Dept, Foster Wheeler Corp, 54-57; fel engr, AIW Proj, 57-61; tech staff gen mgr, 61-66, supvr irradiated components eng, 66-68, mgr adv cores, 68-72, mgr adv submarine proj, 72-74; mgr mat technol, 74-79, CONSULT, BETTIS ATOMIC POWER LAB, WESTINGHOUSE ELEC CORP, 79- *Mem:* Am Soc Mech Engrs. *Res:* Nuclear reactor engineering; heat transfer; power plant design; project management. *Mailing Add:* Bettis Atomic Power Lab Westinghouse Elec Corp PO Box 79 West Mifflin PA 15122

FONG, JEFFREY TSE-WEI, mathematical physics, continuum mechanics, see previous edition

FONG, KEI-LAI LAU, b Hong Kong, May 15, 50; Brit citizen; m 75. MEDICINAL CHEMISTRY, PHARMACOLOGY. *Educ:* Nat Taiwan Univ, BS, 72; Univ Minn, PhD(med chem), 78. *Prof Exp:* Proj investr develop therapeut, M D Anderson Hosp & Tumor Inst, 78-81; ASSOC SR INVESTR DRUG METAB, SMITH KLINE & FRENCH LABS, 81- *Mem:* Am Chem Soc; Am Asn Cancer Res. *Res:* Synthesis and biological evaluation of new antitumor agents, pharmacological studies of antitumor agents; drug metabolism. *Mailing Add:* Smith Kline & French Labs F-31 1500 Spring Garden St Philadelphia PA 19101

FONG, PETER, b Tungshang, China, Sept 3, 24; m 59; c 3. THEORETICAL PHYSICS, MOLECULAR BIOLOGY. *Educ:* Chekiang Univ, BS, 45; Univ Chicago, MS, 50, PhD(physics), 53. *Prof Exp:* Physicist, Inst Nuclear Studies, Univ Chicago, 54; from asst prof to prof physics, Utica Col, Syracuse Univ, 54-66; PROF PHYSICS, EMORY UNIV, 66- *Concurrent Pos:* NSF res grants, 55-66; res assoc, Mass Inst Technol, 56 & 57; res fel, Kellogg Radiation Lab, Calif Inst Technol, 57; vis prof, Cornell Univ, 63-64 & Univ Calif, Berkeley, 65-66. *Mem:* Fel Am Phys Soc; fel Biophys Soc; Am Geophys Union. *Res:* Nuclear physics; astrophysics; quantum mechanics; thermodynamics; DNA functions; brain memory mechanism; origin of ice ages; carbon dioxide greenhouse effect; philosophy and history. *Mailing Add:* Dept Physics Emory Univ Atlanta GA 30322

FONGER, WILLIAM HAMILTON, b Chicago, Ill, Sept 19, 25; m 53; c 3. PHYSICS. *Educ:* Univ Chicago, SB, 48, SM, 50, PhD(physics), 53. *Prof Exp:* MEM TECH STAFF, LABS, RCA CORP, 53- *Mem:* Am Phys Soc. *Res:* Solid state physics. *Mailing Add:* 174 Guyot Ave Princeton NJ 08540

FONKALSRUD, ERIC W, b Baltimore, Md, Aug 31, 32; m 59; c 4. SURGERY. *Educ:* Univ Wash, BA, 53; Johns Hopkins Univ, MD, 57; Am Bd Surg, dipl, 64; Am Bd Thoracic Surg, dipl, 66. *Prof Exp:* Intern surg, Johns Hopkins Hosp, Baltimore, Md, 57-58, asst resident, 58-59; from asst resident to chief resident, 59-63, from asst prof to assoc prof, 63-71, PROF SURG, SCH MED, UNIV CALIF, LOS ANGELES, 71-, CHIEF PEDIAT SURG, 63- *Concurrent Pos:* Instr, Ohio State Univ & resident, Children's Hosp, Columbus, Ohio, 63-65; Mead Johnson grad training award surg, Univ Calif, Los Angeles, Markle scholar, 63-68; USPHS res grants, 65-75; Calif Inst Cancer Res & Los Angeles County Heart Asn grants; James IV surg traveller, Gt Brit, 71; mem surg study sect, NIH, 71-75; mem bd dirs, Martin Mem Found, Am Col Surgeons. *Mem:* Fel Am Col Surg; Am Acad Pediat; Soc Univ Surg (pres), 77); Asn Acad Surg (pres), 72); Am Pediat Surg Asn; Am Asn Thoracic Surg. *Res:* Organ transplantation, experimental and clinical; pulmonary, hepatic and cardiac physiology; studies of neonatal physiology; development of new surgical techniques; inflammatory bowel disease; use of computer assisted instruction in medical education. *Mailing Add:* Dept of Surg Univ of Calif Sch of Med Los Angeles CA 90024

FONKEN, DAVID W(ALTER), b Denver, Colo, Oct 9, 31; m 53; c 3. ENGINEERING HYDROLOGY, IRRIGATION ENGINEERING. *Educ:* Colo State Univ, BS, 53, MCE, 56; Univ Ariz, PhD(civil eng), 74. *Prof Exp:* Hydraul engr, US Bur Reclamation, 56-58; asst prof & asst agr engr, Dept Agr Eng, Univ Ariz, 58-61; hydrometeorologist, Harza Eng Co, 61-68; grad res asst, Dept Agr Eng, Univ Ariz, 68-71; asst prof & dist exten irrig engr, Univ Nebr, 71-75; systs analyst, 75-81, IRRIGATION ENGR & HYDROLOGIST, HARZA ENG CO, 81- Mem: Am Soc Civil Engrs; Am Soc Agr Engrs. Res: Hydrological studies in arid regions; irrigation; hydraulics of irrigation; irrigation scheduling; soil-water-plant relationships. Mailing Add: Harza Eng Co 150 S Wacker Dr Chicago IL 60606

FONKEN, GERHARD JOSEPH, b Ger, Aug 31, 28; nat US; m 52; c 5. ORGANIC CHEMISTRY. Educ: Univ Calif, BS, 54, PhD(chem), 57. Prof Exp: Res chemist, Procter & Gamble Co, 57-58 & Stanford Res Inst, 58-59; from instr to assoc prof, 59-74, exec asst to pres, 76-79, PROF CHEM & ASSOC PROVOST, UNIV TEX, AUSTIN, 74-, VPRES ACAD AFFAIRS & RES, 79- Mem: Am Chem Soc. Res: Natural products; structural determinations of organic compounds; organic photochemical transformations. Mailing Add: Dept of Chem Univ of Tex Austin TX 78712

FONKEN, GUNTHER SIEGFRIED, b Krefeld, Ger, Jan 29, 26; nat US; m 51; c 3. RESEARCH ADMINISTRATION. Educ: Mass Inst Technol, BS, 46; Univ Wis, PhD(chem), 51. Prof Exp: Jr chemist, Res Dept, Merck & Co, Inc, 46-47; res chemist, Chem Dept, 51-60, sect head, Biochem Dept, 60-68, res mgr, Cancer Res Dept, 68-73, res mgr, Exp Biol Res Dept, 73-79, dir, Drug Safety, Planning & Admin Serv, 79-81, GROUP DIR, ADMIN & SUPPORT OPERS, PHARMACEUT RES DEVELOP DIV, UPJOHN CO, 81- Mem: Fel AAAS; Am Soc Microbiol; Am Chem Soc. Res: Pharmaceutical substances. Mailing Add: The Upjohn Co 301 Henrietta St Kalamazoo MI 49001

FONNESBECK, PAUL VANCE, b Weston, Idaho, Aug 4, 31; m 53; c 3. ANIMAL NUTRITION. Educ: Brigham Young Univ, BS, 53; Utah State Univ, MS, 59, PhD(animal nutrit), 62. Prof Exp: Asst prof nutrit, Rutgers Univ, 63-70, asst res prof, 70; res assoc animal sci, 70-77, RES ASST PROF ANIMAL DAIRY & VET SCI, UTAH STATE UNIV, 77- Mem: Am Soc Animal Sci. Res: Nutrient content and utilization of foods and feeds; improving chemical methods for food analysis. Mailing Add: Dept of Animal Sci Utah State Univ Logan UT 84322

FONO, ANDREW, b Budapest, Hungary, Apr 24, 23; nat US; m 58; c 2. ORGANIC CHEMISTRY. Educ: Pazmany Peter Univ, Hungary, PhD(chem), 45. Prof Exp: Asst, Inst Org Chem Res, Stockholm, 46-47; res fel chem, Univ Chicago, 47-51; head res dept, Otto B May Inc, 51-56; indust res assoc, Inst Org Chem, Univ Chicago, 57; sr res scientist, Firestone Tire & Rubber Co, Ohio, 58-60; res dir, Otto B May, Inc, Newark, NJ, 60-75; TECH DIR, ROYCE CHEM CO, 75-, EXEC VPRES, PASSAIC COLOR, 78- Mem: Am Chem Soc; AAAS; Tech Asn Pulp & Paper Indust; Am Asn Textile Chemists & Colorists; NY Acad Sci. Res: Organic reaction mechanism; effect of metal ions and metallo-organic compounds on reactions in solution; polymer and dyestuff chemistry; colloid chemistry; textile chemistry, paper pulping and alkaline battery. Mailing Add: 17 Carlton Ave East Rutherford NJ 07073

FONSECA, ANTHONY GUTIERRE, b Chattanooga, Tenn, Mar 31, 40; m 65; c 2. MINERAL PROCESSING. Educ: Univ Chattanooga, AB, 62; Univ Ga, MS, 66, PhD(inorg chem), 68. Prof Exp: Res scientist, Cent Res Div, 68-74, sr res scientist, Continental Oil Co, 74-75, RES GROUP LEADER, MINING RES DIV, CONOCO INC, 76- Mem: Am Chem Soc; Am Inst Mining, Metall & Petrol Engrs. Res: Investigations of mineral processing systems, plant testing; hydrometallurgical processing of oxide and sulfide materials; slurry transportation; coal and lignite cleaning, desulfurization, processing and preparation; mineral processing and beneficiation, within the general area of mining engineering. Mailing Add: Mining Res Div Conoco Inc ORE Dressing Lab Drawer 1267 Ponca City OK 74603

FONT, WILLIAM FRANCIS, b New Orleans, La, Aug 11, 44; m 68; c 1. PARASITOLOGY. Educ: Tulane Univ, BS, 66; La State Univ, MS, 72, PhD(zool), 75. Prof Exp: ASST PROF BIOL, UNIV WIS, EAU CLAIRE, 75- Honors & Awards: Elon E Byrd Mem Award, Southeastern Soc Parasitologists, 75. Mem: Am Soc Parasitologists; Sigma Xi. Res: Taxonomy and life history of digenetic trematodes. Mailing Add: Dept of Biol Univ of Wis Eau Claire WI 54701

FONTAINE, ARTHUR ROBERT, b Lawrence, Mass, Aug 1, 29; Can citizen; m 52; c 2. MARINE ZOOLOGY. Educ: McGill Univ, BSc, 52; Oxford Univ, DPhil(zool), 61. Prof Exp: Researcher marine biol, Inst Jamaica, Kingston, 52-53; instr biol, Victoria Col, 56-58, asst prof, 58-63; assoc prof, 63-68, assoc dean, 69-70, dean grad studies, 70-72, chmn dept, 77-79, PROF BIOL, UNIV VICTORIA, BC, 68- Concurrent Pos: Vis prof, Friday Harbor Labs, Univ Wash, 64, 65 & 69; vis zoologist, Dove Marine Lab, Newcastle-on-Tyne, 66-67; CIDA prof marine biol, Univ of SPac, Suva, Fiji, 75-77. Mem: AAAS; Soc Syst Zool; Marine Biol Asn UK; sci fel Zool Soc London. Res: Functional morphology and experimental biology of echinoderms. Mailing Add: Dept of Biol Univ of Victoria Victoria BC V8W 2Y2 Can

FONTAINE, GILLES JOSEPH, b Levis, Que, Aug 13, 48; m 69; c 2. ASTROPHYSICS. Educ: Univ Laval, BS, 69; Univ Rochester, PhD(astrophys), 73. Prof Exp: Nat Res Coun Can fel, 73-75, res assoc astrophys, 75-77, asst prof, 77-80, ASSOC PROF DEPT PHYSICS, UNIV MONTREAL, 80- Mem: Am Astron Soc; Can Asn Physicists; Can Astron Soc; Int Astron Union. Res: Stellar structure and stellar evolution; physics of dense matter; interiors and atmospheres of white dwarf stars; pulsating white dwarfs. Mailing Add: Dept of Physics Univ of Montreal PO Box 6128 Montreal PQ H3C 3S7 Can

FONTAINE, JULIA CLARE, b Chattanooga, Tenn, Dec 11, 20. ANATOMY, BIOLOGY. Educ: Nazareth Col, BS, 48; Cath Univ, MS, 56; Univ Louisville, PhD(anat), 69. Prof Exp: Asst prof biol, 59-66, PROF BIOL & CHMN DEPT, SPALDING COL, 69- Mem: AAAS; NY Acad Sci. Res: Fluctuations in amounts of DNA in mammalian peripheral leukocytes; DNA changes in non-replicating cells; circadian rhythms in DNA content of specialized cells. Mailing Add: Dept Biol Spalding Col 851 S Fourth St Louisville KY 40203

FONTAINE, MARC F(RANCIS), b Mexico City, Mex, Mar 27, 26; nat US; m 49; c 3. CHEMICAL ENGINEERING. Educ: La State Univ, BS, 50, MS, 51; Okla State Univ, PhD(chem eng), 54. Prof Exp: Asst chem eng, Okla State Univ, 51-53, instr, 53, instr math, 53-54; res chem engr, Res Ctr, Texaco, Inc, NY, 54-60; sr engr-sci liaison, Texaco UK Ltd, Eng, 60-62, res chem engr, Bellaire Res Labs, Tex, 62-65, group leader, 65-68, sr res chem engr & proj leader, 68-69, SUPVR, BELLAIRE RES LABS, TEXACO, INC, TEX, 69- Mem: AAAS; Am Chem Soc; Am Inst Chem Engrs; Am Inst Mining, Metall & Petrol Engrs. Res: Fuel technology; experimental design; production research, petroleum. Mailing Add: Texaco Inc PO Box 425 Bellaire TX 77401

FONTAINE, THOMAS DAVIS, b Utica, Miss, Apr 12, 16; m 41; c 2. BIOCHEMISTRY. Educ: Miss Col, AB, 37; Univ Pittsburgh, PhD(biochem), 42. Prof Exp: Asst chem, Univ Pittsburgh, 37-38; asst, Cotton Res Found, Mellon Inst, 38-41; asst chemist, Oil, Fat & Protein Div, Southern Regional Res Lab, Bur Agr & Indust Chem, USDA, 41-44, assoc chemist, 44-45, assoc chemist biol, Active Compounds Div, 45-46, chemist, 46-47, sr biochemist, 47-48, prin biochemist & head div, 48-52, prin chemist & head biol active chem compounds div, Eastern Utilization Res Br, 52-55; admin asst to US Sen John C Stennis, 55-57; head fel sect, Sci Personnel & Ed Div, NSF, 57-65, dir, Div Grad Educ Sci, 65-66, assoc dir sci educ, 66-69, dep asst dir, 69-71; asst dir, Div Sponsored Res, Univ Fla, 71-73, assoc dir, 73-75, dir, 75-76; RETIRED. Mem: Am Chem Soc; Am Soc Biol Chem. Res: Proteins; amino acids; enzymes; plant diseases; antibiotics from plants; plant growth modifiers; plant alkaloids; government. Mailing Add: 5306 Brownlee Lane Spring TX 77373

FONTANA, MARIO H, b West Springfield, Mass, Mar 30, 33; m 58; c 2. NUCLEAR SAFETY, HEAT TRANSFER. Educ: Univ Mass, Amherst, BS, 55; Mass Inst Technol, SM, 57; Purdue Univ, PhD(mech eng), 68. Prof Exp: Assoc engr, Oak Ridge Nat Lab, 57-61; sr scientist, High Temp Mat, Inc, Mass, 61-62; mem sr staff nuclear safety, Oak Ridge Nat Lab, 62-63; sr scientist plasma chem, Avco Res & Advan Develop, Mass, 63-64; instr thermodyn, Purdue Univ, 64-65; asst dir, Nuclear Safety Progs, Oak Ridge Nat Lab, 65-71, mgr, Breeder Reactor Safety Progs, 71-80, head, Advan Reactor Systs Sect, 74-81; DIR, NAT INDUST NUCLEAR REACTOR DEGRADED CORE RULEMAKING PROG, TECHNOL ENERGY CORP, 81- Concurrent Pos: Consult, Adv Comt Reactor Safeguards, 68- & Nuclear Regulatory Comm, 76-77. Mem: AAAS; Am Soc Mech Engrs; fel Am Nuclear Soc. Res: Safety of nuclear reactors, both thermal and fast breeders; evaluation of potential reactor accidents and preventive safeguards; director of safety research programs. Mailing Add: 106 Caldwell Dr Oak Ridge TN 37830

FONTANA, MARS G(UY), b Iron Mountain, Mich, Apr 6, 10; m 37; c 4. METALLURGY, CORROSION. Educ: Univ Mich, BS, 31, MS, 32, PhD(metall eng), 35. Hon Degrees: DEng, Univ Mich, 75. Prof Exp: Asst eng res, Univ Mich, 29-34; metall engr & supvr, E I du Pont de Nemours & Co, 34-45; prof, 45-67, regents prof, 67-70, Duriron prof, 70-75, chmn dept metall eng, 48-75, EMER PROF & CHMN METALL ENG, OHIO STATE UNIV, 75- Concurrent Pos: Consult engr, Duriron Co, Ohio, 45-; ed, Corrosion, 62-73. Honors & Awards: Speller Award, Nat Asn Corrosion Engrs, 56; Gold Medal, Am Soc Metals, 79. Mem: Nat Acad Eng; fel & hon mem Am Soc Metals; Nat Asn Corrosion Engrs (pres, 52); Am Inst Chem Engrs; fel Am Inst Mining, Metall & Petrol Engrs. Res: Corrosion; determination of oxygen and nitrogen in iron and steel by vacuum fusion and equilibrium in the system iron-oxygen-hydrogen at 1600 degrees centigrade. Mailing Add: 2086 Elgin Rd Columbus OH 43221

FONTANA, PETER R, b Berne, Switz, Apr 20, 35. THEORETICAL PHYSICS. Educ: Univ Miami, Ohio, MS, 58; Yale Univ, PhD(physics), 60. Prof Exp: Res assoc physics, Univ Chicago, 60-62; asst prof, Univ Mich, Ann Arbor, 62-67; assoc prof, 67-74, PROF PHYSICS, ORE STATE UNIV, 74- Concurrent Pos: Prof, Swiss Inst Technol, Lausanne, Switz, 74-75, 76 & 78. Mem: Am Phys Soc. Res: Interatomic forces; scattering theory; calculation of atomic fine and hyperfine structure; atomic radiative decay processes. Mailing Add: Dept Physics Ore State Univ Corvallis OR 97330

FONTANA, ROBERT E, b Brooklyn, NY, Nov 26, 15; m 45; c 3. SOLID STATE ELECTRONICS, CONTROL SYSTEMS. Educ: NY Univ, BEE, 39; Univ Ill, MS, 47, PhD(elec eng), 49. Prof Exp: Res scientist, Sandia Corp, 49-54, asst for nuclear develop, Hqs, Washington, DC, 54-58, chief nuclear applns, Hq, Air Res & Develop Command, 58-61, dir, Aerospace Res Labs, 61-66; HEAD DEPT ELEC ENG, AIR FORCE INST TECHNOL, 66- Concurrent Pos: Ed joint newslett, Inst Elec & Electronics Engrs-Am Soc Eng Educ, 70- Mem: Am Soc Eng Educ; Inst Elec & Electronics Engrs. Res: Solid state electronics and control systems. Mailing Add: Air Force Inst of Technol AFIT/ENG Wright-Patterson AFB OH 45433

FONTANA, VINCENT J, b New York, NY, Nov 19, 23. IMMUNOLOGY, MEDICINE. Educ: Long Island Col Med, MD, 47. Prof Exp: Fel, NY Univ Hosp, 51-52, assoc prof, 57-69, PROF PEDIAT, SCH MED, NY UNIV, 69- Concurrent Pos: Consult, St Alban's Naval Hosp, 55- & St Mary's Hosp, New York, 60-; med dir, New York Foundling Hosp, 62-; dir pediat, St Vincent's Hosp & Med Ctr, 62-74, emer dir pediat, 74- Mem: Fel Am Acad Pediat; fel Am Acad Allergy; Am Fedn Clin Res; fel NY Acad Med; Harvey Soc. Res: Pediatric allergy and immunology. Mailing Add: 1175 Third Ave New York NY 10021

FONTANELLA, JOHN JOSEPH, b Rochester, Pa, Dec 20, 45; m 78; c 1. SOLID STATE PHYSICS. Educ: Westminster Col, Pa, BS, 67; Case Inst Technol, MS, 69, PhD(physics), 71. Prof Exp: Asst prof, 74-78, ASSOC PROF PHYSICS, US NAVAL ACAD, 78- Mem: Am Phys Soc; Am Asn Physics Teachers; Inst Elec & Electronics Engrs. Res: Real and imaginary parts of the dielectric constant for solids as functions of temperature, pressure and audio frequency. Mailing Add: Dept of Physics US Naval Acad Annapolis MD 21402

FONTENELLE, LYDIA JULIA, b New Orleans, La, May 28, 38. BIOCHEMISTRY. *Educ:* La State Univ, Baton Rouge, BS, 60; Tulane Univ, PhD(biochem), 67. *Prof Exp:* Teacher high schs, La, 60-61; lab technician biochem, Tulane Univ, 61-63; asst prof, 69-73, ASSOC PROF BIOCHEM & PHARMACOL, COL PHARM, IDAHO STATE UNIV, 73- *Concurrent Pos:* Nat Inst Can fel, McEachern Lab, Univ Alta, 67-69; Idaho State Univ fac grant, 70-71. *Mem:* Am Chem Soc; NY Acad Sci. *Res:* Metabolism of drugs and the effects of drugs on control mechanisms of purine biosynthesis de novo. *Mailing Add:* Col of Pharm Idaho State Univ Pocatello ID 83201

FONTENOT, JOSEPH PAUL, b Mamou, La, May 11, 27; m 46; c 6. ANIMAL NUTRITION. *Educ:* Southwestern La Univ, BS, 51; Okla State Univ, MS, 53, PhD(animal nutrit), 54. *Prof Exp:* Instr physiol & pharmacol, Okla State Univ, 54-55; asst prof animal husb, Miss State Univ, 55-56; assoc prof, 56-63, PROF ANIMAL SCI, VA POLYTECH INST & STATE UNIV, 63- *Honors & Awards:* Am Feed Mfrs Asn Nutrit Res Award. *Mem:* AAAS; Am Soc Animal Sci; Am Inst Nutrit; Animal Nutrit Res Coun. *Res:* Ruminant nutrition; nitrogen requirement and metabolism; metabolic disturbances; administration of hormones and other drugs; forage utilization; cellulose digestion; recycling of animal wastes by feeding. *Mailing Add:* Dept of Animal Sci Va Polytech Inst & State Univ Blacksburg VA 24061

FONTEYN, PAUL JOHN, b Williamstown, Mass, Aug 9, 46; m 72; c 2. PLANT ECOLOGY. *Educ:* Univ San Francisco, BS, 68; Univ Calif, Santa Barbara, MA, 74, PhD(biol), 78. *Prof Exp:* ASST PROF PLANT ECOL, SW TEX STATE UNIV, 78- *Mem:* Ecol Soc Am; Sigma Xi. *Res:* Study of individual species distributions, the physiological and abiotic factors influencing these distributions and the dynamic interrelationships such as competition among species. *Mailing Add:* Dept Biol SW Tex State Univ San Marcos TX 78666

FONTHEIM, ERNEST GUNTER, b Berlin, Ger, Oct 23, 22; US citizen; m 50; c 2. PLASMA PHYSICS, SPACE PHYSICS. *Educ:* Southwest Mo State Col, AB & BS, 50; Lehigh Univ, MS, 52, PhD(physics), 60. *Prof Exp:* Assoc res physicist, Radiation Lab, 60-62, RES PHYSICIST, SPACE PHYSICS RES LAB, UNIV MICH, ANN ARBOR, 64- *Concurrent Pos:* Sr res assoc, Goddard Space Flight Ctr, Nat Acad Sci, 72-73. *Mem:* Am Phys Soc; Am Geophys Union; Int Union Radio Sci; Int Asn Geomag & Aeronomy. *Res:* Physics of the ionosphere, magnetosphere and upper atmosphere; kinetic theory. *Mailing Add:* Space Physics Res Lab Univ of Mich Ann Arbor MI 48109

FONTIJN, ARTHUR, b Amsterdam, Neth, Apr 3, 28; nat US; m 77; c 1. PHYSICAL CHEMISTRY, CHEMICAL DYNAMICS. *Educ:* Univ Amsterdam, BSc, 49, DSc(phys chem), 57. *Prof Exp:* Nat Res Coun Can fel, Univ Sask, 55-57; res assoc upper atmosphere chem group, McGill Univ, 57-60; phys chemist, Aerochem Res Labs, Inc, 60-68, head reaction kinetics group, 68-79; sr vis fel, Queen Mary Col, London Univ, 79-81; PROF, DEPT CHEM ENG & ENVIRON ENG, RENSSELAER POLYTECH INST, 81- *Concurrent Pos:* Mem ed adv bd, Combustion & Flame J, 75-; mem, Int Union Pure & Appl Chem, subcomt plasma chem, 75-, exec comt, Phys Chem Div, Am Chem Soc, 79-82. *Honors & Awards:* Silver Medal, Combustion Inst, 74. *Mem:* Royal Soc Chem; Am Chem Soc; Am Phys Soc; Am Geophys Union; Royal Dutch Soc Chem. *Res:* Gas kinetics; chemi-ionization and chemiluminescence; atmospheric chemistry and combustion. *Mailing Add:* Dept Chem Eng Rensselaer Polytech Inst Troy NY 12181

FOODEN, JACK, b Chicago, Ill, May 21, 27; m 50; c 2. ZOOLOGY. *Educ:* Chicago Teachers Col, MEd, 56; Univ Chicago, MA, 51, PhD(zool), 60. *Prof Exp:* Teacher, Chicago Pub Schs, 53-56; NIH res fel primate taxon, Univ Chicago & Chicago Natural Hist Mus, 60-62; PROF ZOOL, CHICAGO STATE UNIV, 62-; RES ASSOC, DIV MAMMALS, FIELD MUS NATURAL HIST, 64- *Concurrent Pos:* Indo-Am Fel, 79-80. *Mem:* AAAS; Am Soc Mammal; Int Primatol Soc. *Res:* Primatology; mammalogy. *Mailing Add:* Div of Mammals Field Mus of Natural Hist Chicago IL 60605

FOOR, W EUGENE, b Wood, Pa, Feb 7, 36; m 58; c 2. ZOOLOGY, PARASITOLOGY. *Educ:* Shippensburg State Col, BSE, 59; Univ Mass, Amherst, PHD(zool), 66. *Prof Exp:* Teacher high schs, Pa, 59-62; fel parasitol, Med Sch, Tulane Univ, 66-67, instr, Sch Pub Health & Trop Med, 67-68, asst prof, 68-70; assoc prof, 70-75, PROF BIOL, WAYNE STATE UNIV, 75- *Mem:* Am Soc Cell Biol; Am Soc Parasitol. *Res:* Ultrastructural studies of reproductive cells in parasitic nematodes; oogenesis, vitellogenesis and shell formation about newly fertilized eggs as well as the mechanism of oocyte penetration employed by spermatozoa. *Mailing Add:* Dept of Biol Wayne State Univ Detroit MI 48202

FOOS, KENNETH MICHAEL, b Bellefontaine, Ohio, Jan 16, 43; m 66; c 1. BOTANY, MYCOLOGY. *Educ:* Ohio State Univ, BS, 65, MS, 70, PhD(bot), 72. *Prof Exp:* Sci teacher, biol & chem, Bowling City Schs, 66-67, bot, Jefferson Local Schs, 67-70; vis asst prof bot, Ohio State Univ, 72-73; asst prof, 73-76, ASSOC PROF BIOL, LAKE ERIE COL, 76- *Concurrent Pos:* Grant proj dir & Lake Erie Col, 76-78. *Mem:* AAAS; Am Inst Biol Sci; Am Soc Microbiologists; Mycol Soc Am; Bot Soc Am. *Res:* Effects of ecological factors on physiology and morphology of zygomycetous fungi; application of numerical approach to fungal systematics; action of chemical agents on fungal growth and reproduction. *Mailing Add:* Lake Erie Col 391 W Washington St Painesville OH 44077

FOOS, RAYMOND ANTHONY, b Bowling Green, Ohio, Sept 30, 28; m 53; c 10. PHYSICAL CHEMISTRY. *Educ:* Xavier Univ, Ohio, BS, 50, MS, 53; Iowa State Univ, PhD(chem), 54. *Prof Exp:* Res chemist, AEC, 51-54; group leader, Union Carbide Metal Co, 54-57; supvr metals & inorg chem, US Indust Chem Co, 57-59, supvr polymer chem, 59-60; mgr extraction & oxide, Brush Beryllium Co, 60-66, mgr, Metal Oxide Dept, 66-69, dir corp res & develop, 69-70, vpres res & develop, 70-74, sr vpres, Friction & Crystal Prod, 74-76, sr vpres, 76-80, EXEC VPRES, BERYLLIUM PROD, BRUSH WELLMAN INC, 80- *Mem:* Am Chem Soc; Am Inst Metall & Petrol Engrs; Am Ceramic

Soc; Soc Automotive Engrs; Int Soc Hybrid Microelectronics. *Res:* Extractive metallurgy of transition elements; sodium chemistry; electro chemistry; patents; liquid extraction; polymers; beryllium chemistry; manufacturing; ceramics; beryllium product metallurgy; powder technology; administration. *Mailing Add:* Brush Wellman Inc 17876 St Clair Ave Cleveland OH 44110

FOOS, ROBERT YOUNG, b Philadelphia, Pa, Nov 20, 22; m 45; c 4. OPHTHALMOLOGY, PATHOLOGY. *Educ:* Univ Calif, Davis, BS, 51, DVM, 53; Univ Calif, Los Angeles, MD, 63. *Prof Exp:* Nat Inst Neurol Dis & Stroke spec fel, 65-66; asst prof, 66-70, assoc prof, 70-76, PROF PATH, SCH MED, UNIV CALIF, LOS ANGELES, 76- DIR OPHTHALMIC PATH LABS, JULES STEIN EYE INST, 67- *Mem:* AAAS. *Res:* Diseases of the retina; experimental ophthalmic pathology. *Mailing Add:* Dept of Path Jules Stein Eye Inst Univ of Calif Los Angeles CA 90024

FOOSE, MICHAEL PETER, b Lancaster, Pa, Jan 9, 48; m 71. STRUCTURAL GEOLOGY. *Educ:* Colby Col, BA, 69; Princeton Univ, MS, 72, PhD(geol), 74. *Prof Exp:* GEOLOGIST, US GEOL SURV, 74- *Mem:* Geol Soc Am; Soc Econ Geologists. *Res:* Rock structures and stratigraphy in upper Michigan with emphasis on locating potential ore deposits; mineral resource investigations in Oregon and Minnesota; examination of the distribution and occurrences of nickel and cobalt throughout the world. *Mailing Add:* Br of Eastern Mineral Resources US Geol Surv Mail Stop 954 Reston VA 22092

FOOSE, RICHARD MARTIN, b Lancaster, Pa, Oct 9, 15; m 43; c 4. GEOLOGY. *Educ:* Franklin & Marshall Col, BS, 37; Northwestern Univ MS, 39; Johns Hopkins Univ, PhD(struct & econ geol), 42. *Prof Exp:* Asst instr geol, Northwestern Univ, 37-39; asst geologist, Pa State Topog & Geol Surv, 39-42, assoc geologist, 42-43; sr geologist, 43-46; prof geol & head dept, Franklin & Marshall Col, 46-57; chmn dept earth sci, Stanford Res Inst, 57-63; prof geol & chmn dept, 63-81, HITCHCOCK PROF GEOL, AMHERST COL, 81- *Concurrent Pos:* Coop geologist, Pa State Turnpike Comn, 41; consult geologist, 42-; deleg, Int Geol Cong, 52, 56, 60, 68; Ford fel, Stanford Univ, 55-56; mem tech work group 2, Nuclear Test Ban Discussions, Geneva, 59; NSF sr fel, Swiss Fed Inst Technol, 62-63; vis prof, Univ Vienna, 68 & Am Univ Beirut, 69; Nat Acad Sci exchange fel, USSR, 69 & 76; mem, Nat Res Coun, 71-75; Nat Acad Sci exchange fel, Bulgaria, 72; mem adv comt, Nat Acad Sci, USSR & Eastern Europe, 72-75. *Mem:* Am Inst Prof Geologists (secy, 68); fel AAAS; fel Geol Soc Am; Soc Econ Geol; fel Explorers Club. *Res:* Origin and occurrence of hialumina clays; manganese minerals of Pennsylvania; groundwater geology; tectonics of middle Rocky Mountains; catastrophic sinkhole development; tectonic evolution of the Mediterranean Basin. *Mailing Add:* Dept of Geol Amherst Col Amherst MA 01002

FOOSE, THOMAS JOHN, b Waynesboro, Pa, Mar 7, 45; m 77; c 4. CONSERVATION BIOLOGY, POPULATION BIOLOGY. *Educ:* Princeton Univ, BA, 69; Univ Chicago, PhD(biol), 82. *Prof Exp:* Res consult, Philadelphia Zool Soc, 75-76; demog consult, Inventory Species Inventory Syst, 76; res asst, Cornell Univ, 77; zool curator, Okla City Zoo, 77-80; CONSERV COORDR, AM ASN ZOOL PARKS & AQUARIUMS, 81- *Concurrent Pos:* Vis researcher, Philadelphia Zool Soc, 75-76 & Toronto Zool Soc, 77; field researcher, Univ Chicago, 76-77; resident researcher, Okla City Zoo, 77-80. *Res:* Population biology, both analysis and management, of endangered species; development of demographic and genetic strategies and programs to propagate and preserve endangered species in captivity; trophic biology of ungulates. *Mailing Add:* Inventory Species Inventory Syst Zool Gardens Apple Valley MN 55124

FOOTE, BENJAMIN ARCHER, b Delaware, Ohio, Oct 25, 28; m 54; c 4. ENTOMOLOGY. *Educ:* Ohio Wesleyan Univ, BA, 50; Ohio State Univ, MS, 52; Cornell Univ, PhD, 61. *Prof Exp:* Asst entom, Ohio State Univ, 50-52; asst limnol, Cornell Univ, 54-58; asst entomologist, Univ Idaho, 58-60; from asst prof to assoc prof, 61-72, PROF ENTOM, KENT STATE UNIV, 72- *Concurrent Pos:* NSF res grant, 69-; Nat Geog Soc grant, 71. *Mem:* Entom Soc Am; Ecol Soc Am; NAm Benthological Soc. *Res:* Ecology of acalyptrate Diptera; biological control of ragweeds. *Mailing Add:* Dept of Biol Sci Kent State Univ Kent OH 44242

FOOTE, BOBBIE LEON, b Spavinaw, Okla, Jan 24, 40; m 68; c 3. INDUSTRIAL ENGINEERING, OPERATIONS RESEARCH. *Educ:* Univ Okla, BS, 61, MA, 63, PhD(eng), 67. *Prof Exp:* Instr math, NE Okla A&M Jr Col, 63-65; prof eng, 67-78, DIR, SCH INDUST ENG, UNIV OKLA, 77- *Concurrent Pos:* Engr, US Post Off Dept, 68; dir modeling studies, Univ Tex, 74-75. *Mem:* Opers Res Soc Am; Inst Mgt Sci; Am Inst Indust Engrs(secy, 73). *Res:* Plant and production planning; quality control; energy distribution; energy systems; math programming. *Mailing Add:* Sch of Indust Eng 202 W Boyd Norman OK 73019

FOOTE, CARLTON DAN, b State Center, Iowa, Jan 16, 35; m 59; c 3. BIOCHEMISTRY, ORGANIC CHEMISTRY. *Educ:* Cent Col, BA, 57; Univ Ill, PhD(biochem), 63. *Prof Exp:* NIH fel, 63-64; asst prof chem, Union Col, Ky, 64-65; asst prof, 65-70, ASSOC PROF CHEM, EASTERN ILL UNIV, 70- *Mem:* Am Chem Soc. *Res:* Steroid biosynthesis; mechanisms of enzymes; cellular differentiation. *Mailing Add:* Dept of Chem Eastern Ill Univ Charleston IL 61920

FOOTE, CHRISTOPHER S, b Hartford, Conn, June 5, 35; m 60; c 2. ORGANIC CHEMISTRY. *Educ:* Yale Univ, BS, 57; Harvard Univ, AM & PhD(org chem), 62. *Prof Exp:* From instr to assoc prof, 61-69, chmn dept, 78-80, PROF CHEM, UNIV CALIF, LOS ANGELES, 69- *Concurrent Pos:* Alfred P Sloan Found fel, 65-67; J S Guggenheim Found fel, 67-68; consult, Procter & Gamble & Occidental Res Corp. *Honors & Awards:* Leo Hendrick Baekeland Medal, Am Chem Soc, 75; Herbert Newby McCoy Award, 77. *Mem:* AAAS; Am Chem Soc; Royal Soc Chem; Ger Chem Soc. *Res:* Organic photochemistry; chemical generation of molecules in excited states; reactions of singlet oxygen; photodynamic effect. *Mailing Add:* Dept of Chem Univ of Calif Los Angeles CA 90024

FOOTE, FLORENCE MARTINDALE, b Montague City, Mass, June 28, 11; wid. ANATOMY, EMBRYOLOGY. *Educ:* Mt Holyoke Col, AB, 32; AM, 34; Univ Iowa, PhD(embryol, endocrinol), 40. *Prof Exp:* Asst zool, Mt Holyoke Col, 32-34, instr, 35-38; instr, Univ Del, 40-41; instr biol, Wagner Col, 42-45, asst prof, 46-47; asst prof zool, 47-50, lectr physiol, 50-62, assoc prof, 63-68, actg chmn dept, 71-72, 75-76, prof, Sch Med, 71-76, prof physiol, 68-76, EMER PROF PHYSIOL, SOUTHERN ILLINOIS UNIV, 76-. *Concurrent Pos:* Guest investr lab exp embryol, Col France, 60-61. *Mem:* AAAS; Am Asn Anat; Soc Develop Biol; Int Inst Embryol. *Res:* Vertebrate embryology. *Mailing Add:* 801 Skyline Dr Carbondale IL 62901

FOOTE, FREEMAN, b Orange, NJ, Nov 8, 08; m 39; c 1. GEOLOGY. *Educ:* Princeton Univ, AB, 31. *Prof Exp:* Asst geol, Columbia Univ, 34-37; from instr to prof geol, 37-68, chmn dept, 64-67, Edward Brust prof geol & mineral, 68-74, EMER PROF GEOL & MINERAL, WILLIAMS COL, 74- *Mem:* AAAS; fel Geol Soc Am; Nat Asn Geol Teachers (secy, 57-60). *Res:* Petrology; structural geology. *Mailing Add:* Cold Spring Rd Williamstown MA 01267

FOOTE, GARVIN BRANT, b Murray, Utah, Oct 30, 42; m 67; c 2. SEVERE STORMS, CLOUD PHYSICS. *Educ:* Univ Ariz, BS, 64, MS, 67, PhD(atmospheric sci), 71. *Prof Exp:* Res assoc cloud physics, Univ Ariz, 67-70; fel, 70-71, scientist, 71-74, PROJ LEADER CLOUD PHYSICS, NAT CTR ATMOSPHERIC RES, 74- *Mem:* Am Meteorol Soc. *Res:* Severe local storms; hail; weather modification; radar meteorology. *Mailing Add:* Nat Ctr Atmospheric Res PO Box 3000 Boulder CO 80307

FOOTE, JAMES HERBERT, b Tacoma, Wash, Dec 13, 29; m 54; c 2. PLASMA PHYSICS, ELEMENTARY PARTICLE PHYSICS. *Educ:* Univ Calif, Berkeley, AB, 53, PhD(physics), 61. *Prof Exp:* PHYSICIST, LAWRENCE LIVERMORE NAT LAB, 60- *Mem:* Am Phys Soc. *Res:* Experimental research and related computer applications; controlled magnetic fusion and high temperature plasma physics, elementary particle scattering. *Mailing Add:* Lawrence Livermore Nat Lab Livermore CA 94550

FOOTE, JOE REEDER, b Amarillo, Tex, Aug 17, 19; m 49; c 4. APPLIED MATHEMATICS. *Educ:* Tex Tech Col, BS, 40; Mass Inst Technol, PhD(math), 49. *Prof Exp:* Instr math, Univ Tex, 40-41; Univ Okla, 45-46 & Mass Inst Technol, 46-49; asst prof, Iowa State Col, 49-51; mathematician, Wright-Patterson AFB, 51-53; asst prof math, Univ Okla, 53-57; assoc prof, Div Eng Sci, Purdue Univ, 57-58; prof math & dir, Holloman Grad Ctr, NMex, 58-66; prof math, Univ Mo-Rolla, 66-70, chmn dept, 67-68; chmn dept, 70-77, PROF MATH, UNIV NEW ORLEANS, 70- *Concurrent Pos:* Mem, Inst Math Sci, NY Univ, 56-57; consult, US Air Force Missile Develop Ctr, 56-65. *Mem:* Math Asn Am; Soc Indust & Appl Math. *Res:* Flight dynamics; differential equations; optimization; calculus of variations; operations research for ICBM defense. *Mailing Add:* Dept of Math Univ of New Orleans New Orleans LA 70122

FOOTE, JOEL LINDSLEY, b Cleveland, Ohio, Jan 11, 28; m 51; c 2. BIOCHEMISTRY. *Educ:* Miami Univ, BS, 52; Case Inst Technol, PhD(org chem), 60. *Prof Exp:* Teacher pub schs, Ohio, 52-56; res assoc biochem, Univ Mich, 60-62, part-time instr, 62-65, asst res biochemist, Ment Health Res Inst, 63-65; ASST ASSOC PROF, DEPT CHEM, WESTERN MICH UNIV, 65- *Concurrent Pos:* NSF fel, 60-62; USPHS trainee, 62-64. *Mem:* Am Chem Soc; Am Soc Biol Chemists; AAAS. *Res:* Lipid biochemistry; biochemistry of phenylketonuria; neurochemistry; glycosphingolipids; atherosclerosis. *Mailing Add:* Dept of Chem Western Mich Univ Kalamazoo MI 49008

FOOTE, KENNETH GERALD, b Cleveland, Ohio, Mar 24, 35; m 59; c 3. BIOLOGY EDUCATION, BRYOPHYTES & LICHENS. *Educ:* Hiram Col, AB, 58; Univ Wis, MS, 62, PhD(bot), 63. *Prof Exp:* Asst prof biol, Sheboygan Ctr, Univ Wis, 63-66; assoc prof, 66-78, PROF BIOL, UNIV WIS-EAU CLAIRE, 78- *Mem:* Am Bryol & Lichenological Soc; Brit Lichenological Soc; Am Inst Biol Sci; Nat Asn Biol Teachers. *Res:* Ecology of saxicolous lichen and bryophyte communities; Bryophytes and lichens of Wisconsin; methods and investigations in biology teaching. *Mailing Add:* Dept of Biol Univ Wis Eau Claire WI 54701

FOOTE, MURRAY WILBUR, b Charlotte, Vt, Mar 22, 16; m 40; c 2. BIOCHEMISTRY. *Educ:* Univ Vt, BS, 38, MS, 50; Univ Conn, PhD, 54. *Prof Exp:* Asst chemist, 40-51, from asst prof biochem to assoc prof biochem, 53-69; assoc biochemist, 53-69, ASSOC PROF MICROBIOL & BIOCHEM, UNIV VT, 69-, ASSOC BIOCHEMIST, AGR EXP STA, 77- *Mem:* Am Soc Plant Physiol. *Res:* Minor elements in plant metabolism; plant proteins and nitrogen metabolism in plants. *Mailing Add:* Agr Exp Sta Univ of Vt Burlington VT 05401

FOOTE, RICHARD HERBERT, b Bozeman, Mont, May 2, 18; m 43, 64; c 5. ENTOMOLOGY. *Educ:* Mont State Col, BS, 42; Johns Hopkins Univ, DSc(parasitol), 52. *Prof Exp:* Asst entom, Univ Minn, 42-43; entomologist, USPHS, 47-49; entomologist, Johns Hopkins Univ, 49-52; entomologist, Entom Res Div, 52-67, asst chief insect identification & parasite introd res br, 67-72, chief syst entom lab, Insect Identification & Beneficial Insect Introd Inst, Sci & Educ Admin-Agr, 72-76, RES ENTOMOLOGIST, INSECT IDENTIFICATION & BENEFICIAL INSECT INTROD INST, SCI & EDUC ADMIN-AGR, USDA, 76- *Concurrent Pos:* Mem coun, Biol Sci Info; mem ed bd, Abstracts Entom. *Honors &. Mem:* Entom Soc Am; Soc Syst Zool; Am Inst Biol Sci; Sigma Xi. *Res:* Taxonomy of Tephritidae; information storage and retrieval for biology. *Mailing Add:* Syst Entom Lab USDA c/o US Nat Mus NHB 168 Washington DC 20560

FOOTE, RICHARD MARTIN, b Chester, Eng, June 22, 50; Can citizen; m 81. MATHEMATICS. *Educ:* Univ Toronto, BSc, 72; Univ Cambridge, Eng, PhD(math), 76. *Prof Exp:* Res fel math, Trinity Col, Cambridge, 76-78; res fel, Trinity Col, Cambridge, 78-79; asst prof, Calif Inst Technol, 76-78; res fel, Trinity Col, Cambridge, 78-79; asst prof, Rutgers Univ, 79-80; ASST PROF MATH, UNIV MINN, 80-; ASST PROF MATH, UNIV VT, 81- *Res:* Finite simple groups; number theory. *Mailing Add:* Dept Math Univ Vt Burlington VT 05405

FOOTE, ROBERT HUTCHINSON, b Gilead, Conn, Aug 20, 22; m 46; c 2. ANIMAL PHYSIOLOGY. *Educ:* Univ Conn, BS, 43; Cornell Univ, MS, 47, PhD(animal breeding), 50. *Prof Exp:* Asst, 46-50, from asst prof to assoc prof, 50-63, PROF ANIMAL PHYSIOL, CORNELL UNIV, 63-, JACOB GOULD SCHURMAN PROF, 80- *Concurrent Pos:* Fulbright scholar, Denmark, 58-59; vis prof, Finland, 74 & Univ Calif, 78. *Honors & Awards:* NY Farmers' Award, 69; Award, Endocrinol & Physiol, 70; Award, Am Dairy Sci Asn, 70. *Mem:* Fel AAAS; Am Fertil Soc; Am Soc Animal Sci; Am Dairy Sci Asn; Soc Study Reproduction. *Res:* Superovulation; cellular preservation and cryogenic effects on sperm cells and embryos; embryo culture; fertility, embryonic mortality and congenital defects; aging and reproductive failure; sexual behavior. *Mailing Add:* Dept of Animal Sci Cornell Univ Ithaca NY 14850

FOOTE, ROBERT S, b Decatur, Ill, June 6, 22; m 53; c 4. PHYSICS. *Educ:* Univ Ill, BS, 48, MS, 49. *Prof Exp:* Mem tech staff, Nat Bur Standards, 49-55; sect head, Cent Res Lab, Tex Instruments, Inc, 57-60, chief geonuclear opers, Sci Serv Div, 61-68; pres, Geosensors Inc, 69-73, PRES, GEODATA INT INC, 73- *Mem:* Am Phys Soc; sr mem Inst Elec & Electronics Engrs. *Res:* Gamma ray spectroscopy; advanced electronic technology; instrumentation. *Mailing Add:* 2853 Claudette Ave Dallas TX 75211

FOOTE, VERNON STUART, JR, b East Grand Rapids, Mich, Dec 13, 24; m 55; c 3. PLASMA PHYSICS, ENGINEERING. *Educ:* George Washington Univ, BME, 51. *Prof Exp:* Armament engr ASW Ord, US Navy Bur Aeronaut, 51-52; sr designer ord, Nav Ord Lab, 52, 53-54; jr mech engr flight simulation, Melpar, Inc, 53; assoc engr, Washington Technol Assocs, Inc, 54-58; sr mech engr, Nat Co, Inc, Nat Radio Co, 58-59; mem prof tech staff, 60-80, SR MEM PROF TECH STAFF, PLASMA PHYSIS LAB, PRINCETON UNIV, 80- *Res:* Mechanisms; control theory; optics; electrooptics; hydraulics. *Mailing Add:* Plasma Physics Lab Princeton Univ 222 Guggenheim Bldg PO Box 451 Princeton NJ 08544

FOOTE, WARREN CHRISTOPHER, b Orderville, Utah, Oct 6, 27; m 49; c 6. ANIMAL PHYSIOLOGY. *Educ:* Utah State Univ, BS, 54; Univ Wis, MS, 55, PhD, 58. *Prof Exp:* From asst prof to assoc prof, 58-69, PROF ANIMAL PHYSIOL, UTAH STATE UNIV, 69- *Concurrent Pos:* Dir, Int Sheep & Goat Inst; consult, US AID, Bolivia, San Marcos Univ & Rockefeller Found. *Mem:* Am Soc Animal Sci. *Res:* Physiology and endocrinology of reproduction, animal behavior; mechanisms involved; influencing factors, their modification and control. *Mailing Add:* Dept Animal Sci Utah State Univ Logan UT 84322

FOOTE, WILFORD DARRELL, b Kanab, Utah, Jan 9, 31; m 53; c 7. ANIMAL PHYSIOLOGY. *Educ:* Utah State Univ, BS, 53; Univ Wis, MS, 56, PhD, 59. *Prof Exp:* Asst genetics & animal husb, Univ Wis, 55-59; PROF ANIMAL SCI & PHYSIOLOGIST, UNIV NEV, RENO, 59- *Mem:* AAAS; Am Soc Animal Sci; Soc Study Reproduction; Int Embryo Transfer Soc. *Res:* Physiology of reproduction. *Mailing Add:* Div Animal Sci Univ Nev Reno NV 89557

FOOTE, WILSON HOOVER, b Nephi, Utah, Jan 30, 20; m 52; c 2. AGRONOMY. *Educ:* Utah State Univ, BS, 42; Univ Minn, MS, 46, PhD, 48. *Prof Exp:* Field foreman, Nephi Dryland Exp Sta, Utah State Univ, 38-42; asst agronomist, Spec Guayule Res Proj, Bur Plant Indust, Soils & Agr Eng, USDA, 43-44; from asst prof to assoc prof, 48-58, PROF AGRON & AGRONOMIST, AGR EXP STA, ORE STATE UNIV, 58-, ASSOC DIR STA, 70- *Mem:* Fel Am Soc Agron. *Res:* Plant breeding; cereal crop production; research administration. *Mailing Add:* Agr Exp Sta Ag 127 Ore State Univ Corvallis OR 97331

FOOTT, WILLIAM HENRY, b Winnipeg, Man, June 6, 21; m 50; c 3. ENTOMOLOGY. *Educ:* Univ Man, BSA, 51; Ont Agr Col, MSA, 53; Univ Minn, PhD(entom), 59. *Prof Exp:* RES SCIENTIST, RES STA, CAN DEPT AGR, 53- *Mem:* Entom Soc Can; Prof Inst Pub Serv Can. *Res:* Ecology and control of insects attacking vegetables and field crops. *Mailing Add:* Res Sta Can Dept of Agr Harrow Can

FOPEANO, JOHN VINCENT, JR, b Ann Arbor, Mich, Jan 29, 28; m 50; c 4. BIOCHEMISTRY. *Educ:* Yale Univ, BA, 50; Univ Mich, MS, 52, PhD(biochem), 55. *Prof Exp:* Instr biochem, State Univ NY, Buffalo, 54-57, from asst to assoc prof, 57-70, consult, Dept Surg, 54-57; PROF MED TECHNOL & CHMN DEPT, CLIN CTR, SCH HEALTH & RELATED PROF, STATE UNIV NY BUFFALO, 70- *Concurrent Pos:* Consult, Mt St Mary's Hosp, Lewiston, NY, 61-78; dir sub-bd I student health serv clin lab, State Univ NY Buffalo, 73-; dir, Health Care Plan Clin Lab, West Seneca, NY, 78- *Mem:* Am Chem Soc; Am Asn Clin Chemists; Am Soc Med Technol. *Mailing Add:* 462 Grider St Clin Ctr Dept Med Tech State Univ of NY Buffalo NY 14215

FORAL, RALPH FRANCIS, b Omaha, Nebr, June 18, 34; m 57; c 5. ENGINEERING MECHANICS, MATERIALS SCIENCE. *Educ:* Univ Nebr, BS, 56; Univ Colo, MS, 58, PhD(eng mech), 63. *Prof Exp:* Assoc engr stress anal, Martin Marietta Corp, 56-58, engr, 58-60, sr engr, 60-62, design specialist, 62-63, res scientist, 63-64; assoc prof, 64-74, PROF ENG MECH, UNIV NEBR-LINCOLN, 74- *Concurrent Pos:* Consult, Martin Marietta Corp, 64-65 & Brunswick Corp, 65- *Honors & Awards:* Skylab Achievement Award, NASA, 74. *Mem:* Am Soc Eng Educ; Am Acad Mech; Am Soc Mech Engrs; Soc Advan Mat & Process Eng. *Res:* Composite materials; analysis and design of structures; pressure vessels; behavior of engineering materials. *Mailing Add:* Dept Eng Mech Univ Nebr Lincoln NE 68588

FORAN, JAMES MICHAEL, b Milwaukee, Wis, Oct 20, 42; m 71; c 1. MATHEMATICS. *Educ:* Marquette Univ, BA, 65; Univ Wis-Milwaukee, MS, 69, PhD(math), 73. *Prof Exp:* Teaching asst math, Univ Wis-Milwaukee, 67-73, lectr, 73-74; asst prof, 74-80, ASSOC PROF MATH, UNIV MO-KANSAS CITY, 80- *Concurrent Pos:* Consult, Archit & Design Graphics

Corp, 73-78; assoc ed, Real Anal Exchange, 76-78. *Mem:* Am Math Soc. *Res:* Functions of a real variable, integration and differentiation theory, measure theory, set theory particularly subsets of the line. *Mailing Add:* Dept of Math Univ of Mo Kansas City MO 64110

FORBES, ALBERT RONALD, b Victoria, BC, Oct 16, 31. ENTOMOLOGY. *Educ:* Univ BC, BA, 52, Ore State Univ, MS, 55; Univ Calif, PhD(entom, zool), 63. *Prof Exp:* Asst entomologist, Field Crop Insect Lab, Victoria, BC, 52-55; assoc entomologist, 56-67, res scientist, 67-73, SR RES SCIENTIST, RES STA, CAN DEPT AGR, 73- *Mem:* Entom Soc Am; Entom Soc Can. *Res:* Economic entomology; systematics of aphidiidae; ultrastructure of insects. *Mailing Add:* Res Sta Can Dept Agr 6660 NW Marine Dr Vancouver BC V6T 1X2 Can

FORBES, ALLAN LOUIS, b Richmond, Va, July 28, 28; m 54; c 3. INTERNAL MEDICINE. *Educ:* McGill Univ, BSc, 49; Med Col Va, MD, 53, MS, 64; Nat War Col, dipl, 68. *Prof Exp:* Intern, Montreal Gen Hosp, 53-54; from jr asst resident to sr asst resident internal med, Med Col Va, 54-56; assoc med & attend physician, Med Ctr, Univ Colo, 56-58; clin investr, Vet Admin Hosp, Richmond, Va, 58-61; asst dir med prog, Interdept Comt Nutrit Nat Defense, NIH, 61-63; med officer, Dept Army, 63-67, chief sci anal br, Life Sci Div, 68-70; dep dir div nutrit, Bur Foods, Food & Drug Admin, 71-73; dir nutrit bur, Health Protection Br, Ottawa, Ont, 73-74; assoc dir, Nutrit & Consumer Sci, 74-79, ASSOC DIR NUTRIT & FOOD SCI, BUR FOODS, FOOD & DRUG ADMIN, 79- *Concurrent Pos:* Intern, King Edward VII Mem Hosp, Bermuda, 53-54; chief clin physiol br, Physiol Div, US Army Med Res & Nutrit Lab, Denver, 56-58; lectr, Med Col Va, 58-73; assoc ed, Am J Clin Nutrit, 79-81; chmn, Food Standards Comn, Int Union Nutrit Sci, 78- *Mem:* Nutrit Soc Can; Am Inst Nutrit; Am Soc Clin Nutrit; Am Fedn Clin Res. *Res:* Clinical nutrition and metabolic disease; international and environmental medicine; food science and technology, food microbiology, food behavior and food marketing. *Mailing Add:* FB-8 Rm 1832 Bur of Foods Food & Drug Admin 200 C St SW Washington DC 20204

FORBES, DONNA JEAN, b Moline, Ill, June 12, 42; m 67; c 2. NEUROSCIENCE. *Educ:* Monmouth Col, BA, 64; Univ Wis-Madison, MS, 67, PhD(physiol), 71. *Prof Exp:* Med res assoc I neurosci, Galesburg State Res Hosp, Ill, 64-65; NIH fel, Dept Anat, Univ Wis-Madison, 70-73, instr, 73; ASST PROF ANAT, UNIV MINN, DULUTH, 73- *Concurrent Pos:* Consult & lectr, Col St Scholastica. *Mem:* Sigma Xi; Soc Neurosci; Cajal Club. *Res:* Neurophysiology and neuroanatomy of somatosensory systems, specifically looking at spinal inputs to thalamus in the squirrel monkey; development of the rat somatosensory system. *Mailing Add:* Dept Biomed Anat Univ of Minn Sch of Med Duluth MN 55812

FORBES, GILBERT BURNETT, b Rochester, NY, Nov 9, 15; m 39; c 2. PEDIATRICS. *Educ:* Univ Rochester, AB, 36, MD, 40. *Prof Exp:* Intern pediat, Strong Mem Hosp, Rochester, 40-41; asst pediatrician, St Louis Children's Hosp, 40-43, resident physician, 41-43; from instr to assoc prof pediat, Washington Univ, 43-50; prof & chmn dept, Univ Tex Southwestern Med Sch, 50-53; assoc prof, 53-57, PROF PEDIAT, SCH MED & DENT, UNIV ROCHESTER, 57-, PROF RADIATION BIOL & BIOPHYS, 70- *Concurrent Pos:* Physician, St Louis Children's Hosp, 41-43, asst pediatrician, 40-43; chief pediatrician, Los Alamos Hosp, 46-47; chief staff pediat, Parkland City-County Hosp & med clin, Children's Med Ctr, Dallas, 50-53; assoc pediatrician, Strong Mem Hosp, 53-57, pediatrician, 57-; guest lectr, Oxford Univ; consult hosps; mem comt infant nutrit, Food & Nutrit Bd, Nat Res Coun; mem sci adv comt, Nutrit Found; res fel, Oxford Univ, 70-71; Nat Inst Child Health & Human Develop res career award; chief ed, Am J Dis Child, 73- *Honors & Awards:* Borden Award, Am Acad Pediat, 64. *Mem:* AAAS; Am Acad Pediat; Am Pediat Soc (vpres, 75-76); Soc Pediat Res (pres, 60-61); AMA. *Res:* Metabolism in infancy and childhood; diagnosis and therapy of clinical pediatrics; pediatric endocrinology; chemical growth; body fluid physiology; infant nutrition. *Mailing Add:* Sch Med & Dent Univ Rochester Rochester NY 14620

FORBES, IAN, b Pittsburgh, Pa, Jan 16, 20; m 44; c 3. AGRONOMY, PLANT BREEDING. *Educ:* Univ Md, BSc, 41, MSc, 49, PhD(plant morphol), 54. *Prof Exp:* Mem res staff, Plant Indust Sta, USDA, Beltsville, 41-42, 45-47, res agronomist, 47-51, res agronomist, Coastal Plain Exp Sta, Univ Ga, 51-63, sr res agronomist, 63-78; RETIRED. *Honors & Awards:* Sears Roebuck Award, 60. *Mem:* Am Soc Agron; Am Genetic Asn; Crop Sci Soc Am. *Res:* Cytogenetics and breeding of forage legumes. *Mailing Add:* 200 Fulwood Blvd Tifton GA 31794

FORBES, JACK EDWIN, b Bloomington, Ill, Dec 11, 28; m 59. MATHEMATICS. *Educ:* Ill Wesleyan Univ, BS, 49; Bradley Univ, MS, 52; Purdue Univ, PhD(math), 57. *Prof Exp:* Instr math, Bradley Univ, 51-52; from instr to asst prof, Purdue Univ, 55-60; dir sec math, Educ Res Coun, Cleveland, Ohio, 60-61; dir res math, Britannica Ctr Studies Learning, Calif, 61-63; math consult, Encycl Britannica Press, 63-64; PROF MATH, PURDUE UNIV, CALUMET CAMPUS, 64- *Concurrent Pos:* Vis prof, Ball State Teachers Col, 58-60. *Mem:* Am Math Soc; Math Asn Am. *Res:* Foundations; mathematics education; programmed instruction; teacher education. *Mailing Add:* Div of Math Sci Purdue Univ Calumet Campus Hammond IN 46323

FORBES, JAMES, b Yonkers, NY, July 9, 10; m 37; c 1. ENTOMOLOGY. *Educ:* Fordham Univ, BS, 32, MS, 34, PhD(entom), 36. *Prof Exp:* From instr to prof, 36-79, EMER PROF, FORDHAM UNIV, 79- *Mem:* Entom Soc Am; Am Soc Zool; Coun Biol Ed. *Res:* Anatomy and histology of the ants. *Mailing Add:* Dept of Biol Fordham Univ Bronx NY 10458

FORBES, JAMES FRANKLIN, b Berwyn, Ill, Feb 9, 41; m 78; c 3. DENTAL MATERIALS. *Educ:* Wheaton Col, BS, 62; Southern Ill Univ, PhD(inorg chem), 68. *Prof Exp:* Instr chem, Drew Univ, 66-68; proj chemist, Ametek Tech Prod, 68-73; res chemist, Lee Pharmaceut, 73-74; proj leader, Am Hosp Supply Corp, 74-77, res chemist, 77-78, proj scientist, Group Technol Ctr,

78-81; SR CHEMIST, UNITEK CORP, 81- *Mem:* Am Chem Soc. *Res:* Formulation of composite dental restorative materials; development of polymeric and mineral systems for preventative and restorative dentistry. *Mailing Add:* 1391 Bryan Ave Tustin CA 92680

FORBES, JERRY WAYNE, b Oquawka, Ill, July 12, 41; m 61; c 2. PHYSICS. *Educ:* Western Ill Univ, BS, 63; Univ Md, MS, 67; Wash State Univ, PhD(physics), 76. *Prof Exp:* RES PHYSICIST, US NAVAL SURFACE WEAPONS CTR, WHITE OAK LAB, 63- *Mem:* Am Phys Soc. *Res:* High pressure physics of solids and liquids, specifically in phase transformations under shock wave loading; also, materials response due to interaction with particle beams. *Mailing Add:* Naval Surface Weapons Ctr Bldg 319 Silver Spring MD 20910

FORBES, MALCOLM HOLLOWAY, b New Haven, Conn, Aug 20, 33; m 63; c 3. ORGANIC CHEMISTRY. *Educ:* Yale Univ, BS, 54; Trinity Col, Conn, MS, 58; Cambridge Univ, PhD(org chem), 60. *Prof Exp:* Res assoc antibiotics, Mass Inst Technol, 60-61, fel, 62-63; consult chem, Ed Serv, Inc, Mass, 63-65; acad dean, Cazenovia Col, 65-70; dean, Col Arts & Sci, Millikin Univ, 70-78; V PRES ACAD AFFAIRS, UNIV EVANSVILLE, 78- *Mem:* Am Asn Higher Educ; AAAS; Am Chem Soc; Sigma Xi. *Res:* College or university administration and improvement of academic programs; curriculum development and evaluation in the sciences. *Mailing Add:* Univ of Evansville Box 329 Evansville IN 47702

FORBES, MARTIN, b Brussels, Belgium, July 25, 20; nat US; m 49; c 2. MICROBIOLOGY. *Educ:* Moravian Col, BS, 47; Univ Pa, MS, 49, PhD(microbiol), 51. *Prof Exp:* US Army res fel microbiol, Univ Hosp, Pa, 51-53, dir animal res proj & res assoc dept microbiol, Sch Med, 53-58; asst prof microbiol, Sch Med, Temple Univ, 58-59; group leader, Dept Chemother, Am Cyanamid Co, 59-65, head, Dept Antimicrobial Ther, 65-69, dir, Infectious Dis Ther Res Sect, Lederle Labs, 69-81; MGR CANCER CHEMOTHER RES, GLENOLDEN LABS, E I DU PONT DE NEMOURS & CO, INC, 82- *Concurrent Pos:* Res assoc, Walter Reed Army Inst Res, 53-58. *Mem:* Am Inst Nutrit; Am Soc Microbiol; NY Acad Sci. *Res:* Antimicrobial agents and chemotherapy. *Mailing Add:* Glenolden Lab E I Du Pont de Nemours & Co Inc Glenolden PA 19036

FORBES, MICHAEL SHEPARD, b Washington, DC, Jan 21, 45; m 70; c 2. BIOLOGICAL STRUCTURE, CELL BIOLOGY. *Educ:* Univ Va, Charlottesville, BA, 66, PhD(biol), 71. *Prof Exp:* Fel physiol, Univ Va, 71-73, res assoc physiol & biol, 73-74; instr, Univ Md, 74-75; asst prof, 76-78; RES ASST PROF PHYSIOL, UNIV VA, 79- *Concurrent Pos:* Res career develop award, NIH, 79-84. *Mem:* Am Soc Zoologists. *Res:* Fine structure and electron cytochemistry of cardiac muscle, skeletal muscle, smooth muscle and blood vessels; filaments and microtubules; sarcoplasmic reticulum; transverse tubules; cell-to-cell attachments. *Mailing Add:* Dept Physiol Univ Va Charlottesville VA 22901

FORBES, MILTON L, b Aruba, Netherlands Antilles, Dec 14, 30; c 4. BIOLOGY. *Educ:* Iowa State Teachers Col, BA, 52, MA, 53; Fla State Univ, PhD(marine biol), 62. *Prof Exp:* Instr biol, Burlington High Sch & Jr Col, Iowa, 53-56 & Ill State Norm Univ, 56-57; assoc prof, Francis State Nicholls Univ, 60-63; assoc prof biol & marine sci, Lamar Univ, 63-70; PROF BIOL & MARINE SCI, COL V I, 70- *Concurrent Pos:* NSF grant investr, 76-77. *Mem:* AAAS; Ecol Soc Am; Marine Biol Asn UK; Nat Sci Teachers Asn. *Res:* Ecology of oysters; science education. *Mailing Add:* Col of V I Kingshill P O St Croix VI 00850

FORBES, OLIVER CLIFFORD, b Eureka, Calif, May 25, 27. GENETICS. *Educ:* Humboldt State Col, AB, 50; Univ Calif, MA, 52, PhD(zool), 58. *Prof Exp:* Instr biol sci, San Francisco State Col, 56-57; from instr to asst prof, 57-68, ASSOC PROF ZOOL, UNIV IDAHO, 68- *Res:* Drosophila genetics; chromosome segregation; mutation. *Mailing Add:* Dept of Biol Sci Univ of Idaho Moscow ID 83843

FORBES, PAUL DONALD, b Binghamton, NY, Mar 3, 36; m 60; c 4. RADIOBIOLOGY. *Educ:* Wheaton Col, Ill, BS, 57; Brown Univ, PhD, 61. *Prof Exp:* Instr anat, Sch Med, Temple Univ, 61-64; assoc prof biol, Barrington Col, 64-68; ASSOC PROF DERMAT, SCH MED, TEMPLE UNIV, 68- *Concurrent Pos:* USPHS traineeship cancer, Sch Med, Temple Univ, 61-64; radiobiologist, Roger Williams Gen Hosp, Providence, RI, 66-68. *Mem:* AAAS; Radiation Res Soc; Am Asn Cancer Res; Soc Invest Dermat; Am Soc Photobiol. *Res:* Chemical and physical carcinogenesis; photobiology of skin. *Mailing Add:* Skin & Cancer Hosp Temple Univ Sch of Med Philadelphia PA 19140

FORBES, RICHARD BRAINARD, b Ellington, NY, Aug 29, 21; m 50; c 2. SOIL FERTILITY, VEGETABLE CROPS. *Educ:* Rollins Col, BS, 43; Univ Fla, MS, 48; Pa State Univ, PhD(agron, soils), 56. *Prof Exp:* Asst soils chemist, Exp Sta, Univ Fla, 48-49, asst prof soils, Univ, 49-53; chemist & agent, US Regional Pasture Res Lab, Pa State Univ, 53-56; asst soils chemist, 56-67, ASSOC SOILS CHEMIST, INST FOOD & AGR SCI, CENT FLA EXP STA, UNIV FLA, 67- *Mem:* Am Soc Agron; Soil Sci Soc Am; Am Inst Chemists. *Res:* Plant nutrients in farm drainage water; soil fertility; plant nutrition; vegetables; soybeans. *Mailing Add:* Agr Res & Educ Ctr Box 909 Univ Fla Sanford FL 32771

FORBES, RICHARD BRYAN, b Correctionville, Iowa, July 29, 36; m 60; c 2. VERTEBRATE ZOOLOGY, ECOLOGY. *Educ:* Univ SDak, AB, 58; Univ NMex, MS, 61; Univ Minn, PhD(ecol), 64. *Prof Exp:* From asst prof to assoc prof, 64-76, PROF BIOL, PORTLAND STATE UNIV, 76- *Mem:* Am Soc Naturalists; AAAS; Am Soc Mammal; Ecol Soc Am. *Res:* Ecology and life histories of terrestrial vertebrates, particularly mammals. *Mailing Add:* Dept Biol Portland State Univ Portland OR 97207

FORBES, RICHARD MATHER, b Wooster, Ohio, Jan 8, 16; m 44; c 3. NUTRITION. *Educ:* Pa State Col, BS, 38, MS, 39; Cornell Univ, PhD(nutrit), 42. *Prof Exp:* Instr biochem, Wayne State Univ, 42; res fel, Cornell Univ, 42-43; asst prof animal husb, Univ Ky, 46-49; assoc prof, 49-55, PROF NUTRIT BIOCHEM, UNIV ILL, URBANA-CHAMPAIGN, 55- *Concurrent Pos:* Mem comn animal nutrit, Nat Res Coun, 61-70; mem nutrit study sect, NIH, 74-78. *Honors & Awards:* Gustav Bohstedt Award, Am Soc Animal Sci, 68; H H Mitchell Award, Univ Ill, 81. *Mem:* AAAS; Am Soc Animal Sci; Am Chem Soc; Am Inst Nutrit. *Res:* Mineral metabolism of animals. *Mailing Add:* 2005 S Vine St Urbana IL 61801

FORBES, ROBERT SHIRLEY, b Moncton, NB, Mar 14, 21; m 45; c 3. FOREST ENTOMOLOGY. *Educ:* Univ NB, BScF, 44, MScF, 49; Ohio State Univ, PhD(entom), 60. *Prof Exp:* Res officer, Forest Insect Surv, Can Dept Agr, 44-55, head, Forest Insect & Dis Surv, Maritime Provs, 55-74, head, Tech Servs Sect, 74-77; res scientist res spruce budworm control, Maritime Forest Res Ctr, Environ Can, 77-80. *Concurrent Pos:* Actg prof forest entom, Fac Forestry, Univ NB, 77-78. *Mem:* Entom Soc Can; Can Inst Forestry. *Res:* Finding ways of increasing the effectiveness of native parasitoids of the spruce budworm, especially Apanteles fumiferanae Vier. and Glypta fumiferanae (Vier.). *Mailing Add:* 1 Acacia Grove Fredericton NB E3B 1Y7 Can

FORBES, THOMAS ROGERS, b New York, NY, Jan 5, 11; m 34; c 2. ANATOMY. *Educ:* Univ Rochester, BA, 33, PhD(anat), 37. *Hon Degrees:* MA, Yale Univ, 62. *Prof Exp:* Asst anat, Sch Med, Johns Hopkins Univ, 37-38, instr, 38-45; tech aide, Div Med Sci, Nat Res Coun & comt med res, Off Sci Res & Develop, 42-45; from instr to assoc prof, 45-62, from asst dean to assoc dean sch med, 48-70, prof, 62-79, EMER PROF ANAT, SCH MED, YALE UNIV, 79- *Concurrent Pos:* Guggenheim fel, 42; fel, Branford Col, Yale Univ, 51-, adv, Yale Med Memorabilia, 74-; mem fac hist & philos of pharm & med, Worshipful Soc Apothecaries, London; sr res fel hist med, Yale Univ, 79- *Honors & Awards:* De Laune lectr & medalist, Worshipful Soc Apothecaries, London. *Mem:* AAAS; Endocrine Soc; Am Asn Hist Med; Am Asn Anatomists; fel Royal Soc Med. *Res:* Endocrinology and embryology of reptilian reproductive system; embryology of human reproductive system; physiology of sex hormones in mammals; history of biology and medicine. *Mailing Add:* Sect of Gross Anat Dept of Surg Yale Univ Sch of Med New Haven CT 06510

FORBES, WARREN C, b New York, NY, Nov 25, 39; m 61; c 3. MINERALOGY. *Educ:* Hofstra Univ, BA, 61; Brown Univ, MSc, 63, PhD(mineral), 66. *Prof Exp:* Asst prof geol, Univ Ga, 65-66; asst prof, 66-74, ASSOC PROF GEOL, UNIV ILL, CHICAGO CIRCLE, 74- *Mem:* Am Mineral Soc. *Res:* Experimental determination of the stability relations of amphiboles and layer-lattice silicates; crystal chemistry. *Mailing Add:* Dept of Geol Sci Univ Ill Chicago Circle Box 4348 Chicago IL 60680

FORBES, WILLIAM FREDERICK, b Can; m 72; c 3. BIOMETRICS. *Educ:* London Univ, BSc, 46, BSc hons, 49, PhD(org chem), 52, DSc(phys org chem), 64. *Prof Exp:* Lectr chem, Univ Nottingham, Eng, 52-53; from assoc prof to prof, Univ Nfld, 53-59; prin res officer, Commonwealth Sci & Indust Res Orgn, Australia, 59-62; prof chem, 62-69, dean fac math, 72-80, PROF STATIST, UNIV WATERLOO, 66- *Concurrent Pos:* Vis prof biochem, Univ Rochester, 64-71; spec consult, Nat Inst Child Health, Develop & Aging, 66-70; mem, Comt Presidents of Univs of Ont, 70-71; chmn bd, Off Comput Coord, Coun Ont Univs, 71-73; hon assoc, Royal Holloway Col, London Univ, 71-; head, Ref Assessment Smoking Habits, WHO Collaborating Ctr, 78- *Mem:* Can Asn Geront (pres, 71-73); Geront Soc (vpres, 71-72). *Res:* Epidemiological studies on aging, in particular the effects of cigarette smoking and trace metals; use of mathematical modelling in the evaluation of risk factors. *Mailing Add:* Fac of Math Univ of Waterloo Waterloo ON N2L 3G1 Can

FORBES-RESHA, JUDITH, b Fullerton, Calif, Sept 27, 42; m 67; c 3. INERTIAL INSTRUMENTATION. *Educ:* Calif State Univ, Fullerton, BA, 74, MS, 79. *Prof Exp:* Engr, Electro Mech Div, Northrop, 75-79; mem tech staff, TRW, Inc, 79-80; PROJ ENGR, ELECTRONICS DIV, NORTHROP, 80- *Concurrent Pos:* Lectr, Univ Southern Calif, Univ Calif, Los Angeles & Univ Ill. *Mem:* Soc Women Engrs; Soc Advan Mat & Process Eng; Am Inst Aeronat & Astronaut. *Res:* Atmospheric radioactivity; biomedical engineering; stress analysis of wire rope cabling; inertial instruments. *Mailing Add:* 7066 Country Club Lane Anaheim CA 92807

FORBIS, ORIE LESTER, JR, b Encinal, Tex, Dec 25, 22; m 46; c 2. PEDIATRICS, PSYCHIATRY. *Educ:* Univ Tex, BA, 51, MD, 53. *Prof Exp:* Res pediat, John Sealy Hosp, Tex, 54-57, res pediat psychiat & neurol, 57-59; child psychiat, Hawthorn Ctr, Mich, 59-61; asst prof psychiat & pediat & dir child guid clin, Med Ctr, Univ Ark, 62-66; psychiatrist dir, Genesee County Ment Health Serv Bd, Mich, 66-67; dir children's serv, Ment Health-Ment Retardation Ctr Austin-Travis County, Austin, 67-69; chief child psychiatrist, Northwest Ment Health Ctr, 69-73; OUTREACH PSYCHIATRIST, SAN ANTONIO STATE HOSP, 73- *Concurrent Pos:* Consult, Northville State Hosp & pub schs, Mich; dir ment health planning, Ark State Health Dept, 63-65; clin assoc prof pediat & psychiat, Med Sch, Univ Tex, San Antonio, 69-73. *Mem:* AMA; Am Acad Ment Deficiency; Am Psychiat Asn. *Res:* Child psychiatry; longitudinal studies of emotional development of children with special reference to socioeconomically-culturally deprived. *Mailing Add:* 314 E Lincoln St New Braunfels TX 78130

FORBRICH, CARL A, JR, b San Antonio, Tex, Nov 5, 39; m 62; c 2. AERONAUTICAL ENGINEERING. *Educ:* Univ Tex, Austin, BS, 61; Univ Okla, MS, 63; Stanford Univ, PhD(aeronaut eng), 67; Univ Colo, Boulder, MBA, 71. *Prof Exp:* Proj engr, Boeing Aircraft Co, Wash, 61; US Air Force, 61-, aerodynamicist, Tinker AFB, Okla, 61-64, from instr to assoc prof aeronaut, US Air Force Acad, 67-71, res assoc, F J Seiler Res Lab, 71-73, proj officer, Chem Laser Br, 73-74, sect chief, 74-75, br chief, Chem Laser Br, Air Force Weapons Lab, 75-79, chief, Munitions Div, Air Force Armament Lab, 79-82, DEP SYST PROG DIR, DEFENSE SATELLITE COMMUN SYST, SPACE DIV, LOS ANGELES, 82- *Mem:* Assoc fel Am Inst Aeronaut & Astronaut; Am Phys Soc. *Res:* Experimental measurement of atomic oscillator strengths in high temperature gases; spectral line broadening; high energy laser research and development. *Mailing Add:* 601 Mooney Rd Ft Walton Beach FL 32548

FORBUSH, BLISS, III, b Pittsburg, Pa, July 1, 45; m 67; c 2. MEMBRANE TRANSPORT. *Educ:* Harvard Col, AB, 67; Johns Hopkins Univ, PhD(physiol), 75. *Prof Exp:* Fel physiol, 75-79, ASST PROF PHYSIOL, YALE UNIV SCH MED, 79- *Res:* Molecular mechanism of solute transport across cell membranes; mechanism of the sodium, potassium-pump, and characterization of a sodium, potassium, chlorine co-transport system. *Mailing Add:* Yale Univ Sch Med 333 Cedar St New Haven CT 06510

FORCE, CARLTON GREGORY, b Gouverneur, NY, Aug 5, 26; m 53; c 4. COLLOID CHEMISTRY. *Educ:* Clarkson Col Technol, BS, 52, PhD(phys chem), 65; Univ Ill, MS, 57. *Prof Exp:* Chemist, Merck & Co, Inc, 52-56; res chemist, Esso Res & Eng Co, 57-59; res chemist, Latex Fiber Industs, Inc, 59-61, sr res chemist, 63-67; res chemist, 67-70, sr res chemist, 70-78, RES ASSOC, WESTVACO CORP, 78- *Mem:* Am Chem Soc. *Res:* Colloid chemistry particularly rubber latex systems and rosin and fatty acid emulsifiers; paper making industry. *Mailing Add:* 239 Hobcaw Dr Mt Pleasant SC 29464

FORCE, DON CLEMENT, b Clear Lake, SDak, July 5, 28; m 53; c 3. ENTOMOLOGY. *Educ:* Fresno State Col, BA, 54; Univ Calif, Davis, MS, 58; Univ Calif, Berkeley, PhD(entom), 63. *Prof Exp:* Entomologist, Stauffer Chem Co, 56-58; lab technologist biol control, Univ Calif, Berkeley, 58-62; entomologist, USDA, 62-65; from asst prof to assoc prof, 65-73, PROF BIOL SCI, CALIF STATE POLYTECH UNIV, 73- *Mem:* AAAS; Am Soc Naturalists; Ecol Soc Am. *Res:* Insect ecology and biological control. *Mailing Add:* Dept of Biol Sci Calif State Polytech Univ Pomona CA 91768

FORCE, LUCY McCARTAN, see McCartan, Lucy

FORCHHEIMER, OTTO LOUIS, b Nurnberg, Ger, Sept 18, 26; US citizen; m 57; c 2. PHYSICAL CHEMISTRY, INORGANIC CHEMISTRY. *Educ:* McGill Univ, BSc, 47; Brown Univ, PhD(chem), 51. *Prof Exp:* Res chemist, Univ Chicago, 51-53; sr res chemist, Gen Abrasive Co, 53-58, asst dir res, 58-59; mgr chem div, Trionics Corp, 59-62; tech dir, 62-67, VPRES & DIR, DOLOMITE BRICK CORP AM, 67-; dir res, 62-80, VPRES MKT & TECH, J E BAKER CO, 80- *Mem:* Am Chem Soc; Am Ceramic Soc; Am Soc Testing & Mat; Refractories Inst; Nat Lime Asn. *Res:* Rates and mechanisms of inorganic reactions; chemistry of abrasives; refractories. *Mailing Add:* J E Baker Co PO Box 1189 York PA 17405

FORCHIELLI, AMERICO LEWIS, b Alpha, NJ, May 28, 22; m 42; c 1. CHEMISTRY. *Educ:* Lafayette Col, BA, 47. *Prof Exp:* Chemist resins, Hercules Powder Co, 47-48; group leader explosives, Picatinny Arsenal, 48-52; res dir waxes, Sure-Seal Corp, 52-53; res chemist, Cent Res Lab, Gen Aniline & Film Corp, 53-54; res chemist, Masury-Young Co, 54-56, dir res & mgr lab, 56-66, res dir, Masury-Columbia Co Div, Alberto-Culver Co, 66-69; prod mgr, Wayland Chem Div, Philip A Hunt Chem Co, Lincoln, 69-74; gen mgr opers, 74-78, exec tech dir, 78-80, VPRES RES & DEVELOP, BUTCHER POLISH CO, 80- *Mem:* Am Chem Soc; fel Am Inst Chem. *Res:* Organic and polymer research; detergents; textile chemicals; lubricants; waxes and specialty products; chemical specialties field. *Mailing Add:* 3 Sherwood Dr Sterling Junction MA 01565

FORCHIELLI, ENRICO HENRY, b West Boylston, Mass, Jan 26, 18; m 47; c 3. BIOCHEMISTRY. *Educ:* Mass Col Pharm, BS, 40; Clark Univ, AB, 51; Boston Univ, MA, 53, PhD(biochem), 56. *Prof Exp:* Res assoc steroid metab, Worcester Found Exp Biol, 47-62, sr scientist, 62-64; head dept steroid metab, 64-72, ASST DIR INST BIOL SCI, SYNTEX RES CTR, 72- *Mem:* Am Soc Biol Chemists; Endocrine Soc. *Res:* Steroid metabolism; biosynthesis enzymology. *Mailing Add:* Inst Biol Sci Syntex Res Ctr Palo Alto CA 94304

FORCIER, GEORGE ARTHUR, b Mapleville, RI, Nov 29, 38; m 64; c 2. ANALYTICAL CHEMISTRY. *Educ:* Providence Col, BS, 60; Univ Mass, MS, 64, PhD(anal chem), 66. *Prof Exp:* Res chemist, 66-71, proj leader, 71-79, mgr, 79-81, ASST DIR, PFIZER, INC, 81- *Res:* Electroanalytical chemistry in acetonitrile; electroanalytical and other instrumental methods of analysis. *Mailing Add:* Pfizer Inc Eastern Pt Rd Groton CT 06340

FORD, ALBERT LEWIS, JR, b Ft Worth, Tex, May 12, 46; m 68; c 2. PHYSICS, MOLECULAR PHYSICS. *Educ:* Rice Univ, BA, 68; Univ Tex, Austin, PhD(chem physics), 72. *Prof Exp:* Res fel atomic & molecular physics, Harvard Col Observ, Harvard Univ, 72-73; asst prof, 73-78, ASSOC PROF PHYSICS, TEX A&M UNIV, 79- *Mem:* Am Phys Soc. *Res:* Ab initio calculations on small diatomic molecules, specifically processes involving a breakdown of the Born-Oppenheimer Approximation; ionization and charge transfer in atom-ion collisions, particularly inner-shell processes. *Mailing Add:* Dept Physics Tex A&M Univ College Station TX 77843

FORD, ARTHUR B, b Seattle, Wash, Sept 4, 32; m 55; c 2. GEOLOGY, PETROLOGY. *Educ:* Univ Wash, BS, 54, MS, 57, PhD(geol), 59. *Prof Exp:* Asst prof geol, San Diego State Col, 58-60; GEOLOGIST, US GEOL SURV, 60- *Mem:* Geol Soc Am. *Res:* Geology of Antarctica and Alaska; metamorphic and igneous petrology; petrology of Dufek intrusion, Antarctica; geology and petrology of Glacier Peak Wilderness Area, North Cascades, Washington. *Mailing Add:* Alaskan Geol Br US Geol Surv 345 Middlefield Rd Menlo Park CA 94025

FORD, C(LARENCE) QUENTIN, b Glenwood, NMex, Aug 6, 23; m 50; c 2. MECHANICAL ENGINEERING. *Educ:* Merchant Marine Acad, BS, 44; NMex State Univ, BSME, 49; Univ Mo, MS, 50; Mich State Univ, PhD, 59. *Prof Exp:* Instr mech eng, Univ Mo, 49-50; from instr to asst prof, Wash State Univ, 50-56; instr, Mich State Univ, 56-59; chmn dept, 60-70, PROF MECH ENG, N MEX STATE UNIV, 59- ASSOC DEAN ENG, 76- *Mem:*

AAAS; Am Soc Mech Engrs; Nat Soc Prof Engrs; Am Soc Eng Educ; Sigma Xi. *Res:* Combustion kinetics; rate of scale formation in boiling processes; heat transfer; thermodynamics. *Mailing Add:* NMex State Univ PO Box 3449 Las Cruces NM 88003

FORD, CLINITA ARNSBY, b Okmulgee, Okla, Sept 23, 28; m 51; c 3. NUTRITION. *Educ:* Lincoln Univ, Mo, BS; Columbia Univ, MS; Kans State Univ, PhD(foods & nutrit). *Prof Exp:* Asst prof home econ, Fla A&M Univ, 49-56; res asst, Kans State Univ, 56-59; prof home econ & chmn dept, 59-77, PROF CONSUMER SCI & TECHNOL & COORDR TITLE III PROG, FLA A&M UNIV, 77- *Concurrent Pos:* Dir & admin consult, Proj Upward Bound, Fla A&M Univ, 65-70; Fla del, White House Conf Aging, 71; mem, Nat Coun Admin Women in Educ. *Mem:* Am Dietetic Asn; Am Home Econ Asn; Am Voc Asn; Inst Food Technol; Am Voc Educ Res Asn. *Res:* Nutritional status of children as determined by dietary and biochemical analysis. *Mailing Add:* 404 Foute-Hilyer Admin Ctr Fla A&M Univ Tallahassee FL 32307

FORD, CLINTON BANKER, b Ann Arbor, Mich, Mar 1, 13; m 40, 61. ASTRONOMY. *Educ:* Univ Mich, AB, 35, MS, 36. *Prof Exp:* Asst astron, Brown Univ, 39-41; instr, Smith Col, 41-42; group leader pure sci, Ordwes Labs, Wesleyan Univ, 46-50, asst dir, 50-53; vpres & res dir, 53-61, TECH CONSULT, NIKOR PROD CO, 61- *Concurrent Pos:* Trustee, Ithaca Col, 67- *Mem:* AAAS; fel Am Astron Soc; Optical Soc Am; Am Inst Aeronaut & Astronaut; Am Asn Variable Star Observers (secy, 48-, pres, 61-62). *Res:* Photometry of variable stars; celestial navigation; highspeed photography; spectroscopy; photo developing equipment. *Mailing Add:* Ten Canterbury Lane Wilton CT 06897

FORD, DANIEL MORGAN, b Medford, Ore, Apr 5, 42; m 65; c 3. SKIN BIOLOGY, TOXICOLOGY. *Educ:* Ore State Univ, BA, 64; Ore Health Sci Univ, PhD(anat), 71. *Prof Exp:* Instr biol, Ore State Univ, 64-66; NIH trainee, Ore Regional Primate Res Ctr, 66-70; scientist, Syntex Res, 70-77; dept head, Int Flavors & Fragrances, Inc, 77-82; VPRES & TECH DIR, HILL TOP RES, INC, 82- *Concurrent Pos:* Consult, Res Inst Fragrance Mat, 78-82, Fragrance Mat Asn, 80-81. *Mem:* Soc Invest Dermat; Am Soc Photobiol; Am Col Toxicol; AAAS; NY Acad Sci. *Res:* Skin as a model for the study of cellular control mechanisms and immunology, as well as practical application in safety evaluation and claims substantiation for pharmaceuticals and consumer products; clinical manifestations of skin allergy, photobiology, and percutaneous absorption; neurobehavioral toxicology. *Mailing Add:* 207 Deepdale Dr Middletown NJ 07748

FORD, DAVID A, b Pasadena, Calif, Oct 25, 35; m 64; c 2. MATHEMATICS. *Educ:* Occidental Col, AB, 56; Univ Utah, MS, 58, PhD(math), 62. *Prof Exp:* Asst prof, 65-71, ASSOC PROF MATH, EMORY UNIV, 71- *Mem:* Am Math Soc; Math Asn Am. *Res:* Functional analysis and ordinary differential equations; applications in the mathematical theory of optimal control. *Mailing Add:* Dept of Math Emory Univ Atlanta GA 30322

FORD, DENYS KENSINGTON, b Newcastle, Eng, Aug 8, 23; Can citizen; m 55; c 3. MEDICINE, RHEUMATOLOGY. *Educ:* Cambridge Univ, BA, 44, MB, 47, MD, 53; FRCPS(C). *Prof Exp:* Registr med, London Hosp Med Col, Eng, 51-53; assoc prof, 60-73, PROF MED, FAC MED, UNIV BC, 73- *Concurrent Pos:* Fel, Fac Med, Univ BC, 54-60. *Mem:* Am Rheumatism Asn; Can Med Asn; Can Soc Clin Invest. *Res:* Arthritis; tissue culture; virology; mycoplasmology. *Mailing Add:* The Arthritis Ctr 895 W Tenth Ave Vancouver BC V5Z 1L7 Can

FORD, DONALD HERBERT, b Kansas City, Mo, Aug 18, 21; m 44; c 1. ANATOMY, PHYSIOLOGY. *Educ:* Wesleyan Univ, BA, 47; Univ Kans, PhD(anat), 52. *Prof Exp:* Asst physiol, Wesleyan Univ, 47-49; asst instr anat, Univ Kans, 49-50; from instr to prof anat, State Univ NY Downstate Med Ctr, 52-77; ASSOC RES DIR, COUN TOBACCO RES, 77- *Concurrent Pos:* Consult, Vet Admin Hosp, Brooklyn, 59- & Long Island Col Hosp. *Mem:* Endocrine Soc; Am Asn Anat; Am Soc Neurochem; Am Physiol Soc; Int Soc Neurochem. *Res:* Interrelationship between the nervous and endocrine system; thyroid-central nervous system interrelations; role of the neurosecretory system as an intermediary between the central nervous system and thyroid; neurochemistry, protein and ribonucleic acid metabolism. *Mailing Add:* Coun Tobacco Res 110 E 59th St New York NY 10022

FORD, DONALD HOSKINS, b Upland, Calif, July 28, 30; m 53; c 3. PLANT PATHOLOGY. *Educ:* Pomona Col, BA, 52; Claremont Col, MA, 54; Univ Calif, PhD(plant path), 58. *Prof Exp:* Asst bot, Rancho Santa Ana Bot Garden, 53-54; res plant pathologist, Forest Serv, US Dept Agr, 54-55; asst plant path, Univ Calif, 55-58; sr plant pathologist, Chem Plant Dis Control, 58-64, plant sci rep, Calif, 64-66; regional coordr, Calif Res Sta, 66-71, res scientist, 71-73, res assoc, 73-80, RES ADV, CALIF RES STA, ELI LILLY & CO, 80- *Mem:* AAAS; Am Phytopath Soc; Am Inst Biol Sci; Sigma Xi. *Res:* fungicides, herbicides and growth regulators; soil fungi in relation to plant roots; mycological interest in the Phycomycetes. *Mailing Add:* Lilly Res Lab 7521 W California Ave Fresno CA 93706

FORD, DWAIN, CHEMISTRY. *Educ:* Andrews Univ, BA, 49; Clark Univ, PhD(chem), 62. *Prof Exp:* Instr sci & math, Wis Acad, 49-58; from asst prof to assoc prof, 62-67, chmn dept, 63-71, PROF CHEM, ANDREWS UNIV, 67-, ACAD DEAN, 71-, DEAN, COL ARTS & SCI, 74- *Mem:* Sigma Xi; Am Asn Higher Educ; Am Chem Soc. *Res:* Chemical carcinogenesis; fatty acid metabolism; organic reaction mechanisms. *Mailing Add:* Col Arts & Sci Andrews Univ Berrien Springs MI 49104

FORD, EMORY A, b South New Berlin, NY, Oct 17, 40; m 63; c 2. ORGANIC POLYMER CHEMISTRY. *Educ:* Hartwick Col, BA, 62; Syracuse Univ, PhD(org chem), 67. *Prof Exp:* Res chemist, 67-72, res group leader polymers, 72-78, technol mgr, 78-81, MGR RES NORTHERN PETROCHEM, MORRIS, ILL, 81- *Mem:* Am Chem Soc; AAAS; Soc Plastics Engrs. *Res:* Synthesis and evaluation of polymeric composites; organic reactions of high polymers. *Mailing Add:* Northern Petrochem Morris FL 60450

FORD, FLOYD MALLORY, b Montgomery Co, Tenn, Feb 21, 21; m 45. ZOOLOGY. *Educ:* Univ Tenn, BS, 49; George Peabody Col, MA, 52; Vanderbilt Univ, PhD(biol), 63. *Prof Exp:* Instr agr, instnl on-the-farm training, 49-50; teacher, Jo Byrns High Sch, 50-51; instr, 52-54, from asst prof to assoc prof, 55-62, PROF BIOL, AUSTIN PEAY STATE UNIV, 63- *Mem:* AAAS; Am Inst Biol Sci; Entom Soc Am; Nat Audubon Soc. *Res:* Taxonomy and ecology of collembola. *Mailing Add:* Dept of Biol Austin Peay State Univ Clarksville TN 37040

FORD, FREDERICK EDDY, chemical engineering, physical chemistry, see previous edition

FORD, GEORGE DUDLEY, b Morgantown, WVa, Aug 18, 40; m 65; c 2. PHYSIOLOGY, BIOPHYSICS. *Educ:* WVa Univ, BS, 61, PhD(pharmacol), 67; Univ Iowa, MS, 64. *Prof Exp:* Instr pharmacol, WVa Univ, 67; AEC fel biophys, Sch Med & Dent, Univ Rochester, 67-70; asst prof, 70-78, ASSOC PROF PHYSIOL, HEALTH SCI DIV, MED COL VA, VA COMMONWEALTH UNIV, 78- *Mem:* Am Physiol Soc; AAAS; Biophys Soc. *Res:* Physiology of vascular smooth muscle; mechanisms of action of adrenergic agonists; mathematical models of membrane transport and adrenergically mediated responses; bioinstrumentation. *Mailing Add:* Dept of Physiol Med Col of Va Va Commonwealth Univ Richmond VA 23298

FORD, GEORGE PRATT, b Leesburg, Ga, Apr 25, 19; m 44; c 2. CHEMISTRY. *Educ:* Ga Inst Technol, BS, 40; Columbia Univ, MA, 48, PhD(chem), 49. *Prof Exp:* Radio chemist, 49-78, CONSULT, LOS ALAMOS SCI LAB, UNIV CALIF, 78- *Mem:* Am Chem Soc; Am Math Soc; Am Phys Soc. *Res:* Aerosols; radio chemistry; fission; statistical treatment of data. *Mailing Add:* 1292 45th St Los Alamos NM 87544

FORD, GEORGE WILLARD, b Detroit, Mich, Jan 25, 27; m 53; c 3. THEORETICAL PHYSICS. *Educ:* Univ Mich, AB, 49, MS, 50, PhD, 55. *Prof Exp:* Asst prof physics, Univ Notre Dame, 54-58; from asst prof to assoc prof, 58-68, PROF PHYSICS, UNIV MICH, ANN ARBOR, 68- *Concurrent Pos:* Mem, Inst Advan Study, 55-56. *Mem:* Am Phys Soc. *Res:* Statistical mechanics; nuclear physics; graph theory. *Mailing Add:* Dept of Physics Univ of Mich Ann Arbor MI 48109

FORD, GILBERT CLAYTON, b Hill City, Kans, Mar 31, 23; m 46; c 3. PHYSICS. *Educ:* Univ Colo, AB, 43; Harvard Univ, MA, 48, PhD(physics), 51. *Prof Exp:* Jr physicist, Manhattan Dist Proj, Univ Calif & Nat Bur Standards, 44-46; fac mem physics, 50-70, V PRES ACAD AFFAIRS, NORTHWEST NAZARENE COL, 70- *Concurrent Pos:* Assoc res physicist, Univ Calif, Berkeley, 58; NSF & Res Corp basic res grants mass spectroscopy, 58-70. *Res:* Mass spectroscopy. *Mailing Add:* Northwest Nazarene Col Nampa ID 83651

FORD, HOLLAND COLE, b Norman, Okla, Apr 12, 40. GALAXIES, PLANETARY NEBULAE. *Educ:* Univ Okla, BS, 62; Univ Wis, PhD(astron), 70. *Prof Exp:* Physicist, US Naval Ord Lab, Corona, 64-65; mem tech staff astrodynamics, TRW, Inc, 65-66; fel astron, Univ Ore, 70-71; asst prof, 71-76, ASSOC PROF ASTRON, UNIV CALIF, LOS ANGELES, 76- *Mem:* Int Astron Union; Am Astron Soc. *Res:* Gaseous nebulae and extragalactic astronomy. *Mailing Add:* Dept Astron Univ Calif Los Angeles CA 90024

FORD, JAMES, b Ryderwood, Wash, Sept 30, 27; m 51; c 4. BIOLOGY, ZOOLOGY. *Educ:* Western Wash State Col, BA(educ) & BA(biol), 51; Ore State Univ, MS, 53, PhD(zool), 62. *Prof Exp:* Instr biol, Wash High Sch, 51-54; instr, Skagit Valley Col, 54-56; instr, Ore Col Educ, 56-57; chmn dept, 57-66, chmn div natural sci, 64-65, dean instr, 65-77, PRES, SKAGIT VALLEY COL, 77- *Mem:* AAAS. *Res:* Chromosome study of pulmonate snails. *Mailing Add:* Skagit Valley Col Mt Vernon WA 98273

FORD, JAMES ARTHUR, b Chicago, Ill, Feb 3, 34. MATERIALS SCIENCE, METALLURGY. *Educ:* Univ Mich, BS(chem eng) & BS(metall eng), 56, MS, 57, PhD(metall eng), 62. *Prof Exp:* Instr metall eng, Univ Mich, 59-61; sr res scientist, Mat Sci Sect, Res Labs, United Aircraft Corp, 61-64; supvr alloy systs group, 65-67, chief chem metall sect, 67-72, assoc dir, Olin Metals Res Labs, Olin Corp, 73-74; vpres res & develop, Conalco, Inc, 74-75; DIR RES & DEVELOP, COMPOSITE CAN DIV, BOISE CASCADE CORP, 75- *Concurrent Pos:* Adj assoc prof metall, Rensselaer Polytech Inst, 61-71. *Mem:* Am Soc Testing Mat; Nat Asn Corrosion Engrs; Electrochem Soc; Am Soc Mech Engrs. *Res:* Research and development of composite cans; development of new and improved alloys; corrosion of alloys. *Mailing Add:* Composite Can Div 13300 Interstate Dr Hazelwood MO 63042

FORD, JAMES L C, JR, b New York, NY, Jan 24, 33; m 59; c 2. PHYSICS. *Educ:* Mont State Univ, BA, 55; Calif Inst Technol, MS, 59, PhD(physics), 62. *Prof Exp:* PHYSICIST, OAK RIDGE NAT LAB, 62- *Mem:* Am Phys Soc. *Res:* Nuclear structure, particularly the medium weight nuclei; study of nuclear structure and nuclear reaction mechanisms by direct interactions and Coulomb excitation. *Mailing Add:* Physics Div Oak Ridge Nat Lab PO Box X Oak Ridge TN 37830

FORD, JOHN ALBERT, JR, b Phoenixville, Pa, Jan 28, 31; m 55; c 3. ORGANIC CHEMISTRY. *Educ:* Hobart Col, BS, 53; Univ Del, MS, 56, PhD, 58. *Prof Exp:* RES CHEMIST, EASTMAN KODAK CO, 58- *Concurrent Pos:* Chmn, Gordon Res Conf Org Reactions & Processes, 75. *Res:* Organic synthesis of organophosphorus compounds, dyes and photographic chemicals; synthesis of organic compounds for color photographic products and processes. *Mailing Add:* 370 Pine Grove Ave Rochester NY 14617

FORD, JOHN L, engineering mechanics, see previous edition

FORD, JOHN PHILIP, b London, Eng, Mar 2, 30; m 58, 76. STRATIGRAPHY, REMOTE SENSING. *Educ:* Univ London, BSc, 59; Ohio State Univ, PhD(geol), 65. *Prof Exp:* engr, A V Roe, Can, 51-56; assoc dir extramural studies, Antioch Col, 60-64; asst prof geol, DePauw Univ, 65-66; from asst prof geol to assoc prof geog & geol, Eastern Ill Univ, 66-77; sr res assoc, 77-79, MEM TECH STAFF, PLANETOLOGY & OCEANOGRAPHY SECT, JET PROPULSION LAB, CALIF INST TECHNOL, 79- *Mem:* Fel Geol Soc Am; Am Asn Petrol Geol; Am Soc Photogram. *Res:* Ordovician stratigraphic geology, paleontology and sedimentation; continental interior of North America; glacial field mapping and survey work, Ill & Ohio; laboratory analysis of field data; geologic interpretation of side-looking airborne radar imagery; landsat multispectral imagery aerial photography, Western US. *Mailing Add:* Jet Propulsion Lab 4800 Oak Grove Dr Pasadena CA 91103

FORD, JOHNY JOE, b Orient, Iowa, Sept 3, 44; m 68; c 2. ENDOCRINOLOGY, ANIMAL REPRODUCTION. *Educ:* Iowa State Univ, BS, 66, PhD(reproductive physics), 72. *Prof Exp:* Fel reproductive physics, Harvard Med Sch, 72-74; res physiologist, Meat Animal Res Ctr, 74-78, RES LEADER, REPRODUCTIVE PHYSICS, US DEPT AGR, 78- *Mem:* Soc Study Reproduction; Endocrine Soc; Am Soc Animal Sci; Soc Study Fertil; Soc Exp Biol Med. *Res:* Reproductive endocrinology in swine with emphasis on endocrine changes associated with sexual differentiation and development. *Mailing Add:* Meat Animal Res Ctr USDA-ARS Box 166 Clay Center NE 68933

FORD, JOSEPH, b Asheville, NC, Dec 18, 27; m 51, 76; c 4. THEORETICAL PHYSICS. *Educ:* Ga Inst Technol, BS, 52; Johns Hopkins Univ, PhD(physics), 56. *Prof Exp:* Res physicist, Electro Metall Res Labs, 56-58; asst prof physics, Univ Miami, 58-60; vis prof, Johns Hopkins Univ, 60-61; from assoc prof to prof, 61-78, REGENT'S PROF PHYSICS, GA INST TECHNOL, 78- *Concurrent Pos:* Consult, Solid State Div, Oak Ridge Nat Lab, 64-66. *Mem:* Fel AAAS; Am Phys Soc. *Res:* Statistical mechanics; solid state physics; nonlinear dynamics; experimental mathematics. *Mailing Add:* Ga Inst of Technol Sch of Physics Atlanta GA 30332

FORD, KENNETH WILLIAM, b West Palm Beach, Fla, May 1, 26; m 53, 62; c 6. THEORETICAL PHYSICS. *Educ:* Harvard Univ, BA, 48; Princeton Univ, PhD(physics), 53. *Prof Exp:* Asst, Los Alamos Sci Lab, 50-51; res assoc, Ind Univ, 53-54; from asst prof to assoc prof physics, 54-57; consult, Los Alamos Sci Lab, 57-58; from assoc prof to prof, Brandeis Univ, 58-64; prof, Univ Calif, Irvine, 64-70; prof, Univ Mass, Boston, 70-75; PRES, N MEX INST MINING & TECHNOL, 75- *Concurrent Pos:* Fulbright fel, Max Planck Inst, Gottingen, 55-56; NSF fel, Mass Inst Technol & Imp Col, London, 61-62; comnr, Col Physics, 68-71. *Mem:* Fel Am Phys Soc; Am Asn Physics Teachers (pres, 72). *Res:* Nuclear theory; elementary particle theory; physics education. *Mailing Add:* NMex Inst Mining & Technol Socorro NM 87801

FORD, LESTER RANDOLPH, JR, b Houston, Tex, Sept 23, 27; m 50, 68; c 9. MATHEMATICS. *Educ:* Univ Chicago, PhB, 49, SM, 50; Univ Ill, PhD(math), 53. *Prof Exp:* Asst, Univ Ill, 50-53; res instr, Duke Univ, 53-54; mathematician, Rand Corp, 54-57; dir opers res, Gen Anal Corp, 57-60; proj mgr, CEIR, Inc, 60-63; head comput sci dept, 63-73, SR SCIENTIST, GEN RES CORP, 73- *Mem:* Soc Indust & Appl Math; Math Asn Am; Opers Res Soc Am. *Res:* Point set topology; operations research; network flow theory; system simulation. *Mailing Add:* 718 Avenida Pequena Santa Barbara CA 93111

FORD, LINCOLN EDMOND, b Boston, Mass, May 14, 38. MEDICAL PHYSIOLOGY. *Educ:* Harvard Univ, AB, 60; Univ Rochester, MD, 65. *Prof Exp:* Intern med & surg, Bassett Hosp, Cooperstown, NY, 65-66; staff assoc physiol, NIH, 66-68; NIH spec fel, Peter Bent Brigham Hosp, Boston, 68-70, res fel cardiovasc sci, 68-69, res assoc, 69-70, asst resident med, 70-71; hon res fel physiol, Univ Col, Univ London, 71-74, NIH spec fel, 71-73; asst prof, 74-80, ASSOC PROF MED & CARDIOL, UNIV CHICAGO, 81- *Concurrent Pos:* adj prof biomed eng, Northwestern Univ. *Mem:* Am Physiol Asn; Soc Gen Physiologist; Biophys Soc. *Res:* Muscle physiology; cardiovascular sciences. *Mailing Add:* Cardiol Sect Dept Med Box 249 Univ Chicago Hosps 950 E 59th St Chicago IL 60637

FORD, LORETTA C, b New York, NY, Dec 28, 20; m; c 1. PUBLIC HEALTH. *Educ:* Univ Colo, BS, 49, MS, 51, EdD, 61. *Prof Exp:* Staff nurse, Pub Health Nursing Serv, Boulder County, Colo, 48-50; supvry nursing dir, Boulder City County Health Dept, 51-55, 56-58; asst prof, Sch Nursing, Univ Colo, 55-56, 60-61, from assoc prof to prof, 62-72; PROF NURSING, UNIV ROCHESTER, 72-, DIR NURSING, UNIV MED CTR & DEAN SCH NURSING, 72- *Concurrent Pos:* Vis prof, Univ Fla, 68 & Univ Wash, 75. *Honors & Awards:* Linda Richards Award, Nat League Nursing, 80. *Mem:* Inst of Med of Nat Acad Sci; fel Acad Nursing; Am Nurses Asn; Am Pub Health Asn; Am Sch Health Asn. *Mailing Add:* Univ Rochester Sch Nursing 601 Elmwood Ave Rochester NY 14642

FORD, MICHAEL EDWARD, b Sunbury, Pa, Dec 27, 48. CHEMISTRY. *Educ:* Lehigh Univ, BA, 70, BA (spanish), 70; Univ EAnglia, PhD(chem), 73. *Prof Exp:* NIH res assoc chem, Colo State Univ, 73-75; RES CHEMIST, AIR PROD & CHEM, PA, 75- *Concurrent Pos:* Adj prof chem, Cedar Crest Col, 81-82. *Mem:* Am Chem Soc; Chem Soc London; Org Reactions Catalysis Soc; Catalysis Club. *Res:* Application of organic and organometallic principles to the discovery and optimization of novel routes to commercially important chemicals. *Mailing Add:* Box 538 Allentown PA 18105

FORD, MILLER CLELL, JR, b Lake Village, Ark, Mar 24, 29; m 61; c 2. CIVIL ENGINEERING. *Educ:* Univ Ark, BSCE, 52, MSCE, 60; Okla State Univ, PhD, 73. *Prof Exp:* Engr, Chance Vought Aircraft Co, 52-55; from asst prof to assoc prof, 59-77, PROF CIVIL ENG, UNIV ARK, FAYETTEVILLE, 77- *Mem:* Am Soc Civil Engrs; Asn Asphalt Paving Technol; Am Soc Testing Mat; Am Cong Surv & Mapping. *Res:* Flexible pavement research on relationship of pavement and soil physical properties with pavement performance; asphalt paving durability and skid resistance investigation; evaluation of asphalt emulsion surface treatment characteristics and performance. *Mailing Add:* 340 Eng Bldg Univ Ark Fayetteville AR 72701

FORD, NEVILLE FINCH, b Greenock, Scotland, Nov 30, 34; US citizen. ORGANIC CHEMISTRY, MEDICINE. *Educ:* Univ Bristol, BSc, 55, PhD(org chem), 58, DSc, 75. *Prof Exp:* Fel, Wayne State Univ, 58-59 & Stanford Univ, 59-60; sr res chemist, Ciba Pharmaceut Co, 60-68, mgr chem res, Ciba-Geigy Corp, 68-69, dir, 69-71, exec dir, Chem Res Pharm Div, 71-80. *Mem:* Am Chem Soc; Royal Soc Chem. *Res:* Synthetic organic and medicinal chemistry. *Mailing Add:* 7146A Dartmouth Ave University City MO 63130

FORD, NORMAN CORNELL, JR, b Springfield, Mass, Feb 9, 32; m 55; c 3. BIOPHYSICS. *Educ:* Mass Inst Technol, BS, 53; Syracuse Univ, MS, 60; Univ Calif, Berkeley, PhD(physics), 64. *Prof Exp:* Mem staff physics, Mass Inst Technol, 64-65; from asst prof to assoc prof, 65-74, PROF PHYSICS, UNIV MASS, AMHERST, 74- *Concurrent Pos:* Guggenheim fel, 71-72; pres, Langley-Ford Instruments, Inc, 77- *Mem:* Am Phys Soc. *Res:* Studies of conformational changes in biological macromolecules. *Mailing Add:* Dept of Physics Univ of Mass Amherst MA 01002

FORD, NORMAN LEE, b Osage City, Kans, Dec 18, 34; m 54; c 3. ORNITHOLOGY, ECOLOGY. *Educ:* Univ Kans, BA, 57; Univ Mich, MS, 62, PhD(zool), 67. *Prof Exp:* Tech asst ornith, Univ Mich Mus Zool, 57-67; from asst prof to assoc prof, 67-78, chmn dept, 72-79, PROF BIOL, ST JOHN'S UNIV, MINN, 78- *Mem:* Am Ornith Union; Wilson Ornith Soc; Cooper Ornith Soc; Evolution Soc Am. *Res:* Anatomy and systematics of owls; reproductive behavior and ecology of passerine birds. *Mailing Add:* Dept of Biol St John's Univ Collegeville MN 56321

FORD, PATRICK LANG, b Lake Charles, La, Sept 23, 27; m 50; c 6. MATHEMATICS. *Educ:* La State Univ, BS, 48, MS, 49; Univ Mo, PhD, 61. *Prof Exp:* Instr math, Kemper Mil Sch, 49-50; asst prof, McNeese State Col, 50-55; instr, Univ Mo, 55-56; assoc prof, 56-65, head dept, 62-80, PROF MATH, MCNEESE STATE UNIV, 65- *Concurrent Pos:* Dir, NSF Inserv Inst. *Mem:* Math Asn Am. *Res:* Algebra; statistics. *Mailing Add:* Dept of Math Sci McNeese State Univ Lake Charles LA 70609

FORD, PETER CAMPBELL, b Salinas, Calif, July 10, 41; m 63; c 2. INORGANIC CHEMISTRY. *Educ:* Calif Inst Technol, BS, 62; Yale Univ, MS, 63, PhD(chem), 66. *Prof Exp:* NSF fel, 66-67; from asst prof to assoc prof, 67-77, PROF CHEM, UNIV CALIF, SANTA BARBARA, 77- *Concurrent Pos:* Camille & Henry Dreyfus Found teacher-scholar grant, 71; vis fel, Res Sch Chem, Australian Nat Univ, 74; guest prof, H C Oasted Inst, Univ Copenhagen, Denmark, 81. *Mem:* Am Chem Soc; Royal Soc Chem. *Res:* Transition metal chemistry; reactions of coordinated ligands; homogeneous catalysis; oxidation mechanisms; photochemistry of metal complexes. *Mailing Add:* Dept Chem Univ Calif Santa Barbara CA 93106

FORD, PETER WILBRAHAM, b Hobart, Australia, Nov 2, 29; m 67. APPLIED PHYSICS. *Educ:* Univ Tasmania, BSc, 54, PhD(physics), 63. *Prof Exp:* Sr physicist, Dept External Affairs, Australia, 55-56; res asst physics, Univ Tasmania, 56-59, actg dir comput installation, 63-64, res physicist, 65; systs analyst, Dept Defense, Australia, 65-66; sr physicist, 66-67; STAFF SCIENTIST, ITEK CORP, 67- *Res:* Design and construction of electromechanical data recorders; computer application to theoretical optics; computer controlled mechanical and optical systems; design of laser graphics machines; design of solid state sensor digitizing machines. *Mailing Add:* Itek Corp 10 Maguire Rd Lexington MA 02173

FORD, RICHARD EARL, b Des Moines, Iowa, May 25, 33; m 54; c 4. VIROLOGY, PLANT PATHOLOGY. *Educ:* Iowa State Univ, BS, 56; Cornell Univ, MS, 59, PhD(plant path), 61. *Prof Exp:* Res technician plant path, Iowa State Univ, 53-55, res technician plant breeding, 55, asst bot, 55-56, instr, 56; asst plant path, Cornell Univ, 56-59, asst plant virol, 59-61; asst prof plant virol, Ore State Univ & res plant pathologist, US Dept Agr, 61-65; from assoc prof to prof plant virol, Iowa State Univ, 65-72; PROF PLANT PATH & HEAD DEPT, UNIV ILL, URBANA, 72- *Concurrent Pos:* Mem, Int Working Group Legume Viruses; int consult plant path & gen agr, Sri Lanka, Thailand, Taiwan, South Korea, Peru, Iran, Yugoslavia, Peoples Repub China. *Mem:* Am Phytopath Soc (secy, 71-74; vpres, 80-81, pres elect, 81-82, pres, 82-83). *Res:* Plant virus; legume and corn viruses; serology; electron microscopy; virus effects on host physiology; interaction of viruses and other pathogens. *Mailing Add:* Dept Plant Path Univ Ill 1102 S Goodwin Ave Urbana IL 61801

FORD, RICHARD FISKE, b Los Angeles, Calif, Mar 7, 34; m 57; c 2. MARINE ECOLOGY, WATER POLLUTION. *Educ:* Pomona Col, BA, 56; Stanford Univ, MA, 59; Scripps Inst Oceanog, Univ Calif, PhD(oceanog), 65. *Prof Exp:* From asst prof to assoc prof, 64-71, PROF ECOL, SAN DIEGO STATE UNIV, 71-, DIR CTR MARINE STUDIES, 74- *Concurrent Pos:* Prin investr, Marine Res Comt Grant, State of Calif, 65-67; NSF Grant, 68-70, 80-81; Nat Oceanic & Atmospheric Agency Grants, 70- & Res Contracts, Res & Develop Prog, Southern Calif Edison Co, 73-78; prin investr & consult, San Diego Gas & Elec Co Res Contracts, 68-; consult, Environ Eng Lab, Inc, 68-72; Bissett-Berman, Inc, 70-71, Ocean Sci & Eng, Inc, 70-, David D Smith & Assocs & Intersea Res Corp, 73- & State of Calif Water Qual Control Bd, 75-76. *Mem:* AAAS; Am Soc Limnol & Oceanog; Ecol Soc Am; Am Asn Univ Professors. *Res:* Population ecology, feeding relationships and related behavior of benthic marine animals; ecological effects and beneficial uses of thermal effluent; ecological effects of marine pollution. *Mailing Add:* Ctr for Marine Studies San Diego State Univ San Diego CA 92182

FORD, RICHARD LYLE, particle physics, see previous edition

FORD, RICHARD WESTAWAY, b London, Ont, Dec 14, 30; m 52; c 2. INDUSTRIAL CHEMISTRY, POLYMER CHEMISTRY. *Educ:* Univ Western Ont, BSc, 52; Queen's Univ, Ont, MA, 54; McMaster Univ, PhD, 57. *Prof Exp:* Chemist, 57-65, group leader polymer chem sect, Res Dept, 65-72, mgr inorg chem prod distrib & planning, 72-74, develop mgr chlor-alkali prod, 74-79, mgr, Plastics Eng, 79-81, MGR PROD FLOW, DOW CHEM CAN, LTD, 81- *Mem:* Fel Chem Inst Can. *Res:* Polymer chemistry. *Mailing Add:* 1371 Indian Rd N Sarnia ON N7V 4C7 Can

FORD, ROBERT SEDGWICK, b Pascagoula, Miss, Aug 8, 16; m 37; c 4. FOOD SCIENCE. *Educ:* Ga Sch Technol, BS, 38. *Prof Exp:* Jr marine engr, Navy Civil Serv, 38-41; chief mech engr, Ingalls Shipbuilding Corp, 41-48; OWNER, ROBERT FORD ASSOCS, 48-; PRES, MAGNOLIA LAB, 61- *Concurrent Pos:* Chief mech engr, Ingalls Shipbuilding Corp, 52-66. *Mem:* AAAS; Am Heart Asn; Int Fedn Food Technol; Am Oil Chemist's Soc; Cereal Chemist's Soc. *Res:* Nutritional pathology; relationship of nutrition to degenerative diseases; engineering research and development; arteriosclerosis; development of internal combustion engines and geophysical power sources. *Mailing Add:* PO Box 1306 Pascagoula MS 39567

FORD, STEPHEN PAUL, b Palo Alto, Calif, Oct 11, 48; m 70; c 3. REPRODUCTIVE PHYSIOLOGY, BIOLOGY. *Educ:* Ore State Univ, BS, 71, PhD(reprod physiol), 77; WVa Univ, MS, 73. *Prof Exp:* Res asst, Dept Animal & Vet Sci, WVa Univ, 71-73 & Dept Animal Sci, Ore State Univ, 74-77; res physiologist, US Meat Animal Res Ctr, Sci & Educ Admin, USDA, 77-79; ASSOC PROF, DEPT ANIMAL SCI, IOWA STATE UNIV, 79- *Mem:* Am Soc Animal Sci; Soc Study Reprod; Sigma Xi. *Res:* Role of the uterus and ovaries in potentiating conceptus survival in domestic animals, specifically, control of uterine and ovarian blood flow by the conceptus. *Mailing Add:* Dept Animal Sci Iowa State Univ Ames IA 50011

FORD, SUSAN HEIM, b New Castle, Ind, May 3, 43; m 68; c 2. BIOCHEMISTRY. DUniv Mich, Ann Arbor, BS, 65; Univ Chicago, PhD(biochem), 69. *Prof Exp:* Grant, Dept Biochem, Univ Chicago, 69-71; instr biol, Kennedy-King Col, 73; res assoc, Dept Biochem, Univ Chicago, 73-77; ASST PROF CHEM, DEPT PHYS SCI, CHICAGO STATE UNIV, 78- *Concurrent Pos:* USPHS grant, Univ Chicago, 70-71; instr gen sci, Loyola Univ, Chicago, 75-77; res grant, Chicago State Univ, 80-83. *Mem:* Sigma Xi; Am Chem Soc. *Res:* Biosynthesis of porphrins, corrins and chlorins; biosynthesis of precursors to these substances and related eyzymology. *Mailing Add:* Dept Phys Sci 95th & King Dr Chicago IL 60628

FORD, THOMAS AVEN, b Washington, DC, Aug 29, 17; m 44; c 4. CHEMISTRY. *Educ:* Univ Wyo, AB, 37; Yale Univ, PhD(chem), 40. *Prof Exp:* Asst chem, Yale Univ, 37-39; res chemist, Exp Sta, E I Du Pont de Nemours & Co Inc, 40-64, supvr pressure res labs, 64-66, mgr, Tech Facil Div, 66-81; RETIRED. *Mem:* AAAS; Am Chem Soc. *Res:* Organic chemistry; fluorine chemistry; polymers. *Mailing Add:* Rt 3 Box 286 Hockessin DE 19707

FORD, THOMAS MATTHEWS, b Cambridge, Ohio, Sept 11, 31; m 59; c 2. VETERINARY MEDICINE. *Educ:* Mich State Univ, BS, 53, DVM, 57, MS, 59; Am Col Lab Animal Med, dipl. *Prof Exp:* Asst, Mich State Univ, 57-58; asst, Res Dept, Kellogg Co, 58-60; instr vet hyg, Iowa State Univ, 60-62; fel, Bowman Gray Sch Med, 62-63; fel, Med Sch, Univ Mich, 63-64, dir, animal diag lab, 64-67; VET, ABBOTT LABS, 67- *Mem:* Am Vet Med Asn; Am Asn Lab Animal Sci. *Res:* Nutrition, pathology and diseases of fur bearing animals; diseases of laboratory animals. *Mailing Add:* D403 Animal Health & Serv 1400 Sheridan Rd North Chicago IL 60064

FORD, WARREN THOMAS, b Kalamazoo, Mich, Mar 22, 42; m 67. ORGANIC CHEMISTRY. *Educ:* Wabash Col, AB, 63; Univ Calif, Los Angeles, PhD(org chem), 67. *Prof Exp:* NSF res fel org chem, Harvard Univ, 67-68; asst prof chem, Univ Ill, Urbana, 68-75; res chemist, Rohm & Haas Co, 75-78; asst prof, 78-80, ASSOC PROF CHEM, OKLA STATE UNIV, 80- *Mem:* Am Chem Soc. *Res:* Polymer and organic chemistry. *Mailing Add:* Chem Dept Okla State Univ Stillwater OK 74078

FORD, WAYNE KEITH, b Buffalo, NY, Dec 21, 53; m 76; c 2. ELECTRONIC STRUCTURE OF POLYMERS. *Educ:* Rochster Inst Technol, BS, 76; Brown Univ, ScM, 78, PhD(physics), 81. *Prof Exp:* RES FEL, XEROX CORP, 80- *Mem:* Am Phys Soc; Am Vacuum Soc. *Res:* Theoretical description of both the electronic properties of organic polymers and the atomic structure of semiconductor surfaces; theory of few-body systems; low energy electron diffraction theory. *Mailing Add:* 52 Aleta Dr Rochester NY 14623

FORD, WILLIAM FRANK, b Rockford, Ill, Jan 27, 34. THEORETICAL PHYSICS, APPLIED MATHEMATICS. *Educ:* John Carroll Univ, BS, 55, MS, 56; Case Inst Technol, PhD(physics), 61. *Prof Exp:* Instr physics, John Carroll Univ, 55-56; engr acoustics, Clevite Corp, 56-57; instr physics, Case Inst Technol, 59-61; engr reactor physics, 61-63, physicist nuclear physics, 63-73, mathematician, 73-75, HEAD MATH ANALYSIS SECT, LEWIS RES CTR, NASA, 75- *Mem:* Am Phys Soc. *Res:* Quantum theory of scattering; approximation theory; fluid mechanics. *Mailing Add:* NASA Lewis Res Ctr 21000 Brookpart Rd MS 142-2 Cleveland OH 44135

FORD, WILLIAM KENT, JR, b Clifton Forge, Va, Apr 8, 31; m 61; c 3. ASTRONOMY. *Educ:* Washington & Lee Univ, BA, 53; Univ Va, MS, 55, PhD(physics), 57. *Prof Exp:* STAFF MEM ASTRON, DEPT TERRESTRIAL MAGNETISM, CARNEGIE INST WASHINGTON, DC, 57- *Concurrent Pos:* Vis resident scientist, Kitt Peak Nat Observ, 73-74. *Mem:* Am Astron Soc; Am Phys Soc. *Res:* Astronomical instrumentation; electronic image intensification; galaxies; rotation of galaxies; redshifts of galaxies. *Mailing Add:* Dept of Terrestrial Magnetism 5241 Broad Branch Rd NW Washington DC 20015

FORD, WILLIAM LIVINGSTONE, b Montreal, Que, Nov 15, 13; m 39; c 2. OCEANOGRAPHY. *Educ:* Univ BC, BA, 36, MA, 37; Northwestern Univ, PhD(phys chem), 40. *Hon Degrees:* DSc, Univ New Brunswick, 78; LLD, Dalhousie Univ, 79. *Prof Exp:* Res chemist, E I du Pont de Nemours & Co, Del, 40-44; oceanogr, Woods Hole Oceanog Inst, Mass, 44-48; asst supt, Naval Res Estab, NS, 49-50, head sect underwater physics, 50-52; dir sci servs, Dept Nat Defence, Ont, 53-55; supt, Pac Naval Lab, BC, 55-59; sci adv to chief naval staff, Nat Defence Hq, 59-63; chief personnel, Defence Res Bd, 63-65; dir Atlantic Oceanog Lab, Bedford Inst, 65-74; dir gen ocean & aquatic sci, Atlantic Region, Fisheries & Marine Serv, Can Dept Environ, 74-78; CONSULT APPL OCEANOG & MGT, 78- *Concurrent Pos:* Mem bd dirs, Nova Scotia Res Found Corp, Assoc Scientists, Woods Hole, Inc. *Mem:* AAAS; Bermuda Biol Sta Res. *Res:* General management of programs in marine ecology, chemical and physical oceanography; air-sea interaction; advanced instrumentation; hydrographic survey and support services including research fleet. *Mailing Add:* 9 Boulderwood Halifax NS B3P 2J3 Can

FORDHAM, CHRISTOPHER COLUMBUS, III, b Greensboro, NC, Nov 28, 26; m 47; c 3. MEDICINE. *Educ:* Harvard Med Sch, MD, 51. *Prof Exp:* From instr to prof med, Sch Med, Univ NC, Chapel Hill, 58-69, asst dean, 65-68, assoc dean clin sci, 68-69; prof med, vpres & dean sch med, Med Col Ga, 69-71; PROF MED & DEAN SCH MED, UNIV NC, CHAPEL HILL, 71- *Mem:* AAAS; fel Am Col Physicians; Am Fedn Clin Res. *Res:* Metabolism; renal physiology and disease; disease and disorders of water and electrolyte homeostasis. *Mailing Add:* Sch of Med Univ of NC Chapel Hill NC 27514

FORDHAM, JAMES LYNN, b Rodney, Ont, Mar 27, 24; m 46; c 4. POLYMER CHEMISTRY. *Educ:* Univ Western Ont, BSc, 46. *Prof Exp:* Chemist, Uniroyal Can, Ltd, Polymer Corp Ltd & Monsanto Co, 46-55; sr res chemist, Diamond Shamrock Corp, 55-56, group leader, 57-59, mgr polymer res & develop, 59-65, from asst dir to dir res, 65-69, vpres res & new bus, 69-81; PRES, FTI CORP, 81- *Mem:* AAAS; NY Acad Sci; Soc Chem Indust; Am Chem Soc. *Res:* Synthesis, structure, properties and uses of biochemicals, electrochemicals, polymers, specialty chemicals and related products; processes; enhanced oil recovery; agritechnology; moniclonal antibodies; mass spectrometry. *Mailing Add:* FTI Corp Suite 219 17000 Dassas Pkwy Dallas TX 75248

FORDHAM, JOSEPH RAYMOND, b Hornell, NY, Sept 1, 37; m 62; c 4. NUTRITIONAL BIOCHEMISTRY. *Educ:* Col Holy Cross, BS, 59; Purdue Univ, MS, 63, PhD(biochem), 66. *Prof Exp:* Asst biochem, Purdue Univ, 60-65; res scientist, Joseph E Seagram & Sons, 65-69; asst prof nutrit & food sci, Univ Ky, 69-76; assoc prof food & nutrit, Ga Southern Col, 76-77; MGR TECH REGULATORY COMPLIANCE, CLINTON CORN PROCESSING CO, 77- *Mem:* Asn Food & Drug Off; Am Feed Mfrs Asn Nutrit Coun; Inst Food Technologists; Am Dietetics Asn; Nutrit Today Soc. *Res:* Carbohydrate metabolism; rumen microbiology; short-chain fatty acid metabolism; diastatic and proteolytic enzymes; flavor chemistry; terpene chemistry; effect of nutrition on lipogenesis; novel plant protein products; nutrition status. *Mailing Add:* 710 Surrey Ct Clinton IA 52732

FORDHAM, WILLIAM DAVID, b Marietta, Ohio, Apr 24, 39; m 64. BIOPHYSICAL CHEMISTRY, BIOCHEMISTRY. *Educ:* Marietta Col, BS, 61; Yale Univ, MS, 62, PhD(biophys chem), 67. *Prof Exp:* Res chemist, Am Cyanamid Co, Bound Brook, 66-71; res assoc, Princeton Univ, 71-73; asst prof, 73-76, ASSOC PROF CHEM, FAIRLEIGH DICKINSON UNIV, 76- *Concurrent Pos:* NIH spec res fel, Princeton Univ, 71-73. *Mem:* Am Chem Soc. *Res:* Biological reaction mechanisms; chemical kinetics; thermochemistry; pigments; surface chemistry; structure of bacterial cell walls; antibiotics; metalloenzymes. *Mailing Add:* Dept of Chem Fairleigh Dickinson Univ Teaneck NJ 07666

FORDON, WILFRED AARON, b New York, NY, Sept 6, 27; m 50; c 2. PATTERN RECOGNITION, ELECTROMAGNETIC THEORY. *Educ:* City Col New York, BEE, 49; Hofstra Univ, MA, 54; Purdue Univ, PhD(elec eng), 76. *Prof Exp:* Jr engr, Link Radio Corp, 50; engr, Airborne Instruments Lab, 51-54, Teletronics Lab, 54-56; mem staff, Lincoln Lab, Mass Inst Technol, 56-58; supvr, Sylvania Electronic Systs, 58-61; mem tech staff, Mitre Corp, 61-67; prin engr, Raytheon Co, 67-69; teaching asst, Purdue Univ, 73-76; vis asst prof, 76-77, ASSOC PROF ELEC ENG, MICH TECHNOL UNIV, 77- *Mem:* Sr mem Inst Elec & Electronics Engrs; AAAS; NY Acad Sci; Sigma Xi. *Res:* Pattern recognition as applied to biomedical engineering; electromagnetic theory as applied to radiowave propagation. *Mailing Add:* Mich Technol Univ Houghton MI 49931

FORDYCE, DAVID BUCHANAN, b Los Angeles, Calif, Oct 15, 24; m 47; c 3. PHYSICAL CHEMISTRY, ANALYTICAL CHEMISTRY. *Educ:* Univ BC, BASc, 46; Univ Wis, PhD(chem), 50. *Prof Exp:* Asst chem, Univ Wis, 47-48; res chemist, 50-56, head lab, 56-63, RES DEPT MGR, ROHM AND HAAS CO, 63- *Mem:* Am Chem Soc. *Res:* Application properties of ion exchange resins, water soluble polymers and surfactants. *Mailing Add:* 313 E Central Ave Moorestown NJ 08057

FORDYCE, JAMES STUART, b London, Eng, Dec 10, 31; nat US; m 54; c 2. PHYSICAL CHEMISTRY, ELECTROCHEMISTRY. *Educ:* Dartmouth Col, AB, 53; Mass Inst Technol, PhD(phys chem), 59. *Prof Exp:* Asst, Mass Inst Technol, 53-59; res chemist, Nat Carbon Co Div, Union Carbide Corp, 58-59, res chemist, Union Carbide Consumer Prod Co Div, 59-63, res chemist develop dept, 63-66; res scientist, 66-68, sect head, Direct Energy Conversion Div, 68-74, chief environ res off, 71-74, mgr environ monitoring systs off, energy conversion & environ systs div, Lewis Res Ctr, 74-76, chief electrochem br, 76-80, dep chief, 80-81, ACTG CHIEF, SOLAR & ELECTROCHEM DIV, NASA, 81- *Concurrent Pos:* Mem environ rev team jetport study, Lake Erie Regional Transp Auth, Cleveland, Ohio, 74-78. *Honors & Awards:* Indust Res-100 Award, 77. *Mem:* AAAS; Am Chem Soc; Electrochem Soc; Fedn Am Scientists. *Res:* Photochemistry; fast reaction kinetics; spectroscopy of molten salts and electrolyte solutions; solid electrolytes; urban air pollution; aircraft pollution; environmental monitoring technology; energy conversion; batteries, fuel cells, bulk energy storage systems; photovoltaic technology and applications. *Mailing Add:* Lewis Res Ctr NASA 21000 Brookpark Rd Cleveland OH 44135

FORE, PAUL LEWIS, fish biology, see previous edition

FOREE, EDWARD G(OLDEN), b Sulphur, Ky, Feb 24, 41; m 62; c 2. ENVIRONMENTAL & CIVIL ENGINEERING. *Educ:* Univ Ky, BS, 64; Stanford Univ, MS, 65, PhD(civil eng), 68. *Prof Exp:* Asst prof, 68-74, assoc prof civil eng, Univ Ky, 74-80; PRES, COMMONWEALTH TECHNOL INC, 80-; VPRES, FTA ENG INC, 81- *Mem:* Am Soc Civil Engrs; Water Pollution Control Fedn; Nat Soc Prof Engrs; Asn Environ Eng Prof. *Res:* Growth and decomposition of algae and related effects on water quality; plant nutrients and eutrophication; acid mine drainage; biological waste treatment. *Mailing Add:* Commonwealth Technol Inc 2520 Regency Rd Suite 104 Lexington KY 40503

FORELLI, FRANK JOHN, b San Diego, Calif, Apr 8, 32; m 59; c 1. MATHEMATICS. *Educ:* Univ Calif, Berkeley, AB, 54, MA, 59, PhD(math), 61. *Prof Exp:* Instr, 61-63, from asst prof to assoc prof, 63-67, PROF MATH, UNIV WIS-MADISON, 67- *Mem:* Am Math Soc. *Res:* Mathematical analysis. *Mailing Add:* Dept of Math Univ of Wis 213 Van Vleeck Hall Madison WI 53706

FOREMAN, BRUCE MILBURN, JR, b Arkadelphia, Ark, Nov 10, 32; m 64; c 1. INFORMATION SCIENCE. *Educ:* Univ Calif, Berkeley, BS, 54, PhD(nuclear chem), 58. *Prof Exp:* Res assoc, Brookhaven Nat Lab, 58-60; res scientist chem, Columbia Univ, 60-64; asst prof physics, Univ Tex, Austin, 64-68; sr scientist, 68-75, SR SYSTS ANALYST, AM INST PHYSICS, 75- *Mem:* Am Phys Soc. *Res:* Mechanisms of nuclear reactions. *Mailing Add:* Publ Div Am Inst of Physics 335 E 45th St New York NY 10017

FOREMAN, CALVIN, b Hannibal, Mo, Aug 15, 10; m 41; c 3. MATHEMATICS. *Educ:* Westminster Col, Mo, AB, 32; Univ Kans, MA, 41, PhD(math), 52. *Prof Exp:* Teacher pub schs, 35-40; asst instr math, Univ Kans, 40-41; instr, Univ Omaha, 41-42; instr, Univ Kans, 46-48, res asst, 48-50; chmn dept math & pre-eng, 50-74, chmn div natural sci, 63-74, prof, 50-80, EMER PROF MATH, BAKER UNIV, 80- *Mem:* Am Math Soc; Math Asn Am. *Res:* Differential geometry; vectors; matrices. *Mailing Add:* Dept of Math Baker Univ Baldwin City KS 66006

FOREMAN, CHARLES FREDERICK, b Blue Rapids, Kans, Nov 9, 20; m 46; c 3. DAIRY SCIENCE. *Educ:* Kans State Col, BS, 48, MS, 49; Univ Mo, PhD, 53. *Prof Exp:* Asst prof dairy exten, Kans State Col, 49-51; asst instr dairy husb, Univ Mo, 51-53; asst prof, Univ Minn, 53-54; from asst prof to prof dairy sci, 55-68, PROF ANIMAL SCI, IOWA STATE UNIV, 68- *Mem:* Am Soc Animal Sci; Am Dairy Sci Asn. *Res:* Dairy cattle nutrition and management. *Mailing Add:* Dept of Animal Sci 123 Kildee Hall Iowa State Univ Ames IA 50011

FOREMAN, CHARLES WILLIAM, b Norman Park, Ga, Nov 2, 23; m 51; c 3. ZOOLOGY, PHYSIOLOGY. *Educ:* Univ NC, BA, 49; Duke Univ, MA, 51, PhD(physiol), 54. *Prof Exp:* Asst prof biol, Wofford Col, 53-55; asst zool, Univ Md, 55-56; from assoc prof to prof biol, Pfeiffer Col, 56-63; from assoc prof to prof, 63-81, WILLIAM HENDERSON PROF BIOL, UNIV OF THE SOUTH, 81-, CHMN DEPT, 76- *Concurrent Pos:* Res partic, Oak Ridge Nat Lab, 60; trustee, Highlands Biol Sta, Univ NC, 61- *Mem:* Fel AAAS; Am Soc Mammalogists; Genetics Soc Am; NY Acad Sci. *Res:* Taxonomic significance and genetic basis of hemoglobin structure. *Mailing Add:* Dept Biol Univ of the South Sewanee TN 37375

FOREMAN, CHARLES WILLIAM, b Lewis, Ind, Mar 18, 23; m 47; c 1. ELECTRICAL ENGINEERING. *Educ:* Rose Polytech Inst, BS, 49. *Prof Exp:* Test engr, Bell Aircraft Corp, 50-51; engr, Goodyear Aircraft Corp, 51-59; staff engr, Melpar, Inc, 59-61; engr, Anal Serv Inc, Falls Church, 61-65, asst independent res, 61-70, DIV MGR, ANAL SERV INC, 70- *Mem:* Inst Elec & Electronics Engrs. *Res:* Systems analysis of military problems. *Mailing Add:* 2525 Flint Hill Rd Vienna VA 22180

FOREMAN, DARHL LOIS, b Idaho Falls, Idaho, May 3, 24. ZOOLOGY, ENDOCRINOLOGY. *Educ:* George Washington Univ, BS, 46; Mt Holyoke Col, MA, 48; Univ Chicago, PhD(zool), 55. *Prof Exp:* From instr to asst prof, 54-70, ASSOC PROF BIOL, CASE WESTERN RESERVE UNIV, 70- *Mem:* Fel AAAS; Am Soc Zoologists; Endocrine Soc; Soc Study Reproduction. *Res:* Ovarian physiology; physiology of annual breeders; animal behavior and endocrine effects; endocrinology of sex and reproduction. *Mailing Add:* Dept of Biol Case Western Reserve Univ Cleveland OH 44106

FOREMAN, DENNIS WALDEN, JR, b Akron, Ohio, Dec 27, 29; m 53; c 2. MINERALOGY, PHYSICAL CHEMISTRY. *Educ:* Mt Union Col, BS, 52; Ohio State Univ, MS, 60, PhD(mineral), 66. *Prof Exp:* Res assoc, 66-68, asst prof, 68-69, assoc prof, 69-76, PROF DENT, OHIO STATE UNIV, 76- *Mem:* AAAS; Am Crystallog Asn; Electron Micros Soc Am; Int Asn Dent Res. *Res:* Crystal structures of hydrogrossular, tin apatite; mineralization in biological environments; bone and tooth structure; crystalline water in human enamel. *Mailing Add:* Rm 407 305 W 12th Ave Ohio State Univ Col of Dent Columbus OH 43210

FOREMAN, HARRY, b Winnipeg, Man, Mar 5, 15; US citizen; m 55; c 2. RADIOLOGICAL HEALTH. *Educ:* Antioch Col, BS, 38; Ohio State Univ, PhD(biochem), 42; Univ Calif, San Francisco, MD, 47. *Prof Exp:* Asst prof biochem, Oglethorpe Univ, 42-43; res chemist, Eldorado Oil Co, 43-44; AEC fel, Univ Calif, Berkeley, 49-51; mem staff, Los Alamos Sci Lab, 51-62; assoc prof pub health, 62-73, assoc dean int progs, 66-69, assoc prof obstet & gynec, 69-73, DIR CTR POP STUDIES, UNIV MINN, MINNEAPOLIS, 69-, PROF OBSTET & GYNEC & PUB HEALTH, 73- *Concurrent Pos:* Mem atomic safety & licensing bd panel, AEC, 71- *Honors & Awards:* McNight Award, Univ Minn Press, 72. *Mem:* Soc Exp Biol & Med; Health Physics Soc; Am Soc Pharmacol & Exp Therapeut; Am Physiol Soc. *Res:* Development of contraceptives; clinical trials, family planning acceptance and administration. *Mailing Add:* Ctr for Pop Studies Univ of Minn Box 395 Mayo Minneapolis MN 55455

FOREMAN, HELEN PULVER, micropaleontology, deceased

FOREMAN, JOHN E(DWARD) K(ENDALL), b Hamilton, Ont, Feb 14, 22; m 47; c 4. MECHANICAL ENGINEERING. *Educ:* Univ Toronto, BASc, 45; Cornell Univ, MME, 52. *Prof Exp:* Spec lectr, Univ Toronto, 46-49; instr & res asst, Cornell Univ, 49-52; res engr, George Kent, Ltd, Eng, 52-54, head res & develop, Can, 54-56; from asst prof to assoc prof eng sci, 56-63, head mech group, 60-72, PROF MECH ENG, UNIV WESTERN ONT, 63-, HEAD, SOUND & VIBRATION LAB, 72- *Concurrent Pos:* Proj coordr, Can Elec Asn, 76- *Mem:* Can Acoust Asn (pres, 72-74); Asn Prof Engrs; Eng Inst Can. *Res:* Biomechanics; mechanical design; noise abatement. *Mailing Add:* Fac Eng Sci Univ Western Ont London Can

FOREMAN, KENNETH M, b New York, NY, July 30, 25; m 54; c 2. AERONAUTICAL ENGINEERING, FLUID DYNAMICS. *Educ:* NY Univ, BAeroEng, 50, MAeroEng, 53; Polytech Inst NY, cert energy policy & technol, 76, MS, 81. *Prof Exp:* Res engr, Bendix Aviation Corp, 51-52; proj engr, Wright Aeronaut Div, Curtiss-Wright Corp, NJ, 52-56; res engr, Engine Div, Fairchild Engine & Airplane Corp, NY, 56-59; specialist & sci res engr, Repub Aviation Corp, 59-65; chief proj engr, Edo Corp, 65-66; staff scientist, 66-80, HEAD, ADVAN FLUID CONCEPTS LAB, GRUMMAN AEROSPACE CORP, BETHPAGE, 80- *Concurrent Pos:* Abstractor, Fire Res Abstr & Revs, Nat Acad Sci. *Mem:* Am Soc Mech Engrs; Am Inst Aeronaut & Astronaut. *Res:* Propulsion; gas dynamics; chemical reactions resulting in heat addition; flow instrumentation; planetary atmospheres; space sciences; air and water pollution instrumentation systems; oceanographic instrumentation; systems engineering; wind energy conversion engineering. *Mailing Add:* 32 Stratford Ct North Bellmore NY 11710

FOREMAN, ROBERT DALE, b Orange City, Iowa, Apr 27, 46; m 69. NEUROPHYSIOLOGY, CARDIOVASCULAR PHYSIOLOGY. *Educ:* Cent Col, Pella, BA, 69; Loyola Univ, Chicago, PhD(physiol), 73. *Prof Exp:* Mem staff neurophysiol, Marine Biomed Inst, Galveston, 75-77; asst prof physiol, Univ Tex Med Br, Galveston, 75-77; asst prof, 77-81, ASSOC PROF NEUROPHYSIOL, UNIV OKLA HEALTH SCI CTR, 81- *Concurrent Pos:* Fel, Marine Biomed Inst, Univ Tex Med Br Galveston, 73-75; asst prof, NIH, Nat Heart, Lung & Blood Inst, 75-80; Am Heart Asn, 75-77 & NIH, 76-77; res career develop award, NIH. *Mem:* Am Physiol Soc; Soc Neurosci; Sigma Xi; Am Sci Affil; AAAS. *Res:* Neural mechanisms underlying the cardiac pain associated with angina pectoris; neural control of heart and blood vessels; neural mechanisms underlying hypertension and arrhythmias. *Mailing Add:* Dept Physiol & Biophysics Col of Med Oklahoma City OK 73190

FOREMAN, ROBERT WALTER, b Flint, Mich, Jan 4, 23; m 45; c 2. METALLURGICAL CHEMISTRY. *Educ:* Univ Mich, BS, 44, MS, 46; Western Reserve Univ, PhD, 55. *Prof Exp:* Asst chem, Manhattan Proj, 44; res assoc eng res, Univ Mich, 44-45; res chemist, Standard Oil Co, 46-66; DIR RES & DEVELOP, PARK CHEM CO, 66-, MEM BD DIRS, 69- *Mem:* Am Chem Soc; Am Soc Metals. *Res:* Metallurgy; organic chemistry; petroleum chemistry; molten salt chemistry; analytical chemistry; absorption spectroscopy. *Mailing Add:* Park Chem Co 8074 Military Ave Detroit MI 48204

FOREMAN, RONALD EUGENE, b Osceola, Iowa, May 28, 38; div; c 1. MARINE ECOLOGY. *Educ:* Univ Colo, BA, 62; Univ Calif, Berkeley, PhD(bot), 70. *Prof Exp:* Asst proj supvr alpine ecol, Inst Arctic & Alpine Res, 58-64; radiation biologist, US Naval Radiol Defense Lab, 65 & 66; teaching assoc bot, Univ Calif, Berkeley, 68-70; asst prof, 70-79, ASSOC PROF BOT & DIR, BAMFIELD MARINE STA, UNIV BC, 79- *Mem:* Ecol Soc Am; Brit Ecol Soc. *Res:* Investigation of spatial-temporal variations in nearshore marine benthic ecosystem structure and function; population dynamics of the kelp Nereocystis leutkeana; phycocolloid production by red algae. *Mailing Add:* Bamfield Marine Sta Bamfield BC V9R 1B0 Can

FOREMAN, RONALD LOUIS, b Chicago, Ill, Oct 26, 37; m 59; c 2. PHARMACOLOGY, TOXICOLOGY. *Educ:* Univ Ill, Chicago, BS, 60, MS, 64, PhD(pharm), 69. *Prof Exp:* NIH trainee pharmacol, 69-71, ASST PROF PHARMACOL, UNIV ILL MED CTR, 71-; TOXICOLOGIST, CHICAGO BD HEALTH LABS, 71- *Mem:* AAAS; Am Chem Soc; Am Pharmaceut Asn. *Res:* Therapeutic and toxicological aspects of drug metabolism and distribution; epoxides as obligatory intermediates in the metabolism of olefins to glycols; public health aspects of drug use and toxicity. *Mailing Add:* Dept of Med Pharmacol Univ of Ill at the Med Ctr Chicago IL 60680

FOREMAN, WILLIAM EDWIN, b Columbus, Ohio, Sept 6, 29; m 57; c 3. MINING ENGINEERING, MINERAL PROCESSING. *Educ:* Ohio State Univ, BEM, 53, Va Polytech Inst, MS, 61; Pa State Univ, PhD(mineral prep), 65. *Prof Exp:* Res engr, Basic Inc, Cleveland, 53-57; ASSOC PROF MINING ENG, VA POLYTECH INST & STATE UNIV, 57- *Concurrent Pos:* Chmn, Inst Coal Mining, Health, Safety & Res, 75-78; Carborundum fel. *Mem:* Am Inst Mining, Petrol & Metall Engrs; Sigma Xi. *Res:* Health and safety in mining and engineering; mineral beneficiation; coal preparation. *Mailing Add:* Dept of Mining & Minerals Engs Va Polytech Inst & State Univ Blacksburg VA 24061

FORENZA, SALVATORE, b Taranto, Italy, June 22, 46; m 73; c 2. MEDICINAL CHEMISTRY. *Educ:* Univ Naples, Italy, Dr org chem, 70. *Prof Exp:* Fel natural prod, Coun Nat Res, 70-71; teach asst org chem, Yale Univ, 71-72; fel natural prod, Univ Wyo, 72-74; fel biosynthetics, Tulane Univ, 74; vis asst prof org chem, Col VI, 75-76; sr res scientist natural prod,

Farmitalia-C-Erba, Italy, 76-80; SR RES SCIENTIST NATURAL PROD, BRISTOL LABS, 80- *Mem:* Am Chem Soc; AAAS. *Res:* Isolation and structure elucidation of naturally occuring antitumoral compounds; semisynthesis of analogs to elucidate structure-activity relationships. *Mailing Add:* Med Chem Dept Bristol Labs PO Box 657 Syracuse NY 13201

FORER, ARTHUR H, b Trenton, NJ, Dec 17, 35; m 64; c 2. CELL BIOLOGY. *Educ:* Mass Inst Technol, BS, 57; Dartmouth Med Sch, PhD(molecular biol), 64. *Prof Exp:* Am Cancer Soc fel, Carlsberg Found, Copenhagen, Denmark, 64-66; Helen Hay Whitney Found fel, Cambridge, Eng & Duke Univ, 67-70; assoc prof molecular biol, Odense Univ, Denmark, 70-72; assoc prof biol, 72-75; PROF BIOL, YORK UNIV, 75- *Concurrent Pos:* Hargitt res fel, Duke Univ, 69-70; mem, Cell Biol & Genetics Grant Selection Panel, Natural Sci & Eng Res Coun Can, 75-78; assoc ed, Can J Biochem & Cell Biol, 80- *Mem:* AAAS; Am Soc Cell Biol; Brit Soc Exp Biol; Can Soc Cell Biol. *Res:* Chromosome movement during cell-division; roles of actin filaments and microtubules in cell motility; ultraviolet microbeam irradiations of living cells. *Mailing Add:* Dept of Biol York Univ Downsview ON M3J 1P3 Can

FOREST, EDWARD, b New York, NY, Mar 6, 33; m 61; c 2. PHYSICAL CHEMISTRY. *Educ:* Brooklyn Col, BS, 55; Princeton Univ, MA, 62, PhD(phys chem), 63. *Prof Exp:* Instr chem, Brooklyn Col, 58-59; asst, Princeton Univ, 59-63; scientist, 63-69, MGR RES DIV, XEROX CORP, 69- *Mem:* Am Chem Soc; Soc Photog Scientists & Engrs. *Res:* Microwave absorption and relaxation in liquid state; liquid crystalline materials; charge transport in organic materials; photo responsive systems; ink jet printing. *Mailing Add:* 16216 Fallkirk Dr Dallas TX 75248

FOREST, HARVEY, b Brooklyn, NY, Jan 23, 37; m 59; c 2. PHYSICAL CHEMISTRY. *Educ:* Brooklyn Col, BS, 58; Columbia Univ, MA, 59, PhD(chem), 64. *Prof Exp:* Staff scientist, Gen Precision Aerospace Res Ctr, 64-66; sr scientist, 66-72, MGR RAULAND TUBE DIV, ZENITH RADIO CORP, 72- *Res:* Luminescence of rare earth activated phosphors. *Mailing Add:* Rauland Tube Div 2407 W North Ave Melrose Park IL 60161

FOREST, HERMAN SILVA, b Chattanooga, Tenn, Feb 18, 21; m 63; c 2. ENVIRONMENTAL BIOLOGY. *Educ:* Univ Tenn, BA, 42; Mich State Univ, MS, 48, PhD(bot), 51. *Prof Exp:* Asst prof biol, Col William & Mary, 53-54; instr bot, Univ Tenn, 55-54; instr bot & biol, Univ Okla, 55-58; dir students mus, Knoxville, 58-60; res asst, Med Ctr, Univ Okla, 60-61; res assoc biol, Univ Rochester, 61-65; PROF BIOL, STATE UNIV NY COL GENESEO, 65- *Concurrent Pos:* NIH fel, 61-62; AEC grant, 62-64; exchange scholar, Univ Moscow, 79, Bot Inst USSR, Leningrad, 64; Czechoslovakia, 80; NSF grant, 65; vis biologist, Am Inst Biol Sci, 69-71; prin scientist, Environ Resource Ctr, 71-81; mem adv panel, Ford Found Prog Assistance Local Conserv Comns, 72-74; fac vis scholar, State Univ NY, 74- *Mem:* AAAS; Am Inst Biol Sci; Ecol Soc Am; Bot Soc Am; Phycol Soc Am. *Res:* Water resources; philosophy of science; non-marine algae and rooted aquatics. *Mailing Add:* Dept Biol State Univ NY Col Geneseo NY 14454

FORESTER, DONALD CHARLES, b Detroit, Mich, Feb 21, 43; m 66; c 1. BEHAVIORAL BIOLOGY, HERPETOLOGY. *Educ:* Tex Tech Univ, BA, 66, MS, 69; NC State Univ, PhD(zool), 74. *Prof Exp:* Instr biol, Hill Jr Col, 68-69, McLennan Community Col, 69-73; vis instr zool, NC State Univ, 73-74; asst prof, 74-80, ASSOC PROF BIOL, TOWSON STATE UNIV, 80- *Mem:* Herpetologists League; Am Soc Ichthyologists & Herpetologists; Soc Study Amphibians & Reptiles; Sigma Xi; Am Soc Zoologists. *Res:* Sexual selection in anurans; parental care in salamanders. *Mailing Add:* Dept of Biol Sci Towson State Univ Baltimore MD 21204

FORESTER, DONALD WAYNE, b Knoxville, Tenn, Apr 7, 37; m 59; c 2. MAGNETISM, MILLIMETER-WAVES. *Educ:* Berea Col, BA, 59; Univ Tenn, MS, 61, PhD(physics), 64. *Prof Exp:* Asst prof physics, Univ Nebr, Lincoln, 64-66; Res Corp grant & asst prof physics, Ga Inst Technol, 66-69; res physicist, solid state div, 69-78, SUPVRY RES PHYSICIST, MAGNETISM BR, ELECTRONICS TECHNOL DIV, NAVAL RES LAB, 78- *Mem:* Am Phys Sco; Sigma Xi. *Res:* Mossbauer experiments; low temperature physics; optical properties of solids; electrical discharges; magnetism in solids; magnetic silencing applications; radar absorbing materials; amorphous materials; thin-film technology. *Mailing Add:* Magnetism Br Naval Res Lab Code 6893 Washington DC 20375

FORESTER, RALPH H, b Chicago, Ill, Apr 11, 28; m 53; c 2. POLYMER CHEMISTRY. *Educ:* Carleton Col, BA, 50. *Prof Exp:* Chemist, G H Tennant Co, 55-66; sr chemist, North Star Div, Midwest Res Inst, 66-78; CHEMIST, FILMTEC CORP, 78- *Res:* Biophysics, low-level bioelectric phenomena; epoxy and urethane coatings; metal fibers, reinforced plastics, abrasives and filters; ultrathin polymer membrane technology; waste water and air pollution technology; reverse osmosis & ultrafiltration. *Mailing Add:* Filmtec Corp 15305 Minnetonka Blvd Minnetonka MN 55343

FORESTER, RICHARD MONROE, b Hancock, NY, Dec 23, 47; m 72. MICROPALEONTOLOGY, PALEOECOLOGY. *Educ:* Syracuse Univ, BS, 69; Univ Ill, MS, 72, PhD(paleoecol), 75. *Prof Exp:* NAT RES COUN ASSOC FEL MICROPALEONT, US GEOL SURV, 75- *Mem:* Paleont Soc; Paleont Asn; Int Paleont Union; AAAS; Geol Soc Am. *Res:* Biostratigraphy, systematics and paleoecology of non-marine ostracodes and charaphytes. *Mailing Add:* Paleont & Stratig Br MS 919 Bldg 25 Denver Fed Ctr Denver CO 80225

FORESTER, ROBERT DONALD, b Los Angeles, Calif, July 27, 24; m 49; c 2. GEOPHYSICS. *Educ:* Calif Inst Technol, BS, 49, MS, 50, PhD, 53. *Prof Exp:* Geophysicist & geologist, Standard Oil Co Calif, 53-58; res assoc, Pan-Am Petrol Corp, 59-65; vpres data processing & res, Petty Labs, Inc, 59-69; mem staff, Indust Opers, TRW, Inc, 69-74; EXPLOR GEOPHYSICIST & GEOLOGIST, TETRA TECH, INC, 74- *Mem:* Soc Explor Geophys. *Res:* Seismology. *Mailing Add:* 201 Vanderpool Houston TX 77024

FORESTI, ROY J(OSEPH), JR, b Baltimore, Md, Mar 25, 25; m 53; c 2. CHEMICAL ENGINEERING. *Educ:* Johns Hopkins Univ, BE, 47; Carnegie Inst Technol, MS, 48; Pa State Univ, PhD(fuel technol), 51. *Prof Exp:* Asst, Pa State Univ, 48-50; res chem engr, US Bur Mines, 51-54; res chem engr, Monsanto Chem Co, 54-55, group leader, 55-59; lectr chem eng, Univ Dayton & sr res scientist, Res Inst, 59-61; assoc prof chem eng, Univ Conn, 61-63; assoc prof chem eng & chmn dept, Cath Univ Am, 63-80; SR ENGR, VITRO LABS, 80- *Mem:* Am Chem Soc; Am Inst Chem Engrs; Am Soc Eng Educ. *Res:* Airborne solid dispersions; gasification of solids; oxidation of gases; nonideal liquids. *Mailing Add:* 301 Willington Dr Silver Spring MD 20904

FORESTIERI, AMERICO F, b Cleveland, Ohio, May 4, 29; m 56; c 3. ENERGY CONVERSION, RESEARCH ADMINISTRATION. *Educ:* Case Inst Technol, BS, 51, MS, 54. *Prof Exp:* Res staff solid state physics, Nat Adv Comt Areonaut, 51-65, HEAD PHOTO-VOLTAICS TECH, NASA, 65- *Concurrent Pos:* Chmn, Photovoltaic Specialists Conf, 75-76, publ chmn, 76-; chmn solar working group, Interagency Advan Power Group, 78-; asst chmn, Intersoc Energy Conversion Eng Conf, 81-82. *Mem:* Inst Elec & Electronics Engrs. *Res:* Develop technology programs to reduce cost and weight and increase efficiency and lifetime of solar cells for space applications. *Mailing Add:* Lewis Res Ctr NASA MS 302-1 21000 Brookpark Rd Cleveland OH 44135

FORET, JAMES A, b Lutcher, La, Sept 3, 21; m 46; c 10. ORNAMENTAL HORTICULTURE, WEED SCIENCE. *Educ:* Univ Southwestern La, BS, 43; Iowa State Univ, MS, 47, PhD(plant physiol), 50. *Prof Exp:* Instr & res asst prof, Iowa State Univ, 46-50; assoc prof, 50-53, head dept gen agr, 53-64, head dept plant indust & gen agr, 69-74, PROF HORT, UNIV SOUTHWESTERN LA, 53-, DEAN COL AGR, 76- *Mem:* Am Soc Hort Sci. *Res:* Disposal of rice hulls; control of Elodea canadensis in lakes of Louisiana; control of alligatorweed in rice irrigation canals; herbicide residue studies in rice irrigation canals; aquatic weed control. *Mailing Add:* Dept of Plant Indust & Gen Agr Univ of Southwestern La Box 487 Lafayette LA 70504

FORET, JOHN EMIL, b New York, NY, Nov 19, 37. DEVELOPMENTAL BIOLOGY. *Educ:* Univ NH, BA, 62, MS, 63; Princeton Univ, AM, 65, PhD(biol), 66. *Prof Exp:* NIH fel, 66-67; asst prof, 67-73, chmn dept, 78-80, ASSOC PROF ZOOL, UNIV NH, 73- *Mem:* Am Soc Zoologists; Am Soc Cell Biol; Soc Develop Biol; AAAS. *Res:* Cellular origins and control mechanisms in limb regeneration. *Mailing Add:* Dept of Zool Univ of NH Durham NH 03824

FORGAC, JOHN MICHAEL, b Lakewood, Ohio, May 30, 49; m 71. CHEMICAL ENGINEERING. *Educ:* Case Western Reserve Univ, BS, 71, MS, 75, PhD(chem eng), 78. *Prof Exp:* res engr coal liquefaction, 77-80, RES ENGR OIL SHALE PROCESSING, AMOCO OIL CO, STANDARD OIL, IND, 80- *Mem:* Am Inst Chem Engrs; Am Chem Soc; AAAS; Sigma Xi; Catalysis Soc. *Res:* Oil shale and coal conversion; heat transfer; heterogeneous chemical reactions; reaction kinetics; crystal growth. *Mailing Add:* Amoco Res Ctr PO Box 400 Naperville IL 60540

FORGACS, JOSEPH, b Nokomis, Ill, Mar 20, 17; m 46; c 5. MEDICAL MICROBIOLOGY. *Educ:* Univ Ill, BS, 40, MS, 42, PhD(bact, hort), 44. *Prof Exp:* Asst hort, Univ Ill, 40-43, asst plant path, 43-44; bacteriologist & chief antibiotics & chemother, Camp Detrick, 46-54; mem staff res div, Am Cyanamid Co, 54-57; dir lab, Spring Valley Gen Hosp, New York, 58-60; mem staff res div, Am Cyanamid Co, 60; staff microbiologist & consult mycotoxocologist, Good Samaritan Hosp, Suffern, NY, 60-69; CONSULT, GEN FOODS CORP, 68-; dir microbiol, Automated Biochem Labs Inc, 69-79; DIR MICROBIOL, DEPT MENT HEALTH, LETCHWORTH DEVELOP CTR, 79- *Concurrent Pos:* Consult microbiologist, Tuxedo Mem Hosp, New York, 60-64; consult mycotoxicologist, Agr Res Serv, USDA, 65-; consult & attend microbiologist, Dept Mental Hyg, State of NY, 73- *Mem:* Am Soc Microbiologists; NY Acad Sci; Int Soc Trop Dermat. *Res:* Food bacteriology and chemistry; antibiotics and chemotherapy; mycology; mycotoxicoses; determine role of fungi in toxicoses of unknown etiology in animals and human beings. *Mailing Add:* 302 N Highland Ave Pearl River NY 10965

FORGACS, OTTO LIONEL, b Berlin, Ger, Jan 4, 31; Can citizen; m 60; c 3. PHYSICAL CHEMISTRY. *Educ:* Manchester Univ, BSc Tech, 55; McGill Univ, PhD(phys chem), 59. *Prof Exp:* Proj supvr, Pulp & Paper Res Inst Can, 58-63; head pulp & paper & allied bldg prod sect, Res Centre, Domtar Ltd, 63-70, mgr prod develop, 70-72, assoc res dir & dir tech planning, 72-73; res dir, 73-77, vpres, Res & Develop, 77-79, SR VPRES, RES & DEVELOP, MACMILLAN BLOEDEL LTD, 79- *Mem:* Fel Tech Asn Pulp & Paper Indust; fel Chem Inst Can; Can Pulp & Paper Asn; Can Forestry Adv Coun. *Res:* Pulp and paper technology. *Mailing Add:* 3350 E Broadway Vancouver Can

FORGASH, ANDREW JOHN, b Dunellen, NJ, Nov 21, 23; m 44; c 4. ENTOMOLOGY. *Educ:* Rutgers Univ, BS, 49, MS, 50, PhD(entom), 52. *Prof Exp:* Asst res specialist chem, 52-54, asst res specialist entom, 54-58, assoc res specialist, 58-61, res specialist, 61-71, RES PROF ENTOM & ECON ZOOL, RUTGERS UNIV, 71- *Mem:* Entom Soc Am. *Res:* Physiology; biochemistry; toxicology. *Mailing Add:* Dept Entom & Econ Zool Rutgers Univ New Brunswick NJ 08903

FORGENG, W(ILLIAM) D(ANIEL), b Scranton, Pa, May 31, 09; m 30; c 2. METALLURGY. *Educ:* Cornell Univ, BCh, 30, PhD(micros), 34. *Prof Exp:* Asst chem, Cornell Univ, 29-34; metallurgist res labs, Union Carbide Corp, 34-53, head metallurgist mining & metals div, 53-77; RETIRED. *Concurrent Pos:* Mem Off Sci Res & Develop, AEC, 44. *Mem:* Fel Am Soc Metals; hon mem Am Soc Test & Mat. *Res:* Metallurgy of ferro-alloys; effect of bismuth as an impurity on the structure and properties of tin. *Mailing Add:* 575 Oakmount Pl Apt 2917 Las Vegas NV 89109

FORGET, BERNARD G, b Fall River, Mass, Mar 23, 39; m 65; c 3. BIOCHEMISTRY, MOLECULAR BIOLOGY. *Educ:* Univ Montreal, BA, 59; McGill Univ, MD, 63; Yale Univ, MA, 78. *Prof Exp:* Clin assoc biochem, Nat Cancer Inst, NIH, 65-67; asst prof, Harvard Med Sch, 72-75, assoc prof pediat, 75-76; assoc prof, 76-77, PROF MED & HUMAN GENETICS, SCH MED, YALE UNIV, 78- *Concurrent Pos:* Spec fel, NIH, 68-69; res fel, Harvard Med Sch, 69-71; fel Med Found, Inc, Boston, 70-72; NIH res career develop award, 72-76. *Mem:* Am Soc Biol Chemists; Am Soc Clin Invest; Am Soc Hematol; Am Fedn Clin Res; Asn Am Physicians. *Res:* Molecular genetics of human hemoglobin synthesis; nucleic acid sequencing; globin gene cloning and structural analysis; molecular basis of thalassemia. *Mailing Add:* Dept of Med 333 Cedar St New Haven CT 06510

FORGHANI-ABKENARI, BAGHER, b Bandar Enzali, Iran, March 10, 36; m 69; c 2. VIROLOGY, IMMUNOLOGY. *Educ:* Justus Liebig Univ, WGer, MS, 61, PhD(virol), 65. *Prof Exp:* Fel virol, Utah State Univ, 65-67; asst prof biol, Nat Univ Iran, 67-69; res assoc virol, Utah State Univ, Logan, 69-70; fel, 70-72, RES SPECIALIST, DIV VIRUS RICKETTSIAL DIS LAB, CALIF STATE DEPT HEALTH SERV, 72- *Mem:* Am Soc Microbiol; Am Acad Microbiol. *Res:* Viruses including, Rubella, Hepatitis, Herpes, Measles, Cytomegalo Varicella-Zoster; degenerative disease; multiple sclerosis: using radio-or enzyme-immunoassay methodology; production and characterization of monoclonal antibody to several viruses. *Mailing Add:* Calif State Dept Health Serv 2151 Berkeley Way Berkeley CA 94704

FORGOTSON, JAMES MORRIS, JR, b Albuquerque, NMex, Mar 17, 30; m 58; c 2. PETROLEUM GEOLOGY, PETROLEUM ENGINEERING. *Educ:* Wash Univ, AB, 51; Univ Tex, BS, 52; Northwestern Univ, MS, 54, PhD(geol), 56. *Prof Exp:* Explor geologist, 53-55; sr res engr, Pan Am Petrol Corp, 56-61, tech group supvr, 61-62, res group supvr, 62-68; vpres, Petrol Info Corp, 68-71; staff geologist, Geophys Serv Inc, 72-74; geologist petrol explor & prod, 74-80, MGR, BURK, BAKWIN & HENRY, 80- *Concurrent Pos:* Adj prof, Univ Tex, Arlington, 74- & Southern Methodist Univ, 75-; pres, Bluebonnet Drilling Inc, 80-, Rosewood Transport Inc, 80- *Honors & Awards:* President's Award, Am Asn Petrol Geol, 64. *Mem:* Am Asn Petrol Geol (secy-treas, 68-70); Soc Econ Paleont & Mineral; Soc Petrol Eng; Soc Explor Geophys; Geol Soc Am. *Res:* Regional stratigraphic studies applied to petroleum exploration; new methods of presenting quantitative geological data; use of electronic computers to process and statistically analyze geological data; well log analysis; interpretation of gravity and magnetic data; data base systems for exploration; petroleum exploration and production; management of geological, land and engineering operations. *Mailing Add:* Slattery Bldg 509 Marshall St 1200 Shreveport LA 71101

FORGY, CHARLES LANNY, b Graham, Tex, Dec 29, 49; m 77. ARTIFICIAL INTELLIGENCE SYSTEMS. *Educ:* Univ Tex, Arlington, BS, 72; Carnegie-Mellon Univ, PhD(comput sci), 79. *Prof Exp:* RES ASSOC COMPUT SCI, CARNEGIE-MELLON UNIV, 78- *Mem:* Asn Comput Mach; Am Asn Artificial Intel. *Res:* Programming languages and computer architectures for artificial intelligence; applications of artificial intelligence. *Mailing Add:* Comput Sci Dept Carnegie-Mellon Univ Pittsburgh PA 15213

FORIST, ARLINGTON ARDEANE, b Lansing, Mich, Oct 14, 22; m 52; c 5. DRUG DEVELOPMENT. *Educ:* Mich State Col, BS, 48, PhD(biochem), 52. *Prof Exp:* Asst, Qm Food & Container Inst, Mich State Col, 48-51; res assoc, 51-60, res sect head, 60-68, res mgr phys & anal chem, 68-79, GROUP MGR PHYS & ANAL CHEM & DRUG METAB RES, UPJOHN CO, 79- *Mem:* AAAS; Am Chem Soc; NY Acad Sci; Am Soc Clin Pharmacol & Therapeut; fel Acad Pharmaceut Sci. *Res:* Multidisciplinary research administration in analytical and physical chemistry; spectroscopy and organic structure elucidation; drug metabolism; biopharmaceutics; pharmacokinetics. *Mailing Add:* Upjohn Co Kalamazoo MI 49001

FORK, DAVID CHARLES, b Detroit, Mich, Mar 4, 29; m 58; c 3. PLANT PHYSIOLOGY. *Educ:* Univ Calif, Berkeley, AB, 51, PhD(bot), 61. *Prof Exp:* BIOLOGIST, DEPT PLANT BIOL, CARNEGIE INST WASHINGTON, 60- *Concurrent Pos:* Courtesy prof, Stanford Univ, 68- *Mem:* AAAS; Am Soc Plant Physiologists; Am Soc Photobiol; Sigma Xi. *Res:* Study of the basic mechanisms of photosynthesis. *Mailing Add:* Dept Plant Biol Carnegie Inst Washington Stanford CA 94305

FORK, RICHARD LYNN, b Dearborn, Mich, Sept 1, 35; m 57, 71; c 4. SOLID STATE PHYSICS, SPECTROSCOPY. *Educ:* Principia Col, BS, 57; Mass Inst Technol, PhD(physics), 62. *Prof Exp:* MEM TECH STAFF, BELL LABS, 62- *Mem:* Fel Am Phys Soc; Optical Soc Am. *Res:* Lasers in magnetic fields; semiconductor luminescence; solid state spectroscopy; femto second spectroscopy; semiconductor microstructures. *Mailing Add:* 191 Holland Rd Middletown NJ 07748

FORKER, E LEE, b Pittsburgh, Pa, Aug 28, 30; m 55; c 4. PHYSIOLOGY, INTERNAL MEDICINE. *Educ:* Haverford Col, BS, 53; Univ Pittsburgh, MD, 57. *Prof Exp:* Intern, Presby Hosp, Denver, Colo, 57-58; resident internal med, Hosp, Col Med, Univ Iowa, 60-63, Iowa Heart Asn fel physiol & biophys, 63-65, asst prof med, 65-69, asst prof physiol & biophys, 67-69, assoc prof internal med, physiol & biophys, 69-73, prof internal med, 73-79; PROF MED & DIR, DIV GASTROENTEROL & LIVER DIS, SCH MED, UNIV MO-COLUMBIA, 80- *Concurrent Pos:* Res assoc, Vet Admin Hosp, Iowa City, 65-67; Markle scholar acad med, 67; NIH res career develop award, 68. *Mem:* Am Soc Clin Invest; Am Asn Study Liver Dis (pres, 83); Soc Math Biol; Am Physiol Soc; Am Gastroenterol Asn. *Res:* Hepatic physiology; bile formation; membrane transport. *Mailing Add:* Gastroenterol & Liver Div Sch Med Univ Mo Columbia MO 65212

FORKEY, DAVID MEDRICK, b Minneapolis, Minn, Apr 9, 40; m 66. ORGANIC CHEMISTRY. *Educ:* St Olaf Col, BA, 62; Univ Wash, PhD(org chem), 67. *Prof Exp:* Nat Res Coun res assoc org synthesis & mass spectrometry, Naval Weapons Ctr, Calif, 67-69; asst prof, 69-74, assoc prof, 74-81, PROF CHEM, CALIF STATE UNIV, SACRAMENTO, 81- *Mem:* Am Chem Soc. *Res:* Syntheses and reactions of heterocyclic compounds; applications of nuclear magnetic resonance and mass spectrometry to organic structural problems; applications of gas chromatography and high-performance liquid chromatography to chemical separations. *Mailing Add:* 4805 Thor Way Carmichael CA 95608

FORLAND, MARVIN, b Newark, NJ, Mar 29, 33; m 65; c 2. INTERNAL MEDICINE, NEPHROLOGY. *Educ:* Colgate Univ, AB, 54; Columbia Univ, MD, 58. *Prof Exp:* Intern & resident internal med, Univ Chicago Hosps, 59-62, asst prof med, Sch Med, Univ Chicago, 64-68; assoc prof med & chief renal & electrolyte sect, 68-72, PROF MED, UNIV TEX MED SCH, SAN ANTONIO, 72-, DEP CHMN DEPT MED, 75- *Mem:* Cent Soc Clin Res; fel Am Col Physicians; Am Soc Nephrol; Int Soc Nephrol. *Res:* Clinical nephrology and metabolism; renal physiology. *Mailing Add:* Univ of Tex Med Sch San Antonio TX 78284

FORLANO, ROBERT J(OSE), b Buenos Aires, Arg, Nov 5, 28; US citizen; m 69; c 1. CERAMICS, METALLURGY. *Educ:* Univ Buenos Aires, BS, 53; Univ Ill, MS, 62, PhD(ceramics eng), 65. *Prof Exp:* CERAMIST, KNOLLS ATOMIC POWER LAB, GEN ELEC CO, 65- *Mem:* Am Ceramic Soc; Am Soc Metals. *Res:* Research in high temperature oxide and materials related with nuclear power applications. *Mailing Add:* Knolls Atomic Power Lab Box 1072 Schenectady NY 12301

FORMAL, SAMUEL BERNARD, b Providence, RI, Aug 28, 23; m 51; c 3. MICROBIOLOGY. *Educ:* Brown Univ, AB, 45, ScM, 48; Boston Univ, PhD(microbiol), 52; Am Bd Microbiol, dipl. *Prof Exp:* Bacteriologist, Food & Drug Admin, 48-49; bacteriologist, 52-56, chief dept appl immunol, 56-76, CHIEF DEPT BACT DIS, WALTER REED ARMY INST RES, 76- *Concurrent Pos:* Mem comn enteric infections, Armed Forces Epidemiol; prof lectr, Sch Med, Georgetown Univ, 73-; mem ed bd, J Reticular Endothelial Soc, 74-, J Infection & Immunity, 78- *Mem:* AAAS; Am Soc Microbiologists; Am Asn Immunologists; Am Acad Microbiol; Infectious Dis Soc Am. *Res:* Pathogenesis and immunity in enteric infections; non-specific immunity. *Mailing Add:* Dept Bact Dis Walter Reed Army Inst of Res Washington DC 20012

FORMAN, DAVID S, b Detroit, Mich, Dec 10, 42. CELL BIOLOGY, NEUROBIOLOGY. *Educ:* Harvard Col, BA, 64; Rockefeller Univ, PhD(life sci), 71. *Prof Exp:* Fel, Lab Neuropharmacol, NIMH, 71-75; res physiologist, Naval Med Res Inst, 75-81; ASST PROF ANAT, UNIFORMED SERV UNIV HEALTH SCI, 81- *Concurrent Pos:* Vis asst prof, Dept Anat, Sch Med, Howard Univ, 75-78; asst prof & lectr, Dept Physiol, Sch Med, George Washington Univ, 77; mem, Merit Rev Bd, neurobiol, Vet Admin, 78-81. *Mem:* Soc Neurosci; Am Soc Cell Biol; Am Soc Neurochem; Int Brain Res Orgn; AAAS. *Res:* Axonal transport, the movement of materials inside neurons; nerve regeneration and non-neural cell motility. *Mailing Add:* Dept Anat Uniformed Serv Univ Health Sci 4301 Jones Bridge Rd Bethesda MD 20814

FORMAN, DONALD T, b New York, NY, Feb 27, 32; m 53; c 3. BIOCHEMISTRY, ANALYTICAL CHEMISTRY. *Educ:* Brooklyn Col, BS, 53; Wayne State Univ, MS, 57, PhD(biochem), 59. *Prof Exp:* Chief biochemist, Hazleton Lab, 59-60; from instr to asst prof, 61-69, ASSOC PROF BIOCHEM, MED SCH, NORTHWESTERN UNIV, EVANSTON, 69-; DIR CLIN BIOCHEM, EVANSTON HOSP, 63- *Concurrent Pos:* NIH & Am Heart Asn res grants, 63-68; dir biochem, Mercy Hosp, 60-63. *Mem:* AAAS; Am Chem Soc; Am Asn Clin Chem. *Res:* Clinical biochemistry, development of better methods, more specific procedures for evaluating disease states; atherosclerosis. *Mailing Add:* Dept of Clin Biochem Evanston Hosp Evanston IL 60201

FORMAN, EARL JULIAN, b Hartford, Conn, June 22, 29; m 53; c 3. ANALYTICAL CHEMISTRY. *Educ:* Wesleyan Univ, BA, 53; Mass Inst Technol, PhD(anal chem), 57. *Prof Exp:* Res chemist, Hercules Powder Co, 57-70; res group leader, 70-77, mgr, Film Div Anal Serv, 78-81, MGR, CORP CHEM INSPECTION, POLAROID CORP, 81- *Mem:* Am Chem Soc. *Mailing Add:* 115 Loring Rd Weston MA 02193

FORMAN, G LAWRENCE, b Hartford, Conn, Nov 13, 42; div; c 3. MAMMALOGY, COMPARATIVE ANATOMY. *Educ:* Univ Kans, BA, 64, MA, 67, PhD(mammal), 69. *Prof Exp:* ASSOC PROF BIOL, ROCKFORD COL, 69-, CHMN DEPT, 71-, CHMN DIV SCI & MATH, 76- *Mem:* AAAS; Am Soc Mammalogists; Sigma Xi; Am Inst Biol Sci; Soc Syst Zool. *Res:* Mammalian systematics; microanatomy of mammals; gastrointestinal morphology in relation to feeding habits; morphology of cellular types in mammals in relation to systematic arrangement; sperm morphology in North American bats; anatomy of lymphoid organs. *Mailing Add:* Dept Biol Rockford Col Rockford IL 61101

FORMAN, GEORGE W, b Salt Lake City, Utah, Dec 9, 19; m 41; c 3. MECHANICAL ENGINEERING, ENGINEERING MECHANICS. *Educ:* Univ Ill, BS, 41; Univ Kans, MS, 58. *Prof Exp:* Design engr & supvr eng training, Hamilton Stand Div, United Aircraft Corp, 41-46; mgr mech eng, Marley Co, 46-53; res mgr, Butler Mfg Co, 53-55; PROF MECH ENG, UNIV KANS, 55- *Concurrent Pos:* Indust consult, 55- *Mem:* Fel Am Soc Mech Engrs. *Res:* Machine design; composite materials research; structural response to impact loads. *Mailing Add:* Dept Mech Eng Univ Kans Lawrence KS 66044

FORMAN, GUY, b Dundee, Ky, Oct 23, 06; m 26. PHYSICS. *Educ:* Western Ky State Col, BS, 29; Ind Univ, MA, 31; Univ Ky, PhD, 50. *Prof Exp:* Assoc prof physics, Western Ky State Col, 29-43; assoc prof, Vanderbilt Univ, 43-62; chmn dept, 62-69, prof, 62-72, EMER PROF PHYSICS, UNIV SOUTH FLA, 72- *Mem:* Am Phys Asn; Optical Soc Am; Am Asn Physics Teachers. *Res:* Action of light on selenium cells as a surface effect; coloration of quartz crystals by radiation with x-rays; x-ray excited phosphorescence of natural crystals; teaching elementary and intermediate physics. *Mailing Add:* Apt 101 10338 Carrollwood Lane Tampa FL 33618

FORMAN, HENRY JAY, b New York, Apr 20, 47; m 79; c 2. BIOCHEMICAL TOXICOLOGY, ENZYMOLOGY. *Educ:* Queens Col, NY, BA, 67; Columbia Univ, PhD(biochem), 71. *Prof Exp:* Res assoc biochem, Duke Univ, 71-73; res investr, Vet Admin Hosp, Kansas City, 73-77; asst prof, 78-81, ASSOC PROF, PHYSIOL, UNIV PA, 81- *Concurrent Pos:* adj asst prof biochem, Univ Kans Med Sch, 77. *Mem:* Am Soc Biol Chemists. *Res:* Function of lung cells; oxygen radicals-generation by mitochondria and macrophages; kinetics and mechanisms. *Mailing Add:* Dept Physiol/G4 Univ Pa Philadelphia PA 19104

FORMAN, J(OSEPH) CHARLES, b Chicago, Ill, Dec 22, 31; m 53; c 3. CHEMICAL & BIOCHEMICAL ENGINEERING. *Educ:* Mass Inst Technol, SB, 53; Northwestern Univ, MS, 57, PhD(chem eng), 60. *Prof Exp:* Mem tech proj training prog, Dow Chem Co, Mich, 53-54; chem engr, Develop Div, Abbott Labs, 56-59; sr chem engr, Eng Develop Dept, 59-63, group leader, Extreme Conditions Lab, 63-67; group leader fermentation eng, Biol Develop Dept, 67-68, sect mgr & proj mgr, 68-74, opers mgr corp procurement, 74-75, dir mfg opers, Agr & Vet Prod Div, 75-77; assoc exec dir, 77-78, EXEC DIR & SECY, AM INST CHEM ENGRS, NEW YORK, 78- *Mem:* Fel Am Inst Chem Engrs; Nat Soc Prof Engrs; Am Chem Soc; Am Soc Assoc Execs; Sigma Xi. *Res:* Association management; technical management; direction and evaluation of technical projects; biochemical engineering; industrial fermentations. *Mailing Add:* Am Inst of Chem Engrs 345 E 47th St New York NY 10017

FORMAN, JAMES, b Watertown, Mass, Dec 23, 39; m 65; c 3. IMMUNOLOGY. *Educ:* Tufts Univ, BS, 61, DMD, 65, PhD(physiol), 71. *Prof Exp:* Fel immunol, Karolinska Inst, Sweden, 71-73; fel, 73-74, asst prof, 74-76, assoc prof, 76-80, PROF IMMUNOL, DEPT MICROBIOL, UNIV TEX HEALTH SCI CTR, DALLAS, 80- *Concurrent Pos:* NIH fel, 71-72. *Mem:* Am Asn Immunologists. *Res:* Cellular immunology; immunogenetics. *Mailing Add:* Dept of Microbiol Univ of Tex Health Sci Ctr Dallas TX 75235

FORMAN, MIRIAM AUSMAN, b San Francisco, Calif, Apr 12, 39; m 64; c 2. SPACE PHYSICS, ASTRONOMY. *Educ:* Univ Chicago, BS, 60, MS, 61; State Univ NY, Stony Brook, PhD(physics), 72. *Prof Exp:* Res scientist, SAfrican Coun Sci & Indust Res, 65-67; res assoc, Lab Space Res, Mass Inst Technol, 67-68; res assoc, 72-73, ADJ PROF SPACE SCI, STATE UNIV NY, STONY BROOK, 73- *Concurrent Pos:* NASA fel, 73-; fel, Max Planck Soc, 78-79. *Mem:* Am Phys Soc; Am Astron Soc; Am Geophys Union. *Res:* Solar effects on cosmic rays in interplanetary effects; carbon-14 variations and solar activity; cosmic physics and high-energy astrophysics; solar terrestrial relations. *Mailing Add:* Dept of Earth & Space Sci State Univ of NY Stony Brook NY 11794

FORMAN, RALPH, b New York, NY, Oct 4, 21; m 43; c 3. PHYSICS. *Educ:* Brooklyn Col, BA, 42; Univ Md, MS, 51, PhD(physics), 54. *Prof Exp:* Physicist, Nat Bur Standards, 42-55 & Union Carbide Corp, 55-64; PHYSICIST, LEWIS RES CTR, NASA, 64- *Mem:* Am Phys Soc. *Res:* irradiated gas plasma; High temperature heat pipes; high temperature thermal conductivity measurements; auger and electron spectroscopy for chemical analysis surface studies of impregnated tungsten thermionic cathodes; studies on the surface reactions involving barium-oxygen-tungsten; secondary-emission measurements on low secondary yield surfaces. *Mailing Add:* Lewis Res Ctr NASA Cleveland OH 44135

FORMAN, RICHARD T T, b Richmond, Va, Nov 10, 35; m 63; c 3. ECOSYSTEM, LANDSCAPE ECOLOGY. *Educ:* Haverford Col, BS, 57; Univ Pa, PhD(bot), 61. *Prof Exp:* Asst instr bot, Univ Pa, 58-59, 60-61 & Duke Univ, 59-60; mem Am Friends Serv Comt agr exten & community develop, Nat Inst Agr, Guatemala, 61-62; asst prof biol, Pan Am Agr Col, Honduras, 62-63; asst prof bot & zool, Univ Wis, 63-66; from asst prof to assoc prof, 66-76, PROF BOT, 76-, DIR, WILLIAM L HUTCHESON MEM FOREST, RUTGERS UNIV, 72-, DIR GRAD PROG BOT & PLANT PHYSIOL, 79- *Concurrent Pos:* Vis scientist, Orgn Trop Studies, Costa Rica, 70; Fulbright scholar, Bogota, Colombia, 70-71; vis scientist, WI Lab, VI, 73, Ft Burgwin Res Ctr, NMex, 76; ed, Ecol & Ecol Monographs, 73-77; CNRS Chercheur, Centre d'Etudes Phytosociologiques et Ecologiques, Montpellier, France; mem comt examrs grad record exam, Educ Testing Serv, 78-80. *Mem:* Fel AAAS; Ecol Soc Am; Am Bryol & Lichenological Soc; Torrey Bot Club (pres, 80-81); Asn Trop Biol. *Res:* Principles of landscape structure and functions; forest communities and ecosystems; responses to stress; biogeography; bryology. *Mailing Add:* Dept Bot Rutgers Univ New Brunswick NJ 08903

FORMAN, WILLIAM, b New York, NY, Oct 16, 14; m 38; c 2. MATHEMATICS. *Educ:* Brooklyn Col, BS, 36, MA, 37; NY Univ, PhD, 53. *Prof Exp:* Lectr, 36-53, from instr to assoc prof, 53-71, PROF MATH, BROOKLYN COL, 71- *Concurrent Pos:* Asst, Inst Math & Mech, NY Univ, 51-52; consult, Systs Res Group, 59-62. *Mem:* Am Math Soc; Math Asn Am; NY Acad Sci. *Res:* Theory of numbers; algebra. *Mailing Add:* Dept of Math Brooklyn Col Brooklyn NY 11210

FORMANEK, EDWARD WILLIAM, b Chicago, Ill, May 6, 42. ALGEBRA. *Educ:* Univ Chicago, BS, 63; DePaul Univ, MS, 65; Rice Univ, PhD(math), 70. *Prof Exp:* Asst prof math, Univ Mo-St Louis, 70-71; fel, Carleton Univ, 71-73; vis mem, Inst Advan Study, 73-74; res assoc, Univ Pisa, 74-75; res assoc math, Univ Chicago, 75-77; res assoc, Hebrew Univ Jerusalem, 77-78; PROF MATH, PA STATE UNIV, 78- *Mem:* Am Math Soc. *Res:* Group theory and ring theory. *Mailing Add:* McAllister Bldg Pa State Univ University Park PA 16802

FORMANEK, R(OBERT) J(OSEPH), b Schenectady, NY, Dec 25, 22; m 46; c 2. CHEMICAL ENGINEERING. *Educ:* Purdue Univ, BSChE, 43. *Prof Exp:* Trainee, B F Goodrich Co, 44-47; compounder, 47-51, textile engr, 51-54; mgr textiles, Dunlop Tire & Rubber Corp, 54-57, mgr compounding & textiles, 57-61, tech mgr, 61-64, asst vpres technol, 64-69, V PRES TECHNOL, DUNLOP TIRE & RUBBER CORP, 69- *Concurrent Pos:* Dir, Am Synthetic Rubber Corp. *Mem:* Rubber Mfg Asn. *Res:* Technical development of tires. *Mailing Add:* Dunlop Tire & Rubber Corp Buffalo NY 14240

FORMICA, JOSEPH VICTOR, b New York, NY, July 3, 29; m 56; c 2. BIOCHEMISTRY. *Educ:* Syracuse Univ, BS, 53, MS, 54; Georgetown Univ, PhD(microbiol), 67. *Prof Exp:* Supvr & bacteriologist, Ft Detrick, Md, 54-58; assoc neurochem, NIH, 58-63; assoc biochem, Georgetown Univ, 63-67, asst prof pediat virol, 67-69; from asst dean to assoc dean, Sch Basic Sci, 77-81, ASSOC PROF MICROBIOL, MED COL VA, 69- *Mem:* Am Chem Soc; Am Soc Microbiol; fel Am Acad Microbiol. *Res:* Biosynthesis of antibiotics; biosynthetic pathway of actinomycin synthesis. *Mailing Add:* Dept Microbiol Box 678 Med Col Va Health Sci Ctr Richmond VA 23298

FORNAESS, JOHN ERIK, b Hamar, Norway, Oct 14, 46; m 73; c 2. MATHEMATICAL ANALYSIS. *Educ:* Univ Oslo, Cand Real, 70; Univ Wash, PhD(math), 74. *Prof Exp:* Instr math, 74-76, asst prof, 76-78, ASSOC PROF MATH, PRINCETON UNIV, 78- *Mem:* Am Math Soc. *Res:* Several complex variables. *Mailing Add:* Dept of Math Fine Hall Princeton Univ Princeton NJ 08544

FORNEFELD, EUGENE JOSEPH, b Sandusky, Ohio, May 4, 20; m 44; c 5. ORGANIC CHEMISTRY. *Educ:* Xavier Univ, Ohio, BS, 41; Univ Detroit, MS, 43; Univ Mich, PhD(org chem), 50. *Prof Exp:* Res assoc pharmacol, Univ Mich, 50-51; RES CHEMIST, ELI LILLY & CO, 51- *Mem:* Am Chem Soc. *Res:* Synthesis of steroids and natural products; structure-activity studies in the acetyl choline and analgesic areas; determination of morphine and physiologically active bases in biological media. *Mailing Add:* Eli Lilly & Co 307 E McCarty St Indianapolis IN 46206

FORNES, RAYMOND EARL, b Greenville, NC, Jan 16, 43; m 66; c 3. POLYMER PHYSICS, TEXTILE PHYSICS. *Educ:* ECarolina Univ, AB, 65; NC State Univ, PhD(physics), 70. *Prof Exp:* asst prof, 70-74, assoc prof textile technol & physics, 74-79, PROF TEXTILE MAT, MGT & PHYSICS, NC STATE UNIV, 79- *Concurrent Pos:* Mem, Nat Sci Comt on Byssinosis, 80-81. *Mem:* Am Phys Soc; The Fiber Soc; AAAS; Sigma Xi. *Res:* Structure and physical properties of fiber forming polymers; composites; x-ray diffraction; cotton dust; nuclear magnetic resonance. *Mailing Add:* Sch of Textiles NC State Univ Raleigh NC 27607

FORNEY, ALBERT J, b Vanport, Pa, July 8, 15; m 42; c 3. CHEMICAL ENGINEERING. *Educ:* Geneva Col, BS, 47; Carnegie Inst Technol, BS, 57. *Prof Exp:* Chemist, US Bur Mines, 47-50, chem engr, 50-59, supvry chem engr, 59-76; RETIRED. *Mem:* Am Chem Soc; Am Inst Chem Engrs. *Res:* Synthetic liquid and gaseous fuels and coal gasification; gas purification, fluidization, steam-iron process; sewage treatment; coal pretreatment; chemicals from coal. *Mailing Add:* 410 Marney Dr Coraopolis PA 15108

FORNEY, FREDERICK WILLIS, b Sioux City, Iowa, Mar 5, 27; m 51; c 4. MICROBIAL PHYSIOLOGY. *Educ:* Univ SDak, BA, 61; Univ Iowa, MS, 66, PhD(microbiol & org chem), 69. *Prof Exp:* Asst microbiol, Univ Iowa, 61-62, NSF res assoc, 68-69; NIH fel, La State Univ, 69-71; asst prof microbiol, Univ Southwestern La, 71-76; res assoc Kans City Med Ctr, 76-77; assoc prof biol, Morningside Col, 77-79; ASSOC PROF BIOL, COL ST TERESA, 79- *Mem:* Sigma Xi; Am Soc Microbiol; Am Chem Soc. *Res:* Development of the microbial degradation of aliphatic methyl ketones by study of the enzymes involved, characterizing them and determining their cellular localizations. *Mailing Add:* Dept Biol Col St Teresa Winona MN 55987

FORNEY, JOHN EDGAR, b Waterloo, Iowa, June 22, 17; m 44, 76; c 3. MICROBIOLOGY, PUBLIC HEALTH. *Educ:* Manchester Col, AB, 38; Stanford Univ, MA, 48, PhD(bact), 49. *Prof Exp:* Asst prof med microbiol, Univ Southern Calif, 49-55; asst dir labs, City Health Dept, Los Angeles, 55-63; asst chief, Lab Consult & Develop Sect, Communicable Dis Ctr, 63-68, chief, Lab Licensure Sect, 68-72, MICROBIOLOGIST CONSULT, LAB TRAINING & CONSULT DIV, CTR DIS CONTROL, US PUB HEALTH SERV, 72- *Concurrent Pos:* Ed, Health Lab Sci, 75-79; consult, Biological Safety, WHO, 80- *Mem:* Am Soc Microbiologists; Am Soc Clin Pathologists; fel Am Acad Microbiol; Sigma Xi; Conf Pub Health Lab Dirs. *Mailing Add:* Ctr for Dis Control Atlanta GA 30333

FORNEY, LARRY J, engineering science, see previous edition

FORNEY, R(OBERT) C(LYDE), b Chicago, Ill, Mar 13, 27; m 48; c 4. CHEMICAL ENGINEERING. *Educ:* Purdue Univ, BS, 47, MS, 48, PhD(chem eng), 50. *Hon Degrees:* Dr Eng, Purdue Univ, 81. *Prof Exp:* Res engr, Textile Fibers Dept, 50-52, group supvr, 52, plant res supvr, 52-56, process supt, 56-59, asst plant mgr, 59-63, tech mgr, 63-64, prod mgr, 64-66, dir prod mkt div, 66-69, asst gen dir mkt div, 69-70, asst gen mgr, 70-75, vpres & gen mgr, 75-77, vpres, Plastics Prod & Resins Dept, 77-78, sr vpres admin dept, 79-81, EXEC VPRES, E I DU PONT DE NEMOURS & CO, INC, 81- *Mem:* Am Chem Soc; Am Inst Chem Engrs. *Res:* Industrial relations; reaction kinetics. *Mailing Add:* Admin Dept 9000 Du Pont Bldg Wilmington DE 19898

FORNEY, ROBERT BURNS, b Ashley, Ind, July 9, 16; m 41; c 2. TOXICOLOGY. *Educ:* Ind Univ, PhD, 48. *Hon Degrees:* LLD, Ind Cent Col, 64. *Prof Exp:* From asst prof to assoc prof toxicol, 48-62, prof pharmacol & toxicol, Sch Med, Ind Univ-Purdue Univ, Indianapolis, 62-77; DISTINGUISHED PROF TOXICOL & DIR STATE TOXICOL LAB, SCH MED, IND UNIV, INDIANAPOLIS, 77- *Concurrent Pos:* Mem traffic safety comt & comt alcohol & drugs, Nat Safety Coun. *Mem:* Am Soc Pharmacol & Exp Therapeut; Soc Toxicol; fel Am Acad Forensic Sci; Am Soc Clin Pharmacol & Therapeut. *Res:* Effects of alcohol, marihuana and other drugs on performance. *Mailing Add:* Sch of Med Ind Univ Indianapolis IN 46202

FOROULIS, Z ANDREW, b Volos, Greece, Dec 6, 26; US citizen; m 62. CHEMICAL & METALLURGICAL ENGINEERING. *Educ:* Nat Univ Athens, Dipl, 54; Mass Inst Technol, MS & ChE, 56, MetE, 60, DSc(metall eng), 61. *Prof Exp:* Chem engr, Dewey & Almy Chem Div, W R Grace & Co, 56-57; engr, 61-62, sr engr, 62-63, eng assoc, 63-68, SR ENG ASSOC,

EXXON RES & ENG CO, 68- *Concurrent Pos:* Adj prof, NY Univ, 68- *Mem:* Am Chem Soc; Am Inst Chem Engrs; Am Inst Mining, Metall & Petrol Engrs; Am Soc Mech Engrs. *Mailing Add:* Exxon Res & Eng Co PO Box 101 Florham Park NJ 07932

FORRAY, MARVIN JULIAN, b New York, NY, Apr 18, 22; m 45; c 4. MATHEMATICS. *Educ:* NY Univ, BA, 43, MS, 44; Columbia Univ, PhD(appl mech), 55. *Prof Exp:* Instr math, Polytech Inst Brooklyn, 44-53; sr engr struct, Repub Aviation Corp, NY, 53-55, prin engr, develop & res, 55-58, design specialist, 58-61, develop engr, 61-66; PROF MATH, C W POST COL, 66- *Concurrent Pos:* Lectr & prof, Adelphi Col, 55-65. *Mem:* Math Asn Am; Am Soc Civil Eng. *Res:* Applied mechanics; elasticity; thermoelasticity; plates and shells; instability of structures; vibrations; heat conduction; calculus of variations; differential equations; functions of a real and complex variable; transform theory. *Mailing Add:* 21 Edward St Lynbrook NY 11563

FORRER, MAX P(AUL), b St Gallen, Switz, Oct 15, 25; nat US; m 52; c 2. ELECTRICAL ENGINEERING. *Educ:* Swiss Fed Inst Technol, dipl ing, 50; Stanford Univ, PhD(elec eng), 59. *Prof Exp:* Develop engr commun, Standard Tel & Radio Corp, Switz, 51-52 & Western Elec Co, NJ, 52-55; proj engr microwave electronics, Microwave Lab, Gen Elec Co, 55-61; proj engr & mgr microwave component, Kane Eng Lab, 61-63; head circuits develop sect, 63-68, vdir, 65-68, DIR, CENTRE ELECTRONIQUE HORLOGER, 68- *Concurrent Pos:* Asst, Hansen Labs, Stanford Univ, 57-58. *Honors & Awards:* Victor Kullberg Medal, Urmakare Ambete, Stockholm, 70. *Mem:* Sr mem Inst Elec & Electronics Engrs. *Res:* Microwave components and tubes; high power klystrons; duplexer devices; microwave secondary emission devices. *Mailing Add:* Centre Electronique Horloger SA 71 Rue Maladiere Neuchatel Switzerland

FORREST, HUGH SOMMERVILLE, b Glasgow, Scotland, Apr 28, 24; m 54; c 3. MOLECULAR BIOLOGY. *Educ:* Glasgow Univ, BSc, 44; Univ London, PhD(chem), 48, DSc, 70; Cambridge Univ, PhD(chem), 51. *Prof Exp:* Mem sci staff, Nat Inst Med Res, Med Res Coun, Gt Brit, 45-48; res fel biol, Calif Inst Technol, 51-54, sr res fel, 55-56; res scientist, 56-57, assoc prof, 57-63, chmn dept, 74-78, PROF ZOOL, UNIV TEX, AUSTIN, 63- *Concurrent Pos:* Co-ed, Biochem Genetics, 70-78, ed, 79- *Mem:* Am Chem Soc; The Chem Soc; Am Soc Biol Chemists. *Res:* Chemistry and biology of pteridines; chemistry of genetic systems and of developmental processes. *Mailing Add:* Dept of Zool Univ of Tex Austin TX 78712

FORREST, IRENE STEPHANIE, b Charlottenburg, Ger, Aug 20, 08; nat US; m 34; c 1. BIOCHEMISTRY. *Educ:* Univ Berlin, PhD(chem), 32. *Prof Exp:* Researcher, microbiol & biochem, Pasteur Inst Paris & Munic Hosp (Hotel Dieu), Paris, France, 32-34; asst chemist, Istanbul, 35-36; researcher biochem, NY Univ, 41-43; researcher, Moraine Prod Div, Gen Motors Corp, Dayton, Ohio, 44; translator, US War Dept, 45-47; nucleic acids res, NY Univ, 48; endocrinol res, St Clare's Hosp, NY, 49-50, consult chem, 51-52; biochem res, Polytech Inst Brooklyn & NY Med Col, 53-56; chief biochem res lab, Vet Admin Hosp, Brockton, Mass, 57-61; chief, Biochem Res Lab, Vet Admin Hosp, Palo Alto, 61-80; RETIRED. *Concurrent Pos:* Res assoc psychiat, Sch Med, Stanford Univ, 61-73; sr res scientist, Inst Chem Biol, Univ San Francisco, 73- *Mem:* AAAS; Am Chem Soc; Soc Exp Biol & Med; Am Soc Pharmacol & Exp Therapeut; Soc Biol Psychiat. *Res:* General biochemistry; psychopharmacology; drug metabolism; phenothiazine drugs. *Mailing Add:* 540 Ringwood Ave Menlo Park CA 94025

FORREST, JAMES BENJAMIN, b Newcastle, NB, Oct 8, 35; m 60, 70; c 3. GEOTECHNOLOGY, STRUCTURES. *Educ:* Univ NB, BSc, 59; Univ BC, MASc, 63; Northwestern Univ, PhD(civil eng), 66. *Prof Exp:* Engr, Dept Nat Health & Welfare, Govt Can, 59-60; design engr, Montreal Eng Ltd, 60-61; asst prof eng, Carleton Univ, 65-68; res assoc engr, Univ NMex, 68-70; SR PROJ ENGR, NAVAL CIVIL ENG LAB, 70- *Concurrent Pos:* Vis lectr, Univ Calif, Los Angeles, 80. *Mem:* Am Soc Civil Engrs; Am Soc Testing & Mat; Soc Am Mil Engrs. *Res:* Yielding of clays subjected to steady state vibratory, quasi-static and impulsive loadings; the constitutive relationships for pavement component materials; soil dynamics, applied mechanics; earthquake induced soil liquefaction; waterfront structures. *Mailing Add:* Naval Civil Eng Lab Code L53 Port Hueneme CA 93043

FORREST, JOHN CHARLES, b Larned, Kans, July 30, 36; m 64; c 2. MEAT SCIENCE. *Educ:* Kans State Univ, BS, 60, MS, 62; Univ Wis, PhD(muscle physiol), 66. *Prof Exp:* Proj asst muscle chem & physiol, Univ Wis, 65-66; asst prof animal sci, Univ Minn, 66-67; assoc prof, 67-77, PROF ANIMAL SCI, PURDUE UNIV, 77- *Mem:* Am Soc Animal Sci; Am Meat Sci Asn; Inst Food Technologists. *Res:* Influence of ante-mortem physiology and stress on the post-mortem metabolism of skeletal and cardiac muscle; effects of temperature on pre-rigor muscle systems. *Mailing Add:* Dept of Animal Sci Purdue Univ West Lafayette IN 47907

FORREST, ROBERT BREWSTER, b Minneapolis, Minn, Mar 24, 34; m 58; c 1. PHOTOGRAMMETRY. *Educ:* Univ Minn, BA, 58; Ohio State Univ, PhD(geod sci), 64. *Prof Exp:* Geod & photogram res asst, Res Found, Ohio State Univ, 58-60, res assoc, 60-63; photogrammetrist, Arecibo Ionospheric Observ, 63-65; sr prin photogrammetrist, Bendix Res Labs, 65-77; MEM STAFF, MECH SUPPORT UTIL, LANGLEY RES CTR, NASA, 77- *Mem:* Am Soc Photogram. *Res:* Computer control applications to photogrammetric instrumentation; geometric modelling of image data; increased non-topographic application of photogrammetry. *Mailing Add:* Mech Support Util M/5387 NASA Langley Res Ctr Hampton VA 23665

FORREST, ROBERT J, b Winnipeg, Man, Dec 21, 28; m 54; c 3. BIOCHEMISTRY, ANIMAL NUTRITION. *Educ:* Univ BC, BSA, 54, MSA, 55; Univ Ill, PhD(biochem), 59. *Prof Exp:* RES SCIENTIST BIOCHEM, CAN DEPT AGR, 59- *Mem:* Am Chem Soc; NY Acad Sci; Am Soc Animal Sci; Can Soc Animal Prod; Agr Inst Can. *Res:* Acid soluble nucleotides of bovine mammary gland; beef production by dairy cattle; beef production; meats research; animal physiology and biochemistry. *Mailing Add:* Res Br Can Dept of Agr Exp Farm Agassiz BC V0M 1A0 Can

FORREST, ROBERT NEAGLE, b Pendleton, Ore, Nov 25, 25; m 51; c 2. OPERATIONS RESEARCH, OPERATIONS ANALYSIS. *Educ:* Univ Ore, BS, 50, MS, 52 & 54, PhD(physics), 59. *Prof Exp:* Nuclear physicist, Lawrence Radiation Lab, Univ Calif, 58-59; mem staff geoastrophysics, Sci Lab, Boeing Airplane Co, 59; asst prof surface physics, Ore State Univ, 59-63; asst prof physics, Southern Ore Col, 63-64; asst prof, 64-80, PROF OPERS ANAL, US NAVAL POSTGRAD SCH, 80- *Mem:* AAAS; Am Asn Physics Teachers; Am Vacuum Soc; Opers Res Soc Am; Sigma Xi. *Mailing Add:* Dept Opers Res US Naval Postgrad Sch Monterey CA 93940

FORREST, THOMAS DOUGLAS, b Murray, Ky, Mar 13, 33; m 64; c 2. MATHEMATICS. *Educ:* Murray State Univ, BS, 54; Univ Tenn, MMath, 63; George Peabody Col, PhD(math), 71. *Prof Exp:* Instr math, Marshall County Schs, Ky, 56-61, Murray High Sch, 63-64 & Murray State Univ, 64-67; ASSOC PROF MATH, MID TENN STATE UNIV, 69- *Concurrent Pos:* NSF panelist, 77. *Mem:* Nat Coun Math Teachers; Math Asn Am. *Mailing Add:* Dept of Math & Comput Sci Mid Tenn State Univ Murfreesboro TN 37130

FORREST, THOMAS PETER, organic chemistry, see previous edition

FORRESTER, ALVIN THEODORE, b Brooklyn, NY, Apr 13, 18; div; c 4. PLASMA PHYSICS. *Educ:* Cornell Univ, AB, 38, AM, 39, PhD(physics), 42. *Prof Exp:* Res assoc, Lawrence Radiation Lab, Univ Calif, 42-45; physicist, RCA Labs, 45-46; from asst prof to assoc prof physics, Univ Southern Calif, 46-55; fel engr, Res Labs, Westinghouse Elec Corp, 55-57, adv physicist, 57-58; nuclear specialist, Atomic Int Div, NAm Aviation, Inc, 58-59, propulsion specialist, Rocketdyne Div, 58-59; mgr ion physics dept, Electro-Optical Systs, Inc, 59-65; prof physics, Univ Calif, Irvine, 65-67; PROF PHYSICS & ENG, UNIV CALIF, LOS ANGELES, 67- *Honors & Awards:* Res Award, Am Rocket Soc, 62. *Mem:* AAAS; fel Am Phys Soc; assoc fel Am Inst Aeronaut & Astronaut; fel Inst Elec & Electronics Engrs; Am Asn Physics Teachers. *Res:* Electron and ion sources; coherence properties of radiation; photoelectric mixing; ion propulsion. *Mailing Add:* Rm 7731 BH Univ Calif Los Angeles CA 90024

FORRESTER, DONALD JASON, b Attleboro, Mass, Jan 31, 37; m 61; c 3. WILDLIFE PARASITOLOGY. *Educ:* Univ Mass, Amherst, BS, 58; Univ Mont, MS, 60; Univ Calif, Davis, PhD(zool), 67. *Prof Exp:* Res assoc zool, Univ Mont, 61-63; asst prof, Clemson Univ, 67-69; asst prof, Div Biol Sci, 69-70, asst prof, Dept Vet Sci, 70-73, assoc prof, 73-79, PROF PARASITOL, COL VET MED, UNIV FLA, 79- *Concurrent Pos:* Ed, Wildlife Dis Asn, 81- *Mem:* Am Soc Parasitologists; Wildlife Disease Asn (vpres, 77-79, pres, 79-81); Wildlife Soc; Can Soc Zool. *Res:* Parasites and diseases of wild animals; epizootiology and ecology of transmission of protozoans and helminths of wild animals. *Mailing Add:* Univ of Fla Col of Vet Med Gainesville FL 32611

FORRESTER, JAY W, b Climax, Neb, July 14, 18; c 3. SYSTEM DYNAMICS. *Educ:* Univ Neb, BSc, 39; Mass Inst Technol, SM, 45. *Hon Degrees:* DEng, Univ Neb, 54, Newark Col Eng, 71, Univ Notre Dame, 74; DSc, Boston Univ, 69, Union Col, 73; DSc Pol, Univ Mannheim, Ger, 79. *Prof Exp:* Mem staff, Servomechanisms Lab, 40-46, Digital Comput Lab, 46-51, head, Digital Comput Div, Lincoln Lab, 52-56, prof mgt, 56-72, GERMESHAUSEN PROF MGT, MASS INST TECHNOL, 77- *Honors & Awards:* Valdemar Poulsen Gold Medal, Danish Acad Tech Sci, 69; Medal of Honor & Systs, Man & Cybernetics Soc Award for Outstanding Accomplishment, Inst Elec & Electronics Engrs, 72; Howard N Potts Award, The Franklin Inst, 74; Harry Goode Mem Award, Am Fedn Info Processing Socs, 77; Computer Pioneer Award, Comput Soc, Inst Elec & Electronics Engrs, 82. *Mem:* Nat Acad Eng; fel Inst Elec & Electronics Engrs; fel Acad Mgt; fel Am Acad Arts & Sci; hon mem Soc Mfg Engrs. *Res:* Random-access; coincident-current magnetic storage used as standard memory device for digital computers; computer modeling to analyze social systems and further develop the field of system dynamics. *Mailing Add:* Syst Dynamics Group Bldg E40 294 Mass Inst Technol Cambridge MA 02139

FORRESTER, SHERRI RHODA, b New York, NY, Aug 8, 36. ORGANIC CHEMISTRY. *Educ:* Duke Univ, BS, 58; Northwestern Univ, PhD(org chem), 62. *Prof Exp:* Asst prof, 62-78, ASSOC PROF CHEM, UNIV NC, GREENSBORO, 78- *Mem:* Am Chem Soc. *Mailing Add:* Dept of Chem Univ of NC Greensboro NC 27412

FORRESTER, WARREN DAVID, b Hamilton, Ont, Mar 4, 25. OCEANOGRAPHY. *Educ:* Univ Toronto, BA, 47; Univ BC, MS, 61; Johns Hopkins Univ, PhD(oceanog), 67. *Prof Exp:* Engr, Geod Surv Can, 47-57 & Can Hydrographic Serv, 57-59; researcher, Bedford Inst Oceanog, 63-75; CHIEF, TIDES CURRENTS & WATER LEVELS, CAN HYDROGRAPHIC SERV, 75- *Concurrent Pos:* Assoc prof, McGill Univ, 69-74 & Dalhousie Univ, 71-75. *Res:* Internal tides in Gulf of St Lawrence; currents and tides in coastal regions; application of geostrophic approximation to transport calculations; circulation in Gulf of St Lawrence. *Mailing Add:* Can Hydrographic Serv Dept of Environ Ottawa ON K1A 1C8 Can

FORRETTE, JOHN ELMER, b Chicago, Ill, Sept 14, 22; m 48; c 1. ANALYTICAL CHEMISTRY. *Educ:* Loyola Univ, Ill, BS, 48; DePaul Univ, MS, 55; Pac Western Univ, PhD, 80. *Prof Exp:* Chemist, Div Hwys, State of Ill, 48-56; from res chemist to sr res chemist, Borg-Warner Corp, 57-63, group leader anal chem, 63-67; group leader, 67-70, MGR ANAL RES, VELSICOL CHEM CO, 70- *Mem:* Sigma Xi; Am Soc Appl Spectros; Am Chem Soc; fel Am Inst Chemists. *Res:* Chemical spectroscopy; gas chromatography; general analytical chemistry; analytical chemistry of agricultural chemicals. *Mailing Add:* Velsicol Chem Co 341 E Ohio St Chicago IL 60611

FORREY, ARDEN W, b Nampa, Idaho, Dec 19, 32; m 61; c 1. BIOCHEMISTRY. *Educ:* Univ Wash, AB, 55, PhD(biochem), 63. *Prof Exp:* Trainee biochem, Univ Wash, 63-64; Nat Inst Arthritis & Metab Dis fel, 64-65; univ fel, Univ Wash, 65-66, lectr biochem, 66-67, res assoc, 67-74, res asst prof, Dept Med, Clin Res Ctr, Harborview Hosp & Univ Wash, 74-77; clin comput specialist, Vet Admin Hosp, Seattle, 78-80; ASST PROF RES, DEPT PEDIAT, GEORGETOWN UNIV, 80- *Mem:* AAAS; Am Chem Soc; Brit Biochem Soc; Am Asn Clin Chem. *Res:* Structure and active sites of proteins, particularly muscle phosphorylase and actin; clinical chemistry; pharmacokinetics; clinical computing. *Mailing Add:* Georgetown Univ Washington DC 20007

FORRO, FREDERICK, JR, b Woonsocket, RI, May 17, 24; m 44; c 4. DNA REPLICATION, RADIATION BIOLOGY. *Educ:* Yale Univ, MD, 49. *Prof Exp:* USPHS fel, Yale Univ, 49-51; assoc biophysicist, Brookhaven Nat Lab, 51-55; from asst prof to assoc prof biophys, Yale Univ, 55-68; chmn dept, 68-77, PROF, DEPT GENETICS & CELL BIOL, UNIV MINN, ST PAUL, 68-, DIR MINORITY AFFAIRS, COL BIOL SCI, 77- *Concurrent Pos:* Agent Europ Atomic Energy Comn, Dept Biol, Univ Brussels, 66-67. *Mem:* AAAS; Genetics Soc Am; Biophys Soc. *Res:* Molecular biology, particularly self-duplication; radiation biology; origin of life. *Mailing Add:* Dept of Genetics & Cell Biol Univ of Minn Col of Biol Sci St Paul MN 55108

FORS, ELTON W, b Drake, NDak, Jan 29, 34; m 61. MATHEMATICS. *Educ:* Univ NDak, BS, 56, MS, 59; Univ Okla, PhD(math educ), 69. *Prof Exp:* Assoc prof, 60-70, PROF MATH, NORTHERN STATE COL, 70- *Mem:* Math Asn Am; Nat Coun Math Teachers. *Mailing Add:* Dept of Math Northern State Col Aberdeen SD 57401

FORSBERG, CECIL WALLACE, b Kinistino, Sask, Mar 24, 42; m 70; c 2. MICROBIAL PHYSIOLOGY. *Educ:* Univ Sask, BSA, 64, MSc, 66; McGill Univ, PhD(microbial physiol), 69. *Prof Exp:* Fel microbial physiol, Nat Inst Med Res, Med Res Coun Eng, 69-71, scientist, 71-73; PROF MICROBIAL ECOL, UNIV GUELPH, 73-, INSTR, PHARMACEUT MICROBIOL & MICROBIOL PHYSIOL, 79- *Mem:* Can Soc Microbiol; Am Soc Microbiol. *Res:* Physiology of anaerobic rumen bacteria, with emphasis on cellulases and proteases of rumen bacteria. *Mailing Add:* Dept Microbiol Col Biol Sci Univ of Guelph Guelph Can

FORSBERG, JOHN HERBERT, b Duluth, Minn, Apr 24, 42; m 66. INORGANIC CHEMISTRY. *Educ:* Univ Minn, Duluth, BA, 64; Univ Ill, MS, 66, PhD(chem), 68. *Prof Exp:* Assoc prof, 68-74, PROF CHEM, ST LOUIS UNIV, 74-, CHMN DEPT, 76- *Concurrent Pos:* Res Corp grant, 68- *Mem:* Am Chem Soc. *Res:* Coordination chemistry in nonaqueous solvent; lanthanide chemistry. *Mailing Add:* Dept of Chem St Louis Univ St Louis MO 63103

FORSBERG, KEVIN, b Oakland, Calif, July 20, 34; m 81; c 3. ENGINEERING MANAGEMENT, SOLID MECHANICS. *Educ:* Mass Inst Technol, SB, 56; Stanford Univ, MS, 58, PhD(eng mech), 61; Stanford Univ Sch Bus Exec Prog, Cert, 79. *Prof Exp:* Scientist, 56-61, res specialist shell dynamics, 62-64, mgr solid mech lab, 64-71, asst dir mat & struct directorate, 71-73, dep prog mgr, Thermal Protection Systs, 73-75, prog mgr thermal protection systs, 75-79, PROG MGR, NEW BUS, LOCKHEED MISSILES & SPACE CO, 79- *Mem:* Fel Am Soc Mech Engrs; Am Inst Aeronautics; NY Acad Sci; Am Inst Aeronaut & Astronaut. *Res:* Static and dynamic behavior of shell structures; application of computer technology and active computer graphics to engineering problems; development and production of thermal protection system for space shuttle orbiter. *Mailing Add:* Dept 61-87 Bldg 577N 1111 Lockheed Way Sunnyvale CA 94086

FORSBERG, ROBERT ARNOLD, b Julesburg, Colo, Nov 6, 30; m 58; c 3. AGRONOMY, PLANT GENETICS. *Educ:* Univ Wis, BS, 52, MS, 57, PhD(agron, plant breeding), 61. *Prof Exp:* Fel statist genetics, NC State Univ, 61-63; from asst prof to assoc prof, 63-73, PROF AGRON, UNIV WIS-MADISON, 73-, CHMN DEPT, 79- *Mem:* Am Soc Agron; Crop Sci Soc Am. *Res:* Interspecific hybridization in Avena; biometrical procedures as applied to quantitative inheritance and plant breeding; breeding and genetics of wheat, oats, barley and rye. *Mailing Add:* Dept of Agron Univ of Wis Madison WI 53706

FORSBLAD, INGEMAR BJORN, b Gothenburg, Sweden, June 18, 27; m 57; c 2. ORGANIC CHEMISTRY. *Educ:* Univ Uppsala, MS, 55, PhD(org chem), 58. *Prof Exp:* Technician chem, Svenska Oljeslageri AB, Sweden, 45-46 & Skanska Attiksfabrik AB, 48; engr org chem, AB Bofors Nobelkrut, 50-51 & Osterreichische Stickstoffweke, Austria, 55; fel, Fla State Univ, 58-59; res assoc, 59-66, head fine chem, 66-71, mgr specialty chem, 71-79, PROD MGR FINE CHEM, UPJOHN CO, 79- *Mem:* Am Inst Chem Engrs; Am Chem Soc; Swedish Chem Soc; Sigma Xi. *Res:* Mechanism of alkylation of beta-ketoesters; process development and production of steroids and aromatic compounds. *Mailing Add:* Upjohn Co 7000 Portage Rd Kalamazoo MI 49001

FORSCHER, BERNARD KRONMAN, b New York, NY, Nov 15, 27; m 48; c 5. BIOCHEMISTRY. *Educ:* NY Univ, BA, 46; Northwestern Univ, PhD(chem), 52. *Prof Exp:* Res chemist, Chas Pfizer & Co, 46-48, chemist, Eng Res & Develop Lab, 47; asst instr, Dent Sch, Northwestern Univ, 48-52; coordr res, Sch Dent, Georgetown Univ, 52-54; chemist, Nat Inst Dent Res, NIH, 54-57; prof biochem & chmn dept, Sch Dent, Univ Kansas City, 57-62; consult, Sect Publ, Mayo Clin, 62-75; ed, Scott & White Mem Hosp, 75-76; MANAGING ED, PROC NAT ACAD SCI, 76- *Mem:* AAAS; Coun Biol Ed. *Res:* Chemistry of inflammation; chemistry of bone. *Mailing Add:* PNAS Nat Acad Sci 2101 Constitution Ave NW Washington DC 20418

FORSCHER, FREDERICK, b Vienna, Austria, May 20, 18; nat US; m 44; c 3. ENGINEERING. *Educ:* Princeton Univ, BS & MS, 47; Columbia Univ, PhD(appl mech), 53. *Prof Exp:* Instr civil eng, Columbia Univ, 47-52; supvr mech metall, Atomic Power Div, Westinghouse Elec Corp, 52-57; vpres, Nuclear Mat & Equip Corp, 57-67; mgr adv fuels, Westinghouse Elec Corp, 67-71; ENERGY MGT CONSULT, 71- *Mem:* Am Soc Metals; Am Soc Mech Engrs; Am Nuclear Soc; hon mem Am Soc Testing & Mat; Am Inst Mining, Metall & Petrol Engrs. *Res:* Social metabolism. *Mailing Add:* 144 N Dithridge St Pittsburgh PA 15213

FORSDYKE, DONALD ROY, b London, Eng, Oct 9, 38; m 64; c 4. BIOCHEMISTRY, IMMUNOLOGY. *Educ:* Univ London, MB, BS, 61; Cambridge Univ, BA, 65, PhD(biochem), 67. *Prof Exp:* House physician, St Mary's Hosp, London, 61; house surgeon, Addenbrooke's Hosp, Cambridge, 63; sci officer exp path, Inst Animal Physiol, Babraham, Cambridge, 67-68; ASSOC PROF BIOCHEM, QUEEN'S UNIV, ONT, 68- *Mem:* Can Biochem Soc; Brit Biochem Soc; Am Asn Immunol. *Res:* Cell control mechanisms, especially lymphoid tissue and nucleic acids; serum factors affecting the transformation of cultured lymphocytes by phytohaemagglutinin and antigens; regulation of gene expression. *Mailing Add:* Dept of Biochem Queen's Univ Fac of Med Kingston Can

FORSEN, HAROLD K(AY), b St Joseph, Mo, Sept 19, 32; m 52; c 3. PLASMA PHYSICS, NUCLEAR ENGINEERING. *Educ:* Calif Inst Technol, BS, 58, MS, 59; Univ Calif, Berkeley, PhD(elec eng), 65. *Prof Exp:* Staff assoc exp physics, Gen Atomic Div, Gen Dynamics Corp, 59-62; res assoc elec eng, Univ Calif, Berkeley, 62-65; assoc prof nuclear eng, Univ Wis-Madison, 65-69, prof, 69-73, dir phys sci lab, 70-72; mgr eng, Exxon Nuclear Co, Bellevue, 73-75, vpres, 75-80, mem bd dir, 78-80; dir, Jersey Nuclear-Avco Isotopes Inc, 73-81, exec vpres, 74-80, pres, 81; MGR ENG & MAT, RES & ENG, BECHTEL GROUP INC, 81- *Concurrent Pos:* Mem tech staff, Hughes Aircraft Co, 58-59; consult, Gen Atomic Div, Gen Dynamics Corp, 62-64, Lawrence Radiation Lab, 64-65, Oak Ridge Nat Lab, 69-72; Argonne Nat Lab, 70-72, Jersey Nuclear Co, 70-73 & Battelle Mem Inst, 71-72; adv to dir, Oak Ridge Nat Lab, 77-, mem, Argonne Univ Asn Spec Comt on Fusion, 80-; mem, Dept Energy Fusion Sr Rev Comt, 77; mem bd trustees, Pac Sci Ctr Found, 77, vpres, 77, pres, 78-80, chmn, 81; mem vis comt, Col Eng, Univ Wash, 81- *Honors & Awards:* Arthur Holly Compton Award, Am Nuclear Soc, 73. *Mem:* Am Phys Soc; Am Nuclear Soc; Inst Elec & Electronics Engrs. *Res:* Plasma physics; ion beams; plasma sources; thermonuclear fusion; reactor concepts; laser isotope separation. *Mailing Add:* 255 Tim Ct Danville CA 94526

FORSHAM, PETER HUGH, b New Orleans, La, Nov 15, 15; m 47; c 3. INTERNAL MEDICINE, ENDOCRINOLOGY. *Educ:* Cambridge Univ, BS, 37, MA, 41; Harvard Med Sch, MD, 43; Am Bd Internal Med, dipl, 51. *Prof Exp:* Res assoc physiol chem, Rockefeller Inst, 40-41; house officer med, Peter Bent Brigham Hosp, Mass, 43-44, asst resident, 44-46, res assoc, 47-49; instr, Harvard Med Sch, 49-51; assoc prof, 51-57, PROF MED & PEDIAT, SCH MED, CHIEF ENDOCRINOL, DEPT MED & DIR METAB RES INST & GEN CLIN RES CTR, MED CTR, UNIV CALIF, SAN FRANCISCO, 57- *Concurrent Pos:* Consult, NIH, chmn metab study sect, 58-60; consult, US Navy, 57-65, Oak Knoll Hosp, Oakland. *Mem:* AAAS; Am Soc Clin Invest; Asn Am Physicians; Soc Exp Biol & Med; Endocrine Soc. *Res:* Metabolic diseases; pathophysiology of the adrenal cortex, mostly in man; relation of pituitary tropic hormones to activity of target glands; metabolic studies of diabetes mellitus; anti-inflammatory agents used in collagen diseases; antiovulatory hormones from the pineal. *Mailing Add:* 267 Hillside Ave Mill Valley CA 94941

FORSHEY, CHESTER GENE, b Salem, Ohio, Mar 21, 25; m 56; c 4. POMOLOGY. *Educ:* Ohio State Univ, BS, 50, PhD(hort), 54. *Prof Exp:* Asst, Ohio Agr Exp Sta, 52-54; from asst prof to prof, 54-66, SUPT, HUDSON VALLEY LAB, NY STATE AGR EXP STA, 69- *Concurrent Pos:* Mem staff, Rockefeller Found Chilean Agr Prog, 63-64; hon mem fac, Cath Univ Chile & Univ Chile. *Mem:* Am Soc Hort Sci; Am Chem Soc. *Res:* Growth regulator effects and nitrogen and mineral nutrition of fruit plants; apple crop production. *Mailing Add:* Hudson Valley Lab NY State Agr Exp Sta Box 727 Highland NY 12528

FORSHEY, WILLIAM OSMOND, JR, b Youngstown, Ohio, Dec 13, 21; m 43; c 2. ORGANIC CHEMISTRY. *Educ:* Grove City Col, BS, 42; Carnegie Inst Technol, MS, 43, DSc, 48. *Prof Exp:* Asst, Carnegie Inst Technol, 44; RES CHEMIST, CENT RES DEPT, EXP STA, E I DU PONT DE NEMOURS & CO, INC, 48- *Mem:* Am Chem Soc. *Res:* Polymer, synthetic organic and high temperature research; inorganic fiber synthesis; composite materials; chemical physics, particularly materials and applications. *Mailing Add:* 313 Village Rd Wilmington DE 19805

FORSLUND, DAVID WALLACE, b Ukiah, Calif, Feb 18, 44; m 68. PLASMA PHYSICS. *Educ:* Univ Santa Clara, BS, 64; Princeton Univ, MA, 67, PhD(astrophys), 69. *Prof Exp:* Fel, 69-71, mem staff plasma physics, 71-78, dep group leader interior confinement, 78-81, LAB FEL, LOS ALAMOS NAT LAB, 81- *Mem:* Am Phys Soc; Fel Am Geophys Union; Am Astron Soc. *Res:* Studying the interaction of intense laser radiation with matter for application to laser fusion with emphasis on parametric instabilities, turbulence theory, linear and nonlinear waves. *Mailing Add:* Group L6-MS 531 Los Alamos Nat Lab Los Alamos NM 87545

FORSMAN, EARL N, b Keuterville, Idaho, Oct 27, 36; m 62; c 3. ATOMIC PHYSICS. *Educ:* Gonzaga Univ, BS, 63; Univ Wash, MS, 65, PhD(physics), 70. *Prof Exp:* Asst prof, 70-77, ASSOC PROF PHYSICS, EASTERN WASH UNIV, 77- *Mem:* Am Inst Physics; Am Asn Physics Teachers. *Res:* Atomic and molecular physics; gas-phase reactions and spectroscopy; uranium exploration techniques. *Mailing Add:* Dept Physics Eastern Wash Univ Cheney WA 99004

FORSMAN, M(ARION) E(DWIN), b Raymondville, Tex, July 19, 12; m 38; c 4. ELECTRICAL ENGINEERING. *Educ:* Univ Tex, BSEE & MSEE, 40; Iowa State Univ, PhD(elec eng), 54. *Prof Exp:* Supt construct, Am Smelting & Refrigeration Co, Tex & Mex, 40-42; field engr, Fischback & Moore of Tex, Inc, 42-43; res dir, Electronic Chem Eng Co, Calif, 46; res lab analyst, Northrop Aircraft, 46-47; assoc prof, Tulane Univ, 47-51; instr, Iowa State Univ, 51-52; elec engr, Gen Elec Co, Wash, 52-55; asst dir, Eng & Indust Exp Sta, 55-64, asst dir eng admin, 64-65, dir, 65-68, prof elec eng & dir eng external progs, 68-74, EMER PROF ELEC ENG, UNIV FLA, 74- *Mem:* Am Soc Eng Educ; Inst Elec & Electronics Engrs; Nat Soc Prof Engrs. *Res:* Electrical power transmission; instrumentation and control; nuclear power. *Mailing Add:* 1644 NW Tenth Ave Gainesville FL 32605

FORSMAN, WILLIAM C(OMSTOCK), b Grand Rapids, Minn, July 24, 29; m 56; c 4. PHYSICAL CHEMISTRY, CHEMICAL ENGINEERING. *Educ:* Univ Minn, BChE, 52; Univ Pa, PhD(phys chem), 61. *Prof Exp:* Chem engr, Hercules Powder Co, 52-54, 56, res chemist, 61-63; from asst prof to assoc prof, 64-77, PROF CHEM ENG, UNIV PA, 77- *Mem:* Am Chem Soc; Am Phys Soc. *Res:* Physics and physical chemistry of high-polymer systems; statistical mechanics. *Mailing Add:* Sch of Chem Eng Univ of Pa Philadelphia PA 19174

FORSSEN, ERIC ANTON, b Los Angeles, Calif, Apr 6, 51. DRUG DEVELOPMENT, DESIGN RESEARCH. *Educ:* Univ Calif, Los Angeles, BS, 73; Univ Southern Calif, Dr Pharm, 77, PhD(pharmaceut sci), 81. *Prof Exp:* Pharmacist, Hosp Good Samaritan, 77-79; RES SCIENTIST, CANCER CHEMOTHER, CANCER CTR, UNIV SOUTHERN CALIF, 79- *Honors & Awards:* Young Investr Award, Am Heart Asn, 81; Life Sci Res Award, IntraSci Res Found, 80. *Mem:* Am Chem Soc; Am Pharmaceut Asn; AAAS. *Res:* Design of new drug molecules and formulations which have reduced toxicity. *Mailing Add:* 18813 Tuba St Northridge CA 91324

FORST, WENDELL, b Trinec, Czech, Sept 28, 26; Can citizen; m 53. PHYSICAL CHEMISTRY, THEORETICAL CHEMISTRY. *Educ:* Prague Tech Univ, BSc, 48; McGill Univ, PhD(phys chem), 55. *Prof Exp:* Res engr, Northeastern Paper Prod, Ltd, Can, 55-56; from asst prof to assoc prof, 56-66, PROF CHEM, LAVAL UNIV, 66- *Concurrent Pos:* Res assoc, Univ NC, 58-61; sabbatical leave, Univ Calif, Berkeley & Free Univ Brussels, 69-70; Commonwealth vis prof, Univ Essex, 75-76. *Mem:* AAAS; Am Chem Soc; Am Phys Soc; Chem Inst Can; Sigma Xi. *Res:* Chemical dynamics; theory of unimolecular reactions. *Mailing Add:* Dept of Chem Laval Univ Quebec PQ G1K 7P4 Can

FORSTALL, WALTON, (JR), b Rosemont, Pa, June 26, 09; m 42; c 2. MECHANICAL ENGINEERING. *Educ:* Lehigh Univ, BS, 31, MS, 43, ME, 51; Mass Inst Technol, ScD(mech eng), 49. *Prof Exp:* Asst test engr, Del Sta, Philadelphia Elec Co, 30; mem sci staff, Franklin Inst, 32-34; eng asst, Philadelphia Gas Works Co, 34-40; instr & asst prof, Lehigh Univ, 40-44; proj engr, Clinton Eng Works, Tenn Eastman Corp, 44-45; res assoc mech eng, Mass Inst Technol, 46-49; assoc prof, 49-57, asst dean eng & sci, 55-57, assoc head dept, 64-77, PROF MECH ENG, CARNEGIE-MELLON UNIV, 57- *Concurrent Pos:* Dir, Klein-Logan Co, Pa, 53-68; mem indust stand adv bd, Commonwealth Pa, 64-68. *Mem:* Fel Am Soc Mech Engrs; Am Soc Eng Educ; Am Phys Soc. *Res:* Momentum, mass and temperature diffusion in a free turbulent boundary layer. *Mailing Add:* Dept Mech Eng Carnegie-Mellon Univ Pittsburgh PA 15213

FORSTAT, HAROLD, b Brooklyn, NY, June 6, 21; m 47; c 4. PHYSICS. *Educ:* Brooklyn Col, BA, 42; Purdue Univ, MS, 50; Univ Conn, PhD(physics), 55. *Prof Exp:* Physicist, Camp Evans Signal Lab, NJ, 42-43; res physicist, SAM Lab, Columbia Univ, 43-46 & Metall Lab, Univ Chicago, 46-48; res physicist, Camp Detrick Biol Lab, Md, 51-53; instr physics, Univ Conn, 54-55; from asst prof to assoc prof, 55-67, PROF PHYSICS, MICH STATE UNIV, 67- *Concurrent Pos:* Fulbright fel, Trinity Col, Dublin, 63-64. *Mem:* Fel Am Phys Soc. *Res:* Hydrodynamics of Helium II; low temperature heat capacities of anti-ferromagnets; magnetism; experimental solid state physics. *Mailing Add:* Dept of Physics Mich State Univ East Lansing MI 48824

FORSTER, D LYNN, b Columbus, Ind, Aug 29, 46; m 65; c 2. AGRICULTURAL ECONOMICS. *Educ:* Purdue Univ, BS, 68, MS, 72; Mich State Univ, PhD(agr econ), 74. *Prof Exp:* Asst prof, 74-77, ASSOC PROF AGR ECON, OHIO STATE UNIV, 77- *Honors & Awards:* Outstanding Doctoral Prog, Am Agr Econ Asn, 75. *Mem:* Am Agr Econ Asn. *Res:* Economic analysis of the control of water pollution in agricultural production; development and application of computer decision making models for agriculture; agricultural productivity. *Mailing Add:* 2120 Fyffe Dept of Agr Econ Ohio State Univ Columbus OH 43210

FORSTER, DENIS, b Newcastle-on-Tyne, Eng, Feb 28, 41; m 64; c 2. INORGANIC CHEMISTRY, CATALYSIS. *Educ:* Univ London, BSc, 62, PhD(inorg chem), 65. *Prof Exp:* Fel, Princeton Univ, 65-66; res chemist, Monsanto Cent Res Dept, 66-70, group leader homogeneous catalysis, 70-74, sr res group leader, 74-75, fel, 75-80, SR FEL, MONSANTO CO, 80- *Honors & Awards:* Chem Pioneer Award, Am Inst Chemists, 80. *Mem:* Am Chem Soc; Royal Soc Chem. *Res:* Transition metal chemistry; vibrational spectroscopy; catalysis. *Mailing Add:* 32 Woodcrest Dr St Louis MO 63124

FORSTER, ERIC OTTO, b Lemberg, Oct 24, 18; nat US; m; c 6. PHYSICAL ORGANIC CHEMISTRY. *Educ:* Columbia Univ, BS, 49, MA, 50, PhD(phys org chem), 51. *Prof Exp:* Res chemist, Standard Oil Develop Co, 51-57, from res assoc to sr res assoc, Esso Res & Eng Co, Standard Oil Co of NJ, 57-75, SCI ADV, EXXON RES & ENG CO, 75- *Concurrent Pos:* Lectr, Columbia Univ, 53-67; adj prof, Rutgers Univ, 67-; bd mem, Nat Acad Sci-Nat Res Coun Conf Elec Insulation & Dielec Phenomena, 72-80. *Mem:* AAAS; Am Chem Soc; fel Inst Elec & Electronics Engrs. *Res:* Electrochemistry applied to hydrocarbon systems; electric properties of petroleum products. *Mailing Add:* 1997 Duncan Dr Scotch Plains NJ 07076

FORSTER, FRANCIS MICHAEL, b Cincinnati, Ohio, Feb 14, 12; m 37; c 5. CLINICAL NEUROLOGY. *Educ:* Univ Cincinnati, BS, 35, BM, 36, MD, 37. *Hon Degrees:* LLD, Xavier Univ, 55. *Prof Exp:* Intern, Good Samaritan Hosp, Mass, 37-38; fel psychiat, Pa Hosp, Philadelphia, 38-39; asst neurol, Harvard Med Sch, 39-40; Rockefeller Found fel & res assoc physiol, Sch Med, Yale Univ, 40-41; instr neurol, Sch Med, Boston Univ, 41-43; from asst prof to assoc prof, Jefferson Med Col, 43-50; prof, Med Ctr, Georgetown Univ, 50-58, dean sch med, 53-58; prof, 58-78, EMER PROF NEUROL, SCH MED, UNIV WIS-MADISON, 78-; DIR EPILEPSY CTR, MADISON VET ADMIN HOSP, 78- *Concurrent Pos:* Resident physician, Boston City Hosp, 39-40; specialist, US Vet Admin, 46-; consult, Hosps, Surg Gen, US Air Force, 56- & Surg Gen, US Navy, 58-; vpres, Am Bd Psychiat & Neurol, 59, pres, 59-60. *Mem:* Am Physiol Soc; Am Neurol Asn; Am Asn Neuropath; fel AMA; Am Acad Neurol (vpres, 53-55, pres, 56-58). *Res:* Epilepsy; vascular accidents; multiple sclerosis; muscular dystrophy. *Mailing Add:* 4020 County M Middleton WI 53562

FORSTER, FRED KURT, b Chicago, Ill, Feb 23, 44. ULTRASONICS, CARDIOVASCULAR DYNAMICS. *Educ:* Univ Ill, BS, 66; Stanford Univ, MS, 68, PhD(aeronaut & astronaut), 72. *Prof Exp:* Res asst bioeng, Inst Biomed Tech Univ & Swiss Fed Inst Technol, Zürich, 71-72; fel bioeng, Ctr Bioeng, 74-77, res engr, 77-79, RES ASST PROF, DEPT MECH ENG, UNIV WASH, 79- *Concurrent Pos:* sr fel, NIH Cardiovascular Technol Traineeship, 74-77; co-investr, NIH prog projs & res grants, 77-79, prin investr, NIH res grants, 80; adj res asst prof, Ctr Bioeng, Univ Wash, 79- *Mem:* Am Inst Ultrasound Med; Inst Elec & Electronics Engrs. *Res:* Medical applications of ultrasound including Doppler and imaging techniques; cardiovascular dynamics including turbulence phenomena in blood and analysis of electrocardiogram signals; medical instrumentation; acoustics; fluid mechanics; time series analysis. *Mailing Add:* Dept Mech Eng MS FU-10 Univ Wash Seattle WA 98195

FORSTER, HARRIET HERTA, b Vienna, Austria; nat US; m 42. PHYSICS. *Educ:* Univ Calif, MA, 47, PhD(physics), 48. *Prof Exp:* Instr, 48-51, from asst prof to assoc prof, 51-64, PROF PHYSICS, UNIV SOUTHERN CALIF, 64- *Mem:* Fel Am Phys Soc. *Res:* Nuclear physics; cosmic rays. *Mailing Add:* Dept of Physics Univ of Southern Calif Los Angeles CA 90007

FORSTER, JEAN LOIS, genetics, cell biology, see previous edition

FORSTER, JOHN HESLOP, b Vancouver, BC, Aug 13, 23; m 51. PHYSICS. *Educ:* Univ BC, BA, 44, MA, 46; Purdue Univ, PhD(physics), 53. *Prof Exp:* Lab asst physics, Univ BC, 43-46; asst instr, Purdue Univ, 46-50, res asst, 50-53; mem tech staff, 53-58, supvr, 58-63, head integrated circuits & Mesa Transistor Dept, 63-68, head bipolar device dept, 68-71, head hybrid assembly techniques dept, 71-73, HEAD INTEGRATED CIRCUIT DEPT, BELL LABS, 73- *Res:* Nucleon irradiation of semiconductors; transistor physics; integrated circuits. *Mailing Add:* Integrated Circuit Dept Bell Labs 555 Union Blvd Allentown PA 18103

FORSTER, KURT, b Vienna, Austria, Mar 17, 15; nat US; c 2. PHYSICS. *Educ:* Univ Vienna, PhD(physics), 38. *Prof Exp:* Sr res engr, Jet Propulsion Lab, Calif Inst Technol, 46-47, res fel physics, 47-48; from asst prof to assoc prof, 48-56; PROF ENG, UNIV CALIF, LOS ANGELES, 56- *Concurrent Pos:* Guggenheim fel, 58-59. *Mem:* AAAS; Am Inst Aeronaut & Astronaut; Am Phys Soc. *Res:* Aerodynamics; heat transfer; space dynamics. *Mailing Add:* Sch of Eng & Appl Sci Univ of Calif Los Angeles CA 90024

FORSTER, LESLIE STEWART, b Chicago, Ill, May 10, 24; m 46; c 2. PHYSICAL CHEMISTRY, BIOPHYSICAL CHEMISTRY. *Educ:* Univ Calif, BS, 47; Univ Minn, PhD(chem), 51. *Prof Exp:* Fel, Univ Rochester, 51-52; instr chem, Bates Col, 52-54; from asst prof to assoc prof, 55-64, PROF CHEM, UNIV ARIZ, 64- *Concurrent Pos:* NSF sci fac fel, Univ Copenhagen, 61-62; consult, NIH, 63-64; USPHS spec fel, Weizmann Inst, Israel, 68-69. *Mem:* Am Chem Soc; Am Phys Soc. *Res:* Luminescence; photophysics of metal complexes; flourescence of biomolecules; intravital monitoring of metabolic activity. *Mailing Add:* Dept of Chem Univ of Ariz Tucson AZ 85721

FORSTER, MICHAEL JAY, b Buffalo, NY, Feb 8, 23; m 48; c 7. POLYMER PHYSICS. *Educ:* Canisius Col, BS, 45; Univ Notre Dame, MS, 50, PhD(physics), 51. *Prof Exp:* Physicist, E I du Pont de Nemours & Co, Inc, 45-46; asst, Univ Notre Dame, 46-51; res physicist, 51-66, group leader, 66-67, mgr textile res, 67-74, RES ASSOC, FIRESTONE TIRE & RUBBER CO, 74- *Mem:* Am Phys Soc; Am Chem Soc; Fiber Soc. *Res:* Fiber structure and properties; fiber morphology; crystalline structure of high polymers. *Mailing Add:* 2541 Ridgewood Rd Akron OH 44313

FORSTER, ROBERT E, II, b St Davids, Pa, Dec 23, 19; m 47; c 4. PHYSIOLOGY. *Educ:* Yale Univ, BS, 41; Univ Pa, MD, 43. *Prof Exp:* Life Ins Med Res Fund fel physiol, Harvard Univ, 48-50; from asst prof to assoc prof physiol, Grad Sch Med, 50-58, chmn dept, 59-70, assoc prof physiol & surg, Sch Med, 57-61, PROF PHYSIOL, GRAD SCH MED, UNIV PA, 58-, ISAAC OTT PROF, 59-, PROF PHYSIOL & SURG, SCH MED, 61-, CHMN DEPT PHYSIOL, 70- *Concurrent Pos:* Lowell M Palmer sr fel, Grad Sch Med, Univ Pa, 54-60; mem cardiovasc study sect, NIH, 60-64 & mem gen clin res ctr comt, 64-71; mem, Nat Adv Heart Coun, 67-71. *Mem:* Nat Acad Sci; Am Physiol Soc (pres, 66-67); Am Soc Clin Invest; Biophys Soc; Soc Gen Physiol. *Res:* Respiratory physiology; gas exchange, rapid exchanges of red cells, tissue oxygenation and temperature regulation. *Mailing Add:* A-201 Richards Bldg G-4 Univ of Pa Dept of Physiol Philadelphia PA 19174

FORSTER, ROY PHILIP, b Milwaukee, Wis, Sept 28, 11; m 35; c 1. PHYSIOLOGY. *Educ:* Marquette Univ, BS, 32; Univ Wis, PhB, 36, PhD(zool), 38. *Hon Degrees:* MA, Dartmouth Col, 48. *Prof Exp:* Asst zool, Marquette Univ, 32-34; asst, Univ Wis, 35-38; from instr to prof biol sci, 38-48, lectr physiol, Med Sch, 64-74, Ira Allen Eastman prof, 64-76, EMER IRA ALLEN EASTMAN PROF, DARTMOUTH COL, 76-, RES PROF BIOL SCI, 76- *Concurrent Pos:* Trustee, Mt Desert Island Biol Lab, 40-, dir, 40-47, vpres, 61-63, pres, 64-70; sect ed, Biol Abstr, 47-; Guggenheim fel, Cambridge Univ, 49; mem, Macy Conf Renal Function, 49-53; Rockefeller Found grant, 50-57; Guggenheim fel, Zool Sta, Univ Naples, 56; grant, NIH, 56-, mem sci rev comt, Health Res Facil, 64-68, mem med biol rev comt & mem ad hoc comt comp pharmacol, 66-67, mem pharmacol-toxicol rev comt, 69-70; vis lectr, Sch Med, George Washington Univ, 59-60 & dir regulatory biol prog, NSF 59-60; consult res biologist, Vet Admin Ctr, Vt, 63-; mem Nat Acad Sci-Nat Res Coun comt eval Nat Sci Found grad fels, 64-65; mem Vet Admin comt res lab sci & med, 64-66; mem coun on circulation, Am Heart Asn; vis prof physiol, Sch Med, Univ Hawaii, 73; adj prof physiol, Dartmouth Med Sch, 74- *Mem:* Fel AAAS; Am Soc Zoologists; Am Physiol Soc; Soc Gen

Physiol; Am Soc Nephrology. *Res:* Cellular and comparative physiology of the kidney; renal hemodynamics; membrane transport processes; nitrogen metabolism and excretion. *Mailing Add:* Dept of Biol Sci Dartmouth Col Hanover NH 03755

FORSTER, SIGMUND, b Lvov, Poland, Feb 11, 06; US citizen; m 45; c 1. PHYSICAL MEDICINE. *Educ:* Univ Naples, MD, 30; Univ Vilno, Poland, MD, 35. *Prof Exp:* Dir sanatorium, Poland, 39-41, dir physiother clin, 41-45; chief dept internal med & physiother, Austria, 45-46; CLIN ASSOC PROF REHAB MED, STATE UNIV NY DOWNSTATE MED CTR, 62-; DIR PHYSIOTHER & REHAB, CONEY ISLAND HOSP, 60-; DIR REHAB MED, MAIMONIDES MED CTR, 67- *Mem:* Fel Am Col Physicians; Acad Phys Med & Rehab; Am Acad Cerebral Palsy; NY Acad Med. *Res:* Physical medicine and rehabilitation. *Mailing Add:* Dept of Rehab Med Maimonides Med Ctr Brooklyn NY 11219

FORSTER, WARREN SCHUMANN, b Denver, Colo, Aug 16, 14; m 41; c 2. ORGANIC CHEMISTRY. *Educ:* Univ Denver, BS, 36; Pa State Univ, MS, 38, PhD(org chem), 40. *Prof Exp:* Asst chem, Pa State Univ, 36-40; res chemist, Bound Brook Lab, Am Cyanamid Co, 40-58, coordr res serv dept, Bus Off, 58-63, tech coordr res & develop dept, 63-81; RETIRED. *Mem:* Am Chem Soc. *Res:* Calorimetry of dimethylamine; aliphatic organic chemistry; fluorescent, vat, soluble vat, synthetic fibre dyestuffs and intermediates; optical bleaches; ultraviolet light absorbers; stabilization of plastics. *Mailing Add:* 62 S Alward Ave Basking Ridge NJ 07920

FORSTER, WILLIAM H(ALL), b Belmar, NJ, July 11, 22; m 45; c 5. COMMUNICATIONS, ELECTRONICS. *Educ:* Harvard Univ, AB, 43, Harvard Bus Sch, AMP. *Prof Exp:* Asst res div, Philco Corp, 43-48, sect engr govt & indust div, 48-50, exec engr, 50-52, exec engr res div, 52-56, assoc dir res solid state electronics, 56-57, dir res, 57-59, dir semiconductor mkt & develop, Philco Int Div, 59-61, dir corp staff, 61-62, dir eng & res commun & electronics div, 62-66; staff asst to pres, Int Tel & Tel Corp, NY, 66 & ITT Europe, Inc, 66-67, vpres & tech dir, 67-76, VPRES PROD GROUP MGR, TELECOMMUN & ELECTRONICS, INT TEL & TEL CORP, NY, 77- *Honors & Awards:* Henri Busignics Award, Radio Club Am. *Mem:* Fel Inst Elec & Electronics Engrs; fel Brit Inst Phys & Phys Soc; fel Radio Club Am; Sigma Xi. *Mailing Add:* Int Tel & Tel Corp 320 Park Ave New York NY 10022

FORSTER, WILLIAM OWEN, b Dearborn, Mich, July 2, 27; m 48; c 3. ANALYTICAL CHEMISTRY, OCEANOGRAPHY. *Educ:* Mich State Univ, BS, 51, MA, 52; Univ Hawaii, PhD(chem), 66. *Prof Exp:* Anal chemist, Buick Motor Car Co, 50-52; teacher, Mich High Sch, 52-56; instr chem, Henry Ford Community Col, 56-61; instr gen sci, Univ Hawaii, 61-66; asst prof chem occeanog, Ore State Univ, 66-72; MEM STAFF, DIV BIOMED & ENVIRON SCI, ENERGY RES & DEVELOP ADMIN, 72- *Concurrent Pos:* Lectr, Kiloani Planetarium, Bishop Mus, 64-66; Oak Ridge Nat Lab fel, PR Nuclear Ctr, Mayaguez, 69-72, head marine biol prog, 70-72; leader marine prog, Div Biomed & Environ Res, Energy Res & Develop Agency, 72-81; sr officer, Div Nuclear Safety & Environ Protection, Int Atomic Energy Agency, 77-81. *Mem:* AAAS; Am Chem Soc; Am Geophys Union; Am Soc Limnol & Oceanog; Soc Appl Spectros. *Res:* Trace element analysis in sea water, biota and sediments; biogeochemistry of marine environments. *Mailing Add:* Div Biomed & Environ Sci Energy Res & Develop Admin Washington DC 20767

FORSTHOEFEL, PAULINUS FREDERICK, b St Sebastian, Ohio, Apr 5, 15. GENETICS. *Educ:* Loyola Univ, Ill, AB, 39; Ohio State Univ, MSc, 51, PhD(zool), 53. *Prof Exp:* Instr math, Loyola Acad, 41-43; instr, Ohio Pvt Sch, 43-44; from instr to assoc prof, 53-63, PROF BIOL, UNIV DETROIT, 63- *Concurrent Pos:* NSF grant, 54-56; USPHS grants, 57-80; judge, Nat Sci Fair, 58 & 68. *Mem:* Fel AAAS; Genetics Soc Am. *Res:* Developmental genetics of mice. *Mailing Add:* 4001 W McNichols Rd Detroit MI 48221

FORSTNER, JAMES LEE, b Chattanooga, Tenn, May 29, 21; m 46; c 2. NUCLEONICS. *Educ:* Univ Calif, Los Angeles, BS, 48, MS, 50; Mass Inst Technol, PhD(anal chem), 53. *Prof Exp:* Res chemist, 53-61, RES CHEMIST NUCLEAR SAFETY, E I DU PONT DE NEMOURS & CO, INC, 61- *Mem:* AAAS; Am Chem Soc. *Res:* Nuclear safety calculations. *Mailing Add:* 1119 Parsons Lane Aiken SC 29801

FORSTNER, JANET FERGUSON, b Toronto, Ont, Nov 14, 37; m 60; c 2. MEDICAL RESEARCH. *Educ:* Univ Toronto, BA, 58, PhD(biochem), 71; Univ BC, MD, 62. *Prof Exp:* Intern med, Toronto Gen Hosp, 62-63; resident pediat, Univ Ill Res & Educ Hosp, 63-64; res fel biochem, Boston Univ, 64-66; res assoc med, 71-72, asst prof biochem, 74-80, ASST PROF MED, TORONTO WESTERN HOSP, UNIV TORONTO, 73-, ASSOC PROF BIOCHEM, 80-; investr, 74-80, ASSOC PROF BIOCHEM, RES INST, HOSP SICK CHILDREN, 74- *Concurrent Pos:* Fel, Can Cystic Fibrosis Found, 71-72; Med Res Coun Can scholar, 72-77. *Mem:* Can Biochem Soc; Asn Women Sci. *Res:* Investigation of the chemical and physical properties and secretion of epithelial mucin glycoproteins from intestine and lung relevance to cystic fibrosis. *Mailing Add:* Hosp for Sick Children 555 University Ave Toronto ON M5G 1X8 Can

FORSYTH, BEN RALPH, b New York, NY, Mar 8, 34; m 62; c 3. INTERNAL MEDICINE, INFECTIOUS DISEASES. *Educ:* NY Univ, MD, 57. *Prof Exp:* Intern & asst res, Yale New Haven Med Ctr, 57-60; res fel bact & immunol, Harvard Med Sch & Boston City Hosp, 60-61; sr investr respiratory virus unit, Lab Infectious Dis, Nat Inst Allergy & Infectious Dis, 63-66; assoc prof, 66-71, actg chmn dept med microbiol, 67, dir infectious dis unit, 66-74, PROF MED, COL MED, UNIV VT, 71-, ASSOC PROF MED MICROBIOL, 67-, ASSOC DEAN LONG RANGE PLANNING, DIV HEALTH SCI, 70- *Concurrent Pos:* Sinsheimer Fund fac fel, 66-71; mem res reagents comt, Nat Inst Allergy & Infectious Dis, 66-68, chmn, 68. *Mem:* Am Fedn Clin Res; Am Soc Microbiol; Infectious Dis Soc Am; Soc Exp Biol & Med. *Res:* Virology; mycoplasma; epidemiology. *Mailing Add:* Given Med Bldg Univ of Vt Col of Med Burlington VT 05401

FORSYTH, DALE MARVIN, b Charles City, Iowa, Feb 4, 45; m 67; c 2. ANIMAL NUTRITION, ANIMAL SCIENCE. *Educ:* Iowa State Univ, BS, 67; Cornell Univ, PhD(nutrit), 71. *Prof Exp:* Asst prof, 72-78, ASSOC PROF ANIMAL NUTRIT, PURDUE UNIV, 78- *Mem:* Am Soc Animal Sci; AAAS. *Res:* Nutrition of the young pig; utilization of feedstuffs, including high moisture, genetically improved, and molded corn; mineral metabolism, especially iron, calcium and fluoride. *Mailing Add:* Dept of Animal Sci Purdue Univ West Lafayette IN 47907

FORSYTH, DOUGLAS JOHN, b Kingston, Ont, Apr 25, 46. ECOTOXICOLOGY, BIOACCUMULATION OF POLLUTANTS. *Educ:* Carleton Univ, BSc, 69; Ohio State Univ, MS, 72, PhD(ecol), 80. *Prof Exp:* Pesticides evaluator, 75-81, WILDLIFE TOXICOLOGIST, CAN WILDLIFE SERV, 82- *Mem:* Am Soc Mammalogists; Soc Environ Toxicol & Chem. *Res:* Impact and bioaccumulation of environmental contaminants in ecosystems; effects of pesticides on wildlife; population dynamics and behavior of mammals; environmental physiology. *Mailing Add:* Can Wildlife Serv 115 Perimeter Rd Saskatoon SK S7N 0X4 Can

FORSYTH, ERIC BOYLAND, b Bolton, Eng, Apr 16, 32; m 58; c 2. ELECTRICAL ENGINEERING. *Educ:* Manchester Univ, BSc, 53; Toronto Univ, MASc, 61. *Prof Exp:* Elec engr particle accelerator, 60-65, chief elec engr, Alternating Gradient Synchrotron Div, 65-67, dep div head, 67-68, proj mgr advan accelerator div, 71-77, DIV HEAD ADVAN TECHNOL APPLICATION, BROOKHAVEN NAT LAB, 77- *Mem:* Inst Elec Engrs, UK; sr mem Inst Elec & Electronics Engrs. *Res:* Development of high power underground transmission systems using superconducting cables. *Mailing Add:* Accelerator Dept Brookhaven Nat Lab Upton NY 11973

FORSYTH, FRANK RUSSELL, b Russell, Ont, Mar 15, 22; m 45; c 5. PLANT PHYSIOLOGY. *Educ:* Queen's Univ, Ont, BA, 49; Univ Toronto, PhD(plant physiol), 52. *Prof Exp:* Res officer agr & plant physiologist, Plant Path Sect, Univ Man, 52-59, res officer, 59-62, res officer agr, Pesticide Res Inst, Kentville Res Sta, Can Dept Agr, 62-78; RETIRED. *Mem:* Can Soc Plant Physiol; Agr Inst Can; Am Soc Hort Sci; Can Soc Hort Sci. *Res:* Biochemical aspects of physiological disorders of fruit in storage. *Mailing Add:* RR 2 Berwick NS B0P 1E0 Can

FORSYTH, J(AMES) S(NEDDON), b Hamilton, Scotland, Dec 11, 16; m 45; c 1. CHEMICAL ENGINEERING. *Educ:* Glasgow Univ, BSc, 38; Univ Leeds, PhD(fuel), 43. *Prof Exp:* Lectr chem eng, Univ Leeds, 45-52; sr lectr, Univ Durham, 52-57; head dept, 57-69, PROF CHEM ENG, UNIV BC, 57- *Honors & Awards:* Moulton Medal, Brit Inst Chem Engrs, 55. *Mem:* Fel Chem Inst Can; Brit Inst Chem Engrs; Royal Inst Chemists. *Res:* Separation operations, especially distillation. *Mailing Add:* Dept of Chem Eng Univ of BC Vancouver Can

FORSYTH, JAMES M, b Niagara Falls, NY, Apr 21, 42; m 68. OPTICS. *Educ:* Univ Rochester, BS, 64, PhD(optics), 69. *Prof Exp:* Asst prof, 68-74, ASSOC PROF OPTICS, INST OPTICS, UNIV ROCHESTER, 74- *Mem:* Fel Optical Soc Am. *Res:* X-ray optics; plasma diagnostics; x-ray lasers. *Mailing Add:* Laser Energetics Univ Rochester River Campus Sta Rochester NY 14627

FORSYTH, JANE LOUISE, b Hanover, NH, Nov 9, 21. GLACIAL GEOLOGY, ENVIRONMENTAL GEOLOGY. *Educ:* Smith Col, AB, 43; Univ Cincinnati, MA, 46; Ohio State Univ, PhD(geol), 56. *Prof Exp:* Asst geol, Univ Cincinnati, 43-46; instr, Miami Univ, 46-47; asst, Univ Calif, Berkeley, 47-48; asst instr, Ohio State Univ, 48-49 & 51-55; Pleistocene geologist, Ohio Geol Surv, 55-65; from asst prof to assoc prof, 65-74, PROF GEOL, BOWLING GREEN STATE UNIV, 74- *Concurrent Pos:* Ed, Ohio J Sci, 64-74. *Mem:* Geol Soc Am; Nat Asn Geol Teachers; Ecol Soc Am. *Res:* Pleistocene geology; Wisconsin chronology in Ohio; soils, particularly as related to glacial geology studies in Ohio; geomorphology; human environmental geology; ecology, especially the relationship between plant distribution and geology in the midwest. *Mailing Add:* Dept of Geol Bowling Green State Univ Bowling Green OH 43403

FORSYTH, JOHN WILEY, b McKinney, Tex, Mar 18, 13; m 43; c 3. EXPERIMENTAL MORPHOLOGY. *Educ:* Tex Christian Univ, BS, 35, MS, 37; Princeton Univ, PhD(exp morphol), 41. *Prof Exp:* Instr, Tex Christian Univ, 36-38; prof, Presby Col (SC), 41-43; adj prof, Univ SC, 46; from asst prof to assoc prof biol, Tex Christian Univ, 46-50, prof, 50-79; RETIRED. *Mem:* AAAS; Am Soc Ichthyol & Herpet; Soc Syst Zool; Am Soc Zool. *Res:* Amphibian limb regeneration; herpetological studies; food habits and distribution in Ft Worth region. *Mailing Add:* Dept of Biol Tex Christian Univ Ft Worth TX 76109

FORSYTH, PAUL FRANCIS, b Ogdensburg, NY, Apr 21, 28; m 51; c 6. INDUSTRIAL CHEMISTRY. *Educ:* Canisius Col, BS, 51, MS, 53. *Prof Exp:* AEC asst, Canisius Col, 51-53; res chemist, Union Carbide Metals Co, 53-61; mat engr, Bell Aerosyst, 61-62; supv engr measurement sect, 62-69, supvr engr, Prod Develop, 69-74, PRIN ENGR, TECH BR, COATED ABRASIVES DIV, CARBORUNDUM CO, 74- *Mem:* Am Chem Soc. *Res:* Inorganic synthesis; vacuum techniques; analytical instrumentation; rheology; particle size analysis; sandpaper product development and processing. *Mailing Add:* Coated Abrasives Div Carborundum Co PO Box 477 Niagara Falls NY 14302

FORSYTH, PETER ALLAN, b Prince Albert, Sask, Mar 20, 22; m 44; c 2. PHYSICS. *Educ:* Univ Sask, BA, 42-46, MA, 47; McGill Univ, PhD(physics), 51. *Prof Exp:* Sci off radio physics lab, Defense Res Telecommun Estab, Can, 51-53, sect leader, Upper Atmospheric Physics Sect, 53-57, supt radio physics lab, 57-58; prof physics, Univ Sask, 58-61; head dept, 61-67, PROF PHYSICS, UNIV WESTERN ONT, 61-, DIR CTR RADIO SCI, 67- *Concurrent Pos:* Mem comt geodet & geophys, Nat Res Coun Can. *Mem:* Can Asn Physicists; fel Royal Soc Can; fel Can Aeronaut & Space Inst. *Res:* Physics of the upper atmosphere; propagation of radio waves in ionized media; scattering of radio waves by inhomogenous media. *Mailing Add:* Dept of Physics Univ of Western Ont London Can

FORSYTH, THOMAS HENRY, b Pikeville, Ky, Nov 8, 42; m 64; c 2. CHEMICAL ENGINEERING, POLYMER SCIENCE. *Educ:* Univ Ky, BS, 64; Va Polytech Inst, MS, 66, PhD(chem eng), 68. *Prof Exp:* Chem engr, Dow Chem Co, Mich, 67-70; from asst prof to assoc prof chem eng, Univ Akron, 70-80, res assoc, Inst Polymer Sci, 76-80; RES ASSOC, B F GOODRICH, 80- *Concurrent Pos:* Lectr, Midland, Mich, 69-70. *Mem:* Am Chem Soc; Am Inst Chem Engrs; Soc Plastic Engrs. *Res:* New plastics and processing of plastics. *Mailing Add:* B F Goodrich Res & Develop Ctr 9921 Brecksville Rd Brecksville OH 44141

FORSYTHE, ALAN BARRY, b Brooklyn, NY, Nov 3, 40; m 62; c 2. BIOSTATISTICS. *Educ:* Brooklyn Col, BS, 62; Columbia Univ, MS, 64; Yale Univ, PhD(biomet), 67. *Prof Exp:* Res asst statist anal, Dept Pediat & Cardiac Res, Yale Univ, 64, statistician, Dept Obstet & Gynec, 66; asst res statistician, 67-68, fels, 70-73, SUPVRY STATISTICIAN, DEPT BIOMATH & SCH MED, UNIV CALIF, LOS ANGELES, 68- *Concurrent Pos:* Consult, Div Perinatol, Dept Obstet & Gynec, Med Sch, Univ Southern Calif, 68-75, Southern Calif Permanente Med Group & Kaiser Found Hosps, 75-; assoc ed, Theory & Methods, J Am Statist Asn; mem, President's Task Force Meetings, Am Statist Asn; assoc ed, J Statist Comput & Simulation, 76-, J Biometrics, J Technomentrics, 78- *Mem:* AAAS; Am Statist Asn; Biomet Soc. *Res:* Robust estimation and hypothesis testing, especially regression; use of computers for statistical analysis and teaching. *Mailing Add:* Dept Biomath Univ Calif Sch Med Los Angeles CA 90024

FORSYTHE, DENNIS MARTIN, b Toledo, Ohio, June 20, 42; m 64; c 2. ORNITHOLOGY. *Educ:* Ohio Univ, BS, 64; Utah State Univ, MS, 67; Clemson Univ, PhD(zool), 74. *Prof Exp:* Res supvr upland game, Minn Div Game & Fish, 68-69; asst prof, 69-75, assoc prof, 75-80, PROF BIOL & DIR, VECTOR BIOL RES PROG, THE CITADEL, 80- *Concurrent Pos:* Vis prof biol, Baptist Col Charleston, 72-79, Prof Activ Continuing Educ Prog, Univ SC, 74-78; res assoc ornith, Charleston Mus, 72-77; res assoc zool, Univ Aberdeen, Scotland, 79; fac grad, Charleston Higher Educ Consortium Marine Sci, 80-; vis prof, Dept Environ Sci, Univ SC, 80- *Mem:* Animal Behav Soc; Am Ornithologists Union; Brit Ornithologists Union; Cooper Ornith Soc; Am Soc Zoologists. *Res:* Behavior and bioacoustics of birds especially shorebirds; solid waste disposal and bird species associated with the bird-aircraft collison hazard; bird populations and community structure in selected plant communities. *Mailing Add:* Dept Biol Citadel Charleston SC 29409

FORSYTHE, HOWARD YOST, JR, b Aiken, SC, Oct 27, 31; m 59; c 4. ENTOMOLOGY. *Educ:* Univ Maine, BS, 58; Cornell Univ, MS, 60, PhD(entom), 62. *Prof Exp:* Asst prof entom, Ohio Agr Exp Sta, 62-66, assoc prof, Ohio Agr Res & Develop Ctr, 66-69; assoc prof, 69-79, PROF ENTOM, UNIV MAINE, ORONO, 79-, CHMN DEPT, 77- *Concurrent Pos:* NSF res grant, 64-66. *Mem:* Entom Soc Am; Entom Soc Can. *Res:* Control and biology of deciduous fruit tree insects and mites; control and biology of insects on blueberries. *Mailing Add:* Dept of Entom Univ of Maine Orono ME 04473

FORSYTHE, RANDALL D, b Durand, Wis, Apr 16, 52. PALEOMAGNETICS, GEOLOGY. *Educ:* Lawrence Univ, BA, 74; Columbia Univ, MS, 76, MPhil, 78, PhD(geol), 81. *Prof Exp:* ASST PROF GEOL, DEPT GEOL SCI, RUTGERS UNIV, 81- *Concurrent Pos:* Vis res scientist geol, Lamont Doherty Geol Observ, Columbia Univ, 81- *Mem:* Geol Soc Am; Am Asn Petrol Geologists; Am Geophys Union. *Res:* Inter-continental correlation of circum Pacific orogenesis, with emphasis on the late paleozoic; generation and testing of hypotheses for orogeny or mountain building. *Mailing Add:* Dept Geol Sci Rutgers Univ New Brunswick NJ 08903

FORSYTHE, WARREN M, b Kingston, Jamaica, June 26, 34. SOIL PHYSICS. *Educ:* Univ Calif, Berkeley, BS, 55, PhD(soil physics), 62. *Prof Exp:* Soil physicist, Sugar Res Dept, Jamaica, 62-63; soil specialist, 64-67, off dir Barbades, 77-80, SOIL SCIENTIST PHYSICS, INTERAM INST AGR, 67-, AGR RES SPECIALIST, TRINIDAD & TOBAGO, 81- *Mem:* Soil Sci Soc Am; Int Soc Soil Sci; Latin Am Soc Agr Sci. *Res:* Soil-water relations; arid zone agriculture; soil management in the wet and dry tropics in relation to irrigation, drainage and soil and water conservation. *Mailing Add:* Interam Inst Agr Sci Turrialba Costa Rica

FORT, RAYMOND CORNELIUS, JR, b Upper Darby, Pa, Mar 28, 38; m 61; c 2. PHYSICAL ORGANIC CHEMISTRY. *Educ:* Drexel Inst, BS, 61; Princeton Univ, PhD(org chem), 65. *Prof Exp:* Fel chem, Princeton Univ, 64-65; asst prof, 65-70, assoc prof, 70-77, PROF CHEM, KENT STATE UNIV, 77- *Concurrent Pos:* Consult crystalloid electronics. *Mem:* Am Chem Soc; The Chem Soc. *Res:* Heteroadamantapes; influence of geometry on the stability of reactive intermediates; FT nuclear magnetic resonance spectroscopy. *Mailing Add:* Dept of Chem Kent State Univ Kent OH 44240

FORT, TOMLINSON, JR, b Sumter, SC, Apr 16, 32; m 56; c 2. SURFACE CHEMISTRY. *Educ:* Univ Ga, BS, 52; Univ Tenn, MS & PhD(surface chem), 57. *Prof Exp:* Stephens res fel, Univ Sydney, 57-58; from res chemist to sr res chemist, E I du Pont de Nemours & Co, Inc, 58-65; from asst prof to prof chem eng sci, Case Western Reserve Univ, 65-73; prof chem eng & chem & head, Dept Chem Eng, Carnegie-Mellon Univ, 73-80; PROF CHEM & CHEM ENG & PROVOST, UNIV MO-ROLLA, 80- *Concurrent Pos:* Vis prof, Univ Copenhagen, 78 & 80. *Mem:* Am Chem Soc; Catalysis Soc; Am Inst Chem Engrs; Am Soc Eng Educ; Sigma Xi. *Res:* Adsorption; monolayers and thin films; catalysis; adhesion; interfaces in composite materials. *Mailing Add:* Off Provost 206 Parker Hall Univ Mo Rolla MO 65401

FORTE, GERTRUDE MARIA, b Philadelphia, Pa, Feb 25, 37; m 61; c 3. BIOLOGY, BIOPHYSICS. *Educ:* Immaculata Col, BA, 58; Univ Pa, PhD(biol), 64. *Prof Exp:* Fel biochem, Univ Southern Calif, Los Angeles, 64-65; fel, 67-68, RES BIOPHYSICIST, DONNER LAB, UNIV CALIF, BERKELEY, 68- *Concurrent Pos:* Prin investr, Nat Heart, Lung & Blood Inst grant, 69-76, prog grant, 76-; prog dir, Nat Res Serv Award Postdoctoral Trainees, 77-; mem Arteriosclerosis Coun, Am Heart Asn. *Mem:* Am Heart Asn; Am Soc Cell Biol; Electron Micros Soc Am; AAAS. *Res:* Structure and function of plasma lipoproteins; electron microscopic analysis of normal and abnormal lipoproteins; synthesis of lipoproteins by liver; relationship between ultrastructure of stomach and process of hydrochloric acid secretion. *Mailing Add:* Donner Lab Univ of Calif Berkeley CA 94720

FORTE, JOHN GAETANO, b Philadelphia, Pa, Dec 23, 34; m 61; c 3. PHYSIOLOGY. *Educ:* Johns Hopkins Univ, AB, 56; Univ Pa, PhD(physiol), 61. *Prof Exp:* Lab instr biol, Univ Pa, 59 & mammalian physiol, 59-61, instr physiol, 61-62, assoc, 62-64; res assoc biochem, Univ Southern Calif, 64-65; from asst prof to assoc prof, 65-74, chmn, Dept Physiol-Anat, 72-79, Miller res professorship, 81-82, PROF PHYSIOL, UNIV CALIF, BERKELEY, 74- *Concurrent Pos:* Mem physiol study sect, NIH, 74-78, chmn, 76-78; sect ed, Ann Rev Physiol, 81- *Mem:* Am Physiol Soc; Biophys Soc; Parietal Cell Club; NY Acad Sci. *Res:* Secretory mechanisms in a variety of tissues, particularly glandular systems of gastrointestinal tract. *Mailing Add:* Dept Physiol-Anat Univ Calif Berkeley CA 94720

FORTE, LEONARD RALPH, b Nashville, Tenn, June 10, 41; m 62; c 3. PHARMACOLOGY. *Educ:* Austin Peay State Col, BS, 63; Vanderbilt Univ, PhD(pharmacol), 69. *Prof Exp:* Res asst pharmacol, Vanderbilt Univ, 63-64, res assoc, 69; from asst prof to assoc prof, 69-81, PROF & CHMN PHARMACOL, UNIV MO-COLUMBIA, 81- *Concurrent Pos:* NIH fel, Vanderbilt Univ, 69; NIH career res develop award, 74-; merit rev bd basic sci res serv, Vet Admin, 78-81; assoc chief staff res, Harry S Truman Vet Admin Hosp, Columbia, 79-81, res pharmacologist, 74- *Mem:* AAAS; Am Soc Pharmacol & Exp Therapeut; Endocrine Soc; Am Soc Bone & Mineral Res. *Res:* Renal pharmacology; calcium homeostasis; characterization of kidney plasma membranes in regard to function and molecular action of parathyroid hormone and calcitonin; physiology of vitamin D; parathyroid hormone during reproductive cycle. *Mailing Add:* Dept of Pharmacol Univ of Mo Columbia MO 65201

FORTIER, CLAUDE, b Montreal, Que, June 11, 21; m 53; c 4. PHYSIOLOGY. *Educ:* Univ Montreal, BA & MA, 41, MD, 48, PhD(exp med surg), 52; FRCP(C), 65. *Hon Degrees:* LLD, Dalhousie Univ, 77; DU, Univ Montreal & Univ Ottawa, 81. *Prof Exp:* Life Ins Med Res Fund res fel, 48-50; asst prof exp med & surg, Univ Montreal, 50-51; res consult med clin, Univ Lausanne, 52-53; res assoc dept neuroendocrinol, Inst Psychiat, Brit Postgrad Med Fedn, Maudsley Hosp, Univ London, 53-55; assoc prof physiol, Baylor Univ Col Med, Houston, 55-60; DIR ENDOCRINE LABS, FAC MED, LAVAL UNIV, 60-, PROF EXP PHYSIOL, 61-, CHMN DEPT, 64- *Concurrent Pos:* Lectr, Inst Psychol, Univ Montreal, 47-51, asst, Inst Exp Med & Surg, 48-51; Am Heart Asn res fels, 51-52 & 53-54; Nat Res Coun Can res fel, 52-53; Commonwealth Fund advan res fel, 54-55; dir, Blue Bird Neuroendocrine Res Labs, Houston, Tex, 55-60; mem, Med Res Coun Can, 63-68, 70-72, vchmn, 65-67; med res adv & coord comts, Defense Res Bd, Can, 67-70; chmn, Nat Comt Can of Int Union Physiol Sci, 69-72, mem, Killam Comt, Can Coun, 67; mem, Nat Cancer Inst Can, 69-72; mem, Prov Med Res Coun Que, 63-70; mem neuroendocrinol panel, Int Brain Res Orgn, 59-; mem adv med bd, Muscular Dystrophy Asn, Can, 62-65; bd dir, Can Found Adv Therapeut, 63-67; consult physician, Hosp Ctr, Univ Laval, 69-; sci adv bd, Montreal Clin Res Inst, 69-; chmn bd, Can Fedn Biol Socs, 73-74; mem bd trustees, Inst Res on Pub Policy, 74-75; mem adv coun, Order of Can, 74-75; vchmn, Sci Coun Can, 75-, chmn task force res in Can, 76- *Honors & Awards:* Companion of the Order of Can, 70; Res Award, French Can Asn Advan Sci, 72; Res Award, Govt Que, 72; Wightman Award, Gairdner Found, 79; Marie Victorin Sci Award, Gov Que, 80. *Mem:* Fel Royal Sc Can (pres, 74-75); Am Physiol Soc; Endocrine Soc; Can Physiol Soc (pres, 66-67); Asn Am Physicians. *Res:* Neurohumoral control of adenohypophysial functions; functional interrelationships between the pituitary, thyroid, adrenal cortex and gonads; biostatistics; biocontrol systems. *Mailing Add:* Dept Physiol Laval Univ Fac of Med Quebec PQ G1K 7P4 Can

FORTIN, ANDRE FRANCIS, b Shawinigan, Que, Dec 29, 51; m 79; c 1. MEATS, BODY COMPOSITION. *Educ:* Macdonald Col, McGill Univ, BSc, 73; Cornell Univ, PhD(nutrit), 77. *Prof Exp:* Teaching asst, Animal Sci Dept, Cornell Univ, 73-76, res asst, 73-77; RES SCIENTIST, ANIMAL RES CTR, AGR CAN, 77- *Concurrent Pos:* Mem, Meat Sci Prog Comt, Am Soc Animal Sci, 82- *Mem:* Am Soc Animal Sci; Am Meat Sci Asn; Can Soc Animal Sci; Agr Inst Can. *Res:* Growth and development of body tissues in beef cattle, swine and sheep; live evaluation of body and carcass composition; hog carcass grading. *Mailing Add:* Animal Res Ctr Agr Can Ottawa ON K1C 0C6 Can

FORTIN, EMERY, solid state physics, see previous edition

FORTIN, J ANDRE, botany, see previous edition

FORTMAN, JOHN JOSEPH, b Dayton, Ohio, Oct 26, 39; m 68. INORGANIC CHEMISTRY, CHEMICAL EDUCATION. *Educ:* Univ Dayton, BS, 61; Univ Notre Dame, PhD(phys Inorg chem), 66. *Prof Exp:* Asst prof, 65-69, ASSOC PROF CHEM, WRIGHT STATE UNIV, 69- *Concurrent Pos:* Res analyst, Aerospace Res Labs, Wright-Patterson Air Force Base, 66-70; vis assoc prof chem, Purdue Univ, 73-74. *Mem:* AAAS; Am Chem Soc; Royal Soc Chem; Sigma Xi. *Res:* Electron paramagnetic resonance; nuclear magnetic resonance of inorganic complexes; coordination chemistry; intramolecular rearrangements of chelate complexes. *Mailing Add:* Dept Chem Wright State Univ Dayton OH 45435

FORTMANN, HENRY RAYMOND, agronomy, deceased

FORTNER, GEORGE WILLIAM, b Middlesboro, Ky, Mar 30, 38; m 77. BIOLOGY, IMMUNOLOGY. *Educ:* Wayne State Univ, BS, 61; Univ Tenn, PhD(microbiol), 73. *Prof Exp:* Res technician microbiol, Oak Ridge Nat Lab, 64-68; investr immunol, Sch Med, Stanford Univ, 73-75; scientist II, Frederick Cancer Res Ctr, 75-77; ASST PROF IMMUNOL, DIV BIOL, KANS STATE UNIV, 77- *Concurrent Pos:* Prin investr grants, Kans State

Univ, 77-78, Mid-Am Cancer Ctr, 77-78 & 79-80 & Nat Cancer Inst, 79-83; assoc scientist, Mid-Am Cancer Ctr, 78- *Mem:* Am Soc Microbiol; AAAS. *Res:* Cellular immunology; immunobiology; tumor immunology; host-parasite relationships. *Mailing Add:* 3426 Chimney Rock Rd Manhattan KS 66502

FORTNER, JOSEPH GERALD, b Bedford, Ind, May 30, 21; m 47; c 2. SURGERY, BIOLOGY. *Educ:* Univ Ill, BS, 44, MD, 45; Univ Birmingham, MSc, 65; Am Bd Surg, dipl. *Prof Exp:* Intern, St Luke's Hosp, Ill, 45-46; resident path, Charity Hosp, La, 48-49; asst resident surg, Bellevue Hosp, NY, 49-51; asst resident surg, Mem Hosp, 51-52, resident, 52-54; from instr surg to assoc prof clin surg, 54-70, assoc prof surg, 70-72, PROF SURG, MED COL, CORNELL UNIV, 72-; ASSOC MEM, SLOAN-KETTERING INST, 61-, DIR, GEN MOTORS SURG RES LAB, 77-, ASSOC CHMN LAB AFFAIRS, 78- *Concurrent Pos:* Nat Cancer Inst trainee, 53-54; attend surgeon, Gastric & Mixed Tumor Serv, Mem Hosp, 69-, Chief, Surg Res Serv, 78-; chief, Div Surg Res, Sloan-Kettering Inst, 68-77, chief, Gastric & Mixed Tumor Serv, 70-78. *Honors & Awards:* Alfred P Sloan Award, 63. *Mem:* Am Radium Soc; Harvey Soc; Soc Univ Surg; Am Asn Cancer Res; fel Am Col Surg. *Res:* Transplantation; experimental surgery; cancer therapy. *Mailing Add:* Mem Hosp Sloan-Kettering Inst New York NY 10021

FORTNER, WENDELL LEE, b Conway, Ark, Nov 17, 35; m 62; c 2. STRATIGRAPHY, HYDROLOGY. *Educ:* Univ Cent Ark, BS, 61. *Prof Exp:* Grad asst, Grad Inst Technol, Univ Ark, 61-62; tech inspector, Martin-Maritta Co, 62-63; chemist, 63-79, CHEM ENGR, PINE BLUFF ARSENAL, US ARMY, 79- *Mem:* Sigma Xi; Am Chem Soc; fel Am Inst Chem Engrs. *Res:* Environmental treatment systems for industrial effluents with continuous chemical and biological monitoring techniques as early warning devices; incineration processes for both bulk chemical and chemical contaminated hardware (fluid-bed, rotary and chain grate); resource recovery operations and techniques. *Mailing Add:* 2113 Mt Vernon Ct Pine Bluff AR 71603

FORTNEY, CECIL GARFIELD, JR, food chemistry, see previous edition

FORTNEY, LLOYD RAY, b Enid, Okla, June 22, 36; m 62; c 2. HIGH ENERGY PHYSICS. *Educ:* NMex State Univ, BS, 58; Univ Wis, PhD(physics), 62. *Prof Exp:* Res assoc high energy physics, Univ Wis, 62-63; res assoc, 63-64, asst prof, 64-70, ASSOC PROF PHYSICS, DUKE UNIV, 70-, DIR, UNDERGRAD STUDIES, 80- *Mem:* Am Phys Soc. *Res:* Experimental high energy physics using hydrogen and heavy liquid bubble chambers. *Mailing Add:* Dept of Physics Duke Univ Durham NC 27706

FORTNUM, DONALD HOLLY, b Berlin, Wis, Apr 2, 32; m 58; c 4. PHYSICAL CHEMISTRY. *Educ:* Carroll Col, Wis, 54; Brown Univ, PhD(chem), 58. *Prof Exp:* Instr chem, Providence Col, 56-57; asst prof, Ursinus Col, 58-65; assoc prof, 65-73, PROF CHEM, GETTYSBURG COL, 73- *Mem:* Am Chem Soc. *Res:* Molecular structure; kinetics of inorganic reactions; computer applications in chemistry. *Mailing Add:* Dept of Chem Gettysburg Col Gettysburg PA 17325

FORTUNATO, FRED ANTHONY, US citizen. CATALYSIS, REACTION KINETICS. *Educ:* Youngstown State Univ, BS, 73; Purdue Univ, MSE, 76, PhD(chem eng), 79. *Prof Exp:* Res chemist, BF Goodrich Res & Develop, 73-74; SR ENGR, EXXON RES & DEVELOP LABS, 79- *Mem:* Am Inst Chem Eng. *Res:* Process development for shale oil upgrading. *Mailing Add:* 12152 Canterbury Dr Baton Rough LA 70814

FORTUNE, H TERRY, b Ramer, Tenn, Feb 16, 41; m 61; c 2. NUCLEAR PHYSICS. *Educ:* Memphis State Univ, BS, 63; Fla State Univ, PhD(physics), 67. *Prof Exp:* Res assoc nuclear physics, Argonne Nat Lab, 67-69; from asst prof to assoc prof, 69-76, PROF PHYSICS, UNIV PA, 76- *Concurrent Pos:* Vis scientist, Argonne Nat Lab, 74; vis fel, Oxford Univ, 77. *Mem:* Am Phys Soc; Am Asn Physics Teachers. *Res:* Nuclear structure physics; reaction mechanisms; reactions induced by heavy ions. *Mailing Add:* Dept of Physics Univ of Pa Philadelphia PA 19104

FORTUNE, JOANNE ELIZABETH, b Watertown, NY, Jan 24, 45; m 74. REPRODUCTIVE ENDOCRINOLOGY. *Educ:* Col New Rochelle, BA, 67; Cornell Univ, MS, 71, PhD(embryol), 75. *Prof Exp:* Fel reproductive physiol, Dept Obstet/Gynec, Univ Western Ont, 75-76; fel reproduction physiol, Dept Animal Sci, 76-77, res assoc, 77-79, sr res assoc, Dept Phys Biol, 79-80, ASST PROF PHYSIOL, SECT PHYSIOL, CORNELL UNIV, 80- *Concurrent Pos:* Co-prin investr, NIH res grant, 78-80, prin investr, 80-; review panel mem, Regulatory Biol Panel, NSF, 81-83. *Mem:* Soc Study Reproduction; Endocrine Soc; Am Soc Zoologists; Soc Develop Biol; Soc Study Fertil. *Res:* Ovarian development and function; hormonal control of steroid production by mammalian and amphibian ovarian cells in vitro, using radioimmunoassay, tissue culture, and microsurgical techniques. *Mailing Add:* 823 Vet Res Tower Cornell Univ Ithaca NY 14853

FORWARD, DOROTHY FLORENCE, b Ottawa, Ont, Apr 15, 03. PLANT PHYSIOLOGY. *Educ:* Univ Toronto, BA, 26, MA, 28, PhD(plant path), 31; Cambridge Univ, PhD(plant physiol), 40. *Prof Exp:* Asst bot, Univ Toronto, 27-33 & 35-37; res fel, Royal Soc Can, 33-34; asst bot, Univ Toronto, 35-37; asst & demonstr plant physiol, 37-41, from lectr to prof, 41-71, assoc chmn dept, 68-71, spec lectr, 71-72, EMER PROF BOT, UNIV TORONTO, 71- *Concurrent Pos:* Spec lectr, McMaster Univ, 36-37. *Mem:* Am Soc Plant Physiol; Can Soc Plant Physiol (secy, 59-61, pres, 62-63); Can Biochem Soc. *Res:* Plant pathology; nature of rust resistance; plant physiology; metabolism; respiration; growth. *Mailing Add:* Dept Bot Univ Toronto Toronto ON M5S 1A1 Can

FORWARD, RICHARD BLAIR, JR, b Washington, DC, Jan 13, 43; m 69; c 2. COMPARATIVE PHYSIOLOGY. *Educ:* Stanford Univ, BA, 65; Univ Calif, Santa Barbara, PhD(biol), 69. *Prof Exp:* From res asst biol to teaching asst, Univ Calif, Santa Barbara, 66-69; res assoc biol, Yale Univ, 69-71; asst prof, 71-77, ASSOC PROF ZOOL, DUKE UNIV, 78- *Mem:* AAAS; Am Soc Photobiol; Am Soc Zoologists; Sigma Xi; Am Soc Limnol & Oceanog. *Res:* Photobehavior and photophysiology of zooplankton. *Mailing Add:* Duke Univ Marine Lab Beaufort NC 28516

FORWARD, ROBERT L, b Geneva, NY, Aug 15, 32; m 54; c 4. EXPERIMENTAL GRAVITATION. *Educ:* Univ Md, BS, 54; Univ Calif, Los Angeles, MS, 58; Univ Md, PhD(physics), 65. *Prof Exp:* Mem tech staff physics, 56-57, assoc dept mgr, Theoret Studies Dept, 67-68, mgr, Explor Studies Dept, 68-74, SR SCIENTIST, HUGHES RES LABS, 75- *Concurrent Pos:* Gravity Res Found awards, 62, 63, 64, 65; ed adv, J Brit Interplanetary Soc, 73- *Mem:* Am Phys Soc; sr mem Inst Elec & Electronics Engrs; sr mem Am Astronaut Soc; assoc fel Inst Aeronaut & Astronaut; fel Brit Interplanetary Soc. *Res:* Experimental investigations of dynamic gravitational fields, gravitational gradient sensors, tests of general theory of relativity and gravitational radiation. *Mailing Add:* Hughes Res Labs 3011 Malibu Canyon Rd Malibu CA 90265

FORYS, LEONARD J, b Buffalo, NY, July 22, 41; m 66; c 2. COMPUTER SCIENCE. *Educ:* Univ Notre Dame, BS, 63; Mass Inst Technol, MS & EE, 65; Univ Calif, Berkeley, PhD(elec eng), 68. *Prof Exp:* Actg asst prof elec eng & comput sci, Univ Calif, Berkeley, 67-68; MEM TECH STAFF, BELL LABS, 68- *Mem:* Inst Elec & Electronics Engrs. *Res:* Control theory; communication theory; teletraffic theory; queueing theory; computer real time performance. *Mailing Add:* Bel Labs 600 Mountain Ave Murray Hill NJ 07974

FORZIATI, ALPHONSE FRANK, b Boston, Mass, Feb 27, 11; m 45. PHYSICAL CHEMISTRY. *Educ:* Harvard Univ, BA, 32, MA, 34, PhD(phys chem), 39. *Prof Exp:* Lab asst chem, Harvard Univ, 32-33 & Radcliffe Col, 33-38; asst phys chem, Harvard Univ, 39-41; Am Petrol Inst res assoc, Nat Bur Stand, 41-50 & Am Dent Asn res assoc, 50-62; electrochemist, Harry Diamond Lab, 62-63; tech prog mgr, Adv Res Proj Agency, US Dept Defense, 63-66; asst chief res div, Fed Water Pollution Control Admin, US Environ Protection Agency, 66-71, chief measurements & instrumentation br, Div Processes & Effects, Off Res & Monitoring, 71-74, staff scientist sci adv bd, 74-77, dir stratospheric modification res staff, Off Res & Develop, 77-80; RETIRED. *Mem:* AAAS; Am Chem Soc; Electrochem Soc; Soc Appl Spectros; Am Dent Asn. *Res:* Electrochemistry; electrode potentials; fuel cells; high vacuum technique; physical properties of hydrocarbons; precise determination of and correlation with molecular structure; fluorescence and phosphorescence; technical program management; instrumentation; monitoring; photobiology; atmospheric chemistry and physics. *Mailing Add:* 15525 Prince Federick Way Silver Spring MD 20906

FOSBERG, MARY DEE HARRIS, computer science, see previous edition

FOSBERG, MAYNARD AXEL, b Turlock, Calif, July 7, 19; m 47; c 2. SOIL GENESIS & CLASSIFICATION. *Educ:* Univ Wis, BS, 48, MS, 49, PhD(soils), 63. *Prof Exp:* From asst prof to assoc prof soils, 58-72, PROF SOIL SCI & SOIL SCIENTIST, UNIV IDAHO, 72- *Mem:* Soil Sci Soc Am; Am Soc Range Mgt; Ecol Soc Am; Sigma Xi. *Res:* Soil genesis and classification; soil-plant relationships. *Mailing Add:* Dept of Plant & Soil Sci Univ of Idaho Moscow ID 83843

FOSBERG, MICHAEL ALLEN, forest meteorology, see previous edition

FOSBERG, THEODORE M(ICHAEL), b Seattle, Wash, Dec 26, 34; m 58; c 5. CHEMICAL ENGINEERING. *Educ:* Univ Wash, BS, 59, MS, 61, PhD(chem eng), 64. *Prof Exp:* Bioscientist, Boeing Co, 64-71; PROCESS ENGR, RESOURCES CONSERV CO, 71- *Mem:* Am Chem Soc; Am Inst Chem Engrs. *Res:* Interphase mass transfer; life support requirements and systems; human factors; process technology for desalination and brine concentrator systems; evaporator technology. *Mailing Add:* 1913 SW 167th Seattle WA 98166

FOSCANTE, RAYMOND EUGENE, b New York, NY, Mar 24, 42; m 64; c 2. ORGANIC CHEMISTRY. *Educ:* Manhattan Col, BS, 62; Seton Hall Univ, PhD(chem), 66. *Prof Exp:* From assoc chemist to sr chemist, 69-71, head org & polymer chem sect, Midwest Res Inst, 71-75; DIR CORP RES & DEVELOP, AMERON, INC, 75- *Mem:* Am Chem Soc; The Chem Soc. *Res:* Propellant chemistry; structure-property relationships; wastewater treatment; corrosion control; polymer cure chemistry; organic and inorganic coatings; polymer synthesis; carcinogen synthesis; research management. *Mailing Add:* 20547 Manzanita Yorba Linda CA 92686

FOSCHINI, GERARD JOSEPH, b Jersey City, NJ, Feb 28, 40; m 62; c 2. APPLIED MATHEMATICS. *Educ:* Newark Col Eng, BSEE, 61; NY Univ, MEE, 63; Stevens Inst Technol, PhD(math), 67. *Prof Exp:* MEM TECH STAFF, BELL TEL LABS, INC, 61- *Mem:* Math Asn Am. *Res:* Computer communications; communication theory; function theory; stochastic processes. *Mailing Add:* 79 Orchard St South Amboy NJ 08879

FOSCOLOS, ANTHONY E, b Cairo, Egypt, May 15, 30; Can citizen; m 58; c 2. SOIL MINERALOGY, SEDIMENTOLOGY. *Educ:* Univ Thessaloniki, BAgE, 53; Univ Calif, Berkeley, MS, 64, PhD(clay physics, chem), 66. *Prof Exp:* Tech officer, Kopaes Orgn, Greece, 53-64; res asst clay mineral, Univ Calif, Berkeley, 63-66; RES SCIENTIST, III, INST SEDIMENTARY & PETROL GEOL, CAN DEPT ENERGY, MINES & RESOURCES, 66- *Concurrent Pos:* Greek Found Scholars grant, 60; NSF grant, 64; lectr & instr, Dept Archaeol, Univ Calgary, 75- *Mem:* Am Soc Agron; NY Acad Sci; Int Soil Sci Soc; Clay Minerals Soc; Sigma Xi. *Res:* Clay physical chemistry, chemistry and mineralogy. *Mailing Add:* 3407 Varal Rd NW Calgary AB T3A 0A3 Can

FOSDICK, LLOYD D(UDLEY), b New York, NY, Jan 18, 28; m 58. COMPUTER SCIENCE. *Educ:* Univ Chicago, PhB, 46, BS, 48; Purdue Univ, MS, 50, PhD(physics), 53. *Prof Exp:* Systs evaluation, Control Systs Lab, 53-54; assoc head, Comput Div, Midwestern Univs Res Asn, 56-57; res asst prof digital comput lab, Univ Ill, 57-61, res assoc prof physics, 61-64, res prof, 64-70; PROF COMPUT SCI, UNIV COLO, BOULDER, 70- *Concurrent Pos:* Guggenheim fel, 64. *Mem:* Asn Comput Mach; Soc Indust & Appl Math. *Res:* Digital computers; statistical mechanics; mathematics of computation. *Mailing Add:* Dept of Comput Sci Univ of Colo Boulder CO 80302

FOSDICK, ROGER L(EE), b Pontiac, Ill, Nov 18, 36; m 56; c 2. APPLIED MATHEMATICS, CONTINUUM MECHANICS. *Educ:* Ill Inst Technol, BS, 59; Brown Univ, PhD(appl math), 63. *Prof Exp:* Asst prof mech, Ill Inst Technol, 62-65, assoc prof, 65-69; PROF MECH, UNIV MINN, MINNEAPOLIS, 69- *Concurrent Pos:* Vis prof, Fed Univ, Rio de Janeiro, Brazil, 77; Erskine fel, Univ Canterbury, Christchurch, NZ, 80. *Mem:* Soc Nat Philos (secy, 72-74, chmn, 79-81); Soc for Rheology; Soc Interaction Mech & Math. *Res:* Continuum mechanics, especially theory of finite elasticity, theory of finite viscoelasticity, and theory of non-linear fluids; continuum thermomechanics. *Mailing Add:* Dept of Aerospace Eng & Mech Univ of Minn Minneapolis MN 55455

FOSGATE, OLIN TRACY, dairy science, deceased

FOSKET, DONALD ELSTON, b Klamath Falls, Ore, July 20, 36. PLANT PHYSIOLOGY, CELL BIOLOGY. *Educ:* Univ Idaho, BA, 58, PhD(plant physiol), 64. *Prof Exp:* Res assoc developmental bot, Brookhaven Nat Lab, 64-65; asst prof biol, Mt Holyoke Col, 65-67; NSF fel, Biol Lab, Harvard Univ, 67-69, Bullard fel, 69-70; asst prof, 70-72, assoc prof develop & cell biol, 72-80, ASSOC PROF BIOL SCI, UNIV CALIF, IRVINE, 80- *Mem:* Am Soc Cell Biol; Soc Develop Biol; AAAS; Bot Soc Am; Soc Exp Biol & Med. *Res:* Regulation of cell division and cell differentiation. *Mailing Add:* Dept of Develop & Cell Biol Univ of Calif Irvine CA 92717

FOSNACHT, DONALD RALPH, b Chicago, Ill, Dec 10, 50; m 72. METALLURGICAL & MINERAL ENGINEERING. *Educ:* MacMurray Col, BS, 73; Columbia Univ, BS, 74, MS, 75; Univ Mo-Rolla, PhD(metall eng), 78. *Prof Exp:* RES ENGR METALL ENG, INLAND STEEL CO, 78- *Mem:* Am Inst Mining, Metall & Petrol Engrs; Sigma Xi. *Res:* Recycling of metallurgical waste materials such as steelmaking dusts, coke breeze, and mill scale; recovery of by-product materials from steelmaking wastes. *Mailing Add:* Inland Steel Res Labs 3001 E Columbus Dr East Chicago IN 46312

FOSS, ALAN STUART, b Stamford, Conn, Sept 9, 29. CHEMICAL ENGINEERING. *Educ:* Worcester Polytech Inst, BS, 52; Univ Del, MChE, 54, PhD(chem eng), 57. *Prof Exp:* Sr res engr, Eng Res Lab, E I du Pont de Nemours & Co, 56-61; from asst prof to assoc prof chem eng, 61-73, vchmn dept, 67-69, PROF CHEM ENG, UNIV CALIF, BERKELEY, 73- *Concurrent Pos:* Fel, Univ Trondheim, 69-70. *Mem:* Am Inst Chem Engrs. *Res:* Chemical process dynamics and control; computer control; energy storage. *Mailing Add:* Dept of Chem Eng Univ of Calif Berkeley CA 94720

FOSS, DONALD C, b Providence, RI, May 3, 38; m 60; c 2. NUTRITION, PHYSIOLOGY. *Educ:* Univ NH, BS, 60; Univ Wis, MS, 61; Univ Mass, PhD(physiol & nutrit), 66. *Prof Exp:* Fel poultry sci, 66-68, from asst prof to assoc prof, 68-80, PROF ANIMAL SCI, UNIV VT, 80- *Concurrent Pos:* Assoc ed, Poultry Sci; consult poulty mgt, Ecuador. *Mem:* Poultry Sci Asn; Am Soc Photobiol; World's Poultry Sci Asn; Sigma Xi; Soc Exp Biol & Med. *Res:* Effects of light quality on growth reproduction and endocrine balance; role of the pineal gland in mediating light effects and circadian rhythms; nutritional and physiological factors influencing poultry growth and egg production. *Mailing Add:* Dept Animal Sci Univ Vt Burlington VT 05405

FOSS, FREDERICK WILLIAM, JR, b Lincoln, Mich, June 3, 33; m 57; c 3. INORGANIC CHEMISTRY. *Educ:* Univ Mich, BS, 55; Univ Minn, Minneapolis, MS, 57; Univ of the Pac, PhD(inorg chem), 64. *Prof Exp:* Instr phys sci, 57-63, from asst prof to assoc prof chem, 63-67, PROF CHEM, WINONA STATE UNIV, 67-, HEAD DEPT, 66- *Mem:* Am Chem Soc. *Res:* Inorganic polarography in non-aqueous solvents; general chemistry, laboratory approaches; chemical lecture demonstrations. *Mailing Add:* Dept of Chem Winona State Univ Winona MN 55987

FOSS, JOHN E, b Whitehall, Wis, May 30, 32; m 53; c 2. SOIL GENESIS, SOIL CLASSIFICATION. *Educ:* Wis State Univ, River Falls, BS, 57; Univ Minn, MS, 59, PhD(soil sci, geol), 65. *Prof Exp:* Asst prof soils, Wis State Univ, River Falls, 60-66; assoc prof soils, Univ MD, 66-73, prof soils, 73-81; PROF & CHMN SOILS, NDAK STATE UNIV, 81- *Concurrent Pos:* Consult, Libby, McNeil & Libby Corp, France, 62, Allied Chem, 73-80, Columbia Gas Corp & A D Little, 75 & Dept Interior, 80-81. *Mem:* AAAS; Am Soc Agron. *Res:* Soil development; interpretation and uses of soil surveys. *Mailing Add:* Dept Soil Sci NDakota State Univ Fargo ND 58102

FOSS, JOHN F, b Washington, Pa, Mar 24, 38; m 60; c 2. FLUID MECHANICS. *Educ:* Purdue Univ, BS, 61, MS, 62, PhD(mech eng), 65. *Prof Exp:* From asst prof to assoc prof, 64-75, PROF MECH ENG, MICH STATE UNIV, 75- *Concurrent Pos:* Fel, Johns Hopkins Univ, 70-71; Humboldt res fel, Univ Karlsruhe, WGer, 78-79. *Mem:* AAAS; Am Soc Mech Engrs; Am Soc Eng Educ; Am Inst Aeronaut & Astronaut; Am Phys Soc. *Res:* Turbulent shear flow and experimental fluid mechanics. *Mailing Add:* Dept of Mech Eng Mich State Univ East Lansing MI 48823

FOSS, JOHN G(ERALD), b Brooklyn, NY, Feb 27, 30; m 57; c 3. BIOPHYSICS. *Educ:* Brooklyn Polytech, BS, 51; Univ Conn, MS, 53; Univ Utah, PhD(phys chem), 56. *Prof Exp:* Assoc phys chem, Univ Minn, 56-57 & Univ Ore, 57-61; PROF BIOPHYS, IOWA STATE UNIV, 61- *Concurrent Pos:* Vis prof, Univ Calif, Berkeley, 63-64; liaison scientist, Off Naval Res, London, 70-72. *Res:* Biophysics; spectroscopic methods in biochemistry. *Mailing Add:* Dept Biochem & Physics Iowa State Univ Ames IA 50011

FOSS, MARTYN (HENRY), b Salt Lake City, Utah, May 28, 18; m 42; c 6. PHYSICS. *Educ:* Univ Chicago, BS, 38; Carnegie Inst Technol, DSc(physics), 48. *Prof Exp:* Shift supvr lab, Ind Ord Works, 40-41, chem engr, 41-43; mem staff, Manhattan Proj, Del, Ill & Los Alamos, 43-46; res physicist, Carnegie Inst Technol, 48-54; sr physicist, Argonne Nat Lab, 55-59, assoc dir, Particle Accelerator Div, 59-62; assoc dir, Nuclear Res Ctr, Carnegie Inst Technol, 62-70, sr physicist, Carnegie-Mellon Univ, 70-74; MEM STAFF, ARGONNE NAT LAB, 74- *Mem:* AAAS; fel Am Phys Soc. *Res:* Particle accelerator. *Mailing Add:* Argonne Nat Lab 9700 S Cass Ave Argonne IL 60439

FOSS, ROBERT PAUL, b Chicago, Ill, Aug 22, 37; m 62; c 2. PHYSICAL ORGANIC CHEMISTRY, POLYMER CHEMISTRY. *Educ:* Northwestern Univ, BA, 58; Calif Inst Technol, PhD(chem), 63. *Prof Exp:* NIH fel chem, Lab Chem Biodynamics, Univ Calif, Berkeley, 63-65; RES CHEMIST, CENT RES DEPT, E I DU PONT DE NEMOURS & CO, INC, 65- *Mem:* Am Chem Soc. *Res:* Photochemistry and energy transfer involving organic and inorganic compounds; polymer chemistry involving general and photopolymerization studies; high energy radiation chemistry of organic and polymer systems. *Mailing Add:* Cent Res & Develop Dept E328 E I du Pont de Nemours & Co Inc Wilmington DE 19898

FOSSAN, DAVID B, b Faribault, Minn, Aug 23, 34; m 64. PHYSICS. *Educ:* St Olaf Col, BA, 56; Univ Wis, MS, 57, PhD(physics), 60. *Prof Exp:* Asst physics, Univ Wis, 60-61; Ford Found grant, Niels Bohr Inst, Copenhagen, 61-62; mem res staff nuclear physics, Van de Graaff Lab, Lockheed Palo Alto Research Lab, 63-65; from asst prof to assoc prof, 65-72, PROF PHYSICS, STATE UNIV NY STONY BROOK, 72- *Concurrent Pos:* Vis physicist, Lawrence Berkeley Lab, Univ Calif, 78-79; mem prof adv comt, Super Heavy Ion Linear Accelerator, Lawrence Berkeley Lab, Univ Calif, 81- *Mem:* Am Phys Soc. *Res:* Nuclear structure via heavy-ion induced reactions and gamma-ray measurements; excited state lifetimes and static moments of nuclei. *Mailing Add:* Dept of Physics State Univ NY Stony Brook NY 11790

FOSSEL, ERIC THOR, b Minneapolis, Minn, Dec 11, 41; m 64; c 2. BIOPHYSICAL CHEMISTRY, CARDIAC METABOLISM. *Educ:* Yale Univ, BA, 64, MS, 66, MPhil, 67; Harvard Univ, PhD(chem), 70. *Prof Exp:* NIH res fel chem, 70-71, NIH res fel biochem, 71-74, lectr biophysics, 74-75, ASST PROF BIOPHYS, MED SCH, HARVARD UNIV, 75- *Concurrent Pos:* Fel, Muscular Dystrophy Asn Am, 72-75; fel, Arthritis Found, 75-78; estab investr, Am Heart Asn, 78- *Mem:* Biophys Soc; Am Heart Asn. *Res:* Thermal rearrangements; enzyme mechanisms; muscle action mechanism; nuclear magnetic resonance in biological systems; cardiac metabolism; ion transport in cardiac tissue. *Mailing Add:* Harvard Med Sch 25 Shattuck St Boston MA 02115

FOSSLAND, ROBERT GERARD, b Winthrop Harbor, Ill, Oct 18, 18; m 60; c 6. REPRODUCTIVE BIOLOGY, EVOLUTIONARY BIOLOGY. *Educ:* Univ Ill, BS, 40; Univ Nebr, PhD(zool), 56. *Prof Exp:* Asst, Univ Nebr, 40-42, from instr to assoc prof dairy sci, Univ Ariz, 45-61; assoc prof zool, Milwaukee-Downer Col, 62; assoc prof biol, 62-65, PROF BIOL, UNIV WIS-EAU CLAIRE, 65- *Res:* Evolutionary biology. *Mailing Add:* Dept of Biol Univ of Wis Eau Claire WI 54701

FOSSUM, GUILFORD O, b Loma, NDak, Dec 17, 18; m 45; c 4. CIVIL & SANITARY ENGINEERING. *Educ:* Univ NDak, BS, 42; Iowa State Univ, MS, 51. *Prof Exp:* Inspector, US Eng Dept, CZ, 42-43; engr, Grand Forks City Eng Dept, 46; from asst prof to assoc prof, 46-61, PROF CIVIL ENG, UNIV NDAK, 61- *Honors & Awards:* Arthur Sidney Bedell Award, Water Pollution Control Fedn, 73. *Mem:* Water Pollution Control Fedn; Am Soc Civil Engrs; Am Soc Eng Educ; Nat Soc Prof Engrs. *Res:* Industrial and municipal wastes and water supplies, including treatment methods. *Mailing Add:* Dept of Civil Eng Univ of NDak Grand Forks ND 58202

FOSSUM, ROBERT, mathematics, statistics, see previous edition

FOSSUM, ROBERT MERLE, b Northfield, Minn, May 1, 38; m 60, 79; c 3. MATHEMATICS. *Educ:* St Olaf Col, BA, 59; Univ Mich, AM, 61, PhD(math), 65. *Prof Exp:* From asst prof to assoc prof, 64-72, PROF MATH, UNIV ILL, URBANA, 72- *Concurrent Pos:* Fulbright res grant, Inst Math, Univ Oslo, 67-68, vis prof, 68-69; vis prof, Univ Aarhus, 71-73; ed, Proc Amer Math Soc, 74-78; vist assoc prof, Univ Copenhagen, 76-77; prof, Univ Paris VI, 78-79. *Mem:* Danish Math Soc; NY Acad Sci; Am Math Soc; Norweg Math Soc. *Res:* Commutative noetherian rings; algebras over commutative noetherian integrally closed integral domains and homological algebra. *Mailing Add:* Dept of Math Univ of Ill Urbana IL 61801

FOSSUM, STEVE P, b Northfield, Minn, Dec 26, 41; m 67; c 1. SURFACE PHYSICS, VACUUM TECHNOLOGY. *Educ:* St Olaf Col, BA, 63; Univ Wis, Madison, MA, 65, PhD(physics), 70. *Prof Exp:* Assoc prof, 66-75, PROF PHYSICS & CHMN DEPT, UNIV WIS-STOUT, 75- *Concurrent Pos:* Exchange lectr, Newcastle Polytech Inst, Eng, 71-72. *Mem:* Am Phys Soc; Am Asn Physics Teachers. *Res:* Atomic hydrogen reactions on metal surfaces in ultra-high vacuums. *Mailing Add:* Dept of Physics Univ Wis-Stout Menomonie WI 54751

FOSSUM, TIMOTHY V, b Northfield, Minn, Oct 29, 42; m 65; c 2. ALGEBRA, COMPUTER SCIENCE. *Educ:* St Olaf Col, BA, 64; Univ Ore, PhD(math), 68. *Prof Exp:* Asst prof math, Univ Utah, 68-74; ASSOC PROF MATH & APPL COMPUT SCI, UNIV WIS-PARKSIDE, 74- *Concurrent Pos:* Vis lectr, Univ Ill, 71-72. *Mem:* Am Math Soc; Math Asn Am. Asn Comput Mach; Orders in semisimple algebras over Dedekind domains, automorphism groups of p-groups. *Mailing Add:* Div of Sci Univ of Wis-Parkside Kenosha WI 53140

FOSTER, ALBERT EARL, b Madison, SDak, Apr 4, 31; m 52; c 2. BARLEY BREEDING & GENETICS. *Educ:* SDak State Univ, BS, 54, MS, 56, PhD(agron), 58. *Prof Exp:* From asst prof to assoc prof, 58-70, PROF AGRON, N DAK STATE UNIV, 70- *Concurrent Pos:* Consult, San Miguel Corp, 76- *Mem:* Am Soc Agron; Sigma Xi. *Res:* Developing of malting barley cultivars for North Dakota and adjacent areas; studies of barley genetics. *Mailing Add:* Dept Agron N Dak State Univ Fargo ND 58105

FOSTER, ALFRED FIELD, b Warren, Ohio, Dec 4, 15; m 40; c 2. PHYSICAL CHEMISTRY. *Educ:* Col of Wooster, BA, 38; Ohio State Univ, MA, 40, PhD, 50. *Prof Exp:* Process engr, US Rubber Co, NC, 42-43; asst prof physics, Davidson Col, 43-44; from asst prof to assoc prof chem, 46-60, actg dean, 68-69, assoc dean col arts & sci, 62-68, assoc dean grad sch, 69-74, PROF CHEM, UNIV TOLEDO, 60- *Concurrent Pos:* Res assoc, Ohio State

Res Found, 48-50; partic, Argonne Nat Lab Conf, 68, 70. *Mem:* AAAS; fel Am Inst Chemists; Am Chem Soc; Am Crystallog Asn; NY Acad Sci. *Res:* X-ray crystal structure; dipole moments of molecules in solutions; radiochemistry. *Mailing Add:* Dept of Chem Univ of Toledo Toledo OH 43606

FOSTER, ALFRED LEON, b New York, NY, July 13, 04; m; c 4. MATHEMATICS. *Educ:* Calif Inst Technol, BS, 26, MS, 27; Princeton Univ, PhD, 30. *Prof Exp:* Instr math, Valparaiso Univ, 27-28 & Princeton Univ, 30-31; int res fel, Univ Gottingen, 31-33; from instr to assoc prof, 33-50, PROF MATH, UNIV CALIF, BERKELEY, 50- *Concurrent Pos:* Vis prof, Inst Math, Univ Ferrara, 68. *Mem:* AAAS; Am Math Soc; Asn Symbolic Logic. *Res:* Abstract algebra; ring theory; universal algebras; structure theory and invariant theory; foundations. *Mailing Add:* Dept of Math Univ of Calif Berkeley CA 94720

FOSTER, ARTHUR R(OWE), b Peabody, Mass, Apr 22, 24; m 47; c 2. MECHANICAL ENGINEERING, NUCLEAR ENGINEERING. *Educ:* Tufts Univ, BS, 45; Yale Univ, MEng, 49. *Prof Exp:* Engr, Mat Develop Lab, Pratt & Whitney Div, United Aircraft Corp, 47-48; chmn dept, 61-75, PROF MECH ENG, NORTHEASTERN UNIV, 49- *Concurrent Pos:* Mem, Gen Elec Profs Conf, 55; Latin Am teaching fel, Escuela Politecnica Nacional, Quito, Ecuador, 75-76. *Honors & Awards:* Fulbright lectr solar energy, Colombia, 79; Centennial Medal, Am Soc Mech Engrs, 81. *Mem:* Am Soc Mech Engrs; Am Soc Eng Educ; Int Solar Eng Soc; Am Nuclear Soc. *Res:* Applied thermodynamics; nuclear engineering; solar engineering. *Mailing Add:* Dept of Mech Eng Northeastern Univ Boston MA 02115

FOSTER, BILLY GLEN, b Canton, Tex, Mar 6, 32; m 54; c 4. MICROBIOLOGY. *Educ:* NTex State Univ, BS, 55, MS, 62; Univ Iowa, PhD(prev med, environ health), 65. *Prof Exp:* Instr biol, NTex State Univ, 60-62; res assoc microbiol, Univ Iowa, 62-65; asst prof, 65-70, ASSOC PROF MICROBIOL, TEX A&M UNIV, 70- *Mem:* AAAS; Am Soc Microbiol; Am Acad Microbiol. *Res:* medical and diagnostic microbiology; epidemiology and serology of infectious disease; humoral and cell medicated immunity; regulation of humoral and cell medicated response; macrophage activation. *Mailing Add:* Dept of Biol Tex A&M Univ College Station TX 77843

FOSTER, BRUCE PARKS, b Mussoorie, India, June 27, 25; US citizen; m 47; c 3. EXPERIMENTAL NUCLEAR PHYSICS. *Educ:* Baldwin-Wallace Col, BS, 49; Yale Univ, MS, 51, PhD(physics), 54. *Prof Exp:* Asst prof, 53-56, ASSOC PROF PHYSICS, NORTH TEX STATE UNIV, 56- *Concurrent Pos:* Fulbright lectr, Peshawar, 60-61; lectr, Forman Christian Col, WPakistan, 61-63; mem vchancellors comt strengthening physics dept, WPakistan Eng Univ, 62-63. *Mem:* Am Phys Soc. *Res:* Investigation and analysis of gamma ray decay schemes in nuclear reactions including the development of computer programs for this purpose; gamma-ray spectroscopy; astronomy. *Mailing Add:* Dept of Physics NTex State Univ Denton TX 76203

FOSTER, C(HARLES) VERNON, b Manzanola, Colo, June 16, 21; m 45; c 3. HEAT TRANSFER. *Educ:* Univ Kans, BSChE, 47, MS, 48; Univ Del, PhD(chem eng), 53. *Prof Exp:* Asst instr math, Univ Kans, 42-43 & 46-47, asst chem eng, 47-48; res engr design methods, C F Braun & Co, Calif, 51-52; process engr process design, Ethyl Corp, La, 52-55; res engr petrochem, Continental Oil Co, 55-56, res group leader, 56-59; consult engr, H C Schutt, 59-60; tech dir, PASA, Petroquimica Arg, SA, 61-64; chief process engr, 64-66, mgr, Process Eng Dept, 66-76, GEN ENG ADV, ENG CTR, CONOCO INC, 76- *Concurrent Pos:* Chmn bd, Heat Transfer Res Inc, 74- *Mem:* Am Chem Soc; Am Inst Chem Engrs. *Res:* Distillation; physical properties; process development of petrochemicals. *Mailing Add:* Conoco Inc Drawer 1267 Ponca City OK 74601

FOSTER, CAXTON CROXFORD, b Ft Bragg, NC, Jan 21, 29; m 59; c 5. COMPUTER ARCHITECTURE. *Educ:* Mass Inst Technol, BS, 50; Univ Mich, MSE, 57, PhD(elec eng), 65. *Prof Exp:* Physicist, Tracer Lab, Inc, Boston, Mass, 51-52; engr, Technol Instrument Corp, Acton, Mich, 53-55; res, Mental Health Res Inst, Univ Mich, 55-64; engr, Goodyear Aerospace Corp, 64-65; dir comput ctr, 65-67, PROF COMPUT SCI, UNIV MASS, 67- *Concurrent Pos:* Vis lectr, Univ Edinburgh, Scotland, 67-68. *Mem:* Asn Comput Mach. *Res:* Design of computer hardware and software. *Mailing Add:* 368 Shays St Amherst MA 01002

FOSTER, CHARLES DAVID OWEN, b London, Ont, Oct 26, 38; m 60; c 2. PHYSIOLOGICAL CHEMISTRY. *Educ:* Western Ont Univ, BSc, 60, MSc, 62; Univ Wis, PhD(biochem), 67. *Prof Exp:* NIH fel biochem, Princeton Univ, 66-68; asst prof, Univ Ill, Urbana-Champaign, 68-72; asst res officer, 72-74, ASSOC RES OFFICER, NAT RES COUN CAN, 75- *Mem:* Sigma Xi. *Res:* Hormonal regulation of enzyme activity; regulation of blood flow in brown adipose tissue; physiology and biochemistry of nonshivering thermogenesis. *Mailing Add:* Biol Sci Div M54 Nat Res Coun Can Ottawa ON K1A 0R6 Can

FOSTER, CHARLES HENRY WHEELWRIGHT, b Boston, Mass, Mar 18, 27; m 53; c 3. NATURAL RESOURCES POLICY, FORESTRY. *Educ:* Harvard Col, BA, 51; Univ Mich, BS, 53, MS, 56; Johns Hopkins Univ, PhD(geog & environ eng), 69; Suffolk Univ, DPA, 71; Yale Univ, MA, 76. *Prof Exp:* Comnr, Mass Dept Natural Resources, 59-66; pres, Nature Conservancy, 66-67; chmn, New Eng Natural Resources Ctr, 69-71; secy, Mass Exec Off Environ Affairs, 71-75; prof environ policy, Univ Mass, 75-76; dean, Sch Forestry & Environ Studies, Yale Univ, 76-81. *Concurrent Pos:* Mem adv coun, Pub Land Law Rev Comn, 67-69; Bullard fel, Harvard Univ, 69-70; mem, Environ Adv Bd, Corps Engrs, 70-72, Task Force Land Use Planning, Coun State Govt, 72-73 & Adv Bd Natural Hazards, NSF, 73-74; US comnr, Int Comn NW Atlantic Fisheries, 73-75; sr staff mem natural resources, Arthur D Little, Inc, 75-76; mem & chmn, N Atlantic Region Adv Comn, Nat Park Serv, 75-77; chmn, Appalachian Nat Scenic Trail Adv Coun, Dept Interior, 75-; mem, Marine Fisheries Adv Comn, Dept Com, 77- *Mem:* Fel AAAS; Soc Am Foresters; Wildlife Soc; Ecol Soc Am; Soil Conservation Soc Am. *Res:* Public administration; environmental impact analysis; land use planning; environmental mediation. *Mailing Add:* 484 Charles River St Needham MA 02192

FOSTER, CHARLES HOWARD, b Greenville, Ky, Sept 8, 47; m 69; c 2. ORGANIC CHEMISTRY. *Educ:* Vanderbilt Univ, BA, 69; Mass Inst Technol, PhD(org chem), 73. *Prof Exp:* Res chemist, 73-75, SR RES CHEMIST, TENN EASTMAN CO, 75- *Mem:* Sigma Xi; Am Chem Soc. *Res:* New synthetic methods; synthesis of natural products; steroid chemistry. *Mailing Add:* Res Labs Bldg 150B Tenn Eastman Co Kingsport TN 37662

FOSTER, CHARLES THOMAS, JR, b Fremont, Ohio, Aug 30, 49; m 75. GEOLOGY, PETROLOGY. *Educ:* Univ Calif, Santa Barbara, BA, 71; Johns Hopkins Univ, MA, 74, PhD(geol), 75. *Prof Exp:* Actg asst prof geol, Univ Calif, Los Angeles, 75-77, res fel, 77; ASST PROF GEOL, UNIV IOWA, 78- *Mem:* Mineral Soc Am; Geol Soc Am; Geol Asn Can; Am Geophys Union. *Res:* Igneous and metamorphic petrology; diagenesis; aqueous geochemistry; irreversible thermodynamic processes in geology, geologic mapping, structural geology. *Mailing Add:* Dept of Geol Univ of Iowa Iowa City IA 52242

FOSTER, DANIEL W, b Marlin, Tex, Mar 4, 30; m 55; c 3. INTERNAL MEDICINE, METABOLISM. *Educ:* Tex Western Col, BA, 51; Univ Tex Southwest Med Sch Dallas, MD, 55. *Prof Exp:* Intern internal med, Parkland Mem Hosp, 55-56, asst resident, 56-58, chief resident, 58-59; fel biochem, Univ Tex Southwestern Med Sch, 59-60; investr, Nat Inst Arthritis & Metab Dis, 60-62; from asst prof to assoc prof, 62-69, PROF INTERNAL MED, UNIV TEX HEALTH SCI CTR DALLAS, 69- *Concurrent Pos:* Mem metab study sect, NIH, 68-70, chmn sect, 70-72; assoc ed, J Clin Invest, 72-77 & J Metab, Clin & Exp, 72-; sr attend physician, Parkland Mem Hosp; ed, J Diabetes, 78-; mem, Nat Diabetes Adv Bd, 81- *Mem:* Am Soc Biol Chemists; Am Soc Clin Invest; Am Diabetes Asn; Asn Am Physicians; Am Fedn Clin Res. *Res:* Endocrinology and metabolism; regulation of fatty acid synthesis and ketone body formation. *Mailing Add:* Dept of Internal Med Univ of Tex Health Sci Ctr Dallas TX 75235

FOSTER, DAVID BERNARD, b Marine City, Mich, May 28, 14; m 38; c 3. NEUROLOGY. *Educ:* Wayne State Univ, AB, 35; Univ Mich, MD, 38, MS, 41. *Prof Exp:* Instr neurol, Med Sch, Univ Mich, 41-44; dir div neurol & neurosurg & instr neurol, Sch Psychiat, Menninger Found, 47-67, sr physician, Div Neurol & Psychiat, Menninger Clin, 67-72; staff neurologist, 72-80, ACTG CHIEF NEUROL, VET ADMIN HOSP, TOPEKA, 81- *Concurrent Pos:* Consult, Topeka Vet Admin Hosp, 47-72, actg chief neurol serv, 67; consult, Topeka State Hosp, 47-; lectr, Med Sch, Univ Kans, 49- *Mem:* Am Neurol Asn; AMA; Am Acad Neurologists. *Res:* Clinical neurology and neuropathology. *Mailing Add:* Topeka Vet Admin Hosp 2200 Gage Blvd Topeka KS 66622

FOSTER, DONALD BARTLEY, b Jackson, Mich, Nov 2, 28; m 57; c 1. DEVELOPMENTAL BIOLOGY, PLANT MORPHOLOGY. *Educ:* Univ Mich, BS, 51, MS, 52; Cornell Univ, PhD(bot), 64. *Prof Exp:* Teacher pub sch, Mich, 51-57; asst prof bot, Ithaca Col, 61-67; assoc prof bot, 67-77, ASSOC PROF BIOL, ELMIRA COL, 77- *Mem:* AAAS; Bot Soc Am. *Res:* Growth and development in the fern genus Botrychium, especially in relation to spore germination, gametophyte and embryo growth processes and phylogenetic relationships; physiological relationship of symbiosis in the gametophytes; tissue culture techniques. *Mailing Add:* 424 W Church Elmira NY 14901

FOSTER, DONALD MYERS, b Mayersville, Miss, Mar 21, 38; m 64; c 2. BIOCHEMISTRY, BIOCHEMICAL PHARMACOLOGY. *Educ:* Delta State Univ, BSE, 61; Univ Houston, MS, 67, PhD(biol sci), 69. *Prof Exp:* Fel biomath, Univ Mich, Ann Arbor, 69-72; res assoc cation transport ATP-phosphatases, Vanderbilt Univ, 72-73; res chemist, Vet Admin Hosp, Minneapolis, 73-76; CHEMIST, O E TEAGUE VET CTR, 76-; ASSOC PROF PATH & BIOCHEM, MED SCH, TEX A&M UNIV, 80- *Concurrent Pos:* Asst prof lab med & path, Med Sch, Univ Minn, Minneapolis, 75-76. *Mem:* Am Chem Soc; Sigma Xi. *Res:* Membrane structure and function as related to actions of drugs and toxic agents; phosphoproteins and mechanisms of active cation transport; clinical chemistry. *Mailing Add:* Lab SVC Vet Admin Ctr Temple TX 76501

FOSTER, DOUGLAS LAYNE, b Brookings, SDak, Apr 15, 44. REPRODUCTIVE ENDOCRINOLOGY, PHYSIOLOGY. *Educ:* Univ Nebr, BS, 66; Univ Ill, PhD(animal sci), 70. *Prof Exp:* NIH fel child health & human develop, 71-72, asst prof, 72-80, ADJ ASST PROF, 72-, ASSOC PROF ANIMAL PHYSIOL, DEPT OBSTET & GYNEC, DIV BIOL SCI, UNIV MICH, ANN ARBOR, 80- *Concurrent Pos:* Fac res grant, 74-75; Nat Inst Child Health & Human Develop grants, 74-77, 75-77, 79-80, 80-84. *Mem:* Soc Study Reproduction; Endocrine Soc. *Res:* Physiology of reproduction; neuroendocrinology; developmental endocrinology; investigation of reproductive neuroendocrine maturation with emphasis on internal and external signals which control onset of puberty in the female; neuroendocrine control of adult ovulatory cycle and seasonality of reproduction. *Mailing Add:* Dept Obstet & Gynec Univ Mich Med Ctr Ann Arbor MI 48109

FOSTER, DUNCAN GRAHAM, JR, b Philadelphia, Pa, Sept 20, 29; m 53; c 4. NUCLEAR PHYSICS, NUCLEAR DATA EVALUATION. *Educ:* Swarthmore Col, 51; Cornell Univ, PhD(exp physics), 56. *Prof Exp:* Res assoc, Pac Northwest Lab, Battelle Mem Inst, 56-69; STAFF MEM, LOS ALAMOS NAT LAB, 69- *Concurrent Pos:* Instr, Ctr Grad Study, Univ Wash, 57-66. *Mem:* Am Phys Soc; Am Nuclear Soc. *Res:* Monoenergetic measurement of neutron age; evaluation of neutron cross sections; fast-neutron total cross sections; medium-energy spallation calculations; post-fission photon and neutron spectra; photon and neutron spectra from actinide decay; neutronic properties of "prompt" fission fragments. *Mailing Add:* MS-243 Los Alamos Nat Lab Box 1663 Los Alamos NM 87545

FOSTER, E(LTON) GORDON, b Milwaukee, Wis, Feb 4, 19; m 41; c 1. CHEMICAL ENGINEERING. *Educ:* Univ Wis, BS, 41, MS, 42, PhD(phys chem & chem eng), 44. *Prof Exp:* Asst phys chem, Univ Wis, 41-43; process engr, E I du Pont de Nemours & Co, 44-46, group leader process engr, 46-51;

asst prof chem eng, Univ Louisville, 51-52; engr, Shell Oil Co, 52-56, supvr, 56-66, mgr process develop dept, Indust Chem Div, Shell Chem Co, NY, 66-68, head, Process Design-Licensing Dept, Shell Develop Co, Calif, 68-70, mgr process eng-licensing dept, 70-74, sr staff res engr, 74-80, res assoc, 80-81, SR RES ASSOC, SHELL DEVELOP CO, SHELL OIL CO, 81- *Mem:* Am Chem Soc; Am Inst Chem Engrs. *Res:* Process evaluation and design of petrochemical processes. *Mailing Add:* Shell Develop Co 2034 Dryden Houston TX 77030

FOSTER, EDWARD STANIFORD, JR, b Port Deposit, Md, June 9, 13; m 36; c 4. APPLIED PHYSICS. *Educ:* Col of Wooster, BA, 35; Wash Univ (St Louis), MS, 37. *Prof Exp:* Field engr, Subterrex-Explor, Geophysicist, 37-39 & Halliburton Oil Well Cementing Co, 39-42; from asst prof to assoc prof, 46-58, PROF ENG PHYSICS UNIV TOLEDO, 58-, PROF PHYSICS, 74- *Concurrent Pos:* Consult, Brush Beryllium Co, 48-58 & Argonne Labs, 64- *Mem:* Am Phys Soc; Am Soc Eng Educ; Am Asn Physics Teachers. *Res:* Applied spectroscopy; peaceful uses of nuclear energy; applied meteorology; atmospheric stability; friction. *Mailing Add:* Dept of Eng Physics Univ of Toledo Toledo OH 43606

FOSTER, EDWIN MICHAEL, b Alba, Tex, Jan 1, 17; m 41; c 1. BACTERIOLOGY. *Educ:* NTex State Teachers Col, BA, 36, MA, 37; Univ Wis, PhD(bact), 40. *Prof Exp:* Instr bact, Univ Wis, 40-41 & Univ Tex, 41-42; from asst prof to assoc prof, 45-52, PROF BACT, UNIV WIS-MADISON, 52-, DIR, FOOD RES INST, 66- *Concurrent Pos:* Mem expert comt food hyg, WHO, 67-; mem, Nat Adv Food & Drug Comn, Food & Drug Admin, 72-76; mem, Food & Nutrit Bd, Nat Acad Sci-Nat Res Coun, 73-76. *Honors & Awards:* Nicholas Appert Award Medal, Inst Food Tech, 69. *Mem:* Am Soc Microbiol (secy, 57-61, pres, 69-70); Am Acad Microbiol (secy-treas, 62-65, pres, 66-67); Inst Food Tech. *Res:* Food borne disease; safety of food additives. *Mailing Add:* Food Res Inst Univ of Wis Madison WI 53706

FOSTER, ELLIS L(OUIS), b Louisville, Ky, Oct 2, 23; m 50; c 2. METALLURGICAL ENGINEERING. *Educ:* Univ Ky, BS, 50. *Prof Exp:* Prin metallurgist, Battelle Mem Inst, 50-56, asst div chief, 56-66, dept tech adv, 66-71, sr adv, 71-73, prog mgr, Thermal Protection System, 73-75; res staff, Inst for Defense Anal, 75-77, MGR, DEFENSE/SPACE SYST MAT REQUIREMENTS PROG OFF, BATTELLE COLUMBUS LABS, 77- *Mem:* Am Soc Metals; Am Vacuum Soc; Am Inst Aeronaut & Astronaut; Am Inst Mining & Metall Engrs. *Res:* Materials and processing research as it applies to reactive and refractory composite materials for use in nuclear, defense, aerospace, and industrial applications. *Mailing Add:* Battelle Columbus Labs 505 King Ave Columbus OH 43201

FOSTER, EUGENE A, b New York, NY, Apr 26, 27; m 52; c 3. PATHOLOGY. *Educ:* Washington Univ, AB, 47, MD, 51. *Prof Exp:* Intern, Salt Lake County Gen Hosp, 51-52; resident path, Peter Bent Brigham Hosp, Boston, 55-58; fel surg path, Barnes Hosp, St Louis, 58-59; from asst prof to assoc prof path, 59-71, prof, Sch Med, Univ Va, 71-76; PROF PATH, SCH MED, TUFTS UNIV, 76- *Concurrent Pos:* Teaching fel, Harvard Med Sch, 57-58; mem exec comt end results group, Nat Cancer Inst, 62-67, chmn, 65-67; Nat Inst Allergy & Infectious Dis res career develop award, 67-72; res worker, Sir William Dunn Sch Path, Univ Oxford, 67-68. *Mem:* Am Asn Pathologists. *Res:* Natural history and epidemiology of cancer; experimental urinary tract infection; pathogenesis of staphylococcal infections. *Mailing Add:* Sch Med Tufts Univ 136 Harrison Ave Boston MA 02111

FOSTER, EUGENE L(EWIS), b Clinton, Mass, Oct 9, 22; m 44; c 4. MECHANICAL ENGINEERING. *Educ:* Univ NH, BS, 44, MS, 51; Mass Inst Technol, MechE, 53, ScD, 54. *Prof Exp:* Proj res engr, Procter & Gamble Co, 46; instr mech eng, Univ NH, 47-49; asst prof, Mass Inst Technol, 50-56; pres, Foster-Miller Assocs, Inc, 56-73; PRES, UTD CORP, 76-, CHIEF EXEC OFFICER & CORP RES OFFICER, 80- *Concurrent Pos:* Instr mech, US Mil Acad, 52-56; chmn, Foster-Miller Assocs, Inc, 56- *Mem:* AAAS; Am Soc Eng Educ; Am Soc Mech Engrs; Am Soc Testing & Mat; NY Acad Sci. *Res:* Heat transfer; thermodynamics. *Mailing Add:* UTD Corp 8425 Frye Rd Alexandria VA 22304

FOSTER, GEORGE A, JR, b Stockton, Kans, Aug 31, 38; m 58; c 3. BIOCHEMISTRY, SCIENCE INFORMATION. *Educ:* Univ Colo, BA, 60; Univ Wis, MS, 62, PhD(biochem), 66. *Prof Exp:* Sr res biochemist, Gen Mills, Inc, 66-69; info scientist, 69-76, patent liaison specialist, 76-78, supvr stability & automation, 78-81, SUPVR PROD & PROJ LIT LIBR, MILES LABS, INC, 81- *Mem:* Am Chem Soc; AAAS. *Res:* Computerized data bases. *Mailing Add:* Miles Labs Inc PO Box 40 Elkhart IN 46515

FOSTER, GERALD LAWRENCE, b Colony, Kans, Dec 27, 27; m 48; c 4. ORGANIC CHEMISTRY. *Educ:* Univ Ottawa, Kans, BS, 50; Kans State Univ, MS, 52. *Prof Exp:* Chemist, Dowell Inc, Okla, 52-54, group leader, 54-58; asst lab dir, Dowell Div, Dow Chem Co, 58-64, sr titled specialist, 64-68; mgr foreign opers, Rainey Corp, 68-69; Europ mkt mgr, T D Williamson, Inc, 69-72, vpres, Williamson Int, 72-5, pres, Williamson Int, 75-78, VPRES, T D WILLIAMSON, INC, 78- *Res:* Inhibition of acid corrosion of ferrous metals; emulsion technology; water desalination. *Mailing Add:* T D Williamson Inc Box 2299 Tulsa OK 74101

FOSTER, GIRAUD VERNAM, b New York, NY, Jan 13, 28; m 52; c 3. ENDOCRINOLOGY. *Educ:* Trinity Col, BS, 52; Univ Md, MD, 56; Univ London, PhD(biochem), 66. *Prof Exp:* Intern, Univ Md Hosp, Baltimore, 56-57, from jr asst resident to sr asst resident med, 57-60; fel physiol chem, Sch Med, Johns Hopkins Univ, 60-62; personal physician to His Majesty Imam Ahmed of Yemen, 62; post med adv to Dept State, Tiaz, Yemen, 62-63; res asst, Dept Med, Royal Postgrad Med Sch, London, 63-64, hon asst lectr, Dept Chem Path, 64-66; hon clin asst med, Hammersmith & St Mark's Hosp, London, 65-68; vis prof med, Univ Ala, Birmingham, 68-72; ASSOC PROF GYNEC, OBSTET, PHYSIOL & MED, SCH MED, JOHNS HOPKINS UNIV, 72- *Concurrent Pos:* Am Heart Asn grants-in-aid, 66-73 & 74-76; Med Res Coun grants, 68-70 & 69-71; NIH grants-in-aid, 72-76; sr lectr, Dept Chem Path, Wellcome Unit Endocrinol & hon sr lectr chem path, Royal Postgrad Med Sch, London, 70- *Mem:* Soc Endocrinol; Biochem Soc; Endocrine Soc; Am Physiol Soc; Am Soc Biol Chemists. *Res:* Hormonal regulation of calcium metabolism; prolactin secretion. *Mailing Add:* Dept Obstet & Gynec Johns Hopkins Hosp Baltimore MD 21205

FOSTER, HAROLD DOUGLAS, b Tunstall, Eng, Jan 9, 43; m 64. GEOMORPHOLOGY, HYDROLOGY. *Educ:* Univ London, BSc, 64, PhD(geog), 67. *Prof Exp:* From instr to asst prof, 67-72, assoc prof, 72-81, PROF GEOG, UNIV VICTORIA, BC, 81- *Concurrent Pos:* Consult, Ottawa Dept Energy, Mines & Resources, UN & Dept Fisheries & Environ, Prov Govt Ont & BC, 68-69; ed, Western Geog Series, 68- *Honors & Awards:* Can Nat Res Coun Award, 67 & 68. *Mem:* Brit Geog Asn; NY Acad Sci; Can Asn Geog; Am Geog Soc; Solar Energy Soc Can. *Res:* Renewable energy resources; natural hazards; water resources; social significance of geomorphology. *Mailing Add:* Dept of Geog Univ of Victoria Victoria Can

FOSTER, HAROLD MARVIN, b Passaic, NJ, Aug 2, 28; m 54; c 4. INDUSTRIAL CHEMISTRY. *Educ:* Lehigh Univ, BS, 50; Univ Ill, PhD(chem), 53. *Prof Exp:* Res chemist, Am Cyanamid Co, 53-61; sr res chemist & proj leader, Mobil Chem Co, 61-66; res group leader, Colors & Chem Dept, Sherwin-Williams Co, Chicago, 66-70, dir pigments lab, Sherwin-Williams Chem Div, 70-72, sr res assoc, 72-73, com develop specialist, Sherwin-Williams Co, Toledo, 73-78; ASST TECH DIR, PIGMENTS DIV, BORDEN CHEM INC, CINCINNATI, 78- CO, TOLEDO, 73- *Mem:* Am Chem Soc. *Res:* Organic synthesis; process research; agricultural chemicals. *Mailing Add:* 10659 Merrick Lane Cincinnati OH 45242

FOSTER, HELEN LAURA, b Adrian, Mich, Dec 15, 19. GEOLOGY. *Educ:* Univ Mich, BS, 41, MS, 43, PhD(geol), 46. *Prof Exp:* Asst geol, Univ Mich, 42-44, instr, Wellesley Col, 46-48; geologist, Mil Geol Br, Tokyo, 48-55, chief Ishigaki field party, 55-57 & DC 57-65, GEOLOGIST, ALASKAN GEOL BR, US GEOL SURV, CALIF, 65- *Concurrent Pos:* Geologist, US Geol Surv, Mich, 43-45; instr, Rocky Mt Field Sta, Univ Mich, 47. *Mem:* AAAS; Fel Geol Soc Am; Am Geophys Union; Arctic Inst; Am Asn Petrol Geologists. *Res:* Volcanoes of Japan; geology of Ryukyu Islands; Yukon-Tanana Upland, Alaska. *Mailing Add:* Alaskan Geol Br US Geol Surv 345 Middlefield Rd Menlo Park CA 94025

FOSTER, HENRY D(ORROH), b Timmonsville, SC, Aug 14, 12; m 42; c 6. CHEMICAL ENGINEERING. *Educ:* Univ SC, BS, 33; Univ Ill, MS, 34, PhD(chem eng), 37. *Prof Exp:* Res chem engr, E I du Pont de Nemours & Co, 37-45, develop chem engr, 45-46, res supvr, 46-47, plant process supvr, Ohio & NJ, 47-48, asst tech supt, NJ & Tex, 48, tech supt, 48-51, asst process mgr, Grasselli Chem Dept, 51-55, process mgr, 55-61, asst mgr plants tech sect, Indust & Biochems Dept, 61-72; RETIRED. *Mem:* Am Chem Soc; Am Inst Chem Engrs. *Res:* Development of chemical manufacturing processes for plastics; insecticides, herbicides, pharmaceuticals, and heavy chemicals; catalytic oxidation in the vapor phase. *Mailing Add:* 1000 Wynnewood Ave Wilmington DE 19803

FOSTER, HENRY LOUIS, b Boston, Mass, Apr 6, 25; m 48; c 3. VETERINARY MEDICINE. *Educ:* Middlesex Col, DVM, 46; dipl, Am Col Lab Animal Med, 61. *Prof Exp:* Consult vet, UNRRA, 46-47; pres dir gen, Soc Des Elevages Charles River France, SA, 64-76, PRES, CHARLES RIVER BREEDING LABS, INC, 47-, CANADA, 70-, ITALY, 71-, CHMN, UK LTD, 70- *Concurrent Pos:* Chmn husb transportation comt, Inst Lab Animal Resources Div, Nat Acad Sci-Nat Res Coun, 58-59, mem prod & stand comts, 58-59, gnotobiotics comt, 59, transportation comt, 60, mem adv coun, 59-64, mem exec comt, 63-64, vpres, Lab Animal Breeders Asn, 58-60, pres, 61-62, secy-treas, 64; mem comt nomenclature randombred animals subcomt gnotobiotes rabbit & rodent procurement stand & stand for qual lab animal feed, Inst Lab Animal Resources, 67; vpres & chmn exec comt, Century Bank & Trust Co, Somerville, Mass, 69-; trustee, Beaver Country Day Sch, 73-75; trustee & fel, Brandeis Univ & mem bd overseers, Rosenstiel Basic Med Sci Res Ctr, 73- *Mem:* Am Vet Med Asn; Am Inst Biol Sci; NY Acad Sci; Am Asn Lab Animal Sci; Am Col Lab Animal Med. *Res:* Commercial production of caesarean-originated, barrier-sustained and gnotobiotic rats, mice, rabbits, hamsters, guinea pigs and non-human primates; production methods; elimination of specific diseases; environmental control. *Mailing Add:* Charles River Breeding Labs Inc 251 Ballardvale St North Wilmington MA 01887

FOSTER, HENRY WENDELL, b Pine Bluff, Ark, Sept 8, 33; m 60; c 2. OBSTETRICS & GYNECOLOGY. *Educ:* Morehouse Col, BS, 54; Univ Ark, MD, 58; Am Bd Obstet & Gynec, dipl. *Prof Exp:* Intern, Receiving Hosp, Detroit, Mich, 58-59; resident, Malden Hosp, Mass, 61-62 & Hubbard Hosp, Nashville, Tenn, 62-65; asst prof, 67-77, PROF OBSTET & GYNEC & CHMN DEPT, MEHARRY MED COL, 77-; CHIEF OBSTET & GYNEC, JOHN A ANDREW MEM HOSP, 65- *Concurrent Pos:* Attend, Macon County Hosp & consult staff, Vet Admin Hosp, Tuskegee, Ala; dir, Maternity & Infant Care Proj 556, John A Andrew Mem Hosp, 70-80; mem, Bd Dirs, Planned Parenthood Fedn Am, 75-; examiner, Am Bd Obstet & Gynec, 76-; mem, Ethics Adv Bd, 77- *Mem:* Inst of Med of Nat Acad Sci; fel Am Col Obstet & Gynec; AMA; Nat Med Asn. *Mailing Add:* Dept of Obstet & Gynec 1005 18th Ave N Nashville TN 37208

FOSTER, IRVING GORDON, b Lynn, Mass, July 15, 12; m 37; c 3. MECHANICS. *Educ:* Va Mil Inst, BS, 35; Univ Wis, PhM, 37; Univ Va, PhD(physics), 48. *Prof Exp:* Res assoc, Weshburn Observ, Univ Wis, 36-37; from instr to prof physics, Va Mil Inst, 37-59; chmn div math & nat sci, Fla Presby Col, 60-73, prof, 60-78, PROF EMER PHYSICS, ECKERD COL, 78- *Concurrent Pos:* Fulbright lectr, Vidyodaya Univ Ceylon; consult, Honeywell, Inc. *Mem:* Am Phys Soc; Am Asn Physics Teachers. *Res:* Theory and design of mechanical devices; coherent radiation. *Mailing Add:* Col of Nat Sci Eckerd Col PO Box 12560 St Petersburg FL 33733

FOSTER, J EARL, b New Albany, Ind, Feb 21, 29; m 55; c 4. MECHANICAL ENGINEERING. *Educ:* US Merchant Marine Acad, BS, 50; Univ Iowa, MS, 55, PhD(mech eng), 58. *Prof Exp:* Engr, Collins Radio Co, Iowa, 57-61; prof mech eng, Univ Wyo, 61-68; prof mech, Univ Mo-Rolla, 68-77; LAB MGR, MOTOROLA COMMUN & ELECTRONICS, 77- *Mem:* Am Soc Mech Engrs; Am Soc Eng Educ. *Res:* Vibrations; dynamics. *Mailing Add:* 4289 Juliet Dr Elgin IL 60120

FOSTER, JAMES HENDERSON, b Chicago, Ill, Feb 21, 46. MATHEMATICS. *Educ:* Northwestern Univ, BA, 68; Univ Southern Calif, PhD(math), 76. *Prof Exp:* Mem tech staff eng, Autonetics Div, Rockwell Int, Inc, 68-70; asst prof math, Univ Santa Clara, 76-80; RES SCIENTIST, LOCKHEED MISSILES & SPACE CO, 80- *Concurrent Pos:* Instr, Univ Calif, Santa Barbara, 76. *Mem:* Am Math Soc; Soc Indust & Appl Math. *Res:* Optimal control theory and differential equations. *Mailing Add:* 243 B Higdon St Mt View CA 94041

FOSTER, JAMES HENRY, b New Haven, Conn, June 24, 30; m 55; c 3. SURGERY. *Educ:* Haverford Col, AB, 50; Columbia Univ, MD, 54. *Prof Exp:* Intern surg, Barnes Hosp, St Louis, Mo, 54-55; asst surg resident, Portland Vet Hosp, Ore, 57-59; asst, Med Sch, Univ Ore, 59-60; chief resident combined serv, Portland Vet Hosp, 60-61, asst chief surg serv, 61-66; from instr to asst prof surg, Med Sch, Univ Ore, 61-65; dir surg serv, Hartford Hosp, 66-78; PROF SURG, SCH MED, UNIV CONN, 73-, CHMN DEPT, 80- *Concurrent Pos:* Consult, Rocky Hill Vet Hosp & Newington Childrens Hosp, 66-, Manchester Mem Hosp, 67- & Norwalk Hosp, 74-; assoc prof surg, Sch Med, Univ Conn, 68-73; examr, Am Bd Surg, 74-; dir, Am Bd Surg. *Mem:* Soc Surg Alimentary Tract; Am Gastroenterol Asn; Am Col Surg; Am Surg Asn. *Mailing Add:* Dept of Surg Univ of Conn Sch of Med Farmington CT 06033

FOSTER, JOHN EDWARD, b Lesterville, Mo, May 22, 40; m 63; c 1. ENTOMOLOGY, PLANT BREEDING. *Educ:* Cent Methodist Col, BA, 64; Univ Mo, MS, 66; Purdue Univ, PhD(entom), 70. *Prof Exp:* Res entom, Agr Res Serv, USDA, 70-76, ASST PROF, AGR EXP STA, PURDUE UNIV, 76- *Concurrent Pos:* Asst prof, Purdue Univ, 70- *Mem:* Entom Soc Am; Sigma Xi. *Res:* Development of insect resistant plant varieties; interrelationship between host plant and insect biotypes; genetics of plant resistance and insect virulence; population management by genetic manipulation. *Mailing Add:* Rm 9 Agr Admin Bldg Purdue Univ West Lafayette IN 47907

FOSTER, JOHN HOSKINS, b Georgetown, Tex, Dec 19, 21; m 45; c 3. SURGERY. *Educ:* Univ Tex, AB, 48; Johns Hopkins Univ, MD, 52. *Prof Exp:* Asst surg, Sch Med, Vanderbilt Univ, 53-57; asst, Univ Lund, 58-59; from asst prof to assoc prof, 60-67, dir, Surg Res Light Lab, 63-69, PROF SURG, SCH MED, VANDERBILT UNIV, 67- *Concurrent Pos:* Surg res fel, Sch Med, Vanderbilt Univ, 54; Am Col Surg J S Kemper Found res scholar, 59-62; surg consult, Thayer Vet Admin Hosp, 59-; attend surgeon, Nashville Gen Hosp, 60-; dir, Specialized Ctr Res in Hypertension; assoc dir, Clin Res Ctr, Vanderbilt Univ Hosp; mem, Inter-Agency Comn Heart Dis, Peripheral Vascular Dis Comt. *Mem:* Int Cardiovasc Soc (pres, 73-); Am Asn Thoracic Surg; Am Col Surgeons; AMA; Am Surg Asn. *Res:* Vascular surgery. *Mailing Add:* Dept of Surg Vanderbilt Univ Sch of Med Nashville TN 37240

FOSTER, JOHN MCGAW, b Philadelphia, Pa, Apr 22, 28; m 51; c 2. BIOCHEMISTRY. *Educ:* Swarthmore Col, BA, 50; Harvard Univ, MA, 53, PhD(biochem), 54. *Prof Exp:* Res assoc biol, Mass Inst Technol, 54-56; asst prof biochem, Sch Med, Boston Univ, 58-67; asst prog dir, Sci Curric Improv Prog, NSF, 67-68, assoc prog dir, 68-69; assoc prof, 69-72, actg dean, Sch Nat Sci, 72-73, PROF BIOL, HAMPSHIRE COL, 72- *Concurrent Pos:* Chief clin chem sect, 406 Med Gen Lab, Japan, 56-57; asst chief, Chem Dept Res & Develop Unit, Fitzsimons Army Hosp, 58; adj prof, Univ Mass, 74- *Mem:* AAAS; Am Inst Biol Sci. *Res:* Energy metabolism of blood cells; biochemical control mechanisms; photosynthetic phosphorylation in green bacteria; nutrient cycling in coniferous forest canopy. *Mailing Add:* Sch of Nat Sci & Math Hampshire Col Amherst MA 01002

FOSTER, JOHN ROBERT, b Washington, DC, Apr 6, 47; m 69; c 2. MARINE BIOLOGY, FISHERIES BIOLOGY. *Educ:* Univ Md, BSc, 69; Univ Toronto, MSc, 71, PhD(behav ecol), 80. *Prof Exp:* Lab technician behav ecol, Dept Zool, Univ Md, 66-69; dir, Univ Toronto, 69-75; environ consult fisheries, Biol Dept, James F MacLaren Ltd, 74-80; environ consult environ protection, Ontario Hydro Ltd, 78-80, fisheries biologist, Res Div, 80-81; ED & RES COORDR MARINE BIOL, HUNTSMAN MARINE LAB, 81- *Mem:* Animal Behav Soc; Ecol Soc Am; Nat Geog Soc. *Res:* Studies of predator-prey relations of moon snails and grass pickered; reproductive behavior in sticklebacks; factors influencing fish entrapment; impringement and entrainment at power plants; stream surveys and the life history of hag fish. *Mailing Add:* Huntsman Marine Lab St Andrews NB E0G 2X0 Can

FOSTER, JOYCE GERALDINE, b Farmville, Va, Oct 10, 51. PLANT METABOLISM, PHOTOSYNTHESIS. *Educ:* Longwood Col, BS, 74; Va Tech, MS, 76, PhD(biochem), 79. *Prof Exp:* Res assoc, Dept Biochem & Nutrit, Va Tech Inst, 79; proj assoc, Dept Hort, Univ Wis, Madison, 80; res assoc, Dept Bot, Wash State Univ, 81; RES BIOCHEMIST, APPALACHIAN SOIL & WATER CONSERV RES LAB, US DEPT AGR, 82- *Concurrent Pos:* Grad teach asst, Dept Biochem & Nutrit, Va Tech, 78. *Mem:* Am Chem Soc; Am Soc Plant Physiologists; Japanese Soc Plant Physiologists; Australian Soc Plant Physiologists; AAAS. *Res:* Mechanisms, enzymology, and regulation of carbon, oxygen, and amino acid metabolism in carbon 3, carbon 4 and crassulacean acid metabolism plants; composition and transport properties of chloroplast envelope membranes; plant stress physiology and biochemistry. *Mailing Add:* USDA Appalachian Lab Airport Rd PO Box 867 Beckley WV 25801

FOSTER, KEN WOOD, b Trenton, NJ, Apr 12, 50; m 72; c 1. CROP GENETICS, BIOMETRY. *Educ:* Colo State Univ, BS, 72; Univ Calif, Davis, MS, 74, PhD(genetics). 76. *Prof Exp:* asst geneticist crops, Univ Calif, Riverside, 76-80, ASST GENETICIST CROPS, UNIV CALIF, DAVIS, 80- *Mem:* Crop Sci Soc Am; Am Soc Agron; Am Soc Plant Physiologists; Genetics Soc Am. *Res:* Improvement of selection methods for quantitative characters. *Mailing Add:* Dept Agron & Range Sci Univ of Calif Davis CA 95616

FOSTER, KENNETH WILLIAM, b Victoria, BC, Jan 8, 44; m 69; c 1. SENSORY PHYSIOLOGY. *Educ:* Univ Victoria, BSc Hons, 65; Calif Inst Technol, PhD(biophysics), 72. *Prof Exp:* Res fel, Biol Div, Calif Inst Technol, 72; res assoc, Dept Molecular, Cellular & Develop Biol, Univ Colo, 72-79; ASST PROF, MT SINAI SCH MED, 80- *Concurrent Pos:* Lectr biophysics, Dept Molecular, Cellular & Develop Biol, Univ Colo, 79. *Mem:* Biophys Soc; Am Soc Photobiologists; NY Acad Sci; AAAS. *Res:* Biophysical, biochemical and genetic analysis of primitive photoreceptor systems, primarily using as models the phototaxis systems of alga, Chlamydomonas; bacterium, Halobacterium and the fungus, Phycomyces; biophysical analysis and systems design of membrane receptor systems. *Mailing Add:* Pharmacol Dept Mt Sinai Med Ctr 1 Gustave L Levy Pl New York NY 10029

FOSTER, KENNITH EARL, b Lamesa, Tex, Jan 20, 45; m 67; c 2. ARID LANDS ECOLOGY, AGRICULTURAL ENGINEERING. *Educ:* Tex Tech Univ, BS, 67; Univ Ariz, MS, 69, PhD(watershed mgt), 72. *Prof Exp:* Res asst agr eng, 67-69, res assoc watershed mgt, 70-71, asst dir, 71-76, ASSOC DIR OFF ARID LANDS STUDIES, UNIV ARIZ, 76-, ASST PROF, 80- *Mem:* AAAS; Int Solar Energy Soc; Inst Environ Sci. *Res:* Possible uses of arid land adapted vegetation; natural resource management using remote sensing. *Mailing Add:* Off of Arid Lands Studies 845 N Park Ave Tucson AZ 85721

FOSTER, KENT ELLSWORTH, b Evergreen Park, Ill, Nov 30, 43; m 71; c 2. MATHEMATICAL ANALYSIS. *Educ:* St Lawrence Univ, NY, BS, 66; Southern Ill Univ, Carbondale, MS, 71, PhD(math), 75. *Prof Exp:* Asst prof math, Mt Allison Univ, 75-78; asst prof math, Emory Univ, 78-79; ASST PROF COMPUT SCI, WINTHROP COL, 79- *Mem:* Am Math Soc; Sigma Xi. *Res:* Oscillation properties of ordinary differential equations; statistical sampling techniques and simulation. *Mailing Add:* Sch Business Winthrop Col Rock Hill SC 29733

FOSTER, LEIGH CURTIS, b Montreal, Que, Aug 24, 25; US citizen; m 48; c 2. SPECTROSCOPY, RESEARCH ADMINISTRATION. *Educ:* McGill Univ, BSc, 50, PhD, 56. *Prof Exp:* Res physicist, Santa Barbara Res Ctr, 50-52 & Calif Res & Develop Co, 52-54; res physicist, Zenith Radio Res Corp, Menlo Park, 56-58, dir res, 58-69, vpres, 60-69, dir, exec vpres & gen mgr, 69-72; vpres & gen mgr, Appl Technol Div ITEK, 72-74; VPRES & CORP DIR ENG, MOTOROLA WORLDQUARTERS, 74- *Honors & Awards:* Bur Ord Develop Award, 45. *Mem:* Inst Elec & Electronics Eng. *Res:* Low noise microwave tubes; ultrasonics; infrared; electron beam devices; laser communications; video recording techniques; coordinate research and development throughout the corporation. *Mailing Add:* RR 2 Crawling Stone Rd Barrington Hills IL 60010

FOSTER, LORRAINE L, b Los Angeles, Calif, Dec 25, 38; m 59; c 3. MATHEMATICS. *Educ:* Occidental Col, BA, 60; Calif Inst Technol, PhD(math), 64. *Prof Exp:* From asst prof to assoc prof, PROF MATH, CALIF STATE UNIV, NORTHRIDGE, 74- *Mem:* Am Math Soc; Math Asn Am; Sigma Xi; Asn Women Math. *Res:* Elementary and algebraic number theory; matrix theories. *Mailing Add:* Dept Math Calif State Univ Northridge CA 91324

FOSTER, M GLENYS, b Cwm Penmachno, Wales; Can citizen. MASS SPECTROMETRY, CHROMATOGRAPHY. *Educ:* Univ London, Eng, BSc, 68; Univ Wales, MSc, 73. *Prof Exp:* Biochemist, Wellsley Hosp, 74-78; CHIEF, MASS SPECTROMETRY SERV, LAB SERV BR, MINISTRY ENVIRON, 81- *Mem:* Am Soc Mass Spectrometry. *Res:* Analytical methodology for the characterization of environmental samples; techniques used include gas chromatography-mass spectrometry with eletron impact and chemical ionisation modes detecting both positive and negative ions; comparitive studies with liquid chromatography-mass spectrometry. *Mailing Add:* Lab Serv Br Ministry Environ PO Box 213 Rexdale ON M9W 5L1 Can

FOSTER, MANUS R, b Canyon, Tex, Mar 10, 27; m 52; c 3. APPLIED MATHEMATICS, GEOPHYSICS. *Educ:* Univ Kans, BS, 48, PhD(math physics), 52. *Prof Exp:* Physicist, Naval Res Lab, 48; asst, Univ Kans, 49-50; sr res technologist, Magnolia Petrol Co, 52-59; from res assoc to sr res assoc, Socony Mobil Oil Co Inc, 59-69, SR SCIENTIST, MOBIL RES & DEVELOP CORP, 69- *Concurrent Pos:* Vis assoc prof, Southern Methodist Univ, 67-70; ed, Soc Explor Geophys, 76-77. *Mem:* Soc Indust & Appl Math; Soc Explor Geophys. *Res:* Geophysical data processing; applied statistics; statistical communication theory. *Mailing Add:* Mobil Res & Develop Corp Field Res Lab Po Box 900 Dallas TX 75221

FOSTER, MARGARET C, b Mar 24, 35. BIOPHYSICS. *Educ:* Univ Richmond, BS, 57; Univ Wis, MS, 60, PhD, 65. *Prof Exp:* Researcher, Europ Orgn Nuclear Res, Geneva, 65-67 & Nuclear Physics Res Lab, Univ Liverpool, Eng, 67-68; asst prof physics, State Univ NY Stony Brook, 68-72, lectr physiol & biophys, 72-73; NIH spec res fel, 73-75, ASST RES BIOLOGIST, UNIV CALIF, SAN DIEGO, 75- *Concurrent Pos:* Spec res fel, NIH, 72; acad career develop award, Nat Eye Inst, 75. *Mem:* Am Phys Soc; Am Asn Physics Teachers; Biophys Soc; AAAS. *Res:* Biophysical studies of membranes from vertebrate and invertebrate photoreceptors. *Mailing Add:* Rm 105 Bldg 2 NIH Bethesda MD 20205

FOSTER, MERCEDES S, ornithology, see previous edition

FOSTER, MICHAEL RALPH, b Indianapolis, Ind, Jan 12, 43; m 66; c 1. FLUID DYNAMICS, AERODYNAMICS. *Educ:* Mass Inst Technol, BS, 65, MS, 66; Calif Inst Technol, PhD(aeronaut eng), 69. *Prof Exp:* Instr math, Mass Inst Technol, 69-70; asst prof, 70-80, ASSOC PROF AERONAUT & ASTRONAUT ENG, OHIO STATE UNIV, 80- *Mem:* Am Phys Soc. *Res:* Theoretical fluid dynamics, especially aspects of geophysical fluid dynamics, rotating and/or stratified fluids, singular perturbation theory. *Mailing Add:* Dept of Aeronaut & Astronaut Eng 2036 Neil Ave Mall Columbus OH 43210

FOSTER, MICHAEL SIMMLER, b Los Angeles, Calif, Sept 4, 42; m 65; c 1. MARINE BIOLOGY, PHYCOLOGY. *Educ:* Stanford Univ, BS, 64, MA, 65; Univ Calif, Santa Barbara, PhD(biol), 72. *Prof Exp:* Res assoc marine bot, Marine Sci Inst, Univ Calif, Santa Barbara, 71-72; asst prof biol sci, Calif State Univ, Hayward, 72-76; ASSOC PROF MARINE SCI, MOSS LANDING MARINE LABS, 76- *Concurrent Pos:* Consult oil pollution effects on marine pop, Off Atty Gen, State of Calif, 74. *Mem:* AAAS; Phycol Soc Am; Ecol Soc Am; Int Phycol Soc; Brit Phycol Soc. *Res:* Population and community ecology of marine macroalgae and the effects of oil pollution on marine organisms. *Mailing Add:* Moss Landing Marine Labs PO Box 223 Moss Landing CA 95039

FOSTER, MORRIS, immunogenetics, oncology, deceased

FOSTER, NEAL ROBERT, b Nyack, NY, Aug 13, 37; m 80. BEHAVIOR-ETHOLOGY, ANIMAL PHYSIOLOGY. *Educ:* Cornell Univ, BA, 59, MS, 61, PhD, 67. *Prof Exp:* Teaching asst zool, Cornell Univ, 58-59, curatorial asst fish collection, 59-60, asst vertebrate zool, 60-65; asst cur, Dept Limnol, Acad Natural Sci, Philadelphia, 65-76; PROJ LEADER PHYSIOL & BEHAV, GREAT LAKES FISHERY LAB, US FISH & WILDLIFE SERV, 77- *Mem:* Am Fisheries Soc; World Maricult Soc; Am Soc Ichthyol & Herpetol; AAAS; Am Inst Fish Res Biologists. *Res:* Bionomic ichthyology; systematics of fishes; comparative ethology, ecology, morphology and evolution of fishes; aquaculture; significance of behavioral phenomena in fish culture and fish management; fish pheromones and olfaction; Great Lakes fish ecology. *Mailing Add:* US Fish & Wildlife Serv 1451 Green Rd Ann Arbor MI 48105

FOSTER, NEIL WILLIAM, b Guelph, Ont, Nov 7, 45; m 69; c 3. SOIL SCIENCE, FORESTRY. *Educ:* Univ Toronto, BScF, 68; Univ Wash, MSc, 71; Univ Guelph, PhD, 79. *Prof Exp:* forestry officer res, 68-79, RES SCIENTIST, CAN FORESTRY SERV, ENVIRON CAN, 80- *Mem:* Soil Sci Soc Am. *Res:* Soil-plant relationships, including the biogeochemical cycling of nutrients especially nitrogen in forest ecosystems, decomposition of plant materials in forest soils in relation to nutrient availability and biological activity. *Mailing Add:* Great Lakes Forest Res Ctr PO Box 490 Sault Ste Marie Can

FOSTER, NORMAN FRANCIS, b Bristol, Eng, Nov 6, 30; m 55; c 2. SEMICONDUCTOR TECHNOLOGY. *Educ:* Bristol Univ, BS, 54, PhD(phys chem), 57. *Prof Exp:* Fel heterogeneous catalysis, Nat Res Coun Can, 57-59; mem tech staff ultrasonics, 60-67, supvr, 67-72, head continuing educ dept, 72-76, HEAD PHOTOMASK & PATTERN GENERATION DEPT, BELL LABS, 76- *Mem:* Inst Elec & Electronics Eng; Am Inst Physics. *Res:* Ultrasonics, mainly in frequency range above 100 megacycles; piezoelectric semiconductors, particularly cadmium sulphide and other II-VI compounds; mechanical filters, mainly 60 to 600 hz; electron beam integrated circuit mask technology. *Mailing Add:* Bell Labs 555 Union Blvd Allentown PA 18103

FOSTER, NORMAN GEORGE, b Chicago, Ill, Dec 23, 19; m 44; c 5. PHYSICAL CHEMISTRY, MASS SPECTROMETRY. *Educ:* Univ Chicago, BS, 42; Univ Ark, MS, 54, PhD(phys chem), 55. *Prof Exp:* Control chemist, Sinclair Ref Co, Ind, 42; anal chemist, Dearborn Chem Co, Ill, 43; res chemist, Whiting Res Labs, Standard Oil Co, Ind, 46-51; asst, Univ Ark, 51-55; res chemist, Cities Serv Res & Develop Co, Okla, 55-57; phys chemist, Bartlesville Petrol Res Ctr, US Bur Mines, 57-65, proj leader, 63; ASSOC PROF CHEM, TEX WOMAN'S UNIV, 65- *Mem:* Fel AAAS; Am Chem Soc; Am Soc Mass Spectrometry; NY Acad Sci; Fel Am Inst Chem. *Res:* Mass spectrometric fragmentations of organo-sulfur compounds, present in petroleum; fragmentation mechanism studies by utilization of isotopically labeled molecules; characterization of complex mixtures by means of mass spectrometry; structure elucidation utilizing mass spectrometry, nuclear magnetic resonance and infrared. *Mailing Add:* Dept of Chem Tex Woman's Univ Box 23973 Denton TX 76204

FOSTER, NORMAN HOLLAND, b Iowa City, Iowa, Oct 2, 34; m 56; c 2. GEOLOGY. *Educ:* Univ Iowa, BA, 57, MS, 60; Univ Kans, PhD(geol), 63. *Prof Exp:* From intermediate geologist to geol specialist & explor team supvr oil & gas, Sinclair Oil Corp & Atlantic Richfield Co, 62-69; from dist geologist to vpres geol explor, Trend Explor Ltd, 69-74; vpres geol explor, Filon Explor Corp, 74-79, mem bd dirs, 77-79; INDEPENDENT GEOLOGIST, 79- *Concurrent Pos:* Distinguished lectr, Am Asn Petrol Geologists, 76-77. *Honors & Awards:* A I Levorsen Award, Am Asn Petrol Geologists, 81. *Mem:* Am Asn Petrol Geologists; fel Geol Soc Am; Soc Econ Paleontologists & Mineralogists; Am Inst Prof Geologists; Soc Independent Prof Earth Scientists. *Res:* Oil and gas exploration in Indonesia and in the Rocky Mountain region and other areas of the United States; use of remote sensing and photogeomorphology in oil, gas and mineral exploration. *Mailing Add:* Filon Explor Corp 1700 Broadway Suite 2216 Denver CO 80202

FOSTER, PERRY ALANSON, JR, b Manchester, NH, May 18, 25; m 47; c 5. PHYSICAL CHEMISTRY. *Educ:* St Anselm's Col, BA, 50; Ga Inst Technol, MS, 55. *Prof Exp:* Asst chem, Ga Inst Technol, 50-52, eng exp sta, 52-55; res chemist, 55-67, sr scientist, 67-76, STAFF SCIENTIST, ALCOA LABS, ALUMINUM CO AM, 76- *Concurrent Pos:* Adj prof, Va Polytech Inst & State Univ, 75-78. *Mem:* Res Soc Am. *Res:* High temperature chemistry; molten salts; phase equilibria in non-metallic systems; electrochemical and process development. *Mailing Add:* Alcoa Labs PO Box 772 New Kensington PA 15068

FOSTER, RAYMOND ORRVILLE, b Gary, Ind, Sept 25, 21; m 43; c 6. CLINICAL BIOCHEMISTRY, REPRODUCTIVE BIOLOGY. *Educ:* Univ Chicago, BS, 50. *Prof Exp:* Res biochemist, Armour Pharmaceut Co, 50-52; asst tech dir, Biol Testing, Rosner-Hixson Labs, 52-60; dir res clin biochem, Weston Labs, Gen Tire & Rubber Co, 60-73; DIR DIAG, FOSTER RES, 74- *Mem:* Am Chem Soc. *Res:* Basic and clinical research in the development of diagnostic tests for the prediction of ovulation in the human female to be used for population control. *Mailing Add:* 1202 Clara St Joliet IL 60435

FOSTER, RICHARD B(ERGERON), b Springdale, Wash, Nov 21, 16; m 55; c 2. ENGINEERING. *Educ:* Univ Calif, BA, 38. *Prof Exp:* Asst supvr, Douglas Aircraft Co, 40-42; dir planning div, Am Aviation, 42-43; chief indust engr, Globe Aircraft Co, 43-44; estimator, Consol Vultee Aircraft Corp, 44; mem staff, Kaiser Shipyards, 44; dist invest chief, US Govt Agencies, 44-47; partner, Foster & Derian, Consults, 47-51, 53-54; exec asst & gen mgr, Marquardt Aircraft, 51-53; DIR STRATEGIC STUDIES CTR, STANFORD RES INST INT, 54- *Mem:* Fel AAAS; Opers Res Soc Am; Sigma Xi; Inst Strategic Studies. *Res:* Philosophy and civil engineering; cost-effectiveness analysis for strategic decisions; values, power and strategy; methods of interdisciplinary research in strategic analysis; comparative strategy. *Mailing Add:* Stanford Res Inst Int 1611 N Kent St Arlington VA 22209

FOSTER, RICHARD N(ORMAN), b Cleveland, Ohio, June 10, 41; m 65. CHEMICAL ENGINEERING. *Educ:* Yale Univ, BE, 63, MS, 65, PhD, 66. *Prof Exp:* Tech rep int mkt develop, Union Carbide Corp, 66, int prod-mkt mgr chem mkt develop, 67-69; mgr tech & financial anal, 69-71, DIR TECHNOL MGT GROUP, TECHNOL TRANSFER, FIRE SAFETY, RES PLANNING & EVAL, ABT ASSOCS, 71- *Mem:* AAAS; Am Inst Chemists; Am Chem Soc. *Res:* Diffusion limited nonisothermal chemical reactions; surface diffusion; semiconductor catalysis; plasma physics; technological transfer; research management. *Mailing Add:* 10 Elmwood Somerville MA 02143

FOSTER, ROBERT EDWARD, II, b Milwaukee, Wis, Feb 4, 20; m 40; c 2. PLANT BREEDING. *Educ:* Univ Calif, BS, 41; Univ Wis, PhD(plant path), 45. *Prof Exp:* Asst plant path, Univ Calif, 41; Alumni Found fel, Univ Wis, 41-46; asst prof, Cornell Univ, 46-50; assoc horticulturist, 50-54, HORTICULTURIST, AGR EXP STA, UNIV ARIZ, 54- *Concurrent Pos:* Inspector, Calif State Dept Agr, 41; plant pathologist, NY Exp Sta, Geneva, 46-50. *Mem:* Am Soc Hort Sci. *Res:* Vegetable breeding; breeding for disease resistance; vegetable genetics; physiology of diseases; seed production; propagation; virus and physiological diseases; melons; lettuce. *Mailing Add:* Dept Plant Sci Univ Ariz Tucson AZ 85721

FOSTER, ROBERT EVERETT, polymer chemistry, research administration, deceased

FOSTER, ROBERT H, b Monroe, Ga, Nov 4, 20; m 42; c 4. BIOGEOGRAPHY. *Educ:* Univ Ga, BS, 63; Brigham Young Univ, MS, 66, PhD(bot), 68. *Prof Exp:* assoc prof, 68-80, EMER PROF GEOG, WESTERN KY UNIV, 80- *Mem:* Asn Am Geog. *Res:* Plant distribution in the United States intermountain region. *Mailing Add:* Dept of Geog & Geol Western Ky Univ Bowling Green KY 42101

FOSTER, ROBERT JOE, b Glendale, Calif, June 6, 24; m 51; c 2. BIOLOGICAL CHEMISTRY. *Educ:* Calif Inst Technol, BS, 48, PhD(chem), 52. *Prof Exp:* Res fel biol, Calif Inst Technol, 53-55; asst chemist & asst prof, 55-61, assoc agr chemist, 61-77, ASSOC PROF CHEM, WASH STATE UNIV, 61- *Mem:* Am Chem Soc; Am Soc Plant Physiol; Am Soc Biol Chem. *Res:* Mechanisms of enzyme action and specificity; comparative enzymology; enzymological photochemistry. *Mailing Add:* Dept of Agr Chem Wash State Univ Pullman WA 99163

FOSTER, ROBERT JOHN, b Cambridge, Mass, Apr 19, 29; m 51; c 2. GEOLOGY. *Educ:* Mass Inst Technol, SB, 51; Univ Wash, MS, 55, PhD(geol), 57. *Prof Exp:* Seismic computer, Geophys Serv, Inc, 51-52; instrumentation engr, Boeing Airplane Co, 53-54; asst, Univ Wash, 55-57; asst prof geol, Mont State Univ, 58-61; assoc prof, 61-67, PROF PHYS SCI, GEOL DEPT, SAN JOSE STATE UNIV, 67- *Mem:* AAAS; Geol Soc Am; Am Asn Petrol Geol; Nat Asn Geol Teachers. *Res:* Petrology; structural geology. *Mailing Add:* Geol Dept Los Gatos CA 95030

FOSTER, ROBERT L, geology, see previous edition

FOSTER, ROBERT SCOTT, medical bacteriology, see previous edition

FOSTER, ROGER SHERMAN, JR, b Washington, DC, Jan 8, 36; m 60; c 4. SURGERY. *Educ:* Haverford Col, AB, 57; Western Reserve Univ, MD, 61; Am Bd Surg, dipl, 69. *Prof Exp:* Res fel, Roswell Park Mem Inst, 66-68; dir, Surg Res Lab, 70-81, dir, Clin Transplant Unit, 72-81, assoc prof, 73-81, PROF SURG, COL MED, UNIV VT, 81- *Concurrent Pos:* Attend surg, Med Ctr Hosp, Vt, 70- *Mem:* Asn Acad Surg; fel Am Col Surgeons; Transplantation Soc; Am Soc Transplant Surgeons. *Res:* Clinical trials to compare treatment programs for breast cancer; laboratory and clinical studies of effects of chemotherapy, immunotherapy and surgery on hematopoiesis. *Mailing Add:* Dept Surg Given Bldg Univ Vt Burlington VT 05401

FOSTER, TERRY LYNN, b Mt Pleasant, Tex, Apr 4, 43; m 64; c 2. MICROBIOLOGY. *Educ:* NTex State Univ, BA, 65, MA, 67; Tex A&M Univ, PhD(microbiol), 73. *Prof Exp:* Assoc prof biol, 67-80, RES PROF, HARDIN-SIMMONS UNIV, 80- *Concurrent Pos:* Prin investr, Hardin-Simmons Univ Sci Res Ctr, 72-80, sr res scientist, 80- *Mem:* Am Soc Microbiol; AAAS. *Res:* Isolation of selected microorganisms from interplanetary spacecraft environments and determination of their response to experimental planetary environments; development and evaluation of new anaerobic procedures and of a new vaccine for bovine brucellosis; evaluation of new clinical diagnostic procedures; evaluation of microbial enhanced oil recovery; development of potential therapeutic for Herpes II. *Mailing Add:* Sci Res Ctr 1249 Ambler Ave Abilene TX 79601

FOSTER, THEODORE DEAN, b Plainfield, NJ, July 25, 29. PHYSICS, OCEANOGRAPHY. *Educ:* Brown Univ, ScB, 52; Univ Colo, MS, 58, MA, 60; Univ Calif, San Diego, PhD(physics), 65. *Prof Exp:* Physicist, Reaction Motors Inc, 52-55; instr phys sci, Univ Colo, 57-60; res physicist, Scripps Inst, Univ Calif, 62-65; asst prof geophys & appl sci, Yale Univ, 65-69; asst res physicist, Scripps Inst Oceanog, 69-71, assoc res oceanogr, 71-77; dean natural sci, 79-80, PROF MARINE SCI, UNIV CALIF, SANTA CRUZ, 77- *Concurrent Pos:* Mem comt polar res, Panel Oceanog, Nat Acad Sci, 71-73; mem working group 38, Sci Comt Oceanic Res, 74-77, convenor, Comt Antarctic Oceanog, 77- *Honors & Awards:* Antarctic Serv Medal, NSF, 73. *Mem:* Am Physical Soc; Int Glaciol Soc; Am Meteorol Soc; Philos Sci Asn; Am Geophys Union. *Res:* Geophysical fluid dynamics; physical oceanography, especially of polar regions; philosophy of science. *Mailing Add:* Ctr for Coastal Marine Studies Univ of Calif Santa Cruz CA 95064

FOSTER, THOMAS SALISBURY, b Stratford, Ont, May 30, 21; m 41; c 2. BIOCHEMISTRY. *Educ:* Univ Western Ont, BSc, 48, MSc, 49, PhD(biochem), 54. *Prof Exp:* RES OFF BIOCHEM, ANIMAL RES INST, CAN DEPT AGR, 53- *Mem:* Can Biochem Soc; Brit Biochem Soc; Can Soc Animal Prod. *Res:* Precursors of deoxyribonucleic acid; pregnancy hormones; adrenal steroid hormones and their relationship to carbohydrate metabolism; adaptation, and metabolism of mucopolysaccharides; pesticides; residues; metabolites; effects on metabolism. *Mailing Add:* Biochem Sect Animal Res Inst Agr Can Ottawa ON K1A 0C6 Can

FOSTER, THOMAS SCOTT, b Gloversville, NY, May 25, 47; m 69; c 2. BIOPHARMACEUTICS, CLINICAL PHARMACOLOGY. *Educ:* State Univ NY, Buffalo, BS, 70; Univ Ky, PharmD(pharm), 73. *Prof Exp:* Assoc prof pharm, Col Pharm, Univ Ky, 73; dir biopharmaceut & pharmacokinetics, Drug Prod Eval Unit, 73-80, ASSOC PROF ANESTHESIOL & PHARM, ALBERT B CHANDLER MED CTR UNIV KY, 80- *Mem:* Am Pharmaceut Asn; Am Soc Hosp Pharmacists; Acad Pharm Pract; Acad Pharmaceut Sci. *Res:* Application of biopharmaceutic and pharmacokinetic principles for adjustment of drug dosage in patients and the critical evaluation of investigational new drugs through design and execution of clinical pharmacology studies. *Mailing Add:* Dept of Pharm C-1148 Univ Ky Med Ctr 800 Rose St Lexington KY 40536

FOSTER, VIRGINIA, b Joseph, Ore, Feb 4, 14. PHYTOPATHOLOGY. *Educ:* Univ Wash, BS, 49, MS, 50; Ohio State Univ, PhD(plant path, bot), 54. *Prof Exp:* Assoc prof biol, Judson Col, 56-58 & Miss State Col W58-59; assoc prof life sci, La Verne Col, 59-60; asst prof biol sci, Calif Western Univ, 60-61; from teacher to asst prof, 61-70, ASSOC PROF BIOL SCI, PENSACOLA JR COL, 70- *Mem:* Am Phytopath Soc; Soc Indust Microbiol. *Res:* Physiological mycology; physiological relations between parasitic fungi and plant hosts, especially the production and action of wilting toxins. *Mailing Add:* Pensacola Jr Col Dept Biol 1000 College Blvd Pensacola FL 32504

FOSTER, WALTER EDWARD, b Cincinnati, Ohio, Oct 6, 24; m 44; c 2. INDUSTRIAL CHEMISTRY, RESEARCH MANAGEMENT. *Educ:* Univ Cincinnati, ChE, 49, MS, 51, PhD(chem), 53. *Prof Exp:* Res chemist, 53-57, res supvr, 57-61, asst dir, 61-63, dir chem res & develop, 63-65 & pioneer res, 65-68, tech dir res & develop, 68-78, GEN MGR RES & DEVELOP, ETHYL CORP, 78- *Mem:* Am Chem Soc. *Res:* Industrial organic, inorganic and organometallic research. *Mailing Add:* Baton Rouge Lab Ethyl Corp Gulf States Rd Baton Rouge LA 70821

FOSTER, WALTER H, JR, b Freehold, NJ, Dec 29, 33. PHYSICAL CHEMISTRY, ANALYTICAL CHEMISTRY. *Educ:* Philadelphia Textile Inst, BS, 55; Mass Inst Technol, PhD(anal chem), 59. *Prof Exp:* Res explor chemist, Org Chem Div, Am Cyanamid Co, Bound Brook, 59-66, from res chemist to sr res chemist, 66-70, sr systs analyst, Res & Develop Dept, 70-81; SYSTS COORDR, RES COMPUTER SYSTS, 81- *Mem:* Am Chem Soc. *Res:* Analytical spectroscopy; physical chemistry of dyeing; photochemistry; laboratory automation systems; scientific computer programming. *Mailing Add:* RR3 Millbrook Lane Colts Neck NJ 07722

FOSTER, WILFRED JOHN DANIEL, b King William Co, Va, May 20, 37; m 69; c 1. PHYSICAL CHEMISTRY. *Educ:* Va State Col, BS, 60; George Washington Univ, MPhil, 72, PhD(chem), 74. *Prof Exp:* Lab technician, 63-67, instr, 67-72, assoc prof, 73-80, PROF CHEM, VA STATE COL, 80- *Mem:* Am Chem Soc. *Res:* Computer assisted investigations of energy transfers that occur when molecules combine, using the Huckle Molecular Orbital Theory. *Mailing Add:* Box 536 Va State Col Petersburg VA 23803

FOSTER, WILFRID RAYMOND, b Fredericton, NB, Feb 14, 13; nat US; m 44. MINERALOGY. *Educ:* Univ NB, BS, 34; Catholic Univ, MS, 36; Univ Chicago, PhD(geol), 40. *Prof Exp:* Instr petrol, Catholic Univ, 40-41; mineral prep, Pa State Col, 41-42; ceramic petrographer, Champion Spark Plug Co, 42-52; assoc prof mineral, 52-57, chmn dept, 57-73, prof, 57-80, EMER PROF GEOL & MINERAL, OHIO STATE UNIV, 80- *Mem:* AAAS; fel Mineral Soc Am; fel Am Ceramic Soc; Am Geophys Union; Mineral Asn Can. *Res:* Petrography and x-ray diffraction of ceramic raw materials and products; solid-phase reactions; froth-flotation; high temperature phase equilibrium of silicates; the sillimanite minerals; thermal behavior of non-metallic minerals. *Mailing Add:* 107 Mendenhall Lab Ohio State Univ 125 S Oval Mall Columbus OH 43210

FOSTER, WILLIAM BURNHAM, b Greenfield, Mass, July 30, 30; m 54; c 1. PARASITOLOGY, INVERTEBRATE ZOOLOGY. *Educ:* Univ Mass, BS, 52, MA, 54; Rice Inst, PhD(parasite physiol), 57. *Prof Exp:* Instr gen biol, invert zool, helminthol & host-parasite relationships, 57-60, from asst prof to assoc prof zool, 64-70, PROF ZOOL, RUTGERS UNIV, 70- *Mem:* Am Soc Trop Med & Hyg; Am Soc Parasitol. *Res:* Physiology and immunology of parasites; ecology; life histories. *Mailing Add:* Dept of Zool Rutgers State Univ New Brunswick NJ 08903

FOSTER, WILLIAM RODERICK, b Springfield, Mo, June 16, 24; m 46; c 5. PHYSICAL CHEMISTRY. *Educ:* Southwestern Mo State Col, BS, 47; Wash Univ, PhD(chem), 50. *Prof Exp:* Sr res tech, Petrol Prod Res, 50-55, res assoc, 55-60, sect supvr, 60-70, mgr reservoir mech res, 70-73, SR RES ASSOC, FIELD RES LAB, MOBIL RES & DEVELOP CORP, 73- *Mem:* Am Chem Soc; Am Inst Chem Eng; Soc Petrol Eng. *Res:* Continuum mechanics; fluid mechanics; in porous media; interfacial phenomena; migration and accumulation of petroleum. *Mailing Add:* 3917 Holliday Rd Dallas TX 75224

FOSTER, WILLIS ROY, b New Orleans, La, Dec 8, 28; m 57; c 3. MEDICAL SCIENCE, INFORMATION SCIENCE. *Educ:* La State Univ, BA, 50, MS & MD, 57. *Prof Exp:* Res assoc pharmacol, George Washington Univ, 57-58; prof assoc, Smithsonian Sci Info Exchange, Washington, DC, 59-63, assoc dir life sci, 64-71, vpres, 72-76; tech dir, Sci Info Serv, Kappa Systs, Inc, Arlington, Va, 76-78; PRES, ADVAN CONCEPTS FOR DEVELOP, INC, BETHESDA, 78- *Concurrent Pos:* Fel, Johns Hopkins Univ, 58-59. *Mem:* Am Chem Soc; AAAS. *Res:* Biochemistry; pharmacology. *Mailing Add:* 6117 Greentree Rd Bethesda MD 20817

FOTH, HENRY DONALD, b Norwalk, Wis, Feb 9, 23; m 48. AGRONOMY, SOIL MORPHOLOGY. *Educ:* Univ Wis, BS, 47, MS, 48; Iowa State Col, PhD, 52. *Prof Exp:* Instr soils, Iowa State Col, 48-52; assoc prof, Agr & Mech Col Tex, 52-55; assoc prof, 55-60, PROF SOILS, MICH STATE UNIV, 60- *Concurrent Pos:* Mem, Int Soil Sci Cong; consult, Encyclopedia Britannica Educ Corp, 74- *Honors & Awards:* Educ Award, Am Soc Agron, 59; Gustav Oahus Award, Nat Sci Teachers Asn, 74; Ensminger-Interstate Distinguished Teacher Award & Teacher-Fel Award, Nat Asn Cols & Teachers of Agr, 75. *Mem:* Fel AAAS; fel Soil Sci Soc Am; Fel Am Soc Agron; Sigma Xi. *Res:* Morphology and genesis of Mollisols; soil fertility and root distribution of field crops; soil geography and land use; teaching programs for soil science. *Mailing Add:* 1800 Ann St East Lansing MI 48823

FOTINO, MIRCEA, b Bucharest, Romania, June 6, 27; US citizen; m 69; c 2. BIOPHYSICS, CYTOLOGY. *Educ:* Univ Paris, Lic-es-sci, 51; Univ Calif, Berkeley, PhD(high-energy physics), 58. *Prof Exp:* Res and teaching asst, Univ Calif, Berkeley, 52-58; charge de recherches, Nat Ctr Sci Res, Polytech Sch, Paris, 58-60; res physicist & lectr physics, Univ Calif, Berkeley, 61; res fel physics, Cambridge Electron Accelerator, Harvard Univ, 61-68, res fel biol, 69-70; dir lab high-volt electron micros, 71-, assoc prof, 71-79, PROF, DEPT MOLECULAR, CELLULAR AND DEVELOP BIOL, UNIV COLO, BOULDER, 79- *Concurrent Pos:* Guest, Dept Physics, Mass Inst Technol, 61-68. *Mem:* Am Phys Soc; NY Acad Sci; Electron Micros Soc Am; Biophys Soc. *Res:* Cosmic-ray pi mesons; beam handling and instrumentation for synchrotrons and particle physics; inverse Compton effect and polarized photons; ultrastructure of biological materials by high-voltage electron microscopy; quantitative cryomicroscopy. *Mailing Add:* Dept Molecular, Cellular & Develop Biol Univ of Colo Boulder CO 80309

FOU, CHENG-MING, b Shanghai, China, May 27, 36; US citizen; m 66; c 2. NUCLEAR PHYSICS, ION-ATOM COLLISION. *Educ:* Nat Taiwan Univ, BS, 56; Univ Munich, dipl physics, 61; Univ Pa, PhD(nuclear exp), 65. *Prof Exp:* Res assoc nuclear struct, Tandem Accelerator Lab, Univ Pa, 65-68; asst prof physics, 68-72, ASSOC PROF PHYSICS, UNIV DEL, 72- *Concurrent Pos:* Vis res prof, Nat Tsing Hua Univ, 74-75. *Mem:* Am Phys Soc. *Res:* Nuclear structure experimental studies using direct reactions and multiparticle final state reactions; particle angular correlation studies for nuclear spectroscopy; inner-shell ionization in ion-atom collision. *Mailing Add:* Dept of Physics Univ of Del Newark DE 19711

FOUBERT, EDWARD LOUIS, JR, b Marquette, Mich, Sept 2, 17; m 39; c 3. ALLERGY. *Educ:* Gonzaga Univ, BS, 39; Univ Wash, MS, 46, PhD(bact), 47. *Prof Exp:* Res chemist, V O D Oil Co, 39-41; instr chem, Gonzaga Univ, 41-42, asst prof biol, 42-44; asst prof bact, Univ Wash, 46-47; assoc prof biol, Gonzaga Univ, 47-50, prof & chmn dept, 50-54; dir res, 53-73, dir spec projs, 73-75, REG AFFAIRS ADMIN, HOLLISTER-STIER, INC, 75- *Concurrent Pos:* Control chemist, Inland Empire Refineries, 41-43. *Mem:* AAAS; Am Soc Microbiol; Am Chem Soc; Am Acad Allergy; NY Acad Sci. *Res:* Taxonomy of anaerobic cocci; bacterial fermentations and ecology; nature of allergens and allergic response. *Mailing Add:* Hollister-Stier Labs Box 3145 Terminal Annex Spokane WA 99220

FOUCHE, CLARENCE ESTES, JR, b Greenville, SC, Sept 23, 46; m 70. ANATOMY. *Educ:* Furman Univ, BS, 68; Univ SC, MS, 71, PhD(biol), 73. *Prof Exp:* Res assoc biochem, 73-75, res assoc microbiol, Sch Med, Vanderbilt Univ, 75-76; asst prof biol, King Faisal Univ, Dannam, Saudi Arabia, 76-77; ASSOC PROF ANAT, SHERMAN COL, 78- *Mem:* Sigma Xi. *Res:* Immunochemistry of schistosomiasis; lipid metabolism in reproductive tissues. *Mailing Add:* 169 Coldstream Dr Spartanburg SC 29303

FOUCHER, WALTER DAVID, JR, b Bennington, Vt, Aug 4, 36; div; c 2. PETROLEUM CHEMISTRY. *Educ:* St Michael's Col, Vt, AB, 58; Univ Vt, MS, 59; Univ Fla, PhD(phys inorg chem), 62. *Prof Exp:* Chemist, Texaco Res Ctr, 62-63, sr chemist, 63-67, res chemist, 67-69, group leader, Lubricants Res, 69-75, group leader, Fuels Res, 75-79, technologist, 79-81, TECHNOLOGIST SCI PLANNING, TEXACO, INC, 81- *Concurrent Pos:* Ed, Mid-Hudson Chemist, Am Chem Soc, 63-69; vis instr, State Univ NY Col New Paltz, 64-68; vis lectr, Marist Col, 67-75; ed, Test Tube Texaco, Inc, 80- *Mem:* Am Chem Soc; Sigma Xi. *Res:* Preparation catalysts and catalyst supports for hydrocarbon conversion; additives and lubricating oils for internal combustion engines, gasoline and diesel; gasoline additive synthesis and development. *Mailing Add:* Texaco Res Ctr Box 509 Beacon NY 12508

FOUGERE, PAUL FRANCIS, b Cambridge, Mass, Feb 29, 32; m 52; c 6. TERRESTRIAL MAGNETISM, MAGNETIC PULSATIONS. *Educ:* Boston Col, BS, 52, MS, 53; Boston Univ, PhD(physics), 65. *Prof Exp:* Physicist, Naval Res Lab, 53-54; tech aircraft engr, Gen Elec Co, Mass, 54-55; PHYSICIST GEOMAGNETISM, AIR FORCE GEOPHYS LAB, 55- *Mem:* Int Asn Geomagnetism & Aeronomy; Am Geophys Union. *Res:*

Spherical harmonic analysis; electronic structure of atoms and of diatomic molecules; space physics; terrestrial magnetic activity; maximum entropy power spectrum analysis; theory and analysis of Air Force Geophysical Lab magnetometer network data. *Mailing Add:* Air Force Geophys Lab Hanscom AFB Bedford MA 01731

FOUGERON, MYRON GEORGE, b Morris, Minn, July 20, 32; m 59; c 2. PHYSIOLOGY, ENDOCRINOLOGY. *Educ:* Sam Houston State Col, BS, 59, MA, 65; Tex A&M Univ, PhD(zool), 67. *Prof Exp:* Teacher jr high sch, Tex, 59-61; partic acad year inst biophys, Col Med, Baylor Univ, 66-67; from asst prof to assoc prof, 67-76, PROF BIOL, KEARNEY STATE COL, 76- *Mem:* Pop Ref Bur; Am Inst Biol Sci. *Res:* Effect of radiation on placental transport; effect of hypophysectomy on the endocrine glands of the American chameleon, Anolis carolinensis. *Mailing Add:* Dept of Biol Kearney State Col Kearney NE 68847

FOUKAL, PETER VOJTA, astrophysics, see previous edition

FOULDS, JOHN DOUGLAS, b Pittsfield, Mass; c 1. BIOCHEMISTRY, MOLECULAR BIOLOGY. *Educ:* Columbia Col, AB, 60, Columbia Univ, PhD(biochem), 66. *Prof Exp:* Asst prof microbiol, Univ Conn Health Ctr, 68-74; RES BIOCHEMIST, NAT INST ARTHRITIS, METAB & DIGESTIVE DIS, 74- *Concurrent Pos:* USPHS fel, Stanford Univ, 66-68. *Mem:* Am Soc Biol Chem; Am Soc Microbiol. *Res:* Membrane structure, assembly, function. *Mailing Add:* Bldg 10/9N 119 NIH-NIAMDD Bethesda MD 20205

FOULIS, DAVID JAMES, b Hinsdale, Ill, July 26, 30; m 56, 62, 77; c 3. MATHEMATICS, QUANTUM PHYSICS. *Educ:* Univ Miami, BA, 52, MS, 53; Tulane Univ, PhD, 58. *Prof Exp:* Asst prof, Lehigh Univ, 58-59; asst prof, Wayne State Univ, 59-63; prof, Univ Fla, 63-65; PROF MATH, GRAD SCH, UNIV MASS, AMHERST, 65- *Mem:* Am Math Soc; Math Asn Am. *Res:* Foundations of statistics; operator algebras; quantum theory. *Mailing Add:* Dept Math & Statist Univ of Mass Amherst MA 01003

FOULK, CLINTON ROSS, b Wichita, Kans, Jan 24, 30; m 58; c 1. COMPUTER SCIENCE, MATHEMATICS. *Educ:* Univ Kans, BA, 51; Univ Ill, Urbana, MA, 58, PhD(math), 63. *Prof Exp:* Res asst comput prog, Digital Comput Lab, Univ Ill, Urbana, 58-62; asst prof math, 63-66, asst prof comput & info sci, 66-68, ASSOC PROF COMPUT & INFO SCI, OHIO STATE UNIV, 68- *Mem:* Asn Comput Mach. *Res:* Computer systems programming. *Mailing Add:* Dept of Comput & Info Sci 2024 Neil Ave Columbus OH 43210

FOULKE, DONALD GARDNER, b Burnham, Pa, Aug 19, 12; m 40; c 4. ORGANIC CHEMISTRY, ELECTROCHEMISTRY. *Educ:* Juniata Col, BS, 34; Rutgers Univ, MS, 37, PhD(chem), 41. *Prof Exp:* Asst, Rutgers Univ, 35-38, instr chem, 38-40; asst prof, Beaver Col, 40-42; res assoc, A Kenneth Graham & Assoc, 41-42; res chemist, Jenkintown Lab, United Eng & Foundry Co, 42; asst chief chemist, Repub Steel Corp, 42-43; chief chemist, Houdaille-Hershey Corp, Ill, 43-45; dir anal lab, Foster D Snell, Inc, NY, 45-46; process electrochemist & chief chemist, Hanson-Van Winkle-Munning Co, NJ, 46-51; mgr electrochem res, Sel-Rex Corp, Nutley, 53-59, dir res, 59-75; CONSULT ELECTROCHEM, 75- *Concurrent Pos:* Assoc chemist bur agr & indust chem, Eastern Regional Res Lab, USDA, 42; tech dir, Laboratorium, 48-; chmn, Nat Task Comt Indust Wastes; ed, Electroplaters Process Control Handbook, 63-75. *Honors & Awards:* Gold Medal, Am Electroplaters Soc, 45, 57 & 64. *Mem:* Am Chem Soc; Am Electroplaters Soc (exec secy, 51-53); Am Soc Metals; Electrochem Soc. *Res:* Electroplating and metal finishing; analytical, colorimetric and instrumental organic chemistry; electroplating of tin from an acid solution; reaction of secondary and tertiary dialkylmagnesiums with epichlorohydrin; reaction of dioxane with the Grignard reagent. *Mailing Add:* 455 Johnston Dr Watchung Plainfield NJ 07060

FOULKES, ERNEST CHARLES, b Ger, Aug 20, 24; US citizen; m 46; c 4. PHYSIOLOGY. *Educ:* Univ Sydney, BSc, 46, MSc, 47; Oxford Univ, DPhil(biochem), 52. *Prof Exp:* Investr, Nat Health Med Res Coun, Australia, 46-49; assoc, May Inst, 52-65; assoc prof, 65-70, PROF ENVIRON HEALTH & PHYSIOL, UNIV CINCINNATI, 70-, ASSOC DIR DEPT ENVIRON HEALTH, 71- *Concurrent Pos:* Estab investr, Am Heart Asn, 56-61; pres adv, Univ Cincinnati, 72-74. *Mem:* Biochem Soc; Biophys Soc; Am Soc Biol Chem; Am Nephrology Soc; Soc Exp Biol & Med. *Res:* Action of heme enzymes; active transport; cell permeability, renal physiology and toxicology. *Mailing Add:* Dept of Environ Health Univ of Cincinnati Col Med Cincinnati OH 45267

FOULKES, ROBERT HUGH, b Wis, Nov 14, 18; m 44; c 1. EXPERIMENTAL ZOOLOGY. *Educ:* Coe Col, AB, 40; Univ Iowa, MS, 47, PhD(zool), 51. *Prof Exp:* Instr zool, Univ Iowa, 47-51; res fel, Edsel Ford Inst Med Res, 51-55; asst prof biol, Northern Ill Univ, 55-56 & St Louis Univ, 56-59; assoc scientist res div, Dr Salsbury's Labs, 59-61; assoc prof biol, 62-69, prof zool, 69-80, PROF BIOL, UNIV WIS, PLATTEVILLE, 80- *Concurrent Pos:* Independent consult, 61- *Mem:* AAAS; Am Soc Zool; Wildlife Dis Asn; Am Inst Biol Sci. *Res:* Regeneration; neoplasms; histochemistry; toxicology; aerobiology. *Mailing Add:* Dept of Zool Univ of Wis Platteville WI 53818

FOULKS, JAMES GRIGSBY, b Bay City, Tex, Sept 18, 16; m 47; c 2. PHARMACOLOGY. *Educ:* Rice Inst, BA, 39; Johns Hopkins Univ, PhD(biol sci), 43; Columbia Univ, MD, 50. *Prof Exp:* Lab asst, Rice Inst, 37-39; lab asst, Univ Rochester, 39-40; lab asst, Johns Hopkins Univ, 40-42; instr anat, Ohio State Univ, 42-43; lab asst pharmacol, Columbia Univ, 50-51; head dept, 51-71, PROF PHARMACOL, UNIV BC, 51- *Concurrent Pos:* Nat Heart Inst fel, Columbia Univ, 50-51. *Mem:* Am Physiol Soc; Soc Exp Biol & Med; Am Soc Pharmacol & Exp Therapeut; Pharmacol Soc Can; Can Physiol Soc. *Res:* Water and electrolyte metabolism; renal and cardiovascular physiology and pharmacology. *Mailing Add:* Dept of Pharmacol Univ of BC Vancouver BC V6T 1W5 Can

FOULKS, SIDNEY MARSHALL, exploration geophysics, see previous edition

FOULSER, DAVID A, b Columbus, Ohio, Apr 10, 33; m 56; c 3. MATHEMATICS. *Educ:* Ohio State Univ, BA, 55; Univ Mich, PhD(math), 63. *Prof Exp:* Instr math, Univ Chicago, 63-65; asst prof, 65-68, assoc prof, 68-74, PROF MATH, UNIV ILL, CHICAGO CIRCLE, 74- *Mem:* Am Math Soc. *Res:* Projective planes; group theory. *Mailing Add:* Dept of Math Col Lib Arts & Sci Univ of Ill at Chicago Circle Chicago IL 60680

FOUNTAIN, CLIFFORD W, b Long Beach, Calif, Sept 12, 30; m 55; c 2. MATERIALS SCIENCE, METAL PHYSICS. *Educ:* Univ Calif, Berkeley, BA, 60; Stanford Univ, MS, 78. *Prof Exp:* Physicist, US Dept Army, DC, 60-62; physicist, US Naval Ord Test Sta, 62-69, physicist, Michelson Lab, 69-78, SUPVRY PHYSICIST, MICHELSON LAB, NAVAL WEAPONS CTR, 78- *Concurrent Pos:* Res assoc, Univ Ore, 62. *Res:* Crystal growth of piezoelectric transducer substrates by hydrothermal techniques. *Mailing Add:* Code 3624 Michelson Lab Naval Weapons Ctr China Lake CA 93555

FOUNTAIN, JOHN CROTHERS, b Berkeley, Calif, May 8, 47. GEOCHEMISTRY. *Educ:* Calif Polytech State Univ, San Luis Obispo, BS, 70; Univ Calif, Santa Barbara, MA, 73, PhD(geol), 75. *Prof Exp:* Asst prof, 75-80, ASSOC PROF GEOL, STATE UNIV NY, BUFFALO, 80- *Mem:* Geol Soc Am; Geochem Soc. *Res:* Trace element and isotope geochemistry; igneous petrology. *Mailing Add:* Dept of Geol 4240 Ridge Lea Rd Buffalo NY 14226

FOUNTAIN, JOHN WILLIAM, b Quincy, Ill, Mar 12, 44. SPACE SCIENCE. *Educ:* Univ Ariz, BS, 66. *Prof Exp:* Res asst, Lunar & Planetary Lab, 65-73, res asst, Lunar & Planetary Lab & Optical Sci Ctr, 73-81, RES ASST, LUNAR & PLANETARY LAB, UNIV ARIZ, 81- *Honors & Awards:* Pub Serv Achievement Award, NASA, 74. *Mem:* Am Astron Soc; AAAS. *Res:* Structure and dynamics of planetary atmospheres; Saturn ring; photometry of planetary atmospheres; astronomical instrumentation; celestial mechanics. *Mailing Add:* Lunar & Planetary Lab Univ of Ariz Tucson AZ 85721

FOUNTAIN, LEONARD DU BOIS, b Missouri Valley, Iowa, Jan 25, 29; m 59; c 1. MATHEMATICAL ANALYSIS. *Educ:* Univ Chicago, AB, 50, MS, 53; Univ Nebr, PhD(math), 60. *Prof Exp:* Instr math, Univ Nebr, 58-60; from asst prof to assoc prof, 60-70, PROF MATH, SAN DIEGO STATE UNIV, 70- *Mem:* Math Asn Am. *Res:* Ordinary differential equations; convex functions and their applications to existence theorems for differential equations. *Mailing Add:* Dept of Math San Diego State Univ San Diego CA 92115

FOUNTAIN, LEWIS SPENCER, b McCrory, Ark, Oct 18, 17; m 46; c 4. GEOSCIENCE, ACOUSTICS. *Educ:* Trinity Univ, BS, 58, MS, 62. *Prof Exp:* Res engr nondestructive testing, 58-64, sr res engr, 64-71, actg mgr & sr res engr, 71-75, SR RES SCIENTIST GEOSCI, SOUTHWEST RES INST, 75- *Mem:* Acoust Soc Am; Inst Elec & Electronics Engrs; Am Soc Nondestructive Testing; Soc Explor Geophysicists; Sigma Xi. *Res:* Subsurface cavity detection studies; detection and disposal activities related to clearing hazardous buried ordnance objects; land mine detector evaluations; global soils studies; chemical, physical, electromagnetic and magnetic analysis of soils; magnetic signature measurement and analysis. *Mailing Add:* Southwest Res Inst PO Drawer 28510 San Antonio TX 78284

FOUNTAIN, ROGER, materials science & engineering, see previous edition

FOUQUETTE, MARTIN JOHN, JR, b Philadelphia, Pa, June 14, 30; div; c 2. HERPETOLOGY. *Educ:* Univ Tex, BA, 51, MA, 53, PhD(zool), 59. *Prof Exp:* interim asst prof zool, Univ Fla, 59-61; asst prof, Univ Southwestern La, 61-65; ASSOC PROF ZOOL, ARIZ STATE UNIV, 65- *Mem:* Am Soc Ichthyologists & Herpetologists; Am Soc Naturalists; Am Soc Zoologists; Sigma Xi; Soc Syst Zool. *Res:* Systematics and ecology of anuran amphibians and squamate reptiles; mechanics of speciation; amphibian bioacoustics; anuran sperm morphology. *Mailing Add:* Dept of Zool Ariz State Univ Tempe AZ 85281

FOURNEY, M(ICHAEL) E(UGENE), b Blue Jay, WVa, Jan 30, 36. AERONAUTICS, MECHANICAL ENGINEERING. *Educ:* Univ WVa, BS, 58; Calif Inst Technol, MS, 59, PhD(aeronaut), 63. *Prof Exp:* Aerospace engr, Bolkow Entwicklungen KG, Ger, 63-64; from res asst prof to res assoc prof aeronaut & astronaut, Univ Wash, 64-72; assoc prof, 72-75, PROF, UNIV CALIF, LOS ANGELES, 75-, CHMN, DEPT MECH & STRUCTURES, 79- *Concurrent Pos:* Consult, Math Sci Northwest Inc, 60-73; pvt consult, 70- *Mem:* Soc Exp Stress Anal (pres, 80-81); Optical Am. *Res:* Solid and experimental mechanics. *Mailing Add:* Dept of Mech & Struct Univ of Calif Los Angeles CA 90024

FOURNIER, MAURILLE JOSEPH, JR, b Montpelier, Vt, Jan 13, 40; m 64; c 2. MOLECULAR BIOLOGY, BIOCHEMISTRY. *Educ:* Univ Vt, BA, 62; Dartmouth Col, PhD(molecular biol), 68. *Prof Exp:* Res biochemist, Walter Reed Army Med Ctr, Walter Reed Army Inst Res, 68-70; Am Cancer Soc fel, Nat Insts Health, 70-72; asst prof, 72-78, ASSOC PROF BIOCHEM, UNIV MASS, AMHERST, 78- *Mem:* Am Soc Biol Chemists; AAAS; Am Soc Microbiol; Biophys Soc. *Res:* Biosynthesis, structure and function of transfer ribonucleic acid, tRNA and other small RNAs; structure and expression of tRNA, 4.5S and 6S RNA genes in Escherichia coli; post-transcriptional modification of tRNA precursors; solution struction of tRNA; biosynthesis of small, stable RNAs in yeast. *Mailing Add:* Dept of Biochem Univ of Mass Amherst MA 01003

FOURNIER, PIERRE WILLIAM, b Sudbury, Ont, Jan 17, 27; m 51; c 3. PATHOLOGY. *Educ:* Univ Ottawa, MD, 53; Royal Col Physicians & Surgeons Can, cert path, 61; FRCP(C), 73. *Prof Exp:* Pathologist, Ottawa Gen Hosp, 60-66; DIR LABS & CHIEF DEPT PATH, RIVERSIDE HOSP OF OTTAWA, 66- *Concurrent Pos:* Lectr, Univ Ottawa, 60-64, asst prof, 65. *Mem:* Can Med Asn; Can Asn Path; Can Soc Forensic Sci; Can Soc Cytol. *Res:* Exfoliative cytology; medico-legal pathology; toxicology. *Mailing Add:* Dept of Path Riverside Hosp 1967 Riverside Dr Ottawa Can

FOURNIER, R E KEITH, b Attlebord, Mass, July 26, 49. CELL GENETICS, MOLECULAR BIOLOGY. *Educ:* Providence Col, BS, 71; Princeton Univ, PhD(biochem), 74. *Prof Exp:* Fel, Dept Biol & Human Genetics, Yale Univ, 75-78; ASST PROF, DEPT MICROBIOL & COMPREHENSIVE CANCER CTR, UNIV SOUTHERN CALIF, 78- *Concurrent Pos:* Adj prof, W Alton Jones Cell Sci Ctr, Lake Placid, NY, 78- *Mem:* Sigma Xi; AAAS. *Res:* Control of eukaryotic gene expression, particularly the genetic and molecular mechanisms which regulate gene activity in higher differentiated mammalian cells. *Mailing Add:* Cancer Res Lab 1303 N Mission Rd Univ Southern Calif Los Angeles CA 90033

FOURNIER, ROBERT ORVILLE, b San Diego, Calif, Jan 14, 32; m 60; c 2. GEOCHEMISTRY. *Educ:* Harvard Univ, AB, 54; Univ Calif, PhD(geol), 58. *Prof Exp:* Assoc prof lectr geol, George Washington Univ, 58-59; GEOLOGIST, US GEOL SURV, 58- *Concurrent Pos:* Chmn, US orgn comt 2nd UN symp develop & use of geothermal energy, 73-75. *Mem:* Geol Soc Am; Mineral Soc Am; Geochem Soc Japan; Int Asn Geochem Cosmochem; Int Asn Gen Ore Deposits. *Res:* Geologic and geochemical aspects of geothermal energy; geochemistry of hydrothermal solutions and hydrothermal alteration; experimental studies of solution mineral reactions at high temperatures and high pressures. *Mailing Add:* Geol Div US Geol Surv 345 Middlefield Rd Menlo Park CA 94025

FOURON, YVES, b Fort-de-France, France, Mar 14, 43; m 68; c 2. ORGANIC CHEMISTRY. *Educ:* Univ Aix-Marseille, Lic es Sci, 67, DEA, 69; Inst Petrochemistry & Indust Org Synthesis, Marseille, Ing Chim, 69; Univ Alta, PhD(org chem), 75. *Prof Exp:* Int Asn Exchange Students Tech Experience fel chem, Kodak Res Labs, 69-70; fel, 75-78, chem prod mgr, 78-79, MKT MGR, CHEMBIOMED LTD, UNIV ALTA, 79- *Res:* Synthetic organic chemistry of nucleic acid compounds and analogs as well as of blood group substances. *Mailing Add:* Chembiomed Ltd W5-56 Chem Bldg Univ Alta Edmonton AB T6G 2E8 Can

FOURTNER, CHARLES RUSSELL, b Hollywood, Calif, Oct 3, 44; m 68; c 3. INVERTEBRATE PHYSIOLOGY. *Educ:* Carroll Col, AB, 66; Mich State Univ, MS, 69, PhD(zool), 71. *Prof Exp:* Fel biol, Univ Miami, 71-72; fel physiol, Univ Alta, 73; asst prof, 74-78, ASSOC PROF BIOL, STATE UNIV NY BUFFALO, 78- *Mem:* Soc Neurosci; Am Soc Zoologists; Soc Exp Biol. *Res:* Structure and function of invertebrate neuromuscular systems; central nervous control of rhythmic behavior patterns such as locomotion and respiration in invertebrates. *Mailing Add:* Dept of Biol Sci State Univ of NY Buffalo NY 14260

FOUSS, JAMES L(AWRENCE), b Warsaw, Ohio, Feb 22, 36; m 57; c 2. AGRICULTURAL ENGINEERING. *Educ:* Ohio State Univ, BAE, 59, MSc, 62, PhD, 71. *Prof Exp:* Res agr engr, USDA, 60-72, lab dir, Coastal Plains Soil & Water Conserv Res Ctr, Agr Res Serv, 72-76; vpres res & new prod develop, 76-81, CHIEF SCIENTIST, HANCOR, INC, 81- *Honors & Awards:* Spec Award, USDA, 62, Performance Awards, 68 & 72, Superior Serv Award, 72. *Mem:* Am Soc Agr Engrs; Soil Conserv Soc Am; Am Soc Testing & Mat. *Res:* Development of new equipment and materials for the high-speed and low-cost installation of subsurface drains in agricultural cropland; plastic septic tank for home sewage disposel systems. *Mailing Add:* 1917 Camelot Lane Findlay OH 45840

FOUST, ALAN S(HIVERS), b Dublin, Tex, June 26, 08; m 39; c 4. CHEMICAL ENGINEERING. *Educ:* Univ Tex, BS, 28, MS, 30; Univ Mich, PhD(chem eng), 38. *Prof Exp:* Tutor chem, Univ Tex, 28-30 & 32-33, instr, 33-35; chemist, Magnolia Petrol Co, 30-32 & Tex Pac Coal & Oil Co, 32-33; assoc prof chem, Col Mines & Metall, Univ Tex, 35-36; from instr to prof chem eng, Univ Mich, 37-52; prof, 52-65, head dept, 52-62, dean col eng, 62-65, McCann prof, 65-77, EMER PROF CHEM ENG, LEHIGH UNIV, 77- *Mem:* Fel Am Inst Chem Engrs. *Res:* Heat transfer; evaporation. *Mailing Add:* Dept of Chem Eng Lehigh Univ Bethlehem PA 18015

FOUTCH, GARY LYNN, b Poplar Bluff, Mo, Aug 26, 54; m 77; c 1. FERMENTATION, CHEMICALS FROM BIOMASS. *Educ:* Univ Mo, Rolla, BS, 75, MS, 77, PhD(chem eng), 80. *Prof Exp:* ASST PROF CHEM ENG, OKLA STATE UNIV, 80- *Concurrent Pos:* Fel, Jet Propulsion Lab, Calif Inst Technol, 81. *Mem:* Am Inst Chem Engrs; Am Chem Soc; Sigma Xi. *Res:* Production of chemicals from biomass by both biological and thermal processes; emphasizing those chemicals which cannot be produced economically from petroleum feedstocks. *Mailing Add:* 423 Eng Okla State Univ Stillwater OK 74078

FOUTCH, HARLEY WAYNE, b Woodlawn, Ill, Sept 29, 44; m 70. AGRONOMY, PLANT PHYSIOLOGY. *Educ:* Southern Ill Univ, BS, 66, MS, 68; Auburn Univ, PhD(agron), 71. *Prof Exp:* ASSOC PROF AGR, MIDDLE TENN STATE UNIV, 70-, ACTG DEPT CHMN, 80- *Mem:* Am Soc Agron; Weed Sci Soc. *Res:* Morphological and physiological response of cool season perennial grasses to temperature; forage crop physiology as affected by management practices; incorporation of herbicides by tillage methods. *Mailing Add:* Box 255 Middle Tenn State Univ Murfreesboro TN 37132

FOUTS, JAMES RALPH, b Macomb, Ill, Aug 8, 29; m 64; c 3. PHARMACOLOGY, TOXICOLOGY. *Educ:* Northwestern Univ, BS, 51, PhD(biochem), 54. *Prof Exp:* Instr & asst chem, Northwestern Univ, 51-54; asst scientist, Nat Heart Inst, 54-56, sr asst scientist, 56; sr res biochemist, Wellcome Res Labs, Burroughs Wellcome & Co, 56-57; from asst prof to prof pharmacol, Col Med, Univ Iowa, 57-70, dir, Oakdale Toxicol Ctr, 68-70; chief pharmacol br, 70-76, sci dir, 76-78, CHIEF LAB PHARMACOL, NAT INST ENVIRON HEALTH SCI, 78- *Concurrent Pos:* Mem comt on anticonvulsant drugs, Nat Inst Neurol Dis & Stroke, 69-75 & 80-83, mem epilepsy adv comt, 72-75 & 80-83; mem sci group on prin of pre-clin testing for drug safety, WHO, 66; Claude Bernard prof, Inst Med & Surg, Univ Mont, 70; adj prof pharmacol, Sch Med, Univ NC, 70-; adj prof entom & toxicol, Sch Agr & Life Sci, NC State Univ, 71-; mem drug interactions contract rev, Nat Inst Drug Abuse, 74-77; mem basic pharmacol adv comt, Pharmaceut Mfrs Asn Found, Inc, 73-78; mem & US rep, Sci Comt Prob Environ, Int Coun Sci Unions, 76-80; chmn, Gordon Res Conf Drug Metab, Plymouth, NH, 77 & 78; vis prof, Univ Zurich, 78-79; vis scientist, Swiss Fed Inst Technol, 78-79; mem coun, Am Soc Pharmacol & Exp Therapeut, 81-84. *Honors & Awards:* Abel Award, Am Soc Pharmacol & Exp Therapeut, 64; NIH Superior Achievement Award, 65. *Mem:* Am Asn Cancer Res; Soc Exp Biol & Med; Am Soc Pharmacol & Exp Therapeut; Soc Toxicol; Sigma Xi. *Res:* Drug metabolizing systems and factors affecting them; correlation of cell structure and enzyme activity; developmental pharmacology and toxicology; comparative and marine pharmacology and toxicology; drug interactions. *Mailing Add:* Nat Inst Environ Health Sci PO Box 12233 Research Triangle Park NC 27709

FOWELL, ANDREW JOHN, b Liverpool, Eng, Sept 27, 36; m 59; c 2. FLUID MECHANICS, ACOUSTICS. *Educ:* Univ Nottingham, BSc, 57, PhD(mech eng), 61. *Prof Exp:* Grad apprentice, English Elec Co, 60-62, develop engr, 62; res scientist, Am Standards Inc, 62-68, supvr acoust, 68-69, mgr adv prod develop, 69-72, mgr fixtures & seats eng, 72-76; chief, Prod Performance Eng Div, 76-81, CHIEF FIRE SAFETY ENG DIV, NAT BUR STANDARDS, 81- *Mem:* Acoust Soc Am; Am Soc Heat, Refrig & Air-Conditioning Engrs; Am Soc Testing & Mat. *Res:* Building technology; pulsating flow; turbulent diffusion; flow through air moving devices; fluid couplings; air conditioner and plumbing noise; consumer product performance; energy conservation; test methods; product safety; fire. *Mailing Add:* 10128 Gravier Ct Gaithersburg MD 20760

FOWKE, LAWRENCE CARROLL, b Toronto, Ont, June 6, 41; m 62; c 3. PLANT CYTOLOGY. *Educ:* Univ Sask, BA, 63; Carleton Univ, PhD(cell biol), 68. *Prof Exp:* Res fel cell biol, Australian Nat Univ, 68-70; from asst prof to assoc prof, 70-79, PROF BIOL, UNIV SASK, 79- *Mem:* Can Soc Cell Biol; Am Soc Cell Biol; Int Asn Plant Tissue Cult; Can Soc Plant Physiologists; Can Bot Asn. *Res:* Light and electron microscope studies of plant protoplasts, especially cell wall regeneration, protoplast fusion and uptake of organelles by protoplasts. *Mailing Add:* Dept Biol Univ Sask Saskatoon SK S7N 0W0 Can

FOWKES, FREDERICK MAYHEW, b Chicago, Ill, Jan 29, 15; m 37; c 4. CHEMISTRY. *Educ:* Univ Chicago, BS, 36, PhD(chem), 38. *Prof Exp:* Chemist, Nat Aluminate Corp, 37; res chemist, Continental Can Co, 38-42 & Shell Develop Co, 46-52, res supvr, 52-59, spec res chemist, Shell Oil Co, 59-61, res supvr, Shell Develop Co, 61-62; dir res, Sprague Elec Co, Mass, 62-68; chmn dept, 68-81, PROF CHEM, LEHIGH UNIV, 68- *Concurrent Pos:* Exchange chemist, Koninklijke Shell Lab, Amsterdam, 55-56. *Mem:* Am Chem Soc; sr mem Inst Elec & Electronics Eng; Electrochem Soc; Am Inst Chem. *Res:* Charge transfer mechanisms at solid-liquid and solid-solid interfaces; electrokinetic phenomena at surfaces and interfaces; surface states of semiconducting solids; dispersion force interactions at interfaces; protons in oxides. *Mailing Add:* Dept of Chem Lehigh Univ Bethlehem PA 18015

FOWLE, CHARLES DAVID, b Victoria, BC, Mar 31, 20; m 44; c 2. VERTEBRATE ECOLOGY, WILDLIFE MANAGEMENT. *Educ:* Univ BC, BA, 42, MA, 44; Univ Toronto, PhD(zool), 53. *Prof Exp:* In-charge wildlife res, Ont Dept Lands & Forest, 47-60; spec lectr, Univ Toronto, 47-62; chmn dept biol, 60-66, master, Vanier Col, 66-71, actg dir ctr res environ qual, 71-72, PROF BIOL, YORK UNIV, 60- *Mem:* Wildlife Soc; Can Soc Zool; Can Soc Wildlife & Fishery Biol. *Mailing Add:* Dept of Biol York Univ Downsview ON M3J 2R3 Can

FOWLER, ALAN B, b Denver, Colo, Oct 15, 28; m 50; c 4. SOLID STATE PHYSICS, SURFACE PHYSICS. *Educ:* Rensselaer Polytech Inst, BS, 51, MS, 52; Harvard Univ, PhD(appl physics), 58. *Prof Exp:* RES STAFF MEM, IBM CORP, 58- *Honors & Awards:* Wetherill Medal, Franklin Inst, 81. *Mem:* AAAS; Sci Res Soc Am; Am Vacuum Soc; fel Am Phys Soc; fel Inst Elec & Electronics Eng. *Res:* Semiconductor research in surface studies; optical properties of heavily doped crystals and photoconductors; injection lasers and thin film devices. *Mailing Add:* Thomas J Watson Res Ctr IBM Corp Yorktown Heights NY 10598

FOWLER, ARNOLD K, b Exeter, NH, Aug 11, 36; m 59; c 2. ANIMAL PHYSIOLOGY, GENETICS. *Educ:* Univ NH, BS, 58; Univ Conn, MS, 60; Ohio State Univ, PhD(animal physiol), 63. *Prof Exp:* Res scientist virol, US Air Force Sch Aerospace Med, 63-64, res scientist cellular biol, 64-69; asst prof animal sci, Univ NH, 69-70; MEM STAFF, NAT CANCER INST, 70- *Mem:* AAAS. *Res:* Mammalian reproductive physiology and genetics; cellular physiology. *Mailing Add:* Nat Cancer Inst Fredrick Cancer Ctr Fredrick MD 21701

FOWLER, AUDREE VERNEE, b Los Angeles, Calif, Oct 7, 33. PROTEIN CHEMISTRY. *Educ:* Univ Calif, Los Angeles, BS, 56, PhD(biochem), 63. *Prof Exp:* Fel, Dept Molecular Biol, Albert Einstein Col Med, 63-65; fel, 65-66, asst, 66-74, assoc res biol chemist, 74-80, RES BIOL CHEMIST, UNIV CALIF, LOS ANGELES, 80- *Mem:* Am Soc Biol Chemists; Sigma Xi. *Res:* Structural studies of protein; sequence, conformation, immunological properties, particularly proteins of the Lac operon. *Mailing Add:* Dept of Biol Chem Univ of Calif Sch of Med Los Angeles CA 90024

FOWLER, BRUCE ANDREW, b Seattle, Wash, Dec 28, 45; m 68; c 2. TOXICOLOGY, ENVIRONMENTAL BIOLOGY. *Educ:* Univ Wash, BS, 68; Univ Ore, PhD(exp path), 72. *Prof Exp:* Staff fel, 72-74, sr staff fel, 74-77, res biologist environ toxicol, 77-80, SR SCIENTIST, LAB PHARMACOL, NAT INST ENVIRON HEALTH SCI, 80- *Concurrent Pos:* Chmn, Steering Comt, Res Triangle Environ Metals Group, 73-; adj asst prof path, Univ NC, Chapel Hill, 74-80, adj assoc prof path, 80-; temp adv, WHO, 78-79; mem, working group, Int Agency for Res Against Cancer, 79. *Mem:* NY Acad Sci; AAAS; Am Asn Pathologists; Soc Toxicol; Am Soc Cell Biol. *Res:* The ultrastructural/biochemical characterization of mechanisms of cell injury from exposure to trace metals in mammals and marine organisms in relation to intracellular binding of both toxic and essential metals. *Mailing Add:* Lab Pharmacol Nat Inst Environ Health Sci Research Triangle Park NC 27709

FOWLER, BRUCE WAYNE, b Gadsden, Ala, Dec 10, 48. VECTOR POTENTIAL THEORY. *Educ:* Univ Ala, BS, 70; Univ Ill, Urbana, MS, 72; Univ Ala, Huntsville, PhD(physics), 78. *Prof Exp:* Syst analyst, Teledyne Brown Eng Co, 72-74; PHYSICIST, US ARMY MISSILE COMMAND, DEPT ARMY, 74- *Concurrent Pos:* Instr & mem grad fac, Univ Ala, Huntsville, 79- *Mem:* Am Chem Soc; Am Phys Soc; Sigma Xi. *Res:* Development of an empirically consistent methodology of technology forecasting; system concept development and analysis including technical, economic and political extrapolation. *Mailing Add:* 202-3 Utica Place Huntsville AL 35806

FOWLER, CHARLES A(LBERT), b Centralia, Ill, Dec 17, 20; m 43; c 2. ELECTRONICS. *Educ:* Univ Ill, BS, 42. *Prof Exp:* Mem staff, Radiation Lab, Mass Inst Technol, 42-45; mem staff, Airborne Instruments Lab, Inc, 45-66; dep dir tactical warfare progs, Off of Dir Defense Res & Eng, Dept Defense, 66-70; vpres & mgr equip develop labs, Equip Div, Raytheon Co, 70-76; V PRES, BEDFORD OPERS, MITRE CORP, BEDFORD, MASS, 76-, GEN MGR, 80- *Mem:* AAAS; fel Inst Elec & Electronics Engrs; assoc fel Am Inst Aeronaut & Astronaut. *Res:* Radar; electronics. *Mailing Add:* Bedford Oper Burlington Rd Bedford MA 01730

FOWLER, CHARLES ARMAN, JR, b Salt Lake City, Utah, Apr 23, 12; m 34; c 2. MAGNETISM. *Educ:* Univ Utah, AB, 33, MS, 34; Univ Calif, PhD(physics), 40. *Prof Exp:* from instr to asst prof, Univ Calif, Berkeley, 40-46; assoc prof, 46-50, chmn dept, 47-72, prof, 50-77, EMER PROF PHYSICS, POMONA COL, 77- *Concurrent Pos:* NSF sr fel, Univ Grenoble, France, 60-61; mem comt physics fac in cols, Am Inst Physics, 62-65; NSF fac fel, 67-68. *Mem:* Am Phys Soc; Am Asn Physics Teachers; Sigma Xi. *Res:* Magnetism; ferromagnetic domains; magneto-optics; molecular spectroscopy; optics; x-ray diffraction. *Mailing Add:* Millikan Lab Pomona Col Claremont CA 91711

FOWLER, CLARENCE MAXWELL, b Centralia, Ill, Nov 26, 18; m 42; c 1. PHYSICS. *Educ:* Univ Ill, BS, 40; Univ Mich, MS & PhD(physics), 49. *Prof Exp:* Asst wire res, Am Steel & Wire Co, 40-43; prof physics, Kans State Col, 49-57; MEM STAFF, LOS ALAMOS NAT LAB, 57- *Mem:* Fel Am Phys Soc. *Res:* Shock waves; high magnetic fields; explosive energy conversion. *Mailing Add:* Los Alamos Nat Lab PO Box 1663 Los Alamos NM 87545

FOWLER, DONA JANE, b Muncie, Ind, May 8, 28; div; c 2. NEUROENDOCRINOLOGY. *Educ:* Purdue Univ, BS, 55, MS, 62, PhD, 65. *Prof Exp:* Res asst plant physiol, Purdue Univ, 54-55, cardiac res, 56-57; assoc res anal chemist, Eli Lilly Co, 57-60; asst zool & biol, Purdue Univ, 60-62 & physiol & ecol, 62-65; from instr to assoc prof, 65-78, PROF BIOL, WESTERN MICH UNIV, 78- *Concurrent Pos:* Guest Scientist, Labs, Genetics, Evolution & Biomet, Nat Ctr Sci Res, Gif-sur-Yvette, France; vis scholar, Biol Dept, Univ Ariz, 80-81. *Mem:* AAAS; Am Inst Biol Sci; Am Soc. Zool; Int Soc Chronobiol; Am Meteorol Soc. *Res:* Metabolic regulation; environmental factors that influence the regulatory functions of invertebrates, chiefly arachnids, experimental parameters involved, including the analysis of neurosecretions and locomotion as cyclic phenomena; monochromatic light receptors in tissue culture. *Mailing Add:* Dept Biol Western Mich Univ Kalamazoo MI 49001

FOWLER, DONALD PAIGE, b Waterbury, Conn, Nov 26, 32; Can citizen; div; c 3. FOREST GENETICS, FORESTRY. *Educ:* Univ NB, BSc, 55; Yale Univ, MS, 56, PhD(forestry), 64. *Prof Exp:* Res scientist forest genetics, Ont Dept Lands & Forests, 56-66; RES SCIENTIST & PROJ LEADER FOREST GENETICS, CAN FORESTRY SERV, 66- *Concurrent Pos:* Sect leader, Can Forestry Serv, 66-; res assoc, Univ NB, 70-; assoc ed, Can J Forest Res, 76- *Mem:* Can Tree Improv Asn; Sigma Xi; Can Inst Forestry. *Res:* Forest genetics and applied tree improvement with special interest in picea and larix; species hybridization; phylogenetic relationships; population structure and development of breeding strategies. *Mailing Add:* Can Forestry Serv PO Box 4000 Fredericton Can

FOWLER, EARLE CABELL, b Bowling Green, Ky, June 10, 21; m 50; c 3. HIGH ENERGY PHYSICS. *Educ:* Univ Ky, BS, 42; Harvard Univ, AM, 47, PhD(physics), 49. *Prof Exp:* Assoc physicist, Brookhaven Nat Lab, 49-52; from asst prof to assoc prof, Yale Univ, 52-62; prof, Duke Univ, 62-70; head dept, 71-77, PROF PHYSICS, PURDUE UNIV, 71- *Concurrent Pos:* Consult, Brookhaven Nat Lab, 52-76; Fulbright lectr, Univ Birmingham, Eng, 58-59; Fulbright scholar, Univ Rome, 67-68; mem bd dirs, Triangle Univ Comput Ctr, 69-71; panel mem, NSF Comput Facil Div, 69-71; chmn exec comt, Nat Accelerator Lab User's Orgn, 72-73; sr physicist, High Energy Physics Br, US Dept Energy, 80- *Mem:* Am Phys Soc. *Res:* Cosmic Rays; high energy particle physics; micrometeorology. *Mailing Add:* ER-22 GTN High Energy Physics US Dept Energy Washington DC 20545

FOWLER, EDWARD HERBERT, b Stoneham, Mass, Oct 25, 36; m 56; c 2. PATHOLOGY. *Educ:* Univ NH, BS, 58; Mich State Univ, MS & DVM, 62; Ohio State Univ, PhD(vet path), 65; Am Col Vet Path, dipl. *Prof Exp:* Asst prof vet path, Ohio State Univ, 66-70, actg asst dean acad affairs, Vet Col, 70; assoc prof oncol, Lab Animal Med & assoc prof path, Sch Med, Univ Rochester, 70-78; CHEM HYG FEL & MGR PATH & ANIMAL CARE, CARNEGIE-MELLON INST RES, 78- *Concurrent Pos:* Consult, Bur Drugs, Food & Drug Admin, 71-72. *Mem:* Am Vet Med Asn; Int Acad Path; Am Soc Vet Clin Path; Histochem Soc; Am Asn Cancer Res. *Res:* Pathogenesis of animal neoplasms; etiology and pathogenesis of steroid hormone dependent animal and human neoplasms; toxicologic pathology. *Mailing Add:* Bushy Run Res Ctr Carnegie Mellon Univ 4400 Fifth Ave Pittsburgh PA 15213

FOWLER, ELIZABETH, b Schenectady, NY, Apr 18, 43. PROTEIN CHEMISTRY, CELL BIOLOGY. *Educ:* Cornell Univ, AB, 65; Harvard Univ, PhD(biol chem), 72. *Prof Exp:* Fel genetics, Univ Wis-Madison, 72-76, asst scientist, 76-77; ASST PROF BACTERIA & IMMUNOL, UNIV NC, CHAPEL HILL, 77- *Mem:* Am Asn Immunologists; Am Soc Cell Biol; AAAS. *Res:* Mechanisms of control of gene activity; functions of chromosomal proteins; structure function studies of abrin and ricin; lymphoblastoid receptors for Epstein Barr virus. *Mailing Add:* Univ NC 424 Swing Bldg 217H Chapel Hill NC 27514

FOWLER, EMIL EUGENE, b Morgantown, WVa, Sept 15, 23; m 49; c 3. CHEMISTRY. *Educ:* WVa Univ, AB, 46, MS, 47. *Prof Exp:* Chief, Radioisotopes Br, Tenn, 47-56, deputy dir, Isotopes Div, 56, dep asst dir, Div Civilian Appln & Off Indust Develop, 56-59, DIR ISOTOPES DEVELOP, US ATOMIC ENERGY COMN, WASHINGTON, DC, 65- *Concurrent Pos:* Dir chem & indust applns, Int Atomic Energy Agency, Vienna, Austria, 75-77; chief tech adv, UN Develop Prog Indust Proj, Vienna, Austria, 80- *Mem:* AAAS; Am Nuclear Soc; Soc Nuclear Med; Health Phys Soc; Am Inst Chem. *Res:* Accelerating development of widespread applications of radioisotopes and high-intensity radiation; radioisotopes production, process development, pricing and marketing; production and distribution of radioisotopes and isotopes technology training. *Mailing Add:* 5124 Westpath Way Bethesda MD 20816

FOWLER, ERIC BEAUMONT, b Milbank, SDak, May 4, 14; m 42; c 3. SOIL CHEMISTRY. *Educ:* Kans State Univ, BS, 42, MS, 44; Iowa State Col, PhD(chem & physiol bact), 50. *Prof Exp:* Prof asst & lab asst bact, Kans State Univ, 39-42; asst soil conserv, Iowa State Col, 42-44, instr bact, 44-50, from asst prof to assoc prof, 50-56; mem staff & alt group leader, Los Alamos Sci Lab, 56-75, mem staff & asst group leader, 75-78, mem staff & prin investr, Soil-Waste Interactions, 78-81; RETIRED. *Concurrent Pos:* Soils element mgr, Nev Appl Ecol Group Energy Res & Develop Admin, 70-78. *Mem:* AAAS; Am Nuclear Soc. *Res:* Chemical and physiological bacteriology; disposal of biological and industrial wastes; plant uptake and control of radio isotopes in the environment; radioactive-soil interactions. *Mailing Add:* Los Alamos Sci Lab Box 1663 Los Alamos NM 87544

FOWLER, FRANK CAVAN, b Kansas City, Mo, June 15, 18; m 43; c 3. CHEMICAL ENGINEERING. *Educ:* Univ Ill, BS, 39; Univ Mich, MS, 40, PhD(chem eng), 43. *Prof Exp:* Chem engr, Phillips Petrol Co, Okla, 43-46; instr univ exten, Univ Okla, 45, from assoc prof to prof chem eng, 46-51; consult chem engr, 51-58; PRES, RES ENGRS, INC, 58- *Concurrent Pos:* Vis prof, Univ Kans, 52-53 & 56-58. *Mem:* Am Chem Soc; Sigma Xi; Am Inst Chem Engrs. *Res:* Fluid flow; heat transfer; distillation; mixing of fluids by successive flow through pipes; process design; thermodynamics. *Mailing Add:* 10000 E 137th Kansas City MO 64149

FOWLER, FRANK WILSON, b Portland, Maine, May 16, 41; m 63. ORGANIC CHEMISTRY. *Educ:* Univ Colo, PhD(chem), 67. *Prof Exp:* Leverhulme vis fel, Univ EAnglia, Eng, 67-68; asst prof, 68-73, assoc prof, 73-80, PROF CHEM, STATE UNIV NY STONY BROOK, 80- *Res:* Synthesis of interesting and unusual heterocyclic molecules; aromaticity; valence tantomerism; natural products. *Mailing Add:* Dept of Chem State Univ of NY Stony Brook NY 11794

FOWLER, GERALD ALLAN, b Tacoma, Wash, June 1, 34; m 62; c 2. MICROPALEONTOLOGY, PALEOECOLOGY. *Educ:* Univ Puget Sound, BS,57; Univ Southern Calif, PhD(geol), 65. *Prof Exp:* Asst prof marine geol, Dept Oceanog, Ore State Univ, 64-72; ASSOC PROF EARTH SCI, DIV SCI, UNIV WIS, PARKSIDE, 72- *Mem:* Geol Soc Am; Soc Econ Paleontologists & Mineralogists. *Res:* Interpretation of paleoenvironments and stratigraphy of marine neogene sediments of continental margin of the Northwest United States using benthic foraminifera. *Mailing Add:* Div Sci Univ Wis Parkside PO Box 2000 Kenosha WI 53141

FOWLER, GREGORY L, b Wichita, Kans, Aug 19, 34; m 67; c 2. GENETICS. *Educ:* Wichita State Univ, BA, 56, MS, 60; Brown Univ, PhD(genetics), 68. *Prof Exp:* Lectr biol, Wichita State Univ, 59-60; instr, Bethany Col, 60-62; asst prof, George Washington Univ, 67-69; assoc & vis asst prof, Univ Ore, 69-71; asst prof, Univ Düsseldorf, 71-74 & Univ Ore, 74-76; ASSOC PROF BIOL, SOUTHERN ORE STATE COL, 76- *Res:* In vitro cytological and biochemical characterization of lampbrush chromosomes in Drosophila hydei testis; light and electron microscope studies of Drosophila spermatogenesis in vitro. *Mailing Add:* Dept of Biol Southern Ore State Col Ashland OR 97520

FOWLER, H(ORATIO) SEYMOUR, b Highland Park, Mich, Mar 1, 19; wid; c 1. BIOLOGY, SCIENCE EDUCATION. *Educ:* Cornell Univ, BS, 41, MS, 46, PhD(sci educ), 51. *Prof Exp:* Teacher pub schs, NY, 46 & 47-49; asst sci educ, Cornell Univ, 49-51; asst prof, Southern Ore Col, 51-52 & biol, Iowa State Teachers Col, 52-57; coordr, Div Acad Curric & Instr, 74-76, PROF SCI EDUC, PA STATE UNIV, 57-, DIR, PA CONSERV LAB, 60-, CHMN SCI EDUC FAC, 69- *Concurrent Pos:* Dir, Iowa teachers conserv camp, 52-57. *Honors & Awards:* Fulbright lectr, Korea, 68-69. *Mem:* Fel AAAS; Am Nature Study Soc (vpres, 64, pres elect, 66, pres, 67); Nat Asn Res Sci Teaching; hon mem Nat Asn Biol Teachers (vpres, 59); Sigma Xi. *Res:* Science education; conservation education. *Mailing Add:* 166 Chambers Bldg Pa State Univ University Park PA 16802

FOWLER, HOWLAND AUCHINCLOSS, b New York, NY, Jan 25, 30; m 62; c 2. PHYSICS, RESEARCH ADMINISTRATION. *Educ:* Princeton Univ, AB, 52; Brown Univ, MSc, 55, PhD(physics), 57. *Prof Exp:* Nat Res Coun assoc, 57-58, physicist, 58-71, PHYS SCI ADMINR, NAT BUR STANDARDS, 71- *Mem:* Am Phys Soc; Soc Indust & Appl Math; Inst Elec & Electronics Engrs. *Res:* Electron physics; electron scattering; electron-optical technique; far-UV optical constants; application of Josephson effect to voltage measurement; applications of computer graphics to physical problems. *Mailing Add:* Ctr for Appl Math Nat Bur Standards Washington DC 20234

FOWLER, IRA, b La, Apr 27, 21; m 52; c 2. EXPERIMENTAL EMBRYOLOGY. *Educ:* La Polytech Inst, BS, 42; Univ La, MS, 49; Northwestern Univ, PhD(zool), 52. *Prof Exp:* Asst, Univ La, 48-50; asst, Northwestern Univ, 50-52, res assoc, 52-53, instr anat, Sch Med, Univ NC, Chapel Hill, 53-55, from asst prof to assoc prof, 55-66, USPHS sr res fel, 57-62; assoc prof, 66-74, PROF ANAT, MED CTR, UNIV KY, 74- *Mem:* Am Inst Biol Sci; Am Soc Zool; Am Asn Anat. *Res:* Cellular responses in auto-immunization. *Mailing Add:* Dept Anat Albert S Chandler Med Ctr Univ Ky Lexington KY 40536

FOWLER, JAMES A, b New York, NY, Jan 30, 23; m 55; c 2. VERTEBRATE EMBRYOLOGY. *Educ:* Princeton Univ, BSE, 44; Columbia Univ, MA, 57, PhD(zool), 61. *Prof Exp:* Power engr, Western Union Tel Co, 47-49; elec engr, St Anthony Mining & Develop Co, 49; lectr embryol, Columbia Univ, 59 & zool, Barnard Col, 59-60; asst dean col arts & sci, 64-69, assoc dean health prof adv, 69-74, ASST PROF BIOL SCI, STATE UNIV NY STONY BROOK, 61- *Mem:* AAAS; Am Soc Zool; Am Soc Naturalists. *Res:* Interaction between evolution and embryology; population genetics of development and its evolutionary history; theoretical analysis of development. *Mailing Add:* Box L Coraway Rd Setauket NY 11733

FOWLER, JAMES LOWELL, b Stephenville, Tex, Oct 20, 35; m 61; c 2. CROP PHYSIOLOGY. *Educ:* Tex Tech Univ, BS, 62, MS, 66; Tex A&M Univ, PhD(plant physiol), 71. *Prof Exp:* Asst prof, 71-79, ASSOC PROF AGRON, NMEX STATE UNIV, 79- *Mem:* Am Soc Agron; Crop Sci Soc Am. *Res:* Cotton production; plant growth and development; environmental physiology; plant water relations; new crops. *Mailing Add:* Box 3Q Dept Agron NMex State Univ Las Cruces NM 88003

FOWLER, JOANNA S, b Aug 9, 42. ORGANIC CHEMISTRY. *Educ:* Univ SFla, BA, 64; Univ Colo, PhD(chem), 68. *Prof Exp:* Res assoc organothallium chem, Univ East Anglia, Eng, 68-69; res assoc org chem, 69-71, CHEMIST, BROOKHAVEN NAT LAB, 71- *Mem:* Soc Nuclear Med; Am Chem Soc. *Res:* Organic synthesis; reactions of molecular fluorine; design and synthesis of radiopharmaceuticals labeled with short-lived nuclides; mechanisms of drug localization. *Mailing Add:* Dept of Chem Brookhaven Nat Lab Upton NY 11973

FOWLER, JOHN ALVIS, b High Point, NC, Oct 17, 21; m; c 6. PSYCHOANALYSIS, PSYCHIATRY. *Educ:* Wake Forest Univ, BS, 43; Bowman Gray Sch Med, MD, 46. *Prof Exp:* Intern, US Naval Hosp, Corpus Christi, Tex, 46-47; resident psychiat, Univ Colo Med Ctr, 49-52; asst prof, 53-61, PROF CHILD PSYCHIAT, MED CTR, DUKE UNIV, 61-, HEAD DIV, 63- *Concurrent Pos:* Resident child psychiat, Univ Colo Med Ctr & Conn Bur Ment Hyg, 51-53; dir, Durham Child Guid Clin, 53-63; training & supv psychoanalyst, Univ NC-Duke Univ Psychoanal Training Prog, 72-; lectr educ, Duke Univ, 73-; mem bd dir, Child Advocacy Comn Durham, Inc, 73-76. *Mem:* Am Psychoanal Asn; Asn Child Psychoanal; Am Psychiat Asn; Am Acad Child Psychiat. *Mailing Add:* Dept of Psychiat Duke Univ Med Ctr Durham NC 27706

FOWLER, JOHN RAYFORD, b Winnfield, La, July 11, 43; m 64; c 2. INORGANIC CHEMISTRY, TEXTILE TECHNOLOGY. *Educ:* McMurry Col, BA, 65; Univ Kans, PhD(inorg chem), 69. *Prof Exp:* Teaching asst chem, Univ Kans, 65-68; res chemist, Textile Res Lab, 69-77, res chemist, 77-79, STAFF CHEMIST, SAVANNAH RIVER LAB, E I DU PONT DE NEMOURS & CO, 80- *Concurrent Pos:* Instr, Aiken TEC, SC, 81- *Mem:* Am Chem Soc. *Res:* Transition metal complexes; nonaqueous solvents; cyano complexes; IR spectroscopy; synthetic textile fibers; textile technology; polymer science; nuclear chemistry; nuclear waste management. *Mailing Add:* 849 Magnolia St SE Aiken SC 29801

FOWLER, JOSEPH LEE, b Springfield, Ohio, Nov 19, 13; m 45; c 2. NUCLEAR PHYSICS. *Educ:* Univ Tenn, AB & MS, 38; Princeton Univ, PhD(physics), 43. *Prof Exp:* Sect leader isotron res, Princeton Univ, 42-43; sect leader & alt group leader bomb physics div, 44-46, group leader in chg cyclotron, Los Alamos, NMex, 46-50; dir high voltage lab, 51-54, from assoc dir to dir, Physics Div, 54-73, RES PHYSICIST, OAK RIDGE NAT LAB, 73-; PROF PHYSICS, UNIV TENN, KNOXVILLE, 74- *Mem:* Fel AAAS; Fel Am Phys Soc. *Res:* Neutron, proton and deuteron interaction with nuclei; fission fragment mass and energy distributions; quarks. *Mailing Add:* Dept of Physics Univ of Tenn Knoxville TN 37916

FOWLER, KENNETH ARTHUR, b Buffalo, NY, Jan 10, 16; m 48; c 2. MATHEMATICS. *Educ:* Cornell Univ, BA, 38; Univ Mich, MA, 47, PhD(math), 52. *Prof Exp:* Asst prof math, Univ Ariz, 51-55; prof, Col Educ, State Univ NY New Paltz, 55-56; asst prof, Union Univ (NY), 56-57; from asst prof to assoc prof, 57-65, PROF MATH, SAN JOSE STATE COL, 65- *Mem:* Am Math Soc; Math Asn Am. *Res:* Algebra; foundations of mathematics; topology. *Mailing Add:* Dept of Math San Jose State Univ San Jose CA 95192

FOWLER, MALCOLM MCFARLAND, b Houston, Tex, Dec 13, 43; m 73; c 2. NUCLEAR & ANALYTICAL CHEMISTRY. *Educ:* Univ NMex, BS, 66; Wash Univ, St Louis, MA, 67, PhD(chem), 72. *Prof Exp:* Fel nuclear chem, McGill Univ, 72-73; fel heavy ion reactions, Lawrence Berkeley Lab, Berkeley, 73-75; STAFF MEM NUCLEAR CHEM, LOS ALAMOS SCI LAB, 75- *Mem:* Am Chem Soc; Am Phys Soc; Sigma Xi. *Res:* Heavy-ion reactions; instrument development; environmental and atmospheric research. *Mailing Add:* 134 Aztec Los Alamos NM 87544

FOWLER, MARY STINECIPHER, see Stinecipher, Mary Margaret

FOWLER, MICHAEL, b Doncaster, Eng, Apr 30, 38; m 65. THEORETICAL PHYSICS. *Educ:* Cambridge Univ, BA, 59, PhD(field theory), 62. *Prof Exp:* Instr physics, Princeton Univ, 62-63; asst prof, Univ Md, 63-65; asst prof, Univ Toronto, 65-68; assoc prof, 68-73, PROF PHYSICS, UNIV VA, 73- *Mem:* Am Phys Soc. *Res:* Analytic methods in potential theory and perturbation theory; electrons in high magnetic fields in metals. *Mailing Add:* Dept of Physics Univ of Va Charlottesville VA 22903

FOWLER, MURRAY ELWOOD, b Glendale, Wash, July 17, 28; m 50; c 5. VETERINARY MEDICINE. *Educ:* Utah State Univ, BS, 52; Iowa State Univ, DVM, 55; Am Bd Vet Toxicol, dipl; Am Col Vet Internists, dipl. *Prof Exp:* Pvt pract vet med, 55-57; from instr to assoc prof, 57-58, PROF VET MED, UNIV CALIF, DAVIS, 58-, CHMN DEPT MED, 73- *Mem:* Am Vet Med Asn; Am Asn Zoo Vets; Wildlife Dis Asn. *Res:* Clinical toxicology; teaching and research in problems of zoo animal medicine and wildlife diseases. *Mailing Add:* Dept of Med Sch of Vet Med Univ of Calif Davis CA 95616

FOWLER, NOBLE OWEN, b Vicksburg, Miss, July 14, 19; m 42; c 3. INTERNAL MEDICINE, CARDIOVASCULAR DISEASE. *Educ:* Univ Tenn, MD, 41. *Prof Exp:* USPHS fel cardiol, Univ Cincinnati, 48-49, trainee, 49-50, Am Heart Asn res fel & asst prof med, 51-52; asst prof med, State Univ NY, 52-54; assoc prof med & chair cardiovasc res, Emory Univ, 54-57; assoc prof clin med, 57-59, assoc prof med, 59-64, PROF INTERNAL MED, UNIV CINCINNATI, 64-; DIR DIV CARDIOL, 70-; DIR CARDIAC RES LAB, CINCINNATI GEN HOSP, 64- *Concurrent Pos:* Consult, Dayton Vet Hosp, 49-52 & Brooklyn Vet Hosp, NY, 54. *Mem:* Fel Am Col Physicians; Am Physiol Soc; Am Clin & Climat Soc. *Res:* Physiology and pharmacology of the pulmonary circulation; physiology of regulation of cardiac output; plasma substitutes; pericardial fuunction. *Mailing Add:* Cardiol Div Rm 3466 Univ of Cincinnati Med Ctr Cincinnati OH 45267

FOWLER, NORMA LEE, b St Louis, Mo, May 29, 52. POPULATION ECOLOGY, POPULATION GENETICS. *Educ:* Univ Chicago, BA, 73; Duke Univ, PhD(bot), 78. *Prof Exp:* Fel, Univ Col NWales, Bangor, UK, 78-79; ASST PROF BOT, UNIV TEX AT AUSTIN, 79- *Mem:* Ecol Soc Am; Soc Study Evolution; British Ecol Soc. *Res:* Herbaceous perennials; plant population dynamics and population regulation, competition, community structure, life histories, and quantitative genetic variation in ecologically relevant characters. *Mailing Add:* Dept Bot Univ Tex Austin TX 78712

FOWLER, RICHARD EDMOND, b Marion, Miss, Dec 20, 23; m 72; c 5. PEDIATRICS. *Educ:* Univ Miss, AB, 43; Duke Univ, MD, 45. *Prof Exp:* Intern, Charity Hosp, New Orleans, 45; resident pediat, Children's Hosp, Birmingham, Ala, 46; resident, La State Serv, Charity Hosp, 48-50; Nat Heart Inst trainee, 50-51, from instr to asst prof, 53-55, PROF PEDIAT & HEAD DEPT, LA STATE UNIV SCH MED, NEW ORLEANS, 55- *Concurrent Pos:* Mem bd, Am Bd Pediat, 75-81, vpres, 79 & 80. *Mem:* Soc Pediat Res; Am Acad Pediat; Am Heart Asn; Am Pediat Soc; fel Am Col Cardiol. *Res:* Various aspects of congenital heart disease. *Mailing Add:* Dept of Pediat La State Univ Sch Med New Orleans LA 70112

FOWLER, RICHARD GILDART, b Albion, Mich, June 13, 16; m 39; c 4. PHYSICS. *Educ:* Albion Col, AB, 36; Univ Mich, MS, 39, PhD(physics), 41. *Prof Exp:* Asst, Dow Chem Co, Mich, 36-38; asst, Univ Mich, 38-40, res physicist, 41 & 42-46; instr physics, NC State Col, 41-42; from asst prof to prof, 46-61, chmn dept, 55-59 & 66-68, res prof, 61-80, EMER PROF PHYSICS, UNIV OKLA, 80- *Concurrent Pos:* Guggenheim fel, 52; Fulbright lectr, Australia, 63; NATO fel, 70. *Mem:* Fel Inst Physics; AAAS; fel Am Phys Soc. *Res:* Ultraviolet spectrochemical analysis; organic structure determination by infrared spectra; plasma physics and electrically generated shock waves; plasma driven shock tubes; purification of graphite; mechanisms involved in the production of radiation. *Mailing Add:* Dept of Physics Univ of Okla 440 W Brooks Norman OK 73069

FOWLER, SCOTT WELLINGTON, b Berkeley, Calif, May 31, 41; m 65; c 2. BIOLOGICAL OCEANOGRAPHY, MARINE RADIOECOLOGY. *Educ:* Univ Calif, Riverside, BA, 64; Ore State Univ, MS, 66, PhD(biol oceanog), 69. *Prof Exp:* Scientist, Battelle-Northwest Labs, 67; Fulbright lectr, Monterrey Inst Technol, Mex, 69-70; SCIENTIST & HEAD BIOL SECT, INT ATOMIC ENERGY AGENCY, INT LAB MARINE RADIOACTIVITY, OCEANOG MUS, MONACO, 70- *Concurrent Pos:* UN Environ Prog Consult, Multidisciplinary Mission, Persian Gulf States, 80 & mission leader, Survey Tar & Oil Pollution, Sultanate Oman, 80; pres marine radioactivity comt, Int Comn Sci, Explor Mediterranean. *Mem:* NY Acad Sci; Am Soc Limnol & Oceanog; Sigma Xi; Int Union Radioecologists. *Res:* Transfer of radionuclides through marine food chains, biokinetics of heavy metals and organic pollutants in marine organisms, zooplankton physiology, marine invertebrate physiology and ecology; vertical flux of marine biogenic particulates. *Mailing Add:* Int Lab of Marine Radioactivity Oceanog Mus Monaco

FOWLER, THOMAS KENNETH, b Thomaston, Ga, Mar 27, 31; m 56; c 3. THEORETICAL PHYSICS. *Educ:* Vanderbilt Univ, BE, 53, MS, 55; Univ Wis, PhD(theoret physics), 57. *Prof Exp:* Physicist, Oak Ridge Nat Lab, 57-65 & gen atomic div, Gen Dynamic Corp, 65-67; head plasma physics div, 67, group leader plasma theory, Lawrence Livermore Lab, 67-69, ASSOC DIR CONTROLLED THERMONUCLEAR RES, LAWRENCE LIVERMORE LAB, 70-, DIV LEADER, 69- *Mem:* Fel Am Phys Soc; Sigma Xi. *Res:* Controlled fusion; plasma and nuclear physics, especially scattering theory. *Mailing Add:* Lawrence Livermore Lab PO Box 808 Livermore CA 94550

FOWLER, TIMOTHY JOHN, b Birmingham, Eng, Jan 11, 38; m 65; c 3. STRUCTURAL ENGINEERING, ENGINEERING MECHANICS. *Educ:* Univ Birmingham, Eng, BSc, 59; Univ London, DIC, 60; Univ Tex, PhD(struct eng), 66. *Prof Exp:* Grad engr civil eng, Binnie, Deacon & Gourley, London, 60-61; design engr civil eng, Binnie & Partners, Kuala Lumpur, Malaya, 62-63; sr engr, eng specialist & prin eng specialist civil, struct & mech eng, 65-71, Monsanto fel, 71-75, SR MONSANTO FEL, CIVIL, STRUCT & MECH ENG, MONSANTO CO, 76- *Mem:* Am Soc Civil Engrs; Am Soc Mech Engrs; Am Concrete Inst; Inst Civil Engrs. *Res:* Acoustic emission; structural mechanics; structural plastics; refractory concrete. *Mailing Add:* Monsanto Co 800 N Lindbergh Blvd St Louis MO 63166

FOWLER, WALLACE T(HOMAS), b Greenville, Tex, Aug 27, 38; m 68; c 2. AEROSPACE ENGINEERING. *Educ:* Univ Tex, Austin, BA, 60, MS, 61, PhD(eng mech), 65. *Prof Exp:* Asst prof eng mech, 65-67, from asst prof to assoc prof aerospace eng, 67-77, PROF AEROSPACE ENG & ENG MECH, UNIV TEX, AUSTIN, 77-, DIR, BUR ENG TEACHING, COL ENG, OFF DEAN, 80- *Concurrent Pos:* Consult, Manned Spacecraft Ctr, 66- & Gen Dynamics/Ft Worth, 67-69. *Mem:* Am Inst Aeronaut & Astronaut. *Res:* Flight mechanics; numerical optimization; guidance and control. *Mailing Add:* Dept of Aerospace Eng & Eng Mech Univ of Tex Austin TX 78712

FOWLER, WARD SCOTT, b Summerfield, Kans, Oct 24, 15; m 40; c 2. PHYSIOLOGY. *Educ:* Swarthmore Col, AB, 37; Harvard Med Sch, MD, 41. *Prof Exp:* Am Col Physicians fel, 47-48; NIH fel, 48-50; assoc prof physiol, Grad Sch Med, Univ Pa, 51-52; from assoc prof to prof, 52-77, EMER PROF PHYSIOL & ASSOC DEAN, MAYO MED SCH, UNIV MINN, 77- *Concurrent Pos:* Consult physician, Mayo Clin, 52- *Mem:* AAAS; Am Physiol Soc; Am Soc Clin Invest; Soc Exp Biol & Med. *Res:* Respiratory physiology, clinical derangements and tests. *Mailing Add:* Mayo Clinic Rochester MN 55901

FOWLER, WILLIAM ALFRED, b Pittsburgh, Pa, Aug 9, 11; m 40; c 2. PHYSICS. *Educ:* Ohio State Univ, BEngPhys, 33; Calif Inst Technol, PhD(physics), 36. *Hon Degrees:* DS, Univ Chicago, 76 & Ohio State Univ, 78, Dr, Univ Liege, 81. *Prof Exp:* Res fel, 36-39, from asst prof to prof, 39-70, INST PROF PHYSICS, CALIF INST TECHNOL, 70- *Concurrent Pos:* Asst dir res, Nat Defense Res Comt, 41-45; tech observ, Off Field Serv & New Develop Div, Dept War, 44; sci dir proj Vista, Dept Defense, 51-52; Guggenheim fel, Cavendish Lab, Cambridge Univ, 54-55, 61-62 & St Johns Col, 61-62; vis prof, Mass Inst Technol, 66; mem nat sci bd, NSF, 68-74; mem bd dirs, Am Friends Cambridge Univ, 70-78; mem space sci bd, Nat Acad Sci, 70-73 & 77-80, mem coun, 74-77, chmn, Off Phys Sci, 81-84; mem gov bd, Am Inst Physics, 74-80. *Honors & Awards:* Naval Ord Develop Award, US Navy, 45; Presidential Medal for Merit, 48; Lamme Medal, Ohio State Univ, 52; Liege Medal, Univ Liege, 55; Barnard Medal, Columbia Univ, 65; Apollo Achievement Award, NASA, 69; Tom W Bonner Prize, Am Phys Soc, 70; G Unger Vetlesen Prize, 73; Nat Medal of Sci, 74; Eddington Medal, Royal Astron Soc, 78. *Mem:* Nat Acad Sci; AAAS; fel Am Phys Soc; Am Astron Soc; Am Philos Soc. *Res:* Studies of nuclear forces and reaction rates; nuclear spectroscopy; structure of light nuclei; thermonuclear sources of stellar energy and element synthesis in stars and supernovae; study of general relativistic effects in quasar and pulsar models. *Mailing Add:* Kellogg Radiation Lab 106-38 Calif Inst of Technol Pasadena CA 91125

FOWLER, WILLIAM MAYO, JR, b Brooklyn, NY, June 16, 26; m 50; c 1. PHYSICAL MEDICINE & REHABILITATION. *Educ:* Springfield Col, BS, 48, MEd, 49; Univ Southern Calif, MD, 57. *Prof Exp:* Instr, Dept Phys Educ, Univ Calif, Los Angeles, 49-52 & United Cerebral Palsy Found grant pediat, 59-60; NIMH training grant neurol, 60-61; lectr phys med & rehab, Univ Calif, Los Angeles, 63-64, asst prof, 64-68, actg chmn dept, 67, chief rehab med, 67-68, assoc prof phys med & rehab & pediat, 68; assoc prof, 68-72, PROF PHYS MED & REHAB & CHMN DEPT, SACRAMENTO MED CTR, UNIV CALIF, DAVIS, 72- *Concurrent Pos:* Dir phys med & rehab, Harbor Gen Hosp, Torrance, Calif, 65; attend physician phys med, Wadsworth Vet Admin Hosp, Los Angeles, 65-68 & Long Beach Vet Admin Hosp, 65-68; consult phys med & rehab, San Fernando Vet Admin Hosp, 67-68; dir, Off Allied Health Sci, Univ Calif, Davis, 69-71. *Mem:* Acad Phys Med & Rehab (pres, 80-81). *Res:* Muscle biology and muscle disease; work physiology; pediatrics. *Mailing Add:* Univ Calif Davis Sacramento Med Ctr Sacramento CA 95817

FOWLER, WYMAN BEALL, JR, b Scranton, Pa, June 18, 37; m 61; c 4. SOLID STATE PHYSICS. *Educ:* Lehigh Univ, BS, 59; Univ Rochester, PhD(physics), 63. *Prof Exp:* Res assoc physics, Univ Rochester, 63 & Univ Ill, 63-66; assoc prof, 66-69, PROF PHYSICS, LEHIGH UNIV, 69-, CHMN DEPT, 78- *Concurrent Pos:* Consult, Argonne Nat Lab, 63-66 & Naval Res Lab, 66-81. *Honors & Awards:* Eastman Kodak Sci Award, 63. *Mem:* AAAS; Fel Am Phys Soc. *Res:* Solid state theory; electronic properties of insulators and semiconductors; color centers; band structures. *Mailing Add:* Dept of Physics Lehigh Univ Bethlehem PA 18015

FOWLES, GEORGE RICHARD, b Glenwood Springs, Colo, Apr 2, 28; m 54; c 4. HIGH PRESSURE PHYSICS. *Educ:* Stanford Univ, BS, 52, MS, 54, PhD(geophysics), 62. *Prof Exp:* Geophysicist, Phelps Dodge Corp, 54-55; physicist, Poulter Labs, Stanford Res Inst, 55-62, group head shock wave physics, 62-63, div dir, 63-66; assoc prof, 66-73, PROF PHYSICS, WASH STATE UNIV, 73- *Concurrent Pos:* Sr staff scientist, Physics Int Co, 69-70; consult, Nat Mat Adv Bd, Nat Res Coun, 70 & 77-78, Inst Cerac, SA, Switzerland, 72, Lawrence Livermore Lab, Stanford Res Inst & Gen Motors Corp, 71- ; Fulbright fel, US Educ Found, NZ, 75. *Mem:* Am Geophys Union; Am Phys Soc. *Res:* Non-linear wave propagation; high pressure physics. *Mailing Add:* Dept of Physics Wash State Univ Pullman WA 99164

FOWLES, GRANT ROBERT, b Fairview, Utah, Sept 19, 19; m 42; c 4. QUANTUM OPTICS. *Educ:* Univ Utah, BS, 41; Univ Calif, PhD(physics), 50. *Prof Exp:* From asst prof to assoc prof, 50-71, PROF PHYSICS, UNIV UTAH, 71- *Mem:* Am Phys Soc; Optical Soc Am. *Res:* Spectroscopy; metal vapor lasers. *Mailing Add:* Dept of Physics Univ of Utah Salt Lake City UT 84112

FOWLES, PATRICK ERNEST, b Harrow, Eng, Nov 7, 38; m 67; c 2. CHEMICAL ENGINEERING, TRIBIOLOGY. *Educ:* Univ London, BSc, 60; Mass Inst Technol, ScD(chem eng, fluid mech), 66. *Prof Exp:* Res chem engr, 66-69, sr res engr, Cent Res Div Lab, 69-74, res assoc, 74-77, mgr lubrication & resources sci group, 77-78, asst mgr, Prod Res & Tech Serv Sect, 78-79, MGR, RESOURCES & PROD RES SECT, MOBIL RES & DEVELOP CORP, 79- *Mem:* Am Soc Lubrication Engrs; Am Inst Chem Engrs. *Res:* Tribology; hydrodynamic and elastohydrodynamic lubrication; rheology of lubricants and related fluids; fluid mechanics; solution mining of uranium; enhanced oil recovery; coal liquefaction; tar sands; oil shale. *Mailing Add:* Mobil Res & Develop Corp PO Box 1025 Princeton NJ 08540

FOWLIS, WILLIAM WEBSTER, b Lanarkshire, Scotland, Jan 21, 37; m 70; c 1. METEOROLOGY, OCEANOGRAPHY. *Educ:* Glasgow Univ, BSc, 59; Univ Durham, PhD(physics), 64. *Prof Exp:* Res staff, Dept Geol & Geophys, Mass Inst Technol, 62-64; res assoc & lectr meteorol, Fla State Univ, 65-68, asst prof & assoc prof meteorol, Geophys Fluid Dynamics Inst, 68-74; assoc prog dir meteorol, Atmospheric Res Sect, NSF, 74-76; MEM SCI STAFF, ATMOSPHERIC SCI DIV, MARSHALL SPACE FLIGHT CTR, NASA, 76- *Concurrent Pos:* Assoc prof meteorol, Fla State Univ, 74-76. *Mem:* AAAS; Am Geophys Union; Am Meteorol Soc; fel Royal Meteorol Soc. *Res:* Geophysical fluid dynamics; experimental and theoretical studies of laboratory models of the general hydrodynamic circulations of planetary atmospheres. *Mailing Add:* NASA Mail Code ES82 Marshall Space Flight Ctr AL 35812

FOWLKES, EDWARD B, II, b Tarboro, NC, Dec 22, 36. STATISTICS. *Educ:* Univ NC, BS, 59; NC State Univ, MS, 64. *Prof Exp:* Qual control engr, Westinghouse Elec Corp, 59-62; MEM TECH STAFF, BELL LABS, 63- *Mem:* Am Statist Asn. *Res:* Ceuster analysis; data analysis; statistical computing. *Mailing Add:* Location 2C-257 Bell Labs Murray Hill NJ 07974

FOX, A(RTHUR) GARDNER, b Syracuse, NY, Nov 22, 12; m 38; c 4. ENGINEERING. *Educ:* Mass Inst Technol, BS, MS & EE, 35. *Prof Exp:* Head, Dept Coherent Wave Physics, Bell Tel Labs, 36-78; RETIRED. *Concurrent Pos:* Ed, J Quantum Electronics. *Honors & Awards:* Quantum Electronics Award & Microwave Career Award, Inst Elec & Electronics Engrs, 78, David Sarnoff Award, 79. *Mem:* Fel Inst Elec & Electronics Engrs; fel Optical Soc Am. *Res:* Coherent optical wave techniques; lasers, resonators, optical beams; microwave techniques in centimeter and millimeter wave length ranges; microwave magnetics. *Mailing Add:* 10 Conover Ln Rumson NJ 07760

FOX, ADRIAN SAMUEL, b Chicago, Ill, Apr 3, 36; m 60; c 2. ORGANIC CHEMISTRY, BIOMEDICAL MATERIALS. *Educ:* Univ Ill, BS, 57; Univ Wash, PhD(org chem), 62. *Prof Exp:* Res fel, Ohio State Univ, 62-63; res chemist, Plastics Div, Union Carbide Corp, NJ, 63-66; staff chemist, Res Dept, Raychem Corp, Calif, 66-68; res chemist, Polymer Res Dept, Pennsalt Chem Corp, 68-70, proj leader, Polymer Res Dept, Pennwalt Corp, 70-76; mgr mat res, Myerson Tooth Corp, Cambridge, Mass, 76-77; mgr mat res, Howmedica Dent Res, Howmedica Div, Pfizer, Inc, 77-79, MGR POLYMER RES, CORP RES & DEVELOP DEPT, HOWMEDICA INC, GROTON, CONN, 79- *Mem:* Am Chem Soc; Int Asn Dent Res. *Res:* Polymer synthesis and post-polymerization chemistry; mechanisms of oxidation reactions; organometallic chemistry; dental materials. *Mailing Add:* Howmedica Inc Eastern Point Rd Groton CT 06340

FOX, ALFRED EARL, b Newark, NJ, Nov 2, 34; m 54; c 3. IMMUNOCHEMISTRY, IMMUNOHEMATOLOGY. *Educ:* Tufts Univ, BS, 56; Rutgers Univ, MS, 65, PhD(microbiol), 72. *Prof Exp:* Bacteriologist, Div Labs & Res, NY State Dept Health, 56-59; sr res assoc immunol, Warner-Lambert Res Inst, 59-74; dir immunohemat res & develop, Dade Div, Am Hosp Supply Corp, 74-77; asst res dir, 77-78, DIR RES, WAMPOLE LABS DIV, CARTER-WALLACE INC, 78- *Concurrent Pos:* Chmn post market surveillance comt, Health Indust Mfg Asn, 75-77; mem comt, Can Blood Bank Stand Comt, 75-77. *Mem:* NY Acad Sci; Am Soc Microbiol; Am Asn Immunologists; Am Soc Histocompatibility Testing; Am Asn Blood Banks. *Res:* Research and development of diagnostic reagents. *Mailing Add:* Wampole Labs Div Carter-Wallace Inc Cranbury NJ 08512

FOX, ARTHUR CHARLES, b Newark, NJ, Sept 16, 26. MEDICINE. *Educ:* NY Univ, MD, 48. *Prof Exp:* Intern med, Bellevue Hosp, 48-49, from asst resident to resident, 49-52; prof asst, Div Med Sci, Nat Res Coun, 53-54; asst, 54-56, from instr to assoc prof, 56-68, PROF MED, SCH MED, NY UNIV, 68- *Concurrent Pos:* Vis physician, Bellevue Hosp & Univ Hosp; Nat Heart Inst res fel, 54-56; consult, Vet Admin Hosp, Manhattan; sect chief cardiol, Med Ctr, NY Univ, 50-52. *Mem:* Fel Am Col Physicians; fel Am Col Cardiol; AAAS; Sigma Xi; Am Fed Clin Res. *Res:* Cardiology; myocardial metabolism and coronary blood flow. *Mailing Add:* Dept of Med NY Univ Sch of Med New York NY 10016

FOX, BENNETT L, b Chicago, Ill, Aug 13, 38. MATHEMATICS. *Educ:* Univ Mich, BA, 60; Univ Chicago, MSc, 62; Univ Calif, Berkeley, PhD(opers res), 65. *Prof Exp:* Mathematician, Rand Corp, 65-71; MEM STAFF, DEPT INFO SCI, UNIV MONTREAL, 71- *Concurrent Pos:* Ford vis prof, Univ Chicago, 71-72. *Mem:* Opers Res Soc Am. *Res:* Reliability theory; dynamic programming. *Mailing Add:* Dept Info Sci CP 6128 Univ of Montreal Montreal Can

FOX, BERNARD LAWRENCE, b Canton, Ohio, Aug 18, 40; m 63. ORGANIC CHEMISTRY. *Educ:* John Carroll Univ, BS, 62; Ohio State Univ, PhD(org chem), 66. *Prof Exp:* Asst prof, 66-71, ASSOC PROF CHEM, UNIV DAYTON, 71- *Concurrent Pos:* Consult, Mat Lab, Wright-Patterson Air Force Base, 67-71. *Mem:* Am Chem Soc. *Res:* Synthesis and reactions of azabicycloalkanes; mechanism of hydrogenolysis of benzylamines; mechanism of lithium aluminum hydride reduction of oxazolidines; drug analysis and clinical chemistry. *Mailing Add:* Dept of Chem Univ of Dayton Dayton OH 45469

FOX, CHARLES JUNIUS, b Detroit, Mich, Nov 22, 26; m 46; c 5. ORGANIC CHEMISTRY. *Educ:* Ohio State Univ, BSc, 47, MSc, 50, PhD(chem), 53. *Prof Exp:* Res assoc, Kettering Lab Appl Physiol, 47-49; res chemist, Durez Plastics Div, Hooker Electrochem Co, 53-55; sr res chemist, 55-61, res assoc, 61-67, LAB HEAD, PHOTOMAT DIV, EASTMAN KODAK CO, 67- *Mem:* Soc Photog Sci & Eng; Am Chem Soc. *Res:* Organic photoconductors; polymers. *Mailing Add:* 623 Oakridge Dr Rochester NY 14617

FOX, CHARLES LEWIS, JR, b New York, NY, Jan 16, 08; m 57; c 3. MICROBIOLOGY, SURGERY. *Educ:* Harvard Univ, AB, 29; State Univ NY Downstate Med Ctr, MD, 34. *Prof Exp:* Intern & house physician-surgeon, Jewish Hosp, Brooklyn, 34-36; asst bact, Harvard Med Sch, 38-39; instr & assoc, Col Physicians & Surgeons, Columbia Univ, 40-46, asst prof, 46-51; assoc prof surg, NY Med Col, Flower & Fifth Ave Hosps, 52-58, assoc prof surg & biochem, 58-60, assoc prof surg & physiol, 60; assoc prof, 60-62, PROF MICROBIOL IN SURG, COL PHYSICIANS & SURGEONS, COLUMBIA UNIV, 62- *Concurrent Pos:* Fel path, Mallory Inst, Boston City Hosp, 34; res fel chem, Mt Sinai Hosp, 36-38; assoc vis surgeon, Metrop Hosp, 53-60; assoc attend surgeon, Flower & Fifth Ave Hosps, 55-60; assoc vis path, Bellevue Hosp, 60-; career scientist, Health Res Coun, 62-; consult, St Barnabas Hosp, NJ, 52-; sr consult, Burn Ctr, Westchester County Med Ctr, Valhalla, NY, 79- *Honors & Awards:* Harvey S Allen Distinguished Serv Award, Am Burn Asn, 77. *Mem:* Am Physiol Soc; Soc Exp Biol & Med; Am Burn Asn; AMA; Am Asn Immunol. *Res:* Discovered silver sulfadiazine, topical therapy burn wound sepsis; fluid and electrolyte physiology; flame photometry; bacterial metabolism; hypertonic fluid for dialysis (kidney falure); hemoglobin spectroscopy and metabolism; microbiology; discovery of silver piperazinyl quinoline carboxylate topical therapy resistant pseudomonas. *Mailing Add:* Col Physicians & Surgeons Columbia Univ 630 W 168th St New York NY 10032

FOX, CHESTER DAVID, b Albany, NY, Apr 8, 31; m 61. PHARMACEUTICAL CHEMISTRY. *Educ:* Union Col NY, BS, 58; Univ Md, MS, 63, PhD(indust pharm), 65. *Prof Exp:* Tech adv prod, 64-78, DIR TECH SERV, AYERST LABS, INC, DIV AM HOME PROD CORP, 78- *Concurrent Pos:* Chmn mfg pract comt, Pharmaceut Mfrs Asn, 73-76. *Mem:* AAAS; Pharmaceut Mfrs Asn; Am Pharmaceut Asn; fel Am Inst Chem; Am Inst Chem Engrs. *Res:* Industrial pharmacy; development of automated industrial pharmaceutical production processes; development and evaluation of new pharmaceutical production equipment and methods. *Mailing Add:* Tech Serv Ayerst Labs Inc 64 Maple St Rouses Point NY 12979

FOX, DALE BENNETT, b Sioux Falls, SDak, May 25, 39; m 64; c 3. HETEROGENEOUS CATALYSIS. *Educ:* Hamline Univ, BS, 61; Univ Iowa, MS, 68, PhD(org chem), 69. *Prof Exp:* Assoc chemist, Res Ctr, Marathon Oil Co, Colo, 62-65; res chemist, Monsanto Co, Mo, 69-71, sr res chemist, 71-75, process specialist, Tex, 75-79, MGR, UNIV RELATIONS & PROFESSIONAL EMPLOYMENT, MONSANTO C0, 79- *Mem:* Am Chem Soc; Catalysis Soc. *Res:* Catalysis; catalysts and catalytic conversions, especially with hydrocarbons; monomer synthesis; general organic and organometallic synthesis. *Mailing Add:* Monsanto Co 800 N Lindbergh Blvd St Louis MO 63166

FOX, DANIEL WAYNE, b Johnstown, Pa, May 14, 23; m 48; c 2. PLASTICS CHEMISTRY, POLYMER CHEMISTRY. *Educ:* Lebanon Valley Col, BS, 49; Univ Okla, MS, 51, PhD(org chem), S3. *Prof Exp:* Chemist, Mat & Process Lab, 53-59, mgr prod develop, Chem Develop Opers, 59-62, res & adv develop, 63-70, MGR CENT RES, PLASTIC DEPT, GEN ELEC CO, 71- *Mem:* Am Chem Soc. *Res:* High performance polymers and plastics. *Mailing Add:* 193 Dawes Ave Pittsfield MA 01201

FOX, DANNY GENE, b West Unity, Ohio, Mar 18, 40; m 60; c 2. RUMINANT NUTRITION. *Educ:* Ohio State Univ, BS, 62, MS, 68, PhD(ruminant nutrit), 70. *Prof Exp:* Asst prof exten beef nutrit, SDak State Univ, 70-72; asst prof beef nutrit, Cornell Univ, 72-74; assoc prof beef cattle res & exten, Mich State Univ, 74-78; MEM FAC DEPT ANIMAL SCI, CORNELL UNIV, 78- *Concurrent Pos:* Proj leader, USDA Exten Serv Proj Mgt Syst Small Beef Herds, 73- *Mem:* Am Soc Animal Sci. *Res:* Protein and energy requirements of varied cattle types; producing beef on high roughage diets; feeding systems for various cattle types. *Mailing Add:* Morrison Hall Cornell Univ Ithaca NY 14853

FOX, DAVID, b Brooklyn, NY, Sept 8, 20; m 38; c 3. THEORETICAL PHYSICS. *Educ:* Univ Calif, Berkeley, BA, 42, MA, 50, PhD(physics), 52. *Prof Exp:* Lectr physics, Israel Inst Technol, 52-55, sr lectr, 55-56; lectr, Hebrew Univ, 55; res assoc, Inst Optics, Univ Rochester, 56-57, asst prof, 57-59; actg dean grad sch, 63-66, PROF PHYSICS, STATE UNIV NY STONY BROOK, 59- *Res:* Theoretical solid state physics; statistical theory of eigenvalues. *Mailing Add:* Dept of Physics State Univ of NY Stony Brook NY 11794

FOX, DAVID WILLIAM, b Dubuque, Iowa, Nov 21, 28; m 50; c 2. MATHEMATICS. *Educ:* Univ Mich, AB, 51, MSE, 52; Univ Md, PhD(math), 58. *Prof Exp:* Sr engr, 53-56, consult, 56-60, mathematician, prin staff, 60-66, SUPVR, APPL MATH RES GROUP, APPL PHYSICS LAB, JOHNS HOPKINS UNIV, 66- *Concurrent Pos:* Res asst prof, Inst Fluid Dynamics & Appl Math, Univ Md, 59-60; consult, Int Div, Battelle Mem Inst, Switz, 60- *Mem:* Am Math Soc. *Res:* Spectral theory of operators and theory of partial differential equations. *Mailing Add:* Appl Math Res Group Appl Physics Lab Johns Hopkins Univ Laurel MD 20810

FOX, DENIS LLEWELLYN, b Udimore, Eng, Dec 22, 01; nat US; m 27, 32; c 4. MARINE BIOLOGY, MARINE BIOCHEMISTRY. *Educ:* Univ Calif, AB, 25; Stanford Univ, PhD(biochem), 31. *Prof Exp:* Chemist, Res Labs, Standard Oil Co Calif, Richmond, 25-29; asst biochem, Stanford Univ, 29-30 & biol, 31; from instr to asst prof physiol, 31-37, from asst prof to prof, marine biochem, 37-69, RES BIOCHEMIST, DIV MARINE BIOL & EMER PROF MARINE BIOCHEM, SCRIPPS INST OCEANOG, UNIV CALIF, SAN DIEGO, 69- *Concurrent Pos:* Res fel, Rockefeller Found, Cambridge Univ, 38-39; mem res comt, San Diego Zoo, 40-80; consult, biochemist, 41-; Guggenheim fel, 45-46; grants, Am Philos Soc, 47, Rockefeller Found, 45-54 & NSF, 62-70; distinguished scholar, Cranbrook Inst Sci, 70-71. *Mem:* Fel AAAS; fel Inst Biol; Am Soc Zool; Am Soc Limnol & Oceanog; Soc Gen Physiol. *Res:* Biochemistry and comparative metabolism of animal biochromes; nutrition, growth and metabolism of marine animals; organic matter in marine waters and sediments; biochemical fossils. *Mailing Add:* Div Mar Biol Scripps Inst Oceanog Univ of Calif San Diego La Jolla CA 92037

FOX, DONALD A, b Cleveland, Ohio, July 1, 48; m 81. NEUROBEHAVIORAL TOXICOLOGY & PHARMACOLOGY. *Educ:* Miami Univ, Oxford, Ohio, BS, 70; Univ Cincinnati Med Ctr, PhD(toxicol), 77. *Prof Exp:* Res pharmacologist, US Environ Protection Agency, 76-77; ASST PROF TOXICOL & PHARMACOL, MED SCH, HEALTH SCI CTR, HOUSTON, 79- *Concurrent Pos:* Consult, US Environ Protection Agency, 79, Nat Comt Air Quality Control, 80; prin investr grant, Lead Neurotoxicity Visual Syst, Nat Inst Environ Health Sci, 81-84. *Mem:* Soc Neurosci; Soc Toxicol; Behav Teratology Soc; Asn Res Vision & Ophthalmol; AAAS. *Res:* Effects of lead exposure on the developing visual system utilizing electrophysiological and psychophysical (behavioral) techniques; visual capacities and the functional bioelectric properties of the scotopic and photopic visual system during development and adulthood. *Mailing Add:* Dept Pharmacol Univ Tex Med Sch Houston TX 77025

FOX, DONALD LEE, b Wichita, Kans, Sept 13, 43. AIR POLLUTION, ATMOSPHERIC CHEMISTRY. *Educ:* Wichita State Univ, BS, 65; Univ Ariz, PhD(phys chem), 71. *Prof Exp:* Environ Protection Agency fel atmospheric chem, 71-73, lectr air hyg, 73, asst prof, 74-80, ASSOC PROF AIR HYG, UNIV NC, CHAPEL HILL, 80- *Concurrent Pos:* Consult, indust, govt & Res Triangle Inst, 74- *Mem:* Air Pollution Control Asn; Am Chem Soc. *Res:* Air pollution chemistry; aerosol formation; kinetics modeling; air monitoring and instrumentation; photochemistry applied to air pollution control devices. *Mailing Add:* Environ Sci & Eng Univ of NC Sch of Pub Health Chapel Hill NC 27514

FOX, DOUGLAS GARY, b New York, NY, July 29, 41; m 64; c 3. METEOROLOGY, AIR POLLUTION. *Educ:* Cooper Union, BCE, 63; Princeton Univ, MA & MSE, 65, PhD(fluid mech), 68. *Prof Exp:* Sr staff scientist meteorol, Nat Ctr Atmospheric Res, 68-72; res meteorologist & br chief, Nat Res Ctr, US Environ Protection Agency, 72-74; RES METEOROLOGIST & PROJ LEADER, ROCKY MOUNTAIN FOREST & RANGE EXP STA, US FOREST SERV, 74- *Concurrent Pos:* Affil prof, Princeton Univ, 69-72; mem panel air pollution modeling, NATO, 73-74; sr mem working group 1 air pollution measurement, modeling & methodology, US-USSR Environ AgreeAgreement, 73-; fac affil, Colo State Univ, 74- *Mem:* AAAS; Am Meteorol Soc; Am Soc Civil Engrs; Am Geophys Union. *Res:* Interactions between the atmosphere and wildland mangement and resource protection, especially associated with air pollution; mountain meteorology and forest meteorology. *Mailing Add:* Rocky Mountain Forest & Range Sta 240 W Prospect St Ft Collins CO 80521

FOX, EDWARD A(LEXANDER), b New York, NY, Aug 7, 20; m 49; c 3. MECHANICS. *Educ:* Harvard Univ, BS, 41; Columbia Univ, BS, 47, PhD(eng mech), 58. *Prof Exp:* From asst prof to assoc prof, 54-65, PROF MECH, RENSSELAER POLYTECH INST, 65- *Mem:* Am Soc Mech Engrs. *Res:* Mathematical theory of elasticity; stress wave propagation; classical mechanics. *Mailing Add:* Dept of Mech Rensselaer Polytech Inst Troy NY 12181

FOX, EDWARD L, b Dayton, Ohio, May 30, 38; m 64; c 2. EXERCISE PHYSIOLOGY. *Educ:* Ohio State Univ, BS, 60, MA, 61, PhD(physiol), 65. *Prof Exp:* NIH fel anat & physiol, Ind Univ, 67-68; from asst prof to assoc prof, 68-73, PROF EXERCISE PHYSIOL & STATIST, OHIO STATE UNIV, 73-, DIR, LAB WORK PHYSIOL, 75- *Mem:* AAAS; NY Acad Sci; Am Physiol Soc; fel, Am Col Sports Med. *Res:* Environmental physiology; effects of heat on exercise tolerance; metabolic responses during exercise; effects of physical conditioning on cardiorespiratory responses during exercise; application of science and medicine to sports. *Mailing Add:* Lab of Work Physiol Ohio State Univ Columbus OH 43210

FOX, EUGENE N, b Chicago, Ill, Dec 9, 27; m 64; c 2. MEDICAL MICROBIOLOGY. *Educ:* Univ Ill, BS, 49, MS, 50; Western Reserve Univ, PhD(microbiol), 55. *Prof Exp:* Instr microbiol, Western Reserve Univ, 58-60; from asst prof prof microbiol, La Rabida Inst, Univ Chicago, 74-77; dir microbiol res & develop, Cutter Labs Inc, 77-80; PRIN, KENSINGTON CONSULT, 81- *Concurrent Pos:* Sr investr, Arthritis & Rheumatism Found, 59-64; consult, Dept Defense, US Army Med Res & Develop Cmnd, 73-77. *Mem:* Am Soc Microbiol; Am Asn Immunol. *Res:* Immunology and infectious diseases. *Mailing Add:* 235 Willamette Ave Kensington CA 94708

FOX, EVA FERNANDEZ, b San Juan, PR, Oct 11, 17; m 45; c 2. RADIOLOGY. *Educ:* Chestnut Hill Col, BS, 39; Med Col Pa, MD, 43. *Prof Exp:* From asst prof to prof, 60-75, chmn dept, 69-75, EMER PROF RADIOL, MED COL PA, 75- *Mem:* Am Col Radiol; AMA; Pan-Am Med Asn; Am Heart Asn. *Mailing Add:* 11853 Paradise Dr Stone Harbor NJ 08247

FOX, FRANCIS HENRY, b Clifton Springs, NY, Mar 11, 23; m 46; c 3. VETERINARY MEDICINE. *Educ:* State Univ NY, DVM, 45. *Prof Exp:* Asst mastitis & vet med, Cornell Univ, 45-46; instr vet med & surg, Ohio State Univ, 46-47; from asst prof to assoc prof, 47-53, chmn dept large animal med obstet & surg & dir ambulatory clin, 72-77, PROF VET MED & OBSTET, NY STATE VET COL, CORNELL UNIV, 53- *Mem:* Am Vet Med Asn. *Res:* Diseases of large domestic animals, especially the bovine. *Mailing Add:* Clin Sci NY State Vet Col Cornell Univ Ithaca NY 14853

FOX, FREDERICK GLENN, b Weyburn, Sask, Mar 6, 18; m 43; c 2. GEOLOGY. *Educ:* Univ Alta, BSc, 40, MSc, 42; Univ Okla, PhD(geol), 48. *Prof Exp:* Geologist, Imperial Oil, Ltd, 42-46 & 48-50; sr geologist, Hudsons Bay Oil & Gas Co, 50-55; sr survey & struct geologist, Triad Oil Co, Ltd, Can, 55-68; SR STRUCT GEOLOGIST, PANARCTIC OILS LTD, 68- *Mem:* Fel Geol Soc Am; fel Geol Asn Can. *Res:* Stratigraphy and structure of Rocky Mountains and the foothills belt; general structural geology; mapping of complex structure. *Mailing Add:* Panarctic Oils Ltd 703 Sixth Ave S W Calgary AB T2P 0T9 Can

FOX, G(EORGE) SIDNEY, b Philadelphia, Pa, Feb 21, 28; m 56; c 2. GEOLOGICAL ENGINEERING. *Educ:* Princeton Univ, BSE, 50. *Prof Exp:* Hydraul engr, US Geol Surv, 51-55; groundwater geologist, 55-67, partner, 67-76, V PRES, LEGGETTE, BRASHEARS & GRAHAM, INC, 76- *Mem:* Geol Soc Am; Am Water Resources Asn; Am Inst Mining, Metall & Petrol Engrs; Am Geophys Union; Asn Prof Geol Scientists. *Mailing Add:* Leggette Brashears & Graham Inc 72 Danbury Rd Wilton CT 06897

FOX, GEORGE EDWARD, b Syracuse, NY, Dec 17, 45; m 73; c 2. MICROBIOLOGY. *Educ:* Syracuse Univ, BSChE, 67, PhD(chem eng), 74. *Prof Exp:* Res assoc genetics & develop, Univ Ill, Urbana, 73-77; ASST PROF BIOPHYS SCI, UNIV HOUSTON, 77- *Mem:* Am Soc Microbiol; Am Chem Soc; Am Inst Chem Engrs; AAAS; NY Acad Sci. *Res:* RNA structure and function; theoretical biology; microbial phylogeny; molecular evolution. *Mailing Add:* Dept of Biophys Sci Univ of Houston Houston TX 77004

FOX, GERALD, b New York, NY, Apr 23, 23; m 55; c 1. INDUSTRIAL CHEMISTRY. *Educ:* Long Island Univ, BSc, 47. *Prof Exp:* Chemist, Fleischmann Labs, NY, 46-49; chief chemist, Consol Laundries Corp, 49-57; secy & dir res, Gold Par Prod Co, Inc, 57-70 & Gold Par Chem, Inc, 70-74; dir chem res, Chemair Corp Am, 75-80; DIR CHEM RES, AM MACHINERY CORP, 80- *Concurrent Pos:* Consult electroplaters & mgrs cosmetic mfrs. *Mem:* Am Chem Soc; Soc Cosmetic Chem; fel Am Inst Chem. *Res:* Sanitary chemicals; chemical specialty items; soaps and detergents for laundry, dry cleaning, textile processing, food and beverage, dairy, dishwashing and metal industries; research and development of new cosmetic products; research and development of new post-harvest processing chemical for the fruit and vegetable industry. *Mailing Add:* 1695 Lee Rd A-103 Miami FL 33172

FOX, HAZEL METZ, b Barton, Md, July 2, 21; m 50; c 5. NUTRITION. *Educ:* Western Md Col, BA, 43; Iowa State Univ, MS, 47, PhD(nutrit), 54. *Hon Degrees:* DSc, Western Md Col, 69. *Prof Exp:* Teacher high sch, Md, 43-45; res assoc, Children's Fund Mich, 47-50; asst, Iowa State Univ, 50-54, instr nutrition, 54-55; from assoc prof to prof, 55-68, GEORGE HOLMES PROF FOOD & NUTRIT, UNIV NEBR-LINCOLN, 68-, CHMN, DEPT HUMAN NUTRIT & FOOD SERV, 63- *Honors & Awards:* Borden Award Human Nutrit, Am Home Econ Asn, 69. *Mem:* AAAS; Am Inst Nutrit; Am Dietetic Asn; Am Home Econ Asn. *Res:* Human nutrition; nutrition education. *Mailing Add:* Dept Human Nutrit & Food Serv Univ Nebr Lincoln NE 68583

FOX, HERBERT, aerospace technology, see previous edition

FOX, HERBERT LEON, b Boston, Mass, Jan 6, 30; m 52; c 4. PHYSICS, ECONOMICS. *Educ:* Boston Univ, BA, 58, MA, 62. *Prof Exp:* Proj engr, Farnsworth-Tamari, 57; chief design engr, Tech Prod Co, 55-57; SR PHYSICIST & ECONOMIST, BOLT BERANEK & NEWMAN, 57- *Concurrent Pos:* Res asst, Boston Univ, 63-64; consult comt, Nat Acad Remote Atmospheric Probing; lectr, Dept Econ, Northeastern Univ; consult econ & physics, Idmon, Inc, 75- *Mem:* AAAS; Am Asn Physics Teachers. *Res:* Atmospheric sound propagation; quantum optics; kinetic theory; nonlinear mechanics; development economics; occupational health and safety; environmental impact. *Mailing Add:* 95 Beacon Hill Ave Lynn MA 01902

FOX, IRVING, b Hartford, Conn, Dec 19, 12; m 41; c 1. MEDICAL ENTOMOLOGY. *Educ:* George Washington Univ, AB, 37, MA, 38; Iowa State Col, PhD, 40; Am Registry Cert Entom, cert med & vet entom. *Prof Exp:* Asst entom, Iowa State Col, 37-40; instr biol, 41-42, from asst prof to assoc prof med entom, 46-62, PROF MED ENTOM, SCH MED, UNIV PR, SAN JUAN, 62- *Concurrent Pos:* Collabr, Bur Entom, USDA, 35-42; prog dir, USPHS Grad Res Training Grant, 57-70. *Mem:* Am Soc Parasitol; Entom Soc Am; Am Soc Trop Med & Hyg; Am Mosquito Control Asn; Am Arachnological Soc. *Res:* Taxonomy, population studies; toxicology, immunology and control of insects and Arachnida such as fleas, mites, ticks, biting flies, mosquitoes and spiders; molluscicides; tardigrada. *Mailing Add:* Dept of Med Zool Univ of PR Sch of Med San Juan PR 00936

FOX, IRVING HARVEY, b Montreal, Que, Dec 7, 43; m 66; c 3. RHEUMATOLOGY, PURINE METABOLISM. *Educ:* McGill Univ, BSc, 65, MDCM, 67. *Prof Exp:* House officer med, Royal Victoria Hosp, 67; fel rheumatology, Duke Univ Med Ctr, 69-72; asst prof med, Univ Toronto, 72-76; assoc prof med, 76-78, asst prof biol chem, 76-80, PROF MED, UNIV MICH, 78-, ASSOC PROF BIOL CHEM, 80-, PROG DIR, CLIN RES CTR, 77- *Mem:* Am Fedn Clin Res; Am Rheumatism Asn; Am Soc Clin Invest; Am Soc Biol Chemists; Cent Soc Clin Res. *Res:* Regulation of human purine nucleotide degradation in normal and disease states. *Mailing Add:* Clin Res Ctr Univ Hosp Ann Arbor MI 48109

FOX, IRWIN J, b Gnoien, Ger, June 26, 26; US citizen; m 64; c 3. CARDIOVASCULAR PHYSIOLOGY. *Educ:* Princeton Univ, AB, 47; NY Med Col, MD, 51; Univ Minn, PhD(physiol), 62. *Prof Exp:* Intern, Michael Reese Hosp, Chicago, 51-52; fel cardiovasc res, 52; fel med & physiol, Mayo Found, 53-59; res assoc, 59-60, from asst prof to assoc prof, 60-72, PROF PHYSIOL, MED SCH, UNIV MINN, MINNEAPOLIS, 72- *Concurrent Pos:* Minn Heart Asn fel, 56-57; USPHS sr res fel, 59-60, USPHS res career develop award, 60-70; mem coun basic sci & circulation, Am Heart Asn; mem, Coun Exp Biol & Med, NIH, 78-81, Cardiovasc & Renal Study Sect, 78-80. *Mem:* AAAS; Soc Exp Biol & Med; Am Physiol Soc. *Res:* Cardiovascular control mechanisms; neural control of the circulation; indicator dilution technics and indocyanine green, methods and application; radionuclide labeled microspheres in regional blood flow measurement, myocardial and intestinal; left ventricular mechanoreceptor reflex in the control of the circulation; coronary circulatory dynamics including effect of drugs. *Mailing Add:* Dept Physiol 440 Millard Hall Univ Minn Sch Med Minneapolis MN 55455

FOX, J EUGENE, b Anderson, Ind, Aug 7, 34; m 60; c 4. PLANT PHYSIOLOGY, PLANT BIOCHEMISTRY. *Educ:* Ind Univ, BS, 56, PhD(bot), 60. *Prof Exp:* Nat Cancer Inst fel bot, Univ Wis, 60-61; from asst prof to assoc prof, 61-70, PROF BIOCHEM & BOT, UNIV KANS, LAWRENCE, 70-, CHMN DEPT BOT, 74- *Concurrent Pos:* Asst dean, Col Arts & Sci, Univ Kans, 67-70, dean, 70-72. *Mem:* AAAS; Am Soc Plant Physiol; Scand Soc Plant Physiol; Japanese Soc Plant Physiol. *Res:* Growth and development of plants; biochemistry of plant growth regulators; plant tissue culture. *Mailing Add:* Dept of Bot Univ of Kans Lawrence KS 66044

FOX, JACK JAY, b New York, NY, Dec 21, 16; m 39; c 2. BIOCHEMISTRY. *Educ:* Univ Colo, BA, 39, PhD(biochem), 50. *Prof Exp:* Nat Res Coun fel, Free Univ Brussels, 50-52; Damon Runyon Mem Fund fel, 52-54, asst chem, 54-58, head medicinal chem, 58-60, assoc mem, 60-64, MEM, SLOAN-KETTERING INST CANCER RES, 64-, CHIEF ORG CHEM, 71- *Concurrent Pos:* From asst prof to assoc prof, Sloan-Kettering Div, Cornell Univ, 56-65, prof, 65- *Honors & Awards:* Alfred P Sloan Award Cancer Res, 56; C S Hudson Award Carbohydrate Chem, 77. *Mem:* Am Chem Soc; Am Soc Biol Chem; Am Asn Cancer Res; Int Soc Heterocyclic Chem. *Res:* Design and syntheses of potential anti-tumor and anti-viral agents and other medicinals; chemistry of carbohydrates, heterocycles, nucleosides and antibiotics. *Mailing Add:* Sloan-Kettering Inst 145 Boston Post Rd Rye NY 10580

FOX, JACK LAWRENCE, b Ann Arbor, Mich, Oct 10, 41; m 61; c 2. BIOCHEMISTRY, BIOPHYSICS. *Educ:* Fla State Univ, BA, 62; Univ Ariz, PhD(chem), 66. *Prof Exp:* Guest investr biochem, Rockefeller Univ, 66-68; asst prof, 68-74, ASSOC PROF ZOOL, UNIV TEX, AUSTIN, 74- *Concurrent Pos:* USPHS fel, 66-68; biol ed, Marcel Dekker, Inc, 73-; Alexander von Humboldt Stiftung fel, 77-78. *Mem:* AAAS; Am Chem Soc; Am Soc Biol Chem; Biophys Soc; Int Union Biochem. *Res:* Enzyme structure and molecular evolution, especially flavoenzymes and phycobiliproteins, chemical and theoretical studies, recombinant DNA. *Mailing Add:* Dept Zool Univ Tex Austin TX 78712

FOX, JAMES DAVID, b Gatesville, Tex, May 11, 43; m 66; c 2. ANIMAL GENETICS, STATISTICS. *Educ:* Tex A&M Univ, BS, 65, MS, 67; Ohio State Univ, PhD(animal breeding), 70. *Prof Exp:* Geneticist, DeKalb Agresearch, Inc, 71-72, DIR SWINE GENETIC RES, DEKALB SWINE BREEDERS INC, 72- *Mem:* Am Soc Animal Sci; Biomet Soc. *Res:* Relationship of mature body weight and efficiency of production in livestock; developing swine breeding stock. *Mailing Add:* DeKalb Swine Breeders Inc 503 Oak St DeKalb IL 60115

FOX, JAMES GAHAN, b Reno, Nev, Mar 8, 43; m 70; c 1. VETERINARY & COMPARATIVE MEDICINE. *Educ:* Colo State Univ, DVM, 68; Stanford Univ MS, 72; Am Col Lab Animal Med, dipl, 74. *Prof Exp:* Resident vet, Biol Lab Animal Div, US Army Vet Corp, Ft Detrick, 68-70; asst prof & staff vet, Med Ctr, Univ Colo, 73-74; inst vet & dir, Animal Care Facil, 74-75, INST VET, ASSOC PROF & DIR DIV LAB ANIMAL MED, MASS INST TECHNOL, 75- *Concurrent Pos:* NIH fel lab animal med & med microbiol, Stanford Univ, 70-72; fac affil, Dept Clins & Surg, Colo State Univ, 73-74; prin investr, NIH Animal Res Diag Lab Grant, 75-78 & Nat Cancer Inst, Animal Res Ctr grant, 77-80; spec consult, Brandeis Univ, Forsyth Dent Ctr & Mass Gen Hosp, 76, West Roxbury Vet Admin Hosp, NIH & Nat Cancer Inst, 77 & US Environ Protection Agency & US Food & Drug Admin, 78. *Mem:* Am Asn Accreditation Lab Animal Care; Am Vet Med Asn; Am Vet Radiol Soc; Am Asn Lab Animal Sci. *Res:* Study of infectious, metabolic or inherited diseases in research animals which adversely affect experimental results; development of animal models as analogs of human disease; animal environment and its role in interpretation of research results. *Mailing Add:* Mass Inst of Technol Div of Lab Animal Med Cambridge MA 02139

FOX, JAY B, JR, b Lincoln, Nebr, July 30, 27; m 52; c 4. BIOCHEMISTRY. *Educ:* Col Puget Sound, BS, 51; Univ Wash, PhD(biochem), 55. *Prof Exp:* Assoc biochemist, Am Meat Inst Found, 55-61, biochemist, 61-64; RES CHEMIST, EASTERN REGION RES CTR, AGR RES SERV, USDA, 64- *Mem:* AAAS; Am Chem Soc; Am Inst Chem; Inst Food Technologists; Am Meat Sci Asn. *Res:* Biochemistry of heme pigments; nitrite chemistry. *Mailing Add:* Eastern Regional Res Ctr Div 600 E Mermaid Lane Philadelphia PA 19118

FOX, JOEL S, b New York, NY, Feb 7, 39; m 63. MECHANICAL ENGINEERING. *Educ:* Polytech Inst Brooklyn, BME, 59, MME, 61, PhD(mech eng), 66. *Prof Exp:* Mem tech staff heat transfer, Hughes Aircraft Co, 61-62; instr mech eng, Polytech Inst Brooklyn, 62-66; asst prof, 66-69, ASSOC PROF MECH ENG, UNIV HAWAII, 69- *Mem:* Am Soc Mech Engrs; Am Soc Eng Educ. *Res:* Electric fields and combustion process interaction; thermal conductivity of polymers; freeze-dry preservation of whole blood. *Mailing Add:* Dept of Mech Eng Univ of Hawaii Honolulu HI 96822

FOX, JOHN ARTHUR, b Toronto, Ont, Feb 8, 24; US citizen; m 46; c 4. MECHANICAL & AEROSPACE ENGINEERING. *Educ:* Univ Mich, BS, 48 & 49; Pa State Univ, MS, 50, PhD(aeronaut eng), 60. *Prof Exp:* Asst, Univ Mich, 49-50; instr aeronaut eng, Pa State Univ, 49-60, assoc prof & actg head dept, 60-61, consult, Ord Res Lab, 57-61; assoc prof mech & aerospace sci, Univ Rochester, 61-67; PROF MECH ENG & CHMN DEPT, UNIV MISS, 67- *Concurrent Pos:* Consult, Piper Aircraft Corp & HRB-Singer, Inc, Pa, 61- & Rochester Appl Sci Assocs, NY, 64- *Mem:* AAAS; Am Soc Eng Educ; Am Inst Aeronaut & Astronaut. *Res:* Mechanical and aerospace science; dynamics and celestial mechanics; aerodynamics; aerospace structures; magnetohydrodynamics. *Mailing Add:* Dept of Mech Eng Univ of Miss University MS 38677

FOX, JOHN DAVID, b Huntington, WVa, Dec 8, 29; div; c 5. NUCLEAR PHYSICS. *Educ:* Mass Inst Technol, SB, 51; Univ Ill, MS, 54, PhD, 60. *Prof Exp:* Asst, Univ Ill, 52-55; asst physicist, Brookhaven Nat Lab, 56-59; from asst prof to assoc prof, 59-65, PROF PHYSICS, FLA STATE UNIV, 65- *Concurrent Pos:* NSF sr fel & guest scientist, Max-Planck Inst Nuclear Physics, Univ Heidelberg, 68-69; sr scientist, Alexander von Humboldt Found, 75. *Mem:* Fel Am Phys Soc. *Res:* Experimental nuclear physics; low energy nuclear physics; neutron physics in resonance region; particle detectors and instrumentation; nuclear isomerism; photonuclear phenomena; isobaric analogue resonances; charged particle induced nuclear reactions. *Mailing Add:* Dept of Physics Fla State Univ Tallahassee FL 32306

FOX, JOHN FREDERICK, b Lakewood, NJ, Aug 22, 45. ECOLOGY, POPULATION BIOLOGY. *Educ:* Johns Hopkins Univ, AB, 67; Univ Chicago, MS, 69, PhD(biol), 74. *Prof Exp:* Programmer, Syst Eng Lab, 69; res assoc, Univ Wyo, 75-77; ASST PROF, UNIV ALASKA, 77- *Mem:* Ecol Soc Am; Soc Study Evolution; Brit Ecol Soc. *Res:* Population biology and community ecology of terrestrial plants; plant animal interactions; fire ecology; bioclimatology; ecosystem modeling. *Mailing Add:* Inst of Arctic Biol Univ of Alaska Fairbanks AK 99701

FOX, JOHN GASTON, b Biggar, Sask, Mar 5, 16; nat US; m 47; c 3. NUCLEAR PHYSICS. *Educ:* Univ Sask, BSc, 35, MSc, 37; Princeton Univ, PhD(physics), 41. *Prof Exp:* Res physicist, Hercules Powder Co, 41-45; res physicist, Manhattan Proj, Los Alamos Nat Lab, NMex, 45-46; from asst prof to assoc prof, 46-56, asst head dept, 50-56, head dept, 56-61, PROF PHYSICS, CARNEGIE-MELLON UNIV, 56- *Concurrent Pos:* Vis mem staff, Joliet Curie Lab, Orsay, France, 62-63; vis prof, Kanpur Indo-Am Prog, Indian Inst Technol, Kanpur, 67-68; prog leader, 71-72; consult, St Francis Hosp, Pittsburgh. *Mem:* Fel Am Phys Soc; Am Asn Physicists Med; Am Asn Physics Teachers; Soc Nuclear Med. *Res:* High energy nuclear physics; relativity; nuclear medicine. *Mailing Add:* Dept of Physics Carnegie-Mellon Univ Pittsburgh PA 15213

FOX, JOHN GERALD, pathology, see previous edition

FOX, JOHN PERRIGO, b Chicago, Ill, Nov 10, 08; m 34, 74; c 4. VIROLOGY, EPIDEMIOLOGY. *Educ:* Haverford Col, BS, 29; Univ Chicago, MD & PhD(path), 36; Columbia Univ, MPH, 48; Am Bd Prev Med, dipl, 50. *Hon Degrees:* LLD, Haverford Col, 77. *Prof Exp:* Asst path, Univ Chicago, 33-36; intern, Evanston Hosp, Ill, 37-38; mem staff, Int Health Div, Rockefeller Found, 38-49; prof epidemiol, Sch Med, Tulane Univ, 49-58, William Hamilton Watkins prof & dir grad pub health div, 58-60; chief epidemiol dept, Pub Health Res Inst of New York, 60-65; prof prev med, Sch Med, 65-70, assoc dean sch pub health & community med, 70-72, prof, 70-76, EMER PROF EPIDEMIOL, UNIV WASH, 76- *Concurrent Pos:* Mem rickettsial dis comn, US Armed Forces Epidemiol Bd, 56-73, mem med comt, Adv Coun, US Army Chem Corps, 57-61; spec consult staff, Ctr Dis Control, USPHS, 56-, consult, Grad Training Grant Comt, Nat Inst Allergy & Infectious Dis, 57-59, mem bd sci counr, 69-73, chmn, 72-73, mem influenza subcomt, 71-73, mem virus & rickettsial study sect, Div Res Grants, 58-64, chmn, 62-64, mem bd sci counr, Div Biol Standards, 59-63, chmn, 62-63, mem epidemiol & biomed training comt, Nat Inst Gen Med Sci, 65-69, mem viral and rickettsial vaccine rev panel, Bur Biologics, 73-79; adj prof, Sch Pub Health, Columbia Univ & Sch Med, NY Univ Univ, 60-65. *Honors & Awards:* John Snow Award, 81. *Mem:* Am Epidemiol Soc; Am Soc Microbiol; Am Soc Trop Med & Hyg; Am Asn Immunol; fel Am Pub Health Asn. *Res:* Active immunization versus yellow fever, rabies, typhus and poliomyelitis; serologic work in typhus, yellow fever and poliomyelitis; chemotherapy in typus; epidemiologic research in poliomyelitis, enterovirus infections, respiratory virus infections and typhus; viral tissue culture with yellow fever. *Mailing Add:* Dept Epidemiol SC 36 Univ Wash Seattle WA 98195

FOX, JOSEPH M(ICKLE), III, b Philadelphia, Pa, Nov 20, 22; m 49; c 6. REFINERY PROCESS DESIGN, PILOT PLANTS. *Educ:* Princeton Univ, BS, 43, MS, 47. *Prof Exp:* Engr tech serv, Pan Am Refining Corp, 43-45; instr chem eng, Princeton Univ, 46-47; res engr, Res & Develop Dept, M W Kellogg Co Div, Pullman, Inc, 47-52, supvr, 52-58, res assoc, 58-61, pilot plant sect head, 61-66; process develop manager, 66-76, asst chief process eng, Process Serv Dept, Refining & Chem Div, 76-80, CHIEF PROCESS ENG, RES & ENG, BECHTEL GROUP, INC, 80- *Concurrent Pos:* Instr, J F Kennedy Univ, 69-70. *Mem:* Fel Am Inst Chem Engrs; Am Chem Soc. *Res:* Process scale-up; petroleum and petrochemical processing; catalysis; heat and mass transfer; unusual separation techniques; environmental control; synthetic fuels; liquified natural gas. *Mailing Add:* Bechtel Group Inc PO Box 3965 San Francisco CA 94119

FOX, KARL RICHARD, b Berkeley, Calif, July 8, 42; c 1. PATHOLOGY, PHYSIOLOGY. *Educ:* Iowa State Univ, BS, 62; Univ Iowa, MD, 67. *Prof Exp:* Fel physiol, Univ Iowa, 67-69; intern path, State Univ NY Upstate Med Ctr, 69-70; NIH fel lab med, Univ Minn, Minneapolis, 70-73; NIH fel & vis asst prof human physiol, Univ Pavia, 73-74; asst prof path, Med Sch, Univ Tex, 74-77; dir hematol, Dept Path, Baylor Univ Med Ctr & asst prof gen path, Baylor Col Dent, 77-81; DIR HEMATOL & CYTOL, GARY METHODIST HOSPS, 81- *Concurrent Pos:* USPHS spec fel, 73. *Mem:* AAAS; Biophys Soc; Am Soc Hemat; Am Physiol Soc; Am Soc Clin Pathologists. *Res:* Biophysics of membrane transport, pathology and physiology of hemostasis. *Mailing Add:* Dept Path Gary Methodist Hosps Gary IN 46402

FOX, KAYE EDWARD, b Caro, Mich, Sept 26, 32; m 58; c 4. PHARMACOLOGY. *Educ:* Univ Mich, BS, 54; Stanford Univ, PhD(pharmacol), 66. *Prof Exp:* From instr to asst prof, 64-71, ASSOC PROF PHARMACOL, MED SCH, ORE HEALTH SCI UNIV, 71- *Mem:* AAAS; Am Soc Pharmacol & Exp Therapeut; Western Pharmacol Soc; Sigma Xi. *Res:* Biochemical pharmacology; drug ototoxicity. *Mailing Add:* Dept Pharmacol Ore Health Sci Univ Portland OR 97201

FOX, KENNETH, b Highland Park, Mich, Aug 16, 35. ATOMIC & MOLECULAR PHYSICS, ASTROPHYSICS. *Educ:* Wayne State Univ, BS, 57; Univ Mich, MS, 58, PhD(physics), 62. *Prof Exp:* Instr physics, Univ Mich, 61-62; vis res physicist, Inst Nuclear Physics Res, Netherlands, 62-63; vis asst prof physics, Vanderbilt Univ, 63-64; asst prof, Univ Tenn, Knoxville, 64-67; Nat Acad Sci-Nat Res Coun sr res assoc, Jet Propulsion Lab, Calif Inst Technol, 67-69; assoc prof, 69-75, PROF PHYSICS, UNIV TENN, KNOXVILLE, 75- *Concurrent Pos:* Consult, Oak Ridge Nat Lab, 64-70 & Jet Propulsion Lab, Calif Inst Technol, 66-67 & 69-71; mem vis staff, Los Alamos Sci Lab, Univ Calif, 74-; Fulbright sr lectrship, Univ Dijon & Univ Paris, France, 75; sr res assoc, Nat Acad Sci-Nat Res Coun, NASA Goddard Space Flight Ctr, 77-78. *Mem:* Am Phys Soc; Sigma Xi; NY Acad Sci; Am Astron Soc; Explorers Club. *Res:* Theoretical and experimental spectroscopy; planetary atmospheres and interstellar gases; observational astronomy; mathematical physics; laser isotope separation. *Mailing Add:* Dept of Physics & Astron Univ of Tenn Knoxville TN 37996

FOX, KENNETH IAN, b Chicago, Ill, Mar 27, 43. FOOD MICROBIOLOGY, FOOD SCIENCE. *Educ:* Univ Ill, Urbana, BS, 65; Mich State Univ, MS, 67, PhD(food sci), 71. *Prof Exp:* Res chemist, J R Short Milling Co, 71-78; RES MGR CITRUS MACH DIV, FMC CORP, 78- *Mem:* Am Soc Microbiol; Inst Food Technol. *Res:* Botulism food poisoning; germination of bacterial spores; dry heat resistance of bacterial spores; citrus juice and by-products. *Mailing Add:* 4906 Liberty Lane Lakeland FL 33803

FOX, KEVIN A, b Nashua, NH, Feb 1, 39; m 66; c 3. BEHAVIORAL PHYSIOLOGY, REPRODUCTIVE BIOLOGY. *Educ:* Univ NH, BA, 60, MS, 62; Univ Vt, PhD(zool), 67. *Prof Exp:* Instr zool, Univ NH, 60-61 & Hebron Acad, 61-64; res technician, Reproductive Physiol, Univ Vt, 65-66; USPHS fel comp path, Penrose Res Lab & Univ Pa, 67-69; res assoc path, Penrose Res Lab, 69-70; from asst prof to assoc prof, 70-77, chmn, Dept Biol, 74-77, assoc acad vpres & dean spec studies, 77-80, PROF, GRAD FAC, STATE UNIV NY COL FREDONIA, 77- *Concurrent Pos:* NIMH grants, 70-74. *Mem:* AAAS; Am Inst Biol Sci; NY Acad Sci. *Res:* Reproductive and behavioral physiology; reproductive and behavioral toxicology. *Mailing Add:* Dept Biol State Univ NY Col Fredonia NY 14063

FOX, LAUREL R, b New York, NY, Jan 5, 46; m 70; c 1. EVOLUTIONARY BIOLOGY. *Educ:* Cornell Univ, BS, 67; Univ Calif, Santa Barbara, MA, 70, PhD(biol), 73. *Prof Exp:* Res fel, Res Sch Biol Sci, Australian Nat Univ, 73-78; asst prof, 78-81, ASSOC PROF, UNIV CALIF, SANTA CRUZ, 81- *Mailing Add:* Biol Bd Studies Univ Calif Santa Cruz CA 95064

FOX, LEONARD P, b Brooklyn, NY, Mar 13, 28; m 50; c 3. ELECTROCHEMISTRY. *Educ:* Lehigh Univ, BS, 48, MS, 49; Franklin & Marshall Col, MS, 56. *Prof Exp:* Develop engr, Tube Div, Radio Corp Am, 49-57, eng group leader, Semiconductor Div, 57-64, mgr prod eng, Integrated Circuit Dept, 64-67, mgr, Printed Circuit Bd Dept, 67-70, res leader chem processing, 70-73, head selectavision process res, 73-77, HEAD APPL PROCESS RES, DAVID SARNOFF RES CTR, RCA CORP, 77- *Mem:* Am Chem Soc; Am Electrochem Soc; Soc Plastics Engrs; Am Electroplaters Soc. *Res:* Electrodeposition; alloys for semiconductor doping and contacts; development of processing techniques for selectavision video disc; corrosion protection; electropolishing of semiconductor surfaces; mechanism of solder adherence to various metals; passivation of semiconductor surfaces and study of surface contamination sources; polymer processing; conductive carbons. *Mailing Add:* David Sarnoff Res Ctr RCA Corp Princeton NJ 08540

FOX, MARTIN, b New York, NY, July 25, 29; m 51; c 3. STATISTICS. *Educ:* Univ Calif, Berkeley, AB, 51, PhD(statist), 59. *Prof Exp:* From asst prof to assoc prof statist, 59-71, actg chmn dept statist & probability, 66-67, PROF STATIST & PROBABILITY, MICH STATE UNIV, 71- *Concurrent Pos:* Fulbright lectr, Tel-Aviv Univ, 62-63; vis res mem, US Army Math Res Ctr, Univ Wis, 67-68; vis prof, Dept Math, Bowling Green State Univ, 75-76. *Mem:* Fel Inst Math Statist (exec secy, 78-81); Am Math Soc; Am Statist Asn; Math Asn Am. *Res:* Mathematical statistics; probability; game theory. *Mailing Add:* Dept of Statist & Probability Mich State Univ East Lansing MI 48824

FOX, MARTIN DALE, b Hackensack, NJ, Oct 18, 46; m 72; c 1. ELECTRICAL ENGINEERING. *Educ:* Cornell Univ, BEE, 69; Duke Univ, PhD(biomed eng), 72. *Prof Exp:* Asst prof, 72-78, ASSOC PROF ELEC ENG & COMPUT SCI, UNIV CONN, 78- *Mem:* Inst Elec & Electronics Engrs; Optical Soc Am; Am Inst Ultrasound Med; Acoust Soc Am. *Res:* Diagnostic ultrasound; ultrasound doppler; medical imaging; holography; computer science. *Mailing Add:* Dept of Elec Eng & Comput Sci Box U-157 Storrs CT 06268

FOX, MARY ELEANOR, b Bellevue, Ky, Aug 14, 19. SOLID STATE PHYSICS. *Educ:* Villa Madonna Col, AB, 42; Cath Univ Am, MS, 44; Univ Cincinnati, PhD(physics), 62. *Prof Exp:* Assoc prof, 44-67, PROF PHYSICS, THOMAS MORE COL, 67- *Mem:* Am Phys Soc; Am Asn Physics Teachers. *Res:* Mathematical and classical physics; nuclear magnetic resonance broad line studies of crystalline materials in relation to motional narrowing; magnetic anisotropy studies in relation to molecular structure. *Mailing Add:* Dept of Physics Thomas More Col PO Box 85 Covington KY 41017

FOX, MARYE ANNE, b Canton, Ohio, Dec 9, 47; m 69; c 3. ORGANIC CHEMISTRY. *Educ:* Notre Dame Col, BS, 69; Cleveland State Univ, MS, 70; Dartmouth Col, PhD(org chem), 74. *Prof Exp:* Instr phys sci, Cuyahoga Community Col, 70-71; fel & res assoc chem, Univ Md, College Park, 74-76; asst prof chem, 76-80, ASSOC PROF CHEM, UNIV TEX, AUSTIN, 81- *Concurrent Pos:* Alfred P Sloan Res fel, 80-82. *Mem:* Am Chem Soc; Interam Photochem Soc. *Res:* Organic photochemistry; photoelectrochemistry; reaction mechanisms. *Mailing Add:* Dept of Chem Univ of Tex Austin TX 78712

FOX, MATTIE RAE SPIVEY, b Joy, Tex, Feb 23, 23; m 54. NUTRITIONAL BIOCHEMISTRY. *Educ:* Tex Woman's Univ, 43; Iowa State Univ, MS, 47; George Washington Univ, PhD(biochem), 53. *Prof Exp:* Chemist, Humble Oil & Ref Co, 43-45; nutrit analyst, USDA, 47-49; biochemist, NIH, 51-62; res biochemist, 62-66, chief micronutrient res br, 66-71, CHIEF NUTRIT INTERACTIONS SECT, DIV NUTRIT, FOOD & DRUG ADMIN, 71- *Honors & Awards:* Prof Achievement Award, Iowa State Univ, 75; Award of Merit, Food & Drug Admin, 75. *Mem:* Fel AAAS; Am Inst Nutrit (treas, 75); Am Chem Soc; NY Acad Sci; Soc Exp Biol & Med. *Res:* Nutrition of man and experimental animals; metabolism of essential and toxic trace elements. *Mailing Add:* Minerals Sect Div Nutrit HFF 268 US Food & Drug Admin 200 C ST SW Washington DC 20204

FOX, MAURICE SANFORD, b New York, NY, Oct 11, 24; m 55; c 3. GENETICS. *Educ:* Univ Chicago, BS, 44, MS, 51, PhD(chem), 51. *Prof Exp:* Res assoc, Univ Chicago, 51-53; asst, Rockefeller Inst, 53-56, from asst prof to assoc prof, 56-62; from assoc prof to prof genetics, 62-79, LESTER WOLFE PROF MOLECULAR BIOL, MASS INST TECHNOL, 79- *Concurrent Pos:* Nuffield res scholar, 57. *Honors & Awards:* Lalor fel award, 59. *Mem:* AAAS; Nat Inst Med-Nat Acad Sci. *Res:* Chemical events following high energy nuclear recoil; mutation; continuous culture of microorganisms; biological properties of deoxyribonucleates; microbial genetics; molecular mechanism of genetic recombination. *Mailing Add:* Dept Biol Mass Inst Technol Cambridge MA 02139

FOX, MICHAEL WILSON, b Bolton, Eng, Aug 13, 37; m 63; c 2. ETHOLOGY. *Educ:* Royal Vet Col, Univ London, BVetMed & MRCVS, 62; Univ London, PhD(med), 67, DSc(behav), 76. *Prof Exp:* Fel, Jackson Lab, Bar Harbor, Maine, 62-64; med res assoc brain & behav develop, State Res Hosp, Galesburg, Ill, 64-67; asst prof biol & psychol, Wash Univ, 67-68, assoc prof psychol, 68-76. *Concurrent Pos:* Dir, Inst Study Animal Problems, US Humane Soc. *Honors & Awards:* Felix Wankle Int Prize in Animal Welfare Res, 81. *Mem:* Animal Behav Soc; Am Vet Med Asn; Am Asn Animal Sci; Am Psychol Asn. *Res:* Animal behavior, development of canines, including wolf, coyote, fox and dog; animal rights philosophy welfare science; comparative psychopathology. *Mailing Add:* 2100 L St NW Washington DC 20037

FOX, NEIL STEWART, b Detroit, Mich, July 21, 45. INDUSTRIAL ORGANIC CHEMISTRY. *Educ:* Wayne State Univ, BS, 67; Iowa State Univ, MS, 70, PhD(chem), 74. *Prof Exp:* Sr chemist, 3M Co, 74-77; res scientist, 77-78, res supvr, 78-81, GROUP LEADER & RES MGR, THIOKOL/DYNACHEM CO, 81- *Mem:* Am Chem Soc; Sigma Xi; Soc Mfg Eng. *Res:* Process and product development of fine chemicals; UV photopolymerization technology; printed circuit boards; graphic arts clear coatings; dry film photoresists; screen inks, solder and etch resists. *Mailing Add:* Thiokol Dynachem Co PO Box 12047 Santa Ana CA 92711

FOX, OWEN FORREST, b Madison, Wis, Jan 11, 44. BIOCHEMISTRY, MOLECULAR BIOLOGY. *Educ:* Ind Inst Technol, BSci, 67; Univ Mo, PhD(biochem), 71. *Prof Exp:* Res asst protein chem, Max Planck Inst Biochem, 72-75; staff scientist biochem, 76-80, SR RES SCIENTIST, OKLA MED RES FOUND, 80- *Mem:* Am Chem Soc; NY Acad Sci; AAAS; Sigma Xi. *Res:* Biochemistry, structure and function of glycoproteins in mucous secretions; metabolism and synthesis of glycoproteins in chemical carcinogenesis. *Mailing Add:* Biomembrane Res Lab 825 NE 13th St Oklahoma City OK 73104

FOX, PAUL JEFFREY, b New York, NY, Dec 6, 41. MARINE GEOLOGY, TECTONOPHYSICS. *Educ:* Ohio Wesleyan Univ, BA, 63; Columbia Univ, PhD(geol), 72. *Prof Exp:* Res asst marine geol, Lamont Doherty Geol Observ, 64-72; asst prof geol, State Univ NY, Albany, 72-77, assoc prof geol, 77-81, ASSOC PROF GEOL, GRAD SCH OCEANOG, UNIV RI, 81- *Concurrent Pos:* Vis res assoc, Lamont Doherty Geol Observ, 72-; mem, Ocean Crust Panel, Deep Earth Sampling Prog, Joint Oceanog Inst, 76-78, chmn, 78-82; panel mem, Adv Comt Ocean Sci, NSF, 78-81. *Mem:* Fel Geol Soc Am; Am Geophys Union; AAAS; Sigma Xi. *Res:* Structure, composition and evolution of ocean crust; the tectonics of ridge-transform-ridge plate boundaries; the geologic history of the Caribbean. *Mailing Add:* Dept of Geol Sci State Univ of NY Albany NY 12222

FOX, PHYLLIS, b Denver, Colo, Mar 13, 23; m 58; c 2. MATHEMATICS, COMPUTER SCIENCE. *Educ:* Wellesley Col, AB, 44; Univ Colo, BS, 48; Mass Inst Technol, MS, 49, ScD(math), 54. *Prof Exp:* ScientAEC, Courant Inst, NY Univ, 54-58; res assoc, Mass Inst Technol, 58-62; assoc prof math, 63-67, prof comput sci, Newark Col Eng, 67-73; MEM TECH STAFF, BELL LABS, 73- em: Soc Indust & Appl Math; Asn Comput Mach. *Res:* Applications of computers; numerical analysis; applied mathematics; development of mathematical subroutine libraries for numerical computation. *Mailing Add:* 66 Old Short Hills Rd Short Hills NJ 07078

FOX, RICHARD CARR, b Lowell, Mass, Oct 3, 33. VERTEBRATE PALEONTOLOGY. *Educ:* Hamilton Col, AB, 55; State Univ NY, MScI, 57; Univ Kans, PhD(zool), 65. *Prof Exp:* Asst prof, 65-69, PROF GEOL & ZOOL, UNIV ALTA, 69- *Mem:* AAAS; Am Soc Zoologists; Am Soc Ichthyologists & Herpetologists; Am Soc Mammalogists; NY Acad Sci. *Res:* Paleozoic reptiles and the origin of reptiles; late Cretaceous and early Tertiary mammals, lizards, salamanders; community evolution of late Cretaceous vertebrates. *Mailing Add:* Dept of Geol Univ of Alta Edmonton AB T6G 2E9 Can

FOX, RICHARD CHARLES, forest entomology, see previous edition

FOX, RICHARD HENRY, b Reno, Nev, Nov 1, 38; m 61; c 2. SOIL FERTILITY. *Educ:* Carleton Col, BA, 61; Univ Ariz, MS, 64, PhD(agr chem & soils), 66. *Prof Exp:* Soils adv to Peru, NC State Univ/USAID Agr Mission Peru, 66-69; asst prof soil fertil & dir opers in PR, Trop Soils Proj, Cornell Univ/USAID/Univ PR, 69-74; ASST PROF SOIL FERTIL, PA STATE UNIV, 75- *Mem:* Soil Sci Soc Am; Am Soc Agron; Int Soil Sci Soc. *Res:* Evaluating soil nitrogen supply capability; studying nitrogen fertilizer transformations, toxicities and losses under field conditions; physiology of phosphorous efficiency in plants; lime requirement testing; magnesium fertility in corn production. *Mailing Add:* Dept of Agron Pa State Univ University Park PA 16802

FOX, RICHARD ROMAINE, b New Haven, Conn, Nov 12, 34; m 55, 81; c 3. LABORATORY ANIMAL SCIENCE, GENETICS. *Educ:* Univ Conn, BS, 56; Univ Minn, MS, 58, PhD(animal breeding, genetics), 59. *Prof Exp:* Actg swine herdsman, Univ Conn, 56; asst animal breeding, Univ Minn, 56-59; fel, 59-60, assoc staff scientist, 60-65, staff scientist, 65-80, SR STAFF SCIENTIST, JACKSON LAB, 80- *Mem:* AAAS; Am Dairy Sci Asn; Am Soc Animal Sci; Genetics Soc Am; Am Genetic Asn. *Res:* Genetics of the rabbit; quantitative genetics; reproductive physiology; germ plasm preservation. *Mailing Add:* Jackson Lab Bar Harbor ME 04609

FOX, RICHARD SHIRLEY, b Lexington, Ky, Feb 20, 43. INVERTEBRATE ZOOLOGY, MARINE ECOLOGY. *Educ:* Univ Fla, BS, 67, MS, 69; Univ NC, Chapel Hill, PhD(zool), 80. *Prof Exp:* Aquatic biologist, Fla Dept Air & Water Pollution Control, 69-71; ASST PROF, DEPT BIOL, LANDER COL, 77- *Concurrent Pos:* Vis prof, NJ Marine Sci Consortium, 76; res assoc, Baruch Inst Marine Biol, Univ SC, 78- *Mem:* Sigma Xi; Am Soc Zoologists; Southeastern Estuarine Res Soc. *Res:* Systematics and ecology of amphipod crustaceans; marine community ecology; island biogeography; faunistic studies of southeastern United States marine invertebrates. *Mailing Add:* Dept Biol Lander Col Greenwood SC 29646

FOX, ROBERT DEAN, b Cass City, Mich, Oct 26, 36; m 66; c 6. AGRICULTURAL ENGINEERING, ATMOSPHERIC PHYSICS. *Educ:* Mich State Univ, BS, 57, MS, 58, PhD(agr eng), 68. *Prof Exp:* Instr agr eng & rural electrification, Mich State Univ, 63-64; AGR ENGR, AGR RES SERV, USDA, 68- *Mem:* Am Soc Agr Engrs; Am Meteorol Soc. *Res:* Diffusion of fine particles in air, specifically the effects of turbulent transport of particles in the region of a plant canopy. *Mailing Add:* Agr Eng Dept Ohio Agr Res & Develop Ctr Wooster OH 44691

FOX, ROBERT KRIEGBAUM, b Covington, Ohio, Apr 1, 07; m 34; c 3. PHYSICAL INORGANIC CHEMISTRY. *Educ:* Ohio State Univ, BA, 29, MA, 30, PhD(inorg & phys chem), 32. *Prof Exp:* Asst chem, Ohio State Univ, 29-32; from instr to asst prof, Bethany Col, WVA, 32-36; asst prof, Hiram Col, 36-41; partner, Fox Chem Co, Ohio, 41-45; pres, Ind Glass Co, 56-74; pres, 45-76, CHMN, LANCASTER GLASS CORP, 76-, VPRES & TREAS, LANCASTER COLONY CORP, 62- *Mem:* Am Chem Soc; Sigma Xi. *Res:* Catalytic oxidation of acetylene black; solubility of manganese hydroxide; fabric treating compounds; crystal and colored glasses. *Mailing Add:* Amanda Rd RD 6 Lancaster OH 43130

FOX, ROBERT LEE, b Moberly, Mo, May 26, 23; m 48; c 5. SOILS. *Educ:* Univ Mo, BS, 47, MA, 50, PhD(soils), 55. *Prof Exp:* Asst prof agron & asst agronomist, Univ Nebr, 50-56; assoc prof, Univ Ankara, 56-58 & Univ Nebr, 58-61; PROF SOIL SCI & SOIL SCIENTIST, UNIV HAWAII, 61- *Mem:* Am Soc Agron; Soil Sci Soc Am. *Res:* Soil fertility and chemistry. *Mailing Add:* Dept of Agron & Soil Sci Univ of Hawaii Honolulu HI 96822

FOX, ROBERT WILLIAM, b Montreal, Que, July 1, 34; m 62; c 2. MECHANICAL ENGINEERING, FLUID MECHANICS. *Educ:* Rensselaer Polytech Inst, BS, 55; Univ Colo, MS, 57; Stanford Univ, PhD(mech eng), 61. *Prof Exp:* Instr mech eng, Univ Colo, 55-57; asst, Stanford Univ, 57-60; from asst prof to assoc prof, 60-66, chmn grad prog, 69-71, asst head, Sch Mech Eng, 71-72, asst dean, Eng for Instr, 72-76, actg head, Sch Mech Eng, 75-76, PROF MECH ENG, PURDUE UNIV, 66-, ASSOC HEAD DEPT, 76- *Concurrent Pos:* Vis prof, Bradley Univ, 64-65; consult, Nat Comt FlUid Mech Films, 63- & Owens Corning Fiberglass Corp, Ohio, 63. *Mem:* Am Soc Eng Educ; Am Soc Mech Engrs. *Res:* Turbulent boundary layers in adverse pressure gradients; diffuser flows. *Mailing Add:* Sch of Mech Eng Purdue Univ Lafayette IN 47907

FOX, RONALD FORREST, b Berkeley, Calif, Oct 1, 43; m 69. THEORETICAL PHYSICS. *Educ:* Reed Col, BA, 64; Rockefeller Univ, PhD(theoret physics), 69. *Prof Exp:* Miller fel theoret physics, Miller Inst Basic Res Sci, Univ Calif, Berkeley, 69-71; from asst prof to assoc prof, 71-79, PROF PHYSICS, GA INST TECH, 79- *Concurrent Pos:* Vis prof chem, Univ Calif, Davis, 81. *Mem:* Am Phys Soc; Sigma Xi. *Res:* Biodynamics; non-equilibrium statistical mechanics; energy conversion; stochastic processes. *Mailing Add:* Sch of Physics Ga Inst of Technol Atlanta GA 30332

FOX, RONALD LEE, fluid mechanics, atomic physics, see previous edition

FOX, RUSSELL ELWELL, b Richmond, Va, Dec 28, 16; m 42; c 3. ATOMIC PHYSICS. *Educ:* Hampden-Sydney Col, BS, 38; Univ Va, MS, 39, PhD(physics), 42. *Prof Exp:* Fel, 42, res physicist, 42-57, mgr, Physics Dept, 57-64, dir atomic & molecular sci res & develop, 64-69, res dir consumer prods, 69-74, RES & DEVELOP DIR INDUST PRODS, RES LAB, WESTINGHOUSE ELEC CORP, 74- *Mem:* AAAS; Am Vacuum Soc; Am Soc Test & Mat (pres, 62-64); fel Am Phys Soc; Illum Eng Soc. *Res:* Mass spectrometry; research planning and administration. *Mailing Add:* Westinghouse Res Labs Beulah Rd Pittsburgh PA 15235

FOX, SALLY INGERSOLL, b Philadelphia, Pa, Oct 19, 25; m 49; c 3. MICROBIOLOGY. *Educ:* Vassar Col, BA, 46; Columbia Univ, MA, 52; Rensselaer Polytech Inst, PhD(biol), 67. *Prof Exp:* Lectr microbiol, Russell Sage Col, 61; asst microbiol, Rensselaer Polytech Inst, 63-66; asst prof, 67-71, assoc prof, 71-80, PROF BIOL, COL ST ROSE, 80- *Mem:* Fedn Am Scientists; Am Soc Microbiol. *Res:* Microflora of acid mine waters, especially leaching areas of copper mines; toxic effects of Bacillus thesingiensis d-endotoxin on cultured cells and Trichuplusiani larvae; interactions between indigenous yeast and copper oxidizing thiobacilli. *Mailing Add:* Dept of Biol Col of St Rose Albany NY 12203

FOX, SAMUEL MICKLE, III, b Andalusia, Pa, Feb 13, 23; m 49; c 4. MEDICINE. *Educ:* Haverford Col, BA, 44; Univ Pa, MD, 47; Am Bd Internal Med, dipl, 55. *Prof Exp:* Intern, resident med, Univ Pa Hosp, 47-50; asst instr med, Univ Pa, 48-50; actg chief gastroenterol, Nat Naval Med Ctr, US Navy, Md, 50-51, from mem staff to chief cardiol serv, 53-54, mem staff, Off Naval Res & Med Off, Eastern Atlantic & Mediterranean, Eng, 51-53; head dept clin invest, Naval Med Res Unit, Cairo, Egypt, 54-56; chief cardiol & officer in chg cardiopulmonary res lab, US Naval Hosp, Portsmouth, Va, 56-57; responsible investr sect cardiodyn, Nat Heart Inst, 57-59, co-chief sect, 59-61, asst dir, 61-62; dep chief heart dis & stroke control prog, USPHS, 63-64, chief, 65-70; prof med, Div Cardiol, Sch Med, George Washington Univ, 70-75; PROD MED, DIV CARDIOL, SCH MED, GEORGETOWN UNIV, 75- *Concurrent Pos:* Res fel med & gastroenterol, Hosp Univ Pa, 48-49; res assoc, Res Inst & Abbassia & Embaba Fever Hosps, Cairo, Egypt, 54-56; vis prof, Ein Shams Univ, 55-56; res assoc, Kasr-el-aini, 55-56; consult, WHO, Inter Am Soc Cardiol & Asian-Pac Soc Cardiol; mem NASA res adv comt biotech & human res, 64-68; fel coun clin cardiol, Am Heart Asn; mem, President's Coun Phys Fitness & Sports, 70- *Mem:* Fel AMA; Am Heart Asn; Am Col Physicians; Am Col Cardiol (pres, 72-73); fel Am Col Sports Med (vpres, 76-79). *Res:* Clinical problems of disturbed cardiopulmonary physiology, prevention, management, and rehabilitation. *Mailing Add:* 3800 Reservoir Rd NW Washington DC 20007

FOX, SERECK HALL, b Philadelphia, Pa, Jan 27, 00; m 26; c 3. PHARMACEUTICAL CHEMISTRY. *Educ:* Philadelphia Col Pharm, PhG, 21. *Hon Degrees:* DSc, Philadelphia Col Pharm, 50. *Prof Exp:* Mem staff, Powers, Weightman & Rosengarten, 19 & H K Mulford Co, 21-29; asst to supt, Sharp & Dohme, Inc, 29-34, dir pharmaceut res, 34-37; tech dir, R P Scherer Corp, 37-53, vpres pharmaceut res & control, 53-57; prof, 57-70, EMER PROF INDUST PHARM, WAYNE STATE UNIV, 70- *Concurrent Pos:* Indust consult, 57- *Mem:* Fel AAAS; Am Chem Soc; Am Pharmaceut Asn; fel Am Inst Chem; fel NY Acad Sci. *Res:* Establishment of standards in foods and drugs; pharmaceutical development; quality control. *Mailing Add:* 12165 Spencer Rd Milford MI 48042

FOX, SIDNEY WALTER, b Los Angeles, Calif, Mar 24, 12; m 37; c 3. BIOCHEMISTRY. *Educ:* Univ Calif, Los Angeles, BA, 33; Calif Inst Technol, PhD(biochem), 40. *Prof Exp:* Asst, Rockefeller Inst, 34-35 & Calif Inst Technol, 35-37; fel, Univ Mich, 41-42; from asst prof to prof chem, Iowa State Col, 43-55, head chem sect, Exp Sta, 49-55; prof chem, Fla State Univ, 55-64, dir oceanog inst, 55-61 & inst space biosci, 61-64; PROF RES & DIR INST MOLECULAR & CELLULAR EVOLUTION, UNIV MIAMI, 64-; DIR REGIONAL LAB, NAT FOUND CANCER RES, 76- *Concurrent Pos:* Consult, AEC, 47-55 & A E Staley Co, 54-60; mem panel selection NSF fels, Nat Acad Sci-Nat Res Coun, 53-55, 60, chmn subcomt nomenclature biochem, Nat Res Coun, 56-57; secy, Nat Comt Biochem, 56-59; subchmn panel selection NSF fac fels, Asn Am Cols, 57-58; Nat Acad Sci deleg, Fourth Int Cong Biochem, Vienna, 58; mem adv panel syst biol, NSF, 58-60 & comn undergrad educ biol sci, 69-71; mem biosci subcomt, NASA, 60-66; Priestman lectr, Univ NB, 64; USA-USSR Interacad lectr, 69; vpres, Int Soc Study Origin Life, 70-74; Shaw lectr, Temple Univ, 75; AAAS lectr, 79-82; vis prof, Tex A&M Univ, 80; Watkins vis prof, Wichita State Univ, 81. *Honors & Awards:* US Dept Com Medal, 62; Fla Award, Am Chem Soc, 74; Camille & Henry Dreyfus lectr, Pomona Col, 81. *Mem:* Fel AAAS; Geochem Soc; Am Chem Soc; Am Soc Biol Chem; Am Soc Cell Biol. *Res:* Thermal proteins; molecular and cellular evolution. *Mailing Add:* IMCE Univ of Miami 521 Anastasia Coral Gables FL 33134

FOX, STANLEY FORREST, b Rockford, Ill, Mar 21, 46; c 2. EVOLUTIONARY ECOLOGY, HERPETOLOGY. *Educ:* Univ Ill, BS, 68; Yale Univ, MPhil, 69, PhD(ecol & evolution), 73. *Prof Exp:* Res asst forest ecol, Brookhaven Lab, 68; biol teacher, Watertown High Sch, 69-70; fel pop biol, Rockefeller Univ, 73-75; asst prof evolution, Boston Univ, 75-77; ASST PROF EVOLUTION, OKLA STATE UNIV, 77- *Concurrent Pos:* Prin investr, NSF res grants, 67, 71-73, 78-80 & 81-83, Am Philos Soc grant, 75 & Sigma Xi grants, 71 & 75; asst cur herpetol, Peabody Mus, Yale Univ, 70, actg cur, 71-73; teaching asst, Yale Univ, 70-71; res assoc, NIH res grant, 75; co-investr, Am Mus Natural Hist & Am Philos res grant, 75. *Mem:* Brit Ecol Soc; Ecol Soc Am; Soc Study Ecolution; Am Soc Naturalists; Am Soc Ichthyologists & Herpetologists. *Res:* Evolutionary ecology of behavior, especially social behavior; ecology of territoriality; population ecology and demography of lizards; natural selection. *Mailing Add:* Dept Zool Okla State Univ Stillwater OK 74078

FOX, STEPHEN SORIN, b New Haven, Conn, July 15, 33; m 59; c 3. PHYSIOLOGICAL PSYCHOLOGY. *Educ:* Univ Pa, BA, 55; Univ Mich, MA, 57, PhD(psychol), 59. *Prof Exp:* Asst physiol psychol, Vision Res Labs, Univ Mich, 55-56; res anatomist, Med Sch, Univ Calif, Los Angeles, 57-59; head animal neurophysiol & behav sect, Schizophrenia & Psychopharmacol Joint Res Proj, Univ Mich, 59-63, assoc res psychobiologist, Ment Health Res Inst, 59-65, asst prof psychol, Univ Mich, 62-65; assoc prof, 65-70, PROF PSYCHOL, UNIV IOWA, 70- *Concurrent Pos:* Res assoc, Ypsilanti State Hosp, Mich, 59-63; investr, Woods Hole Marine Biol Labs, 61- *Mem:* Am Psychol Asn; Biophys Soc; NY Acad Sci; Biofeedback Res Soc; Am Physiol Soc. *Res:* Behavioral neurophysiology; psychobiology; neurophysiological correlates of behavior; electrophysiology; identification of the structural and functional substrate of behavior; neural coding. *Mailing Add:* Dept of Psychol Univ of Iowa Iowa City IA 52240

FOX, THOMAS ALLEN, b Dover, Ohio, Aug 23, 26; m 53; c 2. REACTOR PHYSICS. *Educ:* Univ Ohio, BS, 49, MS, 51. *Prof Exp:* Instr physics, Ohio Univ, 51-52; from res scientist to head, Exp Reactor Physics Sect, 52-68, head, Critical Facil Unit, 68-73, res scientist, Power Amplifier Sect, 73-79, RES SCIENTIST, MICROWAVE AMPLIFIER SECT, LEWIS RES CTR, NASA, 80- *Mem:* Am Nuclear Soc. *Res:* Experimental reactor physics; reactor operations; first analytical studies; reactor critical facilities. *Mailing Add:* Lewis Res Ctr Power Amplifier Sect NASA 21000 Brookpark Cleveland OH 44135

FOX, THOMAS DAVID, b Staten Island, NY, Mar 5, 50. MOLECULAR GENETICS, EXTRACHROMOSOMAL GENETICS. *Educ:* Cornell Univ, BS, 71; Harvard Univ, PhD(biochem & molecular biol), 76. *Prof Exp:* Fel biochem, Biocenter, Univ Basel, 76-78, independent res assoc, 79, asst prof, 79-81; ASST PROF GENETICS, CORNELL UNIV, 81- *Concurrent Pos:* Instr, course on molecular genetics of yeast & molecular biol of membranes, Europ Molecular Biol Orgn, Basel, 80. *Mem:* Genetic Soc Am. *Res:* Study of gene structure and regulation, especially in the mitochondrial genetic system of yeast and higher plants. *Mailing Add:* Sect Genetics & Develop Bradfield Hall Cornell Univ Ithaca NY 14853

FOX, THOMAS OREN, b Ames, Iowa, Nov 24, 45; m 75. BIOCHEMICAL GENETICS, DEVELOPMENTAL NEUROSCIENCE. *Educ:* Pomona Col, BA, 67; Princeton Univ, PHD(biochem sci), 71. *Prof Exp:* Fel develop biol, 71-73, instr biochem genetics, 73-74, asst prof, 74-79, ASSOC PROF NEUROPATH, HARVARD MED SCH, 79- *Concurrent Pos:* Sr res assoc neurosci, Childrens Hosp, Med Ctr, Boston, 79- *Mem:* Soc Neurosci; Endocrine Soc; Am Chem Soc; Tissue Culture Asn; Sigma Xi. *Res:* Biochemical genetics and development of sex steroid receptors; biochemical and behavioral investigations of mammalian mutants with syndromes of androgen-resistance; control mechanisms involved in the sexual differentiation of the brain. *Mailing Add:* Dept Neurosci Childrens Hosp Med Ctr 300 Longwood Ave Boston MA 02115

FOX, THOMAS WALTON, b Pawtucket, RI, Mar 21, 23; m 48; c 2. ANIMAL GENETICS, ANIMAL BREEDING. *Educ:* Univ Mass, BS, 49, MS, 50; Purdue Univ, PhD(genetics, physiol), 52. *Prof Exp:* Asst poultry, Purdue Univ, 50-52; from instr to asst prof, 52-54, prof poultry & head dept, 54-64, head dept vet & animal sci, 64-79, PROF ANIMAL SCI, UNIV MASS, AMHERST, 79- . *Mem:* AAAS; Am Genetics Asn; Poultry Sci Asn; Am Inst Biol Sci; Genetics Soc Am. *Res:* Avian genetics and applied breeding; avian physiology. *Mailing Add:* Dept Vet & Animal Sci Univ Mass Amherst MA 01003

FOX, VIRGIL GRANT, chemical engineering, see previous edition

FOX, WILLIAM, b New Haven, Conn, Mar 15, 14; m 49; c 2. PHYSICAL CHEMISTRY, COLLOID CHEMISTRY. *Educ:* City Col, BS, 35; Columbia Univ, MA, 42, PhD(chem), 44. *Prof Exp:* Patrolman, New York Police Dept, 40-45, detective police lab & field command, 45-52, sgt supvr, 52-57, Lt, Police Acad & Fac Police Sci, City Col New York, 57-62, lt supvr field command, 62-66, capt, 66-77; ASSOC, OAKLAND RES ASSOCS, 56- *Concurrent Pos:* Phys chemist, Petrol Exp Sta, Bur Mines, Okla, 49; mem, Task Force Forensic Chem, Am Chem Soc, 78-80. *Mem:* Am Chem Soc; AAAS; Sigma Xi. *Res:* Physics and chemistry of fluid interfaces; contact angles and force constants of fluid interfaces; surface and interfacial tension; spontaneous mass movements of fluids; surface active agents, emulsions; foams; aerosols; colloids; forensic science. *Mailing Add:* Oakland Res Assocs 657 Oakland Ave Staten Island NY 10310

FOX, WILLIAM B, b Clifton, NJ, Aug 12, 28; m 54; c 1. PHYSICAL INORGANIC CHEMISTRY. *Educ:* Univ Ill, BS, 55; Pa State Univ, PhD(inorg chem), 60. *Prof Exp:* Res chemist, Gen Chem Div, Allied Chem Corp, Morristown, 60-61, sr res chemist, 61-62, tech supvr, 62-66, mgr inorg mat res, Indust Chem Res Lab, 66-68, dir inorg res & develop, 68-71; head, Inorg Chem Br, 71-79, asst dir res, Off Undersecy Defense, Res & Eng, 79-81, HEAD, POLYMERIC MATS BR, NAVAL RES LAB, 81- *Concurrent Pos:* Chmn, Fluorine Div, Am Chem Soc, 80. *Mem:* Am Chem Soc; Royal Soc Chem; Sigma Xi. *Res:* Synthesis of fluorocarbon derivatives of oxygen, nitrogen, sulfur, halogens, and metalloids; isolation and spectroscopy of free radicals; chemical laser systems; high temperature fluids, organic and organometallic polymers, coatings and composites. *Mailing Add:* Polymeric Mats Br Chem Div Naval Res Lab Code 6120 Washington DC 20390

FOX, WILLIAM CASSIDY, b Homestead, Fla, Oct 9, 26; m 55; c 1. MATHEMATICS. *Educ:* Grinnell Col, BA, 49; Univ Mich, MA, 50, PhD(math), 55. *Prof Exp:* CLE Moore res instr, Mass Inst Technol, 54-56; asst prof math, Northwestern Univ, 56-60; res assoc, Tulane Univ, 60-61; ASSOC PROF MATH, STATE UNIV NY STONY BROOK, 61-, DIR GRAD PROG, 75- *Mem:* Am Math Soc; Math Asn Am. *Res:* Topology; analytic and harmonic functions; Riemann surfaces. *Mailing Add:* Dept of Math State Univ of NY Stony Brook NY 11790

FOX, WILLIAM R(OBERT), b Sevierville, Tenn, June 15, 36; m 59; c 3. AGRICULTURAL ENGINEERING, ENGINEERING MECHANICS. *Educ:* Univ Tenn, BS, 58, MS, 59; Iowa State Univ, PhD(agr eng, eng mech), 62. *Prof Exp:* Instr agr eng, Iowa State Univ, 60-62; from asst prof to assoc prof, 62-67, PROF AGR & BIOL ENG & HEAD DEPT, MISS STATE UNIV, 67- *Mem:* AAAS; Am Soc Agr Engrs; Am Soc Eng Educ; Nat Soc Prof Engrs. *Res:* Tillage mechanics and machinery; fundamentals of tillage energy applications. *Mailing Add:* Dept Agr & Biol Eng Miss State Univ Mississippi State MS 39762

FOX, WILLIAM TEMPLETON, b Chicago, Ill, Nov 15, 32; m 59; c 1. GEOLOGY. *Educ:* Williams Col, BA, 54; Northwestern Univ, MS, 60, PhD(geol), 61. *Prof Exp:* From instr to assoc prof, 61-72, PROF GEOL, WILLIAMS COL, 72- *Concurrent Pos:* NSF res Grant, 62-64, fel, Stanford Univ, 66-67; Off Naval Res grant, 69-71; geologist, Shell Oil Co, 61; mem coastal res group, Off Naval Res Contract, 72-78; vis prof, Ore State Univ, 73-74. *Mem:* AAAS; Am Asn Petrol Geol; Geol Soc Am; Soc Econ Paleontologists & Mineralogists. *Res:* Stratigraphy; sedimentation; paleoecology; computer applications to geology. *Mailing Add:* Dept of Geol Williams Col Williamstown MA 01267

FOX, WILLIAM WALTER, JR, b San Diego, Calif, July 18, 45; m 67; c 2. FISHERIES. *Educ:* Univ Miami, BS, 67, MS, 70; Univ Wash, PhD(fisheries), 72. *Prof Exp:* Fisheries biologist pop dynamics, Bur Com Fisheries, Dept Interior, 67-69; fisheries biologist, 72-73, prog leader, 73-75, div chief,

Oceanic Fisheries, 75-78, DIR, SOUTHEAST FISHERIES CTR, NAT MARINE FISHERIES SERV, DEPT COM, 78- *Concurrent Pos:* Mem Sci Comt, Int Whaling Comn, 72; chmn, 27th Ann Tuna Conf, 75-76; mem Sci Comt, Int Comn Conserv Atlantic Tunas, 72-; mem Tuna Stock Assessment Panel, Food & Agr Orgn UN, 74-; contrib ed, Fishery Bulletin, Nat Marine Fisheries Serv, 75-78. *Honors & Awards:* W F Thompson Award, Am Inst Fisheries Res Biologists, 71. *Mem:* Am Fisheries Soc; Am Inst Fisheries Res Biologists. *Res:* Theory and application of quantitative methods to determine the response of natural populations to controlled and uncontrolled exploitation. *Mailing Add:* Nat Marine Fisheries Serv 75 Virginia Beach Dr Miami FL 33149

FOXHALL, GEORGE FREDERIC, b Worcester, Mass, Feb 20, 39; m 61; c 2. SEMICONDUCTOR PHYSICS. *Educ:* Worcester Polytech Inst, BS, 61; Univ Ill, MS, 62. *Prof Exp:* MEM TECH STAFF, BELL TEL LABS, 61- *Mem:* AAAS; sr mem Inst Elec & Electronics Engrs. *Res:* Semiconductor device physics. *Mailing Add:* 5 Plymouth Circle Colony Park Reading PA 19610

FOXMAN, BRUCE MAYER, b Youngstown, Ohio, Mar 12, 42; m 68; c 2. SOLID STATE CHEMISTRY. *Educ:* Iowa State Univ, BS, 64; Mass Inst Technol, PhD(inorg chem), 68. *Prof Exp:* Res fel chem, Australian Nat Univ, 68-72; asst prof, 72-78, ASSOC PROF CHEM, BRANDEIS UNIV, 78- *Concurrent Pos:* Vis prof, T J Watson Res Ctr, IBM CORP, 75; consult, Gen Telephone & Electronics Corp Lab, 81- *Mem:* Am Chem Soc; Am Crystallog Asn; Chem Soc. *Res:* Mechanisms of solid-state reactions; engineering and synthesis of reactive single crystals; x-ray diffraction studies. *Mailing Add:* Dept Chem Brandeis Univ Waltham MA 02254

FOXWORTHY, BRUCE L, b Spokane, Wash, Dec 30, 25; m 56; c 4. HYDROLOGY. *Educ:* Univ Wash, BS, 50. *Prof Exp:* Geologist, Water Resources Div, US Geol Surv, Wash, 51-59, dist geologist, Ore, 59-64, hydrologist in chg, Long Island, NY, 64-68, sub-dist chief, 68-70, asst dist chief, Wash, 70-73, proj chief, Puget Sound Urban Area Studies, 73-82. *Res:* Water resources inventories; artificial recharge; hydrology of volcanic terranes; urban hydrology. *Mailing Add:* US Geol Surv 1201 Pacific Ave Tacoma WA 98402

FOXWORTHY, JAMES E(RNEST), b Los Angeles, Calif, Feb 23, 30; m 50; c 6. ENVIRONMENTAL ENGINEERING, OCEANOGRAPHY. *Educ:* Univ Southern Calif, BS, 55, MS, 58, PhD, 65. *Prof Exp:* Instr civil eng, Univ Wis, 55-56; lectr gen eng, Univ Southern Calif, 56-59; from asst prof to assoc prof civil eng & chmn dept, 58-69, dean col eng, 69-73, dean sci & eng, 73-81, PROF CIVIL ENG, LOYOLA MARYMOUNT UNIV, 69-, EXEC VPRES SCI & ENG, 81- *Concurrent Pos:* Consult, WHO, 74- *Mem:* Am Soc Civil Engrs; Am Soc Eng Educ; Am Asn Prof Environ Engrs; AAAS. *Res:* Waste disposal in the marine environment. *Mailing Add:* Col Sci & Eng 7101 W 80th St Los Angeles CA 90045

FOY, C ALLAN, b Philadelphia, Pa, Jan 27, 44; m 65; c 5. RADAR SYSTEMS. *Educ:* US Naval Acad, Annapolis, Md, BS, 65; Univ Mich, MS, 68, PhD(math), 71. *Prof Exp:* Instr math, US Naval Acad, 77-79; mem res staff, 79-80, asst dir, 80-81, SR PROG MGR, SYST PLANNING CORP, 81- *Mem:* Am Math Soc; Inst Math Statist. *Res:* Radar systems; collection and analysis of radar data; systems level analyses of radar system performance. *Mailing Add:* Syst Planning Corp 1500 Wilson Blvd Arlington VA 22209

FOY, CHARLES DALEY, b Buena Vista, Ky, Aug 19, 23; m 55; c 1. SOIL FERTILITY, PLANT NUTRITION. *Educ:* Univ Tenn, BS, 48; Purdue Univ, MS, 53, PhD(soil fertility), 55. *Prof Exp:* Instr vets inst on farm training, Ind 49-51; asst prof agron, Purdue Univ, 55-57; co-op agent agron, Univ Ark, 57-61, soil scientist, Ark, 57-61, soil scientist, Md, 61-72, RES SOIL SCIENTIST, PLANT STRESS LAB, AGR RES SERV, USDA, 72- *Honors & Awards:* Environ Qual Award, Am Soc Hort Sci, 74. *Mem:* AAAS; Am Soc Agron; Soil Sci Soc Am. *Res:* Causes of acid soil infertility; physiological mechanisms for differential tolerances of plant genotypes to high aluminum and mu manganese and low phosphorus levels in acid soils and mine spoils and low iron availability in calcareous soils; collaboration with plant breeders in tailoring plants for adaptation to soil mineral stresses. *Mailing Add:* Plant Stress Lab Plant Physiol Inst USDA Beltsville MD 20705

FOY, CHESTER LARRIMORE, b Dukedom, Tenn, July 8, 28; m 53; c 2. PLANT PHYSIOLOGY. *Educ:* Univ Tenn, BS, 52; Univ Mo, MS, 53; Univ Calif, PhD(plant physiol), 58. *Prof Exp:* Asst instr field crops, Univ Mo, 52-53; asst specialist chem weed control, Dept Bot, Univ Calif, Davis, 53-56, asst plant physiol, 57-58, asst botanist, 58-64, assoc prof, 66-68, head dept, 74-80, PROF PLANT PHYSIOL, VA POLYTECH INST & STATE UNIV, 68- *Concurrent Pos:* Nat Acad Sci-Nat Res Coun resident res assoc, Ft Detrick, Md, 64-65. *Mem:* Am Soc Agron; Am Soc Plant Physiol; Weed Sci Soc Am; Plant Growth Regulator Soc. *Res:* Agricultural chemicals; chemical weed control; pathways and mechanics of foliar and root absorption, translocation, accumulation; metabolism, mode of action, selectivity and fate of herbicides and surfactants; physiological, biochemical and morphological changes induced by chemicals; detoxification and other plant protective mechanisms; growth regulators and phytotoxicants; pesticides in the environment. *Mailing Add:* Dept Plant Path & Physiol Va Polytech Inst & State Univ Blacksburg VA 24061

FOY, HJORDIS M, b Stockholm, Sweden, June 28, 26; US citizen; m 56; c 3. INFECTIOUS DISEASES, PREVENTIVE MEDICINE. *Educ:* Karolinska Inst, Sweden, MD, 53; Univ Wash, MS, 67, PhD, 68. *Prof Exp:* Mem staff, Hosp Infectious Dis, Stockholm, 53-55; mem staff, Johns Hopkins Hosp, 56-57 & 58-59; sr fel, 63-67, instr, 66-68, asst prof prev med, 68-70, from asst prof to assoc prof epidemiol, 70-76, PROF EPIDEMIOL, SCH PUB HEALTH, UNIV WASH, 76- *Concurrent Pos:* Consult epidemiol & biometry training comt, Nat Inst Gen Med, 71-73; consult bact vaccines & toxoids, Bur Biologics, Food & Drug Admin, 72-; consult allergy, Immunol Res Comt, Nat Inst Allergy & Infectious Dis, 75-77; mem, microbiol & infectious diseases adv comt, Nat Inst Allergy & Infectious Diseases, 78-81. *Mem:* Fel Am Col Prev Med; Am Epidemiol Soc; Int Epidemiol Soc; Soc Epidemiol Res; Infectious Dis Soc Am. *Res:* Epidemiology of infectious diseases, in particular Mycoplasma infections and influenza, chlamydia and influenza infections. *Mailing Add:* Dept of Epidemiol Univ Wash Sch Pub Health Seattle WA 98195

FOY, ROBERT BASTIAN, b Goodland, Ind, June 14, 28; m 50; c 9. BIOCHEMISTRY, CLINICAL CHEMISTRY. *Educ:* Cent Mich Univ, BS, 50; Mich State Univ, MS, 55, PhD(chem), 60. *Prof Exp:* Technologist, Clin Chem, Hurley Hosp, Flint, Mich, 50-52; technologist, Edward W Sparrow Hosp, 52-55, TECH DIR LABS, LAB CLIN MED, 55-, PARTNER, 75- *Concurrent Pos:* Lectr, Mich State Univ, 63-73. *Mem:* AAAS; Am Chem Soc; Am Asn Clin Chemists; Am Soc Clin Pathologists. *Res:* Proteins and enzymes, especially blood coagulation; clinical chemical methodology. *Mailing Add:* Lab Clin Med 930 E Mt Hope Ave Lansing MI 48910

FOY, WADE H(AMPTON), b Richmond, Va, Jan 26, 25; m 52; c 2. ELECTRONICS ENGINEERING. *Educ:* US Naval Acad, BS, 46; NC State Col, BEE, 51; Mass Inst Technol, MSEE, 55; Johns Hopkins Univ, DEng(elec eng), 62. *Prof Exp:* Res engr, Martin Co, Md, 56-62; sr res engr, Stanford Res Inst, 62-67, prog mgr, 68-76, asst lab dir, 76-80, STAFF SCIENTIST, SRI INT, 80- *Concurrent Pos:* Lectr, Martin Exten Prog, Drexel Inst Technol, 57-61; adj prof, 61-62; lectr, Univ Santa Clara, 63-65 & 66- *Mem:* Sr mem Inst Elec & Electronics Engrs. *Res:* Information theory and statistical communication theory; electronic and control system design; applied mathematics. *Mailing Add:* 214 E Edith Ave Los Altos CA 94022

FOY, WALTER LAWRENCE, b West Springfield, Mass, Aug 6, 21; m 63; c 6. PHYSICAL CHEMISTRY. *Educ:* Am Int Col, BS, 41; Clark Univ, MA, 43, PhD(phys chem), 47. *Prof Exp:* Teacher pub sch, Conn, 41-42; res chemist, 47-52, supvr, 52-55, chief supvr, 55-57, tech supt plant, 57-65, mgr prod res, 65-70, mgr graphic arts & printing res, 70-74, lab dir graphic arts & printing prod res, 74-77, LAB DIR PHOTOPOLYMER RES, E I DU PONT DE NEMOURS & CO, 77- *Mem:* AAAS; Am Chem Soc; Soc Photog Scientists & Engrs. *Res:* Electrical conductance of solutions; photographic chemistry; electrical conductance of substituted ammonium salts in ethylidene dichloride. *Mailing Add:* Photo Prod Dept E I du Pont de Nemours & Co Parlin NJ 08859

FOYE, LAURANCE V, JR, b Seattle, Wash, Nov 26, 25; m 51; c 2. MEDICINE. *Educ:* Univ Calif, AB, 49, MD, 52. *Prof Exp:* Asst chief med serv, Vet Admin Hosp, San Francisco, 58-66, chief cancer chemother sect, 60-66; chief cancer ther eval br, Nat Cancer Inst, Md, 66-68, exec secy, Cancer Clin Invest Rev Comt, 66-70, chief clin invests br, 68-70, mem grants assocs bd, NIH, 69-70; dir educ serv & dep asst chief med dir res & educ, 70-73, Vet Admin Cent Off, asst chief med dir acad affairs, 73-74, dep chief med dir, 74-78, DIR, VET ADMIN CTR, SAN FRANCISCO, 78- *Concurrent Pos:* Clin instr, Sch Med, Univ Calif, San Francisco, 57-62, asst clin prof, 62-66, res assoc, Cancer Res Inst, 62-66, assoc clin prof, 79-; prin investr, Vet Admin Cancer Chemother Study Group, 61-66; mem exec comt, Interagency Bd, US Civil Serv Examr, 70-74; mem bd regents, Nat Libr Med, 73-74. *Honors & Awards:* Honor Award, Dept Med & Surg, Vet Admin. *Mem:* AAAS; fel Am Col Physicians; Am Soc Clin Oncol; Asn Am Med Cols. *Res:* Clinical chemotherapy of cancer; evaluation of drugs and disease response. *Mailing Add:* Vet Admin Med Ctr San Francisco CA 94121

FOYE, WILLIAM OWEN, b Athol, Mass, June 26, 23; m; c 1. MEDICINAL CHEMISTRY. *Educ:* Dartmouth Col, AB, 43; Ind Univ, MA, 44, PhD(org chem), 48. *Prof Exp:* Res chemist, E I du Pont de Nemours & Co, 48-49; asst prof pharmaceut chem, Univ Wis, 49-55; assoc prof chem, 55-63, prof, 63-74, chmn dept, 66-71, dean fac, 70-73, dean grad studies, 73-74, DIR RES, MASS COL PHARM, 64-, SAWYER PROF PHARMACEUT SCI, 74- *Concurrent Pos:* vis prof, Univ Cairo, 81. *Honors & Awards:* Res Achievement Award Pharmaceut & Med Chem, Am Pharmaceut Asn Found, 70. *Mem:* Fel AAAS; Am Chem Soc; Am Pharmaceut Asn; fel NY Acad Sci; fel Acad Pharmaceut Sci. *Res:* Cancer chemotherapeutic, antibacterial, antihypertensive, radioprotective agents; biological aspects of metal binding; sulfur-containing molecules of medicinal interest. *Mailing Add:* Mass Col of Pharm 179 Longwood Ave Boston MA 02115

FOYT, ARTHUR GEORGE, JR, b Austin, Tex, June 17, 37; m 60; c 2. ELECTRON DEVICES. *Educ:* Mass Inst Technol, BSEE & MSEE, 60, ScD(Gunn effect), 65. *Prof Exp:* Mem tech staff, Transistor Develop, Bell Tel Labs, NJ, 60-62; mem tech staff, Gunn Effect & Ion Implantation Technol, 62-72, group leader, 72-78, MEM TECH STAFF, OPTICAL SIGNAL PROCESSING, LINCOLN LAB, MASS INST TECHNOL, 78-; MEM TECH & STAFF, OPTICAL SIGNAL PROCESSING, 78- *Mem:* Inst Elec & Electronics Engrs. *Res:* Ion implantation in compound semiconductors; Gunn effect in GaAs and CdTe. *Mailing Add:* Appl Physics Group Lincoln Lab 130 Wood St Lexington MA 02173

FOZDAR, BIRENDRA SINGH, b Hasanpur, India, July 16, 19; m 41; c 2. BIOLOGY, HORTICULTURE. *Educ:* Univ Agra, BSc, 38, MSc, 40; Univ Fla, PhD(veg crops), 62. *Prof Exp:* Asst bot, Indian Agr Res Inst, 41-42; asst plant physiol, Sugarcane Res Inst, 42-43; demonstr bot, Agr Col Agra, 43-44, lectr, 44-47, 48-53; sr asst, Nat Bot Garden, 47-48; asst prof, Cent Col Agr, New Delhi, 53-59; asst geneticist, Indian Agr Res Inst, 59; from instr to asst prof, 62-70, ASSOC PROF BOT, ST ANSELM'S COL, 70- *Concurrent Pos:* Mem, NSF Teacher-Res Partic Prog, Univ Calif, Berkeley, 64-66. *Mem:* AAAS; Am Inst Biol Sci. *Res:* Cytogenetics; plant breeding; horticultural crops and forest trees. *Mailing Add:* Dept of Biol St Anselm's Col Manchester NH 03102

FOZZARD, GEORGE BROWARD, b Jacksonville, Fla, Apr 13, 39; m 69; c 1. ORGANIC CHEMISTRY. *Educ:* Washington & Lee Univ, BS, 61; Univ NC, PhD(org chem), 67. *Prof Exp:* Res asst org chem, Univ NC, 63-66; SR RES CHEMIST, PHILLIPS PETROL CO, 66- *Mem:* Am Chem Soc. *Res:* Conformational analysis; hydrogen bonding; fluorochemicals; laboratory automation; catalytic oxidation. *Mailing Add:* Phillips Petroleum Co Bartlesville OK 74003

FOZZARD, HARRY A, b Jacksonville, Fla, Apr 22, 31; m 54; c 2. PHYSIOLOGY, INTERNAL MEDICINE. *Educ:* Wash Univ, MD, 56. *Prof Exp:* Intern med, Yale Univ, 56-57; asst, Wash Univ, 59-61, from instr to asst prof, 62-66; prof med & physiol, 66-77, OTHO S A SPRAGUE PROF MED SCI, SCH MED, UNIV CHICAGO, 77- *Concurrent Pos:* Nat Heart Inst fels cardiol, Wash Univ, 61-63 & physiol, Univ Berne, 63-64. *Mem:* Am Fedn Clin Res; Biophys Soc; Am Soc Clin Invest; Am Col Cardiol; Am Physiol Soc. *Res:* Intracellular cardiac electrophysiology, especially excitation-contraction coupling; cardiovascular hemodynamics. *Mailing Add:* Dept of Med Univ of Chicago Chicago IL 60637

FRAAD, LEWIS M, b Harrison, NY, Sept 3, 07; m 33; c 3. PEDIATRICS. *Educ:* Univ Vienna, MD, 35. *Prof Exp:* Asst clin prof pediat, Med Col, Cornell Univ, 48-55; assoc prof, 55-59, actg chmn dept, 70-74, PROF PEDIAT, ALBERT EINSTEIN COL MED, 59-, DEP DIR AMBULATORY CARE SERV, 74- *Mem:* Am Pediat Soc; Am Acad Pediat; NY Acad Med. *Res:* Child health; emotional growth and development; problems of pediatric education. *Mailing Add:* Dept of Pediat Albert Einstein Col of Med Bronx NY 10461

FRAAS, ARTHUR P(AUL), b Lakewood, Ohio, Aug 20, 15; m 40; c 2. MECHANICAL ENGINEERING. *Educ:* Case Inst Technol, BS, 38; NY Univ, MS(aeronaut eng), 43. *Prof Exp:* Exp test engr, Wright Aeronaut Corp, 38-40; instr, Aircraft Power Plants, NY Univ, 41-43; exp proj engr, Aircraft Eng Div, Packard Motor Car Co, 43-45; asst prof combustion eng, Case Inst Technol, 45-46; assoc prof, Inst Technol Aeronaut, Brazil, 47-49; mem gen design group, Aircraft Nuclear Propulsion Proj, 50-57, assoc dir, Reactor Div, 57-74, mgr high temperature systs, 74-76, CONSULT, OAK RIDGE NAT LAB, 76- *Concurrent Pos:* Union Carbide Eng fel. *Mem:* Sigma Xi; fel Am Soc Mech Engrs; fel Am Nuclear Soc; Am Inst Aeronaut & Astronaut. *Res:* Heat exchangers; combustion engines; fluidized bed combustion, fossil and nuclear power plants. *Mailing Add:* 1040 Scenic Dr Knoxville TN 37919

FRACHTMAN, HIRSH JULIAN, b Houston, Tex, Sept 2, 13; m 41; c 3. CLINICAL MEDICINE. *Educ:* Rice Univ, BA, 33; Univ Tex, MD, 37; Am Bd Internal Med, dipl. *Prof Exp:* Fel med, Med Sch, Tulane Univ, 38-39; asst prof, 46-64, ASSOC PROF CLIN MED, BAYLOR COL MED, 64- *Concurrent Pos:* Consult physician, St Luke's Hosp; consult physician, Mem Hosp; mem courtesy staff, Hermann, Methodist & Ctr Pavilion Hosps. *Mem:* Am Soc Internal Med; Am Heart Asn; Am Col Cardiol. *Res:* Internal medicine; diagnosis and cardiology. *Mailing Add:* 901 Hermann Prof Bldg Houston TX 77030

FRADE, PETER DANIEL, b Highland Park, Mich, Sept 3, 46. ANALYTICAL TOXICOLOGY. *Educ:* Wayne State Univ, BS, 68, MS, 71, PhD(chem), 78. *Prof Exp:* ANAL CHEMIST & TOXICOLOGIST, DEPT PATH, DIV PHARMACOL & TOXICOL, HENRY FORD HOSP, 68- *Concurrent Pos:* Consult, Inter-Dept, Henry Ford Hosp, 78-; vis scholar, Univ Mich, 80-81 & 81-82; vis lectr, Cranbrook Inst Sci, 82- *Mem:* Sigma Xi; Am Chem Soc; fel Am Inst Chemists; AAAS; NY Acad Sci. *Res:* Investigative and analytical use of high performance liquid chromatography and related techniques as applied to pharmacokinetic studies involving clinical and pre-clinical drugs and their metabolites; development and novel application of pre-column derivatization reagents. *Mailing Add:* 20200 Orleans Detroit MI 48203

FRADIN, FRANK YALE, b Chicago, Ill, May 14, 41; m 63; c 3. PHYSICAL METALLURGY, SOLID STATE PHYSICS. *Educ:* Mass Inst Technol, SB, 63; Univ Ill, MS, 64, PhD(metall, physics), 67. *Prof Exp:* SR SCIENTIST & ASSOC DIR, MAT SCI DIV, ARGONNE NAT LAB, 67- *Concurrent Pos:* Vis prof, Northern Ill Univ, 69-70, 77-78 & 81 & Northwestern Univ, 70. *Mem:* Fel Am Phys Soc; Am Inst Mining, Metall & Petrol Engrs. *Res:* Diffusion in solids; nuclear magnetic resonance in alloys and intermetallic compounds; magnetic and transport properties of alloys and intermetallic compounds; superconductivity. *Mailing Add:* Mat Sci Div Argonne Nat Lab 9700 S Cass Ave Argonne IL 60439

FRADKIN, CHENG-MEI WANG, b China, May 27, 28; nat US; m 52; c 3. GENETICS. *Educ:* Univ Calif, BS, 52; Univ Wis, MS, 53, PhD(genetics), 55. *Prof Exp:* Asst genetics, Univ Wis, 52-55; res assoc, Ohio State Univ, 55-60; fel microbial genetics, Sch Med, Stanford Univ, 60-63; assoc prof, 65-75, head dept, 66-81, PROF BIOL, CHAPMAN COL, 65-, CHMN, NAT SCI DIV, 79- *Res:* Maize genetics and Drosophila genetics; mutation and gene action; hydra development. *Mailing Add:* Dept of Biol Chapman Col Orange CA 92666

FRADKIN, DAVID MILTON, b Los Angeles, Calif, Apr 20, 31; m 59; c 3. THEORETICAL PHYSICS. *Educ:* Univ Calif, Berkeley, BS, 54; Iowa State Univ, PhD(physics), 63. *Prof Exp:* Exploitation engr, Shell Oil Co, 54-56; res assoc theoret physics, Ames Lab, AEC & Iowa State Univ, 63-64; NATO fel, Marconi Inst Physics, Univ Rome, 64-65; from asst prof to assoc prof, 65-75, PROF PHYSICS, WAYNE STATE UNIV, 75-, CHMN DEPT, 81- *Concurrent Pos:* Sr postdoctoral fel, Univ Edinburgh, 77-78. *Mem:* Am Phys Soc. *Res:* Electron polarization operators; coulomb scattering of relativistic electrons; conservation laws and relativistic wave equations; dynamical groups and symmetries; coherent processes in particle beams; particle behavior in intense laser fields. *Mailing Add:* Dept of Physics Wayne State Univ Detroit MI 48202

FRAENKEL, DAN GABRIEL, b London, Eng, May 6, 37; US citizen. BACTERIAL PHYSIOLOGY. *Educ:* Univ Ill, BS, 57; Harvard Univ, PhD(bact), 62. *Prof Exp:* Nat Found fel microbiol, Sch Med, NY Univ, 62-63; res assoc molecular biol, Albert Einstein Col Med, 63-65; from asst prof to assoc prof bact & immunol, 65-73, PROF MICROBIOL & MOLECULAR GENETICS, HARVARD MED SCH, 73- *Mem:* Am Soc Microbiol; Am Soc Biol Chem. *Res:* Physiology and genetics of carbohydrate metabolism in bacteria and in yeast. *Mailing Add:* Microbiol & Molecular Genetics Harvard Med Sch Boston MA 02115

FRAENKEL, GEORGE KESSLER, b Deal, NJ, July 27, 21; m 51, 67. CHEMICAL PHYSICS. *Educ:* Harvard Univ, BA, 42; Cornell Univ, PhD(chem), 49. *Prof Exp:* Res group leader, Nat Defense Res Comt, Oceanog Inst, Woods Hole, 43-46; from instr to assoc prof chem, 49-61, chmn dept, 66-68, PROF CHEM, COLUMBIA UNIV, 61-, DEAN GRAD SCH ARTS & SCI, 68- *Concurrent Pos:* Assoc ed, J Chem Physics, 62-64; mem post-doctoral fel comt, Nat Acad Sci-NSF, 64-65; chmn, Gordon Res Conf Magnetic Resonance, 67. *Honors & Awards:* Army-Navy Cert of Appreciation, 48. *Mem:* Fel AAAS; Am Chem Soc; fel Am Phys Soc. *Res:* Electron spin resonance; free radicals. *Mailing Add:* 450 Riverside Dr New York NY 10027

FRAENKEL, GIDEON, b Frankfurt, Ger, Feb 21, 32; m 61; c 2. CHEMISTRY. *Educ:* Univ Ill, BS, 52; Harvard Univ, MA, 53, PhD(org chem), 57. *Prof Exp:* Res fel chem, Calif Inst Technol, 57-60; from asst prof to assoc prof, 60-69, PROF CHEM, OHIO STATE UNIV, 69- *Concurrent Pos:* Guest prof, Univ Lund, 71; vis prof, Mass Inst Technol, 80-81. *Mem:* Am Chem Soc; Royal Soc Chem; AAAS. *Res:* Reaction mechanisms; nuclear magnetic resonance; organometallic chemistry; kinetics of exchange at equilibrium, reactive intermediates; structure and behavior of carbanions. *Mailing Add:* Dept of Chem Ohio State Univ Columbus OH 43210

FRAENKEL, GOTTFRIED SAMUEL, b Munich, Ger, Apr 23, 01; nat US; m 28; c 2. ENTOMOLOGY, COMPARATIVE PHYSIOLOGY. *Educ:* Univ Munich, PhD(zool), 25. *Hon Degrees:* Hon Dr, Univ Tours, France, 80. *Prof Exp:* Fel, Int Educ Bd, Zool Sta, Univ Naples, 26-27; asst, Dept Zool, Hebrew Univ, 28-30; privatdozent zool, Zool Inst, Univ Fankfurt, 31-33; res assoc, Dept Zool, Univ Col, Univ London, 33-35, lectr zool, Imp Col, Univ London, 36-48; prof, 48-72, EMER PROF ENTOM, UNIV ILL, URBANA, 72- *Concurrent Pos:* Vis prof, Dept Entom, Univ Minn, 47; res career award, USPHS, 62-72. *Mem:* Nat Acad Sci; AAAS; Am Soc Zool; hon mem Royal Entom Soc London; Am Entom Soc. *Res:* Orientation of animals; physiology of insects; comparative physiology and biochemistry. *Mailing Add:* Dept of Entom Univ of Ill Urbana IL 61801

FRAENKEL, STEPHEN JOSEPH, b Berlin, Ger, Nov 28, 17; US citizen; m 41; c 3. STRUCTURAL MECHANICS, MECHANICS OF MATERIALS. *Educ:* Univ Nebr, BS, 40, MS, 41; Ill Inst Technol, PhD(eng mech), 51. *Prof Exp:* Mgr propulsion & struct res, Ill Inst Technol, 46-55; dir res & develop, Stanray Corp, 55-62; dir eng res, Continental Can Co, 62-64; gen mgr, 64-75, DIR RES & DEVELOP, CONTAINER CORP AM, 75- *Mem:* Soc Exp Stress Anal; Tech Asn Pulp & Paper Indust. *Res:* Physical and mechanical properties and materials; stress analysis; behavior of structural and mechanical systems under dynamic loads; instrumented test procedures; statistical design of experiments. *Mailing Add:* 500 E North Ave Carol Stream IL 60187

FRAENKEL-CONRAT, HEINZ LUDWIG, b Breslau, Ger, July 29, 10; nat US; m 39, 64; c 2. MOLECULAR BIOLOGY. *Educ:* Breslau Univ, MD, 33; Univ Edinburgh, PhD(biochem), 36. *Prof Exp:* Asst, Rockefeller Inst, 36-37; res assoc, Butantan Inst, Sao Paulo, Brazil, 37-38; res assoc inst exp biol, Univ Calif, 38-42; from assoc chemist to chemist, Western Regional Res Lab, Bur Agr & Indust Chem, USDA, 42-50; Rockefeller fel, Eng & Denmark, 51; res biochemist, Virus Lab, 52-58, prof virol, 58-63, PROF MOLECULAR BIOL, UNIV CALIF, BERKELEY, 63- *Concurrent Pos:* Guggenheim fel, 63, 67; fac res lectr, Univ Calif, Berkeley, 68. *Honors & Awards:* Lasker Award, Am Pub Health Asn; Calif Scientist of Year Award. *Mem:* Nat Acad Sci; Int Soc Toxinology; Am Acad Arts & Sci; Am Chem Soc; Am Soc Biol Chem. *Res:* Chemistry and structure of proteins and nucleic acids, especially viruses, enzymes, hormones, toxins; structural requirements for activity. *Mailing Add:* Virus Lab Stanley Hall Univ of Calif Berkeley CA 94720

FRAENKEL-CONRAT, JANE E, b Baltimore, Md, Dec 9, 15. BIOCHEMISTRY. *Educ:* Goucher Col, BA, 36; Univ Calif, PhD(biochem), 42. *Prof Exp:* Asst, Sch Med, Johns Hopkins Univ, 36-37; asst, Inst Exp Biol, Univ Calif, 38-42, res assoc, Radiation Lab, 43, res assoc biochem, Univ, 45-47, res chemist, Dept Home Econ, 48-51; res biochemist, Children's Hosp East Bay, Oakland, Calif, 53-63; clin chemist, Mem Hosp, San Leandro, 63-64; sr scientist, Lockheed Missiles & Space Co, 64; dir lab serv & assoc res scientist, Cancer Res Ctr, Ellis Fischel Hosp, Mo, 64-66, dir res labs, 66-67; lectr biol, Seattle Univ, Pine Lake Campus, 67-69; assoc prof chem, St Mary's Sem Col, 69-73; assoc prof, 73-77, PROF CHEM, UNIV MAINE, 77- *Mem:* AAAS; Am Chem Soc; Am Asn Clin Chemists; Am Asn Allied Health; NY Acad Sci. *Res:* Enzyme activity of normal and pathological leukocytes; intermediary protein genetic diseases; metabolism; protein chemistry; development of clinical methods; interpretation of clinical chemistry; effect of irradiation on enzyme activity. *Mailing Add:* Dept of Chem Univ of Maine Machias ME 04654

FRAGA, SERAFIN, b Madrid, Spain, Feb 11, 31; m 56; c 3. THEORETICAL CHEMISTRY. *Educ:* Univ Madrid, Lic Sc, 54, DSc(chem), 57. *Prof Exp:* Res assoc physics, Univ Chicago, 58-61 & chem, Univ Alta, 61-62; asst prof physics, Royal Mil Col, Que, 62-63; from asst prof chem to assoc prof theoret chem, 63-69, PROF THEORET CHEM, UNIV ALTA, 69- *Concurrent Pos:* Juan March Found fel, 58-59; fel, Univ Alta, 61-62. *Mem:* Int Soc Quantum Biol; Chem Inst Can; Royal Span Soc Physics & Chem. *Res:* Quantum chemistry; theoretical research on atomic and molecular structure. *Mailing Add:* Dept of Chem Univ of Alta Edmonton AB T6G 2E8 Can

FRAGASZY, RICHARD J, b New York, NY, June 11, 50. GOETECHNICAL ENGINEERING. *Educ:* Duke Univ, BSE, 72, MS, 74; Univ Calif, Davis, PhD(civil eng), 79. *Prof Exp:* Asst prof, Bucknell Univ, 78-79; ASST PROF CIVIL ENG, SAN DIEGO STATE UNIV, 79- *Mem:* Am Soc Civil Engrs; Int Soc Soil Mech & Found Eng; Sigma Xi; Am Soc Eng Educ. *Res:* Blast-induced liquefaction and use of blasting to compact soils, centrifuge modeling, slope stability, bearing capacity of reinforced earth and dynamic earth pressure. *Mailing Add:* Dept Civil Eng San Diego State Univ San Diego CA 92182

FRAHM, CHARLES PETER, b Mason City, Iowa, July 7, 38; m 58; c 2. THEORETICAL PHYSICS. *Educ:* Ga Inst Technol, BS, 61, PhD(high energy physics), 67. *Prof Exp:* Instr physics, Ga Inst Technol, 65-66; res asst, Univ Tel-Aviv, 66-67; asst prof, Ga Inst Technol, 67-68; from asst prof to assoc prof, 68-75, PROF PHYSICS, ILL STATE UNIV, 75- *Concurrent Pos:* Res asst, Advan Res Corp, 64-68; res physicist, Naval Coastal Systs Lab, 72- *Mem:* Am Asn Physics Teachers; Am Phys Soc. *Res:* Theoretical acoustics; magnetics; general relativity. *Mailing Add:* Dept of Physics Ill State Univ Normal IL 61761

FRAHM, RICHARD R, b Scottsbluff, Nebr, Nov 17, 39; m 61; c 2. POPULATION GENETICS, ANIMAL BREEDING. *Educ:* Univ Nebr, BS, 61; NC State Univ, MS, 63, PhD(genetics), 65. *Prof Exp:* From asst prof to assoc prof, 67-76, PROF ANIMAL BREEDING, OKLA STATE UNIV, 76- *Mem:* Am Soc Animal Sci; Genetics Soc Am; Biomet Soc. *Res:* Population genetics and animal breeding research with beef cattle; research designed to elucidate basic quantitative genetic principles and develop procedures to most effectively incorporate them in breeding programs to improve production efficiency. *Mailing Add:* Dept of Animal Sci Agr Exp Sta Okla State Univ Stillwater OK 74078

FRAILEY, DENNIS J(OHN), b Tulsa, Okla, Mar 5, 44; m 69. COMPUTER SCIENCE. *Educ:* Univ Notre Dame, BS, 66; Purdue Univ, MS, 68, PhD(comput sci), 71. *Prof Exp:* Res scientist comput sci, Ford Motor Co, 66-71; from asst prof to assoc prof, Inst Technol, Southern Methodist Univ, 71-77; mem tech staff, 77-80, SR MEM TECH STAFF & BR MGR, TEX INSTRUMENTS, INC, 80- *Concurrent Pos:* Consult, Tex Instruments, Inc, 74-77; adj assoc prof, Southern Methodist Univ, 77-79; adj assoc prof, Univ Tex, Austin, 81- *Mem:* Asn Comput Mach; Inst Elec & Electronics Engrs, Comput Soc. *Res:* Compilers; operating systems; data structures; microprogramming; scheduling algorithms; code optimization; real-time computing and associated problems. *Mailing Add:* 5303 Musket Ridge Austin TX 78759

FRAIR, WAYNE, b Pittsburgh, Pa, May 23, 26. SYSTEMATIC ZOOLOGY. *Educ:* Houghton Col, BA, 50; Wheaton Col, Ill, BS, 51; Univ Mass, MA(embryol), 55; Rutgers Univ, PhD(serol), 62. *Prof Exp:* Teacher, Ben Lippen Sch, 51-52; asst, Univ Mass, 52-53 & Brown Univ, 54-55; from instr to assoc prof, 55-67, PROF BIOL, KING'S COL, NY, 67- *Concurrent Pos:* Asst, Rutgers Univ, 59-60. *Mem:* Fel AAAS; Sigma Xi; Creation Res Soc (secy, 74-); Am Soc Ichthyologists & Herpetologists; Am Soc Zool. *Res:* Animal relationships; molecular taxonomy. *Mailing Add:* Dept of Biol King's Col Briarcliff Manor NY 10510

FRAJOLA, WALTER JOSEPH, b Chicago, Ill, Nov 2, 16; m 41; c 2. BIOCHEMISTRY. *Educ:* Hamline Univ, BS, 38; Univ Ill, MS, 47, PhD(chem), 50. *Prof Exp:* Instr pub sch, SDak, 38-41; instr pub sch, Minn, 41-42; asst chem, Univ Ill, 46-50; from asst prof to assoc prof physiol chem, Col Med, Ohio State Univ, 50-59, asst prof med res, 53-60, assoc prof path, 59-60, dir, H A Hoster Res Lab, 53-60, chief div clin biochem, 59-62, prof path & physiol chem, 60-68, EMER PROF PHYSIOL CHEM, OHIO STATE UNIV, 77-; PRES, WALTER J FRAJOLA PHD CONSULTING, INC, 80- *Concurrent Pos:* Chief scientist, Columbus Div, NAm Rockwell Corp, 62-66; pres, Lab Anal Blood Studies, Inc, 66-71; pres & lab dir, Community Labs of Ohio, 71-79. *Mem:* Am Chem Soc; Am Asn Clin Chem; Electron Micros Soc Am; NY Acad Sci. *Res:* Enzymes; cancer; clinical chemistry. *Mailing Add:* 2558 Onandaga Dr Columbus OH 43221

FRAKER, ANNA CLYDE, b Chuckey, Tenn, June 25, 35. METALLURGICAL & CERAMICS ENGINEERING. *Educ:* Furman Univ, BS, 57; NC State Univ, MS, 61, PhD(ceramic eng), 67. *Prof Exp:* Res asst metall, NC State Univ, 57-62, res assoc, 63-67; METALLURGIST, NAT BUR STANDARDS, 67- *Mem:* Electron Micros Soc Am; Am Soc Metals; Sigma Xi; Soc Biomat. *Res:* Alloy phase studies; interstitial alloys; recrystallization of aluminum; corrosion of titanium and aluminum; thin foil transmission electron microscopy; corrosion; fatigue. *Mailing Add:* Dept Commerce Nat Bur Standards Washington DC 20234

FRAKER, JOHN RICHARD, b Knoxville, Tenn, Dec 20, 34; m 54; c 3. ENGINEERING MANAGEMENT, INDUSTRIAL ENGINEERING. *Educ:* Univ Tenn, BS, 56, MS, 65; Clemson Univ, PhD(eng mgt), 71. *Prof Exp:* Mfg engr, Westinghouse Elec Corp, 56-57; instr indust eng & opers res, Clemson Univ, 65-72; from asst prof to assoc prof mgt, Western Carolina Univ, 73-75; PROF & CHMN ENG MGT, UNIV DAYTON, 75- *Mem:* Am Inst Indust Engrs; Am Soc Eng Educ; Sigma Xi; Inst Elec & Electronics Engrs. *Res:* Military system simulation; energy and power systems; queueing networks; departure processes. *Mailing Add:* PO Box 613 Dayton OH 45469

FRAKER, PAMELA JEAN, b Williamsport, Ind, Aug 4, 44. IMMUNOBIOLOGY, TRACE ELEMENT NUTRITION. *Educ:* Purdue Univ, BS, 66; Univ Ill, MS, 68, PhD(molecular biol), 71. *Prof Exp:* asst prof, 73-80, ASSOC PROF BIOCHEM, MICH STATE UNIV, 80- *Mem:* Am Inst Nutrit; Am Soc Biol Chem; Am Asn Immunol. *Res:* Study of the effects of nutritional deficiency on the immune capacity. *Mailing Add:* Dept of Biochem Mich State Univ East Lansing MI 48824

FRAKES, ELIZABETH (MCCUNE), b Huron, Kans, Jan 4, 22; m 65. NUTRITION. *Educ:* Univ Kans, BA, 47; Univ Iowa, MS, 48. *Prof Exp:* Dietician, Watkins Mem Hosp & Student Union, Univ Kans, 48-50; from instr to assoc prof, 50-65, PROF NUTRIT, UNIV KANS MED CTR, KANSAS CITY, 66-, CHMN & DIR DEPT DIETETICS & NUTRIT, 72- *Honors & Awards:* Dietary Prod Found Award, Am Dietetic Asn, 66. *Mem:* Am Dietetic Asn. *Res:* Management phase of dietetics and nutrition. *Mailing Add:* Dept of Dietetics & Nutrit Univ of Kans Med Ctr Kansas City KS 66103

FRAKES, LAWRENCE AUSTIN, b Pasadena, Calif, Apr 28, 30; m 54; c 1. SEDIMENTOLOGY, MARINE GEOLOGY. *Educ:* Univ Calif, Los Angeles, BA, 57, MA, 59, PhD(geol), 64. *Prof Exp:* Instr geol, Villanova Univ, 59-60; geologist, Pa Geol Surv, 60-62; asst res geologist, Univ Calif, Los Angeles, 64-67, assoc res geologist, 67-69; assoc prof geol, Univ NMex, 69-70 & Fla State Univ, 70-73; sr lectr, 74-75, READER, MONASH UNIV, 76- *Mem:* Fel AAAS; fel Geol Soc Am; Geol Soc Australia. *Res:* Paleoclimatology; distribution and causes of late Paleozoic glaciation; atmospheric and oceanic circulation patterns during the late Paleozoic, Mesozoic and Cenozoic. *Mailing Add:* Dept of Earth Sci Monash Univ Clayton Victoria 3168 Australia

FRAKES, RODNEY VANCE, b Ontario, Ore, July 20, 30; m 52; c 2. AGRONOMY. *Educ:* Ore State Univ, BS, 56, MS, 57; Purdue Univ, PhD(plant breeding), 60. *Prof Exp:* Instr forage crop res, Purdue Univ, 57-60; from asst prof to assoc prof, 60-69, PROF PLANT BREEDING, DEPT CROP SCI, ORE STATE UNIV, 69-, ASSOC DEAN RES, 81-, ELIZABETH DISTINGUISHED PROF, 80- *Mem:* Am Soc Agron; Crop Sci Soc Am. *Res:* Breeding of legumes, and forage and turf grasses. *Mailing Add:* Dept Crop Sci Ore State Univ Corvallis OR 97331

FRAKNOI, ANDREW GABRIEL, b Budapest, Hungary, Aug 24, 48. ASTRONOMY, SCIENCE EDUCATION. *Educ:* Harvard Univ, BA, 70; Univ Calif, Berkeley, MA, 72. *Prof Exp:* Instr astron & physics, Canada Col, Calif, 72-78; ED, MERCURY & EXEC OFFICER, ASTRON SOC PAC, 78- *Concurrent Pos:* Instr astron, City Col San Francisco, 74-75; instr astron & physics, San Francisco State Univ, 80- *Mem:* Am Astron Soc; Astron Soc Pac; Am Asn Physics Teachers. *Res:* Radio astronomy; astronomy education and communicating science to the public. *Mailing Add:* Astron Soc of the Pac 1290 24th Ave San Francisco CA 94122

FRALEIGH, PETER CHARLES, b New York, NY, Nov 16, 42; m 71; c 2. AQUATIC ECOLOGY. *Educ:* Cornell Univ, BA, 65; Univ Ga, PhD(zool), 71. *Prof Exp:* Res assoc syst sci, Mich State Univ, 71-72; asst prof, 72-80, ASSOC PROF BIOL, UNIV TOLEDO, 80- *Mem:* AAAS; Ecol Soc Am; Am Soc Limnol & Oceanog; Sigma Xi. *Res:* Studies on the environmental regulation of energy flow and community structure in field and laboratory aquatic ecosystems. *Mailing Add:* Dept of Biol Univ of Toledo Toledo OH 43606

FRALEY, ELWIN E, b Sayre, Pa, May 3, 34; c 6. UROLOGY, PATHOLOGY. *Educ:* Princeton Univ, BA, 57; Harvard Med Sch, MD, 61. *Prof Exp:* Instr surg, Mass Gen Hosp, 66-67; investr urol, NIH, 67-69; PROF UROL, UNIV MINN, MINNEAPOLIS, 69-, CHMN DEPT UROL SURGERY, 80- *Honors & Awards:* Soma Weiss Award, Harvard Med Sch, 63; Clin Res Award, Am Urol Asn, 64, Res Essay Awards, 67, Movie Award, 69. *Mem:* AAAS; Am Soc Exp Path; Am Asn Cancer Res; Am Urol Asn; Soc Univ Urol. *Res:* Nucleic acid and protein metabolism in kidney; relation of viruses to development of human genitourinary neoplasms; human tumor immunology; viral oncology; macromolecular pathology. *Mailing Add:* Dept of Urol Surg Univ of Minn Med Ctr Minneapolis MN 55455

FRALEY, ROBERT THOMAS, b Danville, Ill, Jan 25, 53; m 78. PLANT MOLECULAR BIOLOGY, PLANT TISSUE CULTURE. *Educ:* Univ Ill, BS, 74, MS, 76, PhD(microbiol), 78. *Prof Exp:* Res assoc biochem, Univ Calif, San Francisco, 79-81; RES SPECIALIST PLANT MOLECULAR BIOL, MONSANTO CO, 81- *Concurrent Pos:* Fel, Jane Coffin Childs Mem Fund, 80-81; ed, Plant Molecular Biol, 81-; adj prof, Wash Univ, 81- *Mem:* Am Chem Soc. *Res:* Genetic engineering of plants; development of efficient systems for introducing and monitoring the expression of foreign genes in plant cells. *Mailing Add:* U4G Monsanto Co 800 N Lindbeugh St Louis MO 63167

FRALICH, ROBERT WILLIAM, engineering mechanics, aerospace engineering, see previous edition

FRALICK, RICHARD ALLSTON, b Boston, Mass, July 27, 37; m 65; c 2. MARINE PHYCOLOGY. *Educ:* Salem State Col, BA, 67; Univ NH, MS, 70, PhD(bot), 73. *Prof Exp:* Res asst cryptogamic bot, Farlow Herbarium, Harvard Univ, 61-67; instr biol, Austin Prep Sch, 67-69; teaching asst bot & phycol, Univ NH, 69-73; from asst prof to assoc prof, 73-80, PROF NATURAL SCI, PLYMOUTH STATE COL, 80- *Concurrent Pos:* Field asst marine bot, Harvard Univ & Univ Cent Venezuela Exchange Prog, 63, field coordr, Harvard Univ NSF Exped W Antarctica, 64-65; res asst phytoplankton ecol, Water Resources Res Ctr, Univ NH, 69-70, scientist-aquanaut algal ecol & saturation diving, Tektite Exped US VI, 70 & Flare Exped Fla Keys, 72; guest investr, Environ Syst Lab, Woods Hole Oceanog Inst, 73-76; dir, Plymouth State Col Bermuda Prog; consult, US Dept State USAID Prog-Portugal, 77-80. *Honors & Awards:* Cong Bronze Medal, 65; Citation Marine Res, Dept Interior, 70. *Mem:* Sigma Xi; Phycolog Soc Am; Am Polar Soc; AAAS. *Res:* Cultivation of commercially important seaweeds; algal physiological ecology; thermal stress and distribution of marine algae; ecology of nuisance and fouling algae; ecology of Pterocladia and other economically important seaweeds; effects of road-salt on the distribution of marine plants; marine resource management. *Mailing Add:* Dept Natural Sci Plymouth State Col Plymouth NH 03264

FRAM, HARVEY, b Worcester, Mass, Nov 23, 18; m 44; c 2. FOOD SCIENCE. *Educ:* Univ Mass, BS, 40, MS, 42. *Prof Exp:* Asst, Mass Inst Technol, 42-48; group leader, Nat Dairy Res Labs, 48-60; chief food technologist, B Manischewitz Co, Jersey City, 60-70, tech dir, 70-75; tech dir, Joyce Food Prod, 75-76; CHIEF MICROBIOLOGIST, FITELSON LABS, NEW YORK, 76- *Mem:* Inst Food Technol; Am Asn Cereal Chem. *Res:* Radiation sterilization of foods; cultured dairy products; food preservation, canned, baked and frozen. *Mailing Add:* 1108 Belle Ave Teaneck NJ 07666

FRAME, HARLAN D, b Muscatine, Iowa, Jan 1, 33; m 60, 76; c 3. INORGANIC CHEMISTRY, PHYSICAL CHEMISTRY. *Educ:* Univ Wichita, BA, 55; Univ Ill, MS, 58, PhD(inorg chem), 59. *Prof Exp:* Assoc chemist, Argonne Nat Lab, 59-69; asst prof, 69-72, ASSOC PROF CHEM, SOUTHWESTERN STATE COL, OKLA, 72- *Mem:* AAAS; Am Chem Soc. *Res:* Synthetic inorganic chemistry employing nonaqueous solvents; inorganic fluorine chemistry; nonaqueous solvents; high temperature reactions; chromatography; microcomputer software. *Mailing Add:* Dept of Chem Southwestern Okla State Univ Weatherford OK 73096

FRAME, JAMES SUTHERLAND, b New York, NY, Dec 24, 07; m 38; c 4. MATHEMATICS. *Educ:* Harvard Univ, AB, 29, AM, 30, PhD(math), 33. *Prof Exp:* Instr math, Harvard Univ, 30-33; Rogers traveling fel, Univs Harvard, Gottingen & Zurich, 33-34; from instr to asst prof math, Brown Univ, 34-42; assoc prof & chmn dept, Allegheny Col, 42-43; prof math, 43-63, chmn dept, 43-60, proj dir conf bd math sci, 61-62, prof math & eng res, 63-77, EMER PROF MATH & ENG RES, MICH STATE UNIV, 77- *Concurrent Pos:* Mem nat coun, Am Asn Univ Prof, 48-51; mem, Inst Advan Study, 50-51; mem bd gov, Math Asn Am, 50-52 & 58-60; consult, Ford Found, Bangkok, Thailand, 70; consult, Inst fur Quantenchemie, Free Univ Berlin, 72 & 78; vis prof, R W Technische Hochschule, Aachen, WGer, 81. *Honors & Awards:* Sr Res Award, Sigma Xi, 52. *Mem:* AAAS; Am Math Soc; Math Asn Am. *Res:* Theory of representations of finite groups; approximations; matrix theory; continued fractions. *Mailing Add:* 136 Oakland Dr East Lansing MI 48823

FRAME, JOHN W, b Rolla, Mo, Sept 28, 16. METALLURGICAL ENGINEERING. *Educ:* Mo Sch Mines, BS, 37; Lehigh Univ, MS, 38, PhD(metall eng), 61. *Prof Exp:* Mem staff, Metall Dept, Bethlehem Steel Corp, Lackawanna, 38-46, engr res div, 46-56, from supvr to assoc dir res, Phys Metall, 56-64, mgr forming & finishing res, 64-69, mgr prod res, Homer Res Labs, 69-78; RETIRED. *Mem:* Fel Am Soc Metals; Am Inst Mining, Metall & Petrol Engrs; Soc Automotive Engrs. *Res:* Aging, formability and manufacture of sheet steels; corrosion, welding, forming, machining, alloy development, metal physics, fatigue and fracture of steel; organic coating; tin mill products. *Mailing Add:* 733 W Vista Hermosa Dr Green Valley AZ 85614

FRAME, ROBERT ROY, b Oak Park, Ill, Aug 24, 39. INDUSTRIAL ORGANIC CHEMISTRY. *Educ:* Univ Ill, BS, 61, Northwestern Univ, PhD, 65. *Prof Exp:* Fel org chem, Univ Ark, 67-68; vis asst prof, Univ Okla, 68-72; RES CHEMIST, UNIVERSAL OIL PROD CO, 72- *Mem:* Am Chem Soc. *Res:* Research in catalysis. *Mailing Add:* 10 Universal Oil Plaza Des Plaines IL 60016

FRAMPTON, ELON WILSON, b New York, NY, July 27, 24; m 58; c 2. MICROBIOLOGY. *Educ:* Syracuse Univ, BA, 49; Northwestern Univ, MS, 51; Univ Ill, PhD(dairy sci, bact), 59. *Prof Exp:* Lab technician, Hosp, Rockefeller Inst, 42-43; microbilogist, Wilson Labs, Ill, 50-54; asst dairy bact, Univ Ill, 54-58; res fel, M D Anderson Hosp & Tumor Inst, Univ Tex, 59-60, res assoc, 60-62, asst radiation biologist, 62-66, assoc biologist, 66-69; ASSOC PROF BIOL SCI, NORTHERN ILL UNIV, 69- *Mem:* AAAS; Am Soc Microbiol; Radiation Res Soc. *Res:* Radiation and molecular biology; bacterial physiology. *Mailing Add:* Dept of Biol Sci Northern Ill Univ DeKalb IL 60115

FRANCAVILLA, THOMAS LEE, b Buffalo, NY, Dec 3, 39; m 71; c 3. SOLID STATE PHYSICS. *Educ:* Canisius Col, BS, 61; John Carroll Univ, MS, 63; Cath Univ Am, PhD(physics), 73. *Prof Exp:* PHYSICIST, US NAVAL RES LAB, 64- *Mem:* Am Phys Soc; Am Asn Physics Teachers. *Res:* Basic and applied properties of superconducting materials and the phenomenon of superconductivity. *Mailing Add:* US Naval Res Lab Code 6634 Overlook Ave SE Washington DC 20375

FRANCE, EVELYN S (KALAGHER), b East Orange, NJ, May 17, 30; m 68. REPRODUCTIVE TOXICOLOGY, TERATOLOGY. *Educ:* Antioch Col, AB, 53; Wayne State Univ, MS, 55; Boston Univ, PhD(biol), 63. *Prof Exp:* Lab asst nutrit biochem, Univ Rochester, 49-50; asst endocrinol, Ciba Pharmaceut Prod Corp, 51-52; asst, Sch Dent Med, Harvard Univ, 52-53; asst, Wayne State Univ, 53-55; res physiologist, Ortho Res Found, 55-59; res asst endocrinol, Rutgers Univ, 59-61; staff scientist reprod physiol, Worcester Found Exp Biol, 61-67; res biologist, 67-77, SUPVR, TERATOLOGY UNIT, WYETH LABS, 78- *Mem:* AAAS; Am Inst Biol Sci; NY Acad Sci; Soc Study Reproduction. *Res:* Induction and inhibition of ovulation; drugs affecting fetal growth and development. *Mailing Add:* Wyeth Labs PO Box 861 Paoli PA 19301

FRANCE, PETER WILLIAM, b Chicago, Ill, Sept 4, 38; m 65; c 2. SOLID STATE PHYSICS, NUCLEAR MAGNETIC RESONANCE. *Educ:* Wayne State Univ, BS, 62, MS, 64, PhD(physics), 67. *Prof Exp:* Sr res physicist, Bendix Res Labs, 68; asst prof, 68-72, ASSOC PROF PHYSICS, UNIV LOUISVILLE, 72- *Mem:* Am Phys Soc; Am Asn Physics Teachers. *Res:* Application of wide line nuclear magnetic resonance of solids, particularly glass; measurement of physical properties of semiconducting and dielectric glasses, such as resistivities, mobilities and Hall constants. *Mailing Add:* Dept of Physics Univ of Louisville Louisville KY 40208

FRANCE, W(ALTER) DEWAYNE, JR, b New Haven, Conn, Nov 9, 40; m 63; c 3. MATERIALS SCIENCE. *Educ:* Yale Univ, BE, 62; Rensselaer Polytech Inst, PhD(mat eng), 66. *Prof Exp:* Asst corrosion res, Rensselaer Polytech Inst, 63-66; assoc sr res chemist, 66-69, sr res chemist, 69-70, supv specialized activities, 70-73, ASST DEPT HEAD, ANAL CHEM DEPT, RES LABS, GEN MOTORS CORP, 73- *Honors & Awards:* A B Campbell Award, Nat Asn Corrosion Engrs, 70; Appreciation Outstanding Serv Award, Am Soc Testing & Mat, 76. *Mem:* Nat Asn Corrosion Engrs; Am Soc Testing & Mat; Am Soc Metals; Am Chem Soc. *Res:* Management of research on the characterization of materials, including metals, polymers, gases and petroleum products with chemical, instrumental and radioisotopic techniques; evaluation of materials performance in the environment, particularly corrosion. *Mailing Add:* 6455 Bloomfield Glens West Bloomfield MI 48033

FRANCEL, JOSEF, b Olomouc, Czech, Nov 19, 24; m 50; c 7. CHEMISTRY. *Educ:* Tech Univ Brno, Czech, dipl ing, 48; Mass Inst Technol, ScD(ceramics), 53. *Prof Exp:* Asst, Tech Univ Brno, Czech, 46-48; asst, Mass Inst Technol, 50-53; res chemist, Gen Res Div, 53-58, dir appl res sect, Kimble Div, 58-63, RES MGR, CONSUMER & TECH PROD DIV, OWENS-ILL INC, 63- *Concurrent Pos:* Res fel, Naples; consult, 53- *Mem:* AAAS; Am Ceramic Soc. *Res:* High temperature technology; surface chemistry and physics; glass; coatings; refractories; heat transfer; microscopy; interferometry; adhesion; electronics; gas evolution; gas absorption. *Mailing Add:* 1802 Perth St Toledo OH 43607

FRANCES, SAUL, b Brooklyn, NY, Dec 13, 10; m 41; c 2. BACTERIOLOGY. *Educ:* City Col New York, BS, 35; Univ Minn, MS, 37; Columbia Univ, PhD(bact), 46. *Prof Exp:* Bacteriologist, Skin Res Labs, Minn, 37-39; res bacteriologist & asst to dir, Pease Labs, Inc, NY, 40-43; dir, Coconut Processing Labs, 43-44; bacteriologist, Off Sci Res & Develop Contract, Columbia Univ, 44-46, asst bact, Col Physicians & Surgeons, 46-50; dir, 48-72, EXEC DIR, WELLS LABS, INC, 72- *Concurrent Pos:* Fel, Dazian Found Med Res, 44-46; consult, advert agencies & labs, NY, 44- *Mem:* AAAS; Am Chem Soc; Am Soc Microbiol; Sigma Xi; Soc Indust Microbiol. *Res:* Bacteriology of the mouth; physiology of bacteria; anaerobes; antihistaminics; antibiotics; vaccines; chronic infections; cosmetics; cancer research; toxicology. *Mailing Add:* Wells Labs Inc 25-27 Lewis Ave Jersey City NJ 07306

FRANCESCHETTI, DONALD RALPH, b Oceanside, NY, Nov 21, 47. CHEMICAL PHYSICS, SOLID STATE PHYSICS. *Educ:* Brooklyn Col, BS, 69; Princeton Univ, MA, 71, PhD(chem), 74. *Prof Exp:* Res assoc physics, Univ Ill, Urbana-Champaign, 73-75; res assoc, Univ NC, Chapel Hill, 75-77, res asst prof chemistry, 77-79; ASST PROF PHYSICS, MEMPHIS STATE UNIV, TENN, 79- *Concurrent Pos:* NSF energy related fel, 75-76; vis lectr, Dept Chem, State Univ, Utrecht, Neth, 82. *Mem:* Am Phys Soc; Am Chem Soc; Electrochem Soc. *Res:* Solid state electrochemistry, chemisorption and catalysis; hydrogen in metals. *Mailing Add:* Dept Physics Memphis State Univ Memphis TN 38152

FRANCESCHINI, GUY ARTHUR, b North Adams, Mass, Apr 2, 18; m 47; c 1. METEOROLOGY, OCEANOGRAPHY. *Educ:* Univ Mass, BS, 50; Univ Chicago, SM, 52; Tex A&M Univ, PhD(meteorol), 61. *Prof Exp:* Meteorologist, Nat Adv Comt Aeronaut, 45-47; instr, Univ Chicago, 52; asst prof physics, 52-53, asst prof meteorol, 54-60, assoc prof oceanog & meteorol, 61-68, PROF OCEANOG & METEOROL, TEX A&M UNIV, 69-, RES SCIENTIST, RES FOUND, 52- *Mem:* Am Meteorol Soc; Am Geophys Union. *Res:* Air-sea interactions; solar radiation. *Mailing Add:* Rte 2 Box 140 Caldwell TX 77836

FRANCESCHINI, REMO, b New York, NY, Apr 14, 28; m 53; c 3. FOOD SCIENCE, FOOD TECHNOLOGY. *Educ:* Fordham Univ, BS, 49; Univ Mass, MS, 55, PhD(food sci), 59. *Prof Exp:* Mgr new prod, Libby, McNeill & Libby, 58-61; group leader, 61-63, coordr, 63-64, asst dir res, 64-66, dir prod develop, 66-78, DIR RES & DEVELOP, THOMAS J LIPTON, INC, 78- *Mem:* Inst Food Tech; Am Asn Cereal Chem. *Res:* Irradiation of food products; thermal processing; dehydration; utilization of vegetable proteins; new product development; emulsions. *Mailing Add:* 804 Marshall Rd River Vale NJ 07675

FRANCESCONI, RALPH P, b Milford, Mass, Jan 28, 39; m 62; c 3. BIOLOGICAL CHEMISTRY. *Educ:* Amherst Col, AB, 61; Boston Col, MS, 63, PhD(cell biol), 66. *Prof Exp:* USPHS fel biol chem, Harvard Sch Med, 66-68; invest environ biochem, 68-75, RES CHEMIST, US ARMY RES INST ENVIRON MED, 75- *Mem:* AAAS; Sigma Xi; Am Physiol Soc. *Res:* Enzyme development and enzyme regulation in mammals; effects of environmental stress conditions upon enzyme levels; effects of stressors on human amino acid metabolism. *Mailing Add:* Biochem Lab US Army Res Inst of Environ Med Natick MA 01760

FRANCH, ROBERT H, b Bessemer, Mich, June 15, 27; m 58; c 7. CARDIOLOGY, CARDIOVASCULAR PHYSIOLOGY. *Educ:* Univ Colo, AB, 48, MD, 52. *Prof Exp:* Nat Heart Inst trainee cardiovasc dis, 55-56; from instr to assoc prof, 56-70, PROF MED, MED SCH, EMORY UNIV, 70-, DIR, CARDIOVASC LAB, UNIV HOSP, 57- *Concurrent Pos:* Fel cardiol, Med Sch, Emory Univ, 56-57; dir cardiac clin, Grady Hosp, 56-57; examr cardiovasc subspecialty bds, Am Bd Internal Med, 61 & 62; mem panel cardiol specialists, State Div Voc Rehab; cardiac consult heart dis control prog, State Dept Pub Health, Ga, 61-; chmn diag treatment facil sect, Div Community Serv, Nat Conf Cardiovasc Dis, 64; fel coun clin cardiol, Am Heart Asn, 64. *Mem:* Fel Am Col Physicians; fel Am Col Cardiol. *Res:* Physiology of the pulmonary vascular bed; anatomy of pulmonary vascular disease; thermodilution technics for measuring flow and ventricular volumes; natural history of small ventricular septal defect; echocardiography in congenital heart disease. *Mailing Add:* Dept of Med Emory Univ Sch of Med Atlanta GA 30322

FRANCIS, ANTHONY HUSTON, b Philadelphia, Pa, Mar 21, 42; m 65; c 2. CHEMICAL PHYSICS. *Educ:* Yale Univ, BS, 64; Univ Mich, PhD(chem), 69. *Prof Exp:* Asst prof chem, Univ Ill, Chicago Circle, 70-75; asst prof, 76-77, ASSOC PROF CHEM, UNIV MICH, 77- *Mem:* Am Chem Soc. *Res:* Optical and magnetic resonance spectroscopy of impurity centers in crystals; vibrational and electronic spectroscopy of surfaces and surface adsorbates. *Mailing Add:* Dept of Chem Univ of Mich Ann Arbor MI 48109

FRANCIS, AROKIASAMY JOSEPH, b Tiruchirapalli, India, Oct 5, 41; c 3. MICROBIOLOGY, SOIL SCIENCE. *Educ:* Annamalai Univ, BSc, 63, MSc, 65; Cornell Univ, PhD(microbiol), 71. *Prof Exp:* Res assoc microbiol, Cornell Univ, 70-73; microbiologist, Stanford Res Inst, 73-75; assoc scientist, 75-80, MICROBIOLOGIST, NUCLEAR WASTE MGT, BROOKHAVEN NAT LAB, 80- *Concurrent Pos:* Mem tech adv group, Dept Health Serv Nitrogen Pollution, Suffolk County, 75-77. *Mem:* Am Soc Microbiol; Am Nuclear Soc. *Res:* Microbiology of radioactive wastes, microbiol production of sequestering agents of radionuclides and heavy metals, migration of radionuclides and persistence of organoradio nuclide complexes in the environment, biodegradation of pesticides and organic pollutants; nitrogen transformation, biomethylation and effect of acid rain on soil microbial processes; organic chemistry. *Mailing Add:* Dept Energy & Environ Bldg 318 Brookhaven Nat Lab Upton NY 11973

FRANCIS, BETTINA MAGNUS, b Frankfurt, Ger, Sept 3, 43; m 67; c 2. TERATOLOGY, NEUROTOXICOLOGY. *Educ:* NY Univ, BA, 65; Univ Mich, MS, 67, PhD(genetics), 71. *Prof Exp:* res assoc, Environ Toxicol, Ill Natural Hist Surv, 75-76; res assoc, 77-80, asst res biologist, 80-81, ASST PROF, INST ENVIRON STUDIES, UNIV ILL, 81- *Mem:* Teratology Soc; AAAS; Sigma Xi. *Res:* Irreversible health effects of xenobiotics, with particular emphasis on teratogenic and neurological consequences. *Mailing Add:* 801 S Anderson Urbana IL 61801

FRANCIS, CECIL VERNON, b Alma, Mo, Aug 24, 17; m 53. ANALYTICAL CHEMISTRY. *Educ:* Univ Mo, AB, 38. *Prof Exp:* With tech sales & serv, Greene Bros, Inc, 41-43; sect head anal res, 46-57, mgr anal res, 57-79, MGR QUAL ASSURANCE, BASF WYANDOTTE CORP, 79- *Mem:* Am Chem Soc; Am Soc Testing & Mat. *Res:* Optical crystallography; glycols; detergents; carboxymethylcellulose; polyols, amines. *Mailing Add:* 1741 Waverly Rd Trenton MI 48183

FRANCIS, CHESTER WAYNE, b Creston, Iowa, Feb 14, 36; m 63; c 1. SOIL SCIENCE, ECOLOGY. *Educ:* Iowa State Col, BS, 58; Univ Wis, MS, 64, PhD(soils), 67. *Prof Exp:* Soil specialist, IRI Res Inst NY, Brazil, 66-68; SOIL CHEMIST, OAK RIDGE NAT LAB, 69- *Mem:* AAAS; Soil Sci Soc Am; Am Soc Agron. *Res:* Soil chemistry, mineralogy and fertility. *Mailing Add:* Oak Ridge Nat Lab PO Box X Oak Ridge TN 37830

FRANCIS, DAVID W, b New York, NY, Oct 31, 36; m 64; c 2. GENETICS, DEVELOPMENTAL BIOLOGY. *Educ:* Harvard Univ, BA, 57; Univ Wis, MS, 59, PhD(bot), 62. *Prof Exp:* NIH fel biol, Princeton Univ, 62-63, res assoc, 63-65; asst prof, Univ BC, 65-69; assoc prof, 69-77, PROF BIOL SCI, UNIV DEL, 77- *Mem:* Soc Develop Biologists; Soc Microbiologists. *Res:* Cell differentiation in protozoa, especially in Acrasiales. *Mailing Add:* Sch of Life & Health Sci Univ of Del Newark DE 19711

FRANCIS, DAVID WESSON, b New York, NY, Aug 17, 18; m 50, 77; c 3. POULTRY HUSBANDRY. *Educ:* Rutgers Univ, BS, 41; Univ Del, MS, 52; Univ Md, PhD(poultry husb), 55. *Prof Exp:* Technician, Small Animals, Lederle Labs, 41-42; farmer, Soldier Hill Farm, NJ, 42-50; asst poultry sci, Univ Del, 50-51, res instr, 51-53; asst, Univ Md, 53-55; assoc prof, 55-58, prof poultry sci & head dept, 58-77, prof poultry, 77-81, EMER PROF POULTRY, DEPT ANIMAL & RANGE SCI, NMEX STATE UNIV, 81-; CONSULT, 81- *Concurrent Pos:* Consult, NMex State Univ-US Agency Int Develop, Paraguay, 70, 73 & 76. *Honors & Awards:* Distinguished Res Award, Col Agr & Home Econ, NMex State Univ, 68. *Mem:* Fel AAAS; Poultry Sci Asn; Am Asn Avian Path; World Poultry Asn. *Res:* Management; physiology; pathology. *Mailing Add:* Dept Animal & Range Sci N Mex State Univ Las Cruces NM 88003

FRANCIS, DAWN ELIZABETH, coordination chemistry, physical chemistry, see previous edition

FRANCIS, DONALD PINKSTON, b Los Angeles, Calif, Oct 24, 42; m 76; c 2. MEDICAL EPIDEMIOLOGY, VIROLOGY. *Educ:* Northwestern Univ, MD, 68. *Hon Degrees:* DSc, Harvard, 79. *Prof Exp:* Dept HEW int fel, Childrens Bur, Punjab, India, 68; intern-resident pediat, Los Angeles County, Univ Southern Calif Med Ctr, 69-71; state epidemiologist infectious dis, Rivers State, Nigeria, USAID, 71; epidemic intell serv officer, Ctr Dis Control, 71-73; med officer smallpox, WHO, Sudan, 73 & India, 73-75; infectious dis fel, Channing Lab, Harvard Med Sch, 75-77; CHIEF EPIDEMIOL BR, HEPATITIS LABS DIV, CTR DIS CONTROL, 78- *Concurrent Pos:* Microbiol fel, Harvard Sch Pub Health, 76. *Res:* Hepatitis. *Mailing Add:* 4402 N Seventh St Phoenix AZ 85014

FRANCIS, EUGENE A, b Christiansted, VI, Oct 27, 27; m 55. MATHEMATICS. *Educ:* Inter-Am Univ PR, BA, 49; Columbia Univ, MA, 51. *Prof Exp:* From instr to assoc prof math, 51-67, assoc dir, NSF Math Inst, 59-67, chmn dept math, 67-72, assoc dean studies, 72-74, PROF MATH, UNIV PR, MAYAGUEZ, 67- *Concurrent Pos:* Spec lectr, Inter-Am Univ PR, 51, 56, 58. *Mem:* NY Acad Sci; Nat Coun Teachers Math; AAAS; Math Asn Am; Am Math Soc. *Mailing Add:* Dept Math Univ PR Mayaguez PR 00708

FRANCIS, FAITH ELLEN, b Batavia, NY, Dec 28, 29. BIOCHEMISTRY. *Educ:* D'Youville Col, BA, 52; St Louis Univ, PhD(biochem), 57. *Prof Exp:* Res assoc internal med, 57-59, from instr to asst prof, 59-68, asst prof obstet & gynec, 68-72, ASSOC PROF OBSTET & GYNEC, SCH MED, ST LOUIS UNIV, 72-, ASST PROF BIOCHEM, 64- *Mem:* Fel AAAS; Soc Exp Biol & Med; Am Chem Soc; Endocrine Soc; NY Acad Sci. *Res:* Metabolism of steroid hormones. *Mailing Add:* St Louis Univ Sch of Med 1402 S Grand Blvd St Louis MO 63104

FRANCIS, FREDERICK JOHN, b Ottawa, Ont, Oct 9, 21; m 52; c 3. FOOD SCIENCE. *Educ:* Univ Toronto, BA, 46, MA, 48; Univ Mass, PhD, 54. *Prof Exp:* Instr food chem, Univ Toronto, 46-50; lectr hort, Ont Agr Col, 50-54; from asst prof to prof food sci & nutrit, 54-64, Nicolas Appert prof, 64-71, head dept, 71-77, PROF FOOD SCI & NUTRIT, UNIV MASS, AMHERST, 71- *Honors & Awards:* Nicolas Appert Medal, Inst Food Technologists, 79. *Mem:* Fel AAAS; fel Inst Food Technologists (pres, 80-81); Am Soc Hort Sci; Am Chem Soc; NY Acad Sci. *Res:* Plant biochemistry, color and pigments; food preservation; food safety. *Mailing Add:* Dept Food Sci & Nutrit Univ of Mass Amherst MA 01002

FRANCIS, GEORGE KONRAD, b Warnsdorf, Ger, Mar 7, 39; US citizen; m 67; c 1. MATHEMATICS. *Educ:* Univ Notre Dame, BS, 58, Harvard Univ, MA, 60; Univ Mich, PhD(math), 67. *Prof Exp:* Lectr math, Regis Col, 62-63, Boston Col, 63-64 & Newton Col, 64-65; A H Lloyd fel Univ Mich, 67-68; asst prof, 68-73, ASSOC PROF MATH, UNIV ILL, URBANA, 73- *Mem:* Am Math Soc. *Res:* Differential and combinatorial topology of curves and surfaces; control theory and dynamical systems; confidence bounds in multivariate statistics; biomathematics of morphogenesis and evolution; singularities of maps on manifolds; catastrophe theory; pow dimensional manifolds and cell complexes. *Mailing Add:* Dept of Math Univ of Ill Urbana IL 61801

FRANCIS, GERALD PETER, b Seattle, Wash, Feb 15, 36; m 64; c 3. MECHANICAL & MARINE ENGINEERING. *Educ:* Univ Dayton, BME, 58; Cornell Univ, MME, 60, PhD(eng), 65. *Prof Exp:* Instr mech eng, Cornell Univ, 61-64; asst prof, Ga Inst Technol, 64-66; from asst prof to assoc prof, State Univ NY, Buffalo, 66-70, chmn dept, 70-77; prof eng & head dept, US Merchant Marine Acad, 77-80; PROF MECH ENG, UNIV VT, 80-, DEAN, DIV ENG MATH & BUS ADMIN & DEAN, COL ENG & MATH, 80- *Concurrent Pos:* NSF grants, 67-70; Am Heart Asn grants, 69-74. *Mem:* Am Soc Mech Engrs; Am Soc Eng Educ; fel Inst Marine Engrs. *Res:* Turbulent boundary layers; pulsatile blood flow; instrumentation for bio-fluid measurements; turbomachinery. *Mailing Add:* Univ Vt Cols Eng & Math 194 S Prospect Burlington VT 05401

FRANCIS, HOWARD THOMAS, b St Louis, Mo, Oct 22, 17; m 41; c 2. BIOMEDICAL ENGINEERING. *Educ:* Mt Union Col, BS, 38; Pa State Univ, MS, 40, PhD(phys chem), 42. *Prof Exp:* Mgr electrochem, IIT Res Inst, 42-71; DIR BIOMED ENG, COOK COUNTY HOSP, 71- *Mem:* Am Chem Soc; Electrochem Soc; Nat Asn Corrosion Eng; Asn Advan Med Instrumentation; Am Soc Hosp Engrs. *Res:* Electrical safety; medical equipment testing and maintenance; clinical engineering. *Mailing Add:* 107 Walnut St Park Forest IL 60466

FRANCIS, IVOR STUART, b Napier, NZ, Feb 6, 38. STATISTICS. *Educ:* Univ NZ, BSc, 59, MSc, 60; Harvard Univ, PhD(statist), 66. *Prof Exp:* Asst prof statist, Grad Sch Bus Admin, NY Univ, 65-68; asst prof, 68-74, assoc prof, 74-81, PROF STATIST, CORNELL UNIV, 81- *Concurrent Pos:* Vis prof math, Univ Otago, NZ, 72. *Mem:* Am Statist Asn; Inst Math Statist; Biomet Soc; Royal Statist Soc; Asn Comput Mach. *Res:* Multivariate statistical analysis and statistical computing; evaluation of statistical program packages. *Mailing Add:* Statist Ctr 358 Ives Hall Cornell Univ Ithaca NY 14850

FRANCIS, JOHN ELBERT, b Kingfisher, Okla, Mar 14, 37; m 62. MECHANICAL ENGINEERING. *Educ:* Univ Okla, BS, 60, MS, 63, PhD(eng sci), 65. *Prof Exp:* Engr, Allis Chalmers Mfg Co, 60; asst prof mech eng, Univ Mo, Rolla, 64-66; from asst prof to assoc prof, 66-74, asst dean grad col, 68-71, PROF AEROSPACE, MECH & NUCLEAR ENG, UNIV OKLA, 74-, ASSOC DEAN ENG, 81- *Honors & Awards:* Ralph Teetor Award, Soc Automotive Engrs, 69. *Mem:* Am Soc Mech Engrs; Am Inst Aeronaut & Astronaut; Optical Soc Am; Sigma Xi; NY Acad Sci. *Res:* The use of the scanning infrared camera, thermography, in bioengineering and in fatigue studies; experimental and analytical solar energy research. *Mailing Add:* Sch Aerospace Mech & Nuclear Eng 865 Asp Norman OK 73069

FRANCIS, JOHN ELSWORTH, b Toronto, Ont, Jan 25, 32; m 59; c 3. ORGANIC CHEMISTRY. *Educ:* Queen's Univ, Ont, BA, 53, MA, 56; Univ NB, PhD(org chem), 58. *Prof Exp:* Jr res chemist div pure chem, Nat Res Coun Can, 54-55; vis scientist, Nat Inst Arthritis & Metab Dis, 58-60; res chemist, J R Geigy AG, Switz, 60-63 & Geigy Chem Corp, 63-67, res assoc, 67-70, sr staff scientist, 70-71, SR RES FEL, CIBA-GEIGY CORP, 72- *Mem:* Am Chem Soc; Int Soc Heterocyclic Chem. *Res:* Aromatic chemistry; organic deuterium compounds; structure elucidation of lycopodium alkaloids; synthesis and selective cleavage of peptides; thiophene derivatives; sulphonamides; nitrofurans; nitrogen heterocyclic compounds; phenethylamines. *Mailing Add:* Palmer Lane W Pleasantville NY 10570

FRANCIS, LYMAN L(ESLIE), b Alma, Mo, May 17, 20; m 42; c 5. MECHANICAL ENGINEERING. *Educ:* Univ Mo, MS, 50. *Prof Exp:* Design engr, Owen-Ill Glass Co, Ohio, 46-47; jr engr, Toledo Edison Co, 47-48; instr mech eng, Univ Mo, 48-52; assoc prof, Wash State Univ, 52-63; assoc prof, 63-77, PROF ENG, UNIV MO-ROLLA, 77- *Concurrent Pos:* Chmn coun engrs, Coun for Prof Develop, 77-79; bd dir, Soc Mfr Engrs, 78- *Mem:* Am Soc Eng Educ; Soc Mfg Engrs; Am Soc Mech Engrs. *Res:* Manufacturing engineering, materials, and design. *Mailing Add:* Dept Eng Technol Univ Mo Rolla MO 65401

FRANCIS, MARION DAVID, b Campbell River, BC, May 9, 23; m 49; c 2. BIOCHEMISTRY, MEDICAL RESEARCH. *Educ:* Univ BC, BA, 46, MA, 49; Univ Iowa, PhD(biochem), 53. *Prof Exp:* SR SCIENTIST, PROCTER & GAMBLE CO, 52- *Concurrent Pos:* Consult, Am Dent Asn; guest lectr at numerous Am & Europ Univs. *Mem:* Fel AAAS; fel Am Inst Chem; Soc Nuclear Med; NY Acad Sci; Am Chem Soc. *Res:* Diagnostic and therapeutic nuclear medicine; calcium and phosphorus chemistry and metabolism of bones and teeth; biochemistry and physiology of the di- and polyphosphonates; arthritis and inflammatory reactions. *Mailing Add:* Procter & Gamble Co Miami Valley Labs Rm 2N142 Cincinnati OH 45247

FRANCIS, NORMAN, b Rochester, NY, Nov 27, 22; m 47; c 3. THEORETICAL PHYSICS. *Educ:* Univ Rochester, BA, 48, PhD(physics), 52. *Prof Exp:* Res assoc, Ind Univ, 52-55; theoret physicist, 55-64, mgr advan reactor theory, 64-78, CONSULT PHYSICIST, KNOLLS ATOMIC POWER LAB, GEN ELEC CO, 78- *Mem:* Am Phys Soc; fel Am Nuclear Soc. *Res:* Nuclear and reactor theory. *Mailing Add:* Knolls Atomic Power Lab Gen Elec Co River Rd Niskayuna NY 12309

FRANCIS, PETER SCHUYLER, b Youngstown, Ohio, Nov 22, 27; m 51; c 3. PHYSICAL ORGANIC CHEMISTRY. *Educ:* Univ Pa, BA, 51; Univ Del, MS, 53, PhD(org chem), 55. *Prof Exp:* Lab technician chem, Smith Kline & French Labs, 49-51; asst, Univ Del, 52-54; res chemist, Hercules Powder Co, 54-63; sr polymer chemist, North Star Res & Develop Inst, 63-65, dir res polymer chem, 65-67; tech dir chem dept, Franklin Inst Res Labs, 67-69, dir chem dept, 70-71, dir materials & phys sci dept, 71-74; mem bd dir, Germantown Labs, 69-74; dir res, Quaker Chem Corp, 74-76; SR RES CHEMIST, ARCO CHEM CO, 77- *Mem:* Am Chem Soc; Sigma Xi; Am Inst Physics; Soc Plastics Engrs. *Res:* Electrokinetic phenomena; rheology of polymers in bulk and solution; metallizing plastics; polymeric membranes for desalting water; reinforced polymers; flame-retarded polymers; thermoplastics; textile and paper processing. *Mailing Add:* 19 Briarcrest Dr Wallingford PA 19086

FRANCIS, PHILIP HAMILTON, b San Diego, Calif, Apr 13, 38; m; c 4. ENGINEERING MECHANICS, MATERIALS SCIENCE. *Educ:* Calif Polytech State Univ, BS, 59; Univ Iowa, MS, 60, PhD(appl mech), 65; St Mary's Univ, MBA, 72. *Prof Exp:* Stress analyst, Douglas Aircraft Co, Inc, 60-62; sr res engr, Dept Mech Sci, 65-73, mgr, Solid Mech, 73-78, staff engr, Southwest Res Inst, 78-79; PROF & CHMN, DEPT MECH ENG, ILL INST TECHNOL, 79- *Honors & Awards:* Gustas L Larson Award, Am Soc Mech Engrs, 78. *Mem:* Am Soc Mech Engrs; Am Acad Mech; Sigma Xi. *Res:* Composite materials, fracture mechanics, engineering mechanics, technology forecasting, research and development management. *Mailing Add:* Dept of Mat Sci PO Drawer 28510 San Antonio TX 78284

FRANCIS, RAY LLEWELLYN, b Detroit, Mich, Feb 24, 21; m 46; c 3. ORGANIC POLYMER CHEMISTRY. *Educ:* Iowa State Univ, BS, 47; Wayne State Univ, MS, 52; Univ Mich, PD, 75; Int Inst Advan Studies, PhD(chem eng), 81. *Prof Exp:* Develop engr, Uniroyal, 47-52; process engr, Ternstedt, Gen Motors Corp, 52-53; chem engr, 53-57, sr chem engr, 57-63, sr proj chem engr, 63-69, MGR MAT ENG LAB, BURROUGHS CORP, 69- *Mem:* Tech Asn Pulp & Paper Indust; Asn Finishing Processes ; Volunteers Int Tech Assistance; Soc Mfg Engrs. *Res:* Materials and processes for electronics. *Mailing Add:* 34051 N Hampshire Livonia MI 48154

FRANCIS, RICHARD L, b Poplar Bluff, Mo, Feb 5, 33; m 65; c 3. MATHEMATICS. *Educ:* Southeast Mo State Col, BS, 55; Univ Mo, MA, 62, EdD(math educ), 65. *Prof Exp:* Instr math, Kemper Sch, 55-61; PROF MATH, SOUTHEAST MO STATE UNIV, 65- *Mem:* Math Asn Am. *Res:* Mathematics education. *Mailing Add:* Dept of Math Southeast Mo State Univ Cape Girardeau MO 63701

FRANCIS, RICHARD LANE, b Bluefield, WVa, June 9, 38. INDUSTRIAL ENGINEERING, OPERATIONS RESEARCH. *Educ:* Va Polytech Inst, BS, 60; Ga Inst Technol, MS, 62; Northwestern Univ, PhD(indust eng & mgt sci), 67. *Prof Exp:* Systs engr, Eng Res Ctr, Western Elec Co, 62-63; from asst prof to assoc prof indust eng, Ohio State Univ, 66-71; PROF INDUST & SYSTS ENG, UNIV FLA, 71- *Concurrent Pos:* Vis math scientist, Opers Res Div, Nat Bur Standards, 77-78. *Honors & Awards:* Distinguished Serv Award, Am Inst Indust Engrs, 77. *Mem:* Am Inst Indust Engrs; Opers Res Soc Am; Inst Mgt Sci; Sigma Xi. *Res:* Location theory; facility layout; applications of optimization theory. *Mailing Add:* Dept of Indust & Systs Eng Univ of Fla Gainesville FL 32611

FRANCIS, ROBERT COLGATE, b Pittsfield, Mass, Nov 10, 42; m 61; c 2. BIOMATHEMATICS. *Educ:* Univ Calif, Santa Barbara, BA, 64; Univ Wash, MS, 66, PhD(biomath), 70. *Prof Exp:* Asst prof statist & fishery & wildlife biol, Colo State Univ, 69-71; assoc scientist, 71-74, SR SCIENTIST, INTER-AM TROP TUNA COMN, SCRIPPS INST OCEANOG, 74- *Concurrent Pos:* Math modeler & biometrician, Colo State Univ, 69-71; lectr, Scripps Inst Oceanog, 73- *Mem:* Biomet Soc. *Res:* Population dynamics; estimation; experimental design; modeling of biological systems; computer programming and simulation techniques; application of biomathematics in fisheries and wildlife management. *Mailing Add:* Inter-Am Trop Tuna Comn Scripps Inst Oceanog La Jolla CA 92037

FRANCIS, ROBERT DORL, b West Liberty, Ohio, Sept 28, 20; m 43. MEDICAL MICROBIOLOGY, VIROLOGY. *Educ:* Franklin Col, AB, 42; Univ Chicago, MS, 45; Univ Mich, PhD(microbiol), 55. *Prof Exp:* Anal chemist, Swift & Co, 42-44; prin bacteriologist, Emulsol Corp, 47-49; instr bact, Univ Mich, 50-52; sr asst sanitarian, USPHS, 53-55, sr asst scientist, 55-56, scientist, 56; assoc prof dermat, Sch Med & Dent, 71-73, ASSOC PROF MICROBIOL, MED CTR, UNIV ALA, BIRMINGHAM, 56- *Concurrent Pos:* Consult, Emulsol Corp, 49-52 & Bur Labs, Ala State Health Dept, 66-76. *Mem:* AAAS; Am Soc Microbiol. *Res:* Epidemiology and immunology of psittacosis lymphogranuloma venereum, poliomyelitis and enteroviruses; replication and antigens of herpesviruses; molluscum contagiosum; diagnostic virology. *Mailing Add:* Dept of Microbiol Univ of Ala Schs of Med & Dent Birmingham AL 35294

FRANCIS, SAMUEL HOPKINS, b Lancaster, Pa, Jan 27, 43; m 65; c 2. UNDERWATER ACOUSTICS. *Educ:* Yale Univ, BA, 64; Harvard Univ, AM, 68, PhD(physics), 70. *Prof Exp:* mem tech staff, 70-78, TECH GROUP SUPVR, BELL LABS, 78- *Mem:* Am Phys Soc; Acoust Soc Am; Am Geophys Union. *Res:* Atmospheric gravity waves and their ionospheric effects; plasma clouds in the ionosphere; flow noise in sonar systems; use of magnetics for locating and tracking underseas cables. *Mailing Add:* Bell Labs Whippany Rd Whippany NJ 07981

FRANCIS, STANLEY ARTHUR, b Moundsville, WVa, Oct 25, 19; m 44; c 3. PHYSICAL CHEMISTRY. *Educ:* Ohio Univ, BS, 40; Ohio State Univ, PhD(phys chem), 47. *Prof Exp:* Chemist, Monsanto Chem Co, 44-45; res chemist, 47-63, supvr fundamental res, 63-68, dir, 68-71, ASST MGR FUNDAMENTAL RES, TEXACO INC, 71- *Mem:* Am Chem Soc; Am Phys Soc. *Res:* Molecular spectroscopy; administration. *Mailing Add:* 22 Central Ave Wappingers Falls NY 12590

FRANCIS, WARREN C(HARLES), b Rockville, Conn, June 20, 18; m 42; c 2. CHEMICAL ENGINEERING. *Educ:* Mass Inst Technol, BS, 40. *Prof Exp:* Foreman chem processing, Procter & Gamble Co, 40-42, actg chem supvr, 46-48; mgr qual control ceramics, Cambridge Tile Mfg Co, 48-49, dir ceramic eng dept, 49-51, staff asst to pres, 52-53; chem engr, Atomic Energy Div, Phillips Petrol Co, 53-54, group leader eng develop, 55-56, asst sect chief reactor eng, 57-61, sect chief, 61-64, asst res & eng br, 64-66, mgr, Aerojet Nuclear Co, 66-71, mgr reactor eng br, 64-66, mgr, Aerojet Nuclear Co, 66-71, mgr metall & mat sci br, 71-77; dept mgr, Fuels & Mat Div, EG&G Idaho, 77-78; RETIRED. *Concurrent Pos:* Instr radar technol, Coast Artillery Sch, Va, 42-46, exec officer, Artillery Sch, Tex, 51-52. *Res:* Nuclear fuels and reactor materials, including radiation effects. *Mailing Add:* PO Box 146 Teton Village WY 83025

FRANCIS, WILLIAM CONNETT, b Denver, Colo, Dec 23, 22; m 54; c 2. ORGANIC CHEMISTRY. *Educ:* Univ Kans, BS, 47; Ohio State Univ, PhD(org chem), 52; Pepperdine Univ, MBA, 80. *Hon Degrees:* DSc, Cent Methodist Col, 81. *Prof Exp:* Res chemist, Plaskon Div, Libbey-Owens-Ford Glass Co, 47-48; Fulbright grant, Cambridge Univ, 52-53; sr staff mem res dept, Spencer Chem Co, 54-57, group leader org res, 57-60, sect leader, Spencer Chem Div, Gulf Oil Corp, Kans, 60-66, dir res coord chem dept, Tex, 66-69, mgr develop div, 69-71, mgr, Gulf Adhesives Div, 71-73, vpres, Indust & Specialty Chem Div, 73-79, VPRES TECH & DEVELOP SPECIALTY CHEM, GULF OIL CHEM CO, 79- *Mem:* Am Chem Soc. *Res:* Oxidation of organic compounds; synthesis of fluorinated organic compounds and organic compounds of nitrogen; aminoplast resins; high temperature polymers; organic pesticides. *Mailing Add:* Gulf Oil Chem Co PO Box 3766 Houston TX 77001

FRANCIS, WILLIAM PORTER, b St Louis, Mo, Mar 15, 40; m 62; c 3. THEORETICAL PHYSICS, ELEMENTARY PARTICLES. *Educ:* Rensselaer Polytech Inst, BS, 61; Cornell Univ, PhD(physics), 69. *Prof Exp:* Mem tech staff solid state physics, Bell Tel Labs, NJ, 67-68; Nat Res Coun Can fel physics, Univ Windsor, 68-70; asst prof math, 70-77, ASSOC PROF MATH, MICH TECHNOL UNIV, 77- *Mem:* Am Phys Soc; Sigma Xi. *Res:* Gauge theories and the theories of fundamental interactions. *Mailing Add:* Dept of Math Mich Technol Univ Houghton MI 49931

FRANCIS, WILLIAM RANKIN, health care administration, institutional pharmacy, see previous edition

FRANCIS, WILLIAM RICHARD, experimental high energy physics, see previous edition

FRANCISCO, JERRY THOMAS, b Huntingdon, Tenn, Dec 18, 32; m 54; c 2. PATHOLOGY. *Educ:* Univ Tenn, MD, 55. *Prof Exp:* Asst instr path, Univ Tenn, 56-57; dir labs, US Naval Hosp, Memphis, 57-59; from instr to assoc prof, 59-67, PROF PATH, INST PATH, UNIV TENN, MEMPHIS, 67- *Concurrent Pos:* Mem staff, John Gaston Hosp, 60-; med examr, Memphis & Shelby County, Tenn, 60-; chief med examr, 63-66, forensic path consult for chief med examr, 66-70, chief med examr, 70- *Mem:* Am Soc Clin Path; Col Am Path. *Res:* Forensic pathology; effect of sickle cell erythrocytes on the in vitro growth characteristics of certain bacteria. *Mailing Add:* Inst of Path Univ of Tenn Memphis TN 38163

FRANCK, RICHARD W, b Ger, May 15, 36; US citizen; m 58; c 2. ORGANIC CHEMISTRY. *Educ:* Amherst Col, AB, 58; Univ Wis, MA, 60; Stanford Univ, PhD(chem), 63. *Prof Exp:* NIH fel chem, Mass Inst Technol, 62-63; from asst prof to assoc prof, 63-75, PROF CHEM, FORDHAM UNIV, 75- *Mem:* NY Acad Sci; Chem Soc; Am Chem Soc. *Res:* Modern mechanistic and synthetic organic chemistry; bio-organic chemistry. *Mailing Add:* Dept of Chem Fordham Univ New York NY 10458

FRANCK, WALLACE EDMUNDT, b Alexandria, La, Feb 1, 33; m 57; c 2. MATHEMATICAL STATISTICS. *Educ:* La State Univ, BS, 55; Univ NMex, MS, 62, PhD(math), 64. *Prof Exp:* Weapons proj officer, Kirtland AFB, US Air Force, 58-56, programmer math, 58-60; mathematician, US Naval Weapons Eval Facil, 60-62; asst prof, 64-69, ASSOC PROF STATIST, UNIV MO-COLUMBIA, 69- *Mem:* Inst Math Statist. *Res:* Probability; statistics. *Mailing Add:* Dept of Statist Univ of Mo-Columbia Columbia MO 65201

FRANCKE, OSCAR F, b Mexico City, Mex, Mar 1, 50. SYSTEMATICS, BIOGEOGRAPHY. *Educ:* Ariz State Univ, BS, 71, PhD(zool), 76. *Prof Exp:* ASST PROF BIOL & ENTOM, TEX TECH UNIV, 76- *Concurrent Pos:* Ed, J Arachnol, 76-; prin investr faunistic surv, Tex Dept Agr, 77-79. *Mem:* Am Arachnol Soc; AAAS; Am Soc Zoologists; Entom Soc Am; Soc Syst Zool. *Res:* Phylogeny of Arthropoda, particularly chelicerata; biology of Arachnida; systematics, phylogeny, biology and zoogeography of scorpiones; faunistics of formicidae, ants. *Mailing Add:* Dept of Biol Sci Tex Tech Univ Lubbock TX 79409

FRANCKE, UTA, b Wiesbaden, Ger, Sept 9, 42; m 67. HUMAN GENETICS, CYTOGENETICS. *Educ:* Univ Munich Med Sch, MD, 67. *Prof Exp:* Asst prof pediat, Univ Calif, San Diego, 73-78; ASSOC PROF HUMAN GENETICS, MED SCH, YALE UNIV, 78- *Concurrent Pos:* Dir med genetics, San Diego Childrens Hosp, 75-78. *Mem:* Am Soc Human Genetics; Soc Pediat Res; Teratology Soc. *Res:* Human cytogenetics including development of a map for chromosome bands; identification and characterization of new chromosomal syndromes; human gene mapping by somatic cell hybridization; human/mouse comparative chromosome mapping. *Mailing Add:* Dept Human Genetics Yale Sch Med PO Box 3333 New Haven CT 06510

FRANCKO, DAVID ALEX, b Cleveland, Ohio, Aug 15, 52; m 75. LIMNOLOGY, BOTANY. *Educ:* Kent State Univ, BS, 74, MS, 77; Mich State Univ, PhD(bot), 80. *Prof Exp:* Fel, Kellogg Biol Sta, Mich State Univ, 80-81, instr limnol, 80; ASST PROF BOT, OKLA STATE UNIV, 81- *Mem:* AAAS; Am Soc Limnol & Oceanog; Int Soc Theoret Appl Limnol. *Res:* Physiological limnology, especially the molecular ecology of aquatic photoautotrophs; cyclic nucleotide research and nutrient dynamics. *Mailing Add:* Dept Bot Okla State Univ Stillwater OK 74078

FRANCO, NICHOLAS BENJAMIN, b Providence, RI, Apr 26, 38; m 64; c 2. PHYSICAL INORGANIC CHEMISTRY, POLLUTION CHEMISTRY. *Educ:* Providence Col, BS, 59, MS, 62; Univ Miami, PhD(phys chem), 68. *Prof Exp:* Sr res chemist, Olin Corp, 67-69; vpres, treas-mgr water treatment systs, Resource Control, Inc, 69-74; pollution control engr, 74-79, SUPVR RES & DEVELOP, RAW MATS & CHEM PROCESSES, BETHLEHEM STEEL CORP, 79- *Mem:* Asn; Water Pollution Control Fedn. Electroplaters Soc; Am Chem Soc; Air Pollution Control Asn. *Res:* Chemistry of fused salts, propellants, coordination compounds and organometallics; homogeneous catalysis by inorganic salts and organometallics; air and water pollution control; minerals processing. *Mailing Add:* 345 Carver Dr Bethlehem PA 18017

FRANCO, VICTOR, b New York, NY, Dec 15, 37; m 62; c 2. THEORETICAL NUCLEAR PHYSICS, ATOMIC PHYSICS. *Educ:* NY Univ, BS, 58; Harvard Univ, MA, 59, PhD(physics), 64. *Prof Exp:* Instr physics, Mass Inst Technol, 63-64, res assoc, 64-65; fel, Lawrence Radiation Lab, Univ Calif, Berkeley, 65-67 & Los Alamos Sci Lab, 67-69; assoc prof, 69-72, PROF PHYSICS, BROOKLYN COL, 73- *Concurrent Pos:* Consult, Los Alamos Sci Lab; vis scientist, Saclay Nuclear Res Ctr, France, 75-76. *Mem:* Fel Am Phys Soc; Sigma Xi. *Res:* Theoretical medium and high energy nuclear and atomic scattering theory; Glauber approximation; diffraction scattering. *Mailing Add:* Dept of Physics Brooklyn Col Brooklyn NY 11210

FRANCOEUR, ROBERT THOMAS, b Detroit, Mich, Oct 18, 31. EMBRYOLOGY, EVOLUTION. *Educ:* Sacred Heart Col, BA, 53; St Vincent Col, MA, 57; Univ Detroit, MS, 62; Univ Del, PhD(biol), 67. *Prof Exp:* Instr biol & theol, Mt St Agnes Col, 61-62; from asst prof to assoc prof, 65-74, prof embryol, 74-80, PROF BIOL SCI, FAIRLEIGH DICKINSON UNIV, 80- *Honors & Awards:* Buhl Planetarium Award, 60; Educ Found Human Sexuality Award, 78. *Mem:* Nat Coun Family Rels; Am Asn Sex Educr & Counr; Groves Conf Marriage & Family; World Future Soc. *Res:* Interdisciplinary research focusing on the future of human sexuality, the impact of non-reproductive sex on social mores, legal codes, religious values, and politico-economic systems; ethical considerations of reproductive technologies; innovative life styles in practice. *Mailing Add:* Dept of Biol & Allied Health Sci Fairleigh Dickinson Univ Madison NJ 07940

FRANCQ, EDWARD NATHANIEL LLOYD, b Greencastle, Ind, July 5, 34; div; c 2. VERTEBRATE ECOLOGY, MAMMALIAN BEHAVIOR. *Educ:* Univ Md, College Park, BS, 56; Univ Idaho, MS, 62; Pa State Univ, PhD(zool), 67. *Prof Exp:* Instr, 65-67, asst prof, 67-81, ASSOC PROF ZOOL, UNIV NH, 81- *Mem:* AAAS; Am Soc Mammal; Animal Behav Soc. *Res:* Behavior and population ecology of vertebrates, especially small mammals; behavioral responses to environment and stressful situations. *Mailing Add:* Dept of Zool Univ of NH Spaulding Life Sci Bldg Durham NH 03824

FRANDSEN, HENRY, b Chicago, Ill, May 21, 33; m 53; c 3. MATHEMATICS. *Educ:* Univ Ill, BS, 57, MS, 59, PhD(math), 61. *Prof Exp:* Asst math, Univ Ill, 57-61; asst prof, Clark Univ, 61-66; assoc prof, Wheaton Col, 66-67; assoc prof, 67-71, PROF MATH & MATH EDUC, UNIV TENN, KNOXVILLE, 71- *Concurrent Pos:* Mathematician, Mitre Corp, 63-67. *Mem:* AAAS; Am Math Soc; Math Asn Am. *Res:* Algebra; theory of finite groups; mathematics education; secondary school teacher training. *Mailing Add:* Dept of Math Univ of Tenn Knoxville TN 37916

FRANDSEN, JOHN CHRISTIAN, b Salt Lake City, Utah, Aug 25, 33; m 65, 75; c 4. PARASITOLOGY. *Educ:* Univ Utah, BS, 55, MS, 56, PhD, 60. *Prof Exp:* Asst zool, Univ Utah, 55-58, asst NSF & univ res fel, 58-60; res parasitologist, Regional Animal Dis Lab, 61-66, sr res parasitologist, 66-72, dir, Regional Parasite Res Lab, 72-80, SR RES PARASITOLOGIST, AGR RES SERV, USDA, 80- *Concurrent Pos:* Res lectr, Sch Vet Med, Auburn Univ, adj assoc prof zool & entom, Auburn Univ, 71-; vis prof, Sch Vet Med, Tuskegee Inst, 73- *Mem:* Am Soc Parasitol; Am Asn Vet Parasitologists; NY Acad Sci; Soc Protozool. *Res:* Applications of histochemistry in parasitology; host-parasite relationship; ecology of endoparasites; biochemistry of parasites; interrelationships of parasitism and nutrition. *Mailing Add:* Regional Parasite Res Lab Agr Res Serv PO Drawer 952 Auburn AL 36830

FRANDSON, ROWEN DALE, b Fremont, Nebr, July 22, 20; m 50; c 3. ANATOMY. *Educ:* Colo State Univ, BS, 42, DVM, 44, MS, 55. *Prof Exp:* Practicing vet, 47-48; asst from asst prof to assoc prof, 48-62, PROF ANAT, COLO STATE UNIV, 62- *Mem:* AAAS; World Asn Vet Anat; Am Asn Vet Anat; Am Vet Med Asn; Am Asn Anat. *Res:* Microanatomy of hypothalamic region; application of audio-visual techniques to medical and biological education. *Mailing Add:* Dept of Anat Colo State Univ Ft Collins CO 80521

FRANK, ALAN M, b New York, NY, Dec 22, 44; m 68; c 1. OPTICAL PHYSICS, OPTICAL ENGINEERING. *Educ:* NY Univ, BA, 67; Univ Denver, MS, 69. *Prof Exp:* Staff scientist, optics & detectors, Ball Bros Res Corp, 69-73; tech dir atmospheric physics, Colspan Environ Systs, Inc, 73-74; PHYSICIST & OPTICAL SYST ENGR, LAWRENCE LIVERMORE LAB, UNIV CALIF, 74- *Concurrent Pos:* Consult, Skin & Cancer Groups, NY Univ Hosp & Belvue Med Ctr, 63-67; comptroller, Optical Soc Am & Inst Elec & Electronics Engrs Conf on Lasers & Electrooptics. *Mem:* Optic ' Soc Am; Am Phys Soc; Inst Elec & Electronics Engrs Quantum Electronics & Appln Soc. *Res:* Development of optical instrumentation and techniques for plasma physics, remote environmental sensing, astronomy and medicine. *Mailing Add:* Lawrence Livermore Lab L-43 PO Box 808 Livermore CA 94550

FRANK, ALBERT BERNARD, b Fresno, Ohio, July 7, 39; m 62; c 3. PLANT PHYSIOLOGY. *Educ:* Ohio State Univ, BS, 65, MS, 66; NDak State Univ, PhD(agron), 69. *Prof Exp:* PLANT PHYSIOLOGIST, NORTHERN GREAT PLAINS RES CTR, AGR RES SERV, USDA, 69- *Mem:* Am Soc Plant Physiol; Am Soc Agron; Crop Sci Soc Am; Soil Conserv Soc Am. *Res:* Forage grass physiology as it relates to management practices and development of selection criteria for varietal improvement of grasses adapted to the northern Great Plains; effect of environmental and genetic factors on plant water relations as related to the water regime of growing plants in the northern Great Plains; mechanisms of drought tolerance in wheat and forages. *Mailing Add:* USDA-SEA Agr Res Box 459 Northern Great Plains Res Ctr Mandan ND 58554

FRANK, ANDREW JULIAN, b Chicago, Ill, Sept 17, 25; m 48; c 2. COMMUNITY HEALTH. *Educ:* Univ Ill, BS, 48, MS, 49, PhD(anal & inorg chem), 51. *Prof Exp:* Asst prof chem, Tulane Univ, 51-52; res chemist raw mat develop lab, AEC, Mass, 52-54; chief anal res sect, Watertown Arsenal, Mass, 54-56; chief metals chem br, Metall Div, Denver Res Inst, 56-60; res chemist, Allis-Chalmers Mfg Co, Wis, 60-62; from assoc prof to prof chem, Western Wash State Col, 62-70, chmn dept, 62-70; exec dir, Comprehensive Health Planning Coun, Whatcom, Skagit, Island & San Juan Counties, State of Wash, 71-76; asst dir admin, Puget Sound Health Systs Agency, 76-79; ADMINR, JONES, GREY & BAYLEY, 80- *Concurrent Pos:* Instr, Northeastern Univ, 54-56, Denver Res Inst, 57 & Seattle Community Col, 80. *Mem:* AAAS; Fedn Am Scientists; Am Chem Soc; Am Pub Health Asn; Am Hosp Asn. *Res:* Health services utilization; long term care. *Mailing Add:* 2714 9th Ave W Seattle WA 98119

FRANK, ARLEN W(ALKER), b Lima, Peru, Nov 22, 28; US citizen; m 58; C 3. ORGANOPHOSPHORUS CHEMISTRY, TEXTILE CHEMISTRY. *Educ:* Acadia Univ, BSc, 50, cert appl sci, 50; McGill Univ, Can, PhD(chem), 54. *Prof Exp:* Fel, Div Pure Chem, Nat Res Coun, Ottawa, 54-55; res chemist, Exp Sta, E I du Pont de Nemours & Co, 56-69 & Res Ctr, Hooker Chem Corp, 59-66; teaching intern org chem, Chem Dept, Ohio Wesleyan Univ, 66-67; RES CHEMIST, USDA, SOUTHERN REGIONAL RES CTR, NEW ORLEANS, 67- *Mem:* Am Chem Soc; Am Inst Chem; AAAS; Sigma Xi; Am Asn Textile Chemists & Colorists. *Res:* Organophosphorus chemistry; cottonseed proteins; textile fibers; flame retardants for cotton. *Mailing Add:* Southern Regional Res Ctr USDA PO Box 19687 New Orleans LA 70179

FRANK, ARNE, b Drammen, Norway, Feb 1, 25; US citizen; m 51, 75; c 2. MECHANICAL ENGINEERING. *Educ:* Purdue Univ, BSME, 50, MSME, 51. *Prof Exp:* Res asst, Purdue Univ, 51-52; sr engr, Carrier Corp, 52-57; engr, 57-65, mgr eng unitary prod, 65-75, vpres compressor develop, 75-79, VPRES ENG, INT DIV, TRANE CO, 79- *Mem:* Am Soc Heating, Refrig & Air-Conditioning Engrs. *Res:* Efficiency optimization in compressors. *Mailing Add:* Trane Co La Crosse WI 54601

FRANK, ARTHUR JESSE, b Cincinnati, Ohio, Jan 17, 45; m 68; c 2. PHOTOELECTROCHEMISTRY, PHOTOCHEMISTRY. *Educ:* Univ Colo, BA, 68; Univ Fla, PhD(chem), 75. *Prof Exp:* Res asst chem, Univ Fla, 70-75; vis scientist, Hahn-Meitner Inst, Berlin, 75-76; res assoc, Chem Biodyn Div, Lawrence Berkeley Lab, 76-78; staff scientist, 78-82, SR SCIENTIST, PHOTOCONVERSION RES BR, SOLAR ENERGY RES INST, 82- *Mem:* Am Chem Soc; Electrochem Soc; AAAS; Inter-Am Photochem Soc; Int Asn Colloid & Interface Scientists. *Res:* Photochemistry, laser flash photolysis, pulse radiolysis, kinetics, heterogeneous catalysis, micellar systems, redox and free radical processes, conducting polymers, synthetic membranes. *Mailing Add:* Solar Energy Res Inst 1617 Cole Blvd Golden CO 80401

FRANK, BARRY, b Montreal, Que, Mar 26, 41; m 60; c 2. THEORETICAL SOLID STATE PHYSICS. *Educ:* McGill Univ, BS, 61, MS, 62; Univ BC, PhD(theoret physics), 65. *Prof Exp:* Asst prof, 65-71, ASSOC PROF PHYSICS, CONCORDIA UNIV, 71- *Res:* Solid state and particle physics. *Mailing Add:* Dept of Physics Concordia Univ Montreal PQ H3G 1M8 Can

FRANK, BRUCE HILL, b Hartford, Conn, Oct 12, 38; m 61; c 2. BIOCHEMISTRY, BIOPHYSICS. *Educ:* Trinity Col, BS, 60; Northwestern Univ, PhD(phys biochem), 64. *Prof Exp:* RES SCIENTIST PHYS BIOCHEM, ELI LILLY & CO, 66-; ASST PROF BIOCHEM, MED SCH, IND UNIV, INDIANAPOLIS, 69- *Concurrent Pos:* NIH fel, Univ Calif, Berkeley, 64-66. *Mem:* AAAS; Am Chem Soc; Am Soc Biol Chem. *Res:* Physical biochemistry; drug design; diabetes; protein chemistry; ultracentrifugation; self-associating systems. *Mailing Add:* Lilly Res Labs Dept of Biochem Eli Lilly Co Indianapolis IN 46206

FRANK, CHARLES EDWARD, b Philipsburg, Pa, May 1, 14; m 39; c 3. ORGANIC CHEMISTRY. *Educ:* Pa State Col, BS, 35; Ohio State Univ, MS, 36, PhD(org chem), 38. *Prof Exp:* Grad asst, Ohio State Univ, 35-37; res chemist exp sta, E I du Pont de Nemours & Co, 38-48; assoc prof grad dept appl sci, Univ Cincinnati, 48-53; head appl res, Res Div, US Indust Chem Co Div, Nat Distillers & Chem Corp, 53-58, asst dir res, 58-75; CHEM CONSULT, 75- *Concurrent Pos:* Sr tech adv, US Environ Protection Agency, 78- *Mem:* Am Chem Soc. *Res:* Hydrocarbon oxidation; catalysis; carbon monoxide; polymerization; formaldehyde; sodium. *Mailing Add:* 6887 Kenwood Rd Cincinnati OH 45243

FRANK, CHARLES WARREN, cardiology, internal medicine, see previous edition

FRANK, DAVID LEWIS, b Kearny, NJ, Apr 4, 43; m 64; c 2. TOPOLOGY. *Educ:* Columbia Univ, BA, 64; Univ Calif, Berkeley, PhD(math), 67. *Prof Exp:* NSF fel, 67-68; Moore instr math, Mass Inst Technol, 68-70; from asst prof to assoc prof, State Univ NY Stony Brook, 70-75; ASSOC PROF MATH, UNIV MINN, MINNEAPOLIS, 75- *Res:* Vector fields on manifolds; differential structures on manifolds. *Mailing Add:* Sch Math Univ Minn Minneapolis MN 55455

FRANK, DAVID STANLEY, b Brooklyn, NY, Dec 3, 44; m 67; c 2. BIOCHEMISTRY. *Educ:* Univ Pa, BS, 66; Cornell Univ, MS, 68, PhD(org chem), 71. *Prof Exp:* Instr med, State Univ NY Downstate Med Ctr, 71-72; sr res chemist, 72-80, res assoc, 80-81, MKT DIR CLIN CHEM, EASTMAN KODAK CO, 81- *Mem:* AAAS; Am Chem Soc; Soc Anal Cytol. *Res:* Mechanistic enzymology; bioorganic chemistry; immunochemistry. *Mailing Add:* 127 Warrington Dr Rochester NY 14618

FRANK, DONALD JOSEPH, b Cincinnati, Ohio, Nov 9, 26; m 49; c 4. PEDIATRICS. *Educ:* Univ Cincinnati, MD, 51. *Prof Exp:* From instr to asst prof, 54-67, assoc dir, Div Community Pediat, 67-80, ASSOC PROF PEDIAT, COL MED, UNIV CINCINNATI, 67- *Concurrent Pos:* Pvt pract pediat, 54-64; consult, Margaret Mary Hosp, Batesville, Ind, 54- *Mem:* Am Acad Pediat. *Res:* Clinical problems of the newborn; delivery of health care to children; training of pediatric nurse associates. *Mailing Add:* Community Pediat Sect Good Samaritan Hosp Cincinnati OH 45220

FRANK, EVELYN, b Chicago, Ill. MATHEMATICS. *Educ:* Northwestern Univ, PhD, 45. *Prof Exp:* Instr math, Northwestern Univ, 42-46; from asst prof to assoc prof, 46-57, PROF MATH, UNIV ILL, 57- *Mem:* Soc Indust & Appl Math; Am Math Soc; Math Asn Am. *Res:* Analysis; continued fractions; polynomials; location of zeros; stability; special functions; number theory; numerical analysis. *Mailing Add:* PO Box 361 Evanston IL 60204

FRANK, FLOYD WILLIAM, b Fortuna, Calif, Feb 12, 22; m 48; c 2. VETERINARY MEDICINE, VETERINARY MICROBIOLOGY. *Educ:* Wash State Univ, BS & DVM, 51, PhD(vet sci), 63. *Prof Exp:* Vet, Animal Dis Eradication Br, Agr Res Serv, USDA, Ore, 51-53; vet bact, Wyo State Vet Lab, 53-55; assoc vet, Vet Res Lab, 55-63, res vet, 63-67, actg assoc dir agr res, 71, PROF VET SCI & HEAD DEPT, UNIV IDAHO, 67-, DEAN VET MED, 74- *Concurrent Pos:* NIH trainee, 61-62; mem, Tech Comt Vibriosis Sheep & Tech Comt Urolithiasis Cattle & Sheep; dir, Idaho Vet Med Asn, 64-; dir, Intermountain Vet Med Asn, 69-73, pres, 73-74; mem, Nat Adv Bd Wild Horses & Burros, 72-76, chmn, 75-76. *Mem:* Am Vet Med Asn; Am Soc Microbiol; Am Asn Vet Bact; Am Soc Animal Sci. *Res:* Etiology, transmission, treatment and control of vibriosis of sheep; nutritional factors influencing urolithiasis; etiology, transmission and resistance to enteritis in calves and lambs; prophylaxis of enzootic abortion of ewes and epizootic observations regarding tularemia in sheep. *Mailing Add:* Vet Med Univ Idaho Moscow ID 83843

FRANK, FORREST JAY, b Chicago, Ill, Sept 2, 37; m 59; c 1. ORGANIC CHEMISTRY. *Educ:* Grinnell Col, BA, 59; Purdue Univ, PhD(org chem), 64. *Prof Exp:* Res chemist, Rayonier, Inc, 64-65; chairperson dept, 65-80, ASSOC PROF CHEM, ILL WESLEYAN UNIV, 65- *Mem:* Am Asn Advan Sci; Am Chem Soc; Sigma Xi. *Res:* N-alkyl sulfonamide synthesis. *Mailing Add:* Dept of Chem Ill Wesleyan Univ Bloomington IL 61701

FRANK, FRED R, b Chaska, Minn, Aug 13, 26; m 52; c 1. PHYSIOLOGY, BIOCHEMISTRY. *Educ:* Univ Minn, BS, 55, MS, 60, PhD(physiol, biochem), 63. *Prof Exp:* Fel physiol, Univ Calif, Davis, 63-65, res assoc, 65-67; RES ASSOC, UPJOHN CO, 67- *Mem:* AAAS. *Res:* Ion and water metabolism; renal control mechanisms; calcification mechanisms; reversible and irreversible control of reproduction and application of avian and mammalian pest control. *Mailing Add:* Unit 9670 Upjohn Co Kalamazoo MI 49001

FRANK, GEORGE BARRY, b Brooklyn, NY, Feb 1, 29; Can citizen; m 51; c 3. PHYSIOLOGY, PHARMACOLOGY. *Educ:* City Col New York, BS, 50; Ohio State Univ, MSc, 52; McGill Univ, PhD(physiol), 56. *Prof Exp:* Lectr physiol, McGill Univ, 56-57; from asst prof to prof pharmacol, Univ Man, 57-65; PROF PHARMACOL, UNIV ALTA, 65- *Concurrent Pos:* USPHS fel, 56-57; USPHS spec fel physiol, Univ Col, Univ London & USPHS spec fel pharmacol, Univ Lund, 63-64; vis prof pharmacol, Univ Geneva. *Mem:* Am Physiol Soc; Am Soc Pharmacol & Exp Therapeut; Soc Gen Physiol; Can Physiol Soc; Pharmacol Soc Can (treas, 78-81). *Res:* Electrical and mechanical activities of skeletal muscle; physiology and pharmacology of the central nervous system; pharmacology of general central nervous system depressants and narcotic analgesic drugs. *Mailing Add:* Dept Pharmacol Univ Alta Edmonton AB T6G 2E8 Can

FRANK, GLENN WILLIAM, b Mayfield Heights, Ohio, Jan 13, 28; m 49; c 3. GEOLOGY. *Educ:* Kent State Univ, BS, 51; Univ Maine, MS, 53. *Prof Exp:* From asst prof to assoc prof geol, 53-69, mem fac senate, 69-74, secy, 69-70, chmn, 71-72, asst chmn dept, 69-76, PROF GEOL, KENT STATE UNIV, 69-, DANFORTH ASSOC, 71- *Concurrent Pos:* Asst geologist, Maine Geol Surv, 52; consult, Ohio Dept Transp, 73-74; prin investr, NSF grant, 80-82. *Mem:* Sigma Xi; Am Inst Prof Geol; Geol Soc Am; Nat Asn Geol Teachers. *Mailing Add:* Dept of Geol Kent State Univ Kent OH 44242

FRANK, HENRY SORG, b Pittsburgh, Pa, Aug 6, 02; m 27; c 3. PHYSICAL CHEMISTRY, THERMODYNAMICS. *Educ:* Univ Pittsburgh, BChem & MS, 22; Univ Calif, PhD(chem), 28. *Hon Degrees:* LHD, Geneva Col, 69. *Prof Exp:* Instr physics, Canton Christian Col, 22-25; instr chem, Univ Calif, 27-28; from assoc prof to prof, Lingnan Univ, 28-51, chmn dept, 31-47, dean col sci, 38-51, from vprovost to provost, 46-51; prof, 51-70, chmn dept, 51-63, distinguished serv prof, 70-72, EMER PROF CHEM, UNIV PITTSBURGH, 72-; ADJ PROF, POMONA COL, 75- *Concurrent Pos:* Vis prof, Univ Pittsburgh, 39-40; lectr, Univ Calif, 42-45; adj sr fel, Mellon Inst, 63-71; consult, Oak Ridge Nat Lab, 66-71; US adv & spec chair prof, Chem Res Ctr, Nat Taiwan Univ, 68. *Mem:* AAAS; Am Chem Soc; hon mem Chinese Chem Soc. *Res:* Adsorption of gases; thermodynamics; statistical mechanics; theory of solutions; electrolyte theory; structure of water and of aqueous solutions. *Mailing Add:* Dept of Chem Pomona Col Claremont CA 91711

FRANK, HILMER AARON, b St Paul, Minn, Oct 26, 23; m 53; c 1. FOOD MICROBIOLOGY. *Educ:* Univ Minn, BA, 49; Wash State Univ, MS, 52, PhD(food technol), 54. *Prof Exp:* Asst bact, Wash State Univ, 50-51 & hort, 51-55, Nat Cancer Inst res fel, 55-57; bacteriologist indust test lab, US Naval Shipyard, Pa, 57 & eastern regional res lab, USDA, 57-60; from asst prof to assoc prof, 60-68, PROF FOOD SCI, UNIV HAWAII, 68- *Mem:* Am Soc Microbiol; Soc Indust Microbiol; Brit Soc Appl Bact; Brit Soc Gen Microbiol; Sigma Xi. *Res:* food spoilage; spores of anaerobic bacteria; food safety; histamine forming bacteria in fish. *Mailing Add:* Dept Food Sci & Human Nutrit Univ Hawaii 1920 Edmondson Rd Honolulu HI 96822

FRANK, HOWARD, b New York, NY, June 4, 41; m 65; c 3. ELECTRICAL ENGINEERING. *Educ:* Univ Miami, BS, 62; Northwestern Univ, MS, 64, PhD(elec eng), 65. *Prof Exp:* Asst prof elec eng & comput sci, Univ Calif, Berkeley, 65-69, assoc prof, 67-70; exec vpres, 69-70, PRES COMPUT COMMUN, NETWORK ANAL CORP, 70- *Concurrent Pos:* Vis consult, Exec Off President of US, 68-69. *Honors & Awards:* Leonard G Abraham Award, Inst Elec & Electronics Engrs, 69. *Mem:* Fel Inst Elec & Electronics Engrs; AAAS; NY Acad Sci; Opers Res Soc Am. *Res:* Man-machine communications; computer communications; network analysis, system reliability. *Mailing Add:* Network Anal Corp 130 Steamboat Rd Great Neck NY 11024

FRANK, JAMES ANTHONY, plant pathology, plant physiology, see previous edition

FRANK, JEAN ANN, b New York, NY, June 17, 29. ORGANIC CHEMISTRY. *Educ:* Hunter Col, BA, 51; Colo State Univ, MA, 58; Utah State Univ, PhD(chem), 64. *Prof Exp:* Geologist, AEC, 51-57; instr chem, Wis State Col, 58-60; res asst, Brandeis Univ, 63-65; asst prof, 65-68, PROF CHEM & CHMN DEPT, AM INT COL, 68- *Mem:* Am Chem Soc. *Res:* Chemical kinetics of oxidation-reduction type reactions. *Mailing Add:* Dept of Chem Am Int Col Springfield MA 01109

FRANK, JOAN PATRICIA, b New York, NY, May 7, 25; wid. RADIOCHEMISTRY. *Educ:* Univ Mich, BS, 45, MS, 46; Univ Southern Calif, PhD(phys chem), 50. *Prof Exp:* Chemist nuclear chem & radiochem, Brookhaven Nat Lab, 51-56; control chemist anal develop, Parke-Davis & Co, 68-72; staff res assoc radiochem, Univ Calif, Irvine, 73-80; CONSULT, 80- *Mem:* Am Phys Soc; Am Inst Physics. *Res:* Experimental and theoretical aspects of radioactive thermal fluorine atom addition to protonated and deuterated ethylenes with particular emphasis on the isotope effects involved. *Mailing Add:* 2514 Vista Del Oro Newport Beach CA 92660

FRANK, JOHN HOWARD, b Stockton-on-Tees, Eng, Apr 13, 42; m 68; c 3. INSECT ECOLOGY. *Educ:* Durham Univ, BSc, 63; Oxford Univ, DPhil(entom), 67. *Prof Exp:* Fel entom, Univ Alta, 66-68; entomologist, Sugar Mfr Asn Jamaica, Ltd, 68-72; ENTOMOLOGIST, FLA MED ENTOM LAB, FLA DIV HEALTH, 72- *Mem:* Royal Entom Soc London; Entom Soc Am; Brit Ecol Soc; Coleopterists Soc. *Res:* Population ecology and biological control of insect pests; ecology of Staphylinidae, particularly of the Caribbean region. *Mailing Add:* Fla Med Entom Lab PO Box 520 Vero Beach FL 32960

FRANK, LAWRENCE, b Brooklyn, NY, Sept 12, 15; m 40; c 2. MEDICINE. *Educ:* Univ NC, AB, 36; Long Island Col Med, MD, 40; Am Bd Dermat, dipl, 46. *Prof Exp:* Assoc prof, 53-55, PROF DERMAT & DIR DEPT, STATE UNIV NY DOWNSTATE MED CTR, 55-, DIR & HEAD, UNIV HOSP, 68- *Concurrent Pos:* Attend physician, Long Island Col Hosp, 55-, dir dept dermat; attend physician, Kings County Hosp, 57-, dir & head div dermat, 59-; consult, Vet Admin Hosp, Brooklyn, NY, 59-; consult coun drugs, AMA, 59-; consult, Brooklyn Eye & Ear Hosp & Calodonian Hosp. *Mem:* Fel Soc Invest Dermat; fel AMA; fel Am Col Physicians; fel Am Acad Dermat; fel NY Acad Med. *Res:* Dermatology. *Mailing Add:* 125 Argyle Rd Brooklyn NY 11218

FRANK, LEONARD HAROLD, b New York, NY, Jan 24, 30; m 52; c 3. BIOCHEMISTRY. *Educ:* Univ Okla, AB, 50; Johns Hopkins Univ, PhD(biochem), 57. *Prof Exp:* Sr instr biochem, Sch Med, Western Reserve Univ, 57-61; from asst prof to assoc prof, Sch Hyg, Johns Hopkins Univ, 61-67, assoc prof, 67-69, PROF BIOCHEM, SCH MED, UNIV MD, BALTIMORE, 70- *Mem:* Am Soc Biol Chem. *Res:* Amino acid metabolism and metabolic control; microbial physiology. *Mailing Add:* 660 W Redwood St Baltimore MD 21201

FRANK, LOUIS ALBERT, b Chicago, Ill, Aug 30, 38; m 60; c 2. PHYSICS, ASTRONOMY. *Educ:* Univ Iowa, BA, 60, MS, 61, PhD(space sci), 64. *Prof Exp:* From asst prof to assoc prof prof, 64-71, PROF PHYSICS & ASTRON, UNIV IOWA, 71- *Mem:* Am Geophys Union. *Res:* Measurements of planetary magnetic fields, particles and associated atmospheric phenomena; interplanetary medium; solar phenomena. *Mailing Add:* Dept of Physics & Astron Univ of Iowa Iowa City IA 52242

FRANK, MARTIN, b Chicago, Ill, Oct 22, 47; m 70. CELL PHYSIOLOGY, CARDIOVASCULAR PHYSIOLOGY. *Educ:* Univ Ill, Urbana, AB, 69, MS, 71, PhD(physiol), 73. *Prof Exp:* Res assoc cell physiol, Mich Cancer Found, 73-74; res assoc pharmacol, Mich State Univ, 74-75; asst prof, 75-78, ASST PROF LECTR PHYSIOL, GEORGE WASHINGTON UNIV, 78-; HEALTH SCIENTIST ADMINR, PHYSIOL STUDY SECT, NIH, 78- *Concurrent Pos:* Mem res comt, Am Heart Asn, Nation's Capital Affil, 78- *Mem:* Biophys Soc; Am Heart Asn; Am Physiol Soc; AAAS; Sigma Xi. *Res:* Membrane physiology, particularly with respect to small solute and ion transport mechanisms across cell membranes; ion movements associated with myocardial excitation-contraction coupling; nucleocytoplasmic solute exchange and interactions. *Mailing Add:* Physiol Study Sect George Washington Univ Med Ctr Bethesda MD 20037

FRANK, MARTIN J, b Detroit, Mich, June 4, 28; m 50; c 4. INTERNAL MEDICINE, CARDIOLOGY. Educ: Univ Mich, BS & MD, 53; Am Bd Internal Med, dipl, 62. Prof Exp: Intern, Wayne County Gen Hosp, Mich, 53-54, from resident to chief resident med, 56-59; NIH fel cardiol, Wayne State Univ, 59-60; NIH fel, NJ Col Med & Dent, 60-61, from instr to asst prof med, 61-67; assoc prof, 67-69, dir hemodynamic labs, 67-78, PROF MED, MED COL GA, 69-, CHIEF SECT CARDIOL, 78- Concurrent Pos: Staff mem, Eugene Talmadge Mem Hosp, Ga, 67; consult, Vet Admin Hosp, 67, Cent State Hosp, 68 & Univ Hosp, 69. Mem: Am Heart Asn; Am Fedn Clin Res; fel Am Col Cardiol; Am Col Physicians; Fedn Am Socs Exp Biol. Res: Coronary blood flow and myocardial metabolism; left ventricular function in congenital and acquired valvular heart disease; methods for study of circulation by indicator dilution. Mailing Add: Med Col of Ga Eugene Talmadge Mem Hosp Augusta GA 30902

FRANK, MAX, b Detroit, Mich, Feb 25, 27; m 56; c 4. SOLID STATE ELECTRONICS. Educ: Wayne State Univ, BS, 49, MS, 61. Prof Exp: Instr elec eng, Wayne State Univ, 49-50; sr staff engr res solid state electronics, Wayne Eng Res Inst, 51-57; electronics staff engr, Defense Eng Div, Chrysler Corp, 57-59; prin engr solid state radiation effects, 59-79, MGR, TECHNOL FORECASTING EXEC OFFICES, RES LABS DIV, BENDIX CORP, 79- Mem: Sr mem Inst Elec & Electronics Engrs. Res: Prediction of radiation damage in transistors, diodes and microelectronics; radiation effects on magnetic and insulating materials and electronic components; radiation hardening of electronic systems for nuclear and space radiation environments. Mailing Add: 32445 Olde Franklin Dr Farmington Hills MI 48018

FRANK, MICHAEL M, b Brooklyn, NY, Feb 28, 37; m 61; c 3. IMMUNOLOGY. Educ: Univ Wis, AB, 56; Harvard Univ, MD, 60; Am Bd Clin Immunol & Allergy, dipl. Prof Exp: CHIEF, LAB CLIN INVEST & CLIN DIR, NAT INST ALLERGY & INFECTIOUS DIS, NIH, 76- Concurrent Pos: Mem med bd, NIH, 75-, chmn, 78-79. Honors & Awards: Meritorious Serv Award, USPHS, 75. Mem: Am Soc Clin Invest; Asn Am Physicians; Soc Pediat Res; Asn Am Immunologists; Am Fedn Clin Res. Res: Mechanisms of immune damage. Mailing Add: Clin Ctr Nat Inst Health Bethesda MD 20014

FRANK, MORTON HOWARD, b Portland, Maine, Nov 15, 27; m 56; c 2. PHYSIOLOGY. Educ: Bowdoin Col, BA, 48; Univ Ill, MS, 54, PhD, 58. Prof Exp: Asst physiol, Univ Ill, 51-57; fel, Albert Einstein Col Med, 57-59; asst prof psychiat, Col Med, Ohio State Univ, 59-64; asst prof, 64-72, ASSOC PROF PHYSIOL, NEW YORK MED COL, 72- Concurrent Pos: Res assoc, Columbus Psychiat Inst & Hosp, 59-64. Mem: AAAS; Sigma Xi; Am Physiol Soc; Am Heart Asn; assoc fel NY Acad Med. Res: Afferent limb of cardiovascular and respiratory reflexes; visceral afferents; chemoreceptors. Mailing Add: Dept of Physiol Basic Sci Bldg New York Med Col Valhalla NY 10595

FRANK, NEIL LAVERNE, meteorology, see previous edition

FRANK, OSCAR, b Trieste, Italy, Mar 6, 32; US citizen; m 59; c 2. BIOCHEMISTRY, NUTRITION. Educ: Brooklyn Col, BS, 55, MA, 57; NY Univ, PhD(biochem), 61. Prof Exp: Assoc chem, Univ Med Sch, New York, 57-60; instr med, Seton Hall Col Med & Dent, 60-64; asst dir vitamin metab, Dept Med Res, Roosevelt Hosp, New York, 64-66; assoc prof, 66-79, PROF MED, COL MED & DENT NJ, NEWARK, 79- Concurrent Pos: Assoc, Haskins Labs, New York, 56-69. Mem: AAAS; Soc Protozool; Am Inst Biol Sci; Am Soc Clin Nutrit. Res: Development and application to clinical medicine of techniques; demonstrating metabolic disorders, drug effects, nutrition, medicine, dietetics and vitamin metabolism. Mailing Add: 77 Sussex Rd Tenafly NJ 07670

FRANK, PETER WOLFGANG, b Mainz, Ger, Sept 24, 23; nat US; m 46; c 3. ECOLOGY. Educ: Earlham Col, AB, 44; Univ Chicago, PhD, 51. Prof Exp: Seessel fel, Yale Univ, 51-52; asst prof zool, Univ Mo, 52-57; assoc prof, 57-64, PROF BIOL, UNIV ORE, 64- Concurrent Pos: Zool ed, Ecology, 64-70; prog dir gen community ecology, NSF, 76-77; assoc ed, Ann Ref Ecol Syst, 70- Mem: Ecol Soc Am. Res: Population, marine and experimental ecology. Mailing Add: Dept of Biol Univ of Ore Eugene OR 97403

FRANK, RICHARD ERNST, b Stuttgart, Ger, Oct 7, 00; nat US; m 57. ANALYTICAL CHEMISTRY. Educ: Tech Hochsch, Stuttgart, Ger, BS, 21; Univ Freiburg, PhD(chem), 25. Prof Exp: Chemist, Degussa, 25-38 & Harnischfeger Corp, Wis, 39-48; from asst prof to assoc prof, 48-68, assoc dir, Inst Ecol Studies, 71-81, EMER ASSOC PROF CHEM, UNIV NDAK, 68- Concurrent Pos: Mem, NDak Adv Coun Air Pollution Control, 71-80. Mem: Am Chem Soc. Res: Food industry waste recycling; air pollution control; improved teaching of qualitative analysis. Mailing Add: 1020 Boyd Dr Grand Forks ND 58201

FRANK, RICHARD STEPHEN, b Teaneck, NJ, Sept 7, 40; m 64; c 2. FORENSIC SCIENCE, SCIENCE ADMINISTRATION. Educ: Washington Col, BS, 62. Prof Exp: High sch teacher chem, physics & gen sci, Chestertown, Md, 62-63; chemist, US Food & Drug Admin, 63-68; forensic chemist, Bur Narcotics & Dangerous Drugs Admin, 68-70; sect chief forensic drug chem, 70-74; actg chief, 74-77, CHIEF FORENSIC SCI DIV, DRUG ENFORCEMENT ADMIN, 77- Concurrent Pos: Mem comt revise const, Asn Official Anal Chemists, 74-; mem, Crime Lab Info Syst Oper Comt & Criminalistics Cert Study Group. Honors & Awards: Excellence in Performance, Drug Enforcement Admin, 73. Mem: Fel Am Acad Forensic Sci; Am Soc Crime Lab Dirs (secy, 80-81); Asn Official Anal Chemists. Res: Planning laboratories; standardization of forensic drug analyses; proficiency testing. Mailing Add: Drug Enforcement Admin Forensic Sci Div Washington DC 20537

FRANK, ROBERT CARL, b Adams, Wis, Aug 12, 27; m 51; c 3. SOLID STATE SCIENCE. Educ: St Olaf Col, BA, 50; Wayne State Univ, MA, 52, PhD(physics), 59. Prof Exp: Asst, Eng Res Inst, Univ Mich, 52-54; sr res physicist, Res Labs, Gen Motors Corp, 54-64; PROF PHYSICS, AUGUSTANA COL, ILL, 64-, DIR RES, AUGUSTANA RES FOUND, 73- Mem: Am Asn Physics Teachers; Am Phys Soc; Soc Res Adminr; Sigma Xi. Res: Diffusion and trapping of small atoms in solids; internal friction in metals. Mailing Add: Dept of Physics Augustana Col Rock Island IL 61201

FRANK, ROBERT LOEFFLER, b Milwaukee, Wis, Mar 15, 14; m 43; c 2. NUTRITION. Educ: Dartmouth Col, AB, 36; Univ Wis, MA, 38, PhD(org chem), 40. Prof Exp: Asst chem, Univ Wis, 39-40; du Pont asst, Univ Ill, 40-41, instr org chem, 41-42, assoc, 43-45, asst prof, 45-50; dir res, Edwal Labs, Inc, 50-53 & Ringwood Chem Corp, 53-54; vpres, Morton Int, Inc, 55-71, vpres, Morton-Norwich Prod, Inc, 71-76; CONSULT, 76- Concurrent Pos: Vpres, Ringwood Chem Corp, 54-57. Mem: Am Chem Soc. Res: Synthetic organic chemistry; polymer and synthetic rubber chemistry; salt technology; sodium and potassium metabolism. Mailing Add: 700 Lake Shore Dr RR 1 Box 1158 Lake Geneva WI 53147

FRANK, ROBERT MCKINLEY, b Newark, NJ, July 29, 32; m 64; c 2. SILVICULTURE, FOREST MANAGEMENT. Educ: Pa State Univ, BS, 54, MF, 56. Prof Exp: Res forester surv, 57-61, res forester mine spoil reclamation, 61-63, RES FORESTER SPRUCE-FIR SILVICULT, FOREST SERV, USDA, 63- Concurrent Pos: Fac assoc, Univ Maine, 72- Honors & Awards: Meritorious Performance Award, USDA, 63. Mem: Soc Am Foresters. Res: Silviculture and forest management research in northeastern spruce-balsam fir forest types. Mailing Add: USDA Bldg Univ of Maine Orono ME 04469

FRANK, ROBERT MORRIS, b New York, NY, Feb 2, 20; m; c 2. THEORETICAL PHYSICS, DATA PROCESSING. Educ: Cornell Univ, PhD(theoret physics), 51. Prof Exp: Asst prof theoret physics, Fla State Univ, 50-53; mem staff, Los Alamos Sci Lab, Univ Calif, 53-64; assoc, E H Plesset Assocs, Inc, Calif, 62-68; MEM STAFF, LOS ALAMOS SCI LAB, 68- Mem: Am Phys Soc; Asn Comput Mach. Res: Logical design of computing machines. Mailing Add: 155 Monte Rey Dr S White Rock NM 87544

FRANK, SAMUEL B, b Cleveland, Ohio, Sept 7, 09; m 34; c 2. DERMATOLOGY. Educ: Western Reserve Univ, 30, MD, 33; Am Bd Dermat, cert, 40. Prof Exp: Fel, Postgrad Med Sch, Columbia Univ & New York Skin & Cancer Hosp, 35-38, attend physician dermat, 36-38, jr asst, 38-41, asst attend dermatologist, 41-47; instr, 46-48, from asst clin prof to assoc clin prof, 48-63, chief serv, Skin & Cancer Unit, Sch Med, 63-75, chief acne sect, 68-75, PROF CLIN DERMAT, POSTGRAD HOSP, NY UNIV, 63- Concurrent Pos: From asst attend dermatologist to attend dermatologist, White Plains Hosp, 46-71, vis attend dermatologist, 71-; assoc attend dermatologist, Postgrad Med Sch, Columbia Univ & New York Skin & Cancer Hosp, 47-58; attend dermatologist, NY Univ Hosp, 58-; consult, Blythedale Hosp, Valhalla, NY, 47-, Hawthorne Cedar Knolls Sch, 49-, Pleasantville Cottage Sch, 50-, Dobbs Ferry Hosp, 52-, Hillcrest Ctr, Bedford, 58-75 & High Point Hosp, Port Chester, 58-; mem task forces, Nat Prog Dermat, 70-76; trustee, Westchester Health Care Found, 72-79. Mem: Int Soc Trop Dermat (treas, 70-74, secy, 74, exec vpres, 74-79); fel Am Col Physicians. Res: Acne vulgaris. Mailing Add: 3634 Seventh Ave 2D San Diego CA 92103

FRANK, SIDNEY RAYMOND, b Minneapolis, Minn, Mar 16, 19; m 50; c 1. METEOROLOGY. Educ: Univ Minn, BA, 40; Univ Calif, Los Angeles, MA, 41. Prof Exp: Lab asst, Univ Calif, Los Angeles, 41; forecaster, Trans World Airline, Calif, 41-45; res & instr meteorol, Trans World Airline, Kansas City, Mo, 45-52; proj dir, Aerophys Res Found, Calif, 52-56; vpres, Aerometric Res, Inc, 56-68, pres, Aerometric Res Found, 60-68, PRES, SIDNEY R FRANK GROUP & SRF RES INST, 68- Concurrent Pos: Ed, J Aeronaut Meteorol, 45-47; lectr, Univ Kansas City, 49; vpres, NAm Weather Consult, 56-68; pres & dir, Aerometric Res Found, 56-68; assoc ed, J Appl Meteorol, Am Meteorol Soc, 62-67; mem tech rev comt, USPHS, 63-65; lectr & res assoc, Univ Calif, Riverside, 60-65 & Univ Calif, Santa Barbara, 65-; trustee, Santa Barbara Community Col Dist, 65-, pres bd, 71-73; meteorol coordr air pollution control inst, Univ Southern Calif, 67-70. Honors & Awards: Air Transp Asn Awards, 43-49. Mem: AAAS; Air Pollution Control Asn; Am Meteorol Soc; Solar Energy Soc; Am Geophys Union. Res: Meso-scale, transport and diffusion; turbulence, synoptic meteorology and air pollution studies; meteorological aspects of air quality in environmental studies; forensic meterology. Mailing Add: Sidney R Frank Group 444 David Love Pl Goleta CA 93117

FRANK, SIMON, b Orange, NJ, 1921; m 45; c 2. INDUSTRIAL CHEMISTRY. Educ: Drew Univ, AB, 43; Univ Mich, PhD(chem), 50. Prof Exp: From chemist to sr res chemist, 50-60, group leader, 60-67, mgr tech info serv, 67-72, proj leader oil field chem, Stamford Res Lab, 72-76, proj coordr enhanced oil recovery, 76-80, MGR, ENHANCED OIL RECOVERY DEPT & TECH SERV, INDUST PROD DIV, AM CYANAMID CO, 81- Mem: Am Chem Soc; Soc Petrol Engrs. Mailing Add: 34 Hazelwood Lane Stamford CT 06905

FRANK, STANLEY, b New York, NY, Apr 21, 26; m 60. MATHEMATICS EDUCATION. Educ: City Col New York, BS, 50, MA, 53; Univ Fla, PhD(math), 60. Prof Exp: Teacher pub sch, NY, 50-53; teacher math & philos & logic, St John's Col, Fla, 60-61; asst prof math & dir math testing, Univ South Fla, 61-62; systs analyst, Mitre Corp, Mass, 62-64; sr statistician, Dynamics Res, 64-65; systs analyst, Gen Elec Co, 65-67; res dir, Booz-Allen Appl Res, 67-68; proj mgr, TRW Systs, 68-70; PRES & RES DIR, TANGLEWYLDE RES INST, 70; DIR, MATH & MED LEARNING LAB, SANTA FE JR COL, GAINESVILLE, 71- Concurrent Pos: Dir, Div Human Resources, North Fla Conserv Coalition, 81- Mem: Am Statist Asn; Math Asn Am; Opers Res Soc Am; Int Blind Writers Educ Asn. Res: Medical science; navigation; information storage and retrieval; reliability; logic;

autoregressive analysis; management information systems and design of military weapon systems; training of medical personnel; conservation; learning theory; disabilities in reading and quantitative skills. *Mailing Add:* Tanglewylde Res Inst Rte 2 Box 1240 Palatka FL 32077

FRANK, STEVEN NEIL, b Red Oak, Iowa, Feb 15, 47; m 75. ELECTROCHEMISTRY. *Educ:* Colo State Univ, BS, 69; Calif Inst Technol, PhD(electrochem), 74. *Prof Exp:* Assoc electrochem, Calif Inst Technol, 73-74; fel electrochem, Univ Tex, Austin, 74-77; mem tech staff electrochem, 77-80, SR MEM TECH STAFF ELECTROCHEM, TEX INSTRUMENTS INC, 80- *Concurrent Pos:* Robert A Welch fel, Univ Tex, Austin, 74-77. *Mem:* Am Chem Soc; Electrochem Soc. *Res:* Batteries; fuel cells; electrode kinetics; adsorption at electrode surfaces; interfacial phenomena. *Mailing Add:* Cent Res Lab M/S 158 PO Box 225936 Dallas TX 75265

FRANK, SYLVAN GERALD, b San Antonio, Tex, Aug 30, 39; m 64; c 3. SURFACE CHEMISTRY, PHARMACEUTICS. *Educ:* Columbia Univ, BS, 62; Univ Mich, MS, 66, PhD(pharmaceut chem), 68. *Prof Exp:* Asst prof pharm, Duquesne Univ, 68-70; asst prof, 70-73, ASSOC PROF PHARM, OHIO STATE UNIV, 73- *Concurrent Pos:* Vis prof, Swedish Inst Surface Chem, Stockholm, 78-79 78-79. *Honors & Awards:* Award, Mead-Johnson Labs, 69. *Mem:* Am Pharmaceut Asn; Am Heart Asn; Acad Pharmaceut Sci; Int Asn Colloid & Surface Scientists; Sigma Xi. *Res:* Micellar solubilization; emulsions; liquid crystals; application of surface chemistry to biological and pharmaceutical systems; inclusion compounds. *Mailing Add:* Ohio State Univ Col of Pharm 500 W 12th Ave Columbus OH 43210

FRANK, THOMAS STOLLEY, b Milwaukee, Wis, June 26, 31; m 52; c 2. MATHEMATICS, COMPUTER SCIENCE. *Educ:* Lawrence Col, BA, 55; Syracuse Univ, MA, 57, PhD(math), 62. *Prof Exp:* Instr math, Syracuse Univ, 60-62; from asst prof to prof math, 62-77, PROF COMPUT SCI, LE MOYNE COL, NY, 77- *Mem:* Math Asn Am. *Res:* Operating systems. *Mailing Add:* Dept of Comput Sci Le Moyne Col Syracuse NY 13214

FRANK, ULRICH ANTON, b Frankfurt, Ger, June 29, 22; US citizen; m 42; c 3. BIOMEDICAL & MECHANICAL ENGINEERING. *Educ:* Univ NH, BS, 48, BS & MS, 49. *Prof Exp:* Res scientist propulsion, Nat Adv Comt Aeronaut, Cleveland, 48-51; asst chief engr aircraft, Kaiser Metal Prod, Kaiser Indust, 51-58; proj engr radar & nuclear, RCA, Morristown, NJ, 58-68; SR MEM TECH STAFF, ROCHE MED ELECTRONICS INC, HOFFMANN-LA ROCHE, CRANBURY, 68- *Concurrent Pos:* Consult, Pa State Univ, 70-72 & Educ Testing Serv, 71-74. *Honors & Awards:* David Sarnoff Award, RCA, 67. *Mem:* Inst Elec & Electronics Engrs; Soc Eng Med & Biol; Am Soc Cryobiol; Am Soc Mech Engrs; Asn Advan Med Instrumentation. *Res:* Medical sensors, monitoring and closed loop therapy. *Mailing Add:* 945 Stuart Rd Princeton NJ 08540

FRANK, VICTOR SAMUEL, b Hartford, Conn, June 18, 19; m 44; c 3. INDUSTRIAL ORGANIC CHEMISTRY, RESEARCH ADMINISTRATION. *Educ:* Mass Inst Technol, BS, 42, PhD(org chem), 48. *Prof Exp:* Chemist, Dewey & Almy Chem Co, 42-46; asst, Mass Inst Technol, 47-48; sr chemist, Merck & Co, Inc, 49-51; group leader org & polymer res, Dewey & Almy Chem Div, 51-54, res dir org chem, 54-62, dir polymer res, Res Div, 62-67, org & polymer res, 67-68, VPRES RES, RES DIV, W R GRACE & CO, 68- *Concurrent Pos:* Instr, Northeastern Univ, 52-62. *Mem:* Am Chem Soc; fel Am Inst Chemists. *Mailing Add:* W R Grace & Co Res Div 7379 Rte 32 Columbia MD 21044

FRANK, WILLIAM BENSON, b Youngstown, Ohio, July 12, 28. INDUSTRIAL CHEMISTRY, INFORMATION SCIENCE. *Educ:* Thiel Col, BS, 50. *Prof Exp:* Res engr, Phys Chem Div, 53-67, mgr tech info dept, 67-77, SCI ASSOC, PHYS CHEM DIV, ALCOA LABS, ALUMINUM CO AM, 77- *Mem:* AAAS; Am Chem Soc; Electrochem Soc; Am Inst Mining, Metall & Petrol Eng. *Res:* Extractive metallurgy of aluminum. *Mailing Add:* Phys Chem Div Alcoa Labs Alcoa Center PA 15069

FRANK, WILLIAM CHARLES, b Grand Rapids, Mich, Oct 10, 40; m 64; c 2. ORGANIC CHEMISTRY, PHOTOGRAPHIC CHEMISTRY. *Educ:* Valparaiso Univ, BS, 62; Univ Colo, Boulder, PhD(org chem), 65. *Prof Exp:* Sr chemist, Cent Res Lab, 3M Co, 65-66, sr emulsion chemist, Minn 3M Res Ltd, Eng, 66-67, 3M Italia-Ferrania SpA, Italy, 67-68, res specialist photog chem, Photo Prod Div Lab, 68-71, res & develop supvr, 71-73, PROD DEVELOP MGR, PHOTO PROD DIV LAB, 3M CO, 73- *Mem:* Am Chem Soc; Soc Photog Scientists & Engrs. *Res:* Photographic emulsion chemistry; photographic product development; radiographic imaging; phosphors. *Mailing Add:* 3M Co Photo Prod Div Lab 3M Ctr 209-1S St Paul MN 55101

FRANK, WILSON JAMES, b Kansas City, Mo, June 4, 23. PHYSICS. *Educ:* Univ Ill, BS, 48; Univ Calif, PhD(physics), 53. *Prof Exp:* PHYSICIST, LAWRENCE LIVERMORE LAB, UNIV CALIF, 51- *Mem:* Am Phys Soc; Sigma Xi. *Res:* Nuclear physics. *Mailing Add:* Lawrence Livermore Lab Univ of Calif PO Box 808 Livermore CA 94550

FRANKART, WILLIAM A, b Kansas City, Kans, Feb 25, 43. IMMUNOLOGY. *Educ:* Univ Calif, Davis, PhD(biochem), 73. *Prof Exp:* Fel, Fundacion Bariloche/Argentina, 74-75; SR RES BIOCHEMIST, HOLLISTER-STIER LABS, 77- *Mailing Add:* Hollister-Stier Labs PO Box 3145 Ter Annex Spokane WA 99220

FRANKE, CHARLES H, b Jersey City, NJ, Dec 28, 33; m 59; c 3. ALGEBRA. *Educ:* Rutgers Univ, AB, 55, PhD(math), 62; Yale Univ, MA, 56. *Prof Exp:* Instr math, Rutgers Univ, 58-62; mem tech staff, Bell Tel Labs, 62-66; PROF MATH, SETON HALL UNIV, 66-, CHMN DEPT, 71- *Mem:* Math Asn Am; Am Math Soc. *Res:* Galois theory of difference fields obtained by adjoining a fundamental system for a linear homogeneous difference equation to a ground field. *Mailing Add:* Dept of Math Seton Hall Univ Col Arts & Sci South Orange NJ 07079

FRANKE, DONALD EDWARD, b Center, Tex, May 6, 37; m 63; c 3. ANIMAL BREEDING, ANIMAL GENETICS. *Educ:* Stephen F Austin State Univ, BS, 61; La State Univ, MS, 65; Tex A&M Univ, PhD(animal breeding), 69. *Prof Exp:* Teacher voc agr, Little Cypress Sch Dist, Ind, 61-63; asst animal breeding, La State Univ & Tex A&M Univ, 63-69; from asst prof to assoc prof animal sci, Univ Fla, 68-76; PROF ANIMAL SCI, LA STATE UNIV, 76- *Mem:* Am Soc Animal Sci; Am Genetic Asn; Biomet Soc; Sigma Xi. *Res:* Breeding systems for beef production; estimation of genetic parameters associated with growth, reproduction, lactation and efficiencies in beef production; systems analyses for estimating efficiency of red meat production. *Mailing Add:* Animal Sci Dept La State Univ Baton Rouge LA 70803

FRANKE, ERNEST A, b Uvalde, Tex, Oct 22, 39; m 64. ELECTRICAL ENGINEERING. *Educ:* Tex A&I Univ, BS, 61; MS, 63; Case Western Reserve Univ, PhD(eng), 67. *Prof Exp:* From instr to assoc prof, Tex A&I Univ, 62-70, chmn dept, 69-71, prof eng, 70-79, dean, sch eng, 71-79; VPRES RES & DEVELOP, ALPHA ELECTRONICS CO, 79- *Concurrent Pos:* Consult. *Mem:* Inst Elec & Electronics Engrs. *Res:* Computer applications; control systems. *Mailing Add:* Sch of Eng Tex A&I Univ Kingsville TX 78363

FRANKE, ERNST KARL, b Breslau, Ger, Feb 6, 11; nat US; m 47; c 3. BIOPHYSICS. *Educ:* Inst Tech, Breslau, Ger, Dipl Ing, 34; Inst Tech Berlin, Ger, Dr Ing(physics), 39. *Prof Exp:* Physicist, Telefunken Co, Ger, 34-37; asst physics, Inst Tech Berlin, 37-39; res physicist, Helmholtz Inst, 43-47 & Aero Med Lab, Air Develop Ctr, Wright-Patterson AFB, Ohio, 47-56; assoc prof biophys, 56-63, prof, 63-81, EMER PROF PHYSICS, UNIV CINCINNATI, 81- *Concurrent Pos:* Adj prof physics, Thomas More Col, 81- *Mem:* Biophys Soc. *Res:* Electrocardiography; mechanics of human body; viscoelastic properties of muscle tissue; bioacoustics; ballistocardiography. *Mailing Add:* Dept of Physics Univ of Cincinnati Cincinnati OH 45221

FRANKE, FREDERICK RAHDE, b Pittsburgh, Pa, Oct 14, 18; m 43; c 5. MEDICINE. *Educ:* Univ Pittsburgh, BS, 41, MD, 43; Univ Pa, MSc, 50, DSc(med), 52; Am Bd Internal Med, dipl, 50; Am Bd Cardiovasc Dis, dipl, 62. *Prof Exp:* Instr physiol & pharmacol, 48-49, res assoc appl physiol, 49-53, physician in chg therapeut sect, 53-55, ASST PROF MED, MED SCH, UNIV PITTSBURGH, 55-, CLIN PROF PHARMACOL, SCH PHARM, 67- *Concurrent Pos:* Spec fel cardiol & genetics, Johns Hopkins Hosp, 59-60; chief div med, Western Pa Hosp, Pittsburgh, 63-67, chmn dept cardiovasc dis, 66-, med dir, 67-73. *Mem:* Fel Am Col Physicians; Soc Exp Biol & Med; Am Therapeut Soc; Am Heart Asn. *Res:* Cardiovascular diseases; physiologic and pharmacologic research in clinical diseases. *Mailing Add:* Western Pa Hosp 4800 Friendship Ave Pittsburgh PA 15224

FRANKE, JOHN ERWIN, b Belgrade, Minn, Mar 1, 46; m 68. GLOBAL ANALYSIS. *Educ:* Luther Col, Iowa, BA, 68; Northwestern Univ, MS, 71, PhD(math), 73. *Prof Exp:* PROF MATH, NC STATE UNIV, 73- *Concurrent Pos:* Consult, Res Triangle Inst. *Mem:* Am Math Soc; Math Asn Am. *Res:* Global analysis; stability and singularity theory; biomathematics. *Mailing Add:* Dept of Math NC State Univ Raleigh NC 27650

FRANKE, MILTON EUGENE, b Springfield, Ill, Apr 7, 31; m 55; c 2. MECHANICAL ENGINEERING, AERONAUTICS. *Educ:* Univ Fla, BME, 52; Univ Minn, MSME, 54; Ohio State Univ, PhD(mech eng), 67. *Prof Exp:* Engr, Westinghouse Elec Corp, 52; proj engr, US Air Force Wright Air Develop Ctr, 54-56, sr proj engr, 56-57; res engr, E I du Pont de Nemours & Co, 57-59; from asst prof to assoc prof, 59-70, PROF, US AIR FORCE INST TECHNOL, 70- *Concurrent Pos:* Assoc ed, J Dynamic Systs, Measurement & Control, Am Soc Mech Engrs, 79. *Mem:* Am Soc Mech Engrs; Am Soc Eng Educ; Am Inst Aeronaut & Astronaut. *Res:* Acoustics; heat transfer; fluid mechanics; fluidics; gas dynamics; propulsion; effects of electrostatic fields on heat transfer; fuels and lubricants; fuel systems; aerodynamics; dynamic systems; fluid control; hydraulics. *Mailing Add:* Dept of Aeronaut & Astronaut Air Force Inst of Technol Wright-Patterson AFB OH 45433

FRANKE, NORMAN HENRY, pharmacy, deceased

FRANKE, ROBERT G, b Muskegon, Mich, June 27, 33; m 57; c 3. BOTANY. *Educ:* Northern Ill Univ, BS, 56; Northwestern Univ, MS, 61; Univ Tex, PhD(bot), 65. *Prof Exp:* From instr to asst prof natural sci, Mich State Univ, 64-68; assoc prof, 68-73, prof bot & plant path, Iowa State Univ, 73-77; PROF BIOL & HEAD DEPT, UNIV TENN, CHATTANOOGA, 77- *Mem:* Am Inst Biol Sci; Mycol Soc Am; Brit Mycol Soc. *Res:* Taxonomy and natural relationship of Myxomycetes, as disclosed with serological, electrophoretic, and related techniques; ecology of fungi. *Mailing Add:* Dept of Biol Univ of Tenn Chattanooga TN 37402

FRANKEL, ARTHUR IRVING, b Baltimore, Md, Oct 25, 18; m 42; c 2. TESTICULAR REGULATION, MALE SEX BEHAVIOR. *Educ:* Oberlin Col, Ohio, BA, 40; Univ Mo, MA, 41; Univ Ill, PhD(zool), 66. *Prof Exp:* NIH fel endocrinol, Univ Ill, 65-66; NIH fel biochem, Sch Med, Univ Utah, 66-68; from asst prof to assoc prof, 68-81, PROF ENDOCRINOL, STATE UNIV NY, BINGHAMTON, 81- *Concurrent Pos:* Consult, Biochem Endocrinol Study Sect, NIH, 77-81; NIH prin investr, Nat Inst Aging & Nat Inst Child Health & Human Develop, 69- *Mem:* Endocrine Soc; Soc Study Reproduction; Soc Study Fertil. *Res:* Study of the male animal, specializing in regulation of the testis and prostate; androgen receptors; male sex behavior. *Mailing Add:* Dept Biol Sci State Univ NY Binghamton NY 13901

FRANKEL, EDWIN N, b Alexandria, Egypt, July 3, 28; US citizen; m 50; c 5. BIOCHEMISTRY, ORGANIC CHEMISTRY. *Educ:* Mich State Univ, BS, 50; Univ Calif, Davis, MS, 52, PhD(agr chem), 56. *Prof Exp:* Jr specialist dairy chem, Univ Calif, Davis, 53-56; chemist, Northern Regional Res Lab, USDA, Ill, 56-61; group leader food div, Procter & Gamble Co, Ohio, 61-62; RES LEADER, NORTHERN REGIONAL RES CTR, USDA, 62- *Concurrent Pos:* Res fel, Israel Inst Technol, 66-67; assoc ed, Lipids, Am Oil Chemists' Soc, 66-80; sr vis res fel, Queen Mary Col, Univ London, Eng,

75-76. *Honors & Awards:* Superior Serv Award, USDA, 78. *Mem:* Am Oil Chemists' Soc; Am Chem Soc. *Res:* Lipid chemistry; autoxidation and hydrogenation of lipids; homogeneous catalysis and organometallic chemistry. *Mailing Add:* Northern Regional Res Ctr 1815 N University Peoria IL 61604

FRANKEL, FRED HAROLD, b Benoni, SAfrica, Mar 23, 24; US citizen; m 47; c 3. PSYCHIATRY. *Educ:* Univ Witwatersrand, MB, ChB, 48, dipl psychol med, 52; Am Bd Psychiat & Neurol, dipl, 66. *Prof Exp:* Intern surg & med, Johannesburg Gen Hosp, SAfrica, 48-49; resident psychiat, Tara Hosp Nerv Dis, Johannesburg, 50-52; resident psychiat, Mass Gen Hosp, Boston, 52-53; assoc psychiatrist, 68-69, PSYCHIATRIST, BETH ISRAEL HOSP, BOSTON, 69-; ASST PSYCHIATRIST, MASS GEN HOSP, 63-; assoc prof, 76-81, PROF PSYCHIAT, HARVARD MED SCH, 81- *Concurrent Pos:* Consult social serv dept, Transvaal & Orange Free State Chamber of Mines, 54-60; from second asst neuropsychiatrist to asst, Med Sch, Univ Witwatersrand & Johannesburg Gen Hosp, 54-62; hon psychiatrist, Witwatersrand Jewish Aged Home, 59-62; instr psychiat, Harvard Med Sch, 63-68, clin assoc, 68-69, asst prof psychiat, 69-76; asst to comn, Dept Ment Health, Mass, 65-68; consult psychiat, Mass Gen Hosp, 78; med ed, Int J Clin & Exp Hypn, 78- *Mem:* Fel Am Psychiat Asn; fel Royal Soc Med; fel Soc Clin & Exp Hypnosis; fel Am Col Psychiat; Int Soc Hypn (pres, 80-82). *Res:* Psychiatric education; psychosomatic medicine; hypnosis; electroconvulsive therapy. *Mailing Add:* Beth Israel Hosp 330 Brookline Ave Boston MA 02215

FRANKEL, FRED ROBERT, b Baltimore, Md, July 6, 34. MOLECULAR BIOLOGY. *Educ:* Pa State Univ, BS, 55, MS, 57; Univ Fla, PhD, 60. *Prof Exp:* Res assoc, Genetics Res Unit, Carnegie Inst, 60-63; asst prof, 63-69, assoc prof, 69-76, PROF MICROBIOL, SCH MED, UNIV PA, 76- *Mem:* Am Soc Biol Chem; Am Soc Microbiol. *Res:* Action of steroid hormones in target cell nuclei; role of cytoskeleton in cell structure and movement; mechanism of phagocytosis. *Mailing Add:* Dept of Microbiol Sch of Med Univ of Pa Philadelphia PA 19104

FRANKEL, HARRY MEYER, b Baltimore, Md, Oct 11, 27; m 51; c 2. PHYSIOLOGY. *Educ:* Univ Md, BS, 49; Univ Iowa, PhD(physiol), 58. *Prof Exp:* Physiologist, Med Labs, Chem Warfare Lab, Md, 51-55; asst radiation res lab, Univ Iowa, 55-56; physiologist, Chem Warfare Lab, Army Chem Ctr, 58-60; from asst prof to assoc prof, 60-70, chmn dept, 73-79, PROF PHYSIOL, RUTGERS UNIV, NEW BRUNSWICK, 70- *Mem:* AAAS; Am Physiol Soc; Harvey Soc; Soc Exp Biol & Med. *Res:* Environmental and respiratory physiology; comparative pharmacology. *Mailing Add:* Dept of Physiol Rutgers Univ New Brunswick NJ 08903

FRANKEL, HENRY E, physical metallurgy, materials engineering, see previous edition

FRANKEL, HERBERT, b Harrison, NJ, Feb 12, 14; m 41; c 2. ELECTRICAL ENGINEERING. *Educ:* State Univ NY, BA, 40; Washington Univ, St Louis, BS, 47; Rensselaer Polytech Inst, MEE, 53. *Prof Exp:* Engr, DeLaval Separator Co, NY, 47-48; assoc prof elec eng, Rensselaer Polytech Inst, 48-80; SR ENGR, BENDIX FIELD ENG CORP, 80- *Concurrent Pos:* Consult, Watervliet Arsenal, NY, 56- *Mem:* Inst Elec & Electronics Engrs. *Res:* Circuit theory; nondestructive testing of metals. *Mailing Add:* 9250 Rt 108 Space Flight Ctr Bendix Field Eng Corp Columbia MD 21045

FRANKEL, IRWIN, b New Orleans, La, Nov 25, 19; m 45; c 2. CHEMICAL ENGINEERING. *Educ:* Tulane Univ, BChE, 42; Case Inst Technol, MS, 48; Rensselaer Polytech Inst, DChE, 51. *Prof Exp:* Res engr petrochem & gasoline volatility spex, Beacon Res Labs, Texaco, Inc, 47-49; proj leader develop eng fine chem, Chem Div, Corn Prod Co, 51-55; sr engr, Res & Develop Dept, Crown Cork & Seal Co, 55-57; chief technologist, Energy Div, Olin Mathieson Chem Corp, 57-59, mgr liquid fuels develop, 59-60; group leader eng develop org chem, Nat Aniline Div, Allied Chem Corp, 60-65, res supvr, 65-66, proj mgr indust chem div, NJ, 66-69, mgr pilot plants, Fibers Div, Va, 69-70 & opers serv, 70-73; chem engr consult, Versar Inc, 74-78; chem engr consult, Mitre Corp, 78-82; SR ENGR, US SYNTHETIC FUELS CORP, 82- *Concurrent Pos:* Mem, Govt Progs Screening Comt, Am Inst Chem Engrs, 78-81. *Mem:* Am Chem Soc; fel Am Inst Chem Engrs. *Res:* Process development; semiplant production; production. *Mailing Add:* Mitre Corp Metrex Div 1820 Dolly Madison Blvd McLean VA 22120

FRANKEL, JACK WILLIAM, b New York, NY, Feb 15, 25; m 48; c 3. VIROLOGY. *Educ:* Brown Univ, BA, 48; Rutgers Univ, PhD, 51; Am Bd Med Microbiol, dipl. *Prof Exp:* Res fel virol, Pub Health Res Inst, Inc, NY, 51-53; res assoc, Sharp & Dohme Div, Merck & Co, 53-58, res assoc dept microbiol, Sch Med, Temple Univ, 58-59; chief virus diag lab, Dept Res Therapeut, Norristown State Hosp, Pa, 59-61; head virus res, Ciba-Geigy Pharmaceut Co, 61-68; dep dir & dir virus res lab, Life Sci Res Labs, 68-76; ASSOC PROF MED MICROBIOL, COL MED, UNIV S FLA, 76- SCI RES LABS, 68- *Concurrent Pos:* Prof, Hunter Col, 61-68; prof, Drew Univ, 63-68; clin prof med microbiol, Col Med, Univ SFla, 72-76; prof, St Petersburg Col, 74-75. *Mem:* Am Soc Microbiol; Teratology Soc; AAAS; Am Asn Cancer Res; Soc Exp Biol Med. *Res:* Virol oncology. *Mailing Add:* Univ of Fla Col of Med 12901 N 30th St Tampa FL 33612

FRANKEL, JOSEPH, b Vienna, Austria, July 30, 35; US citizen; m 61. DEVELOPMENTAL GENETICS. *Educ:* Cornell Univ, BA, 56; Yale Univ, PhD(zool), 60. *Prof Exp:* NIH fel cell biol, Biol Inst Carlsberg Found, Denmark, 60-62; asst prof, 62-65, assoc prof, 65-71, PROF ZOOL, UNIV IOWA, 71- *Concurrent Pos:* NIH res grants, 63-69, 74-80 & 81-83; NSF res grants, 72-74 & 80-81. *Mem:* Am Soc Zool; Soc Protozool; Genetics Soc Am; Soc Develop Biol. *Res:* Development in ciliated protozoa; pattern formation. *Mailing Add:* Dept of Zool Univ of Iowa Iowa City IA 52242

FRANKEL, JULIUS, b Cernauti, Romania, Dec 10, 35; m 70; c 1. SOLID STATE PHYSICS, ULTRASONICS. *Educ:* Brooklyn Col, BS, 58; Rensselaer Polytech Inst, MS, 65. *Prof Exp:* Res asst physics, NY Univ, 58; grad teaching asst physics, Rensselaer Polytech Inst, 58-60; PHYSICIST PHYSICS & MATH, WATERVLIET ARSENAL, 60- *Concurrent Pos:* Guest scientist, Max Planck Inst-Festkoerper Forschung, Stuttgart, 82. *Honors & Awards:* Siple Award. *Mem:* Am Phys Soc. *Res:* High pressure; equation of state; ultrasonics. *Mailing Add:* Van Leuven Dr S Defreestville Troy NY 12180

FRANKEL, LARRY, b New York, NY, July 8, 28; m 50; c 2. INVERTEBRATE PALEONTOLOGY. *Educ:* Brooklyn Col, BSc, 50; Columbia Univ, AM, 52; Univ Nebr, PhD(geol), 56. *Prof Exp:* Asst, Univ Nebr, 52-54; geologist, US AEC, 54-55; from instr to prof geol, 59-77, PROF GEOL & GEOPHYS, UNIV CONN, 77- *Mem:* Geol Soc Am; Am Asn Petrol Geologists. *Res:* Pleistocene Mollusca and geology; foraminifera, estuarine studies. *Mailing Add:* Dept of Geol Univ of Conn Storrs CT 06268

FRANKEL, LAWRENCE (STEPHEN), b New York, NY, July 26, 41; m 64; c 1. PHYSICAL CHEMISTRY, ANALYTICAL CHEMISTRY. *Educ:* Hofstra Univ, BA, 63; Univ Mass, PhD(phys chem), 67. *Prof Exp:* GROUP LEADER PHYS ANAL CHEM, ROHM AND HAAS CO, 69- *Mem:* Am Chem Soc. *Res:* Transition metal chemistry; kinetics of fast reactions; thermal and spectroscopic characterization of polymers; ion exchange resins and adsorbents; analytical aspects of pollution problems; elastomers. *Mailing Add:* 1110 Delene Rd Jenkintown PA 19046

FRANKEL, MICHAEL JAY, b New York, NY, Feb 20, 47; m 69; c 4. THEORETICAL SOLID STATE PHYSICS, SHOCK WAVE PHYSICS. *Educ:* Yeshiva Univ, BA, 68, MA, 70; NY Univ, PhD(physics), 75. *Prof Exp:* Assoc res scientist theoretical condensed matter physics, City Col, City Univ NY, 75; analyst satellite telemetry, Syst Sci Div, Comput Sci Corp, 75-77; res physicist explosive physics, Energetic Mat Div, Naval Surface Weapons Ctr, US Dept Navy, 77-81; PHYSICIST, SHOCK PHYSICS DIV, US DEFENSE NUCLEAR AGENCY, 81- *Concurrent Pos:* NSF int travel grant & NATO fel, 73, NSF traineeship, NY Univ, 71-74; assoc res scientist & fel, City Univ New York, 75. *Mem:* Am Phys Soc. *Res:* Theory of spatial dispersion and optical properties of solids; radiation and charged particle interaction with matter; experimental and theoretical physics of explosive detonations and shock waves. *Mailing Add:* 11006 Wheeler Dr Silver Spring MD 20901

FRANKEL, RICHARD BARRY, b St Paul, Minn, June 24, 39; m 60; c 2. PHYSICS, CHEMISTRY. *Educ:* Univ Mo, BS, 61; Univ Calif, Berkeley, PhD(chem), 65. *Prof Exp:* Res asst, Lawrence Radiation Lab, Univ Calif, 62-65; res staff mem, 65-79, SR RES SCIENTIST, NAT MAGNET LAB, MASS INST TECHNOL, 79- *Concurrent Pos:* NATO fel, Munich Tech, 67-68. *Mem:* Fel Am Phys Soc; AAAS; Bioelectromagnetic Soc; Explorers Club. *Res:* Mossbauer spectroscopy; magnetic properties of solids; electronic structure of metalloproteins; magnetism in organisms. *Mailing Add:* Nat Magnet Lab Bldg NW 14 Mass Inst of Technol Cambridge MA 02139

FRANKEL, SHERMAN, b USA, Nov 15, 22; div; c 1. HIGH ENERGY PHYSICS. *Educ:* Brooklyn Col, BA, 43; Univ Ill, MS, 47, PhD(physics), 49. *Prof Exp:* Mem staff, Radiation Lab, Mass Inst Technol, 43-46; from asst prof to assoc prof physics, 52-60, PROF PHYSICS, UNIV PA, 60- *Concurrent Pos:* Guggenheim fel, 56-57 & 78-79. *Mem:* Fel Am Phys Soc. *Res:* Elementary particle and nuclear physics. *Mailing Add:* Dept of Physics Univ of Pa Philadelphia PA 19104

FRANKEL, SIDNEY, b New York, NY, Oct 6, 10; m 38; c 1. ELECTRONICS. *Educ:* Rensselaer Polytech Inst, EE, 31, MS, 34, PhD(math), 36. *Prof Exp:* Instr math, Rensselaer Polytech Inst, 31-33; jr engr, Eclipse Aviation Corp, 37-38; engr radio transmitter & head dept, Fed Telecommunications Labs, 38-50; assoc head, Microwave Lab, Hughes Aircraft Co, 50-54; head radar & countermeasures dept, Litton Industs, Inc, 54-58; dir eng, Sierra Div, Philco Corp, 58-60; tech consul & mgr, Sidney Frankel & Assocs, 60-78; ASST PROF ELEC ENG, SAN JOSE STATE UNIV, 79- *Mem:* Fel Inst Elec & Electronics Engrs; Sigma Xi. *Res:* Theory of multiconductor transmission lines and cables. *Mailing Add:* 1165 Saxon Way Menlo Park CA 94025

FRANKEL, THEODORE THOMAS, b Philadelphia, Pa, June 17, 29; m 55; c 3. MATHEMATICS. *Educ:* Univ Calif, AB, 50, PhD, 55. *Prof Exp:* From instr to asst prof math, Stanford Univ, 55-62; assoc prof, Brown Univ, 62-65; PROF MATH, UNIV CALIF, SAN DIEGO, 65- *Concurrent Pos:* Mem, Inst Advan Study, 57-59. *Mem:* Am Math Soc. *Res:* Differential geometry; Morse theory; general relativity. *Mailing Add:* Dept of Math Univ of Calif at San Diego La Jolla CA 92093

FRANKEL, VICTOR H, b Wilmington, Del, May 14, 25; m 58; c 5. ORTHOPEDIC SURGERY, BIOENGINEERING. *Educ:* Swarthmore Col, BA, 46; Univ Pa, MD, 51; Univ Uppsala, DrMed(orthop surg), 60. *Prof Exp:* Attend orthop surgeon, Hosp Joint Dis, New York, 60-66; assoc prof orthop surg, Case Western Reserve Univ, 66-69, prof orthop surg & bioeng, 69-76; PROF & CHMN DEPT ORTHOP SURG, UNIV WASH, SEATTLE, 76- *Concurrent Pos:* Fel, Nelson Nat Found, 58-60; mem comt prosthetics res & develop, Nat Acad Sci, 70- *Mem:* Am Orthop Asn; Asn Bone & Joint Surg; Am Col Surg; Am Soc Test & Mat; Int Soc Orthop Surg & Traumatol. *Res:* Application of engineering techniques to orthopedic surgery; development of biomechanics teaching. *Mailing Add:* Dept of Orthop Surg Univ of Wash Med Sch Seattle WA 98195

FRANKEN, PETER ALDEN, b New York, NY, Nov 10, 28; div; c 3. OPTICAL PHYSICS, QUANTUM OPTICS. *Educ:* Columbia Univ, BA, 48, MA, 50, PhD(physics), 52. *Prof Exp:* Lectr math, Columbia Univ, 48-49, asst physics, 50-52; instr, Stanford Univ, 52-56; from asst prof to prof, Univ Mich, Ann Arbor, 56-73; DIR OPTICAL SCI CTR, UNIV ARIZ, 73-, PROF OPTICAL SCI & PHYSICS, 73- *Concurrent Pos:* Dep dir, Advan Res Projs

Agency, US Dept Defense, Washington, DC, 67-68. *Honors & Awards:* Prize, Am Phys Soc, 67; Wood Prize, Optical Soc Am, 79. *Mem:* Fel Am Phys Soc; fel Optical Soc Am (pres, 77); fel AAAS; Int Soc Optical Eng; Radiol Soc NAm. *Res:* Experimental atomic and electron physics and imaging technology. *Mailing Add:* Optical Sci Ctr Univ of Ariz Tucson AZ 85721

FRANKENBERG, DIRK, b Woodsville, NH, Nov 25, 37; m 60. BIOLOGICAL OCEANOGRAPHY. *Educ:* Dartmouth Col, AB, 59; Emory Univ, MS, 60, PhD(biol), 62. *Prof Exp:* Asst prof zool, Marine Inst, Univ Ga, 62-66 & Univ Del, 66-67; from assoc prof to prof, Univ Ga, 67-74; PROF MARINE SCI & DIR MARINE SCI PROG, UNIV NC, CHAPEL HILL, 74-, CHMN DEPT, 74- *Concurrent Pos:* Dir, Biol Oceanog Prog, NSF, 70-71; dir, Div Ocean Sci, 78-80; mem ocean sci comt, Nat Acad Sci, 73. *Mem:* Ecol Soc Am; Am Inst Biol Sci; Am Soc Limnol & Oceanog. *Res:* Ecology of macro-benthos; oxygen phenomena in estuaries. *Mailing Add:* Dept of Marine Sci Univ of NC Chapel Hill NC 27514

FRANKENBERG, JULIAN MYRON, b Chicago, Ill, Jan 18, 38; m 62; c 1. PALEOBOTANY, PLANT MORPHOLOGY. *Educ:* Univ Ill, BS, 61, PhD(paleobot), 68; Univ Minn, MS, 63. *Prof Exp:* Lab asst, Paleobot Lab, Univ Ill, Urbana, 57-61; teaching asst, Univ Minn, 61-63; teaching asst bot & biol, 63-68, actg asst dean col lib arts & sci, 68, asst dean, 68-70, DIR & ASST DEAN HEALTH PROF INFO OFF, UNIV ILL, URBANA-CHAMPAIGN, 70- *Mem:* AAAS; Bot Soc Am; Am Inst Biol Sci; Asn Am Med Cols; Nat Asn Health Professions (pres, 80-82). *Res:* Study of petrified Stigmaria from North America; coal-ball flora of the Pennsylvania period. *Mailing Add:* Off Dean Students 610 E John St Univ of Ill Health Prof Info Off Champaign IL 61820

FRANKENBURG, PETER EDGAR, b Ludwigshafen on Rhine, Ger, Nov 10, 26; nat US; m 54; c 4. ORGANIC CHEMISTRY. *Educ:* Princeton Univ, AB, 49; Univ Rochester, PhD(org chem), 53. *Prof Exp:* RES ASSOC, E I DU PONT DE NEMOURS & CO, INC, 53- *Mem:* Am Chem Soc; Sigma Xi. *Res:* Polymers for textile use. *Mailing Add:* 2405 Shellpot Dr Wilmington DE 19803

FRANKENFELD, JOHN WILLIAM, b Mesa, Ariz, Oct 29, 32; m 59; c 2. ORGANIC CHEMISTRY. *Educ:* Univ Chicago, BA, 52, SM, 57; Mass Inst Technol, PhD(chem), 62. *Prof Exp:* Res chemist, 61-66, sr res chemist, 66-78, SR STAFF CHEMIST, EXXON RES & ENG CO, 78- *Mem:* Sigma Xi; Am Chem Soc. *Res:* Biological degradation of petroleum hydrocarbons; synthesis of peptides and peptide intermediates; synthetic foods and food additives; synthetic fuels; biological effects of oil pollution. *Mailing Add:* Exxon Res & Eng Co PO Box 8 Linden NJ 07036

FRANKENTHAL, ROBERT PETER, b Berlin, Ger, Sept 11, 30; nat US; m 58; c 1. ELECTROCHEMISTRY, CORROSION. *Educ:* Univ Rochester, BS, 52; Univ Wis, PhD(chem), 56. *Prof Exp:* Res chemist appl res lab, US Steel Corp, 56-60, scientist, Edgar C Bain Lab Fundamental Res, 60-68, sr scientist, 68-72; MEM TECH STAFF, BELL LABS, 72- *Mem:* Am Chem Soc; Electrochem Soc; Nat Asn Corrosion Eng. *Res:* Oxidation and tarnishing of metals and alloys; surface properties of metals and alloys; mechanism of electrode reactions. *Mailing Add:* Bell Labs 600 Mountain Ave Murray Hill NJ 07974

FRANKFATER, ALLEN, b New York, NY, June 23, 41; m 67; c 2. BIOCHEMISTRY. *Educ:* Brooklyn Col, BS, 63; Duke Univ, PhD(biochem), 68. *Prof Exp:* Res assoc biochem, Univ Chicago, 68-70; asst prof, 70-77, ASSOC PROF BIOCHEM, STRITCH SCH MED, LOYOLA UNIV CHICAGO, 77- *Concurrent Pos:* Prin investr, Arthritis Found, 76-77 & Nat Inst Child Health & Human Develop, 77-80. *Mem:* Am Chem Soc; AAAS; Sigma Xi. *Res:* Enzymology; mechanisms of proteolytic enzymes; naturally occurring inhibitors of proteolytic enzymes; intracellular protein degradation and development at the biochemical level of the autonomic nervous system in man. *Mailing Add:* Dept of Biochem 2160 S First Ave Maywood IL 60153

FRANKIE, GORDON WILLIAM, b Albany, Calif, Mar 29, 40; m 69. INSECT ECOLOGY. *Educ:* Univ Calif, Berkeley, BS, 63, PhD(entom), 68. *Prof Exp:* NSF grant & res specialist, Orgn Trop Studies, Inc, Costa Rica, 68-70; asst prof entom, Tex A&M Univ, 70-74; assoc prof, 74-76; assoc prof, 76-81, PROF ENTOM, UNIV CALIF, BERKELEY, 81- *Mem:* AAAS; Soc Study Evolution; Ecol Soc Am; Entom Soc Am. *Res:* Insect-plant relations of insects on ornamental plants; pollination biology in the tropics; biological organization of tropical communities with emphasis on plant reproductive biology; community studies of insects inhabiting insect-induced galls on oak. *Mailing Add:* Dept of Entom Univ of Calif Berkeley CA 94720

FRANKL, DANIEL RICHARD, b New York, NY, Sept 6, 22; m 51; c 2. SURFACE PHYSICS. *Educ:* Cooper Union, BChE, 43; Columbia Univ, PhD(physics), 53. *Prof Exp:* Process develop engr, US Rubber Co, 43-50; res assoc, Columbia Univ, 51-53; eng specialist, Luminescence, Sylvania Elec Prod, Inc, 53-58, semiconductors, Gen Tel & Electronics Labs, Inc, 58-62; vis prof phys metall, Univ Ill, 62-63; PROF PHYSICS, PA STATE UNIV, UNIVERSITY PARK, 63- *Concurrent Pos:* Vis sr res assoc, Univ Sussex, Eng, 69-70; vis res chemist, Univ Calif, San Diego, 78-79. *Mem:* Fel Am Phys Soc; AAAS; Am Vacuum Soc. *Mailing Add:* Dept Physics Pa State Univ University Park PA 16802

FRANKL, WILLIAM S, b Philadelphia, Pa, July 15, 28; m 51; c 2. CARDIOVASCULAR DISEASES. *Educ:* Temple Univ, BA, 51, MD, 55, MS, 61; Am Bd Internal Med, dipl, 62 & 74; Cardiovasc Dis Bd, dipl, 75. *Prof Exp:* Intern med, Buffalo Gen Hosp, 55-56; resident, Temple Univ, 56-57 & 59-61; instr med, Univ Pa, 61-62; instr, Temple Univ, 62-64, assoc, 64-65; from asst prof to assoc prof, 65-68; physician-in-chief dept med, Springfield Hosp Med Ctr, 68-70; prof & dir, Cardiol Div, Med Col Pa, 70-79; PROF MED & ASSOC CHIEF, CARDIOL DIV, THOMAS JEFFERSON UNIV, 79- *Concurrent Pos:* Res fel cardiol, Univ Pa, 61-62; dir EKG sect, Cardiol Div, Temple Univ, 66-68 & Cardiac Care Unit, 67-68; consult cardiol,

Philadelphia Vet Admin Hosp, 70-; fel coun clin cardiol & coun atherosclerosis, Am Heart Asn; Fogarty Int fel, Univ London & Cardiothoracic Inst, 78- *Mem:* Fel Am Col Physicians; fel Am Col Cardiol; Am Soc Clin Pharmacol & Therapeut; NY Acad Sci; Am Fedn Clin Res. *Res:* Cardiac pharmacology, especially beta adrenergic blocking agents; cardiovascular hemodynamics; electrocardiography; vectorcardiography. *Mailing Add:* 536 Moreno Rd Wynnewood PA 19096

FRANKLE, REVA TREELISKY, b Pittsburgh, Pa; c 1. NUTRITION, PUBLIC HEALTH. *Educ:* Carnegie Mellon Inst, BS, 43; Columbia Univ, MS, 63, EdD(nutrit educ), 75. *Prof Exp:* Metab res dietitian, Columbia Univ Col Physicians & Surgeons, 58-63; pub health nutritionist, New York Health Dept, 63-66, Off Econ Opportunity consult, Proj Headstart, 67; nutrit instr, Teachers Col, Columbia, 69-75; DIR NUTRIT, WEIGHT WATCHERS INT, 76- *Concurrent Pos:* Nutrit coordr, Dept Community Med, Mt Sinai Sch of Med, 67-75; consult pub health & nutrit related fields, var orgns, 58- *Mem:* Am Inst Nutrit; Am Dietetic Asn; Soc Nutrit Educators; Am Pub Health Asn; Am Teachers Prev Med. *Res:* Nutrition in medical education; weight loss and maintenance in ambulatory care settings. *Mailing Add:* Weight Watchers Int 800 Community Dr Manhasset NY 11030

FRANKLE, WILLIAM ERNEST, b Baldwin, NY, Mar 10, 44; m 68; c 3. ENVIRONMENTAL SCIENCES. *Educ:* Adelphi Univ, BS, 66; Princeton Univ, MS, 69, PhD(chem), 70. *Prof Exp:* sr res assoc paper chem, 70-77, mgr environ protection sci, 77-81, PROJ MGR ENVIRON COMPLIANCE, CORP RES CTR, INT PAPER CO, 81- *Concurrent Pos:* Chem instr, Harriman Col, 75-76. *Mem:* Am Chem Soc; Am Inst Chemists; NY Acad Sci; Am Forest Asn; Tech Asn Pulp & Paper Indust. *Mailing Add:* Int Paper Co PO Box 797 Tuxedo Park NY 10987

FRANKLIN, ALAN DOUGLAS, b Glenside, Pa, Dec 10, 22; m 43, 60; c 3. SOLID STATE PHYSICS. *Educ:* Princeton Univ, AB, 46, PhD(chem), 49. *Prof Exp:* Sect chief ferromagnetism, Franklin Inst, 49-55; group leader ferroelec, 55-59, chief mineral prod div, 59-63, theoret physicist & asst to dir inst mat res, 63-67, RES CHEMIST, NAT BUR STANDARDS, 67- *Honors & Awards:* Gold Medal, Dept Com, 70. *Mem:* Am Chem Soc; fel Am Phys Soc; Sigma Xi; fel Am Ceramic Soc. *Res:* Theoretical, experimental studies point defects, ion mobility in crystals; solid electrolyte-electrode interfaces; fuel cell materials. *Mailing Add:* Nat Bur of Standards Gaithersburg MD 20234

FRANKLIN, ALLAN DAVID, b Brooklyn, NY, Aug 1, 38; m. PHYSICS. *Educ:* Columbia Univ, AB, 59; Cornell Univ, PhD(physics), 65. *Prof Exp:* Res assoc physics, Princeton Univ, 65-66; instr, 66-67; asst prof, 67-73, ASSOC PROF PHYSICS, UNIV COLO, BOULDER, 73- *Mem:* Am Phys Soc; Hist Sci Soc; Am Asn Physics Teachers. *Res:* History and philosophy of science. *Mailing Add:* Campus Box 390 Univ of Colo Boulder CO 80309

FRANKLIN, BERYL CLETIS, b Colly, Ky, Oct 29, 23; m 47. REPRODUCTIVE PHYSIOLOGY. *Educ:* Ky Wesleyan Col, AB, 48; Univ Ky, MS, 50; Ohio State Univ, PhD, 57. *Prof Exp:* Field rep, Ky Wesleyan Col, 48, instr zool & chem, 49-50; asst zool, Ohio State Univ, 50-52, asst instr, 52-55, supvr grad assts, 54-57, instr, 55-57; instr biol, Del Mar Col, 57-59; asst prof zool, La State Univ, 59-60; from asst prof to assoc prof, 60-67, PROF BIOL, NORTHEAST LA UNIV, 67- *Mem:* AAAS; Am Soc Zool; Sigma Xi. *Res:* Endocrinology; physiological zoology. *Mailing Add:* Dept of Biol Northeast La Univ Monroe LA 71209

FRANKLIN, EDWARD CARLYLE, forest genetics, see previous edition

FRANKLIN, EDWARD CLAUS, medicine, deceased

FRANKLIN, FRED ALDRICH, b Worcester, Mass, July 24, 32. ASTRONOMY. *Educ:* Harvard Univ, AB, 54, MA, 56, PhD, 62. *Prof Exp:* PHYSICIST, SMITHSONIAN ASTROPHYS OBSERV, HARVARD UNIV, 57- *Mem:* Am Astron Soc. *Res:* Photometry and dynamics of planets and satellites. *Mailing Add:* 41 Linnaean St Cambridge MA 02138

FRANKLIN, GENE F(ARTHING), b Banner Elk, NC, July 25, 27; m 52; c 2. ELECTRICAL ENGINEERING. *Educ:* Ga Inst Technol, BEE, 50; Mass Inst Technol, 52; Columbia Univ, EngScD, 55. *Prof Exp:* Instr elec eng, Columbia Univ, 52-55, from asst prof to assoc prof, 5561, PROF ELEC ENG, STANFORD UNIV, 61- *Concurrent Pos:* Consult, indusrs, 58- *Mem:* Inst Elec & Electronics Engrs; Soc Indust & Appl Math. *Res:* Automatic control with emphasis on the control of multivariable nonlinear dynamical systems. *Mailing Add:* Dept of Elec Eng Stanford Univ Stanford CA 94305

FRANKLIN, GEORGE JOSEPH, b Osmond, Nebr. GEOLOGY. *Educ:* Ohio State Univ, PhD(geol), 61. *Prof Exp:* GEOLOGIST, US GEOL SURV, 62- *Mailing Add:* US Geol Surv PO Box 7944 Metairie LA 70010

FRANKLIN, JAMES AUSTIN, aerospace engineering, see previous edition

FRANKLIN, JAMES CURRY, b St Charles, Ky, Nov 11, 33; m 55; c 1. ANALYTICAL CHEMISTRY. *Educ:* Western Ky State Univ, BS, 55; Univ Ala, MS, 62; Univ Tenn, PhD(anal chem), 70. *Prof Exp:* Teacher chem, Union County Bd Educ, 57-58 & Lamar County Bd Educ, 58-59; instr, Univ Ala, 59-61; develop chemist, Y-12 Plant, Oak Ridge, 61-73; res staff chem, Oak Ridge Nat Lab, 73-78; DEPT HEAD Y-12 LAB, NUCLEAR DIV, UNION CARBIDE, 78- *Mem:* Am Chem Soc; Am Soc Mass Spectrometry; Sigma Xi. *Res:* Spark source mass spectrometry and its application to the trace analysis of energy and environmental related materials. *Mailing Add:* Y-12 Plant Bldg 9995 Nuclear Div Union Carbide Oak Ridge TN 37830

FRANKLIN, JAMES MCWILLIE, b North Bay, Ont, Nov 9, 42; m 68. ECONOMIC GEOLOGY, STRATIGRAPHY. *Educ:* Carleton Univ, BS, 64, MS, 67; Univ Western Ont, PhD(geol), 70. *Prof Exp:* From asst prof to assoc prof geol, Lakehead Univ, 69-75; RES SCIENTIST, DEPT ENERGY,

MINES & RESOURCES, GEOL SURV CAN, 75- *Concurrent Pos:* Geologist, Mattagami Lake Mines Ltd, 71; trip coordr, Int Geol Cong, Montreal, 72. *Mem:* Fel Geol Asn Can; Can Inst Mineral & Metall; Mineral Asn Can. *Res:* Precambrian stratigraphy; chemistry of formation of stratabound copper-zinc massive sulphide deposits in Archean volcanic terrains, effects of metamorphism on these deposits; metallogeny of veins associated with Proterozoic sedimentary sequences; lead isotope studies of Archean and Proterozoic mineral deposits; metallogeny of gold deposits in Archean terrains. *Mailing Add:* Dept of Energy Mines & Resources 601 Booth St Ottawa Can

FRANKLIN, JERROLD, b New York, NY, June 19, 30; m 55; c 2. THEORETICAL PHYSICS. *Educ:* Cooper Union, BEE, 52; Univ Ill, MS, 53, PhD(physics), 56. *Prof Exp:* Asst physics, Univ Ill, 52-56; instr, Columbia Univ, 56-59; asst prof, Brown Univ, 59-64, asst to dean, 62-64; physicist, Lawrence Radiation Lab, Univ Calif, 64-67; assoc prof, 67-70, PROF PHYSICS, TEMPLE UNIV, 70- *Concurrent Pos:* Assoc ed, Math Rev, 62-63; vis prof, Israel Inst Technol, 70-71 & 76-77. *Mem:* Am Phys Soc. *Res:* Elementary particle physics; S-matrix theory; quark and parton models. *Mailing Add:* Dept of Physics Temple Univ Philadelphia PA 19122

FRANKLIN, JERRY FOREST, b Waldport, Ore, Oct 27, 36; m 58; c 4. ECOLOGY, FORESTRY. *Educ:* Ore State Univ, BS, 59, MS, 61; Wash State Univ, PhD(bot), 66. *Prof Exp:* Res forester, US Forest Serv, 59-65, plant ecologist, 65-68, prin plant ecologist, 68-73, dept dir coniferous forest biome, 70-73; dir ecosyst anal prog, NSF, 73-75; CHIEF PLANT ECOLOGIST & PROJ LEADER, PAC NORTHWEST FOREST & RANGE EXP STA, US FOREST SERV, 75-, PROF FOREST SCI & BOT, ORE STATE UNIV, 76- *Concurrent Pos:* Bd gov, The Nature Conservancy; nat lectr, Sigma Xi. *Honors & Awards:* Japanese Govt Award, 70; Super Serv Award, USDA, 70; Arthur S Fleming Award, 72. *Mem:* AAAS; Soc Am Foresters; Ecol Soc Am; Brit Ecol Soc. *Res:* Forest community ecology and succession; alpine communities; vegetation-soil relationships, especially Abies-Tsuga forest types. *Mailing Add:* Forestry Sci Lab 3200 Jefferson Way Corvallis OR 97331

FRANKLIN, JOEL NICHOLAS, b Chicago, Ill, Apr 4, 30; m 49; c 1. APPLIED MATHEMATICS. *Educ:* Stanford Univ, BS, 50, PhD(math), 53. *Prof Exp:* Instr math, Inst Math Sci, NY Univ, 53-55; asst prof, Univ Wash, 55-56; sr mathematician, Burroughs Corp, 56-57; assoc prof appl mech, 57-65, prof appl sci, 65-70, PROF APPL MATH, CALIF INST TECHNOL, 70- *Concurrent Pos:* Consult, AEC Radiation Lab, Univ Calif, 55, 57 & Jet Propulsion Lab, NASA, 62- *Mem:* Am Math Soc. *Mailing Add:* Div of Eng & Appl Sci Calif Inst of Technol Pasadena CA 91125

FRANKLIN, KENNETH LINN, b Alameda, Calif, Mar 25, 23; m 58; c 3. ASTRONOMY. *Educ:* Univ Calif, AB, 48, PhD(astron), 53. *Prof Exp:* Lab technician, Lick Observ, Calif, 49-50; asst, Leuschner Observ, 53-54; res fel radio astron, Carnegie Inst, 54-56; asst astronr, 56-57, assoc astronr, 58-63, from asst chmn to chmn, 68-74, ASTRONR, AM MUS-HAYDEN PLANETARIUM, 63- *Concurrent Pos:* Adj prof, Cooper Union, 68; vis prof, Rutgers Univ, 68-72; astron ed, World Almanac, 70-; mem comn five, Int Sci Radio Union; consult, Grumman Aircraft Co, Kearfott Div, Gen Precision, Inc, Eclipse-Pioneer Div, Bendix Corp, AIL Div, Cutler-Hammer Corp, Razdow Labs, Int Tel & Tel, Martin Co, McGraw-Hill Bk Co, Sci Am, NY Times, Time-Life Inc, CBS-TV & NBC-TV. *Mem:* Fel AAAS; Am Astron Soc; Inst Elec & Electronics Engrs; fel Royal Astron Soc; NY Acad Sci. *Res:* Binary stars; galactic structure; radio astronomy; astronomy education. *Mailing Add:* Am Mus-Hayden Planetarium 81st & Central Park W New York NY 10024

FRANKLIN, LUTHER EDWARD, b Birmingham, Ala, Jan 21, 29; m 48; c 2. DEVELOPMENTAL BIOLOGY. *Educ:* Univ Ala, BS, 53; Fla State Univ, PhD(exp biol), 63. *Prof Exp:* Res assoc, Inst Space Biosci, Fla State Univ, 64 & Inst Molecular Evolution, Univ Miami, 64-65; res assoc & adj asst prof, Delta Regional Primate Res Ctr, Tulane Univ, 65-72, assoc prof, 72; ASSOC PROF BIOL, UNIV HOUSTON, 72- *Mem:* Am Soc Cell Biol; Int Soc Develop Biologists; Soc Study Reprod. *Res:* Morphology and physiology of fertilization; aging of the male reproductive system. *Mailing Add:* Dept of Biol Univ of Houston Houston TX 77004

FRANKLIN, MAOMI C, b New York, NY, Mar 25, 29. GENETICS, VIROLOGY. *Educ:* Cornell Univ, BS, 50; Yale Univ, PhD(genetics & biochem), 54. *Prof Exp:* Fel genetics & virol, Calif Inst Technol, 54-56; res assoc, Univ Geneva, Switzerland, 57-59; Mass INst Technol, 59-63; adj prof, Stanford Univ, 74-79; RES PROF GENETICS & VIROL, UNIV UTAH, 79- *Concurrent Pos:* Prin investr res grants, Nat Sci Found, 65-; vis res assoc, Univ Paris, 72-73. *Mem:* Genetics Soc Am; Am Soc Virol; Sigma Xi; Fedn Am Scientists; AAAS. *Res:* Premature termination of lambda transcripts by its E coli host. *Mailing Add:* Dept Biol Unit Utah Salt Lake City UT 84112

FRANKLIN, MERVYN, b Minehead, Eng, Jan 13, 32; Can citizen; m 63. MICROBIOLOGY. *Educ:* Univ Reading, BSc, 55 & 56; McGill Univ, PhD(biochem), 59. *Prof Exp:* From demonstr to sr demonstr bact, McGill Univ, 57-59; J C Childs fel microbiol, Western Reserve Univ, 59-60; lectr bact, McGill Univ, 60-62, asst prof, 62-65; asst prof microbiol, New York Med Col, 65-66, assoc prof, 67-69; prof biol & dean fac sci, Univ NB, Fredericton, 69-75, actg vpres, 75-76, acad vpres, 76-78; PRES, UNIV WINDSOR, ONT, 78- *Concurrent Pos:* Assoc ed, Can J Microbiol, 70-73; mem, Sci Coun Can, 70-76; chmn environ coun, Prov of NB, 72-75; mem, Environ Adv Coun Can, 78-81. *Mem:* Can Asn Deans Arts & Sci; Can Soc Microbiologists (second vpres, 75-76); Am Soc Microbiol. *Res:* Ecology and physiology of aquatic bacteria. *Mailing Add:* Dept of Biol Univ of NB Fredericton Can

FRANKLIN, PHILIP JAQUINS, b Riverside, Calif, Oct 25, 08; m 37; c 1. PHYSICS. *Educ:* Univ Calif, Los Angeles, AB, 31. *Prof Exp:* Teacher pub schs, Calif, 32-42; physicist, Nat Bur Stand, 43-53; physicist & chief components, Diamond Ord Fuze Labs, 53-62, prog mgr adv res proj agency,

US Dept Defense, 62-65; phys sci adminr, Nat Bur Stand, 65-66, Nat Bur Stand chief, Nat Bur Stand-Gen Serv Admin Testing Lab, 66-68; dir mat eval & develop lab, 68-74, actg dir chem & paints div, 74, DIR CHEM & PAINTS DIV, FED SUPPLY SERV, GEN SERV ADMIN, 74- *Mem:* Am Chem Soc; Am Phys Soc; Inst Elec & Electronics Engrs. *Res:* Plastics; electronic instrumentation; components; electrochemistry; casting resins; wax composition; printed circuit techniques; dielectrics; physical science testing. *Mailing Add:* 5907 Massachusetts Ave Bethesda MD 20016

FRANKLIN, RALPH E, b Chicago, Ill, Sept 14, 34; m 57; c 3. OIL SHALE, SYNTHETIC FUELS. *Educ:* Univ Ark, BS, 55, MS, 57; Ohio State Univ, PhD(soil chem, plant nutrit), 61. *Prof Exp:* From asst prof to prof agron, Ohio State Univ & Ohio Agr Res & Develop Ctr, 61-74; soil scientist, US Energy Res & Develop Admin, 74-77; SOIL SCIENTIST, US DEPT ENERGY, 77- *Concurrent Pos:* Int Atomic Energy Agency adv to Peru, 66-67; soil scientist, US AEC, 72-74. *Mem:* AAAS; Am Chem Soc; Soil Sci Soc Am; Am Soc Agron. *Res:* Planning and management of research needed for energy development, expecially oil shale and other sythetic fuel technologies; physical chemistry of soils and plant nutrition; solid waste disposal; agranomic issues. *Mailing Add:* Off of Health & Environ Res US Dept of of Energy Washington DC 20545

FRANKLIN, RICHARD CRAWFORD, b Spokane, Wash, Nov 11, 15; m 42; c 2. ORGANIC CHEMISTRY. *Educ:* Univ Ill, BA, 37; Univ Wis, PhD(chem), 40. *Prof Exp:* Res chemist, 40-41 & 46-64, res supvr, E I du Pont de Nemours & Co, Inc, 64-78; RETIRED. *Mem:* Am Chem Soc. *Res:* Dyes; anthraquinone colors and intermediates; phthalocyanines; rubber chemicals; hydrogenation and organic chemicals; Azo and basic dyes. *Mailing Add:* 1203 Brook Dr Wilmington DE 19803

FRANKLIN, RICHARD MORRIS, b Medford, Mass, Oct 16, 30; m 58; c 2. MOLECULAR BIOPHYSICS, VIROLOGY. *Educ:* Tufts Col, BS, 51; Yale Univ, PhD, 54. *Prof Exp:* Am Cancer Soc res fel, Calif Inst Technol, 54-56; res assoc, Max Planck Inst, Tuebingen, Ger, 56-59; asst prof virol, Rockefeller Inst, 59-63; from assoc prof to prof path, Sch Med, Univ Colo, Denver, 63-67; mem, Pub Health Res Inst, City of New York, 67-71; PROF VIROL, UNIV BASEL, 71- *Concurrent Pos:* Fulbright fel, 56; adj prof, Sch Med, NY Univ, 67-71. *Res:* Techniques of immunohistochemistry; effects of tumor viruses on the immune system; replication of viruses; avian tumor viruses; osteopetrosis and other non-defective and defective leucosis viruses. *Mailing Add:* Biozentrum Univ Basel Klingelbergstrasse 70 Basel Switzerland

FRANKLIN, ROBERT LOUIS, b Salina, Kans, Feb 21, 35; m 61; c 2. BIOCHEMISTRY, ORGANIC CHEMISTRY. *Educ:* Westmar Col, BA, 63; Mich State Univ, PhD(biochem), 67. *Prof Exp:* Asst prof chem, 67-70, ASSOC PROF CHEM, WESTMAR COL, 70- *Mem:* Am Chem Soc; Sigma Xi. *Res:* Synthesis and physiological activity of indolic plant growth regulators; identification and isolation of insect pheromones. *Mailing Add:* Dept of Chem Westmar Col Le Mars IA 51031

FRANKLIN, ROBERT RAY, b Wetumka, Okla, Jan 20, 28; m 51; c 4. OBSTETRICS & GYNECOLOGY. *Educ:* Univ Tex, BA, 49, MD, 53. *Prof Exp:* Assoc prof, 59-70, PROF OBSTET & GYNEC, COL MED, BAYLOR UNIV, 70- *Concurrent Pos:* Mem attend staff, Methodist Hosp, Jeff Davis Hosp & St Luke's Hosp. *Mem:* AMA. *Res:* Endocrinology; bioassay for luteinizing hormone for clinical use; newborn physiology; transitional distress project. *Mailing Add:* 7550 Fannin Houston TX 77054

FRANKLIN, RUDOLPH THOMAS, b Morristown, NJ, Sept 29, 28; m 52; c 5. ENTOMOLOGY. *Educ:* Emory Univ, BA, 50; Univ Ga, MS, 55; Univ Minn, PhD(entom), 64. *Prof Exp:* Forest entomologist, Minn Dept Agr, 58-62; entomologist, Regional Off, Southern Region, US Forest Serv, Ga, 62-63, zone leader entom, NC, 63-65; asst prof entom, 65-70, ASSOC PROF ENTOM & FOREST RESOURCES, UNIV GA, 70- *Mem:* Soc Am Foresters; Entom Soc Am; Entom Soc Can. *Res:* Ecology of forest insects; biology of bark beetles and weevils and hymenopterous parasites of bark beetles. *Mailing Add:* Dept of Entom Univ of Ga Athens GA 30602

FRANKLIN, RUTH ANN, b Dimmitt, Tex, Jan 22, 28. NUTRITION. *Educ:* Tex Tech Univ, BS, 49, MS, 60, EdD(educ & food nutrit), 71. *Prof Exp:* Residence hall dietician, Univ Tex, 50-52; teacher chem & home econ, St Mary of Wasatch Col, 52-54; voc teacher home econ, Albuquerque Pub Schs, 55-68; asst prof food & nutrit, NMex State Univ, 70-72; head dept home econ, Northwestern State Univ, La, 72-74; assoc prof food & nutrit, 74-76, ASSOC PROF HOME ECON, TEX CHRISTIAN UNIV, 76- *Mem:* Soc Nutrit Educ; Am Dietetic Asn; Am Home Econ Asn. *Res:* Lactose tolerance in Mexican Americans and American Indians; obesity in young children; the effects of maternal nutrition on mental development of the infant. *Mailing Add:* 3617 Minot Ave Ft Worth TX 76133

FRANKLIN, SAMUEL GREGG, b Camden, NJ, May 8, 46; m 78. BIOCHEMISTRY. *Educ:* Rutgers Univ, AB, 68; Thomas Jefferson Univ, PhD(biochem), 73. *Prof Exp:* Res asst biochem, Med Col Ga, 68-69; teaching asst, Thomas Jefferson Univ, 69-73; fel, 72-80, SR RES ASSOC, INST CANCER RES, 80- *Mem:* AAAS; Am Chem Soc. *Res:* The primary structure of histone variants; screening and primary structure of human serum albumin variants; biochemistry of hepatitis B virus binding substance. *Mailing Add:* Inst for Cancer Res 7701 Burholme Ave Philadelphia PA 19111

FRANKLIN, STANLEY PHILLIP, b Memphis, Tenn, Aug 14, 31; m 79; c 5. TOPOLOGY. *Educ:* Memphis State Univ, BS, 59; Univ Calif, Los Angeles, MA, 62, PhD(math), 63. *Prof Exp:* NSF fel, Univ Wash, 63-64; asst prof math, Univ Fla, 64-65; from asst prof to prof, Carnegie-Mellon Univ, 65-72; PROF MATH SCI & CHMN DEPT, MEMPHIS STATE UNIV, 72- *Concurrent Pos:* Managing ed, Gen Topology & Its Applns. *Mem:* Am Math Soc; Math Asn Am. *Res:* Categorical topology; computer literacy. *Mailing Add:* Dept of Math Sci Memphis State Univ Memphis TN 38111

FRANKLIN, THOMAS CHESTER, b Birmingham, Ala, Feb 5, 23; m 46; c 4. PHYSICAL CHEMISTRY. *Educ:* Howard Col, BS, 44; Ohio State Univ, PhD(chem), 51. *Prof Exp:* Instr chem, Howard Col, 46-48; asst phys chem, Ohio State Univ, 48-49, asst instr, 49-50; asst prof chem, Richmond Univ, 51-54; assoc prof, 54-62, PROF CHEM, BAYLOR UNIV, 62- *Concurrent Pos:* Chem res worker, Va Inst Sci Res, 52-53. *Mem:* Electrochem Soc; Am Chem Soc; Am Electroplaters Soc. *Res:* Electrochemistry and catalysis. *Mailing Add:* Dept Chem Baylor Univ Waco TX 76703

FRANKLIN, THOMAS DOYAL, JR, b Morganton, NC, Sept 25, 41; m 64; c 2. PHYSIOLOGY, MEDICAL ULTRASOUND. *Educ:* Wake Forest Univ, BS, 63, MS, 67; Univ Ill, Urbana-Champaign, PhD(physiol), 72. *Prof Exp:* Assoc physiologist aerospace med, McDonnell-Douglas Corp, 67-69; res scientist ultrasound, Intersci Res Inst, 69-72; asst dir, 73-80, assoc dir, Fortune-Fry Ultrasound Res Labs, 80-81, asst prof, 72-79, ASSOC PROF RADIOL, SCH MED, IND UNIV, INDIANAPOLIS, 79-, DIR, LIFE SCI RES DIV, INDIANAPOLIS CTR ADVAN RES, 81- *Mem:* AAAS; Am Heart Asn; Am Soc Echocardiography; Sigma Xi; Am Inst Ultrasound in Med. *Res:* Application of ultrasound to soft tissue visualization for diagnosis; potential therapeutic applications of low intensity ultrasound; non-invasive evaluation of the cardiovascular system. *Mailing Add:* Life Sci Res Div Rm A-32 Ind Univ Hosp Indianapolis IN 46223

FRANKLIN, URSULA MARTIUS, b Munich, Ger, Sept 16, 21; Can Citizen; m 52; c 2. PHYSICAL METALLURGY. *Educ:* Tech Univ, Berlin, PhD(appl physics), 49. *Prof Exp:* Fel appl physics, Univ Toronto, 50-52; sr res officer mat eng, Ont Res Found, Toronto, 52-67; PROF MAT SCI, UNIV TORONTO, 67-, AFFIL, INST HIST SCI & TECHNOL, 69- *Concurrent Pos:* Res assoc hist technol, Royal Ont Mus, 69-; mem & comt chmn, Sci Coun Can, 74-77; mem coun & exec, Nat Sci & Eng Res Coun, 77- *Mem:* Am Soc Metal; Can Metall Conf; Soc Archaeol Sci. *Res:* Structure of alloys; archeo-metallurgy; study of ancient metals and alloys; origin and development of bronze technology; metals in early China. *Mailing Add:* Dept of Metall & Mat Sci Univ of Toronto Toronto ON M5S 1A1 Can

FRANKLIN, WILLIAM ELWOOD, b Washington, DC, Nov 22, 31; m 60. TEXTILE CHEMISTRY, POLYMER CHEMISTRY. *Educ:* Univ Nebr, BSc, 53, MSc, 55; Univ Iowa, PhD(org chem), 59. *Prof Exp:* Asst, Univ Iowa, 55-58; from asst prof to assoc prof chem, Loyola Univ, La, 58-65; RES CHEMIST, SOUTHERN REGIONAL RES CTR, RES, SCI & EDUC ADMIN, USDA, 65- *Mem:* Am Chem Soc; Am Inst Chemists; Am Asn Textile Chemists & Colorists. *Res:* Cellulose crosslinking agents; thermally reversable reactions; textile flamability; mass spectrometry. *Mailing Add:* Southern Regional Res Ctr PO Box 19687 New Orleans LA 70179

FRANKLIN, WILLIAM LLOYD, b Santa Monica, Calif, July 31, 41; m 62; c 4. ANIMAL ECOLOGY, MAMMALOGY. *Educ:* Univ Calif, Davis, BS, 64; Humboldt State Univ, MS, 68; Utah State Univ, PhD(wildlife sci), 78. *Prof Exp:* ASST PROF MAMMALIAN WILDLIFE ECOL, DEPT ANIMAL ECOL, IOWA STATE UNIV, 75- *Concurrent Pos:* Prin investr multiple grants, 68-81. *Mem:* Wildlife Soc; Animal Behav Soc; Am Soc Mammalogists; Fauna Preserv Soc. *Res:* Sociobiology and behavioral ecology of mammals; South American wild camelids and ungulate social systems; fish and wildlife sciences. *Mailing Add:* 124 Sci II Iowa State Univ Ames IA 50011

FRANKO, BERNARD VINCENT, b West Brownsville, Pa, June 9, 22; m 46; c 9. PHARMACOLOGY. *Educ:* WVa Univ, BS, 54, MS, 55; Med Col Va, PhD(pharmacol), 58. *Prof Exp:* Instr, 58-60, asst prof, 60-76, ADJ ASST PROF, DEPT PHARMACOL, MED COL, VA COMMONWEALTH UNIV, 76-; pharmacologist, 58-68, assoc dir pharmacol res, 68-71 & 73-76, dir pharmacol res, 71-73, sr monitor qual assurance, 76-78, DIR QUAL ASSURANCE, BIOL RES LABS, A H ROBINS CO, INC, 78- ASST PROF PHARMACOL, MED COL VA, VA COMMONWEALTH UNIV, 60- *Concurrent Pos:* Pharmacologist, 58-68, assoc dir pharmacol res, 68-71 & 73-76, dir pharmacol res, 71-73, sr monitor qual assurance, 78-81, mgr, Res Coord & Training Sect, Biol Res Labs, A H Robins Co, 81-, 76-78, dir qual assurance. *Mem:* Fel AAAS; Am Soc Pharmacol & Exp Therapeut; Soc Exp Biol & Med; Int Soc Biochem Pharmacol. *Res:* Autonomic, cardiovascular and diuretic drugs; toxicology. *Mailing Add:* Biol Res Labs A H Robins Co Inc 1211 Sherwood Ave Richmond VA 23220

FRANKO-FILIPASIC, BORIVOJ RICHARD SIMON, b Zagreb, Yugoslavia, Jan 5, 22; nat US; m 48; c 3. ORGANIC CHEMISTRY. *Educ:* Northwestern Univ, BS, 43, MS, 51, PhD(chem), 52. *Prof Exp:* Res chemist, Pittsburgh Plate Glass Co, 52-53 & Mathieson Chem Corp, 53-56; supvr org res & develop, 56-66, MGR PROCESS RES & DEVELOP, FMC CORP, 66- *Mem:* Am Chem Soc; Royal Soc Chem; Am Inst Chem Eng; Am Soc Test Mat. *Res:* Fats and oils; boron fuels; high pressure reactions; glycerol; flame retardents. *Mailing Add:* FMC Corp PO Box 8 Princeton NJ 08540

FRANKOSKI, STANLEY P, b Suffern, NY, May 24, 44; m 68. PROJECT MANAGEMENT. *Educ:* Villanova Univ, BS, 66; Purdue Univ, MS, 68; Univ Mass, PhD(chem), 72. *Prof Exp:* Res chemist, 72-74, sr res chemist, 74-76, MGR ANAL RES & DEVELOP, GAF CORP, 76- *Mem:* Am Chem Soc. *Res:* Organic functional group analysis; separations; identifications; problem solving; administration. *Mailing Add:* 7 Will Lane Rd #5 West Milford NJ 07480

FRANKS, ALYN P, b Cleveland, Ohio, Nov 12, 36; m 63; c 2. RUBBER CHEMISTRY. *Educ:* Western Reserve Univ, BS, 59, JD, 63. *Prof Exp:* Phys scientist, Crile Vet Admin Hosp, 59-60; chemist, Western Reserve Univ, 61-63; patent attorney, B F Goodrich Co, 63-65; res chemist, PPG Industs, Inc, 65-66; rubber lab mgr & tech dir, Reichhold Chem, Cuyahoga Falls, 66-76; CONSULT & PRES, INST ASTRAL STUDIES, INC, 77-; MGR TECH SALES, SOVEREIGN CHEM CO, 81- *Concurrent Pos:* Chmn bd dirs, Persephone Found, 76-78. *Mem:* Fel Am Chem Soc (secy-treas, 75-78); NY Acad Sci; fel Am Inst Chemists; AAAS. *Res:* Organic synthesis of antioxidants, antiozonants and nucleotides; bioassay of enzymes and hormones; protective coatings; dispersions and lattices. *Mailing Add:* IAS Inc 111 Briny Ave Suite 2411 Pompano Beach FL 33062

FRANKS, EDWIN CLARK, b Chagrin Falls, Ohio, Jan 13, 37; m 58. ZOOLOGY. *Educ:* Ohio State Univ, BSc, 58, MSc, 60, PhD(zool, ornith), 65. *Prof Exp:* Lab technician, Battelle Mem Inst, 59-61, biologist, 61-62; USPHS trainee zool, Pa State Univ, 65-66; asst prof, 66-70, assoc prof, 70-77, PROF BIOL, WESTERN ILL UNIV, 77- *Concurrent Pos:* NSF award, Marine Biol Lab, Woods Hole, 65, NSF grant, Bermuda Biol Sta, 72. *Mem:* Inland Bird Banding Asn; Am Ornith Union; Wilson Ornith Soc; Nat Audubon Soc. *Res:* Bird ecology and behavior; bird life expectancies. *Mailing Add:* Dept of Biol Sci Western Ill Univ Macomb IL 61455

FRANKS, JOHN ANTHONY, JR, b Cleveland, Ohio, Nov 20, 35; m 59; c 3. ORGANIC CHEMISTRY. *Educ:* Univ Notre Dame, BS, 58; Western Reserve Univ, MS, 61, PhD(org chem), 64. *Prof Exp:* Asst chem, Western Reserve Univ, 59-63, fel org chem, Sch Med, 63-64; sr org chemist, Eli Lilly & Co, 64-66; group leader appln res, color & chem res dept, Sherwin-Williams Co, 66-71; factor rep, Parco Sci Co, 71-72; mgr prod develop, Hull-Smith Chem, Inc, 72-74; sr res chemist, 75-80, RES ASSOC, VULCAN MAT CO, 80- *Mem:* Am Chem Soc; Royal Soc Chem; NY Acad Sci; Sigma Xi. *Res:* Investigations on the synthesis and structural elucidations on benzoxazine systems and their derivatives, cyclopentane tetrols plus derivatives and reactions of thebaine type alkaloids; plastisol formulation, extrusion processing, pigments, one package epoxy systems; aluminum dross processing and end use applications, tin chemicals, their processing and applications. *Mailing Add:* 1394 Sanford St Vermilion OH 44089

FRANKS, JOHN JULIAN, b Pueblo, Colo, Apr 9, 29; m 51; c 5. INTERNAL MEDICINE. *Educ:* Univ Colo, BA, 51, MD, 54. *Prof Exp:* Intern, Cornell Med Div, Bellevue Hosp, 54-55; resident internal med, Med Ctr, Univ Colo, 55-58; dep chief dept pharmacol-biochem, Sch Aviation Med, US Air Force, 58-62; staff hematologist, Lackland Air Force Hosp, 62-63; asst prof, Univ Colo, Denver, 63-68, assoc prof med, Med Ctr, 68-77, assoc dir, Clin Res Ctr, 70-77, dir, 77-80; ASSOC CHIEF STAFF, DENVER VET ADMIN MED CTR, 68- *Concurrent Pos:* Res fel med, Sch Med, Harvard Univ & Mass Gen Hosp, 63-64; USPHS res career develop award, 63-69; assoc chief of staff, Denver Vet Hosp. *Mem:* AAAS; Am Fedn Clin Res; Am Physiol Soc; Am Gastroenterol Asn. *Res:* Plasma protein metabolism; oncology; biomathematics. *Mailing Add:* Dept Res & Develop Vet Admin Med Ctr 1055 Clermont St Denver CO 80220

FRANKS, LARRY ALLEN, b Chesterland, Ohio, July 22, 34; m 60; c 2. MOLECULAR SPECTROSCOPY. *Educ:* Hiram Col, AB, 58; Vanderbilt Univ, MS, 60, PhD(physics, math), 68. *Prof Exp:* From scientist to sr scientist, EG&G Inc, 60-68, sci specialist, 68-72; staff scientist, Off Radiation Progs, US Environ Protection Agency, 72-73; sr sci specialist, 73-74, GROUP LEADER, EG&G INC, 74- *Concurrent Pos:* Staff mem, Fed Power Comn-Spec Task Force Natural Gas Technol, 72-73. *Mem:* Health Physics Soc; Am Phys Soc. *Res:* Molecular structure and spectroscopy; development of radiation detection systems. *Mailing Add:* 311 Piedomnt Rd Santa Barbara CA 93105

FRANKS, LEWIS EMBREE, b San Mateo, Calif, Nov 8, 31; m 54; c 3. ELECTRICAL & COMMUNICATIONS ENGINEERING. *Educ:* Ore State Univ, BS, 52; Stanford Univ, MS, 53, PhD(elec eng), 57. *Prof Exp:* Instr elec eng, Stanford Univ, 57-58; mem tech staff, Bell Labs, Inc, 58-62, supvr data syst, 62-69; assoc prof, 69-71, PROF ELEC ENG, UNIV MASS, AMHERST, 71- *Concurrent Pos:* Adj assoc prof, Columbia Univ, 65; adj prof, Northeast Univ, 67-68. *Mem:* Inst Elec & Electronics Engrs. *Res:* Theoretical and design aspects of communication systems, signals, and signal processing equipment; circuit theory and design. *Mailing Add:* Juggler Meadow Rd Amherst MA 01002

FRANKS, NEAL EDWARD, b Canton, Ohio, July 24, 36; m 58; c 2. ORGANIC CHEMISTRY, POLYMER CHEMISTRY. *Educ:* Manchester Col, BA, 58; Ohio State Univ, PhD(org chem), 63. *Prof Exp:* Res assoc biochem, Univ Iowa, 65-66; res biochemist enzyme technol, Procter & Gamble Co, 67-72; res scientist & proj leader synthetic fibers, Am Enka Co, 72-77; GROUP LEADER PULPING TECHNOL, ST REGIS TECH CTR, 77- *Mem:* Am Chem Soc; NY Acad Sci; Tech Asn Pulp & Paper Indust. *Res:* Organic and physical chemistry of natural polymers, particularly fibrous materials, with emphasis on their manufacture and modification. *Mailing Add:* St Regis Tech Ctr W Nyack Rd West Nyack NY 10994

FRANKS, PAUL C, geology, see previous edition

FRANKS, RICHARD LEE, b Portland, Ore, Mar 29, 41; m 66; c 2. COMPUTER PERFORMANCE ANALYSIS. *Educ:* Univ Wash, BSEE, 63; Univ Calif, Berkeley, MS, 69, PhD(elec eng), 70. *Prof Exp:* Mem tech staff, Systs Anal, 70-73, supvr, Systs Anal Group, 73-77, head, Network Mgt Dept, 77-79, HEAD, PERFORMANCE ANAL DEPT, BELL TEL LABS, 79- *Mem:* Inst Elec & Electronics Engrs. *Res:* System theory. *Mailing Add:* 1C-413 Bell Tel Labs Holmdel NJ 07733

FRANKS, STEPHEN GUEST, b Frankstown, Miss, Apr 15, 46; m 77; c 2. GEOLOGY, PETROLOGY. *Educ:* Millsaps Col, BS, 68; Univ Miss, MS, 70; Case Western Reserve Univ, PhD(geol), 76. *Prof Exp:* Res geologist, Atlantic Richfield Co, 74-77, sr res geologist, Geosci Group, 77-80, RES DIR ROCK/FLUID SYSTS, ARCO OIL & GAS, 80- *Honors & Awards:* George C Matson Award, Am Asn Petrol Geol, 78. *Mem:* Am Asn Petrol Geol; Soc Econ Paleontol & Mineral. *Res:* Diagenesis and low-grade metamorphism of clastic sediments, particularly the relationships of tectonism, sedimentation and diagenesis and how these affect the hydrocarbon potential of sedimentary basins. *Mailing Add:* Atlantic Richfield Co PO Box 2819 Exp-116 Dallas TX 75221

FRANKTON, CLARENCE, b Nottingham, Eng, Feb 7, 06; m 48; c 1. WEED SCIENCE. *Educ:* McGill Univ, BSc, 36, PhD(bot), 40. *Prof Exp:* Pasture researcher, Macdonald Col, McGill Univ, 37-44 & Que Civil Serv, 44-46; sr botanist, Plant Res Inst, Can Dept Agr, 46-70; RETIRED. *Honors & Awards:* Lawson Medal, Can Bot Asn, 73. *Res:* Weed biology; taxonomy of weedy plants of Canada; native Rumex and Cirsium. *Mailing Add:* 2297 Fox Crescent Ottawa Can

FRANS, ROBERT EARL, b Louisville, Nebr, Apr 19, 27; m 49; c 3. AGRONOMY. *Educ:* Univ Nebr, BS, 50; Rutgers Univ, MS, 53; Iowa State Univ, PhD(plant physiol), 55. *Prof Exp:* Asst farm crops, Rutgers Univ, 50-53; asst plant physiol, Iowa State Univ, 53-55; from asst prof to prof, 55-75, DISTINGUISHED PROF AGRON, UNIV ARK, FAYETTEVILLE, 75-, ELMS FARMING-RICHARD S BARNETT JR CHMN, WEED SCI, 80- *Mem:* Weed Sci Soc Am. *Res:* Applied physiological usages of growth-active compounds for herbicidal purposes; mechanisms responsible for plant growth inhibition from biologically active compounds. *Mailing Add:* Dept of Agron Univ of Ark Fayetteville AR 72701

FRANSON, J CHRISTIAN, b Manchester, Iowa, Aug 23, 48. CLINICAL PATHOLOGY. *Educ:* Iowa State Univ, BS, 70, MS, 72, DVM, 79. *Prof Exp:* Res assoc vet path, Iowa State Univ, 74-75; wildlife biologist res, 77, RES VET, US FISH & WILDLIFE SERV, 79- *Mem:* Am Vet Med Asn; Wildlife Dis Asn; Am Asn Wildlife Vet. *Res:* Effects of environmental contaminants on wildlife, with particular emphasis on physiological and clinical pathological changes. *Mailing Add:* Patuxent Wildlife Res Ctr Laurel MD 20708

FRANSON, RICHARD CARL, b Woburn, Mass, Dec 14, 43; m 67; c 3. BIOCHEMISTRY. *Educ:* Univ Mass, BS, 65; Bowman Gray Sch Med, MS, 70, PhD(biochem), 72. *Prof Exp:* Instr exp med, Sch Med, NY Univ, 73-75; asst prof biophys, 75-77, asst prof, 77-79, ASSOC PROF BIOPHYS & BIOCHEM, DEPT BIOPHYS, MED COL VA, 79- *Concurrent Pos:* USPHS fel, Sch Med, NY Univ, 72-75; vis scientist, Univ Utrecht, Neth, 79-80; res career develop award, 80-85. *Mem:* AAAS; Harvey Soc; NY Acad Sci; Sigma Xi; Biophys Soc. *Res:* Cell physiology; leukocyte metabolism and function; metabolism of glycerides and phospholipids; role of lysosomes and lysosomal enzymes in cell physiology; lung phospholipid and surfactant metabolism. *Mailing Add:* Dept of Biophys Box 877 Med Col of Va Richmond VA 23298

FRANT, MARTIN S, b NY, July 15, 26; m 48; c 2. ANALYTICAL CHEMISTRY. *Educ:* Brooklyn Col, BS, 49; Western Reserve Univ, MS, 51, PhD(org chem), 53. *Prof Exp:* Asst, Western Reserve Univ, 51-52; sr res chemist, Gallowhur Chem Corp, 52-56; sr res assoc, AMP, Inc, 56-62; asst tech dir, Prototech, Inc, 63-64; from asst dir res to dir res, Orion Res Inc, 64-73, vpres res, 73-78; MGR APPLN SERV, ANAL DIV, FOXBORO CO, 78- *Concurrent Pos:* Co-chmn, Gordon Res Conf Electrodeposition, 61. *Honors & Awards:* Speaker Award, Am Chem Soc, 69. *Mem:* Fel AAAS; Am Electroplaters Soc; Am Chem Soc; Electrochem Soc. *Res:* Aromatic mercury and quaternary ammonium compounds; corrosion of electroplated surfaces; analytical instrumentation for process control; electroanalytical chemistry, ion-sensing electrodes; air and gas measurements. *Mailing Add:* Foxboro Analytical PO Box 435 Burlington MA 01803

FRANTA, WILLIAM ALFRED, b Ligderwood, NDak, Mar 26, 13; m 40; c 3. POLYMER CHEMISTRY, PLASTICS ENGINEERING. *Educ:* Univ NDak, BS, 33, MS, 34; Oxford Univ, AB, 37. *Hon Degrees:* DEng, Univ NDak, 71. *Prof Exp:* Sales engr, Herbert L Brown, Ohio, 37-38; res chemist, Columbia Chem Div, Pittsburgh Plate Glass Co, 38-42; from res chemist to gen lab dir, Polychem Dept, E I du Pont de Nemours & Co, Inc, 46-53, mgr develop & serv, 53-55, mkt, 55-57, prod mgr plastics, 57-60, dir supporting res, Res & Develop Div, 60-64, asst dir, 64, dir res & develop div, Plastics Dept, 64-78; RETIRED. *Mem:* AAAS; Soc Plastics Eng; Am Chem Soc; Am Inst Chem Eng. *Res:* Organic polymers; polymer science; plastics processing and application. *Mailing Add:* 112 W Pembrey Dr Wilmington DE 19803

FRANTA, WILLIAM ROY, b St Paul, Minn, May 21, 42; m 66. MODELING, LOCAL COMPUTER NETWORKS. *Educ:* Inst Technol, Univ Minn, BMath, 64, MS, 66, PhD(comput sci), 70. *Prof Exp:* From asst prof to assoc prof, 70-81, from assoc dir to co-dir, 72-81, PROF COMPUT SCI & ASSOC DIR, INFO SCI CTR, INST TECHNOL, UNIV MINN, 81- *Concurrent Pos:* Vis prof tech, Israel Inst Technol, 82; mem affil fac, Tech Univ Berlin, 79-; consult, Honeywell, Network Systs Corp, Comput Sci Corp & others. *Mem:* Asn Comput Mach; Inst Elec & Electronics Engrs; Inst Mgt Sci. *Res:* Modeling; simulation; local computer networks; statistical analysis. *Mailing Add:* 1401 19th Ave NW New Brighton MN 55112

FRANTI, CHARLES ELMER, b Ewen, Mich, Apr 29, 33; m 56; c 5. APPLIED STATISTICS. *Educ:* Univ Mich, BS, 55, AM, 60; Mich State Univ, MS, 60; Univ Calif, Berkeley, PhD(biostatist), 67. *Prof Exp:* Instr math, biol & phys educ, Suomi Col, 55-59; instr math, Mich Technol Univ, 57-59 & 60-62; actg asst prof biostatist, 66-67, from asst prof to assoc prof, 67-76, assoc prof community health, 72-76, PROF BIOSTATIST, UNIV CALIF, DAVIS, 76-, PROF COMMUNITY HEALTH, 80- *Concurrent Pos:* Consult statist, USDA, 72-76. *Mem:* Am Pub Health Asn; Inst Math Statist; Nat Coun Teachers Math; Soc Indust & Appl Math; Soc Epidemiol Res. *Res:* Mathematical modeling of biomedical phenomena; application of statistical methods in biomedical research; statistical methods in medical surveys; zoonotic diseases. *Mailing Add:* Dept of Community Health Univ of Calif Sch of Med Davis CA 95616

FRANTSI, CHRISTOPHER, b London, Eng, Oct 13, 42; Can citizen; m 66; c 2. AQUACULTURE, FISH DISEASES. *Educ:* Acadia Univ, BSc, 66; Univ Guelph, MSc, 68, PhD(fisheries), 72. *Prof Exp:* Lectr food microbiol, Univ Guelph, 68; biologist, Gov Can Fisheries, 72-75, adv aquacult, 77-78; biologist, Huntsman Marine Lab, 75-77, teaching supvr aquacult, 78-82; PRES, FUNDY ISLES MARINE LTD, 77- *Mem:* Am Fisheries Soc. *Res:* Fish diseases and virology; aquaculture, management and disease. *Mailing Add:* Box 381 St Andrews NB E0G 2X0 Can

FRANTTI, GORDON EARL, b Palmer, Mich, July 28, 28; m 52; c 7. SEISMOLOGY. *Educ:* Mich Technol Univ, BS, 53, MS, 54. *Prof Exp:* Res asst physics, Mich Technol Univ, 53-54; mining engr & geologist, Copper Range Co, 54-55; geologist & geophysicist, Cleveland Cliffs Iron Co, 55-56; geophysicist, US Bur Mines, 56-59; asst prof physics, Mich Technol Univ, 59-60; res assoc, Inst Sci & Technol, Univ Mich, 60-64; lectr geol & mineral, 63-64, assoc res geophysicist, 64-65; ASSOC PROF GEOPHYS, MICH TECHNOL UNIV, 65- *Concurrent Pos:* Consult, US Bur Mines, 59-60 & Gen Elec Co, 62-63. *Mem:* Soc Explor Geophys; Am Geophys Union; Seismol Soc Am. *Res:* Mining and rock mechanics; theoretical and applied seismology; blasting and vibration studies; seismic earth noise. *Mailing Add:* Dept of Geol & Geol Eng Mich Technol Univ Houghton MI 49931

FRANTZ, ANDREW GIBSON, b New York, NY, May 22, 30. ENDOCRINOLOGY. *Educ:* Harvard Univ, AB, 51; Col Physicians & Surgeons, Columbia Univ, MD, 55. *Prof Exp:* Intern resident med, Presbyterian Hosp, NY, 55-58; fel endocrinol, Columbia Univ, 58-60; from instr to assoc med, Harvard Med Sch, 62-66; from asst to assoc prof, 66-71, PROF MED, COL PHYSICIANS & SURGEONS & CHIEF, DIV ENDOCRINOL, DEPT MED, COLUMBIA UNIV, 71- *Concurrent Pos:* Asst med, Mass Gen Hosp, 62-66; attend physician, Presbyterian Hosp, 66-; assoc ed, *Metabolism,* 69-; mem med adv bd, Nat Pituitary Agency, 70-73. *Mem:* Endocrine Soc; Am Soc Clin Invest; Int Soc Neuroendocrinol; Am Fedn Clin Res; NY Acad Sci. *Res:* Endocrinology and neuroendocrinology; characterization, assay, regulation of secretion and mode of action of pituitary hormones, especially prolactin; opioid peptides of hypothalamus and pituitary; diagnosis and treatment of pituitary diseases. *Mailing Add:* Dept Med Columbia Univ Col Physicians & Surgeons New York NY 10032

FRANTZ, BERYL MAY, b Cape Town, SAfrica, June 26, 43; US citizen; m 71; c 1. CLINICAL INFORMATION, DRUG INFORMATION. *Educ:* Univ Cape Town, BSc, 63, Hons, 64; Univ London, PhD(chem), 68. *Prof Exp:* Fel biochem, Med Sch, George Washington Univ, 69; res assoc cardiol, Med Col, Cornell Univ, 69-70; fel, Univ Miami, 70-71; proj assoc biochem, Univ Wis-Madison, 71-73; res investr anal chem, 73-78, SR CLIN INFO SCIENTIST, SQUIBB INST MED RES, 81- *Mem:* Royal Soc Chem; Royal Inst Chem. *Res:* Data generated from clinical studies of new drugs. *Mailing Add:* Squibb Inst Med Res PO Box 4000 Princeton NJ 08540

FRANTZ, IVAN DERAY, JR, b Smithville, WVa, Jan 16, 16; m 42; c 5. BIOCHEMISTRY. *Educ:* Duke Univ, AB, 37; Harvard Univ, MD, 41. *Prof Exp:* Intern, Springfield Hosp, Mass, 41-42; asst to assoc med, Harvard Univ, 48-54, tutor biochem, 47-54, instr med, 50-51; CLARK RES PROF, DEPTS MED & BIOCHEM, MED SCH UNIV MINN, MINNEAPOLIS, 54- *Concurrent Pos:* Res fel med, Harvard Univ, 46-48; Am Cancer Soc fel, Huntington Mem Labs, Mass Gen Hosp, Boston, 46-47; clin fel med, 46-50; asst physician, Mass Gen Hosp, Boston, 50-54; consult, Mass Inst Technol, 47-54; mem coun arteriosclerosis, Am Heart Asn, chmn, 67. *Mem:* Am Soc Biol Chem; Am Soc Clin Invest; Am Asn Cancer Res. *Res:* Bacterial nutrition; enzyme kinetics; protein and lipid metabolism with use of radioactive tracers. *Mailing Add:* Depts of Med & Biochem Univ of Minn Med Sch Minneapolis MN 55455

FRANTZ, JOSEPH FOSTER, b McComb, Miss, Feb 21, 33; m 60; c 3. CHEMICAL ENGINEERING. *Educ:* La State Univ, BS, 55, MS, 56, PhD(chem eng), 58. *Prof Exp:* Res chem engr, Monsanto Co, Ark, 58-60, sr chem engr, Mo, 61-62, eng dept, Hydrocarbons Div, 62-65; mgr develop & mkt, South Hampton Co, Houston, 65-68; PRES, THE FRANTZ CO, 68- *Honors & Awards:* Award, Am Inst Chem Engrs, 63-64. *Mem:* Am Inst Chem Engrs; Am Chem Soc. *Res:* Fluidization; thermal cracking of hydrocarbons; marketing. *Mailing Add:* 6410 Tam O'Shanter Houston TX 77036

FRANTZ, STEPHEN WILLIAM, b Canton, Ohio, Feb 24, 52; m 75; c 2. MOLECULAR TOXICOLOGY. *Educ:* Mich State Univ, BS, 74; Univ Mich, MS, 78, PhD(toxicol), 81. *Prof Exp:* Teaching asst pharm, Col Pharm, Univ Mich, 75-79, res asst toxicol, 79-81; INDUST FEL MOLECULAR TOXICOL, TOXICOL RES LAB, DOW CHEM, CO, 81- *Mem:* Am Chem Soc; Environ Mutagen Soc; Sigma Xi. *Res:* Molecular mechanisms of chemical toxicity in mammalian organisms; mechanisms of skin absorption for toxic industrial solvents wih an interest in improving methods of removal (and/or prevention) of solvent exposures. *Mailing Add:* 2528 S Jefferson Midland MI 48640

FRANTZ, WENDELIN R, b Cleveland, Ohio, Apr 28, 29; m 52; c 3. PETROLEUM GEOLOGY, STRATIGRAPHY. *Educ:* Col Wooster, BA, 52; Univ Pittsburgh, MS, 56, PhD(geol), 63. *Prof Exp:* Explor geologist, Sohio Petrol Co, 56-60; instr geol, Capital Univ, 61-64, asst prof, 64-68; PROF GEOG & EARTH SCI & CHMN DEPT, BLOOMSBURG STATE COL, 68- *Mem:* Am Asn Petrol Geol; Nat Asn Geol Teachers; Geol Soc Am. *Res:* Subsurface stratigraphy and sedimentation, particularly the application to exploration for stratigraphic-type hydrocarbon accumulations. *Mailing Add:* Dept of Geog & Earth Sci Bloomsburg State Col Bloomsburg PA 17815

FRANTZ, WILLIAM LAWRENCE, b Canton, Ohio, Nov 3, 27; m 50; c 3. ZOOLOGY. *Educ:* Kent State Univ, BSc, 51; Ohio State Univ, MSc, 53, PhD, 57. *Prof Exp:* Asst prof biol, Drake Univ, 57-60; asst prof physiol & pharmacol, 60-74, PROF PHYSIOL, MICH STATE UNIV, 74- *Mem:* Am Soc Zool; Am Physiol Soc. *Res:* Cellular physiology; intermediary metabolism; membrane transport. *Mailing Add:* Dept of Physiol Col Natural Sci Mich State Univ East Lansing MI 48824

FRANZ, ANSELM, b Schladming, Austria, Jan 21, 00; nat US; m 29; c 2. MECHANICAL & AERONAUTICAL ENGINEERING. *Educ:* Tech Univ Graz, Austria, MS, 24; Tech Univ Berlin, PhD(eng), 39. *Hon Degrees:* Dr, Tech Univ Graz, Austria, 69. *Prof Exp:* Asst prof turbomachinery, Tech Univ Graz, 24-28; res engr, Schwarzkopff Werke, Berlin, 29-35; vpres eng, Junkers Flugzeug & Motorenwerke, Ger, 36-45; consult jet propulsion, Wright-Patterson Air Force Base, US Air Force, 46-50; vpres & asst gen mgr, 51-68, CONSULT, AVCO LYCOMING DIV, 69- *Honors & Awards:* Klemin Award, Am Helicopter Soc, 66; Austrian Dist Serv Cross for Sci & Art 1st Class, President of Austria, 78. *Mem:* Fel Am Soc Mech Engrs; Soc Automotive Engrs; Am Helicopter Soc; assoc fel Am Inst Aeronaut & Astronaut; Ger Acad Aeronaut Sci. *Res:* Aerodynamics; thermodynamics; combustion; jet-propulsion; gas turbine and jet engine development. *Mailing Add:* 488A Commanche Ln Stratford CT 06497

FRANZ, CURTIS ALLEN, b Gary, Ind, Jan 6, 40; m 69; c 2. ORGANIC CHEMISTRY. *Educ:* Purdue Univ, BS, 62; Ind Univ, MS, 65; Univ Iowa, PhD(org chem), 72. *Prof Exp:* Sr chemist, Ott Chem Co, 70-72; process chemist, 73-75, sr process chemist, 75-77, CHIEF CHEMIST, ORG CHEM DIV, AM CYANAMID CO, 77- *Concurrent Pos:* Chmn, Piscataway Environ Adv Comn, 74- *Mem:* Am Chem Soc. *Res:* Process development in chemistry, process maintenance and profit improvement. *Mailing Add:* Org Chem Div Am Cyanamid Co Bound Brook NJ 08805

FRANZ, DAVID ALAN, b Philadelphia, Pa, Nov 5, 42; m 64; c 2. ANALYTICAL CHEMISTRY. *Educ:* Princeton Univ, AB, 64; Johns Hopkins Univ, MAT, 65; Univ Va, PhD(chem), 70. *Prof Exp:* High sch teacher chem, Baltimore City Pub Schs, 65-66; asst prof, 70-77, ASSOC PROF CHEM, LYCOMING COL, 77- *Concurrent Pos:* Vis scholar, Dept Chem, Univ NMex, 80-81. *Mem:* Am Chem Soc. *Res:* Teaching methods, particularly tested lecture demonstrations; environmental chemical analysis. *Mailing Add:* Dept of Chem Lycoming Col Williamsport PA 17701

FRANZ, DONALD NORBERT, b Indianapolis, Ind, Sept 23, 32; m 58; c 2. NEUROPHARMACOLOGY. *Educ:* Butler Univ, BS, 54, MS, 62; Univ Utah, PhD(pharmacol), 66. *Prof Exp:* Fel vet physiol, Univ Edinburgh, 66-68; asst prof pharmacol, 68-75, ASSOC PROF PHARMACOL, COL MED, UNIV UTAH, 75- *Mem:* AAAS; Am Soc Pharmacol & Exp Therapeut. *Res:* Neurobiology of monoamines in central autonomic transmission; effects of cold and drugs on nerve conduction; pharmacology of central monoaminergic pathways, mechanism of action of antihypertensives and anticonvulsants. *Mailing Add:* Dept of Pharmacol Univ of Utah Col of Med Salt Lake City UT 84132

FRANZ, EDGAR ARTHUR, b Staunton, Ill, Dec 9, 19; m 46; c 4. MATHEMATICS. *Educ:* Univ Iowa, BA, 48, MS, 49. *Prof Exp:* From instr to prof math, Culver-Stockton Col, 49-65; PROF MATH, ILL COL, 65-, HITCHCOCK CHAIR MATH, 80- *Mem:* Math Asn Am. *Res:* General mathematics. *Mailing Add:* 348 Sandusky Jacksonville IL 62650

FRANZ, EDMUND C(LARENCE), b Pittsburgh, Pa, July 8, 20; m 49; c 3. PHYSICAL METALLURGY. *Educ:* Carnegie Inst Technol, BS, 48; Case Inst Technol, MS, 53. *Prof Exp:* Res metallurgist, Cleveland Res Div, 48-53, RES METALLURGIST, ALCOA LABS, ALUMINUM CO AM, 53- *Mem:* Am Soc Metals; Sigma Xi. *Res:* Alloy technology and fabrication of aluminum alloys. *Mailing Add:* 25 Nancy Dr Pittsburgh PA 15235

FRANZ, FRANK ANDREW, b Philadelphia, Pa, Sept 16, 37; m 59; c 1. PHYSICS. *Educ:* Lafayette Col, BS, 59; Univ Ill, MS, 61, PhD(physics), 64. *Prof Exp:* Res assoc physics, Coord Sci Lab, Univ Ill, 64-65; res fel, Swiss Fed Inst Technol, 65-67; from asst prof to assoc prof, 67-74, assoc dean, Col Arts & Sci, 74-76, PROF PHYSICS, IND UNIV, 74-, DEAN FAC, 77- *Concurrent Pos:* NSF fel, 65-67; Alfred P Sloan Found fel, 69-71. *Mem:* AAAS; fel Am Phys Soc; Am Asn Phys Teachers. *Res:* Relaxation phenomena in atomic and solid state physics; optical pumping; collisional interactions between atoms in ground and excited states; magnetic resonance in atomic vapors. *Mailing Add:* Dept of Physics Ind Univ Bloomington IN 47401

FRANZ, GUNTER NORBERT, b Backa Palanka, Yugoslavia, Mar 13, 35; m 65; c 3. PHYSIOLOGY, BIOPHYSICS. *Educ:* Karlsruhe Tech Univ, dipl elec eng, 59; Univ Wash, PhD(physiol, biophys), 68. *Prof Exp:* Asst prof, 68-72, ASSOC PROF PHYSIOL & BIOPHYS, MED CTR, WVA UNIV, 72- *Mem:* AAAS; Inst Elec & Electronics Eng; Biophys Soc; Am Physiol Soc. *Res:* Physiology and biophysics of sensory receptors and muscle membranes; lung mechanics. *Mailing Add:* Dept Physiol & Biophys WVa Univ Med Ctr Morgantown WV 26506

FRANZ, JAMES ALAN, b Seattle, Wash, June 20, 48; m 74; c 2. PHYSICAL ORGANIC CHEMISTRY. *Educ:* Univ Wash, BS, 70; Univ Ill, Champaign-Urbana, PhD(chem), 74. *Prof Exp:* RES SCIENTIST CHEM, PAC NORTHWEST LABS, BATTELLE MEM INST, 74- *Concurrent Pos:* Lectr chem, Wash State Univ, 75- *Mem:* Am Chem Soc. *Res:* Applications of C-13 nuclear magnetic resonance to determination of coal structure; mechanisms of free radical reactions; formation, structure and reactivity of coal. *Mailing Add:* Pac Northwest Lab Battelle Mem Inst PO Box 999 Richland WA 99352

FRANZ, JOHN EDWARD, b Springfield, Ill, Dec 21, 29; m 51; c 4. BIO-ORGANIC CHEMISTRY. *Educ:* Univ Ill, BS, 51; Univ Minn, PhD(chem), 55. *Prof Exp:* Res chemist, Monsanto Co, 55-59, group leader, 59-62, sci fel 62-75, sr sci fel, 75-80, DISTINGUISHED SCI FEL, MONSANTO AGR PROD CO, 80- *Mem:* Am Chem Soc; AAAS. *Res:* Fundamental organic research; reaction mechanisms; coenzyme A antimetabolites; antiauxin chemistry (isothiazoles, isoxazoles, pyrazoles); plant chemistry; cell membrane chemistry (glyceride and phospholipid syntheses, liposomes); phosphonomethylglycine (glyphosate) chemistry and processes; plant hormone chemistry (abscissic acid analogs, ethylene generators). *Mailing Add:* Monsanto Agr Prod Co 800 N Lindberg Blvd St Louis MO 63166

FRANZ, JOHN MATTHIAS, b Oak Park, Ill, May 23, 27; m 51; c 4. BIOCHEMISTRY. *Educ:* Univ Ill, BS, 50; Univ Iowa, MS, 52, PhD(biochem), 55. *Prof Exp:* From instr to asst prof, 55-61, asst chmn dept, 75-76, assoc chmn dept, 76-79, ASSOC PROF BIOCHEM, UNIV MO-COLUMBIA, 61-, DIR UNDERGRAD EDUC, 79- *Concurrent Pos:* Res assoc, Harvard Univ, 65-66. *Res:* Developmental and comparative aspects of metabolic control; tryptophan metabolism; carcinogenesis; use of computers in biochemistry. *Mailing Add:* Univ of Mo Dept of Biochem 322A Chem Bldg Columbia MO 65211

FRANZ, JUDITH ROSENBAUM, b Chicago, Ill, May 3, 38; m 59; c 1. SOLID STATE PHYSICS. *Educ:* Cornell Univ, BA, 59; Univ Ill, MA, 61, PhD(physics), 65. *Prof Exp:* Res physicist, Int Bus Mach Res Lab, Switz, 65-67; vis asst prof, 68-70, from asst prof to assoc prof, 70-79, assoc dean, Col Arts & Sci, 80-82, PROF PHYSICS, IND UNIV, BLOOMINGTON, 79- *Concurrent Pos:* Danforth Assoc, 77-83; Humboldt fel, 78-79. *Mem:* AAAS; Am Phys Soc; Am Asn Physics Teachers. *Res:* Magnetic-field-dependent interactions of ultrasonic waves in metals; nuclear acoustic resonance; metal-nonmetal transition in liquid alloys. *Mailing Add:* Dept of Physics Ind Univ Bloomington IN 47401

FRANZ, NORMAN CHARLES, b Newark, NJ, June 12, 25; m 49; c 1. WOOD SCIENCE, WOOD TECHNOLOGY. *Educ:* State Univ NY, BS, 48; Univ Mich, MWood Tech, 50, PhD, 56. *Prof Exp:* Res engr, Eng Res Inst, 50-54; from instr to assoc prof wood tech, Univ Mich, 54-68; PROF FORESTRY, UNIV BC, 68- *Mem:* Soc Wood Sci & Technol; Forest Prod Res Soc; Am Soc Mech Eng; Int Union Forest Res Orgn. *Res:* Forest products engineering; machining of wood and other materials; ultra-high pressure physics and processing; fluid jet cutting; wood machining. *Mailing Add:* 1203-4665 W 10th Vancouver BC V6H 1J3 Can

FRANZ, OTTO GUSTAV, b Eggenburg, Austria, Feb 14, 31; m 62; c 3. OBSERVATIONAL ASTRONOMY. *Educ:* Univ Vienna, DPhil, 55. *Prof Exp:* Res asst astron, Vienna Univ Observ, 53-55; res assoc, Dearborn Observ, Northwestern Univ, 55-58; astronr, US Naval Observ, 58-65; ASTRONR, LOWELL OBSERV, 65- *Concurrent Pos:* Adj prof, Ohio State Univ, 68- *Mem:* Am Astron Soc; AAAS; Sigma Xi; Int Astron Union. *Res:* Astrometry and photometry of visual binary stars; photometric investigation of planets and planetary satellites; occultation studies of solar system objects; space telescope astrometry. *Mailing Add:* Lowell Observ Flagstaff AZ 86002

FRANZAK, EDMUND GEORGE, b Chicago, Ill, June 27, 30; m 60; c 3. THEORETICAL PHYSICS. *Educ:* Fournier Inst Technol, BS, 52; Univ NMex, MS, 55; Northwestern Univ, MS, 57, PhD(physics), 60. *Prof Exp:* Mem staff, Sandia Corp, 52-55; asst prof physics, Univ Mo, 60-61; head neutron tube develop div, 62-66, mgr, Electronic Components Dept, 66-74, mgr, Integrated Circuit Design Dept, 74-77, MGR, MEASUREMENT STANDARDS DEPT, SANDIA NAT LABS, 77- *Mem:* Inst Elec & Electronic Engrs. *Res:* Neutron and theoretical solid state physics; electron transport in metals. *Mailing Add:* 7000 Vista Del Arroyo NE Albuquerque NM 87109

FRANZBLAU, CARL, b New York, NY, Sept 26, 34; m 58; c 2. BIOCHEMISTRY. *Educ:* Univ Mich, BS, 56; Albert Einstein Col Med, PhD(biochem), 62. *Prof Exp:* From asst prof to assoc prof, 62-71, PROF BIOCHEM, SCH MED, BOSTON UNIV, 71-, CHMN DEPT, 77- *Concurrent Pos:* Res collabr, Brookhaven Nat Lab, 62-72; estab investr, Am Heart Asn, 66-71. *Mem:* Am Chem Soc; Am Soc Biol Chem; NY Acad Sci; Am Heart Asn. *Res:* Chemistry of connective tissue proteins; enzymology. *Mailing Add:* Dept of Biochem Boston Univ Sch of Med Boston MA 02118

FRANZEN, DOROTHEA SUSANNA, b Emporia, Kans, Mar 17, 12. ZOOLOGY. *Educ:* Bethel Col, AB, 37; Univ Kans, MA, 43, PhD(zool), 46. *Prof Exp:* Instr biol, Cedar Crest Col, 46-47; from asst prof to assoc prof, Washburn Univ, 47-52; from assoc prof to prof, 52-71, George C & Ella Beach Lewis prof, 71-77, EMER PROF BIOL, ILL WESLEYAN UNIV, 77- *Concurrent Pos:* Researcher, Univ Reading, Eng, 59-60. *Mem:* Fel AAAS; Am Soc Zool; Soc Syst Zool; Am Malacol Union. *Res:* Distribution and ecology of Cenozoic terrestrial and freshwater Mollusca; fossil and living Pupillidae in Kansas; Succineidae in North America. *Mailing Add:* Dept Biol Ill Wesleyan Univ Bloomington IL 61702

FRANZEN, HUGO FRIEDRICH, b New York, NY, Aug 27, 34; m 56; c 3. PHYSICAL CHEMISTRY. *Educ:* Univ Calif, Berkeley, BS, 57; Univ Kans, PhD(chem), 62. *Prof Exp:* Fel, Inst Inorg Chem, Univ Stockholm, 63-64; asst chemist, AEC, 64-65, assoc chemist, 65-69, chemist, 69-74, SR CHEMIST, AMES LAB, DEPT ENERGY, 74-; PROF CHEM, IOWA STATE UNIV, 74- *Concurrent Pos:* From instr to assoc prof, Iowa State Univ, 64-74. *Mem:* AAAS; Am Chem Soc; Am Crystallog Asn. *Res:* High temperature chemistry; thermodynamics; crystallography; heterogeneous equilibrium; vaporization chemistry. *Mailing Add:* Dept Chem Iowa State Univ Ames IA 50011

FRANZEN, JAMES, b Chicago, Ill, Jan 13, 34; m 61; c 4. BIOCHEMISTRY. *Educ:* Wheaton Col, BS, 55; Univ Ill, MS, 58, PhD(biochem), 60. *Prof Exp:* USPHS fel, Northwestern Univ, 60-61; res assoc biophys chem, Grad Sch Pub Health, 61-62, asst res prof, 62-65, assoc prof biochem, 65-81, PROF BIOCHEM, UNIV PITTSBURGH, 81- *Mem:* Am Chem Soc; Am Soc Biol Chem. *Res:* Structure-function relations in enzymes; cooperative enzyme-substrate interactions. *Mailing Add:* Dept of Biol Sci Fac of Arts & Sci Univ Pittsburgh Pittsburgh PA 15260

FRANZEN, KAY LOUISE, b Minneapolis, Minn, Apr 15, 50. FOOD SCIENCE. *Educ:* Univ Minn, BS, 70, BChem, 71; Cornell Univ, MS, 73, PhD(food chem), 76. *Prof Exp:* Scientist, 75-77, GROUP LEADER RES & DEVELOP, PILLSBURY CO, 77- *Mem:* Inst Food Technologists; AAAS. *Res:* Protein functionality; protein modification; ingredient functionality; cereals; baked goods. *Mailing Add:* Res & Develop 311 Second St SE Minneapolis MN 55414

FRANZEN, WOLFGANG, b Duesseldorf, Ger, Apr 6, 22; nat US; m 43. PHYSICS. *Educ:* Haverford Col, BS, 42; Columbia Univ, MA, 44; Univ Pa, PhD, 49. *Prof Exp:* Instr physics, Princeton Univ, 49-53; asst prof, Univ Rochester, 53-56; sr physicist, Arthur D Little, Inc, 56-61; assoc prof, 61-65, PROF PHYSICS, BOSTON UNIV, 65- *Concurrent Pos:* Exchange fel, Univ Basel, 54-55; NATO sr fel, Toulouse Univ, 69-70; Fulbright lectr, Nat Univ Colombia, 77. *Mem:* Fel Am Phys Soc. *Res:* Nuclear reactions and physics; instrumentation; optical pumping; magnetic resonance; electron resonance scattering and polarization. *Mailing Add:* Dept of Physics Boston Univ Boston MA 02215

FRANZIN, WILLIAM GILBERT, b Powell River, BC, July 11, 46; m 69; c 1. FISH BIOLOGY, ENVIRONMENTAL TOXICOLOGY. *Educ:* Univ BC, BSc Hons, 67; Univ Man, MSc, 70, PhD(zool), 74. *Prof Exp:* Biologist, Environ Can, 73-75, RES SCIENTIST TOXICOL, DEPT FISHERIES & OCEANS, FISHERIES MGT, FISHERIES & OCEANS CAN, 75- *Concurrent Pos:* Sr res award, Sigma Xi, 80. *Mem:* Am Fisheries Soc; Am Soc Ichthyologists & Herpetologists. *Res:* Environmental contamination near smelters; experimental field toxicology of heavy metals; fish population genetics; zoogeography. *Mailing Add:* Fisheries & Marine Serv 501 University Crescent Winnipeg Can

FRANZINI, JOSEPH B(ERNARD), b Las Vegas, NMex, Nov 10, 20; m 46; c 4. CIVIL ENGINEERING. *Educ:* Calif Inst Technol, BS, 42, MS, 43, CE, 44; Stanford Univ, PhD(civil eng), 50. *Prof Exp:* Asst, Calif Inst Technol, 42-44; from instr to assoc prof, 46-62, PROF CIVIL ENG, STANFORD UNIV, 62-, CHMN DEPT, 76- *Mem:* Am Soc Civil Engrs; Am Soc Eng Educ; Am Geophys Union. *Res:* Evaporation suppression; infiltration; porous media flow. *Mailing Add:* Dept of Civil Eng Stanford Univ Stanford CA 94305

FRANZL, ROBERT E, b New York, NY, May 27, 21; m 52; c 1. IMMUNOBIOLOGY. *Educ:* City Col New York, BS, 41; Columbia Univ, MA, 48, PhD(biochem), 52. *Prof Exp:* Asst org chem & biochem, Columbia Univ, 46-52, res assoc biochem, 53-54; res assoc immunochem, Sloan-Kettering Inst, 54-56; res assoc, Rockefeller Univ, 56-59, asst prof immunol, 59-72; chief immunoneurol res, Vet Admin Hosp, Coatesville, 72-76; RES SCIENTIST, UNIV NEV, RENO, 76- *Concurrent Pos:* Vis res assoc, Brookhaven Nat Labs, 52-53. *Mem:* AAAS; Reticuloendothelial Soc; Am Chem Soc; Brit Biochem Soc; AAAS. *Res:* Bacterial enzymes; cyclitols; lipids; immunochemistry; antibody synthesis; drug addiction; cancer. *Mailing Add:* 1445 Blue Spruce Rd Reno NV 89511

FRANZMEIER, DONALD PAUL, b Greenwood, Wis, May 13, 35; m 60; c 3. SOIL GENESIS, SOIL CLASSIFICATION. *Educ:* Univ Minn, BS, 57, MS, 58; Mich State Univ, PhD(soil sci), 62. *Prof Exp:* Soil scientist, Soil Conserv Serv, USDA, 62-67; assoc prof, 67-76, PROF AGRON, PURDUE UNIV, WEST LAFAYETTE, 76-, SOIL SURV LEADER, PURDUE AGR EXP STA, 70- *Mem:* Am Soc Agron; Soil Sci Soc Am; Am Asn Quaternary Res; Soil Conserv Soc Am; Int Soc Soil Sci. *Res:* Soil mineralogy, chemistry and physics in relation to the genesis and classification of soils. *Mailing Add:* Dept Agron Purdue Univ West Lafayette IN 47907

FRANZOSA, EDWARD SYKES, b Boston, Mass, Oct 28, 45. FORENSIC SCIENCE, PHYSICAL CHEMISTRY. *Educ:* Rensselaer Polytech Inst, BS, 67; State Univ NY Binghamton, PhD(phys chem), 75. *Prof Exp:* FORENSIC CHEMIST, DRUG ENFORCEMENT ADMIN, US DEPT JUSTICE, 75- *Concurrent Pos:* Officer & evidence analyst, Whitney Pt Police Dept, NY, 70-75. *Mem:* Am Chem Soc; Am Acad Forensic Sci. *Res:* Pre-resonance raman intensity - quantitative test of theories using vibronically active pyrazine; computerized band contour analysis of laser excited fluorescence of s-tetrazine to determine excited state rotational constants; microscopic and microchemical analysis of illicit and legitimate drug preparations; gas chromatography and mass spectroscopy analysis of synthesis precursors and by-products in clandestinely manufactured drugs. *Mailing Add:* Spec Testing & Res Lab 7704 Old Springhouse Rd McLean VA 22102

FRANZREB, KATHLEEN E, ecology, see previous edition

FRANZUS, BORIS, b Chicago, Ill, July 23, 24; m 48; c 3. PHYSICAL CHEMISTRY, ORGANIC CHEMISTRY. *Educ:* Univ Chicago, MS, 50; Univ Colo, PhD(phys org chem), 54. *Prof Exp:* Res chemist, Phillips Petrol Co, 54-60; sr chemist, Cent Basic Res Labs, Esso Res & Eng Co, 60-67; assoc prof, 67-70, PROF CHEM, E TENN STATE UNIV, 70- *Mem:* Am Chem Soc; Royal Soc Chem. *Res:* Kinetics and mechanisms reactions of organic chemistry. *Mailing Add:* Dept of Chem E Tenn State Univ Johnson City TN 37601

FRAPPIER, ARMAND, b Valleyfield, Que, Nov 26, 04; m 29; c 4. BACTERIOLOGY, HYGIENE. *Educ:* Univ Montreal, BA, 24, MD, 30, Lic-es-Sci, 31; Trudeau Sch, dipl, 32. *Hon Degrees:* Dr, Univ Paris, 64 & Laval Univ, 71. *Prof Exp:* Prof, Fac Med, 33-71, emer founder & dean sch hyg, 45-65, dir & founder, Inst Microbiol & Hyg, 38-74, ADV TO DIR, INST ARMAND-FRAPPIER, UNIV QUEBEC, 74- *Concurrent Pos:* Dir clin labs, St Luke's Hosp, 27-43; consult, Health League, Can, 47-60; mem adv comt med res, Nat Res Coun Can, 52-55; mem panel infection & adv comt biol warfare res, Defence Res Bd, Can; mem adv comt, Pub Health Res, Can, 54-60; mem expert comt tuberc, WHO, 53. *Honors & Awards:* Officer, Order of the Brit Empire, 46; Companion, Order of Can, 69; Jean Toy Prize, Acad Sci, Inst of France, 71. *Mem:* Fel Am Pub Health Asn; Am Asn Path & Bact; fel Royal Soc Can; Can Physiol Soc; Can Soc Microbiol (pres, 54). *Res:* Allergy and immunization in tuberculosis using Bacillus Calmette-Guerin vaccine; development of scarification test; experimental tuberculosis using radio-isotopes; gas gangrene mechanism; role of bacterial surface washings in production of immunity against whooping cough and other agents; infection promoting factors; poliomyelitis; prevention of leukemia with Bacillus Calmette-Guerin. *Mailing Add:* Inst Armand-Frappier CP 100 Laval-des-Rapides PQ H7V 1B7 Can

FRAREY, MURRAY JAMES, b Midland, Ont, Jan 31, 17; m 54; c 2. GEOLOGY. *Educ:* Univ Western Ont, BA, 40; Univ Mich, MSc, 51, PhD(geol), 54. *Prof Exp:* Geologist, Kerr-Addison Gold Mines, Ltd, 41-43; GEOLOGIST, GEOL SURV CAN, 47- *Mem:* Geol Asn Can. *Res:* Precambrian geology. *Mailing Add:* 805-2625 Regina Ottawa ON K2B 5W8 Can

FRARY, SUSAN CATHERINE, b Los Angeles, Calif, May 9, 45; c 1. PHARMACEUTICAL RESEARCH, PROJECT MANAGEMENT. *Educ:* Bennington Col, BA, 66; Univ Vt, PhD(biochem), 72. *Prof Exp:* Res assoc, Scripps Inst Oceanog, Univ Calif, 72-73; res scientist, Lamont-Doherty Geol Observ, Columbia Univ, 73-76; clin res analyst, Med Res Div, 76-79, ASST DIR, MED PROD SURVEILLANCE, LEDERLE LABS, AM CYANAMID CO, 79- *Mem:* AAAS; Am Chem Soc; Drug Info Asn. *Mailing Add:* Lederle Labs Am Cyanamid Co Pearl River NY 10965

FRASCELLA, DANIEL W, b New Brunswick, NJ, July 6, 34; m 56; c 3. PHYSIOLOGY, BIOCHEMISTRY. *Educ:* Rutgers Univ, BS, 60, MS, 62, PhD(physiol, biochem), 68. *Prof Exp:* Pharmacologist, Wallace Labs, 62-63; asst prof physiol, Rutgers Univ, 66-69; sr res fel, Merck Inst Therapeut Res, 69-70; asst prof physiol, St John's Univ, 70-74; asst dir, 74-75, ASSOC DIR SCI MKT, HOECHST-ROUSSEL PHARMACEUT, AM HOECHST CORP, 74- *Concurrent Pos:* Vis lectr, Dept Natural Sci, Pace Col, 66-67; vis assoc prof biol, City Col New York, 72-74. *Mem:* Am Soc Zoologists; AAAS; NY Acad Sci; Sigma Xi; Am Diabetes Asn. *Res:* Tissue biochemical changes induced by stress and cold exposure; whole body and tissue changes induced by stress in diabetics; dietary effect on tissue enzymes; medical - continuing education program development. *Mailing Add:* Hoechst-Roussel Pharmaceut Inc Rte 202-206 N Somerville NJ 08876

FRASCO, DAVID LEE, b Brush, Colo, Apr 8, 31; m 54; c 2. PHYSICAL CHEMISTRY, SPECTROSCOPY. *Educ:* Colo State Col, AB, 53; Wash State Univ, MS, 55, PhD(infrared spectra of solids), 58. *Prof Exp:* Consult, Battelle Pac Northwest Labs, Battelle Mem Inst, 68-78. *Concurrent Pos:* Consult, Battelle NW Labs, Battelle Mem Inst, 68-77. *Concurrent. Mem:* AAAS; Am Chem Soc. *Res:* Physical, chemical and electrical properties of thin lipid membranes, especially artificial cell membranes; infrared spectra of molecular solids. *Mailing Add:* Dept of Chem Whitman Col Walla Walla WA 99362

FRASER, ALAN RICHARD, b Arvida, Que, May 22, 44. INORGANIC CHEMISTRY, BIOCHEMISTRY. *Educ:* McGill Univ, BSc, 66; Sir George Williams Univ, PhD(chem), 74. *Prof Exp:* Fel biochem, Rockefeller Univ, 74-76; res assoc, Univ Toronto, 76-78; asst prof, 78-80, ASSOC PROF CHEM, UNIV MONCTON, 80- *Concurrent Pos:* Med Res Coun Can fel, 74-76; Atkinson Charitable Found fel, 77-78. *Mem:* Chem Inst Can. *Res:* Elongation of protein synthesis; initiation of protein synthesis; chemical derivitization of protein molecules. *Mailing Add:* Dept of Chem Univ of Moncton Moncton NB E1A 3E9 Can

FRASER, ALEX STEWART, b London, UK, Dec 24, 23; m 50; c 6. VISUAL PERCEPTION, GENETICS. *Educ:* Univ Edinburgh, BSc, MSc & PhD, 51. *Prof Exp:* Sr prin res off genetics, Commonwealth Sci & Indust Res Conf, 51-62; prof, Univ Calif, Davis, 62-67; PROF GENETICS, UNIV CINCINNATI, 67- *Res:* Variation of visual perception in humans and the degree to which such variation is genetically determined. *Mailing Add:* Dept Biol Sci Univ Cincinnati Cincinnati OH 45221

FRASER, ALISTAIR BISSON, b Rossland, BC, May 31, 39; m 62; c 2. ATMOSPHERIC PHYSICS, OPTICS. *Educ:* Univ BC, BSc, 62; Univ London, DIC, 68, PhD(meteorol), 68. *Prof Exp:* Meteorol officer, Dept Transp, Govt Can, 62-64; from res assoc to asst prof atmospheric sci, Univ Wash, 68-72; assoc prof, 72-79, PROF METEOROL, PA STATE UNIV, 79- *Mem:* Am Meteorol Soc; Optical Soc Am; Can Meteorol Soc. *Res:* The optical properties of the atmosphere with emphasis on image formation and remote sensing. *Mailing Add:* Dept of Meteorol Pa State Univ University Park PA 16802

FRASER, BLAIR ALLEN, b Rockford, Ill, July 27, 48; m 74. BIOCHEMISTRY, IMMUNOLOGY. *Educ:* Hope Col, AB, 70; Pa State Univ, MS, 72, PhD(biochem), 74. *Prof Exp:* Res assoc immunochem, Rockefeller Univ, 74-77; staff fel, Nat Inst Allergy & Infectious Dis, 77-78; sr staff fel, Biochem Br, Div Bact Prods, 78-79, res chemist, Biochem Br, Div Bact Prods, 79-80, RES CHEMIST, DIV BIOCHEM & BIOPHYS, BUR BIOLOGICS, FED DEPT AGR, 80-, DIR, CHEM BIOL BR, DIV BIOCHEM & BIOPHYS, 81- *Concurrent Pos:* Adj asst prof, The Catholic Univ, 80-; assoc ed, J Immunol, 78-81. *Mem:* Sigma Xi; Am Chem Soc; Harvey Soc; NY Acad Sci; Am Asn Immunologists. *Res:* Structural and immunochemical studies on complex glycoconjugates of microbial cell surface origin; immunological studies of bacteria-host interactions; mass spectrometric methods of structural analysis of biomolecules; investigation of cell surface glycolipids and glycoproteins. *Mailing Add:* Bur of Biologics 8800 Rockville Pike Bethesda MD 20205

FRASER, C E OVID, veterinary immunology, veterinary microbiology, see previous edition

FRASER, CLARENCE MALCOLM, b Hamiota, Man, June 21, 26; m 55; c 5. VETERINARY MEDICINE. *Educ:* Univ Man, BSA, 49; Univ Toronto, DVM, 54, MVSc, 63. *Prof Exp:* Self employed veterinarian, 54-58; ambulatory clinician vet med, Ont Vet Col, 58-63, prof vet med, 63-65; prof vet med & head dept vet clin studies, Univ Sask, 65-70; assoc ed vet manual, Merck & Co, Inc, 70-75; mgr clin res, Pitman Moore, Inc, 75-76; ASSOC ED VET MANUAL, MERCK & CO, INC, 76- *Mem:* Am Vet Med Asn; Can Vet Med Asn. *Res:* Veterinary parasitology; infectious and metabolic diseases. *Mailing Add:* Old Forge Rd 3 Flemington NJ 08822

FRASER, DAVID ALLISON, b Philadelphia, Pa, Aug 29, 22; m 47; c 2. OCCUPATIONAL HEALTH, ELECTRON MICROSCOPY. *Educ:* Univ Pa, BA, 47; Xavier Univ, Ohio, MS, 57; Univ Cincinnati, ScD(indust health), 61. *Prof Exp:* Res chemist, Chem Mfg & Distrib Co, 47-49; chemist, Div Indust Hyg, USPHS, Washington, DC, 49-52, chief aerosol unit, Div Occup Health Prog, Ohio, 52-61; assoc prof, 61-68, PROF INDUST HEALTH, UNIV NC, CHAPEL HILL, 68- *Concurrent Pos:* Lectr, Univ Cincinnati, 58-61; consult, Div Radiol Health, USPHS, 64- *Mem:* Fel AAAS; Am Chem Soc; Electron Micros Soc Am; Am Indust Hyg Asn; fel Royal Micros Soc. *Res:* Industrial health and toxicology; air sampling techniques; physics and sampling of airborne particulates; optical microscopy. *Mailing Add:* Dept of Environ Sci & Eng Univ of NC Chapel Hill NC 27514

FRASER, DAVID WILLIAM, b Abington, Pa, May 10, 44; m 66; c 2. PUBLIC HEALTH. *Educ:* Haverford Col, BA, 65; Harvard Med Sch, MD, 69. *Prof Exp:* Chief special pathogens br, Bacterial Dis Div, Bur Epidemiol, Ctr Dis Control, 75-80; med epidemiol consult, Health Br, Health & Income Maintenance Div, Off Mgt & Budget, 80-81; ASST DIR MED SCI, BACTERIAL DIS DIV, CTR INFECTIOUS DIS, CENTERS DIS CONTROL, 81- *Honors & Awards:* Richard & Hinda Rosenthal Found Award, Am Col Physicians, 79. *Mem:* Am Col Physicians; Am Epidemiol Soc. *Res:* Epidemiology of bacterial diseases, with emphasis on Legionnaires diseases and related diseases; bacterial meningitis and other infections of the respiratory tract. *Mailing Add:* Bldg 1 Rm 5035 Centers for Dis Control Atlanta GA 30333

FRASER, (WILLIAM) DEAN, b Wells River, Vt, Oct 3, 16; m 39, 53, 65; c 7. MOLECULAR BIOLOGY. *Educ:* Harvard Univ, BS, 38; Univ Ill, MS, 39, PhD(org chem), 41. *Prof Exp:* Res chemist, Monsanto Chem Co, Mo, 41-45; res fel, Calif Inst Technol, 46-47; asst prof res, Princeton Univ, 47-48; Nat Res Coun growth fel, Virus Lab, Univ Calif, Berkeley, 48-50, asst res biochemist, 50-52, assoc res biochemist, 52-55; from assoc prof to prof virol, 55-70, chmn dept microbiol, 70-77, PROF MICROBIOL, DEPT BIOL, IND UNIV, BLOOMINGTON, 70- *Mem:* AAAS; Am Chem Soc. *Res:* Mycoplasma viruses; biochemical and genetic resolution. *Mailing Add:* Dept of Biol Ind Univ Bloomington IN 47401

FRASER, DONALD, b Toronto, Ont, Feb 14, 21; m 54; c 1. PHYSIOLOGY. *Educ:* Univ Toronto, MD, 44, MA, 46, PhD(physiol), 50. *Prof Exp:* Res assoc, Hosp for Sick Children, 53-58; assoc pediat, 55-58, asst prof pediat & physiol, 58-77, mem fac physiol, 77-80, RES MEM, RES INST, HOSP FOR SICK CHILDREN, 58- *Honors & Awards:* Medal Med, Royal Col Physicians & Surgeons, Can, 56. *Mem:* AAAS; Soc Pediat Res; fel Am Acad Pediat; Can Pediat Soc. *Res:* Physiology of bone metabolism as applied to children. *Mailing Add:* Res Inst Hospital for Sick Children Toronto ON M5G 1X8 Can

FRASER, DONALD ALEXANDER, b Toronto, Ont, Jan 23, 18; m 53; c 2. BIOGEOGRAPHY, GEOGRAPHY. *Educ:* Univ Toronto, BA, 40, PhD(ecol, plant agr geog), 51; Oak Ridge Inst Nuclear Studies, cert, 55. *Prof Exp:* Demonstr bot, Univ Toronto, 45-48; lectr, Univ Alta, 48-49; sr scientist tree physiol & forest ecol, Petawawa Forest Exp Sta, Chalk River, Ont, 49-70; chmn dept, 70-73, PROF GEOG, CONCORDIA UNIV, 70- *Concurrent Pos:* Vis prof & vdir, Int Atomic Energy Agency-Food & Agr Orgn Courses, Hannover Tech Univ, 65 & Univ Helsinki, 72; consult, James Bay Develop Corp, Que, 74-75. *Mem:* Fel AAAS; Bot Soc Am; Ecol Soc Am; Can Geog Asn. *Res:* Ecology, physiology and morphology of forest trees; radioisotopic techniques in forest research. *Mailing Add:* 617 Berwick Ave Town of Mt Royal Montreal PQ H3R 2A1 Can

FRASER, DONALD ALEXANDER STUART, b Toronto, Ont, Apr 29, 25. STATISTICS. *Educ:* Univ Toronto, BA, 46, MA, 47; Princeton Univ, MA, 48, PhD(math), 49. *Prof Exp:* Instr math, Princeton Univ, 47-49; from asst prof to prof, 49-77, MEM FAC MATH, UNIV TORONTO, 77- *Mem:* Fel AAAS; fel Am Statist Asn; fel Inst Math Statist; fel Royal Statist Soc; fel Royal Soc Can. *Res:* Mathematical statistics. *Mailing Add:* Dept of Math Univ of Toronto Toronto ON M5S 1A1 Can

FRASER, DONALD BOYD, b Teaneck, NJ, Nov 15, 30; c 2. PHYSICAL CHEMISTRY. *Educ:* St Peter's Col, BS, 54; Rutgers Univ, PhD(phys chem), 60. *Prof Exp:* Chemist, Enjay Labs, Esso Res & Eng Co, 60-62; sr develop engr, Celanese Plastics Co, NJ, 62-63, group leader, 63-68; assoc prof, 68-71, PROF CHEM, ESSEX COUNTY COL, 71- CHMN DEPT, 70- *Mem:* Am Chem Soc. *Mailing Add:* Dept of Chem 303 University Ave Newark NJ 07102

FRASER, DOUGLAS FYFE, b Hartford, Conn, June 17, 41. ECOLOGY. *Educ:* Univ Mich, AB, 63; Univ Md, MS, 70, PhD(zool), 74. *Prof Exp:* asst prof, 74-80, ASSOC PROF BIOL, SIENA COL, 80- *Mem:* Am Soc Ichthyologists & Herpetologists; AAAS; Am Fisheries Soc; Ecol Soc Am. *Res:* Population and community ecology of stream dwelling fish and woodland salamanders; systematics of coral snakes. *Mailing Add:* Dept of Biol Siena Col Loudonville NY 12211

FRASER, FRANK CLARKE, b Norwich, Conn, Mar 29, 20; nat Can; m 48; c 4. MEDICAL GENETICS, TERATOLOGY. *Educ:* Acadia Univ, BSc, 40; McGill Univ, MSc, 41, PhD(genetics), 45, MD, CM, 50. *Hon Degrees:* DSc, Acadia Univ, 67. *Prof Exp:* Demonstr genetics, 45-46, from lectr to assoc prof genetics, 46-60, assoc prof pediat, 60-74, PROF MED GENETICS, McGILL UNIV, 60-, PROF PEDIAT, 74- *Concurrent Pos:* Molson-McConnel res fel, 50-51; dir dept med genetics, Montreal Children's Hosp, 50-; clin fel, Royal Victoria Hosp, 50-; teaching fel, McGill Univ, 52-54; consult, Shriners Hosp Crippled Children, 54- *Mem:* Am Soc Human Genetics (vpres, 59, pres, 62); Teratol Soc (pres, 62); Soc Pediat Res; Genetics Soc Can; Royal Soc Can. *Res:* Experimental production of congenital defects; inheritance of human diseases; genetic counseling. *Mailing Add:* Dept of Biol Stewart Bldg McGill Univ Montreal Can

FRASER, GORDON SIMON, b Chicago, Ill, Oct 18, 46. SEDIMENTOLOGY. *Educ:* Univ Ill, BS, 68, MS, 70, PhD(geol), 74. *Prof Exp:* Res asst geol, Ill State Geol Surv, 68-74; Sedimentologist, BP-Alaska, Inc, 74-78; GEOLOGIST, IND GEOL SURV, 78-; ASST PROF GEOL, IND UNIV, 79- *Mem:* Soc Econ Paleontologists & Mineralogists; Int Asn Sedimentologists. *Res:* Resource development and land-use planning; coastal sedimentation; sedimentology of clastic and carbonate rocks; proglacial sedimentation. *Mailing Add:* Ind Geol Surv 611 N Walnut Grove Bloomington IN 47401

FRASER, GRANT ADAM, b New York, NY, Dec 14, 43. MATHEMATICS. *Educ:* Univ Calif, Los Angeles, AB, 64, MA, 69, PhD(math), 70. *Prof Exp:* Asst prof math, Univ San Francisco, 71-72; asst prof, 72-77, ASSOC PROF MATH, UNIV SANTA CLARA, 77- *Mem:* Am Math Soc; Math Asn Am. *Res:* Lattice theory and universal algebra. *Mailing Add:* Dept of Math Univ of Santa Clara Santa Clara CA 95053

FRASER, HARVEY R(EED), b Elizabeth, Ill, Aug 11, 16; m 40; c 3. MECHANICS. *Educ:* US Mil Acad, BS, 39; Calif Inst Technol, MS, 48; Univ Ill, PhD(fluid mech), 56; Von Karman Inst Fluid Dynamics, Belg, dipl, 61. *Prof Exp:* Commanding officer, Eng Co, US Army, Hawaii, 40-43 & eng combat battalion, Europe, 44-45, opers officer, Oak Ridge, Tenn, 45-46, instr mech, US Mil Acad, 48-50, assoc prof, 50-52, prof, 53-65; dean eng, SDak Sch Mines & Technol, 65-66, pres, 66-75; dean acad affairs, Ore Inst Technol, 75-79; DEAN ACAD, CALIF MARITIME ACAD, 79- *Mem:* Soc Am Mil Engrs; Am Soc Eng Educ. *Res:* Fluid mechanics; diffuser flow. *Mailing Add:* Calif Maritime Acad Vallejo CA 94590

FRASER, IAN MCLENNAN, b Victoria, Australia, June 21, 27; m 49; c 3. PHARMACOLOGY. *Educ:* Univ Sydney, BSc, 49; Cambridge Univ, PhD(biol), 52. *Prof Exp:* Lectr physiol, New South Wales Univ Technol, 52-53; from instr to assoc prof, 53-67, chmn dept, 67-70, PROF PHARMACOL, SCH MED, LOMA LINDA UNIV, 67-, CHMN DEPT PHYSIOL & PHARMACOL, 70- *Concurrent Pos:* NIH spec fel, 66-67. *Mem:* Am Soc Pharmacol & Exp Therapeut; Mycol Soc Am; Bot Soc Am. *Res:* Chemotherapy; drug metabolism; pharmacogenetics. *Mailing Add:* Dept of Physiol & Pharmacol Loma Linda Univ Sch of Med Loma Linda CA 92350

FRASER, J(ULIUS) T(HOMAS), b Budapest, Hungary, May 7, 23; US citizen; m 73; c 3. STUDY OF TIME, PHYSICS. *Educ:* Cooper Union, BEE, 50; Univ Hannover, PhD(philos), 70. *Prof Exp:* Engr, Mackay Radio & Tel Co, NY, 50-53; res engr, Westinghouse Elec Corp, 53-55; staff mem, Res Physics Sect, Kearfott Div, Singer Co, 55-58, sr staff mem, 58-62, sr scientist, 62-71; FOUNDER & SECY, INT SOC STUDY TIME, 66- *Concurrent Pos:* Res assoc physics & astron, Mich State Univ, 62-65; vis lectr, Mt Holyoke Col, 67-69; vis prof, Dept Hist, Univ Md, 69-70; assoc prof, Fordham Univ, 71- *Res:* Study of time; philosophy and history of science. *Mailing Add:* Int Soc for the Study of Time PO Box 815 Westport CT 06881

FRASER, JAMES MATTISON, b Bozeman, Mont, July 31, 25; m 51; c 3. PHYSICAL CHEMISTRY, ANALYTICAL CHEMISTRY. *Educ:* Univ Wis, BS, 53, PhD(phys chem), 57. *Prof Exp:* From res chemist to sr res chemist, Res Ctr, Pure Oil Co, 56-60, group supvr phys chem, 60-61, sect supvr instrumental anal, 61-62, from asst dir to dir anal res & serv div, 62-65, supvr spectral anal, 65-69, MGR ANAL RES & SERV, RES DEPT, UNION OIL CO CALIF, 69- *Mem:* Am Chem Soc; Soc Appl Spectros. *Res:* Instrumental and chemical analysis and analytical methods development of petroleum and its products. *Mailing Add:* Union Oil Co of Calif Res Dept PO Box 76 Brea CA 92621

FRASER, JOHN STILES, b Wonsan, Korea, June 23, 21; Can citizen; m 44; c 2. ACCELERATOR PHYSICS. *Educ:* Dalhousie Univ, BSc, 42; McGill Univ, PhD(physics), 49. *Prof Exp:* Asst cyclotron, McGill Univ, 47-49; res physicist nuclear physics, Atomic Energy Can, Ltd, 49-70, sr res officer accelerator physics, 70-81, br head accelerator physics, 78-81; MEM STAFF, ACCELERATOR TECHNOL DIV, LOS ALAMOS NAT LAB, 81- *Mem:* Fel Am Phys Soc; Can Asn Physicists. *Res:* Accelerator design; data processing; nuclear instrumentation; nuclear fission; nuclear reactions. *Mailing Add:* Accelerator Technol Div Los Alamos Nat Lab Los Alamos NM 87545

FRASER, LEMUEL ANDERSON, b Donora, Pa, June 18, 18; m 42; c 1. ZOOLOGY. *Educ:* Am Univ, BA, 39; Univ Wis, MA, 40, PhD(zool), 44. *Prof Exp:* Asst zool, Univ Wis, 41-44; instr, Univ Tex, 46-48, asst prof, 48-49; from asst prof to assoc prof, 49-59, PROF ZOOL, UNIV WIS-MADISON, 59- *Concurrent Pos:* Chmn dept zool, Univ Wis, 57-62 & 64-71. *Mem:* Am Soc Zoologists; Am Micros Soc; Am Soc Limnol & Oceanog. *Res:* Freshwater invertebrates; invertebrate embryology. *Mailing Add:* Dept of Zool Univ of Wis-Madison Madison WI 53706

FRASER, MALCOLM DOUGLAS, chemical engineering, energy engineering, see previous edition

FRASER, MARGARET SHIRLEY, b Biggar, Sask; US citizen. INORGANIC CHEMISTRY. *Educ:* Univ Alta, BS, 48, MS, 50; La State Univ, PhD(inorg chem), 71. *Prof Exp:* Res assoc biochem, Univ Alta, 50-51; proj asst oncol, McArdle Inst, Univ Wis-Madison, 51-52; instr chem, Univ Wis-Racine Col, 52-71; asst prof, 71-78, ASSOC PROF CHEM, UNIV WIS-PARKSIDE, 78- *Mem:* Am Chem Soc; AAAS. *Res:* Olefin and acetylene reactions with hydridoiridium complexes. *Mailing Add:* Dept of Chem Univ of Wis-Parkside Kenosha WI 53141

FRASER, MURRAY JUDSON, biochemical genetics, see previous edition

FRASER, PETER ARTHUR, b Ancon, Ecuador, Aug 26, 28; nat Can; m 52; c 4. PHYSICS. *Educ:* Univ Western Ont, BSc, 50, PhD(physics), 54; Univ Wis, MS, 52. *Prof Exp:* Asst physics, Univ Wis, 50-52; res assoc, Univ Western Ont, 52-54; Nat Res Coun Can fel, Univ Col, Univ London, 54-56; lectr physics, 56-57, from asst prof to prof physics, 57-70, PROF APPL MATH, UNIV WESTERN ONT, 70- *Mem:* Am Asn Physics Teachers; Can Asn Physicists; Brit Inst Physics. *Res:* Low energy atomic collisions. *Mailing Add:* Dept Appl Math Univ Western Ont London ON N6A 5B8 Can

FRASER, ROBERT B, b Plainfield, NJ, Sept 3, 36; m 59; c 4. MATHEMATICS. *Educ:* Rutgers Univ, BA, 62, PhD(math), 67. *Prof Exp:* Instr math, Rutgers Univ, 65-67; asst prof, La State Univ, 67-69; fel, Dalhousie Univ, 69-70; asst prof, La State Univ, 70-71; asst prof math, Marietta Col, 71-77; MGR BUS SYSTS GROUP, OHIO VALLEY DATA CONTROL, 77- *Mem:* Am Math Soc; Math Asn Am. *Res:* Topology and analysis, especially metric geometry; Lipschitz functions; contraction maps. *Mailing Add:* Ohio Valley Data Control 2505 Washington Blvd Belpre OH 45714

FRASER, ROBERT GORDON, b Winnipeg, Man, June 30, 21; m 45; c 4. MEDICINE. *Educ:* Univ Man, LMCC, 45; FRCP(C), 56. *Prof Exp:* Resident radiol, Royal Victoria Hosp, 48-50; demonstr, 51-54, from lectr to assoc prof, McGill Univ, 54-68, prof radiol, 68-76, chmn dept, 71-76; head, Div Gen Diag Radiol, 76-80, PROF DIAG RADIOL, MED CTR, UNIV ALA, BIRMINGHAM, 76- *Concurrent Pos:* Fel radiol, Royal Victoria Hosp, 51, clin asst, 52, assoc radiologist, 54-56, radiologist, 57-64, diag radiologist-in-chief, 64-76; consult radiologist, Royal Can Air Force, 54-59, Montreal Children's Hosp, 54-76 & Montreal Neurol Inst, 55-76; adv, Dept Vet Affairs, Can, 70-76; consult, Can Forces Med Coun. *Mem:* Can Asn Radiol (pres, 70); Fleischner Soc (pres, 70-72); Am Roentgen Ray Soc (1st vpres, 72); Radiol Soc NAm. *Res:* Diagnostic radiology. *Mailing Add:* 3023 Briarcliff Rd Mountain Brook AL 35223

FRASER, ROBERT ROWNTREE, b Ottawa, Ont, Oct 25, 31; m 64; c 4. ORGANIC CHEMISTRY. *Educ:* Univ Western Ont, BSc, 53, MSc, 54; Univ Ill, PhD(org chem), 58. *Prof Exp:* Asst prof org chem, Univ Ottawa, 58-62; sr res chemist, Bristol Labs Div, Bristol-Myers Co, 62-64; assoc prof org chem, 64-70, PROF ORG CHEM, UNIV OTTAWA, 70- *Mem:* Am Chem Soc; Chem Inst Can. *Res:* Stereochemistry and mechanisms of organic reactions; nuclear magnetic resonance spectroscopy. *Mailing Add:* Dept of Chem Univ of Ottawa Ottawa Can

FRASER, ROBERT STEWART, b Nelson, BC, Feb 14, 22; m 49; c 4. INTERNAL MEDICINE, CARDIOLOGY. *Educ:* Univ Alta, BSc, 44, MD, 46, MSc, 50; FRCP(C), 54. *Prof Exp:* Markle scholar, 53-56; Muttart assoc prof med, 55-64, chmn dept, 69-74, prof clin med, 64-78, ASSOC DEAN MED, UNIV ALTA, 78- *Concurrent Pos:* Consult, Charles Camsell Indian Hosp, Edmonton. *Mem:* Can Soc Clin Invest; Can Cardiovasc Soc (pres, 64). *Res:* Clinical cardiology; clinical and experimental hemodynamic studies. *Mailing Add:* Dept of Med Clin Sci Bldg Univ of Alta Edmonton Can

FRASER, ROBERT STUART, b Hiawatha, Utah, May 4, 23; m 50; c 2. METEOROLOGY. *Educ:* Univ Calif, Los Angeles, BA, 49, MA, 52, PhD(meteorol), 60. *Prof Exp:* Res asst atmospheric radiation, Univ Calif, Los Angeles, 52-58; mem tech staff atmospheric physics, TRW Syst, 58-71; SPACE SCIENTIST, NASA, 71- *Mem:* Am Meteorol Soc; Am Optical Soc. *Res:* Measurement of atmospheric characteristics from satellite; effect of Earth's atmosphere on satellite observations; effect of aerosols on Earth's radiation budget. *Mailing Add:* 1901 Kimberly Rd Silver Spring MD 20903

FRASER, RONALD CHESTER, b Portage la Prairie, Man, Nov 6, 19; US citizen; m 44; c 4. DEVELOMENTAL BIOLOGY. *Educ:* Univ Minn, BS, 50, MS, 52, PhD(zool), 53. *Prof Exp:* Asst zool, Univ Minn, 50-53; instr biol, Reed Col, 53-54; from asst prof to assoc prof zool, 54-61, PROF ZOOL, UNIV TENN, KNOXVILLE, 61- *Concurrent Pos:* Asst, Univ Minn, 53-; consult, AEC, 54- *Mem:* Am Soc Zool. *Res:* Morphogenesis; mouse tumor growth; hemoglobins and serum proteins of the chick embryo. *Mailing Add:* Dept of Zool Univ of Tenn Knoxville TN 37916

FRASER, THOMAS HUNTER, b Dansville, NY, Mar 19, 48; m 72; c 2. BIOCHEMISTRY, MOLECULAR BIOLOGY. *Educ:* Univ Rochester, BA, 70; Mass Inst Technol, PhD(biochem), 75. *Prof Exp:* Instr microbiol, Mass Inst Technol, 75-76, res assoc biochem, 76; res assoc biochem, Univ Colo, 76-77; res scientist molecular biol, UpJohn Co, 77-81; VPRES RES & DEVELOP, REPLIGEN CORP, 81- *Concurrent Pos:* Damon Runyon-Walter Winchell Cancer Fund fel, 76-77. *Mem:* AAAS. *Res:* Application of recombinant DNA technology to the production of medically important peptides and proteins. *Mailing Add:* Repligen Corp 101 Binney St Cambridge MA 02142

FRASER-REID, BERTRAM OLIVER, b Christiana, Jamaica, Feb 23, 34; m 63; c 2. ORGANIC CHEMISTRY. *Educ:* Queen's Univ, Ont, BSc, 59, MSc, 61; Univ Alta, PhD(chem), 64. *Prof Exp:* Res fel, Imp Col, Univ London, 64-66; asst prof, 66-71, assoc prof, 71-76, PROF CHEM, UNIV WATERLOO, 76- *Mem:* Am Chem Soc; Chem Inst Can; The Chem Soc. *Res:* Carbohydrate chemistry; photochemistry of imines and related molecules; a synthetic route to spiropentadiene. *Mailing Add:* Dept of Chem Univ of Waterloo Waterloo Can

FRASER-SMITH, ANTONY CHARLES, b Auckland, NZ, July 7, 38; m 68; c 2. SPACE PHYSICS, GEOPHYSICS. *Educ:* Univ NZ, BS, 59, MS, 61; Univ Auckland, PhD(physics), 66. *Prof Exp:* Lectr physics, Univ Auckland, 61-65; assoc res scientist, Lockheed Missiles & Space Co, Calif, 66-68; res assoc, 68-77, SR RES ASSOC, RADIOSCI LAB, STANFORD UNIV, 77- *Concurrent Pos:* Consult, Stanford Res Inst, 70- *Mem:* Fel Brit Inst Physics; Am Geophys Union; Am Inst Physics; Int Union Radio Sci. *Res:* Origin and properties of ultra-low-frequency geomagnetic pulsations and other low-frequency electromagnetic phenomena. *Mailing Add:* Radiosci Lab Stanford Univ Stanford CA 94305

FRASHER, WALLACE G, JR, b Los Angeles, Calif, Dec 2, 20; m 59; c 2. CARDIOVASCULAR PHYSIOLOGY. *Educ:* Univ Southern Calif, AB, 41, MD, 51. *Prof Exp:* Head physician, Los Angeles County Hosp, 55-57; estab investr, Los Angeles County Heart Asn, 58-59; from asst res prof to assoc res prof med, Sch Med Loma Linda Univ, 61-66; from assoc prof to prof physiol, Sch Med Univ Southern Calif, 66-77; DEP EXEC V PRES FOR RES PROG, AM HEART ASN, 77- *Concurrent Pos:* Res fel, Los Angeles County Heart Asn, 57-58; Nat Heart Inst res fel, 60-61, res career develop award, 61-; res fel eng, Calif Inst Technol, 61-63, sr res fel, 63- *Mem:* Am Physiol Soc; Microcirculatory Soc; Soc Rheol; Fedn Am Soc Exp Biol. *Res:* Major artery distensibility; flow properties of blood and its constituents in small tubes; microvascular casting. *Mailing Add:* Am Heart Asn 7320 Greenville Ave Dallas TX 75231

FRASHIER, LOYD DOLA, b Pampa, Tex, Oct 29, 16; m 53; c 3. PHYSICAL CHEMISTRY. *Educ:* Harding Col, BS, 40; Univ Calif, PhD(phys chem), 49. *Prof Exp:* Chemist, E I du Pont de Nemours & Co, Inc, 41-45; assoc prof chem, Ga Inst Technol, 49-58; chmn dept, 58-78, PROF CHEM, PEPPERDINE UNIV, 58- *Mem:* Am Chem Soc. *Res:* Chemical kinetics. *Mailing Add:* Natural Sci Div Pepperdine Univ Malibu CA 90265

FRASIER, GARY WAYNE, b Imperial, Nebr, July 27, 37. RANGELAND HYDROLOGY, WATER HARVESTING. *Educ:* Colo State Univ, BS, 59; Ariz State Univ, MS, 66. *Prof Exp:* Agr engr, 59-67, res hydraulic engr, Water Conserv Lab, Phoenix, 67-78, RES HYDRAULIC ENG, SOUTHWEST RANGELAND WATERSHED RES CTR, AGR RES SERV, USDA, TUCSON, ARIZ, 78- *Concurrent Pos:* Assoc ed, J Range Mgt, 82-85. *Mem:* Am Soc Agr Engrs; Soc Range Mgt; Soil Conserv Soc Am. *Res:* Water harvesting as a means of water supply for livestock, wildlife and households; growing of arid and semiarid plants by water harvesting and runoff farming techniques. *Mailing Add:* 442 E 7th St Tucson AZ 85705

FRASIER, S DOUGLAS, b Los Angeles, Calif, Nov 29, 32; m 56; c 3. PEDIATRIC ENDOCRINOLOGY. *Educ:* Univ Calif, Los Angeles, BA, 54, MD, 58. *Prof Exp:* Asst prof pediat, Sch Med, Univ Calif, Los Angeles, 65-67; from asst prof to assoc prof, 67-74, PROF PEDIAT PHYSIOL & BIOPHYSICS, SCH MED, UNIV SOUTHERN CALIF, 74- *Concurrent Pos:* Fel pediat, Sch Med, Univ Calif, Los Angeles, 63-65. *Mem:* Soc Pediat Res; Endocrine Soc; Am Pediat Soc; Am Acad Pediat. *Res:* Growth hormone physiology in children; growth hormone deficiency and therapeutic effects of growth hormone; antigenicity of human growth hormone; endocrine correlates of puberty. *Mailing Add:* Univ Southern Calif Sch of Med Los Angeles CA 90007

FRATANTONI, JOSEPH CHARLES, b Brooklyn, NY, May 14, 38; m 65; c 3. HEMATOLOGY. *Educ:* Fordham Univ, BS, 59; Harvard Univ, AM, 61; Cornell Univ, MD, 65. *Prof Exp:* From intern to asst resident med, New York Hosp, Cornell Univ, 65-67; staff assoc, Nat Inst Arthritis & Metab Dis, NIH, 67-69; assoc resident med, New York Hosp, Cornell Univ, 69-71; asst prof med & dir coagulation lab, Sch Med, Georgetown Univ, 71-72; staff physician, Hematol Serv, Clin Ctr, Nat Inst Arthritis & Metab Dis, NIH, 72-74; dir, Thrombosis Prog, Nat Heart Lung & Blood Inst, 74-75, chief, blood dis br, div blood dis & resources, 75-77, chief, Blood Resources Br, 77-78; DIR, BLOOD BANK PROD BUR BIOL, FOOD & DRUG ADMIN, 78- *Concurrent Pos:* Mem exec comt, Coun Thrombosis, Am Heart Asn, 75-77; consult & lectr, Nat Naval Med Ctr, 75-; clin asst prof med & pharmacol, Georgetown Univ, 72-76, clin assoc prof, 76-; assoc prof med, Uniformed Servs Univ Health Sci, 77- *Mem:* AAAS; Am Fedn Clin Res; Am Soc Hematol; fel Am Col Physicians; Am Asn Blood Banks. *Res:* Hemostasis; platelets; blood banking. *Mailing Add:* Bur of Biol 8800 Rockville Pike Bethesda MD 20014

FRATER, ROBERT WILLIAM MAYO, b Cape Town, SAfrica, Nov 12, 28; m; c 3. THORACIC SURGERY, CARDIOVASCULAR SURGERY. *Educ:* Univ Cape Town, MB, ChB, 52; Univ Minn, MS, 61; FRCS(E), 61. *Prof Exp:* Intern surg, Groote Schuur Hosp, Cape Town, SAfrica, 53-54; Coun Sci & Indust Res fel, Univ Cape Town, 54-55 & Mayo Found, 55-61; Noble Found award, 61; sr lectr thoracic surg, Univ Cape Town, 62-64; from asst prof to assoc prof thoracic surg, 64-71, actg chmn dept surg, 71-76, PROF THORACIC SURG, ALBERT EINSTEIN COL MED, 71-, CHIEF CARDIO-THORACIC SURG, BRONX MUNIC HOSP CTR, 68-, CHIEF CARDIO-THORACIC SURG, MONTEFIORE HOSP & MED CTR, 76- *Concurrent Pos:* Min Heart Asn fel, Univ Minn, 59-60; sr surgeon, Groote Schuur Hosp & Red Cross War Mem Children's Hosp, Cape Town, 62-64; NIH fels, 65-70; Am Heart Asn grant in aid, 67. *Mem:* Am Asn Thoracic Surg. *Res:* Artificial heart valves; membrane oxygenators; right ventricular growth; cardiovascular toxic factor; ventricular compliance; function natural heart valves; criteria for valve testing; intraortic balloon pumping; left ventricular compliances; myocardial protection. *Mailing Add:* Dept of Surg Albert Einstein Col of Med New York NY 10461

FRATI, WILLIAM, b New York, NY, Sept 14, 31; m 63; c 3. HIGH ENERGY PHYSICS. *Educ:* Polytech Inst Brooklyn, BS, 52; Columbia Univ, MA, 55, PhD(physics), 60. *Prof Exp:* Res assoc physics, Columbia Univ, 60-61; res assoc, 61-65, res specialist, 66-80, ASSOC PROF PHYSICS, RITTENHOUSE LAB, UNIV PA, 81- *Mem:* Am Phys Soc. *Res:* High energy particle physics. *Mailing Add:* Rittenhouse Lab Dept Physics Univ of Pa Philadelphia PA 19104

FRATIANNE, DOUGLAS G, plant physiology, see previous edition

FRATIELLO, ANTHONY, b Providence, RI, Mar 16, 36; m 63; c 3. PHYSICAL CHEMISTRY. *Educ:* Providence Col, BSc, 57; Brown Univ, PhD(chem), 62. *Prof Exp:* Fel & mem tech staff, Bell Tel Labs, 62-63; from asst prof to assoc prof chem, 63-69, PROF CHEM, CALIF STATE UNIV, LOS ANGELES, LOS ANGELES, 69- *Concurrent Pos:* Vis fel, Bell Tel Labs, 69-70; NIH res career develop award, 69-73. *Mem:* Am Chem Soc. *Res:* Nuclear magnetic resonance; solution complexes; ion hydration. *Mailing Add:* Calif State Univ 5151 State Col Dr Los Angeles CA 90032

FRATTALI, VICTOR PAUL, b Scranton, Pa, Mar 23, 38; m 62; c 3. NUTRITIONAL BIOCHEMISTRY, CHEMISTRY. *Educ:* Univ Scranton, BS, 59; Georgetown Univ, PhD(biochem), 65. *Prof Exp:* Chem officer & army res & develop coordr, US Army Missile Command, Ala, 64-66; res chemist, Naval Med Res Inst, Nat Naval Med Ctr, Md, 66-76; nutritionist, 76-80, SUPVRY NUTRITIONIST, BUR FOODS, FOOD & DRUG ADMIN, 80- *Concurrent Pos:* USPHS fel, Naval Med Res Inst, 66, Nat Acad Sci fel, 66-68; res consult, George Washington Univ, 70-75. *Mem:* Am Chem Soc; Undersea Med Soc; Am Inst Nutrit; Am Diabetes Asn; Soc Exp Biol & Med. *Res:* Impact of Federal regulation on nutritional quality of food supply; effect of deep undersea habitation on human nutrient requirements; protein structure and function; protein-protein associating systems; proteinases and proteinase inhibitors. *Mailing Add:* Food & Drug Admin 200 C St SW Washington DC 20204

FRAUENFELDER, HANS (EMIL), b Neuhausen, Switz, July 28, 22; nat US; m 50; c 3. PARTICLE PHYSICS, BIOPHYSICS. *Educ:* Swiss Fed Inst Technol, Dipl, 47, Dr sc nat, 50. *Hon Degrees:* DSc, Univ Penn, Tech Univ Munich. *Prof Exp:* Asst physics, Swiss Fed Inst Technol, 46-52; res assoc, 52, from asst prof to assoc prof, 52-58, PROF PHYSICS, UNIV ILL, URBANA, 58- *Concurrent Pos:* Vis scientist, European Orgn Nuclear Res, 58, 59, 63 & 73; consult, Los Alamos Sci Lab. *Mem:* Nat Acad Sci; fel Am Phys Soc; Swiss Phys Soc; fel AAAS; fel NY Acad Sci. *Res:* Nuclear physics; reactions and dynamics of biomolecules. *Mailing Add:* Dept Physics Univ Ill 1110 W Green St Urbana IL 61801

FRAUENGLASS, ELLIOTT, b Hartford, Conn, Aug 7, 34; m 55; c 3. ORGANIC CHEMISTRY. *Educ:* Univ Conn, BS, 56; Cornell Univ, PhD(org chem), 60. *Prof Exp:* Res chemist, Eastman Kodak Co, 60-65; POLYMER CHEMIST, LOCTITE CORP, 65- *Mem:* Am Chem Soc. *Res:* Synthetic and polymer organic chemistry. *Mailing Add:* Loctite Corp 705 N Mountain Rd Newington CT 06111

FRAUENTHAL, JAMES CLAY, b New York, NY, Nov 25, 44; m 69. APPLIED MATHEMATICS, ENGINEERING MECHANICS. *Educ:* Tufts Univ, BS, 66; Harvard Univ, MS, 67, PhD(appl math), 71. *Prof Exp:* Asst prof mech eng, Tufts Univ, 71-73; res assoc pop sci, Harvard Sch Pub Health, 73-75; ASSOC PROF APPL MATH, STATE UNIV NY STONY BROOK, 75- *Concurrent Pos:* Prin investr, Alfred P Sloan Found, 75-79; ed, Soc Indust & Appl Math News, 75-; trustee, Hosp for Joint Dis-Orthoped Inst, 76-; vis assoc prof math, Harvey Mudd Col, 81-82. *Mem:* Soc Indust & Appl Math; Sigma Xi. *Res:* Population dynamics; structural optimization; elasticity; shell theory; mathematical demography; biomathematics. *Mailing Add:* Dept of Appl Math & Statist State Univ NY Stony Brook NY 11794

FRAUMENI, JOSEPH F, JR, b Boston, Mass, Apr 1, 33. INTERNAL MEDICINE, EPIDEMIOLOGY. *Educ:* Harvard Univ, AB, 54, MScHyg, 65; Duke Univ, MD, 58; Am Bd Internal Med, dipl, 65. *Prof Exp:* Intern med, Johns Hopkins Hosp, 58-59, asst resident, 59-60; sr asst resident, Cornell Second Div, Bellevue Hosp & Mem Ctr, 60-61; chief resident, Mem Sloan-Kettering Cancer Ctr, 61-62; med officer epidemiol, 62-66, head ecol sect, 66-75, assoc chief epidemiol br, 72-76, CHIEF ENVIRON EPIDEMIOL BR, NAT CANCER INST, 76- *Concurrent Pos:* Instr, Med Col, Cornell Univ, 61-62; asst med, Peter Bent Brigham Hosp, 64-65; assoc dir field studies & statist, Nat Cancer Inst, 81- *Mem:* Am Pub Health Asn; Am Col Physicians; Am Epidemiol Soc; Am Asn Cancer Res; Teratol Soc. *Res:* Cancer research, especially epidemiological studies. *Mailing Add:* Rm C307 Landow Bldg Nat Insts Health Bethesda MD 20205

FRAUNFELDER, FREDERICK THEODOR, b Pasadena, Calif, Aug 16, 34; m 59; c 4. OPHTHALMOLOGY. *Educ:* Univ Ore, BS, 56, MD, 60. *Prof Exp:* Intern, Univ Chicago, 61; resident ophthal, Med Sch, Univ Ore, 64-66; from assoc prof to prof ophthal, Med Sch, Univ Ark, Little Rock, 68-78, chmn dept, 68-78; PROF OPHTHAL & CHMN DEPT, MED SCH, UNIV ORE, 78- *Concurrent Pos:* NIH fel ophthal, Univ Ore, 61-62; NIH spec fel ophthal, Wilmer Inst, Johns Hopkins Univ, 67-68; sabbatical, Eye Inst, Univ London, 74-75; consult, Vet Admin Hosp; trustee, Int Serv for Blind, 70-76. *Mem:* Am Acad Ophthal & Otolaryngol; AMA; Asn Univ Prof Ophthal (secy-treas, 73-74); Asn Res Vision & Ophthal; Am Col Surg. *Res:* External eye disease; ocular cancer. *Mailing Add:* Dept of Ophthal Univ of Ore Med Sch Portland OR 97034

FRAUNFELTER, GEORGE H, b Hamburg, Pa, June 2, 27; div. GEOLOGY. *Educ:* Lehigh Univ, BA, 48; Univ Mo, AM, 51, PhD(geol), 64. *Prof Exp:* Cur geol, Univ Mo, 51-55; paleontologist, Creole Petrol Corp, 55-58; cur & asst prof geol, 65-70, assoc prof, 70-73, PROF GEOL, SOUTHERN ILL UNIV, CARBONDALE, 73- *Mem:* AAAS; Am Asn Petrol Geologists; Paleont Soc; Paleont Res Inst; Am Inst Prof Geologists. *Res:* Ichnofossils (Upper Paleozoic); paleontology and stratigraphy of Middle Devonian of Midwestern United States; lower Pennsylvanian megafaunas (invertebrate). *Mailing Add:* Dept of Geol Southern Ill Univ Carbondale IL 62901

FRAUTSCHI, STEVEN CLARK, b Madison, Wis, Dec 6, 33; m 67; c 2. ELEMENTARY PARTICLE PHYSICS. *Educ:* Harvard Univ, BA, 54; Stanford Univ, PhD(physics), 58. *Prof Exp:* NSF fel, Yukawa Hall, Kyoto, 58-59; asst physics, Univ Calif, Berkeley, 59-61; asst prof, Cornell Univ, 61-62; from asst prof to assoc prof, 62-66, PROF PHYSICS, CALIF INST TECHNOL, 66- *Concurrent Pos:* Guggenheim fel, 71-72; vis prof, Univ Paris, Orsay, 77-78. *Mem:* Am Phys Soc. *Res:* Theory of elementary particles. *Mailing Add:* Dept of Physics Calif Inst of Technol Pasadena CA 91125

FRAUTSCHY, JEFFERY DEAN, b Monroe, Wis, June 22, 19; m 48; c 3. GEOLOGY. *Educ:* Univ Minn, BA, 42. *Prof Exp:* Assoc physicist, Div War Res, Univ Calif, 42-46; assoc, Scripps Inst Oceanog, Univ Calif, San Diego, 46-47; geophysicist, US Geol Surv, 47-49; marine geologist, 49-58, ASST DIR, SCRIPPS INST OCEANOG, UNIV CALIF, SAN DIEGO, 58- *Mem:* Geol Soc Am; Am Geophys Union; Am Asn Petrol Geologists; Soc Econ Paleont & Mineral. *Res:* Marine geology; oceanographic field instruments, equipment and methods; oceanographic vessel outfitting and operation; inshore oceanography and shore processes coastline planning; water quality control. *Mailing Add:* 2625 Ellentown Rd La Jolla CA 92037

FRAWLEY, JOHN PAUL, b Washington, DC, Dec 17, 27; m 53; c 2. TOXICOLOGY. *Educ:* Georgetown Univ, BS & MS, 48, PhD(biochem), 50; Am Bd Indust Hyg, dipl. *Prof Exp:* Instr chem, Georgetown Univ, 47-48; res pharmacologist, US Food & Drug Admin, 48-52 & 54-56; lab dir, Surg Res Team in Korea, US Army, 52-54; DIR TOXICOL, HERCULES INC, 56- *Concurrent Pos:* Lectr, Georgetown Univ, 49-52; mem agr bd, Nat Res Coun, 69-72; mem bd dirs, Adria Labs Inc, 74- *Honors & Awards:* Lea Hitchner Award, 68. *Mem:* Am Chem Soc; Soc Toxicol; Am Soc Pharmacol & Exp Therapeut; Am Indust Hyg Asn. *Res:* Toxicity and s drugs, cosmetics and food packaging. *Mailing Add:* 111 Chestnut Ave Edgewood Hills Wilmington DE 19809

FRAWLEY, NILE NELSON, b Madison, Wis, Jan 26, 50; m 72; c 2. INDUSTRIAL CHEMISTRY. *Educ:* Hamline Univ, BA, 72; Univ Minn, PhD(anal chem), 77. *Prof Exp:* Teaching assoc, Univ Minn, 72-77; sr res chemist, 77-80, PROJ LEADER, MICH DIV ANAL LABS, DOW CHEM CO, 80- *Mem:* Am Chem Soc; Sigma Xi. *Res:* Analytical chemistry of potassium cyanate and its determination in biological materials; analytical methodologies for the analysis of agricultural chemicals and the integration of membrane technology into the practice of analytical chemistry. *Mailing Add:* 2212 Belaire St Midland MI 48640

FRAWLEY, THOMAS FRANCIS, b Rochester, NY, June 27, 19; m 47; c 3. MEDICINE. *Educ:* Univ Rochester, AB, 41; Univ Buffalo, MD, 44; Am Bd Internal Med, dipl. *Prof Exp:* Res fel med, Sch Med, Univ Buffalo, 47-49; res fel, Harvard Med Sch, 49-51; head sub-dept endocrinol & metab, Albany Med Col, 51-63, prof med, 59-63; chmn dept, 63-74, prof, 63-80, EMER PROF & CHMN INTERNAL MED, SCH MED, ST LOUIS UNIV, 80-; CHMN GRAD MED EDUC, ST JOHN'S MERCY MED CTR, ST LOUIS, 81- *Concurrent Pos:* Chief endocrine-metab clin, Albany Hosp, 51-63, attend physician, 52-63; consult, Albany Vet Admin Hosp, 51-63; clin investr, Nat Inst Arthritis & Metab Dis, 55-57; physician in chief, St Louis Univ Hosps, 63-74; mem sci rev comt, NIH, 70-74. *Mem:* Endocrine Soc; Am Diabetes Asn; Asn Am Physicians; fel Am Col Physicians; fel NY Acad Sci. *Res:* Clinical and basic investigation of endocrine metabolic disorders, particularly adrenal cortical disorders and carbohydrate metabolism. *Mailing Add:* 12255 DePaul Dr St Louis MO 63044

FRAWLEY, WILLIAM JAMES, b Cleveland, Ohio, Sept 14, 37; c 3. ARTIFICIAL INTELLIGENCE. *Educ:* John Carroll Univ, BS, 58, MS, 60; Univ Okla, PhD(math), 69. *Prof Exp:* Res engr, Lewis Res Ctr, NASA, Ohio, 58-60; instr math, John Carroll Univ, 60-62; sr res mathematician, 62-65, sr res proj mathematician & sect head, 68-76, PROG LEADER COMPUT INTEL, SCHLUMBERGER-DOLL RES CTR, SCHLUMBERGER LTD, 77- *Concurrent Pos:* Lectr, John Carroll Univ, 58-60; comput use consult, Cleveland Elec Illum Co, 60-62. *Mem:* Am Math Soc; Soc Indust & Appl Math. *Res:* Numerical analysis; differential equations; real time analysis and control; design and implementation of knowledge based systems. *Mailing Add:* Schlumberger-Doll Res Ctr Schlumberger Ltd Old Quarry Rd Ridgefield CT 06877

FRAY, ROBERT DUTTON, b Shepherdstown, WVa, Feb 16, 39; m 62. MATHEMATICS. *Educ:* Roanoke Col, BS, 61; Duke Univ, PhD(number theory), 65. *Prof Exp:* Asst prof math, Fla State Univ, 65-71; ASSOC PROF MATH, FURMAN UNIV, 71- *Mem:* Am Math Soc; Math Asn Am. *Res:* Number theory and combinatorial analysis. *Mailing Add:* Dept of Math Furman Univ Greenville SC 29613

FRAYER, WARREN EDWARD, b Manchester, Conn, Sept 22, 39; m 60; c 4. FORESTRY. *Educ:* Pa State Univ, BS, 61; Yale Univ, MF, 62, DF, 65. *Prof Exp:* Res forester, US Forest Serv, Upper Darby, Pa, 63-67; assoc prof forest biomet, Dept Forest & Wood Sci, Colo State Univ, 67-75; supvry res forester, US Forest Serv, Washington, DC, 75-76; HEAD, DEPT FOREST & WOOD SCI,, COLO STATE UNIV, 76- *Concurrent Pos:* Consult fed agencies & companies, 67-; prin invester, various res projs, 68-; vis lectr, Yale Univ, 74. *Res:* Natural resource sampling methods. *Mailing Add:* Dept Forest & Wood Sci Colo State Univ Ft Collins CO 80523

FRAYSER, KATHERINE REGINA, b Lynchburg, Va, Feb 18, 26. PHYSIOLOGY. *Educ:* Randolph-Macon Woman's Col, AB, 46; Duke Univ, AM, 54, PhD(anat), 60. *Prof Exp:* Instr med, Sch Med, Duke Univ, 60-62; asst prof, Sch Med, Ind Univ, 62-63, asst prof med & physiol, 63-65, from assoc prof to prof, 65-73; prof med res & ophthal, 73-78, PROF MED & PHYSIOL, MED UNIV SC, 78- *Concurrent Pos:* Mem, NIH Physiol Study Sect, 72-76, Clin Trails Rev Panel & Sickle Cell Ctr Rev Panel, 75 & 81 & Pulmonary Acad Awards Rev Panel, 75-76. *Mem:* Am Physiol Soc; Am Asn Anat; Microcirculatory Soc. *Res:* Human and experimental pulmonary physiology and pathophysiology, altitude physiology; microcirculation. *Mailing Add:* Dept of Med Med Univ of SC 171 Ashley Ave Charleston SC 29425

FRAZEE, JERRY D, b Wichita Falls, Tex, May 26, 29; div; c 4. PHYSICAL CHEMISTRY. *Educ:* Univ Tex, BS, 51, MA, 57, PhD(chem), 59. *Prof Exp:* Vis scientist phys chem, Rohm & Haas Co, Marshall Space Flight Ctr, 59; asst prof chem, La Polytech Inst, 59-60; from chemist to sr chemist, Rocketdyne Div, NAm Aviation, Inc, 60-67; proj leader & supvr instrumental anal sect, Chem Dept, Gulf Oil Corp, 67-68; SR PAINT CHEMIST, TEX HWY DEPT, 68-; INSTRUMENTAL ANALYSIS CONSULT, SCI-TECH, AUSTIN, 80- *Mem:* AAAS; Am Chem Soc; Brit Oil & Colour Chem Asn; Coblentz Soc; Sigma Xi. *Res:* Organic coatings; pyrolysis of hydrocarbons; analytical chemistry; polymers and resins; spectroscopy; color. *Mailing Add:* M & T Lab 38th & Jackson Sts Austin TX 78703

FRAZER, ALAN, b Philadelphia, Pa, Mar 2, 43; m 68; c 2. PHARMACOLOGY. *Educ:* Philadelphia Col Pharm & Sci, BSc, 64; Univ Pa, PhD(pharmacol), 69. *Prof Exp:* From instr to asst prof, 69-75, ASSOC PROF PHARMACOL, UNIV PA, 75-; RES PHARMACOLOGIST, VET ADMIN HOSP, PHILADELPHIA, 69-, CHIEF, NEUROPSYCHOPHARMACOL UNIT, 81- *Mem:* Am Soc Pharmacol & Exp Therapeut; AAAS. *Res:* Defining the biological basis of affective disorders. *Mailing Add:* Vet Admin Hosp 151E University & Woodland Ave Philadelphia PA 19104

FRAZER, BENJAMIN CHALMERS, b Birmingham, Ala, July 19, 22; m 51; c 3. SOLID STATE PHYSICS. *Educ:* Ala Polytech Inst, BS, 47, MS, 48; Pa State Col, PhD(physcis), 52. *Prof Exp:* Assoc physicist, Brookhaven Nat Lab, 52-55; physicist, Westinghouse Res labs, 55-58; physicist, 58-67, dep chmn dept physics, 67-74, assoc chmn solid state physics, 74-75, SR PHYSICIST, BROOKHAVEN NAT LAB, 67- *Concurrent Pos:* Consult, Westinghouse Res Labs, 55-62; guest scientist, PR Nuclear Ctr, 62-63; assoc ed, J Phys Chem Solids, 64-74; managing ed, The Phys Rev, 74-81. *Mem:* Fel Am Phys Soc; Am Crystallog Asn. *Res:* Structure and dynamics of solids, phase transitions, ferroelectricity, x-ray and neutron scattering, synchotron, radiation. *Mailing Add:* 9529 Ash Hollow Pl Gaithersburg MD 20879

FRAZER, BRYAN DOUGLAS, b Penticton, BC, Feb 17, 42; m 63; c 2. INSECT ECOLOGY. *Educ:* Univ BC, BSc, 65; Univ Calif, Berkeley, PhD(entom), 71. *Prof Exp:* Res officer entom, 65-67, RES SCIENTIST ENTOM, RES BR, AGR CAN, 70- *Concurrent Pos:* Hon lectr plant sci, Univ BC, 72- *Mem:* Am Ecol Soc; Can Entom Soc; Entom Soc Am; Brit Ecol Soc. *Res:* Population dynamics of the aphid vectors of plant virus diseases as an approach to understanding and affecting plant virus epidemiology. *Mailing Add:* Agr Can Res Sta 6660 NW Marine Dr Vancouver BC V6T 1X2 Can

FRAZER, J(OHN) RONALD, b Ottawa, Ont, July 17, 23; US citizen; m 48; c 5. INDUSTRIAL ENGINEERING & MANAGEMENT. *Educ:* Clarkson Col Technol, BME, 45; Iowa State Univ, MS, 50, PhD(eng, econ), 54. *Prof Exp:* Instr mech eng, Clarkson Col Technol, 45-46; from instr to asst prof indust eng, Iowa State Univ, 46-53; from asst prof to prof indust eng & chmn dept, 53-67, dean sch bus admin, 67-70, PROF INDUST MGT, CLARKSON COL TECHNOL, 70- *Mem:* Am Inst Indust Engrs; Acad Mgt; Asn Bus Stimulation Experiential Learning; Am Inst Decision Sci. *Res:* Cost studies; linear programming; operations research; management simulation. *Mailing Add:* Sch of Mgt Clarkson Col Potsdam NY 13676

FRAZER, JACK WINFIELD, b Forest Grove, Ore, Sept 9, 24; m 47; c 3. CHEMISTRY. *Educ:* Hardin-Simmons Univ, BS, 48. *Prof Exp:* Anal chemist, Los Alamos Sci Lab, 48-51, chemist, 51-53; group leader vacuum anal chem, 53-66, from assoc leader to leader gen chem div, 66-74, dept head chem & mat sci, 74-78, SR SCIENTIST, LAWRENCE LIVERMORE LAB, UNIV CALIF, 78- *Concurrent Pos:* Indust prof chem, Ind Univ, 73-77; vis prof elec eng, Colo State Univ, 75; consult, Merck Inc, Universal Oil Prod & Keithley Instruments, Inc. *Honors & Awards:* Instrumentation Award, Am Chem Soc, 73; Award of Merit, Am Soc Testing & Mat, 76. *Mem:* Am Chem Soc; fel Am Soc Testing & Mat; Am Inst Chem Engrs. *Res:* Development of new analytical methods and computer automated instrumentation together with their use in the development of fully computer controlled manufacturing processes, pilot plants and large scale experimental apparatus. *Mailing Add:* 6767 Alisal St Pleasanton CA 94566

FRAZER, JOHN P, b Rochester, NY, Sept 14, 14; m 50; c 2. OTOLARYNGOLOGY. *Educ:* Univ Rochester, MD, 39; Am Bd Otolaryngol, dipl, 44. *Prof Exp:* Instr path, Med Col, Cornell Univ, 39-40; instr surg, Long Island Col Med, 40-41; instr otolaryngol, Sch Med, Yale Univ, 41-46 & 47; consult, Tripler Army Hosp, Hawaii Leprosarium & Leahi Tuberc Hosp, Honolulu, 50-63; PROF OTOLARYNGOL, MED CTR, UNIV ROCHESTER, 63- *Mem:* Am Laryngol, Rhinol & Otol Soc; Am Col Surg; Am Broncho-Esophagol Asn; Am Laryngol Asn. *Mailing Add:* Dept Otolaryngol Univ Rochester Med Ctr Rochester NY 14642

FRAZER, L NEIL, b Courtenay, BC, Apr 7, 48; m 72; c 1. REFLECTION SEISMOLOGY, REFRACTION SEISMOLOGY. *Educ:* Univ BC, BASc, 70; Princeton Univ, PhD(geophysics), 78. *Prof Exp:* Geophysicist, Gulf Oil Can Ltd, 71-72; res assoc, Dept Geol, Princeton Univ, 77-79; asst seismologist, Hawaii Inst Geophysics, 79-81; ASST PROF, DEPT GEOL & GEOPHYSICS, UNIV HAWAII, 82- *Mem:* Seismol Soc Am; Soc Exploration Geophysicists; Am Geophys Union. *Res:* Theoretical body-wave seismology; inversion of relfection and refraction data for earth structure; petroleum exploration; tectonics; geophysics. *Mailing Add:* Dept Geol Univ Hawaii Honolulu HI 96822

FRAZER, MARSHALL EVERETT, b Alva, Okla, Jan 19, 44; m 64; c 1. APPLIED PHYSICS. *Educ:* Northwestern State Col, BS, 64; Univ Tex, Austin, PhD(physics), 74. *Prof Exp:* Instr physics, Northwestern State Col, 64; RES SCIENTIST, APPL RES LABS, UNIV TEX, AUSTIN, 66- *Mem:* Inst Elec & Electronics Engrs; Acoust Soc Am; Sigma Xi. *Res:* Underwater acoustics, acoustic scattering, acoustic propagation; communication theory, decision theory, signal processing, artificial intelligence; multidimensional stochastic processes, spatial and temporal properties of stochastic fields. *Mailing Add:* Appl Res Labs Univ of Tex PO Box 8029 Austin TX 78712

FRAZER, W(ILLIAM) DONALD, b Tampa, Fla, Jan 9, 37; m 61; c 3. COMPUTER SCIENCE. *Educ:* Princeton Univ, BSE, 59; Univ Ill, MS, 61, PhD(elec eng), 63. *Prof Exp:* Res asst, Digital Comput Lab, Univ Ill, 59-61; res staff mem, Thomas J Watson Res Ctr, 63-78, DIR, SYSTS ARCHITECTURE, INFO SYSTS & TECHNOL GROUP, IBM CORP, 79- *Concurrent Pos:* Vis lectr, Princeton Univ, 67-68; adj assoc prof, Courant Inst Math Sci, NY Univ, 70-71. *Mem:* Sigma Xi; Asn Comput Mach. *Res:* Operating systems architecture and design; design and analysis of algorithms for sort, search and optimization; data structures; information theory and coding. *Mailing Add:* Makepeace Hill Waccubuc NY 10597

FRAZER, WILLIAM ROBERT, b Indianapolis, Ind, Aug 6, 33; m 54; c 2. THEORETICAL PHYSICS. *Educ:* Carleton Col, AB, 54; Univ Calif, PhD(physics), 59. *Prof Exp:* Physicist, Lawrence Radiation Lab, Univ Calif, 59; mem physics dept, Inst Advan Study, 59-60; from asst prof to assoc prof physics, 60-67, actg provost, Third Col, 69-70, chmn dept, 75-78, PROF PHYSICS, UNIV CALIF, SAN DIEGO, 67- *Mem:* Am Phys Soc. *Res:* Theoretical physics of the elementary particles. *Mailing Add:* Dept of Physics Univ of Calif at San Diego La Jolla CA 92037

FRAZIER, CLAUDE CLINTON, III, b Hattiesburg, Miss, Aug 27, 48; m 77; c 1. INORGANIC CHEMISTRY, ORGANOMETALLIC CHEMISTRY. *Educ:* Memphis State Univ, BS, 70; Ore Grad Ctr, MS, 72; Calif Inst Technol, PhD(chem), 75. *Prof Exp:* ASST PROF CHEM, UNIV MINN, DULUTH, 78- *Mem:* Am Chem Soc; Sigma Xi. *Res:* Inorganic and organometallic photochemistry; transition metal catalysis. *Mailing Add:* Dept of Chem Univ of Minn Duluth MN 55812

FRAZIER, DONALD THA, b Martin, Ky, Sept 26, 35; m 56; c 3. PHYSIOLOGY, NEUROPHYSIOLOGY. *Educ:* Univ Ky, BS, 58, MS, 60, PhD, 64. *Prof Exp:* From instr to assoc prof neurophysiol, Sch Med, Univ NMex, 64-69; assoc prof, 69-74, PROF PHYSIOL, MED CTR, UNIV KY, 74-, CHMN DEPT, 80- *Concurrent Pos:* NIH res grants, 66-69 & 73-79; dir, Grass Found Fel Prog, 69-79. *Mem:* Neurosci Soc; AAAS; Am Physiol Soc. *Res:* Neurosciences; nature of respiratory neurons; biophysics of nerve membranes. *Mailing Add:* Dept of Physiol Univ of Ky Med Ctr Lexington KY 40506

FRAZIER, EDWARD NELSON, b Los Angeles, Calif, Feb 16, 39; m 68; c 2. ASTROPHYSICS. *Educ:* Univ Calif, Los Angeles, BA, 60; Univ Calif, Berkeley, PhD(astron), 66. *Prof Exp:* Analyst, Aeronutronic Corp, 60-61; res asst astrophys, Kitt Peak Nat Observ, 63; teaching asst astron, Univ Calif, Berkeley, 65-66; scientist astrophys, Univ Heidelberg, 66-67; res astronr, Univ Calif, Berkeley, 67-69; STAFF SCIENTIST SOLAR PHYSICS, AEROSPACE CORP, 69- *Concurrent Pos:* Adj prof, Calif State Univ, Northridge, 76- *Mem:* AAAS; Am Phys Soc; Am Astron Soc; Int Astron Union. *Res:* Mechanical energy transport in solar atmosphere; solar magnetohydrodynamics; properties of interplanetary material. *Mailing Add:* 933 Eighth St Manhattan Beach CA 90266

FRAZIER, GEORGE CLARK, JR, b Cumberland, Va, Apr 14, 30; m 53. CHEMICAL ENGINEERING. *Educ:* Va Polytech Inst, BS, 52; Ohio State Univ, MSc, 56; Johns Hopkins Univ, DEng(chem eng), 62. *Prof Exp:* Engr nuclear reactor design, Atomic Power Div, Westinghouse Elec Corp, 56-59; NATO fel, Cambridge Univ, 62-63; asst prof chem eng, Johns Hopkins Univ, 63-68; assoc prof chem & metall eng, 68-77, PROF CHEM ENG, UNIV TENN, KNOXVILLE, 77- *Concurrent Pos:* Consult, Am Potash & Chem Corp, Calif, 64-70, Direct Reduction Corp, 79- & Union Carbide Corp, 77- *Mem:* Am Inst Chem Engrs; Am Chem Soc; Combustion Inst. *Res:* Combustion; coal processing; heat and mass transfer. *Mailing Add:* Dept Chem Eng Univ Tenn Knoxville TN 37919

FRAZIER, HOWARD STANLEY, b Oak Park, Ill, Jan 16, 26; m 50; c 4. MEDICINE. *Educ:* Univ Chicago, PhB, 47; Harvard Univ, MD, 53. *Prof Exp:* Res fel, Harvard Med Sch, 55-56; res fel, Physiol Lab, Cambridge Univ, 56-57; fel cardiol, Western Reserve Univ, 57-58; res fel, Med Sch, 58-60, asst, 60-62, assoc, Mass Gen Hosp, 62-65, asst prof, 65-68, assoc prof med, Beth Israel Hosp, 68-78, PROF MED, HARVARD MED SCH, 78- *Mem:* Am Physiol Soc; Am Soc Clin Invest; Am Soc Nephrol. *Res:* Health services research. *Mailing Add:* Ctr Anal Health Practices Harvard Sch Pub Health 677 Huntington Ave Boston MA 02115

FRAZIER, J(OHN) EARL, b Houseville, Pa, July 4, 02; m 36; c 2. CERAMICS. *Educ:* Washington & Jefferson Col, BS, 22; Mass Inst Technol, MS, 24; Univ Brazil, ScD, 38. *Prof Exp:* Instr gen chem, Washington & Jefferson Col, 19-20; chem engr, Berney Bond Glass Co Div, Owens-Ill, 24-26; fuel engr, Simplex Eng Co, 26-28, asst secy & treas, 28-31, secy & treas, 31-38, vpres & treas, Frazier-Simplex, Inc, 38-45, PRES, FRAZIER-SIMPLEX, INC, 45-, TREAS, 67- *Concurrent Pos:* Trustee, Washington & Jefferson Col, 60- *Honors & Awards:* Greaves-Walker Roll of Hon Award, Keramos, 67; Albert Victor Bleininger Award, Am Ceramic Soc, 69, John Jeppson Award, 76. *Mem:* Fel AAAS; fel Am Inst Chem; fel Am Ceramic Soc (vpres, 67-68, treas, 68-69, pres elect, 69-70, pres, 70-71); Sigma Xi; Nat Acad Engrs US. *Res:* Melting and annealing of glass by fuel and electric methods; raw materials charging to tank furnaces and to open hearth furnaces, including mixing, handling and storage. *Mailing Add:* Frazier-Simplex Inc PO Box 493 Washington PA 15301

FRAZIER, JAMES LEWIS, b Wadsworth, Ohio, Apr 15, 43; m 73; c 3. NEUROBIOLOGY, BEHAVIORAL PHYSIOLOGY. *Educ:* Ohio State Univ, BS, 66, PhD(entom), 70. *Prof Exp:* From asst prof to assoc prof, Miss Agr & Forestry Exp Sta & Miss State Univ, 70-80, prof, 80-81; SR RES BIOLOGIST, DUPONT EXP STA, E I DU PONT DE NEMOURS & CO, INC, 81- *Mem:* Sigma Xi; Entom Soc Am; Europ Chemoreception Res Org; AAAS. *Res:* Insect behavior, chemoreception, electrophysiology of chemoreceptors. *Mailing Add:* Biochem Dept DuPont Exp Sta Wilmington DE 19898

FRAZIER, JOHN MELVIN, b Greensboro, NC, Apr 24, 44; m 65; c 2. ENVIRONMENTAL MEDICINE. *Educ:* Johns Hopkins Univ, BS, 66, PhD(physics), 71. *Prof Exp:* Res assoc, 70-73, ASST PROF ENVIRON HEALTH SCI, SCH HYG & PUB HEALTH, JOHNS HOPKINS UNIV, 73- *Res:* Physiological and biochemical control of transition metal metabolism in biological systems with particular interests in the toxicokinetics and biliary excretion of cadmium. *Mailing Add:* Dept of Environ Health Sci Johns Hopkins Univ Baltimore MD 21205

FRAZIER, LOY WILLIAM, JR, b Ft Smith, Ark, Aug 14, 38; m 61; c 2. PHYSIOLOGY. *Educ:* Univ Tex, Arlington, BS, 68; Univ Tex Southwestern Med Sch, Dallas, PhD(physiol), 72. *Prof Exp:* Assoc prof, 72-76, PROF PHYSIOL, BAYLOR COL DENT, 76-; ASSOC PROF, GRAD DIV, BAYLOR UNIV, 73- *Concurrent Pos:* Tex Med Found fel, Baylor Col Dent, 73-74; adj assoc prof, Sch Nursing, Baylor Univ, 74-; NIH grant, 75-81. *Mem:* Soc Exp Biol & Med; Am Physiol Soc. *Res:* Electrolyte transport; acid-base balance. *Mailing Add:* Dept of Physiol Baylor Col of Dent Dallas TX 75246

FRAZIER, PATRICIA DIANNE (MURPHY), biochemistry, see previous edition

FRAZIER, ROBERT CARL, b Guilford Co, NC, Feb 14, 32; m 53; c 3. MATHEMATICS. *Educ:* Atlantic Christian Col, AB, 53; ECarolina Univ, MA, 59; Univ Ill, MS, 65; Fla State Univ, EdD(math educ), 69. *Prof Exp:* Teacher high sch, NC, 53-54 & 56-59; assoc prof, 59-69, PROF MATH, ATLANTIC CHRISTIAN COL, 69-, CHMN DEPT, 77- *Mem:* Math Asn Am. *Res:* Comparison of methods of teaching mathematical proof; mathematics education. *Mailing Add:* Dept of Math Atlantic Christian Col Wilson NC 27893

FRAZIER, SHERVERT HUGHES, b Shreveport, La, June 12, 21; m 47; c 4. PSYCHIATRY, PSYCHOANALYSIS. *Educ:* Univ Ill, BS, 41, MD, 43; Am Bd Psychiat & Neurol, dipl, 56; Univ Minn, MS, 57; Columbia Univ, cert psychoanal med, 63; Harvard Univ, MA, 72. *Prof Exp:* Hosp adminr, Harrisburg Med Found, 48-51; fel internal med, Mayo Found, 51-52, asst to staff & fel psychiat, 53-56, consult, 56-58; chief res scientist, NY State Psychiat Inst, 58-61; assoc psychiat, Col Physicians & Surgeons, Columbia Univ, 58-59, asst prof, 59-62; prof & chmn dept, Col Med, Baylor Univ, 62-68; prof, Col Physicians & Surgeons, Columbia Univ, 68-72; PROF PSYCHIAT, HARVARD UNIV, 72-; PSYCHIATRIST IN CHIEF, McLEAN DIV, MASS GEN HOSP, 72- *Concurrent Pos:* Pvt pract, Ill, 46-50 & 53; asst attend psychiatrist, Presby Hosp, New York, 58-63; dir inpatient consult serv psychiat, 61-62, mem med bd & attend psychiat; dir, Houston State Psychiat Inst, 62-65; psychiatrist in chief, Ben Taub Gen Hosp, consult, Vet Admin Hosp & sr attend psychiatrist, Methodist Hosp, Houston, 62-68; consult psychiatrist, Rice Univ, 63-68; state comnr ment health & ment retardation, Tex, 65-66; dir, Am Bd Psychiat & Neurol, 65-73; dep dir, NY Psychiat Inst; attend psychiat, St Luke's Hosp, New York. *Honors & Awards:* Bowis Award, Am Col Psychiat. *Mem:* AMA; Am Psychiat Asn; Am Col Physicians; Am Col Psychiat; Asn Res Nerv & Ment Dis. *Res:* Eating disorders; psychosomatic disorders; headache and pain problems; violence. *Mailing Add:* McLean Hosp 115 Mill St Belmont MA 02178

FRAZIER, STEPHEN EARL, b Spencer, WVa, Oct 21, 39; m 70; c 2. INORGANIC CHEMISTRY. *Educ:* Fla Southern Col, BS, 61; Univ Fla, MS, 63, PhD(chem), 65. *Prof Exp:* Res assoc, Case Western Res Univ, 66-67; res chemist res div, W R Grace & Co, 67-69; prof chem, Polk Jr Col, 70-71; indust consult inorg chem, 71; DIR RES, RUSH-HAMPTON INDUSTS, 71- *Concurrent Pos:* Instr, Baltimore Community Col, 68-69; res assoc, Univ Fla, 70-71. *Mem:* Sigma Xi; NY Acad Sci; Am Chem Soc; Am Soc Heating, Refrig & Air Conditioning Engrs. *Res:* Inorganic phosphorus chemistry; synthesis of organo-silicon chemistry; inorganic polymers; chemistry of chloramine and ammonia; heterogeneous catalysis; inorganic materials science. *Mailing Add:* 3521 Pinetree Rd Orlando FL 32804

FRAZIER, THOMAS VERNON, b Tonopah, Nev, Feb 25, 21; m 64; c 2. PHYSICS. *Educ:* Univ Calif, Los Angeles, AB, 43, MA, 49, PhD(physics), 52. *Prof Exp:* Asst physics, Univ Calif, Los Angeles, 43-44, 45-49; physicist, Naval Ord Lab, 44-45; instr, 50-52, from asst prof to assoc prof, 52-67, PROF PHYSICS, UNIV NEV, RENO, 67- *Concurrent Pos:* Vis Fulbright lectr, Nat Tsing Hua Univ & Taiwan Prov Norm Univ, 59-61. *Mem:* AAAS; Am Asn Physics Teachers; Am Phys Soc; Acoust Soc Am. *Res:* Hearing by bone connection. *Mailing Add:* Dept of Physics Univ of Nev Reno NV 89507

FRAZIER, TODD MEARL, b Lima, Ohio, Nov 9, 25; m; c 4. PUBLIC HEALTH. *Educ:* Kenyon Col, AB, 49; Johns Hopkins Univ, ScM, 57. *Prof Exp:* Statistician, Army Chem Ctr, Md, 51-54; dir biostatist, Baltimore City Health Dept, 54-63; chief div planning, res & statist, DC Dept Pub Health, 63-68; assoc prof biostatist, Sch Pub Health, Harvard Ctr Community Health & Med Care, 68-78; CHIEF SURVEILLANCE BR, DIV SURVEILLANCE, HAZARD EVAL & FIELD STUDIES, NAT INST OCCUP SAFETY & HEALTH, 78- *Res:* Public health administration, planning, research and statistics; occupational health; health program evaluation. *Mailing Add:* 2164 Cablecar Ct Cincinnati OH 45244

FRAZIER, WILLIAM ALLEN, b Carrizo Springs, Tex, Apr 26, 08; m 35; c 3. OLERICULTURE. *Educ:* Agr & Mech Col Tex, BS, 30; Univ Md, MS, 31, PhD, 33. *Prof Exp:* From instr to assoc prof olericult, Univ Md, 33-37; assoc horticulturist, Exp Sta, Univ Ariz, 37-39; olericulturist & head dept veg crops, Univ Hawaii, 39-49; prof & horticulturist, 49-72, EMER PROF HORT, ORE STATE UNIV, 72- *Mem:* AAAS; Am Soc Hort Sci. *Res:* Breeding vegetable crop plants for disease resistance and improved horticultural characters. *Mailing Add:* 3225 NW Crest Dr Corvallis OR 97330

FRAZZA, EVERETT JOSEPH, b NJ, Nov 2, 24; m 46; c 4. ORGANIC CHEMISTRY. *Educ:* Univ Md, BS, 50, PhD(org chem), 54. *Prof Exp:* Chemist, Appl Physics Lab, Johns Hopkins Univ, 51-52; res chemist, 54-58, group leader, Indust Chem Dept, 58-60, group leader, Cent Res Div, 60-69, head biotherapeut dept, Lederle Labs, 69-70, dir res & develop, Davis & Geck Dept, 70-75, assoc dir new prod acquisitions, Med Res Div, 76-80, DIR NEW PROD LICENSING, MED GROUP, AM CYANAMID CO, 80- *Concurrent Pos:* Chmn, Gordon Res Conf Biomat, 76. *Mem:* Am Chem Soc (pres, 50); Soc Biomat; AAAS (pres, 65). *Res:* Aliphatic nitriles; petrochemicals; paper chemicals; monomer and polymer synthesis; medical and biological applications of polymers; surgical sutures; hospital specialties. *Mailing Add:* Med Res Group Am Cyanamid Co Lederle Labs Pearl River NY 10965

FREA, JAMES IRVING, b Sturgeon Bay, Wis, Mar 1, 37; m 59; c 4. BACTERIOLOGY, BIOCHEMISTRY. *Educ:* Univ Wis, BS, 59, MS, 61, PhD(bact, biochem), 63. *Prof Exp:* From asst prof to assoc prof, 65-73, PROF MICROBIOL, OHIO STATE UNIV, 73- *Mem:* AAAS; Am Soc Testing & Mat; Sigma Xi; Am Soc Microbiol; Am Chem Soc. *Res:* Microbial proteins and nucleic acids; actinomycete physiology; microbial ecology; biochemical ecology of microorganisms; microbial methane production and oxidation. *Mailing Add:* Dept Microbiol Ohio State Univ Columbus OH 43210

FREADMAN, MARVIN ALAN, b Pittsfield, Mass, Aug 18, 49. BIOLOGY, COMPARATIVE PHYSIOLOGY. *Educ:* Univ Colo, BA, 71; Col William & Mary, MA, 74; Univ Mass, PhD(zool), 78. *Prof Exp:* NIH fel physiol, John B Pierce Found, Yale Univ, 78-80; RES ASSOC ZOOL, UNIV MASS, AMHERST, 81- *Concurrent Pos:* Vis asst fel, John B Pierce Found, Yale Univ, 81- *Mem:* Am Soc Zoologists; Sigma Xi; AAAS. *Res:* Comparative physiology; function of invertebrate respiratory pigments; gill ventilation and swimming in fishes. *Mailing Add:* John B Pierce Found 290 Congress Ave New Haven CT 06519

FREAR, DONALD STUART, b Wakefield, RI, Sept 5, 29; m 56; c 4. AGRICULTURAL BIOCHEMISTRY. *Educ:* Pa State Univ, BS, 51; Ohio State Univ, MSc, 53, PhD(agr biochem), 55. *Prof Exp:* Res biochemist, Charles F Kettering Found, 55-57; assoc prof to prof biochem, NDak State Univ, 57-76; RES LEADER, AGR RES SER, USDA, 68- *Concurrent Pos:* Res chemist, Sci & Educ Admin-Agr Res, USDA, 64-68. *Mem:* Am Chem Soc. *Res:* Pesticide metabolism in plants. *Mailing Add:* USDA Metab & Radiation Res Lab State Univ Sta Fargo ND 58105

FREAR, GEORGE LEWIS, b State College, Pa, Sept 29, 01; m 28; c 2. APPLIED CHEMISTRY. *Educ:* Pa State Univ, BS, 23; Yale Univ, PhD(phys chem), 26. *Prof Exp:* Fel, Yale Univ, 26-27; res assoc, Am Tin Sheet Plate Co, 27-29; assoc phys chemist, US Bur Mines, 29-33; from assoc chemist to sr chemist, Tenn Valley Authority, 33-45; supvr carbide res, Air Reduction Sales Co, 45-48; phys chemist, Barrett Div, Allied Chem Corp, 48-52, mem staff prod develop, Nitrogen Div, 52-65, mkt analyst, 65-66; CONSULT, 66- *Concurrent Pos:* Spec lectr, Newark Col Eng, 66-71. *Mem:* Am Chem Soc; Chem Mkt Res Asn. *Res:* Chemical research on phosphorus, phosphates, ammonia and ammonium nitrate; wet-process phosphoric acid manufacture. *Mailing Add:* Box 255 RD 1 Flemington NJ 08822

FREAS, ALAN D('YARMETT), b Newark, Ohio, Nov 4, 10; m 34; c 3. ENGINEERING. *Educ:* Univ Wis, BS, 33, MS, 47, CE, 52. *Prof Exp:* Instr civil eng, Univ Wis, 36-39; engr, Forest Prods Lab, US Forest Serv, 33-36, 39-42 & 45-56, asst dir forest prods res, 56-58, asst to dir, 58-67, chief, Div Solid Wood Prod Res, 67-71, asst dir, Timber Utilization Res, 72-74, asst dir, Wood Engr Res, 74-75; ed, Forest Prods Res Soc, 76-77; CONSULT WOOD, 77- *Mem:* Am Soc Civil Engrs; Forest Prod Res Soc. *Res:* Strength of wood, modified wood and plywood; strength of glued, laminated wood structures; processing and protection of forest products; research administration. *Mailing Add:* 2618 Park Pl Madison WI 53705

FREASIER, BEN FOREST, b San Patricio, Tex, May 14, 23; m 44; c 4. PHYSICAL CHEMISTRY. *Educ:* Tex Col Arts & Indust, BS, 47, MS, 50; Tex Tech Col, PhD, 57. *Prof Exp:* Instr chem, Tex Col Arts & Indust, 50-52; instr, Amarillo Col, 53-54; chemist & physicist, Atomic Energy Div, Phillips Petrol Co, 54-55; sr nuclear engr, Convair Div, Gen Dynamics Corp, 55-56; instr chem, Tex Tech Col, 56-57; assoc prof, Tex Col Arts & Indust, 57-60; assoc prof, SDak State Col, 60-61; sr phys chemist, Southwest Res Inst, 61-62; assoc prof, 62-69, PROF CHEM, LA TECH UNIV, 69- *Mem:* Am Chem Soc. *Res:* Kinetics; equilibrium; thermodynamics. *Mailing Add:* Dept of Chem La Tech Univ Ruston LA 71270

FREBERG, C(ARL) ROGER, b Hector, Minn, Mar 17, 16; m 41; c 2. MECHANICAL ENGINEERING. *Educ:* Univ Minn, BME, 38, MS, 40; Purdue Univ, PhD(mech eng), 43. *Prof Exp:* Instr mech eng, Univ Minn, 39-40; Purdue Univ, 40-43, asst prof mech eng & aeronaut eng, 43-45; res engr, Carrier Corp, 45-46; dir eng div, Southern Res Inst, 46-49; head equip res, US Naval Civil Eng Lab, 49-52; assoc dir, Borg Warner Res Ctr, 52-57; PROF MECH ENG, UNIV SOUTHERN CALIF, 57- *Concurrent Pos:* Consult, Studebaker Corp, 44, Carrier Corp, 45 & Hughes Aircraft Corp, 59; lectr, NATO, Paris, France, 58. *Mem:* Am Soc Mech Engrs; Am Soc Eng Educ. *Res:* Vibrations; noise; mechanical design; research management; applied mechanics. *Mailing Add:* OHE 430 Dept of Mech Eng Univ of Southern Calif Los Angeles CA 90007

FREBOLD, HANS (WILHELM LUDWIG AUGUST HERMAN), b Hanover, Ger, July 31, 99; Can citizen; m 26; c 5. GEOLOGY, PALEONTOLOGY. *Educ:* Univ Gottingen, PhD(geol, paleont), 24. *Prof Exp:* Privat-docent geol & paleont, Greifswald, Ger, 26, prof, 31, hon prof, 45; sci res, Geol Inst Copenhagen, 33-41; chief Arctic Div, Ger Sci Inst, 41-45; hon prof, Univ Kiel, 49; consult geologist, Danish Am Prospecting Co, 47-49; geologist, Geol Surv Can, 49, chief div stratig paleont, 51-59, sr res paleontologist, 59-63, prin res scientist, 63-68; CONSULT GEOLOGIST, 69- *Concurrent Pos:* Chief Norwegian Exped, Spitzbergen, 30; party chief Danish exped, NE Greenland, 31; vis prof, Univ Okla, 63-64. *Honors & Awards:* Danish Medal Merit, EGreenland, 35. *Mem:* Fel Royal Soc Can; Danish Geol Soc. *Res:* Stratigraphy and paleontology, particularly of Arctic regions and Canada. *Mailing Add:* 265 Patricia Ave Ottawa ON K1Y 0C6 Can

FRECH, ROGER, b Gary, Ind, Mar 26, 41; c 2. PHYSICAL CHEMISTRY. *Educ:* Mass Inst Technol, BS, 63; Univ Minn, PhD(phys chem), 68. *Prof Exp:* Res assoc phys chem, Ore State Univ, 68-70, instr, 69-70; asst prof phys chem, 70-75, ASSOC PROF CHEM, UNIV OKLA, 75- *Concurrent Pos:* Alexander von Humboldt fel, 81-82. *Mem:* Am Chem Soc; Am Inst Physics. *Res:* Vibrational spectroscopy of crystals and condensed phases; disordered systems; theory of optical and dielectric constants; fast ion conductivity. *Mailing Add:* Dept Chem Rm 211 Univ Okla 620 Parrington Oval Norman OK 73069

FRECHE, JOHN C(HARLES), b Minneapolis, Minn, Apr 29, 23; m 43. METALLURGY, MECHANICAL ENGINEERING. *Educ:* Univ Pittsburgh, BS, 43. *Prof Exp:* Jr engr, Wright Aeronaut Corp, NJ, 43-44; aeronaut res engr, Nat Adv Comt Aeronaut, 44-48, asst head turbine cooling sect, 49-57, head alloys sect, Lewis Res Ctr, 58-63, chief, Fatigue & Alloys Res Br, 63-71, asst chief mat & struct div, 71-74, ASSOC CHIEF MAT & STRUCT DIV, LEWIS RES CTR, NASA, 74- *Honors & Awards:* IR-100 Award, Indust Res Mag, 68, 74 & 78; Except Sci Achievement Medal, NASA, 71. *Mem:* Fel Am Inst Chem; Am Soc Metals; Am Inst Aeronaut & Astronaut; Am Inst Mining, Metall & Petrol Engrs; Soc Exp Stress Anal. *Res:* Materials for air breathing and space propulsion systems; nickel and cobalt base alloys; metal fatigue. *Mailing Add:* NASA Lewis Res Ctr 21000 Brookpark Rd Cleveland OH 44135

FRECHETTE, ALFRED LEO, b Groveton, NH, Aug 22, 09; m 30; c 1. PUBLIC HEALTH. *Educ:* Univ Vt, MD, 34; Harvard Univ, MPH, 39. *Prof Exp:* Instr, Col Med, Univ Vt, 35-36; pvt pract, 36-38; dir venereal dis control, NH Dept Pub Health, 39-42, comnr, 42-45; dir pub health, Brookline, Mass, 45-50; dir health div, United Community Servs Metrop Boston, 50-59; comnr, Mass Dept Pub Health, 59-72; mem staff, Sidney Farber Cancer Ctr, 72-78; COMNR, MASS DEPT PUB HEALTH, 79- *Mem:* Am Pub Health Asn. *Res:* Public health administration. *Mailing Add:* 423 Walnut St Brookline MA 02146

FRECHETTE, (HOWELLS ACHILLE) VAN DERCK, b Ottawa, Ont, Jan 5, 16; nat US; m 40; c 5. CERAMIC SCIENCE, FRACTOLOGY. *Educ:* Alfred Univ, BS, 39; Univ Ill, MS, 40, PhD(ceramic eng), 42. *Prof Exp:* Asst, Eng Exp Sta, Univ Ill, 38-40; res physicist, Corning Glass Works, NY, 42-44; asst instr petrog, 41-42, PROF CERAMIC SCI, NY STATE COL CERAMICS, ALFRED UNIV, 44- *Concurrent Pos:* Chmn solid state studies, Gordon Res Conf, 55; Fulbright prof, Inst Phys Chem, Gottingen, Ger, 55-56; guest prof, Max Planck Inst Silicates, 65-66 & Univ Erlangen-Nurnberg, 73. *Honors & Awards:* Western Elec Award, Am Soc Eng Educ, 68. *Mem:* Nat Inst Ceramic Engrs; fel Am Ceramic Soc; Swedish Royal Soc Arts & Sci; Ger Ceramic Soc. *Res:* Petrography and mineralogy of ceramic materials; color of crystalline inorganic materials; solid state reactivity; refractories; tempering glass products; fractography. *Mailing Add:* NY State Col of Ceramics Alfred Univ Alfred NY 14802

FRECK, PETER G, b Hinsdale, Ill, Aug 14, 34; m 58; c 3. AERONAUTICAL ENGINEERING. *Educ:* Princeton Univ, BSE, 56, MSE, 59; Harvard Univ, MBA, 62. *Prof Exp:* Aerodynamicist, Douglas Aircraft Corp, Calif, 58-60; aeronaut engr, Anal Serv, Inc, Va, 62-64; asst dir, Systs Eval Div, Inst Defense Anal, 64-78; ASSOC TECH DIR, BATTLEFIELD SYSTS, MITRE CORP, 78- *Mem:* Am Inst Aeronaut & Astronaut; Opers Res Soc Am. *Res:* Aircraft performance, stability and control; systems analysis; operations research. *Mailing Add:* MITRE Corp 1820 Dolley Madison Blvd McLean VA 22102

FRECKMAN, DIANA WALL, plant nematology, see previous edition

FRECKMANN, ROBERT W, b Milwaukee, Wis, Dec 5, 39; m 71. PLANT TAXONOMY. *Educ:* Univ Wis-Milwaukee, BS, 62; Iowa State Univ, PhD(plant taxon), 67. *Prof Exp:* Asst cur bot, Milwaukee Pub Mus, 67-68; from asst prof to assoc prof, 68-79, PROF BIOL, UNIV WIS-STEVENS POINT, 79-, CUR HERBARIUM, MUS NATURAL HIST, 69- *Concurrent Pos:* Wis State Univs res fund grant, 69-71. *Mem:* Am Soc Plant Taxon; Bot Soc Am; Int Asn Plant Taxon. *Res:* Taxonomy and biosystematics of Dichanthelium; grasses of Wisconsin; flora of central Wisconsin. *Mailing Add:* Dept of Biol Univ of Wis Stevens Point WI 54481

FRED, EDWIN BROUN, bacteriology, deceased

FRED, MARK SIMON, b Richmond, Ind, June 26, 11; m 41; c 2. PHYSICS. *Educ:* Univ Chicago, BS, 33, MS, 34, PhD(physics), 37. *Prof Exp:* Consult, Standard Oil Co, Ind, 37-43; chemist, Manhattan Dist Proj, Univ Chicago, 42-45; physicist, Armour Res Found, 45-48; consult, Argonne Nat Lab, 45-48, sr res chemist, 48-76; CONSULT, 76- *Honors & Awards:* Meggers Award, Optical Soc Am, 77. *Mem:* Am Chem Soc; fel Optical Soc Am; Am Inst Chem. *Res:* Atomic spectroscopy. *Mailing Add:* 32 Lockport St Plainfield IL 60544

FREDEEN, HOWARD T, b MacRorie, Sask, Dec 10, 21; m 53; c 5. ANIMAL GENETICS, BIOMETRY. *Educ:* Univ Sask, BSc, 43; Univ Alta, MSc, 47; Iowa State Col, PhD(genetics), 52. *Prof Exp:* Lectr animal husb, Univ Sask, 43-45; animal husbandman, 47-55, head livestock res, 55-80, HEAD LIVESTOCK RES, RES SCI ANIMAL BREEDING, MEATS, CAN DEPT AGR, 80- *Concurrent Pos:* Mem, Quinquennial Rev Conf, Commonwealth Agr Bur, Eng, 55; co-developer Lacombe breed of pigs, 59; mem, Nat Animal Breeding Adv Comt, 59-64; sci ed, Can J Genetics & Cytol, 60-64; sci ed, Can J Animal Sci, 63-67, ed, 67-71; chmn, Can Livestock Geneticists Roundtable, 63-64; chmn, Gen Adv Comn Can ROP for Swine, 70-79; tech adv, Can Pork Coun, Can Charolais Asn & Can Lacombe Breeders Asn; adj prof, Univ Alta, 80- *Honors & Awards:* Pub Serv Merit Award, 69; Cert of Merit, Can Soc Animal Sci, 76; Award of Excellence, Genetics Soc Can, 78. *Mem:* AAAS; NY Acad Sci; Am Soc Animal Sci; Poultry Sci Asn; fel Agr Inst Can. *Res:* Genetics of pigs, cattle and poultry, especially factors influencing the effectiveness of selective breeding; meats and carcass evalutation beef and pork. *Mailing Add:* Exp Farm Dept Res Br Can Dept of Agr Lacombe AB T0C 1S0 Can

FREDEN, STANLEY CHARLES, b Far Rockaway, NY, Dec 5, 27; m 57; c 3. SCIENCE ADMINISTRATION, REMOTE SENSING. *Educ:* Univ Calif, Los Angeles, AB, 50, MA, 52, PhD, 56. *Prof Exp:* Asst physics, Univ Calif, Los Angeles, 50-54, assoc, 54-56, instr, 56-57; sr staff physicist, Lawrence Radiation Lab, Livermore, 57-61; sect head, Aerospace Corp, Calif, 61-66, sr staff scientist, 66-68; chief space physics div, Manned Spacecraft Ctr, Tex, 68-70, chief scientist, Lab Meteorol & Earth Sci, 70-74, LANSAT PROJ SCIENTIST, NASA, GOODARD SPACE FLIGHT CTR, 74-, CHIEF MISSIONS UTILIZATION OFF, 74- *Concurrent Pos:* Guest scientist, Max Planck Inst Extraterrestrial Physics, 64-65. *Honors & Awards:* Except Performance Award, Goddard Space Flight Ctr, 73. *Mem:* AAAS; fel Am Phys Soc; Am Geophys Union. *Res:* Particles trapped in the earth's magnetic field; experiments performed with space probes and satellites; acquisition of remotely sensed data and their applications to earth sciences and earth resource survey disciplines, including ecology and environmental quality. *Mailing Add:* Code 902 Goddard Space Flight Ctr NASA Greenbelt MD 20771

FREDENBURG, ROBERT LOVE, b Antwerp, NY, Nov 28, 21; m 42; c 5. SCIENCE EDUCATION. *Educ:* Syracuse Univ, AB, 54, MS, 59, PhD(sci educ), 65. *Prof Exp:* Assoc prof, 59-69, PROF GEOL & PHYS SCI & V PRES ACAD AFFAIRS, CALIF STATE UNIV, CHICO, 69- *Res:* General education physical science courses at the college level and student interest in these courses. *Mailing Add:* Calif State Univ Chico CA 95926

FREDERICK, DANIEL, b Elkhorn, WVa, Apr 29, 25; m 52; c 4. ENGINEERING MECHANICS. *Educ:* Va Polytech Inst, BS, 44, MS, 48; Univ Mich, PhD(eng mech), 55. *Prof Exp:* From instr to prof, 48-74, ALUMNI DISTINGUISHED PROF ENG MECH, VA POLYTECH INST & STATE UNIV, 74-, HEAD DEPT, 70- *Concurrent Pos:* Lectr, Nat Sci Found Adv Mech Inst, Univ Colo, 62-63; consult, Structures Res Div, NASA, Va, Pac Missile Range, Calif, Martin-Marietta Corp, Lord Mfg Co & David Taylor Model Basin; dir conf continuum mech, Nat Sci Found, 65-70. *Honors & Awards:* Award, Am Soc Civil Engrs, 60. *Mem:* Am Soc Civil Engrs; Am Inst Aeronaut & Astronaut; Am Soc Eng Educ; Am Soc Mech Engrs; Soc Eng Sci. *Res:* Aerodynamic stability of bridges; continuum mechanics; elasticity; plasticity; plates and shells; mechanics of composite materials. *Mailing Add:* Dept of Eng Sci & Mech Va Polytech Inst & State Univ Blacksburg VA 24061

FREDERICK, DAVID EUGENE, b Chicago, Ill, June 10, 31; div; c 4. ENGINEERING PHYSICS, COMPUTER SCIENCES. *Educ:* Yale Univ, BS, 52; Univ Ill, PhD(physics), 62. *Prof Exp:* Group leader power plant simulators, Singer Co, 69-71, Harshman Assocs, Inc, 71-72 & Electronic Assocs, Inc, 72-73; consult data acquisition process control systs, 73-77; owner, 77-78, PRES, ARGUS TECHNOL SYSTS, INC, 79- *Mem:* Am Phys Soc; Am Nuclear Soc; Soc Computer Simulation; Sigma Xi; Inst Elec & Electronics Engrs. *Res:* Medium-energy photonuclear physics research. *Mailing Add:* Argus Technol Systs Suite M255 1101 S Winchester Blvd San Jose CA 95128

FREDERICK, DEAN KIMBALL, b Providence, RI, Nov 11, 34; m 57; c 4. ELECTRICAL ENGINEERING. *Educ:* Yale Univ, BE, 55; Brown Univ, ScM, 61; Stanford Univ, PhD(elec eng), 64. *Prof Exp:* Engr, New Departure Div, Gen Motors Corp, 57-58; asst prof elec eng, Clarkson Col Technol, 64; ASSOC PROF ELEC ENG, RENSSELAER POLYTECH INST, 64- *Mem:* Inst Elec & Electronics Engrs. *Res:* Automatic control theory; computer-aided design of control systems; dynamic simulation; computer-aided instruction. *Mailing Add:* Elec Comput & Systs Eng Dept Rensselaer Polytech Inst Troy NY 12181

FREDERICK, EDWARD C, b Mankato, Minn, Nov 17, 30; m 51; c 5. ANIMAL SCIENCE, PHYSIOLOGY. *Educ:* Univ Minn, BS, 54, MS, 55, PhD(reprod), 58. *Prof Exp:* Assoc prof & dairy specialist, Northwest Sch & Exp Sta, 58-64, assoc prof, Southern Sch & Exp Sta, 64-66, prof animal sci, 66-69, supt, Sch & Sta, 64-69, dir, Col, 69-70, PROF ANIMAL SCI, UNIV MINN TECH COL-WASECA, 69-, PROVOST, 70- *Mem:* AAAS; Am DAiry Sci Asn; Am Soc Animal Sci. *Res:* Frozen semen; frequency of semen collection; effects of nutrition on semen production; mastitis; effect of tranquilizers on behavior; fly control studies; dairy-beef feeding trials; high moisture barley studies. *Mailing Add:* Univ of Minn Tech Col Waseca MN 56093

FREDERICK, EDWARD CARROLL, physiology, see previous edition

FREDERICK, GEORGE LEONARD, b Kitchener, Ont, July 15, 30; m 50; c 4. PHARMACOLOGY, TOXICOLOGY. *Educ:* Ont Vet Col, DVM, 52; Univ Western Ont, MSc, 53. *Prof Exp:* Res officer, Animal Res Inst, Can Dept Agr, 54-67; sci adv, Bur Sci Adv Serv, 67-73, sci adv, Br Drugs, 73-80, SCI ADV, BUR HUMAN PRESCRIPTION DRUGS, DEPT NAT HEALTH & WELFARE, CAN, 80- *Mem:* Can Biochem Soc; Nutrit Soc Can; Brit Soc Study Fertil; Can Vet Med Asn. *Res:* Noninfectious causes and prevention of reproductive failures and neonatal mortality in farm animals; role of vitamin B-12 and iron metabolism; evaluation of drug safety and efficacy. *Mailing Add:* Bur Human Prescription Drugs Dept Nat Health & Welfare Vanier K1A 1B8 Can

FREDERICK, HOWARD MASSEY, b Portland, Maine, July 24, 41; m 67; c 2. BIOCHEMISTRY, PHYSIOLOGY. *Educ:* Univ Ariz, BS, 64, MS, 67, PhD(biochem), 74. *Prof Exp:* Nutritionist, Cent Feedmills Israel, 68-69; nutritionist & consult, Syntex Agribusiness, 70-72, NUTRITIONIST, ARIZ FEEDS, 72- *Concurrent Pos:* Mem nutrit coun, Am Feed Mfg Asn, 73-, antibiotic task force, 77-78. *Mem:* Am Asn Vet Nutrit; Am Soc Clin Nutrit; Am Soc Microbiol. *Res:* Control and treatment of infectious diseases in food-producing animals. *Mailing Add:* 1572 W Klamath Dr Tucson AZ 85704

FREDERICK, JOHN EDGAR, b Thursday, WVa, Aug 10, 40. PHYSICAL CHEMISTRY. *Educ:* Glenville State Col, BS, 60; Univ Wis, PhD(phys chem), 64. *Prof Exp:* Chemist, Union Carbide Chem Co, 60; fel phys chem, Stanford Res Inst, 64-66; asst prof chem & polymer sci, 66-72, ASSOC PROF CHEM & POLYMER SCI, UNIV AKRON, 72-, RES ASSOC, INST POLYMER SCI, 66- *Mem:* Am Chem Soc; Soc Rheol. *Res:* High polymer physics; quasielastic light scattering from polymeric systems. *Mailing Add:* Dept Polymer Sci Univ of Akron Akron OH 44325

FREDERICK, JULIAN ROSS, b Sioux Falls, SDak, June 10, 13; m 44; c 5. MECHANICAL ENGINEERING. *Educ:* Iowa State Univ, BS, 35, MS, 36; Univ Mich, PhD(physics), 48. *Prof Exp:* Asst, Univ Mich, 39-41, res assoc ultrasonics, 41-46; asst prof physics, Brown Univ, 47-50; lectr & res physicist, 50-57, from asst prof to assoc prof mech eng, 57-70, PROF MECH ENG, UNIV MICH, 70- *Honors & Awards:* Lester hon lectr, Am Soc Nondestructive Testing. *Mem:* Am Soc Mech Engrs; Am Soc Metals; fel Acoust Soc Am; fel Soc Nondestructive Testing. *Res:* Nondestructive testing; manufacturing engineering; fatigue and fracture of materials. *Mailing Add:* Dept Mech Eng & Appl Mech Univ Mich Ann Arbor MI 48109

FREDERICK, KENNETH JACOB, b Schenectady, NY, Dec 5, 13; m 36, 78; c 3. PHYSICAL CHEMISTRY. *Educ:* Union Col, BS, 36; Univ Calif, PhD(phys chem), 39. *Prof Exp:* Sr res chemist, Solvay Process Div, Allied Chem & Dye Corp, NY, 39-47; group leader, Paraffine Co, Inc, Calif, 47-49; dir res data opers, Abbott Labs, 49-76; RETIRED. *Mem:* AAAS; Am Inst Chemists; Am Chem Soc. *Res:* Physical chemistry of drugs and drug action; scientific instrumentation and mathematics applied to pharmaceutical research; scientific personnel development and facility planning. *Mailing Add:* 1540 N Greenleaf Lake Forest IL 60045

FREDERICK, LAFAYETTE, b Friarspoint, Miss, Mar, 19, 23; m 50; c 3. MYCOLOGY, PLANT PATHOLOGY. *Educ:* Tuskegee Inst, BS, 43; RI State Col, MS, 50; State Col Wash, PhD(plant path), 52. *Prof Exp:* From assoc prof to prof biol, Southern Univ, 52-62; prof biol, Atlanta Univ, 62-76, chmn dept, 63-76; PROF BOT & CHMN DEPT, HOWARD UNIV, 76- *Concurrent Pos:* Carnegie res grant, 53; NSF fac fel, Dept Bot, Univ Ill, 60-61; mem, Comn Undergrad Educ Biol, 70-71; mem, Gen Res Support Adv Comt, NIH & Biol Achievement Test Comt, Educ Testing Serv. *Mem:* AAAS; Am Phytopathological Soc; Mycol Soc Am; Bot Soc Am; Am Inst Biol Sci. *Res:* Vascular wilt diseases of plants; developmental studies on Conidia and ascospores; systematics and ecology of Myxomycetes; systematics of imperfect fungi. *Mailing Add:* Dept of Bot Howard Univ Washington DC 20059

FREDERICK, LLOYD RANDALL, b Ill, Aug 5, 21; m 43; c 3. SOIL MICROBIOLOGY, SOIL FERTILITY. *Educ:* Univ Nebr, BSc, 43; Rutgers Univ, MSc, 47, PhD(microbiol), 50. *Prof Exp:* Asst microbiologist, Purdue Univ, 49-55; from assoc prof to prof soils, 55-78, EMER PROF SOILS, IOWA STATE UNIV, 78-; MICROBIOL SPECIALIST, AID, 78- *Concurrent Pos:* Fulbright res scholar, Ger, 62; consult, W R Grace Inoculant Lab, 67-70 & Res Seeds, Inc, 70-74; microbiol specialist, AID, 75-77. *Mem:* AAAS; fel Am Soc Agron; fel Soil Sci Soc Am; Am Soc Microbiol; Brit Soc Soil Sci. *Res:* Transformations of sulfur compounds by soil microorganisms; decomposition of plant residues and chemicals in soil; factors affecting ammonia retention and oxidation; denitrification; effect of temperature on biological soil changes; biological nitrogen fixation; rhizobia in soils and nodules. *Mailing Add:* AID S&T/AGR-420 RP Washington DC 20523

FREDERICK, MARVIN RAY, b Wadsworth, Ohio, Apr 12, 18; m 41; c 4. ORGANIC CHEMISTRY. *Educ:* Ohio State Univ, BSc, 41; Purdue Univ, PhD(org chem), 47. *Prof Exp:* Lab asst chem, Columbia Chem Div, Pittsburgh Plate Glass Co, Ohio, 36-37; asst, Purdue Univ, 41-43; res chemist, B F Goodrich Co, 46-57, sect leader plastics polymerization, 58-60, mgr chem eng res, 60-69, mgr tech info res, 69-74, mgr, Corp Info Ctr, 74-78; RETIRED. *Mem:* Am Soc Info Sci; Am Chem Soc. *Res:* Organic fluorine chemistry; organic chemicals research; chemistry of monomers and polymerization; chemistry of organic fluorine compounds and their preparation; plastics polymerization. *Mailing Add:* 6827 Westwood Dr Cleveland OH 44141

FREDERICK, SUE ELLEN, b Harrisville, WVa, Feb 25, 46; m 71; c 1. ELECTRON MICROSCOPY, MEMBRANES. *Educ:* Glenville State Col, BS, 66; Univ Wis, Madison, PhD(bot), 70. *Prof Exp:* Fel molecular & cell biol, Univ Colo, Boulder, 70-71; instr biochem, Mich State Univ, 71-72; asst prof, 73-79, ASSOC PROF BIOL SCI, MT HOLYOKE COL, 79- *Mem:* Am Soc Cell Biol; Sigma Xi. *Res:* Ultrastructure and cytochemistry of plant organelles; membranes of plant cells: their flow, cycling, and surface characterstics. *Mailing Add:* Dept Biol Sci Mt Holyoke Col South Hadley MA 01075

FREDERICK, VICTOR RAY, JR, b Springfield, Ohio, Mar 15, 48. BOTANY, LIMNOLOGY. *Educ:* Trinity Univ, BA, 70; Ohio State Univ, MS, 74, PhD(bot), 77. *Prof Exp:* biol coordr & res assoc, 77-80, ASST DIR & SR RES ASSOC, GREAT LAKES LAB, STATE UNIV NY COL BUFFALO, 81- *Mem:* Am Soc Limnol & Oceanog; Bot Soc Am; Phycol Soc Am; Int Asn Great Lakes; Int Phycol Soc. *Res:* Sigma Xi. Res: Phytoplankton ecology; botanical limnology; paleolimnology. *Mailing Add:* Great Lakes Lab State Univ Col 1300 Elmwood Ave Buffalo NY 14222

FREDERICK, WILLIAM GEORGE DEMOTT, b Toledo, Ohio, June 23, 36; m 81; c 3. PHYSICS, MATERIALS SCIENCE. *Educ:* Univ Toledo, BS, 58; Univ Dayton, MS, 68; Univ Cincinnati, PhD(mat sci), 73; Mass Inst Technol, 80. *Prof Exp:* Prof engr magnetic mat, 65-68, tech area mgr electromagnetic mat, 68-73, br chief optical mat, 73-79, CHIEF, MAT LAB PLANS OFF, AIR FORCE MAT LAB, 80- *Concurrent Pos:* Sloan fel, Mass Inst Technol, 79-80. *Honors & Awards:* Arthur Flemming Award, 77. *Mem:* Am Phys Soc; AAAS. *Res:* Infrared transmitting materials; infrared detector materials; magnetic properties of rare earth-cobalt alloys; electromagnetic properties of solids. *Mailing Add:* AF Weapons Aeronaut Lab Mat Lab/XRXM Wright Patterson AFB OH 45433

FREDERICK, WILLIAM JAMES, JR, chemical engineering, see previous edition

FREDERICKS, CHRISTOPHER M, b Detroit, Mich, May 13, 44; m 71; c 2. PHYSIOLOGY. *Educ:* Oberlin Col, BS, 66; Wayne State Univ, PhD(physiol, pharmacol), 71. *Prof Exp:* Fel pharmacol, Sch Pharm, Ore State Univ, 71-72; asst prof physiol, Sch Med, Wayne State Univ, 72-75, assoc urol, 73-75; asst prof physiol, 75-77, ASSOC PROF PHYSIOL, MED UNIV SC, 77- *Mem:* Am Physiol Soc; assoc Pharmacol Soc Can; Soc Study Reprod. *Res:* Urinary and reproductive tract physiology; smooth muscle receptors. *Mailing Add:* Dept of Physiol Med Univ SC Charleston SC 29401

FREDERICKS, ROBERT JOSEPH, b New York, NY, Dec 26, 34. X-RAY CRYSTALLOGRAPHY. *Educ:* Villanova Univ, BS, 57; St Joseph's Col, Pa, MS, 59; Lehigh Univ, PhD(chem), 65. *Prof Exp:* Res chemist, Cent Res Lab, Gen Aniline & Film Corp, 60-65, res specialist, 65-67; res supvr, Cent Res Lab, Allied Chem Corp, 67-72; mgr anal chem, Ethicon Inc, 72-74, dir res serv, 74-76, assoc dir res, 76-78; vpres res & develop, Surgikos, 78-79; VPRES RES & DEVELOP, JOHNSON & JOHNSON DENT PROD CO, 79- *Concurrent Pos:* Am Chem Soc lectr, 71-73. *Mem:* AAAS; Am Chem Soc; Soc Biomat; Sigma Xi; Am Phys Soc. *Res:* Research administration; polymer morphology; polymer structure. *Mailing Add:* Surgikos 501 George St New Brunswick NJ 08903

FREDERICKS, ROBERT W, physics, geophysics, see previous edition

FREDERICKS, WILLIAM JOHN, b San Diego, Calif, Sept 18, 24; m 42. PHYSICAL CHEMISTRY. *Educ:* San Diego State Col, BS, 51; Ore State Col, PhD(phys chem), 55. *Prof Exp:* Fulbright fel, Kamerlingh Onnes Lab, Leiden, Holland, 55-56; chemist, Stanford Res Inst, 56-59, chmn solid state dept, 59-62; assoc prof chem, 62-67, PROF CHEM, ORE STATE UNIV, 67- *Concurrent Pos:* Vis acad, Atomic Energy Res Estab, Harwell, Berkshire, UK, 69-70; vis fel, Ctr Chem Physics, Univ Western Ont, 81. *Mem:* AAAS; Am Phys Soc; Am Chem Soc. *Res:* Solid state chemistry; luminescence; ionic solids; impurity reactions in solids; impurity diffusion; crystal growth and purification. *Mailing Add:* Dept of Chem Ore State Univ Corvallis OR 97331

FREDERICKSEN, JAMES MONROE, b Blackstone, Va, June 25, 19; m 48; c 3. ORGANIC CHEMISTRY. *Educ:* Univ Richmond, BS, 40; Univ Va, PhD(org chem), 47. *Prof Exp:* Chemist, E R Squibb & Co, NJ, 44; sr chemist, Merck & Co, 47-53; prof chem & chmn dept, Davis & Elkins Col, 53-54 & Hampden-Sydney Col, 54-57; PROF CHEM, DAVIDSON COL, 57- *Mem:* Am Chem Soc. *Res:* Quinolines, thiazoles, isoalloxazines and vitamins; synthetic medicinals for tuberculosis and malaria; local anesthetics; synthetic medicinals in the quinoline, isoalloxazines and thiazole series. *Mailing Add:* Dept of Chem Davidson Col Davidson NC 28036

FREDERICKSON, ARMAN FREDERICK, b Winnipeg, Man, May 5, 18; nat US; m 43; c 5. GEOLOGY. *Educ:* Univ Wash, BSc, 40; Mont Sch Mines, MSc, 42; Mass Inst Technol, ScD, 47. *Prof Exp:* Miner western US, 36-40; chief geologist, Cornucopia Gold Mines, Ore, 40-41; instr & asst, Mont Sch Mines, 41-42; engr, Alameda Dry Rock Co, Calif, 42; asst, Mass Inst Technol, 42-43 & 46-47; prof geol, Wash Univ, 47-55; supvr geol res, Pan-Am Petrol Corp, Okla, 55-60; prof earth & planetary sci & chmn dept & dir oceanog prog, Univ Pittsburgh, 60-66; vpres & dir res, King Resources Co, 66-69, sr vpres & dir tech progs, 69-71; pres, Sorbotec, Inc, 71-74; PRES, GLOBAL SURV, INC, 74- *Concurrent Pos:* Consult geologist, geochemist & mining engr, Fulbright res prof, Oslo, 51-52; chmn clay mineral comt, Nat Res Coun; contract negotiator petrol & mining progs, Africa, Mid & Far East, Latin & SAm, US, 81- *Mem:* Fel Geol Soc Am; Soc Econ Geologists; Am Mineral Soc; Am Inst Mining, Metall & Petrol Eng; fel Geol Soc Finland. *Res:* Production of micas from clays; spectrographic, x-ray, diff-thermal and optical research; structure and genesis of ore deposits; isotope and trace geochemistry of sediments; formation fluids; regional stratigraphy and map analysis by computer methods; organization and management of industrial research; mining and petroleum exploration; coal engineering and evaluation; Middle East and North African petroleum exploration; marine geology and geophysics; oceanography. *Mailing Add:* 425 Uvalde McAllen TX 78501

FREDERICKSON, EVAN LLOYD, b Spring Green, Wis, Mar 1, 22; m 46; c 3. ANESTHESIOLOGY. *Educ:* Univ Wis, BS, 47, MD, 50; Univ Iowa, MS, 53. *Prof Exp:* From instr to asst prof anesthesiol, Med Ctr, Univ Kans, 53-56; from asst prof to assoc prof, Univ Wash, 56-59; prof, Med Ctr, Univ Kans, 59-65; PROF ANESTHESIOL, EMORY UNIV, 65- *Mem:* Am Soc Anesthesiol; AMA. *Res:* Effect of drugs on cells; cell membranes; mechanisms of anesthesia. *Mailing Add:* Anesthesia Res Emory Univ Atlanta GA 30322

FREDERICKSON, RICHARD GORDON, b Port Gamble, Wash, June 19, 44; m 70; c 2. ANATOMY, CELL BIOLOGY. *Educ:* Pac Lutheran Univ, BS, 66; Univ NDak, MS, 68, PhD(anat), 70. *Prof Exp:* From instr to asst prof anat, Univ Mich, 70-73; asst prof, 73-76, ASSOC PROF ANAT, WVA UNIV, 76- *Mem:* Am Soc Cell Biologists; Am Asn Anatomists; Soc Neurosci; Sigma Xi. *Res:* Embryonic growth of connective tissue; fine structure of meninges; analytical electron microscopy of heavy metals in cells and tissues; mesenchymal-epittelial interactions in embryonic and adult tissues. *Mailing Add:* Dept Anat WVa Univ Morgantown WV 26505

FREDERIKSE, HANS PIETER ROETERT, b Hague, Neth, July 13, 20; nat US; m 52; c 3. SOLID STATE PHYSICS. *Educ:* Univ Leiden, BS, 41, MS, 45, PhD(physics), 50. *Prof Exp:* Vis lectr physics, Purdue Univ, 50-53; physicist, 53-55, chief solid state physics sect, 55-78, chief, Ceramics, Glass & Solid State Sci Div, 78-81, SR MAT SCIENTIST, NAT BUR STANDARDS, 81- *Concurrent Pos:* Fulbright travel grant, 50-52; Guggenheim fel, 61-62. *Honors & Awards:* Except Serv Award, US Dept Com, 62. *Mem:* Fel Am Phys Soc; Am Ceramic Soc; Fedn Am Scientists; Neth Phys Soc. *Res:* Electrical, optical, and thermal properties of semiconductors, oxides, and polymers; low temperature physics. *Mailing Add:* Nat Bur of Standards US Dept of Com Washington DC 20234

FREDERIKSEN, DIXIE WARD, b San Angelo, Tex, Sept 13, 42; m 63; c 2. PHYSICAL CHEMISTRY, BIOPHYSICS. *Educ:* Tex Technol Col, BA, 63; Wash Univ, AM, 65, PhD(chem), 67. *Prof Exp:* Sr polymer chemist, Eli Lilly & Co, 67; res assoc med, Southwestern Med Sch, Univ Tex, 68-70; res assoc biophys & NIH fel, Kings Col, Univ London, 73-74; asst prof, 74-80, ASSOC PROF BIOCHEM, VANDERBILT UNIV, 80- *Concurrent Pos:* Mellon teacher-scientist fel, Vanderbilt Univ, 74-75; adj assoc prof biol, Rensselaer Polytech Inst, 80- *Mem:* Am Chem Soc; Sigma Xi; Biophys Soc; Am Heart Asn; AAAS. *Res:* Physical chemistry of biological macromolecules, muscle proteins, contraction and cell motility. *Mailing Add:* Dept of Biochem Sch of Med Vanderbilt Univ Nashville TN 37232

FREDERIKSEN, NORMAN OLIVER, palynology, see previous edition

FREDERIKSEN, RICHARD ALLAN, b Renville, Minn, Aug 9, 33; m 58; c 1. PLANT PATHOLOGY, PLANT GENETICS. *Educ:* Univ Minn, BSc, 55, MS, 58, PhD(plant path), 61. *Prof Exp:* Res plant pathologist, USDA, 56-63; from asst prof to assoc prof, 63-73, PROF PLANT PATH, TEX A&M UNIV, 73- *Mem:* Am Phytopath Soc; Indian Phytopath Soc; Int Soc Plant Path. *Res:* Diseases of field crops; genetics of plant pathogens; biological control. *Mailing Add:* Dept of Plant Sci Tex A&M Univ College Station TX 77843

FREDIANI, HAROLD ARTHUR, b New York, NY, Dec 23, 11. ANALYTICAL CHEMISTRY, MICROBIOLOGY. *Educ:* State Univ Iowa, AB, 34, MS, 35; La State Univ, PhD(phys chem), 37. *Prof Exp:* Asst prof anal chem, La State Univ, 37-40; chief chemist reagents, Fisher Sci Co, 40-46; asst dir qual control drugs, Merck & Co, 46-55; asst vpres pharm mfg, Bristol Labs Div, Bristol Myers Co, 55-74; DIR PHARMACEUT COUNR, CAZENOVIA, 74- *Concurrent Pos:* Fulbright prof, USDA, Italy, 51. *Mem:* Am Chem Soc; fel Am Inst Chemists; AAAS; Soc Indust Microbiologists; Am Soc Microbiol. *Res:* Laboratory instrumentation and automation; quality assurance. *Mailing Add:* 2638 Pompey Ctr Rd RD 2 Manlius NY 13104

FREDIN, REYNOLD A, b Greenville, Iowa, Feb 13, 23; m 44; c 2. FISHERIES. *Educ:* Iowa State Univ, BS, 48, MS, 49. *Prof Exp:* Assoc fisheries biologist, NC Wildlife Resources Comn, 49-50; fishery res biologist, Bur Com Fisheries, US Fish & Wildlife Serv, 50-70; dir fisheries data & mgt systs div, Northwest Fisheries Ctr, Nat Marine Fisheries Serv, Nat Oceanic & Atmospheric Admin, 70-78; CONSULT FISHERIES, 78- *Concurrent Pos:* Tech adv, US Sect, Int NPac Fisheries Comn, 56- & US Sect, Int Pac Halibut Comn, 66-; lectr, Univ Wash, 69- *Mem:* Fel Am Inst Fishery Res Biol. *Res:* Population dynamics of North American salmon stocks; biometrics; fisheries and biological statistics of United States salmon stocks; assessment of condition of North Pacific Ocean groundfish stocks; maximum net productivity levels in marine and terrestrial populations of large mammals; potential production of bottomfish in Alaskan waters. *Mailing Add:* 2328 NE 104th St Seattle WA 98125

FREDKIN, DONALD ROY, b New York, NY, Sept 28, 35. PHYSICS. *Educ:* NY Univ, AB, 56; Princeton Univ, PhD(math, physics), 61. *Prof Exp:* Instr physics, Princeton Univ, 59-61; assoc, 61-63, asst prof, 63-69, ASSOC PROF PHYSICS, UNIV CALIF, SAN DIEGO, 69- *Concurrent Pos:* Consult, Bell Tel Labs, Inc, 60-64 & Aerospace Corp, 62-63; Nat Acad Sci-Nat Res Coun fel, Saclay Nuclear Res Ctr, France, 64-65; Sloan res fel, 64-67. *Mem:* Am Phys Soc; Am Math Soc. *Res:* Solid state and low temperature theoretical physics. *Mailing Add:* Dept of Physics Univ of Calif at San Diego La Jolla CA 92038

FREDRICK, JEROME FREDERICK, b New York, NY, Feb 23, 26; m 46; c 3. BIOCHEMISTRY. *Educ:* City Col New York, BSc, 49; NY Univ, MSc, 51, PhD(biol), 55. *Prof Exp:* Instr biol, City Col New York, 48-49; biochemist, Vet Admin Hosp, New York, 49-51; chemist, US Customs Labs, 51-53; asst dir res, 53-60, DIR BIOCHEM RES, DODGE CHEM CO, 60-, ASSOC PROF BIOCHEM, DODGE INST ADVAN STUDIES, 65- *Concurrent Pos:* Consult, Handbook Biol Data Comt, Nat Acad Sci-Nat Res Coun, 57-60. *Mem:* AAAS; Am Chem Soc; fel NY Acad Sci; fel Am Inst Chemists; Am Inst Biol Sci. *Res:* Chelation chemistry; enzymology; chemotherapy of cancer; evolution of isozymes, especially structure and molecular evolution. *Mailing Add:* Dodge Chem Co Res Labs 3425 Boston Post Rd Bronx NY 10469

FREDRICK, LAURENCE WILLIAM, b Stroudsburg, Pa, Aug 27, 27; m 49; c 3. ASTRONOMY. *Educ:* Swarthmore Col, BA, 52, MA, 54; Univ Pa, PhD(astron), 59. *Prof Exp:* Asst astron, Sproul Observ, 52-59; astronr, Lowell Observ, Ariz, 59-63; prof astron, 63-72, dir, Leander McCormick Observ, 63-79, J D HAMILTON PROF ASTRON, UNIV VA, 72- *Concurrent Pos:* Asst, Flower & Cook Observ, 55-59; mem, Nat Res Coun, 65-68; mem, US Nat Comt, Int Astron Union & Spitzer Comt, Nat Space Bd, 65-71. *Honors & Awards:* Fulbright-Hays lectr, Univ Vienna, 72-73. *Mem:* Int Astron Union; Am Astron Soc (secy); Am Meteor Soc (vpres); Royal Astron Soc; Astron Soc Pac. *Res:* Binary stars; infrared spectroscopy; image tubes; instrumentation. *Mailing Add:* Leander McCormick Observ Charlottesville VA 22903

FREDRICKS, WALTER WILLIAM, b Philadelphia, Pa, July 19, 35; m 57, 75; c 3. BIOCHEMISTRY, IMMUNOCHEMISTRY. *Educ:* LaSalle Col, BA, 57; Johns Hopkins Univ, PhD(biochem), 62. *Prof Exp:* USPHS fel, Nat Heart Inst, 62-64; asst prof physiol, Univ Md, 64-65; asst prof biochem, 65-66, asst prof biol, 66-69, ASSOC PROF BIOL, MARQUETTE UNIV, 69- *Mem:* AAAS; Am Soc Biol Chemists. *Res:* Photosynthesis; immunochemistry of hypersensitivity pneumonitis. *Mailing Add:* Dept of Biol Marquette Univ Milwaukee WI 53233

FREDRICKSON, ARNOLD G(ERHARD), b Fairbault, Minn, Apr 11, 32. CHEMICAL ENGINEERING. *Educ:* Univ Minn, BS, 54, MS, 56; Univ Wis, PhD(chem eng, 59. *Prof Exp:* From asst prof to assoc prof, 58-66, PROF CHEM ENG, UNIV MINN, MINNEAPOLIS, 66- *Mem:* Am Chem Soc; Am Inst Chem Engrs. *Res:* Bioengineering; demography. *Mailing Add:* Dept Chem Eng & Mat Sci Univ of Minn Minneapolis MN 55455

FREDRICKSON, DONALD SHARP, b Canon City, Colo, Aug 8, 24; m 50; c 2. CARDIOLOGY, MEDICINE. *Educ:* Univ Mich, BS, 46, MD, 49. *Prof Exp:* Intern, Peter Bent Brigham Hosp, Boston, 49-50, asst med, 50-52; res fel med, Mass Gen Hosp, Boston, 52-53; clin assoc, Nat Heart & Lung Inst, 53-55, investr, Lab Cellular Physiol & Metab, 55-61, clin dir inst, 61-66, dir, 66-68, head sect molecular dis, Lab Metab, 62-66, chief molecular dis br, Div Intramural Res, 66, dir, Div Intramural Res, 68-74; pres, Inst of Med, Nat Acad Sci, 74-75; dir, NIH, 75-81; SCHOLAR IN RESIDENCE, NAT ACAD SCI, 81- *Concurrent Pos:* Clin instr med, Sch Med, George Washington Univ, 56-59, spec lectr internal med, 59-; mem cardiovasc study sect, NIH, 59-62; chmn, Coun Arteriosclerosis, Am Heart Asn, 74; chmn, Fed Interagency Comn Recombining DNA Res, 76-81; chmn, Coun Med, Fed Coord Coun Sci Eng Technol, 78-81; chmn, Fed Comn Res Biol Effects Ion Radiation, 78-81. *Honors & Awards:* Gold Medal Award, Am Col Cardiol, 67; Int Award Heart & Vascular Res, James F Mitchell Found Med Educ & Res, 68; Superior Serv Award, HEW, 70, Distinguished Serv Award, 71; Distinguished Achievement Award, Modern Med, 71; McCollum Award, Am Soc Clin Nutrit & Am Inst Nutrit, 71; Gairdnen Award, 78; Lorenzini Medal, 80. *Mem:* Nat Acad Sci; Inst of Med of Nat Acad Sci; Royal Col Physicians (London); fel Am Col Cardiol; fel Am Col Physicians. *Mailing Add:* Nat Acad Sci 2101 Constitution Ave Washington DC 20418

FREDRICKSON, JAY W(ARREN), metallurgy, deceased

FREDRICKSON, JOHN E, b Chicago, Ill, Sept 12, 19; m 46; c 3. PHYSICS. *Educ:* Univ Calif, Berkeley, BS, 43; Univ Southern Calif, MS, 52, PhD(physics), 56. *Prof Exp:* PROF PHYSICS, CALIF STATE UNIV, LONG BEACH, 62- *Mem:* Am Phys Soc; Am Asn Physics Teachers. *Res:* Solid state physics; infrared spectroscopy. *Mailing Add:* 27526 Eastvale Rd Rolling Hills CA 90274

FREDRICKSON, JOHN MURRAY, b Winnipeg, Man, Mar 24, 31; m 56; c 3. OTOLARYNGOLOGY, NEUROPHYSIOLOGY. *Educ:* Univ BC, BA, 53, MD, 57; Am Bd Otolaryngol, dipl, 66; FRCS(C). *Hon Degrees:* MD, Univ Linkoping, Sweden, 75. *Prof Exp:* Instr surg, Univ Chicago, 63-65; asst prof otolaryngol, Med Ctr, Stanford Univ, 65-68; assoc prof otolaryngol, 68-76, ASST PROF PHYSIOL UNIV TORONTO, 68-, PROF OTOLARYNGOL, 76- *Concurrent Pos:* Vis investr, Univ Freiburg, 64-65; consult, Toronto Gen Hosp, Princess Margaret Cancer Hosp & Hosp for Children. *Honors & Awards:* Res Award, Am Acad Ophthal & Otolaryngol, 64; Hodge Mem Award, Can Otolaryngol Soc, 65. *Mem:* Fel Am Col Surg. *Res:* Vestibular neurophysiology; tissue and organ transplantation. *Mailing Add:* Dept Otolaryngol Med Sci Bldg Univ of Toronto Toronto ON M5S 1A1 Can

FREDRICKSON, LEIGH H, b Sioux City, Iowa, Mar 13, 39; m 65. WILDLIFE ECOLOGY. *Educ:* Iowa State Univ, BS, 61, MS, 63, PhD(zool), 67. *Prof Exp:* Instr zool, Iowa State Univ, 64-65; asst prof biol sci, 67-73, assoc prof wildlife & dir, Gaylord Lab, 73-79, PROF WILDLIFE, SCH FORESTRY, FISHERIES & WILDLIFE, UNIV MO-COLUMBIA, 79- *Mem:* Wildlife Soc; Ecol Soc Am; Am Ornith Union; Wilson Ornith Soc; Cooper Ornith Soc. *Res:* Marsh ecology; behavior and ecology of waterfowl, especially Cairinini and Mergini; behavior of Rallidae; factors influencing clutch size; marsh and swamp ecology, especially lowland hardwoods; ecology of wintering waterfowl. *Mailing Add:* Gaylord Mem Lab Univ Mo Puxico MO 63960

FREDRICKSON, RALPH E, b Minneapolis, Minn, Feb 7, 13; m 39; c 5. CHEMICAL ENGINEERING, ORGANIC CHEMISTRY. *Educ:* Univ Minn, BChE, 35, MS, 37; Columbia Univ, PhD(chem eng), 45. *Prof Exp:* Chem engr, E I du Pont de Nemours & Co, 37-40; chem engr, A E Staley Mfg Co, 42-55, dir eng res, 55-60; spec projs, corp develop, Stepan Chem Co, 61-65; commercial dir, C&I Girdler Inc, 66-69; CONSULT, RAPHAEL KATZEN ASSOCS, 69- *Mem:* Am Chem Soc; Am Inst Chem Engrs. *Res:* Process development; fluidization; phthalic anhydride; organic intermediates; starch and vegetable oil processing. *Mailing Add:* 10260 Pendery Dr Cincinnati OH 45242

FREDRICKSON, RICHARD WILLIAM, b Blakesburg, Iowa, Apr 28, 19; m 47; c 2. ACAROLOGY, ECOLOGY. *Educ:* Univ Kans, AB, 51, MA, 54, PhD(entom), 61. *Prof Exp:* Lectr zool, Southern Ill Univ, 56-58; lectr biol, Queens Col, NY, 61-62, instr, 62-63; from lectr to asst prof, City Col New York, 63-67; assoc prof, 67-75, PROF BIOL, ST JOSEPH'S UNIV, PHILADELPHIA, PA, 75- *Mem:* Acarol Soc Am; Animal Behav Soc. *Res:* Zoogeography and systematics of Acarina; ecology and ethology of Arthropoda, particularly Acarina; symbiotic associations of Acarina. *Mailing Add:* Dept of Biol St Joseph's Univ 5600 City Ave Philadelphia PA 19131

FREDRICKSON, TORGNY NORMAN, veterinary pathology, see previous edition

FREDRIKSEN, RICHARD L, b Spokane, Wash, Feb 20, 30; m 52; c 2. SOILS, FORESTRY. *Educ:* Univ Wash, BSF, 54, MF, 61; Ore State Univ, PhD(forest soils), 75. *Prof Exp:* Forestry aide, Pac Northwest Forest & Range Exp Sta, USDA, 59; technician, Weyerhaeuser Timber Co, 59-60; RES FORESTER, PAC NORTHWEST FOREST & RANGE EXP STA, USDA, 60-, PROF FOREST SOILS, DEPT SOIL SCI & FORESTRY, ORE STATE UNIV. *Concurrent Pos:* Proj leader watershed process, Int Biol Prog, Western Coniferous Forest Biomet, Ore State Univ, 71- *Mem:* AAAS; Am Soc Agron; Soil Sci Soc. *Res:* Soil and nutrient balances and water quality in relation to climate and physical and biological processes and land use in western Oregon. *Mailing Add:* Forestry Sci Lab 3200 Jefferson Way Corvallis OR 97331

FREDRIKSON, KURT A, b Haparanda, Sweden, Apr 9, 26; m 64. GEOCHEMISTRY. *Educ:* Stockholm Inst Technol, Sweden, ChemE, 46; Univ Stockholm, PhD(mineral & geol), 55. *Prof Exp:* Consult engr, Hagconsult Inc, Sweden, 46-52; res asst sediment petrol, Oceanog Inst, Univ Gothenburg, 53-55; res asst meteorite mineral, Univ Stockholm, 55-57; geochemist, Geol Surv Sweden, 58-60; res assoc meteoritics, Univ Calif, San Diego, 60-64; cur-in-chg, 64-67, CUR & SUPVR DIV METEORITES, SMITHSONIAN INST, 67- *Concurrent Pos:* Grants, Australian Nat Univ, 61 & NASA, 64; consult econ geol & inorg & org chem, Sweden, 52-60; prin investr lunar samples, Apollo XI-XVII; Fulbright scholar, Max Planck Inst, Ger, 74-75. *Mem:* Geochem Soc; Meteoritical Soc; Swedish Geol Soc. *Res:* Meteoritics; phase composition in meteorites, particularly chondrites; origin of meteorites and planets; ore mineralogy; electron microprobe analysis. *Mailing Add:* Div of Meteorites Smithsonian Inst Washington DC 20560

FREE, ALFRED HENRY, b Bainbridge, Ohio, Apr 11, 13; m; c 9. BIOCHEMISTRY. *Educ:* Miami Univ, AB, 34; Western Reserve Univ, MS, 36, PhD(biochem), 39. *Prof Exp:* Asst biochem, Cleveland Clin, 34-35; instr, Western Reserve Univ, 39-43, asst prof, 43-46; head biochem sect, Ames Res Lab, 46-59, dir, 59-64, Ames Tech Serv, 64-75, VPRES TECH SERV & SCI RELS, AMES CO, MILES LABS, INC, 75- *Concurrent Pos:* Consult, Ben Venue Labs, Ohio, 43-46. *Mem:* AAAS; Am Soc Biol Chem; Soc Exp Biol & Med; Am Chem Soc; Am Inst Chem. *Res:* Vitamin and protein nutrition; enzymes and gastrointestinal tract; intestinal absorption; antibiotics; clinical biochemistry and laboratory methodology; radioisotope methodology; metabolism of drugs; urinalysis tests. *Mailing Add:* Ames Co Miles Labs Inc Elkhart IN 46514

FREE, CHARLES ALFRED, b Cleveland, Ohio, Apr 19, 36; m 61; c 2. BIOCHEMICAL PHARMACOLOGY, ENZYMOLOGY. *Educ:* Purdue Univ, BS, 57; Univ Calif, Los Angeles, PhD(physiol chem), 62. *Prof Exp:* Res fel, Sloan-Kettering Inst Cancer Res, 62-65; sr res scientist, 65-69, SR RES INVESTR, SQUIBB INST MED RES, 69- *Concurrent Pos:* USPHS fel, 63-65. *Mem:* AAAS; Am Chem Soc. *Res:* Purification and chemistry of anterior pituitary hormones; cyclic nucleotide-mediated biological systems; immediate hypersensitivity; enzyme inhibitors; biochemistry and pharmacology of steroid hormone receptors. *Mailing Add:* Dept of Pharmacol Squibb Inst for Med Res Princeton NJ 08540

FREE, HELEN M, b Feb 20, 23; US citizen; m 47; c 6. CLINICAL CHEMISTRY. *Educ:* Col Wooster, AB, 44; Cent Mich Univ, MA, 78. *Prof Exp:* Control chemist, 44-46, res chemist, Biochem Sect, Miles-Ames, 46-59, assoc res biochemist & group leader, Ames Res Lab, 59-64, Ames Prod Develop Lab, 64-66, Ames Tech Serv, 66-69, new prod mgr clin test systs, Ames Growth & Develop, 69-74, sr new prod mgr microbiol test systs, 74-76, dir spec test systs, Ames Div, 76-78, DIR CLIN LAB, REAGENTS RES DIV, MILES LABS, INC, 78- *Honors & Awards:* Prof Achievement Award Nuclear Med, Am Soc Med Technol, 76. *Mem:* Am Chem Soc; Am Asn Clin Chem; Am Soc Med Technol; fel Am Inst Chemists; fel AAAS. *Mailing Add:* 3764 E Jackson Blvd Elkhart IN 46514

FREE, JOHN ULRIC, b Homestead, Fla, Sept 4, 41; c 1. SOLID STATE PHYSICS, ACOUSTICS. *Educ:* Eastern Nazarene Col, BS, 64; Mass Inst Technol, PhD(physics), 74. *Prof Exp:* ASSOC PROF PHYSICS, EASTERN NAZARENE COL, 70- *Concurrent Pos:* Educ consult, 74-75; mem fac fel prog, NSF, 75. *Mem:* Am Inst Physics; Am Asn Physics Teachers; Acoust Soc Am; Sigma Xi. *Res:* Investigation of fundamental materials using ultrasonic and hypersonic waves; ultrasonic attenuation in metals at low temperatures used to investigate the electron-phonon interaction and the interface between materials. *Mailing Add:* Eastern Nazarene Col 23 E Elm St Quincy MA 02170

FREE, JOSEPH CARL, b Cedar City, Utah, May 14, 35; m 55; c 6. MECHANICAL ENGINEERING. *Educ:* Brigham Young Univ, BES, 58; Calif Inst Technol, MS, 61; Mass Inst Technol, PhD(nonlinear models), 68. *Prof Exp:* Res engr, Autonetics Div, NAm Aviation, Inc, 58-61; from instr to asst prof mech eng, Brigham Young Univ, 61-64; teaching asst, Mass Inst Technol, 64-65; assoc prof, 67-77, PROF MECH ENG, BRIGHAM YOUNG UNIV, 77- *Concurrent Pos:* Consult, Rich Bumper Co, 68 & Lawrence Radiation Lab, 68- *Mem:* Am Soc Mech Engrs. *Res:* Nonlinear system modeling; optimum design of engineering systems; efficient computer simulation; automatic controls. *Mailing Add:* Dept of Mech Eng Brigham Young Univ Provo UT 84602

FREE, MICHAEL JOHN, b Newton Abbot, Eng, Nov 22, 37; m 64; c 2. PHYSIOLOGY. *Educ:* Univ Nottingham, BSc, 64; Ohio State Univ, MSc, 65, PhD(physiol of reprod), 67. *Prof Exp:* Res assoc testis physiol, Animal Reprod Teaching & Res Ctr, Ohio State Univ, 67-69; from asst prof to assoc prof mammalian physiol, Calif State Univ, Hayward, 69-72; SR RES SCIENTIST, BATTELLE, PAC NORTHWEST LAB, 72- *Mem:* Brit Soc Study Fertil; Soc Study Reprod. *Res:* Physiology and biochemistry of the testis and epididymis, particularly effect of temperature and hormones; circulation in vivo metabolism and hormone production and fertility control methods in male and female. *Mailing Add:* Battelle Pac Northwest Lab Richland WA 99352

FREE, SPENCER MICHAEL, JR, biostatistics, see previous edition

FREE, STEPHEN J, b Salt Lake City, Utah, Sept 4, 48; m; c 3. GENETICS, MOLECULAR BIOLOGY. *Educ:* Purdue Univ, BS, 72; Stanford Univ, PhD(genetics), 77. *Prof Exp:* Res assoc, Dept Physiol Chem, Univ Wis, 77-79; ASST PROF GENETICS, DEPT BIOL SCI, STATE UNIV NY AT BUFFALO, 79- *Res:* Mechanisms by which fungi adapt to changes in the environment. *Mailing Add:* Cooke Hall Rm 370 Dept Biol Div Cell & Molecular Biol State Univ NY Buffalo NY 14260

FREEBAIRN, HUGH TAYLOR, plant biochemistry, see previous edition

FREEBERG, FRED E, b Windber, Pa, Nov 5, 37; m 63; c 2. ANALYTICAL CHEMISTRY. *Educ:* Univ Pittsburgh, BS, 59; Pa State Univ, PhD(chem), 65. *Prof Exp:* Asst chemist, Koppers Co, Inc, 59-60; teaching asst, Pa State Univ, 60-65; staff res chemist, 65-80, SECT HEAD, PROCTER & GAMBLE CO, 80- *Mem:* Am Chem Soc. *Res:* General use of thermal methods of analysis to obtain thermodynamic constants as well as application to analysis. *Mailing Add:* Ivorydale Tech Ctr Procter & Gamble Co 5299 Spring Grave Ave Cincinnati OH 45217

FREEBERG, JOHN ARTHUR, b Kenosha, Wis, July 2, 32; m 55. BOTANY. *Educ:* Harvard Univ, AB, 54, PhD(biol), 57. *Prof Exp:* Asst prof biol, Lehigh Univ, 57-62 & Boston Univ, 62-66; ASSOC PROF BIOL, UNIV MASS, BOSTON, 66- *Mem:* Bot Soc Am; AAAS; Int Soc Plant Morphol. *Res:* Morphogenesis of vascular plants. *Mailing Add:* Dept of Biol Univ of Mass Boston MA 02125

FREEBERG, LARRY ROGER, b Loma Linda, Calif, June 2, 41; m 67; c 1. BIOLOGICAL OCEANOGRAPHY. *Educ:* Walla Walla Col, BA, 63; Tex A&M Univ, MS, 71, PhD(oceanog), 76. *Prof Exp:* Chemist qual control, Lockheed Propulsion Co, 63-65; mfg engr solid fuel missiles, 65-67; res assoc phytoplankton ecol, Mote Marine Lab, 74-78; mgr ocean outfall, Dravo Utility Constructors, Inc, 79-80, mgr environ qual, 80-82; MGR ENVIRON AFFAIRS, PETROL OPERS & SUPPORT SERV, INC, 82- *Concurrent Pos:* Consult coral reef ecol, Flower Garden Ocean Res Ctr, 71-73, Univ Tex, 74-77; consult penaeid shrimp, World Life Res Inst, 73-74; prin investr, State of Fla, 74-78 & NASA, 76-78; mem, Ad Hoc Coun Red Tides, Fla, 76-; adj prof, Univ South Fla, 78-79. *Mem:* Am Soc Limnol & Oceanog; Marine Biol Asn UK; Phycol Soc Am. *Res:* Ocean dynamics, especially mesoscale circulation and its influence upon phytoplankton community structure; interrelationships of physical, chemical and biological parameters, which control species dominance and succession; disposal and dispersion of brine and other industrial effluents in near shore marine waters and its effect upon the chemistry and biological community. *Mailing Add:* Petrol Opers & Support Serv Inc 850 S Clearview Pkwy New Orleans LA 70123

FREED, AUBYN, mathematics, see previous edition

FREED, CHARLES, b Budapest, Hungary, Mar 21, 26; US citizen; m 56; c 2. ELECTRICAL ENGINEERING. *Educ:* NY Univ, BEE, 52; Mass Inst Technol, SM, 54, EE, 58. *Prof Exp:* Asst, Res Lab Electronics, Mass Inst Technol, 52-54, Div Indust Co-op, 54-55, Res Lab Electronics, 55-58, consult, Phys Sci Study Comt, 58; sr engr, Res Div, Raytheon Mfg Co, 58-59, Spencer Lab, 59, spec microwave devices oper, 59-62; mem staff, 62-74, SR STAFF, LINCOLN LAB, MASS INST TECHNOL, 78-, LECTR ELEC ENG, 69- *Mem:* Fel Inst Elec & Electronics Engrs. *Res:* Microwave electronics; electron devices; low noise amplification; parametric devices; vacuum theory and techniques; electron beams; laser design and applications, intensity fluctuations and frequency stability; optical detection. *Mailing Add:* Lincoln Lab Wood St Lexington MA 02173

FREED, JACK H, b Brooklyn, NY, Apr 19, 38; m 61; c 2. CHEMICAL PHYSICS. *Educ:* Yale Univ, BE, 58; Columbia Univ, MA, 59, PhD(chem), 62. *Prof Exp:* NSF & Hon US Ramsay Mem fels, 62-63; from asst prof to assoc prof chem, 63-73, PROF CHEM, CORNELL UNIV, 73- *Concurrent Pos:* Alfred P Sloan Found fel, 66-68; vis scientist, US-Japan Coop Sci Prog, Tokyo Univ, 69-70; sr Weizmann fel, Weizmann Inst Sci, 70-; guest prof, Aarhus Univ, Denmark, 74; assoc ed, J Chem Physics, 76-78; vis prof, Geneva Univ, 77 & Delft Tech Univ, 78. *Honors & Awards:* Buck-Whitney Award, Am Chem Soc, 81. *Mem:* Fel Am Phys Soc. *Res:* Applications of magnetic resonance to problems of theoretical chemical interest. *Mailing Add:* Dept Chem Cornell Univ Ithaca NY 14853

FREED, JAMES MELVIN, b Enid, Okla, Apr 6, 39; c 2. CELL PHYSIOLOGY. *Educ:* McPherson Col, BS, 61; Univ Ill, Urbana-Champaign, MS, 63, PhD(physiol), 69. *Prof Exp:* Instr biol, Manchester Col, 63-65; asst prof, 69-76, ASSOC PROF ZOOL, OHIO WESLEYAN UNIV, 76- *Mem:* AAAS; Am Soc Zool; Sigma Xi. *Res:* Biochemical adaptations in poikilotherms to environmental temperature changes. *Mailing Add:* Dept of Zool Ohio Wesleyan Univ Delaware OH 43015

FREED, JEROME JAMES, b New York, NY, May 4, 28; m 51; c 4. CELL BIOLOGY. *Educ:* Yale Univ, BS, 49; Columbia Univ, MA, 51, PhD(zool), 54. *Prof Exp:* Res assoc, 53-62, asst mem, 62-66, assoc mem, 66-78, MEM, INST CANCER RES, 78- *Mem:* AAAS; Tissue Culture Asn; Am Soc Cell Biol; Am Asn Cancer Res. *Res:* Heredity in cultured cells; haploid frog cell cultures; fine structure of cultured cells. *Mailing Add:* Inst for Cancer Res Fox Chase Cancer Ctr Philadelphia PA 19111

FREED, JOHN HOWARD, b New Brighton, Pa, Mar 10, 43; m 71; c 2. TRANSPLANTATION BIOCHEMISTRY, IMMUNOGENETICS. *Educ:* Mass Inst Technol, SB, 65; Stanford Univ, PhD(org chem), 71. *Prof Exp:* Fel immunol, Sch Med, Stanford Univ, 71-73, Albert Einstein Col Med, 73-76; ASST PROF IMMUNOL, SCH MED, JOHNS HOPKINS UNIV, 76- *Mem:* Am Asn Immunologists; AAAS. *Res:* Biochemistry of the membrane antigens encoded by the H-2 complex, the major histocompatibility complex of mice; transplant rejection and regulation of the immune response. *Mailing Add:* Dept Biophysics Sch Med Johns Hopkins Univ 725 N Wolfe St Baltimore MD 21205

FREED, KARL F, b Brooklyn, NY, Sept 25, 42; m 64; c 2. THEORETICAL CHEMISTRY, PHYSICAL CHEMISTRY. *Educ:* Harvard Univ, AM, 65, PhD(chem physics), 67. *Prof Exp:* NATO fel theoret physics, Univ Manchester, 67-68; from asst prof to assoc prof chem, 68-76, PROF CHEM, UNIV CHICAGO, 76- *Concurrent Pos:* Sloan Found res fel, 69-71; Guggenheim Found res fel, 72-73; Dreyfus Found teacher-scholar fel, 72-; sr vis fel, Cavendish Lab, Cambridge, Eng, 72-73; Denkewalter lectr, Loyola Univ Chicago, 76; Phillips lectr, Haverford Col, 76; vis scientist, Centre Nucleaires, Strasbourg, France, 77; adv ed, Chem Physics, 79- & Chemical Rev, 81-; assoc ed, J Chem Physics, 82- *Honors & Awards:* Marlow Medal, Faraday Div, The Chem Soc, 73; Am Chem Soc Award Pure Chem, 76. *Mem:* Am Phys Soc; Royal Soc Chem; Am Chem Soc; Faraday Soc. *Res:* Radiationless processes and photochemistry in polyatomic molecules; electronic structure in disordered systems; statistical mechanics of polymer systems; many-body theory and the electronic structure of molecules; quantum chemistry; polymer chemistry. *Mailing Add:* James Franck Inst Univ Chicago Chicago IL 60637

FREED, MEIER EZRA, b Philadelphia, Pa, Oct 20, 25; m 70. ORGANIC CHEMISTRY. *Educ:* Pa State Univ, BSc, 48, MSc, 49; Univ Pa, PhD(chem), 60. *Prof Exp:* RES CHEMIST, WYETH LABS, INC, 51- *Mem:* Am Chem Soc. *Res:* Pharmaceutical chemistry; heterocyclic and alicyclic derivatives. *Mailing Add:* Wyeth Labs Inc Box 8299 Philadelphia PA 19101

FREED, MURRAY MONROE, b Paterson, NJ, Oct 9, 24; m 48; c 4. REHABILITATION MEDICINE. *Educ:* Harvard Univ, AB, 48; Boston Univ, MD, 52. *Prof Exp:* Nat Found Infantile Paralysis fel phys med, NY Univ-Bellevue Med Ctr, 53-56; instr phys med & rehab, 56-59, assoc, 59-62, from asst prof to assoc prof, 62-67, PROF REHAB MED & CHMN DEPT, SCH MED, BOSTON UNIV, 67- *Concurrent Pos:* Asst chief rehab med, Univ Hosp, Boston, 56-59, chief, 59-; consult, Vet Admin, 62-; mem med adv bd, Mass Sect, Nat Multiple Sclerosis Found, 63-80; physician in chief phys med & rehab, Boston City Hosp, 64-75, sr vis physician, 75-; trustee & mem med sci comt, Mass Sect, Arthritis Found, 64-; deleg, Int Med Soc Paraplegia, 67, 68, 75 & 79; mem med adv bd, Nat Paraplegia Found, 70-; chmn, City Boston Mayor's Comn Physically Handicapped, 72-; mem, Mass Gov Comn Employment Handicapped; dir, Am Bd Phys Med & Rehab, 74- *Mem:* Am

Acad Phys Med & Rehab (pres-elect, 81-82); Am Cong Rehab Med; Am Col Physicians. *Res:* Long term effects of spinal cord trauma; rehabilitation potential of patient with spinal cord trauma; rehabilitation potential of individual with amputation as a result of malignancy. *Mailing Add:* 75 E Newton Boston MA 02118

FREED, MYER, biochemistry, deceased

FREED, NORMAN, b Philadelphia, Pa, June 11, 36; m 60; c 2. THEORETICAL NUCLEAR PHYSICS. *Educ:* Antioch Col, BS, 58; Western Reserve Univ, MS, 61, PhD(theoret physics), 64. *Prof Exp:* Res assoc physics, Univ Nebr, 63-64; Nordic Inst Theoret Atomic Physics res fel, Inst Theoret Physics, Univ Lund, 64-65; Ford Found fel, Bohr Inst, Copenhagen, 65; asst prof, 65-68, asst dean, 78-79, ASSOC PROF PHYSICS, PA STATE UNIV, UNIVERSITY PARK, 68-, ASSOC DEAN, COL SCI, 79- *Concurrent Pos:* On leave, Ctr Nuclear Studies, Saclay, France, 71-72. *Mem:* AAAS; Am Phys Soc; Sigma Xi. *Res:* Intermediate energy nuclear theory; pion photoproduction; nuclear structure theory. *Mailing Add:* 211 Whitmore Lab Pa State Univ University Park PA 16802

FREED, ROBERT LLOYD, b Allentown, Pa, Feb 13, 50. MATERIALS SCIENCE, MATERIALS ENGINEERING. *Educ:* Drexel Univ, BS, 73; Mass Inst Technol, PhD(mat eng), 78. *Prof Exp:* RES ENGR MAT, ENG TECHNOL LAB, E I DU PONT DE NEMOURS & CO, INC, 78- *Mem:* Am Soc Metals; Electron Microscopy Soc Am. *Res:* Application of electron microscopy, transmission electron microscopy/scanning transmission electron microscopy, to materials problems; mechanics of materials; corrosion, wear and the combined corrosion-wear of materials. *Mailing Add:* Bldg E 304 E I du Pont de Nemours & Co Inc Willmington DE 19898

FREED, SIMON, b Lodz, Poland, Nov 11, 99; nat US; m 43. NEUROPHYSIOLOGICAL CHEMISTRY. *Educ:* Mass Inst Technol, SB, 20; Univ Calif, PhD(chem), 27. *Prof Exp:* Instr chem, Univ Calif, 27-28, res assoc, 28-30; Guggenheim fel, Kammerlingh-Onnes Lab, Leiden, 30-31; instr, Univ Chicago, 31-37, asst prof, 37-43 & 45-46; group leader, SAM Lab, Columbia Univ, 43-45; chief chemist, Oak Ridge Nat Lab, 46-49; sr scientist, Brookhaven Nat Lab, 49-65; res prof biochem & neurol, NY Med Col, 67-75; RES COLLABR, BROOKHAVEN NAT LAB, 68- *Concurrent Pos:* Inter-acad exchange, USSR, 66, Czech, 67. *Mem:* AAAS. *Res:* Optical and magnetic properties; symmetry of electric fields about ions in solutions and crystals; chemistry and biochemistry at low temperatures; resolution of states and reactivities in chemistry and biochemistry; endogenous chemistry of animals during learning; radioactivity; physiological chemistry of the nervous system; cryobiochemical analysis of tissue. *Mailing Add:* Brookhaven Nat Lab Upton NY 11973

FREED, VIRGIL HAVEN, b Mendota, Ill, Nov 18, 19; m 44; c 4. BIOCHEMISTRY. *Educ:* Ore State Univ, BS, 43, MS, 48, PhD(chem), 59. *Prof Exp:* Asst prof chem, 44-48, assoc prof chem & farm crops, 48-54, assoc prof chem, 54-59, dir, Environ Health Sci Ctr, 67-81, PROF CHEM, ORE STATE UNIV, 60-, HEAD DEPT AGR CHEM, 61- *Concurrent Pos:* Chmn res comt, USPHS, 47; mem, Western Weed Control Conf, 52; mem, Gordon Res Conf, 58, 65; lectr, Tour Europ Res Ctr, 62; mem, Gov Adv Comt Synthetic Chem in Environ, Ore, 69-; mem toxic substances panel, Nat Acad Sci, 72-73. *Mem:* Fel AAAS; Am Chem Soc; Weed Sci Soc Am. *Res:* Mechanism of action of plant growth regulators and herbicides; physical chemistry of compounds in relation to their biological action. *Mailing Add:* Dept of Agr Chem 337 Weniger Hall Ore State Univ Corvallis OR 97331

FREEDBERG, ABRAHAM STONE, b Salem, Mass, May 30, 08; m 35; c 2. MEDICINE. *Educ:* Harvard Univ, AB, 29; Univ Chicago, MD, 35; Am Bd Internal Med, dipl. *Prof Exp:* House officer med, Mt Sinai Hosp, Ill, 34-35; resident, Cook County Hosp, Ill, 35-36; house officer path, RI Hosp, 36-37; asst med, Beth Israel Hosp, 38-40; res fel, 41-42, asst, 42-46, instr, 46-47, assoc, 47-50, from asst prof to prof, 50-74, EMER PROF MED, HARVARD MED SCH, 74- *Concurrent Pos:* From jr vis physician to physician, Beth Israel Hosp, Boston, 40-69, assoc med res, 40-50, from assoc dir to dir, Cardiol Unit, 50-69; consult & mem thyroid uptake calibration comt, Med Div, Oak Ridge Inst Nuclear Studies, 55-56; Ziskind sr fel, Beth Israel Hosp, Boston, 56; consult metab study sect, USPHS, 56-60; Guggenheim fel, 67-68. *Mem:* Am Physiol Soc; Am Soc Clin Invest; Am Heart Asn; Asn Am Physicians; Am Thyroid Asn (first vpres, 65-66). *Res:* Cardiovascular diseases; thyroid in health and disease. *Mailing Add:* 111 Perkins St Jamaica Plain MA 02130

FREEDLAND, RICHARD A, b Pittsburgh, Pa, May 9, 31; m 58; c 3. PHYSIOLOGICAL CHEMISTRY. *Educ:* Univ Pittsburgh, BS, 53; Univ Ill, MS, 55; Univ Wis, PhD(biochem), 58. *Prof Exp:* Res assoc pediat, Univ Wis, 58-60; lectr biochem, 60-61, from asst prof to assoc prof physiol chem, 61-69, PROF PHYSIOL CHEM, UNIV CALIF, DAVIS, 69-, CHMN DEPT PHYSIOL SCI, 74- *Mem:* Fel AAAS; Am Soc Biol Chem; Am Inst Nutrit; Soc Exp Biol & Med; Am Chem Soc. *Res:* Correlation of enzyme activity and productive capacity in isolated cells after nutritional or hormonal treatment of animals, particularly the mechanisms and physiological interpretations. *Mailing Add:* Dept of Physiol Sci Univ of Calif Sch of Vet Med Davis CA 95616

FREEDMAN, AARON DAVID, b Albany, NY, Jan 4, 22; m 48; c 3. INTERNAL MEDICINE, BIOCHEMISTRY. *Educ:* Cornell Univ, AB, 42; Albany Med Col, MD, 45; Columbia Univ, PhD(biochem), 58; Am Bd Internal Med, dipl. *Prof Exp:* USPHS fel, Columbia Univ, 54-57, instr biochem, 58-59, asst prof med, 59-65; dir dept med, Menorah Med Ctr & dir exp med, Danciger Res Found, 65-69; prof med & assoc dean, Sch Med, Univ Pa, 69-75; dir, 75-79, PROF MED, HERMAN GOLDMAN INST, CITY COL NEW YORK, 75- *Concurrent Pos:* Career investr, Health Res Coun, New York, 64-65; clin prof med, Sch Med, Univ Kans, 66-69; actg vpres health affairs & actg dir, Sophie Davis Sch Biomed Educ, 78-79. *Mem:* Am Soc Biol Chem; Am Soc Cell Biol; Harvey Soc. *Res:* Intermediary metabolism; tricarboxylic acid cycle activity; renal metabolism. *Mailing Add:* City Col of New York 138th St & Convent Ave New York NY 10031

FREEDMAN, ALFRED MORDECAI, b Albany, NY, Jan 7, 17; m 43; c 2. PSYCHIATRY. *Educ:* Cornell Univ, AB, 37; Univ Minn, MB, 41, MD, 42. *Prof Exp:* Intern, Harlem Hosp, NY, 41-42; asst path, Mt Sinai Hosp, 46; physiologist, Med Div, Army Chem Ctr, Md, 46-48; resident, Psychiat Div, NY Univ-Bellevue Med Ctr, 48-49, asst alienist, 49-50, jr psychiatrist, Children's Serv, 50-51, res fel, Univ-Ctr, 51-52, sr psychiatrist, Children's Serv, 53-54, clin instr psychiat, Col Med, 53-55; from asst prof to assoc prof psychiat, State Univ NY Downstate Med Ctr, 55-60; PROF PSYCHIAT & CHMN DEPT, NEW YORK MED COL, 60- *Concurrent Pos:* Child psychiatrist, Inst Phys Med & Rehab, Bellevue Hosp, 52-53, clin asst neuropsychiatrist, 54-55; asst, NY Univ Hosp, 53-55; asst pediatrician, Babies Hosp, 53-60; dir pediat psychiat, Kings County Hosp, 55-60; dir psychiat, Flower & Fifth Ave Hosp, Metrop Hosp & Bird S Coler Hosp, New York; mem bd trustees, Ctr Urban Educ, pres & chmn nat comn confidentiality health records; mem bd dir, Am Bd Psychiat & Neurol; consult, WHO Europ Ment Health Sect. *Mem:* Fel Am Psychiat Asn (pres, 73-74); fel Am Orthopsychiat Asn; fel NY Acad Sci; Am Psychopath Asn (pres, 71-72); Am Col Neuropsychopharmacol (pres, 72-73). *Res:* Effect of anticholinesterases on central nervous system; clinical and biological aspects of child and adult psychiatry; psychiatric education; narcotic addiction. *Mailing Add:* Dept of Psychiat NY Med Col Flower & Fifth Ave Hosp New York NY 10029

FREEDMAN, ALLEN ROY, b Chicago, Ill, Aug 18, 40; m 62; c 2. MATHEMATICS. *Educ:* Univ Calif, Berkeley, AB, 62; Ore State Univ, PhD(math), 65. *Prof Exp:* Asst prof, 65-70, ASSOC PROF MATH, SIMON FRASER UNIV, 70- *Mem:* Am Math Soc. *Res:* Number theory; density theory in additive number theory. *Mailing Add:* Dept of Math Simon Fraser Univ Burnaby Can

FREEDMAN, ARTHUR JACOB, b Brooklyn, NY, Dec 10, 24; m 64; c 6. COOLING WATER TREATMENT, CORROSION CONTROL. *Educ:* NY Univ, BA, 45, MS, 46, PhD(chem), 48. *Prof Exp:* Res assoc, Mass Inst Technol, 48-49; mem staff, Los Alamos Sci Lab, 49-51; res assoc, Univ NMex, 51-54; from asst proj engr to sr proj supvr, Stand Oil Co, Ind, 54-59; sect head, Nalco Chem Co, 59-66, res coordr, 66-67, tech mgr res, 67-69, tech dir, 69-72, mkt mgr, 72-78, tech dir, 78-81; PRES, ARTHUR FREEDMAN ASSOCS, INC, 81- *Mem:* AAAS; Am Chem Soc; Nat Asn Corrosion Engrs. *Res:* Phase rule; radiochemistry; kinetics; corrosion; water treatment; petroleum; wate and air pollution control. *Mailing Add:* Arthur Freedman Assoc Inc PO Box 58 Downers Grove IL 60515

FREEDMAN, DANIEL X, b Lafayette, Ind, Aug 17, 21; m 45. PSYCHIATRY. *Educ:* Harvard Univ, BA, 47; Yale Univ, MD, 51. *Hon Degrees:* DSc, Wabash Col, 74. *Prof Exp:* Intern pediat, Sch Med, Yale Univ, 52-55, resident psychiat, 55, chief resident, 55-56, from instr to prof, 55-66, dir psychopharmacol unit, 58-66; PROF PSYCHIAT & CHMN DEPT, UNIV CHICAGO, 66-, LOUIS BLOCK PROF BIOL SCI, 69- *Concurrent Pos:* Attend psychiatrist, Vet Admin Hosp, West Haven, Conn, 55-66; assoc psychiatrist, Grace-New Haven Community Hosp, 55-66; consult juv courts, 55-57, Fairfield State Hosp, 58-66 & US Dept Army, 65-67; career investr, USPHS, 57-66; consult, NIMH, 60-; chmn panel psychiat drugs efficacy study, Nat Acad Sci-Nat Res Coun, 66-68; mem adv comt, Food & Drug Admin, 67-; dir, Social Sci Res Coun, 67-73; dir, Founds Fund Res in Psychiat, 69-72; chief ed, Arch Gen Psychiat, 70-; mem comt brain sci, Nat Res Coun, 71-73, mem comt probs drug dependence, 71-, Am Psychiat Asn rep to div med sci, 71-73; dir, Drug Abuse Coun, 73; chmn, Pharmacol, Substance Abuse & Environ Toxicol Interdisciplinary Cluster, President's Biomed Res Panel, 75-76; mem selection comt, President's Comn Mental Health, 77 & coordr res task panel, 77-78; mem, Joint Comn Prescription Drug Use, Inc, 77- *Honors & Awards:* Distinguished Achievement Award, Mod Med, 73. *Mem:* Nat Acad Sci; Nat Inst Med; Asn Res Nerv & Ment Dis (pres); fel Am Psychiat Asn (vpres, 75-77); Am Col Neuropsychopharmacol (pres, 70). *Res:* Psychopharmacology; psychoanalytic, neurophysiologic and social investigation in schizophrenia; central nervous system determinants of allergy; drugs, brain function and behavior; methodology of drug studies. *Mailing Add:* Dept of Psychiat Univ of Chicago Chicago IL 60637

FREEDMAN, DANIEL Z, b Hartford, Conn, May 3, 39. THEORETICAL PHYSICS. *Educ:* Wesleyan Univ, BA, 60; Univ Wis, MS, 62, PhD(physics), 64. *Prof Exp:* Res assoc physics, Univ Wis, 64; NSF fel, Imp Col, Univ London, 64-66; res fel, Univ Calif, Berkeley, 65-66, instr, 66-67; mem, Inst Advan Study, Princeton, NJ, 67-68; from asst prof to assoc prof, State Univ NY Stony Brook, 68-74, prof physics, 74-80; PROF APPL MATH, MASS INST TECHNOL, 80- *Concurrent Pos:* Sloan fel, 69-71; vis scientist, Dept Physics, Mass Inst Technol, 70-71; Guggenheim fel, 73-74; vis assoc, Dept Physics, Calif Inst Technol, 77-78. *Mem:* Am Phys Soc. *Res:* Theory of elementary particles and their interactions, particularly as related to the theory of gravitation. *Mailing Add:* Dept Math Mass Inst Technol Cambridge MA 02137

FREEDMAN, DAVID A, b Montreal, Que, Mar 5, 38; div; c 2. STATISTICS. *Educ:* McGill Univ, BSc, 58; Princeton Univ, MA, 59, PhD(probability), 60. *Prof Exp:* Can Coun fel, Imp Col, Univ London, 61-62; PROF STATIST, UNIV CALIF, BERKELEY, 62- *Concurrent Pos:* Sloan fel, Univ Calif, Berkeley, 64-66; vis prof, Hebrew Univ Jerusalem, 68-69; consult various industs & govt, 70-73; vis prof, Nat Free Univ Mexico, 73, Venezuelan Inst Sci Invest, 70-71 & 76 & Univ Kuwait, 81. *Mem:* Inst Math Statist. *Res:* Ergodic theory; Bayesian inference; Martingales; Markov chains; random distribution functions; Brownian motion and diffusion; representation theorems; empirical histograms. *Mailing Add:* Dept of Statist Univ of Calif Berkeley CA 94705

FREEDMAN, DAVID ASA, b Boston, Mass, May 27, 18; m 47; c 4. NEUROLOGY, PSYCHIATRY. *Educ:* Harvard Univ, AB, 39; Tufts Univ, MD, 43. *Prof Exp:* Rockefeller fel neurol, Columbia Univ, 47-48; fel, Tulane Univ, 49, assoc clin prof neurol, 50-65; assoc prof psychiat & neurol, 65-71, PROF PSYCHIAT, BAYLOR COL MED, 71- *Concurrent Pos:* From instr to training & supv analyst, New Orleans Psychoanal Inst, 54-; clin prof psychiat, Med Sch, La State Univ, 69-73; pres & chmn educ comt, Houston-Galveston Psychoanal Inst, Inc, 78- *Mem:* Asn Res Nerv & Ment Dis; Am Acad Neurol; Am Psychiat Asn; Am Psychoanal Asn; Am Col Psychiat. *Res:* Role of congenital and perinatal sensory deprivations in evolution of psychic structure; an approach to the study of ego development. *Mailing Add:* Dept Psychiat Baylor Col Med Houston TX 77025

FREEDMAN, ELI (HANSELL), b Pittsburgh, Pa, Dec 12, 27; m 51; c 2. HIGH TEMPERATURE CHEMISTRY. *Educ:* Carnegie Inst Technol, BS, 47; Cornell Univ, PhD(chem), 52. *Prof Exp:* Res assoc physics, Brown Univ, 52-53, instr chem, 53-56; asst prof, Univ Buffalo, 56-60; res chemist, Chem Br, Ballistic Res Labs, 60-62, chief, Phys Chem Sect, 62-65, chemist, Phys Br, 65-69 & Thermokinetics Group, 69-73, RES CHEMIST, INTERIOR BALLISTICS DIV, BALLISTIC RES LAB, ABERDEEN PROVING GROUND, 73- *Concurrent Pos:* Mem, Eve Col Fac, Johns Hopkins Univ, 65-75. *Mem:* AAAS; Am Chem Soc; Am Phys Soc. *Res:* Chemical reaction in shock tubes; high temperature chemical kinetics; estimation of thermodynamic properties; computing high-temperature equilibria of real gases. *Mailing Add:* Ballistic Res Lab Aberdeen Proving Ground MD 21005

FREEDMAN, GEORGE, b Boston, Mass, Dec 11, 21; m 43; c 2. METALLURGY, PHYSICS. *Educ:* Mass Inst Technol, SB, 43; Boston Univ, MA, 52. *Prof Exp:* Asst metallurgist, 43, plant metallurgist, 43-51, head semiconductor eng & develop sect, 51-55, chief engr adv develop, 55-59, chief process engr, 59-60, mgr mat & tech lab, 62-65, group mgr mat & tech eng, 65-69, mgr, New Prod Ctr, Microwave & Power Tube Div, 69-80, DIR, NEW PROD CTR, RAYTHEON CO, 80-, ADV ED SOLID STATE TECHNOL, 61- *Concurrent Pos:* Pres, Tyco Semiconductor Corp, 60-62; lectr dent mat, Harvard Sch Dent Med, 65-80. *Mem:* Int Microwave Power Inst (chmn, Bd Govs, 76-80). *Res:* Development of new business concepts and new products. *Mailing Add:* 5 Brook Trail Rd Wayland MA 01778

FREEDMAN, HAROLD HERSH, b Malden, Mass, Mar 5, 24; m 51; c 3. ORGANIC CHEMISTRY. *Educ:* Tufts Univ, BS, 49, MS, 50; Boston Univ, PhD(org chem), 56. *Prof Exp:* Chemist, Ionics, Inc, 51-52; res chemist, 56-63, ASSOC SCIENTIST, NEW ENGLAND LAB, DOW CHEM CO, 63- *Mem:* Am Chem Soc; The Chem Soc. *Res:* Mechanism and structure in organic chemistry; organic chemistry of anions in non polar media. *Mailing Add:* Dow Chem USA Cent Res New Eng Lab Box 400 Wayland MA 01778

FREEDMAN, HENRY HILLEL, b New York, NY, Dec 21, 19; m 48; c 1. IMMUNOLOGY. *Educ:* NY Univ, AB, 48, MS, 50, PhD(physiol), 53. *Prof Exp:* Teaching fel biol, Washington Sq Col, NY Univ, 49-52; res assoc, Princeton Labs, Inc, 52-64; res immunologist, Inst Microbiol, Rutgers Univ, 65; sr res assoc, 65-67, mgr dept microbiol, Warner-Lambert Res Inst, 67-68, dir dept, 68-69, dir dept physiol & microbiol, 69-72, dir div biol res, 72-74; dir biomed res dept, ICI United States Inc, 74-76, gen mgr, Pharmaceut Res & Develop, 76-79, vpres, Pharmaceut Res & Develop, 79-81, VPRES, STUART PHARMACEUT DIV, ICI AMERICAS, INC, 81- *Concurrent Pos:* Mem res coun, Univ Del Res Found, 76-79. *Mem:* fel NY Acad Sci; Am Soc Microbiol; Reticuloendothelial Soc (pres, 76); Am Chem Soc; AAAS. *Res:* Immune mechanisms; non-specific host resistance; bacterial lipopolysacchardies; reticuloendothelial system; delayed hypersensitivity; transplantation immunity; immunosuppression. *Mailing Add:* Pharmaceut Res & Develop ICI Americas Inc Wilmington DE 19897

FREEDMAN, HERBERT IRVING, b Winnipeg, Man, Nov 16, 40; m 63; c 4. MATHEMATICAL ANALYSIS, BIOMATHEMATICS. *Educ:* Univ Man, BS, 62; Univ Minn, MA, 64, PhD(math), 67. *Prof Exp:* From asst prof to assoc prof, 67-78, PROF MATH, UNIV ALTA, 78- *Concurrent Pos:* Vis assoc prof math, Univ Minn, 73-74. *Mem:* Am Math Soc; Math Asn Am; Soc Indust & Appl Math; Can Math Cong. *Res:* The existence and stability of periodic oscillations and equilibria of ordinary differential equations; applications to mathematical models of species interactions. *Mailing Add:* Dept of Math Univ of Alta Edmonton Can

FREEDMAN, JEFFREY CARL, b Brooklyn, NY, Sept 24, 45; m 67; c 2. MEMBRANE TRANSPORT, CELL PHYSIOLOGY. *Educ:* Swarthmore Col, BA, 67; Univ Pa, PhD(biol), 73. *Prof Exp:* Asst prof biol, Reed Col, 73-75; fel, physiol & membrane pathol, Sch Med, Yale Univ, 75-79; ASST PROF PHYSIOL, STATE UNIV NY UPSTATE MED CTR, 79- *Concurrent Pos:* Prin investr, res grant, Nat Inst Gen Med Sci, 80- *Mem:* Biophys Soc; Am Physiol Soc; Soc Gen Physiologists; Red Cell Club; NY Acad Sci. *Res:* Red blood cells; ionic and osmotic equilibria; measurement of membrane potentials with fluorescent dyes; effects of calcium on potassium permeability; reconstitution of membrane transport functions into planar lipid bilayers. *Mailing Add:* Dept Physiol Upstate Med Ctr State Univ NY 766 Irving Ave Syracuse NY 13214

FREEDMAN, JEROME, b New York, NY, Aug 16, 16; m 46; c 7. ELECTRICAL ENGINEERING, ELECTRONICS. *Educ:* City Col New York, BS, 38; Polytech Inst Brooklyn, MS, 51. *Prof Exp:* Electronics scientist, Watson Lab, NJ, 46-51; dep chief, Rome Air Develop Ctr, Griffiss Air Force Base, 51-52; staff mem, 52-53, group leader, 53-55, div head, 55-68, ASST DIR, LINCOLN LAB, MASS INST TECHNOL, 68- *Concurrent Pos:* Mem adv comt ballistic missile defense, Adv Res Projs Agency, US Dept Defense, 63-67, chmn, 67-68; mem re-entry progs rev group, US Dept Defense Res & Eng, 63-70; consult, US Arms Control & Disarmament Agency, 65-67 & Inst Defense Anal, 65-; mem avionics panel, Adv Group Aerospace Res & Develop, NATO, 68-79; consult, Joint Chiefs of Staff, 68-; mem, Army Sci Bd, 78- *Honors & Awards:* Editor's Award, Inst Radio Engrs, Inst Elec & Electronics Engrs, 52. *Mem:* AAAS; fel Inst Elec & Electronics Engrs; assoc fel Am Inst Aeronaut & Astronaut. *Res:* Radar system design; signal design theory; microwave technology; systems design and analysis in ballistic missile defense and offense systems; radar system design. *Mailing Add:* Lincoln Lab Mass Inst Technol Lexington MA 02173

FREEDMAN, JULES, b Brooklyn, NY, Feb 3, 33; m 65; c 3. MEDICINAL CHEMISTRY. *Educ:* Brooklyn Col Pharm, BS, 57; Univ Mich, PhD(med chem), 62. *Prof Exp:* Sr res chemist, Lakeside Lab, 62-72, group leader cent nervous syst drugs, 72-75; RES CHEMIST, MERRELL-NAT, INC, 75- *Mem:* Am Chem Soc; NY Acad Sci. *Res:* Development of new synthetic substances useful in treatment of disorders of mental function. *Mailing Add:* Merrell-Nat Inc 2110 E Galbraith Rd Cincinnati OH 45215

FREEDMAN, L(ARRY) A, b Philadelphia, Pa, Mar 29, 27; m 51; c 2. ELECTRICAL ENGINEERING. *Educ:* Drexel Inst Technol, BS, 48; Rutgers Univ, MS, 50. *Prof Exp:* Asst elec eng, Rutgers Univ, 48-50; res engr, David Sarnoff Res Ctr, 50-62, eng leader, Astro-Electronics Div, 62-68, mgr camera develop, 69-75, SR PROJ MGR, ASTRO-ELECTRONICS DIV, RCA CORP, 75- *Mem:* Am Inst Aeronaut & Astronaut; Inst Elec & Electronics Engrs. *Res:* Space electronics; television camera systems. *Mailing Add:* Astro-Electronics Div RCA Corp Princeton NJ 08540

FREEDMAN, LAWRENCE ZELIC, b Gardner, Mass, Sept 4, 19; m 55; c 5. PSYCHIATRY. *Educ:* Tufts Univ, BS, 41, MD, 44; NY Psychoanal Inst, dipl, 50-55. *Prof Exp:* Resident psychiat, New Haven Hosp & Sch Med, Yale Univ, 46-49, assoc clin prof, 49-61; FOUND FUND RES PROF PSYCHIAT, SCH MED, UNIV CHICAGO, 61-, CHMN, INST SOCIAL & BEHAV PATH, 71- *Concurrent Pos:* Vis scholar & sr res assoc, Cambridge Univ, 58-59; fel, Ctr Advan Study Behav Sci, 59-60; fel, Adlai Stevenson Inst Int Affairs, Chicago, 72; vis lectr & mem coop fac, Sch Law, Yale Univ, 49-57, chmn study unit psychiat & law, 53-58; assoc psychiatrist, Grace-New Haven Community Hosp, 49-61; permanent deleg, UN Econ & Social Coun, 49-; psychiat consult, Am Law Inst, 54- & Am Bar Asn, 59-; physician, Billings Hosp, Pritzker Sch Med, Chicago, 61-; med adv bd, Ctr Study Criminal Justice, Sch Law, Univ Chicago, 66-; permanent consult, Comt Environ Design, Nat Housing Ctr, Washington, DC, 66-; psychiatrist, Nat Comn Causes & Prev Violence, 68-70; vis lectr, Child Study Ctr, Yale Univ, 72; vis prof, Univ Tel Aviv, 73. *Mem:* AAAS; Am Psychiat Asn; fel Am Orthopsychiat Asn; NY Acad Sci. *Res:* Psychosomatic medicine; psychosomatic aspects of obstetrics; psychoanalysis; social psychiatry; neurosis and economic factors; non-conformist behavior and social response; delinquent behavior; sex, aggressive and acquisitive deviant behavior. *Mailing Add:* 5741 S Drexel Ave Chicago IL 60637

FREEDMAN, LEON DAVID, b Baltimore, Md, July 19, 21; m 45; c 2. ORGANOMETALLIC CHEMISTRY. *Educ:* Johns Hopkins Univ, AB, 41, MA, 47, PhD(org chem), 49. *Prof Exp:* Anal chemist, Johns Hopkins Hosp, USPHS, 41-44, org chemist, Sch Hyg, 46-48; org chemist, Nat Cancer Inst, 48-49 & Univ NC, 49-61; assoc prof, 61-65, PROF CHEM, NC STATE UNIV, 65- *Concurrent Pos:* Dir, Org Electronic Spectral Data, Inc, 62- *Mem:* AAAS; Am Chem Soc. *Res:* Organophosphorus compounds; oxidation-reduction; relationship between chemical structure and biological activity. *Mailing Add:* 2006 Myron Dr Raleigh NC 27607

FREEDMAN, LEWIS SIMON, b Boston, Mass, Mar 21, 36; m 71. NEUROCHEMISTRY, NEUROPHARMACOLOGY. *Educ:* Harvard Col, AB, 58; Boston Univ, MA, 60; Cornell Univ, PhD(nutrit), 70. *Prof Exp:* NIMH fel neurochem, Dept Psychiat, 69-72, asst prof neurol & pharmacol, 72-78, RES ASSOC PROF NEUROL & PHARMACOL, DEPT NEUROL & PHARMACOL, NY UNIV MED CTR, 78- *Concurrent Pos:* NIMH spec fel neurochem, Dept Psychiat, NY Univ Med Ctr, 72-73. *Mem:* Am Soc Pharmacol & Exp Therapeut; Am Soc Neurochem; Am Asn Cancer Res; Fedn Am Soc Exp Biol. *Res:* Neurotransmitter mechanisms in learning and memory, neonatal undernutrition, neuroblastoma, neurological and psychiatric disorders. *Mailing Add:* NY Univ Med Ctr 550 First Ave New York NY 10010

FREEDMAN, M(ORRIS) DAVID, b Toronto, Ont, May 23, 38; m 62; c 2. ELECTRICAL ENGINEERING. *Educ:* Univ Toronto, BASc, 60; Univ Ill, Urbana, MS, 62, PhD(elec eng), 65. *Prof Exp:* Res assoc elec eng, Biol Comput Lab, Univ Ill, Urbana, 65-66; sr eng, 66-69, staff engr, 70-72, sr staff engr, 72-74, prin engr, 74-75, SR PRIN ENGR, BENDIX RES LABS, 75- *Concurrent Pos:* Adj asst prof, Univ Mich, Dearborn, 72-78, adj assoc prof, 78- *Mem:* Inst Elec & Electronics Engrs; Asn Comput Mach; Soc Mfg Engrs. *Res:* Analysis and synthesis of musical tones; digital computer systems-design and applications; pattern recognition-optical character recognition; computer-aided design systems-multiprocessor computer architecture. *Mailing Add:* Bendix Res Labs Southfield MI 48037

FREEDMAN, MARVIN I, b Boston, Mass, Oct 4, 39; m 66. MATHEMATICS. *Educ:* Mass Inst Technol, BS, 60; Brandeis Univ, MA, 62, PhD(math), 64. *Prof Exp:* Instr math, Univ Calif, Berkeley, 64-66; scientist, Electronic Res Ctr, NASA, 67-70; assoc prof, 70-77, PROF MATH, BOSTON UNIV, 78- *Concurrent Pos:* Vis asst prof, Brown Univ, 68-69. *Honors & Awards:* Co-winner Best Paper Award, Joint Automatic Control Conf, 68. *Mem:* Math Asn Am; Am Math Soc; Soc Indust & Appl Math. *Res:* Stability theory; partial differential equations; harmonic and functional analysis; numerical analysis and system theory; perturbation methods in control; aerodynamics. *Mailing Add:* Dept of Math Boston Univ Boston MA 02215

FREEDMAN, MICHAEL LEWIS, b Hartford, Conn, Dec 30, 42. ORAL MICROBIOL, MICROBIAL PHYSIOLOGY. *Educ:* Brown Univ, AB, 64; State Univ NY Buffalo, PhD(biol), 69. *Prof Exp:* Res assoc, Argonne Nat Lab, 69-71; ASSOC PROF ORAL DIAGNOSIS, SCH DENT MED, UNIV CONN, FARMINGTON, 71- *Mem:* Am Soc Microbiol; Radiol Res Soc; Sigma Xi. *Res:* Genetics and physiology of cariogenic microorganisms. *Mailing Add:* Dept of Oral Diag Univ of Conn Health Ctr Farmington CT 06032

FREEDMAN, MURRAY H, b Toronto, Ont, Nov 3, 36; m 59. BIOCHEMISTRY, IMMUNOLOGY. *Educ:* Univ Toronto, BSc, 59, MSc, 61, PhD(biochem), 64. *Prof Exp:* Med Res Coun overseas fel chem immunol, Weizmann Inst, 64-66; sr cancer res scientist, Roswell Park Mem Inst, 66-68; assoc prof biochem, Fac of Pharm, 68-76, assoc prof, Fac Med, 69-71, PROF BIOCHEM, FAC OF PHARM, UNIV TORONTO, 76-, PROF IMMUNOL, FAC MED, 71-, GRAD CHMN, FAC PHARM, 80- *Concurrent Pos:* Lectr, State Univ NY Buffalo, 67-68; Med Res Coun vis scientist zool, Tumour Immunol Unit, Univ Col, Univ London, 74-75; res scientist, Dept Immunol, Univ Uppsala & Dept Cell Res, Wallenberg Lab, Uppsala, Sweden, 79; res scientist, Dept Path, Harvard Med Sch, 81-82. *Mem:* Am Chem Soc; Am Asn Immunol; Can Soc Immunol; NY Acad Sci; Can Biochem Soc. *Res:* Structural and genetic studies on homogeneous antibodies molecules; structural and functional studies on biological macromolecules using high resolution one-H and thirteen-C; Fourier transform nuclear magnetic resonance spectroscopy; changes in membrane proteins following lymphocyte actuation; fluorescence polarization of 1,6-diphenylhexatriene-labelled cells. *Mailing Add:* Fac of Pharm Univ of Toronto Toronto ON M5S 1A1 Can

FREEDMAN, PHILIP, b London, Eng, June 25, 26; US citizen; m 54; c 5. MEDICINE. *Educ:* Univ London, MB, BS, 48, MD, 51, FRCP. *Prof Exp:* Bilton Pollard fel, Univ Col Hosp Med Sch, Univ London & Dept Med, Univ Ill, 57-59; first asst physician, St George's Hosp, London, 59-60, clin asst physician, Renal Study Clin, 60-63; assoc prof med, Chicago Med Sch, 63, actg chmn dept, 66-67, chmn, 67-74; CHMN DEPT MED, MED CTR, MT SINAI HOSP, 66-, PROF MED, RUSH MED COL, 75- *Concurrent Pos:* Consult physician, Woolwich Hosp Group & Redhill Hosp Group, London, 60-63; chief, Chicago Med Sch Serv, Div Med & dir renal unit, Cook County Hosp, 63-66. *Mem:* Am Fedn Clin Res; Am Soc Nephrology; Soc Exp Biol & Med; fel Am Col Physicians; Med Res Soc London. *Res:* Renal disease, particularly the pathogenesis of glomerulonephritis and the autoimmune diseases; immunologic aspects of renal and systemic disease. *Mailing Add:* Mt Sinai Hosp Med Ctr 2755 W 15th St Chicago IL 60608

FREEDMAN, ROBERT WAGNER, b Newark, NJ, Feb 15, 15; m 46; c 2. ORGANIC CHEMISTRY. *Educ:* Mass Inst Technol, SB, 38; Polytech Inst Brooklyn, PhD(chem), 51. *Prof Exp:* Res chemist, Battelle Mem Inst, 51-52, Balco Res Corp, 52-54 & Colgate Palmolive Co, 54-57; asst plant mgr, Transition Metals, Inc, 57; sect head anal res, Consol Coal Co, 57-65; PROJ COORDR ANAL RES METHODS, US BUR MINES, 65-, SUPVRY RES CHEMIST, 72- *Mem:* Am Chem Soc; Am Inst Chemists; Royal Soc Chem. *Res:* Gas chromatography. *Mailing Add:* 5028 Debra Dr Pittsburgh PA 15236

FREEDMAN, SAMUEL ORKIN, b Montreal, Que, May 8, 28; m 55; c 4. IMMUNOLOGY. *Educ:* McGill Univ, BSc, 49, MD, CM, 53; FRCP(C), 58. *Prof Exp:* From asst prof to assoc prof, 59-65, dean, Fac Med, 77-81, PROF MED, MCGILL UNIV, 65-, VPRIN, 81- *Concurrent Pos:* Dir div clin immunol & allergy, Montreal Gen Hosp, 65-77; chmn grants panel immunol & transplantation, Med Res Coun Can, 68-73; vis prof, London Univ & Chester Beatty Res Inst, 73-74; chmn grants panel immunol, Nat Cancer Inst Can, 75- *Honors & Awards:* Gairdner Int Award for Med Res, 78. *Mem:* Fel Am Col Physicians; Am Soc Clin Invest; Can Acad Allergy (pres, 68-69); fel Royal Soc Can; Can Med Asn. *Res:* Isolation and identification of human tumor antigens by immunological methods; co-discoverer of the CEA test for cancer; tuberculin hypersensitivity and respiratory allergy. *Mailing Add:* F Cyril James Bldg 845 Sherbrooke St W Montreal PQ H3A 2T5 Can

FREEDMAN, STEVEN I(RWIN), b New York, NY, June 5, 35; m 58; c 3. MECHANICAL ENGINEERING, POWER GENERATION. *Educ:* Mass Inst Technol, SB, 56, SM, 57, MechE, 60, PhD(mech eng), 61. *Prof Exp:* From instr to asst prof mech eng, Mass Inst Technol, 59-63; consult engr nuclear space power, Gen Elec Co, 63-68; asst chief engr, Prod Develop Div, Budd Co, 68-70; lectr, Univ Pa, 70-71, chief engr, Nat Ctr Energy Mgt & Power, 71-73; vpres res, IU Energy Systs, 73-74; asst dir combustion & power, Energy Res & Develop Admin, 74-77; asst dir combustion & power, 77-79, CHIEF ENGR COAL UTILIZATION, DEPT ENERGY, 79- *Mem:* Am Soc Mech Engrs. *Res:* Energy conversion, heat transfer, power generation, thermodynamics; magnetohydrodynamics; thermoelectricity; thermionics; fluid mechanics. *Mailing Add:* 7019 Old Cabin Lane Rockville MD 20852

FREEDMAN, STEVEN LESLIE, b Boston, Mass, Mar 3, 35; m 62. NEUROANATOMY, HISTOLOGY. *Educ:* Univ NH, BS, 57; Rutgers Univ, PhD(avian physiol), 62. *Prof Exp:* Res assoc, 64-65, asst prof, 65-71, ASSOC PROF ANAT, COL MED, UNIV VT, 71- *Concurrent Pos:* NIH fel anat, Brain Res Inst, Univ Calif, Los Angeles, 62-63 & Col Med, Univ Vt, 63-64. *Mem:* AAAS; Poultry Sci Asn; Am Asn Anat. *Res:* Neuroanatomical studies of the avian brain stem. *Mailing Add:* Dept of Anat Univ of Vt Burlington VT 05405

FREEDMAN, STUART JAY, b Los Angeles, Calif, Jan 13, 44; m 68; c 1. PHYSICS. *Educ:* Univ Calif, Berkeley, BS, 65, PhD(physics), 71. *Prof Exp:* Instr, Princeton Univ, 72-75, lectr, 75-76; ASST PROF PHYSICS, STANFORD UNIV, 76- *Concurrent Pos:* Sloan fel, 78-82. *Mem:* Am Phys Soc. *Res:* Elementary particle and nuclear physics; fundamental interactions and symmetries. *Mailing Add:* Dept of Physics Stanford Univ Stanford CA 94305

FREEDY, AMOS, b Petach-Tikva, Israel, Oct 11, 38; US citizen; m 65; c 2. ARTIFICIAL INTELLIGENCE, ENGINEERING. *Educ:* Univ Calif, Los Angeles, BS, 65, MS, 67, PhD(eng), 69. *Prof Exp:* EXEC V PRES, PERCEPTRONICS, INC, 70- *Concurrent Pos:* Assoc res engr, Univ Calif, Los Angeles, 70- *Honors & Awards:* Humanitarian Scientist Award, Orgn Rehab Training, 72. *Mem:* Inst Elec & Electronics Engrs; Sigma Xi. *Res:* Artificial limbs control; application of artificial intelligence to man machine system; computer decision aids; man/computer control systems and problem solving. *Mailing Add:* Perceptronics Inc 6271 Variel Ave Woodland Hills CA 91367

FREEH, EDWARD J(AMES), b Pleasant Valley, Pa, Sept 18, 25; m 52; c 5. CHEMICAL ENGINEERING. *Educ:* Univ Dayton, BChE, 48; Mass Inst Technol, MS, 50; Ohio State Univ, PhD(kinetics), 58. *Prof Exp:* Process develop engr nylon mfg, E I du Pont de Nemours & Co, 50-52; res engr, Res Inst, Univ Dayton, 52-55, assoc dir res, 59-62; instr chem eng, Ohio State Univ, 55-58; petrol indust mgr, Indust Nucleonics Corp, 58-59; prof chem eng, Univ Ariz, 62-68 & Ohio State Univ, 68-75; MGR SYSTS, DUVAL CORP, 75- *Concurrent Pos:* Staff consult, Indust Nucleonics Corp, 63- *Mem:* Am Inst Chem Engrs; Am Chem Soc; Am Soc Eng Educ; Instrument Soc Am. *Res:* Application of computers to chemical engineering calculations; instrumentation and process control. *Mailing Add:* Duval Corp 4715 E Fort Lowell Rd Tucson AZ 85712

FREELAND, FORREST DEAN, JR, b Detroit, Mich, June 25, 23; div; c 2. HYDROLOGY, FORESTRY. *Educ:* Univ Mich, BSc, 48, MF, 49; Mich State Univ, PhD(forest hydrol, soils), 56; Humboldt State Univ, BA, 76. *Prof Exp:* Forester, Cent States Forest Exp Sta, US Forest Serv, Ohio, 48-50, res forester, 50-51; teaching asst forestry, Mich State Univ, 51-54; asst prof, Nat Univ Colombia, 54-56 & Mich State Univ, 56-59; res forester, Rocky Mountain Forest & Range Exp Sta, US Forest Serv, Colo, 60-61; consult specialist, Price-Waterhouse & Co, Calif, 61-65; chief hydrologist, Metrop Water Dist Southern Calif, 66-67; assoc prof, 67-72, PROF WATERSHED MGT & HYDROL, HUMBOLDT STATE UNIV, 72- *Concurrent Pos:* Int consult forestry & hydrol. *Mem:* Soc Am Foresters; Am Geophys Union; Am Water Resources Asn. *Res:* Watershed management; forest influences and soils; forest mensuration; statistics; photogrammetry. *Mailing Add:* Dept of Watershed Mgt Humboldt State Univ Arcata CA 95521

FREELAND, MAX, b Browning, Mo, Oct 20, 20; m 55; c 6. ANALYTICAL CHEMISTRY. *Educ:* Northeast Mo State Teachers Col, BS, 41; Iowa State Col, MS, 52, PhD(anal chem), 55. *Prof Exp:* Teacher pub sch, Mo, 46-48; chemist anal method develop, Columbia-Southern Chem Corp, 55-57; assoc prof, 57-66, PROF CHEM, NORTHEAST MO STATE UNIV, 66- *Concurrent Pos:* Fel, Tex A&M Univ, 64-65. *Mem:* Am Chem Soc. *Res:* Spectrophotometric analysis; high precision spectrophotometry; water analysis. *Mailing Add:* Dept of Chem Northeast Mo State Univ Kirksville MO 63501

FREELING, MICHAEL, b Ft Wayne, Ind, Jan 14, 45; m 67; c 2. GENETICS. *Educ:* Univ Ore, BA, 68; Ind Univ, PhD(genetics), 73. *Prof Exp:* ASSOC PROF GENETICS, UNIV CALIF, BERKELEY, 73- *Concurrent Pos:* Guggenheim fel, 80-81. *Res:* Gene regulation and development using plant systems. *Mailing Add:* Dept Genetics Univ Calif Berkeley CA 94702

FREEMAN, ALAN R, b Atlantic City, NJ, Jan 16, 37; m 58; c 2. PHYSIOLOGY, PHARMACOLOGY. *Educ:* Philadelphia Col Pharm, BSc, 58; Hahnemann Med Col, PhD(pharmacol), 62. *Prof Exp:* Instr pharmacol, Hahnemann Med Col, 62-63; Univ fel neurophysiol, Med Ctr, Columbia Univ, 63-66; from asst prof to assoc prof physiol, Med Sch, Rutgers Univ, 66-71; assoc prof psychiat & physiol, Med Ctr & dir neurophysiol sect, Inst Psychiat Res, Ind Univ, Indianapolis, 71-74; PROF PHYSIOL & CHMN DEPT, SCH MED, TEMPLE UNIV, 74- *Mem:* AAAS; Biophys Soc; Am Physiol Soc; Brit Soc Gen Physiol; Soc Neurosci. *Res:* Application of biophysical techniques to electrophysiological, osmotic and permeability studies as an approach to understanding the physiology and pharmacology of the nervous system at the level of the cellular membrane. *Mailing Add:* Dept of Physiol Temple Univ Sch of Med Philadelphia PA 19140

FREEMAN, ALBERT EUGENE, b Lewisburgh, WVa, Mar 16, 31; m 50; c 3. ANIMAL BREEDING. *Educ:* Univ WVa, BS, 52, MS, 54; Cornell Univ PhD(animal breeding), 57. *Prof Exp:* Asst dairy husb, Univ WVa, 52-54; asst animal sci, Cornell Univ, 54-56; from asst prof to assoc prof, 64-65, PROF ANIMAL SCI, IOWA STATE UNIV, 65-, CHARLES F CURTISS DISTINGUISHED PROF AGR, 78- *Concurrent Pos:* Nat assoc animal breeders res, Am Dairy Sci Asn, 75; Fulbright Hays fel, Fulbright Hays Comn, 75; Nat Asn Animal Breeders Res Award, Am Dairy Sci Asn. *Honors & Awards:* Animal Breeding & Genetics Award, Am Soc Animal Sci. *Mem:* Am Soc Animal Sci; Am Dairy Sci Asn; Am Statist Asn. *Res:* Genetic improvement of domestic animals, dairy cattle, beef cattle, swine, poultry and sheep; genetics of populations; statistical genetics. *Mailing Add:* 239 Kildee Hall Iowa State Univ Ames IA 50010

FREEMAN, ARNOLD I, b Toronto, Ont, Sept 26, 37; m; c 3. PEDIATRICS. *Educ:* Univ Toronto, MD, 62; Am Bd Pediat, dipl, 68. *Prof Exp:* Intern, New Mt Sinai Hosp, Toronto, 62-63; resident pediat, Hosp Sick Children, Toronto, 63-65, resident path, 65-66; resident internal med, Sunnybrook Hosp, 66; instr pediat, Univ Tenn, Memphis, 66-68; res asst prof, State Univ NY Buffalo, 68-73; clinician II, 68-71, assoc chief pediat, 71-76, res assoc prof pediat, 73-80, CHIEF PEDIAT, ROSWELL PARK MEM INST, 76-, PROF PEDIAT, 81- *Concurrent Pos:* Res trainee fel, Lab Virol & Oncol, St Jude Res Hosp, Memphis, Tenn, 66-68; chmn electron micros area, Cancer Core Grant, 73; chmn, Acute Leukemia Group B, Nat Study Chemother Brain Tumors. *Mem:* Am Asn Cancer Res; Am Soc Hemat; Am Soc Clin Oncol; NY Acad Sci. *Res:* Treatment of acute lymphocytic leukemia; toxicity to the central nervous system from treatment for acute lymphocytic leukemia; use of interferon and interferon inducers in cancer and in viral or virally related disease. *Mailing Add:* Roswell Park Mem Inst 666 Elm St Buffalo NY 14263

FREEMAN, ARTHUR, b Youngstown, Ohio, Jan 12, 25; m 55; c 2. VETERINARY MEDICINE. *Educ:* Ohio State Univ, DVM, 55. *Prof Exp:* Vet pvt pract, Pac Vet Hosp, Wash, 55-56; dir prof rels, Jensen-Salsbery Labs, Inc, Mo, 56-59; ed, 59-72, ED-IN-CHIEF, J AM VET MED ASN, 72-, ASST EXEC VPRES, 77- *Mem:* Am Vet Med Asn; Coun Biol Ed; Am Asn Equine Practr. *Mailing Add:* 116 Princeton Hinsdale IL 60521

FREEMAN, ARTHUR JAY, b Lublin, Poland, Feb 6, 30; nat US; m 52; c 4. SOLID STATE PHYSICS. *Educ:* Mass Inst Technol, BS, 52, PhD(physics), 56. *Prof Exp:* Asst physics, Mass Inst Technol, 52-56; instr, Brandeis Univ, 55-56; physicist, Ord Mat Res Off, 56-62; assoc dir & head theoret physics group, Nat Magnet Lab, Mass Inst Technol, 62-67; chmn dept, 67-72, PROF PHYSICS, NORTHWESTERN UNIV, EVANSTON, 67- *Concurrent Pos:* Lectr, Northeastern Univ, 59-61; dir, NATO Advan Study Insts, France, 66, Can, 67; Guggenheim fel & Fulbright-Hays fel, Hebrew Univ, Jerusalem, 70-71; ed, Int J Magnetism, 70-74; ed, J Magnet & Magnetic Mat, 75-; Alexander Von Humboldt fel, Tech Univ Munich, 77-78; consult, Argonne Nat Lab, IBM Corp, Nat Magnet Lab, Mass Inst Technol. *Mem:* Fel Am Phys Soc. *Res:* Quantum theory of atoms, molecules and solids; neutron and x-ray scattering; crystalline field theory; electronic band structure of solids; theory of magnetism; hyperfine interactions; theory of electronically driven phase transitions; phonon anomalies in high temperature superconductors; electronic structure of surfaces interfaces, adsorbates on surfaces, and coherent modulated structures. *Mailing Add:* Dept Physics Northwestern Univ Evanston IL 60201

FREEMAN, BOB A, b Eastland, Tex, May 7, 26; m 60; c 4. MICROBIOLOGY. *Educ:* Univ Tex, BA, 49, MA, 50, PhD(bact), 54. *Prof Exp:* Instr biol, Agr & Mech Col Tex, 50-51; instr bact, Univ Ark, 54; from instr to asst prof microbiol, Univ Chicago, 54-64; assoc prof, 64-66, PROF MICROBIOL, UNIV TENN CTR HEALTH SCI, MEMPHIS, 66-, CHMN DEPT, 70- *Concurrent Pos:* USPHS grants, Univ Chicago, 56-64; US Army Res grants, Med Univ, Univ Tenn, 65-71, USPHS grant, 71-74, USDA res grant, 79-81; consult, WHO, 68. *Mem:* AAAS; Am Soc Microbiol; Soc Exp Biol Med; Int Soc Toxinology. *Res:* Effective immunity and mechanisms of pathogenesis in bacterial diseases; microbial toxins. *Mailing Add:* Dept of Microbiol & Immunol Univ of Tenn Ctr for Health Sci Memphis TN 38163

FREEMAN, BRUCE L, JR, b Wharton, Tex, Apr 2, 49. PLASMA PHYSICS, THERMONUCLEAR PHYSICS. *Educ:* Tex A&M Univ, BS, 70; Univ Calif, Davis, MS, 71, PhD(appl sci), 74. *Prof Exp:* STAFF PHYSICIST PLASMA PHYSICS, LOS ALAMOS NAT LAB, 74- *Mem:* Am Phys Soc; AAAS; Inst Elec & Electronics Engrs. *Res:* Application of pulsed power technologies to the achievement of significant fusion energy release from inertial systems; development of increasingly intense pulsed power sources from explosive flux compression generators. *Mailing Add:* 1431 11th St Los Alamos NM 87544

FREEMAN, CAROLYN RUTH, b Kettering, Eng, Jan 2, 50; Can & Brit citizen; m 81; c 1. RADIATION ONCOLOGY. *Educ:* London Univ, MB, ChB, 72; FRCP(C). *Prof Exp:* Asst prof, 78-79, ASSOC PROF & CHMN, DEPT RADIATION ONCOL, MCGILL UNIV, 79- *Concurrent Pos:* Asst radiol oncologist, Mont Gen, Jewish Gen, Royal Victoria & Mont Children's Hosp, 78-79, radiation oncologist-in-chief, 79; consult specialist, Queen Elizabeth, Reddy Mem, St Mary's & Mont Chest Hosps, 78- *Mem:* Can Asn Radiologists; Can Oncol Soc. *Res:* Clinical research in treatment of cancer. *Mailing Add:* Dept Radiation Oncol Mont Gen Hosp 1650 Cedar Ave Montreal PQ H3G 1A4 Can

FREEMAN, CHARLES EDWARD, JR, b Ironton, Mo, Aug 19, 41; m 63; c 4. PLANT ECOLOGY. *Educ:* Abilene Christian Col, BS, 63; NMex State Univ, MS, 66, PhD(plant ecol), 68. *Prof Exp:* Univ Res Inst grants, 68-70, asst prof bot, 68-79, ASSOC PROF BIOL SCI, UNIV TEX, EL PASO, 74- *Res:* Plant autecology; pollination biology. *Mailing Add:* Dept Biol Univ Tex El Paso TX 79968

FREEMAN, DAVID HAINES, b Rochester, NY, June 24, 31; m 56; c 4. PHYSICAL CHEMISTRY, ANALYTICAL CHEMISTRY. *Educ:* Univ Rochester, BS, 52; Carnegie Inst Technol, MS, 54; Mass Inst Technol, PhD(chem), 57. *Prof Exp:* Res assoc phys chem, Mass Inst Technol, 57-60; asst prof chem, Wash State Univ, 60-65; res chemist, Anal Chem Div, Nat Bur Stand, Washington, DC, 65, chief separation & purification sect, 65-74; PROF CHEM, UNIV MD, COLLEGE PARK, 74- *Concurrent Pos:* Chmn, Gordon Res Conf Ion Exchange, 73. *Honors & Awards:* Silver Medal, Dept Com, 69. *Mem:* Am Chem Soc. *Res:* Crosslinked polymers for chromatographic separations; marine chemistry; water-sediment partitioning; high performance liquid chromatography; gel permeation chromatography; ion exchange; chromatographic mechanisms; small particle-classification, metrology and microscopy; ultra-pure chemical reagents. *Mailing Add:* Dept of Chem Univ of Md College Park MD 20742

FREEMAN, DWIGHT CARL, b Salt Lake City, Utah, Mar 7, 51; m 76; c 1. PLANT REPRODUCTION, ECOLOGICAL GENETICS. *Educ:* Univ Utah, BS, 73; Brigham Young Univ, MS, 76, PhD(bot), 77. *Prof Exp:* Res geneticist, US Forest Serv, 77; ASST PROF ECOL, WAYNE STATE UNIV, 77- *Res:* The ecology and evolution of dioecious plant species; the evolution and adaptive significance of sexual lability in dioecious plants; the physiological and genetics of sex determination and sexual lability in dioecious plant species. *Mailing Add:* Dept Biol Wayne State Univ Detroit MI 48202

FREEMAN, EVA CAROL, b Kalamazoo, Mich, May 24, 54. THIN FILM DEVICES. *Educ:* Univ Pa, BA, 74; Harvard Univ, MS, 76, PhD(appl physics), 80. *Prof Exp:* Programmer, Philadelphia Gear Corp, 75; MEM RES STAFF, XEROX CORP, 80- *Mem:* Am Phys Soc; Inst Elec & Electronics Engrs. *Res:* Electrical properties of cadmium selemide and polysilicon thin film transistors. *Mailing Add:* W201-L Xerox Corp Webster NY 14580

FREEMAN, FILLMORE, b Lexington, Miss, Apr 10, 36. ORGANIC CHEMISTRY. *Educ:* Cent State Univ, BSc, 57; Mich State Univ, PhD(phys org chem), 62. *Prof Exp:* Res chemist, Calif Res Corp, 62-64; NIH fel, Yale Univ, 64-65; from asst prof to assoc prof chem, Calif State Univ, Long Beach, 65-73; vis prof, 73, assoc prof, 73-75, PROF CHEM, UNIV CALIF, IRVINE, 75- *Concurrent Pos:* Vis prof, Univ Paris, 71-72; adj prof chem, Univ Ill, Chicago Circle, 76; vis prof chem, Max Planck Inst Biophys Chem, Gottingen, WGer, 77-78; Fulbright-Hays sr res scholar, 77-78; Alexander von Humboldt Found fel, 77-78 & 79. *Mem:* Am Chem Soc; Royal Soc Chem. *Res:* Mechanisms and kinetics of transition metals oxidations; heterocyclic and bio-organic chemistry; organosulphur chemistry. *Mailing Add:* Dept Chem Univ Calif Irvine CA 92717

FREEMAN, FRED W, b Logan, Ohio, Aug 27, 24; m 46; c 3. FORESTRY, HORTICULTURE. *Educ:* Mich State Univ, BS, 49. MS, 51, PhD(forestry), 63. *Prof Exp:* Soil scientist, Fed Bur Reclamation, 50-51; ranger, Ohio Div Forestry, 51-53, forester, 53-55; horticulturist, Hidden Lake Gardens, 55-61, asst prof hort, Univ, 61-68, ASSOC PROF HORT, MICH STATE UNIV, 68-, CUR, HIDDEN LAKE GARDENS, 61- *Concurrent Pos:* Interchange fel hort, Brit Isles, 63. *Mem:* Am Asn Bot Gardens & Arboretums; Am Soc Hort Sci; Royal Hort Soc. *Res:* Arboretum development and management; establishment and maintenance of both woody and herbaceous plant collections in arboretum and conservatory; educational programs in the natural sciences for the visiting public. *Mailing Add:* Hidden Lake Gardens Tipton MI 49287

FREEMAN, GEORGE R(OLAND), b Chattahoochee, Fla, Oct 30, 18; m 43; c 2. AGRICULTURAL ENGINEERING. *Educ:* Univ Fla, BSA, 48, MSA, 57. *Prof Exp:* Asst regional engr, Int Harvester Co, Fla, 48-50; supt field opers, 50-66, asst dir, 66-80, ASST PROF & DIR, AGR EXP STA, UNIV FLA, 80- *Res:* Development of research equipment, tools and buildings for all departments, especially agronomy, animal husbandry, plant pathology and entomology. *Mailing Add:* Agr Exp Sta 1021 McCarty Hall Univ of Fla Gainesville FL 32601

FREEMAN, GORDON RUSSEL, b Hoffer, Sask, Aug 27, 30; m 51; c 2. PHYSICAL CHEMISTRY, RADIATION CHEMISTRY. *Educ:* Univ Sask, BA, 52, MA, 53; McGill Univ, PhD(chem), 55; Oxford Univ, DPhil, 57. *Prof Exp:* Fel, Saclay Ctr Nuclear Studies, France, 57-58; from asst prof to assoc prof, 58-65, chmn div phys chem, 65-75, PROF CHEM, UNIV ALTA, 65- *Mem:* Radiation Res Soc; fel Chem Inst Can; Can Asn Physicists; Am Phys Soc. *Res:* Reaction kinetics; properties and behavior of electrons in fluids. *Mailing Add:* Dept of Chem Univ of Alta Edmonton Can

FREEMAN, GUSTAVE, b New York, NY, July 3, 09; m 38; c 3. MEDICINE. *Educ:* Brown Univ, PhB, 29; Duke Univ, MD, 34. *Prof Exp:* Instr path, Yale Univ, 34-36; from instr to asst prof med, Univ Chicago, 36-47; mem staff, Peter Bent Brigham Hosp, 49-51; chief clin invest, Med Labs, Army Chem Ctr, 51-57; head clin pharmacol & exp therapeut sect, Nat Serv Ctr, Nat Cancer Inst, 57-58; DIR DEPT MED SCI, SRI INT, 58- *Concurrent Pos:* Res assoc, Childrens Hosp, Boston, 49-51, consult, 51-60; asst prof, Johns Hopkins Univ, 52-59; res assoc, Calif Inst Technol, 58-59; consult, NIH, 69-; adv, WHO, 76. *Mem:* Am Soc Trop Med & Hyg; Am Soc Hemat; Am Fedn Clin Res; Int Soc Hemat; Am Asn Cancer Res. *Res:* Thrombocytopenic bleeding; clinical investigation; infectious disease; pathology; cholinesterase biology; cancer chemotherapy; viral tumorigenesis in tissue culture; viral hepatitis; environmental medicine experimental emphysema. *Mailing Add:* Biotechnol Res Dept 333 Ravenswood Ave Menlo Park CA 94025

FREEMAN, HAROLD ADOLPH, b Wilkes-Barre, Pa, July 12, 09; m 35; c 2. STATISTICS. *Educ:* Mass Inst Technol, BS, 31. *Prof Exp:* Asst statist, 33-35, from instr to assoc prof, 35-50, PROF STATIST, MASS INST TECHNOL, 50- *Concurrent Pos:* Guggenheim Mem fel, Princeton Univ, 52-53; NSF fel, Univ NC, 60-61; consult, Urban Inst, 72- *Mem:* Fel Am Statist Asn (vpres, 48-50); fel Am Soc Qual Control; Inst Math Statist; fel Am Acad Arts & Sci. *Res:* Statistical methods; statistical theory; design of experiments. *Mailing Add:* Rm 52-383 Mass Inst of Technol Cambridge MA 02139

FREEMAN, HARRY W, b Mt Pleasant, SC, Jan 19, 23; m 44; c 2. VERTEBRATE ZOOLOGY. *Educ:* Charleston Col, BS, 44; Univ SC, MS, 48; Stanford Univ, PhD(biol), 51. *Prof Exp:* Actg instr biol, Stanford Univ, 50-51; from asst prof to assoc prof, Univ SC, 51-60; PROF BIOL, COL CHARLESTON, 60- *Concurrent Pos:* AEC res assoc invest, 51-53. *Mem:* Am Soc Ichthyol & Herpet. *Res:* Ichthyology; herpetology. *Mailing Add:* Dept of Biol Col of Charleston Charleston SC 29401

FREEMAN, HERBERT, b Frankfurt-am-Main, Ger, Dec 13, 25; US citizen; m 55; c 3. COMPUTER SCIENCE. *Educ:* Union Univ, NY, BSEE, 46; Columbia Univ, MS, 48, DSc(elec eng), 56. *Prof Exp:* Asst elec eng, Columbia Univ, 46-48; head dept advan studies eng, Sperry Gyroscope Co, 48-58, head dept data processing, 59-60; vis prof elec eng, Mass Inst Technol, 58-59; prof elec eng, NY Univ, 60-75, chmn dept, 68-73; PROF COMPUT ENG, RENSSELAER POLYTECH INST, 75- *Concurrent Pos:* Res grant, Air Force Off Sci Res, 61-78; mem cong comt, Int Fedn Info Processing, 64-65, chmn US comt, cong, 71; NASA res grant, 65-; Nat Sci Found fel, 66-67; vis prof, Swiss Fed Inst Echnol, 66-67; dir Cybex Assoc, Inc; vis prof, Comput Sci Inst, Univ Pisa, Italy, 73. *Mem:* Asn Comput Mach; fel Inst Elec & Electronics Engrs; NY Acad Sci; Pattern Recognition Soc; Soc Info Display. *Res:* Digital computers and control systems; logical design, graphical data processing and pattern recognition; computer image processing. *Mailing Add:* Dept of Elec Eng Rensselaer Polytech Inst Troy NY 12181

FREEMAN, HORATIO PUTNAM, b Emmitsburg, Md, Mar 17, 24; m 51; c 3. INORGANIC CHEMISTRY. *Educ:* Dickinson Col, BSc, 47. *Prof Exp:* Res assoc, Bone Char Res Proj, Nat Bur Stand, 48-56; res chemist, Fertilizer Lab, 56-65, RES CHEMIST, SOILS LAB, USDA, 65- *Mem:* Am Chem Soc. *Res:* Cane sugar refining processes; phosphatic fertilizer materials; pesticide chemistry. *Mailing Add:* Soils Lab USDA Beltsville MD 20705

FREEMAN, JAMES HARRISON, b Braddock, Pa, Feb 11, 22; m 44; c 3. ORGANIC CHEMISTRY, POLYMER CHEMISTRY. *Educ:* Juniata Col, BS, 44; Univ Pa, MS, 49, PhD(org chem), 50. *Prof Exp:* Asst instr org chem, Univ Pa, 46-50; res chemist, 50-56, adv chemist, 56-58, mgr org polymer chem sect, Insulation Dept, 58-69, MGR POLYMERS & PLASTICS DEPT, WESTINGHOUSE RES LABS, 69- *Mem:* AAAS; Am Chem Soc. *Res:* Heterocyclic organic compounds; mechanism of phenolformaldehyde resin formation; paper chromatographic analysis; high temperature application of polymers; thermally stable polymers; flat wiring systems; reinforced composites; adhesives; research managment. *Mailing Add:* Polymers & Plastics Dept Westinghouse Res Labs Pittsburgh PA 15235

FREEMAN, JAMES J, b Erie, Pa, Mar 11, 40; m 62; c 3. ELECTRICAL ENGINEERING, BIOENGINEERING. *Educ:* Gannon Col, BS, 62; Univ Detroit, MS, 64, MEng, 68. *Prof Exp:* Instr eng, Univ Detroit, 64-68; NIH Med fel, Carnegie-Mellon Univ, 68-69; from asst prof to assoc prof, 69-80, PROF & CHMN ELEC ENG, UNIV DETRIOT, 80- *Concurrent Pos:* Systs consult, Pan Aura Div, Parke Davis Corp, 66-69; investr, NSF grant, 70-71; res assoc, Providence Hosp, Detroit 71-; NASA grants, 75-80; Air Force Off Sci Res grant, 76-78. *Mem:* Am Soc Eng Educ; Inst Elec & Electronics Engrs. *Res:* Electrical and medical engineering with special emphasis in cardiac ultrasonic diagnosis; microprocessors; blood pressure and flow instrumentation. *Mailing Add:* Dept of Elec Eng Univ of Detroit Detroit MI 48221

FREEMAN, JAMES R, optics, solid state physics, see previous edition

FREEMAN, JEFFREY VANDUYNE, b Orange, NJ, Sept 13, 34; m 56; c 2. ENTOMOLOGY, FORESTRY. *Educ:* State Univ NY Col Environ Sci & Forestry, BS, 57; Rutgers Univ, MS, 60, PhD(entom), 62. *Prof Exp:* Teacher biol, Windham Col, 62-64; from asst prof to assoc prof sci, 64-72, PROF BIOL, CASTLETON STATE COL, 72- *Mem:* Entom Soc Am; Soc Am Foresters; Ecol Soc Am. *Res:* Biology and ecology of horse and deer flies; limnobiological studies, Lake Bomoseen, Vermont and tributaries; big tree survey of Vermont; birds in forests. *Mailing Add:* Dept of Biol Castleton State Col Castleton VT 05735

FREEMAN, JERE EVANS, b Martin, Tenn, Oct 13, 36; m 62; c 4. STRATEGIC PLANNING. *Educ:* Univ Tenn, BS, 58; Univ Ill, MS, 61, PhD(agron), 62; Univ Chicago, MBA, 74. *Prof Exp:* Res asst plant genetics, Univ Ill, 58-62; plant physiologist, CPC Int Inc, 62-67; sect leader res, 67-75, technol forecaster, Off of Pres, 75-76, dir bus environ res, 76-77, cor dir indust res & develop, 77-78, mgr tech planning, CPC NAm, 78-79; VPRES CORP DEVELOP, GOLD KIST INC, 79- *Mem:* Am Soc Agron; Am Asn Cereal Chem; Planning Exec Inst; Asn Corp Growth; Sigma Xi. *Res:* Genetics, physiology and chemistry of cereal grains. *Mailing Add:* Gold Kist Inc PO Box 2210 Atlanta GA 30301

FREEMAN, JEREMIAH PATRICK, b Detroit, Mich, Aug 3, 29; m 53; c 6. ORGANIC CHEMISTRY. *Educ:* Univ Notre Dame, BS, 50; Univ Ill, MS, 51, PhD(chem), 53. *Prof Exp:* Anal chemist, Monsanto Chem Co, 50; asst, Univ Ill, 50-51; sr res chemist, Rohm & Haas Co, 53-57, head org chem group, 57-64; assoc prof, 64-68, chmn dept, 70-79, PROF CHEM, UNIV NOTRE DAME, IND, 68- *Concurrent Pos:* Asst head dept, Univ Notre Dame, 65-70; Sloan fel, 66-68; secy, Organic Syntheses, Inc, 79- *Mem:* Am Chem Soc; The Chem Soc. *Res:* Chemistry of oxidized nitrogen compounds; heterocycles as synthetic intermediates. *Mailing Add:* Dept of Chem Univ of Notre Dame Notre Dame IN 46556

FREEMAN, JOHN A, b Berkeley, Calif, May 7, 38; m 57; c 4. NEUROPHYSIOLOGY, BIOPHYSICS. *Educ:* Trinity Col, BSc, 58; McGill Univ, MD, CM, 62; Mass Inst Technol, PhD(biophys), 67. *Prof Exp:* Lectr physiol, Fac Med, McGill Univ, 61-62; med intern, Wilford Hall US Air Force Hosp, San Antonio, Tex, 62-63; chief in-flight res unit & flight surgeon, US Air Force Sch Aerospace Med, 63-64; fel, Mass Inst Technol, 65-66; fel, Inst Biomed Res, AMA, 67-69; vis scientist, Marine Biol Lab, Woods Hole, 68; res scientist, Aerospace Med Res Lab, Wright-Patterson AFB, 69-71; from asst prof to assoc prof, 71-80, PROF ANAT & OPTHAL, VANDERBILT UNIV, 80- *Concurrent Pos:* Consult biomed electronics, Technol Inc, Ohio. *Mem:* Inst Elec & Electronics Eng; Soc Neurosci; Am Physiol Soc; NY Acad Sci; Asn Res Vision & Ophthal. *Res:* Neurophysiological mechanisms underlying information processing in the vertebrate visual system; molecular mechanisms associated with nurite growth synapse formation; related problems in biomedical engineering involving electronic design, computer applications and mathematical analysis; design of biomedical instrumentation. *Mailing Add:* Dept of Anat Vanderbilt Univ Sch of Med Nashville TN 37232

FREEMAN, JOHN ALDERMAN, b Raleigh, NC, Aug 27, 17; m 41; c 4. ZOOLOGY. *Educ:* Wake Forest Col, BA, 38, MA, 40; Duke Univ, PhD(zool), 49. *Prof Exp:* Prof natural sci, Louisburg Col, 42; asst prof chem, Wake Forest Col, 42-46; instr zool, Duke Univ, 47-48; asst prof biol, Tulane Univ, 48-52; chmn dept, 62-76, PROF BIOL, WINTHROP COL, 52- *Mem:* Am Inst Biol Sci. *Res:* Human blood phospholipids; tissue enzymes; temperature acclimatization in fish; metabolism of the fish brain; mollusk shell growth; differential longevity of sperm. *Mailing Add:* Box 5097 Winthrop Col Rock Hill SC 29733

FREEMAN, JOHN CLINTON, JR, b Houston, Tex, Aug 7, 20; m 47; c 6. METEOROLOGY, MATHEMATICS. *Educ:* Rice Univ, BA, 41; Calif Inst Technol, MS, 42; Univ Chicago, PhD(meteorol), 52. *Prof Exp:* Asst gas & fluid dynamics, Brown Univ, 44-46; meteorologist, US Weather Bur, 48-49; mem res, Inst Adv Study, 49-50; res assoc meteorol, Univ Chicago, 50-52; sr engr, Cook Res Lab, 51-53; assoc prof meteorol & oceanog, Tex A&M Univ, 52-55; owner, Gulf Consult, 55-62; prof math, Univ Houston, 58; prof, 58-66, PROF METEOROL & DIR INST STORM RES, UNIV ST THOMAS, TEX, 66- *Honors & Awards:* Meisinger Award, Am Meteorol Soc, 51, Citation for Work In Estab of the Tornado Warning Radar Network, 61. *Mem:* AAAS; NY Acad Sci; Meteorol Soc Japan; Am Geophys Union; fel Am Meteorol Soc. *Res:* Fluid dynamics; applied mathematics; oceanography. *Mailing Add:* Inst for Storm Res 3812 Montrose Blvd Houston TX 77006

FREEMAN, JOHN DANIEL, b Clarksville, Tenn, Apr 16, 41; m 65; c 2. TAXONOMIC BOTANY. *Educ:* Austin Peay State Univ, BA, 63; Vanderbilt Univ, PhD(biol), 69. *Prof Exp:* Asst prof bot, 68-74, ASSOC PROF BOT, AUBURN UNIV, 74-, CUR HERBARIUM, 68- *Mem:* Am Soc Plant Taxon; Int Asn Plant Taxon. *Res:* Taxonomy and cytogenetics of Trillium; Liliaceae of Alabama; flora of east-central and southeastern Alabama; poisonous plants of Alabama; eastern Asian-eastern North American floristic relationships. *Mailing Add:* Dept of Bot & Microbiol Auburn Univ Auburn AL 36830

FREEMAN, JOHN J, b Washington, DC, Sept 19, 41; m 68; c 2. PHARMACOLOGY. *Educ:* George Washington Univ, BS, 63; Vanderbilt Univ, PhD(pharmacol), 72. *Prof Exp:* Pharmacist, Maxwell & Tennyson, 63-64; fel pharmacol, Univ Calif, Los Angeles, 72-74, res assoc, 74-75; ASST PROF PHARMACOL, UNIV SC, 75- *Res:* Neurotransmitters in both the adrenergic and cholinergic nervous system. *Mailing Add:* Col of Pharmacol Univ SC Columbia SC 29208

FREEMAN, JOHN JEROME, b Arlington Heights, Ill, Sept 28, 33; m 58. PHYSICAL CHEMISTRY. *Educ:* Univ NMex, BSc, 58, PhD(phys chem), 64. *Prof Exp:* Res assoc chem, Brookhaven Nat Lab, 63-66 & Chemstrand Res Ctr, Inc, 66-68; RES CHEMIST, MONSANTO CO, 68- *Mem:* Sigma Xi; NY Acad Sci; Am Phys Soc; Soc Appl Specros; Am Soc Testing Mat. *Res:* Visible absorption and emission spectroscopy of molecules and complexed ions; infrared and Raman spectroscopy; catalyst characterization; polymer characterization. *Mailing Add:* Monsanto Co 800 N Lindbergh Blvd St Louis MO 63166

FREEMAN, JOHN MARK, b Brooklyn, NY, Jan 11, 33; m 56; c 3. PEDIATRIC NEUROLOGY. *Educ:* Amherst Col, AB, 54; Johns Hopkins Univ, MD, 58; Am Bd Pediat, dipl, 63; Am Bd Psychiat & Neurol, dipl, 69. *Prof Exp:* From intern to sr resident pediat, Harriet Lane Home, Johns Hopkins Hosp, 61-64; fel pediat neurol, Columbia Presby Med Ctr, New York, 64-66; asst prof pediat & neurol, Sch Med, Stanford Univ, 66-69; ASSOC PROF PEDIAT & NEUROL, SCH MED, JOHNS HOPKINS UNIV, 69-, DIR PEDIAT-NEUROL SERV & BIRTH DEFECTS TREATMENT CTR, JOHNS HOPKINS HOSP, 69-, DIR PEDIAT SEIZURE CLIN, 74- *Concurrent Pos:* Consult, Perinatal Res Br, Nat Inst Neurol Dis & Stroke & Walter Reed Gen Hosp; exec coun, Child Neurol Soc, 79-81. *Honors & Awards:* Lucy Moses Prize, Columbia Presby Med Ctr, 66. *Mem:* Fel Am Acad Pediat; Am Acad Neurol; Am Pediat Soc; Child Neurol Soc; Asn Prof Child Neurol (pres, 80-82). *Res:* Epilepsy; birth defects; clinical neurology. *Mailing Add:* Dept of Neurol & Pediat Johns Hopkins Univ Sch Med Baltimore MD 21205

FREEMAN, JOHN PAUL, b Washington, DC, Aug 30, 37. PHOTOGRAPHIC CHEMISTRY. *Educ:* Washington & Lee Univ, BSChem, 59; Univ Wash, MS, 64; Ohio State Univ, PhD(org chem), 70. *Prof Exp:* Index ed, Chem Abstr Serv, Am Chem Soc, Columbus, Ohio, 62-64; SR RES CHEMIST, RES LABS, EASTMAN KODAK CO, 71- *Mem:* Am Chem Soc; Soc Photog Scientists & Engrs. *Res:* Sensitizing dye synthesis and behavior in photographic emulsions; mechanism of interaction of organic addenda with photographic systems. *Mailing Add:* 58 Collingwood Dr Rochester NY 14621

FREEMAN, JOHN RICHARDSON, b Murfreesboro, Tenn, Aug 24, 27; m 64; c 3. HERPETOLOGY. *Educ:* Univ NC, AB, 50; George Peabody Col, MA, 53; Univ Fla, PhD(zool), 63. *Prof Exp:* Instr biol, Jacksonville Jr Col, 53-55; from asst prof to assoc prof & head dept, 59-70, PROF BIOL, UNIV TENN, CHATTANOOGA, 70- *Mem:* Am Soc Ichthyol & Herpet. *Res:* Physiological ecology; respiratory behavior in the salamander Pseudobranchus striatus. *Mailing Add:* Dept of Biol Univ of Tenn Chattanooga TN 37401

FREEMAN, JOHN WRIGHT, JR, b Chicago, Ill, July 12, 35; m 57; c 2. SPACE PHYSICS. *Educ:* Beloit Col, BS, 57; Univ Iowa, MS, 61, PhD(physics), 63. *Prof Exp:* Staff scientist, Off Space Sci & Appln, NASA, Washington, DC, 63-64; res assoc space sci, 64-65, from asst prof to assoc prof, 65-72, PROF SPACE PHYSICS & ASTRON, RICE UNIV, 72- *Concurrent Pos:* Consult, NASA, Washington, DC; vis scientist, Royal Inst Technol, Stockholm and Univ Bern, 71-72; prin investr, Apollo Sci Exp; dir, Space Solar Power Res Prog, 77- *Honors & Awards:* Exceptional Sci Achievement Medal, NASA, 73. *Mem:* Am Geophys Union; Int Union Geod & Geophys; Am Asn Physics Teachers; Int Asn Geomag & Aeronomy; Am Inst Aeronaut & Astronaut. *Res:* Space radiation studies, particularly the Van Allen or geomagnetically trapped radiation; low energy particle measurements and magnetospheric dynamics; space solar power; lunar exosphere and solar wind interaction with the moon; solar energy conversion devices. *Mailing Add:* Dept of Space Physics & Astron Rice Univ Houston TX 77001

FREEMAN, KARL BORUCH, b Toronto, Ont, Jan 21, 34; m 55; c 2. BIOCHEMISTRY. *Educ:* Univ Toronto, BA, 56, PhD(biochem), 59. *Prof Exp:* Res assoc, Univ Toronto, 60-61, Nat Inst Med Res, Eng, 61-63 & Ont Cancer Inst, 64-65; from asst prof to assoc prof biochem, 65-72, chmn res unit, 68-72, PROF BIOCHEM, McMASTER UNIV, 72-, CHMN DEPT, 73- *Concurrent Pos:* Vis scientist, London & Edinburgh, 72-73; San Francisco, 80. *Mem:* Am Soc Biol Chem; Can Biochem Soc. *Res:* Biogenesis of mitochondria; function and biosynthesis of mitochondrial nucleic acids and proteins. *Mailing Add:* Dept of Biochem McMaster Univ Health Sci Centre Hamilton ON L8S 4L8 Can

FREEMAN, KELLY CAREY, b Caledonia, Miss, May 27, 19; m 42; c 5. SOILS, FIELD CROPS. *Educ:* Miss State Univ, BS, 41, MS, 61. *Prof Exp:* Res agronomist, 61-70, SUPT LOCATION & RES LEADER, US SUGAR CROPS FIELD STA, USDA, 70- *Mem:* Am Soc Agron. *Res:* Agronomic research in sugarcane and sweet sorghum; breeding and development of sweet sorghum cultivars and sugarcane for syrup and or sugar production. *Mailing Add:* 3714 43rd Meridian MS 39301

FREEMAN, KENNETH ALFREY, b McAllaster, Kans, June 29, 12; m 38; c 2. ORGANIC CHEMISTRY. *Educ:* Stetson Univ, BS, 34, MS, 35; Georgetown Univ, PhD(biochem), 48. *Prof Exp:* Naval stores asst, Univ Fla, 36-38; high sch teacher, Fla, 38-39; chemist, Food & Drug Admin, USDA, La, 39-40; chemist, Fed Security Agency, Washington, DC, 40-42, chief color certification br, 46-53, chief color certification br, Dept Health, Educ & Welfare, 53-57, dep dir div cosmetics, 57-64, dir div color certification & eval, 64-68, dir div colors & cosmetics, 68-70; INDEPENDENT CONSULT, 70- *Concurrent Pos:* Vis lectr, Georgetown Univ, 48-56. *Mem:* Am Chem Soc. *Res:* Terpene chemistry; naval stores; synthetic organic dyes; cosmetics. *Mailing Add:* 6577 Sandspur Lane Ft Myers FL 33907

FREEMAN, LAWRENCE REED, b Nampa, Idaho, Dec 17, 41; m 73. FOOD SCIENCE. *Educ:* Brigham Young Univ, BA, 66, MS, 69; Univ Mass, PhD(food sci), 73. *Prof Exp:* Asst prof, 73-77, ASSOC PROF FOOD SCI, BRIGHAM YOUNG UNIV, 77- *Mem:* Sigma Xi; Am Soc Microbiol; Inst Food Technologists. *Res:* Characterization of compounds produced by microbial metabolism during refrigerated storage of fresh meat and poultry. *Mailing Add:* Dept of Food Sci & Nutrit 2218-SFLC Brigham Young Univ Provo UT 84602

FREEMAN, LEON DAVID, b Minneapolis, Minn, Oct 21, 20; m 43; c 2. THERAPEUTICS, CLINICAL PHARMACOLOGY. *Educ:* Univ Calif, Los Angeles, BA, 43; Univ Southern Calif, PhD(biochem), 62. *Prof Exp:* Lab supvr chem, US Rubber Co, 43-47; chief chemist, Southern Calif Gland Co, 49-60; res dir, Darwin Labs, 55-60; dir biochem sect, Riker Labs, 60-63; assoc dir clin invest, 63-65; vpres & dir biol res, Calbiochem, 66-71; PRES, PHARMAQUEST CORP, 75- *Concurrent Pos:* Tech dir Harvard Labs, 55-60; consult, 71- *Mem:* AAAS; Am Chem Soc; Am Soc Clin Pharmacol & Therapeut. *Res:* Chemistry and biology of heparin and other mucopolysaccharides; mechanism of action and metabolism; lipid metabolism and coronary heart disease; pharmaceutical research and clinical investigation; new drug design and human trials; new methods for isolation of heparin. *Mailing Add:* 48 Alta Way Corte Madera CA 94925

FREEMAN, LESLIE SHERWOOD, b Easton, Pa, Dec 15, 16; m 43; c 2. NEUROPSYCHIATRY. *Educ:* Lafayette Col, BA, 38; NY Univ, MD, 42. *Prof Exp:* Resident med, Easton Hosp, Pa, 42-44; chief psychiat serv, William Beaumont Gen Hosp, 46-47; chief continued treatment serv, Lyons Vet Admin Hosp, NJ, 48-57; dir res & educ, 57-62, chief of staff, 62-75; RETIRED. *Concurrent Pos:* Assoc clin prof psychiat, New York Med Col, 57- & Rutgers Med Sch, 70- *Mem:* fel Am Psychiat. *Mailing Add:* 495 Anlee Rd Somerville NJ 08876

FREEMAN, LOUIS BARTON, b New York, NY, May 12, 35; m 62; c 2. NUCLEAR ENGINEERING, APPLIED MATHEMATICS. *Educ:* Colgate Univ, AB, 55; Harvard Univ, AM, 57; Univ Pittsburgh, PhD(appl math), 65. *Prof Exp:* Assoc scientist, 58-62, scientist, 62-65, sr scientist, 65-71, prin scientist, 71-72, mgr breeder nuclear design, 72-76, ADV SCIENTIST NUCLEAR ENG, BETTIS ATOMIC POWER LAB, WESTINGHOUSE ELEC CORP, 76- *Mem:* Am Nuclear Soc. *Res:* Nuclear reactor calculational methods; analysis of nuclear reactor performance data; nuclear reactor safety calculations. *Mailing Add:* Westinghouse Bettis Atomic Power Lab PO Box 79 West Mifflin PA 15122

FREEMAN, MARC EDWARD, b Philadelphia, Pa, Feb 18, 44; m 70. REPRODUCTIVE ENDOCRINOLOGY. *Educ:* Moravian Col, BS, 65; WVa Univ, MS, 67, PhD(reprod physiol), 70. *Prof Exp:* Res assoc physiol, Sch Med, Emory Univ, 70-71, fel, 71-72; asst prof, 72-80, ASSOC PROF BIOL, FLA STATE UNIV, 80- *Concurrent Pos:* Res career develop award, NIH, 78-83. *Mem:* Endocrine Soc; Am Physiol Soc; Soc Study Reprod; Soc Study Fertility; AAAS. *Res:* The regulation of secretion of luteinizing hormone, follicle stimulating hormone and prolactin. *Mailing Add:* Dept of Biol Sci Fla State Univ Tallahassee FL 32306

FREEMAN, MARK PHILLIPS, b Palembang, Sumatra, June 9, 28; m 49; c 5. PHYSICAL CHEMISTRY. *Educ:* Univ Wash, BS, 53, PhD(chem), 56. *Prof Exp:* Instr chem, Univ Wash, 56 & Univ Calif, 56-58; res chemist, Am Cyanamid Co, 58-64, sr res chemist, 64-65, res assoc, 65-72; sr consult, Tafa Div, IONARC, 72-73; SR SCIENTIST, DOOR OLIVER INC, 73- *Concurrent Pos:* Corp sr educ award, Electrophys Inst, Munich Tech Univ, 63-64; vis prof chem eng, Mass Inst Technol, 67-68. *Mem:* Am Chem Soc; Am Phys Soc; Am Inst Chem Engrs. *Res:* Statistical mechanics of adsorption; extreme high temperature chemistry and physics; plasma state; solid-liquid separations; colloid chemistry. *Mailing Add:* Door Oliver Inc 77 Havemeyer Lane Stamford CT 06904

FREEMAN, MARTIN, computer sciences, see previous edition

FREEMAN, MAX JAMES, b Columbus, Ohio, Aug 28, 34; m 59; c 3. IMMUNOBIOLOGY, IMMUNOPATHOLOGY. *Educ:* Auburn Univ, DVM, 58; Univ Wis, MS, 60, PhD(vet sci path), 61. *Prof Exp:* Asst prof, Ohio Agr Exp Sta, 61-62; fel microbiol, Western Reserve Univ, 62-63, USPHS fel immunol, 63-64; asst prof microbiol, Univ Kans, 64-67; assoc prof, 67-70, PROF IMMUNOL, PURDUE UNIV, 70- *Mem:* Am Vet Med Asn; Am Soc Microbiol; Am Asn Immunologists; Am Soc Exp Path. *Res:* Antibody biosynthesis; function and heterogeneity; immunologic mechanisms in disease. *Mailing Add:* Dept of Vet Microbiol & Path Purdue Univ West Lafayette IN 47906

FREEMAN, MILTON MALCOLM ROLAND, b London, Eng, Apr 23, 34; Can citizen. BIOLOGICAL ANTHROPOLOGY, CULTURAL ANTHROPOLOGY. *Educ:* Univ Reading, BSc, 58; McGill Univ, PhD(physiol ecol), 65. *Prof Exp:* Res asst econ & ecol studies, Arctic Biol Sta, Fisheries Res Bd Can, 61; res demonstr zool, Queen Elizabeth Col, Univ London, 62-64; Dept Northern Affairs & Nat Resources res grant, Northwest Territories & Ottawa, 65-67; asst prof biol, Mem Univ Nfld, 67-68, from asst prof to assoc prof anthrop, 67-72; assoc prof 72-76, PROF ANTHROP,

McMASTER UNIV, 76- *Concurrent Pos:* Nat Mus Can grant, Northwest Territories, 68; Can Coun Killam res grant, Mem Univ Nfld & Northwest Territories, 69-72; dir, Inuit Land Use & Occupancy Res Proj, 73-75; adj prof environ studies, Univ Waterloo, 77- *Mem:* Can Sociol & Anthrop Asn; fel Am Anthrop Asn; fel Arctic Inst NAm; Can Ethnol Soc; Can Pop Soc. *Res:* Human ecological research and public policy issues relating to the Canadian arctic. *Mailing Add:* Dept of Anthrop McMaster Univ Hamilton ON L8S 4K1 Can

FREEMAN, MYRON L, b Fergus Falls, Minn, Nov 2, 30; m 57; c 3. PLANT TAXONOMY. *Educ:* Moorhead State Col, BS, 57; Univ NDak, MS, 62; Univ Northern Colo, DAgr(bot), 70. *Prof Exp:* Instr biol, Univ NDak, 60-62; PROF BIOL, DICKINSON STATE COL, 62-, CHMN DEPT SCI & MATH, 77- *Res:* Identification of western North Dakota plants, especially grasses. *Mailing Add:* Div of Natural Sci & Math Dickinson State Col Dickinson ND 58601

FREEMAN, NEIL JULIAN, b Jersey City, NJ, Nov 25, 39; div; c 2. STRUCTURAL MECHANICS, MOTOR VEHICLE ACCIDENT RECONSTRUCTION. *Educ:* Univ Miami, BS, 62, MS, 65; Northwestern Univ, PhD(theoret & appl mech), 66. *Prof Exp:* Asst prof, 66-69, ASSOC PROF CIVIL ENG, UNIV MIAMI, 70- *Concurrent Pos:* Prin investr, NSF res initiation grant, 68-69 & NSF res grant, 70-72; Nat Comt Vehicle Crashworthiness, Dept Transp, 71-72. *Mem:* Am Soc Civil Engrs; Am Asn Automotive Med; Int Asn Accident & Traffic Med. *Res:* Analytical studies of load transfer, cracks and stress concentrations in composite materials, within the scope of classical elasticity; mixed boundary value problems in elasticity, thermal conductance; multidisciplinary vehicle accident investigation and reconstruction. *Mailing Add:* Dept of Civil Eng Univ of Miami Coral Gables FL 33124

FREEMAN, PETER KENT, b Modesto, Calif, Nov 25, 31; m 55; c 4. ORGANIC CHEMISTRY. *Educ:* Univ Calif, BS, 53; Univ Colo, PhD(chem), 58. *Prof Exp:* Res technologist, Shell Oil Co, 58; res assoc org chem, Pa State Univ, 58-59; from asst prof to prof chem, Univ Idaho, 59-68; PROF CHEM, ORE STATE UNIV, 68- *Mem:* Am Chem Soc. *Res:* Rearrangements; reaction mechanisms. *Mailing Add:* Dept of Chem Ore State Univ Corvallis OR 97331

FREEMAN, RALPH DAVID, b Cleveland, Ohio, Mar 11, 39. PHYSIOLOGICAL OPTICS, NEUROPHYSIOLOGY. *Educ:* Ohio State Univ, BS, 62, OD, 63; Univ Calif, MS, 66, PhD(biophys), 69. *Prof Exp:* Asst prof, 69-74, assoc prof, 74-80, PROF PHYSIOL OPTICS & OPTOM, UNIV CALIF, BERKELEY, 80- *Concurrent Pos:* Nat Eye Inst grant, Univ Calif, Berkeley, 72-; lectr & consult var univs, 72- *Mem:* AAAS; Am Acad Optom. *Res:* Psychophysics of vision; plasticity of visual system; neurophysiology of visual cortex. *Mailing Add:* Sch of Optom Univ of Calif Berkeley CA 94720

FREEMAN, RAYMOND, b Long Eaton, Eng, Jan 6, 32; m 58; c 5. PHYSICAL CHEMISTRY. *Educ:* Oxford Univ, BA, 55, MA & DPhil(nuclear magnetic resonance), 57, DSc(chem), 75. *Prof Exp:* Engr, French AEC, 57-59; sr sci officer, Nat Phys Lab, 59-61; res fel nuclear magnetic resonance, Instrument Div, Varian Assocs, 61-62; sr sci officer, Nat Phys Lab, Eng, 62-63; mgr nuclear magnetic resonance basic res, Instrument Div, Varian Assocs, 64-73; UNIV LECTR, OXFORD UNIV, 73-; FEL, MAGDALEN COL, OXFORD, 73- *Concurrent Pos:* Consult, Varian Assocs, Calif, 74- *Honors & Awards:* Chem Soc Medal, Theoret Chemistry & Spectros, 78. *Mem:* Fel Royal Soc London. *Res:* Nuclear magnetic resonance spectroscopy; double irradiation techniques and relaxation time studies; two-dimensional Fourier transform spectroscopy; nuclear spin echoes. *Mailing Add:* Magdalen Col Oxford England

FREEMAN, REINO SAMUEL, b Virginia, Minn, Aug 20, 19; m 50. HELMINTHOLOGY, PARASITOLOGY. *Educ:* Duluth State Col, BS, 42; Univ Minn, MA, 48, PhD(zool), 50. *Prof Exp:* Asst prof zool, Southern Ill Univ, 50-52; from asst prof to assoc prof parasitol, 52-65, actg chmn dept, 73-75, PROF PARASITOL, UNIV TORONTO, 65- *Concurrent Pos:* Sr res fel, Ont Res Found, 52-64, sr res scientist, 64-66, consult, 66-; Fulbright grant, Finland, 63-64. *Mem:* Am Soc Parasitol; Am Soc Tropical Med & Hyg; Wildlife Dis Asn; Can Soc Zool; Am Inst Biol Sci. *Res:* Taxonomy and life history of cestodes, trematodes and nematodes; life history and ecology of parasitic helminths; parasites of man. *Mailing Add:* Dept of Microbiol & Parasitol Univ of Toronto Fac of Med Toronto ON M5S 1A1 Can

FREEMAN, RICHARD B, b Allentown, Pa, July 24, 31; m 54; c 3. INTERNAL MEDICINE, NEPHROLOGY. *Educ:* Franklin & Marshall Col, BS, 53; Jefferson Med Col, MD, 57. *Prof Exp:* Intern, Pa Hosp, Philadelphia, 57-58, resident med, 59-61; instr, Med Ctr, Georgetown Univ, 64-67; asst prof, 67-69, ASSOC PROF NEPHROLOGY, MED CTR, UNIV ROCHESTER, 69-, HEAD NEPHROLOGY UNIT, 74- *Concurrent Pos:* Fel hypertension, Pa Hosp, Philadelphia, 58-59; fels nephrology, Med Ctr, Georgetown Univ, 61, 63-64; consult, Hosp & Med Facil Div, USPHS, 67-74; mem, Nat Adv Comt Artificial Kidney Chronic Uremia Prog, Nat Insts Arthritis & Metab Dis, 69-74; pres, Nat Kidney Found, 70- *Mem:* AAAS; Am Fedn Clin Res; Am Heart Asn; Am Soc Artificial Internal Organs; Am Soc Nephrology. *Res:* Pathogenesis and course of chronic renal disease; performance characteristics of artificial kidneys; cation metabolism. *Mailing Add:* Univ of Rochester Med Ctr Rochester NY 14620

FREEMAN, RICHARD CARL, b NS, Can, May 8, 29; m 53; c 1. TEXTILE CHEMISTRY. *Educ:* Lowell Technol Inst, BS, 59. *Prof Exp:* From chemist to asst dir res & develop, Joseph Bancroft & Sons Co, 59-70; group mgr wool prod develop, 70-73, VPRES TECH SERV & DEVELOP, THE WOOL BUR INC, WOODBURY, 73- *Mem:* Am Asn Textile Chemists & Colorists; Am Textile Mfrs Inst. *Mailing Add:* Tech Serv & Develop Wool Bur Inc PO Box 430 Woodbury NY 11797

FREEMAN, RICHARD REILING, b Corpus Christi, Tex, Nov 13, 44; m 67; c 2. ATOMIC PHYSICS, X-RAY SCATTERING. *Educ:* Univ Wash, BS, 67; Harvard Univ, AM, 68, PhD(physics), 73. *Prof Exp:* Res engr, Boeing Co, 68-69 & Dynetics Co, 69-70; consult physicist, Calspan Corp, 72-73; instr, Dept Physics, Mass Inst Technol, 73-76; mem tech staff, 76-81, HEAD, ELECTROMAGNETIC PHENOMENA RES DEPT, BELL LABS, 81- *Mem:* Sigma Xi; Am Phys Soc; fel Optical Soc Am. *Res:* Atomic physics; nonlinear optics; x-ray physics. *Mailing Add:* Bell Labs Holmdel NJ 07733

FREEMAN, ROBERT, US citizen. MATHEMATICS. *Educ:* NY Univ, BAE, 47; Univ Calif, Berkeley, PhD(math), 59. *Prof Exp:* Mathematician, Lawrence Radiation Lab, 58-62; from asst prof to assoc prof math, Univ Md, 62-67; ASSOC PROF MATH, UNIV ORE & INST THEORET SCI, 67- *Mem:* NSF grant, 63-65. *Mem:* Am Math Soc; Math Asn Am. *Res:* Spectral and operation theoretic structure of elliptic boundary value problems. *Mailing Add:* Dept of Math Univ of Ore Eugene OR 97403

FREEMAN, ROBERT CLARENCE, b Harrellsville, NC, Oct 14, 27; m 54. ORGANIC CHEMISTRY. *Educ:* NC Col, Durham, BS, 50, MS, 52; Wayne State Univ, PhD(chem), 56. *Prof Exp:* Res chemist, Monsanto Chem Co, 56-62; mem fac, Agr & Tech Col NC, 62-64; res chemist, 64-75, SR RES SPECIALIST, MONSANTO CO, 75- *Mem:* Am Chem Soc. *Res:* Acyloin condensation; ketenimine chemistry; epoxyether chemistry; reactions of phosphorous compounds with alpha halocarbonyl compounds; reactions of enamines; synthesis of radioactive compounds; synthesis of carbon-13 compounds. *Mailing Add:* Monsanto Co Res Lab 800 N Lindberg Blvd St Louis MO 63141

FREEMAN, ROBERT DAVID, b Nicholson, Ga, Feb 7, 30; m 57; c 2. PHYSICAL CHEMISTRY. *Educ:* NGeorgia Col, BS, 48; Purdue Univ, MS, 52, PhD(chem), 54. *Prof Exp:* Phys chemist, Goodyear Atomic Corp, 54-55; from asst prof to assoc prof, 55-79, PROF CHEM, OKLA STATE UNIV, 79- *Mem:* AAAS; Am Chem Soc; Am Phys Soc; Am Asn Physics Teachers. *Res:* Vaporization phenomena and chemistry at high temperatures; molecular flow of rarefied gases; thermochemistry; calorimetry; information theory and thermodynamics. *Mailing Add:* Dept of Chem Okla State Univ Stillwater OK 74075

FREEMAN, ROBERT GLEN, b Kerrville, Tex, Feb 3, 27; m 50; c 4. PATHOLOGY. *Educ:* Baylor Univ, MD, 49. *Prof Exp:* Instr anat, Col Med, Baylor Univ, 50-52; instr, Med Field Serv Sch, Ft San Houston, 52-54; asst prof, Med Br, Univ Tenn, 54-55; resident & asst surg, Vet Admin Hosp, 55-56; resident & instr path, Affil Hosps, Baylor Univ, 57-59, from asst prof to prof, 59-70; prof path & internal med, 70-74, CLIN PROF PATH & INTERNAL MED, UNIV TEX HEALTH SCI CTR, DALLAS, 74- *Concurrent Pos:* Consult dermat, Brooke Army Hosp, Ft Sam Houston, Tex. *Mem:* Col Am Path; Am Acad Dermat; Am Soc Dermatopath; Am Dermat Asn; Soc Invest Dermat. *Res:* Dermatopathology; effects of ultraviolet on the skin. *Mailing Add:* Dept of Path Univ Tex Health Sci Ctr Dallas TX 75235

FREEMAN, ROGER DANTE, b New York, NY, Aug 3, 33; m 59; c 3. CHILD PSYCHIATRY. *Educ:* Swarthmore Col, BA, 54; Johns Hopkins Univ, MD, 58; McGill Univ, dipl psychiat, 63. *Prof Exp:* Rotating intern, Montreal Gen Hosp, 58-59; resident gen psychiat, 59-61; fel child psychiat, Child Study Ctr Philadelphia, 61-63; instr psychiat, Jefferson Med Col, 63-64; from instr to asst prof, Sch Med, Temple Univ, 64-70; assoc prof, 70-77, PROF PSYCHIAT, UNIV BC, 77- *Concurrent Pos:* Dir psychiat serv, Handicapped Children's Unit, St Christopher's Hosp for Children, Philadelphia, 64-69, dir child psychiat clin, 69-70; consult, Upsal Day Sch for Blind Children, Philadelphia, 67-69 & Children's Hosp Diag Ctr, Vancouver, 70- mem active staff, Vancouver Gen Hosp, 70-80, courtesy staff, 80-; consult, US Food & Drug Admin, 72-73; Dept Nat Health & Welfare grant, Univ BC, 72-74; consult, Western Inst Deaf, 74- & Sunny Hill Hosp Children, 75- *Honors & Awards:* Award Merit, Western Inst Deaf, 80. *Mem:* Am Acad Cerebral Palsy; Am Asn Ment Deficiency; Can Med Asn. *Res:* Psychiatry of handicapped children and their families; child psychopharmacology. *Mailing Add:* Dept of Psychiat Univ of BC Vancouver Can

FREEMAN, THOMAS EDWARD, b Laurel, Miss, Jan 29, 30; m 53; c 2. PLANT PATHOLOGY. *Educ:* Millsaps Col, BS, 52; La State Univ, MS, 54, PhD(plant path), 56. *Prof Exp:* Asst, La State Univ, 52-56; asst plant pathologist, 56-63, assoc plant pathologist, 63-68, PLANT PATHOLOGIST & PROF PLANT PATH, UNIV FLA, 68- *Mem:* Am Phytopath Soc. *Res:* Grass diseases; biological control of weed with plant pathogens. *Mailing Add:* Dept of Plant Path Univ of Fla Gainesville FL 32611

FREEMAN, THOMAS J, b Miami, Fla, Sept 30, 32; m 55; c 2. GEOLOGY. *Educ:* Univ Ark, BS, 56, MS, 57; Univ Tex, PhD(geol), 62. *Prof Exp:* Jr geologist, Stand Oil Co, Ohio, 57-58; asst prof geol, Univ Mo, 62-63; field geologist, Ark Geol Comn, 63-64; asst prof, 64-67, assoc prof, 67-80, PROF GEOL, UNIV MO-COLUMBIA, 80- *Concurrent Pos:* Vis prof, Univ Madrid, 69-70; leader, Int Field Inst, Spain, 71. *Mem:* Am Asn Petrol Geologists; Geol Soc Am; Soc Econ Paleont & Mineral. *Res:* Economic aspects of the genesis and diagenesis of carbonate rocks. *Mailing Add:* Dept of Geol Univ of Mo-Columbia Columbia MO 65201

FREEMAN, THOMAS PATRICK, b Denver, Colo, Aug 14, 38; m 63; c 2. PLANT ANATOMY, PLANT MORPHOLOGY. *Educ:* Colo State Univ, BA, 62; Colo State Col, MA, 63; Ariz State Univ, PhD(plant anat), 68. *Prof Exp:* Instr bot, Foothill Col, 63-65; teaching asst, Ariz State Univ, 65-68; ASSOC PROF ANAT, N DAK STATE UNIV, 68-, DIR ELECTRON MICROSCOPE LAB, 77- *Concurrent Pos:* NSF instnl grant, 69. *Mem:* Am Inst Biol Sci; Bot Soc Am; Int Soc Plant Morphol. *Res:* Developmental anatomy of the Cactaceae; effects of water stress on the development of chlorophyll and chloroplast ultrastructure in wheat. *Mailing Add:* Dept of Bot NDak State Univ Fargo ND 58102

FREEMAN, VERNE CRAWFORD, b Bentonville, Ind, Dec 25, 00; m 26; c 1. AGRICULTURE. *Educ:* Purdue Univ, BSA, 23, MSA, 26. *Prof Exp:* Teacher pub sch, Ind, 23-25; instr animal husb & asst to dean, 26-35, from asst dean to assoc dean, 35-69, from asst prof to prof animal husb, 38-69, dir resident instr, 58-69, EMER PROF ANIMAL SCI, SCH AGR, PURDUE UNIV, WEST LAFAYETTE, 80-, EMER DIR RESIDENT INSTR, 69- *Concurrent Pos:* Consult, Bd Fundamental Educ. *Mem:* Am Coun Educ; Farm Econ Asn; fel Am Soc Animal Sci. *Res:* Agricultural personnel and guidance programs. *Mailing Add:* 518 Hillcrest Rd West Lafayette IN 47906

FREEMAN, WADE AUSTIN, b Evanston, Ill, Nov 20, 40; m 75; c 2. INORGANIC CHEMISTRY. *Educ:* Univ Ill, BS, 62; Univ Mich, MS, 64, PhD(chem), 67. *Prof Exp:* Instr chem, 67-70, asst dean, Col Lib Arts, 69-79, ASST PROF CHEM, UNIV ILL, CHICAGO CIRCLE, 70-, DIR FRESHMAN CHEM, 79- *Mem:* Am Chem Soc. *Res:* Relationship of molecular dissymmetry to circular dichroism of inorganic complex compounds. *Mailing Add:* Dept of Chem Box 4348 Univ of Ill Chicago Circle Chicago IL 60680

FREEMAN, WALTER JACKSON, III, b Washington, DC, Jan 30, 27; m 52; c 7. NEUROPHYSIOLOGY. *Educ:* Yale Univ, MD, 54. *Prof Exp:* Intern path, Yale Univ, 54-55; intern med, Hosp, Johns Hopkins Univ, 55-56; asst res physiologist, Univ Calif, Los Angeles, 56-59; from asst prof to assoc prof, 59-67, chmn dept, 67-72, PROF PHYSIOL, CALIF, BERKELEY, 67- *Concurrent Pos:* USPHS fel, Univ Calif, Los Angeles, 56-58; Found Fund Res Psychiat & Guggenheim fels, 65-66; titulane de la chaire solvay, Univ Libre, Bruxelles, 74. *Res:* Neurophysiology. *Mailing Add:* Dept of Physiol-Anat Univ of Calif Berkeley CA 94720

FREEMON, FRANK REED, b Bloomington, Ill, July 18, 38; m 66. NEUROLOGY. *Educ:* Univ Fla, MD, 65. *Prof Exp:* Clin fel neurol, Univ Fla, 66-69; res fel, Wash Univ, 69-70; asst prof neurol, Med Col Wis, 70-72; assoc prof, 72-78, PROF NEUROL, VANDERBILT UNIV, 78- *Mem:* AAAS; Am Acad Neurol. *Res:* Clinical neurology; brain function. *Mailing Add:* 2422 Valleybrook Rd Nashville TN 37215

FREER, RICHARD JOHN, b Poughkeepsie, NY, June 2, 42. PHARMACOLOGY. *Educ:* Marist Col, BA, 64; Columbia Univ, PhD(pharmacol), 69. *Prof Exp:* Instr biochem, Sch Med, Univ Colo, Denver, 69-72; asst prof pharmacol, Univ Conn Health Ctr, Farmington, 72-75; assoc prof, 75-81, PROF PHARMACOL, MED COL VA, 81- *Concurrent Pos:* Estab investr, Am Heart Asn. *Mem:* Am Soc Exp Pharmacol & Ther; Am Heart Asn. *Res:* Synthesis of analogs of vasoactive peptides to study peptide-receptor interactions; study and synthesis of inhibitors of peptide hormones. *Mailing Add:* Dept of Pharmacol Med Col of Va MCV Sta Richmond VA 23298

FREER, STEPHAN T, b Akron, Ohio, May 14, 33; m 59; c 2. BIOCHEMISTRY, PHYSICAL CHEMISTRY. *Educ:* Univ Calif, Berkeley, AB, 59; Univ Wash, PhD(biochem), 64. *Prof Exp:* Asst specialist chem, 64-67, asst res chemist, 67-72, ASSOC RES CHEMIST, UNIV CALIF, SAN DIEGO, 72- *Mem:* AAAS; Am Crystallog Asn. Re Structure and function of biologically significant macromolecules. *Res:* software systems. *Mailing Add:* Dept Chem B-017 Univ Calif San Diego La Jolla CA 92093

FREERKS, MARSHALL CORNELIUS, b Wahpeton, NDak, Sept 2, 12; m 41; c 4. ATOMIC PHYSICS. *Educ:* Carleton Col, BA, 39; Univ Minn, PhD(org & phys chem), 49. *Prof Exp:* Org chemist & res group leader, 49-61; scientist, 61-72, SCI FEL, MONSANTO CO, 72- *Mem:* Am Chem Soc; NY Acad Sci. *Res:* Fundamental nature of catalysis as a function of atomic structure; physical nature of atomic structure; nature of the chemical bond. *Mailing Add:* 339 Greenleaf Dr Kirkwood MO 63122

FREERKSEN, ROBERT WAYNE, b Owatonna, Minn, May 19, 52; m 79. ORGANIC CHEMISTRY. *Educ:* Univ Minn, Minneapolis, BS, 74; Univ Colo, Boulder, PhD(org chem), 78. *Prof Exp:* Res fel chem, Harvard Univ, 78-79; RES CHEMIST, BIOCHEM DEPT, E I DU PONT DE NEMOURS & CO, 79- *Mem:* Am Chem Soc. *Res:* Synthesis of biologically active compounds including naturally occuring polyether ionophores and novel steriods; development of synthetic methods. *Mailing Add:* 2711 Ebright Rd Wilmington DE 19810

FREESE, ERNST, b Dusseldorf, Ger, Sept 27, 25; m 56; c 2. MOLECULAR BIOLOGY. *Educ:* Univ Heidelberg, Vordipl, 48; Univ Gottingen, dipl, 51, PhD(physics), 53. *Prof Exp:* Res fel physics, Max Planck Inst, Gottingen, 53-54; inst nuclear studies, Univ Chicago, 54, biol, Calif Inst Technol, 55-56, biophys, Purdue Univ, 57 & biol, Harvard Univ, 57-59; assoc prof genetics, Univ Wis, 59-62; CHIEF LAB MOLECULAR BIOL, NAT INST NEUROL & COMMUNICATIVE DIS & STROKE, 62- *Mem:* Biophys Soc; Genetics Soc Am; Am Soc Biol Chem; Am Soc Microbiol; Environ Mutagen Soc. *Res:* Quantum theory; molecular mechanisms of mutation; genetic function, cell biology and differentiation. *Mailing Add:* 8300 Whitman Dr Bethesda MD 20014

FREESE, KENNETH BROOKS, experimental plasma physics, computer science, see previous edition

FREESE, RAYMOND WILLIAM, b Foristell, Mo, Dec 17, 34; m 57; c 3. GEOMETRY. *Educ:* Univ Mo, BS, 56 & 58, MA, 58, PhD(math), 61. *Prof Exp:* From asst prof to assoc prof, 61-67, PROF MATH, ST LOUIS UNIV, 67-, CHMN DEPT, 71- *Mem:* Am Math Soc; Math Asn Am. *Res:* Distance geometry. *Mailing Add:* Dept of Math St Louis Univ St Louis MO 63103

FREESE, UWE ERNST, b Bordesholm, WGer, May 11, 25; US citizen; m 61; c 2. OBSTETRICS & GYNECOLOGY. *Educ:* Univ Kiel, MD, 51. *Prof Exp:* From instr to prof, Chicago Lying-in Hosp, Univ Chicago, 71-75, PROF OBSTET & GYNEC & CHMN DEPT, CHICAGO MED SCH-UNIV HEALTH SCI, 75-; DIR OBSTET & GYNEC, COOK COUNTY HOSP, 76-

Mem: Soc Gynec Invest; Perinatal Res Soc; NY Acad Sci; Am Col Obstetricians & Gynecologists. *Res:* Maternal-fetal medicine; morphophysiology of utero-placental unit. *Mailing Add:* Cook County Hosp 1825 W Harrison St Chicago IL 60612

FREESTON, W DENNEY, JR, b Orange, NJ, May 8, 36; m 57; c 2. MECHANICAL ENGINEERING, TEXTILES. *Educ:* Princeton Univ, BS, 57, MS, 58, MA, 59, PhD(mech eng), 61. *Prof Exp:* Asst, Princeton Univ, 57-58; sr res assoc textile mech, Fabric Res Labs, Inc, Dedham, 60-65, asst dir appl mech, 65-69, assoc dir, 69-71; prof, A French Textile Sch, Br 76-80, PROF & DEAN ENG, GA INST TECHNOL, 80- *Honors & Awards:* Distinguished Achievement Award, Fiber Soc, 69. *Mem:* Fiber Soc; Am Soc Testing & Mat. *Res:* Mechanics of flexible fibrous strucures; fabric flammability. *Mailing Add:* Dept of Textile Eng GA Inst of Technol Atlanta GA 30322

FREEZE, ROY ALLAN, b Edmonton, Alta, May 23, 39; m 61; c 4. HYDROLOGY. *Educ:* Queen's Univ, BSc, 61; Univ Calif, Berkeley, MSc, 64, PhD(hydrol), 66. *Prof Exp:* Res scientist, Inland Waters Br, Can Dept Energy, Mines & Resources, 61-69; res staff mem hydrol, Thomas J Watson Res Ctr, IBM Corp, 70-73; assoc prof, 73-77, PROF GEOL SCI, UNIV OF BC, 77- *Honors & Awards:* Horton Award, Am Geophys Union, 70 & 72, Macelwane Award, 73; Meinzer Award, Geol Soc Am, 74. *Mem:* Am Geophys Union; Geol Soc Am. *Res:* Computer simulation of regional groundwater flow systems and hydrologic response models. *Mailing Add:* Dept of Geol Sci Univ BC Vancouver Can

FREGLY, MELVIN JAMES, b Patton, Pa, May 26, 25; m 56. PHYSIOLOGY. *Educ:* Bucknell Univ, BS & MS, 49; Univ Rochester, PhD(physiol), 52. *Prof Exp:* Instr physiol, Harvard Med Sch, 52-56; from asst prof to assoc prof, 56-65, asst dean grad studies, 67-72, prof physiol, 65-79, GRAD RES PROF, COL MED, UNIV FLA, 79- *Concurrent Pos:* Travel fels, Int Physiol Cong, 56, 59 & 62; mem coun high blood pressure, Am Heart Asn; consult, Strasenburgh Pharmaceut Co, NY, 65-67 & Environ Protection Agency, 76- *Mem:* Soc Exp Biol & Med; Am Physiol Soc; Am Soc Zool; Endocrine Soc; Am Thyroid Asn. *Res:* Cardiovascular hypertension; temperature regulation; behavioral physiology. *Mailing Add:* Dept of Physiol Univ of Fla Col of Med Gainesville FL 32610

FREHN, JOHN, b Shippensburg, Pa, Mar 17, 36; m 60; c 2. PHYSIOLOGY. *Educ:* Dickinson Col, BS, 58; Pa State Univ, MS, 60, PhD(zool), 62. *Prof Exp:* From asst prof to assoc prof, 62-70, PROF PHYSIOL, ILL STATE UNIV, 70- *Mem:* AAAS; Am Soc Zoologists. *Res:* Cellular metabolism in cold acclimation and hibernation in various species of mammals. *Mailing Add:* Dept of Biol Sci Ill State Univ Normal IL 61761

FREI, EMIL, III, b St Louis, Mo, Feb 21, 24; m 48; c 5. INTERNAL MEDICINE. *Educ:* Yale Univ, MD, 48. *Prof Exp:* Intern, Univ Hosp, St Louis, 48-49, resident path, 52-53, resident internal med, 53-55; head, Chemother Serv, chief, Med Br & assoc sci dir, Nat Cancer Inst, 55-65; assoc dir, Univ Tex M D Anderson Hosp & Tumor Inst, 65-73; DIR & PHYSICIAN-IN-CHIEF, SIDNEY FARBER CANCER INST, 73-; PROF MED, HARVARD MED SCH, BOSTON, MASS, 80- *Honors & Awards:* Lasker Award, 72. *Mem:* Inst Med-Nat Acad Sci; Am Soc Clin Invest; Am Asn Cancer Res (pres, 71-72); Asn Am Physicians. *Res:* Cancer medicine and chemotherapy - pharmacology. *Mailing Add:* Sidney Farber Cancer Inst 44 Binney St Boston MA 02115

FREI, JAROSLAV VACLAV, b Prague, Czech, Mar 7, 29; Can citizen; m 55; c 5. PATHOLOGY. *Educ:* Charles Univ, Prague, MUC, 49; Queen's Univ, Ont, MD, CM, 56; McGill Univ, MSc, 60, PhD(path), 62; FRCP(C), MRC. *Prof Exp:* Life Ins Med Res Fund fel, McGill Univ, 59-61, Nat Cancer Inst Can fel, 61-62, asst prof path, 62-66; asst prof, Cancer Res Lab, 66-70, assoc prof, Univ, 70-75, PROF PATH, UNIV WESTERN ONT, 75- *Concurrent Pos:* Nat Cancer Inst Can res assoc, 63-66; Eleanor Roosevelt fel, Med Res Coun Toxicol Unit, UK, 66; pathologist, Univ Hosp, London, 72-; vis scientist, Chester Beatty Res Inst, London, 73-74. *Mem:* Am Asn Cancer Res; Am Soc Exp Path; Can Soc Cell Biol; Can Asn Path. *Res:* Experimental carcinogenesis in mice; nitroso compound carcinogenesis; gastroentrological pathology. *Mailing Add:* Dept of Path Univ of Western Ont London Can

FREIBERG, SAMUEL ROBERT, b Staten Island, NY, Apr 14, 24; m 49; c 2. PLANT PHYSIOLOGY, BIOLOGY. *Educ:* Rutgers Univ, BSc, 48, PhD(plant physiol), 51. *Prof Exp:* Res assoc hort, Rutgers Univ, 51-52; plant physiologist div trop res, United Fruit Co, Honduras, 52-57, head plant physiol cent res labs, Mass, 58-60, asst dir res, 60-62, dir labs, 62-65; consult, IRI Res Inst, Inc, 65, dir res, 65-79, vpres, 66-79, MEM BD TRUSTEES, IRI RES INST, INC, 74-; AGRICULTURIST, WORLD BANK, WASHINGTON, DC, 79- *Concurrent Pos:* Vis fel plant physiol, Cornell Univ, 57-58; consult World Bank, Spain 71, Indonesia, 72, Malaysia, 74 & Mexico, 75. *Mem:* AAAS; Am Soc Plant Physiol; Am Soc Hort Sci; Technol; Asn Trop Biol. *Res:* Plant nutrition and growth; post harvest fruit physiology; plant, animal and fruit productivity. *Mailing Add:* World Bank 1818 H St Washington DC 20433

FREIBERGER, WALTER FREDERICK, b Vienna, Austria, Feb 20, 24; nat US; m 56; c 3. APPLIED MATHEMATICS. *Educ:* Univ Melbourne, BA, 47, MA, 49; Cambridge Univ, PhD(math), 53. *Prof Exp:* Sci res officer, Aeronaut Res Lab, Australian Dept Supply, 47-49, sr sci res officer, 53-54; res assoc, 55-56, from asst prof to assoc prof, 56-64, dir ctr comput & info sci, 68-76, PROF APPL MATH, BROWN UNIV, 64-, CHMN DIV, 76- *Concurrent Pos:* Tutor, Dept Math, Univ Melbourne, 47-49; Fulbright fel, 55; Guggenheim fel, Inst Math Statist, Univ Stockholm, 62-63; dir comput lab, Brown Univ, 63-68; managing ed, Quart Appl Math, 66-; ed-in-chief, Int Dictionary Appl Math. *Mem:* Am Math Soc; Asn Comput Mach; Inst Math Statist; Soc Indust & Appl Math. *Res:* Computational probability and statistics; pattern analysis. *Mailing Add:* 24 Alumni Ave Providence RI 02906

FREIBURG, RICHARD EIGHME, b Milwaukee, Wis, Apr 2, 23; m 50; c 4. ZOOLOGY, ECOLOGY. *Educ:* Univ Kans, BA, 49, MA, 51; Ore State Col, PhD(zool), 54. *Prof Exp:* Asst instr zool, Univ Kans, 49-51 & Ore State Col, 51-54; asst prof biol, Washburn Univ, Topeka, 54-57; from asst prof to assoc prof, 57-67, PROF BIOL, MacMURRAY COL, 67-, HEAD DEPT, 70- *Mem:* Am Soc Mammal; Am Soc Ichthyologists & Herpetologists; Ecol Soc Am. *Res:* Herpetology; ecological studies on reptiles and amphibians. *Mailing Add:* Dept of Biol MacMurray Col Jacksonville IL 62650

FREIDBERG, JEFFREY PHILIP, plasma physics, see previous edition

FREIDINGER, ROGER MERLIN, b Pekin, Ill, July 26, 47; m 69. ORGANIC CHEMISTRY, PEPTIDE CHEMISTRY. *Educ:* Univ Ill, Urbana, BS, 69; Mass Inst Technol, PhD(org chem), 75. *Prof Exp:* sr res chemist, 75-80, RES FEL, MERCK & CO INC, 80- *Mem:* Am Chem Soc; AAAS. *Res:* Design and synthesis of biologically active peptides; conformationally constrained peptide analogs. *Mailing Add:* Merck Sharp & Dohme Res Labs West Point PA 19486

FREIDLINE, CHARLES EUGENE, b San Francisco, Calif, Oct 5, 37; m 60. INORGANIC CHEMISTRY, ANALYTICAL CHEMISTRY. *Educ:* Westmont Col, BA, 60; Univ Minn, MS, 63, PhD(inorg chem), 66. *Prof Exp:* ASSOC PROF CHEM, CENT METHODIST COL, 65- *Concurrent Pos:* Nat Acad Sci grant; fel biochem, Univ Mo, 74-75. *Mem:* Am Chem Soc. *Res:* Determination of stability constants of complex ions in solution; stabilized complexes of lead IV; analytical chemistry of biogenic amines and amine oxidation products. *Mailing Add:* Dept of Chem Cent Methodist Col Fayette MO 65248

FREIER, ESTHER FAY, b Hibbing, Minn, Mar 3, 25. PHYSIOLOGICAL CHEMISTRY. *Educ:* Univ Minn, BS, 46, MS, 56. *Prof Exp:* From instr to assoc prof, 51-68, PROF MED TECHNOL, UNIV MINN, MINNEAPOLIS, 68-, CHEMIST, UNIV HOSP, 57- *Mem:* AAAS; Am Chem Soc; Am Soc Med Technol; Am Asn Clin Chemists. *Res:* Clinical chemistry methodology and quality control; proteins and enzymes. *Mailing Add:* Dept of Lab Med Univ of Minn Minneapolis MN 55455

FREIER, GEORGE DAVID, b Ellsworth, Wis, Jan 22, 15; m 43; c 2. ATMOSPHERIC PHYSICS. *Educ:* Wis State Col, River Falls, BS, 38; Univ Minn, MA, 44, PhD(physics), 49. *Prof Exp:* Res physicist, Naval Ord Lab, 44-46; from asst prof to assoc prof, 50-67, PROF PHYSICS, UNIV MINN, MINNEAPOLIS, 67- *Mem:* AAAS; Am Phys Soc; Am Asn Physics Teachers; Am Geophys Union; Am Meteorol Soc. *Res:* Atmospheric electricity. *Mailing Add:* 238 Physics Bldg Univ of Minn Minneapolis MN 55455

FREIER, HERBERT EDWARD, b Delmont, SDak, Mar 19, 21; m 55; c 2. ANALYTICAL CHEMISTRY. *Educ:* Yankton Col, BA, 43; Univ Ill, PhD(org chem), 46. *Prof Exp:* Asst chem, Univ Ill, 43-44, spec asst, 44-46; from asst prof to assoc prof, Univ NDak, 46-50; mem staff, Cent Res, 50-54, supvr anal sect, 54-55 & org sect, 55-57, sect leader tech info serv, 57-60, mgr res serv, 60-74, DIR ANAL & PROPERTIES RES LAB, MINN MINING & MFG CO, 74- *Mem:* Am Chem Soc. *Res:* Organic synthesis and analysis. *Mailing Add:* 3M Ctr PO Box 33221 St Paul MN 55133

FREIER, JEROME BERNARD, b New York, NY, May 6, 16. MATHEMATICS. *Educ:* City Col NY, BS, 39; NY Univ, PhD(math), 58. *Prof Exp:* Asst physics, NY Univ, 47-49; instr math, St Peter's Col, 50-53; asst prof, Rensselaer Polytech Inst, 53-65; ASSOC PROF MATH, SOUTHEASTERN MASS UNIV, 65- *Mem:* AAAS; Am Phys Soc; Am Math Soc. *Res:* Analysis; applied mathematics. *Mailing Add:* Dept of Math Southeastern Mass Univ North Dartmouth MA 02747

FREIER, PHYLLIS S, b Minneapolis, Minn, Jan 19, 21; m 43; c 2. PHYSICS. *Educ:* Univ Minn, BS, 42, MA, 44, PhD(physics), 50. *Prof Exp:* Physicist, Naval Ord Lab, 44-45; res assoc, 50-70, assoc prof, 70-75, PROF PHYSICS, UNIV MINN, MINNEAPOLIS, 75- *Mem:* AAAS; Am Astron Soc; Am Geophys Union; fel Am Phys Soc. *Res:* Cosmic rays. *Mailing Add:* Dept of Physics Univ of Minn Minneapolis MN 55455

FREIFELDER, DAVID, b Philadelphia, Pa, July 19, 35; m 65; c 2. MOLECULAR BIOLOGY. *Educ:* Univ Chicago, BS, 57, PhD(biophys), 59. *Prof Exp:* Physicist, Diamond Ord Lab, 56-58; res assoc biophys, Mass Inst Technol, 60-61; USPHS fel, Univ Inst Microbiol, Copenhagen, 62; res assoc biophys, Mass Inst Technol, 63; Donner Lab, Univ Calif, Berkeley, 63-66; USPHS career develop award, 66-70, assoc prof, 70-74, PROF BIOCHEM, BRANDEIS UNIV, 74- *Res:* Synthesis and physical properties of nucleic acids. *Mailing Add:* Dept of Biochem Brandeis Univ Waltham MA 02154

FREILICH, GERALD, b Brooklyn, NY, Dec 29, 26; m 53; c 2. MATHEMATICS. *Educ:* City Col New York, BS, 46; Brown Univ, MS, 47, PhD(math), 49. *Prof Exp:* Asst math, Brown Univ, 46-48, instr, 49-50; from instr to prof, City Col New York, 50-71, chmn dept, 66-70; PROF MATH, QUEENS COL, NY, 71- *Mem:* Am Math Soc; Math Asn Am. *Res:* Measure theory; theory of convex sets; operations research. *Mailing Add:* 1619 E 21st St Brooklyn NY 11210

FREILICH, JOSEPH KENNETH, b Chicago, Ill, Feb 10, 18; m 46; c 3. INTERNAL MEDICINE. *Educ:* Univ Chicago, MD, 41. *Prof Exp:* From asst prof to prof med, Chicago Med Sch, 48-71; ASSOC PROF MED, STRITCH SCH MED, LOYOLA UNIV, 71-; ATTEND PHYSICIAN & DIR, DEPT OF INHALATION THERAPY & PULMONARY PHYSIOL LAB, ST JOSEPH HOSP, 71- *Concurrent Pos:* Adj, Chest Dept, Michael Reese Hosp, 51-59, attend physician, 59-71; assoc med, Mt Sinai Hosp, 54-71. *Mem:* Fel Am Col Physicians; fel Am Col Chest Physicians. *Res:* Chest diseases. *Mailing Add:* Suite 1345 55 E Washington St Chicago IL 60602

FREILING, EDWARD CLAWSON, b San Francisco, Calif, Aug 11, 22; m 48; c 7. ENVIRONMENTAL SCIENCE. *Educ:* Univ San Francisco, BS, 43; Univ Calif, MS, 47; Stanford Univ, PhD(chem), 51. *Prof Exp:* Asst prof chem, St Mary's Col, Calif, 49-51; sr investr, US Naval Radiol Defense Lab, 51-68, head, Anal Br, 69-74, RES PHYSICIST & CHEMIST, US NAVAL SURFACE WEAPONS CTR, 74- *Honors & Awards:* Super Civilian Serv Award, Chief Naval Mat, 68. *Res:* Ion exchange; radiochemical analysis; nuclear detonation phenomena; fused salt chemistry; kinetics; modeling chemical perturbation of the ionosphere; environmental science, baseline studies, impact assessment; software engineering. *Mailing Add:* US Naval Surface Weapons Ctr Code G-50 Dahlgren VA 22448

FREILING, MICHAEL JOSEPH, b San Francisco, Calif, Mar 19, 50. COMPUTER SCIENCE, ARTIFICIAL INTELLIGENCE. *Educ:* Univ San Francisco, BS, 72; Mass Inst Technol, PhD(appl math), 77. *Prof Exp:* Luce scholar comput sci, Kyoto Univ, 77-78; ASST PROF COMPUT SCI, ORE STATE UNIV, 78- *Mem:* Asn Comput Mach; Sigma Xi; Affil Advert Agencies; Anal & Comput Lab; Inst Int Elec & Electronics Engrs Comput Soc. *Res:* Applications of artificial intelligence techniques to problems of description of mechanical systems and transfer of knowledge between domains of expertise; architecture and development of semantic database systems. *Mailing Add:* Dept of Comput Sci Ore State Univ Corvallis OR 97331

FREIMAN, CHARLES, b New York, NY, June 17, 32; m 55; c 4. COMPUTER SCIENCE. *Educ:* Columbia Univ, AB, 54, BS, 55, MS, 56, ScD(eng), 61. *Prof Exp:* Instr elec eng, Columbia Univ, 56-60; mem res staff, 60-65, develop engr, Systs Develop Div, 65-68, MEM RES STAFF COMPUT SCI, T J WATSON RES CTR, IBM CORP, 68- *Concurrent Pos:* Ed, Info Processing, Int Fedn Info Processing, 71. *Mem:* AAAS; Asn Comput Mach; Inst Elec & Electronic Engrs; Int Fedn Info Processing. *Res:* Discrete information theory; computer arithmetic; computer system maintainability. *Mailing Add:* Palmer Lane Pleasantville NY 10570

FREIMAN, DAVID GALLAND, b New York, NY, July 1, 11; m 49; c 2. PATHOLOGY. *Educ:* City Col New York, AB, 30; Long Island Col Med, MD, 35. *Hon Degrees:* AM, Harvard Univ, 62. *Prof Exp:* Intern & resident path, Montefiore Hosp, 38-43; asst pathologist, Mass Gen Hosp, 44-50; from asst prof to assoc prof path, Col Med, Univ Cincinnati, 50-56; pathologist in chief, Beth Israel Hosp, 56-79; from clin prof to prof, 56-69, MALLINCKRODT PROF PATH, HARVARD MED SCH, 69-; EMER PATHOLOGIST IN CHIEF, BETH ISRAEL HOSP, 79- *Concurrent Pos:* Instr, Med Sch, Tufts Univ, 47 & 48 & Harvard Med Sch, 49 & 50; attend pathologist, Cincinnati Gen & Drake Mem Hosps, 52-56 & Vet Admin Hosps, Ohio & Ky, 54-56; consult, Vet Admin Hosp, Boston, 62-, Cambridge Hosp, 68- & Children's Hosp Med Ctr, 77-; lectr path, Simmons Col, 62-78; Kirstein fel med educ, Harvard Univ, 71-72; mem joint fac, Prog Health Sci & Technol, Harvard Univ-Mass Inst Technol, 75-79; vis prof path, Imperial Med Ctr Iran, 78; spec asst to pres, Beth Israel Hosp, 79- *Mem:* Am Asn Pathologists; Am Soc Clin Path; Histochem Soc; Int Acad Path; Int Soc Thrombosis & Hemostasis. *Res:* Histochemistry; pulmonary disease; sarcoidosis; cardiovascular and thromboembolic disease; medical education. *Mailing Add:* Dept of Path Beth Israel Hosp Boston MA 02215

FREIMAN, STEPHEN WEIL, b Alexandria, La, Jan 21, 42; m 69. CERAMICS. *Educ:* Ga Inst Technol, BChE, 63, MS, 66; Univ Fla, PhD(metall, mat eng), 68. *Prof Exp:* Assoc res scientist, IIT Res Inst, 68-71; mem staff, Ocean Technol Div, Naval Res Lab, 71-78; RES SCIENTIST, NAT BUR STANDARDS, 78- *Mem:* AAAS; Am Ceramic Soc; Sigma Xi; Am Soc Testing & Mat. *Res:* Structure and properties of glass ceramics; structure of glass; mechanical properties of glasses and ceramics; fracture mechanics of glass and ceramics; stress corrosion. *Mailing Add:* Nat Bur Standards Fracture & Deformation Div Washington DC 20234

FREIMANIS, ATIS K, b Riga, Latvia, Mar 28, 25; US citizen; m 51; c 3. RADIOLOGY. *Educ:* Univ Hamburg, Dr Med, 51. *Prof Exp:* From instr to prof, Col Med, Ohio State Univ, 58-70; prof radiol & chmn dept, Med Col Ohio, 70-76; PROF RADIOL & CHMN DEPT, COL MED, OHIO STATE UNIV, 76- *Concurrent Pos:* Consult, Juv Diag Ctr, 51-70, Brown Vet Admin Hosp, Dayton, 63-70 & 76- & Chillicothe Vet Admin Hosp, 64-70. *Mem:* Am Col Radiol; Radiol Soc NAm; Asn Univ Radiol; Am Roentgen Ray Soc; Am Inst Ultrasonics in Med. *Res:* Ultrasonic diagnosis of abdominal diseases; teaching programs in radiology. *Mailing Add:* Dept of Radiol Col of Med Ohio State Univ 410 W 10th Ave Columbus OH 43210

FREIMER, EARL HOWARD, b New York, NY, Nov 15, 26; m 48; c 4. MICROBIOLOGY, INFECTIOUS DISEASES. *Educ:* Univ Mich, AB, 48; State Univ NY, MD, 55; Univ Cambridge, MA, 78. *Prof Exp:* Intern, Columbia Med Serv, Bellevue Hosp, 55-56, asst resident, 56-57; res assoc, Rockefeller Inst & asst physician, Hosp, 57-61; asst prof, Rockefeller Univ & assoc physician, Hosp, 61-68; PROF INTERNAL MED, DIR DIV INFECTIOUS DIS & PROF MICROBIOL & CHMN DEPT, MED COL OHIO, 68- *Concurrent Pos:* Vis assoc prof, State Univ NY Downstate Med Ctr & assoc vis physician, Kings County Hosp, 67-68; vis prof, Col Med, Pa State Univ, 68-69; consult, Toledo Hosp, Ohio, 68-, Mercy Hosp, 70- & St Luke's Hosp, 78-; mem, Adv Panel Infectious Dis, US Pharmacopial Conv, 80-; grants, NIH, Schering-Plough Corp, Lilly Res Labs, Merck & Co, 79-81. *Mem:* AAAS; Am Soc Microbiol; Am Asn Immunol; Infectious Dis Soc Am; fel Am Col Cardiol. *Res:* Biology of group A streptococcus; pathogenesis of rheumatic fever; bacterial L-forms and protoplasts; bacterial cell walls and membranes; immunochemistry of bacterial antigens; mechanisms of action of antimicrobial agents; immunocytochemistry of cardiac muscle; immunology of connective tissue diseases; biology of the pneumococcus. *Mailing Add:* Dept Microbiol Med Col Ohio C S 10008 Toledo OH 43699

FREIMER, MARSHALL LEONARD, b New York, NY, May 6, 32; m 61; c 2. MATHEMATICS. *Educ:* Harvard Univ, AB, 53, AM, 54, PhD(math), 60. *Prof Exp:* Mem staff, Lincoln Lab, Mass Inst Technol, 57-61; mem tech staff, Inst Naval Studies, 61-63; ASSOC PROF BUS ADMIN, GRAD SCH MGT, UNIV ROCHESTER, 63- *Concurrent Pos:* Ford Found fac fel, 65-66. *Mem:* Inst Math Statist; Math Asn Am. *Res:* Operations research, especially mathematical programming and decision analysis. *Mailing Add:* Grad Sch Mgt Univ Rochester Rochester NY 14627

FREIMUTH, HENRY CHARLES, b New York, NY, June 24, 12; wid; c 5. CHEMISTRY, FORENSIC SCIENCE. *Educ:* City Col New York, BS, 32; NY Univ, MS, 33, PhD(chem), 38. *Prof Exp:* Asst instr chem, Wash Sq Col, NY Univ, 37-38, asst therapeut, Sch Med, 38-39; from jr chemist to prin chemist & spec agent, Fed Bur Invest, US Dept Justice, Washington, DC, 39-44; toxicologist, Md State Post-Mortem Examr, 44-72; prof, 72-78, chmn, Dept Chem, 77-78, EMER PROF CHEM, LOYOLA COL, 78- *Concurrent Pos:* Instr, Loyola Col, Md, 46-56, prof lectr, 56-68, adj prof, 68-72; from asst prof to assoc prof legal med, Sch Med, Univ Md, 53-72, adj assoc prof pharmacol & toxicol, Sch Pharm, 70-; consult, Baltimore Poison Control Ctr, 56-; assoc div forensic path, Sch Hyg & Pub Health, Johns Hopkins Univ, 65-72. *Mem:* AAAS; Am Chem Soc; Am Acad Forensic Sci; Int Asn Forensic Toxicologists; Sigma Xi. *Res:* Carbon monoxide poisoning; alcoholic intoxication; detection of organic poisons in tissues; drowning tests; asphyxia; boric acid poisoning. *Mailing Add:* 1402 Gibsonwood Rd Catonsville MD 21228

FREINKEL, NORBERT, b Mannheim, Ger, Jan 26, 26; m 55; c 3. INTERNAL MEDICINE, ENDOCRINOLOGY. *Educ:* Princeton Univ, AB, 47; NY Univ, MD, 49. *Hon Degrees:* MD, Uppsala Univ, Sweden, 81. *Prof Exp:* Intern & asst resident med, Bellevue Hosp, New York, 49-50; from instr to asst prof med, Harvard Med Sch, 56-66; KETTERING PROF MED, CHIEF SECT ENDOCRINOL & METAB & DIR ENDOCRINE CLINS, NORTHWESTERN UNIV-McGAW MED CTR, 66-, PROF BIOCHEM, 69-, DIR CTR ENDOCRINOL, METAB & NUTRIT, 73- *Concurrent Pos:* Am Cancer Soc fel, 53-55; Nat Found Infantile Paralysis fel, 55-56; Agr Res Coun vis scientist, Inst Animal Physiol, Cambridge, Eng, 55-56 & 69-70; investr, Howard Hughes Med Inst, 56-65; asst physician & dir diabetes & metab div, Thorndike Mem Lab, Boston City Hosp, 57-66; consult, Qm Corps, US Army, 57-62, consult, Surgeon Gen, 62-79; vis prof, Wash Univ, 64; mem metab study sect, Div Res Grants, NIH, 67-69, chmn, 70, mem subcomt diabetes, Fogarty Int Ctr, 72-76; mem nat adv coun alcoholism, NIMH, 67-70; vis scientist, Agr Res Coun, Inst Animal Physiol, Cambridge, 69-70; mem comt renal & metab effects of space flight, Space Sci Bd, Nat Acad Sci, 73-74; mem endocrinol & metab adv comt, Bur Drugs, 73-76; consult, FDA, 76-; mem career develop comn, Vet Admin, Washington, DC, 75-77; chmn, Am Zone Prog Comt IX & XI Cong, Int Diabetes Fedn, 76-82. *Honors & Awards:* Lilly Medal & Award, Am Diabetes Asn, 66; Banting Award, Am Diabetes Asn, 78 & 80, Banting lectr, 74 & 80; Kellion Medalist, Australian Diabetes Soc, 81. *Mem:* Asn Am Physicians; Am Soc Clin Invest; Endocrine Soc; Am Diabetes Asn (pres elec, 76-77, pres, 77-78); Soc Exp Biol & Med. *Res:* Hormone transport; gluconeogenic regulation; metabolism of endogenous fuels; alcohol; hypoglycemic disorders; intermediary metabolism in pregnancy; peptide hormone action. *Mailing Add:* Ctr Endocrinol Metab & Nutrit Northwestern Univ Med Sch Chicago IL 60611

FREINKEL, RUTH KIMMELSTIEL, b Hamburg, Ger, Dec 26, 26; US citizen; m 55; c 3. MEDICINE. *Educ:* Randolph Macon Col, AB, 48; Duke Univ, MD, 52; Am Bd Dermat, dipl, 61. *Prof Exp:* Res fel biochem, Harvard Med Sch, 54-55; res fel, Cambridge Univ, 55-56; res fel dermat, Harvard Med Sch, 58-60, instr, 60-61, assoc, 61-64, asst prof, 64-66; assoc prof, 66-72, PROF DERMAT, MED SCH, NORTHWESTERN UNIV, CHICAGO, 72- *Mem:* Am Soc Clin Invest; Soc Invest Dermat; Am Dermat Asn; Am Acad Dermat. *Res:* Intermediate and lipid metabolism of skin; pathogenesis of acne. *Mailing Add:* Dept of Dermat Northwestern Univ Med Sch Chicago IL 60611

FREIRE, ERNESTO I, b Lima, Peru, July 28, 49; m 75; c 1. BIOPHYSICS, BIOCHEMISTRY. *Educ:* Univ Cayetano Heredia, Peru, BS, 72, MS, 73; Univ Va, PhD(biophys), 77. *Prof Exp:* Res assoc biophys, Univ Va, 77-78, vis asst prof, 78-81; ASST PROF BIOCHEM, UNIV TENN, KNOXVILLE, 82- *Mem:* Biophys Soc; Am Chem Soc. *Res:* Statistical mechanics and thermodynamics of conformational transitions in proteins, nucleic acids and model membrane systems; organization and function of biological membranes; computer modeling of biological structures; scanning calorimetry. *Mailing Add:* Dept Biochem Univ Tenn Knoxville TN 37916

FREIREICH, ABRAHAM WALTER, b New York, NY, July 27, 06; m 32; c 2. INTERNAL MEDICINE. *Educ:* City Col New York, BS, 28; NY Univ, MD, 32; Am Bd Internal Med, dipl, 44. *Prof Exp:* Asst toxicologist to Dr A O Gettler, NY, 32-38; toxicologist, 38-66, CHIEF TOXICOLOGIST, NASSAU COUNTY MED EXAMR OFF, 66- *Concurrent Pos:* Asst prof clin med, Post-Grad Med Sch, NY Univ, 46-60, assoc attend physician, Univ Hosp, 52-60; assoc vis physician, Bellevue Hosp, 46-60; chief med, Brunswick Hosp, Amityville, 48-; consult physician, Southside Hosp, Bay Shore, 53-, Nassau Hosp, Mineola, 54-, Long Beach Mem Hosp, 54- & St Francis Hosp & Sanitorium, Roslyn, 56-62; dir div internal med, Meadowbrook Hosp, 56-66, dir & consult toxicologist, Poison Control Ctr, 58-65, chmn dept internal med & emer physician, 66-; consult, Mercy Hosp, Rockville Centre, 62- & South Nassau Community Hosp, Oceanside, 62- *Mem:* Fel Am Col Physicians; Am Acad Forensic Sci (pres, 54-55). *Res:* Toxicology; thrombophlebitis; thiocyanate therapy of hypertension; hydrogen sulfide poisoning; tetanus. *Mailing Add:* 180 Hempstead Ave Malverne NY 11565

FREIREICH, EMIL J, b Chicago, Ill, Mar 16, 27; m 53; c 4. HEMATOLOGY, INTERNAL MEDICINE. *Educ:* Univ Ill, BS, 47, MD, 49; Am Bd Internal Med, dipl, 57. *Prof Exp:* Intern, Cook County Hosp, 49-51; resident internal med, Presby Hosp, Chicago, 51-53; asst med, Boston Univ, 53-55; sr investr, Nat Cancer Inst, 55-65, head leukemia serv, 64-65;

asst head dept develop therapeut, 65-72, PROF MED & CHIEF SECT RES HEMAT, UNIV TEX M D ANDERSON HOSP & TUMOR INST, 65-, HEAD DEPT DEVELOP THERAPEUT, SYST CANCER CTR, 72-, PROF MED, UNIV TEX MED SCH HOUSTON, 75-, RUTH HARRIET AIMSWORTH PROF, 81- *Concurrent Pos:* Asst, Univ Ill, 51-53; res assoc, Evans Mem Hosp, 53-55. *Mem:* Fel Am Col Physicians; Am Soc Hemat; Am Asn Cancer Res; Am Soc Clin Invest; Am Soc Clin Oncol. *Res:* Chemotherapy and natural history of human acute leukemia; platelet and leukocyte transfusion and physiology. *Mailing Add:* Dept of Develop Therapeut M D Anderson Hosp & Tumor Inst Houston TX 77030

FREIS, EDWARD DAVID, b Chicago, Ill, May 13, 12; m 34; c 3. MEDICINE. *Educ:* Univ Ariz, BS, 36; Columbia Univ, MD, 40. *Prof Exp:* Intern med, Mass Mem Hosp, Boston, 40-41; sr intern & house physician, Boston City Hosp, 41-42; asst resident, Evans Mem Hosp, 46-47, res fel cardiovasc dis, 47-49; asst chief med, Vet Admin Hosp, 49-54, chief, 54-59; adj clin prof, 49-57, assoc prof, 57-63, PROF MED, SCH MED, GEORGETOWN UNIV, 63-, CHIEF CARDIOVASC RES LAB, UNIV HOSP, 49-; SR MED INVESTR, VET ADMIN HOSP, 59- *Concurrent Pos:* Instr, Sch Med, Boston Univ, 47-49. *Honors & Awards:* Ciba Award, 81. *Mem:* Am Soc Clin Invest. *Res:* Clinical evaluation and hemodynamic analysis of hypotensive drugs; blood and fluid volume changes in disease; cardiovascular physiology in man. *Mailing Add:* Vet Admin Hosp 50 Irving St NW Washington DC 20422

FREIS, ROBERT P, b San Francisco, Calif, Oct 6, 31; m 55; c 2. COMPUTATIONAL PLASMA PHYSICS. *Educ:* Univ Calif, Los Angeles, BS, 59; Univ Calif, Berkeley, MS, 64. *Prof Exp:* PHYSICIST, LAWRENCE LIVERMORE NAT LAB, 59- *Res:* Computational plasma physics problems related to the magnetic fusion energy program with emphasis on the development and application of numerical simulation techniques. *Mailing Add:* Lawrence Livermore Nat Lab L-630 PO Box 808 Livermore CA 94550

FREISE, EARL J, b Chicago, Ill, Dec 30, 35; m 58; c 4. MATERIALS SCIENCE, METALLURGY. *Educ:* Ill Inst Technol, BS, 58; Northwestern Univ, MS, 59; Cambridge Univ, PhD(metall), 62. *Prof Exp:* From asst prof to assoc prof mat sci, Northwestern Univ, 62-77; adj prof mech eng & dir, Off Res & Prog Develop, Univ NDak, 77-81; ASST VCHANCELLOR RES & PROF MECH ENG, UNIV NEBR, LINCOLN, 82- *Mem:* Am Soc Metals; Am Inst Mining, Metall & Petrol Engrs; Am Soc Eng Educ; Soc Res Adminstrs. *Res:* Phase transformations in materials; physical and mechanical properties of high temperature metallic and nonmetallic materials. *Mailing Add:* Univ Nebr Lincoln NE 68508

FREISER, HENRY, b New York, NY, Aug 27, 20; m 42; c 3. ANALYTICAL CHEMISTRY. *Educ:* City Col New York, BS, 41; Duke Univ, MA, 42, PhD(phys chem), 44. *Prof Exp:* Prof anal & phys chem & chmn dept, NDak State Col, 44-45; res fel, Mellon Inst, 45-46; instr anal chem, Univ Pittsburgh, 46-50, from asst prof to assoc prof, 50-58; head dept, 58-67, PROF CHEM, UNIV ARIZ, 58- *Concurrent Pos:* Mem, Comn Equilibrium Data, Anal Div, Int Union Pure & Appl Chem; O M Smith lectr, 68. *Mem:* Am Chem Soc; Am Soc Testing & Mat; fel The Chem Soc. *Res:* Analytical separations processes and solvent extraction; trace analysis; metal chelates. *Mailing Add:* Dept of Chem Univ of Ariz Tucson AZ 85721

FREISER, MARVIN JOSEPH, b Brooklyn, NY, Feb 9, 26; m 49; c 1. THEORETICAL PHYSICS. *Educ:* Brooklyn Col, BS, 48; Purdue Univ, MS, 51, PhD(physics), 55. *Prof Exp:* Asst prof physics, Worcester Polytech Inst, 55-56; physicist, Midwestern Univs Res Asn, 56-57; assoc physicist, Res Lab, 57-64, RES PHYSICIST, WATSON RES CTR, IBM CORP, 64- *Mem:* Am Phys Soc. *Res:* Solid state physics; theory of magnetism; statistical mechanics; liquid crystals. *Mailing Add:* IBM Watson Res Ctr Box 218 Yorktown Heights NY 10598

FREISHEIM, JAMES HAROLD, b Tacoma, Wash, July 19, 37; m 58; c 2. BIOCHEMISTRY. *Educ:* Pac Lutheran Univ, BA, 60; Univ Wash, PhD(biochem), 66. *Prof Exp:* Res assoc biochem, Scripps Clin & Res Found, 66-69; asst prof, 69-72, assoc prof, 72-77, PROF BIOCHEM, COL MED, UNIV CINCINNATI, 78- *Concurrent Pos:* NIH trainee, 66-67; Am Cancer Soc fel, 67-68. *Mem:* AAAS; Am Soc Biol Chemists; NY Acad Sci; Am Chem Soc; Am Asn Cancer Res. *Res:* Relationship of protein structure to function; molecular properties and mechanism of action of folate-dependent enzymes; mechanism of drug resistance to folate antagonists. *Mailing Add:* Dept of Biochem Univ of Cincinnati Col of Med Cincinnati OH 45267

FREITAG, DEAN R(ICHARD), b Ft Dodge, Iowa, Oct 1, 26; m 52; c 4. CIVIL ENGINEERING, SOIL MECHANICS. *Educ:* Iowa State Univ, BS, 49; Harvard Univ, MS, 51; Auburn Univ, PhD(agr eng), 65. *Prof Exp:* Civil engr, Engr Waterways Exp Sta, US Army, 51-55, supv res civil engr, 55-70, asst tech dir, 70-72, tech dir, Cold Regions Res & Eng Lab, 72-81; ASSOC PROF CIVIL ENG, TENN TECHNOL UNIV, 81- *Concurrent Pos:* Engr, Mat & Res Lab, Calif Div Hwys, 53-54. *Honors & Awards:* US Army Meritorious Civilian Serv Award. *Mem:* Int Soc Terrain-Vehicle Systs; Am Soc Civil Engrs; Am Soc Agr Engrs. *Res:* Mechanics of soil-vehicle systems; behavior of soils under dynamic loading; roads and airfields; cold regions engineering. *Mailing Add:* Tenn Technol Univ Cookeville TN 38501

FREITAG, HARLOW, b New York, NY, Apr 17, 36. COMPUTER SCIENCE. *Educ:* NY Univ, AB, 55; Yale Univ, MS, 57, PhD(chem), 59. *Prof Exp:* Assoc, Data Processing Div, Int Bus Mach Corp, 58-59, mgr chem, Advan Systs Develop Div, 59-61, mem staff, Res Div, 61-63, mgr design automation, Comput Systs Dept, Thomas J Watson Res Ctr, 63-67, mgr subsysts & integration, 67-77, sr mgr tech planning, Res Div, 77-80, MEM INFO SYSTS & TECHNOL GROUP STAFF, IBM CORP, 80- *Mem:* Asn Comput Mach; fel Inst Elec & Electronics Engrs. *Res:* Digital computers. *Mailing Add:* IBM Corp 1000 Westchester Ave White Plains NY 10604

FREITAG, JULIA LOUISE, b Allentown, Pa, Nov 29, 27. PREVENTIVE MEDICINE, EPIDEMIOLOGY. *Educ:* Cornell Univ, AB, 49, MD, 53; Harvard Univ, MPH, 57. *Prof Exp:* Epidemiologist, 57-58, asst dir, Off Epidemiol, 58-66, dir, 66-70, dir, Off Med Manpower, 70-75, ASST COMNR, HEALTH MANPOWER GROUP, NY STATE DEPT HEALTH, 75- *Concurrent Pos:* Lectr, Rensselaer Polytech Inst, 62-70 & Albany Med Col, Uniion Univ, NY, 70-; mem, NY State Adv Coun Voc Educ, 71; mem, Epidemiol & Biomet Adv Comt, Nat Heart & Lung Inst, 72-74. *Res:* Communicable diseases; population studies and outbreak investigation; genetics; inheritance of blood groups. *Mailing Add:* NY State Dept Health Tower Bldg ESP Albany NY 12237

FREITAG, JULIUS HERMAN, b Berkeley, Calif, Jan 6, 08; m 35; c 4. ENTOMOLOGY. *Educ:* Univ Calif, BS, 31, MS, 32, PhD(entom), 35. *Prof Exp:* Jr entomologist, 35-42, from asst entomologist & asst prof to assoc entomologist & assoc prof entom & parasitol, 42-54, entomologist, 54-75, EMER PROF, EXP STA & PROF ENTOM & PARASITOL, UNIV CALIF, BERKELEY, 75- *Concurrent Pos:* Instr, Univ Calif, 39-42. *Mem:* AAAS; Entom Soc Am; Am Phytopath Soc; Am Inst Biol Sci; Brit Asn Appl Biol. *Res:* Insect transmission of plant viruses and mycoplasma; virus and mycoplasma diseases of vegetable crops. *Mailing Add:* Dept of Entom Sci Univ of Calif Berkeley CA 94709

FREITAG, ROBERT FREDERICK, b Jackson, Mich, Jan 20, 20; m 41; c 4. AERONAUTICAL & ASTRONAUTICAL ENGINEERING. *Educ:* Univ Mich, BSE, 41. *Prof Exp:* Aerodyn officer, bur aeronaut, Navy Dept, DC, 42-48; intel officer develop tech intel plans, Off Naval Attache, Eng, 48-49; chief tech systs labs, US Air Force Missile Test Ctr, Cape Canaveral, 49-51; prog plans officer, guided missiles div, bur aeronaut, Navy Dept, 51-53, dir surface launched missiles br, 53-55, dir ballistic missile br, 55, prog officer, off chief naval opers, 55-57, dir plans & requirements, US Navy Pac Missile Range, Calif, 57-59; astronaut officer, bur naval weapons, 59-63; dir launch vehicles & propulsion, 63, manned space flight ctr develop, 63-70, spec asst to assoc adminr manned space flight, 70-72, DEP DIR ADVAN PROGS, OFF MANNED SPACE FLIGHT, NASA, 73- *Concurrent Pos:* Mem subcomt propellers, Nat Adv Comt Aeronaut, 44-46 & spec comt space technol, 58-59; mem, Joint Army-Navy Ballistic Missile Comt, 55-57; mem spec comt adequacy range facilities, Secy Defense, 56-58; mem res adv comt missile & spacecraft aerodyn, NASA, 60-63; mem launch vehicles panel, aeroanut & astronaut coord bd, Joint Defense Dept-NASA, 60-64. *Honors & Awards:* Bronze Medal, Brit Interplanetary Soc, 79. *Mem:* Fel Am Inst Aeronaut & Astronaut; fel Royal Aeronaut Soc. *Res:* Aeronautics and astronautics, especially in aerodynamics, guided missile guidance, rocket propulsion, range testing and instrumentation. *Mailing Add:* Off Space Transportation Systs NASA 600 Independence Ave SW Washington DC 20546

FREIWALD, RONALD CHARLES, b Pittsburgh, Pa, July 21, 43. TOPOLOGY. *Educ:* Washington & Jefferson Col, AB, 65; Univ Rochester, PhD(math), 70. *Prof Exp:* ASSOC PROF MATH, WASHINGTON UNIV, 70- *Mem:* Am Math Soc; Math Asn Am. *Res:* Mapping properties of absolute Borel sets. *Mailing Add:* Dept of Math Washington Univ St Louis MO 63130

FRELINGER, JEFFREY, b Brooklyn, NY, July 16, 48; m 70; c 1. IMMUNOGENETICS, IMMUNOBIOLOGY. *Educ:* Univ Calif, San Diego, BA, 69; Calif Inst Technol, PhD(immunol), 73. *Prof Exp:* Jane Coffin Childs fel immunogenetics, Dept Human Genetics, Univ Mich, 73-75; asst prof, 75-78, ASSOC PROF IMMUNOGENETICS, DEPT MICROBIOL, SCH MED, UNIV SOUTHERN CALIF, 78- *Concurrent Pos:* Fac res award, Am Cancer Soc, 78-; mem, Mammalian Genetics Study Sect, NIH, 79-; vis worker, Radiobiol Unit, Med Res Coun, Horwell, 80. *Mem:* Genetics Soc Am; Sigma Xi; AAAS; Am Asn Immunologists. *Res:* Role of mouse major histocompatibility gene products in the development and regulation of immune responses. *Mailing Add:* Dept of Microbiol Sch of Med 2025 Zonal Los Angeles CA 90033

FREMLING, CALVIN R, b Brainerd, Minn, Nov 13, 29; m 54; c 1. LIMNOLOGY, ENTOMOLOGY. *Educ:* St Cloud State Col, BS, 51, MS, 55; Iowa State Univ, PhD(zool), 59. *Prof Exp:* Sci teacher high sch, Minn, 51-52; ecologist, Univ Utah, Dugway Proving Ground, 52-54; instr zool & bot, Eveleth Jr Col, 55-56; PROF BIOL, WINONA STATE COL, 59- *Concurrent Pos:* Minn Acad Sci vis scientist, High Schs, 50-; NSF res grant, 61-64 & 69-70; consult, USPHS, 62-, Int Joint Comn, 62, Metrop Structures Can, Montreal, 66-69 & Nasco Inc, Wis, 67-; Am Inst Biol Sci vis scientist, Cols, 63-71; Fed Water Pollution Control Admin grant, 66-70. *Mem:* AAAS; Entom Soc Am; Am Soc Limnol & Oceanog; Nat Asn Biol Teachers; Wildlife Soc. *Res:* Ecology of the Mississippi River; biology of Hexagenia mayflies and hydropsychid caddisflies; water pollution and floods. *Mailing Add:* Dept of Biol Winona State Col Winona MN 55987

FREMMING, BENJAMIN DEWITT, b Minneapolis, Minn, Oct 27, 24; m 55; c 2. VETERINARY PHYSIOLOGY. *Educ:* Colo State Univ, DVM, 46; Univ Calif, Berkeley, MPH, 52; Am Col Lab Animal Med, dipl, 56; Am Bd Vet Pub Health, dipl. *Prof Exp:* Scientist virol-serol, Walter Reed Res & Grad Ctr, 52-53; chief radiobiol vet res group, Radiobiol Lab, Univ Tex, 53-56; proj mgr physiol life sci sect, Westinghouse Res Develop Ctr, 61-64; scientist adminr, Nat Univ Tex Med Sch, San Antonio, Heart Inst, 65-67; prof path & dir animal care ctr, 67-71, chmn dept lab animal med, 68-74, prof lab animal med & anesthesiol, 71-77; PROF PHARMACOL, SCHS MED & PHARM & DIR LAB ANIMAL CTR, UNIV MO-KANSAS CITY, 77- *Concurrent Pos:* Mem, Inst Lab Animal Resources, Nat Res Coun, 53-58, chmn coun nonhuman primates, 53-58; pres, Am Col Lab Animal Med, 59-62; consult, Off Inspector Gen, US Dept State, 62-64. *Mem:* fel Am Col Pharm & Therapeut; Am Soc Pharm & Exp Therapeut; Sigma Xi; Am Vet Med Asn; Am Asn Lab Animal Sci. *Res:* Radiobiology; epidemiology; experimental surgery; laboratory animal medicine; reproductive physiology research centered around migration of ova through the fallopian tube, capacation and ova transplantation. *Mailing Add:* Lab Animal Ctr Univ Mo Kansas City MO 64110

FREMONT, CLAUDE, b Que, Aug 18, 22; m 53. PHYSICS. *Educ:* Laval Univ, BA, 43, BAppSci, 47, MSc, 48. *Prof Exp:* Lectr physics, 48-50, assoc prof geophys, 50-53, geophys & physics, 53-63, prof, asst lectr & adj prof, Sch Teacher Orientation, 63-70, PROF PHYSICS, LAVAL UNIV, 70- *Mem:* Can Asn Physicists; French-Can Asn Advan Sci; Royal Astron Soc; Brit Interplanetary Soc. *Res:* Semi-transparent thin films; magnetism. *Mailing Add:* Dept of Physics Laval Univ Quebec PQ G1K 7P4 Can

FREMONT, HERBERT IRWIN, b Brooklyn, NY, Nov 1, 24; m 46; c 2. MATHEMATICS. *Educ:* NY Univ, BA, 49, MA, 51, PhD(math educ), 63. *Prof Exp:* Teacher pub schs, NY, 49-58, chmn dept math, High Sch, 58-61; assoc prof, 61-71, PROF MATH EDUC, QUEENS COL, NY, 71- *Concurrent Pos:* Proj dir, Math Individual Learning Exp, US Off Educ, 60-62; math consult, Bldg Resources Instruct Disadvantaged Groups, Queens Col, NY, 62-63; consult, North Shore Pub Schs, Glen Head, 62-65 & Cold Spring Harbor, NY, 80-82; ed adv, McGraw-Hill Book Co, 63-; curric consult, Huntington Training Proj, Jamaica, NY & US Dept Labor, 64-65; proj dir, Alternatives for Slow Learners in Sec Sch Math, NSF, 78-79 & 81-83. *Mem:* Nat Coun Teachers Math; Math Asn Am. *Res:* Techniques of individualizing instruction in mathematics; new mathematics curriculum based on science concepts; aiding slow learners in mathematics through use of multi-media individualized approach. *Mailing Add:* Dept of Educ Queens Col Flushing NY 11367

FREMOUNT, HENRY NEIL, b Easton, Pa, Sept 29, 33; m 57; c 2. BIOLOGY, MEDICAL PARASITOLOGY. *Educ:* East Stroudsburg State Col, BS, 56, MEd, 64; Columbia Univ, MS, 66, DrPH(parasitic dis), 70. *Prof Exp:* Teacher & co-chmn dept sci, Delaware Valley Joint Sch Syst, 56-58; teacher high sch, Belvidere, NJ, 58-65; assoc prof, 66-71, chmn dept, 74-80, PROF BIOL, EAST STROUDSBURG STATE COL, 71- *Concurrent Pos:* Instr, Sch Pub Health, Columbia Univ, 70-75; fel trop med, Sch Med, La State Univ, 70; vis scientist, Gorgas Mem Lab, Panama, 70; Nat Inst Allergy & Infectious Dis res grant, 71-74; adj assoc prof, Inst Pathobiol & Inst Health Sci, Lehigh Univ, 72-76; consult parasitic dis, Sacred Heart Hosp, Allentown, Pa, 74- *Mem:* AAAS; Royal Soc Trop Med & Hyg; Am Soc Trop Med & Hyg; Am Soc Parasitol. *Res:* Biology and pathophysiology of malaria; ultrastructural changes in the host red cell as induced by the parasite; ultrastructure. *Mailing Add:* Dept of Biol East Stroudsburg State Col East Stroudsburg PA 18301

FREMOUW, EDWARD JOSEPH, b Northfield, Minn, Feb 23, 34; m 60; c 2. AERONOMY, RADIOPHYSICS. *Educ:* Stanford Univ, BS, 57; Univ Alaska, MS, 63, PhD(geophys), 66. *Prof Exp:* Engr, Boeing Co, 57-58; auroral physicist & auroral discipline chief for US Antarctic Res Prog in Antarctica, Arctic Inst NAm, 58-59; engr, Boeing Co, 60; asst elec eng, Univ Alaska, 60-61, asst aeronomy, Geophys Inst, 61-63, res assoc, 63-66, asst prof geophys, Univ, 66-67; physicist, Radio Physics Lab, SRI, Int, 67-70, sr physicist, 70-76, prog mgr, 76-77; STAFF SCIENTIST & VPRES, PHYS DYNAMICS INC, 77- *Concurrent Pos:* Consult, Geophys Inst, Univ Alaska, 67-69. *Mem:* Am Geophys Union; Inst Elec & Electronics Engrs; Int Radio Sci Union. *Res:* Ionospheric and auroral physics; satellite communication, surveillance radars, and navigation; radiowave scattering. *Mailing Add:* Phys Dynamics Inc PO Box 3027 Bellevue WA 98009

FRENCH, ADAM JAMES, b Raton, NMex, Sept 3, 12; c 1. PATHOLOGY. *Educ:* Univ Colo, BS, 33, MS & MD, 36. *Prof Exp:* Intern, Gen Hosp, Kansas City, Mo, 36-37; resident pediat, Children's Hosp, Denver, Colo, 37-38; resident path, St Louis City Hosp, 38-40 & Univ Mich Hosp & Med Sch, 40; instr, 41, from asst prof to assoc prof, 46-53, chmn dept, 56-78, PROF PATH, MED SCH, UNIV MICH, ANN ARBOR, 53- *Concurrent Pos:* Consult path, Vet Admin, Washington, DC, 53-; trustee, Am Bd Path, 62-73, secy-treas, 64-72, pres, 72-73, exec dir, 73-; trustee, Am Bd Path, 62-73, secy-treas, 64-72, pres, 72-73, exec dir, 73-78; mem sci adv bd, Armed Forces Inst Path, 65-70, chmn, 67-69. *Honors & Awards:* Pathologist of Year, Col Am Pathologists, 73; Distinguished Serv Award, Col Am Pathologists & Am Soc Clin Path, 78. *Mem:* Am Asn Path & Bact (secy-treas, 71-74, vpres, 74-75, pres, 75-76); hon mem Am Acad Oral Path; Am Col Physicians; AMA; Am Soc Clin Path. *Mailing Add:* Dept of Path Univ of Mich Ann Arbor MI 48104

FRENCH, ALAN RAYMOND, b Los Angeles, Calif, Dec 17, 46; m 68; c 2. PHYSIOLOGICAL ECOLOGY, CHRONOBIOLOGY. *Educ:* Univ Calif, Berkeley, BA, 68, Los Angeles, PhD(biol), 75. *Prof Exp:* Actg asst prof biol, Univ Calif, Los Angeles, 75-76; res scientist, Dept Biol Sci, Stanford Univ, 76-77; ASST PROF BIOL, UNIV CALIF, RIVERSIDE, 77- *Mem:* Ecol Soc Am; Am Soc Mammalogists; Int Hibernation Soc. *Res:* Vertebrate physiological ecology; timing and energetics of mammalian hibernation; environmental control of reproduction and dormancy; physiology of circadian and circannual rhythms. *Mailing Add:* Dept Biol Univ Calif Riverside CA 92521

FRENCH, ALEXANDER MURDOCH, b New Bedford, Pa, Apr 23, 20; m 47; c 2. PLANT PATHOLOGY. *Educ:* Muskingum Col, BS, 42; Cornell Univ, PhD(plant path), 50. *Prof Exp:* Assoc plant pathologist, 50-59, plant nematologist, 59-71, PRIN STAFF PATHOLOGIST-NEMATOLOGIST, DEPT FOOD & AGR, CALIF, 71- *Mem:* Soc Nematol; Am Phytopath Soc. *Res:* Regulatory plant pathology and plant nematology. *Mailing Add:* Calif Dept of Food & Agr 1220 N St Sacramento CA 95814

FRENCH, ALFRED DEXTER, b Boston, Mass, June 27, 43; m 65. PHYSICAL CHEMISTRY. *Educ:* Iowa State Univ, BS, 65; Ariz State Univ, PhD(phys chem), 71. *Prof Exp:* Res chemist, Northern Lab, USDA, 65-66, Nat Res Coun fel, Southern Lab, 71-73, RES CHEMIST, SOUTHERN LAB, USDA, 73- *Mem:* Am Chem Soc; Am Crystallog Asn. *Res:* Structure of polymers, especially polysaccharides. *Mailing Add:* 201 Central Ave Jefferson LA 70121

FRENCH, ALLEN LEE, b East Grand Rapids, Mich, Jan 19, 39; m 64; c 7. ENTOMOLOGY, ANIMAL PARASITOLOGY. *Educ:* Mich State Univ, BS, 62, MS, 64, PhD(entom), 68. *Prof Exp:* Asst entom, Mich State Univ, 62-68; head entom & parasitol res, 68-75, COORDR BIO-HEALTH RES & REGULATORY COMPLIANCE, MOORMAN MFG CO, 75- *Mem:* Entom Soc Am; Am Soc Parasitologists. *Res:* Evaluation of control procedures for pests and parasites of livestock. *Mailing Add:* Res Dept Moorman Mfg Co Quincy IL 62301

FRENCH, ANTHONY PHILIP, physics, see previous edition

FRENCH, BERLIN CARSON, b Carlton, NY, Oct 5, 04; m 38; c 2. ORGANIC CHEMISTRY. *Educ:* Wesleyan Univ, BS, 26, MA, 28; Yale Univ, MS, 34; Univ NC, PhD(chem), 56. *Prof Exp:* Instr chem, Juniata Col, 30-32 & Arnold Col, 33-34; res chemist, Nat Aniline & Chem Co, NY, 34-35; teacher pub schs, Mass, 35-48; from assoc prof to prof chem, Salem Col, NC, 48-67, chmn dept, 48-67; prof, 67-75, EMER PROF CHEM, CAPE COD COMMUNITY COL, 75- *Concurrent Pos:* NSF fel, Tufts Univ, 59; res grants, Res Corp, 59, 60 & NIH, 60-63; sci consult, Am Chem Soc, 74-76. *Mem:* Am Chem Soc; Nat Sci Teachers Asn; Am Asn Univ Prof; Sigma Xi. *Res:* Chemistry of natural products; naphthylethyl barbiturates; fluoro-riboflavin analogs; polarographic reduction potentials of nitrofluoroxylenes. *Mailing Add:* Cape Cod Community Col West Barnstable MA 02668

FRENCH, BEVAN MEREDITH, b East Orange, NJ, Mar 8, 37; m 67; c 3. GEOCHEMISTRY, ASTROGEOLOGY. *Educ:* Dartmouth Col, AB, 58; Calif Inst Technol, MS, 60; Johns Hopkins Univ, PhD(geol), 64. *Prof Exp:* Nat Acad Sci-Nat Res Coun resident res assoc geochem, Goddard Space Flight Ctr, NASA, 64-65, aerospace technologist, 65-72; prog dir geochem, NSF, 72-75; DISCIPLINE SCIENTIST PLANETARY MAT, NASA, 75- *Concurrent Pos:* Vis prof, Dartmouth Col, 68; co-investr, Apollo XI, XII & XIV Lunar Samples; vis res scientist, Univ Pretoria, SAfrica, 81-82. *Mem:* Meteoritical Soc. *Res:* Shock metamorphism of natural materials; geology of terrestrial meteorite impact craters; mineralogy and shock metamorphism of lunar samples; equilibrium relations in natural and artificial solid-gas systems; experimental synthesis and stability studies of carbonate minerals; sedimentary and metamorphosed iron formations. *Mailing Add:* 7408 Wyndale Lane Chevy Chase MD 20015

FRENCH, CHARLES STACY, b Lowell, Mass, Dec 13, 07; m 38; c 2. PLANT PHYSIOLOGY. *Educ:* Harvard Univ, SB, 30, MA, 32, PhD(biol), 34. *Hon Degrees:* PhD, Univ Goteborg, Sweden, 74. *Prof Exp:* Asst gen physiol, Radcliffe Col, 30-31 & Harvard Univ, 31-33; res fel biol, Calif Inst Technol, 34-35; guest worker, Kaiser Wilhelm Inst, 35-36; Austin teaching fel biochem, Harvard Med Sch, 36-38; instr chem, Univ Chicago, 38-41; from asst prof to assoc prof bot, Univ Minn, 41-47; dir dept plant biol, 47-73, DIR EMER, CARNEGIE INST, 73-, PROF BIOL BY COURTESY, 64- *Honors & Awards:* Award of Merit, Bot Soc Am, 73. *Mem:* Nat Acad Sci; AAAS; Bot Soc Am; Am Soc Plant Physiol; Am Soc Biol Chem. *Res:* Cellular respiration; photosynthesis of purple bacteria, leaves and algae; characteristics, spectroscopy and functions of plant pigments. *Mailing Add:* Dept of Plant Biol Carnegie Inst Stanford CA 94305

FRENCH, DAVID MILTON, b Alexandria, Va, July 11, 14; m; c 3. POLYMER CHEMISTRY. *Educ:* Univ Va, BS, 36, PhD(chem), 40. *Prof Exp:* Chemist, US Rubber Co, 40-46; res engr, Eng Exp Sta, Univ Fla, 46-48, Nat Bur Stand, 49-50, Acme Backing Corp, 53-56 & Wyandotte Chem Corp, 56-59; br head, US Naval Ord Sta, 62-74, group leader, Naval Surface Weapons Ctr, 74-78; CONSULT, 78- *Mem:* Am Chem Soc; AAAS. *Res:* Characterization of prepolymers; physical chemistry of polymers; degradation of crosslinked polymers; polymer network topology; emulsion polymerization; methods and materials of the coatings, adhesives, and solid propellant industries. *Mailing Add:* 703 S Fairfax St Alexandria VA 22314

FRENCH, DAVID N(ICHOLS), b Newton, Mass, Jan 24, 36; m 60; c 4. PHYSICAL METALLURGY, MATERIALS SCIENCE. *Educ:* Mass Inst Technol, BS, 58, MS, 59, ScD(metall), 62. *Prof Exp:* Res metallurgist, Linde Div, Union Carbide Corp, 62-63; mem tech staff, Ingersoll-Rand Res Ctr, 63-68; phys metallurgist, Abex Corp Res Ctr, Mahwah, 68-73; DIR CORP QUAL ASSURANCE, RILEY STOKER CORP, 73- *Mem:* Am Soc Metals; Am Inst Mining, Metall & Petrol Engrs; Nat Asn Corrosion Engrs. *Res:* Mechanical properties and solidification of sea ice; heat flow and transfer; mechanical behavior, x-ray stress analysis and manufacture of composites; ash corrosion; materials for high temperature environments. *Mailing Add:* One Lancaster Rd Northborough MA 01532

FRENCH, DAVID WESTON, b Mason City, Iowa, Nov 10, 21; m 44; c 3. FOREST PATHOLOGY. *Educ:* Univ Minn, BS, 43, MS, 49, PhD, 52. *Prof Exp:* From instr to assoc prof, 50-63, PROF PLANT PATH, UNIV MINN, ST PAUL, 63-, HEAD DEPT, 79- *Mem:* Am Phytopath Soc; Forest Prod Res Soc; Int Soc Arboriculture; Mycol Soc Am. *Res:* Products pathology; mycology. *Mailing Add:* Dept of Plant Path Univ of Minn St Paul MN 55101

FRENCH, DEXTER, b Des Moines, Iowa, Feb 23, 18; m 39; c 6. BIOCHEMISTRY. *Educ:* Univ Dubuque, BA, 38; Iowa State Univ, PhD(plant chem), 42. *Hon Degrees:* DSc, Univ Dubuque, 60. *Prof Exp:* Corn Prod Co fel, Harvard Med Sch, 42-44; res chemist, Corn Prod Co, 44-45; from asst prof to prof chem, 46-60, chmn dept biochem & biophys, 63-71, PROF BIOCHEM, IOWA STATE UNIV, 60-, DISTINGUISHED PROF AGR, 68- *Concurrent Pos:* NSF res fel, Univ London & Univ Paris, 62-63. *Honors & Awards:* Hudson Award, Am Chem Soc, 64; Award of Merit, Japanese Soc Starch Sci, 71; Alsberg-Schoch Award, Am Asn Cereal Chem, 74. *Mem:* Am Chem Soc; Am Soc Biol Chem; Am Asn Cereal Chem; hon mem Japanese Soc Starch Sci. *Res:* Carbohydrates; starch; amylases; mechanism of enzyme action. *Mailing Add:* Dept of Biochem Iowa State Univ Ames IA 50010

FRENCH, EDWARD P(ERRY), b Boise, Idaho, Aug 9, 24; m 49; c 2. SOLAR ENGINEERING, SOLAR POWER. *Educ:* Stanford Univ, BS, 48, MS, 50, PhD(metall), 53. *Prof Exp:* Group supvr ramjet engines, Marquardt Aircraft Co, 52-58; MEM TECH STAFF, ROCKWELL INT, SEAL BEACH, CALIF, 58- *Concurrent Pos:* Instr, eng exten, Univ Calif, Los Angeles, 57 & 62, lectr, col eng, 65-66. *Mem:* Combustion Inst; Am Inst Aeronaut & Astronaut; Sigma Xi; Int Solar Energy Soc. *Res:* Aircraft and space propulsion; aerothermochemistry; thermodynamics; solar engineering. *Mailing Add:* 15988 El Soneto Dr Whittier CA 90603

FRENCH, ERNEST W(EBSTER), b Osnabrock, NDak, July 19, 29; m 54; c 2. AGRICULTURAL ENGINEERING. *Educ:* NDak State Univ, BS, 51, MS, 56. *Prof Exp:* Salesman, Standard Oil Co, 54-55; asst agr engr, 57-59, asst prof agr eng, 59-60, SUPT, WILLISTON BR EXP STA, N DAK STATE UNIV, 60- *Mem:* Am Soc Agr Engrs; Soil Conserv Soc Am. *Res:* Soil and water conservation research and application. *Mailing Add:* Williston Br Exp Sta NDak State Univ Box 1445 Williston ND 58801

FRENCH, F(RANK) E(DWARD), JR, b Cincinnati, Ohio, May 8, 22; m 46; c 3. CHEMICAL ENGINEERING. *Educ:* Mass Inst Technol, BS, 43, ScD(chem eng), 48. *Prof Exp:* Res engr, Grasselli Chem Dept, 48-50, res supvr, 50-53, mgr eng develop sect, 53-54, asst tech supt, 55-56, mem develop dept, 56-59, mgr new prod & mkt develop, 59-61, mkt mgr indust chem, 62-67, mgr tech servs, org chem dept, 67-77, MGR ENVIRON & REGULATORY AFFAIRS, CHEM & PIGMENTS DEPT, E I DU PONT DE NEMOURS & CO, INC, 78- *Mem:* Am Chem Soc; Sigma Xi; Am Inst Chem Engrs. *Res:* Occupational health, safety, environmental protection; regulatory affairs. *Mailing Add:* Chem & Pigments Dept E I du Pont de Nemours & Co Inc Wilmington DE 19898

FRENCH, FRANCIS WILLIAM, b Brooklyn, NY, Dec 28, 27; m 67; c 5. AEROSPACE ENGINEERING, APPLIED MECHANICS. *Educ:* Polytech Inst Brooklyn, BS, 51, MS, 56, PhD(aeronaut eng), 59. *Prof Exp:* Struct draftsman, Grumman Aircraft, 51-52; stress analyst, Aerophys Lab, NAm Aviation, Inc, 52-53; res asst aerospace eng & appl mech, Polytech Inst Brooklyn, 53-55, res assoc, 55-59; sr engr, Technik, Inc, 59-60; sr staff mem, Allied Res Assocs, 60-61, chief appl mech group, 61-62; mem tech staff, Space Systs Dept, Mitre Corp, Mass, 62-65; sr consult engr, Sci Satellite Proj Off, Avco Corp, 65-67, prin res engr, Avco Everett Res Lab, 67-70, sr consult scientist, Avco Systs Div, 70-71, prin res engr, Avco Everett Res Lab, 71-73; PRIN ENGR, W J SCHAFER ASSOCS, 73- *Concurrent Pos:* Assoc ed, J Spacecraft & Rockets. *Mem:* Sr mem Am Astronaut Soc; assoc fel Am Inst Aeronauts & Astronauts. *Res:* Laser systems; manned and unmanned spacecraft; structural mechanics. *Mailing Add:* W J Schafer Assocs 10 Lakeside Office Park Wakefield MA 01880

FRENCH, FRANK ELWOOD, JR, b Lubbock, Tex, Feb 20, 35; m 58; c 2. ENTOMOLOGY, PARASITOLOGY. *Educ:* Tex Tech Col, BS, 57; Iowa State Univ, MS, 58, PhD(entom), 62. *Prof Exp:* Res assoc med entom, Queen's Univ, Ont, 66-68; asst prof, 68-72, ASSOC PROF BIOL, GA SOUTHERN COL, 72- *Mem:* Entom Soc Am. *Res:* Acarina and Insecta of medical and veterinary importance, ectoparasites of mammals; allergic skin reaction to insect bites; Demodex hair follicle mites; life history, host aquisition, host's pathologic response. *Mailing Add:* Dept of Biol Ga Southern Col Statesboro GA 30460

FRENCH, FREDERICK ALEXIS, b Berkeley, Calif, Mar 19, 17; m 37; c 2. CHEMOTHERAPY. *Educ:* Univ Calif, AB, 42. *Prof Exp:* Jr chemist, Shell Develop Co, 40-42, chem engr, 42-45; res chemist chemother, Harold Brunn Res Inst, Mt Zion Hosp & Med Ctr, 44-50, chemother res, 50-56, res assoc cancer chemother, 56-61, dir chemother res, 61-74, RES ASSOC, MT ZION HOSP & MED CTR, SAN FRANCISCO, 75- *Concurrent Pos:* Res chemist, US Naval Radiol Defense Lab, 51-56; mem staff, F A French Assocs, Chem Res & Develop, 70- *Mem:* AAAS; NY Acad Sci; Am Chem Soc; Am Asn Cancer Res. *Res:* Organic analysis and synthesis; organic group analytical research; thermodynamics; chemotherapy of tuberculosis, malaria, cancer, polymers and abrasives. *Mailing Add:* 2 Le Roy Ave Portola Valley CA 94025

FRENCH, GORDON NICHOLS, b Washington, DC, Mar 14, 19; m 42; c 4. INTERNAL MEDICINE. *Educ:* Yale Univ, AB, 41; Tufts Univ, MD, 44. *Prof Exp:* Intern path, Boston City Hosp, 44-45; resident med, Vet Admin Hosp, Boston, 47-48; Bellevue Hosp, New York, 48-49; physician, Green Mountain Clin, Vt, 49-53; instr med, Sch Med, Tufts Univ, 54-59; asst physician, Harvard Univ, 55-59, res assoc, Sch Pub Health, 57-59; dir med, Misericordia Hosp, 59-67; asst prof clin med & assoc dean, Sch Med, Univ Pa, 67-72; DIR MED, NEW BRUNSWICK AFFIL HOSPS, 72- *Concurrent Pos:* Fel pharmacol, Harvard Univ, 46-47; consult, Lemmuel Shattuck Hosp, Boston, 55-59. *Mem:* Fel Am Col Physicians. *Res:* Cardiovascular physiology; ventricular pressure; volume relationships and oxygen consumption in fibrillation and arrest. *Mailing Add:* New Brunswick Affil Hosps PO Box 767 New Brunswick NJ 08903

FRENCH, HARRY TAPLEY, b Hanover, NH, Jan 20, 45. EXPERIMENTAL PHYSICS. *Educ:* Mass Inst Technol, BS, 67; Univ Mich, PhD(physics), 77. *Prof Exp:* RES ASSOC PHYSICS, COLUMBIA UNIV, 77- *Res:* High energy neutron interactions in bubble chambers; experimental particle physics. *Mailing Add:* Nevis Labs PO Box 137 Irvington-on-Hudson NY 10533

FRENCH, J(OHN) BARRY, b Toronto, Ont, Aug 22, 31; m 51; c 4. AEROSPACE ENGINEERING. *Educ:* Univ Toronto, BSc, 55, PhD(low density plasmas), 61; Univ Birmingham, MSc, 57. *Prof Exp:* Attached scientist, Ramjets, Nat Gas Turbine Estab, 55-56; lectr aerospace eng sci, 61-62, from asst prof to assoc prof, 62-68, prof aerospace eng sci, 68-76, ASSOC DIR, INST AEROSPACE STUDIES, UNIV TORONTO, 76- *Concurrent Pos:* Pres, Sciex Inc, 74- *Mem:* Fel Can Aeronaut & Space Inst; fel Royal Soc Arts. *Res:* Development of instrumentation for trace gas analysis; application studies in environmental, medical, military and other areas; quadrupole mass spectroscopy; atmospheric pressure chemical ionization; ion mobility applications; molecular beams; space simulation. *Mailing Add:* Inst for Aerospace Studies 4925 Dufferin St Downsview ON M3H 5T6 Can

FRENCH, JAMES C, b Detroit, Mich, Apr 25, 30; m 56; c 1. ORGANIC CHEMISTRY. *Educ:* Wayne State Univ, BS, 51, PhD(chem), 54. *Prof Exp:* USPHS fel, Harvard Univ, 54-56; RES CHEMIST, PARKE, DAVIS & CO, 56- *Mem:* Am Chem Soc; AAAS; Am Soc Pharmacog; Japan Antibiotics Res Asn. *Res:* Isolation and characterization of antibiotics; peptide synthesis. *Mailing Add:* Warner Lambert/Parke Davis 2800 Plymouth Rd Ann Arbor MI 48106

FRENCH, JAMES EDWIN, b Chicago, Ill, Jan 11, 42. INORGANIC CHEMISTRY, POLYMER CHEMISTRY. *Educ:* Knox Col, BA, 64; Stanford Univ, PhD(chem), 68. *Prof Exp:* NIH fel inorg chem, Mass Inst Technol, 68-69; RES CHEMIST, SR RES CHEMIST, HERCULES INC, 78- *Mem:* Am Chem Soc. *Res:* Transition metal res, electrochemistry of fuel cells and batteries; high temperature polymers; magnetic materials for recording applications. *Mailing Add:* Res Ctr Hercules Inc Wilmington DE 19899

FRENCH, JEAN GILVEY, b Brooklyn, NY, Dec 21, 26. INFECTIOUS DISEASE, POPULATION GENETICS. *Educ:* Cornell Univ, BS, 49; Columbia Univ, MA, 57; John Hopkins Univ, MPH, 61; Univ Mich, DrPH, 66. *Prof Exp:* Epidemiologist, Navajo Cornell Res Proj, 59-60; asst prof, Col Med, Univ Ky, 61-63; asst prof, School Pub Health, Univ Calif, Berkeley, 66-71, assoc prof, Sch Med, Univ Calif, Davis, 71-72; res epidemiol, Environ Protection Agency, 72-77; HEALTH SCIENTIST, NAT CTRS DIS CONTROL, 77- *Concurrent Pos:* Vis prof, Dept Com, Sch Med, Univ Ky, 66; clin assoc prof, Duke Univ, 74-77; vchmn, Interagency Testing Comt, 77-79. *Mem:* NY Acad Sci; AAAS; Asn Teachers Preventive Med. *Res:* Environmental health; chronic disease epidemiology. *Mailing Add:* Ctr Environ Health Ctr Dis Control Atlanta 30333

FRENCH, JEPTHA VICTOR, b Cripple Creek, Colo, Dec 16, 36; m 62; c 2. ENTOMOLOGY, VIROLOGY. *Educ:* Colo State Univ, BSc, 60, MSc, 62; Mich State Univ, PhD(entom), 73. *Prof Exp:* Res assoc, Univ Calif, Riverside, 62-69; fel entom, Mich State Univ, East Lansing, 69-73; asst prof, 73-77, ASSOC PROF ENTOM, CITRUS CTR, TEX A&I UNIV, 77- *Concurrent Pos:* Fel, Mich State Univ, 69-73; consult, S Tex Citrus Growers, 73- *Mem:* Entom Soc Am; Am Registry Prof Entomologists; Int Org Citrus Virologists; Int Soc Citricult. *Res:* Insect transmission of plant pathogenic viruses; biological and chemical control of arthropods attacking citrus. *Mailing Add:* Citrus Ctr Tex A&I Univ Box 2000 Weslaco TX 78596

FRENCH, JOHN DONALD, b New Orleans, La, Feb 19, 23; m 48; c 4. PHYSICS. *Educ:* La State Univ, BS, 48, MS, 52, PhD(physics), 58. *Prof Exp:* Physicist, US Geol Surv, 53-55; asst prof, 58-63, ASSOC PROF PHYSICS, AUBURN UNIV, 63- *Mem:* Am Phys Soc. *Res:* Nuclear physics. *Mailing Add:* Dept Physics Auburn Univ Auburn AL 36849

FRENCH, JOHN DOUGLAS, b Los Angeles, Calif, Apr 11, 11. NEUROSURGERY. *Educ:* Univ Calif, Los Angeles, AB, 33; Univ Southern Calif, MD, 37; Am Bd Surg, dipl, 43; Am Bd Neurol Surg, dipl, 47. *Prof Exp:* Intern internal med, Univ Hosp, Univ Calif, San Francisco, 37-38; asst resident surg, Strong Mem Hosp, 38-41, intern & asst neurosurg, 38-39; instr, Sch Med, Univ Rochester, 41-43, asst prof neurosurg, 43-46; res fel, Neuropsychiat Inst, Univ Ill, 46-47; assoc clin prof surg, 49-58, dir, Brain Res Inst, 60-76, prof, 58-78, EMER PROF ANAT & CLIN PROF SURG, MED SCH, UNIV CALIF, LOS ANGELES, 78-, EMER DIR, BRAIN RES INST, 76- *Concurrent Pos:* Assoc resident, Strong Mem Hosp, 41-42, chief resident surg, 42-43, actg head div neurosurg & asst surgeon, 43-46; chief neurosurg, Vet Admin Hosp, Long Beach, 48-58, assoc dir prof serv for res, 54-58. *Mem:* Am Asn Neurol Surg; Soc Univ Surgeons; AMA; Am Acad Neurol Surg; Soc Neurol Surg. *Res:* Function and disorder of the nervous system. *Mailing Add:* Brain Res Inst Univ of Calif Ctr for Health Sci Los Angeles CA 90024

FRENCH, JOHN ROBERT, plant pathology, see previous edition

FRENCH, JOSEPH H, b Toledo, Ohio, July 4, 28; m; c 4. PEDIATRICS, NEUROLOGY. *Educ:* Ohio State Univ, BA, 50, MD, 54; Am Bd Pediat, dipl, 60; Am Bd Psychiat & Neurol, dipl neurol, 65. *Prof Exp:* Asst prof pediat & neurol, Sch Med, Univ Colo, 61-64; from asst prof to assoc prof, 64-75, PROF PEDIAT & NEUROL, ALBERT EINSTEIN COL MED, 75-; ASST DEAN EDUC, MONTEFIORE HOSP & MED CTR, 70- *Concurrent Pos:* John Hay Whitney Found fel, 54-55; Nat Inst Neurol Dis & Blindness sr clin trainee, 57-61; Commonwealth Fund fel, 70; assoc attend, Montefiore Hosp & Med Ctr, 64-; assoc vis pediatrician, Morrisania City Hosp, 64-; asst vis neurologist, Bronx Munic Hosp, 64-; consult, Jewish Mem Hosp, 66- *Mem:* Fel Am Acad Pediat; fel Am Acad Neurol; Soc Pediat Res. *Res:* Neurochemistry and clinical pediatric neurology. *Mailing Add:* Dept of Pediat 1300 Morris Park Ave Bronx NY 10461

FRENCH, JUDSON CULL, b Washington, DC, Sept 30, 22; m 51; c 1. SOLID STATE ELECTRONICS. *Educ:* Am Univ, BS, 43; Harvard Univ, MS, 49. *Prof Exp:* Instr physics, Johns Hopkins Univ, 43-44; instr, George Washington Univ, 44-47; proj leader gaseous electronics, 48-50, group leader, 51-56, group leader solid state devices, 56-64, from asst chief to chief, Electron Devices Sect, 64-73, chief, Electronic Technol Div, 73-78, DIR, CTR ELECTRONICS & ELEC ENG, NAT BUR STANDARDS, 78- *Honors & Awards:* Silver Medal, Dept Commerce, 64; Edward Bennett Rosa Award, Nat Bur Standards, 71; Gold Medal, Dept Com, 78. *Mem:* Am Phys Soc; fel Inst Elec & Electronics Engrs; Am Soc Testing & Mat. *Res:* Gaseous electronics and semiconductors; microwave gas switching tubes; measurements and research on semiconductor devices and materials. *Mailing Add:* Ctr for Electronics & Elec Eng Nat Bur of Standards Washington DC 20234

FRENCH, KENNETH EDWARD, b Elyria, Ohio, Apr 16, 29; m 58; c 3. AEROSPACE ENGINEERING, MECHANICAL ENGINEERING. *Educ:* Calif Inst Technol, BS, 53; Mass Inst Technol, SM, 57; Univ Santa Clara, Engr, 68. *Prof Exp:* Design engr, Lockheed Aircraft Corp, Calif, 52-55; sr engr design, Sandberg-Serrell Corp, 56-57; chief engr, Irving Air Chute Co,

Inc, 57-58; STAFF ENGR RES & DEVELOP, LOCKHEED MISSILES & SPACE CO, 58- Concurrent Pos: Expert examr mech eng, Calif State Bd Regist Prof Engrs, 67-73; lectr, San Jose State Univ, 74-80. Mem: Am Soc Mech Engrs; Am Inst Aeronaut & Astronaut. Res: Parachute system research, development and design; design of Discoverer parachute system. Mailing Add: Lockheed Missile & Space Co Inc 1111 Lockheed Way Sunnyvale CA 94086

FRENCH, LARRY ROBERT, b Pendleton, Ore, Dec 29, 44; c 1. REPRODUCTIVE PHYSIOLOGY, ENDOCRINOLOGY. Educ: Ore State Univ, BS, 67, MS, 70; Univ Wis-Madison, PhD(endocrinol, reproductive physiol & physiol), 73. Prof Exp: Nat Defense Educ Act fel, Ore State Univ, 67-69; NIH trainee, 69-71, proj specialist, 71-73, res assoc, 73-74, asst prof, 74-81, ASSOC PROF, UNIV WIS-MADISON, 81- Mem: Am Soc Animal Scientist; Sigma Xi; AAAS; Soc Study of Reproduction; Am Dairy Sci Asn. Res: Embryonic and maternal interactions during early pregnancy; control of the corpus luteum; placental hormones; embryonic mortality; intrauterine devices; uterine specific proteins. Mailing Add: 419 E Main Silverton OR 97381

FRENCH, LESLIE HOWSON, b London, Eng, Mar 8, 95; nat US; m 29. PHYSIOLOGY. Educ: George Washington Univ, MD, 24; Am Bd Internal Med, dipl. Prof Exp: Assoc prof embryol & histol, Sch Med, George Washington Univ, 22-24, prof physiol & head dept, 25-33; assoc prof clin med, Sch Med, Georgetown Univ, 34-60; dir med educ & res, Sibley Mem Hosp, 63-66; CONSULT, 66- Concurrent Pos: Chief dept med, Prince Georges Gen Hosp, 45-58, chief cardiologist & dir heart sta, 45-60, consult, 45-75; sr meritorious staff, Dept Internal Med, Prince George's Hosp & Med Ctr, Cheverly, Md, 75-; Ordoneau scholar, George Washington Univ. Mem: Fel Am Col Physicians; fel Am Col Cardiol; Am Col Chest Physicians; fel Am Soc Internal Med; fel Am Col Angiol. Res: Human physiology; electrocardiography; graduate medical education. Mailing Add: 6803 Pineway University Park Hyattsville MD 20782

FRENCH, LYLE ALBERT, b Worthing, SDak, Mar 26, 15; m 41; c 3. NEUROSURGERY. Educ: Univ Minn, BS, 36, MB, 39, MD, 40, MS, 46, PhD(neurosurg), 47; Am Bd Neurol Surg, dipl, 48. Prof Exp: From instr to assoc prof, 47-57, dir div, 60-72, PROF NEUROSURG, MED SCH, UNIV MINN, MINNEAPOLIS, 60-, VPRES HEALTH SCI, UNIV, 70- Mem: AMA. Res: Peripheral nerve injuries; cerebral edema; brain tumors in children. Mailing Add: Univ of Minn Hosps Minneapolis MN 55455

FRENCH, NORMAN ROGER, b Kankakee, Ill, Mar 7, 27; div; c 2. ECOLOGY. Educ: Univ Ill, AB, 49; Univ Colo, MA, 51; Univ Utah, PhD(zool), 54. Prof Exp: Asst, Univ Mus, Univ Colo, 49-51; instr zool, Univ Nebr, 51-52; instr biol, Univ Utah, 54-55; ecologist, Nat Reactor Test Sta, AEC, 55-59; res ecologist, Lab Nuclear Med & Radiation Biol, Univ Calif, Los Angeles, 59-69; prof biol, Nat Resource Ecol Lab, Colo State Univ, 69-81; RES SCIENTIST, RES INST COLO, 81- Concurrent Pos: Cur zool, Nebr State Mus, 51-52; trustee & secy, Biol Abstracts, Biosis, 77-82. Mem: Fel AAAS; Am Inst Biol Sci; Ecol Soc Am; Cooper Ornith Soc; Am Soc Mammalogists. Res: Desert, alpine and grassland ecology, birds and mammals; radiobiology; ecosystem study; computer simulation; consumer ecology African savanna; comparison Union of Soviet Socialist Republic and United States prairie. Mailing Add: 816 Garfield Ft Collins CO 80524

FRENCH, RICHARD COLLINS, b Camden, NJ, Dec 11, 22. PLANT BIOCHEMISTRY. Educ: Rutgers Univ, BS, 47, MS, 48; Purdue Univ, PhD(plant physiol), 53. Prof Exp: Plant physiologist biol warfare labs, Ft Detrick, 53-57; plant physiologist biol sci br agr mkt serv, USDA, 57-62; plant physiologist biol labs crops div, US Army, 62-68, plant physiologist, Plant Sci Lab, 68-71; PLANT PHYSIOLOGIST, PLANT DIS RES LAB, USDA, 71- Mem: Fel Am Inst Chemists; Am Soc Plant Physiol; Bot Soc Am; Mycol Soc Am; Am Soc Hort Sci. Res: Seed and spore physiology. Mailing Add: Plant Dis Res Lab USDA Box 1209 Ft Detrick Frederick MD 21701

FRENCH, ROBERT DEXTER, b Springfield, Mass, Oct 26, 39; m 65; c 2. PHYSICAL METALLURGY, SURFACE PHYSICS. Educ: Northeastern Univ, BSc, 62, MSc, 64; Brown Univ, PhD(eng), 67. Prof Exp: Res asst crystal growth, Northeastern Univ, 62-64; asst phys metall, Brown Univ, 64-67, instr, 67, res assoc, 67-68; metallurgist, 68-77, group leader, 73-78, br chief, 78-79, div chief, 79-81, CHIEF, METALS & CERAMICS LAB, ARMY MAT & MECH RES CTR, 81- Mem: Am Inst Mining & Metall Engrs; Am Soc Metals; Am Crystallog Soc; Metall Soc. Res: Study of metal structure and metal surfaces through electron and field ion microscopy; diffusion of interstitials; creep and stress-rupture in single and two-phase alloys. Mailing Add: Metals Div Army Mat & Mech Res Ctr Watertown MA 02172

FRENCH, ROBERT LEONARD, b Camarillo, Calif, June 13, 33; m 55; c 3. PROJECT MANAGEMENT. Educ: Univ Calif, Los Angeles, BS, 56; Univ Southern Calif, MS, 66. Prof Exp: Supvr, Rocketdyne Div, NAm Rockwell, 56-69; mem tech staff, 69-79, tech mgr salton sea solar pond exp, 79-81, DEP PROJ MGR SOLAR PONDS, JET PROPULSION LAB, CALIF INST TECHNOL, 81- Mem: Int Solar Energy Soc. Res: System design and analysis of salt gradient solar pond power plants; thermodynamic and hydrodynamic behavior, water clarity and measurement and zone boundry control. Mailing Add: 4800 Oak Grove Dr MS 507-228 Pasadena CA 91105

FRENCH, WALTER RUSSELL, JR, b Inman, Nebr, Sept 29, 23; m 45; c 3. PHYSICS. Educ: Nebr Wesleyan Univ, AB, 48; Univ Iowa, MA, 50; Univ Nebr, PhD(physics), 57. Prof Exp: Instr physics, Nebr State Teachers Col, Peru, 50-51; from asst prof to prof, 51-62, chmn sci div, 56-62, E C AMES DISTINGUISHED PROF, PHYSICS, NEBR WESLEYAN UNIV, 62-, HEAD DEPT, 52- Concurrent Pos: NSF fac fel, Univ Wis, 65-66; dir & lectr, NSF-in-Serv Insts, 60-63, dir, 64-65; co-dir, Nebr Acad Sci Vis Scientist Prog, 56-64; consult, Oak Ridge Inst Nuclear Studies, AEC, 62-; participant, Oak Ridge Nat Labs, 63; mem, Cottrell Grants Adv Comt, Res Corp, 71-76; engr

instrument design group, Lawrence Berkeley Lab, Univ Calif, 76-77 & 78; vis prof, Dept Radiation Biol & Biophys, Univ Rochester, 79-81. Mem: Am Phys Soc; Am Asn Physics Teachers. Res: X-ray fluorescence applications; experimental nuclear physics. Mailing Add: Dept Physics Nebr Wesleyan Univ Lincoln NE 68504

FRENCH, WARREN NEIL, b Waverley, Ont, June 27, 35; m 61; c 3. PHARMACEUTICAL CHEMISTRY. Educ: Ont Agr Col, BSA, 56, MSA, 57; McMaster Univ, PhD(org chem), 60. Prof Exp: Univ fel, Univ Toronto, 60-62; CHEMIST PHARMACEUT, HEALTH PROTECTION BR, DEPT NAT HEALTH & WELFARE, 62- Mem: Chem Inst Can. Mailing Add: Health Protection Br Dept of Nat Health & Welfare Ottawa ON K1A 0L2 Can

FRENCH, WILBUR LILE, b Hammond, Ind, Mar 16, 29; m 54; c 3. GENETICS. Educ: Univ Ill, BS, 56, MS, 57, PhD(cytol, genetics), 62. Prof Exp: Instr biol, Eastern Ill Univ, 58-59; res assoc genetics, Univ Ill, 62-63; USPHS fel, Univ Calif, Riverside, 63-64 & Univ Mainz, 64-65; asst prof, 65-70, assoc prof, 70-80, EMER PROF GENETICS, LA STATE UNIV, BATON ROUGE, 80- Mem: AAAS; Genetic Soc Am; Entomol Soc Am; Sigma Xi. Res: Basic molecular mechanisms of life and aging. Mailing Add: 1943 Nicholson Dr Baton Rouge LA 70802

FRENCH, WILLIAM EDWIN, b Jackson, Mich, Nov 17, 36; m 58; c 2. ENVIRONMENTAL MANAGEMENT, MARINE GEOLOGY. Educ: Univ Mich, BS, 58, MS, 60, PhD(oceanog), 65. Prof Exp: Asst res geologist, Great Lakes Res Div, Univ Mich, 59-66; oceanogr, Marine Geophys Surv, US Navy Oceanog Off, DC, 66-68; asst prof geol, Hope Col, 68-72; sr staff consult & vpres logistics, Environ Consult, Inc, 72-80; sr staff consult, Wapora, Inc, 80-81; SR STAFF CONSULT, COASTAL ECOSYSTEM MGT, INC, 81- Mem: Am Soc Limnol & Oceanog; Soc Econ Paleont & Mineral; Geol Soc Am. Res: Measurement of sedimentary activity and near-bottom current regime; lake and estuary circulation; shoreline stabilization; groundwater hydrology of large surface mines. Mailing Add: 914 Wayside Way Richardson TX 75080

FRENCH, WILLIAM GEORGE, b Seattle, Wash, Jan 23, 43; m 65; c 2. PHYSICAL CHEMISTRY, GLASS TECHNOLOGY. Educ: Univ Calif, Riverside, BA, 65; Univ Wis, PhD(phys chem), 69. Prof Exp: mem tech staff chem, Bell Labs, 69-79; SR RES SPECIALIST, 3M CO, ST PAUL, MINN, 79- Mem: Am Chem Soc; Am Ceramic Soc; Optical Soc Am. Res: Physics and chemistry of glass; optical waveguide fibers; high purity materials. Mailing Add: 3M Co 260 5B 04 3m Ctr St Paul MN 55144

FRENCH, WILLIAM STANLEY, b Colfax, Iowa, Sept 17, 40; m 68; c 6. EXPLORATION GEOPHYSICS. Educ: Iowa State Univ, BS, 62; Ore State Univ, PhD(geophys), 70. Prof Exp: Asst phys, Ore State Univ, 62-64, asst geophysics, 64-68; from geophysicist to sr res geophysicist, Gulf Res & Develop Co, Gulf Oil Corp, 68-74; assoc prof geophys, Sch of Oceanog, Ore State Univ, 74-75; res supvr, Tulsa Res Ctr, Amoco Prod Co, Standard Oil Co, Ind, 75-77, consult geophysicist, New Orleans Region, 77-81; PRES, TENSOR GEOPHYS SERV CORP, 81- Mem: Soc Explor Geophys; Am Geophys Union; Seismol Soc Am; Europ Asn Explor Geophysicists. Res: Application of mathematical theory of elastic wave propagation to problems in earthquake seismology and petroleum exploration; oceanographic seismology; gravity and magnetic exploration; ultrasonic modeling. Mailing Add: Tensor Geophys Serv Corp 3510 N Causeway Blvd 501 Metairie LA 70002

FRENKEL, ALBERT W, b Berlin, Ger, Jan 1, 19; nat US; m 48; c 3. PLANT PHYSIOLOGY. Educ: Univ Calif, BA, 39, PhD(plant physiol), 42. Prof Exp: Asst, Univ Calif, 39-42 & Calif Inst Technol, 42-44; assoc radiol, Univ Rochester, US Army, Manhattan Dist & AEC Contract, 45-47; from asst prof to assoc prof bot, 47-55, head dept, 71-75, PROF BOT, UNIV MINN, ST PAUL, 55- Concurrent Pos: Res fel, Mass Gen Hosp, 54; vis scientist, Hopkins Marine Sta, Stanford Univ, 67-68. Mem: Fel AAAS; Am Soc Plant Physiol; Am Chem Soc; Am Soc Microbiol; Am Soc Biol Chem. Res: Biochemistry; photosynthesis; regulation of microbial metabolism. Mailing Add: Dept of Bot Col of Biol Sci 220 Biol Sci Ctr Univ of Minn St Paul MN 55108

FRENKEL, EUGENE PHILLIP, b Detroit, Mich, Aug 27, 29; m 58; c 2. INTERNAL MEDICINE, HEMATOLOGY AND MEDICAL ONCOLOGY. Educ: Wayne State Univ, BS, 49; Univ Mich, MD, 53; Am Bd Internal Med, cert hematol, 62, cert med oncol, 73. Prof Exp: Intern, Wayne County Gen Hosp, Mich, 53-54; resident, Boston City Hosp, 54-55; resident, Med Ctr, Univ Mich, 57-59, res assoc hemat, 59-60, instr, 60-62; from asst prof to assoc prof, 62-69, PROF INTERNAL MED, UNIV TEX HEALTH SCI CTR, DALLAS, 69-, AM CANCER SOC PROF CLIN ONCOL, 73-, CHIEF DIV HEMAT-ONCOL, 62- Concurrent Pos: Consult & chief nuclear med, Dallas Vet Admin Hosp, 62-; consult, St Paul Hosp, 64-, Baylor Univ Med Ctr, Presby Hosp & Brooke Army Hosp, 65- Mem: Fel Am Col Physicians; Am Soc Hemat; Soc Nuclear Med; Am Asn Cancer Res; Am Soc Clin Oncol. Res: Cancer chemotherapy; vitamin Btwelve and folic acid metabolism. Mailing Add: Dept of Internal Med Univ of Tex Health Sci Ctr Dallas TX 75235

FRENKEL, JACOB KARL, b Darmstadt, Ger, Feb 16, 21; nat US; m 54; c 3. PATHOLOGY. Educ: Univ Calif, AB, 42, MD, 46, PhD(comp path), 48. Prof Exp: Asst zool, Univ Calif, 40-42 & 43, asst bact, 42-43, asst anat, 43-44, intern path, Univ Hosp, 46-47, clin asst, Med Sch, 47-48; pathologist, Rocky Mountain Lab, USPHS, 48-50; instr, Med Sch, Univ Tenn, 51-52; from asst prof to assoc prof, 52-60, PROF PATH, SCH MED, UNIV KANS, 60- Concurrent Pos: Fulbright fel & vis prof, Nat Univ Mex, 63-64; researcher, Path Lab, NIH, 50-51; mem, Subcomt Comp Path, Div Med Sci, Nat Res Coun, 65-71; vis prof, Medellin, Colombia, 67 & San Jose, Costa Rica, 71; sci panel mem, Lunar Receiving Lab, 69-72. Honors & Awards: Humboldt Sr Scientist Award, Univ Bonn, Fed Repub Ger, 77. Mem: Am Soc Parasitol;

Soc Exp Biol & Med; Am Asn Pathologists; Infectious Dis Soc Am; Am Soc Trop Med & Hyg. *Res:* Pathogenesis of infection with obligate intracellular organisms; adrenal infection and necrosis; effects of corticoids on immunity and hypersensitivity; cellular immunity; toxoplasmosis. *Mailing Add:* Dept of Path & Oncol Univ of Kans Med Ctr Kansas City KS 66103

FRENKEL, KRYSTYNA, b USSR, Mar 2, 41; US citizen; m 77. CARCINOGENESIS, DNA REPAIR. *Educ:* Univ Warsaw, Poland, MS, 64; NY Univ, PhD(biochem), 74. *Prof Exp:* Asst res scientist org chem, Univ Warsaw, 64-66, sr asst res scientist, 66-68; asst res scientist chem carcinogenesis, Dept Environ Med, Med Ctr, NY Univ, 69-74; fel, Inst Cancer Res Columbia Univ Physicians & Surgeons, 74-76, staff assoc, 76-77; asst res scientist, 77-81, RES ASST PROF, DNA REPAIR, DEPT PATH, MED CTR, NY UNIV, 81- *Concurrent Pos:* Instr, Dept Org Chem, Univ Warsaw, 64-68. *Mem:* Am Chem Soc; Am Asn Cancer Res. *Res:* Modification of nucleic acids by ionizing radiation and by chemical carcinogens and structural and conformational characterization of the products; excision repair mechanisms in normal human cells and repair deficient cells. *Mailing Add:* Dept of Path 550 Fist Ave New York NY 10016

FRENKEL, NIZA B, b Tel Aviv, Israel, June 3, 47; m 68; c 2. VIROLOGY. *Educ:* Univ Chicago, MSc, 70, PhD(virol), 72. *Prof Exp:* Fel genetics, Weizmann Inst Sci, Israel, 72-73; instr virol, 73-74, asst prof biol, 74-80, ASSOC PROF BIOL, DEVELOP BIOL, VIROL & GENETICS, UNIV CHICAGO, 81- *Concurrent Pos:* Prin investr, grants, NIH & NSF, 78- *Mem:* Am Soc Microbiol; Am Soc Microbiol. *Res:* Herpes simplex virus DNA replication and expression; viral mediated cell transformation; eukaryotic gene amplification; viral vectors. *Mailing Add:* 920 E 58th St Chicago IL 60637

FRENKEL, RENE A, b Santiago, Chile, Sept 1, 32; m 59; c 4. BIOCHEMISTRY. *Educ:* Univ Chile, BS & MS, 56; Cornell Univ, PhD(biochem), 64. *Prof Exp:* First asst biochem, Univ Chile, 5657; res asst, Sloan-Kettering Inst Cancer Res, 57-60; res assoc, Univ Pa, 67-68, asst prof 68; asst prof, 68-73, ASSOC PROF BIOCHEM, UNIV TEX HEALTH SCI CTR, DALLAS, 73- *Concurrent Pos:* Johnson Res Found fel biophys, Univ Pa, 64-67. *Mem:* AAAS; Am Soc Biol Chemists. *Res:* Metabolic control; enzyme kinetics and interactions; integrated metabolic sequences. *Mailing Add:* Dept of Biochem Univ of Tex Health Sci Ctr Dallas TX 75235

FRENKIEL, FRANCOIS N, b Warsaw, Poland, Sept 19, 10; nat US; m 62. FLUID DYNAMICS. *Educ:* Univ Ghent, MechEng, 33, AeroEng, 37; Univ Lille, PhD(physics), 46. *Prof Exp:* Res engr, Tech Serv Aeronaut, Belg, 37-38; sci collabr, Univ Ghent, 39; res assoc, Inst Fluid Mech, Univ Lille, 39-40; sci collabr, French Group Aeronaut Res, Toulouse, 40-43, from res assoc to chief lab, Aerodyn Res Ctr, 45-47; mem res staff, Grad Sch Aeronaut Eng, Cornell Univ, 47-48; sr res assoc, US Naval Ord Lab, 48, chief theoret & appl mech subdiv, 49-50; sr res physicist, Res Ctr, Appl Physics Lab, Johns Hopkins Univ, 50-52, mem prin staff, 52-60; consult physicist, 56-60, SR RES SCIENTIST, COMPUT & MATH DEPT, NAVAL SHIP RES & DEVELOP CTR, 60- *Concurrent Pos:* Lectr, Univ Md, 50; consult, US Weather Bur, 52-60 & Appl Physics Lab, Johns Hopkins Univ, 57-60; ed, Physics of Fluids, Am Inst Physics, 57-; prof, Univ Minn, 63-64; chmn, US Nat Comt Theoret & Appl Mech, 65-66, secy, 70-; mem gov bd, Am Inst Physics, 75-77. *Mem:* Fel AAAS; fel Am Phys Soc; Am Meteorol Soc; fel Am Geophys Union; assoc fel Am Inst Aeronaut & Astronaut. *Res:* Atmospheric physics; turbulence; applied mathematics, particularly structure of turbulence and boundary layer. *Mailing Add:* Dept of Comput & Math Naval Ship Res & Develop Ctr Washington DC 20084

FRENSDORFF, H KARL, b Hannover, Ger, Apr 7, 22; nat US. PHYSICAL CHEMISTRY, POLYMER CHEMISTRY. *Educ:* Rensselaer Polytech Inst, BS, 49; Princeton Univ, AM, 51, PhD(phys chem), 52. *Prof Exp:* Res chemist, 52-77, DIV HEAD, E I DU PONT DE NEMOURS & CO, INC, 77- *Concurrent Pos:* Assoc ed, Rubber Chem & Technol, 72-74, 77-, ed, 75-77. *Mem:* AAAS; Am Chem Soc. *Res:* Structure and properties of high polymers; polymerization statistics; sorption and diffusion; macrocyclic polyethers. *Mailing Add:* Polymer Prod Dept Du Pont Exp Sta 353 Wilmington DE 19898

FRENSLEY, WILLIAM ROBERT, b Wichita, Kans. SOLID STATE PHYSICS, SEMICONDUCTORS. *Educ:* Calif Inst Technol, BS, 73; Univ Colo, PhD(physics), 76. *Prof Exp:* Researcher elec eng, Univ Calif, Santa Barbara, 76-77; MEM TECH STAFF, CENT RES LABS, TEX INSTRUMENTS, INC, 77- *Mem:* Am Phys Soc; Inst Elec & Electronics Engrs. *Res:* Semiconductor device physics, particularly gallium arsenide field-effect transistors and heterojunctions. *Mailing Add:* Tex Instruments Inc MS 134 PO Box 225936 Dallas TX 75265

FRENSTER, JOHN H, b Chicago, Ill, Oct 14, 28; m 58; c 3. CELL BIOLOGY, ONCOLOGY. *Educ:* Univ Ill, BS, 50, MD, 54. *Prof Exp:* Intern, Cook County Hosp, Chicago, 55; resident med, Res & Educ Hosps, Univ Ill, 55-58, res fel hemat, 56-57; Am Cancer Soc fel & guest investr cell biol, Rockefeller Inst, 58-60; cell radiobiologist, Walter Reed Army Inst Res, Washington, DC, 60-62; asst prof, Rockefeller Inst, 62-66; CLIN ASSOC PROF MED, SCH MED, STANFORD UNIV, 66-; CHIEF ONCOL, SANTA CLARA VALLEY MED CTR, SAN JOSE, 72- *Concurrent Pos:* Asst hemat, Johns Hopkins Hosp, Md, 60-62; USPHS res career develop award, 62-67. *Mem:* Fel Am Col Physicians; Biophys Soc; Am Soc Hemat; Am Cancer Soc; Am Soc Cell Biol. *Res:* Structure and function of the cell nucleus; clinical and biological aspects of leukemia and lymphomas; control of RNA synthesis; human tumor immunotherapy; quantitation of health or disease within individual human systems. *Mailing Add:* Inst Med Res Santa Clara Valley Med Ctr 751 S Bascom Ave San Jose CA 95128

FRENZEL, HUGH N, b Madison, Wis, Apr 21, 18; m 45; c 4. PETROLEUM GEOLOGY. *Educ:* Univ Wis, BA, 40, MA, 41. *Prof Exp:* Geologist, Standard Oil Co, Tex, 46-49, dist geologist, 49-52; geologist, Ryan, Hayes & Burke, 52-54; from geologist to chief geologist, Ralph Lowe Estate, 54-74; chief geologist & vpres, Flag-Redfern Oil co, 74-80; VPRES EXPLORATION, BISON EXPLORATION CO, 81- *Mem:* Soc Econ Paleont & Mineral; hon life mem Am Asn Petrol Geol; fel Geol Soc Am. *Res:* Petroleum geology, stratigraphy, sedimentation and structure of Permian Basin. *Mailing Add:* 1118 Mogford Midland TX 79701

FRENZEL, LOUIS DANIEL, JR, b San Antonio, Tex, Aug 22, 20; m 45; c 2. BIOLOGY, ECOLOGY. *Educ:* NTex State Col, BS, 47, MS, 48; Univ Minn, PhD(wildlife mgt), 57. *Prof Exp:* Instr biol, Ely Jr Col, Minn, 48-54; asst, Univ Minn, 54-56; prof, Macalester Col, 57-69; PROF ENTOM, FISHERIES & WILDLIFE, UNIV MINN, ST PAUL, 69- *Mem:* Wildlife Soc; Am Soc Mammal; Ecol Soc Am. *Res:* Ecology of terrestrial vertebrates, especially of avian and mammalian populations; field and general biology; wildlife ecology; ecological studies and management of American Bald Eagles. *Mailing Add:* Dept of Entom Fish & Wildlife Univ of Minn St Paul MN 55108

FRENZEN, PAUL, b Oak Park, Ill, Sept 4, 24; m 51; c 4. METEOROLOGY, FLUID DYNAMICS. *Educ:* Univ Chicago, BS, 49, MS, 51, PhD(meteorol), 64. *Prof Exp:* Weather forecaster, Air Weather Serv, US Army Air Force, 44-46; res assoc fluid dynamics, Hydro Lab, Univ Chicago, 51-56; res assoc meteorol, 56-59, assoc meteorologist, 59-78, SR METEOROLOGIST & ASSOC DIV DIR RES & ADMIN, RADIOL & ENVIRON RES DIV, ARGONNE NAT LAB, 78- *Concurrent Pos:* Vis scientist atmospheric physics, Commonwealth Sci & Indust Res Orgn, Melbourne, 62-63 & 68-69. *Mem:* Am Meteorol Soc; Royal Meteorol Soc London; Sigma Xi. *Res:* Atmospheric turbulence; diffusion in air and water. *Mailing Add:* Radiol & Environ Res Div Argonne Nat Lab Bldg 203 Argonne IL 60439

FRERE, MAURICE HERBERT, b Sheridan, Wyo, Sept 8, 32; m 57; c 3. WATERSHED MANAGEMENT, WATER POLLUTION. *Educ:* Univ Wyo, BS, 54, MS, 58; Univ Md, PhD(soils), 62. *Prof Exp:* Res soil scientist, Soil & Water Conserv Div, 58-75, dir, Southern Great Plains Res Watershed, Sci & Educ Admin-Agr Res, 75-79, ASST TO THE REGIONAL ADMINR, AGR RES SERV, USDA, 79- *Mem:* AAAS; Am Soc Agron; Soil Sci Soc Am; Am Chem Soc; Soil Conserv Soc Am. *Res:* Systems analysis of soil-water-plant relations, especially pollution; evaluation of the hydrologic and environmental impact of flood water retarding structures and conservation programs. *Mailing Add:* Sea Agr South Region Hq USDA New Orleans LA 70153

FRERICHS, WAYNE MARVIN, b Bloomington, Nebr, Apr 9, 33; m 57, 72; c 2. VETERINARY SCIENCE, BIOCHEMISTRY. *Educ:* Kans State Univ, BS & DVM, 57; Wash State Univ, PhD(vet sci), 66. *Prof Exp:* Res vet, Animal Parasitol Inst, USDA, 66-82; ANIMAL PROD & HEALTH SECT HEAD, REGIONAL AGR & WATER CTR, RIYADH, SAUDI ARABIA, 82- *Mem:* AAAS; Am Vet Med Asn; Am Soc Microbiol; Animal Health Asn; Am Asn Lab Animal Sci. *Res:* Leptospira antigenic variations; immunology and biology of Babesia caballi, Babesia equi, Babesia rodhaini, Babesia procyoni and Babesia microti; survey of parasitism in Saudi Arabia. *Mailing Add:* 13011 Ingleside Dr Beltsville MD 20705

FRERICHS, WILLIAM EDWARD, b Des Moines, Iowa, Mar 30, 39; m 63; c 2. MICROPALEONTOLOGY. *Educ:* Iowa State Univ, BS & MS, 63; Univ Southern Calif, PhD(geol), 67. *Prof Exp:* Res geologist, Esso Prod Res Co, 66-68; from asst prof to assoc prof, 68-75, PROF GEOL, UNIV WYO, 75- *Concurrent Pos:* NSF grant, 70-72. *Mem:* AAAS. *Res:* Foraminiferal paleoecology; geopolarity history of the Cretaceous; Cretaceous biostratigraphy; vertical movements related to continental drift. *Mailing Add:* Dept of Geol Univ of Wyo Laramie WY 82071

FRERKING, MARGARET ANN, b Jamaica, NY, July 15, 50. ASTROPHYSICS, MILLIMETER AND SUBMILLIMETER INSTRUMENTATION. *Educ:* Mass Inst Technol, BSc, 72, PhD(physics), 77. *Prof Exp:* Consult infrared receivers, Laser Analytics Inc, 76-77; fel radio astron, Bell Labs, 77-80; MEM TECH STAFF MILLIMETER & SUBMILLIMETER WAVE INSTRUMENTATION, JET PROPULSION LABS, 80- *Honors & Awards:* Sigma Xi. *Mem:* Am Astron Soc. *Res:* Millimeter wave and submillimeter wave instrumentation for atmospheric and astrophysical research. *Mailing Add:* Jet Propulsion Lab MS 168-314 4800 Oak Grove Dr Pasadena CA 91103

FRERMAN, FRANK EDWARD, b Louisville, Ky, Feb 7, 42; m 66; c 3. BIOCHEMISTRY, MICROBIOLOGY. *Educ:* Bellarmine Col, BA, 64; Univ Ky, PhD(biochem), 68. *Prof Exp:* Fel biochem, Johns Hopkins Univ, 68-70; asst prof, 70-75, ASSOC PROF MICROBIOL, MED COL WIS, 75- *Res:* Enzymology; lipid metabolism. *Mailing Add:* Dept of Microbiol PO Box 26509 Milwaukee WI 53226

FRESCO, JACQUES ROBERT, b New York, NY, May 30, 28; m 57; c 3. BIOCHEMISTRY, MOLECULAR BIOLOGY. *Educ:* NY Univ, BA, 47, MS, 49, PhD(biochem), 53. *Hon Degrees:* MD, Univ Göteborg, Sweden, 79. *Prof Exp:* Asst, Lebanon Hosp, NY, 47-48; instr chem, Col Med, NY Univ, 53-54; instr pharmacol, 54-56; res fel chem, Harvard Univ, 56-60; from asst prof to assoc prof, 60-65, prof chem, 65-70, chmn dept biochem sci, 74-80, PROF BIOCHEM, PRINCETON UNIV, 70-, PFEIFFER PROF LIFE SCI, 77- *Concurrent Pos:* Fel, Sloan-Kettering Inst Cancer Res & USPHS, 52-54; Lalor tutor biochem sci, Harvard Univ, 57-60; estab investr, Am Heart Asn, 58-63; Guggenheim Found fel, Med Res Coun Lab Molecular Biol, Eng, 69-70. *Mem:* Am Chem Soc; Am Soc Biol Chem. *Res:* Biochemistry of nucleic acids; molecular genetics; conformation of biomacromolecules; mechanisms of mutation; base pairing; protein-nucleic acid recognition; biophysics. *Mailing Add:* Dept Biochem Sci Princeton Univ Princeton NJ 08544

FRESCO, JAMES MARTIN, b Yonkers, NY, Sept 29, 26. ANALYTICAL CHEMISTRY. *Educ:* NY Univ, AB, 49; Polytech Inst Brooklyn, MS, 56; Univ Ariz, PhD(chem), 61. *Prof Exp:* Chemist, Health & Safety Div, NY Opers Off, US AEC, 49-56; res assoc chem, Univ Ariz, 61-62; asst prof, Univ Nev, 62-64; chemist, US Naval Radiol Defense Lab, 64; asst prof, Tex Technol Col, 64-65; asst prof, 65-69, ASSOC PROF CHEM, MCGILL UNIV, 69- *Mem:* Am Chem Soc; The Chem Soc; Chem Inst Can. *Res:* Radiochemistry; infrared spectroscopy; chemistry of coordination compounds; chemical separation processes. *Mailing Add:* Dept of Chem McGill Univ 801 Sherbrooke St W Montreal H3A 2K6 Can

FRESCURA, BERT LOUIS, b Glendale, Calif, Aug 13, 36; div; c 3. MICROELECTRONICS, SOLID STATE PHYSICS. *Educ:* Univ Calif, Los Angeles, BS, 59; Ore State Univ, MS, 63; Stanford Univ, PhD(elec eng), 75. *Prof Exp:* Commun officer, US Air Force, 59-62; engr integrated circuits, Fairchild Semiconductor Res & Develop Labs, 63-67; mem tech staff integrated circuits, Leds & Lasers, Hewlett-Packard Labs, Palo Alto, 67-81, RES & DEVELOP SECT MGR, MICROWAVE SEMICONDUCTOR DIV, HEWLETT-PACKARD, SAN JOSE, 81- *Mem:* Inst Elec & Electronics Engrs; Soc Info Display. *Res:* Bipolar and metal-oxide-silicon integrated circuits; large area led display; double-heterojunction lasers; dynamic model operations section power transistors. *Mailing Add:* 22345 Carta Blanca St Cupertino CA 95014

FRESH, JAMES W, b Toccoa, Ga, Jan 9, 26; m 57; c 2. PATHOLOGY. *Educ:* Lenoir-Rhyne Col, BA, 49; Univ NC, MPH, 50, MD, 57. *Prof Exp:* Instr physiol, Univ NC, 52-54, instr path, 5758; pathologist, Marine Corps Air Facil, US Navy, New River, NC, 58-59 & Naval Hosp, St Albans, NY, 59-62, head path, Naval Med Res Unit 2, Taipei, Taiwan, 62-69, cmndg officer, Naval Med Res Unit 1 & Head path sect, Naval Biomed Res Lab, 69-71, exec officer, Naval Med Res Unit 3, 71-75, chief path, Naval Northwest Regional Med Ctr, Jacksonville, Fla, 75-76; RETIRED. *Concurrent Pos:* Vis prof, Col Med, Taiwan Nat Univ, 62-69, Nat Defense Med Col, Taiwan, 6568 & Taipei Med Col, 65-69; consult, Chinese Navy. *Mem:* Am Soc Clin Path; Col Am Path; Asn Mil Surgeons US; AMA; Am Pub Health Asn. *Res:* Clinical research on malignancies, infectious diseases, nutritional deficiencies and coronary artery disease. *Mailing Add:* 781 Hebernia Rt Green Cove Springs FL 32043

FRESIA, ELMO JAMES, b Pittsfield, Mass, Sept 10, 31; m 58; c 3. ELECTROCHEMISTRY, OXIDE FILMS. *Educ:* Univ Mass, BS, 53; Univ Conn, MS, 59. *Prof Exp:* Proj leader high reliability develop, 59-62, sect head, Solid State Capacitors Res & Develop, 62-69, proj mgr, Electrochem Prod Develop Lab, 69-78, SECT HEAD, DEVICE DEVELOP, RES, DEVELOP & ENG, SPRAGUE ELEC CO, 78- *Mem:* Sigma Xi. *Res:* Preparation and structure determination of ternary oxides; development of solid state capacitors, electrolytic type; dielectric oxide films; corrosion of metals. *Mailing Add:* Res Develop & Eng Sprague Elec Co Marshall St North Adams MA 01247

FRESQUEZ, CATALINA LOURDES, b Socorro, Tex, Feb 11, 37. ZOOLOGY, GENETICS. *Educ:* Incarnate Word Col, BA, 63; Univ Tex, Austin, MA, 69, PhD(zool, genetics), 76. *Prof Exp:* Teacher math, Archbishop Chapelle High Sch, 63-66, chmn dept, 65-66; chmn div natural sci, 78-79, from instr to asst prof, 69-78, ASSOC PROF BIOL, INCARNATE WORD COL, 81- *Concurrent Pos:* Prin investr, Minority Biomed Support Prog, 76-81. *Mem:* Am Soc Cell Biol; Genetics Soc Am. *Res:* Nucleic acid and protein synthesis in polytene chromosomes; regulatory mechanisms; developmental biology. *Mailing Add:* Incarnate Word Col 4301 Broadway San Antonio TX 78209

FRESTON, JAMES W, b Mt Pleasant, Utah, July 20, 36; m 56; c 4. INTERNAL MEDICINE, GASTROENTEROLOGY. *Educ:* Univ Utah, MD, 61, PhD(med), 67. *Prof Exp:* From asst prof to assoc prof, Col Med, Univ Utah, 67-77, prof med & pharmacol, 77-80, chief, Div Clin Pharmacol, 69-80, chmn, Div Gastroenterol, 70-80; PROF & CHMN, DEPT MED, UNIV CONN, 80- *Concurrent Pos:* Nat Inst Arthritis & Metab Dis fel, Dept Med, Royal Free Hosp, London, Eng, 65-67; Burroughs-Wellcome scholar, 69; clin investr, Vet Admin Hosp, Salt Lake City, Utah, 67-69; staff physician, Med Ctr, Univ Utah, 67-; vis prof, Univ Man, 70. *Mem:* AAAS; AMA; Am Asn Study Liver Dis; Am Col Physicians; Am Soc Internal Med. *Res:* Gastrointestinal pharmacology and drug toxicity; peptic ulcer therapy. *Mailing Add:* Dept Med Sch Med Univ Conn Farmington CT 06032

FRETER, KURT RUDOLF, b Hamburg, Ger, Jan 26, 29; Can citizen; m 59; c 4. ORGANIC CHEMISTRY. *Educ:* Univ Frankfurt, Hauptdiplom, 53, Dr rer nat, 55. *Prof Exp:* Vis scientist, NIH, 56-57; group leader med chem, C H Boehringer, Ger, 57-64; head chem dept, Pharma Res Cen Ltd, 64-77; HEAD CHEM DEPT, BOEHRINGER INGELHEIM LTD, 77- *Mem:* Am Chem Soc; Chem Inst Can; Soc Ger Chem. *Res:* Peptides; Heterocyclic Chemistry. *Mailing Add:* 90 East Ridge PO Box 368 Ridgefield CT 06877

FRETER, ROLF GUSTAV, b Hamburg, Ger, Jan 5, 26; US citizen; m 55; c 4. MEDICAL BACTERIOLOGY, IMMUNOLOGY. *Educ:* Univ Frankfurt, PhD(bact), 51. *Prof Exp:* Res assoc bact, Biol Budesanstalt, Braunschweig, Ger, 51; instr, Loyola Univ, Ill, 54-57; assoc prof microbiol, Jefferson Med Col, 57-65; PROF MICROBIOL, UNIV MICH, ANN ARBOR, 65- *Concurrent Pos:* Logan fel & res assoc, Univ Chicago, 52-54. *Mem:* AAAS; Am Soc Microbiol; fel Am Acad Microbiol; Am Asn Immunologists; Soc Exp Biol & Med. *Res:* Oral enteric vaccines; ecology of normal enteric flora of man; bacterial toxins and enzymes; experimental enteric animal infections; anaerobic bacteria. *Mailing Add:* Dept of Microbiol 6734 Med Sci Bldg II Univ Mich Ann Arbor MI 48109

FRETTER, WILLIAM BACHE, b Pasadena, Calif, Sept 28, 16; m 39; c 3. PHYSICS. *Educ:* Univ Calif, AB, 37, PhD(physics), 46. *Prof Exp:* Asst physics, Univ Calif, 37-41; res assoc, Mass Inst Technol, 41; res engr, Westinghouse Elec Co, Pa, 41-44; res engr, Manhattan Dist Proj, Radiation Lab, 45-46, from instr to assoc prof physics, 46-55, dean col lett & sci, 62-67, PROF PHYSICS, UNIV CALIF, BERKELEY, 55- *Concurrent Pos:* Fulbright res scholar, France, 52-53 & 60-61; Guggenheim fel, 60-61. *Honors & Awards:* Chevalier, Legion of Honor, France. *Mem:* Fel Am Phys Soc. *Res:* High power microwaves; isotope separation; cosmic rays; mass of cosmic ray mesotrons; penetrating showers, heavy mesons and hyperons; elementary particle physics. *Mailing Add:* 1120 Cragmont Ave Berkeley CA 94708

FRETWELL, LYMAN JEFFERSON, JR, b Rockford, Ill, Oct 8, 34; m 72; c 5. ACOUSTICS. *Educ:* Calif Inst Technol, BS, 56, PhD(physics), 67. *Prof Exp:* Mem tech staff, 66-68, SUPVR, BELL LABS, INC, 68- *Mem:* AAAS; Am Phys Soc. *Res:* Computational physics techniques in ocean acoustics with modeling of results for practical systems applications. *Mailing Add:* Bell Labs Whippany NJ 07981

FRETWELL, STEVE D, b Harrisonburg, Va, Jan 15, 42; m 63; c 2. POPULATION ECOLOGY. *Educ:* Bucknell Univ, BS, 64; NC State Univ, PhD(biomath), 68. *Prof Exp:* Fel, Princeton Univ, 68-69; from asst prof to assoc prof, 69-80, PROF THEORET ECOL, KANS STATE UNIV, 80- *Mem:* Wilson Ornith Soc; Am Ornith Union. *Res:* Role of behavior in population control; population control in a seasonal environment; role of population control in evolution of behavior. *Mailing Add:* Div of Biol Ackert Hall Kans State Univ Manhattan KS 66502

FRETZ, THOMAS ALVIN, b Buffalo, NY, Oct 9, 42; m 66; c 2. ORNAMENTAL HORTICULTURE. *Educ:* Univ Md, BS, 64; Univ Del, MS, 66, PhD(plant sci), 70. *Prof Exp:* Asst prof hort, Ga Sta, Univ Ga, 69-72; from asst prof to assoc prof hort, Ohio State Univ, 72-81; PROF HORT & HEAD DEPT, VA POLYTECH INST & STATE UNIV, 81- *Mem:* Am Soc Hort Sci; Int Plant Propagators Soc; Am Hort Soc; Agron Soc Am; Crop Sci Soc. *Res:* Chemotaxonomy of ornamental plants; propagation of ornamental plants and utilization of hardwood bark as a growth media for plants. *Mailing Add:* Hutcheson Hall Va Polytech Inst & State Univ Blacksburg VA 24061

FREUD, GEZA, b Budapest, Hungary, Jan 4, 22; m 64; c 3. MATHEMATICAL ANALYSIS. *Educ:* Hungarian Acad Sci, DSc(math), 56; Eotvos Lorand Univ, Budapest, PhD(math), 59. *Prof Exp:* Dep head differential equations, Math Res Inst, Hungarian Acad Sci, 53-64, head res group approximation theory, 64-69, dep head, 70-74; lectr math, Univ Col Dublin, 74; vis prof, 75, PROF MATH, OHIO STATE UNIV, 76- *Concurrent Pos:* Res fel math, Nat Inst Advan Math, Rome, Italy, 59; vis prof math, Univ Giessen, WGer, 62; univ prof math, Univ Rostock, EGer, 63-64; vis prof, Syracuse Univ, 66 & Ohio State Univ, 69; sr res fel, Steklow Inst Math Res, Moscow, 69; vis prof, Univ Montreal, 75 & 76. *Honors & Awards:* Grunwald Prize, First Degree, Hungarian Math Soc, 54; Kossuth Prize, Second Degree, Hungarian Govt, 59. *Mem:* Am Math Soc; Ger Soc Appl Math & Mech; Hungarian Math Soc. *Res:* Theory of approximation in the real field; orthogonal polynomials; theoretical aspects of numerical analysis. *Mailing Add:* Dept of Math Ohio State Univ 231 W 18th Ave Columbus OH 43210

FREUD, PAUL J, b Mineola, NY, Sept 22, 38; m 61; c 3. SOLID STATE PHYSICS. *Educ:* Dartmouth Col, BA, 60; Rutgers Univ, PhD(physics), 64. *Prof Exp:* Sr scientist, Columbus Lab, Battelle Mem Inst, 64-73; prin scientist, 73-80, CORP SCIENTIST, LEEDS & NORTHRUP CORP, 80- *Mem:* Am Phys Soc; Int Soc Hybrid Microelectronics; Am Vacuum Soc. *Res:* Solid state and thin film device research and development; transport properties of thin film metals; semiconductors and alloys. *Mailing Add:* Leeds & Northrup Co Dickerson Rd North Wales PA 19454

FREUDENSTEIN, FERDINAND, b Ger, May 12, 26; nat US; m 59. MECHANICAL ENGINEERING. *Educ:* Harvard Univ, MS, 48; Columbia Univ, PhD(mech eng), 54. *Prof Exp:* Develop engr, Am Optical Co, NY, 48-50; mem tech staff, Bell Tel Labs, Inc, 54; from asst prof to assoc prof mech eng, 54-70, chmn dept, 58-64, PROF MECH ENG, COLUMBIA UNIV, 70- *Concurrent Pos:* Guggenheim fels, 61-62 & 67-68; indust consult. *Honors & Awards:* Jr award, 55 & Machine Design Award, 72, Am Soc Mech Engrs. *Mem:* Nat Acad Eng; fel Am Soc Mech Engrs. *Res:* Engineering design; mechanisms; kinematic analysis and synthesis. *Mailing Add:* Dept of Mech Eng Columbia Univ New York NY 10027

FREUDENTHAL, HUGO DAVID, b Brooklyn, NY, Mar 29, 30; m 55; c 2. ENVIRONMENTAL SCIENCES. *Educ:* Columbia Univ, BS, 53, MS, 55; NY Univ, PhD(protozool), 59. *Prof Exp:* Assoc prof biol, 59-65, chmn dept, 65-73, PROF GRAD MARINE & ENVIRON SCI, POST COL, LONG ISLAND UNIV, 65-; V PRES, H2M CORP, ENVIRON ENGRS & SCIENTISTS, 73- *Concurrent Pos:* Assoc dir, Living Foraminifera Lab, Am Mus Natural Hist, 61-69; mgr life sci, Fairfield Repub Div, Fairchild Industs, Inc, 66-73; res assoc, Nat Bur Standards, 70-72. *Mem:* AAAS; Soc Protozoologists; Am Soc Limnol & Oceanog; Am Micros Soc; Am Soc Microbiol. *Res:* Physiology and ecology of plantonic Foraminifera; calcification and pressure studies on marine microorganisms; ecology and taxonomy of zooxanthellae; photomicrography of planktonic organisms; microbiology of polluted waters; aerospace life sciences; environmental engineering and impact studies. *Mailing Add:* H2M Corp 125 Baylis Rd Melville NY 11747

FREUDENTHAL, PETER, b New York, NY, Aug 12, 34; m 56; c 2. ENVIRONMENTAL HEALTH, METEOROLOGY. *Educ:* NY Univ, BA, 54, MS, 63, PhD(environ health sci), 70; Columbia Univ, BS, 60. *Prof Exp:* Meteorologist, Air Weather Serv, 55-57; asst res scientist, Inst Environ Med, NY Univ Med Ctr, 63-66; phys scientist, Environ Studies Div, Health & Safety Lab, AEC, 66-70; chief, Air Qual Control Eng, 70-75, DIR AIR & NOISE PROGS, CONSOL EDISON CO, NY, 75- *Concurrent Pos:* Asst res scientist, Inst Environ Med, Med Ctr, NY Univ, 66-70; adj assoc prof, Long Island Univ, 68-75; vchmn, Environ Sci Comn, NY Acad Sci, 80-81, chmn, 81- *Mem:* AAAS; Am Meteorol Soc; Air Pollution Control Asn; NY Acad Sci. *Res:* Air pollution; epidemiology; control techniques; cooling tower environmental effects; radioactive fallout transport and deposition; aerosol sizing and deposition; dispersion modeling. *Mailing Add:* Off of Environ Affairs Consol Edison Co 4 Irving Pl New York NY 10003

FREUDENTHAL, RALPH IRA, b New York, NY, Aug 27, 40. BIOCHEMICAL PHARMACOLOGY/TOXICOLOGY. *Educ:* NY Univ, BS, 63; State Univ NY Buffalo, PhD(biochem, pharmacol), 69. *Prof Exp:* Biochem pharmacologist, Res Triangle Inst, 69-73; assoc mgr path, pharmacol/toxicol & animal resources sect, Columbus Labs, Battelle Mem Inst, 73-77; dir, Toxicol Dept, 77-80, DIR, TOXICAL DEPT & ENVIRON HEALTH CTR, STAUFFER CHEM CO, 80- *Mem:* AAAS; Int Soc Biochem Pharmacol; NY Acad Sci; Am Soc Pharmacol & Exp Therapeut; Soc Toxicol. *Res:* Isolation and characterization of enzymes; drug-enzyme interactions; drug metabolism with emphasis on steroidal agents, including the separation and identification of metabolites; whole body autoradiography; mechanisms in carcinogenesis; molecular toxicology. *Mailing Add:* Stauffer Chem Co 400 Farmington Ave Farmington CT 06032

FREUND, GERHARD, b Frankfurt, Ger, Apr 21, 26; US citizen; m 55; c 2. INTERNAL MEDICINE, ENDOCRINOLOGY. *Educ:* Univ Frankfurt, MD, 51; McGill Univ, MS, 57. *Prof Exp:* Resident internal med, Augustana Hosp, Chicago, 52-53; resident, Res & Educ Hosp, Univ Ill, 53-55; clin instr internal med, Col Med, Univ Ill, 57-60, asst clin prof, 60-63; res assoc endocrinol, 63-64, asst prof, 64-70, assoc prof internal med, 70-75, PROF INTERNAL MED, COL MED, UNIV FLA, 75-; CHIEF ENDOCRINOL, VET ADMIN HSOP, GAINESVILLE, 67- *Concurrent Pos:* Res fel endocrinol, McGill Univ, 55-57. *Mem:* AAAS; fel Am Col Physicians; Soc Neurosci; Sigma Xi; Soc Biol Psychiat. *Res:* Effects of intermediary metabolites on systemic diseases; effects of chronic ethanol ingestion and acetaldehyde metabolism on brain function in man and experimental animals. *Mailing Add:* Dept Med Univ Fla Col of Med Gainesville FL 32610

FREUND, HARRY, b Tulsa, Okla, Nov 21, 17; m 45; c 3. ANALYTICAL CHEMISTRY. *Educ:* City Col New York, BS, 40; Univ Mich, MS, 41, PhD(chem), 45. *Prof Exp:* Asst, Anal Lab, Dept Eng Res, Univ Mich, 41-42, res assoc, 42-45, res chemist, 45-47; instr, 47-49, from asst prof to assoc prof, 47-60, prof, 60-80, EMER PROF CHEM, ORE STATE UNIV, 80- *Concurrent Pos:* Chemist, 48- *Honors & Awards:* NY Cocoa Exchange Award, 40. *Mem:* Am Chem Soc. *Res:* Inorganic chemistry; instrumental analysis; chemical instrumentation. *Mailing Add:* Dept of Chem Ore State Univ Corvallis OR 97330

FREUND, HOWARD JOHN, b Philadelphia, Pa, Dec 27, 46; m 71; c 2. COMBUSTION, GAS & SOLID REACTIONS. *Educ:* Pa State Univ, BS, 68; Cornell Univ, PhD(chem), 75. *Prof Exp:* Fel, Fuel Sci Dept, Pa State Univ, 75-76; SR STAFF CHEMIST, EXXON RES & ENG CO, 76- *Mem:* Am Chem Soc; Combustion Inst. *Res:* Mineral effects on coal combustion gasification; interaction of calcium with sulfur species and the reactions of water and carbon dioxide with carbon. *Mailing Add:* Exxon Res & Eng Co PO Box 45 Linden NJ 07036

FREUND, JACK, b New York, NY, Nov 19, 17; m 46; c 3. CLINICAL PHARMACOLOGY. *Educ:* NY Univ, BS, 37; Univ Va, 41-42; Med Col Va, MD, 46. *Prof Exp:* Intern, Hosps, Med Col Va, 46-47; resident path, Beth Israel Hosp, New York, 47-48; asst therapeut, Dept Med, NY Univ-Bellevue Med Ctr, 49; resident med, Vet Admin Hosp, Bronx, 49-50, sr resident chest & cardiol, 50-51; lectr pharmacol & assoc med, 51-58, clin assoc med, 58-61, from asst clin prof to assoc clin prof med, 61-70, ASST PROF PHARMACOL, MED COL VA, 58-, CLIN PROF MED, 70- *Concurrent Pos:* Asst dir clin res, A H Robins Co, Inc, 55-58, dir, 58-60, med dir, 60-62, vpres & med dir, 62-64, vpres res, 64-74, sr vpres res & develop, 74-78; consult pharmaceut indust, 78- *Mem:* Fel Am Col Physicians; fel Am Soc Clin Pharmacol & Therapeut; fel Am Col Cardiol; Soc Toxicol. *Res:* Clinical evaluation of drugs; peripheral vascular disease. *Mailing Add:* 310 Old Bridge Lane Richmond VA 23229

FREUND, JOHN ERNST, b Berlin, Ger, Aug 6, 21; nat US; m 49; c 2. MATHEMATICAL STATISTICS. *Educ:* Univ Calif, Los Angeles, BA, 43, MA, 44; Univ Pittsburgh, PhD(math), 52. *Prof Exp:* Prof math, Alfred Univ, 46-54; prof statist, Va Polytech Inst, 54-57; prof math, 57-71, EMER PROF MATH, ARIZ STATE UNIV, 71- *Mem:* Am Math Soc; Am Statist Asn; Math Asn Am; Inst Math Statist. *Mailing Add:* 7035 20 N 69th Pl Scottsdale AZ 85253

FREUND, LAMBERT BEN, b McHenry, Ill, Nov 23, 42; m 65; c 3. APPLIED MECHANICS, MATERIALS SCIENCE. *Educ:* Univ Ill, Urbana-Champaign, BS, 64, MS, 65; Northwestern Univ, PhD(appl mech), 67. *Prof Exp:* Fel mat, 67-69, from asst prof to assoc prof, 69-75, PROF ENG, BROWN UNIV, 75-, CHMN, DIV ENG, 79- *Concurrent Pos:* Consult, Am Iron & Steel Inst, 72-78; vis prof, Stanford Univ, 74-75. *Honors & Awards:* Henry Hess Award, Am Soc Mech Engrs, 74. *Mem:* Fel Am Soc Mech Engrs; Am Geophys Univ; Am Acad Mech. *Res:* Mechanics of solids; fracture mechanics; stress waves in solids; theoretical seismology. *Mailing Add:* Div of Eng Brown Univ Providence RI 02912

FREUND, MATTHEW J, b New York, NY, Aug 3, 28; m 52; c 2. PHYSIOLOGY, PHARMACOLOGY. *Educ:* NY Univ, BA, 48; Univ Nebr, MSc, 50; Rutgers Univ, PhD(physiol), 57. *Prof Exp:* Asst dairy husb, Rutgers Univ, 55-56; asst anat, Med Col, Cornell Univ, 56-58; instr physiol & pharmacol, 58-60, from asst prof to assoc prof, 60-67, prof pharmacol, New York Med Col, 68-78, assoc prof obstet & gynec, 64-78, res prof urol, 73-78; PROF PHYSIOL, SOUTHERN ILL UNIV, 78-, ASSOC PROF OBSTET & GYNEC, 64-, RES PROF UROL, 73-, CHMN DEPT PHYSIOL, 80- *Concurrent Pos:* Health Res Coun City New York res grant & career scientist, 62- *Mem:* AAAS; Am Physiol Soc; Am Soc Pharmacol & Exp Therapeut; Am Fertil Soc; Am Soc Cell Biol. *Res:* Physiology and pharmacology of reproduction fertility and infertility; cryobiology. *Mailing Add:* Dept of Physiol Southern Ill Univ Carbondale IL 62901

FREUND, PETER GEORGE OLIVER, b Temesvar, Rumania, Sept 7, 36; m 63. THEORETICAL PHYSICS. *Educ:* Polytech Inst Temesvar, dipl eng, 58; Univ Vienna, PhD(physics), 60. *Prof Exp:* Res assoc physics, Inst Theoret Physics, Univ Vienna, 61; res assoc, Inst Theoret Physics, Univ Geneva, 61-62; res assoc, Enrico Fermi Inst Nuclear Studies, 62-64, from asst prof to assoc prof, Inst & Univ, 64-74, PROF PHYSICS, UNIV CHICAGO & ENRICO FERMI INST NUCLEAR STUDIES, 74- *Concurrent Pos:* Mem, Inst Advan Study, Princeton, NJ, 64-65. *Mem:* Fel Am Phys Soc; Austrian Phys Soc; Ital Phys Soc. *Res:* Quantum field theory; dispersion theory; symmetries of elementary particle interactions. *Mailing Add:* Dept of Physics Univ of Chicago Chicago IL 60637

FREUND, PETER RICHARD, b Baltimore, Md, Oct 27, 35; m 59; c 3. FOOD SCIENCE, MICROBIOLOGY. *Educ:* Univ Wis, BS, 57, MS, 58, PhD(food sci), 69. *Prof Exp:* Sr scientist nutrit prod develop, Mead Johnson & Co, 61-65; prod develop mgr candy res, M&M/Mars, 65-67; dir qual control bakery prod mfg, Chapman & Smith Div, DCA Food Industs, 67-68; corp dir qual control & res multi-food mfg, Jewett & Sherman Co, 69-73; tech mgr prod develop, Universal Foods Corp, 73-75, dir tech develop multi-food res, 75-79, mgr res & develop, 79-81; ASST TO THE PRES, MULTI-NATURAL FOOD & AGR INGRED MFG, CHR HANSEN'S LAB, INC, 81- *Mem:* Inst Food Technologists. *Res:* Research and development of microbial cultures and fermentation products, naturally derived enzymes and natural colors. *Mailing Add:* 721 E Wabash Ave Waukesha WI 53186

FREUND, RICHARD A, b New York, NY, Nov 14, 24; m 63. ENGINEERING, STATISTICS. *Educ:* Columbia Univ, BA, 47, MS, 49. *Prof Exp:* Qual control engr, Camera Works, 48-49, statist analyst, Color Tech Div, 49-52, statist engr color print & processing, 53-57, film testing div, 58-60, staff consult, Mgt Systs Develop, 60-76, SR STAFF CONSULT QUAL ASSURANCE, MGT SERV DIV, EASTMAN KODAK CO, 76- *Honors & Awards:* Brumbaugh Award, Am Soc Qual Control, 60 & 62. *Mem:* Fel AAAS; fel Am Soc Qual Control (vpres, 67-70, pres, 72-73); fel Am Statist Asn; Am Soc Testing & Mat; Int Acad Qual. *Res:* Design of experiments; quality assurance systems; statistical quality control. *Mailing Add:* Eastman Kodak Co Kodak Park MSD-B56 Rochester NY 14650

FREUND, ROBERT STANLEY, b Newark, NJ, Jan 26, 39; m 62; c 2. CHEMICAL PHYSICS. *Educ:* Wesleyan Univ, BS, 60; Harvard Univ, MA, 62, PhD(chem physics), 65. *Prof Exp:* Res fel chem, Harvard Univ, 65-66; mem tech staff, 66-76, head dept environ chem, 76-79, HEAD DEPT CHEM KINETICS RES, BELL LABS, 79- *Concurrent Pos:* Mem comt, Atomic & Molecular Scis, Nat Res Coun, 76-; mem, Sci Adv Comt, Gov NJ, 79- *Mem:* Fel Am Phys Soc; Am Chem Soc. *Res:* Molecular spectroscopy; molecular dissociation; high rydberg states; electron collisions with molecules; double resonance and anticrossings. *Mailing Add:* Bell Labs Murray Hill NJ 07974

FREUND, RUDOLF JAKOB, b Kiel, Ger, Mar 3, 27; nat US; m 48; c 3. STATISTICS. *Educ:* Univ Chicago, MA, 51; NC State Univ, PhD(exp statist), 55. *Prof Exp:* From asst prof to assoc prof statist, Va Polytech Inst, 55-62; assoc prof, 62-74, assoc dir inst statist, 62-77, PROF STATIST, TEX A&M UNIV, 74- *Concurrent Pos:* Vis res scholar, Univ Okla, 60. *Mem:* Am Statist Asn; Biometrics Soc. *Res:* Use of computers in statistics; use of statistics and mathematics in economics; use of linear models. *Mailing Add:* Inst Statist Tex A&M Univ College Station TX 77843

FREUND, THOMAS STEVEN, b New York, NY, Jan 11, 44; m 66; c 2. BIOCHEMISTRY. *Educ:* Lehigh Univ, BS, 65, PhD(biochem), 69. *Prof Exp:* Teaching asst chem, Lehigh Univ, 65-66, res asst marine sci & biochem, 66-69; NIH trainee ophthal, Col Physicians & Surgeons, Columbia Univ, 69-70; res assoc oral biol, Sch Dent Med, Univ Conn, 70-75; vis asst prof biol, Trinity Col, Conn, 74-75; asst prof biochem, 75-78, ASSOC PROF BIOCHEM, SCH DENT, FAIRLEIGH DICKINSON UNIV, 78- *Concurrent Pos:* Vis scientist, Nat Inst Med Health Res, Paris, France, 75 & 82. *Mem:* AAAS; NY Acad Sci; Am Chem Soc; Int Asn Den Res; Am Asn Den Res. *Res:* Proteins, their structure and function; hormonal regulation; cellular metal ion requirements and transport; microbial biochemistry and mineral nutrition and development. *Mailing Add:* Sch of Dent Farleigh Dickinson Univ Hackensack NJ 07601

FREUNDLICH, MARTIN, b New York, NY, Dec 15, 30; m 52; c 4. BIOCHEMISTRY, MOLECULAR BIOLOGY. *Educ:* Brooklyn Col, BA, 55; Long Island Univ, MS, 57; Univ Minn, PhD(microbiol), 61. *Prof Exp:* USPHS fel, Cold Spring Harbor Lab Quant Biol, 61-64; asst prof microbiol, Dartmouth Med Sch, 64-66; asst prof biol sci, 66-69, actg chmn dept, 74-75, ASSOC PROF BIOCHEM, STATE UNIV NY STONY BROOK, 69- *Concurrent Pos:* USPHS res grant, 64-67, 69-72 & 73-77 & career develop award, 70-75; Lederle med fel, 65-66; ed, J Bact, 66-70; NY State Res Found grant, 68-69. *Mem:* Am Soc Microbiol; Am Soc Biol Chem. *Res:* Biochemistry and genetic control in branched biosynthetic pathways in microorganisms. *Mailing Add:* Dept of Biochem State Univ of NY Stony Brook NY 11794

FREUNDLICH, MARTIN M, b Goerlitz, Ger, Nov 23, 05; nat US; m 47; c 1. ELECTRONICS. *Educ:* Tech Univ, Berlin, ME, 29, PhD(electronics), 33. *Prof Exp:* Asst, Tech Univ, Berlin, 33-34 & Royal Tech Col, Scotland, 35; mem staff, Pye Radio Ltd, Eng, 35-36, Columbia Broadcasting Syst, 36-49 & NAm Philips, 44-45; asst supv eng consult, AIL Div, Eaton Corp, 49-70; INDEPENDENT CONSULT, 70- *Concurrent Pos:* Adj asst prof, Queensborough Community Col, City Univ New York, 72-78. *Mem:* AAAS; Am Astron Soc; Inst Elec & Electronics Engrs. *Res:* Tube development, oscillographs for lightning investigations, electron microscopes; cathode ray tubes for monochrome and color television, measurements of properties of phosphors; storage tubes; experiments on color television systems; materials in space environments; space lubrication; vacuum technology; exobiology. *Mailing Add:* 16 Suydam Dr Melville NY 11747

FREVEL, LUDO KARL, b Frankfurt am Main, Ger, May 31, 10; nat US; m 37; c 3. CHEMISTRY. *Educ:* Johns Hopkins Univ, PhD(chem), 34. *Prof Exp:* Nat res fel chem, Calif Inst Technol, 34-36; res chemist, Dow Chem Co, 36-74; FEL CHEM, JOHNS HOPKINS UNIV, 74- *Concurrent Pos:* Lab dir chem physics, Dow Chem Co, 69-72; vis res prof mat sci, Pa State Univ, 75. *Mem:* AAAS; Am Chem Soc; Crystallog Asn. *Res:* X-ray studies of substances under pressure; crystal structure; identification of compounds by x-ray and electron diffraction methods; catalysis; iterated functions. *Mailing Add:* 1205 W Park Dr Midland MI 48640

FREVERT, RICHARD KELLER, b Odebolt, Iowa, Feb 26, 14; m 47; c 1. AGRICULTURAL ENGINEERING. *Educ:* Iowa State Col, BS, 37, MS, 40, PhD(agr eng, soils), 48. *Prof Exp:* From instr to prof agr eng, Iowa State Col, 37-58; DIR AGR EXP STA, UNIV ARIZ, 58-, ASSOC DEAN, COL AGR, 72-, PROF AGR ENG, RES SCIENTIST AGR ENG SOILS, WATER & ENG, 80- *Concurrent Pos:* Asst dir, Agr Exp Sta, Iowa State Col, 52-58. *Mem:* Fel AAAS; fel Am Soc Agr Engrs; Soil Conserv Soc Am; Am Geophys Union. *Res:* Permeability of soils; irrigation; drainage; erosion control; soil and water losses from watersheds. *Mailing Add:* Agr Exp Sta Univ of Ariz Tucson AZ 85721

FREY, ALBERT JOSEPH, b Urnaesch, Switz, Apr 23, 27; m 56; c 2. ORGANIC CHEMISTRY, MEDICINAL CHEMISTRY. *Educ:* State Col Trogen, Switz, BS, 47; Swiss Fed Inst Technol, Chem Engr, 51, PhD(steroid synthesis), 53. *Prof Exp:* Res fel, Swiss Fed Inst Technol, 53-55 & Harvard Univ, 55-56; res chemist, Sandoz Ltd, Switz, 56-60, res group leader, 60-62, dir res, Sandoz-Wander, Inc, 62-64, vpres in charge res, 64-70, pres & chief exec officer, 71-81, CHMN BD, SANDOZ, INC, 81- *Mem:* AAAS; Am Chem Soc; Swiss Chem Soc. *Res:* Synthetic organic chemistry especially applied to natural products; drug research in general. *Mailing Add:* Sandoz Inc Route 10 East Hanover NJ 07936

FREY, BRUCE EDWARD, b New York, NY, Jan 29, 45. BIOLOGICAL OCEANOGRAPHY. *Educ:* Cornell Univ, BS, 67; Ore State Univ, MS, 74, PhD(oceanog), 77. *Prof Exp:* res assoc, 77-79, ASST PROF OCEANOG, ORE STATE UNIV, 79- *Concurrent Pos:* Prin investr, Environ Protection Agency grant, 77-79 & Columbia River data develop contract, 79-81. *Mem:* Am Soc Limnol & Oceanog; AAAS; Phycol Soc. *Res:* Phytoplankton ecology and physiology, especially phytoplankton-nutrient interactions. *Mailing Add:* Sch Oceanog Ore State Univ Corvallis OR 97331

FREY, CARL, b New York, NY; m 55; c 3. ENGINEERING. *Educ:* NY Univ, BME, 49; Columbia Univ, MA, 51. *Prof Exp:* Asst exec secy, Eng Manpower Comn, 60, exec secy, 61-64; secy, Engrs Joint Coun, 65-67, exec dir, 67-79; EXEC DIR, AM ASN ENG SOCS, 79- *Concurrent Pos:* Adv, US Dept Labor, 62; mem comt specialized personnel, Off Emergency Planning, Off of the President, 62-64, mem exec res, adv panel select comt govt res, House of Rep, 64-; treas, US Comt Large Dams & US Nat Comt, World Power Conf, 65- *Mem:* AAAS; Am Soc Eng Educ; Am Inst Aeronaut & Astronaut. *Res:* Policies in field of engineering and scientific manpower; professional society. *Mailing Add:* Am Asn Eng Socs 345 E 47th St New York NY 10017

FREY, CHARLES FREDERICK, b New York, NY, Nov 15, 29; m 57; c 5. SURGERY. *Educ:* Amherst Col, BA, 51; Cornell Univ, MD, 55. *Prof Exp:* Instr, New York Hosp, Med Sch, Cornell Univ, 63; from instr to prof surg, Med Ctr, Univ Mich, Ann Arbor, 64-76; PROF & EXEC VCHMN, DEPT SURG, UNIV CALIF, DAVIS, 76- *Concurrent Pos:* Fel, Dept Surg, Univ Mich, 64-65; attend physician surg serv, Vet Admin Hosp, Ann Arbor & Wayne County Gen Hosp, Eloise, 65-71; surg consult, Student Health Serv, 67-70; pres, Univ Asn Emergency Med Serv, 70-71; chmn, Mich Emergency Serv Health Coun, consult to ad hoc adv group on emergency med serv, Vet Admin, 71-72; consult ed, J Am Col Emergency Physicians, 71-74; surg consult, Vet Admin Hosp, 71-76; dir surg, Wayne County Gen Hosp, Eloise, 71-76; mem, Ad Hoc Comt Emergency Med Commun, Nat Acad Sci, 71-72; consult, Ann Arbor Vet Hosp, 71-76; consult & mem, Bd Dirs, Govr's Hwy Safety Res Inst, 73-76; mem, Comt Regional Emergency Med Commun Systs, Nat Acad Sci, Nat Res Coun, 73- chmn, Mich Comt Trauma, 70-74, regional dir, Area V Comt Trauma, 74-76; consult to dir surg, Cent Off, Vet Admin Hosp, 77- *Mem:* Fel Am Col Surgeons; Soc Surg Alimentary Tract; Am Fedn Clin Res; fel Am Asn Surgeons Trauma; Soc Univ Surgeons. *Res:* Pancreatic and biliary pathophysiology; trauma and emergency health service systems. *Mailing Add:* Dept Surg Sch Med Univ Calif 4301 X St Sacramento CA 95817

FREY, CHRIS(TIAN) M(ILLER), b Cumberland, Md, Feb 26, 23; m 43; c 2. MECHANICAL ENGINEERING. *Educ:* Univ Md, BS, 51. *Prof Exp:* Supvr gen design group, Allegany Ballistics Lab, 51-53, design res group, 53-59; chief engr, 59-67, MGR RES & ADVAN TECHNOL DEPT, UNITED TECHNOL CTR, 67- *Concurrent Pos:* Chmn, Missile Booster Mat Comt, 56-59; consult mat adv bd, Nat Acad Sci, 58-60; consult, Nat Aeronaut & Space Admin, 59-60; lectr, Stanford Univ. *Mem:* Am Soc Mech Engrs; Am Soc Testing & Mat; Am Ord Asn. *Res:* Rocket propulsion; high temperature materials; high strength materials, including fiberglass and boron structures; unique fabrication techniques and rocket design. *Mailing Add:* Res & Advan Technol Dept 1890 Newcastle Dr Los Altos CA 94022

FREY, DAVID ALLEN, b Mendota, Ill, Nov 26, 35; m 57; c 2. ORGANIC CHEMISTRY, POLYMER CHEMISTRY. *Educ:* Monmouth Col, Ill, BA, 57; Univ Iowa, MS, 59, PhD(org chem), 61. *Prof Exp:* Fel high temperature polymers under C S Marvel, Univ Ariz, 61-62; res chemist, Phillips Petrol Co, 62-64; res chemist, 64-69, res supvr, 69-75, mgr polymer res, 75-78, QUAL ASSURANCE MGR, MORTON CHEM CO DIV, MORTON-NORWICH PROD, INC, 78- *Mem:* Am Chem Soc. *Res:* Inter-intra polymerizations, high temperature polymers and emulsion and solution polymerizations using free radical and ionic catalysts; quality assurance coatings and adhesives. *Mailing Add:* Morton-Norwich Prod Inc Morton Chem Co Div 1275 Lake Ave Woodstock IL 60098

FREY, DAVID GROVER, b Hartford, Wis, Oct 10, 15; m 48; c 3. LIMNOLOGY. *Educ:* Univ Wis, BA, 36, MA, 38, PhD(zool), 40. *Prof Exp:* Asst, Conserv Dept, Wis, 35-40; jr aquatic biologist, US Fish & Wildlife Serv, Wash, 40-42, asst aquatic biologist, Md, 42-43, assoc aquatic biologist, 43-45; assoc prof zool, Univ NC, 46-50; assoc prof, 50-55, PROF ZOOL, IND UNIV, BLOOMINGTON, 55- *Concurrent Pos:* Fulbright & Guggenheim fels, Austria, 53-54; ed J, Am Soc Limnol & Oceanog & aquatic ed J, Ecol Soc Am; Nat Acad Sci-Nat Res Coun Exchange to Soviet Union, 62; Ford Found consult, Mindanao State Univ, 67-68. *Honors & Awards:* Einar Naumann-August Thienemann Medal, Int Asn Limnol, 80. *Mem:* Am Soc Limnol & Oceanog (pres, 55); Am Micros Soc (vpres, 70); Ecol Soc Am; Am Quaternary Asn (pres, 73-74); Int Asn Limnol (vpres, 80-). *Res:* Development history of lakes and micropaleontology of freshwater deposits; systematics, ecology and evolution of chydorid cladocera. *Mailing Add:* Dept of Zool Ind Univ Bloomington IN 47401

FREY, DENNIS FREDERICK, b Chickasha, Okla, Apr 1, 41; m 62; c 2. ANIMAL BEHAVIOR. *Educ:* Okla State Univ, BS, 63, PhD(zool), 70; Va State Col, MS, 67. *Prof Exp:* ASSOC PROF BIOL SCI, CALIF POLYTECH STATE UNIV, 70- *Concurrent Pos:* Res grant, NIMH, 71-72 & Calif Polytech State Univ, 72-73; researcher, Animal Behav Res Group, Dept Zool, Oxford Univ, 78-79. *Mem:* Animal Behav Soc; Am Soc Zoologists. *Res:* Social Behavior in fishes with particular interest in determinants and consequences of dominance phenomena; time sharing in fish behavior. *Mailing Add:* Dept of Biol Sci Calif Polytech State Univ San Luis Obispo CA 93407

FREY, DONALD N(ELSON), b St Louis, Mo, Mar 13, 23; m 42; c 6. MECHANICAL ENGINEERING. *Educ:* Univ Mich, BS, 47, PhD(metall), 50. *Prof Exp:* Asst eng, Univ Mich, 47-48, res assoc, 48-49, instr metall eng, Col Eng, 49-50, asst prof chem & metall eng, 50-51; assoc dir, Sci Lab, Ford Motor Co, 51-57; asst chief engr, Ford Div, 57-61, prod planning mgr, 61, asst gen mgr, 62-65, vpres & gen mgr, 65-67, vpres prod develop, 67-78; pres, Gen Cable Corp, 68-71; CHMN, BELL & HOWELL CO, 71- *Mem:* Nat Acad Eng; fel Am Soc Metals; Soc Automotive Engrs; Am Inst Mining, Metall & Petrol Engrs. *Res:* Metallurgy of high temperature alloys; general metallurgy including iron and steel making; general automotive engineering; general management. *Mailing Add:* Bell & Howell Co 7100 McCormick Rd Chicago IL 60645

FREY, ELMER JACOB, b Buffalo, NY, Jan, 3, 18; m 45, 63; c 2. SYSTEMS ENGINEERING, INERTIAL INSTRUMENTATION. *Educ:* City Col New York, BS, 37; NY Univ, MS, 40; Mass Inst Technol, PhD(math), 49. *Prof Exp:* Teacher, Pub Sch, NY, 40-41; instr math, Mass Inst Technol, 46-49, mathematician, Instrumentation Lab, 49-53, group leader, 53-55, asst dir, 55-57, dep assoc dir, 57-69, lectr aeronaut & astronaut, 62-72, assoc dir, Measurement Systs Lab, 65-70, mem staff, Ctr Space Res, 70-72; eng mgr satellite systs, Fairchild Space & Electronics Co, 72-75; CONSULT SYSTS ENG, FREY ASSOCS, INC, 75- *Concurrent Pos:* Mem, US Defense Dept Ad Hoc Comt Inertial Guid, 63; vis prof, Spec Sch Aeronaut, Paris, 63-64; consult engr, France, 63-64; consult, US Air Force Sci Adv Bd, 63-65, chief scientist, 64-65; NATO Adv Group Aerospace Res & Develop, 64 & 69; US Dept Transp lectr, Univ Naples, Cath Univ Louvain & Nat Sch Advan Aeronaut Studies, Paris, 69-70. *Mem:* Am Geophys Union; assoc fel Am Inst Aeronaut & Astronaut; Soc Indust & Appl Math. *Res:* Computation systems and borehole instrumentation; railroad automation; transportation safety and cost benefit analysis. *Mailing Add:* Frey Assocs Inc Chestnut Hill Rd RD 4 Amherst NH 03031

FREY, FREDERICK AUGUST, b Milwaukee, Wis, Apr 1, 38. GEOCHEMISTRY. *Educ:* Univ Wis, BS, 60, PhD(phys chem), 66. *Prof Exp:* Res chemist, Hercules Chem Co, 60-61; asst prof, 66-73, assoc prof, 73-80, PROF GEOCHEM, MASS INST TECHNOL, 80- *Mem:* Geol Soc Am; Am Geophys Union; Geochem Soc. *Res:* Elemental distribution in geologic systems. *Mailing Add:* Dept of Earth & Planetary Sci Rm 54-1220 Mass Inst of Technol Cambridge MA 02139

FREY, FREDERICK WOLFF, JR, b New Orleans, La, Sept 30, 30; m 52; c 5. INORGANIC CHEMISTRY. *Educ:* Loyola Univ, La, BS, 50; Tulane Univ, MS, 52, PhD(chem), 54. *Prof Exp:* Chemist, Mallinckrodt Chem Works, 54-55; supvr chem res, 55-73, ASST DIR INDUST CHEM RES, ETHYL CORP, 73- *Mem:* Am Chem Soc. *Res:* Metal hydride chemistry; organometallics. *Mailing Add:* Ethyl Corp Box 341 Baton Rouge LA 70821

FREY, HAROLD JOSEPH, b Benton Harbor, Mich, Oct 9, 20; m 49; c 3. PHYSICAL CHEMISTRY. *Educ:* Loyola Univ, Ill, BS, 41; Catholic Univ, PhD(phys chem), 48. *Prof Exp:* Chemist, Plastics Dept, 48-53, res supvr, 53-58, indust specialist polyolefins, 58-76, MKT PROGS MGR, E I DU PONT DE NEMOURS & CO, INC, 76- *Res:* Polymer chemistry. *Mailing Add:* E I du Pont de Nemours & Co Inc Wilmington DE 19898

FREY, HENRY RICHARD, b New York, NY, July 16, 32; m 60; c 3. PHYSICAL OCEANOGRAPHY, OCEAN ENGINEERING. *Educ:* Queen's Col, BS, 60; NY Univ, MS, 66, PhD(oceanog), 71. *Prof Exp:* Group leader underwater technol, Uniroyal Res Ctr, Uniroyal Inc, 60-66, prog mgr ocean sci & eng, Technol Transfer Div, 66-67; sr res scientist oceanog, Sch Eng & Sci, NY Univ, 67-73 & NY Inst Ocean Resources, 73-74; res assoc prof, Polytech Inst NY, 73-76; tech adv, 77-80, CHIEF MARINE ENVIRON SERVS DIV, NAT OCEANIC & ATMOSPHERIC ADMIN, NAT OCEAN SURV, 80- *Concurrent Pos:* Chmn, Uniroyal Ocean Eng Group, Uniroyal Inc, 60-67; dir ocean eng prog, NY Univ, 71-73 & Polytech Inst NY, 73-76; consult, Ministry of Mining & Nat Resources, Jamaica, Chesapeake Res Consortium & Alpine Geophys Assocs, 76-77. *Mem:* Am Geophys Union; Marine Technol Soc; Sigma Xi. *Res:* Continental shelf and estuarine physical oceanography, especially circulation, mixing, wave climate and transports. *Mailing Add:* Nat Oceanic & Atmospheric Admin 6001 Executive Blvd Rockville MD 20852

FREY, JAMES R, b De Young, Pa, Feb 27, 32; m 53; c 2. BACTERIOLOGY, IMMUNOLOGY. *Educ:* Defiance Col, BS, 52; Miami Univ, Ohio, MA, 57; Mich State Univ, PhD(virol), 61. *Prof Exp:* Asst bact, Tulane Univ, 55-58; asst bact, Mich State Univ, 58-59, virol, 59-61; from asst prof to assoc prof, 61-70, head dept, 68-78, div chmn Natural Systs Studies, 69-78, PROF BIOL, DEFIANCE COL, 70- *Concurrent Pos:* Vis scientist, NSF, 62-64. *Mem:* AAAS; Am Pub Health Asn; Am Soc Microbiol; Am Inst Biol Sci. *Res:* Quantitative study of the enteric viruses in sewage; immuno-genetics approach to study of gene differences. *Mailing Add:* Dept of Biol Defiance Col Defiance OH 43512

FREY, JEFFREY, b New York, NY, Aug 27, 39. ELECTRICAL ENGINEERING, MATERIALS SCIENCE. *Educ:* Cornell Univ, BEE, 60; Univ Calif, Berkeley, MS, 63, PhD(elec eng), 65. *Prof Exp:* Mem tech staff, microwave semiconductor devices, Watkins-Johnson Co, Calif, 65-66; NATO fel, Rutherford High Energy Lab, Eng, 66-67; res assoc ion implantation, UK Atomic Energy Res Estab, Harwell, 67-69; from asst prof to assoc prof, 70-79, PROF ELEC ENG, CORNELL UNIV, 79- *Concurrent Pos:* Japan Soc Promotion Sci fel, Univ Tokyo, 76-77; consult, US Air Force, Carborundum Co & Westinghouse Elec Corp, 77-; mgr device physics & actg mgr advan lithography, Advan Tech Ctr, Signetics Corp, 80-81. *Mem:* Inst Elec & Electronics Engrs. *Res:* Microwave semiconductor devices; microwave integrated circuits; semiconductor materials and devices. *Mailing Add:* Dept Elec Eng Phillips Hall Col Eng Cornell Univ Ithaca NY 14850

FREY, JOHN ERHART, b Chicago, Ill, May 6, 30; m 57; c 4. INORGANIC CHEMISTRY. *Educ:* Northwestern Univ, BS, 52; Univ Ill, MS, 55; Univ Chicago, PhD(inorg chem), 56. *Prof Exp:* Res chemist, Univ Chicago, 56-57; from instr to asst prof chem, Bowdoin Col, 57-60; asst prof, Ill Inst Technol, 60-63 & Western Mich Univ, 63-66; assoc prof, 66-71, asst dean common learning, 69-78, PROF CHEM, NORTHERN MICH UNIV, 78- *Mem:* Am Chem Soc. *Res:* Boron hydrides and halides. *Mailing Add:* Dept of Chem Sch of Arts & Sci Northern Mich Univ Marquette MI 49855

FREY, KENNETH JOHN, b Charlotte, Mich, Mar 23, 23; m 45; c 3. PLANT BREEDING. *Educ:* Mich State Univ, BS, 44, MS, 45; Iowa State Univ, PhD, 48. *Prof Exp:* Asst, Mich State Univ, 44-45, asst prof farm crops, 48-53; from assoc prof to prof agron, 53-70, asst dean grad col, 67-70, actg vpres res & dean grad col, 70-71, C F CURTIS DISTINGUISHED PROF AGR, IOWA STATE UNIV, 70-, PROF AGRON, 80- *Concurrent Pos:* Fulbright scholar, Australia Univ Agr, 68. *Mem:* Fel AAAS; fel Am Soc Agron; Genetics Soc Am. *Res:* Plant breeding methodology for self-pollinated crops; biochemistry of cereal grains. *Mailing Add:* Dept of Agron Iowa State Univ Ames IA 50011

FREY, MARY ANNE BASSETT, b Washington, DC, Dec 15, 34; c 3. MEDICAL PHYSIOLOGY. *Educ:* George Washington Univ, BA, 70, PhD(physiol), 75. *Prof Exp:* Lectr physiol, Montgomery Col, 72-75; Nat Heart & Lung Inst fel, Sch Med, George Washington Univ, 75-76; asst prof physiol, Wright State Univ, 76-80, assoc prof, 80-82; TECH MGR, KENNEDY SPACE CTR, BIONETICS CORP, FLA, 82- *Concurrent Pos:* Consult, Presidents Adv Coun Mgt Improv, 72-73 & US Nat Olympic Men's Volleyball Team; mem, NIH Gen Med Sci Review Comt Access to Res Careers Prog. *Mem:* Asn Women Sci; AAAS; Am Heart Asn; Sigma Xi; Am Physiol Soc. *Res:* Cardiovascular physiology, neural control of the circulation, exercise and stress physiology. *Mailing Add:* Bio-1 Room 3105 O & C Bldg Kennedy Space Ctr Cape Canaveral FL 45431

FREY, MAURICE G, b Cincinnati, Ohio, July 26, 13; m 45; c 2. STRUCTURAL GEOLOGY, PETROLEUM GEOLOGY. *Educ:* Univ Cincinnati, BS, 36; Univ Minn, MS, 37, PhD(geol), 39. *Prof Exp:* Party chief gravity meter crew, Chevron Oil Co Div, Stand Oil Co Calif, 39-41, seismologist, 42-45, supvr geophys, 45-46, dist geologist, 46-47, explor res supvr, 47-48; assoc prof geol, Univ Cincinnati, 48-52; mem staff geol & geophys explor, Chevron Oil Co Div, Standard Oil Co Calif, 52-54, chief geologist, 55-67, asst to vpres, 67-71, consult geologist environ affairs, 71-78; CONSULT, GEOL & GEOPHYS, 78- *Concurrent Pos:* Adj prof earth sci & geophys, Univ New Orleans, 78- *Mem:* Am Asn Petrol Geol; Soc Explor Geophys; fel Geol Soc Am. *Res:* Exploration for oil and gas in relation to origin and development of salt domes; oil in marine environment. *Mailing Add:* 7441 Cameo St New Orleans LA 70124

FREY, MERWIN LESTER, b Manhattan, Kans, Apr 20, 32; m 61; c 2. VETERINARY MICROBIOLOGY. *Educ:* Kans State Univ, BS & DVM, 56; Univ Wis, MS, 61, PhD(vet sci), 66. *Prof Exp:* Res asst vet sci, Univ Wis, 59-61, instr assoc, 61-64; NIH trainee, 64-66; from asst prof to prof vet microbiol, Iowa State Univ, 66-73; prof med & surg & head dept vet parasitol, microbiol & pub health, Col Vet Med, Okla State Univ, 73-77; PROF DEPT VET SCI, UNIV NEBR-LINCOLN, 77- *Mem:* AAAS; Am Vet Med Asn; Am Asn Avian Path; Am Soc Microbiol; Am Asn Vet Lab Diagnosticians. *Res:* Respiratory and other infections of domestic animals, especially mycoplasmas and viruses as causes of pneumonia in cattle. *Mailing Add:* Dept of Vet Sci Univ of Nebr Lincoln NE 68583

FREY, NICHOLAS MARTIN, b Earlham, Iowa, Apr 14, 48; m 71. CROP PHYSIOLOGY. *Educ:* Iowa State Univ, BS, 70; Univ Minn, PhD(plant physiol), 74. *Prof Exp:* Physiologist, Pioneer Hi-Bred Int, Inc, 74-80; COORDR, JOHNSTON RES, 80- *Mem:* Crop Sci Soc Am; Am Soc Agron; Am Soc Plant Physiologists. *Res:* Application of plant physiology research to a plant breeding program; plant development; seed corn production. *Mailing Add:* Pioneer Hi-Bred Int Inc Box 85 Johnston IA 50131

FREY, PERRY ALLEN, b Plain City, Ohio, Nov 14, 35; m 61; c 2. BIOCHEMISTRY. *Educ:* Ohio State Univ, BS, 59; Brandeis Univ, PhD(biochem), 68. *Prof Exp:* Chemist, USPHS, 60-64; NIH res fel chem, Harvard Univ, 67-68; from asst prof to prof chem, Ohio State Univ, 69-81; PROF BIOCHEM, UNIV WIS-MADISON, 81- *Mem:* Am Chem Soc; Am Soc Biol Chemists. *Res:* Chemical mechanism of action of enzymes and coenzymes. *Mailing Add:* Inst Enzyme Res Univ Wis 1710 Univ Ave Madison WI 53706

FREY, SHELDON ELLSWORTH, b Wheelerville, Pa, Apr 29, 21; m 47; c 2. ORGANIC CHEMISTRY. *Educ:* Pa State Col, BS, 43; Univ Tenn, MS, 50; Univ Ill, PhD(chem), 53. *Prof Exp:* Jr engr mass spectrom, Kellex Corp, NY, 43-44, jr engr vacuum test, Tenn, 44; from tech supvr to assoc chemist process control, Carbide & Carbon Chem Div, Union Carbide & Carbon Corp, 44-50; res chemist, E I du Pont de Nemours & Co, 53-62; coordr opers improv, Allied Chem Corp, 62-72; RES CHEMIST & ASST MGR, MONROE CHEM CO, 73- *Mem:* Am Chem Soc. *Res:* Fluorocarbon polymers; organic chemistry of plastics; elastomers; polymers; hindered ketones; products of formaldehyde and hydroxybenzoic acid; fluorinated hydrocarbons; tetraethyl lead; dispersed dyes; cumene hydroperoxide; phenol; phthalic anhydride; benzaldehyde. *Mailing Add:* 404 Kings Hwy Moorestown NJ 08057

FREY, THOMAS G, b Eugene, Ore, Sept 24, 43; m 75; c 2. ORGANIC CHEMISTRY. *Educ:* Univ Ore, BA, 65; Univ Idaho, PhD(org chem), 71. *Prof Exp:* Asst prof, 70-76, assoc prof, 76-80, PROF CHEM, CALIF STATE POLYTECH UNIV, SAN LUIS OBISPO, 80- *Mem:* Am Chem Soc. *Res:* Study of base catalyzed nucleophilic additions to activated acetylenes. *Mailing Add:* Dept of Chem Calif State Polytech Univ San Luis Obispo CA 93407

FREY, WILLIAM ADRIAN, b York, Pa, Jan 1, 51; m 72; c 1. CLINICAL DIAGNOSTICS, IMMUNOCHEMISTRY. *Educ:* King's Col, BS, 72; Pa State Univ, PhD(org chem), 76. *Prof Exp:* Res fel biol chem, Harvard Med Sch, 77-80; RES BIOCHEMIST, CLIN SYSTS DIV, E I DU PONT DE NEMOURS & CO, INC, 80- *Concurrent Pos:* Assoc staff med, Peter Bent Brigham Hosp, Boston, 77-80; fel, Am Cancer Soc, 77-78; traineeship, NIH, 78-80. *Mem:* Am Chem Soc; AAAS; NY Acad Sci; Am Asn Clin Chemists. *Res:* Clinical diagnostics; immunochemistry; enzyme mechanisms. *Mailing Add:* Photo Prod Dept Clin Systs Div E I Du Pont de Nemours & Co Wilmington DE 19898

FREY, WILLIAM CARL, b Newark, NJ, Aug 21, 23; m 47; c 2. STATISTICS, CHEMISTRY. *Educ:* Upsala Col, BA, 43; Rutgers Univ, MS, 54. *Prof Exp:* Control chemist, 43-45, asst to purchasing agent, 45-47, supvr anal unit, Control Dept, 47-53, supvr statist unit, 53-57, head statist serv dept, 57-66, dir rech serv, 66-68, dir qual assurance & regulatory conformance, 68-70, TECH DIR, BRISTOL-MYERS CO, 70- *Concurrent Pos:* Adj instr grad sch, Rutgers Univ, 58- *Honors & Awards:* Ellis R Ott Award, 76. *Mem:* Am Statist Asn; fel Am Soc Qual Control. *Res:* Applied statistics; application of statistical methods in the treatment of experimental data, control of quality, production improvement and in assorted management functions. *Mailing Add:* Bristol-Myers Prod 225 Long Ave Hillside NJ 07207

FREY, WILLIAM FRANCIS, b Bristol, VA, Nov 23, 33; m 55; c 3. EXPERIMENTAL PHYSICS. *Educ:* King Col, AB, 55; Vanderbilt Univ, MS, 57, PhD(physics), 60. *Prof Exp:* Asst prof, 60-64, ASSOC PROF PHYSICS, DAVIDSON COL, 64- *Concurrent Pos:* Consult, Health Physics Div, Oak Ridge Nat Lab, 73- *Res:* Beta-ray spectroscopy; internal conversion coefficients; photoelectric angular distributions; fluorescent yields; multi-photon absorption processes in atoms using tunable dye laser. *Mailing Add:* Dept of Physics Davidson Col Davidson NC 28036

FREYBERGER, WILFRED L(AWSON), b Newark, NJ, Feb 28, 28; m 51; c 3. MINERAL ENGINEERING, SURFACE CHEMISTRY. *Educ:* Mass Inst Technol, SB, 47, ScD(metall), 55. *Prof Exp:* Res engr, NJ Zinc Co, Pa, 55-60; res metallurgist, Am Cyanamid Co, Conn, 60-64; assoc prof metall & res engr, 64-68, dir, Inst Mineral Res, 70-80, PROF METALL ENG, MICH TECHNOL UNIV, 68- *Mem:* AAAS; Am Inst Mining, Metall & Petrol Engrs. *Res:* Flotation collector chemistry; flotation kinetics; developmental studies in the practice of mineral engineering. *Mailing Add:* Inst of Mineral Res Mich Technol Univ Houghton MI 49931

FREYBURGER, WALTER ALFRED, b Philadelphia, Pa, May 14, 20; m 47; c 5. PHARMACOLOGY. *Educ:* Bucknell Univ, BS, 42; Univ Mich, PhD(pharmacol), 51. *Prof Exp:* Asst pharm, Univ Mich, 46-50; pharmacologist, 50-57, sect head cardiovasc-renal pharmacol, 57-68, MGR CARDIOVASC DIS RES, UPJOHN CO, 68- *Concurrent Pos:* Mem, Coun High Blood Pressure Res & Circulation, Am Heart Asn. *Mem:* Am Soc Pharmacol & Exp Therapeut. *Res:* Cardiovascular and autonomic nervous system physiology and pharmacology. *Mailing Add:* Upjohn Co 7000 Portage Rd Kalamazoo MI 49001

FREYD, PETER JOHN, b Evanston, Ill, Feb 5, 36; m 57; c 2. MATHEMATICS. *Educ:* Brown Univ, AB, 58; Princeton Univ, PhD(math), 60. *Prof Exp:* Consult, Batton, Barton, Durstine & Osborn, 58-60; Ritt instr math, Columbia Univ, 60-62; from asst prof to assoc prof, 62-68, PROF MATH, UNIV PA, 68- *Concurrent Pos:* Assoc chmn dept math, Univ Pa, 64-73; vis prof, Univ Chicago, 80; fel, St John's Col, Cambridge, Eng, 80-81; vis prof, Univ Louvain, La Neuve, France, 81. *Mem:* Am Math Soc. *Res:* Categorical algebra & topos theory; theory of functors; Abelian categories and their embeddings; representation in Abelian categories; existence of adjoints; applications to relative homological algebra, stable homotopy, proof theory, model theory and foundations. *Mailing Add:* Dept of Math Univ of Pa Philadelphia PA 19104

FREYER, GUSTAV JOHN, b Ancon, CZ, Nov 11, 31; US citizen; m 57; c 2. SPACE PHYSICS. *Educ:* US Mil Acad, West Point, BS, 54; Air Force Inst Technol, MS, 60; Pa State Univ, PhD(physics), 69. *Prof Exp:* Assoc prof physics, Air Force Inst Technol, 67-71; chief scientist, Air Force Weapons Lab, 73-74, comdr, 75-77; SYST SURVIVABILITY MGR, DENVER DIV, MARTIN MARIETTA AEROSPACE, 77- *Mem:* Am Geophys Union. *Res:* Aurora; magnetospheric physics; nuclear weapon effects. *Mailing Add:* 5959 S Wolff Ct Littleton CO 80123

FREYERMUTH, HARLAN BENJAMIN, b Muscatine, Iowa, Sept 15, 17; m 46; c 1. ORGANIC CHEMISTRY. *Educ:* Univ Iowa, BA, 38, MS, 40, PhD(org chem), 42. *Prof Exp:* Asst, Univ Iowa, 40-42; tech assoc, GAF Corp, 42-69, mgr col rels & tech employment, 69-76; CHEMIST & CONSULT, J T BAKER CHEM CO, 77- *Mem:* Am Chem Soc. *Res:* Organic research in dyes and dye intermediates; formation and properties of uretidinedione; textile finishes; catalytic hydrogenation; diisocyanates; optical bleaching agents; ultra violet absorber; research and process development in inorganic chemicals. *Mailing Add:* 459 Wilkes Barre St Easton PA 18042

FREYGANG, WALTER HENRY, JR, b Jersey City, NJ, Dec 27, 24; m; c 3. PHYSIOLOGY. *Educ:* Stevens Inst Technol, ME, 45; Univ Pa, MD, 49. *Prof Exp:* Intern & asst med resident, Bellevue Hosp, New York, 49-51; asst resident neurol, Columbia-Presby Med Ctr, 51-52, asst neurologist, 52; neurophysiologist, NIH, 52-59; vis scientist, Cambridge Univ, 59; chief, Sect Membrane Physiol, NIMH, 60-67; guest prof, Univ Heidelberg, 67-69; MEM STAFF, DIV BIOL & BIOCHEM RES, NIMH, 69- *Concurrent Pos:* Vis fel neurol & Nat Found Infantile Paralysis fel, Columbia Univ, 52; clin prof neurol, Georgetown Univ; mem, Marine Biol Lab, Woods Hole, Mass. *Mem:* AAAS; Soc Gen Physiol; Biophys Soc; Am Physiol Soc; Asn Res Nerv & Ment Dis. *Res:* Muscle; central nervous system; peripheral nerve. *Mailing Add:* 6247 29th St NW Washington DC 20015

FREYMAN, STANISLAW, b Warsaw, Poland, Feb 4, 36; Can citizen; m 65; c 2. AGRONOMY, CROP PHYSIOLOGY. *Educ:* Univ Pretoria, BSA, 59; Univ BC, MSA, 63, PhD(agron), 67. *Prof Exp:* Lab technician, Univ BC, 62-63; res scientist, Kamloops, BC, 66-69; RES SCIENTIST, AGR CAN RES STA, LETHBRIDGE, ALTA, 69- *Concurrent Pos:* Can adv, All India Coord Res Proj Dryland Agr, 73-75. *Mem:* Crop Sci Soc Am; Am Soc Agron; Can Soc Agron; Agr Inst Can. *Res:* Icesheet and winter injury to crops; increasing productivity of forages on range lands; cultural and ecological aspects of crop production in southern Alberta; intercropping and cropping systems. *Mailing Add:* Agr Can Res Sta Lethbridge AB T1J 4C7 Can

FREYMANN, JOHN GORDON, b Omaha, Nebr, Apr 9, 22; m 50; c 4. MEDICINE. *Educ:* Yale Univ, BS, 44; Harvard Univ, MD, 46; Am Bd Internal Med, dipl, 55, dipl oncol, 75. *Prof Exp:* Intern med, Mass Gen Hosp, 46-47, asst resident med, 50-51; asst, Harvard Med Sch, 54-56, instr, 56-60; asst prof med, Sch Med, Tufts Univ & dir med educ, Mem Hosp, Worcester, Mass, 59-65; gen dir, Boston Hosp Women & lectr prev med, Harvard Med Sch, 65-69; ASSOC PROF FAMILY PRACT & COMMUNITY MED, SCH MED & DENT, UNIV CONN, 69-, PRES, NAT FUND MED EDUC, 75- *Concurrent Pos:* Fel internal med, Mayo Found, Minn, 49-50; res fel, Huntington Lab, 51-53; Damon Runyon fel, Harvard Med Sch, 53-54; asst, Mass Gen Hosp, 54-60, clin assoc, 61-69; pres, Educ Comn Med Grads, 70-76; dir educ, Hartford Hosp, 69-75. *Mem:* Fel Am Col Physicians; Am Asn Cancer Res; Asn Hosp Med Educ (vpres, 70-72); Asn Am Med Cols; Soc Med Adminrs (pres, 79-81). *Res:* Chemotherapy of cancer. *Mailing Add:* Nat Fund of Med Educ 999 Asylum Ave Hartford CT 06105

FREYMANN, MOYE WICKS, b Omaha, Nebr, Sept 2, 25; m 56; c 3. PUBLIC HEALTH. *Educ:* Yale Univ, BS, 45; Johns Hopkins Univ, MD, 48; Harvard Univ, MPH, 56, DrPH, 60. *Prof Exp:* Intern internal med, Univ Hosp, Yale Univ, 49-51; health officer, US Tech Coop Mission, Iran, 52-55; chief consult health & family planning, India Off, Ford Found, 57-66; dir, Carolina Pop Ctr, 66-74, PROF HEALTH ADMIN, SCH PUB HEALTH, UNIV NC, CHAPEL HILL, 66-; SPEC ASST TO ASST SECY HEALTH & SCI AFFAIRS, US HEALTH & SERV, 71- *Concurrent Pos:* Fel virol, Med Sch, Yale Univ, 48-49; USPHS trainee, 51; mem adv comt pop dynamics, Pan-Am Health Orgn; consult, WHO; spec asst to asst secy health & sci affairs, Dept Health, Educ & Welfare, 71-; consult, UN Develop; consult, US Govt Agency Int Develop, NIH, govts of Egypt, Mexico & various UN orgn; med dir, US Public Health Serv Reserve; vis sr scientist, Battella Mem Inst, 81-; bd dir, US Planned Parenthoood Fedn. *Mem:* AAAS; fel Am Pub Health Asn; fel Am Sociol Asn; Soc Int Develop; Int Union for Sci Study of Pop. *Res:* International development theory and practice; population dynamics; public health policy and administration. *Mailing Add:* 269 Rosenau Hall 201 H Univ of NC Sch of Pub Health Chapel Hill NC 27514

FREYMUTH, PETER, b Warmbrunn, Ger, Dec 4, 36; m 65; c 3. AEROSPACE ENGINEERING. *Educ:* Berlin Tech Univ, MPhysics, 62, DrEng, 65. *Prof Exp:* Res assoc aerodynamics, inst turbulence res, Ger Exp Estab Air & Space Res, Berlin, 62-65; res assoc aerospace eng, 65-67, from asst prof to assoc prof, 67-81, PROF AEROSPACE ENG SCI, UNIV COLO, BOULDER, 81- *Honors & Awards:* Erich Trefftz Award, Ger Soc Flight Sci, 66. *Mem:* Am Phys Soc. *Res:* Aerospace engineering sciences, especially radiation effects in quartz crystals, hydrodynamic stability, theory and design of hot-wire anemometers and experimental investigation of turbulent flows; magneto optics. *Mailing Add:* Dept of Aerospace Eng Sci Univ of Colo Boulder CO 80309

FREYRE, RAOUL MANUEL, b Gibara, Cuba, Jan 18, 31. PHYSICS, MATHEMATICS. *Educ:* Inst Holquin, Cuba, BS, 49; Univ Havana, PhD, 55. *Prof Exp:* Asst physics, Inst Holquin, Cuba, 53-54, asst prof math, 54-55, prof & head dept, 55-57; from instr to asst prof physics, NC State Col, 57-63; res physicist, Nat Co, Mass, 63; head dept physics, Col Adv Sci, Canaan, NH, 63-64, dean, 64; asst prof math & physics, Lowell Technol Inst, 64-66; assoc prof, 66, PROF MATH, BOSTON STATE COL, 67- *Mem:* Soc Indust & Appl Math; Am Math Soc; Math Asn Am. *Res:* Lasers. *Mailing Add:* Dept of Math Boston State Col 625 Huntington Ave Boston MA 02115

FREYTAG, PAUL HAROLD, b Laramie, Wyo, Dec 3, 34; m 67; c 2. SYSTEMATIC ENTOMOLOGY. *Educ:* Univ Wyo, BS, 56; Ohio State Univ, MSc, 60, PhD(entom), 63. *Prof Exp:* Res assoc entom, Ohio State Univ, 63-64, asst prof, 64-66; asst prof, Ark State Col, 66-67; ASSOC PROF ENTOM, UNIV KY, 67- *Concurrent Pos:* NSF grant, 64-72. *Mem:* AAAS; Soc Syst Zool; Entom Soc Am; Ecol Soc Am; Am Inst Biol Sci. *Res:* Taxonomic studies of aquatic insects with special reference to the Plecoptera; systematics of leafhoppers (Cicadellidae) and their parasites. *Mailing Add:* Dept Entom Univ Ky Lexington KY 40546

FREZON, SHERWOOD EARL, b Highland Park, Mich, Nov 28, 21. ECONOMIC GEOLOGY. *Educ:* Univ Mich, BS, 50, MS, 63. *Prof Exp:* GEOLOGIST, US GEOL SURV, 51- *Mem:* Am Asn Petrol Geol; Geol Soc Am; Paleont Soc; Soc Econ Paleont & Mineral. *Res:* Paleozoic stratigraphic studies in Oklahoma and Arkansas; domestic oil and gas resource appraisal. *Mailing Add:* Stop 971 Box 25046 Denver Fed Ctr Denver CO 80225

FRIAR, BILLY W(ADE), b Rose Hill, Va, July 18, 31. MECHANICAL ENGINEERING. *Educ:* Berea Col, AB, 53; Va Polytech Inst, BS, 58; Ohio State Univ, MSc, 59, PhD(mech eng), 70. *Prof Exp:* Asst prof mech eng, Va Polytech Inst, 60-62; ASST PROF ENG, WRIGHT STATE UNIV, 70- *Concurrent Pos:* Mech engr, Babcock & Wilcox Co, 60; facilities eng sect, US Army Chem Ctr, 61. *Mem:* AAAS. *Res:* Thermodynamics; measurement of gas density; ionization of gases by beta-particle radiation. *Mailing Add:* Dept of Eng Wright State Univ Dayton OH 45431

FRIAR, JAMES LEWIS, b Mansfield, Ohio, June 26, 40; m 62; c 2. NUCLEAR PHYSICS, THEORETICAL PHYSICS. *Educ:* Case Inst Technol, BS, 62; Stanford Univ, PhD(physics), 67. *Prof Exp:* NATO fel nuclear physics, Europ Orgn Nuclear Res, 67-68; fel, Univ Wash, 68-70; fel, Mass Inst Technol, 70-72; asst prof, Brown Univ, 72-76; MEM STAFF INTERMEDIATE ENERGY NUCLEAR PHYSICS, LOS ALAMOS NAT LAB, 76- *Mem:* Am Phys Soc. *Res:* Electromagnetic nuclear physics; few body problem. *Mailing Add:* Los Alamos Nat Lab MS 454 PO Box 1663 Los Alamos NM 87545

FRIAR, ROBERT EDSEL, b Warren, Ind, Dec 30, 33; m 61; c 3. HUMAN PHYSIOLOGY, BIRTH CONTROL. *Educ:* Purdue Univ, BS, 56, MS, 59, PhD(physiol), 68. *Prof Exp:* Instr high sch, Ind, 56-58, 59-64; from asst prof to assoc prof physiol, 67-74, PROF PHYSIOL, FERRIS STATE COL, 74-, HEAD DEPT BIOL SCI, 71- *Mem:* Am Inst Biol Sci; Soc Study Reprod. *Res:* Affinity of various estrogenic compounds for the estrogen receptor; human physiology; effectiveness of various methods of birth control. *Mailing Add:* Dept Biol Ferris State Col Big Rapids MI 49307

FRIARS, GERALD W, b Sussex, NB, Apr 26, 29; m 54; c 3. POULTRY BREEDING. *Educ:* McGill Univ, BSc, 51; Purdue Univ, MSc, 55, PhD(genetics), 61. *Prof Exp:* Asst genetics, Ont Agr Col, 51-55, lectr, 55-61, res scientist, 61-63, from asst prof to assoc prof, 63-73, PROF GENETICS, UNIV GUELPH, 73- *Concurrent Pos:* Nat Res Coun Can grants quantum genetics, 64-; res grants, Can Dept Agr, Ont Turkey Bd; consult geneticist, Peels Poultry Farm Ltd. *Mem:* Biomet Soc; Poultry Sci Asn; Genetics Soc Can. *Res:* Quantitative genetics of economic and physiological traits of chickens and turkeys; quantitative and population genetics of Tribolium castaneum used as a pilot organism. *Mailing Add:* Dept of Animal & Poultry Sci Univ of Guelph Guelph Can

FRIAUF, ROBERT JAMES, b Pittsburgh, Pa, Mar 31, 26; m 49; c 3. SOLID STATE PHYSICS. *Educ:* Duke Univ, BS, 47; Univ Chicago, SM, 51, PhD(physics), 53. *Prof Exp:* From asst prof to assoc prof, 53-64, PROF PHYSICS, UNIV KANS, 64-, PROF ASTRON, 80- *Concurrent Pos:* Fulbright fel, Univ Stuttgart, 65-66; Argonne Univs Asn distinguished award, Argonne Nat Lab, 78-79. *Mem:* Am Chem Soc; Am Phys Soc; Am Asn Physics Teachers; Sigma Xi. *Res:* Ionic conductivity, diffusion and color centers in ionic crystals. *Mailing Add:* Dept of Physics Univ of Kans Lawrence KS 66045

FRIBERG, JAMES FREDERICK, b Florence, Wis, Aug 27, 43; m 68; c 2. GEOLOGY, SEDIMENTOLOGY. *Educ:* Univ Wis-Milwaukee, BS, 65; Ind Univ, MA, 67, PhD(geol), 70. *Prof Exp:* Res geologist, 70-75, sr res geologist, 75-78, res assoc petrol explor, 78-79, SUPVR, SEDIMENTARY GEOL RES, UNION OIL CO CALIF RES CTR, BREA, 80- *Mem:* Am Asn Petrol Geologists; Soc Econ Paleontologists & Mineralogists. *Res:* Sandstone depositional models; diagenesis of sandstones; exploration methodology for stratigraphic traps; tectonic and sedimentological evolution of fore-arc basins. *Mailing Add:* 20061 Canyon Dr Yorba Linda CA 92686

FRIBERG, LAVERNE MARVIN, b Siren, Wis, Mar 11, 49; m 71; c 2. IGNEOUS PETROLOGY, METAMORPHIC PETROLOGY. *Educ:* Univ Wis, River Falls, BS, 71; Ind Univ, MS, 74, PhD(geol), 76. *Prof Exp:* Asst prof petrol, 76-81, ASSOC PROF, UNIV AKRON, 81- *Mem:* Mineral Soc Am; Geochem Soc; Mineral Asn Can; Microbeam Anal Soc. *Res:* Igneous and metamorphic petrology; utilizing petrography, chemical and cathodoluminescence data in research activities. *Mailing Add:* Dept Geol Univ Akron Akron OH 44325

FRIBOURG, HENRY AUGUST, b Paris, France, Mar 10, 29; nat US; m 56; c 2. CROP ECOLOGY. *Educ:* Univ Wis, BS, 49; Cornell Univ, MS, 51; Iowa State Univ, PhD(agron), 54. *Prof Exp:* From asst agronomist to assoc agronomist forage crop prod res, 56-70, PROF PLANT & SOIL SCI, UNIV TENN, KNOXVILLE, 70- *Concurrent Pos:* Interpreter, Int Grassland Cong, Pa State Univ, 52; chief interpreter, Inter-Am Meeting Livestock Prod, Brazil, 52 & food & agr meeting on exten methods, Caribbean Area, Jamaica, UN, Jamaica, 54; pres, Southern Pasture Forage Crops Improv Conf & Southern Appalachian Sci Fair; vis scientist, Tenn Acad of Sci, 65-; sr lectr & Fulbright-Hays lectr, Ataturk Univ, 73-74. *Mem:* Fel Am Soc Agron; Am Meteorol Soc. *Res:* Digital computer use in agronomic research; forage crop ecology and management; crop climatology. *Mailing Add:* Dept of Plant & Soil Sci Univ of Tenn Knoxville TN 37916

FRIBOURGH, JAMES H, b Sioux City, Iowa, June 10, 26; m 55; c 3. ZOOLOGY, SCIENCE EDUCATION. *Educ:* Univ Iowa, BA & MS, 49, PhD(zool, sci educ), 57. *Prof Exp:* Instr biol, 49-56, assoc prof, 57-59, prof & chmn dept, 59-69, vpres acad affairs, 69-70, vchancellor acad affairs, 70-80, EXEC VCHANCELLOR ACAD AFFAIRS, UNIV ARK, LITTLE ROCK, 80- *Concurrent Pos:* Res biologist, Fish Farming Exp Sta, US Dept Interior, 60-; vis scientist, NSF Vis Scientist Prog, Ark Acad Sci; consult, Radioisotope Serv, Vet Admin Hosp, Little Rock, 60- *Mem:* Fel AAAS; fel Am Inst Fisheries Res Biologists; Am Fisheries Soc; Sigma Xi; Electron Micros Soc Am. *Res:* Fisheries biology and culture; experimental embryology. *Mailing Add:* Univ of Ark 33rd & University Ave Little Rock AR 72204

FRICK, JOHN P, b Kansas City, Mo, Jan 20, 44; m 67; c 2. CORROSION, QUALITY ASSURANCE. *Educ:* Univ Kans, BS, 66; Pa State Univ, MS, 69, PhD(metall), 72. *Prof Exp:* Metallurgist, Wean United, 72-74; res metallurgist, Youngstown Sheet & Tube Co, 74-77; res scientist, Dresser Indust, 78-79; SR RES ENGR, MOBIL OIL CORP, 79- *Mem:* Am Soc Metals; Am Inst Mining, Metall & Petrol Engrs; Nat Asn Corrosion Engrs. *Res:* Corrosion phenomena with particular emphasis on environmental cracking; tribological and metallurgical phenomena. *Mailing Add:* 6924 Middle Cove Dr Dallas TX 75248

FRICK, NEIL HUNTINGTON, b Rockville Centre, NY, July 14, 33; m 60; c 4. PHYSICAL CHEMISTRY, POLYMER CHEMISTRY. *Educ:* Col Wooster, BA, 60; Princeton Univ, MA, 62, PhD(phys chem), 64. *Prof Exp:* Sr res chemist, 64-67, from res assoc to sr res assoc, 67-72, asst dir indust coatings develop, 72-73, mgr coil, appliance & container coatings develop, 73-79, MGR INDUST COATINGS RES, PPG INDUSTS, INC, 79- *Mem:* Am Chem Soc; Fedn Socs Coatings Technol. *Res:* Polymer characterization; electrophoretic deposition of organic coatings; development of new coatings for the coil appliance and container segments of the marketplace; involves the polymer properties, application properties, final film properties and colloidal behavior of systems; research administration, technical management. *Mailing Add:* PPG Industs Inc Coatings & Resins Res Allison Park PA 15101

FRICK, OSCAR L, b New York, NY, Mar 12, 23; m. IMMUNOLOGY, PEDIATRICS. *Educ:* Cornell Univ, AB, 44, MD, 46; Univ Pa, MMedSci, 60; Stanford Univ, PhD(microbiol), 64. *Prof Exp:* Assoc prof, 64-73, PROF PEDIAT, SCH MED, UNIV CALIF, SAN FRANCISCO, 73- *Concurrent Pos:* Mem, Sub-bd allergy, Am Bd Pediat, 67-73. *Mem:* Am Asn Immunologists; Am Acad Allergy (pres, 77-78); Am Acad Pediat; Int Asn Allergol; Am Thoracic Soc. *Res:* Hypersensitivity, especially immediate type related to immunoglobulins and allergy; adaptation of clinical situations to laboratory evaluation. *Mailing Add:* Dept Pediat Sch Med Univ Calif San Francisco CA 94143

FRICK, RICHARD HENRY, b Los Angeles, Calif, Dec 6, 16; m 43; c 2. PHYSICS. *Educ:* Univ Calif, Los Angeles, AB, 37, PhD(physics), 42. *Prof Exp:* Physicist sound transmission, Nat Defense Res Comt, Univ Calif, Los Angeles, 40-42; physicist sound ranging, Duke Univ, 42-45; physicist contact noise, Bell Tel Labs, 45-46; PHYSICIST, AIR FORCE RES, RAND CORP, 46- *Res:* Acoustics; applied mechanics. *Mailing Add:* Rand Corp 1700 Main St Santa Monica CA 90406

FRICKE, ARTHUR LEE, b Huntington, WVa, Mar 6, 34; m 54; c 3. CHEMICAL ENGINEERING. *Educ:* Univ Cincinnati, ChE, 57; Univ Wis, MS, 59, PhD(chem eng), 61. *Prof Exp:* Instr chem eng, Univ Wis, Madison, 59-60; res engr, Shell Develop Co, Calif, 61-63, group leader mech eng res, 63-65, asst dept mgr mkt develop prod, 65-66, sr technologist, process develop, NY, 66-67; from asst prof to assoc prof chem eng, Va Polytech Inst & State Univ, 67-76; PROF CHEM ENG & CHMN DEPT, UNIV MAINE, 76- *Concurrent Pos:* Vpres develop, Polytron Corp, Va, 68-69. *Mem:* Am Chem Soc; Am Inst Chem Engrs; Soc Plastics Engrs; Tech Asn Pulp & Paper Indust. *Res:* Polymer foaming; mass and heat transfer in polymers; phase change in polymers; composities; economic analysis. *Mailing Add:* Dept of Chem Eng Jenness Hall Univ of Maine Orono ME 04473

FRICKE, EDWIN FRANCIS, b Mackay, Idaho, July 25, 10; m 42; c 5. NUCLEAR PHYSICS. *Educ:* Univ Idaho, BS, 35; Univ Calif, Los Angeles, MA, 37, PhD(physics), 40. *Prof Exp:* Design engr, Stone & Webster Engr Corp, Mass, 40-43; engr, Manhattan Proj, Kellex Corp, NY, 43-44; sr engr, Sylvania Elec Prod, Inc, 44-45; phys chemist, Gen Chem Co, 45-46; physicist, Repub Aviation Corp, 46-49; nuclear physicist & staff engr, Argonne Nat Lab, 50-56; sr nuclear physicist, Nuclear Prod Div, ACF Industs, 56-59; sr develop engr & nuclear physicist, Repub Aviation Corp, 59-65; res scientist, Bell Aerosysts Co, 65-66; sr staff scientist, Sanders Assocs, Nashua, 66-68; prin engr, Jackson-Moreland Engrs, 68-70; NUCLEAR ENG CONSULT, 70- *Concurrent Pos:* Instr, Fournier Inst Technol, 50-55. *Mem:* AAAS; Am Chem Soc; Am Nuclear Soc; Sigma Xi; NY Acad Sci. *Res:* Adsorption of sound in five triatomic gases; statistical thermodynamics applied to chemical kinetics. *Mailing Add:* County Rd Merrimack NH 03054

FRICKE, GORDON HUGH, b Buffalo, NY, Apr 18, 37; m 60; c 2. ANALYTICAL CHEMISTRY, CHEMOMETRICS. *Educ:* Goshen Col, BA, 64; State Univ NY Binghamton, MA, 66; Clarkson Col Technol, PhD(chem), 71. *Prof Exp:* Res assoc, State Univ NY Buffalo, 70-71; res fel, Wright State Univ, 71-72; asst prof, 72-75, ASSOC PROF CHEM, IND UNIV-PURDUE UNIV, INDIANAPOLIS, 75- *Concurrent Pos:* Indust fel, Dow Chem Co, 80-81, consult, 81- *Mem:* Am Chem Soc; Sigma Xi. *Res:* New bioselective and solid-state ion-selective electrodes, the miniaturization of the electrodes and the applications of the electrodes to biomedical research and environmental studies; experimental optimization techniques. *Mailing Add:* Dept Chem Ind Univ-Purdue Univ Ind Indianapolis IN 46205

FRICKE, HOWARD HENRY, b Idaho Falls, Idaho, Oct 3, 16; m 47, 80; c 2. INFECTIOUS DISEASES, BIOCHEMISTRY. *Educ:* State Col Wash, BS, 37, MS, 38; Univ Pittsburgh, PhD(biochem), 43. *Prof Exp:* Pharmacist, Owl Drug Co, Wash, 37-38; asst, Pittsburgh Col Pharm, 38-39 & 40-42; res chemist, Abbott Labs, 43-57, biochem group leader, 57-66, sect head microbiol res, 66-70, mgr diag res Abbott Sci Prod Div, 70-74, mgr infectious dis res & develop, Abbott Diag Div, 74-78, mgr, Diag Prod Tech Resources, 80-81; RETIRED. *Concurrent Pos:* Pharmacist drug stores, Pa, 38-43. *Honors & Awards:* Abbott Labs Meritorious Res Award for Sci Achievement, 50, Abbott Presidential Award, 75. *Mem:* AAAS; Am Chem Soc; Am Inst Chem. *Res:* Development of diagnostic test systems for clinical or research laboratories. *Mailing Add:* D-90H Abbott Diag Div Abbott Park Abbott Labs North Chicago IL 60064

FRICKE, MARTIN PAUL, b Franklin, Pa, May 18, 37; m 59. NUCLEAR PHYSICS. *Educ:* Drexel Inst, BS, 61; Univ Minn, MS, 64, PhD(physics & math), 67. *Prof Exp:* Res asst physics, Univ Minn, 61-64; fel, Univ Mich, 67-68; staff physicist, Defense Sci Dept, Gulf Gen Atomic Inc, 68-70, staff physicist & cross sect group leader, Gulf Radiation Technol Div, Gulf Energy & Environ Systs Co, San Diego, 70-74; div mgr, 74-76, asst vpres, 76-77, vpres, 77-79, CORP VPRES, SCI APPL, INC, 79- *Concurrent Pos:* Assoc res scientist, Res Lab, Honeywell Corp, Minn, 62-64. *Mem:* Am Phys Soc. *Res:* Experimental and theoretical research in nuclear reactions. *Mailing Add:* Sci Appl Inc PO Box 2351 1200 Prospect St La Jolla CA 92037

FRICKE, WERNER, b Erfurt, Ger, Sept 7, 06; US citizen; m 34; c 2. ENVIRONMENTAL PHYSICS. *Educ:* Univ Jena, PhD(appl physics), 32. *Prof Exp:* Asst prof appl physics, Univ Jena, 32; res physicist, Fusing Systs, Rheinmetall-Borsig, Ger, 34-35, sect chief ballistic instrumentation, 35-40, sect chief exp ballistics, 40-43, proj mgr missile develop, 43-45; pres, Tool Mach Co, 45-54; sect chief environ studies, Bell Aerosysts Co, 54-68, asst chief engr, Bell Aerospace Co, 68-71, CHIEF ENGR, BELL AIROSYSTEMS CO, TORONTO, 71- *Honors & Awards:* Lilienthal Soc Award, 39. *Mem:* Inst Environ Sci. *Res:* Ballistic instrumentation; stereophotogrammetry; design and testing of guided missiles; induced shock, vibration; noise and space environments. *Mailing Add:* 35 Alamosa Dr Willowdale Can

FRICKE, WILLIAM G(EORGE), JR, b Pittsburgh, Pa, May 10, 26; m 48; c 4. METALLURGY. *Educ:* Pa State Univ, BS, 50, MS, 51; Univ Pittsburgh, PhD(metall eng), 61. *Prof Exp:* Res metallurgist, 52-67, sr res engr, 67-73, STAFF SCIENTIST, ALCOA LABS, ALUMINUM CO AM, 73- *Honors & Awards:* Templin Award, Am Soc Testing & Mat, 55. *Mem:* Am Soc Metals; Am Inst Mining, Metall & Petrol Engrs; Int Soc Stereology; Am Soc Testing & Mat; Microbeam Anal Soc. *Res:* Physical metallurgy and metallography; mechanisms of metal fatigue; deformation and plastic flow; electron microprobe analysis; electron microscopy; auger analysis. *Mailing Add:* Alloy Technol Div Alcoa Labs Aluminum Co of Am Alcoa Center PA 15069

FRICKEN, RAYMOND LEE, b New Orleans, La, June 25, 37. HIGH ENERGY PHYSICS, RESEARCH ADMINISTRATION. *Educ:* Loyola Univ, La, BS, 59; La State Univ, PhD(physics), 63. *Prof Exp:* Physicist, Res Div, US AEC, 63-75, physicist, Div Phys Res, ERDA, 75-77, physicist, Div High Energy Physics, 72-81, CHIEF PROG OPERS BR, US DEPT ENERGY, 81- *Mem:* Am Phys Soc. *Res:* Interactions of primary cosmic rays; high energy particle accelerators. *Mailing Add:* Div High Energy Physics ER-222 US Dept of Energy Washington DC 20545

FRICKEY, PAUL HENRY, b Syracuse, NY, Nov 14, 31; m 56; c 2. MICROBIOLOGY, VIROLOGY. *Educ:* Syracuse Univ, BS, 54, MS, 57; Univ Rochester, PhD(microbiol), 63. *Prof Exp:* Res virologist, Biol Process & Prod Improv Dept, Lederle Labs Div, Am Cyanamid Co, 62-64, res virologist, Virus & Rickettsial Res Sect, 64-70; dir prod & develop, Flow Labs, Inc, 70-73; RES ASSOC, EASTMAN KODAK CO, 73- *Mem:* AAAS; Am Soc Microbiol. *Res:* Factors affecting multiplication of various human respiratory viruses in primate and avian tissues and the development of vaccines from such viruses; identification and anti-viral activity of antibodies in nasal secretions using immunological techniques; development of viral diagnostics. *Mailing Add:* 49 Country Club Rd Rochester NY 14618

FRIDINGER, TOMAS LEE, b Washington, DC, Dec 21, 40; m 63; c 2. PESTICIDE CHEMISTRY, ORGANIC CHEMISTRY. *Educ:* Col William & Mary, BS, 62; Univ Md, PhD(org chem), 67. *Prof Exp:* Sr res chemist, Minn Mining & Mfg Co, 67-70, res specialist, 70-72, supvr synthesis & process chem, 72-74, mgr chem & regulatory affairs, 74-75, tech mgr, 75-79, LAB MGR, 3M CO, 79- *Mem:* Am Chem Soc; Weed Sci Soc Am. *Res:* Synthetic approaches to azirinones; synthesis, formulation and screening of potential agrichemicals, herbicides, plant growth regulators, insecticides, plant disease control agents; agrichemical process, metabolism and environmental chemistry; Environ Protection Agency registration of agrichemicals. *Mailing Add:* 230-B 3M Ctr 3M Co St Paul MN 55101

FRIDLAND, ARNOLD, b Antwerp, Belg; Can citizen; m 63; c 2. BIOCHEMICAL PHARMACOLOGY. *Educ:* Univ Montreal, BS, 63, MS, 64; McGill Univ, PhD(biochem), 68. *Prof Exp:* Fel oncol, McArdle Lab Cancer Res, 68-71; asst mem, 71-76, ASSOC MEM PHARMACOL, ST JUDE CHILDREN'S RES HOSP, 76- *Mem:* Am Chem Soc; Am Asn Cancer Res; Am Soc Biol Chemists. *Res:* Molecular mechanism of action of antimetabolites; DNA replication in eukaryotic cells. *Mailing Add:* St Jude Children's Res Hosp PO Box 318 Memphis TN 38101

FRIDLUND, PAUL RUSSELL, b Minneapolis, Minn, Jan 3, 20; m 49; c 4. PLANT PATHOLOGY. *Educ:* Augsburg Col, BA, 42; Univ Minn, MS, 52, PhD(plant path), 54. *Prof Exp:* Asst, Univ Minn, 46-49; supvr sect plant path, State Dept Agr, Minn, 49-55; assoc plant pathologist, Irrigation Exp Sta, 55-66, PLANT PATHOLOGIST, IRRIGATED AGR RES & EXTEN CTR, WASH STATE UNIV, 66- *Concurrent Pos:* Nat Acad Sci exchange scientist, Romania, 68 & 77. *Mem:* Am Pomol Soc; Am Phytopath Soc. *Res:* Virus diseases of deciduous fruit trees; thermotherapy of virus diseased plants. *Mailing Add:* Irrigated Agr Res & Exten Ctr Wash State Univ Prosser WA 99350

FRIDOVICH, IRWIN, b New York, NY, Aug 2, 29; m 52; c 2. BIOCHEMISTRY, ENZYMOLOGY. *Educ:* City Col New York, BS, 51; Duke Univ, PhD(biochem), 55. *Prof Exp:* Instr, 56-58, from asst prof to assoc prof, 61-71, dir grad stud, 65-67, prof biochem, 71-76, JAMES B DUKE PROF BIOCHEM, DUKE UNIV, 76- *Concurrent Pos:* NIH res fel, 55-56; NIH res career develop award, 59-69; mem, Biochem Study Sect, NIH, 68-71; mem, Nat Bd Med Examrs, 73- *Mem:* Nat Acad Sci; Am Chem Soc; Am Acad Arts & Sci; Am Soc Biol Chemists (pres-elect). *Res:* Generation and scavenging of free radicals in biological systems. *Mailing Add:* Dept of Biochem Duke Univ Med Ctr Durham NC 27710

FRIDY, JOHN ALBERT, b Lancaster, Pa, Sept 30, 37; m 59; c 2. MATHEMATICS. *Educ:* Pa State Univ, BS, 59, MA, 61; Univ NC, PhD(math), 64. *Prof Exp:* Asst prof math, Rutgers Univ, 64-66; assoc prof, 67-77, PROF MATH SCI, KENT STATE UNIV, 77- *Concurrent Pos:* NSF res grant, 65-66. *Mem:* Am Math Soc; Math Asn Am. *Res:* Summability theory; number theory. *Mailing Add:* Dept of Math Kent State Univ Kent OH 44242

FRIEBELE, EDWARD JOSEPH, b New York, NY, Oct 15, 46; m 70; c 2. SOLID STATE PHYSICS, ELECTRICAL ENGINEERING. *Educ:* Davidson Col, BS, 68; Vanderbilt Univ, MS, 70, PhD(solid state physics, elec eng), 73. *Prof Exp:* Nat Res Coun/Naval Res Lab fel, 73-75, RES PHYSICIST SOLID STATE PHYSICS, NAVAL RES LAB, 75-, PROG MGR, DEFENSE ADVAN RES PROJS AGENCY, 80- *Mem:* Am Phys Soc; Inst Elec & Electronics Engrs; Am Ceramic Soc; Sigma Xi; Soc Photog & Instrumentation Engrs. *Res:* Radiation effects in optical fiber waveguides; radiation-induced defect centers in glasses; amorphous ferromagnetism and amorphous antiferromagnetism; preparation of radiation resistant and polarization holding optical fibers; fine grained feromagnetic precipitates. *Mailing Add:* Code 6570 Naval Res Lab Washington DC 20375

FRIED, BERNARD, b New York, NY, Aug 17, 33; m 69; c 1. PARASITOLOGY. *Educ:* NY Univ, AB, 54; Univ NH, MS, 56; Univ Conn, PhD(zool), 61. *Prof Exp:* Asst zool, Univ NH, 54-56; res technician, Archbold Biol Sta, Fla, 57; instr parasitol, Sch Med, Yale Univ, 59; asst zool, Univ Conn, 59-61; NIH res fel parasitol, Emory Univ, 61-63; from asst prof to assoc prof, 63-70, actg head dept, 70-71 & 81-82, KREIDER PROF BIOL, LAFAYETTE COL, 75- *Mem:* Am Soc Parasitol. *Res:* Biology and physiology of endoparasitic trematodes. *Mailing Add:* Dept of Biol Lafayette Col Easton PA 18042

FRIED, BURTON DAVID, b Chicago, Ill, Dec 14, 25; m 47; c 2. PLASMA PHYSICS. *Educ:* Ill Inst Technol, BS, 47; Univ Chicago, MS, 50, PhD(physics), 52. *Prof Exp:* Instr physics, Ill Inst Technol, 48-52; res physicist, Lawrence Berkeley Lab, Univ Calif, 52-54; mem sr staff, TRW Space Tech Labs, Inc, 54-60, dir res Thompson-Ramo-Wooldridge Comput Div, 60-62; assoc prof physics, 63, PROF PHYSICS, UNIV CALIF, LOS ANGELES, 64-; SR STAFF PHYSICIST, TRW SYSTS GROUP, 62- *Concurrent Pos:* Consult, Lawrence Livermore Nat Lab & Sandia Nat Lab; coordr plasma physics & controlled fusion. *Mem:* Fel Am Phys Soc. *Res:* Physics of elementary particles; quantum field theory; theory of ballistic missile trajectories; on-line computing; magnetohydrodynamics; theoretical plasma physics; controlled fusion. *Mailing Add:* Dept of Physics Univ of Calif Los Angeles CA 90024

FRIED, DAVID L, b Brooklyn, NY, Apr 13, 33; div; c 3. OPTICAL PHYSICS. *Educ:* Rutgers Univ, BA, 57, MS, 59, PhD(physics), 62. *Prof Exp:* Engr, Astro-Electronic Div, Radio Corp Am, 57-59; sr tech specialist, Space & Info Systs Div, NAm Rockwell Corp, 61-66, sr tech specialist, Autonetics Div, 66-67, chief, Sensor Technol Sect, Electrooptical Lab, 67-68, mgr, Avionic Systs Sect, 69-70; owner, 70-77, PRES, OPTICAL SCI CO, 77- *Concurrent Pos:* Consult mem, Army Sci Bd, 68-; assoc ed, J Optical Soc Am, 68- & Optics Letters 77-79. *Mem:* Am Phys Soc; fel Optical Soc Am; Inst Elec & Electronics Engr. *Res:* Quantum field theory; optical propagation in stochastic media; electrooptic and mechanooptic interactions; signal processing and noise theory; infrared systems; adaptive optics. *Mailing Add:* PO Box 446 Placentia CA 92670

FRIED, GEORGE H, b New York, NY, Apr 16, 26; m 54; c 3. PHYSIOLOGY. *Educ:* Brooklyn Col, BA, 47; Univ Tenn, MS, 49, PhD(zool), 52. *Prof Exp:* Fel physiol, NY Univ, 53-54; lectr, 57-64, from asst prof to assoc prof, 64-71, PROF BIOL, BROOKLYN COL, 71- *Concurrent Pos:* Res assoc, Levy Found, Beth Israel Hosp, 54-; lectr, Dent Col, NY Univ, 58- *Mem:* AAAS; Am Soc Exp Path; Am Physiol Soc. *Res:* Metabolic studies in obesity; cellular physiology; tissue enzyme levels as a reflection of difference in metabolic intensity in animals of different sizes; enzymatic basis for psychopharmacology; histochemical studies with tetrazolium salts. *Mailing Add:* Dept of Biol Brooklyn Col Brooklyn NY 11210

FRIED, HERBERT MARTIN, b New York, NY, Sept 22, 29; m 52; c 3. THEORETICAL PHYSICS. *Educ:* Brooklyn Col, BS, 50; Univ Conn, MS, 52; Stanford Univ, PhD(physics), 57. *Prof Exp:* NSF fel physics, Univ Paris, 57-58; res lectr, Univ Calif, Los Angeles, 58-63; vis mem, Courant Inst Math Sci, NY Univ, 63-64; from asst prof to assoc prof, 64-69, PROF PHYSICS, BROWN UNIV, 69- *Concurrent Pos:* Consult, Rand Corp, 58- *Mem:* Am Phys Soc. *Res:* Quantum field theory. *Mailing Add:* Dept of Physics Brown Univ Providence RI 02912

FRIED, JERROLD, b New York, NY, Mar 3, 37; m 65; c 2. BIOPHYSICS. *Educ:* Calif Inst Technol, BS, 58; Stanford Univ, MS, 60, PhD(biophys), 64. *Prof Exp:* Res assoc biol, Hunter Col, 64-65; res assoc, 65-67, assoc, 68-76, ASSOC MEM, DEPT HEMATOPOIETIC CELL KINETICS, SLOAN-KETTERING INST CANCER RES, 76- *Concurrent Pos:* Muscular Dystrophy Asn Am, Inc fel, 65; asst prof, Grad Sch Med Sci, Cornell Univ, 68-; Leukemia Soc Am spec fel, 71-73. *Mem:* Cell Kinetics Soc; Soc Anal Cytol; Biophys Soc; Am Asn Cancer Res; Radiation Res Soc. *Res:* Cell proliferation kinetics; mathematical models of cell populations; chemotherapy of acute leukemia; flow microfluorometry. *Mailing Add:* Sloan-Kettering Inst Cancer Res 1275 York Ave New York NY 10021

FRIED, JOEL ROBERT, b Memphis, Tenn, Dec 9, 46. POLYMER CHEMISTRY. *Educ:* Rensselaar Polytech Inst, BS, 68 & 71, ME, 72; Univ Mass, MS, 75, PhD(polymer sci), 76. *Prof Exp:* Assoc staff mem, Gen Elec, 72-73; sr res engr, Monsanto Co, 76-78; ASST PROF CHEM ENG, UNIV CINCINNNATI, 78- *Concurrent Pos:* Consult, Monsanto Co, 79-; dir chem eng labs, Univ Cincinnati, 82- *Mem:* Am Chem Soc; Am Inst Chem Engrs; Am Phys Soc; Soc Plastics Engrs; Soc Rheology. *Res:* Properties of polymer blends; viscoelastic properties of concentrated polymer solutions. *Mailing Add:* Dept Chem & Nuclear Eng ML#171 Univ Cincinnati Cincinnati OH 45221

FRIED, JOHN, b Leipzig, Ger, Oct 7, 29; US citizen; m 55; c 3. ORGANIC CHEMISTRY, MEDICINAL CHEMISTRY. *Educ:* Cornell Univ, AB, 51, PhD(org chem), 55. *Prof Exp:* Fel, Columbia Univ, 55-56; sect head steroid chem, Merck & Co, NJ, 56-64; dept head, Syntex Inst Steroid Chem, 64-65, assoc dir, 65-67, vpres & dir, Inst Org Chem, 67-75, exec vpres, Syntex Res, 75-76, PRES, SYNTEX RES, 76- *Mem:* Am Chem Soc; Royal Soc Chem. *Res:* Organic synthesis; medicinal chemistry; chemistry of natural products. *Mailing Add:* Syntex Res 3401 Hillview Ave Palo Alto CA 94301

FRIED, JOHN H, b Linz, Austria, Oct 9, 24; m 51; c 1. MICROBIOLOGY, CHEMISTRY. *Educ:* Univ Conn, BS, 49; Syracuse Univ, MS, 51. *Prof Exp:* Microbiologist, Stauffer Chem Co, 51-57; microbiologist, Chas Pfizer & Co, 57-71, MICROBIOLOGIST, PFIZER, INC, 71- *Mem:* Am Soc Microbiol; Am Chem Soc; Soc Indust Microbiol. *Res:* Microbiologically derived products; development of commercial fermentation processes. *Mailing Add:* Pfizer Cent Res Groton CT 06340

FRIED, JOSEF, b Przemysl, Poland, July 21, 14; nat US; m 39; c 1. ORGANIC CHEMISTRY. *Educ:* Columbia Univ, PhD(org chem), 41. *Prof Exp:* Eli Lilly fel, Columbia Univ, 40-42; res chemist, Givaudan Res Inst, NY, 43; head dept, Squibb Inst Med Res, NJ, 44-59, dir, Div Org Chem, 59-63; chmn, Dept Chem, 77-79, LOUIS BLOCK PROF, DEPTS CHEM & BIOCHEM, & PROF, BEN MAY LAB CANCER RES, UNIV CHICAGO, 63- *Concurrent Pos:* Chmn, Gordon Res Conf Steroids & Related Natural Prod, 55-57, Conf Med Chem, 81; Knapp Mem lectr, Univ Wis, 58; mem med chem study sect, NIH, 63-67 & 68-72 & comt arrangements, Laurentian Hormone Conf, 64-71. *Honors & Awards:* Med Chem Award, Am Chem Soc, 74. *Mem:* Nat Acad Sci; fel AAAS; Am Chem Soc; Am Soc Biol Chem; fel NY Acad Sci. *Res:* Chemistry of steroids; prostaglandins. *Mailing Add:* Dept of Chem Univ of Chicago Chicago IL 60637

FRIED, MAURICE, b New York, NY, Nov 6, 20; m 43; c 5. PLANT NUTRITION, AGRICULTURE. *Educ:* Cornell Univ, BS, 41, MS, 45; Purdue Univ, PhD(soil chem), 48. *Prof Exp:* Asst soil chem, Cornell Univ, 44-45; instr soils, Purdue Univ, 47-48; prin res scientist, Bur Plant Indust, Soils & Agr Eng, USDA, 48-53 & Agr Res Serv, 53-61; head agr sect, Int Atomic Energy Agency, 61-64; DIR, JOINT FOOD & AGR ORGN-INT ATOMIC ENERGY AGENCY DIV, ATOMIC ENERGY IN AGR, 64- *Concurrent Pos:* Vis res soil scientist & lectr soil sci, Univ Calif, 74-75. *Mem:* Am Soc Agron; Am Soc Plant Physiol; Am Chem Soc; NY Acad Sci; Soil Sci Soc Am. *Res:* Poor crop growth in acid soils; sufficiency of sulfur for plant growth; radioactive tracers in soil and mineral nutrition investigations; nitrogen cycle; denitrification; isotopes in soil; mineral nutrition and fertilizer investigations. *Mailing Add:* Int Atomic Energy Agency VIC PO Box 100 A-1400 Vienna Austria

FRIED, MELVIN, b Brooklyn, NY, May 28, 24; m 47; c 3. BIOCHEMISTRY. *Educ:* Univ Fla, BS, 48, MS, 49; Yale Univ, PhD(biochem), 52. *Prof Exp:* Instr biochem, Washington Univ, 53-56; from asst prof to assoc prof, 56-67, asst dean grad educ, 72-81, PROF BIOCHEM, COL MED, UNIV FLA, 67- *Concurrent Pos:* Childs Fund fel med res, Cambridge Univ, 52-53; NIH sr res fel, 57-62; vis res prof, Inst Biol Chem, Univ Aix-Marseille, 68-69. *Mem:* Am Soc Biol Chemists; Am Chem Soc; Brit Biochem Soc; Soc Exp Biol & Med; Sigma Xi. *Res:* Proteolytic enzymes; protein biosynthesis; nucleic acid chemistry; metal-peptide complexes; chemistry and metabolism of serum lipoproteins; marine biochemistry. *Mailing Add:* Dept Biochem Box J-245 Univ Fla Col Med Gainesville FL 32610

FRIED, RAINER, b Worms, Ger, July 28, 24; US citizen; m 51; c 6. BIOCHEMISTRY. *Educ:* Univ Sao Paulo, BSc, 45, PhD(biochem), 52. *Prof Exp:* From asst prof to assoc prof, Paulist Sch Med, Brazil, 46-50; res assoc biochem, Med Sch, Univ Sao Paulo, 47-57; res assoc, Med Sch, Northwestern Univ, 57-59; res assoc, Vet Admin Hosp, Tupper Lake, NY, 59-61; asst prof, Sch Med, Ind Univ, 61-64; asst prof, 64-65, assoc prof, 65-79, PROF BIOL CHEM, SCH MED, CREIGHTON UNIV, 79- *Concurrent Pos:* Brazilian Nat Res Coun fel, 52-57; Rockefeller Found fel, 54-55; Am Cancer Soc res fel, 55; sr fel, French Nat Res Coun, 73-74; vis prof, Univ Strasbourg, France, 73-74. *Mem:* Res Soc Alcohol; AAAS; Am Neurochem Soc; Int Soc Neurochem. *Res:* Neurochemistry; neurotransmitters; biochemistry free radicals enzymes; purines; biochemical Pharmacology; alcohol metabolic inhibitors. *Mailing Add:* Dept of Biochem Creighton Univ Sch of Med Omaha NE 68178

FRIED, VOJTECH, b Lozin, Czech, Aug 27, 21; m 51; c 1. PHYSICAL CHEMISTRY. *Educ:* Univ Chem Technol, Prague, DrSc, 53, DrChSc, 57, DrSc, 63. *Prof Exp:* From instr to assoc prof phys chem, Univ Chem Technol, Prague, 50-64; PROF CHEM, BROOKLYN COL, 65- *Concurrent Pos:* Vis prof, Arya Mehr Univ Technol, Tehran, Iran, 74-75; Masahiro Yorizane chair professorship, Hiroshima Univ, Japan, 75; vis prof, Jiao Tong Univ, China, 81. *Honors & Awards:* Czech State Prize in Sci, 63. *Mem:* Am Chem Soc; Czech Chem Soc; fel Am Inst Chem; fel Japanese Soc Prom Sci. *Res:* Thermodynamic and statistical theories of solutions of nonelectrolytes; equations of state. *Mailing Add:* Dept Chem Brooklyn Col Brooklyn NY 11210

FRIED, WALTER, b Frauenkirchen, Austria, Mar 21, 35; US citizen; m 65; c 2. INTERNAL MEDICINE, HEMATOLOGY. *Educ:* Univ Chicago, BA, 54, MD, 58. *Prof Exp:* Clin investr, West Side Vet Admin Hosp, Chicago, 65-68; dir hemat labs, Presby St Luke's Hosp, 68-71; dir hemat unit, Univ Ill Hosps, 71-76; dir Div Hemat & Oncol, Michael Reese Hosp, 76-81, actg chmn, dept med, 80-82; ASSOC DEAN, MED SCI & SERV, RUSH PRESBY ST LUKE'S HOSP, 82- *Concurrent Pos:* From assoc prof to prof med, Univ Ill, 67-76; consult staff, Presby St Luke's Hosp, Chicago, 71-82; mem hemat study sect, NIH, 76-80; prof med, Univ Chicago, 76-82 & Rush Med Col, 82- *Mem:* AAAS; Am Soc Clin Invest; Int Soc Exp Hemat (treas, 70-78); Am Soc Hemat; Am Fedn Clin Res. *Res:* Studies on the regulation of erythropoiesis; studies on the regulation of hematopoietic; stem cell kinetics. *Mailing Add:* Univ Chicago Comp Sickle Cell Ctr 950 E 59th St Chicago IL 60637

FRIEDBERG, A(RTHUR) L(EROY), b River Forest, Ill, Mar 25, 19; m 44; c 2. CERAMIC ENGINEERING. *Educ:* Univ Ill, BS, 41, MS, 47, PhD(ceramic eng), 52. *Prof Exp:* From res asst to assoc prof, 46-57, head dept, 63-69, PROF CERAMIC ENG, UNIV ILL, URBANNA-CHAMPAIGN, 57- *Mem:* Fel Am Ceramic Soc. *Res:* Ceramic research; porcelain enamels; high temperature coatings. *Mailing Add:* 65 Ceramic Dr Columbus OH 43214

FRIEDBERG, CARL E, experimental high energy physics, see previous edition

FRIEDBERG, CHARLES BRUCE, experimental solid state physics, low temperature physics, see previous edition

FRIEDBERG, ERROL CLIVE, b Johannesburg, SAfrica, Oct 2, 37; m 61; c 2. BIOCHEMISTRY, PATHOLOGY. *Educ:* Univ Witwatersrand, BSc, 58, MB & BCh, 61; Educ Coun Foreign Med Grad, cert, 69. *Prof Exp:* Intern med & surg, King Edward VIII Hosp, Univ Natal, SAfrica, 62-63; registr path, Univ Witwatersrand, 63-65; resident path, Cleveland Metrop Gen Hosp & Sch Med, Case Western Reserve Univ, 65-66; res investr, Walter Reed Army Inst Res, 69-70; ASSOC PROF PATH, SCH MED, STANFORD UNIV, 70- *Concurrent Pos:* Fel path, Cleveland Metrop Gen Hosp & Sch Med, Case Western Reserve Univ, 65-66; fel biochem, Sch Med, Case Western Reserve Univ, 66-68; AEC, NIH & Am Cancer Soc grants; Josiah Macy Fac Scholar, 78-79; USPHS res develop career award, 74-79; mem, Path B Study Sect, NIH, 78-82. *Mem:* AMA; Biophys Soc; NY Acad Sci; Radiation Res Soc; Am Chem Soc. *Res:* Enzymes in DNA metabolism; repair of radiation damage to DNA; role of DNA repair in carcinogenesis. *Mailing Add:* Dept of Path Stanford Univ Sch of Med Stanford CA 94305

FRIEDBERG, FELIX, b Copenhagen, Denmark, Apr 3, 21; nat US; m 71. BIOCHEMISTRY. *Educ:* Univ Denver, BS, 44; Univ Calif, PhD(biochem), 47. *Prof Exp:* Asst biochem, Univ Calif, 44-46; from instr to assoc prof, 48-61, PROF BIOCHEM, COL MED, HOWARD UNIV, 61- *Concurrent Pos:* USPHS sr fel, 47-48; vis lectr, Cath Univ Am, 50-52; Lederle med fac award, 57; Commonwealth Fund fel, Howard Univ, 62-63. *Mem:* Biophys Soc; Am Soc Biol Chemists. *Res:* Protein metabolism and structure; total amino acid sequence of bacterial alpha amylase. *Mailing Add:* Dept Biochem Howard Univ Col of Med Washington DC 20059

FRIEDBERG, RICHARD MICHAEL, b New York, NY, Oct 8, 35; m 63. THEORETICAL PHYSICS. *Educ:* Harvard Univ, BA, 56; Columbia Univ, MA, 61, PhD(physics), 62. *Prof Exp:* Mem, Inst Adv Study, 62-64; from asst prof to assoc prof, 64-77, PROF PHYSICS, BARNARD COL, COLUMBIA UNIV, 77- *Concurrent Pos:* Sloan res fel, 61-65; visitor, Europ Orgn Nuclear Res, Geneva, Switz, 64-65. *Res:* Elementary particles; mathematical logic; artificial intelligence; quantum optics; statistical mechanics. *Mailing Add:* Dept of Physics Barnard Col Columbia Univ New York NY 10027

FRIEDBERG, SIMEON ADLOW, b Pittsburgh, Pa, July 7, 25; m 50; c 3. LOW TEMPERATURE PHYSICS, MAGNETISM. *Educ:* Harvard Univ, AB, 47; Carnegie Inst Technol, MS, 48, DSc(physics), 51. *Prof Exp:* Fulbright grant, State Univ Leiden, 51-52; res physicist, 52-53, from asst prof to assoc prof, 53-62, chmn dept, 73-80, PROF PHYSICS, CARNEGIE-MELLON UNIV, 62- *Concurrent Pos:* Alfred P Sloan res fel, 57-61; Guggenheim fel, 65-66. *Mem:* Fel Am Phys Soc; AAAS; Sigma Xi. *Res:* Solid state and low temperature physics; thermal, magnetic and transport properties; cooperative behavior in magnetic crystals. *Mailing Add:* Dept Physics Carnegie-Mellon Univ Pittsburgh PA 15213

FRIEDBERG, STEPHEN HOWARD, b Malden, Mass, July 29, 40; m 66; c 3. MATHEMATICAL ANALYSIS. *Educ:* Boston Univ, BA, 62; Northwestern Univ, MS, 64, PhD(math), 67. *Prof Exp:* Instr math, Mass Inst Technol, 67-69; staff mathematician, Comt Undergrad Prog Math, NSF, 69-70; assoc prof, 70-80, PROF MATH, ILL STATE UNIV, NORMAL, 80- *Concurrent Pos:* Lectr math, Royal Holloway Col, Univ London, 74-75. *Mem:* Math Asn Am; Am Math Soc. *Res:* Harmonic analysis of locally compact abelian groups, particularly closed ideals in group algebras. *Mailing Add:* Dept of Math Ill State Univ Normal IL 61761

FRIEDBERG, WALLACE, b New York, NY, Apr 12, 27; m 57; c 3. RADIOBIOLOGY. *Educ:* Hope Col, AB, 49; Mich State Univ, MS, 51, PhD(physiol), 53. *Prof Exp:* Asst, Mich State Univ, 49-53; res assoc, Children's Hosp Philadelphia, Univ Pa, 54-55; res assoc, Biol Div, Oak Ridge Nat Lab, 55-56, from assoc biologist to biologist, 58-60; from asst prof to assoc prof, 61-69, prof parasitol & lab pract, 69-74, PROF RES BIOCHEM & MOLECULAR BIOL, HEALTH SCI CTR, UNIV OKLA, 69-; CHIEF RADIOBIOL RES, AVIATION TOXICOL LAB, CIVIL AEROMED INST, FED AVIATION ADMIN, 60- *Concurrent Pos:* NIH res fels, Ind Univ, 53-54 & Oak Ridge Nat Lab, 57-58; assoc biol, Oklahoma City Univ, 68-70 & 74-75; vis investr, Oak Ridge Nat Lab, 69-79; adj prof zool, Univ Okla, 71- *Mem:* Am Chem Soc; Soc Exp Biol & Med; Am Physiol Soc; Radiation Res Soc; Bioelectromagnetics Soc. *Res:* Biological effects of radiation. *Mailing Add:* Civil Aeromed Inst AAC-114 PO Box 25082 Oklahoma City OK 73125

FRIEDE, REINHARD L, b Jaegerndorf, Czech, May 12, 26; US citizen; m 53; c 2. NEUROPATHOLOGY, HISTOCHEMISTRY. *Educ:* Univ Vienna, MD, 51; Am Bd Path, dipl, 63. *Prof Exp:* Resident, City Hosp, St Poelten, Austria, 51-52; intern, Neurol Inst & Clin, Univ Vienna, 53; mem staff, Clin Neurosurg, Univ Freiburg, 53-57; with civil serv, Wright Air Develop Ctr, Ohio, 57-59; instr psychiat, Univ Mich, 59-60, asst prof histochem, 60-62, assoc prof path, 62-65; prof neuropath, Inst Path, Case Western Reserve Univ, 65-75; prof neuropath, Inst Path, Univ Zurich, Switz, 75-81; PROF NEUROPATH, UNIV GOTTINGEN, GER, 81- *Honors & Awards:* Civil Service Award, 61. *Mem:* Am Asn Neuropath; Ger Asn Neuropath. *Res:* Histochemistry of nervous system; experimental pathology; developmental neuropathology; experimental neuropathology; chemical cytology of nervous system. *Mailing Add:* Univ Gottingen Robert-Koch-StraBe 40 D-3400 Gottingen West Germany

FRIEDEL, ARTHUR W, b Pittsburgh, Pa, Nov 14, 37. INORGANIC CHEMISTRY. *Educ:* Univ Pittsburgh, BS, 59, MEd, 63; Ohio State Univ, PhD(sci educ), 68. *Prof Exp:* Teacher pub schs, Pa, 59-63; asst sci educ, Ohio State Univ, 64-65 & chem, 65-67; from instr to asst prof, 67-72, ASSOC PROF CHEM, IND UNIV-PURDUE UNIV, FT WAYNE, 72- *Concurrent Pos:* Dir, Northeastern Ind Regional Sci Fair, 67- *Mem:* Am Chem Soc; Nat Sci Teachers Asn. *Res:* Chemical education. *Mailing Add:* Dept of Chem Ind Univ-Purdue Univ Ft Wayne IN 46805

FRIEDELL, GILBERT H, b Minneapolis, Minn, Feb 28, 27; m 50; c 5. MEDICINE, PATHOLOGY. *Educ:* Univ Minn, BS, 47, MB, 49, MD, 50; Am Bd Path, dipl, 55. *Prof Exp:* Intern, Minneapolis Gen Hosp, 49-50; asst resident, Mallory Inst Path, 50-52; resident, Salem Hosp, 53-54 & Pondville Hosp, 54-55; from asst to assoc, Mass Mem Hosps, Boston, 57-62; pathologist, New Eng Deaconess Hosp & res assoc, Cancer Res Inst, Boston, 62-67; assoc pathologist, Mallory Inst Path, Boston City Hosp, 67-69; chief dept path, 69-78, MED DIR, ST VINCENT HOSP, 78-; PROF PATH, UNIV MASS, 70- *Concurrent Pos:* Fel, Mallory Inst Path, 50-52; Am Cancer Soc fel path, Free Hosp Women, 52-53; teaching fel, Harvard Med Sch, 52-53; USPHS spec fel, Strangeways Res Lab, Eng, 61-62; asst, Harvard Med Sch, 57-61, instr, 62-67, lectr, 67-; instr, Boston Univ, 62-67, lectr, 67-69, assoc prof, Sch Med, 67-71, lectr, 71-; asst pathologist, Mallory Inst Path, Boston City Hosp, 66-67; clin prof path, Sch Med, Univ Mass, Worcester, 70- *Mem:* Am Asn Cancer Res; Am Soc Exp Path; Am Soc Clin Path; Am Soc Cytol; Am Soc Clin Oncol. *Res:* Clinical and experimental studies of tumor-host relationships with special reference to breast, cervix and bladder cancer. *Mailing Add:* St Vincent Hosp Path Dept 25 Winthrop St Worcester MA 01604

FRIEDELL, HYMER LOUIS, b St Petersburg, Russia, Feb 6, 11; nat US; m 35; c 3. RADIOLOGY. *Educ:* Univ Minn, BS, 31, MB, 35, MD, 36, PhD(radiol), 40. *Prof Exp:* Instr radiol, Univ Calif, 41-42; chmn dept, 46-78, prof, 78-80, EMER PROF RADIOL, SCH MED, CASE WESTERN RESERVE UNIV, 80- *Concurrent Pos:* Nat Cancer Inst fels, Chicago Tumor Inst, Mem Hosp, New York, 3940 & Univ Calif Hosp, 40-41; consult, Nat Adv Comt Aeronaut; chmn, Radiation Study Sect, NIH; chmn, Comt Allocation of Isotopes for Human Use & mem, Reactor Safeguard Comt, AEC; chmn, Subcomt Radiobiol & mem, Comt Radiol, Nat Res Coun; mem, Subcomt Permissable External Dose, Nat Bur Stand; mem, Coun Exec Bd, Argonne Nat Lab, Cent Adv Comt, Radioisotope Sect, Res & Educ Serv, US Vet Admin, Res & Develop Bd, Joint Panel Med Aspects Atomic Warfare & Vis Comt for Med Dept, Brookhaven Nat Lab; partic, Int Cong Radiol; vpres, Nuclear Technol Lab Coun Radiation Protection & Measurements, 77- *Mem:* AAAS; Am Radium Soc; fel Am Col Radiol; Radiation Res Soc (past pres); Radiation Soc NAm. *Res:* Biological effects of radioisotopes; use of radiation and radioisotopes for therapy and diagnosis; radiation protection and radiation hazards. *Mailing Add:* Case Western Reserve Univ Sch Med 2119 Abington Rd Cleveland OH 44106

FRIEDELL, JOHN C, b Dubuque, Iowa, Nov 2, 29. PURE MATHEMATICS. *Educ:* Loras Col, BA, 51; Gregorian Univ, STL, 55; Univ Iowa, MS, 58; Catholic Univ, PhD(math), 62. *Prof Exp:* From instr to assoc prof, 57-75, PROF MATH, LORAS COL, 75- *Mem:* Math Asn Am. *Res:* Linear and topological algebra; Banach algebras. *Mailing Add:* Dept of Math Loras Col Dubuque IA 52001

FRIEDEN, BERNARD ROY, b Brooklyn, NY, Sept 10, 36; m 62; c 2. OPTICAL PHYSICS. *Educ:* Brooklyn Col, BS, 57; Univ Pa, MS, 59; Univ Rochester, PhD(optics), 66. *Prof Exp:* Res asst optics, Univ Rochester, 62-63; from asst prof to assoc prof, 66-74, PROF OPTICAL SCI, UNIV ARIZ, 74- *Concurrent Pos:* Consult, Philco-Ford, Calif, US Navy, Mass, 73, E I du Pont de Nemours & Co, Inc, 74, 78, Can Ctr Remote Sensing, 76 & Kitt Peak Nat Observ, 76-; assoc ed, Optical Soc Am, 78- *Mem:* Fel AAAS; Optical Soc Am. *Res:* Image restoration and enhancement; probability and statistics; active and passive image formation; synthetic aperture radar; apodizing, super-resolving pupils; information theory; numerical, statistical analysis; special mathematical functions. *Mailing Add:* Optical Sci Ctr Univ Ariz Tucson AZ 85721

FRIEDEN, CARL, b New Rochelle, NY, Dec 31, 28; m 53; c 3. BIOCHEMISTRY. *Educ:* Carlton Col, BA, 51; Univ Wis, PhD(chem), 55. *Prof Exp:* Fel, 55-57, from instr to assoc prof, 57-67, PROF BIOCHEM, WASH UNIV, 67- *Honors & Awards:* St Louis Award, Am Chem Soc, 76. *Mem:* AAAS; Am Chem Soc; Am Soc Biol Chem. *Res:* Enzymes and enzyme kinetics; physical chemistry of proteins. *Mailing Add:* Dept Biochem Box 8094 Wash Univ Sch of Med St Louis MO 63110

FRIEDEN, EARL, b Norfolk, VA, Dec 31, 21; m 42; c 2. BIOCHEMISTRY. *Educ:* Univ Calif, Los Angeles, BA, 43; Univ Southern Calif, MS, 47, PhD(biochem), 49. *Prof Exp:* Lab supvr anal chem, Rubber Reserve Co, US Rubber Co, 43-45; res biochemist, Bedwell Labs, 45-47, instr, Univ Southern Calif, 48; from asst prof to assoc prof, 49-57, chmn dept, 62-68, PROF CHEM, FLA STATE UNIV, 57- *Concurrent Pos:* USPHS spec fel, Carlsberg Labs, Denmark, 57-58 & USPHS fel, Univ Calif, La Jolla, 71. *Honors & Awards:* Lalor Award, Inst Enzyme Res, Univ Wis, 55; Fla Award, Am Chem Soc, 68. *Mem:* Am Soc Biol Chem; Am Chem Soc. *Res:* Chemistry and mechanism of enzymes; copper and iron metalloproteins and metalloenzymes; biochemistry of amphibian metamorphosis; role of thyroid hormones in vitro and in vivo systems. *Mailing Add:* Dept Chem Fla State Univ Tallahassee FL 32306

FRIEDEN, EDWARD HIRSCH, b Norfolk, Va, Jan 4, 18; m 41; c 5. BIOCHEMISTRY, ENDOCRINOLOGY. *Educ:* Univ Calif, Los Angeles, AB, 39, MA, 41, PhD(biochem), 42. *Prof Exp:* Asst chem, Univ Calif, Los Angeles, 39-42; Lalor Found fel, Univ Tex, 42-43, instr biochem, Sch Med, 43-44, res assoc, 45-46; res fel, Biol Labs, Harvard Univ, 46-52, instr biol chem, Sch Med, 48-52; from asst prof to assoc prof biochem, Med Sch, Tufts Univ, 52-64; PROF CHEM, KENT STATE UNIV, 64- *Concurrent Pos:*

Guggenheim fel, Univ Calif, Los Angeles, 53; coordr res, Boston Dispensary, 57-64. *Mem:* Am Chem Soc; Am Soc Biol Chem; Endocrine Soc; Soc Exp Biol & Med; Sigma Xi. *Res:* Biochemistry of relaxin; comparative biochemistry. *Mailing Add:* Dept of Chem Kent State Univ Kent OH 44242

FRIEDENBERG, RICHARD M, b New York, NY, 26; m; c 3. RADIOLOGY. *Educ:* Columbia Univ, AB, 46; State Univ NY, MD, 49. *Prof Exp:* Asst prof radiol, Albert Einstein Col Med, 55-66, assoc clin prof, 66-68; prof radiol & chmn dept, New York Med Col, 68-80; chmn, Dept Radiol, Westchester Med Ctr, 74-80; PROF RADIOL & CHMN, DEPT RADIOL SCI, UNIV CALIF, IRVINE, 80- *Concurrent Pos:* Dir & chmn dept radiol, Bronx-Lebanon Hosp Ctr, 57-68. *Mem:* Fel Am Col Radiol; Radiol Soc NAm; Am Roentgen Ray Soc; fel NY Acad Sci. *Mailing Add:* Univ Calif Irvine Med Ctr 101 City Drive S Orange CA 92668

FRIEDENSTEIN, HANNA, b Vienna, Austria; nat US. CHEMISTRY, INFORMATION SCIENCE. *Educ:* Univ London, BSc, 41; Simmons Col, MS, 50. *Prof Exp:* Res chemist, Phillips Elec Ltd, Eng, 42-46; asst intel officer, Brit Oxygen Co, 46-47; res librn, 47-57, head tech info serv, 57-68, MGR, INFO CTR, CABOT CORP, 68- *Mem:* Am Chem Soc; Spec Libr Asn. *Res:* Chemical documentation; communication and retrieval of information; library science. *Mailing Add:* 80 Boundary Rd Malden MA 02148

FRIEDER, GIDEON, b Zvolen, Czech, Sept 30, 37; US citizen; m 60; c 3. COMPUTER SCIENCES. *Educ:* Israel Inst Technol, BS, 59, MS, 61, DSc(quantum physics), 67. *Prof Exp:* Res assoc numerical anal, Sci Dept, Israeli Ministry Defense & Prog, 59-63, res group mgr, 64-67, dep mgr comput sci, 68-69, mgr, 69-70; staff mem, IBM Sci Ctr, 73-75; from asst prof to assoc prof, State Univ NY Buffalo, 75-80, assoc prof comput sci, 75-80, prof, 80-81; PROF & CHMN, DEPT COMPUT & COMMUN SCI, UNIV MICH, ANN ARBOR, 81- *Concurrent Pos:* Nat lectr, Asn Comput Mach, 73 & 77-79; consult microprog & computer archit & system design, 70- *Mem:* Asn Comput Mach; Inst Elec & Electronics Engrs, Comput Soc. *Res:* Distributed architectures of computing system, especially as related to usage of microprogramming methods; nonbinary computers, especially the ternary computer; tomography and computer structures for supporting it; microprogrammed intermediate machines for high-level languages; computer vision via rapid surface recognition. *Mailing Add:* Dept Comput Sci Univ Mich Ann Arbor MI 48109

FRIEDERICH, ALLAN G(EORGE), mechanical engineering, deceased

FRIEDERICI, HARTMANN H R, b Asuncion, Paraguay, Jan 25, 27; US citizen; m 58; c 3. MEDICINE, PATHOLOGY. *Educ:* Goethe Col, Paraguay, BS, 46; Univ La Plata, MD, 53. *Prof Exp:* Asst path, Univ Bonn, 55-56; resident, Univ Ill Col Med, 57-59; from instr to assoc prof, Univ Ill Col Med, 60-69; prof biol sci, Col Arts & Sci, 70-80, PROF PATH, SCH MED, NORWESTERN UNIV, 69-; HEAD DEPT PATH, EVANSTON HOSP, 71- *Concurrent Pos:* Assoc pathologist, Res & Educ Hosp, 61-69. *Mem:* AAAS; Int Acad Path; Am Asn Pathologists; Am Soc Cell Biol. *Res:* Study of ultrastructure of blood and lymphatic capillaries under physiologic and pathologic circumstances in man and experimental animals; cell surfaces. *Mailing Add:* Dept Path Evanston Hosp 2650 Ridge Ave Evanston IL 60201

FRIEDHOFF, ARNOLD JEROME, b Johnstown, Pa, Dec 26, 23; m 46; c 3. PSYCHIATRY. *Educ:* Univ Pa, MD, 47. *Prof Exp:* Intern psychiat, WPa Hosp, 47-48; jr staff psychiatrist, Mayview State Hosp, Pa, 48-51; res psychiat div, Bellevue Hosp & Clin, Med Ctr, 53-54, clin asst psychiat, Col Med, 55-56, clin instr, 56-57, from instr to asst prof, 57-66, PROF PSYCHIAT, COL MED, NY UNIV, 66-, HEAD PSYCHOPHARMACOL RES UNIT, 66-, DIR CTR STUDY PSYCHOTIC DISORDERS, 64- *Concurrent Pos:* Mem, Clin Proj Rev Comt, NIMH, 70-74; dir, Millhauser Labs; jr psychiatrist, NY Univ Hosp & Clin, 54-57, asst vis neuropsychiatrist, 57-; pres, Soc Biol Psychiat, 80-81. *Mem:* Harvey Soc; Asn Res Nerv & Ment Dis (past asst secy); Am Psychiat Asn; Am Psychopath Asn (pres); Am Col Neuropsychopharmacol (past vpres, pres, 77-78 & 79-80). *Res:* Neurochemistry; neuropharmacology. *Mailing Add:* Dept of Psychiat NY Univ Sch of Med New York NY 10016

FRIEDKIN, JOSEPH FRANK, b Brooklyn, NY, Oct 18, 09; m 37; c 2. HYDRAULIC ENGINEERING. *Educ:* Tex Col Mines, BS, 32. *Prof Exp:* Resident engr, San Diego Field Off, 47-52, prin supvr engr, 52-62, COMNR, HQS, EL PASO OFF, US SECT INT BOUNDARY & WATER COMN, US & MEX, 62- *Concurrent Pos:* Mem, Miss River Stabilization Bd, Miss River Comn, 44-45; Bur Reclamation Consult Bd, Colo River Channel Works, Needles, Ariz, 49; Imp Dam Adv Bd, Colo River, 52-60. *Mem:* Fel Am Soc Civil Engrs; Soc Am Mil Engrs. *Res:* Water control and utilization using dams and streams; planning river regulation; surface waters. *Mailing Add:* Int Boundary Comn Exec Ctr 4110 Rio Bravo El Paso TX 79902

FRIEDKIN, MORRIS ENTON, b Kansas City, Mo, Dec 30, 18; m 43; c 3. BIOCHEMISTRY. *Educ:* Iowa State Col, MS, 41; Univ Chicago, PhD(biochem), 48. *Prof Exp:* Chemist penicillin proj, North Regional Res Lab, USDA, 41-45; USPHS fel, Copenhagen Univ, 48-49; from instr to assoc prof pharmacol, Sch Med, Wash Univ, St Louis, 49-58; prof & chmn dept, Sch Med, Tufts Univ, 58-69; provost, Revelle Col, 74-78, PROF BIOL & MEM FAC SCH MED, UNIV CALIF, SAN DIEGO, 69- *Mem:* Am Soc Biol Chem; Am Soc Pharmacol & Exp Therapeut; Am Acad Arts & Sci. *Res:* Enzymology; nucleic acid metabolism; biochemical pharmacology. *Mailing Add:* Dept Biol 2130 Bonner Hall Univ of Calif San Diego B-021 La Jolla CA 92093

FRIEDL, FRANK EDWARD, b Stewart, Minn, May 29, 31; m 56; c 4. ANIMAL PHYSIOLOGY, PARASITOLOGY. *Educ:* Univ Minn, BA, 52, PhD(zool), 58. *Prof Exp:* Asst zool, Univ Minn, 52-58; res fel, USPHS, Rockefeller Inst, 58-60; from asst prof to assoc prof zool, 60-72, PROF, DEPT BIOL, UNIV SFLA, 72- *Mem:* AAAS; Am Soc Parasitol; Am Soc Zool. *Res:* Comparative biochemistry and physiology; metabolism of invertebrates; nitrogen catabolism in molluscs; animal physiology and biochemistry. *Mailing Add:* Dept of Biol Univ of SFla Tampa FL 33620

FRIEDLAENDER, CARLO GOTTHELF IMMANUEL, b Naples, Italy, May 23, 05; Can citizen; m 55; c 2. PETROGRAPHY, MINERALOGY. *Educ:* Univ Zurich, BSc, 23, PhD(geol), 30. *Prof Exp:* Asst mineral & petrog, Inst Eidgenossische Technische Hochsch, 30-34; co-worker, Swiss Geotech Comn, 34-37 & 40-55; geologist, Soc Forminiere, Brussels, 37-40; geologist, Chartered Explor, Rhodesia, 55-56; prof, 57-70, EMER PROF GEOL, DALHOUSIE UNIV, 70- *Mem:* AAAS; Geol Soc Am; fel Geol Asn Can; Mineral Asn Can (secy); Geol Soc SAfrica. *Res:* Petrography of plutonic and metamorphic rocks; geochemistry. *Mailing Add:* 248 Clemow Ave Ottawa ON K0G 1X0 Can

FRIEDLAENDER, FRITZ J(OSEF), b Freiburg, Ger, May 7, 25; nat US; m 69; c 2. MAGNETICS. *Educ:* Carnegie Inst Technol, BS, 51, MS, 52, PhD(elec eng), 55. *Prof Exp:* Asst elec eng, Carnegie Inst Technol, 51-54; asst prof, Columbia Univ, 54-55; from asst prof to assoc prof, 55-62, PROF ELEC ENG, PURDUE UNIV, 62- *Concurrent Pos:* Consult, Gen Elec Co, Ind, 56-58; Components Corp, Ill, 59-61, Lawrence Radiation Lab, Univ Calif, 67-69 & P R Mallory & Co, 74-, Oak Ridge Nat Lab, 79-; guest prof, Max-Planck Inst Metal Res, 64-65, Inst fur Werkstoffe der Elektrotechnik, Ruhr Univ, WGer, 72-73, Nagoya Univ, Japan, 80 & Univ Regensburg, WGer, 81-82; rev ed J, Inst Elec & Electronics Engrs, 75-67. *Honors & Awards:* Humboldt Award, 72. *Mem:* Am Phys Soc; Am Soc Eng Educ; fel Inst Elec & Electronics Engrs; Swiss Elec Eng Soc. *Res:* Magnetics, magnetic devices and memories; high gradient magnetic separation magnetic bubble dynamics; amorphous magnetic films. *Mailing Add:* Sch of Elec Eng Purdue Univ West Lafayette IN 47907

FRIEDLAENDER, JONATHAN SCOTT, b New Orleans, La, Aug 24, 40; m 71; c 2. PHYSICAL ANTHROPOLOGY. *Educ:* Harvard Univ, AB, 62, PhD(anthrop), 69. *Prof Exp:* Pop Coun del demog & pop genetics, Univ Wis-Madison, 68-69, asst prof anthrop, 69-70; from asst prof to assoc prof anthrop, Harvard Univ, 70-76; ASSOC PROF ANTHROP, TEMPLE UNIV, 76- *Mem:* AAAS; Am Asn Phys Anthrop; NY Acad Sci; Brit Soc Study Human Biol; Am Asn Human Genetics. *Res:* Studies of human physical variation over population boundaries; populations on Bougainville Island, Territory of New Guinea. *Mailing Add:* Dept of Anthrop Temple Univ Philadelphia PA 19122

FRIEDLAND, AARON J, chemical & nuclear engineering, see previous edition

FRIEDLAND, BEATRICE L, b New York, NY, Feb 12, 14; m 39; c 2. BIOLOGY. *Educ:* NY Univ, BA, 35, MS, 38, PhD(biol), 43. *Prof Exp:* Instr biol, NY Univ, 43-46 & Hunter Col, 47-51; from instr to prof, 51-79, chmn dept, 55-71, EMER PROF BIOL, STERN COL, YESHIVA UNIV, 79- *Res:* Embryological genetics; action of genes at specific times in development. *Mailing Add:* Yeshiva Univ Col Women 500 W 18th St New York NY 10033

FRIEDLAND, BERNARD, b Brooklyn, NY, May 25, 30; m 59; c 3. ELECTRICAL ENGINEERING, APPLIED MATHEMATICS. *Educ:* Columbia Univ, AB, 52, BS, 53, MS, 54, PhD(elec eng), 57. *Prof Exp:* From instr to asst prof elec eng, Columbia Univ, 54-61; head control systs lab, Melpar, Inc, 61-62; MGR SYSTS RES, KEARFOTT DIV, SINGER CO, 62- *Concurrent Pos:* Adj prof, Columbia Univ, 67-72, NY Univ, 70-73 & Polytech Inst NY, 74- *Mem:* Fel Am Soc Mech Engrs; Inst Elec & Electronics Engrs; Am Inst Aeronaut & Astronaut. *Res:* Modern control theory and application. *Mailing Add:* 36 Dartmouth Rd West Orange NJ 07052

FRIEDLAND, DANIEL, b Columbus, Ohio, Apr 5, 16; m 40; c 2. CHEMICAL ENGINEERING. *Educ:* City Col New York, BChE, 37; Polytech Inst Brooklyn, MChE, 45, DChE, 48. *Prof Exp:* Asst, M W Kellogg Co, 37; chem engr, Cities Serv Oil Co, New York, 38-46; vpres, Truland Chem Co, 46-59; vpres, Trubek Labs, East Rutherford, 59-64, exec vpres, Trubek Chem Co, 64-65; exec vpres, UOP Chem Co, 65-66, vpres mkt, UOP Chem Div, 66-77, pres, Org Chem Div, Crompton & Knowles, 77-78; CONSULT, 78- *Mem:* Am Chem Soc; Am Inst Chem Engrs; Am Inst Chem; Commercial Chem Develop Asn. *Res:* Distillation; extraction; unit operations of chemical engineering; petroleum refining. *Mailing Add:* 1046 Field Ave Plainfield NJ 07060

FRIEDLAND, FRITZ, b Berlin, Ger, Jan 2, 10; nat US; m 38. MEDICINE. *Educ:* Univ Berlin, MD, 34. *Prof Exp:* Chief phys med, Warren City Hosp, Ohio, 43-44; chief phys med & rehab serv, Vet Admin Hosp, Framingham, 46-53 & Boston, 53-73; asst clin prof, 54-61, assoc prof, 61-73, CLIN PROF PHYS & REHAB MED, SCH MED, TUFTS UNIV, 73- *Concurrent Pos:* Consult, Lemuel Shattuck Hosp; mem assoc staff, New Eng Med Ctr Hosps; consult physiatrist, Mass Rehab Hosp, Boston; chief phys med serv, Leonard Morse Hosp, Natick, Mass, 73-81. *Mem:* Fel Am Col Physicians; Am Cong Rehab Med. *Res:* Ultrasound in medicine; medical rehabilitation of paraplegics, amputees, arthritic and poliomyelitic patients, cerebrovascular accidents. *Mailing Add:* Apt 212 Jamaicaway Tower Boston MA 02130

FRIEDLAND, JOAN MARTHA, b Binghamton, NY, Feb 6, 36. BIOCHEMISTRY. *Educ:* Cornell Univ, BS, 59; Univ Ill, MS, 64, PhD(biochem), 68. *Prof Exp:* Res asst, Johns Hopkins Univ, 59-62; res asst, Biol Labs, Harvard Univ, 66-67; res assoc enzym & neurochem, Kingsbrook Jewish Med Ctr, Brooklyn, 68-73; asst physiol & biophys, Mt Sinai Sch Med, 73-74; res assoc, 74-76, ASST PROF, DEPT MED, STATE UNIV NY DOWNSTATE MED CTR, 76- *Concurrent Pos:* Res fel, Harvard Univ, 68. *Mem:* Am Chem Soc. *Res:* Bacterial bioluminescent enzymes; subunit structure; biochemistry of lipid storage diseases, hexosaminidase; isozyme studies on Tay Sachs disease and enzymes; studies in mucopolysacchariodosis; prenatal diagnosis of Tay Sachs disease; Angiotensin converting enzyme in Sarcoidosis and induction of Angiotensin converting enzyme in rabbit and human macrophages. *Mailing Add:* Box 112 Dept of Med 450 Clarkson Ave Brooklyn NY 11203

FRIEDLAND, MELVYN, b Aug 24, 32; m 61; c 2. BIOCHEMISTRY. *Educ:* Univ Calif, Los Angeles, BS, 54; Univ Southern Calif, PhD(biochem), 63. *Prof Exp:* Clin chemist, Bio-Sci Labs, Los Angeles, 63-67; CLIN CHEMIST, UPJOHN CO, 67- *Mem:* AAAS; Am Asn Clin Chem; Am Chem Soc. *Res:* Nucleic acid antimetabolites; development of new tests for clinical chemistry; management of laboratory operations. *Mailing Add:* 3751 Arbutus Trail Portage MI 49002

FRIEDLAND, STEPHEN SHOLOM, b New York, NY, Jan 25, 21; m 45; c 2. MEDICAL PHYSICS. *Educ:* Brooklyn Col, BA, 43; Univ Pa, MA, 47; NY Univ, PhD(physics), 48. *Prof Exp:* Res fel, Sloan-Kettering Inst Cancer Res, 45-48; asst prof physics, Univ NMex, 48-49; prof, Univ Conn, 49-58; scientist, Hughes Aircraft Co, Calif, 58-60; chief exec officer, Solid State Radiations, Inc, 60-68; PROF RADIOL, UNIV SOUTHERN CALIF, 68-; PROF APPL PHYSICS, TEL-AVIV UNIV, 71- *Concurrent Pos:* Prof, San Fernando Valley State Col, 63-68; mem sci specialists, Int Atomic Energy Agency, 69; res fel, Israeli AEC, 69-70. *Mem:* Fel Am Phys Soc; Am Nuclear Soc; Am Geophys Union; Inst Elec & Electronics Engrs. *Res:* Applications of radioisotopes in medicine; holography as applied to tomography. *Mailing Add:* Tel-Aviv Univ Tel Aviv Univ Tel-Aviv Israel

FRIEDLAND, WALDO CHARLES, b Menasha, Wis, Dec 18, 23; m 46; c 6. CHEMISTRY. *Educ:* Iowa State Col, BS, 48, PhD(chem), 51. *Prof Exp:* Res microbiologist, 51-59, sect mgr, 59-63, asst to dir develop, 63-67, dir develop, 67-81, DIR LICENSING, ABBOTT LABS, 81- *Mem:* AAAS; Am Chem Soc. *Res:* Antibiotics and microbial products. *Mailing Add:* 1020 Gracewood Dr Libertyville IL 60048

FRIEDLANDER, ALAN L, b Chicago, Ill, Aug 31, 36; m 58; c 3. ELECTRICAL ENGINEERING. *Educ:* Ill Inst Technol, BS, 58; Case Inst Technol, MS, 63. *Prof Exp:* Aeronaut res engr, Lewis Res Ctr, NASA, 58-63; sr engr, IIT Res Inst, 63-72; SR RES ENGR, SCI APPLN, INC, 72- *Mem:* Am Inst Aeronaut & Astronaut; Sigma Xi; Am Astronaut Soc. *Res:* Theoretical analysis and design of space vehicle guidance and control systems; astronautical engineering; trajectory and space mission analysis. *Mailing Add:* 5041 Wright Terr Skokie IL 60077

FRIEDLANDER, ERIC MARK, b Santurce, PR, Jan 7, 44; US citizen; m 68. ALGEBRAIC K-THEORY. *Educ:* Swarthmore Col, BA, 65; Mass Inst Technol, PhD(math), 70. *Prof Exp:* instr, Princeton Univ, 70-71, lectr, 71-72, asst prof, 72-75; assoc prof, 75-80, PROF MATH, NORTHWESTERN UNIV, 80- *Concurrent Pos:* Res fel, US-France Exchange Scientists, 73-74; vis sr lectr, Sci Res Coun, UK, 77-78; vis mem, Inst Advan Study, Princeton, 81. *Mem:* Sigma Xi; Am Math Soc. *Res:* Techniques from algebraic geometry and topology to exploit newly discovered relationships to obtain results in algebraic geometry, algebraic topology, algebraic K-theory and group theory. *Mailing Add:* Dept Math Northwestern Univ Evanston IL 60201

FRIEDLANDER, GERHART, b Munich, Ger, July 28, 16; nat US; wid; c 2. NUCLEAR CHEMISTRY. *Educ:* Univ Calif, BS, 39, PhD(radiochem), 42. *Prof Exp:* Asst chem, Univ Calif, 42; instr, Univ Idaho, 42-43; chemist & group leader, Los Alamos Sci Lab, Univ Calif, 43-46; res assoc, Res Lab, Gen Elec Co, NY, 46-48; vis lectr chem & physics, Wash Univ, St Louis, 48; chemist, 48-52, chmn dept chem, 68-77, sr chemist, 52-81, CONSULT, BROOKHAVEN NAT LAB, 81- *Concurrent Pos:* Chmn panel future nuclear sci, Nat Acad Sci, 75-77; Humboldt award, 78-79. *Honors & Awards:* Nuclear Applns in Chem Award, Am Chem Soc, 67. *Mem:* AAAS; fel Am Phys Soc; Am Chem Soc; Nat Acad Sci; Am Acad Arts & Sci. *Res:* Nuclear reactions; solar neutrinos; properties of radioactive nuclides. *Mailing Add:* Chem Dept Brookhaven Nat Lab Upton NY 11973

FRIEDLANDER, HENRY Z, b New York, NY, May 18, 25; c 2. ORGANIC CHEMISTRY. *Educ:* Oberlin Col, AB, 48; Univ Ill, MS, 49, PhD(chem), 52; Fordham Law Sch, JD, 74. *Prof Exp:* Res assoc, Case Inst Technol, 48; asst, Univ Ill, 49-52; chemist, Stamford Labs, Am Cyanamid Co, 52-56; sr chemist, Johnson & Johnson, 57-58; sr scientist, Springdale Labs, Am Mach & Found Co, 59-64; res mgr, Dorr-Oliver, Inc, 64-66; mem staff, Union Carbide Corp Res, 66-78; MEM STAFF, STAUFFER CHEM CO, 78- *Mem:* Am Chem Soc. *Res:* Polymerization; synthetic membranes; law. *Mailing Add:* 85 Riverside Ave Stamford CT 06905

FRIEDLANDER, HERBERT NORMAN, b Chicago Heights, Ill, Mar 12, 22; m 43; c 3. PHYSICAL ORGANIC CHEMISTRY, RESEARCH ADMINISTRATION. *Educ:* Univ Chicago, SB, 42, PhD(phys org chem), 47. *Prof Exp:* Lab asst org chem, Univ Chicago, 42-44; jr chemist, Metall Labs, 44, res corp fel & asst, 47-48; jr scientist, Los Alamos Labs, NMex, 44-46; proj chemist, Res Dept, Standard Oil Co, Ind, 48-56; group leader, Res Dept, 59-60; res assoc, Res Dept, Amoco Chem Corp, 61-62; mgr polymer sci, Basic Res Dept, Chemstrand Res Ctr, Inc, 62-65; dir res, 65-66, dir new prod res & develop, 66-67, assoc dir cent res dept, Monsanto Co, 67-68, vpres & dir tech opers, Chemstrand Res Ctr, Inc, 68-74, VPRES & DIR TECH OPERS, MONSANTO TRIANGLE PARK DEVELOP CTR, INC, 74- *Concurrent Pos:* Consult, Nat Coun Res & Develop, State of Israel, 62 & 64; adj assoc prof, Dept Textile Chem, Sch Textiles, NC State Univ, 72-78; adj prof, 81- *Mem:* AAAS; Am Chem Soc. *Res:* Reaction of organic free radicals; slow neutron cross sections; atoms and free radicals in solution; chemicals from petroleum; catalysis and polymerization; stereo-regulated polymerization with solid catalysts; structure and properties of fiber-forming polymers; high performance fibers and fabrics for industrial applications. *Mailing Add:* Monsanto Triangle Park Dev Ctr PO Box 12274 Research Triangle Park NC 27709

FRIEDLANDER, JOHN BENJAMIN, b Toronto, Ont, Oct 4, 41; m 74. NUMBER THEORY. *Educ:* Univ Toronto, BSc, 65; Univ Waterloo, MA, 66; Pa State Univ, PhD(number theory), 72. *Prof Exp:* Vis mem math, Inst Advan Study, 72-74; lectr math, Mass Inst Technol, 74-76; vis prof, Scuola Normale Superiore, Pisa, 76-77; asst prof, 71-79, ASSOC PROF, UNIV TORONTO, 80- *Concurrent Pos:* Vis prof, Univ Ill, Urbana, 80. *Mem:* Am Math Soc. *Res:* Sieve methods; quadratic residues; class numbers; distribution of primes. *Mailing Add:* Phys Sci Group Univ Toronto Scarborough Can

FRIEDLANDER, MICHAEL J, b Miami, Fla, Jan 30, 50; c 1. PHYSIOLOGY. *Educ:* Fla State Univ, BS, 72; Univ Ill, MS, 74, PhD(physiol), 77. *Prof Exp:* NIH fel physiol, Univ Ill, 74-77 & Univ Va, 77-79; res asst prof anat & asst prof neurobiol, State Univ NY Stony Brook, 79-80; ASST PROF PHYSIOL & BIOPHYSICS, UNIV ALA, BIRMINGHAM, 80- *Concurrent Pos:* Co-investr res proj, Nat Eye Inst, 79-80, prin investr, Develop Structure & Function Vis Syst, 81-84. *Mem:* Soc Neurosci; Sigma Xi; Asn Res Vis & Ophthal; AAAS. *Res:* Structural basis of function of individual mammalian brain cells involved in processing visual information in the normal brain and in brains that develop with lack of normal visual input. *Mailing Add:* Dept Physiol & Biophysics Volker Hall Univ Ala Birmingham AL 35294

FRIEDLANDER, MICHAEL WULF, b Cape Town, SAfrica. PHYSICS, ASTROPHYSICS. *Educ:* Univ Cape Town, SAfrica, BSc, 48, MSc, 50; Univ Bristol, Eng, PhD(physics), 55. *Prof Exp:* Jr lectr physics, Univ Cape Town, SAfrica, 51-52; res assoc, Univ Bristol, Eng, 54-56; from asst prof to assoc prof, 56-67, PROF PHYSICS, WASHINGTON UNIV, ST LOUIS, 67- *Concurrent Pos:* Guggenheim fel, 62-63. *Mem:* Am Astron Soc; AAAS; Am Asn Physics Teachers; Int Astron Union; Am Asn Univ Professors (second vpres, 78-80). *Res:* Cosmic rays; infrared astronomy; archaeoastronomy. *Mailing Add:* Dept Physics Washington Univ St Louis MO 63130

FRIEDLANDER, SHELDON K, b New York, NY, Nov 17, 27; m 58; c 4. CHEMICAL & ENVIRONMENTAL ENGINEERING. *Educ:* Columbia Univ, BS, 49; Mass Inst Technol, MS, 51; Univ Ill, PhD(chem eng), 54. *Prof Exp:* Asst prof chem eng, Columbia Univ, 54-57; from asst prof to prof, Johns Hopkins Univ, 57-64; prof chem & environ eng, Calif Inst Technol, 64-78; PROF ENG & V CHMN CHEM ENG, UNIV CALIF, LOS ANGELES, 78- *Concurrent Pos:* Fulbright scholar, France, 60-61; indust & govt consult; mem environ sci & eng study sect, US Pub Health Serv, 65-68; Guggenheim fel, 69-70; chmn panel on abatement particulate emissions, Nat Res Coun, 70-72; mem technol assessment & pollution control adv comt, Environ Protection Agency, 76-79, chmn clean air sci adv comt; mem, Environ Studies Bd, Nat Resource Coun, 77-80. *Honors & Awards:* Colburn Award, Am Inst Chem Engrs, 59; Walker Award, Am Inst Chem Engrs, 79. *Mem:* Nat Acad Eng; Am Inst Chem Engrs; Am Chem Soc. t. *Res:* Aerosol dynamics; diffusion and interfacial transfer; air pollution; bioengineering. *Mailing Add:* 1591 Oakdale St Pasadena CA 91106

FRIEDLANDER, SUSAN JEAN, b London, Eng, Jan 26, 46; m 68. APPLIED MATHEMATICS, GEOPHYSICAL FLUID DYNAMICS. *Educ:* Univ London, BS, 67; Mass Inst Technol, MS, 70; Princeton Univ, PhD(fluid dynamics), 72. *Prof Exp:* Vis mem math, Courant Inst, NY Univ, 72-74; instr, Princeton Univ, 74-75; ASST PROF MATH, UNIV ILL, CHICAGO CIRCLE, 75- *Concurrent Pos:* Consult, Goddard Inst Space Studies, 74-75 & Math Res Ctr, Univ Wis, 80; vis lectr, Math Inst, Oxford Univ, 77-78; res assoc, Univ Calif, Berkeley, 81. *Mem:* Am Math Soc; Soc Indust Appl Math. *Res:* The application of mathematical techniques to problems in geophysical fluid dynamics. *Mailing Add:* Dept Math Univ Ill Chicago Circle Chicago IL 60680

FRIEDLANDER, WALTER JAY, b Los Angeles, Calif, June 6, 19; m 76; c 3. NEUROLOGY. *Educ:* Univ Calif, MD, 45; Am Bd Psychiat & Neurol, dipl. *Prof Exp:* Chief electroencephalog lab, NIH, 52-53; clin instr med, Sch Med, Stanford Univ, 53-55, asst clin prof neurol, 55-56; asst prof, Sch Med, Boston Univ, 57-61; from asst prof to prof, Albany Med Col, 61-66; dir, Ctr Humanities & Med, 75-80, PROF NEUROL, COL MED, UNIV NEBR, 66-, PROF MED JURISP & HUMANITIES & CHMN DEPT, 80-; PROF NEUROL, CREIGHTON UNIV COL MED, 72-, DIR CLIN NEUROL INFO CTR, 72- *Concurrent Pos:* Dir, Clin Neurol Info Ctr, Col Med, Creighton Univ, 72-80. *Mem:* AAAS; fel Am Acad Neurol; Am Electroencephalog Soc; Am Epilepsy Soc; fel Am Col Physicians. *Res:* Neurology; electroencephalography. *Mailing Add:* Dept Med Jurisp & Humanities Univ Nebr Col Med Omaha NE 68105

FRIEDLANDER, WILLIAM SHEFFIELD, b Evanston, Ill, Feb 17, 30; m 51; c 5. ORGANIC CHEMISTRY. *Educ:* Dartmouth Col, AB, 51; Univ Ill, MS, 52, PhD, 54. *Prof Exp:* Sr chemist & group supvr, 54-61, asst mgr, Adv Res Proj Agency Proj, 61-62, head, Polymer Sect, 62-65, dir, Contract Res Lab, 65-67, tech dir, New Bus Ventures Div, 67-73, tech dir, Duplicating Prods Div, 73-75, tech planning mgr, Graphic Systs Group, 3M Co, 75-76, managing dir, Minn 3M Res Ltd, Harlow, Eng, 76-81, DIR TECHNOL EVAL, INDUST & CONSUMER SECTOR, 3M CTR, 81- *Mem:* Am Chem Soc. *Res:* Synthetic organic chemistry; free radical reactions; chemistry of high energy propellants and rocket fuels; polymer science; fluorochemicals; graphic sciences; photographic science; new product development. *Mailing Add:* 3M Ctr St Paul MN 55144

FRIEDLANDER, ZITTA ZIPORA, quantum optics, experimental atomic physics, see previous edition

FRIEDLY, JOHN C, b Glen Dale, WVa, Feb 28, 38; m 62; c 4. CHEMICAL ENGINEERING. *Educ:* Carnegie Inst Technol, BS, 60; Univ Calif, Berkeley, PhD(chem eng), 64. *Prof Exp:* Chem engr, Gen Elec Res Lab, 64-67; asst prof chem eng, Johns Hopkins Univ, 67-68; asst prof, 68-71, assoc prof, 71-81, assoc dean, 79-81, PROF & CHMN CHEM ENG, UNIV ROCHESTER, 81- *Concurrent Pos:* NATO fel, Univ Oxford, 75-76. *Mem:* Am Inst Chem Engrs; Am Chem Soc; Am Soc Eng Educ. *Res:* Dynamics of chemical processes; automatic control as applied to the process industries; heat transfer. *Mailing Add:* Dept of Chem Eng Univ of Rochester Rochester NY 14627

FRIEDMAN, ALAN E, b New Castle, Pa, Apr 18, 45; m 65; c 2. TOXICOLOGY, INFORMATION PROCESSING. *Educ:* Pa State Univ, BS, 66; State Univ NY, Buffalo, PhD(med chem), 73. *Prof Exp:* Asst chem, Res Triangle Inst, 72-74; assoc chem, Sinai Hosp, Baltimore, 74-76; asst state toxicol, Off Chief Med Examr, State Md, 76-77; proj mgr, Tracor Jiteo Inc, 77-79; CLIN PROJ MGR, ALPHA THERAPEUT CORP, 79- *Concurrent Pos:* Instr, Essex Community Col, 77-79. *Mem:* Am Chem Soc. *Res:* Study the safety and effectiveness of new therapeutic agents in animal and human clinical trials. *Mailing Add:* 5555 Valley Blvd Los Angeles CA 90032

FRIEDMAN, ALAN HERBERT, b New York, NY, Sept 24, 37; m 60; c 4. OPHTHALMOLOGY. *Educ:* Cornell Univ, BA, 59; NY Univ, MD, 63. *Prof Exp:* Intern med, Bellevue Hosp, New York, NY, 63-64; resident ophthal, Med Ctr, NY Univ, 66-70; from asst prof to assoc prof ophthal, Albert Einstein Col Med, 70-77, asst prof path, 73-77; CLIN PROF OPHTHAL & ATTEND OPHTHAL PATH, MT SINAI SCH MED, 77- *Concurrent Pos:* Res fel, Royal Postgrad Med Sch London, 72. *Mem:* Asn Res Vision & Ophthal. *Res:* Ocular pathology and histochemistry. *Mailing Add:* Eastern Opthal Path Soc 880 Fifth Ave New York NY 10021

FRIEDMAN, ALEXANDER HERBERT, b Yonkers, NY, July 26, 25; m 61; c 2. PHARMACOLOGY. *Educ:* NY Univ, BA, 48; Univ Ill, MS, 56, PhD(pharmacol), 59. *Prof Exp:* Asst pharmacol, Yale Univ, 53; asst, Col Med, Univ Ill, 55-59; from instr to asst prof, Col Med, Univ Wis, 59-65, actg chmn dept, 63-64; assoc prof, 68-78, PROF PHARMACOL, STRITCH SCH MED, LOYOLA UNIV CHICAGO, 78- *Concurrent Pos:* Lederle med fac award, 66-69; adj prof ophalmol, Stritch Sch Med, Loyola Univ. *Honors & Awards:* Sigma Xi Res Prize, 58. *Mem:* AAAS; Int Soc Chronobiol; Am Soc Photobiol; hon mem NY Acad Sci; Am Soc Pharmacol & Exp Therapeut. *Res:* Neuropharmacology; tremor and rigidity-Parkinsonism; autonomic nervous system pharmacology; muscle spindles; modulator effects of drugs and circadian rhythms of biogenic amines as a basis for drug action; role of neurotransmitters in retinal coding. *Mailing Add:* Dept of Pharmacol & Therapeut Loyola Univ Stritch Sch of Med Maywood IL 60153

FRIEDMAN, AVNER, b Israel, Nov 19, 32; nat US; m 59; c 4. MATHEMATICS. *Educ:* Hebrew Univ, Israel, MSc, 54, PhD, 56. *Prof Exp:* Asst math, Hebrew Univ, Israel, 53-56; res assoc, Univ Kans, 56-57; lectr, Ind Univ, 57-58; asst prof, Univ Calif, 58-59; assoc prof, Univ Minn, 59-61; assoc prof, Stanford Univ, 61-62; PROF MATH, NORTHWESTERN UNIV, 62- *Concurrent Pos:* Sloan fels, 62-65; Guggenheim fel & vis prof, Tel-Aviv Univ, 66-67, vis prof, 70-71. *Mem:* Am Math Soc. *Res:* Mathematical analysis, especially partial differential equations; potential theory; ordinary differential equations; differential games. *Mailing Add:* Dept of Math Northwestern Univ Evanston IL 60201

FRIEDMAN, BEN I, b Cincinnati, Ohio, Oct 18, 26; m 54; c 1. NUCLEAR MEDICINE, INTERNAL MEDICINE. *Educ:* Univ Cincinnati, MD, 48. *Prof Exp:* Instr med, Col Med, Univ Cincinnati, 55-59, asst clin prof, 59-62, from asst prof to assoc prof, 62-68, asst prof radiol, 64-68, assoc dir nuclear med, 66-68; prof radiol, Col Med, Univ Tenn, Memphis, 68-73, prof med, 68-73, prof nuclear med & chmn dept & dir, Div Radiation Sci, 73-77; MEM STAFF, DEPT NUCLEAR MED, MORTON PLANT HOSP, 77- *Concurrent Pos:* Fel hemat & nutrit, Cincinnati Gen Hosp, 53-55; clinician, Outpatient Dept, Cincinnati Gen Hosp, 55-68, from asst attend physician to attend physician, 56-68, asst chief clinician, Hemat Clin, 56-68; attend physician, City Memphis Hosps, 68-77, Doctors Hosp & LeBonheur Childrens Hosp, Memphis. *Mem:* Am Col Nuclear Physicians; Am Col Radiol; AMA; Soc Nuclear Med. *Res:* Hematology; radioisotopes; radiobiology. *Mailing Add:* Dept of Nuclear Med Morton Plant Hosp Box 210 Clearwater FL 33517

FRIEDMAN, BENJAMIN, b Russia, Apr 28, 04; nat US; m 42. MEDICINE. *Educ:* City Col New York, BS, 27; Washington Univ, MD, 31. *Prof Exp:* Instr, Med Col, Cornell Univ, 39-42; from asst prof to prof, Univ Tex Southwest Med Sch, 46-55; prof, Med Col Ala, 55-58; prof, Univ Tex Southwest Med Sch, 58-66; dir, Div Med Educ, 67-70, PROF MED, MED CTR, UNIV ALA, BIRMINGHAM, 66-, VCHMN DEPT, 70- *Concurrent Pos:* Henry res fel endocrinol, Med Col, Cornell Univ, 34; Sutro fel cardiovasc res, Mt Sinai Hosp, New York, 35-39; chief med, Vet Admin Hosp, Dallas, 46- *Mem:* Am Soc Clin Invest; fel Am Col Physicians; Asn Am Physicians. *Res:* Cardiovascular physiology; physiology of blood circulation. *Mailing Add:* Med Ctr Univ of Ala Birmingham AL 35233

FRIEDMAN, BERNARD SAMUEL, b Chicago, Ill, Jan 4, 07; m 38; c 2. PETROLEUM CHEMISTRY. *Educ:* Univ Ill, AB, 30, PhD(org chem), 36. *Prof Exp:* Teacher pub sch, Ill, 30-33; asst instr chem, Univ Ill, 33-36; res chemist, Universal Oil Prods Co, Ill, 36-45; tech dir, Reyam Plastic Prods Co, 45-47; dir chem lab, QM Res & Develop Labs, 47-48; assoc dir org res div, Sinclair Res Labs, Inc, 48-59, res assoc, 59-69; CONSULT, 69- *Concurrent Pos:* Mem, Chicago Bd Educ, 62-77; prof lectr, Univ Chicago, 69-73. *Honors & Awards:* Honor Scroll, Am Inst Chem, 59; Merit Award, Chicago Tech Soc Coun, 63. *Mem:* Am Chem Soc (pres, 74); Am Inst Chem Engrs; fel Am Inst Chem. *Res:* Petroleum and petrochemical catalytic chemistry. *Mailing Add:* 4800 S Chicago Beach Dr Apt 1616 N Chicago IL 60615

FRIEDMAN, CHARLES NATHANIEL, b New York, NY, June 10, 46; m 69; c 2. MATHEMATICS. *Educ:* Cornell Univ, AB, 68; Princeton Univ, PhD(math), 71. *Prof Exp:* C L E Moore instr math, Mass Inst Technol, 71-73; asst prof, 73-78, ASSOC PROF MATH, UNIV TEX, AUSTIN, 78- *Mem:* Am Math Soc. *Res:* Mathematical physics; measurement theory in quantum mechanics; asymptotics of partial differential equations; product integrals. *Mailing Add:* 3408 Pecan Springs Rd Austin TX 78723

FRIEDMAN, CONSTANCE LIVINGSTONE, b Montreal, Que, July 30, 20; m 40. ANATOMY. *Educ:* McGill Univ, BSc, 41, MSc, 42, PhD(anat), 48. *Prof Exp:* Demonstr histol & biochem, McGill Univ, 43-45, res asst & assoc, 45-50; RES ASSOC PROF ANAT, UNIV BC, 50- *Mem:* Can Asn Anat. *Res:* Hypertension; endocrinology; aging. *Mailing Add:* Dept Anat Univ BC Vancouver Can

FRIEDMAN, DANIEL LESTER, b Cleveland, Ohio, Sept 25, 36; div; c 4. MOLECULAR BIOLOGY, BIOCHEMISTRY. *Educ:* Western Reserve Univ, BA, 58, MD & PhD(pharmacol), 65. *Prof Exp:* Fel oncol, McArdel Lab, Univ Wis, 65-67; asst prof, 67-72, ASSOC PROF, VANDERBILT UNIV, 72- *Concurrent Pos:* Mem sci adv panel, NSF, 78-80. *Mem:* Am Soc Cell Biol; Am Soc Bil Chemists; Sigma Xi. *Res:* Biochemistry of growth and cell division; role of cyclic nucleotides in growth. *Mailing Add:* Dept Molecular Biol Vanderbilt Univ Nashville TN 37235

FRIEDMAN, DAVID BELAIS, b Far Rockaway, NY, May 1, 16; m 43; c 3. PEDIATRICS. *Educ:* Univ Mich, AB, 37, MD, 40; Am Bd Pediat, dipl, 50. *Prof Exp:* Intern, Kings County Hosp, Brooklyn, NY, 40-42; resident pediat, Los Angeles County Gen Hosp, Calif, 46-48; staff pediatrician, Permanente Med Group, Oakland, Calif, 48-52, dir outpatient serv, 53-55; from clin instr to clin assoc prof pediat, 55-65, assoc prof, 65-71, dir, Div Family & Child Develop, 65-80, PROF PEDIAT, SCH MED, UNIV SOUTHERN CALIF, 71- *Concurrent Pos:* Teaching fel child psychiat, Sch Med, Univ Pittsburgh, 52-53; pvt practr, Los Angeles, 55-65; chmn, Nat Comt Infant & Presch Child & Task Force Eval Child Abuse Curric; co-dir region IX, Regional Resource Ctr Child Abuse & Neglect, Dept Health Educ & Welfare, 75-78. *Mem:* Am Acad Pediat; Soc Res Child Develop; Am Orthopsychiat Asn. *Res:* Medical education; child behavior and development; pediatric education research. *Mailing Add:* LAC-USC Med Ctr Univ of Southern Calif Sch Med Los Angeles CA 90033

FRIEDMAN, DON GENE, b Long Beach, Calif, May 26, 25; m 49; c 6. METEOROLOGY. *Educ:* Univ Calif, Los Angeles, BA, 50; Mass Inst Technol, MS, 51, ScD(meteorol), 54. *Prof Exp:* Asst meteorol, Mass Inst Technol, 50-54; fel statist, Univ Chicago, 54-55; res assoc appl meteorol & opers res, 55-60, asst dir res, 60-66, assoc dir res, 66-76, DIR, CORP RES DIV, TRAVELERS INS CO, 76- *Concurrent Pos:* Consult, HUD, 66-67, NSF, Assessment Res Natural Hazards Proj, Univ Colo, 73-75, NSF, 75-78, UNESCO & AAAS. *Honors & Awards:* Nat Award for Outstanding Contrib to the Advance of Appl Meteorol, Am Meteorol Soc, 76. *Mem:* Am Meteorol Soc; Am Seismol Soc. *Res:* Operations research; statistics; insurance; applied meteorology; computer simulation for assessment of effects of natural hazards, hurricanes, tornadoes, hailstorms, floods and earthquakes; production of natural disasters. *Mailing Add:* 99 Knollwood Rd Newington CT 06111

FRIEDMAN, EDWARD ALAN, b Bayonne, NJ, Sept 29, 35; m 63; c 2. SOLID STATE PHYSICS, ACADEMIC ADMINISTRATION. *Educ:* Mass Inst Technol, BS, 57; Columbia Univ, PhD(physics), 63. *Prof Exp:* asst prof, 63-69, assoc prof physics, 69-80, PROF AT LARGE, STEVENS INST TECHNOL, 80- *Concurrent Pos:* US Agency Int Develop contract loan, Kabul, Afghanistan, 65-67; chief of party, US Eng Team, Fac Eng, Kabul Univ, 70-73; chmn, Coun for Understanding Technol in Human Affairs, 79-; mem bd dir, Asn Independent Col & Univ, NJ, 78-; sr vpres, Afghanistan Relief Comt, 80- *Honors & Awards:* Res Award, Stevens Inst Technol, 70. *Mem:* AAAS; Am Phys Soc; NY Acad Sci; Am Soc Eng Educ; Am Soc Training & Develop. *Res:* Mossbauer measurements of hyperfine fields; inelastic neutron scattering from magnetic materials; philosophy of technology; studies on role of computers in education and training. *Mailing Add:* Dean of the Col Stevens Inst of Technol Hoboken NJ 07030

FRIEDMAN, EILEEN ANNE, US citizen. CELL BIOLOGY. *Educ:* NY Univ, AB, 67; Johns Hopkins Univ, PhD(molecular biol), 72. *Prof Exp:* Fel cell biol, Albert Einstein Col Med, 74-78; ASSOC GASTROENTEROL, SLOAN-KETTERING CANCER INST, 78- *Concurrent Pos:* Nat Cancer Inst fel, Albert Einstein Col, 75-77. *Mem:* Am Soc Cell Biol. *Res:* Tumor promotion; cell culture; DNA transfection; carcinogenesis. *Mailing Add:* Sloan-Kettering Inst 425 E 68th St New York NY 10021

FRIEDMAN, ELI A, b New York, NY, Apr 9, 33; m 57; c 3. INTERNAL MEDICINE, IMMUNOLOGY. *Educ:* Brooklyn Col, BS, 53; State Univ NY Downstate Med Ctr, MD, 57; Am Bd Internal Med, dipl, 68. *Prof Exp:* Intern med, Peter Bent Brigham Hosp, Boston, 57-58, sr resident, 60-61; instr, Emory Univ, 61-63; from asst prof to assoc prof, 63-71, PROF MED, STATE UNIV NY DOWNSTATE MED CTR, 71- *Concurrent Pos:* Res fel nephrol, Peter Bent Brigham Hosp, Boston, 58-60; consult, Vet Admin & USPHS, 64; coordr regional med prog, USPHS, 76- *Mem:* Fel Am Col Physicians; Transplantation Soc; Am Soc Nephrology; Am Fedn Clin Res; Am Soc Artificial Internal Organs. *Res:* Development and application of artificial kidneys; effect and synergistic relationship of immunosuppressive drugs. *Mailing Add:* Dept of Med State Univ NY Downstate Med Ctr Brooklyn NY 11203

FRIEDMAN, EMANUEL A, b New York, NY, June 9, 26; m 48; c 3. GYNECOLOGY. *Educ:* Brooklyn Col, AB, 47; Columbia Univ, MD, 51, MedScD(physiol), 59; Am Bd Obstet & Gynec, dipl. *Hon Degrees:* AM, Harvard Univ, 69. *Prof Exp:* Intern path, Cornell Med Div, Bellevue Hosp, New York, 51-52; resident obstet & gynec, Columbia-Presby Med Ctr, 52-57; instr, Fac Med, Columbia Univ, 57-59, assoc, 59-60, from asst prof to assoc prof, 60-63; prof & chmn dept, Chicago Med Sch, 63-69; chmn, Div Obstet & Gynec, Michael Reese Hosp & Med Ctr, 63-69; PROF OBSTET & GYNEC, HARVARD MED SCH, 69-; CHMN DEPT OBSTET & GYNEC, BETH ISRAEL HOSP, BOSTON, 69- *Concurrent Pos:* Asst, Columbia-Presby Med Ctr, 57-59, from asst attend to assoc attend, 59-63. *Honors & Awards:* Joseph Mather Smith Award, Columbia Univ, 58, Commemorative Silver Award, 67. *Mem:* AAAS; fel Am Col Obstet & Gynec; fel Am Col Surg; Soc Exp Biol & Med; fel Int Col Surg. *Res:* Physiology and pathophysiology of human labor phenomena; lactation and milk ejection; placental physiology. *Mailing Add:* Dept of Obstet & Gynec Beth Israel Hosp 330 Brookline Ave Boston MA 02215

FRIEDMAN, EMIL MARTIN, b Brooklyn, NY, Feb 15, 48; m 74. RUBBER CHEMISTRY, POLYMER PHYSICS. *Educ:* Mass Inst Technol, SB, 68; Princeton Univ, MA, 70, PhD(phys chem), 73. *Prof Exp:* Vis scientist, Polymer Sci & Eng, Univ Mass, 73-74; SR RES CHEMIST, RES DIV, GOODYEAR TIRE & RUBBER CO, 74- *Mem:* Am Chem Soc. *Res:* Physical properties of uncured rubber; structure-properties relationships; mathematical modeling of chemical processes. *Mailing Add:* Goodyear Tire & Rubber Co Res Div Akron OH 44316

FRIEDMAN, EMILY PERLINSKI, b Atlanta, Ga, Oct 27, 46; m 71. COMPUTER SCIENCE. *Educ:* Cornell Univ, AB, 68; Harvard Univ, SM, 71, PhD(appl math), 74. *Prof Exp:* Assoc programmer, Int Bus Mach, 68-70; asst prof comput sci, 74-80, ASSOC PROF ENG & APPL SCI, UNIV CALIF, LOS ANGELES, 80- *Mem:* Asn Comput Mach; Inst Elec & Electronics Engrs. *Res:* Theory of computation; program schemata; program verification; formal languages and automata; parsing. *Mailing Add:* 3532C Boelter Hall Dept of Comput Sci Univ of Calif Los Angeles CA 90024

FRIEDMAN, EPHRAIM, b Belvedere, Calif, Jan 1, 30; m 54; c 4. OPHTHALMOLOGY. *Educ:* Univ Calif, Los Angeles, BA, 50; Univ Calif, San Francisco, MD, 54. *Prof Exp:* Intern, San Francisco City & County Hosps, 54-55; resident ophthal, Mass Eye & Ear Infirmary, 59-61; instr, Howe Lab Ophthal, 61-64; prof ophthal, Sch Med, Boston Univ, 65-74, dean, 71-74; PROF OPHTHAL & DEAN, ALBERT EINSTEIN COL MED, 74- *Mem:* Asn Res Vision & Ophthal. *Res:* Physiology of the circulation of blood in the eye and related clinical problems. *Mailing Add:* Albert Einstein Col of Med 1300 Morris Park Ave Bronx NY 10461

FRIEDMAN, FRED JAY, b New York, NY, June 28, 51; m 80; c 1. RELATIONAL DATABASES, COMPILERS. *Educ:* Mich State Univ, BS, 71; Yale Univ, MS, 73, MPh, 74. *Prof Exp:* Consult, Naval Underwater Sound Lab & Xerox, 73-74, Advan Comput Techniques, 74, Gen Elec Co, 74-75; mem staff, 75-80, dir, Adv Syst Res, 80-81, CORP SR SCIENTIST, INCO, INC, 81- *Res:* Relational data bases, specifically user-friendly interfaces to back-end data base machines; compilers; computer networks; text editors; software productivity techniques and metrics. *Mailing Add:* INCO Inc 8260 Greensboro Dr McLean VA 22102

FRIEDMAN, GARY DAVID, b Cleveland, Ohio, Mar 8, 34; m 58; c 3. CHRONIC DISEASE EPIDEMIOLOGY. *Educ:* Univ Chicago, BS, 56, MD, 59; Harvard Univ, SM, 65. *Prof Exp:* From intern to asst resident, Harvard Med Serv, Boston City Hosp, 59-61; asst resident, Univ Hosp, Cleveland, 61-62; med officer, Heart Dis Epidemiol Study, US Pub Health Serv, Mass, 61-66, chief, Epidemiol Unit, Epidemiol Field & Training Sta, Heart Dis Control Prog, 66-68; sr epidemiologist, 68-76, ASST DIR EPIDEMIOL & BIOSTATIST, DEPT MED METHODS RES, KAISER-PERMANENTE MED CARE PROG, 76- *Concurrent Pos:* From res fel to res assoc, Dept Prev Med, Med Sch, Harvard Univ, 62-66; asst, Dept Ambulatory & Community Med, Univ Calif, San Francisco, 67-80, assoc clin prof, 80-; lectr, Sch Pub Health, Univ Calif, Berkeley, 68-; prin investr res grants & contracts, 71-; chmn, Comt Criteria & Methods, Coun Epidemiol, Am Heart Asn, 69-71, Prog Comt, 73-76; mem, US-USSR Working Group Sudden Cardia Death, Nat Heart, Lung and Blood Inst, NIH, 75-82. *Mem:* Fel Am Col Physicians; Am Epidemiol Soc; Soc Epidemiol Res; Int Epidemiol Asn. *Res:* Epidemiology of chronic diseases, focusing especially on cardiovascular diseases, cancer, and the effects of smoking, alcohol and medicinal drugs; author or coauthor of over 90 publications. *Mailing Add:* 3451 Piedmont Ave Oakland CA 94611

FRIEDMAN, GEORGE J(ERRY), b New York, NY, Mar 22, 28; m 53; c 3. SYSTEMS ANALYSIS, APPLIED MATHEMATICS. *Educ:* Univ Calif, Berkeley, BS, 49; Univ Calif, Los Angeles, MS, 56, PhD(eng & appl sci), 67. *Prof Exp:* Mech eng assoc, pub utility systs anal, Los Angeles Dept Water & Power, 49-56; res & develop engr, Servomechanisms, Inc, Calif, 56-60; res scientist & mgr adv systs, 60-80, VPRES TECHNICAL, TACTICAL & ELECTRON SYSTS GROUP, NORTHROP, CENTURY CITY, CALIF, 80- *Concurrent Pos:* Lectr, Univ Calif, Los Angeles, 57. *Honors & Awards:* W R G Baker Award, Inst Elec & Electronics Engrs, 70. *Mem:* Soc Gen Systs Res; Inst Elec & Electronics Engrs; Am Inst Aeronaut & Astronaut. *Res:* Operations analysis; constraint theory applied to the analysis of complex, multidimensional math models; computer simulation of evolutionary processes; automata theory; systems analysis methodology; artificial intelligence and multidimensional kinematics. *Mailing Add:* 5084 Gloria Ave Encino CA 91436

FRIEDMAN, GERALD MANFRED, b Berlin, Ger, July 23, 21; nat US; m 48; c 5. SEDIMENTOLOGY, SEDIMENTARY PETROLOGY. *Educ:* Univ London, BSc, 45; Columbia Univ, MA, 50, PhD(geol), 52; DrSci, Univ London, 77. *Prof Exp:* Sr chemist, J Lyons & Co, 45-46; anal chemist, E R Squibb & Sons, 47-49; asst geol, Columbia Univ, 50; from instr to asst prof, Univ Cincinnati, 50-54; consult geologist, Sault Ste Marie, Can, 54-56; sr res geologist, Amoco Prod Co, 56-60, res assoc & supvr sedimentary geology res, 60-64; PROF GEOL, RENSSELAER POLYTECH INST, 64- *Concurrent Pos:* Sect ed, Chem Abstr, 62-69; Fulbright sr vis lectr, Hebrew Univ, 64; ed, J Sedimentary Petrol, 64-70; res scientist, Hudson Labs, Columbia Univ, 65, 66-69, res assoc geol, Univ, 68-71; vis prof mineral, Univ Heidelberg, 67; consult scientist, Inst Petrol Res & Geophys, Israel, 67-71, vis scientist, Geol Surv Israel, 70-73 & 78. *Mem:* Asn Earth Sci Ed (vpres, 70-71, pres, 71-72); Soc Econ Paleontologists & Mineralogists (vpres, 70-71, pres, 74-75); Int Asn Sedimentologists (vpres, 71-75, pres, 75-78); fel AAAS; Nat Asn Geol Teachers (treas, 51-55). *Res:* Carbonate sedimentology; chemistry of sedimentation; petrology and sedimentology of clastic and carbonate sediments. *Mailing Add:* Dept of Geol Rensselaer Polytech Inst Troy NY 12181

FRIEDMAN, HAROLD BERTRAND, b Montgomery, Ala, Oct 13, 04; m 53; c 3. PHYSICAL CHEMISTRY, INDUSTRIAL CHEMISTRY. *Educ:* Univ Ala, AB, 23; Univ Va, PhD(chem), 27. *Prof Exp:* Teacher pub sch, Ala, 23-24; instr phys chem, Univ Maine, 27-28; asst chem, Columbia Univ, 28; from asst prof to assoc prof, Ga Tech, 29-42; chem dir, 45-63, VPRES, ZEP MFG CO, 63- *Concurrent Pos:* Consult chem, 74- *Mem:* Am Chem Soc; fel Am Inst Chem; Sigma Xi. *Res:* Solid-gas catalysis; neutral salt action; reaction velocity and kinetics; activity coefficients of electrolytes; history of chemistry; soaps, waxes and detergents. *Mailing Add:* Zep Mfg Co 1310 Seaboard Industrial Blvd NW Atlanta GA 30301

FRIEDMAN, HAROLD LEO, b New York, NY, Mar 24, 23; m 45; c 2. PHYSICAL CHEMISTRY, CHEMICAL PHYSICS. *Educ:* Univ Chicago, BS, 47, PhD(chem), 49. *Prof Exp:* From instr to assoc prof chem, Univ Southern Calif, 49-59; adv chemist, Res Ctr, Int Bus Mach Corp, 59-65; PROF CHEM, STATE UNIV NY, STONY BROOK, 65- *Concurrent Pos:* Guggenheim fel, 57-58; Alfred P Sloan res fel, 59-61; adj prof, Polytech Inst Brooklyn, 64-65. *Mem:* Am Chem Soc; Am Inst Physics; Royal Soc Chem. *Res:* Equilibrium and dynamic properties of liquid solutions. *Mailing Add:* Dept of Chem State Univ of NY Stony Brook NY 11794

FRIEDMAN, HARRIS LEONARD, b Dover, NJ, Jan 17, 13; m 40; c 2. ORGANIC CHEMISTRY. *Educ:* NY Univ, BS, 34, PhD(org chem), 38. *Prof Exp:* Asst chem, NY Univ, 35-38; res chemist & dir div pure res, Pyridium Corp, 39-47; chief chemist, Reade Mfg Co, NJ, 47-48; chief chem div, Lakeside Labs, Inc, 48-53, dir lab & tech res, 53-59, dir basic res, 59, vpres res, 59-68; PROF MED CHEM, MED COL WIS, 68- *Concurrent Pos:* Consult chemist, Galat Chem Develop Co, 47-48. *Mem:* AAAS; Am Chem Soc; NY Acad Sci; Am Soc Pharmacol & Exp Therapeut; Sigma Xi. *Res:* Chemotherapy; heterocyclic organic chemistry; vitamins; hormones; medicinal chemistry, especially structure activity relationships; bioisosterism. *Mailing Add:* Dept Pharmacol Med Col Wis PO Box 26509 Milwaukee WI 53226

FRIEDMAN, HARRY GEORGE, JR, b New Orleans, La, Aug 12, 38; m 62; c 3. COMPUTER SCIENCE, OPERATING SYSTEMS. *Educ:* Loyola Univ, La, BS, 59; Fla State Univ, PhD(inorg chem), 66. *Prof Exp:* Asst prof, 65-70, ASSOC PROF COMPUT SCI, UNIV ILL, URBANA, 70- *Mem:* Asn Comput Mach. Rer: Compilers; executive systems; computer assisted instruction. *Res:* Computer assisted instruction. *Mailing Add:* 1115 Newbury Champaign IL 61820

FRIEDMAN, HARVEY MARTIN, b Chicago, Ill, Sept 23, 48; m 73. MATHEMATICAL LOGIC, MATHEMATICAL ANALYSIS. *Educ:* Mass Inst Technol, PhD(math), 67. *Prof Exp:* From asst prof to assoc prof logic, Stanford Univ, 67-73; vis prof math, State Univ NY Buffalo, 72-73, prof math, 73-77; PROF MATH, OHIO STATE UNIV, 77- *Concurrent Pos:* Vis assoc prof math, Univ Wis-Madison, 70-71. *Mem:* Am Math Soc; Asn Symbolic Logic. *Res:* Mathematical analysis of informal concepts which arise in the study of mathematics, logic, and philosophy; technical development of mathematical logic. *Mailing Add:* Dept Math Ohio State Univ Columbus OH 43220

FRIEDMAN, HARVEY PAUL, b New York, NY, Dec 31, 35; m 70. EMBRYOLOGY, IMMUNOLOGY. *Educ:* City Col New York, BS, 57; Univ Kans, PhD(anat), 63. *Prof Exp:* Bacteriologist, Sloan-Kettering Inst, 57-58; asst prof microbiol, Meharry Med Col, 65-66; res assoc immunol, Univ Kans, 66-68; asst prof, 68-71, ASSOC PROF, DEPT BIOL, UNIV MO-ST LOUIS, 71- *Concurrent Pos:* NIH fel, Case Western Reserve Univ, 63-65; Nat Inst Neurol Dis & Blindness grant; consult, Vet Admin Hosp, Topeka, Kans. *Mem:* AAAS; Am Soc Neurochem; Soc Study Develop. *Res:* Immunological investigation of embryonic development; in vitro synthesis of antibody. *Mailing Add:* Dept of Biol Univ of Mo 8001 Natural Bridge Rd St Louis MO 63121

FRIEDMAN, HELEN LOWENTHAL, b New York, NY, Jan 25, 24; m 46; c 2. PHYSICAL OPTICS, MEDICAL PHYSICS. *Educ:* Hunter Col, BA, 44; Purdue Univ, MS, 46; Columbia Univ, PhD(physics), 51. *Prof Exp:* Asst physics, Purdue Univ, 44-46; asst, Columbia Univ, 49-51; lectr, Hunter Col, 52-53; instr, Queen's Col, NY, 53-55, lectr, 58-61; asst prof, 61-68, ASSOC PROF PHYSICS, HOFSTRA UNIV, 68- *Mem:* AAAS; Am Phys Soc; Optical Soc Am; Am Asn Physics Teachers; Am Asn Physicists Med. *Res:* Physical optics. *Mailing Add:* Dept of Physics Hofstra Univ Hempstead NY 11550

FRIEDMAN, HENRY DAVID, b New York, NY, June 22, 26. MATHEMATICS. *Educ:* Pa State Col, BS, 48, PhD(math), 53; Columbia Univ, MA, 50. *Prof Exp:* Instr math, City Col New York, 49-51 & Pa State Univ, 51-53; sr mathematician, Haller, Raymond & Brown, 52-53; mathematician, Gen Elec Co, 53-59, Tech Opers, Inc, 59-60, Arcon Corp, 60-62 & Appl Res Lab, Sylvania Electronic Systs Div, Gen Tel & Electronics Corp, 62-65; mgr data processing, Smithsonian Astrophys Observ, 65-66; consult, 66-67; mathematician, Appl Res Lab, Sylvania Electronic Systs Div, Gen Tel & Electronics Corp, 67-71; mathematician, Gen Elec Co, 71-77; SR STAFF ENGR, TRW SYSTS, 78- *Concurrent Pos:* Lectr appl math, Univ Santa Clara, 67-74. *Mem:* Fel AAAS; Asn Comput Mach; Math Asn Am. *Res:* Mathematical statistics; digital computation; operations research. *Mailing Add:* TRW Systs 1145 E Arques Sunnyvale CA 94086

FRIEDMAN, HERBERT, b New York, NY, June 21, 16; m 40; c 2. PHYSICS, ASTRONOMY. *Educ:* Brooklyn Col, BA, 36; Johns Hopkins Univ, PhD(physics), 40. *Hon Degrees:* DSc, Univ Tubingen, 77, Univ Mich, 79. *Prof Exp:* Physicist, 40-43, head electron optics br, 43-58, SUPT, SPACE SCI DIV, US NAVAL RES LAB, 58-, CHIEF SCIENTIST, E O HULBURT CTR SPACE RES, 63- *Concurrent Pos:* Prof, Univ Md, 61-; mem exec comt, Space Sci Bd, Nat Acad Sci, 62-, mem comt sci & pub policy; chmn, Comt Space Res Working Group II for Int Year Quiet Sun, 62-; vchmn, Inter-Union Comt on Ionosphere, 63-; mem exec comt, Int Asn Geomagnesium & Aeronomy, 63-; mem bd trustees, Assoc Univs, Inc, 66-70; mem exec comt, Div Phys Sci, Nat Res Coun-Nat Acad Sci, 69-, mem adv panel atmospheric sci & chmn comt solar-terrestrial res, Geophys Res Bd; mem gen adv comt to US Atomic Energy Comn, 69-74; pres comn 48 on high energy astrophys, Int Astron Union, 70-; mem, President's Sci Adv Comt, 71-73; pres, Inter-Union Comn on Solar-Terrestrial Physics; mem, Space Prog Adv Coun, Nat Aeronaut & Space Admin, 74-77; mem ad hoc adv group on sci progs, President's Sci Adv, NSF, 75-76; mem adv bd, Off Phys Sci, Nat Res Coun, 75-, chmn, Geophys Res Bd, 76-; chmn, X-Ray Astron Comt, Univs Res Asn, Inc, 76-; counr, Nat Res Coun-Nat Acad Sci, 80-, chmn, Assembly Math & Phys Sci, Nat Res Ctr, 80- *Honors & Awards:* Annual Award, Soc Appl

Spectros, 57; Janssen Medal, Fr Photog Soc, 62; Space Sci Award, Am Inst Aeronaut & Astronaut, 63, Dryden Res Award, 73; Capt Robert Dexter Conrad Award, 64; Eddington Medal, Royal Astron Soc, 64; Nat Medal Sci, 68; Albert A Michelson Medal, Franklin Inst, 72; Lovelace Award, Am Astron Soc, 73; William Bowie Medal, Am Geophys Union, 81. *Mem:* Nat Acad Sci; fel AAAS (vpres elect, 71, vpres, 72); fel Am Acad Arts & Sci; fel Am Phys Soc; fel Optical Soc Am. *Res:* X-ray spectroscopy and diffraction; electron diffraction and microscopy; nucleonics; upper atmosphere research; electron tubes; astrophysics; radio astronomy. *Mailing Add:* Code 7100 Space Sci Div Naval Res Lab Washington DC 20375

FRIEDMAN, HERBERT ALTER, b Brooklyn, NY, May 9, 37. CHEMICAL PHARMACOLOGY. *Educ:* Yeshiva Univ, BA, 58; Polytech Inst Brooklyn, PhD(chem), 64. *Prof Exp:* From instr pharmacol to res specialist, Univ Pa Sch Med, 67-76; ASST PROF PHARMACOL, JEFFERSON MED COL, THOMAS JEFFERSON UNIV, 76- *Concurrent Pos:* Fel, Sloan-Kettering Inst Cancer Res, 64-67. *Mem:* Am Chem Soc; Chem Soc London; Am Soc Pharmacol & Exp Therapeut; Sigma Xi. *Res:* Structure-activity relationships; medicinal chemistry; molecular aspects of interactions with muscle; mass spectrometry in pharmacology. *Mailing Add:* Dept of Pharmacol Jefferson Med Col Thomas Jefferson Univ Philadelphia PA 19107

FRIEDMAN, HERMAN, b Philadelphia, Pa, Sept 22, 31; m 58. MICROBIOLOGY, IMMUNOLOGY. *Educ:* Temple Univ, AB, 53, AM, 55; Hahnemann Med Col, PhD(microbiol), 57; Am Bd Microbiol, dipl. *Prof Exp:* Instr microbiol, Hahnemann Med Col, 57-58; res biochemist & chief allergy dept, Vet Admin Hosp, Pittsburgh, 58-59; from asst prof to prof microbiol, Sch Med, Temple Univ, 70-78; head dept, Albert Einstein Med Ctr, 59-78; PROF & CHMN DEPT MICROBIOL, COL MED, UNIV SOUTH FLA, 78- *Concurrent Pos:* Am Heart Found fel, Childrens Hosp, Philadelphia & Hahnemann Med Col, 57-58; NIH & NSF grants, 60-; Am Cancer Soc grants, 65-68 & 72-73; chmn, Comt Immunol, Am Bd Med Microbiol, 67-79; deleg & session chmn, Int Cong Microbiol, Moscow, 66 & Mexico City, 70, Cong Bact, Jerusalem, 73, Immunol, Brighton, Eng, 74, Sydney, Australia, 78 & Transplant Cong, Jerusalem, 74; deleg & session chmn, Virol Cong, Madrd, 75, New York City, 76 & Reticuloendothelial Socs Cong, Panplona, Spain, 75 & Jerusalem, 78; chmn, Int Conf, NY Acad Sci, 71, 73, 74, 75 & 79; consult, Miles Labs, Damon Labs, Smith Kline & French Labs & Wyeth Labs. *Mem:* AAAS; Am Soc Microbiol; fel NY Acad Sci; Brit Soc Gen Microbiol; Am Asn Immunologists. *Res:* Bacterial physiology; tumor virus immunology and oncology; nucleic acid synthesis; immunology and immunochemistry-antibody formation; hypersensitivity and allergy. *Mailing Add:* Dept Microbiol Univ SFla Tampa FL 33612

FRIEDMAN, HOWARD STEPHEN, b Elizabeth, NJ, Mar 31, 48; m 72. ORGANIC CHEMISTRY. *Educ:* NY Univ, AB, 70, MS, 72, PhD(org chem), 76. *Prof Exp:* Scholar & lectr chem, Univ Mich, 75-77; sr res chemist, Goodyear Tire & Rubber Co, 77-79; SR RES CHEMIST, FERRO CORP, BEDFORD, OHIO, 80- *Mem:* Am Chem Soc; Royal Soc Chem; Sigma Xi; Soc Plastics Engrs; NY Acad Sci. *Res:* Research and development of flame retardant, smoke suppressant and intumescent chemicals. *Mailing Add:* 6459 Chiltern Rd NW Canal Fulton OH 44614

FRIEDMAN, IRVING, b New York, NY, Jan 12, 20; m 46. GEOCHEMISTRY. *Educ:* Mont State Col, BS, 42; State Col, Wash, MS, 44; Univ Chicago, PhD(geochem), 50. *Prof Exp:* Chemist, US Naval Res Lab, 46-48; asst geol, Univ Chicago, 48-50, res assoc, Enrico Fermi Inst Nuclear Studies, 50-52; GEOCHEMIST, US GEOL SURV, 52- *Mem:* Geol Soc Am; fel Am Geophys Union; Am Chem Soc; AAAS. *Res:* Phase equilibria in hydrous silicate systems at high temperature and pressure; abundance of stable isotopes applied to earth sciences; volcanology. *Mailing Add:* Br of Isotope Geol US Geol Surv Bldg 21 Denver Fed Ctr Denver CO 80225

FRIEDMAN, IRWIN, b New York, NY, Dec 15, 29; m 53; c 3. MEDICINE. *Educ:* Union Col, BS, 51; NY Univ, MD, 55. *Prof Exp:* DIR PULMONARY FUNCTION LAB, BUFFALO GEN HOSP, 63, RESPIRATORY SERV, 68-; ASSOC PROF INTERNAL MED & PHARMACOL, STATE UNIV NY, BUFFALO, 72- *Concurrent Pos:* Nat Heart Inst fel, 60-61; asst prof internal med, State Univ NY Buffalo, 66-72; pvt practr, 61. *Mem:* Am Thoracic Soc; Am Heart Asn; AMA; Am Col Physicians; Am Col Chest Physicians. *Res:* Clinical pulmonary physiology. *Mailing Add:* 85 High St Buffalo NY 14203

FRIEDMAN, JACK P, b New York, NY, Sept 4, 39; wid; c 2. ENGINEERING PHYSICS, APPLIED MATHEMATICS. *Educ:* Rensselaer Polytech Inst, BS, 60; Univ Chicago, MS, 61, PhD(physics), 65. *Prof Exp:* ENGR COMPUT SCI, APPL MATH & ENG PHYSICS, GEN ELEC KNOLLS ATOMIC POWERLAB, 65- *Mem:* Am Phys Soc; Asn Comput Mach; Am Geophys Union. *Res:* Heat transfer; applied mathematics; computer science; fluid mechanics. *Mailing Add:* 2251 Berkely Ave Schenectady NY 12309

FRIEDMAN, JEROME ISAAC, b Chicago, Ill, Mar 28, 30; m 56; c 3. PHYSICS. *Educ:* Univ Chicago, AB, 50, MS, 53, PhD(physics), 56. *Prof Exp:* Res assoc physics, Univ Chicago, 56-57 & Stanford Univ, 57-60; from asst prof to assoc prof, 60-67, PROF PHYSICS, MASS INST TECHNOL, 67-, DIR, LAB NUCLEAR SCI, 80- *Mem:* Am Phys Soc. *Res:* High energy physics; elementary particles. *Mailing Add:* Dept of Physics Mass Inst of Technol Cambridge MA 02139

FRIEDMAN, JOEL MITCHEL, b Brooklyn, NY, Aug 13, 47; m 71. CHEMICAL PHYSICS, BIOPHYSICS. *Educ:* Brooklyn Col, BS, 69; Univ Pa, MD, 76, PhD(chem), 75. *Prof Exp:* Fel, 75-77, MEM TECH STAFF, BELL LABS, 77- *Mem:* Biophys Soc; Am Phys Soc; Am Chem Soc. *Res:* Experimental and theoretical study of resonant light scattering from molecular systems; application of resonant light scattering to reveal the molecular mechanisms of biological activity. *Mailing Add:* Rm 1A118 Bell Labs Murray Hill NJ 07974

FRIEDMAN, JOYCE BARBARA, b Washington, DC, Jan 5, 28. COMPUTER SCIENCES. *Educ:* Wellesley Col, BA, 49; Radcliffe Col, AM, 52; Harvard Univ, PhD(appl math), 65. *Prof Exp:* Res assoc, Logistics Res Proj, George Washington Univ, 50-51; mathematician, Weapons Syst Eval Group, Off Secy Defense, 52-54 & ACF Indust Inc, 54-56; sr mathematician, Tech Oper Inc, 56-60; mem tech staff, MITRE Corp, 60-65; asst prof comput sci, Stanford Univ, 65-68; assoc prof, 68-71, PROF COMPUT & COMMUN SCI, UNIV MICH, 71- *Concurrent Pos:* Vis scientist, IBM Watson Res Ctr, 70-71; consult, Stanford Res Inst, 74-76. *Mem:* Asn Comput Linguistics (vpres, 70, pres, 71); Asn Comput Mach; Asn Symbolic Logic; Am Math Soc. *Res:* Computational linguistics; computer models of linguistic theories; computer aids to linguistic research; speech understanding systems. *Mailing Add:* Dept of Comput & Commun Sci Univ of Mich Ann Arbor MI 48109

FRIEDMAN, JULES DANIEL, b Poughkeepsie, NY, Oct 24, 28; c 3. GEOLOGY. *Educ:* Cornell Univ, AB, 50; Yale Univ, MS, 52, PhD(geol), 58. *Prof Exp:* Asst dept geol, Yale Univ, 50-53; geologist, DC, 53-69, geologist, Regional Geophys, DC, 69-74, geologist, Theoret & Appl Geophys, Colo, 74-81, GEOLOGIST, PETROPHYS & REMOTE SENSING, US GEOL SURV, COLO, 81- *Concurrent Pos:* Mem panel geodesy & cartography, Comt Polar Res, Nat Acad Sci-Nat Res Coun. *Mem:* Fel Geol Soc Am; Am Geophys Union. *Res:* Geophysics; remote sensing; volcanology; structural geology; geomorphology; application of aerial and satellite infrared thermography to volcanic geology, heat flow, geothermal sources and geomorphology, especially neovolcanic zone of Iceland; Mono Basin, California; Cascade Range, especially Mt St Helens and Lassen volcanic region; lineament analyses and geology of radioactive waste disposal sites; energy resources. *Mailing Add:* US Geol Surv Dept Interior Denver CO 80225

FRIEDMAN, JULIUS JAY, b Brooklyn, NY, Mar 6, 26. PHYSIOLOGY. *Educ:* Tulane Univ, BS, 49, MS, 51, PhD(physiol), 53. *Prof Exp:* Res physiologist, Biophys Lab, Tulane Univ, 53-58; from asst prof to assoc prof, 58-71, PROF PHYSIOL, SCH MED, IND UNIV, INDIANAPOLIS, 71- *Concurrent Pos:* Lederle med fac fel, 60-63. *Mem:* AAAS; Microcirculatory Soc; Am Asn Univ Profs; Am Physiol Soc; Am Inst Biol Sci. *Res:* Tissue blood volumes and hematocrits; hemorrhagic and traumatic shock; peripheral vascular dynamics; microvascular function; trans-capillary exchange; capillary permeability; capillary regulation. *Mailing Add:* Dept of Physiol Ind Univ Med Ctr Indianapolis IN 46202

FRIEDMAN, KENNETH JOSEPH, b Brooklyn, NY, July 28, 43; m 69. PHYSIOLOGY, BIOPHYSICS. *Educ:* Lawrence Col, BA, 64; State Univ NY Stony Brook, PhD(biol sci), 69. *Prof Exp:* Lectr, State Univ NY Stony Brook, 68-69; NIH trainee, Dept Zool, Univ Calif, Los Angeles, 69-70, NIH fel, 70-72, staff fel, 72-75; ASST PROF PHYSIOL, COL MED & DENT, NJ MED SCH, 75- *Mem:* AAAS; Am Physiol Soc; Biophys Soc. *Res:* Role of lipids in determining electrical and transport properties of the cell membrane; neurophysiology and electrophysiology. *Mailing Add:* Dept Physiol NJ Med Sch 100 Bergen St Newark NJ 07103

FRIEDMAN, LAWRENCE BOYD, b Minneapolis, Minn, May 9, 39; m 61; c 2. INORGANIC CHEMISTRY. *Educ:* Univ Minn, Duluth, BA, 61; Harvard Univ, MA, 63, PhD(chem), 66. *Prof Exp:* Asst prof chem, Oakland Univ, 66-68; from asst prof to assoc prof, Wellesley Col, 68-74; lab mgr, 74-80, SR SCIENTIST, POLAROID CORP, 80- *Mem:* Am Chem Soc; Am Crystallog Asn. *Res:* Boron hydride chemistry; x-ray crystallography; analytical techniques; photographic science. *Mailing Add:* 17 Leighton Rd Auburndale MA 02166

FRIEDMAN, LAWRENCE DAVID, b Newark, NJ, Aug 25, 32; m 60; c 3. GENETICS. *Educ:* Rutgers Univ, BA, 54; Northwestern Univ, MS, 55; Univ Wis, PhD(zool, genetics), 60. *Prof Exp:* Asst genetics, Northwestern Univ, 54-55; asst zool, Univ Wis, 55-57, asst genetics, 57-60, proj assoc, 60-61; asst prof biol, Hiram Col, 61-66; ASSOC PROF BIOL, UNIV MO-ST LOUIS, 66- *Mem:* AAAS; Genetics Soc Am; Am Genetic Asn. *Res:* Genetics of Drosophila. *Mailing Add:* Dept of Biol Univ of Mo 8001 Natural Bridge Rd St Louis MO 63121

FRIEDMAN, LEONARD, b Brooklyn, NY, Jan 27, 29; m 64. BIOCHEMISTRY. *Educ:* NY Univ, BA, 51; Rutgers Univ, MS, 53, PhD(biochem), 59. *Prof Exp:* Fel, Iowa State Univ, 59-61; res chemist biochem, NIH, 61-62; res chemist, 62-80, SUPV RES CHEMIST, DIV TOXICOL, FOOD & DRUG ADMIN, 80- *Mem:* AAAS; Soc Toxicol; fel Am Inst Chem; Am Chem Soc. *Res:* Chemical, physical and enzymic nature of proteolytic enzymes, especially rennin and proteinase; metabolism of malaria; effect of nutrition on enzymes and metabolism of tissues. *Mailing Add:* 14805 Waterway Dr Rockville MD 20853

FRIEDMAN, LESTER, b New York, NY, Sept 14, 28; div; c 3. ORGANIC CHEMISTRY. *Educ:* Purdue Univ, BS, 51; Ohio State Univ, PhD(chem), 59. *Prof Exp:* Instr phys chem, Capital Univ, 52-53; asst prof chem, NY Univ, 57-61; from asst prof to assoc prof chem, Case Western Reserve Univ, 61-75; DIR RES & DEVELOP, AMVAC CHEM CORP, 75- *Concurrent Pos:* Consult. *Mem:* AAAS; Am Chem Soc; NY Acad Sci; The Chem Soc. *Res:* Reaction mechanisms and syntheses; reactive intermediates; arynes; carbenes; poorly solvated cations; over crowded molecules; organophosphorus chemistry; insect phermones; chemical basis of olfaction. *Mailing Add:* Amvac Chem Corp 4100 E Washington Blvd Los Angeles CA 90023

FRIEDMAN, LEWIS, b Spring Lake, NJ, Aug 8, 22; m 48; c 3. PHYSICAL CHEMISTRY. *Educ:* Lehigh Univ, AB, 43, AM, 45; Princeton Univ, PhD(chem), 47. *Prof Exp:* Inst Nuclear Studies fel, Univ Chicago, 47-48; assoc chemist, 48-52, chemist, 52-64, SR CHEMIST, BROOKHAVEN NAT LAB, 64- *Concurrent Pos:* Guest scientist, Found Fundamental Res Matter Lab Mass Separation, Amsterdam, Neth, 60-61. *Mem:* Am Soc Mass Spectrometry. *Res:* Electron and ion impact phenomena; high sensitivity and high molecular weight mass spectrometry; chemical studies with isotopes. *Mailing Add:* Brookhaven Nat Lab Upton NY 11973

FRIEDMAN, LIONEL ROBERT, b Philadelphia, Pa, May 8, 33; m 56; c 3. SOLID STATE PHYSICS. *Educ:* Swarthmore Col, BS, 55; Univ Pittsburgh, PhD(physics), 61. *Prof Exp:* Scientist, Westinghouse Atomic Power Div, 55-61; res assoc solid state physics, Univ Pittsburgh, 61-62; mem tech staff, RCA Labs, 62-72; sr res assoc, Sch Math & Physics, Univ East Anglia, Norwich, UK, 72-73; lectr, 73-74, READER DEPT THEORET PHYSICS, UNIV ST ANDREWS, 74- *Concurrent Pos:* Instr, Temple Univ, 64-66; Sci Res Coun sr vis fel, Cavendish Lab, Cambridge Univ, 71-72; contrib lectr physics & technol amorphous mat course, sponsored by Univ Edinburgh, Glasgow, Dundee, Heriot-Watt & St Andrews; mem sci & organizing comt, 7th Int Conf Amorphous & Liquid Semiconductors, Edinburgh, 77; mem tech staff, GTE Labs, 80- *Mem:* Am Phys Soc; Sigma Xi. *Res:* Transport phenomena in solids; small polaron theory; organic semiconduction; amorphous semiconductors; metal-insulator transition. *Mailing Add:* Dept Theoret Physics Univ St Andrews St Andrews Fife Scotland

FRIEDMAN, LORRAINE, b Dawson, NMex, Jan 1, 19. MEDICAL MICROBIOLOGY. *Educ:* Univ NC, MPH, 48; Duke Univ, PhD(microbiol), 51. *Prof Exp:* Bacteriologist, Johns Hopkins Hosp, 46-47; Kellogg Found fel, 47-48; res mycologist, Dept Bact, Naval Biol Lab, Univ Calif, 51-55; PROF MICROBIOL & IMMUNOL, SCH MED, TULANE UNIV, 55- *Concurrent Pos:* Lederle Fac Award, 55-57; consult, USPHS, 62-65, mem study sect, 66-69. *Mem:* Am Pub Health Asn; Am Soc Microbiol; Mycol Soc Am. *Res:* Epidemiology and immunology of mycoses. *Mailing Add:* Mycol Lab Tulane Univ Sch of Med 1430 Tulane Ave New Orleans LA 70112

FRIEDMAN, MARVIN ALAN, toxicology, pharmacology, see previous edition

FRIEDMAN, MARVIN HAROLD, b New York, NY, July 20, 23. PHYSICS. *Educ:* City Col, BS, 43; Univ Ill, MS, 49, PhD(physics), 52. *Prof Exp:* NSF fel, Cornell Univ, 52-53; res assoc physics, Columbia Univ, 53-55; asst prof, Mass Inst Technol, 55-61; assoc prof, 61-66, PROF PHYSICS, NORTHEASTERN UNIV, 66- *Mem:* Fel Am Phys Soc. *Res:* High energy theoretical physics; statistical mechanics. *Mailing Add:* Dept of Physics Northeastern Univ Boston MA 02115

FRIEDMAN, MATTHEW JOEL, b Newark, NJ, Mar 10, 40; c 3. PSYCHIATRY, PHARMACOLOGY. *Educ:* Dartmouth Col, AB, 61; Albert Einstein Col Med, PhD(pharmacol), 67; Univ Ky, MD, 69. *Prof Exp:* Intern, Univ Ky Hosp, 69-70; resident psychiat, Mass Gen Hosp, Boston, 70-72; resident, Dartmouth-Hitchcock Ment Health Ctr, 72-73; ASSOC PROF PSYCHIAT & PHARMACOL, DARTMOUTH MED SCH, 73- *Concurrent Pos:* Chief psychiat, Vet Admin Hosp, White River Junction, Vt, 73- *Mem:* Am Psychiat Asn; Soc Biol Psychiat; Physicians Soc Responsibility. *Res:* Biological basis of affective disorders; hypertension and depression; physical dependence and tolerance; clinical psychopharmacology; blood levels of psychotropic drugs and clinical response; tryptophan metabolism during alcoholism and the abstinent state. *Mailing Add:* Dept of Psychiat Dartmouth Med Sch Hanover NH 03755

FRIEDMAN, MELVIN, b West Orange, NJ, Nov 14, 30; m 54; c 2. ROCK MECHANICS, STRUCTURAL GEOLOGY. *Educ:* Rutgers Univ, BS, 52, MS, 54; Rice Univ, PhD, 61. *Prof Exp:* Res geologist & sect leader, Shell Develop Co, 54-67; assoc prof, 67-69, PROF GEOL, CTR TECTONOPHYS, TEX A&M UNIV, 69-, DIR, CTR TECTONOPHYS, 74- *Concurrent Pos:* Geologist, Bear Creek Mining Co, 53; Consult, numerous companies. *Honors & Awards:* Res Award, Intersoc Comt Rock Mech, 69. *Mem:* Fel AAAS; fel Geol Soc Am; Am Geophys Union. *Res:* Dynamic analysis of tectonic structures through a knowledge of the physical and mechanical properties of minerals and rocks. *Mailing Add:* Ctr Tectonophysics Tex A&M Univ College Station TX 77843

FRIEDMAN, MENDEL, b Pultusk, Poland, Feb 13, 33; US citizen; m 57; c 3. ORGANIC CHEMISTRY, FOOD SCIENCE. *Educ:* Univ Ill, BS, 54; Univ Chicago, MS, 58, PhD(chem), 62. *Prof Exp:* Res assoc, Univ Wis, 61-62; prin chemist, Northern Regional Res Lab, 62-69, res chemist, Western Regional Res Ctr, 69-70, PROF LEADER, US DRUG ADMIN, 70- *Concurrent Pos:* Instr, Bradley Univ, 66-67 & Eureka Col, 67-69; fel, Intra-Sci Found Protein Chem, 71-75. *Mem:* Am Chem Soc; fel AAAS; Am Soc Biol Chemists; Am Inst Nutrit. *Res:* Protein chemistry and biochemistry; bio-organic chemistry; food toxicology and nutrition. *Mailing Add:* 6896 Paseo Grande Moraga CA 94556

FRIEDMAN, MICHAEL E, b Bronx, NY, Aug 17, 37; m 64; c 1. BIOPHYSICAL CHEMISTRY, ANALYTICAL CHEMISTRY. *Prof Exp:* Univ Pa, AB, 59; Polytech Inst Brooklyn, MS, 63; Cornell Univ, PhD(biophys chem), 66. Prof Exp: Technician chem, Pack Med Group, 58-60; staff fel, NIH, 66-68; asst prof chem, 68-78, ASSOC PROF CHEM, AUBURN UNIV, 78- *Mem:* Am Chem Soc. *Res:* Structural studies of biological polymers and their relationship to the body. *Mailing Add:* Dept of Chem Auburn Univ Auburn AL 36830

FRIEDMAN, MISCHA ELLIOT, b Worcester, Mass, Nov 7, 22; m 56; c 2. BACTERIOLOGY. *Educ:* Univ Mass, BS, 48; Univ Ill, MS, 49, PhD(dairy sci), 53. *Prof Exp:* Res assoc dairy sci, Univ Ill, 53; microbiologist, Med Bact Div, US Army Chem Corps, Biol Labs, Ft Detrick, 53-70; exec secy, Allergy & Immunol Study Sect, 70-76, CHIEF, CLIN SCI REV SECT, SCI REV BR, DIV RES GRANTS, NIH, 76- *Concurrent Pos:* Secy Army res & study fel, Hadassah Med Sch, Hebrew Univ, Israel, 64-65; vis lectr, Hadassah Med Sch, Hebrew Univ, Israel, 64-65. *Mem:* AAAS. *Res:* Bacterial nutrition and metabolism; nitrogen metabolism; nutritional inhibitors; bacteriophage; protein synthesis; immunology; science administration. *Mailing Add:* Div of Res Grants Nat Insts of Health Bethesda MD 20205

FRIEDMAN, MORTON (BENJAMIN), b Bayonne, NJ, Mar 14, 28; m 56; c 2. ENGINEERING. *Educ:* NY Univ, BAero Eng, 48, MAero Eng, 50, DEng Sc, 53. *Prof Exp:* Engr aerodyn, Cornell Aeronaut Lab, Inc, 48; res assoc, NY Univ, 53-55; appl mech, Inst Flight Structures, 55-56, asst prof, 56-61, assoc prof, 61-76, PROF AERODYN & APPL MATH, COLUMBIA UNIV, 76- *Concurrent Pos:* Field scholar, Found Instrumentation Educ & Res, 60; Fulbright lectr, Netherlands, 62-63. *Mem:* AAAS. *Res:* Gas dynamics; shock diffraction; acoustics; viscous fluids; applied mathematics and mechanics. *Mailing Add:* Dept of Civil Eng & Eng Mech Columbia Univ New York NY 10027

FRIEDMAN, MORTON HAROLD, b New York, NY, June 18, 35; m 61; c 3. HEMODYNAMICS, BIOLOGICAL TRANSPORT. *Educ:* Cornell Univ, BChE, 57; Univ Mich, MS, 58, PhD(chem eng), 61. *Prof Exp:* Sr chem engr, Cent Res Labs, Minn Mining & Mfg Co, 60-65; sr staff engr, 65-68, prog coordr, Biomed Progs Off, 74-77, supvr theoret probs res, Appl Physics Lab, 75-77, MEM PRIN PROF STAFF, APPL PHYSICS LAB, JOHNS HOPKINS UNIV, 68-, ASSOC PROF OPHTHAL, SCH MED, 71-, ASSOC PROF BIOMED ENG, SCH MED & DEP DIR BIOMED PROGS, APPL PHYSICS LAB, 77- *Honors & Awards:* Nat Capital Award, DC Coun Eng & Archit Soc, 70. *Mem:* AAAS; Biomed Eng Soc; Biophys Soc. *Res:* Physiological transport; membrane biophysics; arterial fluid mechanics. *Mailing Add:* Appl Physics Lab Johns Hopkins Univ Johns Hopkins Rd Laurel MD 20707

FRIEDMAN, MORTON HENRY, b Uniontown, Pa, Apr 16, 38; c 2. HUMAN ANATOMY, MICROSCOPIC ANATOMY. *Educ:* Washington & Jefferson Col, AB, 60; Hofstra Univ, MA, 64; Univ Tenn, PhD(anat), 69. *Prof Exp:* From instr to asst prof, 69-73, ASSOC PROF ANAT, SCH MED, W VA UNIV, 73- *Mem:* NY Acad Sci; AAAS; Am Asn Anatomists; Electron Micros Soc Am; Am Soc Cell Biol. *Res:* Electron microscopy; microanatomy. *Mailing Add:* Dept Anat WVa Univ Sch Med Morgantown WV 26506

FRIEDMAN, NATHAN, b Newark, NJ, May 18, 12; m 39. PERIODONTOLOGY, ORAL PATHOLOGY. *Educ:* Northwestern Univ, BSD & DDS, 36; Am Bd Periodont, dipl. *Prof Exp:* From asst prof to assoc prof periodont & oral path, 51-66, clin prof human behav, Sch Dent, 66, prof human behav & chmn dept, 66-78, CLIN PROF PATH, UNIV SOUTHERN CALIF, 78- *Concurrent Pos:* Consult, Vet Admin, Calif. *Mem:* Am Dent Asn; Am Acad Periodont; Am Acad Oral Path. *Res:* Clinical research and animal experimentation in the field of periodontal surgery and wound healing. *Mailing Add:* 436 N Roxbury Dr Beverly Hills CA 90210

FRIEDMAN, NATHAN BARUCH, b New York, NY, Jan 30, 11; m 42, 60; c 6. PATHOLOGY. *Educ:* Harvard Univ, BS, 30; Cornell Univ, MD, 34. *Prof Exp:* Resident pneumonia serv, Harlem Hosp, NY, 34-35; intern, Montefiore Hosp, New York, 35-37; resident path, Univ Chicago Clins, 38-39; instr, Sch Med, Stanford Univ, 41-42; sr pathologist, Army Inst Path, 46-47; dir labs, Cedars of Lebanon Hosp, 48-71; SR CONSULT, DIV LABS, CEDARS-SINAI MED CTR, 72- *Concurrent Pos:* Littauer fel, Harvard Med Sch, 39-40; prof lectr, George Washington Univ, 47; from assoc clin prof to clin prof, Sch Med, Univ Southern Calif, 52- *Mem:* Endocrine Soc; Am Soc Exp Path; Am Asn Pathologists; Am Asn Cancer Res. *Res:* Pathology of endocrine glands, genitourinary organs and tumors; radiation reactions. *Mailing Add:* Cedars-Sinai Med Ctr 8700 Beverly Blvd Los Angeles CA 90048

FRIEDMAN, ORRIE MAX, b Grenfell, Sask, June 6, 15; nat US; m 59; c 3. RESEARCH ADMINISTRATION, BIO-ORGANIC CHEMISTRY. *Educ:* Univ Man, BSc, 35; McGill Univ, PhD(chem), 44. *Prof Exp:* Asst chem, Nat Res Coun Can, 44-46; res fel chem, Harvard Univ, 46-49; res assoc, Harvard Med Sch, 49-52, asst prof chem, 52-53; from asst prof to prof, Brandeis Univ, 53-56, adj res prof, 56-62, adj res prof, 62-66; dir, Technol Int Ltd, 75-78; PRES & SCI DIR, COLLAB RES, INC, 62- *Concurrent Pos:* Assoc, Beth Israel Hosp, 49-54; consult, Harvard Med Sch, 53-54 & 56-57; spec consult, Nat Cancer Inst, NIH, 65-70; dir, United Chem Co, Ltd, 60- *Mem:* Fel AAAS; Am Chem Soc; Am Asn Cancer Res; fel Chem Soc London; NY Acad Sci. *Res:* Chemistry of high explosives; cancer chemotherapy, psychopharmacology and the chemistry of nucelic acids. *Mailing Add:* 49 Warren St Brookline MA 02146

FRIEDMAN, PAUL, b Brooklyn, NY, Oct 12, 31; m 54; c 2. ORGANIC CHEMISTRY. *Educ:* City Col NY, BS, 53; Brooklyn Col, MA, 57; Stevens Inst Technol, PhD(chem), 63. *Prof Exp:* Sr res chemist, Evans Res & Develop Corp, 55-60; instr chem, Newark Col Eng, 60-61; res assoc, Stevens Inst Technol, 61-63; NSF res assoc, Univ Southern Calif, 63-64; from asst prof to assoc prof, 64-70, PROF CHEM, PRATT INST, 70-, CHMN DEPT MATH & SCI, 75- *Mem:* Fel Royal Soc Chem; Am Chem Soc; Sigma Xi; NY Acad Sci; AAAS. *Res:* Heterocyclic chemistry; non benzenoid aromatics; photochemistry; quantum organic and physical organic chemistry; medicinal chemistry. *Mailing Add:* Dept of Chem Pratt Inst Brooklyn NY 11205

FRIEDMAN, PAUL J, b New York, NY, Jan 20, 37; m 60; c 4. RADIOLOGY, EDUCATIONAL ADMINISTRATION. *Educ:* Univ Wis, BS, 55; Yale Univ, MD, 60. *Prof Exp:* Chief radiol, US Naval Submarine Med Ctr, Conn, 64-66; from asst prof to assoc prof, 68-75, chmn fac, Sch Med, 79-80, PROF RADIOL, UNIV CALIF, SAN DIEGO, 75-, ASSOC DEAN ACAD AFFAIRS, SCH MED, 82- *Concurrent Pos:* James Picker Found advan fel acad radiol, 66-68 & scholar radiol res, 68-69; Markle scholar acad med, 69-74; vchmn, Dept Radiol, Univ Calif, San Diego, 78-82. *Mem:* Am Asn Univ Profs; Fleischner Soc; Asn Univ Radiologists; fel Am Col Radiol; Am Thoracic Soc. *Res:* Pulmonary diseases; pulmonary videodensitometry; radiologic-pathologic correlation; pulmonary radiology; chest computed tomography. *Mailing Add:* Dept of Radiol Univ Calif San Diego La Jolla CA 92093

FRIEDMAN, RICHARD M, b Cleveland, Ohio, Aug 25, 30; m 52; c 4. SPACE PHYSICS. *Educ:* Case Inst Technol, BS, 52; Stanford Univ, MS, 54, PhD(physics), 56. *Prof Exp:* Res scientist, Res Lab, Lockheed Missiles & Space Co, 56-61; mgr nuclear instrumentation, Vela Prog, Aerospace Corp, 61-62, proj leader, infrared measurements, Space Physics Lab, 62-63, staff scientist, 63-66, head space tech support dept, 66-67; proj mgr, TRW Defense & Space Systs Group, 67-69, proj mgr, Viking Lander Biol Instrument, 69-73, advan studies mgr, 73-77, dir, Systs Eng Defense Systs, 77-79, ASST PROJ MGR, DEFENSE SUPPORT PROG, TRW SPACE & TECHNOL GROUP, 79- *Mem:* Am Phys Soc; Am Geophys Union; Am Inst Aeronaut & Astronaut. *Res:* Development of sensor systems for space applications; measurement of solar x-rays; earth's background radiance and nuclear phenomena. *Mailing Add:* Space Systs Div One Space Park Redondo Beach CA 90278

FRIEDMAN, ROBERT BERNARD, b Chicago, Ill, June 9, 38; m 69; c 1. BIOCHEMISTRY, CARBOHYDRATE CHEMISTRY. *Educ:* Northwestern Univ, PhB, 62; Univ Ill, PhD(biochem), 69. *Prof Exp:* Res assoc, Sch Med, Tufts Univ, 68-70; asst prof chem, Boston Univ, 70-71; res fel biochem, Eunice Kennedy Shriver Ctr Ment Retardation, Mass, 71-76; asst prof biochem, Med Sch, Northwestern Univ, 76-79; res biochemist, Vet Admin Lakeside Hosp, 76-79; SECT LEADER, RES AM MAIZE PROD, 79- *Concurrent Pos:* Asst prof chem, Salem State Col, 73-74. *Mem:* AAAS; Sigma Xi; Am Chem Soc; Soc Complex Carbohydrates. *Res:* Study of the structure of glycoproteins and polysaccharides; enzymology; hematology; synthetic and analytic carbohydrate chemistry. *Mailing Add:* 6654 N Mozart Chicago IL 60645

FRIEDMAN, ROBERT DAVID, b New York, NY, Mar 24, 35; c 2. MEDICAL GENETICS, DENTISTRY. *Educ:* Brooklyn Col, BA, 56; NY Univ, DDS, 60; Brandeis Univ, MA, 68; Ind Univ, PhD(med genetics), 72. *Prof Exp:* Asst prof biochem, Sch Dent, Temple Univ, 72-77; ASST PROF ORAL MED, SCH DENT, UNIV PA, 78- *Concurrent Pos:* NIH spec fel med genetics, Ind Univ, 71-72. *Mem:* AAAS; Am Soc Human Genetics; Am Genetics Soc. *Res:* Genetic and biochemical study of the polymorphic proteins in human saliva. *Mailing Add:* 7043 McCallum Philadelphia PA 19119

FRIEDMAN, ROBERT HAROLD, b Sioux City, Iowa, Jan 11, 24; m 45, 66; c 4. PHYSICAL CHEMISTRY. *Educ:* Univ Chicago, PhB, 47, BS, 49; Univ Tex, PhD, 57. *Prof Exp:* Sr res engr, Humble Oil & Ref Co, 56-64; res scientist, Tidewater Oil Co, 64-69; res scientist, 69-76, SR RES SCIENTIST, GETTY OIL CO, 72- *Mem:* Am Phys Soc; Am Chem Soc; Am Inst Mining, Metall & Petrol Eng. *Res:* Theoretical chemistry; operations research; oil recovery from subsurface formations. *Mailing Add:* Getty Oil Co PO Box 42214 Houston TX 77042

FRIEDMAN, ROBERT MORRIS, b New York, NY, Nov 21, 32; m 57; c 2. PATHOLOGY, VIROLOGY. *Educ:* Cornell Univ, BA, 54; NY Univ, MD, 58. *Prof Exp:* Intern Med, Mt Sinai Hosp, New York, 58-59; investr virol, Div Biol Stand, NIH, 59-61, pathologist, Clin Ctr, 61-63; vis scientist virol, Nat Inst Med Res, London, Eng, 63-64; investr, Nat Cancer Inst, 64-70, pathologist, 65-70, chief molecular path sect, Lab Molecular Biol, 70-74; chief, Lab Exp Path, Nat Inst Arthritis, Metab & Digestive Dis, 74-81; PROF & CHMN, DEPT PATH, UNIFORMED SERV UNIV HEALTH SCI, 81- *Concurrent Pos:* Consult, Antiviral Chemother Prog, Nat Inst Allergy & Infectious Dis; McLaughlin lectr, Univ Tex Med Br, Galveston, 71; vis scientist, Biochem Dept, Nat Inst Med Res, London, Eng, 71-73; med dir, USPHS. *Mem:* Am Soc Microbiol; Am Soc Immunologists; Am Soc Exp Path. *Res:* Experimental pathology; virology; interferon studies; immunology. *Mailing Add:* Uniformed Serv Univ Health Sci 4301 Jones Bridge Rd Besthesda MD 20014

FRIEDMAN, RONALD MARVIN, b Brooklyn, NY, Apr 26, 30; c 2. CELL BIOLOGY. *Educ:* Columbia Univ, BS, 60; NY Univ, MS, 67, PhD(cell biol), 76. *Prof Exp:* Fel biochem, Columbia Univ, 75-76 & Yale Univ, 77-78; vis fel, Princeton Univ, 78-79; vis scientist enzym, NY State Inst Basic Res, 79-81; FEL GENETICS, ALBERT EINSTEIN COL MED, 81- *Mem:* Sigma Xi; Am Soc Cell Biol; Harvey Soc; NY Acad Sci. *Res:* Cell culture in serum free medium; transfer of genes from one cell type to another (transfection); cell transformation, its transition point and specific proteins involved in this transition. *Mailing Add:* 3210 Arlington Ave Riverdale NY 10463

FRIEDMAN, SAMUEL ARTHUR, b Brooklyn, NY, Jan 21, 27; div; c 2. GEOLOGY. *Educ:* Brooklyn Col, BS, 50; Ohio State Univ, MS, 52. *Prof Exp:* Geologist, Ind Geol Surv, 52-67; geologist, US Bur Mines, 67-71; GEOLOGIST, OKLA GEOL SURV, 71- *Concurrent Pos:* Adj prof geol, Grad Fac, Univ Okla, 74- *Mem:* Fel Geol Soc Am; Soc Econ Paleont & Mineral; Am Asn Petrol Geologists. *Res:* Coal geology, coal resources and net recoverable reserves; middle Pennsylvanian lithostratigraphy of Indiana and Oklahoma; exploration for low-sulfur coal; depositional environments of coal; fossil river systems. *Mailing Add:* Okla Geol Surv 830 Van Vleet Oval Rm 163 Norman OK 73019

FRIEDMAN, SAMUEL J(OHN), b Cleveland, Ohio, Jan 25, 18; m 51; c 2. CHEMICAL ENGINEERING. *Educ:* Case Inst Technol, BS, 39, MS, 41. *Prof Exp:* Chem engr, 41-47, indust engr, NJ, 47-48, chem engr, Del, 48-50, sr engr, SC, 51-52, group leader, 52-53, res supvr, Va, 53-57, sr tech supvr, 57-62, res mgr, Del, 62-63, tech supt, Old Hickory Res & Develop Lab, 63-69, lab dir, 69-78, RES MGR, TEXTILE RES LAB, E I DU PONT DE NEMOURS & CO, INC, 78- *Mem:* AAAS; Am Chem Soc; Am Soc Mech Engrs; Am Inst Chem Engrs. *Res:* Heat transfer and drying process equipment; synthetic textile fiber products and processes. *Mailing Add:* Textile Res Lab E I du Pont de Nemours & Co Inc Wilmington DE 19898

FRIEDMAN, SELWYN MARVIN, b New York, NY, May 17, 29. BIOCHEMICAL GENETICS, MICROBIOLOGY. *Educ:* Univ Mich, BS, 51; Purdue Univ, MS, 53, PhD(bact), 61. *Prof Exp:* Fel biochem, Western Reserve Univ, 60-61; fel cell biol, Albert Einstein Col Med, 62-63; res fel, Med Col Physicians & Surgeons, Columbia Univ, 63-66; asst prof, 66-69, ASSOC PROF BIOL, HUNTER COL, 69- *Mem:* AAAS; Am Soc Microbiol. *Res:* Protein synthesis and the genetic code; physiology of thermophilic bacteria. *Mailing Add:* Dept of Biol Sci Hunter Col 695 Park Ave New York NY 10021

FRIEDMAN, SEYMOUR K, b New York, NY, July 1, 28; m 56; c 4. ORGANIC CHEMISTRY, COLLOID CHEMISTRY. *Educ:* City Col New York, BS, 48. *Prof Exp:* Group leader chem, Cent Res, Stauffer Chem Co, 53-56; asst mgr develop, Emulsol Div, 57-60, mgr prod appln & planning, Detergent Div, 61-63, CORP DIR COM DEVELOP, 64-76, PROD MGR INDUST SURFACTANTS, WITCO CHEM CO, 76- *Mem:* Com Chem Develop Asn. *Res:* Information techniques; research planning. *Mailing Add:* Witco Chem Co Inc 1000 Convery Perth Amboy NJ 08861

FRIEDMAN, SIDNEY, b Union City, NJ, Jan 24, 26; m 57; c 3. ORGANIC CHEMISTRY. *Educ:* Purdue Univ, BS, 49; Harvard Univ, AM & PhD(org chem), 53. *Prof Exp:* Fel petrol, Mellon Inst, 53-54; res chemist, US Bur Mines, 55-75; res chemist, US Energy Res & Develop Admin, 75-77, BR CHIEF, US DEPT ENERGY, 77- *Concurrent Pos:* Lectr, Duquesne Univ, 56-57. *Honors & Awards:* Bituminous Coal Res Award, 69, 77. *Mem:* Am Chem Soc. *Res:* Organometallic chemistry; catalysis; reaction mechanisms; origin and structure of petroleum and coal; organic spectroscopy; gas chromatography. *Mailing Add:* Pittsburgh Energy Technol Ctr PO Box 10940 Pittsburgh PA 15236

FRIEDMAN, STANLEY, b New York, NY, Dec 11, 25; m; c 4. INSECT PHYSIOLOGY. *Educ:* Univ Ill, BA, 48; Johns Hopkins Univ, PhD(biol), 52. *Prof Exp:* Res assoc entom, Univ Ill, 52-56; biochemist, NIH, 56-58; from asst prof to assoc prof entom, Purdue Univ, 58-64; assoc prof, 64-67, PROF ENTOM, UNIV ILL, URBANA, 67-, HEAD DEPT, 75- *Mem:* Am Soc Zool; Am Soc Biol Chem; Entom Soc Am. *Res:* Biochemistry and physiology of insects. *Mailing Add:* Dept Entom Univ Ill 505 S Goodwin Ave Urbana IL 61801

FRIEDMAN, STEPHEN BURT, b Amsterdam, NY, Mar 23, 31; m 64; c 2. MICROBIOLOGY. *Educ:* Univ Rochester, BA, 53; Syracuse Univ, MS, 55; Univ Ill, PhD(microbiol), 62. *Prof Exp:* NIH fel microbiol, State Univ, Belgium, 62-64; res assoc molecular biol, Cold Spring Harbor Lab Quant Biol, 64-66; ASSOC PROF BIOL, WESTERN MICH UNIV, 66- *Concurrent Pos:* Europ Molecular Biol Orgn fel, Belgium, 72. *Mem:* AAAS; Am Soc Microbiol; Am Inst Biol Sci; NY Acad Sci. *Res:* Bacterial and phage regulation; active transport; membrane structure and function; bacterial isozyme variation and population genetics. *Mailing Add:* Dept of Biomed Sci Western Mich Univ Kalamazoo MI 49008

FRIEDMAN, SYDNEY MURRAY, b Montreal, Que, Feb 17, 16; m 40. MEDICINE. *Educ:* McGill Univ, BA, 38, MD & CM, 40, MSc, 41, PhD(renal physiol), 46. *Prof Exp:* Demonstr histol, McGill Univ, 40-41; from asst prof to assoc prof anat, 44-50; prof anat & head dept, 50-81, PROF ANAT, UNIV BC, 81- *Concurrent Pos:* Asst physician, Royal Victorian Hosp, 48-50; Pfizer traveling fel, Clin Res Inst, Montreal, 71; vis lectr, Can Cardiovasc Soc, 71. *Honors & Awards:* Premier Award Res in Ageing, Ciba Found, 55. *Mem:* Am Physiol Soc; fel Royal Soc Can; Can Asn Anatomists (vpres, 62-64; pres, 65-66); Am Asn Anatomists; Coun High Blood Pressure Res. *Res:* Cardiovascular-renal physiology; endocrinology; hormonal hypertension; aging. *Mailing Add:* Dept Anat Univ of BC Vancouver Can

FRIEDMAN, THOMAS BAER, b Detroit, Mich, Dec 9, 44; m 70; c 2. HUMAN GENETICS, DEVELOPMENTAL GENETICS. *Educ:* Univ Mich, BS, 66, PhD(biol), 71. *Prof Exp:* Staff fel biochem, NIH, 71-74; asst prof develop biol & genetics, Oakland Univ, 74-77; ASSOC PROF GENETICS, MICH STATE UNIV, 78- *Mem:* Genetics Soc Am; AAAS; Soc Develop Biol. *Res:* Galactose metabolism in cultured human cells; regulation of urate oxidase and adenide phosphoribosyl transferase during development of Drosophila Melanogaster. *Mailing Add:* Dept Genetics Mich State Univ East Lansing MI 48824

FRIEDMAN, WILLIAM ALBERT, b Chicago, Ill, May 29, 38; m 61. PHYSICS. *Educ:* Cornell Univ, BEP, 61; Mass Inst Technol, PhD(physics), 66. *Prof Exp:* NSF fel, Niels Boyr Inst, Copenhagen Univ, Denmark, 66-67; instr, Princeton Univ, 67-70; asst prof, 70-73, ASSOC PROF PHYSICS, UNIV WIS-MADISON, 73- *Mem:* Am Phys Soc. *Res:* Theoretical nuclear physics, including nuclear reactions and nuclear structure. *Mailing Add:* Dept of Physics Univ of Wis Madison WI 53706

FRIEDMAN, WILLIAM FOSTER, b New York, NY, July 24, 36; c 2. PEDIATRIC CARDIOLOGY. *Educ:* Columbia Univ, AB, 57; State Univ NY, MD, 61. *Prof Exp:* Intern pediat, Harriet Lane Home, Johns Hopkins Hosp, 61-62, asst & sr resident, 62-64; clin assoc, Cardiol Br & pediat consult, Clin Surg, Nat Heart Inst, 64-66, sr investr & pediat cardiologist, Cardiol Br, 66-68; from asst prof to assoc prof pediat, Sch Med, Univ Calif, San Diego, 68-73, prof, 73-80, chief pediat cardiol, 68-80; PROF PEDIAT CARDIOL & CHMN DEPT PEDIAT, CTR HEALTH SCI, UNIV CALIF, LOS ANGELES, 80- *Concurrent Pos:* Nat Heart Inst res career develop award; consult pediat cardiol, US Naval Hosp, San Diego & Camp Pendleton, 68-; consult pediat cardiologist, Grossmont Hosp, Kaiser Found Hosp, Mercy Hosp, Children's Health Ctr, San Diego, 69-; mem, Cardiovasc Training Comt, Nat Heart & Lung Inst, 71-75; Benjamin Gasul Mem lectr, Hektoen Inst Med Res. *Mem:* Am Soc Clin Invest; Am Fedn Clin Res; Am Heart Asn; Soc Nuclear Med; Soc Pediat Res. *Res:* Physiology, pharmacology and biochemistry of the developing heart. *Mailing Add:* Dept Pediat Univ Calif Ctr Health Sci Los Angeles CA 90024

FRIEDMAN, YOCHANAN, b Chicago, Ill, Feb 25, 45; m 76; c 2. ENDOCRINOLOGY, THYROIDOLOGY. *Educ:* Roosevelt Univ, BS, 67; Univ Ill Med Ctr, PhD(biochem), 73. *Prof Exp:* Instr biochem & immunol, Univ Ill Med Ctr, 72-73; sci investr endocrinol, 73-80, DIR, RADIOIMMUNOASSAY LAB, COOK COUNTY HOSP, CHICAGO, 80- *Mem:* Endocrine Soc; Am Thyroid Asn; Am Fed Clin Res. *Res:* Regulation at the cellular level of thyroid physiology; cyclic adenosine monophosphate adenylate cyclase system. *Mailing Add:* Div Endocrinol 1825 W Harrison St Cook County Hosp Chicago IL 60612

FRIEDMANN, EMERICH IMRE, b Budapest, Hungary, Dec 20, 21. PHYCOLOGY. *Educ:* Sch Agr, Kolozsvar, Hungary, BSc, 43; Sch Agr, Magyarovar, MSc, 49; Univ Vienna, DrPhil(bot), 51. *Prof Exp:* Instr bot, Hebrew Univ, Israel, 52-56, lectr, 57-61, sr lectr, 61-66, assoc prof, 66-67; assoc prof biol, Queen's Univ, Ont, 67-68; assoc prof, 68-76, PROF BIOL SCI, FLA STATE UNIV, 76- *Concurrent Pos:* Res fel, Univ Manchester, 56-58; Dept Sci & Indust Res sr vis res fel, Univ Leeds, 59; res assoc, Queens Col, NY, 65-66; vis assoc prof, Fla State Univ, 66-67; vis prof, Univ Vienna, 75. *Mem:* Am Soc Microbiol; Linn Soc London; Phycol Soc Am; Soc Phycol France; Phycol Soc India. *Res:* Microorganisms of the Antarctic dry valleys; desert algae and cave algae; life history, sexuality, cytology and ecology of marine algae; fine structure of gamete fusion in algae; Phycomycetes parasitic on algae; taxonomy of blue-green algae. *Mailing Add:* Dept of Biol Sci Fla State Univ Tallahassee FL 32306

FRIEDMANN, GERHART B, b Mannheim, Ger, Jan 10, 29; m 59. MEDICAL PHYSICS, OPTICS. *Educ:* Univ Madras, BSc, 49, MA, 51; Univ BC, PhD(physics), 58. *Prof Exp:* Res asst cosmic ray physics, Tata Inst Fundamental Res, 51-54; spec lectr, 58-62, asst prof, 62-70, ASSOC PROF PHYSICS, UNIV VICTORIA, BC, 70- *Concurrent Pos:* Grant radiation physics, BC Cancer Clin, 58-59; physicist, Victoria Cancer Clin, 58-76; radiol health officer, Royal Jubilee Hosp, 63- *Mem:* Can Asn Physicists; Brit Inst Radiol. *Res:* Biological and medical physics. *Mailing Add:* Dept of Physics Univ of Victoria Victoria BC V8W 2Y2 Can

FRIEDMANN, HERBERT, b New York, NY, Apr 22, 00; m 37; c 1. VERTEBRATE ZOOLOGY, ORNITHOLOGY. *Educ:* City Col New York, BS, 20; Cornell Univ, PhD(ornith), 23. *Prof Exp:* Asst ornith, Am Mus Natural Hist, 20; instr zool, Cornell Univ, 22-23; Nat Res Coun fel, Bussey Inst, Harvard Univ, 23-26; instr, Brown Univ, 26-27; instr biol, Amherst Col, 27-29; cur div birds, US Nat Mus, 29-57, head cur zool, 57-61; dir, Los Angeles County Mus, 61-70; RETIRED. *Concurrent Pos:* Expeds, Mex Border, Arg, S, E & Cent Africa; deleg, Int Ornith Cong, Oxford, 34 & Upsala, 50. *Honors & Awards:* Elliot Medal, Nat Acad Sci, 59; Leidy Medal, Acad Nat Sci, Philadelphia, 55; Brewster Medal, Am Ornith Union, 64. *Mem:* Nat Acad Sci; AAAS (pres sect F, 59); Am Soc Naturalists; Am Soc Zool; fel Am Ornith Union (vpres, 32-38, pres, 38-39). *Res:* Systematic ornithology; brood parasitism; natural history symbolism in Medieval and Renaissance art; animal behavior; physiological cycles and cyclical instincts; theoretical biology. *Mailing Add:* 350 S Fuller Ave Apt 12H Los Angeles CA 90036

FRIEDMANN, HERBERT CLAUS, b Mannheim, WGer, June 19, 27; nat US; m 61; c 2. BIOCHEMISTRY. *Educ:* Univ Madras, India, BSc, 47, MSc, 51; Univ Chicago, PhD(biochem), 58. *Prof Exp:* Chemist, Allergic Asthma Enquiry, Govt of Madras, India, 51-54; asst, Univ Chicago, 55-58, res assoc, 58-59; fel, Damon Runyon, McCollum-Pratt Inst, Johns Hopkins Univ, 59-60; res assoc, Dept Physiol, 60-64, asst prof biochem, 64-69, ASSOC PROF BIOCHEM, UNIV CHICAGO, 69- *Mem:* Am Soc Biol Chem; Am Chem Soc; Am Soc Microbiol. *Res:* Enzymes of intermediary metabolism; flavoproteins; vitamin B12; amino acids; porphyrins. *Mailing Add:* Dept Biochem 920 E 58th St Chicago IL 60637

FRIEDMANN, HERMAN H, b New York, NY, Nov 30, 18; m 42; c 2. PHYSICAL CHEMISTRY, SPECTROSCOPY. *Educ:* City Col, BS, 41. *Prof Exp:* Anal chemist, Joseph E Seagram & Sons, 41-44; res biochemist, Schwarz Labs, 46-49; chief chemist, Physiol Chems Co, 49-55; proj leader, 55-63, res specialist, 63-75, sr res specialist, Tech Ctr, 75-80, RES SCIENTIST, GEN FOODS CORP, 80- *Mem:* Am Chem Soc; Soc Appl Spectros; AAAS. *Res:* X-ray diffraction; surface chemistry; infrared and nuclear magnetic resonance spectrometry; structure and function of water in natural products. *Mailing Add:* Tech Ctr Gen Foods Corp 555 S Broadway Tarrytown NY 10591

FRIEDMANN, NAOMI, b Budapest, Hungary, July 4, 33; Israeli citizen; div; c 1. PHYSIOLOGY. *Educ:* Hebrew Univ, Jerusalem, MSc, 60, Hadassah Med Sch, PhD(biochem), 65. *Prof Exp:* Teaching asst biochem, Hadassah Med Sch, Hebrew Univ, 60-65; res assoc med, Columbia Univ, 65-66; res assoc physiol, Vanderbilt Univ, 66-68; instr biochem, Univ Pa, 68-74; asst prof, 74-76, ASSOC PROF PHYSIOL, UNIV TEX MED SCH, HOUSTON, 76- *Res:* Metabolic regulation and the mode of hormone action, especially the role of ions and membrane potential changes in regulatory processes. *Mailing Add:* Dept of Physiol Univ of Tex Med Sch Houston TX 77025

FRIEDMANN, PAUL, b Vienna, Austria, Dec 2, 33; US citizen; m 62; c 2. SURGERY. *Educ:* Univ Pa, AB, 55; Harvard Univ, MD, 59. *Prof Exp:* Asst chief surg, 68-71, CHMN DIV SURG, BAY STATE MED CTR, SPRINGFIELD, 71- *Concurrent Pos:* Asst clin prof, Sch Med, Tufts Univ, 72-75, assoc clin prof, 75-78, clin prof, 78- *Mem:* Am Col Surgeons. *Res:* Clinical research in vascular surgery, alternative techniques in bypass grafting; surgical oncology. *Mailing Add:* Bay State Med Ctr 759 Chestnut St Springfield MA 01107

FRIEDMANN, PERETZ PETER, b Timisoara, Rumania, Nov 18, 38; US citizen; m 64. AEROELASTICITY. *Educ:* Israel Inst Technol, BS, 61, MS, 68; Mass Inst Technol, DSc, 72. *Prof Exp:* Eng off, Air Force, Israel Defence Forces, 61-65; sr engr structures, Israel Aircraft Indust, 65-69; res asst aeroelasticity, Mass Inst Technol, 69-72; asst prof, 72-77, assoc prof, 77-80, PROF MECH STRUCTURES, UNIV CALIF, LOS ANGELES, 80- *Mem:* Am Inst Aeronaut & Astronaut; Am Soc Mech Engrs; Am Helicopter Soc; Am Acad Mech; Soc Eng Sci. *Res:* Rotary-wing aeroelasticity; jet engine blade aeroelastic problems; wind turbine aeroelasticity; fluid-structure interaction problems; structural dynamics; unsteady aerodynamics; numerical methods. *Mailing Add:* 6731G Boelter Hall Univ Calif Los Angeles CA 90024

FRIEDRICH, BENJAMIN C, b Fond du Lac, Wis, Feb 2, 29; m 64. SCIENCE EDUCATION. *Educ:* St Cloud State Col, BS, 54; Univ Ind, MS, 57; Pa State Univ, DEd, 61. *Prof Exp:* Instr chem, Luther Jr Col, 54-56; instr sci educ, Ind Univ, 57-59; asst prof, Northeastern Univ, 61-66; assoc prof, 66-69, prof, Dept Geosci, 69-81, PROF ASTRON, JERSEY STATE COL, 81- *Concurrent Pos:* Chmn dept geosci, Jersey City State Col, 69-73. *Mem:* AAAS. *Mailing Add:* Dept Geosci Jersey City State Col Jersey City NJ 07305

FRIEDRICH, BRUCE H, b Clinton, Okla, Oct 20, 36; m 63; c 1. PHYSICAL CHEMISTRY. *Educ:* Univ Iowa, MS, 61, PhD(chem), 63. *Prof Exp:* Fel phys chem, Univ Calif, Berkeley, 62-63; asst prof chem, Gustavus Adolphus Col, 63-66; from asst prof to assoc prof, 66-76, PROF CHEM, UNIV IOWA, 76- *Mem:* AAAS; Am Chem Soc; Am Phys Soc. *Res:* Infrared spectra of molecular crystals; spectra of donor-acceptor complexes. *Mailing Add:* Dept of Chem Univ of Iowa Iowa City IA 52240

FRIEDRICH, EDWIN CARL, b Woodbury, NJ, Jan 15, 36; m 67. ORGANIC CHEMISTRY. *Educ:* Univ Ill, Urbana, BS, 57; Univ Calif, Los Angeles, PhD(chem), 61. *Prof Exp:* Res assoc chem, Univ Calif, Los Angeles, 61-62; res chemist, Calif Res Corp, 62-64; fel chem, Mass Inst Technol, 64-65; from asst prof to assoc prof, 65-76, PROF CHEM, UNIV CALIF, DAVIS, 76- *Mem:* Am Chem Soc. *Res:* Kinetics, product studies, salt and solvent effects in carbonium ion reactions of cyclopropylcarbinyl and bridged bicyclic systems; free-radical brominations; cyclopropylcarbinyl-allycarbinyl radical rearrangements; organotin and organozinc reaction mechanisms. *Mailing Add:* Dept Chem Univ Calif Davis CA 95616

FRIEDRICH, JAMES WAYNE, b Boonville, Mo, Dec 16, 52. PLANT PHYSIOLOGY, AGRONOMY. *Educ:* Univ Mo, BS, 74; Univ Wis, MS, 75, PhD(agron), 78. *Prof Exp:* Plant physiologist, Univ Calif, Davis, 78-80; TECH SUPVR AGR RES, ALLIED CHEM CORP, 80- *Mem:* Am Soc Plant Physiologists; Am Soc Agron; Crop Sci Soc Am. *Res:* Nitrogen and sulfur metabolism in plants; mineral nutrition. *Mailing Add:* Allied Chem Corp PO Box 6 Solvay NY 13209

FRIEDRICH, JOHN PHILIP, synthetic organic chemistry, see previous edition

FRIEDRICH, LOUIS ELBERT, b Wilmington, Del, Sept 7, 41; m 65. ORGANIC CHEMISTRY. *Educ:* Mass Inst Technol, BS, 63; Univ Calif, Berkeley, PhD(chem), 66. *Prof Exp:* NSF fel chem, Yale Univ, 66-67; from asst prof to assoc prof chem, Univ Rochester, 67-80; SR RES SCIENTIST, EASTMAN KODAK, 80- *Mem:* Am Chem Soc. *Res:* Mechanisms of organic reactions. *Mailing Add:* 36 Corwin Rd Rochester NY 14610

FRIEDRICH, OTTO MARTIN, JR, b Austin, Tex, Jan 29, 39. ELECTRICAL ENGINEERING, ELECTROOPTICS. *Educ:* Univ Tex, Austin, BS, 61, MS, 62, PhD(elec eng), 65. *Prof Exp:* Asst dir electronics res, 71-75, RES ENGR, UNIV TEX, AUSTIN, 65- *Concurrent Pos:* Consult eng, Indust & Govt, 65- *Honors & Awards:* Dr D S Draiper Award, Instrument Soc Am, 72. *Mem:* AAAS; Inst Elec & Electronics Engrs; Instrument Soc Am; Am Phys Soc; Optical Soc Am. *Res:* Electronics; lasers; holography; signal and data processing. *Mailing Add:* 1125 Shady Lane Austin TX 78721

FRIEDRICHS, KURT OTTO, b Kiel, Ger, Sept 28, 01; nat US; m 37; c 5. MATHEMATICS. *Educ:* Univ Gottingen, PhD(math), 25. *Hon Degrees:* PhD, Aachen Tech Univ, 70, Uppsala Univ, 74 & Nat Med Sci, Washington, 76. *Prof Exp:* Asst, Univ Gottingen, 25-27; asst & privat-dozent, Aachen Tech Univ, 27-29; privat-dozent, Univ Gottingen, 29-30; prof math, Brunswick Tech Univ, 30-37; vis prof appl math, 37-39, from assoc prof to prof, 39-74, from assoc dir to dir, 53-67, DISTINGUISHED PROF MATH, COURANT INST MATH SCI, NY UNIV, 74- *Concurrent Pos:* Mem staff, Off Sci Res & Develop, US Navy. *Honors & Awards:* Appl Math & Numerical Anal Award, Nat Acad Sci, 72. *Mem:* Nat Acad Sci; Am Math Soc; fel Am Acad Arts & Sci. *Res:* Partial differential equations, elasticity; fluid dynamics, quantum theory. *Mailing Add:* Courant Inst of Math Sci NY Univ New York NY 10012

FRIEL, DANIEL DENWOOD, b Queenstown, Md, Aug 11, 20; m 43; c 4. CHEMICAL ENGINEERING, PHYSICS. *Educ:* Johns Hopkins Univ, BsChE, 42. *Prof Exp:* Chemist, E I du Pont de Nemours & Co, Inc, 42-43; optics supvr, Manhattan Proj, E I du Pont de Nemours & Co, Inc, Univ Chicago, 43-44 & Manhattan Proj-Hanford Ord Works, 44-45; supvr, Appl Physics Lab, E I du Pont de Nemours & Co, Inc, 45-54, res mgr lab, 54-57, asst lab dir, 57-59, mgr eng prod, 59-60, mgr invest develop dept, 60-69; pres, Holotron Corp, 69-71; mgr, Riston Div, 71-73, dir electronic prods, 73-75, DIR INSTRUMENT PRODS, E I DU PONT DE NEMOURS & CO, INC, 75- *Mem:* Optical Soc Am; Am Phys Soc; Instrument Soc Am. *Res:* Instrumentation. *Mailing Add:* PO Box 3795 Greenville DE 19807

FRIEMAN, EDWARD ALLAN, b New York, NY, Jan 19, 26; m 49, 67; c 5. * PLASMA PHYSICS. *Educ:* Columbia Univ, BS, 45; Polytech Inst Brooklyn, MS, 48, PhD(physics), 51. *Prof Exp:* Instr physics, Polytech Inst Brooklyn, 45-52, res assoc, 47-49; res assoc, Proj Matterhorn, 52-53, head theoret div, 53-64, ASSOC DIR, PLASMA PHYSICS LAB, PRINCETON UNIV, 64-, PROF ASTRON SCI, 61- *Concurrent Pos:* Consult, Lawrence Radiation Lab, Univ Calif, 53-57 & Los Alamos Sci Lab, 53-64; mem res adv comt nuclear energy processes, NASA, 59-; John Simon Guggenheim Mem Found fel, 70. *Mem:* AAAS; Sigma Xi; Am Asn Univ Prof; fel Am Phys Soc; Am Astron Soc. *Res:* Theoretical plasma physics; hydromagnetics; hydrodynamics stability; astrophysics. *Mailing Add:* Sci Appln Inc 1200 Prospect St La Jolla CA 92037

FRIEND, CHARLOTTE, b New York, NY, Mar 11, 21. MEDICAL MICROBIOLOGY. *Educ:* Hunter Col, BA, 44; Yale Univ, PhD(bact), 50. *Prof Exp:* Assoc mem, Sloan-Kettering Inst, 49-66, assoc prof microbiol, Sloan-Kettering Div, Med Col, Cornell Univ, 52-66; PROF & DIR CTR EXP CELL BIOL, MT SINAI SCH MED, 66- *Honors & Awards:* Alfred P Sloan Award, 54, 57 & 62; Am Cancer Soc Award, 62; Presdential Medal Centennial Award, Hunter Col, 70; Virus-Cancer Prog Award, NIH, 74; Prix Griffuel, 79. *Mem:* Nat Acad Sci; Am Asn Cancer Res; Am Asn Immunol; Am Soc Hemat; Tissue Cult Asn. *Res:* Immunology; virology; viruses in relation to cancer. *Mailing Add:* Ctr Exp Cell Biol 100th St & Fifth Ave New York NY 10029

FRIEND, DANIEL S, b Passaic, NJ, Nov 20, 33; c 2. EXPERIMENTAL PATHOLOGY, CELL BIOLOGY. *Educ:* NY Univ, BA, 57; State Univ NY Downstate Med Ctr, MD, 61. *Prof Exp:* Intern, Boston City Hosp, 61-62, resident path, 62-63; res fel anat, Harvard Med Sch, 63-65; res fel, 65-66, lectr, 66-67, from asst prof to assoc prof, 67-78, PROF PATH & VCHMN DEPT, UNIV CALIF, SAN FRANCISCO, 78- *Concurrent Pos:* USPHS career develop award, 67-72 & res grant, 68- *Mem:* AAAS; Am Soc Cell Biol; Soc Study Reproduction; Am Asn Pathologists; Am Asn Anatomists. *Res:* Electron microscopy; structure and function of cell organelles; sperm and male reproductive tract; cell junctions; cytochemistry. *Mailing Add:* Dept Path Univ Calif Sch Med San Francisco CA 94143

FRIEND, JAMES PHILIP, b Hartford, Conn, Nov 30, 29; m 55; c 2. ATMOSPHERIC CHEMISTRY. *Educ:* Mass Inst Technol, SB, 51; Columbia Univ, MA, 53, PhD(chem), 56. *Prof Exp:* Asst chem, Columbia Univ, 53, 55-56; proj engr, Perkin-Elmer Corp, 56-57; sr res scientist, Isotopes, Inc, 57-64, sr scientific adv, 64-67; assoc prof atmospheric chem, NY Univ, 67-72, prof, 72-73; R S HANSON PROF ATMOSPHERIC CHEM, DREXEL UNIV, 73- *Concurrent Pos:* Independent consult; mem, Climatic Impact Comt, Nat Acad Sci, 72-75 & Panel Atmospheric Chem Climatic Impact Comt, 75-; mem biol effects of increased solar ultraviolet radiation comt, Nat Acad Sci, 81-, chem & physics of ozone depletion comt, 81- *Mem:* AAAS; Am Geophys Union; Am Meteorol Soc; Am Chem Soc; Air Pollution Control Asn. *Res:* Atmospheric chemistry and radioactivity; atmospheric diffusion; air pollution chemistry; global cycles and geochemistry of trace materials in the atmosphere; aerosol formation from gas phase reactions; atmospheric chemistry of volcanic plumes. *Mailing Add:* Dept of chem Drexel Univ Philadelphia PA 19104

FRIEND, JONATHON D, US citizen. VETERINARY MEDICINE. *Educ:* Kans State Univ, DVM, 45, MS, 59; Okla State Univ, BS, 49. *Prof Exp:* From asst prof to assoc prof vet anat, 48-58, PROF PHYSIOL SCI, OKLA STATE UNIV, 58- *Mem:* Am Asn Vet Anat; Am Vet Med Asn. *Res:* Regional innervation in the bovine. *Mailing Add:* Dept of Physiol Sci Okla State Univ Stillwater OK 74074

FRIEND, PATRIC LEE, b Iron River, Mich, Sept 4, 38; m 62; c 5. MICROBIOLOGY. *Educ:* Northern Mich Col, BS, 61; Northwestern Univ, PhD(microbiol), 65. *Prof Exp:* Res asst microbiol, Med Sch, Northwestern Univ, 65-66; asst prof, Col Med, Univ Cincinnati, 66-73; MEM STAFF, BETZ LABS INC, TREVOSE, PA, 73- *Mem:* NY Acad Sci; Am Soc Microbiol. *Res:* Aquatic and environmental microbiology, biodegradation and ecological relationships. *Mailing Add:* Betz Labs Inc Somerton Rd Trevose PA 19047

FRIEND, WILLIAM GEORGE, b Toronto, Ont, July 25, 28; m 53. INSECT PHYSIOLOGY. *Educ:* McGill Univ, BSc, 50; Cornell Univ, PhD(insect physiol), 54. *Prof Exp:* Entomologist, Can Dept Agr, 50-59; from asst prof to assoc prof, 59-66, PROF ZOOL, UNIV TORONTO, 66- *Mem:* Entom Soc Am; Entom Soc Can; Can Biochem Soc; Nutrit Soc Can. *Res:* Insect nutrition and biochemistry. *Mailing Add:* Dept of Zool Univ of Toronto Toronto ON M5S 1A1 Can

FRIER, HENRY IRA, nutritional biochemistry, see previous edition

FRIERSON, WILLIAM JOE, b Batesville, Ark, July 8, 07; m 30; c 2. ANALYTICAL CHEMISTRY. *Educ:* Ark Col, AB, 27; Emory Univ, MS, 28; Cornell Univ, PhD(inorg chem), 36. *Prof Exp:* Asst chem, Ark Col, 26-27; from asst prof to assoc prof, Hampden-Sydney Col, 28-44; prof, Birmingham-Southern Col, 44-46; prof, 46-69, William Rand Kenan, Jr prof, 69-75, EMER PROF CHEM, AGNES SCOTT COL, 75- *Concurrent Pos:* Fel, Cornell Univ, 35-36. *Mem:* Am Chem Soc. *Res:* Chemistry of inorganic nitrogen compounds; organic reagents in analytical chemistry; boiling points of pure compounds under varying pressures; paper chromatography of inorganic ions. *Mailing Add:* Dept Chem Agnes Scott Col Decatur GA 30030

FRIES, CARA ROSENDALE, b Toledo, Ohio, Feb 11, 42. COMPARATIVE PATHOBIOLOGY. *Educ:* Univ Del, BA, 66, MS, 69, PhD(comp immunobiol), 77. *Prof Exp:* Instr microbiol & physiol, 68-71, res assoc, 77-79, SCIENTIST, UNIV DEL, 79- *Mem:* AAAS; Am Soc Zoologists; Sigma Xi; Am Soc Microbiol. *Res:* Immunology; microbiology; ultrastructure of marine animals. *Mailing Add:* Sch of Life & Health Sci Univ of Del Newark DE 19711

FRIES, DAVID SAMUEL, b Manassas, Va, June 22, 45; m 65; c 3. MEDICINAL CHEMISTRY. *Educ:* Bridgewater Col, BA, 68; Va Commonwealth Univ, PhD(med chem), 71. *Prof Exp:* Fel med chem, Univ Minn, 71-72; asst prof chem, Winona State Col, 73; ASSOC PROF MED CHEM, UNIV OF THE PAC, 73- *Mem:* AAAS; Int Narcotic Res Club; Am Asn Col Pharm Am Chem Soc. *Res:* The design and synthesis of narcotic antagonist; elucidation of narcotic-receptor topography; design and synthesis of drugs for use in schizophrenia. *Mailing Add:* Sch of Pharm Univ of the Pac Stockton CA 95211

FRIES, JAMES ANDREW, b St Louis, Mo, June 25, 43; m 61; c 2. PHYSICAL CHEMISTRY, ENVIRONMENTAL CHEMISTRY. *Educ:* Univ SDak, BSEd, 65; Univ Iowa, MS, 68, PhD(phys chem), 69. *Prof Exp:* Asst phys chem, Univ Iowa, 65-69; from asst prof to assoc prof chem, 69-75, head dept, 69-78, prof chem, 75-78, ASST to PRES & DIR DEVELOP, NORTHERN STATE COL, 78- *Mem:* Am Chem Soc. *Res:* High temperature mass spectrometric studies of the vaporization and thermodynamics of the lanthanide metal sulfides; water quality studies. *Mailing Add:* Northern State Col Aberdeen SD 57401

FRIES, RALPH JAY, b Lancaster, Pa, Oct 22, 30; m 50; c 3. PHYSICAL CHEMISTRY. *Educ:* Pa State Univ, BSc, 52; Univ Pittsburgh, MLitt, 58, PhD(chem), 59. *Prof Exp:* Res assoc phys chem, Mellon Inst, 55-58; mem staff, 58-73, assoc group leader, Group L-4, 74-77, group leader, Group L-7, 77-81, PROG MGR, LASER-FUSION TARGET FABRICATION PROG, GROUP L-4, LASER DIV, LOS ALAMOS NAT LAB, 73-, GROUP LEADER, GROUP CMB-10, 81- *Concurrent Pos:* Lectr, Univ Pittsburgh, 56-57; vis scientist, Ispra Lab, Europ Atomic Energy Community, Italy, 67-68; vis fel, Inst Laser Eng, Osaka Univ, Japan, 81. *Mem:* Sigma Xi; AAAS; Am Phys Soc; Am Vacuum Soc. *Res:* Surface and high temperature chemistry; physical measurements; diffusion permeation; coatings; microfabrication; laser-fusion target fabrication. *Mailing Add:* MS-528 PO Box 1663 Los Alamos Nat Lab Los Alamos NM 87545

FRIESEL, DENNIS LANE, b Chicago, Ill, July 24, 42; m 64; c 2. EXPERIMENTAL NUCLEAR PHYSICS. *Educ:* St Procopius Col, BS, 64; Univ Notre Dame, PhD(physics), 70. *Prof Exp:* Res assoc, Dept Physics, 70-72, STAFF PHYSICIST, CYCLOTRON FACIL, IND UNIV, BLOOMINGTON, 72- *Mem:* Am Phys Soc. *Res:* Investigation of nuclear structure via (P,2P) and (P,2alpha) experiments on carbon at energies between 100 and 200 mega electron volts; beam development and improved performance of Indiana University Cyclotron Facility 200 mega electron volts separated sector cyclotron. *Mailing Add:* Ind Univ Cyclotron Facil Milo B Sampson Lane Bloomington IN 47401

FRIESEM, ALBERT ASHER, b Haifa, Israel, Jan 18, 36; US citizen; m 56; c 3. APPLIED PHYSICS, ELECTROOPTICS. *Educ:* Univ Mich, BS, 58, PhD(elec optics), 68; Wayne State Univ, MS, 61. *Prof Exp:* Engr, Bell Aircraft Co, NY, 58-59; engr, Res Labs, Bendix Corp, Mich, 59-63; res assoc, Radar & Optics Lab, Inst Sci & Technol, Univ, Mich, 63-66, assoc res engr, 66-68, res engr, 68-69; prin res engr, Electro Optics Ctr, Radiation Inc, 69-73; assoc prof, 73-77, PROF, WEIZMANN INST SCI, 77- *Concurrent Pos:* Vis scholar, Univ Mich, 69-71; sr vis scientist, Weizmann Inst Sci, 72-73; sr res engr, Environ Res Inst Mich, 81-82; vis prof, Univ Mich, 81-82. *Mem:* Sr mem Inst Elec & Electronics Engrs; fel Optical Soc Am. *Res:* Simulation of radar returns with coherent optics; development of image processing; wavefront reconstruction; holographic storage, retrieval and display systems; interferometry; optical memories; optical displays; optical fibers. *Mailing Add:* Dept of Electronics Weizmann Inst of Sci Rehovot Isreal

FRIESEN, BENJAMIN S, b Garden City, Kans, Mar 24, 28; m 53; c 4. RADIATION BIOPHYSICS. *Educ:* Univ Kans, BA, 52, MA, 54; Iowa State Univ, PhD(biophys), 59. *Prof Exp:* USPHS fel, 59-60; from asst prof to assoc prof, 60-70, PROF RADIATION BIOPHYS, UNIV KANS, 70- *Mem:* AAAS; Health Phys Soc; Biophys Soc; Radiation Res Soc; Am Soc Microbiol. *Res:* Biophysical characterization of viruses, viral components and virus-host relationships; radiation effects in microorganisms and tissue culture; deoxyribonucleic acid repair mechanisms. *Mailing Add:* Dept of Radiation Biophys Nuclear Reactor Ctr Univ of Kans Lawrence KS 66044

FRIESEN, DONALD KENT, b Morrison, Ill, Mar 31, 41. ALGEBRA. *Educ:* Knox Col, BA, 63; Dartmouth Col, MA, 65, PhD(math), 66. *Prof Exp:* Res instr math, Dartmouth Col, 66-67; asst prof, 67-74, ASSOC PROF MATH, UNIV ILL, URBANA, 74- *Mem:* Math Asn Am. *Res:* Finite subgroups of orthogonal groups and related problems in theory of finite groups. *Mailing Add:* Dept of Math Univ of Ill Urbana IL 61801

FRIESEN, EARL WAYNE, b Hillsboro, Kans, Jan 8, 27; m 51; c 2. PARTICLE PHYSICS. *Educ:* Univ Calif, AB, 50, PhD, 54. *Prof Exp:* Instr physics, Univ Calif, 54-55; asst prof, Ind Univ, 55-61; assoc prof, 61-66, PROF PHYSICS, SAN FRANCISCO STATE UNIV, 66- *Mem:* Fel Am Phys Soc; Am Asn Physics Teachers. *Res:* Cosmic ray physics; elementary particle physics; high energy nuclear physics. *Mailing Add:* 3 Lower Via Casitas Greenbrae CA 94904

FRIESEN, GEORGE H, weed science, plant physiology, see previous edition

FRIESEN, HENRY GEORGE, b Morden, Man, July 31, 34; m 67; c 2. ENDOCRINOLOGY. *Educ:* Univ Man, MSc & MD, 68. *Prof Exp:* Intern, Winnipeg Gen Hosp, 58-59, asst resident, 59-60; res fel endocrinol, New Eng Ctr Hosp, Boston, 60-61 & 62-63; asst res, Royal Victoria Hosp, Montreal, 61-62 & 63-65; from asst prof med to assoc prof, McGill Univ, 65-71, prof exp med, 72-73; PROF MED & PHYSIOL & HEAD DEPT PHYSIOL, UNIV MAN, 73- *Concurrent Pos:* Asst prof med, Tufts Univ Sch Med, 65-66; assoc, Med Res Coun Can, 68-73; chmn & mem, Med Res Coun Can comts, 70-; assoc ed, Can J Physiol & Pharmacol, 74-78; mem organizing comt, VI Int Endocrine Cong, Hamburg, 75; mem NIH task forces, 75-77 & 78; Sandoz lectr, Can Soc Endocrinol & Metab, 78. *Honors & Awards:* Eli Lilly Award, Endocrine Soc, 74; Gairdner Found Award, Toronto, 77. *Mem:* Can Soc Endocrinol & Metab (pres, 74); Int Soc Neuroendocrinol; fel Can Soc Clin Invest (pres, 78); Royal Soc Can; fel Royal Col Physicians & Surgeans Can. *Res:* Endocrinology, prolactin, placental lactogen and their receptors; growth factors. *Mailing Add:* Dept of Physiol 770 Bannatyne Ave Winnipeg Can

FRIESEN, JAMES DONALD, b Rosthern, Sask, Nov 4, 35; m 58; c 3. MOLECULAR BIOLOGY, MICROBIOLOGY. *Educ:* Univ Sask, BA, 56, MA, 58; Univ Toronto, PhD(med biophysics), 62. *Prof Exp:* Nat Cancer Inst Can fel, Inst Microbiol, Copenhagen Univ, 62-64; vis asst prof physics, Kans State Univ, 64-65, asst prof, 65-67, assoc prof biol, 67-68; assoc prof biol, York Univ, 69-74, prof, 74-81; CHMN, DEPT MED GENETICS, UNIV TORONTO, 81- *Res:* Genetics and regulation of ribosome synthesis and function in microorganisms. *Mailing Add:* Dept Med Genetics Med Sci Bldg Univ Toronto Toronto Can

FRIESEN, RHINEHART F, b Gretna, Man, Jan 6, 14; m 44; c 4. OBSTETRICS & GYNECOLOGY. *Educ:* Univ Man, MD, 44; FRCPS(C), 57. *Prof Exp:* Demonstr obstet & gynec, 58-65, asst pediat, 59-65, lectr & sr res asst, 65-67, asst prof, 67-78, ASSOC PROF OBSTET & GYNEC, UNIV MAN, 67- *Concurrent Pos:* Asst obstetrician & gynecologist, Health Sci Ctr, 59; consult, Man Rehab Hosp. *Mem:* Soc Obstetricians & Gynecologists Can; Can Med Asn; fel Am Col Obstet & Gynec. *Res:* Obstetrics and gynecology; perinatal mortality; fetal transfusions in Rh-sensitized mothers. *Mailing Add:* 1114 Medical Arts Bldg Univ of Man Winnipeg MB R3C 3J5 Can

FRIESEN, STANLEY RICHARD, b Roshern, Sask, Sept 8, 18; US citizen; m 42; c 4. SURGERY. *Educ:* Univ Kans, AB, 40, MD, 43; Univ Minn, PhD(surg), 49; Am Bd Surg, dipl, 50. *Prof Exp:* From asst prof to assoc prof surg & oncol, 49-59, PROF SURG, MED SCH, UNIV KANS, 59- *Concurrent Pos:* Consult, Vet Admin Hosp, Kansas City. *Mem:* AAAS; Soc Exp Biol & Med; Soc Univ Surgeons; Am Surg Asn; fel Am Col Surg. *Res:* Surgical endocrinology and gastroeneterology, specifically acid-peptic ulceration and multiple endocrine adenomatosis. *Mailing Add:* Univ of Kans Med Sch Rainbow Blvd at 39th St Kansas City KS 66103

FRIESEN, WOLFGANG OTTO, b Ger, 42; US citizen. NEUROBIOLOGY, ELECTROPHYSIOLOGY. *Educ:* Bethel Col, Kans, AB, 64; Univ Calif, Berkeley, MA, 66; Univ Calif, San Diego, PhD(neurosci), 74. *Prof Exp:* Res physicist pulmonary physiol, Cardiovasc Res Inst, Univ Calif, San Francisco, 69-70; res biologist neurophysiol, Univ Calif, Berkeley, 74-77; ASST PROF BIOL & NEUROBIOL, UNIV VA, 77- *Concurrent Pos:* NIH fel molecular biol, Univ Calif, Berkeley, 75-77; NIH grant, 78-81; NSF grant, 81-85. *Mem:* AAAS; Soc Neurosci. *Res:* Physiological studies and modeling analysis of the neural basis of animal movements. *Mailing Add:* Dept of Biol Gilmer Hall Univ of Va Charlottesville VA 22901

FRIESER, RUDOLF GRUENSPAN, b Vienna, Austria, Apr 20, 20; US citizen; m 55; c 3. INORGANIC CHEMISTRY, SURFACE CHEMISTRY. *Educ:* Columbia Univ, BS, 50; Brooklyn Polytech Inst, MS, 58. *Prof Exp:* Chem supvr, Path Lab Dr Block, NY, 47-51; anal chemist, Fisher Sci Corp, 51-52; sr chemist, Res Lab, Interchem Corp, 52-58; engr semiconductor chem, RCA Corp, NJ, 58-60; mem tech staff, Bell Tel Lab, 60-65; sr res scientist, Res & Develop Ctr, Sprague Elec Co, 65-68; ADV CHEMIST, IBM CORP, FISHKILL, 68- *Concurrent Pos:* Instr gen chem, North Adams State Col, 66-67; mem bd dir, Electrochem Soc, 78-80. *Mem:* Am Chem Soc; Electrochem Soc; Sigma Xi. *Res:* Characterization and deposition of insulator thin films by chemical vapor deposition, plasma deposition; chemical and plasma etching of semiconductors and insulators; surface chemistry of semiconductors; metals and insulators. *Mailing Add:* Clover Hill Poughkeepsie NY 12603

FRIESINGER, GOTTLIEB CHRISTIAN, b Zanesville, Ohio, July 4, 29; m 52; c 4. MEDICINE, PHYSIOLOGY. *Educ:* Muskingum Col, BS, 51; Johns Hopkins Univ, MD, 55; Am Bd Internal Med, dipl, 65. *Prof Exp:* Intern, Osler Med Serv, Johns Hopkins Univ Hosp, 55-56, asst resident med, 56-57, 59-60, chief resident, 62; from instr to assoc prof med, Sch Med, Johns Hopkins Univ, 63-71; PROF MED & DIR DIV CARDIOL, VANDERBILT UNIV, 71- *Concurrent Pos:* Fel med, Cardiovasc Div, Johns Hopkins Univ, 60-62, Clayton scholar, 63-71; dir myocardial infarction unit, Johns Hopkins Univ, 68-71; mem, Coun Circulation, Am Heart Asn, 66. *Mem:* Am Soc Clin Invest; Am Fedn Clin Res; Am Physiol Soc. *Res:* Applied cardiovascular physiology, especially ischemic heart disease including acute myocardial infarction. *Mailing Add:* Dept of Med Vanderbilt Univ Nashville TN 37203

FRIESS, SEYMOUR LOUIS, b Detroit, Mich, July 1, 22; m 53; c 2. ORGANIC CHEMISTRY. *Educ:* Univ Calif, Los Angeles, AB, 43, MA, 44, PhD(chem), 47. *Prof Exp:* Res chemist, Manhattan Eng Dist, Oak Ridge, 44-45; instr chem, Univ Calif, Los Angeles, 47-48; instr, Univ Rochester, 48-51; res chemist, US Naval Med Res Inst, 51-59, head phys biochem div, 59-68, actg dir, Physiol Sci Dept, 67-68, dir, 68-70, dir, Environ Biosci Dept, 70-80; CONSULT TOXICOL, ARLINGTON, VA, 80- *Concurrent Pos:* Mem comt on toxicol, Nat Res Coun, 67-76 & toxicol info prog comt, 72-75; adj prof pharmacol, Med Sch, Uniformed Serv Univ, 77-; managing dir, Drill, Friess, Hays, Loomis & Shaffer, Inc. *Mem:* Am Chem Soc; Undersea Med Soc; Soc Toxicol. *Res:* Enzymatic topography; kinetics and catalysis; cholinesterase and conduction in nerve; mechanisms of toxic interactions in tissues; hyperbaric pharmacology; marine toxins; chemical hazard assessment and chemical safety evaluation; toxicological mechanisms; pharmacology and toxicology. *Mailing Add:* 6522 Lone Oak Ct Bethesda MD 20017

FRIGERIO, NORMAN ALFRED, oncology, environmental health, deceased

FRIGYESI, TAMAS L, b Budapest, Hungary, June 7, 27; US citizen. NEUROBIOLOGY. *Educ:* Univ Budapest, MD, 51. *Prof Exp:* Asst neurol, Columbia Univ, 65-67; asst prof anat, Albert Einstein Col Med, 67-69; assoc prof physiol, Col Med & Dent NJ, 69-70; assoc prof neurol, Columbia Univ, 70-72; mem staff, Neurosurg Clin, Canton Hosp, Univ Zurich, 72-76; prof physiol & neurol, Sch Med, Tex Tech Univ, Lubbock, 76-79; DIR, EPID RES INST, 79- *Concurrent Pos:* Nat Inst Neurol Dis & Blindness spec fel, 62-65; vis prof, Col Med & Dent NJ, Newark, 70-72; res prof physiol, New York Med Col, 72- *Honors & Awards:* Semmelweis Award, Am-Hungarian Med Asn, 70. *Mem:* Am Physiol Soc; Am Asn Anat; Am Electroencephalog Soc; Soc Neurosci. *Res:* Neurobiology of central integration of sensorimotor activities; synaptic organizations in basal ganglia-diencephalon functional linkages; epilepsy. *Mailing Add:* 2322 17th St Lubbock TX 79401

FRIIHAUF, EDWARD JOE, b Cleveland, Ohio, Apr 29, 36; m 58; c 3. TRIBOLOGY. *Educ:* Kent State Univ, BS, 58; Univ Ill, Urbana, MS, 60, PhD(chem), 61. *Prof Exp:* Chemist, J T Baker Chem Co, 61-62; chemist, Lubrizol Corp, 62-81. *Mem:* Am Chem Soc; Soc Lubrication Engrs. *Res:* Lubricants and related additives. *Mailing Add:* PO Box 678 Manchester VT 05254

FRIMPTER, GEORGE W, b Haverstraw, NY, Mar 17, 28; m 51; c 6. MEDICINE. *Educ:* Williams Col, BA, 48; Cornell Univ, MD, 52. *Prof Exp:* Estab investr, Am Heart Asn, 64-69; from asst prof to assoc prof med, Med Col, Cornell Univ, 61-69; prof med, Univ Tex Med Sch, San Antonio, 69-77; PROF MED & ASSOC CHIEF OF STAFF, AMB CARE,, AUDIE MURPHY VA HOSP, 77- *Concurrent Pos:* Res fel med, USPHS, 58-59; sr res fel, NY Heart Asn, 59-64. *Mem:* Am Fedn Clin Res; Am Soc Clin Invest; fel Am Col Physicians; Aerospace Med Asn. *Res:* Internal medicine; metabolic aspects of kidney disease, especially errors of amino acid metabolism in various inherited conditions. *Mailing Add:* Audie Murphy VA Hosp San Antonio TX 78284

FRIMPTER, MICHAEL HOWARD, b New York, NY, Dec 10, 34; m 62; c 3. GEOLOGY, HYDROLOGY. *Educ:* Williams Col, BA, 57; Boston Univ, MA, 61, PhD(geol), 67. *Prof Exp:* Geologist water resources div, US Geol Surv, 63-68, hydrologist, 68-69; asst prof geol, Wis State Univ, 69-71; hydrologist, 71-79, MASS SUBDIST CHIEF WATER RESOURCES DIV, US GEOL SURV, 79- *Mem:* Geol Soc Am; Nat Waterwell Asn; New Eng Waterworks Asn. *Res:* Geology of the Hudson Highlands; hydrogeology and water chemistry; geochemistry of surface and ground water; glacial geology and ground water resources, New York, New England and Massachusetts. *Mailing Add:* Water Resources Div 150 Causeway St Boston MA 02114

FRINDT, ROBERT FREDERICK, b Edmonton, Alta, March 8, 39; m 63; c 2. ENERGY STORAGE. *Educ:* Univ Alta, BSc, 60; Univ Cambridge, PhD(physics), 63. *Prof Exp:* Sr student, Cavendish Lab, Univ Cambridge, 63-64; asst res officer, Physics Div, Nat Res Coun Can, 64-65; asst prof, 65-67, assoc prof, 67-78, actg dir, Energy Res Inst, 80-81, PROF PHYSICS, SIMON FRASER UNIV, 78- *Concurrent Pos:* Mem, Energy Res Eval Comt, BC Sci Coun, 80- *Mem:* Can Asn Physicists. *Res:* Physical properties of layered materials and intercalated systems. *Mailing Add:* Physics Dept Simon Fraser Univ Burnaby BC V5A 1S6 Can

FRINGS, CHRISTOPHER STANTON, b Birmingham, Ala, Aug 10, 40; m 65; c 2. CLINICAL CHEMISTRY, TOXICOLOGY. *Educ:* Univ Ala, BS, 61; Purdue Univ, PhD(chem), 66. *Prof Exp:* Res assoc biochem, Mayo Clin & Mayo Grad Sch Med, 66-67; DIR CLIN CHEM & TOXICOL, MED LAB ASSOCS & CUNNINGHAM PATH ASSOCS, 67- *Mem:* Am Asn Clin Chem; Am Chem Soc; Am Acad Clin Toxicol. *Res:* Clinical laboratory toxicology and effective therapeutic drug monitoring. *Mailing Add:* Cunningham Path Assocs 1025 S 18th St Birmingham AL 35205

FRINK, CHARLES RICHARD, b Keene, NH, Sept 26, 31; m 53; c 3. SOIL CHEMISTRY. *Educ:* Cornell Univ, BS, 53, PhD(soil chem), 60; Univ Calif, Berkeley, MS, 57. *Prof Exp:* From asst soil chemist to soil chemist, 60-70, CHIEF, DEPT SOIL & WATER, CONN AGR EXP STA, 70-, VDIR, 72- *Mem:* AAAS; Am Chem Soc; Soil Sci Soc Am; NY Acad Sci. *Res:* Aluminum chemistry and clay mineralogy in acid soils; nutrient cycles in soil, water and lake sediments; toxic organic wastes; agricultural production. *Mailing Add:* Conn Agr Exp Sta PO Box 1106 New Haven CT 06504

FRINK, DONALD W, b Madison, Ohio, Apr 25, 33; m 55; c 3. MECHANICAL ENGINEERING. *Educ:* Ohio State Univ, BME, 56, MME, 57. *Prof Exp:* Res engr, 56-60, proj leader, 60-62, proj dir, 62-63, GROUP DIR, BATTELLE MEM INST, 63- *Mem:* Nat Soc Prof Engrs; Am Soc Mech Engrs. *Res:* Kinematics; mechanism; dynamics and statistics; mechanism synthesis and analysis. *Mailing Add:* Battelle Mem Inst 505 King Ave Columbus OH 43201

FRIOU, GEORGE JACOB, b Brooklyn, NY, Oct 5, 19; div; c 4. IMMUNOLOGY, RHEUMATOLOGY. *Educ:* Cornell Univ, BS, 40, MD, 44; Am Bd Internal Med, dipl, 51. *Prof Exp:* Intern internal med, New Haven Hosp, Yale Univ, 44-45, asst resident, 45-46, res fel, 48-49, chief resident, 49-50, instr, Sch Med, 49-50, from clin instr to clin asst prof, 50-58; asst prof med, 58-60, assoc prof med & microbiol, Sch Med, Univ Okla, 60-64; assoc prof med, Sch Med, Univ Southern Calif, 64-68, prof, 68-78, chief immunol & rheumatic dis sect, 64-78; PROF MED, SCH MED, UNIV CALIF, IRVINE, 78-, DIR DIV IMMUNOL & RHEUMATIC DIS, 78- *Mem:* Am Soc Clin Invest; Am Asn Immunologists; Am Rheumatism Asn; fel Am Col Physicians; Am Fedn Clin Res. *Res:* Rheumatic diseases; immunology. *Mailing Add:* Dept of Med Univ of Calif Irvine CA 92717

FRIPP, ARCHIBALD LINLEY, b Columbia, SC, Jan 15, 39; m 63; c 3. MATERIALS SCIENCE, ELECTRICAL ENGINEERING. *Educ:* Univ SC, BS, 66; Univ Va, MS, 69, PhD(mat sci), 74. *Prof Exp:* STAFF MEM PHYSICS, NASA-LANGLEY RES CTR, HAMPTON, 66- *Mem:* Am Asn Crystal Growth; Electrochem Soc; Inst Elec & Electronics Engrs. *Res:* Crystal growth of compound semiconductor materials, which are used to build infrared detector arrays. *Mailing Add:* 125 Little John Rd Williamsburg VA 23185

FRISBIE, RAYMOND EDWARD, b Barstow, Calif, Apr 14, 45; m 72. ENTOMOLOGY. *Educ:* Univ Calif, Riverside, BS, 67, MS, 69, PhD(entom), 72. *Prof Exp:* Res asst entom, Univ Calif, Riverside, 67-72; exten entomologist & pest mgt, 72-75, exten entomologist & pest mgt leader, Tex Agr Exten Serv, 75-77, MEM FAC ENTOM, TEX A&M UNIV, 77-, INTEGRATED PEST MGT COORDR, 79- *Mem:* Entom Soc Am. *Res:* Pest management program designed to reduce production costs to cotton and grain sorghum farmers by using integrated technology to reduce pest populations. *Mailing Add:* Systs Build Rm 312 Tex A&M Univ College Station TX 77843

FRISBY, JAMES CURTIS, b Bethany, Mo, Oct 22, 30; m 69. AGRICULTURAL ENGINEERING. *Educ:* Univ Mo, BS, 52 & 56; Iowa State Univ, MS, 63, PhD(agr eng), 65. *Prof Exp:* Classroom instr math sci, ed & training dept, Caterpillar Tractor Co, Ill, 56-57, tech writer, serv dept, 57-58, mkt analyst, engine div, 58-60; asst mgr, farm serv dept, Iowa State Univ, 61-63, instr agr eng, 63-66; from asst prof to assoc prof, 66-74, PROF AGR ENG, UNIV MO-COLUMBIA, 74- *Mem:* Am Soc Agr Engrs; Am Soc Eng Educ; Nat Asn Col & Teachers Agr; Sigma Xi. *Res:* Application of operations research techniques to machine systems used for agricultural enterprises. *Mailing Add:* Dept Agr Eng 100 Agr Eng Bldg Univ Mo Columbia MO 65201

FRISCH, ALFRED SHELBY, b San Diego, Calif, July 1, 35; m 62; c 2. OCEANOGRAPHY, ATMOSPHERIC SCIENCES. *Educ:* San Diego State Univ, BA, 57; Univ Wash, MS, 64, PhD(geophys), 70. *Prof Exp:* Thermodyn engr mass spectros, Convair Astronaut, 57-59; physicist nuclear physics, Edgerton, Germeshausenire & Griar, Inc, 61-63; oceanogr phys oceanog, Appl Physics Lab, Univ Wash, 65-67; PHYSICIST ATMOSPHERIC SCI & OCEANOG, WAVE PROPAGATION LAB, NAT OCEANIC & ATMOSPHERIC ADMIN, 70- *Honors & Awards:* Group Award, Nat Oceanic & Atmospheric Admin, 75. *Mem:* Am Geophys Union. *Res:* Atmospheric turbulence and air motion using acoustic echo sounding and doppler radars; physical oceanography using high frequency doppler radar for ocean current measurement. *Mailing Add:* Wave Propagation Lab Code R45x5 325 S Broadway Boulder CO 80302

FRISCH, HARRY LLOYD, b Vienna, Austria, Nov 13, 28; nat US; div; c 2. THEORETICAL CHEMISTRY, STATISTICAL MECHANICS. *Educ:* Williams Col, Mass, AB, 47; Polytech Inst Brooklyn, PhD(phys chem), 52. *Prof Exp:* Res assoc phys chem, Polytech Inst Brooklyn, 51-52; res assoc physics, Syracuse Univ, 52-54; from instr to asst prof chem, Univ Southern Calif, 54-56; 56; mem tech staff, Bell Labs, 56-67; assoc dean, Col Arts & prof chem, 67-78, DISTINGUISHED Sci, 69-71, PROF CHEM, STATE UNIV NY ALBANY, 78- *Concurrent Pos:* Vis assoc prof, Yeshiva Univ, 62-; vis mem, Courant Inst Math Sci, NY Univ, 64-65; assoc ed, J Chem Physics, 64-66; mem adv bd, J Adhesion, 70- *Honors & Awards:* Boris Pregel Medal, NY Acad Sci, 73. *Mem:* Am Chem Soc; fel Am Phys Soc. *Res:* Statistical mechanics and kinetic theory; colloid and high polymer chemistry; solid state chemistry and physics. *Mailing Add:* Dept of Chem State Univ of NY Albany NY 12222

FRISCH, HENRY JONATHAN, b Los Alamos, NMex, Aug 21, 44; m 70; c 2. EXPERIMENTAL HIGH ENERGY PHYSICS. *Educ:* Harvard Univ, BA, 66; Univ Calif, Berkeley, PhD(physics), 71. *Prof Exp:* Instr, 71-73, asst prof, 73-77, ASSOC PROF PHYSICS, UNIV CHICAGO, 77- *Res:* Direct lepton and dilepton production and high transverse momentum particle production; very high energy density particle collisions. *Mailing Add:* EFI HEP 320 5640 Ellis Ave Chicago IL 60637

FRISCH, I(VAN) T, b Budapest, Hungary, Sept 21, 37; US citizen; m 62. ELECTRICAL ENGINEERING. *Educ:* Queens Col, NY, BS, 58; Columbia Univ, BS, 58, MS, 59, PhD(elec eng), 62. *Prof Exp:* Asst prof elec eng, Univ Calif, Berkeley, 62-65 & 66-68, assoc prof, 68-69; Ford Found resident eng pract, Bell Tel Labs, 65-66; Guggenheim fel, 69, SR V PRES & GEN MGR, NETWORK ANAL CORP, 71- *Concurrent Pos:* Consult, Collins Radio Co, Inc, 62-; off emergency planning, Exec Off President, 68-; ed-in-chief, Networks; vis prof, State Univ NY, 73-74; adj prof, Columbia Univ, 74-75. *Mem:* Fel Inst Elec & Electronics Engrs. *Mailing Add:* Network Anal Corp 130 Steamboat Rd Great Neck NY 11024

FRISCH, JOSEPH, b Vienna, Austria, Apr 21, 21; nat US; m 57; c 3. MECHANICAL ENGINEERING. *Educ:* Duke Univ, BSME, 46; Univ Calif, MS, 50. *Prof Exp:* Sr engr, dept pub works, Baltimore, 47; from asst prof eng design to prof mech eng, 47-63, asst dir, inst eng res, 63-66, chmn dept mech design, 66-70, assoc dean, 73-76, PROF MECH ENG, UNIV CALIF, BERKELEY, 63- *Concurrent Pos:* A E Taylor distinguished prof, Univ Birmingham, Eng, 70. *Mem:* Fel Am Soc Mech Engrs. *Res:* Mechanical engineering design; materials behavior and processing; computer control. *Mailing Add:* Dept Mech Eng Col Eng Univ Calif Berkeley CA 94720

FRISCH, KURT CHARLES, b Vienna, Austria, Jan 15, 18; nat US; m 46; c 3. CHEMISTRY. *Educ:* Realgymnasium, Austria, BS, 35; Univ Vienna, MA, 38; Columbia Univ, MA, 41, PhD(org chem), 44. *Prof Exp:* Anal & res chemist, Am Dietaids Co, NY, 41; res chemist, Gen Elec Co, 44-52; asst mgr res, E F Houghton & Co, 52-56; dir polymer res & develop, Wyandotte Chem Corp, 56-68; PROF POLYMER ENG & CHEM & DIR POLYMER INST, UNIV DETROIT, 68- *Mem:* Am Chem Soc; NY Acad Sci; fel Am Inst Chem. *Res:* Polymer research on polyurethanes; silicones; phenolics; vinyls; organic synthetic and application research on textile and paper chemicals; synthetic lubricants; antimalarials. *Mailing Add:* Univ of Detroit 4001 McNichols Rd Detroit MI 48221

FRISCH, NORMAN W(ILLIAM), b New York, NY, Dec 8, 23; m 49; c 3. CHEMICAL ENGINEERING. *Educ:* City Col New York, BChE, 48; Yale Univ, DEng(chem eng), 54. *Prof Exp:* Res chem engr, Res Labs, Rohm & Haas Co, 52-60, res assoc, Princeton Chem Res, Inc, 60-64, dir catalyst res, 64-67; mgr chem process develop, Cottrell Environ Systs Div, Res-Cottrell, Inc, 68-70, dir res, 70-74; independent chem consult, 67-81; sr sci consult, Utility Div, Res-Cottrell, Inc, 74-80; VPRES RES & DEVELOP, AFFIL ENERGY & ENVIRON TECHNOLS, INC, 80- *Mem:* Air Pollution Control Asn; AAAS; Am Inst Chem Engrs; Am Chem Soc. *Res:* Air and water pollution control technology; particulate collection mechanisms; electrostatic precipitation; absorption; catalysis; fossil fuel characteristics and combustion; surface chemistry; applied mathematics and mathematical statistics; adsorptions; kinetics; ion exchange. *Mailing Add:* 145 Ridgeview Circle Princeton NJ 08540

FRISCH, P DOUGLAS, b Tiffin, Ohio, Aug 24, 45; m 67; c 2. INORGANIC CHEMISTRY. *Educ:* Ohio Univ, BS, 67; Univ Wis-Madison, PhD(inorg chem), 72. *Prof Exp:* Teaching asst, Univ Wis, 67-70, res assoc, 70-72; Sci Res Coun fel & staff tutor chem, Univ Sheffield, Eng, 72-74; asst prof chem, Univ Maine, Orono, 74-79; res eng specialist, Monsanto Co, St Louis, 79-81; SR CHEMIST, EXXON CHEM CO, LINDEN, NJ, 81- *Mem:* AAAS; Am Chem Soc; Sigma Xi; NY Acad Sci. *Res:* Synthetic inorganic and organometallic chemistry; solid state and solution structural determination; homogeneous and heterogeneous catalysis. *Mailing Add:* 810 Village Green Westfield NJ 07090

FRISCH, ROSE EPSTEIN, b New York, NY, July 7, 18; m 40; c 2. REPRODUCTIVE BIOLOGY, POPULATION SCIENCES. *Educ:* Smith Col, BA, 39; Columbia Univ, MA, 40; Univ Wis, PhD(physiol genetics), 43. *Prof Exp:* Res fel biol, 53-54, res assoc, Ctr Pop Studies, 70-75, MEM, CTR POP STUDIES & LECTR POP SCI, SCH PUB HEALTH, HARVARD UNIV, 75-; RES ASSOC PSYCHIAT, CHILDREN'S HOSP MED CTR, BOSTON, 74- *Concurrent Pos:* Guggenheim Mem Found fel, 75-76. *Mem:* Soc Study Reproduction; Soc Study Fertil; Pop Asn Am; Soc Study Human Biol; Soc Study Social Biol. *Res:* Determinants of puberty and reproductive ability; effects of environmental factors such as nutrition and physicial exercise; fatness, fat/lean ratios and fertility. *Mailing Add:* Harvard Ctr for Pop Studies 9 Bow St Cambridge MA 02138

FRISCHER, HENRI, b Brussels, Belg, Jan 15, 34; US citizen; m 61; c 3. INTERNAL MEDICINE, GENETICS. *Educ:* Santo Domingo Univ, MD, 58; Univ Chicago, PhD(genetics), 65. *Prof Exp:* Intern, Michael Reese Hosp, Chicago, 58-59, from resident to chief resident internal med, 59-62; from instr to asst prof med, Univ Chicago, 64-71; assoc prof hemat, 71-77, DIR, SECT BLOOD GENETICS & PHARMACOGENETICS, DEPT PHARMACOL, RUSH UNIV, 71-, PROF MED & PHARMACOL, RUSH MED COL, 77- *Concurrent Pos:* USPHS spec fel, 65-66; sr attend physician, Rush-Presby St Luke's Med Ctr, 77- *Mem:* AAAS; Am Soc Human Genetics. *Res:* Biochemical genetics; hereditary hemolytic anemias; glucose-6-phosphate dehydroglucose deficiency; disorders and regulation of pentose phosphate shunt; carbohydrate metabolism. *Mailing Add:* Rush Med Ctr Sect of Hemat 1753 W Congress Pkwy Chicago IL 60612

FRISCHKNECHT, FRANK C, b Bicknell, Utah, Oct 12, 28; m 67; c 2. GEOPHYSICS. *Educ:* Univ Utah, BSEE, 50, MS, 53; Univ Colo, MS, 67, PhD(elec eng), 73. *Prof Exp:* Asst engr, Telluride Power Co, 50-51; airways engr, Civil Aeronaut Admin, 51; geologist, 53-54, GEOPHYSICIST, US GEOL SURV, 54- *Mem:* AAAS; Soc Explor Geophys; Am Geophys Union; Am Inst Mining, Metall & Petrol Engrs; Inst Elec & Electronics Engrs. *Res:* Development of electrical exploration methods, chiefly electromagnetic induction methods; development of instruments for airborne and ground electromagnetic and magnetic surveying. *Mailing Add:* US Geol Surv Box 25046 Denver Fed Ctr Denver CO 80225

FRISCHMUTH, ROBERT WELLINGTON, b Cleveland, Ohio, Jan 28, 40. CHEMICAL ENGINEERING. *Educ:* Case Inst Technol, BS, 62; Northwestern Univ, MS, 63. *Prof Exp:* Engr, NASA Lewis Res Ctr, 63-68 & Shell Develop Co, 68-74; group leader, 74-77, MGR RES, OCCIDENTAL RES CORP, 77- *Mem:* Am Inst Chem Engrs; Soc Mining Engrs; Am Chem Soc. *Res:* Coal research; chemicals from coal; management of research. *Mailing Add:* Occidental Res Corp 2100 SE Main St Irvine CA 92714

FRISCO, L(OUIS) J(OSEPH), b Patchogue, NY, Aug 21, 23; m 50; c 2. ELECTRICAL ENGINEERING. *Educ:* Johns Hopkins Univ, BE, 49, MScE, 53. *Prof Exp:* Asst res contract dir, Dielec Lab, Johns Hopkins Univ, 50-58, res contract dir, 58-64; prog mgr dielec mat, Adv Tech Labs, Gen Elec Co, NY, 64-65; mgr, 65-66, dir, Tech Serv Labs, 66-69, dir mfg, 70-77, tech dir, Wire & Cable Div, 77-79, GEN MGR, WIRE & CABLE DIV & CORP DIR PROD REV, RAYCHEM CORP, MENLO PARK, 79- . *Concurrent Pos:* Mem conf elec insulation, Nat Acad Sci-Nat Res Coun; US deleg, Int Electrotechnol Comn. *Mem:* Inst Elec & Electronics Engrs; Am Soc Testing & Mat. *Res:* Electrical insulation and dielectric phenomena. *Mailing Add:* Raychem Corp 300 Constitution Dr Menlo Park CA 94025

FRISELL, WILHELM RICHARD, b Two Harbors, Minn, Apr 27, 20; m 48; c 2. ENZYMOLOGY, METABOLISM. *Educ:* St Olaf Col, BA, 42; Johns Hopkins Univ, MA, 43, PhD(org chem), 46. *Prof Exp:* Jr instr chem, Johns Hopkins Univ, 42-46, res assoc, 46-47, instr, 47-51; from asst prof to prof biochem, Sch Med, Univ Colo, 51-69, assoc dean, Grad Sch, 59-69; prof biochem & chmn dept, NJ Med Sch, Col Med & Dent, NJ, 69-76; PROF BIOCHEM, CHMN DEPT & ASST DEAN GRAD AFFAIRS, EAST CAROLINA UNIV SCH MED, NC, 76- *Concurrent Pos:* Am Scand Found fel, Univ Uppsala, 49-50; mem & chmn, Int Res Fel Comt, Fogarty Int Ctr, NIH, 62-71. *Mem:* Fel AAAS; Am Chem Soc; Am Soc Microbiol; Harvey Soc; Am Soc Biol Chemists. *Res:* One-carbon metabolism; flavin and flavoenzymes; mitochondrial structure and function. *Mailing Add:* Dept Biochem East Carolina Univ Med Sch Greenville NC 27834

FRISHBERG, CAROL, b Brooklyn, NY, Sept 11, 47; m 73; c 1. QUANTUM CHEMISTRY. *Educ:* Brooklyn Col, BS, 68; City Univ NY, PhD(phys chem), 75. *Prof Exp:* Res assoc chem, Univ NC, Chapel Hill, 75-76; ASST PROF CHEM, RAMAPO STATE COL, NJ, 76- *Mem:* Am Chem Soc; Am Phys Soc; Sigma Xi; AAAS. *Res:* Electronic structure of atoms and molecules. *Mailing Add:* Sch Theoret & Appl Sci Ramapo State Col Mahwah NJ 07430

FRISHKOPF, LAWRENCE SAMUEL, b Philadelphia, Pa, June 26, 30; m 60; c 3. BIOPHYSICS. *Educ:* Univ Pa, AB, 51; Mass Inst Technol, PhD(physics), 56. *Prof Exp:* Mem res staff commun biophys, Mass Inst Technol, 55-57; NIH fel biophys, Rockefeller Inst, 57-58; mem tech res staff, Bell Labs, 59-68; PROF ELEC ENG, MASS INST TECHNOL, 68- *Mem:* AAAS; fel Acoust Soc Am; Soc Neurosci. *Res:* Physiology and anatomy of acousticolateralis system; relation to perception and behavior; physiology and anatomy of sensory systems; animal communication. *Mailing Add:* Dept of Elec Eng 36-824 Mass Inst Technol Cambridge MA 02139

FRISHMAN, AUSTIN MICHAEL, b Brooklyn, NY, May 28, 40; m 62; c 2. ENTOMOLOGY. *Educ:* Cornell Univ, BS, 62, MS, 64; Purdue Univ, PhD(entom), 68. *Prof Exp:* Res asst livestock entom, Cornell Univ, 62-64; exten asst entom, Purdue Univ, 64-67, instr pest control & entom, 67-68; from asst prof to assoc prof, 68-75, PROF ENTOM, BOT & BIOL, STATE UNIV NY AGR & TECH COL FARMINGDALE, 75- *Concurrent Pos:* Pvt consult, 68-; NSF res grant & consult, Huntington Comput Proj, Polytech Inst Brooklyn, 68-69; training dir, Copesan Serv, Inc, 69-74 & Southern Mill Creek Prod, Inc, 74-; NSF res grant comput, 70-73. *Mem:* Entom Soc Am. *Res:* Structural and industrial control of pests; extermination; pest control; livestock and medical entomology; extension entomology. *Mailing Add:* Dept of Biol State Univ of NY Agr & Tech Col Farmingdale NY 11735

FRISHMAN, DANIEL, b Brooklyn, NY, Oct 19, 19; m 42; c 4. CHEMISTRY. *Educ:* Brooklyn Col, BA, 40; Cath Univ, MS, 47; Georgetown Univ, PhD, 50. *Prof Exp:* Anal chemist, Navy Yard, Washington, DC, 40-42; asst, Cath Univ, 42-43; res assoc, Textile Found, Nat Bur Standards, 43-44; tech adv, Fercleve Corp, Tenn, 44-45; res assoc, Harris Res Labs, 45-49, proj leader, 51-55; dir res, A Hollander & Son, NJ, 49-51; dir res & develop, Malden Mills, Mass, 55-62; pres & dir res, Fibresearch Corp, 62-65; tech adv, Reid-Meredith Inc, Lawrence, 65-69; PRES, AKKO INC, 74- *Concurrent Pos:* Consult, 69- *Mem:* AAAS; Am Chem Soc; Am Asn Textile Chem & Colorists; Fiber Soc; NY Acad Sci. *Res:* Lead-acid storage batteries; thermal diffusion of uranium isotopes; chemistry and physics of textile fibers, animal fibers, fur and leather; coated and pile fabrics; plastics; synthetic furs. *Mailing Add:* 14 Castle Heights Rd Andover MA 01810

FRISHMAN, FRED, b New York, NY, Aug 4, 23; m 48; c 4. MATHEMATICAL STATISTICS. *Educ:* City Col New York, BBA, 47; George Washington Univ, AB, 56, MA, 57, PhD, 71. *Prof Exp:* Enumerator, US Bur Census, NY, 48; statistician, NY Bd Educ, 48-49; eng statistician, Naval Inspector Ord, 49-51, Bur Ord, Dept Navy, 51-54, head appl math & statist group, US Naval Propellant Plant, 54-60; chief math br, Off Chief Res & Develop, Hq, Dept Army, 60-73; dir, Math Div, Army Res Off, Durham, 73-74; chief, Math Statist Br, US Internal Revenue Serv, 74-79; EXEC SECY COMT APPL & THEORET STATIST, NAT RES COUN-NAT ACAD SCI, 79- *Concurrent Pos:* Assoc statist, Col Gen Studies, George Washington Univ, 55-59, lectr, 60-64; asst prof lectr, 66-73, assoc prof lectr, 74-77, prof lectr, 77-80, adj prof, 80-; chief, Math Br, Army Res Off, London, 71-72. *Mem:* Math Asn Am; Inst Math Statist; fel Am Statist Asn; Int Asn Statist Phys Sci; Int Statist Inst. *Res:* Statistical design of experiments; development of sampling techniques; applications of statistics in the physical sciences. *Mailing Add:* Nat Res Coun 2101 Constitution Ave NW Washington DC 20418

FRISILLO, ALBERT LAWRENCE, b Rome, NY, July 24, 43; m 68; c 3. GEOPHYSICS. *Educ:* Utica Col, BS, 65; Univ Dayton, MS, 67; Pa State Univ, PhD(geophys), 72. *Prof Exp:* Nat Res Coun res assoc, Johnson Spacecraft Ctr, Houston, 72-74; RES SCIENTIST, AMOCO PROD CO RES CTR, 74- *Mem:* Am Geophys Union; Sigma Xi. *Res:* Physical properties of geologic materials as related to the development or improvement of geophysical exploration techniques. *Mailing Add:* Amoco Prod Co Res Ctr PO Box 591 Tulsa OK 74102

FRISINGER, H HOWARD, II, b Ann Arbor, Mich, Feb 28, 33; m 54; c 4. MATHEMATICS, METEOROLOGY. *Educ:* Univ Mich, Ann Arbor, BS & BBA, 56, MS, 61, DEduc(math), 64. *Prof Exp:* assoc prof, 64-76, PROF MATH, COLO STATE UNIV, 76- *Concurrent Pos:* Fac improv comt grant, 64-65. *Mem:* Hist Sci Soc; Am Meteorol Soc; Math Asn Am. *Res:* History of science, especially contributions of mathematics and mathematicians to the development of the science of meteorology. *Mailing Add:* Dept Math Colo State Univ Ft Collins CO 80523

FRISK, GEORGE VLADIMIR, b Schenectady, NY, Apr 3, 46; m 74; c 2. OCEAN ACOUSTICS. *Educ:* Univ Rochester, BA, 67; Brown Univ, ScM, 69; Cath Univ Am, PhD(physics), 75. *Prof Exp:* Physicist acoust, Naval Res Lab, 68-77; asst scientist, 77-81, ASSOC SCIENTIST OCEAN ENG, WOODS HOLE OCEANOG INST, 81- *Mem:* Acoust Soc Am; Sigma Xi. *Res:* Acoustic propagation, reflection, and scattering in the ocean and sea floor; acoustic surface waves; scattering theory of waves; computational physics. *Mailing Add:* Bigelow 208 Woods Hole Oceanog Inst Woods Hole MA 02543

FRISKEN, WILLIAM ROSS, b Hamilton, Ont, May 29, 33; m 56; c 3. PARTICLE PHYSICS. *Educ:* Queen's Univ, Ont, BSc, 56, MSc, 57; Univ Birmingham, PhD(physics), 60. *Prof Exp:* Teaching fel physics, McGill Univ, 60-62, asst prof, 62-64; assoc physicist, Exp Planning Div, Accelerator Dept, Brookhaven Nat Lab, NY, 64-66; assoc prof physics, Case Western Reserve Univ, 66-71; assoc prof, 71-74, PROF PHYSICS, YORK UNIV, 74- *Concurrent Pos:* Adj asst prof, McGill Univ, 64-66. *Mem:* Am Phys Soc; Inst Particle Physics. *Res:* High energy particle physics experiments, particularly with positively and negatively charged electrons and estimated position colliders; design of experimental facilities for new accelerators, storage rings. *Mailing Add:* Dept of Physics York Univ 4700 Keele St Toronto ON M3J 1P3 Can

FRISQUE, ALVIN JOSEPH, b Wis, Jan 27, 23; m 50; c 2. ANALYTICAL CHEMISTRY, PHYSICAL CHEMISTRY. *Educ:* Univ Wis, BS, 48, PhD, 54; Univ Iowa, MS, 51. *Prof Exp:* Chemist, Colgate-Palmolive-Peet Co labs, 48-50; sr chemist, Am Oil Co, 54-61; group leader, 61-69, dir anal facil, 69, vpres indust chem div, 69-73, CORP VPRES RES & DEVELOP, NALCO CHEM CO, 73- *Mem:* Am Chem Soc. *Mailing Add:* 1801 Diehl Rd Naperville IL 60540

FRISQUE, GILLES, b Brussels, Belg, June 18, 43; Can citizen. FORESTRY, RESOURCES MANAGEMENT. *Educ:* Univ Louvain, Belg, BSc, 67; Univ Laval, Can, DSc, 77. *Prof Exp:* Researcher silvicult, Can Forestry Serv, Dept Forestry, 68-74; PROJ LEADER SILVICULT, LAURENTIAN FOREST RES CTR, ENVIRON CAN, 75- *Mem:* Can Inst Forestry. *Res:* Silviculture; boreal forestry; use of biomass for energy production. *Mailing Add:* Laurentian Forest Res Ctr PO Box 3800 Sainte Foy Can

FRISSEL, HARRY FREDERICK, b Alphen aan de Rhine, Netherlands, Mar 29, 20; US citizen; m 43; c 3. NUCLEAR PHYSICS. *Educ:* Hope Col BA, 42; Iowa State Univ, MS, 43, PhD(physics), 54. *Prof Exp:* Res physicist, Cornell Aeronaut Lab, 43-48; chmn dept, 63-75, PROF PHYSICS, HOPE COL, 48- *Concurrent Pos:* Mem, Denver Conf Undergrad Physics, 61- *Mem:* Am Asn Physics Teachers; Sigma Xi; Am Sci Affiliation. *Res:* Area of Walsh-Hadamard transforms and sinc and cosine transforms. *Mailing Add:* Dept of Physics Hope Col Holland MI 49423

FRIST, RAMSEY HUDSON, virology, see previous edition

FRISTOE, HAROLD T(RYON), electrical engineering, deceased

FRISTROM, JAMES W, b Chicago, Ill, July 7, 36; m 66. GENETICS. *Educ:* Reed Col, BA, 59; Rockefeller Univ, PhD(genetics), 64. *Prof Exp:* NSF fel, Biol Div, Calif Inst Technol, 64-65; from asst prof to assoc prof, 65-75, PROF GENETICS, UNIV CALIF, BERKELEY, 75- *Concurrent Pos:* Vis lectr, Univ Sydney, 69; UNESCO expert insect genetics, Biol Res Ctr, Hungarian Acad Sci, 74; Guggenheim fel, 76-77; vis researcher, Genetics Res Labs, CSIRO, Sydney, 76-77. *Res:* Developmental genetics; chemical analysis of morphological mutants and biochemistry of imaginal discs in Drosophila Melanogaster. *Mailing Add:* Dept of Genetics Univ of Calif Berkeley CA 94720

FRISTROM, ROBERT MAURICE, b Portland, Ore, May 26, 22; m 57; c 1. CHEMISTRY, PHYSICS. *Educ:* Reed Col, AB, 43; Univ Ore, AM, 45; Stanford Univ, PhD(chem), 48. *Prof Exp:* Res fel chem, Harvard Univ, 48-51; trustee prod res comt, 74-79, PRIN MEM STAFF CHEM & PHYSICS, APPL PHYSICS LAB, JOHNS HOPKINS UNIV, 51- *Concurrent Pos:* Parson's fel chem eng, Johns Hopkins Univ, 59-60, lectr, 60-61; ed, Fire Res Abstr & Rev, 65 & 78; mem comt fire res, Nat Acad Sci, 70; prin investr fire probs, NSF grant, 70; vis prof, Inst Phys Chem, Univ Gottingen, 73-74; Springer vis prof mech eng, Univ Calif, Berkeley, 80. *Honors & Awards:* Vis Scholar Award, Humboldt Found WGer, 73; Silver Combustion Medal, Combustion Inst, 66. *Mem:* Am Phys Soc; Am Phys Soc; Combustion Inst. *Res:* Microwave spectroscopy; combustion; molecular beams; chemical kinetics; fire research. *Mailing Add:* Appl Physics Lab Johns Hopkins Univ Laurel MD 20810

FRITCHLE, FRANK PAUL, b Chicago, Ill, Aug 27, 22; m 49; c 6. PHYSICS. *Educ:* De Paul Univ, BS, 49, MS, 50; Univ Santa Clara, MBA, 65. *Prof Exp:* Physicist instrument design, Cent Sci Co, 50-53; asst to dir res, 54; group leader prod & equip design, Helipot Div, 55-58, chief equip design engr, 58-59, mgr prod develop, Spinco Div, 59-60, MGR ENG, SPINCO DIV, BECKMAN INSTRUMENTS, INC, 60- *Mem:* AAAS; Am Phys Soc; Inst Elec & Electronics Engrs. *Res:* Design and development of scientific instruments; electronics; precision mechanics; optics; servo systems; precision component design including potentiometers. *Mailing Add:* Spinco Div Beckman Instruments 1117 California Ave Palo Alto CA 94304

FRITCHMAN, HARRY KIER, II, b Portland, Ore, Sept 11, 23; m 55; c 3. INVERTEBRATE ZOOLOGY. *Educ:* Univ Calif, BA, 48, MA, 51, PhD, 53. *Prof Exp:* Actg instr biol, Univ Calif, 53; actg instr zool, Univ Wash, 54; instr, 54-67, chmn dept biol, 68-72, PROF ZOOL, BOISE STATE UNIV, 67- *Concurrent Pos:* Consult, Am Inst Biol Sci Film Series, 60; lectr, NSF Marine Inst, Ore, 62-64. *Res:* Natural history of marine and fresh water invertebrates; aquaculture of Gammarus. *Mailing Add:* Dept Biol Boise State Univ Boise ID 83725

FRITSCH, ARNOLD RUDOLPH, b Passaic, NJ, Mar 28, 32; m 53; c 4. NUCLEAR CHEMISTRY. *Educ:* Univ Rochester, BS, 53; Univ Calif, PhD(chem), 57. *Prof Exp:* Sr engr, Westinghouse Elec Corp, 56-59; br chief, Div Int Affairs, US Atomic Energy Comn, 59-61, spec asst to chmn, 61-68; mgr tech eval dept, Gulf Gen Atomic Inc, Calif, 68-71, pres, Gulf United Nuclear Fuels, Inc, 71-74, DIR NUCLEAR COORD, GULF OIL CORP, 74- *Mem:* Am Phys Soc; Am Chem Soc; Nuclear Soc; Am Inst Chemists. *Res:* Nuclear fuel; reactor technology. *Mailing Add:* Gulf Oil Corp PO Box 1166 Pittsburgh PA 15230

FRITSCH, CARL WALTER, b New York, NY, July 21, 28; m 54; c 2. LIPIDS. *Educ:* Blackburn Col, BA, 52; Ohio State Univ, PhD(agr biochem), 55. *Prof Exp:* Sect leader, Dept Food Processing, 55-67, res assoc, Cereal Develop Dept, 67-76, RES ASSOC CORP RES, JFB TEC CTR, GEN MILLS, INC, 76- *Mem:* Am Oil Chemists' Soc. *Res:* Fats and oils, antioxidants; food deterioration; nutrition. *Mailing Add:* Gen Mills Inc JFB Tech Ctr 9000 Plymouth Ave N Minneapolis MN 55427

FRITSCH, CHARLES A(NTHONY), b Maysville, Ky, Mar 9, 36; m 63; c 5. MECHANICAL ENGINEERING. *Educ:* Univ Dayton, BME, 58; Purdue Univ, MS, 60, PhD(mech eng), 62. *Prof Exp:* Mem tech staff, 61-65, SUPVR, BELL LABS, INC, 65- *Mem:* Am Soc Mech Engrs. *Res:* Thermodynamics and heat transfer; computer aided design. *Mailing Add:* Bell Tel Labs Inc Columbus OH 43213

FRITSCH, EDWARD FRANCIS, molecular biology, virology, see previous edition

FRITSCH, EDWARD FRANCIS, b Pittsburgh, Pa, June 1, 50; m 71; c 2. MOLECULAR CLONING, GENE EXPRESSION. *Educ:* Mass Inst Technol, BS, 72; Univ Wis, PhD(molecular biol), 77. *Prof Exp:* Fel, Univ Southern Calif, 77-78; Calif Inst Technol, 78-80; asst prof biochem, Mich State Univ, 80-82; SR SCIENTIST, GENETICS INST, 82- *Concurrent Pos:* Consult, Genetics Inst, 81-82; instr, Cold Springs Harbor Lab, 80-82. *Res:* Molecular biology of gene expression; isolation and charaterization of eularyotic genes. *Mailing Add:* Genetics Inst 225 Longwood Ave Boston MA 02115

FRITSCH, KLAUS, b Mannheim, WGer, Sept 26, 41; m 65; c 2. ELECTRONICS, ACOUSTICS. *Educ:* Georgetown Univ, BS, 61; Mass Inst Technol, MS, 65; Cath Univ Am, PhD(physics), 68. *Prof Exp:* Asst prof, 67-72, assoc prof, 72-77, PROF PHYSICS, JOHN CARROLL UNIV, 77- *Concurrent Pos:* Guest prof, Univ Saarland, WGer, 79-80. *Mem:* Inst Elec & Electronics Engrs. *Res:* Applications of linear and digital integrated circuits; ultrasonics; fiber optics. *Mailing Add:* 2563 Canterbury Rd Cleveland Heights OH 44118

FRITSCHE, HERBERT AHART, JR, b Houston, Tex, Nov 30, 41; m 69; c 2. CLINICAL CHEMISTRY, ANALYTICAL CHEMISTRY. *Educ:* Univ Houston, BS, 63; Tex A&M Univ, MS, 65, PhD(chem), 68. *Prof Exp:* Asst chief chem div, First US Army Med Lab, Ft Meade, Md, 67-69; CHIEF CLIN CHEM, M D ANDERSON HOSP & TUMOR INST, 69- *Concurrent Pos:* Assoc biochemist & assoc prof biochem, Univ Tex Syst Cancer Ctr, M D Anderson Hosp, 69-; fac mem, Grad Sch, Univ Tex, Houston, 73- *Mem:* Am Asn Clin Chemists. *Res:* Electroanalytical techniques; polarography; immunochemistry; biochemical markers of cancer; automation; computers in the clinical laboratory; alkaline and acid phosphatases; serum isoenzymes; immunoglobulins; carcinoembryonic proteins. *Mailing Add:* Dept Lab Med Rm C3013 M D Anderson Hosp Houston TX 77030

FRITSCHE, RICHARD T, b Dallas, Tex, Jan 29, 36; m 59; c 2. MATHEMATICS. *Educ:* St Louis Univ, BS, 57, MS, 59; Univ Ariz, PhD(math), 67. *Prof Exp:* Instr math, Univ Ariz, 60-61; from instr to asst prof, Univ Dallas, 61-68; ASSOC PROF MATH, NORTHEAST LA UNIV, 68- *Mem:* Am Math Soc; Math Asn Am. *Res:* Topological structures for probabilistic metric spaces. *Mailing Add:* Dept of Math Northeast La Univ Monroe LA 71201

FRITSCHEN, LEO J, b Salina, Kans, Sept 14, 30; m 53; c 7. METEOROLOGY. *Educ:* Kans State Col, BS, 52; Kans State Univ, MS, 58; Iowa State Univ, PhD(agr climat), 60. *Prof Exp:* Res meteorologist, US Water Conserv Lab, USDA, 60-66; assoc prof, 66-73, chmn div biol sci, 73-79, PROF FOREST METEOROL, COL FORESTRY, UNIV WASH, 73-, ADJ PROF ATMOSPHERIC SCI, 73- *Mem:* Am Meteorol Soc; Am Soc Agron; Am Soil Sci Soc. *Res:* Agricultural climatology; micrometeorological research and instrumentation. *Mailing Add:* Col Forestry Univ Wash Seattle WA 98105

FRITSCHEN, ROBERT DAVID, b Mitchell, SDak, Nov 27, 35; m 59; c 2. ANIMAL SCIENCE, BIOLOGY. *Educ:* SDak State Univ, BS, 61, MS, 63. *Prof Exp:* County exten agent agr, 63-65, from asst prof to assoc prof, 65-76, PROF ANIMAL SCI, UNIV NEBR, 76- *Honors & Awards:* Sci Extension Award, Am Soc Animals. *Mem:* Am Regist Cert Animal Scientists; Am Soc Animal Sci. *Res:* Design and management of swine facilities to spare energy; study of factors influencing swine behavior; effect of floor materials on foot and leg lesions. *Mailing Add:* Univ Nebr Marvel Baker Hall Rm 251 Lincoln NE 68583

FRITSCHY, J(OHN) MELVIN, b Tucson, Ariz, Aug 23, 21; m 50; c 2. METALLURGICAL ENGINEERING. *Educ:* Univ Ariz, BS, 44. *Prof Exp:* Asst test engr, Phelps Dodge Corp, 44-45, test engr, 45-46; jr chem engr flotation res, 46-51, chem engr, 51-56, plant res & develop, 56-69, PROCESS ENGR, POTASH CO AM, 69- *Mem:* Am Inst Mining, Metall & Petrol Engrs. *Res:* Mineral beneficiation, especially of potash ores by flotation process. *Mailing Add:* 1118 Thomas Carlsbad NM 88220

FRITTON, DANIEL DALE, b Cheyenne Wells, Colo, Oct 1, 42; m 65; c 6. SOIL PHYSICS. *Educ:* Colo State Univ, BS, 64; Iowa State Univ, MS, 66, PhD(soil physics, agr climat), 68. *Prof Exp:* Res assoc soil physics, Iowa State Univ, 66-68; asst prof, Cornell Univ, 68-71; from asst prof to assoc prof, 71-81, PROF SOIL PHYSICS, PA STATE UNIV, 81- *Mem:* Soil Sci Soc Am; Am Geophys Union; Sigma Xi; Am Soc Agron. *Res:* Heat, water and ion movement in soil; measurement and modification of soil physical properties; simulation of root growth and top growth of corn; physical aspects of waste disposal in soil. *Mailing Add:* Dept of Agron Pa State Univ University Park PA 16802

FRITTS, HAROLD CLARK, b Rochester, NY, Dec 17, 28; wid; c 2. PLANT ECOLOGY, DENDROCHRONOLOGY. *Educ:* Oberlin Col, AB, 51; Ohio State Univ, MSc, 53, PhD(bot), 56. *Prof Exp:* Asst prof bot, Eastern Ill Univ, 56-60; from asst prof to assoc prof, 60-69, PROF DENDROCHRONOL, LAB TREE RING RES, UNIV ARIZ, 69- *Concurrent Pos:* Guggenheim fel, 68-69; mem panel climatic variation, US Comt Global Atmospheric Res Prog, Nat Acad Sci, 72-74; organizer & dir, Int Tree-Ring Data Bank, 75-; mem staff, Nat Defense Univ, 78; mem adv comt on paleoclimat, Climate Dynamics Prog, NSF, 78; mem organizing group, Int Conf Dendroclimat, Eng, 78; fac, North Atlantic Treaty Orgn Advan Study Inst, Italy, 80. *Honors & Awards:* Outstanding Bioclimat Achievement Award, Am Meterol Soc, 82. *Mem:* AAAS; Ecol Soc Am; Tree Ring Soc; Am Meterol Soc; Am Quaternary Asn. *Res:* Tree growth and forest tree physiology; climatology; microenvironment. *Mailing Add:* Lab of Tree Ring Res Univ of Ariz Tucson AZ 85721

FRITTS, HARRY WASHINGTON, JR, b Rockwood, Tenn, Oct 4, 21; m 49; c 3. MEDICINE. *Educ:* Mass Inst Technol, BS, 43; Boston Univ, MD, 51; Am Bd Internal Med, dipl. *Prof Exp:* Mem res staff, Mass Inst Technol, 46-47; instr elec eng, Northeastern Univ, 47-51; assoc, Col Physicians & Surgeons, Columbia Univ, 56-57; from asst prof to Dickinson W Richards prof med, 57-73; PROF MED & CHMN DEPT, SCH MED, STATE UNIV NY STONY BROOK, 73- *Concurrent Pos:* Guggenheim fel, 59; vis physician, Bellevue Hosp, New York, 57-68 & Presby Hosp, 61-73; vis physician & consult, Manhattan Vet Admin Hosp, 57-68; mem, Bd Dirs & Adv Coun Res, NY Heart Asn; mem, Physiol Study Sect & Cardiovasc Training Comt, USPHS; assoc ed, J Clin Invest. *Mem:* Fel Am Col Physicians; Am Physiol Soc; Am Soc Clin Invest; Asn Am Physicians; Am Clin & Climat Soc. *Res:* Diseases of the heart and lungs. *Mailing Add:* Dept of Med Sch of Med State Univ of NY Stony Brook NY 11794

FRITTS, ROBERT WASHBURN, b Rochester, NY, Oct 26, 24; m 47; c 3. PHYSICS. *Educ:* Oberlin Col, AB, 47; Northwestern Univ, MS, 48, PhD(physics), 50. *Prof Exp:* Asst dir res, Milwaukee Gas Specialty Co, Wis, 50-57; supvr thermoelectricity mat group, Minn Mining & Mfg Co, 57-59, mgr thermoelectricity proj, 59-66, sr res specialist energy conversion, 66-68; tech develop mgr, Nat Advert Co, 68-75; MGR ARCHIT MURALS & COM DISPLAY PROJ, GRAPHIC TECHNOL SECTOR DIV, 3M CO, 75- *Mem:* Am Phys Soc. *Res:* Semiconductor research on intermetallic compounds; thermoelectric effects and transport phenomena; thermoelectric generator devices and thermoelectric power supply systems; traffic control devices and systems; optical-electronic color imaging systems; uses for large format graphics. *Mailing Add:* 14733 Hudson Blvd Afton MN 55001

FRITTS, STEVEN HUGH, b Fayetteville, Ark, July 14, 48; m 69; c 2. ECOLOGY OF WOLVES. *Educ:* Univ Ark, BA, 70, MS, 72; Univ Minn, PhD(ecol), 79. *Prof Exp:* WILDLIFE RES BIOLOGIST, PATUXENT WILDLIFE RES CTR, US FISH & WILDLIFE SERV, 79- *Mem:* Sigma Xi; Am Soc Mammalogists; Wildlife Soc. *Res:* Distribution and numbers of wolves (Canis lupus) in north-central and northwestern Minnesota; nature and extent of wolf depredations on domestic animals in Minnesota. *Mailing Add:* NCent Exp Sta Univ Minn Grand Rapids MN 55744

FRITZ, CAROL S, b Gaffney, SC, Nov 9, 40; m 61; c 3. MATHEMATICS. *Educ:* Univ SC, BS, 61, PhD(math), 65. *Prof Exp:* Asst prof math, Calif State Col Hayward, 66-68; from asst prof to assoc prof, 68-78, PROF MATH, MUNDELEIN COL, 78-, CHMN DEPT, 72- *Mem:* Math Asn Am; Am Math Soc. *Res:* Investigations of initial and final structures in categories. *Mailing Add:* Dept of Math Mundelein Col 6363 Sheridan Rd Chicago IL 60660

FRITZ, GAROLD FREDERIC, b Toledo, Ohio, Apr 21, 43; m 64; c 2. SOLID STATE PHYSICS. *Educ:* Univ Toledo, BS, 66; Mich State Univ, MS, 68, PhD(physics), 70. *Prof Exp:* RES PHYSICIST, RES LABS, EASTMAN KODAK CO, 70- *Mem:* Am Phys Soc; Soc Photographic Scientists & Engrs. *Res:* Coupling between pressure and temperature waves in liquid helium; photoconductivity and electrophotographic systems. *Mailing Add:* Eastman Kodak Co Res Labs 1669 Lake Ave Rochester NY 14650

FRITZ, GEORGE JOHN, b New York, NY, Feb 19, 27; m 57. PLANT PHYSIOLOGY. *Educ:* Mont State Univ, BS, 49; Univ Calif, MS, 51; Purdue Univ, PhD(bot), 54. *Prof Exp:* Fel plant physiol, Duke Univ, 54-55; asst prof bot, Pa State Univ, 55-60; ASSOC PROF BOT, UNIV FLA, 60- *Concurrent Pos:* AEC res grant, 57, 61-68; Sigma Xi grant, 58; NSF grant, 62; ed-in-chief, What's New in Plant Physiol, 69- *Mem:* AAAS; Am Soc Plant Physiol; Scand Soc Plant Physiol. *Res:* Oxygen fixation by plants. *Mailing Add:* Dept of Agron Univ of Fla Gainesville FL 32611

FRITZ, GEORGE RICHARD, (JR), b Detroit, Mich, Mar 28, 32; m 60; c 3. PHYSIOLOGY, ENDOCRINOLOGY. *Educ:* Mich State Univ, BS, 54, MS, 58; Univ Ill, PhD(dairy sci), 63. *Prof Exp:* Instr, 65-66, res assoc, 66-67, res asst prof physiol & asst dir primate res lab, 67-71, ASSOC DIR PRIMATE RES LAB, SCH MED, UNIV PITTSBURGH, 72- *Concurrent Pos:* NIH fel physiol, Sch Med, Univ Pittsburgh, 62-65. *Mem:* Am Soc Animal Sci; Brit Soc Study Fertil; Am Asn Lab Animal Sci; Soc Study Reprod. *Res:* Physiology of reproduction, especially regulation of gonadal function and control of parturition. *Mailing Add:* Univ of Pittsburgh Primate Res Lab 709 New Texas Rd Pittsburgh PA 15239

FRITZ, GEORGIA T(HOMAS), b Allentown, Pa, Mar 7, 33; m 57; c 3. ANALYTICAL CHEMISTRY. *Educ:* Ursinus Col, BS, 55; Univ NMex, MS, 77. *Prof Exp:* Asst chem, Cornell Univ, 55-61; res asst anal chem, Molecular Biol Group, 62-69, staff mem, 69-70, 72-75, STAFF MEM ANAL CHEM WX-2, LOS ALAMOS NAT LAB, 75- *Mem:* Am Chem Soc; Am Soc Testing & Mat; AAAS. *Res:* General analytical chemistry; chromatographic and thermal analysis of organic high explosives; thermal analysis of oil shales. *Mailing Add:* Los Alamos Nat Lab PO Box 1663 WX-2 MS 920 Los Alamos NM 87545

FRITZ, GILBERT GEIGER, b Washington, DC, Apr 16, 42; m 71. X-RAY ASTRONOMY, X-RAY INSTRUMENTATION. *Educ:* Johns Hopkins Univ, BA, 64, MA, 65. *Prof Exp:* Physicist, 65-72, SUPVRY ASTROPHYSICIST, US NAVAL RES LAB, 72- *Mem:* AAAS; Sigma Xi. *Res:* X-ray pulsars; soft x-ray background; supernova remnants; x-ray binaries; spectroscopy of x-ray sources; proportional detectors; scintillators; x-ray collimators. *Mailing Add:* Code 4129 US Naval Res Lab Washington DC 20375

FRITZ, HERBERT IRA, b New York, NY, May 31, 35; m 62; c 2. NUTRITION, BIOCHEMISTRY. *Educ:* Univ Calif, Davis, AB, 58, PhD(nutrit), 64. *Prof Exp:* Res asst nutrit, Univ Calif, Davis, 58-64; NIH fel, Univ Pa, 64-66; from asst prof to assoc prof biol sci, 66-74, ASSOC PROF BIOL CHEM, SCH MED, WRIGHT STATE UNIV, 74- *Mem:* AAAS; Teratol Soc; Am Soc Cell Biol; Soc Study Reprod. *Res:* Embryo nutrition; effect of vitamins on development; reproduction of American marsupials; comparative and experimental teratology; fetal alcohol syndrome and hyperactivity. *Mailing Add:* Dept Biol Chem Colonel Glenn Hwy Wright State Univ Dayton OH 45435

FRITZ, IRVING BAMDAS, b Rocky Mount, NC, Feb 11, 27; m 50, 72; c 4. REPRODUCTIVE BIOLOGY, BIOCHEMISTRY. *Educ:* Med Col Va, DDS, 48; Univ Chicago, PhD(physiol), 51. *Prof Exp:* Asst dir dept metab & endocrine res, Med Res Inst, Michael Reese Hosp, 55-56; from asst prof to prof physiol, Univ Mich, Ann Arbor, 56-68; chmn dept, 68-78, PROF MED RES, BANTING & BEST DEPT MED RES, BEST INST, UNIV TORONTO, 68- *Concurrent Pos:* USPHS fel, Inst Med Physiol, Copenhagen, 53-55; Guggenheim fel, 78-79. *Honors & Awards:* Gairdner Award, 80. *Mem:* Am Physiol Soc; Am Biochem Soc; Am Soc Cell Biologists; Endocrine Soc; Soc Study Reprod. *Res:* Spermatogenesis; developmental biology. *Mailing Add:* Banting & Best Dept of Med Univ of Toronto Best Inst Toronto ON M5G 1L6 Can

FRITZ, JAMES CLARENCE, b Berlin, Pa, May 15, 10; m 33; c 2. NUTRITIONAL BIOCHEMISTRY. *Educ:* Pa State Col, BS, 29. *Prof Exp:* Asst, Univ NH, 29-30; jr biologist, Bur Animal Indust, USDA, 30-37, asst biochemist, 37; lab dir, Borden Co, 37-51; dir nutrit res, Dawe's Labs, Inc, 52-65; supvry res chemist, Food & Drug Admin, HEW, 65-78; RETIRED. *Mem:* AAAS; Am Chem Soc; Poultry Sci Asn; Am Dairy Sci Asn; Animal Nutrit Res Coun (chmn, 52, secy-treas, 64-). *Res:* Nitrogen metabolism; physiology of digestion; nutritional requirements; protein quality; vitamin stability; pigmentation of poultry and eggs; nutrient availability; influence of stress on nutritional requirements. *Mailing Add:* 12314 Madeley Lane Bowie MD 20715

FRITZ, JAMES JOHN, b Sunbury, Pa, Sept 21, 20; m 43; c 4. PHYSICAL CHEMISTRY. *Educ:* Pa State Univ, BS, 39; Univ Chicago, MS, 40; Univ Calif, PhD(chem), 48. *Prof Exp:* Asst chem, Univ Calif, 43-48; res assoc phys chem, Ohio State Univ, 48-49; from asst prof to assoc prof, 49-62, PROF CHEM, PA STATE UNIV, 62- *Concurrent Pos:* Guggenheim fel, Oxford Univ, 61-62. *Mem:* Am Chem Soc. *Res:* Low temperature phenomena; solutions of electrolytes. *Mailing Add:* Dept of Chem 218 Pond Lab Pa State Univ University Park PA 16802

FRITZ, JAMES SHERWOOD, b Decatur, Ill, July 20, 24; m 49; c 4. ANALYTICAL CHEMISTRY. *Educ:* James Millikin Univ, BS, 46; Univ Ill, MS, 46, PhD(chem), 48. *Prof Exp:* Asst prof chem, Wayne State Univ, 48-51; from asst prof to assoc prof, 51-60, PROF CHEM, IOWA STATE UNIV, 60- *Honors & Awards:* Chromatography Award, Am Chem Soc, 76. *Mem:* Am Chem Soc. *Res:* Gas, liquid and ion-exchange chromatography; analysis of water for trace organic and inorganic impurities; titrations in nonaqueous solvents. *Mailing Add:* Dept of Chem Iowa State Univ Ames IA 50010

FRITZ, JOSEPH N, solid state physics, see previous edition

FRITZ, K(ENNETH) E(ARL), b Monroeville, Ohio, Oct 17, 18; m 40; c 2. MATERIALS ENGINEERING. *Educ:* Ohio State Univ, BS, 42; Univ Wis, MS, 51. *Prof Exp:* Metall engr, Naval Res Lab, 42-45 & Bucyrus-Erie Co, 45-55; metall engr locomotive & car equip dept, 55-56, mat & process lab, 56-59 & gas turbine dept, 69-73, MGR STRUCT MAT APPLICATIONS, GAS TURBINE DIV, GEN ELEC CO, 73- *Mem:* Am Soc Metals. *Res:* Ultra high strength materials; statistical evaluation of data; precipitation hardening process; high temperature properties of materials. *Mailing Add:* Gas Turbine Div Bldg 53-317 Gen Elec Co One River Rd Schenectady NY 12345

FRITZ, KATHERINE ELIZABETH, b Omaha, Nebr, June 24, 18; m 40; c 2. PATHOLOGY, IMMUNOLOGY. *Educ:* Univ Omaha, BA, 39; Albany Med Col, MS, 61, PhD(path), 66. *Prof Exp:* Res assoc, 61-63, from instr to asst prof, 66-74, assoc prof path, 74-81, RES PROF PATH, ALBANY MED COL, 81- *Concurrent Pos:* Res biologist, Vet Admin Hosp, Albany, NY, 66-; fel, Coun Arteriosclerosis, Am Heart Asn, 71. *Mem:* Am Soc Cell Biol; Electron Micros Soc Am; Am Soc Exp Path. *Res:* Mechanisms influencing the regression of atherosclerotic lesions with emphasis on changes in hydrolytic enzymatic activities and/or phagocytic activities of lesion cells as studied biochemically and histochemically. *Mailing Add:* RD 1 Box 414A Pattersonville NY 12137

FRITZ, LAWRENCE WILLIAM, b Oceanside, NY, Sept 1, 37; m 59; c 3. PHOTOGRAMMETRY, GEODESY. *Educ:* Lafayette Col, AB, 59; Ohio State Univ, MS, 67. *Prof Exp:* Cartogr, US Coast & Geod Surv, 61-67; res phys scientist photogram, Nat Oceanic & Atmospheric Admin, 67-80; SR POLICY ANAL SPACE POLICY, OFF SCI & TECHNOL POLICY, EXEC OFF PRESIDENT, 80- *Concurrent Pos:* Eng reports ed, Photogram Eng & Remote Sensing, 69-73; vis lectr, Va Polytech Inst & State Univ, 81- *Mem:* Am Soc Photogram; AAAS; Int Soc Photogram & Remote Sensing. *Res:* Photogrammetric system for the densification of geodetic networks; precision calibration techniques for mapping cameras and photogrammetric comparators used in the sciences of geodesy and cartography; author or coauthor of more than 30 technical publications. *Mailing Add:* 14833 Lake Terr Rockville MD 20853

FRITZ, MADELEINE ALBERTA, b Saint John, NB. PALEONTOLOGY. *Educ:* McGill Univ, BA, 19; Univ Toronto, PhD(stratig paleont), 26. *Prof Exp:* Asst, 24-35, lectr, 35-37, from asst prof to prof, 37-65, SPEC LECTR & EMER PROF PALEONT, UNIV TORONTO, 65- *Concurrent Pos:* Mus asst, Royal Ont Mus, 27-36, actg dir, 36-37, asst dir invert paleont, 37-43, assoc dir, 45-55, cur, 55-57, res assoc, Dept Invert Paleont, 70- *Mem:* Paleont Soc; Geol Soc Am; Geol Asn Can; fel Royal Soc Can. *Res:* Invertebrate paleontology. *Mailing Add:* Royal Ont Mus 100 Queens Park Toronto ON M4S 2C6 Can

FRITZ, MARC ANTHONY, b Detroit, Mich, Aug 8, 51; m 73. OBSTETRICS & GYNECOLOGY. *Educ:* US Air Force Acad, BS, 73; Tulane Univ Sch, MD, 77. *Prof Exp:* Residency obstet & gynec, Sch Med, Wright State Univ, 77-81; INSTR OBSTET & GYNEC, ORE HEALTH SCI UNIV & FEL, ORE REGIONAL PRIMATE RES CTR, 81- *Mem:* Jr fel Am Col Obstet & Gynec; Am Fertil Soc. *Res:* Investigation of the endocrine vascular relationships of the fetoplacental unit. *Mailing Add:* Ore Regional Primate Res Ctr 505 NW 185th Ave Beaverton OR 97006

FRITZ, MICHAEL E, b Boston, Mass, Feb 26, 38; m 60; c 3. PERIODONTOLOGY, CELL PHYSIOLOGY. *Educ:* Univ Pa, DDS, 63, cert periodont & MS, 65, PhD(physiol), 67. *Prof Exp:* Instr periodont, Sch Dent, Univ Pa, 63-67; assoc prof, 67-73, PROF PERIODONT, SCH DENT, EMORY UNIV, 73-, CHMN DEPT, 67-, CHARLES HOWARD CANDLER PROF, 80. *Concurrent Pos:* Fel physiol, Sch Med, Univ Pa, 63-67; Nat Inst Dent Res grant, 68-; consult, US Vet Admin Hosp, Atlanta, Ga, 67-78 & Ft Benning, Ga, 70-78; Fogarty Int fel, 73-74. *Mem:* AAAS; Int Asn Dent Res; Am Dent Asn; Am Acad Periodont; Fedn Am Socs Exp Biol. *Res:* Physiology of salivary glands; bone pathology; virus infection of cells; clinical dentistry. *Mailing Add:* Dept of Periodont Emory Univ Sch of Dent Atlanta GA 30322

FRITZ, PAUL JOHN, b Belleville, Ill, May 17, 29; m 56; c 4. BIOCHEMISTRY. *Educ:* Washington Univ, AB, 51; Auburn Univ, PhD(biochem), 62. *Prof Exp:* Instr chem, Auburn Univ, 60-62, from asst prof to assoc prof pharmacol, 64-66; asst prof biochem & sr investr, Molecular Biol Lab, Med Ctr, Univ Ala, Birmingham, 6669; ASSOC PROF PHARMACOL, MILTON S HERSHEY MED CTR, PA STATE UNIV, 69- *Concurrent Pos:* USPHS fel biochem, Biol Div, Oak Ridge Nat Lab, 62-64; vis prof pharmacol, Samford Univ, 68-69. *Mem:* AAAS; Am Chem Soc; Am Soc Pharmacol & Exp Therapeut; Am Soc Biol Chemists; Sigma Xi. *Res:* Enzymatic control of metabolism; mechanisms of enzyme action; physical and chemical properties of enzymes; factors controlling synthesis and degradation of enzymes. *Mailing Add:* Dept of Pharmacol Pa State Univ Hershey Med Ctr Hershey PA 17033

FRITZ, PETER, b Stuttgart, Ger, Mar 18, 37; m 66; c 2. GEOLOGY, GEOCHEMISTRY. *Educ:* Univ Stuttgart, dipl, 62, Dr rer nat, 65. *Prof Exp:* NATO res fel, Univ Paris, 65-66; fel, Univ Alta, 66-68, res assoc isotope geol, 68-71; PROF GEOCHEM, UNIV WATERLOO, 71-, CHMN DEPT EARTH SCI, 80- *Mem:* Geochem Soc; Geol Asn Can; Int Asn Geochem & Cosmochem. *Res:* Geochemistry of stable isotopes in groundwater, tritium and carbon-14 dating; quarternary paleoenvironments, marine carbonates and hydrothermal ore deposits; geochemistry in nuclear waste disposal studies. *Mailing Add:* Dept of Earth Sci Univ of Waterloo Waterloo Can

FRITZ, RICHARD BLAIR, b Washington, DC, Jan 23, 36; m 70; c 2. ATMOSPHERIC PHYSICS, IONOSPHERIC PHYSICS. *Educ:* Knox Col, AB, 58; Cornell Univ, MS, 61. *Prof Exp:* Physicist, Gen Elec Res Labs, NY, 58; res asst physics & astron, Cornell Univ, 58-61; PHYSICIST, BOULDER LABS, US DEPT COM, 64- *Concurrent Pos:* Mem US nat comn F & G, Int Union Radio Sci, 74- *Mem:* Am Geophys Union; Air Pollution Control Asn; AAAS. *Res:* Application of optical propagation techniques for remote sensing of atmospheric conditions such as wind and rain; ionospheric monitoring by satellite radio beacon techniques; air pollution meteorology. *Mailing Add:* Wave Propagation Lab NOAA-ERL Dept Com Boulder CO 80303

FRITZ, ROBERT BARTLETT, b Milwaukee, Wis, Nov 16, 37; m 64; c 2. AUTOIMMUNITY, CELLULAR IMMUNOLOGY. *Educ:* Bowdoin Col, AB, 59; Univ Maine, MS, 64; Duke Univ, PhD(microbiol), 67. *Prof Exp:* Res assoc surg, Med Ctr, Duke Univ, 67-69; asst prof, 69-75, ASSOC PROF MICROBIOL, SCH MED, EMORY UNIV, 75- *Concurrent Pos:* Guest investr, Neuroimmunol Br, Nat Inst Neurol & Commun Dis & Stroke, NIH, 80-81. *Mem:* Am Asn Immunologists. *Res:* Characterization of the immune response to neuroantigens responsible for induction of experimental autoimmune disease of the central nervous system. *Mailing Add:* Dept Microbiol & Immunol Sch Med Emory Univ Atlanta GA 30322

FRITZ, ROBERT J(ACOB), b New Orleans, La, June 5, 23; m 47; c 4. MECHANICAL & NUCLEAR ENGINEERING. *Educ:* Tulane Univ, La, BEE, 44; Union Univ, NY, MS, 50, MEE, 52; Rensselaer Polytech Inst, DEng(mech eng), 70. *Prof Exp:* With test prog, 46-47, heat transfer engr, 47-52, mech analyst, 52-53, supvr mech anal, 53-55, sr specialist, 55, supvr eng eval, 55-57, consult eng heat transfer & mech, 57-61, supvr & mgr, reactor core heat transfer sect, 61-63, consult engr, rotating equip & mech, 63-66, CONSULT ENGR STRUCT MECH & DYNAMICS, KNOLLS ATOMIC POWER LAB, GEN ELEC CO, 66- *Mem:* Am Soc Mech Engrs. *Res:* Flow vibrations and mechanics of nuclear reactors and power systems. *Mailing Add:* 2511 Whamer Lane Schenectady NY 12309

FRITZ, RODGER LEE, software & systems engineering, see previous edition

FRITZ, ROY FREDOLIN, b Oakland, Calif, Nov 15, 15; m 39; c 2. ENTOMOLOGY, EPIDEMIOLOGY. *Educ:* Kans State Col, BS, 37, MS, 39; Univ Calif, MPH, 48. *Prof Exp:* Asst entomologist, Agr Exp Sta, Kans State Col, 39-42; asst entomologist, Malaria Control in War Areas, USPHS, 42-43, dist entomologist, 43-44, asst chief entom div, 44-46, typhus control entomologist, 46-47, resident, Univ Calif, 47-49, resident rep commun dis ctr, Region X, 50, chief mosquito control & invest, Eng Br, 51-52, chief vector-borne dis unit, Epidemiol Br, 52-55, actg chief, Surveillance Sect, Ga, 54-55; malariologist adv, Int Coop Admin, Mex Govt, 55-57; malariologist & chief, Malaria Eradication Br, US AID, 58-63; secy, Report Expert Comt Malaria, 62, scientist, Prog & Planning, Malaria Eradication Div, 63-66, scientist, Anopheline Res, Vector Biol & Control, 66-72, MEM EXPERT PANEL MALARIA, WHO, 60- *Concurrent Pos:* Consult, US AID, 74-75. *Mem:* Sigma Xi; Am Soc Prof Biologists (pres, 48); Entom Soc Am; Am Mosquito Control Asn; fel Am Pub Health Asn. *Res:* Medical entomology; epidemiology of vector-borne diseases; ecology; biological control; environmental entomology. *Mailing Add:* 11112 Nocturne Ct Sun City AZ 85351

FRITZ, SIGMUND, b Brooklyn, NY, June 9, 14; m 46; c 2. METEOROLOGY. *Educ:* Brooklyn Col, BS, 34; Mass Inst Technol, MS, 41, ScD, 53. *Prof Exp:* Observer, US Weather Bur, 37-42, meteorologist, Washington, DC, 46-67; meteorologist, Nat Environ Satellite Serv, Nat Oceanic & Atmospheric Admin, 67-75; PROF METEOROL, UNIV MD, 75- *Mem:* Fel Am Meterol Soc; fel Am Geophys Union. *Res:* Solar radiaiton; albedo of ground; albedo and absorption; atmospheric ozone measurements; meteorological satellites; climate. *Mailing Add:* Dept Meterol Space Sci Bldg Univ Md College Park MD 20742

FRITZ, THOMAS EDWARD, b Detroit, Mich, May 24, 33; m 66. PATHOLOGY, RADIOBIOLOGY. *Educ:* Mich State Univ, BS, 55, DVM, 57; Univ Ill, MS, 60. *Prof Exp:* Instr path, Col Vet Med, Univ Ill, 57-62; supvr, Diag Res Lab, Ill State Dept Agr & Univ Ill, 62-63; assoc pathologist, 63-72, asst div dir animal facil, 76-78, PATHOLOGIST, DIV BIOL & MED RES, ARGONNE NAT LAB, 72-, GROUP LEADER RADIATION TOXICITY, 77-, ASSOC DIV DIR, DIV BIOL & MED RES, 79- *Concurrent Pos:* Clin assoc prof path, Loyola Univ, 75-; assoc prof biol,

Northern Ill Univ, 78- *Mem:* AAAS; Am Vet Med Asn; Int Soc Exp Hemat; Am Asn Lab Animal Sci; Radiation Res Soc. *Res:* Comparative pathology of diseases of domestic and laboratory animals; pathology of radiation and isotope toxicity; experimental hematology and leukemogenesis. *Mailing Add:* Div of Biol & Med Res Bldg D-202 Argonne Nat Lab Argonne IL 60439

FRITZ, WILLIAM HAROLD, b Cathlamet, Wash, Aug 24, 28; m 58; c 1. PALEONTOLOGY. *Educ:* Univ Wash, BS, 52, MS, 58, PhD(geol), 60. *Prof Exp:* NSF fel, 60-61; explor geologist, Shell Oil Co, 61-64; CAMBRIAN PALEONTOLOGIST, GEOL SURV CAN, 64- *Concurrent Pos:* Res scientist, NSF, 61- *Mem:* Am Paleont Soc; Brit Paleont Asn. *Res:* Structure and stratigraphy; Cambrian paleontology. *Mailing Add:* Geol Surv of Can 601 Booth St Ottawa Can

FRITZ, WILLIAM J, b Vancouver, Wash, Mar 31, 53; m 73; c 1. VOLCANICLASTIC SEDIMENTATION, PALEOECOLOGY. *Educ:* Walla Walla Col, BS, 75, MS, 77; Univ Mont, PhD(geol), 80. *Prof Exp:* Grad teaching asst paleont & biol labs, Walla Walla Col, 75-77; head grad teaching asst geol labs, Univ Mont, 77-80; petrol geologist oil & gas explor, Amoco Prod Co/Standard Oil, 80-81; ASST PROF GEOL, GA STATE UNIV, 81- *Concurrent Pos:* Petrol consult, Davis Oil Co, 81- *Mem:* Geol Soc Am; Am Asn Petrol Geologists; Soc Econ Paleontologists & Mineralogists; Sigma Xi; Paleont Soc. *Res:* Tertiary sedimentology, paleoecology, and recent depositional environments including the Eocene Yellowstone fossil forest covering both the paleobotany and sedimentology, and the sedimentology of Mt St Helens mud flows; petroleum potential of various tertiary formations in Oregon and Washington. *Mailing Add:* Dept Geol Ga State Univ Atlanta GA 30303

FRITZE, CURTIS W(ILLIAM), b LeSueur, Minn, June 2, 23; m 48; c 3. ELECTRONICS & ELECTRICAL ENGINEERING. *Educ:* Univ Minn, BSEE, 47. *Prof Exp:* Res & design engr, Minn Electronics Corp, 47-50; sr engr, Eng Res Assoc, Inc, 50-54; eng dept mgr, Remington Rand Univac, 54-57; dir spec prod eng, 57-59; vpres & gen mgr, Monarch Electronics Co, 59-60; systs specialist, corp staff mkt, Control Data Corp, 60-62, asst to vpres indust group, 62-65, dir planning, indust & govt group, 65-66, dir corp planning, 66-68, vpres, 68-74, vpres space comput systs, 74-76; V PRES OPERS & ADMIN, CONTROL DATA WORLDTECH, 76- *Concurrent Pos:* Consult, Lab Psychol Hyg, 47-57; mem bd dir, Presby Homes of Minn, & Am Nat Standards Inst, 69-73; mem bd trustees, Sci Mus Minn, 68- *Res:* Technological and corporate planning systems. *Mailing Add:* Control Data Worldtech Box O Minneapolis MN 55440

FRITZE, KLAUS, analytical chemistry, deceased

FRITZELL, ERIK KENNETH, b Grand Forks, NDak, Oct 30, 46; m 73. WILDLIFE BIOLOGY, ECOLOGY. *Educ:* Univ NDak, BS, 68; Southern Ill Univ, MS, 72; Univ Minn, PhD(wildlife), 76. *Prof Exp:* Res assoc ecol, Delta Waterfowl Res Sta, 68-72 & Northern Prairie Wildlife Res Ctr, US Fish & Wildlife, 72-76; lectr wildlife resource, McGill Univ, 76-77; ASST PROF FISHERIES & WILDLIFE, UNIV MO, COLUMBIA, 78- *Mem:* Wildlife Soc; Am Soc Mammalogists. *Res:* Mammalian and avian ecology; sociobiology of carnivores; predator-prey relationships. *Mailing Add:* Dept of Forestry Univ of Mo Columbia MO 65211

FRITZSCHE, ALFRED KEITH, b Hamilton, Ohio, Jan 3, 43. MEMBRANE TRANSPORT. *Educ:* Miami Univ, Ohio, BS, 64; Case Inst Tech, MS, 67; Univ Mass, PhD(polymer sci), 72. *Prof Exp:* Latin Am teaching fel, Univ Simon Bolivar, Venezuela, 72-73; sr res chemist, 74-79, RES SPECIALIST, MONSANTO CO, 79- *Mem:* Am Chem Soc. *Res:* Polymer crstallization kinetics; membrane transport; epoxy sealant technology. *Mailing Add:* 310 Beech St Cary NC 27511

FRITZSCHE, HELLMUT, b Berlin, Ger, Feb 20, 27; US citizen; m 52; c 4. SOLID STATE PHYSICS. *Educ:* Univ Gottingen, dipl, 52; Purdue Univ, PhD(physics), 54. *Prof Exp:* Asst prof physics, Purdue Univ, 55-57; from asst prof to assoc prof, 57-63, dir, Mat Res Lab, 73-77, PROF PHYSICS, UNIV CHICAGO, 63-, CHMN DEPT, 77- *Concurrent Pos:* Mem solid state sci panel, Nat Res Coun-Nat Acad Sci, 74-; vpres & dir, Energy Conversion Devices Inc, 67-; mem adv bd, Encycl Britannica, 67- *Mem:* Fel NY Acad Sci; Fel Am Phys Soc; Am Arbitration Asn. *Res:* Electronic and optical properties of amorphous and crystalline semiconductors and metals; low temperature physics. *Mailing Add:* James Frank Inst Univ of Chicago 5640 Ellis Ave Chicago IL 60637

FRITZSCHE, RONALD ALAN, ichthyology, marine biology, see previous edition

FRIZ, CARL T, b Elmhurst, Ill, July 9, 27; m 63. ANATOMY, BIOCHEMISTRY. *Educ:* Univ Ill, BS, 51, MS, 52; Univ Minn, PhD(anat), 59. *Prof Exp:* USPHS fel biol, Carlsberg Lab, Copenhagen, 59-62; instr anat, Univ Minn, 62-64; asst prof, 64-71, assoc prof, 71-76, PROF ANAT, UNIV BC, 76- *Mem:* Soc Protozool; Am Asn Anat. *Res:* Serological taxonomy and studies of DNA and biochemical analysis of the large, free-living amoebae. *Mailing Add:* Dept of Anat Univ of BC Vancouver BC V6T 1W5 Can

FRIZZELL, LEON ALBERT, b West Stewartstown, NH, Sept 12, 47; m 68; c 1. ELECTRICAL ENGINEERING, BIOENGINEERING. *Educ:* Univ NH, BS, 69; Univ Rochester, MS, 71, PhD(elec eng), 76. *Prof Exp:* Vis asst prof, 75-78, ASST PROF ELEC ENG & BIOENG, UNIV ILL, URBANA, 78- *Mem:* AAAS; Inst Elec & Electronics Engrs; Acoust Soc Am; Am Inst Ultrasound Med. *Res:* Ultrasonic biophysics, bioengineering and dosimetry. *Mailing Add:* Bioacoust Res Lab Univ Ill 1406 W Green St Urbana IL 61801

FROBISH, LOWELL T, b Flanagan, Ill, Aug 3, 40; m 60; c 2. ANIMAL NUTRITION, BIOCHEMISTRY. *Educ:* Univ Ill, Urbana, BS, 62; Iowa State Univ, MS, 64, PhD(animal nutrit), 67. *Prof Exp:* Assoc, Iowa State Univ, 66-67; res animal husbandman, Swine Res Br, Animal Sci Res Div, Agr Res

Serv, USDA, 67-72, chief, Non-Ruminant Animal Nutrit Lab, Animal Sci Inst, 72-81; HEAD, DEPT ANIMAL SCI, CLEMSON UNIV, 81- *Mem:* Am Soc Animal Sci. *Res:* Utilization of energy by gravid animals and the neonatal pig. *Mailing Add:* 120 Ashley Rd Clemson SC 29631

FRODEY, RAY CHARLES, b Pittsburgh, Pa, Sept 6, 23; m 44; c 3. FOOD SCIENCE. *Educ:* Mass Inst Technol, BS & MS, 49. *Prof Exp:* Chemist, 49-51, sr researcher, 51-56, dir new prod, 56-64, VPRES RES & QUAL CONTROL, GERBER PROD CO, 64- *Mem:* Inst Food Technologists; Sigma Xi; AAAS. *Res:* All aspects of food research and engineering including food biochemistry and nutrition, microbiology, packaging, product development and process engineering. *Mailing Add:* 4345 Chippewa Tr Fremont MI 49412

FRODYMA, MICHAEL MITCHELL, b Holyoke, Mass, Mar 3, 20; m 51; c 1. ANALYTICAL CHEMISTRY. *Educ:* Univ Mass, BS, 42; Columbia Univ, AM, 47; Univ Hawaii, MS, 49; George Washington Univ, PhD(chem), 52. *Prof Exp:* Asst chem, Univ Hawaii, 47-49, from asst prof to prof, 52-67; PROG DIR, FAC ORIENTED PROG, DIV SCI PERSONNEL IMPROV, SCI FOUND, 65-66 & 67- *Concurrent Pos:* Exchange asst prof, Vassar Col, 57-58, lectr, 58; fac fel, NSF, 58-61. *Mem:* AAAS; Am Inst Chemists; Am Chem Soc; Royal Soc Chem. *Res:* Microchemistry; oceanographic chemistry; organic polarography; analytical aspects of spectral reflectance. *Mailing Add:* Div Sci Personnel Improv Nat Sci Found Washington DC 20550

FROEDE, HARRY CURT, b Cortez, Colo, Sept 9, 34; m 64; c 3. PHARMACOLOGY, BIOCHEMISTRY. *Educ:* Univ Colo, BS, 58, MS, 61; Washington Univ, PhD(pharmacol), 65. *Prof Exp:* Asst prof pharmacol & toxicol, Sch pharm, 70-77, RES ASSOC, DEPT CHEM, UNIV COLO, BOULDER, 77- RES ASSOC, UNIV COLO, 68- *Concurrent Pos:* Fel pharmacol, Washington Univ, 65-66 & Sch Med, Stanford Univ, 66-69. *Res:* Enzyme mechanisms and control of enzyme activity. *Mailing Add:* Dept of Chem Univ of Colo Boulder CO 80309

FROEHLICH, FRITZ EDGAR, b Ger, Nov 12, 25; nat US; m 49; c 3. PHYSICS. *Educ:* Syracuse Univ, BS, 50, MS, 52, PhD(physics), 55. *Prof Exp:* Asst physics, Syracuse Univ, 50-53, asst instr, 53-54; mem tech staff, Bell Tel Labs, 54-56, supvr commun tech, 56-63, head wideband data & spec systs dept, 63-66, data systs dept, 66-67 & tel technol dept, 67-75, head new sta serv dept, 75-78, head, Bus Terminal Dept, 78-81, HEAD, ADV TERMINAL SYSTS DEPT, BELL LABS, 81- *Concurrent Pos:* Instr, Utica Col, 52-54. *Mem:* AAAS; fel Inst Elec & Electronics Eng; NY Acad Sci; Sigma Xi. *Res:* Techniques of digital and voice communication. *Mailing Add:* Bell Labs Holmdel NJ 07733

FROEHLICH, JEFFREY PAUL, b Milwaukee, Wis, Mar 31, 43; m 65; c 1. BIOPHYSICS. *Educ:* Univ Wis-Madison, BS, 65; Univ Chicago, MD, 69. *Prof Exp:* Fel cancer res, Ben May Lab Cancer Res, Univ Chicago, 65-68, fel biophys, 70-72; USPHS OFFICER, NAT INST AGING, NIH, 72- *Mem:* Am Soc Biol Chemists; Biophys Soc. *Res:* Transient state kinetic properties of enzymes associated with cell membrane cation pumps. *Mailing Add:* Nat Inst Aging Baltimore City Hosps Baltimore MD 21224

FROELICH, ALBERT JOSEPH, b Cleveland, Ohio, Aug 2, 29; m 58; c 2. GEOLOGY. *Educ:* Ohio State Univ, BS, 52, MS, 53. *Prof Exp:* Geologist, US Geol Surv, 53-54; geologist-party chief, San Jose Oil Co, Inc, 56-60; sr geologist, United Canso Oil & Gas, Inc, 60-65; chief geologist, Magellan Petrol Corp, 65-67, geol consult, 67-68; geologist, Ky, 68-71; geologist, Baltimore-Washington Urban Area Proj, Washington, DC, 71-74; chief, Fairfax County Environ Geol Proj, 74-79, CHIEF, CULPEPER BASIN ENVIRON GEOL & HYDROL PROJ, US GEOL SURV, 79- *Mem:* Am Asn Petrol Geol; Geol Soc Am; Am Geophys Union. *Res:* Geology, particularly international petroleum exploration in Philippines, western and northern Canada and Australia; environmental, geophysical and geohydrological studies. *Mailing Add:* STOP 926 Nat Ctr US Geol Surv Reston VA 22092

FROELICH, ERNEST, b Vienna, Austria, Dec 7, 12; nat US; m 47; c 1. MICROBIOLOGY, CHEMOTHERAPY. *Educ:* Univ Zagreb, DVM, 37. *Prof Exp:* Vet asst, Vet Inst, Belgrade, 38-39; head vet, Vet Serum Labs, Zemun, 39-40; head vet, Biol Control Labs, 40-41; UNRRA fel, 46-47; res assoc microbiol & chemother, 48-50, head, Chemother Lab, 50-62, dir res & tech serv, Vet Dept, 62-78, CONSULT, STERLING-WINTHROP RES INST, 78- *Mem:* Am Soc Microbiologists; Am Vet Med Asn; NY Acad Sci. *Res:* Chemotherapy of bacterial, viral and rickettsial diseases; immunological studies of diseases of domestic animals. *Mailing Add:* 174 Tampa Ave Albany NY 12208

FROELICH, PHILIP NISSEN, b Winston-Salem, NC, Apr 12, 46; m 71; c 1. MARINE GEOCHEMISTRY, CHEMICAL OCEANOGRAPHY. *Educ:* Duke Univ, BS, 70; Univ PR, MS, 73; Univ RI, PhD(oceanog), 79. *Prof Exp:* ASST PROF OCEANOG, FLA STATE UNIV, 79- *Mem:* AAAS; Am Geophys Union; Am Soc Limnol & Oceanog; Asn Island Marine Labs Caribbean; Geochem Soc. *Res:* Marine nutrient geochemistry (phosphorus, nitrogen, carbon, silicon); estuarine biogeochemistry; marine geochemistry of intersitial fluids (nutrients, gases and trace metals); germanium geochemistry and paleoceanography. *Mailing Add:* Dept of Oceanog Fla State Univ Tallahassee FL 32306

FROELICH, ROBERT EARL, b St Louis, Mo, July 24, 29; m 54; c 2. PSYCHIATRY. *Educ:* Wash Univ, AB, 51, MD, 55. *Prof Exp:* Resident, Med Col Ga, 58-61; asst prof psychiat, Univ Mo, 61-67; asst prof, Univ Southern Calif, 67-68; assoc prof, Univ Mo, 68-69; from assoc prof to prof psychiat & behav sci, Univ Okla, 69-74; asst dean, 74-76, PROF PSYCHIAT & CHMN DEPT, SCH PRIMARY MED CARE, UNIV ALA, HUNTSVILLE, 74- *Mem:* Health Sci Commun Asn; AMA; Am Psychiat Asn; Asn Educ Commun & Technol. *Res:* Education methods and self instructional packages. *Mailing Add:* Dept of Psychiat Univ of Ala Huntsville AL 35807

FROEMKE, JON, b Sioux Falls, SDak, June 23, 41; m 63; c 1. MATHEMATICS. *Educ:* Univ Nebr, Lincoln, BA, 62, MA, 63; Univ Calif, Berkeley, PhD(math), 67. *Prof Exp:* Asst prof, 67-71, ASSOC PROF MATH, OAKLAND UNIV, 71- *Mem:* AAAS; Am Math Soc; Math Asn Am. *Res:* General algebraic systems. *Mailing Add:* Dept of Math Sci Oakland Univ Rochester MI 48063

FROEMSDORF, DONALD HOPE, b Cape Girardeau, Mo, Mar 4, 34; m 54. ORGANIC CHEMISTRY. *Educ:* Southeast Mo State Univ, BS, 55; Iowa State Univ, PhD(org chem), 59. *Prof Exp:* Asst proj chemist, Res & Develop Dept, Standard Oil Co of Ind, 59-60; assoc prof to prof chem, 66-70, chmn div sci & math, 70-75, DEAN, COL SCI, SOUTHEAST MO STATE COL, 75- *Mem:* AAAS; Am Chem Soc; The Chem Soc. *Res:* Physical organic chemistry; organic reaction mechanisms, especially alpha and beta elimination reactions; structure and properties of high polymers. *Mailing Add:* Col of Sci Southeast Mo State Col Cape Girardeau MO 63701

FROESE, ARNOLD, b Halbstadt, Ukraine, Mar 18, 34; Can citizen; m 69; c 2. IMMUNOCHEMISTRY. *Educ:* Univ Western Ont, BS, 57; McGill Univ, PhD(chem), 63. *Prof Exp:* Lectr, McGill Univ, 63-64; res assoc immunochem, Max Planck Inst Phys Chem, 64-67 & McGill Univ, 67-69; assoc prof, 69-80, PROF IMMUNOL, UNIV MAN, 80- *Concurrent Pos:* Med Res Coun Can & res grant, 68- *Mem:* Chem Inst Can; Can Biochem Soc; Can Soc Immunol, (secty-treas, 77-); Am Asn Immunologists. *Res:* Kinetics of antibody-hapten reactions; structure and function of immunoglobulins; receptors on mast cells. *Mailing Add:* Dept of Immunol Univ of Man Winnipeg MB R3B 2E9 Can

FROESE, GERD, b Saporoshje, USSR, May 18, 26; Can citizen; m 53; c 3. BIOPHYSICS. *Educ:* Univ Sask, 54; Univ Western Ont, MSc, 56, PhD(biophys), 58. *Prof Exp:* PHYSICIST, MANITOBA CANCER TREATMENT & RES FOUND, 60- *Concurrent Pos:* Donner res fel, Max Planck Inst Biophys, Ger, 58-59 & res unit radiobiol, Brit Empire Cancer Campaign, Middlesex, 59-60. *Mem:* Biophys Soc; Can Physiol Soc; Brit Asn Radiation Res. *Res:* Mammalian temperature regulation; radiation physics; radiobiology and cellular biology; experimental tumor immunology. *Mailing Add:* Man Cancer Treatment & Res Found 700 Bannatyne Winnipeg MB R3E 0V9 Can

FROGEL, JAY ALBERT, b New York, NY, Apr 28, 44. INFRARED PHOTOMETRY & SPECTROSCOPY. *Educ:* Harvard Univ, BA, 66; Calif Inst Technol, PhD(astron), 71. *Prof Exp:* Res fel & lectr astron, Harvard Univ, 71-75; STAFF MEM ASTRON, CERRO TOLOLO INTER-AM OBSERV, 75- *Mem:* Am Astron Soc; Astron Soc Pac; Int Astron Union. *Res:* The stellar content of clusters and galaxies; infrared emission from H II regions and galactic nuclei. *Mailing Add:* Cerro Tololo Inter-Am Observ Casilla 603 La Serena Chile

FROHLICH, EDWARD DAVID, b New York, NY, Sept 10, 31; m 59; c 3. INTERNAL MEDICINE. *Educ:* Washington & Jefferson Col, AB, 52; Univ Md, MD, 56; Northwestern Univ, MS, 63. *Prof Exp:* Intern med, DC Gen Hosp, 56, resident internal med, 57-58; resident, Georgetown Univ Hosp, 59-60; clin investr internal med & cardiovasc res, Vet Admin Res Hosp, Northwestern Univ, 62-64; mem staff, Res Div, Cleveland Clin, Ohio, 64-69; assoc prof, Med Ctr, Univ Okla, 69-71, assoc prof pharmacol & prof med & physiol & biophys, 71-75, George Lynn Cross res prof, 75-76; VPRES EDUC & RES, ALTON OCHSNER MED FOUND & DIR, DIV HYPERTENSIVE DIS, OCHSNER CLIN, 76- *Concurrent Pos:* Fel cardiovasc res, Georgetown Univ, 58-59; mem, Med Adv Bds, Coun on Circulation, Am Heart Asn, 64-, Coun High Blood Pressue Res, 68, Coun Basic Sci, 69; ed-in-chief, J Lab & Clin Med. *Mem:* Fel AAAS; Am Soc Clin Pharmacol & Therapeut (pres, 73-74); fel Am Col Cardiol; fel Am Col Physicians; Am Soc Pharmacol & Exp Therapeut. *Res:* Cardiovascular research; hypertension; clinical pharmacology. *Mailing Add:* Off of Vpres Educ & Res 1516 Jefferson Hwy New Orleans LA 70121

FROHLICH, GERHARD J, b Simmern, Ger, Feb 20, 29; US citizen; m 58; c 2. CHEMICAL ENGINEERING, PHYSICAL CHEMISTRY. *Educ:* Darmstadt Tech Univ, dipl chem, 53; Polytech Inst Brooklyn, MChE, 54, DChE, 57. *Prof Exp:* Chem engr, Vulcan-Cincinnati, Inc, Ohio, 55-59; sr chem engr, St Paul Ammonia Prod, Inc, Minn, 59-61, chief process engr, 61-62, mgr res & develop, 62-64; sr chem engr, 64-70, mgr chem eng develop, 70-77, GEN MGR & CORP ENGR, HOFFMANN-LA ROCHE, INC, NUTLEY, 77- *Mem:* Am Inst Chem Engrs; Am Chem Soc; Electrochem Soc; Faraday Soc; Nat Soc Prof Engrs. *Res:* Chemical process design and development; electrochemical engineering; heterogeneous catalysis; liquid-liquid extraction. *Mailing Add:* 669A Mountain Rd Smoke Rise Kinnelon NJ 07405

FROHLIGER, JOHN OWEN, b Indianapolis, Ind, Dec 21, 30; m 52; c 3. ANALYTICAL CHEMISTRY. *Educ:* Purdue Univ, BS, 57; Univ Iowa, MS, 59, PhD(anal chem), 61. *Prof Exp:* Asst prof chem, Duquesne Univ, 61-67; from asst prof to assoc prof indust health & air chem, Grad Sch Pub Health, Univ Pittsburgh, 67-80, actg chmn, Dept Occup Health, 73-75; PRES, INDUST HYG ASSOCS, 80- *Mem:* AAAS; Am Chem Soc; Air Pollution Control Asn; Am Pub Health Asn. *Res:* Analysis of chemical compounds in the environment; liquid chromatography; acid nature of precipitation. *Mailing Add:* Indust Hyg Assocs PO Box 18065 Pittsburgh PA 15236

FROHMAN, CHARLES EDWARD, b Columbus, Ind, Oct 25, 21; m 46; c 4. BIOCHEMISTRY, PHYSIOLOGY. *Educ:* Ind Univ, Bloomington, BS, 47, AM, 48; Wayne State Univ, PhD(physiol chem), 51. *Prof Exp:* Res assoc effect radiation, Kresge Eye Inst, Detroit, 51-52; res assoc, Dept Physiol Chem, 52-55, instr, 55-57, asst prof, 67-69, assoc prof physiol chem, Dept Psychiat, 69-72, PROF BIOCHEM, DEPT PSYCHIAT, WAYNE STATE UNIV, 72-, DIR DEPT BIOCHEM, LAFAYETTE CLIN, 55- *Mem:* Soc Biol Psychiat; Asn Anal Chemists; Am Asn Biol Chemists. *Res:* Mental illness of the brain. *Mailing Add:* Dept of Biochem Lafayette Clin Detroit MI 48207

FROHMAN, LAWRENCE ASHER, b Detroit, Mich, Jan 26, 35. ENDOCRINOLOGY. *Educ:* Univ Mich, Ann Arbor, MD, 58. *Prof Exp:* From asst prof to assoc prof med, State Univ NY Buffalo, 65-73; prof med, sch med, Univ Chicago, 73-81; dir div endocrinol & metab, Michael Reese Med Ctr, 73-81; PROF MED & DIR, DIV ENDOCRINOL METAB, SCH MED, UNIV CINCINNATI, 81- *Concurrent Pos:* Mem endocrinol study sect, NIH, 72-76; mem, Vet Admin Merit Review Bd Endocrinol, 79-; mem adv comt to assoc dir diabetes, endocrinol & metab, NIH, 78- *Mem:* Endocrine Soc; Am Diabetes Asn; Am Soc Clin Invest; Int Soc Neuroendocrinol; Asn Am Physicians. *Res:* Neuroendocrine regulation of anterior pituitary function as related to growth hormone and prolactin secretion; neuropharmacology of hypothalamic releasing and inhibiting hormones; molecular heterogeneity of peptide hormones; neural control of carbohydrate metabolism. *Mailing Add:* Div Endocrinol Univ Cincinnati Med Ctr 231 Bethesda Ave Cincinnati OH 45267

FROHMBERG, RICHARD P, b Newburgh Heights, Ohio, Mar 30, 20; m 45; c 4. ENGINEERING, MATERIALS SCIENCE. *Educ:* Case Inst Technol, BS, 42, MS, 48, PhD(phys metall), 54. *Prof Exp:* Instr phys metall, Case Inst Technol, 48-51, res assoc metals, 51-55; chief prod develop lab, Rocketdyne Div, N Am Aviation, Inc, 55-60, chief mat res, 60-70; CHIEF ENGR, ADVAN DEVELOP & MAT ENG, BENDIX CORP, 70- *Honors & Awards:* Henry Marion Howe Award, 55. *Mem:* AAAS; fel Am Inst Aeronaut & Astronaut; fel Am Soc Metals. *Res:* High temperature materials sciences, including physical metallurgy, fabrication, ceramics and polymer science. *Mailing Add:* Bendix Corp PO Box 1159 Kansas City MO 64141

FROHNSDORFF, GEOFFREY JAMES CARL, b London, Eng, Feb 4, 28; US citizen; m 56; c 3. PHYSICAL CHEMISTRY, MATERIALS SCIENCE. *Educ:* Univ St Andrews, BSc, 53; Lehigh Univ, MS, 56; Univ London, PhD(phys chem) & DIC, 59. *Prof Exp:* Res fel chem, Royal Mil Col, Ont, 59-60; mgr res & develop, Am Cement Corp, 60-70; group leader, Gillette Res Inst, Inc, 70-73; chief, Mat & Composites Sect, 73-80, sr scientist, Structures & Mat Div, 80-81, CHIEF BUILDING MAT DIV, CTR BLDG TECHNOL, NAT BUR STANDARDS, 81- *Concurrent Pos:* Mem comt res cement & concrete, Transp Res Bd, Nat Acad Sci-Nat Res Coun. *Honors & Awards:* P H Bates Award, Am Soc Testing Mat, 78. *Mem:* Fel Am Ceramic Soc (vpres, 81-82); Int Union Mat & Structures Res & Testing Labs; Am Concrete Inst; Am Soc Testing & Mat. *Res:* Performance and durability of building materials; relationships between composition, structure and engineering performance of materials; surface chemistry; cement chemistry; surface coatings; adhesion; corrosion; preservation technology; resource recovery; materials conservation. *Mailing Add:* Ctr for Bldg Technol Nat Bur of Standards Washington DC 20234

FROHRIB, DARRELL A, b Oshkosh, Wis, June 25, 30; m 55; c 3. MECHANICAL & BIOMEDICAL ENGINEERING. *Educ:* Mass Inst Technol, SB, 52, SM, 53; Univ Minn, Minneapolis, PhD(mech), 66. *Prof Exp:* Engr, Sperry Gyroscope Co, NY, 53-59; lectr mech eng, 59-66, asst prof, 66-68, ASSOC PROF MECH ENG, UNIV MINN-MINNEAPOLIS, 68-, DIR DESIGN CTR, 71-, DIR GRAD EDUC IN BIOMED ENG, 78- *Concurrent Pos:* Am Petrol Soc fel, 63-65; Fulbright-Hays sr fel, India, 71; consult, Am Med Systs, 76- & Theradyne Corp, 79- *Mem:* Am Soc Mech Engrs; Am Soc Eng Educ. *Res:* Shock and vibration; engineering design; dynamics; mathematical modeling of regional development systems; automation; urological system implant design; orthopaedic long bone healing prostheses; wheelchair optimization; flywheel energy conservation and retrieval. *Mailing Add:* 2144 Princeton Ave St Paul MN 55105

FROILAND, SVEN GORDON, b Astoria, SDak, May 4, 22; m 43; c 6. BIOLOGY, ECOLOGY. *Educ:* SDak State Univ, BS, 43; Univ Colo, MA, 51, PhD, 57. *Hon Degrees:* DH, Luther Col, 78. *Prof Exp:* Instr biol, Augustana Col, 46-49 & Univ Colo, 49-53; assoc prof, 53-57, chmn, Dept Biol, 53-70 & Div Natural Sci, 59-76, PROF BIOL, AUGUSTANA COL, 57-, FELLOWS CHAIR NATURAL SCI, 80- *Concurrent Pos:* Vis scholar, Univ Ariz, 70-71. *Mem:* AAAS; Ecol Soc Am; Am Inst Biol Sci; Nat Asn Biol Teachers; Soc Study Evolution. *Res:* Morphology of genus betula; taxonomy and ecology of genus salix in Black Hills of South Dakota; natural history of Black Hills. *Mailing Add:* 4808 Arden Ave Sioux Falls SD 57103

FROILAND, THOMAS GORDON, b Henderson, Ky, Dec 9, 43; m 66; c 2. DEVELOPMENTAL GENETICS. *Educ:* Augustana Col, BA, 65; Univ Nebr, MS, 67, PhD(zool), 70. *Prof Exp:* Instr biol, Kans State Univ, 70-71; asst prof, Wayne State Col, 71-72; from asst prof to assoc prof, 72-81, actg dept head, 78-79, PROF BIOL, NORTHERN MICH UNIV, 81-, DEPT HEAD, 79- *Concurrent Pos:* Consult, Upper Peninsula Med Educ Prog, Mich State Univ, 75 & 80. *Mem:* Am Soc Zoologists; Sigma Xi. *Res:* Control of pigmentation in genetic systems; ultrastructural relationships of microtubules to pigment; sex reversal, growth and development in lake trout; copper metabolism in mice. *Mailing Add:* Dept of Biol Northern Mich Univ Marquette MI 49855

FROIX, MICHAEL FRANCIS, b Trinidad, WI, Jan 27, 42; c 2. PHYSICAL CHEMISTRY, POLYMER PHYSICS. *Educ:* Howard Univ, BS, 66, MS, 68, PhD(chem), 71. *Prof Exp:* Chemist, Texaco Res Labs, 66 & Gillette Res Labs, 68; lectr, Community Exten Prog, Fed City Col, 70-71; teaching fel, Howard Univ, 67-71; assoc scientist, 71-73, scientist, Xerox Corp, 73-77; res supvr, Celanese Corp, 77-79; mgr, Mat Sci Dept, 80-82, TECH DIR, PHYSICS SECT, CORP RES & DEVELOP, RAUCHEM CORP, 82- *Mem:* Am Phys Soc; Am Chem Soc; NY Acad Sci; AAAS. *Res:* Property relationships in polymeric materials; structure. *Mailing Add:* Rauchem Corp 300 Constitution Dr Menlo Park CA 94025

FROJMOVIC, MAURICE MONY, b Brussels, Belg, Feb 2, 43; Can citizen; m 66; c 3. SURFACE CHEMISTRY. *Educ:* McGill Univ, PhD(org chem), 67. *Prof Exp:* Nat Res Coun-NATO fel, Chem Biodynamics Lab, 66-68, asst prof, 68-76, ASSOC PROF PHYSIOL, McGILL UNIV, 76- *Mem:* AAAS; Am Chem Soc. *Res:* Interactions at the blood-material interface; platelet structure and function in health and disease; platelet shape change activation in normal human donors, in patients with platelet defect-related bleeding disorders and in patients with thrombotic conditions; platelet-collagen interactions; blood clotting and thrombosis. *Mailing Add:* Dept of Physiol McIntyre Med Bldg McGill Univ Montreal PQ H3A 2T5 Can

FROLANDER, HERBERT FARLEY, b Providence, RI, Sept 29, 22; m 55; c 4. BIOLOGICAL OCEANOGRAPHY. *Educ:* RI Col Educ, EdB, 46; Brown Univ, ScM, 50, PhD(biol), 55. *Prof Exp:* Instr oceanog, Univ Wash, 52-56, asst prof, 57-59; assoc prof, 59-65, asst dean grad sch, 66-67, actg chmn dept oceanog, 67-68, coordr marine sci & technol prog, 68-73, PROF OCEANOG, ORE STATE UNIV, 65- *Concurrent Pos:* Pres-elect, Asn Sea Grant Prog Insts, 70-71, pres, 71- *Mem:* Am Soc Limnol & Oceanog; Am Micros Soc. *Res:* Marine zooplankton; population dynamics. *Mailing Add:* Sch Oceanog Ore State Univ Corvallis OR 97331

FROLIK, ELVIN FRANK, b DeWitt, Nebr, June 9, 09; m 38; c 3. AGRONOMY. *Educ:* Univ Nebr, Lincoln, BS, 30, MS, 32; Univ Minn, PhD, 48. *Prof Exp:* Exten agronomist, 36-45, assoc prof, 46-51, chmn dept agron, 52-55, dir agr exp sta, 55-60, dean col agr, 60-73, prof agron, 51-75, EMER PROF AGRON, UNIV NEBR, LINCOLN, 75- *Concurrent Pos:* Consult, Develop & Resources Corp, Iran, 73-75, USAID, 76-, USDA, 78- & Agr Corp Am, 79- *Mem:* AAAS; Am Soc Agron; Soil Conserv Soc Am; Int Crop Improv Asn (pres, 45-47). *Res:* Maize genetics; radiation genetics of crop plants. *Mailing Add:* 114 Home Econ Bldg East Campus Univ of Nebr Lincoln NE 68583

FROM, ARTHUR HARVEY LEIGH, b South Bend, Ind, Oct 1, 36; m 62. CARDIOVASCULAR PHARMACOLOGY, CLINICAL CARDIOLOGY. *Educ:* Ind Univ, AB, 58, MA, 60, MD(physiol), 61. *Prof Exp:* Asst prof, 69-76, ASSOC PROF MED, MED SCH, UNIV MINN, 76-; STAFF COORDR MED & DIR ECG LAB, MINN VET ADMIN MED CTR, 76- *Mem:* AAAS; Am Fedn Clin Res; Am Heart Asn; Int Soc Heart Res. *Res:* Molecular pharmacology of disitalis. *Mailing Add:* Cardiol Sect Vet Admin Med Ctr 54th St & 48th Ave S Minneapolis MN 55417

FROM, CHARLES A(UGUSTUS), JR, b Chicago, Ill, Apr 12, 15; m 40; c 4. CHEMICAL ENGINEERING. *Educ:* Univ Mich, BS, 36. *Prof Exp:* Anal chemist, E I du Pont de Nemours & Co, 36-37; develop engr raw mat, Western Elec Co, 37-42, plastics develop, 46-55, dept chief, 55-59, non-metallic raw mat develop, 59-61, org finishing, insulating & encapsulation develop, 61-75, chief, Dept Mat, Powder Finishing, Nucleonics & Plastics Develop, Eng & Eng Labs, 75-80; RETIRED. *Concurrent Pos:* Chmn, Environ Comn, Elmhurst, Ill, 81- *Mem:* Am Chem Soc; Am Inst Chem Engrs; Soc Plastics Engrs; Am Watchmakers Inst. *Res:* Plastics; non-metallic raw materials; organic finishing; mechanical finishing; adhesives. *Mailing Add:* 241 Kenmore Ave Elmhurst IL 60126

FROMAGEOT, HENRI PIERRE-MARCEL, b Paris, France, Jan 25, 37; US citizen; m 63; c 3. BIOCHEMESTRY. *Educ:* Nat Sch Advan Chem, Paris, dipl eng, 59; Sorbonne, BS, 60; Cambridge Univ, PhD(chem), 66. *Prof Exp:* Res assoc biochem, Rockefeller Univ, 66-69; staff biochem, Gen Elec Co Res & Develop Ctr, 69-78; sr res assoc, 78-81, RES SCIENTIST, INT PAPER CO, CORP RES CTR, 81- *Mem:* Gesellschaft Deutscher Chem; AAAS. *Res:* Materials for wound healing. *Mailing Add:* Int Paper Co Corp Res Ctr PO Box 797 Tuxedo Park NY 10987

FROMAN, DAROL KENNETH, b Harrington, Wash, Oct 23, 06; m 31; c 2. NUCLEAR PHYSICS. *Educ:* Univ Alta, BSc, 26, MSc, 27; Univ Chicago, PhD(physics), 30. *Hon Degrees:* LLD, Univ Alta, 64. *Prof Exp:* Asst physics, Univ Chicago, 29-30; lectr, Univ Alta, 30-31; lectr, Macdonald Col, McGill Univ, 31-36, asst prof, 36-39 & McGill Univ, 39-41; prof, Univ Denver, 41-42; group leader, Radio & Sound Lab, US Navy, San Diego, 42; res assoc, Manhattan Dist Proj, Metall Lab, Univ Chicago, 42-43; group leader, Los Alamos Sci Labs, 43-45, div leader, 45-48, asst dir weapons develop, 49-51, tech assoc dir, 51-62; PVT CONSULT, 62- *Concurrent Pos:* Dir, Mt Evans High Altitude Lab, 41; sci dir, Atomic Weapons Tests, Eniwetok, 48; consult prof, Univ NMex, 54-61; mem, Sci Adv Comt Ballistic Missiles, Secy Defense, 55-60, Sci Directorate, Douglas Aircraft Co, 63-69 & Gen Adv Comt, AEC, 64- 66; dir develop, Espanola Hosp, 67-70; chmn bd, First Nat Bank Rio Arriba, 71-78. *Mem:* Fel Am Phys Soc; fel Am Nuclear Soc. *Res:* Supersonics; x-rays; cosmic rays; electronics applied to nuclear physics. *Mailing Add:* 250 E Alameda #438 Santa Fe NM 87501

FROMAN, SEYMOUR, b New York, NY, May 19, 20; m 46; c 3. MICROBIOLOGY. *Educ:* NY Univ, BA, 46; Univ Calif, Los Angeles, MA, 49, PhD, 52. *Prof Exp:* Asst clin prof, 64-65, ASSOC PROF-IN-RESIDENCE MICROBIOL & IMMUNOL, SCH MED, UNIV CALIF, LOS ANGELES, 65-; DIR, MICROBIOL RES LAB, OLIVE VIEW HOSP, 64- *Concurrent Pos:* Consult, Tuberc Unit, WHO & Clin Lab, Univ Calif, Los Angeles. *Mem:* Am Soc Microbiologists; Am Thoracic Soc; fel Am Pub Health Asn; NY Acad Sci; Int Union Against Tuberc. *Res:* Microbiology of tuberculosis. *Mailing Add:* Olive View Med Ctr Sylmar CA 91342

FROMHOLD, ALBERT THOMAS, JR, b Birmingham, Ala, Nov 25, 35; m 60; c 2. SOLID STATE PHYSICS. *Educ:* Auburn Univ, BEngPhys, 57, MS, 58; Cornell Univ, PhD(eng physics), 61. *Prof Exp:* Mem res staff, Sandia Corp, 61-65; alumni assoc res prof, 65-69, PROF PHYSICS, AUBURN UNIV, 70- *Concurrent Pos:* Vis scientist, Nat Bur Standards, 69-70, Hokkaido Univ, Sapporo, Japan, 79 & Oak Ridge Nat Lab, 80; NSF Prof Develop Award, 80; res fel, Japan Soc Prom Sci, 79. *Honors & Awards:* Jessie Beams Research Award, Am Phys Soc, 81. *Mem:* Am Phys Soc; Electrochem Soc; Am Asn Physics Teachers. *Res:* Theory of oxide film formation; optical properties of metals; transient nuclear magnetic resonance; nuclear relaxation in metals and magnetic insulators; solid state transport. *Mailing Add:* Dept Physics Auburn Univ Auburn AL 36849

FROMM, DAVID, b New York, NY, Jan 21, 39; m 66; c 3. GASTROINTESTINAL SURGERY. *Educ:* Univ Calif, BS, 60, MD, 64. *Prof Exp:* Intern surg, Univ Calif, 64-65, asst resident, 65-70, chief resident, 70-71; mem staff, Walter Reed Army Inst Res, 71-73; asst prof surg, Harvard Med Sch, 73-77, assoc prof, 77-78; PROF & CHMN, STATE UNIV NY, UPSTATE MED CTR, 78- *Concurrent Pos:* Res fel, NIH grant, Harvard Med Sch, 67-69; Res Career Develop Award, NIH, 75-78. *Mem:* Am Physiol Asn; Am Gastroenterol Asn; Soc Univ Surgeons; Am Surg Asn; Am Col Surgeons. *Res:* Factors influencing gastric mucosal permeability; function of isolated gastric mucosal surface cells. *Mailing Add:* Dept Surg Upstate Med Ctr 750 E Admas St Syracuse NY 13012

FROMM, ELI, b Niedaltdorf, Ger, May 7, 39; US citizen; m 62; c 3. BIOMEDICAL ENGINEERING, PHYSIOLOGY. *Educ:* Drexel Univ, BSEE, 62, MS, 64; Jefferson Med Col, PhD(physiol, biomed eng), 67. *Prof Exp:* Engr, Missile & Space Div, Gen Elec Co, 62-63; engr, Appl Physics Labs, E I du Pont de Nemours & Co, 63; teaching asst physics, 63-64, asst prof, 67-70, assoc prof, 70-80, PROF BIOMED SCI, DEPT BIOL SCI, BIOMED ENG INST, DREXEL UNIV, 80- *Concurrent Pos:* Lalor Found grant, 68-70; NSF grant, 69-71; NIH grant, 69-; consult, var indust co, 68-; lectr, Dept Obstet & Gynec, Sch Med, Univ Pa, 73-; assoc dir, Biomed & Eng Sci Prog, Drexel Univ, 73-74; Staff mem, Comt on Sci & Technol, US House of Representatives, Washington, DC, 80-81. *Mem:* Sr mem Inst Elec & Electronics Engrs; Inst Elec & Electronics Engrs Eng Med & Biol Soc (secy-treas, 73-75, vpres, 76-77, pres, 78-81). *Res:* Physiologic function by telemetry; clinical engineering applications; rhythmic responses of physiologic and biophysical parameters; development of transduction and transmission techniques for biologic variables. *Mailing Add:* Dept of Biol Sci Drexel Univ Philadelphia PA 19104

FROMM, HANS, b Hagenow, Germany, Aug 1, 39; m 68; c 2. GASTROENTEROLOGY. *Educ:* Univ Freiburg, DrMed, 65. *Prof Exp:* Intern, Mem Hosp, Worcester, Mass, 66-67; resident, Lemuel Shattuck Hosp, Boston, Mass, 67-68; resident, Albany Med Col, 68-69, res fel gastroenterol, 69-70; res fel, Gastroenterol Res Unit, Mayo Clin, 70-71; res asst, Div Gastroenterol, Sch Med, Univ Hannover, 71-74, pvt lectr, 74-75; asst head gastroenterol & nutrit unit, Montefiore Hosp, 75-78; asst prof, 75-80, ASSOC PROF MED, UNIV PITTSBURGH, 80-; assoc head gastroenterol & nutrit unit, 78-81, HEAD GASTROENTEROL UNIT, MONTEFIORE HOSP, 81- *Mem:* Am Asn Study Liver Dis; Am Gastroenterol Asn; European Soc Clin Invest; Am Fedn Clin Res; AAAS. *Res:* Bile acid metabolism in cholelithiasis and in inflammatory bowel disease in man; development of new methods of treatment for cholelithiasis and inflammatory bowel disease. *Mailing Add:* Gastroenterol Unit Montefiore Hosp Pittsburgh PA 15213

FROMM, HERBERT JEROME, b New York, NY, Apr 5, 29; m 64; c 4. BIOCHEMISTRY. *Educ:* Mich State Univ, BS, 50; Loyola Univ, Ill, PhD(biochem), 54. *Prof Exp:* From asst prof to prof biochem, Sch Med, Univ NDak, 54-66; PROF BIOCHEM, IOWA STATE UNIV, 66- *Mem:* Am Chem Soc; Am Soc Biol Chemists. *Res:* Enzyme chemistry. *Mailing Add:* Dept of Biochem & Biophys Iowa State Univ Ames IA 50010

FROMM, PAUL OLIVER, b Ramsey, Ill, Dec 2, 23; m 47; c 2. COMPARATIVE PHYSIOLOGY. *Educ:* Univ Ill, Urbana, BS, 49, MS, 51, PhD(physiol), 54. *Prof Exp:* From instr to assoc prof, 54-65, PROF PHYSIOL, MICH STATE UNIV, 65. *Concurrent Pos:* Fulbright res grant, Mus Oceanog, Monaco, 63-64; vis prof, Ariz State Univ, 71, adj prof, 78 & 79. *Mem:* Am Physiol Soc; N Am Benthological Soc; Am Soc Zoologists; Soc Exp Biol & Med. *Res:* Toxic effect of water soluble pollutants on freshwater fish; transfer of materials across isolated-perfused gills of fishes; comparative physiology of vertebrate eyes. *Mailing Add:* Dept of Physiol Mich State Univ East Lansing MI 48824

FROMM, WINFIELD E(RIC), b Haddonfield, NJ, Jan 18, 18; m 44; c 3. ELECTRONIC ENGINEERING. *Educ:* Drexel Inst, BSEE, 40; Polytech Inst Brooklyn, MEE, 48. *Hon Degrees:* DEng, Polytech Inst NY, 74; DHumL, Dowling Col, NY, 74. *Prof Exp:* Aircraft radio engr, Transcontinental & Western Air, Inc, 40-41; mem staff, off sci res & develop, Columbia Univ, 41-45; electronic engr, Airborne Instruments Lab, 45-49, asst supv engr, 49-55, dept head, 55-61, div dir, res syst eng div, 61-64, vpres, 64, group vpres, 64-68; exec vpres, AIL Div Cutler-Hammer, 68-73, pres, 73-77; group vpres, Cutler-Hammer Instruments & Systs Group, 78-79; VPRES, INSTRUMENT & SYSTS OPER, EATON CORP, 79- *Concurrent Pos:* Lectr, Hofstra Col, 51; fel, Polytech Inst NY, 78. *Mem:* Fel Inst Elec & Electronics Engrs; assoc Am Inst Aeronaut & Astronaut. *Res:* Magnetic airborne detection; low and medium frequency vacuum tube circuits; microwave equipment development, including special components and strip transmission lines; electronic and microwave systems for aerospace applications. *Mailing Add:* Instrument & Systs Oper Eaton Corp Melville NY 11747

FROMMER, GABRIEL PAUL, b Budapest, Hungary, Apr 27, 36; US citizen; m 58; c 2. NEUROPSYCHOLOGY. *Educ:* Oberlin Col, BA, 57; Brown Univ, ScM, 59, PhD(psychol), 61. *Prof Exp:* Sr asst scientist neuropsychol, USPHS, 60-62; USPHS fel, Yale Univ, 62-64; from asst prof to assoc prof, 64-79, PROF PSYCHOL, IND UNIV, BLOOMINGTON, 79- *Concurrent Pos:* Vis assoc res scientist physiol, Univ Mich, 73-74 & 75-76, USPHS spec fel, 75-76. *Mem:* Am Psychol Asn; Soc Neurosci; Psychonomic Soc; Sigma Xi; AAAS. *Res:* Neural mechanisms of somesthesis; neural mechanisms of motivation and reinforcement. *Mailing Add:* Dept Psychol Ind Univ Bloomington IN 47405

FROMMER, JACK, b New Haven, Conn, Jan 21, 18; m 44; c 4. ANATOMY. *Educ:* Univ Conn, BS, 40, MS, 46; Brown Univ, PhD(biol), 54. *Prof Exp:* Instr zool, Univ Conn, 47-48; asst res physiol, Yale Univ, 48-49; instr zool, Univ Conn, 49-50; from instr to assoc prof, 53-75, PROF ANAT, MED SCH, TUFTS UNIV, 75- *Mem:* AAAS; Am Asn Anatomists. *Res:* Temporomandibular joint; mandible development; cleft palate; osteoclasts; teratology; radioautography. *Mailing Add:* Med Sch Tufts Univ Boston MA 02111

FROMMER, JANE ELIZABETH, b Providence, RI, Aug 9, 52. CONDUCTING POLYMERS. *Educ:* Tufts Univ, BS, 75; Calif Inst Technol, PhD(chem), 80. *Prof Exp:* Researcher, Mass Inst Technol, 75-76, Mass Gen Hosp, 76 & Lawrence Berkeley Labs, 78-80; RESEARCHER, ALLIED CORP, 80- *Mem:* Am Chem Soc; Asn Women Sci. *Res:* Endocrinology-chemistry and biochemistry of vitamin D; synthetic and mechanistic organic chemistry of acetyl coenzyme A; transition metal thermodynamics; cluster catalysis; conducting polymers. *Mailing Add:* Allied Corp PO Box 1021 R Morristown NJ 07960

FROMMER, PETER LESLIE, b Budapest, Hungary, Feb 13, 32; US citizen; m 53; c 4. CARDIOLOGY, BIOMEDICAL ENGINEERING. *Educ:* Univ Cincinnati, EE, 54; Harvard Med Sch, MD, 58. *Prof Exp:* Intern, Med Ctr, Univ Cincinnati, 58-59, asst resident med, 61-63; jr investr, Lab Tech Develop, 59-61, sr investr, Cardiol Br, 63-66, asst chief, Myocardial Infarction Br, 66-67, chief, Myocardial Infarction Br, 67-72, assoc dir cardiol, Div Heart & Vascular Dis, 72-78, dep dir, 78-81, ACTG DIR, NAT HEART, LUNG & BLOOD INST, NIH, 81- *Concurrent Pos:* Mem, Joint US Comt Eng Med & Biol, Nat Res Coun, 60-65, chmn comt, 64, mem, US Nat Comt Eng Med & Biol, 66-68; mem, Admin Coun, Int Fedn Med & Biol Eng, 65, vpres, 69. *Mem:* Fel Am Col Cardiol; fel Am Col Physicians; Am Fedn Clin Res; Am Heart Asn; Am Physiol Soc. *Res:* Cardiology and cardiovascular physiology; instrumentation; research planning and adminstration. *Mailing Add:* Nat Heart Lung & Blood Inst Bethesda MD 20205

FROMMEYER, WALTER BENEDICT, JR, internal medicine, deceased

FROMMHOLD, LOTHAR WERNER, b Wurzburg, Ger, Apr 20, 30; m 58; c 2. ATOMIC PHYSICS, PLASMA PHYSICS. *Educ:* Univ Hamburg, Dipl, 56, PhD(gas discharges), 61, Dr habil, 64. *Prof Exp:* Res assoc physics, Univ Hamburg, 56-63, instr, 61-63, asst prof, 64; res assoc & instr, Univ Pittsburgh, 64-66, res prof, 66; assoc prof, 66-69, PROF PHYSICS, UNIV TEX, AUSTIN, 69- *Concurrent Pos:* Fulbright travel grant, Univ Pittsburgh, 64, res fel, 64-66. *Mem:* Fel Am Phys Soc. *Res:* Gaseous electronics; atomic and molecular physics; plasma diagnostics; physical chemistry; laser Raman spectroscopy. *Mailing Add:* Dept of Physics Univ of Tex Austin TX 78712

FROMOVITZ, STAN, b Lodz, Poland, May 31, 36; Can citizen. OPERATIONS RESEARCH, APPLIED STATISTICS. *Educ:* Univ Toronto, BASc, 60, MA, 61; Stanford Univ, PhD(statist), 65. *Prof Exp:* Mathematician, Shell Develop Co, 64-67; asst prof statist, Grad Sch Bus, Univ Santa Clara, 67-71; ASSOC PROF MGT SCI, UNIV MD, 71- *Mem:* Opers Res Soc Am; Inst Mgt Sci. *Res:* Mathematical programming; inventory theory; optimization algorithms; applied operations research. *Mailing Add:* Col of Bus & Mgt Univ of Md College Park MD 20742

FRONDEL, CLIFFORD, b New York, NY, Jan 8, 07; m 41; c 2. MINERALOGY. *Educ:* Colo Sch Mines, Geol Eng, 29; Columbia Univ, AM, 36; Mass Inst Technol, PhD(crystallog), 39. *Prof Exp:* Res assoc mineral, Harvard Univ, 39-46, assoc prof, 46-54, prof, 54-77, chmn dept geol sci, 65-69. *Concurrent Pos:* Sr physicist, US War Dept, 42-43; res dir, Reeves Sound Labs & Reeves-Ely Labs, 43-45; corr mem, Am Mus Nat Hist & Hist Mus Vienna; pres, Crystal Res, Inc, 49-72- *Honors & Awards:* Becke Medal, Austrian Mineral Asn, 58; Distinguished Serv Medal, Colo Sch Mines, 64; Roebling Medal, Am Mineral Soc, 64; Boricky Medal, Charles Univ, Prague, 68. *Mem:* Fel Am Mineral Soc (pres, 56); fel Geol Soc Am; Am Acad Arts & Sci; Geochem Soc; Austrian Acad Sci. *Res:* Descriptive mineralogy; crystal synthesis; lunar geochemistry. *Mailing Add:* 20 Beatrice Circle Belmont MA 02178

FRONDEL, JUDITH W, b Philadelphia, Pa, Oct 23, 12; m 49; c 1. GEOLOGY, MINERALOGY. *Educ:* Temple Univ, BA, 34; Bryn Mawr Univ, MA, 45, PhD(geol), 49. *Prof Exp:* Relief investr, Philadelphia County Relief Bd, 34-36; mus docent natural hist, Acad Natural Sci Philadelphia, 36-42; crystallographer, Philadelphia Signal Corps Depot, 42-43; geologist, US Geol Surv, 48-49, part time, 49-61; res assoc, AEC contract, 61-70, res assoc, NASA Contract, Hoffman Lab, 70-74, HON RES ASSOC MINERAL, HARVARD UNIV, 74- *Concurrent Pos:* Fel, Radcliffe Inst Independent Study, 65-66 & 66-67. *Mem:* AAAS; fel Mineral Soc Am; fel Sigma Xi. *Res:* Mineralogical and geochemical investigation of radioactive and rare-earth bearing minerals using optical, x-ray diffraction and x-ray spectographic techniques; investigation of origin of amber, using all mineralogical techniques; investigation of lunar mineralogy. *Mailing Add:* 20 Beatrice Circle Belmont MA 02178

FRONEK, ARNOST, b Topolcany, Czech, Aug 8, 23; m 57; c 2. PHYSIOLOGY. *Educ:* Charles Univ, Prague, MD, 49; Czech Acad Sci, Prague, cert, 55. *Prof Exp:* Intern med, County Hosp, Most, Czech, 49-51; intern, Inst Exp Physiol, Charles Univ, Prague, 51-52; asst prof, Bockus Res Inst, Univ Pa, 65-68, vis asst prof, 62-63; from assoc prof to prof aerospace & mech eng sci, 68-73, PROF BIOENG, SCH MED, UNIV CALIF, SAN DIEGO, 73-, PROF SURG, 76- *Concurrent Pos:* Res fel cardiovasc physiol, Inst Cardiovasc Res, Prague, 52-64. *Mem:* Czech Soc Cardiol (hon secy, 61-64); Czech Soc Physiol; Czech Soc Med Electronics. *Res:* Cardiovascular physiology; local thermodilution; cardiac energetics. *Mailing Add:* Dept of Appl Mech & Eng Sci Univ of Calif Sch of Med La Jolla CA 92093

FRONEK, DONALD KAREL, b Sunnyside, Wash, July 11, 37; m 59; c 2. DIGITAL COMPUTERS, ELECTRICAL ENGINEERING. *Educ:* Wash State Univ, BA, 60, BS, 64; Univ Idaho, MS, 69, PhD(elec eng), 73. *Prof Exp:* Proj officer elec, US Army, 60-62; elec engr, Gen Elec Co, 64-66, Hughes Aircraft Co, Calif, 66-67; instr, Univ Idaho, 68-73; asst prof, Univ Ala, Huntsville, 73-76; ASSOC PROF ELEC, UNIV NEV, RENO, 76- *Concurrent Pos:* Prin investr, NSF, 74-75, Army Res Orgn, 75-76 & 78-79, NASA, 75-76; consult, Battelle Durham, SC, 74-76 & 78- *Mem:* Sigma Xi; Inst Elec & Electronics Engrs. *Res:* Microprocessors; digital switching theory; digital electronics; thick film electronics. *Mailing Add:* Dept of Elec Eng Univ of Nev Reno NV 89557

FRONEK, KITTY, b Grenoble, France, Mar 23, 25; m 51; c 2. HUMAN PHYSIOLOGY. *Educ:* Charles Univ Prague, MD, 51; Czech Acad Sci, CSc(physiol), 60. *Prof Exp:* Instr pharmacol, Med Sch, Charles Univ, Prague, 50-51; sr investr physiol & clin res, Inst Cardiovasc Res, 51-60; head physiol div, Nuclear Lab, Inst Clin & Exp Surg, 60-64; res assoc cardiovasc res, Med Sch, Temple Univ, 65-68; RES BIOENGR, SCH MED, UNIV CALIF, SAN DIEGO, 68- *Concurrent Pos:* Head physiol lab, Episcopal Hosp, Philadelphia, Pa, 67-68. *Mem:* Am Soc Physiol; Am Heart Asn. *Res:* Control and regulation of the cardiovascular system under physiological and pathophysiological conditions; relationship between cardiac output, blood pressure and blood flow in several peripheral regions. *Mailing Add:* Res Physiol Univ Calif San Diego CA 92110

FRONING, GLENN WESLEY, b Gray Summit, Mo, Sept 8, 30; m 62; c 2. POULTRY SCIENCE, FOOD SCIENCE. *Educ:* Univ Mo, BS, 53, MS, 57; Univ Minn, PhD(food tech), 61. *Prof Exp:* Asst prof food sci, Rutgers Univ, 61-63; asst prof poultry sci, Univ Conn, 63-66; prof poultry & wildlife sci, 66-77, chmn dept, 72-77, PROF ANIMAL SCI, UNIV NEBR, LINCOLN, 77- *Mem:* Poultry Sci Asn (secy-treas, 80-); Inst Food Technol; AAAS; Royal Soc Chem. *Res:* Egg white proteins; color and textural properties of poultry meat and poultry meat myoglobin; functional properties of eggs. *Mailing Add:* Dept Animal Sci Univ Nebr Lincoln NE 68583

FRONTERA-REICHARD, JOSE GUILLERMO, b Aguadilla, PR, Jan 20, 19; m 65; c 3. NEUROANATOMY. *Educ:* Univ PR, BS, 40; Univ Mich, MS, 46, PhD(anat), 48. *Prof Exp:* Instr comp vert anat, Nat Univ Panama, 41-43; instr biol sci, Sch Med, Univ PR, San Juan, 43-45, assoc prof biol & chmn dept, 48-50, from asst prof to prof anat, 50-76; PROF & CHAIR, ESC MED UNIV CENT, CARIBE CAYEY, 78- *Concurrent Pos:* USPHS spec fel, Col Physicans & Surgeons, Columbia Univ, 55; consult, Perinatal Physiol Lab, USPHS, San Juan, PR, 56; lectr neurohistol, Free Univ Barcelona & Hosp San Pablo, Barcelona, Spain. *Mem:* Am Asn Anatomists; Am Acad Neurol; Sigma Xi. *Res:* Mammalian vascular anomalies; the anuran diencephalon; function and connections of insular region of macaque's brain; neurohistological techniques; effects of fixatives, storage, and dehydrating fluids on measurements of macaque brains. *Mailing Add:* PO Box 1190 San Juan PR 00936

FROSCH, ROBERT ALAN, b New York, NY, May 22, 28; m 57; c 2. MARINE GEOPHYSICS. *Educ:* Columbia Univ, AB, 47, MA, 49, PhD(theoret physics), 52. *Prof Exp:* Res scientist theoret physics, Hudson Labs, Columbia Univ, 51-53, from asst dir to dir, Theoret Div, 53-63; dir nuclear test detection, Adv Res Proj Agency, Off Secy Defense, 63-65, dep dir, 65-66; asst secy Navy for res & develop, Dept Navy, 66-73; asst exec dir, UN Environ Prog, 73-75; assoc dir, Woods Hole Oceanog Inst, 75-77; adminr, NASA, 77-; PRES, AM ASN ENG SOC, 81- *Concurrent Pos:* Chmn, Interagency Comt Oceanog, 66-67 & US del, Intergovt Oceanog Comt, UNESCO, Paris, 67 & 70; mem, Interagency Comt Marine Res, Educ & Facil, 67-69 & Vis Comt Earth Sci, Mass Inst Technol; Dept Defense mem, Comt Policy & Rev Nat Coun Marine Resources & Eng Develop, 69- *Honors & Awards:* Arthur S Flemming Award, 66. *Mem:* Nat Acad Engrs; fel AAAS; fel Acoust Soc Am; Am Phys Soc; fel Inst Elec & Electronics Engrs. *Res:* Theoretical physics; acoustical oceanography; seismology; system analysis and design; marine physics. *Mailing Add:* Am Asn Eng Soc 345 E 47th St New York NY 10017

FROSCH, WILLIAM ARTHUR, b New York, NY, June 24, 32; m 53; c 2. PSYCHIATRY, PSYCHOANALYSIS. *Educ:* Columbia Univ, AB, 53; NY Univ, MD, 57; NY Psychoanal Inst, cert, 65. *Prof Exp:* From intern to chief resident psychiat, Bellevue Hosp, New York, 57-61; from teaching asst to prof psychiat, Sch Med, NY Univ, 59-74, asst dean, 61-63, dir grad educ, 72-74; PROF PSYCHIAT & VCHMN, NY HOSP-CORNELL UNIV MED CTR, 75-, MED DIR, PAYNE WHITNEY CLINIC, 78- *Concurrent Pos:* USPHS fel psychiat, Bellevue Hosp, New York, from 58-60; from asst dir to assoc dir, Psychiat Div, Bellevue Hosp, 67-72. *Mem:* AAAS; fel Am Psychiat Asn; Asn Res Nerv & Ment Dis. *Res:* Drug abuse; psychopharmacology. *Mailing Add:* NY Hosp-Cornell Univ Med Ctr 525 E 68th St New York NY 10021

FROSETH, JOHN ALLEN, b Eau Claire, Wis, July 18, 42; m 61; c 2. ANIMAL NUTRITION. *Educ:* Wis State Col, BS, 64; Purdue Univ, MS, 66, PhD(animal nutrit), 70. *Prof Exp:* Instr animal sci, Purdue Univ & Nat Univ South, Arg, 67-69; asst prof & asst animal scientist, 69-74, ASSOC PROF ANIMAL SCI & ASSOC ANIMAL SCIENTIST, WASH STATE UNIV, 74- *Concurrent Pos:* Vis prof, Mich State Univ, 81-82. *Mem:* Am Soc Animal Sci; Am Inst Nutrit; Soc Exp Biol Med. *Res:* Mineral and amino acid interrelationships; Northwest grains and by-product feeds for swine; placental composition and transfer of nutrients; swine reproduction in confinement. *Mailing Add:* Dept of Animal Sci Wash State Univ Pullman WA 99164

FROST, ALBERT D(ENVER), b Mass, Feb 12, 22; m 56; c 4. PHYSICAL INSTTRUMENTATION. *Educ:* Tufts Univ, BS, 44; Harvard Univ, AM, 47; Mass Inst Technol, ScD(appl physics), 52. *Prof Exp:* From instr to asst prof physics, Tufts Univ, 47-57; assoc prof elec eng, 57-61, PROF ELEC ENG, UNIV NH, 61-, DIR ANTENNA SYSTS LAB, 58- *Concurrent Pos:* Res assoc acoust lab, Mass Inst Technol, 49-53; engr, Bolt Beranek & Newman, 51-53; consult, Arthur D Little, Inc, 56-57 & Stanford Res Labs, 68-71; asst dir res, Transistor Appln Inc, 59-61; staff scientist, Inst Defense Anal, 63-64; vis prof, Jodrell Bank Radio Astron Lab, Univ Manchester, 64-65, physics dept, Univ Sheffield, 71-72 & Oxford Univ, Res Lab Archaeometry, 78-79; univ fel, US Dept Transportation, 81. *Mem:* Acoust Soc Am; Am Geophys Union; Soc Archaeological Sci. *Res:* Measurement of upper atmosphere tides and winds using meteor trails radar; interferometer observations of ionospheric irregularities; physical acoustics; photoacoustic examination of archaeological materials; atmospheric infrasound; underwater acoustics. *Mailing Add:* Dept of Elec Eng Antenna Systs Lab Univ of NH Durham NH 03824

FROST, ARTHUR ATWATER, b Onarga, Ill, Aug 3, 09; m 34; c 3. PHYSICAL CHEMISTRY. *Educ:* Univ Calif, BS, 31; Princeton Univ, PhD(phys chem), 34. *Prof Exp:* Res fel, Harvard Univ, 34-36; instr, 36-42, from asst prof to assoc prof, 42-54, chmn dept, 57-62, prof, 54-76, EMER PROF CHEM, NORTHWESTERN UNIV, 76- *Concurrent Pos:* Adj prof, Northern Ariz Univ, 76- *Mem:* AAAS; Am Chem Soc; Am Phys Soc. *Res:* Molecular quantum mechanics. *Mailing Add:* 195 Eagle Lane Sedona AZ 86336

FROST, BARRIE JAMES, b Nelson, NZ, June 3, 39; Can/NZ citizen; m 65; c 3. VISION, SENSORY PROCESSES. *Educ:* Univ NZ, BA, 61; Univ Canterbury, MA, 64; Dalhousie Univ, PhD(psychol), 67. *Prof Exp:* Asst res physiologist, Univ Calif, Berkeley, 68-69; asst prof, 68-72, assoc prof, 72-78, PROF PSYCHOL, QUEEN'S UNIV, KINGSTON, 78- *Concurrent Pos:* Vis prof physiol, John Curtin Sch Med Res, Australian Nat Univ, 75-76; mem, Grant Selection Comt, Nat Sci & Eng Res Coun, 79-82; prin investr grants, Med Res Coun, Nat Sci & Eng Res Coun & Nat Health & Welfare. *Mem:* fel Can Psychol Asn; AAAS; Asn Res Vision & Ophthal. *Res:* Single cell recording studies of visual systems; autoradiography development of tactile vocoders for deaf. *Mailing Add:* Dept Psychol Queens Univ Kingston ON K7L 3N6 Can

FROST, BRIAN R T, b London, Eng, Sept 6, 26; US citizen; m 54; c 2. METALLURGY. *Educ:* Univ Birmingham, BSc, 47, PhD(metall), 49; Univ Chicago, MBA, 74. *Prof Exp:* Scientist metall, UK Atomic Energy Authority, 49-69; assoc dir metall, 69-73, DIR MAT SCI DIV, ARGONNE NAT LAB, 73- *Concurrent Pos:* Vis lectr, Queen Mary Col, Univ London, 59-63; vis prof, Northwestern Univ, 76-77. *Mem:* Fel Am Nuclear Soc; Am Soc Metals; Am Inst Metall Engrs; fel Brit Inst Metall; Metals Soc UK. *Res:* Radiation effects; corrosion and mechanical properties of materials for nuclear fission and fusion reactors; materials for non-nuclear energy systems. *Mailing Add:* Argonne Nat Lab 9700 S Cass Ave Argonne IL 60439

FROST, BRUCE WESLEY, b Brunswick, Maine, Mar 8, 41; m 63; c 2. BIOLOGICAL OCEANOGRAPHY. *Educ:* Bowdoin Col, BA, 63; Univ Calif, San Diego, PhD(oceanog), 69. *Prof Exp:* Asst prof, 69-75, assoc prof, 75-80, PROF OCEANOG, UNIV WASH, 80- *Concurrent Pos:* NSF res grant, 70- *Mem:* AAAS; Am Soc Limnol & Oceanog; Soc Syst Zool; Ecol Soc Am; Sigma Xi. *Res:* Ecology and systematics of marine zooplankton. *Mailing Add:* Dept of Oceanog Univ of Wash Seattle WA 98195

FROST, DAVID, b Brooklyn, NY, Dec 19, 25; m 46; c 2. SCIENCE EDITOR, SCIENCE WRITER. *Educ:* City Col New York, BS, 46, MS, 49; NY Univ, MS, 52, PhD, 60. *Prof Exp:* Tutor biol, City Col New York, 46-49; instr, pvt sch, 49-52; from instr to asst prof biol sci, Rutgers Univ, 52-59; sci ed, Squibb Inst Med Res, 59-75; CONSULT ED, 75- *Concurrent Pos:* Adj prof, Rutgers Univ, 53-78. *Mem:* AAAS; NY Acad Sci; Coun Biol Ed. *Res:* Genetic control of axolotl pigmentation; inhibition of lens regeneration in the newt; thin-layer chromatography of antibiotics; writings cover new drugs, surgery, medicine, chemistry and biology. *Mailing Add:* 1229 E Seventh St Plainfield NJ 07062

FROST, DAVID CREGREEN, b Ormskirk, Eng, Mar 27, 29; m 60. PHYSICAL CHEMISTRY. *Educ:* Univ Liverpool, Eng, BSc, 53, PhD(chem), 58, DSc, 79. *Prof Exp:* PROF CHEM, UNIV BC, 59- *Concurrent Pos:* Guggenheim fel, 80. *Mem:* Fel Am Chem Soc; fel Can Inst Chem. *Res:* Photoelectron spectroscopy; ionization and dissociation of molecules by electron and photon impact in the gaseous and solid phases. *Mailing Add:* Dept of Chem Univ of BC Vancouver Can

FROST, H(AROLD) BONNELL, b Ft Washakie, Wyo, Dec 3, 23; m 46; c 4. COMPUTER SCIENCE, ELECTRICAL ENGINEERING. *Educ:* Univ Nebr, BS, 48; Mass Inst Technol, SM, 50, ScD(elec eng), 54. *Prof Exp:* Asst, Lincoln Lab, Mass Inst Technol, 48-54; mem tech staff, NJ, 54-63, MEM TECH STAFF, BELL TEL LABS, PA, 63- *Mem:* AAAS; sr mem Inst Elec & Electronics Engrs. *Res:* Engineering applications of digital computers. *Mailing Add:* Bell Labs 1190 N Pecos St Denver CO 80234

FROST, HAROLD MAURICE, III, b New Haven, Conn, June 4, 42; m 64; c 1. DIELECTRICS, COMPOSITE MATERIALS. *Educ:* Univ Vt, BA, 64, MS, 69, PhD(physics), 74. *Prof Exp:* Scientist biophys, Microbiol Lab, White Sands Missile Range, NMex, 67; Nat Res Coun res assoc ultrasonics, Microwave Physics Lab, Air Force Cambridge Res Labs, 74-75; res physicist, Bur Radiol Health, US Dept HEW, 75-77; proj scientist, Nondestructive Testing & Mat Sci Res & Develop, Pa State Univ, 77-81; CHIEF SCIENTIST, E H V WEIDMANN INDUST, INC, ST JOHNSBURY, VT, 81- *Concurrent Pos:* Consult, 77-; Int ed, Ultrasonics, 77-81. *Mem:* Inst Elec & Electronics Engrs; Acoust Soc Am; Sigma Xi; Am Soc Nondestructive Testing. *Res:* Electromagnetic-ultrasonic transducers; acoustic surface waves as for nondestructive testing; network theory; deformation of polymers; bioeffects of ultrasound; cavitation; torsional and longitudinal acoustic waves in wire; matrix composites and matrix composites; dielectric properties of cellulose; chemistry of cellulose. *Mailing Add:* Appl Res Lab PO Box 30 State College PA 16801

FROST, HERBERT HAMILTON, b New York, NY, Jan 22, 17; m 48; c 5. VERTEBRATE ZOOLOGY. *Educ:* Brigham Young Univ, BA, 41, MS, 47; Cornell Univ, PhD, 55. *Prof Exp:* Teacher & head dept biol sci, Ricks Col, 47-60, chmn div math & natural sci, 55-60; assoc prof, 60-67, PROF ZOOL, BRIGHAM YOUNG UNIV, 67- *Honors & Awards:* Comstock Award, Cornell Univ. *Mem:* AAAS; Sigma Xi. *Res:* Ornithology; natural history; conservation. *Mailing Add:* Dept of Zool Brigham Young Univ Provo UT 84602

FROST, JACKIE GENE, b Feb 18, 37; US citizen; m 63. CHEMISTRY, POLAROGRAPHY. *Educ:* Eastern Ill Univ, BS, 58; Duke Univ, PhD(polarog), 62. *Prof Exp:* Res assoc, Univ NC, 62-63; develop chemist, Anal Instrumentation, 63-66, res chemist, 66-69, sr res chemist, 69-77, RES SUPVR, HALLIBURTON CO, 77- *Mem:* Am Chem Soc; Nat Asn Corrosion Engrs. *Res:* Complex ion chemistry; potentiometry; steel corrosion in alkaline chelating media; steel passivation; stability of metal complex ions; corrosion specialist. *Mailing Add:* Drawer 1431 Halliburton Serv Duncan OK 73533

FROST, JOHN KINGSBURY, b Sioux Falls, SDak, Mar 12, 22; m 49; c 7. IMAGE ANALYSIS, ENVIRONMENTAL & INDUSTRIAL EPIDEMIOLOGY. *Educ:* Univ Calif, Berkeley, BA, 43, Univ Calif, San Francisco MD, 46; Harvard Med Sch, cert, 48; Armed Forces Inst Path, cert, 51; Army Grad Sch Med, cert, 52; Am Bd Path, dipl, 53. *Prof Exp:* Intern, San Francisco Hosp, 47; instr, Sch Med, Univ Calif, 48, instr path & jr res pathologist, Sch Med & Cancer Res Inst, 53-56; assoc prof path & head div cytopath, Sch Med, Univ Md, 56-59; assoc prof & head, Div Cytopath, 59-75, asst prof gynec & obstet, 59-75, PROF PATH & GYNEC, JOHNS HOPKINS, 75-; PATHOLOGIST & HEAD DEPT CYTOPATH, JOHNS HOPKINS HOSP, 59- *Concurrent Pos:* Spec scholar, Calif Dept Pub Health, 48; fel med & path, San Francisco Hosp, 48; consult, Cent Identification Lab, Hawaii, 50-52, US Army, 55-56 & 60-, USPHS, 59- & Am Bd Path, 62- *Honors & Awards:* Papanicolaou Award, Am Soc Cytol, 72. *Mem:* Fel Col Am Pathologists; fel Am Soc Clin Path; Am Soc Cytol (pres, 64-65); fel Int Acad Cytology; Int Acad Path. *Res:* Cytology; cytopathology; automated cytology; computors in cytology; carcinogenesis; hormonal effects; Trichomonas; pulmonary fine structure; bronchoalveolarcytogenesis; early cancer diagnosis; television microscopy and telediagnosis; morphology of developing neoplasia in lung, bladder, cervix and esophagus; early detection, diagnosis and therapy of lung cancer; monitoring hazards and early detection of environmental disease. *Mailing Add:* 610 Path Bldg Johns Hopkins Hosp Baltimore MD 21205

FROST, KENNETH ALMERON, JR, b San Francisco, Calif, Dec 12, 44; m 69; c 1. ORGANIC CHEMISTRY, FUEL SCIENCE. *Educ:* Ind Univ, AB, 66; Univ Calif, Davis, PhD(chem), 71. *Prof Exp:* Res chemist, 71-75, SR RES CHEMIST, CHEVRON RES CO, STANDARD OIL CALIF, 75-, SR RES ASSOC, 80- *Mem:* Am Chem Soc; Am Soc Lubrication Engrs. *Res:* Fuel and lubricant additives; lubrication. *Mailing Add:* Chevron Res Co 576 Standard Ave Richmond CA 94802

FROST, L(ESLIE) S(WIFT), b Pittsburgh, Pa, May 7, 22; m 47; c 2. ELECTRICAL ENGINEERING. *Educ:* Carnegie Inst Technol, BS, 46, MS, 48, DSc(elec eng), 49. *Prof Exp:* Res engr physics, 49-73, ADV ENGR, WESTINGHOUSE RES LABS, 73- *Mem:* Am Phys Soc; Am Inst Elec & Electronics Engrs; Fedn Am Soc Exp Biol. *Res:* Studies of low pressure helium positive column; interpretation of electron transport data; metal vapor arc lamps; experimental and theoretical studies of gas-blast circuit breaker arcs; arc and plasma physics studies. *Mailing Add:* Westinghouse Res Labs 1310 Beulah Rd Pittsburgh PA 15235

FROST, LAWRENCE WILLIAM, b Fredonia, NY, Dec 2, 20; m 42; c 2. POLYMER CHEMISTRY. *Educ:* Allegheny Col, AB, 41; Purdue Univ, PhD(org chem), 44. *Prof Exp:* Res Found fel, Purdue Univ, 44-46; res chemist, 46-59, fel chemist, 59-73, ADV CHEMIST, WESTINGHOUSE ELEC CORP, 73- *Mem:* AAAS; Am Chem Soc. *Res:* Organic fluorine and organo silicon compounds; aromatic polyimides; high temperature electrical varnishes and wire enamels; laminates. *Mailing Add:* Res Labs Westinghouse Elec Corp Pittsburgh PA 15235

FROST, PAUL D(AVIS), b Beverly, Mass, Aug 9, 16; m 43; c 2. PHYSICAL METALLURGY, PROCESS METALLURGY. *Educ:* Rensselaer Polytech Inst, BMetEng, 40. *Prof Exp:* Metallurgist, Republic Steel Corp, NY, 40-43; instr metall, Cornell Univ, 41-45, sr process engr, Airplane Div, Curtiss-Wright, 43-45; res engr, Battelle Mem Inst, 46-53, chief light metals div, 53-60, sr res adv metal prod planning, 60-70, sr adv tech process metall sect, Mat Dept, 70-81, SR TECH ADV, COLUMBUS LABS, BATTELLE MEM INST, 81- *Mem:* Am Soc Metals. *Res:* Ferrous and nonferrous metallurgy; technical economic research in metals, processes and long-range planning. *Mailing Add:* Columbus Div Battelle Mem Inst 505 King Ave Columbus OH 43201

FROST, ROBERT EDWIN, b Gowanda, NY, Feb 1, 32; m 58; c 3. INORGANIC CHEMISTRY. *Educ:* Allegheny Col, BS, 53; Harvard Univ, AM, 55, PhD(chem), 57. *Prof Exp:* Res chemist, Res Ctr, B F Goodrich Co, 57-61; assoc prof, 61-64, PROF CHEM, STATE UNIV NY ALBANY, 64- *Concurrent Pos:* Vis lectr, Univ Ill, 65-66. *Mem:* Am Chem Soc. *Res:* Transition metal complexes; organometallic chemistry. *Mailing Add:* Dept of Chem State Univ of NY Albany NY 12222

FROST, ROBERT HARTWIG, b Riverside, Calif, July 2, 17; m 44; c 2. EXPERIMENTAL PHYSICS. *Educ:* Univ Calif, AB, 39, MA, 45, PhD(physics), 47. *Prof Exp:* Asst physics, Univ Calif, 41-45; asst prof, Univ Mo, 47-53; from asst prof to assoc prof, 53-63, PROF PHYSICS, CALIF POLYTECH STATE UNIV, SAN LUIS OBISPO, 63-, HEAD DEPT, 71- *Mem:* AAAS; Am Asn Physics Teachers; Am Phys Soc. *Res:* Specific ionization of electrons. *Mailing Add:* Dept of Physics Calif Polytech State Univ San Luis Obispo CA 93407

FROST, ROBERT T, b Towson, Md, Sept, 14, 24; m 48; c 5. PHYSICS. *Educ:* Johns Hopkins Univ, AB, 49, PhD, 53. *Prof Exp:* Jr instr physics, Johns Hopkins Univ, 49-51; res assoc, Knolls Atomic Power Lab, 53-55, mgr critical assemblies groups, 55-57, adv reactor physics, 57-59, adv concepts, 59-61, consult, 61-62, mgr space physics, 62-70, mgr earth orbital opers, Space Sci Lab, 70-80, CONSULT ENG, GEN ELEC CO, 80- *Concurrent Pos:* Mem space & atmos physics comt, Am Inst Aeronaut & Astronaut, chmn space processing tech comt. *Mem:* Am Phys Soc; Am Geophys Union. *Res:* Reactions of light nuclei; nuclear reactors; space physics; development of airborne and satellite experiments for remote sensing of earth and atmosphere, electromagnetic levitation and zero gravity metals solidification studies. *Mailing Add:* Gen Elec Co PO Box 8555 Philadelphia PA 19101

FROST, STANLEY H, b Amboy, Ill, May 7, 37; m 62; c 1. GEOLOGY, PALEONTOLOGY. *Educ:* Northern Ill Univ, BS, 61; Univ Ill, MS, 63, PhD(paleont, geol), 66. *Prof Exp:* From asst prof to assoc prof geol, Northern Ill Univ, 69-77; MEM STAFF, GULF RES & DEVELOP CO, HOUSTON, 77- *Mem:* Paleont Soc. *Res:* Carbonate petrology of Silurian and Devonian,

Indiana and Nevada Devonian brachiopods and corals; southeastern Nevada Tertiary larger Foraminifera and corals; northern Central America Tertiary biostratigraphy of western Caribbean. *Mailing Add:* Gulf Res & Develop Co Box 36505 Houston TX 77036

FROST, TERRENCE PARKER, b Concord, NH, Apr 29, 21; m 57; c 2. WATER POLLUTION. *Educ:* Univ NH, BS, 42, MS, 55. *Prof Exp:* Water pollution biologist, 47-67, dir biosyst & basin planning, 73-77, chief aquatic biologist & dir permits & enforcement planning, 67-81, CHIEF AQUATIC BIOLOGIST, NH WATER SUPPLY & POLLUTION CONTROL COMN, 67-, LAB DIR, 81- *Concurrent Pos:* Mem, NH Pesticides Control Bd, 65-79, Gov Adv Comt Oceanog, 66-70, NH Gov Citizens Task Force Subcomt Indust & Domestic Wastes, 69-70, NH Dredge Bd, 67-79, NH Water Resource Res Ctr Adv Bd, 69-, NH Bulk Power Site Eval Comt, 71-, NH Wetlands Bd, 79- & Vt Yankee Nuclear Power Co Tech Adv Bd, 73-; ed, J NH Water Works Asn, 71- *Mem:* AAAS; Water Pollution Control Fedn; Am Soc Limnol & Oceanog; Am Fisheries Soc; Nat Environ Health Asn. *Res:* Travel of underground pollution plumes; deep-lake homogenization for algae control; nutrient removal by duckweed harvest; pollutant removal efficiency of spray irrigation systems on forestlands; acid rainfall; phosphorus rainfall. *Mailing Add:* 37 Clinton St Concord NH 03301

FROST, WALTER, b Edmonton, Alta, Apr 6, 35; m 62; c 2. MECHANICAL ENGINEERING, HEAT TRANSFER. *Educ:* Univ Wash, Seattle, BS, 61, MS, 63, PhD(mech eng), 65. *Prof Exp:* Assoc prof mech eng, 65-76, PROF AVIATION SYSTS, SPACE INST, UNIV TENN, 76- *Mem:* Am Soc Mech Engrs; Am Inst Aeronaut & Astronaut. *Res:* Boiling heat transfer and two phase flow; radiation and convection heat transfer from finned surfaces; natural convection from finite horizontal surfaces; heat transfer in porous media. *Mailing Add:* Space Inst Univ of Tenn Tullahoma TN 37388

FROSTICK, FREDERICK CHARLES, JR, b Maxton, NC, Aug 3, 22; m 53; c 2. ORGANIC CHEMISTRY. *Educ:* Duke Univ, BS, 43, PhD(chem), 51. *Prof Exp:* Res assoc org chem, 50-56, group leader, 56-58, asst to dir res, 58-64, assoc dir admin, 64-70, ASSOC DIR & SITE ADMINR, RES & DEVELOP, UNION CARBIDE CORP, 70- *Concurrent Pos:* Vpres & Trustee, Kanawha Valley Mem Hosp, 71-; pres, Duke Univ Gen Alumni Asn, 75-76; dir, Mountain State Fed Savings & Loan Asn, 81- *Mem:* AAAS; Am Chem Soc; Sigma Xi. *Res:* Oxidations of organic compounds; synthetic organic chemistry; research administration. *Mailing Add:* Union Carbide Corp Tech Ctr PO Box 8361 South Charleston WV 25303

FROTHINGHAM, THOMAS ELIOT, b Boston, Mass, June 21, 26; m 54; c 4. PEDIATRICS, PUBLIC HEALTH. *Educ:* Harvard Med Sch, MD, 51. *Prof Exp:* Asst prof epidemiol, Tulane Univ, 59-60; assoc mem, Pub Health Res Inst, City New York, 60-61; from asst prof to assoc prof trop pub health, Harvard Univ, 61-69; mem staff, Corvallis Clin, 69-73; dir area health educ prog, 73-80, PROF PEDIAT & COMMUNITY & FAMILY MED & DIR, DIV GEN PEDIAT, MED CTR, DUKE UNIV, 73- *Concurrent Pos:* Teaching fel pediat, Harvard Univ, 56-57, res fel, 57-58. *Mem:* Am Soc Trop Med & Hyg; Am Acad Pediat. *Res:* Infectious diseases; clinical, laboratory and public health aspects. *Mailing Add:* Box 3937 Duke Univ Med Ctr Durham NC 27710

FROUNFELKER, ROBERT E, b West Allis, Wis, Apr 20, 25; m 45; c 4. ENGINEERING SCIENCE. *Educ:* Marquette Univ, BME, 45, MS, 48 & 63. *Prof Exp:* Asst physics, Marquette Univ, 46-48, from instr to asst prof math, 48-63; assoc prof, 63-66, PROF ENG SCI, TENN TECHNOL UNIV, 66- *Concurrent Pos:* Consult engr, Bayley Blower Co, 58-63, Sheldons Eng Ltd, 59-63 & Clarage Fan Co, 59-63; comput consult, Johnson Serv Co, 60-63. *Res:* Materials and computer science; computer techniques for rating capacities of air moving equipment; determination of the cohesive and surface energies of ionic crystals. *Mailing Add:* Dept of Eng Sci Tenn Technol Univ Cookeville TN 38501

FROYD, JAMES DONALD, b Brooklyn, NY, May 25, 39; m 63; c 3. PLANT PATHOLOGY. *Educ:* Denison Univ, BS, 61; Univ Minn, MS, 64, PhD(plant path), 67. *Prof Exp:* Res asst plant dis, Univ Minn, St Paul, 61-65, exten plant pathologist, 65-67; SR PLANT PATHOLOGIST, ELI LILLY & CO, 67- *Mem:* Am Phytopath Soc; Int Soc Plant Pathologists; Sigma Xi; Soc Nematologists. *Res:* Ecology of the dissemination of forest pathogens; diseases of ornamentals; chemical control of plant diseases; systemic fungicides. *Mailing Add:* Eli Lilly & Co PO Box 708 Greenfield IN 46140

FRUCHTER, JONATHAN S, b San Antonio, Tex, June 5, 45; m 73; c 2. ENVIRONMENTAL CHEMISTRY, GEOCHEMISTRY. *Educ:* Univ Tex, Austin, BS, 66; Univ Calif, San Diego, PhD(chem), 71. *Prof Exp:* Res asst chem, Univ Calif, San Diego, 66-71; res assoc geochem, Univ Ore, 71-74; SR RES SCIENTIST ENVIRON CHEM & BIOCHEM, PAC NORTHWEST DIV, BATTELLE MEM INST, 74- *Mem:* Am Chem Soc; Geol Soc Am. *Res:* Environmental and analytical chemistry of products and effluents from synthetic fossil fuel plants, especially oil shale; trace elements in igneous rocks and meteorites; interactions of cosmic rays with matter nuclear waste migration. *Mailing Add:* Pac Northwest Div PO Box 999 Richland WA 99352

FRUEH, ALFRED JOSEPH, JR, b Passaic, NJ, Sept 2, 19; m 43; c 3. CRYSTALLOGRAPHY, MINERALOGY. *Educ:* Mass Inst Technol, BS, 42, MS, 47, PhD(mineral), 49. *Prof Exp:* Res assoc, Univ Chicago, 49-52, asst prof mineral & crystallog, 52-58; vis prof, Univ Oslo, 58-59; from asst prof to prof crystallog, McGill Univ, 59-69; chmn dept, 69-78, PROF GEOL, UNIV CONN, 69- *Concurrent Pos:* Chmn, Teaching Comn, Int Union Crystallog, 60-66; Int Union Crystallog rep, Int Coun Sci Unions, 63-66; co-ed, Structures Reports, 60-63 & 69-75; chmn & organizer, Int Mineral Asn, 62 Symp Sulfide Mineralogy; assoc ed, Am Mineralogist, 62-65; mem adv comt crystallog, Nat Res Coun Can, 66-69. *Mem:* Mineral Soc Am; Geol Soc Am; Am Crystallog Asn; Fr Soc Mineral & Crystallog; Brit Mineral Soc. *Res:* X-ray crystallography; mineral structures; solid state physics and chemistry applied to minerals. *Mailing Add:* Dept of Geol Univ of Conn Storrs CT 06268

FRUHMAN, GEORGE JOSHUA, b Boston, Mass, Oct 17, 24. ANATOMY. *Educ:* NY Univ, AB, 48, MS, 52, PhD, 54. *Prof Exp:* Asst prof biol, Stern Col Women, Yeshiva Univ, 55-58; asst prof, 56-70, ASSOC PROF ANAT, ALBERT EINSTEIN COL MED, 70- *Concurrent Pos:* Fel, Damon Runyon Found, NY Univ, 54-56; lectr, NY Univ. *Mem:* Fel NY Acad Sci; Am Asn Anatomists; Am Soc Zoologists; Reticuloendothelial Soc; Soc Exp Biol & Med. *Res:* Experimental hematology; histology. *Mailing Add:* Dept of Anat Albert Einstein Col of Med New York NY 10461

FRUIN, JOHN THOMAS, b Watseka, Ill, April 2, 38; m 64; c 6. TOXICOLOGY, FOOD HYGIENE. *Educ:* Univ Ill, BS, 60, DVM, 62; Purdue Univ, MS, 66, PhD(food technol), 74. *Prof Exp:* Comdr food inspection, US Army Med Detachment, Vietnam, 63-64, chief food res, Qual Assurance Div, Natick Labs, 66-69, chief food hyg group, 76-80, chief toxicol group, 80-81, CHEIF, RES SPECIALITY DIV, TOXICOL RES, US ARMY INST RES, 81- *Concurrent Pos:* Investr, US Army Letterman Army Inst Res, 74-, study dir, 78-; consult, US Army Surgeon Gen, 77- *Mem:* Am Col Vet Prev Med; Am Vet Med Asn; Inst Food Technol; Am Acad Microbiol; Am Asn Food Hyg Vet. *Res:* Conducts basis and applied research in the toxicologic assessment of therapeutic agents; environmental contaminants and food contaminants. *Mailing Add:* 57 Presidio Blvd San Francisco CA 94129

FRUMKES, THOMAS EUGENE, b Rochester, NY, July 25, 41. NEUROSCIENCES, PHYSIOLOGICAL OPTICS. *Educ:* Cornell Univ, AB, 63; Syracuse Univ, PhD(physiol psychol), 67. *Prof Exp:* Asst, Syracuse Univ, 63-64; NIH fel, 67-69, lectr psychol, 68-69, asst prof, 69-74, assoc prof, 74-78, PROF PSYCHOL, QUEENS COL, NY, 78- *Concurrent Pos:* Res assoc, Dept Neurosurg, Mt Sinai Hosp, City Univ New York, 69-70 & Dept Ophthal, Col Physicians & Surgeons, Columbia Univ, 70- *Mem:* AAAS; Optical Soc Am; Asn Res Vision & Ophthal; NY Acad Sci; Soc Neurosci. *Res:* Vision; neurophysiology; psychophysics; sensory processes; central nervous system. *Mailing Add:* Dept of Psychol Queens Col Flushing NY 11367

FRUMP, JOHN ADAMS, b Butterfield, Ark, Oct 1, 21; m 46; c 3. ORGANIC CHEMISTRY. *Educ:* Ind Univ, BS, 50. *Prof Exp:* Chemist, Chrysler Corp, 50-51; plant chemist, Autolite Corp, 51-52; RES CHEMIST, INT MINERALS & CHEM CORP, 52- *Mem:* Am Chem Soc; Am Soc Info Sci. *Res:* Oxazoline and oxazolidine chemistry; emulsion chemistry; nitroparaffin chemistry; process development for recovery of organic compounds. *Mailing Add:* RR 21 Box 701 Terre Haute IN 47802

FRURIP, DAVID J, b Detroit, Mich, Jan 25, 49; m 81. PHYSICAL CHEMISTRY. *Educ:* Eastern Mich Univ, BS, 71; Cornell Univ, PhD(phys chem), 76. *Prof Exp:* ASST CHEMIST PHYSICAL & INORG CHEM, ARGONNE NAT LAB, 76- *Concurrent Pos:* Instr, Aurora Col, 78- *Mem:* Am Chem Soc. *Res:* Nucleation and condensation phenomena; thermal conductivities of associating gases; laser pyrolysis; thermodynamic properties of high temperature vapors. *Mailing Add:* CEN-205 Argonnne Nat Lab 9700 S Cass Ave Argonne IL 60439

FRUSH, CHARLES O(LIN), JR, b Oskaloosa, Iowa, Oct 20, 19; m 41; c 4. MINING ENGINEERING. *Educ:* Iowa State Col, BS, 41, MS, 55. *Prof Exp:* Jr mining engr, Chile Explor Co, 41-44; asst field engr mineral explor, US Smelting, Refining & Mining Co, 44; engr, Frush Mining Co, 44-46; instr mining eng, Iowa State Col, 44-56; asst prof, eng exp sta, 50-56; ASSOC PROF MINING ENG, COLO SCH MINES, 56- *Concurrent Pos:* Fulbright prof mining eng, Univ Liberia, Monrovia, 78-79. *Mem:* Am Inst Mining, Metall & Petrol Engrs. *Res:* Mineral technology. *Mailing Add:* Dept of Mining Eng Colo Sch of Mines Golden CO 80401

FRUSHOUR, BRUCE GEORGE, b Frederick, Md, Sept 27, 47; m 71; c 1. MACROMOLECULAR SCIENCE, PHYSICAL CHEMISTRY. *Educ:* Juniata Col, BS, 69; Case Western Reserve Univ, MS, 72, PhD(macromolecular sci), 74. *Prof Exp:* Sr res chemist, 74-77, res specialist, Textiles Div, 77-80, SR RES SPECIALIST, PLASTICS & RESINS DIV, MONSANTO CO, 80- *Concurrent Pos:* Adj assoc prof, Sch Textiles, NC State Univ, 79- *Mem:* Am Chem Soc; Am Phys Soc. *Res:* Spectroscopy of biopolymers; structure of acrylic and polyester fibers; mechanical properties of plastics. *Mailing Add:* Monsanto Co 730 Worchester St Indian Orchard MA 01151

FRUTH, LESTER SYLVESTER, JR, sedimentology, see previous edition

FRUTHALER, GEORGE JAMES, JR, b New Orleans, La, Aug 8, 25; m 48; c 3. MEDICINE. *Educ:* Tulane Univ, BS, 46, MD, 48; Am Bd Pediat, dipl, 54. *Prof Exp:* Intern, Charity Hosp, La, 48-49 & pediat, Vanderbilt Univ Hosp, 49-50; from instr to assoc prof, 54-68, PROF CLIN PEDIAT, TULANE UNIV, 68-; MEM PEDIAT STAFF, OCHSNER CLIN, 53- *Concurrent Pos:* Ochsner Med Found fel, 50-51 & 53; asst vis physician, Charity Hosp, 50-68, vis physicians, 68-; mem, Am Bd Pediat, 66-72. *Mem:* AMA; Am Acad Pediat. *Res:* Pediatrics; allergy. *Mailing Add:* Ochsner Clin 1514 Jefferson Hwy New Orleans LA 70121

FRUTIGER, ROBERT LESTER, b Harrisburg, Pa, Sept 22, 46; m 72; c 2. MECHANICAL ENGINEERING, SOLID MECHANICS. *Educ:* Univ Pittsburgh, BS, 69, MS, 72, PhD(mech eng), 75. *Prof Exp:* Asst instr, Univ Pittsburgh, 70-75; mem res staff plastics processing, Eng Res Ctr, Western Elec Co, 75-79; SR RES ENGR, ENG MECH, GEN MOTORS RES LABS, 79- *Mem:* Am Soc Mech Engrs; Soc Rheol; Sigma Xi. *Res:* Viscoelasticity; finite elasticity; continuum mechanics; polymer processing. *Mailing Add:* Gen Motors Res Labs Eng Mech Dept Mound & 12 Mile Rd Warren MI 48090

FRUTON, JOSEPH STEWART, b Czestochowa, Poland, May 14, 12; nat US; m 36. BIOCHEMISTRY. *Educ:* Columbia Univ, BA, 31, PhD(biochem), 34. *Hon Degrees:* MA, Yale Univ, 50; DSc, Rockefeller Univ, 76. *Prof Exp:* Asst biochem, Col Physicians & Surgeons, Columbia Univ, 33-34; fel chem,

Rockefeller Inst, 34-35, asst, 35-38, assoc, 38-45; assoc prof physiol chem, 45-50, prof biochem, 50-57, chmn dept, 51-67, dir div sci, 59-62, EUGENE HIGGINS PROF BIOCHEM, YALE UNIV, 57- *Concurrent Pos:* Chmn panel enzymes, Comt Growth, Nat Res Coun, 46-49, mem biochem, Adv Comt, Chem Biol Coord Ctr, 46-51 & Div Chem & Chem Technol, 50-52, fel bd, 53-60, chmn, 58-60, mem, Exec Comt, Div Med Sci, 60-63; spec fel, Rockefeller Found, 48; consult, Anna Fuller Fund, 51-72; Harvey lectr, 55; Dakin lectr, 62; Commonwealth Fund fel, 62-63; mem, Int Union Pure & Appl Chem-Int Union Biochem, 64-69; vis prof, Rockefeller Univ, 68-69; Sarton Lectr, 76 & Xerox, 77. *Honors & Awards:* Lilly Award, Am Chem Soc, 44; Pfizer Award, Hist Sci Soc, 73. *Mem:* Nat Acad Sci; fel AAAS; Am Chem Soc; NY Acad Sci (vpres, 45-46); Benjamin Franklin fel Royal Soc Arts. *Res:* Chemistry and metabolism of amino acids, peptides and proteins; enzymes; history of science. *Mailing Add:* 350 Kline Biol Tower Yale Univ New Haven CT 06520

FRY, ALBERT JOSEPH, b Philadelphia, Pa, May 12, 37; m 66; c 3. ORGANIC CHEMISTRY. *Educ:* Univ Mich, BS, 58; Univ Wis, PhD(org chem), 63. *Prof Exp:* Res fel chem, Calif Inst Technol, 63-64; res fel, 64-65, asst prof, 65-72, assoc prof, 72-77, PROF CHEM, WESLEYAN UNIV, 77- *Mem:* Am Chem Soc; Royal Soc Chem; Int Electrochem Soc. *Res:* Nonbenzenoid aromatic species; synthetic and mechanistic organic electrochemistry. *Mailing Add:* Hall-Atwater Lab of Chem Wesleyan Univ Middletown CT 06457

FRY, ANNE EVANS, b Philadelphia, Pa, Sept 11, 39. ZOOLOGY, DEVELOPMENTAL BIOLOGY. *Educ:* Mt Holyoke Col, AB, 61; Univ Iowa, MS, 63; Univ Mass, PhD(zool), 69. *Prof Exp:* Instr biol, Carleton Col, 63-65; from asst prof to assoc prof, 69-80, PROF ZOOL, OHIO WESLEYAN UNIV, 80- *Mem:* AAAS; Am Inst Biol Sci; Am Soc Zoologists; Soc Develop Biol; Sigma Xi. *Res:* Amphibian limb regeneration, amphibian metamorphosis. *Mailing Add:* Dept of Zool Ohio Wesleyan Univ 70 S Henry St Delaware OH 43015

FRY, ARTHUR JAMES, b Dodson, Mont, Mar 10, 21; m 47; c 3. ORGANIC CHEMISTRY, REACTION MECHANISMS. *Educ:* Mont State Col, BS, 43; Univ Calif, Berkeley, PhD(chem), 51. *Prof Exp:* Assoc chemist, Oak Ridge Nat Lab, 46-48; from asst prof to assoc prof, 51-59, chmn dept, 56-57 & 64-67, PROF CHEM, UNIV ARK, FAYETTEVILLE, 59- *Concurrent Pos:* Consult, Col Chem Consult Serv, 68-; vis prof, Univ Auckland, 69-70 & 78, Univ Adelaide, 70 & Monash Univ, 77. *Mem:* AAAS; Am Chem Soc; The Chem Soc. *Res:* Organic reaction mechanisms; isotope effects on rates of chemical reactions; acid catalyzed ketone rearrangements. *Mailing Add:* Dept of Chem Univ of Ark Fayetteville AR 72701

FRY, CLEOTA GAGE, b Shoshone, Idaho, Dec 30, 10. MATHEMATICS. *Educ:* Reed Col, BA, 33; Purdue Univ, MS, 36, PhD(math), 39. *Prof Exp:* Asst instr math, 39-40, instr physics, 41-45, from instr to asst prof math, 45-55, asst to dean sch sci, 52-61, assoc prof, 55-77, EMER ASSOC PROF MATH, PURDUE UNIV, 77- *Mem:* Am Phys Soc; Am Math Soc. *Res:* Mathematical analysis in field of complex variables; acoustics; theoretical physics; calculation of atomic form factors; applied mathematics. *Mailing Add:* 1100 Hillcrest Rd W Lafayette IN 47906

FRY, DAVID LLOYD GEORGE, b Detroit, Mich, Sept 22, 18; m 42; c 3. PHYSICS. *Educ:* Kalamazoo Col, BA, 40; Ohio State Univ, MS, 42. *Prof Exp:* Asst, Kalamazoo Col, 39-40; res physicist, Gen Motors Corp, 42-48, group leader spectros, 48-52, supvr spectros, 52-56, supvr chem physics, 56-65, supvr chem physics & magnetics, 65-76, dept res scientist, Res Labs, 76-80; RETIRED. *Mem:* Fel AAAS; Am Phys Soc; fel Optical Soc Am. *Res:* Emission and absorption spectroscopy in ultraviolet, visible and infrared; mass spectroscopy; diffusion of gases in solids; nuclear magnetic resonance; internal friction; electro-optics; magnetics; atmospheric physics; combustion physics. *Mailing Add:* 685 Princeton Rd Berkley MI 48072

FRY, DONALD LEWIS, b Des Moines, Iowa, Dec 29, 24; m 57; c 4. PHYSIOLOGY. *Educ:* Harvard Univ, MD, 49. *Prof Exp:* Intern med, Univ Minn Hosps, 49-50, res med, 50-52, res fel, Heart Hosp, 52-53; independent investr, Nat Heart Inst, NIH, 53-61, head, Sect Clin Biophysics, Nat Heart & Lung Inst, 61-71, head, Sect Exp Atherosclerosis, 71-75, chief, Lab Exp Atherosclerosis, Nat Heart & Lung Inst, 75-80; PROF MED PATH & DIR, LAB EXP ATHEROSCLEROSIS, COL MED, OHIO STATE UNIV, COLUMBUS, 80- *Concurrent Pos:* Fel, Var Club Heart Hosp, 52-53. *Mem:* AAAS; Am Physiol Soc; Biophys Soc; Am Soc Clin Invest; NY Acad Sci. *Res:* Physiology and biophysics of the blood-vascular interface, with particular emphasis on mechanochemical events associated with endothelial degeneration, transvascular transport and the genesis of atherosclerosis. *Mailing Add:* Lab Exp Atherosclerosis Ohio State Univ Col Med 2005 Wiseman Hall 400 W 12th Ave Columbus OH 43210

FRY, EDWARD IRAD, b US, Jan 7, 24; m 50. BIOLOGICAL ANTHROPOLOGY. *Educ:* Univ Tex, BA, 49, MA, 50; Harvard Univ, PhD(anthrop), 58. *Prof Exp:* Off coordr, Values Study, Harvard Univ, 50-51; asst prof anthrop & tech dir, Anthropomet Proj, Antioch Col, 55-56; from instr to assoc prof anthrop, Univ Nebr, Lincoln, 56-66; PROF ANTHROP, SOUTHERN METHODIST UNIV, 66- *Concurrent Pos:* Fulbright fel, Univ NZ, Cook Islands, 53-54; field consult, Carnegie Inst, Mex, 55; Fulbright res fel, Univ Hong Kong, 63-64. *Mem:* AAAS; Am Anthrop Asn; Am Asn Phys Anthropologists (pres, 73-75); Soc Study Human Biol; AAAS. *Res:* Human biology, especially growth, skeletal age and bone; Polynesia; United States; Southeast Asia. *Mailing Add:* Dept of Anthrop Southern Methodist Univ Dallas TX 75275

FRY, EDWARD STARUSS, b Meadville, Pa, July 27, 40; m 64; c 3. PHYSICS. *Educ:* Univ Mich, BS, 62, MS, 63, PhD(physics), 69. *Prof Exp:* From asst prof to assoc prof physics, Tex A&M Univ, 69-77; vis assoc prof, Univ Mich, 77-79; ASSOC PROF PHYSICS, TEX A&M UNIV, 79- *Mem:* Optical Soc Am; Am Phys Soc. *Res:* Experimental atomic physics; foundations of quantum mechanics; tests for parity violation; polarized light scattering studies. *Mailing Add:* Dept of Physics Tex A&M Univ College Station TX 77843

FRY, FRANCIS J(OHN), b Johnstown, Pa, Apr 2, 20; m 46; c 9. ELECTRICAL ENGINEERING. *Educ:* Pa State Univ, BS, 40; Univ Pittsburgh, MS, 46. *Prof Exp:* Design engr, Westinghouse Elec Corp, 40-46; res assoc elec eng, Univ Ill, Urbana, 46-50, res asst prof, 50-57, res assoc prof, 57-68, assoc prof, 68-72; assoc dir, 72-78, DIR, ULTRASOUND RES LABS, INDIANAPOLIS CTR ADVAN RES, 78-; ASSOC PROF SURG, IND SCH MED, 72- *Concurrent Pos:* Vpres, Intersci Res Inst, 57-68, pres, 68-70, secy & chmn bd dirs, 70-72; vis assoc prof elec eng, Univ Ill, Urbana, 72- *Honors & Awards:* Pioneer Award, Am Inst Ultrasound Med, 81. *Mem:* Am Inst Ultrasound Med; Am Soc Artificial Internal Organs; Neurosci Soc; Biomed Eng Soc; Acoust Soc Am. *Res:* Application of ultrasound to medical and biological problems; artificial hearts, blood flow; effects of ultrasound on biological systems; ultrasonic soft tissue visualization and tissue modifying systems; neuroscience, quantitative aspects of structural organization in brain; relations between structure and function. *Mailing Add:* Fortune-Fry Ultrasound Res Labs IUPUI 410 Beauty Ave Indianapolis IN 46202

FRY, FREDERICK ERNEST JOSEPH, b Surrey, Eng, Apr 17, 08; Can citizen; m 35; c 3. ECOLOGY. *Educ:* Univ Toronto, AB, 33, AM, 35, PhD(ichthyol), 36; Univ Man, DSc, 70. *Prof Exp:* Assoc prof limnol, Dept Zool, 48-56, prof zool, 56-74, EMER PROF ZOOL, UNIV TORONTO, 74- *Concurrent Pos:* Mem, Fisheries Res Bd Can, 64-69; comnr, Int Great Lakes Fishery Comn, 69-79. *Honors & Awards:* Order of the Brit Empire, 44; Flavelle Medal, Royal Soc Can, 62; Govt Can Centennial Medal, 68; Am Fisheries Soc Medal, 71. *Mem:* Fel Royal Soc Can; Am Soc Limnol & Oceanog (pres, 51); Am Fisheries Soc (pres, 66); Can Soc Zoologists (pres, 66); fel Am Inst Fishery Res Biologists (pres, 73-74). *Res:* Relation of fish to factors in their environment. *Mailing Add:* Dept of Zool Univ of Toronto Toronto ON M5S 1A1 Can

FRY, HAROLD, b Pierce, Colo, Oct 16, 15; m 39; c 2. MECHANICAL ENGINEERING. *Educ:* Colo State Univ, BS, 37; Univ Wyo, ME, 50; Univ Colo, MS, 57. *Prof Exp:* Motor engr, Westinghouse Elec Corp, 37-40; instr machine design, Kans State Univ, 40-42; from asst prof to prof mech eng, Univ Wyo, 42-58; prof, 58-79, EMER ASSOC PROF ENG, ARIZ STATE UNIV, 79- *Concurrent Pos:* Elec engr, Nat Adv Comt Aeronaut, 44-45. *Honors & Awards:* Ralph R Teetor Award, Soc Automotive Engrs, 74. *Mem:* Am Soc Mech Engrs; Soc Automotive Engrs. *Res:* Automotive engines; causes and corrections of bearing failures; wear rates of engine parts under adverse operating conditions. *Mailing Add:* 325 E Broadway Tempe AZ 85282

FRY, JACK L, b Thomas, Okla, Dec 24, 30; m 52; c 3. ACADEMIC ADMINISTRATION, POULTRY SCIENCE. *Educ:* Okla State Univ, BS, 52, MS, 56; Purdue Univ, PhD(food technol), 59. *Prof Exp:* Asst prof, Kans State Univ, 59-64; assoc prof poultry sci, 64-70, fac develop grant, 70, PROF POULTRY SCI, UNIV FLA, 70-, ASST DEAN COL AGR, 75- *Honors & Awards:* Inst Am Poultry Industs Award, 69. *Mem:* Poultry Sci Asn; World Poultry Sci Asn; Inst Food Technologists. *Mailing Add:* Col Agr Univ Fla Gainesville FL 32611

FRY, JAMES LESLIE, b Fostoria, Ohio, May 24, 41; m 64; c 1. ORGANIC CHEMISTRY. *Educ:* Bowling Green State Univ, BS, 63; Mich State Univ, PhD(org chem), 67. *Prof Exp:* NIH fel org chem, Princeton Univ, 67-69; asst prof, 69-73, assoc prof, 73-78, PROF CHEM, UNIV TOLEDO, 78- *Mem:* Am Chem Soc; The Chem Soc; Sigma Xi. *Res:* Kinetic isotope effects; asymmetric syntheses; reaction mechanisms; synthetic applications of carbocation chemistry; organosilicon chemistry. *Mailing Add:* Dept of Chem Univ of Toledo Toledo OH 43606

FRY, JAMES N, b Philadelphia, Pa, Aug 6, 52. THEORETICAL COSMOLOGY. *Educ:* Cornell Univ, BS, 74; Princeton Univ, MA, 76, PhD(physics), 79. *Prof Exp:* McCormick fel, 79-81, RES ASSOC THEORET ASTROPHYS, UNIV CHICAGO, 81- *Mem:* AAAS; Am Phys Soc. *Res:* Nature of the large scale structure of the universe; implications of grand unified theories in the early universe; statistical treatment of the clustering of galaxies. *Mailing Add:* Astron & Astrophys Ctr 5640 S Ellis Ave Chicago IL 60637

FRY, JOHN CRAIG, b Salem, Ore, Dec 11, 26; m 49; c 3. MARINE SCIENCE, SCIENCE POLICY. *Educ:* US Naval Acad, BS, 47; Univ Calif, MS, 52. *Prof Exp:* Prog officer acoust, Naval Underwater Sound Lab, US Navy, 56-59, proj officer, Cruiser Destroyer Flotilla Three, 60-62, head, Requirements Br, Oceanog Div, Off Chief Naval Opers, 62-65; tech asst oceanog, Off Sci & Technol, Exec Off President, 65-67, sr staff mem, Nat Coun Marine Resources & Eng Develop, 67-69; vpres, Ocean Data Systs, Inc, 69-71; dep dir, Off Sci & Technol, AID, 71-76; dir, Off Bilateral & Multilaterial Sci & Technol Affairs, Dept State, 76-78; dep coordr, UN Conf Technol & Sci, 79-80; COUNR SCI & TECHNOL AFFAIRS, US MISSION TO EUROPEAN COMMUNITIES, 81- *Honors & Awards:* Superior Honor Award, Agency Int Develop, 73. *Mem:* NY Acad Sci; Sigma Xi. *Res:* Science technology for international development. *Mailing Add:* US Europ Communities Brussels APO New York NY 09667

FRY, JOHN SEDGWICK, b Philadelphia, Pa, Oct 22, 29; m 51; c 2. ORGANIC CHEMISTRY. *Educ:* Duke Univ, BS, 51, MA, 55. *Prof Exp:* Proj scientist, Plastics Div, 55-68, RES SCIENTIST, RES & DEVELOP DEPT, UNION CARBIDE CORP, 68- *Res:* Polymers and resins and derived products. *Mailing Add:* 14 Westbrook Ave S Somerville NJ 08876

FRY, KENNETH ALVIN, b Topeka, Kans, Oct 20, 14; m 64; c 4. MICROBIOLOGY. *Educ:* Kans State Teachers Col, AB, 35, MS, 36; Purdue Univ, PhD, 60. *Prof Exp:* Teacher pub sch, 36-41, prin, 41-44; instr bact, Martin Col, Univ Tenn, 46-47; asst prof biol, Univ Chattanooga, 47-60, prof & head dept, 60-63; head fel officer, Oak Ridge Inst Nuclear Studies, 64-65; PROF BIOL & CHMN DEPT, TEX WOMEN'S UNIV, 65- *Concurrent Pos:* Consult, Erlanger Hosp, Chattanooga, 50-63 & Chattanooga Med Col & Indust Res Inst, 56-63. *Mem:* Am Acad Microbiol. *Res:* Bacteriology; physiology; biochemistry; radiation. *Mailing Add:* Dept of Biol Tex Women's Univ Denton TX 76204

FRY, KENNETH E, plant physiology, see previous edition

FRY, LOUIS RUMMEL, b New York, NY, Aug 8, 28; m 65. ORTHOPEDIC SURGERY. *Educ:* Denison Univ, BA, 51; Temple Univ, MD, 55; Am Bd Orthop Surg, dipl. *Prof Exp:* Intern, Sch Med, Temple Univ, 56; instr anat, Med Sch, Univ Mich, 57-58, resident, orthop, 61, instr orthop surg, 61-62; from instr to assoc prof orthop surg, Sch Med, Univ Wash, CLIN CONSULT, SCHS MED, UNIV ORE, PORTLAND & UNIV WASH, 75- *Concurrent Pos:* NIH training grant, 64-65; mem staff, Tuality Community Hosp, chief staff, 79-80; adj prof, Pac Univ, Forest Grove, Ore, 77- *Mem:* AAAS; fel Am Col Surg; fel Am Acad Orthop Surg; Orthop Res Soc; AMA. *Res:* Cell morphology; cartilage; ultrastructure; bone ultrastructure. *Mailing Add:* 349 SE 7th St Hillsboro OR 97123

FRY, PEGGY CROOKE, b Conroe, Tex, Oct 24, 28; m 50. NUTRITION. *Educ:* Univ Tex, BS, 49; Harvard Univ, MPH, 55; Univ Nebr, Lincoln, PhD(nutrit), 67. *Prof Exp:* Am Dietetic Asn admin dietetic intern, Aetna Life Ins Co, Hartford, Conn, 49-50; asst dietitian, Rice Univ, 50; asst admin dietitian, Mt Auburn Hosp, Cambridge, Mass, 51; nutritionist, Forsyth Dent Infirmary for Children, Boston, 51-53; org chemist, Charles F Kettering Found, 55-56; from instr to asst prof food & nutrit, Univ Nebr, Lincoln, 56-63; ASST PROF PEDIAT & CHIEF NUTRIT SERV, CHILDREN & YOUTH PROJ, UNIV TEX SOUTHWESTERN MED SCH DALLAS, 68- *Concurrent Pos:* Nutrit consult, Yellow Springs Med Clin, Ohio, 55-56; consult, Interdept Comt Nutrit Nat Defense, NIH, 62-63; Inst Cross-Cult Res, Washington, DC, 68-; Ctr Res & Educ, Denver, Colo, 72- & Diet, Nutrit & Cancer Prog, Nat Cancer Inst, NIH, 75-77; adj prof, Anthrop Dept, Southern Methodist Univ, 78- *Honors & Awards:* Borden Award, Am Home Econ Asn, 49; Effie I Raitt Award, Am Home Econ Asn, 53. *Mem:* Am Inst Nutrit; Am Dietetic Asn. *Res:* Childhood obesity; utilization of amino acids from plant proteins; methodology for determining nutritional status of children; effectiveness of various methods for improving the iron, protein and vitamin A nutriture of preschoolers. *Mailing Add:* Dept Pediat Univ Tex Southwestern Med Sch Dallas TX 75235

FRY, RICHARD JEREMY MICHAEL, b Dublin, Ireland, July 8, 25; m 56; c 3. PHYSIOLOGY, RADIOBIOLOGY. *Educ:* Univ Dublin, BA, 46, MB, BCh & BAO, 49, MD, 62. *Prof Exp:* Lectr physiol, Univ Dublin, 52-59; resident res assoc radiobiol, Argonne Nat Lab, 59-61; lectr physiol, Univ Dublin, 61-63; assoc scientist, Argonne Nat Lab, 63-70; sr scientist radiobiol, Argonne Nat Lab, 70-77; SECT HEAD, CANCER & TOXICOL SECT, BIOL DIV, OAK RIDGE NAT LAB, 77- *Concurrent Pos:* Prof radiol, Univ Chicago, 70-77. *Mem:* Radiation Res Soc; Am Asn Cancer Res; Am Soc Photobiol; Cell Kinetics Soc. *Res:* Cell proliferation and radiation effects; ionizing and ultraviolet radiation carcinogenesis. *Mailing Add:* Biol Div PO Box Y Oak Ridge TN 37830

FRY, THOMAS R, b Franklin, Pa, Dec 10, 23; m 44; c 3. ELECTRICAL UTILITY ENGINEERING. *Educ:* Univ Pittsburgh, BS, 49. *Prof Exp:* Test engr, Porcelain Prods, Inc, WVa, 49-51, chief engr, Parkersburg & Carey plants, 51-59; chief engr, A B Chance Co, 59-67, mgr eng, Utility Systs Div, 67-71; consult, Black & Veatch, Consult Engrs, 71-74; mgr prod develop, Fargo Mfg Co, 74-77; mgr eng, 77-80, DIR FUELS, SOUTH MISS ELEC POWER ASN, 80- *Concurrent Pos:* Consult, Monongahela Power Co, WVa, 53, Am Casualty Co, 53-58 & Puritan Pottery Co, Pa, 57. *Mem:* Nat Soc Prof Engrs; sr mem Inst Elec & Electronics Engrs. *Res:* Generation and transmission of electrical energy. *Mailing Add:* SMiss Elec Power Asn PO Box 1589 Hattiesburg MS 39401

FRY, WAYNE LYLE, b Inwood, Iowa, Oct 6, 22. PALEOBOTANY. *Educ:* Univ Minn, BSc, 47; Cornell Univ, PhD(bot geol), 53. *Prof Exp:* Asst bot, Univ Minn, 47-49; from asst to instr, Cornell Univ, 49-53; geologist, Geol Surv Can, 53-57; asst prof paleont, Univ, 57-61, fac fel, 59-62, dir mus & chmn dept, 69-70, ASSOC PROF PALEONT, UNIV CALIF, BERKELEY, 61-, CUR PALEOBOT, MUS PALEONT, 57- *Concurrent Pos:* Dir, Summer Inst Earth Sci, 65-67 & 69-; assoc prog dir & foreign affairs coordr, Pre-Col Div, NSF, 67-69; ed in chief, J Paleont, 71-77. *Mem:* Fel Geol Soc Am; fel Bot Soc Am; fel Paleont Soc Am. *Res:* Carboniferous and Devonian petrifications; Mesozoic and Tertiary floras of British Columbia; Jurassic floras of western North America. *Mailing Add:* Dept Paleont Univ Calif Berkeley CA 94720

FRY, WILLIAM EARL, b Lincoln, Nebr, July 6, 44; m 70. PLANT PATHOLOGY. *Educ:* Nebr Wesleyan Univ, BA, 66; Cornell Univ, PhD(plant path), 70. *Prof Exp:* Asst prof biol, Cent Conn State Col, 70-71; asst prof, 71-77, ASSOC PROF PLANT PATH, CORNELL UNIV, 77- *Mem:* AAAS; Am Phytopath Soc; Int Soc Plant Path; Potato Asn Am; Am Soc Plant Physiol. *Res:* Biological and physical factors affecting plant disease epidemiology and control; nature of disease resistance in plants. *Mailing Add:* Dept of Plant Path Cornell Univ Ithaca NY 14850

FRY, WILLIAM FREDERICK, b Carlisle, Iowa, Dec 16, 21; m 43; c 2. EXPERIMENTAL PHYSICS. *Educ:* Iowa State Col, BS, 43, PhD(physics), 51. *Prof Exp:* Physicist, Naval Res Lab, 43-47; with AEC, Chicago, 51-52; asst prof, 52-58, PROF PHYSICS, UNIV WIS-MADISON, 58- *Concurrent Pos:* Fulbright lectr, Italy, 56-57. *Mem:* Fel Am Phys Soc. *Res:* Elementary particle physics using bubble chambers; acoustics of violin family. *Mailing Add:* Dept of Physics Univ of Wis Madison WI 53706

FRY, WILLIAM JAMES, b Ann Arbor, Mich, Mar 21, 28; m 49; c 2. SURGERY. *Educ:* Univ Mich, MD, 52; Am Bd Surg, dipl, 60. *Prof Exp:* From instr to prof, Med Sch, Univ Mich, Ann Arbor, 59-74, asst surg, Dept Postgrad Med, 60-66, chief res surg serv, Med Ctr, 64-67, head sect gen surg, 67-76, Frederick A Coller prof surg, 74-76; LEE HUDSON-ROBERT PENN PROF SURG & CHMN DEPT, UNIV TEX SOUTHWESTERN MED SCH, 76- *Concurrent Pos:* Attend physician, Ann Arbor Vet Admin Hosp, 60-61, chief surg, 61-64, consult, 64-76; consult, Wayne Co Gen Hosp, 67-76, Vet Admin Hosp, Dallas, 76- & Med Ctr, Baylor Univ, 76-; mem sr med staff, Parkland Mem Hosp, 76-; USPHS grant. *Mem:* Am Surg Asn; Soc Univ Surg; fel Am Col Surg; Soc Surg Alimentary Tract; Soc Vascular Surg. *Res:* Vascular physiology. *Mailing Add:* Dept Surg Med Sch, Univ Tex Southwestern Dallas TX 75235

FRYBERGER, DAVID, b Duluth, Minn, Feb 22, 31; m 57; c 1. HIGH ENERGY PHYSICS. *Educ:* Yale Univ, BE, 53; Ill Inst Technol, MS, 62; Univ Chicago, PhD(physics), 67. *Prof Exp:* Res engr elec eng, Ill Inst Technol Res Inst, 59-67; ENG PHYSICIST PARTICLE PHYSICS, STANFORD LINEAR ACCELERATOR CTR, 67- *Concurrent Pos:* Hertz fel, Fannie & John Hertz Found, 66-67. *Mem:* Am Phys Soc. *Res:* Elementary particle physics. *Mailing Add:* Stanford Linear Accelerator Ctr PO Box 4349 Stanford CA 94305

FRYBURG, GEORGE CRUMBACK, metallurgical chemistry, see previous edition

FRYDENDALL, MERRILL J, b Portis, Kans, Mar 28, 34; m 59; c 2. VERTEBRATE ECOLOGY, ANIMAL BEHAVIOR. *Educ:* Ft Hays Kans State Col, BS, 56, MS, 60; Utah State Univ, PhD(zool), 67. *Prof Exp:* High sch instr, Kans, 56-57 & 60-62; instr ornith, Utah State Univ, 65; PROF BIOL, MANKATO STATE UNIV, 66- *Mem:* Am Ornithologists Union; Animal Behav Soc; Cooper Ornith Soc; Sigma Xi; Audubon Soc. *Res:* Vertebrate ecology and behavior, especially activity patterns and utilization by mammals and aves; auditory communication especially in aves. *Mailing Add:* Dept of Biol Mankato State Univ Mankato MN 56001

FRYE, ALVA L(EONARD), b Gray, Okla, July 19, 22; m 43; c 2. CHEMICAL ENGINEERING. *Educ:* Iowa State Col, BS, 43. *Prof Exp:* Control chemist, Shell Chem Co, Tex, 43-44; process engr, Nat Synthetic Rubber Co, Ky, 44-47; sect leader, Minn Mining & Mfg Co, 47-57, mgr, cent res pilot plant, 57-62, tech dir paper prod div, 62-68; vpres res & commercial develop, Inmont Corp, 69-70, dir res & develop, 70-71, V PRES RES & DEVELOP, ALADDIN INDUST, INC, 71- *Concurrent Pos:* Dir, ALH, Inc. *Mem:* Am Chem Soc; Am Inst Chem Engrs; Tech Asn Pulp & Paper Indust; Int Platform Asn; Indust Res Inst. *Res:* Synthetic polymers; process development; fluoro-chemical and pilot plant; specialty papers and new products. *Mailing Add:* Aladdin Industs Inc 703 Murfreesboro Rd Nashville TN 37201

FRYE, BILLY EUGENE, developmental biology, zoology, see previous edition

FRYE, C(LIFTON) G(EORGE), b Port Clinton, Ohio, Dec 13, 18; m 43; c 2. CHEMICAL ENGINEERING. *Educ:* Univ Cincinnati, ChE, 41; Mass Inst Technol, MS, 47. *Prof Exp:* Sr chem engr petrochem res, Pan Am Petrol Co, 47-58; sr res eng petrol ref res, Standard Oil Co, Ind, 58-61; res assoc, 61-74, dir, 74-79, MGR RES & DEVELOP, AMOCO OIL CO, 79- *Mem:* Am Meteorol Soc; Am Inst Chem Engrs; Am Chem Soc. *Res:* Application of thermodynamics and kinetics to the development of new catalytic processes. *Mailing Add:* 1305 Heatherton Dr Naperville IL 60540

FRYE, CECIL LEONARD, b Dearborn, Mich, Apr 3, 28; m 52; c 4. ORGANIC CHEMISTRY. *Educ:* Univ Mich, BS, 50, MS, 51; Pa State Univ, PhD(org chem), 60. *Prof Exp:* Res chemist, 51-56, proj leader, Res Dept, 60-63, lab supvr, 63-70, mgr, Sealants Res Unit, 70-72, mgr bio-sci chem res, 73-74, scientist, corp res, 75-80, SCIENTIST, HEALTH & ENVIRON SCI DEPT, DOW CORNING CORP, 80- *Mem:* Am Chem Soc; Sigma Xi. *Res:* Silicon stereochemistry; extra-coordinate silicon compounds; polysiloxanes; environmental chemistry of silicones. *Mailing Add:* Dow Corning Corp Box 1767 2200 W Salzburg Rd Midland MI 48640

FRYE, CHARLES ISAAC, b Peterboro, NH, Dec 15, 35; m 65; c 2. COAL GEOLOGY, STRATIGRAPHY. *Educ:* Univ NH, BA, 58; Univ Mass, Amherst, MS, 60; Univ NDak, PhD(geol), 67. *Prof Exp:* Asst prof, Muskingum Col, 65-70, chmn, Dept Geol-Geog, 69-74, assoc prof geol, 70-79; geologic consult, 79-81, ASSOC PROF GEOL, NW MO STATE UNIV, 81- *Concurrent Pos:* Spec consult, Ohio Environ Protection Agency, 75-78-; consult, Div Reclamation, Ohio Dept Natural Resources, 80-81. *Mem:* Paleont Soc; Geol Soc Am; Am Asn Petrol Geol. *Res:* Stratigraphy and sedimentation of Hell Creek formation and related beds, Montana, North Dakota, South Dakota and of the Conemaugh formation in southeastern Ohio; coal geology, southeast Ohio; reclamation of abandoned coal mine lands in Ohio. *Mailing Add:* Dept Geol-Geog NW Mo State Univ Maryville MO 64468

FRYE, GERALD DALTON, b Winchester, Va, Aug 27, 50; m 71. NEUROPHARMACOLOGY, PHARMACOLOGY. *Educ:* Va Polytech Inst & State Univ, BS, 72; Univ NC, PhD(pharmacol), 77. *Prof Exp:* Res scientist, neuropharmacol, Biol Sci Ctr, 77-79; PHARMACOLOGIST, CTR FOR ALCOHOL STUDIES & RES ASST PROF DEPT PSYCHIAT, UNIV NC, CHAPEL HILL, 79- *Concurrent Pos:* Fel, Nat Inst Alcoholism & Alcohol Abuse, 77-79. *Mem:* AAAS; Soc Neurosci; Res Soc Alcoholism; fel Nat Inst Alcoholism & Alcohol Abuse; Am Soc Pharmacol & Exp Therapeut. *Res:* Neuropsychopharmacology of psychotropic drugs; neuropharmacology of ethanol tolerance and physical dependence; central nervous system mechanisms of GABAergic adaptation. *Mailing Add:* 223 Biol Sci Res Ctr 220H Univ NC Sch Med Chapel Hill NC 27514

FRYE, GLENN MCKINLEY, JR, b Ithaca, Mich, Apr 20, 26; m 48; c 3. PHYSICS. *Educ:* Univ Mich, BSE, 46, MS, 47, PhD(physics), 50. *Prof Exp:* Mem staff, Physics Div, Los Alamos Sci Lab, 51-58; physicist, Physics Br, Res Div, AEC, 58-60; assoc prof, 60-66, PROF PHYSICS, CASE WESTERN RESERVE UNIV, 66- *Concurrent Pos:* Guest lectr, Univ Minn, 57; prof, Univ NMex, 58. *Mem:* Am Phys Soc; AAAS; Am Astron Soc; Int Astron Union. *Res:* Gamma-ray astronomy; high energy astrophysics; neutral cosmic ray secondaries in the atmosphere; cosmic rays. *Mailing Add:* Rockefeller Physics Bldg Case Western Reserve Univ Cleveland OH 44106

FRYE, GRAHAM EUGENE, physics, see previous edition

FRYE, HERSCHEL GORDON, b Long Beach, Calif, Apr 6, 20; m 40; c 2. ANALYTICAL CHEMISTRY. *Educ:* Col of the Pac, AB, 47, MA, 49; Univ Ore, PhD(chem), 57. *Prof Exp:* Chemist, Permanente Metals Corp, 42-44; chief chemist, Kaiser Magnesium Co, 51-52; head sci dept, High Sch, 52-54; from asst prof to assoc prof, 56-62, PROF CHEM, UNIV OF THE PAC, 62- *Concurrent Pos:* Res Corp grants, 58 & 60; Am Philos Soc grants, 59, 63 & 64; gen partner, Anal Consults, 77- *Mem:* AAAS; Am Chem Soc; Am Inst Chemists; Consult Chemists Asn; Am Acad Forensic Sci. *Res:* Absorption spectrophotometry; forensic analytical chemistry; synthesis of coordination compounds. *Mailing Add:* Dept of Chem Univ of the Pac Stockton CA 95207

FRYE, JAMES SAYLER, b Washington, DC, Dec 4, 45; m 67; c 1. NUCLEAR MAGNETIC RESONANCE SPECTROSCOPY. *Educ:* Reed Col, BA, 67; Wash State Univ, PhD(chem), 75. *Prof Exp:* Res chemist, Univ Calif, Davis, 74-76; asst prof chem, Whitman Col, 76-77 & Reed Col, 77-78; RES ASSOC CHEM, COLO STATE UNIV, 78- *Mem:* Am Chem Soc. *Res:* Nuclear magnetic resonance of organic and inorganic compounds in solution and solid phases. *Mailing Add:* Dept Chem Colo State Univ Ft Collins CO 80523

FRYE, JENNINGS BRYAN, JR, b Springhill, La, Sept 3, 18; m 40; c 4. DAIRY SCIENCE. *Educ:* La State Univ, BS, 35; Iowa State Univ, MS, 40, PhD(dairy cattle nutrit), 45. *Prof Exp:* Assoc prof dairy sci, Univ Ga, 45-48; PROF & HEAD DEPT DAIRY SCI, LA STATE UNIV, BATON ROUGE, 48- *Concurrent Pos:* Spec dairy indust consult, Venezuela, 53, spec study, Dairy Indust, 57; Breeding Res, Cuba, 58. *Mem:* Am Forage & Grassland Coun; Am Dairy Sci Asn. *Res:* Dairy cattle management, especially in tropical and subtropical environments; influence of soybeans on the flavor of milk, cream and butter and on the body and texture of butter; bloat in dairy cattle; silage, including use of various preservatives and methods of self feeding; feeding green forage to cattle. *Mailing Add:* Dept of Dairy Sci La State Univ Baton Rouge LA 70803

FRYE, JOHN CHAPMAN, b Marietta, Ohio, July 25, 12; m 36; c 3. GEOLOGY. *Educ:* Marietta Col, AB, 34; Univ Iowa, MS, 37, PhD(geol), 38. *Hon Degrees:* ScD, Marietta Col, 55. *Prof Exp:* Asst geol, Univ Iowa, 35-38; jr geologist, Div Groundwater, US Geol Surv, Kans, 38-40; asst geologist, 40-41; asst state geologist & asst dir, Kans State Geol Surv, 42-45, exec dir, 45-54, state geologist, 52-54; chief, Ill State Geol Surv, 54-74; EXEC DIR, GEOL SOC AM, 74- *Concurrent Pos:* From asst prof to prof, Univ Kans, 42-54; prof geol, Univ Ill, Urbana, 63-74. deleg, Int Geol Cong, Algiers, 52; mem comt geol aspects radioactive waste disposal, Nat Acad Sci-Nat Res Coun, 55-64; chmn, 62-64; chmn adv comt earth resources remote sensing to US Dept Interior, 66-69, mem comt mineral sci & technol to US Bur Mines, 66-70, radioactive waste mgt to US AEC, 68-70, chmn, 70-75, mem bd energy studies & bd mineral resources, Nat Acad Sci, 74-78; ed, Am Asn State Geologists, 56-57; mem, Sci Manpower Comn, 56-58; Am Comn Stratig Nomenclature, 56-57; chmn, 57-59; mem, Nat Res Coun, 58-70; mem adv comt health physics, Oak Ridge Nat Lab, 59-72; adv comt, US Geol Surv, 60-66; exec comt, Ill Ctr Water Resources Res, 63-71; US Nat Comn for UNESCO, 68-71; vchmn, Comt Man & His Environ, 70-71; mem exec adv comt future oil prospects, Nat Petrol Coun, 68-70; spec comt probs environ, Int Coun Sci Unions, 69-71; mem nat adv bd, Desert Res Inst, Univ Nev, 70-76. *Mem:* Nat Acad Eng; fel AAAS; fel Geol Soc Am; Soc Econ Geol; Soc Econ Paleont & Mineral (vpres, 65-66). *Res:* Physiography; Cenozoic and groundwater geology. *Mailing Add:* 4470 Chippewa Dr Boulder CO 80303

FRYE, JOHN H, JR, b Birmingham, Ala, Oct 1, 08; m 35; c 3. PHYSICAL METALLURGY. *Educ:* Howard Col, AB, 30; Lehigh Univ, MS, 34; Oxford Univ, DPhil(phys sci), 42. *Prof Exp:* Engr, Am Cast Iron Pipe Co, Ala, 34-35; instr metall, Lehigh Univ, 35-37, from asst prof to assoc prof, 40-44; res engr, Bethlehem Steel Co, 44-48; dir metall div, Oak Ridge Nat Lab, 48-62, dir, Metals & Ceramics Div, 62-73; PROF METALL ENG, UNIV ALA, 73- *Concurrent Pos:* Lectr, Grad Sch, Univ Tenn, 50; adj prof, Col Eng, Univ Ala, 64-66. *Honors & Awards:* Lincoln Gold Medal, Am Welding Soc, 43. *Mem:* Fel AAAS; fel Am Soc Metals; fel Metall Soc. *Res:* Rates of reaction solids; phase equilibria; nuclear materials. *Mailing Add:* Dept of Chem & Metall Eng PO Box G University AL 35486

FRYE, KEITH, b Columbus, Ohio, July 17, 35; wid. GEOCHEMISTRY, MINERALOGY. *Educ:* Oberlin Col, AB, 57; Univ Minn, MS, 59; Pa State Univ, PhD(geochem), 65. *Prof Exp:* Chemist, Hyman Labs, Inc, 61-62; asst prof geol, Univ Ga, 65-67; ASSOC PROF GEOSCI, OLD DOMINION UNIV, 67- *Mem:* AAAS; Am Geophys Union; fel Geol Soc Am; Mineral Soc Am; Mineral Asn Can. *Res:* Geology and petrology of the central Virginia Blue Ridge; effects of pressure on crystal defects; distribution of trace elements and of minor minerals in granites; interaction between man and his geological environment. *Mailing Add:* Dept of Geophys Sci Old Dominion Univ Norfolk VA 23508

FRYE, ROBERT BRUCE, b Wilmington, Del, Apr 10, 49; m 74; c 1. ORGANIC & SILICONE CHEMISTRY. *Educ:* Univ Del, BS, 71; Mass Inst Technol, PhD(org chem), 76. *Prof Exp:* Sr res chemist dyestuffs, GAF Corp, 76-77; prod develop chemist silicones, 77-80, RES SPECIALIST SILICONES, GEN ELEC CO, 81- *Mem:* AAAS; Am Chem Soc. *Res:* Designing silicones for new and useful applications. *Mailing Add:* Dept Silicone Prod 12-06 Gen Elec Co Waterford NY 12188

FRYE, ROYAL MERRILL, physics, deceased

FRYE, WILBUR WAYNE, b Finger, Tenn, Aug 6, 33; m 57; c 2. SOIL FERTILITY, SOIL CONSERVATION. *Educ:* Univ Tenn, Knoxville, BS, 61, MS, 64; Va Polytech Inst & State Univ, PhD, 69. *Prof Exp:* Instr agron, Tenn Technol Univ, 63-64, asst prof, 64-67, prof & chmn dept, 70-74; ASSOC PROF AGRON, UNIV KY, 74- *Concurrent Pos:* Danforth Assoc, Danforth Found, 81-86. *Mem:* Am Soc Agron; Soil Sci Soc Am; Int Soc Soil Sci; fel Soil Conserv Soc Am; Coun Agr Sci & Technol. *Mailing Add:* Dept of Agron Univ of Ky Lexington KY 40506

FRYE, WILLIAM EMERSON, b Detroit, Mich, June 20, 17; m 42; c 2. SPACE PHYSICS. *Educ:* Univ Ill, AB, 37, MS, 38; Univ Chicago, PhD(physics), 41. *Prof Exp:* Group leader, Airborne Radio Div, Naval Res Lab, Wash, 42-45; asst sect head, 45-46; group leader, Aerophysics Lab, NAm Aviation, Inc, Calif, 46-48; physicist, Rand Corp, 48-56; mgr dept, 56-59, consult scientist, 59-62, 64-68, SR MEM RES LAB, LOCKHEED MISSILE & SPACE CO, 68- *Concurrent Pos:* Mem adv comt control, guid & navig, NASA, 60-64. *Mem:* Am Phys Soc; Am Inst Aeronaut & Astronaut; Am Astronaut Soc. *Res:* Space systems and scientific instrumentation. *Mailing Add:* 536 Lincoln Ave Palo Alto CA 94301

FR14YEN, SVERRE, b Oslo, Norway, June 25, 51. PHYSICS. *Educ:* NTH, Trondheim, Norway, Siv Ing, 76; Stanford Univ, PhD(appl physics), 81. *Prof Exp:* FEL PHYSICS, UNIV CALIF, BERKELEY, 80- *Mem:* Am Phys Soc. *Res:* Theoretical solid state physics; electronic structure and structural properties of semiconductors and metals. *Mailing Add:* Dept Physics Univ Calif Berkeley CA 94720

FRYER, CHARLES W, b Springfield, Mo, May 4, 28; m 53, 76; c 4. GEMOLOGY. *Educ:* Gemol Inst Am, grad gemol, 63. *Prof Exp:* Plant mgr, C Holle Glass Co, 62-64; mgr, R&B Artcraft Co, 64-66; instr, 66-67, LAB SUPVR GEM IDENTIFICATION, GEMOL INST AM, 67- *Res:* X-ray powder diffraction identification of gem materials and their inclusions; optical and physical identification of gem materials and their substitutes; x-ray analysis of pearls to determine natural or cultured origin. *Mailing Add:* 1153 Stanford Santa Monica CA 90404

FRYER, ELSIE BETH, b Kopperl, Tex, June 25, 25; m 66. NUTRITION. *Educ:* Univ NMex, BS, 45; Ohio State Univ, MS, 49; Mich State Univ, PhD(foods & nutrit), 59. *Prof Exp:* High sch teacher, NMex, 45-48; asst prof foods & nutrit, SDak State Col, 49-56; assoc prof, 59-75, PROF NUTRIT, KANS STATE UNIV, 75- *Mem:* Am Dietetic Asn; Am Asn Cereal Chemists; Am Home Econ Asn; Am Inst Nutrit; Inst Food Technologists. *Res:* Food habit and nutritional status surveys of women and children; quality of cereal proteins; human metabolic studies concerned with weight reduction, lipid metabolism and nitrogen balance. *Mailing Add:* Dept of Foods & Nutrit Kans State Univ Manhattan KS 66506

FRYER, HOLLY CLAIRE, b Carlton, Ore, Dec 6, 08; m 34, 66; c 2. BIOLOGICAL STATISTICS. *Educ:* Univ Ore, BS, 31; Ore State Col, MS, 33; Iowa State Col, PhD(statist), 40. *Prof Exp:* Instr math, Iowa State Univ, 37-40; asst prof, Kans State Univ, 40-42, assoc prof & statistician exp sta, 42-44; assoc res mathematician, Columbia Univ, 44-45; prof math, 45-59, head statist dept, 59-75, dir statist lab, 46-75, statistician, exp sta, 40-79, prof statist, 45-79, EMER PROF STATIST, KANS STATE UNIV, 79- *Mem:* Biomet Soc; fel Am Statist Asn; Inst Math Statist; fel Royal Statist Soc. *Res:* Designing biometric experiments; mathematical statistics. *Mailing Add:* Dept of Statist Kans State Univ Manhattan KS 66506

FRYER, JOHN LOUIS, b Ft Worth, Tex, July 4, 29; m 52; c 4. MICROBIOLOGY, FISHERIES. *Educ:* Ore State Univ, BS, 56, MS, 57, PhD(microbiol), 64. *Prof Exp:* Instr fisheries, Ore State Univ, 57-58; fish pathologist, Res Div, Ore Fish Comn, 58-60, state fisheries pathologist, 60-64; from asst prof to assoc prof, 64-73, PROF MICROBIOL & FISHERIES, ORE STATE UNIV, 73-, CHMN MICROBIOL, 77- *Mem:* Am Soc Microbiol; Am Inst Fishery Res Biol; Am Fisheries Soc; Wildlife Dis Asn; Sigma Xi; Am Acad Microbiol. *Res:* Pathogenic microbiology, virology and immunology in relation to infectious diseases of cold blooded animals; methods for prevention, detection and control of diseases in populations of fishes; fish pathology. *Mailing Add:* Dept of Microbiol Ore State Univ Corvallis OR 97331

FRYER, MINOT PACKER, b Conn, Mar 16, 25; m 42; c 2. SURGERY. *Educ:* Brown Univ, AB, 37; Johns Hopkins Univ, MD, 40. *Hon Degrees:* DSc, Brown Univ, 71. *Prof Exp:* Assoc prof clin surg, Med Sch & maxillofacial surg, Dent Sch, 57-67, PROF CLIN SURG, MED SCH & MAXILLOFACIAL SURG, DENT SCH, WASHINGTON UNIV, 67- *Concurrent Pos:* Asst surgeon, Barnes & St Louis Children's Hosps, 48-; mem staff, De Paul Hosp, 48-; consult, Vet Admin Hosp, 49-; vchmn, Am Bd Plastic Surg, 67-68. *Mem:* Am Soc Plastic & Reconstruct Surg; Am Asn Plastic Surg (vpres, 66-67, pres, 67-68); fel Am Asn Surg of Trauma; fel Am Col Surg; Soc Head & Neck Surg. *Res:* Plastic and reconstructive surgery. *Mailing Add:* 4989 Barnes Hosp Plaza St Louis MO 63110

FRYER, RODNEY IAN, b London, Eng, Mar 13, 30; US citizen; m 54; c 4. MEDICINAL CHEMISTRY. *Educ:* Univ Calif, Los Angeles, BS, 57; Univ Manchester, PhD(chem), 60. *Prof Exp:* Sr chemist pharmaceut res, 60-63, asst group chief, 63-65, group chief pharmaceut res, 65-69, sect chief, Res Dept, 70-78, DIR MEDICINAL CHEM, HOFFMANN-LA ROCHE, INC, 79- *Mem:* AAAS; Am Chem Soc; Royal Soc Chem. *Res:* Synthesis and transformations of heterocyclic compounds of potential medicinal interest. *Mailing Add:* Res Dept Hoffmann-La Roche Inc Nutley NJ 07110

FRYKLUND, VERNE CHARLES, JR, b Greeley, Colo, July 2, 20; m 43; c 4. GEOLOGY. *Educ:* Univ Minn, BS, 44, MS, 47, PhD(geol), 49. *Prof Exp:* Field asst, US Geol Surv, 43; jr geologist, 43-45; from instr to asst prof geol, Univ Idaho, 48-51; geologist, US Geol Surv, 51-62; chief lunar & planetary sci br, Manned Space Sci Div, NASA, 62-64; chief mil geol br, US Geol Surv, 64-66; prog mgr, Off Secy Defense, 66-68; dep dir, Nuclear Monitoring Res Off, 68-72; dir technol, Assessments Off, Advan Res Projs Agency, 72-74; CONSULT GEOLOGIST, 74- *Mem:* Fel Geol Soc Am; Soc Econ Geol; Geochem Soc; Am Inst Mining, Metall & Petrol Eng. *Res:* Management; application of geology to national defense matters; arms control problems; economic geology. *Mailing Add:* 6805 Broyhill St McLean VA 22101

FRYLING, ROBERT HOWARD, b Danville, Pa, Nov 17, 21; wid; c 2. MATHEMATICS. *Educ:* Gettysburg Col, BA, 43; Univ Pittsburgh, MS, 51, PhD(math), 72. *Prof Exp:* Instr math, 47-50, dean of men, 52-56, asst prof math, 58-69, assoc prof, 69-77, chmn dept, 74-79, PROF MATH, GETTYSBURG COL, 77- *Mem:* Math Asn Am. *Res:* Theory of random variable centers. *Mailing Add:* Dept of Math Gettysburg Col Gettysburg PA 17325

FRYMAN, LEO RAY, b Noble, Ill, Feb 8, 20; m 41; c 2. DAIRY SCIENCE. *Educ:* Univ Ill, BS, 48, MS, 50; Purdue Univ, PhD, 71. *Prof Exp:* Assoc prof, 48-68, PROF DAIRY SCI EXTEN, UNIV ILL, URBANA, 68- *Mem:* Am Dairy Sci Asn. *Res:* Dairy cattle management, feeding and breeding. *Mailing Add:* 1208 Julie Dr Champaign IL 61820

FRYREAR, DONALD W, b Haxtum, Colo, Dec 8, 36; m 56; c 2. AGRICULTURAL ENGINEERING. *Educ:* Colo State Univ, BS, 59; Kans State Univ, MS, 62. *Prof Exp:* Agr engr, Cent Great Plains Field Sta, USDA, 59-60, agr engr wind erosion lab, 60-62, agr engr, Blackland Conserv Exp Sta, 62-63, res agr engr, 63-65, SUPT & RES AGR ENGR, BIG SPRING FIELD STA, AGR RES SERV, USDA, 65- *Concurrent Pos:* Group mem, World Meteorol Orgn, 76- *Mem:* Am Soc Agr Engrs; Nat Soc Prof Engrs; Sigma Xi. *Res:* Dryland water conservation in Colorado; application of annual barriers for wind erosion control; land modifications for controlling erosion; development of equipment for measuring erosion rates; wind erosion and moisture conservation on sandy soils in a semiarid environment. *Mailing Add:* Agr Res Serv USDA Big Spring Field Sta Big Spring TX 79720

FRYSTAK, RONALD WAYNE, b Chicago, Ill, Sept 25, 41; m 65; c 1. PHYSICAL CHEMISTRY, ENVIRONMENTAL CHEMISTRY. *Educ:* Millikin Univ, BS, 63; Univ Hawaii, PhD(phys chem), 68. *Prof Exp:* asst prof, 68-77, ASSOC PROF CHEM, HAWAII LOA COL, 77- *Mem:* Am Chem Soc. *Res:* Physical interpretation of the He-He interaction through the use of the associated density matrices; saving of Hawaiian beaches in case an accidental oil spillage occurs. *Mailing Add:* Div of Sci & Math Hawaii Loa Col Kaneohe HI 96744

FRYXELL, FRITIOF MELVIN, b Moline, Ill, Apr 27, 00; m 28; c 1. GEOLOGY. *Educ:* Augustana Col, Ill, AB, 22; Univ Ill, MA, 23; Univ Chicago, PhD(geol), 29. *Hon Degrees:* ScD, Wittenberg Univ, 60 & Upsala Col, 60; LLD, Univ Wyo, 79. *Prof Exp:* From asst prof to prof geol, 23-73, cur mus, 29-73, chmn sci div, 46-51, DIR RES FOUND, AUGUSTANA COL, ILL, 47- *Concurrent Pos:* Asst, Univ Chicago, 27-28; naturalist, Grand Teton Nat Park, Wyo, 29-34, geologist, Mus Planning Staff, Nat Park Serv, 35-37; sr geologist, Philippine Govt, 39-40; trustee, Putnam Mus, 41-; geologist, Mil Geol Unit, US Geol Surv, 42-46; Am-Scand traveling fel, 48; lit exec, Francois E Matthes, 49-65; dir, Am Geol Inst, 50-51; Guggenheim Found fel, 54; NSF res grant, Augustana Col, 59-61 & 64. *Honors & Awards:* Miner Award, 53; Meritorious Award, Augustana Col, 58. *Mem:* Fel AAAS; fel Geol Soc Am; fel Am Geog Soc; hon mem Nat Asn Geol Teachers (pres, 38); hon mem Am Alpine Club. *Res:* Geomorphology; glacial and military geology; history of geology. *Mailing Add:* Fryxell Geol Mus Augustana Col Rock Island IL 61201

FRYXELL, GRETA ALBRECHT, b Princeton, Ill, Nov 21, 26; m 47; c 3. BIOLOGICAL OCEANOGRAPHY. *Educ:* Augustana Col, BA, 48; Tex A&M Univ, MEd, 69, PhD(oceanog), 75. *Prof Exp:* Teacher math, Davenport Sch Syst, Iowa, 48-49; teacher sci, Ames Independent Sch Dist, Iowa, 49-52; res assoc, 71-77, asst res scientist, 77-79, assoc res scientist, 79-80, ASST PROF OCEANOG, RES FOUND TEX A&M UNIV, 80- *Concurrent Pos:* Mem, Int Comt Standardize Diatom Terminology, 74-76, Int Diatom Comt, 74-76 & mem arrangements comt, Fifth Symp Living & Fossil Diatoms, Antwerp, 78. *Mem:* Bot Soc Am; Brit Phycol Soc; Int Phycol Soc; Phycol Soc Am; Am Soc Limnol & Oceanog. *Res:* Comparative morphology; systematics; distribution and place in marine ecosystem of phytoplankton, principally diatoms and coccolithophorids; light and electron microscopy on field samples and living cultures. *Mailing Add:* Dept of Oceanog Tex A&M Univ College Station TX 77843

FRYXELL, PAUL ARNOLD, b Moline, Ill, Feb 2, 27; m 47; c 3. SYSTEMATIC BOTANY. *Educ:* Augustana Col, AB, 49; Iowa State Univ, MS, 51, PhD(genetics), 55. *Prof Exp:* Asst agron, Agr Exp Sta, NMex, 52-55; asst prof bot, Univ Wichita, 55-57; from geneticist to prin res geneticist, 57-75, CHIEF RES GENETICIST, SCI EDUC ADMIN, USDA, 75- *Concurrent Pos:* Mem grad fac, Tex A&M Univ; ed, Brittonia, 71-74; dep adminr rep, Plant Germplasm Coord Comt, Sci Educ Admin, 73- *Honors & Awards:* Cotton Genetics Res Award, 67. *Mem:* Fel AAAS; Am Soc Plant Taxonomists; Bot Soc Am; Soc Bot Mexico; Int Asn Plant Taxon. *Res:* Systematics of Malvaceae, especially of the Neotropics, involving revisionary studies of selected genera; floristic treatments of significant regions; experimental and evolutionary studies where revelent. *Mailing Add:* Dept of Soil & Crop Sci Tex A&M Univ College Station TX 77843

FRYXELL, ROBERT EDWARD, b Moline, Ill, Mar 24, 23; m 61; c 3. PHYSICAL INORGANIC CHEMISTRY. *Educ:* Augustana Col, BA, 44; Univ Chicago, MS, 49, PhD(chem), 50. *Prof Exp:* Chemist, Manhattan Proj, Metall Lab, Univ Chicago, 43-44 & Los Alamos Sci Lab, Univ Calif, 44-46; anal chemist, Inst Study Metals, Univ Chicago, 46-50; chemist, M&P Lab, Transformer Div, 50-59, prin engr, Aircraft Nuclear Propulsion Dept, 59-61 & Nuclear Mat & Propulsion Oper, 61-64, mgr high temperature fuels res, 64-69, SR PHYS CHEMIST, AIRCRAFT ENGINE GROUP, GEN ELEC CO, 69- *Mem:* AAAS; Am Chem Soc. *Res:* Separation procedures in analytical chemistry; electrochemistry; reactions of non metallic impurities in metals; high temperature reactions; corrosion. *Mailing Add:* 8430 Old Hickory Dr Cincinnati OH 45243

FRYXELL, RONALD C, b Moline, Ill, Aug 31, 38; m 59; c 1. MATHEMATICS. *Educ:* Augustana Col, Ill, AB, 60; Wash State Univ, MA, 62, PhD(math), 64. *Prof Exp:* Asst prof, 64-70, assoc prof, 70-77, PROF MATH, ALBION COL, 77- *Mem:* Asn Comput Mach; Math Asn Am. *Res:* Finite geometry, particularly finite planes of square order. *Mailing Add:* Dept of Math Albion Col 701 E Porter Albion MI 49224

FTACLAS, CHRIST, b New York, NY. COSMOLOGY, GALAXY STRUCTURE. *Educ:* City Col NY, BS, 65, MA, 71; City Univ NY, PhD(physics), 78. *Prof Exp:* ASST PROF ASTRON, UNIV PA, 78- *Concurrent Pos:* Proj engr, Leesona Mooos Lab, Great Neck Long Island. *Mem:* Am Phys Soc; Am Astron Soc; Int Soc Gen Relativity & Gravitation; NY Acad Sci. *Res:* Relativistic cosmology galaxies; clusters of galaxies; physical cosmology. *Mailing Add:* Dept Astron & Astrophysics Univ Pa Philadelphia PA 19104

FU, HUI-HSING, b Hou-Pei, China, Dec 5, 47; m 70; c 1. NUCLEAR ENGINEERING, SOLID STATE PHYSICS. *Educ:* Nat Tsing Hua Univ, Taiwan, BS, 69; Ohio State Univ, MS, 72, PhD(physics), 74. *Prof Exp:* Res assoc physics, Univ Ill, Urbana-Champaign, 74-76; asst prof physics, Ill State Univ, 76-79; engr, 80-81, SR ENGR, GEN PUB UTILITIES, 81- *Res:* Nuclear fuel management; low temperature physics; many body theory. *Mailing Add:* Gen Pub Utilities 110 Interpace Pkwy Parsippany NJ 07054

FU, JERRY HUI MING, b Hupeh, China, July 15, 32; US citizen; m 64; c 2. PLASMA PHYSICS, SPACE PHYSICS. *Educ:* Univ Taiwan, BS, 56; Northwestern Univ, MS, 61; Univ Mich, PhD(aerospace sci), 67. *Prof Exp:* Fel inst fluid dynamics & appl math, Univ Md, 67-68, res assoc, 67-70; SR SCIENTIST, EG&G, INC, 70- *Mem:* Am Phys Soc; Am Geophys Union. *Res:* Shock wave in collisionless plasma and microstructure of the earth's bow shock; surface potential distribution near a satellite in interplanetary space. *Mailing Add:* 387 Manhattan Loop Los Alamos NM 87544

FU, KING-SUN, b Nanking, China, Oct 2, 30; m 58; c 3. ELECTRICAL ENGINEERING. *Educ:* Nat Taiwan Univ, BS, 53; Univ Toronto, MASc, 56; Univ Ill, PhD(elec eng), 59. *Prof Exp:* Demonstr, Univ Toronto, 54-55; asst, Univ Ill, 55-59; res engr, Boeing Aircraft Co, 59-60; from asst prof to prof elec eng, 60-75, GOSS DISTINGUISHED PROF ENG, PURDUE UNIV, 75- *Concurrent Pos:* Vis prof, Univ Calif, Berkeley, 67-68 & Stanford Univ, 72; Guggenheim fel, 71-72; Sr Res Award, Am Soc Eng Educ, 81. *Mem:* Nat Acad Eng; fel Inst Elec & Electronics Engrs; Am Soc Eng Educ. *Res:* Computer and information sciences; pattern recognition; machine intelligence. *Mailing Add:* Sch of Elec Eng Purdue Univ Lafayette IN 47907

FU, KUAN-CHEN, b Nanking, China, Feb 2, 33; m 63; c 2. CIVIL & STRUCTURAL ENGINEERING. *Educ:* Taiwan Prov Col Eng, BS, 55; Univ Notre Dame, MS, 59, PhD(civil eng), 67. *Prof Exp:* Struct engr, Chas Cole & Sons, 59-63; from asst prof to assoc prof civil eng, 67-78, PROF CIVIL ENG, UNIV TOLEDO, 78- *Concurrent Pos:* Prin investr, NSF res grant, 69-71 & NSF US-China Int res grant, 74-75; chair prof civil eng, Nat Cheng-Kung Univ, Taiwan, 74-75. *Mem:* Am Soc Civil Engrs. *Res:* Optimization of structural configurations under deterministic and probabilistic loading conditions; discrete structural optimization using complex-simplex method. *Mailing Add:* Dept Civil Eng Univ Toledo Toledo OH 43606

FU, LEE LUENG, b Taipei, Taiwan, Oct 10, 50; m 77; c 1. PHYSICAL OCEANOGRAPHY, REMOTE SENSING. *Educ:* Nat Taiwan Univ, BS, 72; Mass Inst Technol, PhD(oceanog), 80. *Prof Exp:* Res assoc, Mass Inst Technol, 80; SR SCIENTIST, JET PROPULSION LAB, CALIF INST TECHNOL, 80- *Mem:* Am Geophys Union; Am Meteorol Soc; Sigma Xi. *Res:* Oceanic internal waves; ocean circulation; geophysical fluid dynamics; geophysical data analysis; oceanic remote sensing with microwave sensors. *Mailing Add:* 183-501 Jet Propulsion Lab 4800 Oak Grove Dr Pasadena CA 91109

FU, LI-SHENG WILLIAM, b China; US citizen. ENGINEERING MECHANICS. *Educ:* Nat Taiwan Univ, BSc, 62; Northwestern Univ, MSc, 65, PhD(theoret & appl mech), 67. *Prof Exp:* Asst prof, 67-71, ASSOC PROF ENG MECH, OHIO STATE UNIV, 71- *Concurrent Pos:* Prin investr, NSF, 69-72 & NASA, 79-82. *Mem:* Am Acad Mech; Am Soc Mech Engrs; Am Soc Testing & Mat; Am Soc Eng Educ; Sigma Xi. *Res:* Fracture and fatigue analysis; crack initiation and growth at elevated temperature; elastic and plastic analysis; non-destructive testing of fracture toughness. *Mailing Add:* Dept of Eng Mech 155 W Woodruff Ave Columbus OH 43210

FU, LORRAINE SHAO-YEN, b China, Jan 7, 39; US citizen; m 67; c 1. MATHEMATICS. *Educ:* Hunter Col, BA, 60; NY Univ, MS, 63; Polytech Inst Brooklyn, PhD(math), 72. *Prof Exp:* Lectr, Hunter Col, 64-67 & 70-71, asst prof math, 71-76; asst prof, 77-80, ASSOC PROF MATH, PACE UNIV, 80- *Concurrent Pos:* Mem, New York City Community Sch Bd, 75-77. *Mem:* Sigma Xi; Am Math Soc; Math Asn Am; Soc Indust & Appl Math. *Res:* Inverse problems. *Mailing Add:* 1 Bellaire Dr Ridge NY 11961

FU, SHOU-CHENG JOSEPH, b Peiping, China, Mar 19, 22; nat US; m 51; c 3. BIOCHEMISTRY. *Educ:* Cath Univ Peiping, China, BS, 41, MS, 44; Johns Hopkins Univ, PhD(chem), 49. *Prof Exp:* Asst chem, Cath Univ Peiping, 42-44; jr instr, Johns Hopkins Univ, 47-49; vis scientist, Nat Cancer Inst, 51-54; chief enzyme & bio-org chem lab, Children's Cancer Res Found, Boston, 56-66; prof chem & chmn chem bd, Chinese Univ Hong Kong, 66-70, vis prof ophthal, Col Physicians & Surgeons, Columbia Univ, 70-71; asst dean, grad sch biomed sci, 75-77, PROF BIOCHEM, COL MED & DENT NJ, 71-, ACTG DEAN, SCH BIOMED SCI, 77- *Concurrent Pos:* Res fel, Nat Cancer Inst, 49-51; Bissing fel from Johns Hopkins Univ to Univ Col, Univ London, 55; res assoc, Children's Hosp Med Ctr & Harvard Med Sch, 56-66; univ dean sci fac, Chinese Univ Hong Kong, 67-69. *Mem:* Fel AAAS; Am Asn Cancer Res; Am Soc Biol Chem; NY Acad Sci; Royal Chem Soc. *Res:* Organic chemistry; chemistry of amino acids and peptides; proteins and enzymes; chemical kinetics and reaction mechanism. *Mailing Add:* Dept Biochem Col Med & Dent of NJ Newark NJ 07103

FU, WALLACE YAMTAK, b Macao, China, June 10, 43; US citizen; m 70. ORGANIC CHEMISTRY. *Educ:* St Johns Univ, BS, 67; Marquette Univ, PhD(org chem), 73. *Prof Exp:* Res assoc chem, Cornell Univ, 73-75; chemist, 75-80, PROJ SCIENTIST, UNION CARBIDE CORP, 80- *Mem:* Am Chem Soc; Sigma Xi; Weed Sci Soc Am. *Res:* Organic photochemistry, organic synthesis and pesticide process development. *Mailing Add:* Union Carbide Agr Prods Co PO Box 12014 Research Triangle Park NC 27709

FU, WEI-NING, b Huang Hsien, China, Feb 24, 25; m 55; c 3. CYTOGENETICS. *Educ:* Nat Honan Univ, China, BS, 49; Okla State Univ, MS, 60, PhD(plant breeding, genetics), 63. *Prof Exp:* Teacher high sch, Taiwan, 49-51; assoc agronomist, Taiwan Tobacco Res Inst, 52-57; asst prof, 63-69, assoc prof, 69-75, PROF GENETICS & CYTOL, CENT CONN STATE COL, 75- NSF grant; fel med, Sch Med, Johns Hopkins Univ, 75. *Mem:* AAAS; Am Genetic Asn; Am Soc Human Genetics; Am Hort Soc. *Res:* Human cytogenetics; oriental vegetables. *Mailing Add:* Dept of Biol Sci Cent Conn State Col New Britain CT 06050

FU, YUAN C(HIN), b Formosa, Feb 16, 30; US citizen; m 60; c 2. FUELS ENGINEERING, CHEMICAL ENGINEERING. *Educ:* Nat Taiwan Univ, BS, 53; Univ Utah, PhD(fuels eng), 61. *Prof Exp:* Res engr, Union Indust Res Inst, Formosa, 53-56; res engr, Phillips Petrol Co, 61-64; res assoc, Univ Southern Calif, 64-65; res chemist, US Bur Mines, 65-75; res engr, ERDA, 75-77; RES ENGR, PITTSBURGH ENERGY TECHNOL CTR, US DEPT ENERGY, 77- *Concurrent Pos:* Instr, Univ Pittsburgh, 67-69. *Honors & Awards:* Bituminous Coal Res Award, Am Chem Soc, 68. *Mem:* Am Chem Soc; Chem Soc Japan; Catalysis Soc. *Res:* Coal liquefaction; coal conversion technology; synfuel technology; acid rain. *Mailing Add:* Pittsburgh Energy Technol Ctr Dept Energy PO Box 10940 Pittsburgh PA 15213

FU, YUN-LUNG, b China, June 12, 42; US citizen; m 70; c 2. ORGANIC CHEMISTRY, POLYMER CHEMISTRY. *Educ:* Nat Taiwan Univ, BSc, 65; State Univ NY Col Environ Sci & Forestry, PhD(chem), 72. *Prof Exp:* Res assoc, Wood Chem Lab, Univ Mont, 72-73; cancer res scientist, Roswell Park Mem Inst, 73-77; res assoc, Int Paper Co, 77-78; res chemist, 78-80, SR RES CHEMIST, AM CYANAMID CO, 80- *Mem:* Am Chem Soc. *Res:* Organic synthesis; polymer synthesis; carbohydrate, cellulose, starch and polysaccharide chemistry; pyrolysis. *Mailing Add:* 50 Tapping Circle Milford CT 06460

FUBINI, EUGENE G(HIRON), b Turin, Italy, Apr 19, 13; nat US; m 45; c 6. ENGINEERING. *Educ:* Univ Rome, Dr Physics, 44. *Hon Degrees:* LLD, Polytech Inst Brooklyn, 68; DEng, Pratt Inst, 67; ScD, Rensselaer Polytech Inst. *Prof Exp:* Res assoc, Nat Inst Electrotechnics, Rome, 35-38; engr in chg microwave & int broadcasting, CBS, Inc, 38-42; res assoc develop electronic countermeasures, Radio Res Lab, Harvard Univ, 42-44; mem staff, Airborne Instruments Lab, 45-61, from div head to vpres, 60-61; asst secy defense & dep dir defense res & eng, 61-65; vpres & group exec, IBM Corp, 65-69; gen dir, 69-79, DIR, TEX INSTRUMENTS, INC, 80-; PRES E G FUBINI CONSULTS LTD, 69- *Concurrent Pos:* Spec lectr, Harvard Univ, 56; mem, President's Sci Adv Comt, 57-61, 69-, Adv Coun Advan Sci Res & Develop, NY State Univ, 58-, Panel Sci Adv Bd, Nat Security Agency, 58-61; chmn, Electromagnetic Warfare Adv Group, Air Res & Develop Command, 58-61; mem, Adv Group Spec Projs, Dept Defense, 58-61, President's Comn Law Enforcement, 65-67, Defense Intel Agency, 65-, chmn, 65-70; mem, Defense Sci Bd, 66-69, Sci Adv Comt, Am Newspaper Publn Asn, 69-; consult, IBM Corp, 69-; mem bd dirs, Volunteers Int Tech Assistance, Inc, 69-; trustee, Urban Inst, 69-; mem, Defense Spec Projs Group, 70-; vis comt, Comput Ctr, Harvard Univ, Sch Eng, Stanford Univ, & George Washington Univ. *Honors & Awards:* Presidential Cert Merit, 46; Defense Medal, Dept Defense, 66; Exceptional Serv Medal, Defense Intel Agency, 70. *Mem:* Nat Acad Eng; fel Inst Elec & Electronics Engrs; NY Acad Sci. *Res:* Advanced development of special electronic devices; nonconventional antennas and microwave devices; radar; radar countermeasures; computers. *Mailing Add:* 1905 N Ft Myer Dr Ste 1120 Arlington VA 22209

FUCALORO, ANTHONY FRANK, physical chemistry, spectrochemistry, see previous edition

FUCCI, DONALD JAMES, b New Kensington, Pa, July 17, 41; m 66; c 2. SPEECH PATHOLOGY. *Educ:* Univ Pittsburgh, BA, 62, MS, 64; Purdue Univ, PhD(speech path), 68. *Prof Exp:* PROF SPEECH PATH, OHIO UNIV, 68- *Mem:* Am Speech & Hearing Asn; Acoust Soc Am. *Res:* Oral vibrotactile sensitivity and perception as related to area of speech and hearing; author or coauthor of over 60 publications. *Mailing Add:* Sch Hearing & Speech Sci Lindley Hall 219 Ohio Univ Athens OH 45701

FUCHIGAMI, LESLIE H, b Lanai City, Hawaii, June 11, 42; m 63; c 5. HORTICULTURE, PLANT PHYSIOLOGY. *Educ:* Univ Hawaii, BS, 64; Univ Minn, St Paul, MS, 66, PhD(plant physiol), 70. *Prof Exp:* assoc prof hort, Ore State Univ, 70-81; PROF HORT, UNIV HAWAII, 81- *Mem:* Am Soc Hort Sci. *Res:* Environmental, physiological and chemical control of cold acclimation in Cornus stolonifera; Meloidogyne hapla versus Treflan; rooting and establishment of Douglas fir; storage of ornamentals; forcing of colored lilies; root regeneration of nursery crops and maturity, dormancy, hardiness, storage and defoliation of deciduous plants; physiology of tropical fruit crops. *Mailing Add:* Dept Hort Univ Hawaii delete this line Honolulu HI 96822

FUCHS, ALBERT FREDERICK, b Philadelphia, Pa, Feb 15, 38; m 63; c 2. BIOMEDICAL ENGINEERING. *Educ:* Drexel Inst, BSEE, 60, MS, 61; Johns Hopkins Univ, PhD(biomed eng), 66. *Prof Exp:* PROF PHYSIOL & BIOPHYS, DEPT PHYSIOL & BIOPHYS & MEM CORE STAFF, REGIONAL PRIMATE RES CTR, UNIV WASH, 69- *Concurrent Pos:* Nat Inst Combat Blindness fel, Johns Hopkins Univ, 66-67; NSF fel, Univ Freiburg, 67-68. *Honors & Awards:* Samuel A Talbot Award, Biomed Eng Group, Inst Elec & Electronics Engrs, 69. *Mem:* Soc Neurosci; assoc Soc Res Vision & Ophthal. *Res:* Oculomotor system of primates. *Mailing Add:* Regional Primate Res Ctr I-421 Hlth Sci Bldg Univ Wash Seattle WA 98195

FUCHS, ANNA-RIITTA, b Helsinki, Finland; c 4. REPRODUCTIVE PHYSIOLOGY. *Educ:* Univ Helsinki, Phil Cand, 48, Phil Mag(chem), 50; Univ Copenhagen, DSc, 78. *Prof Exp:* Fel reproduction, Carnegie Inst Wash Dept Embryol, 50-51; res assoc, Dept Physiol, Univ Copenhagen, 52-54, fel bact, Dept Pub Health, 54-56, res assoc reproduction, Dept Physiol, 57-62, univ adj, 62-65; res assoc reproduction, Biomed Div, Population Coun, NY, 65-70, staff scientist, 70-77; ASSOC PROF REPRODUCTIVE BIOL IN OBSTET & GYNEC, CORNELL UNIV MED COL, 77- *Concurrent Pos:* Adj assoc prof reproductive biol in obstet & gynec, Med Col, Cornell Univ, 71-77, fac mem, Grad Sch Med Sci, 73-; vis prof reproduction, Med Sch, Chulalongkorn Univ, Thailand, 72-73. *Mem:* Endocrine Soc; Soc Gynec Invest; Soc Study Reproduction; Soc Study Fertil; fel NY Acad Sci. *Res:* Endocrinology of gestation and the onset of parturition; uterine physiology; prostaglandins in male and female gonadal function. *Mailing Add:* Dept of Obstet & Gynec S-412 1300 York Ave New York NY 10021

FUCHS, ELAINE V, b Hinsdale, Ill, May 5, 50. GENE EXPRESSION, DIFFERENTIATION. *Educ:* Univ Ill, Champaign-Urbana, BS, 72; Princeton Univ, PhD(biochem), 77. *Prof Exp:* Res fel biochem, Mass Inst Technol, 77-80; ASST PROF BIOCHEM, UNIV CHICAGO, 80- *Concurrent Pos:* Andrew Mellon fel, Univ Chicago, 80; Searle Scholar Award, Searle Corp, 81; career develop award, NIH, 82. *Mem:* Am Soc Cell Biol; Am Soc Biol Chem. *Res:* Molecular biology of gene expression in differentiating human epidermal cells; biochemical changes in the cytoskeletal architecture during differentiation; effect of vitamin A on gene expression in normal and cancerous epithelial cells. *Mailing Add:* Dept Biochem Univ Chicago 920 E 58th St Rm 701 Chicago IL 60637

FUCHS, EWALD FRANZ, b Munderkingen, Ger, Dec 5, 39; m 77. ELECTRICAL ENGINEERING, MATHEMATICS. *Educ:* Univ Stuttgart, BS, 63, dipl eng, 67; Univ Colo, Boulder, PhD(elec eng), 70. *Prof Exp:* Res engr, Siemens AG, Erlangen, Ger, 67; teaching asst, Univ Colo, Boulder, 67-69, res asst, 69-70, res assoc, 70-71, asst prof elec eng, 71; sr engr power indust, Kraftwerk Union AG, Ruhr, Ger, 71-77; ASSOC PROF ELEC ENG, UNIV COLO, BOULDER, 77- *Mem:* Inst Elec & Electronics Engrs; Verein Deutscher Elektrotechniker. *Res:* Investigation of transient and subtransient phenomena in power systems; rotating machine design from a field modeling standpoint. *Mailing Add:* Dept of Elec Eng Univ of Colo Boulder CO 80309

FUCHS, FRANKLIN, b New York, NY, July 1, 31; m 57; c 2. PHYSIOLOGY. *Educ:* Univ Mich, AB, 53; Tufts Univ, PhD(physiol), 62. *Prof Exp:* From instr to asst prof, 64-71, assoc prof physiol, 71-80, PROF SCH MED, UNIV PITTSBURGH, 80- *Concurrent Pos:* Res fel physiol, Sch Med, Tufts Univ, 58-62; USPHS fel, Inst Neurophysiol, Copenhagen, 62-64; Lederle med fac award, 67-70; mem, Physiol Study Sect, NIH, 79-83. *Mem:* AAAS; Soc Gen Physiol; Biophys Soc; Am Physiol Soc. *Res:* Physiology and biochemistry of muscle. *Mailing Add:* Dept of Physiol Univ of Pittsburgh Sch of Med Pittsburgh PA 15261

FUCHS, FRITZ FRIEDRICH, b Frederiksberg, Denmark, Nov 27, 18; m 48; c 4. OBSTETRICS & GYNECOLOGY. *Educ:* Copenhagen Univ, MD, 45, DrMedSci, 57. *Prof Exp:* Second asst surgeon, Kommunehosp, Copenhagen, 53-55; second asst obstetrician & gynecologist, Rigshosp, 55-56, first asst obstetrician & gynecologist, 56-58; gynecologist-in-chief, Kommunehosp, 58-64; Given Found prof, 65-77, dept chmn, 65-78, Harold & Percy Uris prof reprod biol, 77-80, PROF OBSTET & GYNEC, MED COL, CORNELL UNIV, 65- *Concurrent Pos:* Assoc prof, Copenhagen Univ, 56-64; consult, Rockefeller Univ, 68-; consult, WHO, Thailand, 72-73; obstetrician & gynecologist-in-chief, NY Hosp, 65-78, attend obstet & gynecologist, 79- *Mem:* Fel Am Gynec Soc; fel Am Col Obstet & Gynec; fel Am Fertil Soc; fel Endocrine Soc. *Res:* Permeability of placenta; endocrinology of pregnancy; biology of reproduction. *Mailing Add:* Dept of Obstet & Gynec Cornell Univ Med Col New York NY 10021

FUCHS, H(ENRY) O(TTEN), b Strasbourg, France, 1907; US citizen; m 34; c 1. MECHANICAL ENGINEERING. *Educ:* Univ Strasbourg, France, BA, 24; Tech Univ Karlsruhe, Ger, ME, 29, DEng, 33. *Prof Exp:* Sr design engr, Gen Motors Corp, 33-45; chief res engr, Preco Inc, 45-54; pres, Metal Improv Equip Co, 54-61; prof mech eng, 64-72, EMER PROF MECH ENG, STANFORD UNIV, 72- *Honors & Awards:* Da Vinci Medal, Am Soc Mech Engrs, 80. *Mem:* Soc Automotive Engrs; Am Soc Mech Engrs; Am Soc Testing & Mat. *Res:* Metal fatigue; vehicle dynamics; engineering design and development. *Mailing Add:* Dept of Mech Eng Stanford Univ Stanford CA 94305

FUCHS, JACOB, b New York, NY, May 7, 23; m 46; c 2. ANALYTICAL CHEMISTRY, SPECTROCHEMISTRY. *Educ:* NY Univ, AB, 44; Univ Ill, MS, 47, PhD(chem), 50. *Prof Exp:* Asst chem, Univ Ill, 48-52; from asst prof to assoc prof, 52-59, exec officer dept, 61-75, PROF CHEM, ARIZ STATE UNIV, 59-, DIR, MOD INDUST SPECTROS, 56- *Mem:* Am Chem Soc; Soc Appl Spectros; fel Am Inst Chemists. *Res:* X-ray diffraction and spectroscopy; ultraviolet and infrared spectroscopy. *Mailing Add:* Dept of Chem Ariz State Univ Tempe AZ 85287

FUCHS, JAMES ALLEN, b Ballinger, Tex, July 5, 43; m 66; c 2. BIOCHEMISTRY. *Educ:* Tex A&M Univ, BS, 65, MS, 67, PhD(genetics), 70. *Prof Exp:* NSF fel biochem, Univ Enzyme Inst, Copenhagen, 70-71; NIH fel, Nobel Inst Biochem, Sweden, asst prof, 72-78, ASSOC ASST PROF BIOCHEM, UNIV MINN, ST PAUL, 78- *Mem:* Am Soc Microbiol; AAAS. *Res:* Function and regulation of deoxynucleotide metabolism in Escherichia coli. *Mailing Add:* 140 Gortner Lab Univ of Minn St Paul MN 55107

FUCHS, JAMES CLAIBORNE ALLRED, b Coronado, Calif, June 13, 38; m 65; c 1. VASCULAR SURGERY. *Educ:* Princeton Univ, AB, 60; Johns Hopkins Univ, MD, 64. *Prof Exp:* Resident, Duke Univ Med Ctr, 64-66; surgeon, US Pub Health Serv, 66-68; resident, 68-72, asst prof, 74-77, assoc prof, 78-81, PROF SURG, DUKE UNIV MED CTR, 81- *Concurrent Pos:* Chief, Surg Serv, Vet Admin Hosp, 80- *Mem:* Southern Surg Asn; Soc Univ Surgeons; Soc Vascular Surg; Int Cardiovascular Soc; Am Col Surgeons. *Res:* Vascular surgery; the evolution and treatment of atherosclerotic vascular disease; evaluation of postoperative vacular morphology. *Mailing Add:* Dept Surg Box 3351 Duke Univ Med Ctr Durham NC 27710

FUCHS, JULIUS JAKOB, b Monzingen, Ger, Feb 12, 27; US citizen; m 66; c 2. ORGANIC CHEMISTRY. *Educ:* Univ Mainz, PhD, 52. *Prof Exp:* From chemist to res chemist, 53-68, res assoc, 68-79, RES FEL ORG CHEM, E I DU PONT DE NEMOURS & CO, 79- *Concurrent Pos:* Fel, Swiss Fed Inst Technol, 52-53. *Res:* Economical synthesis of biologically active organic compounds. *Mailing Add:* 1104 Greenway Rd Wilmington DE 19803

FUCHS, LASZLO, b Budapest, Hungary, June 24, 24; m 74; c 2. MATHEMATICS. *Educ:* Univ Budapest, MS & PhD(math), 47. *Prof Exp:* Asst math, Eotvos Lorand Univ, Budapest, 49-52, docent, 52-54, prof, 54-68; PROF MATH, TULANE UNIV, 68- *Concurrent Pos:* Vis prof, Tulane Univ, 61-62, Univ New South Wales, 65, Univ Miami, 66-68, Univ de Montpellier, 68, Univ Ariz, 72, Univ di Padova, 77 & 81 & Univ West Australia, 80. *Mem:* Am Math Soc; Math Asn Am; Hungarian Math Soc(treas, 51-63, secy gen, 63-65); Ger Math Asn. *Res:* Abstract algebra, particularly commutative groups, module theory and partially ordered algebraic structure. *Mailing Add:* Dept of Math Tulane Univ New Orleans LA 70118

FUCHS, MORTON S, b New York, NY, Nov 16, 32; m 60; c 2. INSECT ENDOCRINOLOGY. *Educ:* Mich State Univ, BS, 58, MS, 60, PhD(biochem), 67. *Prof Exp:* From asst prof to assoc prof, 66-74, PROF BIOL, UNIV NOTRE DAME, 74-, CHMN, DEPT MICROBIOL, 81- *Concurrent Pos:* Nat Commun Dis Control Ctr grant, 68-71 & NIH grants, 71- *Mem:* AAAS; Entom Soc Am; Am Soc Zool. *Res:* Biochemical and genetic control of differentiation; reproductive physiology of insects. *Mailing Add:* Dept of Biol Univ of Notre Dame Notre Dame IN 46556

FUCHS, NORMAN H, b Newark, NJ, Aug 2, 38; m 59; c 2. THEORETICAL PHYSICS. *Educ:* Carnegie Inst Technol, BS, 59; Mass Inst Technol, PhD(physics), 64. *Prof Exp:* Res assoc physics, Mass Inst Technol, 64; res investr, Univ Pa, 64-66; from asst prof to assoc prof, 66-80, PROF PHYSICS, PURDUE UNIV, 80- *Mem:* Am Phys Soc; Am Asn Physics Teachers. *Res:* Symmetries and their breakdown; elementary particle physics. *Mailing Add:* Dept Physics Purdue Univ West Lafayette IN 47906

FUCHS, RICHARD, b Baltimore, Md, Dec 29, 26. ORGANIC CHEMISTRY. *Educ:* Cornell Univ, AB, 49; Univ Kans, PhD(chem), 53. *Prof Exp:* Asst instr chem, Univ Kans, 49-53; fel, Iowa State Col, 53-54; asst prof chem, Univ Ala, 54-55; from instr to asst prof, Univ Tex, 55-63; assoc prof, 63-72, PROF CHEM, UNIV HOUSTON, 72- *Mem:* Am Chem Soc. *Res:* Solvation effects on rates and equilibria; thermochemistry of strained molecules. *Mailing Add:* Dept of Chem Univ of Houston Houston TX 77004

FUCHS, RICHARD E(ARL), b Milan, Tenn, July 26, 36; m 61; c 2. CHEMICAL ENGINEERING. *Educ:* Univ Tenn, BS, 58; La State Univ, MS, 62, PhD(chem eng), 64. *Prof Exp:* Chem engr, Esso Res Labs, 58-61; asst prof chem eng, Univ Miss, 64; sr res engr, comput processes, Olinkraft, Inc, 64-72; mgr pulp mill systs, Indust Nucleonics Corp, 72-75; develop mgr, paper div, Gulf States Paper Corp, 75-77; SR TECH SERV ENGR, MILL DIV, MANVILLE FOREST PROD CORP, INC, 77- *Mem:* Tech Asn Pulp & Paper Indust. *Res:* Decolorization of pulp mill bleaching effluents; forest products; process control. *Mailing Add:* Manville Forest Prod Corp PO Box 488 West Monroe LA 71291

FUCHS, RONALD, b Los Angeles, Calif, Jan 27, 32; m 63; c 2. SOLID STATE PHYSICS. *Educ:* Calif Inst Technol, BS, 54; Univ Ill, PhD(physics), 57. *Prof Exp:* Fulbright fel, Stuttgart Tech Univ, 57-59; physicist, Div Sponsored Res, Lab Insulation Res, Mass Inst Technol, 59-61; from asst prof to assoc prof, 61-74, PROF PHYSICS, IOWA STATE UNIV, 74- *Mem:* Am Phys Soc. *Res:* Theoretical solid state physics; optical properties; lattice dynamics. *Mailing Add:* Dept of Physics Iowa State Univ Ames IA 50011

FUCHS, VICTOR ROBERT, b New York City, NY, Jan 31, 24; m 48; c 4. MEDICAL SCIENCES. *Educ:* NY Univ, BS, 47; Columbia Univ, MA, 51, PhD(econ), 55. *Prof Exp:* Assoc prof econ, NY Univ, 59-60; prog assoc econ, Ford Found, 60-62; prof community med, Mt Sinai Sch Med & prof econ, City Univ New York Grad Ctr, 68-74; vpres, 68-78, RES ASSOC ECON, NAT BUR ECON RES, 62-; PROF ECON HEALTH, DEPT ECON, STANFORD UNIV & PROF COMMUNITY MED, MED SCH, 74- *Concurrent Pos:* Mem, Pres Comt Mental Retardation, 68-71; bd dir, Banker's Life Co, 81- *Mem:* Inst Med-Nat Acad Sci. *Res:* Economic aspects of health, medical care, family, work, and dimensions of human behavior and social institutions in post-industrial society. *Mailing Add:* 204 Junipero Serra Blvd Stanford CA 94305

FUCHS, WALTER, b Munich, Ger, Dec 29, 32; US citizen. SOLID STATE PHYSICS, COMPUTER SCIENCE. *Educ:* Munich Tech Univ, dipl, 61; Carnegie Mellon Univ, MS, 64, PhD(physics), 68. *Prof Exp:* Asst prof physics, Univ Toledo, 67-68; res assoc, Cornell Univ, 68-70; res physicist energy conversion, 70-79, SUPVRY PHYSICIST, PTTISBURGH ENERGY TECHNOL CTR, US DEPT ENERGY, 79- *Concurrent Pos:* Tech consult, US Dept of Defense, Picatinny Arsenal, 70-72. *Mem:* AAAS; Am Phys Soc; Soc Control & Instrumentation Energy Processes. *Res:* Coal conversion, coal-to-oil, coal-to-gas; instrumentation and control of process facilities; automatic data acquisition and processing; mathematical modeling of conversion processes. *Mailing Add:* US Dept Energy 4800 Forbes Ave Pittsburgh PA 15213

FUCHS, WOLFGANG HEINRICH, b Munich, Germany, May 19, 15; nat US; m 43; c 3. PURE MATHEMATICS. *Educ:* Cambridge Univ, BA, 36, PhD(math), 41. *Prof Exp:* Teacher, Brit Univs, 40-49; assoc prof, 50-58, PROF MATH, CORNELL UNIV, 58- *Concurrent Pos:* Vis assoc prof math, Cornell Univ, 48-49. *Res:* Theory of functions. *Mailing Add:* Dept of Math Cornell Univ Ithaca NY 14850

FUCHSMAN, CHARLES H(ERMAN), b New York, NY, June 12, 17; m 37; c 3. CHEMISTRY. *Educ:* City Col New York, BS, 36; Western Reserve Univ, PhD(org chem), 65. *Prof Exp:* Technologist, US Bur Mines, 42-45; res chemist potash refining, Int Minerals & Chem Corp, 45-51; res group leader, Micro-Pilot Plant Develop, Columbia Southern Chem Corp, 51-56; dir res & develop, Ferro Chem Corp, 56-66, dir res & develop, Ferro Chem Div, Ferro Corp, 66-69, assoc dir res org chem, 69-72; assoc prof, 72-78, PROF ENVIRON STUDIES, BEMIDJI STATE UNIV, 78-, DIR CTR ENVIRON STUDIES, 72- *Mem:* Phytochem Soc NAm; AAAS; Am Chem Soc; Deutsche Ges Moor Torfkunde; NY Acad Sci. *Res:* Organic chemical synthesis; polymer chemistry; history of organic chemistry; reaction mechanisms; chemistry of peat; environmental chemistry; natural products chemistry. *Mailing Add:* 3006 Cedar Lane Bemidji MN 56601

FUCHSMAN, WILLIAM HARVEY, b New York, NY, June 2, 41; m 64; c 3. BIOINORGANIC CHEMISTRY. *Educ:* Harvard Univ, BA, 63; Johns Hopkins Univ, PhD(biochem), 67. *Prof Exp:* Asst prof chem, Univ SFla, 67-68; fel, E I du Pont de Nemours & Co, 68-70; asst prof, 70-76, ASSOC PROF CHEM, OBERLIN COL, 76- *Mem:* AAAS; Am Chem Soc. *Res:* Chemistry of porphyrins, metalloporphyrins and hemeproteins; nitrogen fixation. *Mailing Add:* Dept of Chem Oberlin Col Oberlin OH 44074

FUCIK, EDWARD MONTFORD, b Chicago, Ill, Jan 25, 14; m 43; c 3. CIVIL ENGINEERING. *Educ:* Princeton Univ, BSCE, 35; Harvard Univ, MS, 37. *Prof Exp:* Mem staff, Harza, Consult Engrs, Chicago, 38-40; found engr, Panama Canal, 40-42; mem staff, 45-69, pres, 69-74, chmn bd, 69-77, EMER CHMN BD, HARZA ENG CO, 77- *Concurrent Pos:* Mem consult bd, Kalabagh Dam, Pakistan; mem bd mgrs, Highland Park Hosp, Ill, 66-69; mem adv coun, Ill Inst Technol, 71- *Honors & Awards:* Thomas Fitch Rowland Prize, Am Soc Civil Engrs, 53. *Mem:* Nat Acad Eng; Am Soc Civil Engrs; Soc Am Mil Engrs; Nat Soc Prof Engrs. *Mailing Add:* Harza Eng Co 150 S Wacker Dr Chicago IL 60606

FUCIK, JOHN EDWARD, b Waukegan, Ill, May 30, 28; m 56; c 3. HORTICULTURE, PLANT PHYSIOLOGY. *Educ:* Univ Ill, BS, 49, MS, 57, PhD(hort), 63. *Prof Exp:* Asst prod mgr, Pfister Assoc Growers, Inc, 49-51; supvr & teacher hort, Univ Ill, 57-65; PROF AGR CITRUS CTR, TEX A&I UNIV, 65- *Mem:* Am Soc Hort Sci; Am Soc Plant Physiol; Am Pomol Soc; Int Soc Hort Sci. *Res:* Physiology of horticultural tree crops; tree-soil-environment relationships. *Mailing Add:* Citrus Ctr Tex A&I Univ Weslaco TX 78596

FUDA, MICHAEL GEORGE, b Albany, NY, Oct 31, 38; m 62; c 3. THEORETICAL NUCLEAR PHYSICS. *Educ:* Rensselaer Polytech Inst, BS, 60, PhD(physics), 67. *Prof Exp:* Res physicist, Knolls Atomic Power Lab, 62-64; from asst prof to assoc prof, 67-78, PROF PHYSICS, STATE UNIV NY BUFFALO, 78- *Mem:* Am Phys Soc. *Res:* Scattering theory with applications to nuclear physics; theory of three-particle systems. *Mailing Add:* Dept of Physics State Univ of NY Buffalo NY 14214

FUDALI, ROBERT F, b Minneapolis, Minn, July 7, 33; m 56; c 3. GEOCHEMISTRY, PETROLOGY. *Educ:* Univ Minn, Minneapolis, BA, 56; Pa State Univ, PhD(geochem), 60. *Prof Exp:* Res fel, Pa State Univ, 60-62; staff scientist, Bellcomm Inc, 62-66; RES SCIENTIST, DEPT MINERAL SCI, SMITHSONIAN INST, 66- *Mem:* Meteoritical Soc; Geochem Soc; Mineral Soc Am. *Res:* Genesis of igneous rocks and meteorites; genesis of lunar rocks and landforms; role of large cometary and meteorite impacts in the development of planetary surfaces. *Mailing Add:* Dept Mineral Sci Stop 119 Smithsonian Inst Washington DC 20560

FUDENBERG, H HUGH, b New York, NY, Oct 24, 28; m 55; c 4. HEMATOLOGY, IMMUNOLOGY. *Educ:* Univ Calif, Los Angeles, AB, 49; Univ Chicago, MD, 53; Boston Univ, MA, 57. *Prof Exp:* Intern med, Univ Utah, 53-54; asst resident med, Mt Sinai Hosp, New York, 56-57 & Peter Bent Brigham Hosp, Boston, 57-58; res assoc immunol, Rockefeller Inst, 58-60; from asst prof to prof med, Sch Med, Univ Calif, San Francisco, 66-75, chief hemat unit, 62-75; CHMN DEPT BASIC & CLIN IMMUNOL, MED UNIV SC, 75- *Concurrent Pos:* Fel hemat, Sch Med, Tufts Univ, 54-56; mem, Expert Comt Immunol, WHO, 62-77; prof bact & immunol, Univ Calif, Berkeley, 66-75; chief ed, J Chem Immunol. *Honors & Awards:* Pasteur Medal, Inst Pasteur, Paris, 62; Robert A Cooke Mem Medal, Am Acad Allergy, 67. *Mem:* Fel AAAS; Am Asn Immunologists; Am Soc Human Genetics; Am Soc Clin Invest; Genetics Soc Am. *Res:* Antigenic, biologic, and physico-chemical properties of antibody molecules and related proteins; genetic control of normal antibody synthesis and genetically determined immunologic aberrations predisposing to disease. *Mailing Add:* Dept of Basic & Clin Immunol Med Univ of SC Charleston SC 29403

FUELBERG, HENRY ERNEST, b Brenham, Tex, May 13, 48. METEOROLOGY. *Educ:* Tex A&M Univ, BS, 70, MS, 71, PhD(meteorol), 76. *Prof Exp:* From res asst to res assoc meteorol, Tex A&M Univ, 74-77; asst prof, 77-80, ASSOC PROF METEOROL, ST LOUIS UNIV, 80- *Concurrent Pos:* Prin investr, NASA grants, 78- *Mem:* Am Meteorol Soc. *Res:* Synoptic and dynamic meteorology; atmospheric energetics. *Mailing Add:* Dept of Earth & Atmospheric Sci 221 N Grand St Louis MO 63103

FUELBERTH, JOHN DOUGLAS, algebra, see previous edition

FUENNING, SAMUEL ISAIAH, b Ft Morgan, Colo, Sept 20, 16; m 44; c 5. PREVENTIVE MEDICINE, ATHLETIC MEDICINE. *Educ:* Univ Nebr, BSc, 40, MS, 41, MD, 45. *Prof Exp:* Asst bot, 40-41, assoc prof pub health & assoc cellular res, 50-62, prev med, 62-74, dir, Nebr Ctr Health Educ, 74-77, coordr res & develop, 77-79, PROF PREV MED, UNIV NEBR-LINCOLN, 74-, FAMILY WELLNESS SPECIALIST, 78- *Concurrent Pos:* Chmn, Nebr Voluntary Adv Comn Selective Serv System; med adv, Nebr Govr's Coun Fitness; chmn, Nat Conf Health Col Community, Boston, 70 & Nebr Conf Educ Health & Fitness, 64, 68, 70 & 72; mem, Vis Comt Overseers, Harvard Univ, 70-76; med dir, Univ Nebr Health Serv & Health Ctr, 47-74;

med dir, Athletic Med, 77-; pres, Nebr Interagency Health Coun, 80-; co-chmn, Gov Coun Physical Fitness & Sports, 80- *Honors & Awards:* Phys Fitness Leadership Award, Lincoln Jr Chamber Com, 68 & US Jaycees-Metrop Life Ins Co-President's Coun Phys Fitness & Sports, 69; Hitchcock Award, Am Col Health Asn, Award, 69. *Mem:* Am Col Preventive Med; AMA; Am Col Health Asn (pres, 60-61); Am Public Health Asn; NY Acad Sci. *Res:* Clinical medicine in the college age group; stress; fitness and mental health; sports medicine. *Mailing Add:* Health Educ & Athletic Med Colesium 217 UNL Lincoln NE 68588

FUENTES, RICARDO, JR, b McAllen, Tex, July 28, 48; m 70; c 1. BIOINORGANIC CHEMISTRY. *Educ:* Pan Am Univ, BS, 70; Univ Tex, Austin, PhD(chem), 75. *Prof Exp:* Res assoc biochem, Mich State Univ, 75-77; SR RES CHEMIST, DOW CHEM CO, 77- *Mem:* Am Chem Soc. *Res:* Application of proton, carbon-13 and phosphorus-31 nuclear magnetic resonance to the investigation of metal-enzyme and metal-protein interactions in aqueous solutions; organometallic chemistry of Ziegler-Natta catalysts. *Mailing Add:* Dow Chem Res & Develop PO Box 150 Plaquemine LA 48823

FUERHOLZER, JAMES J, polymer chemistry, organic chemistry, see previous edition

FUERNISS, STEPHEN JOSEPH, b York, Nebr, July 17, 45. ORGANIC CHEMISTRY. *Educ:* Col St Thomas, BA, 67; Univ Nebr, PhD(org chem), 75. *Prof Exp:* Fel, Brandeis Univ, 75-76, Ohio State Univ, 76-77; RES CHEMIST, E I DU PONT DE NEMOURS & CO, INC, 77- *Mem:* Am Chem Soc. *Res:* Photochemistry; polymer chemistry. *Mailing Add:* Photo Prod Dept E I du Pont de Nemours & Co Inc Towanda PA 18840

FUERST, PAUL ANTHONY, b Rockville Centre, NY, June 15, 48; m 70. POPULATION GENETICS, HUMAN GENETICS. *Educ:* Manhattan Col, BA, 70; Brown Univ, ScM, 72, PhD(biol), 75. *Prof Exp:* Res assoc human genetics, Univ Tex Health Sci Ctr Houston, 75-77; asst prof biol, Univ Houston, 76-77; sr res assoc human genetics, Univ Tex Health Sci Ctr, Houston, 77-80; ASST PROF GENETICS, OHIO STATE UNIV, 80- *Mem:* Am Genetics Asn; Genetics Soc Am; Am Soc Human Genetics; Sigma Xi; Am Soc Naturalists. *Res:* Human population genetics especially theoretical genetics including statistical aspects of protein and nucleic acid polymorphism in natural populations; evolutionary genetics. *Mailing Add:* Dept Genetics Ohio State Univ 1735 Neil Ave Columbus OH 43210

FUERST, ROBERT, b Vienna, Austria, Jan 12, 21; nat US; m 46; c 2. GENETICS, MICROBIOLOGY. *Educ:* Univ Houston, BS, 44; Univ Tex, MA, 48, PhD(zool), 55. *Prof Exp:* Res scientist biochem, M D Anderson Hosp & Tumor Inst, 49-52, res scientist, Genetics Found, 52-55, asst biologist chg microbiol sect, 55-57; assoc prof, 57-64, PROF BIOL, TEX WOMAN'S UNIV, 64-, HEAD MICROBIOL RES, 57- *Concurrent Pos:* Asst prof genetics, Univ Tex, 55-57. *Mem:* AAAS; Am Soc Human Genetics; Soc Indust Microbiol; Genetics Soc Am; Sigma Xi. *Res:* Microbial genetics; radiation; biology; author of over one hundred publications. *Mailing Add:* Dept of Biol Tex Woman's Univ Box 22757 Denton TX 76204

FUERSTENAU, D(OUGLAS) W(INSTON), b Hazel, SDak, Dec 6, 28; m 53; c 3. EXTRACTIVE METALLURGY. *Educ:* SDak Sch Mines & Technol, BS, 49; Mont Sch Mines, MS, 50; Mass Inst Technol, ScD(metall), 53. *Prof Exp:* Asst prof mineral eng, Mass Inst Technol, 53-56; res engr, Union Carbide Metals Co, 56-58; mgr mineral eng, Kaiser Aluminum & Chem Corp, 58-59; assoc prof metall, 59-62, chmn deptr mat sci & mineral eng, 70-78, PROF METALL, UNIV CALIF, BERKELEY, 62- *Concurrent Pos:* Mem, Bd Mineral Resources, Nat Resource Coun, 75-77. *Honors & Awards:* Hardy Gold Medal, 57, Raymond Award, 61, Richards Award, 76 & Gaudin Award, 78, Am Inst Mining, Metall & Petrol Engrs. *Mem:* Nat Acad Eng; Am Chem Soc; Am Inst Mining, Metall & Petrol Engrs; Am Inst Chem Engrs. *Res:* Mineral processing; applied colloid and surface chemistry; properties of particulate materials. *Mailing Add:* Dept of Mat Sci & Mineral Eng Univ of Calif Berkeley CA 94720

FUERSTENAU, M(AURICE) C(LARK), b Watertown, SDak, June 6, 33; m 53; c 4. GEOLOGICAL ENGINEERING, METALLURGY. *Educ:* SDak Sch Mines & Technol, BS, 55; Mass Inst Technol, MS, 57, ScD(metall), 61. *Prof Exp:* Res assoc metall, Mass Inst Technol, 60-61; res engr, NMex Bur Mines, 61-63; from asst prof to assoc prof, Colo Sch Mines, 63-68; from assoc prof to prof, Univ Utah, 68-70; PROF METALL ENG & HEAD DEPT, S DAK SCH MINES & TECHNOL, 70- *Honors & Awards:* Arthur F Taggart Award, Soc Mining Engrs, 78; Antoine M Gaudin Award, Soc Mining Engrs, 79. *Mem:* Distinguished mem Soc Mining Engrs; Am Inst Mining, Metall & Petrol Engrs. *Res:* Surface chemistry and adsorption phenomena; kinetics and reaction mechanisms involved in hydrometallurgy; mechanisms involved in froth flotation; fundamentals of sedimentation. *Mailing Add:* Dept of Metall Eng SDak Sch of Mines & Technol Rapid City SD 57701

FUESS, FREDERICK WILLIAM, III, b Syracuse, NY, Nov 5, 27; m 52; c 2. AGRONOMY. *Educ:* Cornell Univ, BS, 52, MEd, 55; Mich State Univ, PhD, 63. *Prof Exp:* Teacher pub sch, 52; asst prof agron, State Univ NY Agr & Tech Inst, Morrisville, 55-60; asst, Mich State Univ, 60-63; from asst prof to assoc prof, 63-69, PROF PLANT & SOIL SCI, ILL STATE UNIV, 69- *Concurrent Pos:* Bk reviewer, AAAS, 70- *Mem:* Am Soc Agron; Crop Sci Soc Am; AAAS; Sigma Xi. *Res:* Crop physiology and management; soybean production. *Mailing Add:* RR 8 Box 7 Normal IL 61761

FUESS, STUART CHARLES, b Batavia, NY, Nov 20, 52; m 80. EXPERIMENTAL PHYSICS. *Educ:* Cornell Univ, BS, 74, MEng, 75; Univ Ill, Urbana-Champaign, PhD(physics), 81. *Prof Exp:* Res asst, Univ Ill, Urbana-Champaign, 81; RES ASSOC, FERMI NAT ACCELERATOR LAB, 81- *Res:* Experimental high energy neutrino physics. *Mailing Add:* Fermi Nat Accelerator Lab MS 122 PO Box 500 Batavia IL 60510

FUGATE, KEARBY JOE, b Dallas, Tex, Aug 6, 34; m 62; c 2. MICROBIOLOGY, BIOCHEMISTRY. *Educ:* Baylor Univ, BA, 56, MS, 63, PhD(microbiol), 67. *Prof Exp:* Res asst microbiol, J K & Susie Wadley Res Inst, 60-63; instr, Dent Sch, Baylor Univ, 64-67; MICROBIOLOGIST, USPHS, 67- *Concurrent Pos:* Br chief hematol & path, Div Clin Lab Devices, Bur Med Devices. *Mem:* AAAS; Am Soc Microbiol; Am Pub Health Asn; fel Am Inst Chemists; Sigma Xi. *Res:* Immunochemistry of bacterial cell wall constituents; immunochemistry of antigen-antibody interactions; immunology of murine leukemia-virus transmission. *Mailing Add:* US Dept of Health Educ & Welfare 8757 Georgia Ave Silver Spring MD 75204

FUGELSO, LEIF ERIK, b Minot, NDak, Oct 29, 35; div; c 3. GEOPHYSICS, APPLIED MATHEMATICS. *Educ:* Univ Chicago, SM, 63, PhD(geophys), 73. *Prof Exp:* Res engr, Mech Res Div, Am Mach & Foundry Co, 59-63, Gen Am Transp Corp, 63-75; seismologist, Portland Cement Asn, 75; STAFF MEM, LOS ALAMOS SCI LAB, 75- *Res:* Seismology; structural dynamics; terminal ballistics; shock waves; weapons and blast effects; explosive safety. *Mailing Add:* Los Alamos Sci Lab PO Box 1663 Los Alamos NM 87544

FUGET, CHARLES ROBERT, b Rochester, Pa, Dec 15, 29; m 56; c 1. PHYSICAL CHEMISTRY, EDUCATIONAL ADMINISTRATION. *Educ:* Geneva Col, BS, 51; Pa State Univ, MS, 53, PhD(phys chem), 56. *Prof Exp:* Res chemist, Esso Res & Eng Co, NJ, 55-56; from asst prof to assoc prof chem, Geneva Col, 56-63; res chemist, Callery Chem Co, 57-59; prof sci, State Univ NY Col Buffalo, 63-64; prof physics & chmn dept, Geneva Col, 64-71; dir div natural sci & math, 71-73, PROF PHYSICS, INDIANA UNIV PA, 71-, assoc dean, 73-76, DEAN SCH NATURAL SCI & MATH, 77- *Mem:* Am Chem Soc; Am Phys Soc. *Res:* Thermodynamic properties; reaction calorimetry; electrochemistry. *Mailing Add:* Sch of Natural Sci & Math 332 Stright Hall Indiana Univ Pa Indiana PA 15705

FUGGER, JOSEPH, b Jesenice, Yugoslavia, Feb 11, 21; nat US; m 53; c 7. INDUSTRIAL CHEMISTRY. *Educ:* Univ Pittsburgh, BS, 46, MS, 48, PhD(chem), 52. *Prof Exp:* Res intern, Northern Regional Lab, USDA, 49-50; asst prof res, Antioch Col, 52-53; res chemist, Buckeye Cellulose Corp, 54-55; fel chem, Harvard Univ, 55-56; res group leader, Thiokol Chem Corp, 57-58; res specialist gas dynamics, Boeing Airplane Co, 58-59; staff scientist res & opers, Aeronutronic Div, Ford Motor Co, 59-60; res scientist, Missiles & Space Div, Lockheed Aircraft Corp, 61-62; res group leader, Westreco, Inc, Nestle Int, 63-64; head basic res sect, 64-67; consult chemist, Hops Extract Corp Am, Wash, 69-70; consult chemist, 70-75; PRES, FUGGER-TECH CONSULTS, 75- *Res:* Organic synthesis; macromolecular systems; beverage and food; solid propellants; materials science. *Mailing Add:* 739 Greenleaf Dr Monroeville PA 15146

FUGLISTER, FREDERICK CHARLES, b New York, NY, Aug 1, 09; m 39; c 3. OCEANOGRAPHY. *Prof Exp:* From observer to physical oceanogr, 40-60, chmn dept phys oceanog, 62-67, SR SCIENTIST, WOODS HOLE OCEANOG INST, 60- *Honors & Awards:* Agassiz Medal, Nat Acad Sci, 69. *Mem:* Fel Am Geophys Union. *Res:* Thermohaline structure of the Atlantic Ocean with special emphasis on the Gulf Stream system; physical oceanography. *Mailing Add:* Woods Hole Oceanog Inst Woods Hole MA 02543

FUGMANN, RUTH ADELE, b Baltimore, Md, Sept 7, 23. IMMUNOLOGY, CHEMOTHERAPY. *Educ:* Johns Hopkins Univ, BS, 50; Univ Miami, MS, 64, PhD(cancer immunol), 68. *Prof Exp:* Technician, Clin Lab, Mercy Hosp, Baltimore, Md, 42-44; sr technician, Army Chem Ctr, 44-48, hematologist, 48-50; res asst cancer, Col Physicians & Surgeons, Columbia Univ, 50-58 & Univ Miami, 58-61; res asst immunochem, Howard Hughes Med Inst, Miami, Fla, 61-65; res asst immunochem, Variety Children's Res Found, 65-68, res assoc cancer immunol, 68-69; co-dir cancer immunol, Cath Med Ctr of Brooklyn & Queens, Inc, 69-76; sr immunologist, 76-80, SCI ADV, IIT RES INST, 80- *Concurrent Pos:* Instr, Univ Miami, 68-70. *Mem:* Am Soc Microbiol; Am Asn Cancer Res; Am Asn Immunol; Reticuloendothelial Soc. *Res:* Cancer and transplantation immunology; cancer chemotherapy. *Mailing Add:* IIT Res Inst 10 W 35th St Chicago IL 60616

FUGO, NICHOLAS WILLIAM, b Syracuse, NY, Sept 15, 13; m 40; c 1. OBSTETRICS & GYNECOLOGY. *Educ:* Syracuse Univ, AB, 35; Univ Iowa, MS, 37, PhD(endocrinol), 40; Univ Chicago, MD, 50; Am Bd Obstet & Gynec, dipl. *Prof Exp:* Res assoc zool, Univ Iowa, 39-40; instr pharmacol, Med Labs, 40-43; res assoc obstet & gynec, Univ Chicago, 46-52, from instr to assoc prof, 52-60; Margaret Higgins Sanger Chair family planning & reproductive physiol, 67-80, EMER PROF OBSTET & GYNEC, SCH MED, WVA UNIV, 80- *Mem:* Soc Exp Biol & Med; Am Soc Pharmacol & Exp Therapeut; Am Fertil Soc; Am Fedn Clin Res; fel Am Col Obstet & Gynec. *Res:* Endocrinology of sex; human reproduction. *Mailing Add:* Dept of Obstet & Gynec WVa Univ Sch of Med Morgantown WV 26506

FUHLHAGE, DONALD WAYNE, b Virgil, Kans, Sept 2, 31; m 61; c 2. ORGANIC CHEMISTRY. *Educ:* Univ Kans, BS, 53, PhD(org chem), 58. *Prof Exp:* Sr res chemist, Tidewater Oil Co, Calif, 58-62; res assoc, Pa, 62-63; supvr process develop, 63-70, sect leader process develop & residue anal, 70-75, SUPVR SYNTHESIS & PILOT PLANT, THOMPSON-HAYWARD CHEM CO, HARRISON & CROSSFIELDS GROUP, 75- *Mem:* Am Chem Soc. *Res:* Pyrrole chemistry; synthesis of pesticides; liquid chromatography; surfactant synthesis. *Mailing Add:* Route 1 Tonganoxie KS 66086

FUHR, IRVIN, b Sharon, Pa, Jan 16, 13; m 40; c 2. BIOPHYSICAL CHEMISTRY. *Educ:* Univ Wis, BS, 37, MS, 39, PhD(biochem), 42. *Prof Exp:* Toxicologist, Army Chem Ctr, US War Dept, 43-48; exec secy, Biochem Study Sect, Div Res Grants, NIH, 48-55, exec secy, Biophysics & Biophys Chem Study Sect, 55-78. *Mem:* Biophys Soc. *Res:* Toxicology of drugs and chemical warfare agents; vitamin and mineral metabolism; anemia and rickets; development of experimental diets and chemical methods; development of rodenticide cartridge. *Mailing Add:* 12925 Crisfield Rd Silver Spring MD 20906

FUHR, JOSEPH ERNEST, b New York, NY, June 30, 36; m 61; c 3. CELL PHYSIOLOGY, HEMATOLOGY. *Educ:* Le Moyne Col, AB, 60; LI Univ, MS, 62; St John's Univ, PhD(biol), 68. *Prof Exp:* Res assoc hemat, Albert Einstein Col Med, 66-68; hemat trainee, Col Physicians & Surgeons, Columbia Univ, 68-70, instr human genetics & develop, 70-71; asst res prof, 71-75, assoc prof med biol, 78-81, ASSOC RES PROF CELL PHYSIOL & HEMAT, MEM RES CTR, UNIV TENN, KNOXVILLE, 75-, PROF MED BIOL & DIR MEM RES CTR, 81- *Concurrent Pos:* Adj assoc prof biol, St John's Univ, NY, 70-71; Leukemia Soc Am spec fel, 70-72; mem ad hoc study sect, Nat Heart, Lung & Blood Inst, 75-76; res career develop award, Nat Inst Arthritis, Metab & Digestive Dis, 76-81; consult sickle cell, Nat Heart, Lung & Blood Int, 81-82. *Mem:* AAAS; Am Soc Hemat; Soc Exp Biol & Med; Int Soc Exp Hemat. *Res:* Erythropoiesis and hemoglobin synthesis; control of protein synthesis. *Mailing Add:* 623 Broome Rd Knoxville TN 37919

FUHRIMAN, D(EAN) K(ENNETH), b Ridgedale, Idaho, June 6, 18; m 41; c 5. CIVIL ENGINEERING. *Educ:* Utah State Col, BS, 41, MS, 50; Univ Wis, PhD(civil eng), 52. *Prof Exp:* Dept asst, exp sta, Utah State Col, 37-41; jr engr, US Corps Engrs, 41; instr, civil eng, Utah State Col, 41-43; asst irrig engr, soil conserv serv, USDA, 46-48, agr engr, PR, 48-50; assoc prof civil eng, Colo Agr & Mech Col, 51-52; assoc prof irrig & drainage engr, Utah State Agr Col, 52-54; assoc prof civil eng, 54-56, chmn dept, 58-61, PROF CIVIL ENG, BRIGHAM YOUNG UNIV, 56- *Concurrent Pos:* Pres & prin engr, Fuhriman, Rollins & Co, 56-66; tech adv, US Water Pollution Control Admin, Washington, DC, 67-68 & Indust Pollution Control Res Div, Environ Protection Admin, 74-75; pres, Fuhriman, Barton & Assoc, Consult Engrs, 70-; mem, US comt Int Comn Irrig, Drainage & Flood Control. *Mem:* Am Soc Civil Engrs; Am Soc Eng Educ; Int Water Resources Asn; Water Pollution Control Fedn. *Res:* Water resources engineering; irrigation; drainage; agricultural engineering; environmental engineering. *Mailing Add:* Col Eng 368L C B Brigham Young Univ Provo UT 84602

FUHRKEN, GEBHARD, b Frankfurt, Ger, Feb 10, 30. MATHEMATICS. *Educ:* Univ Calif, Berkeley, PhD(math), 62. *Prof Exp:* Asst prof, 62-71, ASSOC PROF MATH, UNIV MINN, MINNEAPOLIS, 71- *Mem:* Am Math Soc; Asn Symbolic Logic; Path Asn Am. *Res:* Mathematical logic; theory of models. *Mailing Add:* Sch Math Univ Minn Minneapolis MN 55455

FUHRMAN, ALBERT WILLIAM, b Brooklyn, NY, Jan 13, 21; m 43; c 2. ORGANIC CHEMISTRY. *Educ:* City Col New York, BS, 42; Purdue Univ, MS, 44, PhD(org chem), 48. *Prof Exp:* Res chemist chem div, Glenn L Martin Co, 48-50; res & develop chemist, Naugatuck Chem Div, US Rubber Co, 50-55; plant mgr, Plastics & Chem Div, Great Am Plastics Co, 55-59, vpres, Great Am Chem Corp, 59-81; CONSULT, 81- *Mem:* Am Chem Soc. *Res:* Ketene reactions; vinyl resins; vinyl polymerization; reaction of ketene with certain carbonyl compounds; vinyl compounding. *Mailing Add:* 6847-12 Caminito Mundo San Diego CA 92119

FUHRMAN, FREDERICK ALEXANDER, b Coquille, Ore, Aug 13, 15; m 42. MEDICAL PHYSIOLOGY, TOXINOLOGY. *Educ:* Ore State Col, BS, 37, MS, 39; Stanford Univ, PhD(physiol), 43. *Prof Exp:* Res assoc physiol, 41-44, from instr to prof, 44-59, dir, Fleischmann Labs Med Sci, 59-70, prof exp med, 59-72, prof, 72-81, EMER PROF PHYSIOL, STANFORD UNIV, 81- *Concurrent Pos:* Guggenheim fel, Copenhagen Univ, 51-52; NSF fel, Donner Lab, Univ Calif, 58-59; Commonwealth Fund fel, 65-66; vis investr, Zoophys Lab, Copenhagen Univ, 49, 51-52 & 58-59; consult, Tech Info Div, Libr Cong, 56; vis investr, Hopkins Marine Sta, 71-79, affil prof, 73-79. *Mem:* AAAS; Am Physiol Soc; Am Soc Pharmacol & Exp Therapeut; Soc Gen Physiol; Soc Toxinol. *Res:* Drugs and tissue respiration; temperature and drug action; experimental frostbite; tissue changes following ischemia; ion transport; pharmacology of marine and amphibian toxins. *Mailing Add:* PO Box 313 Pebble Beach CA 93953

FUHRMAN, ROBERT ALEXANDER, b Detroit, Mich, Feb 23, 25; m 49; c 3. AEROSPACE ENGINEERING & TECHNOLOGY. *Educ:* Univ Mich, BS, 45; Univ Md, MS, 52. *Prof Exp:* Proj engr, Naval Air Test Ctr, Patuxent River, Md, 46-53; chief tech eng, Ryan Aeronaut Co, San Diego, 53-58; vpres & asst gen mgr, Missile Systs Div, 58-69, vpres & gen mgr, 69, exec vpres, 73-76, PRES, LOCKHEED MISSILES & SPACE CO, 76- *Concurrent Pos:* Vpres, Lockheed Corp, Burbank, 69-76, sr vpres, 76-, pres, Lockheed Ga Co, Marietta, 70-71, pres, Lockheed Calif Co, Burbank, 71-73; chmn bd, Ventura Mfg Co, 70-71. *Honors & Awards:* Silver Knight Award, Nat Mgt Asn, 69, John J Montgomery Award, 64; Award, Soc Mfg Engrs, 73. *Mem:* Nat Acad Eng; fel Am Inst Aeronaut & Astronaut; Nat Aeronaut Asn; Inst Elec & Electronics Engrs. *Mailing Add:* 1111 Lockheed Sunnyvale CA 94086

FUHS, ALLEN E(UGENE), b Laramie, Wyo, Aug 11, 27; m 51; c 1. MECHANICAL ENGINEERING. *Educ:* Univ NMex, BS, 51; Calif Inst Technol, MS, 55, PhD(mech eng), 58. *Prof Exp:* Asst, Calif Inst Technol, 54-55, lectr jet propulsion, 57-58; asst prof mech eng, Northwestern Univ, 58-59; mem tech staff, phys res lab, space technol labs, Thompson Ramo Wooldridge, Inc, 59-60; staff scientist, plasma res lab, Aerospace Corp, 60-66; prof aeronaut, Naval Postgrad Sch, 66-68, chmn dept, 67-68; chief scientist, Air Force Aero Propulsion Lab, Wright-Patterson AFB, Ohio, 68-70; prof aeronaut, 70-74, chmn, Dept Mech Eng, 75-78, DISTINGUISHED PROF AERONAUT, NAVAL POSTGRAD SCH, 74- *Concurrent Pos:* Private consult, 56-; vis fel, Joint Inst Lab Astrophysics & vis assoc prof, Univ Colo, 64-65. *Honors & Awards:* Ralph R Tector Award, Soc Automotive Engrs, 81. *Mem:* Fel Am Inst Aeronaut & Astronaut; Am Phys Soc; fel Am Soc Mech Engrs; Optical Soc Am; Soc Automotive Engrs. *Res:* Magnetohydrodynamics; spectroscopy; combustion; jet propulsion; re-entry physics; instrumentation for high speed plasma flow; aircraft gas turbines; combustion; high energy lasers. *Mailing Add:* Dept of Aeronaut Naval Postgrad Sch Monterey CA 93940

FUHS, GEORG WOLFGANG, b Cologne, Ger, May 19, 32; m 60; c 3. MICROBIOLOGY, LIMNOLOGY. *Educ:* Univ Bonn, dipl biol & Dr sci nat(biol), 56. *Prof Exp:* Sci employee bot, Univ Frankfurt, 57-58; sci employee hyg & med parasitol, Univ Bonn, 58-63; sr res scientist, 64-68, prin res scientist, 68-73, DIR, DIV LABS & RES, ENVIRON HEALTH INST, NY STATE DEPT HEALTH, 73- *Concurrent Pos:* Res assoc sch pub health, Univ Minn, Minneapolis, 70; Ger Res Asn Career Develop Award Genetics, Univ Cologne, 63-64. *Mem:* Am Soc Microbiol; Int Asn Theoret & Appl Limnol; Am Soc Limnol & Oceanog; Water Pollution Control Fedn; Am Pub Health Asn. *Res:* Cell structure of bacteria and Cyanophyceae; physiological ecology of bacteria and algae; water pollution and eutrophication; sanitary microbiology. *Mailing Add:* Div Labs & Res Empire State Plaza Albany NY 12201

FUJI, HIROSHI, b Sept 26, 30; Japanese citizen; m; c 2. CANCER. *Educ:* Osaka Med Col, MD, 55; Kyoto Univ, DMSc, 60. *Prof Exp:* Res mem, Med Gen Lab, Kanagawaken, Japan, 60-62; USPHS fel, Wistar Inst, Univ Pa, 62-63; res assoc microbiol, Sch Med, Univ Pittsburgh, 63-66; mem guest fac, Sch Med, Univ Frankfurt & Paul Ehrlich Inst, Ger, 66-67; res asst prof & Henry C & Bertha H Buswell fel, Dept Microbiol, Sch Med, State Univ NY, Buffalo, 68-72; SR CANCER RES SCIENTIST, ROSWELL PARK MEM INST, 72- *Res:* Renal graft rejection by humoral antibodies; immunopathology; formation of tranplantation antibodies in mouse parabiosis; cellular immunology; plaque-forming cells; methodology and theory. *Mailing Add:* Roswell Park Mem Inst 666 Elm St Buffalo NY 14263

FUJII, JACK K, b Phoenix, Ariz, June 9, 1940; m 67; c 4. APICULTURE. *Educ:* Univ Calif, Berkeley, BS, 63; Univ Hawaii, Manoa, MS, 68, PhD(entom), 75. *Prof Exp:* State forest entomologist, Hawaii State Div Forestry, 74-76; ASST PROF ENTOM, COL AGR, UNIV HAWAII, HILO, 76- *Mem:* Entom Soc Am; Soc Invertebrate Path; Am Inst Biol Sci. *Res:* Biology, ecology and control of termites; insect pathology. *Mailing Add:* Col Agr Univ Hawaii Hilo HI 96720

FUJII, KOICHI, population ecology, see previous edition

FUJIKAWA, NORMA SUTTON, b Albany, NY, Oct 19, 28; m 68. ANALYTICAL CHEMISTRY. *Educ:* Rutgers Univ, AB, 52; Univ Southern Calif, MS, 68. *Prof Exp:* Chemist, Mallinckrodt Chem Works, NJ, 52-56; assoc scientist, Walter Kidde Nuclear Labs, NY, 56-58; res engr, Rocketdyne Div, NAm Aviation, Inc, 58-62, sr res engr, 62-64, prin scientist, 64-70, mem tech staff, NAm Rockwell Corp, 70-72, supvr, 72-76, MGR, ROCKETDYNE DIV, ROCKWELL INT, 76- *Mem:* Am Chem Soc; MENSA Soc. *Res:* Analytical chemistry of explosives and rocket propellants; propellant and pollution technology; aerospace operations safety investigations; environmental chemistry. *Mailing Add:* Rocketdyne Div Rockwell Int 6633 Canoga Ave Canoga Park CA 91304

FUJIMOTO, ATSUKO ONO, b Japan. PEDIATRICS, GENETICS. *Educ:* Int Christian Univ, Tokyo, BA, 58; Univ Calif, Los Angeles, PhD(chem), 63, MD, 69. *Prof Exp:* Asst biochem, Univ Calif, Los Angeles, 58-62, res biochemist VI, 62-65; from intern to resident, 69-72, asst prof, 74-79, ASSOC PROF PEDIAT, SCH MED, UNIV SOUTHERN CALIF, 79- *Mem:* AAAS; Am Soc Human Genetics; Soc Pediat Res. *Res:* Diagnosis, genetic counseling and prenatal diagnosis of genetic disorders; biochemical disorders. *Mailing Add:* Dept Pediat Sch Med Univ Southern Calif Los Angeles CA 90033

FUJIMOTO, GEORGE IWAO, b Seattle, Wash, July 1, 20; m 49; c 3. BIOCHEMISTRY. *Educ:* Harvard Univ, BA, 42; Univ Mich, MS, 45, PhD(chem), 47. *Prof Exp:* Fel chem, Calif Inst Technol, 47-49; asst res prof biochem, Sch Med, Univ Utah, 49-55; ASSOC PROF BIOCHEM, ALBERT EINSTEIN COL MED, 55- *Mem:* AAAS; Soc Study Reproduction; Am Soc Biol Chem; Endocrine Soc. *Res:* Reproduction biochemistry and endocrinology. *Mailing Add:* 101 Carthage Rd Scarsdale NY 10583

FUJIMOTO, JAMES MASAO, b Vacaville, Calif, May 10, 28. PHARMACOLOGY. *Educ:* Univ Calif, AB, 51, MS, 53, PhD, 56. *Prof Exp:* Asst pharmacol, Univ Calif, 51-55; from instr to prof, Sch Med, Tulane Univ, 56-65, actg chmn dept, 64-65 & 67-68; PROF PHARMACOL, MED COL WIS, 68- *Concurrent Pos:* Res career scientist, Wood Vet Admin Ctr, 78- *Mem:* Soc Exp Biol & Med; Am Soc Pharmacol & Exp Therapeut; Soc Toxicol. *Res:* Drug metabolism; toxicology. *Mailing Add:* Dept of Pharmacol Med Col of Wis Milwaukee WI 53226

FUJIMOTO, MINORU, b Takasago, Japan, Feb 11, 26; m 55; c 3. CHEMICAL PHYSICS. *Educ:* Osaka Univ, BSc, 48; Univ Southampton, PhD(physics), 59. *Prof Exp:* Res assoc physics, Univ Md, 59-61; asst prof, Clark Univ, 61-63 & Univ Man, 63-67; assoc prof, 67-78, PROF PHYSICS, UNIV GUELPH, 78- *Mem:* Am Phys Soc; Phys Soc Japan. *Res:* Physics and chemistry of solids as studied by paramagnetic resonance. *Mailing Add:* Dept of Physics Univ of Guelph Guelph ON N1G 2W1 Can

FUJIMURA, OSAMU, b Tokyo, Japan, Aug 29, 27; m 57; c 2. EXPERIMENTAL PHYSICS, LINGUISTICS. *Educ:* Univ Tokyo, BS, 52, DSc(physics), 62. *Prof Exp:* Speech res mem, Mass Inst Technol, 58-61, Royal Inst Technol, 63-65; prof speech, Univ Tokyo, 65-73; HEAD DEPT LING & SPEECH ANAL, BELL TEL LABS, INC, 73-; RES PROF, HAHNEMANN MED COL & HOSP, 76- *Mem:* Acoust Soc Am; Inst Elec & Electronics Engrs; Ling Soc Am; Phys Soc Japan; Int Asn Phonetic Sci. *Res:* Studies in physical, physiological, psychological and linguistic aspects of speech phenomena. *Mailing Add:* Bell Labs 600 Mountain Ave Murray Hill NJ 07974

FUJIMURA, ROBERT, b Seattle, Wash, July 28, 33; m 62; c 3. BIOCHEMISTRY. *Educ:* Univ Wash, BS, 56; Univ Wis, MS, 59, PhD(biochem), 61. *Prof Exp:* NIH fel biochem, Inst Protein Res, Osaka, Japan, 61-62; fel biophys, Univ Wis, 63; MEM STAFF BIOCHEM, BIOL DIV, OAK RIDGE NAT LAB, 63- *Concurrent Pos:* Lectr, Univ Tenn; res fel, Japan Soc Promotion Sci, 81. *Mem:* Sigma Xi; Am Soc Biol Chem; AAAS. *Res:* Interaction of bacteriophages with their hosts; biosynthesis of small bacteriophages and their nucleic acids; bacteriophage T5 DNA repair and replication; mechanisms of phage T5 DNA polymerase; DNA-protein and protein-protein interactions. *Mailing Add:* Biol Div Oak Ridge Nat Lab Oak Ridge TN 37830

FUJIOKA, ROGER SADAO, b May 11, 38; US citizen; m 66. VIROLOGY, WATER POLLUTION. *Educ:* Univ Hawaii, BS, 60, MS, 66; Univ Mich, PhD(virol), 70. *Prof Exp:* Clin lab officer med technol, US Army, 60-63; res asst microbiol, Univ Hawaii, Honolulu, 63-66; fel virol, Baylor Col Med, 70-71; asst researcher, 72-80, ASSOC RESEARCHER, UNIV HAWAII, HONOLULU, 80-, MEM GRAD FAC, 76- *Mem:* AAAS; Am Soc Microbiol; Water Pollution Control Fed. *Res:* Public health consequences of human viruses in the water environment; technology to improve the disinfection of viruses in water and the mechanism by which viruses are inactivated by disinfectants; use of bacteria to assess hygienic quality of water. *Mailing Add:* Dept of Microbiol Univ of Hawaii Honolulu HI 96822

FUJITA, DONALD J, b Hunt, Idaho, July 2, 43. VIROLOGY, MICROBIOLOGY. *Educ:* Reed Col, BA, 65; Univ Chicago, PhD(microbiol), 71. *Prof Exp:* Fel virol, Sch Med, Stanford Univ, 71-73; vis scientist virol, Sch Med, Univ Southern Calif, 73-74; fel molecular virol, Sch Med, Univ Calif, San Francisco, 74-77; ASST PROF BIOCHEM, CANCER RES LAB & DEPT BIOCHEM, UNIV WESTERN ONT, 78- *Concurrent Pos:* Damon Runyon Found Cancer Res fel, 71-73; Leukemia Soc Am fel, 73-75; trainee, NIH, 75-77; Nat Cancer Inst Can res grants, 78-81 & 81-84; Med Res Coun Can res grants, 79-81 & 81-84; Leukemia Res Fund grant, 79-81; Crusade Against Leukemia res grant, 79-80; sci officer, Res Grant Rev Panel A, Nat Cancer Inst Can, 82. *Mem:* Am Soc Microbiol; AAAS. *Res:* Biochemical and genetic studies on avian RNA tumor viruses; viral gene expression, structure and evolution; cell transformation. *Mailing Add:* Cancer Res Lab Univ of Western Ont London ON N6A 5B8 Can

FUJITA, SHIGEJI, b Oita City, Japan, May 15, 29; m 58; c 4. THEORETICAL PHYSICS. *Educ:* Kyushu Univ, BS, 53. Univ Md, PhD(physics), 60. *Prof Exp:* Res asst physics, Kyushu Univ, 53-56 & Univ Md, 56-58; res assoc, Northwestern Univ, 58-60; sr res assoc phys chem, Univ Brussels, 60-65; vis assoc prof physics, Univ Ore, 65-66; assoc prof, 66-68, PROF PHYSICS, STATE UNIV NY BUFFALO, 68- *Concurrent Pos:* Vis assoc prof, Pa State, 64-65; vis prof, Ctr Math Res, Univ Montreal, 72-73; Nat Univ Mexico, 79 & Univ Zurich, 81. *Mem:* Am Phys Soc; Phys Soc Japan. *Res:* Non-equilibrium statistical mechanics. *Mailing Add:* 247 Cimarand Ct Amherst NY 14068

FUJITA, TETSUYA T, b Japan, Oct 23, 20; m 48; c 1. METEOROLOGY. *Educ:* Meiji Inst Technol, Japan, BS, 43; Univ Tokyo, DSc(meteorol), 53. *Prof Exp:* Asst Meiji Inst Technol, Japan, 43, asst prof, 43-50; asst prof, Kyushu Inst Technol, 50-53; vis prof, 53-56, dir mesometeorol res, 56-61, assoc prof, 61-69, PROF METEOROL, UNIV CHICAGO, 69- *Concurrent Pos:* Consult, Ill State Water Surv, 54-58. *Honors & Awards:* Okada Award, 59; Kamura Award, 65. *Mem:* Am Meteorol Soc; Am Geophys Union; Optical Soc Am; Am Soc Photogram; Meteorol Soc Japan. *Res:* Mesometeorology; severe local storms; aerial photogrammetry; satellite meteorology. *Mailing Add:* Dept of Geophys Sci Univ of Chicago 5734 Ellis Ave Chicago IL 60637

FUJIWARA, KEIGI, b Nita-cho, Shimane, Japan, May 16, 44; m 69; c 1. CELL BIOLOGY. *Educ:* Int Christian Univ, Tokyo, BA, 68; Univ Pa, PhD(biol), 74. *Prof Exp:* Asst biol, Int Christian Univ, 68-69; res fel cell biol, 74-77, ASST PROF ANAT, HARVARD MED SCH, 77- *Mem:* Am Soc Cell Biol; AAAS; NY Acad Sci; Am Asn Anatomists. *Res:* Morphological and biochemical analyses of motile regions of eukaryotic non-muscle cells are being attempted in order to learn mechanisms of cell movements. *Mailing Add:* Dept Anat Harvard Med Sch 25 Shattuck St Boston MA 02115

FUKA, LOUIS RICHARD, b New York City, NY, Dec 19, 37; m 59; c 4. VIBRATION, WAVE PROPAGATION. *Educ:* St Louis Univ, BS, 59; Univ Mo-Rolla, MS, 63; Univ Tex, Austin, PhD(eng), 71. *Prof Exp:* Engr, US Army Corps Engrs, 59-61; engr & scientist specialist, McDonnell Douglas Missiles & Space Systs, 63-67; teaching asst eng mech, Univ Tex, Austin, 69; res engr & scientist, Eng Mech Res Lab, 69-71; staff mem, Los Alamos Nat Lab, 71-80; PRES, LOMAR RES & DEVELOP, 80- *Concurrent Pos:* Consult, Douglas Aircraft Co, 66, Atomic Energy Comn, 72-74; prin investr, Nuclear Regulatory Comn, 72-74; lectr, Am Mgr Asn, 73-74; vis assoc prof, Univ Hawaii, 78-79. *Mem:* Am Soc Mech Engrs. *Res:* Analog digital minicomputer; vibration, shock, wave propagaton, dynamic structural analysis and nuclear weapons effects. *Mailing Add:* 2073 North Rd Los Alamos NM 87544

FUKAI, JUNICHIRO, b Noda, Japan, Mar 6, 38; m 64; c 2. PLASMA PHYSICS. *Educ:* Waseda Univ, Japan, BEngr, 61; Univ Denver, MS, 66; Univ Tenn, Knoxville, PhD(physics), 70. *Prof Exp:* Staff engr design, Tokyo Shibaura Elec Co, 61-64; res assoc physics, Univ Tenn, Knoxville, 70-72; res assoc appl physics, Yale Univ, 72-74; asst prof, 74-78, ASSOC PROF PHYSICS, AUBURN UNIV, 78- *Mem:* Am Phys Soc. *Res:* Theoretical investigations on plasma instabilities and vacuum spark discharges-nonlinear instabilities in a beam plasma and dynamics of plasma discharges; fundamental physics. *Mailing Add:* Dept of Physics Auburn Univ Auburn AL 36849

FUKUHARA, FRANCIS M, b Seattle Wash, Jan 30, 25; m 53; c 4. FISHERIES. *Educ:* Univ Wash, BS, 55, PhD(fisheries), 71. *Prof Exp:* Fishery res biologist, Bur Com Fisheries, 52-66, asst dir, Biol Lab, 66-71, DIR DIV RESOURCE ECOL & FISH MGT, NAT MARINE FISHERIES SERV, 71- *Concurrent Pos:* Scientist mem comt biol & res, Int N Pac Fisheries Comn, 69-; affil prof, Univ Wash, 73- *Mem:* Am Inst Fishery Res Biologists. *Res:* Ecosystem and population dynamics of demersal fish and shellfish communities of the east Bering Sea and east North Pacific Ocean; development of biological bases for management of single species and multiple species complexes. *Mailing Add:* Northwest Fisheries Ctr NMFS 2725 Montlake Blvd E Seattle WA 98112

FUKUI, GEORGE MASAAKI, microbiology, see previous edition

FUKUI, H(ATSUAKI), b Yokohama, Japan, Dec 14, 27; m 54; c 2. ELECTRICAL ENGINEERING. *Educ:* Miyakojima Tech Col, Grad, 49; Osaka Univ, DEng, 61. *Prof Exp:* Res assoc, Osaka City Univ, 49-54; engr, Shimada Phys & Chem Indust Co, 54-55; sr engr, semiconductor div, Sony Corp, 55-59, supvr, 59-61, mgr eng div, 61-62; mem tech staff, 62-69, supvr, 69-73, mem tech staff, 73-81, SUPVR, BELL TEL LABS, MURRAY HILL, 81- *Concurrent Pos:* Lectr, Tokyo Metrop Univ, 62; asst to chmn, Sony Corp, Tokyo, 73; vpres, Sony Corp Am, New York, 73. *Honors & Awards:* Inada Prize, Inst Elec Eng Japan, 59. *Mem:* Sr mem Inst Elec & Electronics Engrs; Microwave Prize, Inst Elec & Electronics Engrs, 80. *Res:* Microwave semiconductor devices: GaAs MESFETs, bipolar transistors, tunnel diodes, avalanche diodes and bulk-effect devices; microwave electron tubes; microwave circuits; image pickup and display devices; videophone subsystems; solid-state consumer electronics; semiconductor lasers. *Mailing Add:* Bell Labs Rm 7F-330 Murray Hill NJ 07974

FUKUI, KATSURA, atomic physics, nuclear physics, see previous edition

FUKUNAGA, KEINOSUKE, b Japan, July 23, 30; m 57; c 2. ELECTRICAL ENGINEERING. *Educ:* Kyoto Univ, BS, 53, PhD(elec eng), 62; Univ Pa, MS, 59. *Prof Exp:* Res engr, res lab, Mitsubishi Elec Co, Amagasaki-shi, Japan, 53-57, sect head res comput control, 59-65, develop of comput, Kamakura-shi, 65-66; asst instr elec eng, Univ Pa, 57-59; assoc prof, 66-73, PROF ELEC ENG, PURDUE UNIV, 73- *Concurrent Pos:* Consult, Lincoln Lab, Mass Inst Technol, 73- & Health Sci Ctr, Univ Okla, 76-78. *Mem:* Fel Inst Elec & Electronics Engrs. *Res:* Information processing; computer system; computer control. *Mailing Add:* Dept of Elec Eng Purdue Univ Lafayette IN 47907

FUKUNAGA, TADAMICHI, b Japan, Mar 21, 31; m 57; c 2. ORGANIC CHEMISTRY, RESEARCH ADMINISTRATION. *Educ:* Osaka Univ, BS, 53, MS, 55; Ohio State Univ, PhD(org chem), 59. *Prof Exp:* Fel, Harvard Univ, 59-62; res staff, E I du Pont de Nemours Co, Inc, 62-65; assoc prof, Tokyo Univ, 65-66; RES STAFF, E I DU PONT DE NEMOURS & CO, INC, 66- *Concurrent Pos:* Vis prof, Univ Ill, Urbana-Champaign, 79. *Mem:* Am Chem Soc. *Res:* Synthetic, physical and theoretical organic chemistry. *Mailing Add:* E I du Pont de Nemours & Co Inc Exp Sta Bldg 328 Wilmington DE 19898

FUKUSHIMA, DAVID KENZO, b Fresno, Calif, Aug 24, 17; m 42; c 2. BIOCHEMISTRY. *Educ:* Whittier Col, BA, 39; Univ Calif, Los Angeles, MA, 43; Univ Rochester, PhD(org chem), 46. *Prof Exp:* Asst, Sloan-Kettering Inst Cancer Res, 47-51, assoc, 51-60, mem, 60-63; sr investr, Montefiore Hosp & Med Ctr, New York, 63-77, dir, Inst Steroid Res, 77-71; RETIRED. *Concurrent Pos:* Fel, Sloan-Kettering Inst, 46-47; prof biochem, Albert Einstein Col Med, 66-81. *Mem:* Am Chem Soc; Endocrine Soc; Am Soc Biol Chemists; Swiss Chem Soc; Brit Soc Endocrinol. *Res:* Biochemistry of steroid hormones in man; steroid chemistry. *Mailing Add:* 1430 N Sharpless St LaHabra CA 90631

FUKUSHIMA, EIICHI, b Tokyo, Japan, June 3, 36; US citizen; m 63; c 3. SOLID STATE PHYSICS, CHEMICAL PHYSICS. *Educ:* Univ Chicago, AB & SB, 57; Dartmouth Col, MA, 59; Univ Wash, PhD(physics), 67. *Prof Exp:* STAFF MEM, LOS ALAMOS SCI LAB, 67- *Concurrent Pos:* Vis prof, Univ Fla, 75-76. *Mem:* Am Phys Soc; Am Asn Physics Teachers. *Res:* Nuclear magnetic resonance studies of solids with emphasis on spinlattice interactions, phase transitions, magnetism, high resolution effects and instrumentation. *Mailing Add:* 4873A Yucca Los Alamos NM 87544

FUKUSHIMA, TOSHIYUKI, b Tacoma, Wash, Sept 26, 21; m 51; c 6. MECHANICAL ENGINEERING. *Educ:* Swarthmore Col, BS, 51; Univ Pa, MS, 59. *Prof Exp:* Engr, Ultra-Mechanisms, Inc, 53, Prewitt Aircraft Corp, 53-54 & Thermal Res & Eng Corp, 54-56; instr mech eng, Swarthmore Col, 56-61; asst prof, Drexel Inst Technol, 61-65; sr engr theoret aerodyn, Dynasci Corp, 65-67; sr engr aerodynamics res, Vertol Div, Boeing Co, Pa, 67-71; TEACHER MATH, DELAWARE COUNTY AREA VOC-TECH SCHS, 71- *Concurrent Pos:* Lectr, Widener Univ, 65- *Res:* Fluid mechanics and heat transfer; thermodynamics and magnetohydrodynamics as applied to energy conversion; helicopter rotor aerodynamics. *Mailing Add:* 218 Lafayette Ave Swarthmore PA 19081

FUKUTA, NORIHIKO, b Tokoname, Japan, May 11, 31; m 66. CLOUD PHYSICS, ATMOSPHERIC SCIENCES. *Educ:* Nagoya Univ, BSc, 54, MSc, 56, PhD(cloud physics), 59. *Prof Exp:* Res asst chemist, Nagoya Univ, 59-61; vis res fel, Commonwealth Sci & Indust Res Orgn, Sydney, Australia, 62-64; head microphys lab, Meteorol Res Inc, Calif, 66-67; dir microphys lab, 67-68; head, Cloud Physics Lab, Denver Res Inst, 68-77; prof environ eng, Col Eng, Univ Denver, 68-75; PROF METEOROL, UNIV UTAH, 77- *Concurrent Pos:* Vis scientist, Imp Col, London, 61-62; assoc ed, J Appl Meteorol, 72-79 & J Atmospheric Sci, 76-; adj prof physics, Univ Denver, 75-77. *Honors & Awards:* Editors' Award, Am Meteorol Soc, 74. *Mem:* Am Meteorol Soc; Meteorol Soc Japan; Am Geophys Union; Sigma Xi; Am Phys Soc. *Res:* Ice nucleation; organic ice nuclei; development of non-AgI cloud seeding generators; convective cloud seeding; ice crystal growth; hydrometeor growth kinetics; hurricane modification; development of cloud condensation and ice nucleus spectrometers. *Mailing Add:* Dept of Meteorol Univ of Utah Salt Lake City UT 84112

FUKUTO, TETSUO ROY, b Los Angeles, Calif, Dec 15, 23; m 53; c 4. ORGANIC CHEMISTRY. *Educ:* Univ Minn, BS, 46; Univ Calif, Los Angeles, PhD, 50. *Prof Exp:* Res fel, Univ Ill, 50-51; develop chemist, Aerojet Eng Corp, 51-52; from asst insect toxicologist to assoc insect toxicologist, 52-63, PROF ENTOM & CHEM & INSECT TOXICOLOGIST, CITRUS RES CTR & AGR EXP STA, UNIV CALIF, RIVERSIDE, 63-, HEAD DIV TOXICOL & PHYSIOL, 74- *Concurrent Pos:* Consult toxicol study sect, USPHS, 62-66. *Mem:* Am Chem Soc; Entom Soc Am. *Res:* Chemistry and mode of action of insecticides. *Mailing Add:* Dept of Entom Univ Calif PO Box 112 Riverside CA 92521

FUKUYAMA, KIMIE, b Tokyo, Japan, Dec 11, 27. DERMATOLOGY. *Educ:* Tokyo Women's Med Col, MD, 49, PhD, 64; Univ Mich, MS, 58. *Prof Exp:* Intern, Tokyo Med Sch, 49-50, resident & asst dermat, 50-56; res assoc, Univ Mich, 58-61; asst, Tokyo Women's Med Col, 61-63, lectr, 64-65; lectr, 65-67, from resident asst prof to resident assoc prof, 67-78, RESIDENT PROF, SCH MED, UNIV CALIF, SAN FRANCISCO, 78- Mem: Soc Invest Dermat; AMA. *Mailing Add:* Dept Dermat HSE 1092 Univ Calif San Francisco CA 94143

FUKUYAMA, THOMAS T, b Juneau, Alaska, Dec 30, 27; m 60; c 3. MICROBIOLOGY, BIOCHEMISTRY. *Educ:* Univ Wash, BS, 50, MS, 53; Univ Pa, PhD(microbiol), 61. *Prof Exp:* Res assoc, Sch Med, 63-64, from instr to asst prof, 64-69, asst prof, Sch Pharm, 69-71, chmn, Grad Educ & Res Coun, 73-76, ASSOC PROF MICROBIOL, SCH PHARM, UNIV SOUTHERN CALIF, 71-, BIOPHARMACY AREA COORDR, 77-, LEVEL II COORDR, 77-, COORDR GRAD PROGS COMT, 75- *Concurrent Pos:* Res fel microbiol, Harvard Med Sch, 60-63; USPHS fel, 61-63 & res grant, 66; Univ Southern Calif gen res support grant, 66. *Mem:* NY Acad Sci; Sigma Xi; AAAS; Am Soc Microbiol. *Res:* Microbial physiology; enzyme action and regulation; mechanisms of action purine nucleoside analogs. *Mailing Add:* Dept of Biochem Univ of So Calif Sch of Pharm Los Angeles CA 90033

FUKUYAMA, TOHRU, b Anjo, Japan, Aug 9, 48; m 77. ORGANIC CHEMISTRY. *Educ:* Nagoya Univ, BA, 71, MA, 73; Harvard Univ, PhD(chem), 77. *Prof Exp:* Fel org chem, Harvard Univ, 77-78; ASST PROF ORG CHEM, RICE UNIV, 78- *Mem:* Am Chem Soc. *Res:* Total synthesis of complex natural products of biological importance. *Mailing Add:* Dept of Chem Rice Univ Houston TX 77001

FULBRIGHT, HARRY WILKS, b Springfield, Mo, Sept 19, 18; m 44. NUCLEAR PHYSICS. *Educ:* Wash Univ, AB, 40, MS, 42, PhD(physics), 44. *Prof Exp:* Physicist in charge cyclotron, Wash Univ, 42-44; physicist & group leader Manhattan dist proj, Calif, Los Alamos, 44-46; asst prof physics, Princeton Univ, 46-50; from asst prof to assoc prof, 50-56, PROF PHYSICS, UNIV ROCHESTER, 56- *Concurrent Pos:* Consult med sch, Univ Rochester, 54-57; Fulbright & Guggenheim fel, Inst Theoret Physics, Copenhagen Univ, 56-57; consult, Gen Atomic Co, 58-60 & Tropel, Inc, 61-64; vis prof, Univ Louis Pasteur, Strasbourg, France, 74-75; vis prof, Punjab Univ, Chandigarh, India, 75. *Mem:* Fel Am Phys Soc. *Res:* Nuclear reactions and structure; nuclear instrumentation. *Mailing Add:* Dept of Physics Univ of Rochester Rochester NY 14627

FULCHER, WILLIAM ERNEST, b Eden, NC, Aug 21, 31; m 56; c 3. BOTANY, PLANT MORPHOLOGY. *Educ:* NC State Univ, BS, 53; Appalachian State Univ, MA, 60; Univ NC, PhD(bot), 71. *Prof Exp:* Teacher biol, Morehead High Sch, Eden, NC, 53-54, 56-62; instr mil subj, Signal Sch, Ft Monmouth, NJ, 54-56; from instr to assoc prof, 62-81, PROF BIOL, GUILFORD COL, 81-, CHMN DEPT, 76- *Mem:* Am Fern Soc; Cactus & Succulent Soc Am; Royal Hort Soc. *Res:* Plant anatomy; plant cell and tissue culture. *Mailing Add:* Dept Biol Guilford Col Greensboro NC 27410

FULCO, ARMAND J, b Los Angeles, Calif, Apr 3, 32; m 55; c 4. BIOCHEMISTRY. *Educ:* Univ Calif, Los Angeles, BS, 57, PhD(lipid biosynthesis), 60. *Prof Exp:* Asst res biochemist, Dept Biol Chem & Dept Biophys & Nuclear Med, 63-70, asst prof in residence, 65-70, assoc prof & assoc res biochemist, 70-76, PROF BIOL CHEM & RES BIOCHEMIST, LAB BIOMED & ENVIRON SCI, UNIV CALIF, LOS AGNELES, 76-, CHIEF, SECT BIOSYNTHETIC CONTROL, 69- *Concurrent Pos:* USPHS res fel, Lipid Labs, Univ Calif, Los Angeles, 6061; NIH res fel chem, Harvard Univ, 61-63; NIH res grants, 70-73, 73-78, 77-82, 78-81 & 82-85. *Mem:* Sigma Xi; AAAS; Am Chem Soc; Am Oil Chemists Soc; Am Soc Biol Chemists. *Res:* Pathways, mechanisms and enzymology of membrane lipid biosynthesis; comparative biochemistry; cytochrome P-450 systems in bacteria; biosynthetic control mechanisms. *Mailing Add:* Lab Biomed & Environ Sci Univ Calif 900 Veteran Ave Los Angeles CA 90024

FULCO, JOSE ROQUE, b Buenos Aires, Arg, Dec 5, 27; m 49; c 5. PHYSICS. *Educ:* Argentine Army Tech Sch, CE, 57; Univ Buenos Aires, PhD(physics), 62. *Prof Exp:* Argentine Army vis fel physics, Lawrence Radiation Lab, Calif, 57-59; prof, Univ Buenos Aires, 59-62; asst res physicist, Univ Calif, San Diego, 62-64; assoc prof, 64-69, assoc dir educ abroad prog, 70-76, PROF PHYSICS, UNIV CALIF, SANTA BARBARA, 69-, CHMN DEPT, 78- *Concurrent Pos:* Prof, La Plata, 62. *Mem:* Fel Am Phys Soc. *Res:* Theoretical high energy physics. *Mailing Add:* Dept of Physics Univ of Calif Santa Barbara CA 93106

FULDA, MYRON OSCAR, b New York, NY, Mar 18, 30; m 61; c 3. ANALYTICAL CHEMISTRY. *Educ:* Iowa State Col, BS, 53, MS, 55. *Prof Exp:* Chemist, 55-64, res chemist, 64-70, sr chemist, 70-78, SR RES CHEMIST, E I DU PONT DE NEMOURS & CO, INC, 78- *Mem:* Am Chem Soc. *Res:* Non-aqueous, complexiometric and electrometric titrimetry; radiochemistry; analytical chemistry of textile fibers; dyeability of acrylic fibers; analysis of air and water pollutants, personnel exposure. *Mailing Add:* 2106 Burns Lane Camden SC 29020

FULDE, ROLAND CHARLES, b Chicago, Ill, Nov 23, 26; m 52; c 2. FOOD SCIENCE. *Educ:* Mich State Univ, BS, 48, MS, 49, PhD, 53. *Prof Exp:* Res bacteriologist, Swift & Co, 53-62; div head, 62-80, MGR, PROCESS BIOCHEM, CAMPBELL SOUP CO, 80- *Mem:* AAAS; Inst Food Technol; Soc Indust Microbiol; Am Soc Microbiol; Am Chem Soc. *Res:* Industrial biochemical processes. *Mailing Add:* Campbell Soup Co Food Sci & Tech Campbell Pl Camden NJ 08101

FULEKI, TIBOR, b Budapest, Hungary, June 28, 31; Can citizen; c 3. FOOD SCIENCE, BIOCHEMISTRY. *Educ:* Col Hort & Viticult, Budapest, BSc, 53; McGill Univ, MSc, 61; Univ Mass, Amherst, PhD(food chem), 67. *Prof Exp:* Res scientist, Res Sta, Agr Can, NS, 61-67 & Res Labs, Health & Welfare Can,

Ont, 67-68; RES SCIENTIST, HORT PROD LAB, HORT RES INST ONT, 68- Mem: Can Inst Food Technol; Inst Food Technol; Am Soc Enologists; Can Soc Hort Sci; Can Soc Oenol. *Res:* Chemical composition of fruits, vegetables and their products; tristimulus colorimetry of horticultural crops; anthocyanin composition of economic plants; chemistry and technology of wine making; food analysis. *Mailing Add:* Hort Prod Lab Hort Res Inst of Ont Vineland Station ON L0R 2E0 Can

FULFORD, MARGARET HANNAH, b Cincinnati, Ohio, June 14, 04. BOTANY. *Educ:* Univ Cincinnati, BA, 26, BE, 27, MA, 28; Yale Univ, PhD(bot), 35. *Prof Exp:* Instr bot & cur, 27-40, from asst prof to prof, 40-76, EMER PROF BOT, UNIV CINCINNATI, 76- *Concurrent Pos:* Fel grad sch, Univ Cincinnati, 58; Guggenheim fel, Harvard Univ, Yale Univ & NY Bot Garden, 41; mem staff biol sta, Univ Mich, 47-53. *Mem:* AAAS; Bot Soc Am; Am Soc Plant Taxon; Am Bryol & Lichenological Soc; Soc Study Evolution. *Res:* Hepatics; leafy hepatics of Latin America; sporeling development and regeneration of hepatics; nutrient studies in a leafy hepatic. *Mailing Add:* Edgecliff Apts 1008 2200 Victory Pkwy Cincinnati OH 45206

FULFORD, PHILLIP JAMES, nuclear engineering, see previous edition

FULGER, CHARLES V, b Budapest, Hungary, Sept 27, 32; US citizen; m 71. FOOD CHEMISTRY, FOOD TECHNOLOGY. *Educ:* Univ Melbourne, BSc, 56; Univ Melbourne, MSc, 60; Univ Mass, PhD(food sci), 67. *Prof Exp:* Anal chemist, Univ Melbourne, 57-60; asst biochem, Univ Calif, 60-63; res fel food res, Univ Mass, 63-67; from proj leader to dir res labs, Kellogg Co, 67-77; CORP RES MGR, GEN FOODS, 77- *Mem:* Am Cereal Chem Soc; Am Chem Soc; Inst Food Technologists. *Res:* Stereochemistry of lipid reactions; experimental design of food systems; cereal chemistry and technology; modification of seed proteins. *Mailing Add:* Gen Foods Tech Ctr 250 North St White Plains NY 10625

FULGHUM, ROBERT SCHMIDT, b Washington, DC, Mar 3, 29; m 53; c 3. BACTERIOLOGY. *Educ:* Roanoke Col, BS, 54; Va Polytech Inst, MS, 59, PhD(bact), 65. *Prof Exp:* Res asst biol, Va Agr Exp Sta, 56-60; from instr to asst prof biol, Susquehanna Univ, 60-64; from asst prof to assoc prof bact, NDak State Univ, 64-68; asst prof oral biol, Col Dent, Univ Ky, 68-71; dir anaerobic prod, Robbin Labs Div, Scott Labs, 71-72; actg chmn, 74-76, ASSOC PROF DEPT MICROBIOL, SCH MED, EAST CAROLINA UNIV, 72- *Concurrent Pos:* Nat Inst Dent Res grant, 71-72; Deafness Res Found grant, 79-81. *Mem:* Am Soc Microbiol; Brit Soc Gen Microbiol; Sigma Xi. *Res:* Anaerobic bacteriology; anaerobic bacteria of medical importance; rumen bacteriology; cecal bacteriology; oral bacteriology; Methodology in anaerobic bacteriology; bacterial nutrition; bacterial flora-host animal ecology; animal models for polymicrobic infection; aerobic and anaerobic bacteriology of otitis media. *Mailing Add:* Dept Microbiol Sch Med East Carolina Univ Greenville NC 27834

FULGINITI, VINCENT ANTHONY, b Philadelphia, Pa, Aug 8, 31; m; c 4. PEDIATRICS, IMMUNOLOGY. *Educ:* Temple Univ, AB, 53, MD, 57, MS, 61. *Prof Exp:* Asst pediat & chief resident, St Christopher's Hosp, Philadelphia, 60-61; from instr to assoc prof, Univ Colo Med Ctr, Denver, 62-68; PROF PEDIAT & HEAD DEPT, COL MED, UNIV ARIZ, 69- *Concurrent Pos:* Fulbright scholar; fel pediat infectious dis, Univ Colo Med Ctr, Denver; Waldo E Nelson lectr, 59; consult, Tucson Med Ctr, Kino Community Hosp & Davis-Monthan Hosp. *Honors & Awards:* First Prize Pediat Res, Philadelphia Pediat Soc, 60; Ross Res Award, Western Soc Pediat Res, 65. *Mem:* AAAS; Infectious Dis Soc Am; Am Soc Microbiol; Am Acad Pediat; AMA. *Res:* Pediatric virology; measles virus, immunization and reaction; smallpox and vaccination. *Mailing Add:* Dept Pediat Col Med Univ Ariz Tucson AZ 85724

FULKERSON, JOHN FREDERICK, microbiology, plant pathology, see previous edition

FULKERSON, ROBERT SERPELL, b Tillonsburg, Ont, Nov 28, 22; m 55; c 2. AGRONOMY. *Educ:* Ont Agr Col, BSA, 46; Univ Toronto, MSA, 48. *Prof Exp:* From lectr to assoc prof, 48-58, PROF CROP SCI, ONT AGR COL, UNIV GUELPH, 58- *Mem:* Am Agron Soc; Agr Inst Can; Am Forage & Grassland Coun. *Res:* Forage management; hay production and utilization; seed production. *Mailing Add:* Dept of Crop Sci Ont Agr Col Univ of Guelph Guelph ON N1G 2W1 Can

FULKERSON, WILLIAM, b Baltimore, Md, May 26, 35; m 57. RESEARCH MANAGEMENT. *Educ:* Rice Univ, BA, 57, PhD(chem eng), 62. *Prof Exp:* Group leader, Metals & Ceramics Div, 69-70, prog mgr, 72-75, sect head, Energy Div, 74-75, DIR ENERGY DIV, OAK RIDGE NAT LAB, 75- *Mem:* AAAS; Sigma Xi. *Res:* Management of energy research and development related to conservation; renewable and environmental effects of energy facilities and programs. *Mailing Add:* Oak Ridge Nat Lab 4500 N PO Box X Oak Ridge TN 37830

FULKS, WATSON, b Ark, Jan 24, 19; m 43; c 3. MATHEMATICS. *Educ:* Ark State Teachers Col, BS, 40; Univ Ark, MS, 41; Univ Minn, PhD(math), 49. *Prof Exp:* Instr math, Univ Ark, 41-44; from instr to assoc prof, Univ Minn, 45-60; prof, Ore State Col, 60-63; PROF MATH, UNIV COLO, BOULDER, 63- *Concurrent Pos:* Asst, Calif Inst Technol, 49-50. *Mem:* AAAS; Am Math Soc; Math Asn Am. *Res:* Partial differential equations; asymptotics. *Mailing Add:* Dept of Math Univ of Colo Boulder CO 80309

FULLAGAR, PAUL DAVID, b Ft Edward, NY, Dec 19, 38; m 59; c 2. GEOCHRONOLOGY. *Educ:* Columbia Univ, AB, 60; Univ Ill, PhD(geol), 63. *Prof Exp:* Asst prof geol, Old Dom Col, 63-67; from asst prof to assoc prof, 67-74, PROF GEOL, UNIV NC, CHAPEL HILL, 74-, CHMN DEPT, 79- *Mem:* Geochem Soc; fel Geol Soc Am. *Res:* Rubidium-strontium geochronology; evolution orogenic belts. *Mailing Add:* Dept of Geol Univ of NC Chapel Hill NC 27514

FULLAM, HAROLD THOMAS, b Tacoma, Wash, June 4, 27. CHEMICAL ENGINEERING. *Educ:* Univ Wash, Seattle, BS, 51, MS, 52, PhD(chem eng), 56. *Prof Exp:* Design engr, Standard Oil Co Calif, 52; res engr, Martinez Refinery, Shell Oil Co Calif, 56-57; group leader, Richmond Res Lab, Stauffer Chem Co, 57-63; sr nuclear engr, Hanford Atomic Prod Opers, Gen Elec Co, 63-65; SR NUCLEAR ENGR, PAC NORTHWEST LAB, BATTELLE MEM INST, 65- *Mem:* Am Chem Soc; Electrochem Soc; Am Ord Asn. *Res:* Fused salt electrochemistry; inorganic process development; high temperature thermodynamics, actinide chemistry and processing. *Mailing Add:* 1500 Torthay Pl Richland WA 99352

FULLER, ALFRED L(EE), b Fullerton, Calif, May 9, 22; m 45; c 3. CHEMICAL ENGINEERING. *Educ:* Univ Southern Calif, BE, 43. *Prof Exp:* Control chemist, A R Maass Chem Co, 46-47; process engr, Gen Elec Co, 47-51; sr res chem engr, Fluor Corp Ltd, 51-60, chief res engr, 60-63; sr engr, Space-Gen Corp, 63-64; sr proj engr, Fluor Corp, Ltd, 64-70, prin mech engr, Fluor Corp, 70-73; chief mech engr, 73-80, MGR MECH ENG, FLUOR ENGRS & CONSTRUCTORS, INC, 80- *Concurrent Pos:* Mem tech adv comt, Heat Transfer Res, Inc & Heat Transfer & Fluid Flow Serv. *Mem:* Am Inst Chem Engrs; fel Am Inst Chem; Am Petrol Inst. *Res:* Evaporative water cooling; heat and mass transfer processes; heat transfer equipment evaluation; conceptual design and evaluation of combustion equipment including fired process heaters and boilers for refining and process industries. *Mailing Add:* Dept Mech Eng 3333 Michelson Dr Irvine CA 92730

FULLER, BARBARA FINK, b Chicago, Ill, Feb 29, 36; m 59, 80; c 2. VERTEBRATE ZOOLOGY, PHYSIOLOGY. *Educ:* Univ Calif, Santa Barbara, BS, 56; Cornell Univ, MS, 58, PhD, 62, RN, 81. *Prof Exp:* Instr biol, Western Reserve Univ, 61-63, NSF instnl grant, 62-63; asst prof zool, Ohio State Univ, 64-68; vis lectr biol, 68-69, lectr, 69-70, assoc prof, 70-73, PROF PHYSIOL, SCH NURSING, UNIV COLO, DENVER, 73- *Concurrent Pos:* NSF res grant, 65-78; isntnl grant, Sch Nursing, Univ Colo, 78-; family nurse practr, 81- *Mem:* NY Acad Sci; AAAS. *Res:* Social Behavior and reproductive physiology; nursing intervention and patient stress. *Mailing Add:* Univ Colo Med Ctr 4200 E Ninth Ave Denver CO 80220

FULLER, BENJAMIN FRANKLIN, JR, b St Paul, Minn, Aug 7, 22; m 45; c 3. MEDICINE. *Educ:* Univ Minn, BA, 43, MD, 45, MS, 50. *Prof Exp:* Clin asst prof internal med, 53-66, from asst prof to assoc prof, 66-70, dir div family med & community health, 66-68, head dept family pract & community health, 68-70, prof med, Med Ctr, 70-76, head sect primary care, Dept Internal Med, 72-76, CLIN PROF MED, UNIV MINN, MINNEAPOLIS, 76- *Mem:* Fel Am Col Physicians. *Res:* Peripheral vascular disease. *Mailing Add:* 3615 Grand Ave White Bear Lake MN 55110

FULLER, DEREK JOSEPH HAGGARD, b London, Eng, June 17, 17; MATHEMATICAL ANALYSIS. *Educ:* Univ SAfrica, BSc, 48, BA, 53, BSc, 56, MSc, 60; Univ Witwatersrand, BSc, 50; Univ Calif, Los Angeles, MA & PhD(math), 63. *Prof Exp:* Lectr math, Pius XII Col, Roma, Basutoland, 50-59 & 63; from lectr to sr lectr, Univ Basutoland, Bechuanaland Protectorate & Swaziland, 64-65; from asst prof to assoc prof, 65-69, actg chmn dept, 66-67, chmn dept, 67-76, PROF MATH, CREIGHTON UNIV, 69- *Mem:* Math Asn Am. *Res:* Analytic functions on Riemann surfaces. *Mailing Add:* Dept of Math Creighton Univ Omaha NE 68178

FULLER, DOROTHY LANGFORD, b Cincinnati, Ohio, Dec 17, 18. BIOLOGY. *Educ:* Stetson Univ, AB, 38, MA, 39. *Prof Exp:* From instr to assoc prof, 41-63, PROF BIOL, STETSON UNIV, 63-, CHMN DEPT, 77- *Concurrent Pos:* NSF grant, 59. *Mem:* AAAS; Am Inst Biol Sci. *Res:* Development of embryo sac and germination in Yucca developmental anatomy. *Mailing Add:* Dept of Biol Stetson Univ De Land FL 32720

FULLER, DUDLEY D(EAN), b Woodhaven, NY, Feb 8, 13; m 45; c 1. MECHANICAL ENGINEERING. *Educ:* City Col New York, BME, 41; Columbia Univ, MS, 45. *Prof Exp:* Instr mech eng, City Col New York, 41-44; from instr to assoc prof, 43-54, chmn dept, 64-70, prof mech eng, 54-81, STEVENS EMER PROF MECH ENG, COLUMBIA UNIV, 81- *Concurrent Pos:* Prin engr, Franklin Inst, 54-69; mem bearing panel, high-temperature bearings, Nat Acad Sci, 59; chmn, Int Gas Bearing Symposium, Off Naval Res, 59; mem bearing panel, Inst Defense Anal, 62; bearing panel, proj forecast, US Army-Air Force, 63; dir, Continuing Educ & Sr Fel Prog, Indust Tribol Inst, Rensselaer Polytech Inst, Troy, NY. *Honors & Awards:* Award, Am Soc Lubrication Engrs, 57; Richards Mem Award, 62 & Mayo D Hersey Tribology Award, 74; Tribology Gold Medal, Inst Mech Engrs, London, 78. *Mem:* Hon mem Am Soc Lubrication Engrs; fel Am Soc Mech Engrs; Soc Automotive Engrs; inst fel, Franklin Inst; Brit Inst Mech Engrs. *Res:* Lubrication and bearing design; gas bearing research. *Mailing Add:* Mink Hollow Rd Lake Hill NY 12448

FULLER, EDWARD C, b Helena, Mont, Aug 8, 07; m 37; c 2. PHYSICAL CHEMISTRY. *Educ:* Mont State Col, BS, 28; Columbia Univ, PhD(phys chem), 41. *Prof Exp:* Instr chem & chem eng, Mont State Col, 28-31; asst chem, Columbia Univ, 31-34; from instr to prof, Bard Col, 35-44; admin aide Manhattan dist atomic energy proj, SAM Labs, Columbia Univ, 44-45; prof chem, Bard Col, 45-46, pres, 46-50; prof chem & dir area natural sci & math, Champlain Col, 50-53; prof & chmn dept, 53-72, EMER PROF CHEM, BELOIT COL, 72- *Mem:* AAAS; Am Chem Soc. *Res:* Teaching chemistry to nonscience students. *Mailing Add:* 920 Park Ave Apt #207 Beloit WI 53511

FULLER, ELLEN ONEIL, b Providence, RI; m 46; c 4. CARDIOVASCULAR PHYSIOLOGY. *Educ:* Med Col Ga, BS, 60; Emory Univ, MN, 60, MSc, 64, PhD(physiol), 68. *Prof Exp:* Assoc prof health sci, Ga State Univ, 68-70; asst prof, 70-80, ASSOC PROF PHYSIOL, EMORY UNIV, 80- *Res:* Hemodynamics of the uterine circulation; effect of exercise-training on heart. *Mailing Add:* Dept of Physiol Emory Univ Atlanta GA 30322

FULLER, EUGENE GEORGE, b Reno, Nev, May 12, 38; m 66; c 2. EMBRYOLOGY, HISTOLOGY. *Educ:* Univ Nevada, BS, 60, MS, 63; Ore State Univ, PhD(zool), 66. *Prof Exp:* Instr zool, Ore State Univ, 66-67; from asst prof to assoc prof, 67-77, PROF ZOOL, BOISE STATE UNIV, 77- *Mem:* AAAS; Am Soc Zoologists. *Res:* Histochemistry of the crustacean antennal gland in relation to its function; histochemistry, histology and morphogenesis of the rodent placenta. *Mailing Add:* Dept of Biol Boise State Univ Boise ID 83725

FULLER, EVERETT G(LADDING), b Springfield, Mass, Dec 6, 20; m 47; c 3. NUCLEAR PHYSICS. *Educ:* Amherst Col, BS, 42; Univ Ill, MA, 47, PhD(physics), 50. *Prof Exp:* Asst physics, Univ Ill, 49-50; physicist, 50-61, section chief, 61-77, dir Photonuclear Data Ctr, 77-81, PHYSICIST, NAT BUR STANDARDS, 81- *Concurrent Pos:* Com Sci Fel, US Dept of Com, 70-71; guest, Inst Theoret Physics, Copenhagen, 64-65; vis guest prof, Inst Theoret Physics, Frankfurt, 67; res assoc prof, Dept Radiol, Sch Med, Univ Md, 71-74; mem, Int Adv Comt to the Pres, Max Planck-Gesellschaft, Ger, 75-80. *Honors & Awards:* Silver Medal for Meritorious Service, US Dept of Com, 58 & Gold Medal for Meritorious Service, 71. *Mem:* Fel Am Phys Soc. *Res:* Photonuclear interaction; interaction of electromagnetic radiation with nuclei. *Mailing Add:* Nuclear Radiation Div Nat Bur Standards Washington DC 20234

FULLER, EVERETT J, b Twin Falls, Idaho, July 3, 29; m 52; c 4. PHYSICAL CHEMISTRY. *Educ:* Idaho State Col, BS, 51; Univ Utah, PhD(chem), 60. *Prof Exp:* Chemisty atomic energy div, Am Cyanamid Co, 51-53 & Phillips Petrol Co, 53; from chemist to sr chemist, 60-67, RES ASSOC, ESSO RES & ENG CO, STANDARD OIL CO, NJ, 70- *Mem:* Am Chem Soc. *Res:* Enzyme model systems; theoretical statistical mechanics; radiochemistry; separations. *Mailing Add:* Corp Res Labs Esso Res & Eng Co Linden NJ 07036

FULLER, FORST DONALD, b Stroh, Ind, Apr 25, 16; m 37; c 2. PHYSIOLOGY. *Educ:* DePauw Univ, BA, 38; Purdue Univ, MS, 41, PhD(zool), 52. *Prof Exp:* Physiologist, Armour Labs, Ill, 42-43; instr zool, Purdue Univ, 46-47; from instr to assoc prof zool, DePauw Univ, 47-58, prof, 58-81, head dept, 73-81; RETIRED. *Concurrent Pos:* Adv premed prog, DePauw Univ, 73- *Res:* Vertebrate and invertebrate physiology. *Mailing Add:* RR 3 Greencastle IN 46135

FULLER, FRANCIS BROCK, b Eugene, Ore, July 8, 27; m 57; c 1. MATHEMATICS. *Educ:* Princeton Univ, AB, 49, PhD, 52. *Prof Exp:* Instr math, Princeton Univ, 51-52; instr, 52-55, from asst prof to assoc prof, 55-66, PROF MATH, CALIF INST TECHNOL, 66- *Concurrent Pos:* Fulbright res scholar, Univ Strasbourg, 67-68. *Mem:* Am Math Soc. *Res:* Applications of algebraic topology, especially fixed point theory; global theory of ordinary differential equations; mechanics of DNA molecules. *Mailing Add:* Caltech 253-37 Pasadena CA 91125

FULLER, GEORGE CHARLES, biochemical pharmacology, see previous edition

FULLER, GERALD MAXWELL, biochemistry, see previous edition

FULLER, GLENN, b Lancaster, Calif, May 18, 29; m 54; c 2. ORGANIC CHEMISTRY. *Educ:* Stanford Univ, BS, 50; Univ Ill, MS, 51, PhD(chem), 53. *Prof Exp:* Chemisty, Shell Develop Co, 53-64; asst prof chem, Mills Col, 64-65; res chemist, 65-71, chief, Fruit Lab, 71-72, RES LEADER PLANT PHYSIOL & CHEM, WESTERN REGIONAL RES LAB, USDA, 72- *Mem:* AAAS; Am Chem Soc; Inst Food Technol; Am Oil Chemists' Soc; The Chem Soc. *Res:* Chemistry of fats and oils; chemistry of free radicals; antioxidants; lubricants; preservation of fruit and fruit products; plant hormones; aflatoxins. *Mailing Add:* 1060 Cragmont St Berkeley CA 94708

FULLER, HAROLD Q, b Waynetown, Ind, Apr 21, 07; m 32; c 3. PHYSICS. *Educ:* Wabash Col, AB, 28; Univ Ill, AM, 30, PhD(physics), 32. *Prof Exp:* Res physics, Univ Ill, 32-33; asst prof math & physics, Ill Col, 33-37; instr physics, Univ Ill, 37-38; from asst prof to prof, Albion Col, 38-47; chmn dept physics, 48-70, actg dean sch sci, 66-67, dean col arts & sci, 70-72, prof 47-77, EMER PROF PHYSICS, UNIV MO-ROLLA, 77-, EMER DEAN COL ARTS & SCI, 72- *Concurrent Pos:* Sr physicist, Process Improv Div, Tenn Eastman Corp, Tenn, 44-45. *Mem:* AAAS; Am Phys Soc; Am Soc Eng Educ; Am Asn Physics Teachers. *Res:* Spectroscopy; photochemistry; soft x-rays. *Mailing Add:* Dept of Physics Univ of Mo Rolla MO 65401

FULLER, HENRY LESTER, b Andreasky, Alaska, June 25, 16; m 46; c 2. POULTRY NUTRITION. *Educ:* State Col Wash, BS, 40; Iowa State Col, MS, 41; Purdue Univ, PhD(poultry nutrit), 51. *Prof Exp:* Salesman livestock feeds, Hales & Hunter Co, 46-48; dir educ sales, Feed Mill Div, Glidden Co, 48-49; assoc prof, 51-57, PROF POULTRY NUTRIT, UNIV GA, 57- *Concurrent Pos:* Indust consult. *Mem:* Poultry Sci Asn; Am Inst Nutrit; World Poultry Sci Asn; Fedn Am Soc Exp Biol. *Res:* Effects of restricted feeding of young chickens on subsequent egg production characterisitics and longevity; nutrition requirements of chickens; effect of diet on heat stress in chickens. *Mailing Add:* 209 Pine Valley Dr Athens GA 30601

FULLER, JACKSON FRANKLIN, JR, b Salt Lake City, Utah, Oct 9, 20; m 42; c 4. ELECTRICAL ENGINEERING, ENERGY CONVERSION. *Educ:* Univ Colo, BSEE, 44. *Prof Exp:* Systs eng elec, Gen Elec Co, 45-69; PROF ELEC, UNIV COLO, 69- *Concurrent Pos:* Consult, US Govt, Pvt Indust, State & Local Govt, 53- *Honors & Awards:* Chas A Coffin Award, Gen Elec Co, 53; Power Educator Award, Edison Elec Inst, 77. *Mem:* Inst Elec & Electronics Engrs; Am Soc Eng Educ. *Res:* Generation; transmission and distribution of electrical energy; energy conversion from nuclear and fossil sources; air quality control from power plants. *Mailing Add:* Dept Elec Eng Univ Colo Boulder CO 80309

FULLER, JAMES OSBORN, b Chaumont, NY, Aug 14, 12; m 39, 74; c 4. 3. GEOLOGY. *Educ:* Lehigh Univ, AB, 34; Columbia Univ, PhD(geol), 41. *Hon Degrees:* LLD, Lehigh Univ, 72. *Prof Exp:* Asst petrol, Columbia Univ, 36-37, asst econ geol, 37-39; asst prof geol, Mt Union Col, 39-41; instr, Ohio State Univ, 41-43; asst prof, WVa Univ, 43-44; asst geologist, US Geol Surv, Va, 44-45; asst prof geol, WVa Univ, 45-46; assoc prof, Ohio State Univ, 46-48, prof, 48-67, acting dean col arts & sci, 51-52, assoc dean, 52-57, secy adv res coun, 55-57, dean col arts & sci, 57-67; pres, Fairleigh Dickinson Univ, 67-74, distinguished prof marine geol, 74; dir of part-time and evening prog & spec asst to president, 74-75, DEAN OF ARTS & PROF GEOL, OHIO STATE UNIV, 75- *Concurrent Pos:* Consult, Nat Sea Grant Adv Panel, 71- *Mem:* AAAS; Am Asn Petrol Geol; fel Geol Soc Am. *Res:* Economic and petroleum geology; field mapping of Sharon conglomerate and Lee County, Virginia, oil field; ore petrography and polishing; water resources of Ohio. *Mailing Add:* 3928 Fairlington Dr Upper Arlington OH 43220

FULLER, KENT RALPH, b Northfield, Minn, Feb 15, 38; m 58; c 1. MATHEMATICS. *Educ:* Mankato State Col, BS, 60, MS, 62; Univ Ore, MA, 65, PhD(math), 67. *Prof Exp:* From asst prof to assoc prof, 67-75, PROF MATH, UNIV IOWA, 75- *Mem:* Am Math Soc. *Res:* Algebra, especially ring theory. *Mailing Add:* Dept of Math Univ of Iowa Iowa City IA 52242

FULLER, LAPHALLE, immunology, see previous edition

FULLER, LEONARD EUGENE, b Casper, Wyo, July 25, 19; m 43. MATHEMATICS. *Educ:* Univ Wyo, BA, 41; Univ Wis, MS, 47, PhD(math), 50. *Prof Exp:* Asst, Univ Wis, 46-50, instr, 50-51; mathematician, Goodyear Aircraft Corp, 51-52; from asst prof to assoc prof, 52-59, PROF MATH, KANS STATE UNIV, 59- *Mem:* Am Math Soc; Math Asn Am; Sigma Xi. *Res:* Applications of matrix theory. *Mailing Add:* Dept Math Kans State Univ Manhattan KS 66502

FULLER, MARIAN JANE, b Scottsbluff, Nebr, Jan 9, 40. PLANT TAXONOMY, GENETICS. *Educ:* Univ Nebr, Lincoln, BS, 62, PhD(plant taxon), 67. *Prof Exp:* Asst prof, 67-70, assoc prof, 70-78, PROF BIOL, MURRAY STATE UNIV, 78- *Mem:* Am Soc Plant Taxon; Int Asn Plant Taxon; Bot Soc Am. *Res:* Relationships among members of the genus Carduus in Nebras; relationships among members of the genus Spiranthes; orchidaceae of Kentucky. *Mailing Add:* Sherwood Forest Murray KY 42071

FULLER, MARK ROY, b Minneapolis, Minn, Sept 8, 46; m 70; c 2. RAPTOR ECOLOGY, PREDATOR-PREY RELATIONSHIPS. *Educ:* Colo State Univ, BS, 68; Cent Wash State Univ MS, 71; Univ Minn, PhD(ecol & behav biol), 79. *Prof Exp:* Res assoc, Bell Mus Nat Hist & Dept Vet Biol, Univ Minn, 76-78; RES BIOLOGIST, US FISH & WILDLIFE SERV, PATUXENT WILDLIFE RES CTR, 78- *Mem:* Am Ornithologists Union; Ecol Soc Am; Sigma Xi; Int Soc Chronobiol. *Res:* Habitat use by birds of prey including minimum area requirements and influence of land-uuse on behavior, density, productivity; raptor population biology, assessment of population status; eco-physiology and predator behavior. *Mailing Add:* Patuxent Wildlife Res Ctr Laurel MD 20708

FULLER, MARTIN EMIL, II, b Inglewood, Calif, Sept 15, 30; m 61; c 2. COMPOSITE POLYMER SYSTEMS. *Educ:* Univ Calif, Los Angeles, BS, 52; Mass Inst Technol, PhD(chem), 56. *Prof Exp:* Asst phys chem, Mass Inst Technol, 52-53; asst prof chem, Pomona Col, 56-61; res asst, Univ Fla, 61-63; assoc prof, Colo Sch Mines, 63-68 & Prescott Col, 68-70; teacher, Colo Rocky Mountain Sch, 70-71; assoc prof chem, Ft Lewis, Colo, 71-73; dir phys chem, 73-80, ASSOC DIR RES & DEVELOP, LEE PHARMACEUT, 80- *Mem:* Am Chem Soc; Am Phys Soc; AAAS; Royal Soc Chem. *Res:* Composite polymer systems; dielectric properties of polypolar polymers and solutions; induced chemical reactions; science education; science and society. *Mailing Add:* Lee Pharmaceut PO Box 3836 South El Monte CA 91733

FULLER, MELVIN STUART, b Livermore Falls, Maine, May 5, 31; m 55; c 3. BOTANY, MYCOLOGY. *Educ:* Univ Maine, BS, 53; Univ Nebr, MS, 55; Univ Calif, PhD, 59; Brown Univ, MS(ad eundem), 63. *Prof Exp:* Instr bot, Brown Univ, 59-60, from asst prof to assoc prof, Brown Univ, 60-64; asst prof, Univ Calif, Berkeley, 64-66, assoc prof & dir electron microscope lab, 66-68; head dept, 68-73, PROF BOT, UNIV GA, 73- *Concurrent Pos:* Consult ed, McGraw-Hill. *Mem:* Mycol Soc Am (vpres, 73-74, pres elect, 74-75, pres, 75-76). *Res:* Biology of the fungi; aquatic Phycomycetes; mitosis in fungi; fungal motile cells. *Mailing Add:* Dept Bot Univ Ga Athens GA 30602

FULLER, MICHAEL D, b London, Eng, June 10, 34. GEOPHYSICS. *Educ:* Cambridge Univ, BA, 58, PhD(geophys), 61. *Prof Exp:* Fel geophys, Scripps Inst, Calif, 61-62; res geophysicist, Gulf Res & Develop Co, Pa, 62-64; assoc prof geophysics, Univ Pittsburgh, 65-69, prof, 69-74; PROF GEOPHYSICS, UNIV CALIF, SANTA BARBARA, 74- *Concurrent Pos:* Mem, NASA Lunar Sci Comts, 69-72 & NSF Earth Sci Panel, 77-79. *Res:* Physical process of magnetization of rocks in nature; paleomagnetic records of secular variation and field reversals; lunar magnetism; seismomagnetism; interpretation of geological structure from aeromagnetic surveys. *Mailing Add:* Dept of Earth & Planetary Sci Univ of Pittsburgh Pittsburgh PA 15213

FULLER, MILTON E, b Mesa, Ariz, Aug 27, 26; m 52; c 3. PHYSICAL CHEMISTRY. *Educ:* Ariz State Univ, BS, 48; Northwestern Univ, PhD(phys chem), 56. *Prof Exp:* Chemist, Shell Develop Co, 56-60; staff chemist, Int Bus Mach Corp, 60-61; asst prof chem, Univ of the Pacific, 61-64; assoc prof, 64-71, chmn dept, 68-69, PROF CHEM, CALIF STATE UNIV, HAYWARD, 71- *Concurrent Pos:* Fulbright lectr, Pakistan, 71-72; consult, Thermex, Inc, 75-77, Lawrence Livermore Nat Lab, 78-80. *Mem:* Am Chem Soc. *Res:* Solid state surface effects; computer applications in teaching chemistry; bring migration in halite. *Mailing Add:* Dept of Chem Calif State Univ Hayward CA 94542

FULLER, PETER MCAFEE, b Grand Rapids, Mich, Jan 24, 43; m 70; c 1. NEUROANATOMY. *Educ:* Olivet Col, BA, 66; Univ Va, PhD(anat), 74. *Prof Exp:* Res assoc, Highway Safety Res Inst, 67-70; asst prof, 74-80, ASSOC PROF ANAT, SCH MED, UNIV LOUISVILLE, 80- *Concurrent Pos:* Consult, Div Prod Safety, Nat Bur Stand, 72-74. *Mem:* Am Asn Anatomists; Am Asn Automotive Med; Aerospace Med Asn; Soc Neurosci. *Res:* Neuroanatomical studies of the vestibular and trigeminal sensory systems in various vertebrate animals in an attempt to understand more fully the sensory input to the central nervous system; accident reconstruction and head injury studies. *Mailing Add:* Dept of Anat Health Sci Ctr Univ of Louisville Louisville KY 40292

FULLER, RAY W, b Dongola, Ill, Dec 16, 35; m 56; c 2. BIOCHEMISTRY. *Educ:* Southern Ill Univ, BA, 57, MA, 58; Purdue Univ, PhD(biochem), 61. *Prof Exp:* Dir biochem res lab, Ft Wayne State Sch, Ind, 61-63; sr pharmacologist, 63-67, res scientist, 67-68, head dept metab res, 68-71, RES res assoc, 71-75, RES ADV RES LABS, ELI LILLY & CO, 76- *Concurrent Pos:* Adj assoc prof biochem, Sch Med, Ind Univ, 74-, vis lectr, Mass Inst Technol, 76-; Pres, The Catecholamine Club, 79-80; mem, Basic Pharmacol Adv Comt, Pharmaceut Mfrs Asn Found, 78-; mem, Basic Psychopharmacol & Neuropsychol Res Rev Comt, Nat Inst Mental Health, 80- *Mem:* AAAS; Am Chem Soc; Am Soc Biol Chemists; Am Soc Pharmacol & Exp Therapeut; Am Soc Neurochem. *Res:* Biochemical mechanism of drug action; neuropsychopharmacology; brain biochemistry; neuroendocrinology; biogenic amine and amino acid metabolism. *Mailing Add:* Res Labs Eli Lilly & Co Indianapolis IN 46206

FULLER, RICHARD CLAIR, theoretical nuclear physics, see previous edition

FULLER, RICHARD KENNETH, b Chicago, Ill, Apr 2, 35; m 60; c 2. GASTROENTEROLOGY. *Educ:* Monmouth Col, BA, 57; Case Western Univ, MD, 62, MS, 71. *Prof Exp:* Instr med, 71-74, ASST PROF BIOMETRY, CASE WESTERN UNIV, 72-, ASST PROF MED, 74- *Mem:* Am Gastroentorol Asn; Am Col Physicians; AAAS. *Res:* Evaluation of treatments for pancreatitis, ascites, hepatic cirrhosis and alcoholism. *Mailing Add:* 10701 East Blvd Cleveland OH 44106

FULLER, RICHARD M, b Crawfordsville, Ind, July 23, 33; m 55; c 3. SOLID STATE PHYSICS. *Educ:* DePauw Univ, BA, 55; Univ Minn, MA, 60; Mich State Univ, PhD(physics), 65. *Prof Exp:* Instr physics, Alma Col, Mich, 59-61, from asst prof to assoc prof, 61-68; assoc prof, 68-70, PROF PHYSICS, GUSTAVUS ADOLPHUS COL, 70- *Concurrent Pos:* Lectr, Mich State Univ, 65 & 68 & Univ Mo-Rolla, 66-67. *Mem:* AAAS; Am Asn Physics Teachers; Am Phys Soc; Sigma Xi. *Res:* Infrared physics; optical and electrical properties of solids particularly ionic crystals and bone. *Mailing Add:* Dept of Physics Gustavus Adolphus Col St Peter MN 56082

FULLER, ROBERT GOHL, b Crawfordsville, Ind, June 7, 35; m 61; c 3. SOLID STATE PHYSICS. *Educ:* Univ Mo-Rolla, BS, 57; Univ Ill, Urbana, MS, 58, PhD(physics), 65. *Prof Exp:* Teacher high sch, Burma, 59-61; res asst physics, Univ Ill, Urbana, 61-65; Nat Res Coun-Nat Acad Sci res fel, Naval Res Lab, 65-67, physicist, 67-69; assoc prof, 69-76, PROF PHYSICS, UNIV NEBR, LINCOLN, 76- *Concurrent Pos:* Vis physicist orthop res, Vet Admin Hosp, Syracuse, NY, 75; vis prof, Univ Calif, Berkeley & Lawrence Hall Sci, 76-77. *Mem:* Am Asn Physics Teachers (vpres, 78, pres-elect, 79, pres, 80-81); Am Phys Soc; Nat Sci Teachers Asn. *Res:* Diffusion, pulse radiolysis, and electrical conductivity of ionic solids; photoconductivity in bone and tendon; physics teaching and Piagetian psychology; faculty development; interactive videodiscs in physics teaching. *Mailing Add:* Dept Physics Univ Nebr Lincoln NE 68588

FULLER, ROY JOSEPH, b Little Rock, Ark, June 19, 39. MATHEMATICS. *Educ:* Univ Ark, BSEE, 61, MS, 63; Princeton Univ, PhD(math), 67. *Prof Exp:* asst prof, 67-80, ASSOC PROF MATH, UNIV ARK, FAYETTEVILLE, 80- *Mem:* Am Math Soc. *Res:* Non-Abelian Gaussian sums and their connection with Hecke operators; estimation of damage to aircraft due to fragmenting-warhead projectiles. *Mailing Add:* Dept of Math Univ of Ark Fayetteville AR 72701

FULLER, RUFUS CLINTON, b Providence, RI, Mar 5, 25; m 46; c 4. MICROBIOLOGY, BIOCHEMISTRY. *Educ:* Brown Univ, AB, 45; Amherst Col, AM, 48; Stanford Univ, PhD(biol), 52. *Hon Degrees:* MA, Dartmouth Col, 61. *Prof Exp:* Teaching asst biol, Brown Univ, 45-46 & Amherst Col, 46-48; teaching asst, Stanford Univ, 48-50, asst microbiol, 51-52; res microbiologist, Lawrence Radiation Lab, Univ Calif, 52-55; assoc plant physiologist, Brookhave Nat Lab, 55-58, plant biochemist, 58-59; prof microbiol & chmn dept, Dartmouth Med Sch, 60-65; prof biomed sci & dir grad sch biomed sci, Univ Tenn, Oak Ridge Nat Lab, 66-71; chmn dept, 71-80, PROF BIOCHEM, UNIV MASS, AMHERST, 71- *Concurrent Pos:* Vis prof life sci, Univ Calif, Riverside, 66; consult biol div, Oak Ridge Nat Lab, 66-72; Sigma Xi sr fel, NSF, Oxford Univ, Eng, 59-60; mem med scientists training comt, Nat Inst Gen Med Sci, 63-65; mem cell biol study sect, NIH, 65-69; mem microbiol training comt, Nat Inst Gen Med Sci, 69-74, consult minority access to res careers training comt, 74-79; US sr scientist award, Alexander von Humboldt Found, Freiburg Univ, Ger, 77-78. *Mem:* AAAS; Am Soc Plant Physiol; Am Soc Microbiol; Am Soc Biol Chem; Am Soc Cell Biol. *Res:* Comparative biochemistry of photosynthesis; cellular biochemistry as related to cellular structures; developmental aspects of microbial ultrastructure; control mechanisms in photosynthesis; membrane structure and function. *Mailing Add:* Dept of Biochem Univ of Mass Amherst MA 01003

FULLER, SAMUEL HENRY, b Detroit, Mich, June 1, 46; m; c 3. COMPUTER SCIENCE, ELECTRICAL ENGINEERING. *Educ:* Univ Mich, BS, 68; Stanford Univ, MS, 69, PhD(elec eng & comput sci), 72. *Prof Exp:* Asst prof comput sci, Carnegie Mellon Univ, 72-74, assoc prof, 74-78; SR GROUP MGR, DIGITAL EQUIP CORP, 78- *Concurrent Pos:* Consult,

Naval Res Lab, 73-77, US Army, Ft Monmouth, 75-77. *Mem:* Inst Elec & Electronics Engrs; Asn Comput Mach. *Res:* Computer architecture; multiple processor structures and performance evaluation; design and evaluation of two experimental multiprocessors; developed techniques for evaluating alternative computer architectures. *Mailing Add:* Digital Equip Corp 77 Reed Rd Hudson MA 01749

FULLER, STEPHEN WILLIAM, b Portchester, NY, Mar 14, 45; m 74; c 1. BOTANY, PHYCOLOGY. *Educ:* Cornell Univ, BS, 67; Univ NH, PhD(bot), 71. *Prof Exp:* Res fel phycol, NY Ocean Sci Lab, 71-72; asst prof, 72-77, ASSOC PROF BIOL, MARY WASHINGTON COL, 77- *Res:* Marine phycology. *Mailing Add:* Dept of Biol Mary Washington Col Fredericksburg VA 22401

FULLER, THOMAS CHARLES, b Evanston, Ill, Aug 2, 18; m 45; c 2. WEED SCIENCE. *Educ:* Northwestern Univ, BS, 40; Univ NMex, MS, 42; Univ Chicago, PhD(cytol), 47. *Prof Exp:* Asst bot & zool, Univ NMex, 40-41; instr bot, RI State Col, 46-48; prof, Hanover Col, 48-49; asst prof, Univ Southern Calif, 49-53; from jr plant pathologist to asst plant pathologist, 53-57, BOTANIST, CALIF DEPT AGR, 57- *Res:* Cytology; mitosis; effects of several sulfa compounds on nuclear and cell division; diseases and culture of ornamentals; distribution of weeds in California. *Mailing Add:* 1220 N St Sacramento CA 95814

FULLER, VERNON JACK, b Washington, DC, Sept 11, 28; m 64; c 2. MEDICAL MICROBIOLOGY. *Educ:* Univ Md, BS, 51; George Washington Univ, MS, 53, PhD(bact), 58. *Prof Exp:* Bacteriologist, Walter Reed Army Inst Res, 56-61; bacteriologist lab germfree animal res, Nat Inst Allergy & Infectious Dis, NIH, 61-63 & lab control activ, Div Biol Standards, 63-72; bacteriologist, Div Control Activ, 72-77, DIR, PROD RELEASE BR, DIV PROD QUAL CONTROL, BUR BIOLOGICS, FOOD & DRUG ADMIN, 78- *Mem:* Am Soc Microbiol. *Res:* Receipt and control of protocols and samples pertaining to biological products. *Mailing Add:* Div Prod Qual Control 8800 Rockville Pike Bethesda MD 20205

FULLER, WALLACE HAMILTON, b Old Hamilton, Alaska, Apr 15, 15; m 39; c 1. BIOCHEMISTRY, BACTERIOLOGY. *Educ:* State Col Wash, BS, 38, MS, 39; Iowa State Col, PhD(soils chem), 42. *Prof Exp:* Res assoc, State Col Wash, 37-39; soil scientist, Soil Conserv Serv, USDA, 39-40; res assoc, Iowa State Col, 40-45; bacteriologist bur plant indust & agr eng, USDA, 45-47; soil scientist, 47-48; biochemist & assoc prof, 48-56, head dept agr chem & soils, 56-72, PROF CHEM & BIOCHEMIST, AGR RES STA, SOILS, WATER & ENG DEPT, UNIV ARIZ, 56- *Mem:* AAAS; Am Soc Agron. *Res:* Soil microbiology; biodegradation of wastes; chemistry of soil organic matter; soil fertilizers; plant nutrition; plant decomposition; soil phosphorus; plant decomposition and nutrient release; waste disposal; metal migration through soils; water quality. *Mailing Add:* 5674 W Flying Circle Tucson AZ 85713

FULLER, WAYNE ARTHUR, b Brooks, Iowa, June 15, 31; m 56; c 2. STATISTICS. *Educ:* Iowa State Univ, BS, 55, MS, 57, PhD(agr econ), 59. *Prof Exp:* Asst agr econ, 55-56, res assoc, 56-59, from asst prof to assoc prof, 59-66, PROF STATIST, IOWA STATE UNIV, 66- *Concurrent Pos:* NSF fel, 64-65. *Mem:* Int Statist Inst; Am Statist Asn; Inst Math Statist; Economet Soc; Biometric Soc. *Res:* Survey sampling, time series, estimation and econometrics. *Mailing Add:* Dept Statist Iowa State Univ Ames IA 50011

FULLER, WENDY WEBB, b Washington, DC, Feb 3, 52. EXPERIMENTAL SOLID STATE PHYSICS. *Educ:* Univ Md, BS, 75; Univ Calif, Los Angeles, MS, 76, PhD(physics), 80. *Prof Exp:* Fel, 80, RES PHYSICIST, NAVAL RES LAB, 80- *Mem:* Am Phys Soc. *Res:* Electronic transport properties of low dimensional materials and superconductivity in thin films. *Mailing Add:* Naval Res Lab Washington DC 20375

FULLER, WILLIAM ALBERT, b Moosomin, Sask, May 10, 24; m 47; c 4. VERTEBRATE ECOLOGY. *Educ:* Univ Sask, BA, 46, MA, 47; Univ Wis, PhD(ecol), 57. *Prof Exp:* Mammalogist, Can Wildlife Serv, 47-59; from asst prof to assoc prof, 59-67, chmn dept, 69-74, PROF ZOOL, UNIV ALTA, 67- *Concurrent Pos:* Mem exec bd, Int Union Conserv Nature & Natural Resources, 64-70. *Mem:* AAAS; Am Soc Mammal; Arctic Inst NAm. *Res:* Ecology of mammals, especially in the taiga in winter. *Mailing Add:* Dept of Zool Univ of Alta Edmonton Can

FULLER, WILLIAM RICHARD, b Indianapolis, Ind, Oct 27, 20; m 43; c 2. MATHEMATICS. *Educ:* Butler Univ, BS, 48; Purdue Univ, MS, 51, PhD(math), 57. *Prof Exp:* Instr math, Butler Univ, 48-49; asst, Purdue Univ, 49-51; mathematician, US Naval Ord Plant, Ind, 51-54; instr math, 54-57, asst prof, 57-59, from assoc prof to actg head, Dept Math & Statist to prof & actg head, Div Math Sci, 59-61 & 63-64, assoc dean, Sch Sci, 65-76, PROF MATH, PURDUE UNIV, 60-, CHANCELLOR, NORTH CENT CAMPUS, 78-82. *Concurrent Pos:* Consult, US Naval Avionics Facility, 58-61, Radio Corp Am Serv Co, Patrick AFB, Fla, 59 & Gen Elec Co, 60-61. *Mem:* Am Math Soc; Math Asn Am; Am Soc Eng Educ. *Res:* Nonlinear differential equations. *Mailing Add:* Div of Math Sci Math Sci Bldg Purdue Univ West Lafayette IN 47906

FULLERTON, ALBERT L, JR, b Boston, Mass, Aug 25, 21; m 44; c 4. DATA PROCESSING. *Educ:* Harvard Univ, AB, 47; Univ Colo, MS, 51. *Prof Exp:* Staff mem commun, Lincoln Lab, Mass Inst Technol, 52-54; proj engr mil systs, Melpar, Inc, 54-57; proj mgr logistic data processing, Sylvania Gen Tel & Electronics Corp, 57-61; tech staff mem commun & data processing, Inst Naval Studies, Franklin Inst Boston, 61-65; tech staff mem commun & data processing, Sanders Assocs, NH, 65-78; MEM TECH STAFF, MITRE CORP, BEDFORD, MASS, 78- *Mem:* Sr mem Inst Elec & Electronics Engrs. *Res:* Naval command, control and communications systems. *Mailing Add:* Blueberry Lane Lincoln Center MA 01773

FULLERTON, CHARLES MICHAEL, b Oklahoma City, Okla, Mar 10, 32; m 54; c 3. ATMOSPHERIC PHYSICS. *Educ:* Univ Okla, BS, 54; NMex Inst Mining & Technol, MSc, 64, PhD(geophys), 66. *Prof Exp:* Instr physics & math, Col St Joseph, NMex, 57-61; from asst prof physics & asst geophysicist to assoc prof physics & assoc geophysicist, 66-74, actg dir, Observ, 69-71, actg provost, Hilo Col, 74, PROF PHYSICS & GEOPHYSICIST, CLOUD PHYSICS OBSERV, HAWAII INST GEOPHYS, UNIV HAWAII, HILO, 74-, DIR OBSERV, 71- *Concurrent Pos:* Prin investr, US Dept Interior Off Water Resources res grant, 71-76. *Mem:* Am Geophys Union; Am Meteorol Soc. *Res:* Precipitation physics; solar coronal emission; electrical effects and coalescence processes in warm rain; ice nuclei concentrations in relation to volcanic activity; microbarometric oscillations; distribution of high intensity rainfall. *Mailing Add:* Cloud Physics Observ Univ of Hawaii Hilo HI 96720

FULLERTON, DAVID STANLEY, b Norwalk, Ohio, Mar 30, 41. QUATERNARY GEOLOGY. *Educ:* Waynesburg Col, BS, 63; Yale Univ, MS, 65; Princeton Univ, AM, 68, PhD(geol & geophys sci), 71. *Prof Exp:* Instr geol, NY Univ, 69-71, asst prof, 71-72; geologist, Ohio State Geol Surv, 72-74; GEOLOGIST, US GEOL SURV, 74- *Res:* Quaternary glaciation and environments in the Montana Plains; holocene environmental changes in the Great Plains; quaternary stratigraphy and chronology in northeast United States. *Mailing Add:* Box 25046 MS 913 Br Cent Env Geol US Geol Surv Fed Ctr Denver CO 80225

FULLERTON, DWIGHT STORY, b Oakland, Calif, June 9, 43; m 64; c 2. MEDICINAL CHEMISTRY. *Educ:* Ore State Univ, BS(chem) & BS(pharm), 67; Univ Calif, Berkeley, PhD(org chem), 71. *Prof Exp:* NIH fel, Univ Va, 71-72; asst prof med chem, Col Pharm, Univ Minn, Minneapolis, 72-76; ASSOC PROF MED CHEM, SCH PHARM, ORE STATE UNIV, 76- *Mem:* Acad Pharmaceut Sci; Am Chem Soc; Sigma Xi; Am Pharmaceut Asn. *Res:* Structure-activity studies of digitalis analogs and of natural product tumor inhibitors; novel synthetic methods. *Mailing Add:* Sch of Pharm Ore State Univ Corvallis OR 97331

FULLERTON, H(ERBERT) P(ALMER), b Philadelphia, Pa, Aug 14, 12; m 34; c 2. MECHANICAL ENGINEERING. *Educ:* Univ Pa, BS, 33, ME, 45; Univ Buffalo, MA, 44. *Prof Exp:* With Gen Elec Co, 33-36 & Am Eng Co, 36-41; assoc prof eng, Univ Buffalo, 41-45; assoc prof mach design, Univ Va, 45-48; develop & design engr, Gen Elec Co, 48-62, proj engr, 62-68, consult engr, 68-75. *Concurrent Pos:* Adj prof, Drexel Inst, 48-64. *Mem:* Am Soc Mech Engrs; Am Soc Eng Educ. *Res:* Mathematical analysis of engineering and business systems. *Mailing Add:* 8 E Franklin St Media PA 19063

FULLHART, LAWRENCE, JR, b Mystic, Iowa, Sept 14, 20; m 42; c 2. CHEMISTRY. *Educ:* William Jewell Col, AB, 42; Iowa State Col, PhD(org chem), 46. *Prof Exp:* Asst, William Jewell Col, 41-42; chemist, 46-57, tech rep, 57-62, develop specialist, 62-70, mkt res rep, 70-72, mkt res specialist, 72-78, MGR MKT RES PROG, E I DU PONT DE NEMOUR & CO, INC, 78- *Mem:* AAAS; Am Chem Soc; NY Acad Sci; Chem Mkt Res Asn. *Res:* Organic sulfur compounds; synthetic antimalarial and antitubercular compounds; synthetic vitamin D; nutritional biochemistry; amino acids and proteins; polymer dispersions; new product opportunities, marketing concepts and strategies. *Mailing Add:* Polymer Prod Dept 1007 Market St Wilmington DE 19898

FULLING, STEPHEN ALBERT, b Evansville, Ind, Apr 29, 45. THEORETICAL PHYSICS, MATHEMATICAL ANALYSIS. *Educ:* Harvard Col, AB, 67; Princeton Univ, MA, 69, PhD(physics), 72. *Prof Exp:* Fel & lectr physics, Univ Wis-Milwaukee, 72-74; res asst appl math, King's Col, Univ London, 74-76; asst prof, 76-79, ASSOC PROF MATH, TEX A&M UNIV, 79- *Concurrent Pos:* Prin investr, NSF res grant, 77- *Mem:* AAAS; Am Asn Physics Teachers; Am Phys Soc; Math Asn Am. *Res:* Quantum field theory; general relativity; spectral and asymptotic analysis of differential operators. *Mailing Add:* Dept of Math Tex A&M Univ College Station TX 77843

FULLMAN, R(OBERT) L(OUIS), b Sewickley, Pa, Sept 13, 22; m 44; c 2. METALLURGY, MATERIALS SCIENCE. *Educ:* Yale Univ, BEng, 43, DEng(metall), 50. *Prof Exp:* Instr metall, New Haven YMCA Jr Col, 47-48; res assoc, 48-55, mgr mat & processes studies, 55-59, mgr metal studies, 60-63, mgr fuel cell studies, 64-65, mgr properties br, 65-68, mgr planning & resources, mat sci & eng, 69-72, METALLURGIST, RES & DEVELOP CTR, GEN ELEC CO, 72- *Concurrent Pos:* Vis lectr, Rensselaer Polytech Inst, 51-56, adj prof, 56-65; secy-treas bd gov, Acta Metallurgica, 65- *Honors & Awards:* Geisler Mem Award, Am Soc Metals, 55. *Mem:* Fel Am Soc Metals; Am Inst Mining, Metall & Petrol Engrs. *Res:* Deformation of metals; interfacial energies in solids; crystal growth; origin of microstructures; recrystallization and grain growth; relationships between microstructure and properties of metals. *Mailing Add:* Corp Res & Develop Ctr Gen Elec Co PO Box 8 Schenectady NY 12301

FULLMER, CURTIS SHERIDAN, physical biology, biochemistry, see previous edition

FULLMER, GEORGE CLINTON, b Tucson, Ariz, Feb 17, 22; m 77; c 2. NUCLEAR ENGINEERING, PHYSICS. *Educ:* Univ Wash, BS, 47. *Prof Exp:* Physicist & supvr pile physics, Hanford Atomic Prod Oper, Gen Elec Co, 47-56, mgr oper physics, 56-65; mgr instrumentation, Pac Northwest Labs, Battelle Mem Inst, 65-66; mgr reactor physics, Hanford Atomic Prod Oper, Gen Elec Co & Douglas United Nuclear, 66-71; mgr core mgt eng, Nuclear Energy Eng Div, 71-76, PROG MGR CORE MGT SERV, NUCLEAR ENERGY ENG DIV, GEN ELEC CO, 76- *Mem:* Am Phys Soc; Am Nuclear Soc. *Res:* Pioneered development and application of techniques for dynamic flux distribution control; operator physics training; international monitoring of shutdown production reactors; and multi-BWR power reactor core management. *Mailing Add:* Nuclear Energy Eng Div M/C 171 San Jose CA 95125

FULLMER, HAROLD MILTON, b Gary, Ind, July 9, 18; m 42; c 2. EXPERIMENTAL PATHOLOGY. *Educ:* Ind Univ, BS, 42, DDS, 44; Am Bd Oral Path, dipl. *Hon Degrees:* Dr, Univ Athens, Greece, 81. *Prof Exp:* Intern & resident, Charity Hosp, New Orleans, 46-48; assoc prof gen & oral path & head dept path, Sch Dent, Loyola Univ, La, 48-53; prin investr lab histol & path, Nat Inst Dent Res, 53-64, chief sect histochem, 65-70, chief exp path br, 68-70; PROF PATH & DENT, ASSOC DEAN SCH DENT & DIR INST DENT RES, MED CTR, UNIV ALA, BIRMINGHAM, 70- *Concurrent Pos:* Mem dent study sect, NIH, 66-70 & dent caries adv comt, 75-79; assoc ed, Oral Surg, Oral Med & Oral Path, 68-76; ed-in-chief, J Oral Path, 72-; assoc ed, J Cutaneous Path, 73-; trustee, Biol Stain Comn, 77-; mem Grants & Allocations Comt, Am Fund Dent Health, 77-; Vet Admin Med Res Career Develop Comt, 77-81; Bd Dir, Nat Soc Med Res, 77-; consult ed, Gerodontology, 81- *Honors & Awards:* Isaac Schour Award, Int Asn Dent Res, 73. *Mem:* Fel AAAS; Histochem Soc; Am Asn Dent Res(vpres, 74-75, pres-elect, 75-76, pres, 76-77); Int Asn Dent Res (vpres, 74-75, pres elect, 75-76, pres, 76-77); Int Asn Oral Pathologists (pres, 78-81). *Res:* Histochemistry and microchemistry of connective tissues, bones and teeth; mechanisms of staining reactions; cytological changes with development and age. *Mailing Add:* Inst of Dent Res Univ of Ala Med Ctr Univ Sta Birmingham AL 35294

FULLMER, JUNE ZIMMERMAN, b Peoria, Ill, Dec 16, 20; m 53. HISTORY OF SCIENCE. *Educ:* Ill Inst Technol, BS, 43, MS, 45; Bryn Mawr Col, PhD, 48. *Prof Exp:* Instr chem, Hood Col, 45-46; asst prof, Pa Col Women, 49-52; res chemist metall eng, Carnegie Inst Technol, 53-54; vis asst prof chem, Newcomb Col, Tulane, 56-57, asst prof, 57-59, assoc prof & head dept, 59-64; vis assoc prof, Ohio Wesleyan Univ, 64-65; from adj assoc prof to assoc prof, 66-71, PROF HIST, OHIO STATE UNIV, 71- *Concurrent Pos:* Berliner fel, Oxford Univ, 48-49; Am Coun Learned Socs fel, 60-61; Guggenheim fel, 63-64; hon fel, Univ Wis, 63-64. *Mem:* Fel AAAS; Hist Sci Soc. *Mailing Add:* 781 Latham Ct Columbus OH 43214

FULLWOOD, RALPH ROY, b Hereford, Tex, Sept 16, 28; m 74; c 3. NUCLEAR ENGINEERING, PHYSICS. *Educ:* Tex Technol Col, BS, 52; Harvard Univ, AM, 55; Rensselaer Polytech Inst, PhD(nuclear eng), 65. *Prof Exp:* Physicist, Knolls Atomic Power Lab, 56-57; res assoc physics, Univ Pa, 57-60; staff mem nuclear eng, Rensselaer Polytech Inst, 60-65, mem fac, 65-66; mem staff physics, Los Alamos Sci Lab, 66-72; mgr, 72-79, ASST VPRES, SCI APPLN INC, 80- *Mem:* Inst Elec & Electronics Engrs; Am Nuclear Soc; Am Phys Soc; Inst Nuclear Mat Mgrs; Int Solar Energy Soc. *Res:* Probabilistic safety analysis applied to nuclear reactor and nuclear fuel cycle; cross section measurements; nuclear spectrum measurements; statistical modeling of failure. *Mailing Add:* 742 Torreya Ct Palo Alto CA 94303

FULMER, CHARLES V, b Council Bluffs, Iowa, Nov 15, 20; m 47; c 4. ENVIRONMENTAL GEOLOGY, GEOLOGICAL ENGINEERING. *Educ:* Univ Wash, BS & MS, 47; Univ Calif, Berkeley, PhD(geol paleont), 56. *Prof Exp:* Geologist, Standard Oil Co, Calif, 51-53, field geologist geol mapping, 53-56, stratigrapher, Wash & Ore, 56-59 & Alaska, 59-60, div stratigrapher, Wash, Ore & Alaska, 60-62; res engr appl res, Boeing Co, 62-64, space explor, 64-72; EARTH SCIENTIST, KING COUNTY DEPT OF LAND USE MGT, 72- *Mem:* Geol Soc Am; Am Asn Petrol Geol; Asn Eng Geol. *Res:* Tertiary stratigraphy of Washington and Oregon; space exploration; environmental analysis for land use management. *Mailing Add:* 6174 NE 187th Pl Seattle WA 98155

FULMER, CLYDE BENSON, b Lowndes Co, Ga, Nov 7, 24; m 54; c 2. PHYSICS. *Educ:* Berry Col, BS, 48; Emory Univ, MS, 49; NC State Col, PhD(eng physics), 57. *Prof Exp:* Asst prof physics, Jacksonville State Col, 49-51; physicist, Redstone Arsenal, 51-52; instr physics, NC State Col, 52-56; PHYSICIST, OAK RIDGE NAT LAB, 56- *Concurrent Pos:* Vis prof physics, Univ Grenoble, France, 74-75. *Mem:* Am Phys Soc; Am Asn Physics Teachers. *Res:* Medium energy nuclear physics. *Mailing Add:* Physics Div Oak Ridge Nat Lab PO Box X Oak Ridge TN 37830

FULMER, GLENN ELTON, b Istanbul, Turkey, Aug 3, 28; US citizen; m 52; c 4. POLYMER PHYSICS, POLYMER CHEMISTRY. *Educ:* Oberlin Col, BA, 49; Johns Hopkins Univ, MA, 56. *Prof Exp:* Chemist, Nalco Chem Co, 49-50; sr engr, Martin Marietta Corp, 56-58; RES ASSOC, RES DIV, W R GRACE & CO, 58- *Concurrent Pos:* Adj prof, Antioch Col, 73- *Mem:* Soc Rheol; Am Soc Testing & Mat; Am Chem Soc. *Res:* Rheological research; failure of materials and development of superior materials; testing of nuclear fuel elements and nuclear fallout; evaluation of ion exchange resings; solar energy conversion. *Mailing Add:* 11505 Crows Nest Clarksville MD 21029

FULMER, HUGH SCOTT, b Syracuse, NY, June 18, 28; m 52; c 3. INTERNAL MEDICINE, PREVENTIVE MEDICINE. *Educ:* Syracuse Univ, AB, 48; State Univ NY, MD, 51; Harvard Univ, MPH, 61. *Prof Exp:* Instr internal med, Sch Med, State Univ NY Syracuse, 57; res assoc pub health & prev med, Cornell Univ, 58-60; from asst prof to prof community med, Col Med, Univ KY, 60-68; tech rep health progs, Peace Corps, Malaysia, 68-69; head, Dept Community & Family Med, 69-77, PROF COMMUNITY & FAMILY MED, COL MED, UNIV MASS, 69-, ASSOC DEAN CLIN EDUC & PRIMARY CARE, 75-, PROF MED, DEPT INTERNAL MED & HEAD, SECT GEN MED, 78- *Mem:* AMA; Am Pub Health Asn; AAAS; Asn Teachers Prev Med (pres, 75-76); Am Inst Community Health (vpres, 78-80). *Res:* Epidemiology of non-infectious disease; medical care. *Mailing Add:* Dept Med Univ of Mass Col of Med Worcester MA 01605

FULMOR, WILLIAM, b Philadelphia, Pa, July 3, 13; m 42; c 3. ORGANIC CHEMISTRY, SPECTROSCOPY. *Educ:* Fairleigh Dickenson Univ, BS, 61. *Prof Exp:* Mem staff, Micro Anal Lab, Am Cyanamid Co, 46-52, supvr, Spectros Lab, 52-63, group leader spectros, Lederle Labs, 63-78; RETIRED. *Mem:* Am Chem Soc; Soc Appl Spectros; Coblentz Soc. *Res:* Application of absorption spectroscopy to elucidation of structures of organic compounds; methods of information retrieval for spectroscopic data. *Mailing Add:* Ferris Lane Nyack NY 10960

FULOP, MILFORD, b New York, NY, Nov 7, 27; m 57; c 2. INTERNAL MEDICINE. *Educ:* Columbia Univ, AB, 46, MD, 49. *Prof Exp:* From asst prof to assoc prof, 56-68, actg chmn dept, 75-80, PROF MED, ALBERT EINSTEIN COL MED, 68-; DIR MED SERV, BRONX MUNIC HOSP CTR, 70- *Mem:* Asn Am Physicians; Am Fedn Clin Res. *Res:* Renal diseases; metabolic disorders. *Mailing Add:* Dept of Med Albert Einstein Col of Med Bronx NY 10461

FULP, RONALD OWEN, b Trinity, NC, June 29, 36; m 59; c 3. ALGEBRA. *Educ:* Wake Forest Col, BS, 58; Univ NC, Chapel Hill, MA, 61; Auburn Univ, PhD(math), 65. *Prof Exp:* Part time instr math, Univ NC, 58-61; instr, Auburn Univ, 61-62; asst prof, Ga State Col, 63-65; from asst prof to assoc prof, Univ Houston, 65-69; assoc prof, 69-76, PROF MATH, NC STATE UNIV, 76- *Mem:* Am Math Soc; Math Asn Am. *Res:* Theory of characters of both algebraic and topological semigroups; homological methods applied to algebraic and topological semigroups, especially theory of extensions and tensor products; homological methods applied to the theory of topological groups. *Mailing Add:* Dept of Math NC State Univ Raleigh NC 27607

FULRATH, RICHARD M(ERLE), ceramics, deceased

FULS, ELLIS, semiconductors, see previous edition

FULTON, CHANDLER MONTGOMERY, b Cleveland, Ohio, Apr 17, 34; m 55, 81; c 3. DEVELOPMENTAL BIOLOGY, CELL BIOLOGY. *Educ:* Brown Univ, BA, 56; Rockefeller Univ, PhD(biol), 60. *Prof Exp:* From instr to assoc prof, 60-76, PROF BIOL, BRANDEIS UNIV, 76-, CHMN DEPT, 81- *Concurrent Pos:* NSF grants, 60-; mem, NSF Adv Panel Develop Biol, 74-77; NIH grant, 78- *Mem:* Soc Develop Biol; Am Soc Cell Biol. *Res:* Analysis of molecular and cellular events of cell differentiation and cell organelle morphogenesis using the amebo-flagellate Naegleria gruberi. *Mailing Add:* Dept of Biol Brandeis Univ Waltham MA 02254

FULTON, DONALD L, b St Louis, Mo, Jan 5, 37; m 57; c 2. ENGINEERING. *Educ:* Parks Col, BS, 61. *Prof Exp:* Proj engr advan technol, Rocketdyn Div, 64-73, mgr mat & processes, 73-75, DIR MAT & PREDICATABILITY, ROCKWELL INT, 75- *Mem:* Nat Mgt Asn; Am Soc Metals; Soc Mgf Engrs. *Res:* Materials and manufacturing for advanced technology aerospace application. *Mailing Add:* 6633 Canoga Ave Canoga Park CA 91304

FULTON, GEORGE PEARMAN, b Milton, Mass, June 3, 14; m 42, 70; c 4. PHYSIOLOGY. *Educ:* Boston Univ, BS, 36, MA, 38, PhD(physiol), 41. *Prof Exp:* Instr biol, Boston Univ, 41-42; res physiologist, Arthur D Little, Inc, Mass, 46-47; from asst prof to prof, 47-60, head dept, 56-74, Shields Warren Prof biol, 60-76, EMER PROF BIOL, BOSTON UNIV, 76-; ASST DIR HEALTH AFFAIRS, SC COMN HIGHER EDUC, 77- *Concurrent Pos:* Vis prof, Sch Med, Stanford Univ, 58-59; mem staff, Childrens Cancer Res Found, Boston, 64-72; consult biophys lab, Aeromed Lab, Wright-Patterson AFB; consult div nursing, USPHS; mem adv bd, Sea Farms Found; mem sci adv bd, New Eng Aquarium; founding ed, Microvascular Res; mem, Marine Adv Bd, SC Wildlife & Marine Resources Comn & SC Nutrit Coun. *Mem:* Fel Am Acad Arts & Sci; Zool; Soc Exp Biol & Med; Radiation Res Soc; Gerontol Soc. *Res:* Blood capillary circulation; innervation of blood vessels; skin temperature and heat tolerance work; topical effects of irritant chemicals on skin; thromboembolism; vascular effects of irradiation; petechial formation; hamster cheek pouch as a site for blood vessel and tumor growth studies. *Mailing Add:* SC Comn on Higher Educ 1429 Senate St Columbia SC 29201

FULTON, J(AMES) C(ALVIN), b Sunbury, Pa, Oct 17, 23; m 46; c 5. METALLURGY. *Educ:* Univ Pa, BS, 50; Mass Inst Technol, SM, 52, ScD(metall), 53. *Prof Exp:* Asst metall, Mass Inst Technol, 50-53; res metallurgist, 53-54, develop metallurgist, 54-56, assoc dir res, 56-57, chief res metallurgist, 57-61, mgr melting technol dept, 61-65, mgr melting res & sci serv dept, 65-71, MGR PROCESS RES & DEVELOP DEPT, ALLEGHENY LUDLUM STEEL CORP, 71- *Mem:* Am Inst Mining, Metall & Petrol Engrs; Am Soc Metals. *Res:* Slag-metal reactions; open hearth and electric furnace development; solidification; vacuum melting. *Mailing Add:* Res & Develop Labs Allegheny Ludlum Steel Corp Brackenridge PA 15014

FULTON, JAMES W(ILLIAM), b Oklahoma City, Okla, Dec 2, 28; m 62; c 2. CHEMICAL ENGINEERING. *Educ:* Harvard Univ, BA, 51; Univ Okla, MS, 61, PhD(chem eng), 64. *Prof Exp:* Serv engr oil well treating, Dowell, Inc, 55-56; process engr, Monsanto Chem Co, 57; instr chem eng, Univ Okla, 58-59; asst prof, Okla State Univ, 63-66; group supvr, 66-77, DESIGN ENGR, MONSANTO CO, 77- *Mem:* Am Inst Chem Engrs. *Res:* Reaction kinetics and catalysis; heterogeneous catalysts; chemical reactor design; biochemical process design; heat and mass transfer in chemical reactors; distillation; applied statistics; economic evaluations. *Mailing Add:* 21 Ridgecrest Dr Chesterfield MO 63017

FULTON, JOHN DAVID, b Norton, Va, Dec 4, 37; m 59; c 1. MATHEMATICS. *Educ:* NC State Univ, BS, 60, MS, 63, PhD(math), 65. *Prof Exp:* Instr math, NC State Univ, 65-66; res assoc math div, Oak Ridge Nat Lab, 66-67; from asst prof to assoc prof, 67-76, PROF MATH, CLEMSON UNIV, 76-, HEAD DEPT MATH SCI, 78- *Mem:* Am Math Soc; Math Asn Am; Soc Indust & Appl Math. *Res:* Combinatorial mathematics. *Mailing Add:* Dept of Math Sci Clemson Univ Clemson SC 29631

FULTON, JOSEPH PATTON, b Princeton, Ind, July 1, 17; m 45; c 2. PLANT PATHOLOGY. *Educ:* Wabash Col, AB, 39; Univ Ill, MA, 41, PhD(plant path), 47. *Prof Exp:* Asst bot, Univ Ill, 39-42 & 46-47; from asst prof to assoc prof, 47-54, PROF PLANT PATH, UNIV ARK, FAYETTEVILLE, 54- *Concurrent Pos:* Head dept plant path, Univ Ark, Fayetteville, 59-64. *Mem:* AAAS; Am Phytopath Soc (pres, 71). *Res:* Diseases of small fruit; virus diseases; beetle vector of virus diseases. *Mailing Add:* Dept of Plant Path Univ of Ark Fayetteville AR 72701

FULTON, PAUL F(RANKLIN), b Irwin, Pa, Mar 28, 16; m 48. PETROLEUM ENGINEERING. *Educ:* Univ Pittsburgh, BS, 38, MS, 51; Pa State Univ, PhD, 64. *Prof Exp:* From instr to assoc prof, 47-56, assoc chmn dept, 65-80, PROF PETROL ENG, UNIV PITTSBURGH, 56-, UNDERGRAD PROG COORDR, DEPT CHEM & PETROL ENG & DIR PETROL ENG CURRIC, 77- *Concurrent Pos:* Res engr, Gulf Res & Develop Co, 49-59; NSF sci faculty fel, 60-61. *Mem:* Am Inst Mining, Metall & Petrol Engrs. *Res:* Petroleum reservoir engineering; core analysis research; thermal methods of oil recovery; role of wettability in oil recovery. *Mailing Add:* Dept of Chem & Petrol Eng Sch of Eng Univ of Pittsburgh Pittsburgh PA 15260

FULTON, ROBERT BURWELL, III, b Washington, DC, Oct 24, 21; m 49; c 5. ECONOMIC GEOLOGY. *Educ:* Johns Hopkins Univ, AB, 43; Stanford Univ, PhD(geol), 49. *Prof Exp:* Asst geologist field mapping, NJ Zinc Co, 47, geologist geochem prospecting, 48-49, geologist gen mineral explor, 49-52, res geologist supv explor, 52-53, asst geol chief, 53-57; geologist, 57-65, asst purchasing agt minerals & ores, 66-68, planning asst purchasing dept, 69, econ geologist & mineral eval, 70-74, RAW MAT PLANNING, E I DU PONT DE NEMOURS & CO, INC, 74- *Concurrent Pos:* Asst, Stanford Univ, 43; indust adv, Int Lead-Zinc Study Group; mem panel on gold, Nat Mat Adv Bd; asst adminr nonmetals, Emergency Minerals Admin, Nat Defense Exec Reserve, 71-; mem panel on demand, Comt on Mineral Resources & Environ, 73-74, mem panel on supply, 74-75. *Mem:* Soc Econ Geologists; Am Inst Mining, Metall & Petrol Engrs; Sigma Xi. *Res:* Investigation and application of geochemical and geophysical methods to mineral exploration; study of occurrence of chemical raw materials; economic evaluation of mineral projects; development of new business ventures; industry-goverment liaison; planning raw materials acquisition strategies. *Mailing Add:* Box 131 RD 3 Kaolin Rd Kennett Square PA 19348

FULTON, ROBERT E(ARLE), b Dothan, Ala, Jan 23, 31; m 53; c 3. STRUCTURAL ENGINEERING, APPLIED MECHANICS. *Educ:* Auburn Univ, BSc, 53; Univ Ill, Urbana, MS, 58, PhD(civil eng), 60. *Prof Exp:* Struct designer, Chicago Bridge & Iron Co, Ala, 53-54; asst prof civil eng, Univ Ill, Urbana, 60-62; aerospace engr, 62-65, head, Automated Methods Sect, 65-76, MGR, INTERGRATED PROG AEROSPACE VEHICLE DESIGN PROJ, LANGLEY RES CTR, NASA, 76- *Concurrent Pos:* Instr, Va Polytech Inst, 62-65 & Univ Va, 62-68; adj prof lectr, George Washington Univ, 68-; adj prof, Old Dominion Univ, 70 & NC State Univ, 71. *Mem:* Am Soc Mech Engrs; Am Inst Aeronaut & Astronaut; Int Asn Shell Struct; Am Soc Civil Engrs; Nat Comput Graphics Asn. *Res:* Structural mechanics including shell structures, stability theory, vibrations and numerical methods; use of computers for analysis and design of complex structures occurring in aerospace and civil engineering; author of over one hundred technical publications and presentations. *Mailing Add:* Struct & Dynamics Div MS246 NASA Langley Res Ctr Hampton VA 23365

FULTON, ROBERT JOHN, b Birtle, Man, May 27, 37; m 63; c 3. GEOLOGY. *Educ:* Univ Man, BSc, 59; Northwestern Univ, PhD(geol), 63. *Prof Exp:* Geologist, 63-67, res scientist Quaternary geol, 67-73, HEAD REGIONAL SURFICIAL GEOL MAPPING, GEOL SURV CAN, 73- *Mem:* Geol Asn Can; Geol Soc Am. *Res:* Mapping of Quaternary deposits; Quaternary history; delta and lake sedimentation. *Mailing Add:* Geol Surv of Can 601 Booth St Ottawa Can

FULTON, ROBERT LESTER, b Weymouth, Mass, May 13, 35; m 65. CHEMICAL PHYSICS. *Educ:* Brown Univ, ScB, 57; Harvard Univ, AM, 60, PhD(chem physics), 64. *Prof Exp:* Res fel chem, Harvard Univ, 64-65; from asst prof to assoc prof, 65-75, PROF CHEM, FLA STATE UNIV, 75- *Mem:* Am Phys Soc. *Res:* Relaxation phenomenon; light scattering by macromolecules; macroscopic quantum electrodynamics; crystal optics; theory of dielectrics. *Mailing Add:* Dept of Chem Fla State Univ Tallahassee FL 32306

FULTON, ROBERT WATT, b Sistersville, WVa, Jan 29, 14. PLANT PATHOLOGY. *Educ:* Wabash Col, AB, 35; Univ Wis, PhD, 40. *Prof Exp:* Instr bot, Wabash Col, 35-37; from asst to asst prof hort, 37-55, fro asst prof to assoc prof, 55-60, PROF PLANT PATH, UNIV WIS-MADISON, 60- *Mem:* AAAS; fel Am Phytopath Soc. *Res:* Viruses and virus diseases of plants. *Mailing Add:* Dept Plant Path Univ Wis Madison WI 53706

FULTON, ROBERT WESLEY, b Blackwell, Okla, Oct 19, 42; m 75. VETERINARY VIROLOGY, VETERINARY MICROBIOLOGY. *Educ:* Okla State Univ, BS, 64, DVM, 66; Wash State Univ, MS, 72; Univ Mo-Columbia, PhD(microbiol), 75; Am Col Vet Microbiologists, dipl, 76. *Prof Exp:* Base vet, US Air Force Vet Serv, 66-70; resident vet clins, Wash State Univ, 70-72; res assoc virol, Univ Mo-Columbia, 72-75; ASSOC PROF VET VIROL, SCH VET MED, LA STATE UNIV, BATON ROUGE, 75- *Mem:* Sigma Xi; Am Vet Med Asn; Am Soc Microbiol. *Res:* Interferon; host defense mechanisms; bovine infectious diseases. *Mailing Add:* Dept of Vet Microbiol & Parasitol La State Univ Sch of Vet Med Baton Rouge LA 70803

FULTON, THOMAS, b Budapest, Hungary, Nov 19, 27; nat US; m 52; c 2. THEORETICAL PHYSICS. *Educ:* Harvard Univ, BA, 50, MA, 51, PhD, 54. *Prof Exp:* Mem & Jewett fel, Inst Adv Study, 54-55, NSF fel, 55-56; from asst prof physics to assoc prof, 56-64, PROF PHYSICS, JOHNS HOPKINS UNIV, 64- *Concurrent Pos:* Consult, Res Inst Advan Study, Inc, 57; vis scientist, Univ Calif, Berkeley, 59; Fulbright sr res scholar & Guggenheim fel, Inst Theoret Physics, Vienna, 64-65; assoc ed, J Math Physics, 68-71; Europ Orgn Nuclear Res, 69-70 & 76-77. *Mem:* Am Phys Soc. *Res:* Quantum theory of fields; elementary particle physics; scattering theory. *Mailing Add:* Dept of Physics Johns Hopkins Univ Baltimore MD 21218

FULTON, WINSTON CORDELL, b Minto, NB, Nov 19, 43. SYSTEMS ANALYSIS. *Educ:* Univ NB, BSc, 72; Mich State Univ, MS, 75, PhD(entom), 78. *Prof Exp:* Asst prof plant path, Mich State Univ, 78-80; ASST PROF ENTOM, PURDUE UNIV, 80- *Mem:* Entom Soc Am; Am Phytopath Soc; AAAS. *Res:* Modelling the effects of Diabrotica damage to roots on grain yield in maize with emphasis on using plant water relations parameters as measures of damage. *Mailing Add:* Dept Entom Purdue Univ West Lafayette IN 47907

FULTYN, ROBERT VICTOR, b Chicago, Ill, Nov 8, 33; m 55; c 1. COMPUTER SCIENCES. *Educ:* Northwestern Univ, BS, 54, MS, 55; Harvard Univ, MS, 58, ScD(indust hyg), 61. *Prof Exp:* STAFF MEM, LOS ALAMOS SCI LAB, UNIV CALIF, 63- *Res:* Design of industrial medical data acquisition and retrieval systems for implementation on small and minicomputer systems. *Mailing Add:* 2 Erie Lane Los Alamos NM 87544

FULTZ, DAVE, b Chicago, Ill, Aug 12, 21; m 46; c 3. DYNAMIC METEOROLOGY, FLUID MECHANICS. *Educ:* Univ Chicago, SB, 41, PhD(meteorol), 47. *Prof Exp:* Asst, US Weather Bur, Chicago Sta, 42; res assoc, Univ Chicago & PR, 42-44; opers analyst, US Air Force, 45; res assoc, 46-47, instr meteorol, 47-48, from asst prof to assoc prof, 48-60, PROF METEOROL, UNIV CHICAGO, 60-, IN CHARGE HYDRODYN LAB, 46- *Concurrent Pos:* Guggenheim fel, 50-51; sr fel, NSF, 57-58; mem sci adv bd, US Air Force, 59-63; Nat Comt Fluid Mech Films, 62-71; res grants adv comt, Air Pollution Control Off, 70-71. *Honors & Awards:* Meisinger Award, Am Meteorol Soc, 51, Rossby Res Medal, 67. *Mem:* Fel Am Meteorol Soc; fel Am Geophys Union; AAAS; Am Astron Soc; Nat Acad Sci. *Res:* Geophysical experimental fluid mechanics; convectional flows in stationary and rotating systems; synoptic study of the upper air, cloud forms; upper air trajectories in weather forecasting. *Mailing Add:* Dept of Geophys Sci Univ of Chicago Chicago IL 60637

FULTZ, R PAUL, b Staunton, Va, Oct 5, 23; m 46; c 4. PUBLIC HEALTH, PEDODONTICS. *Educ:* Med Col Va, DDS, 51; Univ Tex, MPH, 70. *Prof Exp:* Pvt pract pedodont, 53-69; assoc prof prev med, Univ Tex Dent Br Houston, 70-71; PROF COMMUNITY HEALTH & PREV DENT & CHMN DEPT, BAYLOR COL DENT, 71- *Concurrent Pos:* Consult, Region VI Head Start Prog, 72-, Region VI Nat Health Serv Corps, 72- & Tex State Dept Health, 75-; pres, Morcheron Remounts Inc, 77- *Mem:* Am Asn Dent Schs; Am Dent Asn; Am Pub Health Asn; Am Asn Pub Health Dentists. *Res:* Preventive dentistry; dental services delivery. *Mailing Add:* Community Health & Prev Dent 3302 Gaston Ave Dallas TX 75246

FUN, F(AY), b China, July 19, 34; m 60; c 3. CHEMICAL ENGINEERING. *Educ:* Cheng Kung Univ, Taiwan, BS, 56; Case Inst Technol, MS, 61, PhD(chem eng), 63. *Prof Exp:* Res engr, E I du Pont de Nemours & Co, 62-65, sr res engr, 65-69; RES SECT HEAD, RES LAB, US STEEL CORP, 69- *Mem:* Am Inst Chem Engrs; Am Chem Soc; Am Inst Mech Engrs. *Res:* Pyrochemical and plasma reactions; ore beneficiation and reduction; fluidization and fluidized-bed technology; coal preparation and coke making. *Mailing Add:* MS 56 Res Lab US Steel Corp Monroeville PA 15146

FUNCK, DENNIS LIGHT, b Palmyra, Pa, Nov 23, 26; m 49; c 2. POLYMER CHEMISTRY. *Educ:* Lebanon Valley Col, BS, 49; Univ Del, MS, 50, PhD(org chem), 52. *Prof Exp:* Res chemist process develop, 52-62, sr res chemist prod develop, 62-73, RES ASSOC, E I DU PONT DE NEMOURS & CO, 73- *Mem:* Am Chem Soc; Sigma Xi, Soc Plastic Eng. *Res:* Chromic acid oxidation of secondary and tertiary alcohols; free radical chemistry; polymer process and product development, synthesis and oxidation; acoustics; radiation; applications scouting. *Mailing Add:* 104 Monticello Rd Fairfax Wilmington DE 19803

FUNCK, LARRY LEHMAN, b Hershey, Pa, Dec 25, 42; m 64; c 2. INORGANIC CHEMISTRY. *Educ:* Lebanon Valley Col, BS, 64; Lehigh Univ, PhD(inorg chem), 69. *Prof Exp:* Asst prof, 69-77, assoc prof, 77-80, PROF CHEM & SCI COORDR, WHEATON COL, ILL, 80- *Mem:* Am Chem Soc. *Res:* Visible and ultraviolet spectra of transition metal complexes; solution studies of complex equilibria. *Mailing Add:* Dept of Chem Wheaton Col Wheaton IL 60187

FUNDERBURGH, JAMES LOUIS, b Manhattan, Kans, June 30, 45; m 65; c 2. CORNEAL BIOCHEMISTRY, CARBOHYDRATE BIOCHEMISTRY. *Educ:* Univ Tex, Austin, BA, 65; Univ Minn, MS, 69, PhD(biochem), 73. *Prof Exp:* Assoc, Dept Path, Univ Geneva, Switz, 73-75; sr fel, Ophthal Dept, Univ Wash, 73-78; RES ASSOC, SWEDISH HOSP MED CTR, SEATTLE, 79- *Mem:* Asn Res Vision & Ophthal. *Res:* Cellular-extracellular matrix interaction; biochemistry of proteoglycans; corneal biochemistry; early events in herpes virus infection; biochemistry of translation. *Mailing Add:* Corneal Dis Res Lab 1102 Columbia St Seattle WA 98104

FUNDERBURK, HENRY HANLY, JR, b Carrollton, Ala, June 19, 31; m 53; c 2. PLANT PHYSIOLOGY. *Educ:* Auburn Univ, BS, 53, MS, 58; La State Univ, PhD(bot), 61. *Prof Exp:* From asst prof to assoc prof plant physiol, 61-66, alumni assoc prof, 66-68, vpres, 68-78, chancellor, 78-80, PRES, AUBURN UNIV, MONTGOMERY, 80- *Concurrent Pos:* Mem, Weed Res Coun. *Mem:* Weed Sci Soc Am. *Res:* Fate and mode of action of herbicides. *Mailing Add:* Off Pres Auburn Univ Auburn AL 36849

FUNG, ADRIAN K, b Liuchow, Kwangsi, Chin, Dec 25, 36; m 66. ELECTROMAGNETIC WAVES. *Educ:* Nat Taiwan Univ, BSc, 58; Brown Univ, MSc, 61; Univ Kans, PhD(elec eng), 65. *Prof Exp:* PROF ELEC ENG, UNIV KANS, 72- *Concurrent Pos:* NSF grants, 75-77 & 80-82; US Army Res Off grants, 77-79 & 80-; mem, US Comn F, Int Sci Radio Union. *Mem:* Sigma Xi; sr mem Inst Elec & Electronics Engrs. *Res:* Remote sensing of sea, land and vegetations; wave scattering emission and propagation from inhomogeneous media. *Mailing Add:* Dept Elec Eng Univ Kans Lawrence KS 66045

FUNG, DANIEL YEE CHAK, b Hong Kong, May 15, 42; m 68; c 1. MICROBIOLOGY, FOOD TECHNOLOGY. *Educ:* Int Christian Univ, Tokyo, BA, 65; Univ NC, Chapel Hill, MSPH, 67; Iowa State Univ, PhD(food technol), 69. *Prof Exp:* asst prof & dir microbiol, Pa State Univ, 69-78; asst prof, 78-81, ASSOC PROF, DEPT ANIMAL SCI INDUST, KANS STATE UNIV, 80-, CHMN, FOOD SCI GRAD PROG, 79- *Concurrent Pos:* NSF instnl grant & Agr Exp Sta res grant, Pa State Univ, 70-78; Am Pub Health Asn res grants, 74-76; mem NSF-Local Course Improv Proj, 81-83. *Mem:*

AAAS; Am Soc Microbiol; Inst Food Technologists; Int Asn Milk Food & Environ Sanitarians; NY Acad Sci. *Res:* Development of miniaturized microbiological methods for diagnostic microbiology; enterotoxigenesis of Staphylococcus aureus; detection of Salmonella; effects of modern food processing on bacteria survival in foods; Clostridium perfringens sporulation problems. *Mailing Add:* Dept Animal Sci Indust Kans State Univ Manhattan KS 66506

FUNG, HENRY C, JR, b San Francisco, Calif, Feb 5, 39; m 61; c 3. IMMUNOLOGY. *Educ:* Univ Calif, BA, 59; San Francisco State Col, MA, 62; Wash State Univ, PhD(bact), 66. *Prof Exp:* From asst prof to assoc prof, 66-75, PROF MICROBIOL, CALIF STATE UNIV, LONG BEACH, 75- *Concurrent Pos:* Collab scientist, City of Hope Nat Med Ctr; consult, Concept Media, 75- *Mem:* AAAS; Am Pub Health Asn; Am Soc Microbiol; Tissue Cult Asn; NY Acad Sci. *Res:* Cancer immunology; cellular immunity; antigenic mosaic of microorganisms influenced by their environment; immunobiology. *Mailing Add:* Dept of Microbiol 1250 Bellflower Blvd Long Beach CA 90840

FUNG, HENRY YIU-MING, renovascular pharmacology, see previous edition

FUNG, HO-LEUNG, b Hong Kong, Nov 17, 43; m 70; c 2. PHARMACEUTICS. *Educ:* Victorian Col Pharm, Australia, Cert, 66; Univ Kans, PhD(pharmaceut), 70. *Prof Exp:* Asst prof, 70-75, assoc prof, 75-80, PROF PHARMACEUT, STATE UNIV NY BUFFALO, 80-, CHMN DEPT, 78- *Mem:* AAAS; Acad Pharm Sci; Am Pharmaceut Asn. *Res:* Application of physiochemical principles to the optimization of drug delivery in the human body. *Mailing Add:* Dept of Pharmaceut Sch of Pharm State Univ of NY Buffalo NY 14214

FUNG, HONPONG, b Hong Kong, July 29, 20; nat US; m 47; c 2. CIVIL ENGINEERING. *Educ:* Lingnan Univ, BSc, 42; Iowa State Univ, MSc, 48, PhD, 56. *Prof Exp:* Asst mechs surv, Nat Chaio-tung Univ, China, 42-46; res assoc, Eng Exp Sta, Iowa State Univ, 51-55, asst prof res, 55-63, asst prof hwy transp, 55-76, ASSOC PROF RES, BITUMINOUS RES LAB, IOWA STATE UNIV, 63-, ASSOC PROF CIVIL ENG, 76- *Concurrent Pos:* Mem, Hwy Res Bd, 46- *Mem:* Asn Asphalt Paving Technol; Am Road Builders Asn. *Res:* Planning of highway transportation; bituminous paving materials; technology of asphalt pavement construction and quality control of the bituminous paving materials. *Mailing Add:* Dept Civil Eng Iowa State Univ Ames IA 50011

FUNG, LESLIE WO-MEI, b Nanking, China, Sept 23, 46; US citizen. MOLECULAR BIOPHYSICS. *Educ:* Univ Calif, Berkeley, BSc, 68; Mass Inst Technol, PhD(phys chem), 71. *Prof Exp:* Res fel phys chem, Rice Univ, 71-72; lectr chem, Chinese Univ Hong Kong, 72-73; res assoc biophys, Univ Pittsburgh, 73-77; ASST PROF CHEM, WAYNE STATE UNIV, 77- *Honors & Awards:* NIH Nat Res Serv Award, 75-77. *Mem:* AAAS; Am Biophys Soc; Am Chem Soc; Asn Women Sci; Sigma Xi. *Res:* Studies of structural-functional relationship of biological systems by magnetic resonance spectroscopy. *Mailing Add:* Dept of Chem Wayne State Univ Detroit MI 48202

FUNG, SHUN CHONG, b Kwongtung, China, Jan 28, 43; US citizen. CATALYSIS, REACTION KINETICS. *Educ:* Univ Calif, Berkeley, BS, 65; Univ Ill, Urbana, MS, 67, PhD(chem eng), 69. *Prof Exp:* STAFF ENGR, EXXON RES & ENG CO, 69- *Mem:* Am Chem Soc; NAm Catalysis Soc. *Res:* Designing and characterizing new catalysts for petroleum and chemical processes; the understanding of the chemistry of the catalytic reaction via kinetics and mechanism studies of the reaction of interest. *Mailing Add:* Exxon Res & Eng Co PO Box 45 Linden NJ 02036

FUNG, STEVEN, b New Westminster, BC, Oct 31, 51; Can citizen. SYTHETIC ORGANIC CHEMISTRY, MEDICAL CHEMISTRY. *Educ:* Univ BC, BSc, 73; Univ Alta, PhD(org chem), 78. *Prof Exp:* Fel, Zoecon Corp, 78-80; SR SCIENTIST, AYERST LABS, 80- *Mem:* Chem Inst Can; Am Chem Soc. *Res:* Synthetic organic and medicinal chemical research. *Mailing Add:* Ayerst Labs PO Box 6115 Montreal PQ H3C 3J1 Can

FUNG, SUI-AN, b Chekiang, China, Dec 18, 22; m; c 5. MECHANICAL ENGINEERING. *Educ:* Nat Cent Univ NanKing, BS, 48; Univ Rochester, MS, 56; Cornell Univ, PhD, 65. *Prof Exp:* Mech engr, supvr & mgr, Signal Equip Co, 48-52; asst prof mech eng, Univ Evansville, 56-59; assoc prof, Tex Tech Univ, 59-62; MEM STAFF, SPACE DIV, ROCKWELL INT, 65-; PROF, SOUTH BAY UNIV, 79- *Concurrent Pos:* Consult engr, RCA Whirlpool Refrig, Inc, 59. *Mem:* AAAS; Am Soc Mech Engrs; Am Soc Eng Educ; Am Inst Aeronaut & Astronaut. *Res:* Thermodynamic properties; heat transfer; fluid mechanics; applied mathematics and low-g propellant behavior. *Mailing Add:* 325 S Doheny Dr Beverly Hills CA 90211

FUNG, YUAN-CHENG B(ERTAAM), b China, Sept 15, 19; m 49; c 2. BIOENGINEERING, STRUCTURAL DYNAMICS. *Educ:* Nat Cent Univ, China, BS, 41, MS, 43; Calif Inst Technol, PhD(aeronaut), 48. *Prof Exp:* Instr mech, Nat Cent Univ, China, 41-43; from asst prof to prof aeronaut, Calif Inst Technol, 51-66; PROF BIOENG & APPL MECH, UNIV CALIF, SAN DIEGO, 66- *Concurrent Pos:* Ed, J Biomech Eng, 79- *Honors & Awards:* Landis Award for Res, Microcirculatory Soc, 75; Von Karman Medal, Am Soc Engrs, 76; Lissner Award, Am Soc Mech Engrs, 78. *Mem:* Am Inst Aeronaut & Astronaut; Am Soc Mech Engrs; Am Physiol Engrs; Int Soc Biorheol (vpres, 74-); Microcirculatory Soc. *Res:* Physiology; circulation; respiration; elasticity; aeroelasticity; dynamics; author or coauthor of over 200 scientific papers. *Mailing Add:* Dept Bioeng & Appl Mech Univ Calif San Diego La Jolla CA 92093

FUNICELLI, NICHOLAS ANTHONY, b New York, NY, Aug 31, 48; m 69. FISHERIES, MARINE ECOLOGY. *Educ:* C W Post Col, BA, 70, MS, 72; Univ Southern Miss, PhD(marine biol), 75. *Prof Exp:* Intern, Miss Marine Resources Coun, 73-74; fisheries biologist, US Corp Engrs, Savannah Dist, 74-75; proj biologist, Consolidated Edison Co NY, 75-77; sr ecologist, Environ Protection Agency, 77-78; asst prof, Dept Environ & Marine Sci, C W Post Col, 77-78; proj officer, 78-79, leader, Contract Admin, 79-80, FISHERIES RES BIOLOGIST, NAT COASTAL ECOSYST TEAM, US FISH & WILDLIFE SERV, AUSTIN, TEX, 81- *Mem:* Am Fisheries Soc; Am Littoral Soc. *Res:* Life histories of batoid fishes. *Mailing Add:* US Fish & Wildlife Serv 300 E Eighth St Rm G 121 Austin TX 78701

FUNK, CYRIL REED, JR, b Richmond, Utah, Sept 20, 28; m 51; c 3. PLANT BREEDING. *Educ:* Utah State Univ, BS, 52, MS, 55; Rutgers Univ, PhD(plant breeding), 62. *Prof Exp:* Instr farm crops, 56-61, from asst res specialist to assoc res specialist turfgrass breeding, 61-69, RES PROF TURFGRASS BREEDING, RUTGERS UNIV, 69- *Mem:* Am Soc Agron; Am Genetic Asn; AAAS; Sigma Xi; NY Acad Sci. *Res:* Field corn breeding, production and management; ecology of crop mixtures; seed quality; turfgrass breeding and genetics; apomixis; author or co author of many scientific publications. *Mailing Add:* Dept Soils & Crops Cook Col Rutgers Univ New Brunswick NJ 08903

FUNK, DAVID CROZIER, b Wilmington, Del, Sept 24, 22; m 47; c 4. CARDIOLOGY. *Educ:* Emory Univ, BS, 43, MD, 46. *Prof Exp:* Intern, Hosps, 46-47, resident, 49-52, from clin instr to clin assoc prof, Col Med, 52-70, ASSOC PROF INTERNAL MED, COL MED, UNIV IOWA, 70- *Concurrent Pos:* Clin investr, Vet Admin, 57-60; trainee, Cardiovascular Res Inst, Univ Calif, San Francisco, 59-60; chief cardiovasc lab, Vet Admin Hosp, Iowa City, 57-; fel coun cardiol, Am Heart Asn. *Mem:* AAAS; fel Am Col Physicians; fel Am Col Cardiol. *Res:* Cardiovascular and pulmonary physiology. *Mailing Add:* Dept of Internal Med Univ of Iowa Col of Med Iowa City IA 52240

FUNK, DAVID TRUMAN, b Greensburg, Ind, Oct 17, 29; m 56; c 1. FOREST GENETICS. *Educ:* Purdue Univ, BS, 51, MS, 56; Mich State Univ, PhD, 71. *Prof Exp:* Res forester, Cent States Forest Exp Sta, 56-65, plant geneticist, 65-70, prin plant geneticist, NCent Forest Exp Sta, 70-79, ASST DIR, NORTHEAST FOREST EXP STA, US FOREST SERV, 79- *Concurrent Pos:* Chmn, Cent States Forest Tree Improv Conf, 68-71; co-chmn working party breeding nut species, Int Union Forestry Res Orgns, 73- *Mem:* AAAS; Soc Am Foresters; Fedn Am Scientists. *Res:* Strip-mine reclamation and reforestation research; population genetics; hardwood tree breeding. *Mailing Add:* Forestry Sci Lab PO Box 640 Durham NH 03824

FUNK, EMERSON GORNFLOW, JR, b Highland Park, Mich, Jan 27, 31; m 53; c 3. NUCLEAR PHYSICS. *Educ:* Wayne State Univ, AB, 53; Univ Mich, MA, 54, PhD(physics), 58. *Prof Exp:* Instr physics, Univ Mich, 58; from asst prof to assoc prof, 58-71, PROF PHYSICS, UNIV NOTRE DAME, 71- *Mem:* Am Phys Soc; Am Asn Physics Teachers. *Res:* Nuclear spectroscopy; investigation of nuclear level schemes by gamma and beta ray spectroscopy and nuclear reaction techniques. *Mailing Add:* Dept of Physics Univ of Notre Dame Notre Dame IN 46556

FUNK, GLENN ALBERT, b Highland Park, Mich, Feb 28, 42; m 66; c 2. MEDICAL VIROLOGY, MEDICAL MICROBIOLOGY. *Educ:* Univ Calif, Berkeley, BA, 63; Univ Calif, Los Angeles, MS, 65; Stanford Univ, PhD(med microbiol), 75. *Prof Exp:* Mental health trainee med microbiol, NIH, 63-65; dir, Clin Virol Lab, Naval Med Res Unit 2, Taipei, Taiwan, 66-69, mem staff res microbiol, Naval Biosci Lab, Oakland, Calif, 70; res assoc med virol, Baylor Col Med, 74-76; asst prof, 76-81, ASSOC PROF MICROBIOL & MED VIROL, SAN JOSE STATE UNIV, 81-; MGR RES, INT DIAGNOSTIC TECHNOL, SANTA CLARA, CALIF, 81- *Concurrent Pos:* Asst, Sch Med, Stanford Univ, 72-74, USPHS fel med microbiol, 69-74; fel, Baylor Col Med, 75-76; consult, Microbiol Assoc, Rockville, Md. *Mem:* Am Soc Microbiol; Soc Wine Educrs. *Res:* Biochemical and biophysical characterization of animal viruses; virology and immunology of hepatitis; biomedical instrumentation and computer interfacing; viral immunodiagnosis. *Mailing Add:* Dept of Biol Sci San Jose State Univ San Jose CA 95192

FUNK, HELEN BEATRICE, b Waverly, Iowa, May 23, 13. MICROBIOLOGY. *Educ:* Iowa State Teachers Col, BA, 35; Univ Iowa, MS, 36; Univ Wis, PhD(bact), 55. *Prof Exp:* Teacher pub sch, Ill, 36-43; instr bact & zool, Milwaukee-Downer Col, 43-46; teaching fel, Univ Wis, 46-48 & 49-50; asst prof bot, Barnard Col, Columbia Univ, 50-56; assoc prof, 56-61, chmn dept, 58-61, prof, 61-78, EMER PROF BIOL SCI, GOUCHER COL, 78- *Concurrent Pos:* Fulbright lectr, Univ Tehran, 61-62; res leprosy unit, Dept Pathobiol, Sch Hygiene & Pub Health, Johns Hopkins Univ, 78-, vis prof, 78-79, res assoc, 79-81. *Mem:* AAAS; Am Soc Microbiol; Soc Protozool. *Res:* Physiology; soil microbiology; vitamin metabolism; host dependent agents; cultivation of bacteria that cause leprosy. *Mailing Add:* 414 Forest Ave Waterloo IA 50702

FUNK, JAMES ELLIS, b Cincinnati, Ohio, Nov 8, 32; m 55; c 5. MECHANICAL & CHEMICAL ENGINEERING. *Educ:* Univ Cincinnati, ChemE, 55; Univ Pittsburgh, MS, 58, PhD(chem eng), 60. *Prof Exp:* Sr engr, Bettis Atomic Power Lab, Westinghouse Elec Corp, 55-63; group leader, Allison Div, Gen Motors Corp, 63-64; from assoc prof to prof mech eng & assoc dean grad progs, Univ Ky, 64-70; dir tech activities, indust group, Combustion Eng, Inc, 70-71; dean, Col Eng, Univ Ky, 71-79, assoc vpres, Acad Affairs & coordr, Energy Res Educ, 79-81; DIR, ADV TECH CTR, ALLIS-CHALMERS CORP, 81- *Concurrent Pos:* Consult, NSF & Nat Bur Standards. *Mem:* AAAS; Am Inst Chem Engrs. *Res:* Chromatography; systems analysis; thermochemical hydrogen production; thermodynamics. *Mailing Add:* Adv Technol Ctr Allis-Chalmers Corp Box 512 Milwaukee WI 53201

FUNK, JOHN LEON, b Coschocton, Ohio, Nov 15, 09; m 33; c 1. ECOLOGY, FISH BIOLOGY. *Educ:* Kent State Univ, BS, 32; Univ Mich, MA, 39. *Prof Exp:* Aquatic biologist, Inst Fisheries Res, Mich Dept Conserv, 40-44 & Wash State Pollution Control Cmn, 44-45; fishery biologist, Mo Dept Conserv, 45-52, supvr steam res, 52-59, supt fisheries res & training, 59-72, staff specialist, 72-74; ECOL CONSULT, 74- *Mem:* Am Fisheries Soc; fel Am Inst Fishery Res Biol. *Res:* Warm water stream fisheries; ecology of fishes of warm water streams; migration of fishes; populations and ecology of streams and associated fauna. *Mailing Add:* 1025 Hickory Hill Dr Columbia MO 65201

FUNK, RICHARD CULLEN, b Omaha, Nebr, Sept 22, 34; m 57; c 4. ACAROLOGY, INVERTEBRATE ZOOLOGY. *Educ:* Colo State Univ, BS, 57, MS, 60; Univ Kans, PhD(entom), 68. *Prof Exp:* From asst prof to assoc prof, 65-78, PROF ZOOL, EASTERN ILL UNIV, 78- *Mem:* Am Acarological Soc; Am Arachnological Soc; Entom Soc Am; Am Micros Soc; Soc Syst Zool. *Res:* Systematics, zoogeography and biology of celaenopsoid, fedrizzioid and other taxa of phoretic mites. *Mailing Add:* Dept of Zool Eastern Ill Univ Charleston IL 61920

FUNK, WILLIAM HENRY, b Ephraim, Utah, June 10, 33; m 64; c 1. LIMNOLOGY, SANITARY BIOLOGY. *Educ:* Univ Utah, BS, 55, MS, 63, PhD(zool), 66. *Prof Exp:* Instr high schs, Utah, 57-63; assoc prof sanit sci, 66-75, PROF CIVIL & ENVIRON ENG, WASH STATE UNIV, 75- *Concurrent Pos:* Ed, Newsletter, Pac Northwest Sect, Water Pollution Control Fedn, 68-77; consult lake asns & industries on water qual; consult, US Civil Serv Comn, 73-75; Nat dir, Pac Northwest Pollution Control Asn, 78- *Honors & Awards:* Arthur Sidney Bedell Award for serv in water pollution control. *Mem:* Water Pollution Control Fedn; Am Soc Limnol & Oceanog; Am Micros Soc; Sigma Xi. *Res:* Nature and causes of eutrophication of lakes and reservoirs; development of multidisciplinary research and inter-university cooperation on water research. *Mailing Add:* Dept Environ Eng 141 Sloan Hall Wash State Univ Pullman WA 99164

FUNKE, PHILLIP T, b Bend, Ore, Nov 1, 32; m 70. MASS SPECTROMETRY, ORGANIC CHEMISTRY. *Educ:* Univ Puget Sound, BS, 54; Stevens Inst Technol, MS, 56, PhD(phys chem), 62. *Prof Exp:* Instr chem, Newark Col, Eng, 60-63; res scientist mass spectrometry, Stevens Inst Technol, 63-70; res investr, Squibb Inst Med Res, 70-72, RES FEL MASS SPECTROMETRY, E R SQUIBB & SONS, 72- *Concurrent Pos:* Vis lectr, Stevens Inst Technol, 63-70; consult, Sandoz Pharmaceut, Inc, 66-69. *Mem:* Am Chem Soc; Am Soc Mass Spectrometry. *Res:* Organic structure determination by mass spectrometry; ion-molecule reactions; analysis of thermal degradation products of polymers; gas chromatography; quantitative analysis of drugs in body fluids; positive and negative chemical ionization. *Mailing Add:* PO Box 4000 Lawrenceville Princeton Rd Princeton NJ 08540

FUNKENBUSCH, WALTER WILLIAM, b Canton, Mo, Feb 13, 18; m 45; c 4. MATHEMATICS. *Educ:* Culver-Stockton Col, BA, 40; Ore State Col, MS, 50. *Prof Exp:* Asst math, Ore State Col, 40-41, inst, 42-44; seismograph comput, W Geophys Co, 44; instr math, Mich Col Mining & Technol, 44-45 & 45-49; from asst prof to assoc prof, 49-67, PROF MATH, MICH TECHNOL UNIV, 67- *Concurrent Pos:* Instr, Mich State Col, 45; Proj dir undergrad partic, NSF, 59-60. *Mem:* Math Asn Am. *Res:* Probability and game theory. *Mailing Add:* Dept of Math Mich Technol Univ Houghton MI 49931

FUNKHOUSER, EDWARD ALLEN, b Trenton, NJ, Sept 30, 45; m 68; c 2. PLANT PHYSIOLOGY, PLANT BIOCHEMISTRY. *Educ:* Del Valley Col, BS, 67; Rutgers Univ, MS, 69, PhD(plant physiol), 72. *Prof Exp:* Instr biol, Del Valley Col Sci & Agr, 69-72; res assoc plant biochem, State Univ NY Buffalo, 72-74; sci asst plant physiol, Vennesland res dept, Max Planck Soc Advan Sci, 74-76; asst prof, 76-81, ASSOC PROF PLANT PHYSIOL, DEPT PLANT SCI, TEX A&M UNIV, 82- *Mem:* AAAS; NY Acad Sci; Am Soc Plant Physiologists; Japanese Soc Plant Physiologists; Sigma Xi. *Res:* Mineral nutrition in plants; control of nitrate utilization in plants and factors which control nitrate reductase activity. *Mailing Add:* Dept Plant Sci Tex A&M Univ College Station TX 77843

FUNKHOUSER, JOHN TOWER, b Paterson, NJ, Dec 19, 28; m 55; c 3. ANALYTICAL CHEMISTRY. *Educ:* Princeton Univ, AB, 50; Mass Inst Technol, PhD(chem), 54. *Prof Exp:* Chemist, E I du Pont de Nemours & Co, 54-62; chemist, 62-63, group leader anal res, 63-69, dir, Environ Sci Res & Develop Div, Cambridge, 71-73, MGR CONSULT, ARTHUR D LITTLE, INC, 73-; DIR, CTR ENVIRON ASSURANCE, 78- *Mem:* AAAS; Am Chem Soc. *Mailing Add:* 68 Westland Rd Weston MA 02193

FUNNELL, JOHN E(ESLEY), materials engineering. mineral technology, deceased

FUNT, B LIONEL, b Jan 20, 24; Can citizen; m 47; c 3. POLYMER CHEMISTRY. *Educ:* Dalhousie Univ, BSc, 44, MSc, 46; McGill Univ, PhD(phys chem), 49. *Prof Exp:* Lectr chem, Dalhousie Univ, 46-47; from asst prof to prof, Univ Man, 50-68, dean grad studies, 64-68; dean sci, 68-71, PROF CHEM, SIMON FRASER UNIV, 68- *Concurrent Pos:* Res consult, Nuclear Enterprises, 54-76, dir, UK, 56-76, Can, 60-, US, 68-76; mem bd dirs, Asn Univs & Cols Can, 66-69 & Univs Grants Comn Man, 67-69; mem bd gov, Simon Fraser Univ, 75-78. *Mem:* Fel Chem Inst Can. *Res:* Photoelectrochemical solar energy conversion; organic scintillators and scintillation mechanisms; kinetics of polymerization; electrically initiated polymerizations. *Mailing Add:* Dept of Chem Simon Fraser Univ Burnaby Can

FUOSS, RAYMOND MATTHEW, b Bellwood, Pa, Sept 28, 05; m 26, 47; c 1. PHYSICAL CHEMISTRY. *Educ:* Harvard Univ, ScB, 25; Brown Univ, PhD(chem), 32. *Prof Exp:* Res instr, Skinner, Sherman & Esselen, Inc, Mass, 27-30; res instr, Brown Univ, 32-33; int res fel, Leipzig & Cambridge, 33-34; asst res prof chem, Brown Univ, 34-36; res chemist, Gen Elec Co, NY, 36-45; Sterling prof, 45-74, EMER PROF CHEM, YALE UNIV, 74- *Concurrent Pos:* Mem, Off Sci Res & Develop, Nat Defense Res Comt & Off Naval Res, 44. *Honors & Awards:* Award, Am Chem Soc, 35. *Mem:* Nat Acad Sci; Am Chem Soc; Am Acad Arts & Sci. *Res:* Experimental and theoretical studies of properties of electrolytes, dielectrics and polymers. *Mailing Add:* Dept of Chem Yale Univ New Haven CT 06520

FUQUA, MARY ELIZABETH, b Dresden, Tenn, Sept 12, 22. EDUCATIONAL ADMINISTRATION, NUTRITION. *Educ:* Univ Tenn, BS, 44; Ohio State Univ, MS, 48, PhD(food & nutrit), 52. *Prof Exp:* Therapeut dietician med ctr, Univ Ind, 45-47; instr foods & nutrit, Ohio State Univ, 48-49; asst prof, Univ Ill, 51-53; assoc prof, Pa State Univ, 53-63; head dept, 63-66, assoc dean exten, 73-78, PROF FOODS & NUTRIT, PURDUE UNIV, 63-, ASSOC DEAN, 78- *Mem:* Am Dietetic Asn; Sigma Xi; Am Inst Nutrit. *Res:* Calcium metabolism. *Mailing Add:* Stone Hall Purdue Univ West Lafayette IN 47906

FUQUAY, JAMES JENKINS, b Montesano, Wash, May 18, 24; m 46; c 4. METEOROLOGY, CLIMATOLOGY. *Educ:* Univ Wash, BS, 50, MS, 52. *Prof Exp:* Jr res meteorologist atmospheric diffusion, Univ Wash, 50-51, res meteorologist, 51-52; res meteorologist, Atmospheric Physics Oper, Hanford Labs, Gen Elec Co, 52-60, mgr, 60-65; mgr atmospheric physics sect, Physics & Instruments Dept, 65-66 & Environ & Radiol Sci Dept, 66-68, assoc mgr environ & life sci div, 68-74, asst dir, Prog Support, 75-80, DIR LAB SUPORT, PAC NORTHWEST LAB, BATTELLE MEM INST, 80- *Mem:* Am Meteorol Soc; Am Geophys Union; Air Pollution Control Asn. *Res:* Micrometeorology; microclimatology; application of meteorology in industrial plant operation and dispersing of stack effluents. *Mailing Add:* Pac Northwest Labs PO Box 999 3000 Stevens Dr Richland WA 99352

FUQUAY, JOHN WADE, b Burlington, NC, July 31, 33; m 70; c 2. ANIMAL PHYSIOLOGY. *Educ:* NC State Univ, BS, 55, MS, 66; Pa State Univ, PhD(dairy sci), 69. *Prof Exp:* Herd mgr dairy cattle, Fuquay's Jersey Farm, 59-64; asst dairy cattle physiol, NC State Univ, 64-66; asst dairy cattle nutrit, Pa State Univ, 66-69; asst prof, 69-72, assoc prof, 72-79, PROF DAIRY CATTLE PHYSIOL, MISS STATE UNIV, 79- *Concurrent Pos:* Vis prof, Univ Calif, Davis, 79; chmn, Am Dairy Sci Asn Educ Comn, 81-82. *Mem:* Am Dairy Sci Asn; AAAS; Am Soc Animal Sci. *Res:* Dairy cattle, especially endocrine regulation of estrous cycle and causes of reproductive failure, environmental stress or effects on physiology and performance; regulation of oviduct motility and blood flow. *Mailing Add:* Dept of Dairy Sci Drawer DD Miss State Univ Mississippi State MS 39762

FURBERG, CURT DANIEL, b Skelleftea, Sweden, May 30, 36; m 65; c 3. CARDIOLOGY. *Educ:* Univ Uppsala, Sweden, MK, 58; Univ Umea, Sweden, ML, 63. *Prof Exp:* Resident, Dept Clin Physiol, Umea Univ Hosp, Sweden, 63-66, co-dir, 67-68; dir, Dept Clin Physiol, Boden Cent Hosp, 68-74; med officer, 74-79, CHIEF, CLIN TRIALS BR, DIV HEART & VASCULAR DIS, NAT HEART, LUNG & BLOOD INST, 79- *Concurrent Pos:* Assoc prof, Univ Umea, Sweden, 68-82; prin investr, WHO, Swit, 70-75; consult, Hassle Pharmaceut Co, Sweden, 71-75; lectr, NIH, 81-82 & Food & Drug Admin, 82; mem, Am Heart Asn. *Mem:* Soc Clin Trials; Swedish Soc Cardiol. *Res:* Clinical trials; preventive cardiology. *Mailing Add:* 6619 Sulky Lane Rockville MD 20852

FURBISH, FRANCIS SCOTT, b Portland, Maine, Mar 25, 40; m 69; c 1. BIOCHEMISTRY. *Educ:* Univ Maine, BS, 63; Iowa State Univ, PhD(biochem), 69. *Prof Exp:* Chief chem sect, US Army, Valley Forge Gen Hosp, 69-72; guest worker biochem, 75-76, SR STAFF FEL BIOCHEM, NIH, 76- *Mem:* AAAS; Am Chem Soc; NY Acad Sci; Soc Exp Biol & Med. *Res:* Enzyme replacement therapy; protein purification and modification; glycoprotein receptors in mammalian systems; analytical biochemistry; coenzymes, enzymology. *Mailing Add:* NIH Bldg 10 Rm 4N-248 Bethesda MD 20205

FURBY, NEAL WASHBURN, b Hanford, Calif, Apr 20, 12; m 37; c 3. CHEMISTRY. *Educ:* Univ Calif, BS, 39. *Prof Exp:* From res chemist to sr res chemist, Chevron Res Co, 39-58, supvry res chemist, 58-64, sr res assoc, 64-77; V PRES, INT LUBRICATION CONSULTS, 77- *Mem:* Am Chem Soc; Am Soc Test & Mat; Am Soc Lubrication Eng. *Res:* Petroleum chemistry; lubricating oils; lubricants; hydraulic fluids; engine oils; synthetic fluids. *Mailing Add:* 34 Highgate Rd Berkeley CA 94707

FURCHGOTT, ROBERT FRANCIS, b Charleston, SC, June 4, 16; m 41; c 3. PHARMACOLOGY, BIOCHEMISTRY. *Educ:* Univ NC, BS, 37; Northwestern Univ, PhD(biochem), 40. *Prof Exp:* Res fel med, Med Col, Cornell Univ, 40-43, res assoc, 43-47, instr physiol, 43-48, asst prof med biochem, 47-49; from asst prof to assoc prof pharmacol, Med Sch, Washington Univ, 49-56; PROF PHARMACOL & CHMN DEPT, STATE NY DOWNSTATE MED CTR, 56- *Concurrent Pos:* Ed, J Am Soc Pharmacol & Exp Therapeut, 53-62; mem pharmacol training comt, USPHS, 61-64; mem pharmacol-toxicol rev comt, 65-68; Commonwealth fel, 62-63; vis prof, Univ Geneva, 62-63; mem bd sci coun, Nat Heart Inst, 64-68; ed, Pharmacol Rev, 64-69; mem metab rev panel, New York City Health Res Coun, 65-70; USPHS spec fel, 71-72; vis prof, Univ Calif, San Diego, 71-72; ed, Molecular Pharmacol, 72- & Blood Vessels, 72-; vis prof, Med Univ SC, 80 & Univ Calif, 80. *Mem:* AAAS; Am Chem Soc; Am Soc Biol Chemists; Am Soc Pharmacol & Exp Therapeut (pres, 71-72); Harvey Soc. *Res:* Physical chemistry of red cell structure; circulatory shock and hypertension; pharmacology and biochemistry of cardiac and smooth muscle; adrenergic mechanisms; theory of drug-receptor interactions; mechanisms of vasodilitation. *Mailing Add:* Dept of Pharmacol State Univ of NY Downstate Med Ctr Brooklyn NY 11203

FURCINITTI, PAUL STEPHEN, b Milford, Mass, Mar 8, 49; m 78. RADIATION BIOLOGY, ATOMIC PHYSICS. *Educ:* Worcester Polytech Inst, BS, 71; Univ NH, MS, 74, PhD(physics), 75. *Prof Exp:* Res assoc laser physics, Worcester Polytech Inst, 76; res assoc radiation biol, Pa State Univ,

76-78; res assoc, Carrcinogenesis Risk Assessment, Div Health & Safety Res, Oak Ridge Nat Lab, 78-79; RES ASSOC, RADIATION BIOPHYSICS, COLUMBIA UNIV, 79-; RES COLLABR, BROOKHAVEN NAT LAB, 79- *Mem:* AAAS; Sigma Xi; Tissue Cult Asn; Optical Soc Am; Radiation Res Soc. *Res:* Cellular radiation biology; analytical cell electrophoresis; laser light scattering; laser theory; chemical carcinogenesis. *Mailing Add:* 80 N Country Rd PO Box 159 Shoreham NY 11786

FURDYNA, JACEK K, b Kamionka, Poland, Sept 6, 33; US citizen; m 60; c 4. SOLID STATE PHYSICS. *Educ:* Loyola Univ, Chicago, BS, 55; Northwestern Univ, PhD(physics), 60. *Prof Exp:* Res assoc, Northwestern Univ, 60-62; res physicist, Francis Bitter Nat Magnet Lab, Mass Inst Technol, 62-66; assoc prof, 66-72, PROF PHYSICS, PURDUE UNIV, 72- *Mem:* Am Phys Soc. *Res:* Physics of semiconductors and metals; galvano-magnetic phenomena; magneto-optical phenomena at microwave frequencies; plasma effect in solids. *Mailing Add:* Dept of Physics Purdue Univ West Lafayette IN 47907

FURESZ, JOHN, b Miskolc, Hungary, Oct 13, 27; Can citizen; m 64; c 3. VIROLOGY. *Educ:* Univ Budapest, MD, 51 & McGill Univ, 61. *Prof Exp:* Med officer virol, State Inst Hyg, Budapest, 51-56; biologist, Lab of Hyg, Ottawa, 56-64; med officer, Can Commun Dis Ctr, 64-73; dir, Bur Viral Dis, 73-74, DIR BUR BIOL, DRUGS DIRECTORATE, 74- *Mem:* Fel Am Acad Microbiol; Can Soc Microbiol; Can Asn Med Microbiol; Am Soc Microbiol; Int Asn Microbiol Socs. *Res:* Antigenic structure of influenza viruses; genetic markers of polioviruses; measles, German measles and mumps vaccines in the laboratory and field trials; slow virus infections. *Mailing Add:* Bur Biol Drugs Directorate Tunney's Pasture Ottawa Can

FUREY, ROBERT LAWRENCE, b Canton, Ohio, June 25, 41; m 64; c 2. ORGANIC CHEMISTRY. *Educ:* Kent State Univ, BS, 63, PhD(org chem), 67. *Prof Exp:* Res chemist, Res Labs, Edgewood Arsenal, Md, 67-69; assoc sr res chemist, 69-73, sr res chemist fuels, 73-80, STAFF RES SCIENTIST, GEN MOTORS RES LABS, 80- *Mem:* Am Chem Soc; Soc Automotive Eng. *Res:* Organic photochemistry of N-substituted imines; effects of conventional and alternative automotive fuels on vehicle emissions and durability. *Mailing Add:* Fuels & Lubricants Dept Gen Motors Res Labs Warren MI 48090

FURFINE, CHARLES STUART, b St Louis, Mo, Apr 26, 36; m 58; c 2. BIOLOGICAL CHEMISTRY. *Educ:* Wash Univ, St Louis, BA, 57, PhD(biochem), 62. *Prof Exp:* Res fel biochem, Albert Einstein Col Med, 62-63, from instr to asst prof, 63-68; asst prof biochem, Georgetown Univ, 68-75; CHEMIST, FOOD & DRUG ADMIN, 75- *Concurrent Pos:* NIH grant, 65-72. *Mem:* Am Chem Soc. *Res:* Effect of substrates on the physical chemical parameters of proteins; nature of allosteric effects and its relation to phenomena observed in vivo. *Mailing Add:* Food & Drug Admin BMD 8757 Georgia Ave Silver Spring MD 20910

FURGASON, ROBERT ROY, b Spokane, Wash, Aug 2, 35; m 64. CHEMICAL ENGINEERING. *Educ:* Univ Idaho, BS, 56, MS, 58; Northwestern Univ, PhD(chem eng), 61. *Prof Exp:* From instr to assoc prof chem eng, 57-67, chmn dept, 63-74, dean, Col Eng, 74-78, PROF CHEM ENG, UNIV IDAHO, 67-, VPRES ACAD AFFAIRS & RES, 78- *Concurrent Pos:* Consult, Minute Maid Corp, 58-59, J R Simplot Co, 63-; NSF grant, 64-; develop consult, B F Goodrich Chem Co, 69-70, continuing consult, 70- *Mem:* Am Inst Chem Engrs; Am Chem Soc; Am Soc Eng Educ; Sigma Xi. *Res:* Heat transfer in chemically reacting systems, especially nitrogen tetroxide-nitrogen dioxide and ozone-oxygen decomposing systems; physical properties of reacting systems. *Mailing Add:* Dept of Chem Eng Univ of Idaho Moscow ID 83843

FURGIUELE, ANGELO RALPH, b Washington, Pa, Apr 14, 29; m 52; c 2. PHARMACOLOGY. *Educ:* Duquesne Univ, BS, 51; Univ Pittsburgh, MS, 59, PhD(pharmacol), 62. *Prof Exp:* Sr res scientist, Squibb Inst Med Res, 62-64, sci coordr biol, Squibb-Int Div, Olin Mathieson Chem Corp, 64-67, dir biol res, E R Squibb & Sons Inc, 67-72; DIR, INT NEW PROD DEVELOP, McNEIL LABS INC, 72- *Mem:* AAAS; NY Acad Sci; Am Pharmaceut Asn; Am Soc Pharmacol & Exp Therapeut; Am Soc Toxicol. *Res:* Central nervous system pharmacology; toxicology; new product planning, development, marketing; product acquisition/licensing; research management. *Mailing Add:* McNeil Labs Inc 500 Off Ctr Fort Washington PA 19034

FURIA, THOMAS EDWARD, b New York, NY, May 5, 34. FOOD SCIENCES, ORGANIC CHEMISTRY. *Educ:* NY Univ, BS, 56. *Prof Exp:* Chemist metal finishing, Oakite Corp, 55-56; tech mgr specialty chem, Ciba-Geigy Corp, 56-73; PRES, INTECHMARK CORP, 72-; e. *Concurrent Pos:* dir food sci, Dynapol, 73-79; sr indust consult, Sambos Restaurants Inc, Int, 79- *Honors & Awards:* Anal Chem Award, Bausch & Lomb, 52; Bond Award, Am Oil Chemists' Soc, 75 & 76. *Mem:* Inst Food Technologists; Am Chem Soc; Am Soc Microbiol; Am Oil Chemists' Soc; Am Soc Enologists. *Res:* Food additives; food ingredients; antioxidants; dyes; antimicrobial agents; chelating agents; flavor and fragrances; functional polymers. *Mailing Add:* PO Box 11201 Palo Alto CA 94306

FURLONG, CLEMENT EUGENE, biochemistry, see previous edition

FURLONG, IRA E, b June 2, 31; US citizen. GEOLOGY. *Educ:* Boston Univ, AB, 53, MS, 54, PhD(geol), 60. *Prof Exp:* Instr geol, Marshall Univ, 58-59; lectr, Boston Univ, 59-60; from instr to assoc prof, 60-69, PROF GEOL, BRIDGEWATER STATE COL, 69- *Mem:* AAAS; Asn Am Geographers; Geol Soc Am; Nat Asn Geol Teachers (vpres, 65, pres, 66). *Res:* Genesis of granite plutons and their relationship on resulting geomorphology. *Mailing Add:* Dept of Geol Bridgewater State Col Bridgewater MA 02324

FURLONG, NORMAN BURR, JR, b Norwalk, Ohio, Jan 6, 31; m 56; c 3. BIOCHEMISTRY. *Educ:* Southern Methodist Univ, AB & BS, 52; Stanford Univ, MS, 54; Univ Tex, PhD(chem), 60. *Prof Exp:* USPHS fels, Biol Div, Oak Ridge Nat Lab, 60-61 & Univ Tex M D Anderson Hosp & Tumor Inst, 61-62; asst biochemist, 62-66, asst prof, 64-66, assoc dean curriculum develop, 68-73, ASSOC PROF BIOCHEM, GRAD SCH BIOMED SCI & ASSOC BIOCHEMIST, UNIV TEX M D ANDERSON HOSP & TUMOR INST, 66- *Mem:* AAAS; Am Asn Cancer Res; Sigma Xi. *Res:* Biosynthesis of DNA, enzymology and mechanism of DNA replication; tumor-host relationships; oligonucleotide biochemistry; nonaqueous subcellular separation methods; mechanisms of carcinogenesis; mechanisms of anti-tumor agents; biomolecular information theory; interdisciplinary curricula in the sciences. *Mailing Add:* Dept Biochem Univ Tex M D Anderson Hosp & Tumor Inst Houston TX 77025

FURLONG, RICHARD W, b Norwalk, Ohio, Mar 30, 29; m 51; c 2. STRUCTURAL ENGINEERING. *Educ:* Southern Methodist Univ, BS, 52; Washington Univ, St Louis, MS, 57; Univ Tex, PhD(struct), 63. *Prof Exp:* Engr, McDonnell Aircraft Corp, Mo, 52-53, Petrol Equip Co, 53-55 & F Ray Martin, Inc, 55-58; from asst prof civil eng & struct to assoc prof civil eng, 58-71, PROF CIVIL ENG, UNIV TEX, AUSTIN, 71- *Concurrent Pos:* Lectr, Washington Univ, 54-56; Erskine fel, Univ Canterbury, New Zealand, 73. *Mem:* Am Soc Civil Engrs; Nat Soc Prof Engrs; Am Concrete Inst. *Res:* Analysis and design of structures, especially reinforced concrete and limit analysis of continuous frames; composite steel-concrete construction; design of metal and concrete structures. *Mailing Add:* Dept of Civil Eng Univ of Tex Austin TX 78712

FURLONG, ROBERT B, b Malone, NY, Jan 19, 34; m 60. MINERALOGY, GEOCHEMISTRY. *Educ:* Harpur Col, BA, 62; Univ Ill, Urbana, MS, 65, PhD(clay mineral), 67. *Prof Exp:* From asst prof to assoc prof, 66-81, PROF GEOL, WAYNE STATE UNIV, 81-, CHMN DEPT, 74- *Mem:* Clay Minerals Soc; Mineral Soc Am; Geochem Soc. *Res:* Use of electron microscopy and electron diffraction to study high temperature changes in the clay minerals; clay mineralogy of deep sea sediment; heavy metal contamination in lake waters; erosion of airless planetary bodies and asteroids by meteorite impact (with Luciano Ronca); computer sciences. *Mailing Add:* Dept Geol Wayne State Univ Detroit MI 48202

FURMAN, DEANE PHILIP, b Richardton, NDak, June 4, 15; m 38; c 3. ENTOMOLOGY, PARASITOLOGY. *Educ:* Univ Calif, BS, 37, PhD(med entom), 42. *Prof Exp:* Entomologist, USPHS, 46; asst prof parasitol & asst entomologist, 46-52, assoc prof & assoc entomologist, 52-58, chmn, div parasitol, 63-72, chmn, Div Entomol & Parasitol, 73-75, PROF & ENTOMOLOGIST, EXP STA, UNIV OF CALIF, BERKELEY, 58- *Concurrent Pos:* NIH spec fel, 64-65; guest investr, US Naval Med Res Unit-3, Egypt, 64-65; chmn, Interdisciplinary Grad Group Parasitol. *Mem:* AAAS; Am Soc Parasitol; Entom Soc Am; Am Soc Trop Med & Hyg; Wildlife Dis Asn. *Res:* Control of parasitic arthropods; systematics of parasitic mites and ticks; biology of helminths; arthropod vectors of diseases and parasites of man and animals. *Mailing Add:* Div of Entom & Parasitol Univ of Calif Berkeley CA 94720

FURMAN, ROBERT HOWARD, b Schenectady, NY, Oct 23, 18; m 45; c 4. RESEARCH ADMINISTRATION. *Educ:* Union Col, NY, AB, 40; Yale Univ, MD, 43. *Prof Exp:* Asst med, Sch Med, Yale Univ, 44-45, from intern to asst resident physician, 44-45; instr physiol & asst med, Sch Med, Vanderbilt Univ, 46-48, from asst resident physician to resident physician, 48-50, from instr to asst prof med, 49-52; from assoc prof to prof res med, Sch Med, Univ Okla, 52-70, head cardiovasc sect, Okla Med Res Found, 52-70, assoc dir res, 58-70; exec dir clin res, Eli Lilly & Co, 70-73, vpres, Lilly Res Labs, 73-76, V PRES, CORP MED AFFAIRS, ELI LILLY & CO, 76-; PROF MED, SCH MED, IND UNIV, INDIANAPOLIS, 70- *Concurrent Pos:* Lilly fel, Sch Med, Vanderbilt Univ, 46-47, Nat Res Coun fel med sci, 47-48; mem cardiovasc study sect, NIH, 60-63; mem heart spec proj comt, Adv Heart Coun, Coun Arteriosclerosis, Am Heart Asn. *Mem:* Endocrine Soc; Soc Exp Biol & Med; Am Physiol Soc; Cent Soc Clin Res; Am Heart Asn. *Res:* Nutritional-endocrinologic-lipid metabolic interrelationships in atherogenesis; clinical pharmacology research. *Mailing Add:* Eli Lilly & Co 307 E McCarty St Indianapolis IN 46285

FURMAN, ROLAND WILLIAM, II, b Albany, NY, Sept 7, 38; m 63; c 2. CLIMATOLOGY. *Educ:* Va Polytech Inst, BS, 64; Colo State Univ, MS, 67, PhD(earth resources), 74. *Prof Exp:* METEOROLOGIST, ROCKY MOUNTAIN FOREST & RANGE EXP STA, 71- *Mem:* Am Meteorol Soc; Sigma Xi. *Res:* Behavioral characteristics of meteorological variables in mountainous terrain. *Mailing Add:* Rocky Mt Forest & Range Exp Sta 240 W Prospect Ft Collins CO 80526

FURMAN, SEYMOUR, b New York, NY, July 12, 31; m 57; c 3. SURGERY. *Educ:* State Univ NY, MD, 55. *Prof Exp:* Intern med, Montefiore Hosp & Med Ctr, NY, 55-56, resident surg, 56-60; resident thoracic surg, Baylor Univ, 62-63; adj attend surgeon, Montefiore Hosp & Med Ctr, 63; from asst prof to assoc prof, 68-77, PROF SURG, ALBERT EINSTEIN COL MED, 77- *Concurrent Pos:* Instr, Dept Surg, Baylor Univ, 63; clin assoc surg, Montefiore Hosp & Med Ctr, 64-66, assoc surgeon, 66-67, assoc attend surgeon, 70-78, attend surgeon, 78-; assoc attend surgeon, Polyclin Med Sch & Hosp, 66-67. *Mem:* AMA; Am Soc Artificial Internal Organs; fel Am Col Surg; Asn Advan Med Instrumentation; Am Heart Asn. *Res:* Cardiothoracic surgery; cardiac pacemaker; cardiac support systems. *Mailing Add:* 111 E 210th St Bronx NY 10467

FURMAN, WALTER L, b Charlotte, NC, Nov 30, 13. MATHEMATICS, PHYSICS. *Educ:* The Citadel, BS, 33; Univ Fla, MS, 41, PhD(math), 61; Univ St Louis, STL, 51. *Prof Exp:* Teacher high sch, SC, 33-34; teacher, Rugby Acad, La, 36-37; instr physics, Spring Hill Col, 43-46 & 51-53; instr phys sci, Univ Fla, 55-57; asst prof, 57-63, assoc prof, 63-66, prof, 66-79, EMER PROF MATH, SPRING HILL COL, PA, 79- *Concurrent Pos:* US State Dept fel, Jesuit Univ, Bogota, 59-60. *Mem:* AAAS; Math Asn Am; Soc Indust & Appl Math; Am Math Soc. *Res:* Mathematics in the Latin American universities. *Mailing Add:* Dept of Math Spring Hill Col Mobile AL 36608

FURNAS, DAVID WILLIAM, b Caldwell, Idaho, Apr 1, 31; m 56; c 3. PLASTIC SURGERY, RECONSTRUCTIVE SURGERY. *Educ:* Univ Calif, AB, 52, MD, 55, MS, 57; Am Bd Surg, dipl, 66; Am Bd Plastic Surg, dipl. *Prof Exp:* Asst pharmacol, Univ Calif, 55, from intern to asst resident surg, Univ Hosp, 55-57; asst resident psychiat, Langley Porter Neuropsychiat Inst, 57-60; resident surg, Gorgas Hosp, CZ, 60-61; resident plastic surg, NY Hosp-Cornell Univ, 61-63; registr, Glasgow Royal Infirmary, 63-64; assoc prof surg, Univ Iowa, 64-69; from assoc prof to prof, 69-80, CLIN PROF, DIV PLASTIC SURG, UNIV CALIF, IRVINE, 80-, CHIEF, DIV PLASTIC SURG, 69- *Concurrent Pos:* NIMH fel psychiat, Langley Porter Neuropsychiat Inst, 57-60; surgeon, African Med & Res Found, Kenya, 72-73; with Balakbayan Med Mission, Mindanao, Philippines, 80, 81. *Honors & Awards:* Res Award, Am Soc Surg of Hand, 70. *Mem:* Soc Maxillofacial Surg; Asn Surg EAfrica; Am Soc Surg of the Hand; Am Soc Plastic & Reconstruct Surg; Am Asn Plastic Surg. *Res:* Surgery and growth of the facial skeleton; microsurgery; nasoorbital surgery; hand surgery; surgery in the tropics; surgical anatomy; experimental transplantation surgery; technology and psychology of esthetic surgery of the face. *Mailing Add:* Univ Calif Div of Plastic Surg Irvine Med Ctr 101 City Dr S Irvine CA 92717

FURNER, RAYMOND LYNN, b Parkersburg, WVa, May 19, 43. PHARMACOLOGY, CHEMOTHERAPY. *Educ:* WVa Univ, BA, 65, MS, 67, PhD(pharmacol), 68. *Prof Exp:* Alexander von Humboldt Stiftung res assoc pharmacol, Univ Tübingen, 69; Nat Acad Sci res assoc, Ames Res Ctr, NASA, Moffett Field, Calif, 70-71; sr pharamacologist, Southern Res Inst, 71-79; DIR GAS CHROMATOGRAPHY/MASS SPECTROMETRY LAB, NEUROSCI PROG, UNIV ALA, BIRMINGHAM, 81- *Concurrent Pos:* Assoc prof pharmacol, Univ Ala, Birmingham, 73- *Mem:* Am Soc Pharmacol & Exp Therapeut; Sigma Xi; AAAS; Am Asn Cancer Res. *Res:* Absorption, distribution, metabolism, excretion and pharmacokinetics of chemotherapeutics used in the treatment of cancer or malaria; analytical biochemistry. *Mailing Add:* Neurosci Prog Univ Ala Birmingham AL 35294

FURNESS, GEOFFREY, b Blackburg, Eng, Aug 2, 19; m 41; c 2. MICROBIOLOGY, SEXUALLY TRANSMITTED DISEASES. *Educ:* Univ Leeds, BSc, 48; Univ Manchester, dipl bact, 49, PhD(microbiol), 51. *Prof Exp:* Lectr microbiol, Trinity Col, Dublin, 52-54; sr scientist, Wright-Fleming Inst, London, 54-59 & Med Res Coun London, 59-62; head dept virol, Twyford Lab, Guinness Brewers, 62-66; PROF MICROBIOL, NJ MED SCH, COL MED & DENT NJ, 66- *Concurrent Pos:* Vis scientist, Dept Microbiol, Univ Pittsburgh, 57-59; vis prof, Commonwealth Sci & Indust Orgn, Parkville, Australia, 71; ed, Vet Microbiol. *Mem:* Am Soc Microbiol; Soc Gen Microbiol; Brit Soc Cell Biol; Brit Inst Biol; Am Asn Univ Prof. *Res:* Classical mycoplasmas; discovered the pathogenic Cory bacterium genitalium and non pathogenic Coryne bacterium pseudogenitalium; discovered the toxic T-inactivator produced by ureaplasmas. *Mailing Add:* Dept of Microbiol NJ Med Sch Col of Med & Dent of NJ Newark NJ 07103

FURNIVAL, GEORGE MASON, b Johnson City, Tenn, May 1, 25; m 46; c 2. FORESTRY. *Educ:* Univ Ga, BSF, 48; Duke Univ, MF, 52, DF, 57. *Prof Exp:* Res forester, Miss State Col, 48-50 & US Forest Serv, 52-55; instr forest mensuration, Sch Forestry, Yale Univ, 55-57, from asst prof to assoc prof, 57-64; dir biomet studies, US Forest Serv, 64-65; PROF FOREST BIOMET, YALE UNIV, 65-, WEYERHAUSER PROF FOREST MGT, 71-, DIR GRAD STUDIES, 77- *Mem:* Soc Am Foresters; Am Statist Asn. *Res:* Application of statistical methods in forestry. *Mailing Add:* Dept of Forest Biomet Yale Univ 1303 A New Haven CT 06520

FURNIVAL, GEORGE MITCHELL, b Winnipeg, Man, July 25, 08; m 37; c 4. GEOLOGY, PETROLEUM. *Educ:* Univ Man, BSc, 29; Queen's Univ, Can, MA, 34; Mass Inst Technol, PhD(econ geol, mining eng), 35. *Prof Exp:* In-chg field parties, Nipissing Mining Co, 29-30; asst geol, Univ Man, 30-31; geol asst, Man Dept Mines, 31; asst geol, Queen's Univ Can, 31-33; geologist, Geol Surv Can, 31-32, Bear Explor & Radium Ltd, 33, Ont Dept Mines, 34 & O'Brien Gold Mines, 35-36; asst supt, Cline Lake Gold Mines, 36-39; geologist, Geol Surv Can, 39-42; sr geologist, Stand Oil Co, BC, Ltd, 42-43; dist geologist, Dom Oil Co, Ltd, 43; dist geologist, Calif Stand Co, 43-45, field supt, 45-46; dir mines, Prov Man, 46-48; supt land & lease, Calif Stand Co, 48-49, mgr land & lease, 49-50, vpres land & legal dir, 50-54, dir & vpres in-chg legal, crude oil sales & pub rels, 54-55, vpres explor & dir, Calif Explor Co, Stand Oil Co, Calif, 55-63; chmn bd & managing dir, W Australian Petrol Pty, Ltd, 63-70; consult, 70-72; vpres opers & dir, 73-75, sr vpres & dir, Brascan Resources Ltd, 75-77. *Concurrent Pos:* Mem, Dom Prov Comt Aerial Photog, Topog, Geol & Geophys Surv, 46-48; secy, Inter-Prov Mines Minister's Conf, Winnipeg, 46; mem Man deleg, Mines Minister's Conf, NS, 47; Alta deleg, BC, 50 & Sask, 51; pres, Dom Oil Co, Ltd, Trinidad, 52-60; vpres & dir, Richmond Co, Peru, 55-63; Cuba Calif Co, Bahama Calif Co, Richmond Oil Co, Columbia, Calif Petrol Guatemala, Calif Ecuador Co & Bolivia Calif Co. *Honors & Awards:* Distinguished Serv Award, Petrol Soc, Can Inst Mining & Metall, 74; Selwyn G Blaylock Gold Medal, Can Inst Mining & Metall, 79. *Mem:* Hon mem Can Inst Mining & Metall; hon mem Eng Inst Can; Am Asn Petrol Geol; fel Royal Soc Can; fel Geol Soc Am. *Res:* Gold, silver, uranium and base metal; ore deposits of the Canadian Precambrian rocks; petroleum geology; sedimentary and structural geology of Western Canada, Caribbean area, Central and South America, Australia, East Indies, Middle East, North and West Africa and Western Europe; coal mines of Western Canada and Sydney Basin, Australia. *Mailing Add:* 1315 Baldwin Crescent SW Calgary Can

FURR, AARON KEITH, b Salisbury, NC, Mar 5, 32; m 58; c 4. NUCLEAR PHYSICS, HEALTH PHYSICS. *Educ:* Catawba Col, BA, 54; Emory Univ, MS, 55; Duke Univ, PhD(nuclear physics), 62. *Prof Exp:* Asst prof physics, 60-63, assoc prof, 63-70, prof physics & nuclear eng, 70-71, dir, Nuclear Lab, 72-75, PROF NUCLEAR SCI & ENG, VA POLYTECH INST & STATE UNIV, 71-, DIR, OFF HEALTH & SAFETY REGULATORY PROGS, 75- *Mem:* Nat Fire Protection Asn; Health Phys Soc; Sigma Xi. *Res:* Nuclear level measurements; neutron spectroscopy; activation analysis. *Mailing Add:* Off Health & Safety Va Polytech Inst & State Univ Blacksburg VA 24061

FURR, HOWARD L(EE), b Pontotoc, Miss, Oct 31, 15; m 46; c 3. CIVIL ENGINEERING. *Educ:* Miss State Col, BS, 41; Agr & Mech Col, Tex, MS, 48; PhD(civil eng), 58. *Prof Exp:* Designer & detailer, Sverdrup & Parcel, Inc, Mo, 49-51; asst prof civil eng, Univ Miss, 51-55, prof, 56-59; prof, Mo Sch Mines, 59-61; PROF CIVIL ENG, TEX A&M UNIV, 62- *Honors & Awards:* Recog Award, Gen Dynamics, 69. *Mem:* Am Soc Civil Engrs; Am Soc Eng Educ; Am Concrete Inst. *Res:* Structural design and mechanics. *Mailing Add:* Dept Civil Eng Tex A&M Univ College Station TX 77843

FURRER, JOHN D, b Walton, Nebr, Jan 23, 20; m 51; c 4. AGRONOMY. *Educ:* Univ Nebr, BS, 47, MS, 52. *Prof Exp:* Exten agronomist, 47-64, exten specialist & assoc prof, 65-70, PESTICIDE SPECIALIST & PROF AGRON, UNIV NEBR, LINCOLN, 70- *Mem:* Weed Sci Soc Am. *Res:* Herbicides for perennial weed control; pre-emergence herbicides for annual weed control in corn, sorghum and soybeans and for lawn weed control. *Mailing Add:* Dept of Agron E Campus Univ of Nebr Lincoln NE 68583

FURROW, STANLEY DONALD, b Bangor, Maine, Mar 6, 34; m 61; c 2. PHYSICAL CHEMISTRY. *Educ:* Univ Maine, BS, 56, MS, 62, PhD(chem), 65. *Prof Exp:* Instr chem, Univ Maine, 63-64; res asst, Exeter Univ, 65-66; asst prof chem, Univ Maine, 66-69; ASST PROF CHEM, PA STATE UNIV, 69- *Mem:* Am Chem Soc. *Res:* Non-electrolyte solution thermodynamics; calorimetry; oscillating chemical reactions. *Mailing Add:* Dept Chem Berks Campus Pa State Univ PO Box 2150 Reading PA 19608

FURRY, BENJAMIN K, b Wadsworth, Ohio, Nov 21, 23; m 45; c 3. RUBBER CHEMISTRY. *Educ:* Muskingum Col, BS, 44. *Prof Exp:* Lab technician adhesives, Firestone Tire & Rubber Co, 44-46; asst chemist, Seiberling Latex Prod, 46-51, chief chemist latex polymers, 51-67; develop scientist, B F Goodrich Chem Co, 67-68; vpres res & develop, Seiberling Latex Prod, 68-73; vpres res, MCM Hosp Supplies Inc, El Reno, 73-79; TECH DIR, LATEX INDUSTS, CHIPPEWA LAKE, OHIO, 79- *Mem:* Am Chem Soc. *Res:* Dipping compounds in natural and synthetic lactices; foam polymers; dipping plastisols; catheters and hospital devices. *Mailing Add:* 751 W St Wadsworth OH 44281

FURRY, DONALD EDWARD, b Cleveland, Ohio, Feb 8, 34; m 60; c 2. ANATOMY, PHYSIOLOGY. *Educ:* John Carroll Univ, BS, 56, MS, 57. *Prof Exp:* Res assoc, Children's Hosp, Cincinnati, 59; aviation physiologist, US Naval Sch Aviation Med, 59-64; instr appl physiol, Col Med, Univ Cincinnati, 64-65; res aviation physiologist, Naval Med Res Inst, 65-69, aerospace physiologist, 69-74; sr physiologist, Naval Regional Med Ctr, 74-76, asst dir training, 76-80, EXEC OFFICER, NAVAL AEROSPACE MED INST, 80- *Mem:* Fel Aerospace Med Asn. *Res:* Microanatomy; primate anatomy; pulmonary physiology; hyperbaric-radiation biology; decompression sickness. *Mailing Add:* Naval Aerospace Med Inst Pensacola FL 32508

FURRY, RONALD B(AY), b Niagara Falls, NY, Oct 22, 31; m 53; c 3. AGRICULTURAL ENGINEERING. *Educ:* Cornell Univ, BS, 53, MS, 55; Iowa State Univ, PhD, 65. *Prof Exp:* Engr drawing & descriptive geometry, 53-56, asst prof agr exten eng, 56-60; from asst prof to assoc prof agr eng, 60-72, teaching & dir planning serv, 60-63, grad field rep & coordr grad instr, 69-73, PROF AGR ENG, CORNELL UNIV, 72- *Concurrent Pos:* NSF sci fac fel, 63-65. *Mem:* Am Soc Agr Engrs; Am Soc Eng Educ. *Res:* Plant and animal structures and environments; controlled atmosphere storage of fruits and vegetables; similitude methodology. *Mailing Add:* Dept of Agr Eng Riley-Robb Hall Cornell Univ Ithaca NY 14853

FURSE, CLARE TAYLOR, b Salt Lake City, Utah, May 18, 31; m 55; c 5. ANALYTICAL CHEMISTRY. *Educ:* Univ Utah, BS, 57, PhD(anal chem), 61. *Prof Exp:* Res chemist, Esso Res & Eng Co, 61-64; assoc prof, 64-74, PROF CHEM, MERCER UNIV, 74- *Mem:* Am Chem Soc. *Res:* Square-wave polarography; electrode kinetics; ultraviolet and fluorescence spectroscopy; separation and identification of polynuclear aromatics. *Mailing Add:* Dept of Chem Mercer Univ Macon GA 31207

FURSHPAN, EDWIN JEAN, b Hartford, Conn, Apr 18, 28; m 57; c 3. NEUROBIOLOGY. *Educ:* Univ Conn, BA, 50; Calif Inst Technol, PhD(animal physiol), 55. *Hon Degrees:* AM, Harvard Med Sch, 67. *Prof Exp:* Fel & hon asst, Univ Col, Univ London, 55-58; instr neurophysiol, Med Sch, Johns Hopkins Univ, 58-59; assoc neurophysiol & neuropharmacol, 59-62; from asst prof to assoc prof, 62-69, PROF NEUROBIOL, HARVARD MED SCH, 69- *Mem:* Soc Neurosci; Am Acad Arts & Sci; hon mem Harvey Soc. *Res:* Electrophysiology and chemistry of excitable cells; cell interaction; development of neuronal properties; control of transmitter choice in neurons. *Mailing Add:* Dept of Neurobiol Harvard Med Sch Boston MA 02115

FURST, ARTHUR, b Minneapolis, Minn, Dec 25, 14; m 40; c 4. CANCER, TOXICOLOGY. *Educ:* Univ Calif, Los Angeles, AB, 37, MA, 40; Stanford Univ, PhD(chem), 48. *Prof Exp:* Asst, Univ Calif, Los Angeles, 38-39; teacher, Pac Mil Acad, 39-40; teacher petrol inspection & org chem, Univ Calif, 41-45; teacher chem, City Col of San Francisco, 40-47; from asst prof to assoc prof, Univ San Francisco, 47-52; from assoc prof to prof med chem, Sch Med, Stanford Univ, 52-61; prof chem & dir, Inst Chem Biol, Univ San Francisco, 61-80, dean, Grad Div, 76-80; CONSULT TOXICOL, 81- *Concurrent Pos:* Res assoc, Mt Zion Hosp, 50-82; clin prof, Col Physicians & Surgeons, Columbia Univ, 69-70; vis fel, Battelle Res Ctr, 74; grants, Res Corp, USPHS & Am Cancer Soc. *Mem:* AAAS; Am Chem Soc; Am Asn Cancer Res; Am Soc Pharmacol & Exp Therapeut; Soc Toxicol. *Res:* Synthesis of possible growth inhibitors; chemotherapy of cancer and virus; carcinogenesis; metals and hydrocarbons. *Mailing Add:* Inst of Chem Biol Univ of San Francisco San Francisco CA 94117

FURST, MERRICK LEE, b New York, NY, Jan 18, 55. COMPUTER THEORY. *Educ:* Bucknell Univ, BS & MS, 76; Cornell Univ, MS & PhD(comput sci), 80. *Prof Exp:* ASST PROF COMPUT SCI, CARNEGIE-MELLON UNIV, 80- *Mem:* Am Math Soc; Asn Comput Mach. *Res:* Algorithm design and computational complexity with an emphasis on graph algorithms; isomorphism testing and proving lower bounds. *Mailing Add:* Hall Sci Dept Comput Sci Carnegie-Mellon Univ Pittsburgh PA 15213

FURST, MILTON, b New York, NY, Sept 10, 21; m 45; c 2. PHYSICS. *Educ:* City Col New York, BS, 42; NY Univ, BS, 48, PhD, 52. *Prof Exp:* Physicist, NY Naval Shipyard, 47-50; asst physics, NY Univ, 50-52; from instr to assoc prof, 55-67, PROF PHYSICS, HUNTER COL, 67- *Concurrent Pos:* Res assoc, NY Univ, 52-63, res scientist, 63-67; consult & researcher, Saclay Nuclear Res Ctr, France, 61-62; vis res prof, Oakland Univ, 74-75. *Mem:* AAAS; Am Phys Soc. *Res:* Fluorescence and energy transfer in liquid organic systems under high energy and light excitations. *Mailing Add:* Dept of Physics Hunter Col New York NY 10021

FURST, ULRICH RICHARD, b Vienna, Austria, Jan 18, 13; nat US; m 44; c 2. PHYSICS. *Educ:* Inst Tech, Vienna, EE, 35, PhD(physics), 38. *Prof Exp:* Engr, Keystone Mfg Co, Mass, 38-40 & Rehtron Corp, Ill, 40-41; electronic engr, Offner Electronics, 41-42; chief electronic engr, Russell Elec Co, 42-46; pres, Furst Electronics, Inc, 46-56; chief electronics engr, Elec Eye Equip Co, 56-58; chief missile opers unit, Bomarc Proj, Aero-Space Div, Boeing Co, 58-62; sect mgr, Syst Eng Dept, Missile Systs Div, 62-73, SR STAFF ENGR, ELECTRO-OPTICAL & DATA SYSTS GROUP, HUGHES AIRCRAFT CO, 73- *Concurrent Pos:* Lectr, Northwestern Univ, 46-49. *Mem:* Sr mem Inst Elec & Electronics Eng. *Res:* Military electronics systems. *Mailing Add:* 3620 Weslin Ave Sherman Oaks CA 91623

FURSTMAN, LAWRENCE L, b Chicago, Ill, Feb 28, 09; m 33; c 2. ORTHODONTICS, ANATOMY. *Educ:* Univ Southern Calif, DDS, 29, MS, 64, PhD(anat), 69; Univ Ill, cert, 34. *Prof Exp:* Instr histol, Sch Dent, Univ Southern Calif, 34-36, spec lectr, Grad Sch Orthod, 61-69, res assoc anat, 69-70; lectr, 70-71, adj prof anat, 71-80, RES ANATOMIST, SCH DENT, CTR HEALTH SCI, UNIV CALIF, LOS ANGELES, 80- *Concurrent Pos:* Fel anat, Sch Med, Univ Southern Calif, 61-69; consult, Cedars Sinai Hosp, 66-; res assoc, Univ Southern Calif, 69- *Honors & Awards:* Los Angeles County Health Dept Medal, 29; Milo Hellman Res Award, Am Asn Orthod, 63. *Mem:* Am Asn Orthod; fel Am Col Dent; Am Asn Anatomists; Int Asn Dent Res; Int Soc Cranio-facial Biol. *Res:* Growth and development of the face and head; retrograde axonal transport; development and normal age changes in the temporo-mandibular joint and hormonal, nutritional and functional disturbances. *Mailing Add:* 6-3-048 Ctr for Health Sci Univ of Calif Sch of Dent Los Angeles CA 90024

FURTADO, DOLORES, b West Warwick, RI, July 4, 38. MEDICAL MICROBIOLOGY. *Educ:* Cornell Univ, BS, 60; Univ Mich, MS, 63, PhD(bact), 66. *Prof Exp:* Asst prof, 70-76, ASSOC PROF MICROBIOL, MED SCH, UNIV KANS, 76- *Concurrent Pos:* NIH fel, Guy's Hosp Med Sch, London, 66-67 & Yale Univ Sch Med, 67-70; fel, Nat Kidney Found, 69; mem kidney coun, Am Heart Asn. *Mem:* Am Soc Microbiol; Am Soc Nephrol; Int Soc Nephrol. *Res:* Pathogenesis of bacterial infections; experimental urinary tract infections; host-parasite interactions during bactermia; asymptomatic bacterial infections. *Mailing Add:* Dept of Microbiol Univ of Kans Med Ctr Kansas City KS 66103

FURTADO, VICTOR CUNHA, b Elizabeth, NJ, Mar 21, 37; m 58; c 4. HEALTH PHYSICS, ENVIRONMENTAL HEALTH ENGINEERING. *Educ:* Newark Col Eng, BSCE, 58; Univ Calif, Berkeley, MBiorad, 63; NY Univ, PhD(civil eng, environ health sci), 71. *Prof Exp:* Sanit & indust hyg engr, 810th Med Group, Fairchild AFB, Wash, 58-61, health physicist, 392nd Med Group, Vandenberg AFB, Calif, 63-64 & 6595th Aerospace Test Wing, 64-65, bioenviron engr, Aerospace Med Div, Brooks AFB, Tex, 65-66, Health Physicist, Radiol Health Lab, Wright-Patterson AFB, 69-72, bioenviron engr, 1st Med Serv Wing, Clark AB, Philippines, 72-75, Sch Aerospace Med, 75-78, SR BIOENVIRON ENG, OFF AIR FORCE SURG GEN, US AIR FORCE, BROOKS AFB, TEX, 78-, ASSOC CHIEF, BIOMED SCI CORPS, 79- *Mem:* Health Physics Soc; Am Conf Govt Indust Hygienists. *Res:* Evaluation of low levels of iodine-131 in nuclear power reactor environments. *Mailing Add:* Air Force Med Serv Ctr Wright-Patterson AFB Brooks AFB TX 78235

FURTAK, THOMAS ELTON, b Ord, Nebr, May 23, 49; m 71; c 3. SURFACE PHYSICS. *Educ:* Univ Nebr, Lincoln, BS, 71; Iowa State Univ, PhD(solid state physics), 75. *Prof Exp:* Res fel photoelectrochem physics, Ames Lab, ERDA, 75-77; leader electrochem group, Solid State Physics Div, Ames Lab, Dept Energy, 77-80; ASSOC PROF PHYSICS, RENSSELAER POLYTECH INST, 80- *Mem:* Am Phys Soc; Am Chem Soc; Electrochem Soc; Sigma Xi. *Res:* Physics of interfaces, particularly the solid and aqueous-solution interface; monochromatic light as a quantum probe in the surface; in situ photoemission; electrochemical modulation spectroscopy; Raman spectroscopy; photoelectrocatalysis. *Mailing Add:* Rensselaer Polytech Inst Troy NY 12181

FURTER, W(ILLIAM) F(REDERICK), b North Bay, Ont, Apr 5, 31; m 66; c 3. CHEMICAL ENGINEERING. *Educ:* Royal Mil Col Can, RMC, 53; Univ Toronto, BASc, 54; Mass Inst Technol, SM, 55; Univ Toronto, PhD(chem eng), 58; Nat Defence Col Can, NDC, 70. *Prof Exp:* Asst instr, Mass Inst Technol, 54-55 & Univ Toronto, 55-58; res engr & sr tech investr, Res & Develop Dept, Du Pont of Can Ltd, 58-60; from asst prof to assoc prof chem eng, 60-66, head, Chem Eng Div, Dept Chem & Chem Eng, 60-80, secy, Grad Sch, 67-80, actg dean grad studies & res, 78-79, PROF CHEM ENG, ROYAL MIL COL CAN, 66-, DEAN, CAN FORCES MIL COL & CHMN, EXTEN DIV, 80- *Concurrent Pos:* Spec lectr, Royal Mil Col Can, 58-60; consult engr, 60-; res grant, Defence Res Bd Can, 63-, NSF & Petrol Res Fund; Dominion scholar; consult engr, Hexcel Corp, Calif, Air Liquide Ltd, Can & Union Carbide Corp, WVa. *Honors & Awards:* Eng Inst Can Prize; Royal Can Sch Mil Eng Prize. *Mem:* Fel Chem Inst Can; Can Soc Chem Engrs; Can Nuclear Asn; Am Nuclear Soc. *Res:* Vapor-liquid phase equilibria; solution thermodynamics; extractive distillation; gas-liquid tray design; packed tower design; nuclear chemical engineering; engineering economics and administration. *Mailing Add:* Dept of Chem Eng Royal Mil Col of Can Kingston Can

FURTH, DAVID GEORGE, b Cleveland, Ohio, May 10, 45. BIO-SYSTEMATICS. *Educ:* Miami Univ, BA, 67; Ohio State Univ, MS, 69; Cornell Univ, PhD(entomol), 76. *Prof Exp:* Teaching asst zool, Ohio State Univ, 67-69; nusery inspector plant pests, Ohio Dept Agr, 70; teaching asst entmol, Cornell Univ, 70-72; cur insects entomol, Tel Aviv Univ, 72-74; lectr biol, Yale Univ, 76-77; fel entomol, Hebrew Univ Jerusalem, 77-79; consult, aquatic entomol, Nature Reserve Authority Israel, 80-81; MUS ASST, CUR ENTOMOL, PEABODY MUS NATURAL HIST, YALE UNIV, 81- *Mem:* Sigma Xi; Entomol Soc Am; Coleopterist's Soc; Xerces Soc. *Res:* Systematics; food plant ecology; biogeography; evolution of Leaf Beetles (Chrysomelidae); general biogeography of the Middle East; faunistics and ecology of aquatic insects, especially Hemiptera; insect co-evolution with plants, including ferns. *Mailing Add:* Dept Entomol Peabody Mus Natural Hist Yale Univ PO Box 6666 New Haven CT 06511

FURTH, EUGENE DAVID, b Philadelphia, Pa, Jan 25, 29; m 52; c 2. MEDICINE, ENDOCRINOLOGY. *Educ:* Wesleyan Univ, AB, 50; Cornell Univ, MD, 54; Am Bd Internal Med, dipl. *Prof Exp:* Asst prof med & radiobiol, Col Med, Cornell Univ, 63-67, asst dir radioisotope lab, NY Hosp, 62-67; from assoc prof to prof med, Albany Med Col, 67-75; PROF & CHMN, DEPT MED, SCH MED, E CAROLINA UNIV, 75- *Mem:* Am Fedn Clin Res; Am Thyroid Asn; Endocrine Soc. *Res:* Thyroid gland physiology and pathophysiology. *Mailing Add:* Dept of Med E Carolina Univ Greenville NC 27834

FURTH, F(REDERICK) R(AYMOND), b Seattle, Wash, Oct 13, 01; m. ELECTRONICS. *Educ:* US Naval Acad, BS, 24; Yale Univ, MS, 32. *Prof Exp:* Ship assignments, US Navy, 24-30, radio off, battleship div, 32-35, naval commun, 35-37, US Fleet Commun Off, 38-40, Off Chief Naval Opers, 40-43, radar mission, UK, 43, dep chief electronics, 44-46, electronics off, Puget Sound Naval Shipyard, 46-48, dir, Naval Res Lab, 49-52; asst chief, Bur Ships, 52-53, chief, Naval res, 54-56; vpres, Farnsworth Electronics Co, 56-57; asst dir res & develop, Int Tel & Tel Co, 57-58, vpres & dir res & develop, 58-60, vpres for mil electronics develop & gen mgr, Farnsworth Res Corp, 60-62, vchmn & gen mgr, 62-67; independent consult, 68-78; RETIRED. *Concurrent Pos:* Mem, Inst Aeronaut Sci. *Mem:* Fel AAAS; Am Inst Aeronaut & Astronaut; Sigma Xi; Soc Naval Archit & Marine Engrs; Inst Elec & Electronics Engrs. *Mailing Add:* Penic Mem Home Box 2001 Southern Pines NC 28387

FURTH, FRANK WILLARD, b Trenton, NJ, Sept 27, 22; m 45; c 4. INTERNAL MEDICINE, HEMATOLOGY. *Educ:* Rutgers Univ, BS, 43; Univ Rochester, MD, 47; Am Bd Internal Med, dipl, 56. *Prof Exp:* Instr radiation biol, Univ Rochester, 50-52, instr internal med, 54-56; asst prof & coordr cancer ed, Col Med, State Univ NY Upstate Med Ctr, 56-62; dir med serv & educ, Community Gen Hosp Greater Syracuse, 62-67; assoc prof med, State Univ NY Upstate Med Ctr, 67-68; asst regional health dir, Syracuse Regional Off, NY State Dept Health, 68-77; dir pharmaceut med serv, 77-79, VPRES, DRUG REGULATORY AFFAIRS, MEAD JOHNSON PHARMACEUT DIV, MEAD JOHNSON & CO, 79- *Mem:* Am Col Physicians. *Mailing Add:* Mead Johnson Pharmaceut Div 2404 Pennsylvania St Evansville IN 47721

FURTH, HAROLD PAUL, b Vienna, Austria, Jan 13, 30; nat US; div; c 1. PHYSICS. *Educ:* Harvard Univ, AB, 51, PhD, 60. *Prof Exp:* Physicist, Lawrence Radiation Lab, Univ Calif, Berkeley, 56-67; co-head, Exp Div, 67-78, assoc dir & head res dept, 78-80, prog dir, 80-81, DIR, PLASMA PHYSICS LAB, PRINCETON UNIV, 81-, PROF ASTROPHYS SCI, 67- *Concurrent Pos:* Assoc Ed, Review of Modern Physics, 75- *Honors & Awards:* E O Lawrence Mem Award, AEC, 74. *Mem:* Nat Acad Sci; Fel Am Phys Soc. *Res:* Plasma physics; controlled thermonuclear research, particularly toroidal confinement experiments, theory of nonideal magneto-hydrodynamic stability, optimization of magnetic confinement configurations, design of toroidal magnetic fusion reactors. *Mailing Add:* Plasma Physics Lab Princeton Univ Princeton NJ 08544

FURTH, JACOB, b Miskolcz, Hungary, 96; nat US. CANCER, EXPERIMENTAL PATHOLOGY. *Educ:* Ger Univ, Prague, MD, 21; Am Bd Path, dipl. *Hon Degrees:* DSc, Univ Pa, 68. *Prof Exp:* Asst hyg inst, Ger Univ, 21-22; fel Henry Phipps Inst, Pa, 24-25, from asst to assoc, 25-32; pathologist med col, Cornell Univ, 32-33, from asst prof to assoc prof, 33-45, prof, 45-49; chief lab, Br 10, US Vet Admin, 47-49, chief path & physiol sect, Biol Div, AEC, Oak Ridge Nat Lab, 49-53; assoc dir res, Children's Cancer Res Found, Harvard Med Sch, 54-59; dir exp path, Roswell Park Mem Inst, Buffalo, 59-61; prof, 61-67, EMER PROF PATH & SPEC LECTR, COLUMBIA UNIV, 67- *Concurrent Pos:* Clin prof, Harvard Med Sch, 58-59; dir path lab, Francis Delafield Hosp, 61-68; actg dir inst cancer res, Columbia Univ, 68-69. *Honors & Awards:* AMA Gold Medal, 31; Bertner Award, MD, Anderson Hosp & Tumor Inst, 58; Robert Roessler de Villiers Award, 59; Semmelweis Medal, 62; Clowes Medal, Am Asn Cancer Res, 62; Rosenthal Award, AAAS, 67; Alessandro Pascoli Prize, Perugia Int Cancer Conf, 73; Rovs-Whipple Award, Am Asn Pathologists & Bacteriologists, 74. *Mem:* Nat Acad Sci; AAAS; Am Asn Cancer Res (pres, 57-58); Am Soc Exp Path (pres, 59-60). *Res:* Typhoid; tuberculosis; antigens; leukemia; blood; tumors; general pathology; radiation biology; endocrine neoplasia. *Mailing Add:* Inst of Cancer Res 99 Ft Washington Ave New York NY 10032

FURTH, JOHN J, b Philadelphia, Pa, Jan 25, 29; m 59; c 2. BIOCHEMISTRY, PATHOLOGY. *Educ:* Cornell Univ, BA, 50. *Prof Exp:* Intern med path, Cornell Univ, 58-59; resident path, NY Univ, 59-60; fel biochem, Sch Med, NY Univ, 60-62; assoc, 62-65, asst prof, 65-68, assoc prof, 68-79, PROF PATH, SCH MED, UNIV PA, 79- *Concurrent Pos:* USPHS fel, 60-62, res career develop award, 62-71; mem path B study sect, NIH, 73-77; Eleanor Roosevelt fel, Am Cancer Soc-Int Union Against Cancer, 77-78; vis prof biochem, Aberdeen Univ, 77-78; assoc ed, Cancer Res, 77- *Honors & Awards:* Roche Award, Sch Med, Duke Univ, 56. *Res:* Enzymic synthesis of RNA and DNA. *Mailing Add:* Dept of Path Univ of Pa Sch of Med Philadelphia PA 19174

FURTH, MARK EDWARD, molecular biology, genetics, see previous edition

FURUKAWA, DAVID HIROSHI, b San Pedro, Calif, Mar 26, 38; m 64; c 5. CHEMICAL ENGINEERING. *Educ:* Univ Colo, BSChE, 60. *Prof Exp:* Chem engr saline water demineralization sect, Bur Reclamation, 60-64, supvr sect, 64-66, head sect, 66-69; mgr res & develop, Havens Int, 69-70, mgr com develop dept, Calgon-Havens Systs, 70-73; mgr com develop, UOP, Inc, Fluid Systs Div, 73-76; consult chem engr, Furukawa & Assocs, 76-78; prin chem engr, Boyle Eng Corp, 78-81; DIR MKT, RESOURCES CONSERV CO, 81- *Mem:* Am Inst Chem Engrs; Am Chem Soc; Am Water Works Asn; Water Pollution Control Fedn; Int Desalination & Environ Asn. *Res:* Desalting, particularly reverse osmosis but also electrodialysis and transport depletion; characterization of permselective and semipermeable membranes. *Mailing Add:* Resources Conserv Co 9747 Business Park Ave San Diego CA 92131

FURUKAWA, GEORGE TADAHARU, b Calif, May 25, 21; m 51; c 2. THERMODYNAMICS. *Educ:* Cent Col, Mo, AB, 43; Univ Wis, PhD(chem), 48. *Prof Exp:* Instr chem & physics, Cent Col, Mo, 43-45; PHYSICIST, BUR STANDARDS, 48- *Concurrent Pos:* Prof lectr, George Washington Univ, 64-68. *Mem:* Am Chem Soc; Am Phys Soc; Calorimetry Conf (secy-treas, 60-63). *Res:* Low temperature heat capacity; vapor pressure; latent heats; surface tension; gas heat capacity; heterogeneous phase equilibria; temperature scale and thermometry; investigation of platinum resistance thermometry and thermometric fixed points. *Mailing Add:* 1712 Evelyn Dr Rockville MD 20852

FURUKAWA, TOSHIHARU, b Japan, Mar 22, 48; m 77. MATERIALS SCIENCE, MATERIALS ENGINEERING. *Educ:* Osaka Univ, Japan, BS, 70; Pa State Univ, MS, 73, PhD PhD(solid state sci), 77. *Prof Exp:* Proj assoc mat sci, Pa State Univ, 77-80; MEM STAFF, IBM CORP, EFISHKILL, 80- *Mem:* Am Ceramic Soc. *Res:* Structure and crystallization of amorphous materials; characterizations and engineering applications of refractory, luminescence and semiconducting materials; surface and interfacial science; interactions of organic and inorganic materials. *Mailing Add:* Dept 49F Bldg 300-40E IBM Corp Hopewell Junction NY 12533

FURUMOTO, AUGUSTINE S, b Honolulu, Hawaii, Aug 12, 27; m 65; c 2. SEISMOLOGY. *Educ:* Univ Dayton, BS, 49; Univ Tokyo, MSc, 55; St Louis Univ, PhD(geophys), 61. *Prof Exp:* Asst prof geophys & seismol, 61-67, assoc prof geophys, 67-71, PROF GEOPHYS & SEISMOLOGIST, INST GEOPHYS, UNIV HAWAII, HONOLULU, 71- *Mem:* AAAS; Am Geophys Union; Seismol Soc Am; Nat Asn Corrosion Engrs; Sigma Xi. *Res:* Crustal and upper mantle exploration by explosion methods in the Pacific area; seismicity of Hawaii; geophysical exploration for geothermal resources. *Mailing Add:* Univ of Hawaii Inst of Geophys 2525 Correa Rd Honolulu HI 96822

FURUMOTO, HORACE WATARU, b Honolulu, Hawaii, Dec 13, 31; m 59; c 2. PHYSICS. *Educ:* Calif Inst Technol, BSc, 55; Ohio State Univ, PhD(physics), 63. *Prof Exp:* Mem staff physics, Avco Systs Div, Avco Corp, 63-66 & NASA, 66-70; mem staff elec eng, US Dept Transp, 70-72; mem staff physics, Avco Everett Res Lab, Inc, 72-77; PRES, CANDELA CORP, NATICK, MASS, 77- *Mem:* AAAS; Am Phys Soc; Optical Soc Am; Inst Elec & Electronics Engrs. *Res:* Laser research; laser applications; tunable dye lasers; pulsed discharge circuits. *Mailing Add:* 14 Woodridge Rd Wellesley MA 02181

FURUMOTO, WARREN AKIRA, b Honolulu, Hawaii, Dec 17, 34; m 62. PLANT SCIENCE. *Educ:* Calif Inst Technol, BS, 57; Univ Calif, Los Angeles, PhD(bot sci), 61. *Prof Exp:* Instr bot, Univ Chicago, 60-62; from asst prof to assoc prof, 62-70, PROF BIOL, CALIF STATE UNIV, NORTHRIDGE, 70- *Concurrent Pos:* NSF res grants, 60-65. *Mem:* AAAS. *Res:* Studies on the infective process of tobacco mosaic virus. *Mailing Add:* Dept of Biol Calif State Univ Northridge CA 91324

FURUSAWA, EIICHI, b Japan, Jan 25, 28; m; c 1. CHEMOTHERAPY, VIROLOGY. *Educ:* Osaka Univ, MD, 54, PhD, 59. *Prof Exp:* Res assoc, Res Inst Microbial Dis, Osaka Univ, 55-59; fel microbiol, Stanford Univ, 59-61, res assoc, 61-64; assoc pharmacologist, Pac Biomed Ctr, 64-65, assoc prof, 65-69, PROF PHARMACOL, SCH MED, UNIV HAWAII, MANOA, 69- *Concurrent Pos:* Fel microbiol, Columbia Univ, 60; NIH res grant, 67-79; Leukemia Soc res grant, 70-71; AMA res grant, 71-75; Am Cancer Soc res grant, 71-78. *Mem:* Soc Exp Biol & Med; Am Asn Cancer Res; Am Soc Microbiol; Soc Japanese Virol. *Res:* Virus and cancer chemotherapy and search for antiviral and anticancer agents from natural products. *Mailing Add:* Sch of Med Univ of Hawaii Honolulu HI 96822

FURUTA, TOKUJI, b La Mesa, Calif, Mar 3, 25. ENVIRONMENTAL HORTICULTURE. *Educ:* Ohio State Univ, BS, 48, MSc, 49, PhD(hort), 51. *Prof Exp:* Asst, Ohio State Univ, 49-51; assoc prof hort, Auburn Univ, 51-62, prof, 62-65; EXTEN SPECIALIST ORNAMENTAL HORT, UNIV CALIF, RIVERSIDE, 65- *Concurrent Pos:* Assoc horticulturist, Agr Exp Sta, Auburn Univ, 51-62, horticulturist, 62-65; indust consult. *Mem:* Fel AAAS; Int Plant Propagators Soc; Am Soc Hort Sci. *Res:* Plants for environmental plantings and maintenance; human behavior as a basis for use of plants in human environments; nutrition and propagation of floricultural and ornamental plants; systems analysis for plant production; economics of production and marketing; management of nursery businesses. *Mailing Add:* Batchelor Hall Exten Univ Calif Riverside CA 92502

FUSARO, BERNARD A, b Charleston, WVa, Aug 9, 24; m 66. MATHEMATICS. *Educ:* Swarthmore Col, BA, 50; Columbia Univ, MA, 54; Univ Md, PhD(math), 65. *Prof Exp:* Instr physics & math, Ripon Col, 51-52; asst math, Columbia Univ, 52-54; instr, Middlebury Col, 54-57 & Univ Md, 57-61; vis asst prof, Univ Okla, 61-62; asst prof to assoc prof, Univ SFla, 62-67; prof & chmn dept, Queens Col, NC, 67-69, Dana prof, 69-74; PROF MATH & CHMN DEPT, SALISBURY STATE COL, MD, 74- *Concurrent Pos:* Lectr, NSF Inst, Univ Okla, 61-62; Fulbright prof, Nat Taiwan Univ, 70-71; vis adj prof, Dept Environ Eng Sci, Univ Fla, 80-81. *Mem:* Am Math Soc; Math Asn Am; Soc Indust & Appl Math. *Res:* Linear and hyperbolic second order differential equations, particularly the generalized Euler-Poisson-Darboux equation; harmonic Riemannian spaces. *Mailing Add:* Dept of Math Sci Salisbury State Col Salisbury MD 21801

FUSARO, CRAIG ALLEN, b San Jose, Calif, July 19, 48. POPULATION BIOLOGY. *Educ:* San Jose State Univ, BA, 70; Univ Calif, Santa Barbara, MA, 73, PhD(biol), 77. *Prof Exp:* Assoc scientist, Ecomar, Inc, 78- *Mem:* Crustacean Soc. *Res:* Population ecology of marine intertidal crustaceans; community ecology of marine subtidal kelp beds and reefs; fate-and-effects studies of exploratory drilling fluids discharge. *Mailing Add:* 435 El Sueno Santa Barbara CA 93110

FUSARO, RAMON MICHAEL, b Brooklyn, NY, Mar 6, 27; m 51; c 2. DERMATOLOGY. *Educ:* Univ Minn, BA, 49, BS, 51, MD, 53, MS, 58, PhD, 65. *Prof Exp:* Intern, Minneapolis Gen Hosp, Minn, 53-54; resident, Minneapolis Gen Hosp-Univ Minn Hosp, 54-57; from instr to assoc prof dermat, Med Sch, Univ Minn, 57-70; prof & chmn dept, Med Ctr, Univ Nebr-Omaha, 70-75; PROF DERMAT & CHMN DEPT, CREIGHTON UNIV & DIR DERMAT PROG, CREIGHTON-NEBR UNIVS HEALTH FOUND, 75- *Mem:* Am Acad Dermat; Am Fedn Clin Res; AMA; Soc Invest Dermat. *Res:* Clinical dermatology; carbohydrate metabolism; photosensitivity, immunology. *Mailing Add:* Dermat Prog 4004 Conkling Hall Creighton-Nebr Univs Health Found Omaha NE 68105

FUSCALDO, ANTHONY ALFRED, b New York, NY, Nov 11, 39; m 63; c 2. VIROLOGY, GENETICS. *Educ:* St John's Univ, NY, BS, 61, MS, 63; Ind Univ, Bloomington, PhD(microbiol), 67. *Prof Exp:* Prin investr viral genetics, US Army Biol Labs, 67-71; res assoc, Merrell Nat Labs Div, Richardson-Merrell, Inc, 71-74; asst prof & head res labs, Dept Med Hemat & Oncol & asst prof, Dept Biol Chem, 74-80, PROF & ADMINR, DEPT HEMAT & ONCOL, HAHNEMANN MED COL & HOSP, 80- *Mem:* AAAS; Tissue Culture Asn; Soc Occup & Environ Health; Am Soc Microbiol. *Res:* Biochemical and biophysical analysis of viruses; viral replication, morphogenesis and genetics; virus purification; isolation and characterization of oncornaviruses from human tissue specimens; tissue culture growth of human leukemic cells. *Mailing Add:* 230 N Broad St Philadelphia PA 19102

FUSCALDO, KATHRYN ELIZABETH, b New York, NY, Jan 4, 31. GENETICS, MEDICAL CYTOGENETICS. *Educ:* Queens Col, NY, BS, 52; Hofstra Col, MA, 55; Mich State Univ, PhD, 60. *Prof Exp:* Jr bacteriologist immunol, NY State Dept Health, 52-53; asst, Carnegie Inst, 55-56; asst genetics, Mich State Univ, 56-60; asst prof, St John's Univ, NY, 60-63; asst prof genetics, 63-65, assoc prof med, 74-76, assoc prof anat, 65-77, res assoc prof microbiol, 66-75, PROF MED ONCOL, HEMATOL & PATH, HAHNEMANN MED COL, 78-, ASSOC DIR & ADMINR CANCER INST, 73- & DIR MED GENETICS, 73- *Concurrent Pos:* Instr, Hofstra Col, 55-56; guest investr, Carnegie Inst, 61-63; vis lectr, Med Col Pa, 71-74. *Mem:* Am Asn Cancer Inst; Am Asn Cancer Res; AAAS; Genetics Soc Am; Am Soc Microbiol. *Res:* Cytogenetics of myeloproliferative diseases; biochemical genetics; oncogenetics; immunogenetics; genetic control of protein synthesis. *Mailing Add:* Div of Genetics Hahnemann Med Col Philadelphia PA 19102

FUSCO, GABRIEL CARMINE, b Pittsburgh, Pa, Nov 11, 36; m 60; c 3. ORGANIC CHEMISTRY. *Educ:* Duquesne Univ, BS, 58, MS, 60; Univ Colo, PhD(org chem), 65. *Prof Exp:* Res chemist, Jackson Lab, E I du Pont de Nemours & Co, NJ, 65-67; asst prof, 67-68, assoc prof, 68-71, PROF CHEM, CALIFORNIA STATE COL, 71- *Mem:* Am Chem Soc; The Chem Soc. *Res:* Carbonium ion rearrangements; addition and elimination reactions; substitution reactions of saturated carbons. *Mailing Add:* Dept of Chem California State Col California PA 15419

FUSCO, MADELINE M, b Waterbury, Conn, Nov 7, 24. PHYSIOLOGY. *Educ:* Ohio State Univ, BS, 48, MS, 49; Univ Pa, PhD(physiol), 59. *Prof Exp:* Vis lectr physiol, Goucher Col, 49-50, instr, 50-52; asst instr, Univ Pa, 52-55; instr, Vassar Col, 54-55; from instr to assoc prof, Univ Mich, 59-67; assoc prof, Med Col Pa, 67-71; PROF ANAT SCI, SCH BASIC SCI, STATE UNIV NY STONY BROOK, 71-, ASSOC DEAN, 77- *Mem:* AAAS; Am Physiol Soc. *Res:* Animal calorimetry; temperature regulation, especially in hypothalamus; temperature regulation; neural control of energy exchange; behavior; neurophysiology. *Mailing Add:* Dept of Anat Sch of Basic Sci State Univ of NY Stony Brook NY 11790

FUSCO, ROBERT ANGELO, b Middletown, NY, Aug 22, 41; m 64; c 2. ENTOMOLOGY. *Educ:* Univ Ky, BS, 64, MS, 67; Pa State Univ, PhD(entom), 71. *Prof Exp:* Entomologist, Md State Bd Agr, 71-72; ENTOMOLOGIST, PA DEPT ENVIRON RESOURCES, 72- *Mem:* Sigma Xi; Entom Soc Am; Soc Am Foresters. *Res:* Parasitoid-host interactions; parasitoid behavior; parasitoid biology; laboratory rearing and colonization techniques. *Mailing Add:* Pa Dept Environ Resources 34 Airport Dr Middletown PA 17057

FUSELER, JOHN WILLIAM, b Columbia, SC, May 3, 43; m 73. CELL BIOLOGY. *Educ:* Ga Inst Technol, BS, 67; Univ Pa, PhD(biol), 73. *Prof Exp:* Res assoc cell biol, Univ Pa, 73-75; SR RES INVESTR CELL BIOL, UNIV TEX MED BR, 75-; MEM FAC CELL BIOL, UNIV TEX HEALTH SCI CTR DALLAS, 78- *Mem:* Am Soc Cell Biol; Am Inst Biol Sci; Bot Soc Am. *Res:* Mechanism of Mitosis in mammalian tissue culture cells; effect of temperature and various drugs on the microtubule assembly-disassembly process involved in chromosome movement. *Mailing Add:* Dept of Cell Biol 5323 Harry Hine Blvd Dallas TX 75235

FUSHIMI, FRED CHIKASHI, computer science, see previous edition

FUSHTEY, STEPHEN GEORGE, b Wasel, Alta, Sept 17, 24; m 51; c 4. PLANT PATHOLOGY. *Educ:* Univ Alta, BSc, 47, MSc, 50; Univ London, PhD(plant path), 53. *Prof Exp:* Asst plant pathologist, Plant Path Lab, Can Dept Agr, 47-51; lectr bot & plant path, Univ Guelph, 53-57, from asst prof to assoc prof, 64-80; RES SCIENTIEST, AGR CAN, 80- *Mem:* Am Phytopath Soc; Soc Nematol; Can Phytopath Soc; Agr Inst Can. *Res:* Diseases of cereal crops; nematology; turf grass diseases. *Mailing Add:* Agr Can Res Sta PO Box 1000 Agassiz BC V0M 1A0 Can

FUSON, ERNEST WAYNE, b Cawood, Ky, Oct 13, 47; m 69; c 2. IMMUNOLOGY. *Educ:* Lee Col, Tenn, BS, 69; Univ Tenn, Knoxville, MS, 72, PhD(zool), 75. *Prof Exp:* ASST PROF MED BIOL, MEM RES CTR, UNIV TENN, KNOXVILLE, 78- *Concurrent Pos:* Nat Res Serv award, Nat Cancer Inst-NIH, 77-78. *Mem:* Am Asn Immunologists; Int Soc Exp Hemat; Soc Exp Biol & Med. *Res:* Immune response, cellular and humoral to tumor induction and development; mechanisms of tissue damage in autoimmune diseases; mechanisms of leukocyte-mediated cytotoxicity, including target recognition; effector cell activation and suppression; mechanisms of catalysis. *Mailing Add:* Univ Tenn Mem Res Ctr 1924 Alcoa Hwy Knoxville TN 37920

FUSON, NELSON, b Canton, China, Sept 4, 13; US citizen; m 45; c 2. MOLECULAR SPECTROSCOPY. *Educ:* Col Emporia, AB, 34; Univ Kans, MA, 35; Univ Mich, PhD(physics), 39. *Prof Exp:* Lab instr physics, Univ Mich, 35-37; instr, Rutgers Univ, 38-41; res physicist, Off Sci Res & Develop, Univ Mich, 45; res assoc, Rockefeller Found Proj, Johns Hopkins Univ, 46-48; asst prof physics, Howard Univ, 48-49; assoc prof, 49-52, PROF PHYSICS, FISK UNIV, 52-, DIR FISK INFRARED SPECTROS INST, 50- Concurrent Dir, Fisk Infrared Spectros Res Lab, 52-69; dir, Latin Am Fisk Infrared Spectros Inst, Sao Paulo, Brazil, 65; consult, AMP, Inc, Pa, 55-57; res assoc, Univ Bordeaux, 56-57, vis prof, Fac of Sci, 57-59; vis prof, Vanderbilt Univ, 60; dir coop study, Nashville Univ Ctr Coun, 69-70, exec secy, 70-72. *Concurrent Pos:* co-prin investr, Fisk Univ/Vanderbilt Univ physics consortium, NSF res prog, 80-83. *Mem:* Fel AAAS; Am Chem Soc; Am Phys Soc: Am Soc Physics Teachers; Coblentz Soc. *Res:* Applications of infrared spectroscopy to problems in chemical physics such as inter-molecular interactions, carcinogenic properties, inorganic ions in alkali halide matrices; biophysics; teaching of infrared spectroscopy short courses. *Mailing Add:* Dept Physics Fisk Univ Nashville TN 37203

FUSON, ROBERT L, b Indianapolis, Ind, Mar 12, 23; m 59; c 2. THORACIC SURGERY, CARDIOVASCULAR SURGERY. *Educ:* DePauw Univ, MA, 56, MA, 57; Ind Univ, MD, 61; Am Bd Surg, dipl, 70. *Prof Exp:* Vpres res, Hemathermatrol Corp, 58-62; resident, Med Ctr, Duke Univ, 62-69; mgr surg prod res & develop dept, Ethicon, Inc, NJ, 69-73, dir prod develop, 73-75; SR VPRES, ZIMMER USA, 75- *Concurrent Pos:* Intern, Med Ctr, Ind Univ, 61-62; asst prof surg, Rutgers Univ, 71-75. *Mem:* Am Soc Artificial Internal Organs. *Res:* Development of biomedical devices; clinical and experimental surgical research; medical product regulatory and quality affairs. *Mailing Add:* Zimmer USA Warsaw IN 46580

FUSON, ROGER BAKER, b Hazard, Ky, Mar 7, 16; m 48. IMMUNOLOGY, ANATOMY. *Educ:* Univ Ky, BS, 39; Univ Utah, BS, 51, MS, 52, PhD(anat, microbiol), 58. *Prof Exp:* Res bacteriologist, Vet Admin Hosp, Salt Lake City, 52-58; assoc dir exp med lab, Deaconess Hosp, Great Falls, Mont, 58-61; scientist adminr res grants br, 61-63, head predoctoral fels sect, 63-74, FELS OFFICER, NAT INST GEN MED SCI, 74- *Mem:* AAAS; Am Soc Cell Biol; Am Soc Microbiol; NY Acad Sci; Am Asn Anat. *Res:* Inhibition of hyaluronidase activity by blood sera as a function of neoplasia and Cytotoxins elicited by transplanted tumors and normal tissues. *Mailing Add:* Nat Inst of Gen Med Sci Bethesda MD 20014

FUSSELL, CATHARINE PUGH, b Philadelphia, Pa, July 13, 19. CELL BIOLOGY, BOTANY. *Educ:* Colby Col, AB, 41; Cornell Univ, MS, 58; Columbia Univ, PhD(cell biol), 66. *Prof Exp:* Admin asst, Shipping & Purchasing Dept, Am Friends Serv Comt, Philadelphia, 47-55; res asst biol, Brookhaven Nat Lab, 57-60; res assoc, Inst Cancer Res, Philadelphia, 66-67; NIH res fel, Fels Res Inst, Sch Med, Temple Univ, 67-68; from asst prof to assoc prof, McKeesport Campus, 68-77, ASSOC PROF BIOL, OGONTZ CAMPUS, PA STATE UNIV, 77- *Concurrent Pos:* NSF instnl res grant, Pa State Univ, 69-70, small cols prog, 81, marine biol lab, Woods Hole, Mass. *Mem:* AAAS; Am Soc Cell Biol; Bot Soc Am; Genetics Soc Am. *Res:* Chromosome position in interphase nuclei in relation to differentiation; relationship between chromosome structure and chromosome function; changes in macromolecular components of chromosomes and nuclei during cell division, cell differentiation and embryonic development. *Mailing Add:* Dept Biol Pa State Univ Abington PA 19001

FUSSELL, DELBERT DEAN, b Geneva, Nebr, Aug 17, 37; m 75; c 2. CHEMICAL & PETROLEUM ENGINEERING. *Educ:* Univ Nebr, Lincoln, BS, 60, MS, 61; Rice Univ, PhD(chem eng), 65. *Prof Exp:* res supvr, 67-80, DIR, RES DEPT, AMOCO PROD CO, 80- *Mem:* Am Inst Chem Engrs; Am Inst Mining, Metall & Petrol Engrs; Soc Petrol Engrs. *Res:* Numerical solution of the boundary layer equations; effect of ultrasonics on heat and mass transfer; numerical solution of reservoir fluid flow equations including compositional effects on phase properties; carbon dioxide and micellar flooding processes. *Mailing Add:* Res Dept Amoco Prod Co PO Box 591 Tulsa OK 74102

FUSTER, JOAQUIN MARIA, b Barcelona, Spain, Aug 17, 30; m 57; c 3. NEUROPHYSIOLOGY. *Educ:* Univ Barcelona, MD, 53; Univ Granada, PhD, 67. *Prof Exp:* Intern psychiat, Sch Med, Univ Barcelona, 52-53; asst resident, Neuropsychiat Clin, Innsbruck Univ, 54; asst resident, Inst Prev Psychiat, Univ Barcelona, 55-56; from assoc res psychiatrist to res psychiatrist, 57-67, PROF PSYCHIAT, MED CTR, UNIV CALIF, LOS ANGELES, 67- *Concurrent Pos:* Balmes fel, Neuropsychiat Clin, Innsbruck Univ, 54; Del Amo fel, 56; NIMH career develop award, 60-70, career scientist award, 70- *Mem:* AAAS; NY Acad Sci; Soc Neurosci; Am Psychiat Asn. *Res:* Neurophysiological basis of behavior; biological psychiatry. *Mailing Add:* Dept of Psychiat Univ of Calif Med Ctr Los Angeles CA 90024

FUTCH, ARCHER HAMNER, b Monroe NC, Mar 21, 25; m 53; c 3. PHYSICS. *Educ:* Univ NC, BS, 49, MS, 51; Univ Md, PhD(physics), 56. *Prof Exp:* Physicist, E I du Pont de Nemours & Co, 55-58; PHYSICIST, LAWRENCE RADIATION LAB, 59- *Mem:* Am Phys Soc; Am Nuclear Soc. *Res:* Atomic and nuclear physics; controlled fusion research including plasma diagnostics and numerical computations. *Mailing Add:* Lawrence Livermore Lab PO Box 808 Livermore CA 94550

FUTCH, DAVID GARDNER, b Schofield Barracks, Hawaii, Aug 31, 32; m 67; c 1. GENETICS, EVOLUTION. *Educ:* Univ NC, BA, 55; Univ Tex, MA, 61, PhD(zool), 64. *Prof Exp:* Res fel genetics, Calif Inst Technol, 64-65, Inst Animal Genetics, Edinburgh, 65-67 & City of Hope Med Ctr, 67; asst prof, 67-72, ASSOC PROF BIOL, SAN DIEGO STATE UNIV, 72- *Mem:* Genetics Soc Am; Soc Study Evolution; Am Genetic Asn. *Res:* Population genetics and evolution; genetic and cytological studies of evolution in Drosophila; genetics of parthenogenesis and sexual isolation in Drosophila. *Mailing Add:* Dept Biol San Diego State Univ San Diego CA 92182

FUTCHER, ANTHONY GRAHAM, b Rugby, Eng, Jan 18, 41; m 64; c 2. BIOSYSTEMATICS, NATURAL HISTORY. *Educ:* Columbia Union Col, BA, 62; Loma Linda Univ, PhD(biol), 74. *Prof Exp:* High sch teacher, Md, 62-63; from instr to assoc prof, 66-80, PROF BIOL, COLUMBIA UNION COL, 80-, DIR, BIOL STA, 74- *Mem:* Soc Syst Zool; Am Ornithologists Union; Am Soc Mammalogists. *Res:* Mammalian and avian biosystematics and karyology. *Mailing Add:* Dept of Biol Columbia Union Col Takoma Park MD 20912

FUTCHER, PALMER HOWARD, b Baltimore, Md, Sept 13, 10; m 42; c 2. MEDICINE. *Educ:* Harvard Univ, AB, 32; Johns Hopkins Univ, MD, 36. *Prof Exp:* Intern, Johns Hopkins Hosp, 36-39; fel & asst res physician, Rockefeller Inst Hosp, 39-41; resident, Johns Hopkins Hosp, 41; asst prof med, Sch Med, Washington Univ, 46-48; assoc prof, Johns Hopkins Univ, 48-66, dir personnel health clin, Hopkins Med Insts, 62-66; ASSOC CLIN PROF MED, SCH MED, UNIV PA, 67- *Concurrent Pos:* Exec dir, Am Bd Internal Med, 67-75. *Mem:* Am Soc Clin Invest; Endocrine Soc; Am Diabetes Asn; AMA; Am Col Physicians. *Res:* Evaluation of clinical competence of physicians, clinical medicine. *Mailing Add:* 273 S Third St Philadelphia PA 19106

FUTRELL, JEAN H, b Dry Prong, La, Oct 20, 33; m 77; c 2. PHYSICAL CHEMISTRY. *Educ:* La Polytech Inst, BS, 55; Univ Calif, PhD(chem), 58. *Prof Exp:* Res chemist, Humble Oil & Refining Co, 58-59; sr res chemist & group leader, Aero-Space Res Labs, Ohio, 61-68; PROF CHEM, UNIV UTAH, 68- *Concurrent Pos:* Sloan fel, 68-72; NIH Career Development Award, 69-74; Fulbright fel, Austria, 80-81. *Mem:* AAAS; Am Chem Soc; Am Phys Soc; Am Soc Mass Spectros (pres, 76-78). *Res:* Chemical kinetics; mass spectrometry; ion-molecule reactions. *Mailing Add:* Dept Chem Univ Utah Salt Lake City UT 84112

FUTRELL, MARY FELTNER, b Cadiz, Ky, Jan 5, 24; m 47; c 2. BIOCHEMISTRY, HUMAN NUTRITION. *Educ:* Austin Peay State Univ, BS, 44; Univ Wis, MS, 49, PhD(human nutrit), 52. *Prof Exp:* Grade sch teacher, Tenn, 42-43; high sch teacher, Tenn, 44-46 & Ky, 47-49; res asst nutrit, Univ Wis, 48-52; res assoc biochem, Tex A&M Univ, 52-54, asst prof home econ, 54-56; lectr, Ahmadu Bello Univ, Nigeria, 64-66; prof nutrit, 67-80, PROF HOME ECON, MISS STATE UNIV, 80- *Mem:* Fel Am Inst Chemists; Am Home Econ Asn; Am Dietetic Asn. *Res:* Amino acids in self-selected diets; ascorbic acid requirements; nutritional status of preschool children. *Mailing Add:* PO Drawer DT Mississippi State MS 39762

FUTRELLE, ROBERT PEEL, b Washington, DC, Apr 23, 37; m 62. DEVELOPMENTAL BIOLOGY, COMPUTER SCIENCES. *Educ:* Mass Inst Technol, BS, 59, PhD(physics), 66. *Prof Exp:* Mem tech staff theoret physics, Sci Ctr, NAm Rockwell Corp, 65-69, staff engr optical physics, Electrooptical Lab, Autonetics Div, 69-71; vis fel, Joint Inst Lab Astrophys, Univ Colo-Nat Bur Standards, 71-72; res assoc biophysics & theoret biol, Univ Chicago, 72-75; ASST PROF GENETICS & DEVELOP, UNIV ILL, 75- *Concurrent Pos:* Chmn, Gordon Res Conf Atomic & Molecular Interactions, 70-71. *Mem:* AAAS; Asn Comput Mach; Inst Elec & Electronics Eng; Soc Develop Biol. *Res:* Developmental genetics and pattern formation in the cellular slime molds; mathematical biology; analysis of motion and behavior using real-time interactive and automated computer image analysis; foundations of interactive computer graphics. *Mailing Add:* Dept Genetics & Develop Morrill 515 Univ Ill Urbana IL 61820

FUTTERMAN, SIDNEY, biochemistry, deceased

FUTUYMA, DOUGLAS JOEL, b New York, NY, Apr 24, 42. POPULATION BIOLOGY. *Educ:* Cornell Univ, BS, 63; Univ Mich, MS, 66, PhD(zool), 69. *Prof Exp:* asst prof, 69-76, PROF ECOL & EVOLUTION, STATE UNIV NY, STONY BROOK, 76- *Concurrent Pos:* Mem fac, Orgn Trop Studies, 66, 69, 71, 74 & 81. *Mem:* Soc Study Evolution; Genetic Soc Am; Ecol Soc Am; Am Soc Naturalists; Soc Syst Zool. *Res:* Analysis of mechanisms of coevolution and its effects on community structure; genetic and ecological dynamics of coevolution of terrestrial plants and herbivores. *Mailing Add:* Dept of Ecol & Evolution State Univ of NY Stony Brook NY 11794

FUXA, JAMES RODERICK, b Lincoln, Nebr, Jan 26, 49; m 72. ENTOMOLOGY, INSECT PATHOLOGY. *Educ:* Univ Nebr, BS, 71; Ore State Univ, MS, 75; NC State Univ, PhD(entom), 78. *Prof Exp:* asst prof entom, 78-81, ASSOC PROF ENTOM, LA STATE UNIV, BATON ROUGE, 81- *Mem:* Soc Invert Path; Entom Soc Am; Nat Asn Advan Sci; Sigma Xi. *Res:* Insect pathology, primarily epizootiology and microbial control of lepidopterous pests of field crops. *Mailing Add:* Dept of Entom La State Univ Baton Rouge LA 70803

FUZEK, JOHN FRANK, b Knoxville, Tenn, Dec 21, 21; m 43; c 3. PHYSICAL CHEMISTRY. *Educ:* Univ Tenn, BS, 43, MS, 45, PhD(phys chem), 47. *Prof Exp:* Chem eng aide, Tenn Valley Authority, 40-42, chemist, Hercules Powder Co, Wilmington, 43-44; Off Naval Res fel, Tenn, 47-48; res chemist, Beaunit Fibers Div, Beaunit Corp, 48-55, head res physics, 55-66; sr res chemist, 66-70, RES ASSOC, TENN EASTMAN CO, 70- *Honors & Awards:* Oak Ridge Inst Res Award, 49. *Mem:* Fel AAAS; Am Chem Soc; Am Crystallog Asn; fel Am Inst Chem; Am Asn Textile Chem & Colorists. *Res:* Catalysis; kinetics; absorption; cellulose chemistry; physical chemistry of polymers; x-ray diffraction of polymers; analytical instrumentation; fiber science. *Mailing Add:* Res Labs Tenn Eastman Co Kingsport TN 37662

FYE, PAUL MCDONALD, b Johnstown, Pa, Aug 6, 12; m 42; c 2. PHYSICAL CHEMISTRY. *Educ:* Albright Col, BS, 35; Columbia Univ, PhD(phys chem), 39. *Hon Degrees:* ScD, Albright Col, 55, Tufts Univ, 70, Southeastern Mass Univ, 70, Fla Inst Technol, 73 & Southampton Univ, 78; LLD, Northeastern Univ, 74. *Prof Exp:* Statutory asst chem, Columbia Univ, 35-39; asst prof, Hofstra Col, 39-41; res assoc high explosives, Nat Defense Res Comt Proj, Carnegie Inst Technol, 41-42; res supvr underwater explosives res lab, Woods Hole Oceanog Inst, 42-44, from dep res dir to res dir, 44-47; assoc prof chem, Univ Tenn, 47-48; dep chief, Naval Ord Lab, 48-51, chief explosives res dept, 51-56, assoc tech dir res, 56-58; dir, 58-77, PRES, WOODS HOLE OCEANOG INST, 61- *Concurrent Pos:* Mem steering task group, Polaris, 56-58; ad hoc group long range res & develop, 60-65; mem, Undersea Res & Develop Planning Coun, 59-76; mem comt oceanog, Nat Acad Sci, 61-70; bd trustees, State Cols Mass, 66; vis comt dept geol sci, Harvard Univ, 67-73 & dept astron, 74-77; US rep sci comn, NATO Res Ctr, La Spezia, Italy, 68-73; bd dirs, A D Little, Inc, 69-, Textron, Inc, 69- & Develop Sci, Inc, 77-; mem corp, Marine Biol Lab; trustee, Bermuda Biol Sta, Woods Hole Oceanog Inst; mem, President's Task Force Oceanog, 69; mem ocean sci comt, Nat Acad Sci, 70-, chmn, 80-; dir, Charles Stark Draper Lab, 74-; mem bd trustees, Mass Maritime Acad, 80-; presiding officer, Law of the Sea Inst, Ocean Energy Systs Coun, Dept Educ, 79- *Honors & Awards:* Presidential Cert of Merit, 48; Bur Ord Develop Award, 46; Asn Govt Account Ann Achievement Award, 77. *Mem:* AAAS; Am Chem Soc; Am Phys Soc; Am Geophys Union; Marine Technol Soc (pres, 68-69). *Res:* Oceanography; gas kinetics; photochemistry; purification of gases; high explosives; underwater photography; liquid state. *Mailing Add:* Woods Hole Oceanog Inst Woods Hole MA 02543

FYE, ROBERT EATON, b Cresco, Iowa, Jan 19, 24. ENTOMOLOGY. *Educ:* Iowa State Col, BS, 49; Wash State Univ, MS, 51; Univ Wis, PhD, 54. *Prof Exp:* Asst entomologist, NMex State Univ, 54-55; entomologist entom res div, Agr Res Serv, USDA, 55-59; res officer, Can Dept Forestry, 60-65; entomologist, Cotton Insect Biol Control Lab, Ariz-NMex Area, 65-77, RES ENTOMOLOGIST, YAKIMA AGR RES LAB, WASH-ORE AREA, WESTERN REGION, AGR RES SERV, USDA, 77- *Concurrent Pos:* Assoc prof, Univ Ariz, 67-77; vis scientist, Cotton Res Unit, Commonwealth Sci & Indust Res Orgn, Australia, 74-75. *Mem:* Entom Soc Am; Ecol Soc Am. *Res:* Biology and ecology of cotton insects, pear psylla, lygus bugs, pollinators, native bees and wasps; predation; insect population dynamics; bioclimatology. *Mailing Add:* Yakima Agr Res Lab 3706 W Nob Hill Blvd Yakima WA 98902

FYFE, FOREST WILLIAM, b Aberdeen, Scotland, June 21, 13; m 43; c 4. ANATOMY. *Educ:* Aberdeen Univ, MA, 33, MB & ChB, 37. *Prof Exp:* House physician & surgeon, Royal Infirmary, Blackburn, Eng, 37-38; house surgeon, Royal Nat Orthop Hosp, Stanmore, Eng, 38-39; from asst to lectr anat, Aberdeen Univ, 39-55; from assoc prof to prof anat, Fac Med, Dalhousie Univ, 64-78; RETIRED. *Mailing Add:* 1447 Edward St Halifax NS B3H 3H5 Can

FYFE, I(AN) MILLAR, b Glen Ridge, NJ, Nov 13, 25; m 51; c 1. AERONAUTICAL ENGINEERING, APPLIED MECHANICS. *Educ:* Royal Col Sci & Technol, ARTC, 51; Univ Del, MME, 54; Stanford Univ, PhD(mech), 58. *Prof Exp:* Res engr dynamics, Boeing Co, 57-60; from asst prof to assoc prof aeronaut, 60-69, PROF AERONAUT & ASTRONAUT, UNIV WASH, 69- *Concurrent Pos:* NATO sr fel, 68. *Mem:* Am Soc Mech Engrs; Am Inst Aeronaut & Astronaut; Soc Exp Stress Anal. *Res:* Wave propagation in solids and fluids; impact dynamics. *Mailing Add:* 206 Guggenheim Hall Univ Wash Seattle WA 98105

FYFE, JAMES ARTHUR, b Woodstock, Ill, Mar 16, 41; m 64; c 3. ENZYMOLOGY, MECHANISMS OF ANTIHERPES COMPOUNDS. *Educ:* Carleton Col, BA, 63; Univ Chicago, PhD(biochem), 68. *Prof Exp:* Asst prof biochem & chem, Trinity Univ, Tex, 68-70; RES BIOCHEMIST, WELLCOME RES LABS, BURROUGHS WELLCOME CO, 70- *Mem:* Am Chem Soc. *Res:* Mechanisms of action and substrate-inhibitor specificities of purine and pyrimidine metabolizing enzymes; enzymology of antiviral chemotherapy. *Mailing Add:* Wellcome Res Labs 3030 Cornwallis Rd Research Triangle Park NC 27709

FYFE, RICHARD ROSS, b Binghamton, NY, Nov 19, 41; m 66; c 2. CHEMICAL ENGINEERING, ELECTROCHEMISTRY. *Educ:* Lafayette Col, BS & BA, 64; Columbia Univ, MS, 66, DEngSc(chem eng), 69. *Prof Exp:* Chem engr, Alcorn Combustion Co, 68-69; res chem engr, Picatinny Arsenal, US Army, 69-72; staff chemist, Lawrence Livermore Lab, Univ Calif, 72-74; res scientist, Union Camp Corp, NJ, 74-79; SR RES ENGR, KOPPERS CO, INC, 79- *Mem:* Am Inst Chem Engrs; Am Chem Soc. *Res:* Colloid chemistry; kinetics; electrostatics; shock waves; metastable and explosive materials characterization; surface chemistry; tall oil and fatty acid processes; terpene processes; coal tar processes. *Mailing Add:* Koppers Co Inc 440 College Park Dr Monroeville PA 15146

FYFE, WILLIAM SEFTON, b Ashburton, NZ, June 4, 27; Can citizen; m 52; c 3. GEOLOGY. *Educ:* Univ Otago, BSc, 48, MSc, 49, PhD(chem), 52. *Prof Exp:* Prof geol, Univ Calif, Berkeley, 58-66 & Manchester, UK, 66-72; PROF & CHMN GEOL, UNIV WESTERN ONTARIO, CAN, 72- *Honors & Awards:* Logan Medal, Geol Asn Can, 81. *Mem:* Geol Soc Am; Minerals Soc Am; Royal Soc London; Geol Asn Can; Chem Soc UK. *Res:* Geology; geochemistry; environmental science. *Mailing Add:* 1197 Richmond St London ON N6A 3L3 Can

FYFFE, DAVID EUGENE, b Washington, Ind, June 29, 25; m 65; c 3. INDUSTRIAL ENGINEERING, OPERATIONS RESEARCH. *Educ:* Purdue Univ, BSME, 50, MSIE, 55; Northwestern Univ, PhD, 64. *Prof Exp:* Mgr qual control, Appliance Motor Dept, Gen Elec Co, 57-61; assoc prof indust eng, 64-67, PROF INDUST ENG, GA INST TECHNOL, 67- *Concurrent Pos:* Consult indust eng & mgt. *Mem:* Am Inst Indust Engrs; Am Soc Eng Educ; Am Soc Qual Control; Inst Mgt Sci. *Res:* Production, inventory and distribution systems; project feasibility analysis; quality control. *Mailing Add:* Dept of Indust Eng Ga Inst of Technol Atlanta GA 30332

FYLES, JAMES THOMAS, b Vancouver, BC, Dec 22, 24; m 50; c 4. GEOLOGY. *Educ:* Univ BC, BASc, 47, MASc, 49; Columbia Univ, PhD(geol), 54. *Prof Exp:* Asst geologist, 48-54, Geologist, 54-72; dep minister, BC Dept Mines & Petrol Resources, 72-81; CONSULT, 81- *Mem:* Can Inst Min & Metall; Geol Asn Can; fel Soc Econ Geologists. *Res:* Economic geology of metallic mineral deposits; structural geology; mineral resources and land use in British Columbia; mineral resource management and administration. *Mailing Add:* 1720 Kingsberry Crescent Victoria BC V8P 2A7 Can

FYLES, JOHN GLADSTONE, b Vancouver, BC, Feb 27, 23; m 50; c 3. ENVIRONMENTAL GEOLOGY, ENVIRONMENTAL MANAGEMENT. *Educ:* Univ BC, BASc, 46, MASc, 50; Ohio State Univ, PhD(geol), 56. *Prof Exp:* Tech officer, Dept Energy, Mines & Resources, Geol Surv Can, 50-56, geologist, 56-68, chief terrain sci div, 68-73, environ eng adv, 73-77; dir gen, Northern Pipelines Br, Dept Indian Affairs & Northern Develop, 77-79; CHIEF GEOLOGIST, GEOL SURV CAN, 79- *Concurrent Pos:* coord for Dept Energy, Mines & Resources, Environ-Social Prog, Northern Pipelines of Task Force on Northern Oil Develop, 71-74, head pipeline appln assessment group, 74; head inquiry appraisal team, Mackenzie Valley Pipeline Inquiry, 75-77. *Mem:* Geol Soc Am. *Res:* Pleistocene geology; geomorphology; engineering geology. *Mailing Add:* 965 Kingsmere Ave Ottawa Can

FYMAT, ALAIN L, b Casablanca, Morocco, Dec 7, 38; m 60; c 2. METEOROLOGY, PLANETARY ATMOSPHERES. *Educ:* Nat Super Sch Meteorol, Paris, BA, 59; Sorbonne, MA, 60; Univ Bordeaux, MS, 63; Univ Calif, Los Angeles, PhD(meteorol), 67. *Prof Exp:* Staff engr, weather Bur Morocco, 60-63; res meteorologist, Univ Calif, Los Angeles, 64-67; sr res scientist, 67-70, MEM TECH STAFF, SPACE SCI DIV, JET PROPULSION LAB, CALIF INST TECHNOL, 70- *Concurrent Pos:* Asst prof & lectr meteorol, Univ Calif, Los Angeles, 67-70; prof geol, Univ Southern Calif, 70; vis prof physics, Univ Lille, 70-71; adv, Int Radiation Comn, 73-; assoc ed, Int J Appl Math & Comput, 74-; vis prof physics, Univ Leningrad, 78; vis prof atmospheric sci, Univ Calif, Los Angeles, 79. *Honors & Awards:* NASA Awards for Sci Inventions, 71 & 75. *Mem:* Am Inst Physics; Am Astron Soc; Optical Soc Am; Am Geophys Union; Am Meteorol Soc. *Res:* Hydrogen lyman alpha geocorona; radiative transfer in planetary atmospheres; interferometric polarimetry; spectral line formation in scattering atmospheres; integral equations theory; differential equations theory; system identification; optimization; environmental pollution; societal aspects and implications. *Mailing Add:* Jet Propulsion Lab Space Sci Div 4800 Oak Grove Dr Pasadena CA 91125

FYSTROM, DELL O, b Minneapolis, Minn, Aug 29, 37; div; c 3. ATOMIC PHYSICS. *Educ:* St Olaf Col, BA, 59; Univ Colo, Boulder, PhD(physics), 69. *Prof Exp:* Chmn dept, 70-73, ASSOC PROF PHYSICS, UNIV WIS-LA CROSSE, 69- *Concurrent Pos:* Chmn dept physics, Haile Sellassie Univ, 74-75. *Mem:* Am Asn Physics Teachers. *Res:* Magnetic moment; precision measurements; proton moment; nuclear magnetons. *Mailing Add:* Dept of Physics Univ of Wis-La Crosse La Crosse WI 54601

FYTELSON, MILTON, b Bridgeport, Conn, Nov 15, 17; m 46; c 2. CHEMISTRY. *Educ:* Yale Univ, BS, 37, PhD(org chem), 41. *Prof Exp:* Pfizer fel, Columbia Univ, 41-42; res chemist, Yale Univ, 42-43; chemist, Am Quinine Co, Bogota, Colombia, SAm, 43; fel, Mellon Inst, 44-45; res chemist, E I du Pont de Nemours & Co, 46-58; group leader, Toms River Chem Corp, 58-67; mgr process develop, Otto B May, Inc, 67-68; pres, Fytelson & Assocs, Chem & Eng Consult, 68-74; plant mgr pigments, 74-79, ASST TO VPRES MFG, SANDOZ COLORS & CHEM, 79- *Concurrent Pos:* Mem, Off Sci Res & Develop; mem, Bd Econ Warfare, 44. *Mem:* Am Chem Soc. *Res:* Synthesis of vitamin A; synthesis of synthetic lubricants; synthesis and applications of organic pigments; metallo-organic complexes; process development and engineering; sulfur and chromium chemistry. *Mailing Add:* 859 Dewey St Union NJ 07083